2018
Harris
Ohio
Services Directory

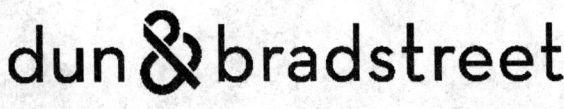

 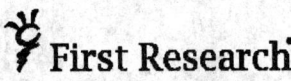 

Published July 2018 next update July 2019

WARNING: Purchasers and users of this directory may not use this directory to compile mailing lists, other marketing aids and other types of data, which are sold or otherwise provided to third parties. Such use is wrongful, illegal and a violation of the federal copyright laws.

CAUTION: Because of the many thousands of establishment listings contained in this directory and the possibilities of both human and mechanical error in processing this information, Mergent Inc. cannot assume liability for the correctness of the listings or information on which they are based. Hence, no information contained in this work should be relied upon in any instance where there is a possibility of any loss or damage as a consequence of any error or omission in this volume.

Publisher
Mergent Inc.
444 Madison Ave
New York, NY 10022

©Mergent Inc All Rights Reserved
2018 Mergent Business Press
ISSN 1080-2614
ISBN 978-1-68200-805-8

TABLE OF CONTENTS

Summary of Contents & Explanatory Notes 4
User's Guide to Listings 6

Geographic Section
County/City Cross-Reference Index 9
Firms Listed by Location City 13

Standard Industrial Classification (SIC) Section
SIC Alphabetical Index 885
SIC Numerical Index 887
Firms Listed by SIC 889

Alphabetic Section
Firms Listed by Firm Name 1095

Services Section
Services Index 1371
Firms Listed by Service Category 1389

SUMMARY OF CONTENTS

Number of Companies 20,561
Number of Decision Makers 58,422
Minimum Number of Employees 25

EXPLANATORY NOTES

How to Cross-Reference in This Directory

Sequential Entry Numbers. Each establishment in the Geographic Section is numbered sequentially (G-0000). The number assigned to each establishment is referred to as its "entry number." To make cross-referencing easier, each listing in the Geographic, SIC, Alphabetic and Product Sections includes the establishment's entry number. To facilitate locating an entry in the Geographic Section, the entry numbers for the first listing on the left page and the last listing on the right page are printed at the top of the page next to the city name.

Source Suggestions Welcome

Although all known sources were used to compile this directory, it is possible that companies were inadvertently omitted. Your assistance in calling attention to such omissions would be greatly appreciated. A special form on the facing page will help you in the reporting process.

Analysis

Every effort has been made to contact all firms to verify their information. The one exception to this rule is the annual sales figure, which is considered by many companies to be confidential information. Therefore, estimated sales have been calculated by multiplying the nationwide average sales per employee for the firm's major SIC/NAICS code by the firm's number of employees. Nationwide averages for sales per employee by SIC/NAICS codes are provided by the U.S. Department of Commerce and are updated annually. All sales—sales (est)—have been estimated by this method. The exceptions are parent companies (PA), division headquarters (DH) and headquarter locations (HQ) which may include an actual corporate sales figure—sales (corporate-wide) if available.

Types of Companies

Descriptive and statistical data are included for companies in the entire state. These comprise manufacturers, machine shops, fabricators, assemblers and printers. Also identified are corporate offices in the state.

Employment Data

This directory contains companies with 25 or more employees in the service industry. The actual employment shown in the Geographic Section includes male & female employees and embraces all levels of the company. This figure is for the facility listed and does not include other offices or branches. It should be recognized that these figures represent an approximate year-round average. These employment figures are broken into codes A-E and used in the SIC and Services Sections to further help you in qualifying a company. Be sure to check the footnotes on the bottom of the page for the code breakdowns.

Standard Industrial Classification (SIC)

The Standard Industrial Classification (SIC) system used in this directory was developed by the federal government for use in classifying establishments by the type of activity they are engaged in. The SIC classifications used in this directory are from the 1987 edition published by the U.S. Government's Office of Management and Budget. The SIC system separates all activities into broad industrial divisions (e.g., manufacturing, mining, retail trade). It further subdivides each division. The range of manufacturing industry classes extends from two-digit codes (major industry group) to four-digit codes (product).

For example:

Industry Breakdown	Code	Industry, Product, etc.
*Major industry group	20	Food and kindred products
Industry group	203	Canned and frozen foods
*Industry	2033	Fruits and vegetables, etc.

*Classifications used in this directory

Only two-digit and four-digit codes are used in this directory.

Arrangement

1. The **Geographic Section** contains complete in-depth corporate data. This section is sorted by cities listed in alphabetical order and companies listed alphabetically within each city. A County/City Index for referencing cities within counties precedes this section.

> IMPORTANT NOTICE: It is a violation of both federal and state law to transmit an unsolicited advertisement to a facsimile machine. Any user of this product that violates such laws may be subject to civil and criminal penalties, which may exceed $500 for each transmission of an unsolicited facsimile. Mergent Inc. provides fax numbers for lawful purposes only and expressly forbids the use of these numbers in any unlawful manner.

2. The **Standard Industrial Classification (SIC) Section** lists companies under approximately 500 four-digit SIC codes. An alphabetical and a numerical index precedes this section. A company can be listed under several codes. The codes are in numerical order with companies listed alphabetically under each code.

3. The **Alphabetic Section** lists all companies with their full physical or mailing addresses and telephone number.

4. The **Services Section** lists companies under unique Harris categories. An index precedes this section. Companies can be listed under several categories.

USER'S GUIDE TO LISTINGS

GEOGRAPHIC SECTION

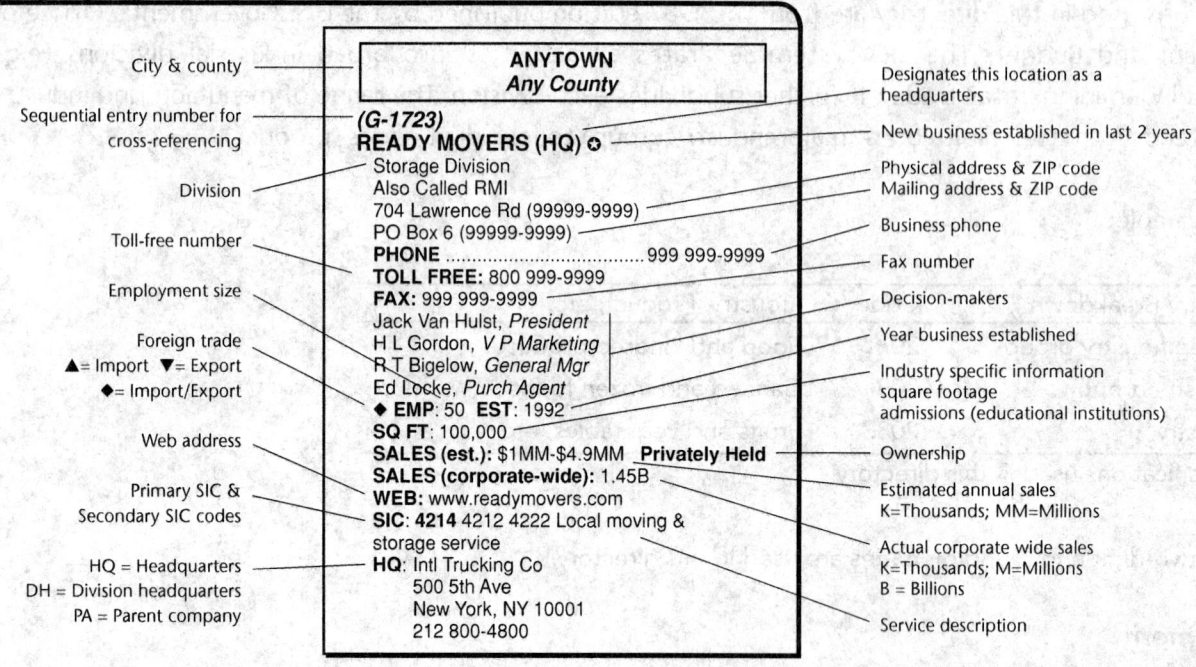

SIC SECTION

ALPHABETIC SECTION

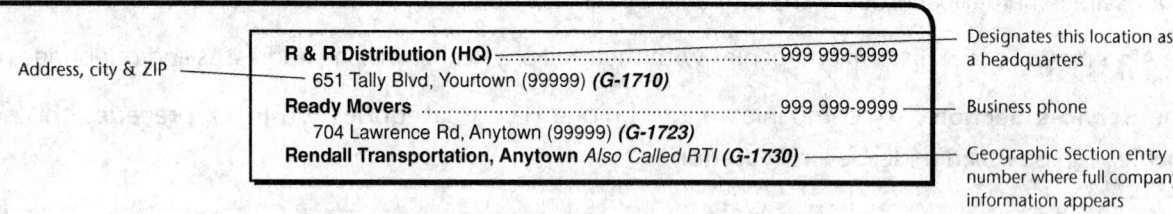

SERVICES SECTION

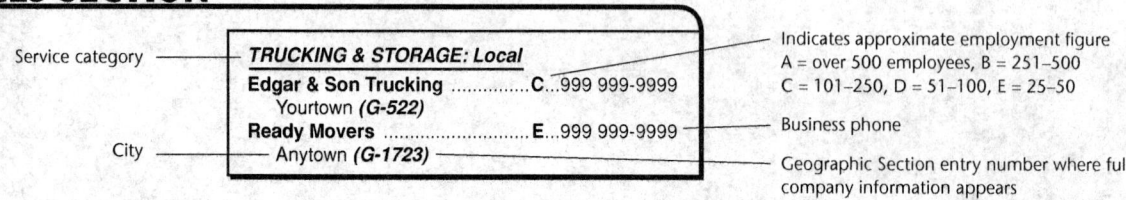

GEOGRAPHIC SECTION
Companies sorted by city in alphabetical order
In-depth company data listed

STANDARD INDUSTRIAL CLASSIFICATIONS
Alphabetical index of classifcation descriptions
Numerical index of classifcation descriptions
Companies sorted by SIC product groupings

ALPHABETIC SECTION
Company listings in alphabetical order

SERVICES INDEX
Service categories are listed in alphabetical order

SERVICES SECTION
Companies sorted by service classifications

Ohio
County Map

COUNTY/CITY CROSS-REFERENCE INDEX

Adams
City	Entry #
Manchester	(G-13255)
Peebles	(G-15938)
Seaman	(G-16818)
West Union	(G-19271)
Winchester	(G-19798)

Allen
City	Entry #
Beaverdam	(G-1288)
Bluffton	(G-1726)
Delphos	(G-10137)
Elida	(G-10586)
Harrod	(G-11813)
Lima	(G-12729)
Spencerville	(G-17107)

Ashland
City	Entry #
Ashland	(G-649)
Hayesville	(G-11834)
Jeromesville	(G-12333)
Loudonville	(G-13088)
Perrysville	(G-16077)
Polk	(G-16230)

Ashtabula
City	Entry #
Andover	(G-609)
Ashtabula	(G-710)
Austinburg	(G-865)
Conneaut	(G-9037)
Geneva	(G-11357)
Jefferson	(G-12328)
North Kingsville	(G-15391)
Rock Creek	(G-16558)
Windsor	(G-19805)

Athens
City	Entry #
Albany	(G-519)
Athens	(G-771)
Glouster	(G-11434)
Millfield	(G-14632)
Nelsonville	(G-14960)
The Plains	(G-17664)

Auglaize
City	Entry #
Cridersville	(G-9151)
Lima	(G-12926)
Minster	(G-14659)
New Bremen	(G-15016)
New Knoxville	(G-15052)
Saint Marys	(G-16670)
Wapakoneta	(G-18792)

Belmont
City	Entry #
Barnesville	(G-987)
Bellaire	(G-1361)
Belmont	(G-1428)
Bethesda	(G-1485)
Bridgeport	(G-1859)
Flushing	(G-11104)
Martins Ferry	(G-13599)
Powhatan Point	(G-16356)
Saint Clairsville	(G-16616)
Shadyside	(G-16849)

Brown
City	Entry #
Aberdeen	(G-1)
Fayetteville	(G-10984)
Georgetown	(G-11383)
Lake Waynoka	(G-12463)
Mount Orab	(G-14867)
Ripley	(G-16547)
Sardinia	(G-16812)

Butler
City	Entry #
College Corner	(G-6838)
Fairfield	(G-10814)
Fairfield Township	(G-10924)
Hamilton	(G-11689)
Liberty Township	(G-12717)
Liberty Twp	(G-12725)
Middletown	(G-14410)
Monroe	(G-14687)
Oxford	(G-15810)
Ross	(G-16603)
Shandon	(G-16873)
Somerville	(G-17071)
Trenton	(G-18340)
West Chester	(G-19011)

Carroll
City	Entry #
Carrollton	(G-2611)
Malvern	(G-13250)
Mechanicstown	(G-14031)
Sherrodsville	(G-16905)

Champaign
City	Entry #
Saint Paris	(G-16686)
Urbana	(G-18573)
Woodstock	(G-19821)

Clark
City	Entry #
Enon	(G-10726)
Medway	(G-14140)
New Carlisle	(G-15020)
South Charleston	(G-17075)
South Vienna	(G-17100)
Springfield	(G-17145)

Clermont
City	Entry #
Amelia	(G-571)
Batavia	(G-994)
Bethel	(G-1482)
Cincinnati	(G-2900)
Felicity	(G-10985)
Goshen	(G-11437)
Loveland	(G-13109)
Miamiville	(G-14374)
Milford	(G-14501)
New Richmond	(G-15124)
Owensville	(G-15809)
Point Pleasant	(G-16218)
Williamsburg	(G-19629)

Clinton
City	Entry #
Blanchester	(G-1514)
New Vienna	(G-15132)
Sabina	(G-16615)
Wilmington	(G-19740)

Columbiana
City	Entry #
Columbiana	(G-6853)
East Liverpool	(G-10513)
East Palestine	(G-10537)
Hanoverton	(G-11787)
Kensington	(G-12349)
Leetonia	(G-12661)
Lisbon	(G-12931)
Negley	(G-14958)
New Waterford	(G-15137)
Salem	(G-16687)
Salineville	(G-16722)
Wellsville	(G-19006)

Coshocton
City	Entry #
Conesville	(G-9035)
Coshocton	(G-9086)
Warsaw	(G-18936)
West Lafayette	(G-19257)

Crawford
City	Entry #
Bucyrus	(G-2023)
Crestline	(G-9142)
Galion	(G-11288)
New Washington	(G-15133)

Cuyahoga
City	Entry #
Bay Village	(G-1038)
Beachwood	(G-1044)
Bedford	(G-1291)
Bedford Heights	(G-1345)
Berea	(G-1445)
Brecksville	(G-1810)
Broadview Heights	(G-1873)
Brooklyn	(G-1904)
Brooklyn Heights	(G-1908)
Brookpark	(G-1934)
Chagrin Falls	(G-2688)
Cleveland	(G-4917)
Cleveland Heights	(G-6786)
Euclid	(G-10741)
Garfield Heights	(G-11351)
Gates Mills	(G-11355)
Highland Heights	(G-11868)
Independence	(G-12177)
Lakewood	(G-12469)
Maple Heights	(G-13398)
Mayfield Heights	(G-13998)
Mayfield Village	(G-14010)
Middleburg Heights	(G-14378)
Moreland Hills	(G-14839)
Newburgh Heights	(G-15250)
North Olmsted	(G-15409)
North Royalton	(G-15479)
Oakwood Village	(G-15625)
Olmsted Falls	(G-15673)
Olmsted Twp	(G-15675)
Parma	(G-15897)
Pepper Pike	(G-15955)
Richmond Heights	(G-16536)
Rocky River	(G-16567)
Seven Hills	(G-16825)
Shaker Heights	(G-16855)
Solon	(G-16967)
Strongsville	(G-17437)
Walton Hills	(G-18789)
Warrensville Heights	(G-18931)
Westlake	(G-19454)

Darke
City	Entry #
Ansonia	(G-619)
Arcanum	(G-629)
Dayton	(G-9248)
Greenville	(G-11489)
New Madison	(G-15072)
New Weston	(G-15140)
Osgood	(G-15791)
Rossburg	(G-16604)
Union City	(G-18500)
Versailles	(G-18722)
Yorkshire	(G-20092)

Defiance
City	Entry #
Defiance	(G-10020)
Hicksville	(G-11862)

Delaware
City	Entry #
Columbus	(G-6868)
Delaware	(G-10064)
Galena	(G-11277)
Lewis Center	(G-12665)
Ostrander	(G-15793)
Powell	(G-16323)
Sunbury	(G-17549)
Westerville	(G-19282)

Erie
City	Entry #
Berlin Heights	(G-1481)
Castalia	(G-2630)
Huron	(G-12159)
Kelleys Island	(G-12348)
Milan	(G-14492)
Sandusky	(G-16723)
Vermilion	(G-18708)

Fairfield
City	Entry #
Baltimore	(G-948)
Carroll	(G-2607)
Lancaster	(G-12506)
Millersport	(G-14629)
Pickerington	(G-16083)
Rushville	(G-16613)
Stoutsville	(G-17349)
Sugar Grove	(G-17540)

Fayette
City	Entry #
Washington Court Hou	(G-18937)
Wshngtn CT Hs	(G-20013)

Franklin
City	Entry #
Blacklick	(G-1499)
Brice	(G-1858)
Canal Winchester	(G-2150)
Columbus	(G-6912)
Dublin	(G-10231)
Etna	(G-10728)
Gahanna	(G-11232)
Galloway	(G-11342)
Grove City	(G-11527)
Groveport	(G-11621)
Hilliard	(G-11873)
Lockbourne	(G-12944)
New Albany	(G-14970)
Obetz	(G-15663)
Reynoldsburg	(G-16423)
Upper Arlington	(G-18546)
Urbancrest	(G-18604)
Westerville	(G-19360)
Worthington	(G-19937)

Fulton
City	Entry #
Archbold	(G-632)
Delta	(G-10155)
Lyons	(G-13185)
Metamora	(G-14264)
Pettisville	(G-16082)
Swanton	(G-17562)
Wauseon	(G-18948)

Gallia
City	Entry #
Bidwell	(G-1494)
Cheshire	(G-2789)
Crown City	(G-9155)
Gallipolis	(G-11308)
Patriot	(G-15926)
Rio Grande	(G-16546)
Thurman	(G-17670)
Vinton	(G-18744)

Geauga
City	Entry #
Burton	(G-2059)
Chagrin Falls	(G-2712)
Chardon	(G-2738)
Chesterland	(G-2792)
Huntsburg	(G-12156)
Middlefield	(G-14393)
Newbury	(G-15253)
Novelty	(G-15601)

Greene
City	Entry #
Beavercreek	(G-1142)
Beavercreek Township	(G-1265)
Bellbrook	(G-1370)
Cedarville	(G-2631)
Dayton	(G-9249)
Fairborn	(G-10782)
Jamestown	(G-12326)
Spring Valley	(G-17109)
Wright Patterson Afb	(G-20012)
Xenia	(G-20039)
Yellow Springs	(G-20088)

Guernsey
City	Entry #
Buffalo	(G-2053)
Byesville	(G-2069)
Cambridge	(G-2092)
Kimbolton	(G-12446)
Lore City	(G-13086)
Pleasant City	(G-16213)
Salesville	(G-16720)
Senecaville	(G-16823)

Hamilton
City	Entry #
Arlington Heights	(G-648)
Blue Ash	(G-1520)
Cincinnati	(G-2939)
Cleves	(G-6797)
Harrison	(G-11788)
Hooven	(G-12076)
Miamitown	(G-14370)
Montgomery	(G-14725)
Mount Saint Joseph	(G-14871)
North Bend	(G-15317)
Norwood	(G-15598)
Sharonville	(G-16881)
Symmes Twp	(G-17629)
Terrace Park	(G-17662)
Walnut Hills	(G-18787)
West Chester	(G-19188)

Hancock
City	Entry #
Arlington	(G-647)
Findlay	(G-10986)
Mc Comb	(G-14021)

Hardin
City	Entry #
Ada	(G-3)

COUNTY/CITY CROSS-REFERENCE

Name	ENTRY #
Dunkirk	(G-10501)
Forest	(G-11107)
Kenton	(G-12408)
Mc Guffey	(G-14025)
Mount Victory	(G-14929)

Harrison
Name	ENTRY #
Bowerston	(G-1754)
Cadiz	(G-2073)
Freeport	(G-11181)
Hopedale	(G-12078)
Scio	(G-16816)

Henry
Name	ENTRY #
Deshler	(G-10169)
Holgate	(G-12003)
Liberty Center	(G-12716)
Mc Clure	(G-14020)
Napoleon	(G-14934)
Ridgeville Corners	(G-16545)

Highland
Name	ENTRY #
Greenfield	(G-11482)
Hillsboro	(G-11968)
Lynchburg	(G-13184)

Hocking
Name	ENTRY #
Logan	(G-12967)
Rockbridge	(G-16560)

Holmes
Name	ENTRY #
Berlin	(G-1477)
Big Prairie	(G-1498)
Holmesville	(G-12070)
Killbuck	(G-12445)
Millersburg	(G-14582)
Mount Hope	(G-14866)
Walnut Creek	(G-18784)
Winesburg	(G-19806)

Huron
Name	ENTRY #
Bellevue	(G-1402)
Collins	(G-6839)
Greenwich	(G-11526)
Monroeville	(G-14720)
New Haven	(G-15051)
New London	(G-15065)
North Fairfield	(G-15380)
Norwalk	(G-15561)
Plymouth	(G-16216)
Wakeman	(G-18774)
Willard	(G-19617)

Jackson
Name	ENTRY #
Jackson	(G-12305)
Oak Hill	(G-15618)
Wellston	(G-18997)

Jefferson
Name	ENTRY #
Adena	(G-7)
Amsterdam	(G-607)
Bergholz	(G-1476)
Bloomingdale	(G-1517)
Brilliant	(G-1865)
Dillonvale	(G-10173)
East Springfield	(G-10543)
Hammondsville	(G-11786)
Mingo Junction	(G-14653)
Rayland	(G-16417)
Richmond	(G-16535)
Steubenville	(G-17302)
Stratton	(G-17403)
Toronto	(G-18334)
Wintersville	(G-19807)

Name	ENTRY #
Yorkville	(G-20093)

Knox
Name	ENTRY #
Centerburg	(G-2666)
Danville	(G-9245)
Fredericktown	(G-11178)
Gambier	(G-11347)
Howard	(G-12081)
Mount Vernon	(G-14877)

Lake
Name	ENTRY #
Concord Township	(G-9032)
Concord Twp	(G-9033)
Eastlake	(G-10544)
Grand River	(G-11455)
Kirtland	(G-12457)
Madison	(G-13220)
Mentor	(G-14141)
Mentor On The Lake	(G-14261)
Painesville	(G-15832)
Perry	(G-15958)
Wickliffe	(G-19591)
Willoughby	(G-19640)
Willoughby Hills	(G-19728)
Willowick	(G-19737)

Lawrence
Name	ENTRY #
Chesapeake	(G-2781)
Coal Grove	(G-6826)
Ironton	(G-12280)
Pedro	(G-15937)
Proctorville	(G-16357)
South Point	(G-17080)
Willow Wood	(G-19736)

Licking
Name	ENTRY #
Buckeye Lake	(G-2021)
Croton	(G-9154)
Etna	(G-10731)
Granville	(G-11458)
Heath	(G-11835)
Hebron	(G-11845)
Homer	(G-12075)
Johnstown	(G-12335)
Kirkersville	(G-12455)
Newark	(G-15141)
Pataskala	(G-15920)
Saint Louisville	(G-16668)
Utica	(G-18610)

Logan
Name	ENTRY #
Belle Center	(G-1373)
Bellefontaine	(G-1374)
De Graff	(G-10016)
East Liberty	(G-10507)
Lakeview	(G-12467)
West Liberty	(G-19260)
West Mansfield	(G-19266)

Lorain
Name	ENTRY #
Amherst	(G-585)
Avon	(G-874)
Avon Lake	(G-921)
Columbia Station	(G-6840)
Elyria	(G-10590)
Grafton	(G-11440)
Lagrange	(G-12460)
Lorain	(G-13010)
North Ridgeville	(G-15452)
Oberlin	(G-15637)
Sheffield Village	(G-16883)
South Amherst	(G-17073)
Wellington	(G-18989)

Lucas
Name	ENTRY #
Holland	(G-12005)
Maumee	(G-13870)
Oregon	(G-15721)
Ottawa Hills	(G-15806)
Sylvania	(G-17575)
Toledo	(G-17732)
Waterville	(G-18941)
Whitehouse	(G-19583)

Madison
Name	ENTRY #
London	(G-12992)
Mount Sterling	(G-14873)
Plain City	(G-16178)
West Jefferson	(G-19247)

Mahoning
Name	ENTRY #
Austintown	(G-867)
Beloit	(G-1432)
Berlin Center	(G-1480)
Boardman	(G-1737)
Campbell	(G-2138)
Canfield	(G-2182)
Lowellville	(G-13170)
New Middletown	(G-15074)
New Springfield	(G-15129)
North Jackson	(G-15381)
North Lima	(G-15395)
Petersburg	(G-16081)
Poland	(G-16219)
Sebring	(G-16820)
Struthers	(G-17526)
Youngstown	(G-20094)

Marion
Name	ENTRY #
La Rue	(G-12459)
Marion	(G-13522)
Morral	(G-14840)
Prospect	(G-16363)
Waldo	(G-18782)

Medina
Name	ENTRY #
Brunswick	(G-1967)
Chippewa Lake	(G-2899)
Hinckley	(G-11994)
Lodi	(G-12964)
Medina	(G-14032)
Seville	(G-16837)
Sharon Center	(G-16874)
Spencer	(G-17105)
Valley City	(G-18614)
Wadsworth	(G-18745)
Westfield Center	(G-19451)

Meigs
Name	ENTRY #
Long Bottom	(G-13009)
Middleport	(G-14406)
Pomeroy	(G-16231)
Racine	(G-16371)
Syracuse	(G-17632)

Mercer
Name	ENTRY #
Burkettsville	(G-2058)
Celina	(G-2633)
Coldwater	(G-6827)
Fort Recovery	(G-11113)
Maria Stein	(G-13427)
Rockford	(G-16561)
Saint Henry	(G-16665)

Miami
Name	ENTRY #
Bradford	(G-1806)
Covington	(G-9135)
Piqua	(G-16133)

Name	ENTRY #
Tipp City	(G-17710)
Troy	(G-18347)
West Milton	(G-19268)

Monroe
Name	ENTRY #
Beallsville	(G-1139)
Lewisville	(G-12714)
Sardis	(G-16815)
Woodsfield	(G-19812)

Montgomery
Name	ENTRY #
Beavercreek	(G-1225)
Beavercreek Township	(G-1287)
Brookville	(G-1958)
Centerville	(G-2669)
Clayton	(G-4911)
Dayton	(G-9291)
Englewood	(G-10696)
Farmersville	(G-10983)
Germantown	(G-11399)
Huber Heights	(G-12094)
Kettering	(G-12426)
Miamisburg	(G-14267)
Moraine	(G-14749)
Oakwood	(G-15620)
Trotwood	(G-18344)
Union	(G-18498)
Vandalia	(G-18655)
Washington Township	(G-18938)
West Carrollton	(G-19009)

Morgan
Name	ENTRY #
Malta	(G-13249)
Mc Connelsville	(G-14022)
McConnelsville	(G-14026)
Stockport	(G-17346)

Morrow
Name	ENTRY #
Chesterville	(G-2806)
Marengo	(G-13423)
Mount Gilead	(G-14851)

Muskingum
Name	ENTRY #
Dresden	(G-10230)
Duncan Falls	(G-10498)
East Fultonham	(G-10505)
Frazeysburg	(G-11174)
Nashport	(G-14951)
New Concord	(G-15034)
Roseville	(G-16600)
South Zanesville	(G-17103)
Zanesville	(G-20440)

Noble
Name	ENTRY #
Caldwell	(G-2082)
Dexter City	(G-10170)

Ottawa
Name	ENTRY #
Clay Center	(G-4910)
Elmore	(G-10587)
Genoa	(G-11374)
Lakeside	(G-12464)
Lakeside Marblehead	(G-12466)
Marblehead	(G-13421)
Oak Harbor	(G-15605)
Port Clinton	(G-16237)
Put In Bay	(G-16366)
Rocky Ridge	(G-16566)
Williston	(G-19639)

Paulding
Name	ENTRY #
Antwerp	(G-620)
Oakwood	(G-15623)
Paulding	(G-15927)

Perry
Name	ENTRY #
Crooksville	(G-9153)
Glenford	(G-11433)
New Lexington	(G-15053)
Somerset	(G-17070)
Thornville	(G-17666)

Pickaway
Name	ENTRY #
Ashville	(G-769)
Circleville	(G-4875)
Orient	(G-15760)
Williamsport	(G-19637)

Pike
Name	ENTRY #
Beaver	(G-1141)
Piketon	(G-16108)
Waverly	(G-18965)

Portage
Name	ENTRY #
Atwater	(G-823)
Aurora	(G-824)
Deerfield	(G-10017)
Diamond	(G-10172)
Garrettsville	(G-11352)
Hiram	(G-12002)
Kent	(G-12350)
Mantua	(G-13384)
Mogadore	(G-14669)
Randolph	(G-16372)
Ravenna	(G-16374)
Rootstown	(G-16597)
Streetsboro	(G-17404)
Windham	(G-19803)

Preble
Name	ENTRY #
Camden	(G-2136)
Eaton	(G-10552)
Gratis	(G-11473)
Lewisburg	(G-12711)
New Paris	(G-15075)
West Alexandria	(G-19007)
West Manchester	(G-19265)

Putnam
Name	ENTRY #
Columbus Grove	(G-9029)
Continental	(G-9049)
Fort Jennings	(G-11108)
Glandorf	(G-11432)
Kalida	(G-12346)
Leipsic	(G-12663)
Ottawa	(G-15796)
Ottoville	(G-15808)
Pandora	(G-15889)

Richland
Name	ENTRY #
Bellville	(G-1421)
Butler	(G-2067)
Lexington	(G-12715)
Mansfield	(G-13257)
Ontario	(G-15682)
Shelby	(G-16897)

Ross
Name	ENTRY #
Bainbridge	(G-941)
Chillicothe	(G-2807)
Frankfort	(G-11145)
Kingston	(G-12450)

Sandusky
Name	ENTRY #
Burgoon	(G-2057)

COUNTY/CITY CROSS-REFERENCE

	ENTRY #
Clyde	(G-6808)
Fremont	(G-11182)
Gibsonburg	(G-11402)
Vickery	(G-18733)
Woodville	(G-19823)

Scioto
Franklin Furnace	(G-11168)
Lucasville	(G-13176)
Mc Dermott	(G-14023)
Minford	(G-14652)
New Boston	(G-15011)
Portsmouth	(G-16262)
South Webster	(G-17102)
Wheelersburg	(G-19570)

Seneca
Alvada	(G-567)
Attica	(G-821)
Bascom	(G-993)
Bloomville	(G-1519)
Flat Rock	(G-11103)
Fostoria	(G-11122)
Green Springs	(G-11474)
Kansas	(G-12347)
Tiffin	(G-17671)

Shelby
Anna	(G-616)
Botkins	(G-1751)
Fort Loramie	(G-11110)
Jackson Center	(G-12322)
Russia	(G-16614)
Sidney	(G-16909)

Stark
Alliance	(G-521)
Beach City	(G-1043)
Brewster	(G-1854)
Canal Fulton	(G-2140)
Canton	(G-2219)

	ENTRY #
East Canton	(G-10502)
East Sparta	(G-10540)
Hartville	(G-11814)
Louisville	(G-13093)
Magnolia	(G-13239)
Massillon	(G-13780)
Minerva	(G-14641)
Navarre	(G-14954)
North Canton	(G-15320)
North Lawrence	(G-15392)
Paris	(G-15895)
Uniontown	(G-18506)
Waynesburg	(G-18979)
Wilmot	(G-19797)

Summit
Akron	(G-9)
Barberton	(G-949)
Bath	(G-1033)
Clinton	(G-6807)
Copley	(G-9051)
Coventry Township	(G-9122)
Cuyahoga Falls	(G-9158)
Fairlawn	(G-10937)
Hudson	(G-12100)
Macedonia	(G-13186)
Munroe Falls	(G-14931)
New Franklin	(G-15042)
Northfield	(G-15508)
Norton	(G-15554)
Peninsula	(G-15946)
Richfield	(G-16493)
Silver Lake	(G-16962)
Stow	(G-17350)
Tallmadge	(G-17633)
Twinsburg	(G-18389)

Trumbull
Bristolville	(G-1871)
Brookfield	(G-1896)

	ENTRY #
Burghill	(G-2056)
Cortland	(G-9072)
Fowler	(G-11144)
Girard	(G-11406)
Hubbard	(G-12082)
Kinsman	(G-12452)
Masury	(G-13866)
Mc Donald	(G-14024)
Mesopotamia	(G-14263)
Mineral Ridge	(G-14635)
Newton Falls	(G-15272)
Niles	(G-15280)
Southington	(G-17104)
Vienna	(G-18735)
Warren	(G-18813)
West Farmington	(G-19246)

Tuscarawas
Baltic	(G-944)
Bolivar	(G-1746)
Dennison	(G-10163)
Dover	(G-10175)
Dundee	(G-10499)
Midvale	(G-14489)
Mineral City	(G-14633)
New Philadelphia	(G-15080)
Newcomerstown	(G-15266)
Port Washington	(G-16260)
Strasburg	(G-17401)
Sugarcreek	(G-17543)
Uhrichsville	(G-18487)

Union
Marysville	(G-13605)
Milford Center	(G-14575)
Raymond	(G-16420)
Richwood	(G-16544)

Van Wert
Convoy	(G-9050)
Middle Point	(G-14376)

	ENTRY #
Van Wert	(G-18626)

Vinton
Creola	(G-9141)
Hamden	(G-11687)
Mc Arthur	(G-14015)

Warren
Carlisle	(G-2602)
Franklin	(G-11147)
Kings Mills	(G-12448)
Lebanon	(G-12585)
Maineville	(G-13240)
Mason	(G-13658)
Middletown	(G-14472)
Morrow	(G-14843)
Oregonia	(G-15757)
Pleasant Plain	(G-16214)
South Lebanon	(G-17078)
Springboro	(G-17112)
Waynesville	(G-18982)

Washington
Belpre	(G-1433)
Beverly	(G-1487)
Cutler	(G-9156)
Little Hocking	(G-12943)
Lowell	(G-13167)
Marietta	(G-13430)
Reno	(G-16421)
Vincent	(G-18743)
Waterford	(G-18939)

Wayne
Apple Creek	(G-623)
Burbank	(G-2054)
Creston	(G-9150)
Dalton	(G-9239)
Doylestown	(G-10223)
Fredericksburg	(G-11177)
Kidron	(G-12440)

	ENTRY #
Marshallville	(G-13597)
Mount Eaton	(G-14850)
Orrville	(G-15763)
Rittman	(G-16550)
Shreve	(G-16907)
Smithville	(G-16966)
West Salem	(G-19270)
Wooster	(G-19825)

Williams
Alvordton	(G-570)
Bryan	(G-2000)
Edgerton	(G-10581)
Edon	(G-10585)
Montpelier	(G-14736)
Stryker	(G-17536)
West Unity	(G-19280)

Wood
Bowling Green	(G-1755)
Bradner	(G-1808)
Cygnet	(G-9238)
Grand Rapids	(G-11447)
Luckey	(G-13183)
Millbury	(G-14577)
North Baltimore	(G-15312)
Northwood	(G-15526)
Pemberville	(G-15941)
Perrysburg	(G-15970)
Portage	(G-16261)
Rossford	(G-16606)
Stony Ridge	(G-17347)
Walbridge	(G-18775)
Wayne	(G-18977)

Wyandot
Carey	(G-2596)
Nevada	(G-14969)
Upper Sandusky	(G-18557)

GEOGRAPHIC SECTION

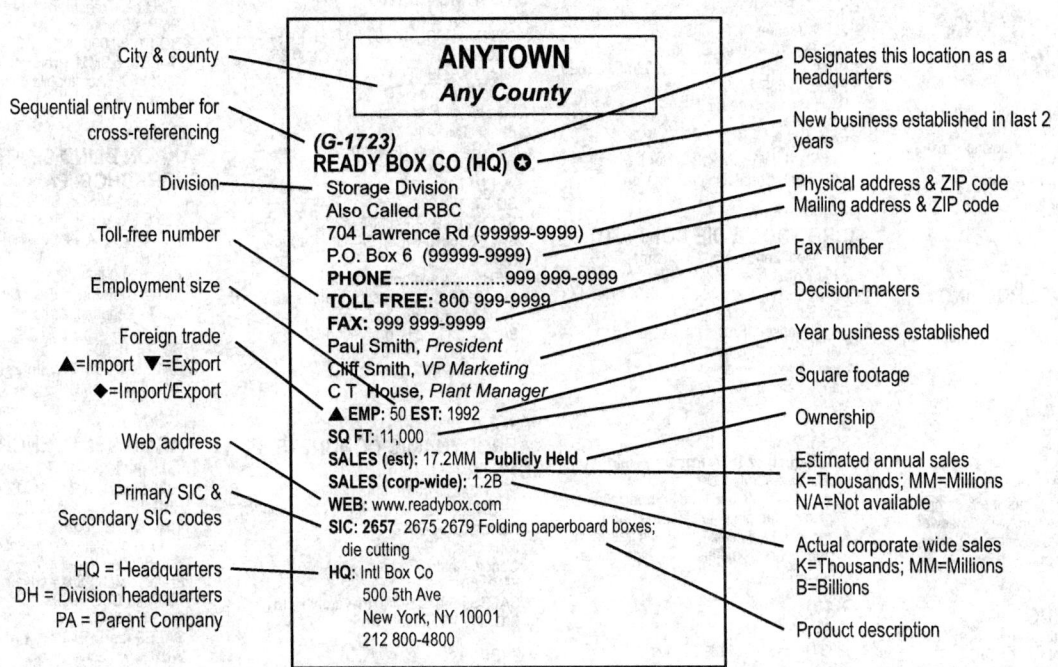

See footnotes for symbols and codes identification.
- This section is in alphabetical order by city.
- Companies are sorted alphabetically under their respective cities.
- To locate cities within a county refer to the County/City Cross Reference Index.

IMPORTANT NOTICE: It is a violation of both federal and state law to transmit an unsolicited advertisement to a facsimile machine. Any user of this product that violates such laws may be subject to civil and criminal penalties which may exceed $500 for each transmission of an unsolicited facsimile. Harris InfoSource provides fax numbers for lawful purposes only and expressly forbids the use of these numbers in any unlawful manner.

Aberdeen
Brown County

(G-1)
BEVERLY HILLS INN LA LLC
1830 Us Highway 52 (45101-2503)
PHONE.................................859 494-9151
Anette Mineer, *Mng Member*
EMP: 30
SALES: 1MM **Privately Held**
SIC: 7011 5812 7231 Hotels & motels; American restaurant; unisex hair salons

(G-2)
DAYTON POWER AND LIGHT COMPANY
Also Called: DPL
Us Rte 52 (45101)
P.O. Box 468 (45101-0468)
PHONE.................................937 549-2641
Fax: 937 549-3774
John Hughes, *Plant Mgr*
Robyn Dillow, *Project Mgr*
Craig Spangler, *Opers Mgr*
Troy Willia, *Safety Mgr*
Cliff Waits, *Production*
EMP: 400
SQ FT: 1,040
SALES (corp-wide): 10.5B **Publicly Held**
WEB: www.waytogo.com
SIC: 4911 ; generation, electric power
HQ: The Dayton Power And Light Company
1065 Woodman Dr
Dayton OH 45432
937 224-6000

Ada
Hardin County

(G-3)
BRENT BURRIS TRUCKING LLC
2445 County Road 75 (45810-9786)
P.O. Box 227 (45810-0227)
PHONE.................................419 759-2020
Brent Burris,
EMP: 50
SALES (est): 4.3MM **Privately Held**
SIC: 4213 Trucking, except local

(G-4)
COMMUNITY HLTH PRFSSIONALS INC
Also Called: Ada Visiting Nurses
1200 S Main St (45810-2616)
PHONE.................................419 634-7443
Fax: 419 634-7447
Claudia Crawford, *Manager*
Vicki Southward, *Manager*
EMP: 25
SALES (corp-wide): 14MM **Privately Held**
SIC: 8082 8051 Visiting nurse service; skilled nursing care facilities
PA: Community Health Professionals, Inc.
1159 Westwood Dr
Van Wert OH 45891
419 238-9223

(G-5)
COUNTY OF HARDIN
Also Called: Ada Lberty Joint Ambulance Dst
530 N Gilbert St (45810-1012)
P.O. Box 204 (45810-0204)
PHONE.................................419 634-7729
Fax: 419 634-5290
Keith Shaw, *Chief*
EMP: 27 **Privately Held**
WEB: www.kenton.com
SIC: 4119 Ambulance service
PA: County Of Hardin
1 Court House Sq Rm 100
Kenton OH 43326
419 674-2205

(G-6)
MIDWEST REHAB INC
118 E Highland Ave (45810-1120)
PHONE.................................419 238-3405
Fax: 419 238-3612
Steve Zuber, *President*
EMP: 60
SALES (est): 2.8MM **Privately Held**
SIC: 8093 Rehabilitation center, outpatient treatment

Adena
Jefferson County

(G-7)
ADENA NH LLC
Also Called: Adena Hlth Rehabilitation Ctr
213 U S Route 250 (43901-7925)
PHONE.................................740 546-3620
Ronald Swartz, *CFO*
Mordecai Rosenberg, *Mng Member*
Lisa Schwartz, *Admin Sec*
Dawn Wozniak, *Exec Sec*
EMP: 40
SALES (est): 450.8K **Privately Held**
SIC: 8051 8322 Skilled nursing care facilities; rehabilitation services

(G-8)
SIENNA HILLS NURSING & REHAB
73841 Pleasant Grove Rd (43901-9514)
PHONE.................................740 546-3013
Oscar Jarnicke, *President*
EMP: 45
SALES (est): 1.2MM **Privately Held**
SIC: 8051 Skilled nursing care facilities

Akron
Summit County

(G-9)
21ST CENTURY FINANCIAL INC
130 Springside Dr Ste 100 (44333-4543)
PHONE.................................330 668-9065
Fax: 330 668-9066
Charlie Parks, *President*
Paul Bullaraii, *Senior VP*
Mike Sarver, *Vice Pres*
Brett Sarver, *VP Finance*
Daniel Dammon, *CIO*
EMP: 40 **EST:** 1996
SALES (est): 15.5MM **Privately Held**
SIC: 6311 Life insurance

Akron - Summit County (G-10)

(G-10)
50 X 20 HOLDING COMPANY INC
779 White Pond Dr (44320-1136)
PHONE..................330 865-4663
Walt Myers, *General Mgr*
Guy Robinson, *Branch Mgr*
EMP: 40
SALES (corp-wide): 80.4MM Privately Held
SIC: 1521 Single-family housing construction
PA: 50 X 20 Holding Company, Inc.
2715 Wise Ave Nw
Canton OH 44708
330 478-4500

(G-11)
A CRANO EXCAVATING INC
1505 Industrial Pkwy (44310-2603)
PHONE..................330 630-1061
Fax: 330 630-1117
James V Riter, *President*
Anthony Riter, *Vice Pres*
Mike Jones, *Opers Staff*
Raymond Riter, *Treasurer*
Jenny Vincent, *Manager*
EMP: 40
SALES (est): 8.6MM Privately Held
SIC: 1623 1794 Oil & gas line & compressor station construction; water & sewer line construction; excavation & grading, building construction

(G-12)
A TO ZOFF CO INC
Also Called: Zoff Heating & Plumbing
1105 Canton Rd (44312-3320)
PHONE..................330 733-7902
Fax: 330 733-2418
Elizabeth Zofchak, *President*
Joseph Zofchak Jr, *Vice Pres*
EMP: 25
SQ FT: 4,800
SALES (est): 3.1MM Privately Held
SIC: 1711 Warm air heating & air conditioning contractor

(G-13)
A-A BLUEPRINT CO INC
2757 Gilchrist Rd (44305-4400)
PHONE..................330 794-8803
Fax: 330 794-8348
John Scalia, *President*
Daisy Scalia, *Principal*
Joseph Brown, *Production*
Velvet Taylor, *Sales Staff*
EMP: 32
SQ FT: 30,000
SALES (est): 5.7MM Privately Held
WEB: www.aablueprint.com
SIC: 2791 7334 2752 2789 Typesetting; photocopying & duplicating services; commercial printing, offset; bookbinding & related work; letterpress printing

(G-14)
ABACUS CHILD CARE CENTERS INC
839 S Arlington St (44306-2452)
P.O. Box 7333 (44306-0333)
PHONE..................330 773-4200
Fax: 330 773-4396
Kim Herburgh, *President*
Talisa Salaam, *Director*
Kimberly Herbuhl, *Director*
EMP: 32
SALES (est): 785.9K Privately Held
SIC: 8351 Child day care services

(G-15)
ACC AUTOMATION CO INC
475 Wolf Ledges Pkwy (44311-1199)
PHONE..................330 928-3821
Frank Rzicznek, *Vice Pres*
William Howe, *Vice Pres*
William T Mars, *Vice Pres*
EMP: 25
SQ FT: 7,500
SALES (est): 2.3MM Privately Held
SIC: 8711 3536 Consulting engineer; cranes, overhead traveling

(G-16)
ACCESS INC
Also Called: AKRON CITIZEN'S COALITION FOR
230 W Market St (44303-2197)
P.O. Box 1007 (44309-1007)
PHONE..................330 535-2999
Fax: 330 535-2999
Silvia Hines, *Exec Dir*
EMP: 30
SQ FT: 9,050
SALES: 1.4MM Privately Held
SIC: 8699 Charitable organization

(G-17)
ACRO TOOL & DIE COMPANY
Also Called: Landscape & Christmas Tree
325 Morgan Ave (44311-2494)
PHONE..................330 773-5173
Fax: 330 773-6317
T T Thompson, *President*
Mark Weigand, *General Mgr*
Steve Wilcox, *Purchasing*
Randy Farnsworth, *QC Mgr*
M A Ross, *Engineer*
▲ EMP: 60
SQ FT: 27,000
SALES (est): 9.1MM Privately Held
WEB: www.acrotool.com
SIC: 3544 3469 0781 0811 Special dies & tools; stamping metal for the trade; landscape services; Christmas tree farm; machine tools, metal cutting type; sheet metalwork

(G-18)
ACRT INC (PA)
1333 Home Ave (44310-2512)
PHONE..................800 622-2562
Michael Weidner, *CEO*
Todd Jones, *Vice Pres*
Cliff Benedict, *Opers Mgr*
Colleen Costa, *Opers Mgr*
Nathan Holmen, *Opers Mgr*
EMP: 35
SQ FT: 7,200
SALES: 68MM Privately Held
WEB: www.acrtinc.com
SIC: 8748 Environmental consultant

(G-19)
ACRT SERVICES INC
1333 Home Ave (44310-2512)
PHONE..................330 945-7500
Michael Weidner, *President*
EMP: 1100
SALES: 80MM Privately Held
SIC: 8748 Business consulting

(G-20)
ACTIONLINK LLC
286 N Cleveland Massillon (44333-2492)
PHONE..................888 737-8757
Bruce Finn, *President*
Miguel Gonzalez, *Regional Mgr*
Delbert Tanner, *COO*
Annette Baker, *QA Dir*
Dede Meilinger, *Human Resources*
EMP: 2000
SQ FT: 12,000
SALES (est): 78MM
SALES (corp-wide): 8.7B Privately Held
WEB: www.actionlink.com
SIC: 8748 Business consulting
PA: Acosta Inc.
6600 Corporate Ctr Pkwy
Jacksonville FL 32216
904 332-7986

(G-21)
ADVANCED AUTO GLASS INC (PA)
44 N Union St (44304-1347)
PHONE..................412 373-6675
Fax: 330 376-6110
Greg Pattakos, *President*
Christina Pattakos, *Vice Pres*
▲ EMP: 29
SQ FT: 4,400
SALES (est): 12.2MM Privately Held
WEB: www.advancedautoglass.com
SIC: 7536 1793 Automotive glass replacement shops; glass & glazing work

(G-22)
ADVANCED ELASTOMER SYSTEMS LP (HQ)
Also Called: AES
388 S Main St Ste 600 (44311-1065)
PHONE..................800 352-7866
Fax: 330 849-5599
Rogerf Sellew, *CEO*
Loic Vivier, *President*
Angie Hall, *Safety Mgr*
Paul Gallagher, *Treasurer*
Charles Foster, *Sales Mgr*
▲ EMP: 150
SQ FT: 150,000
SALES (est): 130.6MM
SALES (corp-wide): 244.3B Publicly Held
WEB: www.santoprene.com
SIC: 5162 5085 Plastics materials & basic shapes; rubber goods, mechanical
PA: Exxon Mobil Corporation
5959 Las Colinas Blvd
Irving TX 75039
972 444-1000

(G-23)
AERODYNAMIC CONCRETE & CNSTR
1726 Massillon Rd (44312-4207)
PHONE..................330 906-7477
Fax: 330 794-9916
John Chafe, *Partner*
Geneie Chafe, *Partner*
EMP: 50
SALES (est): 3.8MM Privately Held
SIC: 1771 Concrete work

(G-24)
AFM EAST ARCHWOOD OIL INC
745 E Archwood Ave (44306-2657)
PHONE..................330 786-1000
EMP: 46 EST: 2010
SALES: 46.2MM Privately Held
SIC: 5172 Whol Petroleum Products

(G-25)
AIRBORN ELECTRONICS INC
2230 Picton Pkwy (44312-4269)
PHONE..................330 245-2630
Brian Kerns, *Purch Mgr*
Brian Selzer, *Administration*
EMP: 27
SALES (corp-wide): 106MM Privately Held
SIC: 5065 Electronic parts
PA: Airborn Electronics, Inc.
3500 Airborn Cir
Georgetown TX 78626
512 863-5585

(G-26)
AKRON AREA COMMERCIAL CLEANING
1264 Copley Rd (44320-2748)
PHONE..................330 434-0767
Fax: 330 434-0102
Annamarie Frederick, *President*
Jeffrey Frederick, *Vice Pres*
EMP: 50
SQ FT: 5,000
SALES: 500K Privately Held
SIC: 7349 Janitorial service, contract basis

(G-27)
AKRON ART MUSEUM
1 S High St (44308-1801)
PHONE..................330 376-9185
Fax: 330 376-1180
Mitchell Kahan, *President*
Sherry Streb, *General Mgr*
Susan Schweitzer, *Vice Pres*
Michael Murphy, *Opers Staff*
Arnold Tunstall, *Credit Mgr*
EMP: 75
SQ FT: 3,312
SALES: 3.1MM Privately Held
WEB: www.akronartmuseum.org
SIC: 8412 Museum

(G-28)
AKRON AUTOMOBILE ASSOCIATION (PA)
Also Called: AKRON AUTOMOBILE CLUB
100 Rosa Parks Dr (44311-2015)
PHONE..................330 762-0631
Fax: 330 798-4136
Brian Thomas, *President*
Daniel Zinni, *Vice Pres*
Gail Lee, *Treasurer*
EMP: 83
SQ FT: 20,000
SALES: 6.9MM Privately Held
SIC: 8699 Automobile owners' association; travel club

(G-29)
AKRON BLIND CENTER & WORKSHOP (PA)
Also Called: VISON SUPPORT SERVICES
325 E Market St (44304-1340)
P.O. Box 1864 (44309-1864)
PHONE..................330 253-2555
Fax: 330 996-4088
Kristen Baysinger, *Exec Dir*
James Lenahan, *Director*
EMP: 53
SQ FT: 15,000
SALES: 91.6K Privately Held
SIC: 8331 Job training services

(G-30)
AKRON CENTL ENGRV MOLD MCH INC
1625 Massillon Rd (44312-4204)
PHONE..................330 794-8704
Fax: 330 794-0571
John Kaeberlein, *President*
Bob Simone, *Plant Mgr*
Frank R Muhl, *Shareholder*
EMP: 50 EST: 1969
SQ FT: 15,000
SALES (est): 10.8MM Privately Held
WEB: www.acemm.com
SIC: 3544 8742 4213 Industrial molds; new products & services consultants; automobiles, transport & delivery

(G-31)
AKRON CITICENTER HOTEL LLC
Also Called: Ramada Plaza Akron
20 W Mill St (44308-1407)
PHONE..................330 253-8355
Fax: 330 434-6619
Jack Saheid, *Manager*
Mohamed Saheid,
EMP: 55
SALES (est): 2.8MM Privately Held
SIC: 1522 Renovation, hotel/motel

(G-32)
AKRON CITY HOSPITAL INC
525 E Market St (44304-1698)
PHONE..................330 253-5046
Fax: 330 375-3050
Barbara Hiney, *Ch of Bd*
Albert F Gilbert, *President*
Beth O'Brien, *Exec VP*
James B Pickering, *Vice Pres*
David H Wilhoite, *Treasurer*
EMP: 2900
SQ FT: 850,000
SALES (est): 152.2MM Privately Held
SIC: 8062 General medical & surgical hospitals

(G-33)
AKRON CMNTY SVC CTR URBAN LEAG
Also Called: Akron Community Serv Center
440 Vernon Odom Blvd (44307-2108)
PHONE..................234 542-4141
Fax: 330 434-2716
Fred Wright, *President*
Tracey Lane, *Director*
EMP: 28
SALES: 1.9MM Privately Held
SIC: 8399 Community action agency

(G-34)
AKRON COCA-COLA BOTTLING CO
1560 Triplett Blvd (44306-3306)
PHONE..................330 784-2653
Matt Cartaglia, *General Mgr*
Tish Cross, *Purch Mgr*
Alisa Morris, *Manager*
Barbara Pfeiffer, *Manager*
Matt Tarcaglia, *Manager*
▲ EMP: 1300 EST: 1985

GEOGRAPHIC SECTION
Akron - Summit County (G-56)

SALES (est): 164.4MM
SALES (corp-wide): 35.4B Publicly Held
WEB: www.colasic.net
SIC: 5149 Soft drinks
HQ: Coca-Cola Refreshments Usa, Inc.
2500 Windy Ridge Pkwy Se
Atlanta GA 30339
770 989-3000

(G-35)
AKRON CONCRETE CORP
910 White Pond Dr (44320-1502)
PHONE..................330 864-1188
Fax: 330 864-1189
David Ochsenhirt, President
Mary Cavalier, Human Resources
EMP: 40
SALES (est): 4.1MM Privately Held
WEB: www.akronconcrete.com
SIC: 1771 Concrete pumping

(G-36)
AKRON COUNCIL OF ENGINEERING
411 Wolf Ledges Pkwy (44311-1028)
P.O. Box 2993 (44309-2993)
PHONE..................330 535-8835
Michael B Dowell, Principal
EMP: 30
SALES (est): 1.1MM
SALES (corp-wide): 2.7MM Privately Held
SIC: 8621 Professional membership organizations
PA: Akron Council Of Engineering & Scientific Societies
411 Wolf Ledges Pkwy # 105
Akron OH 44311
330 535-8835

(G-37)
AKRON ELECTRIC INC
1025 Eaton Ave (44303-1313)
PHONE..................330 745-8891
George Ostich, President
Pragnesh Patel, Engineer
EMP: 65
SQ FT: 13,000
SALES (est): 14.5MM
SALES (corp-wide): 22MM Privately Held
WEB: www.akronelectric.com
SIC: 5063 Boxes & fittings, electrical
PA: Akron Foundry Co.
2728 Wingate Ave
Akron OH 44314
330 745-3101

(G-38)
AKRON ENERGY SYSTEMS LLC
226 Opportunity Pkwy (44307-2232)
PHONE..................330 374-0600
Marc Divis, President
Donald J Hoffman, Chairman
Steve Durgala, Opers Mgr
Paul Conlon, Controller
Robert Douglas, Controller
EMP: 54
SALES (est): 11.1MM Privately Held
SIC: 4961 Steam heating systems (suppliers of heat)

(G-39)
AKRON ERECTORS INC
8098 W Waterloo Rd (44314)
P.O. Box 3710 (44314-0710)
PHONE..................330 745-7100
Dennis Stump, CEO
EMP: 25
SQ FT: 1,000
SALES (est): 1.3MM Privately Held
SIC: 1791 Structural steel erection

(G-40)
AKRON FOUNDRY CO (PA)
2728 Wingate Ave (44314-1300)
P.O. Box 27028 (44319-7028)
PHONE..................330 745-3101
Fax: 330 745-7999
George Ostich, President
Ronald C Allan, Principal
Geraldine Ostich, Vice Pres
Michael Ostich, VP Opers
Gene Jarvis, Purch Agent
EMP: 175 EST: 1969
SQ FT: 100,000
SALES (est): 22MM Privately Held
WEB: www.akronfoundry.com
SIC: 3369 5063 3365 3363 Castings, except die-castings, precision; boxes & fittings, electrical; aluminum foundries; aluminum die-castings

(G-41)
AKRON GENERAL FOUNDATION
Also Called: AKRON GENERAL HEALTH SYSTEM
400 Wabash Ave (44307-2433)
PHONE..................330 344-6888
Karen Bozzelli, President
Janna Ford, Opers-Prdtn-Mfg
Andrea Hinton, Opers-Prdtn-Mfg
Shannon Edelen, Executive Asst
Vicki Brockman, Planning
EMP: 45
SALES: 3MM
SALES (corp-wide): 8B Privately Held
SIC: 8322 Individual & family services
HQ: Akron General Medical Center Inc
1 Akron General Ave
Akron OH 44307
330 344-6000

(G-42)
AKRON GENERAL HEALTH SYSTEM
4125 Medina Rd Ste 104 (44333-4514)
PHONE..................330 665-8200
Doris Volk, Principal
Peggy Blodgett, General Ptnr
EMP: 30
SALES (corp-wide): 8B Privately Held
SIC: 8011 Surgeon
HQ: Akron General Health System
1 Akron General Ave
Akron OH 44307
330 344-6000

(G-43)
AKRON GENERAL MEDICAL CENTER (DH)
Also Called: Edwin Shaw Rehabilitation Hosp
1 Akron General Ave (44307-2432)
PHONE..................330 344-6000
Fax: 330 376-4835
F William Steere, Ch of Bd
Robert Stefanko, Vice Chairman
Carl R Martino, Ch Radiology
William Gardner, Exec VP
Penny Walberg, Senior VP
EMP: 56
SQ FT: 1,027,000
SALES: 544.4MM
SALES (corp-wide): 8B Privately Held
SIC: 8322 Rehabilitation services
HQ: Akron General Health System
1 Akron General Ave
Akron OH 44307
330 344-6000

(G-44)
AKRON GENERAL MEDICAL CENTER
224 W Exchange St Ste 330 (44302-1715)
PHONE..................330 344-1980
David Baumgardner, Principal
Rex Street, CFO
Denise Mercer, Office Mgr
Eric Jenison, Med Doctor
Mark Leeson, Med Doctor
EMP: 103
SQ FT: 79,879
SALES (corp-wide): 8B Privately Held
SIC: 8062 General medical & surgical hospitals
HQ: Akron General Medical Center Inc
1 Akron General Ave
Akron OH 44307
330 344-6000

(G-45)
AKRON GENERAL MEDICAL CENTER
Akron Gen Employee Hlth Dept
1 Akron General Ave (44307-2432)
PHONE..................330 344-1444
Ken Bulen MD, Director
EMP: 103
SALES (corp-wide): 8B Privately Held
SIC: 8062 General medical & surgical hospitals
HQ: Akron General Medical Center Inc
1 Akron General Ave
Akron OH 44307
330 344-6000

(G-46)
AKRON GENERAL MEDICAL CENTER
Also Called: Akron Gen Hlth & Wellness Ctr
4125 Medina Rd Ste 1 (44333-4505)
PHONE..................330 665-8000
Doug Ribley, Manager
EMP: 200
SALES (corp-wide): 8B Privately Held
SIC: 8062 8093 7991 General medical & surgical hospitals; specialty outpatient clinics; health club
HQ: Akron General Medical Center Inc
1 Akron General Ave
Akron OH 44307
330 344-6000

(G-47)
AKRON HARDWARE CONSULTANTS INC (PA)
1100 Killian Rd (44312-4730)
PHONE..................330 644-7167
Fax: 330 644-6368
Roy Crute, President
Thomas Orihel, COO
Bill Jubara, Vice Pres
Randy Floyd, Facilities Dir
Tim Kane, Warehouse Mgr
EMP: 60
SQ FT: 28,000
SALES (est): 27.6MM Privately Held
SIC: 5072 Builders' hardware

(G-48)
AKRON MANAGEMENT CORP
Also Called: Firestone Country Club
452 E Warner Rd (44319-1925)
PHONE..................330 644-8441
Fax: 330 645-2556
Mark Gore, General Mgr
Larry Napora, Director
Dick Robbins,
EMP: 260 EST: 1950
SQ FT: 3,700
SALES (est): 15.4MM
SALES (corp-wide): 433.7MM Privately Held
WEB: www.firestonecountryclub.com
SIC: 7997 5941 5812 5813 Golf club, membership; golf goods & equipment; eating places; cocktail lounge
HQ: Clubcorp Usa, Inc.
3030 Lyndon B Johnson Fwy
Dallas TX 75234
972 243-6191

(G-49)
AKRON NEONATOLOGY INC
300 Locust St (44302-1821)
PHONE..................330 379-9473
Anand D Kantak MD, President
William H Considine, Principal
EMP: 30
SALES (est): 1.2MM Publicly Held
WEB: www.pediatrix.com
SIC: 8011 Specialized medical practitioners, except internal; physical medicine, physician/surgeon; pediatrician
PA: Mednax, Inc.
1301 Concord Ter
Sunrise FL 33323

(G-50)
AKRON PLASTIC SURGEONS INC
Also Called: Parker, Michael G MD
1 Park West Blvd Ste 350 (44320-4226)
P.O. Box 1706, Stow (44224-0706)
PHONE..................330 253-9161
Fax: 330 253-5933
James Lehman Jr, President
Michael G Parker MD, Principal
Douglas S Wagner MD, Principal
Frank Quirk, Corp Secy
M D Tantri MD, Vice Pres
EMP: 37
SQ FT: 6,800
SALES (est): 3.9MM Privately Held
WEB: www.akronplasticsurgeons.com
SIC: 8011 Plastic surgeon

(G-51)
AKRON PUBLIC SCHOOL MAINT SVCS
Also Called: Facility Services
515 Grant St (44311-1109)
PHONE..................330 761-2640
Mike Critchfield, Principal
John Pierson, Treasurer
Ken Phares, Administration
EMP: 62
SALES (est): 1.1MM Privately Held
SIC: 7349 Building maintenance services

(G-52)
AKRON PUBLIC SCHOOLS
70 N Broadway St (44308-1911)
PHONE..................330 761-1660
David James, Exec Dir
EMP: 300
SALES (corp-wide): 259MM Privately Held
WEB: www.akronschools.com
SIC: 1541 Industrial buildings & warehouses
PA: Akron Public Schools
70 N Broadway St
Akron OH 44308
330 761-1661

(G-53)
AKRON RADIOLOGY INC
525 E Market St (44304-1619)
PHONE..................330 375-3043
Fax: 330 375-7932
Edward Bury, President
Sue Pavloff, Vice Pres
Darrell Berger, Engineer
Kimberly Holm, Marketing Staff
Frederick Kraus MD, Med Doctor
EMP: 28
SALES (est): 3.8MM Privately Held
WEB: www.akronradiology.com
SIC: 8011 Radiologist

(G-54)
AKRON RUBBER DEV LAB INC (PA)
2887 Gilchrist Rd (44305-4415)
PHONE..................330 794-6600
Fax: 330 794-6610
Charles R Samples, CEO
Jerry Leyden, President
Tim Samples, Principal
Jim Drummond, Business Mgr
Bill Sanderson, Safety Mgr
EMP: 65
SALES (est): 17.2MM Privately Held
WEB: www.ardl-india.com
SIC: 8731 Commercial research laboratory

(G-55)
AKRON SCHOOL TRNSP SVCS
500 E North St (44304-1220)
PHONE..................330 761-1390
Fax: 330 761-1399
Kathy Kiel, Principal
EMP: 80
SALES (est): 1.6MM Privately Held
SIC: 4151 School buses

(G-56)
AKRON SUMMIT CMNTY ACTION AGCY
Also Called: Foster Grandparent Program
670 W Exchange St (44302-1300)
PHONE..................330 572-8532
Fax: 330 253-8836
Sonia Williams, Manager
Rebecca Davison, Personnel Assit
Jessica Hurst, Assistant
EMP: 150
SALES (corp-wide): 22.1MM Privately Held
WEB: www.ascainc.org
SIC: 8399 8361 Antipoverty board; group foster home
PA: Akron Summit Community Action Agency
55 E Mill St
Akron OH 44308
330 376-7730

Akron - Summit County (G-57)

GEOGRAPHIC SECTION

(G-57)
AKRON SUMMIT CMNTY ACTION AGCY
1335 Massillon Rd (44306-4137)
PHONE..................330 733-2290
Fax: 330 733-2291
Alice Owen, *Manager*
EMP: 56
SALES (corp-wide): 22.1MM **Privately Held**
SIC: 8399 8351 Antipoverty board; child day care services
PA: Akron Summit Community Action Agency
55 E Mill St
Akron OH 44308
330 376-7730

(G-58)
AKRON SUMMIT CMNTY ACTION AGCY (PA)
55 E Mill St (44308-1405)
P.O. Box 2000 (44309-2000)
PHONE..................330 376-7730
Fax: 330 996-4040
Malcolm J Costa, *President*
Gay Evans, *General Mgr*
Malcolm Costa, *Vice Pres*
Richard Nelson, *Financial Exec*
Allyson Lee, *Human Res Dir*
EMP: 331
SQ FT: 8,908
SALES (est): 22.1MM **Privately Held**
WEB: www.ascainc.org
SIC: 8399 Antipoverty board

(G-59)
AKRON WOMANS CITY CLUB INC
732 W Exchange St (44302-1308)
PHONE..................330 762-6261
Fax: 330 762-5744
Judith Wishnek, *General Mgr*
Diane Vukovich, *Asst Treas*
Patricia Mitchen, *Office Mgr*
Patti Mitchen, *Office Mgr*
EMP: 25
SQ FT: 32,897
SALES: 925.4K **Privately Held**
SIC: 8641 Social club, membership

(G-60)
AKRON ZOOLOGICAL PARK
500 Edgewood Ave (44307-2199)
PHONE..................330 375-2550
Fax: 330 375-2575
L Patricia Simmons, *CEO*
Patricia Waickman, *Senior VP*
Charles Craig, *Vice Pres*
Doug Piekarz, *Vice Pres*
Carl Roxbury, *Vice Pres*
EMP: 50
SQ FT: 35,000
SALES: 12.1MM **Privately Held**
WEB: www.akronzoo.com
SIC: 8422 Zoological garden, noncommercial

(G-61)
AKRON-CANTON REGIONAL FOODBANK (PA)
350 Opportunity Pkwy (44307-2234)
PHONE..................330 535-6900
Fax: 330 996-5337
Daniel R Flowers, *CEO*
Richard Wilson, *Vice Chairman*
Peggy Susniskas, *COO*
Laura Bennett, *Vice Pres*
Patricia Gibbs, *Treasurer*
EMP: 50
SQ FT: 87,000
SALES: 38.4MM **Privately Held**
WEB: www.akroncantonfoodbank.com
SIC: 8699 Charitable organization

(G-62)
AKRON-SUMMIT CONVENTION
Also Called: John S Knight Center
77 E Mill St (44308-1459)
PHONE..................330 374-7560
Fax: 330 374-8971
Gregg Mervis, *President*
Vicky Killian, *Finance Dir*
Raven Gayheart, *Sales Mgr*
Jill Raymond, *Sales Mgr*

Jennifer Eckman, *Office Mgr*
EMP: 35 **EST:** 1973
SALES: 6.8MM **Privately Held**
WEB: www.johnsknightcenter.com
SIC: 7389 Convention & show services; tourist information bureau

(G-63)
ALBERT GUARNIERI & CO
61 S Seiberling St (44305-4216)
PHONE..................330 794-9834
EMP: 56
SALES (corp-wide): 30MM **Privately Held**
SIC: 5194 5145 5141 Tobacco & tobacco products; confectionery; groceries, general line
PA: Albert Guarnieri & Co.
1133 E Market St
Warren OH 44483
330 394-5636

(G-64)
ALCO-CHEM INC (PA)
45 N Summit St (44308-1933)
PHONE..................330 253-3535
Fax: 330 253-9219
Anthony Mandala Jr, *President*
Bart Mandala, *Vice Pres*
Robert Mandala, *Vice Pres*
John Mandala, *Opers Mgr*
Joanne Anderson, *Accounts Mgr*
▲ **EMP:** 34
SQ FT: 22,000
SALES (est): 26.7MM **Privately Held**
WEB: www.alco-chem.com
SIC: 5087 2869 2842 Janitors' supplies; industrial organic chemicals; specialty cleaning, polishes & sanitation goods

(G-65)
ALCOHOL DRUG ADDICTION
100 W Cedar St Ste 300 (44307-2572)
PHONE..................330 564-4075
Tom Leffler, *Principal*
William Zumbar, *Senior VP*
Gerald Craig, *Manager*
EMP: 57 **Privately Held**
SIC: 9431 6513 Administration of public health programs; apartment building operators

(G-66)
ALL STAR TRAINING CLUB
3108 Sparrows Crst (44319-5401)
PHONE..................330 352-5602
Catherine Lancianese, *Principal*
EMP: 25
SALES (est): 395.3K **Privately Held**
SIC: 8322 Individual & family services

(G-67)
ALLAN HUNTER CONSTRUCTION LLC
931 Evans Ave (44305-1041)
P.O. Box 1552 (44309-1552)
PHONE..................330 634-9082
Chris Moore, *Owner*
EMP: 25 **EST:** 2007
SQ FT: 4,000
SALES: 2.6MM **Privately Held**
SIC: 1521 4212 New construction, single-family houses; local trucking, without storage

(G-68)
ALLIED INFOTECH CORPORATION
2170 Romig Rd (44320-3879)
PHONE..................330 745-8529
Michael Zulia, *President*
Sam Vulia, *Opers Staff*
Scott Thayer, *Sales Mgr*
Sam Zulia, *Sales Mgr*
Pam Fretz, *Info Tech Mgr*
EMP: 51
SQ FT: 18,000
SALES (est): 5.1MM **Privately Held**
WEB: www.alliedinfotech.com
SIC: 7389 Document storage service

(G-69)
ALMOST FAMILY INC
1225 E Waterloo Rd (44306-3805)
PHONE..................330 724-7545
Fax: 330 724-8727

Renea Thompson, *Branch Mgr*
EMP: 30
SALES (corp-wide): 796.9MM **Publicly Held**
SIC: 8082 Home health care services
PA: Almost Family, Inc.
9510 Ormsby Station Rd
Louisville KY 40223
502 891-1000

(G-70)
ALPHA PHI ALPHA HOMES INC
730 Callis Dr (44311-1313)
PHONE..................330 376-2115
Fax: 330 376-9905
Beverly Lomax, *General Mgr*
EMP: 57
SALES (corp-wide): 5.6MM **Privately Held**
SIC: 7299 6513 Apartment locating service; apartment building operators
PA: Alpha Phi Alpha Homes Incorporated
662 Wolf Ledges Pkwy
Akron OH
330 376-8787

(G-71)
AMERICAN MED
1265 Triplett Blvd (44306-3162)
PHONE..................330 762-8999
Jerry Key, *CEO*
Kim Hamilton, *Manager*
EMP: 300
SALES (corp-wide): 7.8B **Publicly Held**
WEB: www.amr-inc.com
SIC: 4119 8741 Ambulance service; management services
HQ: American Medical Response, Inc.
6363 S Fiddlers Green Cir # 1400
Greenwood Village CO 80111

(G-72)
AMERICAN NATIONAL RED CROSS
501 W Market St (44303-1842)
PHONE..................330 535-6131
Craig Chaffinch, *CEO*
Margie Green, *Exec Dir*
EMP: 33
SALES (corp-wide): 2.5B **Privately Held**
WEB: www.redcross.org
SIC: 8322 Individual & family services
PA: The American National Red Cross
430 17th St Nw
Washington DC 20006
202 737-8300

(G-73)
AMERICAS BEST MEDICAL EQP CO
Also Called: Americas Best Medical Eqp
1566 Akron Peninsula Rd # 2 (44313-7980)
PHONE..................330 928-0884
Fax: 330 928-5250
Jeffrey E Gregory, *President*
Sharon Gregory, *Vice Pres*
EMP: 40
SQ FT: 12,000
SALES (est): 6.4MM **Privately Held**
SIC: 5169 7352 5047 Oxygen; invalid supplies rental; medical & hospital equipment

(G-74)
AMERIPRISE FINANCIAL SVCS INC
3333 Massillon Rd Ste 110 (44312-5993)
PHONE..................330 494-9300
Kile Lewis, *Chairman*
EMP: 50
SALES (corp-wide): 12B **Publicly Held**
WEB: www.amps.com
SIC: 6282 Investment advisory service
HQ: Ameriprise Financial Services Inc.
500 2nd St S Ste 101
La Crosse WI 54601
608 783-2639

(G-75)
AMPERSAND GROUP LLC
1946 S Arlington St (44306-4285)
PHONE..................330 379-0044
Jim Martin, *Manager*
Todd Mellon,

EMP: 46
SALES: 13.6MM **Privately Held**
SIC: 5961 7389 ; financial services

(G-76)
ANESTHESIOLOGY ASSOC OF AKRON
224 W Exchange St Ste 220 (44302-1726)
PHONE..................330 344-6401
Fax: 330 384-1714
Paul Korytkowski, *President*
Joseph Kirk, *Anesthesiology*
Eric Regula, *Anesthesiology*
Dr Michael Di Cioccio,
Kathryn Leininger, *Hematology*
EMP: 50
SALES (est): 4.6MM **Privately Held**
SIC: 8011 Anesthesiologist

(G-77)
ANSTINE DRYWALL INC
2215 E Waterloo Rd # 403 (44312-3857)
PHONE..................330 784-3867
Fax: 330 784-3965
Danny Anstine, *President*
EMP: 30 **EST:** 1987
SALES (est): 2.8MM **Privately Held**
SIC: 1742 Drywall

(G-78)
APPLE GROWTH PARTNERS INC (PA)
1540 W Market St (44313-7114)
PHONE..................330 867-7350
Harold Gaar, *CEO*
Ivan Mahovlic, *President*
Rick Archer, *Principal*
James Gornik, *Principal*
Sean McKiernan, *Principal*
▲ **EMP:** 70
SQ FT: 2,500
SALES (est): 20.1MM **Privately Held**
SIC: 8748 8721 Business consulting; certified public accountant

(G-79)
ARCADIA SERVICES INC
Also Called: Arcadia Health Care
1650 W Market St Ste 27 (44313-7007)
PHONE..................330 869-9520
Fax: 330 869-9524
Kathy Kozachenko, *Manager*
EMP: 51
SALES (corp-wide): 156.6MM **Privately Held**
SIC: 7363 8082 Medical help service; home health care services
PA: Arcadia Services, Inc.
20750 Civic Center Dr # 100
Southfield MI 48076
248 352-7530

(G-80)
ARCADIS US INC
222 S Main St (44308-1533)
PHONE..................330 434-1995
Gary Johnson, *Branch Mgr*
Dan Furgason, *Info Tech Dir*
EMP: 61
SALES (corp-wide): 2.6B **Privately Held**
SIC: 8711 Sanitary engineers
HQ: Arcadis U.S., Inc.
630 Plaza Dr Ste 200
Highlands Ranch CO 80129
720 344-3500

(G-81)
ARDMORE INC
981 E Market St (44305-2443)
PHONE..................330 535-2601
Fax: 330 535-7911
Michael Sharphouse, *Research*
Deborah Dutton, *Finance*
Sarah Menke, *Human Res Mgr*
Joyce Fox, *Manager*
Tonia Morris, *Manager*
EMP: 180 **EST:** 1975
SQ FT: 12,000
SALES: 5.9MM **Privately Held**
SIC: 8361 8699 Home for the mentally retarded; home for the physically handicapped; charitable organization

GEOGRAPHIC SECTION
Akron - Summit County (G-104)

(G-82)
AT&T CORP
3890 Medina Rd Ste B (44333-2470)
PHONE 330 665-3100
Derek Swan, *Branch Mgr*
EMP: 69
SALES (corp-wide): 160.5B **Publicly Held**
WEB: www.sbc.com
SIC: 4813 Local & long distance telephone communications
HQ: At&T Corp.
   1 At&T Way
   Bedminster NJ 07921
   800 403-3302

(G-83)
AT&T CORP
45 E Market St (44308-2009)
PHONE 330 752-7776
Randall Stephenson, *Branch Mgr*
Chad Elwell, *Manager*
EMP: 109
SALES (corp-wide): 160.5B **Publicly Held**
SIC: 4813 Local & long distance telephone communications
HQ: At&T Corp.
   1 At&T Way
   Bedminster NJ 07921
   800 403-3302

(G-84)
ATHENS MOLD AND MACHINE INC
1461 Industrial Pkwy (44310-2601)
PHONE 740 593-6613
Fax: 740 594-7355
Jack D Thornton, *President*
Mark Thornton, *Vice Pres*
David Wickham, *Purch Agent*
Larry Pinkerton, *Sales Staff*
Marcia Wilson, *Office Mgr*
EMP: 81
SQ FT: 70,000
SALES (est): 10.5MM **Privately Held**
SIC: 3544 3599 7692 Special dies & tools; machine shop, jobbing & repair; welding shop

(G-85)
AUTOMOTIVE DISTRIBUTORS CO INC
1329 E Archwood Ave (44306-2832)
PHONE 330 785-7290
Fax: 330 785-7295
Robert Yeoman, *Owner*
Carol Moorehead, *Financial Exec*
Jeff Lang, *Manager*
Sam Watkins, *Manager*
EMP: 40
SALES (corp-wide): 132.8MM **Privately Held**
WEB: www.adw1.com
SIC: 5013 Automotive supplies
PA: Automotive Distributors Co., Inc.
   2981 Morse Rd
   Columbus OH 43231
   614 476-1315

(G-86)
AXESSPOINTE CMNTY HLTH CTR INC (PA)
Also Called: Axesspointe Community Hlth Ctr
1400 S Arlington St # 38 (44306-3750)
P.O. Box 7695 (44306-0695)
PHONE 330 724-5471
Fax: 330 724-5694
Mark Batson, *CEO*
Pat Divoky, *Ch of Bd*
Gary Collins, *CFO*
Ron Reel, *Accounting Mgr*
Michelle Moreno, *Family Practiti*
EMP: 25
SALES (est): 4.3MM **Privately Held**
SIC: 8011 Clinic, operated by physicians

(G-87)
B F G FEDERAL CREDIT UNION (PA)
445 S Main St Ste B (44311-1056)
PHONE 330 374-2990
Fax: 330 374-2984
Owen Dibert, *Ch of Bd*
Betty Phillips, *President*
Cheryl Foster, *Exec VP*
Paul Bush, *Credit Mgr*
EMP: 64
SQ FT: 29,000
SALES: 4.5MM **Privately Held**
WEB: www.bfgcu.net
SIC: 6061 Federal credit unions

(G-88)
B G TRUCKING & CONSTRUCTION
1280 Superior Ave (44307-1131)
P.O. Box 308, North Lima (44452-0308)
PHONE 330 620-8734
Fax: 330 535-6258
Bernard Lewis, *President*
Alicia Lewis, *Corp Secy*
Geneva Lewis, *Vice Pres*
EMP: 50
SALES (est): 9MM **Privately Held**
SIC: 1771 5211 Blacktop (asphalt) work; concrete repair; masonry materials & supplies

(G-89)
BARBICAS CONSTRUCTION CO
124 Darrow Rd Ste 1 (44305-3835)
PHONE 330 733-9101
Fax: 330 864-9059
Carla Barbicas, *President*
Elia Barbicas, *Corp Secy*
Joe Vayak, *Vice Pres*
Alan Potter, *Safety Dir*
EMP: 36
SQ FT: 9,600
SALES: 9.1MM **Privately Held**
SIC: 1771 1611 Blacktop (asphalt) work; surfacing & paving; grading; highway & street paving contractor; general contractor, highway & street construction

(G-90)
BATH MANOR LIMITED PARTNERSHIP
Also Called: BATH MANOR SPECIAL CARE CENTRE
2330 Smith Rd (44333-2927)
PHONE 330 836-1006
Fax: 330 836-1870
Morton J Weisburg, *President*
Vernie Venture, *Education*
EMP: 50
SALES: 10MM
SALES (corp-wide): 68.5MM **Privately Held**
SIC: 8051 Skilled nursing care facilities
PA: Saber Healthcare Group, L.L.C.
   26691 Richmond Rd Frnt
   Bedford OH 44146
   216 292-5706

(G-91)
BATTERED WOMENS SHELTER (PA)
Also Called: B W S
974 E Market St (44305-2445)
PHONE 330 374-0740
Fax: 330 374-0119
Tiffany Wiles, *Finance*
Terri Heckman, *Director*
EMP: 75
SQ FT: 5,542
SALES: 2.5MM **Privately Held**
WEB: www.scmcbws.org
SIC: 8322 Emergency shelters

(G-92)
BBS & ASSOCIATES INC
130 Springside Dr Ste 200 (44333-4553)
PHONE 330 665-5227
Dale Berkey, *President*
Jim Alexander, *Vice Pres*
Phyllis Laskowski, *CFO*
Amy Nicely, *Sr Project Mgr*
Kim Lint, *Manager*
EMP: 32
SALES (est): 2.6MM **Privately Held**
SIC: 7389 7311 8748 Fund raising organizations; advertising agencies; business consulting

(G-93)
BCG SYSTEMS THAT WORK INC
Also Called: B C G Systems
1735 Merriman Rd Ste 3000 (44313-9005)
PHONE 330 864-4816
Fax: 330 864-6003
Mark Goodson, *President*
Jim Coats, *Vice Pres*
Richard Spann, *Engineer*
Jason Kline, *Sales Staff*
Dustin Miller, *Manager*
EMP: 35
SQ FT: 12,000
SALES (est): 5.6MM **Privately Held**
WEB: www.systemsthatwork.com
SIC: 7379 Computer related consulting services
PA: Brockman, Coats, Gedelian & Co.
   1735 Merriman Rd Ste 300
   Akron OH

(G-94)
BDO USA LLP
301 Springside Dr (44333-2434)
PHONE 330 668-9696
Fax: 330 668-2538
James Dannemiller, *Partner*
Jerry Justice, *Manager*
Diana Rogers, *Technology*
Jennifer Rickenbacker, *Executive Asst*
Kimberly Nelson, *Admin Asst*
EMP: 90
SALES (corp-wide): 1.2B **Privately Held**
SIC: 8721 Accounting, auditing & bookkeeping
PA: Bdo Usa, Llp
   330 N Wabash Ave Ste 3200
   Chicago IL 60611
   312 240-1236

(G-95)
BEACON COMPANY (PA)
Also Called: Northeast Furniture Rental
2350 Gilchrist Rd (44305-3810)
PHONE 330 733-8322
Fax: 330 733-9382
Jerry Karkowski, *President*
Jean Conrad, *Corp Secy*
Rick Macken, *Controller*
EMP: 26
SQ FT: 12,000
SALES (est): 4.3MM **Privately Held**
SIC: 7359 5712 Furniture rental; furniture stores

(G-96)
BELL MUSIC COMPANY
533 W Market St (44303-1892)
PHONE 330 376-6337
Fax: 330 376-3776
EMP: 25
SQ FT: 12,000
SALES (est): 1.3MM **Privately Held**
SIC: 7993 Amusement Device Operator

(G-97)
BENEFICIAL BUILDING SERVICES (PA)
1830 13th St Sw (44314-2907)
PHONE 330 848-2556
Fax: 330 848-3554
James Lawson, *President*
Paul Carnifac, *Vice Pres*
Tom Lesiczka, *Vice Pres*
Jim Neininger, *Vice Pres*
EMP: 55
SQ FT: 500
SALES (est): 1.6MM **Privately Held**
SIC: 7349 Building cleaning service; building maintenance, except repairs; janitorial service, contract basis; window cleaning

(G-98)
BERMEX INC
1333 Home Ave (44310-2512)
PHONE 330 945-7500
Todd Jones, *President*
David Mack, *Manager*
EMP: 271
SALES: 12.3MM
SALES (corp-wide): 68MM **Privately Held**
SIC: 7389 Meter readers, remote

PA: Acrt, Inc.
   1333 Home Ave
   Akron OH 44310
   800 622-2562

(G-99)
BERNARD BUSSON BUILDER
Also Called: Timbertop Apartments
1551 Treetop Trl (44313-4986)
PHONE 330 929-4926
Fax: 330 929-3629
Bernard D Busson, *Owner*
EMP: 41
SQ FT: 4,000
SALES (est): 3.5MM **Privately Held**
SIC: 1522 1531 8741 1521 Apartment building construction; speculative builder, multi-family dwellings; management services; single-family housing construction

(G-100)
BERNS ONEILL SEC & SAFETY LLC
Also Called: Boss Investigations
1000 N Main St (44310-1452)
PHONE 330 374-9133
Dan O'Neill, *Mng Member*
Cheryl Zehnder, *Manager*
Maurice Berns,
EMP: 30
SQ FT: 2,000
SALES (est): 55K
SALES (corp-wide): 6.4MM **Privately Held**
SIC: 7361 Placement agencies
PA: Professional Placement Services Llc
   34200 Solon Rd
   Solon OH 44139
   440 914-0090

(G-101)
BEST WESTERN EXECUTIVE INN
2677 Gilchrist Rd Unit 1 (44305-4439)
PHONE 330 794-1050
Fax: 330 794-8495
Dilu Dinani, *Partner*
Haider Ladha, *Partner*
EMP: 25
SQ FT: 73,823
SALES (est): 1.3MM **Privately Held**
SIC: 7011 Hotels

(G-102)
BIO-MDCAL APPLCATIONS OHIO INC
Also Called: Greater Akron Dialysis Center
345 Bishop St (44307-2401)
PHONE 330 376-4905
Fax: 330 376-4060
Dottie Sample, *Exec Dir*
Natthavat Tanphaichitr, *Nephrology*
EMP: 28
SQ FT: 2,000
SALES (corp-wide): 20.9B **Privately Held**
WEB: www.fresenius.org
SIC: 8092 Kidney dialysis centers
HQ: Bio-Medical Applications Of Ohio, Inc.
   920 Winter St
   Waltham MA 02451

(G-103)
BLICK CLINIC INC (PA)
640 W Market St (44303-1465)
PHONE 330 762-5425
Fax: 330 702-4019
Karin Loper-Orr, *President*
Michelle Clark, *Purchasing*
Gayle Breedlove, *Bookkeeper*
Larry Gladden, *Human Res Mgr*
Judy Colvin, *Med Doctor*
EMP: 215
SQ FT: 15,600
SALES: 14.1MM **Privately Held**
WEB: www.blickclinic.org
SIC: 8093 8322 Mental health clinic, outpatient; individual & family services

(G-104)
BLICK CLINIC INC
682 W Market St (44303-1414)
PHONE 330 762-5425
Dr G Lafoarme, *Exec Dir*
EMP: 60
SQ FT: 11,400

Akron - Summit County (G-105)

GEOGRAPHIC SECTION

SALES (corp-wide): 14.1MM **Privately Held**
WEB: www.blickclinic.org
SIC: **8093** Mental health clinic, outpatient
PA: Blick Clinic, Inc.
   640 W Market St
   Akron OH 44303
   330 762-5425

(G-105)
BLUELINX CORPORATION
550 Munroe Falls Rd (44305)
P.O. Box 218, Mogadore (44260-0218)
PHONE.................................330 794-1141
Bob Jacobus, *Manager*
EMP: 30
SALES (corp-wide): 32.6B **Publicly Held**
WEB: www.bluelinx.com
SIC: **5031** Building materials, exterior; doors & windows; building materials, interior
HQ: Bluelinx Corporation
   4300 Wildwood Pkwy
   Atlanta GA 30339
   770 953-7000

(G-106)
BOGIE INDUSTRIES INC LTD
Also Called: Weaver Fab & Finishing
1100 Home Ave (44310-3504)
PHONE.................................330 745-3105
Jim Lauer, *President*
Marian Lauer, *Owner*
Fuzzy Helton, *Vice Pres*
Diana Helton, *Office Mgr*
EMP: 38
SQ FT: 40,000
SALES (est): 10.7MM **Privately Held**
WEB: www.weaverfab.com
SIC: **3444** 1799 3399 Sheet metalwork; coating of metal structures at construction site; powder, metal

(G-107)
BRAKEFIRE INCORPORATED
Also Called: Akron Welding & Spring Co
451 Kennedy Rd (44305-4423)
PHONE.................................330 535-4343
Kenneth G May, *Manager*
EMP: 34
SALES (corp-wide): 26.5MM **Privately Held**
WEB: www.silcofireprotection.com
SIC: **5087** Firefighting equipment
PA: Brakefire, Incorporated
   10765 Medallion Dr
   Cincinnati OH 45241
   513 733-5655

(G-108)
BRAUN & STEIDL ARCHITECTS INC (HQ)
Also Called: Studio of Prime Ae Group
1041 W Market St (44313-7143)
PHONE.................................330 864-7755
Fax: 330 864-3691
Kumar Buvanendaran, *President*
EMP: 25
SQ FT: 7,000
SALES (est): 3.5MM **Privately Held**
WEB: www.bsa-net.com
SIC: **8712** Architectural engineering

(G-109)
BRENNAN MANNA & DIAMOND LLC (PA)
75 E Market St (44308-2010)
PHONE.................................330 253-5060
Fax: 330 253-1977
Nancy Grams, *President*
Rita Putaturo, *Marketing Mgr*
Joy Westfall, *Office Mgr*
Dee Botzer, *Manager*
Danny Wyszynski, *Technology*
EMP: 50
SQ FT: 6,800
SALES (est): 7.9MM **Privately Held**
WEB: www.bmdllc.com
SIC: **8111** General practice law office

(G-110)
BRIDGESTONE RESEARCH LLC
Also Called: Bridgestone Americas Center
1655 S Main St (44301-2035)
PHONE.................................330 379-7570
H Mouri, *President*
Hank Hara, *Exec VP*
Yutaka Yamaguchi, *Vice Pres*
Chris Olson, *Opers Staff*
Ray Madonia, *Accountant*
EMP: 2623
SALES (est): 98.4MM
SALES (corp-wide): 32.5B **Privately Held**
WEB: www.bridgestone-firestone.com
SIC: **8731** Commercial physical research
HQ: Bridgestone Americas Tire Operations, Llc
   200 4th Ave S Ste 100
   Nashville TN 37201
   615 937-1000

(G-111)
BRIGHT HORIZONS CHLD CTRS LLC
475 Ohio St (44304-1421)
PHONE.................................330 375-7633
Fax: 330 375-6425
Cindy Usner, *Director*
EMP: 27
SALES (corp-wide): 1.7B **Publicly Held**
WEB: www.atlantaga.ncr.com
SIC: **8351** Group day care center
HQ: Bright Horizons Children's Centers Llc
   200 Talcott Ave
   Watertown MA 02472
   617 673-8000

(G-112)
BRINKS INCORPORATED
1601 Industrial Pkwy (44310-2695)
PHONE.................................330 633-5351
Fax: 330 633-3875
Steve Seredich, *General Mgr*
Mike Nace, *Manager*
EMP: 40
SALES (corp-wide): 3.3B **Publicly Held**
WEB: www.brinksinc.com
SIC: **7381** Armored car services
HQ: Brink's, Incorporated
   1801 Bayberry Ct Ste 400
   Richmond VA 23226
   804 289-9600

(G-113)
BROOKDALE LVING CMMUNITIES INC
100 Brookmont Rd Ofc (44333-9268)
PHONE.................................330 666-4545
Debra Haueter, *Manager*
Carol Shemenski, *Hlthcr Dir*
EMP: 50
SALES (corp-wide): 4.7B **Publicly Held**
WEB: www.parkplace-spokane.com
SIC: **6513** Retirement hotel operation
HQ: Brookdale Living Communities, Inc.
   515 N State St Ste 1750
   Chicago IL 60654

(G-114)
BROOKDALE SENIOR LIVING INC
101 N Clvland Mssillon Rd (44333-2422)
PHONE.................................330 666-7011
John Rijos, *Branch Mgr*
EMP: 61
SALES (corp-wide): 4.7B **Publicly Held**
SIC: **8059** Convalescent home
PA: Brookdale Senior Living
   111 Westwood Pl Ste 400
   Brentwood TN 37027
   615 221-2250

(G-115)
BROTT MARDIS & CO
1540 W Market St (44313-7114)
PHONE.................................330 762-5022
Fax: 330 762-2727
Denise M Griggs, *President*
Donald A Brott, *President*
William B Mardis, *Vice Pres*
Kevin L Snyder, *Asst Treas*
Robert A Kazar, *Admin Sec*
EMP: 30
SQ FT: 4,300
SALES (est): 2MM **Privately Held**
WEB: www.brottmardis.com
SIC: **8721** Accounting services, except auditing

(G-116)
BUCKEYE CMNTY THIRTY FIVE LP
2228 11th St Sw (44314-2437)
PHONE.................................614 942-2020
Steve Boone, *Partner*
Trenda Cooper, *Clerk*
EMP: 99 EST: 2013
SALES (est): 3.8MM **Privately Held**
SIC: **6513** Apartment building operators

(G-117)
BUCKEYE STATE CREDIT UNION (PA)
197 E Thornton St (44311-1537)
P.O. Box 848 (44309-0848)
PHONE.................................330 253-9197
Fax: 330 253-1908
Norma Sue Preston, *CEO*
Susan Preston, *Mfg Staff*
Jon Boley, *VP Finance*
Micheal Devine, *Financial Analy*
Kathy Hammond, *Marketing Staff*
EMP: 65
SALES: 3.1MM **Privately Held**
WEB: www.buckeyecu.com
SIC: **6062** State credit unions, not federally chartered

(G-118)
BUCKINGHAM DLTTLE BRROUGHS LLC (PA)
3800 Embassy Pkwy (44333-8387)
PHONE.................................330 376-5300
Nicholas T George, *President*
Chelsea Gehring, *President*
Terry Lehner, *President*
Leanne Svihlik, *President*
Pat Zellia, *President*
EMP: 165
SQ FT: 70,000
SALES (est): 40.6MM **Privately Held**
SIC: **8111** General practice law office

(G-119)
BUREAU VERITAS NORTH AMER INC
520 S Main St Ste 2444 (44311-1087)
PHONE.................................330 252-5100
Fax: 330 252-5105
Barb Hana, *President*
EMP: 30
SALES (corp-wide): 316.4MM **Privately Held**
SIC: **8748** Environmental consultant
HQ: Bureau Veritas North America, Inc.
   1601 Sawgrs Corp Pkwy
   Sunrise FL 33323
   954 236-8100

(G-120)
CANAL PHYSICIAN GROUP
1 Akron General Ave (44307-2432)
PHONE.................................330 344-4000
Fax: 330 253-2349
Lakshman Negi, *Med Doctor*
Kim Roberts, *Practice Mgr*
Colin Moorhead, *Director*
EMP: 25
SALES (est): 2MM **Privately Held**
SIC: **8011** General & family practice, physician/surgeon

(G-121)
CARDINAL ENVIRONMENTAL SVC INC
180 E Miller Ave (44301-1349)
PHONE.................................330 252-0220
Daniel Pohl, *President*
David Dubravetz, *General Mgr*
Ray Brophy, *Vice Pres*
Dan Brynelsen, *Project Mgr*
Allen Linger, *Manager*
EMP: 25
SQ FT: 10,000
SALES (est): 3.1MM **Privately Held**
SIC: **1799** Asbestos removal & encapsulation

(G-122)
CARDINAL MAINTENANCE & SVC CO
180 E Miller Ave (44301-1349)
PHONE.................................330 252-0282
Dan Pohl, *President*
Doug Wilson, *Sales Associate*
Greg Wilson, *Sales Associate*
Erika Phares, *Maintence Staff*
Andrea Pohl, *Maintence Staff*
EMP: 120
SQ FT: 7,000
SALES (est): 5.5MM **Privately Held**
SIC: **7349** 8748 1761 Janitorial service, contract basis; business consulting; roofing, siding & sheet metal work

(G-123)
CARTER-JONES LUMBER COMPANY
Also Called: Carter Lumber
172 N Case Ave (44305-2599)
PHONE.................................330 784-5441
Fax: 330 784-7467
Mike Smead, *Manager*
Chuck Bryant, *Manager*
EMP: 70
SALES (corp-wide): 1.2B **Privately Held**
SIC: **5211** 5031 5251 Lumber products; lumber, plywood & millwork; hardware
HQ: The Carter-Jones Lumber Company
   601 Tallmadge Rd
   Kent OH 44240
   330 673-6100

(G-124)
CBIZ ACCOUNTING TAX
4040 Embassy Pkwy Ste 100 (44333-8354)
PHONE.................................330 668-6500
Terri Albertson, *Managing Dir*
Betty Isler, *Managing Dir*
Tracey McDonald, *Managing Dir*
Laura Plotner, *Managing Dir*
Lewis Taub, *Managing Dir*
EMP: 60
SALES (est): 4MM **Publicly Held**
WEB: www.cbizinc.com
SIC: **8721** Accounting, auditing & bookkeeping
PA: Cbiz, Inc.
   6050 Oak Tree Blvd # 500
   Cleveland OH 44131

(G-125)
CEDARWOOD CONSTRUCTION COMPANY
1765 Merriman Rd (44313-9003)
PHONE.................................330 836-9971
Fax: 330 836-2280
Anthony Petrarca, *President*
Michael W Pelech Jr, *Vice Pres*
EMP: 100
SQ FT: 15,500
SALES (est): 6.3MM **Privately Held**
SIC: **8741** 1542 Construction management; commercial & office building, new construction

(G-126)
CELLCO PARTNERSHIP
Also Called: Verizon Wireless
50 W Bowery St (44308-1102)
PHONE.................................330 376-8275
EMP: 71
SALES (corp-wide): 126B **Publicly Held**
SIC: **4812** Cellular telephone services
HQ: Cellco Partnership
   1 Verizon Way
   Basking Ridge NJ 07920

(G-127)
CENTER 5
Also Called: Suma Health Sys St Thomas Hosp
444 N Main St (44310-3110)
PHONE.................................330 379-5900
Fax: 330 379-5515
EMP: 85
SALES (est): 3MM **Privately Held**
SIC: **8093** Specialty Outpatient Clinic

(G-128)
CENTER FOR UROLOGIC HEALTH LLC (PA)
Also Called: Physicians Urology Centre
95 Arch St Ste 165 (44304-1488)
PHONE.................................330 375-0924
Fabian Breaux MD, *President*
Joseph Dankoff, *Corp Secy*

GEOGRAPHIC SECTION

Akron - Summit County (G-152)

John Chulik MD, *Vice Pres*
Ray Bologna, *Med Doctor*
Todd Breaux, *Med Doctor*
EMP: 36
SALES (est): 7.6MM **Privately Held**
WEB: www.physiciansurology.com
SIC: 8011   Medical centers

(G-129)
CHAPEL HILL MANAGEMENT INC
2000 Brittain Rd Ste 830 (44310-4303)
PHONE 330 633-7100
Fax: 330 633-1353
Richard B Buchholzer, *President*
Robert P Dunn, *Vice Pres*
Joe McKelvey, *Opers Mgr*
Mildred R Blount, *Admin Sec*
EMP: 65
SQ FT: 12,590
SALES (est): 4.3MM **Privately Held**
SIC: 6512   Shopping center, community (100,000 - 300,000 sq ft)

(G-130)
CHEMSTRESS CONSULTANT COMPANY (PA)
39 S Main St (44308-1844)
PHONE 330 535-5591
Fax: 330 434-3400
James Kehres, *President*
Frank Fodor, *General Mgr*
Paul K Christoff, *Principal*
Rod Clark, *Principal*
Wiliam R Ferguson, *Principal*
EMP: 150
SQ FT: 70,000
SALES (est): 27.7MM **Privately Held**
WEB: www.chemstress.com
SIC: 8711 8712 8741 Consulting engineer; architectural services; construction management

(G-131)
CHESTER WEST DENTISTRY
1575 Vernon Odom Blvd (44320-4091)
PHONE 330 753-7734
Dr Jeffrey S Rosenthal, *President*
EMP: 30
SALES (est): 274.1K **Privately Held**
SIC: 8011 8021 Offices & clinics of medical doctors; dentists' office

(G-132)
CHICAGO TITLE INSURANCE CO
799 White Pond Dr Ste A (44320-1189)
PHONE 330 873-9393
Fax: 330 873-9222
Lorie Finney, *Banking Exec*
Shelly Maggard, *Manager*
EMP: 80
SALES (corp-wide): 7.6B **Publicly Held**
WEB: www.goldleaf-tech.com
SIC: 6361   Real estate title insurance
HQ: Chicago Title Insurance Company
 601 Riverside Ave
 Jacksonville FL 32204

(G-133)
CHILDREN MEDICAL GROUP INC
3800 Embassy Pkwy (44333-8387)
PHONE 330 762-9033
Fax: 330 996-7031
D Douglas Hackenberg, *President*
Lorie D'Avello, *Vice Pres*
Sherrie Brooks, *Manager*
Susan Vargo, *Admin Sec*
EMP: 25
SALES (est): 3.1MM **Privately Held**
SIC: 8011   Pediatrician

(G-134)
CHILDRENS HOME CARE GROUP
185 W Cedar St Ste 203 (44307-2447)
PHONE 330 543-5000
Fax: 330 543-3084
Meredith Slosberg, *Vice Pres*
Polly Herchek, *Director*
EMP: 280
SALES (est): 11.2MM **Privately Held**
SIC: 8082 Home health care services

(G-135)
CHILDRENS HOSP MED CTR AKRON (PA)
Also Called: Akron Children's Hospital
1 Perkins Sq (44308-1063)
PHONE 330 543-1000
Fax: 330 543-3808
William Considine, *CEO*
Michael Holder, *Dean*
Grace Wakulchik, *COO*
Daniel McMahon, *Trustee*
Michael Rubin, *Ch Radiology*
EMP: 3462
SQ FT: 356,000
SALES: 747.4MM **Privately Held**
SIC: 8069   Children's hospital

(G-136)
CHILDRENS HOSP MED CTR AKRON
Also Called: Ask Childrens
1 Perkins Sq (44308-1063)
PHONE 330 543-8004
Fax: 330 543-3754
Cheryl Ballentine, *Principal*
Kristene Nagy, *Manager*
Ron Tharp, *Nurse*
EMP: 40
SALES (corp-wide): 747.4MM **Privately Held**
SIC: 8069 8011 Children's hospital; offices & clinics of medical doctors
PA: Childrens Hospital Medical Center Of Akron
 1 Perkins Sq
 Akron OH 44308
 330 543-1000

(G-137)
CIOFFI & SON CONSTRUCTION
1001 Eastwood Ave (44305-1127)
PHONE 330 794-9448
Fax: 330 794-2858
Frank Cioffi, *President*
Dominic Cioffi, *Vice Pres*
Maria Palcko, *Admin Sec*
EMP: 30 EST: 1975
SQ FT: 5,000
SALES (est): 4.4MM **Privately Held**
SIC: 1771   Sidewalk contractor; curb construction; driveway contractor

(G-138)
CITY OF AKRON
Also Called: Good Park Golf Course
530 Nome Ave (44320-1234)
PHONE 330 864-0020
Fax: 330 375-2136
Dante Deandrea, *Branch Mgr*
EMP: 30 **Privately Held**
SIC: 7992 Public golf courses
PA: City Of Akron
 166 S High St Rm 502
 Akron OH 44308
 330 375-2720

(G-139)
CITY OF AKRON
Also Called: Akron Water Distribution Div
1460 Triplett Blvd (44306-3304)
PHONE 330 375-2420
Fax: 330 375-2114
David Crundell, *Principal*
EMP: 120 **Privately Held**
SIC: 4941 Water supply
PA: City Of Akron
 166 S High St Rm 502
 Akron OH 44308
 330 375-2720

(G-140)
CITY OF AKRON
Sewer Department
2460 Akron Peninsula Rd (44313-4710)
PHONE 330 375-2666
Fax: 330 375-2399
Jim Six, *Branch Mgr*
EMP: 50
SQ FT: 240 **Privately Held**
SIC: 4952   Sewerage systems
PA: City Of Akron
 166 S High St Rm 502
 Akron OH 44308
 330 375-2720

(G-141)
CITY OF AKRON
Also Called: Traffic Engineering
1420 Triplett Blvd (44306-3304)
PHONE 330 375-2851
David Gester, *Manager*
EMP: 33 **Privately Held**
SIC: 8748 9111 Traffic consultant; mayors' offices
PA: City Of Akron
 166 S High St Rm 502
 Akron OH 44308
 330 375-2720

(G-142)
CITY OF AKRON
Bureau of Engineering
166 S High St Rm 701 (44308-1627)
PHONE 330 375-2355
Jim Hewitt, *Office Mgr*
EMP: 80 **Privately Held**
SIC: 8711 9111 Engineering services; mayors' offices
PA: City Of Akron
 166 S High St Rm 502
 Akron OH 44308
 330 375-2720

(G-143)
CITY SCRAP & SALVAGE CO
760 Flora Ave (44314-1755)
PHONE 330 753-5051
Fax: 330 753-9288
Steven Katz, *CEO*
Randy Katz, *Vice Pres*
Ron Jones, *Site Mgr*
EMP: 31
SQ FT: 10,000
SALES (est): 7.7MM
SALES (corp-wide): 869.5MM **Publicly Held**
SIC: 5093 3341 Ferrous metal scrap & waste; nonferrous metals scrap; secondary nonferrous metals
HQ: Tsb Metal Recycling Llc
 1835 Dueber Ave Sw
 Canton OH 44706

(G-144)
CITY YELLOW CAB COMPANY
650 Home Ave (44310-4102)
PHONE 330 253-3141
Fax: 330 253-2135
Derek McClenathen, *President*
Derek Mc Clenathen, *President*
Cornelius P Chima, *Corp Secy*
Judy Portman, *Accounts Exec*
Daniel Schlichting, *Sales Executive*
EMP: 30 EST: 1933
SQ FT: 6,000
SALES (est): 2.7MM **Privately Held**
SIC: 7515 4121 Passenger car leasing; taxicabs

(G-145)
CLEARPATH HM HLTH HOSPICE LLC
475 Wolf Ledges Pkwy (44311-1199)
PHONE 330 784-2162
Fax: 330 784-2197
Ruth Self, *Mng Member*
EMP: 90
SALES (est): 3.5MM **Privately Held**
SIC: 8082 Visiting nurse service

(G-146)
CLEARWATER SERVICES INC
Also Called: Clearwater Systems
1411 Vernon Odom Blvd (44320-4086)
PHONE 330 836-4946
Jerome P Kovach Jr, *CEO*
EMP: 61 EST: 2014
SQ FT: 13,000
SALES (est): 7.4MM **Privately Held**
SIC: 4941 7389 Water supply; water softener service

(G-147)
CLEVELAND ELC ILLUMINATING CO (HQ)
76 S Main St (44308-1812)
PHONE 800 589-3101
John E Skory, *President*
L L Vespoli, *Exec VP*
Leila Vespoli, *Exec VP*

Harvey L Wagner, *Vice Pres*
Mark T Clark, *CFO*
EMP: 91 EST: 1892
SALES: 928.4MM **Publicly Held**
SIC: 4911   Generation, electric power; transmission, electric power

(G-148)
CLIFTONLARSONALLEN LLP
388 S Main St Ste 403 (44311-4407)
PHONE 330 376-0100
Fax: 330 376-0658
Sheila Gabriel, *Human Resources*
Mike Markowski, *Manager*
EMP: 26
SALES (corp-wide): 755.1MM **Privately Held**
WEB: www.brunercox.com
SIC: 8721   Accounting services, except auditing
PA: Cliftonlarsonallen Llp
 220 S 6th St Ste 300
 Minneapolis MN 55402
 612 376-4500

(G-149)
CLUBCORP USA INC
600 Swartz Rd (44319-1332)
PHONE 330 724-4444
Mark Gore, *Manager*
EMP: 25
SALES (corp-wide): 433.7MM **Privately Held**
WEB: www.remington-gc.com
SIC: 7999 Golf driving range
HQ: Clubcorp Usa, Inc.
 3030 Lyndon B Johnson Fwy
 Dallas TX 75234
 972 243-6191

(G-150)
COHEN & COMPANY LTD
3500 Embassy Pkwy (44333-8373)
PHONE 330 374-1040
Fax: 330 535-0111
J Michael Kolk, *Partner*
Rachel Roan, *Accountant*
Tracy Campbell, *Manager*
Sean Detwiler, *Manager*
Bryan McShane, *Manager*
EMP: 100
SALES (corp-wide): 36MM **Privately Held**
WEB: www.cohencpa.com
SIC: 8721 Certified public accountant
PA: Cohen & Company, Ltd.
 1350 Euclid Ave Ste 800
 Cleveland OH 44115
 216 579-1040

(G-151)
COLEMAN PROFESSIONAL SVCS INC
Sage Computer
3043 Sanitarium Rd Ste 2 (44312-4600)
PHONE 330 628-2275
Mike Hallett, *VP Mktg*
Sandra Randall, *Supervisor*
Susie Ruffin, *Supervisor*
Debra Prioletti, *Director*
EMP: 220
SALES (corp-wide): 43.8MM **Privately Held**
SIC: 7374 Data entry service
PA: Coleman Professional Services, Inc.
 5982 Rhodes Rd
 Kent OH 44240
 330 673-1347

(G-152)
COMMERCIAL TIME SHARING INC
Also Called: C T I
2740 Cory Ave (44314-1339)
PHONE 330 644-3059
Fax: 330 644-8110
David L Poling, *Ch of Bd*
Ronald Symens, *President*
Susan Mikulin, *Purchasing*
Tom Gambone, *Manager*
Sean McCloskey, *Engineer*
EMP: 29
SQ FT: 8,000

Akron - Summit County (G-153)   **GEOGRAPHIC SECTION**

SALES (est): 6MM **Privately Held**
WEB: www.ipobox.net
SIC: **7373** 7371 5045 Systems integration services; computer software development; computer software

(G-153)
COMMUNITY DRUG BOARD INC (PA)
725 E Market St (44305-2421)
PHONE..............................330 315-5590
Fax: 330 434-7125
Theodore P Ziegler, *CEO*
Janet Wagner, *COO*
Pamela J Crislip, *CFO*
Jess E Tarr, *Exec Dir*
EMP: 90
SQ FT: 17,000
SALES: 12.5MM **Privately Held**
SIC: **8093** 8322 Substance abuse clinics (outpatient); substance abuse counseling

(G-154)
COMMUNITY DRUG BOARD INC
Also Called: Ramar-Genesis
380 S Portage Path (44320-2326)
PHONE..............................330 996-5114
Fax: 330 434-7885
Rozanne Hindman, *Branch Mgr*
EMP: 90
SALES (corp-wide): 12.5MM **Privately Held**
SIC: **8322** Rehabilitation services
PA: Community Drug Board, Inc.
   725 E Market St
   Akron OH 44305
   330 315-5590

(G-155)
COMMUNITY HBILITATION SVCS INC (PA)
Also Called: University of Individuality
493 Canton Rd (44312-1647)
P.O. Box 1028 (44309-1028)
PHONE..............................234 334-4288
Fax: 330 753-1905
Wanda Haines, *President*
EMP: 25
SALES: 40.5MM **Privately Held**
SIC: **8361** Home for the mentally retarded

(G-156)
COMMUNITY LEGAL AID SERVICES (PA)
Also Called: Western Reserve Legal Services
50 S Main St Ste 800 (44308-1823)
PHONE..............................330 535-4191
Fax: 330 535-0728
Nancy Grim, *President*
Ereka Langford, *Office Mgr*
Linda Duffy, *Manager*
Dan Ragan, *Info Tech Mgr*
Andrea Sandej, *Exec Dir*
EMP: 70
SALES: 4.7MM **Privately Hold**
SIC: **8111** Legal aid service; general practice attorney, lawyer

(G-157)
COMMUNITY SUPPORT SERVICES INC (PA)
150 Cross St (44311-1026)
PHONE..............................330 253-9388
Fax: 330 376-6726
Terry Dalton, *CEO*
Terrence B Dalton, *President*
James E Bournival, *Vice Pres*
Jon Garey, *Vice Pres*
Frank Sepetauc, *Vice Pres*
EMP: 201
SQ FT: 45,000
SALES: 18.6MM **Privately Held**
WEB: www.cssbh.org
SIC: **8093** 8331 8361 Mental health clinic, outpatient; vocational rehabilitation agency; home for the emotionally disturbed

(G-158)
COMMUNITY SUPPORT SERVICES INC
Also Called: Work Tech
150 Cross St (44311-1026)
PHONE..............................330 253-9675
Frank Sepetauc, *Manager*

EMP: 75
SALES (corp-wide): 18.6MM **Privately Held**
WEB: www.cssbh.org
SIC: **8093** Mental health clinic, outpatient
PA: Community Support Services, Inc.
   150 Cross St
   Akron OH 44311
   330 253-9388

(G-159)
COMMUNITY SUPPORT SERVICES INC
Also Called: Keebler Hall
403 Canton Rd (44312-1603)
PHONE..............................330 733-6203
Fax: 330 733-5045
Rebecca Sandlin, *Manager*
EMP: 74
SALES (corp-wide): 18.6MM **Privately Held**
WEB: www.cssbh.org
SIC: **8093** Mental health clinic, outpatient
PA: Community Support Services, Inc.
   150 Cross St
   Akron OH 44311
   330 253-9388

(G-160)
CONCORD TESTA HOTEL ASSOC LLC
Also Called: Courtyard By Marriott
41 Furnace St (44308-1914)
PHONE..............................330 252-9228
Dena St Clair,
EMP: 99
SALES (est): 587.2K **Privately Held**
SIC: **7011** Hotels & motels

(G-161)
CONSULTANTS COLLECTIONS
310 N Clvland Mssillon Rd (44333-9302)
PHONE..............................330 666-6900
Joseph R Harris, *President*
EMP: 35
SQ FT: 500
SALES (est): 823.6K **Privately Held**
SIC: **8748** Business consulting

(G-162)
CONTITECH NORTH AMERICA INC
1144 E Market St Ste 543 (44316-1001)
PHONE..............................440 225-5363
Dave Maguire, *President*
Tim Jarvis, *Branch Mgr*
EMP: 28
SALES (corp-wide): 51.9B **Privately Held**
WEB: www.veyance.com
SIC: **5531** 7538 5013 3011 Automotive & home supply stores; general automotive repair shops; motor vehicle supplies & new parts; tires & inner tubes; rubber & plastics hose & beltings
HQ: Contitech North America, Inc.
   703 S Clvlnd Massillon Rd
   Fairlawn OH 44333

(G-163)
CONWED PLAS ACQUISITION V LLC
Also Called: Filtrexx International
61 N Clevlnd Msslln Rd (44333-4558)
PHONE..............................440 926-2607
Chris Hatzenbuhler, *CEO*
Ray Swartzwelder, *President*
Mike Younken, *VP Sales*
Rocky Owens, *Marketing Staff*
Doug Schumaker, *Marketing Staff*
EMP: 99
SQ FT: 1,000
SALES (est): 17.6MM **Publicly Held**
SIC: **8731** Environmental research
PA: Schweitzer-Mauduit International, Inc.
   100 N Point Ctr E Ste 600
   Alpharetta GA 30022

(G-164)
COOPER BROTHERS TRUCKING LLC (PA)
1355 E Archwood Ave (44306-2832)
P.O. Box 7725 (44306-0725)
PHONE..............................330 784-1717
Suzie Miter, *Opers Mgr*
Annalee Cooper, *Mng Member*

Mark Cooper, *Manager*
EMP: 29
SQ FT: 60,000
SALES: 7MM **Privately Held**
WEB: www.cooperbrostrucking.com
SIC: **4213** Heavy hauling

(G-165)
CORNERSTONE MEDICAL ASSOCIATES
453 S High St Ste 201 (44311-4417)
PHONE..............................330 374-0229
Jessica Deluke,
EMP: 35
SQ FT: 11,000
SALES (est): 5MM **Privately Held**
SIC: **7352** 5047 Medical equipment rental; medical equipment & supplies

(G-166)
COTTER MDSE STOR OF OHIO
1564 Firestone Pkwy (44301-1626)
P.O. Box 808 (44309-0808)
PHONE..............................330 773-9177
Chris Geib, *President*
Gary Medvets, *General Mgr*
Howard D Heater, *Vice Pres*
Gary Medvetz, *Opers Mgr*
Tonya Bridgeland, *Financial Exec*
EMP: 45
SQ FT: 500,000
SALES (est): 4.1MM
SALES (corp-wide): 12.8MM **Privately Held**
SIC: **4225** General warehousing
PA: The Cotter Merchandise Storage Company
   1564 Firestone Pkwy
   Akron OH 44301
   330 315-2755

(G-167)
COTTER MOVING & STORAGE CO (PA)
Also Called: A-Advnced Mvg Stor Systms-Self
265 W Bowery St (44308-1034)
P.O. Box 529 (44309-0529)
PHONE..............................330 535-5115
Fax: 330 535-5137
Harry L Bord, *President*
Fred Bord, *Vice Pres*
William C Bord, *Treasurer*
EMP: 25
SQ FT: 250,000
SALES (est): 1.6MM **Privately Held**
SIC: **4213** 4225 4212 Trucking, except local; general warehousing & storage; local trucking, without storage

(G-168)
COUNTY OF SUMMIT
Also Called: Summit County Probation Offs
25 N Main St (44308-1919)
PHONE..............................330 643-2300
Fax: 330 643-2691
Arian Davis, *Manager*
Jackie Fink, *Manager*
Pete Hoost, *Director*
EMP: 62
SQ FT: 29,236 **Privately Held**
WEB: www.cpcourt.summitoh.net
SIC: **8322** 9111 Probation office; county supervisors' & executives' offices
PA: County Of Summit
   650 Dan St
   Akron OH 44310
   330 643-2500

(G-169)
COUNTY OF SUMMIT
Also Called: Summit Cnty Juvenile CT
650 Dan St (44310-3909)
PHONE..............................330 643-2943
Fax: 330 379-3647
Dave Alexander, *Administration*
EMP: 150 **Privately Held**
WEB: www.cpcourt.summitoh.net
SIC: **8361** 9211 Juvenile correctional facilities; courts
PA: County Of Summit
   650 Dan St
   Akron OH 44310
   330 643-2500

(G-170)
COUNTY OF SUMMIT
538 E South St (44311-1848)
PHONE..............................330 643-2850
Gene Esser, *General Mgr*
Allan Brubaker, *Branch Mgr*
Geordie Kissos, *Manager*
Robert Starosto, *Supervisor*
Patrick Dobbins, *Asst Director*
EMP: 120
SQ FT: 1,368 **Privately Held**
WEB: www.cpcourt.summitoh.net
SIC: **8711** 9111 Engineering services; county supervisors' & executives' offices
PA: County Of Summit
   650 Dan St
   Akron OH 44310
   330 643-2500

(G-171)
COUNTY OF SUMMIT
Also Called: Highway Maintenance
601 E Crosier St (44311-1808)
PHONE..............................330 643-2860
Fax: 330 374-6961
Tim Boley, *Manager*
Gary Ellison, *Director*
EMP: 200 **Privately Held**
WEB: www.cpcourt.summitoh.net
SIC: **1611** Highway & street maintenance
PA: County Of Summit
   650 Dan St
   Akron OH 44310
   330 643-2500

(G-172)
COUNTY OF SUMMIT
Social Services
47 N Main St (44308-1925)
PHONE..............................330 643-7217
Fax: 330 643-7144
Dr Daisy Alfred Smith, *Director*
EMP: 500 **Privately Held**
WEB: www.cpcourt.summitoh.net
SIC: **8322** Individual & family services
PA: County Of Summit
   650 Dan St
   Akron OH 44310
   330 643-2500

(G-173)
COUNTY OF SUMMIT BOARD OF MNTL
636 W Exchange St (44302-1306)
PHONE..............................330 634-8100
Tom Armstrong, *Superintendent*
Dennis Spisak, *Sales Staff*
Brock Arrington, *Admin Asst*
Tiffany Benedict, *Admin Asst*
Maryanne Buchanan, *Admin Asst*
EMP: 700
SALES (est): 5MM **Privately Held**
SIC: **8699** Charitable organization

(G-174)
CRAFTSMEN RESTORATION LLC (PA)
Also Called: Village Handyman, The
2013 N Clvland Msslln Rd (44333-1258)
PHONE..............................877 442-3424
Jeffrey Sartori, *Mng Member*
Michael Farist,
EMP: 26
SALES: 12.6MM **Privately Held**
SIC: **1521** General remodeling, single-family houses

(G-175)
CRAIN COMMUNICATIONS INC
Also Called: Rubber & Plastics News
1725 Merriman Rd Ste 300 (44313-5283)
PHONE..............................330 836-9180
Fax: 330 836-1005
Jeannie Reall, *Editor*
Lisa Sarkis, *Editor*
Robert S Simmons, *Vice Pres*
Mary Kramer, *Vice Pres*
Ja Lewellen, *Research*
EMP: 90

GEOGRAPHIC SECTION

Akron - Summit County (G-198)

SALES (corp-wide): 225MM **Privately Held**
WEB: www.crainsnewyork.com
SIC: 2711 2721 7389 Newspapers: publishing only, not printed on site; periodicals; advertising, promotional & trade show services
PA: Crain Communications, Inc.
  1155 Gratiot Ave
  Detroit MI 48207
  313 446-6000

(G-176)
CRAWFORD GROUP INC
3960 Medina Rd (44333-2445)
PHONE 330 665-5432
EMP: 54
SALES (corp-wide): 6.1B **Privately Held**
SIC: 7514 Passenger car rental
PA: The Crawford Group Inc
  600 Corporate Park Dr
  Saint Louis MO 63105
  314 512-5000

(G-177)
CRYSTAL ARTHRITIS CENTER INC
3975 Embassy Pkwy Ste 101 (44333-8325)
PHONE 330 668-4045
Fax: 330 668-2492
Raymond Federman MD, *President*
Lori Stockert, *Superintendent*
EMP: 36
SQ FT: 2,200
SALES (est): 3.8MM **Privately Held**
SIC: 8011 Rheumatology specialist, physician/surgeon

(G-178)
CRYSTAL CLINIC SURGERY CTR INC
3975 Embassy Pkwy Ste 202 (44333-8395)
PHONE 330 668-4040
Ronald R Suntken, *President*
Holli Cholley, *President*
Gregory P Zolton, *President*
Gordon L Bennett MD, *Vice Pres*
Jim Bell, *Project Mgr*
EMP: 700
SQ FT: 6,800
SALES (est): 45.1MM **Privately Held**
WEB: www.crystalclinic.com
SIC: 8011 Surgeon

(G-179)
CRYSTAL CLNIC ORTHPDIC CTR LLC (PA)
3925 Embassy Pkwy Ste 250 (44333-1799)
PHONE 330 668-4040
Ronald R Suntken, *President*
Holli Cholley, *Opers Staff*
Daniel Ferry, *CFO*
Gregg Zolton, *CIO*
EMP: 99 **EST:** 2007
SALES (est): 19.7MM **Privately Held**
SIC: 8069 Orthopedic hospital

(G-180)
CRYSTAL CLNIC ORTHPDIC CTR LLC
20 Olive St Ste 200 (44310-3169)
PHONE 330 535-3396
EMP: 62
SALES (corp-wide): 19.7MM **Privately Held**
SIC: 8069 Orthopedic hospital
PA: Crystal Clinic Orthopaedic Center, Llc
  3925 Embassy Pkwy Ste 250
  Akron OH 44333
  330 668-4040

(G-181)
CSL PLASMA INC
727 Grant St Lowr (44311-2128)
PHONE 330 535-4338
Jane Mueller, *Branch Mgr*
EMP: 65
SALES (corp-wide): 6.9B **Privately Held**
WEB: www.zlbplasma.com
SIC: 8099 Blood donor station

HQ: Csl Plasma Inc.
  900 Broken Sound Pkwy # 4
  Boca Raton FL 33487
  561 981-3700

(G-182)
CUTLER AND ASSOCIATES INC
Also Called: Cutler Realtor
971 E Turkeyfoot Lake Rd (44312-5240)
PHONE 330 896-1680
Bonnie Wagler, *Manager*
EMP: 55
SALES (corp-wide): 9.3MM **Privately Held**
WEB: www.cutlerhomes.com
SIC: 6531 Real estate agents & managers
PA: Cutler And Associates, Inc
  4618 Dressler Rd Nw
  Canton OH 44718
  330 493-9323

(G-183)
CUTLER REAL ESTATE
971 E Turkeyfoot Lake Rd A (44312-5240)
PHONE 330 644-0644
Bonnie Wagler, *Manager*
EMP: 40
SALES (corp-wide): 6.9MM **Privately Held**
SIC: 6531 Real estate agents & managers
PA: Cutler Real Estate
  2800 W Market St
  Fairlawn OH 44333
  330 836-9141

(G-184)
CYO & COMMUNITY SERVICES INC (PA)
795 Russell Ave (44307-1115)
PHONE 330 762-2961
Fax: 330 762-2001
Celeste Thayer, *Office Mgr*
Amanda Leitner, *Psychologist*
Donald P Finn, *Exec Dir*
Linda Biermann, *Nurse*
Todd Dockrill,
EMP: 40
SALES (est): 1.2MM **Privately Held**
SIC: 8661 8322 Religious organizations; individual & family services

(G-185)
CYPRESS COMPANIES INC (PA)
670 W Market St (44303-1448)
PHONE 330 849-6500
Fax: 330 762-5855
Rollie Bauer, *CEO*
Dennis Raney, *Exec VP*
Matt McGinnes, *Vice Pres*
Nancy Allshouse, *Executive Asst*
EMP: 50
SALES (est): 7.2MM **Privately Held**
WEB: www.cypresscos.com
SIC: 8741 Management services

(G-186)
DAN MARCHETTA CNSTR CO INC
525 N Cleveland Massillon (44333-3332)
PHONE 330 668-4800
Fax: 330 668-2972
Daniel T Marchetta Jr, *President*
Joseph Marchetta, *Vice Pres*
Michael Marchetta, *Vice Pres*
Linda Kinsey, *Manager*
EMP: 30
SQ FT: 3,000
SALES (est): 7.9MM **Privately Held**
SIC: 1542 1521 Commercial & office building, new construction; commercial & office buildings, renovation & repair; new construction, single-family houses

(G-187)
DATZAP LLC
1520 S Arlington St (44306-3863)
PHONE 330 785-2100
Donald Jacob, *Mng Member*
Teressa Struckman, *Administration*
EMP: 30 **EST:** 2002
SALES (est): 868.5K **Privately Held**
SIC: 4813

(G-188)
DAVITA INC
73 Massillon Rd (44312-1028)
PHONE 330 733-1861
Candi Willoughby, *Branch Mgr*
EMP: 33 **Publicly Held**
SIC: 8092 Kidney dialysis centers
PA: Davita Inc.
  2000 16th St
  Denver CO 80202

(G-189)
DENTAL HEALTH GROUP PA
Also Called: Great Expressions
2000 Brittain Rd Ste 91 (44310-4320)
PHONE 330 630-9222
Fax: 330 630-8029
Sam Jaffe, *Manager*
EMP: 30
SALES (corp-wide): 113.5MM **Privately Held**
SIC: 8021 Dentists' office
PA: Dental Health Group, P.A.
  29777 Telg Rd St 3000
  Southfield MI 48034
  248 203-2330

(G-190)
DETROIT WESTFIELD LLC
Also Called: Holiday Inn
4073 Medina Rd (44333-2476)
PHONE 330 666-4131
Fred Lami, *Partner*
Louie Lemaster, *General Mgr*
Deborah Smith, *Vice Pres*
K A McFalls, *Admin Sec*
Theodore Sahley,
EMP: 60
SQ FT: 106,335
SALES (est): 3.1MM **Privately Held**
SIC: 7011 5812 Motels; restaurant, family: independent

(G-191)
DI FEO & SONS POULTRY INC
1075 Grant St (44301-1434)
P.O. Box 530 (44309-0530)
PHONE 330 564-8172
Fax: 330 773-5194
Robert Di Feo, *President*
John Di Feo, *Vice Pres*
Edward Di Feo, *Treasurer*
EMP: 30
SQ FT: 7,000
SALES (est): 11.5MM **Privately Held**
SIC: 5144 5499 Poultry: live, dressed or frozen (unpackaged); eggs; eggs & poultry

(G-192)
DIET CENTER WORLDWIDE INC (PA)
395 Springside Dr (44333-2434)
PHONE 330 665-5861
Charles E Sekeres, *President*
Linda Maksim, *Manager*
Tammi Deharpart, *Plan/Corp Dev D*
EMP: 40
SQ FT: 53,684
SALES (est): 1.7MM **Privately Held**
SIC: 7299 6794 Diet center, without medical staff; franchises, selling or licensing

(G-193)
DIGITAL COLOR INTL LLC
Also Called: D C I
1653 Merriman Rd Ste 211 (44313-5276)
PHONE 330 762-6959
Fax: 330 762-6919
Christopher Che, *CEO*
Cindy Christian, *Prdtn Mgr*
Elaine Salyer, *Accounts Mgr*
Michael Osborne, *Manager*
David Fusselman,
EMP: 43
SQ FT: 38,000
SALES (est): 8.5MM **Privately Held**
WEB: www.digitalcolorinternational.com
SIC: 7336 2653 7319 7331 Creative services to advertisers, except writers; display items, solid fiber: made from purchased materials; display advertising service; transit advertising services; direct mail advertising services; commercial printing, lithographic

(G-194)
DIVERSIFIED AIR SYSTEMS INC
1201 George Wash Blvd (44312-3007)
PHONE 330 784-3366
John Smelko, *Manager*
EMP: 35
SALES (corp-wide): 12.2MM **Privately Held**
WEB: www.diversifiedair.com
SIC: 5075 7699 Compressors, air conditioning; compressor repair
PA: Diversified Air Systems, Inc.
  4760 Van Epps Rd
  Brooklyn Heights OH 44131
  216 741-1700

(G-195)
DLZ OHIO INC
1 Canal Square Plz # 1300 (44308-1037)
PHONE 330 923-0401
Thomas Sisley, *Senior VP*
Matt Roberts, *Project Mgr*
Geary A Visc, *Finance Mgr*
Geary Visca, *Finance Mgr*
Tom Sisley, *Manager*
EMP: 25
SQ FT: 11,667
SALES (corp-wide): 93MM **Privately Held**
SIC: 8711 Consulting engineer
HQ: Dlz Ohio, Inc.
  6121 Huntley Rd
  Columbus OH 43229
  614 888-0040

(G-196)
DON DRUMM STUDIOS & GALLERY
437 Crouse St (44311-1220)
PHONE 330 253-6840
Fax: 330 253-4014
Don Drumm, *President*
Jill Parr, *General Mgr*
Elizabeth B Drumm, *Treasurer*
Judy Kelly, *Bookkeeper*
Ann Whittenberger, *Sales Executive*
EMP: 32
SALES (est): 4.1MM **Privately Held**
WEB: www.dondrummstudios.com
SIC: 5999 5199 8999 7336 Artists' supplies & materials; art goods; sculptor's studio; commercial art & graphic design

(G-197)
DONZELLS FLOWER & GRDN CTR INC
Also Called: Donzell's
937 E Waterloo Rd (44306-3996)
PHONE 330 724-0550
Sam Donzelli, *President*
Wm Gale, *Principal*
Harold D Parker, *Principal*
Susan Hale, *Human Resources*
Marie Lavendar, *Executive*
▲ **EMP:** 30
SQ FT: 52,000
SALES (est): 4.5MM **Privately Held**
WEB: www.donzells.com
SIC: 5999 5181 Christmas lights & decorations; beer & ale

(G-198)
DOUG BIGELOW CHEVROLET INC
Also Called: Doug Chevrolet
3281 S Arlington Rd (44312-5215)
PHONE 330 644-7500
Fax: 330 644-8172
Doug Bigelow, *CEO*
Christopher Bigelow, *Principal*
Patricia Bigelow, *Corp Secy*
Tracie Baumgardner, *Manager*
EMP: 75
SQ FT: 10,000
SALES (est): 29.5MM **Privately Held**
WEB: www.dougchevrolet.com
SIC: 5511 5521 7538 7532 Automobiles, new & used; used car dealers; general automotive repair shops; top & body repair & paint shops; automobiles & other motor vehicles

---

(PA)=Parent Co (HQ)=Headquarters (DH)=Div Headquarters
✪ = New Business established in last 2 years

2018 Harris Ohio Services Directory

Akron - Summit County (G-199)

GEOGRAPHIC SECTION

(G-199)
DOWNTOWN AKRON PARTNERSHIP INC
Also Called: DAT
103 S High St Fl 4 (44308-1461)
PHONE.................................330 374-7676
Clair Dickinson, *Ch of Bd*
Holly Mattucci, *Business Mgr*
Linda Fry, *Project Dir*
Beth Klaes, *Controller*
Lisa Knapp, *Comms Dir*
EMP: 50
SALES: 1.3MM **Privately Held**
WEB: www.downtownakron.com
SIC: 8699 Charitable organization

(G-200)
DRB SYSTEMS LLC (PA)
3245 Pickle Rd (44312-5333)
P.O. Box 550, Uniontown (44685-0550)
PHONE.................................330 645-3299
Fax: 330 645-2299
Dale Brott, *President*
Vincent Scovern, *Technical Mgr*
William Dietz, *Research*
James Flesher, *Engineer*
Kenneth Brott, *Treasurer*
EMP: 85
SALES (est): 33.8MM **Privately Held**
WEB: www.drbsystems.com
SIC: 7373 7371 7372 Systems software development services; custom computer programming services; prepackaged software

(G-201)
DSI EAST
73 Massillon Rd (44312-1028)
PHONE.................................330 733-1861
EMP: 29
SALES (est): 309.1K **Publicly Held**
SIC: 8092 Kidney dialysis centers
PA: Davita Inc.
   2000 16th St
   Denver CO 80202

(G-202)
DUER CONSTRUCTION CO INC
70 E North St (44304-1203)
PHONE.................................330 848-9930
Fax: 330 848-9931
Lawrence Griebel, *President*
Tom Griebel, *Vice Pres*
Karen Thomas, *Buyer*
EMP: 75
SQ FT: 20,000
SALES (est): 4.5MM **Privately Held**
WEB: www.duerconstructioncompany.com
SIC: 1741 Bricklaying

(G-203)
E & V VENTURES INC (PA)
Also Called: Two Men and A Truck
1511 E Market St (44305-4208)
PHONE.................................330 794-6683
Fax: 330 794-6684
Victoria Slama, *President*
Kenneth Slama Jr, *Vice Pres*
Eric Voth, *Vice Pres*
Jerry Dennison, *Manager*
EMP: 46
SALES (est): 6.5MM **Privately Held**
SIC: 4212 Moving services

(G-204)
EARTH N WOOD PRODUCTS INC
2436 S Arlington Rd (44319-2029)
PHONE.................................330 644-1858
EMP: 49
SALES (corp-wide): 15.4MM **Privately Held**
SIC: 5099 Whol Durable Goods
PA: Earth 'n Wood Products, Inc.
   5335 Strausser St Nw
   Canton OH 44720
   330 499-8309

(G-205)
EAST AKRON NEIGHBORHOOD DEV
Also Called: Akron Lead Base Program
550 S Arlington St (44306-1740)
PHONE.................................330 773-6838
Laura Hengoed, *Property Mgr*

Grady Appleton, *Exec Dir*
Fred Vaughn, *Deputy Dir*
Charles Small, *Maintence Staff*
EMP: 45
SQ FT: 1,701
SALES (est): 4.9MM **Privately Held**
SIC: 8699 Charitable organization

(G-206)
ECHOGEN POWER SYSTEMS DEL INC
365 Water St (44308-1044)
PHONE.................................234 542-4379
Philip Brennan, *CEO*
Timothy Held, *Principal*
Mark Terzola, *COO*
Edward Zdankiewicz,
▲ **EMP:** 36 **EST:** 2011
SALES: 30.4MM **Privately Held**
SIC: 4911 Generation, electric power

(G-207)
EMERGE COUNSELING SERVICE
900 Mull Ave (44313-7502)
PHONE.................................330 865-8351
John Palmer, *President*
Lee Wetherbee, *Principal*
EMP: 30
SALES (est): 124.2K **Privately Held**
SIC: 8049 8093 8322 Clinical psychologist; mental health clinic, outpatient; family counseling services

(G-208)
EMERGE MINISTRIES INC
900 Mull Ave (44313-7597)
PHONE.................................330 865-8351
Fax: 330 873-3439
Clayton Glickert, *President*
Richard D Dobbins, *President*
Dr Donald A Lichi, *Vice Pres*
Julie Carpenter, *Treasurer*
Norma Rowe, *Treasurer*
EMP: 44
SQ FT: 25,000
SALES (est): 2.2MM **Privately Held**
WEB: www.emerge.org
SIC: 8322 7841 5942 General counseling services; video disk/tape rental to the general public; books, religious

(G-209)
EPIPHANY MANAGEMENT GROUP LLC
283 E Waterloo Rd (44319-1238)
PHONE.................................330 706-4056
Suranjan Shome, *Principal*
Doug Jones, *COO*
Joe Bukovina, *Finance Mgr*
Craig Main, *Accounts Mgr*
Scott Lazur, *Consultant*
EMP: 30
SALES (est): 5.5MM **Privately Held**
WEB: www.epiphanymgmt.com
SIC: 8742 Business consultant

(G-210)
EXECUTIVE INSURANCE AGENCY (PA)
130 Springside Dr Ste 300 (44333-2489)
PHONE.................................330 576-1234
Lawrence S Rybka, *Ch of Bd*
Joseph Pilla, *Vice Pres*
Troy Crook, *Opers Staff*
Sarah Lee, *Manager*
Benjamin Rovee, *CIO*
EMP: 28
SQ FT: 7,000
SALES (est): 3.8MM **Privately Held**
SIC: 6411 Insurance agents

(G-211)
EXECUTIVE PROPERTIES INC (PA)
733 W Market St Ste 102 (44303-1088)
PHONE.................................330 376-4037
Fax: 330 376-8669
Thomas J Dillon, *President*
Francis Dillon Kline, *Vice Pres*
Kathy Lloyd, *Manager*
Linda Reynolds, *Manager*
EMP: 30
SQ FT: 600

SALES (est): 5.1MM **Privately Held**
WEB: www.execprop.com
SIC: 6531 Real estate managers; rental agent, real estate

(G-212)
EXONIC SYSTEMS LLC
380 Water St (44308-1045)
P.O. Box 1030 (44309-1030)
PHONE.................................330 315-3100
Richard Rogers, *President*
Don Vulgamore, *Office Mgr*
EMP: 35
SQ FT: 17,000
SALES: 12MM **Privately Held**
SIC: 5065 Electronic parts & equipment

(G-213)
FAIRLAWN COUNTRY CLUB COMPANY
200 N Wheaton Rd (44313-3963)
P.O. Box 5423 (44334-0423)
PHONE.................................330 836-5541
Fax: 330 873-2572
Kelly Butler, *President*
Mike Balso, *Vice Pres*
Elizabeth Wecker, *Marketing Mgr*
Eileen Benson, *Director*
EMP: 70 **EST:** 1917
SQ FT: 40,000
SALES: 5.4MM **Privately Held**
WEB: www.fairlawncountryclub.com
SIC: 7997 5813 5812 Country club, membership; drinking places; eating places

(G-214)
FALLSWAY EQUIPMENT CO INC (PA)
1277 Devalera St (44310-2454)
P.O. Box 4537 (44310-0537)
PHONE.................................330 633-6000
Fax: 330 633-6080
Jeffrey Zimmer, *President*
Harry Fairhurst, *Owner*
Gregory Fairhurst, *COO*
Teresa Forwalder, *Manager*
Tom McGuire, *Manager*
▲ **EMP:** 114
SQ FT: 92,140
SALES (est): 65.1MM **Privately Held**
WEB: www.fallsway.com
SIC: 5084 5511 7699 7359 Trucks, industrial; lift trucks & parts; trucks, tractors & trailers: new & used; industrial truck repair; industrial truck rental

(G-215)
FAMOUS DISTRIBUTION INC (HQ)
Also Called: Famous Supply Companies
2620 Ridgewood Rd Ste 200 (44313-3507)
P.O. Box 951344, Cleveland (44193-0011)
PHONE.................................330 762-9621
Jay Blaushild, *CEO*
Marc Blaushild, *President*
Nick Ezzone, *Vice Pres*
Callie St Clair, *Opers Mgr*
Brian Blaushild, *Purch Dir*
EMP: 60
SQ FT: 200,000
SALES (est): 210.7MM **Privately Held**
WEB: www.famous-supply.com
SIC: 5074 5075 5085 5023 Plumbing & hydronic heating supplies; furnaces, warm air; warm air heating equipment & supplies; valves & fittings; kitchenware

(G-216)
FAMOUS DISTRIBUTION INC
Also Called: Johnson Contrls Authorized Dlr
166 N Union St (44304-1355)
PHONE.................................330 434-5194
Fax: 330 434-9358
Cari Sutton, *Plant Mgr*
Steve Greer, *Manager*
Dave Pappas, *Manager*
EMP: 50 **Privately Held**
WEB: www.famous-supply.com
SIC: 5075 5074 Furnaces, warm air; plumbing & hydronic heating supplies
HQ: Famous Distribution Inc
   2620 Ridgewood Rd Ste 200
   Akron OH 44313
   330 762-9621

(G-217)
FAMOUS ENTERPRISES INC (PA)
Also Called: Famous Manufacturing
2620 Ridgewood Rd Ste 200 (44313-3507)
PHONE.................................330 762-9621
Fax: 330 762-8722
Marc Blaushild, *President*
Jay Blaushild, *Chairman*
Dale J Newman, *Treasurer*
Anthony Panas, *Sales Staff*
Naomi Baity, *Manager*
EMP: 45
SQ FT: 20,000
SALES (est): 292.4MM **Privately Held**
WEB: www.jfgood.com
SIC: 5075 5031 5074 7699 Warm air heating equipment & supplies; lumber, plywood & millwork; plumbing & hydronic heating supplies; industrial equipment services

(G-218)
FAMOUS II INC (PA)
Also Called: Pittsburgh Plumbing & Htg Sup
2620 Ridgewood Rd Ste 200 (44313-3507)
PHONE.................................330 762-9621
Jay Blaushild, *President*
Richard Newman, *Shareholder*
EMP: 55
SALES (est): 56.3MM **Privately Held**
WEB: www.famoussupply.com
SIC: 5075 5074 Furnaces, heating: electric; plumbing & hydronic heating supplies

(G-219)
FAMOUS INDUSTRIES INC (HQ)
Also Called: Johnson Contrls Authorized Dlr
2620 Ridgewood Rd Ste 200 (44313-3507)
PHONE.................................330 535-1811
Fax: 330 353-5057
Jay Blaushild, *President*
Marc Blaushild, *Vice Pres*
CAM Jordan, *Technical Mgr*
EMP: 50
SALES (est): 77.3MM **Privately Held**
WEB: www.jfgoodco.com
SIC: 5074 3444 5065 Plumbing & hydronic heating supplies; plumbing & heating valves; metal ventilating equipment; telephone equipment; intercommunication equipment, electronic

(G-220)
FAMOUS INDUSTRIES INC
Also Called: J F Good Co
166 N Union St (44304-1355)
PHONE.................................330 535-1811
Jim Vinson, *Manager*
Mike Palermo, *Manager*
David Ross, *Manager*
Rick Wank, *Director*
EMP: 40 **Privately Held**
WEB: www.jfgoodco.com
SIC: 5074 Plumbing & hydronic heating supplies
HQ: Famous Industries, Inc.
   2620 Ridgewood Rd Ste 200
   Akron OH 44313
   330 535-1811

(G-221)
FC 1346 LLC
118 Hollywood Ave (44313-6724)
PHONE.................................330 864-8170
Edward Pelavin,
EMP: 47
SALES (est): 2MM
SALES (corp-wide): 3.7MM **Privately Held**
SIC: 1542 Nonresidential construction
PA: Epdl, Llc
   118 Hollywood Ave
   Akron OH 44313
   330 864-8170

(G-222)
FC SCHWENDLER LLC
724 Canton Rd (44312-2607)
P.O. Box 6341 (44312-0341)
PHONE.................................330 733-8715
Fred Schwendler, *Partner*
Anne Schwendler,
EMP: 27
SQ FT: 29,000

▲ = Import ▼=Export
◆ =Import/Export

GEOGRAPHIC SECTION — Akron - Summit County (G-246)

SALES: 526K Privately Held
SIC: 8741 Management services

(G-223)
FEDEX FREIGHT INC
678 Killian Rd (44319-2528)
PHONE..................................330 645-0879
EMP: 80
SALES (corp-wide): 47.4B Publicly Held
SIC: 4213 4212 Trucking Operator-Nonlocal Local Trucking Operator
HQ: Fedex Freight, Inc.
    2200 Forward Dr
    Harrison AR 72601
    870 741-9000

(G-224)
FIRST AMRCN CASH ADVNCE SC LLC
3100 Manchester Rd (44319-1464)
PHONE..................................330 644-9144
Fax: 330 644-9144
EMP: 52 Privately Held
SIC: 6361 Title Insurance Carrier
HQ: First American Cash Advance Of South Carolina, Llc
    1603 N Longstreet St
    Kingstree SC

(G-225)
FIRSTENERGY CORP (PA)
76 S Main St Bsmt (44308-1817)
PHONE..................................800 736-3402
George M Smart, *Ch of Bd*
Charles E Jones, *President*
K Jon Taylor, *Vice Pres*
James F Pearson, *CFO*
Ebony L Yeboah-Amankwah, *Officer*
EMP: 1618
SALES: 14B Publicly Held
WEB: www.firstenergycorp.com
SIC: 4911 Electric services; distribution, electric power; generation, electric power; transmission, electric power

(G-226)
FIRSTENERGY NUCLEAR OPER CO
76 S Main St Bsmt (44308-1817)
PHONE..................................800 646-0400
Fax: 330 384-3856
Anthony J Alexander, *CEO*
James H Lash, *President*
Garry Leidich, *President*
Lew Myers, *COO*
Charles E Jones, *Exec VP*
EMP: 13000
SQ FT: 250,000
SALES (est): 1.2B Publicly Held
SIC: 4911 Electric services
PA: Firstenergy Corp.
    76 S Main St Bsmt
    Akron OH 44308

(G-227)
FLEXSYS AMERICA LP (DH)
260 Springside Dr (44333-4554)
PHONE..................................330 666-4111
Fax: 330 688-8345
Enrique Bolanos, *CEO*
James Voss, *President*
Steve Wiliamson, *Purchasing*
Frederick Ignatz-Hoover, *Adv Mgr*
Dennis Hay, *Manager*
▼ EMP: 65
SQ FT: 85,000
SALES (est): 22MM Publicly Held
SIC: 3069 8731 2899 2823 Reclaimed rubber & specialty rubber compounds; commercial physical research; chemical preparations; cellulosic manmade fibers; synthetic rubber; plastics materials & resins
HQ: Solutia Inc.
    575 Maryville Centre Dr
    Saint Louis MO 63141
    423 229-2000

(G-228)
FORMU3 INTERNATIONAL INC (PA)
395 Springside Dr (44333-2434)
PHONE..................................330 668-1461
Charles Sekeres, *President*
EMP: 35

SALES (est): 1.4MM Privately Held
SIC: 8093 7299 Weight loss clinic, with medical staff; diet center, without medical staff

(G-229)
FRED MARTIN NISSAN LLC
3388 S Arlington Rd (44312-5257)
PHONE..................................330 644-8888
Fax: 330 564-2042
Michael Patton, *General Mgr*
Fred Kodroff, *Finance Mgr*
Duane Huff,
Adam Huff,
EMP: 45
SALES (est): 12.5MM Privately Held
SIC: 5511 7539 Automobiles, new & used; automotive repair shops

(G-230)
FRED W ALBRECHT GROCERY CO
Also Called: Acme
3979 Medina Rd (44333-2444)
PHONE..................................330 666-6781
Fax: 330 666-8015
Denny Hoover, *Branch Mgr*
Bill Haliko, *Manager*
EMP: 180
SALES (corp-wide): 339.6MM Privately Held
WEB: www.acmefreshmarket.com
SIC: 5411 5912 7384 Grocery stores, chain; drug stores & proprietary stores; photofinish laboratories
PA: The Fred W Albrecht Grocery Company
    2700 Gilchrist Rd Ste A
    Akron OH 44305
    330 733-2861

(G-231)
FRITO-LAY NORTH AMERICA INC
1460 E Turkeyfoot Lake Rd (44312-5349)
PHONE..................................330 786-6000
Fax: 330 786-6050
Jessica Wolf, *Sales Mgr*
Papo Ray, *Marketing Staff*
Doug Evans, *Branch Mgr*
EMP: 40
SQ FT: 14,832
SALES (corp-wide): 63.5B Publicly Held
WEB: www.fritolay.com
SIC: 4225 General warehousing
HQ: Frito-Lay North America, Inc.
    7701 Legacy Dr
    Plano TX 75024

(G-232)
G & O RESOURCES LTD
96 E Crosier St (44311-2342)
PHONE..................................330 253-2525
Robert Nelson, *CEO*
Chuck Will, *Manager*
EMP: 60
SALES (est): 3.4MM Privately Held
WEB: www.goresources.com
SIC: 4932 Gas & other services combined

(G-233)
GBC DESIGN INC
565 White Pond Dr (44320-1123)
PHONE..................................330 283-6870
Sy Cymerman, *President*
EMP: 37
SQ FT: 10,000
SALES (est): 5.1MM Privately Held
WEB: www.gbcdesign.com
SIC: 8711 8712 Consulting engineer; architectural services

(G-234)
GENERAL TRANSPORT INCORPORATED
1100 Jenkins Blvd (44306-3754)
P.O. Box 7727 (44306-0727)
PHONE..................................330 786-3400
Harold Joseph Ostrowske, *President*
Michelle Troy, *Corp Secy*
John Troy, *Vice Pres*
Brian Bianchi, *Opers Mgr*
EMP: 200
SQ FT: 5,000

SALES (est): 14.9MM Privately Held
WEB: www.generaltrans.com
SIC: 4213 Trucking, except local

(G-235)
GENESIS CORP
Also Called: Genesis 10
1 Cascade Plz Ste 1230 (44308-1144)
PHONE..................................330 597-4100
Nate Gram, *Branch Mgr*
EMP: 85
SALES (corp-wide): 179.7MM Privately Held
SIC: 7379
PA: Genesis Corp.
    950 3rd Ave Ste 900
    New York NY 10022
    212 688-5522

(G-236)
GIRONDA VITO & BROS INC
1130 Brittain Rd (44305-1005)
PHONE..................................330 630-9399
Fax: 330 630-3866
Frank Gironda, *President*
Pamela Gironda, *Vice Pres*
Jon Romesberg, *Manager*
EMP: 40
SQ FT: 7,200
SALES (est): 4.2MM Privately Held
WEB: www.vgconstruction.com
SIC: 1771 Concrete work

(G-237)
GLENCOE RESTORATION GROUP LLC
Also Called: Grgstormpro
575 Canton Rd (44312-2511)
PHONE..................................330 752-1244
Whitney Philips, *Mng Member*
EMP: 32
SQ FT: 1,600
SALES: 500K Privately Held
SIC: 1531 Operative builders

(G-238)
GLOBAL EXEC SLUTIONS GROUP LLC
Also Called: Mri Network
3505 Embassy Pkwy Ste 200 (44333-8404)
PHONE..................................330 666-3354
Fax: 330 666-5655
Scott Chadbourne, *Managing Dir*
Patricia Nicklaus, *Transportation*
John Davis, *Senior Mgr*
Jeff Friess, *Senior Mgr*
Keith Gardner, *Senior Mgr*
EMP: 27 EST: 2001
SQ FT: 14,000
SALES (est): 2.5MM Privately Held
WEB: www.mriexecutivesolutions.com
SIC: 7361 Executive placement

(G-239)
GMI HOLDINGS INC
Genie Company, The
2850 Gilchrist Rd (44305-4444)
PHONE..................................330 794-0846
EMP: 55
SALES (corp-wide): 2.8B Privately Held
SIC: 4225 5072 General Warehouse/Storage Whol Hardware
HQ: Gmi Holdings, Inc.
    1 Door Dr
    Mount Hope OH 44660
    330 821-5360

(G-240)
GOLDEN LIVING LLC
Also Called: Beverly
721 Hickory St (44303-2213)
PHONE..................................330 762-6486
Fax: 330 762-1862
Michael Jordan, *Manager*
Linda Sullivan Rn, *Nursing Dir*
EMP: 200
SALES (corp-wide): 7.4MM Privately Held
SIC: 8059 8051 Convalescent home; skilled nursing care facilities
PA: Golden Living Llc
    5220 Tennyson Pkwy # 400
    Plano TX 75024
    972 372-6300

(G-241)
GOODWILL INDUSTRIES INC
Also Called: Pic
570 E Waterloo Rd (44319-1223)
PHONE..................................330 724-6995
Fax: 330 786-2507
Nan McClenagham, *President*
Laura Mervine, *Payroll Mgr*
Jim Bouplon, *CTO*
Gail Ball, *Executive*
Brenda Baum, *Executive*
EMP: 50
SALES (est): 5MM Privately Held
SIC: 8322 8331 7361 Individual & family services; job training & vocational rehabilitation services; employment agencies

(G-242)
GOODWILL INDUSTRIES OF AKRON (PA)
570 E Waterloo Rd (44319-1223)
PHONE..................................330 724-6995
Nancy Ellis McClenaghan, *CEO*
M M Montis, *Principal*
Hester Allison, *Vice Pres*
Janet Morrison, *Vice Pres*
Greg Morton, *Vice Pres*
EMP: 150
SQ FT: 112,000
SALES: 17.3MM Privately Held
WEB: www.goodwillakron.org
SIC: 8331 Vocational rehabilitation agency

(G-243)
GOODYEAR TIRE & RUBBER COMPANY (PA)
200 E Innovation Way (44316-0001)
PHONE..................................330 796-2121
Fax: 330 796-3183
Richard J Kramer, *Ch of Bd*
Carol Archer, *President*
Chris Delaney, *President*
Jean-Claude Kihn, *President*
Stephen R McClellan, *President*
◆ EMP: 3000 EST: 1898
SALES: 15.3B Publicly Held
WEB: www.goodyear.com
SIC: 3011 3052 7534 7538 Tires & inner tubes; inner tubes, all types; pneumatic tires, all types; tire & inner tube materials & related products; rubber & plastics hose & beltings; automobile hose, rubber; rubber belting; tire retreading & repair shops; rebuilding & retreading tires; general automotive repair shops; truck engine repair, except industrial; automotive repair shops; brake services; shock absorber replacement; tune-up service, automotive; motor vehicle supplies & new parts; automotive servicing equipment; automotive supplies & parts

(G-244)
GPD SERVICES COMPANY INC (PA)
Also Called: Gpd Associates
520 S Main St Ste 2531 (44311-1073)
PHONE..................................330 572-2100
Fax: 330 434-1331
David B Granger, *President*
Darrin Kotecki, *President*
EMP: 62
SALES (est): 20MM Privately Held
SIC: 8712 Architectural services

(G-245)
GREAT LAKES HOME HLTH SVCS INC
1530 W Market St (44313-7141)
PHONE..................................888 260-9835
EMP: 50 Privately Held
SIC: 8082 Home health care services
PA: Great Lakes Home Health Services, Inc.
    900 Cooper St
    Jackson MI 49202

(G-246)
GREATER AKRON MUSICAL ASSN
Also Called: AKRON SYMPHONY
92 N Main St (44308-1932)
PHONE..................................330 535-8131
Fax: 330 535-7302
Robert L Culp Jr, *Vice Pres*

Akron - Summit County (G-247)   **GEOGRAPHIC SECTION**

Orzella Matherson, *Vice Pres*
Robert Mollard, *Persnl Mgr*
Paul Jarrett, *Mktg Dir*
Bill Walz, *Director*
EMP: 88
SQ FT: 22,000
SALES: 1.7MM **Privately Held**
SIC: 7929 Symphony orchestras

(G-247)
GREENLEAF FAMILY CENTER (PA)
580 Grant St (44311-9910)
PHONE...................330 376-9494
Judy Joyce, *President*
Naomi Sciulli, *Facilities Mgr*
James M Athans, *Psychologist*
Karen McKeighen, *Manager*
Pamela Meredith, *Program Dir*
EMP: 28
SQ FT: 8,000
SALES: 2.6MM **Privately Held**
WEB: www.greenleafctr.org
SIC: 8322 Family service agency; family counseling services

(G-248)
GREENSTAR MID-AMERICA LLC
1535 Exeter Rd (44306-3889)
PHONE...................330 784-1167
Tom Jackson, *Branch Mgr*
EMP: 25
SALES (corp-wide): 14.4B **Publicly Held**
SIC: 4953 Recycling, waste materials
HQ: Greenstar Mid-America, Llc
   1001 Fannin St Ste 4000
   Houston TX 77002

(G-249)
GUYS PARTY CENTER
Also Called: Guy's Party Ctr
500 E Waterloo Rd (44319-1272)
PHONE...................330 724-6373
Fax: 330 724-4070
Rocky Zimbardi, *President*
Anthony Zimbardi, *General Mgr*
Michael Nyeste, *Sales Executive*
EMP: 50
SALES (est): 1.3MM **Privately Held**
WEB: www.guyspartycenter.com
SIC: 7299 5812 Banquet hall facilities; eating places

(G-250)
H&R BLOCK INC
Also Called: H & R Block
1400 S Arlington St # 18 (44306-3772)
PHONE...................330 773-0412
Mary Joe Hicks, *Manager*
Donna Carter, *Manager*
EMP: 30
SALES (corp-wide): 3B **Publicly Held**
WEB: www.hrblock.com
SIC: 7291 Tax return preparation services
PA: H&R Block, Inc.
   1 H&R Block Way
   Kansas City MO 64105
   816 854-3000

(G-251)
HAND REHABILITATION ASSOCIATES
3925 Embassy Pkwy Ste 200 (44333-8400)
PHONE...................330 668-4055
Fax: 330 668-4077
Joyce E Baldwin, *President*
Adele L Wargo, *Corp Secy*
EMP: 25
SQ FT: 4,000
SALES (est): 662.8K **Privately Held**
SIC: 8011 Orthopedic physician

(G-252)
HANNA CAMBELL & POWELL
3737 Embassy Pkwy Ste 100 (44333-8380)
PHONE...................330 670-7300
Fax: 330 670-0977
Timothy Campbell, *Partner*
Timothy Campbell, *Partner*
David Hanna, *Partner*
Donald Powell, *Partner*
Juliana Gall, *Editor*
EMP: 50

SALES (est): 8.2MM **Privately Held**
WEB: www.hcplaw.net
SIC: 8111 Corporate, partnership & business law

(G-253)
HARRY C LOBALZO & SONS INC (PA)
Also Called: Hobart Sales & Service
61 N Cleveland Ste A (44333)
PHONE...................330 666-6758
Fax: 330 666-8645
Harry C Lobalzo, *President*
Rick Lobalzo, *Exec VP*
Douglas Fox, *Financial Exec*
Dina Saprido, *Manager*
▲ **EMP:** 45
SQ FT: 20,000
SALES (est): 20.5MM **Privately Held**
WEB: www.lobalzo.com
SIC: 5046 7699 3556 Commercial cooking & food service equipment; bakery equipment & supplies; restaurant equipment repair; food products machinery

(G-254)
HARTVILLE GROUP INC (PA)
1210 Massillon Rd (44306-3327)
PHONE...................330 484-8166
Nicholas J Leighton, *Ch of Bd*
Dennis C Rushovich, *President*
Chris Chaney, *President*
Scott Taylor, *President*
Liz Watson, *President*
EMP: 39
SQ FT: 12,395
SALES (est): 35.5MM **Privately Held**
WEB: www.hartvillegroup.com
SIC: 6399 Health insurance for pets

(G-255)
HARWICK STANDARD DIST CORP (PA)
60 S Seiberling St (44305-4217)
P.O. Box 9360 (44305-0360)
PHONE...................330 798-9300
Fax: 330 798-0214
Ernie Pouttu, *CEO*
Jeffrey J Buda, *President*
Richard A Chenoweth, *Principal*
Brian Johnson, *Principal*
Bill Knezevich, *Principal*
♦ **EMP:** 60
SQ FT: 160,000
SALES (est): 80MM **Privately Held**
WEB: www.harwickstandard.com
SIC: 5169 Chemicals, industrial & heavy

(G-256)
HASENSTAB ARCHITECTS INC (PA)
190 N Union St Ste 400 (44304-1362)
PHONE...................330 434-4464
Fax: 330 434-8546
Dennis Check, *President*
Robert Medziuch, *Treasurer*
Julie Todich, *Admin Sec*
Nadja Barnett,
David Marino,
EMP: 37
SALES (est): 7.5MM **Privately Held**
WEB: www.hainc.cc
SIC: 8712 Architectural engineering

(G-257)
HAT WHITE MANAGEMENT LLC (PA)
Also Called: Life Skills Center
121 S Main St Ste 200 (44308-1426)
PHONE...................800 525-7967
Fax: 330 535-5055
Rodd Coker, *Vice Pres*
Robert L Fox, *Vice Pres*
Kerry Jupina, *Vice Pres*
Wendy Rydarowicz, *Vice Pres*
Nathan Flaker, *Accountant*
EMP: 40
SALES (est): 24.1MM **Privately Held**
WEB: www.whitehatmgmt.com
SIC: 4142 8741 Bus charter service, except local; business management

(G-258)
HAVEN REST MINISTRIES INC (PA)
175 E Market St (44308-2011)
P.O. Box 547 (44309-0547)
PHONE...................330 535-1563
Fax: 330 535-8917
James Cummins, *President*
Dr Forest Crocker, *Vice Pres*
Emil A Voelz Jr, *Vice Pres*
Kathy Wells, *Controller*
L J Dalton, *Manager*
EMP: 90
SQ FT: 45,851
SALES (est): 3.7MM **Privately Held**
WEB: www.havenofrest.org
SIC: 8661 8322 Non-denominational church; individual & family services

(G-259)
HCR MANORCARE MED SVCS FLA LLC
Also Called: Arden Courts of Akron Bath
171 N Clvland Mssillon Rd (44333-2422)
PHONE...................330 668-6889
Fax: 330 668-6242
Richard Winslow, *Exec Dir*
EMP: 60
SQ FT: 25,448
SALES (corp-wide): 3.6B **Publicly Held**
WEB: www.manorcare.com
SIC: 8051 Convalescent home with continuous nursing care
HQ: Hcr Manorcare Medical Services Of Florida, Llc
   333 N Summit St Ste 100
   Toledo OH 43604
   419 252-5500

(G-260)
HEALTHCARE FACILITY MGT LLC
Also Called: Wyant Woods Care Center
200 Wyant Rd (44313-4228)
PHONE...................330 836-7953
Jim Burke, *Administration*
EMP: 115
SALES (corp-wide): 103.9MM **Privately Held**
WEB: www.communicarehealth.com
SIC: 8051 8052 Skilled nursing care facilities; intermediate care facilities
PA: Communicare Health Services, Inc.
   4700 Ashwood Dr Ste 200
   Blue Ash OH 45241
   513 530-1654

(G-261)
HEALTHSPAN INTEGRATED CARE
Also Called: Kaiser Foundation Health Plan
1260 Independence Ave (44310-1812)
PHONE...................330 633-8400
EMP: 29
SALES (corp-wide): 4.2B **Privately Held**
SIC: 6324 Hospital & medical service plans
HQ: Healthspan Integrated Care
   1001 Lakeside Ave E # 1200
   Cleveland OH 44114
   216 621-5600

(G-262)
HERITAGE TRUCK EQUIPMENT INC
1600 E Waterloo Rd (44306-4103)
P.O. Box 189, Uniontown (44685-0189)
PHONE...................330 699-4491
Fax: 330 564-0756
Eric Bontrager, *President*
Brian Bontrager, *Vice Pres*
Robert Shenefield, *Plant Mgr*
Bob Shenefield, *Prdtn Mgr*
Al Morris, *Parts Mgr*
EMP: 40
SQ FT: 15,000
SALES (est): 12.2MM **Privately Held**
WEB: www.heritagetruck.com
SIC: 5531 7539 Truck equipment & parts; trailer repair

(G-263)
HICKORY HEALTH CARE INC
721 Hickory St (44303-2213)
PHONE...................330 762-6486
Brian Colleran, *President*

Shelly Bacon, *Nursing Dir*
Allie Kozick, *Social Dir*
January Wells, *Food Svc Dir*
Stephanie Potter, *Admin Asst*
EMP: 99
SALES (est): 2.1MM **Privately Held**
SIC: 8059 Nursing home, except skilled & intermediate care facility

(G-264)
HIGH LINE CORPORATION
Also Called: Casnet
45 Goodyear Blvd (44305-4032)
PHONE...................330 848-8800
Fax: 330 848-8866
Bradley D Bowers, *President*
Mike Leeders, *Vice Pres*
Matt Golz, *Controller*
Jeff Comer, *CTO*
Terry Starkey, *Director*
EMP: 50
SQ FT: 30,000
SALES (est): 5.9MM **Privately Held**
WEB: www.gotocasnet.com
SIC: 7389 5999 7629 4226 Microfilm recording & developing service; telephone & communication equipment; electrical repair shops; document & office records storage

(G-265)
HILLANDALE FARMS CORPORATION (PA)
1330 Austin Ave (44306-3106)
PHONE...................330 724-3199
Fax: 330 243-4999
Orland Bethel, *President*
Gary Bethel, *Corp Secy*
Keven Patton, *Facilities Mgr*
EMP: 45
SQ FT: 10,000
SALES (est): 27.5MM **Privately Held**
WEB: www.hillandalefarms.com
SIC: 5144 5143 5147 5141 Eggs; butter; cheese; meats & meat products; groceries, general line

(G-266)
HITCHCOCK FLEMING & ASSOC INC
Also Called: H F A
500 Wolf Ledges Pkwy (44311-1080)
PHONE...................330 376-2111
Fax: 330 376-2220
Jack Deleo, *CEO*
Nick Betro, *President*
Charles Abraham, *Managing Prtnr*
Heith Busch, *Vice Pres*
Sandi Nelson, *Production*
EMP: 90
SQ FT: 16,000
SALES: 19MM **Privately Held**
SIC: 7311 Advertising consultant

(G-267)
HOC TRANSPORT COMPANY
1569 Industrial Pkwy (44310-2603)
PHONE...................330 630-0100
Fax: 330 630-0108
Carl Hummel, *Principal*
Dale Costilow, *Supervisor*
EMP: 26
SALES (est): 4.1MM **Privately Held**
SIC: 4789 Cargo loading & unloading services

(G-268)
HOGLUND CHWLKOWSKI MROZIK PLLC
Also Called: Hoglund Law
520 S Main St (44311-1072)
PHONE...................330 252-8009
Robert Hoglund, *Branch Mgr*
EMP: 119 **Privately Held**
SIC: 8111 Legal services
PA: Hoglund, Chwialkowski & Mrozik Pllc
   1781 County Road B W
   Saint Paul MN 55113

(G-269)
HOLLAND OIL COMPANY (PA)
1485 Marion Ave (44313-7625)
PHONE...................330 835-1815
Lisa M Holland-Toth, *President*
Lynn Gorman, *Exec VP*

▲ = Import ▼ = Export
♦ = Import/Export

GEOGRAPHIC SECTION

Akron - Summit County (G-293)

Michael J Toth, *Senior VP*
Carl Hummel, *VP Opers*
James Bartlebaugh, *Human Res Dir*
EMP: 70
SQ FT: 20,000
SALES: 179.2MM **Privately Held**
WEB: www.hollandoil.com
SIC: 5541 5172 5411 Gasoline service stations; gasoline; service station supplies, petroleum; convenience stores

(G-270)
HOLUB IRON & STEEL COMPANY
470 N Arlington St (44305-1604)
PHONE.................................330 252-5655
Stephen Carroll, *President*
EMP: 25 **EST:** 1924
SQ FT: 7,500
SALES (est): 2.8MM **Privately Held**
SIC: 5093 5051 Ferrous metal scrap & waste; nonferrous metals scrap; steel

(G-271)
HOME DEPOT USA INC
Also Called: Home Depot, The
2811 S Arlington Rd (44312-4715)
PHONE.................................330 245-0280
Fax: 330 245-2187
Eric Hilgert, *Branch Mgr*
EMP: 200
SQ FT: 119,856
SALES (corp-wide): 100.9B **Publicly Held**
WEB: www.homerentalsdepot.com
SIC: 5211 7359 Home centers; tool rental
HQ: Home Depot U.S.A., Inc.
   2455 Paces Ferry Rd Se
   Atlanta GA 30339

(G-272)
HOWARD HANNA SMYTHE CRAMER
2603 W Market St Ste 100a (44313-4214)
PHONE.................................216 447-4477
Fax: 330 836-5966
Cris Burdick, *Manager*
George Crumlich, *Administration*
Janis Brenneman, *Real Est Agnt*
Marilyn M Close, *Real Est Agnt*
Michael E Latine, *Real Est Agnt*
EMP: 70
SALES (corp-wide): 76.4MM **Privately Held**
WEB: www.smythecramer.com
SIC: 6531 Real estate brokers & agents
HQ: Howard Hanna Smythe Cramer
   6000 Parkland Blvd
   Cleveland OH 44124
   216 447-4477

(G-273)
HUNTINGTON NATIONAL BANK
Iii Cascade Plz Fl 7 (44308)
PHONE.................................330 996-6300
Marta Mazurczak, *VP Finance*
EMP: 4814
SALES (corp-wide): 4.7B **Publicly Held**
SIC: 6021 National commercial banks
HQ: The Huntington National Bank
   17 S High St Fl 1
   Columbus OH 43215
   614 480-4293

(G-274)
HUNTINGTON NATIONAL BANK
Also Called: Firstmerit
106 S Main St Fl 5 (44308-1412)
PHONE.................................330 384-7201
Dave Humbel, *Senior VP*
Joseph Kwasny, *Senior VP*
Michael Mason, *Senior VP*
Craig Schurr, *Senior VP*
Scott Terryn, *Senior VP*
EMP: 2836
SALES (corp-wide): 4.7B **Publicly Held**
SIC: 6021 National commercial banks
HQ: The Huntington National Bank
   17 S High St Fl 1
   Columbus OH 43215
   614 480-4293

(G-275)
HUNTINGTON NATIONAL BANK
121 S Main St Ste 200 (44308-1426)
PHONE.................................330 384-7092
Fax: 330 384-7321
EMP: 25
SALES (corp-wide): 4.7B **Publicly Held**
SIC: 6021 National commercial banks
HQ: The Huntington National Bank
   17 S High St Fl 1
   Columbus OH 43215
   614 480-4293

(G-276)
IACOMINIS PAPA JOES INC
1561 Akron Peninsula Rd (44313-5159)
PHONE.................................330 923-7999
Judith Amato, *President*
Jeffrey Bruno, *Treasurer*
EMP: 89
SALES (est): 3.8MM **Privately Held**
WEB: www.lopico.com
SIC: 7299 5812 5921 Banquet hall facilities; eating places; wine

(G-277)
INFO LINE INC
703 S Main St Ste 200 (44311-1098)
PHONE.................................330 252-8064
Richard Stahl, *President*
EMP: 47
SALES: 4MM **Privately Held**
SIC: 8322 Referral service for personal & social problems

(G-278)
INFOCISION MANAGEMENT CORP (PA)
325 Springside Dr (44333-4504)
PHONE.................................330 668-1411
Fax: 330 668-1401
Craig Taylor, *CEO*
Gary Taylor, *Ch of Bd*
Steve Boyazis, *President*
Mike Langenfeld, *COO*
Steve Brubaker, *Senior VP*
EMP: 356
SQ FT: 38,000
SALES (est): 242.3MM **Privately Held**
WEB: www.infocision.com
SIC: 7389 Telemarketing services

(G-279)
INFOCISION MANAGEMENT CORP
250 N Clvland Mssillon Rd (44333-2479)
PHONE.................................330 668-6615
Marshal Larsen, *Branch Mgr*
Jennifer Opphile, *Manager*
EMP: 227
SALES (corp-wide): 242.3MM **Privately Held**
WEB: www.infocision.com
SIC: 7389 Telemarketing services
PA: Infocision Management Corporation
   325 Springside Dr
   Akron OH 44333
   330 668-1411

(G-280)
INSTALLED BUILDING PDTS LLC
Also Called: Nooney & Moses
2783 Gilchrist Rd Unit B (44305-4406)
PHONE.................................330 798-9640
Fax: 330 798-9641
James Pope, *Principal*
Terrill Dillinger, *Manager*
EMP: 30
SALES (corp-wide): 1.1B **Publicly Held**
WEB: www.dwdcpa.com
SIC: 1742 Insulation, buildings
HQ: Installed Building Products Llc
   495 S High St Ste 50
   Columbus OH 43215
   614 221-3399

(G-281)
INTERNAL MEDICINE OF AKRON
150 Springside Dr 320c (44333-2486)
PHONE.................................330 376-2728
Fax: 330 376-0130
Erwin A Maseelall MD, *President*
Jeffrey Eckman, *Principal*
Michael Giddeon, *Principal*
Philip Wilcox, *Med Doctor*
EMP: 25
SALES (est): 3MM **Privately Held**
SIC: 8011 Internal medicine, physician/surgeon

(G-282)
INTERNATIONAL CHEM WKRS CR UN (PA)
1655 W Market St Fl 6 (44313-7004)
PHONE.................................330 926-1444
Fax: 330 867-0544
Frank Cyphers, *Principal*
Randy Vehar, *Counsel*
Eric Bray, *Treasurer*
Susan Moore, *Financial Exec*
Sandy Noble, *Director*
EMP: 40
SQ FT: 60,000
SALES (est): 4.6MM **Privately Held**
SIC: 8631 Labor union

(G-283)
IRACE INC
Also Called: Irace Automotive
2265 W Market St (44313-6907)
PHONE.................................330 836-7247
Jim Irace, *Principal*
EMP: 25 **EST:** 2001
SQ FT: 2,448
SALES (est): 4.4MM **Privately Held**
SIC: 5541 7538 7539 Filling stations, gasoline; general automotive repair shops; automotive repair shops

(G-284)
ISD RENAL INC
Also Called: Akron Renal Center
525 E Market St Bldg 50 (44304-1619)
P.O. Box 102407, Atlanta GA (30368-2407)
PHONE.................................330 375-6848
James K Hilger,
EMP: 85 **Publicly Held**
SIC: 8092 Kidney dialysis centers
HQ: Isd Renal, Inc.
   2000 16th St
   Denver CO 80202

(G-285)
J F BERNARD INC
359 Stanton Ave (44301-1468)
PHONE.................................330 785-3830
Fax: 330 785-3840
Joseph Bernard Jr, *President*
Eric Bernard, *Vice Pres*
Rob Hampton, *Project Mgr*
Johnathan Meade, *Project Mgr*
Steve Noffert, *Accounts Mgr*
EMP: 30
SALES (est): 4.3MM **Privately Held**
WEB: www.jfbinc.com
SIC: 1711 Warm air heating & air conditioning contractor

(G-286)
J W DIDADO ELECTRIC INC
1033 Kelly Ave (44306-3143)
PHONE.................................330 374-0070
Fax: 330 374-0620
Gary Didado, *President*
Rhonda Didado, *Corp Secy*
Tony Didado, *Vice Pres*
Dan Orha, *Project Mgr*
Steve McDeditt, *Controller*
EMP: 40
SQ FT: 6,500
SALES (est): 35.6MM
SALES (corp-wide): 9.4B **Publicly Held**
WEB: www.jwdidadoelectric.com
SIC: 1731 General electrical contractor
PA: Quanta Services, Inc.
   2800 Post Oak Blvd # 2600
   Houston TX 77050
   713 629-7600

(G-287)
J W GEOPFERT CO INC
Also Called: Geopfert Company, The
1024 Home Ave (44310-3579)
PHONE.................................330 762-2293
Fax: 330 762-2293
Thomas Geopfert Jr, *President*
Thomas Geopfert Sr, *Chairman*
Joseph Geopfert, *Vice Pres*
Jean Geopfert, *Treasurer*
Terry Elmert, *Maintence Staff*
EMP: 32 **EST:** 1953
SQ FT: 6,100
SALES (est): 6.7MM **Privately Held**
WEB: www.geopfert.com
SIC: 1711 Warm air heating & air conditioning contractor

(G-288)
J&B SPRAFKA ENTERPRISES INC (PA)
1430 Goodyear Blvd (44305-4168)
PHONE.................................330 733-4212
Brian Sprafka, *President*
Jennifer Sprafka, *Vice Pres*
EMP: 28
SQ FT: 4,000
SALES (est): 1.1MM **Privately Held**
WEB: www.colourourrainbow.com
SIC: 8351 8211 7999 Preschool center; kindergarten; day camp

(G-289)
JACKSON KELLY PLLC
17 S Main St 1 (44308-1803)
PHONE.................................330 252-9060
Cheryl Green, *Branch Mgr*
Andrew N Schock, *Associate*
EMP: 56
SALES (corp-wide): 80.4MM **Privately Held**
SIC: 8111 General practice attorney, lawyer
PA: Jackson Kelly Pllc
   500 Lee St E Ste 1600
   Charleston WV 25301
   304 340-1000

(G-290)
JC PENNEY CORPORATION INC
Also Called: JC Penney
2000 Brittain Rd Ste 600 (44310-1814)
PHONE.................................330 633-7700
Fax: 330 633-4274
Carton Sanders, *Manager*
EMP: 300
SALES (corp-wide): 12.5B **Publicly Held**
SIC: 5311 7231 Department stores, non-discount; beauty shops
HQ: J. C. Penney Corporation, Inc.
   6501 Legacy Dr
   Plano TX 75024
   972 431-1000

(G-291)
JE CARSTEN COMPANY (PA)
Also Called: Vita Pup
61 S Seiberling St (44305-4216)
PHONE.................................330 794-4440
Fax: 330 794-9847
J M Carsten, *President*
James E Carsten, *Corp Secy*
Peter Carsten, *Vice Pres*
Don Thacker, *Info Tech Mgr*
EMP: 36 **EST:** 1947
SQ FT: 22,000
SALES (est): 4.9MM **Privately Held**
SIC: 5194 5145 Cigarettes; cigars; smoking tobacco; confectionery

(G-292)
JEFF PLUMBER INC (PA)
1100 Tower Dr (44305-1090)
PHONE.................................330 940-2600
Jeffrey L Thompson, *CEO*
Kevin Thompson, *Treasurer*
Jordy Skovborg, *Financial Exec*
EMP: 25
SQ FT: 6,000
SALES (est): 4.1MM **Privately Held**
WEB: www.jefftheplumber.com
SIC: 1711 Plumbing contractors

(G-293)
JENNINGS HEATING COMPANY INC
Also Called: Jennings Heating & Cooling
1671 E Market St (44305-4210)
P.O. Box 9442 (44305-0442)
PHONE.................................330 784-1286
Fax: 330 784-6980
Mike Foraker, *President*
Fred S Jennings, *Vice Pres*
Marshall Jennings, *Vice Pres*
Mike Catalano, *Manager*
EMP: 38
SQ FT: 10,000
SALES (est): 6.9MM **Privately Held**
WEB: www.jenningsheating.com
SIC: 1711 Warm air heating & air conditioning contractor

(PA)=Parent Co (HQ)=Headquarters (DH)=Div Headquarters
✪ = New Business established in last 2 years

Akron - Summit County (G-294) GEOGRAPHIC SECTION

(G-294)
JERSEY CENTRAL PWR & LIGHT CO (HQ)
76 E Main St (44308-1812)
PHONE..................................800 736-3402
Donald M Lynch, *President*
Chad Hampson, *General Mgr*
Leila L Vespoli, *Exec VP*
Charles E Jones, *Senior VP*
David C Luff, *Senior VP*
▲ **EMP:** 170 **EST:** 1925
SALES: 1.8B **Publicly Held**
WEB: www.jersey-central-power-light.mon-mouth.n
SIC: 4911 Electric services; distribution, electric power; generation, electric power; transmission, electric power

(G-295)
JOHN DELLAGNESE & ASSOC INC
4000 Embassy Pkwy Ste 400 (44333-8357)
PHONE..................................330 668-4000
Regina Shaw, *President*
Christina Kallio, *Accountant*
EMP: 25
SQ FT: 8,600
SALES: 1MM **Privately Held**
WEB: www.dellagnese.com
SIC: 6531 Real estate managers

(G-296)
JOHN P NOVATNY ELECTRIC CO
955 Evans Ave (44305-1041)
PHONE..................................330 630-8900
Fax: 330 603-8909
Mark Trudics, *President*
Nick Sich, *Superintendent*
Mike Panaciulli, *Vice Pres*
EMP: 50 **EST:** 1920
SQ FT: 10,000
SALES (est): 10.4MM **Privately Held**
SIC: 1731 General electrical contractor

(G-297)
JONES GROUP INTERIORS INC
701 S Broadway St Ste 200 (44311-1500)
PHONE..................................330 253-9180
Fax: 330 253-2585
Robert J Jones, *President*
Robert F Linton, *Principal*
Linda E Miller, *Principal*
Patricia Wendling, *Principal*
Shirley Jones, *Admin Sec*
EMP: 25
SQ FT: 64,575
SALES (est): 3.4MM **Privately Held**
WEB: www.bie1.com
SIC: 7389 8748 5021 Interior designer; lighting consultant; office furniture

(G-298)
JPMORGAN CHASE BANK NAT ASSN
1805 Brittain Rd (44310-1803)
PHONE..................................330 972-1915
Eric Vanhorn, *Branch Mgr*
EMP: 26
SALES (corp-wide): 99.6B **Publicly Held**
WEB: www.chase.com
SIC: 6021 National commercial banks
HQ: Jpmorgan Chase Bank, National Association
    1111 Polaris Pkwy
    Columbus OH 43240
    614 436-3055

(G-299)
KAISER FOUNDATION HOSPITALS
Also Called: Chapel Hill Medical Offices
1260 Independence Ave (44310-1812)
PHONE..................................330 633-8400
EMP: 593
SALES (corp-wide): 82.6B **Privately Held**
SIC: 8011 Offices & clinics of medical doctors
HQ: Kaiser Foundation Hospitals Inc
    1 Kaiser Plz
    Oakland CA 94612
    510 271-6611

(G-300)
KALLAS ENTERPRISES INC
Also Called: Custom Trim of America
916 E Buchtel Ave (44305-2337)
PHONE..................................330 253-6893
Fax: 330 258-1469
Alex Kallas, *President*
Michelle Brannon, *Office Mgr*
Glenn Criss, *Manager*
EMP: 26
SQ FT: 20,000
SALES (est): 2MM **Privately Held**
SIC: 7532 Upholstery & trim shop, automotive; tops (canvas or plastic), installation or repair: automotive

(G-301)
KANDY KANE CHILDRENS LRNG CTR (PA)
Also Called: Kandy Kane Chrstn Day Care Ctr
1010 S Hawkins Ave (44320-2615)
P.O. Box 3395 (44309-3395)
PHONE..................................330 864-6642
Mamie Gardner, *President*
Morris Gardner, *Vice Pres*
Willie Oden, *Administration*
EMP: 30 **EST:** 1974
SQ FT: 9,796
SALES: 0 **Privately Held**
SIC: 8351 Group day care center

(G-302)
KEEPTRYAN INC
55 E Exchange St (44308-1521)
PHONE..................................330 319-1866
Daniel Dubiel, *CEO*
Ryan Shambaugh, *COO*
EMP: 99
SALES (est): 1.7MM **Privately Held**
SIC: 5088 4725 8731 9661 Aircraft & space vehicle supplies & parts; arrangement of travel tour packages, wholesale; commercial physical research; food research;

(G-303)
KENMORE CONSTRUCTION CO INC (PA)
700 Home Ave (44310-4190)
PHONE..................................330 762-8936
William A Scala, *President*
Bill Scala, *Superintendent*
Matt Moravec, *Vice Pres*
Thomas Postak, *Vice Pres*
Paul Scala, *Vice Pres*
▲ **EMP:** 151
SQ FT: 3,000
SALES (est): 93MM **Privately Held**
WEB: www.kenmorecompanies.com
SIC: 1611 5032 General contractor, highway & street construction; sand, construction

(G-304)
KENNY OBAYASHI JOINT VENTURE V
144 Cuyahoga St (44304-1067)
PHONE..................................703 969-0611
Michael Stoecker, *Vice Pres*
Lisa Wheeler, *Admin Asst*
EMP: 150
SALES (est): 4.4MM **Privately Held**
SIC: 1542 Commercial & office building, new construction

(G-305)
KEVIN C MCDONNELL MD
224 W Exchange St Ste 220 (44302-1726)
PHONE..................................330 344-6401
Kevin McDonnell MD, *Co-Owner*
EMP: 77 **EST:** 2013
SALES (est): 94.4K **Privately Held**
SIC: 8011 Anesthesiologist

(G-306)
KEYSTONE TECHNOLOGY CONS
Also Called: Keystone Business Solutions
787 Wye Rd (44333-2268)
PHONE..................................330 666-6200
Greg Cordray, *President*
Brian Fontanella, *Vice Pres*
David Howard, *Vice Pres*
Scott Foos, *Engineer*
Jared Wesley, *Engineer*
EMP: 25
SALES (est): 4.7MM **Privately Held**
SIC: 7371 Computer software development & applications

(G-307)
KINDRED HEALTHCARE OPERATING
Also Called: Ridgepark Center
145 Olive St (44310-3236)
PHONE..................................330 762-0901
Fax: 330 762-0905
Corie Cross, *Purchasing*
Karen Page, *CFO*
Jim Kallevig, *Admin Director*
EMP: 172
SALES (corp-wide): 6B **Publicly Held**
WEB: www.salemhaven.com
SIC: 8051 Skilled nursing care facilities
HQ: Kindred Healthcare Operating, Inc.
    680 S 4th St
    Louisville KY 40202
    502 596-7300

(G-308)
KNOTICE LLC
526 S Main St Ste 705 (44311-4402)
PHONE..................................800 801-4194
Fax: 330 922-0859
Tina Shepard, *Opers Staff*
Brian Deagan, *Human Res Dir*
Elizabeth Huebner, *Accounts Exec*
Nicole Piccolomini, *Marketing Staff*
Daniel Spohn, *Database Admin*
EMP: 60
SALES (est): 1.7MM
SALES (corp-wide): 150MM **Privately Held**
SIC: 7373 Systems software development services
PA: Ignitionone, Inc.
    470 Park Ave S Fl 6
    New York NY 10016
    888 744-6483

(G-309)
KRUMROY-COZAD CNSTR CORP
376 W Exchange St (44302-1703)
PHONE..................................330 376-4136
Fax: 330 376-8681
Daniel J Cozad, *President*
EMP: 50
SQ FT: 3,226
SALES (est): 12.3MM **Privately Held**
WEB: www.krumroy-cozad.com
SIC: 1542 Commercial & office building, new construction

(G-310)
KURTZ BROS COMPOST SERVICES
2677 Riverview Rd (44313-4719)
PHONE..................................330 864-2621
Thomas Kurtz, *President*
Chuck Turner, *Director*
EMP: 30
SALES (est): 4.3MM **Privately Held**
WEB: www.kbcompost.com
SIC: 2875 8741 Compost; management services

(G-311)
LABORATORY CORPORATION AMERICA
1 Park West Blvd Ste 290 (44320-4231)
PHONE..................................330 865-3624
Fax: 330 865-3543
Barb Hoskinson, *Manager*
EMP: 25 **Publicly Held**
SIC: 8071 Testing laboratories
HQ: Laboratory Corporation Of America
    358 S Main St Ste 458
    Burlington NC 27215
    336 229-1127

(G-312)
LAKE ERIE ELECTRIC INC
1888 Brown St (44301-3143)
PHONE..................................330 724-1241
Fax: 330 724-1792
Jeff Hendershot, *Project Mgr*
Kim Stueber, *Project Mgr*
Gregg Juchum, *Warehouse Mgr*
John Kellamis, *Branch Mgr*
EMP: 33
SALES (corp-wide): 137.9MM **Privately Held**
SIC: 1731 General electrical contractor
PA: Erie Lake Electric Inc
    25730 1st St
    Westlake OH 44145
    440 835-5565

(G-313)
LAWRENCE A CERVINO MD
Also Called: Wells, Mark D MD
3975 Embassy Pkwy Ste 203 (44333-8396)
PHONE..................................330 668-4065
Lawrence A Cervino MD, *Owner*
EMP: 25
SALES (est): 632.7K **Privately Held**
SIC: 8011 Plastic surgeon

(G-314)
LAWYERS TITLE COMPANY
799 White Pond Dr Ste A (44320-1189)
PHONE..................................330 376-0000
Fax: 330 762-2349
Terry Endress, *Manager*
EMP: 29
SALES (corp-wide): 7.6B **Publicly Held**
SIC: 6361 6541 Real estate title insurance; title & trust companies
HQ: Lawyers Title Company
    7530 N Glenoaks Blvd
    Burbank CA 91504
    818 767-0425

(G-315)
LEVEL 3 COMMUNICATIONS INC
520 S Main St Ste 2435 (44311-1071)
PHONE..................................330 256-8999
Scott Farley, *Manager*
EMP: 50
SALES (corp-wide): 17.6B **Publicly Held**
WEB: www.level3.com
SIC: 4813 Telephone communication, except radio
HQ: Level 3 Parent, Llc
    1025 Eldorado Blvd
    Broomfield CO 80021
    720 888-1000

(G-316)
LEVEL 3 TELECOM LLC
Also Called: Time Warner Cable
1019 E Turkeyfoot Lake Rd (44312-5242)
PHONE..................................234 542-6279
EMP: 29
SALES (corp-wide): 17.6B **Publicly Held**
SIC: 4813
HQ: Level 3 Telecom, Llc
    10475 Park Meadows Dr
    Lone Tree CO 80124
    303 566-1000

(G-317)
LHA DEVELOPMENTS
910 Eller Ave (44306-3705)
PHONE..................................330 785-3219
Kathy McCormick, *Manager*
EMP: 25
SALES (est): 977.4K **Privately Held**
SIC: 6552 Subdividers & developers

(G-318)
LIFE INSURANCE MKTG CO INC
91 Mayfield Ave (44313-6827)
PHONE..................................330 867-1707
Lawrence S Rybka, *President*
Elaine Pressler, *Treasurer*
EMP: 50
SALES (est): 5.2MM **Privately Held**
SIC: 6411 Insurance agents, brokers & service

(G-319)
LIFELINE SYSTEMS COMPANY
703 S Main St Ste 211 (44311-1098)
PHONE..................................330 762-5627
Richard Stahal, *CEO*
Leverda Wallace, *Surgery Dir*
EMP: 50
SALES (corp-wide): 25.9B **Privately Held**
SIC: 8399 Social service information exchange

GEOGRAPHIC SECTION   Akron - Summit County (G-342)

HQ: Lifeline Systems Company
    111 Lawrence St
    Framingham MA 01702
    508 988-1000

(G-320)
LINCARE INC
Also Called: America's Best Medical
1566 Akron Peninsula Rd # 2
(44313-7980)
PHONE....................330 928-0884
Rob Dellaposta, *Manager*
EMP: 35
SALES (corp-wide): 20.1B **Privately Held**
WEB: www.lincare.com
SIC: 8399 Advocacy group
HQ: Lincare Inc.
    19387 Us Highway 19 N
    Clearwater FL 33764
    727 530-7700

(G-321)
LINDSEY CNSTR & DESIGN INC
2151 S Arlington Rd (44306-4207)
PHONE....................330 785-9931
Fax: 330 899-9179
Eric Lindsey, *CEO*
Anthony Luttrell, *General Mgr*
George Noussias, *Comptroller*
EMP: 26
SQ FT: 2,400
SALES (est): 6.4MM **Privately Held**
SIC: 7389 5033 Design services; roofing, siding & insulation

(G-322)
LKQ CORPORATION
1435 Triplett Blvd (44306-3303)
PHONE....................330 733-6333
EMP: 34
SALES (corp-wide): 9.7B **Publicly Held**
WEB: www.lkqcorp.com
SIC: 5093 Scrap & waste materials
PA: Lkq Corporation
    500 W Madison St Ste 2800
    Chicago IL 60661
    312 621-1950

(G-323)
LKQ TRIPLETTASAP INC (HQ)
Also Called: Triplett ASAP
1435 Triplett Blvd (44306-3303)
P.O. Box 7667 (44306-0667)
PHONE....................330 733-6333
Fax: 330 733-3629
Stuart Willen, *President*
Brad Willen, *Vice Pres*
Todd Willen, *Vice Pres*
Marsha Flight, *Accounts Mgr*
EMP: 120
SQ FT: 25,000
SALES (est): 31.8MM
SALES (corp-wide): 9.7B **Publicly Held**
WEB: www.triplettasap.com
SIC: 5015 5521 Automotive supplies, used; used car dealers
PA: Lkq Corporation
    500 W Madison St Ste 2800
    Chicago IL 60661
    312 621-1950

(G-324)
LOCAL UNION 856 UAW BLDG CORP
1155 George Wash Blvd (44312-3005)
PHONE....................330 733-6231
Fax: 330 733-6233
Gene Steele, *President*
Renee Kaplinger, *Admin Sec*
EMP: 25
SQ FT: 2,100
SALES (est): 1.1MM **Privately Held**
SIC: 8631 Labor union

(G-325)
LOCKHART CONCRETE CO (PA)
800 W Waterloo Rd (44314-2150)
PHONE....................330 745-6520
Robert Lockart, *President*
Alexander R Lockhart, *Principal*
Jill Lockhart, *Vice Pres*
Amy McDougal, *Manager*
Rick Stanley, *Admin Sec*
EMP: 55
SALES (est): 7.1MM **Privately Held**
SIC: 1771 Concrete work

(G-326)
LOCKHEED MARTIN
Also Called: Aerospace Simulations
1210 Massillon Rd (44315-0001)
PHONE....................330 796-2800
Dan Fiest, *Manager*
EMP: 600 **Publicly Held**
SIC: 7374 Data processing & preparation
HQ: Lockheed Martin Integrated Systems, Llc
    6801 Rockledge Dr
    Bethesda MD 20817

(G-327)
LOCUST DENTAL CENTER
Also Called: Locust Dental Ctr
300 Locust St Ste 430 (44302-1880)
PHONE....................330 535-7876
Fax: 330 535-7878
Gail Kamlowski, *Office Mgr*
EMP: 25
SALES (est): 1.6MM **Privately Held**
SIC: 8021 Dentists' office

(G-328)
LOWES HOME CENTERS LLC
186 N Clvland Mssillon Rd (44333-2467)
PHONE....................330 665-9356
Fax: 330 665-9372
Mike Hoffmeier, *Manager*
EMP: 150
SALES (corp-wide): 68.6B **Publicly Held**
SIC: 5211 5031 5722 5064 Home centers; building materials, exterior; building materials, interior; household appliance stores; electrical appliances, television & radio
HQ: Lowe's Home Centers, Llc
    1605 Curtis Bridge Rd
    Wilkesboro NC 28697
    336 658-4000

(G-329)
LOWES HOME CENTERS LLC
940 Interstate Pkwy (44312-5286)
PHONE....................330 245-4300
Fax: 330 245-4304
Scott Adkins, *Manager*
EMP: 150
SALES (corp-wide): 68.6B **Publicly Held**
SIC: 5211 5031 5722 5064 Lumber & other building materials; building materials, exterior; building materials, interior; household appliance stores; electrical appliances, television & radio
HQ: Lowe's Home Centers, Llc
    1605 Curtis Bridge Rd
    Wilkesboro NC 28697
    336 658-4000

(G-330)
LUMBERJACKS INC (PA)
Also Called: Lumberjack's Creative Bldg Ctr
723 E Tallmadge Ave Ste 1 (44310-2419)
PHONE....................330 762-2401
Fax: 330 762-2851
Jack D Allen, *President*
Tim Manocchio, *Sales Associate*
EMP: 50
SQ FT: 31,500
SALES (est): 10.3MM **Privately Held**
WEB: www.lumberjacks.com
SIC: 5211 5031 Cabinets, kitchen; millwork & lumber; lumber: rough, dressed & finished; kitchen cabinets

(G-331)
M & R FREDERICKTOWN LTD INC
Also Called: Spectra Medical Distribution
895 Home Ave (44310-4115)
PHONE....................440 801-1563
Mike Houska, *President*
Clarence Palgua, *Partner*
Chris Gifford, *Controller*
EMP: 25
SQ FT: 4,000
SALES (est): 3.7MM **Privately Held**
SIC: 5139 5047 Footwear; medical equipment & supplies

(G-332)
MANOR CARE OF AMERICA INC
1211 W Market St (44313-7180)
PHONE....................330 867-8530
Fax: 330 867-9159
Kim Nelson, *Manager*
Joseph Iemma, *Director*
Nancy Wisner, *Administration*
EMP: 110
SALES (corp-wide): 3.6B **Publicly Held**
WEB: www.trisunhealthcare.com
SIC: 8051 Convalescent home with continuous nursing care
HQ: Manor Care Of America, Inc.
    333 N Summit St Ste 103
    Toledo OH 43604
    419 252-5500

(G-333)
MCDONALDS 3490
578 E Market St (44304-1660)
PHONE....................330 762-7747
V Gorsmith, *General Mgr*
Victoria Gorsmith, *General Mgr*
EMP: 46
SALES (est): 970K **Privately Held**
SIC: 5812 7389 Fast-food restaurant, independent;

(G-334)
MCKINLEY EARLY CHILDHOOD CTR
440 Vernon Odom Blvd (44307-2108)
PHONE....................330 252-2552
Fax: 330 252-5752
Dianna Sigmon, *Administration*
EMP: 25
SALES (est): 446K
SALES (corp-wide): 1.9MM **Privately Held**
SIC: 8351 Group day care center
PA: Mckinley Early Childhood Ctr
    1350 Cherry Ave Ne
    Canton OH 44714
    330 454-4800

(G-335)
MED ASSIST PRGRAM OF INFO LINE
703 S Main St Ste 211 (44311-1098)
PHONE....................330 762-0609
Elaine Woloshyn, *Director*
EMP: 40
SALES (est): 577.2K **Privately Held**
SIC: 8399 Social service information exchange

(G-336)
MEDIC MANAGEMENT GROUP LLC (PA)
275 Springside Dr (44333-4548)
PHONE....................330 670-5316
Thomas Ferkovic, *President*
Sarah Scroggins, *Controller*
Cristi Jackson, *Practice Mgr*
Lynette Cutler, *Manager*
Tamiya Williams, *Senior Mgr*
EMP: 87
SALES (est): 5.4MM **Privately Held**
SIC: 8721 Billing & bookkeeping service

(G-337)
MEDLINK OF OHIO INC
Also Called: Nursefinders
1225 E Waterloo Rd (44306-3805)
PHONE....................330 773-9434
Fax: 330 773-9502
Doti Johnson, *Manager*
EMP: 300
SALES (corp-wide): 796.9MM **Publicly Held**
SIC: 8049 7363 Nurses, registered & practical; temporary help service
HQ: Medlink Of Ohio, Inc
    20600 Chagrin Blvd # 290
    Cleveland OH 44122
    216 751-5900

(G-338)
MERRILL LYNCH PIERCE FENNER
4000 Embassy Pkwy Ste 300
(44333-8357)
PHONE....................330 670-2400
Fax: 330 722-4077
Barbara Krkamer, *Opers Mgr*
Talva Burns, *Personnel*
Michael Siriani, *Sales Mgr*
Sid Jones, *Manager*
James B Springer, *Manager*
EMP: 40
SALES (corp-wide): 100.2B **Publicly Held**
WEB: www.merlyn.com
SIC: 6211 Security brokers & dealers
HQ: Merrill Lynch, Pierce, Fenner & Smith Incorporated
    111 8th Ave
    New York NY 10011
    800 637-7455

(G-339)
MERRILL LYNCH PIERCE FENNER
4000 Embassy Pkwy Ste 300
(44333-8357)
PHONE....................330 670-2400
Fax: 330 253-3299
Fredric Chopko, *Vice Pres*
Bryan Jones, *Vice Pres*
Jerry Huffman, *Branch Mgr*
Patricia Papes, *Agent*
Robert Wright, *Director*
EMP: 100
SALES (corp-wide): 100.2B **Publicly Held**
WEB: www.merlyn.com
SIC: 6211 8742 6282 6221 Security brokers & dealers; management consulting services; investment advice; commodity contracts brokers, dealers
HQ: Merrill Lynch, Pierce, Fenner & Smith Incorporated
    111 8th Ave
    New York NY 10011
    800 637-7455

(G-340)
METALICO AKRON INC (HQ)
Also Called: Metalico Annaco
943 Hazel St (44305-1609)
P.O. Box 1148 (44309-1148)
PHONE....................330 376-1400
Fax: 330 376-9696
Jeffery Bauer, *General Mgr*
Melinda Ryanfield, *Controller*
Jesse Stuart, *Manager*
EMP: 35 **EST:** 1930
SQ FT: 30,000
SALES: 9.9MM
SALES (corp-wide): 476MM **Privately Held**
WEB: www.annaco.com
SIC: 5093 4953 3341 Ferrous metal scrap & waste; nonferrous metals scrap; refuse systems; secondary nonferrous metals
PA: Metalico, Inc.
    135 Dermody St
    Cranford NJ 07016
    908 497-9610

(G-341)
METRO REGIONAL TRANSIT AUTH (PA)
416 Kenmore Blvd (44301-1099)
PHONE....................330 762-0341
Fax: 330 762-0804
Bernard Bear, *President*
Saundra Foster, *President*
Scott C Meyer, *Vice Pres*
Troy Webb, *Facilities Mgr*
Dean J Harris, *CFO*
EMP: 365
SQ FT: 300,000
SALES (est): 26.8MM **Privately Held**
SIC: 4111 Bus transportation

(G-342)
METROPOLITAN EDISON COMPANY (HQ)
Also Called: MET-ED
76 S Main St (44308-1812)
PHONE....................800 736-3402
Charles E Jones, *President*
Leila L Vespoli, *Exec VP*
Harvey L Wagner, *Vice Pres*
Mark T Clark, *CFO*
James F Pearson, *Treasurer*
EMP: 134 **EST:** 1922
SALES: 837.1MM **Publicly Held**
SIC: 4911 Electric services; generation, electric power; distribution, electric power; transmission, electric power

Akron - Summit County (G-343) — GEOGRAPHIC SECTION

(G-343)
METROPOLITAN SECURITY SVCS INC
Also Called: Walden Security
2 S Main St (44308-1813)
PHONE..................................330 253-6459
EMP: 439 **Privately Held**
SIC: 7381 Guard services
PA: Metropolitan Security Services, Inc.
100 E 10th St Ste 400
Chattanooga TN 37402

(G-344)
MID-OHIO FORKLIFTS INC
1336 Home Ave (44310-2551)
PHONE..................................330 633-1230
Fax: 330 630-2424
Art Sherwood, *President*
Matthew Welhouse, *Opers Mgr*
Patty Heaton, *Parts Mgr*
Cory Rolph, *Regl Sales Mgr*
Roger Wright, *Marketing Staff*
EMP: 25
SQ FT: 17,250
SALES (est): 14.8MM **Privately Held**
WEB: www.midohioforklift.com
SIC: 5084 Materials handling machinery

(G-345)
MILLERS RENTAL AND SLS CO INC (PA)
2023 Romig Rd (44320-3819)
PHONE..................................330 753-8600
Fax: 330 753-9990
John J Miller, *CEO*
Steven C Bittel, *CFO*
Kim Pietrosanti, *Controller*
Kerry Klein, *VP Finance*
Tracy Smith, *Sales Staff*
EMP: 95
SQ FT: 14,000
SALES (est): 20.5MM **Privately Held**
WEB: www.millers.com
SIC: 5999 7352 Hospital equipment & supplies; medical equipment rental

(G-346)
MOBILE MEALS INC (PA)
1357 Home Ave (44310-2549)
PHONE..................................330 376-7717
Fax: 330 253-3115
Kathleen Downing, *Director*
EMP: 88
SQ FT: 6,500
SALES: 3.6MM **Privately Held**
SIC: 8399 Community development groups

(G-347)
MORGAN STANLEY
3700 Embassy Pkwy Ste 340 (44333-8339)
PHONE..................................330 670-4600
Fax: 330 670-4660
Teri Deal, *Manager*
EMP: 25
SALES (corp-wide): 43.6B **Publicly Held**
SIC: 6153 Short-term business credit
PA: Morgan Stanley
1585 Broadway
New York NY 10036
212 761-4000

(G-348)
MYERS INDUSTRIES INC (PA)
1293 S Main St (44301-1339)
PHONE..................................330 253-5592
Fax: 330 253-0035
F Jack Liebau Jr, *Ch of Bd*
R David Banyard, *President*
Chris Dupaul, *President*
Virgil Jules, *Business Mgr*
Robert Sadinski, *Engineer*
◆ EMP: 45
SQ FT: 129,000
SALES: 547MM **Publicly Held**
WEB: www.myersind.com
SIC: 3089 3086 3069 3052 Pallets, plastic; stock shapes, plastic; boxes, plastic; blow molded finished plastic products; plastics foam products; packaging & shipping materials, foamed plastic; insulation or cushioning material, foamed plastic; padding, foamed plastic; rubber automotive products; automobile hose, rubber; tools & equipment, automotive; tire & tube repair materials

(G-349)
NATIONWIDE CHILDRENS HOSPITAL
Also Called: Central Billing Office
1 Canal Square Plz # 110 (44308-1037)
PHONE..................................330 253-5200
Melanie Polack, *Manager*
EMP: 38
SALES (corp-wide): 1.3B **Privately Held**
SIC: 8069 8721 Children's hospital; billing & bookkeeping service
PA: Nationwide Children's Hospital
700 Childrens Dr
Columbus OH 43205
614 722-2000

(G-350)
NEUROLOGY NROSCIENCE ASSOC INC (PA)
701 White Pond Dr (44320-1155)
PHONE..................................330 572-1011
Lawrence M Saltis, *Principal*
EMP: 29
SALES (est): 6.1MM **Privately Held**
SIC: 8011 Neurologist

(G-351)
NEWTOWN NINE INC
568 E Crosier St (44311-1809)
PHONE..................................330 376-7741
Fax: 330 376-4657
Kevin Akers, *Branch Mgr*
EMP: 49
SALES (corp-wide): 40MM **Privately Held**
WEB: www.ohiomaterialshandling.com
SIC: 7538 5084 Truck engine repair, except industrial; materials handling machinery
PA: Newtown Nine, Inc.
8155 Roll And Hold Pkwy
Macedonia OH 44056
440 781-0623

(G-352)
NIGHTINGALE HOLDINGS LLC (PA)
Also Called: Pebble Creek
670 Jarvis Rd (44319-2538)
PHONE..................................330 645-0200
Jim Egli,
Betty Snyder, *Administration*
EMP: 441
SALES (est): 10.3MM **Privately Held**
SIC: 8051 Convalescent home with continuous nursing care

(G-353)
NORTHAST OHIO EYE SURGEONS INC
1 Park West Blvd Ste 310 (44320-4226)
PHONE..................................330 836-8545
Todd E Woodruff, *Principal*
Erin Schellenberger, *Physician Asst*
EMP: 37
SALES (corp-wide): 1.1MM **Privately Held**
SIC: 8011 Ophthalmologist
PA: Northeast Ohio Eye Surgeons, Inc.
2013 State Route 59
Kent OH 44240
330 678-0201

(G-354)
NORTHAST OHIO ORTHPEDICS ASSOC
224 W Exchange St Ste 440 (44302-1718)
PHONE..................................330 344-1980
Fax: 330 384-6038
Michael J Smith, *Principal*
Linda Donohew, *Office Mgr*
EMP: 50
SALES (est): 3.4MM **Privately Held**
SIC: 8011 Orthopedic physician

(G-355)
NORTHAST OHIO SSTNBLE CMMNTIES
146 S High St Ste 800 (44308-1432)
PHONE..................................216 410-7698
EMP: 55
SALES (est): 262.8K **Privately Held**
SIC: 8699 Charitable organization

(G-356)
NORTHEAST OHIO CARDIOLOGY SVCS
95 Arch St Ste 300350 (44304-1437)
PHONE..................................330 253-8195
Alexander Ormond, *President*
Dr Vincent Johnson Jr, *Corp Secy*
Dr William Bauman, *Vice Pres*
Stephen M Heupler, *Cardiovascular*
EMP: 34
SQ FT: 8,200
SALES (est): 3.1MM **Privately Held**
SIC: 8011 Cardiologist & cardio-vascular specialist

(G-357)
NORTHERN DATACOMM CORP
3700 Embassy Pkwy Ste 141 (44333-8384)
PHONE..................................330 665-0344
Michael D Sheers, *President*
EMP: 25
SALES (est): 2.3MM **Privately Held**
SIC: 7373 Systems integration services

(G-358)
NORTHERN STYLE CNSTR LLC
344 Lease St Ste 104 (44306-1021)
PHONE..................................330 412-9594
Burton Pierce, *Mng Member*
James Pierce,
EMP: 60
SQ FT: 3,000
SALES: 2.1MM **Privately Held**
SIC: 1521 Single-family housing construction

(G-359)
NSA TECHNOLOGIES LLC
3867 Medina Rd Ste 256 (44333-4525)
PHONE..................................330 576-4600
Kristen Lavender, *Finance Mgr*
Vincent E Fischer,
Victor J Bierman III,
Mark W Jenney,
EMP: 150
SALES (est): 7MM **Privately Held**
SIC: 7372 8742 8731 Publishers' computer software; marketing consulting services; commercial physical research; biological research

(G-360)
OAK ASSOCIATES LTD
3875 Embassy Pkwy Ste 250 (44333-8355)
PHONE..................................330 666-5263
Fax: 330 668-2901
Robert D Stimpson, *Opers Staff*
Carol Zollars, *Financial Exec*
James D Oelschlager, *Mng Member*
Vanita B Oelschlager,
Vanita Oelschlager,
EMP: 45
SQ FT: 35,000
SALES (est): 12.9MM **Privately Held**
SIC: 6282 Investment advisory service

(G-361)
OBSTETRICS GYNCLOGY OF RESERVE
799 Wye Rd (44333-2268)
PHONE..................................330 666-1166
Ross Marchetta, *President*
EMP: 35
SQ FT: 1,600
SALES (est): 2.8MM **Privately Held**
SIC: 8011 Gynecologist; obstetrician

(G-362)
OFFICEMAX NORTH AMERICA INC
37 N Clvland Massillon Rd (44333-2420)
PHONE..................................330 666-4550
Mike Chomatics, *Manager*
Bob Gasior, *Manager*
Mike Jamatic, *Manager*
John Linder, *Manager*
EMP: 25
SALES (corp-wide): 10.2B **Publicly Held**
WEB: www.copymax.net
SIC: 5112 Office supplies
HQ: Officemax North America, Inc.
263 Shuman Blvd
Naperville IL 60563
630 717-0791

(G-363)
OHIO CHAMBER BALLET
Also Called: Ohio Ballet
354 E Market St (44325-0036)
PHONE..................................330 972-7900
Fax: 330 972-7902
Stephen Newenhisen, *Principal*
EMP: 35
SALES (est): 497.3K **Privately Held**
SIC: 7922 7911 Ballet production; dance studios, schools & halls

(G-364)
OHIO DEPT OF JOB & FMLY SVCS
Also Called: Job Service of Ohio
161 S High St Ste 300 (44308-1615)
PHONE..................................330 484-5402
Barbara Frank, *Director*
EMP: 60 **Privately Held**
WEB: www.job.com
SIC: 9441 7361 Administration of social & manpower programs; ; employment agencies
HQ: The Ohio Department Of Job And Family Services
30 E Broad St Fl 32
Columbus OH 43215

(G-365)
OHIO EDISON COMPANY (HQ)
76 S Main St Bsmt (44308-1817)
PHONE..................................800 736-3402
Fax: 330 384-5396
Charles E Jones Jr, *President*
Leila Vespoli, *Exec VP*
Harvey L Wagner, *Vice Pres*
R H Marsh, *CFO*
James F Pearson, *CFO*
EMP: 154 EST: 1930
SALES: 1.3B **Publicly Held**
SIC: 4911 Electric services; generation, electric power; transmission, electric power; distribution, electric power

(G-366)
OHIO GASKET AND SHIM CO INC (PA)
Also Called: Ogs Industries
976 Evans Ave (44305-1019)
PHONE..................................330 630-0626
Fax: 330 630-2075
John S Bader, *President*
Jack Lenhart, *Facilities Mgr*
Pam Varner, *Accounting Mgr*
Shelly Penrod, *Human Res Mgr*
Andrew Bader, *Sales Staff*
▲ EMP: 45 EST: 1959
SQ FT: 84,000
SALES (est): 21.6MM **Privately Held**
WEB: www.ogsindustries.com
SIC: 3469 3053 3599 3499 Stamping metal for the trade; gaskets, all materials; machine shop, jobbing & repair; shims, metal; packaging & labeling services

(G-367)
OHIO MAINT & RENOVATION INC (PA)
Also Called: Commercial Maintenance & Repr
124 Darrow Rd (44305-3835)
PHONE..................................330 315-3101
Fax: 330 315-3112
Steven Harvey, *CEO*
Steven E Harvey, *CEO*
Mike Abel, *Vice Pres*
EMP: 40

SALES (est): 6.4MM **Privately Held**
SIC: 1542 Commercial & office building contractors

(G-368)
OHIO PRESBT RETIREMENT SVCS
Also Called: Rockynol Retirtment Community
1150 W Market St (44313-7129)
PHONE.................................330 867-2150
Michelle Brummage, *Human Res Mgr*
Thomas R Miller, *Branch Mgr*
Frank P Bevilacqua II, *Bd of Directors*
EMP: 150 **Privately Held**
WEB: www.nwo.oprs.org
SIC: 8051 Skilled nursing care facilities
PA: Ohio Living
1001 Kingsmill Pkwy
Columbus OH 43229

(G-369)
OHIO REHABILITATION SVCS COMM
Also Called: Bureau Vctional Rehabilitation
161 S High St Ste 103 (44308-1615)
PHONE.................................330 643-3080
Fax: 330 643-3084
Bonita Susko, *Branch Mgr*
Marie Lishick, *Manager*
EMP: 35 **Privately Held**
WEB: www.rsc.ohio.gov
SIC: 9441 8331 ; vocational rehabilitation agency
HQ: Opportunities For Ohioans With Disabilities Agency
400 E Campus View Blvd
Columbus OH 43235
614 438-1200

(G-370)
OID ASSOCIATES
Also Called: Springside Racquet Fitnes CLB
215 Springside Dr (44333-2432)
PHONE.................................330 666-3161
Ken Channels, *General Mgr*
Val Murphy, *Manager*
EMP: 25
SQ FT: 86,000
SALES (est): 1.1MM **Privately Held**
SIC: 7991 Health club

(G-371)
OMNOVA SOLUTIONS INC
2990 Gilchrist Rd (44305-4418)
PHONE.................................330 794-6300
Tim Tinson, *Safety Mgr*
Chris Soulsby, *Engineer*
Sonya Varga, *Engineer*
Bill Beers, *Manager*
Brian Grant, *Manager*
EMP: 65
SQ FT: 117,299
SALES (corp-wide): 783.1MM **Publicly Held**
WEB: www.omnova.com
SIC: 8731 Commercial physical research
PA: Omnova Solutions Inc.
25435 Harvard Rd
Beachwood OH 44122
216 682-7000

(G-372)
ORIANA HOUSE INC
941 Sherman St (44311-2467)
P.O. Box 1501 (44309-1501)
PHONE.................................330 374-9610
James Lawrence, *President*
Christine Wilson, *Sales Executive*
EMP: 700
SALES (corp-wide): 48.4MM **Privately Held**
SIC: 7389 Personal service agents, brokers & bureaus
PA: Oriana House, Inc.
885 E Buchtel Ave
Akron OH 44305
330 535-8116

(G-373)
ORIANA HOUSE INC (PA)
885 E Buchtel Ave (44305-2338)
P.O. Box 1501 (44309-1501)
PHONE.................................330 535-8116
Fax: 330 996-2233
James Lawrence, *President*
William Scheub, *Managing Dir*

Gina D'Aurelio, *Principal*
Anne Connell-Freund, *Exec VP*
Bernard Rochford, *Exec VP*
EMP: 1513 EST: 1981
SALES: 48.4MM **Privately Held**
WEB: www.orianahouse.org
SIC: 8322 9111 Alcoholism counseling, nontreatment; rehabilitation services; county supervisors' & executives' offices

(G-374)
ORIANA HOUSE INC
Also Called: A D M Crisis Center
15 Frederick Ave (44310-2904)
PHONE.................................330 996-7730
Fax: 330 996-7742
Tammy Johnson, *Manager*
EMP: 60
SALES (corp-wide): 48.4MM **Privately Held**
WEB: www.orianahouse.org
SIC: 8322 8069 Emergency social services; drug addiction rehabilitation hospital
PA: Oriana House, Inc.
885 E Buchtel Ave
Akron OH 44305

(G-375)
ORIANA HOUSE INC
Also Called: Summit County Jail
205 E Crosier St (44311-2351)
PHONE.................................330 643-2171
Steven Finical, *Branch Mgr*
EMP: 200
SALES (est): 1.9MM
SALES (corp-wide): 48.4MM **Privately Held**
WEB: www.orianahouse.org
SIC: 8322 Alcoholism counseling, nontreatment
PA: Oriana House, Inc.
885 E Buchtel Ave
Akron OH 44305
330 535-8116

(G-376)
ORIN GROUP LLC
537 N Clvland Mssillon Rd (44333-2457)
PHONE.................................330 630-3937
Fax: 330 325-0087
Charlene Gibson, *Project Dir*
John Krusinski,
EMP: 35
SQ FT: 7,888
SALES (est): 2MM **Privately Held**
WEB: www.oringroup.com
SIC: 8748 Environmental consultant

(G-377)
PARKLANE MANOR OF AKRON INC
Also Called: Rti
744 Colette Dr (44306-2208)
PHONE.................................330 724-3315
Robert Abassi, *President*
Robert Goehler, *Manager*
EMP: 50
SALES: 1.8MM **Privately Held**
SIC: 6513 Apartment building operators

(G-378)
PASTORAL COUNSELING SVC SUMMIT
Also Called: P C S
611 W Market St (44303-1406)
PHONE.................................330 996-4600
Fax: 330 643-0767
Byron Arledge, *CEO*
Marvin Sharpless, *Senior VP*
Kris Remark, *Finance Mgr*
Sandra Clawson, *Accounts Mgr*
Janet Sparrow, *Office Mgr*
EMP: 140
SALES: 8.1MM **Privately Held**
SIC: 8322 8049 General counseling services; psychiatric social worker

(G-379)
PEBBLE CREEK CNVLSCNT CTR
Also Called: Communicare
670 Jarvis Rd (44319-2538)
PHONE.................................330 645-0200
Dave Murphy, *Senior VP*

Jim Egli, *Administration*
EMP: 220
SQ FT: 60,000
SALES (est): 2.1MM
SALES (corp-wide): 10.3MM **Privately Held**
SIC: 8051 Skilled nursing care facilities
PA: Nightingale Holdings, Llc
670 Jarvis Rd
Akron OH 44319
330 645-0200

(G-380)
PEDIATRICS OF AKRON INC
300 Locust St Ste 200 (44302-1889)
PHONE.................................330 253-7753
Fax: 330 253-4611
Rajneefh Jain, *President*
Dr Robert Sobieski, *Vice Pres*
Dr William Ginther, *Treasurer*
Angie Price, *Practice Mgr*
Martin Dicintio, *Assistant*
EMP: 25
SALES (est): 5.3MM **Privately Held**
SIC: 8011 Pediatrician

(G-381)
PENN MUTUAL LIFE INSURANCE CO
130 Springside Dr Ste 100 (44333-4543)
PHONE.................................330 668-9065
Charles R Parks, *Manager*
Joseph Dazey, *Advisor*
EMP: 50
SALES (corp-wide): 2.8B **Privately Held**
WEB: www.thepfggroup.com
SIC: 6311 Life insurance
PA: The Penn Mutual Life Insurance Co
600 Dresher Rd
Horsham PA 19044
215 956-8000

(G-382)
PENNSYLVANIA ELECTRIC COMPANY (HQ)
76 S Main St Bsmt (44308-1817)
PHONE.................................800 545-7741
Charles E Jones, *President*
Leila L Vespoli, *Exec VP*
Harvey L Wagner, *Vice Pres*
Mark T Clark, *CFO*
James F Pearson, *Treasurer*
EMP: 80
SALES: 893.8MM **Publicly Held**
SIC: 4911 Electric services

(G-383)
PENNSYLVANIA POWER COMPANY (DH)
Also Called: PENN POWER
76 S Main St Bsmt (44308-1817)
PHONE.................................800 720-3600
Fax: 330 384-4796
Anthony D Alexander, *President*
T M Welsh, *Senior VP*
W Reeher, *Vice Pres*
Robert Wuschinske, *Vice Pres*
Harvey Wagner, *Finance Other*
EMP: 140 EST: 1930
SQ FT: 40,000
SALES: 243.8MM **Publicly Held**
SIC: 4911 Distribution, electric power; generation, electric power; transmission, electric power
HQ: Ohio Edison Company
76 S Main St Bsmt
Akron OH 44308
800 736-3402

(G-384)
PENSKE TRUCK LEASING CO LP
3000 Fortuna Dr (44312-5252)
PHONE.................................330 645-3100
Fax: 330 645-3120
John Kushan, *Manager*
James Weyrick, *Executive*
EMP: 25
SQ FT: 9,520
SALES (corp-wide): 2.9B **Privately Held**
WEB: www.pensketruckleasing.com
SIC: 7513 Truck leasing, without drivers; truck rental, without drivers

PA: Penske Truck Leasing Co., L.P.
2675 Morgantown Rd
Reading PA 19607
610 775-6000

(G-385)
PERKINELMER HLTH SCIENCES INC
520 S Main St Ste 2423 (44311-1086)
PHONE.................................330 825-4525
Susan Monaco, *Human Res Mgr*
Chritine Gradisher, *Manager*
Jim Bailey, *Manager*
Paul Dudley, *Manager*
Aniket Parekh, *Software Engr*
EMP: 32
SALES (corp-wide): 2.2B **Publicly Held**
SIC: 2835 2836 5049 In vitro & in vivo diagnostic substances; biological products, except diagnostic; laboratory equipment, except medical or dental
HQ: Perkinelmer Health Sciences, Inc.
940 Winter St
Waltham MA 02451
781 663-6900

(G-386)
PERRIN ASPHALT CO INC
525 Dan St (44310-3987)
PHONE.................................330 253-1020
Fax: 330 253-1042
Charles W Perrin, *President*
Pamela J Perrin, *Corp Secy*
Keith D Perrin, *Vice Pres*
Kimberly A Perrin, *Vice Pres*
Michael A Perrin, *Vice Pres*
EMP: 100
SALES: 25MM **Privately Held**
WEB: www.perrinasphalt.com
SIC: 1771 Blacktop (asphalt) work

(G-387)
PETER M KOSTOFF
222 S Main St Fl 4 (44308-1533)
PHONE.................................330 849-6681
Peter M Kostoff, *Principal*
EMP: 65
SALES (est): 3.1MM **Privately Held**
SIC: 8111 General practice attorney, lawyer

(G-388)
PETERS TSCHANTZ & ASSOC INC
275 Springside Dr Ste 300 (44333-4550)
PHONE.................................330 666-3702
James Peters, *President*
Dave Tzchantz, *Corp Secy*
Tom Bandwin, *Vice Pres*
Tom Myers, *Engineer*
Steve Bishauzi, *Human Res Mgr*
EMP: 25 EST: 1954
SQ FT: 120,000
SALES (est): 3.4MM **Privately Held**
WEB: www.ptbengineering.com
SIC: 8711 Electrical or electronic engineering

(G-389)
PHYSICIANS WEIGHT LS CTR AMER (PA)
395 Springside Dr (44333-2434)
PHONE.................................330 666-7952
Fax: 330 666-2197
Charles E Sekeres, *President*
Michelle Michael, *Director*
EMP: 25
SQ FT: 45,000
SALES (est): 124MM **Privately Held**
SIC: 5141 5122 6794 Groceries, general line; vitamins & minerals; franchises, selling or licensing

(G-390)
PINNACLE RECYCLING LLC
2330 Romig Rd (44320-3825)
P.O. Box 3857 (44314-0857)
PHONE.................................330 745-3700
Jack Washam, *Accounts Mgr*
Jeff Burke, *Sales Staff*
Gary M Dalessandro,
EMP: 33 EST: 2010
SALES (est): 7.2MM **Privately Held**
SIC: 4953 Recycling, waste materials

Akron - Summit County (G-391)

(G-391)
PLANNED PRENTHOOD GREATER OHIO
Also Called: Akron Health Center
444 W Exchange St (44302-1711)
PHONE....................330 535-2671
Fax: 330 535-7145
Stephanie Kight, *CEO*
EMP: 48
SALES (corp-wide): 20.7MM **Privately Held**
SIC: 8093 Family planning clinic
PA: Planned Parenthood Of Greater Ohio
206 E State St
Columbus OH 43215
614 224-2235

(G-392)
PLATINUM TECHNOLOGIES
121 S Main St Ste 200 (44308-1426)
PHONE....................216 926-1080
Jody Anderson, *Principal*
Jacqueline Agnello, *Finance*
EMP: 38
SALES (est): 2.5MM **Privately Held**
SIC: 7379

(G-393)
PLUS ONE COMMUNICATIONS LLC
1115 S Main St (44301-1205)
PHONE....................330 255-4500
Robert Madden, *CEO*
Bobby Cart, *President*
Jill Madden, *Vice Pres*
EMP: 500 EST: 2008
SQ FT: 50,000
SALES: 20MM **Privately Held**
SIC: 7379 Computer related maintenance services

(G-394)
PNC BANK NATIONAL ASSOCIATION
Also Called: National City Bank
1 Cascade Plz Ste 200 (44308-1198)
PHONE....................330 375-8342
Fax: 330 375-8018
Cecilia Frew, *Portfolio Mgr*
Susan Brenner, *Branch Mgr*
Dennis Galvon, *MIS Dir*
EMP: 125
SALES (corp-wide): 18B **Publicly Held**
WEB: www.allegiantbank.com
SIC: 6021 National commercial banks
HQ: Pnc Bank, National Association
222 Delaware Ave
Wilmington DE 19801
877 762-2000

(G-395)
POLISH AMERICAN CITIZENS CLUB
Also Called: Polish-American Club
472 E Glenwood Ave (44310-3421)
P.O. Box 414, Tallmadge (44278-0414)
PHONE....................330 253-0496
Tom Buehl, *President*
Stan Oziomek, *Admin Sec*
EMP: 50
SQ FT: 9,665
SALES (est): 1MM **Privately Held**
SIC: 8641 Fraternal associations

(G-396)
PORTAGE COUNTRY CLUB COMPANY
240 N Portage Path (44303-1299)
PHONE....................330 836-8565
Fax: 330 836-3115
Robert J Le Fever, *General Mgr*
Jim Albanese, *Facilities Mgr*
Greg Relyea, *Controller*
Nicole Johnson, *Manager*
Stephen Goczo, *Director*
EMP: 80
SQ FT: 52,275
SALES: 4MM **Privately Held**
WEB: www.portagecc.com
SIC: 7997 Country club, membership

(G-397)
PORTAGE PATH BEHAVIORAL HEALTH (PA)
340 S Broadway St (44308-1529)
PHONE....................330 253-3100
Fax: 330 376-8002
Jerome Kraker, *President*
Tim Morgan, *President*
Jeffrey Moore, *Vice Pres*
Phil Heislman, *VP Opers*
Jessica Bahry, *Accounting Dir*
EMP: 68
SQ FT: 12,000
SALES: 12.2MM **Privately Held**
WEB: www.portagepath.org
SIC: 8093 Mental health clinic, outpatient

(G-398)
PORTAGE PATH BEHAVORIAL HEALTH
Also Called: Emergency Psychiatric Svc
10 Penfield Ave (44310-2912)
PHONE....................330 762-6110
Candy Pallante, *Financial Exec*
Antonio Montinola, *Manager*
Tracy M Dawyduk, *Manager*
Melissa Stokes, *Admin Asst*
Timothy L Gannon, *Psychiatry*
EMP: 60
SALES (corp-wide): 12.2MM **Privately Held**
WEB: www.portagepath.org
SIC: 8093 4119 Mental health clinic, out-patient; ambulance service
PA: Portage Path Behavorial Health
340 S Broadway St
Akron OH 44308
330 253-3100

(G-399)
POWER ENGINEERS INCORPORATED
Also Called: P E I
1 S Main St Ste 501 (44308-1867)
PHONE....................234 678-9875
EMP: 49
SALES (corp-wide): 398.7MM **Privately Held**
SIC: 8711 Consulting engineer
PA: Power Engineers, Incorporated
3940 Glenbrook Dr
Hailey ID 83333
208 788-3456

(G-400)
PRAXAIR DISTRIBUTION INC
1760 E Market St (44305-4245)
PHONE....................330 376-2242
Howard Horn, *Finance Mgr*
Brian McCormick, *Branch Mgr*
EMP: 30
SALES (corp-wide): 11.4B **Publicly Held**
SIC: 5084 Welding machinery & equipment
HQ: Praxair Distribution, Inc.
10 Riverview Dr
Danbury CT 06810
203 837-2000

(G-401)
QT EQUIPMENT COMPANY (PA)
151 W Dartmore Ave (44301-2462)
PHONE....................330 724-3055
Daniel Root, *President*
Dave Root, *Treasurer*
Kelly Stewart, *Sales Mgr*
Aimee Jesse, *Administration*
▼ EMP: 35
SQ FT: 20,000
SALES (est): 6.3MM **Privately Held**
SIC: 7532 5531 3713 Body shop, trucks; automotive tires; utility truck bodies

(G-402)
R & R TRUCK SALES INC
1650 E Waterloo Rd (44306-4103)
P.O. Box 7309 (44306-0309)
PHONE....................330 784-5881
Fax: 330 784-4392
George Ralich, *President*
Steven Ralich, *Corp Secy*
Daniel Ralich, *Vice Pres*
Larry Chapman, *Parts Mgr*
Vickie Sayre, *Controller*
EMP: 30
SQ FT: 30,000
SALES (est): 14.5MM **Privately Held**
WEB: www.rrtrucksales.com
SIC: 5511 5012 Trucks, tractors & trailers: new & used; trucks, commercial

(G-403)
R B STOUT INC
1285 N Clvland Mssllon Rd (44333-1805)
PHONE....................330 666-8811
Fax: 330 666-7448
Rodney B Stout, *CEO*
Jerry Kusar, *President*
Allen D Keefer, *Vice Pres*
Steve Baker, *Project Mgr*
Paul Revoldt, *Sales Staff*
EMP: 50
SQ FT: 3,500
SALES (est): 6MM **Privately Held**
SIC: 0782 5261 Landscape contractors; lawn & garden supplies

(G-404)
RADIOLOGY & IMAGING SERVICES
Also Called: Risi
2603 W Market St Ste 110 (44313-4231)
P.O. Box 910, Hudson (44236-5910)
PHONE....................330 864-0832
Tom Schmidlin, *President*
Donna Gemmell, *CFO*
Marie Pickle, *Manager*
Sherrie Larm, *Exec Dir*
EMP: 50
SALES (est): 3.7MM **Privately Held**
SIC: 8011 Physicians' office, including specialists

(G-405)
RAY BERTOLINI TRUCKING CO
2070 Wright Rd (44320-2440)
P.O. Box 8155 (44320-0155)
PHONE....................330 867-0666
Fax: 330 867-0181
Joseph F Bertolini, *President*
Skip Mears, *Vice Pres*
EMP: 26
SQ FT: 14,000
SALES (est): 3.8MM **Privately Held**
SIC: 4212 4213 1611 1794 Local trucking, without storage; trucking, except local; general contractor, highway & street construction; excavation work; wrecking & demolition work; demolition, buildings & other structures

(G-406)
REGAL CINEMAS INC
Also Called: Montrose Cinema 12
4020 Medina Rd Ste 100 (44333-4524)
PHONE....................330 666-9373
Fax: 330 665-1654
Mandy Hught, *Manager*
EMP: 30
SALES (corp-wide): 982.1MM **Privately Held**
WEB: www.regalcinemas.com
SIC: 7832 Motion picture theaters, except drive-in
HQ: Regal Cinemas, Inc.
101 E Blount Ave Ste 100
Knoxville TN 37920
865 922-1123

(G-407)
REGAL CINEMAS INC
Also Called: Independence 10
1210 Independence Ave (44310-1812)
PHONE....................330 633-7668
Fax: 330 633-7364
Mark Schneider, *Branch Mgr*
EMP: 35
SALES (corp-wide): 982.1MM **Privately Held**
WEB: www.regalcinemas.com
SIC: 7832 Motion picture theaters, except drive-in
HQ: Regal Cinemas, Inc.
101 E Blount Ave Ste 100
Knoxville TN 37920
865 922-1123

(G-408)
REGENCY SEATING INC
Also Called: Regency Office Furniture
2375 Romig Rd (44320-3824)
PHONE....................330 848-3700
Fax: 330 848-6260
John Summerville, *CEO*
John Kryska, *General Mgr*
Aaron Summerville, *CFO*
Donald Reagan, *Manager*
▲ EMP: 35
SQ FT: 100,000
SALES: 10.1MM **Privately Held**
WEB: www.regencyseating.com
SIC: 5021 Office furniture

(G-409)
RELIABLE APPL INSTALLATION INC
2850 Gilchrist Rd Ste 1b (44305-4431)
PHONE....................330 784-7474
EMP: 75
SALES (corp-wide): 10.7MM **Privately Held**
SIC: 4212 Local trucking, without storage
PA: Reliable Appliance Installation, Inc.
604 Office Pkwy
Westerville OH 43082
614 794-3307

(G-410)
RENNER KENNER GRIEVE BOBAK (PA)
106 S Main St (44308-1417)
PHONE....................330 376-1242
Fax: 330 376-9646
Edward Grieve, *Partner*
Donald J Bobak, *Partner*
Phillip Kenner, *Partner*
Reese Taylor, *Partner*
Martha Hastings, *Corp Counsel*
EMP: 37
SQ FT: 4,500
SALES: 7.2MM **Privately Held**
SIC: 8111 General practice attorney, lawyer

(G-411)
REPRODUCTIVE GYNECOLOGY INC
95 Arch St Ste 250 (44304-1496)
PHONE....................330 375-7722
Fax: 330 253-6708
Richard Moretuzzo, *President*
Brad Hambert, *Branch Mgr*
Summer L James, *OB/GYN*
EMP: 25
SALES (est): 4.3MM **Privately Held**
WEB: www.reproductivegynecologyinc.com
SIC: 8011 Gynecologist

(G-412)
REPUBLIC SERVICES INC
964 Hazel St (44305-1610)
PHONE....................330 434-9183
Al Marino, *Manager*
Nancy Gump, *Administration*
EMP: 34
SALES (corp-wide): 10B **Publicly Held**
WEB: www.republicservices.com
SIC: 4953 Garbage: collecting, destroying & processing; non-hazardous waste disposal sites; recycling, waste materials; sanitary landfill operation
PA: Republic Services, Inc.
18500 N Allied Way # 100
Phoenix AZ 85054
480 627-2700

(G-413)
RESERVE
3636 Yellow Creek Rd (44333-2269)
PHONE....................330 666-1166
Ross Marchetta, *Owner*
EMP: 30
SALES (est): 889.5K **Privately Held**
WEB: www.reserveinc.org
SIC: 8011 Gynecologist

(G-414)
RGIS LLC
767 E Turkey Foot Lake Rd (44319)
PHONE....................330 896-9802
Fax: 330 896-2537
Frank Altir, *Branch Mgr*
EMP: 90
SALES (corp-wide): 7.1B **Publicly Held**
WEB: www.rgisinv.com
SIC: 7389 Inventory computing service

GEOGRAPHIC SECTION
Akron - Summit County (G-438)

HQ: Rgis, Llc
2000 Taylor Rd
Auburn Hills MI 48326
248 651-2511

(G-415)
RICHARDS WHL FENCE CO INC
Also Called: RICHARD'S FENCE COMPANY
1600 Firestone Pkwy (44301-1659)
PHONE..................330 773-0423
Fax: 330 773-3513
Richard Peterson, *President*
Bill Peterson, *Vice Pres*
▲ EMP: 30
SQ FT: 235,000
SALES: 10.8MM **Privately Held**
SIC: 3315 5039 Chain link fencing; wire fence, gates & accessories

(G-416)
RICOH USA INC
Also Called: Nightrider Overnite Copy Svc
80 W Center St (44308-1037)
PHONE..................330 384-9111
Fax: 330 384-8955
Mike Perkins, *Manager*
EMP: 25
SALES (corp-wide): 17.8B **Privately Held**
WEB: www.ikon.com
SIC: 7334 Photocopying & duplicating services
HQ: Ricoh Usa, Inc.
70 Valley Stream Pkwy
Malvern PA 19355
610 296-8000

(G-417)
RODERICK LINTON BELFANCE LLP
50 S Main St Fl 10 (44308-1849)
PHONE..................330 434-3000
Katherine Belfance, *Partner*
Brenda Schwartz, *Counsel*
Sonya Ward, *Legal Staff*
Daniel Bache, *Associate*
Brian Bremer, *Associate*
EMP: 43
SALES (est): 1.7MM **Privately Held**
SIC: 8111 General practice law office

(G-418)
ROETZEL AND ANDRESS A LEGAL P (PA)
222 S Main St Ste 400 (44308-1500)
PHONE..................330 376-2700
Robert E Blackham, *CEO*
Anita Gill, *President*
Paul L Jackson, *President*
Lou Crocco, *Counsel*
John Heer, *Counsel*
EMP: 130 EST: 1872
SQ FT: 115,000
SALES (est): 53.4MM **Privately Held**
WEB: www.ralaw.com
SIC: 8111 General practice law office

(G-419)
RUBBER CITY MACHINERY CORP
Also Called: R C M
1 Thousand Sweitzer Ave (44311)
P.O. Box 2043 (44309-2043)
PHONE..................330 434-3500
Fax: 330 434-2244
George B Sobieraj, *President*
Daniel Abraham, *General Mgr*
Bernie Sobieraj, *Vice Pres*
Robert J Westfall, *Vice Pres*
Scott Ross, *Engineer*
▲ EMP: 32
SQ FT: 100,000
SALES (est): 7.7MM **Privately Held**
SIC: 3559 5084 7629 Rubber working machinery, including tires; plastics working machinery; industrial machinery & equipment; electrical repair shops

(G-420)
RUBBER CITY RADIO GROUP (PA)
Also Called: Wqmx 94.9 FM
1795 W Market St (44313-7001)
PHONE..................330 869-9800
Thomas Mandel, *President*
Amani Abraham, *Editor*
Mark Biviano, *Vice Pres*
Henry Zelman, *Vice Pres*
Nancy Bittner, *Accounts Exec*
EMP: 79
SALES (est): 16.7MM **Privately Held**
SIC: 4832 Radio broadcasting stations; rock

(G-421)
RUBBER CITY REALTY INC
942 Kenmore Blvd (44314-2148)
PHONE..................330 745-9034
Fax: 330 745-9036
George W Turchin, *President*
Helen Turchin, *Vice Pres*
Chris Cerino, *Opers Staff*
EMP: 70
SQ FT: 2,500
SALES (est): 3.3MM **Privately Held**
SIC: 6531 1521 1522 Real estate brokers & agents; general remodeling, single-family houses; remodeling, multi-family dwellings

(G-422)
S & K ASPHALT & CONCRETE
2275 Manchester Rd (44314-3745)
PHONE..................330 848-6284
Nick Skeriotis, *CEO*
EMP: 25 EST: 2008
SALES (est): 2.7MM **Privately Held**
SIC: 1771 1611 Blacktop (asphalt) work; surfacing & paving

(G-423)
SABER HEALTHCARE GROUP LLC
Also Called: Windsong Care Center
120 Brookmont Rd (44333-3057)
PHONE..................216 292-5706
Teresa Lane, *Administration*
EMP: 40
SALES (corp-wide): 68.5MM **Privately Held**
WEB: www.parkplace-spokane.com
SIC: 8051 Skilled nursing care facilities
PA: Saber Healthcare Group, L.L.C.
26691 Richmond Rd Frnt
Bedford OH 44146
216 292-5706

(G-424)
SACS CNSLTING TRAINING CTR INC
Also Called: Sacs Cnslting Invstigative Svc
520 S Main St Ste 2516 (44311-1073)
PHONE..................330 255-1101
Timothy Dimoff, *President*
Lori Ann Crowe, *Business Mgr*
Anthony Wellendorf, *COO*
Michelle Dimoff, *CFO*
Alma Glasper, *Office Mgr*
EMP: 25
SALES (est): 287.1K **Privately Held**
WEB: www.sacsconsulting.com
SIC: 8742 Management consulting services

(G-425)
SADGURU KRUPA LLC
897 Arlington Rdg E (44312-5276)
PHONE..................330 644-2111
Naresh Patel,
EMP: 35 EST: 2008
SALES (est): 541.5K **Privately Held**
SIC: 7011 Hotels & motels

(G-426)
SALOMA INTL CO SINCE 1978
Also Called: Salomanetics
430 Grant St (44311-1190)
P.O. Box 24370, Fort Lauderdale FL (33307-4370)
PHONE..................440 941-1527
Henry Drake Stull, *Owner*
EMP: 27
SALES (est): 747.7K **Privately Held**
SIC: 8748 Business consulting

(G-427)
SALVATION ARMY
190 S Maple St (44302-1603)
PHONE..................330 762-8481
Fax: 330 762-0205
Karla Clark, *Manager*
Jackie Keller, *Exec Dir*
EMP: 30
SALES (corp-wide): 4.3B **Privately Held**
WEB: www.salvationarmy-usaeast.org
SIC: 8399 Advocacy group
HQ: The Salvation Army
440 W Nyack Rd Ofc
West Nyack NY 10994
845 620-7200

(G-428)
SALVATION ARMY
1006 Grant St (44311-2442)
P.O. Box 1743 (44309-1743)
PHONE..................330 773-3331
Fax: 330 773-3335
Gregory Cole, *Branch Mgr*
EMP: 102
SALES (corp-wide): 4.3B **Privately Held**
WEB: www.salvationarmy-usaeast.org
SIC: 8069 5932 8741 Specialty hospitals, except psychiatric; used merchandise stores; administrative management
HQ: The Salvation Army
440 W Nyack Rd Ofc
West Nyack NY 10994
845 620-7200

(G-429)
SBM BUSINESS SERVICES INC (DH)
Also Called: GMAC Insurance
333 S Main St Ste 200 (44308-1205)
PHONE..................330 396-7000
Fax: 330 762-4636
Steven B Shechter, *President*
Ron Buzek, *Vice Pres*
Scott Gill, *Vice Pres*
Edward Morrison, *Vice Pres*
Donna Syroid, *Vice Pres*
EMP: 26
SQ FT: 9,000
SALES (est): 5.2MM **Privately Held**
SIC: 6411 Insurance agents, brokers & service
HQ: Dawson Insurance, Inc.
3900 Kinross Lakes Pkwy
Richfield OH 44286
440 333-9000

(G-430)
SCHOMER GLAUS PYLE (PA)
Also Called: GPD GROUP
520 S Main St Ste 2531 (44311-1073)
PHONE..................330 572-2100
Darrin Kotecki, *President*
Jim Riche, *President*
Jeff Evans, *Senior VP*
Jeffrey D Evans, *Senior VP*
Brad Cramer, *Vice Pres*
EMP: 270
SQ FT: 20,000
SALES (est): 93.9MM **Privately Held**
WEB: www.gpdgroup.com
SIC: 8711 8712 Consulting engineer; architectural services

(G-431)
SEGMINT INC
365 Water St (44308-1044)
PHONE..................330 594-5379
Russel Heiser, *CEO*
EMP: 33
SQ FT: 8,000
SALES (est): 5MM **Privately Held**
SIC: 7313 Electronic media advertising representatives

(G-432)
SELECT MEDICAL CORPORATION
Select Specialty Hosp Akron
200 E Market St (44308-2015)
PHONE..................330 761-7500
Doug McGee, *COO*
Keith Janus, *Opers Staff*
Candi Bourn, *Human Res Dir*
Merv Tierney, *Director*
Brian Blocker, *Pharmacy Dir*
EMP: 88
SALES (corp-wide): 3.7B **Publicly Held**
WEB: www.selectmedicalcorp.com
SIC: 8062 General medical & surgical hospitals
HQ: Select Medical Corporation
4714 Gettysburg Rd
Mechanicsburg PA 17055
717 972-1100

(G-433)
SELECT SPCLTY HSPTAL-AKRON LLC
200 E Market St (44308-2015)
P.O. Box 2090 (44309-2090)
PHONE..................330 761-7500
Fax: 330 375-4218
Jeffrey Houck, *Principal*
William Powel, *Vice Pres*
Gary Elliot, *Director*
EMP: 100 EST: 2000
SALES (est): 4.3MM
SALES (corp-wide): 3.7B **Publicly Held**
SIC: 8069 8361 8051 Alcoholism rehabilitation hospital; residential care; skilled nursing care facilities
HQ: Sempercare, Inc
4716 Old Gettysburg Rd
Mechanicsburg PA 17055
717 972-1100

(G-434)
SERVICE CORPS RETIRED EXECS
Also Called: S C O R E 81
1 Cascade Plz Fl 18 (44308-1166)
PHONE..................330 379-3163
Ron Stallings, *Chairman*
EMP: 42
SALES (corp-wide): 13.1MM **Privately Held**
WEB: www.score199.mv.com
SIC: 8748 Business consulting
PA: Service Corps Of Retired Executives Association
1175 Herndon Pkwy Ste 900
Herndon VA 20170
703 487-3612

(G-435)
SERVICE EXPERTS LLC
847 Home Ave (44310-4114)
PHONE..................330 577-3918
EMP: 27
SALES (corp-wide): 736.6MM **Privately Held**
SIC: 1711 Heating & air conditioning contractors
HQ: Service Experts Llc
3820 American Dr Ste 200
Plano TX 75075

(G-436)
SH-91 LIMITED PARTNERSHIP
Also Called: Spring Hill Apartments
1221 Everton Dr (44307-1468)
PHONE..................330 535-1581
Fax: 330 535-3675
Gerald A Krueger, *Partner*
Janice Rubrich, *Principal*
EMP: 26
SALES (est): 1MM **Privately Held**
SIC: 6513 Apartment building operators

(G-437)
SHAW JEWISH COMMUNITY CENTER
750 White Pond Dr (44320-1128)
PHONE..................330 867-7850
Fax: 330 867-7856
Michael Wise, *CEO*
Irving Sugerman, *President*
EMP: 105 EST: 1924
SQ FT: 100,000
SALES: 4.9MM **Privately Held**
SIC: 8322 Community center

(G-438)
SIGNET MANAGEMENT CO LTD
19 N High St (44308-1912)
PHONE..................330 762-9102
Anthony S Manna, *Chairman*
Martin Berry,
Patrick James,
EMP: 200
SALES (est): 21.2MM **Privately Held**
WEB: www.signet-enterprises.com
SIC: 8742 Management consulting services

Akron - Summit County (G-439) GEOGRAPHIC SECTION

(G-439)
SIRPILLA RECRTL VHCL CTR INC
Also Called: Freedom Rv
1005 Interstate Pkwy (44312-5285)
PHONE..................................330 494-2525
Fax: 330 645-3560
John A Sirpilla Jr, *President*
Todd Bleichrodt, *Site Mgr*
Wayde Henry, *Sales Executive*
Lenny Girardi, *Manager*
Karen Snyder, *Executive*
EMP: 74
SQ FT: 23,000
SALES (est): 17MM Privately Held
WEB: www.sirpillarv.com
SIC: 5561 7699 Travel trailers: automobile, new & used; motor homes; campers (pickup coaches) for mounting on trucks; mobile home repair

(G-440)
SKYCASTERS LLC
1520 S Arlington St # 100 (44306-3863)
PHONE..................................330 785-2100
Fax: 330 818-1978
Thomas Reed, *General Mgr*
Don Jacobs, *COO*
Ed Richards, *Manager*
Julie Long, *Web Dvlpr*
Sam Corbin, *Technical Staff*
▼ EMP: 32
SQ FT: 1,608
SALES: 7.1MM Privately Held
WEB: www.satellite-asp.com
SIC: 4813

(G-441)
SMITHERS GROUP INC (PA)
121 S Main St Ste 300 (44308-1426)
PHONE..................................330 762-7441
Volker Bornemann, *President*
Michael J Hochschwender, *President*
Prasad Raje, *President*
Gregory J Dziak, *Principal*
Steve Mihnovets, *Vice Pres*
EMP: 55
SALES (est): 63.6MM Privately Held
WEB: www.smithersgroup.com
SIC: 8742 Business consultant

(G-442)
SMITHERS QUALITY ASSESSMENTS
Also Called: Sqa
121 S Main St Ste 300 (44308-1426)
PHONE..................................330 762-4231
Jeanette Preston, *President*
EMP: 25
SALES (est): 2.6MM
SALES (corp-wide): 63.6MM Privately Held
WEB: www.smithersregistrar.com
SIC: 8742 8734 8748 Quality assurance consultant; product testing laboratories; testing services; test development & evaluation service
PA: The Smithers Group Inc
  121 S Main St Ste 300
  Akron OH 44308
  330 762-7441

(G-443)
SMITHERS RAPRA INC (HQ)
425 W Market St (44303-2044)
PHONE..................................330 762-7441
Fax: 330 762-7447
J Michael Hochschwender, *President*
Bruce D Lambillotte, *General Mgr*
Dan Rogers, *Editor*
Douglas Domeck, *Vice Pres*
Rikki Lamba, *Vice Pres*
EMP: 51
SQ FT: 20,000
SALES: 1MM
SALES (corp-wide): 63.6MM Privately Held
WEB: www.smithersconsulting.com
SIC: 8734 8742 Product testing laboratories; business consultant
PA: The Smithers Group Inc
  121 S Main St Ste 300
  Akron OH 44308
  330 762-7441

(G-444)
SMITHERS TIRE & AUTO TESTNG TX
Also Called: Smithers Trnsp Test Ctrs
425 W Market St (44303-2044)
PHONE..................................330 762-7441
J Hoschschwender, *President*
Steve Mihnovets, *Controller*
EMP: 47
SALES (est): 133.5K
SALES (corp-wide): 63.6MM Privately Held
WEB: www.smitherstiretest.com
SIC: 8734 Product testing laboratories; automobile proving & testing ground
HQ: Smithers Rapra Inc.
  425 W Market St
  Akron OH 44303
  330 762-7441

(G-445)
SPANO BROTHERS CNSTR CO
2595 Pressler Rd (44312-5553)
PHONE..................................330 645-1544
Fax: 330 645-1404
Vito Spano, *President*
EMP: 30
SQ FT: 20,000
SALES (est): 4.7MM Privately Held
SIC: 1794 1771 Excavation work; concrete work

(G-446)
SPECTRUM MGT HOLDG CO LLC
530 Suth Main St Ste 1751 (44311)
PHONE..................................330 208-9028
Jodi Drake, *Human Resources*
Steve Frey, *Branch Mgr*
Charles Bona, *Senior Mgr*
EMP: 27
SALES (corp-wide): 41.5B Publicly Held
SIC: 4841 Cable television services
HQ: Spectrum Management Holding Company, Llc
  400 Atlantic St
  Stamford CT 06901
  203 905-7801

(G-447)
ST GEORGE & CO INC
Also Called: St George Company
2586 Robindale Ave (44312-1653)
PHONE..................................330 733-7528
Fax: 330 794-1044
John Stgeorge, *CEO*
EMP: 32
SALES (est): 1.8MM Privately Held
WEB: www.stgeorgeco.com
SIC: 8741 Business management

(G-448)
ST PAULS CATHOLIC CHURCH (PA)
433 Mission Dr (44301-2710)
PHONE..................................330 724-1263
Fax: 330 724-7680
Ralph Thomas, *Pastor*
EMP: 50
SQ FT: 2,000
SALES: 450K Privately Held
SIC: 8661 8351 8211 Catholic Church; preschool center; Catholic elementary school

(G-449)
STAN HYWET HALL AND GRDNS INC
714 N Portage Path (44303-1399)
PHONE..................................330 836-5533
Fax: 330 836-2680
Harry Lynch, *CEO*
Dianne Ketler, *General Mgr*
William Binnie, *COO*
Sean Joyce, *Exec VP*
Gailmarie Fort, *Vice Pres*
EMP: 62
SQ FT: 5,000
SALES: 8MM Privately Held
WEB: www.stanhywet.org
SIC: 8412 8422 Museum; arboreta & botanical or zoological gardens

(G-450)
STARK KNOLL
3475 Richwood Rd (44333)
PHONE..................................330 376-3300
Fax: 330 376-6237
Michael L Stark, *Principal*
EMP: 40
SALES (est): 3.4MM Privately Held
SIC: 8111 General practice law office

(G-451)
STONEHEDGE ENTERPRISES INC
Also Called: Stonehedge Place
580 E Cuyahoga Falls Ave (44310-1540)
PHONE..................................330 928-2161
Fax: 330 928-0038
Fred Borden, *President*
Frank Bevilacqua, *Sr Exec VP*
Ron Winer, *Vice Pres*
Shelly Siegenthaler, *Financial Exec*
EMP: 48
SQ FT: 50,000
SALES (est): 1.7MM Privately Held
SIC: 7933 5813 7948 7999 Ten pin center; cocktail lounge; race track operation; miniature golf course operation; snack bar; coin-operated amusement devices

(G-452)
SUMMA HEALTH
1 Park West Blvd Ste 130 (44320-4230)
PHONE..................................330 873-1518
Barb Pisaneli, *Branch Mgr*
EMP: 655
SALES (corp-wide): 1B Privately Held
SIC: 8011 Offices & clinics of medical doctors
PA: Summa Health System
  525 E Market St
  Akron OH 44304
  330 375-3000

(G-453)
SUMMA HEALTH SYSTEM
Also Called: Summa Care
168 E Market St Ste 208 (44308-2014)
PHONE..................................330 535-7319
Charles Vignos, *Branch Mgr*
Linda Eitner, *Supervisor*
Greg Journey, *CIO*
Dave Orr, *Director*
Rose Gearhart, *Analyst*
EMP: 52
SALES (corp-wide): 1B Privately Held
WEB: www.summahealth.org
SIC: 8062 General medical & surgical hospitals
PA: Summa Health System
  525 E Market St
  Akron OH 44304
  330 375-3000

(G-454)
SUMMA HEALTH SYSTEM
Also Called: Summa Rehabilitation Services
750 White Pond Dr Ste 500 (44320-1128)
PHONE..................................330 836-9023
EMP: 737
SALES (corp-wide): 1B Privately Held
SIC: 8099 Blood related health services
PA: Summa Health System
  525 E Market St
  Akron OH 44304
  330 375-3000

(G-455)
SUMMA HEALTH SYSTEM
1077 Gorge Blvd (44310-2408)
PHONE..................................330 252-0095
William Powel III, *Vice Pres*
Elizabeth Bender, *Surgeon*
EMP: 246
SALES (corp-wide): 1B Privately Held
SIC: 8011 Physical medicine, physician/surgeon
PA: Summa Health System
  525 E Market St
  Akron OH 44304
  330 375-3000

(G-456)
SUMMA HEALTH SYSTEM
Also Called: Summa Akron City Hospital
525 E Market St (44304-1698)
PHONE..................................330 375-3000
Gregory Cloyd, *Anesthesiology*
Tia Castaldi,
EMP: 45
SALES (corp-wide): 1B Privately Held
SIC: 8062 General medical & surgical hospitals
PA: Summa Health System
  525 E Market St
  Akron OH 44304
  330 375-3000

(G-457)
SUMMA HEALTH SYSTEM
Also Called: Family Practice Center Akron
75 Arch St Ste 303 (44304-1432)
PHONE..................................330 375-3584
Jaki Mills, *Manager*
Dr Richard Hines, *Director*
Justin D Catlett, *Family Practiti*
EMP: 70
SALES (corp-wide): 1B Privately Held
WEB: www.summahealth.org
SIC: 8062 8011 General medical & surgical hospitals; general & family practice, physician/surgeon
PA: Summa Health System
  525 E Market St
  Akron OH 44304
  330 375-3000

(G-458)
SUMMA HEALTH SYSTEM
Also Called: Internal Medical Center
75 Arch St Ste 302 (44304-1432)
PHONE..................................330 375-3315
Fax: 330 375-7779
Ken Waters, *Project Mgr*
Samantha Williams, *Pub Rel Dir*
Steven M Radwany, *Manager*
Thomas Briggle, *Director*
EMP: 130
SALES (corp-wide): 1B Privately Held
WEB: www.summahealth.org
SIC: 8062 8093 8011 General medical & surgical hospitals; specialty outpatient clinics; offices & clinics of medical doctors
PA: Summa Health System
  525 E Market St
  Akron OH 44304
  330 375-3000

(G-459)
SUMMA HEALTH SYSTEM
Also Called: Akron City Hospital
55 Arch St Ste 1b (44304-1436)
PHONE..................................330 375-3315
Fax: 330 375-7720
Larry Meklenburg, *Database Admin*
Steven Radwany, *Director*
Ken Komorny, *Admin Sec*
Darrell Berger, *Technician*
EMP: 200
SALES (corp-wide): 1B Privately Held
WEB: www.summahealth.org
SIC: 8011 Internal medicine, physician/surgeon
PA: Summa Health System
  525 E Market St
  Akron OH 44304
  330 375-3000

(G-460)
SUMMA HEALTH SYSTEM
Also Called: Family Mdcine Ctr At St Thomas
444 N Main St (44310-3110)
PHONE..................................330 375-3000
Fax: 330 379-5527
Michael Rutherford, *CFO*
Todd Hampton, *Pharmacist*
Carrie Tucker, *Manager*
Michael Canterbury, *Info Tech Mgr*
Dr J Flanagan, *Director*
EMP: 25
SALES (corp-wide): 1B Privately Held
WEB: www.summahealth.org
SIC: 8062 8011 General medical & surgical hospitals; offices & clinics of medical doctors
PA: Summa Health System
  525 E Market St
  Akron OH 44304
  330 375-3000

GEOGRAPHIC SECTION
Akron - Summit County (G-486)

(G-461)
SUMMA HEALTH SYSTEM
Also Called: Summa Park West
1 Park West Blvd Ste 130 (44320-4230)
PHONE.................................330 864-8060
Deanna Frye, *Branch Mgr*
Anita Dash-Modi, *Ophthalmology*
EMP: 491
SALES (corp-wide): 1B **Privately Held**
SIC: 8011 Radiologist
PA: Summa Health System
 525 E Market St
 Akron OH 44304
 330 375-3000

(G-462)
SUMMA INSURANCE COMPANY INC (DH)
Also Called: Summacare
10 N Main St (44308-1958)
P.O. Box 3620 (44309-3620)
PHONE.................................800 996-8411
Fax: 330 996-8746
Claude Vincenti, *CEO*
Martin P Hauser, *President*
Charles R Vignos, *Vice Chairman*
Annette M Ruby, *Vice Pres*
Yvonne Damico, *Admin Asst*
EMP: 290
SALES (est): 346.8MM
SALES (corp-wide): 1B **Privately Held**
SIC: 6321 6311 Health insurance carriers; life insurance

(G-463)
SUMMA REHAB HOSPITAL LLC
29 N Adams St (44304-1641)
PHONE.................................330 572-7300
Fax: 330 572-7310
Pam Mackintosh, *Director*
William A Powel III,
Derek Steele,
EMP: 25
SALES (est): 2.2MM **Privately Held**
SIC: 8049 Physiotherapist

(G-464)
SUMMACARE INC
10 N Main St Unit 1 (44308-1958)
PHONE.................................330 996-8410
Martin Hauser, *President*
Autumn Love, *Opers Mgr*
Jim Mc Nutt, *Financial Exec*
Debbie Boop, *Sales Executive*
Timothy P Colligan, *Manager*
EMP: 325
SALES (est): 6.5MM
SALES (corp-wide): 1B **Privately Held**
WEB: www.summacare.com
SIC: 8099 Medical services organization
HQ: Summa Insurance Company, Inc.
 10 N Main St
 Akron OH 44308
 330 996-8411

(G-465)
SUMMIT CNTY DEPT JOB FMLY SVCS
1180 S Main St Ste 102 (44301-1253)
PHONE.................................330 643-8200
Michelle Moore, *Principal*
EMP: 99
SALES (est): 1.5MM **Privately Held**
SIC: 8322 Family counseling services

(G-466)
SUMMIT CNTY INTERNISTS & ASSOC (PA)
55 Arch St Ste 1a (44304-1424)
PHONE.................................330 375-3690
Fax: 330 375-4939
Dale P Murphy MD, *Owner*
EMP: 37
SALES (est): 3.3MM **Privately Held**
SIC: 8011 Internal medicine, physician/surgeon

(G-467)
SUMMIT HAND CENTER INC
3975 Embassy Pkwy Ste 201 (44333-8393)
PHONE.................................330 668-4055
William McCue, *President*
John X Biondi MD, *Principal*
John W Dietrich MD, *Principal*
William Mc Cue MD, *Principal*
Nina M Njus MD, *Principal*
EMP: 30
SALES (est): 1.7MM **Privately Held**
SIC: 8011 Orthopedic physician

(G-468)
SUMMIT OPTHOMOLOGY OPTICAL
Also Called: West Market Optical Service
1 Park West Blvd Ste 150 (44320-4230)
PHONE.................................330 864-8060
Dr J Cannatti, *Partner*
EMP: 50
SALES (est): 846.4K **Privately Held**
SIC: 8011 5995 Ophthalmologist; optical goods stores

(G-469)
SUPERR-SPDIE PORTABLE SVCS INC
1050 Killian Rd (44312-4744)
PHONE.................................330 733-9000
Jeffrey M Grubbs, *President*
Patrick Flynn, *Vice Pres*
Shelley Grubbs, *Treasurer*
Scott Savage, *Marketing Staff*
Brian Rayl, *Manager*
EMP: 32
SQ FT: 24,000
SALES (est): 6.5MM **Privately Held**
SIC: 7359 5099 Portable toilet rental; toilets, portable

(G-470)
SWS EQUIPMENT SERVICES INC
Also Called: S W S
712 Palisades Dr (44303-1708)
PHONE.................................330 806-2767
Loyd McCoy, *President*
◆ EMP: 30
SALES (est): 1.4MM **Privately Held**
SIC: 1799 Rigging & scaffolding

(G-471)
TASTY PURE FOOD COMPANY (PA)
1557 Industrial Pkwy (44310-2603)
PHONE.................................330 434-8141
Jim K Heilmeier, *President*
Bill Heilmeier, *CFO*
William Heilmeier, *CFO*
Andrew Heilmeier, *Sales Staff*
EMP: 34
SQ FT: 20,000
SALES (est): 28.9MM **Privately Held**
WEB: www.tastypure.com
SIC: 5147 5142 5141 Meats, fresh; packaged frozen goods; groceries, general line

(G-472)
TECH CENTER INC
265 S Main St Ste 200 (44308-1223)
PHONE.................................330 762-6212
Fax: 330 762-2035
Doug Eilertson, *President*
EMP: 25
SALES (est): 1.3MM **Privately Held**
WEB: www.techcenterinc.com
SIC: 7361 Executive placement

(G-473)
TECH PRO INC
3030 Gilchrist Rd (44305-4420)
PHONE.................................330 923-3546
Fax: 330 923-6335
John Putman, *President*
Kay Putman, *Vice Pres*
Caroline Glaeser, *Purch Mgr*
▲ EMP: 28
SQ FT: 30,000
SALES (est): 2.6MM **Privately Held**
WEB: www.techpro-usa.com
SIC: 7699 3821 3829 3825 Laboratory instrument repair; laboratory apparatus & furniture; measuring & controlling devices; instruments to measure electricity; computer peripheral equipment

(G-474)
TENNIS UNLIMITED INC
Also Called: TOWPATH RACQUET CLUB
2108 Akron Peninsula Rd (44313-4804)
PHONE.................................330 928-8763
Fax: 330 928-1093
Dallas Aleman, *President*
Nancy Aleman, *Vice Pres*
Kristianne Bontempo, *Manager*
EMP: 30
SQ FT: 50,000
SALES (est): 1MM **Privately Held**
WEB: www.towpathtennis.com
SIC: 7997 5941 Tennis club, membership; tennis goods & equipment

(G-475)
TERMINAL WAREHOUSE INC (HQ)
1779 Marvo Dr (44306-4331)
P.O. Box 20109, Canton (44701-0109)
PHONE.................................330 773-2056
Fax: 330 773-6132
Douglas J Sibila, *CEO*
Ronald R Goson, *Ch of Bd*
William Hanlon, *President*
Chuck Bridwell, *General Mgr*
Bill Hanlon, *COO*
EMP: 64
SQ FT: 1,700,000
SALES (est): 17.5MM **Privately Held**
WEB: www.terminalwhse.com
SIC: 4225 General warehousing

(G-476)
THE FAMOUS MANUFACTURING CO
2620 Ridgewood Rd Ste 200 (44313-3507)
PHONE.................................330 762-9621
Jay Blaushild, *President*
EMP: 35 EST: 2001
SALES (est): 4.3MM **Privately Held**
SIC: 5075 5074 Furnaces, heating: electric; furnaces, warm air; air conditioning & ventilation equipment & supplies; plumbing & hydronic heating supplies
PA: Famous Enterprises, Inc.
 2620 Ridgewood Rd Ste 200
 Akron OH 44313

(G-477)
TIME WARNER CABLE INC
1919 Brittain Rd (44310-1843)
PHONE.................................330 800-3874
John Duran, *Director*
Stephen Fry, *Director*
EMP: 25
SALES (corp-wide): 41.5B **Publicly Held**
SIC: 4841 4813 Cable television services;
HQ: Spectrum Management Holding Company, Llc
 400 Atlantic St
 Stamford CT 06901
 203 905-7801

(G-478)
TOLEDO EDISON COMPANY (HQ)
Also Called: Toledo Railways and Light Co
76 S Main St Bsmt (44308-1817)
PHONE.................................800 447-3333
Anthony J Alexander, *CEO*
C E Jones, *President*
Jasmine Witherspoon, *Principal*
L L Vespoli, *Exec VP*
Harvey L Wagner, *Vice Pres*
EMP: 117
SALES: 484.3MM **Publicly Held**
SIC: 4911 Distribution, electric power; transmission, electric power

(G-479)
TPUSA INC
Also Called: Teleperformance USA
150 E Market St (44308-2014)
PHONE.................................330 374-1232
EMP: 500
SALES (corp-wide): 74.7MM **Privately Held**
SIC: 7389 Telemarketing services
HQ: Tpusa, Inc.
 5295 S Commerce Dr # 600
 Murray UT 84107
 801 257-5800

(G-480)
TRANSITWORKS LLC
1090 W Wilbeth Rd (44314-1945)
PHONE.................................330 861-1118
Ken Richards, *Business Mgr*
Dennis Summers, *Vice Pres*
Thomas Habib, *Prdtn Mgr*
Rick Cook, *Purchasing*
Jim Fazio, *Regl Sales Mgr*
▲ EMP: 99
SALES (est): 16MM
SALES (corp-wide): 408MM **Privately Held**
WEB: www.mobilityworks.net
SIC: 5511 7532 Automobiles, new & used; customizing services, non-factory basis
PA: Wmk, Llc
 4199 Kinross Lakes Pkwy # 300
 Richfield OH 44286
 234 312-2000

(G-481)
TRI-COUNTY PALLET RECYCL INC
Also Called: Tri-County Mulch
900 Flora Ave (44314-1722)
PHONE.................................330 848-0313
William C Bowling, *President*
EMP: 40
SALES (est): 6.3MM **Privately Held**
SIC: 5031 Lumber, plywood & millwork

(G-482)
TW TELECOM INC
Also Called: Time Warner Cable
1019 E Turkeyfoot Lake Rd (44312-5242)
PHONE.................................234 542-6279
EMP: 29
SALES (corp-wide): 1.4B **Publicly Held**
SIC: 4813 Telephone Communications
PA: Tw Telecom Inc.
 10475 Park Meadows Dr
 Littleton CO 80124
 303 566-1000

(G-483)
UNIFIED CNSTR SYSTEMS LTD (PA)
1920 S Main St (44301-2851)
PHONE.................................330 773-2511
Jason Haws,
Scott Wyler,
EMP: 30
SQ FT: 6,000
SALES (est): 4.3MM **Privately Held**
WEB: www.foundsystems.com
SIC: 1742 1799 Insulation, buildings; waterproofing

(G-484)
UNITED DENTAL LABORATORIES (PA)
261 South Ave (44302)
P.O. Box 428, Tallmadge (44278-0428)
PHONE.................................330 253-1810
Fax: 330 253-1669
Richard Delapa Jr, *President*
R J Delapa, *Manager*
Lenny Nigh, *Manager*
EMP: 35
SQ FT: 15,000
SALES (est): 4.9MM **Privately Held**
WEB: www.uniteddentallab.com
SIC: 8072 3843 Denture production; dental equipment & supplies

(G-485)
UNITED DISABILITY SERVICES INC (PA)
701 S Main St (44311-1019)
PHONE.................................330 374-1169
Shelley Morris, *Business Mgr*
Kevin Foote, *Sales Staff*
Heidi Imhoff, *Program Mgr*
Beth Macmillian, *Manager*
Marianne Riggenbach, *Manager*
EMP: 160 EST: 1949
SQ FT: 78,000
SALES: 11.5MM **Privately Held**
SIC: 8093 8331 8322 Specialty outpatient clinics; rehabilitation center, outpatient treatment; job training & vocational rehabilitation services; social services for the handicapped

(G-486)
UNITED WAY OF SUMMIT COUNTY
90 N Prospect St (44304-1273)
PHONE.................................330 762-7601

Akron - Summit County (G-487) — GEOGRAPHIC SECTION

Robert A Kulinski, *President*
Brett Kimmell, *CFO*
Michele Stanovic, *Financial Exec*
Steven L Farnsworth, *Bd of Directors*
Valerie A Geiger, *Bd of Directors*
EMP: 29
SQ FT: 13,000
SALES: 12.7MM **Privately Held**
SIC: 8399 Fund raising organization, non-fee basis

(G-487)
UNIVERSAL NURSING SERVICES (PA)
483 Augusta Dr (44333-9214)
PHONE 330 434-7318
Fax: 330 434-2567
Gloria Rookard, *President*
Derrick Rookard, *Vice Pres*
David Rookard, *Treasurer*
EMP: 50
SQ FT: 4,800
SALES (est): 7.6MM **Privately Held**
SIC: 8082 Home health care services

(G-488)
UNIVERSITY OF AKRON
Also Called: College Polymr Science & Engrg
170 University Ave (44325-0044)
PHONE 330 972-6008
Steven Cheng, *Dean*
Kumar Nanjundiah, *Professor*
Shi Q Wang, *Professor*
EMP: 60
SALES (corp-wide): 549.7MM **Privately Held**
WEB: www.uakron.edu
SIC: 8221 8711 University; engineering services
PA: The University Of Akron
   302 Buchtel Mall
   Akron OH 44325
   330 972-7111

(G-489)
UNIVERSITY OF AKRON
Also Called: Center For Child Development
108 Fir Hl (44325-0004)
PHONE 330 972-8210
Ryan Brosnahan, *Research*
Sophia Kraun, *Director*
Nancy Somerick, *Director*
EMP: 30
SALES (corp-wide): 549.7MM **Privately Held**
WEB: www.uakron.edu
SIC: 8351 8221 Child day care services; university
PA: The University Of Akron
   302 Buchtel Mall
   Akron OH 44325
   330 972-7111

(G-490)
URS GROUP INC
564 White Pond Dr (44320-1100)
PHONE 330 836-9111
Fax: 330 836-9115
Eric Smith, *General Mgr*
Scott Buchanan, *Engineer*
Ryan Schuster, *Engineer*
Rohn Noirot, *Security Mgr*
Michael Burgess, *Manager*
EMP: 90
SALES (corp-wide): 18.2B **Publicly Held**
SIC: 8712 8711 Architectural engineering; professional engineer
HQ: Urs Group, Inc.
   300 S Grand Ave Ste 1100
   Los Angeles CA 90071
   213 593-8000

(G-491)
USIC LOCATING SERVICES LLC
441 Munroe Falls Rd (44312)
PHONE 330 733-9393
Fax: 330 278-1846
Shaun Corrin, *Manager*
Rob Dorman, *Manager*
EMP: 125 **Privately Held**
WEB: www.sm-p.com
SIC: 8713 Surveying services
HQ: Usic Locating Services, Llc
   9045 River Rd Ste 300
   Indianapolis IN 46240
   317 575-7800

(G-492)
VALMARK INSURANCE AGENCY LLC
130 Springside Dr Ste 300 (44333-2489)
PHONE 330 576-1234
Lawrence J Rybka, *President*
Caleb Callahan, *COO*
Kathleen Meyer, *Manager*
Mark White, *Executive*
EMP: 60
SQ FT: 15,000
SALES (est): 9MM **Privately Held**
WEB: www.abellassociates.com
SIC: 6411 6211 Insurance agents, brokers & service; security brokers & dealers

(G-493)
VALMARK SECURITIES INC (HQ)
130 Springside Dr Ste 300 (44333-2489)
PHONE 330 576-1234
Lawrence J Rybka, *President*
Brenda L Hood, *Vice Pres*
David K Critzer, *CFO*
Erika Blockson, *Human Res Mgr*
Sheila Jelinek, *Manager*
EMP: 28
SALES (est): 6.6MM
SALES (corp-wide): 3.8MM **Privately Held**
SIC: 6211 Security brokers & dealers
PA: Executive Insurance Agency Inc
   130 Springside Dr Ste 300
   Akron OH 44333
   330 576-1234

(G-494)
VAN DEVERE INC (PA)
Also Called: Van Devere Buick
300 W Market St (44303-2185)
PHONE 330 253-6137
Fax: 330 253-1370
Michael Van Devere, *President*
Chris Bender, *General Mgr*
Shirley A Van Devere, *Corp Secy*
Cory Kanis, *Finance Mgr*
Brian Vandevere, *Finance Mgr*
EMP: 77
SALES (est): 98.9MM **Privately Held**
WEB: www.vandevere.com
SIC: 5511 7515 Automobiles, new & used; passenger car leasing

(G-495)
VANTAGE AGING (PA)
2279 Romig Rd (44320-3823)
PHONE 330 253-4597
Karen Hrdlicka, *President*
Melinda Smith Yeargin, *Chairman*
William Morgan, *CFO*
Kiesha Butler, *Manager*
Dena Haswell, *Info Tech Mgr*
EMP: 67 **EST:** 1975
SQ FT: 17,000
SALES: 13.1MM **Privately Held**
SIC: 8322 Senior citizens' center or association

(G-496)
VANTAGE AGING
1155 E Tallmadge Ave (44310-3529)
PHONE 330 785-9770
Catherine Lewis, *President*
EMP: 620
SALES (corp-wide): 13.1MM **Privately Held**
SIC: 8999 Artists & artists' studios
PA: Vantage Aging
   2279 Romig Rd
   Akron OH 44320
   330 253-4597

(G-497)
VIP HOMECARE INC
Also Called: VIP Home Care
545 E Cuyahoga Falls Ave (44310-1550)
PHONE 330 929-2838
Fax: 330 929-9901
Diane Johnson, *President*
EMP: 85
SALES (est): 1.2MM **Privately Held**
SIC: 8082 Home health care services

(G-498)
VIRTUAL HOLD TECHNOLOGY LLC (PA)
3875 Embassy Pkwy Ste 350 (44333-8343)
PHONE 330 666-1181
Fax: 330 670-2269
Wes Hayden, *CEO*
Thomas Jameson, *Exec VP*
Ted Bray, *Vice Pres*
Kevin Shinseki, *Vice Pres*
James Pavlic, *Engineer*
EMP: 78
SQ FT: 18,000
SALES (est): 21.1MM **Privately Held**
WEB: www.virtualhold.com
SIC: 7371 7372 Computer software development; prepackaged software

(G-499)
VISITING NURSE SERVICE INC (PA)
1 Home Care Pl (44320-3999)
PHONE 330 745-1601
Karen Talbott, *President*
Jerry Bauman, *Vice Pres*
John Janoso, *Vice Pres*
Tom Lyzen, *Vice Pres*
Pat Waickman, *Vice Pres*
EMP: 325
SQ FT: 20,000
SALES: 21.8MM **Privately Held**
WEB: www.vnsa.com
SIC: 8082 Visiting nurse service

(G-500)
VULCAN MACHINERY CORPORATION
20 N Case Ave (44305-2598)
PHONE 330 376-6025
Fax: 330 376-2172
David Jacobs, *President*
Bradley J Acobs, *Vice Pres*
Bradley J Jacobs, *Vice Pres*
Gary Bradford, *Plant Mgr*
Kim Caetty, *Purch Mgr*
EMP: 25
SALES (est): 3.9MM **Privately Held**
WEB: www.vulcanmachinery.com
SIC: 3559 7299 Plastics working machinery; banquet hall facilities

(G-501)
W G LOCKHART CONSTRUCTION CO
800 W Waterloo Rd (44314-1528)
PHONE 330 745-6520
Fax: 330 745-5711
Alexander R Lockhart, *President*
Richard Stanley, *Admin Sec*
EMP: 100
SQ FT: 5,000
SALES (est): 8.1MM **Privately Held**
SIC: 1611 3273 Highway & street construction; ready-mixed concrete

(G-502)
WAIDS RAINBOW RENTAL INC
1050 Killian Rd (44312-4744)
PHONE 216 524-3736
Fax: 216 524-4207
Patricia Waid, *President*
Ron Waid, *Treasurer*
Bernadette Waid, *Shareholder*
Claire Waid, *Admin Sec*
EMP: 25
SQ FT: 3,400
SALES (est): 2.2MM **Privately Held**
SIC: 7359 Portable toilet rental

(G-503)
WALGREEN CO
Also Called: Walgreens
302 Canton Rd (44312-1544)
PHONE 330 733-4237
Fax: 330 733-4203
Jess Roeger, *Branch Mgr*
Jim Cetnrawski, *Manager*
EMP: 30
SALES (corp-wide): 118.2B **Publicly Held**
WEB: www.walgreens.com
SIC: 5912 7384 Drug stores; photofinishing laboratory
HQ: Walgreen Co.
   200 Wilmot Rd
   Deerfield IL 60015
   847 315-2500

(G-504)
WALNUT RIDGE MANAGEMENT
520 S Main St Ste 2457 (44311-1095)
PHONE 234 678-3900
Jeanette M Thomas, *Principal*
EMP: 70 **EST:** 2010
SALES (est): 6.7MM **Privately Held**
SIC: 8741 Business management

(G-505)
WEAVER INDUSTRIES INC
636 W Exchange St (44302-1306)
PHONE 330 379-3606
Jean Fish, *Manager*
EMP: 120
SALES (corp-wide): 5.4MM **Privately Held**
SIC: 7389 Packaging & labeling services
PA: Weaver Industries Inc.
   520 S Main St Ste 2441
   Akron OH 44311
   330 379-3660

(G-506)
WEAVER INDUSTRIES INC (PA)
520 S Main St Ste 2441 (44311-1071)
PHONE 330 379-3660
Fax: 330 376-2066
Jack Skinner, *General Mgr*
Jim Weaver, *Exec VP*
Bill Richards, *Sales Executive*
Jeff Johnson, *Exec Dir*
Denise Balko, *Admin Asst*
EMP: 30
SQ FT: 20,000
SALES: 5.4MM **Privately Held**
WEB: www.weaverindustries.org
SIC: 7389 8331 Packaging & labeling services; job training & vocational rehabilitation services

(G-507)
WEAVER INDUSTRIES INC
340 N Clvland Mssillon Rd (44333-9302)
PHONE 330 666-5114
Fax: 330 634-8222
Shirley Nemec, *Mfg Staff*
John Irvine, *Sales Staff*
Claire Poirer-Keys, *Manager*
Bob Craven, *Asst Mgr*
EMP: 175
SALES (corp-wide): 5.4MM **Privately Held**
SIC: 7389 8331 Packaging & labeling services; job training & vocational rehabilitation services
PA: Weaver Industries Inc.
   520 S Main St Ste 2441
   Akron OH 44311
   330 379-3660

(G-508)
WEAVER INDUSTRIES INC
Also Called: Weaver Secure Shred
2337 Romig Rd Ste 2 (44320-3824)
PHONE 330 745-2400
Jack Skinner, *Branch Mgr*
EMP: 127
SALES (corp-wide): 5.4MM **Privately Held**
SIC: 7389 Document & office record destruction
PA: Weaver Industries Inc.
   520 S Main St Ste 2441
   Akron OH 44311
   330 379-3660

(G-509)
WHITE POND GARDENS INC
Also Called: Graf Growers
1015 White Pond Dr (44320-1503)
PHONE 330 836-2727
Fax: 330 836-0476
Lisa Graf, *President*
Craig Graf, *Corp Secy*
Scott Graf, *Vice Pres*
EMP: 32
SQ FT: 5,000

GEOGRAPHIC SECTION

Alliance - Stark County (G-531)

SALES (est): 4.2MM **Privately Held**
WEB: www.grafgrowers.com
SIC: **0182** 0181 5261 0161 Food crops grown under cover; flowers: grown under cover (e.g. greenhouse production); nurseries & garden centers; vegetables & melons

(G-510)
WHITESPACE DESIGN GROUP INC
Also Called: Whitespace Creative
243 Furnace St (44304)
PHONE..................330 762-9320
Fax: 330 762-9323
Keeven White, *President*
Greg Kiskadden, *Vice Pres*
Gregory Kiskadden, *Vice Pres*
Alan Ashby, *Director*
Samantha Warnock, *Admin Asst*
EMP: 30
SQ FT: 6,000
SALES (est): 10.7MM **Privately Held**
WEB: www.whitespace-creative.com
SIC: **7311** 8743 7336 Advertising agencies; advertising consultant; public relations services; public relations & publicity; sales promotion; commercial art & graphic design; graphic arts & related design

(G-511)
WOLFF BROS SUPPLY INC
1200 Kelly Ave (44306-3735)
PHONE..................330 786-4140
Fax: 330 773-2153
Robert Doherty, *Business Mgr*
Bob Doherty, *Sales & Mktg St*
Denise Alt, *Consultant*
Todd Ennemoser, *Consultant*
Diane Gilles, *Consultant*
EMP: 30
SALES (corp-wide): 114.4MM **Privately Held**
WEB: www.wolffbros.com
SIC: **5063** 5074 5075 Electrical apparatus & equipment; plumbing & hydronic heating supplies; warm air heating & air conditioning
PA: Wolff Bros. Supply, Inc
6078 Wolff Rd
Medina OH 44256
330 725-3451

(G-512)
WQMX LOVE FUND
1795 W Market St (44313-7001)
PHONE..................330 869-9800
Thomas Mandel, *President*
EMP: 75
SALES (est): 824.5K **Privately Held**
SIC: **4832** Radio broadcasting stations

(G-513)
WYANT LEASING CO LLC
Also Called: Wyant Woods Care Center
200 Wyant Rd (44313-4228)
PHONE..................330 836-7953
Fax: 330 836-6806
Stephen Rosedale,
EMP: 270
SALES (est): 9MM **Privately Held**
SIC: **8051** Skilled nursing care facilities

(G-514)
WZ MANAGEMENT INC
3417 E Waterloo Rd (44312-4036)
P.O. Box 6258 (44312-0258)
PHONE..................330 628-4881
Fax: 330 628-0948
Sidney Zetzer, *President*
John Miskar, *Parts Mgr*
Robert Zetzer, *Executive*
Shirley Zetzer, *Admin Sec*
◆ EMP: 32 **EST**: 1946
SALES (est): 9.8MM **Privately Held**
WEB: www.samwinermotors.com
SIC: **5013** 5531 Truck parts & accessories; truck equipment & parts

(G-515)
YOUNG MENS CHRISTIAN ASSOC
Also Called: Phoenix School Program
888 Jonathan Ave (44306-3607)
PHONE..................330 784-0408

Wendy Neloms, *Principal*
EMP: 25
SQ FT: 17,127
SALES (corp-wide): 16.8MM **Privately Held**
WEB: www.campynoah.com
SIC: **8641** 7991 8351 7032 Youth organizations; physical fitness facilities; child day care services; youth camps; individual & family services
PA: The Young Men's Christian Association Of Akron Ohio
50 S Mn St Ste Ll100
Akron OH 44308
330 376-1335

(G-516)
YOUNG MENS CHRISTIAN ASSOC
Also Called: YMCA
350 E Wilbeth Rd (44301-2624)
PHONE..................330 724-1255
Fax: 330 724-4303
Jodi Kovacik, *Business Mgr*
Patrick Gillihan, *Property Mgr*
Gary Lake, *Director*
Kristy Liggett, *Program Dir*
Melissa Roddy, *Executive*
EMP: 35
SALES (corp-wide): 16.8MM **Privately Held**
WEB: www.campynoah.com
SIC: **8641** 8351 Youth organizations; child day care services
PA: The Young Men's Christian Association Of Akron Ohio
50 S Mn St Ste Ll100
Akron OH 44308
330 376-1335

(G-517)
YOUNG MENS CHRISTIAN ASSOC
Also Called: Canal Square Branch
80 W Center St (44308-1037)
PHONE..................330 376-1335
Douglas R Kohl, *President*
Jill Doerner, *Vice Pres*
Laura Merritt, *Mktg Dir*
Vivian Cullen, *Director*
Missy Denault, *Director*
EMP: 550
SALES (corp-wide): 16.8MM **Privately Held**
WEB: www.campynoah.com
SIC: **8641** 8351 Recreation association; child day care services
PA: The Young Men's Christian Association Of Akron Ohio
50 S Mn St Ste Ll100
Akron OH 44308
330 376-1335

(G-518)
YRS INC
Also Called: Service Plus
4100 Embassy Pkwy (44333-1783)
PHONE..................330 665-3906
Bruce Finn, *President*
Cynthia Fitzgibbons, *Vice Pres*
EMP: 60
SQ FT: 1,948
SALES (est): 1.3MM **Privately Held**
SIC: **7363** Help supply services

Albany
Athens County

(G-519)
FARM CREDIT MID-AMERICA
2368 Blizzard Ln (45710-9287)
PHONE..................740 441-9312
Donna Crabtree, *Manager*
EMP: 42
SALES (corp-wide): 469.9MM **Privately Held**
SIC: **6029** 6141 6162 Commercial banks; personal credit institutions; mortgage bankers & correspondents
PA: Farm Credit Mid-America
1601 Ups Dr
Louisville KY 40223
502 420-3700

(G-520)
OASIS THRPTIC FSTER CARE NTWRK
34265 State Route 681 S (45710-9083)
PHONE..................740 698-0340
Fax: 740 698-0821
Kay Wheeler, *President*
Charles Wheeler, *President*
Brian Michael, *Manager*
Sue Hagaman, *Asst Admin*
EMP: 25
SALES (est): 2.2MM **Privately Held**
SIC: **8361** Group foster home

Alliance
Stark County

(G-521)
A J OSTER FOILS LLC
2081 Mccrea St (44601-2793)
PHONE..................330 823-1700
Fax: 330 823-1705
Kevin Bense, *President*
Alexander B Jourdan, *General Mgr*
Beth Tirey, *COO*
Robert M James, *Vice Pres*
Beth Riordan, *Safety Mgr*
▲ EMP: 53
SQ FT: 80,000
SALES (est): 14.9MM **Publicly Held**
SIC: **3341** 3353 3471 3497 Secondary nonferrous metals; aluminum sheet, plate & foil; plating & polishing; metal foil & leaf; metals service centers & offices
HQ: A.J. Oster, Llc
301 Metro Center Blvd # 204
Warwick RI 02886
401 736-2600

(G-522)
AARONS INC
2102 W State St (44601-3527)
PHONE..................330 823-1879
Fax: 330 823-3019
Anthony Hunter, *Manager*
EMP: 25
SALES (corp-wide): 3.3B **Publicly Held**
WEB: www.aaronrents.com
SIC: **7359** Furniture rental
PA: Aaron's, Inc.
400 Galleria Pkwy Se # 300
Atlanta GA 30339
678 402-3000

(G-523)
ALLIANALCE HOSPITALIST GROUP
200 E State St (44601-4936)
PHONE..................330 823-5626
Stan Jonas, *Principal*
Bart Brine, *Ophthalmology*
Ashraf Ahmed, *Internal Med*
Michelle Ahmed, *Internal Med*
Karamjitc Bhullar, *Internal Med*
EMP: 25
SALES: 63.6K **Privately Held**
SIC: **8062** General medical & surgical hospitals

(G-524)
ALLIANCE CITIZENS HEALTH ASSN
200 E State St (44601-4936)
PHONE..................330 596-6000
Stan Jonas, *CEO*
Stacy Garber, *Recruiter*
EMP: 1200
SQ FT: 30,000
SALES: 109.9MM **Privately Held**
SIC: **8062** General medical & surgical hospitals

(G-525)
ALLIANCE HOT STOVE BASEBALL L
1127 Forest Ave (44601-3261)
P.O. Box 2681 (44601-0681)
PHONE..................330 823-7034
Bill Fast, *President*
Jim Newman, *Vice Pres*
William Clark, *Treasurer*
Brian Whitlatch, *Commissioner*

Barry Benedict, *Admin Sec*
EMP: 25
SALES: 83.4K **Privately Held**
SIC: **7941** Baseball club, professional & semi-professional

(G-526)
ALLIANCE TOWERS LLC
350 S Arch Ave Apt 106 (44601-2677)
PHONE..................330 823-1063
Leeann Morein, *Partner*
David Robertson, *Principal*
Jennifer Hardee, *Admin Sec*
EMP: 3924
SALES (est): 33.1MM **Publicly Held**
WEB: www.aimco.com
SIC: **6513** Apartment building operators
HQ: Aimco Properties, L.P.
4582 S Ulster St Ste 1100
Denver CO 80237

(G-527)
BEL AIR CARE CENTER
2350 Cherry Ave (44601-5022)
PHONE..................330 821-3939
Fax: 330 821-9402
David Childs, *Owner*
Kenneth Biros, *Director*
Arnold Yost, *Administration*
EMP: 90
SALES (est): 2.6MM **Privately Held**
SIC: **8052** 8059 8051 Intermediate care facilities; convalescent home; skilled nursing care facilities

(G-528)
BROOKDALE SENIOR LIVING COMMUN
Also Called: Sterling House of Alliance
1277 S Sawburg Ave (44601-5755)
PHONE..................330 829-0180
Fax: 330 821-5587
Andrea Williams, *Director*
EMP: 34
SALES (corp-wide): 4.7B **Publicly Held**
WEB: www.assisted.com
SIC: **8059** Rest home, with health care
HQ: Brookdale Senior Living Communities, Inc.
6737 W Wa St Ste 2300
Milwaukee WI 53214
414 918-5000

(G-529)
CANTERBURY VILLA OF ALLIANCE
1785 N Freshley Ave (44601-8770)
PHONE..................330 821-1391
Fax: 330 821-6127
Brian Colleran, *President*
Joe Piesciuk, *Maintence Staff*
EMP: 100
SALES: 7.1MM
SALES (corp-wide): 11.5MM **Privately Held**
SIC: **8051** Skilled nursing care facilities
PA: Ballantrae Healthcare, Llc
1128 Pennsylvania St Ne
Albuquerque NM 87110
505 366-5200

(G-530)
CARING HANDS INC
885 S Sawburg Ave Ste 107 (44601-5905)
PHONE..................330 821-6310
Fax: 330 821-6313
Malenda Sever, *Director*
EMP: 150
SALES: 1.5MM **Privately Held**
SIC: **8082** Home health care services

(G-531)
CELLCO PARTNERSHIP
Also Called: Verizon
2700 W State St (44601-5611)
PHONE..................330 823-7758
Fax: 330 823-4510
William Sanford, *Branch Mgr*
EMP: 71
SALES (corp-wide): 126B **Publicly Held**
SIC: **4812** Cellular telephone services
HQ: Cellco Partnership
1 Verizon Way
Basking Ridge NJ 07920

Alliance - Stark County (G-532)

(G-532)
CINTAS CORPORATION
12445 Rockhill Ave Ne (44601-1065)
PHONE.................................330 821-2220
Joe Caruthers, *General Mgr*
EMP: 100
SQ FT: 38,000
SALES (corp-wide): 5.3B **Publicly Held**
WEB: www.cintas-corp.com
SIC: 7218 Industrial launderers
PA: Cintas Corporation
6800 Cintas Blvd
Cincinnati OH 45262
513 459-1200

(G-533)
CITY ALLIANCE WATER SEWER DST
1015 Walnut Ave (44601-1367)
PHONE.................................330 823-5216
Doug Hastings, *Superintendent*
EMP: 31
SQ FT: 4,048
SALES (est): 2MM **Privately Held**
SIC: 4941 Water supply

(G-534)
CLEM LUMBER AND DISTRG CO
16055 Waverly St Ne (44601-1441)
P.O. Box 2238 (44601-0238)
PHONE.................................330 821-2130
Fax: 330 821-6143
Don McAlister, *President*
James McAlister, *President*
David McAlister, *Corp Secy*
Rich Wollaim, *Purch Agent*
Tom Quinn, *Sales Staff*
▲ **EMP:** 65 **EST:** 1946
SQ FT: 60,000
SALES (est): 43.3MM **Privately Held**
SIC: 5031 Millwork; building materials, interior; building materials, exterior

(G-535)
CONCORDE THERAPY GROUP INC
Also Called: Concord Therapy Group
2484 W State St (44601-5608)
PHONE.................................330 493-4210
Fax: 330 829-2376
Marcy Woost, *Manager*
Mary Rusznak, *Manager*
Jason Ruznak, *OB/GYN*
EMP: 30 **Privately Held**
WEB: www.concordehealth.com
SIC: 8049 8011 Physical therapist; offices & clinics of medical doctors
PA: Concorde Therapy Group Inc
4645 Belpar St Nw
Canton OH 44718

(G-536)
COPE FARM EQUIPMENT INC (PA)
Also Called: John Deere Authorized Dealer
24915 State Route 62 (44601-9000)
PHONE.................................330 821-5867
Fax: 330 821-3542
Alan W Cope, *President*
Evan W Morris Jr, *Principal*
Mike Knam, *Sales Mgr*
Ben Johnston, *Manager*
Carol A Ricci, *Admin Sec*
EMP: 26 **EST:** 1967
SQ FT: 20,000
SALES (est): 4.2MM **Privately Held**
WEB: www.copefarm.com
SIC: 7699 5999 5082 Farm machinery repair; farm equipment & supplies; construction & mining machinery

(G-537)
D A PETERSON INC
Also Called: Wdpn
393 Smyth Ave (44601-1562)
P.O. Box 2356 (44601-0356)
PHONE.................................330 821-1111
Donald A Peterson Jr, *President*
Jill P Mc Carty, *Treasurer*
Josephine H Peterson, *Admin Sec*
EMP: 35
SQ FT: 3,500
SALES (est): 2.5MM **Privately Held**
WEB: www.dapeterson.com
SIC: 4832 Radio broadcasting stations, music format

(G-538)
DINO PERSICHETTI
Also Called: Perkins Family Restaurant
20040 Hrrsburg Wstvlle Rd (44601)
PHONE.................................330 821-9600
Fax: 330 821-8042
Dino Persichetti, *President*
Richard Fielgar, *General Mgr*
Phillip Constantine, *Corp Secy*
Richard Felgar, *Manager*
EMP: 40
SQ FT: 2,788
SALES (est): 1.5MM **Privately Held**
SIC: 5812 7011 Restaurant, family: chain; motor inn

(G-539)
FIDELITY PROPERTIES INC
220 E Main St (44601-2423)
P.O. Box 2055 (44601-0055)
PHONE.................................330 821-9700
Fax: 330 821-1970
Paul D Boggs, *President*
Gregory A Robb, *Treasurer*
James E Thorpe Jr, *Admin Sec*
EMP: 37
SQ FT: 10,000
SALES (est): 3.3MM **Privately Held**
SIC: 7322 Collection agency, except real estate

(G-540)
IMMEDIATE MEDICAL SERVICE INC
2461 W State St Ste E (44601-5609)
PHONE.................................330 823-0400
EMP: 25
SQ FT: 12,000
SALES: 200K
SALES (corp-wide): 103.2MM **Privately Held**
SIC: 8011 Freestanding Emergency Medical Center
PA: Alliance Community Hospital
200 E State St
Alliance OH 44601
330 596-6000

(G-541)
INTERNTIONAL ASSN FIREFIGHTERS
Also Called: Alliance Fire Dept
63 E Broadway St (44601-2646)
PHONE.................................330 823-5222
Fax: 330 821-4716
Jim Reese, *Chief*
EMP: 30
SALES (corp-wide): 56.3MM **Privately Held**
WEB: www.sjff.org
SIC: 8631 Labor union
PA: International Association Of Firefighters
1750 New York Ave Nw # 300
Washington DC 20006
202 737-8484

(G-542)
J C MASONRY CONSTRUCTION INC
Also Called: J C Construction
7450 Parks Ave Ne (44601-8136)
PHONE.................................330 823-9795
James Menegay, *Partner*
James Upperman, *Principal*
EMP: 30
SALES (est): 1.3MM **Privately Held**
SIC: 1741 Masonry & other stonework

(G-543)
KUNTZMAN TRUCKING INC (PA)
13515 Oyster Rd (44601-2064)
PHONE.................................330 821-9160
Virgil Waters, *Ch of Bd*
Kenneth Boatright, *President*
EMP: 47 **EST:** 1997
SQ FT: 32,000
SALES (est): 6.9MM **Privately Held**
SIC: 4213 4212 Contract haulers; local trucking, without storage

(G-544)
LAVERY CHEVROLET-BUICK INC (PA)
Also Called: Lavery Buick
1096 W State St (44601-4694)
P.O. Box 3545 (44601-7545)
PHONE.................................330 823-1100
Fax: 330 823-8754
Thomas C Lavery, *Ch of Bd*
William Lavery, *President*
Larry Hadit, *Business Mgr*
Pat Bland, *Treasurer*
Larry Haidet, *Sales Mgr*
EMP: 33
SQ FT: 31,000
SALES (est): 11MM **Privately Held**
WEB: www.laverychevy.com
SIC: 5511 7538 7532 7515 Automobiles, new & used; pickups, new & used; general automotive repair shops; top & body repair & paint shops; passenger car leasing; used car dealers

(G-545)
LOWES HOME CENTERS LLC
2595 W State St (44601-5604)
PHONE.................................330 829-2700
Fax: 330 829-2719
Keith Fosse, *Manager*
EMP: 150
SALES (corp-wide): 68.6B **Publicly Held**
SIC: 5211 5031 5722 5064 Home centers; building materials, exterior; building materials, interior; household appliance stores; electrical appliances, television & radio
HQ: Lowe's Home Centers, Llc
1605 Curtis Bridge Rd
Wilkesboro NC 28697
336 658-4000

(G-546)
MAC MANUFACTURING INC (PA)
14599 Commerce St Ne (44601-1003)
PHONE.................................330 823-9900
Michael Conny, *Principal*
Jenny Conny, *Corp Secy*
Dan Tubbs, *Vice Pres*
▲ **EMP:** 700
SALES (est): 270.9MM **Privately Held**
SIC: 3715 5012 Truck trailers; trailers for trucks, new & used; truck bodies

(G-547)
MAC TRAILER MANUFACTURING INC (PA)
14599 Commerce St Ne (44601-1003)
PHONE.................................330 823-9900
Fax: 330 823-0232
Mike Conny, *President*
Ben Childers, *Vice Pres*
Tay Griffith, *Vice Pres*
David Sandor, *Vice Pres*
Matt Arnato, *Engineer*
▲ **EMP:** 214
SQ FT: 220,000
SALES (est): 143.8MM **Privately Held**
SIC: 3715 5012 5013 5015 Truck trailers; trailers for trucks, new & used; truck bodies; motor vehicle supplies & new parts; motor vehicle parts, used; trailer repair

(G-548)
MAC TRAILER SERVICE INC
14504 Commerce St Ne (44601-1000)
PHONE.................................330 823-9190
Fax: 330 823-9193
Michael Conny, *President*
John Pierce, *General Mgr*
Ed Mansell, *Vice Pres*
Ralph Brooks, *Engineer*
Robin Ward, *Controller*
EMP: 40 **EST:** 1997
SALES (est): 8.9MM **Privately Held**
SIC: 7539 Trailer repair

(G-549)
MILLER PRODUCTS INC
Also Called: Mpi Label Systems Eqp Rfid Div
1421 W Main St (44601-2153)
PHONE.................................330 238-4200
Shauna Bardo, *General Mgr*
Carey Weingart, *Branch Mgr*
Patrick Stalling, *Manager*
Matt Hoopes, *Technician*
Danielle Steer, *Services*
EMP: 35
SALES (corp-wide): 33.1MM **Privately Held**
SIC: 7389 Packaging & labeling services
PA: Miller Products, Inc.
450 Courtney Rd
Sebring OH 44672
330 938-2134

(G-550)
OHIO EYE ALLIANCE (PA)
985 S Sawburg Ave (44601-3515)
PHONE.................................330 823-1680
Fax: 330 823-3831
Sanjeev Dewan MD, *President*
Richard Lehrer MD, *President*
Tammy Ulbricht, *Financial Exec*
EMP: 32 **EST:** 1892
SQ FT: 8,000
SALES (est): 5MM **Privately Held**
WEB: www.ohioeye.com
SIC: 8011 Ophthalmologist

(G-551)
OREILLY AUTOMOTIVE INC
1805 W State St (44601-3538)
PHONE.................................330 238-1416
EMP: 35 **Publicly Held**
SIC: 7389 Automobile recovery service
PA: O'reilly Automotive, Inc.
233 S Patterson Ave
Springfield MO 65802

(G-552)
QBS INC
Also Called: Fedvendor
1548 S Linden Ave (44601-4211)
PHONE.................................330 821-8801
Fax: 330 821-2616
Jim Franks, *President*
Craig Larson, *Superintendent*
Bob Rauckhorst, *Project Mgr*
EMP: 31
SQ FT: 6,000
SALES (est): 9.5MM **Privately Held**
WEB: www.qbsinc.com
SIC: 1542 1541 Commercial & office building, new construction; commercial & office building contractors; industrial buildings, new construction

(G-553)
ROBERTSON HEATING SUP CO OHIO (PA)
2155 W Main St (44601-2190)
P.O. Box 2448 (44601-0448)
PHONE.................................800 433-9532
Scott Robertson, *President*
Ed Robertson, *Vice Pres*
Darel Miller, *Human Res Mgr*
Gary Bush, *VP Sales*
Susan Neil, *Admin Sec*
EMP: 41 **EST:** 1946
SQ FT: 137,000
SALES (est): 36.4MM **Privately Held**
SIC: 5075 5074 Warm air heating & air conditioning; plumbing & hydronic heating supplies

(G-554)
ROBERTSON HTG SUP ALIANCE OHIO (PA)
2155 W Main St (44601-2190)
P.O. Box 2448 (44601-0448)
PHONE.................................330 821-9180
Scott Robertson, *President*
Edward Robertson, *Vice Pres*
Larry Smith, *Manager*
Susan Neil, *Admin Sec*
▲ **EMP:** 110 **EST:** 1946
SALES (est): 19.5MM **Privately Held**
SIC: 5074 5999 5722 Plumbing fittings & supplies; plumbing & heating supplies; air conditioning room units, self-contained

(G-555)
ROBERTSON HTG SUP CANTON OHIO (PA)
2155 W Main St (44601-2190)
P.O. Box 2448 (44601-0448)
PHONE.................................330 821-9180
John J Robertson, *Principal*
Phil Braisted, *Vice Chairman*

GEOGRAPHIC SECTION

Sue Snode, *Vice Chairman*
Ed Robertson, *Exec VP*
Kevin Duro, *Vice Pres*
EMP: 35
SQ FT: 137,000
SALES (est): 11.8MM **Privately Held**
WEB: www.rhs1.com
SIC: 5074 Plumbing fittings & supplies

(G-556)
ROBERTSON HTG SUP CLUMBUS OHIO (PA)
2155 W Main St (44601-2190)
P.O. Box 2448 (44601-0448)
PHONE.................330 821-9180
Fax: 330 821-8251
Scott Robertson, *President*
Geoff Alpert, *Vice Pres*
Kevin Duro, *Vice Pres*
Scott Middleton, *Vice Pres*
Ed Robertson, *Vice Pres*
EMP: 105
SQ FT: 60,000
SALES (est): 88.5MM **Privately Held**
SIC: 5074 Plumbing fittings & supplies

(G-557)
ROGER S PALUTSIS MD
Also Called: Carnation Clinic
1401 S Arch Ave (44601-4288)
PHONE.................330 821-0201
Fax: 330 821-1924
Roger S Palutsis MD, *Owner*
Roger S Paluti, *Surg-Orthopdc*
EMP: 25
SALES (est): 2MM **Privately Held**
WEB: www.carnationclinic.com
SIC: 8011 Internal medicine, physician/surgeon

(G-558)
ROSELAWN HEALTH SERVICES CORP
Also Called: Roselawn Terrace
11999 Klinger Ave Ne (44601-1116)
PHONE.................330 823-0618
Jeffrey Donner, *President*
Brian Colleran, *President*
Gamal Elmo-Basher, *Director*
EMP: 50
SQ FT: 3,824
SALES (est): 2MM **Privately Held**
WEB: www.roselawn-terrace.net
SIC: 8059 Nursing home, except skilled & intermediate care facility

(G-559)
RUHL ELECTRIC CO
6428 Union Ave Ne (44601-8140)
PHONE.................330 823-7230
Fax: 330 821-0155
Kenneth W Ruhl Jr, *President*
Tracy Ruhl, *Vice Pres*
Patricia Ruhl, *Treasurer*
Angel Ruhl, *Office Mgr*
Paula Baum, *Manager*
EMP: 25
SQ FT: 30,000
SALES (est): 3.2MM **Privately Held**
WEB: www.ruhlelectric.com
SIC: 1731 General electrical contractor

(G-560)
SSOE INC
22831 State Route 62 (44601-9026)
PHONE.................330 821-7198
Michael Hickman, *Principal*
EMP: 27
SALES (corp-wide): 138.2MM **Privately Held**
SIC: 8711 8712 8741 Structural engineering; architectural engineering; management services
PA: Ssoe, Inc.
1001 Madison Ave Ste A
Toledo OH 43604
419 255-3830

(G-561)
STARK COUNTY CMNTY ACTION AGCY
Also Called: Alliance Franklin Head Start
321 Franklin Ave (44601-1908)
PHONE.................330 821-5977
Fax: 330 821-4580

Betty Thompson, *Office Mgr*
EMP: 35
SALES (est): 483.3K
SALES (corp-wide): 11.4MM **Privately Held**
SIC: 8351 Head start center, except in conjunction with school
PA: Stark County Community Action Agency
1366 Market Ave N
Canton OH 44714
330 454-1676

(G-562)
STARK METAL SALES INC
Also Called: SMS
432 Keystone St (44601-1722)
PHONE.................330 823-7383
Fax: 330 823-5949
Mark Popovec, *Sales Associate*
Charle B Reiber, *Incorporator*
EMP: 35
SQ FT: 70,000
SALES (est): 32MM **Privately Held**
WEB: www.starkmetal.com
SIC: 5051 Steel

(G-563)
STEEL EQP SPECIALISTS INC (PA)
Also Called: S.E.S.
1507 Beeson St Ne (44601-2142)
PHONE.................330 823-8260
Fax: 330 821-6350
James R Boughton, *CEO*
T Virgil Huggett, *Ch of Bd*
Doris Gulyas, *Principal*
Said S Kabalan, *Principal*
Richard G Pinkett, *Principal*
▲ **EMP:** 72 **EST:** 1976
SQ FT: 32,000
SALES (est): 24.3MM **Privately Held**
WEB: www.seseng.com
SIC: 7699 3599 7629 3593 Industrial machinery & equipment repair; custom machinery; electrical repair shops; fluid power cylinders & actuators; rolling mill machinery; fabricated structural metal

(G-564)
TRAFFIC CTRL SAFETY SVCS LLC
8970 Allen Dr Ne (44601-9702)
PHONE.................330 904-2732
Donald Peterson, *President*
EMP: 30 **EST:** 2012
SQ FT: 2,500
SALES (est): 1.1MM **Privately Held**
SIC: 7389 Flagging service (traffic control)

(G-565)
WINKLE INDUSTRIES INC
2080 W Main St (44601-2187)
PHONE.................330 823-9730
Fax: 330 823-9788
Joe Schatz, *CEO*
Gary Pittman, *Plant Mgr*
Jeff McCartney, *Engineer*
Dave Bentz, *Electrical Engi*
Jeffrey Parimuha, *Electrical Engi*
▲ **EMP:** 55
SQ FT: 85,000
SALES (est): 12.8MM **Privately Held**
WEB: www.winkleindustries.com
SIC: 7699 3499 5063 Industrial machinery & equipment repair; magnets, permanent: metallic; control & signal wire & cable, including coaxial

(G-566)
YMCA
205 S Union Ave (44601-2593)
PHONE.................330 823-1930
Fax: 330 823-0305
Dale Nissley, *Director*
EMP: 50
SQ FT: 12,000
SALES: 1.2MM **Privately Held**
SIC: 8641 7991 8351 7032 Youth organizations; physical fitness facilities; child day care services; youth camps; individual & family services

Alvada
Seneca County

(G-567)
ACI CONST CO INC
Also Called: Alvada Trucking
2959 S Us Highway 23 (44802-9713)
PHONE.................419 595-4284
Fax: 419 595-4282
Richard C Kirk, *Principal*
Tammy Sessions, *Controller*
Dianne Arbegast, *Administration*
EMP: 25 **EST:** 2003
SALES (est): 4MM **Privately Held**
SIC: 4212 Dump truck haulage

(G-568)
ALVADA CONST INC
Also Called: Alvada Construction
2959 S Us Highway 23 (44802-9713)
PHONE.................419 595-4224
Fax: 419 595-2801
Richard Kirk, *President*
Roger Bishop, *General Mgr*
Kevin Kurtz, *Project Mgr*
Vicky Coppus, *Accountant*
Brendle Chuck, *CTO*
EMP: 150
SQ FT: 1,500
SALES (est): 32.3MM **Privately Held**
SIC: 1542 Commercial & office building contractors

(G-569)
KIRK BROS CO INC
11942 Us Highway 224 (44802-9609)
P.O. Box 49 (44802-0049)
PHONE.................419 595-4020
Fax: 419 595-4019
Richard C Kirk, *President*
Robert Kirk, *Treasurer*
Tress Philips, *Controller*
EMP: 65 **EST:** 1969
SQ FT: 4,000
SALES (est): 22.8MM **Privately Held**
SIC: 1629 1623 Waste water & sewage treatment plant construction; water & sewer line construction

Alvordton
Williams County

(G-570)
KUNKLE FARM LIMITED
20674 Us Highway 20 (43501-9753)
PHONE.................419 237-2748
Richard Kuncle, *President*
Don Kunkle, *Principal*
EMP: 80
SALES: 2.4MM **Privately Held**
SIC: 0191 General farms, primarily crop

Amelia
Clermont County

(G-571)
A & A SAFETY INC (PA)
1126 Ferris Rd Bldg A (45102-2376)
PHONE.................513 043 6100
Fax: 513 943-6106
Ruth H Luttmer, *CEO*
William N Luttmer, *Vice Pres*
T R O'Bian, *Purch Agent*
Francis Luttmer, *Treasurer*
Carol Burchfield, *Accountant*
EMP: 50
SQ FT: 12,300
SALES (est): 20.4MM **Privately Held**
WEB: www.aasafetyinc.com
SIC: 7359 3993 5084 1721 Work zone traffic equipment (flags, cones, barrels, etc.); signs & advertising specialties; safety equipment; painting & paper hanging; highway & street sign installation

(G-572)
AMELIA DAVITA DIALYSIS CENTER
1761 E Ohio Pike (45102-2007)
PHONE.................513 797-0713
Donald Wolfer, *Manager*
EMP: 29
SALES (est): 336.2K **Publicly Held**
SIC: 8092 Kidney dialysis centers
PA: Davita Inc.
2000 16th St
Denver CO 80202

(G-573)
AMERICAN FAMILY HOME INSUR CO
7000 Midland Blvd (45102-2608)
P.O. Box 5323, Cincinnati (45201-5323)
PHONE.................513 943-7100
Fax: 513 943-0436
Thomas J Rohs, *President*
John W Hayden, *Senior VP*
Brad Fisher, *Vice Pres*
Jeff Martin, *Vice Pres*
Sandy Wagner, *Vice Pres*
EMP: 51
SALES (est): 6.8MM **Privately Held**
SIC: 6411 Insurance agents
HQ: American Modern Insurance Group, Inc.
7000 Midland Blvd
Amelia OH 45102

(G-574)
AMERICAN MODERN HOME INSUR CO (DH)
Also Called: American Mdrn Srpls Lnes Insur
7000 Midland Blvd (45102-2608)
P.O. Box 5323, Cincinnati (45201-5323)
PHONE.................513 943-7100
Fax: 513 943-1502
John Hayden, *President*
Timothy S Hogan, *Principal*
W Gary King, *Principal*
William McD Kite, *Principal*
Ken Boberg, *Exec VP*
EMP: 60 **EST:** 1965
SALES (est): 156.6MM **Privately Held**
WEB: www.americanmodernhomeinsurancecompany.com
SIC: 6331 Fire, marine & casualty insurance

(G-575)
AMERICAN MODERN HOME SVC CO
7000 Midland Blvd (45102-2608)
PHONE.................513 943-7100
W Todd Gray, *President*
Steve Smith, *Prgrmr*
Kelli Woosley, *Associate*
EMP: 28
SALES (est): 9MM **Privately Held**
SIC: 6321 Reinsurance carriers, accident & health
HQ: American Modern Insurance Group, Inc.
7000 Midland Blvd
Amelia OH 45102

(G-576)
AMERICAN MODRN INSUR GROUP INC (DH)
Also Called: American Modern Home Insur Co
7000 Midland Blvd (45102-2608)
P.O. Box 5323, Cincinnati (45201-5323)
PHONE.................800 543-2644
Fax: 513 943-7200
John W Hayden, *President*
Kevin Barber, *President*
Tony Dirksing, *President*
Eric Hunziker, *President*
Kim Loos, *President*
EMP: 108
SALES (est): 599.6MM **Privately Held**
WEB: www.amig.com
SIC: 6321 6411 Accident & health insurance carriers; insurance agents & brokers
HQ: Midland-Guardian Co.
7000 Midland Blvd
Amelia OH 45102
513 943-7100

Amelia - Clermont County (G-577)

(G-577)
AMERICAN WESTERN HOME INSUR CO
7000 Midland Blvd (45102-2608)
PHONE..................513 943-7100
Joseph P Hayden Jr, *Ch of Bd*
Thomas Rohs, *President*
Michael Conaton, *Exec VP*
Ken Boberg, *Senior VP*
Bob Fulcher, *Senior VP*
EMP: 428
SALES (est): 105.4MM **Privately Held**
WEB: www.amig.com
SIC: 6331 Fire, marine & casualty insurance
HQ: American Modern Home Insurance Company
7000 Midland Blvd
Amelia OH 45102
513 943-7100

(G-578)
BANTAM LEASING INC
2291 State Route 125 (45102-9700)
P.O. Box 249, Bethel (45106-0249)
PHONE..................513 734-6696
Shanda Douglas, *President*
EMP: 25
SQ FT: 1,050
SALES (est): 2.4MM **Privately Held**
SIC: 4213 Trucking, except local

(G-579)
CLERMONT COUNSELING CENTER (PA)
Also Called: Lifepoint Solutions
43 E Main St (45102-1993)
PHONE..................513 947-7000
Fax: 513 947-7001
Arlene Herman, *CEO*
Mark Evans, *Asst Controller*
Annette Cook, *Manager*
Christy Raleigh, *Program Dir*
EMP: 30
SALES: 2.9MM **Privately Held**
WEB: www.clermontcounseling.org
SIC: 8322 General counseling services

(G-580)
EGER PRODUCTS INC (PA)
1132 Ferris Rd (45102-1020)
PHONE..................513 753-4200
Fax: 513 753-9888
Reva Eger, *President*
Jerome Schildmeyer, *Principal*
Richard Koebbe, *Vice Pres*
Sherry Sandusjy, *Finance Mgr*
Kent Willie, *Manager*
EMP: 60
SQ FT: 38,400
SALES: 28MM **Privately Held**
WEB: www.egerproducts.com
SIC: 3644 3544 5039 Insulators & insulation materials, electrical; forms (molds); for foundry & plastics working machinery; ceiling systems & products

(G-581)
INTERPHACE PHTGRPHY CMMNCTIONS
Also Called: Awis Designs
1365 Meadowlark Ln (45102-2612)
PHONE..................254 289-6270
Todd A Fair, *President*
Todd Fair, *President*
EMP: 25
SALES (est): 1.1MM **Privately Held**
WEB: www.awisdesigns.com
SIC: 7335 Commercial photography

(G-582)
MIDLAND-GUARDIAN CO (HQ)
7000 Midland Blvd (45102-2608)
P.O. Box 5323, Cincinnati (45201-5323)
PHONE..................513 943-7100
Andreas Kleiner, *President*
John Von Lehman, *Exec VP*
Larry Compton, *Senior VP*
Todd Gray, *CFO*
Matt McConnell, *Treasurer*
EMP: 650 EST: 1952
SALES: 733.4MM **Privately Held**
SIC: 6311 6331 Life insurance carriers; fire, marine & casualty insurance: stock

PA: Munchener Ruckversicherungs-Gesellschaft Ag In Munchen
Koniginstr. 107
Munchen 80802
893 891-0

(G-583)
SUNRISE MANOR CONVALESCENT CTR
3434 State Route 132 (45102-2012)
P.O. Box 54923, Cincinnati (45254-0923)
PHONE..................513 797-5144
Fax: 513 797-4627
Howard L Meeker, *President*
Steve Meeker, *Principal*
Florel Meeker, *Vice Pres*
Jyoti Mehta, *Director*
Patricia Meeker, *Administration*
EMP: 80
SALES (est): 2.8MM **Privately Held**
SIC: 8052 Intermediate care facilities

(G-584)
WHITT INC
Also Called: Whitt Plumbing
1152 Ferris Rd (45102-1020)
PHONE..................513 753-7707
Fax: 513 753-7768
Richard Whitt, *President*
Lila Whitt, *Corp Secy*
EMP: 25
SQ FT: 8,500
SALES (est): 3.1MM **Privately Held**
WEB: www.whitt.com
SIC: 1711 Plumbing contractors

Amherst
Lorain County

(G-585)
AMHERST ANIMAL HOSPITAL INC
1425 Cooper Foster Pk Rd (44001-1297)
PHONE..................440 282-5220
Fax: 440 282-9422
Thomas Gigliotti, *President*
Jerome Gigliotti, *Vice Pres*
EMP: 30
SQ FT: 6,000
SALES (est): 1.3MM **Privately Held**
SIC: 0742 Veterinarian, animal specialties

(G-586)
AMHERST EXEMPTED VLG SCHOOLS
Also Called: Bus Garage
225 Washington St (44001-1526)
PHONE..................440 988-2633
Kathy Moyer, *Supervisor*
EMP: 48 **Privately Held**
SIC: 7521 Parking garage
PA: Amherst Exempted Village Schools
185 Forest St
Amherst OH 44001

(G-587)
AMHERST HOSPITAL ASSOCIATION
Also Called: E M H Regional Medical Center
254 Cleveland Ave (44001-1699)
PHONE..................440 988-6000
Fax: 440 988-3016
Kristi Sink, *President*
David Cook, *CFO*
Sharon Shafer, *Marketing Staff*
Frank Szollsky Jr, *Manager*
Gary Wharton, *Manager*
EMP: 152 EST: 1917
SQ FT: 90,000
SALES (est): 7.4MM **Privately Held**
WEB: www.emh-healthcare.org
SIC: 8011 Freestanding emergency medical center

(G-588)
AMHERST MANOR NURSING HOME
175 N Lake St (44001-1332)
P.O. Box 260 (44001-0260)
PHONE..................440 988-4415
Fax: 440 988-3008
Donel Sprenger, *President*

Anthony Sprenger, *Vice Pres*
Itri Eren, *Director*
EMP: 70
SQ FT: 30,000
SALES (est): 2.3MM **Privately Held**
WEB: www.sprengerretirement.com
SIC: 8052 Intermediate care facilities
PA: Sprenger Enterprises, Inc.
2198 Gladstone Ct
Glendale Heights IL 60139

(G-589)
BUTCHKO ELECTRIC INC
7333 S Dewey Rd (44001-2507)
PHONE..................440 985-3180
Fax: 440 985-5826
Gary A Butchko, *President*
Bill Butchko, *Vice Pres*
Linda Hambly, *Manager*
Brinda Click, *Admin Asst*
EMP: 25
SQ FT: 2,000
SALES (est): 1.8MM **Privately Held**
WEB: www.butchkoelectric.com
SIC: 7349 1731 Building maintenance, except repairs; general electrical contractor

(G-590)
CELLCO PARTNERSHIP
Also Called: Verizon Wireless
7566 Oak Point Rd (44001-9658)
PHONE..................440 984-5200
Andrew Schimd, *Branch Mgr*
EMP: 25
SALES (corp-wide): 126B **Publicly Held**
SIC: 4813 4812 Telephone communication, except radio; cellular telephone services
HQ: Cellco Partnership
1 Verizon Way
Basking Ridge NJ 07920

(G-591)
ED MULLINAX FORD LLC
Also Called: Autonation Ford Amherst
8000 Leavitt Rd (44001-2712)
P.O. Box 280 (44001-0280)
PHONE..................440 984-2431
Fax: 440 984-2837
Michael J Jackson, *Ch of Bd*
Dennis Pritt, *General Mgr*
EMP: 250
SALES (est): 37.7MM
SALES (corp-wide): 21.5B **Publicly Held**
SIC: 5511 7538 7532 5521 Automobiles, new & used; general automotive repair shops; top & body repair & paint shops; used car dealers
HQ: An Dealership Holding Corp.
200 Sw 1st Ave
Fort Lauderdale FL 33301
954 769-7000

(G-592)
EDWARDS LAND CLEARING INC
Also Called: Edwards Tree Service
49090 Cooper Foster Pk Rd (44001-9649)
PHONE..................440 988-4477
Fax: 440 988-4480
Jaret Kopocs, *Principal*
EMP: 40
SALES: 1.2MM **Privately Held**
SIC: 0781 Landscape services

(G-593)
ENVIROTEST SYSTEMS CORP
205 Sandstone Blvd (44001-1273)
PHONE..................330 963-4464
EMP: 34 **Privately Held**
WEB: www.il.etest.com
SIC: 7549 Emissions testing without repairs, automotive
HQ: Envirotest Systems Corp.
7 Kripes Rd
East Granby CT 06026

(G-594)
FIFTH THIRD BANK
309 N Leavitt Rd (44001-1126)
PHONE..................440 984-2402
Tina Graham, *Branch Mgr*
EMP: 109
SALES (corp-wide): 7.7B **Publicly Held**
SIC: 6021 National trust companies with deposits, commercial

HQ: The Fifth Third Bank
38 Fountain Square Plz
Cincinnati OH 45202
513 579-5203

(G-595)
GRACE HOSPITAL
254 Cleveland Ave (44001-1620)
PHONE..................216 687-4013
Fax: 440 988-6148
Vickie Kayatin, *Principal*
EMP: 90
SALES (est): 618.9K
SALES (corp-wide): 17.4MM **Privately Held**
SIC: 8062 General medical & surgical hospitals
PA: Grace Hospital
2307 W 14th St
Cleveland OH 44113
216 687-1500

(G-596)
H&R BLOCK INC
1980 G Coper Foster Pk Rd (44001)
PHONE..................440 282-4288
Fax: 440 282-4365
Sharon Griffith, *Director*
EMP: 27
SALES (corp-wide): 3B **Publicly Held**
SIC: 7291 Tax return preparation services
PA: H&R Block, Inc.
1 H&R Block Way
Kansas City MO 64105
816 854-3000

(G-597)
HOWARD HANNA SMYTHE CRAMER
1711 Cooper Foster Pk Rd (44001-1205)
PHONE..................440 282-8002
Rick Edler, *Branch Mgr*
Roger Farr, *Branch Mgr*
EMP: 30
SALES (corp-wide): 76.4MM **Privately Held**
WEB: www.smythecramer.com
SIC: 6531 Real estate brokers & agents
HQ: Howard Hanna Smythe Cramer
6000 Parkland Blvd
Cleveland OH 44124
216 447-4477

(G-598)
KTM NORTH AMERICA INC (PA)
1119 Milan Ave (44001-1319)
PHONE..................855 215-6360
Di Stefan Pierer, *CEO*
Rod Bush, *President*
Brian Doran, *Area Mgr*
Jeremy Ketchum, *Area Mgr*
Jakob Branner, *Vice Pres*
▲ EMP: 87
SQ FT: 5,000
SALES (est): 36.8MM **Privately Held**
SIC: 5012 3751 Motorcycles; motorcycles, bicycles & parts

(G-599)
LORAIN CNTY STY OFF EQP CO INC
1953 Cooper Foster Pk Rd (44001-1207)
PHONE..................440 960-7070
Pamelynn C Carver, *President*
James A Adkins, *Vice Pres*
Alan T Shaffstall, *Vice Pres*
EMP: 40
SQ FT: 33,000
SALES (est): 11.2MM **Privately Held**
WEB: www.bobels.com
SIC: 5044 5943 Office equipment; office forms & supplies

(G-600)
MERCY HEALTH
578 N Leavitt Rd (44001-1131)
PHONE..................440 988-1009
Marsha Heuring, *Branch Mgr*
EMP: 35
SALES (corp-wide): 4.2B **Privately Held**
SIC: 8099 Blood related health services
PA: Mercy Health
1701 Mercy Health Pl
Cincinnati OH 45237
513 639-2800

GEOGRAPHIC SECTION

Antwerp - Paulding County (G-622)

(G-601)
PET CENTRAL LODGE & GROOMING
1425 C Foster Pk Rd C (44001)
PHONE....................440 282-1811
Dawn Roberts, *Manager*
EMP: 25
SALES (est): 670K **Privately Held**
SIC: 0752 Grooming services, pet & animal specialties

(G-602)
RAK CORROSION CONTROL INC
7455 S Dewey Rd (44001-2509)
PHONE....................440 985-2171
Fax: 216 985-2174
Clinton Reph, *Ch of Bd*
Guy A Reph, *President*
Tari Reph, *Vice Pres*
EMP: 25
SQ FT: 20,000
SALES (est): 4.1MM **Privately Held**
SIC: 1799 1742 Sandblasting of building exteriors; corrosion control installation; insulation, buildings

(G-603)
REALTY ONE INC
Also Called: Realty One Amherst 59
1711 Cooper Foster Park (44001-1205)
PHONE....................440 282-8002
Toll Free:........................877 -
Fax: 440 282-8727
Rick Edler, *Branch Mgr*
Liz Concar, *Manager*
Angie Callaway, *Manager*
EMP: 55
SALES (corp-wide): 67.8MM **Privately Held**
WEB: www.realty-1st.com
SIC: 6531 Real estate agents & managers
HQ: Realty One, Inc.
800 W Saint Clair Ave
Cleveland OH 44113
216 328-2500

(G-604)
SLIMANS SALES & SERVICE INC
Also Called: Slimans Chrysler Plymouth Dodge
7498 Leavitt Rd (44001-2457)
PHONE....................440 988-4484
Fax: 440 988-4487
Paul Sliman, *President*
Barbara Sliman, *Treasurer*
Jim Bucher, *Sales Mgr*
Ben Gray, *Director*
Mark Sinegar, *Director*
EMP: 42
SQ FT: 20,000
SALES (est): 17.7MM **Privately Held**
SIC: 5511 5012 Automobiles, new & used; pickups, new & used; automobiles & other motor vehicles

(G-605)
SPITZER AUTO WORLD AMHERST
200 N Leavitt Rd (44001-1125)
PHONE....................440 988-4444
Alan Spitzer, *President*
Joe Garrett, *Marketing Mgr*
Sam Young, *Executive*
EMP: 55 EST: 1995
SALES (est): 17MM
SALES (corp-wide): 51.3MM **Privately Held**
WEB: www.spitzerauto.com
SIC: 5511 7515 5521 Automobiles, new & used; passenger car leasing; used car dealers
PA: Spitzer Management, Inc.
150 E Bridge St
Elyria OH 44035
440 323-4671

(G-606)
STAR BUILDERS INC
46405 Telegraph Rd (44001-2855)
P.O. Box 109 (44001-0109)
PHONE....................440 986-5951
Fax: 440 986-3360
Richard Molder, *CEO*
Kalyn Wise, *President*

Todd Mealwitz, *Vice Pres*
EMP: 45
SQ FT: 30,000
SALES (est): 11.4MM **Privately Held**
SIC: 1542 1541 Commercial & office building contractors; farm building construction; industrial buildings & warehouses; warehouse construction

Amsterdam
Jefferson County

(G-607)
APEX ENVIRONMENTAL LLC
11 County Road 78 (43903-7942)
PHONE....................740 543-4389
Antony Rosso, *CEO*
Tim Loveland, *General Mgr*
EMP: 90
SQ FT: 2,500
SALES (est): 14.3MM **Privately Held**
SIC: 1629 Waste disposal plant construction

(G-608)
EDISON LOCAL SCHOOL DISTRICT
Also Called: Edison Bus Garage
8235 Amsterdam Rd Se (43903-9794)
PHONE....................740 543-4011
Fax: 740 543-4360
Florence Mader, *Manager*
EMP: 33
SALES (corp-wide): 21.2MM **Privately Held**
SIC: 8211 7514 Public senior high school; passenger car rental
PA: Edison Local School District
14890 State Route 213
Hammondsville OH 43930
740 282-0065

Andover
Ashtabula County

(G-609)
ANDOVER BANCORP INC (PA)
19 Public Sq (44003-9316)
P.O. Box 1300 (44003-1300)
PHONE....................440 293-7605
Larry W Park, *President*
James Greenfield, *Vice Pres*
Diana Englehardt, *CFO*
Terri McKinley, *Branch Mgr*
EMP: 50
SALES (est): 16.8MM **Privately Held**
WEB: www.andoverbancorp.com
SIC: 6022 State commercial banks

(G-610)
ANDOVER VLG RETIREMENT CMNTY
486 S Main St (44003-9602)
PHONE....................440 293-5416
Carol Timko, *Facilities Dir*
Kim Bish, *Director*
Hannah Curtis, *Director*
Michael J Namey Jr, *Director*
Debbie Leese, *Nursing Dir*
EMP: 235
SALES (est): 10.8MM **Privately Held**
WEB: www.andoverretirement.com
SIC: 8051 Convalescent home with continuous nursing care

(G-611)
DAVITA INC
Also Called: Davita Kidney Dialysis
486 S Main St (44003-9602)
PHONE....................440 293-6028
Tracy Meure, *Branch Mgr*
Michael Andrews, *Admin Asst*
EMP: 25 **Publicly Held**
SIC: 8322 Community center
PA: Davita Inc.
2000 16th St
Denver CO 80202

(G-612)
FRATERNAL ORDER EAGLES INC
Also Called: Foe 4035
6210 State Route 85 (44003-9702)
P.O. Box 1175 (44003-1175)
PHONE....................440 293-5997
Marlene Waters, *Branch Mgr*
EMP: 26
SQ FT: 1,248
SALES (corp-wide): 11MM **Privately Held**
WEB: www.fraternalorderofeagles.tribe.net
SIC: 8641 Fraternal associations
HQ: Fraternal Order Of Eagles Inc.
1623 Gateway Cir
Grove City OH 43123
614 883-2200

(G-613)
PYMATUNING AMBULANCE SERVICE
153 Station St (44003)
P.O. Box 1509 (44003-1509)
PHONE....................440 293-7991
EMP: 25 EST: 1997
SALES: 101.2K **Privately Held**
SIC: 4119 Ambulance Service

(G-614)
SEELEY ENTERPRISES COMPANY (PA)
Also Called: Seeley Medical
104 Parker Dr (44003-9481)
PHONE....................440 293-6600
Fax: 440 293-7395
Mario Lacute, *CEO*
Joe Petrolla, *President*
Glenna Gallagher, *Principal*
Ron Adamov, *Vice Pres*
Donald Bellante, *Vice Pres*
EMP: 35
SQ FT: 12,000
SALES (est): 18MM **Privately Held**
WEB: www.seeleymedical.com
SIC: 5999 7352 Medical apparatus & supplies; medical equipment rental

(G-615)
SEELEY MEDICAL OXYGEN CO (HQ)
104 Parker Dr (44003-9481)
PHONE....................440 255-7163
Mario Lacute, *President*
Donald Bellante, *Vice Pres*
Ann Lacute, *Vice Pres*
EMP: 45 EST: 1955
SQ FT: 15,000
SALES (est): 12.9MM
SALES (corp-wide): 18MM **Privately Held**
SIC: 5047 7352 Medical equipment & supplies; medical equipment rental
PA: Seeley Enterprises Company
104 Parker Dr
Andover OH 44003
440 293-6600

Anna
Shelby County

(G-616)
AGRANA FRUIT US INC
16197 County Road 25a (45302-9498)
PHONE....................937 693-3821
Nancy Jager, *Vice Pres*
Phillip Bokar, *Project Mgr*
Jeff Elliott, *Opers Staff*
Alice Rindler, *Personnel*
Jeff Elliott, *Manager*
EMP: 150
SALES (corp-wide): 51.7MM **Privately Held**
SIC: 8734 2099 2087 Food testing service; food preparations; flavoring extracts & syrups
HQ: Agrana Fruit Us, Inc.
6850 Southpointe Pkwy
Brecksville OH 44141
440 546-1199

(G-617)
ANNA RESCUE SQUAD
203 S Linden St (45302-8712)
P.O. Box 201 (45302-0201)
PHONE....................937 394-7377
Fax: 937 394-7477
Melinda Gerlich, *President*
Jessica Rickart, *Administration*
EMP: 25
SALES: 276.8K **Privately Held**
SIC: 4119 Ambulance service

(G-618)
WELLS BROTHER ELECTRIC INC
Also Called: Honeywell Authorized Dealer
105 Shue Dr (45302-8402)
PHONE....................937 394-7559
Fax: 937 394-7632
Curt Wells, *President*
Andy Haag, *Business Mgr*
Scott Robinson, *Business Mgr*
Ken Steinke, *Vice Pres*
Jerry Wells, *Vice Pres*
EMP: 82
SALES: 27MM **Privately Held**
SIC: 1731 1711 General electrical contractor; plumbing contractors

Ansonia
Darke County

(G-619)
ANSONIA AREA EMERGENCY SERVICE
225 W Elroy Ansonia Rd (45303-9786)
P.O. Box 171 (45303-0171)
PHONE....................937 337-2651
Fax: 937 337-2345
Ron Thompson, *President*
Kris Eb, *Chief*
EMP: 30
SALES: 264.3K **Privately Held**
SIC: 8322 Emergency social services

Antwerp
Paulding County

(G-620)
SCHROEDER ASSOCIATES INC (PA)
5554 County Road 424 (45813-9420)
PHONE....................419 258-5075
Fax: 419 258-2112
Easther H Schroeder, *Principal*
Charles Schroeder, *Principal*
EMP: 30
SQ FT: 10,000
SALES (est): 4.3MM **Privately Held**
SIC: 4212 4789 4213 Local trucking, without storage; pipeline terminal facilities, independently operated; trucking, except local

(G-621)
VILLAGE OF ANTWERP (PA)
118 N Main St (45813-8402)
P.O. Box 1046 (45813-1046)
PHONE....................419 258-7422
Fax: 419 258-2241
Ray Delong, *Mayor*
Sarah Keerman, *Administration*
EMP: 42 EST: 1846 **Privately Held**
SIC: 9111 8611 City & town managers' offices; business associations

(G-622)
VILLAGE OF ANTWERP
Also Called: Fire Department
203 S Cleveland St (45813)
P.O. Box 1046 (45813-1046)
PHONE....................419 258-6631
Ray Friend, *Chief*
EMP: 25 **Privately Held**
SIC: 4119 9224 Ambulance service; fire department, not including volunteer;
PA: Village Of Antwerp
118 N Main St
Antwerp OH 45813
419 258-7422

Apple Creek
Wayne County

(G-623)
APPLE CREEK BANKING CO (INC) (PA)
3 W Main St (44606-9549)
PHONE.................330 698-2631
Fax: 330 698-4770
Carol Meek, *CEO*
Leo Miller, *Senior VP*
Ginny Allen, *Accounts Mgr*
Margo Broehl, *Admin Sec*
EMP: 43
SQ FT: 12,000
SALES: 5.4MM **Privately Held**
WEB: www.applecreekbank.com
SIC: 6022 State commercial banks

(G-624)
ESPT LIQUIDATION INC
339 Mill St (44606-9541)
P.O. Box 458 (44606-0458)
PHONE.................330 698-4711
Fax: 330 698-1254
Leonard Buckner, *President*
Gloria Edmonson, *Sales Executive*
Paul C Rodusky, *Program Dir*
EMP: 75 **EST:** 1960
SQ FT: 88,000
SALES (est): 21.1MM **Privately Held**
WEB: www.euclidspiral.com
SIC: 5047 5113 Medical & hospital equipment; paper tubes & cores

(G-625)
GROSS LUMBER INC
8848 Ely Rd (44606-9799)
PHONE.................330 683-2055
Fax: 330 682-7565
Don Grossniklaus, *President*
Rick Grossniklaus, *Vice Pres*
Connie Duncan, *Manager*
EMP: 35 **EST:** 1957
SQ FT: 30,000
SALES (est): 5MM **Privately Held**
SIC: 2448 5031 5099 2426 Pallets, wood; lumber: rough, dressed & finished; wood & wood by-products; hardwood dimension & flooring mills; sawmills & planing mills, general

(G-626)
PRECISION PRODUCTS GROUP INC
Also Called: Euclid Medical Products
339 Mill St (44606-9541)
PHONE.................330 698-4711
Ray Schroeder, *Manager*
EMP: 75
SALES (est): 2.2MM **Privately Held**
SIC: 5047 5113 Medical & hospital equipment; paper tubes & cores
PA: Precision Products Group, Inc.
10201 N Illinois St # 390
Indianapolis IN 46290

(G-627)
TROYERS HOME PANTRY (PA)
668 W Main St (44606-9092)
PHONE.................330 698-4182
Fax: 330 698-3537
Abe Troyer, *Owner*
Penni Vacca, *Manager*
EMP: 25
SQ FT: 5,000
SALES (est): 1.5MM **Privately Held**
SIC: 5149 5461 Bakery products; bakeries

(G-628)
WESTHAFER TRUCKING INC
6333 E Messner Rd (44606-9642)
PHONE.................330 698-3030
Glen Westhafer, *President*
Terri Sinder, *Admin Sec*
EMP: 30
SALES (est): 2.7MM **Privately Held**
SIC: 4212 Local trucking, without storage

Arcanum
Darke County

(G-629)
BRUMBAUGH CONSTRUCTION INC
3520 State Route 49 (45304-9731)
P.O. Box 309 (45304-0309)
PHONE.................937 692-5107
Fax: 937 692-5678
Scott Myers, *President*
Fred A Garber, *Principal*
Jason Willis, *Executive*
Ralph Brumbaugh, *Shareholder*
Diane Wills, *Admin Sec*
▲ **EMP:** 43 **EST:** 1961
SQ FT: 3,000
SALES (est): 14.7MM **Privately Held**
WEB: www.brumbaughconstruction.com
SIC: 1542 1622 Commercial & office building, new construction; bridge construction

(G-630)
MIKESELL TRANSPORTATION BROKER
Also Called: Beach Golf Course
1476 State Route 503 (45304-9237)
PHONE.................937 996-5731
Bruce Mikesell, *President*
Terri Mikesell, *Corp Secy*
EMP: 35
SALES (est): 912.6K **Privately Held**
SIC: 4789 Transportation services

(G-631)
TROUTWINE AUTO SALES INC
9 N Main St (45304-1300)
PHONE.................937 692-8373
Fax: 937 692-8628
James L Troutwine, *President*
J Todd Troutwine, *Corp Secy*
F Scott Troutwine, *Vice Pres*
EMP: 30
SQ FT: 90,000
SALES: 13.4MM **Privately Held**
SIC: 5511 5983 5172 Automobiles, new & used; fuel oil dealers; fuel oil

Archbold
Fulton County

(G-632)
ARCHBOLD ELEVATOR INC
3265 County Road 24 (43502-9415)
PHONE.................419 445-2451
Fax: 419 446-9472
William Fricke, *President*
Carolyn Fricke, *Corp Secy*
EMP: 30
SQ FT: 4,000
SALES (est): 4.8MM **Privately Held**
WEB: www.archboldelevator.com
SIC: 5153 5191 Grain elevators; farm supplies

(G-633)
BLACK SWAMP EQUIPMENT LLC (PA)
700 E Lugbill Rd (43502-1566)
PHONE.................419 445-0030
Jeff Fryman, *Principal*
Kearen S Burkholder,
EMP: 32
SQ FT: 3,500
SALES (est): 5.2MM **Privately Held**
WEB: www.blackswampequipment.com
SIC: 7359 Tool rental

(G-634)
COMMUNITY HLTH PRFSSIONALS INC
230 Westfield Dr (43502-1047)
PHONE.................419 445-5128
Fax: 419 445-6314
Brent Tow, *Branch Mgr*
Sally Osborn,
EMP: 46
SALES (corp-wide): 14MM **Privately Held**
SIC: 8082 Visiting nurse service
PA: Community Health Professionals, Inc.
1159 Westwood Dr
Van Wert OH 45891
419 238-9223

(G-635)
COMMUNITY HSPTALS WLLNESS CTRS
Also Called: Archbold Hospital
121 Westfield Dr Ste 1 (43502-1005)
PHONE.................419 445-2015
Fax: 419 445-8102
Greg Flattery, *President*
Rusty O Brunicardi, *COO*
Shawna L Leupp, *Office Mgr*
EMP: 76
SALES (corp-wide): 77.2MM **Privately Held**
SIC: 8062 General medical & surgical hospitals
PA: Community Hospitals And Wellness Centers
433 W High St
Bryan OH 43506
419 636-1131

(G-636)
FARMERS & MERCHANTS STATE BANK (HQ)
307-11 N Defiance St (43502)
P.O. Box 216 (43502-0216)
PHONE.................419 446-2501
Fax: 419 446-2982
Paul S Siebenmorgen, *CEO*
Todd Graham, *Exec VP*
Rex D Rice, *Exec VP*
John Kundo, *Assistant VP*
Brenda Mossing, *Assistant VP*
EMP: 115 **EST:** 1897
SALES: 47.7MM
SALES (corp-wide): 51.9MM **Publicly Held**
WEB: www.fm-bank.com
SIC: 6022 State trust companies accepting deposits, commercial
PA: Farmers & Merchants Bancorp, Inc.
307 N Defiance St
Archbold OH 43502
419 446-2501

(G-637)
LIECHTY INC (HQ)
1701 S Defiance St (43502-9798)
P.O. Box 67 (43502-0067)
PHONE.................419 445-1565
Fax: 419 445-1779
Orval Jay Beck, *President*
Linda Schnitkey, *Accountant*
Randy Baughman, *Sales Staff*
EMP: 30
SALES (est): 26.1MM **Privately Held**
WEB: www.liechtyfarmequipment.com
SIC: 5083 Agricultural machinery & equipment

(G-638)
MBC HOLDINGS INC (PA)
1613 S Defiance St (43502-9488)
P.O. Box 30 (43502-0030)
PHONE.................419 445-1015
Dean E Miller, *President*
Steven A Everhart, *Corp Secy*
Robert Miller, *Vice Pres*
Ryan Bernath, *Project Mgr*
Dave Lersch, *Manager*
EMP: 721
SALES (est): 60.3MM **Privately Held**
WEB: www.mbcholdings.com
SIC: 1622 1611 Bridge construction; highway & street paving contractor

(G-639)
MILLER BROS CONST INC
1613 S Defiance St (43502-9488)
P.O. Box 30 (43502-0030)
PHONE.................419 445-1015
Bradley D Miller, *President*
Terry Moore, *Corp Secy*
Mark F Murray, *Exec VP*
Keith Fletcher, *Vice Pres*
Scott Jaskela, *Vice Pres*
EMP: 30 **EST:** 1945
SQ FT: 48,000
SALES (est): 14.7MM **Privately Held**
WEB: www.millerbrosconst.com
SIC: 1611 Highway & street paving contractor
PA: Mbc Holdings, Inc.
1613 S Defiance St
Archbold OH 43502

(G-640)
NORTHWEST OHIO COMPUTER ASSN (PA)
Also Called: Northern Bckeye Edcatn Council
209 Nolan Pkwy (43502-8404)
PHONE.................419 267-5565
Fax: 419 267-5222
Beverly Hoagland, *Superintendent*
Marc Robinson, *Superintendent*
Ken Jones, *Exec VP*
Jeff Zsigrai, *Vice Pres*
Matt Dick, *Opers Staff*
EMP: 69
SQ FT: 6,000
SALES (est): 7.9MM **Privately Held**
SIC: 7374 8211 Data processing service; elementary & secondary schools

(G-641)
PROGRESSIVE FURNITURE INC (HQ)
Also Called: Progressive International
502 Middle St (43502-1559)
P.O. Box 308 (43502-0308)
PHONE.................419 446-4500
Fax: 419 825-3146
Kevin Sauder, *President*
Dan Kendrick, *Exec VP*
Mike France, *Vice Pres*
John Boring, *VP Finance*
Janys Etts, *Credit Mgr*
▲ **EMP:** 25
SQ FT: 8,000
SALES (est): 23.8MM
SALES (corp-wide): 500MM **Privately Held**
WEB: www.progressivefurniture.com
SIC: 2511 2517 5021 Bed frames, except water bed frames: wood; dressers, household: wood; home entertainment unit cabinets, wood; tables, occasional; beds; dining room furniture
PA: Sauder Woodworking Co.
502 Middle St
Archbold OH 43502
419 446-3828

(G-642)
QUADCO REHABILITATION CENTER
Also Called: Northwest Products Div
600 Oak St (43502-1579)
PHONE.................419 445-1950
Fax: 419 446-2984
John D Miller, *Project Dir*
Phillip Zuver, *Branch Mgr*
Shannon Zellers, *Program Mgr*
Melody Weaver, *Supervisor*
EMP: 90
SALES (corp-wide): 247.7K **Privately Held**
SIC: 8331 2448 Vocational rehabilitation agency; wood pallets & skids
PA: Quadco Rehabilitation Center Inc
427 N Defiance St
Stryker OH 43557
419 682-1011

(G-643)
SAUDER HARITAGE INN
22611 State Route 2 (43502-9452)
PHONE.................419 445-6408
Debbie David, *CEO*
EMP: 40
SALES (est): 687.9K **Privately Held**
SIC: 7011 Tourist camps, cabins, cottages & courts

(G-644)
SAUDER VILLAGE
22611 State Route 2 (43502-9452)
PHONE.................419 446-2541
Fax: 419 445-5251
Maynard Sauder, *President*
Harold Plassman, *Vice Pres*
Greg Bontrager, *Treasurer*
Denny Shanon, *Accounts Mgr*
Debbie Sauder David, *Exec Dir*

GEOGRAPHIC SECTION

Ashland - Ashland County (G-665)

EMP: 300
SQ FT: 20,000
SALES (est): 6.5MM **Privately Held**
SIC: 5812 7299 8412 5947 Restaurant, family: independent; banquet hall facilities; museum; gift shop

(G-645)
SAUDER WOODWORKING CO (PA)
502 Middle St (43502-1500)
P.O. Box 156 (43502-0156)
PHONE.................................419 446-3828
Fax: 419 446-2654
Kevin J Sauder, *President*
Amy Robison, *Principal*
Maynard Sauder, *Chairman*
Wes Graber, *Area Mgr*
Kevin Lamb, *Exec VP*
◆ EMP: 2100
SALES: 500MM **Privately Held**
WEB: www.sauder.com
SIC: 2519 5021 Furniture, household: glass, fiberglass & plastic; furniture

(G-646)
SONIT SYSTEMS LLC
130 Westfield Dr (43502-1060)
PHONE.................................419 446-2151
Lana Rising, *Purch Mgr*
Brenda Farnsworth, *CFO*
Douglas Nofziger, *Accounts Exec*
Sue Scott, *Accounts Exec*
Klein Gnagey, *Sales Staff*
EMP: 41
SALES (est): 6.6MM **Privately Held**
SIC: 7379

Arlington
Hancock County

(G-647)
EVANGELICAL LUTHERAN
Also Called: Good Samaritan Soc - Arlington
100 Powell Dr (45814-9688)
P.O. Box 5038, Sioux Falls SD (57117-5038)
PHONE.................................419 365-5115
Fax: 419 365-1234
Rayenae Nylander, *Treasurer*
Karan Keeran, *Office Mgr*
Sara Nowlan, *Office Mgr*
Teresa Buck, *Director*
Stephen Freshwater, *Director*
EMP: 95
SALES (corp-wide): 1B **Privately Held**
WEB: www.good-sam.com
SIC: 8059 8051 Nursing home, except skilled & intermediate care facility; skilled nursing care facilities
PA: The Evangelical Lutheran Good Samaritan Society
4800 W 57th St
Sioux Falls SD 57108
866 928-1635

Arlington Heights
Hamilton County

(G-648)
MITER MASONRY CONTRACTORS
421 Maple Ave (45215-5425)
PHONE.................................513 821-3334
Fax: 513 821-3364
Thomas Krallman, *President*
Anne M Krallman, *Corp Secy*
EMP: 40
SQ FT: 8,000
SALES (est): 3.9MM **Privately Held**
SIC: 1741 Masonry & other stonework

Ashland
Ashland County

(G-649)
ABERS GARAGE INC (PA)
Also Called: Aber's Truck Center
1729 Claremont Ave (44805-3594)
PHONE.................................419 281-5500
Fax: 419 281-3693
Danny Aber, *President*
Frances Aber, *Corp Secy*
Allen Aber, *Vice Pres*
Jerry Aber, *Vice Pres*
EMP: 45 EST: 1950
SQ FT: 26,000
SALES (est): 22.6MM **Privately Held**
WEB: www.aberstrucks.com
SIC: 5511 7538 7549 5012 Trucks, tractors & trailers: new & used; general truck repair; towing service, automotive; automobiles & other motor vehicles

(G-650)
ANDERSON PRESS INCORPORATED
Also Called: Dalmatian Press
1840 Baney Rd S (44805-3524)
PHONE.................................615 370-9922
Chad Wiggins, *General Mgr*
Cindy Waters, *Traffic Mgr*
Rich Hilicki, *Branch Mgr*
EMP: 25
SALES (corp-wide): 31.3MM **Privately Held**
SIC: 5092 5192 5094 Toys & hobby goods & supplies; books, periodicals & newspapers; coins
PA: Anderson Press Incorporated
4001 Helton Dr
Florence AL 35630
404 214-4300

(G-651)
APPLESEED CMNTY MNTAL HLTH CTR
Also Called: APPLESEED COUNSELING
2233 Rocky Ln (44805-4701)
PHONE.................................419 281-3716
Fax: 419 281-4605
Brandy Barone, *Info Tech Mgr*
Jerry Strausaugh, *Director*
EMP: 25
SALES: 4.3MM **Privately Held**
WEB: www.appleseedcmhc.org
SIC: 8049 8093 Clinical psychologist; specialty outpatient clinics

(G-652)
ASHLAND CITY SCHOOL DISTRICT
Also Called: Reagan Elementary School
850 Jackson Dr (44805-4254)
PHONE.................................419 289-7967
Fax: 419 281-4233
Stephen McDonnell, *Principal*
EMP: 50
SALES (corp-wide): 4.8MM **Privately Held**
SIC: 8211 8351 Public junior high school; public elementary school; preschool center
PA: Ashland City School District
1407 Claremont Ave
Ashland OH 44805
419 289-1117

(G-653)
ASHLAND CLEANING LLC
48 W Main St (44805-2237)
PHONE.................................419 281-1747
Melinda Turk, *President*
EMP: 40
SQ FT: 1,800
SALES (est): 230.8K **Privately Held**
SIC: 7349 Building & office cleaning services; floor waxing; janitorial service, contract basis; maid services, contract or fee basis

(G-654)
ASHLAND CLEANING LLC
Also Called: Ahsland Cleaning
48 W Main St (44805-2237)
PHONE.................................419 281-1747
Melinda Turk, *Principal*
EMP: 50
SALES: 600K **Privately Held**
SIC: 7699 Cleaning services

(G-655)
ASHLAND CNTY COUNCIL ON AGING
240 E 3rd St (44805-2405)
PHONE.................................419 281-1477
Fax: 419 281-7871
James A Dalenberg, *Exec Dir*
EMP: 50
SALES: 926K **Privately Held**
SIC: 8322 Old age assistance

(G-656)
ASHLAND COMFORT CONTROL INC (PA)
Also Called: Honeywell Authorized Dealer
805 E Main St (44805-2620)
PHONE.................................419 281-0144
Fax: 419 281-6971
Jeffrey Reep, *President*
Joy Reep, *Corp Secy*
EMP: 29
SQ FT: 17,000
SALES (est): 5MM **Privately Held**
WEB: www.ashlandcomfortcontrol.com
SIC: 1711 Warm air heating & air conditioning contractor; refrigeration contractor

(G-657)
ASHLAND GOLF CLUB
1333 Center St (44805-4142)
PHONE.................................419 289-2917
Fax: 419 281-0816
Cindy Mitchell, *General Mgr*
Tim Haag, *Superintendent*
David Huckabee, *Manager*
EMP: 35
SQ FT: 3,500
SALES (est): 25.1K **Privately Held**
WEB: www.ccashland.com
SIC: 7997 Golf club, membership

(G-658)
ASHLAND LLC
Also Called: Ashland Distribution
1745 Cottage St (44805-1237)
PHONE.................................419 289-9588
Teresa Kennedy, *Engineer*
David Thomas, *Plant Engr*
Norma Malcolm, *Controller*
David A Tobolski, *Branch Mgr*
Sarah Humphrey, *Administration*
EMP: 100
SALES (corp-wide): 3.2B **Publicly Held**
WEB: www.ashland.com
SIC: 5169 Alkalines & chlorine
HQ: Ashland Llc
50 E Rivercenter Blvd # 1600
Covington KY 41011
859 815-3333

(G-659)
ASPEN MANAGEMENT USA LLC (PA)
1566 County Road 1095 (44805-9592)
PHONE.................................419 281-3367
David Wurster, *President*
Thomas Wurster, *Vice Pres*
Ann Wurster, *Treasurer*
EMP: 43
SALES (est): 3.8MM **Privately Held**
SIC: 6513 Apartment building operators

(G-660)
ATLAS BOLT & SCREW COMPANY LLC (DH)
Also Called: Atlas Fasteners For Cnstr
1628 Troy Rd (44805-1398)
PHONE.................................419 289-6171
Fax: 419 289-2564
Robert W Moore, *President*
Robert C Gluth, *Treasurer*
Ed Kreitner, *Sales Executive*
Jim Gerhart, *Manager*
Robert Webb, *Admin Sec*
▲ EMP: 175
SQ FT: 75,000
SALES (est): 30.1MM
SALES (corp-wide): 242.1B **Publicly Held**
WEB: www.atlasfasteners.com
SIC: 3452 5085 5051 5072 Washers, metal; screws, metal; fasteners, industrial: nuts, bolts, screws, etc.; metals service centers & offices; hardware
HQ: Marmon Group Llc
181 W Madison St Ste 2600
Chicago IL 60602
312 372-9500

(G-661)
BALL BOUNCE AND SPORT INC (PA)
Also Called: Hedstrom Fitness
1 Hedstrom Dr (44805-3586)
PHONE.................................419 289-9310
Fax: 419 281-3371
James Braeunig, *CEO*
John Williams, *Vice Pres*
Scott Fickes, *CFO*
Michael Kelly, *CFO*
Vicky Gingery, *Controller*
◆ EMP: 270
SQ FT: 187,000
SALES (est): 158.8MM **Privately Held**
SIC: 5092 5091 3089 Toys; fitness equipment & supplies; plastic processing

(G-662)
BALL BOUNCE AND SPORT INC
Also Called: Hedstrom Plastics
100 Hedstrom Dr (44805-3586)
PHONE.................................419 289-9310
Dave Braeunig, *General Mgr*
EMP: 50
SALES (corp-wide): 158.8MM **Privately Held**
SIC: 5092 Toys
PA: Ball, Bounce And Sport, Inc.
1 Hedstrom Dr
Ashland OH 44805
419 289-9310

(G-663)
BCU ELECTRIC INC
1019 Us Highway 250 N (44805-9474)
PHONE.................................419 281-8944
Fax: 419 289-6239
Bennie Uselton, *President*
Gary Baumberger, *Project Mgr*
Aaron Brenneman, *Engineer*
Brenda Uselton, *Treasurer*
EMP: 40
SQ FT: 6,000
SALES (est): 10.5MM **Privately Held**
WEB: www.bcuelectric.com
SIC: 1731 General electrical contractor

(G-664)
BENDON INC (PA)
1840 Baney Rd S (44805-3524)
PHONE.................................419 207-3600
Fax: 419 207-3605
Benjamin Ferguson, *President*
Terry Gerwig, *Exec VP*
Jenny Hastings, *Exec VP*
Michelle Manning, *Senior VP*
Don Myers II, *Senior VP*
▲ EMP: 54
SQ FT: 220,000
SALES (est): 31.6MM **Privately Held**
WEB: www.bendonpub.com
SIC: 2731 5999 5961 5092 Books: publishing only; educational aids & electronic training materials; educational supplies & equipment, mail order; educational toys

(G-665)
BOOKMASTERS INC (PA)
Also Called: Atlasbooks
30 Amberwood Pkwy (44805-9765)
PHONE.................................419 281-1802
Deb Keets, *President*
Tony Proe, *President*
Raymond Sevin, *President*
Chris Ashdown, *Publisher*
Larisa Elt, *Publisher*
EMP: 122
SQ FT: 180,000

Ashland - Ashland County (G-666)

GEOGRAPHIC SECTION

SALES (est): 58.4MM **Privately Held**
WEB: www.atlasbooks.com
SIC: 7389 2752 2731 2791 Printers' services: folding, collating; commercial printing, lithographic; book publishing; typesetting; books, periodicals & newspapers

(G-666)
BRETHREN CARE INC
Also Called: Bloomfield Cottages
2140 Center St Ofc (44805-4380)
PHONE..........................419 289-0803
Fax: 419 289-0803
Jay Brooks, *CEO*
Matthew McFarland, *CFO*
Pat Long, *Office Mgr*
Tina Massie, *Director*
Mehrdad Tavallaee, *Director*
EMP: 200
SQ FT: 38,000
SALES: 14.7MM **Privately Held**
WEB: www.brethrencarevillage.org
SIC: 8052 6513 8051 Intermediate care facilities; apartment building operators; skilled nursing care facilities

(G-667)
BRETHREN CARE VILLAGE LLC
2140 Center St (44805-4376)
PHONE..........................419 289-1585
Troy Snyder, *CEO*
Michael Watkins, *Technology*
EMP: 99
SQ FT: 49,810
SALES (est): 299.2K **Privately Held**
SIC: 8059 Personal care home, with health care

(G-668)
BUREN INSURANCE GROUP INC (PA)
Also Called: Padgett-Young & Associates
1101 Sugarbush Dr (44805-9400)
PHONE..........................419 281-8060
Fax: 419 281-7119
Tim Buren, *President*
Jeffrey Buren, *Vice Pres*
Dale Roberts, *CFO*
Holly Stevens, *Sales Mgr*
Lora Copley, *Manager*
EMP: 38
SQ FT: 1,200
SALES (est): 12.8MM **Privately Held**
WEB: www.barnardagency.com
SIC: 6411 Insurance agents

(G-669)
CASTLE CONSTRUCTION CO INC
588 Us Highway 250 E (44805-8919)
PHONE..........................419 289-1122
Fax: 330 289-1100
John Makuch, *President*
Kris Cranston, *Manager*
EMP: 38
SALES (est): 3.7MM **Privately Held**
SIC: 1751 Framing contractor

(G-670)
CATHOLIC CHARITIES CORPORATION
Also Called: Catholic Charities Services
34 W 2nd St Ste 18 (44805-2201)
PHONE..........................419 289-1903
Fax: 419 281-8342
Cathy Themens, *Director*
Terese Holm, *Director*
John Klee, *Director*
Mary A Beckman, *Program Dir*
EMP: 25 **Privately Held**
WEB: www.catholic-action.org
SIC: 8399 8322 Fund raising organization, non-fee basis; child related social services
PA: Catholic Charities Corporation
7911 Detroit Ave
Cleveland OH 44102

(G-671)
CATHOLIC DIOCESE OF CLEVELAND
Also Called: Saint Edward's Church
501 Cottage St (44805-2125)
PHONE..........................419 289-7224
Fax: 419 289-0515
James J Cassidy, *Pastor*
EMP: 30
SALES (corp-wide): 79.9MM **Privately Held**
WEB: www.oce-ocs.org
SIC: 8661 6512 Catholic Church; auditorium & hall operation
PA: Catholic Diocese Of Cleveland
1404 E 9th St Ste 201
Cleveland OH 44114
216 696-6525

(G-672)
CENTERRA CO-OP (PA)
813 Clark Ave (44805-1967)
PHONE..........................419 281-2153
Jean Bratton, *CEO*
Gary Besancon, *Vice Pres*
Bill Rohrbaugh, *Vice Pres*
John Runion, *Opers Mgr*
Bob Mole, *Site Mgr*
EMP: 30
SALES: 174.6MM **Privately Held**
WEB: www.tc-feed.com
SIC: 5983 5261 5999 2048 Fuel oil dealers; fertilizer; feed & farm supply; bird food, prepared; gases, liquefied petroleum (propane)

(G-673)
CHANDLER SYSTEMS INCORPORATED
Also Called: Best Controls Company
710 Orange St (44805-1725)
PHONE..........................888 363-9434
Fax: 419 289-2535
William Chandler III, *President*
Bill Chandler, *Principal*
Debra Vogel, *Manager*
Polly Chandler, *Admin Sec*
▲ EMP: 65
SQ FT: 52,000
SALES (est): 25.3MM **Privately Held**
WEB: www.chandlersystemsinc.com
SIC: 5074 3625 3823 Water purification equipment; relays & industrial controls; industrial instrmnts msrmnt display/control process variable

(G-674)
CHARLES RIVER LABS ASHLAND LLC (DH)
1407 George Rd (44805-8946)
PHONE..........................419 282-8700
David Spaight, *CEO*
Evelyn Tanchevski, *Project Mgr*
Robert Wally, *Opers Mgr*
Joelle Lucarell, *Research*
Katy McQuate, *Research*
EMP: 103
SALES (est): 124.3MM
SALES (corp-wide): 1.8B **Publicly Held**
SIC: 8733 Research institute
HQ: Charles River Laboratories Sa Usa, Inc.
30 Two Bridges Rd Ste 200
Fairfield NJ 07004
919 245-3114

(G-675)
COMPAK INC
605 Westlake Dr (44805-4710)
PHONE..........................419 207-8888
Fax: 419 207-8884
Jerry Baker, *President*
Jeff Baker, *Manager*
▲ EMP: 50
SQ FT: 240,000
SALES (est): 3.6MM **Privately Held**
SIC: 1541 7699 Industrial buildings & warehouses; pumps & pumping equipment repair

(G-676)
COMPANIONS OF ASHLAND LLC (PA)
1241 E Main St (44805-2810)
PHONE..........................419 281-2273
Fax: 419 207-1737
Tiffany Behrendsen,
EMP: 42
SALES (est): 3.1MM **Privately Held**
SIC: 8082 Home health care services

(G-677)
CRYSTAL CARE CENTERS INC
1251 E Main St (44805-2810)
PHONE..........................419 281-9595
Fax: 419 282-9609
Jerry Smith, *Owner*
Dennis Reynolds, *Envir Svcs Dir*
Connie Weaver, *Office Mgr*
Mike Stencel, *Director*
Heidi Beachler, *Hlthcr Dir*
EMP: 40 **Privately Held**
SIC: 8051 Convalescent home with continuous nursing care
PA: Crystal Care Centers Inc
1159 Wyandotte Ave
Mansfield OH 44906

(G-678)
D-R TRAINING CENTER & WORKSHOP
Also Called: Dale-Roy School & Training Ctr
1256 Center St (44805-4139)
PHONE..........................419 289-0470
Jerry Simon, *Ch of Bd*
Ron Pagano, *Superintendent*
Jim Huntington, *Superintendent*
Kathy Wallace, *Principal*
EMP: 185
SQ FT: 5,000
SALES: 253.8K **Privately Held**
WEB: www.daleroy.org
SIC: 8211 8331 8361 School for the retarded; school for physically handicapped; public special education school; sheltered workshop; residential care

(G-679)
DONLEY FORD-LINCOLN INC (PA)
1641 Claremont Ave (44805-3536)
P.O. Box 405 (44805-0405)
PHONE..........................419 281-3673
Fax: 419 281-6147
Scott Donley, *President*
Jim Farley, *Vice Pres*
Andy Thomas, *Sales Mgr*
Ryan Fair, *Sales Associate*
Michael Jackson, *Sales Associate*
EMP: 45
SQ FT: 25,000
SALES (est): 19.8MM **Privately Held**
WEB: www.donleyford.com
SIC: 5511 5012 Automobiles, new & used; automobiles & other motor vehicles

(G-680)
GOOD SHEPHERD HOME FOR AGED
Also Called: The Good Shepherd
622 Center St (44805-3343)
PHONE..........................614 228-5200
Fax: 419 281-0656
Marshall G Moore, *CEO*
Larry Crowell, *President*
Phil Helser, *CFO*
Frank Duffy, *VP Finance*
Henry Kassab, *Accounting Mgr*
EMP: 170
SQ FT: 82,651
SALES: 10.8MM **Privately Held**
SIC: 8051 Convalescent home with continuous nursing care

(G-681)
GUENTHER MECHANICAL INC
1248 Middle Rowsburg Rd (44805-2813)
P.O. Box 97 (44805-0097)
PHONE..........................419 289-6900
Fax: 419 281-0750
Herbert E Guenther, *President*
James B Andrews, *Vice Pres*
Jim Cutright, *Vice Pres*
Andrews Isolde, *Treasurer*
EMP: 120
SQ FT: 35,000
SALES (est): 32.2MM **Privately Held**
SIC: 1711 Mechanical contractor

(G-682)
HOSPICE OF NORTH CENTRAL OHIO (PA)
1050 Dauch Dr (44805-8845)
PHONE..........................419 281-7107
Fax: 419 281-8427
Larry McConnell, *COO*
Betty Hennessey, *Marketing Staff*
Ruth Lindsey, *Exec Dir*
Linda Hickey, *Exec Dir*
EMP: 40
SQ FT: 6,500
SALES: 8.4MM **Privately Held**
WEB: www.hospiceofnorthcentralohio.org
SIC: 8082 8051 8059 Home health care services; skilled nursing care facilities; rest home, with health care

(G-683)
IHEARTCOMMUNICATIONS INC
1197 Us Highway 42 (44805-4575)
PHONE..........................419 289-2605
Diana Coon, *General Mgr*
Bill Clark, *General Mgr*
Monica Tovar, *Business Mgr*
Jim Ryan, *Senior VP*
Gregory Capogna, *Vice Pres*
EMP: 26 **Publicly Held**
SIC: 4832 Radio broadcasting stations
HQ: Iheartcommunications, Inc.
20880 Stone Oak Pkwy
San Antonio TX 78258
210 822-2828

(G-684)
KINGSTON HEALTHCARE COMPANY
Also Called: Kingston of Ashland
20 Amberwood Pkwy (44805-9765)
PHONE..........................419 289-3859
Fax: 419 281-6357
Sandy Liederbach, *Purch Agent*
Cathy Bowman, *Envir Svcs Dir*
Timothy Callahan, *Branch Mgr*
Michael Stencel, *Director*
Judy Clyburn, *Nursing Dir*
EMP: 114
SALES (corp-wide): 95.5MM **Privately Held**
WEB: www.kingstonhealthcare.com
SIC: 8051 Convalescent home with continuous nursing care
PA: Kingston Healthcare Company
1 Seagate Ste 1960
Toledo OH 43604
419 247-2880

(G-685)
LABORATORY CORPORATION AMERICA
53 Sugarbush Ct (44805-9737)
PHONE..........................419 281-7100
Dan Phillip, *Branch Mgr*
EMP: 25 **Publicly Held**
SIC: 8071 Testing laboratories
HQ: Laboratory Corporation Of America
358 S Main St Ste 458
Burlington NC 27215
336 229-1127

(G-686)
LUTHERAN SCIAL SVCS CENTL OHIO
Also Called: Good Shepard, The
622 Center St (44805-3343)
PHONE..........................419 289-3523
Sandra Hempfield, *Business Mgr*
Michele Cenci, *Vice Pres*
Deb Mitchell, *Maintenance Dir*
Alice Hawley, *Chf Purch Ofc*
Joe Abraham, *Manager*
EMP: 165
SALES (corp-wide): 49.2MM **Privately Held**
SIC: 8051 Skilled nursing care facilities
PA: Lutheran Social Services Of Central Ohio
500 W Wilson Bridge Rd
Worthington OH 43085
419 289-3523

(G-687)
MCGRAW-HILL SCHOOL EDUCATION H
Also Called: Mc Graw-Hill Educational Pubg
1250 George Rd (44805-8916)
PHONE..........................419 207-7400
Fax: 419 207-7401
Maryellen Valaitis, *Principal*
Gary Curtiss, *Maintence Staff*
Angela Oxley, *Assistant*
EMP: 401

SALES (est): 27.6MM
SALES (corp-wide): 750MM Privately Held
WEB: www.mcgraw-hill.com
SIC: 2731 5192 Books: publishing & printing; books, periodicals & newspapers
PA: Mcgraw-Hill School Education Holdings, Llc
2 Penn Plz Fl 20
New York NY 10121
646 766-2000

(G-688)
MEDICAL ASSOCIATES OF MID-OHIO
2109 Claremont Ave (44805-3547)
PHONE...................................419 289-1331
Michael Stencel MD, *President*
Christopher D Boyd, *Family Practiti*
EMP: 25
SALES (est): 1.8MM Privately Held
SIC: 8011 Offices & clinics of medical doctors

(G-689)
MITCHELL & SONS MOVING & STOR
1217 Township Road 1153 (44805-3474)
PHONE...................................419 289-3311
Mitchell Goshinski Jr, *President*
John Atkins, *Vice Pres*
Jennifer McQuellan, *Vice Pres*
Sue Goshinki, *CFO*
EMP: 25
SQ FT: 12,000
SALES (est): 1.4MM Privately Held
WEB: www.mitchellandsons.com
SIC: 4214 4213 Household goods moving & storage, local; household goods transport

(G-690)
MOWRY CONSTRUCTION & ENGRG INC
2105 Claremont Ave (44805-3590)
P.O. Box 188 (44805-0188)
PHONE...................................419 289-2262
Fax: 419 281-8307
Michael Dana Mowry, *President*
Ronald Lee Mowry, *Vice Pres*
Norma Allen, *Manager*
EMP: 25
SQ FT: 6,660
SALES: 5MM Privately Held
SIC: 1542 1541 Commercial & office building, new construction; commercial & office buildings, renovation & repair; industrial buildings, new construction; renovation, remodeling & repairs: industrial buildings

(G-691)
NATIONAL ASSN LTR CARRIERS
530 Claremont Ave (44805-3177)
PHONE...................................419 289-8359
Kim Dellinger, *Manager*
EMP: 50
SALES (corp-wide): 1.4B Privately Held
WEB: www.nalc.org
SIC: 8631 Labor union
PA: National Association Of Letter Carriers
100 Indana Ave Nw Ste 709
Washington DC 20001
202 393-4695

(G-692)
PUMP HOUSE MINISTRIES
400 Orange St (44805-2216)
PHONE...................................419 207-3900
Fax: 419 207-3910
Gerald Bruce Wilkinson, *President*
Rich Pate, *Manager*
Rebecca Zickefoose, *Manager*
Simon Kimaru, *Director*
Pete Snyder, *Director*
EMP: 35
SALES (est): 1.1MM Privately Held
WEB: www.pumphouseministries.com
SIC: 8322 Social service center

(G-693)
RANDALL R LEAB
Also Called: Accessibility
1895 Township Road 1215 (44805-9414)
PHONE...................................330 689-6263
Randall R Leab, *CFO*
EMP: 45
SALES (est): 434.8K Privately Held
SIC: 8399 Community development groups

(G-694)
RETURN POLYMERS INC
400 Westlake Dr (44805-1397)
PHONE...................................419 289-1998
David Foell, *President*
Nicki Mikolajczyk, *Manager*
EMP: 65
SQ FT: 26,000
SALES (est): 1.4MM Privately Held
WEB: www.returnpolymers.com
SIC: 7389 Personal service agents, brokers & bureaus

(G-695)
RPG INC
400 Westlake Dr (44805-1397)
PHONE...................................419 289-2757
William Hutira, *President*
Michael Hutira, *Vice Pres*
EMP: 60
SQ FT: 50,000
SALES (est): 5.3MM Privately Held
SIC: 4953 Recycling, waste materials

(G-696)
SAMARITAN PROFESSIONAL CORP
1025 Center St (44805-4011)
PHONE...................................419 289-0491
Fax: 419 289-2831
Danny Boggs, *President*
EMP: 50
SALES: 8.3MM Privately Held
SIC: 8011 Gastronomist

(G-697)
SAMARITAN REGIONAL HEALTH SYS
Also Called: Samaritan Health & Rehab Ctr
2163 Claremont Ave (44805-3547)
PHONE...................................419 281-1330
Fax: 419 281-4850
Mary Griest, *CFO*
Don Harris, *Director*
EMP: 30
SALES (corp-wide): 74.6MM Privately Held
WEB: www.samaritanhospital.org
SIC: 8062 8049 General medical & surgical hospitals; occupational therapist
PA: Samaritan Regional Health System
1025 Center St
Ashland OH 44805
419 289-0491

(G-698)
SAMARITAN REGIONAL HEALTH SYS (PA)
Also Called: PEOPLES HOSPITAL
1025 Center St (44805-4097)
PHONE...................................419 289-0491
Danny L Boggs, *CEO*
Mary Macdonald, *President*
Karin Schwan, *COO*
Matthew Bernhard, *Vice Pres*
Philip Myers, *Vice Pres*
EMP: 349
SQ FT: 128,700
SALES: 74.6MM Privately Held
WEB: www.samaritanhospital.org
SIC: 8062 General medical & surgical hospitals

(G-699)
SIMONSON CONSTRUCTION SVCS INC
2112 Troy Rd (44805-1396)
PHONE...................................419 281-8299
Fax: 419 281-6150
Robert M Simonson, *President*
Doug Beattie, *Superintendent*
Ron Lantz, *Superintendent*
Daniel Moore, *Vice Pres*
Jay Myers, *Vice Pres*
EMP: 72
SQ FT: 11,532

SALES (est): 22.3MM Privately Held
SIC: 1542 1521 8741 8712 Commercial & office building, new construction; new construction, single-family houses; construction management; architectural services

(G-700)
SUNSHINE HOMECARE
320 Pleasant St (44805-2029)
P.O. Box 450 (44805-0450)
PHONE...................................419 207-9900
Fax: 419 207-1300
Wendy Maust, *Partner*
Tim Maust, *Partner*
EMP: 25
SALES (est): 936K Privately Held
SIC: 8082 Home health care services

(G-701)
THIELS REPLACEMENT SYSTEMS INC
Also Called: Cabinet Restylers
419 E 8th St (44805-1953)
PHONE...................................419 289-6139
Fax: 419 281-4884
Eric Thiel, *President*
Denise Appleby, *Vice Pres*
Anthony Thiel, *Wholesale*
Bobbie Browne, *Manager*
EMP: 56
SQ FT: 50,000
SALES (est): 7.7MM Privately Held
SIC: 1751 2541 5211 1799 Window & door (prefabricated) installation; cabinet & finish carpentry; cabinets, lockers & shelving; cabinets, kitchen; bathtub refinishing; gutter & downspout contractor

(G-702)
TRANSFORMATION NETWORK (PA)
1310 Claremont Ave Unit A (44805-3529)
PHONE...................................419 207-1188
Dan Phillip, *President*
Lindsey Plushnik, *Manager*
Bob Bufford, *Administration*
Wayne Mullet, *Administration*
EMP: 28
SALES: 4.3MM Privately Held
WEB: www.transformationnetwork.org
SIC: 8322 Individual & family services

(G-703)
TRINITY LUTH CHILD CARE
Also Called: Trinity Lutheran Church of Ash
508 Center St (44805-3341)
PHONE...................................419 289-2126
Fax: 419 289-1381
Sanford Mitchell, *Pastor*
Anne Seiss, *Exec Dir*
EMP: 27
SALES (est): 1.4MM Privately Held
WEB: www.trinityashland.org
SIC: 8661 8351 Lutheran Church; child day care services

(G-704)
VALLEY TRANSPORTATION INC
Also Called: Valley Fleet
1 Valley Dr (44805)
P.O. Box 305 (44805-0305)
PHONE...................................419 289-6200
Fax: 419 281-0864
Steven Aber, *President*
Karen Aber, *Corp Secy*
Shawn Aber, *Vice Pres*
Robert Peck, *Manager*
EMP: 150
SQ FT: 20,000
SALES (est): 22.6MM Privately Held
WEB: www.valleytransportation.com
SIC: 4213 Contract haulers

(G-705)
VERIZON COMMUNICATIONS INC
1041 Commerce Pkwy (44805-8953)
PHONE...................................419 281-1714
Fax: 419 289-7943
Courtney Shaw, *Sales Associate*
EMP: 51
SALES (corp-wide): 126B Publicly Held
SIC: 4812 Cellular telephone services

PA: Verizon Communications Inc.
1095 Ave Of The Americas
New York NY 10036
212 395-1000

(G-706)
VISITING NRSE ASSN OF CLVELAND
Also Called: Visiting Nurse Assn Ashland
1165 E Main St (44805-2831)
PHONE...................................419 281-2480
EMP: 257
SALES (corp-wide): 18.6MM Privately Held
SIC: 8082 Visiting nurse service
PA: The Visiting Nurse Association Of Cleveland
2500 E 22nd St
Cleveland OH 44115
216 931-1400

(G-707)
WARD REALESTATE INC
Also Called: Coldwell Banker
600 E Main St (44805-2699)
PHONE...................................419 281-2000
Fax: 419 281-2004
Robert Ward II, *President*
Polly Ward Chandler, *Vice Pres*
Lisa Lang, *Sales Associate*
Stacy Patton, *Sales Associate*
Janet J Enzor, *Real Est Agnt*
EMP: 25 EST: 1943
SQ FT: 1,800
SALES (est): 2.1MM Privately Held
WEB: www.wardrealestate.com
SIC: 6531 Real estate agent, residential

(G-708)
WHITCOMB & HESS INC
1020 Cleveland Ave (44805-2710)
PHONE...................................419 289-7007
Fax: 419 281-7432
Jim Hess, *President*
Allison Smith, *Accounting Dir*
Beau Carpenter, *Accountant*
Chris Bevington, *Manager*
Tracy Wells, *Planning*
EMP: 25
SALES (est): 2MM Privately Held
SIC: 8721 Certified public accountant

(G-709)
Y M C A OF ASHLAND OHIO INC
Also Called: YMCA
207 Miller St (44805-2484)
PHONE...................................419 289-0626
Fax: 419 289-9121
Teri Augenstein, *VP Mktg*
Pamela Garrett, *Comms Dir*
Jerry Seiter, *Exec Dir*
Abby Majesky, *Director*
Tiffany Roberts, *Director*
EMP: 55
SQ FT: 443,000
SALES: 1MM Privately Held
WEB: www.ashlandymcaoh.org
SIC: 8641 7991 8351 7032 Youth organizations; physical fitness facilities; child day care services; youth camps; individual & family services

Ashtabula
Ashtabula County

(G-710)
ABC CHILD CARE & LEARNING CTR
Also Called: ABC Day Care
2012 W 11th St (44004-2625)
PHONE...................................440 964-8799
Lireena Spring, *Director*
Jodi Vantveer, *Administration*
EMP: 38
SALES (est): 1MM Privately Held
WEB: www.abc-childcare.com
SIC: 8351 Preschool center

(G-711)
ASH CRAFT INDUSTRIES INC
5959 Green Rd (44004-4746)
PHONE...................................440 224-2177
Fax: 440 224-2375

Ashtabula - Ashtabula County (G-712)

GEOGRAPHIC SECTION

Linda Perry, *Director*
EMP: 220
SQ FT: 45,000
SALES: 89.6K **Privately Held**
SIC: 8331 Vocational rehabilitation agency; sheltered workshop

(G-712)
ASHTABULA AREA CITY SCHOOL DST
Also Called: Transportation Department
5921 Gerald Rd (44004-9450)
PHONE 440 992-1221
Al Peck, *Principal*
EMP: 35
SALES (corp-wide): 50.5MM **Privately Held**
SIC: 8211 7538 Public senior high school; general automotive repair shops
PA: Ashtabula Area City School District
2630 3rd Dr N
Ashtabula OH 44004
440 992-1200

(G-713)
ASHTABULA BROADCASTING STATION
Also Called: Wzoo-FM
3226 Jefferson Rd (44004-9112)
P.O. Box 980 (44005-0980)
PHONE 440 993-2126
Fax: 440 993-1025
Dana Schulte, *Principal*
EMP: 50
SALES (est): 1.5MM **Privately Held**
SIC: 4832 Radio broadcasting stations, music format

(G-714)
ASHTABULA CHEMICAL CORP
Also Called: Green Leaf Motor Express
4606 State Rd (44004-6210)
P.O. Box 667 (44005-0667)
PHONE 440 998-0100
Mark Jarvis, *President*
Jack Jarvis, *Vice Pres*
David Jarvis, *Treasurer*
EMP: 25
SQ FT: 150,000
SALES (est): 1.3MM **Privately Held**
SIC: 4789 6512 Cargo loading & unloading services; commercial & industrial building operation

(G-715)
ASHTABULA CLINIC INC (PA)
2422 Lake Ave (44004-4982)
PHONE 440 997-6980
Fax: 440 992-5053
Morris Wasylenki MD, *President*
Glenn E Eippert MD, *Vice Pres*
Suk K Choi, *Treasurer*
Robert Dlwgosh, *Med Doctor*
John Lee MD, *Med Doctor*
EMP: 81
SQ FT: 13,000
SALES (est): 7.9MM **Privately Held**
WEB: www.ashtabulaclinic.com
SIC: 8011 Clinic, operated by physicians

(G-716)
ASHTABULA COMMUNITY COUNSELING
Also Called: Friendship Home
2801 C Ct Unit 2 (44004-4578)
PHONE 440 998-6032
Dale Brinker, *Exec Dir*
Stephen Cervas, *Director*
EMP: 55
SALES: 3.8MM **Privately Held**
SIC: 8322 Individual & family services

(G-717)
ASHTABULA COUNTY COMMISSIONERS
Also Called: Ashtabula Welfare Department
2924 Donahoe Dr (44004-4540)
P.O. Box 1650 (44005-1650)
PHONE 440 994-1206
Joanne Gonzalez, *MIS Staff*
Paul Fuller, *Director*
EMP: 100 **Privately Held**
SIC: 6371 Pension, health & welfare funds

PA: Ashtabula County Commissioners
25 W Jefferson St
Jefferson OH 44047
440 576-3649

(G-718)
ASHTABULA COUNTY COMMNTY ACTN (PA)
Also Called: ACCAA
6920 Austinburg Rd (44004-9393)
P.O. Box 2610 (44005-2610)
PHONE 440 997-1721
Steve Cervas, *CFO*
Richard J Pepperney, *Exec Dir*
Judith Barris, *Admin Sec*
EMP: 168
SQ FT: 17,380
SALES: 92.1K **Privately Held**
SIC: 8399 Antipoverty board

(G-719)
ASHTABULA COUNTY COMMNTY ACTN
4510 Main Ave (44004-6925)
PHONE 440 993-7716
Stephanie Patriarco, *Branch Mgr*
EMP: 78
SALES (corp-wide): 92.1K **Privately Held**
SIC: 8399 Antipoverty board
PA: Ashtabula County Community Action Agency Properties Corporation
6920 Austinburg Rd
Ashtabula OH 44004
440 997-1721

(G-720)
ASHTABULA COUNTY COMMNTY ACTN
3215 Lake Ave (44004-5758)
PHONE 440 997-5957
David Jordan, *Branch Mgr*
EMP: 73
SALES (corp-wide): 92.1K **Privately Held**
SIC: 8399 Community action agency
PA: Ashtabula County Community Action Agency Properties Corporation
6920 Austinburg Rd
Ashtabula OH 44004
440 997-1721

(G-721)
ASHTABULA COUNTY COMMUNITY
6920 Austinburg Rd (44004-9393)
PHONE 440 997-1721
Fax: 440 992-3319
Richard Pepperney, *CEO*
Lori Pawlowski, *Trustee*
Steve Cervas, *Director*
EMP: 180
SALES: 9.3MM **Privately Held**
SIC: 8322 Social service center

(G-722)
ASHTABULA COUNTY MEDICAL CTR (PA)
2420 Lake Ave (44004-4970)
PHONE 440 997-2262
Fax: 440 997-6487
Michael Habowski, *CEO*
Mohammad Varghai, *Managing Dir*
Joe Giangola, *Chairman*
Bill Dingleden, *Corp Secy*
Kathy Crawford, *COO*
EMP: 750
SQ FT: 270,000
SALES: 119.6MM **Privately Held**
WEB: www.ashtabulacountymedicalcenter.com
SIC: 8062 General medical & surgical hospitals

(G-723)
ASHTABULA COUNTY MEDICAL CTR
2422 Lake Ave (44004-4985)
PHONE 440 997-6960
Patricia Parco, *Vice Pres*
Edward Wiese, *Med Doctor*
David Alpeter, *Manager*
EMP: 200

SALES (corp-wide): 119.6MM **Privately Held**
WEB: www.ashtabulacountymedicalcenter.com
SIC: 8062 8011 General medical & surgical hospitals; offices & clinics of medical doctors
PA: Ashtabula County Medical Center
2420 Lake Ave
Ashtabula OH 44004
440 997-2262

(G-724)
ASHTABULA DENTAL ASSOCIATES
Also Called: Laukhuf, Gary DDS
5005 State Rd (44004-6265)
PHONE 440 992-3146
Fax: 440 992-6948
William Sockman, *President*
Gregory Seymour DDS, *Vice Pres*
▲ **EMP:** 45
SQ FT: 7,700
SALES (est): 4.2MM **Privately Held**
SIC: 8021 Dentists' office

(G-725)
ASHTABULA JOB AND FAMILY SVCS
2924 Donahoe Dr (44004-4540)
PHONE 440 994-2020
Fax: 440 994-2025
Ronald Smith, *CFO*
Patrick Arcaro, *Director*
EMP: 170
SALES (est): 2.1MM **Privately Held**
SIC: 8322 Senior citizens' center or association

(G-726)
ASHTABULA RGIONAL HM HLTH SVCS
3949 Jefferson Rd (44004-9117)
P.O. Box 1428 (44005-1428)
PHONE 440 992-4663
Fax: 440 992-0687
Kerry Gerken, *President*
Pat Throckmorton, *Manager*
Sue Shadle, *Info Tech Dir*
Connie Forinash, *Executive*
EMP: 80 **EST:** 1974
SQ FT: 1,200
SALES: 5.3MM **Privately Held**
SIC: 8082 Home health care services

(G-727)
ASHTABULA STEVEDORE COMPANY
Also Called: Pinney Doc Co
1149 E 5th St (44004-3513)
PHONE 440 964-7186
Maynard B Walker, *President*
Joe Del Priore, *Vice Pres*
Lee Demers, *Manager*
EMP: 40
SQ FT: 120
SALES (est): 1.1MM **Privately Held**
SIC: 7363 Help supply services

(G-728)
AYRSHIRE INC
1432 E 21st St (44004-4062)
PHONE 440 992-0743
Ed Furman, *Manager*
EMP: 70
SALES (est): 4MM **Privately Held**
SIC: 1711 7359 Mechanical contractor; equipment rental & leasing

(G-729)
BEATITUDE HOUSE
3404 Lake Ave (44004-5700)
PHONE 440 992-0265
Sarah Masek, *Branch Mgr*
EMP: 26 **Privately Held**
SIC: 8322 Emergency shelters
PA: Beatitude House
238 Tod Ln
Youngstown OH

(G-730)
C TED FORSBERG
5005 State Rd (44004-6265)
PHONE 440 992-3145
C Ted Forsberg, *Owner*

EMP: 40
SALES (est): 1.3MM **Privately Held**
SIC: 8021 Offices & clinics of dentists

(G-731)
CELLCO PARTNERSHIP
Also Called: Verizon Wireless
3315 N Ridge Rd E (44004-4300)
PHONE 440 998-3111
Fax: 440 998-3120
EMP: 76
SALES (corp-wide): 126B **Publicly Held**
SIC: 4812 Cellular telephone services
HQ: Cellco Partnership
1 Verizon Way
Basking Ridge NJ 07920

(G-732)
CHALK BOX GET FIT LLC
5521 Main Ave (44004-7037)
PHONE 440 992-9619
Fax: 440 992-9619
Kathy Speelman, *Mng Member*
David Speelman,
EMP: 25
SALES: 250K **Privately Held**
SIC: 5941 5699 7991 Gymnasium equipment; sports apparel; physical fitness facilities

(G-733)
CHS-LAKE ERIE INC
Also Called: CARINGTON PARK
2217 West Ave (44004-3107)
PHONE 440 964-8446
Fax: 440 964-2652
Brian Colleran, *President*
Kelly Johnson,
EMP: 200
SALES: 11.8MM **Privately Held**
SIC: 8051 Mental retardation hospital

(G-734)
CITY TAXICAB & TRANSFER CO
Also Called: Black Eagle Transfer Company
1753 W Prospect Rd (44004-6621)
P.O. Box 3076 (44005-3076)
PHONE 440 992-2156
Fax: 440 992-9376
Bill Peek, *President*
EMP: 30
SQ FT: 600
SALES (est): 2.1MM **Privately Held**
SIC: 4111 4121 4215 Local & suburban transit; taxicabs; package delivery, vehicular

(G-735)
COMMUNITY CARE AMBLANCE NETWRK (PA)
115 E 24th St (44004-3417)
P.O. Box 1340 (44005-1340)
PHONE 440 992-1401
Tiffany Fisher, *Manager*
Julie Rose, *Exec Dir*
Michael Sass, *Director*
Ashtabula County Medical Cente, *Shareholder*
Memorial Hospital of Geneva, *Shareholder*
EMP: 75
SQ FT: 36,000
SALES: 16.3MM **Privately Held**
WEB: www.ccan.org
SIC: 4119 Ambulance service

(G-736)
COMMUNITY COUNSLNG CTR ASHTABU (PA)
2801 C Ct Unit 2 (44004-4578)
PHONE 440 998-4210
Fax: 440 998-6489
Kathy L Regal, *CEO*
Karen Fronczak, *Opers Spvr*
Jennifer Keefner, *CFO*
Patrick Arcaro, *Manager*
Ed Palagyi, *Maintece Staff*
EMP: 85 **EST:** 1961
SALES: 5.5MM **Privately Held**
SIC: 8093 Mental health clinic, outpatient

(G-737)
CONTINUUM HOME CARE INC
Also Called: Home Health Care
1100 Lake Ave (44004-2930)
PHONE 440 964-3332
Fax: 440 964-7972

GEOGRAPHIC SECTION

Ashtabula - Ashtabula County (G-760)

Robert L Huff, *President*
Lynne Huff, *President*
Tim Day, *COO*
Karen Farrow, *Mktg Dir*
Debbie Boyle, *Case Mgr*
EMP: 37
SALES (est): 1.6MM **Privately Held**
SIC: 8082 Home health care services

(G-738)
COUNTRY CLUB RETIREMENT CENTER
Also Called: Country Club Center III
925 E 26th St (44004-5061)
PHONE.................440 992-0022
Fax: 440 992-7423
Gabriella Vendetti, *Manager*
Paul Mikulin, *Info Tech Mgr*
Suk Choi, *Director*
EMP: 70
SALES (corp-wide): 5.4MM **Privately Held**
SIC: 8059 Nursing home, except skilled & intermediate care facility
PA: Country Club Retirement Center, Inc
  55801 Conno Mara Dr
  Bellaire OH 43906
  740 671-9330

(G-739)
COUNTY OF ASHTABULA
Also Called: Ashtabula Cnty Chldren Svcs Bd
3914 C Ct (44004-4572)
P.O. Box 1175 (44005-1175)
PHONE.................440 998-1811
Fax: 440 992-6828
Diane Solembrino, *Director*
Diana Bloom, *Executive*
EMP: 80
SALES (est): 2.7MM **Privately Held**
WEB: www.help-a-child.com
SIC: 8322 Child related social services
PA: County Of Ashtabula
  2505 S Ridge Rd E
  Ashtabula OH 44004
  440 224-2155

(G-740)
CSX TRANSPORTATION INC
1709 E Prospect Rd (44004-5815)
PHONE.................440 992-0871
EMP: 39
SALES (corp-wide): 11.4B **Publicly Held**
SIC: 4011 Railroads, line-haul operating
HQ: Csx Transportation, Inc.
  500 Water St
  Jacksonville FL 32202
  904 359-3100

(G-741)
DELTA RAILROAD CNSTR INC (PA)
2648 W Prospect Rd Frnt (44004-6372)
P.O. Box 1398 (44005-1398)
PHONE.................440 992-2997
Fax: 440 992-1311
Larry F Laurello, *President*
Lawrence C Laurello, *General Mgr*
Michael A Laurello, *Vice Pres*
Paul J Laurello, *Vice Pres*
Rick R Ryel, *Vice Pres*
▲ **EMP:** 100
SQ FT: 82,000
SALES: 44.3MM **Privately Held**
WEB: www.deltarr.com
SIC: 1629 Railroad & railway roadbed construction

(G-742)
DENTURE CENTER
Also Called: Hobby Smile Center
2010 W 19th St (44004-9709)
PHONE.................440 964-0542
Martin Crombie DDS, *Principal*
Scott Ball, *Vice Pres*
Debra Crombie, *Vice Pres*
Scott Maclean, *Vice Pres*
Peat Thorne, *Vice Pres*
EMP: 26
SALES (est): 711.9K **Privately Held**
SIC: 8021 Offices & clinics of dentists

(G-743)
EAST OHIO GAS COMPANY
Also Called: Dominion Energy Ohio
7001 Center Rd (44004-8948)
PHONE.................216 736-6120
Dave Findley, *Branch Mgr*
EMP: 59
SALES (corp-wide): 12.5B **Publicly Held**
SIC: 4924 Natural gas distribution
HQ: The East Ohio Gas Company
  19701 Libby Rd
  Maple Heights OH 44137
  800 362-7557

(G-744)
GAP RADIO BROADCASTING LLC
3226 Jefferson Rd (44004-9112)
P.O. Box 738 (44005-0738)
PHONE.................440 992-9700
Dana Schoulty, *Manager*
EMP: 40
SALES (corp-wide): 7.2MM **Privately Held**
SIC: 4832 Radio broadcasting stations
PA: Gap Radio Broadcasting Llc
  2525 Kell Blvd Ste 200
  Wichita Falls TX

(G-745)
GOODWILL INDS OF ASHTABULA (PA)
Also Called: Goodwill Industry
621 Goodwill Dr (44004-3232)
P.O. Box 2926 (44005-2926)
PHONE.................440 964-3565
Fax: 440 964-3257
Tom Richter, *Opers Mgr*
Alexandra Vanallen, *Marketing Staff*
Beth Oliver, *Manager*
Dorthey Altonen, *Exec Dir*
EMP: 106
SQ FT: 35,000
SALES: 3.4MM **Privately Held**
SIC: 8331 5932 Vocational rehabilitation agency; used merchandise stores

(G-746)
HAPPY HEARTS SCHOOL
Also Called: Ashtabula Board of Mental
2505 S Ridge Rd E (44004-4493)
PHONE.................440 224-2157
Fax: 440 224-0678
Patrick Guliano, *Principal*
EMP: 125 **Privately Held**
WEB: www.help-a-child.com
SIC: 8322 Rehabilitation services
PA: County Of Ashtabula
  2505 S Ridge Rd E
  Ashtabula OH 44004
  440 224-2155

(G-747)
HEALTH SMILE CENTER
Also Called: Healthy Smile Center The
2010 W 19th St (44004-9709)
PHONE.................440 992-2700
Martin Crombie, *Owner*
EMP: 25
SALES (est): 1.3MM **Privately Held**
SIC: 8072 8021 Artificial teeth production; offices & clinics of dentists

(G-748)
HOSPICE OF THE WESTERN RESERVE
1166 Lake Ave (44004-2930)
PHONE.................440 997-6619
Fax: 440 997-6478
Cindy Baker, *Manager*
Cathy Westcott, *Manager*
Mary Temperney, *Director*
EMP: 57
SALES (corp-wide): 89.8MM **Privately Held**
SIC: 8082 8322 Home health care services; individual & family services
PA: Hospice Of The Western Reserve, Inc
  17876 Saint Clair Ave
  Cleveland OH 44110
  216 383-2222

(G-749)
ID NETWORKS INC
7720 Jefferson Rd (44004-9025)
P.O. Box 2986 (44005-2986)
PHONE.................440 992-0062
Douglas G Blenman, *President*
Bonnie Blenman, *Corp Secy*
Patrick Foster, *Project Mgr*
Corey Yovich, *Project Mgr*
Travis Malin, *Manager*
EMP: 31
SALES (est): 5.9MM **Privately Held**
WEB: www.idnetworks.com
SIC: 7373 Systems software development services

(G-750)
JBJ ENTERPRISES INC
Also Called: Top Performance
2450 W Prospect Rd (44004-6358)
PHONE.................440 992-6051
James Monday Jr, *President*
Elizabeth Monday, *Vice Pres*
John Monday, *Treasurer*
EMP: 45
SQ FT: 2,000
SALES (est): 1.3MM **Privately Held**
WEB: www.jbjenterprises.com
SIC: 7231 Hairdressers

(G-751)
JERSEY CENTRAL PWR & LIGHT CO
Also Called: Firstenergy
2210 S Ridge W (44004-9047)
PHONE.................440 994-8271
Bill Larson, *Manager*
Bill Shears, *Supervisor*
EMP: 67 **Publicly Held**
WEB: www.jersey-central-power-light.monmouth.n
SIC: 4911 Electric services
HQ: Jersey Central Power & Light Company
  76 S Main St
  Akron OH 44308
  800 736-3402

(G-752)
LOWES HOME CENTERS LLC
2416 Dillon Dr (44004-4102)
PHONE.................440 998-6555
Fax: 440 998-6553
Bob Caguin, *Office Mgr*
John Matras, *Manager*
EMP: 150
SALES (corp-wide): 68.6B **Publicly Held**
SIC: 5211 5031 5722 5064 Home centers; building materials, exterior; building materials, interior; household appliance stores; electrical appliances, television & radio
HQ: Lowe's Home Centers, Llc
  1605 Curtis Bridge Rd
  Wilkesboro NC 28697
  336 658-4000

(G-753)
LT HARNETT TRUCKING INC
2440 State Rd (44004-4163)
PHONE.................440 997-5528
Chuck Hughes, *Branch Mgr*
EMP: 50
SALES (corp-wide): 20.8MM **Privately Held**
SIC: 4212 4213 Local trucking, without storage; trucking, except local
PA: L.T. Harnett Trucking, Inc.
  7431 State Route 7
  Kinsman OH 44428
  330 876-2701

(G-754)
LT TRUCKING INC
Also Called: Harnett Vision Transportation
2440 State Rd (44004-4163)
PHONE.................440 997-5528
Fax: 440 997-5640
David Harnett, *President*
Chuck Hughes, *Manager*
Kevin Rybaik, *Manager*
EMP: 50
SALES: 15MM **Privately Held**
SIC: 4213 Contract haulers

(G-755)
MOHAWK FINE PAPERS INC
6642 Center Rd (44004-8945)
PHONE.................440 969-2049
EMP: 218
SALES (corp-wide): 233.6MM **Privately Held**
SIC: 5111 Fine paper
PA: Mohawk Fine Papers Inc.
  465 Saratoga St
  Cohoes NY 12047
  518 237-1740

(G-756)
NEW AVENUES TO INDEPENDENCE
4230 Lake Ave (44004-6845)
PHONE.................888 853-8905
Fax: 440 964-0172
Carol Blaasco, *President*
EMP: 25
SALES (corp-wide): 14.5MM **Privately Held**
SIC: 8361 Home for the mentally handicapped
PA: New Avenues To Independence Inc
  17608 Euclid Ave
  Cleveland OH 44112
  216 481-1907

(G-757)
NORFOLK SOUTHERN CORPORATION
645 E 6th St (44004-3517)
PHONE.................440 992-2274
Ben Johnson, *Manager*
EMP: 40
SALES (corp-wide): 10.5B **Publicly Held**
WEB: www.nscorp.com
SIC: 4011 Railroads, line-haul operating
PA: Norfolk Southern Corporation
  3 Commercial Pl Ste 1a
  Norfolk VA 23510
  757 629-2680

(G-758)
NORFOLK SOUTHERN CORPORATION
Also Called: Norfolk Sthern Ashtbula Cltock
2886 Harbor Sta (44004)
PHONE.................440 992-2215
Brian Johnson, *Manager*
EMP: 55
SALES (corp-wide): 10.5B **Publicly Held**
WEB: www.nscorp.com
SIC: 4011 Railroads, line-haul operating
PA: Norfolk Southern Corporation
  3 Commercial Pl Ste 1a
  Norfolk VA 23510
  757 629-2680

(G-759)
PARK HAVEN INC
Also Called: Park Haven Home
6434 Lee Road Ext (44004-4814)
PHONE.................440 992-9441
Fax: 440 992-7592
Beatrice Knowlson, *President*
Bill Knowlson Jr, *President*
EMP: 50
SALES (est): 1.5MM **Privately Held**
WEB: www.parkhavenhomeskillednursing.com
SIC: 8059 Nursing home, except skilled & intermediate care facility

(G-760)
PINNEY DOCK & TRANSPORT LLC
1149 E 5th St (44004-3513)
P.O. Box 41 (44005-0041)
PHONE.................440 964-7186
Fax: 440 964-5210
Ricki Seaman, *Terminal Mgr*
John Mead, *Finance*
Lee Demers,
Bradley Frank,
◆ **EMP:** 33
SQ FT: 20,000
SALES (est): 7.4MM **Publicly Held**
SIC: 3731 4491 5032 Drydocks, floating; docks, piers & terminals; limestone
PA: Kinder Morgan Inc
  1001 La St Ste 1000
  Houston TX 77002

Ashtabula - Ashtabula County (G-761)

(G-761)
SAFETY-KLEEN SYSTEMS INC
1302 W 38th St (44004-5434)
PHONE............................440 992-8665
Kevin Gozzard, *Branch Mgr*
EMP: 27
SALES (corp-wide): 2.9B **Publicly Held**
SIC: 7359 Equipment rental & leasing
HQ: Safety-Kleen Systems, Inc.
  2600 N Central Expy # 400
  Richardson TX 75080
  972 265-2000

(G-762)
SALUTARY PROVIDERS INC
Also Called: Carington Park
2217 West Ave (44004-3107)
PHONE............................440 964-8446
Mindy Rizzo, *Purch Mgr*
Diana Walton, *Office Mgr*
Cindy Woodburn, *Manager*
Robert Whitehouse, *Director*
EMP: 203
SALES (corp-wide): 2.1MM **Privately Held**
SIC: 8059 8052 8051 Convalescent home; intermediate care facilities; skilled nursing care facilities
PA: Salutary Providers Inc
  8230 Beckett Park Dr
  West Chester OH

(G-763)
SHAWNEE OPTICAL INC
3705 State Rd (44004-5957)
PHONE............................440 997-2020
Bob Leonardi, *Branch Mgr*
EMP: 51
SALES (corp-wide): 2.4MM **Privately Held**
SIC: 8042 5995 5049 Contact lense specialist optometrist; optical goods stores; optical goods
PA: Shawnee Optical Inc
  2240 E 38th St Ste 2
  Erie PA 16510
  814 824-3937

(G-764)
SPECTRUM MGT HOLDG CO LLC
2904 State Rd (44004-5328)
PHONE............................440 319-3271
Valentin Vargas, *Branch Mgr*
EMP: 83
SALES (corp-wide): 41.5B **Publicly Held**
SIC: 4841 Cable television services
HQ: Spectrum Management Holding Company, Llc
  400 Atlantic St
  Stamford CT 06901
  203 905-7801

(G-765)
UNION INDUSTRIAL CONTRACTORS
Also Called: UIC General Contractors
1800 E 21st St (44004-4012)
P.O. Box 1718 (44005-1718)
PHONE............................440 998-7871
Fax: 440 998-0026
Kim Kidner, *President*
Ryan Cochran, *Admin Sec*
EMP: 40 EST: 1978
SQ FT: 22,000
SALES: 10.9MM **Privately Held**
WEB: www.uicconstruction.com
SIC: 1542 1541 Commercial & office building, new construction; commercial & office buildings, renovation & repair; industrial buildings, new construction; renovation, remodeling & repairs: industrial buildings

(G-766)
VETERANS HEALTH ADMINISTRATION
Also Called: Ashtabula County V A Clinic
4314 Main Ave Frnt (44004-6894)
PHONE............................866 463-0912
EMP: 264 **Publicly Held**
WEB: www.veterans-ru.org
SIC: 8011 9451 Clinic, operated by physicians; psychiatric clinic;
HQ: Veterans Health Administration
  810 Vermont Ave Nw
  Washington DC 20420

(G-767)
VOLPONE ENTERPRISES INC
Also Called: Ziggler Heating
5223 N Ridge Rd W Ste 2 (44004-8851)
PHONE............................440 969-1141
Tim Volpone, *President*
EMP: 27
SALES (est): 1.3MM **Privately Held**
SIC: 1711 Warm air heating & air conditioning contractor

(G-768)
YMCA OF ASHTABULA COUNTY INC
Also Called: ASHTABULA COUNTY FAMILY Y
263 W Prospect Rd (44004-5841)
PHONE............................440 997-5321
Fax: 440 992-5899
Stacy Herr, *Vice Pres*
Henri De Villiers, *Finance*
Trevor Sprague, *Exec Dir*
Carol Molnar, *Director*
Annette Griffin, *Director*
EMP: 75
SALES: 1.2MM **Privately Held**
SIC: 8641 7997 Social associations; recreation association; membership sports & recreation clubs

Ashville
Pickaway County

(G-769)
CITIZENS BANK OF ASHVILLE OHIO (PA)
26 Main St E (43103-1512)
P.O. Box 227 (43103-0227)
PHONE............................740 983-2511
Fax: 740 983-2515
Calvin Gebhart, *President*
Amanda Triplet, *Assistant VP*
Lafern Bailey, *Vice Pres*
Geralyn Martin, *Vice Pres*
David Moody, *Vice Pres*
EMP: 27
SALES: 4.4MM **Privately Held**
SIC: 6022 State trust companies accepting deposits, commercial

(G-770)
NOXIOUS VEGETATION CONTROL INC
Also Called: Novco
14923 State Route 104 (43103-9411)
P.O. Box 21757, Columbus (43221-0757)
PHONE............................614 486-8994
Charles W Thomas, *President*
Clarence Wissinger, *General Mgr*
Donna Thomas, *Vice Pres*
Todd Thomas, *Vice Pres*
Clarence Wissiner, *Vice Pres*
EMP: 100
SQ FT: 8,000
SALES (est): 29.1MM **Privately Held**
WEB: www.helicopterminitmen.com
SIC: 5191 Herbicides

Athens
Athens County

(G-771)
AMERICAN ELECTRIC POWER CO INC
9135 State Route 682 (45701-9102)
PHONE............................740 594-1988
Dave Corrigan, *Principal*
Charles Spires, *Opers Mgr*
EMP: 45
SALES (corp-wide): 15.4B **Publicly Held**
SIC: 4911 Distribution, electric power
PA: American Electric Power Company, Inc.
  1 Riverside Plz Fl 1 # 1
  Columbus OH 43215
  614 716-1000

(G-772)
APPALACHIAN COMMUNITY VISI
444 W Union St Ste C (45701-2340)
PHONE............................740 594-8226
Deborah Sechkar, *Vice Pres*
Margaret Frey, *Director*
Patty Mercer, *Director*
EMP: 75
SQ FT: 8,000
SALES: 3.5MM **Privately Held**
WEB: www.acvna.org
SIC: 8082 Visiting nurse service

(G-773)
ATCO INC
21 Campbell St (45701-2697)
PHONE............................740 592-6659
Fax: 740 594-7814
Jodi Harris, *Superintendent*
Laurie Gregg, *Business Mgr*
EMP: 150
SQ FT: 18,000
SALES: 466.7K **Privately Held**
WEB: www.atcoinc.org
SIC: 8331 7331 Sheltered workshop; direct mail advertising services

(G-774)
ATHENS GOLF & COUNTRY CLUB (PA)
Also Called: ATHENS COUNTRY CLUB
7606 Country Club Rd (45701-8844)
PHONE............................740 592-1655
Fax: 740 592-3475
Rick Oremus, *President*
Rick Frame, *General Mgr*
Mark Felcman, *Vice Pres*
EMP: 50
SQ FT: 5,000
SALES: 924.6K **Privately Held**
SIC: 7997 Country club, membership

(G-775)
ATHENS MEDICAL ASSOCIATES LLC
Also Called: River Rose Obstetrics & Gyneco
75 Hospital Dr Ste 216 (45701-2859)
PHONE............................740 594-8819
Richard F Castrop, *Mng Member*
Terry Seath, *Administration*
EMP: 51
SALES (est): 4.9MM **Privately Held**
SIC: 8099 Medical services organization

(G-776)
ATHENS OH 1013 LLC
Also Called: Fairfield Inn
924 E State St (45701-2116)
PHONE............................740 589-5839
Jack Bortle, *Mng Member*
EMP: 25
SQ FT: 47,613
SALES (est): 785.6K **Privately Held**
SIC: 7011 Hotels & motels

(G-777)
ATHENS-HCKING CNTY RECYCL CTRS
Also Called: Refuse / Recycling
5991 Industrial Park Rd (45701-8736)
P.O. Box 2607 (45701-5407)
PHONE............................740 797-4208
Fax: 740 797-4604
Joe Kalser, *Principal*
Joe Kasler, *Manager*
EMP: 26
SQ FT: 150,000
SALES: 2.4MM **Privately Held**
SIC: 4953 Recycling, waste materials

(G-778)
ATTRACTIONS
19 N Court St (45701-2420)
PHONE............................740 592-5600
Leslie Cornwell, *Owner*
EMP: 29
SALES (est): 690K **Privately Held**
SIC: 7231 7299 7241 Hairdressers; tanning salon; barber shops

(G-779)
CORPORATION FOR OH APPALACHIAN (PA)
Also Called: Coad
1 Pinchot Pl (45701-2135)
P.O. Box 787 (45701-0787)
PHONE............................740 594-8499
Fax: 740 592-5994
Owen Yoder, *CFO*
Mary Lewis, *Manager*
Alvin Norris, *Exec Dir*
Richard Roller, *Exec Dir*
Ronald Rees, *Director*
EMP: 32 EST: 1972
SQ FT: 168
SALES: 25.3MM **Privately Held**
WEB: www.coadinc.org
SIC: 8322 Individual & family services

(G-780)
COUNTY OF ATHENS
Also Called: County Engineers Office
16000 Canineville Rd (45701)
PHONE............................740 593-5514
Fax: 740 592-4616
Archie Stanley, *Principal*
EMP: 27
SQ FT: 20,000 **Privately Held**
SIC: 8711 9111 Consulting engineer; county supervisors' & executives' offices
PA: County Of Athens
  15 S Court St Rm 234
  Athens OH 45701
  740 592-3219

(G-781)
COUNTY OF ATHENS
Also Called: Athens County Childrens Svcs
18 Stonybrook Dr (45701-1451)
P.O. Box 1046 (45701-1046)
PHONE............................740 592-3061
Fax: 740 593-3880
Catherine Hill, *Director*
EMP: 80 **Privately Held**
WEB: www.opd.state.oh.us
SIC: 8351 9111 Child day care services; county supervisors' & executives' offices
PA: County Of Athens
  15 S Court St Rm 234
  Athens OH 45701
  740 592-3219

(G-782)
DAVID R WHITE SERVICES INC (PA)
Also Called: David White Services
5315 Hebbardsville Rd (45701-8973)
P.O. Box 250 (45701-0250)
PHONE............................740 594-8381
Fax: 740 593-6326
Gayman Chambers, *President*
Emily Jefferf, *Accounts Mgr*
EMP: 38
SQ FT: 16,000
SALES (est): 6.9MM **Privately Held**
SIC: 1711 Warm air heating & air conditioning contractor

(G-783)
DON WOOD BCK OLDSMBLE PNTIAC C
900 E State St (45701-2116)
PHONE............................740 593-6641
Don Wood, *CEO*
Chad Hixenbaugh, *Sales Mgr*
EMP: 100
SQ FT: 10,000
SALES (est): 18.5MM **Privately Held**
SIC: 5511 7538 Automobiles, new & used; general automotive repair shops

(G-784)
DON WOOD INC
Also Called: Don Wood GMC & Toyota
900 E State St (45701-2116)
PHONE............................740 593-6641
Fax: 740 593-8092
Donald Wood, *President*
Jeff Wood, *President*
Ryan Leadbetter, *General Mgr*
Brent Hanson, *Business Mgr*
Bob Swain, *Business Mgr*
EMP: 70

GEOGRAPHIC SECTION
Athens - Athens County (G-806)

SALES (est): 29.9MM Privately Held
WEB: www.donwood.com
SIC: 5511 7538 5521 Automobiles, new & used; general automotive repair shops; used car dealers

(G-785)
ECHOING HILLS VILLAGE INC
Also Called: Echoing Meadows
528 1/2 Richland Ave (45701-3748)
PHONE...................740 594-3541
Fax: 740 593-5270
Heather Buckley, Social Dir
Mark Hutchinson, Administration
DEA Bartlett, Admin Sec
EMP: 65
SALES (est): 1.3MM
SALES (corp-wide): 25.3MM Privately Held
WEB: www.echoinghillsvillage.org
SIC: 7032 8361 Sporting & recreational camps; residential care
PA: Echoing Hills Village, Inc.
   36272 County Road 79
   Warsaw OH 43844
   740 327-2311

(G-786)
EDISON BIOTECHNOLOGY INSTITUTE
101 Konneker The Rdgs (45701)
PHONE...................740 593-4713
Shiyong Wu, Director
EMP: 45
SALES (est): 1.9MM Privately Held
SIC: 8731 Biological research

(G-787)
ERIC HASEMEIER DO
Also Called: On Call Medical
510 W Union St Ste A (45701-2331)
PHONE...................740 594-7979
Fax: 740 594-5090
Eric Hasemeier Do, Owner
EMP: 25
SALES (est): 780K Privately Held
SIC: 8031 8011 Offices & clinics of osteopathic physicians; offices & clinics of medical doctors

(G-788)
G & J PEPSI-COLA BOTTLERS INC
2001 E State St (45701-2125)
PHONE...................740 593-3366
Fax: 740 592-2971
Curt Allison, Branch Mgr
EMP: 51
SALES (corp-wide): 475.8MM Privately Held
WEB: www.gjpepsi.com
SIC: 4225 5149 2086 General warehousing; beverages, except coffee & tea; carbonated beverages, nonalcoholic: bottled & canned
PA: G & J Pepsi-Cola Bottlers Inc
   9435 Waterstone Blvd # 290
   Cincinnati OH 45249
   513 785-6060

(G-789)
GENESIS RESPIRATORY SVCS INC
25 E Stimson Ave (45701-2644)
PHONE...................740 456-4363
Rosalie K Williams, Branch Mgr
EMP: 30
SALES (corp-wide): 14MM Privately Held
SIC: 7389 Personal service agents, brokers & bureaus
PA: Genesis Respiratory Services, Inc.
   4132 Gallia St
   Portsmouth OH 45662
   740 354-4363

(G-790)
HAVAR INC (PA)
396 Richland Ave (45701-3204)
P.O. Box 460 (45701-0460)
PHONE...................740 594-3533
Fax: 740 593-3894
Jerrad Willis, Business Mgr
Mitch Daugherty, Program Mgr
Barb Mugrage, Program Mgr
Lisa Simpson, Program Mgr
Carla Perry, Manager
EMP: 75
SQ FT: 3,300
SALES (est): 3.6MM Privately Held
WEB: www.havar.com
SIC: 8361 8322 Residential care; individual & family services

(G-791)
HEALTH RECOVERY SERVICES INC (PA)
224 Columbus Rd Ste 102 (45701-1350)
P.O. Box 724 (45701-0724)
PHONE...................740 592-6720
Fax: 740 592-6728
Virginia Smith, Finance Dir
Lisa Betts, Manager
Steve Coates, Manager
Tony Deluca, Manager
Kim Gebura, Manager
EMP: 185 EST: 1975
SALES (est): 13.2MM Privately Held
WEB: www.hrs.org
SIC: 8069 8361 Alcoholism rehabilitation hospital; rehabilitation center, residential: health care incidental

(G-792)
HOCKING VLY BNK OF ATHENS CO (PA)
7 W Stimson Ave (45701-2649)
PHONE...................740 592-4441
Fax: 740 594-3147
Benedict Weissenrieder, CEO
Tammy Bobo, Vice Pres
M Nisley, Loan Officer
EMP: 45 EST: 1963
SALES (est): 10.3MM Privately Held
SIC: 6022 State trust companies accepting deposits, commercial

(G-793)
HOLZER CLINIC LLC
2131 E State St (45701-2138)
PHONE...................740 589-3100
Sue Campbell, Manager
Judith Lubbers, Family Practiti
EMP: 112
SALES (corp-wide): 323.8MM Privately Held
SIC: 8011 Clinic, operated by physicians
HQ: Holzer Clinic Llc
   90 Jackson Pike
   Gallipolis OH 45631
   740 446-5411

(G-794)
INTEGRATED SERVICES OF APPALA
11 Graham Dr (45701-1430)
P.O. Box 132 (45701-0132)
PHONE...................740 594-6807
Fax: 740 594-9967
Susan Isaac, President
Karen Kaufman, Area Mgr
Cheryl Brooks, Finance
Stephen Poling, Personnel Exec
Kevin Gillespie, Director
EMP: 80
SQ FT: 1,000
SALES: 12.9MM Privately Held
WEB: www.integratedservice.org
SIC: 8322 8399 8331 Individual & family services; health systems agency; job training & vocational rehabilitation services

(G-795)
JOEY BOYLE
Also Called: Athens Bicycle Club
11 Garfield Ave (45701-1650)
P.O. Box 624 (45701-0624)
PHONE...................216 273-8317
Joey Boyle, Owner
EMP: 30
SALES (est): 114K Privately Held
SIC: 8641 Civic social & fraternal associations

(G-796)
KAL ELECTRIC INC
5265 Hebbardsville Rd (45701-8973)
PHONE...................740 593-8720
Fax: 740 767-3602
Dirk Walton, CEO
Kay Proffitt, Vice Pres
Laurie Walton, Treasurer
Katlyn Walton, Admin Sec
EMP: 46
SALES (est): 6.1MM Privately Held
WEB: www.kalelectric.com
SIC: 1731 General electrical contractor

(G-797)
KIMES CONVALESCENT CENTER
75 Kimes Ln (45701-3899)
PHONE...................740 593-3391
Fax: 740 594-3053
Richard Buckley, Owner
EMP: 45
SALES: 4.5MM Privately Held
SIC: 8051 Convalescent home with continuous nursing care

(G-798)
LAUGHLIN MUSIC & VENDING SVC (PA)
Also Called: Laughlin Music and Vending Svc
148 W Union St (45701-2728)
P.O. Box 547 (45701-0547)
PHONE...................740 593-7778
Fax: 740 593-7770
Harold D Laughlin, President
Dewey Laughlin, Corp Secy
Naomi Laughlin, Vice Pres
EMP: 29
SQ FT: 100,000
SALES (est): 4.3MM Privately Held
SIC: 5962 5063 5087 Sandwich & hot food vending machines; electrical apparatus & equipment; laundry equipment & supplies

(G-799)
LOWES HOME CENTERS LLC
983 E State St (45701-2117)
PHONE...................740 589-3750
Fax: 740 589-3753
Dave Matter, Principal
Mike Grueser, Store Mgr
EMP: 150
SALES (corp-wide): 68.6B Publicly Held
SIC: 5211 5031 5722 5064 Home centers; building materials, exterior; building materials, interior; household appliance stores; electrical appliances, television & radio
HQ: Lowe's Home Centers, Llc
   1605 Curtis Bridge Rd
   Wilkesboro NC 28697
   336 658-4000

(G-800)
MALONE WAREHOUSE TIRE INC
5239 Hebbardsville Rd (45701-8973)
PHONE...................740 592-2893
Fax: 740 592-6048
Deslar Malone, President
Sandra M Malone, Principal
Darrin Malone, Vice Pres
▲ EMP: 35
SQ FT: 14,200
SALES (est): 15.3MM Privately Held
SIC: 5014 Automobile tires & tubes

(G-801)
MENTAL HEALTH AND ADDI SERV
Also Called: Appalchian Bhvioral Healthcare
100 Hospital Dr (45701-2301)
PHONE...................740 594-5000
Fax: 740 592-6707
David Myles, Safety Mgr
Corrie Callaghan, QA Dir
Kelly Sole, CFO
Don Bowers, Director
Lori Brown, Director
EMP: 35 Privately Held
SIC: 8093 9431 Mental health clinic, outpatient;
HQ: Ohio Department Of Mental Health And Addiction Services
   30 E Broad St Fl 8
   Columbus OH 43215

(G-802)
MOTEL PARTNERS LLC
Also Called: Baymont Inn & Suites
20 Home St (45701-2039)
PHONE...................740 594-3000
Thomas Parfitt, Managing Prtnr
Brent Hayes, Managing Prtnr
Glena Smith, Info Tech Mgr
EMP: 25
SALES (est): 963.8K Privately Held
SIC: 7011 Inns

(G-803)
OHIO STATE UNIVERSITY
Also Called: Southeast Asia Collection
1 Park Pl (45701-5005)
PHONE...................740 593-2657
Fax: 740 593-2692
Jeff Ferrier, Manager
John Howell, Assoc Prof
EMP: 100
SALES (corp-wide): 5.5B Privately Held
WEB: www.ohio-state.edu
SIC: 8732 8221 Educational research; university
PA: The Ohio State University
   Student Acade Servi Bldg
   Columbus OH 43210
   614 292-6446

(G-804)
OHIO UNIVERSITY
Also Called: Computer Services
3 Station St Apt D (45701-2760)
PHONE...................740 593-1000
Marlo M Tinkham, Managing Dir
Dewayne Starkey, Principal
Karin Sandell, Top Exec
Paul Pettit, Transportation
Ryan Rawas, Engineer
EMP: 60
SALES (corp-wide): 531.5MM Privately Held
WEB: www.zanesville.ohiou.edu
SIC: 7371 8221 Custom computer programming services; university
PA: Ohio University
   1 Ohio University
   Athens OH 45701
   740 593-1000

(G-805)
OHIO UNIVERSITY
Also Called: Woub Public Media
Woub 35 S Cllg St 395 (45701)
PHONE...................740 593-1771
Cheri Russo, Editor
Tom Hodson, Director
EMP: 38
SQ FT: 120,982
SALES (corp-wide): 531.5MM Privately Held
SIC: 4833 4832 Television broadcasting stations; radio broadcasting stations, except music format
PA: Ohio University
   1 Ohio University
   Athens OH 45701
   740 593-1000

(G-806)
OHIO UNIVERSITY
Also Called: Woub Channel 20 & 44
35 S College St (45701-2933)
PHONE...................740 593-1771
Fax: 740 593-0240
Mark Brower, General Mgr
Jean Cunningham, Marketing Mgr
Tim Sharp, Director
Christopher France, Professor
Ashok Gupta, Professor
EMP: 35
SALES (corp-wide): 531.5MM Privately Held
WEB: www.zanesville.ohiou.edu
SIC: 4832 4833 Radio broadcasting stations; television broadcasting stations
PA: Ohio University
   1 Ohio University
   Athens OH 45701
   740 593-1000

(PA)=Parent Co (HQ)=Headquarters (DH)=Div Headquarters
✪ = New Business established in last 2 years

Athens - Athens County (G-807)   GEOGRAPHIC SECTION

(G-807)
OHIO UNIVERSITY
Also Called: Medical Office
227 W Washington St Apt 1 (45701-2442)
PHONE..................................740 593-2195
Peter Dane, *Principal*
Michael H Rowe, *Otolaryngology*
Ellen Fultz, *Assistant*
EMP: 52
SALES (corp-wide): 531.5MM **Privately Held**
WEB: www.zanesville.ohiou.edu
SIC: 8011 8211 Medical centers; elementary & secondary schools
PA: Ohio University
  1 Ohio University
  Athens OH 45701
  740 593-1000

(G-808)
OHIO UNIVERSITY
Ohio Univ Student Health Svcs
2 Health Center Dr Rm 110 (45701-2907)
PHONE..................................740 593-1660
James Kemper, *VP Human Res*
Jacqueline Legg, *Manager*
Gerardine Botte, *Manager*
Dave Steortz, *Manager*
Alfred Weiner, *Director*
EMP: 35
SALES (corp-wide): 531.5MM **Privately Held**
WEB: www.zanesville.ohiou.edu
SIC: 8011 8221 Offices & clinics of medical doctors; university
PA: Ohio University
  1 Ohio University
  Athens OH 45701
  740 593-1000

(G-809)
OHIO VALLEY HOME HEALTH INC
2097 E State St Ste B1 (45701-2156)
PHONE..................................740 249-4219
Donna Williams, *Mktg Dir*
Summer Atkinson, *Branch Mgr*
April Burgette, *Administration*
EMP: 31
SALES (corp-wide): 5MM **Privately Held**
SIC: 8082 Home health care services
PA: Ohio Valley Home Health Inc
  1480 Jackson Pike
  Gallipolis OH 45631
  740 441-1393

(G-810)
PARKS RECREATION ATHENS
Also Called: Community Center
701 E State St (45701-2110)
PHONE..................................740 592-0046
Richard Campitelli, *Director*
EMP: 50 **EST:** 2000
SALES (est): 1.7MM **Privately Held**
SIC: 7033 Recreational vehicle parks

(G-811)
SHELTERING ARMS HOSPITAL FOUND
Also Called: OHIOHEALTH O'BLENESS HOSPITAL
55 Hospital Dr (45701-2302)
PHONE..................................740 592-9300
Fax: 740 592-9200
Larry Thornhill, *CEO*
Mark Seckinger, *President*
Greg Long, *President*
Clifford Young, *Principal*
Lynn Anastas, *Vice Pres*
EMP: 368 **EST:** 1948
SQ FT: 127,500
SALES: 96.3MM
SALES (corp-wide): 3.7B **Privately Held**
SIC: 8062 General medical & surgical hospitals
PA: Ohiohealth Corporation
  180 E Broad St
  Columbus OH 43215
  614 788-8860

(G-812)
SPECTRUM MGT HOLDG CO LLC
28 Station St (45701-2757)
PHONE..................................740 200-3385
Steve Hewitt, *Branch Mgr*
EMP: 83
SALES (corp-wide): 41.5B **Publicly Held**
SIC: 4841 Cable television services
HQ: Spectrum Management Holding Company, Llc
  400 Atlantic St
  Stamford CT 06901
  203 905-7801

(G-813)
SUNPOWER INC
2005 E State St Ste 104 (45701-2125)
PHONE..................................740 594-2221
Fax: 740 593-7531
Thomas Matros, *Business Mgr*
Jeffrey Hatfield, *Vice Pres*
Michael Kienitz, *Vice Pres*
Bill Hammer, *Research*
Steven Carpenter, *Electrical Engi*
EMP: 95
SQ FT: 16,000
SALES (est): 15.6MM
SALES (corp-wide): 4.3B **Publicly Held**
WEB: www.sunpower.com
SIC: 8731 8711 8733 3769 Commercial physical research; engineering services; physical research, noncommercial; scientific research agency; guided missile & space vehicle parts & auxiliary equipment
HQ: Advanced Measurement Technology, Inc.
  801 S Illinois Ave
  Oak Ridge TN 37830
  865 482-4411

(G-814)
TASC OF SOUTHEAST OHIO
86 Columbus Rd (45701-1300)
PHONE..................................740 594-2276
Fax: 740 594-3105
Stephen Thomas, *CEO*
Cherilyn Warner, *President*
EMP: 28 **EST:** 2003
SALES (est): 175.9K **Privately Held**
SIC: 8322 Individual & family services

(G-815)
TRI COUNTY MENTAL HEALTH SVCS (PA)
Also Called: TRAC
90 Hospital Dr (45701-2301)
PHONE..................................740 592-3091
Toll Free:..........................888 -
Fax: 740 594-5642
George P Weigly, *CEO*
Gary Cordingley, *Med Doctor*
George Weigly, *Exec Dir*
EMP: 204
SALES: 150.4K **Privately Held**
WEB: www.epilepsyservices.org
SIC: 8093 8361 8011 Mental health clinic, outpatient; home for the mentally handicapped; offices & clinics of medical doctors

(G-816)
TRI COUNTY MENTAL HEALTH SVCS
90 Hospital Dr (45701-2301)
PHONE..................................740 594-5045
George Weigly, *Branch Mgr*
Terry Hayes, *Officer*
EMP: 99
SALES (corp-wide): 150.4K **Privately Held**
SIC: 8093 Mental health clinic, outpatient
PA: Tri County Mental Health Services Inc
  90 Hospital Dr
  Athens OH 45701
  740 592-3091

(G-817)
TS TECH AMERICAS INC
TS Tech North America
10 Kenny Dr (45701-9406)
PHONE..................................740 593-5958
Dave Snapp, *Engineer*
Bill Hass, *Manager*
Bill Hess, *Manager*
EMP: 43
SALES (corp-wide): 3.7B **Privately Held**
SIC: 5099 Child restraint seats, automotive
HQ: Ts Tech Americas, Inc.
  8458 E Broad St
  Reynoldsburg OH 43068
  614 575-4100

(G-818)
UNITED PARCEL SERVICE INC OH
Also Called: UPS
1 Kenny Dr (45701-9406)
PHONE..................................740 592-4570
Matthew Kazmirski, *Manager*
EMP: 50
SALES (corp-wide): 65.8B **Publicly Held**
WEB: www.upsscs.com
SIC: 4215 Parcel delivery, vehicular
HQ: United Parcel Service, Inc. (Oh)
  55 Glenlake Pkwy
  Atlanta GA 30328
  404 828-6000

(G-819)
UNIVERSITY MEDICAL ASSOC INC
350 Parks Hall (45701-1359)
PHONE..................................740 593-0753
Scott Jenkinson, *Principal*
Melinda Ford, *Family Practiti*
EMP: 150
SALES: 11MM **Privately Held**
SIC: 8011 Offices & clinics of medical doctors

(G-820)
WHITE & CHAMBERS PARTNERSHIP
Also Called: Manufactured Comfort
5315 Hebbardsville Rd (45701-8973)
P.O. Box 250 (45701-0250)
PHONE..................................740 594-8381
David R White, *Partner*
Gayman Chambers, *Partner*
Sandra White, *Partner*
EMP: 40
SALES (est): 1.9MM **Privately Held**
WEB: www.davidwhiteservices.com
SIC: 6512 Commercial & industrial building operation

Attica
Seneca County

(G-821)
CLAY DISTRIBUTING CO
15025 E Us 224 (44807)
P.O. Box 581 (44807-0581)
PHONE..................................419 426-3051
Fax: 419 426-7325
Doug Beck, *President*
Dean Beck, *Corp Secy*
Brian Beck, *Vice Pres*
Ed Willman, *Vice Pres*
EMP: 30
SALES (est): 8.7MM
SALES (corp-wide): 209.2MM **Privately Held**
WEB: www.beckoil.com
SIC: 5172 Petroleum products
PA: Beck Suppliers, Inc.
  1000 N Front St
  Fremont OH 43420
  419 332-5527

(G-822)
NORTH CENTRAL ELC COOP INC
350 Stump Pike Rd (44807-9571)
P.O. Box 475 (44807-0475)
PHONE..................................800 426-3072
Fax: 419 426-1245
Richard Reichert, *President*
Markus I Bryant, *General Mgr*
Denny Schendler, *Vice Pres*
Duane E Frankard, *Treasurer*
Richard Lease, *Treasurer*
EMP: 44 **EST:** 1936
SQ FT: 27,000
SALES: 25.4MM **Privately Held**
WEB: www.ncelec.org
SIC: 4911 Distribution, electric power

Atwater
Portage County

(G-823)
ZENITH SYSTEMS LLC
9627 Price St Ne (44201-9602)
PHONE..................................216 406-7916
Paul Francisco, *President*
EMP: 367 **Privately Held**
SIC: 1731 Electrical work
PA: Zenith Systems, Llc
  5055 Corbin Dr
  Cleveland OH 44128

Aurora
Portage County

(G-824)
ANNA MARIA OF AURORA INC (PA)
Also Called: Kensington Care Center
889 N Aurora Rd (44202-9537)
PHONE..................................330 562-6171
Fax: 330 562-3572
Robert J Norton Jr, *President*
George Norton, *VP Admin*
Diane Barben, *Sls & Mktg Exec*
Ken Moss, *Controller*
Mindy Hershey, *Human Res Mgr*
EMP: 200
SQ FT: 100,000
SALES (est): 20.4MM **Privately Held**
WEB: www.annamariaofaurora.com
SIC: 8051 Skilled nursing care facilities

(G-825)
ANNA MARIA OF AURORA INC
849 Rural Rd (44202)
PHONE..................................330 562-3120
Robert J Norton Jr, *President*
EMP: 100
SALES (corp-wide): 20.4MM **Privately Held**
WEB: www.annamariaofaurora.com
SIC: 8051 Skilled nursing care facilities
PA: Anna Maria Of Aurora, Inc.
  889 N Aurora Rd
  Aurora OH 44202
  330 562-6171

(G-826)
AURORA HOTEL PARTNERS LLC
Also Called: Aurora Inn Hotel & Event Ctr
30 Shawnee Trl (44202-9385)
PHONE..................................330 562-0767
Stephen Mansfield,
EMP: 50
SQ FT: 42,682
SALES (est): 184.9K **Privately Held**
SIC: 7011 6513 5812 Resort hotel, franchised; residential hotel operation; American restaurant

(G-827)
AURORA MANOR SPECIAL CARE
101 S Bissell Rd (44202-9170)
PHONE..................................440 424-4000
Fax: 330 562-5181
Lenore Barnick, *Nursing Dir*
Joann Hall, *Executive*
Christa Mayes, *Administration*
EMP: 40
SALES (est): 3.4MM
SALES (corp-wide): 68.5MM **Privately Held**
WEB: www.nursehome.com
SIC: 8051 8093 Skilled nursing care facilities; rehabilitation center, outpatient treatment
PA: Saber Healthcare Group, L.L.C.
  26691 Richmond Rd Frnt
  Bedford OH 44146
  216 292-5706

GEOGRAPHIC SECTION
Aurora - Portage County (G-851)

(G-828)
B & I HOTEL MANAGEMENT LLC
Also Called: Bertram Inn
600 N Aurora Rd (44202-7107)
PHONE..................330 995-0200
Fax: 330 562-9163
Chris Papp, *Research*
Liss Cowell, *Controller*
Dale A Bradford, *Mng Member*
EMP: 150
SALES (est): 10.1MM **Privately Held**
WEB: www.thebertraminn.com
SIC: 7011 7991 5813 5812 Inns; physical fitness facilities; drinking places; eating places

(G-829)
BARRINGTON GOLF CLUB INC (PA)
350 N Aurora Rd (44202-7104)
PHONE..................330 995-0600
Fax: 330 562-9122
Dave Roberts, *General Mgr*
Jack Nicklaus, *Principal*
Richard A Rosner, *Principal*
Bill Thrush, *Comptroller*
Jeff Broer, *Manager*
EMP: 55
SALES (est): 8.9MM **Privately Held**
SIC: 7997 Golf club, membership

(G-830)
BARRINGTON GOLF CLUB INC
680 N Aurora Rd (44202-7107)
PHONE..................330 995-0821
EMP: 65
SALES (corp-wide): 8.9MM **Privately Held**
SIC: 7997 Golf club, membership
PA: Barrington Golf Club, Inc.
    350 N Aurora Rd
    Aurora OH 44202
    330 995-0600

(G-831)
BREEZY POINT LTD PARTNERSHIP
Also Called: Barrington Golf Club
350 N Aurora Rd (44202-7104)
PHONE..................330 995-0600
James A Schoff, *Branch Mgr*
Kathy Schneider, *Manager*
EMP: 40 **Privately Held**
SIC: 7997 7991 5813 5812 Golf club, membership; physical fitness facilities; drinking places; eating places
PA: Breezy Point Limited Partnership
    30575 Bnbridge Rd Ste 100
    Solon OH 44139

(G-832)
CABIN RESTAURANT
34 N Chillicothe Rd (44202-7780)
PHONE..................330 562-9171
Mario Liuzzo, *President*
EMP: 40
SALES (est): 215.2K **Privately Held**
SIC: 5812 7299 7011 Italian restaurant; miscellaneous personal service; hotels & motels

(G-833)
CALVIN KLEIN INC
549 S Chilcthe Rd Ste C11 (44202-8875)
PHONE..................330 562-2746
Fax: 330 562-2474
Mary Jo Mullins, *Branch Mgr*
EMP: 50
SALES (corp-wide): 8.9B **Publicly Held**
SIC: 7699 Cleaning services
HQ: Calvin Klein, Inc.
    205 W 39th St Lbby 2
    New York NY 10018
    212 719-2600

(G-834)
CERRUTI LLC
Also Called: Aurora Inn and Conference Ctr
30 Shawnee Trl (44202-9385)
PHONE..................330 562-0120
Fax: 330 562-5249
Nina Parson, *Manager*
Manu Patel,
EMP: 25

SALES (est): 1.6MM **Privately Held**
SIC: 7011 Hotels

(G-835)
CERTANTEED GYPS CILING MFG INC
1192 S Chillicothe Rd (44202-9201)
PHONE..................800 233-8990
EMP: 40
SALES (est): 5.1MM
SALES (corp-wide): 185.8MM **Privately Held**
SIC: 1742 Acoustical & ceiling work
HQ: Certanteed Corporation
    20 Moores Rd
    Malvern PA 19355
    610 893-5000

(G-836)
CITY OF AURORA
158 W Pioneer Trl (44202-9103)
PHONE..................330 562-8662
Fax: 330 562-1306
Ann Womer Benjamin, *Mayor*
Leah Cellura, *Asst Director*
EMP: 99 **Privately Held**
SIC: 1611 9111 Highway & street maintenance;
PA: City Of Aurora
    130 S Chillicothe Rd
    Aurora OH 44202
    330 562-6131

(G-837)
ELECTROVATIONS INC
350 Harris Dr (44202-7536)
PHONE..................330 274-3558
Fax: 330 995-3684
R Charles Vermerris, *President*
EMP: 25
SQ FT: 4,500
SALES (est): 1.9MM **Privately Held**
SIC: 8711 7389 3357 Electrical or electronic engineering; design, commercial & industrial; nonferrous wiredrawing & insulating

(G-838)
FINE- LINE COMMUNICATIONS INC
400 Walnut Ridge Trl (44202-7676)
P.O. Box 91 (44202-0091)
PHONE..................330 562-0731
Fax: 330 405-4762
Barbara Hoover, *President*
Curt Hoover, *Vice Pres*
EMP: 30
SALES (est): 2.4MM **Privately Held**
WEB: www.finelinecomm.com
SIC: 1731 Communications specialization

(G-839)
FUNTIME PARKS INC
Also Called: Six Flags Ohio
1060 N Aurora Rd (44202-8749)
PHONE..................330 562-7131
Gary Story, *President*
James Dannhauser, *CFO*
Todd Sasala, *MIS Dir*
John Gannon, *Director*
James Coughlin, *Admin Sec*
EMP: 175
SQ FT: 20,000
SALES (est): 2.2MM
SALES (corp-wide): 64.8MM **Privately Held**
WEB: www.six-flags.com
SIC: 7996 Theme park, amusement
PA: Six Flags Theme Parks Inc.
    924 E Avenue J
    Grand Prairie TX 75050
    972 595-5000

(G-840)
GODFREY & WING INC (PA)
220 Campus Dr (44202-6663)
PHONE..................330 562-1440
Christopher Gilmore, *President*
Brad Welch, *Corp Secy*
Karen Gilmore, *Vice Pres*
Denise Bidgood, *Accountant*
Barb Fetzer, *Accountant*
▲ EMP: 50
SQ FT: 68,000

SALES (est): 19.3MM **Privately Held**
SIC: 3479 8734 Coating of metals with plastic or resins; testing laboratories

(G-841)
HOWARD HANNA SMYTHE CRAMER
195 Barrington Town Sq Dr (44202-7790)
PHONE..................330 562-6188
Fax: 330 562-6352
Dottie Dupree, *Manager*
Dotty Dupuy, *Manager*
Laura Bejger, *Executive*
Mary Strimple, *Real Est Agnt*
EMP: 55
SALES (corp-wide): 76.4MM **Privately Held**
WEB: www.smythecramer.com
SIC: 6531 Real estate agents & managers
HQ: Howard Hanna Smythe Cramer
    6000 Parkland Blvd
    Cleveland OH 44124
    216 447-4477

(G-842)
ILPEA INDUSTRIES INC
OEM/Miller
1300 Danner Dr (44202-9284)
PHONE..................330 562-2916
Fax: 330 562-7635
John Gourley, *Opers Mgr*
Jim Severt, *Warehouse Mgr*
Mike Frys, *Purchasing*
Darrell Carson, *QC Dir*
Kathy Goode, *Personnel*
EMP: 135
SALES (corp-wide): 212.4MM **Privately Held**
WEB: www.holmindustries.com
SIC: 3089 5162 3083 Plastic containers, except foam; plastics sheets & rods; laminated plastics plate & sheet
PA: Ilpea Industries, Inc.
    745 S Gardner St
    Scottsburg IN 47170
    812 752-2526

(G-843)
JIT PACKAGING AURORA INC
1250 Page Rd (44202-6666)
PHONE..................330 562-8080
Rick Macdonald, *President*
Albert N Salvatore, *Principal*
Marian Maulis, *Purch Dir*
Kenneth Ddagg, *CFO*
Stefana Popobiciu, *Controller*
EMP: 27
SALES (est): 11.1MM **Privately Held**
SIC: 5113 Corrugated & solid fiber boxes

(G-844)
KAPSTONE CONTAINER CORPORATION
Also Called: Filmco
1450 S Chillicothe Rd (44202-9282)
P.O. Box 239 (44202-0239)
PHONE..................330 562-6111
Reed Kimbell, *Production*
Sue Burkholder, *Purchasing*
John Vamosi, *QC Dir*
Richard Pohland, *Branch Mgr*
Marianne Martone, *Director*
EMP: 106
SQ FT: 20,000
SALES (corp-wide): 3.3B **Publicly Held**
SIC: 3081 5199 2671 Packing materials, plastic sheet, packaging materials, packaging paper & plastics film, coated & laminated
HQ: Kapstone Container Corporation
    1601 Blairs Ferry Rd Ne
    Cedar Rapids IA 52402
    319 393-3610

(G-845)
MARC GLASSMAN INC
Also Called: Marc's 45
300 Aurora Commons Cir (44202-8828)
PHONE..................330 995-9246
Fax: 330 995-9259
Michael Lamay, *Manager*
EMP: 160

SALES (corp-wide): 1.3B **Privately Held**
WEB: www.marcs.com
SIC: 5331 7384 5912 Variety stores; photofinish laboratories; drug stores & proprietary stores
PA: Marc Glassman, Inc.
    5841 W 130th St
    Cleveland OH 44130
    216 265-7700

(G-846)
MARIOS INTERNATIONAL SPA & HT (PA)
Also Called: Mario's Beauty Salon
34 N Chillicothe Rd (44202-7780)
PHONE..................330 562-5141
Fax: 330 562-5380
Mario Liuzzo, *President*
Sheryl Greve, *Corp Secy*
Joanne Liuzzo, *Vice Pres*
Bryon Miller, *Controller*
EMP: 140
SALES (est): 2.2MM **Privately Held**
SIC: 7231 7991 7011 5812 Cosmetology & personal hygiene salons; spas; hotels; Italian restaurant; health food restaurant

(G-847)
MARK DURA INC
11384 Chamberlain Rd (44202)
P.O. Box 868 (44202-0868)
PHONE..................330 995-0883
Fax: 330 995-0884
Curtis Britton, *CEO*
Frank Gibson, *CFO*
EMP: 30
SQ FT: 13,000
SALES: 8MM **Privately Held**
SIC: 1721 Pavement marking contractor

(G-848)
MILL DISTRIBUTORS INC
45 Aurora Industrial Pkwy (44202-8088)
PHONE..................330 995-9200
Fax: 330 995-9207
Thomas H Wieder, *President*
Mark Blace, *President*
Douglas M Wieder, *Corp Secy*
Chris Sorna, *Purch Mgr*
Jennifer Whitacre, *Buyer*
▲ EMP: 53 EST: 1926
SQ FT: 40,000
SALES (est): 44.3MM **Privately Held**
WEB: www.milldist.com
SIC: 5023 5021 Blankets; bedspreads; sheets, textile; pillowcases; furniture; mattresses; chairs

(G-849)
PARTSSOURCE INC
777 Lena Dr (44202-8025)
PHONE..................330 562-9900
Fax: 330 562-9901
Philip Settimi, *President*
Mike Maguire, *Senior VP*
Mark Critchfield, *Vice Pres*
Mike Poling, *Vice Pres*
Stephen Smeyak, *Vice Pres*
EMP: 210
SQ FT: 75,000
SALES (est): 141.8MM **Privately Held**
WEB: www.partssource.com
SIC: 5047 Medical equipment & supplies

(G-850)
PNC BANK NATIONAL ASSOCIATION
7044 N Aurora Rd (44202-9626)
PHONE..................330 562-9700
Fax: 330 562-9733
Jeff Dyrlund, *Branch Mgr*
EMP: 162
SALES (corp-wide): 18B **Publicly Held**
SIC: 6029 6021 Commercial banks; national commercial banks
HQ: Pnc Bank, National Association
    222 Delaware Ave
    Wilmington DE 19801
    877 762-2000

(G-851)
REALTY ONE INC
195 Barrington Town Sq Dr (44202-7790)
PHONE..................330 562-2277
Fax: 330 562-2282
Diane Barbin, *Manager*

Aurora - Portage County (G-852)

GEOGRAPHIC SECTION

EMP: 44
SALES (corp-wide): 67.8MM Privately Held
WEB: www.realty-1st.com
SIC: 6531 Real estate agents & managers
HQ: Realty One, Inc.
  800 W Saint Clair Ave
  Cleveland OH 44113
  216 328-2500

(G-852)
ROBECK FLUID POWER CO
350 Lena Dr (44202-8098)
PHONE..................330 562-1140
Fax: 330 562-1141
Peter Becker, President
Ken Traeger, Corp Secy
Sherri Meloy, Purchasing
Robert Long, Engineer
Dave Nagle, Engineer
▲ EMP: 65
SQ FT: 6,000
SALES (est): 71.1MM Privately Held
WEB: www.robeckfluidpower.com
SIC: 5084 3593 3594 3494 Hydraulic systems equipment & supplies; fluid power cylinders & actuators; fluid power pumps & motors; valves & pipe fittings

(G-853)
ROVISYS BUILDING TECH LLC (PA)
Also Called: Rovisys Building Tech Rbt
260 Campus Dr (44202-6663)
PHONE..................330 954-7600
Derek Drayer, Managing Prtnr
Peter Madonia, Controller
EMP: 32
SQ FT: 1,000
SALES (est): 1.3MM Privately Held
SIC: 7373 Computer integrated systems design

(G-854)
ROVISYS COMPANY (PA)
1455 Danner Dr (44202-9273)
PHONE..................330 562-8600
Fax: 330 562-8688
John W Robertson, President
Freda Keelin, Vice Pres
Melanie Bukovec, Engineer
Christopher Evans, Engineer
Josh Fellows, Engineer
EMP: 146
SQ FT: 35,000
SALES (est): 77.4MM Privately Held
WEB: www.rovisys.com
SIC: 8711 Consulting engineer

(G-855)
SEAWORLD ENTERTAINMENT INC
1100 Squires Rd (44202-8706)
PHONE..................330 562-8101
Fax: 330 995-2091
EMP: 32
SALES (corp-wide): 1.3B Publicly Held
SIC: 7996 Marine Theme Park
PA: Seaworld Entertainment, Inc.
  9205 Southpark Center Loo
  Orlando FL 32819
  407 226-5011

(G-856)
TECHNICAL CONSUMER PDTS INC
Also Called: T C P
325 Campus Dr (44202-6662)
PHONE..................800 324-1496
Kaj Den Daas, CEO
Solomon Yan, President
Rebecca Harmon, Business Mgr
Jim Connolly, Senior VP
Bill Tortora, Senior VP
▲ EMP: 292
SQ FT: 159,000
SALES (est): 219.7MM Privately Held
WEB: www.technicalconsumerproducts.com
SIC: 5063 Lighting fittings & accessories

(G-857)
TWO-X ENGNERS CONSTRUCTERS LLC
570 Club Dr (44202-6305)
P.O. Box 906 (44202-0906)
PHONE..................330 995-0592
Kenneth Finnerty, Mng Member
Sam Waren, Mng Member
EMP: 45
SALES: 7.8MM Privately Held
SIC: 1521 Single-family housing construction

(G-858)
UNITED TECHNICAL SUPPORT SVCS
206 E Garfield Rd (44202-9301)
PHONE..................330 562-3330
Fax: 330 562-2988
James Cecil, CEO
Jeannete Giovanielli, Opers Mgr
Doug Szygenda, Opers Mgr
Larry Cornell, Admin Sec
EMP: 75
SQ FT: 5,000
SALES (est): 12.6MM Privately Held
SIC: 7373 Local area network (LAN) systems integrator

(G-859)
UNITED TECHNICAL SUPPORT SVCS
206 E Garfield Rd (44202-9301)
PHONE..................330 562-3330
EMP: 50
SQ FT: 5,000
SALES (est): 3MM
SALES (corp-wide): 13.4MM Privately Held
SIC: 7699 Repair Services
PA: United Technical Support Services, Inc
  206 E Garfield Rd
  Aurora OH 44202
  330 562-3330

(G-860)
VWR CHEMICALS LLC
Also Called: VWR International
220 Lena Dr (44202-9244)
PHONE..................330 425-2522
EMP: 36
SALES (corp-wide): 4.5B Privately Held
SIC: 5169 Chemicals & allied products
HQ: Vwr Chemicals, Llc
  3 Lincoln Blvd
  Rouses Point NY 12979
  518 297-4444

(G-861)
WALDEN CLUB
1119 Aurora Hudson Rd (44202-7512)
PHONE..................330 995-7162
Manuel Barenholtz, President
EMP: 80 EST: 1969
SQ FT: 10,000
SALES (est): 2.4MM Privately Held
SIC: 7997 5941 5812 Golf club, membership; tennis club, membership; golf goods & equipment; tennis goods & equipment; eating places

(G-862)
WALDEN COMPANY LTD
Also Called: Walden Country Club
1119 Aurora Hudson Rd (44202-7512)
PHONE..................330 562-7145
Fax: 330 562-5051
Robert J Rosencrans, Managing Prtnr
Manuel Barenholtz, Partner
Heather Thoman, Sales Mgr
Brenda Dye, Manager
Barrie Rosencrans, Director
EMP: 135
SALES (est): 5MM Privately Held
SIC: 5812 7997 Eating places; country club, membership

(G-863)
WALDEN TURF CENTER
375 Deer Island Dr (44202-8202)
PHONE..................330 995-0023
Rob Rosencrans, Owner
EMP: 50
SALES (est): 657.9K Privately Held
SIC: 0782 Turf installation services, except artificial

(G-864)
WATERWAY GAS & WASH COMPANY
7010 N Aurora Rd (44202-9626)
PHONE..................330 995-2900
Shayne Roche, General Mgr
Cathy Hemp, Manager
EMP: 47
SALES (corp-wide): 350.2MM Privately Held
SIC: 7542 Washing & polishing, automotive
PA: Waterway Gas & Wash Company
  727 Goddard Ave
  Chesterfield MO 63005
  636 537-1111

Austinburg
Ashtabula County

(G-865)
NASSIEF AUTOMOTIVE INC
Also Called: Nassief Honda
2920 Gh Dr (44010-9793)
PHONE..................440 997-5151
Fax: 440 992-9330
George Nassief, CEO
Todd Nassief, President
Ann Nassief, Corp Secy
Helen Nassief, Vice Pres
Denise Didonato, Sales Mgr
EMP: 32
SQ FT: 10,000
SALES (est): 10.4MM Privately Held
WEB: www.nassief.com
SIC: 5511 7538 Automobiles, new & used; trucks, tractors & trailers: new & used; general automotive repair shops

(G-866)
UNITED PARCEL SERVICE INC OH
Also Called: UPS
1553 State Route 45 (44010-9749)
PHONE..................440 275-3301
Carol Bianchi, Manager
EMP: 65
SALES (corp-wide): 65.8B Publicly Held
WEB: www.upsscs.com
SIC: 4215 Parcel delivery, vehicular
HQ: United Parcel Service, Inc. (Oh)
  55 Glenlake Pkwy
  Atlanta GA 30328
  404 828-6000

Austintown
Mahoning County

(G-867)
44444 LLC
Also Called: Target Trans-Logic
5783 Norquest Blvd (44515-2201)
P.O. Box 4043 (44515-0043)
PHONE..................330 502-2023
George Rood Jr, Mng Member
EMP: 38
SALES: 200K Privately Held
SIC: 4212 Mail carriers, contract

(G-868)
BROOKDALE SNIOR LVING CMMNTIES
Also Called: Brookdale Austintown
1420 S Canfield Niles Rd (44515-4040)
PHONE..................330 249-1071
Fax: 330 270-0400
Anna Jannecti, Manager
Charles Rupert, Exec Dir
EMP: 36
SALES (corp-wide): 4.7B Publicly Held
WEB: www.assisted.com
SIC: 8059 8051 Rest home, with health care; extended care facility
HQ: Brookdale Senior Living Communities, Inc.
  6737 W Wa St Ste 2300
  Milwaukee WI 53214
  414 918-5000

(G-869)
CHCC HOME HEALTH CARE
Also Called: Community Home Health
60 N Canfield Niles Rd # 50 (44515-2340)
PHONE..................330 759-4069
Brad Contel, Administration
EMP: 40
SALES (est): 94.9K Privately Held
SIC: 8082 8049 8059 Home health care services; occupational therapist; convalescent home

(G-870)
OHIO DEPARTMENT OF HEALTH
Also Called: Wic Program
50 Westchester Dr Ste 202 (44515-3991)
PHONE..................330 792-2397
EMP: 269 Privately Held
SIC: 8322 Individual & family services
HQ: Department Of Health Ohio
  246 N High St
  Columbus OH 43215

(G-871)
PRIMO PROPERTIES LLC
5555 Cerni Pl (44515-1159)
PHONE..................330 606-6746
Frank Pasqualetti, Owner
EMP: 36 EST: 2009
SQ FT: 50,400
SALES: 20MM Privately Held
SIC: 6512 Nonresidential building operators

(G-872)
R L LIPTON DISTRIBUTING LLC
425 Victoria Rd Ste B (44515-2029)
PHONE..................800 321-6553
Fax: 330 629-8726
Martin Lipton, President
Edward Carissimi, Manager
Leonard Ganley, Manager
Jim Gill, Info Tech Dir
Kraig Barth, Associate
EMP: 70
SALES (est): 14.6MM Privately Held
WEB: www.rllipton.com
SIC: 5149 Beverages, except coffee & tea

(G-873)
RHIEL SUPPLY CO INC (PA)
Also Called: Rhiel Supply Co, The
3735 Oakwood Ave (44515-3050)
PHONE..................330 799-7777
Fax: 330 799-2451
Toby Mirto, CEO
Daniel F Mirto, President
J D Mirto, Vice Pres
James Wade, Sales Mgr
Karen Blasko, Cust Mgr
EMP: 35
SQ FT: 30,000
SALES (est): 10.6MM Privately Held
WEB: www.rhiel.com
SIC: 5087 5169 Janitors' supplies; swimming pool & spa chemicals

Avon
Lorain County

(G-874)
ALL PRO FREIGHT SYSTEMS INC (PA)
1200 Chester Indus Pkwy (44011-1081)
PHONE..................440 934-2222
Fax: 440 934-2255
Chris Haas, President
Ken Gruman, Vice Pres
Matt Demyan, VP Opers
Matt Seedhouse, VP Opers
Ken Haas, Opers Mgr
EMP: 80
SQ FT: 109,000

GEOGRAPHIC SECTION

Avon - Lorain County (G-899)

SALES (est): 41.3MM **Privately Held**
WEB: www.allprofreight.com
SIC: **4225** 4214 4213 General warehousing & storage; general warehousing; local trucking with storage; trucking, except local; contract haulers

(G-875)
APEX INTERIORS INC
3233 Waterford Way (44011-2910)
PHONE..................330 327-2226
Tom Hershey, *President*
EMP: 26
SALES: 1.5MM **Privately Held**
SIC: **1742** Drywall

(G-876)
AVON OAKS COUNTRY CLUB
32300 Detroit Rd Ste A (44011-2097)
PHONE..................440 892-0660
Fax: 440 892-0660
Barb Russell, *Controller*
Ann Patterson, *Mktg Coord*
Judd Stevenson, *Director*
EMP: 65
SQ FT: 30,000
SALES (est): 4.3MM **Privately Held**
WEB: www.avonoakscc.com
SIC: **7997** Country club, membership

(G-877)
AVON PROPERTIES INC
Also Called: Bob O Link Golf Course
4141 Center Rd (44011-2347)
PHONE..................440 934-6217
Fax: 440 934-6398
William Fitch, *President*
Donna Fitch, *Treasurer*
EMP: 35
SQ FT: 1,500
SALES (est): 2.5MM **Privately Held**
SIC: **7992** 5941 Public golf courses; golf goods & equipment

(G-878)
AVONDALE GOLF CLUB
3111 Moon Rd (44011-1743)
PHONE..................440 934-4398
Fax: 440 934-4398
Jane K Egger, *President*
Carol Noll, *Partner*
George Noll, *Partner*
Linda Aery,
EMP: 32 EST: 1972
SALES (est): 1.2MM **Privately Held**
WEB: www.avondalegolfclub.com
SIC: **7992** 7997 Public golf courses; membership sports & recreation clubs

(G-879)
BEARING TECHNOLOGIES LTD (PA)
1141 Jaycox Rd (44011-1366)
PHONE..................440 937-4770
Fax: 440 937-4771
Laz Tromler, *CEO*
David Maxwell, *Accounts Mgr*
▲ EMP: 60 EST: 1997
SQ FT: 230,000
SALES (est): 32.8MM **Privately Held**
SIC: **5085** Bearings

(G-880)
BRADY HOMES INC
36741 Chester Rd (44011-1065)
PHONE..................440 937-6255
Fax: 440 937-6257
Shaun P Brady, *President*
Trevor Miller, *Pub Rel Dir*
EMP: 40
SQ FT: 900
SALES (est): 2.7MM **Privately Held**
WEB: www.bradyhomesinc.com
SIC: **1521** New construction, single-family houses; general remodeling, single-family houses

(G-881)
BRAMHALL ENGRG & SURVEYING CO (PA)
801 Moore Rd (44011-4051)
PHONE..................440 934-7878
Fax: 440 934-7879
Michael Bramhall, *President*
Chris Howard, *Vice Pres*
Valerie Kilmer, *Project Mgr*
Nicholas Sheffield, *Research*
James Scott, *Project Engr*
EMP: 33
SQ FT: 11,000
SALES: 3MM **Privately Held**
WEB: www.bramhall-engineering.com
SIC: **8711** 8713 Civil engineering; surveying services

(G-882)
BRIGHTVIEW LANDSCAPES LLC
1051 Lear Industrial Pkwy A (44011-1386)
PHONE..................440 937-5126
Fax: 440 937-2231
Matt Krems, *Manager*
Jim Louth, *Executive*
EMP: 47
SALES (corp-wide): 914MM **Privately Held**
SIC: **0781** Landscape services
HQ: Brightview Landscapes, Llc
  401 Plymouth Rd Ste 500
  Plymouth Meeting PA 19462
  484 567-7204

(G-883)
CARAVON GOLF COMPANY LTD
Also Called: Red Tail Golf Club
4400 Nagel Rd (44011-2736)
PHONE..................440 937-6018
Fax: 440 937-6275
Bob Buck, *General Mgr*
Robin Harabin, *Sales Staff*
Alex Katsaras, *Manager*
EMP: 61
SALES (est): 3.1MM
SALES (corp-wide): 4.6MM **Privately Held**
WEB: www.redtailgolfclub.com
SIC: **7997** Golf club, membership
PA: Caravon Golf Company, Ltd.
  27500 Detroit Rd Ste 300
  Cleveland OH 44145
  440 892-6800

(G-884)
CARROLL MANUFACTURING & SALES
Also Called: CMS
35179 Avon Commerce Pkwy (44011-1374)
PHONE..................440 937-3900
Chris Carroll, *President*
Colleen Carroll, *General Mgr*
Ron Mitchell, *CFO*
Ken Hynes, *VP Sales*
Jessica Neal, *Sales Staff*
▲ EMP: 50
SALES (est): 11MM **Privately Held**
WEB: www.carrollmfg.com
SIC: **5046** Commercial cooking & food service equipment

(G-885)
CELLCO PARTNERSHIP
Also Called: Verizon Wireless
36050 Detroit Rd (44011-1683)
PHONE..................440 934-0576
EMP: 71
SALES (corp-wide): 126B **Publicly Held**
SIC: **4812** Cellular telephone services
HQ: Cellco Partnership
  1 Verizon Way
  Basking Ridge NJ 07920

(G-886)
CHAMBERLAIN HR
36368 Detroit Rd Ste A (44011-2843)
PHONE..................216 589-9280
Henry Chamberlain, *Branch Mgr*
EMP: 102
SALES (corp-wide): 56.4MM **Privately Held**
SIC: **8111** General practice attorney, lawyer
PA: Chamberlain, Hrdlicka, White, Williams & Aughtry, P.C.
  1200 Smith St
  Houston TX 77002
  713 658-1818

(G-887)
CHAPMAN & CHAPMAN INC
36711 American Way Ste 2f (44011-4061)
PHONE..................440 934-4102
Walter K Chapman, *CEO*
Karen Spiewacki, *Admin Asst*
EMP: 35 EST: 1963
SALES (est): 3.6MM **Privately Held**
SIC: **6411** 8742 Insurance information & consulting services; financial consultant

(G-888)
CHEMTRON CORPORATION
35850 Schneider Ct (44011-1298)
PHONE..................440 937-6348
Fax: 440 937-6845
Andrew Kuhar, *President*
Michael Guenther, *Vice Pres*
Dawnn Perry, *Accountant*
Kathy Cook, *Administration*
EMP: 50
SQ FT: 16,500
SALES (est): 25.7MM **Privately Held**
WEB: www.chemtron-corp.com
SIC: **4953** 4959 Recycling, waste materials; refuse collection & disposal services; environmental cleanup services

(G-889)
CITY OF AVON
36080 Chester Rd (44011-1070)
PHONE..................440 937-5740
Jerry Plas, *Director*
EMP: 30 **Privately Held**
WEB: www.cityofavon.com
SIC: **1611** Highway & street maintenance
PA: City Of Avon
  36080 Chester Rd
  Avon OH 44011
  440 937-7800

(G-890)
CLEVELAND WHEELS
Also Called: Aircraft Wheels and Breaks
1160 Center Rd (44011-1208)
PHONE..................440 937-6211
Manny Nnay Bajakfoujian, *CEO*
George Brick, *Purchasing*
Joe Mendise, *Engineer*
Otto Miller, *Engineer*
Steve Myers, *Manager*
EMP: 99
SALES (est): 6.5MM **Privately Held**
SIC: **5088** 3799 Aircraft equipment & supplies; transportation equipment

(G-891)
COCHIN TECHNOLOGIES LLC
Also Called: Delight Connection
37854 Briar Lakes Dr (44011-3105)
PHONE..................440 941-4856
Robin Roy, *Principal*
EMP: 50
SALES: 2MM **Privately Held**
SIC: **7371** Computer software development

(G-892)
EMH REGIONAL MEDICAL CENTER
Also Called: Fitness Center
1997 Healthway Dr (44011-2834)
PHONE..................440 988-6800
Fax: 440 988-6810
Connie Hurst, *Buyer*
Sabarras George, *Manager*
Brad Calabrese, *Manager*
Sylvia Fedro, *Manager*
Sharon Kaczmarczyk, *Manager*
EMP: 100
SALES (corp-wide): 2.3B **Privately Held**
SIC: **8062** 7991 Hospital, affiliated with AMA residency; physical fitness facilities
HQ: Emh Regional Medical Center
  630 E River St
  Elyria OH 44035
  440 329-7500

(G-893)
FREEMAN MANUFACTURING & SUP CO (PA)
1101 Moore Rd (44011-4043)
PHONE..................440 934-1902
Fax: 440 934-7200
Gerald W Rusk, *Ch of Bd*
Lou Turco, *President*
Turco Matthew, *Vice Pres*
Matthew Turco, *Vice Pres*
Gene Horning, *Plant Mgr*
EMP: 50
SQ FT: 110,000
SALES (est): 70.2MM **Privately Held**
WEB: www.freemansupply.com
SIC: **5084** 3087 3543 2821 Industrial machinery & equipment; custom compound purchased resins; industrial patterns; plastics materials & resins

(G-894)
GODDARD SCHOOL OF AVON
2555 Hale St (44011-1856)
PHONE..................440 934-3300
Fax: 440 934-7037
John Keshock, *Owner*
Mark Reinhart, *Director*
EMP: 25
SALES (est): 517.4K **Privately Held**
SIC: **8351** Preschool center

(G-895)
GREAT LAKES COMPUTER CORP
33675 Lear Indus Pkwy (44011-1370)
PHONE..................440 937-1100
Jim Manco, *CEO*
Robert Martin, *Vice Pres*
David Doucette, *Opers Mgr*
Lorna Blair, *Human Res Dir*
Scot Ferris, *Manager*
EMP: 60
SQ FT: 20,000
SALES (est): 5MM **Privately Held**
WEB: www.grlakes.com
SIC: **7378** 5734 Computer peripheral equipment repair & maintenance; computer & software stores

(G-896)
HANNA HOLDINGS INC
Also Called: Howard Hanna Real Estate
2100 Center Rd Ste L (44011-1892)
PHONE..................440 933-6195
Meghan Kopp, *Branch Mgr*
EMP: 25
SALES (corp-wide): 76.4MM **Privately Held**
SIC: **6531** Real estate agent, residential
PA: Hanna Holdings, Inc.
  1090 Freeport Rd Ste 1a
  Pittsburgh PA 15238
  412 967-9000

(G-897)
HEALTHSPAN INTEGRATED CARE
Also Called: Kaiser Foundation Health Plan
36711 American Way Fl 1 (44011-4061)
PHONE..................440 937-2350
Melanie B Rolsen, *Branch Mgr*
EMP: 25
SALES (corp-wide): 4.2B **Privately Held**
SIC: **6324** Health maintenance organization (HMO), insurance only
HQ: Healthspan Integrated Care
  1001 Lakeside Ave E # 1200
  Cleveland OH 44114
  216 621-5600

(G-898)
HOME DEPOT USA INC
Also Called: Home Depot, The
35930 Detroit Rd (44011-1653)
PHONE..................440 937-2240
Fax: 440 937-0102
Ronald W Salazar, *Manager*
EMP: 100
SALES (corp-wide): 100.9B **Publicly Held**
WEB: www.homerentalsdepot.com
SIC: **5211** 7359 Home centers; tool rental
HQ: Home Depot U.S.A., Inc.
  2455 Paces Ferry Rd Se
  Atlanta GA 30339

(G-899)
J WAY LEASING LTD
1284 Miller Rd (44011-1004)
PHONE..................440 934-1020
Alan N Johnson,
Susan Lutz,
EMP: 30 EST: 1997
SQ FT: 26,000
SALES (est): 2.9MM **Privately Held**
SIC: **1629** 7359 Marine construction; equipment rental & leasing

Avon - Lorain County (G-900)

(G-900)
JENNE INC
33665 Chester Rd (44011-1307)
PHONE.....................440 835-0040
Fax: 440 835-2788
Dave Johnson, *CEO*
Rose M Jenne, *Ch of Bd*
Dean M Jenne, *President*
Ray Jenne Jr, *President*
Andrew Dominick, *Business Mgr*
▲ EMP: 200
SQ FT: 126,000
SALES (est): 270.4MM **Privately Held**
WEB: www.jenne.com
SIC: 7371 7382 Software programming applications; security systems services

(G-901)
KAISER FOUNDATION HOSPITALS
Also Called: Avon Medical Offices
36711 American Way (44011-4062)
PHONE.....................216 524-7377
Fax: 440 937-2313
EMP: 593
SALES (corp-wide): 82.6B **Privately Held**
SIC: 8011 Offices & clinics of medical doctors
HQ: Kaiser Foundation Hospitals Inc
1 Kaiser Plz
Oakland CA 94612
510 271-6611

(G-902)
KASSOUF COMPANY
2231 Lilac Ln (44011-2610)
PHONE.....................216 651-3333
Fax: 216 651-3839
Robert J Kassouf, *President*
Rocco A Dipuccio, *Treasurer*
Rocco Dipuccio, *Treasurer*
Michael Martin, *Controller*
Natalie Strouse, *CIO*
EMP: 25 EST: 1927
SQ FT: 10,000
SALES (est): 2.7MM **Privately Held**
SIC: 1622 Tunnel construction

(G-903)
KMU TRUCKING & EXCVTG INC
4436 Center Rd (44011-2369)
PHONE.....................440 934-1008
Fax: 440 934-1908
Kevin Urig, *President*
Lorie Urig, *Vice Pres*
Connie Lanenga, *Manager*
Keith Urig, *Admin Sec*
EMP: 30
SALES (est): 20MM **Privately Held**
SIC: 1794 4212 Excavation & grading, building construction; local trucking, without storage

(G-904)
KUNO CREATIVE GROUP LLC
36901 American Way Ste 2a (44011-4058)
PHONE.....................440 225-4144
Martha Neff, *Editor*
Jarrick Cooper, *Accounts Mgr*
Maren Dickey, *Accounts Mgr*
Jackie Meter, *Accounts Mgr*
Cassandra Renner, *Accounts Mgr*
EMP: 27
SALES (est): 1.9MM **Privately Held**
WEB: www.kunocreative.com
SIC: 7374 7311 Computer graphics service; advertising agencies

(G-905)
LE CHAPERON ROUGE (PA)
1504 Travelers Pt (44011-4046)
PHONE.....................440 934-0296
Marie Bentley, *Director*
EMP: 41
SALES (est): 4.3MM **Privately Held**
SIC: 8351 Child day care services

(G-906)
LOWES HOME CENTERS LLC
1445 Center Rd (44011-1238)
PHONE.....................440 937-3500
Fax: 440 937-3503
James Collier, *Office Mgr*
Greg Fillar, *Manager*
EMP: 130
SALES (corp-wide): 68.6B **Publicly Held**
SIC: 5211 5031 5722 5064 Home centers; building materials, exterior; building materials, interior; household appliance stores; electrical appliances, television & radio
HQ: Lowe's Home Centers, Llc
1605 Curtis Bridge Rd
Wilkesboro NC 28697
336 658-4000

(G-907)
MERCY HEALTH
1480 Center Rd Ste A (44011-1239)
PHONE.....................440 937-4600
John W Escolas Do, *Principal*
EMP: 48
SALES (corp-wide): 4.2B **Privately Held**
SIC: 8011 General & family practice, physician/surgeon
PA: Mercy Health
1701 Mercy Health Pl
Cincinnati OH 45237
513 639-2800

(G-908)
NORTH COAST BEARINGS LLC
Also Called: After Market Products
1050 Jaycox Rd (44011-1312)
PHONE.....................440 930-7600
William Hagy, *President*
▲ EMP: 50
SQ FT: 30,000
SALES (est): 35.9MM **Privately Held**
SIC: 5085 Bearings

(G-909)
NORTH OHIO HEART CENTER INC
Also Called: Ohio Medical Group
1220 Moore Rd Ste B (44011-4044)
P.O. Box 714363, Columbus (43271-4363)
PHONE.....................440 204-4000
Ali N Assaad MD, *Med Doctor*
Philip D Wenschuh MD, *Med Doctor*
Gary Thome, *Manager*
EMP: 40
SALES (corp-wide): 13.5MM **Privately Held**
WEB: www.nohc.com
SIC: 8011 Cardiologist & cardio-vascular specialist
PA: North Ohio Heart Center, Inc
3600 Kolbe Rd Ste 127
Lorain OH 44053
440 204-4000

(G-910)
NVR INC
2553 Palmer Ln (44011-2048)
PHONE.....................440 933-7734
EMP: 33 **Publicly Held**
SIC: 1521 New construction, single-family houses
PA: Nvr, Inc.
11700 Plaza America Dr # 500
Reston VA 20190

(G-911)
OUR LADY OF WAYSIDE INC (PA)
38135 Colorado Ave (44011-1028)
PHONE.....................440 934-6152
Fax: 440 934-6327
Terry Davis, *CEO*
N Lindsey Smith, *Chairman*
Chris Zito, *Treasurer*
Laura Yates, *Human Resources*
Pam Barker, *Mktg Dir*
EMP: 360
SQ FT: 3,700
SALES (est): 27MM **Privately Held**
SIC: 8361 Home for the mentally handicapped; home for the physically handicapped

(G-912)
PAT YOUNG SERVICE CO INC
1260 Moore Rd Ste K (44011-4021)
PHONE.....................440 891-1550
Kirk Young, *Branch Mgr*
EMP: 40
SALES (corp-wide): 55.8MM **Privately Held**
WEB: www.pysfederated.com
SIC: 5013 Motor vehicle supplies & new parts
PA: Pat Young Service Co Inc
6100 Hillcrest Dr
Cleveland OH 44125
216 447-8550

(G-913)
PERSONAL LAWN CARE INC
3910 Long Rd (44011-2244)
PHONE.....................440 934-5296
Fax: 440 934-5328
Thomas Brunner, *President*
EMP: 30
SQ FT: 4,500
SALES (est): 2.7MM **Privately Held**
SIC: 0781 0782 Landscape architects; lawn care services

(G-914)
PHOENIX COSMOPOLITAN GROUP LLC
36550 Chester Rd Apt 1505 (44011-4003)
PHONE.....................814 746-4863
Tamarah Black, *CEO*
Michele Zieziula, *COO*
Leon Wilson, *CFO*
Stanislav Kostenko, *Controller*
EMP: 26
SALES (est): 2.1MM **Privately Held**
SIC: 8742 Management consulting services

(G-915)
R & J INVESTMENT CO INC
Also Called: Avon Oaks Nursing Home
37800 French Creek Rd (44011-1763)
PHONE.....................440 934-5204
Fax: 440 934-4787
Joan E Reidy, *President*
Juliette Reidy, *Corp Secy*
Karen Ortiz, *Vice Pres*
Richard J Reidy, *Vice Pres*
Paula Orchowski, *Office Mgr*
EMP: 130
SQ FT: 75,000
SALES (est): 8.1MM **Privately Held**
WEB: www.avonoaks.net
SIC: 8051 8351 Convalescent home with continuous nursing care; child day care services

(G-916)
RIVER PLUMBING INC
Also Called: River Plumbing & Supply
1756 Moore Rd (44011-1024)
P.O. Box 270 (44011-0270)
PHONE.....................440 934-3720
David Dobos, *President*
John Janner, *General Mgr*
Douglas Vaught, *Vice Pres*
Greg Talor, *Manager*
EMP: 38
SQ FT: 8,000
SALES: 3.5MM **Privately Held**
SIC: 1711 Plumbing contractors

(G-917)
SWEDA SWEDA ASSOCIATES INC
Also Called: GMAC Real Estate
5329 N Abbey (44011)
PHONE.....................419 433-4841
Fax: 440 934-1003
Richard Sweda, *President*
EMP: 40
SQ FT: 2,500
SALES (est): 1.9MM **Privately Held**
SIC: 6531 Real estate brokers & agents

(G-918)
WHITTGUARD SECURITY SERVICES
37435 Colorado Ave (44011-1531)
PHONE.....................440 288-7233
James Whitt, *Owner*
Art Keller, *Opers Mgr*
EMP: 130
SQ FT: 3,000
SALES: 1MM **Privately Held**
SIC: 7381 Security guard service

(G-919)
WICKENS HRZER PNZA COOK BTISTA
35765 Chester Rd (44011-1262)
PHONE.....................440 695-8000
Fax: 440 447-0998
David L Herzer, *President*
Corri Burns, *President*
Matthew Nakon, *Principal*
Joseph Cirigliano, *Vice Pres*
Rochelle Kuznicki, *Vice Pres*
EMP: 75
SQ FT: 30,000
SALES (est): 9.9MM **Privately Held**
SIC: 8111 General practice law office; general practice attorney, lawyer

(G-920)
WILLOWAY NURSERIES INC (PA)
4534 Center Rd (44011-2368)
P.O. Box 299 (44011-0299)
PHONE.....................440 934-4435
Fax: 440 934-4738
Tom Demaline, *President*
Cathy Kowalczyk, *Vice Pres*
Dale Hammersmith, *Prdtn Mgr*
Nicholas Moser, *Opers Staff*
Tim Cullinan, *Purchasing*
▲ EMP: 101
SQ FT: 5,000
SALES (est): 31.7MM **Privately Held**
WEB: www.willowaynurseries.com
SIC: 0181 Shrubberies grown in field nurseries; nursery stock, growing of; foliage, growing of

Avon Lake
Lorain County

(G-921)
APL LOGISTICS LTD
32608 Surrey Ln (44012-1643)
PHONE.....................440 930-2822
EMP: 245
SALES (corp-wide): 4.1B **Privately Held**
SIC: 4412 Deep sea foreign transportation of freight
HQ: Apl Logistics, Ltd.
17600 N Perimeter Dr # 150
Scottsdale AZ 85255
602 357-9100

(G-922)
AVON LAKE ANIMAL CLINIC INC
Also Called: Avon Lake Animal Care Center
124 Miller Rd (44012-1015)
PHONE.....................440 933-5297
Fax: 440 933-3258
James Haddad, *President*
John H Simpson Dvm, *Principal*
Frank J Krpuka Jr,
EMP: 45
SQ FT: 2,000
SALES (est): 5MM **Privately Held**
SIC: 0742 0752 Animal hospital services, pets & other animal specialties; veterinarian, animal specialties; grooming services, pet & animal specialties

(G-923)
AVON LAKE SHEET METAL CO
33574 Pin Oak Pkwy (44012-2320)
P.O. Box 64 (44012-0064)
PHONE.....................440 933-3505
Fax: 440 933-7160
Carl Wetzig Jr, *President*
Gary Wightman, *Corp Secy*
Dennis Lightfoot, *Draft/Design*
EMP: 38
SQ FT: 32,000
SALES (est): 8.8MM **Privately Held**
WEB: www.avonlakesheetmetal.com
SIC: 3444 1761 Sheet metalwork; sheet metalwork

(G-924)
CATAMARAN HOME DLVRY OHIO INC
Also Called: Ips
33381 Walker Rd (44012-1463)
PHONE.....................440 930-5520
Fax: 440 930-5540

GEOGRAPHIC SECTION

Baltic - Tuscarawas County (G-945)

Douglas Boodjeh, *Chairman*
Thomas Mc Connell, *VP Finance*
Stacy Kendeigh Cain, *Cust Mgr*
Brandon Hardin, *Pharmacist*
Christopher Simmons, *Pharmacy Dir*
EMP: 65
SALES (est): 7.6MM
SALES (corp-wide): 201.1B **Publicly Held**
WEB: www.ipsrx.com
SIC: 5961 5122 Pharmaceuticals, mail order; drugs, proprietaries & sundries
HQ: Catamaran Health Solutions Llc
800 King Farm Blvd # 400
Rockville MD 20850

(G-925)
CITY OF AVON LAKE
Also Called: Water & Sewer Department
201 Miller Rd (44012-1004)
PHONE.................................440 933-6226
Fax: 440 933-3854
Todd A Danielson, *Branch Mgr*
EMP: 36 **Privately Held**
WEB: www.sunsetshoresbb.com
SIC: 4941 4952 Water supply; sewerage systems
PA: City Of Avon Lake
150 Avon Belden Rd
Avon Lake OH 44012
440 933-6141

(G-926)
CLEVELAND CLINIC FOUNDATION
450 Avon Belden Rd (44012-2282)
PHONE.................................440 930-6800
Michael Iott, *Marketing Staff*
Katelyn Legros, *Marketing Staff*
Toby Cosgrove, *Manager*
Cassandra Indries, *Manager*
Miranda Kosik, *Consultant*
EMP: 85
SALES (corp-wide): 8B **Privately Held**
SIC: 6733 Trusts
PA: The Cleveland Clinic Foundation
9500 Euclid Ave
Cleveland OH 44195
216 636-8335

(G-927)
COMPREHENSIVE LOGISTICS CO INC
1200 Chester Indus Pkwy (44012)
PHONE.................................330 233-2627
Daryl Legg, *Branch Mgr*
EMP: 33 **Privately Held**
SIC: 8742 Management consulting services
PA: Comprehensive Logistics Co., Inc.
4944 Belmont Ave Ste 202
Youngstown OH 44505

(G-928)
DMR MANAGEMENT INC
Also Called: Fast Track Auction Sales
109 Brookfield Rd (44012-1504)
PHONE.................................513 771-1700
Ray Donsante, *President*
Carmen Donsante, *Vice Pres*
Michael Vescio, *Vice Pres*
EMP: 50
SALES: 12MM **Privately Held**
SIC: 7389 Auction, appraisal & exchange services

(G-929)
ED TOMKO CHRYSLR JEP DGE INC
33725 Walker Rd (44012-1010)
PHONE.................................440 835-5900
Fax: 440 933-7740
Edward P Tomko, *President*
Dolores Tomko, *Vice Pres*
Paul E Tomko, *Admin Sec*
EMP: 30
SQ FT: 8,000
SALES (est): 10.9MM **Privately Held**
SIC: 5511 7538 7515 5012 Automobiles, new & used; general automotive repair shops; passenger car leasing; automobiles & other motor vehicles

(G-930)
FLUID MECHANICS LLC (PA)
760 Moore Rd (44012-2317)
PHONE.................................216 362-7800
Thomas Koenig, *Treasurer*
Herwig Flug, *Mng Member*
James Stevenot, *Admin Sec*
Joanna Vardas, *Asst Sec*
EMP: 25 EST: 2015
SQ FT: 10,000
SALES (est): 9.7MM **Privately Held**
SIC: 5084 Engines & parts, diesel

(G-931)
H & B WINDOW CLEANING INC
753 Avon Belden Rd Ste D (44012-2253)
P.O. Box 42, Avon (44011-0042)
PHONE.................................440 934-6158
John Aunspaw, *President*
Donna Aunspaw, *Vice Pres*
EMP: 25
SQ FT: 1,777
SALES (est): 743.2K **Privately Held**
SIC: 7349 Window cleaning

(G-932)
HALL CONTRACTING SERVICES INC
33540 Pin Oak Pkwy (44012-2320)
P.O. Box 144, Florissant CO (80816-0144)
PHONE.................................440 930-0050
Richard Palmer, *President*
Graham Hall, *Chairman*
Judy Beiser, *Controller*
Tom Julius, *Manager*
▲ **EMP:** 55
SQ FT: 24,000
SALES (est): 5.4MM **Privately Held**
WEB: www.grhall.com
SIC: 7699 Printing trades machinery & equipment repair

(G-933)
KOPF CONSTRUCTION CORPORATION
Also Called: Aqua Marine Luxury Apartments
750 Aqua Marine Blvd (44012-2585)
PHONE.................................440 933-0250
David Klima, *Branch Mgr*
EMP: 73
SALES (corp-wide): 22.5MM **Privately Held**
SIC: 6513 Apartment building operators
PA: Kopf Construction Corporation
420 Avon Belden Rd Ste A
Avon Lake OH 44012
440 933-6908

(G-934)
LUBRIZOL ADVANCED MTLS INC
550 Moore Rd (44012-2313)
P.O. Box 134 (44012-0134)
PHONE.................................440 933-0400
Michael Mazur, *Opers Staff*
Rick Corry, *Mfg Staff*
Lawrence Thayer, *Chief Engr*
Joeri Plusnin, *Engineer*
Dmitry Shuster, *Engineer*
EMP: 50
SALES (corp-wide): 242.1B **Publicly Held**
WEB: www.pharma.noveoninc.com
SIC: 8731 2821 2899 Commercial physical research; plastics materials & resins; chemical preparations
HQ: Lubrizol Advanced Materials Inc.
9911 Brecksville Rd
Brecksville OH 44141
216 447-5000

(G-935)
M T BUSINESS TECHNOLOGIES
Also Called: Mt Business Technologies
33588 Pin Oak Pkwy (44012-2320)
PHONE.................................440 933-7682
Donald Cole, *Manager*
Rob Austin, *Manager*
Tom Fumich, *Manager*
EMP: 45
SALES (corp-wide): 10.2B **Publicly Held**
WEB: www.mtbustech.com
SIC: 5044 Office equipment

HQ: Mt Business Technologies, Inc.
1150 National Pkwy
Mansfield OH 44906
419 529-6100

(G-936)
NRG POWER MIDWEST LP
Also Called: Avon Lake Generating Station
33570 Lake Rd (44012-1108)
PHONE.................................440 930-6401
Fax: 440 930-6444
Kim Povolka, *Human Res Mgr*
Dan Rogatto, *Branch Mgr*
Robert Laeng, *Agent*
EMP: 54 **Publicly Held**
SIC: 4911 Generation, electric power
HQ: Nrg Power Midwest Lp
1000 Main St
Houston TX 77002

(G-937)
POLYONE CORPORATION (PA)
33587 Walker Rd (44012-1145)
PHONE.................................440 930-1000
Robert M Patterson, *Ch of Bd*
Richard N Altice, *President*
Mark D Crist, *President*
Craig M Nikrant, *President*
John V Van Hulle, *President*
◆ **EMP:** 73
SALES: 3.2B **Publicly Held**
WEB: www.polyone.com
SIC: 2821 3087 5162 3081 Thermoplastic materials; polyvinyl chloride resins (PVC); vinyl resins; custom compound purchased resins; resins; plastics basic shapes; unsupported plastics film & sheet

(G-938)
RAIL LOGISTICS INC (PA)
32861 Pin Oak Pkwy Ste D (44012-3502)
PHONE.................................440 933-6500
Thomas Novak, *President*
Dave Mahaney, *Regional Mgr*
Jennifer Young, *Human Resources*
Ruth Fritz, *Office Mgr*
Steven Dennis, *Manager*
EMP: 80
SQ FT: 1,500
SALES: 8MM **Privately Held**
WEB: www.raillogistics.com
SIC: 4013 Railroad terminals

(G-939)
SEMINOLE THEATER CO LLC
Also Called: Seminole 8 Theaters
32818 Walker Rd (44012-1473)
PHONE.................................440 934-6998
EMP: 25
SALES: 1.9MM **Privately Held**
SIC: 7832 Motion Picture Theater

(G-940)
WATTEREDGE LLC (DH)
567 Miller Rd (44012-2304)
PHONE.................................440 933-6110
Joseph P Langhenry, *President*
Erin Kobunski, *General Mgr*
Ken Ferrence, *Purchasing*
Benjamin Gontarz, *Engineer*
George Sass, *Project Engr*
◆ **EMP:** 64 EST: 1970
SQ FT: 65,000
SALES (est): 41.1MM
SALES (corp-wide): 2.5B **Privately Held**
WEB: www.watteredge.com
SIC: 5085 3643 5051 3052 Industrial supplies; current-carrying wiring devices; metals service centers & offices; rubber & plastics hose & beltings; miscellaneous metalwork
HQ: Coleman Cable, Llc
1530 S Shields Dr
Waukegan IL 60085
847 672-2300

Bainbridge
Ross County

(G-941)
COUNTRYSIDE RENTALS INC (PA)
Also Called: Rent To Own
210 S Quarry St (45612-9482)
P.O. Box 547 (45612-0547)
PHONE.................................740 634-2666
Fax: 740 634-2667
Michael D Tissot, *President*
James D Hapner, *Principal*
Ronald L Magee, *Principal*
Jane Tissot, *Corp Secy*
Heather Buchanan, *Purch Dir*
EMP: 26
SQ FT: 8,000
SALES (est): 31.1MM **Privately Held**
WEB: www.r2o.com
SIC: 7359 Television rental; electronic equipment rental, except computers; furniture rental

(G-942)
LIGHTHOUSE YOUTH SERVICES INC
Also Called: Paint Creek Youth Center
1071 Tong Hollow Rd (45612-1500)
P.O. Box 586 (45612-0586)
PHONE.................................740 634-3094
Fax: 740 634-3047
Merri J Layne, *Manager*
Renee Hagan, *Director*
EMP: 60
SALES (corp-wide): 25.2MM **Privately Held**
SIC: 8322 8361 Youth center; juvenile correctional facilities
PA: Lighthouse Youth Services, Inc.
401 E Mcmillan St
Cincinnati OH 45206
513 221-3350

(G-943)
W K H R RADIO
Also Called: FM 91 Point 5
17425 Snyder Rd (45612)
PHONE.................................440 708-0915
Rowland Shepard, *Vice Pres*
Bill Weisinger, *Engineer*
EMP: 30 EST: 1999
SALES (est): 122.8K **Privately Held**
SIC: 4832 Radio broadcasting stations

Baltic
Tuscarawas County

(G-944)
BALTIC HEALTH CARE CORP
Also Called: Oakponte Nrsing Rehabilitation
130 Buena Vista St (43804-9091)
PHONE.................................330 897-4311
Brian Colleran, *President*
Melanie Patrello, *Manager*
Bob Speelman, *Manager*
EMP: 99
SALES (est): 2.8MM **Privately Held**
SIC: 8099 Health & allied services

(G-945)
FLEX TECHNOLOGIES INC
Also Called: Poly Flex
3430 State Route 93 (43804-9705)
P.O. Box 300 (43804-0300)
PHONE.................................330 897-6311
Fax: 330 897-7000
Gglenn Burket, *Division Mgr*
Brian Harrison, *Manager*
Ken Ziegembusch, *Info Tech Mgr*
EMP: 35
SQ FT: 20,000
SALES (corp-wide): 65.3MM **Privately Held**
WEB: www.flextechnologies.com
SIC: 2821 5169 3087 Molding compounds, plastics; synthetic resins, rubber & plastic materials; custom compound purchased resins

Baltic - Tuscarawas County (G-946)

PA: Flex Technologies, Inc.
5479 Gundy Dr
Midvale OH 44653
740 922-5992

(G-946)
KEIM LUMBER COMPANY
State Rte 557 (43804)
PHONE................................330 893-2251
Bill Keim, *Branch Mgr*
EMP: 41
SALES (corp-wide): 37.3MM **Privately Held**
WEB: www.keimlumber.com
SIC: 5211 5031 Planing mill products & lumber; lumber: rough, dressed & finished
PA: Keim Lumber Company
4465 St Rte 557
Charm OH 44617
330 893-2251

(G-947)
SCHLABACH WOOD DESIGN INC
52567 State Route 651 (43804-9520)
PHONE................................330 897-2600
Fax: 330 897-8000
Willis Schlabach, *President*
Jonas Miller, *Purch Mgr*
Greg McElroy, *Sales Staff*
EMP: 32
SQ FT: 9,000
SALES (est): 3.3MM **Privately Held**
WEB: www.schlabachwooddesign.com
SIC: 1751 5211 Cabinet & finish carpentry; cabinets, kitchen

Baltimore
Fairfield County

(G-948)
MICRO CONSTRUCTION LLC
Also Called: Micro Roll Off Containers
8675 Lncster Newark Rd Ne (43105-9659)
P.O. Box 202 (43105-0202)
PHONE................................740 862-0751
Rusty Mock, *Mng Member*
John Dust, *Manager*
Tony P Mock,
EMP: 25
SALES (est): 1.7MM **Privately Held**
SIC: 4953 5032 Garbage: collecting, destroying & processing; granite building stone

Barberton
Summit County

(G-949)
AKROCHEM CORPORATION
2845 Newpark Dr (44203-1047)
PHONE................................330 535-2108
Jack Hale, *Branch Mgr*
EMP: 25
SALES (corp-wide): 106.1MM **Privately Held**
SIC: 5169 Chemicals & allied products
PA: Akrochem Corporation
3770 Embassy Pkwy
Akron OH 44333
330 535-2100

(G-950)
AKRON FOUNDRY CO
Also Called: Akron Electric
1025 Eagon St (44203-1603)
PHONE................................330 745-3101
Mike Pancoe, *General Mgr*
Sukhwant Puri, *Mfg Mgr*
Lawren Hamilton, *Production*
Predrag Djeric, *Engineer*
George Sam, *Accounts Mgr*
EMP: 40
SALES (corp-wide): 22MM **Privately Held**
WEB: www.akronfoundry.com
SIC: 1731 3699 3644 3444 Electrical work; electrical equipment & supplies; noncurrent-carrying wiring services; sheet metalwork; aluminum foundries

PA: Akron Foundry Co.
2728 Wingate Ave
Akron OH 44314
330 745-3101

(G-951)
AKRON PORCELAIN & PLASTICS CO
83 E State St (44203-2755)
P.O. Box 15157, Akron (44314-5157)
PHONE................................330 745-2159
George H Lewis III, *President*
M Dunphy, *Vice Pres*
EMP: 26
SQ FT: 47,900
SALES (est): 1.6MM
SALES (corp-wide): 21.1MM **Privately Held**
WEB: www.akronporcelain.com
SIC: 4225 General warehousing & storage
PA: The Akron Porcelain & Plastics Co
2739 Cory Ave
Akron OH 44314
330 745-2159

(G-952)
APPLE HEATING INC (PA)
Also Called: Apple Electric
344 4th St Nw (44203-2212)
PHONE................................440 997-1212
Fax: 440 992-6320
Scott Robinson, *President*
David Pinelli, *Vice Pres*
Barbara English, *Bookkeeper*
Rick Crowell, *Consultant*
Linda Hoffmann, *Director*
EMP: 26
SQ FT: 8,000
SALES (est): 3.1MM **Privately Held**
WEB: www.appleheating.com
SIC: 1711 Warm air heating & air conditioning contractor; hydronics heating contractor

(G-953)
ARIS HORTICULTURE INC (PA)
Also Called: Yoder Trading Company
115 3rd St Se (44203-4208)
PHONE................................330 745-2143
Fax: 330 753-5294
William Rasbach, *President*
Thomas D Doak, *Principal*
G Ramsey Yoder, *Chairman*
William Riffey, *Vice Pres*
Scott Schaefer, *CFO*
▲ **EMP:** 85
SQ FT: 28,000
SALES (est): 206.3MM **Privately Held**
WEB: www.yoder.com
SIC: 0181 Plants, foliage & shrubberies; florists' greens & flowers

(G-954)
BABCOCK & WILCOX CNSTR CO INC (DH)
74 Robinson Ave (44203-2630)
PHONE................................330 860-6301
Fax: 330 753-9354
E James Ferland, *CEO*
Mark S Low, *Senior VP*
D Paul Scavuzzo, *Senior VP*
Rod Carlson, *Vice Pres*
Robert Harrison, *Materials Mgr*
EMP: 94
SALES (est): 457.4MM
SALES (corp-wide): 1.5B **Publicly Held**
SIC: 1629 Power plant construction
HQ: The Babcock & Wilcox Company
20 S Van Buren Ave
Barberton OH 44203
330 753-4511

(G-955)
BABCOCK & WILCOX COMPANY (HQ)
20 S Van Buren Ave (44203-3585)
P.O. Box 351 (44203-0351)
PHONE................................330 753-4511
Fax: 330 860-1093
Leslie C Kass, *President*
Gregory Calvin, *President*
Leonard Bossart, *Regional Mgr*
Kevin Brolly, *Regional Mgr*
Fred Untch, *Regional Mgr*
◆ **EMP:** 1000 **EST:** 1867
SQ FT: 16,000

SALES (est): 831.8MM
SALES (corp-wide): 1.5B **Publicly Held**
SIC: 1629 1711 3443 7699 Industrial plant construction; power plant construction; plumbing, heating, air-conditioning contractors; fabricated plate work (boiler shop); boilers: industrial, power, or marine; boiler & heating repair services; management services; auto controls regulating residntl & coml environmt & applncs
PA: Babcock & Wilcox Enterprises, Inc.
13024 Balntyn Corp Pl # 700
Charlotte NC 28277
704 625-4900

(G-956)
BARBERTON AREA FAMILY PRACTICE
155 5th St Ne (44203-3332)
PHONE................................330 615-3205
Jon Elias, *Supervisor*
James Randall Richard, *Director*
Mary A Gesaman,
EMP: 40
SALES (est): 1.3MM **Privately Held**
SIC: 8011 General & family practice, physician/surgeon

(G-957)
BARBERTON JAYCEES
541 W Tuscarawas Ave # 104 (44203-2568)
P.O. Box 148 (44203-0148)
PHONE................................330 745-3733
Teri Dwyer, *President*
EMP: 45
SALES: 39.1K **Privately Held**
SIC: 8611 Junior Chamber of Commerce

(G-958)
BARBERTON LAUNDRY & CLEANING
Also Called: Liniform Service
1050 Northview Ave (44203-7197)
PHONE................................330 825-6911
Fax: 330 825-0920
Bertha Jenkins, *President*
A Edward Good, *Chairman*
Patricia Shultz, *Vice Pres*
EMP: 40
SQ FT: 35,000
SALES (est): 4.1MM **Privately Held**
WEB: www.liniform.com
SIC: 7213 7299 Uniform supply; clothing rental services

(G-959)
BLIND & SON LLC
Also Called: Tri-County Heating & Cooling
344 4th St Nw (44203-2212)
PHONE................................330 753-7711
Fax: 330 753-7522
William Blind, *Mng Member*
Joe Bilota,
John Hartman,
David Zahn,
EMP: 80
SQ FT: 15,000
SALES (est): 16.4MM **Privately Held**
SIC: 1711 Warm air heating & air conditioning contractor

(G-960)
CASEGOODS INC
130 31st St Nw (44203-7238)
PHONE................................330 825-2461
Mitchell Volk, *President*
Denise Volk, *Corp Secy*
EMP: 30
SALES (est): 2.8MM **Privately Held**
WEB: www.casegoods.com
SIC: 1751 Cabinet & finish carpentry

(G-961)
CHRISTIAN HEALTHCARE
127 Hazelwood Ave (44203-1316)
PHONE................................330 848-1511
Roger Kittelson, *CFO*
Norma Mull, *Supervisor*
Ron Betson, *Technology*
Chris Lavoie, *Technology*
Howard Russell, *Exec Dir*
EMP: 40

SALES: 220.3MM **Privately Held**
WEB: www.christianbrotherhood.org
SIC: 8011 Offices & clinics of medical doctors

(G-962)
CORPORATE ELECTRIC COMPANY LLC
Also Called: Electrical Construction
378 S Van Buren Ave (44203-4014)
P.O. Box 390, Akron (44309-0390)
PHONE................................330 331-7517
Crystal Bowers, *Office Mgr*
Marcus Sabo,
Rachel Collins,
EMP: 33
SALES (est): 2.7MM **Privately Held**
SIC: 1731 General electrical contractor

(G-963)
FOUR CORNERS CLEANING INC
3479 E Tuscarawas Ext (44203-3843)
PHONE................................330 644-0834
Timothy Horvath, *President*
Rebecca Horvath, *Vice Pres*
EMP: 50
SALES (est): 1.1MM **Privately Held**
SIC: 7349 Cleaning service, industrial or commercial

(G-964)
GENERAL PLASTEX INC
35 Stuver Pl (44203-2417)
PHONE................................330 745-7775
Fax: 330 745-6939
Renee Hershberger, *President*
Oscar Toris, *General Mgr*
David Mantyla, *VP Sales*
Anita Bader, *Executive*
EMP: 31
SQ FT: 52,500
SALES (est): 6.1MM **Privately Held**
SIC: 3452 7699 Bolts, nuts, rivets & washers; screws, metal; industrial machinery & equipment repair

(G-965)
HCR MANORCARE MED SVCS FLA LLC
Also Called: Manor Care
85 3rd St Se (44203-4208)
PHONE................................330 753-5005
Fax: 330 753-0820
Sara Fielding-Russell, *Director*
Mark Pluskota, *Director*
Lori Gardner, *Food Svc Dir*
Sara Filding-Russell, *Administration*
Kirby Long, *Maintence Staff*
EMP: 150
SQ FT: 31,749
SALES (corp-wide): 3.6B **Publicly Held**
WEB: www.manorcare.com
SIC: 8051 Convalescent home with continuous nursing care
HQ: Hcr Manorcare Medical Services Of Florida, Llc
333 N Summit St Ste 100
Toledo OH 43604
419 252-5500

(G-966)
INTEGRITY PROCESSING LLC
1055 Wooster Rd N (44203-1327)
P.O. Box 342, Chagrin Falls (44022-0342)
PHONE................................330 285-6937
Gerald F Robinson,
EMP: 30
SALES (est): 1.1MM **Privately Held**
SIC: 7699 Plastics products repair

(G-967)
JOSEPH R HARRISON COMPANY LPA
36 37th St Sw (44203-7321)
PHONE................................330 666-6900
Fax: 330 668-1013
Joseph R Harrison, *President*
Lazar John,
EMP: 42
SQ FT: 5,500
SALES (est): 3.7MM **Privately Held**
WEB: www.jrhlpa.com
SIC: 8111 General practice law office

GEOGRAPHIC SECTION

Barnesville - Belmont County (G-991)

(G-968)
JR ENGINEERING INC
123 9th St Nw (44203-2455)
P.O. Box 189 (44203-0189)
PHONE...................................330 848-0960
Louis Bilinovich Jr, *President*
EMP: 115
SQ FT: 725,000
SALES (corp-wide): 70.6MM **Privately Held**
SIC: 5084 5013 Industrial machinery & equipment; motor vehicle supplies & new parts
PA: Jr Engineering, Inc.
123 9th St Nw
Barberton OH 44203
330 848-0960

(G-969)
LABCARE
165 5th St Se Ste A (44203-9001)
PHONE...................................330 753-3649
Fax: 330 753-3643
Bobbi Butterfield, *Principal*
Linda Soto, *Manager*
EMP: 30
SALES (est): 419.4K **Privately Held**
SIC: 8071 8011 Medical laboratories; medical centers

(G-970)
LENNYS AUTO SALES INC
Also Called: Lenny's Collision Center
893 Wooster Rd N (44203-1637)
PHONE...................................330 848-2993
Fax: 330 848-4478
Leonard K Eicher, *President*
Brenda L Eicher, *Vice Pres*
EMP: 25
SQ FT: 7,000
SALES: 1MM **Privately Held**
WEB: www.lennyscollision.com
SIC: 7532 Collision shops, automotive; lettering & painting services

(G-971)
LOYAL OAK GOLF COURSE INC
2909 Clvland Massillon Rd (44203-5228)
PHONE...................................330 825-2904
Arthur Gruber, *President*
Katheryn Gruber, *Vice Pres*
Harold Corzin, *Admin Sec*
EMP: 30 **EST:** 1938
SALES (est): 1.3MM **Privately Held**
SIC: 7992 5813 5812 5941 Public golf courses; bar (drinking places); snack bar; golf goods & equipment

(G-972)
PLEASANT VIEW NURSING HOME (PA)
Also Called: Pleasant View Health Care Ctr
401 Snyder Ave (44203-4131)
PHONE...................................330 745-6028
Fax: 330 861-1200
Richard Morris, *President*
Phillip Gilcrest, *Director*
David Collins, *Maintence Staff*
Eileen Morris,
EMP: 99
SALES (est): 9.3MM **Privately Held**
SIC: 8051 Convalescent home with continuous nursing care

(G-973)
PLEASANT VIEW NURSING HOME
220 3rd St Se (44203-4235)
PHONE...................................330 848-5028
Fax: 330 848-5035
Richard Morris, *Branch Mgr*
EMP: 50
SALES (corp-wide): 9.3MM **Privately Held**
SIC: 8052 Personal care facility
PA: Pleasant View Nursing Home
401 Snyder Ave
Barberton OH 44203
330 745-6028

(G-974)
PSC METALS INC
284 7th St Nw (44203-2125)
PHONE...................................234 208-2331
EMP: 51

SALES (corp-wide): 21.7B **Publicly Held**
SIC: 5093 Metal scrap & waste materials
HQ: Psc Metals, Inc.
5875 Landerbrook Dr # 200
Mayfield Heights OH 44124
440 753-5400

(G-975)
PSC METALS INC
701 W Hopocan Ave (44203-2159)
PHONE...................................330 794-8300
Kim Mattler, *General Mgr*
Kris Coffield, *Manager*
Jim Vargo, *Manager*
EMP: 45
SALES (corp-wide): 21.7B **Publicly Held**
WEB: www.pscmetals.com
SIC: 5093 Metal scrap & waste materials
HQ: Psc Metals, Inc.
5875 Landerbrook Dr # 200
Mayfield Heights OH 44124
440 753-5400

(G-976)
PSC METALS INC
701 W Hopocan Ave (44203-2159)
PHONE...................................330 745-4437
Fax: 330 745-4137
Dave Casalinova, *Manager*
EMP: 42
SQ FT: 16,000
SALES (corp-wide): 21.7B **Publicly Held**
WEB: www.pscmetals.com
SIC: 5093 Metal scrap & waste materials
HQ: Psc Metals, Inc.
5875 Landerbrook Dr # 200
Mayfield Heights OH 44124
440 753-5400

(G-977)
RONDY FLEET SERVICES INC
255 Wooster Rd N (44203-8206)
PHONE...................................330 745-9016
Donald Rondy, *President*
Ronna Rondy, *Corp Secy*
Frank Moore, *Vice Pres*
EMP: 150
SALES (est): 13.5MM
SALES (corp-wide): 33.1MM **Privately Held**
WEB: www.rondy.net
SIC: 4731 7538 Freight transportation arrangement; general automotive repair shops
HQ: Tahoma Rubber & Plastics, Inc.
255 Wooster Rd N
Barberton OH 44203
330 745-9016

(G-978)
RT80 EXPRESS INC
4409 Clvland Massillon Rd (44203-5703)
P.O. Box 269 (44203-0269)
PHONE...................................330 706-0900
David Bilinovich, *President*
Pam Bilinovich, *Vice Pres*
Jeff Ellebruch, *Project Mgr*
Jason Presutto, *Traffic Mgr*
Christy Curtis, *Manager*
EMP: 30
SQ FT: 140,000
SALES (est): 4.7MM **Privately Held**
SIC: 4212 4213 Local trucking, without storage; trucking, except local

(G-979)
SKILLED NURSE CTR OF
155 5th St Ne (44203-3332)
PHONE...................................330 615-3717
Kevin McMan, *Administration*
EMP: 45 **EST:** 2013
SALES (est): 552.9K **Privately Held**
SIC: 8062 General medical & surgical hospitals

(G-980)
SUMMA HEALTH
Also Called: Lab Care
165 5th St Se Ste A (44203-9001)
PHONE...................................330 753-3649
Fran Royer, *Manager*
EMP: 70
SALES (corp-wide): 1B **Privately Held**
WEB: www.barbhosp.com
SIC: 8062 8071 General medical & surgical hospitals; medical laboratories

PA: Summa Health System
525 E Market St
Akron OH 44304
330 375-3000

(G-981)
SUMMA HEALTH
Also Called: Summa Barberton Hospital
155 5th St Ne (44203-3332)
PHONE...................................330 615-3000
Fax: 330 848-7820
Ronald J Elder, *Principal*
Sandra L Bailey Do, *Osteopathy*
Stephen A Dabreau Do, *Osteopathy*
EMP: 2701
SALES (corp-wide): 1B **Privately Held**
SIC: 8062 General medical & surgical hospitals
PA: Summa Health System
525 E Market St
Akron OH 44304
330 375-3000

(G-982)
TAHOMA ENTERPRISES INC (PA)
255 Wooster Rd N (44203-2560)
PHONE...................................330 745-9016
William P Herrington, *CEO*
Steven Strouse, *Managing Dir*
Warren Flathers, *Maint Mgr*
Charles Daugherty, *Opers Staff*
Marcia Berlin, *Manager*
EMP: 100
SALES (est): 33.1MM **Privately Held**
SIC: 3069 3089 5199 5162 Reclaimed rubber (reworked by manufacturing processes); plastic processing; foams & rubber; plastics products

(G-983)
TAHOMA RUBBER & PLASTICS INC (HQ)
Also Called: Rondy & Co.
255 Wooster Rd N (44203-2560)
PHONE...................................330 745-9016
Fax: 330 745-4886
William P Herrington, *CEO*
Steven Strouse, *Managing Dir*
Bob McGovern, *Plant Mgr*
Warren Flathers, *Maint Mgr*
Charles Daugherty, *Opers Staff*
▼ **EMP:** 100
SQ FT: 750,000
SALES: 23.8MM
SALES (corp-wide): 33.1MM **Privately Held**
WEB: www.rondy.net
SIC: 3069 3089 5199 5162 Reclaimed rubber (reworked by manufacturing processes); plastic processing; foams & rubber; plastics products
PA: Tahoma Enterprises, Inc.
255 Wooster Rd N
Barberton OH 44203
330 745-9016

(G-984)
WALGREEN CO
Also Called: Walgreens
900 Wooster Rd N (44203-1659)
PHONE...................................330 745-2674
Fax: 330 745-7398
Steve Krausa, *Manager*
EMP: 30
SALES (corp-wide): 118.2B **Publicly Held**
WEB: www.walgreens.com
SIC: 5912 7384 Drug stores; photofinishing laboratory
HQ: Walgreen Co.
200 Wilmot Rd
Deerfield IL 60015
847 315-2500

(G-985)
WESTERN & SOUTHERN LF INSUR CO
4172 Clvland Massillon Rd (44203-5704)
PHONE...................................330 825-9935
Fax: 330 825-9945
Joseph Parker, *Marketing Mgr*
Roger Sanford, *Branch Mgr*
EMP: 34 **Privately Held**
SIC: 6411 Life insurance agents

HQ: The Western & Southern Life Insurance Company
400 Broadway St
Cincinnati OH 45202
513 629-1800

(G-986)
YERMAN & YOUNG PAINTING INC
811 Brady Ave (44203-6661)
PHONE...................................330 861-0022
Fax: 330 861-0033
Michael Yerman, *President*
Beth Yerman, *Corp Secy*
EMP: 30
SALES (est): 2.5MM **Privately Held**
SIC: 1721 Commercial painting

Barnesville
Belmont County

(G-987)
BARNESVILLE HEALTHCARE REHAB
Also Called: Astoria Place of Barnesville
400 Carrie Ave (43713-1317)
PHONE...................................740 425-3648
Joseph Brandman,
Jeremy Goldberg,
Matt Gotter,
Michael Nudell,
EMP: 78 **EST:** 2012
SALES (est): 2.2MM **Privately Held**
SIC: 8051 Skilled nursing care facilities

(G-988)
BARNESVILLE HOSPITAL ASSN INC
639 W Main St (43713-1039)
P.O. Box 309 (43713-0309)
PHONE...................................740 425-3941
Fax: 740 425-9213
Richard Doan, *CEO*
David Phillips, *COO*
Willie Cooper-Lohr, *CFO*
Lala Miller, *Director*
David Stephen, *Food Svc Dir*
EMP: 330
SQ FT: 60,000
SALES: 19.5MM **Privately Held**
WEB: www.barnesvillehospital.com
SIC: 8062 Hospital, affiliated with AMA residency

(G-989)
BARNESVILLE LIVESTOCK SALES CO
Also Called: Barnesville Live Stock Ofc
315 S Gardner St (43713-1379)
P.O. Box 166, New Concord (43762-0166)
PHONE...................................740 425-3611
Fax: 740 425-3612
Mike N Morris, *Owner*
Gary Fogle, *Owner*
EMP: 25
SQ FT: 3,600
SALES (est): 1.5MM **Privately Held**
SIC: 5154 Auctioning livestock

(G-990)
OHIO HILLS HEALTH SERVICES (PA)
101 E Main St (43713-1005)
PHONE...................................740 425-5165
William E Chaney, *President*
Charles Bardell, *Vice Pres*
Candy Lendon, *Treasurer*
Linda Tacosik, *Admin Sec*
Theodre Koler, *Administration*
EMP: 80
SALES: 4.5MM **Privately Held**
SIC: 8059 Personal care home, with health care

(G-991)
SOUTH CENTRAL POWER COMPANY
Also Called: Belmont Division
37801 Brnsvlle Bthesda Rd (43713)
PHONE...................................740 425-4018
Fax: 740 425-4552
Ajit Kadakia, *Exec VP*

Barnesville - Belmont County (G-992) — GEOGRAPHIC SECTION

Jim Meyers, *Branch Mgr*
EMP: 30
SALES (corp-wide): 282.1MM **Privately Held**
WEB: www.southcentralpower.com
SIC: 4911 Distribution, electric power
PA: South Central Power Company Inc
2780 Coonpath Rd Ne
Lancaster OH 43130
740 653-4422

(G-992)
WESBANCO BANK INC
230 E Main St (43713-1006)
PHONE..................740 425-1927
EMP: 53
SALES (corp-wide): 284.5MM **Publicly Held**
SIC: 6022 State Commercial Bank
HQ: Wesbanco Bank, Inc.
1 Bank Plz
Wheeling WV 26003
304 234-9000

Bascom
Seneca County

(G-993)
COUNTY OF SENECA
P.O. Box 119 (44809-0119)
PHONE..................419 937-2340
EMP: 25 **Privately Held**
SIC: 4119 Ambulance service
PA: County Of Seneca
111 Madison St
Tiffin OH 44883
419 447-4550

Batavia
Clermont County

(G-994)
AECOM TECHNICAL SERVICES INC
4386 Haskell Ln (45103-2958)
P.O. Box 24099, Dayton (45424-0099)
PHONE..................937 233-1898
Todd Webster, *Branch Mgr*
EMP: 35
SALES (corp-wide): 18.2B **Publicly Held**
WEB: www.earthtech.com
SIC: 8711 Sanitary engineers
HQ: Aecom Technical Services, Inc.
300 S Grand Ave Ste 1100
Los Angeles CA 90071
213 593-8000

(G-995)
BACHMANS INC
Also Called: Honeywell Authorized Dealer
4058 Clough Woods Dr (45103-2586)
PHONE..................513 943-5300
Fax: 513 943-5310
Marc E Bachman, *President*
Rod E Bachman, *Exec VP*
Hubert Acton, *Sales Staff*
EMP: 30 EST: 1955
SQ FT: 16,500
SALES (est): 6.1MM **Privately Held**
WEB: www.bachmansinc.com
SIC: 1711 Warm air heating & air conditioning contractor; refrigeration contractor

(G-996)
BURD BROTHERS INC (PA)
4005 Borman Dr (45103-1684)
P.O. Box 324 (45103-0324)
PHONE..................800 538-2873
Fax: 513 735-0328
Dick Burdick, *CEO*
Tyler Burdick, *President*
Gayle Burdick, *Chairman*
Ron Inabnitt, *Warehouse Mgr*
Ryan Meiers, *Warehouse Mgr*
EMP: 78
SQ FT: 30,000
SALES: 7.2MM **Privately Held**
WEB: www.burdbrothers.com
SIC: 4213 4225 Contract haulers; general warehousing

(G-997)
CARINGTON HEALTH SYSTEMS
Also Called: Batavia Nrsing Cnvalescent Inn
4000 Golden Age Dr (45103-1913)
PHONE..................513 732-6500
Fax: 513 732-0343
Powell Glyndolyn, *Manager*
Lora Pruitt, *Manager*
Steve Chaney, *Administration*
EMP: 300
SALES (corp-wide): 85.7MM **Privately Held**
SIC: 8051 Convalescent home with continuous nursing care
PA: Carington Health Systems
8200 Beckett Park Dr
Hamilton OH 45011
513 682-2700

(G-998)
CHILD FOCUS INC
2337 Clermont Center Dr (45103-1959)
PHONE..................513 732-8800
Fax: 513 732-8806
Jim Carter, *Branch Mgr*
Rebecca Neavill, *Exec Dir*
EMP: 32
SALES (corp-wide): 15.7MM **Privately Held**
WEB: www.childfocus.com
SIC: 8322 Child related social services
PA: Child Focus, Inc.
4629 Aicholtz Rd Ste 2
Cincinnati OH 45244
513 752-1555

(G-999)
CLERMONT CNTY WTR RSURCES DEPT
Also Called: Clermont County Wtr Resources
4400 Haskell Ln (45103-2990)
PHONE..................513 732-7970
Sukie Scheetz, *Controller*
Tom Yeager, *Director*
EMP: 97
SQ FT: 11,000
SALES: 27.9MM **Privately Held**
SIC: 4952 Sewerage systems

(G-1000)
CLERMONT COUNTY COMMUNITY SVCS (PA)
3003 Hospital Dr (45103-2689)
PHONE..................513 732-2277
Joyce A Richardson, *President*
Billie Kuntz, *Director*
Joe Spaulding, *Director*
EMP: 35
SQ FT: 10,000
SALES: 2.4MM **Privately Held**
WEB: www.clermontsupportskids.org
SIC: 8322 9111 Individual & family services; county supervisors' & executives' offices

(G-1001)
CLERMONT COUNTY GEN HLTH DST
2275 Bauer Rd Ste 300 (45103-1914)
PHONE..................513 732-7499
Fax: 513 732-7936
Timothy Kelly, *Principal*
Julianne Nesbit, *Commissioner*
Tim Kelly, *Asst Director*
EMP: 49 **Privately Held**
WEB: www.clermontauditor.org
SIC: 9431 8748 ; business consulting

(G-1002)
CLERMONT NORTH EAST SCHOOL DST (PA)
2792 Us Highway 50 (45103-8532)
PHONE..................513 625-8283
Neil Leist, *Superintendent*
Fred Feltz, *Psychologist*
Scott Wells, *Athletic Dir*
Wade Reeves, *Maintence Staff*
Rhonda Campbell, *Teacher*
EMP: 43
SALES (est): 7.4MM **Privately Held**
SIC: 8211 8741 Public elementary & secondary schools; management services

(G-1003)
CLERMONT RECOVERY CENTER INC
1088 Wasserman Way Ste C (45103-1974)
PHONE..................513 735-8100
Fax: 513 735-8103
Steve Goldsberry, *President*
Cathy McClain, *Opers Spvr*
Scott Stiver, *Treasurer*
Larae Roach, *Psychologist*
Doris Sigel, *Psychologist*
EMP: 50
SALES: 5.9MM **Privately Held**
SIC: 8093 Drug clinic, outpatient

(G-1004)
CLERMONT SENIOR SERVICES INC (PA)
Also Called: Clermont Senior Services
2085 James E Sauls Sr Dr (45103-3255)
PHONE..................513 724-1255
Fax: 513 724-6012
Cynthia Jenkins-Gramke, *CEO*
Gregory Carson, *CFO*
Greg Shivener, *Info Tech Dir*
Liz Atwell, *Exec Dir*
Barb Wiedenbein, *Director*
EMP: 45
SQ FT: 33,000
SALES: 8.1MM **Privately Held**
WEB: www.clermontseniors.com
SIC: 8322 Senior citizens' center or association

(G-1005)
COLLOTYPE LABELS USA INC
4053 Clough Woods Dr (45103-2587)
PHONE..................513 381-1480
David Buse, *President*
William Schult, *Accountant*
EMP: 100
SALES (est): 9.3MM
SALES (corp-wide): 923.3MM **Publicly Held**
SIC: 5131 Labels
PA: Multi-Color Corporation
4053 Clough Woods Dr
Batavia OH 45103
513 381-1480

(G-1006)
COUNTY OF CLERMONT
Also Called: Information Systems Dept
2279 Clermont Center Dr (45103-1956)
PHONE..................513 732-7661
Fax: 513 732-1325
Steve Rybolt, *Manager*
James Owens, *Exec Dir*
EMP: 35
SQ FT: 1,320 **Privately Held**
WEB: www.clermontauditor.org
SIC: 8999 9121 Information bureau; county commissioner;
PA: County Of Clermont
177 E Main St
Batavia OH 45103
513 732-7980

(G-1007)
COUNTY OF CLERMONT
Also Called: Division of Water Resources
4400 Haskell Ln (45103-2990)
PHONE..................513 732-7970
Lyle Bloom, *Director*
EMP: 45 **Privately Held**
SIC: 1623 Water, sewer & utility lines
PA: County Of Clermont
177 E Main St
Batavia OH 45103
513 732-7980

(G-1008)
CURTISS-WRIGHT FLOW CONTROL
Also Called: Qualtech NP
750 Kent Rd (45103-1704)
PHONE..................513 735-2538
EMP: 85
SALES (corp-wide): 2.1B **Publicly Held**
SIC: 3491 3443 3599 1799 Mfg Industrial Valves Mfg Fabricated Plate Wrk Mfg Industrial Machinery Special Trade Contractor
HQ: Curtiss-Wright Flow Control Service Corporation
2950 E Birch St
Brea CA 92821
714 982-1898

(G-1009)
DEVELOPMENTAL DISABILITIES (PA)
2040 Us Highway 50 (45103-8694)
PHONE..................513 732-7000
Sharon Woodrow, *Superintendent*
Monica Vanscoy, *HR Admin*
Lisa Davis, *Pub Rel Dir*
Alice Fricke, *Manager*
David Paudill, *Manager*
EMP: 200
SQ FT: 25,000
SALES (est): 7.1MM **Privately Held**
WEB: www.ccmrdd.org
SIC: 8322 Individual & family services

(G-1010)
DEVELPMNTAL DSBLTIES OHIO DEPT
Also Called: Southwest Ohio Dvlopmental Ctr
4399 E Bauman Ln (45103-1685)
PHONE..................513 732-9200
Fax: 513 735-8242
Nancy McAvoy, *Principal*
James Krumer, *Manager*
Andrew Willcoxon, *Director*
EMP: 225 **Privately Held**
SIC: 9431 8322 Administration of public health programs; ; family counseling services
HQ: Ohio Department Of Developmental Disabilities
30 E Broad St Fl 13
Columbus OH 43215

(G-1011)
EDUCATIONAL AND COMMUNITY RDO
Rr 276 (45103)
P.O. Box 338, Owensville (45160-0338)
PHONE..................513 724-3939
Mel Riffen, *President*
Paul Bodde, *Treasurer*
Don Littman, *Admin Sec*
EMP: 45
SALES: 180.5K **Privately Held**
SIC: 4832 Radio broadcasting stations

(G-1012)
EDWARD ROSE ASSOCIATES INC
Also Called: Eastgate Woods Apts
4412 Eastwood Dr (45103-2440)
PHONE..................513 752-2727
Fax: 513 752-2937
Gary Mounts, *Manager*
EMP: 25
SALES (corp-wide): 7.1MM **Privately Held**
SIC: 6513 Apartment building operators
PA: Edward Rose Associates, Inc.
38525 Woodward Ave
Bloomfield Hills MI 48304
248 539-2255

(G-1013)
FIRST TRANSIT INC
2040 Us Highway 50 (45103-8694)
PHONE..................513 732-1206
Fax: 513 732-1207
Carolyn Kelley, *Principal*
EMP: 86
SALES (corp-wide): 7B **Privately Held**
SIC: 4131 Intercity & rural bus transportation
HQ: First Transit, Inc.
600 Vine St Ste 1400
Cincinnati OH 45202
513 241-2200

(G-1014)
GC AT STONELICK HILLS
3155 Sherilyn Ln (45103-8674)
PHONE..................513 735-4653
Fax: 513 735-4338
Jeff Osterfeld, *Owner*
Mike Sowards, *General Mgr*
EMP: 40

SALES (est): 1.5MM Privately Held
SIC: 7992 Public golf courses

(G-1015)
GLOBAL SCRAP MANAGEMENT INC (PA)
Also Called: G S M
4340 Batavia Rd (45103-3342)
PHONE..................513 576-6600
Chris Hamm, *President*
Pat Bowden, *Vice Pres*
Dave Chodos, *Vice Pres*
Kathy Luccasen, *CFO*
EMP: 26
SALES (est): 21.9MM Privately Held
SIC: 4953 Recycling, waste materials

(G-1016)
HEALTHSOURCE OF OHIO INC
2055 Hospital Dr Ste 320 (45103-1978)
PHONE..................513 707-1997
EMP: 48
SALES (corp-wide): 38.7MM Privately Held
SIC: 8093 Specialty outpatient clinics
PA: Healthsource Of Ohio, Inc.
  5400 Dupont Cir Ste A
  Milford OH 45150
  513 576-7700

(G-1017)
J & B SYSTEMS COMPANY INC
5055 State Route 276 (45103-1211)
P.O. Box 56, Owensville (45160-0056)
PHONE..................513 732-2000
Fax: 513 735-1014
Jerrilyn Kearney, *President*
William Kearney, *Owner*
Melia Calvert, *Purchasing*
EMP: 120
SQ FT: 45,000
SALES (est): 4MM Privately Held
SIC: 7389 Packaging & labeling services

(G-1018)
JEFF WYLER CHEVROLET INC
Also Called: Jeff Wyler Mazda
1117 State Route 32 (45103-2380)
P.O. Box 345 (45103-0345)
PHONE..................513 752-3447
Fax: 513 753-2290
Jeffrey L Wyler, *President*
David Wyler, *Vice Pres*
James Simon, *Mktg Dir*
Mike Brees, *Manager*
Rachel Lykins, *Manager*
EMP: 300
SQ FT: 90,000
SALES (est): 71.8MM Privately Held
SIC: 5511 7539 7538 3714 Automobiles, new & used; automotive repair shops; general automotive repair shops; motor vehicle parts & accessories; top & body repair & paint shops

(G-1019)
LEHN PAINTING INC (PA)
4175 Taylor Rd (45103-9792)
PHONE..................513 732-1515
William R Lehn, *President*
Kimberly E Lehn, *Corp Secy*
David Lehn, *Director*
EMP: 46
SQ FT: 8,000
SALES (est): 5.1MM Privately Held
SIC: 1721 Residential painting

(G-1020)
PAK LAB
5069 State Route 276 (45103-1211)
P.O. Box 550, Owensville (45160-0550)
PHONE..................513 735-4777
Fax: 513 735-4888
Rick Zellen, *General Mgr*
Jackie Schmidt, *Accountant*
William Kearney, *Mng Member*
Albert Brantley, *Manager*
Kerry Cotter,
EMP: 45
SQ FT: 17,000
SALES (est): 5.2MM Privately Held
SIC: 7389 Packaging & labeling services

(G-1021)
PERRY INTERIORS INC
4054 Clough Woods Dr (45103-2586)
PHONE..................513 761-9333
Karen Perry, *President*
Rick Perry, *Vice Pres*
EMP: 30 EST: 1999
SQ FT: 3,500
SALES (est): 2.6MM Privately Held
SIC: 1721 Residential painting

(G-1022)
R & R WIRING CONTRACTORS INC
1269 Clough Pike (45103-2501)
PHONE..................513 752-6304
Fax: 513 753-2182
Mark Rettinger, *President*
Rick Rettinger, *Vice Pres*
Deborah Rettinger, *Admin Sec*
EMP: 34
SQ FT: 5,000
SALES (est): 4.2MM Privately Held
SIC: 1731 General electrical contractor

(G-1023)
RECORD EXPRESS LLC
4295 Armstrong Blvd (45103-1697)
PHONE..................513 685-7329
Nadine Albenze-Smith, *CEO*
Keith D'Ambra, *COO*
EMP: 25
SALES (est): 2.4MM Privately Held
SIC: 7374 Optical scanning data service

(G-1024)
SISTER OF MERCY OF CLERM COUNT (DH)
Also Called: Clermont Mercy Hospital
3000 Hospital Dr (45103-1921)
PHONE..................513 732-8200
Fax: 513 732-8537
Mark Shuagerman, *President*
Bonna Bauer, *Vice Pres*
Arlene Cooper, *Vice Pres*
Mel Fritz, *CFO*
Raytier Angeli, *CIO*
EMP: 71
SQ FT: 230,000
SALES: 119.6MM
SALES (corp-wide): 4.2B Privately Held
SIC: 8062 8011 General medical & surgical hospitals; clinic, operated by physicians
HQ: Mercy Health Cincinnati Llc
  1701 Mercy Health Pl
  Cincinnati OH 45237
  513 952-5000

(G-1025)
SPORTSMANS MARKET INC
Also Called: SPORTY'S WRIGHT BROTHERS COLLE
2001 Sportys Dr (45103-9719)
PHONE..................513 735-9100
Harold Shevers Jr, *Ch of Bd*
Michael J Wolf, *President*
Marc A Liggett, *Exec VP*
John P Lynch, *Exec VP*
Bill Anderson, *Senior VP*
▲ EMP: 172 EST: 1961
SQ FT: 120,000
SALES (est): 71.8MM Privately Held
WEB: www.sportys.com
SIC: 5599 5088 Aircraft instruments, equipment or parts; aircraft equipment & supplies

(G-1026)
STRICKER BROS INC
Also Called: Stricker Auto Sales
4955 Benton Rd (45103-1203)
PHONE..................513 732-1152
Fax: 513 732-2451
John M Stricker, *President*
Arthur J Stricker, *Vice Pres*
Kelley Simpson, *Manager*
▼ EMP: 50 EST: 1956
SQ FT: 2,500
SALES (est): 11.8MM Privately Held
WEB: www.gmusedpartsonline.com
SIC: 5521 5015 5531 Automobiles, used cars only; automotive supplies, used; automobile & truck equipment & parts

(G-1027)
THREE D GOLF LLC
Also Called: Elks Run Golf Club
2000 Elklick Rd (45103-9401)
PHONE..................513 732-0295
Daryll Landrum, *Mng Member*
Kim Day,
William Landrum,
David Shearer,
EMP: 40
SALES (est): 1.1MM Privately Held
SIC: 7999 Miniature golf course operation

(G-1028)
TOWNE CONSTRUCTION SVCS LLC
Also Called: Towne Properties Machine Group
500 Kent Rd Ste A (45103-1703)
PHONE..................513 561-3700
Christopher Bortz, *President*
Shane Bordwine, *Vice Pres*
Thad Stall, *Opers Mgr*
Greg McCarren, *CFO*
Neil Bortz,
EMP: 150 EST: 2005
SALES: 14.5MM
SALES (corp-wide): 16.7MM Privately Held
SIC: 1771 Concrete work
PA: Original Partners Limited Partnership
  1055 Saint Paul Pl
  Cincinnati OH 45202
  513 381-8696

(G-1029)
UNIVERSAL PACKG SYSTEMS INC
Also Called: Paklab
5055 State Route 276 (45103-1211)
PHONE..................513 732-2000
Richard Burton, *Branch Mgr*
EMP: 388
SALES (corp-wide): 423.8MM Privately Held
SIC: 2844 7389 3565 2671 Cosmetic preparations; packaging & labeling services; bottling machinery: filling, capping, labeling; plastic film, coated or laminated for packaging
PA: Universal Packaging Systems, Inc.
  380 Townline Rd Ste 130
  Hauppauge NY 11788
  631 543-2277

(G-1030)
UNIVERSAL PACKG SYSTEMS INC
5069 State Route 276 (45103-1211)
PHONE..................513 735-4777
Rick Zellen, *Site Mgr*
EMP: 40
SALES (corp-wide): 423.8MM Privately Held
SIC: 2844 7389 3565 2671 Cosmetic preparations; packaging & labeling services; bottling machinery: filling, capping, labeling; plastic film, coated or laminated for packaging
PA: Universal Packaging Systems, Inc.
  380 Townline Rd Ste 130
  Hauppauge NY 11788
  631 543-2277

(G-1031)
UTILITY TRAILER MFG CO
4225 Curliss Ln (45103-3217)
PHONE..................513 436-2600
Jason Pautvein, *Cust Mgr*
Del Eastman, *Manager*
Wendy Doyle, *Admin Asst*
EMP: 30
SALES (corp-wide): 228.8MM Privately Held
WEB: www.utm.com
SIC: 4225 General warehousing & storage
PA: Utility Trailer Manufacturing Company
  17295 Railroad St Ste A
  City Of Industry CA 91748
  626 964-7319

(G-1032)
YMCA OF CLERMONT COUNTY INC
2075 James E Sauls Sr Dr (45103-3256)
PHONE..................513 724-9622
Fax: 513 724-5511
Whit Hitckmin, *Principal*
EMP: 40
SQ FT: 33,000
SALES: 750K Privately Held
SIC: 8641 7991 8351 7032 Youth organizations; physical fitness facilities; child day care services; youth camps; individual & family services

Bath
Summit County

(G-1033)
ADMIRAL TRUCK PARTS INC
7941 Ranger Rd (44210)
PHONE..................330 659-6311
Eugene H Gerhart, *President*
Mary Gerhart, *Treasurer*
EMP: 30
SQ FT: 3,000
SALES (est): 1.7MM
SALES (corp-wide): 11.3MM Privately Held
SIC: 5531 5013 Automobile & truck equipment & parts; truck parts & accessories
PA: Ohio Transport Refrigeration, Inc.
  2225 N Cleve Mass Rd
  Bath OH 44210
  330 659-6311

(G-1034)
MERRILL LYNCH PIERCE FENNER
4000 Embassy Pkwy Ste 210 (44210)
PHONE..................330 670-2400
Fax: 330 668-1521
Peter J Calleri, *Manager*
Joseph Danniballe, *Manager*
EMP: 26
SALES (corp-wide): 100.2B Publicly Held
WEB: www.merlyn.com
SIC: 6211 Security brokers & dealers
HQ: Merrill Lynch, Pierce, Fenner & Smith Incorporated
  111 8th Ave
  New York NY 10011
  800 637-7455

(G-1035)
OLD TRAIL SCHOOL
2315 Ira Rd (44210)
PHONE..................330 666-1118
Fax: 330 666-2187
John Farber, *Headmaster*
Karen Andrews, *Headmaster*
Laurie Arnold, *Headmaster*
Steve Hopkins, *Dept Chairman*
Robert Morgan, *Facilities Dir*
EMP: 95
SQ FT: 100,000
SALES: 11.5MM Privately Held
WEB: www.oldtrail.org
SIC: 8211 8351 Private elementary school; preschool center

(G-1036)
WESTERN RESERVE HISTORICAL SOC
Also Called: Hale Farm & Village
2686 Oak Hill Dr (44210)
P.O. Box 296 (44210-0296)
PHONE..................330 666-3711
Fax: 330 666-9497
Margaret Tramontine, *Director*
EMP: 75
SALES (corp-wide): 6.6MM Privately Held
SIC: 8412 Museum
PA: Western Reserve Historical Society
  10825 East Blvd
  Cleveland OH 44106
  216 721-5722

Bath - Summit County (G-1037)

(G-1037)
WILLORY LLC
1970 N Cleveland Mssilln (44210-5367)
P.O. Box 50 (44210-0050)
PHONE.................................330 576-5486
John Bernatovicz,
EMP: 37
SALES: 3MM **Privately Held**
SIC: 7361 Executive placement

Bay Village
Cuyahoga County

(G-1038)
BRADLEY BAY ASSISTED LIVING
605 Bradley Rd (44140-1670)
PHONE.................................440 871-4509
Fax: 440 808-5687
John O'Neal, *Owner*
John O' Neal, *Owner*
Dianna White, *Manager*
EMP: 25
SALES (est): 442.8K **Privately Held**
SIC: 8361 8082 Rest home, with health care incidental; home health care services

(G-1039)
BRADLEY ROAD NURSING HOME
605 Bradley Rd (44140-1698)
PHONE.................................440 871-3474
Fax: 440 871-4743
John O'Neill, *Administration*
EMP: 130
SALES (est): 3.5MM **Privately Held**
SIC: 8051 Skilled nursing care facilities

(G-1040)
LAKE ERIE NATURE & SCIENCE CTR
28728 Wolf Rd (44140-1350)
PHONE.................................440 871-2900
Fax: 440 871-2901
Patrick J Mazur, *Ch of Bd*
Larry D Richardson, *Principal*
Catherine Timko, *Exec Dir*
Dale Brogan, *Education*
Darci Sanders, *Advisor*
EMP: 36
SQ FT: 22,240
SALES: 1.6MM **Privately Held**
WEB: www.lensc.org
SIC: 8299 0752 8412 Educational service, nondegree granting: continuing educ.; animal specialty services; planetarium

(G-1041)
REALTY ONE INC
Also Called: Realty One Bay Village
600 Dover Center Rd Ste C (44140-3310)
PHONE.................................440 835-6500
Toll Free:..............................877 -
Fax: 440 835-1780
Bill Conrad, *Manager*
EMP: 70
SALES (corp-wide): 67.8MM **Privately Held**
WEB: www.realty-1st.com
SIC: 6531 Real estate agents & managers
HQ: Realty One, Inc.
   800 W Saint Clair Ave
   Cleveland OH 44113
   216 328-2500

(G-1042)
US SWIMMING LAKE ERIE SWIMMING
301 Rockledge Dr (44140-2712)
PHONE.................................330 423-0485
Edward L Bettendorf, *Principal*
EMP: 25
SALES: 191.2K **Privately Held**
SIC: 7997 Swimming club, membership

Beach City
Stark County

(G-1043)
GRABILL PLUMBING & HEATING
Also Called: Graybill Gallery Kitchens Bath
10235 Manchester Ave Sw (44608-9756)
PHONE.................................330 756-2075
Fax: 330 756-2399
Luke Grabill, *President*
Karla Ferguson, *Principal*
Grant Grabill, *Vice Pres*
EMP: 28 EST: 1965
SALES (est): 6MM **Privately Held**
WEB: www.grabill.com
SIC: 1711 Plumbing contractors

Beachwood
Cuyahoga County

(G-1044)
A+ SOLUTIONS LLC
Also Called: Ohiosolutions.org
3659 Green Rd Ste 112 (44122-5715)
PHONE.................................216 896-0111
Hadassa Meyers, *Mng Member*
Oren Meyers,
EMP: 49
SQ FT: 1,877
SALES (est): 911.9K **Privately Held**
SIC: 8049 8093 8299 Speech therapist; clinical psychologist; occupational therapist; mental health clinic, outpatient; educational services

(G-1045)
ABB INC
23000 Harvard Rd (44122-7234)
PHONE.................................440 585-7804
Jerry Fuller, *Manager*
EMP: 30
SALES (corp-wide): 33.8B **Privately Held**
WEB: www.elsterelectricity.com
SIC: 5063 8711 5084 Switchgear; engineering services; industrial machinery & equipment
HQ: Abb Inc.
   305 Gregson Dr
   Cary NC 27511

(G-1046)
ADVANCE PAYROLL FUNDING LTD
Also Called: Advance Partners
3401 Entp Pkwy Fl 5 (44122)
PHONE.................................216 831-8900
Fax: 216 831-8819
Joel Adelman, *CEO*
Adam C Stern, *President*
David Garson, *Vice Pres*
Jack Terrana, *Vice Pres*
Danny Goldstein, *Opers Staff*
EMP: 114
SQ FT: 4,000
SALES (est): 16.5MM
SALES (corp-wide): 3.1B **Publicly Held**
WEB: www.advancepayroll.com
SIC: 8721 Payroll accounting service
PA: Paychex, Inc
   911 Panorama Trl S
   Rochester NY 14625
   585 385-6666

(G-1047)
ADVANTAGE IMAGING LLC (PA)
Also Called: Advantage Diagnostic
3733 Park East Dr Ste 100 (44122-4334)
PHONE.................................216 292-9998
Jonathan Metzler MD, *Principal*
Doreene Zelch, *Marketing Staff*
Kristina Van Deusen, *Mng Member*
EMP: 25
SALES (est): 1.9MM **Privately Held**
SIC: 8099 Health screening service

(G-1048)
AERODYNAMICS INC ARDYNAMICS INC
25700 Science Park Dr # 210 (44122-7319)
PHONE.................................404 596-8751
Scott Beale, *CEO*
EMP: 30
SALES (est): 2.9MM **Privately Held**
SIC: 4522 Flying charter service

(G-1049)
ALTRUISM SOCIETY INC
3695 Green Rd Unit 22896 (44122-7945)
PHONE.................................877 283-4001
James Abrams, *CEO*
Jaicynthia Farmer, *Vice Pres*
EMP: 99
SALES (est): 2.1MM **Privately Held**
SIC: 6732 Trusts: educational, religious, etc.

(G-1050)
ALZHEIMERS DISEASE AND
23215 Commerce Park # 300 (44122-5803)
PHONE.................................216 721-8457
Fax: 216 721-1629
Valerie Mencer, *Sales Staff*
Christine Stevens, *Manager*
Nancy B Udelson, *Exec Dir*
EMP: 25 EST: 1980
SALES (est): 2.2MM **Privately Held**
SIC: 8621 Health association

(G-1051)
APOLLO PROPERTY MANAGEMENT LLC (PA)
25825 Science Park Dr # 150 (44122-7300)
PHONE.................................216 468-0050
Jason Wasserbauer, *Vice Pres*
Gary Murphy, *CFO*
Steve Pogozelski, *Accounting Dir*
Joyce Nelson, *Accountant*
Ross Stephan, *Office Mgr*
EMP: 33
SALES (est): 5.8MM **Privately Held**
SIC: 8741 Management services

(G-1052)
ATLANTIC HOSPITALITY & MGT LLC
26300 Chagrin Blvd (44122-4229)
PHONE.................................216 454-5450
Theodore A Sahley,
EMP: 44
SALES (est): 3.6MM **Privately Held**
WEB: www.atlantichospitalityinc.com
SIC: 8741 Hotel or motel management

(G-1053)
ATTEVO INC
24500 Chagrin Blvd # 300 (44122-5646)
PHONE.................................216 928-2800
David Snyder, *CEO*
John Frankovich, *Vice Pres*
Joe Burmester, *CFO*
Michael Deh, *Controller*
Phillip Trem, *Controller*
EMP: 70
SALES (est): 6MM **Privately Held**
SIC: 8742 7373 7379 Management consulting services; computer integrated systems design; computer related consulting services

(G-1054)
AVNET INC
Also Called: Avnet Computers
2000 Auburn Dr Ste 200 (44122-4328)
PHONE.................................440 349-7600
Kimberly Marriott, *Accounts Mgr*
Melinda Hicks, *Manager*
Billy Sevel, *Technology*
EMP: 27
SALES (corp-wide): 17.4B **Publicly Held**
WEB: www.avnet.com
SIC: 5065 Electronic parts
PA: Avnet, Inc.
   2211 S 47th St
   Phoenix AZ 85034
   480 643-2000

(G-1055)
BEACHWOOD PROF FIRE FIGHTERS C
P.O. Box 221250 (44122-0996)
PHONE.................................216 292-1968
Mark Russo, *President*
EMP: 42
SALES: 32.4K **Privately Held**
SIC: 8699 Membership organizations

(G-1056)
BRE DDR PARKER PAVILIONS LLC
3300 Enterprise Pkwy (44122-7200)
PHONE.................................216 755-6451
Daniel Hurwitz, *CEO*
EMP: 50 EST: 2012
SALES (est): 1.8MM
SALES (corp-wide): 921.5MM **Privately Held**
SIC: 6531 Real estate agent, commercial
PA: Ddr Corp.
   3300 Enterprise Pkwy
   Beachwood OH 44122
   216 755-5500

(G-1057)
BRYDEN PLACE INC
25201 Chagrin Blvd # 190 (44122-5633)
PHONE.................................614 258-6623
Roger King, *President*
Glyndon Powell, *President*
Edward L Byington, *Vice Pres*
Kenneth Writesel, *Director*
Ashley Eblin, *Administration*
EMP: 150
SALES (est): 5.8MM **Privately Held**
SIC: 8051 Convalescent home with continuous nursing care

(G-1058)
BUCKEYE RUBBER & PACKING CO
23940 Mercantile Rd (44122-5989)
PHONE.................................216 464-8900
Fax: 216 464-8900
Donaldcatlin, *Principal*
Donald Catlin, *Exec VP*
Irene Papp, *Exec VP*
James Sampson, *Vice Pres*
Ted Kasper, *Sales Mgr*
▲ EMP: 45 EST: 1937
SQ FT: 30,000
SALES: 20.2MM **Privately Held**
WEB: www.buckeyerubber.com
SIC: 5085 Gaskets & seals; gaskets

(G-1059)
BUFFALO-GTB ASSOCIATES LLC
Also Called: Hampton Inn and Suites
3840 Orange Pl (44122-4488)
PHONE.................................216 831-3735
Fax: 216 831-3738
Ryan Matllack, *Manager*
Dana Burtanger, *CTO*
EMP: 28
SALES (corp-wide): 3MM **Privately Held**
WEB: www.buffalolodging.com
SIC: 7011 Hotels
PA: Buffalo-Gtb Associates, Llc
   570 Delaware Ave
   Buffalo NY 14202
   781 344-4435

(G-1060)
CARLISLE MCNELLIE RINI KRAM
24755 Chagrin Blvd (44122-5682)
PHONE.................................216 360-7200
Fax: 216 360-7210
Richard McNellie, *President*
Herbert Kramer, *Vice Pres*
William Rini, *Vice Pres*
James Sassano, *Vice Pres*
Phyllis Ulrich, *Vice Pres*
EMP: 40 EST: 1979
SQ FT: 5,000
SALES (est): 6.1MM **Privately Held**
SIC: 8111 Real estate law; debt collection law; bankruptcy law; will, estate & trust law

GEOGRAPHIC SECTION
Beachwood - Cuyahoga County (G-1086)

(G-1061)
CELLCO PARTNERSHIP
Also Called: Verizon Wireless
27460 Chagrin Blvd (44122-4423)
PHONE 216 765-1444
Greg Howell, *Engineer*
Paul Tirri, *Engineer*
Joe Gizzi, *Finance*
James Manning, *Accounts Mgr*
Richard Feacher, *Accounts Exec*
EMP: 138
SALES (corp-wide): 126B **Publicly Held**
SIC: 4812 Cellular telephone services
HQ: Cellco Partnership
1 Verizon Way
Basking Ridge NJ 07920

(G-1062)
CHAMPION OPTICAL NETWORK
Also Called: Champion One
23645 Mercantile Rd Ste A (44122-5936)
PHONE 216 831-1800
John Jutila, *CEO*
Lish Engel, *Controller*
Karen Zimmerman, *Accounts Mgr*
Cushing Kim, *Sales Staff*
Keith Lewis, *Mktg Dir*
EMP: 33
SQ FT: 5,000
SALES (est): 8.6MM **Privately Held**
WEB: www.cctupgrades.com
SIC: 5049 Optical goods

(G-1063)
CLEVELAND BCHWOOD HSPTLITY LLC
Also Called: Hilton Cleveland/Beachwood
3663 Park East Dr (44122-4315)
PHONE 216 464-5950
Jock Litris, *Vice Pres*
Steve Degutis, *Controller*
Scott Schmelzer, *Manager*
Scott Schmeozer, *Admin Mgr*
EMP: 99
SALES (est): 5.1MM **Privately Held**
SIC: 7011 Hotels

(G-1064)
CLEVELAND CENTER FOR ETNG DSOR
25550 Chagrin Blvd # 200 (44122-5638)
PHONE 216 765-2535
Mark Warren, *Principal*
Lucene Wisniewski, *Director*
EMP: 28
SALES: 950K **Privately Held**
SIC: 8322 General counseling services

(G-1065)
CLEVELAND CLINIC FOUNDATION
25875 Science Park Dr (44122-7304)
PHONE 216 448-0116
Lisa Cummins, *Manager*
Amy Cossette, *Consultant*
Pamela Holmes, *Director*
Sarah Brawner, *Associate*
EMP: 2931
SALES (corp-wide): 8B **Privately Held**
SIC: 8062 General medical & surgical hospitals
PA: The Cleveland Clinic Foundation
9500 Euclid Ave
Cleveland OH 44195
216 636-8335

(G-1066)
CLUB LIFE ENTERTAINMENT LLC
2000 Auburn Dr Ste 200 (44122-4328)
PHONE 216 831-1134
Ryan Gossekin,
EMP: 27
SALES (est): 82.4K **Privately Held**
SIC: 7929 8742 Entertainment service; marketing consulting services

(G-1067)
COMMUNITY HEALTH CENTERS OHIO
3355 Richmond Rd Ste 225a (44122-4180)
PHONE 216 831-1494
Arun Chattree, *Exec Dir*
EMP: 54
SALES: 800K **Privately Held**
SIC: 8093 Specialty outpatient clinics

(G-1068)
CORNELIA C HODGSON - ARCHITEC (PA)
23240 Chagrin Blvd # 300 (44122-5405)
PHONE 216 593-0057
Cornelia Hodgson, *President*
Bonnie Brodnik, *Executive Asst*
EMP: 47
SQ FT: 5,000
SALES (est): 5.7MM **Privately Held**
SIC: 8712 Architectural engineering

(G-1069)
CTPARTNERS EXEC SEARCH INC
28601 Chagrin Blvd # 600 (44122-4557)
PHONE 216 464-8710
Fax: 216 464-6172
EMP: 65
SALES (corp-wide): 176.8MM **Publicly Held**
SIC: 7361 Employment Agency
PA: Ctpartners Executive Search Inc.
1166 Avenue Of The Amrcs
New York NY 10036
212 588-3500

(G-1070)
CW FINANCIAL LLC
Also Called: Press Wood Management
23550 Commerce Park # 5000 (44122-5862)
PHONE 941 907-9490
Johanna Brooks, *Principal*
Stephanie Webb, *Human Resources*
EMP: 325 **EST:** 1991
SALES (est): 38.1MM **Privately Held**
SIC: 6282 Investment advice

(G-1071)
DDR CORP (PA)
3300 Enterprise Pkwy (44122-7200)
PHONE 216 755-5500
Fax: 216 755-1500
Terrance R Ahern, *Ch of Bd*
David R Lukes, *President*
William Kern, *COO*
William T Ross, *COO*
Michele K Boal, *Counsel*
EMP: 150
SALES (est): 921.5MM **Privately Held**
WEB: www.ddrc.com
SIC: 6798 Real estate investment trusts

(G-1072)
DDR TUCSON SPECTRUM I LLC
3300 Enterprise Pkwy (44122-7200)
PHONE 216 755-5500
Daniel Hurwitz, *President*
EMP: 25 **EST:** 2012
SALES (est): 1.5MM
SALES (corp-wide): 921.5MM **Privately Held**
SIC: 6798 Real estate investment trusts
PA: Ddr Corp.
3300 Enterprise Pkwy
Beachwood OH 44122
216 755-5500

(G-1073)
DEALERS GROUP LIMITED
Also Called: Scher Group
23240 Chagrin Blvd # 802 (44122-5404)
PHONE 440 352-4970
Robert Scher, *CFO*
Jan Benroth, *Treasurer*
Pete Hallahan ME, *Director*
David Stenstrom,
EMP: 25
SQ FT: 12,500
SALES: 4MM **Privately Held**
WEB: www.dlrgrp.com
SIC: 8742 7514 Industry specialist consultants; rent-a-car service

(G-1074)
EATON CORPORATION
1000 Eaton Blvd (44122-6058)
PHONE 440 523-5000
Fax: 216 523-6498
Mark Tudor,
Brian Braley, *Project Mgr*
Matthew Reinhardt, *Engineer*
John Schindler, *Branch Mgr*
James Biggins, *Manager*
EMP: 400 **Privately Held**
WEB: www.eaton.com
SIC: 7549 Automotive maintenance services
HQ: Eaton Corporation
1000 Eaton Blvd
Cleveland OH 44122
216 523-5000

(G-1075)
EATON CORPORATION
Eastlake Office
1000 Eaton Blvd (44122-6058)
PHONE 216 523-5000
Robert Decaro, *Project Mgr*
Manuel Prieto, *Project Mgr*
Keith Cozart, *Purch Mgr*
Bernie Beier, *Engineer*
Sell Craig, *Engineer*
EMP: 260 **Privately Held**
WEB: www.eaton.com
SIC: 3714 5084 Hydraulic fluid power pumps for auto steering mechanism; hydraulic systems equipment & supplies
HQ: Eaton Corporation
1000 Eaton Blvd
Cleveland OH 44122
216 523-5000

(G-1076)
ENVIRNMENTAL RESOURCES MGT INC
Also Called: Erm Midatlantic
3333 Richmond Rd Ste 160 (44122-4196)
PHONE 216 593-5200
Cheryl Garson, *Branch Mgr*
EMP: 31
SALES (corp-wide): 215.5K **Privately Held**
SIC: 8748 Environmental consultant
HQ: Environmental Resources Management, Inc.
75 Valley Stream Pkwy
Malvern PA 19355
484 913-0300

(G-1077)
EXPERT SYSTEM APPLICATIONS
26700 Alsace Ct Apt 302 (44122-7576)
PHONE 440 248-0110
Fax: 440 248-0199
Virginia Ngo, *President*
EMP: 25
SALES (est): 2.7MM **Privately Held**
WEB: www.expert-system.com
SIC: 7373 8243 Local area network (LAN) systems integrator; operator training, computer

(G-1078)
EZRA HEALTH CARE INC
Also Called: Beachwood Nrsing Hlthcare Ctr
23258 Fernwood Dr (44122-1569)
PHONE 440 498-3000
Will Grunspan, *President*
Sharona Grunspan, *Vice Pres*
EMP: 130
SQ FT: 160,000
SALES: 963.6MM **Privately Held**
WEB: www.ezrahealthcareinc.com
SIC: 8051 Extended care facility

(G-1079)
FEDEX OFFICE & PRINT SVCS INC
27450 Chagrin Blvd (44122-4423)
PHONE 216 292-2679
Bobby Stager, *Manager*
EMP: 25
SALES (corp-wide): 60.3B **Publicly Held**
WEB: www.kinkos.com
SIC: 7334 Photocopying & duplicating services
HQ: Fedex Office And Print Services, Inc.
7900 Legacy Dr
Plano TX 75024
214 550-7000

(G-1080)
FOX INTERNATIONAL LIMITED INC (PA)
23645 Merc Rd Ste B (44122)
PHONE 216 454-1001
Fax: 440 439-8893
Ronald D Ordway, *CEO*
David Heiden, *President*
Murray Fox, *Principal*
Richard H Siegel, *Principal*
Greg Osborn, *CFO*
▼ **EMP:** 47
SQ FT: 50,000
SALES (est): 24.7MM **Privately Held**
WEB: www.fox-intl.com
SIC: 5065 7389 5087 Electronic parts & equipment; telemarketing services; fire-fighting equipment

(G-1081)
FRANKLIN & SEIDELMANN INC (PA)
3700 Park East Dr Ste 300 (44122-4399)
PHONE 216 255-5700
Fax: 216 255-5701
Peter Franklin, *President*
Clayton T Larsen, *Senior VP*
Frank Seidelmann, *Vice Pres*
Michele Leoni, *Mktg Dir*
Mireille Michalak, *Manager*
EMP: 26
SALES (est): 4.9MM **Privately Held**
WEB: www.franklin-seidelmann.com
SIC: 8011 Radiologist

(G-1082)
FRANKLIN & SEIDELMANN LLC
3700 Park East Dr Ste 300 (44122-4399)
PHONE 216 255-5700
Bill O' Neal, *Controller*
Frank E Seidelmann MD,
Peter D Franklin MD,
EMP: 80
SQ FT: 11,508
SALES (est): 4.4MM **Privately Held**
SIC: 8741 Management services

(G-1083)
GCI CONSTRUCTION LLC (PA)
25101 Chagrin Blvd (44122-5643)
PHONE 216 831-6100
Larry Goldberg, *President*
EMP: 33
SALES (est): 28.1MM **Privately Held**
SIC: 1522 1521 Multi-family dwelling construction; single-family housing construction

(G-1084)
HEALTH DATA MGT SOLUTIONS INC
3201 Enterprise Pkwy (44122-7330)
PHONE 216 595-1232
Fax: 216 595-9688
Denise Zeman, *Branch Mgr*
Sonal Sheth, *Manager*
Steve Young, *Technology*
Marilyn Morrow, *Director*
Kim Buschlen, *Administration*
EMP: 86 **Privately Held**
SIC: 8099 Blood related health services
PA: Health Data & Management Solutions, Inc.
123 N Wacker Dr Ste 650
Chicago IL 60606

(G-1085)
HEMODIALYSIS SERVICES INC
Also Called: Hsi Hemodialysis Services
25550 Chagrin Blvd # 404 (44122-4640)
P.O. Box 22330 (44122-0330)
PHONE 216 378-2691
Fax: 216 378-2819
Charles Wilson, *President*
Steven Lovelace, *CFO*
EMP: 43 **EST:** 1991
SALES (est): 4.3MM **Privately Held**
WEB: www.hsihd.com
SIC: 8092 Kidney dialysis centers

(G-1086)
HOWARD HANNA SMYTHE CRAMER
28879 Chagrin Blvd (44122-4603)
PHONE 216 831-0210

Beachwood - Cuyahoga County (G-1087)

Tiffany Majkowski, *Financial Exec*
Howard Hanna, *Branch Mgr*
Peggy Garr, *Real Est Agnt*
Susan Hennenberg, *Real Est Agnt*
EMP: 30
SALES (corp-wide): 76.4MM **Privately Held**
SIC: 6531 Real estate brokers & agents
HQ: Howard Hanna Smythe Cramer
6000 Parkland Blvd
Cleveland OH 44124
216 447-4477

(G-1087)
HOWARD HANNA SMYTHE CRAMER
24465 Greenwich Ln (44122-1646)
PHONE..................216 751-8550
Fax: 216 751-2804
Len Okuly, *Branch Mgr*
Benjamin K Chmielewski, *Real Est Agnt*
Jackie Collesi, *Real Est Agnt*
Dorothy Schechter, *Real Est Agnt*
Susan C Sloan, *Real Est Agnt*
EMP: 30
SALES (corp-wide): 76.4MM **Privately Held**
SIC: 6531 Real estate agent, residential
HQ: Howard Hanna Smythe Cramer
6000 Parkland Blvd
Cleveland OH 44124
216 447-4477

(G-1088)
IA URBAN HTELS BCHWOOD TRS LLC
Also Called: Embassy Suites
3775 Park East Dr (44122-4307)
PHONE..................216 765-8066
Fax: 216 765-0930
Lari Stih, *General Mgr*
Monica Gambino, *Sls & Mktg Exec*
Chuck Willson, *Manager*
Tulio Garonzi, *Director*
Mark Herron,
EMP: 99
SQ FT: 66,940
SALES (est): 5.8MM **Privately Held**
SIC: 7011 Hotels & motels

(G-1089)
INTELLICORP RECORDS INC
3000 Auburn Dr Ste 410 (44122-4340)
PHONE..................216 450-5200
Fax: 216 450-5201
Todd Carpenter, *President*
Michael Krassner, *Vice Pres*
Thomas Mitchell, *Project Mgr*
Joe Petrecca, *Engineer*
Kelly Georgiou, *Finance*
EMP: 65
SQ FT: 16,000
SALES (est): 11.6MM **Publicly Held**
WEB: www.intellicorp.net
SIC: 7375 Information retrieval services
HQ: Insurance Services Office, Inc.
545 Washington Blvd Fl 12
Jersey City NJ 07310
201 469-2000

(G-1090)
JACOBS REAL ESTATE SERVICES
2000 Auburn Dr Ste 120 (44122-4328)
PHONE..................216 514-9830
Doug Miller, *Mng Member*
EMP: 39
SALES (est): 557.7K **Privately Held**
SIC: 6531 6512 Real estate brokers & agents; commercial & industrial building operation

(G-1091)
JEWISH COMMUNITY CTR CLEVELAND
Also Called: MANDEL JEWISH COMMUNITY OF CLE
26001 S Woodland Rd (44122-3367)
PHONE..................216 831-0700
Michael Hyman, *CEO*
Deborah Ackerman, *Vice Pres*
Lauri Baker, *Accountant*
CJ Nalepa, *Sales Staff*
Debra Posner, *VP Mktg*
EMP: 225 EST: 1948
SQ FT: 93,000
SALES: 14.1MM **Privately Held**
SIC: 8322 Social service center

(G-1092)
JOSEPH AND FLORENCE MANDEL
26500 Shaker Blvd (44122-7116)
PHONE..................216 464-4055
Fax: 216 464-3229
Jerry D Isaac-Shapiro, *Principal*
Bennet Kleinman, *Principal*
L C Sherman, *Principal*
Bennett Yanowitz, *Principal*
Janet Keane, *CFO*
EMP: 90
SQ FT: 28,600
SALES (est): 5.9MM **Privately Held**
WEB: www.agnon.org
SIC: 8211 8351 Catholic elementary & secondary schools; Catholic combined elementary & secondary school; private elementary school; preschool center

(G-1093)
KALYPSO LP (PA)
3659 Green Rd Ste 100 (44122-5715)
PHONE..................216 378-4290
Bill Poston, *Managing Prtnr*
Greg Adkins, *Partner*
Mick Broekhof, *Partner*
Niels Ebbing, *Partner*
Michael Friedman, *Partner*
EMP: 70
SALES (est): 7.1MM **Privately Held**
SIC: 8742 Business consultant

(G-1094)
KINDRED HEALTHCARE INC
23333 Harvard Rd (44122-6232)
PHONE..................216 593-2200
EMP: 64
SALES (corp-wide): 6B **Publicly Held**
SIC: 8322 Rehabilitation services
PA: Kindred Healthcare, Inc.
680 S 4th St
Louisville KY 40202
502 596-7300

(G-1095)
KING GROUP INC
25550 Chagrin Blvd # 300 (44122-4640)
PHONE..................216 831-9330
Fax: 216 831-8879
Donald M King, *President*
EMP: 25
SQ FT: 3,500
SALES (est): 1.5MM **Privately Held**
SIC: 6512 Nonresidential building operators

(G-1096)
LINCOLN FINCL ADVISORS CORP
28601 Chagrin Blvd # 300 (44122-4500)
PHONE..................216 765-7400
Drew Adler, *Financial Exec*
Lawrence Kronick, *Branch Mgr*
Karen Lasher, *Manager*
Kathryn Addison, *Agent*
Hooman Omidpanah, *Agent*
EMP: 50
SALES (corp-wide): 14.2B **Publicly Held**
WEB: www.lfaonline.com
SIC: 6282 Investment advisory service
HQ: Lincoln Financial Advisors Corporation
1300 S Clinton St
Fort Wayne IN 46802
800 237-3813

(G-1097)
MARSH BERRY & COMPANY INC (PA)
28601 Chagrin Blvd # 400 (44122-4556)
PHONE..................440 354-3230
John Wepler, *President*
Douglas A Yoh, *President*
Dale Myer, *Managing Dir*
Lawrence J Marsh, *Chairman*
Rob Lieblein, *Exec VP*
EMP: 27
SALES (est): 11.2MM **Privately Held**
SIC: 8742 8741 Business consultant; management services

(G-1098)
MCM CAPITAL PARTNERS
25201 Chagrin Blvd # 360 (44122-5600)
PHONE..................216 514-1840
Mark Mansour, *Managing Prtnr*
Fred Disanto, *Managing Prtnr*
Robert Kingsbury, *Vice Pres*
Gregory Meredith, *Vice Pres*
Kevin F Hayes, *Marketing Mgr*
EMP: 343
SQ FT: 5,000
SALES (est): 45.8MM **Privately Held**
WEB: www.mcmcapital.com
SIC: 6211 Investment bankers

(G-1099)
MEDICAL MUTUAL OF OHIO
Also Called: Antares Management Solutions
23700 Commerce Park (44122-5827)
PHONE..................216 292-0400
Paul Apostle, *Vice Pres*
Monica Klag, *Purch Agent*
Jim Page, *Purch Agent*
Eric Lazar, *Engineer*
Jay Hader, *Auditor*
EMP: 300
SALES (corp-wide): 1.4B **Privately Held**
SIC: 6411 6321 Insurance agents; accident & health insurance carriers
PA: Medical Mutual Of Ohio
2060 E 9th St Frnt Ste
Cleveland OH 44115
216 687-7000

(G-1100)
MENORAH PARK CENTER FOR SENIO
Also Called: Rh Meyers Apartments
27200 Cedar Rd (44122-8104)
PHONE..................216 831-6515
Kimberly Kootsouradis, *Office Mgr*
Stewart Collins, *Branch Mgr*
Sandy Valtman, *Records Dir*
EMP: 50
SQ FT: 195,000
SALES (est): 2.3MM
SALES (corp-wide): 71.1MM **Privately Held**
WEB: www.menorahpark.org
SIC: 6513 Retirement hotel operation
PA: Menorah Park Center For Senior Living Bet Moshav Zekenim Hadati
27100 Cedar Rd
Cleveland OH 44122
216 831-6500

(G-1101)
METROHEALTH SYSTEM
Also Called: Metrohealth Beachwood Hlth Ctr
3609 Park East Dr Ste 300 (44122-4309)
PHONE..................216 765-0733
Michael Phillips, *Officer*
Judy Butler,
Mary Luebke,
Jeff Rubel,
Dave Wloch,
EMP: 26
SALES (corp-wide): 888.4MM **Privately Held**
SIC: 8062 General medical & surgical hospitals
PA: The Metrohealth System
2500 Metrohealth Dr
Cleveland OH 44109
216 398-6000

(G-1102)
METROHEALTH SYSTEM
Also Called: Metrohlth Pepper Pike Hlth Ctr
29125 Chagrin Blvd # 110 (44122-4622)
PHONE..................216 591-0523
Fax: 216 591-1496
Frances Ballo, *Branch Mgr*
EMP: 26
SALES (corp-wide): 888.4MM **Privately Held**
SIC: 8062 General medical & surgical hospitals
PA: The Metrohealth System
2500 Metrohealth Dr
Cleveland OH 44109
216 398-6000

(G-1103)
MIM SOFTWARE INC (PA)
25800 Science Park Dr # 180 (44122-7339)
PHONE..................216 896-9798
Dennis Nelson, *President*
Jerimy Brockway, *President*
Pete Simmelink, *COO*
Pete Zimmelink, *COO*
Alexandra Jorgensen, *Counsel*
EMP: 49
SALES (est): 16.3MM **Privately Held**
WEB: www.mimvista.com
SIC: 7372 Application computer software

(G-1104)
MONTEFIORE HOME
1 David N Myers Pkwy (44122)
PHONE..................216 360-9080
Fax: 216 360-9080
Lauren B Rock, *CEO*
Mark Weiss, *CFO*
Althea Johnson, *Human Res Dir*
Jacqulyn Gutowski, *Manager*
Marge Brown, *Director*
EMP: 450
SQ FT: 180,000
SALES: 29.7MM **Privately Held**
SIC: 8051 Skilled nursing care facilities

(G-1105)
MR MAGIC CARNEGIE INC
Also Called: Mr Magic Car Wash & Detail Ctr
23511 Chagrin Blvd # 306 (44122-5528)
PHONE..................440 461-7572
Fax: 216 881-7737
Sterling Kassoff, *President*
EMP: 25
SQ FT: 7,800
SALES (est): 967.5K **Privately Held**
SIC: 7542 Washing & polishing, automotive; carwash, automatic

(G-1106)
MURWOOD REAL ESTATE GROUP LLC
Also Called: Keller Williams Realtors
29225 Chagrin Blvd # 360 (44122-4645)
PHONE..................216 839-5500
Fax: 216 839-1705
Laird Wynn, *Manager*
John Ludwick,
Marcy Capadona, *Real Est Agnt*
Robert A Cugini II, *Real Est Agnt*
Colleen L Hart, *Real Est Agnt*
EMP: 50
SALES (est): 3.9MM **Privately Held**
SIC: 6531 Real estate agent, residential

(G-1107)
NORTH EAST OHIO HEALTH SVCS (PA)
Also Called: Connections Hlth Wlns Advo
24200 Chagrin Blvd # 126 (44122-5529)
P.O. Box 22955 (44122-0955)
PHONE..................216 831-6466
Fax: 216 766-6084
Esther Pla, *CEO*
James Nagle, *CFO*
Ronald Nowak, *CFO*
Laurie Waller, *Human Res Dir*
Donna Ellison, *Office Mgr*
EMP: 61
SQ FT: 12,000
SALES: 18.3MM **Privately Held**
WEB: www.neohs.org
SIC: 8322 8093 General counseling services; specialty outpatient clinics

(G-1108)
NORTHCOAST HEALTHCARE MGT INC
23611 Chagrin Blvd # 380 (44122-5540)
PHONE..................216 591-2000
Fran Voll, *President*
Dr Kenneth Weiner, *President*
Jack Koenig, *Vice Pres*
David Geller, *CFO*
R W Brockman, *Treasurer*
EMP: 120
SQ FT: 22,000

GEOGRAPHIC SECTION
Beachwood - Cuyahoga County (G-1133)

SALES (est): 6.5MM
SALES (corp-wide): 198.5B Publicly Held
SIC: 8741 8721 Management services; billing & bookkeeping service
HQ: Ndchealth Corporation
1564 Northeast Expy Ne
Brookhaven GA 30329
404 728-2000

(G-1109)
NPA ASSOCIATES
Also Called: Nelson Park Apartments
23875 Commerce Park # 120 (44122-5835)
PHONE..................614 258-4053
Fax: 614 258-0575
Angelica Stoves, *Principal*
Mira Debevc, *Principal*
Larry Looney, *Principal*
Angelica Hoda, *Manager*
EMP: 99
SALES: 950K Privately Held
SIC: 6513 Apartment building operators

(G-1110)
OHIO CLLBRTIVE LRNG SLTONS INC (PA)
Also Called: Smart Solutions
24700 Chagrin Blvd # 104 (44122-5647)
PHONE..................216 595-5289
Anand Julka, *President*
Dale Mesnick, *Opers Staff*
Griffith Beck, *Accounts Mgr*
Jonathan Pittman, *Manager*
Chris Wnoroski, *Consultant*
EMP: 50
SQ FT: 6,000
SALES (est): 15MM Privately Held
WEB: www.smartsolutionsonline.com
SIC: 7372 8741 Business oriented computer software; business management

(G-1111)
OHIO DESIGN CENTRE
23533 Mercantile Rd (44122-5959)
PHONE..................216 831-1245
Fax: 216 831-3770
Jeffery Davis, *Owner*
Davis Development, *Mng Member*
EMP: 100
SQ FT: 100,000
SALES (est): 4.8MM Privately Held
SIC: 7389 Interior designer

(G-1112)
ORACLE SYSTEMS CORPORATION
3333 Richmond Rd Ste 420 (44122-4198)
PHONE..................216 328-9100
Fax: 216 328-9100
Vijaya Godugu, *Technical Mgr*
Jeff Sedam, *Engineer*
Stewart Flemming, *Manager*
EMP: 94
SALES (corp-wide): 37.8B Publicly Held
WEB: www.forcecapital.com
SIC: 8748 5045 Systems analysis & engineering consulting services; computers, peripherals & software
HQ: Oracle Systems Corporation
500 Oracle Pkwy
Redwood City CA 94065
650 506-7000

(G-1113)
ORPHAN FOUNDATION OF AMERICA
Also Called: Foster Care To Success
23811 Chagrin Blvd # 210 (44122-5525)
PHONE..................571 203-0270
Gina Stracuzzi, *President*
Laura Adkins, *Engineer*
Gordon Bonhart, *Treasurer*
Tanya Noble, *Info Tech Dir*
Eileen McCaffrey, *Director*
EMP: 26
SALES: 12.7MM Privately Held
WEB: www.orphan.org
SIC: 8399 Fund raising organization, non-fee basis

(G-1114)
PENSKE LOGISTICS LLC
3000 Auburn Dr Ste 100 (44122-4333)
PHONE..................216 765-5475
Peter Smith, *Ch of Bd*
Robert Daymon, *General Mgr*
Joe Reilman, *General Mgr*
Caleb Soetanto, *Project Mgr*
Dennis Suhadolnik, *Project Mgr*
EMP: 75
SALES (corp-wide): 2.9B Privately Held
WEB: www.penskelogistics.com
SIC: 4213 Contract haulers
HQ: Penske Logistics Llc
Green Hls Rr 10
Reading PA 19603
800 529-6531

(G-1115)
PREFERRED MEDICAL GROUP INC
23600 Commerce Park (44122-5817)
PHONE..................404 403-8310
EMP: 189
SALES (corp-wide): 11.3MM Privately Held
SIC: 8082 Home health care services
PA: Preferred Medical Group, Inc.
9140 Crsea Del Fntana Way
Naples FL 34109
239 597-2010

(G-1116)
PSYCHLGCAL BEHAVIORAL CONS LLC (PA)
25101 Chagrin Blvd # 100 (44122-5643)
PHONE..................216 456-8123
Donald Sykes, *Managing Dir*
EMP: 25
SQ FT: 12,719
SALES: 13MM Privately Held
SIC: 8093 Mental health clinic, outpatient

(G-1117)
QUALCHOICE INC
Also Called: University Hospitals Hlth Sys
3605 Warrensville Ctr Rd (44122-5203)
PHONE..................330 656-1231
Thomas A Sullivan, *President*
Rebecca N Ho, *Vice Pres*
Bryan A James, *Vice Pres*
Gaye Massey, *Vice Pres*
Karen Fifer Ferry, *CFO*
EMP: 300
SQ FT: 17,000
SALES (est): 20MM
SALES (corp-wide): 2.3B Privately Held
WEB: www.qchp.com
SIC: 6411 Medical insurance claim processing, contract or fee basis
PA: University Hospitals Health System, Inc.
3605 Warrensville Ctr Rd
Shaker Heights OH 44122
216 767-8900

(G-1118)
RCT ENGINEERING INC (PA)
24880 Shaker Blvd (44122-2356)
PHONE..................561 684-7534
James V Burphy, *President*
Ralph S Tyler Jr, *Chairman*
Carol Anderson, *Manager*
EMP: 28
SQ FT: 3,800
SALES (est): 3.1MM Privately Held
WEB: www.rctengineering.com
SIC: 8711 Engineering services

(G-1119)
RETINA ASSOCIATE OF CLEVELAND (PA)
3401 Entp Pkwy Ste 300 (44122)
PHONE..................216 831-5700
Dr Lawrence J Singerman, *President*
David Miller, *President*
Dr Michael Novak, *Vice Pres*
Dianne Himmelman, *Ophthalmology*
Vicki Gunter, *Manager*
EMP: 35
SQ FT: 5,000
SALES (est): 10.8MM Privately Held
SIC: 8011 Ophthalmologist

(G-1120)
ROBOTS AND PENCILS LP ✪
24245 Mercantile Rd (44122)
PHONE..................587 350-4095
Dave Aikenhead, *CFO*
EMP: 63 EST: 2017
SALES (est): 1.6MM Privately Held
SIC: 7373 Systems software development services

(G-1121)
RODDY GROUP INC
24500 Chagrin Blvd # 200 (44122-5646)
PHONE..................216 763-0088
Matthew Roddy, *President*
EMP: 30
SALES (est): 158.4K Privately Held
SIC: 7322 Adjustment bureau, except insurance

(G-1122)
RURALOGIC INC
24500 Chagrin Blvd # 300 (44122-5646)
PHONE..................419 630-0500
Jim Armstead, *Principal*
EMP: 55
SALES (est): 3.3MM Privately Held
SIC: 8742 Management consulting services

(G-1123)
SHIELDS CAPITAL CORPORATION
20600 Chagrin Blvd # 800 (44122-5327)
PHONE..................216 767-1340
Robert Snapper, *Principal*
EMP: 55
SALES (corp-wide): 26.3MM Privately Held
SIC: 6799 Investors
PA: Shields Capital Corporation
140 Broadway Ste 4400
New York NY 10005
212 320-3000

(G-1124)
SIEGEL SIEGEL J & JENNINGS CO (PA)
23425 Commerce Park # 103 (44122-5848)
PHONE..................216 763-1004
Fax: 216 241-1006
Fred Siegel, *President*
J K Jennings,
EMP: 29
SALES (est): 3.5MM Privately Held
SIC: 8111 General practice attorney, lawyer

(G-1125)
SIGNATURE BOUTIQUE HOTEL LP
1010 Eaton Blvd (44122-6058)
PHONE..................216 595-0900
J T Norville, *Managing Prtnr*
Alan Feuerman, *General Mgr*
EMP: 36
SQ FT: 70,176
SALES (est): 686.5K Privately Held
SIC: 7011 Hotels

(G-1126)
SIGNATURE OPTICAL INC
2000 Auburn Dr Ste 140 (44122-4328)
PHONE..................216 831-6299
Fax: 216 292-5544
David Sholitan MD, *Corp Secy*
Rosemary Perl,
Diane L Tucker,
Jackie Decapite, *Ophthalmic Tech*
EMP: 32 EST: 1971
SALES (est): 1.8MM Privately Held
WEB: www.clevelandclinic.org
SIC: 8011 Ophthalmologist

(G-1127)
STRATOS WEALTH PARTNERS LTD
3750 Park East Dr (44122-4348)
PHONE..................440 519-2500
Fax: 440 248-1942
Jeffrey Concepcion, *CEO*
Blake Rawson, *Managing Prtnr*
John Turcotte, *Managing Dir*
Linda Roth, *Vice Pres*
Tracy Dalby, *Opers Mgr*
EMP: 56
SALES (est): 789.8K
SALES (corp-wide): 401K Privately Held
SIC: 6282 Investment advisory service
PA: Man On The Moon, Llc
6241 Riverside Dr Ste 1n
Dublin OH 43017
614 886-9395

(G-1128)
SUNSTORM GAMES LLC
23245a Mercantile Rd (44122-5911)
PHONE..................216 403-4820
Ron Laneve, *COO*
Anthony Campiti,
Len Tagon,
EMP: 38
SALES: 10MM Privately Held
SIC: 7371 Computer software development

(G-1129)
SURESITE CONSULTING GROUP LLC (PA)
3659 Green Rd Ste 214 (44122-5715)
PHONE..................216 593-0400
Kelly Warsaw, *CEO*
Jerry Warsaw, *President*
Courtney Schmidt, *Exec VP*
Jerald Warsaw,
EMP: 30
SALES (est): 11.5MM Privately Held
WEB: www.sure-site.com
SIC: 1541 Industrial buildings, new construction

(G-1130)
TELARC INTERNATIONAL CORP (PA)
23412 Commerce Park (44122-5813)
PHONE..................216 464-2313
Fax: 216 360-9663
Jack Renner, *Ch of Bd*
Robert Woods, *President*
Kajo Paukert, *Vice Pres*
Scott Peplin, *Vice Pres*
Nick Phillips, *Vice Pres*
EMP: 42
SQ FT: 14,000
SALES (est): 6.5MM Privately Held
WEB: www.telarc.com
SIC: 5099 7389 Compact discs; music recording producer

(G-1131)
TOA TECHNOLOGIES INC (PA)
3333 Richmond Rd Ste 420 (44122-4198)
PHONE..................216 360-8106
Fax: 216 378-7881
Yuval Brisker, *President*
Irad Carmi, *President*
Bruce Grainger, *Senior VP*
Jennifer Friedman, *Vice Pres*
Steven Gershik, *Vice Pres*
EMP: 73
SALES (est): 204.2K Privately Held
WEB: www.toatechnologies.com
SIC: 7371 Computer software development

(G-1132)
TODD ASSOCIATES INC (PA)
23825 Commerce Park Ste A (44122-5837)
PHONE..................440 461-1101
Edward J Hyland Jr, *President*
Wayne Dilinovic, *COO*
Wayne A Leach, *Vice Pres*
Jared Rukin, *Accountant*
Kathy Doorley, *Broker*
EMP: 55
SQ FT: 5,000
SALES (est): 15.8MM Privately Held
WEB: www.toddassociates.com
SIC: 6411 Insurance agents

(G-1133)
TREMCO INCORPORATED (HQ)
3735 Green Rd (44122-5730)
PHONE..................216 292-5000
Fax: 216 765-6716
Jeffrey L Korach, *CEO*
Randall J Korach, *President*
Deryl Kratzer, *Division Pres*
Moorman Scott, *Division Pres*
Kevin Rooney, *District Mgr*

Beachwood - Cuyahoga County (G-1134)

◆ **EMP:** 300
SQ FT: 93,000
SALES (est): 596.8MM
SALES (corp-wide): 4.9B **Publicly Held**
WEB: www.tremcoinc.com
SIC: 2891 2952 1761 1752 Sealants; caulking compounds; adhesives; epoxy adhesives; roofing materials; coating compounds, tar; asphalt saturated board; roofing contractor; floor laying & floor work; paints & allied products; specialty cleaning, polishes & sanitation goods
PA: Rpm International Inc.
2628 Pearl Rd
Medina OH 44256
330 273-5090

(G-1134)
UNITED INSURANCE COMPANY AMER
23215 Commerce Park # 310 (44122-5843)
PHONE.................................216 514-1904
Fax: 216 514-1666
Chris Powell, *General Mgr*
EMP: 30
SALES (corp-wide): 2.7B **Publicly Held**
WEB: www.unitedinsure.com
SIC: 6411 Insurance agents, brokers & service
HQ: United Insurance Company Of America
12115 Lackland Rd
Saint Louis MO 63146
314 819-4300

(G-1135)
UNIVERSITY HOSPITALS CLEVELAND
Also Called: Alzheimer Center
23215 Commerce Park # 300 (44122-5803)
PHONE.................................216 721-8457
Fax: 216 831-8585
Karl Herrup, *Principal*
Harry Menegay PHD, *IT/INT Sup*
EMP: 60
SALES (corp-wide): 2.3B **Privately Held**
SIC: 8062 8011 General medical & surgical hospitals; offices & clinics of medical doctors
HQ: University Hospitals Of Cleveland
11100 Euclid Ave
Cleveland OH 44106
216 844-1000

(G-1136)
WEATHERPROOFING TECH INC (DH)
3735 Green Rd (44122-5705)
PHONE.................................216 292-5000
Fax: 216 292-5038
Robert Beckner, *President*
Deryl Kratzer, *President*
Jeffrey L Korach, *Principal*
Mike Drumm, *CFO*
Jim Lohmann, *Sales Mgr*
EMP: 66
SALES (est): 70.7MM
SALES (corp-wide): 4.9B **Publicly Held**
WEB: www.wtiservices.com
SIC: 1761 Roofing contractor
HQ: Tremco Incorporated
3735 Green Rd
Beachwood OH 44122
216 292-5000

(G-1137)
WEATHERPROOFING TECH INC
3735 Green Rd (44122-5705)
PHONE.................................281 480-7900
Marty Billingsly, *Branch Mgr*
EMP: 550
SALES (corp-wide): 4.9B **Publicly Held**
WEB: www.wtiservices.com
SIC: 1761 Roofing contractor
HQ: Weatherproofing Technologies, Inc.
3735 Green Rd
Beachwood OH 44122
216 292-5000

(G-1138)
ZINNER & CO
3201 Entp Pkwy Ste 410 (44122)
PHONE.................................216 831-0733
Fax: 216 765-7118

Robin Baum, *Managing Prtnr*
Michael Jennings, *Senior Partner*
Donald J Zinner, *Partner*
David Antine, *Partner*
Sidney Brode, *Partner*
EMP: 41 **EST:** 1939
SQ FT: 5,000
SALES (est): 3.3MM **Privately Held**
WEB: www.zinnerco.com
SIC: 8721 Certified public accountant

Beallsville
Monroe County

(G-1139)
AMERICAN ENERGY CORPORATION
43521 Mayhugh Hill Rd (43716-9641)
PHONE.................................740 926-2430
Fax: 740 926-9138
Murray Ryant, *Principal*
Tim Eddy, *Maintence Staff*
▲ **EMP:** 485
SALES (est): 40.1MM **Privately Held**
SIC: 1241 1222 Coal mining services; bituminous coal-underground mining

(G-1140)
EMORY ROTHENBUHLER & SONS
47126 Sunfish Creek Rd (43716-9592)
PHONE.................................740 458-1432
Fax: 740 458-1470
Joyce Bonar, *President*
Gene Rothenbuhler, *Vice Pres*
EMP: 35
SQ FT: 8,000
SALES (est): 644.2K **Privately Held**
SIC: 4212 Local trucking, without storage

Beaver
Pike County

(G-1141)
D G M INC
1881 Adams Rd (45613-3500)
P.O. Box 207 (45613-0207)
PHONE.................................740 226-1950
Fax: 740 820-8816
Gerry Salsibury, *President*
Denny Salisbury, *Vice Pres*
Janet Salisbury, *Vice Pres*
Mark Salisbury, *Vice Pres*
Thomas Salisbury, *Vice Pres*
EMP: 61
SALES (est): 11.6MM **Privately Held**
SIC: 1611 General contractor, highway & street construction

Beavercreek
Greene County

(G-1142)
22ND CENTURY TECHNOLOGIES INC
2601 Commons Blvd Ste 130 (45431-3830)
PHONE.................................866 537-9191
Satvinder Singh, *President*
EMP: 62
SALES (corp-wide): 81.7MM **Privately Held**
SIC: 7371 Computer software systems analysis & design, custom
PA: 22nd Century Technologies Inc.
220 Davidson Ave Ste 100b
Somerset NJ 08873
732 537-9191

(G-1143)
A M MANAGEMENT INC
2000 Zink Rd (45324-2018)
PHONE.................................937 426-6500
Diana Spiegel, *Branch Mgr*
EMP: 44

SALES (corp-wide): 3.1MM **Privately Held**
SIC: 7021 Dormitory, commercially operated
PA: A M Management Inc
2871 Heinz Rd Ste B
Iowa City IA 52240
319 354-1961

(G-1144)
AAA CLUB ALLIANCE INC
3321 Dayton Xenia Rd (45432-2728)
PHONE.................................937 427-5884
EMP: 151
SALES (corp-wide): 487.4MM **Privately Held**
SIC: 6411 Insurance agents
PA: Aaa Club Alliance Inc.
1 River Pl
Wilmington DE 19801
302 299-4700

(G-1145)
ADVANT-E CORPORATION (PA)
2434 Esquire Dr (45431-2573)
PHONE.................................937 429-4288
Fax: 937 429-4309
Jason K Wadzinski, *Ch of Bd*
James E Lesch, *CFO*
Jason Boone, *Accounting Dir*
EMP: 60 **EST:** 1994
SQ FT: 19,000
SALES: 12.6MM **Publicly Held**
WEB: www.advant-e.com
SIC: 7372 7375 Application computer software; information retrieval services

(G-1146)
APPLIED OPTIMIZATION INC
3040 Presidential Dr # 100 (45324-6272)
PHONE.................................937 431-5100
Anil Chaudhary, *President*
Katy Keenan, *Marketing Staff*
Jessica Piekenbrock, *Comp Scientist*
Derek Boone, *Network Enginr*
EMP: 101
SQ FT: 1,450
SALES (est): 8MM **Privately Held**
WEB: www.appliedo.com
SIC: 8733 Physical research, noncommercial

(G-1147)
ARCADIA SERVICES INC
Arcadia Health Care
2440 Dayton Xenia Rd C (45434-7124)
PHONE.................................937 912-5800
Cathy Sparling, *COO*
EMP: 51
SALES (corp-wide): 156.6MM **Privately Held**
SIC: 7363 8082 Medical help service; home health care services
PA: Arcadia Services, Inc.
20750 Civic Center Dr # 100
Southfield MI 48076
248 352-7530

(G-1148)
ASSURED INFORMATION SEC INC
3500 Pentagon Blvd # 310 (45431-2374)
PHONE.................................937 427-9720
Charles Green, *CEO*
Shannon Secor, *Controller*
Shannon M Secor, *Branch Mgr*
EMP: 54
SALES (corp-wide): 27.5MM **Privately Held**
SIC: 7371 7373 8733 Computer software development & applications; computer integrated systems design; physical research, noncommercial
PA: Assured Information Security, Inc.
153 Brooks Rd Ste 8
Rome NY 13441
315 336-3306

(G-1149)
AT&T GOVERNMENT SOLUTIONS INC
2940 Presidential Dr # 390 (45324-6762)
PHONE.................................937 306-3030
Kirk Dunker, *General Mgr*
David Browder, *Director*
EMP: 75

SQ FT: 1,500
SALES (corp-wide): 160.5B **Publicly Held**
SIC: 3829 8742 Measuring & controlling devices; management consulting services
HQ: At&T Government Solutions, Inc.
1900 Gallows Rd Ste 105
Vienna VA 22182
703 506-5000

(G-1150)
BEAVER-VU BOWL
1238 N Fairfield Rd (45432-2634)
PHONE.................................937 426-6771
Fax: 937 426-4994
Doug Wilson, *President*
Ron Rentz, *Principal*
Tom Wilson, *Principal*
Bob Rentz, *Corp Secy*
Bob Wilson, *Vice Pres*
EMP: 40
SQ FT: 5,500
SALES: 1.2MM **Privately Held**
WEB: www.daytonbowling.com
SIC: 7933 7999 5091 Ten pin center; bowling instruction; bowling equipment

(G-1151)
BEAVERCREEK CHURCH OF NAZARENE
1850 N Fairfield Rd (45432-2714)
PHONE.................................937 426-0079
Fax: 937 426-2490
Debbie Black, *Director*
EMP: 50
SALES (est): 2.4MM **Privately Held**
SIC: 8351 Preschool center

(G-1152)
BEAVERCREEK MEDICAL CENTER
2510 Commons Blvd Ste 120 (45431-3821)
PHONE.................................937 558-3000
Fax: 937 558-3008
Ann Hopkins, *Manager*
EMP: 71
SALES (est): 2MM
SALES (corp-wide): 1.7B **Privately Held**
SIC: 8062 General medical & surgical hospitals
HQ: Dayton Osteopathic Hospital
405 W Grand Ave
Dayton OH 45405
937 762-1629

(G-1153)
BEAVERCREEK MEDICAL CENTER
2510 Commons Blvd Ste 120 (45431-3821)
PHONE.................................937 558-3000
EMP: 52
SALES (est): 269K
SALES (corp-wide): 1.7B **Privately Held**
SIC: 8062 General medical & surgical hospitals
HQ: Dayton Osteopathic Hospital
405 W Grand Ave
Dayton OH 45405
937 762-1629

(G-1154)
BOOZ ALLEN HAMILTON INC
3800 Pentagon Blvd # 110 (45431-2199)
PHONE.................................937 429-5580
Fax: 937 429-9795
Keith Welsh, *Treasurer*
Charles Flowers, *Branch Mgr*
Hayward Learn, *Manager*
EMP: 50 **Publicly Held**
WEB: www.arinc.com
SIC: 8711 Engineering services
HQ: Booz Allen Hamilton Inc.
8283 Greensboro Dr # 700
Mc Lean VA 22102
703 902-5000

(G-1155)
BTAS INC (PA)
Also Called: Business Tech & Solutions
4391 Dayton Xenia Rd (45432-1803)
PHONE.................................937 431-9431
Fax: 937 431-9413
Angela Fronista, *President*

GEOGRAPHIC SECTION
Beavercreek - Greene County (G-1179)

Charles Dyer, *Vice Pres*
John Sotman, *Vice Pres*
George Vlahos, *Vice Pres*
Chad Rayburn, *CFO*
EMP: 185
SQ FT: 7,500
SALES (est): 23.4MM **Privately Held**
WEB: www.btas.com
SIC: 8742 7374 7371 Business consultant; data processing & preparation; custom computer programming services

(G-1156)
C H DEAN INC (PA)
Also Called: Dean Financial Management
3500 Pentagon Blvd # 200 (45431-2376)
PHONE..............................937 222-9531
Fax: 937 227-9304
Dennis D Dean, *CEO*
Stephen M Miller, *President*
Mark E Schutter, *Exec VP*
Ron Best, *Vice Pres*
Ronald Best, *Vice Pres*
EMP: 60
SQ FT: 26,000
SALES (est): 11.8MM **Privately Held**
WEB: www.chdean.com
SIC: 6282 8721 8742 Investment counselors; accounting services, except auditing; management consulting services

(G-1157)
CADX SYSTEMS INC
2689 Commons Blvd Ste 100 (45431-3832)
PHONE..............................937 431-1464
EMP: 71
SALES (est): 789.9K
SALES (corp-wide): 26.3MM **Publicly Held**
SIC: 8071 Research And Development Of Computer Aided Detection Systems
PA: Icad, Inc.
  98 Spit Brook Rd Ste 100
  Nashua NH 03062
  603 882-5200

(G-1158)
CELLCO PARTNERSHIP
Also Called: Verizon
2755 Fairfield Cmns (45431-3777)
PHONE..............................937 429-4000
Steve Hamlin, *Branch Mgr*
EMP: 30
SALES (corp-wide): 126B **Publicly Held**
SIC: 4812 5999 Cellular telephone services; mobile telephones & equipment
HQ: Cellco Partnership
  1 Verizon Way
  Basking Ridge NJ 07920

(G-1159)
CHOICE HEALTHCARE LIMITED
1257 N Fairfield Rd (45432-2633)
PHONE..............................937 254-6220
Fax: 937 254-6292
Cammy Burns, *Principal*
Dana Albaugh, *Asst Director*
EMP: 60 **EST:** 2000
SALES (est): 2MM **Privately Held**
SIC: 8082 Visiting nurse service

(G-1160)
CISCO SYSTEMS INC
2661 Commons Blvd Ste 133 (45431-3704)
PHONE..............................937 427-4204
Helen Yep, *Principal*
EMP: 691
SALES (corp-wide): 48B **Publicly Held**
SIC: 3577 7379 Data conversion equipment, media-to-media: computer;
PA: Cisco Systems, Inc.
  170 W Tasman Dr
  San Jose CA 95134
  408 526-4000

(G-1161)
CITY OF BEAVERCREEK
2800 New Germany Trebein (45431-8531)
PHONE..............................937 320-0742
Fax: 937 431-0552
Mike Gafkjen, *Superintendent*
Zachary Wike, *Asst Supt*
Steve Click, *Manager*
Leslie Heller, *Manager*

Steve Klick, *Director*
EMP: 60 **Privately Held**
SIC: 7992 7299 Public golf courses; banquet hall facilities
PA: City Of Beavercreek
  1368 Research Park Dr
  Beavercreek OH 45432
  937 427-5510

(G-1162)
COMPUTERS UNIVERSAL INC
2850 Presidential Dr # 150 (45324-7201)
PHONE..............................614 543-0473
Peter L Cannon, *President*
Gregory Hurst, *Info Tech Mgr*
David Linnenkohl, *Director*
Tod Robbins, *Admin Asst*
EMP: 140 **EST:** 1998
SALES (est): 9.1MM **Privately Held**
WEB: www.computers-universal.com
SIC: 7373 Systems integration services

(G-1163)
CREEK TECHNOLOGIES COMPANY
2372 Lakeview Dr Ste H (45431-2566)
PHONE..............................937 272-4581
Lee Allen Culver, *President*
EMP: 120
SQ FT: 16,000
SALES: 14.8MM **Privately Held**
SIC: 7379 Computer related maintenance services

(G-1164)
CSRA LLC
3560 Pentagon Blvd (45431-1706)
PHONE..............................937 429-9774
Prakash Raj, *Engineer*
David Edmondson, *Branch Mgr*
David Dodds, *Director*
Katherine Mann, *Director*
EMP: 320
SALES (corp-wide): 30.9B **Publicly Held**
WEB: www.csc.com
SIC: 7376 Computer facilities management
HQ: Csra Llc
  3170 Fairview Park Dr
  Falls Church VA 22042
  703 641-2000

(G-1165)
DAUGWOOD INC
Also Called: Right At Home
3183 Beaver Vu Dr Ste B (45434-6385)
PHONE..............................937 429-9465
Lynn Daugherty, *President*
EMP: 35
SALES (est): 498.4K **Privately Held**
SIC: 8082 4729 Home health care services; carpool/vanpool arrangement

(G-1166)
DAVITA INC
3070 Presidential Dr A (45324-6273)
PHONE..............................937 426-6475
Tony Herd, *Principal*
EMP: 27 **Publicly Held**
SIC: 8092 Kidney dialysis centers
PA: Davita Inc.
  2000 16th St
  Denver CO 80202

(G-1167)
DAYTON ROOF & REMODELING CO
418 Merrick Dr (45434-5812)
PHONE..............................937 224-7667
Fax: 937 224-7669
William A Landefeld, *President*
Terryl Oyer, *Vice Pres*
EMP: 25 **EST:** 1948
SQ FT: 2,500
SALES (est): 1.9MM **Privately Held**
SIC: 1521 1761 New construction, single-family houses; roofing, siding & sheet metal work

(G-1168)
DESIGN KNOWLEDGE COMPANY
3100 Presidential Dr # 103 (45324-7145)
PHONE..............................937 320-9244
James R McCracken, *CEO*
Daniel Schiavone, *President*

Eric Loomis, *Vice Pres*
Daniel P Schaivone, *Engineer*
Jeff Walrath, *Senior Engr*
EMP: 63
SQ FT: 13,000
SALES (est): 8.8MM **Privately Held**
WEB: www.tdkc.com
SIC: 8711 Engineering services

(G-1169)
DRS SIGNAL TECHNOLOGIES INC
4393 Dayton Xenia Rd (45432-1803)
PHONE..............................937 429-7470
Leo Torresani, *President*
Peter Oberbeck, *Vice Pres*
Bob Taylor, *Vice Pres*
Roger Witkemper, *Vice Pres*
Louis Duchesheau, *Engineer*
EMP: 30
SALES (est): 10.3MM
SALES (corp-wide): 8.3B **Privately Held**
WEB: www.drs-st.com
SIC: 3825 7371 Electrical energy measuring equipment; custom computer programming services
HQ: Leonardo Drs, Inc.
  2345 Crystal Dr Ste 1000
  Arlington VA 22202
  703 416-8000

(G-1170)
DYN MARINE SERVICES INC
3040 Presidential Dr (45324-6294)
PHONE..............................937 427-2663
Ernie Carrillo, *Manager*
EMP: 40
SALES (corp-wide): 32.6B **Publicly Held**
SIC: 7376 Computer facilities management
HQ: Dyn Marine Services, Inc.
  3190 Frview Pk Dr Ste 350
  Falls Church VA 22042

(G-1171)
E&I SOLUTIONS LLC
3610 Pentagon Blvd # 220 (45431-6700)
PHONE..............................937 912-0288
David Judson, *President*
EMP: 30
SALES (est): 612.1K **Privately Held**
SIC: 7373 7376 7379 Computer integrated systems design; computer facilities management; computer related maintenance services

(G-1172)
EDICT SYSTEMS INC
2434 Esquire Dr (45431-2573)
PHONE..............................937 429-4288
Fax: 937 429-4309
Ason K Wadzinski, *Ch of Bd*
David McDonald, *QA Dir*
James Lesch, *CFO*
David J Rike, *VP Sales*
Michael Byers, *Accounts Exec*
EMP: 45
SQ FT: 12,000
SALES: 11.5MM
SALES (corp-wide): 12.6MM **Publicly Held**
WEB: www.retailec.com
SIC: 7372 Prepackaged software
PA: Advant-E Corporation
  2434 Esquire Dr
  Beavercreek OH 45431
  937 429-4288

(G-1173)
FITNESS INTERNATIONAL LLC
2500 N Fairfield Rd Ste F (45431-1781)
PHONE..............................937 427-0700
Fax: 937 306-0076
Christina Watson, *Branch Mgr*
EMP: 29
SALES (corp-wide): 176.8MM **Privately Held**
SIC: 7991 Physical fitness clubs with training equipment
PA: Fitness International, Llc
  3161 Michelson Dr Ste 600
  Irvine CA 92612
  949 255-7200

(G-1174)
G M A SURGERY INC
3359 Kemp Rd Ste 120 (45431-2565)
PHONE..............................937 429-7350
Larry Gault, *Administration*
EMP: 26
SALES (est): 1.2MM **Privately Held**
SIC: 8062 General medical & surgical hospitals

(G-1175)
GREENE MEMORIAL HOSPITAL INC
Also Called: Beavercreek Health Park
3359 Kemp Rd (45431-2565)
PHONE..............................937 458-4500
Fax: 937 458-4419
Larry Gault, *Branch Mgr*
EMP: 45
SQ FT: 1,782
SALES (corp-wide): 1.7B **Privately Held**
WEB: www.greenememorialhospital.com
SIC: 8062 Hospital, affiliated with AMA residency
HQ: Greene Memorial Hospital Inc.
  1141 N Monroe Dr
  Xenia OH 45385
  937 352-2000

(G-1176)
HJ FORD ASSOCIATES INC
2940 Presidential Dr # 150 (45324-6762)
PHONE..............................937 429-9711
Frank Grosso, *Vice Pres*
EMP: 125 **Publicly Held**
WEB: www.hjford.com
SIC: 8711 8742 7361 Industrial engineers; management consulting services; employment agencies
HQ: H.J. Ford Associates, Inc.
  2900 Presidential Dr # 150
  Beavercreek OH 45324
  937 490-1482

(G-1177)
HOME DEPOT USA INC
Also Called: Home Depot, The
3775 Presidential Dr (45324-9095)
PHONE..............................937 431-7346
Fax: 937 431-7326
Serenity McKenzie, *Editor*
Tiffany A Collinsworth, *Manager*
EMP: 95
SALES (corp-wide): 100.9B **Publicly Held**
WEB: www.homerentalsdepot.com
SIC: 5211 7359 Home centers; tool rental
HQ: Home Depot U.S.A., Inc.
  2455 Paces Ferry Rd Se
  Atlanta GA 30339

(G-1178)
ILLUMINATION WORKS LLC
2689 Cmmons Blvd Ste 120 (45431)
PHONE..............................937 938-1321
Leeanna Scovil, *Business Mgr*
Jonathon J Mitchell, *Mng Member*
Sandra Simpson, *Manager*
Kim Buchhalter, *Consultant*
Loran Peoples, *Technology*
EMP: 80
SQ FT: 6,200
SALES: 12.1MM **Privately Held**
WEB: www.illuminationworksllc.com
SIC: 7379 7374 Data processing consultant; data processing & preparation

(G-1179)
INTERNATIONAL BUS MCHS CORP
Also Called: IBM
3000 Presidential Dr # 300 (45324-6208)
PHONE..............................917 406-7400
EMP: 381
SALES (corp-wide): 79.1B **Publicly Held**
WEB: www.ibm.com
SIC: 7379 Computer related consulting services
PA: International Business Machines Corporation
  1 New Orchard Rd Ste 1 # 1
  Armonk NY 10504
  914 499-1900

Beavercreek - Greene County (G-1180)

(G-1180)
JJR SOLUTIONS LLC
3610 Pentagon Blvd # 220 (45431-6700)
PHONE..................................937 912-0288
Fax: 937 912-0299
David Judson, *General Mgr*
Linda Skinner, *COO*
Joe Skinner, *Office Mgr*
David L Judson Jr, *Mng Member*
Jean Kuns, *Database Admin*
EMP: 35
SALES: 4MM **Privately Held**
WEB: www.jjrsolutions.com
SIC: 8742 7371 7376 8711 Management information systems consultant; computer software development & applications; computer facilities management; engineering services; computer related maintenance services; physical research, noncommercial

(G-1181)
KETTERING MEDICAL CENTER
Also Called: Soin Medical Center
3535 Pentagon Park Blvd (45431)
PHONE..................................937 702-4000
Donna Taylor, *Purchasing*
Dawn Myers, *Case Mgr*
EMP: 54
SALES (corp-wide): 1.7B **Privately Held**
SIC: 8062 General medical & surgical hospitals
HQ: Kettering Medical Center
3535 Southern Blvd
Kettering OH 45429
937 298-4331

(G-1182)
KEYW CORPORATION
1415 Research Park Dr (45432-2842)
PHONE..................................937 702-9512
Robert Day, *Controller*
EMP: 30 **Publicly Held**
SIC: 8711 8748 Engineering services; testing services
HQ: The Keyw Corporation
7740 Milestone Pkwy # 400
Hanover MD 21076

(G-1183)
KNOLLWOOD FLORISTS INC
Also Called: Knollwood Garden Center
3766 Dayton Xenia Rd (45432-2887)
P.O. Box 517, Dayton (45434-0517)
PHONE..................................937 426-0861
Fax: 937 426-3330
Robert Scott, *President*
John Scott, *Vice Pres*
EMP: 35 EST: 1930
SQ FT: 35,000
SALES (est): 4MM **Privately Held**
WEB: www.knollwoodgardens.com
SIC: 5261 0181 Garden supplies & tools; flowers; grown under cover (e.g. greenhouse production)

(G-1184)
KNOLLWOOD FLORISTS INC
3766 Dayton Xenia Rd (45432-2887)
PHONE..................................937 426-0861
Robert Scott, *President*
John Scott, *Vice Pres*
EMP: 50
SQ FT: 900
SALES (est): 2.9MM **Privately Held**
SIC: 0782 0781 Landscape contractors; landscape counseling services

(G-1185)
LEIDOS INC
3745 Pentagon Blvd (45431-2369)
PHONE..................................937 431-2220
Fax: 937 429-9557
John Jumper, *CEO*
Daniel Shrum, *Principal*
R Overdorf, *Engineer*
Mike Ritter, *MIS Dir*
Phyllis Turvey, *Director*
EMP: 304
SALES (corp-wide): 10.1B **Publicly Held**
WEB: www.saic.com
SIC: 8732 8731 Market analysis or research; commercial physical research

HQ: Leidos, Inc.
11951 Freedom Dr Ste 500
Reston VA 20190
571 526-6000

(G-1186)
LIBERTY INSULATION CO INC (PA)
2903 Kant Pl (45431-8573)
PHONE..................................513 621-0108
Denver Smith, *President*
Nancy Smith, *Corp Secy*
Laura Meo, *Vice Pres*
EMP: 60
SALES (est): 4.8MM **Privately Held**
SIC: 1742 Insulation, buildings

(G-1187)
LIFECYCLE SOLUTIONS JV LLC ◆
2689 Cmmons Blvd Ste 120 (45431)
PHONE..................................937 938-1321
Jonathon Mitchell, *Partner*
Leeanna Scovil, *Business Mgr*
EMP: 99 EST: 2017
SALES (est): 1.4MM **Privately Held**
SIC: 7371 Custom computer programming services

(G-1188)
LOCKHEED MARTIN CORPORATION
2940 Presidential Dr # 290 (45324-6564)
PHONE..................................937 429-0100
Anney Harris, *Branch Mgr*
Ronney Harris, *Manager*
EMP: 232 **Publicly Held**
SIC: 8711 Aviation &/or aeronautical engineering
PA: Lockheed Martin Corporation
6801 Rockledge Dr
Bethesda MD 20817

(G-1189)
LOWES HOME CENTERS LLC
2850 Centre Dr Ste I (45324-2675)
PHONE..................................937 427-1110
Fax: 937 427-6438
Brian Oletti, *Branch Mgr*
EMP: 150
SALES (corp-wide): 68.6B **Publicly Held**
SIC: 5211 5031 5722 5064 Home centers; building materials, exterior; building materials, interior; household appliance stores; electrical appliances, television & radio
HQ: Lowe's Home Centers, Llc
1605 Curtis Bridge Rd
Wilkesboro NC 28697
336 658-4000

(G-1190)
MATRIX RESEARCH INC (PA)
Also Called: Matrix Research & Engineering
1300 Research Park Dr (45432-2818)
PHONE..................................937 427-8433
Robert J Puskar, *Ch of Bd*
Robert W Hawley, *President*
James E Lutz, *CFO*
Carl Mentzer, *Manager*
William Pierson, *Admin Sec*
EMP: 47
SQ FT: 4,000
SALES (est): 9.1MM **Privately Held**
SIC: 3829 8711 Measuring & controlling devices; engineering services

(G-1191)
MCKEEVER & NIEKAMP ELC INC
1834 Woods Dr (45432-2261)
PHONE..................................937 431-9363
Fax: 937 431-9364
Larry A McKeever, *President*
Doug Niekamp, *Vice Pres*
Tyler Homan, *Manager*
EMP: 25
SQ FT: 3,000
SALES (est): 4.4MM **Privately Held**
WEB: www.mckeeverniekamp.com
SIC: 1731 General electrical contractor

(G-1192)
MCR LLC
2601 Missi Point Blvd Ste (45431)
PHONE..................................937 879-5055

Kurt Gwaltney, *Manager*
EMP: 100
SALES (corp-wide): 55.6MM **Privately Held**
WEB: www.innolog.com
SIC: 8741 Administrative management
PA: Mcr, Llc
2010 Corp Rdg Ste 350
Mclean VA 22102
703 506-4600

(G-1193)
N & C ACTIVE LEARNING LLC
1380 N Fairfield Rd (45432-2644)
PHONE..................................937 545-1342
Colleen Clemens,
Nathan Clemens,
EMP: 30
SALES (est): 315.7K **Privately Held**
SIC: 8351 Child day care services

(G-1194)
NOVA TECHNOLOGY SOLUTIONS LLC
3100 Presidential Dr # 310 (45324-9039)
PHONE..................................937 426-2596
Fax: 937 426-2909
Milt Hamilton, *Project Mgr*
Rick Denezza,
Brad Hart,
EMP: 48
SQ FT: 4,000
SALES: 3.9MM **Privately Held**
WEB: www.novatechsol.com
SIC: 7379

(G-1195)
ORACLE CORPORATION
3610 Pentagon Blvd # 205 (45431-6700)
PHONE..................................513 826-5632
Peter Burton, *Principal*
EMP: 191
SALES (corp-wide): 37.7B **Publicly Held**
SIC: 7372 Business oriented computer software
PA: Oracle Corporation
500 Oracle Pkwy
Redwood City CA 94065
650 506-7000

(G-1196)
PERDUCO GROUP INC
3610 Pentagon Blvd # 110 (45431-6700)
PHONE..................................937 401-0271
Toyzanne Mason, *President*
Stephen Chambal, *Exec VP*
Christopher Mason, *Vice Pres*
John Myers, *Research*
Paul Auclair, *Consultant*
EMP: 44
SQ FT: 4,580
SALES: 500K **Privately Held**
SIC: 8741 8742 Management services; management consulting services

(G-1197)
PH FAIRBORN HT OWNER 2800 LLC
Also Called: Holiday Inn
2800 Presidential Dr (45324-6296)
PHONE..................................937 426-7800
Fax: 937 426-1284
Nathaniel Hamilton, *General Mgr*
EMP: 85
SALES (est): 1.1MM **Privately Held**
SIC: 7011 Hotels & motels

(G-1198)
PREMIER RADIOLOGY GROUP INC
2145 N Fairfield Rd Ste A (45431-2783)
P.O. Box 1365, Springfield (45501-1365)
PHONE..................................937 431-9729
Robin E Osborn, *President*
Dr Crystl Osborne, *Shareholder*
Marry Ellen Beckman, *Administration*
EMP: 27
SQ FT: 16,000
SALES (est): 5MM **Privately Held**
SIC: 8011 Radiologist

(G-1199)
PRIMARY CR NTWRK PRMR HLTH PRT
722 N Fairfield Rd (45434-5918)
PHONE..................................937 208-7000
Fax: 937 208-7010
H Kepler, *Family Practiti*
EMP: 56
SALES (corp-wide): 33.7MM **Privately Held**
SIC: 8049 Acupuncturist
PA: Primary Care Network Of Premier Health Partners
110 N Main St Ste 350
Dayton OH 45402
937 226-7085

(G-1200)
PUPPY PALS RESCUE INC
4241 Country Glen Cir (45432-4129)
PHONE..................................937 426-2643
Linda Klopfenstein, *President*
EMP: 25
SALES: 37K **Privately Held**
SIC: 0752 Dog pounds

(G-1201)
QBASE LLC (PA)
3725 Pentagon Blvd # 100 (45431-2775)
PHONE..................................888 458-0345
Steve Baldwin, *President*
Brian Nightingale, *Exec VP*
Scott Reynolds, *Exec VP*
Steve Schlosser, *Exec VP*
Louis Grever, *Senior VP*
EMP: 32
SQ FT: 9,000
SALES (est): 28.9MM **Privately Held**
WEB: www.qbase.us
SIC: 7379 Data processing consultant

(G-1202)
RAINBOW DATA SYSTEMS INC
2358 Lakeview Dr Ste A (45431-2569)
PHONE..................................937 431-8000
Fax: 937 431-8090
John H Kim, *President*
David Reynolds, *Business Mgr*
Tom Steuer, *Business Mgr*
Doug Mummert, *COO*
Sam Morgan, *Vice Pres*
EMP: 34
SQ FT: 7,100
SALES: 5.9MM **Privately Held**
WEB: www.rainbowdata.com
SIC: 7379 7371 7373 Computer related consulting services; custom computer programming services; computer software development; computer integrated systems design

(G-1203)
REGAL CINEMAS INC
Also Called: Hollywood 20
2651 Fairfield Cmns (45431-3775)
PHONE..................................937 431-9418
Gwen Watts, *Manager*
EMP: 35
SALES (corp-wide): 982.1MM **Privately Held**
WEB: www.regalcinemas.com
SIC: 7832 Motion picture theaters, except drive-in
HQ: Regal Cinemas, Inc.
101 E Blount Ave Ste 100
Knoxville TN 37920
865 922-1123

(G-1204)
RESIDENCE INN BY MARRIOTT BEAV
2779 Frfield Commons Blvd (45431)
PHONE..................................937 427-3914
Carroll Hamann, *Manager*
Ryann McCoy, *Manager*
EMP: 50
SALES (est): 1.3MM **Privately Held**
SIC: 7011 Hotels

(G-1205)
RIVERSIDE RESEARCH INSTITUTE
2640 Hibiscus Way (45431-1798)
PHONE..................................937 431-3810
Fax: 937 431-3811

GEOGRAPHIC SECTION

Beavercreek - Montgomery County (G-1228)

Steve Omick, *President*
Brian O'Connor, *Manager*
Jeffrey D Pursel, *Director*
William Cooley,
EMP: 99
SALES (corp-wide): 88.1MM **Privately Held**
SIC: 8733 Research institute
PA: Riverside Research Institute
 156 William St Fl 9
 New York NY 10038
 212 563-4545

(G-1206)
ROUND ROOM LLC
Also Called: Unknown
3301 Dayton Xenia Rd (45432-2758)
PHONE 937 429-2230
EMP: 44 **Privately Held**
SIC: 4813 Local & long distance telephone communications
PA: Round Room, Llc
 525 Congressional Blvd
 Carmel IN 46032

(G-1207)
SEARS ROEBUCK AND CO
Also Called: Sears Auto Center
2727 Fairfield Cmns (45431-3778)
PHONE 937 427-8528
Fax: 937 427-8516
Mark Cokely, *Manager*
EMP: 25
SALES (corp-wide): 16.7B **Publicly Held**
SIC: 7549 Automotive maintenance services
HQ: Sears, Roebuck And Co.
 3333 Beverly Rd
 Hoffman Estates IL 60179
 847 286-2500

(G-1208)
SIBCY CLINE INC
2476 Commons Blvd Ste E (45431-3808)
PHONE 937 429-2101
Fax: 937 429-2102
Rob Sibcy, *Owner*
Martha E Donges, *COO*
EMP: 42
SALES (corp-wide): 2.1B **Privately Held**
SIC: 6531 Real estate agent, residential
PA: Sibcy Cline, Inc.
 8044 Montgomery Rd # 300
 Cincinnati OH 45236
 513 984-4100

(G-1209)
SOLUTIONS THROUGH INNOVATIVE T
Also Called: STI Technologies
3152 Presidential Dr (45324-2039)
PHONE 937 320-9994
Dr Alvin E Hall Sr, *President*
Charles A Colon III, *Vice Pres*
Joe Blume, *Web Dvlpr*
David Dunning, *Program Dir*
Shawn Castle, *Analyst*
EMP: 65 **EST:** 2000
SQ FT: 2,000
SALES (est): 6.3MM **Privately Held**
WEB: www.sti-tec.com
SIC: 7371 Computer software development & applications

(G-1210)
SUMARIA SYSTEMS INC
3164 Presidential Dr (45324-2039)
PHONE 937 429-6070
Fax: 937 429-6073
Don Kurtz, *President*
Ron Goerges, *Branch Mgr*
C H Bolton, *Manager*
EMP: 80
SALES (corp-wide): 31.8MM **Privately Held**
WEB: www.sumaria.com
SIC: 7373 8711 7374 7371 Computer integrated systems design; consulting engineer; data processing & preparation; custom computer programming services
PA: Sumaria Systems, Inc.
 99 Rosewood Dr Ste 140
 Danvers MA 01923
 978 739-4200

(G-1211)
SYTRONICS INC
4433 Dayton Xenia Rd # 1 (45432-1805)
PHONE 937 431-6100
Fax: 937 431-6400
Barrett Myers, *President*
Sonja Johannes, *Corp Secy*
Scott Grigsby, *Vice Pres*
Steve Myers, *Vice Pres*
Gregory Hubbard, *Engineer*
EMP: 35
SQ FT: 22,000
SALES: 5MM **Privately Held**
WEB: www.sytronics.com
SIC: 7373 8731 8732 Computer integrated systems design; computer systems analysis & design; commercial physical research; commercial nonphysical research

(G-1212)
TACG LLC (PA)
3725 Pentagon Blvd # 110 (45431-2775)
PHONE 937 203-8201
Brian Chaney, *President*
Todd Vikan, *COO*
Joel Schell, *Opers Staff*
Keith Harvey, *Engineer*
Erin O'Brien, *Mktg Dir*
EMP: 66
SALES (est): 7.4MM **Privately Held**
SIC: 8742 Management consulting services

(G-1213)
UES INC (PA)
4401 Dayton Xenia Rd (45432-1805)
PHONE 937 426-6900
Fax: 937 252-6373
Nina Joshi, *CEO*
Johnson Tang, *Managing Dir*
John Gruenwald, *Vice Pres*
Ronda Boles, *Purch Agent*
E E Boakye, *Research*
EMP: 180
SQ FT: 80,000
SALES (est): 38.8MM **Privately Held**
WEB: www.ues.com
SIC: 8731 Biotechnical research, commercial

(G-1214)
UES METALS GROUP
4401 Dayton Xenia Rd (45432-1805)
PHONE 937 255-9340
T Parthaswrthy, *Office Mgr*
Triplicane Parthaswrthy, *Office Mgr*
EMP: 30 **EST:** 2008
SALES (est): 1.6MM **Privately Held**
SIC: 6411 Research services, insurance

(G-1215)
UNISON INDUSTRIES LLC
Also Called: Elano Div
2070 Heller Dr (45434-7210)
PHONE 937 427-0550
Robert Hessel, *Branch Mgr*
EMP: 400
SALES (corp-wide): 122B **Publicly Held**
WEB: www.unisonindustries.com
SIC: 3728 4581 Aircraft parts & equipment; aircraft servicing & repairing
HQ: Unison Industries, Llc
 7575 Baymeadows Way
 Jacksonville FL 32256
 904 739-4000

(G-1216)
UNIVERSAL TECHNOLOGY CORP (PA)
Also Called: U T C
1270 N Fairfield Rd (45432-2600)
PHONE 937 426-2808
Fax: 937 426-8755
Bob Gran, *CEO*
Donna Walker, *General Mgr*
Norman C Carey, *Principal*
Charles J Giemza, *Principal*
Robert D Guyton, *Principal*
EMP: 72 **EST:** 1961
SQ FT: 24,000
SALES (est): 48.4MM **Privately Held**
WEB: www.utcdayton.com
SIC: 8711 7812 7221 Engineering services; audio-visual program production; photographic studios, portrait

(G-1217)
VANA SOLUTIONS LLC
4027 Col Glenn Hwy 110 (45431)
PHONE 937 242-6399
Josh Garcia, *Opers Staff*
David Baldwin, *Business Anlyst*
Eric Gruss, *Manager*
Maria Mamitag, *Consultant*
Tim Schlabach, *Consultant*
EMP: 50
SALES (est): 2.7MM **Privately Held**
SIC: 7379 Computer related maintenance services

(G-1218)
VOSS TOYOTA INC
2110 Heller Dr (45434-7211)
P.O. Box 340100, Dayton (45434-0100)
PHONE 937 427-3700
Fax: 937 431-2130
John E Voss, *President*
Rob George, *Sales Mgr*
Tim Brown, *Sales Staff*
Ryan Kahler, *Sales Staff*
Mary Voench, *Executive*
EMP: 40
SQ FT: 23,000
SALES (est): 13MM **Privately Held**
WEB: www.vosstoyota.com
SIC: 5511 7538 5531 5521 Automobiles, new & used; general automotive repair shops; automotive & home supply stores; used car dealers; automobiles & other motor vehicles

(G-1219)
WRIGHT EXECUTIVE HT LTD PARTNR (PA)
Also Called: Holiday Inn
2800 Presidential Dr (45324-6296)
PHONE 937 426-7800
Western and Southern Life Insu, *Partner*
Steve Groppe, *General Mgr*
Kenneth D Reid, *Exec VP*
David Dixon, *Accountant*
Karl Williard, *Director*
EMP: 180
SALES (est): 6.1MM **Privately Held**
WEB: www.hwdaytonfairborn.com
SIC: 7011 Hotels & motels

(G-1220)
WRIGHT EXECUTIVE HT LTD PARTNR
Also Called: Homewood Suites
2750 Presidential Dr (45324-6262)
PHONE 937 429-0600
Fax: 937 429-0600
Jamie Walters, *General Mgr*
Stephen Brown, *Sales Mgr*
Janelle Richards, *Branch Mgr*
EMP: 128 **Privately Held**
WEB: www.hwdaytonfairborn.com
SIC: 7011 Hotels & motels
PA: Wright Executive Hotel Limited Partnership
 2800 Presidential Dr
 Beavercreek OH 45324

(G-1221)
WRIGHT STATE PHYSCANS DRMTLOGY (PA)
725 University Blvd (45324-2640)
PHONE 937 224-7546
Sheena Geoghegan, *Med Doctor*
Larry Lawhorne, *Geriatrics*
Jeffrey Travers, *Dermatology*
Marc Raslich, *Pediatrics*
EMP: 45
SALES (est): 8.1MM **Privately Held**
SIC: 8011 Dermatologist

(G-1222)
WRIGHT STATE UNIVERSITY
Also Called: Quest Diagnostics
3640 Colonel Glenn Hwy (45324-2096)
PHONE 937 775-3333
Fax: 937 775-2181
Simone Polk, *Manager*
Jeffrey A Vernooy, *Director*
EMP: 1177
SALES (corp-wide): 238.1MM **Privately Held**
SIC: 5063 8221 Electrical apparatus & equipment; university

PA: Wright State University
 3640 Colonel Glenn Hwy
 Dayton OH 45435
 937 775-3333

(G-1223)
WRIGHT-PATT CREDIT UNION INC (PA)
3560 Pentagon Blvd (45431-1706)
P.O. Box 286, Fairborn (45324-0286)
PHONE 937 912-7000
Fax: 937 429-3484
Doug Fecher, *President*
Kim Test, *Principal*
Eric Bugger, *Vice Pres*
Pam Cima, *Vice Pres*
Jennifer Ogden, *Vice Pres*
EMP: 254
SQ FT: 46,000
SALES: 117.3MM **Privately Held**
WEB: www.wrightpattcu.com
SIC: 6062 State credit unions, not federally chartered

(G-1224)
WYLE LABORATORIES INC
2601 Mission Point Blvd # 300 (45431-6600)
PHONE 937 912-3470
Gabe Lemaster, *Opers Mgr*
Rush Kester, *Manager*
Ed Osiadacz, *Info Tech Mgr*
Douglas Van Kirk, *Admin Sec*
EMP: 40 **Publicly Held**
WEB: www.wylelabs.com
SIC: 8734 Testing laboratories
HQ: Wyle Laboratories, Inc.
 1960 E Grand Ave Ste 900
 El Segundo CA 90245

Beavercreek
Montgomery County

(G-1225)
APPLIED RESEARCH SOLUTIONS INC (PA)
51 Plum St Ste 240 (45440-1397)
PHONE 937 912-6100
Gary Wittinger, *CEO*
Kevin Sullivan, *President*
Gary Wittlinger, *General Mgr*
Jaclyn Schmidt, *Research*
Juan Lopez, *Engineer*
EMP: 85
SALES (est): 6.9MM **Privately Held**
WEB: www.arsiresearch.com
SIC: 8733 Research institute

(G-1226)
AT&T CORP
4467 Walnut St (45440-1379)
PHONE 937 320-9648
Jonathon Gohmann, *Branch Mgr*
EMP: 69
SALES (corp-wide): 160.5B **Publicly Held**
WEB: www.att.com
SIC: 4813 Local & long distance telephone communications
HQ: At&T Corp.
 1 At&T Way
 Bedminster NJ 07921
 800 403-3302

(G-1227)
AT&T INC
4467 Walnut St Ste A120 (45440-1379)
PHONE 937 320-9648
EMP: 30
SALES (corp-wide): 160.5B **Publicly Held**
SIC: 4812 Cellular telephone services
PA: At&T Inc.
 208 S Akard St
 Dallas TX 75202
 210 821-4105

(G-1228)
ATK SPACE SYSTEMS INC
1365 Technology Ct (45430-2212)
PHONE 937 490-4121
James Dillon, *General Mgr*
Mark Cottle, *Principal*

Beavercreek - Montgomery County (G-1229)

Joseph Scheckel, *Principal*
Blake Larson, *COO*
Todd Henrich, *Vice Pres*
EMP: 50
SALES (corp-wide): 4.7B **Publicly Held**
WEB: www.psi-pci.com
SIC: 8731 Commercial physical research
HQ: Atk Space Systems Inc.
6033 Bandini Blvd
Commerce CA 90040
323 722-0222

(G-1229)
BIG HILL REALTY CORP
Also Called: Suzie Roselius Real Estate
4011 Danern Dr (45430-2040)
PHONE 937 426-4420
Suzie Roselius, *Branch Mgr*
EMP: 75
SALES (est): 1.2MM
SALES (corp-wide): 9.3MM **Privately Held**
WEB: www.bighillgmac.com
SIC: 6531 Real estate brokers & agents
PA: Big Hill Realty Corp
5580 Far Hills Ave
Dayton OH 45429
937 435-1177

(G-1230)
BIG HILL REALTY CORP
Also Called: Better Homes and Gardens
3944 Indian Ripple Rd (45440-3450)
PHONE 937 429-2200
Fax: 937 429-3655
Tamara M Peacock, *COO*
Stephen Gum, *Broker*
Sherry Stevens, *Broker*
Diana Kuck, *Sales Executive*
Jeff Mayberry, *Sales Executive*
EMP: 29
SALES (est): 1.4MM
SALES (corp-wide): 9.3MM **Privately Held**
WEB: www.bighillgmac.com
SIC: 6531 Real estate agent, residential
PA: Big Hill Realty Corp
5580 Far Hills Ave
Dayton OH 45429
937 435-1177

(G-1231)
BROOKDALE SENIOR LIVING COMMUN
Also Called: Brookdale Beavercreek
3839 Indian Ripple Rd (45440-3468)
PHONE 937 203-8443
Chris Mattox, *Manager*
Kay Keish, *Director*
EMP: 25
SALES (corp-wide): 4.7B **Publicly Held**
WEB: www.assisted.com
SIC: 8059 Rest home, with health care
HQ: Brookdale Senior Living Communities, Inc.
6737 W Wa St Ste 2300
Milwaukee WI 53214
414 918-5000

(G-1232)
CENTRE COMMUNICATIONS CORP
70 Birch Aly Ste 240 (45440-1477)
PHONE 440 454-3262
Eman Shawkey Kailini, *President*
Rick Stadelman, *Principal*
Eric Denis Weiss, *Director*
EMP: 25
SQ FT: 15,000
SALES (est): 249K **Privately Held**
SIC: 8999 Communication services

(G-1233)
CITIGROUP GLOBAL MARKETS INC
Also Called: Smith Barney
4380 Buckeye Ln Ste 200 (45440-7310)
PHONE 860 291-4181
Fax: 937 223-4010
James Tracy, *Div Sub Head*
Rusty Clark, *Branch Mgr*
Russel Clark, *Branch Mgr*
EMP: 70

SALES (corp-wide): 71.4B **Publicly Held**
WEB: www.salomonsmithbarney.com
SIC: 6211 Security brokers & dealers; stock brokers & dealers
HQ: Citigroup Global Markets Inc.
388 Greenwich St Fl 18
New York NY 10013
212 816-6000

(G-1234)
COMPUNET CLINICAL LABS LLC
75 Sylvania Dr (45440-3237)
PHONE 937 427-2655
Fax: 937 320-5061
Linda Blumme, *Manager*
EMP: 57
SALES (corp-wide): 354MM **Privately Held**
SIC: 8071 Medical laboratories
HQ: Compunet Clinical Laboratories, Llc
2308 Sandridge Dr
Moraine OH 45439
937 296-0844

(G-1235)
CONTECH-GDCG
4197 Research Blvd (45430-2203)
PHONE 937 426-3577
Greg Thompson, *Partner*
EMP: 40
SQ FT: 14,000
SALES (est): 1.5MM **Privately Held**
SIC: 8741 Construction management

(G-1236)
DAYTON EYE SURGERY CENTER
81 Sylvania Dr (45440-3271)
PHONE 937 431-9531
Fax: 937 431-9532
Charles Kidwell Jr, *Principal*
Judith L Doell, *Administration*
EMP: 40
SALES (est): 5.4MM **Privately Held**
SIC: 8011 Medical centers

(G-1237)
DEDICATED NURSING ASSOC INC
70 Birch Aly Ste 240 (45440-1477)
PHONE 888 465-6929
EMP: 165 **Privately Held**
SIC: 8051 7361 7363 Skilled nursing care facilities; nurses' registry; medical help service
PA: Dedicated Nursing Associates, Inc.
6536 State Route 22
Delmont PA 15626

(G-1238)
DIGESTIVE CARE INC
75 Sylvania Dr (45440-3237)
PHONE 937 320-5050
Fax: 937 320-5060
Jonhathan Saxe MD, *President*
William Wilson, *Principal*
Richard C Cammerer MD, *Vice Pres*
George M Chioran MD, *Med Doctor*
Giti Rostami MD, *Med Doctor*
EMP: 100
SALES (est): 9.3MM **Privately Held**
WEB: www.digestivecare.net
SIC: 8011 Gastronomist

(G-1239)
ENDOSCOPY CENTER OF DAYTON (PA)
4200 Indian Ripple Rd (45440-3248)
PHONE 937 320-5050
Dr Larry Weprin, *President*
Christopher Wille, *Managing Prtnr*
Tammy Hafer, *Administration*
EMP: 32
SQ FT: 10,000
SALES (est): 2.1MM **Privately Held**
SIC: 8011 Gastronomist

(G-1240)
FARMERS FINANCIAL SERVICES
3888 Indian Ripple Rd (45440-3448)
PHONE 937 424-0643
Fax: 937 424-0666
Pete Dutton, *Owner*
Roger Gilbert, *Manager*

EMP: 40
SALES (est): 1.9MM **Privately Held**
SIC: 6411 Insurance agents, brokers & service

(G-1241)
FIRST COMMAND FINCL PLG INC
51 Plum St Ste 260 (45440-1397)
PHONE 937 429-4490
John Deraper, *Manager*
EMP: 30
SALES (corp-wide): 473.5MM **Privately Held**
SIC: 6211 Mutual funds, selling by independent salesperson
HQ: First Command Financial Planning, Inc.
1 Firstcomm Plz
Fort Worth TX 76109
817 731-8621

(G-1242)
GLOBAL MILITARY EXPERT CO
Also Called: Spotlight Labs
275 Palmetto Ct (45440-3583)
PHONE 800 738-9795
Nathaniel C Dickman,
Bradford Everman,
EMP: 50
SALES (est): 3.8MM **Privately Held**
SIC: 8711 8742 Engineering services; electrical or electronic engineering; aviation &/or aeronautical engineering; training & development consultant

(G-1243)
GREATER DAYTON CNSTR LTD
Also Called: Oberer Thompson Co
4197 Research Blvd (45430-2203)
PHONE 937 426-3577
Fax: 937 256-6368
Greg Thompson, *Partner*
Robin Collier, *Partner*
Kevin Hess, *Vice Pres*
Gene Tartell, *Vice Pres*
Eugene Tartell, *VP Opers*
EMP: 74
SQ FT: 13,500
SALES (est): 42.6MM **Privately Held**
SIC: 1542 1521 1522 Commercial & office building, new construction; specialized public building contractors; new construction, single-family houses; residential construction; apartment building construction; multi-family dwellings, new construction; remodeling, multi-family dwellings

(G-1244)
GREENTOWN CENTER LLC
Also Called: Greene, The
4452 Buckeye Ln (45440-3100)
PHONE 937 490-4990
David Lukes, *CEO*
Andrea Olshan, *President*
Kelli Kooken, *Marketing Staff*
Steve Willshaw, *Manager*
EMP: 90
SALES (est): 4.8MM **Privately Held**
SIC: 6531 Real estate agents & managers

(G-1245)
HAROLD J BECKER COMPANY INC
3946 Indian Ripple Rd (45440-3499)
P.O. Box 340970, Dayton (45434-0970)
PHONE 614 279-1414
Fax: 937 429-4521
Kevin L Bechtel, *President*
Nicholas Bechtel, *Vice Pres*
Dave Fromma, *Project Mgr*
Naomi Terry, *Controller*
Christina Bailey, *Admin Asst*
EMP: 30 **EST:** 1949
SQ FT: 12,000
SALES (est): 5.1MM **Privately Held**
WEB: www.hjbecker.com
SIC: 1761 1799 Roofing contractor; waterproofing

(G-1246)
HCF OF CRESTVIEW INC
Also Called: Village At The Greene
4381 Tonawanda Trl (45430-1961)
PHONE 937 426-5033

Fax: 937 426-9044
Patrice Gerber, *Principal*
Jerome Demmings, *Administration*
EMP: 99
SQ FT: 26,580
SALES (est): 3.7MM **Privately Held**
SIC: 8051 Convalescent home with continuous nursing care

(G-1247)
ITS FINANCIAL LLC
Also Called: Instant Tax Service
51 Plum St Ste 260 (45440-1397)
PHONE 937 425-6889
Peter Samborsky, *CFO*
James Mowery, *CIO*
Mark Makkas, *Database Admin*
Fesum Ogbazion,
EMP: 77
SQ FT: 4,000
SALES (est): 8.8MM **Privately Held**
SIC: 8742 Franchising consultant

(G-1248)
LARUE ENTERPRISES INC
Also Called: Merry Maids
3331 Seajay Dr (45430-1365)
PHONE 937 438-5711
Fax: 937 438-4594
Judith Larue, *Owner*
EMP: 35
SALES: 1MM **Privately Held**
SIC: 7349 7363 Maid services, contract or fee basis; domestic help service

(G-1249)
LEWIS P C JACKSON
70 Birch Aly (45440-1479)
PHONE 937 306-6304
EMP: 38
SALES (corp-wide): 340.5MM **Privately Held**
SIC: 8111 General practice law office
PA: Lewis P C Jackson
1133 Weschester Ave
White Plains NY 10604
914 872-8060

(G-1250)
LOFINOS INC
Also Called: Lofino's Investment
3255 Seajay Dr (45440-1356)
PHONE 937 431-1662
Fax: 937 426-0065
Michael D Lofino, *President*
Charles Lofino, *Chairman*
John Mantia, *Corp Secy*
John Alge, *COO*
Martin Sloan, *Controller*
EMP: 80
SQ FT: 45,000
SALES (est): 6.9MM **Privately Held**
WEB: www.lofinos.com
SIC: 5411 6512 Supermarkets, independent; shopping center, property operation only

(G-1251)
MACAULAY-BROWN INC (PA)
Also Called: Macb
4021 Executive Dr (45430-1062)
PHONE 937 426-3421
Fax: 937 426-5364
Sid Fuchs, *CEO*
Sidney E Fuchs, *President*
Mike Beauchamp, *Senior VP*
Mark Chadason, *Senior VP*
Fred Norman, *Senior VP*
EMP: 400 **EST:** 1979
SQ FT: 64,000
SALES (est): 313.6MM **Privately Held**
WEB: www.macaulaybrown.com
SIC: 8711 8733 Consulting engineer; research institute

(G-1252)
MANATRON INC (DH)
4105 Executive Dr (45430-1071)
PHONE 937 431-4000
Allen Peat, *President*
Nan W Warner, *Regional Mgr*
Ruel Williamson, *COO*
EMP: 34
SQ FT: 12,000

GEOGRAPHIC SECTION — Beavercreek Township - Greene County (G-1275)

SALES (est): 3.5MM
SALES (corp-wide): 3.1B **Publicly Held**
SIC: 7373 5045 Turnkey vendors, computer systems; local area network (LAN) systems integrator; computer peripheral equipment; computers & accessories, personal & home entertainment
HQ: Manatron, Inc.
510 E Milham Ave
Portage MI 49002
269 567-2900

(G-1253)
MANATRON SABRE SYSTEMS AND SVC (DH)
4105 Executive Dr (45430-1071)
PHONE.............................937 431-4000
Fax: 937 431-4001
Dan Muthard, *President*
Barb Sloan, *Manager*
EMP: 68
SALES (est): 7.7MM
SALES (corp-wide): 3.1B **Publicly Held**
WEB: www.manatron.com
SIC: 5045 6531 Computer software; appraiser, real estate
HQ: Manatron, Inc.
510 E Milham Ave
Portage MI 49002
269 567-2900

(G-1254)
MINI UNIVERSITY INC (PA)
115 Harbert Dr Ste A (45440-5117)
PHONE.............................937 426-1414
Fax: 937 426-5650
Julie Thorner, *President*
Donna Mowles, *Human Res Dir*
Sarah Cannon, *Mktg Coord*
Catina Anderson, *Director*
Bess John, *Director*
EMP: 125
SALES (est): 1MM **Privately Held**
WEB: www.miniuniversity.net
SIC: 8351 Preschool center

(G-1255)
NORTHROP GRUMMAN SYSTEMS CORP
4020 Executive Dr (45430-1061)
PHONE.............................937 429-6450
Mel Meadows, *Branch Mgr*
Karen Sadri-Lonbani, *Info Tech Mgr*
Thomas Seibert, *Director*
Jeffrey Wood, *Administration*
EMP: 45 **Publicly Held**
SIC: 7373 Computer systems analysis & design
HQ: Northrop Grumman Systems Corporation
2980 Fairview Park Dr
Falls Church VA 22042
703 280-2900

(G-1256)
POND-WOOLPERT LLC
4454 Idea Center Blvd (45430-1500)
PHONE.............................937 461-5660
David Ziegman,
EMP: 60
SALES (est): 1MM **Privately Held**
SIC: 8712 Architectural engineering

(G-1257)
RE/MAX
51 Plum St Ste 220 (45440-1397)
PHONE.............................937 477-4997
Stan Haper, *Owner*
Marsha Conner, *Broker*
Kathryn Dixon, *Broker*
Cheri Knedler, *Broker*
Jill Aldineh, *Consultant*
EMP: 45 EST: 2011
SALES: 150K **Privately Held**
SIC: 6531 Real estate agent, residential

(G-1258)
RICHARD L LISTON MD
Also Called: Danton Eye Associates
89 Sylvania Dr (45440-3281)
PHONE.............................937 320-2020
Dr R Liston, *Partner*
EMP: 52
SALES (est): 925K **Privately Held**
SIC: 8011 General & family practice, physician/surgeon

(G-1259)
SAWDEY SOLUTION SERVICES INC (PA)
1430 Oak Ct Ste 304 (45430-1065)
PHONE.............................937 490-4060
Constance Sawdey, *President*
Jeffrey Sawdey, *Vice Pres*
Rick Noll, *Opers Mgr*
Joseph Pmp, *Opers Staff*
Marcus Smith, *Manager*
EMP: 29 EST: 2001
SALES: 16MM **Privately Held**
WEB: www.sawdeysolutionservices.com
SIC: 7371 8748 Custom computer programming services; systems engineering consultant, ex. computer or professional

(G-1260)
TAITECH INC (PA)
1430 Oak Ct Ste 301 (45430-1065)
PHONE.............................937 431-1007
Fax: 937 431-1008
Tzong Chen, *President*
Ryan Milligan, *Engineer*
Sherree Reed, *Human Res Dir*
EMP: 43
SQ FT: 1,000
SALES (est): 3.7MM **Privately Held**
WEB: www.taitech.com
SIC: 8731 Biological research

(G-1261)
UNITED CHURCH HOMES INC
Also Called: Trinity Community
3218 Indian Ripple Rd (45440-3637)
PHONE.............................937 426-8481
Fax: 937 426-3043
Timothy Hackett, *Vice Pres*
Tami Woodall, *Chf Purch Ofc*
Tom Lee, *Info Tech Dir*
Laura Farrell, *Director*
EMP: 200
SALES (corp-wide): 78.1MM **Privately Held**
WEB: www.altenheimcommunity.org
SIC: 8051 8052 8361 Convalescent home with continuous nursing care; intermediate care facilities; geriatric residential care
PA: United Church Homes Inc
170 E Center St
Marion OH 43302
740 382-4885

(G-1262)
WERNLI REALTY INC
1300 Grange Hall Rd (45430-1013)
PHONE.............................937 258-7878
Richard L Schaefer, *President*
Norman Miller, *Vice Pres*
John Miltenberger, *Asst Sec*
EMP: 75
SQ FT: 20,000
SALES (est): 8.6MM **Privately Held**
SIC: 3441 6512 Building components, structural steel; nonresidential building operators

(G-1263)
WOOLPRT-MRRICK JOINT VENTR LLP
4454 Idea Center Blvd (45430-1500)
PHONE.............................937 461-5660
David Ziegman, *Principal*
Janice James, *Office Mgr*
EMP: 50 EST: 2014
SQ FT: 1,800
SALES (est): 1.7MM **Privately Held**
SIC: 8712 Architectural engineering

(G-1264)
WYLE LABORATORIES INC
2700 Indian Ripple Rd (45440-3638)
PHONE.............................937 320-2712
Mike Gilkey, *Branch Mgr*
Francis Smith, *Info Tech Mgr*
EMP: 150 **Publicly Held**
WEB: www.wylelabs.com
SIC: 8731 Commercial physical research
HQ: Wyle Laboratories, Inc.
1960 E Grand Ave Ste 900
El Segundo CA 90245

Beavercreek Township
Greene County

(G-1265)
AZIMUTH CORPORATION
4027 Colonel Glenn Hwy # 230 (45431-1695)
PHONE.............................937 256-8571
James Michael Livingston, *CEO*
Valerie Rossi, *President*
Charles Rossi, *Vice Pres*
EMP: 49
SQ FT: 3,286
SALES: 8.5MM **Privately Held**
WEB: www.azimuth-corp.com
SIC: 8711 8731 8742 Consulting engineer; commercial physical research; management consulting services

(G-1266)
COLDWELL BNKR HRITG RLTORS LLC
4139 Colonel Glenn Hwy (45431-1652)
PHONE.............................937 426-6060
Bruce Doldeer, *Manager*
Bruce Dolbeer, *Manager*
EMP: 32
SALES (corp-wide): 7.5MM **Privately Held**
WEB: www.coldwellbankerdayton.com
SIC: 6531 Real estate agent, residential
PA: Coldwell Banker Heritage Realtors Llc
2000 Hewitt Ave
Dayton OH 45440
937 434-7600

(G-1267)
DAVE DNNIS CHRYSLER JEEP DODGE
Also Called: Dave Dennis Auto Group
4232 Colonel Glenn Hwy (45431-1604)
PHONE.............................937 429-5566
Fax: 937 429-2210
Jason Dennis, *President*
Ulysses Ponder, *Treasurer*
Jerry Hecht, *Finance Mgr*
Virginia Purdin, *Human Res Mgr*
Ryan McGee, *Sales Mgr*
EMP: 60
SQ FT: 31,000
SALES (est): 25.7MM **Privately Held**
WEB: www.davedennis.com
SIC: 5511 7532 7538 5531 Automobiles, new & used; body shop, automotive; general automotive repair shops; automotive parts; automotive accessories

(G-1268)
DAYTON AEROSPACE INC
4141 Colonel Glenn Hwy # 252 (45431-5102)
PHONE.............................937 426-4300
Fax: 937 426-1352
Robert Matthews, *President*
Charles Craw Jr, *Vice Pres*
Bob Matthews, *Vice Pres*
Gary Poleskey, *Vice Pres*
Robert Raggio, *Vice Pres*
EMP: 30
SQ FT: 6,337
SALES (est): 5.5MM **Privately Held**
WEB: www.daytonaero.com
SIC: 8742 Business consultant

(G-1269)
FRONTIER TECHNOLOGY INC (PA)
Also Called: Fti
4141 Colonel Glenn Hwy # 140 (45431-1662)
PHONE.............................937 429-3302
Fax: 937 429-3704
Ron Shroder, *CEO*
Donald Conroy, *Vice Pres*
Eric Styron, *Project Mgr*
Carmen Barone, *Controller*
Thomas P Karmondy, *Manager*
EMP: 30
SQ FT: 3,834
SALES (est): 30.2MM **Privately Held**
WEB: www.fti-net.com
SIC: 8711 7371 Consulting engineer; computer software development & applications

(G-1270)
INFOSCITEX CORPORATION
4027 Colonel Glenn Hwy # 210 (45431-1661)
PHONE.............................937 429-9008
Lori Walton, *Branch Mgr*
EMP: 27
SALES (corp-wide): 277.4MM **Privately Held**
SIC: 8711 Engineering services
HQ: Infoscitex Corporation
295 Foster St Ste 1
Littleton MA 01460
781 419-6370

(G-1271)
JACOBS TECHNOLOGY INC
Also Called: Advanced Systems Group
4027 Colonel Glenn Hwy (45431-1673)
PHONE.............................937 429-5056
EMP: 40
SALES (corp-wide): 12.1B **Publicly Held**
SIC: 8711 Engineering Services
HQ: Jacobs Technology Inc.
600 William Northern Blvd
Tullahoma TN 37388
931 455-6400

(G-1272)
JOES LDSCPG BEAVERCREEK INC
2500 National Rd (45324-2011)
PHONE.............................937 427-1133
Fax: 937 427-1955
Joe Leopard, *President*
Jannet Leopard, *Office Mgr*
EMP: 30
SQ FT: 5,000
SALES (est): 3MM **Privately Held**
WEB: www.joeslandscaping.com
SIC: 0781 Landscape services

(G-1273)
LANE CHEVROLET
635 S Orchard Ln (45434-6163)
P.O. Box 340910, Dayton (45434-0910)
PHONE.............................937 426-2313
Jason Laughlin, *Principal*
Keith Bockbrader, *Purch Mgr*
Jaime Holbrook, *Sales Mgr*
EMP: 92
SALES (est): 11.3MM **Privately Held**
SIC: 5511 7538 Automobiles, new & used; general automotive repair shops

(G-1274)
LANG CHEVROLET CO
Also Called: Lang Chevrolet Geo
635 Orchard Ln (45434-6163)
P.O. Box 340910, Dayton (45434-0910)
PHONE.............................937 426-2313
Fax: 937 426-6254
Richard F Lang, *Owner*
Joe Carrico, *Division Mgr*
Gerry Laughlin, *General Mgr*
Keith Bockbrader, *Co-Owner*
Judy Lang, *Co-Owner*
EMP: 100
SQ FT: 35,000
SALES (est): 32.8MM **Privately Held**
WEB: www.langs.com
SIC: 5511 7538 7532 7515 Automobiles, new & used; trucks, tractors & trailers: new & used; general automotive repair shops; top & body repair & paint shops; passenger car leasing; used car dealers

(G-1275)
MODERN TECH SOLUTIONS INC
Also Called: Mtsi
4141 Colonel Glenn Hwy # 115 (45431-5100)
PHONE.............................937 426-9025
Scott Coale, *Principal*
EMP: 65
SALES (est): 5.7MM **Privately Held**
WEB: www.mtsi-va.com
SIC: 8711 8731 Consulting engineer; commercial physical research

Beavercreek Township - Greene County (G-1276)

GEOGRAPHIC SECTION

PA: Modern Technology Solutions, Inc.
5285 Shawnee Rd Ste 400
Alexandria VA 22312

(G-1276)
NORTHROP GRUMMAN TECHNICAL
Also Called: Ngts
4065 Colonel Glenn Hwy (45431-1601)
PHONE..........................937 320-3100
Dale A Brookhart, *Principal*
Barry Cothran, *Research*
Dave Johns, *Engineer*
Saju Kuruvilla, *Branch Mgr*
Garin Clint, *Program Mgr*
EMP: 150 **Publicly Held**
WEB: www.afqrc.com
SIC: **8732** 8711 7373 Market analysis or research; engineering services; computer integrated systems design
HQ: Northrop Grumman Technical Services, Inc.
2340 Dulles Corner Blvd
Herndon VA 20171
703 713-4096

(G-1277)
OASIS SYSTEMS INC
4141 Colonel Glenn Hwy (45431-1600)
PHONE..........................937 426-1295
Tome Challea, *President*
EMP: 48
SALES (est): 2.2MM **Privately Held**
SIC: **7379** Computer related consulting services

(G-1278)
OPTIMETRICS INC
4027 Colonel Glenn Hwy (45431-1673)
PHONE..........................937 306-7180
EMP: 28
SALES (corp-wide): 277.4MM **Privately Held**
SIC: **8711** Engineering services
HQ: Optimetrics, Inc.
100 Walter Ward Blvd
Abingdon MD 21009
734 330-2190

(G-1279)
PEERLESS TECHNOLOGIES CORP
2300 National Rd (45324-2009)
PHONE..........................937 490-5000
Fax: 937 490-5001
Michael C Bridges, *President*
Tom Reinhardt, *Senior Partner*
Doug Burkett, *Senior VP*
Don Greiman, *Senior VP*
Julie Jones, *Senior VP*
EMP: 60
SQ FT: 17,000
SALES (est): 15.1MM **Privately Held**
WEB: www.epeerless.com
SIC: **7373** Computer systems analysis & design

(G-1280)
PHILLIPS COMPANIES
Also Called: Phillips Sand & Gravel Co
620 Phillips Dr (45434-7230)
PHONE..........................937 426-5461
Richard L Phillips II, *President*
Larry Phillips, *Vice Pres*
EMP: 29
SALES (corp-wide): 13.3MM **Privately Held**
WEB: www.phillipscompanies.com
SIC: **3273** 1771 Ready-mixed concrete; concrete pumping
PA: Phillips Companies
620 Phillips Dr
Beavercreek Township OH 45434
937 426-5461

(G-1281)
PHILLIPS READY MIX CO
620 Phillips Dr (45434-7230)
P.O. Box 187, Alpha (45301-0187)
PHONE..........................937 426-5151
Fax: 937 426-0659
Rick Phillips, *President*
Dennis Phillips, *Treasurer*
Larry Phillips, *Asst Sec*
EMP: 100

SALES (est): 4.2MM **Privately Held**
SIC: **1771** 3273 7353 5191 Concrete pumping; ready-mixed concrete; heavy construction equipment rental; farm supplies; excavation work; construction sand & gravel

(G-1282)
PRIORITY BUILDING SERVICES INC
2370 National Rd (45324-2009)
P.O. Box 1881, Fairborn (45324-7881)
PHONE..........................937 233-7030
Fax: 937 320-9606
Oscar Blair, *President*
Gwen Blair, *Vice Pres*
EMP: 65
SQ FT: 7,500
SALES (est): 2.6MM **Privately Held**
WEB: www.prioritybldgservs.com
SIC: **7349** Janitorial service, contract basis

(G-1283)
QUANTECH SERVICES INC
4141 Colonel Glenn Hwy # 273 (45431-1676)
PHONE..........................937 490-8461
Maryanne E Cromwell, *Principal*
EMP: 133
SALES (corp-wide): 81MM **Privately Held**
SIC: **8999** Artists & artists' studios
PA: Quantech Services Inc.
91 Hartwell Ave Ste 3
Lexington MA 02421
781 271-9757

(G-1284)
SMITH CONSTRUCTION GROUP INC
731 Orchard Ln (45434-7214)
PHONE..........................937 426-0500
Fax: 937 426-0505
Sean Smith, *President*
Herb Hall, *Project Mgr*
Ben Pike, *Project Mgr*
Cody Smith, *Project Mgr*
Madonna Evans, *Manager*
EMP: 25
SALES (est): 10.7MM **Privately Held**
SIC: **1542** Commercial & office building, new construction

(G-1285)
SONOCO PRODUCTS COMPANY
Sonoco Consumer Products
761 Space Dr (45434-7171)
PHONE..........................937 429-0040
Norwood Bizzell, *Manager*
EMP: 60
SALES (corp-wide): 5B **Publicly Held**
WEB: www.sonoco.com
SIC: **2655** 5113 2891 Cans, fiber: made from purchased material; paper tubes & cores; adhesives & sealants
PA: Sonoco Products Company
1 N 2nd St
Hartsville SC 29550
843 383-7000

(G-1286)
STANLEY STEEMER INTL INC
Also Called: Stanley Steemer Carpet Clr 09
824 Space Dr (45434-7163)
PHONE..........................937 431-3205
Fax: 937 431-3210
Brad Martin, *Branch Mgr*
Anthony Mohler, *Manager*
EMP: 30
SALES (est): 241.9MM **Privately Held**
WEB: www.stanley-steemer.com
SIC: **7217** Carpet & furniture cleaning on location
PA: Stanley Steemer International, Inc.
5800 Innovation Dr
Dublin OH 43016
614 764-2007

Beavercreek Township
Montgomery County

(G-1287)
BROOKDALE SENIOR LIVING INC
Also Called: Brookdale Kettering
280 Walden Way Ofc (45440-4402)
PHONE..........................937 203-8596
Lynn Fugate, *Corp Comm Staff*
Sharon Bristow, *Manager*
EMP: 65
SALES (corp-wide): 4.7B **Publicly Held**
WEB: www.grandcourtlifestyles.com
SIC: **6513** Retirement hotel operation
PA: Brookdale Senior Living
111 Westwood Pl Ste 400
Brentwood TN 37027
615 221-2250

Beaverdam
Allen County

(G-1288)
BEAVERDAM FLEET SERVICES INC
424 E Main St (45808-9724)
PHONE..........................419 643-8880
Joe Seeling, *President*
Mary Hrach, *Admin Sec*
EMP: 31
SQ FT: 11,000
SALES (est): 2.3MM **Privately Held**
WEB: www.beaverdamfleetservice.com
SIC: **7538** 7549 General truck repair; towing service, automotive

(G-1289)
BLUE BEACON USA LP II
Also Called: Blue Beacon of Beaverdam
413 E Main St (45808-9728)
PHONE..........................419 643-8146
Mike Kreager, *Branch Mgr*
EMP: 30
SALES (corp-wide): 88.4MM **Privately Held**
SIC: **7542** Truck wash
PA: Blue Beacon U.S.A., L.P. Ii
500 Graves Blvd
Salina KS 67401
785 825-2221

(G-1290)
LOVES TRAVEL STOPS
416 Village Ave (45808-9704)
PHONE..........................419 643-8482
Adam Chandler, *Principal*
EMP: 31
SALES (corp-wide): 5.5B **Privately Held**
SIC: **7538** Truck engine repair, except industrial
PA: Love's Travel Stops & Country Stores, Inc.
10601 N Pennsylvania Ave
Oklahoma City OK 73120
405 302-6500

Bedford
Cuyahoga County

(G-1291)
1ST GEAR AUTO INC
Also Called: North Coast Auto Mall
333 Broadway Ave (44146-2602)
PHONE..........................216 458-0791
Igor Grinberg, *CEO*
Michael Dorenkott, *Sales Associate*
Christian Spivey, *Sales Associate*
EMP: 26
SALES (est): 4.6MM **Privately Held**
SIC: **7538** General automotive repair shops

(G-1292)
A M CASTLE & CO
Also Called: Oliver Steel Plate
26800 Miles Rd (44146-1405)
PHONE..........................330 425-7000
Scott J Dolan, *Branch Mgr*
EMP: 65
SALES (corp-wide): 533.1MM **Publicly Held**
SIC: **5051** 3444 3443 3398 Metals service centers & offices; sheet metalwork; fabricated plate work (boiler shop); metal heat treating
PA: A.M. Castle & Co.
1420 Kensington Rd # 220
Oak Brook IL 60523
847 455-7111

(G-1293)
AKE MARKETING
503 Broadway Ave (44146-2723)
PHONE..........................440 232-1661
Jennifer Marriott, *Manager*
EMP: 30 EST: 2001
SALES (est): 1.9MM **Privately Held**
SIC: **8742** Marketing consulting services

(G-1294)
BEDFORD CHURCH OF NAZARENE
Also Called: Bedford Nurs Schl Kindergarden
365 Center Rd (44146-2237)
PHONE..........................440 232-7440
Fax: 440 232-0683
Stephen Ley, *Treasurer*
Bradley Taylor, *Administration*
Linda Bartlett, *Administration*
EMP: 26
SQ FT: 100,000
SALES: 500K **Privately Held**
WEB: www.bcn.org
SIC: **8351** Nursery school

(G-1295)
BEDFORD HEIGHTS CITY WASTE
Also Called: Bedford Heights City Waste Wtr
25301 Solon Rd (44146-4727)
PHONE..........................440 439-5343
Dave Pocaro, *Director*
EMP: 25
SALES (est): 1MM **Privately Held**
SIC: **7699** Waste cleaning services

(G-1296)
BELLE TIRE
205 Oak Leaf Oval (44146-6156)
PHONE..........................440 735-0800
Don Barn, *President*
Stacey White, *Office Mgr*
EMP: 25
SQ FT: 3,000
SALES (est): 1.9MM **Privately Held**
SIC: **7534** Tire retreading & repair shops

(G-1297)
BOEHRINGER INGELHEIM USA CORP
Also Called: Ben Venue Laboratories
300 Northfield Rd (44146-4650)
P.O. Box 2075, Ridgefield CT (06877-6675)
PHONE..........................440 232-3320
Don Whiteaker, *Materials Mgr*
Gary Price, *CFO*
Ignacio Ruelas, *Business Anlyst*
Paul Kersten, *Marketing Staff*
▲ EMP: 28
SALES (est): 11.2MM
SALES (corp-wide): 16.7B **Privately Held**
SIC: **5122** Pharmaceuticals
PA: C.H. Boehringer Sohn Ag & Co. Kg
Binger Str. 173
Ingelheim Am Rhein 55218
613 277-0

(G-1298)
CBF INDUSTRIES INC
Also Called: Cleveland Business Furniture
23600 Aurora Rd (44146-1712)
PHONE..........................216 229-9300
Fax: 216 229-7310
Gary Bunge, *President*
Joe Fixler, *Vice Pres*
Joe Sixler, *Vice Pres*

Terry Kopania, *Treasurer*
Joseph Adato, *Manager*
EMP: 30
SQ FT: 92,000
SALES (est): 5.7MM
SALES (corp-wide): 5.9MM **Privately Held**
WEB: www.ebo.com
SIC: 5046 5021 5712 Shelving, commercial & industrial; office furniture; office furniture
PA: E.B.O. Inc
   23600 Aurora Rd
   Bedford OH 44146
   216 229-9300

(G-1299)
CHAGRIN VALLEY DISPATCH
88 Center Rd Ste B100 (44146-2700)
PHONE..................440 247-7321
Nick Dicicco, *Director*
EMP: 39
SQ FT: 5,000
SALES: 4.2MM **Privately Held**
SIC: 8322 Hotline

(G-1300)
COMFORT SYSTEMS USA OHIO INC (HQ)
7401 First Pl Ste A (44146-6723)
PHONE..................440 703-1600
Fax: 440 703-1601
Daniel Lemons, *President*
Mike Barnhart, *CFO*
EMP: 50
SQ FT: 21,000
SALES (est): 17.6MM
SALES (corp-wide): 1.7B **Publicly Held**
SIC: 1711 Warm air heating & air conditioning contractor
PA: Comfort Systems Usa, Inc.
   675 Bering Dr Ste 400
   Houston TX 77057
   713 830-9600

(G-1301)
COMMUNITY HOSPITAL OF BEDFORD
Also Called: University Hospitals Hlth Sys
44 Blaine Ave (44146-2709)
PHONE..................440 735-3900
Fax: 440 232-0776
Arlene Rak, *President*
Nancy De Santis, *Sls & Mktg Exec*
Don Paulson, *CFO*
Velibor Drobnjak, *Pharmacist*
Ron Broadus, *Director*
EMP: 425
SQ FT: 155,000
SALES (est): 28.3MM
SALES (corp-wide): 2.3B **Privately Held**
WEB: www.uhhsbmc.com
SIC: 8062 General medical & surgical hospitals
PA: University Hospitals Health System, Inc.
   3605 Warrensville Ctr Rd
   Shaker Heights OH 44122
   216 767-8900

(G-1302)
CUNNINGHAM PAVING COMPANY
20814 Aurora Rd (44146-1006)
PHONE..................216 581-8600
Fax: 216 581-8683
Timothy Cunningham, *President*
EMP: 30
SALES: 9MM **Privately Held**
SIC: 1611 Highway & street paving contractor

(G-1303)
DEUFOL WORLDWIDE PACKAGING LLC
19800 Alexander Rd (44146-5346)
PHONE..................440 232-1100
EMP: 54
SALES (est): 1MM **Privately Held**
SIC: 4783 5113 Packing And Crating, Nsk

(G-1304)
DONE-RITE BOWLING SERVICE CO (PA)
Also Called: Paragon Machine Company
20434 Krick Rd (44146-4422)
PHONE..................440 232-3280
Fax: 440 232-3635
Robert W Gable, *CEO*
Glenn Gable, *President*
Gale Burns, *Vice Pres*
Dave Patz, *Vice Pres*
Ann Gable, *Shareholder*
▲ **EMP:** 25 **EST:** 1950
SQ FT: 20,000
SALES (est): 2.6MM **Privately Held**
WEB: www.donerite.com
SIC: 3949 1752 5091 Bowling equipment & supplies; floor laying & floor work; bowling equipment

(G-1305)
EBO INC (PA)
Also Called: Cbf
23600 Aurora Rd (44146-1712)
PHONE..................216 229-9300
Gary Bunge, *President*
Joe Fixler, *Vice Pres*
Terry Kopania, *Treasurer*
Gary Grecar, *Admin Sec*
EMP: 26
SQ FT: 100,000
SALES (est): 5.9MM **Privately Held**
WEB: www.ebo.com
SIC: 5046 5021 5712 Shelving, commercial & industrial; office furniture; office furniture

(G-1306)
FEDERAL EXPRESS CORPORATION
Also Called: Fedex
5313 Majestic Pkwy (44146-1743)
PHONE..................800 463-3339
Fred Laskovics, *District Mgr*
EMP: 150
SALES (corp-wide): 60.3B **Publicly Held**
WEB: www.federalexpress.com
SIC: 4212 Local trucking, without storage
HQ: Federal Express Corporation
   3610 Hacks Cross Rd
   Memphis TN 38125
   901 369-3600

(G-1307)
FOWLER ELECTRIC CO
26185 Broadway Ave (44146-6512)
PHONE..................440 735-2385
Fax: 440 786-9780
Tim Phillips, *Project Mgr*
Richard Trela, *Mng Member*
Scott Jordan, *Mng Member*
Tim Fowler, *Sr Project Mgr*
EMP: 53
SALES: 24MM **Privately Held**
SIC: 1711 1731 Mechanical contractor; general electrical contractor

(G-1308)
GRACE HOSPITAL
44 Blaine Ave (44146-2709)
PHONE..................216 687-1500
EMP: 55
SALES (corp-wide): 17.4MM **Privately Held**
SIC: 8062 General medical & surgical hospitals
PA: Grace Hospital
   2307 W 14th St
   Cleveland OH 44113
   216 687-1500

(G-1309)
HANDL-IT INC
7120 Krick Rd Ste 1a (44146-4444)
PHONE..................440 439-9400
Fax: 440 439-9463
Jerry Peters, *Branch Mgr*
Jeannie Sureck, *Manager*
EMP: 100 **Privately Held**
WEB: www.handlit.net
SIC: 5063 Light bulbs & related supplies
PA: Handl-It, Inc
   360 Highland Rd E 2
   Macedonia OH 44056

(G-1310)
HAVSCO INC
5018 Richmond Rd (44146-1329)
PHONE..................440 439-8900
Fax: 440 439-0974
Rick Coates, *General Mgr*
Bob Haines, *Service Mgr*
Phil Wike, *Manager*
EMP: 40
SQ FT: 10,000
SALES (est): 2.4MM **Privately Held**
SIC: 1711 Warm air heating & air conditioning contractor; ventilation & duct work contractor

(G-1311)
HAWTHORNE VALLEY COUNTRY CLUB
25250 Rockside Rd Ste 1 (44146-1839)
PHONE..................440 232-1400
Fax: 440 439-6856
Bob Zeman, *General Mgr*
Terri Weglicki, *Accounting Mgr*
EMP: 100
SQ FT: 46,500
SALES (est): 2.8MM **Privately Held**
SIC: 7997 5941 Country club, membership; sporting goods & bicycle shops

(G-1312)
ILLINOIS TOOL WORKS INC
Anchor Fasteners
26101 Fargo Ave (44146-1305)
PHONE..................216 292-7161
Fax: 216 292-3699
Frank Lieberman, *Plant Mgr*
Mary Frabotta, *Purchasing*
Judi Sandbrook, *Personnel*
Ray Belcher, *Branch Mgr*
EMP: 35
SALES (corp-wide): 14.3B **Publicly Held**
SIC: 5063 Electronic wire & cable
PA: Illinois Tool Works Inc.
   155 Harlem Ave
   Glenview IL 60025
   847 724-7500

(G-1313)
INDUSTRIAL FIRST INC (PA)
25840 Miles Rd Ste 2 (44146-1426)
PHONE..................216 991-8605
Steven F Lau, *President*
Frank Burkosky, *Exec VP*
Dale Leboda, *Project Mgr*
Mitch Gelofsack, *Department Mgr*
Greg Klik, *Department Mgr*
EMP: 125
SQ FT: 6,400
SALES (est): 33.2MM **Privately Held**
WEB: www.industrialfirst.com
SIC: 1741 1761 1791 Masonry & other stonework; siding contractor; structural steel erection

(G-1314)
KBJ-SUMMIT LLC
7817 First Pl (44146-6707)
PHONE..................440 232-3334
Kyle Jones, *Principal*
EMP: 60
SALES (est): 2.9MM **Privately Held**
SIC: 1542 Nonresidential construction

(G-1315)
KOLTCZ CONCRETE BLOCK CO
7660 Oak Leaf Rd (44146-5554)
PHONE..................440 232-3030
Fax: 440 232-4506
Stanley M Koltcz, *President*
EMP: 26 **EST:** 1938
SQ FT: 55,000
SALES (est): 5MM **Privately Held**
WEB: www.koltcz.com
SIC: 3271 5032 5211 Blocks, concrete or cinder: standard; masons' materials; masonry materials & supplies

(G-1316)
LEGACY CONSULTANT PHARMACY
Also Called: Autumn
26691 Richmond Rd (44146-1421)
PHONE..................336 760-1670
April Jones, *Human Res Dir*
Jessica Fountain, *Cert Phar Tech*
Ann Lemmons, *Cert Phar Tech*
Kimberly Mabe, *Manager*
Mary Thomas, *Consultant*
EMP: 40
SALES (est): 3.3MM **Privately Held**
SIC: 8748 Business consulting

(G-1317)
LOVEMAN STEEL CORPORATION
5455 Perkins Rd (44146-1856)
PHONE..................440 232-6200
Fax: 440 232-0914
Anthony Murru, *CEO*
James Loveman, *COO*
David Loveman, *Exec VP*
Rob Loveman, *Vice Pres*
John Steagall, *Vice Pres*
▼ **EMP:** 75
SQ FT: 80,000
SALES: 17MM **Privately Held**
WEB: www.lovemansteel.com
SIC: 5051 3443 Plates, metal; weldments

(G-1318)
LOWES HOME CENTERS LLC
24500 Miles Rd (44146-1314)
PHONE..................216 831-2860
Fax: 216 831-1935
John Lerch, *Manager*
EMP: 300
SALES (corp-wide): 68.6B **Publicly Held**
SIC: 5211 5031 5722 5064 Home centers; building materials, exterior; building materials, interior; household appliance stores; electrical appliances, television & radio
HQ: Lowe's Home Centers, Llc
   1605 Curtis Bridge Rd
   Wilkesboro NC 28697
   336 658-4000

(G-1319)
MAINES PAPER & FOOD SVC INC
199 Oak Leaf Oval (44146-6156)
PHONE..................216 643-7500
Christina Grau, *Cust Mgr*
Dennis Kee, *Manager*
EMP: 50
SALES (corp-wide): 1.9B **Privately Held**
WEB: www.maines.net
SIC: 5142 5169 5149 5113 Packaged frozen goods; chemicals & allied products; groceries & related products; industrial & personal service paper
PA: Maines Paper & Food Service, Inc.
   101 Broome Corporate Pkwy
   Conklin NY 13748
   607 779-1200

(G-1320)
MANTUA MANUFACTURING CO (PA)
Also Called: MANTUA BED FRAMES
7900 Northfield Rd (44146-5525)
PHONE..................800 333-8333
David Jaffe, *CEO*
Charles Bastien, *Vice Pres*
Dirk Smith, *Vice Pres*
Jeff Wick, *Vice Pres*
Frank Barkley, *Plant Mgr*
▲ **EMP:** 120 **EST:** 1952
SQ FT: 67,500
SALES (est): 101.7MM **Privately Held**
WEB: www.bedframes.com
SIC: 5021 2514 Bedsprings; frames for box springs or bedsprings: metal

(G-1321)
MCCARTHY BURGESS & WOLFF INC (PA)
26000 Cannon Rd (44146-1807)
PHONE..................440 735-5100
Fax: 440 735-5110
Freida M Wolff, *President*
Brian Nagle, *General Mgr*
Stephen Wolff, *Principal*
Monica Ziman, *CFO*
James Tournas, *Credit Mgr*
EMP: 140
SQ FT: 21,000

Bedford - Cuyahoga County (G-1322)

SALES (est): 19.1MM Privately Held
WEB: www.mbandw.com
SIC: 7322 Collection agency, except real estate

(G-1322)
MEDICAL SERVICE COMPANY (PA)
24000 Broadway Ave (44146-6329)
PHONE..............................440 232-3000
Fax: 440 232-3411
Joel D Marx, *President*
Darrel Lowery, *President*
John Geller, *Vice Pres*
Dana McLaughlin, *Vice Pres*
Seth Weinstein, *Business Anlyst*
EMP: 62
SQ FT: 4,000
SALES (est): 25.7MM Privately Held
WEB: www.medicalserviceco.com
SIC: 5912 7352 Drug stores; medical equipment rental

(G-1323)
NORFOLK SOUTHERN RAILWAY CO
7847 Northfield Rd (44146-5522)
PHONE..............................440 439-1827
Allan Carter, *Superintendent*
EMP: 57
SALES (corp-wide): 10.5B Publicly Held
SIC: 4011 Railroads, line-haul operating
HQ: Norfolk Southern Railway Company
3 Commercial Pl Ste 1a
Norfolk VA 23510
757 629-2680

(G-1324)
NPK CONSTRUCTION EQUIPMENT INC (HQ)
7550 Independence Dr (44146-5541)
PHONE..............................440 232-7900
Fax: 440 232-4382
Dan Tyrell, *President*
Marga Parker, *Accountant*
◆ EMP: 60
SQ FT: 150,000
SALES (est): 45.5MM
SALES (corp-wide): 85.8MM Privately Held
WEB: www.npkce.com
SIC: 5082 3599 3546 3532 General construction machinery & equipment; machine shop, jobbing & repair; power-driven handtools; mining machinery; construction machinery; cutlery
PA: Nippon Pneumatic Manufacturing Co.,Ltd.
4-11-5, Kamiji, Higashinari-Ku
Osaka OSK 537-0
669 739-100

(G-1325)
OAKWOOD HOSPITALITY CORP
Also Called: Holiday Inn
23303 Oakwood Commons Dr (44146-5700)
PHONE..............................440 786-1998
Fax: 440 786-2779
Vinu Patel, *President*
Chris Ellis, *Manager*
EMP: 25
SALES (est): 1.1MM Privately Held
SIC: 7011 Hotels

(G-1326)
OHIO CONCRETE RESURFACING INC (PA)
Also Called: Nature Stone
15 N Park St (44146-3634)
PHONE..............................440 786-9100
Fax: 440 786-1927
Antonia Masetta, *President*
Larry Degennaro, *Sales Staff*
Sean Burton, *Lab Dir*
Russell Masetta, *Admin Sec*
EMP: 30
SQ FT: 8,000
SALES (est): 12.9MM Privately Held
WEB: www.naturestonefloors.com
SIC: 1799 Epoxy application

(G-1327)
OLYMPIC STEEL INC
5080 Richmond Rd (44146-1329)
PHONE..............................216 292-3800
Jim Heyerdahl, *Sales Staff*
Rich Manson, *Branch Mgr*
Coady Barrie, *Manager*
EMP: 156
SALES (corp-wide): 1.3B Publicly Held
WEB: www.olysteel.com
SIC: 5051 Steel; sheets, metal; plates, metal; aluminum bars, rods, ingots, sheets, pipes, plates, etc.
PA: Olympic Steel, Inc.
22901 Millcreek Blvd # 650
Cleveland OH 44122
216 292-3800

(G-1328)
OWNERS MANAGEMENT COMPANY
25250 Rockside Rd (44146-1838)
PHONE..............................440 439-3800
Paul T Wilms, *Controller*
EMP: 40
SALES (est): 734.4K Privately Held
SIC: 6513 6531 Apartment building operators; real estate agents & managers

(G-1329)
PARTNERS AUTO GROUP BDFORD INC
Also Called: Mazda Saab of Bedford
11 Broadway Ave (44146-2001)
PHONE..............................440 439-2323
Fax: 440 439-8977
Chris Hudak, *President*
Jerald Loretitsch, *Corp Secy*
Bill Klonaris, *Sales Mgr*
Daniel Harris, *Sales Staff*
Milo Milosevic, *Sales Staff*
EMP: 52
SQ FT: 30,000
SALES (est): 20.9MM Privately Held
WEB: www.saabofbedford.com
SIC: 5511 7515 Automobiles, new & used; passenger car leasing

(G-1330)
PENSKE TRUCK LEASING CO LP
7600 First Pl (44146-6700)
PHONE..............................440 232-5811
Mike Mackerty, *Safety Dir*
Daniel O Florig, *Manager*
O Florig, *Manager*
EMP: 30
SQ FT: 15,068
SALES (corp-wide): 2.9B Privately Held
WEB: www.pensketruckleasing.com
SIC: 7513 Truck leasing, without drivers
PA: Penske Truck Leasing Co., L.P.
2675 Morgantown Rd
Reading PA 19607
610 775-6000

(G-1331)
RENAISSANCE HOME HEALTH CARE
5311 Northfield Rd (44146-1188)
PHONE..............................216 662-8702
Patricia Eady, *President*
EMP: 95
SALES (est): 1.5MM Privately Held
SIC: 8099 Health screening service

(G-1332)
ROSELAND LANES INC
26383 Broadway Ave (44146-6516)
PHONE..............................440 439-0097
Fax: 440 439-7199
Peter Scimone, *President*
Rosalie Scimone, *Corp Secy*
Anna Marie Slaby, *Vice Pres*
EMP: 60 EST: 1961
SQ FT: 20,000
SALES (est): 2.5MM Privately Held
WEB: www.roselandlanes.com
SIC: 7933 5812 Ten pin center; snack bar; caterers

(G-1333)
SABER HEALTHCARE GROUP LLC (PA)
26691 Richmond Rd Frnt (44146-1422)
PHONE..............................216 292-5706
Fax: 216 292-5709
Peter Holmes, *Purchasing*
Miranda Fox, *Mktg Dir*
William Weisberg, *Mng Member*
Timothy Rieder, *Director*
Julie Burnett, *Social Dir*
EMP: 50
SQ FT: 3,600
SALES (est): 68.5MM Privately Held
SIC: 8051 8741 Convalescent home with continuous nursing care; nursing & personal care facility management

(G-1334)
SAFELY HOME INC
121 Center Rd Ofc (44146-2758)
PHONE..............................440 232-9310
George Purgert, *Exec Dir*
EMP: 25
SALES (est): 1.8MM Privately Held
SIC: 8322 Child related social services

(G-1335)
SERVICEMASTER CLEAN
Also Called: ServiceMaster By McCastle
26496 Broadway Ave (44146-6526)
P.O. Box 39175, Solon (44139-0175)
PHONE..............................440 349-0979
Fax: 440 349-9055
Larry McCastle, *President*
EMP: 32
SALES (est): 910K Privately Held
WEB: www.servicemasterclean.com
SIC: 7349 Building maintenance services

(G-1336)
SIGNATURE HEALTHCARE LLC
5386 Majestic Pkwy (44146-1784)
PHONE..............................440 232-1800
EMP: 140 Privately Held
SIC: 8011 6321 Offices & clinics of medical doctors; accident & health insurance
PA: Signature Healthcare, Llc
12201 Bluegrass Pkwy
Louisville KY 40299

(G-1337)
SMITH & OBY SERVICE CO
7676 Northfield Rd (44146-5519)
PHONE..............................440 735-5322
Gary Y Klie, *President*
Matthew Kittenberger, *Manager*
EMP: 30
SALES (est): 3.3MM Privately Held
WEB: www.smithandoby.com
SIC: 1711 7699 7623 Warm air heating & air conditioning contractor; ventilation & duct work contractor; boiler & heating repair services; air conditioning repair

(G-1338)
SMYLIE ONE HEATING & COOLING
Also Called: Honeywell Authorized Dealer
5108 Richmond Rd (44146-1331)
PHONE..............................440 449-4328
Fax: 440 729-7104
Shari Rosen, *President*
Steven Smiley, *Vice Pres*
Scott Fisher, *Warehouse Mgr*
Gary Rosen, *Sales Mgr*
Ralph Doran, *Manager*
EMP: 25
SALES (est): 5.1MM Privately Held
SIC: 1711 Warm air heating & air conditioning contractor

(G-1339)
SOUTHEAST AREA LAW ENFORCEMENT
165 Center Rd (44146-2738)
PHONE..............................216 475-1234
Thomas P Murphy, *Director*
EMP: 30
SALES (est): 489.7K Privately Held
SIC: 8611 Business associations

(G-1340)
STATE CREST CARPET & FLOORING (PA)
5400 Perkins Rd (44146-1857)
PHONE..............................440 232-3980
Fax: 440 232-3994
Dennis Chiancone, *President*
Janice Redina, *Corp Secy*
◆ EMP: 30
SQ FT: 36,000
SALES (est): 10.7MM Privately Held
SIC: 5023 Carpets; resilient floor coverings: tile or sheet

(G-1341)
TOYOTA OF BEDFORD
18151 Rockside Rd (44146-2039)
PHONE..............................440 439-8600
Mike Damato, *Partner*
Greg Figueroa, *General Mgr*
Lynn Combs, *CFO*
Rob Kessler, *Controller*
Nick Snyder, *Finance Mgr*
EMP: 56
SALES (est): 16.5MM Privately Held
WEB: www.toyotaofbedford.com
SIC: 5511 7515 5521 Automobiles, new & used; passenger car leasing; used car dealers

(G-1342)
TRUGREEN LIMITED PARTNERSHIP
Also Called: Tru Green-Chemlawn
20375 Hannan Pkwy (44146-5354)
P.O. Box 46429, Cleveland (44146-0429)
PHONE..............................440 786-7200
Fax: 440 786-7202
Jim Jeffers, *Sales Executive*
Lorrie Smith, *Office Mgr*
Steve Chaney, *Manager*
EMP: 100
SALES (corp-wide): 4B Privately Held
SIC: 0782 Lawn care services
HQ: Trugreen Limited Partnership
1790 Kirby Pkwy
Memphis TN 38138
901 251-4128

(G-1343)
UNIVERSITY MEDNET
22750 Rockside Rd Ste 210 (44146-1576)
PHONE..............................440 285-9079
Fax: 440 786-2723
Yvonne Maret, *Manager*
EMP: 50
SALES (corp-wide): 11.6MM Privately Held
SIC: 8011 Clinic, operated by physicians
PA: University Mednet
18599 Lake Shore Blvd
Euclid OH 44119
216 383-0100

(G-1344)
WINDOW FACTORY OF AMERICA (PA)
21600 Alexander Rd (44146-5509)
PHONE..............................440 439-3050
Fax: 440 232-6416
Sheldon Fromson, *Ch of Bd*
Scott Berman, *President*
Cindy Obringer, *CFO*
EMP: 100
SQ FT: 20,000
SALES (est): 8.3MM Privately Held
WEB: www.wadf.com
SIC: 5211 5031 1751 Door & window products; windows; window & door (prefabricated) installation

Bedford Heights
Cuyahoga County

(G-1345)
ALLOY METAL EXCHANGE LLC
Also Called: Dynamic Metal Services
26000 Corbin Dr (44128)
PHONE..............................216 478-0200
Brian Ducovna, *President*
Ben Henson, *Vice Pres*
Bill Mills, *Vice Pres*
George Smolinski, *Opers Staff*

Kevin Lamar, *CFO*
EMP: 25
SQ FT: 40,000
SALES (est): 11.2MM **Privately Held**
SIC: 1081 Metal mining services

(G-1346)
AMERICAS FLOOR SOURCE LLC
26000 Richmond Rd Ste 1 (44146-1420)
PHONE.................................216 342-4929
Glenn Gould, *Branch Mgr*
EMP: 41 **Privately Held**
SIC: 7217 5713 Carpet & upholstery cleaning; floor covering stores
PA: America's Floor Source, Llc
3442 Millennium Ct
Columbus OH 43219

(G-1347)
BASS SECURITY SERVICES INC (PA)
26701 Richmond Rd (44146-1449)
PHONE.................................216 755-1200
Dale Bass, *CEO*
Ron Brown, *COO*
Paul Fisher, *Vice Pres*
Kenneth Kossin Jr, *Vice Pres*
Ken Koffin, *CFO*
EMP: 82
SQ FT: 31,000
SALES (est): 45.2MM **Privately Held**
WEB: www.bass-security.com
SIC: 5251 7382 Door locks & lock sets; security systems services

(G-1348)
BUCKEYE HEATING AND AC SUP INC (PA)
5075 Richmond Rd (44146-1384)
PHONE.................................216 831-0066
John Wortendyke, *President*
Louis Tisch, *Vice Pres*
Chris Wortendyke, *Sales Mgr*
Tammy Cochran, *Manager*
EMP: 35
SQ FT: 30,000
SALES (est): 10.3MM **Privately Held**
SIC: 5078 5075 Refrigeration equipment & supplies; warm air heating & air conditioning

(G-1349)
CHAPEL STEEL CORP
26400 Richmond Rd (44146-1444)
PHONE.................................800 570-7674
EMP: 25
SALES (corp-wide): 9.7B **Publicly Held**
SIC: 5051 Steel
HQ: Chapel Steel Corp.
590 N Bethlehem Pike
Ambler PA 19002
215 793-0899

(G-1350)
CHORES UNLIMITED INC
Also Called: Cui
26150 Richmond Rd Unit C (44146-1438)
P.O. Box 46760, Bedford (44146-0760)
PHONE.................................440 439-5455
Robin Gray, *Vice Pres*
Bryan Gray, *Vice Pres*
Gary Gray, *Vice Pres*
Linda Tylek, *Manager*
EMP: 85
SQ FT: 10,000
SALES: 3.8MM **Privately Held**
SIC: 0782 Mowing services, lawn

(G-1351)
EDELMAN PLUMBING SUPPLY INC (PA)
26201 Richmond Rd Ste 4 (44146-1454)
PHONE.................................216 591-0150
Fax: 216 591-0471
Alan Edelman, *Ch of Bd*
Sheldon Edelman, *President*
Anna Salerno, *Sales Mgr*
Steve Caldwell, *Sales Staff*
Jessica Geisler, *Sales Staff*
EMP: 30 **EST:** 1953
SQ FT: 40,000
SALES (est): 10.1MM **Privately Held**
WEB: www.edelmanplumbing.com
SIC: 5074 Plumbing fittings & supplies

(G-1352)
GIANT EAGLE INC
5300 Richmond Rd (44146-1335)
PHONE.................................216 292-7000
Charles Rego, *Vice Pres*
Anthony Rego, *Branch Mgr*
Bill Hohmann, *Manager*
Carl Lowe, *Manager*
EMP: 37
SALES (corp-wide): 7.6B **Privately Held**
SIC: 5411 5141 5147 5148 Supermarkets, chain; groceries, general line; meats, fresh; fresh fruits & vegetables; dairy products, except dried or canned; franchises, selling or licensing
PA: Giant Eagle, Inc.
101 Kappa Dr
Pittsburgh PA 15238
800 362-8899

(G-1353)
INTERGRATED CONSULTING
Also Called: ICM
5311 Northfield Rd (44146-1188)
PHONE.................................216 214-7547
Cynthia Weston,
Joe Fouche,
EMP: 40
SALES (est): 1.7MM **Privately Held**
WEB: www.integrated-consulting.net
SIC: 8741 Management services

(G-1354)
J B HUNT TRANSPORT INC
26235 Cannon Rd (44146-1802)
PHONE.................................440 786-8436
EMP: 167
SALES (corp-wide): 7.1B **Publicly Held**
SIC: 4213 Trucking, except local
HQ: J. B. Hunt Transport, Inc.
615 J B Hunt Corporate Dr
Lowell AR 72745
479 820-0000

(G-1355)
KINDRED HEALTHCARE INC
Also Called: Kindred At Home
5386 Majestic Pkwy Ste 1 (44146-6907)
PHONE.................................440 232-1800
EMP: 116
SALES (corp-wide): 6B **Publicly Held**
SIC: 8082 8049 Home health care services; nurses & other medical assistants
PA: Kindred Healthcare, Inc.
680 S 4th St
Louisville KY 40202
502 596-7300

(G-1356)
PLANNED PRENTHOOD GREATER OHIO
Also Called: Bedford Heights Health Center
25350 Rockside Rd (44146-7110)
PHONE.................................216 961-8804
Tara Broderick, *Manager*
Laszlo N Sogor, *Obstetrician*
EMP: 50
SALES (corp-wide): 20.7MM **Privately Held**
SIC: 8093 Family planning clinic
PA: Planned Parenthood Of Greater Ohio
206 E State St
Columbus OH 43215
614 224-2235

(G-1357)
PUBLIC STORAGE
22800 Miles Rd (44128-5447)
PHONE.................................216 220-7978
Barbara Lawrence, *Manager*
EMP: 50
SQ FT: 80,050
SALES (corp-wide): 2.6B **Publicly Held**
WEB: www.publicstorage.com
SIC: 4225 Miniwarehouse, warehousing
PA: Public Storage
701 Western Ave
Glendale CA 91201
818 244-8080

(G-1358)
R J MARTIN ELEC SVCS INC
22841 Aurora Rd (44146-1244)
PHONE.................................216 662-7100
Robert J Martin Jr, *President*
Diane Martin, *Vice Pres*
Marie Schenkel, *CFO*
Charlie Taylor, *Sales Executive*
EMP: 51
SQ FT: 50,000
SALES (est): 3.1MM **Privately Held**
SIC: 1731 General electrical contractor

(G-1359)
RISER FOODS COMPANY (HQ)
Also Called: American Seaway
5300 Richmond Rd (44146-1389)
PHONE.................................216 292-7000
Fax: 216 292-7000
Laura Shapira Karet, *CEO*
John Lucot, *President*
David S Shapira, *Chairman*
Mark Minnaugh, *CFO*
Pam Claffey, *Executive Asst*
EMP: 100
SQ FT: 1,000,000
SALES (est): 63.1MM
SALES (corp-wide): 7.6B **Privately Held**
SIC: 5411 5141 5146 5199 Supermarkets, chain; groceries, general line; seafoods; general merchandise, nondurable; druggists' sundries
PA: Giant Eagle, Inc.
101 Kappa Dr
Pittsburgh PA 15238
800 362-8899

(G-1360)
THE MAIDS
23480 Aurora Rd Ste 1 (44146-1757)
PHONE.................................440 735-6243
Fax: 440 735-9631
Michael Manhoff, *Owner*
EMP: 60
SALES (est): 97.1K **Privately Held**
SIC: 7349 Maid services, contract or fee basis

Bellaire
Belmont County

(G-1361)
BELLAIRE HARBOR SERVICE LLC
Also Called: Harbor Services
4102 Jefferson St (43906-1282)
P.O. Box 29 (43906-0029)
PHONE.................................740 676-4305
Charles Appleby, *Manager*
Bob Harrison,
EMP: 43
SALES (est): 5.5MM **Privately Held**
SIC: 4491 Marine loading & unloading services

(G-1362)
BELMONT COMMUNITY HOSPITAL (HQ)
4697 Harrison St (43906-1338)
P.O. Box 653 (43906-0653)
PHONE.................................740 671-1200
Fax: 740 671-1265
Terry L L Stake, *Ch Radiology*
Colleen Matkovich, *Opers Mgr*
Jim Holden, *CFO*
Pat Bulkle, *Human Res Mgr*
Sharon Hartman, *Med Doctor*
EMP: 259
SQ FT: 98,000
SALES: 19.7MM
SALES (corp-wide): 375.6MM **Privately Held**
SIC: 8062 General medical & surgical hospitals
PA: Wheeling Hospital, Inc.
1 Medical Park
Wheeling WV 26003
304 243-3000

(G-1363)
BELMONT FEDERAL SAV & LN ASSN (PA)
3301 Guernsey St (43906-1527)
P.O. Box 654 (43906-0654)
PHONE.................................740 676-1165
Fax: 740 676-1185
Thomas Poe, *President*
Nancy Veres, *Vice Pres*
Ray Wise, *Vice Pres*
James Trouten, *Admin Sec*
EMP: 48 **EST:** 1885
SQ FT: 5,000
SALES: 13.4MM **Privately Held**
SIC: 6035 Federal savings & loan associations

(G-1364)
COMMUNITY ACTION COMSN BELMONT
Also Called: Indian Learning Head Start
4129 Noble St (43906-1246)
PHONE.................................740 676-0800
Fax: 740 676-5191
Michelle Davidson, *Principal*
EMP: 93
SALES (corp-wide): 3.9MM **Privately Held**
SIC: 8351 Head start center, except in conjunction with school
PA: Community Action Commission Of Belmont County
153 1/2 W Main St
Saint Clairsville OH 43950
740 695-0293

(G-1365)
COUNTRY CLUB RETIREMENT CENTER (PA)
55801 Conno Mara Dr (43906-9698)
PHONE.................................740 671-9330
Fax: 740 676-1277
David Taylor, *Principal*
Mark Bradley, *Principal*
John E Holland, *Principal*
EMP: 169
SALES (est): 5.4MM **Privately Held**
SIC: 8059 8052 8051 Nursing home, except skilled & intermediate care facility; intermediate care facilities; skilled nursing care facilities

(G-1366)
JPMORGAN CHASE BANK NAT ASSN
3201 Belmont St Ste 100 (43906-1547)
P.O. Box 10 (43906-0010)
PHONE.................................740 676-2671
Fax: 740 671-9586
Beth Kaufman, *Principal*
Larry Gautschi, *Office Mgr*
EMP: 26
SALES (corp-wide): 99.6B **Publicly Held**
SIC: 6021 National commercial banks
HQ: Jpmorgan Chase Bank, National Association
1111 Polaris Pkwy
Columbus OH 43240
614 436-3055

(G-1367)
S-L DISTRIBUTION COMPANY INC
Also Called: Snyder's Potato Chips
3157 Guernsey St (43906-1541)
PHONE.................................740 676-6932
Dennis Delbert, *Partner*
EMP: 100
SALES (corp-wide): 7.8B **Publicly Held**
SIC: 5145 Potato chips
HQ: S-L Distribution Company, Llc
1250 York St
Hanover PA 17331
717 632-4477

(G-1368)
WHEELING HOSPITAL INC
Also Called: Belmont Community Hlth Ctr
3000 Guernsey St (43906-1540)
PHONE.................................740 676-4623
Sherri Harvey, *Vice Pres*
Diane Patt, *QA Dir*
Jim Holden, *Finance Mgr*
Gurbachan Chawla, *Branch Mgr*
Sean D Loy, *Info Tech Dir*
EMP: 100
SALES (corp-wide): 375.6MM **Privately Held**
SIC: 8099 Blood related health services
PA: Wheeling Hospital, Inc.
1 Medical Park
Wheeling WV 26003
304 243-3000

Bellaire - Belmont County (G-1369)

(G-1369)
XTO ENERGY INC
2358 W 23rd St (43906-9614)
PHONE 740 671-9901
EMP: 73
SALES (corp-wide): 244.3B **Publicly Held**
SIC: **1311** Crude petroleum production
HQ: Xto Energy Inc.
   810 Houston St Ste 2000
   Fort Worth TX 76102

Bellbrook
Greene County

(G-1370)
BELLBROOK RHBLTTION HEALTHCARE
Also Called: Bellbrook Rhbltttion Healthcare
1957 N Lakeman Dr (45305-1245)
PHONE 937 848-8421
Fax: 937 848-5683
Brian Guthrie, *Envir Svcs Dir*
Christine Campbell, *Personnel*
Kalene Gordon, *Office Mgr*
Leslie Hicks, *Manager*
Aimee Hollinsworth, *Director*
EMP: 99
SQ FT: 21,950
SALES: 10MM **Privately Held**
SIC: **8051** Convalescent home with continuous nursing care

(G-1371)
LIBERTY HEALTH CARE CENTER INC
4336 W Franklin St 100 (45305-1551)
PHONE 937 296-1550
Amber Hyman, *Superintendent*
Linda Black, *Principal*
EMP: 25
SALES (est): 1.8MM **Privately Held**
SIC: **8082** Home health care services

(G-1372)
LITTLE MIAMI RIVER CATERING CO
80 E Franklin St (45305-2005)
PHONE 937 848-2464
Fax: 937 845-5170
Glen Penquite, *President*
Molly McCowell, *Manager*
Joan Emttite, *Admin Sec*
EMP: 50
SALES (est): 1.6MM **Privately Held**
WEB: www.lmrcatering.com
SIC: **5812 7299** Caterers; banquet hall facilities

Belle Center
Logan County

(G-1373)
WALMART INC
11040 Pear Ln (43310-9771)
PHONE 937 843-3681
EMP: 283
SALES (corp-wide): 500.3B **Publicly Held**
SIC: **4225** General warehousing & storage
PA: Walmart Inc.
   702 Sw 8th St
   Bentonville AR 72716
   479 273-4000

Bellefontaine
Logan County

(G-1374)
ACUSPORT CORPORATION (PA)
1 Hunter Pl (43311-3001)
PHONE 937 593-7010
Fax: 937 592-5625
William L Fraim, *Ch of Bd*
Steve Reed, *Vice Pres*
Julie Nystrom, *Opers Mgr*
David Crilly, *QA Dir*
Jordan Guck, *QA Dir*
EMP: 120
SQ FT: 120,000
SALES (est): 312MM **Privately Held**
WEB: www.acusport.com
SIC: **5091** Firearms, sporting; archery equipment; ammunition, sporting; hunting equipment & supplies

(G-1375)
AGC AUTOMOTIVE AMERICAS
1465 W Sandusky Ave (43311-1082)
PHONE 937 599-3131
Fax: 937 599-3322
Arkady Doorman, *Vice Pres*
Dean Wright, *Plant Mgr*
Arcadie Dorman, *Opers Staff*
Kazuhiro Sako, *Treasurer*
Dick Huber, *Controller*
▲ EMP: 81
SALES (est): 11.4MM **Privately Held**
SIC: **7549 1793 1799 3231** Automotive customizing services, non-factory basis; glass & glazing work; glass tinting, architectural or automotive; products of purchased glass

(G-1376)
ALLIED WASTE SYSTEMS INC
Also Called: Site 046
2946 Us Highway 68 N (43311-9218)
PHONE 937 593-3566
Randy Traub, *General Mgr*
EMP: 60
SALES (corp-wide): 10B **Publicly Held**
WEB: www.fennellgrp.com
SIC: **4953** Garbage: collecting, destroying & processing
HQ: Allied Waste Systems, Inc.
   18500 N Allied Way # 100
   Phoenix AZ 85054
   480 627-2700

(G-1377)
BELLEFONTAINE PHYSICAL THERAPY
711 Rush Ave (43311-2250)
PHONE 937 592-1625
Fax: 937 592-3489
Rodney Kerns, *President*
EMP: 25
SALES (est): 1.2MM **Privately Held**
WEB: www.bellefonainept.com
SIC: **8049** Physiotherapist

(G-1378)
BELLETECH CORP (HQ)
700 W Lake Ave (43311-9647)
P.O. Box 790 (43311-0790)
PHONE 937 599-3774
Fax: 937 599-5478
Masaaki Mori, *President*
Mark Mc Intyre, *COO*
Mark McIntyre, *COO*
Teresa Cummins, *Purch Mgr*
Andy Fleming, *QA Dir*
▲ EMP: 75
SQ FT: 100,000
SALES (est): 17.2MM
SALES (corp-wide): 13B **Privately Held**
WEB: www.belletechcorp.com
SIC: **7536** Automotive glass replacement shops
PA: Asahi Glass Company,Limited
   1-5-1, Marunouchi
   Chiyoda-Ku TKY 100-0
   332 185-741

(G-1379)
CITIZENS FEDERAL SAV & LN ASSN
110 N Main St (43311-2084)
PHONE 937 593-0015
Charles Earick, *President*
Christi Skidmore, *Assistant VP*
Paul Gillespie, *Vice Pres*
Kim Norton, *Bd of Directors*
Niki Ropp, *Bd of Directors*
EMP: 30
SALES: 4.7MM **Privately Held**
WEB: www.citizensfederalsl.com
SIC: **6035** Federal savings & loan associations

(G-1380)
COUNTY OF LOGAN
Also Called: Logan Cnty Prbate Juvenile Crt
101 S Main St Rm 1 (43311-2055)
PHONE 937 599-7252
Fax: 937 599-7297
Annette Deao, *General Mgr*
Linda Brunke, *Principal*
Brandie Stonerock, *Manager*
EMP: 35 **Privately Held**
WEB: www.co.logan.oh.us
SIC: **8743 9211** Public relations services; courts
PA: County Of Logan
   100 S Madriver St
   Bellefontaine OH 43311
   937 599-7209

(G-1381)
COUNTY OF LOGAN
121 S Opera St Rm 12 (43311-2057)
PHONE 937 599-4221
Sara J Tracey, *Branch Mgr*
EMP: 38 **Privately Held**
SIC: **8999** Artists & artists' studios
PA: County Of Logan
   100 S Madriver St
   Bellefontaine OH 43311
   937 599-7209

(G-1382)
COUNTY OF LOGAN
Also Called: Logan Acres
2739 County Road 91 (43311-9007)
PHONE 937 592-2901
Fax: 937 592-2763
Corey Topp, *Human Res Dir*
Andrew Hershderger, *Manager*
James Lawler, *Director*
Liz Salyer, *Nursing Dir*
EMP: 115 **Privately Held**
WEB: www.co.logan.oh.us
SIC: **8361 8051** Home for the aged; skilled nursing care facilities
PA: County Of Logan
   100 S Madriver St
   Bellefontaine OH 43311
   937 599-7209

(G-1383)
COUNTY OF LOGAN
Also Called: Logan County Childrens Svcs
1100 S Detroit St (43311-9702)
PHONE 937 599-7290
Fax: 937 599-7296
John Holtkamp, *Director*
EMP: 26 **Privately Held**
WEB: www.co.logan.oh.us
SIC: **8322** Child related social services
PA: County Of Logan
   100 S Madriver St
   Bellefontaine OH 43311
   937 599-7209

(G-1384)
HEALTH CARE RTREMENT CORP AMER
Also Called: Heartland of Bellefontaine
221 School St (43311-1078)
PHONE 937 599-5123
Cindy Anderson, *Personnel*
Iva Dewitt-Hoblit, *Manager*
Michele Jones, *Director*
Mellanie Ridenour, *Director*
EMP: 100
SALES (corp-wide): 3.6B **Publicly Held**
WEB: www.hrc-manorcare.com
SIC: **8051** Convalescent home with continuous nursing care
HQ: Health Care And Retirement Corporation of America
   333 N Summit St Ste 103
   Toledo OH 43604
   419 252-5500

(G-1385)
LINK CONSTRUCTION GROUP INC
895 County Road 32 N (43311-9210)
PHONE 937 292-7774
Fax: 937 292-7958
David Link, *President*
Jennifer Bell, *Project Mgr*
Nicholas Fuoco, *Project Mgr*
Aaron Hinkle, *Foreman/Supr*
Richard Dyer, *Treasurer*
EMP: 40
SQ FT: 1,500
SALES: 14.2MM **Privately Held**
SIC: **1542** Commercial & office building contractors

(G-1386)
LOGAN COUNTY ENGINEERING OFF
1991 County Road 13 (43311-9322)
PHONE 937 592-2791
Fax: 937 599-2658
Scott Coleman, *President*
EMP: 39 EST: 1819
SALES (est): 4.7MM **Privately Held**
SIC: **8711** Engineering services

(G-1387)
LOGAN HOUSING CORP INC
Also Called: Logan County Board of Mrdd
1973 State Route 47 W (43311-9328)
P.O. Box 710 (43311-0710)
PHONE 937 592-2009
Joy Badenhop, *Principal*
Sean Keagan, *Manager*
Susan Jones, *Director*
Susan Holycross, *Director*
EMP: 80
SALES (est): 83.8K **Privately Held**
WEB: www.mrdd.co.logan.oh.us
SIC: **8351** Preschool center

(G-1388)
LOWES HOME CENTERS LLC
2168 Us Highway 68 S (43311-8904)
PHONE 937 599-4000
Fax: 937 599-4018
Jeremy Givens, *Manager*
EMP: 150
SALES (corp-wide): 68.6B **Publicly Held**
SIC: **5211 5031 5722 5064** Home centers; building materials, exterior; building materials, interior; household appliance stores; electrical appliances, television & radio
HQ: Lowe's Home Centers, Llc
   1605 Curtis Bridge Rd
   Wilkesboro NC 28697
   336 658-4000

(G-1389)
MARY RTAN HLTH ASSN LOGAN CNTY (PA)
Also Called: Mary Rutan Hospital
205 E Palmer Rd (43311-2281)
PHONE 937 592-4015
Fax: 937 592-6007
Mandy Goble, *President*
Mary Rutan, *COO*
Chuck Earick, *Trustee*
Nancy Knight, *Trustee*
Mary Montgomery, *Trustee*
EMP: 44
SQ FT: 145,000
SALES: 4.1MM **Privately Held**
WEB: www.maryrutanhospital.com
SIC: **8741** Hospital management

(G-1390)
MARY RUTAN HOSPITAL (HQ)
205 E Palmer Rd (43311-2298)
PHONE 937 592-4015
Thomas Simon, *Ch of Bd*
Ron Carmen, *Vice Pres*
Glenn Durfor, *Opers Mgr*
Tammy Bowen, *CFO*
Tamara A Allison, *Controller*
EMP: 650
SQ FT: 90,000
SALES: 96MM
SALES (corp-wide): 4.1MM **Privately Held**
WEB: www.maryrutan.org
SIC: **8062** General medical & surgical hospitals
PA: Mary Rutan Health Association Of Logan County
   205 E Palmer Rd
   Bellefontaine OH 43311
   937 592-4015

GEOGRAPHIC SECTION

Bellevue - Huron County (G-1414)

(G-1391)
MOBILE INSTR SVC & REPR INC (PA)
333 Water Ave (43311-1733)
PHONE..................937 592-5025
Fax: 937 592-7004
Dwight E Reed, *President*
Joyce Warnecke, *General Mgr*
Charles Reed, *Corp Secy*
Ann Reed, *Vice Pres*
Pam Wasson, *CFO*
EMP: 160
SQ FT: 85,000
SALES (est): 28MM **Privately Held**
WEB: www.mobileinstrument.com
SIC: 7699 Surgical instrument repair

(G-1392)
REPUBLIC SERVICES INC
2946 Us Rt 68 N (43311)
PHONE..................937 593-3566
Matthew Evans, *Opers Mgr*
Jim Speirs, *Controller*
EMP: 34
SALES (corp-wide): 10B **Publicly Held**
SIC: 4953 Sanitary landfill operation
PA: Republic Services, Inc.
  18500 N Allied Way # 100
  Phoenix AZ 85054
  480 627-2700

(G-1393)
ROBINSON INVESTMENTS LTD
811 N Main St (43311-2376)
P.O. Box 508 (43311-0508)
PHONE..................937 593-1849
Fax: 937 593-6582
Mark Robinson, *President*
Matt Robinson, *President*
Rusty Bingham, *General Mgr*
Jerry Robinson,
Penny Robinson,
EMP: 37
SQ FT: 70,000
SALES (est): 6.2MM **Privately Held**
SIC: 6512 Commercial & industrial building operation

(G-1394)
ROSS TRAINING CENTER INC
36 County Road 32 S (43311-1152)
PHONE..................937 592-0025
Brian Reimes, *President*
Joe Mancufl, *Superintendent*
Brian Reames, *Exec Dir*
EMP: 90
SALES (est): 1.4MM **Privately Held**
SIC: 8331 Sheltered workshop

(G-1395)
RTC INDUSTRIES INC
Also Called: RTC EMPLOYMENT SERVICES
36 County Road 32 S (43311-1152)
P.O. Box 710 (43311-0710)
PHONE..................937 592-0534
Fax: 937 592-3001
Helen Manns, *Prdtn Mgr*
Nancy Evans Donley, *Manager*
Christy McGill, *Manager*
EMP: 50
SALES: 2.3MM **Privately Held**
SIC: 8331 Sheltered workshop

(G-1396)
SHAW GROUP INC
2940 Us I lighway 68 N (43311-9218)
PHONE..................937 593-2022
EMP: 502
SALES (corp-wide): 10.6B **Publicly Held**
SIC: 8734 Provides Services To Environmental And Infrastructure
HQ: The Shaw Group Inc
  4171 Essen Ln
  Baton Rouge LA 70809

(G-1397)
SPARTANNASH COMPANY
Fame
4067 County Road 130 (43311-9359)
P.O. Box 219 (43311-0219)
PHONE..................937 599-1110
Fax: 937 592-8032
Glenn Curtis, *Division Mgr*
Gary Bickmore, *Managing Dir*
Tom Keller, *Vice Pres*
Jim Donnely, *Plant Mgr*

David Tuttle, *Opers Staff*
EMP: 675
SALES (corp-wide): 8.1B **Publicly Held**
SIC: 5141 Food brokers
PA: Spartannash Company
  850 76th St Sw
  Byron Center MI 49315
  616 878-2000

(G-1398)
SPARTANNASH COMPANY
Also Called: Bellefontaine Distribution Ctr
4067 County Road 130 (43311-9359)
PHONE..................937 599-1110
Glenn Curtis, *Manager*
EMP: 93
SALES (corp-wide): 8.1B **Publicly Held**
WEB: www.nashfinch.com
SIC: 5141 Groceries, general line
PA: Spartannash Company
  850 76th St Sw
  Byron Center MI 49315
  616 878-2000

(G-1399)
STEVE AUSTIN AUTO GROUP
Also Called: Steve Austins of Hardin County
2500 S Main St (43311)
P.O. Box 247 (43311-0247)
PHONE..................937 592-3015
Steve Austin, *President*
Jack Dewitt, *Opers Mgr*
EMP: 40
SALES (est): 2MM **Privately Held**
WEB: www.steveaustins.com
SIC: 7549 High performance auto repair & service

(G-1400)
VIEIRA INC
Also Called: Cherokee Hills Golf Course
4622 County Road 49 (43311-9038)
PHONE..................937 599-3221
Fax: 937 593-0711
James Vieira, *President*
Michael A Vieira, *Vice Pres*
EMP: 27
SQ FT: 3,000
SALES (est): 1.1MM **Privately Held**
WEB: www.cherokeehillsgolfclub.com
SIC: 7992 Public golf courses

(G-1401)
YOUNG MENS CHRISTIAN ASSOC
Also Called: Camp Willson
2732 County Road 11 (43311-9306)
PHONE..................937 593-9001
Fax: 937 593-6194
Brian Kridler, *Senior VP*
Anne Brienza, *Branch Mgr*
Jean Fry, *Director*
Malik W Moore, *Director*
Bobbie Shannon, *Director*
EMP: 50
SALES (corp-wide): 44.9MM **Privately Held**
WEB: www.ymca-columbus.com
SIC: 8641 7991 8351 7032 Youth organizations; physical fitness facilities; child day care services; youth camps; individual & family services
PA: Young Men's Christian Association Of Central Ohio
  40 W Long St
  Columbus OH 43215
  614 389-4409

Bellevue
Huron County

(G-1402)
AMRSTRONG DISTRIBUTORS INC
Also Called: Hart-Greer
421 Monroe St (44811-1730)
PHONE..................419 483-4840
Fax: 419 483-3557
John W Norris Jr, *Ch of Bd*
EMP: 35 **EST:** 1999

SALES (corp-wide): 3.8B **Publicly Held**
WEB: www.magicpak.com
SIC: 6719 Personal holding companies, except banks
HQ: Armstrong Air Conditioning Inc.
  215 Metropolitan Dr
  West Columbia SC 29170
  803 738-4000

(G-1403)
AUDRICH INC
Also Called: Bellevue Care Center
1 Audrich Sq (44811-9700)
PHONE..................419 483-6225
Fax: 419 483-0215
Robert Tebeau, *President*
Ernest Tebeau, *Vice Pres*
James Tebeau, *Vice Pres*
Ronald Tebeau, *Vice Pres*
Mary Tebeau, *Treasurer*
EMP: 169
SQ FT: 40,000
SALES: 7.8MM **Privately Held**
SIC: 8093 8051 8052 Rehabilitation center, outpatient treatment; skilled nursing care facilities; intermediate care facilities

(G-1404)
BELLEVUE HOSPITAL (PA)
1400 W Main St Unit Front (44811-9088)
PHONE..................419 483-4040
Fax: 419 483-6384
Mike Winthrop, *President*
Dr Valerie Hepburn, *President*
Sara Brokow, *COO*
David West, *Ch Radiology*
Alan Ganci, *Exec VP*
EMP: 400 **EST:** 1915
SQ FT: 70,000
SALES: 46.2MM **Privately Held**
SIC: 8062 General medical & surgical hospitals

(G-1405)
BELLEVUE HOSPITAL
811 Northwest St (44811-1028)
PHONE..................419 547-0074
Fax: 419 483-1304
Michael Winthrop, *Principal*
Tony Lombardi, *Human Res Dir*
Kara Seamon, *Manager*
Barbara B Swartz, *Manager*
Janet Runner, *Director*
EMP: 307
SALES (corp-wide): 46.2MM **Privately Held**
SIC: 8062 General medical & surgical hospitals
PA: The Bellevue Hospital
  1400 W Main St Unit Front
  Bellevue OH 44811
  419 483-4040

(G-1406)
BENCHMARK NATIONAL CORPORATION
400 N Buckeye St (44811-1210)
PHONE..................419 660-1100
Gary A Cooper, *Branch Mgr*
EMP: 30
SALES (corp-wide): 11.2MM **Privately Held**
SIC: 8748 8742 7389 Business consulting; quality assurance consultant; inspection & testing services
PA: Benchmark National Corporation
  3161 N Republic Blvd
  Toledo OH 43615
  419 843-6691

(G-1407)
CROGAN COLONIAL BANK
1 Union Sq (44811-1400)
P.O. Box 150 (44811-0150)
PHONE..................419 483-2541
EMP: 45 **EST:** 1930
SALES (est): 4.8MM **Privately Held**
SIC: 6022 State Commercial Bank

(G-1408)
DONALD E DIDION II
Also Called: Didion's Mechanical
1027b County Road 308 (44811)
PHONE..................419 483-2226
Fax: 419 483-4382
Donald E Didion II, *Principal*

EMP: 25
SQ FT: 20,000
SALES: 1.4MM **Privately Held**
WEB: www.didionsmech.com
SIC: 3499 8711 Fire- or burglary-resistive products; engineering services

(G-1409)
FIRELANDS FEDERAL CREDIT UNION (PA)
221 E Main St (44811-1410)
P.O. Box 8005 (44811-8005)
PHONE..................419 483-4180
Fax: 419 483-7100
Kevin L Wadsworth, *President*
Deborah Houle, *Vice Pres*
Jacquelyn Wells, *Vice Pres*
EMP: 47
SQ FT: 10,000
SALES: 10.8MM **Privately Held**
SIC: 6061 6163 Federal credit unions; loan brokers

(G-1410)
FIRST NATIONAL BANK BELLEVUE (HQ)
120 North St (44811-1452)
P.O. Box 210 (44811-0210)
PHONE..................419 483-7340
Fax: 419 483-0006
Dean Miller, *President*
Vickie Smith, *Assistant VP*
Valerie Bumb, *Vice Pres*
Jeff Geary, *Vice Pres*
Deborah Hawkins, *Vice Pres*
EMP: 30
SQ FT: 10,000
SALES: 10.4MM **Privately Held**
WEB: www.fnblifetime.com
SIC: 6021 National commercial banks

(G-1411)
GREAT LAKES PACKERS INC
400 Great Lakes Pkwy (44811-1165)
P.O. Box 366 (44811-0366)
PHONE..................419 483-2956
Fax: 419 483-6922
Jerome Fritz, *President*
Anna Bloomberg, *Admin Asst*
EMP: 50
SQ FT: 31,500
SALES: 16MM **Privately Held**
SIC: 0723 Vegetable packing services; fruit (fresh) packing services

(G-1412)
LIFETOUCH NAT SCHL STUDIOS INC
102 Commerce Park Dr (44811-9095)
PHONE..................419 483-8200
Douglas Barr, *Branch Mgr*
EMP: 41
SALES (corp-wide): 856.2MM **Privately Held**
SIC: 7221 School photographer
HQ: Lifetouch National School Studios Inc.
  11000 Viking Dr Ste 300
  Eden Prairie MN 55344
  952 826-4000

(G-1413)
NEW BEGINNINGS PEDIATRICS INC
Also Called: Trippe, Glen MD
1400 W Main St Ste G (44811-9088)
PHONE..................419 483-4122
Glen Trippe MD, *Director*
EMP: 25 **Privately Held**
SIC: 8011 Pediatrician
PA: New Beginnings Pediatrics Inc
  282 Benedict Ave Ste B
  Norwalk OH 44857

(G-1414)
NORFOLK SOUTHERN CORPORATION
24424 N Prairie Rd (44811)
PHONE..................419 483-1423
Chris Buttermore, *Foreman/Supr*
Paula Stiffler, *Manager*
EMP: 133
SALES (corp-wide): 10.5B **Publicly Held**
WEB: www.nscorp.com
SIC: 4011 Railroads, line-haul operating

Bellevue - Huron County (G-1415)

PA: Norfolk Southern Corporation
3 Commercial Pl Ste 1a
Norfolk VA 23510
757 629-2680

(G-1415)
PLOGER TRANSPORTATION LLC (PA)
15581 County Road 46 (44811-9507)
PHONE 419 465-2100
Fax: 419 465-2981
Jerry Morrow, *Office Mgr*
Tanya Morrow,
EMP: 40
SQ FT: 2,000
SALES (est): 9.3MM **Privately Held**
SIC: 4731 Transportation agents & brokers

(G-1416)
QUALITY WELDING INC
104 Ronald Ln (44811)
P.O. Box 273 (44811-0273)
PHONE 419 483-6067
Fax: 419 483-3551
Charles Tinnel, *President*
Jessica Gilbert, *Manager*
EMP: 25
SQ FT: 2,800
SALES: 1.5MM **Privately Held**
SIC: 7692 Welding repair

(G-1417)
ROYAL COLOR INC
Also Called: Ohio School Pictures
550 Goodrich Rd (44811-1139)
P.O. Box 769, Berea (44017-0769)
PHONE 440 234-1337
Adam Barr, *CEO*
Douglas H Barr, *President*
Elaine Barr, *Vice Pres*
EMP: 490
SQ FT: 7,500
SALES: 8MM **Privately Held**
WEB: www.ohioschoolpictures.com
SIC: 7221 Photographer, still or video

(G-1418)
SABER HEALTHCARE GROUP LLC
Also Called: Bellevue Care Center
1 Audrich Sq (44811-9700)
PHONE 419 483-6225
Cindy Starkey, *Administration*
EMP: 36
SALES (corp-wide): 68.5MM **Privately Held**
SIC: 8051 Skilled nursing care facilities
PA: Saber Healthcare Group, L.L.C.
26691 Richmond Rd Frnt
Bedford OH 44146
216 292-5706

(G-1419)
WILBERT INC
Also Called: Wilbert Plastic Services
635 Southwest St (44811-9314)
PHONE 419 483-2300
Wendell Casteel, *Project Engr*
Greg Botner, *Branch Mgr*
EMP: 85
SALES (corp-wide): 1B **Privately Held**
SIC: 5162 Plastics products
PA: Wilbert, Inc.
2001 Oaks Pkwy
Belmont NC 28012
704 247-3850

(G-1420)
WOODARD PHOTOGRAPHIC INC (HQ)
550 Goodrich Rd (44811-1163)
P.O. Box 8001 (44811-8001)
PHONE 419 483-3364
Fax: 419 483-5505
George Woodard, *President*
Marc Woodard, *President*
Roger Wilburn, *Vice Pres*
Cheryl Sangeory, *Human Res Dir*
Wesley Westlund, *Executive*
EMP: 40
SQ FT: 18,763
SALES (est): 6MM
SALES (corp-wide): 856.2MM **Privately Held**
WEB: www.woodardphoto.com
SIC: 7335 7221 Commercial photography; school photographer
PA: Lifetouch Inc.
11000 Viking Dr
Eden Prairie MN 55344
952 826-4000

Bellville
Richland County

(G-1421)
BELLVILLE HOTEL COMPANY
Also Called: Quality Inn
1000 Comfort Plaza Dr (44813-8820)
PHONE 419 886-7000
Dan Galat, *Owner*
Steve Hering, *Partner*
Jim Hering, *Partner*
EMP: 30 EST: 1996
SQ FT: 40,000
SALES: 1.2MM **Privately Held**
SIC: 7011 Hotels & motels

(G-1422)
COMPETITIVE TRANSPORTATION
7086 State Route 546 (44813-9316)
P.O. Box 1177, Mansfield (44901-1177)
PHONE 419 529-5300
Fax: 419 529-5490
Merle D Shaffner, *President*
Jeffery Shaffner, *Corp Secy*
Robin Shaffner, *Vice Pres*
EMP: 42
SQ FT: 27,500
SALES: 3.2MM **Privately Held**
SIC: 4212 4213 Local trucking, without storage; trucking, except local

(G-1423)
CONSULATE MANAGEMENT CO LLC
Also Called: Country Meadow Care Center
4910 Algire Rd (44813-9263)
PHONE 419 886-3922
Phil Critcher, *Director*
EMP: 55
SALES (corp-wide): 581.9MM **Privately Held**
WEB: www.tandemhealthcare.com
SIC: 8051 Skilled nursing care facilities
PA: Consulate Management Company, Llc
800 Concourse Pkwy S
Maitland FL 32751
407 571-1550

(G-1424)
COUNTRY MDOW FCLTY OPRTONS LLC
Also Called: Country Meadow Care Center
4910 Algire Rd (44813-9263)
PHONE 419 886-3922
Fax: 419 886-9826
Denise Conn, *Executive*
Joe Conte,
Carla Naegele,
EMP: 53
SALES (est): 2.3MM **Privately Held**
SIC: 8051 Skilled nursing care facilities

(G-1425)
COUNTRY MEADOW CARE CENTER LLC ◆
Also Called: Country Meadow Rehabilitation
4910 Algire Rd (44813-9263)
PHONE 419 886-3922
Carol Keen, *Manager*
Phil Kritcher, *Exec Dir*
EMP: 47 EST: 2017
SALES (est): 631.6K **Privately Held**
SIC: 8093 8059 Rehabilitation center, outpatient treatment; nursing home, except skilled & intermediate care facility

(G-1426)
VALLEYVIEW MANAGEMENT CO INC
Also Called: Comfort Inn
855 Comfort Plaza Dr (44813-1267)
PHONE 419 886-4000
Fax: 419 886-3813
James W Haring, *President*
Daniel Galat, *Vice Pres*
EMP: 29
SALES (est): 1.5MM **Privately Held**
SIC: 7011 Hotels & motels

(G-1427)
WADE & GATTON NURSERIES
1288 Gatton Rock Rd (44813-9106)
PHONE 419 883-3191
Fax: 419 883-3677
Van R Wade, *Owner*
EMP: 65
SQ FT: 1,000
SALES (est): 3.4MM **Privately Held**
SIC: 0181 5261 Nursery stock, growing of; nurseries & garden centers

Belmont
Belmont County

(G-1428)
50 X 20 HOLDING COMPANY INC
Also Called: Schumacher Homes
41201 Bond Dr (43718-7502)
PHONE 740 238-4262
Greg McQuaid, *Branch Mgr*
EMP: 27
SALES (corp-wide): 80.4MM **Privately Held**
SIC: 1521 Single-family housing construction
PA: 50 X 20 Holding Company, Inc.
2715 Wise Ave Nw
Canton OH 44708
330 478-4500

(G-1429)
RECO EQUIPMENT INC (PA)
Also Called: Bobcat of Pittsburgh
41245 Reco Rd (43718-9542)
P.O. Box 160, Morristown (43759-0160)
PHONE 740 619-8071
Fax: 740 782-1020
Reed B Mahany, *President*
Paul Di Tullio, *Vice Pres*
Josh Gasber, *Vice Pres*
Paul D Tullio, *Vice Pres*
James Bentley, *Controller*
▲ EMP: 25
SQ FT: 26,000
SALES (est): 61.3MM **Privately Held**
WEB: www.recoequip.com
SIC: 5082 Cranes, construction; excavating machinery & equipment; power shovels

(G-1430)
STINGRAY PRESSURE PUMPING LLC (PA)
42739 National Rd (43718-9669)
PHONE 405 648-4177
Tom Davis, *Superintendent*
Jack Tarver, *Vice Pres*
Jeremy Parker, *Opers Mgr*
John Paxson, *Purch Mgr*
Tiffany Smith, *Office Mgr*
▲ EMP: 42
SALES (est): 130.1MM **Privately Held**
SIC: 1389 Gas field services

(G-1431)
VALLEY HARLEY DAVIDSON CO (PA)
Also Called: Valley Harley Davidson-Buell
41255 Reco Rd (43718-9542)
PHONE 740 695-9591
Fax: 740 782-1527
William Paul Jr, *President*
EMP: 42
SQ FT: 16,000
SALES (est): 8.1MM **Privately Held**
SIC: 5571 7699 Motorcycles; motorcycle repair service

Beloit
Mahoning County

(G-1432)
STRATTON CHEVROLET CO
16050 State Route 14a (44609-9734)
PHONE 330 537-3151
Fax: 330 537-3650
Don L Stratton Jr, *President*
Theresa Stratton, *Corp Secy*
Don L Stratton Sr, *Shareholder*
EMP: 25 EST: 1928
SQ FT: 7,800
SALES (est): 146.4K **Privately Held**
SIC: 5511 7538 5012 Automobiles, new & used; pickups, new & used; vans, new & used; general automotive repair shops; automobiles & other motor vehicles

Belpre
Washington County

(G-1433)
BELPRE HISTORICAL SOCIETY
Also Called: FARMERS CASTLE MUSEUM EDUCATIO
509 Ridge St (45714-2454)
P.O. Box 731 (45714-0731)
PHONE 740 423-7588
Nancy Sams, *President*
John King, *Vice Pres*
EMP: 40
SALES: 171K **Privately Held**
WEB: www.belprehistory.org
SIC: 8412 Museum

(G-1434)
BLENNERHASSETT YACHT CLUB INC
800 Oneal St (45714-1754)
PHONE 740 423-9062
David Ruble, *CEO*
EMP: 45
SALES: 68.6K **Privately Held**
SIC: 7997 Yacht club, membership

(G-1435)
DAVITA INC
Also Called: Da Vita
2906 Washington Blvd (45714-1848)
PHONE 740 401-0607
Traci Lancaster, *Branch Mgr*
EMP: 37 **Publicly Held**
SIC: 8092 Kidney dialysis centers
PA: Davita Inc.
2000 16th St
Denver CO 80202

(G-1436)
ENTERPRISE SERVICES LLC
2505 Washington Blvd Frnt (45714-1982)
P.O. Box 219 (45714-0219)
PHONE 740 423-9501
Max Ptrpton, *Branch Mgr*
Don Best, *Systems Mgr*
EMP: 78
SALES (corp-wide): 23.5B **Publicly Held**
WEB: www.eds.com
SIC: 7374 Data processing service
HQ: Enterprise Services Llc
5400 Legacy Dr
Plano TX 75024
703 245-9675

(G-1437)
ESTES EXPRESS LINES INC
12140 State Road 7 (45714)
PHONE 740 401-0410
Sam Kirbe, *Manager*
EMP: 26
SALES (corp-wide): 2.4B **Privately Held**
WEB: www.estes-express.com
SIC: 4213 Contract haulers
PA: Estes Express Lines, Inc.
3901 W Broad St
Richmond VA 23230
804 353-1900

GEOGRAPHIC SECTION
Berea - Cuyahoga County (G-1462)

(G-1438)
FRONTIER BASSMASTERS INC
904 Boulevard Dr (45714-1210)
PHONE.................740 423-9293
Jerry Burkhart, *President*
Tim William, *Corp Secy*
John Trunk, *Vice Pres*
EMP: 25
SALES (est): 443K **Privately Held**
SIC: 7997 Outdoor field clubs

(G-1439)
JPMORGAN CHASE BANK NAT ASSN
321 Main St (45714-1613)
P.O. Box 710 (45714-0710)
PHONE.................740 423-4111
Fax: 740 423-4156
Drew Smith, *Branch Mgr*
EMP: 32
SALES (corp-wide): 99.6B **Publicly Held**
SIC: 6099 Check clearing services
HQ: Jpmorgan Chase Bank, National Association
1111 Polaris Pkwy
Columbus OH 43240
614 436-3055

(G-1440)
JUSTICE & BUSINESS SVCS LLC
210 Florence St (45714-1757)
PHONE.................740 423-5005
Gary L Justice,
EMP: 40
SALES: 2MM **Privately Held**
SIC: 1541 1542 Industrial buildings, new construction; commercial & office building, new construction

(G-1441)
KRATON POLYMERS US LLC
2419 State Rd 618 (45714)
P.O. Box 235 (45714-0235)
PHONE.................740 423-7571
Dave Cuppett, *Safety Mgr*
Tim Buttermore, *Engineer*
John Dietz, *Engineer*
Dave Mongilio, *Engineer*
Vaneese Bell, *Corp Comm Staff*
EMP: 400 **Publicly Held**
WEB: www.kraton.com
SIC: 2822 5169 2821 Synthetic rubber; synthetic resins, rubber & plastic materials; plastics materials & resins
HQ: Kraton Polymers U.S. Llc
15710 John F Kennedy Blvd # 300
Houston TX 77032
281 504-4700

(G-1442)
MARIETTA MEMORIAL HOSPITAL
809 Farson St (45714-1066)
PHONE.................740 401-0362
EMP: 470
SALES (corp-wide): 400.4MM **Privately Held**
SIC: 8062 General medical & surgical hospitals
PA: Marietta Memorial Hospital Inc
401 Matthew St
Marietta OH 45750
740 374-1400

(G-1443)
OHIO VALLY AMBULATORY SURGERY
608 Washington Blvd (45714-2465)
P.O. Box 369 (45714-0369)
PHONE.................740 423-4684
David Catalino Mendoza, *Principal*
Tracey Hood, *Financial Exec*
EMP: 29
SALES (est): 4.2MM **Privately Held**
SIC: 8011 Ambulatory surgical center

(G-1444)
STONEGATE CONSTRUCTION INC
1378 Way Rd (45714-9633)
PHONE.................740 423-9170
Karen Hiehle, *President*
Michael Hiehle, *Corp Secy*
James Robertson, *Vice Pres*
Alan Litman, *Asst Treas*
EMP: 70
SQ FT: 1,800
SALES (est): 12.8MM **Privately Held**
SIC: 1611 1794 General contractor, highway & street construction; excavation work

Berea
Cuyahoga County

(G-1445)
AMERICAN INTERNATIONAL CNSTR
1180 Berea Indus Pkwy (44017-2947)
PHONE.................440 243-5535
Fax: 440 243-7745
Michael Petrasek, *President*
William Perry, *Vice Pres*
Joel Garn, *Project Mgr*
Lynn Tess, *Manager*
Michelle Petrasek, *Admin Sec*
EMP: 25 **EST:** 1978
SQ FT: 9,000
SALES (est): 3MM **Privately Held**
SIC: 1799 1741 Caulking (construction); waterproofing; coating of concrete structures with plastic; exterior cleaning, including sandblasting; tuckpointing or restoration

(G-1446)
BALDWIN WALLACE UNIVERSITY
Also Called: Recreational Sports & Svc
136 E Bagley Rd (44017-2011)
PHONE.................440 826-2285
Fax: 440 826-6868
Tim Miller, *Director*
Susan C Warner, *Director*
Jim Wojtkun, *Recruiter*
EMP: 30
SALES (corp-wide): 103.2MM **Privately Held**
WEB: www.baldwinw.edu
SIC: 7999 8221 Recreation center; college, except junior
PA: Baldwin Wallace University
275 Eastland Rd
Berea OH 44017
440 826-2900

(G-1447)
BEREA B O E TRNSP DEPT
235 Riveredge Pkwy (44017-1123)
PHONE.................216 898-8300
Al Fiekle, *Manager*
EMP: 80
SALES (est): 2.5MM **Privately Held**
SIC: 4151 School buses

(G-1448)
BEREA LAKE TOWERS INC
4 Berea Commons Ste 1 (44017-2524)
PHONE.................440 243-9050
Fax: 440 243-9178
Michael Coury, *President*
John Coury, *Corp Secy*
Phillip Coury, *Vice Pres*
EMP: 50
SQ FT: 60,000
SALES (est): 3.2MM **Privately Held**
SIC: 8361 Home for the aged

(G-1449)
BEREA LK TWERS RTIREMENT CMNTY
3 Berea Commons (44017-2524)
PHONE.................440 243-9050
Fax: 440 891-0196
Tammy Cummins, *CEO*
Fran Reynolds, *Manager*
Joan Gainer, *Manager*
David Lash, *Director*
EMP: 45
SALES (est): 846.5K **Privately Held**
SIC: 8059 Rest home, with health care

(G-1450)
CHARLIE TOWING SERVICE INC
Also Called: Charlie's Towing Svc
55 Lou Groza Blvd (44017-1237)
PHONE.................440 234-5300
Fax: 440 234-5317
Charles Valentine, *President*
EMP: 30
SQ FT: 8,000
SALES (est): 2.8MM **Privately Held**
SIC: 7549 Towing service, automotive

(G-1451)
CITY OF BEREA
Also Called: Berea Service Garage
400 Barrett Rd (44017-1021)
PHONE.................440 826-5853
Fax: 440 243-3339
Russ Frank, *Superintendent*
Cyril Kleem, *Mayor*
EMP: 40
SQ FT: 23,124
SALES (est): 1.5MM **Privately Held**
SIC: 7538 9532 General automotive repair shops; county planning & development agency, government
PA: City Of Berea
11 Berea Commons
Berea OH 44017
440 826-5800

(G-1452)
CLEVELAND BROWNS FOOTBALL LLC
76 Lou Groza Blvd (44017-1269)
PHONE.................440 891-5000
Fax: 440 891-5009
Joe Banner, *CEO*
Andrew Berry, *President*
Alec Scheiner, *President*
Bob Kain, *Vice Chairman*
Sashi Brown, *Exec VP*
EMP: 150
SQ FT: 10,000
SALES (est): 18.4MM **Privately Held**
WEB: www.clevelandbrowns.com
SIC: 7941 Football club

(G-1453)
COMMUNICARE HEALTH SVCS INC
Also Called: Berea Alzheimer's Care Center
49 Sheldon Rd (44017-1136)
PHONE.................440 234-0454
Fax: 440 234-0494
Haleigh Niece, *Exec Dir*
Geoff Byrne, *Exec Dir*
EMP: 100
SALES (corp-wide): 103.9MM **Privately Held**
SIC: 8051 Skilled nursing care facilities
PA: Communicare Health Services, Inc.
4700 Ashwood Dr Ste 200
Blue Ash OH 45241
513 530-1654

(G-1454)
CUYAHOGA COUNTY AG SOC
Also Called: Cuyahoga County Fair
164 Eastland Rd (44017-2066)
P.O. Box 135 (44017-0135)
PHONE.................440 243-0090
Timothy Fowler, *President*
Joyce Woycitzky, *Bookkeeper*
EMP: 30
SALES (est): 1.2MM **Privately Held**
WEB: www.cuyfair.com
SIC: 8641 7999 Civic associations; agricultural fair

(G-1455)
CYPRESS HOSPICE LLC
2 Berea Commons Ste 1 (44017-2535)
PHONE.................440 973-0250
Jay Coury,
Amber Sekerak, *Associate*
EMP: 25
SALES (est): 286.2K **Privately Held**
SIC: 8052 Personal care facility

(G-1456)
ENVIROTEST SYSTEMS CORP
1291 W Bagley Rd (44017-2911)
PHONE.................330 963-4464
EMP: 34
SQ FT: 7,545 **Privately Held**
WEB: www.il.etest.com
SIC: 7549 Emissions testing without repairs, automotive
HQ: Envirotest Systems Corp.
7 Kripes Rd
East Granby CT 06026

(G-1457)
ESTABROOK CORPORATION (PA)
700 W Bagley Rd (44017-2900)
P.O. Box 804 (44017-0804)
PHONE.................440 234-8566
Fax: 440 234-3966
Kelly Sutula, *Ch of Bd*
Jeffrey W Tarr, *President*
Brad Tarr, *Accounts Mgr*
Kevin McKenzie, *Sales Engr*
Ed Tondra, *Sales Engr*
EMP: 30
SQ FT: 25,000
SALES (est): 44.9MM **Privately Held**
WEB: www.estabrookcorp.com
SIC: 5084 7699 Pumps & pumping equipment; industrial machinery & equipment repair

(G-1458)
ETB UNIVERSITY PROPERTIES LLC
343 W Bagley Rd (44017-1370)
PHONE.................440 826-2212
Robert C Helmer, *President*
EMP: 142
SQ FT: 40,000
SALES: 110K
SALES (corp-wide): 103.2MM **Privately Held**
SIC: 6519 Real property lessors
PA: Baldwin Wallace University
275 Eastland Rd
Berea OH 44017
440 826-2900

(G-1459)
FASTENER INDUSTRIES INC
Also Called: Ohio Nut & Bolt Company Div
33 Lou Groza Blvd (44017-1237)
PHONE.................440 891-2031
Fax: 440 243-4006
Linda Kerekas, *CFO*
Tim Morgan, *Manager*
EMP: 50
SALES (corp-wide): 42.3MM **Privately Held**
WEB: www.on-b.com
SIC: 3452 5084 Bolts, nuts, rivets & washers; lift trucks & parts
PA: Fastener Industries, Inc.
1 Berea Commons Ste 209
Berea OH 44017
440 243-0034

(G-1460)
FRONT LEASING CO LLC
Also Called: Aristocrat Berea Skilled
255 Front St (44017-1943)
PHONE.................440 243-4000
Fax: 440 234-0819
David W Trimble, *CPA*
Stephen L Rosedale,
Charles Stoltz,
EMP: 245
SALES (est): 6.6MM **Privately Held**
SIC: 8051 Convalescent home with continuous nursing care

(G-1461)
INTERCNNECT CBLING NETWRK SVCS
125 Pelret Indus Pkwy (44017-2940)
PHONE.................440 891-0465
Fax: 440 891-0478
Diana O Fretwell, *President*
Sarah Mitchell, *Business Mgr*
Jim Fretwell, *Corp Secy*
Todd Penna, *Info Tech Mgr*
EMP: 32
SALES (est): 4.2MM **Privately Held**
WEB: www.icns-interconnect.com
SIC: 1731 Computer installation; telephone & telephone equipment installation

(G-1462)
L O G TRANSPORTATION INC
Also Called: Eagle Freight
120 Blaze Industrial Pkwy (44017-2930)
PHONE.................440 891-0850
Kelly Hoban, *President*
EMP: 25
SQ FT: 46,000

Berea - Cuyahoga County (G-1463)

SALES (est): 2.7MM **Privately Held**
SIC: 4213 Heavy hauling

(G-1463)
MERRICK BODY SHOP
520 Front St (44017-1758)
PHONE..................440 243-6700
Robert Serpentini, *Owner*
Ray Cieslak, *Finance*
EMP: 25
SALES (est): 1.5MM **Privately Held**
SIC: 5511 5521 7532 Automobiles, new & used; automobiles, used cars only; paint shop, automotive

(G-1464)
NORTHSTAR ALLOYS & MACHINE CO
631 Wyleswood Dr (44017-2264)
P.O. Box 684 (44017-0684)
PHONE..................440 234-3069
Jane Wagner, *President*
EMP: 40
SQ FT: 3,000
SALES (est): 732K **Privately Held**
SIC: 5051 Steel

(G-1465)
OHIO TPK & INFRASTRUCTURE COMM (DH)
Also Called: EXECUTIVE OFFICE
682 Prospect St (44017-2711)
P.O. Box 460 (44017-0460)
PHONE..................440 234-2081
Fax: 440 234-4618
Randy Cole, *CEO*
Jerry N Hruby, *Chairman*
Sandy Barber, *Corp Secy*
Martin S Seekely, *CFO*
James Steiner, *CFO*
EMP: 125
SQ FT: 55,000
SALES: 313.1MM **Privately Held**
WEB: www.ohioturnpike.net
SIC: 4785 Toll road operation

(G-1466)
OHIO TPK & INFRASTRUCTURE COMM
Also Called: Amherst Maintenance Bldg
682 Prospect St (44017-2711)
PHONE..................440 234-2081
Dan Castrigano, *Chief*
EMP: 160 **Privately Held**
WEB: www.ohioturnpike.net
SIC: 1611 0782 9621 Highway & street maintenance; highway lawn & garden maintenance services; regulation, administration of transportation;
HQ: Ohio Turnpike And Infrastructure Commission
    682 Prospect St
    Berea OH 44017
    440 234-2081

(G-1467)
OHIOGUIDESTONE (PA)
434 Eastland Rd (44017-1217)
PHONE..................440 234-2006
Fax: 440 234-8319
Richard Frank, *CEO*
Becky Volle, *Business Mgr*
Donna Keegan, *Vice Pres*
Kelly Stofko, *HR Admin*
Anissa Miranda, *Human Resources*
EMP: 50
SQ FT: 53,000
SALES: 58.6MM **Privately Held**
WEB: www.bchfs.org
SIC: 8322 8361 8351 8051 Child related social services; home for the emotionally disturbed; child day care services; skilled nursing care facilities

(G-1468)
ROCKY RIVER LEASING CO LLC
Also Called: Northwestern Healthcare Center
570 N Rocky River Dr (44017-1613)
PHONE..................440 243-5688
Fax: 440 243-4314
Stephen L Rosedale, *Chairman*
David W Trimble, *CPA*
EMP: 150

SALES (est): 5.3MM **Privately Held**
SIC: 8051 Skilled nursing care facilities

(G-1469)
SOUND COM CORPORATION
Also Called: Sound Com System
227 Depot St (44017-1860)
PHONE..................440 234-2604
Fax: 440 234-2614
Paul Winkler, *President*
Paul Fussner, *President*
Jim Averweg, *General Mgr*
Carl McLaughlin, *COO*
Mike Decarlo, *Project Mgr*
EMP: 70 EST: 1974
SQ FT: 10,500
SALES (est): 63.8MM **Privately Held**
SIC: 5065 Communication equipment; sound equipment, electronic

(G-1470)
SUBURBAN COLLISION CENTERS
Also Called: Surburan Collision Ctr
1151 W Bagley Rd (44017-2909)
PHONE..................440 243-5533
Fax: 440 243-5532
Angelo Papotto, *Owner*
EMP: 36
SQ FT: 8,617
SALES (est): 2.2MM **Privately Held**
WEB: www.suburbancollision.com
SIC: 7532 Body shop, automotive

(G-1471)
T & L ENTERPRISES INC
Also Called: ServiceMaster
1060 W Bagley Rd Ste 101 (44017-2938)
PHONE..................440 234-5900
Fax: 440 234-5660
Terry D Litt, *President*
Elizabeth Litt, *Corp Secy*
EMP: 30
SQ FT: 3,000
SALES (est): 900K **Privately Held**
SIC: 7349 Building maintenance services

(G-1472)
T ALLEN INC
200 Depot St (44017-1810)
PHONE..................440 234-2366
Fax: 440 234-5722
Thomas Krivos, *President*
Randy Hamilton, *Vice Pres*
EMP: 30
SQ FT: 4,500
SALES (est): 7MM **Privately Held**
WEB: www.rogue-cavern.net
SIC: 1542 Commercial & office building contractors

(G-1473)
TIMCO RUBBER PRODUCTS INC (PA)
125 Blaze Industrial Pkwy (44017-2930)
PHONE..................216 267-6242
Fax: 216 267-6245
John Kuzmick, *CEO*
Joe Hoffman, *President*
Randy Dahlke, *Vice Pres*
Joe Budd, *Project Mgr*
Bill Rainey, *Project Mgr*
EMP: 27
SQ FT: 4,500
SALES (est): 16MM **Privately Held**
WEB: www.timcorubber.com
SIC: 5085 Rubber goods, mechanical

(G-1474)
TRICOR EMPLYMENT SCREENING LTD
110 Blaze Industrial Pkwy (44017-2950)
PHONE..................800 818-5116
Charlotte Kaufman, *Cust Mgr*
Mary Morrison,
EMP: 39
SQ FT: 7,200
SALES (est): 2.5MM **Privately Held**
SIC: 7389 Personal investigation service

(G-1475)
WEEKLEYS MAILING SERVICE INC
1420 W Bagley Rd (44017-2935)
PHONE..................440 234-4325

Fax: 440 234-6502
Thomas Weekley, *President*
Gerald Milton, *Vice Pres*
Vera Rutz, *Treasurer*
Bob Edmonds, *Manager*
EMP: 100
SQ FT: 63,000
SALES (est): 15.1MM **Privately Held**
WEB: www.weekleysmailing.com
SIC: 7331 Mailing service

Bergholz
Jefferson County

(G-1476)
ROSEBUD MINING COMPANY
Also Called: Bergholz 7
9076 County Road 53 (43908-7948)
PHONE..................740 768-2097
William Denoon, *Branch Mgr*
EMP: 33
SALES (corp-wide): 672.6MM **Privately Held**
SIC: 1222 1221 Bituminous coal-underground mining; bituminous coal & lignite-surface mining
PA: Rosebud Mining Company
    301 Market St
    Kittanning PA 16201
    724 545-6222

Berlin
Holmes County

(G-1477)
BERLIN CONTRACTORS
Also Called: Holmes Crane
5233 Township Rd 359 (44610)
P.O. Box 257 (44610-0257)
PHONE..................330 893-2904
Fax: 330 893-4614
Perry Chupp, *Owner*
EMP: 25
SALES (est): 2.3MM **Privately Held**
SIC: 1771 Concrete work

(G-1478)
DUTCH HERITAGE FARMS INC
Also Called: Amish Farm, The
Hc 39 (44610)
P.O. Box 270 (44610-0270)
PHONE..................330 893-3232
Fax: 330 893-3158
John Schrock, *President*
James Schrock, *Corp Secy*
EMP: 40
SALES (est): 1.4MM **Privately Held**
SIC: 7999 5947 Tourist attraction, commercial; gift shop

(G-1479)
ZINCKS INN (PA)
4703 State Rt 39 (44610)
P.O. Box 441 (44610-0441)
PHONE..................330 893-6600
Fax: 330 893-0401
Alan Zincks, *Owner*
EMP: 25
SALES (est): 810.9K **Privately Held**
SIC: 7011 Hotels

Berlin Center
Mahoning County

(G-1480)
BECDIR CONSTRUCTION COMPANY
15764 W Akron Canfield Rd (44401-9786)
PHONE..................330 547-2134
Fax: 330 547-7109
David Dirusso, *President*
Rebecca Dirusso, *Vice Pres*
Joe Breddick, *Accountant*
Lynda Feichtenbiner, *Manager*
EMP: 50
SQ FT: 6,000

SALES (est): 10.5MM **Privately Held**
SIC: 1622 1611 Bridge construction; highway & street construction

Berlin Heights
Erie County

(G-1481)
DANIELS BASEMENT WATERPROOFING
Also Called: Daniel's Construction
10407 Main Rd (44814-9585)
PHONE..................440 965-4332
Fax: 440 965-4153
Daniel Polling, *Owner*
EMP: 30
SALES (est): 1.1MM **Privately Held**
WEB: www.danielswaterproofing.com
SIC: 1799 Waterproofing

Bethel
Clermont County

(G-1482)
BASTIN HOME INC
656 W Plane St (45106-9721)
PHONE..................513 734-2662
Debbie Bastin, *CEO*
EMP: 35
SALES (est): 1.6MM **Privately Held**
SIC: 8361 Home for the mentally handicapped

(G-1483)
M M CONSTRUCTION
1924 St Routee 222 (45106)
PHONE..................513 553-0106
Mark Sturgill, *President*
EMP: 50
SALES (est): 100K **Privately Held**
SIC: 1521 Single-family housing construction

(G-1484)
UTTER CONSTRUCTION INC
1302 State Route 133 (45106-8449)
PHONE..................513 876-2246
Doug Utter, *President*
Jim Messmer, *President*
Steve Turner, *COO*
Dwayne K Utter, *Vice Pres*
Chris McIntyre, *Opers Mgr*
EMP: 150
SALES (est): 41.7MM **Privately Held**
WEB: www.utterconstruction.net
SIC: 1794 Excavation work

Bethesda
Belmont County

(G-1485)
NEW HORIZON YOUTH CENTER CO
40060 National Rd (43719-9763)
PHONE..................740 782-0092
Fax: 740 782-1510
Tom Perrone, *President*
EMP: 50
SQ FT: 1,296
SALES (est): 1.8MM **Privately Held**
SIC: 8322 Youth center

(G-1486)
RES-CARE INC
39555 National Rd (43719-9762)
PHONE..................740 782-1476
Gloria Llewellyn, *Exec Dir*
EMP: 37
SALES (corp-wide): 24.5B **Privately Held**
SIC: 8082 Home health care services
HQ: Res-Care, Inc.
    9901 Linn Station Rd
    Louisville KY 40223
    502 394-2100

Beverly
Washington County

(G-1487)
APPALACHIAN RESPITE CARE LTD
Also Called: Dayspring Healthcare Center
501 Pinecrest Dr (45715-8909)
PHONE.................................740 984-4262
Meg Suermondt, *Partner*
Brian Casey, *Administration*
EMP: 75
SQ FT: 17,000
SALES: 441.2MM **Privately Held**
SIC: 8051 Skilled nursing care facilities

(G-1488)
CITIZENS BANK COMPANY (PA)
501 5th St (45715-8916)
PHONE.................................740 984-2381
Todd A Hilverding, *CEO*
Loretta Linn, *Vice Pres*
Josh Arnold, *Marketing Mgr*
Lisa Keeney, *Officer*
Linda Flowers, *Administration*
EMP: 28
SALES: 9.2MM **Privately Held**
WEB: www.thecitizens.com
SIC: 6022 State trust companies accepting deposits, commercial

(G-1489)
DAY SPRING HEALTH CARE CORP
501 Pinecrest Dr (45715-8909)
PHONE.................................740 984-4262
Brian Colleran, *President*
EMP: 62
SALES (est): 669.1K **Privately Held**
SIC: 8051 Skilled nursing care facilities

(G-1490)
DYNEGY WASHINGTON II LLC
859 State Route 83 (45715-9301)
PHONE.................................713 507-6400
Rick Barton, *Branch Mgr*
EMP: 26
SALES (corp-wide): 4.8B **Publicly Held**
SIC: 4911 Distribution, electric power
HQ: Dynegy Washington Ii, Llc
    601 Travis St Ste 1400
    Houston TX 77002
    713 507-6400

(G-1491)
LARRY LANG EXCAVATING INC
19371 State Route 60 (45715-5055)
PHONE.................................740 984-4750
Fax: 740 984-2871
Larry D Lang, *President*
Wanda Hall, *Office Mgr*
EMP: 30
SALES: 3MM **Privately Held**
SIC: 1794 Excavation & grading, building construction

(G-1492)
MUSKINGUM VLY NRSING RHBLTTION
501 Pinecrest Dr (45715-8909)
PHONE.................................740 984-4262
Gary Waters, *Director*
Clay Enslen, *Administration*
Steven Pleli, *Administration*
EMP: 65 EST: 2007
SALES (est): 1.6MM **Privately Held**
SIC: 8322 Rehabilitation services

(G-1493)
STEPHENS-MATTHEWS MKTG INC
605 Center St (45715-2504)
P.O. Box 1208 (45715-1208)
PHONE.................................740 984-8011
Fax: 740 984-8011
David Stephens, *President*
Jarod Kesselring, *Vice Pres*
Larry L Mathews, *Treasurer*
Vincent Mahoney, *Agent*
Dave Russell, *Director*
EMP: 32
SQ FT: 3,500
SALES: 7.3MM **Privately Held**
SIC: 6411 Insurance brokers

Bidwell
Gallia County

(G-1494)
CARMICHAEL EQUIPMENT INC (PA)
668 Pinecrest Dr (45614-9275)
PHONE.................................740 446-2412
Fax: 740 446-9104
John Carmichael, *President*
Loralee Carmichael, *Vice Pres*
Jessica Stanley, *Controller*
EMP: 35
SQ FT: 39,000
SALES (est): 11.1MM **Privately Held**
WEB: www.careq.com
SIC: 5999 5261 5082 Farm equipment & supplies; lawn & garden equipment; contractors' materials

(G-1495)
FOSTER SALES & DELIVERY INC
35 Corporate Dr (45614)
P.O. Box 5 (45614-0005)
PHONE.................................740 245-0200
Fax: 740 245-9731
Robert D Foster, *President*
Mary Pope, *Controller*
Dave Casto, *Manager*
Richard Lewis, *Manager*
Howard Joseph Foster, *Admin Sec*
EMP: 55
SQ FT: 5,000
SALES (est): 10.1MM **Privately Held**
SIC: 4213 Trucking, except local

(G-1496)
TRIMAT CONSTRUCTION INC
13621 State Route 554 (45614-9425)
P.O. Box 10 (45614-0010)
PHONE.................................740 388-9515
Fax: 740 388-9530
Matthew Toler, *President*
Patrica Toler, *Treasurer*
EMP: 50
SQ FT: 3,000
SALES (est): 7.1MM **Privately Held**
WEB: www.trimatconstruction.com
SIC: 1521 1794 New construction, single-family houses; excavation work; excavation & grading, building construction

(G-1497)
VRABLE III INC
Also Called: Abbyshire Place Skilled Nurse
311 Buck Ridge Rd (45614-8018)
PHONE.................................740 446-7150
Al Vrable, *President*
James Merrill, *CFO*
EMP: 81
SALES: 5.6MM **Privately Held**
SIC: 8082 Home health care services
PA: Vrable Healthcare, Inc.
    3248 Henderson Rd
    Columbus OH 43220

Big Prairie
Holmes County

(G-1498)
MANSFIELD PLUMBING PDTS LLC
13211 State Route 226 (44611-9584)
P.O. Box 68 (44611-0068)
PHONE.................................330 496-2301
Fax: 330 496-4475
Paul Conrad, *Manager*
EMP: 40 **Privately Held**
SIC: 1711 3088 Plumbing contractors; plastics plumbing fixtures
HQ: Mansfield Plumbing Products Llc
    150 E 1st St
    Perrysville OH 44864
    419 938-5211

Blacklick
Franklin County

(G-1499)
AMERISCAPE INC
6751 Taylor Rd Unit D1 (43004-8313)
P.O. Box 663, New Albany (43054-0663)
PHONE.................................614 863-5400
Fax: 614 797-9276
Bill Duraney, *President*
EMP: 45
SALES (est): 2.1MM **Privately Held**
SIC: 0782 Landscape contractors; lawn care services

(G-1500)
ATRIUM BUYING CORPORATION
Also Called: David Hirsh
1010 Jackson Hole Dr # 100 (43004-6050)
PHONE.................................740 966-8200
David Hirsh, *President*
Douglas Tu, *CFO*
Jason Tu, *CFO*
Brittany Baker, *Sales Staff*
Jennifer Hanes, *Manager*
▲ EMP: 100
SQ FT: 25,000
SALES: 100MM **Privately Held**
SIC: 5137 Handbags

(G-1501)
BUCKEYE LANDSCAPE SERVICE INC
6608 Taylor Rd (43004-8661)
PHONE.................................614 866-0088
Fax: 614 866-1188
Kevin McIntyre, *President*
Garry Schwartzkopf, *Chairman*
Rachel Marks, *Accountant*
Paul Barlow, *Manager*
Joyce Kasper, *Admin Sec*
▲ EMP: 100
SQ FT: 4,000
SALES (est): 5.8MM **Privately Held**
WEB: www.buckeyelandscape.com
SIC: 0781 1629 0782 1711 Landscape services; golf course construction; lawn care services; seeding services, lawn; sodding contractor; irrigation sprinkler system installation

(G-1502)
BUCKEYE POWER SALES CO INC (PA)
Also Called: Bps Superstore
6850 Commerce Court Dr (43004-9297)
P.O. Box 489 (43004-0489)
PHONE.................................513 755-2323
Fax: 614 861-2291
Donald E Bohls, *President*
Greggory R Bohls, *Vice Pres*
Thomas E Bohls, *Vice Pres*
Jane Bohls, *Purchasing*
Craig Casdorph, *Controller*
EMP: 53
SQ FT: 40,000
SALES: 66.4MM **Privately Held**
WEB: www.bpssuperstore.com
SIC: 5063 Generators

(G-1503)
CBRE INC
860 Taylor Station Rd (43004-9540)
PHONE.................................014 419-7429
EMP: 29
SALES (corp-wide): 14.2B **Publicly Held**
SIC: 6531 Real estate agent, commercial
HQ: Cbre, Inc.
    400 S Hope St Ste 25
    Los Angeles CA 90071
    310 477-5876

(G-1504)
CINTAS CORPORATION NO 2
1275 Research Rd (43004-9534)
P.O. Box 400 (43004-0400)
PHONE.................................614 860-9152
Fax: 614 860-9644
Matt Schwinghammer, *Manager*
EMP: 120
SQ FT: 27,948
SALES (corp-wide): 5.3B **Publicly Held**
WEB: www.cintas-corp.com
SIC: 7213 7218 Uniform supply; industrial launderers
HQ: Cintas Corporation No 2
    6800 Cintas Blvd
    Mason OH 45040

(G-1505)
COAST TO COAST STUDIOS LLC
7522 Blacklick Ridge Blvd (43004-9144)
PHONE.................................614 861-9800
Bobby Killian, *Manager*
Charles H Morgan,
EMP: 45
SQ FT: 3,000
SALES (est): 1.3MM **Privately Held**
SIC: 7389 Personal service agents, brokers & bureaus

(G-1506)
DISMAS DISTRIBUTION SERVICES
6772 Kilowatt Cir (43004-9553)
PHONE.................................614 861-2525
Fax: 614 866-5248
Terry Smith, *President*
EMP: 50
SQ FT: 10,000
SALES (est): 3.4MM **Privately Held**
WEB: www.dismas.net
SIC: 7319 Sample distribution

(G-1507)
HENLEY & ASSOC SEC GROUP LLC
967 Jefferson Chase Way (43004-9154)
PHONE.................................614 378-3727
Camika Jones, *CEO*
EMP: 25
SQ FT: 10,000
SALES (est): 719.2K **Privately Held**
SIC: 7382 Security systems services

(G-1508)
JEFFERSON GOLF & COUNTRY CLUB
7271 Jefferson Meadows Dr (43004-9811)
PHONE.................................614 759-7500
Fax: 614 759-0447
Earl Berry, *President*
Rick Moling, *CFO*
EMP: 35
SQ FT: 7,980
SALES (est): 3.6MM **Privately Held**
WEB: www.jeffersoncountryclub.com
SIC: 7997 Golf club, membership; country club, membership

(G-1509)
JESS HOWARD ELECTRIC COMPANY
6630 Taylor Rd (43004-8661)
P.O. Box 400 (43004-0400)
PHONE.................................614 864-2167
Fax: 614 861-1830
Jess E Howard, *CEO*
John Howard, *President*
Bill Walt, *Exec VP*
Mel Haywood, *Vice Pres*
Tim Howard Sr, *Vice Pres*
EMP: 140
SQ FT: 70,000
SALES (est): 45.6MM **Privately Held**
WEB: www.jesshoward.com
SIC: 1731 General electrical contractor

(G-1510)
MANHATTAN MORTGAGE GROUP LTD
6833 Clark State Rd (43004-7500)
PHONE.................................614 933-8955
Fax: 614 933-8956
Michael Matalka, *President*
Anthony Brusadin, *Manager*
EMP: 60
SQ FT: 7,500
SALES (est): 5.7MM **Privately Held**
WEB: www.manhattanmortgagegroup.com
SIC: 6163 Loan brokers

Blacklick - Franklin County (G-1511)
GEOGRAPHIC SECTION

(G-1511)
UNIFIRST CORPORATION
211 Reynoldsburg New Albn (43004-8700)
PHONE..........................614 575-9999
Fax: 614 575-9799
Ryan West, *Site Mgr*
Douglas Parfker, *Branch Mgr*
EMP: 50
SALES (corp-wide): 1.5B **Publicly Held**
WEB: www.unifirst.com
SIC: 7218 7213 Work clothing supply; uniform supply
PA: Unifirst Corporation
     68 Jonspin Rd
     Wilmington MA 01887
     978 658-8888

(G-1512)
VESCO OIL CORPORATION
254 Business Center Dr (43004-9240)
PHONE..........................614 367-1412
EMP: 27
SALES (corp-wide): 233.6MM **Privately Held**
SIC: 5172 Crude oil
PA: Vesco Oil Corporation
     16055 W 12 Mile Rd
     Southfield MI 48076
     800 527-5358

(G-1513)
YARDMASTER OF COLUMBUS INC
570 Reynldsbrg New Albany (43004-9688)
PHONE..........................614 863-4510
Robert Slingluff, *President*
Rick Colwell, *Corp Secy*
Kurt Kluznik, *Vice Pres*
Paul Goodwill, *Sales Executive*
EMP: 30
SALES (est): 1.8MM **Privately Held**
SIC: 0781 4959 Landscape architects; landscape planning services; snowplowing

Blanchester
Clinton County

(G-1514)
FIRST RICHMOND CORP
Also Called: Continental Manor
820 E Center St (45107-1310)
PHONE..........................937 783-4949
Fax: 937 783-4398
Ron Spatafora, *Mktg Dir*
Howard W Reifsteck, *Branch Mgr*
Bruce Staley, *Director*
Samantha Fox, *Records Dir*
EMP: 57
SALES (corp-wide): 7.5MM **Privately Held**
SIC: 8051 Skilled nursing care facilities
PA: First Richmond Corp
     900 N E St
     Richmond IN 47374
     765 962-2947

(G-1515)
J-C-R TECH INC
936 Cherry St (45107-1318)
P.O. Box 65 (45107-0065)
PHONE..........................937 783-2296
Rick Carmean, *President*
Larry Hinz, *Electrical Engi*
Caleb Maxwell, *Electrical Engi*
▲ EMP: 27
SQ FT: 18,000
SALES (est): 4.5MM **Privately Held**
WEB: www.jcrtech.com
SIC: 3541 7629 3544 Machine tool replacement & repair parts, metal cutting types; electrical repair shops; special dies, tools, jigs & fixtures

(G-1516)
RUTHMAN PUMP AND ENGINEERING
Fulflo Specialties Co
459 E Fancy St (45107-1462)
PHONE..........................937 783-2411
David Locaputo, *Manager*
EMP: 25

SALES (corp-wide): 45.4MM **Privately Held**
WEB: www.ruthmannpumpen.de
SIC: 3494 5085 3491 Valves & pipe fittings; valves & fittings; industrial valves
PA: Ruthman Pump And Engineering, Inc
     1212 Streng St
     Cincinnati OH 45223
     513 559-1901

Bloomingdale
Jefferson County

(G-1517)
KUESTER IMPLEMENT COMPANY INC
Also Called: John Deere Authorized Dealer
1436 State Route 152 (43910-7997)
PHONE..........................740 944-1502
Fax: 740 944-1511
Dave Boring, *President*
Dean Boring, *Manager*
EMP: 25
SQ FT: 13,360
SALES (est): 3.8MM **Privately Held**
WEB: www.kuesterimplement.com
SIC: 5999 5261 5082 Farm machinery; nurseries & garden centers; construction & mining machinery

(G-1518)
WILLIAM WOOD
8392 County Road 39 (43910-7808)
PHONE..........................740 543-4052
William Wood, *CEO*
EMP: 37
SALES (est): 4MM **Privately Held**
SIC: 5051 Steel

Bloomville
Seneca County

(G-1519)
ELMCO TRUCKING INC
30 Railroad St (44818-9108)
P.O. Box 218 (44818-0218)
PHONE..........................419 983-2010
Fax: 419 983-3806
Elmer Cole, *President*
Wendy Seyer, *Principal*
EMP: 25
SALES (est): 1.1MM **Privately Held**
SIC: 4213 Trucking, except local

Blue Ash
Hamilton County

(G-1520)
1 FINANCIAL CORPORATION
10123 Alliance Rd Ste 110 (45242-4714)
PHONE..........................513 936-1400
William V Carroll, *President*
EMP: 25
SALES: 2MM **Privately Held**
SIC: 7389 Financial services

(G-1521)
4MYBENEFITS INC
4665 Cornell Rd Ste 331 (45241-2455)
PHONE..........................513 891-6648
Gerald A Peter, *President*
Justin Peter, *Principal*
Linda Peter, *Principal*
Jason Peter, *Vice Pres*
Paul Eldridge, *Natl Sales Mgr*
▲ EMP: 25
SALES (est): 1.5MM **Privately Held**
WEB: www.4mybenefits.com
SIC: 4813

(G-1522)
5901 PFFFER RD HTELS SITES LLC
Also Called: Clarion Hotel Suites
5901 Pfeiffer Rd (45242-4821)
PHONE..........................513 793-4500
Jose Machuca, *General Mgr*
EMP: 80

SALES (est): 2.6MM **Privately Held**
SIC: 7011 5812 Hotels; eating places

(G-1523)
ADVANCED COMPUTER GRAPHICS
10895 Indeco Dr (45241-2926)
PHONE..........................513 936-5060
Fax: 513 936-4184
Tony Butrum, *CEO*
Mary Sue Harpenau, *Vice Pres*
Kelly Flerlage, *Controller*
EMP: 25
SQ FT: 11,564
SALES (est): 2.4MM **Privately Held**
WEB: www.acgmultimedia.com
SIC: 8742 Marketing consulting services

(G-1524)
ADVANCED INTGRTED SLUTIONS LLC
11140 Deerfield Rd (45242-2022)
PHONE..........................313 724-8600
Vanessa Willett, *President*
EMP: 30
SALES (corp-wide): 12MM **Privately Held**
SIC: 1542 Commercial & office buildings, renovation & repair
PA: Advanced Integrated Solutions, Llc
     27016 Princeton St
     Inkster MI 48141
     313 724-8600

(G-1525)
ADVANCED TESTING LAB INC
Also Called: Advanced Testing Laboratories
6954 Cornell Rd Ste 200 (45242-3001)
PHONE..........................513 489-8447
Fax: 513 489-9291
Greg Neal, *President*
Renee Downey, *Accounting Mgr*
Paula Brooks, *Manager*
Nicholas Tatum, *Manager*
EMP: 250
SALES (est): 41.3MM **Privately Held**
SIC: 8734 Testing laboratories

(G-1526)
ADVANCED TESTING MGT GROUP INC
6954 Cornell Rd Ste 200 (45242-3001)
PHONE..........................513 489-8447
Greg Neal, *President*
Dorothy S Stammer, *Corp Secy*
Elizabeth Horton, *Vice Pres*
Dieter Stammer, *Vice Pres*
Sherry Kirschner, *Manager*
EMP: 250
SQ FT: 6,000
SALES (est): 15.5MM **Privately Held**
WEB: www.advancedtesting.net
SIC: 8734 Testing laboratories

(G-1527)
ADVANTAGE SALES & MKTG LLC
Also Called: Advantage Sales & Mktg
10300 Alliance Rd Ste 400 (45242-4761)
PHONE..........................513 841-0500
Fax: 513 841-0554
John Mazza, *President*
Dave Weeks, *Manager*
EMP: 80
SALES (corp-wide): 8.9B **Privately Held**
SIC: 5141 Food brokers
HQ: Advantage Sales & Marketing Llc
     18100 Von Karman Ave # 900
     Irvine CA 92612
     949 797-2900

(G-1528)
ADVANTECH CORPORATION
Also Called: Advantech Indus Automtn Group
11380 Reed Hartman Hwy (45241-2430)
PHONE..........................513 742-8895
Fax: 513 742-8892
Eric Chen, *Vice Pres*
Nicolas Gonthier, *Project Mgr*
Donald Appel, *Opers Staff*
Matrix Choong, *Technical Mgr*
Sean Wu, *Engineer*
EMP: 70
SALES (corp-wide): 1.3B **Privately Held**
SIC: 5045 Computer peripheral equipment

HQ: Advantech Corporation
     380 Fairview Way
     Milpitas CA 95035
     408 519-3800

(G-1529)
ALPHA & OMEGA BLDG SVCS INC
11250 Cornell Park Dr # 200 (45242-1827)
PHONE..........................513 429-5082
Fax: 513 429-5088
Jim Baker, *CEO*
EMP: 38
SALES (corp-wide): 9.5MM **Privately Held**
SIC: 7349 Janitorial service, contract basis
PA: Alpha & Omega Building Services, Inc.
     2843 Culver Ave Ste B
     Dayton OH 45429
     937 298-2125

(G-1530)
ALS GROUP USA CORP
4388 Glendale Milford Rd (45242-3706)
PHONE..........................513 733-5336
James Baxter, *Branch Mgr*
EMP: 26
SQ FT: 5,645
SALES (corp-wide): 975.4MM **Privately Held**
WEB: www.paragonlabs.com
SIC: 8734 8748 Testing laboratories; environmental consultant
HQ: Als Group Usa, Corp.
     10450 Stncliff Rd Ste 210
     Houston TX 77099
     281 530-5656

(G-1531)
AMEC FSTR WHLR ENVRNMNT INFRST
4460 Lake Forest Dr # 200 (45242-3741)
PHONE..........................513 489-6611
Rick Campbell, *Manager*
EMP: 30
SALES (corp-wide): 6.7B **Privately Held**
SIC: 8711 Consulting engineer
HQ: Amec Foster Wheeler Environment & Infrastructure, Inc.
     1105 Lakewood Pkwy # 300
     Alpharetta GA 30009
     770 360-0600

(G-1532)
AMERIGROUP OHIO INC
10123 Alliance Rd Ste 140 (45242-4714)
P.O. Box 62509, Virginia Beach VA (23466-2509)
PHONE..........................513 733-2300
Fax: 513 733-0516
Gary Radke, *Principal*
Sharon Brumley, *Manager*
Essie Matthews, *Manager*
EMP: 35
SALES (est): 12.7MM
SALES (corp-wide): 90B **Publicly Held**
WEB: www.amerigroupcorp.com
SIC: 6324 Hospital & medical service plans
HQ: Amerigroup Corporation
     4425 Corp Ln Ste 160
     Virginia Beach VA 23462

(G-1533)
AMERIPATH CINCINNATI INC
Also Called: Richfield Labs
9670 Kenwood Rd (45242-6141)
PHONE..........................513 745-8330
Fax: 513 745-8335
David R Barron MD, *President*
EMP: 35
SALES (est): 2.6MM
SALES (corp-wide): 7.7B **Publicly Held**
WEB: www.ameripath.com
SIC: 8011 Physicians' office, including specialists
HQ: Ameripath, Inc.
     7111 Fairway Dr Ste 101
     Palm Beach Gardens FL 33418
     561 712-6200

(G-1534)
APRECIA PHARMACEUTICALS CO
10901 Kenwood Rd (45242-2813)
PHONE..........................513 864-4107

GEOGRAPHIC SECTION

Blue Ash - Hamilton County (G-1559)

Don Wetherhold, *CEO*
Mike Rohlfs, *CFO*
EMP: 112
SQ FT: 14,000 **Privately Held**
SIC: 6719 Investment holding companies, except banks

(G-1535)
ARDUS MEDICAL INC
9407 Kenwood Rd (45242-6811)
P.O. Box 42122, Cincinnati (45242-0122)
PHONE..................................855 592-7387
Fax: 513 469-2329
Kevin Williams, *President*
George Pettesch, *Purch Mgr*
Mark Gleis, *Personnel Exec*
Tracey Roberts, *Sales Staff*
Chis Thomas, *Manager*
EMP: 78
SQ FT: 23,000
SALES (est): 8.2MM **Privately Held**
WEB: www.ardusmedical.com
SIC: 5047 Medical equipment & supplies

(G-1536)
ARSZMAN & LYONS LLC
Also Called: A&L Imaging
9933 Alliance Rd Ste 2 (45242-5662)
PHONE..................................513 527-4900
William Lyons,
Jason Arszman,
EMP: 25
SQ FT: 8,000
SALES (est): 1.6MM **Privately Held**
WEB: www.alimaging.com
SIC: 7379

(G-1537)
AXIOM PRODUCT DEVELOPMENT LLC
Also Called: Axiom Consulting
4370 Creek Rd (45241-2924)
PHONE..................................513 791-2425
Giri Lakshimada, *President*
EMP: 46
SALES (est): 4.6MM
SALES (corp-wide): 1.8MM **Privately Held**
SIC: 8748 Business consulting
PA: Axiom Consulting Private Limited
    307, Shree Chambers, 100 Feet Ring Road, 1st Floor,
    Bengaluru KA 56008
    802 679-9570

(G-1538)
BELCAN LLC (PA)
10200 Anderson Way (45242-4718)
PHONE..................................513 891-0972
Fax: 513 793-8618
Lance H Kwasniewski, *CEO*
Lee Shabe, *President*
Joe Triompo, *President*
Harold Pope, *General Mgr*
Scott Briggs, *Senior VP*
EMP: 3000
SQ FT: 104,000
SALES (est): 666.9MM **Privately Held**
SIC: 7363 8711 Engineering help service; engineering services

(G-1539)
BELCAN CORPORATION
Multimedia Services Division
10200 Anderson Way (45242-4718)
PHONE..................................513 985-7777
Fax: 513 985-7276
Patrick Wagonfield, *Principal*
Steve Rengers, *Vice Pres*
Carolyn Garner, *Project Mgr*
Steve M Houghtaling, *Opers Mgr*
Steven Struckman, *Opers Staff*
EMP: 749
SALES (corp-wide): 666.9MM **Privately Held**
SIC: 7363 Engineering help service
PA: Belcan, Llc
    10200 Anderson Way
    Blue Ash OH 45242
    513 891-0972

(G-1540)
BELCAN ENGINEERING GROUP LLC (HQ)
10200 Anderson Way (45242-4718)
PHONE..................................513 891-0972
Fax: 513 985-7251
Lance Kwasniewski, *CEO*
Neal Montour, *Senior VP*
Russell Lubik, *QC Mgr*
Joseph Sebben, *QC Mgr*
John Peter, *Research*
EMP: 1100 **EST:** 1991
SQ FT: 104,000
SALES (est): 327MM
SALES (corp-wide): 666.9MM **Privately Held**
SIC: 8711 Engineering services
PA: Belcan, Llc
    10200 Anderson Way
    Blue Ash OH 45242
    513 891-0972

(G-1541)
BELCAN SVCS GROUP LTD PARTNR (HQ)
10200 Anderson Way (45242-4718)
PHONE..................................513 891-0972
Arnold Johnson, *Partner*
John Kuprionis, *Partner*
Michael McCaw, *Partner*
Candace McCaw, *General Ptnr*
Mike Wirth, *CFO*
EMP: 200
SALES: 260.6MM
SALES (corp-wide): 666.9MM **Privately Held**
SIC: 7363 Engineering help service
PA: Belcan, Llc
    10200 Anderson Way
    Blue Ash OH 45242
    513 891-0972

(G-1542)
BEST & DONOVAN N A INC
5570 Creek Rd (45242-4004)
P.O. Box 42235, Cincinnati (45242-0235)
PHONE..................................513 791-9180
Scott Andre, *CEO*
L George Andre, *Chairman*
Keith Jameson, *Purch Dir*
George Andre, *Sls & Mktg Exec*
Tim Park, *CFO*
▲ **EMP:** 25
SQ FT: 50,000
SALES: 5MM **Privately Held**
SIC: 5084 Industrial machinery & equipment

(G-1543)
BG HOLDING LLC
4620 Carlynn Dr (45241-2202)
PHONE..................................513 489-1023
Beth Frondorf, *Human Res Dir*
EMP: 6565 **Privately Held**
SIC: 0781 Landscape services
PA: Bg Holding Llc
    2275 Res Blvd Ste 600
    Rockville MD 20850

(G-1544)
BLUE ASH FIRE DEPARTMENT
10647 Kenwood Rd (45242-3846)
PHONE..................................513 745-8534
Fax: 513 794-3496
Richard Brown, *Chief*
EMP: 46 **EST:** 2011 **Privately Held**
SIC: 9224 8049 Fire department, not including volunteer; ; paramedic

(G-1545)
BLUE CHIP MAILING SERVICES INC
9933 Alliance Rd Ste 1 (45242-5662)
PHONE..................................513 541-4800
Lisa Ruttenberg, *President*
Pamela Kremp, *Finance*
Joe Engel, *Manager*
EMP: 35
SQ FT: 35,000
SALES (est): 4.3MM **Privately Held**
WEB: www.bluechipmail.net
SIC: 7331 7299 Mailing service; stitching, custom

(G-1546)
BLUE-KENWOOD LLC
Also Called: Hilton Garden Blue Ash
5300 Cornell Rd (45242-2002)
PHONE..................................513 469-6900
Greg Culey Od, *Principal*
Peter Winchester, *Director*
EMP: 40
SALES (est): 428K **Privately Held**
SIC: 7011 Hotels

(G-1547)
BLUESPRING SOFTWARE INC (PA)
10290 Alliance Rd (45242-4710)
PHONE..................................513 794-1764
Fax: 513 794-1764
Blaine Clark, *President*
Mahendra Vora, *Chairman*
Micah Zimmerman, *CFO*
EMP: 41
SQ FT: 9,000
SALES: 5MM **Privately Held**
WEB: www.bluespringsw.com
SIC: 7371 4813 7375 Computer software development; ; information retrieval services

(G-1548)
BRAND BUILD INC
Also Called: EMI Network
9933 Alliance Rd (45242-5661)
PHONE..................................513 579-1950
Lisa Licker, *President*
Jeffrey Eads, *Project Mgr*
Jeff Levinson, *Project Mgr*
Mark Arnett, *CFO*
Archie Walker, *Sales Mgr*
EMP: 37
SALES (est): 5.9MM **Privately Held**
SIC: 7311 Advertising consultant

(G-1549)
BRIGHTSTAR HEALTHCARE
10999 Reed Hartman Hwy # 209 (45242-8331)
PHONE..................................513 321-4688
John Apler,
EMP: 25
SALES (est): 443.8K **Privately Held**
SIC: 8082 Home health care services

(G-1550)
BUCKEYE HOME HEALTH CARE
10921 Reed Hartman Hwy # 312 (45242-2849)
PHONE..................................513 791-6446
EMP: 120 **Privately Held**
SIC: 9431 8082 Administration of public health programs; home health care services
PA: Buckeye Home Health Care
    7700 Paragon Rd Ste A
    Dayton OH 45459

(G-1551)
CASSADY SCHILLER & ASSOCIATES
4555 Lake Forest Dr # 400 (45242-3732)
PHONE..................................513 483-6699
Fax: 513 483-6680
David Cassady, *President*
Robert Schiller, *Managing Prtnr*
Betsy Cassady, *Accountant*
Shannon Louis, *Accountant*
Jeffrey Stautberg, *Manager*
EMP: 40
SALES (est): 3.9MM **Privately Held**
WEB: www.csa-cpa.com
SIC: 8721 Certified public accountant

(G-1552)
CAVALIER DISTRIBUTING COMPANY
4650 Lake Forest Dr # 580 (45242-3756)
PHONE..................................513 247-9222
George T Fisher, *President*
Bob McCall, *Regional Mgr*
Larry Coblentz, *Opers Mgr*
Kiel Weber, *Warehouse Mgr*
Ian Sroufe, *Purch Mgr*
▲ **EMP:** 70
SQ FT: 12,000
SALES (est): 43.3MM **Privately Held**
SIC: 5181 Beer & other fermented malt liquors

(G-1553)
CEI PHYSICIANS INC
Also Called: Cincinnati Eye Institute
1945 Cei Dr (45242-5664)
PHONE..................................513 984-5133
Richard Kerstine MD, *President*
John Cohen MD, *Principal*
James D Faulkner MD, *Principal*
William Faulkner MD, *Principal*
Robert H Osher MD, *Principal*
EMP: 400
SALES (est): 19.7MM **Privately Held**
SIC: 8011 Ophthalmologist

(G-1554)
CEI PHYSICIANS PSC INC (PA)
Also Called: Cincinnati Eye Institute
1945 Cei Dr (45242-5664)
PHONE..................................513 984-5133
Clyde Bell, *President*
Robert E Brant, *Principal*
Kerry McGehee, *COO*
Carry McGehee, *Vice Pres*
Mhsa M Dressler, *Project Mgr*
EMP: 160
SQ FT: 44,000
SALES (est): 46.4MM **Privately Held**
SIC: 8011 Ophthalmologist

(G-1555)
CINCINNATI COLLISION CENTER
Also Called: Carstar
9323 Blue Ash Rd (45242-6818)
PHONE..................................513 984-4445
Fax: 513 984-1831
Greg Theobald, *President*
EMP: 30
SQ FT: 29,239
SALES (est): 2.5MM **Privately Held**
SIC: 7532 Body shop, automotive

(G-1556)
CINCINNATI COPIERS INC (PA)
Also Called: Prosource
4720 Glendale Milford Rd (45242-3847)
PHONE..................................513 769-0606
Fax: 513 769-0080
Benjamin J Russert, *Chairman*
Kendall Cox, *Opers Mgr*
Randy Abramovic, *Facilities Mgr*
Chris Shersky, *CFO*
Geoff Griffiths, *Controller*
EMP: 110
SQ FT: 26,000
SALES (est): 52.1MM **Privately Held**
WEB: www.totalprosource.com
SIC: 7378 5999 Computer maintenance & repair; business machines & equipment

(G-1557)
CINCINNATI OCCUPATIONAL THERAP (PA)
Also Called: Coti
4440 Carver Woods Dr # 200 (45242-5524)
PHONE..................................513 791-5688
Kathryn Reese, *COO*
Michael Dixon, *Manager*
Linda Campbell, *Supervisor*
Deborah Whitcomb, *Exec Dir*
Rachel Pettibone, *Exec Dir*
EMP: 26
SALES (est): 2.5MM **Privately Held**
WEB: www.cintiotinstitute.com
SIC: 8049 Occupational therapist

(G-1558)
CITY OF BLUE ASH
Also Called: Blue Ash Golf Course
4040 Cooper Rd (45241-3331)
PHONE..................................513 745-8577
David Waltz, *Manager*
EMP: 32
SQ FT: 3,756
SALES (est): 671.6K **Privately Held**
SIC: 7992 Public golf courses
PA: City Of Blue Ash
    4343 Cooper Rd
    Cincinnati OH 45242
    513 745-8500

(G-1559)
CLIPPER MAGAZINE LLC
4601 Malsbary Rd 1 (45242-5632)
PHONE..................................513 794-4100
EMP: 60 **Privately Held**
SIC: 7331 Direct mail advertising services
HQ: Clipper Magazine, Llc
    3708 Hempland Rd
    Mountville PA 17554
    717 569-5100

Blue Ash - Hamilton County (G-1560)

(G-1560)
CLUBESSENTIAL LLC (PA)
4600 Mcauley Pl Ste 350 (45242-4765)
PHONE.....................800 448-1475
William Ivers Jr, *Owner*
Kate Iver, *Principal*
Tom Iver, *Exec VP*
Jim Dies, *Vice Pres*
Conner Erwin, *Vice Pres*
EMP: 41
SQ FT: 6,341
SALES: 8.2MM **Privately Held**
SIC: 7371 7374 Computer software development; computer graphics service

(G-1561)
CMP I BLUE ASH OWNER LLC
Also Called: Courtyard Cincinnati Blue Ash
4625 Lake Forest Dr (45242-3729)
PHONE.....................513 733-4334
Fax: 513 733-5711
Rick Kimmel, *Manager*
Ronnie Nicholes, *Manager*
EMP: 26
SALES (est): 1.6MM
SALES (corp-wide): 50.6MM **Privately Held**
SIC: 7011 Hotels
PA: Cmp I Owner-T, Llc
    399 Park Ave Fl 18
    New York NY 10022
    212 547-2609

(G-1562)
CMP I OWNER-T LLC
4625 Lake Forest Dr (45242-3729)
PHONE.....................513 733-4334
Rick Kimmel, *Manager*
EMP: 26
SALES (corp-wide): 50.6MM **Privately Held**
SIC: 8741 Hotel or motel management
PA: Cmp I Owner-T, Llc
    399 Park Ave Fl 18
    New York NY 10022
    212 547-2609

(G-1563)
COLUMBUS HOTEL PARTNERS
4243 Hunt Rd (45242-6645)
PHONE.....................513 891-1066
Mike Conway, *President*
Todd Garvin, *Sales Mgr*
EMP: 40
SALES (est): 5.8MM **Privately Held**
SIC: 7011 Hotels

(G-1564)
COMMUNICARE HEALTH SVCS INC (PA)
4700 Ashwood Dr Ste 200 (45241-2424)
PHONE.....................513 530-1654
Stephen L Rosedale, *President*
Beatrice Rosedale, *Vice Pres*
Jahan Ketabchi, *CIO*
Michele Hoft, *Exec Dir*
Misty Clapsaddle, *Executive Asst*
EMP: 40
SALES (est): 103.9MM **Privately Held**
WEB: www.communicarehealth.com
SIC: 8741 Hospital management; nursing & personal care facility management

(G-1565)
COMPLETE MECHANICAL SVCS LLC
11399 Grooms Rd (45242-1405)
PHONE.....................513 489-3080
Fax: 513 489-0105
Felicia Duncan, *Manager*
Tom Blaha,
Bruce Ducker,
Daniel G Dulle,
Wyane Miller,
EMP: 86
SQ FT: 20,000
SALES: 17.4MM **Privately Held**
WEB: www.completemech.com
SIC: 1711 Mechanical contractor

(G-1566)
CORNERSTONE MED SVCS MIDWEST
4570 Cornell Rd (45241-2425)
PHONE.....................513 554-0222
EMP: 40
SALES (est): 1.4MM **Privately Held**
SIC: 5047 Medical equipment & supplies

(G-1567)
CORNERSTONE MEDICAL SERVICES
4570 Cornell Rd (45241-2425)
PHONE.....................513 554-0222
Tom Sayre, *President*
EMP: 40
SALES (est): 6.2MM **Privately Held**
WEB: www.cornerstoneonecall.com
SIC: 5047 Medical equipment & supplies

(G-1568)
CORPS SECURITY AGENCY INC
Also Called: Csa
9475 Kenwood Rd Ste 14 (45242-6830)
PHONE.....................513 631-3200
Fax: 513 631-3525
William Brodberger, *President*
Diane Dektas, *Manager*
EMP: 100
SQ FT: 900
SALES: 2.2MM **Privately Held**
SIC: 7381 7323 Security guard service; private investigator; credit investigation service

(G-1569)
COUNSELING SOURCE INC
Also Called: Rehab Continuum, The
10921 Reed Hartman Hwy # 134 (45242-2881)
PHONE.....................513 984-9838
Fax: 513 984-8075
David Turner, *President*
OH Akron, *President*
Eric Poklar, *Vice Pres*
Catherine Staskavich, *Manager*
Merilee Wale, *Social Worker*
EMP: 40
SALES (est): 3MM **Privately Held**
WEB: www.thecounselingsource.com
SIC: 8093 Mental health clinic, outpatient

(G-1570)
CREATIVE CRAFTS GROUP LLC
10151 Carver Rd Ste 200 (45242-4760)
PHONE.....................303 215-5600
Joe Collette, *Controller*
Tina Battock,
EMP: 85
SALES (est): 4.8MM **Privately Held**
SIC: 7313 Radio, television, publisher representatives

(G-1571)
CRESTLINE HOTELS & RESORTS LLC
11435 Reed Hartman Hwy (45241-2418)
PHONE.....................513 489-3666
April Collins, *Manager*
EMP: 26 **Publicly Held**
SIC: 8741 Hotel or motel management
HQ: Crestline Hotels & Resorts, Llc
    3950 University Dr # 301
    Fairfax VA 22030
    571 529-6100

(G-1572)
CROSSGATE LANES INC
Also Called: Crossgate Bowling Lanes
4230 Hunt Rd (45242-6612)
PHONE.....................513 891-0310
Fax: 513 792-3105
Ronald C Bedinghaus, *President*
Rosemary Bedinghaus, *Vice Pres*
Chuckie Chiara, *Vice Pres*
Sam Mizener, *Vice Pres*
Andrew Moore, *Vice Pres*
EMP: 30
SQ FT: 27,000
SALES (est): 1.4MM **Privately Held**
WEB: www.crossgatelanes.com
SIC: 7933 5812 Ten pin center; eating places

(G-1573)
CT CONSULTANTS INC
11120 Kenwood Rd (45242-1818)
PHONE.....................513 791-1700
Mark Brueggemann, *Vice Pres*
EMP: 44
SALES (corp-wide): 43.6MM **Privately Held**
SIC: 8711 8712 8713 Consulting engineer; architectural engineering; surveying services
PA: C.T. Consultants, Inc.
    8150 Sterling Ct
    Mentor OH 44060
    440 951-9000

(G-1574)
CURATOR VIDEO LLC
10250 Alliance Rd Ste 226 (45242-4737)
PHONE.....................513 842-6605
Mark Schrantz,
EMP: 50
SALES (est): 713.7K **Privately Held**
SIC: 8732 Market analysis or research

(G-1575)
DAYTON/CNCINNATI TECH SVCS LLC (PA)
Also Called: Dcts
5757 Cornell Rd (45242-2009)
PHONE.....................513 892-3940
Fax: 513 892-3492
Richard Grinstead, *Mng Member*
Theodore Dehoff, *Network Enginr*
Brandon Hawley, *Director*
Julie Grinstead,
Dave Hendren,
EMP: 30
SQ FT: 3,500
SALES (est): 9.9MM **Privately Held**
WEB: www.daycintech.com
SIC: 7373 1731 Value-added resellers, computer systems; computer installation

(G-1576)
DENMARK CONSULTANTS INC
6000 Cornell Rd (45242-2016)
PHONE.....................513 530-9984
Fax: 513 530-9965
Mark Hoskins, *President*
John Wilcox, *Consultant*
EMP: 28
SQ FT: 6,000
SALES (est): 2.5MM **Privately Held**
WEB: www.dennmark.com
SIC: 8711 Electrical or electronic engineering; mechanical engineering

(G-1577)
DESIGN CENTER
Also Called: Architechs Plus
10816 Millington Ct # 100 (45242-4025)
PHONE.....................513 618-3133
Rick Koehler, *Partner*
Nora Wiley, *Vice Pres*
EMP: 30
SALES (est): 3.8MM **Privately Held**
SIC: 8712 Architectural services

(G-1578)
DHL SUPPLY CHAIN (USA)
4550 Creek Rd (45242-2804)
PHONE.....................513 745-7445
Dave Pendeton, *Branch Mgr*
EMP: 25
SALES (corp-wide): 71.2B **Privately Held**
WEB: www.exel-logistics.com
SIC: 4225 General warehousing
HQ: Exel Inc.
    570 Polaris Pkwy
    Westerville OH 43082
    614 865-8500

(G-1579)
DUGAN & MEYERS CONSTRUCTION CO (HQ)
11110 Kenwood Rd (45242-1818)
PHONE.....................513 891-4300
Francis Dugan, *CEO*
Jerome E Meyers Jr, *President*
Keith Hall, *Superintendent*
Tim Dugan, *Vice Pres*
Jeffrey Kelly, *Treasurer*
EMP: 150
SQ FT: 20,000
SALES (est): 59.1MM
SALES (corp-wide): 103.1MM **Privately Held**
WEB: www.dugan-meyers.com
SIC: 1541 1542 1522 Industrial buildings, new construction; commercial & office building, new construction; institutional building construction; condominium construction
PA: Dugan & Meyers Interests, Inc.
    11110 Kenwood Rd
    Blue Ash OH 45242
    513 891-4300

(G-1580)
DUGAN & MEYERS INTERESTS INC (PA)
11110 Kenwood Rd (45242-1818)
PHONE.....................513 891-4300
Fax: 513 891-0704
Jerome E Meyers Jr, *CEO*
Jeffrey Kelly, *CFO*
Steve Desalvo, *Manager*
Traci Thomas, *Exec Sec*
EMP: 25
SQ FT: 15,100
SALES (est): 103.1MM **Privately Held**
SIC: 1541 1542 1522 Industrial buildings, new construction; commercial & office building, new construction; condominium construction

(G-1581)
DUGAN & MEYERS LLC
11110 Kenwood Rd (45242-1818)
PHONE.....................513 891-4300
Jeff Kelly, *CFO*
Cherryl Sammons, *Accountant*
EMP: 250
SALES: 100MM **Privately Held**
SIC: 1542 Commercial & office building contractors

(G-1582)
EASTER SEALS TRISTATE (HQ)
4300 Rossplain Dr (45236-1208)
PHONE.....................513 985-0515
Fax: 513 793-5211
Pamela Green, *President*
Peter Bloch, *President*
Mary Miller, *Trustee*
Rich Davis, *Vice Pres*
Clark Earick, *Vice Pres*
EMP: 115
SQ FT: 30,000
SALES: 9.5MM
SALES (corp-wide): 17.2MM **Privately Held**
SIC: 8331 8322 Vocational rehabilitation agency; individual & family services
PA: Easter Seals Tristate Llc
    2901 Gilbert Ave
    Cincinnati OH 45206
    513 281-2316

(G-1583)
ELIASSEN GROUP LLC
10101 Alliance Rd Ste 195 (45242-4715)
PHONE.....................781 205-8100
Donna Yuenger, *Accounts Exec*
EMP: 49
SALES (corp-wide): 124.2MM **Privately Held**
SIC: 7371 7374 Custom computer programming services; data processing & preparation
PA: Eliassen Group, Llc
    55 Walkers Brook Dr # 600
    Reading MA 01867
    781 246-1600

(G-1584)
EMC CORPORATION
9825 Kenwood Rd Ste 300 (45242-6252)
PHONE.....................513 794-9624
Fax: 513 745-0324
Mike Lagermann, *Accounts Exec*
Stephen Swanson, *Sales Staff*
Debbie B Phipps, *Marketing Mgr*
Jack Garrahan, *Branch Mgr*
Steve Becker, *Manager*
EMP: 55
SALES (corp-wide): 78.6B **Publicly Held**
WEB: www.emc.com
SIC: 3572 7372 Computer storage devices; prepackaged software

HQ: Emc Corporation
176 South St
Hopkinton MA 01748
508 435-1000

(G-1585)
EMPLOYERS MUTUAL CASUALTY CO
Also Called: EMC Insurance Companies
11311 Cornell Park Dr # 500 (45242-1889)
PHONE..................513 221-6010
Phil Goedde, *Manager*
Sean Pelletier, *Officer*
EMP: 77
SALES (corp-wide): 1.1B Publicly Held
SIC: 6411 6321 6311 6519 Insurance agents; reinsurance carriers, accident & health; life insurance carriers; real property lessors
PA: Employers Mutual Casualty Company
717 Mulberry St
Des Moines IA 50309
515 280-2511

(G-1586)
ENERVISE INCORPORATED (PA)
Also Called: Engineering Excellence
4360 Glendale Milford Rd (45242-3706)
PHONE..................513 761-6000
Fax: 513 761-7741
Daniel J Temming, *CEO*
Andrew Beto, *General Mgr*
Ann Moran, *Senior VP*
Tina Wheelwright, *VP Opers*
Mary Ann Cianciolo, *Controller*
EMP: 104
SQ FT: 22,000
SALES (est): 40.9MM Privately Held
WEB: www.engineeringexcellence.com
SIC: 1711 Mechanical contractor

(G-1587)
ENGINEERING EXCELLENCE
Blue Ash Business Park (45242)
PHONE..................972 535-3756
Andy Beto, *General Mgr*
Holly Baas, *Manager*
Scott Boxer,
EMP: 85 EST: 2008
SALES: 2.5MM Privately Held
SIC: 1711 Heating & air conditioning contractors

(G-1588)
ENTERPRISE DATA MANAGEMENT INC (DH)
Also Called: Datalliance
4380 Malsbary Rd Ste 250 (45242-5648)
PHONE..................513 791-7272
Fax: 513 794-4461
Carl Hall, *President*
Doug Bethea, *Vice Pres*
Collins Don, *Vice Pres*
Jennifer Warner, *Vice Pres*
Jeff Weaver, *Vice Pres*
EMP: 32
SALES (est): 8.6MM Privately Held
WEB: www.edm1.com
SIC: 7379 8742 7378 7374 Computer related consulting services; management consulting services; computer maintenance & repair; data processing & preparation
HQ: True Commerce, Inc.
800 Cranberry Woods Dr
Cranberry Township PA 16066
724 940-5520

(G-1589)
ENVIRNMENTAL RESOURCES MGT INC
9825 Kenwood Rd Ste 100 (45242-6252)
PHONE..................513 830-9030
Fax: 513 830-9031
Jodi Keller, *Branch Mgr*
EMP: 31
SALES (corp-wide): 215.5K Privately Held
SIC: 8748 Environmental consultant
HQ: Environmental Resources Management, Inc.
75 Valley Stream Pkwy
Malvern PA 19355
484 913-0300

(G-1590)
EQUIPMENT DEPOT OHIO INC (DH)
4331 Rossplain Dr (45236-1207)
PHONE..................513 891-0600
Fax: 513 794-2728
Edward Neyer, *President*
John Ventre, *Vice Pres*
Joe Spriggs, *Materials Mgr*
Dale Hockenberry, *Parts Mgr*
Mike Melloy, *Parts Mgr*
▲ EMP: 25
SQ FT: 106,000
SALES (est): 90.2MM
SALES (corp-wide): 7.3B Privately Held
WEB: www.portmanpeople.com
SIC: 5084 Materials handling machinery
HQ: Pon North America, Inc.
840 Gessner Rd Ste 950
Houston TX 77024
713 365-2547

(G-1591)
F+W MEDIA INC (HQ)
Also Called: Novel Writing Workshop
10151 Carver Rd Ste 200 (45242-4760)
P.O. Box 78000, Detroit MI (48278-0001)
PHONE..................513 531-2690
David Nussbaum, *Ch of Bd*
Sara Domville, *President*
Allison Dolan, *Publisher*
Gary Lynch, *Publisher*
Jamie Markle, *Publisher*
▲ EMP: 265 EST: 2005
SQ FT: 250,000
SALES (est): 242MM Privately Held
WEB: www.decorativeartist.com
SIC: 2721 2731 4813 Magazines: publishing only, not printed on site; trade journals: publishing only, not printed on site; books: publishing only; book clubs: publishing only, not printed on site;
PA: New Publishing Holdings, Llc
10151 Carver Rd Ste 200
Blue Ash OH 45242
513 531-2690

(G-1592)
FEG CONSULTING LLC
3587 Tiffany Ridge Ln (45241-3810)
PHONE..................412 224-2263
Adam Stalczynski, *Principal*
Christa Lachenmayr, *Business Mgr*
Tanya Boudreau,
EMP: 25
SALES (est): 2MM Privately Held
WEB: www.feg-consulting.com
SIC: 8748 Agricultural consultant

(G-1593)
FEINTOOL EQUIPMENT CORPORATION
6833 Creek Rd (45242-4121)
PHONE..................513 791-1118
Fax: 513 791-1589
Lars Reich, *General Mgr*
Mark Rowlett, *Facilities Mgr*
Allison Smith, *Production*
Beat Andres, *Sls & Mktg Exec*
Lynn Petreman, *Human Res Mgr*
▲ EMP: 35
SQ FT: 29,000
SALES (est): 8.1MM
SALES (corp-wide): 2.9B Privately Held
SIC: 5084 Industrial machinery & equipment
HQ: Feintool U.S. Operations, Inc.
11280 Cornell Park Dr
Blue Ash OH 45242
513 247-4061

(G-1594)
FIRST DATA GVRNMENT SLTIONS LP
11311 Cornell Park Dr (45242-1889)
PHONE..................513 489-9599
Fax: 513 530-8155
Jeffrey D Myers, *Partner*
Chris Stevens, *Manager*
Yan Xian, *Technology*
EMP: 93
SALES (est): 15.6MM Privately Held
SIC: 6099 8742 Electronic funds transfer network, including switching; business planning & organizing services

(G-1595)
FIRST DATA GVRNMNT SOLUTNS INC (HQ)
11311 Cornell Park Dr (45242-1889)
PHONE..................513 489-9599
Michael D Capellas, *CEO*
Grant McKay, *Business Anlyst*
Srilatha Lingam, *Software Engr*
EMP: 125
SALES (est): 8.7MM
SALES (corp-wide): 12B Publicly Held
WEB: www.fdgs.com
SIC: 7371 Custom computer programming services
PA: First Data Corporation
225 Liberty St Fl 29
New York NY 10281
800 735-3362

(G-1596)
FISHBECK THMPSON CARR HBER INC
11353 Reed Hartman Hwy # 500 (45241-2443)
PHONE..................513 469-2370
Fax: 513 469-2372
Peter Soltys, *Manager*
EMP: 27
SALES (corp-wide): 78.1MM Privately Held
SIC: 8711 Consulting engineer
PA: Fishbeck, Thompson, Carr & Huber, Inc.
1515 Arboretum Dr Se
Grand Rapids MI 49546
616 575-3824

(G-1597)
FUSION ALLIANCE LLC
4555 Lake Forest Dr # 325 (45242-3785)
PHONE..................513 563-8444
Fax: 513 563-2270
Julie Kimmel, *Principal*
Jason Lee, *Consultant*
Rob Pfister, *Consultant*
EMP: 27
SALES (corp-wide): 59.5MM Privately Held
SIC: 8742 Management information systems consultant
HQ: Fusion Alliance, Llc
301 Pennsylvania Pkwy 2
Carmel IN 46032
317 955-1300

(G-1598)
G & G INVESTMENT LLC
4901 Hunt Rd Ste 300 (45242-6990)
PHONE..................513 984-0300
Stephen Guttman, *President*
EMP: 65
SALES (est): 5.3MM Privately Held
SIC: 6162 Mortgage companies, urban

(G-1599)
GENERAL ELECTRIC COMPANY
11240 Cornell Park Dr # 114 (45242-1800)
PHONE..................513 530-7107
Fax: 513 755-6983
Gary Ernst, *Branch Mgr*
EMP: 30
SALES (corp-wide): 122B Publicly Held
SIC: 5084 Industrial machinery & equipment
PA: General Electric Company
41 Farnsworth St
Boston MA 02210
617 443-3000

(G-1600)
GFK CUSTOM RESEARCH LLC
11240 Cornell Park Dr (45242-1800)
PHONE..................513 562-1507
EMP: 112
SALES (corp-wide): 1.5B Privately Held
SIC: 8732 Commercial Nonphysical Research
HQ: Gfk Custom Research, Llc
200 Liberty St Fl 4
New York NY 10281
212 240-5300

(G-1601)
GINGERBREAD INC
Also Called: Gingerbread Academy
4215 Malsbary Rd (45242-5509)
PHONE..................513 793-4122
Fax: 513 793-0085
Louise Yakubisin, *President*
EMP: 35
SALES (est): 910.3K Privately Held
WEB: www.gingerbread.net
SIC: 8351 Group day care center

(G-1602)
GIRL SCOUTS OF WESTERN OHIO (PA)
4930 Cornell Rd (45242-1804)
PHONE..................513 489-1025
Fax: 513 489-1417
Barbara J Bonifas, *CEO*
EMP: 47 EST: 1963
SQ FT: 6,000
SALES: 12.4MM Privately Held
WEB: www.grgsc.org
SIC: 8641 Girl Scout organization

(G-1603)
GLOBALTRANZ ENTERPRISES INC
10945 Reed Hartman Hwy (45242-2828)
PHONE..................513 745-0138
EMP: 103
SALES (corp-wide): 484MM Privately Held
SIC: 4731 Freight Transportation Arrangement
PA: Globaltranz Enterprises, Inc.
7350 N Dobson Rd Ste 135
Scottsdale AZ 85256
480 339-5600

(G-1604)
GOETTSCH INT INC (PA)
9852 Redhill Dr (45242-5627)
PHONE..................513 563-6500
Edith Goettsch, *Ch of Bd*
Eric Goettsch, *President*
Mike Goettsch, *Vice Pres*
Rick D Rogers, *Controller*
Sandy Goettsch, *Financial Exec*
◆ EMP: 25
SQ FT: 11,500
SALES (est): 11.3MM Privately Held
WEB: www.goettsch.com
SIC: 5084 Paper manufacturing machinery

(G-1605)
GROUNDSYSTEMS INC (PA)
11315 Williamson Rd (45241-2232)
PHONE..................800 570-0213
Rachel Rorie, *President*
Michael Rorie, *Vice Pres*
Mike Graves, *Accounts Mgr*
EMP: 35 EST: 2013
SALES (est): 22.3MM Privately Held
SIC: 0782 Landscape contractors

(G-1606)
HAL HOMES INC (PA)
9545 Kenwood Rd Ste 401 (45242-6100)
PHONE..................513 984-5360
Harold Silverman, *President*
Tori Hyatt, *Accountant*
EMP: 25
SQ FT: 30,000
SALES (est): 5.7MM Privately Held
WEB: www.halhomes.com
SIC: 1542 Commercial & office building, new construction

(G-1607)
HARRIS & BURGIN
9545 Kenwood Rd Ste 301 (45242-6100)
PHONE..................513 891-3270
Fax: 513 891-3266
Jerald D Harris, *Partner*
Lester J Burgin, *Partner*
EMP: 30
SALES (est): 1.8MM Privately Held
WEB: www.harris-burgin.com
SIC: 8111 General practice attorney, lawyer

Blue Ash - Hamilton County (G-1608) GEOGRAPHIC SECTION

(G-1608)
HEALTH CARE FACILITY MGT LLC (HQ)
Also Called: Communicare Family of Company
4700 Ashwood Dr Ste 200 (45241-2424)
PHONE...................513 489-7100
Stephen L Rosedale, *CEO*
Connie Forgraze, *Manager*
Stacy Henry, *Manager*
Kathy Havel, *Info Tech Mgr*
EMP: 65
SALES (est): 13.3MM
SALES (corp-wide): 103.9MM **Privately Held**
SIC: 8082 Home health care services
PA: Communicare Health Services, Inc.
4700 Ashwood Dr Ste 200
Blue Ash OH 45241
513 530-1654

(G-1609)
HEALTHCARE HOLDINGS INC
4700 Ashwood Dr Ste 200 (45241-2424)
PHONE...................513 530-1600
Steve Rosedale, *President*
EMP: 60
SALES (est): 1.5MM **Privately Held**
SIC: 8082 Home health care services

(G-1610)
HENNINGSON DRHAM RICHARDSON PC
9987 Carver Rd Ste 200 (45242-5552)
PHONE...................513 984-7500
Brad Hyre, *Vice Pres*
Melissa Kiscoan, *Manager*
EMP: 66
SALES (est): 2.3MM **Privately Held**
SIC: 8711 Designing: ship, boat, machine & product

(G-1611)
HILLS COMMUNITIES INC
4901 Hunt Rd Ste 300 (45242-6990)
PHONE...................513 984-0300
Fax: 513 618-7681
Stephen Guttman, *President*
Harold Guttman, *Vice Pres*
Jerry Stanislaw, *CFO*
Louis Guttman, *Treasurer*
Laurie Kamphaus, *Controller*
EMP: 120
SQ FT: 5,000
SALES (est): 15.8MM **Privately Held**
WEB: www.hillscommunities.com
SIC: 1522 Condominium construction

(G-1612)
HILLS DEVELOPERS INC
4901 Hunt Rd Ste 300 (45242-6990)
PHONE...................513 984-0300
Murray Guttman, *Ch of Bd*
Stephen Guttman, *President*
Christa Heiser, *District Mgr*
Louis Guttman, *Corp Secy*
Harold Guttman, *Vice Pres*
EMP: 175
SQ FT: 16,000
SALES: 50MM **Privately Held**
WEB: www.hillsinc.com
SIC: 8741 Construction management

(G-1613)
HILLS PROPERTY MANAGEMENT INC (PA)
Also Called: Hills Real Estate Group
4901 Hunt Rd Ste 300 (45242-6990)
PHONE...................513 984-0300
Steve Guttman, *President*
Louis Guttman, *Vice Pres*
Kevin Junker, *Vice Pres*
Rusty Lykes, *Vice Pres*
James Dooley, *Accountant*
EMP: 70
SQ FT: 2,000
SALES (est): 11.4MM **Privately Held**
SIC: 6513 6512 Apartment building operators; nonresidential building operators

(G-1614)
ILLINOIS TOOL WORKS INC
Paxton Products
10125 Carver Rd (45242-4719)
PHONE...................513 891-7474
Tony King, *Principal*
Margaret W Comey, *Principal*
Barbara Stefel, *Business Mgr*
Tom Long, *Controller*
Karyn Ranz, *Human Resources*
EMP: 28
SALES (corp-wide): 14.3B **Publicly Held**
SIC: 8741 Management services
PA: Illinois Tool Works Inc.
155 Harlem Ave
Glenview IL 60025
847 724-7500

(G-1615)
INNOVTIVE CLLECTN CONCEPTS INC
Also Called: National Child Support Center
11353 Reed Hartman Hwy # 100 (45241-2443)
P.O. Box 42437, Cincinnati (45242-0437)
PHONE...................513 489-5500
Fax: 513 605-3090
Michael T Higgins, *CEO*
James Durham, *President*
EMP: 25
SQ FT: 5,500
SALES (est): 2.7MM **Privately Held**
WEB: www.nationalchildsupport.com
SIC: 7322 Adjustment & collection services

(G-1616)
INTERACT ONE INC
4665 Cornell Rd Ste 255 (45241-2455)
PHONE...................513 469-7042
Fax: 513 469-8799
Maryellen Dwyer, *Ch of Bd*
Brian Dwyer, *President*
Zach Stutzman, *Vice Pres*
Joe Williams, *Vice Pres*
Barb Scales, *Project Mgr*
EMP: 32
SALES (est): 2.5MM **Privately Held**
WEB: www.interactone.com
SIC: 7374 Computer graphics service

(G-1617)
IRON MOUNTAIN INFO MGT LLC
11350 Deerfield Rd (45242-2105)
PHONE...................513 247-2183
Jay Geisler, *General Mgr*
EMP: 30
SALES (corp-wide): 3.8B **Publicly Held**
SIC: 4226 Document & office records storage
HQ: Iron Mountain Information Management, Llc
1 Federal St
Boston MA 02110
800 899-4766

(G-1618)
ITCUBE LLC
10999 Reed Hartman Hwy # 136 (45242-8331)
PHONE...................513 891-7300
Fax: 513 891-7307
Surajit Mitra, *Project Mgr*
Hiten Patel,
EMP: 99
SALES (est): 4.6MM **Privately Held**
WEB: www.itcube.net
SIC: 7371 Computer software systems analysis & design, custom

(G-1619)
J PETERMAN COMPANY LLC
Also Called: J. Peterman
5345 Creek Rd (45242-3935)
PHONE...................888 647-2555
Mark Richardson, *Controller*
John Peterman,
Tim Peterman,
▲ **EMP**: 35
SQ FT: 15,000
SALES (est): 7.3MM **Privately Held**
SIC: 5136 5611 5621 5137 Apparel belts, men's & boys'; men's & boys' clothing stores; women's clothing stores; women's & children's clothing

(G-1620)
JOHNSON MIRMIRAN THOMPSON INC
4600 Mcauley Pl Ste 150 (45242-4765)
PHONE...................614 714-0270
Andrew Barr, *Manager*
EMP: 86
SALES (corp-wide): 224.9MM **Privately Held**
SIC: 8711 Civil engineering
PA: Johnson, Mirmiran & Thompson, Inc.
40 Wight Ave
Hunt Valley MD 21030
410 329-3100

(G-1621)
JPMORGAN CHASE BANK NAT ASSN
9019 Plainfield Rd (45236-1201)
PHONE...................513 826-2317
EMP: 26
SALES (corp-wide): 99.6B **Publicly Held**
SIC: 6021 National commercial banks
HQ: Jpmorgan Chase Bank, National Association
1111 Polaris Pkwy
Columbus OH 43240
614 436-3055

(G-1622)
KINDER GARDEN SCHOOL
10969 Reed Hartman Hwy (45242-2821)
PHONE...................513 791-4300
Fax: 513 792-0006
Tami Lanham, *Owner*
EMP: 45
SALES: 800K **Privately Held**
WEB: www.kindergardenschool.com
SIC: 8351 Preschool center

(G-1623)
L J F MANAGEMENT INC
Also Called: Oxford Square
4719 Alma Ave Ofc 200 (45242-6172)
P.O. Box 54844, Cincinnati (45254-0844)
PHONE...................513 688-0104
Fax: 513 792-9997
Aristide Belfiore, *President*
Linda Fox, *Corp Secy*
EMP: 25
SALES (est): 1.3MM **Privately Held**
SIC: 6531 Real estate managers

(G-1624)
LAN SOLUTIONS INC
Also Called: Intrust It
9850 Redhill Dr (45242-5627)
PHONE...................513 469-6500
Fax: 513 469-5385
Timothy J Rettig, *President*
Jeff Andrews, *President*
Marc Reiter, *Opers Mgr*
Charlene Fennimore, *Accounting Mgr*
EMP: 30
SQ FT: 4,300
SALES (est): 4.9MM **Privately Held**
SIC: 7379

(G-1625)
LANDRUM & BROWN INCORPORATED (PA)
11279 Cornell Park Dr (45242-1811)
PHONE...................513 530-5333
Fax: 513 530-5333
Jeff Thomas, *CEO*
Mark Perryman, *President*
Rob Adams, *Exec VP*
Dennis E Peters, *CFO*
Jason Cox, *Med Doctor*
EMP: 60 **EST**: 1949
SQ FT: 16,500
SALES (est): 20.6MM **Privately Held**
SIC: 8742 8748 Management consulting services; transportation consultant; business consulting

(G-1626)
LANG FINANCIAL GROUP INC
4225 Malsbary Rd Ste 100 (45242-5561)
PHONE...................513 699-2966
Stanford L Lang, *Ch of Bd*
Steven J McAbee, *COO*
EMP: 26
SQ FT: 8,700
SALES (est): 5.6MM **Privately Held**
WEB: www.langgroup.com
SIC: 6411 8742 6282 Insurance agents; financial consultant; investment advice

(G-1627)
LEADEC CORP (DH)
9395 Kenwood Rd Ste 200 (45242-6819)
PHONE...................513 731-3590
Fax: 513 731-3659
William Bell, *CEO*
Rob Wright, *Regional Mgr*
Donald G Morsch, *Treasurer*
Betsy Wallis, *Controller*
Kim Saylor, *Human Resources*
EMP: 34
SQ FT: 18,000
SALES (corp-wide): 265.7MM **Privately Held**
WEB: www.premiermss.com
SIC: 7349 8741 3714 Building cleaning service; management services; motor vehicle parts & accessories
HQ: Leadec Holding Bv & Co. Kg
Meitnerstr. 11
Stuttgart 70563
711 784-10

(G-1628)
LIBERTY MUTUAL INSURANCE CO
4747 Lake Forest Dr # 150 (45242-3861)
PHONE...................513 984-0550
Fax: 513 984-3109
Ross Hern, *Auditor*
Morgan Terrill, *Sales Staff*
Denise Carroll, *Underwriter*
Deborah Chikar, *Underwriter*
David Elliott, *Underwriter*
EMP: 70
SALES (corp-wide): 38.3B **Privately Held**
WEB: www.libertymutual.com
SIC: 6331 Fire, marine & casualty insurance
HQ: Liberty Mutual Insurance Company
175 Berkeley St
Boston MA 02116
617 357-9500

(G-1629)
LITERATURE FULFILLMENT SVCS
11400 Grooms Rd Ste 112 (45242-1435)
PHONE...................513 774-8600
Rank Grande, *President*
Francesco Grande, *President*
Perry Frey, *Vice Pres*
EMP: 25
SALES (est): 3.1MM **Privately Held**
WEB: www.lfsmail.com
SIC: 7331 Mailing service

(G-1630)
LODGE STONE WOOD
11350 Swing Rd (45241-2227)
PHONE...................513 769-4325
Fax: 513 769-0843
Sandy Johnson, *Director*
EMP: 39
SALES (est): 215.2K **Privately Held**
SIC: 7996 Theme park, amusement

(G-1631)
LSI INDUSTRIES INC
LSI Midwest Lighting
10000 Alliance Rd (45242-4706)
PHONE...................913 281-1100
Steve Dennis, *Opers Mgr*
Terry Winton, *Purch Agent*
Dennis Oberling, *Manager*
Mike Brewer, *CIO*
EMP: 200
SALES (corp-wide): 331.3MM **Publicly Held**
WEB: www.lsi-industries.com
SIC: 3646 5063 Commercial indusl & institutional electric lighting fixtures; lighting fixtures
PA: Lsi Industries Inc.
10000 Alliance Rd
Blue Ash OH 45242
513 793-3200

(G-1632)
LUMINEX HOME DECOR (PA)
Also Called: Luminex HD&f Company
10521 Millington Ct (45242-4022)
PHONE...................513 563-1113
Calvin Johnston, *CEO*
Dawn Enright, *Manager*
EMP: 709

GEOGRAPHIC SECTION
Blue Ash - Hamilton County (G-1658)

SALES (est): 259.4MM **Privately Held**
SIC: **5023** 2844 Decorative home furnishings & supplies; toilet preparations

(G-1633)
MAPP BUILDING SERVICE LLC
11367 Deerfield Rd 200 (45242-2121)
PHONE.................513 253-3990
Fax: 513 679-5743
Curtis Mapp,
Joette Mapp,
EMP: 30
SQ FT: 4,400
SALES (est): 740K **Privately Held**
SIC: **7349** 5087 Janitorial service, contract basis; cleaning & maintenance equipment & supplies

(G-1634)
MARKET INQUIRY LLC
5825 Creek Rd (45242-4009)
PHONE.................513 794-1088
Cathy Noyes, *Owner*
John Ganster, *Controller*
David Cohavi, *Marketing Staff*
Lee Anne Adams, *Director*
Cindy McGownd, *Director*
EMP: 30
SALES (est): 2.5MM **Privately Held**
WEB: www.marketinquiry.com
SIC: **8732** Market analysis or research

(G-1635)
MARKETVISION RESEARCH INC (PA)
5151 Pfeiffer Rd Ste 300 (45242-4854)
PHONE.................513 791-3100
Jon Pinnell, *President*
Donald Mc Mullen, *Chairman*
Chad Davis, *Vice Pres*
Brian Dundon, *Vice Pres*
Michelle Jefferys, *Vice Pres*
EMP: 70
SQ FT: 20,500
SALES (est): 15.2MM **Privately Held**
WEB: www.copyvision.com
SIC: **8732** Market analysis or research

(G-1636)
MARRIOTT INTERNATIONAL INC
Also Called: Residence Inn By Marriott
11401 Reed Hartman Hwy (45241-2418)
PHONE.................513 530-5060
Fax: 513 530-0133
Tina Honican, *VP Finance*
John Secola, *Branch Mgr*
EMP: 167
SALES (corp-wide): 22.8B **Publicly Held**
SIC: **7011** Hotels & motels
PA: Marriott International, Inc.
10400 Fernwood Rd
Bethesda MD 20817
301 380-3000

(G-1637)
MD BUSINESS SOLUTIONS INC
9825 Kenwood Rd Ste 108 (45242-6252)
P.O. Box 630110, Cincinnati (45263-0110)
PHONE.................513 872-4500
Fax: 513 527-0400
Mark S Grossman, *President*
Tom Merchant, *Controller*
Annette Shepherd, *Mktg Dir*
Eric Anderson, *Info Tech Dir*
Joseph E Bernstein MD, *Director*
EMP: 40
SQ FT: 10,000
SALES (est): 3.3MM **Privately Held**
WEB: www.mdbiz.com
SIC: **8721** 8741 Billing & bookkeeping service; management services

(G-1638)
MEDICAL SOLUTIONS LLC
9987 Carver Rd Ste 510 (45242-5563)
PHONE.................513 936-3468
Kelly Anderson, *Branch Mgr*
EMP: 60 **Privately Held**
SIC: **7361** Nurses' registry
PA: Medical Solutions, L.L.C.
1010 N 102nd St Ste 300
Omaha NE 68114

(G-1639)
MERCHANDISING SERVICES CO
10999 Reed Hartman Hwy (45242-8331)
PHONE.................866 479-8246
Mike Buschelmann, *President*
EMP: 62
SALES (corp-wide): 5.2MM **Privately Held**
SIC: **8742** Merchandising consultant
PA: Merchandising Services, Co.
9891 Montgomery Rd # 320
Cincinnati OH 45242
866 479-8246

(G-1640)
MERCY HEALTH
9403 Kenwood Rd Ste D203 (45242-6878)
PHONE.................513 686-8100
EMP: 42
SALES (corp-wide): 4.2B **Privately Held**
SIC: **8011** Offices & clinics of medical doctors
PA: Mercy Health
1701 Mercy Health Pl
Cincinnati OH 45237
513 639-2800

(G-1641)
MERCY HEALTH PARTNERS
4600 Mcauley Pl Ste A (45242-4765)
PHONE.................513 981-5056
EMP: 58
SALES (corp-wide): 4.5B **Privately Held**
SIC: **8062** General Hospital
HQ: Mercy Health Partners
4600 Mcauley Pl Ste A
Blue Ash OH 45237
513 981-6000

(G-1642)
MERRILL LYNCH BUSINESS
5151 Pfeiffer Rd Ste 100 (45242-8400)
PHONE.................513 791-5700
Fax: 513 791-5685
EMP: 44
SQ FT: 9,000
SALES (corp-wide): 95.1B **Publicly Held**
SIC: **6021** Business Credit Institution
HQ: Merrill Lynch Business Financial Services Inc.
540 W Madison St Fl 1
Chicago IL 60661
312 325-2625

(G-1643)
META MANUFACTURING CORPORATION
8901 Blue Ash Rd Ste 1 (45242-7809)
PHONE.................513 793-6382
Fax: 513 793-6390
David Mc Swain, *President*
Bruce Fille, *QC Mgr*
Pete Van Curen, *Sales Mgr*
Jeff Theis, *Manager*
Mike Fennen, *Director*
EMP: 50
SQ FT: 54,000
SALES (est): 9.2MM **Privately Held**
WEB: www.metamfg.com
SIC: **3599** 7692 Machine shop, jobbing & repair; welding repair

(G-1644)
MODERN OFFICE METHODS INC (PA)
Also Called: M.O.M.
4747 Lake Forest Dr # 200 (45242-3853)
PHONE.................513 791-0909
Robert J McCarthy, *Ch of Bd*
Kevin P McCarthy, *President*
Steven Bandy, *Vice Pres*
Silas P Rose, *Vice Pres*
Ken Staubitz, *Vice Pres*
EMP: 85 EST: 1957
SQ FT: 10,000
SALES (est): 28.8MM **Privately Held**
WEB: www.momnet.com
SIC: **7359** 7629 5044 Office machine rental, except computers; business machine repair, electric; office equipment

(G-1645)
MOLLOY ROOFING COMPANY
11099 Deerfield Rd (45242-4111)
PHONE.................513 791-7400
Fax: 513 791-7418
Donald A Molloy, *President*
Joyce Molloy, *Corp Secy*
EMP: 45
SQ FT: 10,000
SALES (est): 6.6MM **Privately Held**
SIC: **1761** Roofing contractor

(G-1646)
MORPHICK INC
4555 Lake Forest Dr # 150 (45242-3781)
PHONE.................844 506-6774
Brian Minick, *Principal*
Brian Gittinger, *Sales Engr*
Kody McLaughlin, *Manager*
Tushar Shah, *Sr Software Eng*
EMP: 32
SALES (est): 2.2MM **Privately Held**
SIC: **7371** Computer software development

(G-1647)
MPF SALES AND MKTG GROUP LLC
11243 Cornell Park Dr (45242-1811)
PHONE.................513 793-6241
Mike Marek, *Mng Member*
Jamie Jackson, *Admin Asst*
EMP: 200 EST: 2010
SALES (est): 140.2K **Privately Held**
SIC: **5141** Food brokers

(G-1648)
MTM TECHNOLOGIES (TEXAS) INC
10653 Techwood Cir # 100 (45242-2833)
PHONE.................513 786-6600
Jeff Grahm, *General Mgr*
EMP: 27 **Privately Held**
SIC: **5045** Computers, peripherals & software
HQ: Mtm Technologies (Texas) Inc
12600 Northborough Dr # 200
Houston TX 77067
203 975-3700

(G-1649)
MURRAY GUTTMAN
Also Called: M G Management
4901 Hunt Rd Ste 300 (45242-6990)
PHONE.................513 984-0300
Murray Guttman, *Chairman*
EMP: 70
SQ FT: 2,000
SALES (est): 3MM **Privately Held**
SIC: **6513** Apartment building operators

(G-1650)
MYCA MLTMDIA TRNNG SLTONS LLC
4555 Lake Forest Dr # 650 (45242-3785)
PHONE.................513 544-2379
Laura Davies, *Project Mgr*
Joan Hickey, *Prdtn Mgr*
Patricia Massey, *Mng Member*
Bobby Childers, *Director*
Carol Kirschbaum, *Director*
EMP: 35
SALES: 700K **Privately Held**
SIC: **7379**

(G-1651)
N SERVICES INC
Also Called: A Miracle Home Care
10901 Reed Hartman Hwy (45242-2831)
PHONE.................513 793-2000
Fax: 513 712-3514
Natalya Chernova, *President*
EMP: 55
SALES: 140K **Privately Held**
SIC: **7349** Building maintenance services

(G-1652)
NIELSEN CONSUMER INSIGHTS INC
Also Called: Answer Group, The
4665 Cornell Rd Ste 160 (45241-2455)
PHONE.................513 489-9000
Fax: 513 489-9130
Jack Korte, *Vice Pres*
EMP: 100
SALES (corp-wide): 6.5B **Privately Held**
WEB: www.harrisi.com
SIC: **8732** Market analysis or research
HQ: Nielsen Consumer Insights, Inc.
155 Corporate Woods
Rochester NY 14623
585 272-8400

(G-1653)
NIGHTNGL-ALAN MED EQP SVCS LLC
11418 Deerfield Rd Bldg 1 (45242-2116)
PHONE.................513 247-8200
Fax: 513 247-8207
Steve Steigelman, *CFO*
Paul Meyer, *Mng Member*
Tiffany Galloway, *Info Tech Mgr*
Richard Almasy,
EMP: 33
SQ FT: 4,000
SALES (est): 7.6MM **Privately Held**
WEB: www.namedinc.com
SIC: **5047** Medical equipment & supplies

(G-1654)
NORMANDY GROUP LLC
5151 Pfeiffer Rd Ste 210 (45242-4854)
PHONE.................513 745-0990
Peter Von Nessi, *Managing Dir*
Jane Burke, *Marketing Staff*
Charles C Burke, *Mng Member*
EMP: 25
SALES (est): 4.2MM **Privately Held**
WEB: www.thenormandygroup.com
SIC: **8742** Business consultant

(G-1655)
OHIO VALLEY ELEC SVCS LLC
4585 Cornell Rd (45241-2439)
PHONE.................513 771-2410
Fax: 513 771-2690
Steve Ortner, *President*
Brent Foster, *Project Mgr*
Ronald Kelly, *Project Mgr*
Darren Jones, *Foreman/Supr*
Roger Brockman, *Cust Mgr*
EMP: 85
SQ FT: 8,000
SALES: 17.3MM **Privately Held**
SIC: **1731** General electrical contractor

(G-1656)
OHS LLC
Also Called: Ohs Media Group
11427 Reed Hartman Hwy (45241-2418)
PHONE.................513 252-2249
Chris Schlueter,
EMP: 43
SALES: 950K **Privately Held**
SIC: **7319** Advertising

(G-1657)
OMYA INDUSTRIES INC (HQ)
9987 Carver Rd Ste 300 (45242-5563)
PHONE.................513 387-4600
Anthony Colak, *President*
John Suddarth, *Vice Pres*
John Yockey, *VP Opers*
Dean Borud, *Project Mgr*
Roland Meier, *Facilities Mgr*
◆ EMP: 85 EST: 1977
SQ FT: 21,700
SALES (est): 279.8MM
SALES (corp-wide): 3.9B **Privately Held**
SIC: **1422** Crushed & broken limestone
PA: Omya Ag
Baslerstrasse 42
Oftringen AG 4665
627 892-929

(G-1658)
ORACLE SYSTEMS CORPORATION
9987 Carver Rd Ste 250 (45242-5553)
PHONE.................513 826-6000
Fax: 614 280-6573
Dale Weideling, *Vice Pres*
Adam Scott, *Accounts Exec*
Carol Beebe, *Manager*
Steve Seger, *Senior Mgr*
EMP: 50
SALES (corp-wide): 37.7B **Publicly Held**
WEB: www.forcecapital.com
SIC: **7372** Prepackaged software

Blue Ash - Hamilton County (G-1659)

HQ: Oracle Systems Corporation
500 Oracle Pkwy
Redwood City CA 94065
650 506-7000

(G-1659)
ORTHOPAEDIC OFFICES INC
Also Called: Freiberg Spine Institute
9825 Kenwood Rd Ste 200 (45242-6252)
PHONE..................513 221-5500
Michael Swank, *Branch Mgr*
EMP: 29
SALES (corp-wide): 2.9MM **Privately Held**
WEB: www.freibergortho.com
SIC: 8011 Orthopedic physician
PA: Orthopaedic Offices, Inc
8250 Kenwood Crossing Way # 100
Cincinnati OH 45236
513 221-5500

(G-1660)
ORTHOPEDIC CONS CINCINNATI (PA)
Also Called: Wellington Orthpd Spt Medicine
4701 Creek Rd Ste 110 (45242-8330)
PHONE..................513 733-8894
Fax: 513 733-8588
Robert S Heidt MD Sr, *President*
Edward Miller, *Chairman*
Judy George, *Purchasing*
Joe Udepohl, *CFO*
Michael Welch, *Treasurer*
▲ **EMP:** 224
SQ FT: 14,000
SALES (est): 18MM **Privately Held**
SIC: 8011 Orthopedic physician

(G-1661)
OSCAR RBRTSN DOC MGMT SVCS
Also Called: Ordms
10999 Reed Hartman Hwy # 208 (45242-8331)
PHONE..................800 991-4611
Barbara Wofford, *Accountant*
Oscar Robertson, *Mng Member*
Tia Robertson,
EMP: 50
SALES: 950K **Privately Held**
SIC: 7334 7359 Photocopying & duplicating services; office machine rental, except computers

(G-1662)
PATRIOT ROOFING COMPANY INC (PA)
Also Called: Patriot Roofing & Restoration
11524 Grooms Rd Ste A (45242-1416)
PHONE..................513 469-7663
Cesar Sanchez, *CEO*
Jenny Sanchez, *President*
EMP: 30
SALES: 11.5MM **Privately Held**
SIC: 1522 1761 Hotel/motel & multi-family home renovation & remodeling; roof repair

(G-1663)
PCM SALES INC
Also Called: Educational Services
4600 Mcauley Pl Ste 200 (45242-4775)
PHONE..................513 842-3500
Fax: 513 842-3501
Brian Koehl, *General Mgr*
Julie Coalfleet, *Accounts Mgr*
John McGoff, *Accounts Exec*
Chris Stegman, *Sales Executive*
Tammy Burns, *VP Mktg*
EMP: 150
SALES (corp-wide): 2.1B **Publicly Held**
WEB: www.sarcom.com
SIC: 5045 Computers
HQ: Pcm Sales, Inc.
1940 E Mariposa Ave
El Segundo CA 90245
310 354-5600

(G-1664)
PREMIER HEALTH CARE MGT INC
4750 Ashwood Dr Ste 300 (45241-2453)
PHONE..................248 644-5522
Fax: 513 561-4029
Harold Sosna, *President*

Kris Rolfsen, *Director*
EMP: 30
SALES: 3.1MM **Privately Held**
SIC: 8051 Skilled nursing care facilities

(G-1665)
PRIORITY DISPATCH INC (PA)
4665 Malsbary Rd (45242-5645)
PHONE..................513 791-3900
Fax: 513 985-1090
R Jeffrey Thomas, *President*
David Castator, *General Mgr*
Scott Schmidt, *General Mgr*
Beth Dusha, *Treasurer*
Beth Duscha, *VP Finance*
EMP: 40 **EST:** 1972
SQ FT: 20,000
SALES (est): 16.1MM **Privately Held**
SIC: 4212 Delivery service, vehicular

(G-1666)
PROCAMPS INC
4600 Mcauley Pl Fl 4 (45242-4773)
PHONE..................513 745-5855
Gregg Darbyshire, *President*
Andy Danner, *Vice Pres*
Bill Zembrodt, *Controller*
EMP: 30
SQ FT: 2,000
SALES (est): 4.8MM **Privately Held**
SIC: 7032 Sporting & recreational camps

(G-1667)
PROCTER & GAMBLE DISTRG LLC
11510 Reed Hartman Hwy (45241-2422)
PHONE..................513 626-2500
Fax: 513 626-1203
Constantin Farah, *Research*
Felipe Stortini, *Engineer*
Sherry Schmidt, *Human Resources*
Tony Burns, *Branch Mgr*
Anthony Watkins, *Manager*
EMP: 273
SALES (corp-wide): 65B **Publicly Held**
SIC: 5169 5122 5149 5113 Detergents; laundry soap chips & powder; drugs, proprietaries & sundries; groceries & related products; coffee, green or roasted; napkins, paper; towels, paper; dishes, disposable plastic & paper; diapers
HQ: Procter & Gamble Distributing Llc
1 Procter And Gamble Plz
Cincinnati OH 45202
513 983-1100

(G-1668)
PROFESSIONAL DATA RESOURCES INC (PA)
4555 Lake Forest Dr # 220 (45242-3761)
PHONE..................513 792-5100
Fax: 513 792-5105
Phyllis Adams, *President*
EMP: 101
SQ FT: 5,000
SALES (est): 3.9MM **Privately Held**
WEB: www.pdrinc.com
SIC: 7379 7361 Data processing consultant; employment agencies

(G-1669)
QVIDIAN CORPORATION
10260 Alliance Rd Ste 210 (45242-4743)
PHONE..................513 631-1155
Fax: 513 791-4580
Lewis Miller, *President*
Stella Chistyakov, *Accountant*
Alexander Kozlovsky, *Technology*
EMP: 50
SQ FT: 5,500 **Publicly Held**
SIC: 7371 Computer software development
HQ: Qvidian Corporation
1 Executive Dr Ste 302
Chelmsford MA 01824

(G-1670)
R L B INC (PA)
Also Called: Blue Ash Educational Building
10149 Kenwood Rd (45242-5712)
PHONE..................513 793-3758
Fax: 513 891-7816
Robert L Bucciere, *President*
Tonya Briggs, *Vice Pres*
Paul Hartinger, *Director*
Russell L Bucciere, *Admin Sec*

EMP: 27
SQ FT: 2,000
SALES (est): 2.3MM **Privately Held**
SIC: 8351 Child day care services

(G-1671)
RA CONSULTANTS LLC
10856 Kenwood Rd (45242-2812)
PHONE..................513 469-6600
Fax: 513 469-2684
John P Allen, *President*
Marijo Flamm, *Admin Asst*
EMP: 30
SALES (est): 4.5MM **Privately Held**
WEB: www.raconsultsllc.com
SIC: 8711 3679 Civil engineering; commutators, electronic

(G-1672)
RACO INDUSTRIES LLC (HQ)
5481 Creek Rd (45242-4001)
PHONE..................513 984-2101
Don Mech, *President*
David Pepin, *Business Mgr*
Johnnie Johnson, *COO*
Rob Deubell, *Vice Pres*
Tina Shuemake, *Purch Mgr*
EMP: 85
SQ FT: 82,000
SALES (est): 23.5MM
SALES (corp-wide): 44.8MM **Privately Held**
SIC: 5045 5199 7389 Printers, computer; badges; packaging & labeling services
PA: Raco Industries, Inc.
5481 Creek Rd
Blue Ash OH 45242
513 984-2101

(G-1673)
RACO WIRELESS LLC (HQ)
4460 Carver Woods Dr # 100 (45242-5520)
PHONE..................513 870-6480
Brian Johnson, *Business Mgr*
Ariel Gonzalez, *VP Opers*
Bob Bruner, *Technical Mgr*
Allan Abram, *CFO*
Ray Brien, *Controller*
EMP: 51
SALES (est): 26.8MM
SALES (corp-wide): 5.7MM **Privately Held**
WEB: www.racoindustries.com
SIC: 4813 7371 ; computer software development & applications
PA: Kore Wireless Group, Inc.
3700 Mansell Rd Ste 300
Alpharetta GA 30022
416 621-1232

(G-1674)
RANDSTAD PROFESSIONALS US LLC
Also Called: Randstad Engineering
4555 Lake Forest Dr # 300 (45242-3785)
PHONE..................513 792-6658
Ed Anderson, *General Mgr*
EMP: 39
SALES (corp-wide): 27.4B **Privately Held**
SIC: 7363 Temporary help service
HQ: Randstad Professional Us, Lp
150 Presidential Way Fl 4
Woburn MA 01801

(G-1675)
RANDSTAD PROFESSIONALS US LP
Also Called: Mergis Group, The
5151 Pfeiffer Rd Ste 120 (45242-4854)
PHONE..................513 791-8600
EMP: 39
SALES (corp-wide): 21.7B **Privately Held**
SIC: 7363 Help Supply Services
HQ: Randstad Professionals Us, Lp
150 Presidential Way # 300
Woburn MA 01801
781 213-1500

(G-1676)
RAY HAMILTON COMPANIES
Also Called: Ray Hamilton Company
11083 Kenwood Rd (45242-1815)
PHONE..................513 641-5400
Jay Wallis, *President*
Lorna Vinsant, *Controller*

Linda Waltz, *Admin Asst*
Dean Gallo,
EMP: 43
SQ FT: 67,000
SALES (est): 374.7K **Privately Held**
WEB: www.rayhamilton.com
SIC: 4214 4226 4212 4731 Local trucking with storage; furniture moving & storage, local; document & office records storage; safe moving, local; freight transportation arrangement; domestic freight forwarding

(G-1677)
RAYMOND STORAGE CONCEPTS INC (PA)
5480 Creek Rd Unit 1 (45242-4029)
PHONE..................513 891-7290
Fax: 513 891-7299
Scott Wolcott, *President*
Tim Crowe, *Vice Pres*
Paul Beatty, *Opers Mgr*
Elliott Stephen, *Design Engr*
Nancy Delong, *Accounting Mgr*
▲ **EMP:** 50
SQ FT: 15,000
SALES: 50MM **Privately Held**
SIC: 5084 7699 Materials handling machinery; industrial equipment services

(G-1678)
REED HARTMAN CORPORATE CENTER
10925 Reed Hartman Hwy # 200 (45242-2836)
PHONE..................513 984-3030
Robert Blatt, *President*
David Wolfe, *Vice Pres*
Barbara Dizenhuz,
EMP: 50
SALES (est): 1.7MM **Privately Held**
SIC: 6512 Commercial & industrial building operation

(G-1679)
REHAB CONTINUUM INC
Also Called: Rehab Continuum, The
10921 Reed Hartman Hwy # 133 (45242-2830)
P.O. Box 428666, Cincinnati (45242-8666)
PHONE..................513 984-8070
David Turner, *President*
EMP: 30
SQ FT: 500
SALES (est): 927.3K **Privately Held**
SIC: 8049 8011 8063 Physical therapist; offices & clinics of medical doctors; hospital for the mentally ill

(G-1680)
REPUBLIC BANK
9683 Kenwood Rd (45242-6128)
PHONE..................513 793-7666
EMP: 460
SALES (corp-wide): 202.1MM **Privately Held**
SIC: 6029 Commercial Bank
PA: Republic Bank
328 S Saginaw St Lbby
Flint MI 48502
810 257-2506

(G-1681)
REQ/JQH HOLDINGS INC (PA)
Also Called: International Merchants
4243 Hunt Rd Ste 2 (45242-6645)
PHONE..................513 891-1066
Fax: 513 891-2821
J Erik Kamfjord, *Ch of Bd*
John Q Hammons, *Vice Ch Bd*
Roy E Winegardner, *Vice Ch Bd*
Keith W Daub, *President*
Jennifer Porter, *General Mgr*
EMP: 90
SQ FT: 24,000
SALES (est): 84.3MM **Privately Held**
WEB: www.wihotels.com
SIC: 8741 6552 Hotel or motel management; land subdividers & developers, commercial

(G-1682)
RESOURCE INTERNATIONAL
4480 Lake Forest Dr # 308 (45242-3753)
PHONE..................513 769-6998
Fax: 513 769-7055

Farah Majadzadeh, *President*
Steve Johnson, *Vice Pres*
Cameron Majadzadeh, *Vice Pres*
Darin Crain, *QA Dir*
George Yousef, *Research*
EMP: 100
SALES (est): 4.9MM **Privately Held**
SIC: 8711 Consulting engineer

(G-1683)
RICOH USA INC
10300 Alliance Rd Ste 350 (45242-4764)
PHONE..................513 984-9898
Nicholas Guerriero, *Accounts Exec*
Jack Busmeyer, *Sales Staff*
Charles Dews, *Branch Mgr*
EMP: 70
SALES (corp-wide): 17.8B **Privately Held**
WEB: www.ikon.com
SIC: 5044 5065 7359 5112 Photocopy machines; copying equipment; facsimile equipment; office machine rental, except computers; photocopying supplies; photo-copying & duplicating services; machinery & equipment finance leasing
HQ: Ricoh Usa, Inc.
  70 Valley Stream Pkwy
  Malvern PA 19355
  610 296-8000

(G-1684)
ROBERT HALF INTERNATIONAL INC
10300 Alliance Rd Ste 220 (45242-4764)
PHONE..................513 563-0770
Fax: 614 629-0099
Donna Connor, *Branch Mgr*
EMP: 92
SALES (corp-wide): 5.2B **Publicly Held**
SIC: 7361 Placement agencies
PA: Robert Half International Inc.
  2884 Sand Hill Rd Ste 200
  Menlo Park CA 94025
  650 234-6000

(G-1685)
RUN JUMP-N-PLAY
5897 Pfeiffer Rd (45242-4819)
PHONE..................513 701-7529
David E Powell, *Owner*
Jennifer Morgan-Mccane, *Controller*
EMP: 30
SALES (est): 499.8K **Privately Held**
SIC: 7929 Entertainment service

(G-1686)
SAMUELS PRODUCTS INC
9851 Redhill Dr (45242-5694)
PHONE..................513 891-4456
Fax: 513 891-4520
Millard Samuels, *President*
Thomas J Samuels, *Vice Pres*
Timothy Kroger, *Sales Mgr*
William Fitzpatric, *Admin Sec*
EMP: 30 **EST:** 1903
SQ FT: 61,000
SALES (est): 4.3MM **Privately Held**
WEB: www.samuelsproducts.com
SIC: 2759 5122 Flexographic printing; bags, plastic: printing; druggists' sundries

(G-1687)
SCHULMAN ASSOCS INSTL REVIEW (PA)
Also Called: Sairb
4445 Lake Forest Dr # 300 (45242-3739)
PHONE..................513 761-4100
Michael Woods, *President*
Eli Alford, *COO*
Lynn McLaren, *Human Res Mgr*
Bob Berold, *Accounts Mgr*
Mary Harris, *Manager*
EMP: 160
SQ FT: 29,000
SALES: 32MM **Privately Held**
SIC: 8621 Professional standards review board

(G-1688)
SERVICE EXPERTS HTG & AC LLC
Also Called: Stevenson Service Experts
4610 Carlynn Dr (45241-2202)
PHONE..................513 489-3361
EMP: 30

SALES (corp-wide): 736.6MM **Privately Held**
SIC: 1711 Plumbing, heating, air-conditioning contractors
HQ: Service Experts Heating & Air Conditioning Llc
  3820 American Dr Ste 200
  Plano TX 75075
  972 535-3800

(G-1689)
SOGETI USA LLC
4445 Lake Forest Dr # 550 (45242-3734)
PHONE..................513 824-3000
Shiva Agolla, *Vice Pres*
Mike Buob, *Vice Pres*
Azfar Mallick, *Vice Pres*
Kevin Finke, *Opers Staff*
Patrick Keyser, *Opers Staff*
EMP: 50
SALES (corp-wide): 353.3MM **Privately Held**
WEB: www.sogeti-usa.com
SIC: 7379
HQ: Sogeti Usa Llc
  10100 Innovation Dr # 200
  Miamisburg OH 45342
  937 291-8100

(G-1690)
SONOCO PRODUCTS COMPANY
4747 Lake Forest Dr # 100 (45242-3853)
PHONE..................513 381-2088
Mike Ackerson, *Opers Staff*
Amber Aufderbeck, *Administration*
Shiloh Marinich, *Administration*
Sarah Kornegay, *Graphic Designe*
EMP: 40
SALES (corp-wide): 5B **Publicly Held**
SIC: 7389 Packaging & labeling services
PA: Sonoco Products Company
  1 N 2nd St
  Hartsville SC 29550
  843 383-7000

(G-1691)
SUGAR CREEK PACKING CO
4360 Creek Rd (45241-2924)
PHONE..................513 551-5255
EMP: 25
SALES (corp-wide): 767.9MM **Privately Held**
SIC: 4783 Packing & crating
PA: Sugar Creek Packing Co.
  2101 Kenskill Ave
  Wshngtn Ct Hs OH 43160
  740 335-7440

(G-1692)
SYCAMORE SENIOR CENTER (PA)
Also Called: Mt View Terrace
4455 Carver Woods Dr (45242-5560)
PHONE..................513 984-1234
Fax: 513 686-1040
Jim Formal, *President*
Ray Kingsbury, *Vice Pres*
Bill Young, *Marketing Staff*
Cynthia Holloway, *Director*
EMP: 90
SALES (est): 4MM **Privately Held**
SIC: 8322 Senior citizens' center or association

(G-1693)
TECHNCAL SLTONS SPCIALISTS INC
4250 Creek Rd (45241-2956)
PHONE..................513 792-8930
George D Mihal, *President*
George Mihal, *President*
Robin Mihal, *Admin Sec*
EMP: 25 **EST:** 1990
SALES (est): 1.5MM **Privately Held**
SIC: 8742 Business planning & organizing services

(G-1694)
THERAPY SUPPORT INC
4351 Creek Rd (45241-2923)
PHONE..................513 469-6999
Brain Pavlin, *Owner*
Ted Sowards, *Branch Mgr*
EMP: 100

SALES (corp-wide): 259.4MM **Privately Held**
WEB: www.therapysupport.com
SIC: 5047 Medical & hospital equipment
HQ: Therapy Support, Inc.
  2803 N Oak Grove Ave
  Springfield MO 65803

(G-1695)
TIME WARNER CABLE ENTPS LLC
11325 Reed Hartman Hwy # 110 (45241-2493)
PHONE..................513 489-5000
Mary Egloff, *Manager*
Jim Price, *Manager*
Jeannette Richardson, *Recruiter*
EMP: 900
SALES (corp-wide): 41.5B **Publicly Held**
SIC: 4841 Cable television services
HQ: Time Warner Cable Enterprises Llc
  400 Atlantic St Ste 6
  Stamford CT 06901

(G-1696)
TIME WARNER CABLE INC
9825 Kenwood Rd Ste 102 (45242-6252)
PHONE..................513 354-1100
Micall Phillips, *Accounts Exec*
Mike Barbetta, *Manager*
Yvette Badua, *Manager*
Susie V Boom, *Manager*
Bob Krall, *Manager*
EMP: 25
SALES (corp-wide): 41.5B **Publicly Held**
SIC: 4899 Data communication services
HQ: Spectrum Management Holding Company, Llc
  400 Atlantic St
  Stamford CT 06901
  203 905-7801

(G-1697)
TIME WARNER CABLE INC
11252 Cornell Park Dr (45242-1886)
PHONE..................513 489-5000
Hans Fischmann, *General Mgr*
Wilfredo Juan R Baez, *Pastor*
Jane F Sautter, *Pastor*
Mike Roudi, *Vice Pres*
Nancy Sanders, *Vice Pres*
EMP: 83
SQ FT: 7,038
SALES (corp-wide): 41.5B **Publicly Held**
SIC: 4841 Cable television services
HQ: Spectrum Management Holding Company, Llc
  400 Atlantic St
  Stamford CT 06901
  203 905-7801

(G-1698)
TOYOTA MOTOR CREDIT CORP
Also Called: Lexus Financial Services
1945 Cei Dr (45242-5664)
PHONE..................513 984-7100
Patrick Bunker, *Manager*
EMP: 70
SALES (corp-wide): 242.8B **Privately Held**
WEB: www.toyota.com
SIC: 6141 Automobile & consumer finance companies
HQ: Toyota Motor Credit Corporation
  6565 Headquarters Dr
  Plano TX 75024
  310 468 1310

(G-1699)
TRADESMEN INTERNATIONAL LLC
4398 Glendale Milford Rd (45242-3706)
PHONE..................513 771-1115
Fax: 937 890-3856
Keith McNeely, *Branch Mgr*
Dave Henderson, *Manager*
EMP: 80 **Privately Held**
WEB: www.tradesmen-intl.com
SIC: 7363 Temporary help service
PA: Tradesmen International, Llc
  9760 Shepard Rd
  Macedonia OH 44056

(G-1700)
TREMOR LLC
9545 Kenwood Rd Ste 303 (45242-6270)
PHONE..................513 983-1100
Paulette Yarosz, *Vice Pres*
Herb Robinson, *Opers Staff*
Eric Thompson, *Design Engr*
Geoffry Schroeder, *Manager*
Cory Cusmano, *Analyst*
EMP: 30
SALES (est): 1.2MM **Privately Held**
WEB: www.tremor.com
SIC: 4813

(G-1701)
TRI-CON INCORPORATED
11160 Kenwood Rd Ste 200 (45242-1818)
P.O. Box 498457, Cincinnati (45249-7457)
PHONE..................513 530-9844
Raymond A Conn, *President*
Camilla Warren, *Vice Pres*
Joan Conn, *Admin Sec*
EMP: 25
SALES (est): 6.7MM **Privately Held**
SIC: 1542 Commercial & office building, new construction

(G-1702)
TRIHEALTH INC
11121 Kenwood Rd (45242-1817)
PHONE..................513 891-1627
Jodie McCalla, *Sr Project Mgr*
Stacey Bodenstein, *Manager*
Linda Hogel, *Manager*
Rick Hassler, *Director*
Kelly Lang, *Director*
EMP: 35 **Privately Held**
WEB: www.trihealth.com
SIC: 8741 8011 Hospital management; offices & clinics of medical doctors
HQ: Trihealth, Inc.
  619 Oak St
  Cincinnati OH 45206
  513 569-6111

(G-1703)
TRIPLEFIN LLC (PA)
11333 Cornell Park Dr (45242-1813)
PHONE..................855 877-5346
Gregory T Lalonde, *CEO*
Joseph Conda, *President*
Rick Randall, *President*
Michael Eckstein, *COO*
Steve Gatton, *Vice Pres*
▲ **EMP:** 100 **EST:** 1983
SALES (est): 81.9MM **Privately Held**
WEB: www.triplefin.com
SIC: 5122 Pharmaceuticals

(G-1704)
TRIPLEFIN LLC
11333 Cornell Park Dr (45242-1813)
PHONE..................513 794-9870
Fax: 513 793-1828
Joe Hauck, *Exec VP*
Wendy Ficke, *Branch Mgr*
Geri Mittelhauser, *Executive*
EMP: 40
SALES (corp-wide): 81.9MM **Privately Held**
WEB: www.triplefin.com
SIC: 7389 Telemarketing services
PA: Triplefin Llc
  11333 Cornell Park Dr
  Blue Ash OH 45242
  855 877-5346

(G-1705)
TRUEPOINT INC
4901 Hunt Rd Ste 200 (45242-6990)
PHONE..................513 792-6648
Michael J Chasnoff, *President*
Janel Carroll, *General Mgr*
Christopher L Sheldon Jr, *Accountant*
Katrina Harsel, *Manager*
John Azens, *Director*
EMP: 27
SALES (est): 3.9MM **Privately Held**
WEB: www.acsadvisors.com
SIC: 8742 Financial consultant

(G-1706)
TRUSTAFF MANAGEMENT INC
Also Called: Trustaff Travel Nurses
4675 Cornell Rd (45241-2461)
PHONE..................513 272-3999

Blue Ash - Hamilton County (G-1707) — GEOGRAPHIC SECTION

Brent Loring, *CEO*
Pam Oliver, *COO*
Doug Dean, *Vice Pres*
Michelle Filipkowski, *Vice Pres*
Larry Hoelscher, *Vice Pres*
EMP: 2000
SQ FT: 40,000
SALES: 305.7MM **Privately Held**
WEB: www.trustaff.com
SIC: 8741 Personnel management

(G-1707)
TSG-CINCINNATI LLC
11243 Cornell Park Dr (45242-1811)
PHONE 513 793-6241
Paul E Towle,
EMP: 60
SALES (est): 9.4MM **Privately Held**
SIC: 5147 Meat brokers

(G-1708)
ULTIMATE REHAB LTD
11305 Reed Hartman Hwy # 226
(45241-2435)
PHONE 513 563-8777
Fax: 513 563-8770
Lorie Macdonald, *CEO*
Kelley Robinson, *Vice Pres*
Sheryl Marler, *VP Opers*
Thomas Macdonald, *CFO*
Brandi Fedkow, *Office Mgr*
EMP: 85
SALES (est): 2.8MM **Privately Held**
SIC: 8093 Rehabilitation center, outpatient treatment

(G-1709)
UNIFUND CCR LLC
10625 Techwood Cir (45242-2846)
PHONE 513 489-8877
David G Rosenberg, *CEO*
Mike Grdina, *Finance Mgr*
EMP: 100
SALES (est): 11.7MM **Privately Held**
SIC: 6153 Buying of installment notes

(G-1710)
UNIFUND CORPORATION
Also Called: Rushcard
10625 Techwood Cir (45242-2846)
PHONE 513 489-8877
Fax: 513 489-7511
David G Rosenberg, *CEO*
Susan Appel, *Counsel*
Michael Schwartz, *Exec VP*
Robert Schofield, *Vice Pres*
Jeffrey Shaffer, *Vice Pres*
EMP: 50
SQ FT: 12,000
SALES (est): 36.9MM **Privately Held**
SIC: 6153 Buying of installment notes

(G-1711)
UNIQUE CONSTRUCTION SVCS INC
10999 Reed Hartman Hwy # 313
(45242-8331)
PHONE 513 608-1363
EMP: 33
SALES: 850K **Privately Held**
SIC: 1721 Contractor Of Commercial And Residentail Painting

(G-1712)
UNIRUSH LLC (HQ)
Also Called: Babyphat
4701 Creek Rd Ste 200 (45242-8330)
P.O. Box 42482, Cincinnati (45242-0482)
PHONE 866 766-2229
Ron Hynes, *CEO*
Douglas McGann, *President*
Jason Miles, *Senior VP*
Chris Ruppel, *Senior VP*
Rob Eisenstein, *Project Mgr*
EMP: 68
SALES (est): 25.1MM
SALES (corp-wide): 890.1MM **Publicly Held**
SIC: 7389 Financial services
PA: Green Dot Corporation
3465 E Foothill Blvd # 100
Pasadena CA 91107
626 765-2000

(G-1713)
UNITED HEALTHCARE OHIO INC
5151 Pfeiffer Rd Ste 400 (45242-4854)
PHONE 513 603-6200
Dorothy Coleman, *CEO*
EMP: 250
SALES (corp-wide): 201.1B **Publicly Held**
WEB: www.uhc.com
SIC: 6324 Health maintenance organization (HMO), insurance only
HQ: United Healthcare Of Ohio, Inc.
9200 Worthington Rd
Columbus OH 43085
614 410-7000

(G-1714)
UNIVERSAL WORK AND POWER LLC
Also Called: Kemper Shuttle Services
4620 Carlynn Dr (45241-2202)
PHONE 513 981-1111
Miko Eminyan, *Mng Member*
Mkrtich Eminyan, *Mng Member*
EMP: 30
SALES (est): 261.7K **Privately Held**
SIC: 4111 4119 Local & suburban transit; local rental transportation

(G-1715)
VARIOUS VIEWS RESEARCH INC
11353 Reed Hartman Hwy # 200
(45241-2443)
PHONE 513 489-9000
Mirjana Popovich, *CEO*
Sharon Lally, *President*
Kevin Vaselakes, *President*
Janet Pauciulo, *Accounting Mgr*
Brendan Burns, *Marketing Staff*
EMP: 55
SQ FT: 13,788
SALES (est): 6.4MM **Privately Held**
SIC: 8732 Market analysis or research

(G-1716)
VORA VENTURES LLC
10290 Alliance Rd (45242-4710)
PHONE 513 792-5100
Kevin Dooley, *Exec VP*
David Porter, *Assoc VP*
Mahendra B Vora, *Mng Member*
Karen Conrade, *Admin Sec*
EMP: 200
SALES (est): 14MM **Privately Held**
SIC: 8741 Business management; financial management for business

(G-1717)
W & H REALTY INC (PA)
Also Called: Holiday Inn
4243 Hunt Rd (45242-6645)
PHONE 513 891-1066
J Erik Kamfjord, *Ch of Bd*
John J Slaboch, *Corp Secy*
Amy Tepton, *Accounts Mgr*
EMP: 50
SALES (est): 15MM **Privately Held**
SIC: 7011 Hotels & motels

(G-1718)
WJCB LLC
9475 Kenwood Rd Ste 14 (45242-6830)
PHONE 513 631-3200
Diane Wainscott, *Manager*
William Brodberger,
EMP: 50
SQ FT: 900
SALES (est): 1MM **Privately Held**
WEB: www.wjcb.com
SIC: 7361 Executive placement

(G-1719)
WOLF MACHINE COMPANY (PA)
5570 Creek Rd (45242-4004)
PHONE 513 791-5194
Fax: 513 791-0925
Scott E Andre, *President*
Greg Russell, *Vice Pres*
Keith Jameson, *Purch Agent*
EMP: 160 **EST:** 1888
SQ FT: 50,000
SALES (est): 41.3MM **Privately Held**
WEB: www.wolfmachine.com
SIC: 8741 3552 3556 3546 Machine tools & accessories; textile machinery; food products machinery; power-driven handtools

(G-1720)
WOLF SENSORY INC
Also Called: Wolf Group, The
10860 Kenwood Rd (45242-2812)
PHONE 513 891-9100
Fax: 513 792-3533
Mona Wolf, *President*
Cheryl Volk, *Senior VP*
EMP: 50
SQ FT: 17,000
SALES (est): 4.9MM **Privately Held**
WEB: www.wolfsensory.com
SIC: 8732 Market analysis or research

(G-1721)
WOODWARD CONSTRUCTION INC
11425 Deerfield Rd (45242-2106)
PHONE 513 247-9241
Fax: 513 247-9240
Jeff Woodward, *President*
Brent Sebesy, *Vice Pres*
Wally Szymanski, *Project Mgr*
Jana Swart, *Exec Sec*
EMP: 26
SQ FT: 5,000
SALES (est): 3MM **Privately Held**
SIC: 1542 Commercial & office building, new construction

(G-1722)
WW GRAINGER INC
Also Called: Grainger 152
4420 Glendale Milford Rd (45242-3708)
PHONE 513 563-7100
Fax: 513 563-6929
Gary Brown, *General Mgr*
Scott Wells, *Sales Staff*
Marty Jamieson, *Manager*
EMP: 25
SQ FT: 2,450
SALES (corp-wide): 10.4B **Publicly Held**
WEB: www.grainger.com
SIC: 5084 5063 Industrial machinery & equipment; motors, electric
PA: W.W. Grainger, Inc.
100 Grainger Pkwy
Lake Forest IL 60045
847 535-1000

(G-1723)
WWS ASSOCIATES INC (PA)
Also Called: 2trg
11093 Kenwood Rd Ste 7 (45242-1815)
PHONE 513 761-5333
Elli Workum, *CEO*
Stuart Shaffer, *Exec VP*
Carol Weinstein, *CFO*
▼ **EMP:** 117
SQ FT: 90,000
SALES (est): 53.5MM **Privately Held**
SIC: 4953 Recycling, waste materials

(G-1724)
XEROX CORPORATION
10560 Ashview Pl (45242-3735)
PHONE 513 554-3200
Fax: 513 554-3267
Lonnie Stiff, *Plant Mgr*
Dennis Pauley, *Info Tech Mgr*
EMP: 500
SALES (corp-wide): 10.2B **Publicly Held**
WEB: www.xerox.com
SIC: 3861 5044 Photocopy machines; office equipment
PA: Xerox Corporation
201 Merritt 7
Norwalk CT 06851
203 968-3000

(G-1725)
YOUNG MENS CHRISTIAN
Also Called: Blue Ash YMCA
5000 Ymca Dr (45242-7444)
PHONE 513 791-5000
Fax: 513 792-5309
Jonathan Eicher, *Facilities Mgr*
Juley Lawson, *Purchasing*
Annie Worobetz, *Treasurer*
Paul Waldsmith, *Exec Dir*
Alan Geans, *Exec Dir*
EMP: 150
SQ FT: 16,506
SALES (corp-wide): 33.6MM **Privately Held**
WEB: www.cincinnatiymca.org
SIC: 8641 7336 8351 7997 Civic social & fraternal associations; commercial art & graphic design; child day care services; membership sports & recreation clubs
PA: Young Mens Christian Association Of Greater Cincinnati
1105 Elm St
Cincinnati OH 45202
513 651-2100

Bluffton
Allen County

(G-1726)
A TO Z PORTION CTRL MEATS INC
201 N Main St (45817-1283)
PHONE 419 358-2926
Fax: 419 358-8876
Lee Ann Kagy, *President*
Sean Kagy, *COO*
Jessica Strahm, *QC Mgr*
EMP: 25 **EST:** 1945
SQ FT: 20,000
SALES (est): 9.4MM **Privately Held**
SIC: 5147 5142 5421 2013 Meats, fresh; meat, frozen: packaged; meat markets, including freezer provisioniers; sausages & other prepared meats

(G-1727)
BLANCHARD VLY RGIONAL HLTH CTR
Also Called: Bluffton Campus
139 Garau St (45817-1027)
P.O. Box 48 (45817-0048)
PHONE 419 358-9010
Fax: 419 358-1532
Clifford Harmon, *COO*
Barbara Plaugher, *QC Dir*
Deb Miller, *Med Doctor*
Gary Blosser, *Supervisor*
William Watkins, *Director*
EMP: 150
SALES (corp-wide): 32.5MM **Privately Held**
SIC: 8011 Health maintenance organization
HQ: Blanchard Valley Regional Health Center
1900 S Main St
Findlay OH 45840
419 423-4500

(G-1728)
BLUFFTON FAMILY RECREATION
Also Called: BFR
215 Snider Rd (45817-9572)
PHONE 419 358-6978
Fax: 419 358-4708
Mandy Kinn, *President*
Maranda Miller, *Manager*
Carole Enneking, *Director*
EMP: 30
SALES: 331.7K **Privately Held**
WEB: www.bfronline.com
SIC: 8641 Recreation association

(G-1729)
CARPE DIEM INDUSTRIES LLC
Also Called: Diamond Machine and Mfg
505 E Jefferson St (45817-1349)
PHONE 419 358-0129
Fax: 419 358-0196
Tammy Whitlow, *Human Res Mgr*
Ryan Smith, *Manager*
EMP: 30
SQ FT: 271,000

SALES (corp-wide): 18.1MM **Privately Held**
WEB: www.colonialsurfacesolutions.com
SIC: 3471 3398 3479 1799 Cleaning & descaling metal products; sand blasting of metal parts; tumbling (cleaning & polishing) of machine parts; metal heat treating; tempering of metal; painting of metal products; coating of metal structures at construction site
PA: Carpe Diem Industries, Llc
4599 Campbell Rd
Columbus Grove OH 45830
419 659-5639

(G-1730)
CITIZENS NAT BNK OF BLUFFTON (HQ)
102 S Main St (45817-1250)
P.O. Box 88 (45817-0088)
PHONE.................419 358-8040
J Michael Romey, *President*
Darrell Buroker, *Exec VP*
Robert D Everett, *Exec VP*
Michael Comer, *Senior VP*
Bob Inniger, *Vice Pres*
EMP: 48
SALES: 38.4MM **Privately Held**
WEB: www.cnbohio.com
SIC: 6021 National commercial banks

(G-1731)
GROB SYSTEMS INC
Also Called: Machine Tool Division
1070 Navajo Dr (45817-9666)
PHONE.................419 358-9015
Fax: 419 369-3332
Ralf Bronnenmeier, *CEO*
Jason Cartright, *President*
Michael Hutecker, *President*
William Vejnovic, *Vice Pres*
Thomas Ruf, *Project Mgr*
◆ EMP: 198
SQ FT: 262,000
SALES (est): 151MM
SALES (corp-wide): 276.6MM **Privately Held**
WEB: www.grobsystems.com
SIC: 3535 7699 Robotic conveyors; industrial equipment services
PA: Grob-Werke Burkhart Grob E.K.
Industriestr. 4
Mindelheim 87719
826 199-60

(G-1732)
J W J INVESTMENTS INC
Also Called: Richland Manor
7400 Sweeney Rd (45817)
PHONE.................419 643-3161
Fax: 419 643-4702
William J Mc Clellan, *President*
Terri Schneider, *Principal*
Stephanie Theis, *Principal*
David Woodruff, *Director*
Kari Berens, *Executive*
EMP: 112
SALES (corp-wide): 2.6MM **Privately Held**
WEB: www.jwjinvestments.com
SIC: 8059 8051 Nursing home, except skilled & intermediate care facility; skilled nursing care facilities
PA: J W J Investments Inc
300 Cherry St
Genoa OH
419 855-7755

(G-1733)
JPMORGAN CHASE BANK NAT ASSN
135 S Main St (45817-1249)
PHONE.................419 358-4055
Chad Grieser, *Branch Mgr*
EMP: 26
SALES (corp-wide): 99.6B **Publicly Held**
SIC: 6021 National commercial banks
HQ: Jpmorgan Chase Bank, National Association
1111 Polaris Pkwy
Columbus OH 43240
614 436-3055

(G-1734)
MENNONITE MEMORIAL HOME INC (PA)
Also Called: MAPLE CREST SENIOR LIVING VILL
410 W Elm St (45817-1122)
PHONE.................419 358-1015
David Lynn Thompson, *CEO*
Kris Reese, *Director*
David Woodruff, *Director*
Pat Emery, *Nursing Dir*
Nancy Crawford, *Admin Asst*
EMP: 250
SQ FT: 65,000
SALES: 5.5MM **Privately Held**
SIC: 8052 8059 8051 Intermediate care facilities; personal care home, with health care; skilled nursing care facilities

(G-1735)
MENNONITE MEMORIAL HOME INC
Also Called: Maple Crest
700 Maple Crest Ct (45817-8552)
PHONE.................419 358-7654
Fax: 419 358-7644
Daren Lee, *Manager*
Heather Clum, *Nursing Dir*
EMP: 40
SALES (corp-wide): 5.5MM **Privately Held**
SIC: 8059 Convalescent home
PA: Mennonite Memorial Home Inc
410 W Elm St
Bluffton OH 45817
419 358-1015

(G-1736)
TRILOGY HEALTHCARE ALLEN LLC
7400 Swaney Rd (45817-9551)
PHONE.................419 643-3161
Kathy Corbinn,
EMP: 76
SALES (est): 921.6K **Privately Held**
SIC: 8051 Skilled nursing care facilities

Boardman
Mahoning County

(G-1737)
ASHLEY ENTERPRISES LLC (PA)
Also Called: Briarfield At Ashley Circle
1419 Boardman Canfield Rd (44512-8062)
PHONE.................330 726-5790
Rob Rupeka, *CFO*
Edward Reese, *Mng Member*
Diane Reese,
EMP: 93
SQ FT: 33,991
SALES (est): 3.1MM **Privately Held**
SIC: 8051 Skilled nursing care facilities

(G-1738)
BEEGHLY OAKS OPERATING LLC
Also Called: Beeghly Oaks Center For Rehabi
6505 Market St Bldg D (44512-3459)
PHONE.................330 884-2300
Fax: 330 726-0182
Mark Friedman, *Mng Member*
Linda Day, *Administration*
EMP: 130 EST: 2014
SALES (est): 85.8K **Privately Held**
SIC: 8322 8052 Rehabilitation services; home for the mentally retarded, with health care

(G-1739)
FINANCIAL ENGINES INC
1449 Boardman Canfield Rd (44512-8061)
PHONE.................330 726-3100
Ronald Tabus, *Branch Mgr*
EMP: 49
SALES (corp-wide): 480.5MM **Publicly Held**
SIC: 6282 Investment advice
PA: Financial Engines, Inc.
1050 Enterprise Way Fl 3
Sunnyvale CA 94089
408 498-6000

(G-1740)
GORANT CHOCOLATIER LLC (PA)
Also Called: Gorant's Yum Yum Tree
8301 Market St (44512-6257)
PHONE.................330 726-8821
Gary Weiss, *President*
Jack Peluse, *Plant Mgr*
Joseph M Miller, *Mng Member*
EMP: 120 EST: 1946
SQ FT: 60,000
SALES (est): 27.9MM **Privately Held**
SIC: 5441 5947 5145 3999 Candy; greeting cards; gift shop; candy; candles; chocolate & cocoa products

(G-1741)
HOME DEPOT USA INC
Also Called: Home Depot, The
7001 Southern Blvd (44512-4637)
PHONE.................330 965-4790
Fax: 330 965-4826
Audrey Elias, *Manager*
EMP: 160
SALES (corp-wide): 100.9B **Publicly Held**
WEB: www.homerentalsdepot.com
SIC: 5211 7359 Home centers; tool rental
HQ: Home Depot U.S.A., Inc.
2455 Paces Ferry Rd Se
Atlanta GA 30339

(G-1742)
OREILLY AUTOMOTIVE INC
8308 Market St (44512-6256)
PHONE.................330 318-3136
EMP: 58 **Publicly Held**
SIC: 5531 5013 Batteries, automotive & truck; automotive supplies & parts
PA: O'reilly Automotive, Inc.
233 S Patterson Ave
Springfield MO 65802

(G-1743)
RAPHAELS SCHL BUTY CULTURE INC (PA)
615 Boardman Canfield Rd (44512-4748)
P.O. Box 238, Girard (44420-0238)
PHONE.................330 782-3395
Fax: 330 652-2179
Jacquilyn Eusanio, *President*
Michelle Benson, *Admin Sec*
EMP: 25
SQ FT: 9,000
SALES (est): 1.1MM **Privately Held**
WEB: www.raphaelsbeautyschool.com
SIC: 7231 Cosmetology school

(G-1744)
RL BEST COMPANY
723 Bev Rd (44512-6423)
PHONE.................330 758-8601
Fax: 330 758-9413
Ted A Best, *President*
Ted Best, *President*
Mark Best, *Vice Pres*
William Kavanaugh, *Vice Pres*
Jeffrey Best, *Engineer*
◆ EMP: 26
SQ FT: 35,000
SALES: 9MM **Privately Held**
WEB: www.rlbest.com
SIC: 3599 7539 Machine shop, jobbing & repair; machine shop, automotive

(G-1745)
VECTOR SECURITY INC
970 Windham Ct Ste 2 (44512-5084)
PHONE.................330 726-9841
Fax: 330 726-9826
John Zaboroski, *Opers Mgr*
Chris Toombs, *Sales Mgr*
Jennifer Petrock, *Branch Mgr*
Jim Lorah, *Branch Mgr*
Robert Zagorsky, *Consultant*
EMP: 26
SALES (corp-wide): 438MM **Privately Held**
WEB: www.vectorsecurity.com
SIC: 7382 1731 Burglar alarm maintenance & monitoring; fire detection & burglar alarm systems specialization

HQ: Vector Security Inc.
2000 Ericsson Dr Ste 250
Warrendale PA 15086
724 741-2200

Bolivar
Tuscarawas County

(G-1746)
ELEET CRYOGENICS INC
11132 Industrial Pkwy Nw (44612-8993)
PHONE.................330 874-4009
Garry Sears, *President*
Tenia Sears, *Vice Pres*
Andrew Reeves, *Project Mgr*
Karrisa Reeves, *Prdtn Mgr*
Ray Himes, *Manager*
▲ EMP: 33
SQ FT: 47,000
SALES (est): 9.3MM **Privately Held**
WEB: www.eleetcryogenics.com
SIC: 3443 7353 2761 5088 Cryogenic tanks, for liquids & gases; oil field equipment, rental or leasing; manifold business forms; tanks & tank components; trailer rental; management services

(G-1747)
FSRC TANKS INC
11029 Industrial Pkwy Nw (44612-8992)
PHONE.................234 221-2015
Andrew Feucht, *President*
Ryan Lowers, *Project Mgr*
EMP: 35
SALES (est): 1.5MM **Privately Held**
SIC: 1791 3443 Storage tanks, metal; erection; reactor containment vessels, metal plate

(G-1748)
HARRIS BATTERY COMPANY INC (PA)
10708 Industrial Pkwy Nw (44612-8429)
PHONE.................330 874-0205
Fax: 330 874-0416
Jerry Harris, *CEO*
Christopher Harris, *President*
Reid Geibel, *General Mgr*
Sidney Geibel, *Vice Pres*
Adam Humphrey, *Warehouse Mgr*
▲ EMP: 39 EST: 1979
SQ FT: 41,000
SALES (est): 40.5MM **Privately Held**
WEB: www.harrisbattery.com
SIC: 5013 5065 Automotive batteries; electronic parts & equipment

(G-1749)
MEGCO MANAGEMENT INC
Also Called: Hennis Care Center of Bolivar
300 Yant St (44612-9712)
PHONE.................330 874-9999
Shirley Billman, *Director*
James Martin, *Director*
David Hennis, *Administration*
EMP: 120 EST: 1999
SALES (est): 5.4MM **Privately Held**
SIC: 8051 Convalescent home with continuous nursing care

(G-1750)
OHIO MACHINERY CO
Also Called: Caterpillar Authorized Dealer
10955 Industrial Pkwy Nw (44612-8991)
PHONE.................330 874-1003
Fax: 330 874-1103
Janie Rogers, *Branch Mgr*
Denis Fox, *Manager*
Matt Mole, *Manager*
EMP: 38
SALES (corp-wide): 222.7MM **Privately Held**
WEB: www.enginesnow.com
SIC: 7699 5082 Hydraulic equipment repair; construction & mining machinery
PA: Ohio Machinery Co.
3993 E Royalton Rd
Broadview Heights OH 44147
440 526-6200

Botkins
Shelby County

(G-1751)
BEEM CONSTRUCTION INC
225 S Mill St (45306-8023)
P.O. Box 208 (45306-0208)
PHONE.....................937 693-3176
Roger Barlage, *President*
Dean Alstaetter, *Vice Pres*
Tim Butcher, *Vice Pres*
Steven Eilerman, *Vice Pres*
Donald Eilerman, *Treasurer*
EMP: 45 **EST:** 1977
SQ FT: 8,000
SALES (est): 8.6MM **Privately Held**
WEB: www.beemconstruction.com
SIC: 1541 Industrial buildings, new construction; warehouse construction

(G-1752)
BROWN INDUSTRIAL INC
311 W South St (45306-8019)
P.O. Box 74 (45306-0074)
PHONE.....................937 693-3838
Fax: 937 693-4121
Christopher D Brown, *President*
Ruth C Brown, *Corp Secy*
Craig D Brown, *Vice Pres*
Pat Meyers, *Accountant*
EMP: 45
SQ FT: 32,000
SALES (est): 12.8MM **Privately Held**
WEB: www.brownindustrial.com
SIC: 3713 5012 5084 7692 Truck bodies (motor vehicles); truck bodies; industrial machinery & equipment; packaging machinery & equipment; automotive welding

(G-1753)
SCHNIPPEL CONSTRUCTION INC
302 N Main St (45306-8039)
P.O. Box 477 (45306-0477)
PHONE.....................937 693-3831
Fax: 937 693-6481
Thomas J Schnippel, *President*
Daniel Rider, *Superintendent*
Tracy Cooper, *Corp Secy*
Keith Schnippel, *Marketing Staff*
EMP: 30
SQ FT: 9,000
SALES: 3.5MM **Privately Held**
WEB: www.schnippelconstruction.com
SIC: 1522 1541 1542 Multi-family dwelling construction; industrial buildings, new construction; commercial & office building, new construction

Bowerston
Harrison County

(G-1754)
CARRIAGE INN OF BOWERSTON INC
Also Called: Sunny Slope Nursing Home
102 Boyce Dr (44695-9701)
PHONE.....................740 269-8001
Fax: 740 269-1733
Bob Huff, *President*
Anna Clark, *Manager*
Martha Yeager, *Director*
Keven Case, *Administration*
EMP: 65
SQ FT: 9,700
SALES (est): 3.7MM **Privately Held**
SIC: 8052 Personal care facility

Bowling Green
Wood County

(G-1755)
AA GREEN REALTY INC
1045 N Main St Ste 2 (43402-1360)
PHONE.....................419 352-5331
Fax: 419 352-0770
Allen A Green, *President*
Larry Davies, *Executive*
EMP: 32
SALES: 1.1MM **Privately Held**
WEB: www.aagreen.com
SIC: 6531 Real estate agent, residential

(G-1756)
ADVANCED SPECIALTY PRODUCTS
428 Clough St (43402-2914)
P.O. Box 210 (43402-0210)
PHONE.....................419 882-6528
Fax: 419 352-9663
Kenneth T Kujawa, *President*
Eugene Kujawa, *Vice Pres*
▼ **EMP:** 60
SQ FT: 24,000
SALES (est): 7.8MM **Privately Held**
SIC: 5082 7389 2759 Construction & mining machinery; packaging & labeling services; commercial printing

(G-1757)
AL-MAR LANES
Also Called: Cj's Sports Bar
1010 N Main St (43402-1301)
PHONE.....................419 352-4637
Fax: 419 352-1673
Bill Wammes, *Owner*
Mike Ackley, *Sales Staff*
Pancha Melendrez, *Director*
EMP: 36
SQ FT: 16,500
SALES: 980K **Privately Held**
SIC: 7933 5941 7389 6531 Ten pin center; sporting goods & bicycle shops; auction, appraisal & exchange services; appraiser, real estate; cocktail lounge; warehousing, self-storage

(G-1758)
ARGO-HYTOS INC
1835 N Research Dr (43402)
P.O. Box 28 (43402-0028)
PHONE.....................419 353-6070
Christian H Kienzle, *President*
Larry Gerken, *Vice Pres*
Patrick Green, *Vice Pres*
Walter Bader, *CFO*
George Hartwell, *Sales Staff*
▲ **EMP:** 1200
SQ FT: 6,200
SALES (est): 213.6MM **Privately Held**
WEB: www.argo-hytos.com
SIC: 5084 Hydraulic systems equipment & supplies
PA: Fsp Fluid Systems Partners Holding Ag
Rebmattli 20
Baar ZG
417 632-905

(G-1759)
B G NEWS
Also Called: Bg News
214 W Hall Bgsu (43403-0001)
PHONE.....................419 372-2601
Fax: 419 372-6967
EMP: 50
SALES (est): 2MM **Privately Held**
SIC: 2711 7313 2741 Newspapers-Publishing/Printing Advertising Representative Misc Publishing

(G-1760)
BEHAVRAL CNNCTIONS WD CNTY INC (PA)
280 S Main St (43402-3053)
P.O. Box 29 (43402-0029)
PHONE.....................419 352-5387
Richard Goldberg, *CEO*
Sajid Khan, *President*
Deborah Smith, *CFO*
Michelle Klement, *Treasurer*
Lisa Boyd, *Controller*
EMP: 171
SQ FT: 5,500
SALES: 4.8MM **Privately Held**
SIC: 8093 Alcohol clinic, outpatient

(G-1761)
BEHAVRAL CNNCTIONS WD CNTY INC
320 W Gypsy Lane Rd Ste A (43402-4571)
PHONE.....................419 352-5387
Fax: 419 352-5439
Richard Goldberg, *Director*
EMP: 26
SALES (corp-wide): 4.8MM **Privately Held**
SIC: 8093 8069 Alcohol clinic, outpatient; drug addiction rehabilitation hospital
PA: Behavioral Connections Of Wood County, Inc.
280 S Main St
Bowling Green OH 43402
419 352-5387

(G-1762)
BEHAVRAL CNNCTIONS WD CNTY INC
1010 N Prospect St (43402-1335)
P.O. Box 8970, Toledo (43623-0970)
PHONE.....................419 352-5387
John Betts, *Manager*
Marlys Reetz, *Exec Dir*
Galina D Zhurakovski, *Psychiatry*
Jeanne A Jagodzinski, *Nurse Practr*
EMP: 150
SALES (corp-wide): 4.8MM **Privately Held**
SIC: 8093 Mental health clinic, outpatient
PA: Behavioral Connections Of Wood County, Inc.
280 S Main St
Bowling Green OH 43402
419 352-5387

(G-1763)
BETCO CORPORATION (PA)
400 Van Camp Rd (43402-9062)
PHONE.....................419 241-2156
Fax: 419 241-1327
Paul C Betz, *CEO*
Jeff Satterfield, *Division Mgr*
Fred Corder, *Regional Mgr*
Greg Gangelhoff, *Regional Mgr*
David Saenz, *Regional Mgr*
EMP: 200 **EST:** 1950
SQ FT: 90,000
SALES (est): 138.8MM **Privately Held**
WEB: www.betco.com
SIC: 6719 Investment holding companies, except banks

(G-1764)
BOWLING GREEN COOP NURS SCHL
Also Called: Bright Beginnings Preschool
315 S College Dr (43402-4001)
PHONE.....................419 352-8675
Kelly McHugh, *President*
EMP: 32
SALES (est): 40.5K **Privately Held**
SIC: 8351 Nursery school

(G-1765)
BOWLING GREEN LNCLN-MRCURY INC
Also Called: Bowling Green Lincoln Auto SL
1079 N Main St (43402-1302)
PHONE.....................419 352-2553
Fax: 419 353-0453
John Heffernan, *President*
Carl Heffernan Jr, *President*
Kay C Heffernan, *Vice Pres*
Jesse Lane, *Store Mgr*
Lisa Kline, *Finance Mgr*
EMP: 35
SQ FT: 37,000
SALES (est): 13.5MM **Privately Held**
WEB: www.bglmj.com
SIC: 5511 7538 Automobiles, new & used; general automotive repair shops

(G-1766)
BOWLING GREEN STATE UNIV FDN
Also Called: UNIVERSITY ADVANCEMENT
Mileti Alumni Center (43403-0001)
PHONE.....................419 372-2551
Tim Koder, *Vice Pres*
EMP: 40
SALES: 24.9MM **Privately Held**
SIC: 7389 Fund raising organizations

(G-1767)
BOWLING GREEN STATE UNIVERSITY
Also Called: Wbgu FM 88 1
120 W Hall (43403-0001)
PHONE.....................419 372-8657
Fax: 419 372-0202
Jon Meinhold, *Manager*
Wendy Manning, *Professor*
EMP: 60
SALES (corp-wide): 253.3MM **Privately Held**
WEB: www.bgsu.edu
SIC: 4832 8221 Radio broadcasting stations; university
PA: Bowling Green State University
110 Mcfall Ctr
Bowling Green OH 43403
419 372-2311

(G-1768)
BOWLING GREEN STATE UNIVERSITY
Also Called: College of Musical Arts
516 Admin Bldg (43403-0001)
PHONE.....................419 372-2186
Fax: 419 372-2938
Richard Tennell, *Principal*
EMP: 80
SALES (corp-wide): 253.3MM **Privately Held**
WEB: www.bgsu.edu
SIC: 8221 8641 University; civic social & fraternal associations
PA: Bowling Green State University
110 Mcfall Ctr
Bowling Green OH 43403
419 372-2311

(G-1769)
BOWLING GREEN STATE UNIVERSITY
W B G U TV
245 Troup Ave (43402-3158)
PHONE.....................419 372-2700
Fax: 419 372-7048
Patrick Fitzgerald, *Opers-Prdtn-Mfg*
Tina Simon, *Mktg Dir*
EMP: 45
SALES (corp-wide): 253.3MM **Privately Held**
WEB: www.bgsu.edu
SIC: 4833 8221 Television broadcasting stations; university
PA: Bowling Green State University
110 Mcfall Ctr
Bowling Green OH 43403
419 372-2311

(G-1770)
BROOKDALE SNIOR LVING CMMNTIES
Also Called: Sterling House Bowling Green
121 N Wintergarden Rd Ofc (43402-2199)
PHONE.....................419 354-5300
Fax: 419 354-1177
Cynthia Walsh, *Manager*
Nicole Schutt, *Admin Asst*
EMP: 40
SALES (corp-wide): 4.7B **Publicly Held**
WEB: www.assisted.com
SIC: 8059 Rest home, with health care
HQ: Brookdale Senior Living Communities, Inc.
6737 W Wa St Ste 2300
Milwaukee WI 53214
414 918-5000

(G-1771)
CELLCO PARTNERSHIP
Also Called: Verizon Wireless
1530 E Wooster St (43402-3338)
PHONE.....................419 353-0904
Fax: 419 352-0797
EMP: 76
SALES (corp-wide): 126B **Publicly Held**
SIC: 4812 Cellular telephone services
HQ: Cellco Partnership
1 Verizon Way
Basking Ridge NJ 07920

(G-1772)
CENTURY MARKETING CORPORATION (HQ)
Also Called: Centurylabel
12836 S Dixie Hwy (43402-9230)
PHONE.....................419 354-2591
Fax: 419 352-9567
Albert J Caperna, *President*
Craig E Dixon, *President*
Robert Petrie, *General Mgr*

▲ = Import ▼ =Export
◆ =Import/Export

William Horner, *Corp Secy*
Jeffery Palmer, *VP Admin*
▼ **EMP:** 150
SQ FT: 58,000
SALES (est): 21.2MM
SALES (corp-wide): 78.8MM **Privately Held**
WEB: www.centurylabel.com
SIC: 2759 2679 5046 5199 Labels & seals; printing; flexographic printing; tags & labels, paper; price marking equipment & supplies; packaging materials; commercial printing, lithographic
PA: Cmc Group, Inc.
12836 S Dixie Hwy
Bowling Green OH 43402
419 352-9567

(G-1773)
CMC DAYMARK CORPORATION
Also Called: Daymark Security Systems
12830 S Dixie Hwy (43402-9697)
PHONE....................419 354-2591
Jeffery Palmer, *General Mgr*
Estra Miller, *Manager*
▲ **EMP:** 140
SALES (est): 24.9MM
SALES (corp-wide): 78.8MM **Privately Held**
WEB: www.centurylabel.com
SIC: 2679 5046 Labels, paper: made from purchased material; commercial equipment
PA: Cmc Group, Inc.
12836 S Dixie Hwy
Bowling Green OH 43402
419 352-9567

(G-1774)
DAYMARK FOOD SAFETY SYSTEMS
12830 S Dixie Hwy Bldg B (43402-9697)
PHONE....................419 353-2458
Jeff Palmer, *President*
Lynn Elington, *Manager*
EMP: 140
SALES (est): 12.8MM **Privately Held**
WEB: www.daymarklabel.com
SIC: 8734 Food testing service

(G-1775)
FALCON PLAZA LLC
Also Called: Best Western Falcon Plaza Mtl
1450 E Wooster St Ste 401 (43402-3260)
PHONE....................419 352-4671
Fax: 419 352-4671
Jacob C Bishop, *President*
EMP: 27
SALES (est): 992.6K **Privately Held**
SIC: 7011 Hotels & motels

(G-1776)
FIRST DEFIANCE FINANCIAL CORP
209 W Poe Rd (43402-1767)
PHONE....................419 353-8611
EMP: 42 **Publicly Held**
SIC: 6035 6411 Savings institutions, federally chartered; insurance agents, brokers & service
PA: First Defiance Financial Corp.
601 Clinton St
Defiance OH 43512

(G-1777)
GKN DRIVELINE NORTH AMER INC
Also Called: GKN Driveline Bowling Green
2223 Wood Bridge Blvd (43402-8873)
PHONE....................419 354-3955
Hideo Miyagi, *Branch Mgr*
Scott Sanner, *Manager*
EMP: 65
SALES (corp-wide): 10.8B **Privately Held**
WEB: www.gknai.com
SIC: 5013 Motor vehicle supplies & new parts
HQ: Gkn Driveline North America, Inc.
2200 N Opdyke Rd
Auburn Hills MI 48326
248 296-7000

(G-1778)
GREENLINE FOODS INC (DH)
12700 S Dixie Hwy (43402-9697)
PHONE....................419 354-1149
Fax: 419 352-2146
George Benson, *CEO*
Thomas Harteis, *Opers Staff*
Michael Salsbury, *Production*
Mervyn McCulloch, *CFO*
Jamie Peters, *Controller*
EMP: 65
SQ FT: 10,000
SALES (est): 67.9MM
SALES (corp-wide): 532.2MM **Publicly Held**
SIC: 5148 Vegetables, fresh
HQ: Apio, Inc.
4575 W Main St
Guadalupe CA 93434
800 454-1355

(G-1779)
H & R BLOCK
241 S Main St (43402-3026)
PHONE....................419 352-9467
Fax: 419 352-7747
Judy McGraw, *Owner*
EMP: 25
SALES (est): 456.4K **Privately Held**
SIC: 7291 Tax return preparation services

(G-1780)
HARTUNG BROTHERS INC
815 S Dunbridge Rd (43402-8720)
PHONE....................419 352-3000
Neil Schilling, *Branch Mgr*
EMP: 50
SALES (corp-wide): 120MM **Privately Held**
WEB: www.hartungbrothers.com
SIC: 0115 Corn
PA: Hartung Brothers, Inc.
708 Heartland Trl # 2000
Madison WI 53717
608 829-6000

(G-1781)
HCF OF BOWL GREEN CARE CTR INC
850 W Poe Rd (43402-1219)
PHONE....................419 352-7558
Fax: 419 354-9501
Tom Blakely, *CEO*
Tammy Caldwell, *Facilities Dir*
Rick Mertes, *Office Mgr*
Julie Naftzger, *Office Mgr*
Jalon Helton, *Director*
EMP: 82
SALES (est): 1.9MM
SALES (corp-wide): 154.8MM **Privately Held**
SIC: 8051 Convalescent home with continuous nursing care
PA: Hcf Management, Inc.
1100 Shawnee Rd
Lima OH 45805
419 999-2010

(G-1782)
HCF OF BOWLING GREEN INC
1021 W Poe Rd (43402-9362)
PHONE....................419 352-4694
Fax: 419 352-4233
Tara Woggon, *Sls & Mktg Exec*
Ellen Treen, *Office Mgr*
Maranda Hafner, *Director*
EMP: 102
SALES (est): 2.4MM
SALES (corp-wide): 154.8MM **Privately Held**
SIC: 6513 Apartment building operators
PA: Hcf Management, Inc.
1100 Shawnee Rd
Lima OH 45805
419 999-2010

(G-1783)
ISHIKAWA GASKET AMERICA INC
828 Van Camp Rd (43402-9379)
PHONE....................419 353-7300
Gary Stasiak, *Manager*
EMP: 190

SALES (corp-wide): 54MM **Privately Held**
WEB: www.ishikawaamerica.com
SIC: 3053 5085 3714 Gaskets & sealing devices; gaskets; motor vehicle parts & accessories
HQ: Ishikawa Gasket America, Inc.
828 Van Camp Rd
Bowling Green OH 43402

(G-1784)
LANE WOOD INDUSTRIES
Also Called: Work Leads To Independence
991 S Main St (43402-4708)
PHONE....................419 352-5059
Vic Gable, *CEO*
Richard Harris, *Principal*
Virginia Melchert, *Principal*
Melinda Kale, *CFO*
EMP: 350
SALES (est): 6MM **Privately Held**
SIC: 7361 Employment agencies

(G-1785)
MACK INDUSTRIES
507 Derby Ave (43402-3973)
PHONE....................419 353-7081
Betsie Mack, *President*
Jeff Colvin, *Opers-Prdtn-Mfg*
Tom Setzer, *Credit Mgr*
EMP: 173
SALES (est): 19.3MM
SALES (corp-wide): 160.1MM **Privately Held**
WEB: www.mackconcrete.com
SIC: 3272 5211 1711 Burial vaults, concrete or precast terrazzo; masonry materials & supplies; septic system construction
PA: Mack Industries, Inc.
1321 Industrial Pkwy N # 500
Brunswick OH 44212
330 460-7005

(G-1786)
NEWELL BRANDS INC
Also Called: Calphalon
20750 Midstar Dr (43402-9215)
PHONE....................419 662-2225
Zachary Graffice, *Branch Mgr*
EMP: 200
SALES (corp-wide): 14.7B **Publicly Held**
SIC: 5023 Kitchen tools & utensils
PA: Newell Brands Inc.
221 River St
Hoboken NJ 07030
201 610-6600

(G-1787)
NORTHWESTERN WATER & SEWER DST
12560 Middleton Pike (43402-8289)
P.O. Box 348 (43402-0348)
PHONE....................419 354-9090
Steve Arnold, *Vice Chairman*
Mark Davis, *Project Mgr*
Dick Heyman, *Project Mgr*
Mike Curtis, *Opers Staff*
Tom Stalter, *Engineer*
EMP: 49
SQ FT: 30,000
SALES (est): 25MM **Privately Held**
WEB: www.nwwsd.org
SIC: 4952 4941 Sewerage systems; water supply

(G-1788)
OHIO BILIFFS CRT OFFICERS ASSN
Also Called: Obaco
1 Court House Sq (43402-2427)
PHONE....................419 353-9302
Tom Chidester,
EMP: 99
SALES (est): 4.1MM **Privately Held**
SIC: 8611 Business associations

(G-1789)
PHOENIX TECHNOLOGIES INTL LLC
Also Called: Pti
1098 Fairview Ave (43402-1233)
PHONE....................419 353-7738
Fax: 419 354-7738
Don Hayward, *General Mgr*
Jack Ritchie, *Plant Supt*

Dennis Velkov, *Plant Mgr*
Dennis Balduff, *Project Mgr*
Jesse Pine, *Maint Spvr*
▲ **EMP:** 50
SQ FT: 100,000
SALES (est): 15.1MM **Privately Held**
WEB: www.phoenixtechnologies.net
SIC: 3085 5169 Plastics bottles; synthetic resins, rubber & plastic materials

(G-1790)
PIONEER PACKING CO
510 Napoleon Rd (43402-4821)
P.O. Box 171 (43402-0171)
PHONE....................419 352-5283
Fax: 419 352-2416
Brian Contris, *President*
EMP: 70 **EST:** 1945
SQ FT: 30,000
SALES (est): 7.3MM **Privately Held**
WEB: www.pioneeroakland.com
SIC: 5147 Meats & meat products

(G-1791)
POGGEMEYER DESIGN GROUP INC (PA)
Also Called: PDG
1168 N Main St (43402-1352)
PHONE....................419 244-8074
Fax: 419 353-0187
Michael Atherine, *Principal*
Jack A Jones, *Chairman*
Teri Gutierrez, *Business Mgr*
Richard Heyman, *Exec VP*
Tom Borck, *Vice Pres*
EMP: 110
SQ FT: 50,000
SALES (est): 36.2MM **Privately Held**
WEB: www.poggemeyer.com
SIC: 8711 8712 8713 8748 Professional engineer; architectural services; surveying services; city planning

(G-1792)
R & Y HOLDING
Also Called: Hampton Inn
142 Campbell Hill Rd (43402-3458)
PHONE....................419 353-3464
Fax: 419 352-7327
Jabbar Youssif, *Owner*
Sami Abou-Dahech, *Manager*
EMP: 25
SALES (est): 1MM **Privately Held**
SIC: 7011 Hotels & motels

(G-1793)
SAM BS RESTAURANT
163 S Main St (43402-2910)
PHONE....................419 353-2277
Fax: 419 352-7800
Jim Ferell, *Owner*
EMP: 45
SQ FT: 4,000
SALES (est): 1MM **Privately Held**
WEB: www.sambs.com
SIC: 5812 7299 American restaurant; banquet hall facilities

(G-1794)
SPECK SALES INCORPORATED
17746 N Dixie Hwy (43402-9324)
PHONE....................419 353-8312
Fax: 419 353-1717
Esther Speck, *President*
Terry Speck, *Corp Secy*
Bruce Speck, *Vice Pres*
▲ **EMP:** 27
SQ FT: 6,000
SALES (est): 6.7MM **Privately Held**
WEB: www.specksales.com
SIC: 5014 5531 5083 7539 Automobile tires & tubes; automotive tires; agricultural machinery; wheel alignment, automotive

(G-1795)
TOLEDO MOLDING & DIE INC
515 E Gypsy Lane Rd (43402-8739)
PHONE....................419 354-6050
Fax: 419 352-0525
Zachary Graber, *Maint Spvr*
Doug Crowley, *Production*
Bruce Romstad, *Engineer*
Kyle Schmenk, *Engineer*
Tom Pasche, *Manager*
EMP: 100

Bowling Green - Wood County (G-1796)

SALES (corp-wide): 377.7MM **Privately Held**
WEB: www.tmdinc.com
SIC: 5031 Molding, all materials
PA: Toledo Molding & Die, Inc.
1429 Coining Dr
Toledo OH 43612
419 470-3950

(G-1796)
USF HOLLAND LLC
20820 Midstar Dr (43402-8611)
PHONE.....................419 354-6633
Fax: 419 354-6623
Tod Weadock, *Manager*
EMP: 100
SALES (corp-wide): 4.8B **Publicly Held**
WEB: www.usfc.com
SIC: 4213 Less-than-truckload (LTL) transport
HQ: Usf Holland Llc
700 S Waverly Rd
Holland MI 49423
616 395-5000

(G-1797)
WIRELESS SOURCE ENTPS LLC
16545 Euler Rd (43402-9709)
PHONE.....................419 266-5556
Don Stichler, *Mng Member*
Donald Stichler, *Mng Member*
Lisa Sticher, *Administration*
EMP: 35
SALES: 2MM **Privately Held**
SIC: 8999 Communication services

(G-1798)
WOOD COUNTY CHLD SVCS ASSN
Also Called: CHILDREN'S RESOURCE CENTER
1045 Klotz Rd (43402-4820)
P.O. Box 738 (43402-0738)
PHONE.....................419 352-7588
Toll Free:....................888 -
Fax: 419 354-4977
Timothy Scherer, *Exec Dir*
EMP: 90
SQ FT: 29,900
SALES: 5.3MM **Privately Held**
WEB: www.crc.wcnet.org
SIC: 8322 8361 8093 Child related social services; residential care; specialty outpatient clinics

(G-1799)
WOOD COUNTY COMMITTEE ON AGING (PA)
305 N Main St (43402-2424)
PHONE.....................419 353-5661
Fax: 419 352-7448
Sandy Abke, *Site Mgr*
Cheryl Fix, *Site Mgr*
Mary Tebbe, *Site Mgr*
Barbara Becker, *Manager*
Katie Troutner, *Technology*
EMP: 32
SALES: 2.8MM **Privately Held**
WEB: www.bowlinggreenhomeinfo.com
SIC: 8322 Senior citizens' center or association

(G-1800)
WOOD COUNTY HOSPITAL ASSOC (PA)
Also Called: WCH
960 W Wooster St (43402-2644)
PHONE.....................419 354-8900
Fax: 419 354-8200
Stanley Korducki, *President*
Gregory Johnson, *Ch OB/GYN*
John EBY, *Vice Pres*
Tom Makley, *Opers Mgr*
Diani Sonoras, *Materials Mgr*
EMP: 530
SQ FT: 130,000
SALES: 109.8MM **Privately Held**
WEB: www.wch.net
SIC: 8062 General medical & surgical hospitals

(G-1801)
WOOD COUNTY OHIO
1 Court House Sq (43402-2427)
PHONE.....................419 354-9201
Fax: 419 354-9376
James Carter, *Branch Mgr*
EMP: 200 **Privately Held**
WEB: www.woodmrdd.org
SIC: 8322 Probation office
PA: Wood County Ohio
1 Court House Sq
Bowling Green OH 43402
419 354-9100

(G-1802)
WOOD COUNTY OHIO
Also Called: Wood Haven Health Care
1965 E Gypsy Lane Rd (43402-9396)
PHONE.....................419 353-8411
Fax: 419 353-2394
David Cecil, *Administration*
EMP: 125
SQ FT: 400,000 **Privately Held**
WEB: www.woodmrdd.org
SIC: 8051 9111 Convalescent home with continuous nursing care; county supervisors' & executives' offices
PA: Wood County Ohio
1 Court House Sq
Bowling Green OH 43402
419 354-9100

(G-1803)
WOOD COUNTY OHIO
Also Called: Wood County Health Department
1840 E Gypsy Lane Rd (43402-9173)
PHONE.....................419 353-6914
Fax: 419 353-9680
Jan Pelot, *Manager*
Greg Johnson, *Obstetrician*
Pam Butler, *Director*
Vickie Askins, *Bd of Directors*
Mary Gardner, *Officer*
EMP: 61 **Privately Held**
WEB: www.woodmrdd.org
SIC: 9431 8399 ; health systems agency
PA: Wood County Ohio
1 Court House Sq
Bowling Green OH 43402
419 354-9100

(G-1804)
WOOD COUNTY OHIO
Also Called: Community Emplyment Svcs WD Ln
705 W Newton Rd (43402-9026)
PHONE.....................419 352-5059
Fax: 419 354-4320
Vic Gable, *Director*
Kyle Clark, *Director*
EMP: 30 **Privately Held**
WEB: www.woodmrdd.org
SIC: 7361 8331 Placement agencies; job training & vocational rehabilitation services
PA: Wood County Ohio
1 Court House Sq
Bowling Green OH 43402
419 354-9100

(G-1805)
WRYNECK DEVELOPMENT LLC
Also Called: Stone Ridge Golf Club
1553 Muirfield Dr (43402-5230)
PHONE.....................419 354-2535
Joe Ghesquiere, *General Mgr*
Joann Whittaker, *Accountant*
Tara Batey, *Manager*
Kara Higdon, *Director*
Ryan Noone, *Executive*
EMP: 25
SQ FT: 20,000
SALES (est): 4.5MM **Privately Held**
SIC: 6552 Land subdividers & developers, residential

Bradford
Miami County

(G-1806)
DICK LAVY TRUCKING INC
8848 State Route 121 (45308-9631)
PHONE.....................937 448-2104
Fax: 937 448-2312
Richard Lavy, *President*
Ray Lavy, *Vice Pres*
Steve Burke, *Maintenance Dir*
Heather Applegate, *Opers Mgr*
Mike Schaefer, *Opers Staff*
EMP: 243
SQ FT: 18,000
SALES (est): 48.1MM **Privately Held**
WEB: www.dicklavytrucking.com
SIC: 4213 4731 Contract haulers; freight transportation arrangement

(G-1807)
METCON LTD (PA)
6730 Greentree Rd (45308-9756)
PHONE.....................937 447-9200
Fax: 937 447-9201
Glen Garber, *President*
Kirby Crist, *Vice Pres*
Simon King, *Vice Pres*
Anthony Miller, *Vice Pres*
Cody Mikesell, *Project Mgr*
EMP: 33
SALES (est): 9.7MM **Privately Held**
SIC: 1771 Foundation & footing contractor

Bradner
Wood County

(G-1808)
AMERICAN WARMING AND VENT
120 Plin St (43406-7735)
P.O. Box 677 (43406-0677)
PHONE.....................419 288-2703
Stewart E Reed, *President*
John Reed, *President*
Mike Almaguer, *Sales Staff*
EMP: 75
SALES (est): 21.2MM **Privately Held**
SIC: 5031 5039 Doors & windows; air ducts, sheet metal

(G-1809)
DAVIDSON TRUCKING INC
1227 Bowling Green Rd E (43406-9789)
P.O. Box 162 (43406-0162)
PHONE.....................419 288-2318
Fax: 419 288-3845
Dan Davidson, *President*
Jessica Davidson, *Corp Secy*
Kayla Davidson, *Manager*
Phillip Davidson, *Manager*
EMP: 25
SALES (est): 3.1MM **Privately Held**
SIC: 4212 4213 Local trucking, without storage; trucking, except local

Brecksville
Cuyahoga County

(G-1810)
AB RESOURCES LLC
6802 W Snowville Rd Ste E (44141-3296)
PHONE.....................440 922-1098
Fax: 440 922-1251
Chris Halvorson, *CFO*
Gordon O Yonel,
EMP: 25
SQ FT: 7,500
SALES (est): 3.5MM **Privately Held**
SIC: 1311 Crude petroleum & natural gas production

(G-1811)
AHOLA CORPORATION
6820 W Snowville Rd (44141-3214)
PHONE.....................440 717-7620
Fax: 440 717-7690
Mark Ahola, *President*
Craig Pollman, *Controller*
Karen Hajtinger, *CPA*
Paula Tresger, *Sales Associate*
Tim Yonek, *Sales Associate*
EMP: 60
SQ FT: 21,000
SALES (est): 6.3MM **Privately Held**
WEB: www.ahola.com
SIC: 8721 Payroll accounting service

(G-1812)
ANGEL CARE INC
7033 Oakes Rd (44141-2737)
PHONE.....................440 736-7267
Peggy Haladyna, *President*
EMP: 25
SALES (est): 800K **Privately Held**
SIC: 8351 Child day care services

(G-1813)
APPLIED MEDICAL TECHNOLOGY INC (PA)
Also Called: Amt
8006 Katherine Blvd (44141-4202)
PHONE.....................440 717-4000
George J Picha, *President*
Robert J Crump, *Principal*
Tim Austin, *Manager*
Lisa Robbins, *Manager*
Dana Kaiser, *Admin Asst*
EMP: 30
SQ FT: 14,000
SALES (est): 8.4MM **Privately Held**
SIC: 3841 3083 8731 Surgical & medical instruments; laminated plastics plate & sheet; medical research, commercial

(G-1814)
ARISE INCORPORATED
7000 S Edgerton Rd # 100 (44141-3199)
PHONE.....................440 746-8860
Fax: 440 746-8955
William Ramonas, *President*
Laura Fagan, *Director*
Doris Burnhill, *Admin Sec*
EMP: 30
SALES (est): 2.9MM **Privately Held**
WEB: www.globalriskconsultants.com
SIC: 1711 Boiler maintenance contractor
HQ: Tuv Sud America Inc.
10 Centennial Dr Ste 207
Peabody MA 01960
978 573-2500

(G-1815)
BPI INFRMTION SYSTEMS OHIO INC
6055 W Snowville Rd (44141-3245)
PHONE.....................440 717-4112
Gary Ellis, *President*
George Stoll, *Vice Pres*
Travis Breedlove, *Engineer*
Scott D'Amore, *Engineer*
Rich Engelhardt, *Engineer*
EMP: 50
SQ FT: 12,000
SALES (est): 6.7MM **Privately Held**
WEB: www.bpiohio.com
SIC: 7378 7373 Computer maintenance & repair; computer integrated systems design; systems engineering, computer related; value-added resellers, computer systems

(G-1816)
BRECKSVLLE HALTHCARE GROUP INC
Also Called: Oaks of Brecksville, The
8757 Brecksville Rd (44141-1919)
P.O. Box 8757 (44141)
PHONE.....................440 546-0643
Repchick S George, *President*
EMP: 98
SALES (est): 2.1MM **Privately Held**
SIC: 8093 8099 Rehabilitation center, outpatient treatment; physical examination & testing services

(G-1817)
CINTAS CORPORATION NO 2
55 Andrews Cir Ste 1a (44141-3270)
PHONE.....................440 746-7777
EMP: 88
SALES (corp-wide): 5.3B **Publicly Held**
SIC: 7218 Industrial uniform supply
HQ: Cintas Corporation No. 2
6800 Cintas Blvd
Mason OH 45040

(G-1818)
CITY OF BRECKSVILLE
Also Called: Brecksville City Service Dept
9069 Brecksville Rd (44141-2367)
PHONE.....................440 526-1384
Fax: 440 526-7721
Robert Pech, *Director*
EMP: 40 **Privately Held**
SIC: 1611 Highway & street maintenance

GEOGRAPHIC SECTION
Brecksville - Cuyahoga County (G-1842)

PA: City Of Brecksville
9069 Brecksville Rd
Cleveland OH 44141
440 526-4351

(G-1819)
CITY OF BRECKSVILLE
Also Called: Brecksville Community Center
1 Community Dr (44141-2326)
PHONE..................440 526-4109
Fax: 440 546-2000
Jack Abbruzzese, Manager
Tom Tupa, Exec Dir
EMP: 80 Privately Held
SIC: 8322 7991 Community center; physical fitness facilities
PA: City Of Brecksville
9069 Brecksville Rd
Cleveland OH 44141
440 526-4351

(G-1820)
CLEVELAND METROPARKS
Also Called: Sleepy Hollow Golf Course
9445 Brecksville Rd (44141-2711)
PHONE..................440 526-4285
Fax: 440 526-2298
John Fiander, Manager
EMP: 60
SALES (corp-wide): 57.3MM Privately Held
WEB: www.clemetparks.com
SIC: 7992 Public golf courses
PA: Cleveland Metroparks
4101 Fulton Pkwy
Cleveland OH 44144
216 635-3200

(G-1821)
CLINICAL TECHNOLOGY INC
7005 S Edgerton Rd (44141-4203)
PHONE..................440 526-0160
Fax: 440 526-4139
Dennis Forchione, President
Dennis A Forchione, President
Michelle Grimes, General Mgr
Michael Guzzo, Area Mgr
Dominic Verrilli, Vice Pres
EMP: 40
SQ FT: 11,000
SALES (est): 15.1MM Privately Held
SIC: 5047 Patient monitoring equipment

(G-1822)
CSI MANAGED CARE INC
Also Called: Csi Network Services
6955 Treeline Dr Ste A (44141-3373)
PHONE..................440 717-1700
Ed Rivalsky, CEO
Rob Leonhardt, Manager
Anthony Krajcik, Info Tech Mgr
EMP: 99
SALES (est): 2.4MM Privately Held
SIC: 8059 Nursing & personal care

(G-1823)
ELLISON TECHNOLOGIES INC
6955 Treeline Dr Ste J (44141-3373)
PHONE..................440 546-1920
Tim Kilty, COO
Matt Bujoll, Branch Mgr
Kurt Schaldach, Manager
EMP: 30
SALES (corp-wide): 38.4B Privately Held
WEB: www.ellisonmw.com
SIC: 5084 Machine tools & metalworking machinery
HQ: Ellison Technologies, Inc.
9912 Pioneer Blvd
Santa Fe Springs CA 90670
562 949-8311

(G-1824)
GENERATIONS COFFEE COMPANY LLC
60100 W Snowell (44141)
PHONE..................440 546-0901
Michael Caruso, General Mgr
EMP: 30
SALES (est): 3.1MM
SALES (corp-wide): 77.1MM Publicly Held
WEB: www.coffeeholding.com
SIC: 2095 5149 5499 Roasted coffee; groceries & related products; coffee

PA: Coffee Holding Co., Inc.
3475 Victory Blvd Ste 4
Staten Island NY 10314
718 832-0800

(G-1825)
GLOBAL RISK CONSULTANTS CORP
7000 S Edgerton Rd # 100 (44141-3172)
PHONE..................440 746-8861
Fax: 440 746-8995
Doris Barnhouse, Administration
EMP: 31 Privately Held
WEB: www.globalriskconsultants.com
SIC: 8711 Consulting engineer
HQ: Global Risk Consultants Corp.
100 Walnut Ave Ste 501
Clark NJ 07066
732 680-1370

(G-1826)
HASTINGS WATER WORKS INC (PA)
10331 Brecksville Rd (44141-3335)
PHONE..................440 832-7700
Fax: 440 546-0377
David J Hastings, President
Rick Norris, General Mgr
Brian McEntee, District Mgr
Jerry Rowell, COO
Marianne Jones, Finance
EMP: 35
SQ FT: 17,000
SALES (est): 4.6MM Privately Held
WEB: www.hastingswaterworks.com
SIC: 7389 Swimming pool & hot tub service & maintenance

(G-1827)
HOUSE OF LA ROSE CLEVELAND
6745 Southpointe Pkwy (44141-3267)
PHONE..................440 746-7500
Fax: 440 271-0674
Thomas A La Rose, Ch of Bd
Joseph F La Rose, Vice Ch Bd
James P La Rose, President
Peter C La Rose, Vice Pres
Art Sunday, Sales Mgr
EMP: 210 EST: 1979
SQ FT: 153,000
SALES (est): 105MM Privately Held
WEB: www.la-rose.com
SIC: 5181 Beer & other fermented malt liquors

(G-1828)
HUDEC DENTAL ASSOCIATES INC (PA)
6700 W Snowville Rd (44141-3285)
PHONE..................216 485-5788
Fax: 216 741-3131
John Hudec, Principal
John A Hudec, Principal
Gail Sandish, Administration
EMP: 64
SALES (est): 11MM Privately Held
SIC: 8021 Dental clinic

(G-1829)
JERSEY CENTRAL PWR & LIGHT CO
Also Called: Firstenergy
6896 Miller Rd (44141-3222)
PHONE..................440 546-8609
Dennis Chack, President
Ben Baquero, Project Mgr
Laura Redenshek, Human Res Dir
Craig Hakenson, Manager
Mark Myers, Manager
EMP: 980
SQ FT: 48,531 Publicly Held
WEB: www.jersey-central-power-light.monmouth.n
SIC: 4911 Distribution, electric power
HQ: Jersey Central Power & Light Company
76 S Main St
Akron OH 44308
800 736-3402

(G-1830)
JOHNSON CNTRLS SEC SLTIONS LLC
6650 W Snowville Rd Ste K (44141-4301)
PHONE..................440 262-1084
Fax: 440 838-5595
Mark Altsman, General Mgr
Laura Peffer, Sales Staff
Jay Johnson, Manager
EMP: 65
SQ FT: 4,000 Privately Held
WEB: www.adt.com
SIC: 7382 5063 Burglar alarm maintenance & monitoring; fire alarm maintenance & monitoring; electrical apparatus & equipment
HQ: Johnson Controls Security Solutions Llc
4700 Exchange Ct Ste 300
Boca Raton FL 33431
561 264-2071

(G-1831)
JONES LANG LSALLE AMERICAS INC
Also Called: J.L.L.
9921 Brecksville Rd (44141-3201)
PHONE..................216 447-5276
Ed Prabucki, General Mgr
EMP: 37
SALES (corp-wide): 7.9B Publicly Held
WEB: www.am.joneslanglasalle.com
SIC: 6531 Real estate agents & managers
HQ: Jones Lang Lasalle Americas, Inc.
200 E Randolph St # 4300
Chicago IL 60601
312 782-5800

(G-1832)
LUCE SMITH & SCOTT INC
Also Called: Allstate
6860 W Snwvlle Rd Ste 110 (44141)
PHONE..................440 746-1700
Fax: 440 746-1130
William Killea, CEO
Daniel Skaljac, President
Janice M Dwyer, Vice Pres
Belinda Lipcsik, Vice Pres
Greg Skaljac, Vice Pres
EMP: 28 EST: 1923
SALES: 2.8MM Privately Held
WEB: www.lucesmithscott.com
SIC: 6411 Insurance agents, brokers & service

(G-1833)
MEDIQUANT INC
6900 S Edgerton Rd # 100 (44141-3193)
PHONE..................440 746-2300
Tony Papalera, President
Jennifer Spencer, Manager
EMP: 57
SALES (est): 15.1MM Privately Held
WEB: www.mediquant.com
SIC: 5045 Computer software

(G-1834)
MICHAEL BENZA AND ASSOC INC
6860 W Snowville Rd # 100 (44141-3279)
P.O. Box 469, Richfield (44286-0469)
PHONE..................440 526-4206
Fax: 440 546-2691
Steven Benza, President
Brenda Funk, Corp Secy
Paul Hawkins, Engineer
Jamie Dayton, Office Mgr
EMP: 26
SALES (est): 3.5MM Privately Held
WEB: www.mbenzaengr.com
SIC: 8711 Consulting engineer; civil engineering; pollution control engineering

(G-1835)
NATIONAL STAFFING GROUP LTD
8221 Brecksville Rd # 202 (44141-1390)
P.O. Box 41444 (44141-0444)
PHONE..................440 546-0800
Kim Barnett, President
EMP: 42
SALES (est): 1.8MM Privately Held
WEB: www.nsgl.com
SIC: 7361 Executive placement

(G-1836)
NEOPOST USA INC
6670 W Snowville Rd Ste 2 (44141-4300)
PHONE..................440 526-3196
John Moss, Manager
EMP: 25
SALES (corp-wide): 47.4MM Privately Held
WEB: www.neopostinc.com
SIC: 5084 Meters, consumption registering
HQ: Neopost Usa Inc.
478 Wheelers Farms Rd
Milford CT 06461
203 301-3400

(G-1837)
NGN ELECTRIC CORP
10310 Brecksville Rd (44141-3338)
P.O. Box 1119, Hudson (44236-6319)
PHONE..................330 923-2777
Fax: 330 923-2275
Gene Piscitello, President
Tom Hinkle, CTO
▼EMP: 40
SALES (est): 4.7MM Privately Held
WEB: www.ngnelectric.com
SIC: 1731 General electrical contractor

(G-1838)
NVR INC
6770 W Snowville Rd 100 (44141-3212)
PHONE..................440 584-4250
Fax: 440 979-2001
Michael Gould, President
EMP: 36 Publicly Held
SIC: 1521 New construction, single-family houses
PA: Nvr, Inc.
11700 Plaza America Dr # 500
Reston VA 20190

(G-1839)
PAUL DENNIS
Also Called: Chippewa Place
7005 Stadium Dr Ofc (44141-1843)
PHONE..................440 746-8600
Fax: 440 526-0335
Paul Dennis, Owner
Alison Ciccarello, Office Mgr
Laurie Weiser, Manager
EMP: 30
SQ FT: 28,910
SALES (est): 1.5MM Privately Held
SIC: 8361 6513 Home for the aged; apartment building operators

(G-1840)
PITNEY BOWES INC
6910 Treeline Dr Ste C (44141-3366)
PHONE..................203 426-7025
Brian Philbin, Director
EMP: 75
SALES (corp-wide): 3.5B Publicly Held
SIC: 3579 7359 Postage meters; business machine & electronic equipment rental services
PA: Pitney Bowes Inc.
3001 Summer St Ste 3
Stamford CT 06905
203 356-5000

(G-1841)
PNC BANK NATIONAL ASSOCIATION
National City Bank
6750 Miller Rd (44141-3239)
PHONE..................440 546-6760
Lynne Sheley Baker, Branch Mgr
EMP: 77
SALES (corp-wide): 18B Publicly Held
WEB: www.allegiantbank.com
SIC: 6141 Personal credit institutions
HQ: Pnc Bank, National Association
222 Delaware Ave
Wilmington DE 19801
877 762-2000

(G-1842)
POMEROY IT SOLUTIONS SLS INC
6670 W Snowville Rd Ste 3 (44141-4300)
PHONE..................440 717-1364
Hal Loughry, General Mgr
Bret Durisin, Manager
Susan Summers, Analyst

Brecksville - Cuyahoga County (G-1843)

EMP: 25
SALES (corp-wide): 62.6MM **Privately Held**
WEB: www.pomeroy.com
SIC: 5045 1731 7373 8243 Computers, peripherals & software; computer peripheral equipment; computers; computer installation; voice, data & video wiring contractor; computer integrated systems design; systems software development services; computer systems analysis & design; data processing schools; computer maintenance & repair; computer rental & leasing
HQ: Pomeroy It Solutions Sales Company, Inc.
1020 Petersburg Rd
Hebron KY 41048

(G-1843)
PROMERUS LLC
9921 Brecksville Rd (44141-3201)
PHONE 440 922-0300
Nobuaki Sugimoto, *CEO*
Robert Shick, *President*
Geert Casteleyn, *CFO*
EMP: 42
SQ FT: 40,000
SALES (est): 7.1MM
SALES (corp-wide): 1.7B **Privately Held**
WEB: www.promerus.com
SIC: 8731 Electronic research
HQ: Sumitomo Bakelite North America Holding, Inc.
46820 Magellan Dr Ste C
Novi MI 48377
248 313-7000

(G-1844)
PROVATO LLC
8748 Brecksville Rd # 125 (44141-1988)
PHONE 440 546-0768
Kevin Marquirt, *President*
EMP: 50
SQ FT: 1,400
SALES (est): 1.6MM **Privately Held**
SIC: 8999 Information bureau

(G-1845)
RAMBUS INC
6611 W Snowville Rd (44141-3209)
PHONE 440 397-2549
Becky Saldivar, *Branch Mgr*
Tony Mazzola, *Director*
EMP: 29
SALES (corp-wide): 393.1MM **Publicly Held**
SIC: 8731 Electronic research
PA: Rambus Inc.
1050 Entp Way Ste 700
Sunnyvale CA 94089
408 462-8000

(G-1846)
REALTY ONE INC
8805 Brecksville Rd (44141-1948)
PHONE 440 526-2900
Fax: 440 526-6613
Connie Rockey, *Manager*
EMP: 60
SALES (corp-wide): 67.8MM **Privately Held**
WEB: www.realty-1st.com
SIC: 6531 Real estate brokers & agents
HQ: Realty One, Inc.
800 W Saint Clair Ave
Cleveland OH 44113
216 328-2500

(G-1847)
RICHFIELD FINANCIAL GROUP INC
8223 Brecksville Rd # 201 (44141-1367)
PHONE 440 546-4288
Fax: 440 546-0988
Maura Prentiss, *Administration*
EMP: 30
SALES (est): 3MM **Privately Held**
SIC: 6411 Insurance brokers

(G-1848)
SABER HEALTHCARE GROUP LLC
Also Called: Oaks of Brecksville, The
8757 Brecksville Rd (44141-1919)
PHONE 440 546-0643

Sue Doherty, *Administration*
EMP: 36
SALES (corp-wide): 68.5MM **Privately Held**
SIC: 8051 Skilled nursing care facilities
PA: Saber Healthcare Group, L.L.C.
26691 Richmond Rd Frnt
Bedford OH 44146
216 292-5706

(G-1849)
SCG FIELDS LLC
10303 Brecksville Rd (44141-3335)
PHONE 440 546-1200
Michael Sherman, *CEO*
Joseph Smith, *COO*
Nancy Gammalo, *Controller*
Christopher Franks, *Director*
EMP: 50
SALES (est): 242.1K **Privately Held**
SIC: 1629 Athletic field construction

(G-1850)
SIEMENS INDUSTRY INC
Also Called: Rapistan Systems
6930 Treeline Dr Ste A (44141-3367)
PHONE 440 526-2770
Fax: 440 526-0931
Charles McBride, *Manager*
EMP: 30
SALES (corp-wide): 97.7B **Privately Held**
WEB: www.sea.siemens.com
SIC: 5084 3535 Industrial machinery & equipment; conveyors & conveying equipment
HQ: Siemens Industry, Inc.
100 Technology Dr
Alpharetta GA 30005
770 740-3000

(G-1851)
SOFTWARE ANSWERS INC
6770 W Snowville Rd 200 (44141-3212)
PHONE 440 526-0095
Paul Chaffee, *President*
Scott Miller, *Vice Pres*
Lia Hardy, *QA Dir*
Paul Chassey, *Office Mgr*
Craig Munyon, *Manager*
EMP: 30
SQ FT: 7,700
SALES (est): 3MM **Privately Held**
SIC: 8742 Industry specialist consultants

(G-1852)
SPORTS SURFACES CNSTR LLC
Also Called: Sports Construction Group
10303 Brecksville Rd (44141-3335)
PHONE 440 546-1200
Nancy Gammalo, *Controller*
Steve Hines, *Asst Controller*
Kelly Strine, *Accountant*
Joel Desguin, *Sales Staff*
Keith Froelich, *Sales Associate*
EMP: 25
SALES (est): 6.3MM **Privately Held**
SIC: 1629 Athletic field construction

(G-1853)
TRUE NORTH ENERGY LLC (PA)
10346 Brecksville Rd (44141-3338)
PHONE 877 245-9336
Mark E Lyden, *President*
Joe Sahdala, *District Mgr*
Ryan Howard, *COO*
Mary B Lyden, *Vice Pres*
Keith A McIntyre, *Vice Pres*
EMP: 35
SQ FT: 18,000
SALES (est): 274.9MM **Privately Held**
WEB: www.case.edu
SIC: 5541 5172 Filling stations, gasoline; gasoline; engine fuels & oils; service station supplies, petroleum

Brewster
Stark County

(G-1854)
BREWSTER PARKE INC
Also Called: Brewster Convalescent Center
264 Mohican St Ne (44613-1126)
PHONE 330 767-4179
Fax: 330 767-3907

David E Childs, *President*
Cheryl Childs, *Vice Pres*
Ann Toney, *Persnl Dir*
EMP: 84
SQ FT: 9,000
SALES (est): 6.2MM **Privately Held**
SIC: 8059 8052 8051 Convalescent home; intermediate care facilities; skilled nursing care facilities

(G-1855)
HEALTHSPAN INTEGRATED CARE
Also Called: Kaiser Foundation Health Plan
360 Wabash Ave N (44613-1042)
PHONE 330 767-3436
Charles Cather, *Principal*
EMP: 29
SALES (corp-wide): 4.2B **Privately Held**
SIC: 6324 Hospital & medical service plans
HQ: Healthspan Integrated Care
1001 Lakeside Ave E # 1200
Cleveland OH 44114
216 621-5600

(G-1856)
MIKE MORRIS
Also Called: Five Star Power Clg & Pntg
505 Wabash Ave N (44613-1045)
PHONE 330 767-4122
Fax: 330 767-4331
Mike Morris, *Owner*
EMP: 28
SQ FT: 5,000
SALES (est): 1.4MM **Privately Held**
SIC: 1799 1721 Exterior cleaning, including sandblasting; exterior commercial painting contractor; interior commercial painting contractor; industrial painting

(G-1857)
WHEELING & LAKE ERIE RLWY CO (HQ)
100 1st St Se (44613-1202)
P.O. Box 96 (44613-0096)
PHONE 330 767-3401
Fax: 330 767-3483
Larry R Parsons, *CEO*
William Callison, *President*
Jonathan Chastek, *Exec VP*
James I Northcraft, *Vice Pres*
Mike Mokodean, *Vice Pres*
EMP: 303
SQ FT: 33,000
SALES: 100.6MM
SALES (corp-wide): 103.3MM **Privately Held**
WEB: www.wlerwy.com
SIC: 4011 Railroads, line-haul operating
PA: Wheeling Corporation
100 1st St Se
Brewster OH 44613
330 767-3401

Brice
Franklin County

(G-1858)
K RAY HOLDING CO
Also Called: Ken-Ray Electric
3121 Brice Rd (43109)
PHONE 614 861-4738
Fax: 614 861-4738
Kenneth W Ray, *President*
Janice Ray, *Vice Pres*
EMP: 25
SALES (est): 2MM **Privately Held**
SIC: 1731 General electrical contractor

Bridgeport
Belmont County

(G-1859)
BELMONT CNTY FIRE & SQUAD OFFI
69604 Sunset Hts (43912-1688)
PHONE 740 312-5058
Allan Ketzell III, *President*
Jim Delman, *Treasurer*
EMP: 30

SALES (est): 400.3K **Privately Held**
SIC: 0851 Fire fighting services, forest

(G-1860)
BRIDGEPORT AUTO PARTS INC (PA)
890 National Rd (43912-1444)
P.O. Box 390 (43912-0390)
PHONE 740 635-0441
Fax: 740 635-3486
Tim Conway, *President*
Timothy A Conway, *President*
Daniel Vandi, *Controller*
Timothy Conway Jr, *Administration*
EMP: 35
SQ FT: 19,000
SALES (est): 3.3MM **Privately Held**
SIC: 5013 5531 Automotive supplies & parts; automotive parts

(G-1861)
COMCAST CORPORATION
908 National Rd (43912-1532)
PHONE 740 633-3437
Paul Luicart, *Principal*
EMP: 57
SALES (corp-wide): 84.5B **Publicly Held**
WEB: www.comcast.com
SIC: 4841 Cable television services
PA: Comcast Corporation
1701 Jfk Blvd
Philadelphia PA 19103
215 286-1700

(G-1862)
ERB ELECTRIC CO
500 Hall St Ste 1 (43912-1324)
PHONE 740 633-5055
Fax: 740 633-5127
Tom Knight, *President*
Marianne Knight, *Vice Pres*
John Satkowski, *Foreman/Supr*
Paul Simmons, *Engineer*
Kathy Heil, *Treasurer*
EMP: 200 EST: 1958
SALES (est): 30.9MM **Privately Held**
WEB: www.erbelectric.com
SIC: 1731 General electrical contractor

(G-1863)
HEALTH CARE RTREMENT CORP AMER
Also Called: Heartland - Lansing
300 Commercial Dr (43912)
PHONE 740 635-4600
Jamie Dangelo, *Manager*
EMP: 100
SALES (corp-wide): 3.6B **Publicly Held**
WEB: www.hrc-manorcare.com
SIC: 8051 Skilled nursing care facilities
HQ: Health Care And Retirement Corporation Of America
333 N Summit St Ste 103
Toledo OH 43604
419 252-5500

(G-1864)
LASH PAVING INC
70700 Swingle Rd (43912-8800)
P.O. Box 296, Colerain (43916-0296)
PHONE 740 635-4335
David Lash, *President*
Brian Barrato, *Vice Pres*
Daniel Lash, *Vice Pres*
EMP: 70
SALES (est): 8.4MM **Privately Held**
SIC: 1611 Surfacing & paving

Brilliant
Jefferson County

(G-1865)
AMERICAN ELECTRIC POWER CO INC
306 County Road 7e (43913-1079)
PHONE 740 598-4164
Thomas Marosi, *Plant Mgr*
Jeffrey Gremelspacher, *Chief Engr*
Bill Gilson, *Engineer*
Dwight Pittenger, *Branch Mgr*
EMP: 46
SALES (corp-wide): 15.4B **Publicly Held**
SIC: 4911 Distribution, electric power

GEOGRAPHIC SECTION
Broadview Heights - Cuyahoga County (G-1888)

PA: American Electric Power Company, Inc.
1 Riverside Plz Fl # 1
Columbus OH 43215
614 716-1000

(G-1866)
BUCKEYE POWER INC
Also Called: Cardinal Plant
306 County Road 7e (43913-1079)
PHONE..............................740 598-6534
Doug Shearn, *Manager*
EMP: 300
SALES (corp-wide): 575.9MM **Privately Held**
WEB: www.buckeyepower.com
SIC: 4911 Generation, electric power
PA: Buckeye Power, Inc.
6677 Busch Blvd
Columbus OH 43229
614 781-0573

(G-1867)
CARDINAL OPERATING COMPANY
Also Called: American Electric Power
306 County Road 7e (43913-1079)
PHONE..............................740 598-4164
Douglas Shearn, *Plant Mgr*
Joel Milliken, *Production*
Douglas Shern, *Manager*
Gale Nation, *Manager*
Dwight Pittenger, *Manager*
EMP: 250 **Privately Held**
SIC: 4911 Electric services

(G-1868)
FRALEY & SCHILLING INC
708 Dandy Ln (43913)
PHONE..............................740 598-4118
Fax: 740 598-3923
Jon Patton, *Manager*
EMP: 115
SALES (corp-wide): 86.1MM **Privately Held**
SIC: 4213 4212 Contract haulers; local trucking, without storage
PA: Fraley & Schilling Inc
1920 S State Road 3
Rushville IN 46173
765 932-5977

(G-1869)
TRUGREEN LIMITED PARTNERSHIP
Also Called: Tru Green-Chemlawn
198 Penn St (43913-1232)
P.O. Box 157 (43913)
PHONE..............................740 598-4724
EMP: 30
SALES (corp-wide): 3.3B **Privately Held**
SIC: 0782 Lawn/Garden Services
PA: Trugreen Limited Partnership
860 Ridge Lake Blvd G02
Memphis TN 38138
901 681-1800

(G-1870)
UNITED PARCEL SERVICE INC OH
Also Called: UPS
500 Labelle St (43913-1165)
PHONE..............................740 598-4293
EMP: 158
SALES (corp-wide): 65.8B **Publicly Held**
WEB: www.upsscs.com
SIC: 4215 Parcel delivery, vehicular
HQ: United Parcel Service, Inc. (Oh)
55 Glenlake Pkwy
Atlanta GA 30328
404 828-6000

Bristolville
Trumbull County

(G-1871)
FINLAW CONSTRUCTION INC
5213 State Route 45 (44402-9608)
PHONE..............................330 889-2074
Judy Finlaw, *President*
Scott Finlaw, *Vice Pres*
EMP: 25
SALES (est): 2.9MM **Privately Held**
SIC: 1623 Underground utilities contractor

(G-1872)
K M B INC
Also Called: King Bros Feed & Supply
1306 State Route 88 (44402-8740)
P.O. Box 240 (44402-0240)
PHONE..............................330 889-3451
Fax: 330 889-9608
Marlene King, *President*
Rex King, *Vice Pres*
EMP: 35 **EST:** 1956
SQ FT: 4,200
SALES (est): 6.2MM **Privately Held**
WEB: www.kingbrosracing.com
SIC: 3273 5211 5261 5191 Ready-mixed concrete; lumber & other building materials; fertilizer; feed; concrete products

Broadview Heights
Cuyahoga County

(G-1873)
BUCKEYE DISTRIBUTING INC
215 Ken Mar Indus Pkwy (44147-4606)
PHONE..............................440 526-6668
Fax: 440 526-8234
J Troy Bigham, *Owner*
Jim Gilbride, *Owner*
Terry Bigham, *Principal*
James Gilbride, *Vice Pres*
Scott Wiseman, *Sales Mgr*
▲ **EMP:** 125
SQ FT: 45,000
SALES (est): 1MM **Privately Held**
WEB: www.buckeyedist.com
SIC: 5149 Soft drinks

(G-1874)
CLEVELAND CLINIC FOUNDATION
Also Called: Broadview Heights
2001 E Royalton Rd (44147-2811)
PHONE..............................440 986-4000
Mark Lang, *Manager*
EMP: 2656
SALES (corp-wide): 8B **Privately Held**
SIC: 8062 General medical & surgical hospitals
PA: The Cleveland Clinic Foundation
9500 Euclid Ave
Cleveland OH 44195
216 636-8335

(G-1875)
CLINICL OTCMS MNGMNT SYST LLC
Also Called: Coms Interactive
9200 S Hills Blvd Ste 200 (44147-3520)
PHONE..............................330 650-9900
Edward J Tromczynski, *CEO*
Frederick T Croft, *Ch of Bd*
Tom Mohney, *Vice Pres*
Bill Stuart, *CFO*
Jackie Dreher, *Manager*
EMP: 59
SQ FT: 1,400
SALES (est): 9.5MM **Privately Held**
WEB: www.comsllc.com
SIC: 7372 Business oriented computer software

(G-1876)
CT MEDICAL ELECTRONICS CO
1 Corporation Ctr (44147-3265)
PHONE..............................440 526-3551
Dennis Forchione, *President*
EMP: 40
SALES (est): 3.3MM **Privately Held**
SIC: 5047 Medical & hospital equipment

(G-1877)
DANA LAUREN SALON & SPA
8076 Broadview Rd (44147-1204)
PHONE..............................440 262-1092
Dana Lauren,
EMP: 30
SALES (est): 445.2K **Privately Held**
SIC: 7231 Hairdressers

(G-1878)
DEUTSCHE BANK SECURITIES INC
3152 Oakwood Trl (44147-3918)
PHONE..............................440 237-0188
Charles Dunham, *Branch Mgr*
EMP: 43
SALES (corp-wide): 11.5B **Privately Held**
SIC: 6211 Brokers, security
HQ: Deutsche Bank Securities Inc.
60 Wall St Bsmt 1
New York NY 10005
212 250-2500

(G-1879)
FAMILY HERITG LF INSUR CO AMER (HQ)
6001 E Royalton Rd # 200 (44147-3527)
P.O. Box 470608 (44147-0608)
PHONE..............................440 922-5200
Fax: 440 922-5201
Howard Lewis, *CEO*
Tracey Bell, *President*
Dave Deliz, *President*
Ken Matson, *President*
Dave Erinakes, *Vice Pres*
EMP: 44
SQ FT: 16,000
SALES (est): 53.7MM
SALES (corp-wide): 4.1B **Publicly Held**
SIC: 6411 Insurance agents
PA: Torchmark Corporation
3700 S Stonebridge Dr
Mckinney TX 75070
972 569-4000

(G-1880)
GREAT LAKES ENERGY
332 Clearview Ct (44147-3091)
PHONE..............................440 582-4662
Michael Kennedy, *Principal*
EMP: 50
SALES (est): 3.9MM **Privately Held**
SIC: 4911 Electric services

(G-1881)
HARBORSIDE CLVELAND LTD PARTNR
Also Called: Harborside Healthcarebroadview
2801 E Royalton Rd (44147-2827)
PHONE..............................440 526-4770
Fax: 440 526-0165
George Topalsky, *Director*
Joe Garrett, *Administration*
John Devaul, *Administration*
EMP: 150 **Publicly Held**
SIC: 8051 Convalescent home with continuous nursing care
HQ: Harborside Of Cleveland Limited Partnership
101 Sun Ave Ne
Albuquerque NM

(G-1882)
KONICA MINOLTA BUSINESS SOLUTI
9150 S Hills Blvd Ste 100 (44147-3511)
PHONE..............................440 546-5795
Fax: 216 265-1060
Mark Bares, *Financial Exec*
Brian Whitford, *Sales Staff*
Chris Kaskey, *Manager*
Julian Hill, *Manager*
Mike Gadomski, *Consultant*
EMP: 75
SALES (corp-wide): 8.4B **Privately Held**
WEB: www.konicabt.com
SIC: 5065 Electronic parts & equipment
HQ: Konica Minolta Business Solutions U.S.A., Inc.
100 Williams Dr
Ramsey NJ 07446
201 825-4000

(G-1883)
METROPOLITAN LIFE INSUR CO
Also Called: MetLife
9200 S Hills Blvd Ste 100 (44147-3507)
PHONE..............................440 746-8699
Fax: 440 526-5240
Michael Connole, *Manager*
Ron Olesinski, *Agent*
Joseph Miller, *Director*
EMP: 50
SQ FT: 5,036
SALES (corp-wide): 63.4B **Publicly Held**
SIC: 6411 Insurance agents & brokers
HQ: Metropolitan Life Insurance Company (Inc)
501 Us Highway 22
Bridgewater NJ 08807
212 578-2211

(G-1884)
MUTUAL SHAREHOLDER SVCS LLC
8000 Town Centre Dr # 400 (44147-4030)
PHONE..............................440 922-0067
Fax: 440 526-4446
Dave Kocurkovic, *Opers Staff*
Tanya Vegera, *Accountant*
Greg Getts,
EMP: 27
SQ FT: 7,000
SALES (est): 6.1MM **Privately Held**
WEB: www.mutualss.com
SIC: 6282 8721 Manager of mutual funds, contract or fee basis; accounting services, except auditing

(G-1885)
NORTHAST OHIO MED RSERVE CORPS
3612 Ridge Park Dr (44147-2042)
P.O. Box 33524, Cleveland (44133-0524)
PHONE..............................216 789-6653
Thomas J Powell, *President*
EMP: 50
SALES (est): 931.6K **Privately Held**
WEB: www.neomrc.org
SIC: 8099 Medical services organization

(G-1886)
OHIO MACHINERY CO (PA)
Also Called: Caterpillar Authorized Dealer
3993 E Royalton Rd (44147-2898)
PHONE..............................440 526-6200
Fax: 440 526-9513
Ken Taylor, *President*
Janie Hovan, *Division Mgr*
Gabe Hoffa, *General Mgr*
Klaus Dobrowa, *Managing Dir*
Eric W Emch, *Vice Pres*
◆ **EMP:** 160
SQ FT: 92,000
SALES (est): 222.7MM **Privately Held**
WEB: www.enginesnow.com
SIC: 7513 6159 7699 5082 Truck rental, without drivers; machinery & equipment finance leasing; aircraft & heavy equipment repair services; construction equipment repair; general construction machinery & equipment; mining machinery & equipment, except petroleum; heavy construction equipment rental

(G-1887)
OHIO MACHINERY CO
Also Called: Caterpillar
900 Ken Mar Indus Pkwy (44147-2992)
PHONE..............................440 526-0520
Fax: 440 526-4609
Jeff Dress, *Accounts Mgr*
Mike Graham, *Sales Staff*
Chuck Vorhees, *Sales Staff*
Greg Deanna, *Manager*
Dan Bonnes, *Manager*
EMP: 80
SALES (corp-wide): 222.7MM **Privately Held**
WEB: www.enginesnow.com
SIC: 5082 General construction machinery & equipment
PA: Ohio Machinery Co.
3993 E Royalton Rd
Broadview Heights OH 44147
440 526-6200

(G-1888)
OMNI FASTENERS INC
909 Towpath Trl (44147-3676)
PHONE..............................440 838-1800
Fax: 440 524-0544
Ron Kuczmarski, *President*
Lynn Kuczmarski, *Vice Pres*
Jon Goodman, *Purchasing*
Roman Didytch, *Sales Staff*
Kathy Gavo, *Manager*
▲ **EMP:** 25
SQ FT: 23,000

SALES (est): 8.2MM **Privately Held**
WEB: www.omnifasteners.com
SIC: 5072 Nuts (hardware); bolts; screws

(G-1889)
PEAK PERFORMANCE CENTER INC
1 Eagle Valley Ct (44147-2982)
PHONE..................................440 838-5600
Fax: 440 838-1884
John Collis PHD, *President*
Roy Napoli, *Director*
EMP: 50
SQ FT: 45,000
SALES (est): 1.6MM **Privately Held**
WEB: www.peakperformancecenter.com
SIC: 8093 Rehabilitation center, outpatient treatment

(G-1890)
RAM CONSTRUCTION SERVICES
100 Corporation Ctr # 4 (44147-3265)
PHONE..................................440 740-0100
Robert Mazur, *President*
Eric Blaine, *Foreman/Supr*
Katy Lansteary, *Accountant*
Kevin Houle, *Finance*
Larry Roberts, *Director*
EMP: 50
SALES (est): 2MM
SALES (corp-wide): 107.9MM **Privately Held**
SIC: 1799 Waterproofing
PA: Ram Construction Services Of Michigan, Inc.
13800 Eckles Rd
Livonia MI 48150
734 464-3800

(G-1891)
SEASON CONTRACTORS INC
55 Eagle Valley Ct (44147-2982)
PHONE..................................440 717-0188
Fax: 440 717-0189
Don Cacciacarne, *President*
Sharon Vasickanin, *IT/INT Sup*
▲ EMP: 30
SQ FT: 8,000
SALES (est): 3.7MM **Privately Held**
WEB: www.bxohio.net
SIC: 1521 1542 1751 New construction, single-family houses; commercial & office building, new construction; framing contractor

(G-1892)
T M C SYSTEMS LLC
7655 Town Centre Dr (44147-4032)
PHONE..................................440 740-1234
Martin Camloh,
Theresa Camloh,
EMP: 28
SALES (est): 869.5K **Privately Held**
SIC: 8351 Preschool center

(G-1893)
THYSSENKRUPP ELEVATOR CORP
9200 Market Pl (44147-2863)
PHONE..................................440 717-0080
Lou Cozza, *Sales Staff*
Phil Resparc, *Office Mgr*
EMP: 40
SALES (corp-wide): 48.7B **Privately Held**
WEB: www.tyssenkrupp.com
SIC: 5084 7699 Elevators; elevators: inspection, service & repair
HQ: Thyssenkrupp Elevator Corporation
11605 Haynes Bridge Rd # 650
Alpharetta GA 30009
678 319-3240

(G-1894)
UNITED FD & COML WKRS INTL UN
9199 Market Pl (44147-2869)
PHONE..................................216 241-2828
Tom Robertson, *Principal*
Fatima Azeez, *Executive Asst*
Deidra Lawson, *Admin Sec*
EMP: 50
SALES (corp-wide): 238MM **Privately Held**
SIC: 8631 Labor union

PA: United Food And Commercial Workers International Union
1775 K St Nw
Washington DC 20006
202 223-3111

(G-1895)
WARWICK COMMUNICATIONS INC (PA)
Also Called: C C I
405 Ken Mar Indus Pkwy (44147-4614)
PHONE..................................216 787-0300
Fax: 216 263-1717
Steve Leopold, *CEO*
Laura Green, *Sales Pres*
Heidi Murphy, *Vice Pres*
Tonia Earley, *Project Mgr*
Samuel Kalb, *Accounting Mgr*
EMP: 30
SQ FT: 25,000
SALES (est): 8.1MM **Privately Held**
WEB: www.warwickinc.com
SIC: 7359 5065 Electronic equipment rental, except computers; telephone equipment

Brookfield
Trumbull County

(G-1896)
A TARA TIFFANYS PROPERTY
Also Called: Tiffany's Banquet Center
601 Bedford Rd Se (44403-9756)
PHONE..................................330 448-0778
Fax: 330 448-0775
James Winner, *Owner*
Sandy Superak, *Manager*
EMP: 50
SQ FT: 20,000
SALES (est): 1.3MM **Privately Held**
WEB: www.tiffanysbanquet.com
SIC: 7299 5812 Banquet hall facilities; caterers

(G-1897)
K-Y RESIDENTIAL COML INDUS DEV
Also Called: Kirila Realty
505 Bedford Rd Se (44403-9750)
P.O. Box 179 (44403-0179)
PHONE..................................330 448-4055
Ronald Kirila, *President*
David Pringle, *Executive*
EMP: 75
SQ FT: 40,000
SALES (est): 5.8MM **Privately Held**
SIC: 1542 1522 Shopping center construction; apartment building construction

(G-1898)
KIRILA CONTRACTORS INC
505 Bedford Rd Se (44403-9750)
P.O. Box 179 (44403-0179)
PHONE..................................330 448-4055
Fax: 330 448-4054
Ronald Kirila Jr, *President*
Paul Kirila, *Vice Pres*
Robert Kirila, *Vice Pres*
William Kirila Jr, *Vice Pres*
EMP: 70
SQ FT: 50,000
SALES: 19.7MM **Privately Held**
WEB: www.kirila.com
SIC: 1611 1542 Highway & street paving contractor; commercial & office building contractors

(G-1899)
KIRILA FIRE TRNING FCLTIES INC
509 Bedford Rd Se (44403-9750)
P.O. Box 2 (44403-0002)
PHONE..................................724 854-5207
Jerry Kirila, *President*
Theresa Delaney, *Controller*
EMP: 25
SQ FT: 30,000
SALES (est): 6.4MM **Privately Held**
SIC: 8748 Safety training service

(G-1900)
NICK STRIMBU INC (PA)
3500 Parkway Dr (44403-9755)
P.O. Box 268 (44403-0268)
PHONE..................................330 448-4046
Fax: 330 448-1672
William Strimbu, *President*
Nicholas Strimbu III, *Exec VP*
Elizabeth Murray, *Senior VP*
Tom Nesbit, *Vice Pres*
Cory Knowlton, *Opers Staff*
EMP: 72
SQ FT: 200,000
SALES (est): 23.9MM **Privately Held**
WEB: www.nickstrimbu.com
SIC: 4213 Trucking, except local

(G-1901)
T R L INC
3500 Parkway Dr (44403-9755)
P.O. Box 268 (44403-0268)
PHONE..................................330 448-4071
William Strimbu, *President*
EMP: 150
SQ FT: 200,000
SALES (est): 11.1MM **Privately Held**
WEB: www.trl.com
SIC: 4212 Truck rental with drivers

(G-1902)
UNITED STEEL SERVICE LLC (PA)
Also Called: Uniserv
4500 Parkway Dr (44403-8720)
P.O. Box 149 (44403-0149)
PHONE..................................330 448-4057
Fax: 330 448-1304
Steven A Friedman, *CEO*
Mark Jones, *Safety Mgr*
Joel Miller, *Treasurer*
Gary Komsa, *Controller*
Kelly Williams, *Credit Mgr*
▲ EMP: 120
SQ FT: 50,000
SALES (est): 26.8MM **Privately Held**
WEB: www.uniserv.com
SIC: 5051 Steel

(G-1903)
YANKEE RUN GOLF COURSE
7610 Warren Sharon Rd (44403-9626)
PHONE..................................330 448-8096
Fax: 330 448-0554
Paul McMullen, *President*
William Gary McMullen, *Treasurer*
EMP: 53 EST: 1931
SALES (est): 1.8MM **Privately Held**
WEB: www.yankeerun.com
SIC: 7992 5941 Public golf courses; sporting goods & bicycle shops

Brooklyn
Cuyahoga County

(G-1904)
AMC ENTERTAINMENT INC
4788 Ridge Rd (44144-3327)
PHONE..................................216 749-0260
Paul Gellott, *Branch Mgr*
EMP: 27 **Publicly Held**
WEB: www.amctheatres.com
SIC: 7832 Motion picture theaters, except drive-in
HQ: Amc Entertainment Inc.
11500 Ash St
Leawood KS 66211
913 213-2000

(G-1905)
CRESTVIEW PARTNERS II GP LP
4900 Tiedeman Rd Fl 4 (44144-2338)
PHONE..................................216 898-2400
David C Brown, *Ch of Bd*
EMP: 276
SALES (est): 6.3MM **Privately Held**
SIC: 6282 Investment advisory service

(G-1906)
FERROUS METAL TRANSFER
11103 Memphis Ave (44144-2055)
PHONE..................................216 671-8500
Fax: 216 883-5225

Eduardo Gonzalez, *President*
Reed McGivney, *Exec VP*
Anthony Potelicki, *Vice Pres*
Jim Stratton, *Vice Pres*
David Hill, *Treasurer*
EMP: 36
SQ FT: 1,000
SALES (est): 3.1MM **Privately Held**
SIC: 4212 4213 1541 1611 Lumber & timber trucking; steel hauling, local; heavy hauling; steel building construction; general contractor, highway & street construction

(G-1907)
VICTORY CAPITAL MANAGEMENT INC (HQ)
Also Called: Cemp
4900 Tiedeman Rd Fl 4 (44144-2338)
PHONE..................................216 898-2400
David Brown, *CEO*
Kelly S Cliff, *President*
Kelly Cliff, *President*
Mannik S Dhillon, *President*
Jason Dahl, *Managing Dir*
EMP: 219
SALES (est): 297.8MM **Publicly Held**
SIC: 6282 Investment advice
PA: Victory Capital Holdings, Inc.
4900 Tiedeman Rd Fl 4
Brooklyn OH 44144
216 898-2400

Brooklyn Heights
Cuyahoga County

(G-1908)
ABC PIPING CO
1277 E Schaaf Rd Ste 5 (44131-1336)
PHONE..................................216 398-4000
Fax: 216 398-0507
Aldo Campellone, *President*
Lisa Backo, *General Mgr*
Robert Campellone, *Vice Pres*
John Frabotta, *Sales Executive*
Ramona Vanni, *Manager*
EMP: 34
SQ FT: 15,000
SALES (est): 13.2MM **Privately Held**
WEB: www.abcpipingco.com
SIC: 1623 1711 Pipeline construction; plumbing contractors

(G-1909)
ADELMOS ELECTRIC SEWER CLG CO
4917 Van Epps Rd (44131-1017)
PHONE..................................216 641-2301
Joseph Di Franco, *President*
EMP: 35
SALES (est): 2.5MM **Privately Held**
SIC: 7699 1711 1799 Sewer cleaning & rodding; plumbing contractors; waterproofing

(G-1910)
AIR SYSTEMS OF OHIO INC (PA)
4760 Van Epps Rd (44131-1014)
PHONE..................................216 741-1700
Vince Lisi, *President*
Bob Lisi, *Treasurer*
EMP: 26
SQ FT: 10,000
SALES (est): 4.3MM **Privately Held**
SIC: 5084 5075 Compressors, except air conditioning; compressors, air conditioning

(G-1911)
BRILLIANT ELECTRIC SIGN CO LTD
4811 Van Epps Rd (44131-1082)
PHONE..................................216 741-3800
Fax: 216 741-3800
Rob Kraus, *Plant Mgr*
Patty Molnar, *Project Mgr*
Skip Huber, *Foreman/Supr*
Lee Rodenfels, *Accounts Exec*
John Walsh, *Sales Staff*
EMP: 55
SQ FT: 55,000

GEOGRAPHIC SECTION

Brooklyn Heights - Cuyahoga County (G-1933)

SALES (est): 7.6MM **Privately Held**
WEB: www.brilliantsign.com
SIC: 3993 1799 Electric signs; sign installation & maintenance

(G-1912)
CI DISPOSITION CO
1000 Valley Belt Rd (44131-1433)
PHONE..................................216 587-5200
Fax: 216 587-5210
Richard N Bean, *Senior VP*
Gary Tarnowski, *Vice Pres*
Jeffrey Bahner, *Vice Pres*
Eric Lautzenheizer, *VP Sales*
Victor W Seifried, *Adv Mgr*
EMP: 38
SQ FT: 56,000
SALES (est): 8MM **Privately Held**
WEB: www.comptrolinc.com
SIC: 3699 5085 Linear accelerators; industrial supplies

(G-1913)
CLEVELAND CONCRETE CNSTR INC (PA)
Also Called: Cleveland Cement Contractors
4823 Van Epps Rd (44131-1015)
PHONE..................................216 741-3954
Fax: 216 741-9278
Ronald Simonetti, *CEO*
Michael H Simonetti, *President*
Tim Moennich, *Business Mgr*
Steven Murphy, *Vice Pres*
Jim Simonetti, *Vice Pres*
EMP: 100 **EST:** 1944
SQ FT: 10,000
SALES (est): 22.7MM **Privately Held**
WEB: www.clevelandcement.com
SIC: 1771 Foundation & footing contractor

(G-1914)
DEDICATED TRANSPORT LLC (HQ)
700 W Resource Dr (44131-1836)
PHONE..................................216 641-2500
Fax: 216 641-2525
Tom McDermott, *President*
David Molzan, *Opers Mgr*
Joel Niewald, *Opers Mgr*
F Fred Price, *CFO*
Franklin Price, *CFO*
EMP: 120
SQ FT: 6,000
SALES (est): 22.3MM **Privately Held**
WEB: www.dedicatedtransport.com
SIC: 4212 4213 Local trucking, without storage; contract haulers

(G-1915)
ELECTRICAL APPL REPR SVC INC
5805 Valley Belt Rd (44131-1423)
PHONE..................................216 459-8700
Fax: 216 459-8707
Tom Roberts, *President*
Kenneth Roberts, *Treasurer*
Gloria Crist, *Admin Sec*
EMP: 26
SQ FT: 12,500
SALES (est): 3.1MM **Privately Held**
WEB: www.electapplrep.com
SIC: 7629 7623 Electrical equipment repair services; refrigeration service & repair

(G-1916)
FLAVORFRESH DISPENSERS INC
4705 Van Epps Rd (44131-1013)
PHONE..................................216 641-0200
Stanley Klein, *President*
Michael O'Malley, *Corp Secy*
EMP: 50
SALES (est): 3.2MM **Privately Held**
SIC: 5149 Beverage concentrates; juices; soft drinks; water, distilled

(G-1917)
JANTECH BUILDING SERVICES INC
4963 Schaaf Ln (44131-1034)
PHONE..................................216 661-6102
Fax: 216 739-2219
William Rosby, *President*
Jeff Thayer, *Vice Pres*
Mike Nichols, *QA Dir*
EMP: 200
SQ FT: 3,000
SALES (est): 6.5MM **Privately Held**
WEB: www.jantechinc.com
SIC: 7349 Janitorial service, contract basis

(G-1918)
KAISER FOUNDATION HOSPITALS
Also Called: Bedford Medical Offices
5400 Lancaster Dr (44131-1832)
PHONE..................................216 524-7377
Fax: 440 786-3841
EMP: 593
SALES (corp-wide): 82.6B **Privately Held**
SIC: 8011 Offices & clinics of medical doctors
HQ: Kaiser Foundation Hospitals Inc
  1 Kaiser Plz
  Oakland CA 94612
  510 271-6611

(G-1919)
KAISER FOUNDATION HOSPITALS
Also Called: Parma Medical Center
5400 Lancaster Dr (44131-1832)
PHONE..................................800 524-7377
Fax: 216 265-4385
EMP: 593
SALES (corp-wide): 82.6B **Privately Held**
SIC: 8011 Medical centers
HQ: Kaiser Foundation Hospitals Inc
  1 Kaiser Plz
  Oakland CA 94612
  510 271-6611

(G-1920)
MULTI FLOW TRANSPORT INC
4705 Van Epps Rd (44131-1013)
PHONE..................................216 641-0200
Stanley Klein, *President*
EMP: 50
SALES (est): 2.1MM **Privately Held**
WEB: www.mftransport.net
SIC: 4789 Cargo loading & unloading services

(G-1921)
MULTI-FLOW DISPENSERS OHIO INC (PA)
4705 Van Epps Rd (44131-1013)
PHONE..................................216 641-0200
Stanley Klein, *President*
Bill Fazzone, *Vice Pres*
Tim Baird, *Finance Mgr*
Michelle Frankiewicz, *Technology*
EMP: 100
SQ FT: 17,000
SALES (est): 46.8MM **Privately Held**
SIC: 5145 7359 Syrups, fountain; vending machine rental

(G-1922)
OHIO DESK CO
4851 Van Epps Rd Ste B (44131-1052)
PHONE..................................216 623-0600
Fax: 216 623-0213
Ralph Gervasi, *Manager*
Randy Spence, *Consultant*
EMP: 45
SALES (corp-wide): 39.6MM **Privately Held**
WEB: www.ohiodesk.com
SIC: 4225 General warehousing & storage
PA: The Ohio Desk Company
  1122 Prospect Ave E
  Cleveland OH 44115
  216 623-0600

(G-1923)
PEN BRANDS LLC (HQ)
220 Eastview Dr Ste 102 (44131-1040)
PHONE..................................216 447-1199
Fax: 216 447-1137
Scott Rickert, *CEO*
Anne Marie Thomas, *President*
Bruce Vereecken, *President*
Krish RAO, *Vice Pres*
Bruce Bereeckes, *CFO*
EMP: 42
SQ FT: 19,200
SALES (est): 1.8MM
SALES (corp-wide): 8.1MM **Publicly Held**
WEB: www.nanofilm.cc
SIC: 8731 5995 Commercial physical research; biological research; chemical laboratory, except testing; optical goods stores
PA: Pen Inc.
  701 Brickell Ave Ste 1550
  Miami FL 33131
  844 273-6462

(G-1924)
RENTOKIL NORTH AMERICA INC
1240 Valley Belt Rd (44131-1437)
PHONE..................................216 328-0700
Fax: 216 321-3374
J Ehrlich, *Principal*
EMP: 26
SALES (corp-wide): 2.6B **Privately Held**
SIC: 7342 Pest control in structures
HQ: Rentokil North America, Inc.
  1125 Berkshire Blvd # 150
  Wyomissing PA 19610
  610 372-9700

(G-1925)
RENTOKIL NORTH AMERICA INC
Also Called: Ambius
1240 Valley Belt Rd (44131-1437)
PHONE..................................216 739-0200
Connie Brock, *Branch Mgr*
EMP: 33
SALES (corp-wide): 2.6B **Privately Held**
SIC: 5193 Plants, potted
HQ: Rentokil North America, Inc.
  1125 Berkshire Blvd # 150
  Wyomissing PA 19610
  610 372-9700

(G-1926)
SOLAR TESTING LABORATORIES INC (PA)
1125 Valley Belt Rd (44131-1434)
PHONE..................................216 741-7007
Fax: 216 741-7011
George J Ata, *President*
Anthony Kichurchak, *Exec VP*
Edward A Zielinski, *Exec VP*
Michael Kichurchak, *Vice Pres*
Mark Recktenwald, *Vice Pres*
EMP: 135
SQ FT: 20,000
SALES (est): 11.6MM **Privately Held**
WEB: www.solartestinglabs.com
SIC: 8748 Testing services

(G-1927)
SPECIALTY EQUIPMENT SALES CO
Also Called: Sesco
5705 Valley Belt Rd (44131-1421)
PHONE..................................216 351-2559
Fax: 216 898-9999
Edward Ahern, *President*
Scott Reitano, *President*
Steve Wright, *President*
Karen Ksiezyk, *Regional Mgr*
Kevin Leonard, *Regional Mgr*
▲ **EMP:** 26
SQ FT: 15,000
SALES (est): 10.2MM **Privately Held**
SIC: 5046 Restaurant equipment & supplies

(G-1928)
TOP DAWG GROUP LLC
220 Eastview Dr Ste 103 (44131-1040)
PHONE..................................216 398-1066
Fax: 216 351-3425
George A Sagaris, *President*
Antoinette Koleno, *Vice Pres*
Tony Koleno, *Vice Pres*
Anthony Sagaris, *Vice Pres*
Patrick McCabe, *Opers Mgr*
EMP: 25
SQ FT: 12,000
SALES (est): 4.9MM **Privately Held**
WEB: www.topdawgdelivery.com
SIC: 4212 4225 Delivery service, vehicular; general warehousing & storage

(G-1929)
TOWLIFT INC (PA)
1395 Valley Belt Rd (44131-1474)
PHONE..................................216 749-6800
Fax: 216 749-0873
David H Cannon, *President*
David Bongorno, *Vice Pres*
Len Tober, *Vice Pres*
Brian Tighe, *Parts Mgr*
Bill McDowell, *Engineer*
▲ **EMP:** 121
SQ FT: 28,000
SALES (est): 106.6MM **Privately Held**
WEB: www.towlift.com/about_towlift.html
SIC: 5084 7699 7359 Materials handling machinery; industrial machine parts; industrial truck repair; equipment rental & leasing

(G-1930)
UPTIME CORPORATION
4820 Van Epps Rd (44131-1016)
PHONE..................................216 661-1655
Fax: 216 661-9443
Jay Ross, *President*
Steve Haic, *Sales Mgr*
EMP: 30
SQ FT: 25,000
SALES (est): 1.7MM
SALES (corp-wide): 12MM **Privately Held**
SIC: 7378 Computer maintenance & repair
PA: Ultimate Technology Corporation
  100 Rawson Rd Ste 210
  Victor NY 14564
  585 924-9500

(G-1931)
VIRGINIA TILE COMPANY
4749 Spring Rd (44131-1025)
PHONE..................................216 741-8400
Jeff Dudzik, *Branch Mgr*
EMP: 29
SALES (corp-wide): 117.8MM **Privately Held**
SIC: 1743 Tile installation, ceramic
PA: Virginia Tile Company
  28320 Plymouth Rd
  Livonia MI 48150
  248 476-7850

(G-1932)
VISTA COLOR IMAGING INC
4770 Van Epps Rd Ste 1 (44131-1058)
PHONE..................................216 651-2830
Fax: 216 651-5004
Paul E Gallo, *CEO*
Kevin Vesely, *President*
Herb Byers, *Vice Pres*
Joanne Mociolek, *Vice Pres*
Sal Cribari, *Accounts Mgr*
EMP: 25 **EST:** 1970
SALES (est): 3.7MM **Privately Held**
WEB: www.vistacolorlab.com
SIC: 7384 Photograph developing & retouching; photograph enlarging; photographic services

(G-1933)
WELTMAN WEINBERG & REIS CO LPA
965 Keynote Cir (44131-1829)
PHONE..................................216 739-5100
Fax: 216 739-5072
Alan Weinberg, *Managing Prtnr*
Robert B Weltman, *Senior Partner*
Shawna Gentile, *Plant Mgr*
Todd Herrick, *Project Mgr*
Richard Humrick, *Opers Mgr*
EMP: 240
SALES (est): 35.5MM
SALES (corp-wide): 98.4MM **Privately Held**
SIC: 8111 General practice law office
PA: Weltman, Weinberg & Reis Co., L.P.A.
  323 W Lkeside Ave Ste 200
  Cleveland OH 44113
  216 685-1000

Brookpark
Cuyahoga County

(G-1934)
16644 SNOW RD LLC
Also Called: Howard Johnson
16644 Snow Rd (44142-2767)
PHONE..................................216 676-5200
Fax: 216 676-6044
Praveeen Auror,
EMP: 28
SALES (est): 2.3MM **Privately Held**
SIC: 7011 Hotels & motels

(G-1935)
AM INDUSTRIAL GROUP LLC (PA)
16000 Commerce Park Dr (44142-2023)
PHONE..................................216 433-7171
Reginald Wyman, *Owner*
Luke Wootten, *Opers Mgr*
Curtis Wyman, *Sales Staff*
Robert Wootten, *Marketing Staff*
▲ EMP: 40
SQ FT: 5,000
SALES (est): 23.6MM **Privately Held**
WEB: www.amindustrial.com
SIC: 5084 3541 1799 Machine tools & accessories; sawing & cutoff machines (metalworking machinery); rigging & scaffolding

(G-1936)
AVALON PRECISION CAST CO LLC
Also Called: Avalon Precision Metalsmiths
15583 Brookpark Rd (44142-1618)
PHONE..................................216 362-4100
Fax: 216 362-4108
David Palivec, *President*
Norm Hammerer, *VP Sales*
Lindsey Krauth, *Senior Mgr*
EMP: 238 EST: 2012
SALES (est): 91.8MM
SALES (corp-wide): 51.3MM **Privately Held**
SIC: 5051 Steel
PA: Xapc, Co.
   15583 Brookpark Rd
   Cleveland OH 44142
   216 362-4100

(G-1937)
CAR PARTS WAREHOUSE INC (PA)
Also Called: C P W
5200 W 130th St (44142-1804)
PHONE..................................216 281-4500
Fax: 216 676-5516
Tony Difiore, *President*
Carmelina Di Fiore, *Corp Secy*
Don Ujccu, *Manager*
▲ EMP: 30
SQ FT: 70,000
SALES (est): 91.4MM **Privately Held**
WEB: www.carpartswarehouse.com
SIC: 5013 5531 Automotive supplies; automotive parts

(G-1938)
CEC COMBUSTION SAFETY LLC (DH)
2100 Apollo Dr (44142-4103)
PHONE..................................216 749-2992
Fax: 216 398-8403
Tim Romance, *Project Engr*
Karen Brown, *Financial Exec*
EMP: 43
SQ FT: 25,000
SALES: 12MM
SALES (corp-wide): 40.5B **Publicly Held**
WEB: www.cec-consultants.com
SIC: 8711 7389 Consulting engineer; mechanical engineering; industrial & commercial equipment inspection service
HQ: Eclipse, Inc.
   1665 Elmwood Rd
   Rockford IL 61103
   815 877-3031

(G-1939)
CHU AIRPORT INN INC
Also Called: Quality Inn
16161 Brookpark Rd (44142-1624)
PHONE..................................216 267-5100
Fax: 216 267-2428
Sangiv Bansal, *President*
EMP: 25
SQ FT: 33,000
SALES (est): 1.1MM
SALES (corp-wide): 1.7MM **Privately Held**
SIC: 7011 Hotels & motels
PA: Chu Management Co Inc
   2875 Medina Rd
   Medina OH 44256
   330 725-4571

(G-1940)
CLP TOWNE INC
Also Called: Towne Air Freight
5160 W 161st St (44142-1603)
PHONE..................................440 234-3324
Fax: 440 234-2281
Jay Searls, *Manager*
EMP: 50
SALES (corp-wide): 1.1B **Publicly Held**
WEB: www.towneair.com
SIC: 4513 4215 4213 4212 Package delivery, private air; courier services, except by air; trucking, except local; local trucking, without storage
HQ: Clp Towne Inc.
   24805 Us Highway 20
   South Bend IN 46628
   574 233-3183

(G-1941)
CREDIT FIRST NA
Also Called: AMTS
6275 Eastland Rd (44142-1399)
PHONE..................................216 362-5000
Alfred Policy, *CEO*
Alan Meier, *CFO*
Donald Maier, *Finance*
Matt Kurilec, *Marketing Mgr*
Alex Scutea, *Technology*
EMP: 199
SQ FT: 25,000
SALES: 44.2MM
SALES (corp-wide): 32.5B **Privately Held**
WEB: www.bfis.com
SIC: 6021 National commercial banks
HQ: Bridgestone Retail Operations, Llc
   333 E Lake St Ste 300
   Bloomingdale IL 60108
   630 259-9000

(G-1942)
CUSA LL INC
Also Called: A Coach USA Company
13315 Brookpark Rd (44142-1822)
P.O. Box 81172, Cleveland (44181-0172)
PHONE..................................216 267-8810
Tom Goebel, *President*
Mike Goebel, *Corp Secy*
Jack Goebel, *Vice Pres*
EMP: 200
SQ FT: 48,000
SALES (est): 372.7K **Privately Held**
WEB: www.lakefrontlines.com
SIC: 4119 4142 4141 Local passenger transportation; bus charter service, except local; local bus charter service

(G-1943)
DISTRIBUTION DATA INCORPORATED (PA)
Also Called: Ddi
16101 Snow Rd Ste 200 (44142-2817)
P.O. Box 818019, Cleveland (44181-8019)
PHONE..................................216 362-3009
Fax: 216 362-3043
Robert W Hartig, *President*
Charles C Deems, *Exec VP*
Lynn M Hartig, *Vice Pres*
Debbie Zillich, *Vice Pres*
Randy Davis, *Manager*
EMP: 38
SQ FT: 34,000
SALES (est): 66.2MM **Privately Held**
WEB: www.ddiservices.com
SIC: 5199 7371 8742 4731 Art goods & supplies; custom computer programming services; transportation consultant; freight forwarding; management services

(G-1944)
EDUCATION ALTERNATIVES (PA)
5445 Smith Rd (44142-2026)
PHONE..................................216 332-9360
Gerald Swartz, *CEO*
Wil Soto, *Business Mgr*
Robyn Arbogast, *Exec VP*
Sandra Lymon, *Transptn Dir*
Mara Kampe, *Opers Mgr*
EMP: 87
SALES: 9.1MM **Privately Held**
SIC: 8211 8093 Private special education school; rehabilitation center, outpatient treatment

(G-1945)
FOSBEL INC (HQ)
Also Called: Cetek
20600 Sheldon Rd (44142-1319)
PHONE..................................216 362-3900
Fax: 216 362-3901
Derek Scott, *President*
Sarah Burton, *CFO*
Kathlene Stevens, *CFO*
June Toddy, *CFO*
▲ EMP: 120
SALES (est): 27MM **Privately Held**
SIC: 7629 7692 Electrical repair shops; welding repair
PA: Fosbel Holding, Inc.
   20600 Sheldon Rd
   Cleveland OH 44142
   216 362-3900

(G-1946)
HOPKIN ARPRT LMSINE SHTTLE SVC
Also Called: Hopkin S Airport Limosine Svc
1315 Brookpark Rd (44142)
PHONE..................................216 267-8282
Fax: 216 362-4934
Mary Goebel, *President*
EMP: 30
SALES (est): 418.6K **Privately Held**
SIC: 4119 Limousine rental, with driver

(G-1947)
J & R ASSOCIATES
Also Called: Windsor Construction
14803 Holland Rd (44142-3065)
PHONE..................................440 250-4080
John Coury Sr, *President*
EMP: 1000
SALES (est): 53.3MM **Privately Held**
SIC: 1542 8361 6514 Institutional building construction; home for the aged; dwelling operators, except apartments

(G-1948)
K-M-S INDUSTRIES INC
Also Called: K.M.S.
6519 Eastland Rd Ste 1 (44142-1347)
PHONE..................................440 243-6680
Fax: 440 243-5667
Gerald Korman, *President*
Richard Malone Jr, *Vice Pres*
Diane Malone, *Treasurer*
Kay Teresa, *Controller*
Kay Bailey, *Manager*
EMP: 30
SQ FT: 25,000
SALES (est): 5.6MM **Privately Held**
SIC: 3599 5531 7692 Machine shop, jobbing & repair; automotive parts; automotive accessories; welding repair

(G-1949)
LAKEFRONT LINES INC (DH)
13315 Brookpark Rd (44142-1822)
P.O. Box 81172, Cleveland (44181-0172)
PHONE..................................216 267-8810
Fax: 216 267-8264
Chris Goebel, *CEO*
Christopher Goebel, *General Mgr*
Tom Goebel, *General Mgr*
Sam Rodriguez, *Maintenance Dir*
Barb Ruess, *Accountant*
EMP: 175
SQ FT: 48,000
SALES (est): 31.7MM
SALES (corp-wide): 4.9B **Privately Held**
SIC: 4119 4142 4141 Local passenger transportation; bus charter service, except local; local bus charter service

(G-1950)
LAKEWOOD CHRYSLER-PLYMOUTH
Also Called: Spitzer Lakewood
13001 Brookpark Rd (44142-1819)
PHONE..................................216 521-1000
Fax: 216 521-7650
Allan Spitzer, *President*
William Burke, *Vice Pres*
EMP: 30
SQ FT: 30,000
SALES (est): 7.2MM **Privately Held**
SIC: 5511 7538 7515 Automobiles, new & used; general automotive repair shops; passenger car leasing

(G-1951)
MCPC INC (PA)
Also Called: McPc Tech Pdts & Solutions
21500 Aerospace Pkwy (44142-1071)
PHONE..................................440 238-0102
Michael Trebilcock, *CEO*
Lance Frew, *President*
Andy Jones, *President*
Joe Sierra, *Business Mgr*
Peter Dimarco, *Exec VP*
EMP: 120
SQ FT: 80,000
SALES (est): 445.3MM **Privately Held**
WEB: www.mcpc.com
SIC: 5045 Computers, peripherals & software

(G-1952)
NORTH COAST LOGISTICS INC (PA)
18901 Snow Rd Frnt (44142-1471)
PHONE..................................216 362-7159
Patricia A Gazey, *President*
Dante Granados, *General Mgr*
Bob Hamill, *General Mgr*
Gary Medvitz, *General Mgr*
William Harrison, *Vice Pres*
EMP: 40
SQ FT: 575,000
SALES: 18.5MM **Privately Held**
WEB: www.northcoastlogistics.com
SIC: 4225 General warehousing

(G-1953)
NORTH PARK CARE CENTER LLC
14803 Holland Rd (44142-3065)
PHONE..................................440 250-4080
Charles Calabrase, *Accountant*
John P Coury III, *Mng Member*
EMP: 65
SQ FT: 66,000
SALES (est): 2.5MM **Privately Held**
SIC: 6514 Dwelling operators, except apartments

(G-1954)
ROBERT ERNEY
Also Called: Elite Proofing
14830 Larkfield Dr (44142-3005)
P.O. Box 5087, Chicago IL (60680-5087)
PHONE..................................312 788-9005
Robert Erney, *President*
EMP: 25
SQ FT: 1,500
SALES: 250K **Privately Held**
SIC: 7338 Proofreading service

(G-1955)
STANDARD CONTG & ENGRG INC
Also Called: S C E
6356 Eastland Rd (44142-1302)
PHONE..................................440 243-1001
Fax: 440 243-1415
Russell Metzger, *President*
Brad Metzger, *General Mgr*
George Clevenger, *Superintendent*
Gary Barnhill, *Vice Pres*
George Wonkovich, *Vice Pres*
EMP: 75
SQ FT: 6,000
SALES (est): 17.4MM **Privately Held**
WEB: www.standardcontracting.com
SIC: 1541 1771 1794 1796 Industrial buildings, new construction; renovation, remodeling & repairs: industrial buildings; concrete work; excavation work; machine moving & rigging

GEOGRAPHIC SECTION

Brunswick - Medina County (G-1981)

(G-1956)
SWX ENTERPRISES INC
5231 Engle Rd (44142-1531)
PHONE..................216 676-4600
Dean Armanini, *President*
EMP: 50
SQ FT: 25,000
SALES (est): 8.3MM **Privately Held**
SIC: 4213 Trucking, except local

(G-1957)
VANTAGE PARTNERS LLC
3000 Aerospace Pkwy (44142-1001)
PHONE..................216 925-1302
Joseph Polk, *President*
Walter Lendel, *Electrical Engi*
EMP: 25
SALES (est): 5.5MM **Privately Held**
SIC: 8711 Aviation &/or aeronautical engineering

Brookville
Montgomery County

(G-1958)
A BROWN & SONS NURSERY (PA)
11506 Dyton Grnville Pike (45309-8652)
P.O. Box 427, Phillipsburg (45354-0427)
PHONE..................937 836-5826
Kenneth Brown, *President*
Harry Brown, *Vice Pres*
John Brown, *Vice Pres*
Michael Brown, *Vice Pres*
EMP: 33
SALES (est): 6.1MM **Privately Held**
SIC: 0181 5431 Nursery stock, growing of; vegetable stands or markets

(G-1959)
BROOK HAVEN HOME HEALTH CARE
Also Called: Brookhaven Home Health Care
850 Albert Rd (45309-9275)
PHONE..................937 833-6945
Dale Baughman, *President*
EMP: 40
SALES (est): 1.2MM **Privately Held**
SIC: 8071 8082 Medical laboratories; home health care services

(G-1960)
BROOKVILLE ENTERPRISES INC
Also Called: BROOKHAVEN NURSING & CARE CENT
1 Country Ln (45309-8260)
PHONE..................937 833-2133
Fax: 937 833-3944
Dale Baughman, *President*
Terry Miller, *Treasurer*
Carolyn Hoff, *Corp Comm Staff*
Mike McKinniss, *Exec Dir*
EMP: 255 **EST**: 1972
SQ FT: 32,500
SALES: 13.2MM **Privately Held**
SIC: 8052 8051 Intermediate care facilities; skilled nursing care facilities

(G-1961)
BROOKVILLE ROADSTER INC
718 Albert Rd (45309-9202)
PHONE..................937 833-4605
Ray Gollahon, *President*
Lisa Lengerich, *Financial Exec*
Alan George, *Sales Staff*
Pete George, *Sales Staff*
EMP: 40
SALES (est): 5.8MM **Privately Held**
WEB: www.brookvilleroadster.com
SIC: 3711 5013 Automobile assembly, including specialty automobiles; automotive supplies & parts

(G-1962)
DAYTON TALL TIMBERS RESORT
Also Called: KOA Dayton Tall Timbers Resort
7796 Wellbaum Rd (45309-9214)
PHONE..................937 833-3888
Rhonda Landis, *President*
Joseph Landis, *Vice Pres*
EMP: 25
SALES: 630K **Privately Held**
SIC: 7033 Campgrounds; campsite

(G-1963)
IMAGE PAVEMENT MAINTENANCE
425 Carr Dr (45309-1935)
P.O. Box 157 (45309-0157)
PHONE..................937 833-9200
Fax: 937 833-9400
Michael Gartrell, *President*
EMP: 42
SALES (est): 3.9MM **Privately Held**
SIC: 1611 2951 1799 1771 Surfacing & paving; asphalt paving mixtures & blocks; parking lot maintenance; driveway contractor; sweeping service: road, airport, parking lot, etc.; tennis court construction

(G-1964)
MACKIL INC
Also Called: Rob's Restaurant & Catering
705 Arlington Rd (45309-9728)
PHONE..................937 833-3310
Fax: 937 833-6764
Joe Schwartzberger, *President*
Gerard Schwartz, *President*
EMP: 45
SALES (est): 1.7MM **Privately Held**
SIC: 7299 5812 Banquet hall facilities; American restaurant

(G-1965)
PROVIMI NORTH AMERICA INC (HQ)
Also Called: Cargill Premix and Nutrition
10 Collective Way (45309-8878)
P.O. Box 69 (45309-0069)
PHONE..................937 770-2400
Thomas Taylor, *President*
Terrence Quinlan, *President*
Brett Heiting, *Area Mgr*
Kenneth Bryant, *Vice Pres*
Mark Hemrick, *Safety Mgr*
◆ EMP: 253
SALES (est): 516.9MM
SALES (corp-wide): 109.7B **Privately Held**
WEB: www.vigortone.com
SIC: 5191 2048 Animal feeds; prepared feeds
PA: Cargill, Incorporated
 15407 Mcginty Rd W
 Wayzata MN 55391
 952 742-7575

(G-1966)
SHILOH GROUP
Also Called: Shiloh Springs Care Center
14336 Amity Rd (45309-8764)
PHONE..................937 833-2219
Joe Hardy, *Partner*
Joe Barnett, *Partner*
Margaret Barnett, *Partner*
Katherine Gibson, *Partner*
Debra Hardy, *Partner*
EMP: 120
SQ FT: 30,000
SALES (est): 3.4MM **Privately Held**
SIC: 8059 Nursing home, except skilled & intermediate care facility

Brunswick
Medina County

(G-1967)
ALL CONSTRUCTION SERVICES INC
Also Called: All Construction/Mooney Moses
945 Industrial Pkwy N (44212-4321)
PHONE..................330 225-1653
Fax: 330 220-6826
David J Le Hotan, *President*
Michael J Fox, *Vice Pres*
David Lehotan, *Manager*
EMP: 40
SQ FT: 12,000
SALES (est): 3.7MM
SALES (corp-wide): 1.1B **Publicly Held**
WEB: www.dwdcpa.com
SIC: 1742 Insulation, buildings
HQ: Installed Building Products Llc
 495 S High St Ste 50
 Columbus OH 43215
 614 221-3399

(G-1968)
ALLSTATE PAINTING & CONTG CO
1256 Industrial Pkwy N # 2 (44212-2369)
P.O. Box 369 (44212-0369)
PHONE..................330 220-5533
Fax: 330 642-0440
Elias Kafantaris, *President*
George Rodits, *Vice Pres*
EMP: 90 **EST**: 1962
SQ FT: 5,000
SALES (est): 3.4MM **Privately Held**
SIC: 1721 1799 Exterior commercial painting contractor; sandblasting of building exteriors

(G-1969)
BRUNSWICK CITY SCHOOLS (PA)
3643 Center Rd (44212-3619)
PHONE..................330 225-7731
Fax: 330 273-0507
James Hayas, *Superintendent*
Tracy Wheeler, *Asst Supt*
Richard Nowak, *School Board Pr*
Nancy Zelei, *Vice Pres*
Robert Kelly, *Facilities Dir*
EMP: 811
SQ FT: 10,000
SALES: 84.3MM **Privately Held**
SIC: 8211 8351 Public elementary & secondary schools; secondary school; child day care services

(G-1970)
BRUNSWICK FOOD PANTRY INC
2876 Center Rd (44212)
PHONE..................330 225-0395
Kathryn Pick, *Director*
EMP: 30
SALES: 44.1K **Privately Held**
SIC: 8699 Charitable organization

(G-1971)
CARLSON AMBLNCE TRNSPT SVC INC
1642 Pearl Rd (44212-3406)
PHONE..................330 225-2400
Neil Carlson, *President*
EMP: 32
SQ FT: 7,000
SALES (est): 967.5K
SALES (corp-wide): 1.2MM **Privately Held**
SIC: 4119 Ambulance service
PA: Carlson-Brunswick Funeral Home Inc
 1642 Pearl Rd
 Brunswick OH 44212
 330 225-2400

(G-1972)
CITY OF BRUNSWICK
Animal Control
4095 Center Rd (44212-2944)
PHONE..................330 225-9144
Sam Scaffide, *Director*
EMP: 200 **Privately Held**
SIC: 8699 Animal humane society
PA: City Of Brunswick
 4095 Center Rd
 Brunswick OH 44212
 330 225-9144

(G-1973)
CONTROL CLEANING SOLUTIONS
780 Pearl Rd (44212-2177)
PHONE..................330 220-3333
Nicholas Cummings, *CEO*
EMP: 45
SQ FT: 3,000
SALES (est): 1.2MM **Privately Held**
SIC: 7349 Cleaning service, industrial or commercial

(G-1974)
DEED REALTY CO
4600 Center Rd (44212-3345)
PHONE..................330 225-5220
Fax: 440 888-8203
Bonnie Scahel, *President*
Thomas Scahel, *Corp Secy*
EMP: 29
SALES (est): 1.4MM **Privately Held**
WEB: www.deedrealty.com
SIC: 6531 Real estate brokers & agents

(G-1975)
DIGESTIVE DISEASE CONSULTANTS
1299 Industrial Pkwy N # 110 (44212-6366)
PHONE..................330 225-6468
David Myers, *Owner*
Helen Sharma, *Office Mgr*
Fadi Bashour, *Med Doctor*
EMP: 25
SALES (est): 2.8MM **Privately Held**
SIC: 4959 Disease control

(G-1976)
DW TOGETHER LLC
Also Called: H & R Block Brunswick
3698 Center Rd (44212-3620)
PHONE..................330 225-8200
Joseph Destro, *President*
Debra Destro, *Treasurer*
EMP: 32
SALES (est): 850K **Privately Held**
SIC: 7291 Tax return preparation services

(G-1977)
ESBI INTERNATIONAL SALON
4193 Center Rd (44212-2935)
PHONE..................330 220-3724
Fax: 440 878-8723
Nuccio Basilisco, *Partner*
Cheryl Basilisco, *Partner*
EMP: 35
SALES (est): 656.2K **Privately Held**
SIC: 7231 Manicurist, pedicurist

(G-1978)
FOOD SAMPLE EXPRESS LLC
2945 Carquest Dr (44212-4447)
PHONE..................330 225-3550
Jeffrey M Wood, *Mng Member*
Judi Flynn,
EMP: 90
SALES (est): 12MM **Privately Held**
WEB: www.imtco.com
SIC: 5141 Groceries, general line

(G-1979)
FUTURE UNLIMITED INC
1407 Jefferson Ave (44212-3321)
PHONE..................330 273-6677
Geraldine Moner, *President*
Patrick Moner, *Vice Pres*
Pauline St Denis, *Vice Pres*
Carolyn Touchet, *Vice Pres*
EMP: 50
SQ FT: 1,200
SALES (est): 2.4MM **Privately Held**
SIC: 7361 7363 Employment agencies; temporary help service

(G-1980)
GENERAL PARTS INC
Also Called: Advance Auto Parts
2830 Carquest Dr (44212-4352)
PHONE..................330 220-6500
Tom Kenney, *Manager*
EMP: 80
SALES (corp-wide): 9.3B **Publicly Held**
WEB: www.carquest.com
SIC: 5013 Automotive supplies & parts
HQ: General Parts, Inc.
 2635 E Millbrook Rd Ste C
 Raleigh NC 27604
 919 573-3000

(G-1981)
HOME DEPOT USA INC
Also Called: Home Depot, The
3330 Center Rd (44212-6510)
PHONE..................330 220-2654
Fax: 330 220-2813
Jason Werny, *Branch Mgr*
EMP: 150
SALES (corp-wide): 100.9B **Publicly Held**
WEB: www.homerentalsdepot.com
SIC: 5211 7359 Home centers; tool rental
HQ: Home Depot U.S.A., Inc.
 2455 Paces Ferry Rd Se
 Atlanta GA 30339

(G-1982)
INTEGRATED MARKETING TECH INC
Also Called: IMT
2945 Carquest Dr (44212-4447)
PHONE..................................330 225-3550
Jeff Wood, *President*
Judy Carrie, *Controller*
Judi Carrie, *Executive*
EMP: 100
SQ FT: 120,000
SALES (est): 8.9MM **Privately Held**
SIC: 7363 7374 Labor resource services; data processing service

(G-1983)
JOSEPH SCHMIDT REALTY INC
47 Pearl Rd (44212-1114)
PHONE..................................330 225-6688
Fax: 330 273-4463
Joseph Schmidt, *President*
EMP: 29
SQ FT: 1,904
SALES (est): 1.4MM **Privately Held**
WEB: www.josephschmidtrealty.com
SIC: 6531 Real estate brokers & agents

(G-1984)
JPMORGAN CHASE BANK NAT ASSN
3191 Center Rd (44212-3819)
PHONE..................................330 225-1330
Fax: 330 225-6026
Laurie Kadlac, *Manager*
EMP: 26
SALES (corp-wide): 99.6B **Publicly Held**
SIC: 6021 National commercial banks
HQ: Jpmorgan Chase Bank, National Association
1111 Polaris Pkwy
Columbus OH 43240
614 436-3055

(G-1985)
KHM CONSULTING INC
Also Called: Khm Travel Group
1152 Pearl Rd (44212-2888)
PHONE..................................330 460-5635
Richard Zimmerman, *President*
Carolyn M Sekerak, *Mktg Dir*
EMP: 45 EST: 2007
SALES (est): 13.8MM **Privately Held**
SIC: 4724 Tourist agency arranging transport, lodging & car rental

(G-1986)
LOU-RAY ASSOCIATES INC
1378 Pearl Rd Ste 201 (44212-3469)
PHONE..................................330 220-1999
John Herman, *CEO*
Murray Herman, *President*
Doug Fabian, *Vice Pres*
Scott Katzenmeyer, *Consultant*
Joseph M Herman, *Shareholder*
EMP: 25
SQ FT: 7,500
SALES (est): 2.4MM **Privately Held**
WEB: www.louray.com
SIC: 7374 Data processing & preparation

(G-1987)
MAPLESIDE VALLEY LLC (PA)
Also Called: Mapleside Bakery
294 Pearl Rd (44212-1118)
PHONE..................................330 225-5576
William Eyssen Jr, *Principal*
David Eyssen, *Principal*
Robert Romph, *Manager*
Joshua Schmidt, *Manager*
EMP: 150
SQ FT: 9,900
SALES (est): 8.3MM **Privately Held**
WEB: www.mapleside.com
SIC: 0175 0172 5947 5812 Apple orchard; peach orchard; plum orchard; grapes; gift shop; novelties; eating places; bakeries; fruit stands or markets

(G-1988)
PRECISION SUPPLY COMPANY INC
2845 Interstate Pkwy (44212-4326)
PHONE..................................330 225-5530
Alfred J Koch, *CEO*
Bob Koch, *President*
Tracy Lehnecker, *CFO*
Doug Pearce, *Manager*
EMP: 75 EST: 1973
SQ FT: 18,630
SALES (est): 42.9MM **Privately Held**
WEB: www.precisionsupply.com
SIC: 5084 5085 Machine tools & accessories; industrial supplies
PA: Blackhawk Industrial Distribution, Inc.
1501 Sw Expressway Dr
Broken Arrow OK 74012

(G-1989)
ROLLING HLLS RHAB WELLNESS CTR
4426 Homestead Dr (44212-2506)
P.O. Box 70 (44212-0070)
PHONE..................................330 225-9121
Fax: 330 220-5536
Dan Shiller, *President*
Basil Gaitanaros, *Vice Pres*
Mary Traczyk, *Vice Pres*
Michael Traczyk, *Vice Pres*
EMP: 125
SQ FT: 15,000
SALES (est): 5MM **Privately Held**
SIC: 8051 Extended care facility

(G-1990)
SUBURBAN TRANSPORTATION CO INC
Also Called: Suburban School
1289 Pearl Rd (44212-2868)
PHONE..................................440 846-9291
Fax: 440 846-9294
James Ondrejcak, *Principal*
Debbie Bezak, *Human Resources*
Deb Koch, *Supervisor*
EMP: 26
SALES (corp-wide): 4.8MM **Privately Held**
SIC: 4151 School buses
PA: Suburban Transportation Company, Inc.
26 River Rd
Hinckley OH 44233
440 582-5553

(G-1991)
SYMATIC INC
Also Called: Ancom Business Products
2831 Center Rd (44212-2331)
PHONE..................................330 225-1510
Fax: 330 225-3434
Walter H Tanner, *President*
Cindy Holton, *Vice Pres*
Jackie Wolford, *Controller*
EMP: 35
SALES (est): 5.4MM **Privately Held**
WEB: www.ancom-filing.com
SIC: 3579 5044 2541 2521 Paper handling machines; office equipment; wood partitions & fixtures; wood office furniture

(G-1992)
TMR INC
2945 Carquest Dr (44212-4447)
PHONE..................................330 220-8564
Peter Howe, *Ch of Bd*
Jason Atkins, *President*
Marjorie Zychowski, *Founder*
Jennifer Hamilton, *Human Res Mgr*
Casandra Wright, *Accounts Mgr*
EMP: 120
SQ FT: 210,000
SALES (est): 10.2MM **Privately Held**
WEB: www.themailroom.com
SIC: 7334 7331 Photocopying & duplicating services; direct mail advertising services

(G-1993)
TOTAL MARKETING RESOURCES LLC
Also Called: T M R
2811 Carquest Dr (44212-4332)
PHONE..................................330 220-1275
Jeff Wood,
Linda Wood,
EMP: 27
SQ FT: 125,000
SALES (est): 2.2MM **Privately Held**
SIC: 8742 Business planning & organizing services

(G-1994)
VOESTLPINE PRECISION STRIP LLC (HQ)
3052 Interstate Pkwy (44212-4324)
PHONE..................................330 220-7800
Udo Koehler, *Mng Member*
◆ **EMP:** 100
SALES (est): 15.6MM
SALES (corp-wide): 11.9B **Privately Held**
SIC: 5051 Iron or steel semifinished products
PA: Voestalpine Ag
Voest-Alpine-StraBe 1
Linz 4020
503 041-50

(G-1995)
W W WILLIAMS COMPANY LLC
Also Called: Midwest Division - Brunswick
1176 Industrial Pkwy N (44212-2342)
PHONE..................................330 225-7751
Alan Gatlin, *CEO*
Megan Wajda, *Administration*
EMP: 50
SALES (corp-wide): 2.1B **Privately Held**
SIC: 5084 7538 7537 Industrial machinery & equipment; engines & parts, diesel; diesel engine repair: automotive; automotive transmission repair shops
HQ: The W W Williams Company Llc
835 Goodale Blvd
Columbus OH 43212
614 228-5000

(G-1996)
WHITAKER MASONRY INC
4910 Grafton Rd (44212-1002)
PHONE..................................330 225-7970
Frank Whitaker, *President*
EMP: 48 EST: 2000
SALES: 2.6MM **Privately Held**
SIC: 1741 Masonry & other stonework

(G-1997)
WILLOWOOD CARE CENTER
Also Called: Sand T Nursing Home
1186 Hadcock Rd (44212-3061)
PHONE..................................330 225-3156
Fax: 330 273-4876
Edward Telle, *President*
Michael Lanese, *Human Resources*
Jackie Snook, *Human Resources*
Lori Miner, *Pub Rel Dir*
Neil Grabenstetter, *Director*
EMP: 121
SQ FT: 27,150
SALES (est): 6.1MM **Privately Held**
WEB: www.willowoodcare.com
SIC: 8051 8742 Convalescent home with continuous nursing care; management consulting services

(G-1998)
WINKING LIZARD INC
3634 Center Rd (44212-4446)
PHONE..................................330 220-9944
Jim Callam, *Branch Mgr*
EMP: 90
SALES (corp-wide): 101.4MM **Privately Held**
SIC: 5812 7299 Fast food restaurants & stands; banquet hall facilities
PA: Winking Lizard, Inc.
25380 Miles Rd
Bedford OH 44146
216 831-0022

(G-1999)
WOLVERTON INC
3048 Nationwide Pkwy (44212-2360)
PHONE..................................330 220-3320
Fax: 330 273-4361
EMP: 25
SALES (corp-wide): 663.9MM **Privately Held**
SIC: 5199 Whol Pet Supplies
HQ: Wolverton, Inc.
5542 W Grand River Ave
Lansing MI 48906
517 327-0738

Bryan
Williams County

(G-2000)
AIRMATE COMPANY
16280 County Road D (43506-9552)
PHONE..................................419 636-3184
Fax: 419 636-4210
Carol Schreder Czech, *President*
Carol Schreder, *President*
Neil Oberlin, *Vice Pres*
Ed Dewitt, *Prdtn Mgr*
Kelli Entenman, *Prdtn Mgr*
▲ **EMP:** 57
SQ FT: 24,000
SALES (est): 6.8MM **Privately Held**
WEB: www.airmatecompany.com
SIC: 3823 7311 Industrial instrmnts msrmnt display/control process variable; advertising consultant

(G-2001)
ALLIED WASTE SYSTEMS INC
Also Called: Site 091b
12604 County Road G (43506-9596)
PHONE..................................419 636-2242
Fax: 419 636-5507
Chris Carpenter, *Manager*
EMP: 49
SALES (corp-wide): 10B **Publicly Held**
WEB: www.fennellgrp.com
SIC: 4953 Garbage: collecting, destroying & processing
HQ: Allied Waste Systems, Inc.
18500 N Allied Way # 100
Phoenix AZ 85054
480 627-2700

(G-2002)
ANDERSON & VREELAND INC
Also Called: Anderson Vreeland Midwest
15348 State Rte 127 E (43506)
P.O. Box 527 (43506-0527)
PHONE..................................419 636-5002
Fax: 419 636-4334
Graig Sanderson, *Buyer*
Gary Goll, *Purchasing*
Mitch Male, *Research*
Keith Vreeland, *Engineer*
Gene Lockhart, *Design Engr*
EMP: 80
SQ FT: 3,000
SALES (corp-wide): 72.7MM **Privately Held**
WEB: www.andersonvreeland.com
SIC: 5084 3555 3542 2796 Printing trades machinery, equipment & supplies; printing trades machinery; machine tools, metal forming type; platemaking services
PA: Anderson & Vreeland, Inc.
8 Evans St
Fairfield NJ 07004
973 227-2270

(G-2003)
BUCKEYE GOLF CLUB CO INC
Also Called: Orchard Hills Country Club
10277 County Road D (43506-9548)
PHONE..................................419 636-6984
Fax: 419 633-3663
Rob Vogelsong, *President*
Diana Amstutz, *Manager*
Terry Snyder, *Manager*
EMP: 35
SQ FT: 7,000
SALES (est): 1MM **Privately Held**
WEB: www.orchardhillscountryclub.com
SIC: 7997 Country club, membership

(G-2004)
COMMUNITY HSPTALS WLLNESS CTRS (PA)
Also Called: Chwc
433 W High St (43506-1690)
PHONE..................................419 636-1131
Fax: 419 636-3100
Phil Ennen, *CEO*
Mike Culler, *COO*
Usha Sharma, *Ch Radiology*
Chad Tinkel, *Vice Pres*
Dan Shuck, *Purch Agent*
EMP: 101
SQ FT: 50,000

GEOGRAPHIC SECTION

Bucyrus - Crawford County (G-2027)

SALES: 77.2MM **Privately Held**
SIC: **8062** General medical & surgical hospitals

(G-2005)
COUNTY OF WILLIAMS
Also Called: Williams Conty Hllsd Cntry Lvg
9876 County Road 16 (43506-9781)
PHONE.................................419 636-4508
Fax: 419 636-1269
Marcia Hauer, *Manager*
Clarence Bell, *Director*
EMP: 120 **Privately Held**
SIC: **8051** 9111 Skilled nursing care facilities; county supervisors' & executives' offices
PA: County Of Williams
1 Courthouse Sq Ste L
Bryan OH 43506
419 636-2059

(G-2006)
GEORGE GARDNER
Also Called: Custom Cleaners
1420 W High St (43506-1595)
PHONE.................................419 636-4277
George Gardner, *Owner*
EMP: 65
SQ FT: 10,500
SALES (est): 913.7K **Privately Held**
SIC: **7216** 7211 7349 Drycleaning plants, except rugs; power laundries, family & commercial; janitorial service, contract basis

(G-2007)
HARBORSIDE HEALTHCARE NW OHIO
1104 Wesley Ave (43506-2579)
PHONE.................................419 636-5071
Fax: 419 636-3894
Kevin Park, *Director*
Katy Hithcock, *Administration*
EMP: 180 EST: 1976
SALES (est): 2.5MM **Privately Held**
SIC: **8059** 8051 Nursing home, except skilled & intermediate care facility; skilled nursing care facilities

(G-2008)
INGERSOLL-RAND COMPANY
209 N Main St (43506-1319)
P.O. Box 151 (43506-0151)
PHONE.................................419 633-6800
Robbie Robinson, *Vice Pres*
Kim Ford, *Finance Mgr*
J Haas, *Human Res Dir*
Larry White, *Manager*
Rick Burch, *Manager*
EMP: 50 **Privately Held**
WEB: www.ingersoll-rand.com
SIC: **3546** 4225 3823 3594 Power-driven handtools; general warehousing & storage; industrial instrmnts msrmnt display/control process variable; fluid power pumps & motors; pumps & pumping equipment; hoists, cranes & monorails
HQ: Ingersoll-Rand Company
800 Beaty St Ste B
Davidson NC 28036
704 655-4000

(G-2009)
LE SMITH COMPANY (PA)
1030 E Wilson St (43506-9358)
P.O. Box 766 (43506-0766)
PHONE.................................419 636-4555
Fax: 419 636-3744
Laura Juarez, *President*
Steve Smith, *Principal*
Craig Francisco, *COO*
Mari Ivan, *COO*
Aaron Walz, *Facilities Mgr*
▲ EMP: 100 EST: 1950
SQ FT: 90,000
SALES (est): 18.8MM **Privately Held**
WEB: www.lesmith.com
SIC: **2431** 5072 2541 Interior & ornamental woodwork & trim; builders' hardware; wood partitions & fixtures

(G-2010)
MAJAAC INC
Also Called: Brust Pipeline
820 E Edgerton St (43506-1412)
P.O. Box 624 (43506-0624)
PHONE.................................419 636-5678
Fax: 419 636-3639
Nicholas Arnold II, *President*
EMP: 25 EST: 1940
SQ FT: 7,000
SALES (est): 1.8MM **Privately Held**
WEB: www.majaac.com
SIC: **1623** Gas main construction

(G-2011)
MANUFACTURED HOUSING ENTPS INC
Also Called: MANSION HOMES
9302 Us Highway 6 (43506-9516)
PHONE.................................419 636-4511
Mary Jane Fitzcharles, *CEO*
Janet Rice, *Corp Secy*
Nathan Kimpel, *Vice Pres*
Robert Confer, *Purch Agent*
John Bailey, *Engineer*
EMP: 150
SQ FT: 250,000
SALES: 28.1MM **Privately Held**
WEB: www.mheinc.com
SIC: **2451** 1521 Mobile homes, except recreational; single-family housing construction

(G-2012)
MIDWEST CMNTY HLTH ASSOC INC (HQ)
Also Called: Parkview Physicians Group
442 W High St Ste 3 (43506-1685)
PHONE.................................419 633-4034
Randall Bauman, *President*
James Hamilton, *COO*
Holly Geren, *Purch Dir*
Stacey Beck, *CFO*
Sharon A Ransom, *Obstetrician*
EMP: 175
SALES (est): 18.7MM **Privately Held**
SIC: **8011** Medical centers

(G-2013)
OHIO GAS COMPANY (HQ)
200 W High St (43506-1677)
P.O. Box 528 (43506-0528)
PHONE.................................419 636-1117
Fax: 419 636-2134
Richard Hallett, *President*
Bob Eyre, *Vice Pres*
Douglas Saul, *Vice Pres*
Dee Swanson, *Vice Pres*
Kim Watkins, *Vice Pres*
EMP: 30 EST: 1914
SQ FT: 15,000
SALES (est): 38.3MM
SALES (corp-wide): 44.9MM **Publicly Held**
WEB: www.ohiogas.com
SIC: **4924** Natural gas distribution
PA: Nwo Resources Inc
200 W High St
Bryan OH 43506
419 636-1117

(G-2014)
OHIO GAS COMPANY
715 E Wilson St (43506-1848)
P.O. Box 528 (43506-0528)
PHONE.................................419 636-3642
Doug Saul, *Director*
EMP: 30
SALES (corp-wide): 44.9MM **Publicly Held**
WEB: www.ohiogas.com
SIC: **4922** Natural gas transmission
HQ: Ohio Gas Company
200 W High St
Bryan OH 43506
419 636-1117

(G-2015)
OREILLY AUTOMOTIVE INC
1116 S Main St (43506-2439)
PHONE.................................419 630-0811
EMP: 46 **Publicly Held**
SIC: **5531** 5013 Batteries, automotive & truck; automotive supplies & parts
PA: O'reilly Automotive, Inc.
233 S Patterson Ave
Springfield MO 65802

(G-2016)
PEOPLEWORKS DEV OF HR LLC
3440 County Road 9 (43506-9708)
PHONE.................................419 636-4637
John Murray,
Sam Stuck,
EMP: 27
SALES (est): 1.7MM **Privately Held**
SIC: **8742** Human resource consulting services

(G-2017)
POTTER INC (PA)
630 Commerce Dr (43506-8864)
P.O. Box 685 (43506-0685)
PHONE.................................419 636-5624
Dave Gorzelanczyk, *President*
Marie Campbell Watkins, *Vice Pres*
Pam Klein, *Analyst*
▲ EMP: 30
SQ FT: 37,000
SALES (est): 26MM **Privately Held**
WEB: www.potter-inc.com
SIC: **5199** Baskets; gifts & novelties

(G-2018)
POWER TRAIN COMPONENTS INC
509 E Edgerton St (43506-1315)
P.O. Box 805 (43506-0805)
PHONE.................................419 636-4430
Fax: 419 636-5852
Delton R Nihart, *Ch of Bd*
Jack Nihart, *President*
Jeff Drinnon, *Warehouse Mgr*
Linda McClellan, *Treasurer*
▲ EMP: 55
SQ FT: 60,000
SALES (est): 19.4MM **Privately Held**
WEB: www.ptcauto.com
SIC: **5013** Truck parts & accessories

(G-2019)
PULASKI HEAD START
Also Called: Northwest Cmmuntiy Action Comm
6678 Us Highway 127 (43506-8607)
PHONE.................................419 636-8862
Fax: 419 636-8964
Deb Gerken, *President*
Carmen Coy, *Manager*
EMP: 25
SALES (est): 444.9K **Privately Held**
SIC: **8351** Head start center, except in conjunction with school

(G-2020)
REPUBLIC SERVICES INC
Also Called: Williams County Landfill
12359 County Road G (43506-9596)
PHONE.................................419 636-5109
John Bolyard, *Branch Mgr*
EMP: 34
SALES (corp-wide): 10B **Publicly Held**
SIC: **4953** Sanitary landfill operation
PA: Republic Services, Inc.
18500 N Allied Way # 100
Phoenix AZ 85054
480 627-2700

Buckeye Lake
Licking County

(G-2021)
BUCKEYE LAKE YACHT CLUB INC
5019 Northbank Rd (43008-7862)
P.O. Box 867 (43008-0867)
PHONE.................................740 929-4466
Fax: 740 929-2123
Fritz Riderman, *General Mgr*
Fritz Reiterman, *Manager*
EMP: 30
SALES: 824.8K **Privately Held**
WEB: www.buckeyelakeyc.com
SIC: **7997** Yacht club, membership

(G-2022)
NORTONE SERVICE INC
164 Slocum Ave (43008-7826)
P.O. Box 82, Canal Winchester (43110-0082)
PHONE.................................740 527-2057
William Hubbard, *President*
Aaron Sott, *Vice Pres*
EMP: 42 EST: 1989
SALES (est): 968K **Privately Held**
SIC: **7349** Janitorial service, contract basis

Bucyrus
Crawford County

(G-2023)
ALTERCARE OF BUCYRUS INC
1929 Whetstone St (44820-3564)
PHONE.................................419 562-7644
Fax: 419 562-8442
Stephanie Shannon, *Personnel Exec*
Cathy Rox, *Administration*
Gregory A Potts, *Administration*
Josh Snyder, *Administration*
EMP: 130
SALES (est): 5.4MM **Privately Held**
SIC: **8051** Convalescent home with continuous nursing care

(G-2024)
BROKEN ARROW INC
1649 Marion Rd (44820-3116)
PHONE.................................419 562-3480
Fax: 419 562-3480
Jayne Hanning, *Exec Dir*
EMP: 32
SALES: 1.2MM **Privately Held**
SIC: **8322** 8699 8059 Social services for the handicapped; charitable organization; personal care home, with health care

(G-2025)
BUCKEYE DRAG RACING ASSN LLC
201 Penn Ave (44820-2032)
PHONE.................................419 562-0869
Fred Nolen, *President*
EMP: 30
SALES (est): 440.5K **Privately Held**
SIC: **8699** Automobile owners' association

(G-2026)
BUCYRUS COMMUNITY HOSPITAL INC
629 N Sandusky Ave (44820-1821)
PHONE.................................419 562-4677
Jerry Morasko, *Principal*
Andrew Daniels, *COO*
Jerry Klein, *CFO*
Todd L Gallentine, *Pharmacist*
Carrie Coleman, *Manager*
EMP: 165 EST: 1956
SQ FT: 75,000
SALES (est): 27MM
SALES (corp-wide): 22.9MM **Privately Held**
WEB: www.bchonline.org
SIC: **8062** Hospital, affiliated with AMA residency
PA: Avita Health System
269 Portland Way S
Galion OH 44833
419 468-4841

(G-2027)
BUCYRUS COMMUNITY HOSPITAL LLC
629 N Sandusky Ave (44820-1821)
PHONE.................................419 562-4677
Fax: 419 562-5598
Jerome Morasko, *Mng Member*
Andy Daniels,
Eric Draime,
Shirley Fitz,
Traci Oswald,
EMP: 95
SALES: 53.5MM
SALES (corp-wide): 22.9MM **Privately Held**
SIC: **8062** General medical & surgical hospitals

Bucyrus - Crawford County (G-2028) **GEOGRAPHIC SECTION**

PA: Avita Health System
269 Portland Way S
Galion OH 44833
419 468-4841

(G-2028)
CARLES BRATWURST INC
1210 E Mansfield St (44820-1943)
PHONE...................419 562-7741
Fax: 419 562-2027
Chris Berry, *President*
Gary Aluk, *Manager*
EMP: 25 EST: 1929
SQ FT: 4,000
SALES (est): 1.8MM **Privately Held**
WEB: www.carlesbrats.com
SIC: 5421 5147 Meat markets, including freezer provisioners; meats, fresh

(G-2029)
CITY OF BUCYRUS
Also Called: Crawford Cnty Council On Aging
200 S Spring St (44820-2227)
P.O. Box 166 (44820-0166)
PHONE...................419 562-3050
Margaret Wells, *Director*
EMP: 45 **Privately Held**
WEB: www.crawfordcountyaging.com
SIC: 8322 Senior citizens' center or association
PA: City Of Bucyrus
500 S Sandusky Ave
Bucyrus OH 44820
419 562-6767

(G-2030)
CNB BANK
105 Washington Sq (44820-2252)
PHONE...................419 562-7040
Joseph B Bower, *Branch Mgr*
EMP: 60
SALES (corp-wide): 130.3MM **Publicly Held**
SIC: 6022 State commercial banks
HQ: Cnb Bank
1 S 2nd St
Clearfield PA 16830
814 765-4577

(G-2031)
COMMUNITY COUNSELING SERVICES
2458 Stetzer Rd (44820-2066)
P.O. Box 765 (44820-0765)
PHONE...................419 468-8211
Fax: 419 468-4720
Paul Sipes, *Controller*
Tom Saccenti, *Director*
Thomas Saccenti, *Executive*
EMP: 35
SQ FT: 4,600
SALES: 3.2MM **Privately Held**
SIC: 8093 8322 8069 Mental health clinic, outpatient; crisis intervention center; alcoholism rehabilitation hospital

(G-2032)
COMMUNITY INVSTORS BANCORP INC
119 S Sandusky Ave (44820-2220)
PHONE...................419 562-7055
Phillip Gerber, *President*
David M Auck, *Principal*
Brent D Fissel, *Principal*
Phillip E Harris, *Principal*
Dale C Hoyles, *Principal*
EMP: 42
SALES: 7.4MM **Privately Held**
WEB: www.ffcb.com
SIC: 6712 Bank holding companies

(G-2033)
COUNTY OF CRAWFORD
Also Called: Crawford Cnty Job & Fmly Svcs
224 Norton Way (44820-1831)
PHONE...................419 562-0015
Fax: 419 562-1056
Melinda Crall-Cauley, *Manager*
Thomas M O'Leary, *Director*
EMP: 75 **Privately Held**
SIC: 8331 Job training services
PA: County Of Crawford
112 E Mansfield St Ste A
Bucyrus OH 44820
419 562-5871

(G-2034)
COUNTY OF CRAWFORD
815 Whetstone St (44820-3359)
PHONE...................419 562-7731
Tim Marcom, *Principal*
Mark Baker, *Manager*
EMP: 44 **Privately Held**
SIC: 8711 Engineering services
PA: County Of Crawford
112 E Mansfield St Ste A
Bucyrus OH 44820
419 562-5871

(G-2035)
CRAWFORD COUNTY CHILDREN SVCS (PA)
Also Called: Children's Service Board
224 Norton Way (44820-1831)
PHONE...................419 562-1200
Fax: 419 468-6771
Brian Star, *Principal*
Kathy Scott, *Director*
EMP: 28
SALES (est): 937.3K **Privately Held**
SIC: 8322 Child related social services

(G-2036)
CRAWFORD COUNTY COUNCIL ON AGI
200 S Spring St (44820-2227)
PHONE...................419 562-3050
Fax: 419 562-0759
Bruce Grafmiller, *Manager*
Margaret Wells, *Director*
EMP: 45
SALES: 1.7MM **Privately Held**
SIC: 8322 Senior citizens' center or association

(G-2037)
FARMERS CITIZENS BANK (DH)
105 Washington Sq (44820-2252)
P.O. Box 567 (44820-0567)
PHONE...................419 562-7040
Fax: 419 562-8322
Coleman Clougherty, *CEO*
Robert D Hord, *Chairman*
Carol Aurand, *Vice Pres*
Terry Gernert, *Vice Pres*
Bill Holden, *Vice Pres*
EMP: 43 EST: 1907
SQ FT: 24,000
SALES (est): 14.3MM
SALES (corp-wide): 130.3MM **Publicly Held**
WEB: www.farmerscitizensbank.com
SIC: 6022 State commercial banks
HQ: Cnb Bank
1 S 2nd St
Clearfield PA 16830
814 765-4577

(G-2038)
HEALTH CARE RTREMENT CORP AMER
Also Called: Heartland of Bucyrus
1170 W Mansfield St (44820-8509)
PHONE...................419 562-9907
Tiffany Remmert, *Principal*
EMP: 99
SALES (corp-wide): 3.6B **Publicly Held**
WEB: www.hrc-manorcare.com
SIC: 8051 Skilled nursing care facilities
HQ: Health Care And Retirement Corporation Of America
333 N Summit St Ste 103
Toledo OH 43604
419 252-5500

(G-2039)
HEBCO PRODUCTS INC
1232 Whetstone St (44820-3539)
PHONE...................419 562-7987
Fax: 419 562-8577
Andrew Ason, *President*
Ralph Reins, *Vice Pres*
Matt Barringer, *Engineer*
EMP: 862
SALES (est): 76.2MM
SALES (corp-wide): 182.1MM **Privately Held**
WEB: www.hebcoproducts.com
SIC: 3714 3451 3429 5013 Motor vehicle brake systems & parts; screw machine products; manufactured hardware (general); automotive supplies & parts
PA: Qualitor, Inc.
1840 Mccullough St
Lima OH 45801
248 204-8600

(G-2040)
HOMECARE MTTERS HM HLTH HSPICE
133 S Sandusky Ave (44820-2220)
P.O. Box 327, Galion (44833-0327)
PHONE...................419 562-2001
B Maglott, *Exec Dir*
Bertha Maglott, *Exec Dir*
EMP: 73 EST: 2007
SALES (est): 1MM **Privately Held**
SIC: 8082 Visiting nurse service

(G-2041)
HORD LIVESTOCK COMPANY INC
887 State Route 98 (44820-8646)
PHONE...................419 562-0277
Robert Hord, *Principal*
EMP: 46
SALES (corp-wide): 10.8MM **Privately Held**
SIC: 5154 Livestock
PA: Hord Livestock Company Inc.
911 State Route 98
Bucyrus OH 44820
419 562-9885

(G-2042)
J & F CONSTRUCTION AND DEV INC
2141 State Route 19 (44820-9569)
PHONE...................419 562-6662
Fax: 419 562-9167
James Mayes, *President*
Steve Bridgford, *Vice Pres*
Brock Mayes, *Vice Pres*
Sherry Colver, *Accounts Mgr*
Ronda Scott, *Manager*
EMP: 28
SQ FT: 5,000
SALES (est): 9.3MM **Privately Held**
WEB: www.jfconstruction.com
SIC: 1542 1541 Commercial & office building, new construction; industrial buildings & warehouses

(G-2043)
MAPLECRST ASISTD LVG INTL ORDR
Also Called: Maple Crest Assisted Living
717 Rogers St (44820-2735)
PHONE...................419 562-4988
Fax: 419 562-4883
Judy Wilkins, *Director*
EMP: 25
SALES: 584.3K **Privately Held**
SIC: 8082 5812 Home health care services; eating places

(G-2044)
NATIONAL LIME AND STONE CO
4580 Bethel Rd (44820-9754)
P.O. Box 69 (44820-0069)
PHONE...................419 562-0771
Fax: 419 562-8574
Eric Johnson, *Principal*
Rick Dehays, *Purch Agent*
Delmo Arend, *Sales Staff*
Roger Nye, *Maintence Staff*
EMP: 62
SALES (corp-wide): 3.2B **Privately Held**
WEB: www.natlime.com
SIC: 1411 3281 1422 Limestone, dimension-quarrying; cut stone & stone products; crushed & broken limestone
PA: The National Lime And Stone Company
551 Lake Cascade Pkwy
Findlay OH 45840
419 422-4341

(G-2045)
OBERLANDERS TREE & LDSCP LTD
1874 E Mansfield St (44820-2018)
PHONE...................419 562-8733
Fax: 419 562-3207
Roger Oberlander, *Principal*
Marie Frey, *Admin Sec*
EMP: 25
SALES (est): 1.4MM **Privately Held**
SIC: 0781 0783 Landscape services; ornamental shrub & tree services

(G-2046)
OHIO MUTUAL INSURANCE COMPANY (PA)
1725 Hopley Ave (44820-3596)
P.O. Box 111 (44820-0111)
PHONE...................419 562-3011
Fax: 419 562-0995
Jim Kennedy, *President*
Brad McCormack, *President*
Todd Albert, *Vice Pres*
Michael Brogan, *Vice Pres*
Marsha Clady, *Vice Pres*
EMP: 186 EST: 1901
SQ FT: 26,000
SALES (est): 71.1MM **Privately Held**
SIC: 6411 6331 Insurance brokers; fire, marine & casualty insurance: mutual

(G-2047)
SUBURBAN GALA LANES INC (PA)
975 Hopley Ave (44820-3506)
PHONE...................419 468-7488
David Skaggs, *President*
Sherry Ransom, *Treasurer*
EMP: 40 EST: 1962
SALES (est): 600K **Privately Held**
SIC: 7933 Ten pin center

(G-2048)
TOTAL WAREHOUSING SERVICES
115 Crossroads Blvd (44820-1362)
P.O. Box 149 (44820-0149)
PHONE...................419 562-2878
Fax: 419 562-3937
Jason McMullen, *President*
Justin McMullen, *Vice Pres*
EMP: 60
SQ FT: 71,000
SALES (est): 4.7MM **Privately Held**
SIC: 4225 General warehousing

(G-2049)
UNITED BANK NATIONAL ASSN (HQ)
Also Called: United Bank N A
401 S Sandusky Ave (44820-2624)
P.O. Box 568 (44820-0568)
PHONE...................419 562-3040
Fax: 419 562-9948
Don Stone, *President*
Glen Chase, *Vice Pres*
David Lauthers, *Vice Pres*
Monica Sinney, *Controller*
Jennifer Buchanan, *Branch Mgr*
EMP: 25
SQ FT: 5,000
SALES (est): 1.3MM
SALES (corp-wide): 367MM **Publicly Held**
WEB: www.unitedbankna.com
SIC: 6021 National commercial banks
PA: Park National Corporation
50 N 3rd St
Newark OH 43055
740 349-8451

(G-2050)
UNITED OHIO INSURANCE COMPANY
1725 Hopley Ave (44820-3569)
P.O. Box 111 (44820-0111)
PHONE...................419 562-3011
James Kennedy, *President*
Randu O'Conner, *Vice Pres*
David Hendrix, *CFO*
Patty Hughes, *Accountant*
EMP: 150
SQ FT: 15,000

GEOGRAPHIC SECTION

Byesville - Guernsey County (G-2072)

SALES (est): 5.9MM
SALES (corp-wide): 71.1MM **Privately Held**
SIC: 6411 Insurance agents, brokers & service
PA: Ohio Mutual Insurance Company
1725 Hopley Ave
Bucyrus OH 44820
419 562-3011

(G-2051)
WAYCRAFT INC (PA)
118 River St (44820-1536)
PHONE..................419 563-0550
Fax: 419 563-0551
Mark Barron, *President*
James Ward, *Production*
W Michael Miller, *Exec Dir*
EMP: 55
SQ FT: 44,000
SALES (est): 1.3MM **Privately Held**
SIC: 8331 Job training & vocational rehabilitation services

(G-2052)
WAYCRAFT INC
118 River St (44820-1536)
PHONE..................419 562-3321
Nancy Whiteamire, *Branch Mgr*
EMP: 70
SALES (est): 1MM
SALES (corp-wide): 1.3MM **Privately Held**
SIC: 8331 Job training & vocational rehabilitation services
PA: Waycraft, Inc.
118 River St
Bucyrus OH 44820
419 563-0550

Buffalo
Guernsey County

(G-2053)
UNITED HSPTALITY SOLUTIONS LLC
11998 Clay Pike Rd (43722-9900)
P.O. Box 98 (43722-0098)
PHONE..................800 238-0487
John Givens, *Controller*
Jennifer Yontz-Orlando, *Mng Member*
Marc Orlando,
Hugo Vargas,
Marieclaire Yontz,
EMP: 600
SQ FT: 1,200
SALES (est): 7.9MM **Privately Held**
SIC: 7011 Hotels & motels

Burbank
Wayne County

(G-2054)
4TH AND GOAL DISTRIBUTION LLC
9911 Avon Lake Rd (44214-9631)
PHONE..................440 212-0769
Chris Mares,
EMP: 25
SALES (est): 374.2K **Privately Held**
SIC: 5091 Sporting & recreation goods

(G-2055)
RON BURGE TRUCKING INC
Also Called: Burge, Ron
1876 W Britton Rd (44214-9729)
PHONE..................330 624-5373
Fax: 330 624-0122
Mike Burge, *President*
Annette Burge, *Corp Secy*
Scott Burge, *Vice Pres*
Sandra Burge, *Shareholder*
EMP: 30
SQ FT: 2,000
SALES (est): 6.5MM **Privately Held**
WEB: www.ronburgetrucking.com
SIC: 4213 Contract haulers

Burghill
Trumbull County

(G-2056)
WILLIAM KERFOOT MASONRY INC
4948 State Route 7 (44404-9778)
PHONE..................330 772-6460
Fax: 330 772-6460
William Kerfoot, *President*
EMP: 26
SALES (est): 983.6K **Privately Held**
SIC: 1741 Masonry & other stonework

Burgoon
Sandusky County

(G-2057)
ECI INC
2704 County Road 13 (43407-9750)
PHONE..................419 986-5566
EMP: 273
SALES (corp-wide): 3.8MM **Privately Held**
SIC: 6513 8361 Retirement hotel operation; geriatric residential care
PA: Eci Inc
207 State St
Bettsville OH

Burkettsville
Mercer County

(G-2058)
KLINGSHIRN & SONS TRUCKING
Also Called: Klingshirn, Tom & Sons Trckng
14884 St Rt 118 S (45310)
P.O. Box 98 (45310-0098)
PHONE..................937 338-5000
Thomas P Klingshirn, *President*
Paul Klingshirn, *Vice Pres*
Robert Klingshirn, *Vice Pres*
Joe Klingshirn, *Treasurer*
Mary Ann Klingshirn, *Admin Sec*
EMP: 40
SALES (est): 5.8MM **Privately Held**
SIC: 4213 4212 Contract haulers; local trucking, without storage

Burton
Geauga County

(G-2059)
AMERICAN LEGION
Also Called: Atwood Mock Post 459
14052 Goodwin St (44021-9522)
P.O. Box 261 (44021-0261)
PHONE..................440 834-8621
Bob Hams, *Vice Pres*
EMP: 25
SALES (est): 302.5K **Privately Held**
SIC: 8641 Veterans' organization

(G-2060)
BAMA MASONRY INC
14379 Aquilla Rd (44021-9558)
PHONE..................440 834-4175
Susan Saurman, *President*
EMP: 25
SALES (est): 2MM **Privately Held**
SIC: 1741 Masonry & other stonework

(G-2061)
BFG SUPPLY CO LLC (DH)
Also Called: Tricor Pacific Capital Partner
14500 Kinsman Rd (44021-9423)
P.O. Box 479 (44021-0479)
PHONE..................440 834-1883
Fax: 440 834-1885
Rob Glockner, *President*
Doug Scott, *President*
Daniel Dignan, *General Mgr*
Tim Gallagher, *Vice Pres*
Nicole Krizner, *Vice Pres*
▲ EMP: 30
SQ FT: 32,000
SALES (est): 166.9MM
SALES (corp-wide): 1.5MM **Privately Held**
WEB: www.bfgsupply.com
SIC: 5191 5261 Garden supplies; garden supplies & tools

(G-2062)
HEXPOL COMPOUNDING LLC
Also Called: Burton Rubber Processing
14330 Kinsman Rd (44021-9648)
PHONE..................440 834-4644
Fax: 440 834-5524
Len McCleain, *Vice Pres*
Steven Strouse, *Vice Pres*
D Thomas, *Traffic Mgr*
John Gorrell, *Manager*
Debbie Christian, *Clerk*
EMP: 200
SALES (corp-wide): 1.1B **Privately Held**
SIC: 3087 2865 5162 2899 Custom compound purchased resins; dyes & pigments; resins; plastics basic shapes; chemical preparations; adhesives & sealants; paints & allied products
HQ: Hexpol Compounding Llc
14330 Kinsman Rd
Burton OH 44021
440 834-4644

(G-2063)
IMPULLITTI LANDSCAPING INC
Also Called: Impullitti & Sons Landscaping
14659 Ravenna Rd (44021-9713)
PHONE..................440 834-1866
Fax: 440 834-1867
Wayne Impullitti, *President*
EMP: 50
SALES: 2.5MM **Privately Held**
SIC: 0782 0781 Landscape contractors; landscape planning services

(G-2064)
MIDEAST BAPTIST CONFERENCE
14282 Butternut Rd (44021-9572)
PHONE..................440 834-8984
Tim Nelson, *Treasurer*
Dave Scull, *Director*
John Lundwall, *Director*
EMP: 50 EST: 1956
SQ FT: 1,296
SALES (est): 438.6K **Privately Held**
WEB: www.campburton.org
SIC: 7032 8661 Sporting & recreational camps; religious organizations

(G-2065)
STEPHEN M TRUDICK
Also Called: Hardwood Lumber Co
13813 Station Rd (44021)
P.O. Box 15 (44021-0015)
PHONE..................440 834-1891
Fax: 440 834-0243
Stephen M Trudick, *Owner*
Nancy Taddie, *Financial Exec*
Dawn Pauletter, *Office Mgr*
Jayne Shaffer, *Director*
▲ EMP: 41
SQ FT: 80,000
SALES (est): 5.6MM **Privately Held**
WEB: www.hardwood-lumber.com
SIC: 3991 2426 5031 3442 Brooms & brushes; dimension, hardwood; lumber: rough, dressed & finished; metal doors, sash & trim; millwork; sawmills & planing mills, general

(G-2066)
WINDSOR HOUSE INC
Also Called: Burton Health Care Center
14095 E Center St (44021-9651)
PHONE..................440 834-0544
Fax: 440 834-9824
Robert Evans, *Director*
Clara Brown, *Food Svc Dir*
Erin Kostas, *Administration*
EMP: 40
SALES (corp-wide): 25.7MM **Privately Held**
SIC: 8741 8051 Nursing & personal care facility management; skilled nursing care facilities
PA: Windsor House, Inc.
101 W Liberty St
Girard OH
330 545-1550

Butler
Richland County

(G-2067)
OTS-NJ LLC
21 Traxler St (44822-8827)
PHONE..................732 833-0600
James T O Connor, *Owner*
James White,
EMP: 55
SQ FT: 1,700
SALES (est): 7.8MM **Privately Held**
WEB: www.vikingelectronics.com
SIC: 1623 Water, sewer & utility lines

(G-2068)
SUSAN A SMITH CRYSTAL CARE
5375 Teeter Rd (44822-9623)
PHONE..................419 747-2666
Jerry Smith, *President*
Kyann Miner, *Vice Pres*
Jennifer Coile, *Treasurer*
Mindy Caudill, *Controller*
Susan Smith, *Admin Sec*
EMP: 45 EST: 1993
SALES (est): 670.6K **Privately Held**
SIC: 8059 7542 Nursing home, except skilled & intermediate care facility; carwashes

Byesville
Guernsey County

(G-2069)
ALEXANDER J ABERNETHY
Also Called: Cambridge Country Club
60755 Southgate Rd (43723-9643)
PHONE..................740 432-2107
Alexander J Abernethy, *Principal*
EMP: 40
SALES (est): 603.7K **Privately Held**
SIC: 7997 Country club, membership

(G-2070)
CAMBRIDGE COUNTRY CLUB COMPANY
60755 Southgate Rd (43723-9643)
PHONE..................740 439-2744
Gary Farmer, *President*
Tom Fischer, *Vice Pres*
EMP: 25
SQ FT: 25,000
SALES (est): 890K **Privately Held**
SIC: 7997 7992 5941 5813 Country club, membership; golf club, membership; swimming club, membership; tennis club, membership; public golf courses; sporting goods & bicycle shops; drinking places; eating places

(G-2071)
KEN HARPER
Also Called: GUERNSEY INDUSTRIES
60772 Southgate Rd (43723-9731)
PHONE..................740 439-4452
Susie Mathia, *Bookkeeper*
Kon Harper, *Exec Dir*
EMP: 110
SALES: 1MM **Privately Held**
SIC: 8331 2511 2448 Sheltered workshop; wood household furniture; wood pallets & skids

(G-2072)
VILLAGE OF BYESVILLE
221 Main St (43723-1338)
P.O. Box 8 (43723-0008)
PHONE..................740 685-5901
Jay Jackson, *Mayor*
Annette Whealdon, *Treasurer*
EMP: 25
SALES: 852.1K **Privately Held**
SIC: 8721 Billing & bookkeeping service

Cadiz
Harrison County

(G-2073)
CARRIAGE INN OF CADIZ INC
308 W Warren St (43907-1077)
PHONE.................................740 942-8084
Fax: 740 942-8204
Ken Bernsen, *President*
Lynne Huff, *Vice Pres*
Bobbi Darios, *VP Finance*
Gloria Croland, *VP Mktg*
Tina Phillips, *Executive*
EMP: 32 EST: 1982
SALES (est): 4.3MM **Privately Held**
SIC: **8051** 8322 Convalescent home with continuous nursing care; rehabilitation services

(G-2074)
DARON COAL COMPANY LLC
40580 Cadiz Piedmont Rd (43907-9514)
PHONE.................................614 643-0337
Fax: 740 942-2904
Charles C Ungurean,
EMP: 159
SALES (est): 5.6MM
SALES (corp-wide): 1.3B **Publicly Held**
SIC: **1221** Bituminous coal surface mining
HQ: Oxford Mining Company, Inc.
544 Chestnut St
Coshocton OH 43812
740 622-6302

(G-2075)
HARRISON CO COUNTY HOME
41500 Cadiz Dennison Rd (43907-9575)
PHONE.................................740 942-3573
Fax: 740 942-3663
William G Rogers, *Superintendent*
EMP: 30
SALES (est): 686K **Privately Held**
SIC: **8361** Home for the aged

(G-2076)
HARRISON COMMUNITY HOSP INC (PA)
951 E Market St (43907-9799)
PHONE.................................740 942-4631
Fax: 740 942-2749
Terry M Carson, *CEO*
Randall C Hunt, *Principal*
Donald Liming, *Purch Dir*
Dean Sloane, *CFO*
Frank Bohach, *Technology*
EMP: 197
SQ FT: 52,390
SALES: 11MM **Privately Held**
WEB: www.harrisoncommunity.com
SIC: **8062** Hospital, affiliated with AMA residency

(G-2077)
HARRISON INDUSTRIES INC
82460 Cadiz Jewett Rd (43907-9427)
PHONE.................................740 942-2988
Fax: 740 942-2150
C L Strahl, *Dir Ops-Prd-Mfg*
Dawn Barnhart, *Manager*
F Scott Brace, *Director*
EMP: 55
SQ FT: 8,000
SALES (est): 230.3K **Privately Held**
WEB: www.harrisonindustries.com
SIC: **8331** 5712 7349 Sheltered workshop; outdoor & garden furniture; building maintenance services

(G-2078)
ISI SYSTEMS INC (PA)
43029 Industrial Park Rd (43907-9621)
P.O. Box 156, Bellaire (43906-0156)
PHONE.................................740 942-0050
Christine Wallace, *President*
William Wallace, *Exec VP*
EMP: 30
SQ FT: 10,000
SALES (est): 1.5MM **Privately Held**
WEB: www.isisystems.net
SIC: **1629** Industrial plant construction

(G-2079)
MANNIK & SMITH GROUP INC
Also Called: Mannik Smith Group, The
104 S Main St (43907-1171)
PHONE.................................740 942-4222
EMP: 38
SALES (est): 1.8MM
SALES (corp-wide): 34.3MM **Privately Held**
SIC: **8711** Consulting engineer
PA: The Mannik & Smith Group Inc
1800 Indian Wood Cir
Maumee OH 43537
419 891-2222

(G-2080)
OHIO MACHINERY CO
Also Called: Ohio Cat
1016 E Market St (43907-9728)
PHONE.................................740 942-4626
Fax: 740 942-4029
Frank Keller, *Manager*
Kandy Buhl-Raney, *Manager*
Jesmine Smith, *Manager*
EMP: 50
SALES (corp-wide): 222.7MM **Privately Held**
WEB: www.enginesnow.com
SIC: **5082** General construction machinery & equipment
PA: Ohio Machinery Co.
3993 E Royalton Rd
Broadview Heights OH 44147
440 526-6200

(G-2081)
VERIZON NORTH INC
994 E Market St (43907-9799)
PHONE.................................740 942-2566
Jim Woods, *President*
EMP: 25
SALES (corp-wide): 126B **Publicly Held**
SIC: **4813** Local telephone communications; long distance telephone communications
HQ: Verizon North Inc
140 West St
New York NY 10007
212 395-1000

Caldwell
Noble County

(G-2082)
BRADEN MED SERVICES INC
Also Called: Gillespie Drug
44519 Marietta Rd (43724-9209)
PHONE.................................740 732-2356
James Scott Braden, *President*
Kyle Huck, *General Mgr*
Diane R Braden, *Treasurer*
Kyle Cook, *Treasurer*
John Turner, *Sales Executive*
EMP: 35
SQ FT: 5,000
SALES (est): 2.2MM **Privately Held**
WEB: www.bradenmed.com
SIC: **8082** 7352 5122 5169 Home health care services; medical equipment rental; pharmaceuticals; oxygen; hospital equipment & furniture

(G-2083)
COMMUNITY IMPRV CORP NBLE CNTY
44523 Marietta Rd (43724-9209)
P.O. Box 41 (43724-0041)
PHONE.................................740 509-0248
Scott Braden, *President*
EMP: 99
SALES (est): 68.1K **Privately Held**
SIC: **8399** Community development groups

(G-2084)
CROCK CONSTRUCTION CO
17990 Woodsfield Rd (43724-9435)
PHONE.................................740 732-2306
Edward Crock, *CEO*
Brandon Crock, *Vice Pres*
Leander Crock, *Vice Pres*
Chandler Sherry, *Financial Exec*
EMP: 25 EST: 1948
SQ FT: 15,000
SALES (est): 4.3MM **Privately Held**
SIC: **1542** 1521 Commercial & office building, new construction; new construction, single-family houses

(G-2085)
G M N TRI CNTY COMMUNTY ACTION (PA)
615 North St (43724-1123)
PHONE.................................740 732-2388
Debbie Brown, *Manager*
Gary Ricer, *Exec Dir*
William Schmidt, *Exec Dir*
EMP: 150
SQ FT: 4,000
SALES: 6.7MM **Privately Held**
WEB: www.gmncac.org
SIC: **8322** Social service center

(G-2086)
IEH AUTO PARTS LLC
218 West St (43724-1337)
PHONE.................................740 732-2395
Wally Olson, *Branch Mgr*
EMP: 27
SALES (corp-wide): 21.7B **Publicly Held**
SIC: **5013** Automotive supplies & parts
HQ: Ieh Auto Parts Llc
108 Townpark Dr Nw
Kennesaw GA 30144
770 701-5000

(G-2087)
NOBEL LEARNING CENTER
44135 Marietta Rd (43724-9124)
PHONE.................................740 732-4722
Lashona D Volld, *Director*
EMP: 30
SALES: 775.3K **Privately Held**
SIC: **8351** Preschool center

(G-2088)
NOBLE CNTY NBLE CNTY CMMSONERS
Also Called: Noble County Health Department
44069 Marietta Rd (43724-9124)
PHONE.................................740 732-4958
Fax: 740 732-5043
Shawn Ray, *Branch Mgr*
EMP: 32 **Privately Held**
SIC: **8093** 9111 Family planning & birth control clinics; county supervisors' & executives' offices
PA: Noble, County Of Noble County Comisioners
200 Court House Fl 2
Caldwell OH 43724
740 732-4044

(G-2089)
SUMMIT ACRES INC (PA)
Also Called: Summit Acres Nursing Home
44565 Sunset Rd (43724-9731)
PHONE.................................740 732-2364
Fax: 740 732-7816
Leander Crock, *President*
Malcolm Parks, *Treasurer*
Edward Hupp, *Admin Sec*
Donald Crock, *Administration*
EMP: 200
SQ FT: 54,000
SALES (est): 5.9MM **Privately Held**
SIC: **8093** 8052 8082 Rehabilitation center, outpatient treatment; intermediate care facilities; home health care services

(G-2090)
TLC HOME HEALTH CARE INC
43 Kennedy Dr (43724-9004)
PHONE.................................740 732-5211
Betty Postelwait, *President*
EMP: 40
SALES (est): 1.3MM **Privately Held**
SIC: **8082** Home health care services

(G-2091)
UNITED AMBULANCE SERVICE
523 Main St (43724-1324)
PHONE.................................740 732-5653
Maria Higgins, *Office Mgr*
Jim Starr, *Director*
EMP: 40
SALES (est): 604.4K **Privately Held**
SIC: **4119** Ambulance service

Cambridge
Guernsey County

(G-2092)
AFC CABLE SYSTEMS INC
829 Georgetown Rd (43725)
PHONE.................................740 435-3340
Fax: 740 435-9731
Bob Koscoe, *Branch Mgr*
EMP: 52 **Publicly Held**
WEB: www.afcweb.com
SIC: **5063** Wire & cable
HQ: Afc Cable Systems, Inc.
16100 Lathrop Ave
Harvey IL 60426
508 998-1131

(G-2093)
ALL FOR KIDS INC
1405 E Wheeling Ave (43725-2563)
P.O. Box 1266 (43725-6266)
PHONE.................................740 435-8050
Fax: 740 435-3178
Lisa Brown, *President*
EMP: 25
SALES (est): 681.7K **Privately Held**
SIC: **8351** Child day care services

(G-2094)
ALLWELL BEHAVIORAL HEALTH SVCS
Also Called: Guernsy Counseling Center
2500 Glenn Hwy (43725-9028)
PHONE.................................740 439-4428
Fax: 740 439-3389
Samantha Lanning, *Office Mgr*
Karen Stanley, *Office Mgr*
Barbara Stclair, *Manager*
EMP: 25
SALES (est): 453.8K
SALES (corp-wide): 11.5MM **Privately Held**
SIC: **8093** 8322 Mental health clinic, outpatient; family counseling services
PA: Allwell Behavioral Health Services
2845 Bell St
Zanesville OH 43701
740 454-9766

(G-2095)
ANN CORBETT DESIGN INC
534 N 1st St (43725-1206)
PHONE.................................740 432-2969
Fax: 740 432-8865
Julie Leyshon, *CEO*
Melissa Work, *Manager*
EMP: 25
SQ FT: 10,000
SALES (est): 3.3MM **Privately Held**
WEB: www.lmidesign.com
SIC: **8711** Engineering services

(G-2096)
AREA AGENCY ON AGING REG 9 INC
1730 Southgate Pkwy (43725-3024)
PHONE.................................740 439-4478
Fax: 740 432-1060
James Endly, *CEO*
Joan Cannon, *Officer*
EMP: 98 EST: 1975
SQ FT: 15,000
SALES: 42.4MM **Privately Held**
WEB: www.aaa9.org
SIC: **8322** Outreach program

(G-2097)
ASPLUNDH TREE EXPERT CO
4362 Glenn Hwy (43725-9447)
PHONE.................................740 435-4300
EMP: 363
SALES (corp-wide): 4.3B **Privately Held**
SIC: **5211** 0783 Lumber products; ornamental shrub & tree services
PA: Asplundh Tree Expert Llc
708 Blair Mill Rd
Willow Grove PA 19090
215 784-4200

Cambridge - Guernsey County (G-2122)

(G-2098)
CAMBRIDGE ASSOCIATES LTD
Also Called: Holiday Inn
2248 Southgate Pkwy (43725-3038)
P.O. Box 15395, Columbus (43215-0395)
PHONE..................740 432-7313
Ralph Ray, *General Mgr*
EMP: 50
SALES (corp-wide): 1.4MM Privately Held
SIC: 7011 Hotels & motels
PA: Cambridge Associates Ltd
2002 Richard Jones Rd 105c
Nashville TN 37215
615 385-4946

(G-2099)
CAMBRIDGE HOME HEALTHCARE
1300 Clark St Unit 7 (43725-8875)
PHONE..................740 432-6191
Fax: 740 439-2780
Connie Stone, *Manager*
EMP: 50
SALES (est): 1.5MM Privately Held
SIC: 8051 Skilled nursing care facilities

(G-2100)
CAMBRIDGE NH LLC
Also Called: Greystone Health and
66731 Old Twenty One Rd (43725-8987)
PHONE..................740 432-7717
Mordecai Rosenberg, *President*
Ronald Swartz, *CFO*
Lisa Schwartz, *Admin Sec*
Dawn Wozniak, *Exec Sec*
EMP: 80
SALES (est): 264.1K Privately Held
SIC: 8051 Skilled nursing care facilities

(G-2101)
CAMBRIDGE PACKAGING INC
Also Called: Cambridge Box & Gift Shop
60794 Southgate Rd (43725-9414)
PHONE..................740 432-3351
Fax: 740 439-5890
Larry Knellinger, *President*
Bill Knellinger, *Vice Pres*
Rick Knellinger, *Vice Pres*
Dave Garvin, *Prdtn Mgr*
John Common, *Purch Mgr*
EMP: 31
SQ FT: 26,000
SALES (est): 8MM Privately Held
WEB: www.cambridgepackaging.com
SIC: 2653 5199 Boxes, corrugated: made from purchased materials; packaging materials

(G-2102)
CAMBRIDGE PROPERTY INVESTORS
Also Called: Holiday Inn
2248 Southgate Pkwy (43725-3038)
P.O. Box 96, Byesville (43723-0096)
PHONE..................740 432-7313
Fax: 740 432-2337
Richard Lenhart, *Partner*
Kelly Lenhart,
EMP: 47
SALES (est): 1.9MM Privately Held
SIC: 7011 Hotels & motels

(G-2103)
CELLCO PARTNERSHIP
Also Called: Verizon Wireless
2103 Southgate Pkwy (43725-3080)
PHONE..................740 439-3509
Fax: 740 439-3509
Jeff Fluharty, *Principal*
EMP: 71
SALES (corp-wide): 126B Publicly Held
SIC: 4812 Cellular telephone services
HQ: Cellco Partnership
1 Verizon Way
Basking Ridge NJ 07920

(G-2104)
CHILDRENS ADVOCACY CENTER
274 Highland Ave (43725-2571)
P.O. Box 1725 (43725-6725)
PHONE..................740 432-6581
Melissa Kaylor, *Director*
EMP: 32

SALES (est): 705.1K Privately Held
SIC: 8322 Child related social services

(G-2105)
COLUMBIA GAS TRANSMISSION LLC
Also Called: Columbia Energy
11296 E Pike Rd (43725-9669)
PHONE..................740 432-1612
Fax: 740 432-1606
Rod Graham, *Manager*
EMP: 45
SALES (corp-wide): 9.2B Privately Held
SIC: 4923 Gas transmission & distribution
HQ: Columbia Gas Transmission, Llc
200 Cizzic Ctr Dr
Columbus OH 43216
614 460-6000

(G-2106)
COUNTY OF GUERNSEY
Also Called: Guernsey Cnty Children Svcs Bd
274 Highland Ave (43725-2571)
PHONE..................740 439-5555
Kelly Lynch, *Exec Dir*
EMP: 35 Privately Held
WEB: www.visitguernseycounty.com
SIC: 8351 9111 Child day care services; county supervisors' & executives' offices
PA: County Of Guernsey
627 Wheeling Ave Rm 301
Cambridge OH 43725
740 432-9243

(G-2107)
COUNTY OF GUERNSEY
Also Called: Guernsey Co Public Info Agency
324 Highland Ave (43725-2530)
PHONE..................800 307-8422
Kathy Jamiel, *Director*
EMP: 80 Privately Held
WEB: www.visitguernseycounty.com
SIC: 8743 Public relations services
PA: County Of Guernsey
627 Wheeling Ave Rm 301
Cambridge OH 43725
740 432-9243

(G-2108)
COUNTY OF GUERNSEY
Also Called: Department of Jobs & Family
324 Highland Ave (43725-2530)
PHONE..................740 432-2381
Fax: 740 432-1952
Kathy Jamiel, *Director*
EMP: 82 Privately Held
WEB: www.visitguernseycounty.com
SIC: 7361 8322 Employment agencies; community center
PA: County Of Guernsey
627 Wheeling Ave Rm 301
Cambridge OH 43725
740 432-9243

(G-2109)
COUNTY OF GUERNSEY
Also Called: Guernsey County Senior Center
1022 Carlisle Ave (43725-2420)
PHONE..................740 439-6681
Fax: 740 439-7478
Shon Gress, *Director*
EMP: 50 Privately Held
WEB: www.visitguernseycounty.com
SIC: 8322 Individual & family services
PA: County Of Guernsey
627 Wheeling Ave Rm 301
Cambridge OH 43725
740 432-9243

(G-2110)
DUNNING MOTOR SALES INC
9108 Southgate Rd (43725-8005)
PHONE..................740 439-4465
Fax: 740 439-2692
John Dunning Jr, *General Mgr*
Nancy S Dunning, *Vice Pres*
Sal Gard, *Parts Mgr*
Craig Abner, *Sales Mgr*
Dwight Abner, *Sales Mgr*
EMP: 45
SALES (est): 18.8MM Privately Held
WEB: www.dunningmotorsales.com
SIC: 5511 7538 7515 Automobiles, new & used; general automotive repair shops; passenger car leasing

(G-2111)
DYNO NOBEL TRANSPORTATION
Also Called: Dyno Transportation
850 Woodlawn Ave (43725-2959)
PHONE..................740 439-5050
Fax: 740 432-2456
Bobby Bickford, *Branch Mgr*
EMP: 30
SALES (corp-wide): 2.7B Privately Held
SIC: 4212 Delivery service, vehicular
HQ: Dyno Nobel Transportation, Inc
2795 E Cottonwood Pkwy # 500
Salt Lake City UT 84121
801 364-4800

(G-2112)
FAMILY PLANNING CENTER
326 Highland Ave (43725-2530)
PHONE..................740 439-3340
Maryland Moorehead, *Partner*
EMP: 25
SALES (est): 596.8K Privately Held
SIC: 8093 Family planning clinic

(G-2113)
FEDERAL-MOGUL LLC
6420 Glenn Hwy (43725-9755)
PHONE..................740 432-2393
Steve Grilliot, *Plant Mgr*
Rick Kunko, *Controller*
Robb Junker, *Branch Mgr*
EMP: 210
SALES (corp-wide): 21.7B Publicly Held
SIC: 3053 3592 3562 5085 Gaskets & sealing devices; oil seals, rubber; gaskets, all materials; pistons & piston rings; ball bearings & parts; bearings; motor vehicle parts & accessories; bearings, motor vehicle; transmission housings or parts, motor vehicle; steering mechanisms, motor vehicle; motor vehicle lighting equipment
HQ: Federal-Mogul Llc
27300 W 11 Mile Rd # 101
Southfield MI 48034

(G-2114)
FOOD DISTRIBUTORS INC
449 N 1st St (43725-1256)
P.O. Box 607 (43725-0607)
PHONE..................740 439-2764
Fax: 740 439-5980
Charles E Smith, *President*
Tina Baily, *General Mgr*
Darla Perkins, *Manager*
EMP: 25 EST: 1973
SQ FT: 25,000
SALES (est): 5.3MM Privately Held
SIC: 5149 5142 5113 Canned goods: fruit, vegetables, seafood, meats, etc.; packaged frozen goods; industrial & personal service paper

(G-2115)
GEORGETOWN VINEYARDS INC
62920 Georgetown Rd (43725-9749)
PHONE..................740 435-3222
Fax: 740 432-2427
John Nicolozakes, *President*
Kay Nicolozakes, *Vice Pres*
Sam Nicolozakes, *Treasurer*
Emma McVicker, *Admin Sec*
EMP: 25
SQ FT: 600
SALES (est): 113.3K Privately Held
SIC: 0721 2084 5812 2082 Vines, cultivation of; wine cellars, bonded: engaged in blending wines; pizza restaurants; near beer

(G-2116)
GOODWILL INDS CENTL OHIO INC
1712 Southgate Pkwy (43725-3024)
PHONE..................740 439-7000
Fax: 740 439-7000
Vickie Frick, *Manager*
EMP: 50
SALES (corp-wide): 45.1MM Privately Held
SIC: 8699 8331 5932 Charitable organization; vocational rehabilitation agency; used merchandise stores

PA: Goodwill Industries Of Central Ohio, Inc.
1331 Edgehill Rd
Columbus OH 43212
614 294-5181

(G-2117)
GUERNSEY COUNTY CMNTY DEV CORP
Also Called: Guernsey County Cdc
905 Wheeling Ave (43725-2318)
P.O. Box 1175 (43725-6175)
PHONE..................740 439-0020
Dan Speedy, *Exec Dir*
EMP: 36
SALES: 942.5K Privately Held
SIC: 8399 Community development groups

(G-2118)
GUERNSEY HEALTH ENTERPRISES
1341 Clark St (43725-9614)
P.O. Box 610 (43725-0610)
PHONE..................740 439-3561
Fax: 740 439-8175
Raymond Shorey, *President*
EMP: 700
SQ FT: 211,000
SALES (est): 1.9MM
SALES (corp-wide): 2MM Privately Held
SIC: 4119 8059 5912 Ambulance service; rest home, with health care; drug stores
PA: Guernsey Health Systems Inc
1341 Clark St
Cambridge OH 43725
740 439-3561

(G-2119)
GUERNSEY HEALTH SYSTEMS INC (PA)
1341 Clark St (43725-9614)
P.O. Box 610 (43725-0610)
PHONE..................740 439-3561
Philip Hearing, *CEO*
Donald P Huelskamp, *CFO*
EMP: 650
SQ FT: 211,000
SALES: 2MM Privately Held
SIC: 4119 8062 8052 Local passenger transportation; general medical & surgical hospitals; intermediate care facilities

(G-2120)
HIGGINS BUILDING COMPANY INC
11342 E Pike Rd (43725-9669)
PHONE..................740 439-5553
James R Higgins, *President*
Darlene Higgins, *Corp Secy*
Martin Higgins, *Vice Pres*
EMP: 40
SQ FT: 11,000
SALES (est): 5.2MM Privately Held
WEB: www.higginsbuildinginc.org
SIC: 1541 1542 Industrial buildings, new construction; commercial & office building, new construction

(G-2121)
I A R INC (PA)
220 N 8th St (43725-1840)
PHONE..................740 432-3371
Kevin Siedling, *President*
Terry Mc Vey, *Admin Sec*
EMP: 46
SALES (est): 1.1MM Privately Held
WEB: www.riamusic.org
SIC: 8361 Home for the mentally handicapped

(G-2122)
KINDRED HEALTHCARE OPER INC
Also Called: Kindred Nursing
1471 Wills Creek Vly Dr (43725-8620)
PHONE..................740 439-4437
Fax: 740 439-2606
Debbie Morse, *Manager*
Tony Starr, *Director*
Margaret Gerdau, *Nursing Dir*
Mary Jo Yonker, *Receptionist*
EMP: 140
SALES (corp-wide): 6B Publicly Held
WEB: www.salemhaven.com
SIC: 8051 Skilled nursing care facilities

Cambridge - Guernsey County (G-2123)

HQ: Kindred Healthcare Operating, Inc.
680 S 4th St
Louisville KY 40202
502 596-7300

(G-2123)
MEDICAL ASSOC CAMBRIDGE INC
1515 Maple Dr Ste 1 (43725-1162)
PHONE......................740 439-3515
Fax: 740 432-4427
Mark T Goggin, *Principal*
Patrick D Goggin, *Principal*
Kayode Ojedele, *Principal*
Douglas A Rush, *Principal*
Mark Kimpton, *Family Practiti*
EMP: 34
SALES (est): 2.8MM Privately Held
SIC: 8011 Clinic, operated by physicians; psychiatrists & psychoanalysts; surgeon

(G-2124)
NICOLOZAKES TRCKG & CNSTR INC
8555 Georgetown Rd (43725-8866)
P.O. Box 670 (43725-0670)
PHONE......................740 432-5648
Fax: 740 439-4205
William A Nicolozakes, *President*
Basil J Nicolozakes, *Vice Pres*
Dean S Nicolozakes, *Vice Pres*
James A Nicolozakes, *Vice Pres*
Rida Darcolay, *Accountant*
EMP: 30 EST: 1953
SQ FT: 32,600
SALES: 5.1MM Privately Held
WEB: www.nicolozakes.com
SIC: 1541 4212 4213 1794 Industrial buildings, new construction; light haulage & cartage, local; heavy machinery transport; excavation & grading, building construction

(G-2125)
OHIO BRIDGE CORPORATION
Also Called: U.S. Bridge
201 Wheeling Ave (43725-2256)
P.O. Box 757 (43725-0757)
PHONE......................740 432-6334
Daniel Rogovin, *CEO*
Richard Rogovin, *Chairman*
Dan Rogovin, *Vice Pres*
Bob Huhn, *Plant Mgr*
Scott Flaten, *Project Engr*
▼EMP: 140 EST: 1952
SQ FT: 250,000
SALES (est): 60.4MM Privately Held
SIC: 1622 3449 Bridge construction; bars, concrete reinforcing; fabricated steel

(G-2126)
PEOPLES BANKING AND TRUST CO
845 Wheeling Ave (43725-2316)
PHONE......................740 439-2767
Fax: 740 432-2750
Larry Miller, *Manager*
Nathan Larrick, *Advisor*
EMP: 27
SALES (corp-wide): 182.1MM Publicly Held
SIC: 6022 State trust companies accepting deposits, commercial
HQ: The Peoples Banking And Trust Company
138 Putnam St
Marietta OH 45750
740 373-3155

(G-2127)
RED CARPET HEALTH CARE CENTER
8420 Georgetown Rd (43725-9770)
PHONE......................740 439-4401
Fax: 740 439-0636
Arnold Tuber, *Corp Secy*
Dale Shonk, *Vice Pres*
William Shade, *Director*
Vern Beynon, *Administration*
EMP: 130
SQ FT: 35,000
SALES (est): 4.9MM
SALES (corp-wide): 10.3MM Privately Held
WEB: www.redcarpethcc.com
SIC: 8059 8051 Rest home, with health care; skilled nursing care facilities
PA: S.F.T. Health Care Inc
5890 Mayfair Rd
Canton OH 44720
330 499-6358

(G-2128)
SOUTHEAST DIVERSIFIED INDS
1401 Burgess Ave (43725-3003)
PHONE......................740 432-4241
Fax: 740 439-0141
Ed Rolan Dee, *Chairman*
Daniel Duniver, *Manager*
EMP: 70
SQ FT: 20,000
SALES: 78K Privately Held
SIC: 8322 4783 8331 Association for the handicapped; packing & crating; job training & vocational rehabilitation services

(G-2129)
SOUTHSTERN OHIO RGONAL MED CTR (PA)
Also Called: Southeastern Med
1341 Clark St (43725-9614)
P.O. Box 610 (43725-0610)
PHONE......................740 439-3561
Fax: 740 439-8399
Raymond Chorey, *President*
Doug Gotschall, *Materials Dir*
Donald Huelskamp, *CFO*
Nabiel Alkhouri, *Med Doctor*
Benny McCullough, *Supervisor*
EMP: 40
SQ FT: 211,000
SALES: 105.5MM Privately Held
SIC: 8062 General medical & surgical hospitals

(G-2130)
SUPERIOR MED INC (PA)
1251 Clark St (43725-9612)
P.O. Box 501 (43725-0501)
PHONE......................740 439-8839
Fax: 740 439-8996
Cindy Heller, *Principal*
Carrie Gunn, *Manager*
EMP: 37
SALES (est): 6.1MM Privately Held
WEB: www.superiormed.com
SIC: 8011 8721 Medical centers; billing & bookkeeping service

(G-2131)
THE C-Z COMPANY (PA)
Also Called: C-Z Realtors
201 Wheeling Ave (43725-2256)
P.O. Box 757 (43725-0757)
PHONE......................740 432-6334
Arthur Rogovin, *Vice Pres*
Casey Frame, *Accountant*
Casey Rich, *Accountant*
Nate Wutrick, *Regl Sales Mgr*
Josep Costa, *Sales Staff*
EMP: 40 EST: 1947
SQ FT: 4,000
SALES (est): 3.9MM Privately Held
SIC: 6512 4225 Commercial & industrial building operation; general warehousing & storage

(G-2132)
UNITED AMBLNCE SVC OF CMBRIDGE (HQ)
1331 Campbell Ave (43725-2928)
P.O. Box 1118 (43725-6118)
PHONE......................740 439-7787
Raymond Chorey, *President*
Andrew D Eddy, *Vice Pres*
James Michael Starr, *Director*
EMP: 26
SQ FT: 1,500
SALES (est): 92.4K
SALES (corp-wide): 2MM Privately Held
SIC: 4119 Ambulance service
PA: Guernsey Health Systems Inc
1341 Clark St
Cambridge OH 43725
740 439-3561

(G-2133)
VICTORIAN OAKS LLC
Also Called: Victorian Oaks Asst Lvng/Demta
1480 Deerpath Dr (43725-9098)
PHONE......................740 432-2262
Fax: 740 439-3464
Stephanie Brandon, *Marketing Staff*
Christopher Randall, *Mng Member*
Shenea Craeighton, *Exec Dir*
Charles E Randall, *
EMP: 45
SQ FT: 24,000
SALES: 1.3MM Privately Held
SIC: 8059 Rest home, with health care

(G-2134)
XANTERRA PARKS & RESORTS INC
Also Called: Salt Fork Rsort Conference Ctr
Us Rte 22 E (43725)
P.O. Box 7 (43725-0007)
PHONE......................740 439-2751
Keith Cook, *Branch Mgr*
EMP: 137
SALES (corp-wide): 414.9MM Privately Held
WEB: www.amfac.com
SIC: 7011 5813 5812 Resort hotel; drinking places; eating places
HQ: Parks Xanterra & Resorts Inc
6312 S Fiddlers Green Cir 600n
Greenwood Village CO 80111
303 600-3400

(G-2135)
ZEKELMAN INDUSTRIES INC
Also Called: Wheatland Tube Company
9208 Jeffrey Dr (43725-9417)
PHONE......................740 432-2146
Ned Feeney, *President*
Kelly Saling, *Opers Staff*
John Parks, *Mfg Staff*
Michael Welsh, *Purchasing*
Fred Schneider, *Controller*
EMP: 104
SQ FT: 58,000 Privately Held
SIC: 3317 3498 5074 3644 Pipes, seamless steel; fabricated pipe & fittings; plumbing fittings & supplies; noncurrent-carrying wiring services; plumbing fixture fittings & trim; blast furnaces & steel mills
PA: Zekelman Industries, Inc.
227 W Monroe St Ste 2600
Chicago IL 60606

Camden
Preble County

(G-2136)
BARNETS INC
Also Called: G & J Kartway
1619 Barnetts Mill Rd (45311-9728)
PHONE......................937 452-3275
Fax: 937 452-1219
Gary Gregg, *President*
Jane Simpson, *Vice Pres*
Travis Gregg, *Treasurer*
Elaine Gregg, *Admin Sec*
EMP: 48
SQ FT: 25,000
SALES: 9MM Privately Held
SIC: 5153 4213 Grain elevators; trucking, except local

(G-2137)
COUNCIL ON RUR SVC PRGRAMS INC
8263 Us Route 127 (45311-8798)
PHONE......................937 452-1090
EMP: 97
SALES (corp-wide): 14.7MM Privately Held
SIC: 8351 Head start center, except in conjunction with school
PA: Council On Rural Service Programs, Inc.
201 Robert M Davis Pkwy B
Piqua OH 45356
937 778-5220

Campbell
Mahoning County

(G-2138)
APBN INC
670 Robinson Rd (44405-2031)
P.O. Box 637 (44405-0637)
PHONE......................724 964-8252
Diane Katsourakis, *President*
Nikita Katsourakis, *Vice Pres*
Vasalis Katsourakis, *Vice Pres*
Frank Molfi, *Controller*
EMP: 37
SALES (est): 3.1MM Privately Held
SIC: 1721 Bridge painting

(G-2139)
LIBERTY-ALPHA III JV
24 Madison St (44405-1800)
PHONE......................330 755-7711
Emanouel Frangos, *Principal*
Joshua Bowley, *Manager*
EMP: 40
SALES: 950K Privately Held
SIC: 1721 Bridge painting

Canal Fulton
Stark County

(G-2140)
AVALON FOODSERVICE INC
1 Avalon Dr (44614-8893)
P.O. Box 536 (44614-0536)
PHONE......................330 854-4551
Fax: 330 854-7108
Andrew Schroer, *President*
Jeff Fix, *President*
John Holdren, *President*
Tim Weisend, *President*
Bob Egan Sr, *Superintendent*
EMP: 120 EST: 1957
SQ FT: 100,000
SALES (est): 188.3MM Privately Held
WEB: www.avalonfoods.com
SIC: 5142 5149 5169 5113 Packaged frozen goods; canned goods: fruit, vegetables, seafood, meats, etc.; chemicals & allied products; industrial & personal service paper; individual & family services; eating places

(G-2141)
BJAAM ENVIRONMENTAL INC
472 Elm Ridge Ave (44614-9369)
P.O. Box 523 (44614-0523)
PHONE......................330 854-5300
Fax: 330 854-5340
Brett Urian, *President*
Williams Pidcock, *Principal*
Troy Schultz, *Vice Pres*
Dan Lovesy, *Project Mgr*
Aimee Ritter, *Project Mgr*
EMP: 50
SQ FT: 26,000
SALES (est): 6.9MM Privately Held
WEB: www.bjaam.com
SIC: 8748 Environmental consultant

(G-2142)
CLARK SON ACTN LIQUIDATION INC
4500 Erie Ave Nw (44614-8598)
PHONE......................330 837-9710
Clark Barkheimer, *President*
EMP: 25
SALES (est): 5.7MM Privately Held
SIC: 5031 Kitchen cabinets

(G-2143)
GASLITE VILLA CONVALESCENT CTR
7055 High Mill Ave Nw (44614-9344)
PHONE......................330 494-4500
Corita C Childs, *President*
EMP: 95 EST: 1964
SQ FT: 22,000
SALES (est): 4.5MM Privately Held
WEB: www.gaslitevilla.com
SIC: 8059 8052 Convalescent home; intermediate care facilities

GEOGRAPHIC SECTION

(G-2144)
NORTHWEST LOCAL SCHOOL DST (PA)
2309 Locust St S (44614-9389)
PHONE..................330 854-2291
M Shreffler, *Superintendent*
Michael Shreffler, *Superintendent*
John Hexamer, *Asst Supt*
Bruce Beadle, *School Board Pr*
Sam Birche, *Transptn Dir*
EMP: 57
SALES: 23.6MM **Privately Held**
SIC: **8211** 8741 Elementary & secondary schools; public elementary & secondary schools; management services

(G-2145)
PNC BANK NATIONAL ASSOCIATION
420 Beverly Ave (44614-9338)
P.O. Box 289 (44614-0289)
PHONE..................330 854-0974
Doug Choven, *Manager*
EMP: 162
SALES (corp-wide): 18B **Publicly Held**
WEB: www.allegiantbank.com
SIC: **6029** Commercial banks
HQ: Pnc Bank, National Association
    222 Delaware Ave
    Wilmington DE 19801
    877 762-2000

(G-2146)
SKIPCO FINANCIAL ADJUSTERS (PA)
2306 Locust St S (44614-9388)
P.O. Box 606 (44614-0606)
PHONE..................330 854-4800
Fax: 330 854-5559
Robert Blowers, *President*
Cynthia Blowers, *Vice Pres*
David Jackson, *Finance Mgr*
Joseph Bernstein, *Manager*
Seung Bathrick, *Director*
EMP: 60
SQ FT: 17,000
SALES (est): 8MM **Privately Held**
WEB: www.skipcoautoauction.com
SIC: **7389** 5521 Auctioneers, fee basis; used car dealers

(G-2147)
TOWN OF CANAL FULTON (PA)
155 Market St E Ste A (44614-1305)
PHONE..................330 854-9448
John Grogan, *Mayor*
Scott M Svab, *Finance Dir*
Patricia Schauwecker, *Council Mbr*
EMP: 42 EST: 1840
SQ FT: 2,145 **Privately Held**
SIC: **9121** 8611 Town council; ; business associations

(G-2148)
UNITED CHURCH HOMES INC
12200 Strausser St Nw (44614-9479)
PHONE..................330 854-4177
Lynnette Wright, *Counsel*
Susan Strutner, *Administration*
EMP: 150
SALES (corp-wide): 78.1MM **Privately Held**
WEB: www.altenheimcommunity.org
SIC: **8051** Convalescent home with continuous nursing care
HQ: United Church Homes Inc
    170 E Center St
    Marion OH 43302
    740 382-4885

(G-2149)
ZVN PROPERTIES INC
957 Cherry St E (44614-9609)
P.O. Box 583 (44614-0583)
PHONE..................330 854-5890
Bryan Lysikowski, *CEO*
Rick Hoback, *President*
Richard Hoback, *President*
David Dolan, *COO*
EMP: 65 EST: 2007
SQ FT: 5,000
SALES (est): 7MM **Privately Held**
SIC: **6512** Nonresidential building operators

Canal Winchester
Franklin County

(G-2150)
A FOX CONSTRUCTION
6478 Winchester Blvd # 156 (43110-2004)
PHONE..................614 506-1685
Lisa M Fox, *Owner*
EMP: 40
SALES: 300K **Privately Held**
SIC: **8611** Business associations

(G-2151)
A K ATHLETIC EQUIPMENT INC
8015 Howe Industrial Pkwy (43110-7890)
PHONE..................614 920-3069
Angela Katz, *President*
EMP: 25
SQ FT: 32,000
SALES (est): 4.2MM **Privately Held**
WEB: www.akathletics.com
SIC: **3086** 5091 Plastics foam products; gymnasium equipment

(G-2152)
AERO ELECTRICAL CONTRACTORS
8020 Dove Pkwy Ste A (43110-9559)
PHONE..................614 834-8181
Fax: 740 862-5509
George R Wolfenbarker, *President*
Caren Wolfenbarker, *Corp Secy*
Paul Hollingshead, *Vice Pres*
Sherry Hollingshead, *Manager*
EMP: 36
SALES (est): 4.7MM **Privately Held**
SIC: **1731** General electrical contractor

(G-2153)
BERWICK ELECTRIC COMPANY
6863 Eliza Dr (43110-1338)
P.O. Box 241 (43110-0241)
PHONE..................614 834-2301
Theodore Philput, *President*
EMP: 37
SALES (est): 2.7MM **Privately Held**
SIC: **1731** General electrical contractor

(G-2154)
CAMGEN LTD
6693 Axtel Dr (43110-8417)
PHONE..................330 204-8636
William Genkins,
EMP: 35
SALES: 5MM **Privately Held**
SIC: **7371** 8711 Custom computer programming services; electrical or electronic engineering

(G-2155)
CATERPILLAR INC
8170 Dove Pkwy (43110-9674)
PHONE..................614 834-2400
Kelly Orr, *Facilities Mgr*
Roy Fonseca, *Engineer*
Jay Kautz, *Engineer*
Eric Ruth, *Engineer*
Kelley Maxwell, *Sales Staff*
EMP: 63
SALES (corp-wide): 45.4B **Publicly Held**
WEB: www.cat.com
SIC: **4225** General warehousing & storage
PA: Caterpillar Inc.
    510 Lake Cook Rd Ste 100
    Deerfield IL 60015
    224 551-4000

(G-2156)
CENTRAL OHIO PRIMARY CARE
6201 Gender Rd (43110-2007)
PHONE..................614 834-8042
EMP: 37 **Privately Held**
SIC: **8011** Pediatrician
PA: Central Ohio Primary Care Physicians, Inc.
    570 Polaris Pkwy Ste 250
    Westerville OH 43082

(G-2157)
CITY OF CANAL WINCHESTER
22 S Trine St (43110-1230)
PHONE..................614 837-8276
Jennifer Paswell, *Director*
EMP: 26 **Privately Held**
WEB: www.cwcvb.com
SIC: **8322** 9111 Senior citizens' center or association; mayors' offices
PA: City Of Canal Winchester
    36 S High St
    Canal Winchester OH 43110
    614 837-6937

(G-2158)
FEECORP CORPORATION (PA)
Also Called: F E E
7995 Allen Rd Nw (43110-9206)
P.O. Box 447, Pickerington (43147-0447)
PHONE..................614 837-3010
Fax: 614 837-3019
Karen Fee, *President*
Dawn Fee, *Vice Pres*
Casandra Fee, *Admin Sec*
EMP: 50
SQ FT: 2,400
SALES (est): 16.1MM **Privately Held**
SIC: **1799** Exterior cleaning, including sandblasting; petroleum storage tanks, pumping & draining; petroleum storage tank installation, underground

(G-2159)
GENERAL TEMPERATURE CTRL INC
970 W Walnut St (43110-9757)
PHONE..................614 837-3888
Fax: 614 837-5434
Bob Billings, *CEO*
Brenda Billings, *President*
L R Billings Jr, *Principal*
Brian Ray Woodard, *Principal*
Patricia Ann Woodard, *Principal*
EMP: 30
SQ FT: 10,000
SALES (est): 7.9MM **Privately Held**
WEB: www.gtc.cc
SIC: **1711** Warm air heating & air conditioning contractor

(G-2160)
GODDARD SCHOOL
6405 Canal St (43110-2044)
PHONE..................614 920-9810
Eric Park, *Principal*
EMP: 26 EST: 2015
SALES (est): 215K **Privately Held**
SIC: **8351** Group day care center

(G-2161)
JPMORGAN CHASE BANK NAT ASSN
6314 Gender Rd (43110-2052)
PHONE..................614 920-4182
Steve Rouch, *Branch Mgr*
EMP: 26
SALES (corp-wide): 99.6B **Publicly Held**
WEB: www.chasebank.com
SIC: **6021** National commercial banks
HQ: Jpmorgan Chase Bank, National Association
    1111 Polaris Pkwy
    Columbus OH 43240
    614 436-3055

(G-2162)
KEN HEIBERGER PAVING INC
458 W Waterloo St (43110-1019)
PHONE..................614 837-0290
Fax: 614 837-3765
Kenneth Heiberger, *President*
EMP: 70
SALES (est): 175.6K **Privately Held**
SIC: **1611** Highway & street paving contractor

(G-2163)
KESSLER HEATING & COOLING
Also Called: Honeywell Authorized Dealer
9793 Basil Western Rd Nw (43110-9278)
P.O. Box 245 (43110-0245)
PHONE..................614 837-9961
Fax: 614 837-5787
Ervin Kessler, *Owner*
EMP: 30
SALES (est): 3MM **Privately Held**
WEB: www.kesslerheating.com
SIC: **1711** Warm air heating & air conditioning contractor

(G-2164)
KINDRED NURSING CENTERS E LLC
Also Called: MGM Health Care Winchstr
36 Lehman Dr (43110-1006)
PHONE..................614 837-9666
Raymond Pongonis, *Director*
Seth White, *Administration*
EMP: 150
SALES (corp-wide): 6B **Publicly Held**
WEB: www.salemhaven.com
SIC: **8051** Convalescent home with continuous nursing care
HQ: Kindred Nursing Centers East, L.L.C.
    680 S 4th St
    Louisville KY 40202
    502 596-7300

(G-2165)
ONEIL AWNING AND TENT INC
895 W Walnut St (43110-9436)
PHONE..................614 837-6352
Fax: 614 837-1220
Dennis Ritchey, *President*
Tim Ritchey, *Vice Pres*
Fred Waller, *Vice Pres*
Mark Ritchey, *VP Sales*
Suzanne Wagner, *Sales Staff*
EMP: 65
SQ FT: 40,000
SALES (est): 8.3MM **Privately Held**
WEB: www.oneiltents.com
SIC: **7359** Tent & tarpaulin rental

(G-2166)
REHRIG PENN LOGISTICS INC
8200 Dove Pkwy (43110-7718)
PHONE..................614 833-2564
Matt Fissel, *Principal*
EMP: 36 **Privately Held**
SIC: **4731** Freight transportation arrangement
HQ: Rehrig Penn Logistics, Inc.
    7800 100th St
    Pleasant Prairie WI 53158

(G-2167)
REI TELECOM INC (PA)
7890 Robinett Way (43110-8165)
PHONE..................614 255-3100
Tim Roehrenbeck, *President*
EMP: 25 EST: 1999
SQ FT: 4,000
SALES: 1.5MM **Privately Held**
WEB: www.reitelecom.com
SIC: **1731** Telephone & telephone equipment installation; general electrical contractor

(G-2168)
RENTOKIL NORTH AMERICA INC
Also Called: I P S Interior Landscaping
6300 Cmmerce Ctr Dr Ste G (43110)
PHONE..................614 837-0099
Monica Desch, *Manager*
EMP: 30
SALES (corp-wide): 2.6B **Privately Held**
WEB: www.primescapeproducts.com
SIC: **7389** Plant care service
HQ: Rentokil North America, Inc.
    1125 Berkshire Blvd # 150
    Wyomissing PA 19610
    610 372-9700

(G-2169)
RUDOLPH BROTHERS & CO
6550 Oley Speaks Way (43110-8274)
PHONE..................614 833-0707
Fax: 614 833-0456
Kevin Rudolph, *CEO*
Rick Rudolph, *President*
William Coontz Jr, *Vice Pres*
Brain Stump, *Plt & Fclts Mgr*
Eric Watson, *Purch Mgr*
EMP: 31 EST: 1966
SQ FT: 25,000
SALES (est): 18.9MM **Privately Held**
WEB: www.rudolphbros.com
SIC: **5169** Chemicals & allied products; adhesives, chemical; sealants; adhesives & sealants

Canal Winchester - Franklin County (G-2170)

(G-2170)
SEALS CONSTRUCTION INC
10283 Busey Rd Nw (43110-9629)
PHONE..................................614 836-7200
Andy Seals, *President*
Matt Stibich, *Project Mgr*
EMP: 47 **EST:** 1999
SQ FT: 12,000
SALES (est): 7.4MM **Privately Held**
WEB: www.sealsinc.com
SIC: 1794 Excavation & grading, building construction

(G-2171)
SOUTH CENTRAL POWER COMPANY
10229 Busey Rd Nw (43110-9629)
PHONE..................................614 837-4351
Tom Musick, *President*
Cyndi Arledge, *Principal*
Cathy Bilter, *Sales & Mktg St*
Rebecca Witt, *CFO*
Amanda Babbert, *Advisor*
EMP: 35
SALES (corp-wide): 282.1MM **Privately Held**
WEB: www.southcentralpower.com
SIC: 4911 Distribution, electric power
PA: South Central Power Company Inc
2780 Coonpath Rd Ne
Lancaster OH 43130
740 653-4422

(G-2172)
TNT MOBILE POWERWASH INC
260 Pfeifer Dr (43110-2031)
PHONE..................................614 402-7474
Seth Bromberg, *President*
EMP: 25
SALES (est): 922.7K **Privately Held**
SIC: 1799 Steam cleaning of building exteriors

(G-2173)
TRI COUNTY FAMILY PHYSICIANS
11925 Lithopolis Rd Nw (43110-9535)
PHONE..................................614 837-6363
Fax: 614 837-0425
Fred Hennis, *Principal*
EMP: 40
SALES (est): 2.4MM **Privately Held**
SIC: 8011 General & family practice, physician/surgeon

(G-2174)
UNITED CHURCH RESIDENCES OF
Also Called: CANAL VILLAGE
85 Covenant Way (43110-1080)
P.O. Box 1806, Marion (43301-1806)
PHONE..................................614 837-2008
Brian Allen, *President*
Erin Redd, *Executive Asst*
EMP: 60
SQ FT: 20,000
SALES: 525.4K **Privately Held**
SIC: 6513 Apartment building operators

(G-2175)
VOGEL DIALYSIS LLC
Also Called: Canal Winchester Dialysis
3568 Gender Rd (43110-8007)
PHONE..................................614 834-3564
James K Hilger,
EMP: 37
SALES (est): 548.5K **Publicly Held**
SIC: 8092 Kidney dialysis centers
PA: Davita Inc.
2000 16th St
Denver CO 80202

(G-2176)
WAIBEL HEATING COMPANY
2840 Cedar Hill Rd Nw (43110-8947)
PHONE..................................614 837-7615
Tim Waibel, *President*
Marsha Waibel, *Corp Secy*
EMP: 25
SQ FT: 6,200
SALES: 2MM **Privately Held**
SIC: 1711 Warm air heating & air conditioning contractor

(G-2177)
WASTE MANAGEMENT OHIO INC
1006 W Walnut St (43110-9757)
PHONE..................................614 382-6342
Troy Cuttingham, *Sr Corp Ofcr*
Mike Lavengco, *Sr Corp Ofcr*
Bill Truback, *Sr Corp Ofcr*
Rob Smith, *Vice Pres*
Ron Deterese, *Opers Staff*
EMP: 61
SALES (corp-wide): 14.4B **Publicly Held**
WEB: www.wm.com
SIC: 8611 Business associations
HQ: Waste Management Of Ohio, Inc.
1700 N Broad St
Fairborn OH 45324

(G-2178)
WASTE MANAGEMENT OHIO INC
1046 W Walnut St (43110-9757)
PHONE..................................614 833-5290
Karen Factor, *Principal*
Steven Mignone, *Safety Mgr*
Ginger Kaladas, *Credit Staff*
Lee Hicks, *Contract Law*
Kiki Lee,
EMP: 99
SALES (corp-wide): 14.4B **Publicly Held**
WEB: www.wm.com
SIC: 4953 Refuse systems
HQ: Waste Management Of Ohio, Inc.
1700 N Broad St
Fairborn OH 45324

(G-2179)
WINCHESTER PLACE LEASING LLC
Also Called: Winchester Care Rehabilitation
36 Lehman Dr (43110-1099)
PHONE..................................614 834-2273
Eli Gunzburg, *Manager*
Jody Kupchik, *Assistant*
EMP: 99
SQ FT: 52,214
SALES (est): 819.5K
SALES (corp-wide): 1.5MM **Privately Held**
SIC: 8051 Mental retardation hospital
PA: Aspenwood Holdings, Llc
29225 Chagrin Blvd # 230
Cleveland OH 44122
216 367-1214

(G-2180)
WORLD HARVEST CHURCH INC (PA)
Also Called: Breakthrough Media Ministries
4595 Gender Rd (43110-9149)
P.O. Box 428 (43110-0428)
PHONE..................................614 837-1990
Fax: 614 834-1276
Rodney Parsley, *Pastor*
Darrin Endicott, *Maintenance Dir*
Andrew Sturdon, *Controller*
Kym Wimbish, *Human Res Dir*
Wayne Haseleu, *Manager*
EMP: 300
SQ FT: 200,000
SALES (est): 13.1MM **Privately Held**
WEB: www.breakthrough.net
SIC: 8661 7812 2731 Non-denominational church; video tape production; books; publishing & printing

(G-2181)
YOUNG MENS CHRISTIAN ASSOC
Also Called: Jerry L Garver Branch
6767 Refugee Rd (43110-8682)
PHONE..................................614 834-9622
Fax: 614 834-9625
Mike Sabin, *Branch Mgr*
Marcus Parham, *Director*
Tamala Perryman, *Director*
Jacob Hittle, *Assistant*
EMP: 200
SALES (corp-wide): 44.9MM **Privately Held**
WEB: www.ymca-columbus.com
SIC: 8641 8661 8322 7997 Youth organizations; religious organizations; individual & family services; membership sports & recreation clubs; physical fitness facilities

PA: Young Men's Christian Association Of Central Ohio
40 W Long St
Columbus OH 43215
614 389-4409

Canfield
Mahoning County

(G-2182)
ALLY FINANCIAL INC
Also Called: GMAC
3731 Boardman Canfield Rd (44406-9013)
PHONE..................................330 533-7300
Steve Hidell, *Branch Mgr*
EMP: 45
SALES (corp-wide): 9.8B **Publicly Held**
WEB: www.gmacfs.com
SIC: 6153 Short-term business credit
PA: Ally Financial Inc.
500 Woodward Ave Fl 10
Detroit MI 48226
866 710-4623

(G-2183)
BODINE PERRY LLC (PA)
3711 Strrs Cntre Dr Ste 2 (44406)
PHONE..................................330 702-8100
Fax: 330 702-8781
Matthew Bodine, *COO*
Justin Yost, *Accountant*
Mathew Bodine,
Jim Hunter,
Daniel Perry,
EMP: 50
SALES (est): 9MM **Privately Held**
WEB: www.bodineperry.com
SIC: 8721 8742 Certified public accountant; financial consultant

(G-2184)
CANFIELD METAL COATING CORP
460 W Main St (44406-1434)
PHONE..................................330 702-3876
Ronald W Jandrokovic, *President*
Paul Pirko, *Vice Pres*
Clarence Newhouse Jr, *Plant Mgr*
Phil Widomski, *Controller*
George S Bokros, *Finance Dir*
EMP: 52
SALES (est): 1MM
SALES (corp-wide): 1.3B **Publicly Held**
WEB: www.coilcoat.com
SIC: 3479 5051 Galvanizing of iron, steel or end-formed products; metals service centers & offices
HQ: Handy & Harman Ltd.
590 Madison Ave Rm 3202
New York NY 10022

(G-2185)
CASALS HAIR SALON INC (PA)
Also Called: Casal Day Spa and Salon
4030 Boardman Canfield Rd (44406-9505)
PHONE..................................330 533-6766
Fax: 330 533-6677
Thomas Ciarniello, *President*
EMP: 35
SALES (est): 2.3MM **Privately Held**
SIC: 7231 Manicurist, pedicurist

(G-2186)
CENTER FOR DLYSIS CRE OF CNFLD
3695 Stutz Dr Ste 1 (44406-9144)
PHONE..................................330 702-3040
Fax: 330 702-3050
Kim Blankenship, *Manager*
Erdal Sarac, *Director*
EMP: 30
SALES (est): 1.5MM **Privately Held**
SIC: 8011 Clinic, operated by physicians

(G-2187)
COY BROTHERS INC
433 Fairground Blvd (44406-1551)
PHONE..................................330 533-6864
Fax: 330 533-6902
Arlan Coy, *President*
Danielle McCown, *Manager*
Patricia Coy, *Admin Sec*
EMP: 32 **EST:** 1920

SALES: 3MM **Privately Held**
SIC: 4213 Trucking, except local

(G-2188)
DANIELS LUMBER CO INC
Also Called: Bernard Daniels Lumber Co
250 Railroad St (44406-1443)
PHONE..................................330 533-2211
Paul B Daniels, *President*
Tom Paranzino, *President*
Mike Harmond, *Business Mgr*
EMP: 60
SQ FT: 100,000
SALES (est): 8.9MM **Privately Held**
SIC: 5031 5211 5251 Lumber, plywood & millwork; lumber & other building materials; hardware

(G-2189)
FACILITY PRODUCTS & SVCS LLC
330 Newton St (44406-1435)
PHONE..................................330 533-8943
Fax: 330 533-8944
John Christopher, *Principal*
Mike Carlozzi, *Manager*
Edward Petruzzi, *Supervisor*
EMP: 44
SALES (est): 6.5MM **Privately Held**
SIC: 1761 Roofing, siding & sheet metal work

(G-2190)
FARMERS NAT BNK OF CANFIELD (HQ)
20 S Broad St (44406-1401)
P.O. Box 555 (44406-0555)
PHONE..................................330 533-3341
Fax: 330 533-6365
Kevin Helmick, *President*
Gregg Strollo, *Principal*
Carl D Culp, *Exec VP*
Don Lukas, *Senior VP*
James R Vansickle, *Senior VP*
EMP: 127
SQ FT: 25,000
SALES: 87.1MM
SALES (corp-wide): 104.5MM **Publicly Held**
SIC: 6021 National commercial banks
PA: Farmers National Banc Corp.
20 S Broad St
Canfield OH 44406
330 533-3341

(G-2191)
GATEWAYS TO BETTER LIVING INC
3220 S Raccoon Rd (44406-9359)
PHONE..................................330 797-1764
EMP: 25
SALES (corp-wide): 17.3MM **Privately Held**
SIC: 8361 Home for the mentally retarded
PA: Gateways To Better Living Inc
6000 Mahoning Ave Ste 234
Youngstown OH 44515
330 792-2854

(G-2192)
GREEN HAVEN MEMORIAL GARDENS
3495 S Canfield Niles Rd (44406-9698)
PHONE..................................330 533-6811
Fax: 330 533-1261
Merrill O Fisher, *Principal*
EMP: 30
SALES (est): 1.6MM **Privately Held**
SIC: 6553 Cemeteries, real estate operation

(G-2193)
HILL BARTH & KING LLC (PA)
6603 Summit Dr (44406-9509)
P.O. Box 3406, Youngstown (44513-3406)
PHONE..................................330 758-8613
Fax: 330 758-0357
Christopher M Allegretti, *CEO*
Leannah Hostetler, *CFO*
Leannah Hostetler, *CFO*
Doug Stahl, *CFO*
Tom Tomaszewski, *Controller*
EMP: 50
SQ FT: 15,000

GEOGRAPHIC SECTION
Canfield - Mahoning County (G-2216)

SALES (est): 49.7MM **Privately Held**
WEB: www.hbkcpa.com
SIC: 8721 8741 Certified public accountant; financial management for business

(G-2194)
HILL BARTH & KING LLC
Also Called: Hbk
6603 Summit Dr (44406-9509)
PHONE..................330 747-1903
Fax: 330 747-5805
Richard A Keyse, *Principal*
Steven Steer, *Principal*
Annemarie Hopkins, *Accountant*
Rose Depinet-Foss, *CPA*
William T Poole, *Finance*
EMP: 27
SALES (corp-wide): 49.7MM **Privately Held**
WEB: www.hbkcpa.com
SIC: 8721 Certified public accountant
PA: Hill, Barth & King Llc
6603 Summit Dr
Canfield OH 44406
330 758-8613

(G-2195)
HOWARD HANNA SMYTHE CRAMER
4374 Boardman Canfield Rd (44406-8092)
PHONE..................800 656-7356
Fax: 330 702-8560
Gina Shutrump, *Principal*
Michele Lux, *Finance Mgr*
Cindy Lautzenheiser, *Real Est Agnt*
Pamela Porter, *Real Est Agnt*
Nancy L Zatchok, *Real Est Agnt*
EMP: 30
SALES (corp-wide): 76.4MM **Privately Held**
SIC: 6531 Real estate agents & managers
HQ: Howard Hanna Smythe Cramer
6000 Parkland Blvd
Cleveland OH 44124
216 447-4477

(G-2196)
IES SYSTEMS INC
464 Lisbon St (44406-1423)
P.O. Box 89 (44406-0089)
PHONE..................330 533-6683
Fax: 330 533-7293
Mark Brucoli, *President*
Kelly Weiss, *Corp Secy*
Rob McAndrew, *Exec VP*
David Wigal, *Exec VP*
Bill Yobi, *Exec VP*
EMP: 45
SQ FT: 27,000
SALES (est): 7.5MM **Privately Held**
WEB: www.ies-us.com
SIC: 7389 3821 Design, commercial & industrial; laboratory apparatus & furniture

(G-2197)
J A DONADEE CORPORATION (PA)
535 N Broad St Ste 5 (44406-8221)
PHONE..................330 533-3305
John A Donadee, *President*
Bill Burnside, *Plant Supt*
Jane Donadee, *Treasurer*
Billie Delull, *Controller*
Maureen Russo, *Office Mgr*
EMP: 39
SQ FT: 4,200
SALES (est): 3.6MM **Privately Held**
SIC: 1611 General contractor, highway & street construction

(G-2198)
L CALVIN JONES & COMPANY
3744 Starrs Centre Dr (44406-8001)
P.O. Box 159 (44406-0159)
PHONE..................330 533-1195
Alvin Miller Jr, *President*
Jean Veauthier, *Accounting Mgr*
Mercy Komar, *Psychologist*
Richard Wisnoskey, *Consultant*
Cynthia Spencer, *Admin Sec*
EMP: 25
SALES (est): 7MM **Privately Held**
WEB: www.lcalvinjones.com
SIC: 6331 Fire, marine & casualty insurance & carriers

(G-2199)
MEANDER HOSPITALITY GROUP INC
Also Called: Staybridge Suites
6599 Seville Dr Ste 100 (44406-7010)
PHONE..................330 702-0226
Bill Kovas, *President*
Bill Puglise, *General Mgr*
Tim Dehnart, *Manager*
EMP: 35 EST: 1998
SALES (est): 2.3MM **Privately Held**
SIC: 7011 Hotels & motels

(G-2200)
MERRILL LYNCH PIERCE FENNER
4137 Boardman Canfield Rd (44406-8087)
PHONE..................330 702-7300
Fax: 330 702-7301
Gordon Raynor, *Manager*
EMP: 40
SALES (corp-wide): 100.2B **Publicly Held**
SIC: 6211 Stock brokers & dealers
HQ: Merrill Lynch, Pierce, Fenner & Smith Incorporated
111 8th Ave
New York NY 10011
800 637-7455

(G-2201)
MERRILL LYNCH PIERCE FENNER
4137 Boardman Canfield Rd # 201 (44406-7004)
PHONE..................330 702-0535
Fax: 330 702-7301
EMP: 27
SALES (corp-wide): 95.1B **Publicly Held**
SIC: 6211 Security Broker/Dealer
HQ: Merrill Lynch, Pierce, Fenner & Smith Incorporated
111 8th Ave
New York NY 10011
800 637-7455

(G-2202)
MYERS BUS PARTS AND SUPS CO
Also Called: Myers Equipment
8860 Akron Canfield Rd (44406-8770)
PHONE..................330 533-2275
David Myers, *President*
Richard Myers, *Vice Pres*
Clark Myers, *Purchasing*
EMP: 40
SALES (est): 2.9MM **Privately Held**
SIC: 5015 Automotive parts & supplies, used

(G-2203)
MYERS EQUIPMENT CORPORATION
8860 Akron Canfield Rd (44406-8770)
PHONE..................330 533-5556
David Myers, *President*
Doug Spencer, *Parts Mgr*
Allan Swift, *Sales Mgr*
Ryan Schmidt, *Sales Staff*
Rob Spencer, *Sales Staff*
▼ EMP: 40
SQ FT: 40,000
SALES (est): 15.1MM **Privately Held**
WEB: www.myersequip.com
SIC: 5083 Farm equipment parts & supplies

(G-2204)
NADLER NADLER & BURDMAN CO LPA
6550 Seville Dr Ste B (44406-9138)
PHONE..................330 533-6195
Fax: 330 744-8690
Jay Skolnick, *President*
Michael A Gallo, *Treasurer*
Robert S Hartford Jr,
William A Myers,
Donn D Rosenblum,
EMP: 35
SQ FT: 12,000
SALES (est): 3.7MM **Privately Held**
WEB: www.nnblaw.com
SIC: 8111 General practice law office

(G-2205)
OHIO DEPARTMENT TRANSPORTATION
Also Called: Odot District 4
501 W Main St (44406)
PHONE..................330 533-4351
Fax: 330 533-1471
Charles Miner, *Manager*
Joe Maslach, *Manager*
EMP: 34 **Privately Held**
SIC: 9621 1611 Regulation, administration of transportation; ; highway & street maintenance
HQ: Ohio Department Of Transportation
1980 W Broad St
Columbus OH 43223

(G-2206)
OHIO STRUCTURES INC (HQ)
535 N Broad St Ste 5 (44406-8221)
PHONE..................330 533-0084
Fax: 330 533-0191
John Donadee, *President*
Julie Hlebovy, *Corp Secy*
Sean Giblin, *Vice Pres*
David Spurio, *Treasurer*
Thomas Kostelic, *Admin Sec*
EMP: 50
SALES (est): 13.2MM
SALES (corp-wide): 3.6MM **Privately Held**
SIC: 3441 8711 Fabricated structural metal; engineering services
PA: J A Donadee Corporation
535 N Broad St Ste 5
Canfield OH 44406
330 533-3305

(G-2207)
PAUL HRNCHAR FORD-MERCURY INC
Also Called: Hrnchar's Fairway Ford
366 W Main St (44406-1477)
PHONE..................330 533-3673
Paul J Hrnchar, *President*
Jimmy Himes, *Sales Staff*
Jeff Stockman, *Information Mgr*
EMP: 40
SQ FT: 30,000
SALES (est): 16.5MM **Privately Held**
SIC: 5511 7539 7532 Automobiles, new & used; trucks, tractors & trailers: new & used; automotive repair shops; body shop, automotive

(G-2208)
ROHOLT VISION INSTITUTE INC
25 Manor Hill Dr (44406-1596)
PHONE..................330 702-8755
Philip Roholt, *President*
EMP: 30
SALES (est): 1.8MM
SALES (corp-wide): 2MM **Privately Held**
SIC: 8733 Noncommercial research organizations
PA: Roholt Vision Institute Inc
5890 Mayfair Rd
Canton OH 44720
330 305-2200

(G-2209)
SCHROEDEL SCULLIN & BESTIC LLC
196 N Broad St Ste A (44406-1291)
PHONE..................330 533-1131
Fax: 330 533-2050
Karl Schroedel, *Principal*
Mark R Heagerty, *Principal*
John Pulliam, *Vice Pres*
Brian Frederick, *Manager*
Donna Seiser, *Manager*
EMP: 40
SALES (est): 2.5MM **Privately Held**
WEB: www.ssb-cpa.com
SIC: 8721 Certified public accountant

(G-2210)
SEBASTIANI TRUCKING INC
61 Railroad St (44406-1440)
PHONE..................330 286-0059
Daniel Sebastiani, *CEO*
Emilio Sebastiani, *President*
Angelica Sebastiani, *Corp Secy*
EMP: 56
SQ FT: 2,500
SALES (est): 6.6MM **Privately Held**
SIC: 4212 Dump truck haulage

(G-2211)
TALMER BANK AND TRUST
2 S Broad St (44406-1401)
PHONE..................330 726-3396
EMP: 38
SALES (corp-wide): 321.3MM **Publicly Held**
SIC: 6035 Savings Bank
HQ: Talmer Bank And Trust
2301 W Big Beaver Rd # 525
Troy MI 48084
248 649-2301

(G-2212)
THOMAS PACKER & CO (PA)
6601 Westford Pl Ste 101 (44406-7005)
PHONE..................330 533-9777
Fax: 330 533-1734
Phillip Dennison, *President*
Patricia Czechowski, *Opers Staff*
Steven Kacerski, *Tax Mgr*
Bridgette Bukofchan, *Accountant*
Kim Murphy, *Accountant*
EMP: 40
SALES (est): 7.8MM **Privately Held**
SIC: 8721 Certified public accountant

(G-2213)
TIPPECANOE COUNTRY CLUB INC
Also Called: TIPPECANOE PRO SHOP
5870 Tippecanoe Rd (44406-9538)
P.O. Box 86 (44406-0086)
PHONE..................330 758-7518
Fax: 330 758-4844
Adnan Folloum, *Manager*
Stacey Owen, *Manager*
EMP: 35
SQ FT: 34,000
SALES: 3MM **Privately Held**
SIC: 7997 5941 7991 5812 Country club, membership; golf club, membership; swimming club, membership; tennis club, membership; golf goods & equipment; physical fitness facilities; eating places

(G-2214)
UNITED SRGCAL PRTNERS INTL INC
4147 Westford Dr (44406-8086)
PHONE..................330 702-1489
John Wellik, *Senior VP*
Jeff Kober, *Materials Mgr*
Cheryl Lambros, *Branch Mgr*
Shawn P Bannon, *Manager*
Delores Powell, *Manager*
EMP: 30
SALES (corp-wide): 19.3B **Publicly Held**
WEB: www.surgisinc.com
SIC: 8011 Ambulatory surgical center
HQ: United Surgical Partners International, Inc.
15305 Dallas Pkwy # 1600
Addison TX 75001
972 713-3500

(G-2215)
WHITE HOUSE FRUIT FARM INC
9249 Youngstown Salem Rd (44406-9482)
PHONE..................330 533-4161
Fax: 330 533-7953
David J Hull, *President*
Phyllis Hull, *Vice Pres*
Deborah Hull, *Admin Sec*
Deborah Hull Pifer, *Admin Sec*
EMP: 30
SALES: 3.5MM **Privately Held**
WEB: www.whitehousefruitfarm.com
SIC: 0175 Apple orchard

(G-2216)
WSB REHABILITATION SVCS INC (PA)
Also Called: Blue Sky Therapy
510 W Main St Ste B (44406-1454)
PHONE..................330 533-1338
Fax: 330 702-0510
Renee Bucci Halfhill, *President*
Mellisa Urioste, *Finance*
Michael Yatsco, *Sales Associate*
Rosalie Nolfi, *Mktg Coord*
Kelly Jenkins, *Manager*

Canfield - Mahoning County (G-2217)

EMP: 60
SALES (est): 26.6MM Privately Held
WEB: www.blueskytherapy.net
SIC: 8049 Physical therapist

(G-2217)
YOUNGSTOWN ORTHOPAEDIC ASSOC
6470 Tippecanoe Rd Ste A (44406-9568)
PHONE....................330 726-1466
Fax: 330 758-0466
Rick Peaslee, *Engineer*
Jami Toot, *Human Res Mgr*
Robert Cutticakuo, *Director*
James Jamison, *Director*
James Kerrigan, *Director*
EMP: 30
SQ FT: 2,000
SALES (est): 6MM Privately Held
SIC: 8011 Orthopedic physician; surgeon

(G-2218)
ZINNI GOLF CO INC
9866 Lisbon Rd (44406-9498)
P.O. Box 676 (44406-0676)
PHONE....................330 533-7155
James Zinni, *President*
Tim Zinni, *Vice Pres*
Marcia Zinni, *Admin Sec*
EMP: 30
SQ FT: 8,000
SALES (est): 2.7MM Privately Held
SIC: 1629 Golf course construction

Canton
Stark County

(G-2219)
415 GROUP INC (PA)
4100 Holiday St Nw # 100 (44718-2589)
P.O. Box 35334 (44735-5334)
PHONE....................330 492-0094
Frank Monaco, *President*
Scott Whetstone, *Vice Pres*
Kelby Kraft, *Accountant*
Patricia Metz, *Accountant*
Kathleen Krohn, *CPA*
EMP: 38
SQ FT: 13,000
SALES: 3.5MM Privately Held
WEB: www.415group.com
SIC: 8721 Certified public accountant

(G-2220)
50 X 20 HOLDING COMPANY INC (PA)
Also Called: Schumacher Homes
2715 Wise Ave Nw (44708-1641)
PHONE....................330 478-4500
Fax: 330 477-6197
Paul T Schumacher, *President*
Larry Scheetz, *President*
Keith Fluharty, *General Mgr*
Greg Pacholski, *General Mgr*
Tim Reese, *General Mgr*
EMP: 57
SQ FT: 250,000
SALES (est): 80.4MM Privately Held
SIC: 1521 New construction, single-family houses

(G-2221)
A CHILDS PLACE NURSERY SCHOOL
4770 Higbee Ave Nw (44718-2550)
PHONE....................330 493-1333
EMP: 55
SQ FT: 6,100
SALES (est): 978K Privately Held
SIC: 8351 Nursery School

(G-2222)
ABBOTT ELECTRIC (PA)
1935 Allen Ave Se (44707-3605)
PHONE....................330 452-6601
James D Abbott, *President*
Michael C Abbott, *Vice Pres*
Nancy Abbott, *Vice Pres*
John Dale, *Project Mgr*
Al Columbo, *Opers Mgr*
EMP: 63
SQ FT: 5,000
SALES: 19MM Privately Held
SIC: 1731 General electrical contractor

(G-2223)
ABCD INC (PA)
Also Called: A B C D
1225 Gross Ave Ne (44705-1605)
PHONE....................330 455-6385
Fax: 330 455-3913
William Dent, *CEO*
Larry Bell, *Director*
Amanda Webb, *Director*
EMP: 30
SQ FT: 114,000
SALES: 1.4MM Privately Held
SIC: 8399 Community action agency

(G-2224)
ACUTE CARE SPECIALTY HOSPITAL
2600 6th St Sw (44710-1702)
PHONE....................330 363-4860
Ileen Good, *Principal*
EMP: 638 **EST:** 2009
SALES: 7.3MM Privately Held
SIC: 8062 General medical & surgical hospitals

(G-2225)
ADELMANS TRUCK PARTS CORP (PA)
Also Called: Adelman's Truck Sales
2000 Waynesburg Dr Se (44707-2194)
PHONE....................330 456-0206
Fax: 330 456-3959
Carl Adelman, *President*
Larry Adelman, *Vice Pres*
◆ **EMP:** 30
SQ FT: 120,000
SALES (est): 8.8MM Privately Held
WEB: www.adelmans.com
SIC: 5013 3714 Truck parts & accessories; power transmission equipment, motor vehicle; differentials & parts, motor vehicle

(G-2226)
ADVANTAGE APPLIANCE SERVICES
Also Called: Absolute Health Services
7235 Whipple Ave Nw (44720-7137)
P.O. Box 2279, North Canton (44720-0279)
PHONE....................330 498-8101
Gereld Schroer Sr, *President*
Kevin Fearon, *COO*
Jerry Schroer Jr, *Vice Pres*
Renee Steurer, *Accounts Exec*
Pam Babics, *Manager*
EMP: 175
SQ FT: 27,000
SALES (est): 10.9MM Privately Held
WEB: www.abshealth.com
SIC: 5047 Medical equipment & supplies

(G-2227)
ADVENT DRILLING INC
366 Rose Lane St Sw (44720-3556)
P.O. Box 2562 (44720-0562)
PHONE....................330 497-2533
Charles Keeney Jr, *President*
Gary Yarnell, *Vice Pres*
Laurie Keeney, *Admin Sec*
EMP: 27
SALES: 1.9MM Privately Held
SIC: 1381 Drilling oil & gas wells

(G-2228)
ADVENTURE CMBAT OPERATIONS LLC
4501 Hlls Dls Rd Nw A (44708-1572)
P.O. Box 35063 (44735-5063)
PHONE....................330 818-1029
Travis Krauss, *Owner*
Melissa Laskovski, *Manager*
EMP: 30
SQ FT: 2,300
SALES (est): 450K Privately Held
SIC: 7929 7389 Entertainers & entertainment groups;

(G-2229)
AEEA LLC
Also Called: Meriprise Financial
4383 Executive Cir Nw (44718-2999)
PHONE....................330 497-5304

Mike Dougherty, *Partner*
EMP: 30
SALES (est): 1.7MM Privately Held
SIC: 8742 Planning consultant

(G-2230)
ALCO-CHEM INC
1303 Park Ave Sw (44706-5403)
PHONE....................330 833-8551
Alco Chem, *President*
EMP: 34
SALES (corp-wide): 26.7MM Privately Held
SIC: 7629 5113 5087 Electrical household appliance repair; paper & products, wrapping or coarse; janitors' supplies
PA: Alco-Chem, Inc.
  45 N Summit St
  Akron OH 44308
  330 253-3535

(G-2231)
ALLEN-KEITH CONSTRUCTION CO (PA)
Also Called: Service Master By Allen Keith
2735 Greensburg Rd (44720-1423)
PHONE....................330 266-2220
Daniel Hanlon, *CEO*
Thomas Hocking, *Vice Pres*
Tammy Verman, *Manager*
EMP: 57
SQ FT: 38,000
SALES (est): 8MM Privately Held
WEB: www.allenkeith.com
SIC: 7349 1541 7217 Building maintenance services; industrial buildings & warehouses; carpet & upholstery cleaning

(G-2232)
ALLIANCE IMAGING INC
4825 Higbee Ave Nw # 201 (44718-2567)
PHONE....................330 493-5100
Fax: 330 493-5372
Shawn Smith, *Vice Pres*
Steven J Ossakow, *Vice Pres*
Jason Evans, *Opers Mgr*
Dennis Updike, *Opers Mgr*
Randy Skiles, *Treasurer*
EMP: 115
SQ FT: 5,000
SALES (est): 3.6MM Privately Held
WEB: www.mvhs.org
SIC: 8071 8731 X-ray laboratory, including dental; commercial physical research
HQ: Alliance Healthcare Services, Inc.
  18201 Von Karman Ave
  Irvine CA 92612
  949 242-5300

(G-2233)
ALLIANCE PETROLEUM CORPORATION (HQ)
4150 Belden Village Mall (44718-2502)
PHONE....................330 493-0440
Fax: 330 493-3409
Dora L Silvis, *COO*
Tim Altier, *Senior VP*
Nick Armstrong, *Vice Pres*
David Dean, *VP Opers*
Martin L Miller, *VP Opers*
EMP: 61
SQ FT: 2,900
SALES (est): 75.2MM Privately Held
WEB: www.alliancepetroleumcorp.com
SIC: 1311 1382 Crude petroleum production; natural gas production; oil & gas exploration services
PA: Diversified Gas & Oil Corporation
  1100 Corporate Dr Ste 100
  Birmingham AL 35242
  205 408-0909

(G-2234)
ALLIED TRUCK PARTS CO
4216 Southway St Sw (44706-1876)
PHONE....................330 477-8127
Fax: 330 477-6359
Lorel L Molder, *President*
Lee Hochstetler, *Vice Pres*
William Rudner, *Treasurer*
EMP: 35
SQ FT: 35,000

SALES: 4.7MM Privately Held
SIC: 5013 5511 7538 Truck parts & accessories; trucks, tractors & trailers: new & used; truck engine repair, except industrial

(G-2235)
ALTERCARE NOBLES POND INC
Also Called: Altercare of Ohio
7006 Fulton Dr Nw (44718-1521)
PHONE....................330 834-4800
Fax: 330 834-4894
Brenda Pedro, *Administration*
EMP: 70
SQ FT: 38,892
SALES (est): 2.7MM Privately Held
SIC: 8052 8051 Intermediate care facilities; skilled nursing care facilities

(G-2236)
ALTERNATIVE RESIDENCES TWO
Also Called: Canton Group Home
2832 34th St Ne (44705-3886)
PHONE....................330 453-0200
Fax: 330 453-3895
EMP: 45
SALES (corp-wide): 5K Privately Held
SIC: 8361 8052 Residential Care Services Intermediate Care Facility
PA: Alternative Residences Two, Inc
  67051 Executive Dr
  Saint Clairsville OH 43950
  740 526-0514

(G-2237)
AMERICAN ELECTRIC POWER CO INC
Also Called: AEP Texas North Company
301 Cleveland Ave Sw (44702-1623)
P.O. Box 24400 (44701-4400)
PHONE....................330 438-7024
Jack Kincaid, *Project Mgr*
Rich Tharp, *Safety Mgr*
John Fabian, *Engineer*
Michael Ickes, *Engineer*
Dave Miller, *Engineer*
EMP: 208
SALES (corp-wide): 15.4B Publicly Held
WEB: www.myenviroassistant.com
SIC: 4911 Electric services; distribution, electric power; generation, electric power; transmission, electric power
PA: American Electric Power Company, Inc.
  1 Riverside Plz Fl 1 # 1
  Columbus OH 43215
  614 716-1000

(G-2238)
AMERICAN ELECTRIC POWER CO INC
Also Called: AEP
5300 Navarre Rd Sw (44706-3315)
PHONE....................330 580-5085
EMP: 46
SALES (corp-wide): 15.4B Publicly Held
SIC: 4911 Distribution, electric power
PA: American Electric Power Company, Inc.
  1 Riverside Plz Fl 1 # 1
  Columbus OH 43215
  614 716-1000

(G-2239)
AMERICAN PRPRTY-MNAGEMENT CORP
Also Called: Marriott McKinley Grande Hotel
320 Market Ave S (44702-2108)
PHONE....................330 454-5000
Fax: 330 454-5494
Keith Johnson, *General Mgr*
Kevin Goebel, *Manager*
EMP: 100
SALES (corp-wide): 156.6MM Privately Held
WEB: www.americanpropertymanagement-corp.com
SIC: 7011 Hotels & motels
PA: American Property-Management Corporation
  8910 University Center Ln # 100
  San Diego CA 92122
  858 964-5500

GEOGRAPHIC SECTION

Canton - Stark County (G-2262)

(G-2240)
AMERIDIAL INC
4877 Higbee Ave Nw (44718-2566)
PHONE....................................800 445-7128
Michael McCarthy, *Branch Mgr*
Janine Jones, *Info Tech Dir*
EMP: 350
SALES (corp-wide): 40MM **Privately Held**
SIC: 7389 Telemarketing services
PA: Ameridial, Inc.
4535 Strausser St Nw
North Canton OH 44720
330 497-4888

(G-2241)
ANSWERCARE LLC
4150 Belden Village St Nw # 307 (44718-2539)
PHONE....................................855 213-1511
Jordan P Bucar, *Mng Member*
EMP: 55
SQ FT: 1,500
SALES: 502K **Privately Held**
SIC: 8082 Home health care services

(G-2242)
ANTHEM INSURANCE COMPANIES INC
Also Called: Blue Cross
4150 Belden Village St Nw # 506 (44718-2595)
PHONE....................................330 492-2151
Fax: 330 493-2148
Eloise Walls, *Branch Mgr*
EMP: 30
SALES (corp-wide): 90B **Publicly Held**
WEB: www.anthem-inc.com
SIC: 6324 Group hospitalization plans
HQ: Anthem Insurance Companies, Inc.
120 Monument Cir Ste 200
Indianapolis IN 46204
317 488-6000

(G-2243)
APPALACHIAN POWER COMPANY
301 Cleveland Ave Sw (44702-1623)
P.O. Box 24400 (44701-4400)
PHONE....................................330 438-7102
EMP: 98
SALES (corp-wide): 15.4B **Publicly Held**
SIC: 4911 Electric services
HQ: Appalachian Power Company
1 Riverside Plz
Columbus OH 43215
614 716-1000

(G-2244)
ARCHER CORPORATION
Also Called: Archer Sign
1917 Henry Ave Sw (44706-2941)
PHONE....................................330 455-9995
Jerry Archer, *CEO*
Michael Minor, *Vice Pres*
Paul Petro, *Project Mgr*
Scott Hughes, *Engineer*
Beth Watson, *Manager*
EMP: 40
SQ FT: 70,000
SALES (est): 6.4MM **Privately Held**
WEB: www.archersign.com
SIC: 1799 3993 Sign installation & maintenance; signs & advertising specialties

(G-2245)
ARTHUR MIDDLETON CAPITAL HOLDN
8000 Freedom Ave Nw (44720-6912)
PHONE....................................330 966-3033
Monica Wallace, *Branch Mgr*
EMP: 203 **Privately Held**
SIC: 6799 Investors
PA: Arthur Middleton Capital Holdings, Inc.
8000 Freedom Ave Nw
North Canton OH 44720

(G-2246)
ASAP HOMECARE INC
4150 Belden Village St Nw (44718-2595)
PHONE....................................330 491-0700
Fax: 330 491-0725
Roy Batista, *Manager*
EMP: 56
SALES (corp-wide): 6.9MM **Privately Held**
SIC: 8059 Convalescent home
PA: Asap Homecare Inc
1 Park Centre Dr Ste 107
Wadsworth OH 44281
330 334-7027

(G-2247)
ASW GLOBAL LLC
Also Called: Asw Akron Logistic
2150 International Pkwy (44720-1373)
PHONE....................................330 899-1003
Bruce Paisley, *Branch Mgr*
EMP: 60
SALES (corp-wide): 84.5MM **Privately Held**
WEB: www.aswservices.com
SIC: 4225 General warehousing
PA: Asw Global, Llc
3375 Gilchrist Rd
Mogadore OH 44260
330 733-6291

(G-2248)
ATLANTIC FISH & DISTRG CO
Also Called: Atlantic Food Distributors
430 6th St Se (44702-1158)
PHONE....................................330 454-1307
Fax: 330 452-6622
Debbi Vinton, *Vice Pres*
Bob Tomczak, *Buyer*
Victoria Johanning, *Purchasing*
Jim Cooke, *Manager*
June Kauffman, *Manager*
EMP: 41
SQ FT: 3,000
SALES (est): 37.2MM **Privately Held**
SIC: 5141 Food brokers

(G-2249)
AULTCARE CORP
2600 6th St Sw (44710-1702)
PHONE....................................330 363-6360
Rick Haines, *President*
Allen Rovner MD, *President*
Andrea Finley, *Vice Pres*
Frank Getz, *Vice Pres*
Mike Novelli, *Vice Pres*
EMP: 300
SALES (est): 185.1MM **Privately Held**
SIC: 6324 Group hospitalization plans

(G-2250)
AULTCARE INSURANCE COMPANY
2600 6th St Sw (44710-1702)
P.O. Box 6910 (44706-0910)
PHONE....................................330 363-6360
Rick Haines, *President*
Melissa Shelton, *Vice Pres*
Syed Fayyaz, *Info Tech Mgr*
EMP: 400
SALES (est): 117.4MM **Privately Held**
WEB: www.aultcare.com
SIC: 6321 Health insurance carriers

(G-2251)
AULTMAN HEALTH FOUNDATION
6100 Whipple Ave Nw (44720-7618)
PHONE....................................330 305-6999
Cindy Spondsellar, *Manager*
EMP: 150
SALES (corp-wide): 1.1MM **Privately Held**
SIC: 8011 Health maintenance organization
PA: Aultman Health Foundation
2600 6th St Sw
Canton OH 44710
330 452-9911

(G-2252)
AULTMAN HEALTH FOUNDATION (PA)
2600 6th St Sw (44710-1702)
PHONE....................................330 452-9911
Christopher Remark, *CEO*
Joseph R Halter Jr, *Vice Chairman*
Michael Soehnlen, *Ch Radiology*
Elizabeth Edmunds, *Vice Pres*
Anne Gunther, *Vice Pres*
EMP: 37
SQ FT: 1,000,000
SALES: 1.1MM **Privately Held**
SIC: 8011 Health maintenance organization

(G-2253)
AULTMAN HOSPITAL (PA)
2600 6th St Sw (44710-1799)
PHONE....................................330 452-9911
Fax: 330 588-2607
Christopher E Remark, *CEO*
Edward J Roth III, *President*
Chris Parrish, *Assistant VP*
Angela Williams, *Assoc VP*
Cheryl Carpenter, *Buyer*
EMP: 2900 EST: 1891
SQ FT: 700,000
SALES: 315.1MM **Privately Held**
WEB: www.aultmanresidencies.com
SIC: 8062 8069 8221 General medical & surgical hospitals; specialty hospitals, except psychiatric; colleges universities & professional schools

(G-2254)
AULTMAN HOSPITAL
2600 6th St Sw (44710-1799)
PHONE....................................330 452-9911
Doug Kirby, *Supervisor*
EMP: 272
SALES (corp-wide): 315.1MM **Privately Held**
WEB: www.aultmanresidencies.com
SIC: 8062 8069 General medical & surgical hospitals; specialty hospitals, except psychiatric
PA: The Aultman Hospital
2600 6th St Sw
Canton OH 44710
330 452-9911

(G-2255)
AULTMAN HOSPITAL
Also Called: Primetime
2600 6th St Sw (44710-1799)
PHONE....................................330 363-6262
Edward Ross, *President*
EMP: 2100
SALES (corp-wide): 315.1MM **Privately Held**
WEB: www.aultmanresidencies.com
SIC: 8062 6324 8322 General medical & surgical hospitals; hospital & medical service plans; geriatric social service
PA: The Aultman Hospital
2600 6th St Sw
Canton OH 44710
330 452-9911

(G-2256)
AULTMAN HOSPITAL
Also Called: Child Care Center
125 Dartmouth Ave Sw (44710-1716)
PHONE....................................330 452-2273
Fax: 330 452-2650
Julie A Httery, *Manager*
Keri Gollbach, *Exec Dir*
Kerri Gollbach, *Director*
EMP: 30
SALES (corp-wide): 315.1MM **Privately Held**
WEB: www.aultmanresidencies.com
SIC: 8062 8351 General medical & surgical hospitals; group day care center
PA: The Aultman Hospital
2600 6th St Sw
Canton OH 44710
330 452-9911

(G-2257)
AULTMAN NORTH CANTON MED GROUP (PA)
Also Called: Ncmf
6046 Whipple Ave Nw (44720-7616)
PHONE....................................330 433-1200
Fax: 330 305-5001
Nicholas Cleary, *CEO*
Carol Pontius, *COO*
Tmothy Murphy, *CFO*
Kirk Zinke, *VP Mktg*
Randy Wittmer, *Marketing Staff*
EMP: 300
SQ FT: 93,398
SALES: 30.5MM **Privately Held**
WEB: www.ncmf.com
SIC: 8011 Clinic, operated by physicians

(G-2258)
AULTMAN NORTH INC
6100 Whipple Ave Nw (44720-7618)
PHONE....................................330 305-6999
Fax: 330 305-6871
Edward Roth, *President*
David Thiel, *Vice Pres*
Mark Wright, *CFO*
Cindy Sponseller, *Manager*
Lori Hatton,
EMP: 40
SALES (est): 2.4MM
SALES (corp-wide): 315.1MM **Privately Held**
WEB: www.aultmanresidencies.com
SIC: 8062 8011 General medical & surgical hospitals; ophthalmologist
PA: The Aultman Hospital
2600 6th St Sw
Canton OH 44710
330 452-9911

(G-2259)
B-TEK SCALES LLC
1510 Metric Ave Sw (44706-3088)
PHONE....................................330 471-8900
Fax: 330 471-8909
Kraig F Brechbuhler, *President*
Eric Wolfe, *Regional Mgr*
Rei Tritt, *Corp Secy*
Andrew Brechbuhler, *Vice Pres*
Jeff Graham, *Vice Pres*
◆ EMP: 50
SQ FT: 65,000
SALES (est): 18.6MM
SALES (corp-wide): 48.1MM **Privately Held**
WEB: www.b-tek.com
SIC: 3325 7371 Steel foundries; software programming applications
PA: Brechbuhler Scales, Inc.
1424 Scales St Sw
Canton OH 44706
330 458-3060

(G-2260)
BAKER DBLKAR BECK WLEY MATHEWS
Also Called: Baker Dublikar
400 S Main St (44720-3028)
PHONE....................................330 499-6000
Fax: 330 499-6423
Jack Baker, *Partner*
Gregory Beck, *Partner*
Ralph Dublikar, *Partner*
Daniel Funk, *Partner*
James Hanratti, *Partner*
EMP: 30
SALES (est): 3.9MM **Privately Held**
WEB: www.bakerfirm.com
SIC: 8111 General practice attorney, lawyer

(G-2261)
BEAVER CONSTRUCTORS INC
2000 Beaver Place Ave Sw (44706-1963)
P.O. Box 6059 (44706-0059)
PHONE....................................330 478-2151
W Mark Sterling, *President*
Jeffrey W Sterling, *Vice Pres*
Richard Williams, *CFO*
EMP: 80
SALES: 48.3MM **Privately Held**
SIC: 1741 1611 Masonry & other stonework; general contractor, highway & street construction

(G-2262)
BETHANY NURSING HOME INC
626 34th St Nw (44709-2977)
PHONE....................................330 492-7171
Fax: 330 492-0779
John Baum, *President*
Susan Kelly, *Business Mgr*
Elizabeth Baum, *Treasurer*
Mary Meyer, *Systems Mgr*
Nancy Engle, *Social Dir*
EMP: 50 EST: 1968
SQ FT: 16,000
SALES (est): 4.7MM **Privately Held**
WEB: www.bethanynh.com
SIC: 8051 Convalescent home with continuous nursing care

Canton - Stark County (G-2263) — GEOGRAPHIC SECTION

(G-2263)
BILFINGER WESTCON INC
4525 Vliet St Sw (44710-1311)
PHONE.................................330 818-9734
EMP: 26
SALES (corp-wide): 4.7B Privately Held
SIC: 1541 Industrial buildings & warehouses
HQ: Bilfinger Westcon Inc.
    7401 Yukon Dr
    Bismarck ND 58503
    701 222-0076

(G-2264)
BIOTECH MEDICAL INC
7800 Whipple Ave Nw (44767-0001)
PHONE.................................330 494-5504
Michael Giorgio, *CFO*
Samuel Parker, *Controller*
Mark Collins, *Marketing Staff*
Suarez Corporation Industries, *Mng Member*
Benjamin Suarez,
◆ EMP: 800
SQ FT: 50,000
SALES (est): 108.7MM Privately Held
SIC: 5047 Medical equipment & supplies

(G-2265)
BITZEL EXCAVATING INC
4141 Southway St Sw (44706-1809)
PHONE.................................330 477-9653
Fax: 330 477-9594
Pete Bitzel Jr, *President*
Robert Marraccini, *Vice Pres*
Lee Ann Cush, *Admin Sec*
EMP: 30 EST: 1982
SQ FT: 5,000
SALES (est): 3.3MM Privately Held
SIC: 1623 Sewer line construction; water main construction

(G-2266)
BLUE TECHNOLOGIES INC
5701 Mayfair Rd (44720-1546)
PHONE.................................330 499-9300
Keith Stump, *Manager*
EMP: 25 Privately Held
SIC: 7629 5044 5045 Business machine repair, electric; copying equipment; word processing equipment
PA: Blue Technologies, Inc.
    5885 Grant Ave
    Cleveland OH 44105

(G-2267)
BOLER COMPANY
Also Called: Hendrickson Trailer Commercial
2070 Industrial Pl Se (44707-2641)
PHONE.................................330 445-6728
Thomas Marcus, *Materials Mgr*
Hoby R Solo, *Engineer*
Joseph Mahler, *Accounting Dir*
Perry Bale, *Branch Mgr*
Don Hayes, *Manager*
EMP: 250
SALES (corp-wide): 1B Privately Held
SIC: 5084 Safety equipment
PA: The Boler Company
    500 Park Blvd Ste 1010
    Itasca IL 60143
    630 773-9111

(G-2268)
BRAWNSTONE SECURITY LLC
6986 Fenwick Ave Ne (44721-2560)
PHONE.................................330 800-9006
Daniel Unsworth, *President*
EMP: 71
SALES (est): 2.1MM
SALES (corp-wide): 822.1K Publicly Held
SIC: 7382 Security systems services
PA: Fastfunds Financial Corp
    7315 E Peakview Ave
    Centennial CO 80111
    561 514-9042

(G-2269)
BRECHBUHLER SCALES INC (PA)
1424 Scales St Sw (44706-3096)
PHONE.................................330 458-3060
Fax: 330 453-5322
Kraig Brechbuhler, *President*
Jason Ammerman, *Regional Mgr*
Dave Boeck, *Regional Mgr*
Bob Musgrove, *Regional Mgr*
Jerry Konchar, *Exec VP*
EMP: 50
SQ FT: 90,000
SALES (est): 48.1MM Privately Held
WEB: www.brechbuhler.com
SIC: 5046 7699 Scales, except laboratory; scale repair service

(G-2270)
BROOKSIDE COUNTRY CLUB INC
1800 Canton Ave Nw (44708-1803)
PHONE.................................330 477-6505
Fax: 330 477-3566
Andrew Grove, *General Mgr*
Troy Grove, *Director*
EMP: 60
SQ FT: 70,000
SALES (est): 3.7MM Privately Held
SIC: 7997 Country club, membership

(G-2271)
BROOKWOOD MANAGEMENT COMPANY (PA)
Also Called: Versailles Gardens Apts
1201 S Main St Ste 220 (44720-4283)
PHONE.................................330 497-6565
Fax: 330 497-8050
William Lemmon, *President*
EMP: 32
SQ FT: 4,800
SALES (est): 7.3MM Privately Held
WEB: www.brookwoodmgnt.com
SIC: 6531 Condominium manager

(G-2272)
BUCKEYE PAPER CO INC
5233 Southway St Sw # 523 (44706-1943)
P.O. Box 711, Massillon (44648-0711)
PHONE.................................330 477-5925
Fax: 330 477-2256
Edward N Bast Sr, *President*
Rob Bolanz, *General Mgr*
Edward Bast Jr, *Vice Pres*
Debby Olson, *Manager*
▼ EMP: 32
SQ FT: 54,000
SALES (est): 8.9MM Privately Held
WEB: www.buckeyepaper.com
SIC: 2679 5113 Paper products, converted; industrial & personal service paper

(G-2273)
BUCKEYE PROF IMAGING INC
5143 Stoneham Rd (44720-1585)
PHONE.................................800 433-1292
Fax: 330 499-7403
Steven J Troup, *President*
Sandra Troup, *Corp Secy*
Darryl Shinaberry, *Sales Mgr*
Ronna McArthur, *Accounts Mgr*
Larry Pindel, *Manager*
EMP: 25
SQ FT: 27,000
SALES (est): 2.7MM Privately Held
WEB: www.buckeyecolor.com
SIC: 7384 Photofinishing laboratory

(G-2274)
BUCKEYE PROTECTIVE SERVICE
2215 6th St Sw (44706-1379)
P.O. Box 6416 (44706-0416)
PHONE.................................330 456-2671
Fax: 330 453-1502
Donald G Jones, *Ch of Bd*
Richard Jacobsen, *President*
Susan Jones, *Consultant*
James Dibianca, *Executive*
Raymond Jones, *Admin Sec*
EMP: 400
SQ FT: 12,500
SALES (est): 7.7MM Privately Held
WEB: www.buckeyeprotective.com
SIC: 7381 Security guard service

(G-2275)
BUCKINGHAM DLTTLE BRROUGHS LLC
4518 Fulton Dr Nw (44718-2391)
PHONE.................................888 811-2825
Joseph L Ackerman, *Partner*
Ronald C Allan, *Partner*
Samuel A Peppers, *Partner*
Michael Mopsick, *Vice Pres*
Robert Briggs, *Branch Mgr*
EMP: 73
SALES (corp-wide): 40.6MM Privately Held
SIC: 8111 General practice attorney, lawyer
PA: Buckingham, Doolittle & Burroughs, Llc
    3800 Embassy Pkwy
    Akron OH 44333
    330 376-5300

(G-2276)
BUCKINGHAM DLTTLE BRROUGHS LLC
4518 Fulton Dr Nw (44718-2391)
P.O. Box 35548 (44735-5548)
PHONE.................................330 492-8717
Fax: 330 492-9625
Jeffery A Halm, *Partner*
Kim Dornack, *Legal Staff*
EMP: 60
SALES (corp-wide): 40.6MM Privately Held
SIC: 8111 General practice law office
PA: Buckingham, Doolittle & Burroughs, Llc
    3800 Embassy Pkwy
    Akron OH 44333
    330 376-5300

(G-2277)
BUCKINGHAM DLTTLE BRROUGHS LLC
4518 Fulton Dr Nw (44718-2391)
P.O. Box 35548 (44735-5548)
PHONE.................................330 492-8717
Linda Pannok, *Branch Mgr*
EMP: 60
SALES (corp-wide): 40.6MM Privately Held
SIC: 8111 General practice attorney, lawyer
PA: Buckingham, Doolittle & Burroughs, Llc
    3800 Embassy Pkwy
    Akron OH 44333
    330 376-5300

(G-2278)
CA-MJ HOTEL ASSOCIATES LTD
Also Called: Courtyard By Marriott Canton
4375 Metro Cir Nw (44720-7715)
PHONE.................................330 494-6494
Richard Jabara, *General Ptnr*
William Meyer, *General Ptnr*
Thomas Gephart, *Human Res Dir*
Angela Gallik, *Web Dvlpr*
Jeff Hach, *Director*
EMP: 61
SALES (est): 2.4MM Privately Held
SIC: 7011 Hotels
PA: Meyer Jabara Hotels
    7 Kenosia Ave Ste 2a
    Danbury CT 06810

(G-2279)
CAEP-DUNLAP LLC
2600 6th St Sw (44710-1702)
PHONE.................................330 456-2695
Timothy M O'Toole, *Principal*
EMP: 35
SALES (est): 247K Privately Held
SIC: 8062 General medical & surgical hospitals

(G-2280)
CAIN MOTORS INC
Also Called: Cain B M W
6527 Whipple Ave Nw (44720-7339)
PHONE.................................330 494-5588
Fax: 330 494-8709
David Cain, *President*
Greg Haines, *Business Mgr*
Brian Cain, *Vice Pres*
Brian Conner, *Parts Mgr*
Tim Barnes, *Sales Mgr*
EMP: 49
SQ FT: 17,000
SALES (est): 23.3MM Privately Held
SIC: 5511 7538 5521 Automobiles, new & used; pickups, new & used; vans, new & used; general automotive repair shops; used car dealers

(G-2281)
CANTON ALTMAN EMRGNCY PHYSCANS
2600 6th St Sw (44710-1702)
PHONE.................................330 456-2695
Fax: 330 452-9037
Paul Ricks, *President*
Timothy O'Toole, *Executive*
EMP: 36
SALES (est): 4MM Privately Held
SIC: 8011 Clinic, operated by physicians

(G-2282)
CANTON ASSISTED LIVING
836 34th St Nw (44709-2947)
PHONE.................................330 492-7131
Max Hagee, *CEO*
Deanna Gilbert, *Director*
Katie Owens, *Director*
Mark Stachel, *Director*
Anne Halm, *Social Dir*
EMP: 200
SALES (est): 1.9MM Privately Held
SIC: 8051 8052 Convalescent home with continuous nursing care; intermediate care facilities

(G-2283)
CANTON CHRISTIAN HOME INC
Also Called: C C H
2550 Cleveland Ave Nw (44709-3306)
PHONE.................................330 456-0004
Fax: 330 452-9951
Mary Huff, *CFO*
Mike Kerr, *Controller*
David L Coss, *Human Res Mgr*
Janet Whitlatch, *Pub Rel Dir*
Tom K Strobl, *Exec Dir*
EMP: 180
SQ FT: 154,000
SALES: 12.1MM Privately Held
WEB: www.cantonchristianhome.org
SIC: 8322 Senior citizens' center or association

(G-2284)
CANTON CITY SCHOOL DISTRICT
Also Called: Fairmount Elementary School
2701 Coventry Blvd Ne (44705-4165)
PHONE.................................330 456-3167
Fax: 330 588-2151
Marilyn Vanalmen, *Principal*
Nick Demetro, *Teacher*
Charla Malone, *Assistant*
EMP: 30
SALES (corp-wide): 55.5MM Privately Held
SIC: 8351 Preschool center
PA: Canton City School District
    305 Mckinley Ave Nw
    Canton OH 44702
    330 438-2500

(G-2285)
CANTON CITY SCHOOL DISTRICT
Also Called: Canton School Trnsp Dept
2030 Cleveland Ave Sw (44707-3657)
PHONE.................................330 456-6710
Fax: 330 453-6346
Connie Dickon, *Supervisor*
Sheena Miller, *Director*
EMP: 100
SALES (corp-wide): 55.5MM Privately Held
SIC: 4151 School buses
PA: Canton City School District
    305 Mckinley Ave Nw
    Canton OH 44702
    330 438-2500

(G-2286)
CANTON COUNTRY DAY SCHOOL
3000 Demington Ave Nw (44718-3399)
PHONE.................................330 453-8279
Fax: 330 453-6038
Doug Donavan, *Business Mgr*
Dody Nahas, *Dean*
David Costello, *Headmaster*
Pam Shaw, *Headmaster*
Matthew McCaffrey, *Ch Admin Ofcr*
EMP: 48
SQ FT: 30,000

▲ = Import ▼ = Export
◆ = Import/Export

GEOGRAPHIC SECTION

Canton - Stark County (G-2310)

SALES: 2.9MM **Privately Held**
WEB: www.cantoncountryday.org
SIC: 8211 8351 Private elementary school; child day care services

(G-2287)
CANTON ERECTORS INC
Also Called: C E I
2009 Quimby Ave Sw (44706-2491)
PHONE..................................330 453-7363
Fax: 330 453-5937
Brian Selinsky, *President*
Susan Smith, *Corp Secy*
Bryan Grove, *Vice Pres*
Christine Gordon, *Manager*
▲ EMP: 30
SQ FT: 18,500
SALES (est): 6.7MM **Privately Held**
WEB: www.cantonerectors.com
SIC: 1796 7353 Machine moving & rigging; cranes & aerial lift equipment, rental or leasing

(G-2288)
CANTON FLOORS INC
Also Called: CFI Interiors
3944 Fulton Dr Nw (44718-3094)
PHONE..................................330 492-1121
Fax: 330 492-9921
Rollie L Layfield, *President*
I K Sapienza, *Principal*
Wayne Kroll, *Exec VP*
Gary W Frank, *Vice Pres*
Steve Folger, *Project Mgr*
EMP: 40
SQ FT: 15,200
SALES (est): 10MM **Privately Held**
WEB: www.cfiinteriors.com
SIC: 1542 Commercial & office buildings, renovation & repair

(G-2289)
CANTON HOTEL HOLDINGS INC
Also Called: Comfort Inn
5345 Broadmoor Cir Nw (44709-4026)
PHONE..................................330 492-1331
Mike Koker, *Manager*
EMP: 30
SALES (est): 1MM
SALES (corp-wide): 198.1MM **Privately Held**
WEB: www.sunbursthospitality.com
SIC: 7011 Hotels
PA: Sunburst Hospitality Corporation
10750 Columbia Pike # 300
Silver Spring MD 20901
301 592-3800

(G-2290)
CANTON INVENTORY SERVICE
2204 38th St Ne (44705-2822)
P.O. Box 9068 (44711-9068)
PHONE..................................330 453-1633
Michael Pierce, *Owner*
EMP: 30
SALES (est): 1.2MM **Privately Held**
SIC: 7389 Inventory computing service

(G-2291)
CANTON JEWISH COMMUNITY CENTER
Also Called: CANTON JEWISH COMMUNITY FEDERA
432 30th St Nw (44709-3108)
PHONE..................................330 452-6444
Fax: 330 452-4487
Paul Spiegal, *Director*
Bonnie Manello, *Asst Director*
EMP: 55
SQ FT: 70,000
SALES: 538.5K **Privately Held**
WEB: www.jewishcanton.org
SIC: 8322 Community center

(G-2292)
CANTON MED EDUCATN FOUNDATION
Also Called: C M E F
2600 6th St Sw (44710-1702)
PHONE..................................330 363-6783
Clifford Johnson, *Med Doctor*
Carol Young, *Director*
Kathleen Senger, *Director*
EMP: 50 EST: 1977
SQ FT: 100

SALES: 4.3MM **Privately Held**
SIC: 8732 Educational research

(G-2293)
CANTON MONTESSORI ASSOCIATION
Also Called: Canton Montessori School
125 15th St Nw (44703-3207)
PHONE..................................330 452-0148
Jennifer Deuble, *Vice Pres*
Maryann McLellan, *Manager*
EMP: 39
SALES (corp-wide): 903.3K **Privately Held**
WEB: www.cantonmontessori.org
SIC: 8351 Montessori child development center
PA: Canton Montessori Association, Inc
125 15th St Nw
Canton OH 44703
330 452-0148

(G-2294)
CANTON OPHTHALMOLOGY ASSOC
2600 Tuscarawas St W # 200 (44708-4693)
PHONE..................................330 994-1286
Fax: 330 456-9308
Frank J Weinstock MD, *President*
Dr Jamie Zucker, *Corp Secy*
Joy Elliott, *Ophthalmic Tech*
EMP: 25
SALES (est): 1.9MM **Privately Held**
WEB: www.coaeye.com
SIC: 8011 Ophthalmologist

(G-2295)
CANTON PUBLIC WORKS
Also Called: Canton Street Department
2436 30th St Ne (44705-2568)
PHONE..................................330 489-3030
Fax: 330 580-1950
Michael Roar, *Superintendent*
Linda Patterson, *Executive*
EMP: 37
SALES (est): 2MM **Privately Held**
SIC: 1611 Highway & street construction

(G-2296)
CANTON REG CHAM OF COMM FDN
222 Market Ave N (44702-1418)
PHONE..................................330 456-7253
Dennis Saunier, *President*
EMP: 40
SALES: 555.8K **Privately Held**
SIC: 8611 Chamber of Commerce

(G-2297)
CANTON RGNAL CHMBER OF CMMERCE
222 Market Ave N Ste 122 (44702-1418)
PHONE..................................330 456-7253
Fax: 330 489-6005
Dennis Saunier, *President*
Linnea Gallagher-Olbon, *Principal*
John A Murphy Jr, *Vice Chairman*
Steve Katz, *Vice Pres*
Robert Fonte, *Director*
EMP: 40 EST: 2009
SALES (est): 5.7MM **Privately Held**
SIC: 8611 Community affairs & services

(G-2298)
CANTON SCHOOL EMPLOYEES FED CR (PA)
1380 Market Ave N (44714-2606)
PHONE..................................330 452-9801
Robert Hallier, *President*
Jeannie Fye, *COO*
Bill Wittig, *Vice Pres*
Kara Chambers, *Loan Officer*
Steve Pflugh, *Broker*
EMP: 40
SALES (est): 12.4MM **Privately Held**
WEB: www.csefcu.com
SIC: 6061 Federal credit unions

(G-2299)
CARDIOLOGY CONSULTANTS INC
2600 Tuscarawas St W # 600 (44708-4644)
PHONE..................................330 454-8076
Fax: 330 454-3927
Alan Kamen MD, *President*
Ira Friedlander MD, *Principal*
Srinivasu Paranandi MD, *Principal*
Dennis Ruff MD, *Principal*
Henry Seto MD, *Principal*
EMP: 60
SALES (est): 1.6MM **Privately Held**
SIC: 8011 Cardiologist & cardio-vascular specialist

(G-2300)
CARDIOVASCULAR CONSULTANTS INC
2600 6th St Sw Ste A2710 (44710-1702)
PHONE..................................330 454-8076
Milan Dopirak, *President*
Marla Metzger, *Office Mgr*
Alan Kamen, *Med Doctor*
Nicholas Roberts, *Surgeon*
Ramana R Podugu, *Cardiovascular*
EMP: 70
SALES (est): 6.5MM **Privately Held**
SIC: 8011 Cardiologist & cardio-vascular specialist

(G-2301)
CARPET SERVICES PLUS INC
Also Called: Carpet Restoration Plus
1807 Allen Ave Se Ste 8 (44707-3696)
PHONE..................................330 458-2409
Fax: 330 458-2423
Andrew C Miller, *President*
EMP: 47
SQ FT: 2,500
SALES (est): 1.4MM **Privately Held**
SIC: 7217 Carpet & furniture cleaning on location

(G-2302)
CELLCO PARTNERSHIP
Also Called: Verizon
4926 Dressler Rd Nw (44718-2557)
PHONE..................................330 493-7979
Rick Pawlack, *Branch Mgr*
Diane Bach, *Manager*
Matt Reed, *Manager*
EMP: 30
SALES (corp-wide): 126B **Publicly Held**
SIC: 4812 5999 Cellular telephone services; telephone equipment & systems
HQ: Cellco Partnership
1 Verizon Way
Basking Ridge NJ 07920

(G-2303)
CHASE PHIPPS
2993 Perry Dr Sw (44706-2269)
PHONE..................................330 754-0467
Mike Madal, *General Mgr*
EMP: 40 EST: 2010
SALES (est): 2.4MM **Privately Held**
SIC: 7359 Tool rental

(G-2304)
CHILD ADLSCENT BEHAVIORAL HLTH (PA)
919 2nd St Ne (44704-1132)
PHONE..................................330 454-7917
Fax: 330 454-1476
Lillian Blosfield, *CFO*
Kenneth Hammer, *Manager*
Susan Finsel, *Supervisor*
Michael Johnson, *Exec Dir*
Sally Sutterfield, *Director*
EMP: 50
SALES: 8.7MM **Privately Held**
WEB: www.casrv.org
SIC: 8322 Child guidance agency

(G-2305)
CHILD ADLSCENT BEHAVIORAL HLTH
4641 Fulton Dr Nw (44718-2384)
PHONE..................................330 433-6075
Fax: 330 433-1843
Sandy Vaughn, *Manager*
Susan Ishiyama, *Child Psychology*
Rebecca M Zarko, *Child Psycholgy*

Mary Frazier, *Exec Dir*
Amelia Kocher, *Director*
EMP: 65
SALES (corp-wide): 8.7MM **Privately Held**
WEB: www.casrv.org
SIC: 8322 Child guidance agency
PA: Child And Adolescent Behavioral Health
919 2nd St Ne
Canton OH 44704
330 454-7917

(G-2306)
CHILDRENS PHYSICIAN INC
4575 Everhard Rd Nw (44718-2406)
PHONE..................................330 494-5600
Fax: 330 966-1644
Michael Motz, *President*
Douglas Blocker, *Vice Pres*
Douglas L Bocker, *Manager*
Laura Hemphill, *Nurse*
EMP: 31
SALES (est): 3.7MM **Privately Held**
SIC: 8011 Pediatrician

(G-2307)
CHRISTIAN PERRY PRE SCHOOL
139 Perry Dr Nw (44708-5048)
PHONE..................................330 477-7262
Fax: 330 477-0539
Sarah Modlin, *Director*
Sharon Skogen, *Director*
EMP: 30
SALES (est): 675.2K **Privately Held**
SIC: 8211 8351 Private elementary & secondary schools; group day care center

(G-2308)
CINEMARK USA INC
Also Called: Cinemark Movies 10
6284 Dressler Rd Nw (44720-7608)
PHONE..................................330 497-9118
Jeremy Thomas, *Manager*
EMP: 40 **Publicly Held**
SIC: 7832 Motion picture theaters, except drive-in
HQ: Cinemark Usa, Inc.
3900 Dallas Pkwy Ste 500
Plano TX 75093
972 665-1000

(G-2309)
CINTAS CORPORATION NO 2
3865 Highland Park Nw (44720-4537)
P.O. Box 3010 (44720-8010)
PHONE..................................330 966-7800
Fax: 330 966-7888
Allen Kocsis, *Manager*
Dawn Hlass, *Manager*
Dixie King, *Manager*
Cheryl Mitch, *Manager*
EMP: 100
SQ FT: 17,084
SALES (corp-wide): 5.3B **Publicly Held**
WEB: www.cintas-corp.com
SIC: 7218 2326 2337 Industrial uniform supply; treated equipment supply: mats, rugs, mops, cloths, etc.; wiping towel supply; work uniforms; uniforms, except athletic: women's, misses' & juniors'
HQ: Cintas Corporation No. 2
6800 Cintas Blvd
Mason OH 45040

(G-2310)
CITIZENS BANK NATIONAL ASSN
400 Tuscarawas St W Ste 1 (44702-2044)
PHONE..................................330 580-1913
Fax: 330 580-1917
Tom Hollister, *Vice Chairman*
Robert Brown, *Pastor*
David Curtis, *Exec VP*
Randall Stickler, *Exec VP*
Cindy Schulze, *Senior VP*
EMP: 100
SALES (corp-wide): 6.4B **Publicly Held**
SIC: 6021 National commercial banks
HQ: Citizens Bank, National Association
1 Citizens Plz Ste 1 # 1
Providence RI 02903
401 282-7000

Canton - Stark County (G-2311)   GEOGRAPHIC SECTION

(G-2311)
CITY OF CANTON
Also Called: Water Pollution Control Ctrl
3530 Central Ave Se (44707-1338)
PHONE...................................330 489-3080
Fax: 330 489-3084
Tracy Mills, *Superintendent*
Kelly Berta, *Manager*
Doug Dickerhoff, *Senior Mgr*
EMP: 42 Privately Held
WEB: www.cantonincometax.com
SIC: 4953
PA: City Of Canton
   218 Cleveland Ave Sw
   Canton OH 44702
   330 438-4300

(G-2312)
CLAYS HERITAGE CARPET INC (PA)
Also Called: Heritage Carpet & HM Dctg Ctrs
1440 N Main St (44720-1640)
PHONE...................................330 497-1280
Fax: 330 497-8077
Dennis Clay, *President*
Paula Clay, *Admin Sec*
EMP: 38
SQ FT: 3,850
SALES (est): 6.5MM Privately Held
WEB: www.heritage-carpet.com
SIC: 5713 5211 1752 Carpets; rugs; lumber & other building materials; floor laying & floor work

(G-2313)
CLEARMOUNT ELEMENTARY SCHOOL
150 Clearmount Ave Se (44720-3214)
PHONE...................................330 497-5640
Beth Humbert, *President*
Mary Lynn Grande, *Vice Pres*
Rickie Irwin, *Treasurer*
Paula Guiler, *Librarian*
Sue Roush, *Admin Sec*
EMP: 48
SALES: 15.8K Privately Held
SIC: 8641 Parent-teachers' association

(G-2314)
CLIFTONLARSONALLEN LLP
4505 Stephens Cir Nw (44718-3683)
PHONE...................................330 497-2000
Steven Pittman, *Partner*
EMP: 100
SALES (corp-wide): 755.1MM Privately Held
SIC: 8721 Certified public accountant
PA: Cliftonlarsonallen Llp
   220 S 6th St Ste 300
   Minneapolis MN 55402
   612 376-4500

(G-2315)
COLUMBIA-CSA/HS GREATER CANTON
Also Called: Columbia Mercy Medical Center
1320 Mercy Dr Nw 30 (44708-2614)
PHONE...................................330 489-1000
Jack Topoleski, *CEO*
Csa Health Network, *General Ptnr*
Columbia HCA Healthcare Corp, *Ltd Ptnr*
Michael Rieger, *CFO*
Fran Vojir, *Accounts Mgr*
EMP: 2185
SQ FT: 652,760
SALES (est): 15.3MM Privately Held
SIC: 8062 General medical & surgical hospitals

(G-2316)
COMMQUEST SERVICES INC
Also Called: COMMUNITY SERVICES OF STARK CO
625 Cleveland Ave Nw (44702-1805)
PHONE...................................330 455-0374
Fax: 330 821-8506
Keith Hochadel, *CEO*
John Kaminiski, *President*
Richard Craig, *President*
Shannon English-Hexamer, *Vice Pres*
Jennifer Peveich, *CFO*
EMP: 103
SQ FT: 8,500
SALES: 7.5MM Privately Held
SIC: 8322 8742 Family service agency; management consulting services

(G-2317)
COMMUNICARE HEALTH SVCS INC
Also Called: Pines Healthcare Center, The
3015 17th St Nw (44708-6004)
PHONE...................................330 454-6508
Fax: 330 454-7716
Brigitte Hurney, *Human Res Mgr*
Tad Gamboni, *Manager*
Brian McClain, *Director*
Kim Frankberger, *Administration*
EMP: 25
SALES (corp-wide): 103.9MM Privately Held
WEB: www.atriumlivingcenters.com
SIC: 6531 Real estate agents & managers
PA: Communicare Health Services, Inc.
   4700 Ashwood Dr Ste 200
   Blue Ash OH 45241
   513 530-1654

(G-2318)
COMMUNICARE HEALTH SVCS INC
Also Called: Canton Healthcare Center
1223 Market Ave N (44714-2603)
PHONE...................................330 454-2152
Fax: 330 454-2543
Kim Frankieberger, *Administration*
EMP: 200
SQ FT: 38,794
SALES (corp-wide): 103.9MM Privately Held
WEB: www.atriumlivingcenters.com
SIC: 6531 8051 Real estate agents & managers; skilled nursing care facilities
PA: Communicare Health Services, Inc.
   4700 Ashwood Dr Ste 200
   Blue Ash OH 45241
   513 530-1654

(G-2319)
CONCORDE THERAPY GROUP INC (PA)
4645 Belpar St Nw (44718-3602)
PHONE...................................330 493-4210
Fax: 330 493-4744
Timothy C Murphy, *President*
Paul McGhee, *Vice Pres*
Joseph Salvo, *CFO*
Mark Mottice, *Shareholder*
EMP: 180
SQ FT: 21,000
SALES (est): 6.7MM Privately Held
WEB: www.concordehealth.com
SIC: 8049 8021 Physiotherapist; speech specialist; occupational therapist; offices & clinics of dentists

(G-2320)
CONCORDE THERAPY GROUP INC
5156 Whipple Ave Nw (44718-2663)
PHONE...................................330 478-1752
Fax: 330 478-1763
Janet Murphy, *Branch Mgr*
EMP: 30 Privately Held
SIC: 8049 Physical therapist
PA: Concorde Therapy Group Inc
   4645 Belpar St Nw
   Canton OH 44718

(G-2321)
CONSOLIDATED COMMUNICATIONS
Also Called: C.C.i
7015 Sunset Strip Ave Nw (44720-7078)
PHONE...................................330 896-3905
Fax: 330 479-5944
Richard Lutz, *Principal*
Melissa Leasure, *VP Finance*
Nick Shaheen, *Sales Mgr*
Christine McDonnell, *Sales Associate*
EMP: 28
SALES (est): 1.7MM Privately Held
WEB: www.cci-solutions.com
SIC: 7622 5065 Communication equipment repair; communication equipment

(G-2322)
COUNTY OF STARK
Also Called: Higgins Sheltered Workshop
3041 Cleveland Ave S (44707-3625)
PHONE...................................330 484-4814
Candace Fontes, *Sales Dir*
Margalie Belivaire, *Manager*
Ed Allar, *Manager*
Scott Marsh, *Database Admin*
EMP: 100 Privately Held
WEB: www.starkadas.org
SIC: 9431 8331 Mental health agency administration, government; job training & vocational rehabilitation services
PA: County Of Stark
   110 Central Plz S Ste 240
   Canton OH 44702
   330 451-7371

(G-2323)
COUNTY OF STARK
Also Called: Stark County Sewer Dept
1701 Mahoning Rd Ne (44705-1471)
PHONE...................................330 451-2303
Fax: 330 453-9044
Mike Armogida, *Manager*
EMP: 790
SQ FT: 17,924 Privately Held
WEB: www.starkadas.org
SIC: 4952 Sewerage systems
PA: County Of Stark
   110 Central Plz S Ste 240
   Canton OH 44702
   330 451-7371

(G-2324)
COUNTY OF STARK
Also Called: Stark County Engineer
5165 Southway St Sw (44706-1962)
PHONE...................................330 477-6781
Fax: 330 477-3926
Keith Bennett, *Principal*
Stephen Gronow, *Safety Mgr*
EMP: 105
SQ FT: 20,626 Privately Held
WEB: www.starkadas.org
SIC: 8711 Engineering services
PA: County Of Stark
   110 Central Plz S Ste 240
   Canton OH 44702
   330 451-7371

(G-2325)
COUNTY OF STARK
Also Called: Mhrs Board of Stark County
121 Cleveland Ave Sw (44702-1903)
PHONE...................................330 455-6644
Fax: 330 455-4242
Donna Edwards, *Program Mgr*
Karen Jepsen, *Manager*
Erica Thom, *Manager*
Aaron Kutcher, *Technology*
Andy Gray, *Analyst*
EMP: 36 Privately Held
WEB: www.starkadas.org
SIC: 8069 Drug addiction rehabilitation hospital
PA: County Of Stark
   110 Central Plz S Ste 240
   Canton OH 44702
   330 451-7371

(G-2326)
COURTVIEW JUSTICE SOLUTIONS (DH)
4825 Higbee Ave Nw # 101 (44718-2567)
PHONE...................................330 497-0033
John H Hines III, *President*
Barbara Petroc, *General Mgr*
Tor Gudmundsen, *Managing Dir*
Jeffrey Harmon, *Managing Dir*
Jason Badik, *Project Dir*
EMP: 35
SALES (est): 15.8MM
SALES (corp-wide): 2.1B Privately Held
SIC: 7373 Systems software development services

(G-2327)
CRISIS INTERVENTION & RCVY CTR
832 Mckinley Ave Nw (44703-2463)
PHONE...................................330 455-9407
Fax: 330 455-8706
Jim Wicxson, *Data Proc Dir*
Bernard Jesiolowski, *Director*
Jeff Allen, *Director*
Sharon Saunier, *Admin Sec*
EMP: 59
SALES: 6.8MM Privately Held
SIC: 8322 8049 Crisis center; psychologist, psychotherapist & hypnotist

(G-2328)
CRISIS INTVNTN CTR STARK CNTY
2421 13th St Nw (44708-3116)
PHONE...................................330 452-9812
Ryan McNair, *Info Tech Dir*
Jim Wicxson, *Technology*
Bernard Jesiolowski, *Director*
EMP: 90
SQ FT: 7,570
SALES: 6.6MM Privately Held
WEB: www.cicstark.org
SIC: 8322 Crisis intervention center

(G-2329)
CROSS TRUCK EQUIPMENT CO INC
1801 Perry Dr Sw (44706-1923)
P.O. Box 80509 (44708-0509)
PHONE...................................330 477-8151
Fax: 330 477-8426
M Lucille Cross, *President*
Glenn G Cross, *Principal*
Ivan Bruce Hart, *Principal*
John Cross, *Vice Pres*
William Cross, *Purch Agent*
EMP: 30 EST: 1950
SQ FT: 45,000
SALES (est): 18.2MM Privately Held
WEB: www.crosstruck.com
SIC: 5084 5013 Trucks, industrial; truck parts & accessories

(G-2330)
CROXTON REALTY COMPANY
410 47th St Nw (44709-1417)
PHONE...................................330 492-1697
Fax: 330 492-6314
Elaine Croxton, *CEO*
Beau Croxton, *Real Est Agnt*
EMP: 25
SQ FT: 3,500
SALES (est): 1.3MM Privately Held
WEB: www.croxtonrealty.com
SIC: 6531 Real estate agents & managers

(G-2331)
CUTLER AND ASSOCIATES INC (PA)
Also Called: Cutler/Gmac Real Estate
4618 Dressler Rd Nw (44718-2500)
PHONE...................................330 493-9323
Fax: 330 492-1831
James L Bray, *President*
James H Camp, *Vice Pres*
Jay L Cutler, *Vice Pres*
Cassie Walters, *Controller*
EMP: 25 EST: 1947
SQ FT: 9,500
SALES (est): 9.3MM Privately Held
WEB: www.cutlerhomes.com
SIC: 6531 Buying agent, real estate; selling agent, real estate

(G-2332)
CUTLER REAL ESTATE (PA)
Also Called: Cutler G M A C Real Estate
4618 Dressler Rd Nw (44718-2500)
PHONE...................................330 492-7230
James Bray, *President*
James Camp, *Principal*
Jay Cutler, *Vice Pres*
EMP: 90
SALES (est): 4.2MM Privately Held
SIC: 6531 Real estate brokers & agents

(G-2333)
DAMARC INC
Also Called: Harding Park Cycle
4330 Kirby Ave Ne (44705-4348)
PHONE...................................330 454-6171
Fax: 330 454-4260
Daniel Harding, *President*
Danette Harding, *Controller*
EMP: 43
SQ FT: 40,000

GEOGRAPHIC SECTION   **Canton - Stark County (G-2358)**

SALES (est): 11.9MM **Privately Held**
WEB: www.hardingsparkcycle.com
SIC: 5571 7699 Motorcycles; motorcycle repair service

(G-2334)
DAVID W STEINBACH INC
Also Called: Steinbach Painting
6824 Wise Ave Nw (44720-7359)
PHONE.................330 497-5959
David Steinbach, *President*
EMP: 31
SALES: 900K **Privately Held**
SIC: 1721 Painting & paper hanging

(G-2335)
DAVITA INC
Also Called: Da Vita
4685 Fulton Dr Nw (44718-2379)
PHONE.................330 494-2091
James Jenni, *Branch Mgr*
EMP: 25 **Publicly Held**
SIC: 8092 Kidney dialysis centers
PA: Davita Inc.
   2000 16th St
   Denver CO 80202

(G-2336)
DAY KETTERER LTD (PA)
200 Market Ave N Ste 300 (44702-1436)
P.O. Box 24213 (44701-4213)
PHONE.................330 455-0173
Fax: 330 455-2633
Blake Gerney, *Managing Prtnr*
Robert Roland, *Managing Prtnr*
James R Blake, *Partner*
Scott A Scherff, *Counsel*
Steve Moser, *Facilities Mgr*
EMP: 73
SQ FT: 35,000
SALES (est): 10.2MM **Privately Held**
WEB: www.dayketterer.com
SIC: 8111 General practice law office

(G-2337)
DDR CORP
5539 Dressler Rd Nw (44720-7750)
PHONE.................216 755-5547
Scott Woolstine, *President*
EMP: 50
SALES (corp-wide): 921.5MM **Privately Held**
WEB: www.ddrc.com
SIC: 6531 Real estate brokers & agents
PA: Ddr Corp.
   3300 Enterprise Pkwy
   Beachwood OH 44122
   216 755-5500

(G-2338)
DELTA MEDIA GROUP INC
4726 Hills And Dales Rd N (44708-1571)
PHONE.................330 493-0350
Mike Minard, *President*
Brian Jorris, *Accounts Exec*
EMP: 40
SALES (est): 4.3MM **Privately Held**
WEB: www.deltagroup.com
SIC: 7372 Application computer software

(G-2339)
DETROIT DIESEL CORPORATION
515 11th St Se (44707-3811)
PHONE.................330 430-4300
Fax: 330 430-4395
Craig Cartmill, *Sales/Mktg Mgr*
Cathy Bradshaw, *Human Res Mgr*
Jerry Reaves, *Manager*
Greg France, *Manager*
Jerry Palmreuter, *Manager*
EMP: 264
SALES (corp-wide): 193.7B **Privately Held**
WEB: www.detroitdeisel.com
SIC: 5084 Engines & parts, diesel
HQ: Detroit Diesel Corporation
   13400 W Outer Dr
   Detroit MI 48239
   313 592-5000

(G-2340)
DIEBOLD INCORPORATED
217 2nd St Nw Fl 6 (44702-1567)
PHONE.................330 588-3619
Fax: 330 489-4199
William T Blair, *Exec VP*
Michael J Hillock, *Senior VP*
Alben W Warf, *Senior VP*
Warren Dettinger, *Vice Pres*
Donald Eagon, *Vice Pres*
EMP: 125
SALES (corp-wide): 4.6B **Publicly Held**
SIC: 5049 1731 Bank equipment & supplies; banking machine installation & service
PA: Diebold Nixdorf, Incorporated
   5995 Mayfair Rd
   North Canton OH 44720
   330 490-4000

(G-2341)
DIGNITY HEALTH
Also Called: Emergency Physicians Med Group
4535 Dressler Rd Nw (44718-2545)
PHONE.................330 493-4443
Josh Rubin, *Principal*
Euthym Kontaxis, *Director*
Robert P Kozel, *Director*
Sarah Vogel, *Director*
EMP: 150
SALES (corp-wide): 7.1B **Privately Held**
WEB: www.chw.edu
SIC: 8011 8621 Medical centers; professional membership organizations
PA: Dignity Health
   185 Berry St Ste 300
   San Francisco CA 94107
   415 438-5500

(G-2342)
DLHBOWLES INC (PA)
2422 Leo Ave Sw (44706-2344)
PHONE.................330 478-2503
John W Saxon, *CEO*
SRI Sridhara, *President*
Matthew Reese, *Vice Pres*
Dennis Whittington, *Buyer*
Melissa Stutler, *QC Mgr*
EMP: 450
SQ FT: 107,000
SALES (est): 185.4MM **Privately Held**
WEB: www.dlh-inc.com
SIC: 8711 3089 3082 Engineering services; injection molding of plastics; tubes, unsupported plastic

(G-2343)
DOMESTIC VIOLENCE PROJECT INC
720 19th St Ne (44714-2213)
P.O. Box 9459 (44711-9459)
PHONE.................330 445-2000
Fax: 330 445-2007
Connie Kincaid, *CFO*
Jonda Carnes, *Human Resources*
Cheli Curran, *Exec Dir*
Elizabeth Bretz, *Director*
EMP: 33
SQ FT: 24,575
SALES: 1.6MM **Privately Held**
SIC: 8322 8361 Emergency shelters; hot-line; residential care

(G-2344)
DOWNTOWN FORD LINCOLN INC
1423 Tuscarawas St W (44702-2037)
PHONE.................330 456-2781
Fax: 330 456-2786
Donald Schneider, *President*
Jayne A Montgomery, *Corp Secy*
Brad A Black, *Vice Pres*
Cindy Loudon, *Finance Mgr*
Randy Upperman, *Sales Staff*
EMP: 98
SQ FT: 35,000
SALES (est): 35.2MM **Privately Held**
SIC: 5511 5012 7538 7532 Automobiles, new & used; trucks, tractors & trailers: new & used; vans, new & used; automobiles & other motor vehicles; general automotive repair shops; collision shops, automotive

(G-2345)
EAST OHIO GAS COMPANY
Dominion Energy Ohio
4725 Southway St Sw (44706-1936)
PHONE.................330 477-9411
Nancy McClenaghan, *Branch Mgr*
EMP: 120
SALES (corp-wide): 12.5B **Publicly Held**
SIC: 4923 Gas transmission & distribution
HQ: The East Ohio Gas Company
   19701 Libby Rd
   Maple Heights OH 44137
   800 362-7557

(G-2346)
EAST OHIO GAS COMPANY
Dominion Energy Ohio
7015 Freedom Ave Nw (44720-7381)
PHONE.................330 499-2501
Fax: 330 266-2180
Greg Theirl, *Branch Mgr*
EMP: 90
SALES (corp-wide): 12.5B **Publicly Held**
SIC: 4923 Gas transmission & distribution
HQ: The East Ohio Gas Company
   19701 Libby Rd
   Maple Heights OH 44137
   800 362-7557

(G-2347)
EAST OHIO GAS COMPANY
Also Called: Dominion Energy Ohio
332 2nd St Nw (44702-1704)
P.O. Box 26666, Richmond VA (23261-6666)
PHONE.................330 478-1700
Fax: 330 478-3157
Nancy Mc Lanihan, *Branch Mgr*
EMP: 200
SALES (corp-wide): 12.5B **Publicly Held**
SIC: 4924 4923 Natural gas distribution; gas transmission & distribution
HQ: The East Ohio Gas Company
   19701 Libby Rd
   Maple Heights OH 44137
   800 362-7557

(G-2348)
EASTBURY BOWLING CENTER
3000 Atl Blvd Ne Unit A (44705-3908)
PHONE.................330 452-3700
Fax: 330 452-0716
Rocco Ferruccio, *President*
Rocco Ferruccio, *President*
EMP: 30
SQ FT: 86,000
SALES (est): 945.7K **Privately Held**
SIC: 7933 5813 Ten pin center; cocktail lounge

(G-2349)
EBSCO INDUSTRIES INC
Also Called: Ebsco Teleservice
4150 Belden Village Mall (44718-2502)
PHONE.................330 478-0281
EMP: 337
SALES (corp-wide): 2.3B **Privately Held**
SIC: 7389 Business Services
PA: Ebsco Industries, Inc.
   5724 Highway 280 E
   Birmingham AL 35242
   205 991-6600

(G-2350)
ECKINGER CONSTRUCTION COMPANY
2340 Shepler Ch Ave Sw (44706-3093)
PHONE.................330 453-2566
Fax: 330 453-0647
Tom Eckinger, *CEO*
Philip Eckinger, *President*
Janice Holdsworth, *Corp Secy*
Jeremy Eckinger, *Vice Pres*
Fred Eckhardt, *Project Mgr*
EMP: 47 EST: 1923
SQ FT: 18,740
SALES (est): 24.7MM **Privately Held**
WEB: www.eckinger.com
SIC: 1542 Shopping center construction

(G-2351)
EDCO CLEANERS INC
Also Called: Dutch Girl Cleaners
2455 Whipple Ave Nw (44708-1513)
PHONE.................330 477-3357
Fax: 330 477-7749
Mark Edwards, *President*
Linda Edwards, *Corp Secy*
EMP: 35
SQ FT: 3,400
SALES (est): 1.4MM **Privately Held**
SIC: 7216 Drycleaning plants, except rugs

(G-2352)
EDGE HAIR DESIGN & SPA
4655 Dressler Rd Nw (44718-3657)
PHONE.................330 477-2300
Patti Bower Chaney, *Owner*
EMP: 25
SALES (est): 126.1K **Privately Held**
SIC: 7231 Hairdressers

(G-2353)
EMERITUS CORPORATION
Also Called: Emeritus Assisted Living
4507 22nd St Nw Apt 33 (44708-6211)
PHONE.................330 477-5727
Fax: 330 477-5327
Sue Rohr, *Branch Mgr*
EMP: 35
SALES (corp-wide): 4.7B **Publicly Held**
WEB: www.emeraldestatesslc.com
SIC: 8399 Health systems agency
HQ: Emeritus Corporation
   3131 Elliott Ave Ste 500
   Milwaukee WI 53214

(G-2354)
EMP HOLDINGS LTD
4535 Dressler Rd Nw (44718-2545)
PHONE.................330 493-4443
David Peppard,
Peter Rome,
EMP: 900
SALES (est): 57.7MM **Privately Held**
SIC: 7363 Medical help service

(G-2355)
EMP MANAGEMENT GROUP LTD
Also Called: Emergency Medicine Physicians
4535 Dressler Rd Nw (44718-2545)
PHONE.................330 493-4443
Fax: 330 493-8677
Dominic J Bagnoli Jr, *CEO*
David C Packo MD, *President*
William B White MD, *Partner*
Broida Robert I, *COO*
Denise Works, *Exec VP*
EMP: 60
SQ FT: 24,000
SALES (est): 9.8MM **Privately Held**
SIC: 8741 8011 Hospital management; nursing & personal care facility management; offices & clinics of medical doctors

(G-2356)
ENVIRITE OF OHIO INC
Also Called: Eq Ohio
2050 Central Ave Se (44707-3540)
PHONE.................330 456-6238
Fax: 330 456-2801
Jeffrey R Feeler, *President*
Simon Bell, *Vice Pres*
Eric Gerratt, *Treasurer*
Ellen Riley, *Manager*
Wayne Ipsen, *Admin Sec*
EMP: 50
SALES (est): 12MM
SALES (corp-wide): 504MM **Publicly Held**
WEB: www.envirite.com
SIC: 4953 8734 Recycling, waste materials; hazardous waste testing
PA: Us Ecology, Inc.
   101 S Capitol Blvd # 1000
   Boise ID 83702
   208 331-8400

(G-2357)
ERIE INDEMNITY COMPANY
4690 Munson St Nw (44718-3636)
PHONE.................330 433-6300
EMP: 75
SALES (corp-wide): 1.6B **Publicly Held**
WEB: www.erieinsurance.com
SIC: 6411 8741 Insurance agents; management services
PA: Erie Indemnity Company
   100 Erie Insurance Pl
   Erie PA 16530
   814 870-2000

(G-2358)
ERIE INSURANCE EXCHANGE
1120 Valleyview Ave Sw (44710-1426)
PHONE.................330 479-1010
EMP: 67

Canton - Stark County (G-2359)

GEOGRAPHIC SECTION

SALES (corp-wide): 374.1MM **Privately Held**
WEB: www.erie-insurance.com
SIC: **6331** Reciprocal interinsurance exchanges: fire, marine, casualty
PA: Erie Insurance Exchange
 100 Erie Insurance Pl
 Erie PA 16530
 800 458-0811

(G-2359)
ERIE INSURANCE EXCHANGE
4690 Munson St Nw Ste A (44718-3636)
P.O. Box 9031 (44711-9031)
PHONE..................................330 433-1925
Fax: 330 433-6447
Mark Hammerstein, *Manager*
Rhonda McHenry, *Director*
EMP: 100
SALES (corp-wide): 374.1MM **Privately Held**
WEB: www.erie-insurance.com
SIC: **6331** Reciprocal interinsurance exchanges: fire, marine, casualty
PA: Erie Insurance Exchange
 100 Erie Insurance Pl
 Erie PA 16530
 800 458-0811

(G-2360)
ESBER BEVERAGE COMPANY
2217 Bolivar Rd Sw (44706-3099)
PHONE..................................330 456-4361
Fax: 330 456-6207
Gary Esber, *President*
Patricia McCrimmon, *Manager*
Fred Nida, *Manager*
Cindy Esber, *Info Tech Mgr*
▲ EMP: 50
SQ FT: 40,000
SALES (est): 26.7MM **Privately Held**
WEB: www.esberbeverage.com
SIC: **5181** **5182** **5149** Ale; beer & other fermented malt liquors; wine & distilled beverages; beverages, except coffee & tea

(G-2361)
EXTENDED FAMILY CONCEPTS INC
Also Called: Heather Ridge Commons
913 Pittsburg Ave Nw (44720-1814)
PHONE..................................330 966-2555
Fax: 330 499-1950
Gloria Prose, *President*
Pamela Koury, *Manager*
Coleen Neifeldt, *Director*
EMP: 50
SALES (est): 1.9MM **Privately Held**
SIC: **8361** Residential care

(G-2362)
EYE CENTERS OF OHIO INC
800 Mckinley Ave Nw (44703-2463)
PHONE..................................330 966-1111
John Malik, *Branch Mgr*
EMP: 30
SALES (est): 996K
SALES (corp-wide): 4.7MM **Privately Held**
WEB: www.eyecentersofohio.com
SIC: **8011** Ophthalmologist
PA: Eye Centers Of Ohio Inc
 1330 Mercy Dr Nw Ste 310
 Canton OH 44708
 330 489-1441

(G-2363)
FAMILY MEDICINE STARK COUNTY
6512 Whipple Ave Nw (44720-7340)
PHONE..................................330 499-5600
Fax: 330 499-4190
Gust Pantelas MD, *President*
Matthew L Cause MD, *Vice Pres*
Michelle Moulin, *Office Mgr*
EMP: 25
SALES (est): 3.5MM **Privately Held**
SIC: **8011** General & family practice, physician/surgeon

(G-2364)
FAMILY PHYSICIANS INC
4860 Frank Ave Nw (44720-7498)
PHONE..................................330 494-7099
Fax: 330 494-2147

Thomas Shemory, *President*
Melanie Mirande, *Principal*
Dr Gregory A Haban, *Vice Pres*
Dr Howard Marshall, *Treasurer*
Dr Paul Bortos, *Admin Sec*
EMP: 38
SQ FT: 20,000
SALES (est): 6.3MM **Privately Held**
SIC: **8011** Physicians' office, including specialists

(G-2365)
FEDERAL EXPRESS CORPORATION
Also Called: Fedex
3301 Bruening Ave Sw (44706-4100)
PHONE..................................800 463-3339
EMP: 34
SALES (corp-wide): 60.3B **Publicly Held**
WEB: www.fedex.com
SIC: **4513** Package delivery, private air
HQ: Federal Express Corporation
 3610 Hacks Cross Rd
 Memphis TN 38125
 901 369-3600

(G-2366)
FEDEX GROUND PACKAGE SYS INC
8033 Pittsburg Ave Nw (44720-5673)
PHONE..................................330 244-1534
EMP: 40
SALES (corp-wide): 47.4B **Publicly Held**
SIC: **4215** Courier Service
HQ: Fedex Ground Package System, Inc.
 1000 Fed Ex Dr
 Coraopolis PA 15108
 412 269-1000

(G-2367)
FIRST CHRISTIAN CHURCH
6900 Market Ave N (44721-2437)
PHONE..................................330 445-2700
John Hampton, *Pastor*
Brad Hammond, *Pastor*
Bill Webster, *Facilities Dir*
Rikki Kadri, *Office Admin*
Diane Chenevey, *Director*
EMP: 50
SQ FT: 107,000
SALES: 2.5MM **Privately Held**
WEB: www.trychurchagain.com
SIC: **8661** **8351** Miscellaneous denomination church; preschool center

(G-2368)
FIRSTMERIT MORTGAGE CORP
4455 Hills & Dales Rd Nw (44718-1505)
PHONE..................................330 478-3400
Fax: 330 478-3490
Stephen D Steinour, *President*
George Carrick, *Administration*
EMP: 85
SALES (est): 16.9MM
SALES (corp-wide): 4.7B **Publicly Held**
WEB: www.firstmerit.com
SIC: **6162** Mortgage bankers
HQ: The Huntington National Bank
 17 S High St Fl 1
 Columbus OH 43215
 614 480-4293

(G-2369)
FLAMOS ENTERPRISES INC
Also Called: Stark Sandblasting & Pntg Co
1501 Raff Rd Sw Ste 1 (44710-2356)
PHONE..................................330 478-0009
Fax: 330 478-0005
Stelio Flamos, *President*
William Cotopolis, *Vice Pres*
Nathan Barr, *Safety Mgr*
Nathaniel Addessi, *Finance Mgr*
David Patterson, *Manager*
EMP: 50
SQ FT: 30,000
SALES (est): 7MM **Privately Held**
WEB: www.sandblastandpaint.com
SIC: **1799** **7389** **1721** Sandblasting of building exteriors; waterproofing; interior decorating; industrial painting

(G-2370)
FRATERNAL ORDER EAGLES INC
Also Called: Foe 2370
5024 Monticello Ave Nw (44708-3445)
P.O. Box 80032 (44708-0032)
PHONE..................................330 477-8059
Tom Preda, *Manager*
EMP: 32
SALES (corp-wide): 11MM **Privately Held**
WEB: www.fraternalorderofeagles.tribe.net
SIC: **8641** Fraternal associations
HQ: Fraternal Order Of Eagles Inc.
 1623 Gateway Cir
 Grove City OH 43123
 614 883-2200

(G-2371)
FREEDOM HARLEY-DAVIDSON INC
7233 Sunset Strip Ave Nw (44720-7038)
PHONE..................................330 494-2453
Fax: 330 305-6575
David M Smith Sr, *President*
Kathy Hartmann, *General Mgr*
Josephine Smith, *Corp Secy*
Kathy Hartman, *Vice Pres*
Sam Huff, *Sales Mgr*
EMP: 33
SQ FT: 22,000
SALES: 3.1MM **Privately Held**
WEB: www.freedomharley.com
SIC: **5571** **7699** Motorcycle dealers; motorcycle parts & accessories; motorcycle repair service

(G-2372)
FRIEND-SHIP CHILD CARE CTR LLC
425 45th St Sw (44706-4429)
PHONE..................................330 484-2051
Susan Neading, *Director*
Joan Gray,
EMP: 28
SALES (est): 539.3K **Privately Held**
SIC: **8351** Child day care services

(G-2373)
FURBAY ELECTRIC SUPPLY CO (PA)
208 Schroyer Ave Sw (44702-2039)
P.O. Box 6268 (44706-0268)
PHONE..................................330 454-3033
Fax: 330 454-6816
Timothy Furbay, *President*
Jean Furbay, *Vice Pres*
Homer Miller, *Warehouse Mgr*
Jeff Kutz, *Purch Mgr*
Cheryl Manko, *Controller*
EMP: 52
SQ FT: 35,000
SALES (est): 46.8MM **Privately Held**
SIC: **5063** Electrical supplies; lighting fixtures

(G-2374)
G E G ENTERPRISES INC
Also Called: Gary's Place Salon & Spa
4080 Fulton Dr Nw (44718-2866)
PHONE..................................330 494-9160
Jeff Scott, *Manager*
EMP: 34
SQ FT: 960
SALES (corp-wide): 887.9K **Privately Held**
WEB: www.garysplacesalons.com
SIC: **7231** Beauty shops
PA: G E G Enterprises Inc
 4345 Tuscarawas St W
 Canton OH 44708
 330 477-3133

(G-2375)
G E G ENTERPRISES INC (PA)
Also Called: Gary's Place
4345 Tuscarawas St W (44708-5461)
PHONE..................................330 477-3133
Fax: 330 477-7102
Jeff Scott, *President*
Shelly Talbot, *Vice Pres*
Doris Self, *Financial Exec*
Steve Gerber, *Info Tech Dir*
EMP: 25
SQ FT: 2,500

SALES: 887.9K **Privately Held**
WEB: www.garysplacesalons.com
SIC: **7231** **5999** **5122** **7299** Unisex hair salons; facial salons; manicurist, pedicurist; hair care products; hair preparations; massage parlor

(G-2376)
GASPAR INC
1545 Whipple Ave Sw (44710-1373)
PHONE..................................330 477-2222
Gary W Gaspar, *President*
Wesley M Morgan, *Managing Dir*
Chuck Clark, *Editor*
Bob Frederick, *Purch Mgr*
Judy Gaspar, *Admin Sec*
EMP: 55
SQ FT: 36,000
SALES (est): 15.6MM **Privately Held**
WEB: www.gasparinc.com
SIC: **3443** **7692** **3444** Tanks, standard or custom fabricated: metal plate; heat exchangers, condensers & components; welding repair; sheet metalwork

(G-2377)
GASTROENTEROLOGY ASSOCIATES
4665 Belpar St Nw (44718-3602)
P.O. Box 36329 (44735-6329)
PHONE..................................330 493-1480
Fax: 330 493-6805
Sanjiv Khetarpal, *President*
Linda Snyder, *Office Mgr*
Kathy Farley-White, *Manager*
EMP: 38 EST: 1971
SQ FT: 4,500
SALES (est): 4MM **Privately Held**
SIC: **8011** Gastronomist

(G-2378)
GENERAL ELECTRIC COMPANY
4500 Munson St Nw (44718-3607)
P.O. Box 36960 (44735-6960)
PHONE..................................330 433-5163
Ken Scheller, *Vice Pres*
Chad Hartman, *Engineer*
Lisa Moore, *Technology*
John Weber, *Technology*
Susan Ullman, *Administration*
EMP: 1200
SQ FT: 73,234
SALES (corp-wide): 122B **Publicly Held**
WEB: www.gecapital.com
SIC: **6141** Installment sales finance, other than banks
PA: General Electric Company
 41 Farnsworth St
 Boston MA 02210
 617 443-3000

(G-2379)
GERDAU MACSTEEL ATMOSPHERE ANN
Also Called: Advanced Bar Technology
1501 Raff Rd Sw (44710-2356)
PHONE..................................330 478-0314
Fax: 330 478-6554
Saminathan Ramaswamy, *Principal*
Scott C Pence, *Principal*
Barb Mraz, *Personnel*
EMP: 80
SQ FT: 31,316 **Privately Held**
WEB: www.aaimac.com
SIC: **7389** **3398** Metal cutting services; metal heat treating
HQ: Gerdau Macsteel Atmosphere Annealing
 209 W Mount Hope Ave # 1
 Lansing MI 48910
 517 782-6415

(G-2380)
GLENMOOR COUNTRY CLUB INC
4191 Glenmoor Rd Nw Lowr (44718-4077)
PHONE..................................330 966-3600
Fax: 330 966-3611
Iris Wolstein, *Ch of Bd*
Myron Vernis, *General Mgr*
Bob Hon, *COO*
Dewayne Foster, *Maintenance Dir*
Pat Haag, *Human Res Dir*
EMP: 120
SQ FT: 167,000

Canton - Stark County (G-2405)

SALES (est): 11.8MM Privately Held
WEB: www.glenmoorcc.com
SIC: 7997 Country club, membership

(G-2381)
GLOBAL INSULATION INC (PA)
Also Called: Chempower Sheetmetal
4450 Belden Village St Nw # 306 (44718-2588)
PHONE...................330 479-3100
Fax: 330 479-1866
Patrick F Byrne, *President*
Dale Crumley, *Vice Pres*
Ron Collins, *Information Mgr*
EMP: 38
SQ FT: 1,200
SALES (est): 11.7MM Privately Held
SIC: 1742 1761 Insulation, buildings; sheet metalwork

(G-2382)
GOLDEN KEY CTR FOR EXCPTNL CHL
1431 30th St Nw (44709-2926)
PHONE...................330 493-4400
Terry Frank, *Exec Dir*
EMP: 40
SALES (est): 1.1MM Privately Held
SIC: 8351 Preschool center

(G-2383)
GOODWILL IDSTRS GRTR CLVLND L (PA)
408 9th St Sw (44707-4714)
PHONE...................330 454-9461
Anne Richards, *President*
Craig Chaffinch, *CFO*
Laurel Schafrath, *Accountant*
Teri Streator, *Sales Executive*
Robyn Steinmetz, *Mktg Dir*
EMP: 100
SQ FT: 96,000
SALES (est): 27.6MM Privately Held
SIC: 8331 Vocational rehabilitation agency

(G-2384)
GOODWILL INDS RHBILITATION CTR (PA)
408 9th St Sw (44707-4799)
PHONE...................330 454-9461
Fax: 330 454-9461
Ken Weber, *CEO*
Gene Dechellis, *CFO*
Anne Richards, *VP Human Res*
Crista Adamczyk, *Manager*
Harold G Oswald, *Exec Dir*
EMP: 276
SQ FT: 76,000
SALES (est): 8MM Privately Held
WEB: www.goodwillcanton.org
SIC: 8322 8331 Rehabilitation services; community service employment training program

(G-2385)
GRACO OHIO INC
Also Called: Profiol
8400 Port Jackson Ave Nw (44720-5464)
PHONE...................330 494-1313
Paul Fisher, *Business Mgr*
Brad Smith, *Business Mgr*
Rance Robenstine, *Opers Mgr*
Brent R Kaiser, *Production*
Tim Knisely, *Buyer*
EMP: 100
SQ FT: 832
SALES (corp-wide): 1.4B Publicly Held
WEB: www.dispensit.com
SIC: 5084 Pumps & pumping equipment
HQ: Graco Ohio Inc.
8400 Port Jackson Ave Nw
North Canton OH 44720
330 494-1313

(G-2386)
H & H AUTO PARTS INC (PA)
300 15th St Sw (44707-4095)
P.O. Box 6440 (44706-0440)
PHONE...................330 456-4778
Fax: 330 456-1425
James Green, *President*
Richard Green, *Vice Pres*
EMP: 55
SQ FT: 10,000
SALES (est): 10.6MM Privately Held
SIC: 5013 5531 Automotive supplies & parts; automotive parts

(G-2387)
H & H AUTO PARTS INC
6434 Wise Ave Nw (44720-7385)
PHONE...................330 494-2975
Fax: 330 494-0932
Curt Price, *Manager*
EMP: 25
SALES (corp-wide): 10.6MM Privately Held
SIC: 5013 5531 Automotive supplies & parts; automotive accessories; automotive parts
PA: H & H Auto Parts Inc
300 15th St Sw
Canton OH 44707
330 456-4778

(G-2388)
HAIR SHOPPE INC
6460 Wise Ave Nw (44720-7351)
PHONE...................330 497-1651
Fax: 330 497-3627
Karen Volzer, *President*
EMP: 60
SALES (est): 1.2MM Privately Held
WEB: www.thehairshoppe.com
SIC: 7231 Hairdressers

(G-2389)
HAMMOND CONSTRUCTION INC
1278 Park Ave Sw (44706-1599)
PHONE...................330 455-7039
Fax: 330 455-9460
William A Schurman, *President*
Joe Daugherty, *Superintendent*
Victor Gramoy Jr, *Corp Secy*
John Kirkpatrick, *Exec VP*
Bill Schurman, *Vice Pres*
EMP: 80 EST: 1973
SQ FT: 20,000
SALES (est): 32.7MM Privately Held
WEB: www.hammondconstruction.com
SIC: 1542 1541 8741 Commercial & office building contractors; industrial buildings & warehouses; construction management

(G-2390)
HAMMONTREE & ASSOCIATES LTD (PA)
5233 Stoneham Rd (44720-1594)
PHONE...................330 499-8817
Fax: 330 499-0149
Bruce Bair, *Partner*
Barbara H Bennett, *Partner*
Keith A Bennett, *Partner*
Charles F Hammontree, *Partner*
Greg Mencer, *Sales Mgr*
EMP: 46
SQ FT: 10,800
SALES (est): 8.6MM Privately Held
WEB: www.hammontree-engineers.com
SIC: 8711 8713 Consulting engineer; surveying services

(G-2391)
HAMPTON INNS LLC
5335 Broadmoor Cir Nw (44709-4097)
PHONE...................330 492-0151
Fax: 330 492-4636
Jeremiah Louden, *Manager*
Linda Battista, *Manager*
EMP: 29
SALES (corp-wide): 9.1B Publicly Held
WEB: www.premierhotels.us
SIC: 7011 Hotels & motels
HQ: Hampton Inns, Llc
755 Crossover Ln
Memphis TN 38117
901 374-5000

(G-2392)
HANCO INTERNATIONAL
Also Called: Hannon Co, The
1605 Waynesburg Dr Se (44707-2196)
PHONE...................330 456-9407
Tom Hannan, *Chairman*
EMP: 75
SALES (est): 1.5MM Privately Held
SIC: 7389 Design, commercial & industrial

(G-2393)
HANNON COMPANY (PA)
Also Called: Charles Rewinding Div
1605 Waynesburg Dr Se (44707-2137)
PHONE...................330 456-4728
Fax: 330 456-3323
Christopher Meister, *President*
Gary Gonzalez, *Plant Mgr*
Mike McAllister, *Foreman/Supr*
Gary Griswold, *CFO*
Cindy Keyes, *Human Resources*
EMP: 75 EST: 1926
SQ FT: 65,000
SALES (est): 25.8MM Privately Held
WEB: www.hanco.com
SIC: 3621 3825 5084 3699 Motors, electric; test equipment for electronic & electrical circuits; transformers, portable; instrument; industrial machinery & equipment; electrical equipment & supplies; transformers, except electric; industrial furnaces & ovens

(G-2394)
HARBOR FREIGHT TOOLS USA INC
2905 Whipple Ave Nw (44708-1533)
PHONE...................330 479-9852
Al Williams, *Manager*
EMP: 90
SALES (corp-wide): 2.3B Privately Held
SIC: 8742 Retail trade consultant
PA: Harbor Freight Tools Usa, Inc.
26541 Agoura Rd
Calabasas CA 91302
818 836-5001

(G-2395)
HARMON MEDIA GROUP
4501 Hills & Dales Rd Nw (44708-1572)
PHONE...................330 478-5325
Ernest Blood, *CEO*
Karen Hought, *Vice Pres*
EMP: 49
SALES (est): 3.3MM Privately Held
SIC: 7319 Media buying service

(G-2396)
HART ROOFING INC
Also Called: (PARENT COMPANY IS HART, EDWARD R COMPANY)
437 Mcgregor Ave Nw (44703-2831)
P.O. Box 6207 (44706-0207)
PHONE...................330 452-4055
Harry Rennecker, *Ch of Bd*
Michael McAndrew, *Manager*
Michael Mc Andrew, *President*
EMP: 25
SALES (est): 1.2MM Privately Held
SIC: 1761 Roofing, siding & sheet metal work

(G-2397)
HEARTBEATS TO CITY INC
1352 Market Ave S (44707-4811)
PHONE...................330 452-4524
EMP: 36
SQ FT: 5,000
SALES: 774.3K Privately Held
SIC: 8699 8299 Membership Organization School/Educational Services

(G-2398)
HIGHPOINT HOME HEALTHCARE AGCY
4767 Higbee Ave Nw (44718-2551)
PHONE...................330 491-1805
Fax: 330 491-1809
Joseph Kuntz,
EMP: 37
SALES (est): 674.7K Privately Held
WEB: www.hphomecare.net
SIC: 8099 Health & allied services

(G-2399)
HILAND GROUP INCORPORATED (PA)
Also Called: Delano Foods
7600 Supreme St Nw (44720-6920)
P.O. Box 36737 (44735-6737)
PHONE...................330 499-8404
EMP: 65 EST: 1955
SQ FT: 10,000
SALES (est): 8.3MM Privately Held
SIC: 5149 2099 Whol Groceries Mfg Food Preparations

(G-2400)
HILSCHER-CLARKE ELECTRIC CO (PA)
519 4th St Nw (44703-2699)
PHONE...................330 452-9806
Fax: 330 452-5867
Ronald Becker, *CEO*
Ronald D Becker, *CEO*
Scott A Goodspeed, *President*
Scott Goodspeed, *President*
Mike Davis, *Division Mgr*
EMP: 30
SQ FT: 26,000
SALES (est): 48.2MM Privately Held
WEB: www.hilscher-clarke.com
SIC: 1731 General electrical contractor

(G-2401)
HILTON GARDEN INN AKRON
5251 Landmark Blvd (44720-1575)
PHONE...................330 966-4907
Fax: 330 966-5265
Lindsey Misconish, *General Mgr*
Robyn Ewing, *Sales Executive*
EMP: 35
SALES (est): 1.2MM Privately Held
SIC: 7011 Hotels

(G-2402)
HOME DEPOT USA INC
Also Called: Home Depot, The
4873 Portage St Nw (44720-7246)
PHONE...................330 497-1810
Fax: 330 649-4017
Jay Hissom, *Branch Mgr*
EMP: 150
SQ FT: 111,806
SALES (corp-wide): 100.9B Publicly Held
WEB: www.homerentalsdepot.com
SIC: 5211 7359 Home centers; tool rental
HQ: Home Depot U.S.A., Inc.
2455 Paces Ferry Rd Se
Atlanta GA 30339

(G-2403)
HOME HELPERS IN HOME CARE
2510 Blake Ave Nw (44708-2525)
PHONE...................330 455-5440
Ted Burkholder, *President*
EMP: 70
SALES (est): 564.8K Privately Held
SIC: 8082 Home health care services

(G-2404)
HOSPITALISTS MGT GROUP LLC (DH)
Also Called: Cogent-Hmg
4535 Dressler Rd Nw (44718-2545)
PHONE...................866 464-7497
Andrea Funk, *Vice Pres*
David Hess, *Vice Pres*
Elizabeth Yanko, *Vice Pres*
Cindy Berry, *Opers Staff*
Marisa Stoll, *Opers Staff*
EMP: 560
SQ FT: 8,000
SALES (est): 42.5MM
SALES (corp-wide): 20.9B Privately Held
SIC: 8741 Hospital management
HQ: Hmg Holding Corporation
920 Winter St
Waltham MA 02451
781 699-9000

(G-2405)
HOUSE OF LORETO
2812 Harvard Ave Nw (44709-3195)
PHONE...................330 453-8137
Fax: 330 453-8140
Sister Claire Batterson, *Vice Pres*
Sister Gladis, *Exec Dir*
Mark Stachel, *Director*
EMP: 75
SQ FT: 350,000
SALES: 2.3MM Privately Held
WEB: www.houseofloreto.com
SIC: 8051 Extended care facility

Canton - Stark County (G-2406) — GEOGRAPHIC SECTION

(G-2406)
HOWARD HANNA SMYTHE CRAMER
4758 Dressler Rd Nw (44718-2555)
PHONE..................330 493-6555
Fax: 330 493-5385
Ron Tomblin, *Branch Mgr*
Antonise Jackson, *Real Est Agnt*
EMP: 45
SALES (corp-wide): 76.4MM **Privately Held**
WEB: www.smythecramer.com
SIC: 6531 Real estate agents & managers
HQ: Howard Hanna Smythe Cramer
6000 Parkland Blvd
Cleveland OH 44124
216 447-4477

(G-2407)
HUGHES KITCHENS AND BATH LLC
1258 Cleveland Ave Nw (44703-3147)
PHONE..................330 455-5269
Fax: 330 452-2240
Anthony Pierce, *Opers Mgr*
Nancy Gardner, *Office Mgr*
Michael Pierce,
EMP: 30
SQ FT: 80,000
SALES (est): 3.2MM **Privately Held**
SIC: 1799 Kitchen & bathroom remodeling

(G-2408)
HUMANA INC
4690 Munson St Nw Ste C (44718-3636)
PHONE..................330 498-0537
EMP: 701
SALES (corp-wide): 53.7B **Publicly Held**
SIC: 8062 General medical & surgical hospitals
PA: Humana Inc.
500 W Main St Ste 300
Louisville KY 40202
502 580-1000

(G-2409)
HUNTINGTON INSURANCE INC
Also Called: Canton Insurance
220 Market Ave S Ste 40 (44702-2182)
PHONE..................330 430-1300
Scott Dodds, *Branch Mgr*
EMP: 37
SALES (corp-wide): 4.7B **Publicly Held**
SIC: 6411 Insurance agents
HQ: Huntington Insurance, Inc.
519 Madison Ave
Toledo OH 43604
419 720-7900

(G-2410)
INCEPT CORPORATION
4150 Belden Village St Nw # 205 (44718-3643)
PHONE..................330 649-8000
Fax: 330 649-8007
Jeffrey White, *President*
Sam Falletta, *President*
Adam Snyder, *COO*
Wendy Afee, *Vice Pres*
Billie Johnson, *Vice Pres*
EMP: 200
SQ FT: 10,000
SALES (est): 22.2MM **Privately Held**
WEB: www.inceptcorp.com
SIC: 7389 Telemarketing services

(G-2411)
INDUSTRIAL PARTS & SERVICE CO
Also Called: Industrial Parts and Service
6440 Promler St Nw (44720-7625)
PHONE..................330 966-5025
Fax: 330 966-5033
Edwin Mauser Sr, *President*
Mark Mauser, *Treasurer*
Tony Delibero, *Sales Mgr*
Nicole Calabris, *Sales Staff*
Jason Schoeppner, *Sales Staff*
◆ EMP: 26
SQ FT: 19,000
SALES (est): 14.8MM **Privately Held**
SIC: 5084 7699 Materials handling machinery; industrial equipment services

(G-2412)
INTEGRITY GLOBAL MARKETING LLC
4735 Belpar St Nw (44718-3648)
PHONE..................330 492-9989
Paul Monea,
▲ EMP: 40
SALES (est): 1.1MM **Privately Held**
SIC: 7999 Gymnastic instruction, non-membership

(G-2413)
INTERNATIONAL ASSOCIATION OF (PA)
Also Called: Iaitam
4848 Munson St Nw (44718-3631)
PHONE..................330 628-3012
Barbara Rembiesa, *President*
Regina Hoskin, *General Mgr*
Glenn Wilson, *Exec VP*
William Harwood, *CFO*
Alan Barbish, *Sales Mgr*
EMP: 30
SQ FT: 3,000
SALES (est): 4.6MM **Privately Held**
SIC: 7379 8249 ; business training services

(G-2414)
INTERSTATE FIRE & SEC SYSTEMS
3271 Bruening Ave Sw (44706-4191)
PHONE..................330 453-9495
Fax: 330 453-1610
Rodney Crilow, *President*
Chad Crilow, *General Mgr*
Dave Check, *Prgrmr*
Barb Betts, *Admin Sec*
EMP: 35
SQ FT: 13,000
SALES (est): 9MM **Privately Held**
WEB: www.interstatefands.com
SIC: 5063 1731 Burglar alarm systems; fire alarm systems; electrical work

(G-2415)
INTRIGUE SALON & DAY SPA
4762 Dressler Rd Nw (44718-2555)
PHONE..................330 493-7003
Yevonne Reese, *Owner*
EMP: 26
SALES (est): 440.1K **Privately Held**
SIC: 7231 Manicurist, pedicurist

(G-2416)
J M T CARTAGE INC
4925 Southway St Sw (44706-1939)
PHONE..................330 478-2430
Fax: 330 478-0720
Jeffrey M Tomich, *President*
EMP: 35
SQ FT: 11,000
SALES (est): 3.1MM **Privately Held**
WEB: www.jmtcartage.com
SIC: 4212 4213 Light haulage & cartage, local; contract haulers

(G-2417)
JANSON INDUSTRIES
1200 Garfield Ave Sw (44706-1639)
P.O. Box 6090 (44706-0090)
PHONE..................330 455-7029
Fax: 330 455-5919
Richard Janson, *Partner*
Eric H Janson, *Partner*
Erin Goss, *Project Mgr*
Tim Brindack, *Design Engr*
Herman Sayre, *Sales Mgr*
EMP: 100
SQ FT: 120,000
SALES (est): 13.6MM **Privately Held**
WEB: www.jansonindustries.com
SIC: 1799 2391 3999 Rigging & scaffolding; curtains & draperies; stage hardware & equipment, except lighting

(G-2418)
JMW WELDING AND MFG
512 45th St Sw (44706-4432)
PHONE..................330 484-2428
Fax: 330 484-2021
John Slutz, *President*
Michael Slutz, *Vice Pres*
Neal Slutz, *Treasurer*
Janet McDonald, *Human Res Mgr*
EMP: 30
SQ FT: 12,000
SALES (est): 6MM **Privately Held**
SIC: 3443 7692 Industrial vessels, tanks & containers; dumpsters, garbage; welding repair

(G-2419)
JOHNSON CNTRLS SEC SLTIONS LLC
5590 Lauby Rd Ste 6 (44720-1500)
PHONE..................330 497-0850
Fax: 330 494-3684
Brad Wilamson, *General Mgr*
Michele Ruetty, *Manager*
EMP: 110 **Privately Held**
WEB: www.adt.com
SIC: 7382 Burglar alarm maintenance & monitoring; fire alarm maintenance & monitoring
HQ: Johnson Controls Security Solutions Llc
4700 Exchange Ct Ste 300
Boca Raton FL 33431
561 264-2071

(G-2420)
K & L FLOORMASTERS LLC
1518 Cadney St Ne (44714-1189)
PHONE..................330 493-0869
Fax: 330 493-0872
Kenneth D Wallace Sr, *Mng Member*
Cheyene Aliasss, *Admin Sec*
EMP: 29
SALES (est): 703.7K **Privately Held**
SIC: 7349 Janitorial service, contract basis

(G-2421)
K HOVNANIAN SUMMIT HOMES LLC (HQ)
2000 10th St Ne (44705-1414)
PHONE..................330 454-4048
Fax: 330 454-4677
Mark Tournoux, *Purch Dir*
Deena Dervin, *Sales Staff*
Ferman Yoder, *Manager*
Burce Grosse,
Ricky Haney,
EMP: 50
SALES (est): 46.9MM
SALES (corp-wide): 2.4B **Publicly Held**
SIC: 1521 New construction, single-family houses
PA: Hovnanian Enterprises, Inc.
90 Matawan Rd Fl 5
Matawan NJ 07747
732 747-7800

(G-2422)
KEMPTHORN AUTOMALL (PA)
Also Called: Jaguar Volvo
1449 Cleveland Ave Nw (44703-3138)
PHONE..................800 451-3877
Richard Kempthorn, *President*
Marilyn Kempthorn, *Vice Pres*
Ian Franz, *Sales Staff*
Ruth Franz, *Sales Staff*
Dan Paridon, *Sales Associate*
EMP: 100
SQ FT: 25,000
SALES (est): 29MM **Privately Held**
SIC: 5511 5521 7538 7515 Automobiles, new & used; vans, new & used; pickups, new & used; used car dealers; general automotive repair shops; passenger car leasing; truck rental & leasing, no drivers

(G-2423)
KEMPTHORN AUTOMALL
1449 Cleveland Ave Nw (44703-3138)
PHONE..................330 456-8287
Richard Kempthorn, *President*
James Kempthorn, *Vice Pres*
Eric Kempthorn, *Admin Sec*
EMP: 150
SALES (est): 17.3MM **Privately Held**
SIC: 5511 7538 7515 7513 Automobiles, new & used; general automotive repair shops; passenger car leasing; truck rental & leasing, no drivers; used car dealers; automobiles & other motor vehicles

(G-2424)
KEMPTHORN MOTORS INC
1449 Cleveland Ave Nw (44703-3181)
PHONE..................330 452-6511
Fax: 330 455-9716
Richard Kempthorn, *President*
Fran Stoiber, *Parts Mgr*
Dwayne Holbrook, *Sales Mgr*
Mike Lyons, *Sales Mgr*
Bob Malloy, *Sales Mgr*
EMP: 100 EST: 1938
SALES (est): 23.2MM **Privately Held**
SIC: 6159 Automobile finance leasing

(G-2425)
KIDNEY & HYPERTENSION CON
4689 Fulton Dr Nw (44718-2379)
PHONE..................330 649-9400
Fax: 330 649-8059
Jehad Yusef Asfoura, *Principal*
Dan Nye, *Financial Exec*
Tami Cromley, *Med Doctor*
Debbie King, *Manager*
EMP: 28 EST: 2001
SALES (est): 6.7MM **Privately Held**
SIC: 6211 Security brokers & dealers

(G-2426)
KIDS-PLAY INC
1651 Boettler Rd (44721)
PHONE..................330 896-2400
David Schipper, *President*
EMP: 31
SALES (est): 125.8K
SALES (corp-wide): 4.8MM **Privately Held**
SIC: 8351 Preschool center
PA: Kids-Play Inc
388 S Main St Ste 100
Akron OH 44311
330 253-2373

(G-2427)
KLASE ENTERPRISES INC (PA)
Also Called: United Sales Co
713 12th St Ne (44704-1315)
PHONE..................330 452-6300
Fax: 330 452-4385
Marlin Klase, *President*
David D Klase, *Vice Pres*
Sue Street, *Manager*
EMP: 42 EST: 1970
SQ FT: 3,000
SALES (est): 7.5MM **Privately Held**
SIC: 5013 Body repair or paint shop supplies, automotive

(G-2428)
KNOCH CORPORATION
1015 Schneider St Se 1a (44720-3800)
PHONE..................330 244-1440
James B Fenske, *President*
David J Walker, *Vice Pres*
Mike Jirele, *Sr Project Mgr*
Annette Destefano, *Admin Sec*
EMP: 53 EST: 1983
SQ FT: 3,000
SALES (est): 13.8MM **Privately Held**
SIC: 1542 1541 Commercial & office building, new construction; industrial buildings, new construction

(G-2429)
KOZMIC KORNER
8282 Port Jackson Ave Nw (44720-5471)
PHONE..................330 494-4148
Fax: 330 494-4148
Barb Hanna, *Owner*
EMP: 25
SALES (est): 626.9K **Privately Held**
SIC: 8351 Group day care center

(G-2430)
KRUGLIAK WILKINS GRIFIYHD & (PA)
4775 Munson St Nw (44718-3612)
P.O. Box 36963 (44735-6963)
PHONE..................330 497-0700
Fax: 330 497-4020
Gregory Watts, *COO*
Sue Wilson, *Accountant*
David Lewis, *Corp Counsel*
Cynthia Nolte, *Manager*
Scott Miller, *CTO*
EMP: 68 EST: 1965
SQ FT: 23,000
SALES (est): 11.2MM **Privately Held**
WEB: www.kwgd.com
SIC: 8111 General practice law office

GEOGRAPHIC SECTION

Canton - Stark County (G-2455)

(G-2431)
LED TRANSPORTATION
4645 Monica Ave Sw (44706-4525)
PHONE....................330 484-2772
Gregg Elliott, *Principal*
EMP: 25
SALES: 1MM **Privately Held**
SIC: 4111 Local & suburban transit

(G-2432)
LEO A DICK & SONS CO (PA)
935 Mckinley Ave Nw (44703-2072)
PHONE....................330 452-5010
Fax: 330 452-0527
Leo A Dick, *President*
Lawrence J Dick, *Corp Secy*
Donna Widford, *Accountant*
Victoria Harper, *Executive Asst*
▲ **EMP:** 30 **EST:** 1922
SQ FT: 50,000
SALES (est): 22.8MM **Privately Held**
SIC: 5149 Specialty food items

(G-2433)
LEONARD INSUR SVCS AGCY INC (DH)
4244 Mount Pleasant St Nw (44720-5469)
P.O. Box 9160 (44711-9160)
PHONE....................330 266-1904
Fax: 330 498-9946
W Fred Kloots Jr, *President*
Paul Cruciani, *Vice Pres*
Richard Martindale, *Vice Pres*
W Todd Witham, *Vice Pres*
Robin Loomis, *Accounts Mgr*
EMP: 30
SQ FT: 8,500
SALES (est): 16.4MM **Privately Held**
WEB: www.leonardinsurance.com
SIC: 6411 Insurance agents, brokers & service
HQ: Dawson Insurance, Inc.
  3900 Kinross Lakes Pkwy
  Richfield OH 44286
  440 333-9000

(G-2434)
LEPPO INC
Also Called: Leppo Equipment
1534 Shepler Ch Ave Sw (44706-3017)
PHONE....................330 456-2930
Fax: 330 456-7614
Jeff Ulman, *Branch Mgr*
EMP: 26
SQ FT: 1,890
SALES (corp-wide): 70.6MM **Privately Held**
WEB: www.leppos.com
SIC: 7353 7699 Heavy construction equipment rental; construction equipment repair
PA: Leppo, Inc.
  176 West Ave
  Tallmadge OH 44278
  330 633-3999

(G-2435)
LG FUEL CELL SYSTEMS INC
Also Called: Royce-Rollins Fuel Cell System
6065 Strip Ave Nw (44720-9207)
PHONE....................330 491-4800
Chung In-Jae, *CEO*
Andrew J Marsh, *President*
Gary Hyman, *Principal*
Rodger McKain, *Vice Pres*
Tom Jones, *Engineer*
EMP: 38
SALES (est): 9.1MM **Privately Held**
SIC: 8731 Energy research

(G-2436)
LIBERTY HEALTHSHARE INC
4845 Fulton Dr Nw Ste 1 (44718-2300)
PHONE....................855 585-4237
Dale Bellis, *Exec Dir*
Matthew Bellis, *Director*
EMP: 26
SALES: 1.9MM **Privately Held**
SIC: 7389 Financial services

(G-2437)
LIFECARE FMLY HLTH & DNTL CTR
2725 Lincoln St E (44707-2769)
PHONE....................330 454-2000
Fax: 330 454-2202
Kay Seeberger, *CEO*
Janet McPeek, *CFO*
Eric D Riley, *Director*
EMP: 35
SQ FT: 16,552
SALES (est): 7.4MM **Privately Held**
SIC: 8011 Clinic, operated by physicians

(G-2438)
LIFETOUCH NAT SCHL STUDIOS INC
1300 S Main St Ste 300 (44720-4252)
PHONE....................330 497-1291
Fax: 330 497-8296
Barry Weber, *Manager*
EMP: 40
SALES (corp-wide): 856.2MM **Privately Held**
SIC: 7221 School photographer
HQ: Lifetouch National School Studios Inc.
  11000 Viking Dr Ste 300
  Eden Prairie MN 55344
  952 826-4000

(G-2439)
LOCKER MOVING & STORAGE INC (PA)
131 Perry Dr Nw (44708-5048)
PHONE....................330 784-0477
Fax: 330 477-2732
Gregory Stephens, *President*
Wendy Menegay, *Principal*
Kenneth Keller, *Vice Pres*
Sherry L Stephens, *Treasurer*
Jackie Pinter, *Admin Sec*
EMP: 25
SQ FT: 22,000
SALES (est): 2.1MM **Privately Held**
SIC: 4214 4213 4226 4212 Local trucking with storage; household goods transport; special warehousing & storage; local trucking, without storage; general warehousing & storage

(G-2440)
LOWES HOME CENTERS LLC
6375 Strip Ave Nw (44720-7097)
PHONE....................330 497-2720
Fax: 330 497-4058
Jim Weirick, *General Mgr*
Brett Bailey, *District Mgr*
Bill Micklos, *Manager*
EMP: 150
SALES (corp-wide): 68.6B **Publicly Held**
SIC: 5211 5031 5722 5064 Home centers; building materials, exterior; building materials, interior; household appliance stores; electrical appliances, television & radio
HQ: Lowe's Home Centers, Llc
  1605 Curtis Bridge Rd
  Wilkesboro NC 28697
  336 658-4000

(G-2441)
LUIS F SOTO MD
Also Called: Asfoura, Jehad MD
4689 Fulton Dr Nw (44718-2379)
PHONE....................330 649-9400
Luis F Soto MD, *Principal*
Asfoura Jehad MD, *Principal*
EMP: 25
SALES (est): 484K **Privately Held**
SIC: 8011 Offices & clinics of medical doctors

(G-2442)
M CONLEY COMPANY (PA)
Also Called: Network
1312 4th St Se (44707-3243)
P.O. Box 21270 (44701-1270)
PHONE....................330 456-8243
Fax: 330 588-2572
Robert Stuart III, *CEO*
Eric Conley, *President*
Michael Conley, *Principal*
Ernest A Gerber, *Principal*
Robert H Stewart III, *COO*
EMP: 100
SQ FT: 75,000
SALES (est): 80MM **Privately Held**
WEB: www.conleypackaging.com
SIC: 5113 5087 5084 Industrial & personal service paper; paper & products, wrapping or coarse; janitors' supplies; safety equipment

(G-2443)
MALONEY & ASSOCIATES INC
Also Called: Canton Chair Rental
4850 Southway St Sw (44706-1947)
PHONE....................330 479-7084
Tim Moloney Sr, *President*
R C Maloney, *Vice Pres*
Dean Cecconi, *Opers Mgr*
Peggy Monnot, *Sls & Mktg Exec*
Anna Holsinger, *Sales Associate*
EMP: 40
SQ FT: 20,000
SALES (est): 6.4MM **Privately Held**
WEB: www.cantonchairrental.com
SIC: 7359 Party supplies rental services

(G-2444)
MANO LOGISTICS LLC
1934 Navarre Rd Sw (44706-1570)
PHONE....................330 454-1307
Tiffany Manolakis, *Manager*
Stan Manolakis,
EMP: 34
SALES (est): 1.2MM **Privately Held**
SIC: 4214 Local trucking with storage

(G-2445)
MANOR CARE OF AMERICA INC
5005 Higbee Ave Nw (44718-2521)
PHONE....................330 492-7835
Fax: 330 492-7839
Megan Lublin, *Manager*
Daniel Cannone, *Director*
EMP: 110
SALES (corp-wide): 3.6B **Publicly Held**
WEB: www.trisunhealthcare.com
SIC: 8051 Convalescent home with continuous nursing care
HQ: Manor Care Of America, Inc.
  333 N Summit St Ste 103
  Toledo OH 43604
  419 252-5500

(G-2446)
MARATHON PETROLEUM COMPANY LP
3500 21st St Sw (44706-2457)
PHONE....................330 479-5688
Brad McKain, *General Mgr*
EMP: 350 **Publicly Held**
SIC: 5172 Gasoline
HQ: Marathon Petroleum Company Lp
  539 S Main St
  Findlay OH 45840

(G-2447)
MARGARET B SHIPLEY CHILD HLTH (PA)
919 2nd St Ne (44704-1132)
PHONE....................330 478-6333
Fax: 330 453-2362
Steve Muckley, *President*
Dr Allison Oprandi, *Vice Pres*
James Rossi, *Treasurer*
Laurie Inskeep, *Exec Dir*
Angela Vagotis, *Admin Sec*
EMP: 30
SALES (est): 809K **Privately Held**
SIC: 8011 Clinic, operated by physicians

(G-2448)
MARQUIS MOBILITY INC
4051 Whipple Ave Nw Ste E (44718-2967)
PHONE....................330 497-5373
Rick Worstell, *President*
EMP: 100
SALES (est): 11.3MM **Privately Held**
SIC: 5047 Medical equipment & supplies

(G-2449)
MARRIOTT INTERNATIONAL INC
Also Called: Fairfield Inn
4025 Greentree Ave Sw (44706-4016)
PHONE....................330 484-0300
Jennifer Ruiz, *Manager*
EMP: 25
SALES (corp-wide): 22.8B **Publicly Held**
SIC: 7011 Hotels
PA: Marriott International, Inc.
  10400 Fernwood Rd
  Bethesda MD 20817
  301 380-3000

(G-2450)
MARTIN LOGISTICS INC
4526 Louisville St Ne (44705-4850)
PHONE....................330 456-8000
Alice F Martin, *President*
EMP: 51 **EST:** 1997
SQ FT: 30,000
SALES (est): 6.8MM **Privately Held**
SIC: 4731 Freight forwarding

(G-2451)
MATRIX MANAGEMENT SOLUTIONS
5200 Stoneham Rd (44720-1584)
PHONE....................330 470-3700
Mark Terpylak, *President*
EMP: 140
SALES (est): 8.7MM
SALES (corp-wide): 509.6MM **Publicly Held**
SIC: 7372 7373 Prepackaged software; computer integrated systems design
PA: Quality Systems, Inc.
  18111 Von Karman Ave # 700
  Irvine CA 92612
  949 255-2600

(G-2452)
MAYFLOWER NURSING HOME INC
Also Called: Sumser Health Care Center
836 34th St Nw (44709-2947)
PHONE....................330 492-7131
Shirley Armstrong, *President*
EMP: 150
SQ FT: 55,000
SALES (est): 1.4MM **Privately Held**
SIC: 8051 8059 Convalescent home with continuous nursing care; personal care home, with health care

(G-2453)
MCKINLEY AIR TRANSPORT INC
5430 Lauby Rd Bldg 4 (44720-1576)
P.O. Box 2406 (44720-0406)
PHONE....................330 497-6956
Fax: 330 499-0444
Don J Armen, *President*
Sandy Soemisch, *Administration*
EMP: 40 **EST:** 1934
SQ FT: 38,000
SALES (est): 6.5MM **Privately Held**
SIC: 5599 4581 5172 4522 Aircraft, self-propelled; aircraft cleaning & janitorial service; aircraft fueling services; flying charter service

(G-2454)
MCKINLEY EARLY CHILDHOOD CTR (PA)
1350 Cherry Ave Ne (44714-2529)
PHONE....................330 454-4800
Fax: 330 454-8564
Kevin Goeble, *Manager*
Kathie McDonald, *Director*
Michelle Wiggin, *Administration*
EMP: 37
SQ FT: 5,000
SALES (est): 1.9MM **Privately Held**
SIC: 8351 Group day care center; preschool center

(G-2455)
MCKINLEY LIFE CARE CENTER LLC
800 Market Ave N Ste 1560 (44702-2303)
PHONE....................330 456-1014
Fax: 330 430-2177
Bob Knapp,
EMP: 100 **EST:** 1999
SALES (est): 4.9MM
SALES (corp-wide): 26.7MM **Privately Held**
SIC: 8051 Extended care facility

Canton - Stark County (G-2456)

PA: Extended Care Consulting, Llc
2201 Main St Ste A
Evanston IL 60202
847 905-3000

(G-2456)
MEADOWLAKE CORPORATION
Also Called: Golf and Swim Club
1211 39th St Ne Ste A (44714-1237)
PHONE.................330 492-2010
Fax: 330 492-2011
Roy Barr, *President*
EMP: 25
SQ FT: 1,500
SALES (est): 1.1MM **Privately Held**
SIC: 7992 5941 Public golf courses; sporting goods & bicycle shops

(G-2457)
MEDLINE DIAMED LLC (HQ)
3800 Commerce St Sw (44706-3367)
PHONE.................330 484-1450
Scott Wakser, *Mng Member*
Howard Fried,
Jerry Fried,
Michael Fried,
Douglas Sharpe,
▲ EMP: 46
SQ FT: 15,000
SALES (est): 7.7MM
SALES (corp-wide): 8B **Privately Held**
WEB: www.diamedinc.com
SIC: 5047 Medical equipment & supplies
PA: Medline Industries, Inc.
3 Lakes Dr
Northfield IL 60093
847 949-5500

(G-2458)
MERCY MEDICAL CENTER INC
Also Called: Mercy Medical Center Hospice
4369 Whipple Ave Nw (44718-2643)
PHONE.................330 649-4380
Fax: 330 966-8099
Maria Thompson, *Director*
EMP: 60
SALES (corp-wide): 321.4MM **Privately Held**
SIC: 8011 Clinic, operated by physicians
HQ: Mercy Medical Center, Inc.
1320 Mercy Dr Nw
Canton OH 44708
330 489-1000

(G-2459)
MERCY MEDICAL CENTER INC (HQ)
1320 Mercy Dr Nw (44708-2641)
PHONE.................330 489-1000
Fax: 330 430-2794
Thomas E Cecconi, *President*
Christopher J Swift, *Principal*
David D Cemate, *COO*
William Murphy, *Ch Radiology*
Sister Carolyn Capuano, *Vice Pres*
EMP: 40
SQ FT: 1,000,000
SALES: 309MM
SALES (corp-wide): 321.4MM **Privately Held**
WEB: www.cantonmercy.com
SIC: 8062 General medical & surgical hospitals
PA: The Sisters Of Charity Of St Augustine Health System Inc
2475 E 22nd St
Cleveland OH 44115
216 696-5560

(G-2460)
MERRILL LYNCH PIERCE FENNER
4678 Munson St Nw (44718-3647)
PHONE.................330 497-6600
Fax: 330 497-6648
Anastasia Cozer, *Manager*
Gregory Dinarda, *Manager*
Debbie Hall, *Manager*
Benjamin O Kirksey, *Agent*
George Merrill, *Administration*
EMP: 50
SALES (corp-wide): 100.2B **Publicly Held**
WEB: www.merlyn.com
SIC: 6211 Security brokers & dealers

HQ: Merrill Lynch, Pierce, Fenner & Smith Incorporated
111 8th Ave
New York NY 10011
800 637-7455

(G-2461)
MICHAEL BAKER INTL INC
101 Cleveland Ave Nw # 106 (44702-1707)
PHONE.................330 453-3110
Kurt Bergman, *CEO*
Louis Levner, *Assistant VP*
Michael Baker, *Branch Mgr*
EMP: 140
SALES (corp-wide): 592.9MM **Privately Held**
SIC: 8711 8741 Civil engineering; management services
HQ: Baker Michael International Inc
500 Grant St Ste 5400
Pittsburgh PA 15219
412 269-6300

(G-2462)
MIDLANDS MILLROOM SUPPLY INC
1911 36th St Ne (44705-5023)
P.O. Box 7007 (44705-0007)
PHONE.................330 453-9100
Fax: 330 453-6644
Fred Clark, *President*
Rod Cunningham, *Mfg Mgr*
Tonia Bove, *Purch Mgr*
Tim Ruppelli, *Sales Engr*
Yoshi Terada, *Sales Executive*
▲ EMP: 28
SQ FT: 17,000
SALES: 15MM **Privately Held**
WEB: www.batch-off.com
SIC: 5084 3061 Materials handling machinery; mechanical rubber goods

(G-2463)
MILLER & CO PORTABLE TOIL SVCS
2400 Shepler Ch Ave Sw (44706-4112)
PHONE.................330 453-9472
Fax: 330 453-9476
Ronald Miller Jr, *President*
EMP: 30 EST: 1999
SQ FT: 40,000
SALES (est): 4MM **Privately Held**
WEB: www.millerandcompany.com
SIC: 7359 Portable toilet rental

(G-2464)
MIRACLE PLUMBING & HEATING CO
Also Called: Honeywell Authorized Dealer
2121 Whipple Ave Nw (44708-2361)
PHONE.................330 477-2402
Fax: 330 477-6661
Steven J Brown, *President*
John Dewees, *General Mgr*
Michelle Hargis, *Marketing Mgr*
Bob Braler, *Director*
EMP: 35
SALES (est): 5.4MM **Privately Held**
WEB: www.miracleplumbing.com
SIC: 1711 1623 Warm air heating & air conditioning contractor; plumbing contractors; irrigation sprinkler system installation; water main construction

(G-2465)
MORROW CONTROL AND SUPPLY INC (PA)
Also Called: Johnson Contrls Authorized Dlr
810 Marion Motley Ave Ne (44705-1430)
PHONE.................330 452-9791
Fax: 330 452-8306
Richard Schwane, *President*
Jack Baltzly, *Warehouse Mgr*
Milton Baltzly, *Warehouse Mgr*
Janice Ritenour, *Purchasing*
Calvin Ratliff, *Sales Mgr*
EMP: 35
SQ FT: 100,000
SALES: 13MM **Privately Held**
SIC: 5074 Heating equipment (hydronic)

(G-2466)
MPLX TERMINALS LLC
2408 Gambrinus Ave Sw (44706-2365)
PHONE.................330 479-5539

Sue Kreinen, *VP Opers*
Mike Armebrester, *Plant Mgr*
Julie Vinci, *Purch Agent*
Linda Martin, *QC Dir*
Sue Krienen, *Engineer*
EMP: 350
SALES (corp-wide): 3.8B **Publicly Held**
WEB: www.mapllc.com
SIC: 5172 2951 Gasoline; asphalt paving mixtures & blocks
HQ: Mplx Terminals Llc
200 E Hardin St
Findlay OH

(G-2467)
MPW INDUSTRIAL SERVICES INC
Also Called: Industrial Cleaning
907 Belden Ave Se (44707-2613)
PHONE.................330 454-1898
Kevin Smith, *Branch Mgr*
Ivan Gorowitz, *Manager*
Tim S Tarry Jr, *Manager*
EMP: 70
SALES (corp-wide): 257.9MM **Privately Held**
SIC: 7349 Building component cleaning service
HQ: Mpw Industrial Services, Inc.
9711 Lancaster Rd
Hebron OH 43025
800 827-8790

(G-2468)
MULLINAX FORD NORTH CANTON INC
Also Called: Autonation Ford North Canton
5900 Whipple Ave Nw (44720-7614)
PHONE.................330 238-3206
Fax: 330 497-3123
Charles E Mullinax, *President*
Larry Mullinax, *Treasurer*
David Spradlin, *Sales Associate*
Brian Gilmore, *Manager*
Dale Greagory, *MIS Dir*
EMP: 125
SQ FT: 40,000
SALES (est): 38.6MM
SALES (corp-wide): 21.5B **Publicly Held**
WEB: www.mullinaxfordcanton.com
SIC: 5511 5521 7515 Automobiles, new & used; pickups, new & used; vans, new & used; used car dealers; passenger car leasing
HQ: An Dealership Holding Corp.
200 Sw 1st Ave
Fort Lauderdale FL 33301
954 769-7000

(G-2469)
MULTI-CNTY JVNILE ATTNTION SYS (PA)
815 Faircrest St Sw (44706-4844)
PHONE.................330 484-8112
Fax: 330 484-8112
Mellissa Clark, *General Mgr*
Donald Thernes, *Superintendent*
Donna J Ogrisseg, *Persnl Dir*
Theresa Metzger, *Supervisor*
Cathy Fithian, *Director*
EMP: 100
SALES: 12.5MM **Privately Held**
SIC: 8361 Juvenile correctional home

(G-2470)
NATIONAL FOOTBALL MUSEUM INC
Also Called: Professional Football Hall Fame
2121 George Halas Dr Nw (44708-2630)
PHONE.................330 456-8207
Fax: 330 456-8175
John Muhlbach Jr, *Chairman*
Brian Proud, *COO*
Anne Graffice, *Vice Pres*
Muhlbach John, *Vice Pres*
Brock Richards, *Vice Pres*
EMP: 31
SQ FT: 83,000
SALES: 30.4MM **Privately Held**
WEB: www.profootballhof.com
SIC: 7941 Football club

(G-2471)
NATIONWIDE CORPORATION
1000 Market Ave N (44702-1025)
P.O. Box 8379 (44711-8379)
PHONE.................330 452-8705
Larry Ray, *Manager*
EMP: 600
SALES (corp-wide): 26.6B **Privately Held**
WEB: www.nationwide.com
SIC: 6411 Insurance agents
HQ: Nationwide Corporation
1 Nationwide Plz
Columbus OH 43215
614 249-7111

(G-2472)
NATIONWIDE MUTUAL INSURANCE CO
1000 Market Ave N (44702-1025)
P.O. Box 8379 (44711-8379)
PHONE.................330 489-5000
Barbara Moses, *Manager*
Jeff Elliot, *Senior Mgr*
EMP: 520
SALES (corp-wide): 26.6B **Privately Held**
WEB: www.nirassn.com
SIC: 6411 Insurance agents
PA: Nationwide Mutual Insurance Company
1 Nationwide Plz
Columbus OH 43215
614 249-7111

(G-2473)
NIMISHILLEN & TUSCARAWAS LLC
2633 8th St Ne (44704-2311)
PHONE.................330 438-5821
Fax: 330 438-5866
Steve Sinnott, *General Mgr*
EMP: 32
SALES (est): 2.4MM **Privately Held**
SIC: 4011 Railroads, line-haul operating
HQ: Republic Steel Inc.
2633 8th St Ne
Canton OH 44704
330 438-5435

(G-2474)
NORCIA BAKERY
624 Belden Ave Ne (44704-2229)
PHONE.................330 454-1077
Donald C Horne, *President*
Jim Butler, *Vice Pres*
EMP: 25 EST: 1920
SQ FT: 3,200
SALES (est): 3MM **Privately Held**
SIC: 2051 5461 5149 2052 Bakery: wholesale or wholesale/retail combined; bread; groceries & related products; cookies & crackers

(G-2475)
NORTH CANTON CITY SCHOOL DST
Also Called: North Canton Schl Transprtatn
387 Pershing Ave Ne (44720-2582)
PHONE.................330 497-5615
Fax: 330 305-5465
Thomas Shoup, *Superintendent*
EMP: 66
SALES (corp-wide): 51.2MM **Privately Held**
WEB: www.northcantoncityschools.com
SIC: 4151 School buses
PA: North Canton City School District
525 7th St Ne
Canton OH 44720
330 497-5600

(G-2476)
NORTHEAST PROFESSIONAL HM CARE (PA)
1177 S Main St Ste 11 (44720-4200)
PHONE.................330 966-2311
Fax: 330 966-2381
Anthony John Vallone, *President*
Eusnook Vallone, *Corp Secy*
EMP: 46 EST: 1995
SALES (est): 4.5MM **Privately Held**
SIC: 8082 Visiting nurse service

GEOGRAPHIC SECTION
Canton - Stark County (G-2501)

(G-2477)
NUEROCARE CENTER INC
4105 Holiday St Nw (44718-2531)
P.O. Box 35006 (44735-5006)
PHONE...................330 494-2917
EMP: 70 EST: 2002
SALES (est): 3MM **Privately Held**
SIC: 8011 Medical Doctor's Office

(G-2478)
OHIO AUTO SUPPLY COMPANY
Also Called: Professional Detailing Pdts
1128 Tuscarawas St W (44702-2086)
PHONE...................330 454-5105
Fax: 330 454-5130
Michael Dickson, *President*
Angie Piper, *Manager*
Stanley R Rubin, *Admin Sec*
EMP: 29 EST: 1933
SQ FT: 15,000
SALES (est): 6.7MM **Privately Held**
WEB: www.ohioautosupply.com
SIC: 5013 2842 5531 3714 Automotive supplies & parts; cleaning or polishing preparations; automotive parts; motor vehicle parts & accessories

(G-2479)
OHIO FARMERS INSURANCE COMPANY
1801 Faircrest St Se (44707-1243)
PHONE...................330 484-5660
Willian Edwards, *Owner*
EMP: 242
SALES (corp-wide): 1.6B **Privately Held**
SIC: 6411 6399 Property & casualty insurance agent; health insurance for pets
PA: Ohio Farmers Insurance Company
1 Park Cir
Westfield Center OH 44251
800 243-0210

(G-2480)
OHIO HEAD & NECK SURGEONS INC (PA)
Also Called: Canton Allergy Lab
4912 Higbee Ave Nw # 200 (44718-2599)
PHONE...................330 492-2844
Fax: 330 492-0840
Steven J Ossakow, *President*
Julie Farley, *Manager*
Chuck Bogdan, *Surgeon*
EMP: 36
SALES (est): 4.7MM **Privately Held**
SIC: 8011 Ears, nose & throat specialist: physician/surgeon; physicians' office, including specialists; surgeon; allergist

(G-2481)
OHIO MACHINERY CO
Also Called: Caterpillar Authorized Dealer
4731 Corporate St Sw (44706-1906)
PHONE...................330 478-6525
Fax: 330 478-6529
Gabe Hoffa, *Manager*
EMP: 40
SALES (corp-wide): 222.7MM **Privately Held**
WEB: www.enginesnow.com
SIC: 5082 General construction machinery & equipment
PA: Ohio Machinery Co.
3993 E Royalton Rd
Broadview Heights OH 44147
440 526-6200

(G-2482)
OHIO POOLS & SPAS INC (PA)
6815 Whipple Ave Nw (44720-7335)
PHONE...................330 494-7755
Fax: 330 494-7925
Richard A Annis, *President*
Steve Oliver, *Sls & Mktg Exec*
Gary Hilbert, *Human Res Mgr*
▲ EMP: 31
SQ FT: 8,000
SALES (est): 5.9MM **Privately Held**
WEB: www.ohiopools.com
SIC: 1799 Swimming pool construction

(G-2483)
OHIO POWER COMPANY
1 Riverside Plz (44701)
P.O. Box 24421 (44701-4421)
PHONE...................888 216-3523
Thomas Nohl, *Branch Mgr*
EMP: 30
SALES (corp-wide): 15.4B **Publicly Held**
SIC: 1731 Electrical work
HQ: Ohio Power Company
1 Riverside Plz
Columbus OH 43215
614 716-1000

(G-2484)
OHIO RETINA ASSOCIATES INC (PA)
4690 Munson St Nw Ste D (44718-3636)
PHONE...................330 966-9800
Fax: 330 966-9803
Thomas Tsai, *President*
Jeffery C Lamkin, *Principal*
Arnold F Nothnagel, *Corp Secy*
EMP: 25
SQ FT: 3,300
SALES (est): 3.8MM **Privately Held**
SIC: 8011 Eyes, ears, nose & throat specialist: physician/surgeon

(G-2485)
OHIO STATE UNIVERSITY
Also Called: Stark and Summit Regional EXT
5119 Lauby Rd (44720-1544)
PHONE...................330 263-3725
Ernest Oelker, *Branch Mgr*
EMP: 25
SALES (corp-wide): 5.5B **Privately Held**
WEB: www.ohio-state.edu
SIC: 8221 8731 University; agricultural research
PA: The Ohio State University
Student Acade Servi Bldg
Columbus OH 43210
614 292-6446

(G-2486)
OHIO STEEL SLITTERS INC
1401 Raff Rd Sw (44710-2319)
P.O. Box 80168 (44708-0168)
PHONE...................330 477-6741
Fax: 330 447-6410
Warren Selinsky, *President*
Craig Selinsky, *President*
Sally Stang, *Manager*
Florence Selinsky, *Admin Sec*
EMP: 25
SQ FT: 165,000
SALES: 400K **Privately Held**
SIC: 7389 Metal slitting & shearing

(G-2487)
ORTHORPDICS MLTSPCIALTY NETWRK (PA)
4760 Belpar St Nw (44718-3603)
PHONE...................330 493-1630
Stephen A Lohr, *CEO*
Ray Cinicola, *CFO*
Michael D London, *Admin Sec*
EMP: 50
SALES (est): 3.5MM **Privately Held**
SIC: 8011 Orthopedic physician; surgeon

(G-2488)
PARK CENTRE LANES INC
7313 Whipple Ave Nw (44720-7179)
PHONE...................330 499-0555
Fax: 330 499-0556
Timmy Brendle, *President*
Annie Case, *Principal*
EMP: 40 EST: 1976
SQ FT: 12,000
SALES: 800.7K **Privately Held**
WEB: www.parkcentrelanes.com
SIC: 7933 Ten pin center

(G-2489)
PATHWAY CARING FOR CHILDREN (PA)
4895 Dressler Rd Nw Ste A (44718-2571)
PHONE...................330 493-0083
Eric Belden, *CEO*
Gregg Umberger, *CFO*
Jim Bridges, *Director*
Crystal Schneiders, *Director*
Julie Davis, *Training Spec*
EMP: 60
SQ FT: 21,000
SALES: 4.6MM **Privately Held**
SIC: 8361 Children's home; group foster home

(G-2490)
PEOPLES SERVICES INC (PA)
2207 Kimball Rd Se (44707-3631)
P.O. Box 20109 (44701-0109)
PHONE...................330 453-3709
Fax: 330 453-5171
Ronald R Sibila, *Ch of Bd*
Douglas J Sibila, *President*
Chuck Bridwell, *General Mgr*
Jeff Choquette, *General Mgr*
James Morgan, *General Mgr*
EMP: 25
SQ FT: 110,000
SALES: 70.7MM **Privately Held**
SIC: 4225 4213 4212 General warehousing; trucking, except local; local trucking, without storage

(G-2491)
POWELL ELECTRICAL SYSTEMS INC
Also Called: Pemco North Canton Division
8967 Pleasantwood Ave Nw (44720-4761)
PHONE...................330 966-1750
Fax: 330 966-1787
Sharon James, *Project Mgr*
Donald Vrudney, *Mfg Staff*
Paula Myers, *Purchasing*
Peter Crombie, *Engineer*
Allen Marshall, *Engineer*
EMP: 92
SQ FT: 41,600
SALES (corp-wide): 395.9MM **Publicly Held**
WEB: www.powl.com
SIC: 3678 5063 3699 Electronic connectors; electrical apparatus & equipment; electrical equipment & supplies
HQ: Powell Electrical Systems, Inc.
7232 Airport Blvd
Houston TX 77061
713 770-2131

(G-2492)
PREFERRED TEMPORARY SERVICES
4791 Munson St Nw (44718-3612)
PHONE...................330 494-5502
Charles Hill, *CEO*
Douglas Hill, *Executive*
EMP: 30
SALES (est): 1.4MM **Privately Held**
SIC: 7363 Temporary help service

(G-2493)
PRIMARY CARE PHYSICIANS ASSN
4575 Stephens Cir Nw (44718-3629)
PHONE...................330 499-9944
Karin Triggs, *Partner*
Karin T Riggs, *Partner*
Lynn Ferry, *Manager*
EMP: 25
SALES (est): 3.3MM **Privately Held**
SIC: 8011 Pediatrician

(G-2494)
PRIME COMMUNICATIONS LP
Also Called: Unknown
4232 Belden Village Mall (44718-2504)
PHONE...................281 240-7800
EMP: 40
SALES (corp-wide): 280MM **Privately Held**
SIC: 4812 Cellular telephone services
PA: Prime Communications, L P
12550 Reed Rd Ste 100
Sugar Land TX 77478
281 240-7800

(G-2495)
PROJECT REBUILD INC
406 Shorb Ave Nw (44703-2617)
PHONE...................330 639-1559
Jake Martin, *Manager*
Trisha Postlewait, *Manager*
Joanna James, *Exec Dir*
Carolyn Hess, *Director*
Don Brighenti, *Director*
EMP: 25
SQ FT: 3,600
SALES: 756.9K **Privately Held**
WEB: www.projectrebuild.com
SIC: 8331 Community service employment training program

(G-2496)
PROTECH SECURITY INC
Also Called: Protech Alarm Systems
7026 Sunset Strip Ave Nw (44720-7077)
P.O. Box 35034 (44735-5034)
PHONE...................330 499-3555
Fax: 330 499-8327
Daniel Mc Kimm, *President*
Laura Mc Kimm, *Corp Secy*
Laura M Kimm, *Admin Sec*
Daniel McKimm, *Administration*
EMP: 27 EST: 1980
SQ FT: 7,500
SALES (est): 5MM **Privately Held**
WEB: www.protech-security.com
SIC: 1731 7382 Fire detection & burglar alarm systems specialization; closed circuit television installation; security systems services

(G-2497)
PSC METALS INC
237 Tuscarawas St E (44702-1214)
P.O. Box 21070 (44701-1070)
PHONE...................330 455-0212
EMP: 42
SALES (corp-wide): 19.1B **Publicly Held**
SIC: 5093 Wholesales Scrap Metals
HQ: Psc Metals, Inc.
5875 Landerbrook Dr # 200
Mayfield Heights OH 44124
216 752-4000

(G-2498)
PSC METALS INC
3101 Varley Ave Sw (44706-3544)
PHONE...................330 484-7610
Fax: 330 484-0516
Carol Seifert, *Office Mgr*
Andrew Luntz, *Branch Mgr*
Carol Seifirt, *Administration*
EMP: 42
SALES (corp-wide): 21.7B **Publicly Held**
WEB: www.pscmetals.com
SIC: 5093 Metal scrap & waste materials
HQ: Psc Metals, Inc.
5875 Landerbrook Dr # 200
Mayfield Heights OH 44124
440 753-5400

(G-2499)
QUEST RECOVERY PREVENTION SVCS (PA)
1341 Market Ave N (44714-2624)
PHONE...................330 453-8252
Fax: 330 453-6716
Keith Hochadel, *CEO*
Ivan Rosa, *COO*
Beth Devitt, *CFO*
Kristen Petrilla, *Mktg Dir*
Scott Harhager, *Director*
EMP: 111
SQ FT: 12,000
SALES: 13MM **Privately Held**
WEB: www.questrecoveryservices.com
SIC: 8322 Substance abuse counseling; outreach program

(G-2500)
QUICK DELIVERY SERVICE INC (HQ)
2207 Kimball Rd Se (44707-3631)
P.O. Box 20109 (44701-0109)
PHONE...................330 453-3709
Douglas J Sibila, *President*
Larry Kelley, *CFO*
EMP: 30
SALES (est): 2.7MM **Privately Held**
SIC: 4212 Delivery service, vehicular

(G-2501)
R E RICHARDS INC
Also Called: Eecutive Directions
9701 Cleveland Ave Nw # 100 (44720-9833)
P.O. Box 3006 (44720-8006)
PHONE...................330 499-1001
Fax: 330 499-2579
Paul Richards, *President*
EMP: 25
SALES (est): 1.5MM **Privately Held**
SIC: 7361 Executive placement

Canton - Stark County (G-2502)

(G-2502)
R S SEWING INC
1387 Clarendon Ave Sw # 10 (44710-2190)
PHONE..................................330 478-3360
Fax: 330 478-3365
Richard Spencer, *President*
EMP: 25
SALES (est): 5.2MM **Privately Held**
SIC: 5131 Sewing supplies & notions

(G-2503)
RADIOLOGY ASSOC CANTON INC
2600 6th St Sw (44710-1702)
PHONE..................................330 363-2842
John Vizzuso, *CEO*
EMP: 50
SALES (est): 1.9MM **Privately Held**
SIC: 8721 Billing & bookkeeping service

(G-2504)
RED CARPET CAR WASH INC
4546 Tuscarawas St W (44708-5337)
PHONE..................................330 477-5772
Fax: 330 477-1966
Jonathan Shaw, *President*
EMP: 41
SQ FT: 10,000
SALES (est): 1.4MM **Privately Held**
SIC: 7542 Washing & polishing, automotive

(G-2505)
RED ROBIN GOURMET BURGERS INC
6522 Strip Ave Nw (44720-9203)
PHONE..................................330 305-1080
Fax: 330 305-1768
Jason Myers, *Manager*
EMP: 65
SALES (corp-wide): 1.3B **Publicly Held**
SIC: 5812 6794 Restaurant, family: chain; franchises, selling or licensing
PA: Red Robin Gourmet Burgers Inc
6312 S Fiddlers Green Cir 200n
Greenwood Village CO 80111
303 846-6000

(G-2506)
RENTWEAR INC
7944 Whipple Ave Nw (44720-6992)
PHONE..................................330 535-2301
Roger Clay, *President*
Patricia Clay, *Corp Secy*
Christopher Clay, *Vice Pres*
Daniel Clay, *Vice Pres*
Tadd Clay, *Vice Pres*
EMP: 72 EST: 1972
SQ FT: 31,000
SALES (est): 5.6MM **Privately Held**
SIC: 7218 Industrial uniform supply; wiping towel supply; laundered mat & rug supply

(G-2507)
REPRODUCTIVE GYNECOLOGY INC
2600 Tuscarawas St W # 560 (44708-4699)
PHONE..................................330 452-6010
Richard Moretuzzo, *President*
EMP: 35
SALES (est): 780.8K **Privately Held**
SIC: 8011 Endocrinologist; fertility specialist, physician

(G-2508)
REPUBLIC N&T RAILROAD INC
2633 8th St Ne (44704-2311)
PHONE..................................330 438-5826
Jim Murphy, *Manager*
EMP: 110
SALES (est): 8.8MM **Privately Held**
SIC: 4011 Railroads, line-haul operating
HQ: Republic Steel Inc.
2633 8th St Ne
Canton OH 44704
330 438-5435

(G-2509)
REPUBLIC TELCOM WORLDWIDE LLC (HQ)
3939 Everhard Rd Nw (44709-4004)
PHONE..................................330 966-4586
Aaron Stryker, *General Mgr*
EMP: 150
SALES (est): 8.2MM **Privately Held**
SIC: 7389 Telephone services

(G-2510)
RES-CARE INC
2915 33rd St Ne (44705-3827)
PHONE..................................330 453-4144
Molly Maher, *Branch Mgr*
EMP: 48
SALES (corp-wide): 24.5B **Privately Held**
WEB: www.rescare.com
SIC: 8052 Home for the mentally retarded, with health care
HQ: Res-Care, Inc.
9901 Linn Station Rd
Louisville KY 40223
502 394-2100

(G-2511)
RESCARE OHIO INC
2821 Whipple Ave Nw # 100 (44708-6215)
PHONE..................................330 479-9841
Lisa Javersak, *Branch Mgr*
EMP: 39
SALES (corp-wide): 24.5B **Privately Held**
SIC: 8361 Self-help group home
HQ: Rescare Ohio Inc
348 W Main St
Williamsburg OH 45176

(G-2512)
RESERVE FTL LLC
Also Called: Reserve Iron Ohio
1451 Trump Ave Ne (44730-1651)
PHONE..................................773 721-8740
Guy Peake, *Branch Mgr*
EMP: 30 **Privately Held**
SIC: 5093 Ferrous metal scrap & waste
PA: Reserve Ftl, Llc
11600 S Burley Ave
Chicago IL 60617

(G-2513)
REXS AIR CONDITIONING COMPANY
Also Called: Rex Reliable
7801 Freedom Ave Nw (44720-6907)
P.O. Box 1030, Uniontown (44685-1030)
PHONE..................................330 499-8733
Scott Seifert, *President*
Chuck Lenhart, *Controller*
Eugene Seifert, *Shareholder*
EMP: 25
SALES (est): 1.8MM **Privately Held**
SIC: 1711 Plumbing, heating, air-conditioning contractors

(G-2514)
RICK ALLMAN
Also Called: Primerica
4450 Belden Village St Nw Nw800 (44718-2552)
PHONE..................................330 699-1660
Fax: 330 244-1875
Rick Allman, *Owner*
EMP: 40
SALES (est): 4.1MM **Privately Held**
SIC: 6411 Insurance agents & brokers

(G-2515)
ROMAN PLUMBING COMPANY
2411 Shepler Ch Ave Sw (44706-4199)
PHONE..................................330 455-5155
Fax: 330 455-5190
Scott Kocher, *President*
Doug Kocher, *Vice Pres*
Jeannette Pattrill, *Manager*
EMP: 55
SQ FT: 2,500
SALES (est): 7.5MM **Privately Held**
SIC: 1711 Plumbing contractors; warm air heating & air conditioning contractor

(G-2516)
RORICKS INC
Also Called: Roricks Ceiling Center
4701 Eagle St Nw (44720-7083)
PHONE..................................330 497-6888
Fax: 330 497-6761
Richard L Rorick, *President*
Michael Arters, *Opers Mgr*
Krissy Greene, *Controller*
Lewis W Devore, *Manager*
Floyd E Oryszak, *Manager*
EMP: 50
SQ FT: 23,000

SALES (est): 5.7MM **Privately Held**
WEB: www.roricks.com
SIC: 1742 Drywall; plastering, plain or ornamental

(G-2517)
ROYAL SHEEN SERVICE CENTER
Also Called: Royal Car Wash
6857 Whipple Ave Nw (44720-7335)
PHONE..................................330 966-7200
Fax: 330 966-7171
Scott Walker, *General Mgr*
Lonn Swinehart, *Vice Pres*
Pam Walker, *Admin Sec*
EMP: 25
SQ FT: 5,720
SALES (est): 1MM **Privately Held**
SIC: 7542 Carwash, automatic

(G-2518)
RUKH-JAGI HOLDINGS LLC
Also Called: Holiday Inn Canton
4520 Everhard Rd Nw (44718-2407)
PHONE..................................330 494-2770
Rupen Patel,
EMP: 100
SALES (est): 6.1MM **Privately Held**
WEB: www.hicanton.com
SIC: 7011 Hotels & motels

(G-2519)
RUNT WARE & SANITARY SERVICE
7944 Whipple Ave Nw (44720-6930)
PHONE..................................330 494-5776
Fax: 330 494-4852
Roger Clay, *General Mgr*
Chris Clay, *Principal*
Tadd Clay, *Principal*
Dan Clay, *Manager*
EMP: 50
SALES (est): 598.7K **Privately Held**
WEB: www.saniserv.biz
SIC: 7218 Industrial uniform supply

(G-2520)
RUSSELL D ENS DO
Also Called: Ohio Anestisia
4665 Douglas Cir Nw # 101 (44718-3673)
PHONE..................................330 499-5700
Mark Fellow, *Owner*
Amanda Gillis, *Admin Sec*
David W Lehman, *Administration*
EMP: 50
SALES (est): 142.6K **Privately Held**
SIC: 8011 Anesthesiologist

(G-2521)
S&S CAR CARE INC
5340 Mayfair Rd (44720-1533)
PHONE..................................330 494-9535
Fax: 330 966-0400
Lonn Swinehart, *President*
Peter Denissoff, *Director*
EMP: 25
SQ FT: 20,000
SALES (est): 1.3MM **Privately Held**
SIC: 7539 Automotive repair shops

(G-2522)
SAFETY RESOURCES COMPANY OHIO
4650 Southway St Sw (44706-1935)
P.O. Box 80425 (44708-0425)
PHONE..................................330 477-1100
Curt Speck, *President*
Gordon Hanlan, *Purch Agent*
Gordon Snyder, *Consultant*
Justin Snyder, *Consultant*
EMP: 33
SALES (est): 4.5MM **Privately Held**
SIC: 8742 Quality assurance consultant

(G-2523)
SCHAUER GROUP INCORPORATED
200 Market Ave N Ste 100 (44702-1435)
PHONE..................................330 453-7721
David T Schauer, *President*
Tim Pentivegna, *Vice Pres*
Ronald Repp, *Vice Pres*
William T Schauer, *Treasurer*
Carolyn Nupp, *Financial Exec*
EMP: 40

SQ FT: 11,000
SALES (est): 6.7MM **Privately Held**
WEB: www.schauergroup.com
SIC: 6411 Insurance agents; advisory services, insurance

(G-2524)
SECURITY SAVINGS MORTGAGE CORP
Also Called: Mortgage Service Center
300 Tuscarawas St W Fl 8 (44702-1914)
P.O. Box 8469 (44711-8469)
PHONE..................................330 455-2833
Fax: 330 455-7726
Clara E Preston, *President*
Libe Preston, *President*
Joan Ickes, *Vice Pres*
Gary Palombo, *Treasurer*
Pam Milhoan, *Human Resources*
EMP: 60
SQ FT: 22,100
SALES (est): 8MM
SALES (corp-wide): 276.9MM **Privately Held**
WEB: www.dollarbank.com
SIC: 6162 Mortgage bankers
PA: Dollar Bank, Federal Savings Bank
401 Liberty Ave
Pittsburgh PA 15222
412 261-4900

(G-2525)
SELINSKY FORCE LLC
4015 23rd St Sw (44706-2313)
PHONE..................................330 477-4527
Don Kelley, *Project Mgr*
Scott Selinsky, *Project Mgr*
Steve Miller, *Branch Mgr*
Kevin Price, *Manager*
EMP: 200
SALES (est): 27.7MM **Privately Held**
SIC: 5085 Industrial supplies
HQ: The Selinsky Force Llc
4244 Mount Pleasant St Nw # 100
North Canton OH 44720

(G-2526)
SERVICEMASTER BY STEINBACH
6824 Wise Ave Nw (44720-7359)
PHONE..................................330 497-5959
Fax: 330 497-8714
Dave Steinbach, *President*
Thomas Baer, *President*
EMP: 25
SQ FT: 3,000
SALES: 750K **Privately Held**
SIC: 7349 Janitorial service, contract basis

(G-2527)
SHARED PET IMAGING LLC
4825 Higbee Ave Nw # 201 (44718-2567)
PHONE..................................330 491-0480
Fax: 330 491-0488
Randy Skiles,
Steven J Ossakow,
Raymond Rosedale,
EMP: 175 EST: 1999
SQ FT: 10,000
SALES (est): 3.6MM **Privately Held**
WEB: www.sharedpet.com
SIC: 8071 Medical laboratories
HQ: Alliance Healthcare Services, Inc.
18201 Von Karman Ave
Irvine CA 92612
949 242-5300

(G-2528)
SIMPLY YOUTH LLC
123 Cleveland Ave Nw (44702-1707)
PHONE..................................330 284-2537
Chip Conde, *Treasurer*
Terrance Jones, *Exec Dir*
EMP: 89
SALES (est): 300.6K **Privately Held**
SIC: 8322 Child related social services

(G-2529)
SIRAK FINANCIAL SERVICES
Also Called: Guardian Life Insurance
4700 Dressler Rd Nw (44718-2511)
PHONE..................................330 493-3211
Mark L Sirak, *Vice Pres*
Edward Pryor, *Executive*
EMP: 90
SQ FT: 5,000

GEOGRAPHIC SECTION
Canton - Stark County (G-2554)

SALES (est): 19.4MM **Privately Held**
SIC: 6311 Life insurance

(G-2530)
SIRAK FINANCIAL SERVICES INC (PA)
Also Called: Sirak Financial Companies
4700 Dressler Rd Nw (44718-2511)
PHONE..................330 493-0642
Fax: 330 493-5939
Gary D Sirak, *President*
Wayne E S Arnold, *CFO*
EMP: 60 EST: 1956
SQ FT: 22,000
SALES (est): 10.4MM **Privately Held**
WEB: www.sirakfinancial.com
SIC: 6211 6411 Stock brokers & dealers; pension & retirement plan consultants; insurance agents

(G-2531)
SIRAK-MOORE INSURANCE AGCY INC
Also Called: Kemper Insurance
4700 Dressler Rd Nw (44718-2511)
PHONE..................330 493-3211
Corbin Moore, *President*
Jim Evans, *General Mgr*
John Hamilton, *Vice Pres*
Mark L Sirak, *Vice Pres*
Wayne Arnold, *CFO*
EMP: 30
SQ FT: 20,000
SALES (est): 4.2MM **Privately Held**
SIC: 6411 Insurance agents, brokers & service

(G-2532)
SLESNICK IRON & METAL CO
Also Called: Auto Crushers
927 Warner Rd Se (44707-3337)
PHONE..................330 453-8475
W Stanley Slesnick, *President*
Edward Slesnick, *Vice Pres*
Jeffrey Slesnick, *Admin Sec*
EMP: 50 EST: 1920
SQ FT: 3,000
SALES (est): 13.3MM **Privately Held**
WEB: www.autocrushers.com
SIC: 5093 Junk & scrap

(G-2533)
SOUTHWAY FENCE COMPANY
5156 Southway St Sw (44706-1944)
PHONE..................330 477-5251
Fax: 330 477-0521
Peter Williams Sr, *President*
Pam Ohman, *Bookkeeper*
EMP: 30
SQ FT: 8,800
SALES (est): 4.2MM **Privately Held**
WEB: www.southwayfence.com
SIC: 1799 Fence construction

(G-2534)
SPAULDING CONSTRUCTION CO INC
7640 Whipple Ave Nw (44720-6924)
PHONE..................330 494-1776
EMP: 52 EST: 1987
SALES (est): 5.1MM **Privately Held**
SIC: 1771 Cement Contractor

(G-2535)
SPITZER CHEVROLET COMPANY
7111 Sunset Strip Ave Nw (44720-7080)
PHONE..................330 966-9524
Alan Spitzer, *President*
Kevin Spitzer, *Vice Pres*
EMP: 40 EST: 1959
SQ FT: 7,140
SALES (est): 12.8MM **Privately Held**
SIC: 5511 7514 Automobiles, new & used; vans, new & used; pickups, new & used; passenger car rental

(G-2536)
SPRAYWORKS EQUIPMENT GROUP LLC
215 Navarre Rd Sw (44707-4046)
P.O. Box 20388 (44701-0388)
PHONE..................330 587-4141
Debra Davidson,
James Davidson,
EMP: 30 EST: 2008
SALES (est): 9MM **Privately Held**
SIC: 5046 Commercial equipment

(G-2537)
STANDARD PLUMBING & HEATING CO (PA)
435 Walnut Ave Se (44702-1348)
P.O. Box 20650 (44701-0650)
PHONE..................330 453-5150
David Grabowsky, *President*
Herman C Grabowsky, *Principal*
May C Grabowsky, *Principal*
Robert W Grabowsky, *Principal*
Bruce Humbert, *Project Mgr*
EMP: 75
SQ FT: 20,000
SALES (est): 25.7MM **Privately Held**
WEB: www.standardpandh.net
SIC: 1711 Plumbing contractors; warm air heating & air conditioning contractor; ventilation & duct work contractor; process piping contractor

(G-2538)
STAR COUNTY HOME CONSORTIUM
201 3rd St Ne Fl 2201 (44702-1212)
PHONE..................330 451-7395
EMP: 25
SALES (est): 940.9K **Privately Held**
SIC: 8748 Urban planning & consulting services

(G-2539)
STARK AREA REGIONAL TRNST AUTH (PA)
Also Called: Sarta
1600 Gateway Blvd Se (44707-3544)
PHONE..................330 477-2782
Fax: 330 454-5476
Tom Williams, *Transptn Dir*
Kieth Bennett, *Engineer*
Carole Kuczynski, *Finance*
Kristie Maher-Petty, *Marketing Mgr*
Tammy Brown, *Manager*
EMP: 207
SQ FT: 100,000
SALES (est): 18.7MM **Privately Held**
WEB: www.sartaonline.com
SIC: 4131 4111 Intercity & rural bus transportation; local & suburban transit

(G-2540)
STARK CNTY DEPT JOB FMLY SVCS
221 3rd St Se (44702-1302)
PHONE..................330 451-8400
Fax: 330 451-8499
Jane Bethel, *Finance*
Susan Lenigar, *Director*
Nedra Petro, *Director*
Rob Pierson, *Director*
Julie Barnes, *Administration*
EMP: 485
SQ FT: 121,700
SALES (est): 9.8MM **Privately Held**
SIC: 8322 Public welfare center
PA: County Of Stark
110 Central Plz S Ste 240
Canton OH 44702
330 451-7371

(G-2541)
STARK CNTY EMRGNCY PHYSICIANS
5154 Fulton Dr Nw (44718-2365)
PHONE..................330 492-7950
Frank Kaeberlien, *President*
David Gormsen, *Vice Pres*
Melanie Butera, *Manager*
Brenda Wessles, *Administration*
EMP: 26 EST: 2007
SALES (est): 1.3MM **Privately Held**
SIC: 8011 Medical centers

(G-2542)
STARK CNTY HISTORICAL SOC INC
Also Called: MCKINLEY NATIONAL MEMORIAL
800 Mckinley Monu Dr Nw (44708-4832)
PHONE..................330 455-7043
Raelynn Mays, *Manager*
Cindy Sober, *Manager*

Scott Courtney, *Info Tech Dir*
Kimberly Kenney, *Info Tech Mgr*
Joyce Yut, *Director*
EMP: 25
SALES (est): 875.6K **Privately Held**
WEB: www.mckinleymuseum.org
SIC: 8412 Museum; historical society

(G-2543)
STARK COUNTY BOARD OF DEVELOPM
Also Called: Workshops, The
2950 Whipple Ave Nw (44708-1534)
PHONE..................330 477-5200
H Michael Miller, *CEO*
Gary Braun, *President*
Robert Spence, *Purch Dir*
Trish Faist, *Purchasing*
Eric Wenhardt, *Engineer*
EMP: 600
SALES (est): 17.7MM **Privately Held**
WEB: www.theworkshopsinc.com
SIC: 8331 8093 Sheltered workshop; mental health clinic, outpatient

(G-2544)
STARK COUNTY NEUROLOGISTS INC
4105 Holiday St Nw (44718-2531)
P.O. Box 35006 (44735-5006)
PHONE..................330 494-2097
Fax: 330 494-9750
Alok Bhagap, *President*
Dr Morris Kinast, *Vice Pres*
Dr Leon Rosenberg, *Treasurer*
Dr Jay P Berke, *Admin Sec*
EMP: 56
SQ FT: 3,100
SALES (est): 2.9MM **Privately Held**
WEB: www.neurocarecenter.com
SIC: 8011 Neurologist; physical medicine, physician/surgeon

(G-2545)
STARK COUNTY PARK DISTRICT
5300 Tyner Ave Nw (44708-5041)
PHONE..................330 477-3552
Rob Hoover, *Opers Spvr*
Bob Fonte, *Director*
EMP: 60
SQ FT: 2,912
SALES (est): 5.3MM **Privately Held**
SIC: 7999 Recreation services

(G-2546)
STARK COUNTY WOMENS CLINIC INC
5000 Higbee Ave Nw (44718-2582)
PHONE..................330 493-0313
Fax: 330 493-9349
William Alford Do, *President*
Carl Schlech MD, *Principal*
Melissa Patton, *Med Doctor*
Kenneth Shranko, *Manager*
EMP: 70 EST: 1971
SQ FT: 11,000
SALES (est): 9.9MM **Privately Held**
SIC: 8011 Gynecologist; obstetrician

(G-2547)
STARK FEDERAL CREDIT UNION (PA)
4100 Dressler Rd Nw (44718-2754)
PHONE..................330 493-8325
Fax: 330 493-8328
Nino Gemma, *CEO*
Karen Mathes, *Opers Spvr*
EMP: 31
SQ FT: 4,000
SALES (est): 3.5MM **Privately Held**
WEB: www.starkcu.org
SIC: 6141 Personal credit institutions

(G-2548)
STB ENTERPRISES
4417 17th St Nw (44708-2709)
PHONE..................330 478-0044
Fax: 330 478-0060
Bernice Guist, *Owner*
EMP: 25
SQ FT: 1,700
SALES (est): 763K **Privately Held**
SIC: 7349 Office cleaning or charring

(G-2549)
STEELE W W JR AGENCY INC
Also Called: Schauer Indpendence Insur Agcy
200 Market Ave N Ste 100 (44702-1435)
PHONE..................330 453-7721
David Shauer, *President*
Aimee B Belden, *Assoc VP*
EMP: 40
SQ FT: 2,500
SALES (est): 5.8MM **Privately Held**
SIC: 6411 Insurance agents

(G-2550)
STOLLE MACHINERY COMPANY LLC
4150 Belden Village St Nw (44718-2595)
PHONE..................330 493-0444
Jim McClung, *Branch Mgr*
EMP: 50
SALES (corp-wide): 262.3MM **Privately Held**
WEB: www.stollemachinery.com
SIC: 5084 Industrial machinery & equipment
PA: Stolle Machinery Company, Llc
6949 S Potomac St
Centennial CO 80112
303 708-9044

(G-2551)
STONE CROSSING ASSISTED LIVING
Also Called: Glenwood Assisted Living
820 34th St Nw (44709-2966)
PHONE..................330 492-7131
Tracy Imhoff, *Administration*
EMP: 250
SALES (est): 561.8K **Privately Held**
SIC: 8051 Skilled nursing care facilities

(G-2552)
STONE PRODUCTS INC (HQ)
Also Called: GREY STONE
3105 Varley Ave Sw (44706-3544)
P.O. Box 6059 (44706-0059)
PHONE..................800 235-6088
Fax: 330 484-3314
W Mark Sterling, *President*
Thomas Kovesci, *General Mgr*
Jeff Sterling, *Vice Pres*
Jeffrey Sterling, *Vice Pres*
Richard Williams, *CFO*
▼ EMP: 25
SQ FT: 5,000
SALES: 11MM
SALES (corp-wide): 186.1MM **Privately Held**
WEB: www.stonepro.com
SIC: 5082 Construction & mining machinery
PA: The Beaver Excavating Co
2000 Beaver Place Ave Sw
Canton OH 44706
330 478-2151

(G-2553)
STONEMOR PARTNERS LP
4450 Belden Village St Nw # 802 (44718-2552)
PHONE..................330 491-8001
Eleanor Masalko, *Human Resources*
Cathy Konen, *Manager*
EMP: 50
SALES (corp-wide): 326.2MM **Publicly Held**
WEB: www.stonemor.com
SIC: 6553 Cemetery subdividers & developers
PA: Stonemor Partners L.P.
3600 Horizon Blvd Ste 100
Trevose PA 19053
215 826-2800

(G-2554)
SUAREZ CORPORATION INDUSTRIES
Biotech Research Division
7800 Whipple Ave Nw (44767-0002)
PHONE..................330 494-4282
Benjamin Suarez, *Manager*
Peggy Kerchner, *Manager*
Michael Schumacher, *MIS Dir*
Jenny Bradshaw, *Director*
EMP: 75

Canton - Stark County (G-2555) — GEOGRAPHIC SECTION

SALES (corp-wide): 138.3MM **Privately Held**
WEB: www.suarez.com
SIC: 3841 5091 2834 5122 Veterinarians' instruments & apparatus; fitness equipment & supplies; vitamin, nutrient & hematinic preparations for human use; vitamins & minerals
PA: Suarez Corporation Industries
  7800 Whipple Ave Nw
  North Canton OH 44720
  330 494-5504

(G-2555)
SUNSET HILLS CEMETERY CORP
5001 Everhard Rd Nw (44718-2473)
PHONE 330 494-2051
Victor M Evans, *President*
Floyd E Bennett, *Treasurer*
E Keith Payne, *Admin Sec*
EMP: 35
SQ FT: 12,600
SALES (est): 1.4MM
SALES (corp-wide): 3.1B **Publicly Held**
WEB: www.sci-corp.com
SIC: 6553 Cemetery association
PA: Service Corporation International
  1929 Allen Pkwy
  Houston TX 77019
  713 522-5141

(G-2556)
SUPERIOR PAVING & MATERIALS
5947 Whipple Ave Nw (44720-7613)
PHONE 330 499-5849
Marlene Oster, *President*
EMP: 35
SQ FT: 3,000
SALES (est): 4.6MM **Privately Held**
SIC: 1611 Highway & street paving contractor

(G-2557)
TAB CONSTRUCTION COMPANY INC
530 Walnut Ave Ne (44702-1273)
P.O. Box 20657 (44701)
PHONE 330 454-5228
William E Richardson III, *President*
EMP: 50
SQ FT: 3,900
SALES (est): 9.5MM **Privately Held**
WEB: www.tab-construction.com
SIC: 1611 1542 Highway & street construction; nonresidential construction

(G-2558)
TEBO FINANCIAL SERVICES INC
4740 Belpar St Nw Ste A (44718-3685)
PHONE 234 207-2500
Robert L Bowman, *President*
Roy A Baker Jr, *CFO*
Robert M James, *Admin Sec*
EMP: 48
SALES: 10.6MM **Privately Held**
WEB: www.tebofinancialservices.com
SIC: 6141 Personal credit institutions

(G-2559)
TERMINAL WAREHOUSE INC
2207 Kimball Rd Se (44707-3631)
PHONE 330 453-3709
Douglas J Sibila, *President*
EMP: 25
SALES (est): 1.8MM **Privately Held**
SIC: 4225 General warehousing & storage
PA: People's Services, Inc.
  2207 Kimball Rd Se
  Canton OH 44707

(G-2560)
TERMINIX INTL CO LTD PARTNR
2680 Roberts Ave Nw Ste A (44709-3484)
PHONE 978 744-2402
Fax: 330 307-5071
Sam Bodila, *Manager*
EMP: 30
SALES (corp-wide): 2.9B **Publicly Held**
SIC: 7342 Pest control services
HQ: The Terminix International Company Limited Partnership
  860 Ridge Lake Blvd A3-4008
  Memphis TN 38120
  901 766-1400

(G-2561)
THOMAS AND ASSOCIATES
1421 Portage St Nw Ste C (44720-2289)
PHONE 330 494-2111
Fax: 330 494-1947
Dr Michael L Thomas, *President*
EMP: 30
SQ FT: 3,920
SALES (est): 3.1MM **Privately Held**
SIC: 8021 Dentists' office

(G-2562)
TIME WARNER CABLE INC
5520 Whipple Ave Nw (44720-7700)
P.O. Box 8559 (44711-8559)
PHONE 330 494-9200
Fax: 330 490-2257
Ken Fuchs, *Vice Pres*
Jim Nicholas, *Mktg Dir*
Catherine Byrd, *Supervisor*
Wells Ferdinand, *Exec Dir*
EMP: 83
SQ FT: 30,000
SALES (corp-wide): 41.5B **Publicly Held**
SIC: 4841 Cable television services
HQ: Spectrum Management Holding Company, Llc
  400 Atlantic St
  Stamford CT 06901
  203 905-7801

(G-2563)
TOM BAIER & ASSOC INC
Also Called: Coldwell Banker
4686 Douglas Cir Nw (44718-3619)
PHONE 330 497-3115
Fax: 330 497-0085
Thomas Baier, *President*
Adam Mondl, *Sales Staff*
Patricia Adolph, *Manager*
Ben Emerick, *Agent*
Lori L Ford, *Real Est Agnt*
EMP: 25
SALES (est): 1.2MM **Privately Held**
WEB: www.ohiohomesbypat.com
SIC: 6531 Real estate agent, residential

(G-2564)
TOP ECHELON CONTRACTING INC
4883 Dressler Rd Nw # 200 (44718-3665)
PHONE 330 454-3508
Debra M Fledderjohann, *President*
Todd Schmitt, *Controller*
Diane Marzec, *Hum Res Coord*
Julie Majors, *Personnel*
Lisa Kovac, *Manager*
EMP: 364
SQ FT: 1,095
SALES: 26.7MM **Privately Held**
WEB: www.topecheloncontracting.com
SIC: 8742 8721 7363 Materials mgmt. (purchasing, handling, inventory) consultant; payroll accounting service; engineering help service

(G-2565)
TRUGREEN LIMITED PARTNERSHIP
Also Called: Tru Green-Chemlawn
6302 Promway Ave Nw (44720-7620)
P.O. Box 36120 (44735-6120)
PHONE 330 409-2861
Bill Brown, *Manager*
EMP: 40
SALES (corp-wide): 4B **Privately Held**
SIC: 0782 Lawn care services
HQ: Trugreen Limited Partnership
  1790 Kirby Pkwy
  Memphis TN 38138
  901 251-4128

(G-2566)
TYCOR ROOFING INC
1704 Warner Rd Se (44707-2276)
PHONE 330 452-8150
Bruce Martin, *President*
Cynthia Soos, *Treasurer*
Cinde L Martin, *Admin Sec*
EMP: 25 EST: 1974
SQ FT: 5,664
SALES (est): 4.3MM **Privately Held**
WEB: www.haljones.com
SIC: 1761 Roofing contractor

(G-2567)
UNITED FOOD & COMMERCIAL WKR
Also Called: LOCAL 17A
1800 Cleveland Ave Nw (44709-3602)
PHONE 330 452-4850
Sonja Campbell, *President*
Gary Feiock, *Principal*
EMP: 40
SALES: 671.5K **Privately Held**
SIC: 8631 Labor union

(G-2568)
UNITED GL & PANL SYSTEMS INC
4250 Strausser St Nw (44720-7114)
PHONE 330 244-9745
Fax: 330 433-9250
Thomas M Nesbitt, *President*
Shelly M Nesbitt, *Corp Secy*
Derek Cobb, *Project Mgr*
Maria Liossis, *Controller*
Lori Koehler, *Accountant*
EMP: 42
SQ FT: 36,000
SALES (est): 9MM **Privately Held**
WEB: www.ugps.com
SIC: 1793 1761 Glass & glazing work; roofing, siding & sheet metal work

(G-2569)
UNITED HEALTH NETWORK LTD
4455 Dressler Rd Nw (44718-2785)
PHONE 330 492-2102
Jeff Russell, *President*
EMP: 48
SALES: 2.1MM **Privately Held**
WEB: www.unitedhealthnetwork.com
SIC: 8011 Offices & clinics of medical doctors

(G-2570)
UNITED PARCEL SERVICE INC OH
Also Called: UPS
4850 Navarre Rd Sw (44706-2238)
PHONE 330 478-1007
Roger Mattock, *Branch Mgr*
EMP: 152
SALES (corp-wide): 65.8B **Publicly Held**
WEB: www.upsscs.com
SIC: 4215 Parcel delivery, vehicular
HQ: United Parcel Service, Inc. (Oh)
  55 Glenlake Pkwy
  Atlanta GA 30328
  404 828-6000

(G-2571)
UNITED STATES COMMEMRTV ART GA
7800 Whipple Ave Nw (44767-0001)
PHONE 330 494-5504
Fax: 330 497-6807
EMP: 25
SALES (est): 3.4MM **Privately Held**
SIC: 5094 Whol Jewelry/Precious Stones

(G-2572)
UNITED STEELWORKERS OF AMERICA
Also Called: Uswa
4069 Bradley Cir Nw (44718-2565)
PHONE 330 493-7721
Fax: 330 493-7870
Dennis Brommer, *Manager*
Dave McCall, *Director*
EMP: 111
SALES (corp-wide): 61.5K **Privately Held**
WEB: www.uswa.org
SIC: 8631 Labor union
PA: United Steelworkers
  60 Bolevard Of The Allies
  Pittsburgh PA 15222
  412 562-2400

(G-2573)
UNITED WAY GREATER STARK CNTY
401 Market Ave N Ste 300 (44702-1502)
PHONE 330 491-0445
Maria Heege, *President*
Merele Kinsey, *Project Mgr*
Diane Dukat, *Director*
Robin Seemann, *Director*
EMP: 25
SALES: 6.7MM **Privately Held**
SIC: 8399 Fund raising organization, non-fee basis

(G-2574)
US TECH AROSPC ENGRG CORP (PA)
Also Called: US Technology Aerospace
4200 Munson St Nw (44718-2981)
PHONE 330 455-1181
Raymond F Williams, *President*
Robert Putnam, *Vice Pres*
John Socotch, *Vice Pres*
Nimmie E Wasson, *Vice Pres*
Maryann Amigo, *Accountant*
EMP: 70
SALES (est): 7.9MM **Privately Held**
WEB: www.ustae.com
SIC: 8711 Engineering services

(G-2575)
USAM INC
Also Called: United Studios of America
4450 Belden Village St Nw # 305 (44718-2552)
PHONE 330 244-8782
Fax: 330 832-6201
Dean Nelson, *President*
Jolynn Buettell, *Manager*
Robert Humphries, *Admin Sec*
EMP: 75 EST: 1996
SQ FT: 35,000
SALES (est): 1.6MM **Privately Held**
WEB: www.unitedstudiosofamerica.com
SIC: 7221 Photographer, still or video

(G-2576)
VERVASI VINEYARD & ITLN BISTRO
Also Called: Gervasi Vineyard
1700 55th St Ne (44721-3401)
PHONE 330 497-1000
Ted Swaldo, *Principal*
Paul Cincotta, *Opers Staff*
Jan Prengaman, *Director*
Jerry Risner, *Executive*
Rachel Reda, *Relations*
EMP: 31
SALES (est): 10.1MM **Privately Held**
SIC: 5182 Wine

(G-2577)
VETERANS HEALTH ADMINISTRATION
Also Called: Veterans Clinic
733 Market Ave S (44702-2165)
PHONE 330 489-4600
Fax: 330 489-4684
Nancye Jackson, *Branch Mgr*
EMP: 70 **Publicly Held**
WEB: www.veterans-ru.org
SIC: 8011 9451 Clinic, operated by physicians;
HQ: Veterans Health Administration
  810 Vermont Ave Nw
  Washington DC 20420

(G-2578)
VICTORY SQ APRTMNTS LTD PARTNR
1206 Lppert Rd Ne Apt 211 (44705)
PHONE 330 455-8035
George Buchanan, *Principal*
Leeann Morein, *Manager*
EMP: 99
SALES: 950K **Privately Held**
SIC: 6513 Apartment building operators

(G-2579)
VISUAL EDGE TECHNOLOGY INC (PA)
3874 Highland Park Nw (44720-4538)
PHONE 330 494-9694
Austin Vanchieri, *Ch of Bd*

Les Beyeler, *Vice Chairman*
Yvonne Brown, *CFO*
Jennifer Weiland, *Accounting Mgr*
Lisa Stinson, *Sales Associate*
EMP: 123
SQ FT: 52,000
SALES (est): 52.8MM **Privately Held**
WEB: www.visualedgetechnology.com
SIC: 5044 5065 Copying equipment; facsimile equipment

(G-2580)
W L LOGAN TRUCKING COMPANY
Also Called: Logan Logistics
3224 Navarre Rd Sw (44706-1897)
PHONE 330 478-1404
Fax: 330 478-0557
William L Logan Sr, *Ch of Bd*
Betty Jane Logan, *President*
Robert Logan, *Corp Secy*
William L Logan Jr, *Vice Pres*
Paul Quinn, *Traffic Mgr*
EMP: 125
SQ FT: 30,000
SALES (est): 41.7MM **Privately Held**
WEB: www.logantrucking.com
SIC: 4213 4212 Trucking, except local; contract haulers; local trucking, without storage

(G-2581)
W W SCHAUB ELECTRIC CO
501 Applegrove St Nw (44720-1619)
PHONE 330 494-3560
Fax: 330 494-7315
Wesley W Schaub III, *President*
Bob Schaub, *Vice Pres*
Robert Schaub, *Vice Pres*
Pam Hess, *Purchasing*
Helen Gortney, *Manager*
EMP: 40
SQ FT: 16,000
SALES (est): 4MM **Privately Held**
WEB: www.wwschaub.com
SIC: 1731 General electrical contractor

(G-2582)
WARSTLER BROTHERS LANDSCAPING
4125 Salway Ave Nw (44718-2953)
PHONE 330 492-9500
Fax: 330 492-3987
Shawn Warstler, *President*
Shawn Warstler, *President*
Howard Davis, *Sales Mgr*
EMP: 33
SQ FT: 3,360
SALES (est): 3.6MM **Privately Held**
SIC: 0782 4959 Landscape contractors; snowplowing

(G-2583)
WASTE MANAGEMENT OHIO INC
1800 9th St Ne (44705-1404)
PHONE 330 452-9000
Dave Bower, *Opers Staff*
Don Leisure, *Manager*
Lee Hicks, *Contract Law*
EMP: 30
SALES (corp-wide): 14.4B **Publicly Held**
WEB: www.metrodisposal.com
SIC: 4953 Garbage: collecting, destroying & processing; waste materials, disposal at sea
HQ: Waste Management Of Ohio, Inc.
1700 N Broad St
Fairborn OH 45324

(G-2584)
WERN-RAUSCH LOCKE ADVERTISING
Also Called: Wrl Advertising
4470 Dressler Rd Nw (44718-2716)
PHONE 330 493-8866
Todd Locke, *President*
Robert Isenberg, *Principal*
Charles T Locke, *Vice Pres*
Thomas Locke, *Vice Pres*
David Rausch, *Vice Pres*
EMP: 28 **EST:** 1956
SQ FT: 5,500

SALES (est): 6.4MM **Privately Held**
WEB: www.wrladv.com
SIC: 7311 Advertising agencies

(G-2585)
WESTERN BRANCH DIESEL INC
Also Called: John Deere Authorized Dealer
1616 Metric Ave Sw (44706-3087)
PHONE 330 454-8800
Fax: 330 454-6126
Mike McElwain, *Branch Mgr*
EMP: 28
SQ FT: 22,400
SALES (corp-wide): 84MM **Privately Held**
WEB: www.westernbranchdiesel.com
SIC: 5084 5531 5063 3714 Engines & parts, diesel; truck equipment & parts; generators; motor vehicle parts & accessories; power transmission equipment; internal combustion engines
PA: Western Branch Diesel, Incorporated
3504 Shipwright St
Portsmouth VA 23703
757 673-7000

(G-2586)
WESTFIELD BELDEN VILLAGE
4230 Belden Village Mall (44718-2504)
PHONE 330 494-5490
Katrina Barton, *General Mgr*
EMP: 40
SALES (est): 2.5MM **Privately Held**
SIC: 8611 Merchants' association

(G-2587)
WINDSOR MEDICAL CENTER INC
1454 E Maple St (44720-2634)
PHONE 330 499-8300
Thomas Sawllen, *President*
Steven Weaver, *Director*
EMP: 100
SQ FT: 10,000
SALES (est): 7.1MM **Privately Held**
SIC: 8059 8661 8052 8051 Personal care home, with health care; religious organizations; intermediate care facilities; skilled nursing care facilities

(G-2588)
WORKFORCE INITIATIVE ASSN (PA)
822 30th St Nw (44709-2902)
PHONE 330 433-9675
Fax: 330 491-2600
Sharon Parry, *Controller*
Jennifer M Eells, *Manager*
Alice Stephens, *Director*
Michelle Moore, *Administration*
EMP: 25
SQ FT: 15,000
SALES (est): 10.6MM **Privately Held**
WEB: www.eswork.org
SIC: 8331 Job training services

(G-2589)
WORKFORCE SERVICES INC (PA)
Also Called: Wf Services
6245 Sherman Ch Ave Sw (44706-3770)
PHONE 330 484-2566
John Kissell, *President*
Francesca Nicoletti, *Vice Pres*
Debbie Klimczyk, *Admin Dir*
EMP: 40
SQ FT: 2,400
SALES (est): 4.2MM **Privately Held**
SIC: 7538 General truck repair

(G-2590)
Y M C A CENTRAL STARK COUNTY
Also Called: YMCA Child Care
200 Charlotte St Nw (44720-2404)
PHONE 330 305-5437
Fax: 330 305-5435
Sherry Sampson, *Branch Mgr*
EMP: 45

SALES (corp-wide): 16.5MM **Privately Held**
WEB: www.ymcastark.org
SIC: 8641 7991 8351 7032 Youth organizations; physical fitness facilities; child day care services; youth camps; individual & family services
PA: Y M C A Of Central Stark County
1201 30th St Nw Ste 200a
Canton OH 44709
330 491-9622

(G-2591)
Y M C A CENTRAL STARK COUNTY
Also Called: Gymnastics Center
7241 Whipple Ave Nw (44720-7137)
PHONE 330 498-4082
Fax: 330 498-4084
Colleen Ekle, *Branch Mgr*
EMP: 33
SALES (corp-wide): 16.5MM **Privately Held**
WEB: www.ymcastark.org
SIC: 8641 7991 8351 7032 Youth organizations; physical fitness facilities; child day care services; youth camps; individual & family services
PA: Y M C A Of Central Stark County
1201 30th St Nw Ste 200a
Canton OH 44709
330 491-9622

(G-2592)
YOUNG TRUCK SALES INC (PA)
Also Called: Jay-Mac
4970 Southway St Sw (44706-1940)
P.O. Box 6118 (44706-0118)
PHONE 330 477-6271
Fax: 330 477-9106
Richard A Young, *Ch of Bd*
Craig Young, *President*
Nellie M Young, *Principal*
Robert P Young, *Vice Pres*
Craig Johns, *Sales Associate*
EMP: 50
SQ FT: 31,000
SALES (est): 39.5MM **Privately Held**
SIC: 5511 5013 7538 Automobiles, new & used; truck parts & accessories; general automotive repair shops

(G-2593)
YOUNG WOMNS CHRSTN ASSC CANTON (PA)
Also Called: YWCA OF CANTON
231 6th St Ne (44702-1035)
PHONE 330 453-7644
Fax: 330 453-2735
Kelly Bah, *CEO*
Darcy Anderson, *Mktg Dir*
Dan Hennon, *Case Mgr*
Lisa Snyder, *Case Mgr*
Barbara Payne, *Manager*
EMP: 55
SQ FT: 71,749
SALES: 5.1MM **Privately Held**
SIC: 8322 Child related social services

(G-2594)
YOUNG WOMNS CHRSTN ASSC CANTON
1700 Gateway Blvd Se (44707-3518)
PHONE 330 453-0789
Sandy Markert, *Branch Mgr*
EMP: 51
SALES (corp-wide): 5.1MM **Privately Held**
SIC: 8641 7991 8351 7032 Youth organizations; physical fitness facilities; child day care services; youth camps; individual & family services
PA: The Young Women's Christian Association Of Canton Ohio
231 6th St Ne
Canton OH 44702
330 453-7644

(G-2595)
ZIEGLER BOLT & PARTS CO (PA)
Also Called: Ziegler Bolt & Nut House
4848 Corporate St Sw (44706-1907)
P.O. Box 80369 (44708-0369)
PHONE 330 478-2542

Fax: 330 478-2031
William A Ziegler Jr, *President*
Glen Arner, *Purch Agent*
Jim Spadone, *Purch Agent*
Janet Hanacek, *Treasurer*
Tina Carl, *Accountant*
EMP: 86
SQ FT: 80,000
SALES (est): 34MM **Privately Held**
WEB: www.zieglerbolt.com
SIC: 5085 5072 Fasteners, industrial: nuts, bolts, screws, etc.; hardware

Carey
Wyandot County

(G-2596)
NATIONAL LIME AND STONE CO
370 N Patterson St (43316-1057)
P.O. Box 8 (43316-0008)
PHONE 419 396-7671
Fax: 419 396-3534
J Kinsler, *Exec VP*
R Kruse, *Vice Pres*
Tim Horn, *Plant Mgr*
Rick Dehays, *Purchasing*
Chris Beeman, *VP Finance*
EMP: 130
SALES (corp-wide): 3.2B **Privately Held**
WEB: www.natlime.com
SIC: 1422 3291 3281 3274 Lime rock, ground; abrasive products; cut stone & stone products; lime; alkalies & chlorine; construction sand & gravel
PA: The National Lime And Stone Company
551 Lake Cascade Pkwy
Findlay OH 45840
419 422-4341

(G-2597)
REPUBLIC SERVICES INC
11164 County Highway 4 (43316-9750)
PHONE 419 396-3581
Thomas Weelden V, *Branch Mgr*
EMP: 34
SALES (corp-wide): 10B **Publicly Held**
SIC: 4953 Refuse collection & disposal services
PA: Republic Services, Inc.
18500 N Allied Way # 100
Phoenix AZ 85054
480 627-2700

(G-2598)
SHELLY COMPANY
1794 County Highway 99 (43316-9722)
PHONE 419 396-7641
Marc Bader, *Branch Mgr*
EMP: 42
SALES (corp-wide): 29.7B **Privately Held**
SIC: 1611 Surfacing & paving
HQ: Shelly Company
80 Park Dr
Thornville OH 43076
740 246-6315

(G-2599)
VAUGHN INDUSTRIES LLC (PA)
1201 E Findlay St (43316-9686)
P.O. Box 96 (43316-0096)
PHONE 419 396-3900
Todd Fisher, *Regional Mgr*
Jason Arend, *Project Mgr*
Ryan Clouse, *Project Mgr*
Jay Kitzler, *Project Mgr*
Ryan Loveridge, *Project Mgr*
▲ **EMP:** 500
SQ FT: 12,800
SALES (est): 158.5MM **Privately Held**
SIC: 1731 1711 General electrical contractor; mechanical contractor

(G-2600)
VULCAN ENTERPRISES INC
Also Called: Vulcan Fire Protection
2600 State Highway 568 A (43316-1178)
PHONE 419 396-3535
Fax: 419 396-7581
Joyce Hunter, *CEO*
Larry Walters, *President*
Armando A Madrigal, *Principal*
Michael Kenn, *Vice Pres*
EMP: 37
SQ FT: 10,000

SALES (est): 5.9MM **Privately Held**
SIC: **1711** Fire sprinkler system installation

(G-2601)
WAGNER LINCOLN-MERCURY INC
1200 S Vance St (43316-7502)
PHONE.....................................419 435-8131
Fax: 419 435-7432
Rick Wagner, *President*
Joe Craven, *General Mgr*
Ralph Mitchell, *Manager*
EMP: 28
SALES (est): 9.6MM **Privately Held**
SIC: **5511** 7538 5521 Automobiles, new & used; general automotive repair shops; used car dealers

Carlisle
Warren County

(G-2602)
CARLISLE HEALTH CARE INC
730 Hillcrest Ave (45005-3305)
PHONE.....................................937 746-2662
Fax: 937 746-8204
Aaron Handler, *President*
Abe Wagshal, *President*
Abe Wagschal, *Director*
Scott Zollett, *Director*
EMP: 45 EST: 1981
SQ FT: 36,338
SALES: 2.7MM **Privately Held**
WEB: www.carlislemanor.com
SIC: **8051** Convalescent home with continuous nursing care

(G-2603)
DEBELLO MASONRY INC
30 Eagle Ct (45005-6334)
PHONE.....................................937 235-2096
Donald F Debello, *President*
EMP: 30
SALES (est): 2.1MM **Privately Held**
SIC: **1741** Masonry & other stonework

(G-2604)
MPS GROUP INC
512 Linden Ave (45005-3345)
PHONE.....................................937 746-2117
Charlie Williams, *Ch of Bd*
EMP: 100 **Privately Held**
SIC: **1799** Cleaning new buildings after construction
PA: Mps Group, Inc.
    38755 Hills Tech Dr
    Farmington Hills MI 48331

(G-2605)
NARROW WAY CUSTOM TECHNOLOGY
100 Industry Dr (45005-6304)
PHONE.....................................937 743-1611
Fax: 937 743-1688
Timothy Williams, *President*
Cindy Williams, *Vice Pres*
EMP: 29 EST: 1998
SQ FT: 5,600
SALES (est): 5.3MM **Privately Held**
SIC: **3599** 7629 Custom machinery; electrical repair shops

(G-2606)
SOCIETY FOR HANDICAPPED CITZNS
Also Called: FAIRVIEW HOMES
624 Fairview Dr (45005-3145)
PHONE.....................................937 746-4201
Bobby Seebach, *Exec Dir*
EMP: 33
SALES: 1.2MM **Privately Held**
SIC: **8322** 8361 Social services for the handicapped; residential care

Carroll
Fairfield County

(G-2607)
AMERICAN BORING INC
6895 Pickerington Rd (43112-9614)
PHONE.....................................740 969-8000
Rocky E Roark, *President*
EMP: 35
SQ FT: 4,800
SALES: 2.6MM **Privately Held**
SIC: **1623** Underground utilities contractor

(G-2608)
FAIRFIELD INDUSTRIES INC
4465 Coonpath Rd (43112-9705)
PHONE.....................................740 652-7230
Fax: 740 756-7857
Anthony Fortkamp, *Director*
EMP: 190
SQ FT: 108,000
SALES: 821.4K **Privately Held**
SIC: **8331** Sheltered workshop

(G-2609)
THOMPSON CONCRETE LTD
6182 Winchester Rd (43112-9764)
P.O. Box 440 (43112-0440)
PHONE.....................................740 756-7256
Fax: 740 756-7965
Scott Thompson, *Partner*
Zach Craiglow, *Project Mgr*
Jay Segura, *Opers Mgr*
Erik Avesil, *Foreman/Supr*
Nathan Morgan, *Manager*
EMP: 124
SQ FT: 4,000
SALES (est): 25.1MM **Privately Held**
WEB: www.thompsonconcrete.com
SIC: **1771** Concrete work

(G-2610)
WRENCH LTD COMPANY (PA)
4805 Scooby Ln (43112-9446)
PHONE.....................................740 654-5304
Fax: 740 756-7004
Cameron Gabbard, *President*
Deborah Agee, *COO*
Jason Templeton, *Vice Pres*
Brett Angus, *Parts Mgr*
Clay Bentley, *Parts Mgr*
▲ EMP: 65 EST: 1999
SQ FT: 40,000
SALES: 70MM **Privately Held**
WEB: www.companywrench.com
SIC: **5082** General construction machinery & equipment

Carrollton
Carroll County

(G-2611)
CARROLL ELECTRIC COOP INC
250 Canton Rd Nw (44615-8403)
P.O. Box 67 (44615-0067)
PHONE.....................................330 627-2116
Fax: 330 627-7050
Lary Sanders, *President*
Harol Hutton, *General Mgr*
Diane Smith, *Opers Staff*
Tim Dingess, *Engineer*
Bill Meese, *Supervisor*
EMP: 33 EST: 1937
SQ FT: 11,000
SALES: 22.4MM **Privately Held**
WEB: www.carrollelectriccoop.com
SIC: **4911** Distribution, electric power

(G-2612)
CARROLL GOLDEN AGE RETREAT
2202 Kensington Rd Ne (44615-8678)
PHONE.....................................330 627-4665
Fax: 330 627-5103
Ollie Hawkins, *Superintendent*
EMP: 40
SALES (est): 951K **Privately Held**
SIC: **8059** 8052 Rest home, with health care; intermediate care facilities

(G-2613)
CARROLL HEALTH CARE CENTER
Also Called: Carroll Healthcare Center
648 Longhorn St Nw (44615-9469)
PHONE.....................................330 627-5501
Fax: 330 627-9793
Erma Mc Cullough, *Corp Secy*
Pam King, *Purchasing*
Mark Lamielle, *Director*
Alan Miller, *Administration*
EMP: 110
SQ FT: 27,000
SALES (est): 6.5MM **Privately Held**
SIC: **8051** 8052 Convalescent home with continuous nursing care; intermediate care facilities

(G-2614)
CARROLL HILLS INDUSTRIES INC
540 High St Nw (44615-1116)
P.O. Box 567 (44615-0567)
PHONE.....................................330 627-5524
Fax: 330 627-6605
Matt Champbell, *Superintendent*
Rich Pizzoferrato, *Exec Dir*
Shannan Boone, *Administration*
Vicki Brumback, *Administration*
Diana Strader, *Administration*
EMP: 60
SQ FT: 4,640
SALES: 253.5K **Privately Held**
SIC: **8331** 3999 Sheltered workshop; barber & beauty shop equipment

(G-2615)
COUNTY OF CARROLL
P.O. Box 98 (44615-0098)
PHONE.....................................330 627-4866
Robert Wirkner, *Vice Pres*
Nick Cascarelli, *Branch Mgr*
Melanie Campbell, *Hlthcr Dir*
Charles Collier, *Admin Asst*
Rachel Rinkes, *Admin Asst*
EMP: 30 **Privately Held**
SIC: **8099** Blood related health services
PA: County Of Carroll
    119 S Lisbon St Ste 203
    Carrollton OH 44615
    330 627-2250

(G-2616)
COUNTY OF CARROLL
Also Called: Board of Mental Retardation
2167 Kensington Rd Ne (44615-8626)
P.O. Box 429 (44615-0429)
PHONE.....................................330 627-7651
Fax: 330 627-6606
Alicia Hall, *Principal*
Amy Swaim, *Editor*
Steve Defilippo, *Director*
Tonya Hawk, *Assistant*
EMP: 34 **Privately Held**
SIC: **9431** 8093 Mental health agency administration, government; rehabilitation center, outpatient treatment
PA: County Of Carroll
    119 S Lisbon St Ste 203
    Carrollton OH 44615
    330 627-2250

(G-2617)
CPX CARROLLTON ES LLC
Also Called: Candlewood Carrollton
1296 Canton Rd Nw (44615-9453)
PHONE.....................................330 627-1200
Paul Stanton, *Vice Pres*
Jennifer Schneider, *Marketing Staff*
EMP: 25 EST: 2014
SQ FT: 80,000
SALES (est): 680.2K **Privately Held**
SIC: **7011** Hotels & motels

(G-2618)
EAST CARROLL NURSING HOME
Also Called: Countryview Manor
2193 Commerce Dr (44615-8677)
PHONE.....................................330 627-6900
Thelma Miller, *Owner*
Sheryl Wallace, *Co-Owner*
EMP: 55

SALES (est): 1.5MM **Privately Held**
SIC: **8051** 8059 Convalescent home with continuous nursing care; home for the mentally retarded, exc. skilled or intermediate

(G-2619)
EFFICIENT SERVICES OHIO INC
Also Called: Eso
277 Steubenville Rd Se (44615-9601)
PHONE.....................................330 627-4440
Bryan T Shaw, *CEO*
Wanda Wilson, *Office Mgr*
EMP: 30
SALES (est): 7.2MM **Privately Held**
SIC: **5039** Soil erosion control fabrics

(G-2620)
FUSION CERAMICS INC
237 High St Sw (44615-1523)
P.O. Box 127 (44615-0127)
PHONE.....................................330 627-5821
Dick Hannon Jr, *Manager*
EMP: 30
SALES (corp-wide): 8.2MM **Privately Held**
WEB: www.fusionceramics.com
SIC: **4225** General warehousing & storage
PA: Fusion Ceramics, Inc.
    160 Scio Rd Se
    Carrollton OH 44615
    330 627-5821

(G-2621)
GRADY RENTALS LLC
4094 Canton Rd Nw (44615-9340)
PHONE.....................................330 627-2022
Michael Pence,
EMP: 36 EST: 2011
SALES: 5.6MM **Privately Held**
SIC: **7353** Oil equipment rental services

(G-2622)
GUESS MOTORS INC (PA)
457 Steubenville Rd Se (44615-9608)
PHONE.....................................866 890-0522
Toll Free:....................................888   -
Fax: 330 627-3460
Paul Guess, *President*
Michael Guess, *Vice Pres*
Vic Power, *Sales Mgr*
Kate Poole, *Sales Staff*
Chris Eick, *Office Mgr*
EMP: 30
SQ FT: 12,000
SALES (est): 12.5MM **Privately Held**
WEB: www.guessmotors.com
SIC: **5511** 7538 Automobiles, new & used; general automotive repair shops

(G-2623)
MERCY MEDICAL CENTER INC
Also Called: Timken Mercy Health Center
125 Canton Rd Nw (44615-1009)
Rural Route 125 (44615)
PHONE.....................................330 627-7641
Fax: 330 627-5796
Jack Topeleski, *Owner*
EMP: 25
SALES (corp-wide): 321.4MM **Privately Held**
WEB: www.cantonmercy.com
SIC: **8011** 8093 Clinic, operated by physicians; specialty outpatient clinics
HQ: Mercy Medical Center, Inc.
    1320 Mercy Dr Nw
    Canton OH 44708
    330 489-1000

(G-2624)
NORTH AMERICAN PLAS CHEM INC
Also Called: Noramco
750 Garfield Ave Nw (44615-1114)
PHONE.....................................330 627-2210
John Boggs, *Manager*
EMP: 35
SALES (est): 5.3MM
SALES (corp-wide): 39.6MM **Privately Held**
WEB: www.nap-bag.com
SIC: **5113** Bags, paper & disposable plastic

GEOGRAPHIC SECTION Celina - Mercer County (G-2647)

PA: North American Plastics Chemicals Incorporated
1400 E 222nd St
Euclid OH 44117
216 531-3400

(G-2625)
OHIO F F A CAMPS INC
Also Called: F F A Camp Muskingum
3266 Dyewood Rd Sw (44615-9246)
PHONE..................330 627-2208
Fax: 330 627-4485
Billy Plessel, *IT Specialist*
Todd Davis, *Director*
EMP: 35
SQ FT: 1,000
SALES: 2MM Privately Held
SIC: 7032 Recreational camps

(G-2626)
RES-CARE INC
Also Called: RES Care OH
520 S Lisbon St (44615-9582)
PHONE..................330 627-7552
Jenny Brendel, *Manager*
EMP: 47
SALES (corp-wide): 24.5B Privately Held
SIC: 8052 Home for the mentally retarded, with health care
HQ: Res-Care, Inc.
9901 Linn Station Rd
Louisville KY 40223
502 394-2100

(G-2627)
ROSEBUD MINING COMPANY
Also Called: Kensington Prep Plant
95 N Lisbon St (44615-1325)
PHONE..................330 222-2334
Randy Michell, *Manager*
EMP: 25
SALES (corp-wide): 672.6MM Privately Held
WEB: www.lore.com
SIC: 1222 1241 Bituminous coal-underground mining; coal mining services
PA: Rosebud Mining Company
301 Market St
Kittanning PA 16201
724 545-6222

(G-2628)
SAINT JOHNS VILLA
Also Called: Villa Restaurant
701 Crest St Nw (44615-8425)
P.O. Box 457 (44615-0457)
PHONE..................330 627-4662
Fax: 330 627-4826
Sister Elaine Weber, *President*
EMP: 145
SQ FT: 60,000
SALES: 4.4MM Privately Held
WEB: www.stjohnsvilla.net
SIC: 8361 5812 8351 8052 Residential care; home for the mentally handicapped; home for the physically handicapped; eating places; child day care services; intermediate care facilities

(G-2629)
SALVATION ARMY
5037 Edgewood Rd Sw (44615-9278)
PHONE..................330 735-2671
Fax: 330 735-2815
Josh Lyle, *Director*
EMP: 80
SALES (corp-wide): 4.3B Privately Held
WEB: www.salvationarmy-usaeast.org
SIC: 7032 Sporting & recreational camps
HQ: The Salvation Army
440 W Nyack Rd Ofc
West Nyack NY 10994
845 620-7200

Castalia
Erie County

(G-2630)
HANSON AGGREGATES EAST LLC
9220 Portland Rd (44824-9260)
PHONE..................419 483-4390
Gregory Russell, *Plant Mgr*
Tera Thornhill, *Manager*
EMP: 67
SQ FT: 3,200
SALES (corp-wide): 16B Privately Held
SIC: 1422 3274 Limestones, ground; lime
HQ: Hanson Aggregates East Llc
3131 Rdu Center Dr
Morrisville NC 27560
919 380-2500

Cedarville
Greene County

(G-2631)
APPLIED SCIENCES INC (PA)
141 W Xenia Ave (45314-9529)
P.O. Box 579 (45314-0579)
PHONE..................937 766-2020
Fax: 937 766-5886
Max Lake, *President*
Inga Lake, *Vice Pres*
EMP: 32
SQ FT: 6,600
SALES (est): 5MM Privately Held
SIC: 8731 3624 Commercial research laboratory; carbon & graphite products

(G-2632)
DALES TRUCK PARTS INC
2891 Us Route 42 E (45314-9443)
P.O. Box 2 (45314-0002)
PHONE..................937 766-2551
Fax: 937 766-2439
Edward Dale Hughes, *President*
Mark Beddinger, *Finance*
Ron Staker, *Finance*
Chris Hoskins, *Sales Executive*
Criss Snider, *Manager*
▼ EMP: 28 EST: 1968
SQ FT: 6,000
SALES (est): 7.1MM Privately Held
WEB: www.dalestruckparts.com
SIC: 5015 5531 Motor vehicle parts, used; truck equipment & parts

Celina
Mercer County

(G-2633)
ALLIED WASTE SYSTEMS INC
6141 Depweg Rd (45822-9573)
PHONE..................419 925-4592
Fax: 419 925-4487
Randy Traub, *Sales/Mktg Mgr*
EMP: 30
SQ FT: 1,000
SALES (corp-wide): 10B Publicly Held
SIC: 4953 Garbage: collecting, destroying & processing
HQ: Allied Waste Systems, Inc.
18500 N Allied Way # 100
Phoenix AZ 85054
480 627-2700

(G-2634)
AMERI INTERNTL TRADE GRP INC
Also Called: Aitg
1 Visions Pkwy (45822-7500)
PHONE..................419 586-6433
Murray L Dorfman, *President*
Joan C Dorfman, *Exec VP*
Leslie C Dorfman, *Exec VP*
William Dorfman, *Exec VP*
▲ EMP: 25
SQ FT: 25,000
SALES (est): 2.6MM Privately Held
WEB: www.aitginc.com
SIC: 5199 Gifts & novelties

(G-2635)
ASSISTED LIVING CONCEPTS INC
Also Called: Miller House
1506 Meadowview Dr Ofc (45822-4101)
PHONE..................419 586-2484
Fax: 419 586-2820
Celena Wolff, *Branch Mgr*
Bryan R Davenport, *Manager*
EMP: 25
SALES (corp-wide): 380.5MM Privately Held
WEB: www.assistedlivingconcepts.com
SIC: 8051 Skilled nursing care facilities
HQ: Assisted Living Concepts, Llc
330 N Wabash Ave Ste 3700
Chicago IL 60611

(G-2636)
BRIDGESTONE RET OPERATIONS LLC
Also Called: Michel Tires Plus 227571
1109 N Main St (45822-1076)
PHONE..................419 586-1600
Stephan Brancaleone, *Manager*
EMP: 30
SALES (corp-wide): 32.5B Privately Held
WEB: www.tiresplus.com
SIC: 7534 Tire retreading & repair shops
HQ: Bridgestone Retail Operations, Llc
333 E Lake St Ste 300
Bloomingdale IL 60108
630 259-9000

(G-2637)
CA GROUP
Also Called: CA INDUSTRIES
4980 Mud Pike Rd (45822-9274)
PHONE..................419 586-2137
Fax: 419 586-6415
Beth Butler, *CEO*
Bradley Niekamp, *Development*
EMP: 40
SQ FT: 8,000
SALES: 1.3MM Privately Held
WEB: www.caindustries.com
SIC: 8322 Adult day care center

(G-2638)
CELINA MUTUAL INSURANCE CO (PA)
Also Called: Celina Insurance Group
1 Insurance Sq (45822-1659)
PHONE..................419 586-5181
Fax: 419 586-6068
Donald W Montgomery, *Ch of Bd*
William W Montgomery, *President*
Philip Fullenkamp, *Vice Pres*
Theodore Wissman, *Vice Pres*
Phil Fullenkemp, *CFO*
EMP: 130 EST: 1919
SQ FT: 75,000
SALES (est): 97.3MM Privately Held
WEB: www.celinagroup.com
SIC: 6331 Fire, marine & casualty insurance: mutual

(G-2639)
CITY OF CELINA
Also Called: Celina Waste Water Plant
1125 S Elm St (45822-2375)
PHONE..................419 586-2451
Fax: 419 586-3414
Kerry Duncan, *Manager*
Jason Andrews, *Lab Dir*
EMP: 45 Privately Held
WEB: www.celinaohio.org
SIC: 4941 Water supply
PA: City Of Celina
225 N Main St
Celina OH 45822
419 586-5823

(G-2640)
COMCAST CORPORATION
812 N Main St (45822-1045)
PHONE..................419 586-1458
Rick Whaley, *Branch Mgr*
EMP: 57
SALES (corp-wide): 84.5B Publicly Held
WEB: www.comcast.com
SIC: 4841 Cable television services
PA: Comcast Corporation
1701 Jfk Blvd
Philadelphia PA 19103
215 286-1700

(G-2641)
COMMUNITY HLTH PRFSSIONALS INC
Also Called: Celina Visting Nurses
816 Pro Dr (45822-1360)
PHONE..................419 586-1999
Fax: 419 586-4727
Deb Garwood, *Manager*
EMP: 40
SALES (corp-wide): 14MM Privately Held
SIC: 8082 Visiting nurse service
PA: Community Health Professionals, Inc.
1159 Westwood Dr
Van Wert OH 45891
419 238-9223

(G-2642)
COMMUNITY HLTH PRFSSIONALS INC
Also Called: Private Duty & Visiting Nurses
816 Pro Dr (45822-1360)
PHONE..................419 586-6266
Caprice Smith, *Manager*
EMP: 60
SALES (corp-wide): 14MM Privately Held
SIC: 8082 7361 Visiting nurse service; nurses' registry
PA: Community Health Professionals, Inc.
1159 Westwood Dr
Van Wert OH 45891
419 238-9223

(G-2643)
COUNTY OF MERCER
Also Called: Cheryl Ann Special Olympics
4980 Mud Pike Rd (45822-9274)
PHONE..................419 586-2369
Fax: 419 586-6375
Tonya Brooks-Clark, *General Mgr*
Mike Overman, *Superintendent*
Tim Wilson, *Manager*
EMP: 60 Privately Held
WEB: www.mercercountyohio.org
SIC: 8322 8351 8331 Association for the handicapped; child day care services; job training & vocational rehabilitation services
PA: County Of Mercer
220 W Livingston St A201
Celina OH 45822
419 586-3178

(G-2644)
COUNTY OF MERCER
220 W Livingston St # 10 (45822-1670)
PHONE..................419 586-5106
Fax: 419 586-5643
Dale Borger, *Director*
EMP: 30 Privately Held
WEB: www.mercercountyohio.org
SIC: 8322 9111 Individual & family services; county supervisors' & executives' offices
PA: County Of Mercer
220 W Livingston St A201
Celina OH 45822
419 586-3178

(G-2645)
DELTA KAPPA GAMMA SOCIETY
Also Called: Beta PHI
1030 Canterbury Dr (45822-1169)
PHONE..................419 586-6016
Dolores Irish, *President*
Eline Marbaugh, *Treasurer*
Jenny Jamison, *Admin Sec*
EMP: 50 EST: 2001
SALES (est): 276.4K Privately Held
WEB: www.betaphi.com
SIC: 8641 Civic social & fraternal associations

(G-2646)
DOCTORS URGENT CARE
950 S Main St Ste 10 (45822-2475)
PHONE..................419 586-1611
James Wermert, *President*
Lisa Klenke, *Vice Pres*
Cindy Berning, *CFO*
EMP: 30 EST: 2007
SALES (est): 809.3K Privately Held
SIC: 8011 Clinic, operated by physicians

(G-2647)
FOUNDTION BEHAVIORAL HLTH SVCS
4761 State Route 29 (45822-8216)
PHONE..................419 584-1000
Fax: 419 584-1825
Brian Angle, *Director*
EMP: 30

Celina - Mercer County (G-2648)

SALES: 2.6MM **Privately Held**
SIC: 8093 Mental health clinic, outpatient

(G-2648)
JPMORGAN CHASE BANK NAT ASSN
205 W Market St (45822-2122)
PHONE.....................419 586-6668
Curt Cramer, *Site Mgr*
Ken Watts, *Manager*
EMP: 26
SALES (corp-wide): 99.6B **Publicly Held**
WEB: www.chase.com
SIC: 6021 National commercial banks
HQ: Jpmorgan Chase Bank, National Association
1111 Polaris Pkwy
Columbus OH 43240
614 436-3055

(G-2649)
KERNS CHEVROLET-BUICK-GMC INC
Also Called: Kerns Chevrolet Buick GMC
218 S Walnut St (45822-2145)
P.O. Box 27 (45822-0027)
PHONE.....................419 586-5131
Fax: 419 586-1198
Michael Kerns, *President*
George Heiser, *Principal*
J J Kerns, *Principal*
Mary Ellen Kerns, *Principal*
Chris Kerns, *Vice Pres*
EMP: 27
SQ FT: 10,000
SALES (est): 7.7MM **Privately Held**
WEB: www.kernschevyolds.com
SIC: 5511 7515 5521 Automobiles, new & used; passenger car leasing; used car dealers

(G-2650)
KIDS KASTLE DAY CARE
6783 Staeger Rd (45822-2800)
PHONE.....................419 586-0903
Jodi Will,
EMP: 35
SALES (est): 266.5K **Privately Held**
SIC: 8351 Preschool center

(G-2651)
MCKIRNAN BROS INC
Also Called: McKirnan Bros. Inc.
530 Schunk Rd (45822-2429)
P.O. Box 267 (45822-0267)
PHONE.....................419 586-2428
Fax: 419 586-6772
Robert D McKirnan, *President*
Robert J McKirnan, *President*
Bob McKirnan, *Owner*
Betty J McKirnan, *Principal*
Daniel M McKirnan, *Principal*
EMP: 29
SQ FT: 14,000
SALES (est): 4.7MM **Privately Held**
SIC: 5962 5194 Merchandising machine operators; tobacco & tobacco products

(G-2652)
MERCELINA MOBILE HOME PARK
424 Elmgrove Dr (45822-1804)
PHONE.....................419 586-5407
Jerry Brandts, *President*
Verdice Brandts, *Manager*
EMP: 64
SALES (est): 1.6MM **Privately Held**
SIC: 6515 Mobile home site operators

(G-2653)
MERCER CNTY JOINT TOWNSHP HOSP
Mercer Health Home Care
909 E Wayne St Ste 126 (45822-3304)
PHONE.....................419 584-0143
Lisa Muhlenkamp, *Branch Mgr*
EMP: 50
SALES (corp-wide): 50.6MM **Privately Held**
SIC: 8082 Home health care services
PA: Mercer County Joint Township Community Hospital
800 W Main St
Coldwater OH 45828
419 678-2341

(G-2654)
MERCER CNTY JOINT TOWNSHIP HOSP
Also Called: Community Medical Center
950 S Main St (45822-2413)
PHONE.....................419 586-1611
Fax: 419 586-4170
Vivian Hillwaret, *Manager*
Vivian Hellwarth, *Manager*
EMP: 30
SALES (corp-wide): 50.6MM **Privately Held**
WEB: www.mercerhospital.com
SIC: 8062 8011 General medical & surgical hospitals; offices & clinics of medical doctors
PA: Mercer County Joint Township Community Hospital
800 W Main St
Coldwater OH 45828
419 678-2341

(G-2655)
MERCER LANDMARK INC
417 W Market St (45822-2126)
PHONE.....................419 586-7443
Fax: 419 586-9717
Scott Boulis, *Manager*
EMP: 40
SALES (corp-wide): 242.8MM **Privately Held**
SIC: 4221 Grain elevator, storage only
PA: Mercer Landmark, Inc.
426 W Market St
Celina OH 45822
419 628-3093

(G-2656)
MERCER RESIDENTIAL SERVICES
Also Called: Mud Pike Group Home The
334 Godfrey Ave (45822-2120)
P.O. Box 603 (45822-0603)
PHONE.....................419 586-4709
Fax: 419 586-1432
Garry Mosier, *Director*
EMP: 50
SALES (est): 1.6MM **Privately Held**
WEB: www.mrsinc.org
SIC: 8059 Nursing home, except skilled & intermediate care facility; personal care home, with health care

(G-2657)
MERCER RESIDENTIAL SVCS INC
420 S Sugar St (45822-2431)
P.O. Box 603 (45822-0603)
PHONE.....................419 586-4709
Fax: 419 586-4777
Garry Mosier, *CEO*
EMP: 65
SQ FT: 1,500
SALES: 2.4MM **Privately Held**
SIC: 8052 Personal care facility

(G-2658)
MIDWEST LOGISTICS SYSTEMS
8779 State Route 703 (45822-2936)
PHONE.....................419 584-1414
F Edward Voelker, *President*
James Duvall, *Principal*
Andrew Roettger, *Trustee*
Bill Russell, *Trustee*
Ellen Welker, *Vice Pres*
EMP: 389
SALES (est): 78.6MM **Privately Held**
SIC: 4213 4212 Trucking, except local; local trucking, without storage

(G-2659)
PEREGRINE HEALTH SERVICES INC
Also Called: Gardens At Celina The
1301 Myers Rd (45822-4114)
PHONE.....................419 586-4135
Ed Fodrea, *Branch Mgr*
EMP: 54
SALES (corp-wide): 7MM **Privately Held**
SIC: 8099 Blood related health services
PA: Peregrine Health Services, Inc.
1661 Old Henderson Rd
Columbus OH 43220
614 459-2656

(G-2660)
RAF CELINA LLC
1915-1955 Haveman Rd (45822)
PHONE.....................216 464-6626
Andrew Kline, *Vice Pres*
Chad Gardner, *Controller*
EMP: 25
SALES (est): 396.5K **Privately Held**
SIC: 6512 Shopping center, community (100,000 - 300,000 sq ft)

(G-2661)
RAYMOND JAMES FINCL SVCS INC
225 N Main St (45822-1601)
PHONE.....................419 586-5121
Deny Knapschaefer, *Branch Mgr*
EMP: 30
SALES (corp-wide): 6.5B **Publicly Held**
SIC: 6211 6733 6029 Brokers, security; trusts; commercial banks
HQ: Raymond James Financial Services, Inc.
880 Carillon Pkwy
Saint Petersburg FL 33716
727 567-1000

(G-2662)
REPUBLIC SERVICES INC
6141 Depweg Rd (45822-9573)
PHONE.....................419 925-4592
Dan Jackson, *Branch Mgr*
EMP: 34
SALES (corp-wide): 10B **Publicly Held**
SIC: 4953 Sanitary landfill operation
PA: Republic Services, Inc.
18500 N Allied Way # 100
Phoenix AZ 85054
480 627-2700

(G-2663)
SAMPLES CHUCK-GENERAL CONTR
1460 E Wayne St (45822-9394)
PHONE.....................419 586-1434
Charles E Samples, *President*
Sue Minch, *Project Mgr*
EMP: 28
SQ FT: 6,000
SALES (est): 2.9MM **Privately Held**
SIC: 1611 Highway & street construction

(G-2664)
TOMS INSTALLATION CO INC
5349 State Route 29 (45822-9210)
P.O. Box 30 (45822-0030)
PHONE.....................419 584-1218
Tom Slusser, *President*
Samuel Slusser, *Vice Pres*
Toni Slusser, *CFO*
EMP: 30
SALES (est): 1.2MM **Privately Held**
WEB: www.tomsinstallationco.com
SIC: 7389 Telephone services

(G-2665)
UNITED PARCEL SERVICE INC OH
Also Called: UPS
1851 Industrial Dr (45822-1377)
PHONE.....................419 586-8556
Steve Hoyne, *Branch Mgr*
EMP: 200
SALES (corp-wide): 65.8B **Publicly Held**
WEB: www.upsscs.com
SIC: 4215 Parcel delivery, vehicular
HQ: United Parcel Service, Inc. (Oh)
55 Glenlake Pkwy
Atlanta GA 30328
404 828-6000

Centerburg
Knox County

(G-2666)
CENTERBURG TWO LLC
Also Called: Centerburg Resp & Spclty Rehab
212 Fairview St (43011-8314)
PHONE.....................740 625-5774
William Weisberg,
EMP: 73
SALES (est): 294.7K
SALES (corp-wide): 68.5MM **Privately Held**
SIC: 8051 Skilled nursing care facilities
PA: Saber Healthcare Group, L.L.C.
26691 Richmond Rd Frnt
Bedford OH 44146
216 292-5706

(G-2667)
RESCARE OHIO INC
Also Called: Canterbury Villa
80 Miller St (43011-7023)
P.O. Box 10, Marengo (43334-0010)
PHONE.....................740 625-6873
Fax: 740 625-6872
Lisa Wood, *Branch Mgr*
EMP: 50
SALES (corp-wide): 24.5B **Privately Held**
WEB: www.schoenbrunnhealthcare.com
SIC: 8051 Skilled nursing care facilities
HQ: Rescare Ohio Inc
348 W Main St
Williamsburg OH 45176

(G-2668)
SHREDDED BEDDING CORPORATION (PA)
Also Called: SBC Recycling
6589 Bennington Chapel Rd (43011-9312)
PHONE.....................740 893-3567
Fax: 614 893-3568
D Lynn Hatfield, *President*
Betty L Hatfield, *Corp Secy*
Michael Hatfield, *Vice Pres*
Ryan Hatfield, *Vice Pres*
EMP: 50
SQ FT: 25,000
SALES (est): 9.5MM **Privately Held**
WEB: www.sbcrecycling.com
SIC: 7389 4953 5093 Brokers' services; document & office record destruction; recycling, waste materials; scrap & waste materials

Centerville
Montgomery County

(G-2669)
AGJ KIDZ LLC
Also Called: Kidz Watch
101 E Alexville 1 Rd 110 Ste 110 1st (45459)
PHONE.....................937 350-1001
Emily W Weaner, *Mng Member*
Bradley W Weaner,
EMP: 25 **EST:** 2013
SALES (est): 185.1K **Privately Held**
SIC: 8351 Group day care center

(G-2670)
AISLING ENTERPRISES LLC
9747 Crooked Creek Dr (45458-3029)
PHONE.....................937 203-1757
Jason Terry, *President*
EMP: 30 **EST:** 2014
SALES (est): 1.9MM **Privately Held**
SIC: 7373 Systems software development services

(G-2671)
ALL ABOUT KIDS
1300 E Social Row Rd (45458-4718)
PHONE.....................937 885-7480
Lisa Rizzo, *Director*
EMP: 30 **EST:** 2012
SALES (est): 365K **Privately Held**
SIC: 8351 Preschool center

(G-2672)
ALLERGY & ASTHMA CENTRE DAYTON (PA)
Also Called: Allergy & Asthma Centre Dayton
8039 Wash Vlg Dr Ste 100 (45458-1877)
PHONE.....................937 435-8999
Fax: 937 435-4211
Joyce Smith, *Office Mgr*
Arturo J Bonnin, *Med Doctor*
Kelly Careher, *Gnrl Med Prac*
EMP: 29
SALES (est): 3.6MM **Privately Held**
SIC: 8011 Allergist

GEOGRAPHIC SECTION
Chagrin Falls - Cuyahoga County (G-2696)

(G-2673)
AMERICAN CUTTING EDGE INC
480 Congress Park Dr (45459-4144)
PHONE..................................937 438-2390
Chuck Biehn Jr, *President*
Sharon Drewry, *Human Res Mgr*
Danielle Holley, *Accounts Mgr*
Grahame Poferl, *Sales Staff*
Dominique Ballmann, *Manager*
▲ **EMP:** 122
SQ FT: 4,000
SALES (est): 5.1MM
SALES (corp-wide): 41.4MM **Privately Held**
WEB: www.americancuttingedge.com
SIC: 5122 Razor blades
PA: Cb Manufacturing & Sales Co., Inc.
    4455 Infirmary Rd
    Miamisburg OH 45342
    937 866-5986

(G-2674)
AT&T MOBILITY LLC
199 E Alex Bell Rd # 418 (45459-2797)
PHONE..................................937 439-4900
Brad Wimsatt, *Manager*
EMP: 26
SALES (corp-wide): 160.5B **Publicly Held**
WEB: www.cingular.com
SIC: 4812 Cellular telephone services
HQ: At&T Mobility Llc
    1025 Lenox Park Blvd Ne
    Brookhaven GA 30319
    800 331-0500

(G-2675)
CENTERVILLE FITNESS INC
Also Called: Club 51 Fitness
51 E Spring Valley Pike (45458-3801)
PHONE..................................937 291-7990
Michael Brunett, *President*
EMP: 35
SQ FT: 40,000
SALES (est): 182.5K **Privately Held**
SIC: 7991 Physical fitness facilities

(G-2676)
CLYO INTERNAL MEDICINE INC
7073 Clyo Rd (45459-4816)
PHONE..................................937 435-5857
R Jeffrey Taylor, *President*
EMP: 75
SALES (est): 2.4MM
SALES (corp-wide): 287.4MM **Privately Held**
SIC: 8011 Physicians' office, including specialists
HQ: Ipc Healthcare, Inc.
    4605 Lankershim Blvd
    North Hollywood CA 91602
    888 447-2362

(G-2677)
DAYTON OB GYN
330 N Main St Ste 200 (45459-4459)
PHONE..................................937 439-7550
Fax: 937 439-7552
Ahmed Moezzi, *President*
Brent Imbody, *Vice Pres*
Michael Thesing, *Vice Pres*
Debbie Oxner, *Office Mgr*
EMP: 25
SQ FT: 46,000
SALES (est): 2.9MM **Privately Held**
SIC: 8011 Fertility specialist, physician; specialized medical practitioners, except internal; gynecologist

(G-2678)
GRISMER TIRE COMPANY (PA)
1099 S Main St (45458-3840)
P.O. Box 337, Dayton (45401-0337)
PHONE..................................937 643-2526
Fax: 937 643-2532
Charles L Marshall II, *President*
Robert Hupp, *Treasurer*
Carolyn Houk, *Controller*
John L Marshall, *Admin Sec*
▲ **EMP:** 28 **EST:** 1932
SQ FT: 40,000
SALES (est): 25.5MM **Privately Held**
WEB: www.grismertire.com
SIC: 5531 7538 5014 7534 Automotive tires; general automotive repair shops; automobile tires & tubes; truck tires & tubes; rebuilding & retreading tires

(G-2679)
HCR MANORCARE MED SVCS FLA LLC
Also Called: Manor Care Hlth Svcs Cntrville
1001 E Alex Bell Rd (45459-2637)
PHONE..................................937 436-9700
Fax: 937 436-1495
Jerry Wright, *Human Resources*
Lee Elliot, *Administration*
EMP: 200
SALES (corp-wide): 3.6B **Publicly Held**
WEB: www.manorcare.com
SIC: 8051 Convalescent home with continuous nursing care
HQ: Hcr Manorcare Medical Services Of Florida, Llc
    333 N Summit St Ste 100
    Toledo OH 43604
    419 252-5500

(G-2680)
IRONGATE INC (PA)
Also Called: Irongate Realtors
122 N Main St (45459-4621)
PHONE..................................937 433-3300
Fax: 937 433-1374
Steven Brown, *President*
Steve Joslin, *COO*
Karen Abrams, *Vice Pres*
Greg Gillen, *Vice Pres*
Scot Sutherland, *Broker*
EMP: 225
SALES (est): 12.9MM **Privately Held**
WEB: www.irongate-realtors.com
SIC: 6531 6311 Real estate agent, residential; selling agent, real estate; mutual association life insurance

(G-2681)
KETTERING ADVENTIST HEALTHCARE
1989 Miamisbg Cntrvll Rd (45459-3859)
PHONE..................................937 401-6306
EMP: 40
SALES (corp-wide): 1.7B **Privately Held**
SIC: 8099 Blood related health services
PA: Kettering Adventist Healthcare
    3535 Southern Blvd
    Dayton OH 45429
    937 298-4331

(G-2682)
KGBO HOLDINGS INC
6525 Centervl Bus Pkwy (45459-2686)
PHONE..................................800 580-3101
Matt Howard, *Principal*
EMP: 39
SALES (corp-wide): 2.3B **Privately Held**
SIC: 6211 Investment firm, general brokerage
PA: Kgbo Holdings, Inc
    4289 Ivy Pointe Blvd
    Cincinnati OH 45245
    513 831-2600

(G-2683)
ORTHOPEDIC ASSOCIATES (PA)
7677 Yankee St Ste 110 (45459-3475)
PHONE..................................937 415-9100
Fax: 937 428-0440
Jan E Faunders, *President*
H Brent Bamberger, *Treasurer*
Jessica Weihrauch, *Mktg Dir*
Rowland Andrea, *Manager*
Chad Weber, *Orthopedist*
EMP: 30
SALES (est): 10.9MM **Privately Held**
WEB: www.oaswo.com
SIC: 8011 Orthopedic physician

(G-2684)
PREMIER INTEGRATED MED ASSOC (PA)
Also Called: Primed Physicians
6520 Acro Ct (45459-2679)
PHONE..................................937 291-6813
Mark Couch, *President*
EMP: 67
SQ FT: 16,345
SALES (est): 4.4MM **Privately Held**
SIC: 8011 Internal medicine, physician/surgeon; oncologist; hematologist; cardiologist & cardio-vascular specialist

(G-2685)
SELECTTECH SERVICES CORP
8045 Washington Vlg Dr (45458-1847)
PHONE..................................937 438-9905
Fax: 937 438-9920
Robert B Finch, *CEO*
Scott A Sullivan, *President*
Maxine Orum, *Chairman*
Linda Vikmanis, *Vice Pres*
Lisa Eglad, *Treasurer*
EMP: 140
SQ FT: 4,300
SALES (est): 19.8MM **Privately Held**
WEB: www.selecttechservices.com
SIC: 8744 7376 Facilities support services; computer facilities management

(G-2686)
SUPPORT FINCL RESOURCES INC
830 E Franklin St Ste A (45459-5621)
P.O. Box 291767, Dayton (45429-0767)
PHONE..................................800 444-5465
EMP: 40
SQ FT: 5,000
SALES: 1MM
SALES (corp-wide): 4.9MM **Privately Held**
SIC: 8742 Management Consulting Services
PA: Support Insurance Systems Agency, Inc.
    830 E Franklin St Ste A
    Centerville OH 45459
    937 434-5700

(G-2687)
SUPPORT INSUR SYSTEMS AGCY INC (PA)
830 E Franklin St Ste A (45459-5621)
P.O. Box 291767, Dayton (45429-0767)
PHONE..................................937 434-5700
Rhonda Sheets, *President*
Helen Salas, *Vice Pres*
Faith Patrick, *Accountant*
Dave Hilbig, *Manager*
Howard Sheets, *Director*
EMP: 40
SALES: 4.9MM **Privately Held**
SIC: 6411 Insurance agents

Chagrin Falls
Cuyahoga County

(G-2688)
ACTIVE CHIROPRACTIC
1 S Main St Ste 1 (44022-3225)
PHONE..................................440 893-8800
Fax: 440 893-9422
George Heathcote, *Owner*
Rose Heathcote, *Manager*
EMP: 46
SQ FT: 34,354
SALES (est): 2.1MM **Privately Held**
SIC: 8041 Offices & clinics of chiropractors

(G-2689)
ALTHANS INSURANCE AGENCY INC
543 Washington St (44022-4446)
P.O. Box 570 (44022-0570)
PHONE..................................440 247-6422
Fax: 440 247-6422
James C Althans, *President*
Susan Barriball, *Vice Chairman*
Michael A Althans, *COO*
Mike Fiala, *Vice Pres*
John S Althans, *CFO*
EMP: 40
SQ FT: 15,000
SALES (est): 14.7MM **Privately Held**
WEB: www.althans.com
SIC: 6411 Insurance agents

(G-2690)
BARKLEY OF CLEVELAND LLC
Also Called: Barkley Pet Hotel & Day Spa
27349 Miles Rd (44022-2133)
PHONE..................................440 248-2275
Howard Perlmuter,
Howard J Babrow,
EMP: 30
SALES (est): 1.1MM **Privately Held**
SIC: 0752 Boarding services, kennels

(G-2691)
CHAGRIN FALLS HISTORICAL SOC
87 E Washington St (44022-3001)
PHONE..................................440 247-4695
Fax: 440 247-5331
Carolyn Sihler, *Treasurer*
Pat Zalba, *Manager*
Jane Babinksy, *Director*
EMP: 35
SALES: 284.2K **Privately Held**
SIC: 8412 Museum

(G-2692)
CHAGRIN VALLEY COUNTRY CLUB CO
4700 Som Center Rd (44022-2399)
PHONE..................................440 248-4310
Fax: 440 248-4310
Alan Matta, *CFO*
Jack Goldberg, *Exec Dir*
EMP: 100
SQ FT: 30,000
SALES: 5MM **Privately Held**
WEB: www.cvcclub.com
SIC: 7997 Country club, membership

(G-2693)
CLEVELND CLNC CHAGRN FLLS FMLY
551 Washington St (44022-4403)
PHONE..................................440 893-9393
Kim Reidel, *Principal*
Lisa Ramage, *Manager*
Susan Belley, *Manager*
Nicole Vaughn,
EMP: 35
SALES (est): 1.8MM
SALES (corp-wide): 8B **Privately Held**
SIC: 8099 Health screening service
PA: The Cleveland Clinic Foundation
    9500 Euclid Ave
    Cleveland OH 44195
    216 636-8335

(G-2694)
CLUB AT HILLBROOK INC
14800 Hillbrook Dr (44022-2634)
P.O. Box 603 (44022-0603)
PHONE..................................440 247-4940
Fax: 440 247-4518
Jim Kaufman, *President*
Angel Burton, *Sales Dir*
EMP: 25
SALES (est): 1.1MM **Privately Held**
WEB: www.clubhillbrook.com
SIC: 7997 Country club, membership

(G-2695)
D E WILLIAMS ELECTRIC INC
168 Solon Rd Ste B (44022-3100)
P.O. Box 180 (44022-0180)
PHONE..................................440 543-1222
Fax: 440 543-1227
Dan E Williams, *Ch of Bd*
Briana Harper, *President*
Douglas Williams, *Vice Pres*
Ted Williams, *Vice Pres*
Stan Newell, *Manager*
EMP: 50 **EST:** 1952
SQ FT: 12,000
SALES (est): 8.7MM **Privately Held**
WEB: www.dewilliamselectric.com
SIC: 1731 General electrical contractor

(G-2696)
FOR WOMEN LIKE ME INC (PA)
Also Called: Fwlm
46 Shopping Plz Ste 155 (44022-3022)
PHONE..................................407 848-7339
Arline Burks, *CEO*
Dakkota Gant, *President*
Marsha Robles, *Vice Pres*
Kathy Chislom, *Treasurer*

Chagrin Falls - Cuyahoga County (G-2697)

Jamie Johnston, *Executive Asst*
◆ **EMP:** 42
SQ FT: 5,000
SALES: 53MM **Privately Held**
WEB: www.forwomenlikeme.com
SIC: 7812 5137 5621 5136 Television film production; women's & children's clothing; women's clothing stores; men's & boys' clothing; men's & boys' clothing stores

(G-2697)
GARFIELD HTS COACH LINE INC
Also Called: Cleveland Southeastern Trails
119 Manor Brook Dr (44022-4163)
P.O. Box 46670, Bedford (44146-0670)
PHONE.................................440 232-4550
Anthony J Walters, *President*
Diane Hyland, *Corp Secy*
Patrick J Hyland, *Vice Pres*
Frank D Walters, *Vice Pres*
EMP: 75
SQ FT: 85,000
SALES (est): 3.4MM **Privately Held**
SIC: 4142 Bus charter service, except local

(G-2698)
GOLDEN LIVING LLC
Also Called: Hamlet Manor
150 Cleveland St (44022-2985)
PHONE.................................440 247-4200
Michael Booth, *Controller*
Marilyn McKinnie, *Sales Mgr*
Bartlett T Bell, *Branch Mgr*
EMP: 185
SQ FT: 41,000
SALES (corp-wide): 7.4MM **Privately Held**
SIC: 8059 Convalescent home
PA: Golden Living Llc
5220 Tennyson Pkwy # 400
Plano TX 75024
972 372-6300

(G-2699)
HAMLET VILLAGE IN CHAGRIN FLS
Also Called: Hamlet Nursing Home
150 Cleveland St (44022-2985)
PHONE.................................440 247-4200
Fax: 440 247-7597
John Eigen, *Branch Mgr*
Janet Johnson, *Nursing Dir*
EMP: 72
SALES (corp-wide): 10.8MM **Privately Held**
SIC: 8059 Rest home, with health care
PA: Hamlet Village In Chagrin Falls
200 Hamlet Hills Dr Ofc
Chagrin Falls OH 44022
216 263-6033

(G-2700)
HAMLET VILLAGE IN CHAGRIN FLS (PA)
200 Hamlet Hills Dr Ofc (44022-2838)
PHONE.................................216 263-6033
Fax: 440 247-1291
Victor Nccallum, *Facilities Dir*
Rita Stickle, *Office Mgr*
John Eigen, *Exec Dir*
Lawrence Gray, *Director*
Molly Spencer, *Director*
EMP: 78
SALES (est): 10.8MM **Privately Held**
WEB: www.hamletretirement.com
SIC: 8051 Convalescent home with continuous nursing care

(G-2701)
INVESTMERICA LIMITED
547 Washington St Ste 10 (44022-4436)
PHONE.................................216 618-3296
Monty Warren,
EMP: 67
SQ FT: 1,500
SALES (est): 5.2MM **Privately Held**
SIC: 6798 1521 Real estate investment trusts; single-family housing construction

(G-2702)
LAKE HORRY ELECTRIC (PA)
Also Called: Hirsch Division
255 Bramley Ct (44022-3613)
PHONE.................................440 808-8791
Ronald Hirsch, *President*
Michael Simon, *Vice Pres*
Birdie Hirsch, *Admin Sec*
EMP: 100
SQ FT: 12,000
SALES (est): 6.5MM **Privately Held**
SIC: 1731 Electrical work

(G-2703)
OPINIONS LTD (PA)
33 River St (44022-3020)
PHONE.................................440 893-0300
Qasim Butt, *Opers Mgr*
Rick Hammar, *Opers Mgr*
Jaime Rexroat, *Facilities Mgr*
Anita Evans, *Opers Staff*
Erika Harris, *Research*
EMP: 50 **EST:** 1998
SALES (est): 12.6MM **Privately Held**
WEB: www.opinionsltd.com
SIC: 8732 Market analysis or research

(G-2704)
REAL ESTATE MORTGAGE CORP
200 Jackson Dr (44022-1556)
PHONE.................................440 356-5373
Fax: 440 356-3410
Mark Johnston, *President*
EMP: 100
SQ FT: 4,000
SALES (est): 7.1MM
SALES (corp-wide): 23.2MM **Privately Held**
WEB: www.remcorp.com
SIC: 6163 Mortgage brokers arranging for loans, using money of others
PA: The American Eagle Mortgage Co Llc
6145 Park Square Dr Ste 4
Lorain OH 44053
440 988-2900

(G-2705)
SNAVELY BUILDING COMPANY (PA)
7139 Pine St Ste 110 (44022-3401)
PHONE.................................440 585-9091
John P Snavely, *President*
Joe Sullens, *Superintendent*
Peter Snavely, *Principal*
Paul Snavely, *Vice Pres*
Kay Neubert, *Project Mgr*
EMP: 30
SQ FT: 6,000
SALES (est): 19MM **Privately Held**
WEB: www.benefit-svcs.com
SIC: 1542 1521 1522 Commercial & office building contractors; new construction, single-family houses; general remodeling, single-family houses; apartment building construction; multi-family dwellings, new construction; remodeling, multi-family dwellings

(G-2706)
SNAVELY DEVELOPMENT COMPANY (PA)
7139 Pine St (44022-3401)
PHONE.................................440 585-9091
Peter Snavely, *President*
John P Snavely, *Chairman*
Paul Snavely, *Vice Pres*
Dennis Zanath, *Project Mgr*
Brad Lohan, *Financial Exec*
EMP: 40
SQ FT: 6,000
SALES: 75MM **Privately Held**
SIC: 1521 1522 New construction, single-family houses; multi-family dwellings, new construction

(G-2707)
SNL DESIGNS LTD
13 N Franklin St (44022-3009)
PHONE.................................440 247-2344
Nancy Lyons, *Owner*
EMP: 30
SALES (est): 1.4MM **Privately Held**
SIC: 7389 Design services

(G-2708)
SUNPOINT SENIOR LIVING HAMLET
150 Cleveland St (44022-2985)
PHONE.................................440 247-4200
Alan Rosenfield, *Principal*
EMP: 50
SALES (est): 981.6K **Privately Held**
SIC: 6513 Retirement hotel operation

(G-2709)
VERTICAL KNOWLEDGE LLC (PA)
8 E Washington St Ste 200 (44022-3057)
PHONE.................................216 920-7790
Matt Carpenter, *CEO*
EMP: 55
SALES (est): 6.8MM **Privately Held**
SIC: 7379

(G-2710)
WESTERN RESERVE REALTY LLC
Also Called: Remax Traditions
26 S Main St Ste 100 (44022-3268)
PHONE.................................440 247-3707
Fax: 440 247-3660
Janeann Bell,
Dwight Milko,
Ann Sords, *Real Est Agnt*
Mark Baughman, *Associate*
EMP: 38
SQ FT: 3,000
SALES (est): 2.1MM **Privately Held**
SIC: 6531 Real estate agent, residential

(G-2711)
WESTERN RSRVE LAND CONSERVANCY (PA)
3850 Chagrin River Rd (44022-1131)
PHONE.................................440 729-9621
Richard Cochran, *CEO*
James Spira, *President*
Joanie O'Brien, *General Mgr*
Chris Szell, *General Mgr*
Julia Musson, *Principal*
EMP: 32
SALES: 15.5MM **Privately Held**
SIC: 8641 Environmental protection organization

Chagrin Falls
Geauga County

(G-2712)
CHAGRIN VALLEY ATHLETIC CLUB
17260 Snyder Rd (44023-2724)
PHONE.................................440 543-5141
Fax: 440 543-5141
James M Rosenberger, *President*
Hollis H Rosenberger, *Treasurer*
Annie Bartlett, *Controller*
Jane Clarke, *Sales Staff*
Kate Lukwinski, *Manager*
EMP: 100
SALES (est): 4MM **Privately Held**
WEB: www.cvaclub.com
SIC: 7991 Athletic club & gymnasiums, membership

(G-2713)
CUSTOM MATERIALS INC
Also Called: C M I Group
16865 Park Circle Dr (44023-4591)
PHONE.................................440 543-8284
Fax: 440 543-7636
Debby Shaw, *General Mgr*
Anthony D Borrelli, *Principal*
Jesse Dowdle, *Plant Mgr*
Dave Fisher, *Plant Mgr*
Tony Reiss, *QC Mgr*
EMP: 65
SQ FT: 50,000
SALES (est): 13.5MM **Privately Held**
WEB: www.custommaterials.com
SIC: 8711 Engineering services

(G-2714)
EASTON SALES AND RENTAL LLC (PA)
16750 Hilltop Park Pl (44023-4500)
PHONE.................................440 708-0099
David Udelson, *Mng Member*
EMP: 25
SALES (est): 8.4MM **Privately Held**
SIC: 7359 Equipment rental & leasing

(G-2715)
ENDO-SURGICAL CENTER FLA LLC
8185 Washington St (44023-4574)
PHONE.................................440 708-0582
Fax: 440 708-0583
Jean Neading, *Administration*
Rami Abbass, *Assistant*
EMP: 370
SALES (corp-wide): 14.2MM **Privately Held**
SIC: 8011 Endocrinologist
PA: Endo-Surgical Center Of Florida, Llc
2500 York Rd Ste 300
Jamison PA 18929
877 442-3687

(G-2716)
ENVIROTEST SYSTEMS CORP
17202 Munn Rd (44023-5417)
PHONE.................................330 963-4464
Steve Peterson, *Branch Mgr*
EMP: 34 **Privately Held**
WEB: www.il.etest.com
SIC: 7549 Emissions testing without repairs, automotive
HQ: Envirotest Systems Corp.
7 Kripes Rd
East Granby CT 06026

(G-2717)
GENERAL ENVIRONMENTAL MGT LLC
16533 Chillicothe Rd (44023-4327)
PHONE.................................216 621-3694
Scott Forster,
Eric Lofquist,
EMP: 53
SQ FT: 6,000
SALES (est): 4.7MM **Privately Held**
SIC: 4953 Recycling, waste materials

(G-2718)
GOLDFISH SWIM SCHOOL
4670 Richmond Rd Ste 100 (44023)
PHONE.................................216 364-9090
Soneli Morris, *General Mgr*
Andrew Joseph, *General Mgr*
Emily Ryan, *General Mgr*
Jessie Dejongh, *Manager*
Lauren Ledford, *Manager*
EMP: 45
SALES (est): 1MM **Privately Held**
SIC: 7999 7299 Swimming instruction; facility rental & party planning services

(G-2719)
HEMLOCK LANDSCAPES INC
7209 Chagrin Rd Ste A (44023-1129)
PHONE.................................440 247-3631
Fax: 440 247-7957
Dennis Barriball, *President*
Mark Lefelhoc, *Opers Mgr*
Lauren Barriball, *Treasurer*
Emily Barriball, *Executive Asst*
Brian Barriball, *Admin Asst*
EMP: 25
SQ FT: 4,500
SALES (est): 1.3MM **Privately Held**
WEB: www.hemlocklandscapes.com
SIC: 0781 0782 Landscape services; landscape contractors

(G-2720)
IMS COMPANY
Also Called: Injection Molders Supply
10373 Stafford Rd (44023-5296)
PHONE.................................440 543-1615
Fax: 440 543-1069
Brad G Morse, *CEO*
Mary Ann Morris, *Co-CEO*
Jeffrey Sawicki, *COO*
Rhonda Horan, *Purch Mgr*
Laura Fisher, *Purch Agent*
◆ **EMP:** 60 **EST:** 1960

GEOGRAPHIC SECTION

Chardon - Geauga County (G-2743)

SQ FT: 62,000
SALES (est): 43.6MM **Privately Held**
SIC: 5084 Industrial machinery & equipment; plastic products machinery

(G-2721)
INDUSTRIAL MAINT SVCS INC
9824 Washington St Ste A (44023-5455)
P.O. Box 265, Chesterland (44026-0265)
PHONE.................................440 729-2068
Bryce Vasko, *President*
Shane Dangy, *Vice Pres*
Dan Okay, *Admin Sec*
EMP: 47
SQ FT: 2,000
SALES (est): 3.3MM **Privately Held**
SIC: 7699 5084 Printing trades machinery & equipment repair; paper manufacturing machinery

(G-2722)
LOWES GREENHOUSE & GIFT SHOP
Also Called: Lowe's Greenhouses Flor Ldscp
16540 Chillicothe Rd (44023-4328)
PHONE.................................440 543-5123
Fax: 440 543-5123
Jeffrey B Griff, *President*
Bernard A Griff, *President*
EMP: 35
SQ FT: 40,000
SALES: 1MM **Privately Held**
WEB: www.lowesgreenhouse.com
SIC: 5992 0181 5947 Flowers, fresh; foliage, growing of; nursery stock, growing of; plants, potted; growing of; flowers: grown under cover (e.g. greenhouse production); gift shop

(G-2723)
M&C HOTEL INTERESTS INC
Also Called: Pine Lake Trout Club
17021 Chillicothe Rd (44023-4617)
P.O. Box 23282 (44023-0282)
PHONE.................................440 543-1331
Fax: 440 543-1026
Sandra Hughes, *Branch Mgr*
EMP: 30 **Privately Held**
WEB: www.richfield.com
SIC: 8741 7997 Hotel or motel management; membership sports & recreation clubs
HQ: M&C Hotel Interests, Inc.
    6560 Greenwood Plaza Blvd # 300
    Greenwood Village CO 80111

(G-2724)
MANOR CARE OF AMERICA INC
Also Called: Arden Courts of Bainbridge
8100 Washington St (44023-4506)
PHONE.................................440 543-6766
Erin Tfenning, *Manager*
Mark McBride, *Manager*
Allan Rosenfield, *Director*
EMP: 60
SALES (corp-wide): 3.6B **Publicly Held**
WEB: www.trisunhealthcare.com
SIC: 8051 Extended care facility
HQ: Manor Care Of America, Inc.
    333 N Summit St Ste 103
    Toledo OH 43604
    419 252-5500

(G-2725)
MEDHURST MASON CONTRACTORS INC
17111 Munn Rd Ste 1 (44023-5427)
PHONE.................................440 543-8885
Fax: 440 543-5029
Robert Medhurst, *President*
Carol Medhurst, *Treasurer*
Irene Taparone, *Controller*
Joyce Cavanaugh, *Manager*
Bob Medhurst, *Manager*
EMP: 115 EST: 1976
SQ FT: 7,900
SALES (est): 10MM **Privately Held**
WEB: www.medhurstmason.com
SIC: 1741 Bricklaying

(G-2726)
NEW WEMBLEY LLC
Also Called: Wembley Club, The
8345 Woodberry Blvd (44023-4520)
PHONE.................................440 543-8171
Fax: 440 543-9246
Marc Duvin, *President*
Justin Kolanz, *General Mgr*
Sandy Cadman, *Manager*
Jane Copper, *Director*
Vera Hoyle, *Director*
EMP: 50
SALES (est): 1.8MM **Privately Held**
SIC: 7997 Country club, membership

(G-2727)
OHIO VALLEY GROUP INC
16965 Park Circle Dr (44023-6502)
PHONE.................................440 543-0500
Andrew F Dangelo, *President*
Kathleen Dangelo, *Vice Pres*
Beverly Ries, *Office Admin*
Mike Rossi, *Maintence Staff*
EMP: 25
SALES (est): 3.9MM **Privately Held**
SIC: 0781 Landscape services

(G-2728)
PARK PLACE INTERNATIONAL LLC
8401 Chagrin Rd Ste 15a (44023-4702)
PHONE.................................877 991-1991
Fax: 440 247-2604
Erik Littlejohn, *President*
David Sullivan, *Vice Pres*
Steve Larabee, *Engineer*
Barb Brooks, *Accountant*
Jim Sutton, *VP Sales*
EMP: 55
SALES (corp-wide): 43.1MM **Privately Held**
WEB: www.parkplaceintl.com
SIC: 5045 Computer peripheral equipment
PA: Park Place International, Llc
    100 Crowley Dr
    Marlborough MA 01752
    877 991-1991

(G-2729)
PRINTING SERVICES
16750 Park Circle Dr (44023-4563)
PHONE.................................440 708-1999
Robert Roulan, *President*
Brian Pottinger, *Manager*
EMP: 25
SQ FT: 16,000
SALES (est): 1.2MM **Privately Held**
SIC: 7389 2752 Printers' services: folding, collating; commercial printing, lithographic

(G-2730)
PROS FREIGHT CORPORATION
16687 Hilltop Park Pl (44023-4500)
PHONE.................................440 543-7555
Elaine R Moore, *President*
Russell Moore, *Manager*
EMP: 30 EST: 1975
SQ FT: 2,000
SALES (est): 3.6MM **Privately Held**
SIC: 4213 Contract haulers

(G-2731)
ROUNDTABLE ONLINE LEARNING LLC
8401 Chagrin Rd Ste 6 (44023-4702)
PHONE.................................440 220-5252
Fax: 216 932-4700
Dan Grajzl, *President*
James Lorentz, *Partner*
Jim Wenger, *Exec VP*
Tanya Loncar, *Vice Pres*
Colleen Kline, *Sls & Mktg Exec*
EMP: 25
SQ FT: 3,500
SALES: 1.5MM **Privately Held**
WEB: www.knowbasenetworks.com
SIC: 8299 4813 Educational services;

(G-2732)
RURAL/METRO CORPORATION
8401 Chagrin Rd Ste 15a (44023-4702)
PHONE.................................440 543-3313
Fax: 440 543-3361
EMP: 110
SALES (corp-wide): 431.3MM **Privately Held**
SIC: 4119 Local Passenger Transportation
HQ: Rural/Metro Corporation
    9221 E Via De Ventura
    Scottsdale AZ 85258
    480 606-3886

(G-2733)
SCHNEIDER SADDLERY LLC
Also Called: Billy Royal
8255 Washington St (44023-4507)
PHONE.................................440 543-2700
Fax: 440 543-2710
Donald Schneider, *President*
Stanley Schneider, *Vice Pres*
John Berzanske, *Inv Control Mgr*
Tammy Plants, *Buyer*
Erin Aldrich, *Purchasing*
▲ EMP: 35 EST: 1966
SQ FT: 40,000
SALES (est): 16.2MM **Privately Held**
WEB: www.sstack.com
SIC: 5941 5699 5091 5961 Saddlery & equestrian equipment; riding apparel; western apparel; sporting & recreation goods; mail order house; women's accessory & specialty stores

(G-2734)
SOUTH FRANKLIN CIRCLE
16575 S Franklin St (44023-1002)
PHONE.................................440 247-1300
Bill Fehrenbach, *Vice Pres*
Rob Lucarelli, *Director*
EMP: 140
SALES (est): 2.7MM
SALES (corp-wide): 13.5MM **Privately Held**
SIC: 6513 Retirement hotel operation
PA: South Franklin Circle
    16600 Warren Ct
    Chagrin Falls OH 44023
    440 247-1300

(G-2735)
STOCK FAIRFIELD CORPORATION
Also Called: Stock Equipment Company
16490 Chillicothe Rd (44023-4326)
PHONE.................................440 543-6000
Robert Ciavarella, *President*
EMP: 170 EST: 2007
SALES (est): 45.4MM **Privately Held**
WEB: www.stockequipment.com
SIC: 5063 8711 3535 3823 Power transmission equipment, electric; electrical or electronic engineering; conveyors & conveying equipment; industrial instrmnts msrmnt display/control process variable; relays & industrial controls; industrial trucks & tractors
HQ: Stock Equipment Company, Inc.
    16490 Chillicothe Rd
    Chagrin Falls OH 44023
    440 543-6000

(G-2736)
THERAPEUTIC RIDING CENTER INC
Also Called: Fieldstone Farms Theraptic Rid
16497 Snyder Rd (44023-4313)
PHONE.................................440 708-0029
Fax: 440 708-0029
Linette Stuart, *Exec Dir*
James B Rucker Jr,
John H Wilharm Jr,
EMP: 29
SQ FT: 1,901
SALES: 1MM **Privately Held**
WEB: www.fieldstonefarmtrc.com
SIC: 7999 8093 Riding stable; rehabilitation center, outpatient treatment

(G-2737)
ULL INC (PA)
9812 Washington St (44023-5486)
P.O. Box 23399 (44023-0399)
PHONE.................................440 543-5195
Marilyn Ullman, *President*
Joshua R Cilley, *President*
Kim Ullman, *Vice Pres*
Lucy Kelley, *Manager*
Bernd O Bryant, *Admin Sec*
EMP: 35
SQ FT: 20,000
SALES (est): 18.6MM **Privately Held**
WEB: www.ullmanoil.com
SIC: 5172 5983 Petroleum products; fuel oil dealers

Chardon
Geauga County

(G-2738)
ADVANCE AUTO PARTS INC
230 Center St (44024-1122)
PHONE.................................440 226-3150
EMP: 30
SALES (corp-wide): 9.3B **Publicly Held**
SIC: 5531 5015 5013 Automobile & truck equipment & parts; motor vehicle parts, used; automotive supplies & parts
PA: Advance Auto Parts, Inc.
    5008 Airport Rd Nw
    Roanoke VA 24012
    540 362-4911

(G-2739)
ALLTEL COMMUNICATIONS CORP
205 S Hambden St (44024-1228)
P.O. Box 428 (44024-0428)
PHONE.................................330 656-8000
Dennis McGiles, *Branch Mgr*
EMP: 42
SALES (corp-wide): 160.5B **Publicly Held**
SIC: 4813 Local & long distance telephone communications
HQ: Alltel Communications Corp
    66 N 4th St
    Newark OH 43055
    740 349-8551

(G-2740)
AYRSHIRE INC
191 Fifth Ave (44024-1005)
P.O. Box 172 (44024-0172)
PHONE.................................440 286-9507
Fax: 440 285-8262
Randall Darling, *President*
H W Bernstein, *Principal*
D M Dworken, *Principal*
M E Resnick, *Principal*
Ken Jamison, *Vice Pres*
EMP: 50 EST: 1975
SQ FT: 5,000
SALES (est): 12.9MM **Privately Held**
WEB: www.ayrshireinc.com
SIC: 1541 Industrial buildings, new construction

(G-2741)
BASS LAKE TAVERN INC
Also Called: Bass Lake Inn
426 South St (44024-1448)
PHONE.................................440 285-3100
Fax: 440 285-9393
Thomas Lutz, *President*
Erik Heatwole, *Vice Pres*
EMP: 60
SQ FT: 8,000
SALES (est): 1.5MM **Privately Held**
WEB: www.basslakeinn.com
SIC: 5812 5813 7011 American restaurant; bar (drinking places); bed & breakfast inn

(G-2742)
CHARDON LAKES GOLF COURSE INC (PA)
470 South St (44024-2804)
PHONE.................................440 285-4653
Jerry Peterson, *President*
Rick Heterstrom, *General Mgr*
Tom Bond, *Manager*
Bob Acquaviva, *Asst Mgr*
EMP: 40
SQ FT: 300
SALES (est): 1.2MM **Privately Held**
SIC: 7992 Public golf courses

(G-2743)
CHARDON TOOL & SUPPLY CO INC
115 Parker Ct (44024-1112)
P.O. Box 291 (44024-0291)
PHONE.................................440 286-6440
Fax: 440 286-7165
Weldon Bennett, *President*
Donna Blewett, *Principal*
Marshall Meadows, *Principal*
Andrew O'Dell, *Principal*

Chardon - Geauga County (G-2744)

Mazie Smith, *Office Mgr*
EMP: 35
SQ FT: 4,800
SALES: 3MM **Privately Held**
SIC: 3545 5085 Diamond cutting tools for turning, boring, burnishing, etc.; diamonds, industrial: natural, crude

(G-2744)
CLEMSON EXCAVATING INC
9954 Old State Rd (44024-9521)
P.O. Box 224 (44024-0224)
PHONE.................................440 286-4757
Bill Clemson, *President*
Shirley Clemson, *Corp Secy*
Murl Clemson, *Vice Pres*
Bonnie Clemson, *Manager*
EMP: 25
SQ FT: 2,500
SALES (est): 2.8MM **Privately Held**
SIC: 1794 Excavation & grading, building construction

(G-2745)
COUNTY OF GEAUGA
107 South St Ste 5 (44024-1375)
PHONE.................................440 286-6264
Linda Reed, *Director*
EMP: 123 Privately Held
SIC: 8093 Mental health clinic, outpatient
PA: County Of Geauga
470 Center St Bldg 4
Chardon OH 44024
440 285-2222

(G-2746)
COUNTY OF GEAUGA
Also Called: Job and Family Service
12480 Ravenwood Dr (44024-9009)
P.O. Box 309 (44024-0309)
PHONE.................................440 564-2246
EMP: 85 Privately Held
SIC: 8331 8322 Job Training/Related Services Individual/Family Services
PA: County Of Geauga
470 Center St Bldg 4
Chardon OH 44024

(G-2747)
COUNTY OF GEAUGA
Also Called: Geauga County Jobs & Fmly Svcs
12480 Ravenwood Dr (44024-9009)
P.O. Box 309 (44024-0309)
PHONE.................................440 285-9141
Fax: 440 286-6654
Tim Taylor, *Director*
EMP: 80 Privately Held
SIC: 8322 Public welfare center
PA: County Of Geauga
470 Center St Bldg 4
Chardon OH 44024
440 285-2222

(G-2748)
E2B TEKNOLOGIES INC (PA)
521 5th Ave (44024-1088)
PHONE.................................440 352-4700
Fax: 440 352-9342
William Henslee, *President*
Mark Hanson, *General Mgr*
Lauren Sweeney, *Accounts Mgr*
Lynne L Henslee, *Branch Mgr*
Angela Harris, *Manager*
EMP: 45
SQ FT: 10,000
SALES: 6MM **Privately Held**
WEB: www.e2btek.com
SIC: 7379 Computer related consulting services

(G-2749)
ENVIROTEST SYSTEMS CORP
10632 Auburn Rd (44024-9646)
PHONE.................................330 963-4464
Mike Hensley, *Branch Mgr*
EMP: 34 Privately Held
WEB: www.il.etest.com
SIC: 7549 Emissions testing without repairs, automotive
HQ: Envirotest Systems Corp.
7 Kripes Rd
East Granby CT 06026

(G-2750)
GEAUGA MECHANICAL COMPANY
12585 Chardon Windsor Rd (44024-8968)
PHONE.................................440 285-2000
Fax: 440 285-2006
Bruce Berman, *President*
Ted R Beman, *Vice Pres*
Ted R Berman, *Vice Pres*
Bryan Wadsworth, *Project Mgr*
Jeff Fishman, *Foreman/Supr*
EMP: 72
SQ FT: 15,000
SALES (est): 15.1MM **Privately Held**
WEB: www.geaugamechanical.com
SIC: 1711 1761 Warm air heating & air conditioning contractor; sheet metalwork

(G-2751)
GEM ELECTRIC
12577 Gar Hwy (44024-9201)
PHONE.................................440 286-6200
Patrick Nusrala, *Owner*
Gregory Harriss, *Admin Asst*
EMP: 25
SQ FT: 3,000
SALES: 4MM **Privately Held**
SIC: 1731 General electrical contractor

(G-2752)
HEATHERHILL CARE COMMUNITIES
12340 Bass Lake Rd (44024-8327)
PHONE.................................440 285-4040
Fax: 440 285-7278
Jim Homa, *President*
Andy Bragalone, *Principal*
Beejadi Makunda, *COO*
Lynette Gesicki, *HR Admin*
Margaret Milyo, *Human Resources*
EMP: 47
SALES (est): 3.6MM **Privately Held**
SIC: 8051 Skilled nursing care facilities

(G-2753)
JPMORGAN CHASE BANK NAT ASSN
100 Center St Ste 100 (44024-1181)
PHONE.................................440 286-6111
Lisa Timms, *Manager*
Lisa Tims, *Manager*
EMP: 26
SALES (corp-wide): 99.6B **Publicly Held**
WEB: www.chase.com
SIC: 6021 National commercial banks
HQ: Jpmorgan Chase Bank, National Association
1111 Polaris Pkwy
Columbus OH 43240
614 436-3055

(G-2754)
JUST 4 KIDZ CHILDCARE
13896 Gar Hwy (44024-9251)
PHONE.................................440 285-2221
Fax: 440 279-0152
Tina Prince, *Director*
EMP: 25
SALES (est): 636.3K **Privately Held**
SIC: 8351 Child day care services

(G-2755)
LANXESS CORPORATION
145 Parker Ct (44024-1112)
PHONE.................................440 279-2367
EMP: 250
SALES (corp-wide): 11.4B **Privately Held**
SIC: 3069 5169 Reclaimed rubber & specialty rubber compounds; industrial chemicals
HQ: Lanxess Corporation
111 Parkwest Dr
Pittsburgh PA 15275
800 526-9377

(G-2756)
LEGEND LAKE GOLF CLUB INC
11135 Auburn Rd (44024-9306)
PHONE.................................440 285-3110
Fax: 440 285-3136
Lou Alexander, *President*
Jim Jevnikar, *General Mgr*
Orion McCarty, *General Mgr*
Mike Mucciarone, *General Mgr*
Sandy Danison, *Manager*
EMP: 40
SQ FT: 5,400
SALES (est): 1.7MM **Privately Held**
SIC: 7997 Golf club, membership

(G-2757)
MCI COMMUNICATIONS SVCS INC
Also Called: Verizon Business
12956 Taylor Wells Rd (44024-7910)
PHONE.................................440 635-0418
Dane Oneill, *Branch Mgr*
EMP: 450
SALES (corp-wide): 126B **Publicly Held**
SIC: 4813 Long distance telephone communications
HQ: Mci Communications Services, Inc.
22001 Loudoun County Pkwy
Ashburn VA 20147
703 886-5600

(G-2758)
MOUNTAIN FOODS INC
9761 Ravenna Rd (44024-9114)
PHONE.................................440 286-7177
John Youdath, *President*
Sandra Youdath, *Vice Pres*
◆ **EMP:** 30
SQ FT: 20,000
SALES (est): 12.1MM **Privately Held**
SIC: 5141 Groceries, general line

(G-2759)
NMS INC CERTIF PUB ACCOUNTANTS (PA)
121 South St (44024-1306)
PHONE.................................440 286-5222
Fax: 440 286-4300
Shawn Neece, *President*
George Malec, *Vice Pres*
Brian Seifert, *Treasurer*
Jessica Marker, *Controller*
Michael Duffy, *CPA*
EMP: 31
SQ FT: 9,000
SALES (est): 3.5MM **Privately Held**
WEB: www.neececpa.com
SIC: 8721 Certified public accountant

(G-2760)
NOTRE DAME COLLEGE OF OHIO
Also Called: Notre Dame Pre-School
13000 Auburn Rd (44024-9337)
PHONE.................................440 279-1127
David Bellini, *Psychologist*
Jennifer Hanna, *Director*
Grace Corbett, *Teacher*
Cassandra Long, *Teacher*
Christine Nemecek, *Teacher*
EMP: 25
SALES (est): 1MM
SALES (corp-wide): 50.5MM **Privately Held**
SIC: 8351 Preschool center
PA: The Notre Dame College Of Ohio
4545 College Rd
Cleveland OH 44121
216 381-1680

(G-2761)
PARKSIDE CARE CORPORATION
Also Called: Hospice of Care
831 South St (44024-1438)
PHONE.................................440 286-2273
Fax: 440 286-7662
Jason Baker, *CEO*
Cindy Brostek, *Office Mgr*
EMP: 80
SALES (est): 3.1MM **Privately Held**
SIC: 8082 Home health care services

(G-2762)
PENTAIR RSDNTIAL FLTRATION LLC
220 Park Dr (44024-1091)
PHONE.................................440 286-4116
Kevin Williams, *Principal*
◆ **EMP:** 32 **EST:** 2008
SALES (est): 4.5MM **Privately Held**
SIC: 4971 Irrigation systems

(G-2763)
RAVENWOOD MENTAL HLTH CTR INC (PA)
Also Called: Ravenwood Health
12557 Ravenwood Dr (44024-9009)
PHONE.................................440 285-3568
Fax: 440 285-4552
Vicki Clark, *CEO*
Elisa Gagliardi, *Accountant*
Deanna Brant, *Director*
EMP: 35
SALES: 7.4MM **Privately Held**
SIC: 8093 Mental health clinic, outpatient

(G-2764)
RESIDENCE ARTISTS INC
220 5th Ave (44024-1075)
PHONE.................................440 286-8822
Fax: 440 286-8218
Keith Landies, *President*
Tina Vankan, *Admin Sec*
EMP: 40
SALES (est): 3.7MM **Privately Held**
WEB: www.residenceartists.com
SIC: 1721 1521 1542 Residential painting; exterior commercial painting contractor; new construction, single-family houses; commercial & office buildings, renovation & repair

(G-2765)
RESIDENCE OF CHARDON
Also Called: Residents of Chardon
501 Chardon Windsor Rd (44024-8944)
PHONE.................................440 286-2277
Fax: 440 286-2249
Debbie Bowman, *Financial Exec*
Christin Johnson, *Administration*
EMP: 60 **EST:** 2000
SALES (est): 1.9MM **Privately Held**
SIC: 8052 Intermediate care facilities

(G-2766)
SAINT MARY PARISH
Also Called: Church of St Mary Catholic
401 North St (44024-1035)
PHONE.................................440 285-7051
Fax: 440 286-3886
Tom Behrend, *Principal*
Sandy Nativio, *Principal*
Daniel P Redmond, *Pastor*
Thomas C Gilles, *Pastor*
Jeanette Stone, *Senior Mgr*
EMP: 55
SALES (est): 2.1MM **Privately Held**
SIC: 8661 8611 Catholic Church; community affairs & services

(G-2767)
SAND RIDGE GOLF CLUB
12150 Mayfield Rd (44024-8448)
PHONE.................................440 285-8088
Peter Conway, *President*
Bill Conway, *Chairman*
Mary Samide, *Info Tech Mgr*
EMP: 100
SALES (est): 5.2MM **Privately Held**
SIC: 7997 5941 5812 Golf club, membership; sporting goods & bicycle shops; box lunch stand

(G-2768)
SOMMERSET DEVELOPMENT LTD
10585 Somerset Dr (44024-8946)
P.O. Box 1102 (44024-5102)
PHONE.................................440 286-6194
Sharon Sommers, *President*
EMP: 155
SQ FT: 1,000
SALES (est): 10.5MM **Privately Held**
SIC: 6552 7353 Land subdividers & developers, commercial; heavy construction equipment rental

(G-2769)
STAT INTEGRATED TECH INC (PA)
Also Called: Aqua Doc Lake & Pond MGT
10779 Mayfield Rd (44024-9323)
P.O. Box 625, Chesterland (44026-0625)
PHONE.................................440 286-7663
Fax: 440 286-1300
Jeanine Wilson, *President*
Beverly Sherley, *Manager*

EMP: 34
SALES (est): 7.8MM Privately Held
SIC: 8741 Management services

(G-2770)
STEMBANC INC
100 7th Ave Ste 200 (44024-7805)
PHONE 440 332-4279
Fax: 440 286-7575
Archibald Grabinski, *CEO*
Edward Cup, *CFO*
Debbie Richards, *Director*
EMP: 40
SALES (est): 2.3MM Privately Held
WEB: www.stembanc.com
SIC: 8071 8731 Biological laboratory; biological research

(G-2771)
THRASHER DINSMORE & DOLAN (PA)
Also Called: Thrasher Dinsmore & Doland
100 7th Ave Ste 150 (44024)
PHONE 440 285-2242
Fax: 440 285-9423
Lawrence J Dolan, *President*
Matthew J Dolan, *Principal*
Brandon Dynes, *Counsel*
David E Lowe, *Vice Pres*
Dale H Markowitz, *Treasurer*
EMP: 25
SALES (est): 4.1MM Privately Held
WEB: www.dolan.law.pro
SIC: 8111 General practice law office

(G-2772)
UAHS HEATHER HILL HOME HEALTH
12340 Bass Lake Rd (44024-8327)
PHONE 440 285-5098
Fax: 440 285-0946
Danielle Lynce, *Human Res Mgr*
Louise McKorkell, *Director*
Lori Rust, *Director*
Kurt Meyer, *Administration*
EMP: 50
SQ FT: 7,915
SALES (est): 3.3MM
SALES (corp-wide): 19.4MM Privately Held
WEB: www.heatherhill.com
SIC: 8082 Home health care services
PA: University Hospitals Health System-Heather Hill, Inc.
12340 Bass Lake Rd
Chardon OH 44024
440 285-4040

(G-2773)
UNIVERSAL DISPOSAL INC
9954 Old State Rd (44024-9521)
P.O. Box 1065 (44024-5065)
PHONE 440 286-3153
Fax: 440 285-7239
Murl Clemson, *President*
Shirley Clemson, *Corp Secy*
Bill Clemson, *Vice Pres*
EMP: 50
SQ FT: 1,500
SALES (est): 6.3MM Privately Held
SIC: 4212 Garbage collection & transport, no disposal

(G-2774)
UNIVERSITY HOSPITALS
Also Called: Uhhs-Geauga Regional Hospital
13207 Ravenna Rd (44024-7032)
PHONE 440 285-6000
Fax: 440 286-7219
Steven Jones, *President*
Judy Ernest, *Editor*
Robert Forino, *Vice Chairman*
Amitabh Goel, *Dept Chairman*
Dichai Duangjak, *Ch OB/GYN*
EMP: 613 EST: 1952
SQ FT: 280,000
SALES: 140.4MM
SALES (corp-wide): 2.3B Privately Held
SIC: 8062 General medical & surgical hospitals
PA: University Hospitals Health System, Inc.
3605 Warrensville Ctr Rd
Shaker Heights OH 44122
216 767-8900

(G-2775)
UNIVERSITY HOSPITALS HEALTH (PA)
Also Called: Heather HI Rehabilitation Hosp
12340 Bass Lake Rd (44024-8327)
PHONE 440 285-4040
Fax: 440 285-4378
Louise Alexander, *Ch of Bd*
Susan Juris, *President*
Alan Lerner, *General Mgr*
Linton Sharpnack, *COO*
David Pasco, *Vice Pres*
EMP: 550 EST: 1935
SQ FT: 39,000
SALES: 19.4MM Privately Held
SIC: 8069 8059 8052 8051 Specialty hospitals, except psychiatric; convalescent home; rest home, with health care; intermediate care facilities; skilled nursing care facilities

(G-2776)
VISITING NURSE SERVICE INC
Also Called: Geauga Cnty Visiting Nurse Svc
13221 Ravenna Rd Ste 1 (44024-9016)
PHONE 440 286-9461
Fax: 440 286-9695
Pat Stagner, *Principal*
EMP: 30
SALES (corp-wide): 21.8MM Privately Held
WEB: www.vnsa.com
SIC: 8082 Visiting nurse service
PA: Visiting Nurse Service, Inc.
1 Home Care Pl
Akron OH 44320
330 745-1601

(G-2777)
WASTE MANAGEMENT OHIO INC
10237 Cutts Rd (44024-9185)
PHONE 440 286-7116
Fax: 216 286-5400
Vince Crawford, *Plant Mgr*
Ginger Kaladas, *Credit Staff*
Elmer Hershfield, *Manager*
Bill Skidmore, *Manager*
Marlyn Gallus, *Director*
EMP: 49
SQ FT: 866
SALES (corp-wide): 14.4B Publicly Held
WEB: www.wm.com
SIC: 4953 4212 Refuse systems; local trucking, without storage
HQ: Waste Management Of Ohio, Inc.
1700 N Broad St
Fairborn OH 45324

(G-2778)
WATER LEASING CO LLC
Also Called: Chardon Healthcare Center
620 Water St (44024-1149)
PHONE 440 285-9400
David W Trimble, *CPA*
Stephen L Rosedale, *Mng Member*
Ronald S Wilheim, *Mng Member*
Becky Warren, *Food Svc Dir*
EMP: 150
SALES (est): 5.9MM Privately Held
SIC: 8051 Convalescent home with continuous nursing care

(G-2779)
WOODWORKERS OUTLET
510 Center St (44024-1004)
P.O. Box 1099 (44024-5099)
PHONE 440 286-3942
Dan Walter, *Owner*
EMP: 30
SALES (est): 2MM Privately Held
SIC: 5084 Industrial machinery & equipment

(G-2780)
YOUNG MNS CHRSTN ASSN CLVELAND
Also Called: YMCA
12460 Bass Lake Rd (44024-8315)
PHONE 440 285-7543
Alexandria Nichols, *Branch Mgr*
EMP: 90
SALES (corp-wide): 29.2MM Privately Held
SIC: 8641 7991 8351 7032 Youth organizations; physical fitness facilities; child day care services; youth camps; individual & family services
PA: Young Men's Christian Association Of Cleveland
1801 Superior Ave E # 130
Cleveland OH 44114
216 781-1337

Chesapeake
Lawrence County

(G-2781)
BIG SANDY FURNITURE INC
Also Called: Big Sandy Superstore
45 County Rd 407 (45619)
PHONE 740 894-4242
Fax: 740 894-3026
Buck Ellis, *Manager*
EMP: 50 Privately Held
WEB: www.bigsandyfurniture.com
SIC: 4225 5712 General warehousing & storage; furniture stores
HQ: Big Sandy Furniture, Inc.
8375 Gallia Pike
Franklin Furnace OH 45629
740 574-2113

(G-2782)
COLLINS CAREER CENTER
11627 State Route 243 (45619-7962)
PHONE 740 867-6641
Fax: 740 867-2009
Gerald Love, *President*
Steve Dodgion, *Superintendent*
Harold Shafer, *Superintendent*
Perry Walls, *Superintendent*
Jim Howard, *Principal*
EMP: 90
SALES (est): 5.7MM Privately Held
WEB: www.collinscareercenter.com
SIC: 8331 Job training & vocational rehabilitation services

(G-2783)
CONNECTLINK INC
406 2nd Ave (45619-1026)
P.O. Box 740 (45619-0740)
PHONE 740 867-5095
Phil Henson, *President*
Amy Henson, *CFO*
Amy Henson, *Marketing Staff*
EMP: 25
SALES (est): 1.8MM Privately Held
SIC: 4813

(G-2784)
G BIG INC (PA)
Also Called: Pickett Concrete
441 Rockwood Ave (45619-1120)
PHONE 740 867-5758
Fax: 740 867-5758
John W Galloway, *President*
James W Galloway, *Vice Pres*
Todd A Galloway, *Vice Pres*
William Smith, *Manager*
EMP: 25
SQ FT: 2,000
SALES (est): 3.8MM Privately Held
WEB: www.gbig.com
SIC: 3273 1771 Ready-mixed concrete; concrete work

(G-2785)
KLLEE TRUCKING INC
1714 Township Road 278 (45619-7606)
PHONE 740 867-6454
Sandra Adkins, *President*
David Stump, *Manager*
Kelly Stump, *Admin Sec*
EMP: 55
SALES (est): 2.5MM Privately Held
SIC: 4213 Trucking, except local

(G-2786)
PREMIER MANAGEMENT CO INC
805 3rd Ave (45619-1045)
P.O. Box 274 (45619-0274)
PHONE 740 867-2144
Fax: 740 867-2141
Jon Barker, *President*
Becki Carpenter, *Office Mgr*
Teffaney Barker, *Admin Sec*
EMP: 25
SQ FT: 3,500
SALES (est): 1.2MM Privately Held
SIC: 8741 Management services

(G-2787)
RESCARE
11090 County Road 1 (45619-7019)
PHONE 740 867-3051
Fax: 740 867-3181
Coleen Houck, *General Mgr*
Coleen Hauk, *Manager*
Angela Halfhill, *Nursing Dir*
EMP: 30
SALES (est): 617.8K
SALES (corp-wide): 24.5B Privately Held
SIC: 8361 8052 Group foster home; intermediate care facilities
HQ: Rescare Homecare
9901 Linn Station Rd
Louisville KY 40223
502 394-2100

(G-2788)
RESCARE OHIO INC
1107 Us Hwy 52 (45619)
PHONE 740 867-4568
Sherrie Carter, *Manager*
Don Barickman, *Manager*
Karen Gunter, *Manager*
EMP: 25
SALES (corp-wide): 24.5B Privately Held
SIC: 8082 Home health care services
HQ: Rescare Ohio Inc
348 W Main St
Williamsburg OH 45176

Cheshire
Gallia County

(G-2789)
DISABLED AMERICAN VETERANS
Also Called: Dav Chapter 53
28051 State Route 7 (45620-9603)
PHONE 740 367-7973
Danver Curtis, *Principal*
EMP: 374
SALES (corp-wide): 202.6MM Privately Held
SIC: 8641 Veterans' organization
PA: Disabled American Veterans
3725 Alexandria Pike
Cold Spring KY 41076
859 441-7300

(G-2790)
GALLIA-MEIGS COMMUNITY ACTION (PA)
8010 State Route 7 N (45620-7700)
P.O. Box 272 (45620-0272)
PHONE 740 367-7341
Fax: 740 367-7343
Michael Davenport, *Ch of Bd*
Tony Gallagher, *Vice Pres*
Tarissa Beaver, *Finance*
Tom Reed, *Exec Dir*
Linda Lester, *Admin Sec*
EMP: 28
SQ FT: 3,600
SALES: 3.1MM Privately Held
SIC: 8322 Individual & family services

(G-2791)
GAVIN AEP PLANT
7397 State Route 7 N (45620-7500)
P.O. Box 271 (45620-0271)
PHONE 740 925-3166
EMP: 26
SALES (est): 14.4MM Privately Held
SIC: 4911 Electric services

Chesterland
Geauga County

(G-2792)
AMERICAN GOLF CORPORATION
Also Called: Fowlers Mill Golf Course
13095 Rockhaven Rd (44026-3311)
PHONE......................440 286-9544
Fax: 440 286-7595
Mike Mucciarone, *General Mgr*
Keith Goodge, *Superintendent*
Erin Frank, *Sales Staff*
David Scull, *Manager*
Matthew Baca, *Manager*
EMP: 55
SALES (corp-wide): 621.9MM **Privately Held**
WEB: www.americangolf.com
SIC: 7997 Country club, membership
PA: American Golf Corporation
6080 Center Dr Ste 500
Los Angeles CA 90045
310 664-4000

(G-2793)
BRIGHTVIEW LANDSCAPES LLC
7901 Old Ranger Rd (44026)
PHONE......................440 729-2302
Fax: 440 729-2407
Tim Korte, *Manager*
EMP: 50
SALES (corp-wide): 914MM **Privately Held**
SIC: 0781 0782 Landscape services; lawn services
HQ: Brightview Landscapes, Llc
401 Plymouth Rd Ste 500
Plymouth Meeting PA 19462
484 567-7204

(G-2794)
CREATIVE LEARNING CHILD CARE
7654 Sherman Rd (44026-2026)
PHONE......................440 729-9001
REA Wedekamm, *President*
Donald Wedekamm, *Vice Pres*
EMP: 35
SALES: 508.4K **Privately Held**
WEB: www.creativelearningchildcare.com
SIC: 8351 Group day care center

(G-2795)
FAIRMOUNT MINERALS LLC
Also Called: Fairmount Santrol
8834 Mayfield Rd Ste A (44026-2696)
P.O. Box 400 (44026-0400)
PHONE......................269 926-9450
Jenniffer Deckard, *CEO*
EMP: 200
SALES: 988MM
SALES (corp-wide): 959.8MM **Publicly Held**
SIC: 1446 Industrial sand
HQ: Fairmount Santrol Inc.
8834 Mayfield Rd Ste A
Chesterland OH 44026
440 214-3200

(G-2796)
FML RESIN LLC
8834 Mayfield Rd (44026-2690)
PHONE......................440 214-3200
Jenniffer D Deckard, *President*
EMP: 27
SALES (est): 23.2MM
SALES (corp-wide): 959.8MM **Publicly Held**
SIC: 1442 Construction sand & gravel
PA: Fairmount Santrol Holdings Inc.
8834 Mayfield Rd Ste A
Chesterland OH 44026
800 255-7263

(G-2797)
FML TERMINAL LOGISTICS LLC (DH)
8834 Mayfield Rd (44026-2690)
PHONE......................440 214-3200
Jennifer Deckard, *President*
EMP: 71
SALES (est): 3.6MM
SALES (corp-wide): 959.8MM **Publicly Held**
SIC: 1442 Construction sand & gravel
HQ: Fairmount Santrol Inc.
8834 Mayfield Rd Ste A
Chesterland OH 44026
440 214-3200

(G-2798)
G H A INC
Also Called: Turney's
12670 W Geauga Plz (44026-2505)
PHONE......................440 729-2130
Howard Adelman, *President*
Ann Adelman, *Vice Pres*
EMP: 30
SQ FT: 34,000
SALES (est): 873.3K **Privately Held**
SIC: 6531 Real estate managers

(G-2799)
MATO INC
Also Called: Avanti Salon
8027 Mayfield Rd (44026-2438)
PHONE......................440 729-9008
Fax: 440 729-1512
Marisa Paterniti, *President*
Tony Paterniti, *Vice Pres*
EMP: 30
SQ FT: 1,450
SALES (est): 1MM **Privately Held**
SIC: 7231 Cosmetology & personal hygiene salons

(G-2800)
METZENBAUM SHELTERED INDS
Also Called: MSI
8090 Cedar Rd (44026-3400)
PHONE......................440 729-1919
Robert Preston, *Chairman*
Keith Redfern, *Sales Mgr*
Robert Voss, *Manager*
Keith Werbeach, *Exec Dir*
Diane Buehner, *Admin Sec*
EMP: 160
SQ FT: 12,000
SALES: 2.4MM **Privately Held**
SIC: 8331 7389 3672 Sheltered workshop; packaging & labeling services; presorted mail service; printed circuit boards

(G-2801)
PROFESSIONAL HSE CLG SVCS INC
8228 Mayfield Rd Ste 1b (44026-2542)
PHONE......................440 729-7866
Shawn Day, *President*
EMP: 30
SQ FT: 1,200
SALES (est): 797.5K **Privately Held**
SIC: 7349 Cleaning service, industrial or commercial

(G-2802)
RES-CARE INC
Also Called: Raise
8228 Mayfield Rd Ste 5b (44026-2542)
PHONE......................440 729-2432
Kevin Cook, *Director*
EMP: 34
SALES (corp-wide): 24.5B **Privately Held**
WEB: www.rescare.com
SIC: 8082 Home health care services
HQ: Res-Care, Inc.
9901 Linn Station Rd
Louisville KY 40223
502 394-2100

(G-2803)
SPORTY EVENTS
8430 Mayfield Rd (44026-2580)
PHONE......................440 342-5046
David Gordon, *COO*
EMP: 25
SALES: 1.1MM **Privately Held**
WEB: www.sportyevents.com
SIC: 8699 5999 Amateur sports promotion; trophies & plaques

(G-2804)
SYCAMORE LAKE INC
Also Called: Alpine Valley Ski Area
10620 Mayfield Rd (44026-2738)
PHONE......................440 729-9775
Fax: 440 285-4844
Thomas Apthorp, *President*
Kent Young, *General Mgr*
S Sandy Sutlo, *Treasurer*
EMP: 200 EST: 1963
SQ FT: 22,000
SALES (est): 5.4MM **Privately Held**
WEB: www.alpinevalleyohio.com
SIC: 7011 5812 Ski lodge; caterers

(G-2805)
TOWNSHIP OF CHESTER
Also Called: Chester Township Fire Rescue
8552 Parkside Dr (44026-2643)
PHONE......................440 729-9951
John Wargelin, *Chief*
EMP: 40 **Privately Held**
SIC: 9224 7363 ; medical help service
PA: Township Of Chester
12701 Chillicothe Rd
Chesterland OH 44026
440 729-7058

Chesterville
Morrow County

(G-2806)
LEVERING MANAGEMENT INC
Also Called: Morrow Manor Nursing Home
115 N Portland St (43317)
PHONE......................419 768-2401
Fax: 419 768-9060
Matthew Hintz, *Director*
Darlene Yake, *Administration*
EMP: 50
SALES (corp-wide): 32.8MM **Privately Held**
SIC: 8741 8059 Management services; nursing home, except skilled & intermediate care facility
PA: Levering Management, Inc.
201 N Main St
Mount Vernon OH 43050
740 397-3897

Chillicothe
Ross County

(G-2807)
ACCURATE HEATING & COOLING
3001 River Rd (45601-8178)
PHONE......................740 775-5005
Tom White, *Owner*
EMP: 40
SALES (est): 2.6MM **Privately Held**
WEB: www.accuratehvac.com
SIC: 1711 Warm air heating & air conditioning contractor

(G-2808)
ADENA HEALTH SYSTEM
Also Called: Parks Ob Gyn Assoc
4439 State Route 159 # 120 (45601-8207)
PHONE......................740 779-7201
Fax: 740 779-7279
Susan Rowe, *Office Mgr*
Heidi Streitenberger, *Manager*
Lee H Parks, *Obstetrician*
Kristen Vickers, *Executive*
EMP: 29
SALES (corp-wide): 111.9MM **Privately Held**
WEB: www.adena.org
SIC: 8062 8031 Hospital, medical school affiliated with nursing & residency; offices & clinics of osteopathic physicians
PA: Adena Health System
272 Hospital Rd
Chillicothe OH 45601
740 779-7360

(G-2809)
ADENA HEALTH SYSTEM (PA)
Also Called: Greenfield Area Medical Center
272 Hospital Rd (45601-9031)
PHONE......................740 779-7360
Fax: 740 779-7463
Jeffrey J Graham, *President*
Eric Cecava, *COO*
Dale Hume, *Ch Radiology*
Nick Alexander, *Vice Pres*
James West, *Vice Pres*
EMP: 1130
SQ FT: 690,000
SALES: 111.9MM **Privately Held**
WEB: www.adena.org
SIC: 8062 Hospital, medical school affiliated with nursing & residency

(G-2810)
ADENA HEALTH SYSTEM
85 River Trce (45601-2686)
PHONE......................740 779-8995
EMP: 213
SALES (corp-wide): 111.9MM **Privately Held**
SIC: 8062 Hospital, medical school affiliated with nursing & residency
PA: Adena Health System
272 Hospital Rd
Chillicothe OH 45601
740 779-7360

(G-2811)
ADENA HEALTH SYSTEM
Also Called: Adena Rhblitation Wellness Ctr
445 Shawnee Ln (45601-4145)
PHONE......................740 779-4801
Fax: 740 779-7388
R Sorrell, *Manager*
EMP: 25
SALES (corp-wide): 111.9MM **Privately Held**
WEB: www.adena.org
SIC: 8062 Hospital, medical school affiliated with nursing & residency
PA: Adena Health System
272 Hospital Rd
Chillicothe OH 45601
740 779-7360

(G-2812)
ADENA HEALTH SYSTEM
Also Called: Adena Counseling Center
455 Shawnee Dr Ln (45601)
PHONE......................740 779-4888
Fax: 740 779-4898
R Sorrell, *Branch Mgr*
Young Lee, *Med Doctor*
EMP: 25
SALES (corp-wide): 111.9MM **Privately Held**
WEB: www.adena.org
SIC: 8322 General counseling services
PA: Adena Health System
272 Hospital Rd
Chillicothe OH 45601
740 779-7360

(G-2813)
ADENA PCKWY-ROSS FMLY PHYSCANS
100 N Walnut St (45601-2420)
PHONE......................740 779-4500
April Dollison, *General Mgr*
EMP: 30 EST: 2010
SALES (est): 110.4K **Privately Held**
SIC: 8011 General & family practice, physician/surgeon

(G-2814)
AMERICAN ELECTRIC POWER CO INC
701 Hardin Dr (45601-2780)
PHONE......................740 779-5261
Jeff Frazier, *Safety Dir*
EMP: 44
SALES (corp-wide): 15.4B **Publicly Held**
SIC: 4911 Generation, electric power
PA: American Electric Power Company, Inc.
1 Riverside Plz Fl 1 # 1
Columbus OH 43215
614 716-1000

GEOGRAPHIC SECTION
Chillicothe - Ross County (G-2839)

(G-2815)
B & B ROOFING INC
150 Cooks Hill Rd (45601-8220)
P.O. Box 6351 (45601-6351)
PHONE.................................740 772-4759
James Butt, *President*
Joe Zupi, *Vice Pres*
Melissa Butt, *Treasurer*
Jennifer Grooms, *Admin Sec*
EMP: 25
SQ FT: 9,000
SALES: 5.6K **Privately Held**
WEB: www.bandbroofing.com
SIC: 1761 Roofing contractor

(G-2816)
BIG SANDY FURNITURE INC
1404 N Bridge St (45601-4101)
PHONE.................................740 775-4244
Fax: 740 775-4354
Annette Dickess, *Financial Exec*
Mike Farmer, *Branch Mgr*
Marvin Jordan, *Executive*
EMP: 30 **Privately Held**
WEB: www.bigsandyfurniture.com
SIC: 4225 5722 5712 General warehousing & storage; electric household appliances, major; furniture stores
HQ: Big Sandy Furniture, Inc.
8375 Gallia Pike
Franklin Furnace OH 45629
740 574-2113

(G-2817)
CHILLICOTHE BOWLING LANES INC
Also Called: Shawnee Trophies & Sptg Gds
1680 N Bridge St (45601-4105)
PHONE.................................740 773-3300
Fax: 740 773-3311
John Corcoran, *President*
Walter Highland, *Treasurer*
Kenneth De Long, *Admin Sec*
EMP: 26
SQ FT: 39,600
SALES: 1.2MM **Privately Held**
SIC: 7933 5812 5813 5941 Ten pin center; snack bar; cocktail lounge; bowling equipment & supplies

(G-2818)
CHILLICOTHE CITY SCHOOL DST
Also Called: Chillicothe Cty Sch Trans Off
89 Riverside St (45601-2547)
PHONE.................................740 775-2936
Bobbi Lowry, *Director*
EMP: 26
SALES (est): 601.7K
SALES (corp-wide): 52.2MM **Privately Held**
SIC: 4151 7521 7538 School buses; automobile storage garage; general automotive repair shops
PA: Chillicothe City School District
425 Yoctangee Pkwy
Chillicothe OH 45601
740 775-4250

(G-2819)
CHILLICOTHE COUNTRY CLUB CO
Woodbridge Ave & Arch St (45601)
PHONE.................................740 775-0150
Fax: 740 775-0752
Bill Jones, *President*
Chris Frey, *General Mgr*
Carvel Simmons, *Vice Pres*
Noble Yoshida, *Treasurer*
Beth Gilmore, *Manager*
EMP: 30
SALES: 1MM **Privately Held**
SIC: 7997 Country club, membership

(G-2820)
CHILLICOTHE FAMILY PHYSICIANS
60 Capital Dr (45601-1186)
PHONE.................................740 779-4100
Fax: 740 779-4149
Paul Mc Carter, *President*
Wayne W Beam Jr, *Family Practiti*
EMP: 25
SALES (est): 1.5MM **Privately Held**
SIC: 8011 General & family practice, physician/surgeon

(G-2821)
CHILLICOTHE LONG TERM CARE
Also Called: Westmoreland Place
230 Cherry St (45601-2301)
PHONE.................................740 773-6161
Fax: 740 773-6165
Ron Alltop, *Facilities Dir*
Ellen Wallace, *Facilities Dir*
Diane Rau, *Human Res Dir*
Julie Decamp, *Pub Rel Dir*
Diana Cole, *Office Mgr*
EMP: 140
SALES (est): 5.2MM
SALES (corp-wide): 970.6MM **Privately Held**
WEB: www.westmorelandplace.com
SIC: 8051 Extended care facility
PA: Chillicothe Long Term Care Inc
7265 Kenwood Rd Ste 300
Cincinnati OH 45236
513 793-8804

(G-2822)
CHILLICOTHE MOTEL LLC
Also Called: Comfort Inn
20 N Plaza Blvd (45601-1757)
PHONE.................................740 773-3903
Fax: 740 775-3588
John Woods, *General Mgr*
Patrick K McCalister,
Wen F Chen MD,
Ron Fewster,
Tom White,
EMP: 34
SQ FT: 40,000
SALES (est): 1.3MM **Privately Held**
SIC: 7011 7991 Hotel, franchised; physical fitness facilities

(G-2823)
CHILLICOTHE OPCO LLC
60 Marietta Rd (45601-9433)
PHONE.................................740 772-5900
William D Orand, *CEO*
Kimberly Russell, *Asst Mgr*
Scott Burleyson,
EMP: 99
SALES (est): 2MM **Privately Held**
SIC: 8051 Skilled nursing care facilities
PA: Signature Healthcare, Llc
12201 Bluegrass Pkwy
Louisville KY 40299

(G-2824)
CHILLICOTHE RACQUET CLUB
Also Called: Csrc
1245 Western Ave (45601-1169)
PHONE.................................740 773-4928
Fax: 740 773-4930
Aaron Koch, *Partner*
Charles Halm, *Partner*
EMP: 30
SQ FT: 32,000
SALES (est): 672.6K **Privately Held**
SIC: 7997 7991 Tennis club, membership; racquetball club, membership; physical fitness facilities

(G-2825)
CHILLICOTHE TELEPHONE COMPANY (HQ)
68 E Main St (45601-2503)
P.O. Box 480 (45601-0480)
PHONE.................................740 772-8200
Fax: 740 775-7606
William Mc Kell, *CEO*
David Polk, *Vice Pres*
Chris Glassburn, *Human Res Dir*
Pamela Cox, *Benefits Mgr*
Tom Krouse, *Mktg Dir*
EMP: 130 EST: 1927
SQ FT: 80,000
SALES (est): 71.8MM **Privately Held**
SIC: 4813 4841 Local telephone communications; cable television services

(G-2826)
CHILLICOTHE TELEPHONE COMPANY
861 Orange St (45601-1341)
P.O. Box 480 (45601-0480)
PHONE.................................740 772-8361
Fax: 740 779-9307
Greg Haas, *Manager*
Rick Mitten, *Network Tech*
EMP: 75
SALES (est): 2.7MM **Privately Held**
SIC: 4813 5999 Local telephone communications; telephone equipment & systems
HQ: The Chillicothe Telephone Company
68 E Main St
Chillicothe OH 45601
740 772-8200

(G-2827)
CLARY TRUCKING INC
1177 Eastern Ave (45601-9102)
PHONE.................................740 702-4242
Jesse Clary, *President*
EMP: 49
SALES (est): 693.7K **Privately Held**
SIC: 4212 Local trucking, without storage

(G-2828)
CORPORATE HEALTH DIMENSIONS
Also Called: Mead Family Medical Ctr
311 Caldwell St (45601-3332)
PHONE.................................740 775-6119
Fax: 740 775-6999
Roy E Manning, *Med Doctor*
Dawn Limle, *Manager*
EMP: 25
SALES (corp-wide): 630.3MM **Privately Held**
SIC: 8741 8011 Hospital management; general & family practice, physician/surgeon
HQ: Corporate Health Dimensions, Inc
40 British American Blvd # 2
Latham NY 12110
518 843-2300

(G-2829)
COUNTY ENGINEERS OFFICE
Also Called: Garage, The
755 Fairgrounds Rd (45601-9702)
PHONE.................................740 702-3130
Fax: 740 702-3135
Charles Ortman, *Engineer*
EMP: 25 EST: 1800
SALES (est): 3.2MM **Privately Held**
SIC: 8711 7538 Engineering services; general automotive repair shops

(G-2830)
COUNTY OF ROSS
Also Called: South Cntrl OH Rgnl Juv Dtn CT
182 Cattail Rd (45601-9404)
PHONE.................................740 773-4169
Fax: 740 773-6630
Cathy Fenner, *Superintendent*
EMP: 36 **Privately Held**
WEB: www.rosscountycommissioners.com
SIC: 8361 9223 Juvenile correctional facilities; detention center, government
PA: County Of Ross
2 N Paint St Ste H
Chillicothe OH 45601
740 702-3085

(G-2831)
COURT DIALYSIS LLC
Also Called: Adena Dialysis
1180 N Bridge St (45601-1793)
PHONE.................................740 773-3733
Jim Hilger, *Principal*
EMP: 37
SALES (est): 707.1K **Publicly Held**
SIC: 8092 Kidney dialysis centers
PA: Davita Inc.
2000 16th St
Denver CO 80202

(G-2832)
D E HUDDLESTON INC
283 S Paint St (45601-3829)
P.O. Box 207 (45601-0207)
PHONE.................................740 773-2130
Fax: 740 775-6268
Don Huddleston, *President*
Don Anderson, *Vice Pres*
Jeff Huddleston, *Admin Sec*
EMP: 25
SQ FT: 2,000
SALES (est): 3.8MM **Privately Held**
WEB: www.dehuddleston.com
SIC: 1541 1542 Industrial buildings, new construction; commercial & office building, new construction

(G-2833)
DANBARRY LINEMAS INC
119 Pawnee Rd (45601-1770)
PHONE.................................740 779-6115
Danny Heilbrun, *President*
EMP: 30
SALES (est): 374.7K **Privately Held**
SIC: 7832 Exhibitors, itinerant: motion picture

(G-2834)
DAVE PINKERTON
Also Called: Advance Services
221 Renick Ave (45601-2852)
PHONE.................................740 477-8888
Fax: 740 773-6245
Dave Pinkerton, *Owner*
Ronda Valentine, *Administration*
EMP: 25
SALES (est): 2.6MM **Privately Held**
SIC: 1711 Heating & air conditioning contractors

(G-2835)
DETILLION LANDSCAPING CO INC
20337 State Route 104 (45601-8489)
PHONE.................................740 775-5305
Fax: 740 773-3490
Randy Detillion, *President*
Cynthia Detillion, *Corp Secy*
EMP: 40
SQ FT: 800
SALES (est): 2.7MM **Privately Held**
SIC: 0781 0782 Landscape planning services; lawn care services

(G-2836)
FAMILY NURSING SERVICES INC
24 Star Dr (45601-9845)
PHONE.................................740 775-5463
Fax: 740 775-5464
Randy Rush, *President*
Renee Hatton, *Manager*
EMP: 50
SALES (est): 1.4MM **Privately Held**
WEB: www.familynursingservices.com
SIC: 8082 Visiting nurse service

(G-2837)
FEDEX FREIGHT CORPORATION
377 Gateway Dr (45601-3976)
PHONE.................................800 979-9232
Tim Rush, *Manager*
Jon Dorfmeyer, *Manager*
EMP: 34
SALES (corp-wide): 60.3B **Publicly Held**
SIC: 4513 Air courier services
HQ: Fedex Freight Corporation
1715 Aaron Brenner Dr
Memphis TN 38120

(G-2838)
FEDEX GROUND PACKAGE SYS INC
1415 Industrial Dr (45601-3977)
PHONE.................................800 463-3339
Brian Lowther, *Office Mgr*
EMP: 34
SALES (corp-wide): 60.3B **Publicly Held**
WEB: www.fedex.com
SIC: 4513 Package delivery, private air
HQ: Fedex Ground Package System, Inc.
1000 Fed Ex Dr
Coraopolis PA 15108
412 269-1000

(G-2839)
FIRST CAPITAL BANCSHARES INC
33 W Main St (45601-3131)
P.O. Box 463 (45601-0463)
PHONE.................................740 775-6777
Thomas Beard, *President*

Chillicothe - Ross County (G-2840) — GEOGRAPHIC SECTION

John H Kochensparger III, *Chairman*
EMP: 55 **Privately Held**
SIC: 6712 6021 Bank holding companies; national commercial banks

(G-2840)
FIRST CAPITAL ENTERPRISES INC
505 E 7th St (45601-3632)
PHONE 740 773-2166
Fax: 740 773-2167
Howard Percival, *General Mgr*
Ron Sarrar, *Director*
James Lambert, *Admin Asst*
EMP: 60
SQ FT: 18,000
SALES: 2.8MM **Privately Held**
WEB: www.fce-mrdd.net
SIC: 8331 8699 Sheltered workshop; charitable organization

(G-2841)
G & J PEPSI-COLA BOTTLERS INC
Also Called: Pepsico
400 E 7th St (45601-3455)
PHONE 740 774-2148
Fax: 740 774-1160
Henry Thrapp, *Sales & Mktg St*
John Miller, *Finance Mgr*
EMP: 45
SALES (corp-wide): 475.8MM **Privately Held**
WEB: www.gjpepsi.com
SIC: 5149 2086 Starch; bottled & canned soft drinks
PA: G & J Pepsi-Cola Bottlers Inc
  9435 Waterstone Blvd # 390
  Cincinnati OH 45249
  513 785-6060

(G-2842)
GOOD SMARITAN NETWRK ROSS CNTY
133 E 7th St (45601-3352)
P.O. Box 1781 (45601-5781)
PHONE 740 774-6303
Steve Delmoe, *Chairman*
EMP: 25
SALES (est): 164.8K **Privately Held**
SIC: 8322 Individual & family services

(G-2843)
GOODWILL INDS OF S CENTL OHIO
457 E Main St (45601-3578)
PHONE 740 702-4000
Jarrod Depugh, *Pub Rel Dir*
Wanda Lanzer, *Office Mgr*
Keith Alcorn, *Director*
Tracy Brown, *Director*
Beverly Jeffirey, *Director*
EMP: 99
SQ FT: 6,000
SALES: 5.4MM **Privately Held**
SIC: 8331 8322 Sheltered workshop; individual & family services

(G-2844)
HANSON AGGREGATES EAST LLC
Hanson Aggregates Davon
33 Renick Ave (45601-2895)
PHONE 740 773-2172
Steve Guill, *Opers Mgr*
Leonard McFerren, *Manager*
Paul J Roeder, *Director*
EMP: 25
SALES (corp-wide): 16B **Privately Held**
SIC: 3273 3271 3272 1442 Ready-mixed concrete; blocks, concrete or cinder: standard; concrete products; construction sand & gravel
HQ: Hanson Aggregates East Llc
  3131 Rdu Center Dr
  Morrisville NC 27560
  919 380-2500

(G-2845)
HEALTH CARE RTREMENT CORP AMER
Also Called: Heartland of Chillicothe
1058 Columbus St (45601-2810)
PHONE 740 773-5000
Fax: 740 772-4491
Mike Armstrong, *Branch Mgr*
EMP: 100
SALES (corp-wide): 3.6B **Publicly Held**
WEB: www.hrc-manorcare.com
SIC: 8051 Skilled nursing care facilities
HQ: Health Care And Retirement Corporation Of America
  333 N Summit St Ste 103
  Toledo OH 43604
  419 252-5500

(G-2846)
HERRNSTEIN CHRYSLER INC (PA)
Also Called: Herrnstein Auto Group
133 Marietta Rd (45601-9433)
P.O. Box 266 (45601-0266)
PHONE 740 773-2203
Fax: 740 773-2203
Bart Herrnstein, *President*
Linda Herrnstein, *Corp Secy*
William B Herrnstein, *Vice Pres*
Lucille Herrnstein, *Treasurer*
Bob Tillis, *Sales Mgr*
EMP: 72
SQ FT: 11,500
SALES (est): 17.7MM **Privately Held**
SIC: 5511 7549 Automobiles, new & used; automotive maintenance services

(G-2847)
HOMELAND CREDIT UNION INC (PA)
310 Caldwell St (45601-3331)
P.O. Box 1974 (45601-5974)
PHONE 740 775-3024
Michael Spindler, *CEO*
Shane Poe, *CFO*
Teresa Jones, *Marketing Staff*
EMP: 65
SQ FT: 3,500
SALES: 10.8MM **Privately Held**
WEB: www.homelandcreditunion.com
SIC: 6062 State credit unions, not federally chartered

(G-2848)
HOMELAND CREDIT UNION INC
25 Consumer Center Dr (45601-2676)
P.O. Box 1974 (45601-5974)
PHONE 740 775-3331
Shayne Poe, *CEO*
EMP: 31
SALES (est): 2.6MM
SALES (corp-wide): 10.8MM **Privately Held**
WEB: www.homelandcreditunion.com
SIC: 6062 6141 State credit unions, not federally chartered; personal finance licensed loan companies, small
PA: Homeland Credit Union, Inc.
  310 Caldwell St
  Chillicothe OH 45601
  740 775-3024

(G-2849)
HOPEWELL HEALTH CENTERS INC (PA)
Also Called: LINCOLN PARK MEDICAL CENTER
1049 Western Ave (45601-1104)
P.O. Box 188 (45601-0188)
PHONE 740 773-1006
Fax: 740 775-7855
Mark Bridenbaugh, *CEO*
Diane Lewe, *President*
Kathy Cecil, *Vice Pres*
Brad Nelson, *CFO*
Amanda Putnam, *Human Res Dir*
EMP: 50
SALES: 33.1MM **Privately Held**
SIC: 8099 Medical services organization

(G-2850)
HORIZON PCS INC (HQ)
68 E Main St (45601-2503)
PHONE 740 772-8200
William A McKell, *Ch of Bd*
Steven Burkhardt, *Corp Secy*
Alan G Morse, *COO*
Kate L Gayord, *Vice Pres*
Joseph J Watson, *Sls & Mktg Exec*
EMP: 200
SALES (est): 39MM **Privately Held**
SIC: 4812 Radio telephone communication

(G-2851)
HORIZON TELCOM INC (PA)
68 E Main St (45601-2503)
PHONE 740 772-8200
Robert Mc Kell, *Ch of Bd*
Thomas Mc Kell, *President*
Narty Forde, *General Mgr*
Joe Corbin, *VP Opers*
Jack Thompson, *CFO*
EMP: 285
SQ FT: 80,000
SALES (est): 32.5MM **Privately Held**
WEB: www.horizontel.com
SIC: 4813 Local telephone communications

(G-2852)
HUNTINGTON NATIONAL BANK
Also Called: Home Mortgage
445 Western Ave (45601-2243)
PHONE 740 773-2681
Fax: 740 772-2265
Delbert Bochard, *President*
EMP: 50
SALES (corp-wide): 4.7B **Publicly Held**
WEB: www.huntingtonnationalbank.com
SIC: 6029 6162 6021 Commercial banks; mortgage bankers; national commercial banks
HQ: The Huntington National Bank
  17 S High St Fl 1
  Columbus OH 43215
  614 480-4293

(G-2853)
INGLE-BARR INC (PA)
Also Called: Ibi
20 Plyleys Ln (45601-2005)
P.O. Box 874 (45601-0874)
PHONE 740 702-6117
Fax: 740 702-6116
Wilbur B Poole, *President*
Jeffrey Poole, *Vice Pres*
Rod Poole, *Vice Pres*
Ken Krebs, *Manager*
Howard Loel, *Manager*
EMP: 100
SQ FT: 6,500
SALES (est): 40.5MM **Privately Held**
WEB: www.4ibi.com
SIC: 1541 1521 1542 Renovation, remodeling & repairs: industrial buildings; general remodeling, single-family houses; commercial & office buildings, renovation & repair

(G-2854)
J B EXPRESS INC
27311 Old Route 35 (45601-8110)
P.O. Box 91 (45601-0091)
PHONE 740 702-9830
Jon Bell, *President*
Josh Bell, *Vice Pres*
Deana Bell, *Treasurer*
EMP: 60
SQ FT: 24,440
SALES (est): 12.1MM **Privately Held**
WEB: www.jbexpress.com
SIC: 4731 1623 4225 Transportation agents & brokers; oil & gas pipeline construction; general warehousing & storage

(G-2855)
J L SWANEY INC
975 Vigo Rd (45601-8993)
PHONE 740 884-4450
Jared Swaney, *President*
EMP: 27
SALES (est): 3.2MM **Privately Held**
SIC: 5094 Beads

(G-2856)
J W ENTERPRISES INC (PA)
Also Called: ERA
159 E Main St (45601-2507)
P.O. Box 2066 (45601-8066)
PHONE 740 774-4500
Wayne Martin Jr, *CEO*
Mark Cenci, *President*
EMP: 80
SQ FT: 6,000
SALES (est): 4.5MM **Privately Held**
WEB: www.benchmarkrealtyllc.com
SIC: 6531 1521 Real estate agent, residential; appraiser, real estate; auction, real estate; new construction, single-family houses

(G-2857)
KINDRED NURSING CENTERS E LLC
Also Called: Kindred Transitional
60 Marietta Rd (45601-9433)
PHONE 740 772-5900
William Altman, *Vice Pres*
Joseph Landenwich, *Vice Pres*
Christina Schramm, *Director*
Christopher Skocik, *Director*
EMP: 113
SALES (corp-wide): 6B **Publicly Held**
WEB: www.salemhaven.com
SIC: 8052 Personal care facility
HQ: Kindred Nursing Centers East, L.L.C.
  680 S 4th St
  Louisville KY 40202
  502 596-7300

(G-2858)
KITCHEN COLLECTION LLC
133 Redd St (45601-3400)
PHONE 740 773-9150
Mike White, *Branch Mgr*
EMP: 40
SALES (corp-wide): 1.1B **Publicly Held**
WEB: www.kitchencollection.com
SIC: 4226 Special warehousing & storage
HQ: The Kitchen Collection Llc
  71 E Water St
  Chillicothe OH 45601
  740 773-9150

(G-2859)
LCNB NATIONAL BANK
33 W Main St Frnt (45601-3132)
PHONE 740 775-6777
Ryan Adams, *Assoc VP*
EMP: 49
SALES (corp-wide): 54.9MM **Publicly Held**
SIC: 6021 National trust companies with deposits, commercial
HQ: Lcnb National Bank
  2 N Broadway St Lowr
  Lebanon OH 45036
  513 932-1414

(G-2860)
LITTER BOB FUEL & HEATING CO (HQ)
Also Called: Litter Quality Propane
524 Eastern Ave (45601-3471)
P.O. Box 297 (45601-0297)
PHONE 740 773-2196
Fax: 740 773-9230
Robert W Litter, *President*
Anna Roseberry, *Corp Secy*
Scott Dyke, *Manager*
EMP: 32
SQ FT: 1,500
SALES (est): 9.3MM **Privately Held**
SIC: 5984 1711 Propane gas, bottled; liquefied petroleum gas, delivered to customers' premises; plumbing, heating, air-conditioning contractors

(G-2861)
LITTER DISTRIBUTING CO INC
Also Called: Classic Brands
656 Hospital Rd (45601-9030)
PHONE 740 774-2831
Fax: 740 774-2838
Ken Bartley, *Warehouse Mgr*
John Lodge, *Manager*
EMP: 53 **Privately Held**
SIC: 5181 Beer & other fermented malt liquors
HQ: Litter Distributing Company, Inc.
  656 Hospital Rd
  Chillicothe OH 45601
  740 775-2063

(G-2862)
LOWES HOME CENTERS LLC
867 N Bridge St (45601-1775)
PHONE 740 773-7777
Fax: 740 773-6724
Denny Gray, *Office Mgr*

GEOGRAPHIC SECTION
Chillicothe - Ross County (G-2887)

EMP: 150
SALES (corp-wide): 68.6B **Publicly Held**
SIC: 5211 5031 5722 5064 Home centers; building materials, exterior; building materials, interior; household appliance stores; electrical appliances, television & radio
HQ: Lowe's Home Centers, Llc
  1605 Curtis Bridge Rd
  Wilkesboro NC 28697
  336 658-4000

(G-2863)
MAXIM HEALTHCARE SERVICES INC
220 N Plaza Blvd (45601-1787)
PHONE 740 772-4100
Rachel Fuller, *Branch Mgr*
EMP: 93
SALES (corp-wide): 1.3B **Privately Held**
SIC: 8099 8049 Blood related health services; nurses & other medical assistants
PA: Maxim Healthcare Services, Inc.
  7227 Lee Deforest Dr
  Columbia MD 21046
  410 910-1500

(G-2864)
MPW INDUSTRIAL SERVICES INC
65 Kenworth Dr (45601-8829)
PHONE 740 774-5251
EMP: 89
SALES (corp-wide): 257.9MM **Privately Held**
SIC: 7349 Cleaning service, industrial or commercial
HQ: Mpw Industrial Services, Inc.
  9711 Lancaster Rd
  Hebron OH 43025
  800 827-8790

(G-2865)
OAKWOOD MANAGEMENT COMPANY
402 W Main St (45601-3049)
PHONE 740 774-3570
Fred Carlisle, *Branch Mgr*
EMP: 46
SALES (corp-wide): 4.3MM **Privately Held**
SIC: 6513 Apartment hotel operation
PA: Oakwood Management Company Inc
  6950 Americana Pkwy Ste A
  Reynoldsburg OH 43068
  614 866-8702

(G-2866)
OHIO EYE SPECIALISTS INC
Also Called: Vision America of Ohio
50 N Plaza Blvd (45601-1757)
PHONE 800 948-3937
Harmet Chawla, *President*
Debbie Clark, *Manager*
EMP: 30 **Privately Held**
SIC: 8042 Offices & clinics of optometrists
PA: Ohio Eye Specialists, Inc.
  955 Circle Dr
  Circleville OH 43113

(G-2867)
OVERBROOK PARK LTD
Also Called: Overbrook Park
2179 Anderson Station Rd (45601-8856)
PHONE 740 773-1159
Fax: 740 773-1159
Leeann Morein, *Principal*
Jennifer Hardee, *Principal*
EMP: 99
SALES (est): 3.2MM **Privately Held**
SIC: 6513 Apartment building operators

(G-2868)
OYER ELECTRIC INC
Also Called: S.O.S. Electric
14650 Pleasant Valley Rd (45601-4049)
P.O. Box 1800 (45601-5800)
PHONE 740 773-2828
Fax: 740 775-5184
Larry Oyer, *President*
Betty Oyer, *Vice Pres*
Scott Oyer, *Vice Pres*
Phil Scherer, *Project Mgr*
Lisa Sagraves, *Bookkeeper*
EMP: 60

SQ FT: 11,000
SALES: 3MM **Privately Held**
WEB: www.soselectric.net
SIC: 1731 General electrical contractor

(G-2869)
PACE INTERNATIONAL UNION
Also Called: Paper Alied Indus Chem & Enrgy
170 S Hickory St (45601-3336)
PHONE 740 772-2038
Keith Staggs, *President*
EMP: 35
SALES (corp-wide): 26.9MM **Privately Held**
SIC: 8631 Labor unions & similar labor organizations
PA: Pace International Union
  5 Gateway Ctr
  Pittsburgh PA 15222
  412 562-2400

(G-2870)
PETLAND INC (PA)
250 Riverside St (45601-2611)
P.O. Box 1606 (45601-5606)
PHONE 740 775-2464
Edward R Kunzelman, *President*
Greg Hudson, *COO*
Rondon Bettin, *Exec VP*
Steve Huggins, *Vice Pres*
Tony Samples, *Vice Pres*
EMP: 100
SQ FT: 40,000
SALES (est): 53MM **Privately Held**
WEB: www.petland.com
SIC: 5199 6794 Pet supplies; franchises, selling or licensing

(G-2871)
PINNACLE BUILDING SERVICES INC
776 Rinkliff Ln (45601-8185)
PHONE 614 871-6190
Michael Meade, *President*
Beth Wright, *Assistant*
EMP: 125
SQ FT: 500
SALES: 2.2MM **Privately Held**
SIC: 7349 Cleaning service, industrial or commercial

(G-2872)
R L S CORPORATION
Also Called: R L S Recycling
990 Eastern Ave (45601-3658)
P.O. Box 327 (45601-0327)
PHONE 740 773-1440
Charles Stevens, *President*
EMP: 25 EST: 1923
SQ FT: 14,000
SALES (est): 3.3MM **Privately Held**
SIC: 5093 3341 Metal scrap & waste materials; waste paper; secondary nonferrous metals

(G-2873)
RECORDING WORKSHOP
Also Called: Recording Workshop, The
455 Massieville Rd (45601-9395)
PHONE 740 663-1000
Fax: 740 663-2427
William Joseph Waters, *Owner*
Paul Pollard, *Mktg Dir*
Jim Rosebrook, *Director*
EMP: 30
SQ FT: 10,500
SALES (est): 1.6MM **Privately Held**
WEB: www.recordingworkshop.com
SIC: 8249 7389 Trade school; recording studio, noncommercial records

(G-2874)
REHABCARE GROUP MGT SVCS INC
230 Cherry St (45601-2301)
PHONE 740 779-6732
EMP: 26
SALES (corp-wide): 6B **Publicly Held**
SIC: 8093 Rehabilitation center, outpatient treatment
HQ: Rehabcare Group Mgt Svcs Inc
  680 S 4th St
  Louisville KY 40202
  502 596-7300

(G-2875)
RLS DISPOSAL COMPANY INC
990 Eastern Ave (45601-3658)
PHONE 740 773-1440
Charlies N Stevens, *President*
Vincent Stevens, *Manager*
EMP: 50
SALES: 950K **Privately Held**
SIC: 4953 Refuse systems

(G-2876)
RON NEFF REAL ESTATE (PA)
Also Called: Ron Neff Her Realtors
153 S Paint St (45601-3215)
PHONE 740 773-4670
Fax: 740 774-6333
Ron Neff, *Owner*
EMP: 27
SQ FT: 2,500
SALES: 650K **Privately Held**
SIC: 6531 Real estate agents & managers

(G-2877)
ROSS CNTY CMMITTEE FOR ELDERLY
Also Called: Senior Center
1824 Western Ave (45601-1036)
PHONE 740 773-3544
Fax: 740 773-4730
Jodi Riley, *Director*
Janet Elliott, *Director*
EMP: 45 EST: 1975
SALES: 1.4MM **Privately Held**
SIC: 8322 Outreach program; referral service for personal & social problems

(G-2878)
ROSS COUNTY CHILDREN SVCS CTR (PA)
Also Called: Ross Cnty Job & Family Svcs
150 E 2nd St (45601-2525)
P.O. Box 469 (45601-0469)
PHONE 740 773-2651
Fax: 740 772-7648
Robert Gallagher, *CEO*
Thomas E Williamson, *Director*
EMP: 100
SALES (est): 2.3MM **Privately Held**
SIC: 8322 Individual & family services

(G-2879)
ROSS COUNTY COMMUNITY (PA)
603 Central Ctr (45601-2249)
PHONE 740 702-7222
Ed Alexinas, *Principal*
EMP: 34
SALES: 4.8MM **Privately Held**
WEB: www.rossccac.com
SIC: 8322 Individual & family services

(G-2880)
ROSS COUNTY HEALTH DISTRICT
150 E 2nd St (45601-2295)
PHONE 740 775-1114
Fax: 740 772-2597
Donna Higgins, *General Mgr*
Lisa Flowers, *Manager*
Wanda Medcalf, *Director*
Michelle Long, *Asst Director*
EMP: 133
SALES (est): 3.5MM **Privately Held**
SIC: 8082 Home health care services

(G-2001)
ROSS COUNTY WATER COMPANY INC
Also Called: RURAL WATER UTILITY
663 Fairgrounds Rd (45601-9715)
P.O. Box 1690 (45601-5690)
PHONE 740 774-4117
Fax: 740 774-2090
Michael Riffle, *President*
Todd W Metzger, *General Mgr*
William Neal, *Corp Secy*
Clyde Hawkins, *Vice Pres*
Clint Martz, *Sls & Mktg Exec*
EMP: 33
SQ FT: 3,000
SALES: 7.8MM **Privately Held**
WEB: www.rosscowater.org
SIC: 4941 Water supply

(G-2882)
ROSS COUNTY YMCA
100 Mill St (45601-1662)
PHONE 740 772-4340
Fax: 740 774-1734
Debby White, *Exec Dir*
Steve Clever, *Exec Dir*
Zack Lynch, *Associate Dir*
Samantha Daniels,
EMP: 65
SALES: 902.7K **Privately Held**
SIC: 8641 8611 8351 8661 Youth organizations; business associations; child day care services; religious organizations; individual & family services; physical fitness facilities

(G-2883)
RUMPKE/KENWORTH CONTRACT
Also Called: Kenworth Truck Co
65 Kenworth Dr (45601-8829)
PHONE 740 774-5111
Fax: 740 774-5330
Robert Brown, *Facilities Mgr*
Carl Carter, *Facilities Mgr*
John Auxter, *Engineer*
Brian Rooney, *Engineer*
Judy Nctigue, *Branch Mgr*
▲ EMP: 69
SALES (est): 46.7MM **Privately Held**
SIC: 5084 5511 Trucks, industrial; trucks, tractors & trailers: new & used

(G-2884)
SCIOTO PNT VLY MENTAL HLTH CTR (PA)
4449 State Route 159 (45601-8620)
P.O. Box 6179 (45601-6179)
PHONE 740 775-1260
Fax: 740 775-0292
Sue Frey, *Treasurer*
Gary Kreuchauf, *Exec Dir*
Carol Anderson, *Exec Dir*
Jacki Byers, *Associate Dir*
Julius Roberts, *Psychiatry*
EMP: 220
SQ FT: 25,000
SALES: 14.2MM **Privately Held**
SIC: 8322 8093 General counseling services; mental health clinic, outpatient

(G-2885)
SIOTO PAINTSVILLE MENTAL HLTH
Also Called: Crisis Center
4449 State Route 159 (45601-8620)
P.O. Box 6179 (45601-6179)
PHONE 740 775-1260
Ed Sythe, *Director*
Robyn Lett, *Director*
EMP: 26
SALES (est): 315.5K **Privately Held**
SIC: 8322 Crisis center

(G-2886)
SOUTHERN OHIO EYE ASSOC LLC (PA)
159 E 2nd St (45601-2526)
PHONE 740 773-6347
Toll Free: .... 888 -
Stephen Demick,
Linda Brushart, *Administration*
Cynthia Adamiec, *Technician*
EMP: 42
SALES (est): 5.7MM **Privately Held**
SIC: 8011 Ophthalmologist

(G-2887)
SOUTHERN OHIO WNS CANCER PRJ
Also Called: Bccp
150 E 2nd St (45601-2525)
PHONE 740 775-7332
Timothy Angel, *Commissioner*
Jamie Eselgroth, *Commissioner*
Frank Hirsch, *Commissioner*
EMP: 100
SALES (est): 1.5MM **Privately Held**
SIC: 8011 Offices & clinics of medical doctors

Chillicothe - Ross County (G-2888) GEOGRAPHIC SECTION

(G-2888)
SPECTRUM MGT HOLDG CO LLC
Also Called: Time Warner
32 Enterprise Pl (45601-8600)
PHONE..................740 762-0291
Jim Cavender, *Manager*
EMP: 83
SALES (corp-wide): 41.5B **Publicly Held**
SIC: 4841 Cable television services
HQ: Spectrum Management Holding Company, Llc
400 Atlantic St
Stamford CT 06901
203 905-7801

(G-2889)
SUNRUSH CONSTRUCTION CO INC (PA)
1988 Western Ave (45601-1048)
PHONE..................740 775-1300
Fax: 740 775-1347
Greg Wells, *President*
Michael Long, *Vice Pres*
Annette Stinson, *Manager*
EMP: 30
SQ FT: 10,000
SALES (est): 7.2MM **Privately Held**
WEB: www.sunrushconstruction.com
SIC: 1541 1542 Industrial buildings, new construction; commercial & office building, new construction

(G-2890)
TRADITIONS OF CHILLICOTHE
Also Called: Assisted Living Facilities
142 University Dr Ofc (45601-2119)
PHONE..................740 773-8107
Fax: 740 773-5113
Pat Nichols, *Director*
EMP: 30
SALES (est): 1.3MM **Privately Held**
WEB: www.traditionshealth.org
SIC: 8059 Nursing home, except skilled & intermediate care facility

(G-2891)
TRANSPORTATION OHIO DEPARTMENT
Also Called: State Highway Garage
255 Larrick Ln (45601-4067)
PHONE..................740 773-3191
Aaron Mitten, *Director*
EMP: 30 **Privately Held**
SIC: 1611 9621 Highway & street maintenance; bureau of public roads
HQ: Ohio Department Of Transportation
1980 W Broad St
Columbus OH 43223

(G-2892)
UNITED PARCEL SERVICE INC
Also Called: UPS
1536 N Bridge St (45601-4104)
PHONE..................800 742-5877
EMP: 38
SALES (corp-wide): 65.8B **Publicly Held**
SIC: 4215 Package delivery, vehicular; parcel delivery, vehicular
PA: United Parcel Service, Inc.
55 Glenlake Pkwy
Atlanta GA 30328
404 828-6000

(G-2893)
UNITED STEELWORKERS
Also Called: Uswa
196 Burbridge Ave (45601-3358)
PHONE..................740 772-5988
James Bowers, *President*
EMP: 45
SALES (corp-wide): 61.5K **Privately Held**
SIC: 8631 Labor union
PA: United Steelworkers
60 Bolevard Of The Allies
Pittsburgh PA 15222
412 562-2400

(G-2894)
VA MEDICAL CENTER AUTOMATED RE
17273 State Route 104 (45601-9718)
PHONE..................740 772-7118
Sheila E Jordan, *Principal*
Roslyn Cross, *Persnl Dir*

Deborah Meesig, *Persnl Dir*
EMP: 31
SALES (est): 3.8MM **Privately Held**
SIC: 8062 General medical & surgical hospitals

(G-2895)
VETERANS HEALTH ADMINISTRATION
Also Called: Chillicothe VA Medical Center
17273 State Route 104 (45601-9718)
PHONE..................202 461-4800
Kitty Hess, *Principal*
Gary Mack, *Principal*
Michael Murphy, *Principal*
John Tribuiano, *Principal*
Jack Wilkins, *Principal*
EMP: 1100 **Publicly Held**
WEB: www.veterans-ru.org
SIC: 8011 9451 Medical centers; psychiatric clinic;
HQ: Veterans Health Administration
810 Vermont Ave Nw
Washington DC 20420

(G-2896)
WASTE MANAGEMENT OHIO INC
675 Chamber Dr (45601-8257)
PHONE..................800 356-5235
Ginger Kaladas, *Credit Staff*
Paul Pistono, *Manager*
Gerri Kitzmiller, *Manager*
Lee Hicks, *Contract Law*
EMP: 99
SALES (corp-wide): 14.4B **Publicly Held**
WEB: www.wm.com
SIC: 4953 Refuse systems
HQ: Waste Management Of Ohio, Inc.
1700 N Broad St
Fairborn OH 45324

(G-2897)
WHITED SEIGNEUR SAMS & RAHE
Also Called: Wssr Cpas
213 S Paint St (45601-3828)
PHONE..................740 702-2600
Fax: 740 702-2610
Kathleen M Alderman, *Partner*
Barry Rhea, *Partner*
John Sams, *Partner*
Donald Seigneur, *Partner*
Jerry Whited, *Partner*
EMP: 25
SALES (est): 2MM **Privately Held**
WEB: www.wssrcpa.com
SIC: 8721 Certified public accountant

(G-2898)
WISE MEDICAL STAFFING INC (PA)
80 E 2nd St (45601-2523)
PHONE..................740 775-4108
Milton Clegg, *President*
Patricia Pannell, *Vice Pres*
Deborah Wolfe, *Vice Pres*
Heather Beavers, *Manager*
Jamie Maddy, *Manager*
EMP: 70
SALES: 2MM **Privately Held**
WEB: www.wisemedicalstaffing.com
SIC: 7361 Nurses' registry

Chippewa Lake
Medina County

(G-2899)
THE OAKS LODGE
5878 Longacre Ln (44215-9778)
P.O. Box 32 (44215-0032)
PHONE..................330 769-2601
Fax: 330 769-4434
Bonnie Druschel, *President*
Donald R Casper, *President*
EMP: 50 **EST:** 1949
SQ FT: 10,393
SALES: 1MM **Privately Held**
WEB: www.theoakslodge.com
SIC: 5812 5813 7299 Restaurant, family; independent; cocktail lounge; banquet hall facilities

Cincinnati
Clermont County

(G-2900)
5ME LLC
4270 Ivy Pointe Blvd # 100 (45245-0004)
PHONE..................513 719-1600
William A Horwarth, *President*
Jeffery Price, *Vice Pres*
Chris Chapman, *CFO*
EMP: 45
SALES (est): 9.1MM
SALES (corp-wide): 9.9MM **Privately Held**
SIC: 3544 8742 Special dies, tools, jigs & fixtures; business consultant
PA: 5me Holdings Llc
4270 Ivy Pointe Blvd # 100
Cincinnati OH 45245
859 534-4872

(G-2901)
ABILITY NETWORK INC
4357 Ferguson Dr Ste 100 (45245-1684)
PHONE..................513 943-8888
Fax: 513 943-8878
James Donaldson, *Principal*
Jerry Nichols, *Manager*
EMP: 30
SALES (corp-wide): 449.3MM **Publicly Held**
SIC: 7376 6411 Computer facilities management; insurance agents, brokers & service
HQ: Ability Network Inc.
100 N 6th St Ste 900a
Minneapolis MN 55403
612 460-4301

(G-2902)
AIRTRON LP
756 Cincinnati Batavia Pi (45245-1277)
PHONE..................513 860-5959
EMP: 77 **Privately Held**
SIC: 1711 Warm air heating & air conditioning contractor
HQ: Airtron, Inc.
9260 Marketpl Dr
Miamisburg OH 45342
937 898-0826

(G-2903)
AMERATHON LLC (HQ)
671 Ohio Pike Ste K (45245-2136)
PHONE..................513 752-7300
Debbie Martin, *President*
Christopher Martin, *Vice Pres*
Tom Kaylor, *CFO*
Jim Jackson, *Admin Sec*
EMP: 450 **EST:** 2014
SQ FT: 25,000
SALES: 82MM
SALES (corp-wide): 57MM **Privately Held**
SIC: 8071 Ultrasound laboratory
PA: American Health Associates, Inc.
15712 Sw 41st St Ste 16
Davie FL 33331
954 919-5005

(G-2904)
BEECHMONT FORD INC (PA)
600 Ohio Pike (45245-2118)
PHONE..................513 752-6611
Fax: 513 752-7373
Mark Williams, *President*
Jeff Fithen, *General Mgr*
Mitch Allison, *Business Mgr*
Dan Rapier, *Corp Secy*
Lorine Williams, *Vice Pres*
EMP: 120
SQ FT: 25,000
SALES (est): 54.8MM **Privately Held**
SIC: 5511 7538 7515 5531 Automobiles, new & used; pickups, new & used; vans, new & used; general automotive repair shops; passenger car leasing; automotive & home supply stores; motor vehicle supplies & new parts

(G-2905)
CGH-GLOBAL EMERG MNGMT STRATEG
Also Called: Cgh Global
851 Ohio Pike Ste 203 (45245-2203)
PHONE..................800 376-0655
Andrew Glassmeyer, *CEO*
Eric Mitchell, *President*
EMP: 48 **EST:** 2011
SALES (est): 180.2K
SALES (corp-wide): 8MM **Privately Held**
SIC: 8711 8322 1389 0851 Fire protection engineering; emergency social services; fire fighting, oil & gas field; fire fighting services, forest; fire prevention services, forest
PA: Cgh-Global, Llc
851 Ohio Pike Ste 203
Cincinnati OH 45245
800 376-0655

(G-2906)
CHILDRENS HOSPITAL MEDICAL CTR
796 Cncnnati Batavia Pike (45245-1262)
PHONE..................513 636-6036
Jean Kinman, *Branch Mgr*
Brian Wildman, *Manager*
Raymond Troy, *Child Psychlgy*
EMP: 920
SALES (corp-wide): 1.6B **Privately Held**
SIC: 8069 Children's hospital
PA: Children's Hospital Medical Center
3333 Burnet Ave
Cincinnati OH 45229
513 636-4200

(G-2907)
CINCINNATI DENTAL SERVICES
4360 Ferguson Dr Ste 140 (45245-1683)
PHONE..................513 753-6446
Sherry Gifford, *Branch Mgr*
EMP: 45
SALES (corp-wide): 5.8MM **Privately Held**
SIC: 8021 Dentists' office
PA: Cincinnati Dental Services Inc
121 E Mcmillan St
Cincinnati OH 45219
513 721-8888

(G-2908)
CLERMONT HILLS CO LLC
Also Called: Holiday Inn
4501 Eastgate Blvd (45245-1201)
PHONE..................513 752-4400
Fax: 513 753-3178
Jacquie A Dowdy, *Mng Member*
Dennis Flannigan, *Director*
EMP: 80
SALES (est): 2.5MM **Privately Held**
SIC: 7011 Hotels & motels

(G-2909)
CURTISS-WRIGHT FLOW CONTROL
Qualtech NP
4600 E Tech Dr (45245-1000)
PHONE..................513 528-7900
Mark Chatham, *Opers Staff*
Tim Geers, *Engineer*
Marion Mitchell, *Branch Mgr*
Mike Wooldridge, *Manager*
Tami Cann, *Admin Asst*
EMP: 88
SALES (corp-wide): 2.2B **Publicly Held**
WEB: www.et.curtisswright.com
SIC: 3491 3599 3443 1799 Industrial valves; machine shop, jobbing & repair; plate work for the nuclear industry; diamond drilling & sawing
HQ: Curtiss-Wright Flow Control Service Corporation
2950 E Birch St
Brea CA 92821
714 982-1898

(G-2910)
CURTISS-WRIGHT FLOW CONTROL
Also Called: Qualtech NP
4600 E Tech Dr (45245-1000)
PHONE..................513 528-7900
Kurt Mitchell, *Branch Mgr*
EMP: 88

Cincinnati - Clermont County (G-2933)

(G-2910 cont.)
SALES (corp-wide): 2.2B Publicly Held
SIC: 3491 8734 3441 Industrial valves; testing laboratories; fabricated structural metal
HQ: Curtiss-Wright Flow Control Service Corporation
2950 E Birch St
Brea CA 92821
714 982-1898

(G-2911)
CURTISS-WRIGHT FLOW CTRL CORP
Also Called: Qualtech NP
4600 E Tech Dr (45245-1000)
PHONE.................513 528-7900
Dwaine A Godfrey, *Vice Pres*
Lucy Miller, *Safety Mgr*
John D Clark, *Sales Executive*
Don Clark, *Marketing Mgr*
Marion Mitchell, *Branch Mgr*
EMP: 82
SALES (corp-wide): 2.2B Publicly Held
SIC: 3443 8734 Fabricated plate work (boiler shop); testing laboratories
HQ: Curtiss-Wright Flow Control Corporation
1966 Broadhollow Rd Ste E
Farmingdale NY 11735
631 293-3800

(G-2912)
DAVID M SCHNEIDER MD INC (PA)
Also Called: Midwest Eye Center
4452 Estgate Blvd Ste 305 (45245)
PHONE.................513 752-5700
Fax: 513 752-5716
David M Schneider MD, *President*
Lauri Walters, *Office Mgr*
Annie Taylor, *Nursing Dir*
Phillip G Kies,
Jeannie Butler, *Receptionist Se*
EMP: 33
SALES (est): 6.4MM Privately Held
SIC: 8011 Eyes, ears, nose & throat specialist; physician/surgeon; ophthalmologist; surgeon

(G-2913)
EASTGATE HEALTH CARE CENTER
4400 Glen Este Withamsvil (45245)
PHONE.................513 752-3710
Fax: 513 752-8112
Henry Schneider, *President*
Barry Bortz, *Vice Pres*
Lynn Sennett, *Nursing Dir*
Michael Hamilton, *Records Dir*
EMP: 211
SQ FT: 87,000
SALES (est): 7.3MM
SALES (corp-wide): 74MM Privately Held
WEB: www.carespring.com
SIC: 8051 Skilled nursing care facilities
PA: Carespring Health Care Management, Llc
390 Wards Corner Rd
Loveland OH 45140
513 943-4000

(G-2914)
EASTGATE PROFESSIONAL OFF PK V
4357 Ferguson Dr Ste 220 (45245-1689)
PHONE.................513 943-0050
Greg Crowelo, *President*
Gregory K Crowell, *Partner*
Jerry Stanislaw, *CFO*
EMP: 25
SALES (est): 793.3K Privately Held
SIC: 6531 Real estate agent, commercial

(G-2915)
EASTGATE VILLAGE
776 Cincinnati Batavia Pi (45245-1260)
PHONE.................513 753-4400
Fax: 513 753-8019
Oscar Jarnicki, *President*
Jon Trowbridge, *General Mgr*
Brooke Singleton, *Manager*
John Trowbridge, *Administration*
EMP: 40
SQ FT: 500,000
SALES (est): 2.2MM Privately Held
WEB: www.eastgatevillage.com
SIC: 8361 Home for the aged

(G-2916)
GENERAL DATA COMPANY INC (PA)
4354 Ferguson Dr (45245-1667)
P.O. Box 541165 (45254-1165)
PHONE.................513 752-7978
Fax: 513 752-6947
Peter Wenzel, *President*
Jim Burns, *Vice Pres*
Rick Cmar, *Vice Pres*
Jeffrey Kenny, *Vice Pres*
Dave Laurash, *VP Mfg*
▲ EMP: 230
SQ FT: 45,000
SALES (est): 61.8MM Privately Held
WEB: www.general-data.com
SIC: 2679 5046 5084 2759 Labels, paper; made from purchased material; commercial equipment; printing trades machinery, equipment & supplies; commercial printing; surgical & medical instruments; unsupported plastics film & sheet

(G-2917)
GENERAL FNCL TAX CNSULTING LLC
1004 Seabrook Way (45245-1963)
P.O. Box 541032 (45254-1032)
PHONE.................888 496-2679
Sarah Gelter, *COO*
Mike Cunningham, *Exec VP*
Jessica Brown, *Senior VP*
Jason Walter, *Senior VP*
Mark Austin, *Vice Pres*
EMP: 32
SALES (est): 2.1MM Privately Held
SIC: 8742 Financial consultant

(G-2918)
JEFF WYLER AUTOMOTIVE FMLY INC (PA)
Also Called: Wyler, Jeff, Dealer Group
829 Eastgate South Dr (45245-1547)
PHONE.................513 752-7450
Jeff Wyler, *CEO*
Kathryn Collier, *Business Mgr*
Doug Kurzynski, *Business Mgr*
Darryl Barnhouse, *Store Mgr*
Bruce Hix, *Parts Mgr*
EMP: 26
SQ FT: 4,400
SALES (est): 7.8MM Privately Held
SIC: 8741 5511 Business management; new & used car dealers

(G-2919)
JEFF WYLER FT THOMAS INC
829 Eastgate South Dr (45245-1547)
PHONE.................513 752-7450
Jeffrey L Wyler, *Principal*
EMP: 80
SALES (est): 1.3MM Privately Held
SIC: 7532 Body shop, automotive

(G-2920)
JENKINS ENTERPRISES LLC
Also Called: Janiking
849 Locust Corner Rd (45245-3111)
PHONE.................513 752-7896
Pat Jenkins, *President*
EMP: 50
SALES (est): 1.3MM Privately Held
SIC: 7349 Janitorial service, contract basis

(G-2921)
JOE DODGE KIDD INC
1065 Ohio Pike (45245-2329)
PHONE.................513 752-1804
Fax: 513 752-1808
Ron Kidd, *CEO*
Trudi Schwarz, *Corp Secy*
Barney Bryant, *Sales Staff*
EMP: 39 EST: 1978
SQ FT: 20,000
SALES (est): 13.8MM Privately Held
WEB: www.joekidddodge.com
SIC: 5511 7538 7532 7515 Automobiles, new & used; general automotive repair shops; top & body repair & paint shops; passenger car leasing; automotive & home supply stores

(G-2922)
KGBO HOLDINGS INC (PA)
4289 Ivy Pointe Blvd (45245-0002)
P.O. Box 799, Milford (45150-0799)
PHONE.................513 831-2600
Kenneth Oaks, *President*
Kerry Byrne, *Exec VP*
Matt McConnell, *Vice Pres*
Kurt Carman, *Opers Mgr*
Kate Lucas Stump, *Controller*
EMP: 32
SQ FT: 100,000
SALES (est): 2.3B Privately Held
WEB: www.totalqualitylogistics.com
SIC: 4731 Truck transportation brokers

(G-2923)
LNS AMERICA INC (DH)
4621 E Tech Dr (45245-1044)
PHONE.................513 528-5674
Fax: 513 528-5733
John Tolasky, *CEO*
Eve Scemama, *President*
John Stone, *Regional Mgr*
Sraj Frank, *Vice Pres*
Kirby Gehrum, *Engineer*
▲ EMP: 70
SQ FT: 52,000
SALES (est): 32.4MM Privately Held
SIC: 5084 Industrial machinery & equipment
HQ: Lns Sa
Route De Frinvillier
Orvin BE
323 580-200

(G-2924)
LOWES HOME CENTERS LLC
618 Mount Moriah Dr (45245-2113)
PHONE.................513 753-5094
Fax: 513 943-7079
Mark Houndshed, *Manager*
EMP: 300
SQ FT: 1,753
SALES (corp-wide): 68.6B Publicly Held
SIC: 5211 5031 5722 5064 Home centers; building materials, exterior; building materials, interior; household appliance stores; electrical appliances, television & radio
HQ: Lowe's Home Centers, Llc
1605 Curtis Bridge Rd
Wilkesboro NC 28697
336 658-4000

(G-2925)
NATIONWIDE CHILDRENS HOSPITAL
796 Old State Route 74 # 200 (45245-1262)
PHONE.................513 636-6000
Fax: 513 636-6007
Kenneth G Massey, *Vice Pres*
Donna Kinnemeyer, *Manager*
EMP: 473
SALES (corp-wide): 1.3B Privately Held
SIC: 8069 Children's hospital
PA: Nationwide Children's Hospital
700 Childrens Dr
Columbus OH 43205
614 722-2000

(G-2926)
ORTHOPEDIC CONS CINCINNATI
4440 Glnste Wthmsville Rd (45245-1318)
PHONE.................513 752-7488
Robert S Hiedt Sr, *President*
EMP: 30
SALES (corp-wide): 18MM Privately Held
SIC: 8011 Orthopedic physician
PA: Orthopedic Consultants Of Cincinnati
4701 Creek Rd Ste 110
Blue Ash OH 45242
513 733-8894

(G-2927)
PEDIATRICS ASSOC OF MT CARMEL
4371 Ferguson Dr (45245-1668)
PHONE.................513 752-3650
Fax: 513 752-3387
Robert Carson MD, *Principal*
Helene Blitzer, *Principal*
Emanuel O Doyne, *Principal*
Cathryn Yost, *Principal*
Christopher Peltier, *Pediatrics*
EMP: 30 EST: 1973
SQ FT: 1,040
SALES (est): 4MM Privately Held
SIC: 8011 Pediatrician

(G-2928)
PETSMART INC
650 Eastgate South Dr B (45245-1772)
PHONE.................513 752-8463
Fax: 513 752-9387
Scott King, *Manager*
EMP: 28
SALES (corp-wide): 12.7B Privately Held
WEB: www.petsmart.com
SIC: 5999 0752 Pet food; animal specialty services
HQ: Petsmart, Inc.
19601 N 27th Ave
Phoenix AZ 85027
623 580-6100

(G-2929)
PRESSLEY RIDGE FOUNDATION
4355 Ferguson Dr Ste 125 (45245-5149)
PHONE.................513 752-4548
Matthew Mitchell, *Branch Mgr*
EMP: 584 Privately Held
SIC: 8093 Mental health clinic, outpatient
PA: Pressley Ridge Foundation
5500 Corporate Dr Ste 400
Pittsburgh PA 15237

(G-2930)
SCHNELLER HEATING AND AC CO
1079 Ohio Pike (45245-2339)
PHONE.................859 341-1200
Fax: 513 753-3105
Kris Knochelmann, *President*
Jacob C Grisham, *President*
Chris Knochelmann, *President*
Pete Knochelmann, *Manager*
EMP: 25
SQ FT: 4,500
SALES (est): 3.9MM Privately Held
WEB: www.schnellerheating.com
SIC: 1711 Warm air heating & air conditioning contractor

(G-2931)
SIBCY CLINE INC
792 Eastgate South Dr # 800 (45245-1563)
PHONE.................513 752-4000
Fax: 513 752-4315
Lori Schlagheck, *Financial Exec*
Mary Stone, *Manager*
EMP: 45
SALES (corp-wide): 2.1B Privately Held
WEB: www.sibcycline.com
SIC: 6531 Real estate agent, residential
PA: Sibcy Cline, Inc.
8044 Montgomery Rd # 300
Cincinnati OH 45236
513 984-4100

(G-2932)
SPIRIT WOMEN HEALTH NETWRK LLC
Also Called: Spirit Health
4270 Ivy Pointe Blvd # 220 (45245-0003)
PHONE.................561 544-2004
John Hopper, *Exec VP*
Julie Burt, *Opers-Prdtn-Mfg*
Fey Ruback, *Comptroller*
Rosina Lacomb, *Program Mgr*
Brian Debooth, *Network Analyst*
EMP: 30 EST: 2006
SALES (est): 3.3MM Privately Held
SIC: 8742 Hospital & health services consultant

(G-2933)
STEWART ADVNCED LAND TITLE LTD (PA)
4355 Ferguson Dr Ste 190 (45245-5137)
PHONE.................513 753-2800
Fax: 513 753-2805
Gregory Traynor,
Jane King, *Admin Asst*
EMP: 37
SALES (est): 6.3MM Privately Held
SIC: 6361 Title insurance

Cincinnati - Clermont County (G-2934)

(G-2934)
SURGERY CENTER CINCINNATI LLC
4415 Aicholtz Rd (45245-5140)
PHONE..................513 947-1130
Fax: 513 947-8541
Donna Crenshaw, *Manager*
Nestor Aquino,
Sabino Baluyout Et Al,
Sabino Al,
Rolando Go,
EMP: 100
SALES (est): 4.5MM **Privately Held**
WEB: www.phcps.com
SIC: 8011 Surgeon

(G-2935)
THARALDSON HOSPITALITY MGT
Also Called: Fairfield Inn
4521 Eastgate Blvd (45245-1201)
PHONE..................513 947-9402
Fax: 513 947-9402
Brittany Yeargan, *Marketing Staff*
Joyce Jabornick, *Manager*
EMP: 25 **Privately Held**
SIC: 7011 Inns
PA: Tharaldson Hospitality Management
1201 Page Dr S Ste 200
Fargo ND 58103

(G-2936)
TOTAL QUALITY LOGISTICS LLC (HQ)
Also Called: Tql
4289 Ivy Pointe Blvd (45245-0002)
P.O. Box 799, Milford (45150-0799)
PHONE..................513 831-2600
Kenneth G Oaks, *CEO*
Kerry Bryne, *President*
Kerry Byrne, *Exec VP*
Jeff Montelisciani, *Senior VP*
Tim Enos, *Opers Mgr*
EMP: 201
SQ FT: 100,000
SALES: 2.3B **Privately Held**
WEB: www.totalqualitylogistics.com
SIC: 4731 Truck transportation brokers
PA: Kgbo Holdings, Inc
4289 Ivy Pointe Blvd
Cincinnati OH 45245
513 831-2600

(G-2937)
ULTA BEAUTY INC
700 Estgate S Dr Ste 250 (45245)
PHONE..................513 752-1472
EMP: 99
SALES (corp-wide): 4.8B **Publicly Held**
SIC: 7241 Barber shops
PA: Ulta Beauty, Inc.
1000 Remington Blvd # 120
Bolingbrook IL 60440
630 410-4800

(G-2938)
WILLIS ONE HOUR HEATING & AC
756 Cncnnati Batavia Pike (45245-1276)
PHONE..................513 752-2512
Joseph Gertz, *General Mgr*
EMP: 75
SALES (est): 5MM **Privately Held**
SIC: 1711 Warm air heating & air conditioning contractor

Cincinnati
Hamilton County

(G-2939)
16 BIT BAR
1331 Walnut St (45202-7120)
PHONE..................513 381-1616
Mike Bowling, *General Mgr*
EMP: 45
SALES (est): 65.6K **Privately Held**
SIC: 7993 5813 Arcades; tavern (drinking places)

(G-2940)
1ST CHOICE SECURITY INC
2245 Gilbert Ave Ste 400 (45206-3000)
PHONE..................513 381-6789
Alan Grissinger, *President*
Brandon Finke, *Human Resources*
EMP: 175
SQ FT: 1,200
SALES: 4MM **Privately Held**
SIC: 7381 Security guard service

(G-2941)
2060 DIGITAL LLC
2060 Reading Rd (45202-1454)
PHONE..................513 699-5012
James Bryant, *President*
Robin Griteman, *Marketing Staff*
Jenna Shoemaker, *Manager*
EMP: 41
SALES (est): 1.4MM **Privately Held**
SIC: 8742 Marketing consulting services

(G-2942)
21C CINCINNATI LLC
Also Called: 21c Museum Hotel Cincinnati
609 Walnut St Ste 2 (45202-1191)
PHONE..................513 578-6600
Gerry Link Cha, *General Mgr*
Laura Lee Brown,
Steve Wilson,
EMP: 60
SALES (est): 5.8MM **Privately Held**
SIC: 7011 Hotel, franchised

(G-2943)
2444 MDSON RD CNDO OWNERS ASSN
Also Called: Regency, The
2444 Madison Rd Ste 101 (45208-1278)
PHONE..................513 871-0100
Fax: 513 871-5804
Mary Lawson, *President*
James R Schafer, *General Mgr*
Jane Royse, *Accountant*
Anita Saylor, *Accountant*
EMP: 30
SALES: 300K **Privately Held**
WEB: www.homebuildingpitfalls.com
SIC: 8641 Condominium association

(G-2944)
2780 AIRPORT DRIVE LLC
2135 Dana Ave Ste 200 (45207-1327)
PHONE..................513 563-7555
Jeff Tell, *CFO*
William Sayer, *Clerk*
EMP: 30 **EST:** 2015
SQ FT: 104,069
SALES (est): 437.2K **Privately Held**
SIC: 6531 Real estate agents & managers

(G-2945)
36 E SEVENTH LLC
2135 Dana Ave Ste 200 (45207-1327)
PHONE..................513 699-2279
Will Sayer, *Clerk*
EMP: 30 **EST:** 2016
SALES (est): 480.9K **Privately Held**
SIC: 6531 Real estate agents & managers

(G-2946)
506 PHELPS HOLDINGS LLC
Also Called: Residnce Inn Cincinnati Dwntwn
506 E 4th St (45202-3303)
PHONE..................513 651-1234
Fax: 513 651-1004
John Slaboch, *Vice Pres*
EMP: 42
SALES (est): 3.3MM **Privately Held**
SIC: 7011 Hotels

(G-2947)
6300 SHARONVILLE ASSOC LLC
Also Called: Doubletree Hotel
6300 E Kemper Rd (45241-2360)
PHONE..................513 489-3636
David Sundermann, *Principal*
Donna Seeley, *Sales Dir*
EMP: 182
SALES (est): 5.1MM **Privately Held**
WEB: www.dtwarrenplace.com
SIC: 7011 Hotels & motels

(G-2948)
722 REDEMPTION FUNDING INC
Also Called: Newstart Loan, The
169 Northland Blvd Ste 2 (45246-3154)
PHONE..................513 679-8302
Fax: 513 721-2822
Stan Zappin, *President*
Greg Sweeny, *Chairman*
Bob Freppon, *CFO*
Maryanne Kenner, *Manager*
Jake Sweeney, *Shareholder*
EMP: 35
SQ FT: 3,000
SALES: 22MM **Privately Held**
WEB: www.722redemption.com
SIC: 6141 Financing: automobiles, furniture, etc., not a deposit bank

(G-2949)
8451 LLC (HQ)
100 W 5th St (45202-2704)
PHONE..................513 632-1020
Fax: 513 632-1021
Simon Hay, *CEO*
Dave Palm, *Senior VP*
Piyush Zaveri, *Vice Pres*
Michael Whelan, *CFO*
Mary S Findley, *Human Res Dir*
EMP: 124
SQ FT: 40,000
SALES (est): 61.3MM
SALES (corp-wide): 122.6B **Publicly Held**
WEB: www.dunnhumby.com
SIC: 8732 Market analysis or research
PA: The Kroger Co
1014 Vine St Ste 1000
Cincinnati OH 45202
513 762-4000

(G-2950)
A & A WALL SYSTEMS INC
11589 Deerfield Rd (45242-1419)
PHONE..................513 489-0086
Fax: 513 489-0544
Michele McIntyre, *President*
Dale Adkins, *Vice Pres*
EMP: 45
SQ FT: 6,000
SALES (est): 7.4MM **Privately Held**
SIC: 1542 Commercial & office building, new construction; commercial & office buildings, renovation & repair

(G-2951)
A AND A MLLWRIGHT RIGGING SVCS
2205 Langdon Farm Rd (45237-4712)
PHONE..................513 396-6212
Fax: 513 396-6609
Clifford Applegate, *President*
EMP: 50
SQ FT: 28,959
SALES: 2MM **Privately Held**
SIC: 1796 7353 7699 Machinery installation; millwright; machine moving & rigging; cranes & aerial lift equipment, rental or leasing; industrial machinery & equipment repair

(G-2952)
A BETTER CHILD CARE CORP
6945 Harrison Ave (45247-3205)
PHONE..................513 353-5437
Alice Osborne, *Manager*
EMP: 25 **EST:** 2009
SALES (est): 357.9K **Privately Held**
SIC: 8351 Preschool center

(G-2953)
A C LEASING COMPANY
Also Called: A C Trucking
3023 E Kemper Rd Bldg 9 (45241-1509)
PHONE..................513 771-3676
Fax: 513 326-2344
Joseph Zembrodt, *President*
John Zembrodt, *Corp Secy*
Robert Schutzman, *Controller*
Harry Roth, *Director*
EMP: 42
SQ FT: 525,000
SALES (est): 6MM **Privately Held**
WEB: www.acleasing.net
SIC: 4214 4213 Local trucking with storage; trucking, except local

(G-2954)
A CCS DAY CARE CENTERS INC
1705 Section Rd (45237-3313)
PHONE..................513 841-2227
Jamica Thomas, *President*
Derek Edwards, *General Mgr*
EMP: 28 **EST:** 2013
SALES (est): 142.6K **Privately Held**
SIC: 8351 Child day care services

(G-2955)
A ONE FINE DRY CLEANERS INC (PA)
6223 Montgomery Rd (45213-1403)
PHONE..................513 351-2663
Mark Folzenlogen, *President*
EMP: 65
SALES (est): 1.8MM **Privately Held**
WEB: www.a-onecleaners.com
SIC: 7216 Cleaning & dyeing, except rugs

(G-2956)
A-1 QUALITY LABOR SERVICES LLC
Robertson Ave Ste 3021 (45209)
PHONE..................513 678-0724
William J Foster III,
EMP: 25
SALES: 450K **Privately Held**
SIC: 4491 Marine cargo handling

(G-2957)
A1 QUALITY LABOR SVC
3055 Blue Rock Rd (45239-6302)
PHONE..................513 353-0173
William Foster, *Owner*
Richard Mursinna, *Opers Mgr*
EMP: 50
SALES (est): 1.8MM **Privately Held**
SIC: 4225 General warehousing & storage

(G-2958)
AAA ALLIED GROUP INC (PA)
Also Called: World Wide Travel Service
15 W Central Pkwy (45202-1005)
PHONE..................513 762-3100
Fax: 513 762-5441
James L Pease III, *President*
Jane Jones, *General Mgr*
Mark Gabbard, *Regional Mgr*
Tom Beidleman, *Vice Pres*
Kim Knochelman, *Accounting Mgr*
EMP: 300
SQ FT: 50,000
SALES (est): 143.9M **Privately Held**
WEB: www.aaacincinnati.com
SIC: 4724 8699 Travel agencies; automobile owners' association

(G-2959)
AAA CINCINNATI INSURANCE SVC
15 W Central Pkwy (45202-1005)
PHONE..................513 345-5600
Fax: 513 381-0970
David Mc Millon, *President*
Stephen Wilson, *Treasurer*
Phil Dupont, *Telecomm Mgr*
EMP: 30
SALES (est): 184.7K **Privately Held**
SIC: 6411 Insurance agents

(G-2960)
ABCO FIRE LLC
Also Called: Abco Fire Protection
510 W Benson St (45215-3106)
PHONE..................800 875-7200
Meghan Cunningham, *Manager*
EMP: 46
SALES (corp-wide): 14.2MM **Privately Held**
SIC: 5099 7389 Safety equipment & supplies; fire extinguisher servicing
HQ: Abco Fire, Llc
4545 W 160th St
Cleveland OH 44135
216 433-7200

(G-2961)
ABM FACILITY SERVICES INC
Also Called: ABM Engineering
3087 B Terminal Dr (45275)
P.O. Box 75338 (45275-0338)
PHONE..................859 767-4393
Jeff Evans, *Accounts Exec*

GEOGRAPHIC SECTION

Cincinnati - Hamilton County (G-2984)

EMP: 36
SALES (corp-wide): 5.4B **Publicly Held**
SIC: **7349** Building maintenance services
HQ: Abm Facility Services, Inc.
1266 14th St Ste 103
Oakland CA 94607

(G-2962)
ABM JANITORIAL SERVICES INC
354 Gest St (45203-1822)
PHONE..................513 731-1418
Brian Planicka, *Manager*
EMP: 105
SALES (corp-wide): 5.4B **Publicly Held**
SIC: **7349** Janitorial service, contract basis
HQ: Abm Janitorial Services, Inc.
1111 Fannin St Ste 1500
Houston TX 77002
713 654-8924

(G-2963)
ACCENTURE LLP
201 E 4th St Ste 1600 (45202-4249)
PHONE..................513 455-1000
Nathan Beadle, *Manager*
Giovanni Molina, *Consultant*
Sandhya Nair, *Consultant*
David Zalla, *Associate*
EMP: 62 **Privately Held**
WEB: www.wavesecurities.com
SIC: **8742** Business consultant
HQ: Accenture Llp
161 N Clark St Ste 1100
Chicago IL 60601
312 693-0161

(G-2964)
ACCENTURE LLP
425 Walnut St Ste 1200 (45202-3928)
PHONE..................513 651-2444
Anderson Jeff, *Engineer*
Edward Harbach, *Branch Mgr*
Jorge Barreto, *Manager*
EMP: 85 **Privately Held**
SIC: **8742** Business consultant
HQ: Accenture Llp
161 N Clark St Ste 1100
Chicago IL 60601
312 693-0161

(G-2965)
ACCOUNTANTS TO YOU LLC
Also Called: Consultants To You
430 Reading Rd Ste 100 (45202-1477)
PHONE..................513 651-2855
Fax: 513 651-5866
Jason Oswald, *Vice Pres*
Andrea Thorn, *Vice Pres*
Rachel Schulz, *Sales Staff*
Gary Merrifield,
Kt Russell, *Recruiter*
EMP: 35
SALES (est): 2MM **Privately Held**
WEB: www.accountantstoyou.com
SIC: **7361** Executive placement

(G-2966)
ACE DORAN HAULING & RIGGING CO (DH)
1601 Blue Rock St (45223-2579)
PHONE..................513 681-7900
Fax: 513 681-7900
Daniel J Doran, *President*
Bob Doran, *Vice Pres*
Dennis Nelson, *Asst Director*
EMP: 34
SQ FT: 3,000
SALES (est): 5.9MM **Privately Held**
HQ: Bennett Motor Express, Llc
1001 Industrial Pkwy
Mcdonough GA 30253
770 957-1866

(G-2967)
ACE-MERIT LLC
30 Garfield Pl Ste 540 (45202-4366)
PHONE..................513 241-3200
Fax: 513 241-7958
Brenda Worrell, *General Mgr*
Alicia Hardin,
Angelia Portune,
EMP: 30
SQ FT: 3,000

SALES (est): 2.2MM **Privately Held**
WEB: www.acemerit.com
SIC: **7338** Court reporting service

(G-2968)
ACPI SYSTEMS INC
1440 Kemper Meadow Dr (45240-1636)
P.O. Box 368, Ross (45061-0368)
PHONE..................513 738-3840
Fax: 513 738-3841
Laura L Meyer, *President*
James J Meyer, *Vice Pres*
Ken Brock, *Project Mgr*
EMP: 45
SQ FT: 5,000
SALES (est): 12.3MM **Privately Held**
WEB: www.acpi-systems.com
SIC: **1731** **8711** Electrical work; electrical or electronic engineering

(G-2969)
ACS ACQCO CORP
201 E 4th St Ste 900 (45202-4160)
PHONE..................513 719-2600
Elizabeth A Haley, *President*
EMP: 121 EST: 2014
SALES (est): 342.8K
SALES (corp-wide): 184.7B **Publicly Held**
SIC: **5122** Drugs, proprietaries & sundries
HQ: Omnicare, Inc.
900 Omnicare Ctr 201e4t
Cincinnati OH 45202
513 719-2600

(G-2970)
ACTION ENGNEERED LOGISTICS LLC
Also Called: Ace Brokerage, LLC
1601 Blue Rock St (45223-2502)
PHONE..................513 681-7900
Daniel Doran, *President*
EMP: 93
SQ FT: 8,000
SALES (est): 11.7MM **Privately Held**
SIC: **4731** Transportation agents & brokers
HQ: Bennett Motor Express, Llc
1001 Industrial Pkwy
Mcdonough GA 30253
770 957-1866

(G-2971)
ACUREN INSPECTION INC
502 W Crescentville Rd (45246-1222)
PHONE..................513 671-7073
Mike Ross, *District Mgr*
EMP: 27
SALES (corp-wide): 1.6B **Privately Held**
SIC: **1389** Testing, measuring, surveying & analysis services
HQ: Acuren Inspection, Inc.
30 Main St Ste 402
Danbury CT 06810
203 702-8740

(G-2972)
ADDICTION SERVICES COUNCIL
Also Called: CASA
2828 Vernon Pl (45219-2414)
PHONE..................513 281-7880
Fax: 513 281-7884
Nan Franks, *CEO*
Daina Dennis, *COO*
EMP: 32
SQ FT: 4,000
SALES: 1.8MM **Privately Held**
WEB: www.alcoholismcouncil.org
SIC: **8322** Alcoholism counseling, nontreatment; drug abuse counselor, nontreatment

(G-2973)
ADLETA INC
Also Called: Adleta Construction
389 S Wayne Ave (45215-4522)
PHONE..................513 554-1469
Fax: 513 554-1221
Robert Adleta Sr, *President*
Bob Adleta, *Vice Pres*
Robert Adleta II, *Vice Pres*
Tim Adleta, *Vice Pres*
Bob Dunn, *Vice Pres*
EMP: 35
SQ FT: 2,000

SALES (est): 6.9MM **Privately Held**
SIC: **1771** **1623** Concrete work; sewer line construction

(G-2974)
ADVANCE IMPLANT DENTISTRY INC
5823 Wooster Pike (45227-4505)
PHONE..................513 271-0821
Fax: 513 271-0621
Scott E Sayre, *President*
Janet Sayre, *Vice Pres*
Robert Buechner, *Admin Sec*
EMP: 40
SQ FT: 1,600
SALES (est): 3.2MM **Privately Held**
WEB: www.advanced-dentistry.net
SIC: **8021** Dentists' office

(G-2975)
ADVANCE TRNSP SYSTEMS INC
Also Called: Ats Transportation Services
10558 Taconic Ter (45215-1125)
PHONE..................513 818-4311
Fax: 513 771-4877
Robert L Wyenandt, *President*
Ryan Burke, *Opers Mgr*
Kelly Gardner, *Sales Staff*
Dan Hicks, *Sales Staff*
Dave Tawney, *Sales Staff*
EMP: 25
SQ FT: 10,000
SALES: 50MM **Privately Held**
WEB: www.atslogistics.com
SIC: **4731** Truck transportation brokers

(G-2976)
ADVANTAGE RESOURCING AMER INC (HQ)
Also Called: Advantage Staffing
201 E 4th St Ste 800 (45202-4248)
PHONE..................781 472-8900
Stacey Lane, *Exec VP*
Erin Kamenoff, *Senior VP*
Tom Schmidt, *Senior VP*
Matt Anderson, *Vice Pres*
Judy Culpepper, *Vice Pres*
EMP: 30
SALES (est): 745.9M
SALES (corp-wide): 16.1B **Privately Held**
SIC: **7361** Labor contractors (employment agency)
PA: Recruit Holdings Co.,Ltd.
1-9-2, Marunouchi
Chiyoda-Ku TKY 100-0
368 351-111

(G-2977)
AFFINITY DISP EXPOSITIONS INC
Also Called: Adex International
1301 Glendale Milford Rd (45215-1210)
PHONE..................513 771-2339
Tim Murphy, *President*
EMP: 110
SALES (corp-wide): 24.3MM **Privately Held**
WEB: www.adex-intl.com
SIC: **7389** Trade show arrangement
PA: Affinity Displays & Expositions, Inc.
1301 Glendale Milford Rd
Cincinnati OH 45215
513 771-2339

(G-2978)
AIC CONTRACTING INC (PA)
12100 Mosteller Rd # 100 (45241-6405)
PHONE..................513 881-5900
Michael Ansari, *Principal*
Tina Ansari, *Principal*
Richard Baumann, *Project Mgr*
Mary Vesper, *Controller*
Sam Sharif, *Admin Sec*
EMP: 38
SQ FT: 18,000
SALES (est): 6.8MM **Privately Held**
WEB: www.aiccontracting.com
SIC: **1799** Home/office interiors finishing, furnishing & remodeling

(G-2979)
AIRGAS USA LLC
Also Called: Linde Gas
10031 Cncnnati Dyton Pike (45241-1003)
PHONE..................513 563-8070

Hal Magers, *Branch Mgr*
EMP: 35
SALES (corp-wide): 163.9MM **Privately Held**
WEB: www.us.linde-gas.com
SIC: **5084** **5169** Industrial machinery & equipment; chemicals & allied products
HQ: Airgas Usa, Llc
259 N Radnor Chester Rd # 100
Radnor PA 19087
610 687-5253

(G-2980)
AL NEYER LLC (PA)
302 W 3rd St Ste 800 (45202-3426)
PHONE..................513 271-6400
Molly North, *President*
Rob Gage, *Vice Pres*
Scott Jones, *Human Resources*
Rob Marks, *Sr Project Mgr*
Kathy Feller, *Payroll Mgr*
EMP: 56
SQ FT: 22,570
SALES (est): 9.1MM **Privately Held**
SIC: **6531** Real estate managers

(G-2981)
AL NEYER LLC
302 W 3rd St Ste 800 (45202-3426)
PHONE..................513 271-6400
Molly North, *President*
David F Neyer, *President*
William L Neyer, *Exec VP*
Cassie J Belmonte, *Vice Pres*
Mildred Curtis, *Vice Pres*
EMP: 80
SQ FT: 17,837
SALES (est): 15MM **Privately Held**
WEB: www.neyer.com
SIC: **6552** **1522** **1541** **1542** Land subdividers & developers, commercial; land subdividers & developers, residential; multi-family dwelling construction; industrial buildings & warehouses; commercial & office building contractors

(G-2982)
ALBERT MIKE LEASING INC (PA)
10340 Evendale Dr (45241-2512)
PHONE..................513 563-1400
Fax: 513 956-2954
Robert Betagole, *CEO*
Marty Betagole, *President*
Brad Area, *Area Mgr*
Mexico Arizona, *Area Mgr*
Barb Powell, *Area Mgr*
▼ EMP: 169
SQ FT: 56,000
SALES (est): 32.8MM **Privately Held**
WEB: www.cvgrentacar.com
SIC: **7515** **7513** **5521** **5012** Passenger car leasing; truck leasing, without drivers; automobiles, used cars only; trucks, tractors & trailers: used; automobiles; trucks, noncommercial; automotive & home supply stores; new & used car dealers

(G-2983)
ALEXANDER & ASSOCIATES CO (PA)
360 Mclean Dr (45237-1643)
PHONE..................513 731-7800
Fax: 513 366-4520
Thomas Luebbe, *President*
Victor Mohoney, *Senior VP*
Russell Miller, *Vice Pres*
Thomas Rowe, *Vice Pres*
Kevin McCormick, *Project Mgr*
EMP: 160
SQ FT: 15,000
SALES (est): 24.9MM **Privately Held**
WEB: www.alexanderandassoc.com
SIC: **8711** Consulting engineer

(G-2984)
ALL ABOUT HEATING COOLING
7861 Palace Dr (45249-1635)
PHONE..................513 621-4620
DOT Braun, *Owner*
EMP: 30 EST: 2012
SALES (est): 901.6K **Privately Held**
SIC: **1711** Warm air heating & air conditioning contractor

Cincinnati - Hamilton County (G-2985)

(G-2985)
ALL OCCASIONS EVENT RENTAL
10629 Reading Rd (45241-2526)
PHONE...................513 563-0600
Fax: 513 563-6757
Elizabeth Wilson, *President*
Sheryl Barker, *Accountant*
Eric Easterling, *Manager*
Bethany Jones, *Manager*
Jenn Mercer, *Manager*
EMP: 25
SALES (est): 4.7MM **Privately Held**
SIC: 7359 Party supplies rental services

(G-2986)
ALLAN PEACE & ASSOCIATES INC
Also Called: C A I Insurance Agency
2035 Reading Rd (45202-1415)
PHONE...................513 579-1700
Carl Schloteman, *President*
EMP: 40
SALES (est): 3.2MM **Privately Held**
WEB: www.allanpeace.com
SIC: 6411 Insurance agents, brokers & service

(G-2987)
ALLCAN GLOBAL SERVICES INC (PA)
11235 Sebring Dr (45240-2714)
PHONE...................513 825-1655
Anthony Lacey, *CEO*
EMP: 48
SQ FT: 50,000
SALES (est): 3MM **Privately Held**
SIC: 1731 8741 7361 Electrical work; management services; placement agencies

(G-2988)
ALLGEIER & SON INC (PA)
6386 Bridgetown Rd (45248-2933)
PHONE...................513 574-3735
Fax: 513 598-2163
Michael Allgeier, *Owner*
Margaret A Steigerwald, *Treasurer*
EMP: 40
SQ FT: 800
SALES (est): 5MM **Privately Held**
SIC: 1794 1422 1795 Excavation & grading, building construction; crushed & broken limestone; wrecking & demolition work

(G-2989)
ALLIED BUILDING PRODUCTS CORP
1735 Eastern Ave (45202-1710)
PHONE...................513 784-9090
Fax: 513 784-9024
Robert Braun, *Opers Mgr*
Jim Francis, *Manager*
EMP: 25
SQ FT: 20,000
SALES (corp-wide): 4.3B **Publicly Held**
WEB: www.alliedbuilding.com
SIC: 5033 5031 Roofing & siding materials; windows
HQ: Allied Building Products Corp.
  15 E Union Ave
  East Rutherford NJ 07073
  201 507-8400

(G-2990)
ALLIED CAR WASH INC
Also Called: AAA Auto Wash
3330 Central Pkwy (45225-2307)
PHONE...................513 559-1733
Emina Short, *Finance Dir*
Jennifer Fulks, *Accountant*
EMP: 45
SALES (est): 177.2K **Privately Held**
SIC: 7542 Carwash, automatic

(G-2991)
ALLIED CASH HOLDINGS LLC (PA)
Also Called: Allied Cash Advance
7755 Montgomery Rd # 400 (45236-4197)
PHONE...................305 371-3141
David Davis, *President*
Douglas Clark, *Vice Pres*
Scott Kitchen, *Vice Pres*
Shannon Obrien, *Vice Pres*
Roger Dean, *CFO*
EMP: 58
SQ FT: 5,400
SALES (est): 138.4MM **Privately Held**
SIC: 6099 Check cashing agencies

(G-2992)
ALLIED SECURITY LLC
110 Boggs Ln Ste 140 (45246-3143)
PHONE...................513 771-3776
Fax: 513 771-3537
Tim Cember, *Manager*
Gary Jones, *Manager*
EMP: 430
SALES (corp-wide): 13MM **Privately Held**
WEB: www.alliedsecurity.com
SIC: 7381 Security guard service
HQ: Allied Security, Llc
  161 Washington St
  Conshohocken PA 19428
  610 239-1100

(G-2993)
ALMOST FAMILY INC
2135 Dana Ave Ste 220 (45207-1342)
PHONE...................513 662-3400
EMP: 30
SALES (corp-wide): 796.9MM **Publicly Held**
SIC: 7389 Automobile recovery service
PA: Almost Family, Inc.
  9510 Ormsby Station Rd
  Louisville KY 40223
  502 891-1000

(G-2994)
ALPHA INVESTMENT PARTNERSHIP (PA)
Also Called: Cincinnati Equitable Insurance
525 Vine St Ste 1925 (45202-3125)
P.O. Box 3428 (45201-3428)
PHONE...................513 621-1826
Peter Alpaugh, *President*
Greg Baker, *President*
Steve Lavdas, *Engineer*
James Orwig, *Advisor*
EMP: 58
SALES (est): 13.3MM **Privately Held**
SIC: 6411 Insurance agents, brokers & service

(G-2995)
ALPS SERVICES INC
10653 Chester Rd (45215-1205)
PHONE...................513 671-6300
Fax: 513 346-4122
Eddie Sinkfield, *President*
Wesla Brown, *Vice Pres*
Denise Barone, *Manager*
EMP: 40
SQ FT: 8,500
SALES: 2.1MM **Privately Held**
WEB: www.alpsservices.com
SIC: 8742 Hospital & health services consultant

(G-2996)
ALSTOM SIGNALING OPERATION LLC
25 Merchant St (45246-3700)
PHONE...................513 552-6485
Bill Dwyer, *Branch Mgr*
EMP: 259
SALES (corp-wide): 1.6B **Privately Held**
WEB: www.proyard.com
SIC: 4789 Cargo loading & unloading services
PA: Alstom Signaling Operation, Llc
  2901 E Lake Rd Bldg 122
  Erie PA 16531
  800 825-3178

(G-2997)
ALTERNATIVE HOME CARE & STFFNG
7759 Montgomery Rd (45236-4201)
PHONE...................513 794-0571
Kelly Wickline, *Principal*
EMP: 40 EST: 2012
SALES (est): 225.7K **Privately Held**
SIC: 8082 Home health care services

(G-2998)
ALTERNATIVE HOME HEALTH CARE
5150 E Galbraith Rd # 200 (45236-2872)
PHONE...................513 794-0555
Fax: 513 794-1539
Kelly Wickline, *President*
EMP: 40
SALES (est): 2.3MM **Privately Held**
WEB: www.alternativehomehealthcare.com
SIC: 8741 8082 Nursing & personal care facility management; home health care services

(G-2999)
ALVEO HEALTH LLC
700 W Pete Rose Way # 426 (45203-1892)
PHONE...................513 557-3502
Jeff Loney, *CEO*
EMP: 25 EST: 1988
SQ FT: 3,600
SALES (est): 113.6K **Privately Held**
SIC: 8099 Physical examination service, insurance

(G-3000)
AMENITY HOME HEALTH CARE LLC
3025 W Galbraith Rd (45239-4222)
PHONE...................513 931-3689
Fax: 513 931-4230
Patricia Carter, *Partner*
EMP: 40
SALES (est): 591.6K **Privately Held**
SIC: 8082 Home health care services

(G-3001)
AMERICAN CONTRS INDEMNITY CO
7794 5 Mile Rd (45230-2368)
PHONE...................513 688-0800
Paul Abrams, *Branch Mgr*
EMP: 34
SALES (corp-wide): 46B **Privately Held**
SIC: 6399 Bank deposit insurance
HQ: American Contractors Indemnity Company
  801 S Figueroa St Ste 700
  Los Angeles CA 90017

(G-3002)
AMERICAN EMPIRE SURPLUS LINES
Also Called: American Empire Insurance
515 Main St (45202-3223)
PHONE...................513 369-3000
Bob Nelson, *President*
Thomas Matthew Held, *Assistant VP*
Chet Nalepa, *Vice Pres*
Matt Held, *Admin Sec*
EMP: 43
SQ FT: 20,000
SALES (est): 4.3MM **Publicly Held**
SIC: 6411 Insurance agents
HQ: American Empire Surplus Lines Insurance Company
  580 Walnut St
  Cincinnati OH 45202
  513 369-3000

(G-3003)
AMERICAN EMPRIE SRPLS LINES IN (DH)
580 Walnut St (45202-3127)
PHONE...................513 369-3000
Fax: 513 369-3062
Robert A Nelson, *Ch of Bd*
Mark R Lonneman, *President*
Carl H Lindner III, *Officer*
EMP: 57
SQ FT: 33,000
SALES (est): 23.9MM **Publicly Held**
SIC: 6331 Fire, marine & casualty insurance: stock; property damage insurance
HQ: Great American Insurance Company
  301 E 4th St Fl 8
  Cincinnati OH 45202
  513 369-5000

(G-3004)
AMERICAN FEDERATION OF GOV
3200 Vine St (45220-2213)
P.O. Box 29093 (45229-0093)
PHONE...................513 861-6047
Fax: 513 861-6120
EMP: 25
SALES (corp-wide): 42.4MM **Privately Held**
SIC: 8631 Labor union
PA: American Federation Of Government Employees, Afl-Cio
  80 F St Nw Fl 7
  Washington DC 20001
  202 737-8700

(G-3005)
AMERICAN FINANCIAL CORPORATION
580 Walnut St Fl 9 (45202-3193)
PHONE...................513 579-2121
Fax: 513 369-3655
James Evans, *Principal*
Howard Baird, *Vice Pres*
Robert Dobbs, *Vice Pres*
Mark Weiss, *Vice Pres*
Brian Hertzman, *Controller*
EMP: 92
SALES (est): 1MM **Publicly Held**
SIC: 8111 General practice attorney, lawyer
HQ: Afc Holding Company Inc
  1 E 4th St
  Cincinnati OH 45202

(G-3006)
AMERICAN FINANCIAL GROUP INC (PA)
301 E 4th St (45202-4245)
PHONE...................513 579-2121
Fax: 513 579-0110
Carl H Lindner III, *CEO*
S Craig Lindner, *President*
Matthew Washington, *COO*
Alicia Yoo, *Exec VP*
Vito C Peraino, *Senior VP*
EMP: 146
SQ FT: 675,000
SALES: 6.8B **Publicly Held**
WEB: www.amfnl.com
SIC: 6331 6311 6321 Fire, marine & casualty insurance; life insurance; life insurance carriers; accident & health insurance; accident associations, mutual

(G-3007)
AMERICAN GEN LF INSUR CO DEL
Also Called: AIG
250 E 5th St Ste 1500 (45202-4252)
PHONE...................513 762-7807
Fax: 513 762-7811
Robert Adams, *Principal*
Dale Connor, *Vice Pres*
Brook Syers, *Auditor*
Judy Storey-Cantu, *Business Anlyst*
Susan Adams, *Manager*
EMP: 49
SALES (corp-wide): 49.5B **Publicly Held**
WEB: www.aiglifeinsurancecompany.com
SIC: 6411 Insurance agents, brokers & service
HQ: American General Life Insurance Company Of Delaware
  2727 Allen Pkwy Ste A
  Houston TX 77019
  713 522-1111

(G-3008)
AMERICAN MONEY MANAGEMENT CORP
301 E 4th St Fl 27 (45202-4245)
PHONE...................513 579-2592
S Craig Lindner, *Ch of Bd*
John B Berding, *President*
David Meyer, *Senior VP*
Sandra W Heimann, *Vice Pres*
EMP: 38
SQ FT: 2,000
SALES (est): 6MM **Publicly Held**
WEB: www.amfnl.com
SIC: 6282 Investment advisory service

GEOGRAPHIC SECTION

Cincinnati - Hamilton County (G-3032)

PA: American Financial Group, Inc.
301 E 4th St
Cincinnati OH 45202

(G-3009)
AMERICAN NURSING CARE INC
4750 Wesley Ave Ste Q (45212-2273)
PHONE.................513 731-4600
Fax: 513 458-5632
Amy Owens, Manager
EMP: 40 Privately Held
WEB: www.americannursingcare.com
SIC: 8051 8082 Skilled nursing care facilities; home health care services
HQ: American Nursing Care, Inc.
1700 Edison Dr Ste 300
Milford OH 45150
513 576-0262

(G-3010)
AMERICAN NURSING CARE INC
4460 Red Bank Rd Ste 100 (45227-2173)
PHONE.................513 245-1500
Victoria Dixon, Principal
EMP: 68 Privately Held
SIC: 8051 Skilled nursing care facilities
HQ: American Nursing Care, Inc.
1700 Edison Dr Ste 300
Milford OH 45150
513 576-0262

(G-3011)
AMERICAN PARA PROF SYSTEMS INC
Also Called: A P P S
6056 Montgomery Rd (45213-1612)
P.O. Box 36166 (45236-0166)
PHONE.................513 531-2900
Fax: 513 531-3366
Sarah Swisher, Manager
EMP: 30
SQ FT: 350
SALES (corp-wide): 9.3MM Privately Held
WEB: www.appsms.com
SIC: 8011 Medical insurance plan
PA: American Para Professional Systems, Inc.
1 Jericho Plz Ste 101
Jericho NY 11753
516 822-6230

(G-3012)
AMERICAN RED CROSS (HQ)
Also Called: Cincinnati Area Chapter
2111 Dana Ave (45207-1303)
PHONE.................513 579-3000
Fax: 513 579-3953
Trish Smitson, CEO
Becky Willis, Accounts Mgr
C Hazel, Marketing Mgr
Nikki Williams, Corp Comm Staff
Delbert Felix, Office Mgr
EMP: 75
SQ FT: 26,147
SALES (est): 7MM
SALES (corp-wide): 2.5B Privately Held
SIC: 8322 Disaster service; first aid service; youth center
PA: The American National Red Cross
430 17th St Nw
Washington DC 20006
202 737-8300

(G-3013)
AMERICAN RISK SERVICES LLC
1130 Congress Ave Ste A (45246-4485)
PHONE.................513 772-3712
Robert Simpson III, Principal
EMP: 27
SALES: 3.5MM Privately Held
WEB: www.americanriskservices.com
SIC: 6411 Insurance brokers

(G-3014)
AMERIDIAN SPECIALTY SERVICES
11520 Rockfield Ct (45241-1919)
PHONE.................513 769-0150
Betty Owens, President
Derek Wehman, Vice Pres
Jim Owens, Project Mgr
Tom Owens, VP Sales
Mike Barney, Manager

EMP: 50
SQ FT: 32,000
SALES (est): 7.3MM Privately Held
WEB: www.ameridiansvcs.com
SIC: 8741 1761 3441 Construction management; architectural sheet metal work; gutter & downspout contractor; fabricated structural metal

(G-3015)
AMERITAS LIFE INSURANCE CORP
1876 Waycross Rd (45240-2825)
P.O. Box 40888 (45240-0888)
PHONE.................513 595-2334
Joann M Martin, CEO
Steven J Valerius, President
Tim L Stonehocker, Exec VP
J Thomas Burkhard, Senior VP
Cheryl L Heilman, Senior VP
EMP: 40
SALES (est): 27.7MM Privately Held
SIC: 6311 Life insurance

(G-3016)
AMP ADVERTISING INC
700 Walnut St Ste 500 (45202-2011)
PHONE.................513 333-4100
George Sabert, President
Jim Browning, Vice Pres
Lewis Cresta, Pub Rel Mgr
EMP: 38
SALES (est): 3.1MM Privately Held
WEB: www.sunriseadvertising.com
SIC: 7311 Advertising agencies

(G-3017)
AMPAC HOLDINGS LLC (DH)
Also Called: Proampac
12025 Tricon Rd (45246-1719)
PHONE.................513 671-1777
James Baker, Senior VP
Kathy Hale, Credit Mgr
Greg Tucker, Mng Member
Doug Andersen, Manager
Eric Bradford,
◆ EMP: 700 EST: 2001
SQ FT: 220,000
SALES (est): 365.9MM
SALES (corp-wide): 90.7K Privately Held
WEB: www.ampaconline.com
SIC: 2673 2677 3081 2674 Plastic bags: made from purchased materials; pliofilm bags: made from purchased materials; envelopes; unsupported plastics film & sheet; shopping bags: made from purchased materials; investment holding companies, except banks
HQ: Proampac Holdings Inc.
12025 Tricon Rd
Cincinnati OH 45246
513 671-1777

(G-3018)
AMPACET CORPORATION
4705 Duke Dr 400 (45249)
PHONE.................513 247-5400
Fax: 513 247-5415
Vicky Willsey, Manager
EMP: 25
SALES (corp-wide): 631.1MM Privately Held
WEB: www.ampacet.com
SIC: 3089 5162 Coloring & finishing of plastic products; plastics materials & basic shapes
PA: Ampacet Corporation
660 White Plains Rd # 360
Tarrytown NY 10591
914 631-6600

(G-3019)
AMPLE TRAILER LEASING & SALES
610 Wayne Park Dr (45215-2847)
PHONE.................513 563-2550
Edward Focke, President
EMP: 27
SQ FT: 6,000
SALES (est): 1.8MM Privately Held
SIC: 7519 Trailer rental

(G-3020)
AMS INC
1608 Elmore St (45223-2619)
PHONE.................513 244-8500

Fax: 513 244-8504
David Aberman, President
▼ EMP: 25
SALES (est): 3.8MM Privately Held
SIC: 1542 Commercial & office building, new construction

(G-3021)
ANARK INC
Also Called: Animal Ark Pet Resort
2150 Struble Rd (45231-1736)
PHONE.................513 825-7387
Fax: 513 674-9489
Vicki Gumpbush, President
Dave Gump, Vice Pres
George Gump, Treasurer
Jan Gump, Admin Sec
EMP: 30
SQ FT: 12,768
SALES (est): 697K Privately Held
WEB: www.anark.com
SIC: 0752 5999 Animal boarding services; animal training services; grooming services, pet & animal specialties; pets & pet supplies

(G-3022)
ANDERSON HEALTHCARE LTD
Also Called: Anderson, The
8139 Beechmont Ave (45255-3152)
P.O. Box 541084 (45254-1084)
PHONE.................513 474-6200
Fax: 513 388-3000
Ross Darrell, Telecom Exec
Darrell Ross, Telecom Exec
Akiva Wagschal,
Linda Wagschal,
EMP: 96
SQ FT: 44,000
SALES (est): 6.6MM Privately Held
SIC: 8051 8069 Convalescent home with continuous nursing care; specialty hospitals, except psychiatric

(G-3023)
ANDERSON HILLS PEDIATRICS INC
7400 Jager Ct (45230-4344)
PHONE.................513 232-8100
Fax: 513 624-3191
Roger Herman, President
Laura K White MD, Med Doctor
Brian Vanderhorst, Manager
Petra Bauer, Manager
EMP: 70
SQ FT: 4,750
SALES (est): 10.6MM Privately Held
WEB: www.ahpediatrics.com
SIC: 8011 Pediatrician

(G-3024)
ANDERSON JEFFERY R RE INC
3805 Edwards Rd Ste 700 (45209-1955)
PHONE.................513 241-5800
Jeffrey R Anderson, President
Ryan Garlitz, Controller
Christ Wesselkamper, Property Mgr
Tony Cook, Manager
Mindy Heizer, Director
EMP: 50
SQ FT: 30,000
SALES (est): 3.1MM Privately Held
WEB: www.anderson-realestate.com
SIC: 6512 Commercial & industrial building operation

(G-3025)
ANDERSON LITTLE
8516 Beechmont Ave (45255-4708)
PHONE.................513 474-7800
Fax: 513 474-0333
Robin Beier, Director
Robin L Beier, Director
EMP: 38
SALES (est): 823.3K Privately Held
SIC: 8351 Group day care center

(G-3026)
ANDERSON TWNSHIP HSTORICAL SOC
6550 Clough Pike (45244-4029)
P.O. Box 30174 (45230-0174)
PHONE.................513 231-2114
Sue A Wettstein, President
Carol Voorhees, Corp Secy
Albert Wettstein, COO

Robert Radcliffe, Exec VP
Bruce Bromen,
EMP: 45 EST: 1975
SALES: 92.3K Privately Held
SIC: 8412 Historical society

(G-3027)
ANDREW BELMONT SARGENT (PA)
Also Called: ABS Business Products
10855 Medallion Dr (45241-4829)
PHONE.................513 769-7800
Fax: 513 351-0112
James Donnellon, President
Ross Winslow, Sales Staff
Terry Dunigan, Office Mgr
Grant Hilty, Consultant
EMP: 31
SQ FT: 17,000
SALES (est): 23.1MM Privately Held
WEB: www.absproducts.com
SIC: 5044 7699 Copying equipment; office equipment & accessory customizing

(G-3028)
ANESTHSIA ASSOC CINCINNATI INC
2139 Auburn Ave (45219-2906)
P.O. Box 40574 (45240-0574)
PHONE.................513 585-0577
Mark Manley, President
Kim McCinnell, Practice Mgr
Matthew Ciotti, Anesthesiology
Shanaka R Peiris, Anesthesiology
EMP: 60
SALES (est): 3.8MM
SALES (corp-wide): 287.4MM Privately Held
SIC: 8011 Anesthesiologist
HQ: Team Health Holdings, Inc.
265 Brookview Centre Way
Knoxville TN 37919
865 693-1000

(G-3029)
ANGELS 4 LIFE LLC
431 Ohio Pike Ste 182s (45255-3717)
PHONE.................513 474-5683
Shellie Fischer,
EMP: 30
SALES: 1MM Privately Held
SIC: 8082 8052 Home health care services; home for the mentally retarded, with health care

(G-3030)
ANGELS TOUCH NURSING CARE
3619 Harrison Ave (45211-5540)
PHONE.................513 661-4111
Fax: 513 661-4068
Bonnie Perrino, President
Beverly Rosemeyer, Assistant
EMP: 30
SALES (est): 846.7K Privately Held
SIC: 8082 Visiting nurse service

(G-3031)
ANHEUSER-BUSCH LLC
600 Vine St Ste 1002 (45202-2400)
PHONE.................513 381-3927
Dirk Disper, Branch Mgr
EMP: 113
SALES (corp-wide): 57.4K Privately Held
SIC: 5181 Beer & other fermented malt liquors
HQ: Anheuser-Busch, Llc
1 Busch Pl
Saint Louis MO 63118
314 632-6777

(G-3032)
AP CCHMC
3333 Burnet Ave (45229-3026)
PHONE.................513 636-4200
Amy Snow, Pastor
Betsy Gerrein, Project Mgr
Diane Wall, Human Res Mgr
Lois Curtwright, Director
Michael Grau, Director
EMP: 45
SALES (est): 8.4MM Privately Held
SIC: 8011 Pediatrician

(PA)=Parent Co (HQ)=Headquarters (DH)=Div Headquarters
✪ = New Business established in last 2 years

2018 Harris Ohio Services Directory

Cincinnati - Hamilton County (G-3033)

(G-3033)
APC2 INC (PA)
Also Called: Appearance Plus
6812 Clough Pike (45244-4037)
PHONE................513 231-5540
Fax: 513 624-3856
Jonathon Lindy, *President*
EMP: 63
SALES (est): 4.4MM **Privately Held**
WEB: www.appearanceplus.com
SIC: 7216 7212 Cleaning & dyeing, except rugs; laundry & drycleaner agents

(G-3034)
APEX ENVIRONMENTAL SVCS LLC
295 Northland Blvd (45246-3603)
PHONE................513 772-2739
Fax: 513 772-4739
Bill Evans,
EMP: 85 EST: 1998
SALES (est): 2.3MM **Privately Held**
WEB: www.apexservicesllc.com
SIC: 7349 Janitorial service, contract basis

(G-3035)
APEX RESTORATION CONTRS LTD (PA)
6315 Warrick St (45227-2540)
P.O. Box 80850, Rochester MI (48308-0850)
PHONE................513 489-1795
Fax: 513 489-1588
Laeron Evans, *Vice Pres*
Daniel P Mc Neil, *Mng Member*
Amy Trotta, *Manager*
EMP: 30
SQ FT: 10,200
SALES (est): 4.6MM **Privately Held**
WEB: www.apexrest.com
SIC: 1521 1542 General remodeling, single-family houses; commercial & office buildings, renovation & repair

(G-3036)
APOLLO HEATING AND AC INC
Also Called: Three Rivers Heating & Air
1730 Tennessee Ave (45229-1202)
PHONE................513 271-3600
James Gerdsen, *President*
EMP: 35
SQ FT: 6,700
SALES (est): 6.6MM **Privately Held**
WEB: www.apollo-hvac.com
SIC: 1711 1731 Warm air heating & air conditioning contractor; electrical work

(G-3037)
APPLIED MECHANICAL SYSTEMS INC
12082 Champion Way (45241-6406)
PHONE................513 825-1800
Fax: 513 825-5759
Shane Drinnon, *Project Mgr*
Drew Mitakides, *Branch Mgr*
Brenda Glover, *Data Proc Exec*
EMP: 75
SQ FT: 3,500
SALES (corp-wide): 33.5MM **Privately Held**
WEB: www.appliedmechanicalsys.com
SIC: 1711 Plumbing contractors; warm air heating & air conditioning contractor
PA: Applied Mechanical Systems, Inc.
5598 Wolf Creek Pike
Dayton OH 45426
937 854-3073

(G-3038)
APTIM CORP
5050 Section Ave (45212-2055)
PHONE................513 782-4700
William Pier, *Manager*
Patricia Olson, *Manager*
EMP: 40
SALES (corp-wide): 2B **Privately Held**
WEB: www.shawgrp.com
SIC: 8711 Engineering services
HQ: Aptim Corp.
10001 Woodloch Forest Dr # 450
The Woodlands TX 77380
832 823-2700

(G-3039)
ARAMARK UNF & CAREER AP LLC
P.O. Box 12131 (45212-0131)
PHONE................513 533-1000
Rick Lachrop, *General Mgr*
Kathy Dukich, *Director*
EMP: 62 **Publicly Held**
SIC: 7218 Industrial uniform supply; treated equipment supply: mats, rugs, mops, cloths, etc.; wiping towel supply
HQ: Aramark Uniform & Career Apparel, Llc
115 N First St Ste 203
Burbank CA 91502
818 973-3700

(G-3040)
ARC DOCUMENT SOLUTIONS INC
7157 E Kemper Rd (45249-1028)
PHONE................513 326-2300
Joe Hipps, *Manager*
EMP: 27
SALES (corp-wide): 394.5MM **Publicly Held**
SIC: 7334 Photocopying & duplicating services
PA: Arc Document Solutions, Inc.
1981 N Broadway Ste 385
Walnut Creek CA 94596
925 949-5100

(G-3041)
ARCHDIOCESE OF CINCINNATI
Also Called: St Bartholomew Cons School
9375 Winton Rd (45231-3967)
PHONE................513 729-1725
Fax: 513 728-3110
Leanora Roach, *Principal*
Chip Burwinkel, *Administration*
EMP: 55
SALES (corp-wide): 229.4MM **Privately Held**
WEB: www.catholiccincinnati.org
SIC: 7032 Girls' camp
PA: Archdiocese Of Cincinnati
100 E 8th St Fl 8
Cincinnati OH 45202
513 421-3131

(G-3042)
ARCHDIOCESE OF CINCINNATI
Also Called: Altercrest
274 Sutton Rd (45230-3521)
PHONE................513 231-8651
Fax: 513 231-8651
Robert Wehr, *Exec Dir*
EMP: 50
SALES (corp-wide): 229.4MM **Privately Held**
WEB: www.catholiccincinnati.org
SIC: 8361 Residential care
PA: Archdiocese Of Cincinnati
100 E 8th St Fl 8
Cincinnati OH 45202
513 421-3131

(G-3043)
ARCHIABLE ELECTRIC COMPANY
3803 Ford Cir (45227-3403)
PHONE................513 621-1307
Fax: 513 621-8487
James D Schroth, *President*
Vickie Bradhold, *Vice Pres*
Jan Praechter, *Foreman/Supr*
Howie Vollmer, *Purch Mgr*
Larry Rahe, *Executive*
EMP: 65 EST: 1919
SQ FT: 10,000
SALES (est): 9.5MM **Privately Held**
SIC: 1731 General electrical contractor

(G-3044)
ARCHITECTURAL METAL ERECTORS
869 W North Bend Rd (45224-1340)
P.O. Box 24 (45224)
PHONE................513 242-5106
Fax: 513 242-7933
Chris Geiger, *President*
EMP: 25
SQ FT: 10,000

SALES (est): 1.6MM
SALES (corp-wide): 9.2MM **Privately Held**
SIC: 1799 Ornamental metal work
PA: Geiger Construction Products Inc.
869 W North Bend Rd
Cincinnati OH 45224
513 242-5106

(G-3045)
ARENA MANAGEMENT HOLDINGS LLC
Also Called: U S Bank Arena
100 Broadway St (45202-3514)
PHONE................513 421-4111
Fax: 513 333-3040
Jim Moehring, *Vice Pres*
Kristin Ropp, *Vice Pres*
Kimberly Barry, *Store Mgr*
Ian Adkins, *Prdtn Mgr*
Mary Reed, *Personnel Exec*
EMP: 600
SQ FT: 123,208
SALES (est): 20.3MM **Privately Held**
WEB: www.usbankarena.com
SIC: 7941 6531 Sports field or stadium operator, promoting sports events; real estate agents & managers

(G-3046)
ARGUS INTERNATIONAL INC
4240 Airport Rd Ste 300 (45226-1623)
PHONE................513 852-1010
Kathy Tyler, *Principal*
Scott Liston, *Exec VP*
Aaron Greenwald, *Senior VP*
Shirley Mason, *Senior VP*
Josh Olds, *VP Opers*
EMP: 25 EST: 1999
SALES (est): 3.9MM **Privately Held**
SIC: 4785 7389 Transportation inspection services; industrial & commercial equipment inspection service

(G-3047)
ARLINGTON MEMORIAL GRDNS ASSN
2145 Compton Rd (45231-3009)
PHONE................513 521-7003
Fax: 513 728-4574
Leroy Meier, *Ch of Bd*
Edwin Friedhoff, *Ch of Bd*
Daniel Applegate, *President*
Julie Hoffman, *Vice Pres*
EMP: 35
SQ FT: 10,000
SALES: 3.7MM **Privately Held**
WEB: www.amgardens.org
SIC: 6553 Cemeteries, real estate operation

(G-3048)
ARLITT CHILD DEVELOPMENT CTR
44 W Corry St (45219)
PHONE................513 556-3802
Larry Johnson, *Exec Dir*
EMP: 60
SALES (est): 540.5K **Privately Held**
SIC: 8351 Child day care services

(G-3049)
ARS OHIO LLC
947 Sundance Dr (45233-4567)
PHONE................513 327-7645
Karen Finn, *Accountant*
EMP: 25
SALES (est): 1.9MM **Privately Held**
SIC: 7389

(G-3050)
ART HAUSER INSURANCE INC
Also Called: Hauser Group, The
8260 Northcreek Dr # 200 (45236-2296)
PHONE................513 745-9200
Fax: 513 745-9219
Mark J Hauser, *President*
Gary L Morgan, *COO*
Paul M Swanson, *Exec VP*
Jim Hyer, *Senior VP*
Jeri S Harrison, *Vice Pres*
EMP: 54
SALES (est): 18.1MM **Privately Held**
SIC: 6411 Insurance agents

(G-3051)
ARTHUR J GALLAGHER & CO
Also Called: Gallagher Sks
201 E 4th St Ste 99 (45202-4248)
PHONE................513 977-3100
Bob Murphy, *Vice Pres*
Sarah Hill, *Accounts Mgr*
Thomas Dietz, *Branch Mgr*
Brad Cooley, *Info Tech Dir*
EMP: 25
SALES (corp-wide): 6.1B **Publicly Held**
SIC: 6411 Insurance brokers
PA: Arthur J. Gallagher & Co.
2850 Golf Rd Ste 1000
Rolling Meadows IL 60008
630 773-3800

(G-3052)
AT HOSPITALITY LLC
5375 Medpace Way (45227-1543)
PHONE................513 527-9962
Stephanie Boles, *Finance Dir*
August J Troendle,
EMP: 100
SALES: 13MM **Privately Held**
SIC: 7011 Hotels

(G-3053)
AT&T CORP
3612 Stonecreek Blvd (45251-1450)
PHONE................513 741-1700
Gary Goldstein, *Branch Mgr*
EMP: 85
SALES (corp-wide): 160.5B **Publicly Held**
SIC: 4813 Local & long distance telephone communications
HQ: At&T Corp.
1 At&T Way
Bedminster NJ 07921
800 403-3302

(G-3054)
AT&T CORP
221 E 4th St (45202-4124)
PHONE................513 629-5000
Fax: 513 421-1483
Jan Ojdana, *Technical Mgr*
Dennis Beck, *Branch Mgr*
EMP: 800
SALES (corp-wide): 160.5B **Publicly Held**
WEB: www.att.com
SIC: 4813 4822 4812 Long distance telephone communications; telegram services; radio telephone communication
HQ: At&T Corp.
1 At&T Way
Bedminster NJ 07921
800 403-3302

(G-3055)
AT&T MOBILITY LLC
1605 Western Ave (45214-2001)
PHONE................513 381-6800
EMP: 26
SALES (corp-wide): 160.5B **Publicly Held**
WEB: www.cingular.com
SIC: 4812 Radio telephone communication
HQ: At&T Mobility Llc
1025 Lenox Park Blvd Ne
Brookhaven GA 30319
800 331-0500

(G-3056)
ATC GROUP SERVICES LLC
Also Called: Atc Associates
11121 Canal Rd (45241-1861)
PHONE................513 771-2112
Fax: 513 782-6918
Keith Arend, *Branch Mgr*
EMP: 56 **Privately Held**
WEB: www.atc-enviro.com
SIC: 8711 8734 Sanitary engineers; testing laboratories
HQ: Atc Group Services Llc
221 Rue De Jean Ste 300
Lafayette LA 70508
337 234-8777

(G-3057)
ATKINS & STANG INC
1031 Meta Dr (45237-5007)
PHONE................513 242-8300
Fax: 513 482-7054

Fred Stang, *President*
Randall Stortz, *Vice Pres*
Susan Ochs, *Treasurer*
James Wessel, *Treasurer*
Linda McCormick, *Admin Sec*
EMP: 69
SQ FT: 28,000
SALES (est): 9.6MM **Privately Held**
WEB: www.atkinsandstang.com
SIC: 1731 General electrical contractor

(G-3058)
ATLANTIC FOODS CORP
1999 Section Rd (45237-3343)
PHONE.................................513 772-3535
Gary Grefer, *President*
Jeff Busch, *COO*
Stuart Berning, *Vice Pres*
Stuart Goret, *Vice Pres*
Amy Pray, *Sales Staff*
▲ **EMP:** 65
SALES (est): 36.4MM **Privately Held**
SIC: 5149 Specialty food items

(G-3059)
ATLANTIC GREYHOUND LINES
600 Vine St Ste 1400 (45202-2426)
PHONE.................................513 721-4450
David S Leach, *CEO*
Michael Kuzmich, *Info Tech Dir*
Dave Murphy, *Info Tech Dir*
EMP: 29
SALES (est): 1.3MM **Privately Held**
SIC: 4131 Intercity & rural bus transportation

(G-3060)
ATLAS TOWING SERVICE
5675 Glenway Ave (45238-2130)
PHONE.................................513 451-1854
Mike Kaeser, *Owner*
EMP: 26
SALES (est): 421.2K **Privately Held**
SIC: 7549 Towing services

(G-3061)
ATM SOLUTIONS INC (PA)
551 Northland Blvd (45240-3212)
PHONE.................................513 742-4900
Fax: 513 674-2175
Paul Scott, *President*
Mike Hines, *President*
Christy McMurry, *President*
Chris Fryer, *Vice Pres*
Lou Masur, *Accounts Exec*
EMP: 100 **EST:** 1996
SALES (est): 18.5MM **Privately Held**
WEB: www.atm-solutions.com
SIC: 7699 Automated teller machine (ATM) repair

(G-3062)
ATRIA SENIOR LIVING GROUP INC
Also Called: Northgate Pk Retirement Cmnty
9191 Round Top Rd Ofc (45251-2465)
PHONE.................................513 923-3711
Natalie May, *Principal*
EMP: 50
SALES (corp-wide): 3.5B **Publicly Held**
WEB: www.atriacom.com
SIC: 6513 Retirement hotel operation
HQ: Atria Senior Living Group Inc
300 E Market St Ste 100
Louisville KY 40202

(G-3063)
AUGUST FOOD & WINE LLC
Also Called: Nate
1214 Vine St (45202-7298)
PHONE.................................513 421-2020
Lana Wright,
EMP: 40 **EST:** 2010
SALES (est): 3.7MM **Privately Held**
SIC: 5182 Wine

(G-3064)
AUGUST GROH & SONS INC
8832 Reading Rd (45215-4815)
PHONE.................................513 821-0090
Fax: 513 679-4062
Jo Groh, *President*
August Groh, *Vice Pres*
Richard T Groh, *Vice Pres*
EMP: 30 **EST:** 1926
SQ FT: 10,000
SALES (est): 2.8MM **Privately Held**
WEB: www.groh.com
SIC: 1721 7349 Commercial painting; janitorial service, contract basis

(G-3065)
AUTO AFTERMARKET CONCEPTS
Also Called: Calafonia Dream By AAC
1031 Redna Ter (45215-1114)
PHONE.................................513 942-2535
John Miller, *Partner*
Mike Eckel, *Partner*
Judy Kin, *Admin Sec*
▲ **EMP:** 25
SQ FT: 24,720
SALES: 4MM **Privately Held**
SIC: 5013 Automotive engines & engine parts

(G-3066)
AUTO CENTER USA INC
Also Called: Kings Mazda Kia
4544 Kings Water Dr (45249-8201)
PHONE.................................513 683-4900
Fax: 513 683-5759
Robert C Reichert, *President*
Louis K Galbraith, *Corp Secy*
Gerald Carmichael, *Vice Pres*
Mark Pittman, *Vice Pres*
James Andersen, *Sales Mgr*
EMP: 49
SALES (est): 25MM **Privately Held**
SIC: 5511 7538 7515 5521 Automobiles, new & used; pickups, new & used; general automotive repair shops; passenger car leasing; used car dealers

(G-3067)
AUTO CONCEPTS CINCINNATTI LLC
3428 Hauck Rd Ste I (45241-4603)
PHONE.................................513 769-4540
Thomas Reader, *Principal*
Charles Deringer, *Mng Member*
Joseph Hart, *Mng Member*
Thomas Richards, *Mng Member*
Wayne Maupin, *Manager*
EMP: 30 **EST:** 2000
SQ FT: 20,000
SALES (est): 1MM **Privately Held**
SIC: 7549 Automotive customizing services, non-factory basis

(G-3068)
AWRS LLC
Also Called: Ekomovers USA
10866 Newmarket Dr (45251-1027)
PHONE.................................888 611-2292
Aaron Williams,
EMP: 40
SALES (est): 2.5MM **Privately Held**
SIC: 4213 Household goods transport

(G-3069)
AXA ADVISORS LLC
4000 Smith Rd Ste 300 (45209-1967)
PHONE.................................513 762-7705
Susan Hisle, *Marketing Mgr*
Chris Dolly, *Branch Mgr*
Hank Shields,
Donald Hughett, *Advisor*
Marc Wagner, *Advisor*
EMP: 40
SALES (corp-wide): 3.8B **Publicly Held**
WEB: www.axacs.com
SIC: 6411 Insurance agents
HQ: Axa Advisors, Llc
1290 Ave Of Amrcs Fl Cnc1
New York NY 10104
212 554-1234

(G-3070)
AXCESS RCVERY CR SOLUTIONS INC
4540 Cooper Rd Ste 305 (45242-5649)
PHONE.................................513 229-6700
Jerry R Williams, *President*
Robert W Neu, *Treasurer*
Stephen J Schaller, *Admin Sec*
EMP: 50
SALES (est): 3MM **Privately Held**
SIC: 7322 Adjustment & collection services

(G-3071)
AZTEC SERVICES GROUP INC
3814 William P Dooley Byp (45223-2664)
PHONE.................................513 541-2002
Albert C Meininger, *President*
Tom Coon, *Vice Pres*
Kim Meininger, *Administration*
EMP: 100 **EST:** 2013
SQ FT: 2,000
SALES: 1.6MM **Privately Held**
SIC: 8744 1795 ; wrecking & demolition work

(G-3072)
B & J ELECTRICAL COMPANY INC
6316 Wiehe Rd (45237-4214)
PHONE.................................513 351-7100
Fax: 513 351-7101
Debbie Janzen, *President*
Gary Lee Janzen, *Chairman*
Shannon Ernst, *Chairman*
Peggy Deorger, *Vice Pres*
Kirsten Janzen, *Vice Pres*
EMP: 45
SQ FT: 1,000
SALES: 8MM **Privately Held**
WEB: www.bjelectrical.com
SIC: 1731 General electrical contractor

(G-3073)
BAJON SALON MONTGOMERY
7840 Cooper Rd (45242-7639)
PHONE.................................513 984-8880
Mark Welch, *President*
EMP: 50
SALES (est): 316.9K **Privately Held**
WEB: www.bajonsalon.com
SIC: 7231 Beauty shops

(G-3074)
BAKER & HOSTETLER LLP
312 Walnut St Ste 3200 (45202-4074)
PHONE.................................513 929-3400
Fax: 513 929-0303
David G Holcombe, *Managing Prtnr*
Joan Finlin, *Credit Mgr*
Marie Chomyk, *Marketing Mgr*
Kathy Dean, *Marketing Mgr*
Sharon Jesse, *Manager*
EMP: 41
SALES (corp-wide): 313.3MM **Privately Held**
SIC: 8111 General practice attorney, lawyer; bankruptcy law; labor & employment law; real estate law
PA: Baker & Hostetler Llp
127 Public Sq Ste 2000
Cleveland OH 44114
216 621-0200

(G-3075)
BANQUETS UNLIMITED
Also Called: Briarwood Banquet Center
1320 Ethan Ave (45225-1810)
P.O. Box 461, Hebron KY (41048-0461)
PHONE.................................859 689-4000
EMP: 25
SQ FT: 19,000
SALES (est): 353.3K **Privately Held**
SIC: 7299 Miscellaneous Personal Services, Nec, Nsk

(G-3076)
BAPTIST HOME AND CENTER
Also Called: Judson Village
2373 Harrison Ave (45211-7927)
PHONE.................................513 662-5880
Roland S Sedziol, *President*
Rev Michael Brandy, *Vice Pres*
Al Meyer, *Treasurer*
Tom Pille, *Finance*
Mary Loesch, *Admin Sec*
EMP: 150
SQ FT: 8,500
SALES: 63.4K **Privately Held**
WEB: www.judsonvillage.com
SIC: 6513 8052 8051 Retirement hotel operation; intermediate care facilities; skilled nursing care facilities

(G-3077)
BARBARA S DESALVO INC
800 Compton Rd Unit 18 (45231-3846)
PHONE.................................513 729-2111
Barbara S Desalvo, *President*
EMP: 30
SALES (est): 2.9MM **Privately Held**
SIC: 8748 Educational consultant

(G-3078)
BAREFOOT LLC
700 W Pete Rose Way (45203-1892)
PHONE.................................513 861-3668
Douglas Worple, *President*
Sean Brown, *Partner*
Fran Dicari, *Partner*
Jodi Greene, *Partner*
Steve Kissing, *Partner*
EMP: 47
SALES (est): 82.8K **Privately Held**
SIC: 7311 Advertising agencies

(G-3079)
BARNES DENNIG & CO LTD (PA)
150 E 4th St Ste 300 (45202-4186)
PHONE.................................513 241-8313
Fax: 513 241-8303
Richard L Batterbery, *Partner*
Alan E Bieber, *Partner*
Bradley S Chaffin, *Partner*
Alvin B Denning Jr, *Partner*
James A Donnellon, *Partner*
EMP: 70
SQ FT: 19,549
SALES: 8MM **Privately Held**
SIC: 8721 Certified public accountant

(G-3080)
BARRETT CENTER FOR CANCER PREV
234 Goodman St (45219-2364)
PHONE.................................513 558-3200
EMP: 100
SALES (est): 3.8MM **Privately Held**
SIC: 8733 Research Institute

(G-3081)
BARTLETT & CO LLC
600 Vine St Ste 2100 (45202-3896)
PHONE.................................513 621-4612
Fax: 513 621-4612
Kelley J Downing, *President*
Thomas Steele, *CFO*
David P Francis, *Portfolio Mgr*
Rick Reynolds, *Portfolio Mgr*
Troy Snider, *Portfolio Mgr*
EMP: 56
SQ FT: 28,000
SALES (est): 9.4MM **Privately Held**
WEB: www.bartlett1898.com
SIC: 6282 Investment advisory service

(G-3082)
BAXTER BURIAL VAULT SERVICE
Also Called: Baxter-Wilbert Burial Vault
909 E Ross Ave (45217-1159)
PHONE.................................513 641-1010
R Douglas Baxter, *President*
Tom Frondorf, *Manager*
Jane Minges, *Manager*
Tammy Richards, *Manager*
EMP: 25
SALES: 2.4MM **Privately Held**
SIC: 5087 3272 Concrete burial vaults & boxes; funeral directors' equipment & supplies; concrete products

(G-3083)
BAXTER HODELL DONNELLY PRESTON (PA)
Also Called: Bhdp Architecture
302 W 3rd St Ste 500 (45202-3434)
PHONE.................................513 271-1634
Michael J Habel, *CEO*
Thomas Arends, *Vice Pres*
Barry J Bayer, *Vice Pres*
Anthony E Berger, *Vice Pres*
Larry Digennaro, *Vice Pres*
EMP: 101 **EST:** 1937
SQ FT: 24,000
SALES: 30.1MM **Privately Held**
WEB: www.bhdp.com
SIC: 8741 8712 8742 7373 Construction management; architectural engineering; management consulting services; computer integrated systems design

Cincinnati - Hamilton County (G-3084)   GEOGRAPHIC SECTION

(G-3084)
BBDO WORLDWIDE INC
700 W Pete Rose Way (45203-1892)
PHONE 513 861-3668
Fax: 513 487-6855
Sean Brown, *President*
Tessa Smith, *General Mgr*
David Otting, *Editor*
Micky Osterman, *Project Mgr*
Jodi Shipp, *Project Mgr*
EMP: 47
SALES (corp-wide): 15.2B **Publicly Held**
WEB: www.bbdo.com
SIC: 7311 Advertising agencies
HQ: Bbdo Worldwide Inc.
1285 Ave Of The Amer
New York NY 10019
212 459-5000

(G-3085)
BDO USA LLP
221 E 4th St Ste 2600 (45202-4100)
PHONE 513 592-2400
Fax: 513 984-9634
David Wozniak, *VP Opers*
Brian Berning, *Branch Mgr*
Leah Hollstegge, *Manager*
EMP: 35
SALES (corp-wide): 1.2B **Privately Held**
SIC: 8721 7389 Accounting, auditing & bookkeeping; financial services
PA: Bdo Usa, Llp
330 N Wabash Ave Ste 3200
Chicago IL 60611
312 240-1236

(G-3086)
BDS INC (PA)
3500 Southside Ave (45204-1138)
PHONE 513 921-8441
William Lindsey, *President*
Mark Pickering, *Terminal Mgr*
EMP: 35
SALES (est): 3.3MM **Privately Held**
WEB: www.bds.net
SIC: 4226 4225 Liquid storage; general warehousing & storage

(G-3087)
BEACON ELECTRIC COMPANY
Also Called: Beacon Electrical Contractors
7815 Redsky Dr (45249-1636)
PHONE 513 851-0711
Fax: 513 851-0721
William K Schubert, *CEO*
Joe Mellencamp, *President*
Kenneth K Butler, *Vice Pres*
David Earlywine, *Vice Pres*
Bonnie Klein, *Vice Pres*
EMP: 100
SQ FT: 10,000
SALES (est): 30.6MM **Privately Held**
WEB: www.beacon-electric.com
SIC: 1731 General electrical contractor

(G-3088)
BEECH ACRES PARENTING CENTER (PA)
Also Called: Beech Acres Thrptic Fster Care
6881 Beechmont Ave (45230-2907)
PHONE 513 231-6630
John C Bloomstorm, *Ch of Bd*
James Mason, *President*
Dianne Jordan Grizzard, *COO*
Richard Sorg, *Vice Pres*
Tom Gormley, *Chief Mktg Ofcr*
EMP: 190
SQ FT: 25,000
SALES: 9MM **Privately Held**
WEB: www.beechacres.net
SIC: 8322 Adoption services

(G-3089)
BEECHMONT MOTORS INC (PA)
Also Called: Beechmont Porsche
8639 Beechmont Ave (45255-4709)
PHONE 513 388-3883
William Woeste Jr, *President*
Margo Woeste, *Treasurer*
Bryan Hendricks, *Sales Mgr*
Bob Kendrach, *Sales Mgr*
Jan Borchelt, *Sales Staff*
EMP: 30
SQ FT: 60,000
SALES (est): 25.8MM **Privately Held**
WEB: www.beechmontvolvo.com
SIC: 5511 7539 5012 5013 Automobiles, new & used; pickups, new & used; automotive repair shops; automobiles; motor vehicle supplies & new parts

(G-3090)
BEECHMONT PET HOSPITAL INC
6400 Salem Rd (45230-2811)
PHONE 513 232-0300
Fax: 513 232-4782
Stewart Smith Dvm, *President*
Sharon Hajek, *Manager*
EMP: 30
SALES (est): 1MM **Privately Held**
SIC: 0742 Veterinarian, animal specialties

(G-3091)
BEECHMONT RACQUET CLUB INC
Also Called: Beechmont Racquet and Fitness
435 Ohio Pike (45255-3712)
PHONE 513 528-5700
Fax: 513 528-5704
William Atkins, *President*
Bradon Atkins, *Manager*
Jerry Howard, *Manager*
Helen Atkins, *Admin Sec*
EMP: 40
SQ FT: 160,000
SALES (est): 1.9MM **Privately Held**
WEB: www.beechmontracquetclub.com
SIC: 7991 7997 Health club; racquetball club, membership

(G-3092)
BEECHMONT TOYOTA INC
8667 Beechmont Ave (45255-4709)
PHONE 513 388-3800
Fax: 513 388-3752
William F Woeste Jr, *President*
Cynthia Mac Connell, *Corp Secy*
Margot Woeste, *Vice Pres*
James Woodall, *VP Opers*
Bob Wilder, *Parts Mgr*
EMP: 70
SQ FT: 20,000
SALES (est): 23.6MM **Privately Held**
WEB: www.beechmonttoyota.com
SIC: 5511 7539 5012 5013 Automobiles, new & used; pickups, new & used; automotive repair shops; automobiles; motor vehicle supplies & new parts

(G-3093)
BEECHWOOD HOME
2140 Pogue Ave (45208-3299)
PHONE 513 321-9294
Fax: 513 321-4664
Patricia Clark, *CEO*
Tim Owens, *CFO*
Denice Hertlein, *Treasurer*
Dorothy Echoles, *Persnl Dir*
Mauer Rosen, *Manager*
EMP: 150
SQ FT: 53,000
SALES: 5.9MM **Privately Held**
WEB: www.beechwoodhome.com
SIC: 8051 Skilled nursing care facilities

(G-3094)
BEECHWOOD TERRACE CARE CTR INC
Also Called: Forest Hills Care Center
8700 Moran Rd (45244-1986)
PHONE 513 578-6200
Harold Sosna, *President*
Kris Rolfsen, *Director*
EMP: 160 EST: 2007
SALES: 11.5MM **Privately Held**
SIC: 8051 Skilled nursing care facilities

(G-3095)
BELCAN CORPORATION
Also Called: Belcan Engineering Services
7785 E Kemper Rd (45249-1611)
PHONE 513 277-3100
Fax: 513 277-3102
RG Lee, *Principal*
Dan Gregorich, *Engineer*
Robert Rost, *Engineer*
Scott Daniels, *Program Mgr*
Melody Spurlock, *Technology*
EMP: 250
SALES (corp-wide): 666.9MM **Privately Held**
SIC: 8711 Engineering services
PA: Belcan, Llc
10200 Anderson Way
Blue Ash OH 45242
513 891-0972

(G-3096)
BELFLEX STAFFING NETWORK LLC (PA)
11591 Goldcoast Dr (45249-1633)
PHONE 513 488-8588
Mike McCaw, *CEO*
Todd Cross, *President*
Candace McCaw, *Chairman*
Bob Baer, *Vice Pres*
Tim Mueller, *CFO*
EMP: 125
SALES: 110.1MM **Privately Held**
SIC: 7361 7363 Labor contractors (employment agency); help supply services

(G-3097)
BELTING COMPANY OF CINCINNATI (PA)
Also Called: Cbt Company
5500 Ridge Ave (45213-2516)
P.O. Box 14639 (45250-0639)
PHONE 513 621-9050
Fax: 513 621-0549
James E Stahl Jr, *President*
Pat Cullen, *General Mgr*
Jerry Perkins, *General Mgr*
Daryl A Albrecht, *Managing Dir*
Mike Kiniyalocts, *Vice Pres*
▲ EMP: 110
SQ FT: 95,000
SALES: 198.2MM **Privately Held**
WEB: www.cinbelt.com
SIC: 5085 5063 Bearings; power transmission equipment, electric

(G-3098)
BENCO DENTAL SUPPLY CO
10014 Intl Blvd Bldg 9 (45246)
PHONE 513 874-2990
Fax: 513 874-2998
Charles Chen, *Owner*
EMP: 98
SALES (corp-wide): 512.1MM **Privately Held**
SIC: 5047 Dental equipment & supplies
PA: Benco Dental Supply Co.
295 Centerpoint Blvd
Pittston PA 18640
570 602-7781

(G-3099)
BERNSTEIN ALLERGY GROUP INC
8444 Winton Rd (45231-4927)
PHONE 513 931-0775
Fax: 513 931-0779
Jonathan A Bernstein, *President*
David I Bernstein, *Vice Pres*
Cheryl Bernstein, *Manager*
Justin C Greiwe, *Admin Sec*
Barbara Mirlisena, *Administration*
EMP: 26
SALES (est): 3.1MM **Privately Held**
SIC: 8011 Allergist

(G-3100)
BESL TRANSFER CO
5700 Este Ave (45232-1435)
PHONE 513 242-3456
Fax: 513 242-4013
David Rusch, *CEO*
John M Smith, *Ch of Bd*
Kelly M Dehan, *General Mgr*
Jim Collins, *Vice Pres*
Michael J Meyer, *Controller*
EMP: 25
SQ FT: 8,500
SALES (est): 9.8MM
SALES (corp-wide): 2.1B **Privately Held**
WEB: www.besl.com
SIC: 4213 4212 Contract haulers; local trucking, without storage
PA: Crst International, Inc.
201 1st St Se
Cedar Rapids IA 52401
319 396-4400

(G-3101)
BEST EXPRESS FOODS INC
2368 Victory Pkwy Ste 410 (45206-2810)
P.O. Box 8039 (45208-0039)
PHONE 513 531-2378
Fax: 513 531-0766
Allan Berliant, *President*
Joni Kelly, *Human Resources*
Sarah Nicholas, *Marketing Staff*
Sharon Salter, *Manager*
EMP: 60
SQ FT: 2,600
SALES (est): 27.5MM **Privately Held**
WEB: www.bestexpressfoods.com
SIC: 5142 Packaged frozen goods

(G-3102)
BEST UPON REQUEST CORP INC
8170 Corp Pk Dr Ste 300 (45242)
PHONE 513 605-7800
Fax: 513 605-7805
Tillie Hidalgo Lima, *President*
Katie Stout, *Controller*
Erika Destefano, *Human Res Mgr*
Ginger Stumpf, *Business Anlyst*
Matthew Dollard, *Manager*
EMP: 93
SALES (est): 7.4MM **Privately Held**
WEB: www.bestuponrequest.com
SIC: 7299 Consumer buying service

(G-3103)
BETA RHO HOUSE ASSOC KAPPA
2801 Clifton Ave (45220-2401)
PHONE 513 221-1280
Betsy Kampman, *Principal*
EMP: 60
SALES (est): 298.5K **Privately Held**
SIC: 8641 Fraternal associations

(G-3104)
BETHESDA FOUNDATION INC
619 Oak St (45206-1613)
PHONE 513 569-6575
John Prout, *Principal*
EMP: 33
SALES: 7.1MM **Privately Held**
SIC: 8051 Skilled nursing care facilities

(G-3105)
BETHESDA HOSPITAL INC (DH)
Also Called: Bethesda North Hospital
619 Oak St (45206-1690)
PHONE 513 569-6100
Fax: 513 631-0796
John Prout, *President*
Sher A Mc Clanahan, *COO*
Alan P Oltman, *Ch OB/GYN*
Craig Rucker, *CFO*
Michael Croftoon, *Controller*
EMP: 1390
SALES: 551.9MM **Privately Held**
SIC: 8062 General medical & surgical hospitals
HQ: Bethesda, Inc.
619 Oak St 7n
Cincinnati OH 45206
513 569-6400

(G-3106)
BETHESDA HOSPITAL INC
Also Called: Bethesda North Hospital
10500 Montgomery Rd (45242-4402)
P.O. Box 422410 (45242-2410)
PHONE 513 745-1111
Fax: 513 745-1134
John Prout, *President*
Kenneth R Bass, *Senior VP*
Rick Moore, *Vice Pres*
Michael Mattingly, *Consultant*
Chris Swallow, *Consultant*
EMP: 1500 **Privately Held**
SIC: 8062 General medical & surgical hospitals
HQ: Bethesda Hospital, Inc.
619 Oak St
Cincinnati OH 45206
513 569-6100

GEOGRAPHIC SECTION
Cincinnati - Hamilton County (G-3131)

(G-3107)
BETHESDA HOSPITAL INC
Bethesda Care-Sharonville
3801 Hauck Rd Frnt (45241-4607)
PHONE................513 563-1505
Fax: 513 769-4776
Jay Fultz, *Principal*
EMP: 35 **Privately Held**
SIC: 8011 8062 Primary care medical clinic; general medical & surgical hospitals
HQ: Bethesda Hospital, Inc.
  619 Oak St
  Cincinnati OH 45206
  513 569-6100

(G-3108)
BILLS BATTERY COMPANY INC
5221 Crookshank Rd (45238-3392)
P.O. Box 58305 (45258-0305)
PHONE................513 922-0100
Fax: 513 922-2566
Michael F Hartoin, *President*
Michael Hartoin, *President*
Ronald Hartoin, *Vice Pres*
Helen Hartoin, *Admin Sec*
EMP: 28 **EST:** 1946
SQ FT: 40,000
SALES: 12MM **Privately Held**
SIC: 5013 Automotive supplies

(G-3109)
BIORX LLC (HQ)
Also Called: Thriverx
7167 E Kemper Rd (45249-1028)
PHONE................866 442-4679
Fax: 513 792-3838
Paul Costello, *Business Mgr*
Jennifer Arms, *Vice Pres*
Barb Leitow, *Project Mgr*
Derrick Loudermilk, *Materials Mgr*
Justin Dent, *Opers Staff*
EMP: 95
SALES (est): 90.8MM
SALES (corp-wide): 4.4B **Publicly Held**
WEB: www.biorx.net
SIC: 5122 8748 2834 5047 Pharmaceuticals; business consulting; pharmaceutical preparations; medical & hospital equipment; skilled nursing care facilities
PA: Diplomat Pharmacy, Inc.
  4100 S Saginaw St Ste A
  Flint MI 48507
  888 720-4450

(G-3110)
BIZ COM ELECTRIC INC
2867 Stanton Ave (45206-1122)
PHONE................513 961-7200
Fax: 513 961-7306
Bruce M Cummins, *President*
Larry Ayer, *Vice Pres*
EMP: 35
SQ FT: 7,000
SALES (est): 5.5MM **Privately Held**
WEB: www.bizcomelec.com
SIC: 1731 General electrical contractor

(G-3111)
BKD LLP
312 Walnut St Ste 3000 (45202-4025)
P.O. Box 5367 (45202)
PHONE................513 621-8300
Lindsay Field, *CPA*
Judy Haefling, *Office Mgr*
J Scott Golan, *Administration*
EMP: 54
SALES (corp-wide): 472.3MM **Privately Held**
SIC: 8721 8748 Certified public accountant; business consulting
PA: Bkd, Llp
  910 E Saint Louis St # 400
  Springfield MO 65806
  417 831-7283

(G-3112)
BLACK STONE CINCINNATI LLC (PA)
Also Called: Assisted Care By Black Stone
4700 E Galbraith Rd Fl 3 (45236-2754)
PHONE................513 924-1370
Fax: 513 924-3620
David Tramontana, *CEO*
Christine Doggett, *Vice Pres*
Phil Sexton, *Vice Pres*
Brandy Keith, *Manager*
Jenny Sand, *Office Admin*
EMP: 45
SALES (est): 13.8MM **Privately Held**
SIC: 8082 Home health care services

(G-3113)
BLACKBIRD CAPITAL GROUP LLC
312 Walnut St Ste 1600 (45202-4038)
PHONE................513 762-7890
John P Vota,
EMP: 210
SALES (est): 8.9MM **Privately Held**
SIC: 6799 Investors

(G-3114)
BLEUX HOLDINGS LLC
7257 Wooster Pike (45227-3830)
PHONE................859 414-5060
Jon Henson, *Principal*
EMP: 35 **Privately Held**
SIC: 6719 Holding companies

(G-3115)
BLUE & CO LLC
720 E Pete Rose Way # 100 (45202-3583)
PHONE................513 241-4507
Stephen Mann, *Branch Mgr*
EMP: 149
SALES (corp-wide): 37.6MM **Privately Held**
SIC: 8721 Certified public accountant
PA: Blue & Co., Llc
  12800 N Meridian St # 400
  Carmel IN 46032
  317 848-8920

(G-3116)
BLUE ASH BUSINESS ASSOCIATION
P.O. Box 429277 (45242-9277)
PHONE................513 253-1006
Larry Bresko, *Vice Pres*
EMP: 100
SALES (est): 1.1MM **Privately Held**
SIC: 8611 Business associations

(G-3117)
BLUE ASH DISTRIBUTION CTR LLC
2135 Dana Ave Ste 200 (45207-1327)
PHONE................513 699-2279
Will Sayer, *Finance*
EMP: 30
SALES (est): 397.4K **Privately Held**
SIC: 6531 Real estate agents & managers

(G-3118)
BLUE ASH HEALTHCARE GROUP INC
Also Called: Blue Ash Care Center
4900 Cooper Rd (45242-6915)
PHONE................513 793-3362
Fax: 513 791-8268
George Repchick, *President*
EMP: 40
SALES (est): 3.1MM
SALES (corp-wide): 68.5MM **Privately Held**
WEB: www.saberhealth.com
SIC: 8051 8059 Skilled nursing care facilities; nursing home, except skilled & intermediate care facility
PA: Saber Healthcare Group, L.L.C.
  26691 Richmond Rd Frnt
  Bedford OH 44146
  216 292-5706

(G-3119)
BLUE CHIP 2000 COML CLG INC
Also Called: Blue Chip Pros
7250 Edington Dr (45249-1063)
PHONE................513 561-2999
Daniel F Hopkins, *President*
Gary J Hopkins, *Vice Pres*
Debbie Gadberry, *CFO*
Bill Faulhaber, *Director*
EMP: 450
SALES (est): 18.2MM **Privately Held**
SIC: 7349 Cleaning service, industrial or commercial

(G-3120)
BLUE CHIP PLUMBING INC
1950 Waycross Rd (45240-2827)
PHONE................513 941-4010
Bryan Gilbert, *President*
EMP: 60
SALES (est): 559K **Privately Held**
SIC: 1711 Plumbing contractors

(G-3121)
BLUE CHP SRGCL CTR PTNS LLC
4760 Red Bank Rd Ste 222 (45227-1549)
P.O. Box 42666 (45242-0666)
PHONE................513 561-8900
Fax: 513 561-8901
Jay Rom, *President*
Beth Johnson, *Vice Pres*
Jan Diedrich, *VP Opers*
Kim Esteph, *VP Opers*
Donna Smith, *VP Opers*
EMP: 51
SALES (est): 7.8MM **Privately Held**
WEB: www.bluechipsurgical.com
SIC: 8062 General medical & surgical hospitals

(G-3122)
BLUE STAR LUBRICATION TECH LLC
3630 E Kemper Rd (45241-2011)
PHONE................847 285-1888
Fax: 847 285-1894
Tam Lavarich, *Technical Mgr*
Andrea Kasiewicz, *Office Mgr*
Jeff Worth, *Mng Member*
Tim Davis,
EMP: 28
SQ FT: 3,200
SALES (est): 13.2MM **Privately Held**
WEB: www.bluestarlt.com
SIC: 5172 Lubricating oils & greases

(G-3123)
BOB SUMEREL TIRE CO INC
471 Ohio Pike (45255-3337)
PHONE................513 528-1900
Fax: 513 688-8213
Chris Anderson, *Manager*
EMP: 29
SALES (corp-wide): 87.3MM **Privately Held**
SIC: 8999 Artists & artists' studios
PA: Bob Sumerel Tire Co., Inc.
  1257 Cox Ave
  Erlanger KY 41018
  859 283-2700

(G-3124)
BOB SUMEREL TIRE CO INC
5977 Harrison Ave (45248-1605)
PHONE................513 598-2300
Bob Sumerel, *Branch Mgr*
EMP: 25
SALES (corp-wide): 87.3MM **Privately Held**
SIC: 8999 Artists & artists' studios
PA: Bob Sumerel Tire Co., Inc.
  1257 Cox Ave
  Erlanger KY 41018
  859 283-2700

(G-3125)
BOB SUMEREL TIRE CO INC
2540 Annuity Dr (45241-1502)
PHONE................513 792-6600
Fax: 513 792-6605
Bill Mountford, *Manager*
EMP: 35
SALES (corp-wide): 87.3MM **Privately Held**
WEB: www.bobsumereltire.com
SIC: 5012 5014 Trucks, commercial; automobile tires & tubes; truck tires & tubes
PA: Bob Sumerel Tire Co., Inc.
  1257 Cox Ave
  Erlanger KY 41018
  859 283-2700

(G-3126)
BONNEVILLE INTERNATIONAL CORP
2060 Reading Rd Ste 400 (45202-1456)
PHONE................513 699-5102
Duke Hamilton, *Branch Mgr*
EMP: 83
SALES (corp-wide): 2.8B **Privately Held**
WEB: www.boncom.com
SIC: 4832 Radio broadcasting stations
HQ: Bonneville International Corporation
  7800 E Orchard Rd Ste 400
  Greenwood Village CO 80111
  303 321-0950

(G-3127)
BORDEN DAIRY CO CINCINNATI LLC
Also Called: H. Meyer Dairy
415 John St (45215-5481)
PHONE................513 948-8811
Fax: 513 948-8837
David R Meyer, *President*
Michael Campe, *Controller*
EMP: 154 **EST:** 1976
SALES (est): 60MM **Privately Held**
WEB: www.meyerdairy.com
SIC: 2026 2086 5143 5144 Milk processing (pasteurizing, homogenizing, bottling); bottled & canned soft drinks; dairy products, except dried or canned; poultry & poultry products

(G-3128)
BOY SCOUTS OF AMERICA (PA)
Also Called: Dan Beard Council
10078 Reading Rd (45241-4833)
PHONE................513 961-2336
Fax: 513 961-2688
Laura Brunner, *President*
Barb Griffin, *Office Mgr*
Sherry Siddall, *Administration*
EMP: 50
SQ FT: 13,400
SALES (est): 6.5MM **Privately Held**
WEB: www.danbeard.org
SIC: 8641 Boy Scout organization

(G-3129)
BRENDAMOUR MOVING & STOR INC
2630 Glendale Milford Rd D (45241-4835)
PHONE................800 354-9715
Fax: 513 860-2177
Jack Brendamour, *CEO*
Michael Brendamour, *President*
Paul Brendamour, *General Mgr*
Joan Brendamour, *Vice Pres*
Chuck Wolfe, *Treasurer*
EMP: 65
SALES (est): 7.7MM **Privately Held**
WEB: www.brendamourmoving.com
SIC: 4214 4213 Household goods moving & storage, local; trucking, except local

(G-3130)
BRG REALTY GROUP LLC (PA)
Also Called: Berkshire Realty Group
7265 Kenwood Rd Ste 111 (45236-4411)
PHONE................513 936-5960
Fax: 513 936-5960
Robin Hinchliffe, *Portfolio Mgr*
Bob Kohlman, *Portfolio Mgr*
Jennifer Young, *Manager*
Andrew R Giannelli,
Kellie Davis, *Executive Asst*
EMP: 156
SALES (est): 17.5MM **Privately Held**
SIC: 6531 Rental agent, real estate

(G-3131)
BRICKER & ECKLER LLP
201 E 5th St Ste 1110 (45202-4135)
PHONE................513 870-6700
Kurt Tunnell, *Managing Prtnr*
Paramila A Kamath, *Associate*
EMP: 163
SALES (corp-wide): 46.5MM **Privately Held**
SIC: 8111 9222 General practice attorney, lawyer; Attorney General's office
PA: Bricker & Eckler Llp
  100 S 3rd St Ste B
  Columbus OH 43215
  614 227-2300

Cincinnati - Hamilton County (G-3132)

(G-3132)
BRIDGESTONE RET OPERATIONS LLC
Also Called: Michel Tires Plus 227550
8398 Winton Rd (45231-5919)
PHONE.....................513 522-2525
Marcus Johnson, *Manager*
EMP: 30
SALES (corp-wide): 32.5B Privately Held
WEB: www.tiresplus.com
SIC: 7534 Tire retreading & repair shops
HQ: Bridgestone Retail Operations, Llc
333 E Lake St Ste 300
Bloomingdale IL 60108
630 259-9000

(G-3133)
BRIDGESTONE RET OPERATIONS LLC
Also Called: Michel Tires Plus 227554
9820 Colerain Ave (45251-1429)
PHONE.....................513 741-9701
Jim Phelps, *Branch Mgr*
EMP: 30
SALES (corp-wide): 32.5B Privately Held
WEB: www.tiresplus.com
SIC: 7534 Tire retreading & repair shops
HQ: Bridgestone Retail Operations, Llc
333 E Lake St Ste 300
Bloomingdale IL 60108
630 259-9000

(G-3134)
BRIDGESTONE RET OPERATIONS LLC
Also Called: Michel Tires Plus 227553
5907 Wooster Pike (45227-4507)
PHONE.....................513 271-7100
Christopher Stout, *Manager*
Charlie Thomas, *Manager*
EMP: 30
SALES (corp-wide): 32.5B Privately Held
WEB: www.tiresplus.com
SIC: 7534 Tire retreading & repair shops
HQ: Bridgestone Retail Operations, Llc
333 E Lake St Ste 300
Bloomingdale IL 60108
630 259-9000

(G-3135)
BRINKS INCORPORATED
1105 Hopkins St (45203-1119)
PHONE.....................513 621-9310
Fax: 513 421-6525
Mike Moorman, *Manager*
EMP: 65
SALES (corp-wide): 3.3B Publicly Held
WEB: www.brinksinc.com
SIC: 7381 Armored car services
HQ: Brink's, Incorporated
1801 Bayberry Ct Ste 400
Richmond VA 23226
804 289-9600

(G-3136)
BROADBAND EXPRESS LLC
11359 Mosteller Rd (45241-1827)
PHONE.....................513 834-8085
Dusty Banks, *Branch Mgr*
EMP: 48
SALES (corp-wide): 3B Publicly Held
SIC: 1731 Cable television installation
HQ: Broadband Express, Llc
374 Westdale Ave Ste B
Westerville OH 43082
614 823-6464

(G-3137)
BROOKDALE DEER PARK
3801 E Galbraith Rd Ofc (45236-1585)
PHONE.....................513 745-7600
Noreen Bouley, *Manager*
EMP: 57
SQ FT: 20,075
SALES (est): 1MM Privately Held
SIC: 8059 Domiciliary care

(G-3138)
BROOKDALE SENIOR LIVING INC
9101 Winton Rd (45231-3829)
PHONE.....................855 308-2438
Christine Butler, *Director*
EMP: 85

SALES (corp-wide): 4.7B Publicly Held
SIC: 6282 Investment advice
PA: Brookdale Senior Living
111 Westwood Pl Ste 400
Brentwood TN 37027
615 221-2250

(G-3139)
BROOKDALE SENIOR LIVING INC
9090 Montgomery Rd (45242-7712)
PHONE.....................513 745-9292
Mark Ohlendorf, *Branch Mgr*
EMP: 42
SALES (corp-wide): 4.7B Publicly Held
SIC: 8082 Home health care services
PA: Brookdale Senior Living
111 Westwood Pl Ste 400
Brentwood TN 37027
615 221-2250

(G-3140)
BROOKDALE SENIOR LIVING INC
3801 E Galbraith Rd Ofc (45236-1585)
PHONE.....................513 745-7600
EMP: 73
SALES (corp-wide): 4.7B Publicly Held
SIC: 8351 Montessori child development center
PA: Brookdale Senior Living
111 Westwood Pl Ste 400
Brentwood TN 37027
615 221-2250

(G-3141)
BROTHERS PROPERTIES CORP
Also Called: Cinncinnatian Hotel, The
601 Vine St Ste 1 (45202-2408)
PHONE.....................513 381-3000
Victor Fuller, *President*
Denise Vandersall, *General Mgr*
Stephen Fuller, *Vice Pres*
EMP: 125
SALES: 9.5MM Privately Held
WEB: www.cincinnatianhotel.com
SIC: 7011 5812 5813 Hotels; eating places; bar (drinking places)

(G-3142)
BROWER PRODUCTS INC (DH)
Also Called: Cabinet Solutions By Design
401 Northland Blvd (45240-3210)
PHONE.....................937 563-1111
Daniel C Brower, *Ch of Bd*
William Brower, *President*
Mark Frericks, *Vice Pres*
John Anderson, *Sales Staff*
Rod Kirby, *Administration*
EMP: 80
SQ FT: 125,000
SALES (est): 9.7MM Privately Held
SIC: 5031 2434 5211 3281 Kitchen cabinets; windows; doors; molding, all materials; wood kitchen cabinets; cabinets, kitchen; door & window products; lumber products; cut stone & stone products; wood partitions & fixtures
HQ: Nisbet, Inc.
11575 Reading Rd
Cincinnati OH 45241
513 563-1111

(G-3143)
BRUCE M ALLMAN
312 Walnut St Ste 1400 (45202-4029)
PHONE.....................513 352-6712
Bruce M Allman, *Partner*
EMP: 80 EST: 1999
SALES (est): 2.1MM Privately Held
SIC: 8111 General practice attorney, lawyer

(G-3144)
BRUCE R BRACKEN
Also Called: Uc Physician
222 Piedmont Ave (45219-4231)
PHONE.....................513 558-3700
Bruce R Bracken, *Owner*
Gary Kelm, *Director*
EMP: 30
SALES (est): 649.1K Privately Held
SIC: 8011 Urologist

(G-3145)
BSI ENGINEERING LLC (PA)
300 E Bus Way Ste 300 (45241)
PHONE.....................513 201-3100
Phil Beirne, *President*
Blake Leclair, *Project Mgr*
Michael Swift, *Project Mgr*
Jessica Walker, *Project Mgr*
Jake Davis, *Engineer*
EMP: 130
SQ FT: 17,000
SALES (est): 36.2MM Privately Held
SIC: 8711 Consulting engineer

(G-3146)
BUDCO GROUP INC (PA)
Also Called: O/B Leasing Company
1100 Gest St (45203-1114)
PHONE.....................513 621-6111
Fax: 513 621-4330
Otto Budig Jr, *President*
George J Budig, *Vice Pres*
Brian Schwartz, *Controller*
EMP: 25
SQ FT: 55,000
SALES: 195.1MM Privately Held
SIC: 7359 Equipment rental & leasing

(G-3147)
BUILDERS FIRSTSOURCE INC
10059 Princeton Glendale (45246-1223)
PHONE.....................513 874-9950
Mike Stimpfl, *Branch Mgr*
EMP: 28
SALES (corp-wide): 7B Publicly Held
WEB: www.hopelumber.com
SIC: 5211 5031 Home centers; lumber, plywood & millwork
PA: Builders Firstsource, Inc.
2001 Bryan St Ste 1600
Dallas TX 75201
214 880-3500

(G-3148)
BUILDING 8 INC
Also Called: J & N
10995 Canal Rd (45241-1886)
PHONE.....................513 771-8000
Fax: 513 771-6502
Thomas J Kuechly, *President*
David W Blocker, *Vice Pres*
Nick Kuechly, *Vice Pres*
Rich Mitchell, *Warehouse Mgr*
Jederson De Cezaro, *Purch Mgr*
▲ EMP: 27 EST: 1954
SQ FT: 68,000
SALES (est): 47.9MM
SALES (corp-wide): 301.1MM Privately Held
WEB: www.jnae.com
SIC: 5013 Automotive supplies & parts; alternators
HQ: Arrowhead Electrical Products, Inc.
3787 95th Ave Ne
Circle Pines MN 55014
763 255-2555

(G-3149)
BURGESS & NIPLE INC
312 Plum St Ste 1210 (45202-2678)
PHONE.....................513 579-0042
Fax: 513 579-0321
Roger Huston, *Engineer*
Michelle Sefton, *Engineer*
Robert Draper, *IT/INT Sup*
Barry Y Dixon, *Director*
Milton Bosworth, *Director*
EMP: 105
SALES (corp-wide): 122.1MM Privately Held
WEB: www.burgessniple.com
SIC: 8712 8711 Architectural engineering; consulting engineer
PA: Burgess & Niple, Inc.
5085 Reed Rd
Columbus OH 43220
502 254-2344

(G-3150)
BURKE INC (PA)
Also Called: Burke Institute
500 W 7th St (45203-1543)
PHONE.....................513 241-5663
Fax: 513 684-7733
Jeff Miller, *CEO*
Micheal H Baumgardner, *President*

Linda L Harlow, *Publisher*
Mary B Mapstone, *Senior VP*
Stacy McWhorter, *Senior VP*
EMP: 202
SQ FT: 51,000
SALES (est): 50MM Privately Held
SIC: 8732 8742 Market analysis or research; management consulting services

(G-3151)
BURKE & SCHINDLER PLLC
901 Evans St (45204)
PHONE.....................859 344-8887
Lynnda Kasanicky, *Consultant*
Gene Schindler,
Sharon Enderle, *Admin Asst*
Jeanne Watson, *Administration*
Patrick Burke,
EMP: 30
SALES (est): 1.1MM Privately Held
SIC: 8721 Certified public accountant

(G-3152)
BURKE MANLEY LPA
225 W Court St (45202-1012)
PHONE.....................513 721-5525
Fax: 513 721-4268
Robert Manley, *President*
Kathie Thomas, *President*
Bonnie Hill, *Office Mgr*
Bonnie Bockelman, *Manager*
Theresa McGoron, *Legal Staff*
EMP: 27
SALES (est): 3MM Privately Held
WEB: www.mbl-law.com
SIC: 8111 General practice attorney, lawyer

(G-3153)
BURLINGTON HOUSE INC
2222 Springdale Rd (45231-1805)
PHONE.....................513 851-7888
Fax: 513 589-3444
Stephen L Rosedale, *President*
Beatrice W Rosedale, *Vice Pres*
Thomas Van Hook, *Director*
Thomas V Hook, *Social Dir*
Chris C Newman, *Food Svc Dir*
EMP: 100
SQ FT: 2,682
SALES (est): 2.9MM Privately Held
SIC: 8051 Convalescent home with continuous nursing care

(G-3154)
BURTONS COLLISION
Also Called: Burtons Collision & Auto Repr
4384 E Galbraith Rd (45236-2618)
PHONE.....................513 984-3396
Fax: 513 984-1351
Duane Burton, *Owner*
Kathy Penter, *Asst Mgr*
EMP: 35
SALES (est): 2.2MM Privately Held
WEB: www.burtonscollision.com
SIC: 7532 7538 7539 Body shop, automotive; general automotive repair shops; engine repair; engine rebuilding: automotive; frame & front end repair services; powertrain components repair services; electrical services; brake services

(G-3155)
BUSINESS BACKER LLC
10856 Reed Hartman Hwy # 100 (45242-2820)
PHONE.....................513 792-6866
Jim Salters, *President*
Robert Billhorn, *Business Mgr*
Steve Tosh, *COO*
Candace Levine, *VP Finance*
Chelsea Franklin, *Human Resources*
EMP: 25
SALES (est): 7.7MM
SALES (corp-wide): 843.7MM Publicly Held
SIC: 6153 7389 Working capital financing; financial services
PA: Enova International, Inc.
175 W Jackson Blvd Fl 10
Chicago IL 60604
312 568-4200

GEOGRAPHIC SECTION

Cincinnati - Hamilton County (G-3179)

(G-3156)
BUSINESS EQUIPMENT CO INC
Also Called: Beco Legal Systems
175 Tri County Pkwy # 120 (45246-3237)
PHONE..................513 948-1500
Michael Brookbank, *President*
Jeff Austin, *Vice Pres*
John Brookbank, *Vice Pres*
EMP: 25
SQ FT: 10,000
SALES (est): 4.5MM **Privately Held**
SIC: 7371 Computer software development

(G-3157)
BUSKEN BAKERY INC (PA)
2675 Madison Rd (45208-1389)
PHONE..................513 871-2114
Fax: 513 871-2662
D Page Busken, *President*
Marilyn Buskirk, *General Mgr*
Brian Busken, *Senior VP*
Tina Toole, *Vice Pres*
Suzan Kelly, *VP Opers*
EMP: 90 EST: 1928
SQ FT: 21,000
SALES (est): 12.7MM **Privately Held**
WEB: www.busken.com
SIC: 5461 5149 Bread; bakery products

(G-3158)
BYER STEEL RECYCLING INC (PA)
Also Called: Byer Steel Division
200 W North Bend Rd (45216-1728)
P.O. Box 1817 (45201-1817)
PHONE..................513 948-0300
Fax: 513 948-1534
Burke Byer, *President*
Jay Binder, *COO*
Jonas Allen, *Vice Pres*
Larry Byer, *Vice Pres*
Shawn Eddy, *Vice Pres*
EMP: 38
SQ FT: 100,000
SALES (est): 20.8MM **Privately Held**
WEB: www.acomsteel.com
SIC: 5093 Ferrous metal scrap & waste

(G-3159)
BYRNES-CONWAY COMPANY
21 Byrneslake Ct (45216-1661)
PHONE..................513 948-8882
Fax: 513 948-0161
Robert M Sanders, *President*
EMP: 65 EST: 1997
SALES (est): 3.9MM **Privately Held**
SIC: 1629 Trenching contractor

(G-3160)
C J & L CONSTRUCTION INC
11980 Runyan Dr (45241-1623)
PHONE..................513 769-3600
James J Kossen Jr, *President*
Matt Brannigan, *Marketing Staff*
Marc Rees, *Manager*
EMP: 25
SQ FT: 2,100
SALES (est): 5MM **Privately Held**
WEB: www.cjlconstruction.com
SIC: 1611 Highway & street maintenance

(G-3161)
C K OF CINCINNATI INC
Also Called: Comfort Keepers
7525 State Rd Ste B (45255-6406)
PHONE..................513 752-5533
Fax: 513 752-9944
Veronica Disimile, *President*
Chris Disimile, *Vice Pres*
EMP: 105 EST: 2001
SALES (est): 2.7MM **Privately Held**
SIC: 8082 Home health care services

(G-3162)
C MICAH RAND INC
Also Called: Brookwood Retirement Community
12100 Reed Hartman Hwy (45241-6071)
PHONE..................513 605-2000
Fax: 513 605-2040
Steve Boymel, *President*
Wilkins Teresa, *Sls & Mktg Exec*
Michael Smith, *Accountant*
Loretta Hoerst, *Finance*
Peggy McShane, *Nursing Dir*
EMP: 150
SQ FT: 180,000
SALES: 15.5MM **Privately Held**
SIC: 8361 Rest home, with health care incidental

(G-3163)
C&C CLEAN TEAM ENTERPRISES LLC
Also Called: Widmer's
2016 Madison Rd (45208-3238)
PHONE..................513 321-5100
Fax: 513 321-7547
Rob Roy, *Division Mgr*
Jack Kilgore, *Opers Mgr*
Chris Nida, *Controller*
Steve Carico, *VP Finance*
Andy Lawrence, *Manager*
EMP: 250
SALES (est): 13.5MM **Privately Held**
SIC: 7212 7217 Garment pressing & cleaners' agents; carpet & upholstery cleaning

(G-3164)
CADRE COMPUTER RESOURCES CO (PA)
Also Called: Cadre Information Security
201 E 5th St Ste 1800 (45202-4162)
PHONE..................513 762-7350
Fax: 513 762-6502
Sandra E Laney, *CEO*
Steven W Snider, *President*
Stephen M Krumpelman, *Vice Pres*
Jim Burkardt, *Sales Staff*
Katherine Viancourt, *Sales Staff*
EMP: 48
SQ FT: 8,000
SALES (est): 43.3MM **Privately Held**
WEB: www.cadre.net
SIC: 7379

(G-3165)
CAI/INSURANCE AGENCY INC (PA)
Also Called: ACTUARIAL & EMPLOYEE BENEFIT S
2035 Reading Rd (45202-1415)
PHONE..................513 221-1140
Fax: 513 872-7519
Carl R Schlotman III, *CEO*
Michael Schlotman, *COO*
Jimmie Foster, *Senior VP*
Kevin Schlotman, *Senior VP*
Bill Luning, *Vice Pres*
EMP: 42
SQ FT: 17,000
SALES: 7MM **Privately Held**
SIC: 6411 Insurance agents

(G-3166)
CALFEE HALTER & GRISWOLD LLP
255 E 5th St (45202-4700)
PHONE..................513 693-4880
Shelli Spine, *Office Mgr*
Meghan Glynn, *Manager*
Sean Suder, *Consultant*
EMP: 192
SALES (corp-wide): 49.3MM **Privately Held**
SIC: 8111 General practice attorney, lawyer
PA: Calfee, Halter & Griswold Llp
1405 E 6th St Ste 1
Cleveland OH 44114
216 831-2732

(G-3167)
CAMARGO CLUB
8605 Shawnee Run Rd (45243-2811)
PHONE..................513 561-9292
Joseph Beech III, *Vice Pres*
John Lawrence, *Vice Pres*
Doug Postler, *Treasurer*
Kerry Chandler, *Controller*
Jamy Barter, *Manager*
EMP: 105
SQ FT: 7,000
SALES: 3.8MM **Privately Held**
SIC: 7997 Country club, membership

(G-3168)
CAMARGO CONSTRUCTION COMPANY
6801 Shawnee Run Rd (45243-2417)
PHONE..................513 248-1500
Fax: 513 576-8344
Harry W Adler Jr, *President*
Rita Adler, *Manager*
EMP: 35
SQ FT: 1,200
SALES (est): 3.7MM **Privately Held**
WEB: www.camargoconstruction.com
SIC: 1611 1794 1542 Surfacing & paving; excavation work; commercial & office building, new construction

(G-3169)
CAMARGO MANOR INC
Also Called: Pavillion At Camargo, The
12100 Reed Hartman Hwy (45241-6071)
PHONE..................513 605-3000
Fax: 513 561-6304
Henry Schneider, *President*
Steven Boymel, *Vice Pres*
Jerry Stanislaw, *Treasurer*
James E Lark, *Director*
EMP: 80
SQ FT: 10,000
SALES (est): 1.2MM **Privately Held**
SIC: 8051 8052 Skilled nursing care facilities; intermediate care facilities

(G-3170)
CAMARGO RENTAL CENTER INC
8149 Camargo Rd (45243-2203)
PHONE..................513 271-6510
Fax: 513 271-6564
David Murphy, *CEO*
Natalie S Currin, *President*
EMP: 28
SQ FT: 30,000
SALES (est): 3MM **Privately Held**
WEB: www.camargorental.com
SIC: 7299 7359 7389 Facility rental & party planning services; party planning service; party supplies rental services; decoration service for special events

(G-3171)
CAMDEN MANAGEMENT INC
Also Called: Real Estate
463 Ohio Pike Ste 304 (45255-3722)
P.O. Box 960, Milford (45150-0960)
PHONE..................513 383-1635
Robert Camden, *President*
Owen Liske, *Regional Mgr*
EMP: 26
SALES (est): 966.4K **Privately Held**
SIC: 8741 Business management

(G-3172)
CAMPBELL SALES COMPANY
8805 Governors Hill Dr # 300 (45249-3318)
PHONE..................513 697-2900
Keith Olscamp, *Manager*
EMP: 30
SALES (corp-wide): 7.8B **Publicly Held**
WEB: www.campbellsoup.com
SIC: 8743 Sales promotion
HQ: Campbell Sales Company
1 Campbell Pl
Camden NJ 08103
856 342-4800

(G-3173)
CAMPEON ROOFG & WATERPROOFING
3535 Round Bottom Rd (45244-3025)
PHONE..................513 271-8972
Fax: 513 271-3181
Mary B Barnes, *President*
Peter A Barnes, *Treasurer*
Mike Rohe, *Technology*
EMP: 50
SQ FT: 10,000
SALES (est): 5.2MM **Privately Held**
WEB: www.campeon.com
SIC: 1761 Roofing contractor; sheet metalwork

(G-3174)
CAPITAL INVESTMENT GROUP INC
226 E 8th St (45202-2104)
PHONE..................513 241-5090
David Bastos, *President*
EMP: 40
SALES (est): 1.9MM **Privately Held**
SIC: 6799 Investors

(G-3175)
CAR WASH PLUS LTD
12105 Montgomery Rd (45249-1730)
PHONE..................513 683-4228
Fax: 513 469-8039
Bill Austin, *Owner*
EMP: 30
SQ FT: 5,000
SALES (est): 660.5K **Privately Held**
SIC: 7542 Carwashes

(G-3176)
CARACOLE INC
4138 Hamilton Ave (45223-2293)
PHONE..................513 761-1480
Fax: 513 761-3377
Mark McComas, *CFO*
Cheryl Damon-Greiner, *Accounts Mgr*
Dean Clevenger, *Office Mgr*
John Conboy, *Manager*
Whitney O'Neal, *Manager*
EMP: 41
SQ FT: 4,800
SALES: 4.2MM **Privately Held**
WEB: www.caracole.org
SIC: 8361 8322 Home for destitute men & women; referral service for personal & social problems

(G-3177)
CARDIAC VSCLAR THRCIC SURGEONS
4030 Smith Rd Ste 300 (45209-1974)
PHONE..................513 421-3494
Steven Park, *President*
Creighton Wright, *Vice Pres*
Karen A Gersch, *Surgeon*
Loren F Hiratzka, *Surgeon*
Eric J Okum, *Surgeon*
EMP: 38
SALES (est): 5MM
SALES (corp-wide): 4.2B **Privately Held**
WEB: www.cvts.com
SIC: 8011 Cardiologist & cardio-vascular specialist
PA: Mercy Health
1701 Mercy Health Pl
Cincinnati OH 45237
513 639-2800

(G-3178)
CARDINAL PACELLI SCHOOL
927 Ellison Ave (45226-1287)
PHONE..................513 321-1048
Fax: 513 533-6114
Terri Canto, *Principal*
Teri Haught, *Vice Pres*
Emily Daley, *Corp Comm Staff*
Mary L Groenke, *Librarian*
Jennie Clark, *Manager*
EMP: 360 EST: 2012
SALES (est): 3.1MM **Privately Held**
SIC: 8211 8351 Catholic elementary school; preschool center

(G-3179)
CARDINAL SOLUTIONS GROUP INC (PA)
7755 Montgomery Rd # 510 (45236-7923)
PHONE..................513 984-6700
Fax: 513 792-2835
Kelly P Conway, *President*
Michael A York, *Vice Pres*
Todd McCoain, *Finance*
Kristi Lell, *Human Res Mgr*
Dan Lange, *Practice Mgr*
EMP: 81 EST: 1996
SALES (est): 23.5MM **Privately Held**
WEB: www.cardinalsolutions.com
SIC: 7379

Cincinnati - Hamilton County (G-3180)
GEOGRAPHIC SECTION

(G-3180)
CARDIOLOGY CTR OF CINCINNATI (PA)
Also Called: Cardiology Center Cincinnati
10525 Montgomery Rd A (45242-4401)
P.O. Box 631834 (45263-0001)
PHONE.................513 745-9800
Fax: 513 985-2905
Edward J Loughery, *President*
Najamul Ansari, *Cardiovascular*
Richard L Callihan Jr, *Cardiovascular*
Simon Jung, *Cardiovascular*
EMP: 30
SALES (est): 6.7MM Privately Held
WEB: www.thecardiologycenter.com
SIC: 8011 Cardiologist & cardio-vascular specialist

(G-3181)
CARE CONNECTION OF CINCINNATI
7265 Kenwood Rd Ste 363 (45236-4411)
PHONE.................513 842-1101
Fax: 513 842-1105
Bob James,
Tony Izquierdo,
EMP: 70
SALES (est): 3MM Privately Held
WEB: www.ccohomecare.com
SIC: 8082 Visiting nurse service

(G-3182)
CAREGIVERS HEALTH NETWORK INC
2135 Dana Ave Ste 200 (45207-1327)
PHONE.................513 662-3400
Fax: 513 662-3071
Mary S Allen, *Principal*
Rebecca Miars, *Vice Pres*
EMP: 70
SALES (est): 1.5MM
SALES (corp-wide): 796.9MM Publicly Held
WEB: www.caregivershealthnetwork.com
SIC: 8082 Home health care services
PA: Almost Family, Inc.
    9510 Ormsby Station Rd
    Louisville KY 40223
    502 891-1000

(G-3183)
CARESTAR INC (PA)
5566 Cheviot Rd (45247-7094)
PHONE.................513 618-8300
Fax: 513 245-6132
Thomas J Gruber, *President*
Sharon Higgins, *Vice Pres*
Katrina Kunkel, *Opers Spvr*
Tanya Golding, *Human Res Mgr*
Susan Werner, *HR Admin*
EMP: 124
SQ FT: 15,000
SALES (est): 23.5MM Privately Held
SIC: 7361 8082 Nurses' registry; home health care services

(G-3184)
CAREW REALTY INC
441 Vine St Ste 3900 (45202-3011)
PHONE.................513 241-3888
Stewart Warm, *Ch of Bd*
Alex Warm, *Vice Ch Bd*
Steven N Stein, *President*
Stewart Fahrnbach, *Vice Pres*
James F Bastin, *CFO*
EMP: 45
SALES (est): 3.8MM Privately Held
SIC: 6512 Commercial & industrial building operation

(G-3185)
CARINGTON HEALTH SYSTEMS
Also Called: Glencare Center
3627 Harvey Ave (45229-2005)
PHONE.................513 961-8881
Fax: 513 872-7916
Bob Bishop, *Administration*
EMP: 110
SALES (corp-wide): 85.7MM Privately Held
SIC: 8051 8049 Convalescent home with continuous nursing care; physical therapist

PA: Carington Health Systems
    8200 Beckett Park Dr
    Hamilton OH 45011
    513 682-2700

(G-3186)
CAROL A & RALP V H US B FDN TR
425 Walnut St Fl 11f (45202-3944)
PHONE.................513 632-4426
Chris McKim, *Assistant VP*
Kevin Beck, *Financial Analy*
Chris Darby, *Cust Mgr*
Amy Hitch, *Manager*
Audra Matthews, *Manager*
EMP: 39
SALES: 15.5MM Privately Held
SIC: 8699 Charitable organization

(G-3187)
CAROL REESE
Also Called: Center Service
421 Anderson Ferry Rd (45238-5228)
PHONE.................513 347-0252
Carol Reese, *Owner*
Carol Mefford, *Owner*
EMP: 25
SALES (est): 642.3K Privately Held
SIC: 7389 Telephone answering service

(G-3188)
CARUSO INC (PA)
3465 Hauck Rd (45241-1601)
PHONE.................513 860-9200
Jim Caruso, *CEO*
James S Caruso, *Principal*
Steve Caruso, *Exec VP*
Mike Caruso, *Vice Pres*
Wayne Kramer, *Vice Pres*
▲ EMP: 105 EST: 1926
SQ FT: 155,000
SALES (est): 83.2MM Privately Held
WEB: www.carusofoods.com
SIC: 5148 Fruits, fresh; vegetables, fresh

(G-3189)
CARVAKA INC
1404 Race St Ste 302 (45202-7366)
PHONE.................513 381-1531
Beau Necco, *President*
EMP: 25
SALES (est): 910K Privately Held
SIC: 8322 Child related social services

(G-3190)
CAS-KER COMPANY INC
2550 Civic Center Dr (45231-1310)
PHONE.................513 674-7700
Fax: 513 647-0600
Patrick J Cassedy, *President*
Daniel B Cassedy, *Corp Secy*
Thomas J Cassedy, *Vice Pres*
Richard Foster, *Vice Pres*
▲ EMP: 38
SQ FT: 21,750
SALES (est): 8.6MM Privately Held
WEB: www.casker.com
SIC: 5094 Clocks, watches & parts

(G-3191)
CASCO MFG SOLUTIONS INC
3107 Spring Grove Ave (45225-1821)
PHONE.................513 681-0003
Fax: 513 853-3612
Melissa Mangold, *President*
Thomas Mangold, *Chairman*
Terri Mangold, *Vice Pres*
Jim Moore, *Opers Mgr*
Jeff Hummeldorf, *Prdtn Mgr*
▲ EMP: 60 EST: 1959
SQ FT: 72,000
SALES (est): 10.6MM Privately Held
WEB: www.cascosolutions.com
SIC: 2515 7641 3841 2522 Mattresses, containing felt, foam rubber, urethane, etc.; upholstery work; surgical & medical instruments; office furniture, except wood; household furnishings

(G-3192)
CASSIDY TRLEY COML RE SVCS INC
Also Called: Colliers Turley Martin Tucker
300 E Bus Way Ste 190 (45241)
PHONE.................513 771-2580
Marnie Castleberry, *Branch Mgr*

Melaine Murphy, *Manager*
EMP: 25
SALES (corp-wide): 5.5B Privately Held
SIC: 6531 Real estate agent, commercial
HQ: Cassidy Turley Commercial Real Estate Services Inc.
    7700 Forsyth Blvd Ste 900
    Saint Louis MO 63105
    314 862-7100

(G-3193)
CATALINA MARKETING CORPORATION
525 Vine St Ste 2200 (45202-3123)
PHONE.................513 564-8200
Kriss Jones, *Manager*
EMP: 36 Privately Held
WEB: www.catalinamktg.com
SIC: 7319 Coupon distribution
HQ: Catalina Marketing Corporation
    200 Carillon Pkwy
    Saint Petersburg FL 33716
    727 579-5000

(G-3194)
CATHOLIC CHARITIES OF SW OHIO (PA)
7162 Reading Rd Ste 604 (45237-3819)
PHONE.................513 241-7745
Fax: 513 241-4333
M Kathleen Donnellan, *Exec Dir*
Giovanna Alvarez, *Director*
Gene Johnson, *Asst Director*
Leslie New, *Admin Sec*
EMP: 90
SALES: 17.2MM Privately Held
SIC: 8322 4119 Social service center; local passenger transportation

(G-3195)
CATHOLIC RESIDENTIAL SERVICE
100 E 8th St Ste 5 (45202-2195)
PHONE.................513 784-0400
Steve Schulte, *Treasurer*
Christy Hoekzema, *Director*
EMP: 30
SALES: 3.1MM Privately Held
SIC: 8322 Social services for the handicapped

(G-3196)
CBRE INC
201 E 5th St Ste 2200 (45202-4113)
PHONE.................513 369-1300
Fax: 513 241-2291
David Lockard, *Vice Pres*
Michael McMillan, *Vice Pres*
Bill Wiebe, *Vice Pres*
Chris Carey, *Research*
Robert Calhoun, *Engineer*
EMP: 71
SALES (corp-wide): 14.2B Publicly Held
SIC: 6531 Real estate agent, commercial
HQ: Cbre, Inc.
    400 S Hope St Ste 25
    Los Angeles CA 90071
    310 477-5876

(G-3197)
CBS CORPORATION
2060 Reading Rd Fl 34 (45202-1454)
PHONE.................513 749-1035
Jim Bryant, *Manager*
EMP: 130
SALES (corp-wide): 13.7B Publicly Held
SIC: 4832 Radio broadcasting stations
HQ: Cbs Corporation
    51 W 52nd St Bsmt 1
    New York NY 10019
    212 975-4321

(G-3198)
CBS RADIO INC
2060 Reading Rd (45202-1454)
PHONE.................513 699-5105
Fax: 513 562-3030
Christine Mello, *Sales Executive*
Jim Bryant, *Manager*
Tim Closson, *Manager*
Grover Collins, *Manager*
Julie Evans, *Manager*
EMP: 60

SALES (corp-wide): 592.8MM Publicly Held
WEB: www.infinityradio.com
SIC: 4832 Radio broadcasting stations, music format
HQ: Cbs Radio Inc.
    345 Hudson St Fl 10
    New York NY 10014
    212 314-9200

(G-3199)
CDW TECHNOLOGIES LLC
9349 Waterstone Blvd (45249-8320)
PHONE.................513 677-4100
Fax: 513 677-4101
Sean Eveslage, *Accounts Exec*
Dominic Wisler, *Accounts Exec*
Chris Ashcraft, *Branch Mgr*
Adam Childers, *Manager*
David Gates, *Manager*
EMP: 52 Publicly Held
WEB: www.berbee.com
SIC: 7373 Systems integration services
HQ: Cdw Technologies Llc
    5520 Research Park Dr
    Fitchburg WI 53711

(G-3200)
CEI PHYSICIANS PSC INC
7794 5 Mile Rd Ste 270 (45230-2369)
PHONE.................513 233-2700
Wendy Lippert, *Admin Mgr*
EMP: 31
SALES (corp-wide): 46.4MM Privately Held
SIC: 8011 Ophthalmologist
PA: Cei Physicians, P.S.C., Inc.
    1945 Cei Dr
    Blue Ash OH 45242
    513 984-5133

(G-3201)
CEI PHYSICIANS PSC INC
4760 Red Bank Rd Ste 108 (45227-1549)
PHONE.................513 531-2020
Heather Statton, *Branch Mgr*
EMP: 31
SALES (corp-wide): 46.4MM Privately Held
SIC: 8011 Eyes, ears, nose & throat specialist: physician/surgeon
PA: Cei Physicians, P.S.C., Inc.
    1945 Cei Dr
    Blue Ash OH 45242
    513 984-5133

(G-3202)
CELLCO PARTNERSHIP
Also Called: Verizon
9674 Colerain Ave (45251-2006)
PHONE.................513 923-2700
Fax: 513 923-3575
Ralph Wright, *Manager*
EMP: 71
SALES (corp-wide): 126B Publicly Held
SIC: 4812 Cellular telephone services
HQ: Cellco Partnership
    1 Verizon Way
    Basking Ridge NJ 07920

(G-3203)
CELLCO PARTNERSHIP
8650 Governors Hill Dr (45249-1372)
PHONE.................513 697-1190
EMP: 71
SALES (corp-wide): 126B Publicly Held
SIC: 4812 Cellular telephone services
HQ: Cellco Partnership
    1 Verizon Way
    Basking Ridge NJ 07920

(G-3204)
CELLCO PARTNERSHIP
Also Called: Verizon
482 Ohio Pike Ste 1 (45255-7300)
PHONE.................513 688-1300
Fax: 513 688-1429
Matthew Hoog, *Accounts Exec*
Pam Baird, *Branch Mgr*
EMP: 25
SALES (corp-wide): 126B Publicly Held
SIC: 4812 5731 Cellular telephone services; radio, television & electronic stores
HQ: Cellco Partnership
    1 Verizon Way
    Basking Ridge NJ 07920

GEOGRAPHIC SECTION
Cincinnati - Hamilton County (G-3228)

(G-3205)
CELLCO PARTNERSHIP
Also Called: Verizon
55 E Kemper Rd (45246-3224)
PHONE.....................513 671-2200
Fax: 513 671-0597
Lyn Boigt, *Branch Mgr*
EMP: 25
SALES (corp-wide): 126B **Publicly Held**
SIC: 4812 5999 Cellular telephone services; mobile telephones & equipment
HQ: Cellco Partnership
  1 Verizon Way
  Basking Ridge NJ 07920

(G-3206)
CELLCO PARTNERSHIP
Also Called: Verizon
9040 Union Cemetery Rd (45249-2016)
PHONE.....................513 697-0222
Fax: 513 697-8414
Sue Milam, *Branch Mgr*
EMP: 30
SALES (corp-wide): 126B **Publicly Held**
SIC: 4812 5999 Cellular telephone services; mobile telephones & equipment
HQ: Cellco Partnership
  1 Verizon Way
  Basking Ridge NJ 07920

(G-3207)
CENTER FOR CHEMICAL ADDICTIONS
830 Ezzard Charles Dr (45214-2525)
PHONE.....................513 381-6672
Nancy Blamer, *Manager*
Gladys Evans, *Supervisor*
Sandra L Keuhn, *Exec Dir*
EMP: 70
SQ FT: 31,000
SALES (est): 4.1MM **Privately Held**
SIC: 8069 8093 8063 Alcoholism rehabilitation hospital; drug addiction rehabilitation hospital; specialty outpatient clinics; psychiatric hospitals

(G-3208)
CENTER FOR FOOT & ANKLE CARE
25 Merchant St Ste 220 (45246-3740)
PHONE.....................513 533-1199
Dave Gibson, *Manager*
EMP: 48
SALES (est): 3.1MM **Privately Held**
WEB: www.cfac.net
SIC: 8043 Offices & clinics of podiatrists

(G-3209)
CENTRAL ACCOUNTING SYSTEMS
Also Called: Health Care Management Group
12500 Reed Hartman Hwy (45241-1892)
PHONE.....................513 605-2700
Fax: 513 489-2408
Steven Boymel, *President*
Evan Boymel, *Vice Pres*
Gregory Miller, *VP Opers*
Allan Acheson, *CFO*
Lynn Spirs, *Controller*
EMP: 26
SALES (est): 4.8MM **Privately Held**
WEB: www.hcmg.com
SIC: 8721 Accounting, auditing & bookkeeping

(G-3210)
CENTRAL BUSINESS EQUIPMENT CO (HQ)
Also Called: Patterson Pope
10321 S Medallion Dr (45241-4825)
PHONE.....................513 891-4430
Fax: 513 891-7029
Dennis Hammack, *President*
Glen Kalley, *Regional Mgr*
Gene Rouse, *Vice Pres*
Steve Streight, *Sales Mgr*
EMP: 27
SALES (est): 7.5MM
SALES (corp-wide): 100.4MM **Privately Held**
WEB: www.centralbusinessgroup.com
SIC: 5021 Filing units

PA: Patterson Pope, Inc.
  3001 N Graham St
  Charlotte NC 28206
  704 523-4400

(G-3211)
CENTRAL COMMNTY HLTH BRD OF HA (PA)
532 Maxwell Ave (45219-2408)
PHONE.....................513 559-2000
Fax: 513 559-2020
Deborah Smith, *Accounting Mgr*
Ed Shelleby, *Psychologist*
Larry Sykes, *Manager*
Charlie Bogenschutz, *MIS Dir*
Andy McCleese, *Software Engr*
EMP: 146
SQ FT: 2,500
SALES: 10.1MM **Privately Held**
SIC: 8063 8093 Hospital for the mentally ill; specialty outpatient clinics

(G-3212)
CENTRAL COMMNTY HLTH BRD OF HA
3020 Vernon Pl (45219-2418)
PHONE.....................513 559-2981
Fax: 513 559-2077
Bennett Cooper, *Director*
EMP: 50
SALES (corp-wide): 10.1MM **Privately Held**
SIC: 8093 Drug clinic, outpatient
PA: Central Community Health Board Of Hamilton County, The Inc.
  532 Maxwell Ave
  Cincinnati OH 45219
  513 559-2000

(G-3213)
CENTRAL COMMUNITY
Also Called: Crisis Stablization Center
3007 Vernon Pl (45219-2417)
PHONE.....................513 559-2000
Venessa Jetters, *Manager*
EMP: 100
SQ FT: 8,114
SALES (corp-wide): 10.1MM **Privately Held**
SIC: 8063 Hospital for the mentally ill
PA: Central Community Health Board Of Hamilton County, The Inc.
  532 Maxwell Ave
  Cincinnati OH 45219
  513 559-2000

(G-3214)
CENTRAL INSULATION SYSTEMS INC
300 Murray Rd (45217-1011)
PHONE.....................513 242-0600
Fax: 513 482-3717
Steve Kirby, *President*
Kathy Kirby, *Vice Pres*
Larry Kissel, *Vice Pres*
Jerry Lichtenfeld, *Project Mgr*
EMP: 50
SQ FT: 30,000
SALES (est): 8.9MM **Privately Held**
WEB: www.centralinsulation.com
SIC: 1799 1742 Asbestos removal & encapsulation; insulation, buildings

(G-3215)
CENTRAL PARKING SYSTEM INC
303 Broadway St Lot A (45202-4220)
PHONE.....................513 381-2621
EMP: 35
SALES (corp-wide): 1.5B **Publicly Held**
SIC: 7521 Parking lots
HQ: Central Parking System, Inc.
  1225 I St Nw Ste C100
  Washington DC 20005
  202 496-9650

(G-3216)
CENTRAL READY MIX LLC (PA)
6310 E Kemper Rd Ste 125 (45241-2370)
P.O. Box 70, Monroe (45050-0070)
PHONE.....................513 402-5001
Toll Free:.....................888 -
Fax: 937 743-0651
John Dales, *Controller*
Ashish Goel, *Manager*

Robert Cherry,
EMP: 30 EST: 1934
SQ FT: 8,000
SALES (est): 12.4MM **Privately Held**
WEB: www.morainematerials.com
SIC: 3273 1442 Ready-mixed concrete; sand mining

(G-3217)
CENTRAL STEEL AND WIRE COMPANY
525 Township Ave (45216-2399)
PHONE.....................513 242-2233
Fax: 513 242-1524
Mike Staggs, *Warehouse Mgr*
Larry Henry, *Purchasing*
William Bessler, *Sales Staff*
Tom Rogina, *Branch Mgr*
EMP: 150
SALES (corp-wide): 599.1MM **Publicly Held**
WEB: www.centralsteel.com
SIC: 5051 Steel
PA: Central Steel And Wire Company
  3000 W 51st St
  Chicago IL 60632
  773 471-3800

(G-3218)
CENTRAL USA WIRELESS LLC
11210 Montgomery Rd (45249-2311)
PHONE.....................513 469-1500
Angie Flottemesch, *Opers Staff*
EMP: 28
SALES (est): 2.9MM **Privately Held**
SIC: 7622 3663 Antenna repair & installation; household antenna installation & service; antennas, transmitting & communications

(G-3219)
CENTRIC CONSULTING LLC
9380 Montgomery Rd # 207 (45242-7756)
PHONE.....................513 791-3061
Dawn Nyomo, *Business Anlyst*
Dan Driscoll, *Manager*
Brad Clark, *Consultant*
Stacy Brogden, *Senior Mgr*
Maurice Faison, *Senior Mgr*
EMP: 33
SALES (corp-wide): 37.5MM **Privately Held**
SIC: 8999 Scientific consulting
PA: Centric Consulting, Llc
  1215 Lyons Rd F
  Dayton OH 45458
  888 781-7567

(G-3220)
CENTURY MECH SOLUTIONS INC
Also Called: Honeywell Authorized Dealer
1554 Chase Ave (45223-2146)
PHONE.....................513 681-5700
Thomas Lienhart Pe, *President*
Margaret Lienhart, *Corp Secy*
Doug S Nerhaus, *Vice Pres*
Kenneth J Miller, *Vice Pres*
Jeff Wilmink, *VP Sales*
EMP: 31 EST: 1938
SQ FT: 4,500
SALES (est): 8MM **Privately Held**
SIC: 1711 Warm air heating & air conditioning contractor

(G-3221)
CFM RELIGION PUBG GROUP LLC (PA)
8805 Governors Hill Dr # 400 (45249-3319)
PHONE.....................513 931-4050
Matthew Thibeau, *President*
Don Puterbaugh, *Manager*
EMP: 31
SALES (est): 34.4MM **Privately Held**
SIC: 2721 8741 Magazines: publishing only, not printed on site; management services

(G-3222)
CFS CONSTRUCTION INC
2170 Gilbert Ave Ste 100 (45206-3019)
PHONE.....................513 559-4500
Fax: 513 793-2345
Dan Scullin, *President*

Gary Osterback, *Controller*
EMP: 46
SQ FT: 5,000
SALES (est): 2.9MM **Privately Held**
WEB: www.cfsoh.com
SIC: 1522 1542 Hotel/motel & multi-family home renovation & remodeling; multi-family dwellings, new construction; commercial & office buildings, renovation & repair; commercial & office building, new construction

(G-3223)
CGH-GLBAL OPERATIONS LOGISTICS
4957 Cinnamon Cir (45244-1210)
PHONE.....................800 376-0655
Andrew Glassmeyer, *CEO*
Matthew Holmes, *COO*
EMP: 32
SALES (est): 218.9K **Privately Held**
SIC: 8049 Paramedic

(G-3224)
CGH-GLOBAL SECURITY LLC
4957 Cinnamon Cir (45244-1210)
PHONE.....................800 376-0655
Andrew Glassmeyer, *CEO*
Matthew Holmes, *COO*
EMP: 32 EST: 2016
SALES (est): 496.4K
SALES (corp-wide): 8MM **Privately Held**
SIC: 7389
PA: Cgh-Global, Llc
  851 Ohio Pike Ste 203
  Cincinnati OH 45245
  800 376-0655

(G-3225)
CGH-GLOBAL TECHNOLOGIES LLC
4957 Cinnamon Cir (45244-1210)
PHONE.....................800 376-0655
Andrew Glassmeyer, *CEO*
Matthew Holmes, *COO*
EMP: 32 EST: 2016
SALES (est): 524.3K
SALES (corp-wide): 8MM **Privately Held**
SIC: 8748 Business consulting
PA: Cgh-Global, Llc
  851 Ohio Pike Ste 203
  Cincinnati OH 45245
  800 376-0655

(G-3226)
CH2M HILL INC
400 E Bus Way Ste 400 (45241)
PHONE.....................513 243-5070
Mike Bartlett, *Principal*
EMP: 77
SALES (est): 22.3MM **Privately Held**
SIC: 8711 Consulting engineer

(G-3227)
CHAMPION CLG SPECIALISTS INC
8391 Blue Ash Rd (45236-1986)
PHONE.....................513 871-2333
Toll Free:.....................888 -
Fax: 513 871-6959
Chris Kurtz, *President*
Pat Kurtz, *Vice Pres*
Deedee Long, *Office Mgr*
EMP: 30 EST: 1982
SQ FT: 12,000
SALES (est): 1.5MM **Privately Held**
WEB: www.championcleaning.net
SIC: 7349 Cleaning service, industrial or commercial; air duct cleaning

(G-3228)
CHAMPION OPCO LLC (PA)
Also Called: Champion Windows Manufacturing
12121 Champion Way (45241-6419)
PHONE.....................513 924-4858
Fax: 513 346-4614
Jim Mishler, *CEO*
Donald R Jones, *President*
Martin Hiedet, *VP Admin*
Joe Faisant, *CFO*
Lisa Brumfield, *Controller*
▲ **EMP:** 300 EST: 1953
SQ FT: 500,000

Cincinnati - Hamilton County (G-3229)

SALES (est): 515.7MM **Privately Held**
WEB: www.championfactorydirct.com
SIC: 3089 1761 3442 Window frames & sash, plastic; siding contractor; storm doors or windows, metal

(G-3229)
CHAMPLIN HAUPT ARCHITECTS INC (PA)
Also Called: Champlin Architecture
720 E Pete Rose Way # 140 (45202-3375)
PHONE..................513 241-4474
Fax: 859 331-5594
Robert A Schilling Jr, *President*
Jay D Derenthal, *Principal*
Melissa M Lutz, *Principal*
Joan Tepe Wurtenberger, *Vice Pres*
Mike Anderson, *Project Mgr*
EMP: 52
SQ FT: 6,900
SALES (est): 9.3MM **Privately Held**
WEB: www.charchitects.com
SIC: 8712 Architectural engineering

(G-3230)
CHARLES V FRANCIS TRUST
Also Called: Metro Recycling
19 W Vine St (45215-3233)
PHONE..................513 528-5600
Charles V Francis, *Owner*
EMP: 40
SALES (est): 2.8MM **Privately Held**
SIC: 6733 Personal investment trust management

(G-3231)
CHARLES W POWERS & ASSOC INC
Also Called: Powers Agency
1 W 4th St Ste 500 (45202-3610)
PHONE..................513 721-5353
Lori Powers, *CEO*
Charles W Powers, *President*
Jennifer King, *Vice Pres*
Stacey Martin, *Vice Pres*
Mark Wesling, *Vice Pres*
EMP: 30
SALES (est): 5.6MM **Privately Held**
WEB: www.powersagency.com
SIC: 7311 Advertising consultant

(G-3232)
CHAS G BUCHY PACKING COMPANY
Also Called: Buchy Food Service
10510 Evendale Dr (45241-2516)
PHONE..................800 762-1060
G James Buchy, *President*
Sharon Buchy, *Vice Pres*
Kate Kerg, *Vice Pres*
EMP: 38 EST: 1878
SQ FT: 30,000
SALES (est): 10.6MM **Privately Held**
WEB: www.buchyfoods.com
SIC: 5141 Groceries, general line

(G-3233)
CHE INTERNATIONAL GROUP LLC (PA)
Also Called: Cig
9435 Waterstone Blvd # 140 (45249-8229)
PHONE..................513 444-2072
Christopher Che, *CEO*
EMP: 44 **Privately Held**
SIC: 6719 Investment holding companies, except banks

(G-3234)
CHECK IT OUT 4 ME LLC
7709 Greenland Pl Ste 1 (45237-2711)
PHONE..................513 568-4269
Carlton Eddins,
EMP: 25
SALES (est): 392.5K **Privately Held**
SIC: 8748 Business consulting

(G-3235)
CHECK N GO OF IOWA INC (HQ)
7755 Montgomery Rd # 400 (45236-4197)
PHONE..................563 359-7800
Fax: 563 359-5337
Jennifer Wulf, *Manager*
EMP: 50

SALES (est): 13.2MM
SALES (corp-wide): 664.6MM **Privately Held**
WEB: www.check-n-go.com
SIC: 6099 Check cashing agencies
PA: Cng Financial Corporation
    7755 Montgomery Rd # 400
    Cincinnati OH 45236
    513 336-7735

(G-3236)
CHEEK-O INC
639 Northland Blvd (45240-5202)
PHONE..................513 942-4880
Fax: 513 742-8039
Rebecca Callahan, *President*
Tim Vale, *Accountant*
EMP: 25
SALES (est): 3.7MM **Privately Held**
SIC: 5137 Women's & children's clothing

(G-3237)
CHEMED CORPORATION (PA)
255 E 5th St Ste 2600 (45202-4138)
PHONE..................513 762-6690
Fax: 513 762-6919
George J Walsh III, *Ch of Bd*
Kevin J McNamara, *President*
Spencer S Lee, *Exec VP*
Nicholas M Westfall, *Exec VP*
Michael D Witzeman, *Vice Pres*
EMP: 64
SALES: 1.6B **Publicly Held**
WEB: www.chemed.com
SIC: 8082 1711 7699 Home health care services; visiting nurse service; plumbing, heating, air-conditioning contractors; plumbing contractors; sewer cleaning & rodding

(G-3238)
CHEMICAL BANK
7373 Beechmont Ave # 100 (45230-4100)
PHONE..................513 232-0800
Jim Sollars, *Manager*
EMP: 39
SALES (corp-wide): 776.1MM **Publicly Held**
SIC: 6035 Federal savings & loan associations
HQ: Chemical Bank
    333 E Main St
    Midland MI 48640
    989 631-9200

(G-3239)
CHERRY GROVE SPORTS CENTER
Also Called: Cherry Grove Lanes
4005 Hopper Hill Rd (45255-4945)
PHONE..................513 232-7199
Fax: 513 528-4588
Jack Betts, *President*
Larry Roberts, *Principal*
EMP: 30
SQ FT: 852
SALES (est): 1.1MM **Privately Held**
WEB: www.cglanes.com
SIC: 7933 Ten pin center

(G-3240)
CHESAPEAKE RESEARCH REVIEW LLC
9380 Main St (45242-7657)
PHONE..................410 884-2900
Jeffrey Wendel,
EMP: 30
SALES (corp-wide): 7.1MM **Privately Held**
SIC: 8621 Professional standards review board
PA: Chesapeake Research Review, Llc
    6940 Columbia Gateway Dr
    Columbia MD 21046
    410 884-2900

(G-3241)
CHESTER WEST HOLDINGS INC
Also Called: West Chester Protective Gear
11500 Canal Rd (45241-1862)
PHONE..................800 647-1900
Fax: 513 539-2827
Tim Fogarty, *CEO*
Mark J Jahnke, *President*
Ken Meyer, *President*
Robert W Fisher, *Corp Secy*

Vincent Wu, *Senior VP*
▲ EMP: 110
SQ FT: 200,000
SALES (est): 81.3MM
SALES (corp-wide): 25.3MM **Privately Held**
SIC: 3842 2381 5136 5137 Clothing, fire resistant & protective; gloves, work: woven or knit, made from purchased materials; men's & boys' clothing; women's & children's clothing; safety equipment & supplies
PA: Wcm Holdings, Inc.
    11500 Canal Rd
    Cincinnati OH 45241
    513 705-2100

(G-3242)
CHEVIOT MUTUAL HOLDING COMPANY
3723 Glenmore Ave (45211-4720)
PHONE..................513 661-0457
Thomas J Linneman, *President*
EMP: 52
SALES (est): 3.5MM **Privately Held**
SIC: 6035 Federal savings & loan associations

(G-3243)
CHILD FOCUS INC (PA)
4629 Aicholtz Rd Ste 2 (45244-1560)
PHONE..................513 752-1555
Fax: 513 753-2144
James Carter, *CEO*
Sandy Lock, *COO*
Matt McConnell, *Treasurer*
Glen Welling, *Human Res Mgr*
Tara Keith, *Marketing Staff*
EMP: 75
SQ FT: 27,000
SALES: 15.7MM **Privately Held**
WEB: www.child-focus.org
SIC: 8322 8093 8351 Child related social services; child guidance agency; family (marriage) counseling; mental health clinic, outpatient; head start center, except in conjunction with school

(G-3244)
CHILDRENS HM OF CNCINNATI OHIO
Also Called: CHILDREN'S HOME SCHOOL
5050 Madison Rd (45227-1491)
PHONE..................513 272-2800
Fax: 513 527-7300
Ellen Johnson, *CEO*
Roderick Hinton, *Vice Pres*
Shannon Taylor, *Vice Pres*
Reggie Hill, *Assistant*
EMP: 200
SQ FT: 84,000
SALES (est): 21.2MM **Privately Held**
WEB: www.thechildrenshomecinti.org
SIC: 8322 Child related social services

(G-3245)
CHILDRENS HOSPITAL
3373 Burnet Ave (45229-3026)
PHONE..................513 636-4051
Fax: 513 636-7844
Diane Holbrook, *Principal*
Melissa Stamper, *Pharmacist*
Jackqueline May, *Admin Asst*
EMP: 25
SALES (est): 1.6MM **Privately Held**
SIC: 8069 Children's hospital

(G-3246)
CHILDRENS HOSPITAL MEDICAL CTR
2750 Beekman St (45225-2049)
PHONE..................513 541-4500
Fax: 513 541-4544
Tiffany Whatley, *Manager*
EMP: 766
SALES (corp-wide): 1.6B **Privately Held**
SIC: 8322 Neighborhood center
PA: Children's Hospital Medical Center
    3333 Burnet Ave
    Cincinnati OH 45229
    513 636-4200

(G-3247)
CHILDRENS HOSPITAL MEDICAL CTR
Also Called: Cincinnati Chld Hosp Med Ctr
3333 Burnet Ave (45229-3039)
PHONE..................513 636-4200
Jill Guilfoile, *Principal*
Janet Majors, *Admin Asst*
EMP: 657
SALES (corp-wide): 1.6B **Privately Held**
SIC: 8011 Medical centers
PA: Children's Hospital Medical Center
    3333 Burnet Ave
    Cincinnati OH 45229
    513 636-4200

(G-3248)
CHILDRENS HOSPITAL MEDICAL CTR
Heart Institute Diagnostic Lab
240 Albert Sabin Way (45229-2842)
PHONE..................513 803-1751
Gina Schoenling, *Project Mgr*
John L Jefferies, *Med Doctor*
Wenying Zhang, *Director*
Jennifer Hembree, *Admin Asst*
EMP: 1840
SALES (corp-wide): 1.6B **Privately Held**
SIC: 8733 Medical research
PA: Children's Hospital Medical Center
    3333 Burnet Ave
    Cincinnati OH 45229
    513 636-4200

(G-3249)
CHILDRENS HOSPITAL MEDICAL CTR
2900 Vernon Pl (45219-2436)
PHONE..................513 636-4200
Erica Clark, *Research*
Korie Counts, *Manager*
Eric Schloss, *Network Analyst*
EMP: 788
SALES (corp-wide): 1.6B **Privately Held**
SIC: 8069 Children's hospital
PA: Children's Hospital Medical Center
    3333 Burnet Ave
    Cincinnati OH 45229
    513 636-4200

(G-3250)
CHILDRENS HOSPITAL MEDICAL CTR
Cincinnati Chld Hosp Med Ctr
2800 Winslow Ave Fl 3 (45206-1144)
PHONE..................513 636-4366
Fax: 513 861-2275
Sheila M Johnson, *Business Mgr*
Neva C Davis, *Project Mgr*
Mary Shinkle, *Project Mgr*
Michael S Chua, *Med Doctor*
A G Del Rey, *Med Doctor*
EMP: 766
SALES (corp-wide): 1.6B **Privately Held**
SIC: 8011 Physical medicine, physician/surgeon
PA: Children's Hospital Medical Center
    3333 Burnet Ave
    Cincinnati OH 45229
    513 636-4200

(G-3251)
CHILDRENS HOSPITAL MEDICAL CTR
Also Called: Outpatient Anderson
7495 State Rd Ste 355 (45255-6402)
PHONE..................513 636-6100
Fax: 513 636-6118
Mark Potticary, *Opers Staff*
Vince Paradisco, *Manager*
Chris Mayhew, *Co-Director*
Jean Kinman DDS, *Fmly & Gen Dent*
EMP: 40
SALES (corp-wide): 1.6B **Privately Held**
WEB: www.cincinnatichildrens.org
SIC: 8733 8093 Medical research; specialty outpatient clinics
PA: Children's Hospital Medical Center
    3333 Burnet Ave
    Cincinnati OH 45229
    513 636-4200

Cincinnati - Hamilton County

(G-3252)
CHILDRENS HOSPITAL MEDICAL CTR (PA)
Also Called: Children's Home Healthcare
3333 Burnet Ave (45229-3039)
PHONE.................................513 636-4200
Fax: 513 475-3928
Michael Fisher, *President*
Michael K Farrell, *Chief*
Laura Coorey, *Business Mgr*
Mark Lindenmeyer, *Business Mgr*
Deborah Neumann, *Business Mgr*
EMP: 3543
SQ FT: 1,803,000
SALES: 1.6B Privately Held
WEB: www.cincinnatichildrens.org
SIC: **8733** 8011 8069 8731 Medical research; clinic, operated by physicians; children's hospital; biotechnical research, commercial

(G-3253)
CHILDRENS HOSPITAL MEDICAL CTR
Also Called: Cincinnati Children's Hospital
3350 Elland Ave (45229-3039)
PHONE.................................513 636-4200
Mark McDonald, *Assoc VP*
Anita Brentley, *QA Dir*
Eric Brandt, *Research*
Jane Howie, *Marketing Staff*
Walter Flynn, *Branch Mgr*
EMP: 3417
SALES (corp-wide): 1.6B Privately Held
SIC: **4225** General warehousing
PA: Children's Hospital Medical Center
   3333 Burnet Ave
   Cincinnati OH 45229
   513 636-4200

(G-3254)
CHILDRENS HOSPITAL MEDICAL CTR
3333 Burnet Ave (45229-3039)
PHONE.................................513 636-8778
Michelle Stultz, *Branch Mgr*
EMP: 526
SALES (corp-wide): 1.6B Privately Held
SIC: **8011** Pediatrician
PA: Children's Hospital Medical Center
   3333 Burnet Ave
   Cincinnati OH 45229
   513 636-4200

(G-3255)
CHILDRENS HOSPITAL MEDICAL CTR
3333 Burnet Ave (45229-3039)
PHONE.................................513 636-8778
Robby Thompson, *Branch Mgr*
EMP: 920
SALES (corp-wide): 1.6B Privately Held
SIC: **8062** General medical & surgical hospitals
PA: Children's Hospital Medical Center
   3333 Burnet Ave
   Cincinnati OH 45229
   513 636-4200

(G-3256)
CHILLICOTHE LONG TERM CARE (PA)
Also Called: Westmoreland Place
7265 Kenwood Rd Ste 300 (45236-4414)
PHONE.................................513 793-8804
James Farley, *President*
Michael Scharfenberger, *Exec VP*
Kerry Grever, *Executive Asst*
EMP: 80
SQ FT: 50,000
SALES: 970.6MM Privately Held
WEB: www.westmorelandplace.com
SIC: **8051** Skilled nursing care facilities

(G-3257)
CHIRST HOSPITAL SURGERY CENTER
4850 Red Bank Rd Fl 1 (45227-1546)
PHONE.................................513 272-3448
Fax: 513 272-3449
Tammy Wood,
Mary Ann,
Cindy Law,
EMP: 35

SALES (est): 2.8MM Privately Held
WEB: www.redbanksurgery.com
SIC: **8011** Surgeon

(G-3258)
CHP AP SHARED SERVICES
P.O. Box 5203 (45201-5203)
PHONE.................................513 981-6704
EMP: 26
SALES (est): 1.9MM Privately Held
SIC: **8999** Services

(G-3259)
CHRIST HOSPITAL
2139 Auburn Ave (45219-2989)
PHONE.................................513 721-8272
Sandra L Miller, *Surgeon*
EMP: 53
SALES (est): 517.6K
SALES (corp-wide): 929.7MM Privately Held
SIC: **8011** General & family practice, physician/surgeon
PA: The Christ Hospital
   2139 Auburn Ave
   Cincinnati OH 45219
   513 585-2000

(G-3260)
CHRIST HOSPITAL
7545 Beechmont Ave Ste F (45255-4238)
PHONE.................................513 564-4000
Richard F Kammerer, *Branch Mgr*
EMP: 35
SALES (corp-wide): 929.7MM Privately Held
SIC: **8062** 8011 General medical & surgical hospitals; gynecologist
PA: The Christ Hospital
   2139 Auburn Ave
   Cincinnati OH 45219
   513 585-2000

(G-3261)
CHRIST HOSPITAL
11140 Montgomery Rd (45249-2309)
PHONE.................................513 561-7809
EMP: 123
SALES (corp-wide): 929.7MM Privately Held
SIC: **8062** 8031 8011 General medical & surgical hospitals; offices & clinics of osteopathic physicians; offices & clinics of medical doctors
PA: The Christ Hospital
   2139 Auburn Ave
   Cincinnati OH 45219
   513 585-2000

(G-3262)
CHRIST HOSPITAL
Also Called: Spectrum Rehabilitation
7545 Beechmont Ave Ste E (45255-4238)
PHONE.................................513 688-1111
Fax: 513 688-1000
Raymond C Rost, *Principal*
Ann Dardzinski, *Manager*
EMP: 311
SALES (corp-wide): 929.7MM Privately Held
SIC: **8062** 8049 Hospital, medical school affiliated with nursing & residency; physical therapist
PA: The Christ Hospital
   2139 Auburn Ave
   Cincinnati OH 45219
   513 585-2000

(G-3263)
CHRIST HOSPITAL
4440 Red Bank Rd Ste 100 (45227-2177)
PHONE.................................513 564-1340
Lisa Jarman, *Office Mgr*
EMP: 236
SALES (corp-wide): 929.7MM Privately Held
SIC: **7389** Inspection & testing services
PA: The Christ Hospital
   2139 Auburn Ave
   Cincinnati OH 45219
   513 585-2000

(G-3264)
CHRIST HOSPITAL
Also Called: Surgery Center
4850 Red Bank Rd Fl 1 (45227-1546)
PHONE.................................513 272-3448
EMP: 311
SALES (corp-wide): 929.7MM Privately Held
SIC: **8062** General medical & surgical hospitals
PA: The Christ Hospital
   2139 Auburn Ave
   Cincinnati OH 45219
   513 585-2000

(G-3265)
CHRIST HOSPITAL
2123 Auburn Ave Ste 341 (45219-2906)
PHONE.................................513 585-0050
Karthikeyan Kanagarajan, *Med Doctor*
EMP: 53
SALES (corp-wide): 929.7MM Privately Held
SIC: **8011** Radiologist
PA: The Christ Hospital
   2139 Auburn Ave
   Cincinnati OH 45219
   513 585-2000

(G-3266)
CHRIST HOSPITAL (PA)
Also Called: CHRIST HOSPITAL HEALTH NETWORK
2139 Auburn Ave (45219-2989)
PHONE.................................513 585-2000
Fax: 513 585-2673
Jack Cook, *CEO*
Allan Jones, *President*
Mike Keating, *President*
Mike Schwebler, *COO*
Heather Adkins, *Vice Pres*
EMP: 1500
SALES: 929.7MM Privately Held
SIC: **8062** Hospital, medical school affiliated with nursing & residency

(G-3267)
CHRIST HOSPITAL
4803 Montgomery Rd # 114 (45212-1153)
PHONE.................................513 631-3300
Mona Fry, *Branch Mgr*
EMP: 96
SALES (corp-wide): 929.7MM Privately Held
SIC: **8011** General & family practice, physician/surgeon
PA: The Christ Hospital
   2139 Auburn Ave
   Cincinnati OH 45219
   513 585-2000

(G-3268)
CHRIST HOSPITAL
Also Called: Christ Hospital, The
2355 Norwood Ave Ste 1 (45212-2750)
PHONE.................................513 351-0800
EMP: 105
SALES (corp-wide): 929.7MM Privately Held
SIC: **8011** Radiologist
PA: The Christ Hospital
   2139 Auburn Ave
   Cincinnati OH 45219
   513 585-2000

(G-3269)
CHRIST HOSPITAL CORPORATION
Also Called: Glenway Family Medicine
5885 Harrison Ave # 2900 (45248-1728)
PHONE.................................513 347-2300
Fax: 513 451-2135
EMP: 184
SALES (corp-wide): 929.7MM Privately Held
SIC: **8011** Internal medicine, physician/surgeon
PA: The Christ Hospital
   2139 Auburn Ave
   Cincinnati OH 45219
   513 585-2000

(G-3270)
CHRIST HOSPITAL SPINE SURGERY
4020 Smith Rd (45209-1936)
PHONE.................................513 619-5899
Fax: 513 619-5897
Mike Judge, *General Mgr*
EMP: 28
SALES (est): 4.4MM Privately Held
SIC: **8062** 8093 General medical & surgical hospitals; specialty outpatient clinics

(G-3271)
CHRISTIAN BENEVOLENT ASSOCN (PA)
8097 Hamilton Ave (45231-2321)
PHONE.................................513 931-5000
J Donald Sams, *CEO*
David Bickel, *Controller*
EMP: 200
SALES: 1.7MM Privately Held
SIC: **8741** Nursing & personal care facility management

(G-3272)
CHRISTIAN COMMUNITY HLTH SVCS
Also Called: Crossroad Health Center
5 E Liberty St Ste 4 (45202-8202)
PHONE.................................513 381-2247
Fax: 513 381-2256
Anne Scheid, *Manager*
Sally Stewart, *Exec Dir*
Andrew D Grubbs, *Director*
▲ EMP: 37
SALES (est): 4.2MM Privately Held
WEB: www.crossrd.org
SIC: **8011** Clinic, operated by physicians

(G-3273)
CHS NORWOOD INC
Also Called: WOODS EDGE POINT
1171 Towne St (45216-2227)
PHONE.................................513 242-1360
Floyd Brown, *Facilities Dir*
Lois Scheider, *Bookkeeper*
Carol Bottonari, *Director*
Nick Jones, *Executive*
Phil Wolven, *Maintence Staff*
EMP: 70
SALES: 7MM Privately Held
SIC: **8051** Skilled nursing care facilities

(G-3274)
CHS-NORWOOD INC
Also Called: Harmony Court
6969 Glenmeadow Ln (45237-3001)
PHONE.................................513 351-7007
Glyndon Powell, *Principal*
Kim Brooks, *Office Mgr*
Susan Stokes, *Executive*
Laurie Westermeyer, *Administration*
EMP: 160
SALES: 8.7MM
SALES (corp-wide): 85.7MM Privately Held
SIC: **8051** Convalescent home with continuous nursing care
PA: Carington Health Systems
   8200 Beckett Park Dr
   Hamilton OH 45011
   513 682-2700

(G-3275)
CIMCOOL INDUSTRIAL PDTS LLC (DH)
3000 Disney St (45209-5028)
PHONE.................................888 246-2665
Fax: 513 458-8298
Tom Goeke, *CEO*
Robert McKee, *President*
John Molnar, *Managing Dir*
Michael Crawford, *District Mgr*
Richard Marrone, *District Mgr*
▲ EMP: 56
SALES (est): 161.1MM
SALES (corp-wide): 1.2B Publicly Held
SIC: **5169** Chemicals & allied products

(G-3276)
CIMX LLC
Also Called: Cimx Software
4625 Red Bank Rd Ste 200 (45227-1552)
PHONE.................................513 248-7700
Fax: 513 248-7711

Cincinnati - Hamilton County (G-3277)   GEOGRAPHIC SECTION

Anthony Cuilwik, *Principal*
Kristin Cuilwik, *Manager*
Comfort Wendel, *Director*
EMP: 30
SQ FT: 12,000
SALES (est): 3.3MM Privately Held
WEB: www.cimx.com
SIC: 7372 7371 Prepackaged software; custom computer programming services

(G-3277)
CINCILINGUA INC
322 E 4th St (45202-4202)
PHONE...................513 721-8782
Hubert Collet, *President*
Edda Collet, *Corp Secy*
Sylvie Sum, *Program Mgr*
EMP: 45
SQ FT: 4,257
SALES (est): 1.6MM Privately Held
WEB: www.cincilingua.com
SIC: 8299 7389 Language school; translation services

(G-3278)
CINCINNATI - VULCAN COMPANY
5353 Spring Grove Ave (45217-1026)
PHONE...................513 242-5300
Fax: 513 242-4488
Garry C Ferraris, *President*
Kathy Hughes, *Office Mgr*
EMP: 60
SQ FT: 6,000
SALES (est): 12.9MM Privately Held
WEB: www.vulcanoil.com
SIC: 5983 2992 5171 2899 Fuel oil dealers; oils & greases, blending & compounding; petroleum bulk stations; petroleum terminals; chemical preparations; specialty cleaning, polishes & sanitation goods; soap & other detergents
PA: Coolant Control, Inc.
 5353 Spring Grove Ave
 Cincinnati OH 45217
 513 471-8770

(G-3279)
CINCINNATI AIR CONDITIONING CO
Also Called: Honeywell Authorized Dealer
2080 Northwest Dr (45231-1700)
PHONE...................513 721-5622
Fax: 513 345-2544
Mark Radtke, *President*
Michael Geiger, *Corp Secy*
Sherry Leadbetter, *Safety Dir*
Ken Wietmarschen, *Project Mgr*
Bill Wolf, *Project Mgr*
EMP: 55 EST: 1939
SQ FT: 30,000
SALES (est): 17.2MM Privately Held
WEB: www.cincinnatiair.com
SIC: 1711 3822 Warm air heating & air conditioning contractor; refrigeration contractor; auto controls regulating residntl & coml environmt & applncs

(G-3280)
CINCINNATI ANML RFRRL
Also Called: Care Center
6995 E Kemper Rd (45249-1024)
PHONE...................513 530-0911
Fax: 513 530-0811
Angie Gleason, *Sales Staff*
Douglas Hoffman,
Daniel Carey,
Michelle Muldoon,
Sharmila Ruparel,
EMP: 85 EST: 2000
SALES (est): 7.3MM Privately Held
SIC: 0742 Veterinary services, specialties

(G-3281)
CINCINNATI AREA SENIOR SVCS (PA)
2368 Victory Pkwy Ste 300 (45206-2810)
PHONE...................513 721-4330
Fax: 513 721-8304
Jim Boesch, *CFO*
Claudia Harrod, *Manager*
Elizabeth Patterson, *Exec Dir*
David Gunn, *Director*
Tracy Collins, *Deputy Dir*
EMP: 130 EST: 1966
SQ FT: 9,000
SALES: 3.8MM Privately Held
WEB: www.senserv.org
SIC: 8322 Senior citizens' center or association

(G-3282)
CINCINNATI ASSN FOR THE BLIND
2045 Gilbert Ave (45202-1403)
PHONE...................513 221-8558
Toll Free:....................888   -
Fax: 513 221-2995
John Mitchell, *CEO*
Fred Newman, *COO*
Amy Scrivner, *Development*
Jennifer Dubois, *Finance*
Judy Hale, *Info Tech Mgr*
EMP: 125
SQ FT: 88,000
SALES: 7.3MM Privately Held
SIC: 8331 8322 2891 Sheltered workshop; association for the handicapped; adhesives & sealants

(G-3283)
CINCINNATI BALLET COMPANY INC
1555 Central Pkwy (45214-2863)
PHONE...................513 621-5219
Fax: 513 621-4844
Victoria Morgan, *CEO*
Melissa Santomo, *COO*
Julie Sunderland, *Transptn Dir*
Melinda Dobson, *Production*
David Bickel, *Finance*
EMP: 30 EST: 1958
SQ FT: 27,595
SALES: 8.3MM Privately Held
WEB: www.cincinnatiballet.com
SIC: 7911 Dance studios, schools & halls

(G-3284)
CINCINNATI BAR ASSOCIATION
225 E 6th St Fl 2 (45202-3213)
PHONE...................513 381-8213
Chad Levin, *Treasurer*
Carol Branch, *Comms Dir*
Catherine Glover, *Exec Dir*
Terrie Minniti, *Director*
Angela Harris, *Administration*
EMP: 28
SQ FT: 37,000
SALES: 2.9MM Privately Held
WEB: www.cincybar.org
SIC: 8621 Bar association

(G-3285)
CINCINNATI BELL INC (PA)
221 E 4th St Ste 700 (45202-4118)
P.O. Box 2301 (45201-2301)
PHONE...................513 397-9900
Fax: 513 421-5973
Theodore H Torbeck, *CEO*
Phillip R Cox, *Ch of Bd*
Leigh R Fox, *President*
Joshua T Duckworth, *Vice Pres*
Chris Elma, *Vice Pres*
▲ **EMP:** 100
SALES: 1.2B Publicly Held
WEB: www.broadwing.com
SIC: 4813 7373 7374 7379 Telephone communication, except radio; local & long distance telephone communications; local telephone communications; ; systems software development services; data processing service; computer related consulting services;

(G-3286)
CINCINNATI BELL TECHNO
4600 Montgomery Rd # 400 (45212-2600)
PHONE...................513 841-6700
Maureen Westin, *Sales/Mktg Mgr*
John Burns, *Manager*
Krishna Meruga, *IT/INT Sup*
Bob Gau, *Director*
EMP: 100
SALES (corp-wide): 1.2B Publicly Held
SIC: 7379 5045 Computer related consulting services; computer peripheral equipment
HQ: Cincinnati Bell Technology Solutions Inc.
 221 E 4th St Ste 700
 Cincinnati OH 45202

(G-3287)
CINCINNATI BELL TECHNO (HQ)
Also Called: Cbts
221 E 4th St Ste 700 (45202-4118)
P.O. Box 2301 (45201-2301)
PHONE...................513 841-2287
Fax: 513 841-5072
Theodore H Torbeck, *CEO*
John Burns, *President*
Jeff Betteker, *Vice Pres*
Dave Burns, *Vice Pres*
Leigh Fox, *Vice Pres*
▼ **EMP:** 300
SQ FT: 10,000
SALES (est): 157.5MM
SALES (corp-wide): 1.2B Publicly Held
SIC: 7379 5734 Computer related consulting services; computer peripheral equipment
PA: Cincinnati Bell Inc.
 221 E 4th St Ste 700
 Cincinnati OH 45202
 513 397-9900

(G-3288)
CINCINNATI BELL TELE CO LLC (HQ)
209 W 7th St Fl 1 (45202-2394)
P.O. Box 2301 (45201-2301)
PHONE...................513 565-9402
Fax: 513 241-1264
Rodney D Dir, *COO*
David Stahl, *Opers Mgr*
Brian A Ross, *CFO*
Gary J Wotaszek, *CFO*
Mark Peterson, *Treasurer*
EMP: 142 EST: 1873
SQ FT: 100,000
SALES (est): 834.5MM
SALES (corp-wide): 1.2B Publicly Held
SIC: 4813 Telephone communication, except radio; local telephone communications; long distance telephone communications; data telephone communications
PA: Cincinnati Bell Inc.
 221 E 4th St Ste 700
 Cincinnati OH 45202
 513 397-9900

(G-3289)
CINCINNATI BENGALS INC (PA)
1 Paul Brown Stadium (45202-3492)
PHONE...................513 621-3550
Fax: 513 621-3570
Michael Brown, *CEO*
Andrew R Berger, *Ch of Bd*
Bill Sacanlon, *CFO*
William Scanlom, *CFO*
William Connelly, *Marketing Staff*
EMP: 50
SALES (est): 7.6MM Privately Held
SIC: 7941 Football club

(G-3290)
CINCINNATI BULK TERMINALS LLC
895 Mehring Way (45203-1906)
PHONE...................513 621-4800
Fax: 513 621-5182
Jack Weiss, *Mng Member*
EMP: 50
SALES (est): 9.6MM Privately Held
WEB: www.progressfuels.com
SIC: 4491 Marine terminals

(G-3291)
CINCINNATI CENTRAL CR UN INC (PA)
1717 Western Ave (45214-2007)
P.O. Box 14699 (45250-0699)
PHONE...................513 241-2050
Fax: 513 241-8018
William A Herring, *President*
John Nunns, *President*
Jeff Meyer, *Marketing Staff*
Karen Rokich,
EMP: 55
SQ FT: 15,000
SALES: 4.7MM Privately Held
WEB: www.cincinnaticentralcreditunion.com
SIC: 6061 Federal credit unions

(G-3292)
CINCINNATI CIRCUS COMPANY LLC
Also Called: Amazing Portable Circus, The
6433 Wiehe Rd (45237-4215)
PHONE...................513 921-5454
Heather Mason, *Asst Mgr*
Dave Willacker,
EMP: 85
SALES (est): 158.7K Privately Held
SIC: 7929 Entertainment service

(G-3293)
CINCINNATI CNSLTING CONSORTIUM
220 Wyoming Ave (45215-4308)
PHONE...................513 233-0011
Fax: 513 232-3226
Richard Bruder, *President*
Ed Kruszynski, *Exec VP*
Margaret Swallow, *Marketing Staff*
EMP: 35
SALES (est): 2.5MM Privately Held
WEB: www.cincconsult.com
SIC: 8748 Business consulting

(G-3294)
CINCINNATI COML CONTG LLC
4760 Red Bank Rd Ste 226 (45227-1549)
PHONE...................513 561-6633
John Westheimer, *President*
Lawrence Knasel, *Vice Pres*
Heather Moore, *Vice Pres*
Jason Manni, *CFO*
Amy Westheimer, *Sales Dir*
EMP: 25
SQ FT: 6,000
SALES (est): 7.8MM Privately Held
SIC: 1542 6531 Commercial & office building, new construction; real estate agents & managers

(G-3295)
CINCINNATI COUNTRY CLUB
2348 Grandin Rd (45208-3399)
PHONE...................513 533-5200
Fax: 513 533-5232
Pat O'Callaghan, *General Mgr*
Rob Snider, *Controller*
EMP: 125
SQ FT: 75,000
SALES: 9.2MM Privately Held
SIC: 7997 Country club, membership

(G-3296)
CINCINNATI CTR/PSYCHOANALYSIS
3001 Highland Ave (45219-2315)
PHONE...................513 961-8484
Fax: 513 961-1530
Lance White, *Treasurer*
Katherine Miller, *Marketing Staff*
Phyllis Donovan, *Manager*
Marcia Kaplan, *Bd of Directors*
EMP: 25
SALES (est): 2.1MM Privately Held
WEB: www.cps-i.org
SIC: 8322 Family counseling services

(G-3297)
CINCINNATI DENTAL SERVICES
8111 Cheviot Rd Ste 102 (45247-4013)
PHONE...................513 741-7779
Judy Farrell, *Office Mgr*
EMP: 45
SALES (corp-wide): 5.8MM Privately Held
SIC: 8021 Dental clinic
PA: Cincinnati Dental Services Inc
 121 E Mcmillan St
 Cincinnati OH 45219
 513 721-8888

(G-3298)
CINCINNATI DENTAL SERVICES (PA)
121 E Mcmillan St (45219-2606)
PHONE...................513 721-8888
Fax: 513 721-2398
Larry Faust, *President*
Missy Garvin, *Vice Pres*
Steve Jones, *Vice Pres*
Darlene Foster, *Manager*
Fred White Jr, *Manager*
EMP: 75

GEOGRAPHIC SECTION

Cincinnati - Hamilton County (G-3320)

SQ FT: 18,500
SALES (est): 5.8MM Privately Held
SIC: 8021 Dentists' office

(G-3299)
CINCINNATI DRYWALL INC
659 Wilmer Ave (45226-1859)
PHONE..................513 321-7322
Michael W Mott, *President*
David Mott, *Treasurer*
Christy Alfieri, *Admin Sec*
EMP: 50 EST: 1973
SQ FT: 7,800
SALES (est): 3.7MM Privately Held
WEB: www.cincinnatidrywall.net
SIC: 1742 Drywall

(G-3300)
CINCINNATI EARLY LEARNING CTR (PA)
1301 E Mcmillan St (45206-2222)
PHONE..................513 961-2690
Fax: 513 961-1160
Tracey Rowe, *Vice Pres*
Patricia Gleason, *Exec Dir*
Jennifer Armstrong, *Director*
Kathy Benkert, *Director*
Linda Doyle, *Director*
EMP: 30
SALES: 5.1MM Privately Held
SIC: 8351 Preschool center

(G-3301)
CINCINNATI EQUITABLE INSUR CO (DH)
525 Vine St Ste 1925 (45202-3125)
P.O. Box 3428 (45201-3428)
PHONE..................513 621-1826
Fax: 513 621-4531
Greg Baker, *CEO*
Gregory Baker, *President*
Peter Alpaugh, *Chairman*
Michelle Wegman, *Purchasing*
Don Reynolds, *Manager*
▲ EMP: 40
SQ FT: 5,000
SALES (est): 14.3MM Privately Held
WEB: www.1826.com
SIC: 6331 6321 Fire, marine & casualty insurance: stock; property damage insurance; health insurance carriers
HQ: Cincinnati Equitable Companies, Inc
  525 Vine St Ste 1925
  Cincinnati OH 45202
  513 621-1826

(G-3302)
CINCINNATI FEDERAL (PA)
6581 Harrison Ave (45247-2810)
PHONE..................513 574-3025
Fax: 513 921-8749
Joe Bunke, *President*
Edward H Kopf, *Principal*
Bob Bedinghaus, *Chairman*
Bradley Kopf, *Vice Pres*
Herb Brinkman, *CFO*
EMP: 33
SQ FT: 3,000
SALES: 4.6MM Privately Held
WEB: www.cincinnatifederal.com
SIC: 6035 Federal savings & loan associations

(G-3303)
CINCINNATI FIFTH STREET HT LLC
Also Called: Cincinnati Hyatt Regency
151 W 5th St (45202-2703)
PHONE..................513 579-1234
Fax: 513 579-0107
Hank Artime, *Agent*
Lakeisha Walker, *Agent*
EMP: 99
SQ FT: 100,000
SALES (est): 382.2K Privately Held
SIC: 7041 Membership-basis organization hotels

(G-3304)
CINCINNATI FILL INC
900 Kieley Pl (45217-1153)
PHONE..................513 242-7526
Steve Roth, *Manager*
EMP: 30

SALES (est): 2.2MM Privately Held
WEB: www.cincinnatireadymix.com
SIC: 1611 General contractor, highway & street construction

(G-3305)
CINCINNATI FLOOR COMPANY INC (PA)
5162 Broerman Ave (45217-1140)
PHONE..................513 641-4500
Fax: 513 482-4204
Douglas J Drenik, *CEO*
Charle Maricle, *President*
Jill Drenik, *Treasurer*
EMP: 50 EST: 1894
SQ FT: 12,000
SALES (est): 9.2MM Privately Held
WEB: www.cincifloor.com
SIC: 1752 Wood floor installation & refinishing

(G-3306)
CINCINNATI GEARING SYSTEMS INC
5757 Mariemont Ave (45227-4216)
PHONE..................513 527-8600
Fax: 513 271-3510
Dan Thomas, *Plant Supt*
Ty Cooper, *Site Mgr*
Kent Kiehl, *Manager*
Jack Artopoeus, *Manager*
Eileen Vinson, *Manager*
EMP: 75
SALES (corp-wide): 33.5MM Privately Held
WEB: www.steeltreating.com
SIC: 5085 Gears
PA: Cincinnati Gearing Systems Incorporated
  5757 Mariemont Ave
  Cincinnati OH 45227
  513 527-8600

(G-3307)
CINCINNATI HAND SURGERY CONS (PA)
10700 Montgomery Rd # 150 (45242-3255)
PHONE..................513 961-4263
Peter Stern, *President*
Andrew Markiewitz, *COO*
Dr John Mc Donough, *Vice Pres*
Mary K Busch, *Office Mgr*
Sarah Auxier, *Supervisor*
EMP: 32
SQ FT: 9,000
SALES: 2.5MM Privately Held
SIC: 8011 Surgeon

(G-3308)
CINCINNATI HEAD AND NECK INC (PA)
Also Called: Cincinnati Better Hearing Ctr
2123 Auburn Ave (45219-2906)
PHONE..................513 232-3277
Fax: 513 632-5804
Michael Wood MD, *President*
Joseph Hellmann, *Corp Secy*
Thomas Kereiakes, *Vice Pres*
Roxanne Reed, *Administration*
EMP: 25
SQ FT: 1,300
SALES: 500K Privately Held
SIC: 8011 Ears, nose & throat specialist: physician/surgeon

(G-3309)
CINCINNATI HEALTH NETWORK INC
2825 Burnet Ave Ste 232 (45219-2426)
PHONE..................513 961-0600
Kate Bennett, *CEO*
Austin Maddox, *CFO*
Valarie Dowell, *Director*
Susan Bartels, *Admin Asst*
EMP: 25
SQ FT: 2,200
SALES: 3.6MM Privately Held
WEB: www.cincihomeless.org
SIC: 8741 8699 Hospital management; nursing & personal care facility management; charitable organization

(G-3310)
CINCINNATI HUMN RELATIONS COMM
Also Called: CHRC
801 Plum St Rm 158 (45202-5704)
PHONE..................513 352-3237
Fax: 513 352-2496
Sherry Taylor, *Office Mgr*
Ericka King-Betts, *Director*
EMP: 33
SALES: 900.6K Privately Held
SIC: 8699 Charitable organization

(G-3311)
CINCINNATI INDUS ACTONEERS INC
2020 Dunlap St (45214-2310)
PHONE..................513 241-9701
Fax: 513 241-6760
Jerome A Luggen, *President*
Jeffrey Duggen, *Vice Pres*
Jeffrey L Luggen, *Vice Pres*
Amy Given, *Adv Mgr*
EMP: 25
SQ FT: 20,000
SALES: 16MM Privately Held
WEB: www.cia-auction.com
SIC: 7389 Auction, appraisal & exchange services

(G-3312)
CINCINNATI INSTITUTE FINE ARTS (PA)
Also Called: ARTSWAVE
20 East Central Pkwy # 2 (45202-7239)
PHONE..................513 871-2787
Fax: 513 871-2706
Mary McCullough-Hudson, *CEO*
Sue Reichelderfer, *Principal*
Alecia Kintner, *COO*
Theresa Haught, *Vice Pres*
Sarah Ditlinger, *Manager*
EMP: 27
SQ FT: 4,000
SALES: 14.7MM Privately Held
WEB: www.taftmuseum.org
SIC: 8399 Fund raising organization, non-fee basis

(G-3313)
CINCINNATI INSTITUTE FINE ARTS
Also Called: Taft Museum
316 Pike St (45202-4214)
PHONE..................513 241-0343
Fax: 513 241-7762
Phillip C Long, *Director*
EMP: 25
SQ FT: 7,880
SALES (est): 654K
SALES (corp-wide): 14.7MM Privately Held
WEB: www.taftmuseum.org
SIC: 8412 Museum
PA: Cincinnati Institute Of Fine Arts
  20 East Central Pkwy # 2
  Cincinnati OH 45202
  513 871-2787

(G-3314)
CINCINNATI MEDICAL BILLING SVC
8160 Corp Pk Dr Ste 330 (45242)
P.O. Box 42417 (45242-0417)
PHONE..................513 965-8041
Beverly Shelton, *President*
K D Charles, *Vice Pres*
Charles K D, *Vice Pres*
EMP: 50
SQ FT: 7,500
SALES (est): 2.7MM Privately Held
SIC: 8721 Billing & bookkeeping service

(G-3315)
CINCINNATI METRO HSING AUTH
Also Called: Cmha
1635 Western Ave (45214-2001)
PHONE..................513 421-2642
Gene Reed, *Manager*
EMP: 32

SALES (corp-wide): 116.8MM Privately Held
WEB: www.cmha.com
SIC: 6513 Apartment building operators
PA: Cincinnati Metropolitan Housing Authority
  1635 Western Ave
  Cincinnati OH 45214
  513 421-8190

(G-3316)
CINCINNATI METRO HSING AUTH (PA)
1635 Western Ave (45214-2001)
PHONE..................513 421-8190
Fax: 513 977-5616
Joy Gazaway, *Counsel*
Angela Stearns, *Counsel*
Pamela Stephens, *Accountant*
Michael Durr, *Auditor*
Reema Ruberg, *Finance*
EMP: 42
SQ FT: 10,000
SALES: 116.8MM Privately Held
WEB: www.cintimha.com
SIC: 6514 Dwelling operators, except apartments

(G-3317)
CINCINNATI METRO HSING AUTH
Also Called: Section 8
1627 Western Ave (45214-2001)
PHONE..................513 333-0670
Fax: 513 333-0681
Joan Roark, *Director*
EMP: 48
SQ FT: 10,347
SALES (corp-wide): 116.8MM Privately Held
WEB: www.cintimha.com
SIC: 6513 6514 Apartment building operators; dwelling operators, except apartments
PA: Cincinnati Metropolitan Housing Authority
  1635 Western Ave
  Cincinnati OH 45214
  513 421-8190

(G-3318)
CINCINNATI MUSEUM ASSOCIATION (PA)
Also Called: Cincinnati Art Museum
953 Eden Park Dr (45202-1557)
PHONE..................513 721-5204
Fax: 513 721-0129
Andrew Dewitt, *President*
Valerie Newell, *Vice Pres*
Ted Forrest, *Human Res Dir*
Laura Biaglow, *Human Res Mgr*
Roberto Henriquez, *Info Tech Mgr*
▲ EMP: 170
SQ FT: 300,000
SALES: 31.1MM Privately Held
WEB: www.artacademy.edu
SIC: 8412 8299 Museum; art gallery, non-commercial; art school, except commercial

(G-3319)
CINCINNATI MUSEUM CENTER (PA)
250 W Court St Ste 300e (45202-1095)
PHONE..................513 287-7000
Fax: 513 287-7079
Douglass McDonald, *President*
Susan Anthe, *Division Mgr*
Larry Sisk, *VP Admin*
Lee Finke, *Vice Pres*
Glenn Storrs, *Research*
EMP: 286
SQ FT: 504,000
SALES: 42.6MM Privately Held
WEB: www.cincymuseum.com
SIC: 7832 8412 8231 Motion picture theaters, except drive-in; museums & art galleries; libraries

(G-3320)
CINCINNATI NETHERLAND HT LLC
Also Called: Hilton Cncnnati Netherland Plz
35 W 5th St (45202-2801)
PHONE..................513 421-9100

Cincinnati - Hamilton County (G-3321)

GEOGRAPHIC SECTION

Kent Heinlien, *Purchasing*
Greg Power,
EMP: 350
SALES (est): 12.5MM **Privately Held**
SIC: 7011 Hotels

(G-3321)
CINCINNATI OPERA ASSOCIATION
1243 Elm St (45202-7531)
PHONE..................513 768-5500
Fax: 513 678-5552
Patricia K Beggs, *CEO*
Robert W Olson, *President*
Cathy Crain, *Chairman*
Glenn Plott, *Opers Staff*
Sarah Clark, *Production*
EMP: 27
SALES: 7.7MM **Privately Held**
WEB: www.cincinnatiopera.org
SIC: 7922 Theatrical companies

(G-3322)
CINCINNATI POOL MANAGEMENT INC
3461 Mustafa Dr (45241-1668)
P.O. Box 603, West Chester (45071-0603)
PHONE..................513 777-1444
Gary Toner, *President*
Lindsay Ferguson, *CTO*
EMP: 507
SQ FT: 15,000
SALES (est): 7.6MM **Privately Held**
WEB: www.cincinnatipoolmgmt.com
SIC: 7999 Lifeguard service

(G-3323)
CINCINNATI PUBLIC RADIO INC
Also Called: W G U C-FM Radio
1223 Central Pkwy (45214-2834)
PHONE..................513 241-8282
Fax: 513 241-8456
Richard Eiswerth, *President*
Don Danko, *Vice Pres*
Chris Phelps, *Vice Pres*
Mark Heyne, *Opers Mgr*
Stephen Baum, *Engineer*
EMP: 36
SQ FT: 20,000
SALES: 7.5MM **Privately Held**
WEB: www.cinradio.org
SIC: 4832 Radio broadcasting stations, music format

(G-3324)
CINCINNATI REDS LLC (PA)
100 Joe Nuxhall Way (45202-4109)
PHONE..................513 765-7000
Robert Castellini, *CEO*
Brian Kearney, *Vice Pres*
Doug Healey, *CFO*
Tina Schweier, *CFO*
Carl Lindnert,
▼ **EMP:** 125 **EST:** 1869
SQ FT: 5,000
SALES (est): 2.3MM **Privately Held**
WEB: www.cincinnatireds.com
SIC: 7941 Baseball club, professional & semi-professional

(G-3325)
CINCINNATI REDS LLC
100 Main St (45202)
PHONE..................513 765-7923
Anthony V Ward, *Principal*
EMP: 92
SALES (corp-wide): 2.3MM **Privately Held**
SIC: 7941 Baseball club, professional & semi-professional
PA: The Cincinnati Reds Llc
100 Joe Nuxhall Way
Cincinnati OH 45202
513 765-7000

(G-3326)
CINCINNATI SENIOR CARE LLC
4001 Rosslyn Dr (45209-1111)
PHONE..................513 272-0600
John E Marshall,
Karen Marshall,
EMP: 28
SALES (est): 1.4MM **Privately Held**
SIC: 8051 Convalescent home with continuous nursing care

(G-3327)
CINCINNATI SHAKESPEARE COMPANY
217 W 12th St (45202-7501)
PHONE..................513 381-2273
Fax: 513 381-2298
Vicky Reynolds, *Trustee*
Brian Phillips, *Exec Dir*
Jay Woffington, *Exec Dir*
Kelly Bollinger, *Director*
Joeliene Magoto, *Director*
EMP: 35
SALES: 10.6MM **Privately Held**
WEB: www.cincyshakes.com
SIC: 7922 Theatrical companies

(G-3328)
CINCINNATI SPEECH HEARING CTR (PA)
2825 Burnet Ave Ste 401 (45219-2426)
PHONE..................513 221-0527
Fax: 513 221-1703
Bob Nogg, *Finance Mgr*
Carol P Leslie, *Exec Dir*
Brigid Mercer, *Director*
EMP: 34
SQ FT: 9,000
SALES (est): 1.1MM **Privately Held**
WEB: www.hearingspeechdeaf.com
SIC: 8099 8093 Hearing testing service; speech defect clinic

(G-3329)
CINCINNATI SPORTS MALL INC
Also Called: Cincinnati Sports Club
3950 Red Bank Rd Ste A (45227-3430)
PHONE..................513 527-4000
Fax: 513 527-5030
Christopher L Fister, *President*
Daniel A Funk MD, *Owner*
Monica Rayburn, *Office Mgr*
Eric Hawkins, *Executive*
Charles Reynolds, *Admin Sec*
EMP: 60
SQ FT: 100,000
SALES (est): 6.2MM **Privately Held**
WEB: www.cincinnatisportsclub.com
SIC: 6512 7991 7997 Nonresidential building operators; athletic club & gymnasiums, membership; membership sports & recreation clubs

(G-3330)
CINCINNATI STEEL PRODUCTS CO
4540 Steel Pl (45209-1161)
PHONE..................513 871-4444
Fax: 513 321-9608
James S Todd, *CEO*
Tom Brown, *President*
Thomas Rutter, *Corp Secy*
Ralph Freiberger, *Credit Mgr*
Steve Hirschauer, *Manager*
EMP: 50 **EST:** 1933
SQ FT: 75,000
SALES: 14.5MM **Privately Held**
WEB: www.cincinnatisteel.com
SIC: 5051 Steel

(G-3331)
CINCINNATI SUB-ZERO PDTS LLC
Also Called: E S S C
12011 Mosteller Rd (45241-1528)
PHONE..................800 989-7373
Jerry G Silvertooth, *Vice Pres*
Lesley Durik, *QC Mgr*
Russ Pennavaria, *Sales Mgr*
Steve Berke, *Manager*
Steve Hoekzema, *Manager*
EMP: 240
SALES (corp-wide): 985.6MM **Publicly Held**
WEB: www.cszinc.com
SIC: 8734 Testing laboratories
HQ: Cincinnati Sub-Zero Products, Llc
12011 Mosteller Rd
Cincinnati OH 45241
513 719-3264

(G-3332)
CINCINNATI SYMPHONY ORCHESTRA (PA)
Also Called: Riverbend Music Center
1241 Elm St (45202-7531)
PHONE..................513 621-1919
Fax: 513 621-2132
Melody Sawyer Richardson, *Chairman*
Teresa Ahrenholz, *Vice Pres*
Jennifer Damiano, *Vice Pres*
Kenneth A Goode, *Development*
Christopher Pinelo, *Pub Rel Mgr*
EMP: 150
SQ FT: 10,000
SALES: 75.6MM **Privately Held**
WEB: www.cincinnatisymphony.org
SIC: 7929 Symphony orchestras

(G-3333)
CINCINNATI TAE KWON DO INC
Also Called: Cincinnati Tae Kwon Do Cntr
4325 Red Bank Rd Ste A (45227-2175)
PHONE..................513 271-6900
Fax: 513 271-6904
Paul Korchak, *President*
EMP: 30
SQ FT: 4,200
SALES (est): 768.8K **Privately Held**
WEB: www.cincytaekwondo.com
SIC: 7999 Martial arts school

(G-3334)
CINCINNATI USA RGIONAL CHAMBER
3 E 4th St Ste 200 (45202-3746)
PHONE..................513 579-3100
Fax: 513 579-6956
Jill P Meyer, *President*
Tom Farrell, *President*
Ellen Van Der Horst, *President*
Kevin Canafax, *General Mgr*
Brendon J Cull, *COO*
EMP: 75 **EST:** 1839
SQ FT: 24,900
SALES: 17.7MM **Privately Held**
WEB: www.cincinnatichamber.com
SIC: 8611 Chamber of Commerce

(G-3335)
CINCINNATI YOUTH COLLABORATIVE
301 Oak St (45219-2508)
PHONE..................513 475-4165
Jenny Keller, *Vice Pres*
Bill Russel, *Vice Pres*
Myrtis Powell, *Exec Dir*
Ed Owens III,
John Pepper Jr,
EMP: 25
SQ FT: 800
SALES: 3.1MM **Privately Held**
WEB: www.cycyouth.org
SIC: 8322 Youth center

(G-3336)
CINCINNATIAN HOTEL
Also Called: Cincinnatian Hotel, The
601 Vine St (45202-2408)
PHONE..................513 381-3000
Fax: 513 651-0256
Rick Foreman, *Controller*
EMP: 140
SQ FT: 105,160
SALES (est): 11.9MM **Privately Held**
SIC: 6512 Commercial & industrial building operation

(G-3337)
CINCINNATIS OPTIMUM RES ENVIR
Also Called: Core
75 Tri County Pkwy (45246-3218)
PHONE..................513 771-2673
Fax: 513 326-6075
Timothy Wells, *CTO*
Martha A Adams, *Exec Dir*
Cathy Graf, *Asst Director*
EMP: 150
SALES: 6.9MM **Privately Held**
WEB: www.coreinc.org
SIC: 8361 Home for the mentally handicapped; residential care for the handicapped

(G-3338)
CINCINNATUS SAVINGS & LOAN (PA)
3300 Harrison Ave (45211-5697)
PHONE..................513 661-6903
Steven E Shultz, *President*
Michael St John, *Vice Pres*
Terry Todd, *Vice Pres*
Jeffery Beerman, *CFO*
Bud Dornette, *Loan Officer*
EMP: 25 **EST:** 1885
SALES: 4.1MM **Privately Held**
WEB: www.cincinnatussl.com
SIC: 6035 Federal savings & loan associations

(G-3339)
CINCINNTI EDUC & RES FOR VETRN
Also Called: Biomedical Research & Educatn
3200 Vine St (45220-2213)
PHONE..................513 861-3100
Ronn Hayks, *CEO*
Sam Denham, *Executive*
EMP: 25
SQ FT: 3,502
SALES (est): 1.5MM **Privately Held**
SIC: 8733 Educational research agency

(G-3340)
CINCITI BL ETD TRTS LLC
221 E 4th St Fl 1290 (45202-4124)
PHONE..................513 397-0963
Rochelle Brown, *Principal*
Michael Holmes, *Manager*
EMP: 99
SALES (est): 4.1MM
SALES (corp-wide): 1.2B **Publicly Held**
SIC: 4813 Telephone communication, except radio
PA: Cincinnati Bell Inc.
221 E 4th St Ste 700
Cincinnati OH 45202
513 397-9900

(G-3341)
CINCO CREDIT UNION (PA)
Also Called: CINCO FAMILY FINANCIAL CENTER
49 William Howard Taft Rd (45219-1760)
PHONE..................513 281-9988
William C Page, *President*
Peggy Bartlett, *COO*
Bob Niehaus, *Senior VP*
Terry Tracey, *VP Admin*
Mark Schweinfurth, *CFO*
EMP: 50
SQ FT: 17,400
SALES: 3.5MM **Privately Held**
SIC: 6061 Federal credit unions

(G-3342)
CINCOM INTRNATIONAL OPERATIONS (HQ)
55 Merchant St Ste 100 (45246-3761)
PHONE..................513 612-2300
Thomas M Nies, *Ch of Bd*
Gerald Shawhan, *Treasurer*
Brian Jackson, *Assoc Editor*
Will Dyer, *CIO*
Kenneth L Byrne, *Admin Sec*
EMP: 350
SALES (est): 26.2MM
SALES (corp-wide): 121.7MM **Privately Held**
SIC: 7371 7373 Computer software development; computer integrated systems design
PA: Cincom Systems, Inc.
55 Merchant St Ste 100
Cincinnati OH 45246
513 612-2300

(G-3343)
CINCOM SYSTEMS INC (PA)
55 Merchant St Ste 100 (45246-3761)
PHONE..................513 612-2300
Fax: 513 389-2080
Thomas M Nies, *Ch of Bd*
Greg Mills, *President*
Sandy Truitt, *Business Mgr*
Lori Gelter, *Vice Pres*
James Ross, *Vice Pres*
EMP: 300
SQ FT: 180,000

Cincinnati - Hamilton County (G-3365)

SALES (est): 121.7MM Privately Held
SIC: 7373 Systems software development services

(G-3344)
CINCOM SYSTEMS INC
Also Called: Cincom Helpdesk
2300 Montana Ave Ste 235 (45211-3890)
PHONE..................513 389-2344
Fax: 513 481-8332
Mike Aichele, Branch Mgr
EMP: 30
SALES (corp-wide): 121.7MM Privately Held
SIC: 7379 Computer related consulting services
PA: Cincom Systems, Inc.
   55 Merchant St Ste 100
   Cincinnati OH 45246
   513 612-2300

(G-3345)
CINCYSMILES FOUNDATION INC
Also Called: GREATER CINCINNATI ORAL HEALTH
635 W 7th St Ste 405 (45203-1549)
PHONE..................513 621-0248
Kristen Gasperetti, Manager
Lawrence F Hill, Director
Sonya Dreves, Director
EMP: 35
SQ FT: 800
SALES: 1.6MM Privately Held
SIC: 8322 Individual & family services

(G-3346)
CINERGY CORP (DH)
139 E 4th St (45202-4003)
P.O. Box 960 (45201-0960)
PHONE..................513 421-9500
Fax: 513 287-3116
David L Hauser, President
John Campbell, President
M Harkness, Exec VP
Jaim De La Espriella, Vice Pres
Steven Schrader, CFO
▲ EMP: 1700
SQ FT: 300,000
SALES (est): 2.1B
SALES (corp-wide): 23.5B Publicly Held
WEB: www.cinergy.com
SIC: 4911 4924 Distribution, electric power; generation, electric power; transmission, electric power; natural gas distribution
HQ: Duke Energy Carolinas, Llc
   526 S Church St
   Charlotte NC 28202
   704 382-3853

(G-3347)
CINERGY PWR GNERATION SVCS LLC
139 E 4th St (45202-4003)
PHONE..................513 421-9500
Bernard Roberts, Controller
EMP: 1362 EST: 1997
SALES (est): 1.3B
SALES (corp-wide): 23.5B Publicly Held
WEB: www.cinergy.com
SIC: 4911 Transmission, electric power
HQ: Cinergy Corp.
   139 E 4th St
   Cincinnati OH 45202

(G-3348)
CINFED FEDERAL CREDIT UNION (PA)
Also Called: CINFED CREDIT UNION
550 Main St Ste 5510 (45202-5230)
PHONE..................513 333-3800
Fax: 513 333-3889
Jay Sigler, CEO
Christine Kunnen, President
Eric Ketcham, COO
Elizabeth Dodd, Senior VP
Scott Federle, Senior VP
EMP: 93
SQ FT: 1,500
SALES: 14.7MM Privately Held
SIC: 6061 Federal credit unions

(G-3349)
CINTAS CORPORATION (PA)
6800 Cintas Blvd (45262)
P.O. Box 625737 (45262-5737)
PHONE..................513 459-1200
Fax: 513 573-4035
Scott D Farmer, Ch of Bd
J Phillip Holloman, President
Tom Cato, General Mgr
Steve Prince, Business Mgr
Thomas E Frooman, Senior VP
◆ EMP: 1500
SALES: 5.3B Publicly Held
WEB: www.cintas-corp.com
SIC: 7218 2337 2326 5084 Industrial uniform supply; uniforms, except athletic: women's, misses' & juniors'; work uniforms; safety equipment

(G-3350)
CINTAS CORPORATION
Also Called: Cintas Uniforms AP Fcilty Svcs
5570 Ridge Ave (45213-2516)
PHONE..................513 631-5750
Marie Seng, Branch Mgr
EMP: 100
SALES (corp-wide): 5.3B Publicly Held
SIC: 2326 2337 7218 5084 Work uniforms; uniforms, except athletic: women's, misses' & juniors'; industrial uniform supply; wiping towel supply; treated equipment supply: mats, rugs, mops, cloths, etc.; safety equipment
PA: Cintas Corporation
   6800 Cintas Blvd
   Cincinnati OH 45262
   513 459-1200

(G-3351)
CINTAS CORPORATION
690 E Crscntvlle Rd Ste A (45246)
PHONE..................513 671-7717
Evan S Fee, Principal
Mark Schmitt, Plant Mgr
Cloressa Davis, Accounts Mgr
Bob Eichenhofer, Accounts Mgr
Megan McGlothen, Accounts Mgr
EMP: 60
SALES (corp-wide): 5.3B Publicly Held
SIC: 7218 Industrial uniform supply
PA: Cintas Corporation
   6800 Cintas Blvd
   Cincinnati OH 45262
   513 459-1200

(G-3352)
CINTAS R US INC
6800 Cintas Blvd (45262)
PHONE..................513 459-1200
Scott Farmer, CEO
Richard T Farmer, President
EMP: 1500
SALES (est): 8.3MM
SALES (corp-wide): 5.3B Publicly Held
SIC: 7218 Industrial uniform supply
PA: Cintas Corporation
   6800 Cintas Blvd
   Cincinnati OH 45262
   513 459-1200

(G-3353)
CINTAS SALES CORPORATION (HQ)
6800 Cintas Blvd (45262)
PHONE..................513 459-1200
Richard T Farmer, Ch of Bd
Robert J Kohlhepp, Vice Ch Bd
Scott Farmer, President
Bradley Beyer, Opers Mgr
Terri Hansen, Opers Mgr
EMP: 450
SALES (est): 32.2MM
SALES (corp-wide): 5.3B Publicly Held
SIC: 7218 5136 5137 Industrial uniform supply; work clothing supply; work uniforms; uniforms, men's & boys'; uniforms, women's & children's
PA: Cintas Corporation
   6800 Cintas Blvd
   Cincinnati OH 45262
   513 459-1200

(G-3354)
CINTECH LLC
3280 Hageman Ave (45241-1907)
PHONE..................513 731-6000
Fax: 513 923-5274
William Ammerman, VP Sls/Mktg
Racheal McLaaese, Accountant
Travis O'Keefe, Sales Staff
Lewis Bonadies, VP Mktg
Darren Sargent, Network Enginr
EMP: 82
SALES (est): 3.5MM
SALES (corp-wide): 1.2B Publicly Held
SIC: 7371 Computer software development
HQ: Cincinnati Bell Technology Solutions Inc.
   221 E 4th St Ste 700
   Cincinnati OH 45202

(G-3355)
CITIGROUP GLOBAL MARKETS INC
Also Called: Smithbarney
4030 Smith Rd Ste 200 (45209-1937)
PHONE..................513 579-8300
Fax: 513 579-5005
John A Whalen, Manager
John T Coggins, Consultant
EMP: 100
SALES (corp-wide): 71.4B Publicly Held
WEB: www.salomonsmithbarney.com
SIC: 6211 Security brokers & dealers; stock brokers & dealers
HQ: Citigroup Global Markets Inc.
   388 Greenwich St Fl 18
   New York NY 10013
   212 816-6000

(G-3356)
CITIZENS FINANCIAL SVCS INC
9620 Colerain Ave # 60 (45251-2018)
PHONE..................513 385-3200
EMP: 97
SALES (corp-wide): 56.7MM Publicly Held
SIC: 7389 Financial services
PA: Citizens Financial Services, Inc.
   15 S Main St
   Mansfield PA 16933
   570 662-2121

(G-3357)
CITY DASH INC
949 Laidlaw Ave (45237-5003)
PHONE..................513 562-2000
Troy Burt, President
Robert Harshbarger, Exec VP
Jeff Fine, Vice Pres
John Janesch, Opers Mgr
Jason Stumin, Opers Staff
EMP: 120
SQ FT: 10,000
SALES: 19.3MM Privately Held
SIC: 4213 4215 4212 Less-than-truckload (LTL) transport; courier services, except by air; local trucking, without storage

(G-3358)
CITY GOSPEL MISSION
1805 Dalton Ave (45214-2055)
PHONE..................513 241-5525
Fax: 513 345-1079
Sterling Hawks, Director
Stephanie Downs, Director
Doug Dunlap, Director
Mike Meece, Director
EMP: 45
SALES: 8MM Privately Held
WEB: www.citygospelmission.com
SIC: 8322 Individual & family services

(G-3359)
CLARK SCHAEFER HACKETT & CO (PA)
1 E 4th St Ste 1200 (45202-4294)
PHONE..................513 241-3111
Fax: 513 241-1212
Thomas D Hazelbaker, Ch of Bd
Carl R Coburn, President
David Eichert, Managing Dir
Neil O'Connor, Chairman
Kyle Brandon, Business Mgr
EMP: 45
SQ FT: 8,700
SALES (est): 40.4MM Privately Held
WEB: www.cshco.com
SIC: 8721 Certified public accountant

(G-3360)
CLARKE POWER SERVICES INC (PA)
3133 E Kemper Rd (45241-1516)
PHONE..................513 771-2200
Mark Andreae, CEO
Kirk Andreae, President
Riley Asher, Vice Pres
Don Bixler, Vice Pres
Randy Keach, Vice Pres
▲ EMP: 100
SQ FT: 62,000
SALES: 252.9MM Privately Held
WEB: www.clarkedda.com
SIC: 5084 Engines & parts, diesel

(G-3361)
CLEAN HARBORS ENVMTL SVCS INC
Also Called: Ohio Valley Technical Services
4880 Spring Grove Ave (45232-1933)
PHONE..................513 681-6242
Eugene Cookson, Vice Pres
Stephen Dovell, Vice Pres
William Geary, Vice Pres
Floyd Williams, Safety Mgr
Benjamin Hostler, Research
EMP: 33
SALES (corp-wide): 2.9B Publicly Held
SIC: 4953 Refuse systems
HQ: Clean Harbors Environmental Services, Inc.
   42 Longwater Dr
   Norwell MA 02061
   781 792-5000

(G-3362)
CLEAN LIVING LAUNDRY LLC
Also Called: Super Laundry
2437 Gilbert Ave (45206-2518)
PHONE..................513 569-0439
Lara Krupp, Manager
Benjamin Krupp,
Paul Meise,
Daniel Wente,
EMP: 25
SALES (est): 871.4K Privately Held
SIC: 7219 Laundry, except power & coin-operated

(G-3363)
CLERMONT COUNSELING CENTER
3730 Glenway Ave (45205-1354)
PHONE..................513 345-8555
Arlene Herman, Branch Mgr
Monica Bailey, Manager
EMP: 25
SALES (est): 397.2K
SALES (corp-wide): 2.9MM Privately Held
SIC: 8322 General counseling services
PA: Clermont Counseling Center
   43 E Main St
   Amelia OH 45102
   513 947-7000

(G-3364)
CLIFF NORTH CONSULTANTS INC
3747 Warsaw Ave (45205-1773)
PHONE..................513 251-4930
Fax: 513 557-3732
Paul Mc Osker, President
Paul McOsker, Sales Executive
Lizebeth Mc Osker, Admin Sec
EMP: 25
SQ FT: 12,123
SALES (est): 2.5MM Privately Held
SIC: 8748 8734 Testing services; product testing laboratories

(G-3365)
CLIFTON CARE CENTER INC
Also Called: Communicare of Clifton
463 Warner St (45219-1167)
PHONE..................513 530-1600
Fax: 513 281-2559
Stephen L Rosedale, President
Charles R Stoltz, Exec VP
Ronald S Wilhelm, Exec VP
Joe Hancock, Facilities Dir
Katherine Allen, Project Mgr
EMP: 200
SQ FT: 26,000

Cincinnati - Hamilton County (G-3366)

SALES: 950K
SALES (corp-wide): 103.9MM Privately Held
WEB: www.communicarehealth.com
SIC: 8051 Skilled nursing care facilities
PA: Communicare Health Services, Inc.
4700 Ashwood Dr Ste 200
Blue Ash OH 45241
513 530-1654

(G-3366)
CLINICAL RESEARCH CENTER
3333 Burnet Ave Rm 3641 (45229-3026)
PHONE.................513 636-4412
Jim Heubi, Principal
Donna Lyons, Business Mgr
EMP: 60
SALES (est): 18.4MM Privately Held
SIC: 6324 8062 Hospital & medical service plans; general medical & surgical hospitals

(G-3367)
CLIPPARD INSTRUMENT LAB INC (PA)
Also Called: Clippard Minimatic
7390 Colerain Ave (45239-5396)
PHONE.................513 521-4261
Fax: 513 521-4464
Harriet H Clippard, Principal
◆ EMP: 200 EST: 1941
SQ FT: 84,000
SALES: 1.7MM Privately Held
WEB: www.clippard.com
SIC: 5085 Pistons & valves; diamonds, industrial: natural, crude

(G-3368)
CLOPAY TRANSPORTATION COMPANY
312 Walnut St Ste 1600 (45202-4038)
PHONE.................513 381-4800
Frank Smith, Vice Pres
Pete Lawrence, Natl Sales Mgr
Craig Stephens, Natl Sales Mgr
Cheryl Kirk, Business Anlyst
EMP: 100
SALES (est): 8.5MM Publicly Held
SIC: 4213 Trucking, except local
HQ: Clopay Building Products Company, Inc.
8585 Duke Blvd
Mason OH 45040

(G-3369)
CLOVERNOOK INC (PA)
Also Called: CLOVERNOOK HEALTH CARE PAVILIO
7025 Clovernook Ave (45231-5557)
P.O. Box 246, Mason (45040-0246)
PHONE.................513 605-4000
Steve Boymel, President
Tamara Bell, Accountant
EMP: 120
SQ FT: 15,000
SALES: 11MM Privately Held
SIC: 8051 Skilled nursing care facilities

(G-3370)
CLOVERNOOK CENTER FOR THE BLI (PA)
7000 Hamilton Ave (45231-5240)
PHONE.................513 522-3860
Fax: 513 728-3950
Robin Usalis, President
Christopher Faust, President
Beasy Baugh, Vice Pres
Betsy Baugh, Vice Pres
Jacqueline L Conner, Vice Pres
EMP: 150
SQ FT: 40,000
SALES: 8.5MM Privately Held
WEB: www.clovernook.org
SIC: 2656 8322 7389 Paper cups, plates, dishes & utensils; rehabilitation services; fund raising organizations

(G-3371)
CLOVERNOOK COUNTRY CLUB
2035 W Galbraith Rd (45239-4364)
PHONE.................513 521-0333
Fax: 513 521-6369
Leslie Huesman, President
EMP: 70
SQ FT: 12,000
SALES: 2.4MM Privately Held
SIC: 7997 Country club, membership

(G-3372)
CM-GC LLC
1810 Section Rd (45237-3306)
PHONE.................513 527-4141
Fax: 513 527-5555
Schuyler Murdock,
EMP: 39
SQ FT: 5,000
SALES (est): 3.9MM Privately Held
WEB: www.cm-gc.com
SIC: 1541 1542 Industrial buildings & warehouses; renovation, remodeling & repairs: industrial buildings; commercial & office building, new construction; commercial & office buildings, renovation & repair

(G-3373)
CMTA INC
222 E 14th St (45202-7385)
PHONE.................502 326-3085
Fax: 513 621-5473
Jeff Millard, Opers-Prdtn-Mfg
Thom Anderson, Engineer
Tim Morris, CFO
Stephen Heckman, Admin Sec
EMP: 150
SALES (corp-wide): 29.5MM Privately Held
SIC: 8711 Engineering services
PA: Cmta, Inc.
10411 Meeting St
Prospect KY
502 326-3085

(G-3374)
CNG FINANCIAL CORP
7755 Montgomery Rd # 400 (45236-4197)
PHONE.................513 336-7735
David Davis, President
Debbie Kessen, Executive Asst
EMP: 3000
SALES (est): 442.8K Privately Held
SIC: 6282 Investment advice

(G-3375)
CNG FINANCIAL CORPORATION (PA)
Also Called: Check N Go
7755 Montgomery Rd # 400 (45236-4197)
PHONE.................513 336-7735
Fax: 513 573-4680
Jared A Davis, President
Robert M Beck Jr, Principal
David Davis, Exec VP
Charles Becker, Site Mgr
Luke Williamson, Financial Analy
EMP: 300 EST: 1994
SQ FT: 66,000
SALES (est): 664.6MM Privately Held
WEB: www.checkngo.com
SIC: 6099 Check cashing agencies

(G-3376)
CNSLD HUMACARE- EMPLOYEE MGT (PA)
9435 Waterstone Blvd # 250 (45249-8226)
PHONE.................513 605-3522
Fax: 513 605-3523
William B Southerland, CEO
Jim Barrie, Director
Ashley Meuser, Director
EMP: 45 EST: 1995
SALES (est): 4.7MM Privately Held
SIC: 7361 Employment agencies

(G-3377)
COFFEE BREAK CORPORATION
Also Called: Restaurant Refreshment Service
1940 Losantiville Ave (45237-4106)
PHONE.................513 841-1100
Fax: 513 458-8468
Robert Walter, Principal
Robert C Porter Jr, Principal
Edward Walter, Vice Pres
Mary A Walter, Vice Pres
Jocelyn Caster, Accounts Mgr
EMP: 35
SQ FT: 7,500
SALES (est): 10.7MM Privately Held
WEB: www.coffeebreakroasting.com
SIC: 5149 5962 Coffee, green or roasted; beverage vending machines

(G-3378)
COHEN TODD KITE STANFORD LLC
250 E 5th St Ste 2350 (45202-5136)
PHONE.................513 205-7286
Fax: 513 241-4490
Maria Masterson, Marketing Staff
Joan Willis, Office Mgr
Robin Fischer, Executive
Terrence E Mire,
John G Cobey,
EMP: 40 EST: 1894
SALES (est): 5.4MM Privately Held
WEB: www.ctks.com
SIC: 8111 General practice law office

(G-3379)
COHO CREATIVE LLC
2331 Victory Pkwy (45206-2888)
PHONE.................513 751-7500
Fax: 513 751-7775
Daniel Brod, Principal
Julie Knight, VP Finance
Erin Wilson, Sr Project Mgr
Liz Grimsley, Manager
Lisa McGraw, Director
EMP: 26
SALES (est): 2.7MM Privately Held
WEB: www.cohocreative.com
SIC: 8742 Marketing consulting services

(G-3380)
COLAS SOLUTIONS INC
7374 Main St (45244-3015)
PHONE.................513 272-5348
Roger Hayner, President
EMP: 25
SALES (est): 4.2MM
SALES (corp-wide): 95.5MM Privately Held
SIC: 1611 1622 Highway & street construction; bridge construction
HQ: Colas Inc.
73 Headquarters Plz 10t
Morristown NJ 07960
973 290-9082

(G-3381)
COLDSTREAM COUNTRY CLUB
400 Asbury Rd (45255-4657)
PHONE.................513 231-3900
Fax: 513 624-2781
Mike Haehnle, General Mgr
Greg Skibinski, Executive
EMP: 50
SQ FT: 5,000
SALES: 3.5MM Privately Held
SIC: 7997 Country club, membership

(G-3382)
COLDWELL BANKER
2721 Erie Ave (45208-2103)
PHONE.................513 321-9944
Fax: 513 321-9944
EMP: 50
SALES (est): 146.2K Privately Held
SIC: 6531 Real Estate Agent/Manager

(G-3383)
COLDWELL BANKER WEST SHELL
3260 Westbourne Dr (45248-5107)
PHONE.................513 922-9400
Fax: 513 347-2514
Judith Jones, Branch Mgr
Kevin Kelly, Manager
Anne Bedinghaus, Real Est Agnt
Jane Deller, Real Est Agnt
Chris Fay, Real Est Agnt
EMP: 53
SALES (corp-wide): 15.3MM Privately Held
SIC: 6531 Real estate agent, residential
PA: Coldwell Banker West Shell
9321 Montgomery Rd Ste C
Cincinnati OH 45242
513 794-9494

(G-3384)
COLDWELL BANKER WEST SHELL
6700 Ruwes Oak Dr (45248-1032)
PHONE.................513 385-9300
Rakesh Ram, Vice Pres
Lisa McCarthy, Sales Staff
Janet Davis, Office Mgr
Anne Bedinghaus, Branch Mgr
Steve Oyler, Manager
EMP: 90
SALES (corp-wide): 15.3MM Privately Held
WEB: www.coldwellbankerwestshell.com
SIC: 6531 Real estate agent, residential
PA: Coldwell Banker West Shell
9321 Montgomery Rd Ste C
Cincinnati OH 45242
513 794-9494

(G-3385)
COLDWELL BANKER WEST SHELL
7203 Wooster Pike (45227-3830)
PHONE.................513 271-7200
Fax: 513 527-3054
Ogle Annett, Sales Associate
Beth Rouse, Branch Mgr
Ashley Langenerunner, Admin Sec
Ed Annett, Real Est Agnt
Mary H Arkeilpane, Real Est Agnt
EMP: 30
SALES (corp-wide): 15.3MM Privately Held
WEB: www.coldwellbankerwestshell.com
SIC: 6531 Real estate agent, residential
PA: Coldwell Banker West Shell
9321 Montgomery Rd Ste C
Cincinnati OH 45242
513 794-9494

(G-3386)
COLE + RUSSELL ARCHITECTS INC (PA)
Also Called: Cr Architecture and Design
600 Vine St Ste 2210 (45202-2491)
PHONE.................513 721-8080
Fax: 513 721-8181
John Russell, President
David Johnson, COO
Mark Bischoff, Project Mgr
Shannon Duffy, Project Mgr
Eric Fortner, Project Mgr
EMP: 30
SALES (est): 7.3MM Privately Held
WEB: www.colerussell.com
SIC: 8712 Architectural engineering

(G-3387)
COLERAIN DRY RDGE CHLDCARE LTD
Also Called: ABC Early Childhood Lrng Ctr
3998 Dry Ridge Rd (45252-1910)
PHONE.................513 923-4300
David Maumey,
Lawrence Day,
David Mauney,
Kimmy Mauney,
EMP: 29
SQ FT: 8,700
SALES (est): 1.1MM Privately Held
SIC: 8351 Preschool center

(G-3388)
COLLINS KAO INC
8911 Rossash Rd (45236-1209)
PHONE.................513 948-9000
EMP: 29 Privately Held
SIC: 5043 5946 Photographic equipment & supplies; camera & photographic supply stores
PA: Kao Collins Inc
1201 Edison Dr
Cincinnati OH 45216

(G-3389)
COLUMBUS EQUIPMENT COMPANY
712 Shepherd Ave (45215-3118)
PHONE.................513 771-3922
Fax: 513 771-1377
Jeff McVey, Branch Mgr
Al Shepherd, Manager
Ben Sutkamp, Manager
EMP: 28
SQ FT: 3,000
SALES (corp-wide): 84.2MM Privately Held
WEB: www.colsequipment.com
SIC: 5082 5084 General construction machinery & equipment; industrial machinery & equipment

GEOGRAPHIC SECTION

Cincinnati - Hamilton County (G-3413)

PA: The Columbus Equipment Company
2323 Performance Way
Columbus OH 43207
614 437-0352

(G-3390)
COLUMBUS LIFE INSURANCE CO
400 E 4th St (45202-3302)
P.O. Box 5737 (45201-5737)
PHONE.................513 361-6700
Fax: 513 361-6717
Jj Miller, *CEO*
Cynthia Funcheon, *President*
Sharon Lunsford, *President*
Kelly Anderson, *Editor*
Lawrence Grypp, *COO*
EMP: 52
SALES (est): 21.4MM **Privately Held**
WEB: www.columbuslife.com
SIC: 6311 6411 Life insurance carriers; insurance agents, brokers & service
HQ: The Western & Southern Life Insurance Company
400 Broadway St
Cincinnati OH 45202
513 629-1800

(G-3391)
COMEY & SHEPHERD LLC
7870 E Kemper Rd Ste 100 (45249-1675)
PHONE.................513 489-2100
Jonathan Amster, *Branch Mgr*
EMP: 28
SALES (est): 1.5MM
SALES (corp-wide): 19.7MM **Privately Held**
SIC: 6531 Real estate agent, residential
PA: Comey & Shepherd, Llc
6901 Wooster Pike
Cincinnati OH 45227
513 561-5800

(G-3392)
COMEY & SHEPHERD LLC (PA)
Also Called: Comey & Shepherd Realtors
6901 Wooster Pike (45227-4491)
PHONE.................513 561-5800
Fax: 513 561-8050
Alan Young, *COO*
Kathy Kelley, *Vice Pres*
Sandy Peters, *Vice Pres*
Patricia A Williams, *Project Mgr*
Evelyn Black, *Broker*
EMP: 224
SQ FT: 15,000
SALES (est): 19.7MM **Privately Held**
WEB: www.comey.com
SIC: 6531 Real estate agent, residential

(G-3393)
COMEY & SHEPHERD LLC
2716 Observatory Ave (45208-2108)
PHONE.................513 321-4343
Fax: 513 321-5606
Bonnie Casper, *Vice Pres*
Carol Harris, *Vice Pres*
Jennifer Heidlage, *Vice Pres*
Chris Nicholson, *Vice Pres*
Marc Grafton, *Sales Associate*
EMP: 50
SALES (est): 1.9MM
SALES (corp-wide): 19.7MM **Privately Held**
WEB: www.comey.com
SIC: 6531 Real estate agent, residential
PA: Comey & Shepherd, Llc
6901 Wooster Pike
Cincinnati OH 45227
513 561-5800

(G-3394)
COMEY & SHEPHERD LLC
7333 Beechmont Ave (45230-4118)
PHONE.................513 231-2800
Amy Minor, *Vice Pres*
Charlene Pfingstag, *Vice Pres*
Jack Wolking, *VP Sales*
Cindy Aiken, *Manager*
Bobbi Hart, *CIO*
EMP: 35
SALES (est): 1.1MM
SALES (corp-wide): 19.7MM **Privately Held**
WEB: www.comey.com
SIC: 6531 Real estate agent, residential

PA: Comey & Shepherd, Llc
6901 Wooster Pike
Cincinnati OH 45227
513 561-5800

(G-3395)
COMEY & SHEPHERD LLC
9857 Montgomery Rd (45242-6424)
PHONE.................513 891-4444
Fax: 513 891-5307
Bob Dorger, *Vice Pres*
Chris Behm, *Buyer*
Robert Neal, *Broker*
Marsha Schraffenberger, *Broker*
Linda Ashley, *Bookkeeper*
EMP: 38
SALES (est): 1.3MM
SALES (corp-wide): 19.7MM **Privately Held**
WEB: www.comey.com
SIC: 6531 Real estate agent, residential
PA: Comey & Shepherd, Llc
6901 Wooster Pike
Cincinnati OH 45227
513 561-5800

(G-3396)
COMFORT INN NORTHEAST
9011 Fields Ertel Rd (45249-8261)
P.O. Box 498278 (45249-7278)
PHONE.................513 683-9700
Gregory Roetting, *General Mgr*
Subhash Patel, *Principal*
Patel Subhas, *Director*
EMP: 30
SALES (est): 791.2K **Privately Held**
SIC: 7011 Hotels & motels

(G-3397)
COMM LTD CARE DIALYSIS CENTER
2109 Reading Rd (45202-1417)
PHONE.................513 784-1800
Fax: 513 723-2355
Brenda SIS, *Director*
EMP: 30
SALES (est): 88.9K **Privately Held**
SIC: 8092 Kidney dialysis centers

(G-3398)
COMMERCE HOLDINGS INC
312 Elm St Ste 1150 (45202-2763)
PHONE.................513 579-1950
V Daniel Magarian, *President*
Jeff Levinson, *Project Mgr*
Jim Schmidt, *Marketing Staff*
EMP: 40
SQ FT: 12,000
SALES (est): 5.5MM **Privately Held**
WEB: www.eminetwork.com
SIC: 7311 Advertising agencies

(G-3399)
COMMERCIAL HVAC INC
Also Called: Honeywell Authorized Dealer
5240 Lester Rd Ste 200 (45213-2522)
PHONE.................513 396-6100
Fax: 513 531-3744
Roger Clark, *President*
EMP: 30
SALES (est): 4MM
SALES (corp-wide): 11.4MM **Privately Held**
WEB: www.commhvac.com
SIC: 1711 Mechanical contractor
PA: Grote Enterprises Llc
5240 Lester Rd
Cincinnati OH 45213
513 731-5700

(G-3400)
COMMITTED TO CARE INC
155 Tri County Pkwy # 220 (45246-3238)
PHONE.................513 245-1190
Naomi Sim, *CEO*
Brenda Sims-Caldwell, *CFO*
EMP: 28
SQ FT: 1,000
SALES (est): 916.9K **Privately Held**
SIC: 8082 Visiting nurse service

(G-3401)
COMMUNITY INSURANCE COMPANY
Also Called: Anthem
1351 Wm Howard Taft (45206-1721)
PHONE.................859 282-7888
Fax: 513 872-8174
Jeff Hammer, *General Mgr*
Karen Bass, *Corp Comm Staff*
Karen Stevenson, *Corp Comm Staff*
Jennifer Chambers, *Business Anlyst*
Dawn Caudill, *Manager*
EMP: 25
SALES (corp-wide): 90B **Publicly Held**
SIC: 6324 Hospital & medical service plans
HQ: Community Insurance Company
4361 Irwin Simpson Rd
Mason OH 45040

(G-3402)
COMPEL FITNESS LLC
10711 Princeton Pike Ste 341 (45246)
PHONE.................216 965-5694
William Dane, *Mng Member*
EMP: 150
SALES (est): 448.2K **Privately Held**
SIC: 7991 Physical fitness clubs with training equipment

(G-3403)
COMPLETE BUILDING MAINT LLC
3629 Wabash Ave (45207-1223)
PHONE.................513 235-7511
Anthony Boulding, *President*
EMP: 35
SALES: 250K **Privately Held**
SIC: 7349 Building maintenance services

(G-3404)
COMPLETE QLTY TRNSP SLTONS LLC
3055 Blue Rock Rd Ste T (45239-6302)
PHONE.................513 914-4882
Richard Mursinna,
William Foster,
EMP: 25
SALES (est): 2.3MM **Privately Held**
SIC: 4731 Brokers, shipping

(G-3405)
COMPREHENSIVE CMNTY CHILD CARE (PA)
Also Called: 4C FOR CHILDREN
2100 Sherman Ave Ste 300 (45212-2775)
PHONE.................513 221-0033
Fax: 513 221-0393
Vanessa Freytag, *President*
Elaine Wart, *COO*
Tracy Carter, *Vice Pres*
Karen Hurley, *Vice Pres*
Luke Wiley, *Vice Pres*
EMP: 37
SQ FT: 12,000
SALES (est): 9.6MM **Privately Held**
WEB: www.4c-cinci.org
SIC: 8322 Child guidance agency

(G-3406)
COMPREHENSIVE HEALTH CARE SVCS
Also Called: Comprehensive Health Care Svcs
4580 Springdale Rd (45251-1417)
PHONE.................513 245-0100
Fax: 513 245-0301
Belinda Schraer, *President*
Patricia Kesselring, *Financial Exec*
Sandy Wolff, *Med Doctor*
EMP: 200
SALES (est): 5.5MM **Privately Held**
WEB: www.comphomecare.com
SIC: 8082 7361 Home health care services; employment agencies

(G-3407)
COMPREHENSIVE MANAGED CARE SYS
Also Called: C M C S
3380 Erie Ave (45208-1626)
PHONE.................513 533-0021
Fax: 513 533-2841
Jose L Chavez MD, *President*
EMP: 40

SQ FT: 2,500
SALES (est): 2.7MM **Privately Held**
WEB: www.ohiomco.com
SIC: 8741 Management services

(G-3408)
COMPRHENSIVE CARDIOLOGIST CONS
4760 E Galbraith Rd # 212 (45236-6703)
PHONE.................513 936-9191
Ned Mehlman MD, *Owner*
Stuart Steinberg, *Med Doctor*
EMP: 50
SALES (est): 1.2MM **Privately Held**
SIC: 8011 Offices & clinics of medical doctors

(G-3409)
CONCORDIA PROPERTIES LLC
Also Called: Tri County Mall Promotion Fund
11700 Princeton Pike B213 (45246-2535)
PHONE.................513 671-0120
Fax: 513 671-2931
Sandra Holzwarth, *Director*
EMP: 25 EST: 1960
SQ FT: 50
SALES (est): 2.7MM **Privately Held**
WEB: www.concordiaproperties.com
SIC: 8742 Marketing consulting services

(G-3410)
CONEY ISLAND INC
6201 Kellogg Ave (45230-7199)
PHONE.................513 232-8230
Fax: 513 231-1352
Victor W Nolting, *CEO*
Linda Layton, *Senior VP*
Tom Chase, *Maint Spvr*
Jennifer Reder, *Treasurer*
Deb Weaver, *Accounts Exec*
▲ **EMP:** 36
SQ FT: 2,560
SALES (est): 4.7MM **Privately Held**
WEB: www.coneyislandpark.com
SIC: 7999 Tourist attractions, amusement park concessions & rides

(G-3411)
CONSOLIDATED GRAIN & BARGE CO
Also Called: Anderson Ferry
4837 River Rd (45233-1634)
PHONE.................513 941-4805
EMP: 30 **Privately Held**
SIC: 4221 5153 4449 4491 Grain elevator, storage only; grain & field beans; canal barge operations; marine cargo handling
HQ: Consolidated Grain & Barge Company
1127 Hwy 190 E Service Rd
Covington LA 70433
985 867-3500

(G-3412)
CONTEMPORARY ARTS CENTER
44 E 6th St (45202-3998)
PHONE.................513 721-0390
Fax: 513 721-7418
Gale Beckett, *Vice Pres*
Glen Gruber, *CFO*
Margaux Higgins, *Controller*
Chris Perbix, *Corp Comm Staff*
Raphaela Platow, *Director*
EMP: 40
SQ FT: 80,000
SALES: 3.9MM **Privately Held**
WEB: www.cacmail.org
SIC: 8412 Arts or science center

(G-3413)
CONTRACTORS MATERIALS COMPANY
Also Called: Mmi of Kentucky
10320 S Medallion Dr (45241-4836)
P.O. Box 621227 (45262-1227)
PHONE.................513 733-3000
Fax: 513 956-3173
Martha C Luken, *President*
David L Friedman, *Vice Pres*
Daniel P King, *Vice Pres*
Vincent Ferrara, *Facilities Mgr*
Laurie Kamphaus, *Controller*
▲ **EMP:** 50
SQ FT: 95,000

Cincinnati - Hamilton County (G-3414) GEOGRAPHIC SECTION

SALES (est): 29.6MM **Privately Held**
WEB: www.cmcmmi.com
SIC: 5211 5051 Lumber & other building materials; concrete reinforcing bars

(G-3414)
CONTROLLED CREDIT CORPORATION
644 Linn St Ste 1101 (45203-1742)
P.O. Box 5154 (45205-0154)
PHONE.................513 921-2600
Fax: 513 921-6995
Daniel J Heisel, *President*
Robert W Leuenberger, *Vice Pres*
Becky Kelly, *Accounting Mgr*
Patty Olberding, *Manager*
Paul E Heisel, *Director*
EMP: 42 **EST:** 1967
SQ FT: 7,000
SALES (est): 5.7MM **Privately Held**
WEB: www.controlledcredit.com
SIC: 7322 Collection agency, except real estate

(G-3415)
CONTROLS CENTER INC (PA)
Also Called: Johnson Contrls Authorized Dlr
1640 E Kemper Rd Ste 2 (45246-2806)
PHONE.................513 772-2665
Fax: 513 772-4355
Gregory E Grimme, *President*
Mark J Grimme, *Vice Pres*
Andrew Verey, *Vice Pres*
EMP: 65
SQ FT: 45,000
SALES (est): 29.1MM **Privately Held**
WEB: www.johnstonecincinnati.com
SIC: 5075 5078 Air conditioning equipment, except room units; warm air heating equipment & supplies; refrigeration equipment & supplies

(G-3416)
CONVERGINT TECHNOLOGIES LLC
Also Called: Post Browning
7812 Redsky Dr (45249-1632)
PHONE.................513 771-1717
Mike Caron, *Vice Pres*
EMP: 130
SALES (corp-wide): 469.1MM **Privately Held**
SIC: 5065 7699 Security control equipment & systems; industrial machinery & equipment repair
PA: Convergint Technologies Llc
1 Commerce Dr
Schaumburg IL 60173
847 620-5000

(G-3417)
CONVERGYS CORPORATION (PA)
201 E 4th St (45202-4206)
P.O. Box 1895 (45201-1895)
PHONE.................513 723-7000
Jeffrey H Fox, *Ch of Bd*
Andrea J Ayers, *President*
Marjorie M Connelly, *COO*
Vicki Sweeda, *Project Mgr*
Marla Warburton, *Project Mgr*
EMP: 800 **EST:** 1996
SALES: 2.7B **Publicly Held**
WEB: www.convergys.com
SIC: 7374 7373 Data processing service; computer integrated systems design

(G-3418)
CONVERGYS CSTMER MGT GROUP INC (HQ)
201 E 4th St Bsmt (45202-4206)
P.O. Box 1638 (45201-1638)
PHONE.................513 723-6104
David F Dougherty, *President*
Ronald E Schultz, *COO*
Andre S Valentine, *CFO*
Michael Bockelman, *Mktg Dir*
David J Smith, *Analyst*
EMP: 300
SQ FT: 100,000
SALES (est): 331.6MM
SALES (corp-wide): 2.7B **Publicly Held**
SIC: 7389 8732 Telemarketing services; market analysis or research

PA: Convergys Corporation
201 E 4th St
Cincinnati OH 45202
513 723-7000

(G-3419)
CONVERGYS GVRNMENT SLTIONS LLC
201 E 4th St Ste Bsmt (45202-4248)
PHONE.................513 723-7006
Linda T Drumright, *Vice Pres*
Michael Schroeder, *Vice Pres*
Robert J Krolik, *CFO*
Earl C Shanks, *CFO*
David Dougherty, *Mng Member*
EMP: 99
SQ FT: 60,000
SALES (est): 11MM
SALES (corp-wide): 2.7B **Publicly Held**
WEB: www.convergys.com
SIC: 7374 Data processing & preparation
PA: Convergys Corporation
201 E 4th St
Cincinnati OH 45202
513 723-7000

(G-3420)
CONVERSA LANGUAGE CENTER INC
817 Main St Ste 600 (45202-2183)
PHONE.................513 651-5679
Jerry Thiemann, *President*
Dave Kaufman, *Director*
Gerry Thiemann, *Director*
EMP: 25
SQ FT: 5,000
SALES (est): 1.5MM **Privately Held**
WEB: www.conversa1.com
SIC: 7389 Translation services

(G-3421)
CORCORAN AND HARNIST HTG & AC
Also Called: Honeywell Authorized Dealer
1457 Harrison Ave (45214-1605)
PHONE.................513 921-2227
Fax: 513 921-1101
Tim Corcoran, *President*
Greg Harnist, *Vice Pres*
EMP: 35
SQ FT: 300,000
SALES: 3.5MM **Privately Held**
WEB: www.corcoranharnist.com
SIC: 1711 Warm air heating & air conditioning contractor

(G-3422)
CORE RESOURCES INC
7795 5 Mile Rd (45230-2355)
PHONE.................513 731-1771
Fax: 513 731-8885
Paul Kitzmiller, *CEO*
David Kitzmiller, *COO*
Jennifer Abbott, *Project Mgr*
Kevin Kappes, *Controller*
Mike Willis, *Sales Staff*
EMP: 52
SQ FT: 7,000
SALES (est): 9.6MM **Privately Held**
WEB: www.core-1.com
SIC: 8741 Construction management

(G-3423)
CORNERSTONE BROKER INS SVCS AG (PA)
Also Called: Cornerstone Brkrg Ins Svc Agn
2101 Florence Ave (45206-2426)
PHONE.................513 241-7675
Fax: 513 241-7668
John Carroll, *CEO*
John Clark, *Vice Pres*
Steve Geis, *Vice Pres*
Colleen Baird, *Broker*
Kristen Fields, *Broker*
EMP: 40
SALES (est): 11MM **Privately Held**
SIC: 6411 Insurance agents

(G-3424)
CORS & BASSETT LLC (PA)
537 E Pete Rose Way # 400 (45202-3578)
PHONE.................513 852-8200
Janet Houston, *Partner*
Hans Zimmer, *Partner*
David L Barth, *Business Mgr*

Kenneth B Bassett, *Counsel*
Frank Diedrichs, *Counsel*
EMP: 75
SALES (est): 12.1MM **Privately Held**
SIC: 8111 General practice attorney, lawyer

(G-3425)
COSTELLO PNTG BLDG RESTORATION
1113 Halpin Ave (45208-2907)
PHONE.................513 321-3326
John Costello, *President*
Pam Kesselring, *Project Mgr*
EMP: 25
SQ FT: 800
SALES (est): 1.3MM **Privately Held**
SIC: 1721 Exterior commercial painting contractor

(G-3426)
COTTINGHAM RETIREMENT CMNTY
3995 Cottingham Dr # 102 (45241-1680)
PHONE.................513 563-3600
Fax: 513 563-3601
Barbara Thomas, *Facilities Dir*
Lisa Day-Dean, *Persnl Dir*
Margaret Unger, *Personnel*
Jan Shirley, *Nursing Dir*
Margie Berryman, *Store Dir*
EMP: 160
SALES: 10.2MM **Privately Held**
SIC: 8051 Skilled nursing care facilities

(G-3427)
COUNCIL ON AGING OF SOUTHWESTE
175 Tri County Pkwy # 200 (45246-3237)
PHONE.................513 721-1025
Paul Booth, *Vice Pres*
Kimberly Easley, *Vice Pres*
Becky Knight, *Vice Pres*
Jacqueline Golston, *Human Res Dir*
Melita Ellington, *Human Resources*
EMP: 200
SQ FT: 31,000
SALES (est): 78.3MM **Privately Held**
WEB: www.help4seniors.org
SIC: 8399 8322 Council for social agency; individual & family services

(G-3428)
COUNTY OF HAMILTON
Also Called: Mental Retardation & Dev
2600 Civic Center Dr (45231-1312)
PHONE.................513 742-1576
Fax: 513 742-6634
Michael Bailey, *Manager*
William Hinkle, *Exec Dir*
Charles Altenau, *Director*
EMP: 359
SQ FT: 3,000 **Privately Held**
WEB: www.mhrecovery.com
SIC: 8331 8431 8322 Sheltered workshop; mental health agency administration, government; ; individual & family services
PA: County Of Hamilton
138 E Court St Rm 607
Cincinnati OH 45202
513 946-4400

(G-3429)
COUNTY OF HAMILTON
Also Called: Hillcrest Training School
246 Bonham Rd (45215-2054)
PHONE.................513 552-1200
Dennis Johnson, *Principal*
EMP: 150
SQ FT: 3,192 **Privately Held**
WEB: www.mhrecovery.com
SIC: 8361 9411 9211 Training school for delinquents; administration of educational programs; ; courts;
PA: County Of Hamilton
138 E Court St Rm 607
Cincinnati OH 45202
513 946-4400

(G-3430)
COUNTY OF HAMILTON
138 E Court St Rm 700 (45202-1224)
PHONE.................513 946-4250
Fax: 513 946-4288

Teodore Hubbard, *Chief*
Michael Carr, *Director*
EMP: 100 **Privately Held**
WEB: www.mhrecovery.com
SIC: 8711 9511 Civil engineering; air, water & solid waste management;
PA: County Of Hamilton
138 E Court St Rm 607
Cincinnati OH 45202
513 946-4400

(G-3431)
COUNTY OF HAMILTON
Also Called: Mental Retardation & Dev
5884 Bridgetown Rd (45248-3106)
PHONE.................513 598-2965
Elizabeth Bellew, *Branch Mgr*
Charles Altenau, *Director*
EMP: 260 **Privately Held**
WEB: www.mhrecovery.com
SIC: 8093 9431 Mental health clinic, outpatient; mental health agency administration, government;
PA: County Of Hamilton
138 E Court St Rm 607
Cincinnati OH 45202
513 946-4400

(G-3432)
COUNTY OF HAMILTON
Also Called: Hamilton County Coroner
3159 Eden Ave (45219-2274)
PHONE.................513 221-4524
Fax: 513 221-0307
Pat Hanrahan, *Program Mgr*
EMP: 48 **Privately Held**
WEB: www.mhrecovery.com
SIC: 8049 ; psychiatric social worker
PA: County Of Hamilton
138 E Court St Rm 607
Cincinnati OH 45202
513 946-4400

(G-3433)
COUNTY OF HAMILTON
Also Called: Health Dept
7162 Reading Rd Ste 800 (45237-3845)
PHONE.................513 821-6946
Patsy Matillar, *Program Dir*
EMP: 45 **Privately Held**
WEB: www.mhrecovery.com
SIC: 8322 9431 Child related social services; administration of public health programs;
PA: County Of Hamilton
138 E Court St Rm 607
Cincinnati OH 45202
513 946-4400

(G-3434)
COUPLE TO COUPLE LEAG INTL INC (PA)
Also Called: Foundation For The Family
4290 Delhi Rd (45238-5829)
P.O. Box 111184 (45211-1184)
PHONE.................513 471-2000
Fax: 513 557-2449
Sheila K Kippley, *Principal*
Mike Manhart, *Exec Dir*
EMP: 25
SQ FT: 13,500
SALES: 1.4MM **Privately Held**
SIC: 8322 Family service agency

(G-3435)
COURT STRET CENTER ASSOCIATES
Also Called: Parking Company of America
250 W Court St Ste 200e (45202-1064)
PHONE.................513 241-0415
Martin Chavez, *President*
Pedro Fiadini, *Agent*
EMP: 42
SQ FT: 105,000
SALES (est): 1.9MM **Privately Held**
WEB: www.pca-star.com
SIC: 6512 Commercial & industrial building operation

(G-3436)
COWAN SYSTEMS LLC
10801 Evendale Dr (45241-7508)
PHONE.................513 769-4774
EMP: 129 **Privately Held**
SIC: 4213 Trucking, except local

GEOGRAPHIC SECTION
Cincinnati - Hamilton County (G-3461)

PA: Cowan Systems, Llc
4555 Hollins Ferry Rd
Baltimore MD 21227

(G-3437)
CRAFTSMAN ELECTRIC INC
3855 Alta Ave Ste 1 (45236-3932)
PHONE.................513 891-4426
Fax: 513 891-5434
Kathleen Fischer, *President*
Charles Fischer, *Vice Pres*
William Hungler, *Project Mgr*
Ryan West, *Accountant*
▲ **EMP:** 55
SQ FT: 16,000
SALES (est): 8.4MM **Privately Held**
SIC: 1731 General electrical contractor

(G-3438)
CRANE HEATING & AC CO
Also Called: Honeywell Authorized Dealer
24 Clay St (45217-1193)
PHONE.................513 641-4700
Fax: 513 641-4702
Frank J Crane III, *President*
Edward Crane, *Vice Pres*
Jim Lohbeck, *Sales Mgr*
Karen Crane, *Admin Sec*
EMP: 40 **EST:** 1953
SQ FT: 6,000
SALES (est): 5.8MM **Privately Held**
WEB: www.crane-htg-air.com
SIC: 1711 Warm air heating & air conditioning contractor

(G-3439)
CRANLEY SURGICAL ASSOCIATES
3747 W Fork Rd (45247-7548)
PHONE.................513 961-4335
Fax: 513 961-4227
L R Roedersheimer, *President*
James J Arbough, *Principal*
John J Cranley, *Principal*
Robert Cranley, *Principal*
EMP: 33
SALES (est): 2.6MM **Privately Held**
WEB: www.cranleysurgical.com
SIC: 8011 Cardiologist & cardio-vascular specialist

(G-3440)
CRONINS INC
Also Called: Joseph Northland Porsche Audi
9847 Kings Auto Mall Rd (45249-8245)
PHONE.................513 851-5900
Ronald Joseph, *President*
Greg Joseph, *General Mgr*
EMP: 37
SQ FT: 13,000
SALES (est): 9.3MM **Privately Held**
SIC: 5511 5531 7389 Automobiles, new & used; automotive & home supply stores; drive-a-way automobile service

(G-3441)
CROOKED TREE GOLF COURSE
1250 Springfield Pike # 100 (45215-2148)
PHONE.................513 398-3933
Fax: 513 398-3950
Joe Bischoff, *Manager*
Cheryl Bonk, *Manager*
Jack Eisert, *Manager*
EMP: 40
SQ FT: 8,500
SALES (est): 1.1MM **Privately Held**
SIC: 7992 Public golf courses

(G-3442)
CROSSROADS CENTER
311 Mrtin Lther King Dr W (45220)
PHONE.................513 475-5300
Janice Bishop, *Senior VP*
Debi Gadberry, *VP Human Res*
Carl Tucker, *Manager*
Jacqueline P Butler, *Exec Dir*
Roberto Soria, *Director*
EMP: 150
SALES (est): 5.1MM **Privately Held**
SIC: 8069 8361 8093 Alcoholism rehabilitation hospital; drug addiction rehabilitation hospital; residential care; specialty outpatient clinics

(G-3443)
CRYSTALWOOD INC
Also Called: Alois Alzheimer Center, The
70 Damon Rd (45218-1041)
PHONE.................513 605-1000
Fax: 513 825-2998
Stephen Boymel, *President*
Gregg Miller, *VP Opers*
Jon Rarick, *Exec Dir*
EMP: 85
SQ FT: 30,000
SALES (est): 123.9K **Privately Held**
WEB: www.alois.com
SIC: 8059 8361 8052 Rest home, with health care; residential care; intermediate care facilities

(G-3444)
CSX TRANSPORTATION INC
3601 Geringer St (45223-2405)
PHONE.................513 369-5514
Bob Babcock, *Branch Mgr*
Lance Hensley, *Clerk*
EMP: 38
SALES (corp-wide): 11.4B **Publicly Held**
WEB: www.csxt.com
SIC: 4011 Railroads, line-haul operating
HQ: Csx Transportation, Inc.
500 Water St
Jacksonville FL 32202
904 359-3100

(G-3445)
CTS CONSTRUCTION INC
Also Called: CTS Telecommunications
6661 Cooper Rd (45242)
PHONE.................513 489-8290
Fax: 513 489-8298
Rick Stezer, *President*
John Diss, *Superintendent*
Bill Coate, *COO*
William Coate, *Vice Pres*
Andrew Rotunno, *Vice Pres*
EMP: 100
SQ FT: 15,000
SALES (est): 15.6MM **Privately Held**
WEB: www.ctstelecomm.com
SIC: 7378 8748 1796 1731 Computer maintenance & repair; telecommunications consultant; installing building equipment; electrical work

(G-3446)
CUMBERLAND GAP LLC
Also Called: Ramada Inn Cumberland Hotel
2285 Banning Rd (45239-6611)
PHONE.................513 681-9300
Toni Winston, *President*
Jackie Iovine, *General Mgr*
EMP: 30
SALES (est): 1.1MM **Privately Held**
SIC: 7011 Hotels & motels

(G-3447)
CUMULUS BROADCASTING LLC
4805 Montgomery Rd (45212-2198)
PHONE.................850 243-7676
Chris Huneke, *Branch Mgr*
EMP: 38
SALES (corp-wide): 1.1B **Publicly Held**
SIC: 4832 Radio broadcasting stations
HQ: Cumulus Broadcasting, Llc
3280 Peachtree Rd Nw Ste
Atlanta GA 30305
404 949-0700

(G-3448)
CUMULUS MEDIA INC
Also Called: Warm 98
4805 Montgomery Rd # 300 (45212-2198)
PHONE.................513 241-9898
Fax: 513 357-2945
Joe Wickman, *Sales Mgr*
Karrie Subbrick, *Manager*
Keith Mitchell, *Program Dir*
Tina Cleman, *Executive*
EMP: 65
SALES (corp-wide): 1.1B **Publicly Held**
WEB: www.cumulusmedia.com
SIC: 4832 Radio broadcasting stations
PA: Cumulus Media Inc.
3280 Peachtree Rd Ne # 2300
Atlanta GA 30305
404 949-0700

(G-3449)
CURIOSITY LLC
Also Called: Curiosity Advertising
35 E 7th St Ste 800 (45202-2411)
PHONE.................513 744-6000
Gregory Livingston, *COO*
Stephanie Anglavar, *Vice Pres*
Jeff Jones, *Vice Pres*
Sarah Aicklen, *Project Mgr*
Kevin Clark, *Project Mgr*
EMP: 62
SQ FT: 14,000
SALES (est): 4MM **Privately Held**
WEB: www.Curiosity360.com
SIC: 7311 Advertising consultant

(G-3450)
CUSO CORPORATION
10485 Reading Rd (45241-2523)
PHONE.................513 984-2876
Fax: 513 554-0570
Patrick Taylor, *CEO*
Tim Ballinger, *President*
Tina Wander, *COO*
EMP: 100
SALES (est): 6.1MM **Privately Held**
SIC: 6062 State credit unions

(G-3451)
CUSTOM DESIGN BENEFITS INC
5589 Cheviot Rd (45247-7020)
PHONE.................513 598-2929
Fax: 513 598-2901
M Steven Chapel, *CEO*
Julie Muller, *President*
EMP: 38
SQ FT: 10,000
SALES (est): 22.3MM **Privately Held**
WEB: www.customdesignbenefits.com
SIC: 6324 Hospital & medical service plans

(G-3452)
CUSTOM MAID CLEANING SERVICES
3840 Burwood Ave (45212-3944)
P.O. Box 12688 (45212-0688)
PHONE.................513 351-6571
Walter H Ford, *President*
EMP: 50 **EST:** 1972
SALES (est): 1.1MM **Privately Held**
SIC: 7349 Janitorial service, contract basis

(G-3453)
D & D ADVERTISING ENTERPRISES
801 Evans St Ste 203 (45204-2075)
PHONE.................513 921-6827
Fax: 513 921-6909
Diane Carpenter, *President*
Edwin D Hottinger, *President*
Doug Hottinger, *Financial Exec*
Christopher Arnette, *Manager*
EMP: 25
SALES (est): 2MM **Privately Held**
WEB: www.coverads.com
SIC: 7311 Advertising consultant

(G-3454)
D B A INC
Also Called: Active Detective Bureau
4239 Hamilton Ave (45223-2088)
PHONE.................513 541-6600
Fax: 513 541-6690
Celine M Estill, *President*
Bari Mairose, *Network Mgr*
Bari Venn Mairose, *Web Proj Mgr*
EMP: 50
SALES (est): 2MM **Privately Held**
SIC: 7381 1731 7382 Private investigator; security guard service; fire detection & burglar alarm systems specialization; security systems services

(G-3455)
D H PACKAGING CO (PA)
Also Called: Wrap & Send Services Co.
8005 Plainfield Rd Ste 20 (45236-2500)
PHONE.................513 791-2022
Fax: 513 791-2701
Mike Jamali, *President*
Denise Dehan, *VP Admin*
Tom Sizer, *Manager*
EMP: 600
SALES (est): 8.3MM **Privately Held**
SIC: 7299 7389 Gift wrapping services; packaging & labeling services

(G-3456)
D JAMES INCORPORATED
Also Called: HILLEBRAND NURSING AND REHABIL
4320 Bridgetown Rd (45211-4428)
PHONE.................513 574-4550
Fax: 513 598-3970
James Glass, *President*
Cindy Donesi, *COO*
Dan Suer, *Plant Mgr*
DOT Kemper, *Finance Other*
Donna Masminster, *Mktg Dir*
EMP: 200
SQ FT: 2,953
SALES (est): 12.4MM **Privately Held**
WEB: www.hillebrandhealth.com
SIC: 8051 Convalescent home with continuous nursing care

(G-3457)
D-G CUSTOM CHROME LLC
5200 Lester Rd (45213-2522)
PHONE.................513 531-1881
Alex Wyatt, *President*
Don Gorman, *President*
Victoria Gorman, *Vice Pres*
EMP: 58
SQ FT: 10,162
SALES (est): 7.2MM **Privately Held**
WEB: www.dgcustomchrome.com
SIC: 5013 3471 Automotive supplies & parts; plating & polishing

(G-3458)
DACIA R CRUM
Also Called: Ulmer & Berne
600 Vine St (45202-2400)
PHONE.................513 698-5000
Fax: 513 762-6250
Janine Gumbert, *President*
Sheryl Ritter, *President*
Dacia R Crum, *Principal*
Randy Lindner, *Purch Dir*
Debra Wade, *Corp Counsel*
EMP: 75
SALES (est): 3.5MM **Privately Held**
SIC: 8111 General practice attorney, lawyer

(G-3459)
DAG CONSTRUCTION CO INC
4924 Winton Rd (45232-1505)
PHONE.................513 542-8597
Fax: 513 542-9286
Dale S White Sr, *CEO*
Stephanie A Hall, *President*
Lindsay A Wilhelm, *President*
Gregory J Webb, *COO*
Dale White Jr, *Vice Pres*
EMP: 40
SALES (est): 11.9MM **Privately Held**
WEB: www.dag-cons.com
SIC: 1541 1542 Industrial buildings & warehouses; renovation, remodeling & repairs: industrial buildings; commercial & office building, new construction; commercial & office buildings, renovation & repair

(G-3460)
DALTON ROOFING CO
4477 Eastern Ave (45226-1803)
PHONE.................513 871-2800
Fax: 513 871-2842
John Dalton, *President*
Frank Dalton, *Vice Pres*
Patty Loew, *Manager*
Martha Dalton, *Admin Sec*
EMP: 60
SQ FT: 8,000
SALES (est): 6.4MM **Privately Held**
WEB: www.daltonroofing.net
SIC: 1761 Roofing contractor

(G-3461)
DAMON TAX SERVICE
6572 Glenway Ave (45211-4410)
PHONE.................513 574-9087
Fax: 513 574-9087
Damon Robins, *President*
Sue Volker, *Manager*
EMP: 40

Cincinnati - Hamilton County (G-3462)

SQ FT: 1,400
SALES: 200K **Privately Held**
WEB: www.damontaxservice.com
SIC: 7291 Tax return preparation services

(G-3462)
DANSON INC
Also Called: Aegis Protective Services
3033 Robertson Ave (45209-1233)
PHONE.....................513 948-0066
Fax: 513 948-0766
Justin Dutro, *President*
Daniel G Dutro, *Vice Pres*
Dee Dutro, *Manager*
Rod Hale, *Director*
EMP: 210
SQ FT: 2,400
SALES (est): 7.3MM **Privately Held**
WEB: www.danson.com
SIC: 7381 Security guard service

(G-3463)
DAVID L BARTH LWYR
537 E Pete Rose Way (45202-3567)
PHONE.....................513 852-8228
David Barth, *Principal*
EMP: 60
SALES (est): 1.5MM **Privately Held**
SIC: 8111 General practice attorney, lawyer

(G-3464)
DAVIS CATERING INC
30 Garfield Pl Ste 10 (45202-4375)
PHONE.....................513 241-3464
Fax: 513 333-2553
Robert Dawson, *President*
Robert L Dawson, *Corp Secy*
Nils Dawson, *Vice Pres*
EMP: 80
SQ FT: 50,000
SALES (est): 2.7MM **Privately Held**
SIC: 5812 7299 Caterers; banquet hall facilities

(G-3465)
DAVITA INC
2109 Reading Rd (45202-1417)
PHONE.....................513 784-1800
Barbara Frommeyer, *Branch Mgr*
Joshua Creamer, *Director*
Julie Skoog, *Administration*
EMP: 27 **Publicly Held**
SIC: 8092 Kidney dialysis centers
PA: Davita Inc.
    2000 16th St
    Denver CO 80202

(G-3466)
DAVITA INC
7502 State Rd (45255-2596)
PHONE.....................513 624-0400
Laurie Johnson, *Branch Mgr*
Donna Wolfer, *Manager*
Patricia E Cook, *Gnrl Med Prac*
EMP: 27 **Publicly Held**
SIC: 8092 Kidney dialysis centers
PA: Davita Inc.
    2000 16th St
    Denver CO 80202

(G-3467)
DAY SHARE LTD
5915 Glenway Ave (45238-2008)
PHONE.....................513 451-1100
Fax: 513 347-2850
Jeff Gault, *COO*
Thoams Gault, *Mng Member*
Thomas Gault, *Mng Member*
Patricia Gault,
EMP: 48
SALES (est): 1.1MM **Privately Held**
WEB: www.dayshare.com
SIC: 8322 Senior citizens' center or association

(G-3468)
DAYTON HEIDELBERG DISTRG CO
1518 Dalton Ave (45214-2018)
PHONE.....................513 421-5000
Fax: 513 421-5194
Lee Oberlag, *President*
Toby Coston, *General Mgr*
Ken Lelley, *COO*
Harry Johnson, *Vice Pres*
Greg Michalec, *Vice Pres*
EMP: 98
SALES (corp-wide): 369.4MM **Privately Held**
SIC: 5181 Beer & other fermented malt liquors
PA: Dayton Heidelberg Distributing Co.
    3601 Dryden Rd
    Moraine OH 45439
    937 222-8692

(G-3469)
DCS SANITATION MANAGEMENT INC (PA)
7864 Camargo Rd (45243-4300)
P.O. Box 43215 (45243-0215)
PHONE.....................513 891-4980
Fax: 513 271-5710
Lance White, *CEO*
Thomas Murray, *President*
James Gillespie, *CFO*
Joice Hatic, *Credit Mgr*
Joyce Schehl, *Human Res Dir*
EMP: 85
SQ FT: 3,000
SALES (est): 42.4MM **Privately Held**
SIC: 7349 7342 Building cleaning service; disinfecting services

(G-3470)
DE FOXX & ASSOCIATES INC (PA)
Also Called: Validex
324 W 9th St Fl 5 (45202-2043)
PHONE.....................513 621-5522
Fax: 513 241-1634
David E Foxx, *President*
P Swigart, *CFO*
Tony Patton, *Human Res Dir*
Jason Redar, *CTO*
Crosby Jeff, *Programmer Anys*
EMP: 350
SQ FT: 25,000
SALES (est): 124.9MM **Privately Held**
WEB: www.xlcservices.com
SIC: 8742 8741 Business consultant; general management consultant; construction management

(G-3471)
DEACONESS ASSOCIATIONS INC (PA)
615 Elsinore Pl Bldg B (45202-1459)
PHONE.....................513 559-2100
E Anthony Woods, *President*
Dave Mc Adams, *CFO*
Marlene Reynolds, *Supervisor*
EMP: 300
SALES: 23.6MM **Privately Held**
SIC: 6324 Hospital & medical service plans

(G-3472)
DEACONESS HOSPITAL OF CINCINNA (PA)
615 Elsinore Pl Bldg B (45202-1459)
PHONE.....................513 559-2100
Fax: 513 475-5076
James L Pahls, *Ch of Bd*
E Anthony Woods, *Chairman*
Chowdry Bashir MD, *Med Doctor*
Scott Woods MD, *Med Doctor*
Ben Carpenter, *Manager*
EMP: 87 EST: 1888
SQ FT: 649,000
SALES: 4.3MM **Privately Held**
SIC: 8062 General medical & surgical hospitals

(G-3473)
DEACONESS LONG TERM CARE INC (HQ)
330 Straight St Ste 310 (45219-1068)
P.O. Box 198027 (45219-8027)
PHONE.....................513 861-0400
Fax: 513 487-3644
Bryan Burklow, *President*
Lesa Dean, *Facilities Mgr*
Kenneth Raupach, *CFO*
William Hostler, *Controller*
EMP: 99
SQ FT: 1,891

SALES: 2.8K
SALES (corp-wide): 23.6MM **Privately Held**
SIC: 8741 Nursing & personal care facility management
PA: The Deaconess Associations Inc
    615 Elsinore Pl Bldg B
    Cincinnati OH 45202
    513 559-2100

(G-3474)
DEACONESS LONG TERM CARE OF MI (PA)
Also Called: Camden Health Center
330 Straight St Ste 310 (45219-1068)
PHONE.....................513 487-3600
Ken Raupach, *COO*
Pam Lund, *Manager*
EMP: 1500
SALES: 22K **Privately Held**
WEB: www.deaconessltc.org
SIC: 8059 8361 8052 8051 Nursing home, except skilled & intermediate care facility; residential care; intermediate care facilities; skilled nursing care facilities

(G-3475)
DEANHOUSTON CREATIVE GROUP INC (PA)
310 Culvert St Ste 300 (45202-2229)
PHONE.....................513 421-6622
Fax: 513 562-3522
Dale Dean, *President*
Walter Bonnett, *Exec VP*
Andy Dean, *Vice Pres*
Greg Houston, *Vice Pres*
James Molloy, *Vice Pres*
EMP: 33
SQ FT: 4,100
SALES (est): 7.3MM **Privately Held**
SIC: 7311 Advertising consultant

(G-3476)
DEBRA-KUEMPEL INC (HQ)
Also Called: De Bra - Kuempel
3976 Southern Ave (45227-3562)
P.O. Box 701620 (45270-1620)
PHONE.....................513 271-6500
Joe D Clark, *CEO*
Fred B De Bra, *Ch of Bd*
Morris H Reed, *Corp Secy*
Robert E Cupp, *Vice Pres*
John Kuempel Jr, *Vice Pres*
EMP: 80 EST: 1944
SQ FT: 20,079
SALES (est): 29.3MM
SALES (corp-wide): 7.6B **Publicly Held**
SIC: 3446 1711 3443 3441 Architectural metalwork; mechanical contractor; fabricated plate work (boiler shop); fabricated structural metal
PA: Emcor Group, Inc.
    301 Merritt 7 Fl 6
    Norwalk CT 06851
    203 849-7800

(G-3477)
DEDICATED NURSING ASSOC INC
11542 Springfield Pike (45246-3516)
PHONE.....................866 450-5550
EMP: 41 **Privately Held**
SIC: 7361 7363 8051 Nurses' registry; medical help service; skilled nursing care facilities
PA: Dedicated Nursing Associates, Inc.
    6536 State Route 22
    Delmont PA 15626

(G-3478)
DEER PARK ROOFING INC (PA)
7201 Blue Ash Rd (45236-3665)
PHONE.....................513 891-9151
Fax: 513 891-9152
Nicholas A Sabino, *President*
Katie Teufel, *Human Res Dir*
Rodney Calhoun, *Sales Staff*
Angie Broughton, *Office Mgr*
EMP: 45
SQ FT: 23,000
SALES (est): 13.5MM **Privately Held**
WEB: www.deerparkroofing.com
SIC: 1761 Roofing contractor

(G-3479)
DEFINITIVE SOLUTIONS CO INC
Also Called: DSC Consulting
8180 Corp Pk Dr Ste 305 (45242)
PHONE.....................513 719-9100
Fax: 513 719-9130
Tim Osborn, *President*
Tony Manzo, *Vice Pres*
Ken Reece, *Vice Pres*
Roy Neal, *Manager*
EMP: 82
SQ FT: 6,000
SALES (est): 6.3MM **Privately Held**
SIC: 7389 7379 7374 7373 Trade show arrangement; data processing consultant; data processing & preparation; computer integrated systems design

(G-3480)
DEI INCORPORATED
1550 Kemper Meadow Dr (45240-1638)
PHONE.....................513 825-5800
Fax: 513 825-1947
Richard D Grow, *Ch of Bd*
Nedd Compton, *President*
Don Neill, *President*
David Welsh, *President*
David Cochran, *Regional Mgr*
EMP: 74
SQ FT: 15,000
SALES (est): 14.5MM **Privately Held**
WEB: www.dei-corp.com
SIC: 8712 Architectural engineering

(G-3481)
DELHI TOWNSHIP (PA)
934 Neeb Rd (45233-4101)
PHONE.....................513 922-0060
Fax: 513 922-9315
Ken Ryan, *Principal*
Douglas Campbell, *Fire Chief*
Michael Davis, *Trustee*
Al Duebber, *Trustee*
Jerome Luebbers, *Trustee*
EMP: 70 **Privately Held**
SIC: 9111 8322 City & town managers' offices; ; senior citizens' center or association

(G-3482)
DELOITTE & TOUCHE LLP
Also Called: Deloitte Consulting
250 E 5th St Fl 1600 (45202-4263)
P.O. Box 5340 (45201-5340)
PHONE.....................513 784-7100
Fax: 513 784-7202
Clifford L Oppenheim, *Principal*
Reynolds Thomas, *Personnel Exec*
Sandi Stavermann, *Manager*
Dennis Krysmalski, *Senior Mgr*
Greg Bier, *IT/INT Sup*
EMP: 440
SALES (corp-wide): 5.9B **Privately Held**
WEB: www.deloitte.com
SIC: 8721 8748 8742 7291 Certified public accountant; business consulting; management consulting services; tax return preparation services
HQ: Deloitte & Touche Llp
    30 Rockefeller Plz # 4350
    New York NY 10112
    212 492-4000

(G-3483)
DELTA ELECTRICAL CONTRS LTD
4890 Gray Rd (45232-1512)
PHONE.....................513 421-7744
Fax: 513 421-8400
Dale Scheidt, *Owner*
Brad Scheidt, *Project Mgr*
Eric Scheidt, *Project Mgr*
EMP: 31
SQ FT: 18,000
SALES: 1MM **Privately Held**
SIC: 1731 Electronic controls installation

(G-3484)
DESKEY ASSOCIATES INC
120 E 8th St (45202-2118)
PHONE.....................513 721-6800
Fax: 513 639-7575
Michael Busher, *President*
Douglas Studer, *Vice Pres*
Rob Anthony, *Design Engr*
Becky Hyde, *Controller*

GEOGRAPHIC SECTION

Cincinnati - Hamilton County (G-3508)

EMP: 90 EST: 1925
SALES (est): 9.5MM Privately Held
WEB: www.deskey.com
SIC: 8711 8732 Designing; ship, boat, machine & product; market analysis or research

(G-3485)
DETOX HEALTH CARE CORP OHIO
Also Called: Vitas Healthcare Corp of Ohio
11500 Northlake Dr # 400 (45249-1650)
PHONE..................513 742-6310
Kim Toole, President
EMP: 350
SALES (est): 5.8MM Privately Held
SIC: 8621 Health association

(G-3486)
DHL SUPPLY CHAIN (USA)
401 Murray Rd (45217-1012)
PHONE..................513 482-6015
Ron Kohorst, Vice Pres
EMP: 55
SALES (corp-wide): 71.2B Privately Held
SIC: 4225 General warehousing
HQ: Exel Inc.
570 Polaris Pkwy
Westerville OH 43082
614 865-8500

(G-3487)
DHL SUPPLY CHAIN (USA)
10121 Princtn Glndle Rd B (45246-1211)
PHONE..................513 942-1575
Fax: 513 942-1673
Skip Riley, Branch Mgr
EMP: 30
SALES (corp-wide): 71.2B Privately Held
WEB: www.exel-logistics.com
SIC: 4225 4213 General warehousing; trucking, except local
HQ: Exel Inc.
570 Polaris Pkwy
Westerville OH 43082
614 865-8500

(G-3488)
DIA ELECTRIC INC
3326 Reading Rd (45229-3114)
PHONE..................513 281-0783
Thomas Gangloff, President
Sandy Morelli, General Mgr
Joyce Gangloff, Admin Sec
EMP: 25 EST: 1951
SQ FT: 3,000
SALES (est): 2.3MM Privately Held
SIC: 1731 General electrical contractor

(G-3489)
DIALYSIS CLINIC INC
499 E Mcmillan St (45206-1924)
PHONE..................513 281-0091
Fax: 513 221-3425
Roy Danfro, Manager
Heather Duncan, Manager
Susie Tallarico, Manager
Jerry Moody, Director
Natalie Lawrence, Admin Sec
EMP: 60
SQ FT: 3,840
SALES (corp-wide): 736.2MM Privately Held
WEB: www.dciinc.org
SIC: 8092 Kidney dialysis centers
PA: Dialysis Clinic, Inc.
1633 Church St Ste 500
Nashville TN 37203
615 327-3061

(G-3490)
DICKINSON FLEET SERVICES LLC
11536 Gondola St Ste B (45241-5802)
PHONE..................513 772-3629
Fax: 513 772-2492
Robert Siemers, Sales Executive
John Demers, Manager
Mike Hubbard, Manager
EMP: 25 Privately Held
WEB: www.dickinsonfleetservices.com
SIC: 7538 General truck repair
PA: Dickinson Fleet Services, Llc
4709 W 96th St
Indianapolis IN 46268

(G-3491)
DINSMORE & SHOHL LLP (PA)
255 E 5th St Ste 1900 (45202-1971)
PHONE..................513 977-8200
Fax: 937 977-8141
Peter Georgiton, Managing Prtnr
Kirk Wall, Managing Prtnr
Patrick D Lane, Counsel
Harry Riggs, Counsel
Jan H Steinher, Counsel
EMP: 406
SQ FT: 158,000
SALES: 2.4MM Privately Held
SIC: 8111 General practice law office

(G-3492)
DIRECT EXPRESS DELIVERY SVC
Also Called: Direct-X
2841 Colerain Ave (45225-2205)
P.O. Box 14028 (45250-0028)
PHONE..................513 541-0600
Fax: 513 541-0676
Joseph Griffin, President
John C Griffin, Vice Pres
Reno Runck, Accounts Mgr
EMP: 30
SQ FT: 10,000
SALES (est): 5.6MM Privately Held
SIC: 4213 Trucking, except local

(G-3493)
DIRECTIONS RESEARCH INC (PA)
401 E Court St Ste 200 (45202-1379)
PHONE..................513 651-2990
Fax: 513 651-2998
Randolph Brooks, President
Betsy Sutherland, Senior VP
Janice Brinker, Vice Pres
Lisa Butler, Vice Pres
Beth Daush, Vice Pres
EMP: 125
SQ FT: 46,374
SALES (est): 18.6MM Privately Held
WEB: www.i-dri.com
SIC: 8732 Market analysis or research

(G-3494)
DIVERSCARE HEALTHCARE SVCS INC
Also Called: Diversicare of St. Theresa
7010 Rowan Hill Dr (45227-3380)
PHONE..................513 271-7010
Brenda Wimsatt, Director
EMP: 36
SALES (corp-wide): 574.7MM Publicly Held
SIC: 8051 Skilled nursing care facilities
PA: Diversicare Healthcare Services, Inc.
1621 Galleria Blvd
Brentwood TN 37027
615 771-7575

(G-3495)
DIVERSIPAK INC (PA)
Also Called: Questmark
838 Reedy St (45202-2216)
PHONE..................513 321-7884
Dan Kunkemoeller, CEO
Jennifer Kunkemoeller, Principal
Douglas Hearn, Project Mgr
Ted Trammel, CFO
Sherry Birkhold, Personnel Exec
EMP: 125
SQ FT: 15,000
SALES (est): 22.4MM Privately Held
WEB: www.diversipak.com
SIC: 2631 7336 Container, packaging & boxboard; package design

(G-3496)
DJJ HOLDING CORPORATION (HQ)
Also Called: David J Joseph Company, The
300 Pike St (45202-4222)
PHONE..................513 621-8770
Craig A Feldman, President
Pat Wells, General Mgr
Robert L Angotti, Exec VP
Mark D Schaefer, Exec VP
Karen A Arnold, Senior VP
▼ EMP: 175
SQ FT: 160,000
SALES (est): 1.2B
SALES (corp-wide): 20.2B Publicly Held
SIC: 5093 5088 4741 Ferrous metal scrap & waste; nonferrous metals scrap; railroad equipment & supplies; rental of railroad cars
PA: Nucor Corporation
1915 Rexford Rd Ste 400
Charlotte NC 28211
704 366-7000

(G-3497)
DOMAJAPARO INC (PA)
Also Called: Thompson Hall & Jordan Fnrl HM
11400 Winton Rd (45240-2354)
PHONE..................513 742-3600
Fax: 513 674-2467
Katherine Jordan, President
Donald H Jordan, Corp Secy
Jon Patterson, Vice Pres
EMP: 44 EST: 1935
SQ FT: 3,536
SALES (est): 7.8MM Privately Held
SIC: 7261 Funeral home

(G-3498)
DONNELLON MC CARTHY INC
4141 Turrill St (45223-2200)
PHONE..................513 681-3200
EMP: 35
SALES (corp-wide): 34.3MM Privately Held
SIC: 5044 Photocopy machines
PA: Donnellon Mc Carthy, Inc.
10855 Medallion Dr
Cincinnati OH 45241
513 769-7800

(G-3499)
DONTY HORTON HM CARE DHHC LLC
2692 Madison Rd Ste N1192 (45208-1321)
PHONE..................513 463-3442
Darnetta Metcalf, Director
Donty Horton,
EMP: 35
SALES (est): 986.1K Privately Held
SIC: 8361 7381 4119 Residential care for the handicapped; fingerprint service; local passenger transportation

(G-3500)
DOTLOOP LLC
700 W Pete Rose Way # 436 (45203-1919)
PHONE..................513 257-0550
Austin Allison, CEO
Daivak Shah, President
Michael Graham, COO
Jeffrey Mills, Senior VP
Marnie Blanco, Vice Pres
EMP: 170
SALES (est): 3MM
SALES (corp-wide): 1B Publicly Held
SIC: 7371 Computer software development
HQ: Zillow, Inc.
1301 2nd Ave Fl 31
Seattle WA 98101
206 470-7000

(G-3501)
DRAKE CENTER LLC
151 W Galbraith Rd (45216-1015)
PHONE..................513 418-2500
Fax: 513 418-2501
Jerome Keller, CFO
Jerry Poppe, Client Mgr
Bradlee Carman, Marketing Staff
Paul Newman, Psychologist
Amaresh Nath, Med Doctor
EMP: 800
SQ FT: 400,000
SALES: 57MM Privately Held
WEB: www.drakecenter.com
SIC: 8051 Skilled nursing care facilities
PA: Uc Health, Llc.
3200 Burnet Ave
Cincinnati OH 45229

(G-3502)
DRAKE DEVELOPMENT INC
Also Called: Bridgeway Pointe
165 W Galbraith Rd Ofc (45216-1034)
PHONE..................513 418-4370
Fax: 513 948-4379
W Wexler, Exec Dir
Daphne U Glenn, Exec Dir
William Wexler, Exec Dir
EMP: 65
SQ FT: 94,256
SALES: 2.9MM Privately Held
SIC: 8361 Residential care

(G-3503)
DRURY HOTELS COMPANY LLC
Also Called: Drury Inn Suites Cincinnati N
2265 E Sharon Rd (45241-1870)
PHONE..................513 771-5601
Kam Siu, Branch Mgr
EMP: 29
SALES (corp-wide): 397.4MM Privately Held
WEB: www.druryhotels.com
SIC: 7011 Hotels
PA: Drury Hotels Company, Llc
721 Emerson Rd Ste 400
Saint Louis MO 63141
314 429-2255

(G-3504)
DRY RUN LIMITED PARTNERSHIP
Also Called: Ivy Hills Country Club
7711 Ivy Hills Dr (45244-2575)
P.O. Box 44086 (45244-0086)
PHONE..................513 561-9119
Fax: 513 561-6432
Ron Townsend, General Mgr
William Hines, General Mgr
E Michael Zicka, Ltd Ptnr
EMP: 30
SALES (est): 2.4MM Privately Held
SIC: 7997 Country club, membership

(G-3505)
DSS INSTALLATIONS LTD
Also Called: Dss/Direct TV
6717 Montgomery Rd (45236-3816)
P.O. Box 36520 (45236-0520)
PHONE..................513 761-7000
Fax: 513 891-0067
Allen Sheff, Partner
EMP: 30 EST: 1990
SQ FT: 12,000
SALES: 2.8MM Privately Held
SIC: 5731 1731 7622 Antennas, satellite dish; cable television installation; antenna repair & installation

(G-3506)
DUKE ENERGY BECKJORD LLC
139 E 4th St (45202-4034)
PHONE..................513 287-2561
Charles Whitlock, Principal
Tracy Hemsink,
EMP: 1963
SALES (est): 71.8MM
SALES (corp-wide): 23.5B Publicly Held
SIC: 4911 Electric services
HQ: Duke Energy Ohio, Inc.
139 E 4th St
Cincinnati OH 45202
704 382-3853

(G-3507)
DUKE ENERGY KENTUCKY INC
Also Called: DUKE ENERGY OHIO
139 E 4th St (45202-4034)
PHONE..................704 594-6200
James Rogers, CEO
Michael Gribler, General Mgr
Robert Hall, General Mgr
David Knue, General Mgr
Jackson H Randolph, Chairman
EMP: 200
SQ FT: 300,000
SALES: 440.7MM
SALES (corp-wide): 23.5B Publicly Held
SIC: 4932 4931 Gas & other services combined; electric & other services combined
HQ: Duke Energy Ohio, Inc.
139 E 4th St
Cincinnati OH 45202
704 382-3853

(G-3508)
DUKE ENERGY OHIO INC (HQ)
139 E 4th St (45202-4034)
PHONE..................704 382-3853
Lynn J Good, CEO

Cincinnati - Hamilton County (G-3509)

Kimberly Timmons, *General Mgr*
Brian D Savoy, *Senior VP*
Patti Resor, *Buyer*
Clararesa Toney, *Engineer*
▲ **EMP:** 100
SALES: 1.9B
SALES (corp-wide): 23.5B **Publicly Held**
SIC: 4911 4922 4924 4931 Electric services; distribution, electric power; generation, electric power; transmission, electric power; natural gas transmission; natural gas distribution; electric & other services combined
PA: Duke Energy Corporation
550 S Tryon St
Charlotte NC 28202
704 382-3853

(G-3509)
DUKE ENERGY OHIO INC
Also Called: Montfort Heights
5445 Audro Dr (45247-7001)
PHONE.................................800 544-6900
Rick Hicks, *Project Mgr*
John L King, *Opers Staff*
Eric Stolzenberger, *Branch Mgr*
EMP: 129
SALES (corp-wide): 23.5B **Publicly Held**
SIC: 4911 Electric services
HQ: Duke Energy Ohio, Inc.
139 E 4th St
Cincinnati OH 45202
704 382-3853

(G-3510)
DUKE ENERGY OHIO INC
Also Called: Brecon Distribution Center
7600 E Kemper Rd (45249-1610)
P.O. Box 5385 (45201-5385)
PHONE.................................513 287-1120
Darrell Ingel, *Branch Mgr*
EMP: 25
SALES (corp-wide): 23.5B **Publicly Held**
SIC: 4911 Electric services
HQ: Duke Energy Ohio, Inc.
139 E 4th St
Cincinnati OH 45202
704 382-3853

(G-3511)
DUKE ENERGY OHIO INC
Also Called: Duke Enrgy Ohio Cstmer Svc Ctr
3300 Central Pkwy (45225-2307)
PHONE.................................513 421-9500
Barb Stang, *Manager*
EMP: 200
SALES (corp-wide): 23.5B **Publicly Held**
SIC: 8742 Management consulting services
HQ: Duke Energy Ohio, Inc.
139 E 4th St
Cincinnati OH 45202
704 382-3853

(G-3512)
DUNBAR ARMORED INC
1257 W 7th St (45203-1001)
PHONE.................................513 381-8000
Fax: 513 381-0511
Brian Baker, *Manager*
EMP: 40
SALES (corp-wide): 700.1MM **Privately Held**
WEB: www.dunbararmored.com
SIC: 7381 Armored car services
PA: Dunbar Armored, Inc.
50 Schilling Rd
Hunt Valley MD 21031
410 584-9800

(G-3513)
DUNCAN AVIATION INC
358 Wilmer Ave 121 (45226-1832)
PHONE.................................513 873-7523
Jeremy Rutherford, *Branch Mgr*
EMP: 66
SALES (corp-wide): 240.9MM **Privately Held**
SIC: 4581 Aircraft maintenance & repair services
PA: Duncan Aviation, Inc.
3701 Aviation Rd
Lincoln NE 68524
402 475-2611

(G-3514)
DUNNHUMBY INC
3825 Edwards Rd Ste 600 (45209-1293)
PHONE.................................513 579-3400
Simon Hay, *CEO*
Linda David, *Vice Pres*
Bill Sandman, *Technology*
Joann Wright, *Associate Dir*
EMP: 59
SALES (est): 15.7MM
SALES (corp-wide): 69.9B **Privately Held**
SIC: 8742 Marketing consulting services
PA: Tesco Plc
Tesco House
Welwyn Garden City HERTS AL7 1
800 505-555

(G-3515)
DURGA LLC
11320 Chester Rd (45246-4003)
PHONE.................................513 771-2080
Vijaya K Vemulapalli, *Mng Member*
Sasikala Vemulapalli,
EMP: 99
SALES (est): 4MM **Privately Held**
SIC: 7011 5812 5091 Hotels; American restaurant; water slides (recreation park)

(G-3516)
DVA HEALTHCARE - SOUTH
Also Called: Western Hills Dialysis
3267 Westbourne Dr (45248-5110)
PHONE.................................513 347-0444
Theresa Underwood, *Principal*
EMP: 25 **Publicly Held**
WEB: www.us.gambro.com
SIC: 8092 Kidney dialysis centers
HQ: Dva Healthcare - Southwest Ohio, Llc
1210 Hicks Blvd
Fairfield OH 45014

(G-3517)
DXP ENTERPRISES INC
5177 Spring Grove Ave (45217-1050)
PHONE.................................513 242-2227
Scott McCarthy, *Site Mgr*
EMP: 28 **Publicly Held**
SIC: 5084 5063 Industrial machinery & equipment; electrical apparatus & equipment
PA: Dxp Enterprises, Inc.
7272 Pinemont Dr
Houston TX 77040

(G-3518)
DYNCORP
26 W Mrtin Lther King Dr (45220-2242)
PHONE.................................513 569-7415
Dennis M McMullen, *Prgrmr*
Michael Johnson,
EMP: 70
SALES (corp-wide): 16.3B **Privately Held**
WEB: www.dyncorp.com
SIC: 7373 Systems integration services
PA: Dyncorp Llc
1700 Old Meadow Rd
Mc Lean VA 22102
571 722-0210

(G-3519)
E & A PEDCO SERVICES INC (PA)
11499 Chester Rd Ste 501 (45246-4012)
PHONE.................................513 782-4920
Fax: 513 782-4950
Kenneth Hover, *CEO*
William Giesler, *President*
Jerome W Doerger, *Vice Pres*
Philip Lambing, *Vice Pres*
Steve Weidner, *Vice Pres*
EMP: 75
SQ FT: 12,250
SALES (est): 10.7MM **Privately Held**
WEB: www.pedcoea.com
SIC: 8711 8712 7389 Consulting engineer; architectural engineering; interior designer

(G-3520)
E & J GALLO WINERY
125 E Court St (45202-1212)
PHONE.................................513 381-4050
Holly McClelland, *Manager*
Julie Fisher, *Manager*
EMP: 38
SALES (corp-wide): 2.1B **Privately Held**
SIC: 5182 Wine
PA: E. & J. Gallo Winery
600 Yosemite Blvd
Modesto CA 95354
209 341-3111

(G-3521)
E & J TRAILER LEASING INC
610 Wayne Park Dr Ste 5 (45215-2847)
PHONE.................................513 563-7366
Edward John Focke, *President*
Edward John Focke Jr, *Vice Pres*
EMP: 30
SALES (est): 2MM **Privately Held**
SIC: 7519 Trailer rental

(G-3522)
E & J TRAILER SALES & SERVICE
610 Wayne Park Dr Ste 5 (45215-2847)
PHONE.................................513 563-2550
Fax: 513 563-4391
Edward Focke, *President*
Connie Cornelius, *Treasurer*
EMP: 35
SQ FT: 40,000
SALES (est): 1.4MM **Privately Held**
WEB: www.ejtrailer.com
SIC: 7519 Trailer rental

(G-3523)
E A ZICKA CO
2714 East Tower Dr Ofc (45238-2699)
PHONE.................................513 451-1440
Fax: 513 451-1499
EMP: 50 **EST:** 1938
SQ FT: 1,500
SALES (est): 1.8MM **Privately Held**
SIC: 6513 1521 6531 Apartment Building Operator Single-Family House Construction Real Estate Agent/Manager

(G-3524)
E J ROBINSON GLASS CO
Also Called: Andy's Mirror and Glass
5618 Center Hill Ave (45216-2306)
PHONE.................................513 242-9250
Fax: 513 482-3764
Robert Diers, *CEO*
Rick Schiller, *President*
EMP: 30
SQ FT: 22,000
SALES: 4MM **Privately Held**
WEB: www.andysmirror.com
SIC: 1793 Glass & glazing work

(G-3525)
E&I CONSTRUCTION LLC
1210 Sycamore St Ste 200 (45202-7321)
PHONE.................................513 421-2045
EMP: 35 **EST:** 2001
SQ FT: 6,000
SALES (est): 2.6MM **Privately Held**
SIC: 1771 Concrete Contractors

(G-3526)
EA VICA CO
Also Called: Four Towers Apts
2714 E Twr Dr Ofc Ste 007 (45238)
PHONE.................................513 481-3500
Edwin Vica, *Owner*
EMP: 30 **EST:** 2001
SALES (est): 906.3K **Privately Held**
SIC: 6513 Apartment building operators

(G-3527)
EAGLE FINANCIAL BANCORP INC (PA)
6415 Bridgetown Rd (45248-2934)
PHONE.................................513 574-0700
James W Braun, *Ch of Bd*
Gary J Koester, *President*
Patricia L Walter, *Exec VP*
Kevin R Schramm, *CFO*
EMP: 28
SALES: 6.4MM **Publicly Held**
SIC: 6035 Savings institutions, federally chartered

(G-3528)
EAGLE REALTY GROUP LLC (DH)
421 E 4th St (45202-3317)
P.O. Box 1091 (45201-1091)
PHONE.................................513 361-7700
Fax: 513 361-7701
Mario San Marco, *President*
Thomas M Stapleton, *Senior VP*
Cynthia Bucco, *Assistant VP*
Andrew Stclair, *Assistant VP*
Rob Alpern, *Vice Pres*
EMP: 37
SQ FT: 49,200
SALES (est): 8.1MM **Privately Held**
SIC: 6531 6552 Real estate managers; land subdividers & developers, commercial
HQ: The Western & Southern Life Insurance Company
400 Broadway St
Cincinnati OH 45202
513 629-1800

(G-3529)
EAGLEBURGMANN KE INC (DH)
Also Called: Eagle Burgmann EXT Joint Sol
3478 Hauck Rd (45241-4604)
PHONE.................................859 746-0091
Juergem Peschla, *CEO*
Hans Hansford, *Vice Pres*
Jose Antunes, *CFO*
Shannon Sweeney, *Controller*
Hans V Hansen, *Director*
▲ **EMP:** 37
SQ FT: 6,000
SALES (est): 5.7MM
SALES (corp-wide): 8.3B **Privately Held**
SIC: 7699 Industrial equipment services
HQ: Eagleburgmann Ke A/S
Park Alle 34
Vejen 6600
753 649-88

(G-3530)
EARLE M JORGENSEN COMPANY
Also Called: EMJ Cincinnati
601 Redna Ter (45215-1108)
PHONE.................................513 771-3223
Fax: 513 771-6734
James Stewart, *Mfg Staff*
Pat Byrne, *Personnel*
Matt Hinkel, *Sales Staff*
Larry Johantgen, *Sales Associate*
Jeff Stethens, *Branch Mgr*
EMP: 30
SQ FT: 10,000
SALES (corp-wide): 9.7B **Publicly Held**
WEB: www.emjmetals.com
SIC: 5051 Steel
HQ: Earle M. Jorgensen Company
10650 Alameda St
Lynwood CA 90262
323 567-1122

(G-3531)
EAST GALBRAITH HEALTH CARE CTR (PA)
3889 E Galbraith Rd (45236-1514)
PHONE.................................513 984-5220
Henry Schneider, *President*
Raymond Schneider, *Treasurer*
Debbie Spicer, *Human Resources*
Bud Walters, *Marketing Staff*
Craig Smith, *Info Tech Dir*
EMP: 252
SQ FT: 7,245
SALES (est): 6.3MM **Privately Held**
SIC: 8059 Nursing home, except skilled & intermediate care facility

(G-3532)
EAST GALBRAITH NURSING HOME
3889 E Galbraith Rd (45236-1597)
PHONE.................................513 984-5220
Henry Schneider, *President*
Jodie Watson, *Personnel*
Tammy Griffen, *Nursing Dir*
Penny Coffey, *Hlthcr Dir*
Brian Hill, *Administration*
EMP: 250
SQ FT: 48,000

GEOGRAPHIC SECTION
Cincinnati - Hamilton County (G-3557)

SALES (est): 4.8MM **Privately Held**
SIC: 8052 8051 Intermediate care facilities; skilled nursing care facilities

(G-3533)
EASTER SEALS TRISTATE LLC (PA)
2901 Gilbert Ave (45206-1211)
PHONE..................513 281-2316
Greg McGruder, *Prdtn Mgr*
David Wolfzorn, *CFO*
Christina Wolnitzek, *Accountant*
Pam Green, *Mng Member*
David Dreith, *Manager*
EMP: 60
SQ FT: 22,000
SALES (est): 17.2MM **Privately Held**
SIC: 8331 Sheltered workshop

(G-3534)
EASTER SEALS TRISTATE LLC
Also Called: Walnut Hills Center Location
447 Morgan St (45206-2347)
PHONE..................513 475-6791
Fax: 513 861-6248
David Dreith, *Manager*
Calista Stone, *Manager*
EMP: 120
SQ FT: 4,000
SALES (corp-wide): 17.2MM **Privately Held**
SIC: 8322 Individual & family services
PA: Easter Seals Tristate Llc
2901 Gilbert Ave
Cincinnati OH 45206
513 281-2316

(G-3535)
EASTERN HILL INTERNAL MEDICINE
8000 5 Mile Rd Ste 305 (45230-2188)
PHONE..................513 232-3500
Fax: 513 624-2704
David G Wilson MD, *Owner*
EMP: 25
SALES (est): 1.5MM **Privately Held**
SIC: 8011 Internal medicine, physician/surgeon

(G-3536)
EASTERN HILLS PEDIATRIC ASSOC
Also Called: Eastern Hills Pediatrics
7502 State Rd Ste 3350 (45255-2801)
PHONE..................513 231-3345
Fax: 513 231-6739
John E Furby, *Principal*
Nancy Chabot, *Administration*
Jennifer McCachran, *Administration*
EMP: 35
SALES (est): 4.2MM **Privately Held**
WEB: www.ehpeds.com
SIC: 8011 Pediatrician

(G-3537)
EASTGATE ANIMAL HOSPITAL INC
459 Old State Route 74 (45244-4210)
PHONE..................513 528-0700
Fax: 513 528-3149
Todd A Phillips, *President*
EMP: 25
SALES (est): 1.2MM **Privately Held**
WEB: www.eastgateanimal.com
SIC: 0742 Veterinarian, animal specialties

(G-3538)
EASTSIDE BODY SHOP
7636 Beechmont Ave (45255-4202)
PHONE..................513 624-1145
Bill Woeste, *President*
EMP: 25
SALES (est): 1.2MM **Privately Held**
SIC: 7532 Body shop, automotive

(G-3539)
EASTSIDE ROOFG RESTORATION CO
417 Purcell Ave (45205-2245)
PHONE..................513 471-0434
James Connaire, *Owner*
EMP: 30
SALES (est): 855.1K **Privately Held**
SIC: 1761 Roof repair

(G-3540)
EBENEZER ROAD CORP
Also Called: Western Hills Retirement Vlg
6210 Cleves Warsaw Pike (45233-4510)
PHONE..................513 941-0099
Barry A Kohn, *President*
Sam Boymel, *Chairman*
Harold Sosna, *Vice Pres*
Tammy Gates, *Human Res Mgr*
Keith Vogelsang, *Info Tech Mgr*
EMP: 250
SQ FT: 150,000
SALES (est): 17.8MM **Privately Held**
SIC: 6513 8052 8051 Retirement hotel operation; intermediate care facilities; skilled nursing care facilities

(G-3541)
ECKERT FIRE PROTEC
510 W Benson St (45215-3106)
PHONE..................513 948-1030
Fax: 513 948-1039
Don Eckert, *President*
Alyson Nahrup, *Manager*
Mary Ann Eckert, *Admin Sec*
EMP: 50
SQ FT: 6,000
SALES (est): 7.5MM **Privately Held**
WEB: www.eckertfireprotection.com
SIC: 1711 Sprinkler contractors

(G-3542)
ECKSTEIN ROOFING COMPANY
264 Stille Dr (45233-1647)
PHONE..................513 941-1511
Fax: 513 941-1572
James Eckstein Jr, *President*
Jane Gruber, *Manager*
EMP: 30
SQ FT: 12,000
SALES (est): 5.6MM **Privately Held**
SIC: 1761 Sheet metalwork; roofing contractor

(G-3543)
ECO ENGINEERING INC
Also Called: Consolidated Lighting Svcs Co
11815 Highway Dr Ste 600 (45241-2065)
PHONE..................513 985-8300
Thomas Kirkpatrick, *President*
Garry G Buttermann I, *Manager*
Clint Gonzales, *Manager*
Susan Kirkpatrick, *Admin Sec*
EMP: 58
SQ FT: 11,000
SALES (est): 16MM **Privately Held**
WEB: www.ecoengineering.com
SIC: 1731 General electrical contractor

(G-3544)
ECOTAGE
11700 Princeton Pike # 4 (45246-2535)
PHONE..................513 782-2229
Teggy Sova, *Manager*
EMP: 40
SALES (est): 293.7K **Privately Held**
SIC: 7231 Beauty shops

(G-3545)
ELBE PROPERTIES (PA)
Also Called: Janus Hotel and Resort
8534 E Kemper Rd (45249-3701)
PHONE..................513 489-1955
Fax: 513 489-1224
Louis S Beck, *Partner*
Harry Yeaggy, *Partner*
EMP: 700
SQ FT: 6,000
SALES (est): 19.4MM **Privately Held**
SIC: 7011 7033 Motels; campgrounds

(G-3546)
ELECTRIC MOTOR TECH LLC (PA)
Also Called: Emt
5217 Beech St (45217-1021)
PHONE..................513 821-9999
Fax: 513 821-9960
F Daniel Freshley, *Mng Member*
Kennie Hennery, *Manager*
Andy Butz,
Dwaine York,
EMP: 42 EST: 1999
SQ FT: 30,000
SALES (est): 9.3MM **Privately Held**
WEB: www.electricmotortech.com
SIC: 7629 5063 Electrical repair shops; motors, electric

(G-3547)
ELECTRIC SERVICE CO INC
5331 Hetzzel St (45227-1513)
PHONE..................513 271-6387
Fax: 513 271-0543
Helen Snyder, *President*
Todd Benadum, *Manager*
EMP: 34
SQ FT: 35,000
SALES (est): 6.1MM **Privately Held**
WEB: www.electricservice.com
SIC: 7629 3677 3621 Electronic equipment repair; transformers power supply, electronic type; phase or rotary converters (electrical equipment)

(G-3548)
ELECTROL SYSTEMS INC
1380 Kemper Meadow Dr (45240-1634)
PHONE..................513 942-7777
Fax: 513 942-7818
David C Staiger, *President*
John Hughes, *Accounts Mgr*
Terry Childers, *Manager*
Dewayne Scudder, *Manager*
EMP: 25
SQ FT: 13,750
SALES (est): 4MM **Privately Held**
WEB: www.electrolsystems.cc
SIC: 8711 Electrical or electronic engineering

(G-3549)
ELECTRONIC REGISTRY SYSTEMS
155 Tri County Pkwy # 110 (45246-3238)
PHONE..................513 771-7330
Fax: 513 771-5277
Ashok Ramaswamy, *President*
Todd Carter, *Manager*
Elijah Bialik, *Software Dev*
EMP: 25
SQ FT: 1,000
SALES (est): 2.6MM **Privately Held**
WEB: www.ers-can.com
SIC: 7371 Computer software development

(G-3550)
ELEVAR DESIGN GROUP INC
Also Called: Sfa Architects
300 W 4th St (45202-2665)
PHONE..................513 721-0600
Fax: 513 721-0611
Emilio Thomas Fernandez, *CEO*
Kim Patton, *COO*
Greg Otis, *Senior VP*
Evan Eagle, *Project Mgr*
Matthew King, *Project Mgr*
EMP: 49
SQ FT: 2,000
SALES (est): 4.8MM **Privately Held**
WEB: www.sfa-architects.com
SIC: 8712 7389 Architectural engineering; design services

(G-3551)
ELLIOTT DAVIS LLC
201 E 5th St Ste 2100 (45202-4230)
PHONE..................513 579-1717
Fax: 513 579-1729
Kathy Mitts,
EMP: 25
SALES (corp-wide): 60.8MM **Privately Held**
SIC: 8721 Accounting services, except auditing; certified public accountant
PA: Elliott Davis, Llc
200 E Broad St Ste 500
Greenville SC 29601
864 242-3370

(G-3552)
EMCOR FACILITIES SERVICES INC (HQ)
Also Called: Viox Services
9655 Reading Rd (45215-3513)
PHONE..................888 846-9462
Fax: 513 679-3310
Mike Viox, *President*
Bob Harris, *General Mgr*
Ed Fagaly, *Superintendent*
Matthew Fetters, *Regional Mgr*
Mike Orebaugh, *Business Mgr*
EMP: 100 EST: 1946
SQ FT: 38,000
SALES: 307.4MM
SALES (corp-wide): 7.6B **Publicly Held**
WEB: www.viox-services.com
SIC: 8744 Facilities support services
PA: Emcor Group, Inc.
301 Merritt 7 Fl 6
Norwalk CT 06851
203 849-7800

(G-3553)
EMERSION DESIGN LLC
310 Culvert St Ste 100 (45202-2229)
PHONE..................513 841-9100
Fax: 513 841-9222
Alan Hautman,
James Cheng,
Roger Curran,
Chad Edwards,
Steve Kimball,
EMP: 28
SQ FT: 5,000
SALES (est): 3.3MM **Privately Held**
WEB: www.emersiondesign.com
SIC: 8711 7389 8748 8712 Structural engineering; design services; urban planning & consulting services; architectural services; architectural engineering

(G-3554)
EMPOWER MEDIAMARKETING INC (PA)
15 E 14th St (45202-7001)
PHONE..................513 871-7779
Jim Price, *President*
Natalie Dalton, *Vice Pres*
Julie Pahutski, *Vice Pres*
Lori Glover, *Buyer*
Amy Lorensen, *Buyer*
EMP: 150
SQ FT: 40,000
SALES (est): 18.4MM **Privately Held**
WEB: www.empowermm.com
SIC: 7319 Media buying service

(G-3555)
ENCLOSURE SUPPLIERS LLC
Also Called: Champion
12119 Champion Way (45241-6419)
PHONE..................513 782-3900
Fax: 513 782-3903
Dennis Manes,
Keith Vermilyea, *Relations*
▲ EMP: 30
SQ FT: 160,000
SALES (est): 12.1MM
SALES (corp-wide): 515.7MM **Privately Held**
SIC: 3448 5031 3231 Prefabricated metal buildings; lumber, plywood & millwork; products of purchased glass
PA: Champion Opco, Llc
12121 Champion Way
Cincinnati OH 45241
513 924-4858

(G-3556)
ENCOMPASS HEALTH CORPORATION
Also Called: HealthSouth
151 W Galbraith Rd (45216-1015)
PHONE..................513 418-5600
Sholloy Borry, *Mktg Dir*
Joseph Steger, *Branch Mgr*
Deana Barone, *Case Mgr*
Yvette Jackson, *Nursing Dir*
Joe Walsh, *Pharmacy Dir*
EMP: 113
SALES (corp-wide): 3.9B **Publicly Held**
SIC: 8069 Specialty hospitals, except psychiatric
PA: Encompass Health Corporation
3660 Grandview Pkwy
Birmingham AL 35243
205 967-7116

(G-3557)
ENERFAB INC (PA)
4955 Spring Grove Ave (45232-1925)
PHONE..................513 641-0500
Fax: 513 641-1821
Wendell R Bell, *CEO*

Cincinnati - Hamilton County (G-3558)

Jeffrey P Hock, *President*
Dave Herche, *Chairman*
Jeffrey R Aasch, *Exec VP*
Mark Schoettmer, *Vice Pres*
▲ **EMP:** 330
SQ FT: 180,000
SALES (est): 621.1MM **Privately Held**
WEB: www.enerfab.com
SIC: 3443 1629 1541 1711 Tanks, standard or custom fabricated; metal plate; power plant construction; land reclamation; industrial buildings & warehouses; mechanical contractor; process piping contractor; painting, coating & hot dipping

(G-3558)
ENGLE MANAGEMENT GROUP
867 Yarger Dr (45230-3540)
PHONE.................................513 232-9729
EMP: 51
SALES (est): 1.7MM **Privately Held**
SIC: 7299 Misc Personal Services

(G-3559)
ENTERPRISE HOLDINGS INC
Also Called: Enterprise Rent-A-Car
3670 Park 42 Dr (45241-2072)
PHONE.................................937 879-0023
Fax: 513 956-3811
Mike Cullen, *Controller*
Leandra Carlfeldt, *Manager*
Madeline Stoddard, *Supervisor*
EMP: 40
SALES (corp-wide): 6.1B **Privately Held**
SIC: 7514 7515 Rent-a-car service; passenger car leasing
HQ: Enterprise Holdings, Inc.
   600 Corporate Park Dr
   Saint Louis MO 63105
   314 512-5000

(G-3560)
ENTERPRISE VENDING INC
895 Glendale Milford Rd (45215-1136)
PHONE.................................513 772-1373
Fax: 513 791-7180
Ron Patiya, *Manager*
EMP: 30
SALES (corp-wide): 14MM **Privately Held**
SIC: 4225 7699 General warehousing & storage; vending machine repair
PA: Enterprise Vending, Inc.
   895 Glendale Milford Rd
   Cincinnati OH
   513 791-7070

(G-3561)
ENVIRONMENTAL ENTERPRISES INC
Also Called: Eei-Plant
4650 Spring Grove Ave (45232-1920)
PHONE.................................513 541-1823
Fax: 513 541-1638
Gary Brunner, *Info Tech Mgr*
Dan McCabe, *Systems Staff*
EMP: 82
SALES (corp-wide): 24.7MM **Privately Held**
WEB: www.eeienv.com
SIC: 4953 Recycling, waste materials
PA: Environmental Enterprises Inc
   10163 Cncinnati Dayton Rd
   Cincinnati OH 45241
   513 772-2818

(G-3562)
ENVIRONMENTAL QUALITY MGT (HQ)
Also Called: E Q M
1800 Carillion Blvd 100 (45240-2788)
PHONE.................................513 825-7500
Fred Nichols, *President*
Brenda Reid, *General Mgr*
Ronald L Hawks, *Vice Pres*
John R Kominsky, *Vice Pres*
Robert G McCullough, *Vice Pres*
EMP: 88
SQ FT: 30,000
SALES (est): 47.1MM **Publicly Held**
WEB: www.eqm.com
SIC: 8711 Consulting engineer

(G-3563)
ENVIRONMENTAL SOLUTIONS (PA)
4525 Este Ave (45232-1762)
PHONE.................................513 451-1777
Virgil Brack Jr, *President*
Bryan Bayer, *Regional Mgr*
Taina Pankiewicz, *COO*
Casey Swecker, *Vice Pres*
Taina Brack, *CFO*
EMP: 34
SQ FT: 8,000
SALES: 5.4MM **Privately Held**
WEB: www.environmentalsi.com
SIC: 8748 Environmental consultant

(G-3564)
ENVISION CORPORATION
Also Called: Envision Children
8 Enfield St Ste 4 (45218-1433)
PHONE.................................513 772-5437
Matthew Hughes, *Exec Dir*
EMP: 53
SQ FT: 2,000
SALES: 248K **Privately Held**
SIC: 8748 Testing service, educational or personnel

(G-3565)
EPIPHEO INCORPORATED
Also Called: Epipheo Studios
700 W Pete Rose Way 450 (45203-1892)
PHONE.................................888 687-7620
John Herman, *CEO*
Lucas Cole, *Principal*
Chris Molnar, *Editor*
Dan Chaney, *Controller*
Daniel Chaney, *Accountant*
EMP: 40 **EST:** 2009
SALES: 20MM **Privately Held**
SIC: 7311 8742 Advertising agencies; marketing consulting services

(G-3566)
EPISCOPAL RETIREMENT HOMES
3870 Virginia Ave Ste 2 (45227-3427)
PHONE.................................513 271-9610
Kathleen Ison-Lind,
EMP: 68
SALES (est): 897.2K **Privately Held**
SIC: 6513 Retirement hotel operation

(G-3567)
EPISCOPAL RETIREMENT HOMES INC (PA)
3870 Virginia Ave Ste 2 (45227-3427)
PHONE.................................513 271-9610
Fax: 513 271-9648
R Douglas Spitler, *CEO*
Kathy Ison, *Vice Pres*
Nel Paul Scheper, *Vice Pres*
Paul Scheper, *CFO*
Paul J Scheper, *CFO*
EMP: 25
SQ FT: 6,900
SALES: 32.8MM **Privately Held**
WEB: www.erhinc.com
SIC: 8361 8322 8051 Home for the aged; senior citizens' center or association; old age assistance; skilled nursing care facilities

(G-3568)
EPISCOPAL RETIREMENT HOMES INC
3939 Erie Ave (45208-1954)
PHONE.................................513 561-6363
Fax: 513 561-2064
Laura Lamb, *Branch Mgr*
EMP: 36
SALES (corp-wide): 32.8MM **Privately Held**
WEB: www.erhinc.com
SIC: 8361 Home for the aged
PA: Episcopal Retirement Homes, Inc.
   3870 Virginia Ave Ste 2
   Cincinnati OH 45227
   513 271-9610

(G-3569)
EPISCOPAL RETIREMENT HOMES INC
Also Called: Marjorie P Lee Rtirement Cmnty
3550 Shaw Ave Ofc (45208-1416)
PHONE.................................513 871-2090
Fax: 513 871-4993
Mary Collins, *Manager*
Donald Nunlist-Young, *Director*
Ginny Uehlin, *Administration*
EMP: 180
SQ FT: 2,850
SALES (corp-wide): 32.8MM **Privately Held**
WEB: www.erhinc.com
SIC: 8361 Home for the aged
PA: Episcopal Retirement Homes, Inc.
   3870 Virginia Ave Ste 2
   Cincinnati OH 45227
   513 271-9610

(G-3570)
EQUITY DIAMOND BROKERS INC (PA)
Also Called: Eddie Lane's Diamond Showroom
9301 Montgomery Rd (45242-7701)
PHONE.................................513 793-4760
Fax: 513 793-3538
Edmund Lane, *President*
Ted Bevis, *Corp Secy*
Patrick Higgins, *Vice Pres*
Cindy Lange, *Vice Pres*
EMP: 45
SQ FT: 7,000
SALES (est): 11MM **Privately Held**
WEB: www.edbsonline.com
SIC: 5094 5944 Jewelry; jewelry stores

(G-3571)
EQUITY RESOURCES INC
130 Tri County Pkwy # 108 (45246-3212)
PHONE.................................513 518-6318
Ed Rivor, *President*
EMP: 100
SALES (est): 78.9K **Privately Held**
SIC: 8742 6211 Business planning & organizing services; mortgages, buying & selling

(G-3572)
ERHAL INC
3870 Virginia Ave (45227-3431)
PHONE.................................513 272-5555
Paul Scheper, *CFO*
Elizabeth Ison, *Accountant*
EMP: 30
SALES (est): 1.3MM **Privately Held**
SIC: 6531 Cooperative apartment manager

(G-3573)
ERIC MOWER AND ASSOCIATES INC
830 Main St Fl 10 (45202-2186)
PHONE.................................513 381-8855
Karen Newman, *Business Mgr*
Jeff Everllein, *Branch Mgr*
Amanda Teemley, *Admin Asst*
EMP: 40
SALES (corp-wide): 32.1MM **Privately Held**
SIC: 7311 Advertising consultant
PA: Eric Mower And Associates, Inc.
   211 W Jefferson St Ste 1
   Syracuse NY 13202
   315 466-1000

(G-3574)
ERNEST V THOMAS JR (PA)
Also Called: Thomas & Thomas
2323 Park Ave (45206-2711)
PHONE.................................513 961-5311
Fax: 513 961-0075
Ernest V Thomas III, *Owner*
EMP: 50
SQ FT: 4,500
SALES (est): 4.4MM **Privately Held**
WEB: www.thomaslawfirm.com
SIC: 8111 General practice law office

(G-3575)
ERNST & YOUNG LLP
Also Called: Ey
312 Walnut St Ste 1900 (45202-4028)
PHONE.................................513 612-1400
Steven Beinlich, *Managing Prtnr*
Tom O'Neil, *Managing Prtnr*
Stanley Brown, *Partner*
Mark Doll, *Partner*
Steven Krekeler, *Partner*
EMP: 200
SALES (corp-wide): 5.3B **Privately Held**
WEB: www.ey.com
SIC: 8721 8742 Certified public accountant; auditing services; business consultant; management information systems consultant
PA: Ernst & Young Llp
   5 Times Sq Fl Conlv1
   New York NY 10036
   212 773-3000

(G-3576)
ERNST CORPORATION
9175 Governors Way (45249-2037)
PHONE.................................513 697-6970
Richard Geier, *President*
EMP: 30 **EST:** 1998
SALES (est): 404.1K **Privately Held**
SIC: 8351 Preschool center

(G-3577)
ESTREAMZ INC
1311 Vine St (45202-7118)
PHONE.................................513 278-7836
Travis Bea, *President*
EMP: 30
SQ FT: 15,000
SALES (est): 664.4K **Privately Held**
SIC: 7379 7372 7812 ; home entertainment computer software; motion picture production & distribution, television

(G-3578)
EUCLID HEALTH CARE INC (PA)
Also Called: Madeira Health Care Center
6940 Stiegler Ln (45243-2635)
PHONE.................................513 561-4105
Fax: 513 561-2450
Harold Sosna, *President*
Cindy Wagner, *Data Proc Staff*
Kris Rolfsen, *Director*
EMP: 128
SALES: 8MM **Privately Held**
SIC: 8051 Skilled nursing care facilities

(G-3579)
EVANSTON BULLDOGS YOUTH FOOTBA
3060 Durrell Ave (45207-1716)
PHONE.................................513 254-9500
Peterson Mingo, *Principal*
Milan Lanier, *Vice Pres*
EMP: 30
SALES (est): 428.9K **Privately Held**
SIC: 7389

(G-3580)
EVERGREEN PHARMACEUTICAL LLC (DH)
201 E 4th St Ste 900 (45202-4160)
PHONE.................................513 719-2600
Carl Wood, *President*
EMP: 300
SQ FT: 40,000
SALES (est): 66.4MM
SALES (corp-wide): 184.7B **Publicly Held**
SIC: 5122 Pharmaceuticals
HQ: Omnicare Holding Company
   1105 Market St Ste 1300
   Cincinnati OH 45215
   513 719-2600

(G-3581)
EVERGREEN PHRM CAL INC (DH)
201 E 4th St Ste 900 (45202-4160)
PHONE.................................513 719-2600
Elizabeth A Haley, *President*
Vickey Summers, *Supervisor*
EMP: 38 **EST:** 2004
SALES (est): 20.6MM
SALES (corp-wide): 184.7B **Publicly Held**
WEB: www.omnicare.com
SIC: 5122 Pharmaceuticals

GEOGRAPHIC SECTION
Cincinnati - Hamilton County (G-3603)

HQ: Omnicare Holding Company
1105 Market St Ste 1300
Cincinnati OH 45215
513 719-2600

(G-3582)
EVERS WELDING CO INC
4849 Blue Rock Rd (45247-5504)
P.O. Box 53426 (45253-0426)
PHONE..................................513 385-7352
Fax: 513 385-7322
Edward G Evers, *President*
Jacqueline Evers, *Corp Secy*
EMP: 40
SQ FT: 3,000
SALES (est): 4.5MM **Privately Held**
WEB: www.everssteel.com
SIC: 1791 3441 Structural steel erection; fabricated structural metal

(G-3583)
EVERY CHILD SUCCEEDS
3333 Burnet Ave (45229-3026)
PHONE..................................513 636-2830
Fax: 513 636-2460
Judith Van Ginkle, *President*
David Clark, *Vice Pres*
Jodie Short, *Research*
Julie Massie, *Consultant*
Margaret Clark, *Program Dir*
EMP: 150
SALES: 9.3MM **Privately Held**
WEB: www.everychildsucceeds.com
SIC: 8082 Home health care services

(G-3584)
EVOLUTION CRTIVE SOLUTIONS LLC
7107 Shona Dr Ste 110 (45237-3808)
PHONE..................................513 681-4450
Cathy Lindemann, *President*
Cathy Welz, *Accounting Mgr*
EMP: 25
SQ FT: 14,000
SALES: 3MM **Privately Held**
SIC: 7336 2759 5199 7389 Graphic arts & related design; commercial printing; advertising specialties; embroidering of advertising on shirts, etc.; screen printing; manmade fiber & silk broadwoven fabrics

(G-3585)
EXCELLENCE ALLIANCE GROUP INC
700 Walnut St Ste 210 (45202-2015)
PHONE..................................513 619-4800
Fax: 513 619-4801
Michael Baker, *President*
Justin Baker, *Marketing Staff*
EMP: 25
SQ FT: 20,000
SALES (est): 1.5MM **Privately Held**
WEB: www.eainet.com
SIC: 8742 1711 Business consultant; mechanical contractor

(G-3586)
EXECUTIVE JET MANAGEMENT INC (DH)
4556 Airport Rd (45226-1601)
PHONE..................................513 979-6600
Fax: 513 979-6720
Robert Molsbergen, *President*
Diane McLoughlin, *Regional Mgr*
Rebecca Bursk, *Senior VP*
Rob Schalk, *Senior VP*
Jeff Cropper, *Vice Pres*
EMP: 280
SQ FT: 78,000
SALES (est): 67.8MM
SALES (corp-wide): 242.1B **Publicly Held**
WEB: www.executivejetmanagement.com
SIC: 4522 8741 4581 4512 Flying charter service; management services; airports, flying fields & services; air transportation, scheduled
HQ: Netjets Inc.
4111 Bridgeway Ave
Columbus OH 43219
614 239-5500

(G-3587)
FACILITIES MGT SOLUTIONS LLC
250 W Court St (45202-1088)
PHONE..................................513 639-2230
Alex Riveira, *Executive*
Ben Kaplan,
Mike Murdock,
EMP: 25
SALES (est): 1.6MM
SALES (corp-wide): 1.5B **Privately Held**
WEB: www.hochtief.de
SIC: 8742 Administrative services consultant
HQ: Hochtief Ag
Opernplatz 2
Essen 45128
201 824-0

(G-3588)
FACTORY MUTUAL INSURANCE CO
Also Called: FM Global
9 Woodcrest Dr (45246-2363)
PHONE..................................513 742-9516
Mary Breighner, *Branch Mgr*
Mary Brighner, *Manager*
EMP: 90
SALES (corp-wide): 4B **Privately Held**
SIC: 6411 Insurance agents
PA: Factory Mutual Insurance Co
270 Central Ave
Johnston RI 02919
401 275-3000

(G-3589)
FAMILY MEDICAL GROUP
6331 Glenway Ave (45211-6301)
PHONE..................................513 389-1400
Linda Behlmer, *Principal*
EMP: 26
SALES (est): 2.2MM **Privately Held**
SIC: 8011 General & family practice, physician/surgeon

(G-3590)
FAMILY MOTOR COACH ASSN INC (PA)
8291 Clough Pike (45244-2756)
PHONE..................................513 474-3622
Fax: 513 474-2332
Lana Makin, *CEO*
Kathie Balogh, *Vice Pres*
Bill Mallory, *Vice Pres*
Daniel Ball, *Project Mgr*
Pamela Kay, *Comms Dir*
EMP: 46
SQ FT: 22,000
SALES: 3.1MM **Privately Held**
WEB: www.fmca.com
SIC: 8641 2721 Social associations; magazines: publishing & printing

(G-3591)
FAMILY SERVICE (PA)
Also Called: United Way
3730 Glenway Ave (45205-1354)
PHONE..................................513 381-6300
Fax: 513 921-8222
Arlene Herman, *President*
John Sarra, *Vice Pres*
Mark Schneider, *Vice Pres*
Lauren Brown, *Marketing Staff*
Tim Barney, *Info Tech Mgr*
EMP: 50
SQ FT: 10,500
SALES (est): 5.7MM **Privately Held**
WEB: www.mricinci.com
SIC: 8322 Social service center

(G-3592)
FARM INC
239 Anderson Ferry Rd (45238-5638)
PHONE..................................513 922-7020
Fax: 513 922-7020
Dan Elsaesser, *President*
Dolores Elsaesser, *Chairman*
Sam Hendricks, *Purchasing*
Michael Honald, *Treasurer*
Michael Siebert, *Admin Sec*
EMP: 40
SQ FT: 21,600

SALES: 100K **Privately Held**
WEB: www.theplacetohaveaparty.com
SIC: 7299 5812 Banquet hall facilities; eating places

(G-3593)
FASCOR INC
11260 Chester Rd Ste 100 (45246-4079)
PHONE..................................513 421-1777
John Klare Jr, *President*
John Klare Sr, *Chairman*
Andrew Klare, *Vice Pres*
Ed Sachsendorfer, *Controller*
Dale Hogeback, *CTO*
EMP: 40 EST: 1978
SQ FT: 4,625
SALES (est): 4.7MM **Privately Held**
WEB: www.fascor.com
SIC: 7371 Computer software systems analysis & design, custom; computer software development

(G-3594)
FAY LIMITED PARTNERSHIP
Also Called: Fay Apartments
3710 President Dr (45225-1016)
PHONE..................................513 542-8333
Fax: 513 542-8764
Jerry Bowen, *Manager*
EMP: 35
SQ FT: 2,501
SALES (corp-wide): 2.3MM **Privately Held**
SIC: 6513 Apartment building operators
PA: Fay Limited Partnership
36 E 4th St 1320
Cincinnati OH 45202
513 241-1911

(G-3595)
FAY LIMITED PARTNERSHIP (PA)
36 E 4th St 1320 (45202-3725)
PHONE..................................513 241-1911
David Hendy, *Partner*
Ken Kerr, *Partner*
EMP: 35
SQ FT: 1,000,000
SALES (est): 2.3MM **Privately Held**
SIC: 6513 6531 Apartment building operators; real estate agents & managers

(G-3596)
FEDERAL HOME LN BNK CINCINNATI (PA)
600 Atrium Two # 2 (45201)
P.O. Box 598 (45201-0598)
PHONE..................................513 852-7500
Donald J Mullineaux, *Ch of Bd*
James A England, *Vice Ch Bd*
Andrew S Howell, *President*
Donald R Able, *COO*
R Kyle Lawler, *Exec VP*
EMP: 600
SQ FT: 79,000
SALES: 1.6B **Privately Held**
WEB: www.fhlbcin.com
SIC: 6019 Federal home loan banks

(G-3597)
FEDERAL HOME LN BNK CINCINNATI
1000 Atrium 2 (45202)
P.O. Box 598 (45201-0598)
PHONE..................................513 852-5719
Charles Thiemann, *Manager*
Mark Russell, *Manager*
Fermin Chavez, *Administration*
EMP: 80
SALES (corp-wide): 1.6B **Privately Held**
SIC: 6022 State commercial banks
PA: Federal Home Loan Bank Of Cincinnati
600 Atrium Two # 2
Cincinnati OH 45201
513 852-7500

(G-3598)
FEDERAL INSURANCE COMPANY
Also Called: Chubb
312 Walnut St Ste 2100 (45202-4083)
PHONE..................................513 721-0601
Fax: 513 651-6088
John Lafrance, *Opers Mgr*
Jeff Barton, *Marketing Mgr*

Gary Delong, *Manager*
Doug Daillie, *Manager*
Amy Kendall, *Manager*
EMP: 80
SALES (corp-wide): 28.7B **Privately Held**
WEB: www.federalinsurancecompany.com
SIC: 6411 Insurance agents, brokers & service
HQ: Federal Insurance Company
15 Mountainview Rd
Warren NJ 07059
908 903-2000

(G-3599)
FEDERAL RSRVE BNK OF CLEVELAND
150 E 4th St Fl 3 (45202-4181)
P.O. Box 999 (45201-0999)
PHONE..................................513 721-4787
Fax: 513 455-4583
James M Anderson, *Ch of Bd*
Barbara Henshaw, *General Mgr*
Kay Schimdt, *Opers Staff*
Nadine Wallman, *Property Mgr*
Glenn D Leveridge, *Director*
EMP: 225 **Privately Held**
WEB: www.clevelandfed.com
SIC: 6011 Federal reserve branches
HQ: The Federal Reserve Bank Of Cleveland
1455 E 6th St
Cleveland OH 44114
216 579-2000

(G-3600)
FELDKAMP ENTERPRISES INC
Also Called: Honeywell Authorized Dealer
3642 Muddy Creek Rd (45238-2044)
PHONE..................................513 347-4500
Fax: 513 347-4506
James E Feldkamp Jr, *President*
Bob Damron, *Project Mgr*
Scott Davis, *Project Mgr*
Dan Gindele, *Project Mgr*
Dan Lewis, *Project Mgr*
EMP: 200
SQ FT: 40,000
SALES (est): 70.5MM **Privately Held**
SIC: 1711 Ventilation & duct work contractor

(G-3601)
FELDYS
8060 Beechmont Ave (45255-3145)
PHONE..................................513 474-2212
Fax: 513 474-4867
Brian Feldkamp, *Owner*
EMP: 70
SALES (est): 501.5K **Privately Held**
SIC: 8641 Bars & restaurants, members only

(G-3602)
FENTON RIGGING & CONTG INC
2150 Langdon Farm Rd (45237-4791)
PHONE..................................513 631-5500
Michael Besl, *President*
Doug Hollstegge, *COO*
William C Besl, *Vice Pres*
Bryan Erickson, *Project Mgr*
David Williams, *Project Mgr*
▲ EMP: 150 EST: 1893
SQ FT: 6,800
SALES (est): 78.5MM **Privately Held**
WEB: www.fentonrigging.com
SIC: 1622 1796 Bridge, tunnel & elevated highway; machine moving & rigging

(G-3603)
FERN EXPOSITION SERVICES LLC (PA)
Also Called: George Fern Company
645 Linn St (45203-1722)
PHONE..................................513 621-6111
Fax: 513 562-0462
Aaron Bludworth, *President*
David Pulford, *General Mgr*
Nick Stammler, *General Mgr*
Michael Cox, *Exec VP*
Mark Epstein, *Vice Pres*
EMP: 30
SQ FT: 500,000
SALES (est): 44.5MM **Privately Held**
WEB: www.geofern.com
SIC: 7359 Electronic equipment rental, except computers

Cincinnati - Hamilton County (G-3604)

(G-3604)
FIELDS MARKETING RESEARCH INC
Also Called: Fields Research
3814 West St Ste 110 (45227-3743)
PHONE 513 821-6266
Fax: 513 679-5300
Ken Fields, *President*
EMP: 55
SQ FT: 4,000
SALES (est): 4.1MM **Privately Held**
WEB: www.fieldsresearch.com
SIC: 8732 Market analysis or research

(G-3605)
FIFTH THIRD BANCORP (PA)
38 Fountain Square Plz (45202-3102)
PHONE 800 972-3030
Fax: 513 579-4312
Greg D Carmichael, *Ch of Bd*
Lars C Anderson, *COO*
Philip R McHugh, *Exec VP*
Timothy N Spence, *Exec VP*
Mark D Hazel, *Senior VP*
EMP: 62 EST: 1975
SALES: 7.7B **Publicly Held**
WEB: www.53.com
SIC: 6022 State trust companies accepting deposits, commercial

(G-3606)
FIFTH THIRD BANK
5830 Harrison Ave (45248-1623)
PHONE 513 574-4457
Fax: 513 598-2464
Jason Beccaccio, *Manager*
EMP: 117
SALES (corp-wide): 7.7B **Publicly Held**
SIC: 6021 National commercial banks
HQ: The Fifth Third Bank
38 Fountain Square Plz
Cincinnati OH 45202
513 579-5203

(G-3607)
FIFTH THIRD BANK (DH)
38 Fountain Square Plz (45202-3191)
PHONE 513 579-5203
Fax: 513 744-6701
George A Schaefer, *CEO*
Greg Carmichael, *President*
Thomas R Quinn Jr, *President*
Eric Smith, *President*
Hal Clemmer, *Regional Pres*
EMP: 1800
SALES: 6.8B
SALES (corp-wide): 7.7B **Publicly Held**
WEB: www.53rd.com
SIC: 6022 State trust companies accepting deposits, commercial

(G-3608)
FIFTH THIRD BANK
Fifth 3rd Ctr 38 Fountain (45263-0001)
PHONE 513 579-5203
George Schaefer, *Principal*
Mark Hendrix, *Senior VP*
Amy Donovan, *Assistant VP*
Jeffrey Rouse, *Assistant VP*
James Carty, *Vice Pres*
EMP: 100
SALES (corp-wide): 7.7B **Publicly Held**
SIC: 6162 Mortgage bankers & correspondents
HQ: The Fifth Third Bank
38 Fountain Square Plz
Cincinnati OH 45202
513 579-5203

(G-3609)
FIFTH THIRD EQUIPMENT FIN CO (DH)
38 Fountain Square Plz (45202-3102)
PHONE 800 972-3030
Fax: 513 744-6706
George Schaefer Jr, *President*
Jina Jayanetti, *Top Exec*
Heather R Koenig, *Exec VP*
David Jackson, *Senior VP*
Vinay Jha, *Senior VP*
EMP: 44
SQ FT: 1,000
SALES (est): 20.3MM
SALES (corp-wide): 7.7B **Publicly Held**
SIC: 7359 Equipment rental & leasing

HQ: The Fifth Third Bank
38 Fountain Square Plz
Cincinnati OH 45202
513 579-5203

(G-3610)
FINANCIAL NETWORK GROUP LTD
Also Called: Simply Money
7890 E Kemper Rd Ste 200 (45249-1657)
PHONE 513 469-7500
Fax: 513 469-1234
Nathan J Bachrach, *CEO*
Edward Finke, *President*
Dee House, *Managing Dir*
Richard Mayer, *Vice Pres*
Jean Plumley, *Vice Pres*
EMP: 37
SQ FT: 8,500
SALES (est): 3.7MM **Privately Held**
SIC: 8742 6282 Financial consultant; investment advisory service

(G-3611)
FINIT GROUP LLC
Also Called: Finit Solutions
8050 Hosbrook Rd Ste 326 (45236-2907)
PHONE 513 793-4648
Suyen Lee, *Human Res Mgr*
Jason Hampton, *Consultant*
Randy Scott, *Consultant*
Angie Apple,
EMP: 60
SALES (est): 243.9K **Privately Held**
SIC: 8742 Business consultant

(G-3612)
FINNEYTOWN CONTRACTING CORP
Also Called: Universal Contracting
5151 Fishwick Dr (45216-2215)
PHONE 513 482-2700
Fax: 513 482-2707
Philip Neumann, *President*
Greg Neumann, *Vice Pres*
EMP: 40
SQ FT: 7,500
SALES (est): 4.8MM **Privately Held**
SIC: 1542 Commercial & office building, new construction

(G-3613)
FIRST ACCEPTANCE CORPORATION
6150 Colerain Ave (45239-6418)
PHONE 513 741-0811
Deana Hayes, *Principal*
EMP: 31
SALES (corp-wide): 347.5MM **Publicly Held**
SIC: 6411 Insurance agents, brokers & service
PA: First Acceptance Corporation
3813 Green Hills Vlg Dr
Nashville TN 37215
615 844-2800

(G-3614)
FIRST CHOICE MEDICAL STAFFING
Also Called: First Choice Cincinnati Branch
1008 Marshall Ave Frnt (45225-2347)
PHONE 513 631-5656
Sheena Bell, *Branch Mgr*
EMP: 76
SALES (corp-wide): 4.6MM **Privately Held**
SIC: 8099 Blood related health services
PA: First Choice Medical Staffing Of Ohio, Inc.
1457 W 117th St
Cleveland OH 44107
216 521-2222

(G-3615)
FIRST FINANCIAL BANCORP
225 Pictoria Dr Ste 700 (45246-1620)
PHONE 513 551-5640
Fax: 513 705-4600
Bard Diaz, *Vice Pres*
Chris Hart, *Vice Pres*
Jon McClure, *Vice Pres*
Jerry Begley, *Manager*
EMP: 200

SALES (corp-wide): 409.2MM **Publicly Held**
WEB: www.ffbc-oh.com
SIC: 6035 6021 Savings institutions, federally chartered; national commercial banks
PA: First Financial Bancorp.
255 E 5th St Ste 700
Cincinnati OH 45202
877 322-9530

(G-3616)
FIRST FINANCIAL BANK
255 E 5th St Ste 2900 (45202-4704)
PHONE 513 979-5800
Ray Beck, *Senior VP*
Cathy Belding, *Assistant VP*
Benjamin Cornist, *Assistant VP*
Misty Lawrence, *Assistant VP*
Donna Schneider, *Assistant VP*
EMP: 30
SALES (corp-wide): 409.2MM **Publicly Held**
SIC: 6021 National commercial banks
HQ: First Financial Bank
255 E 5th St Ste 700
Cincinnati OH 45202
877 322-9530

(G-3617)
FIRST FINANCIAL BANK (HQ)
255 E 5th St Ste 700 (45202-4700)
PHONE 877 322-9530
Fax: 513 867-4515
Claude E Davis, *President*
Michael R Teone, *COO*
Ed Hensley, *Senior VP*
Glenn Boone, *Vice Pres*
Eddie Phillips, *Engineer*
EMP: 228
SALES: 406.3MM
SALES (corp-wide): 409.2MM **Publicly Held**
WEB: www.firstfb.com
SIC: 6022 State commercial banks
PA: First Financial Bancorp.
255 E 5th St Ste 700
Cincinnati OH 45202
877 322-9530

(G-3618)
FIRST GROUP INVESTMENT PARTNR (DH)
600 Vine St Ste 1200 (45202-2474)
PHONE 513 241-2200
Alton Sloan, *Partner*
Phil Crookes, *Partner*
EMP: 100
SALES (est): 212.7MM
SALES (corp-wide): 7B **Privately Held**
SIC: 7513 4212 4213 4225 Truck leasing, without drivers; truck rental, without drivers; local trucking, without storage; trucking, except local; general warehousing; school buses; local & suburban transit
HQ: Firstbus Investments Limited
Oldmixon Crescent
Weston-Super-Mare BS24
122 465-0100

(G-3619)
FIRST SERVICES INC
600 Vine St Ste 1200 (45202-2474)
PHONE 513 241-2200
Brad Thomas, *President*
Wayne Johnson, *CFO*
EMP: 5006
SALES (est): 135.8K
SALES (corp-wide): 7B **Privately Held**
SIC: 8741 7539 Management services; automotive repair shops
HQ: Firstgroup Usa, Inc.
600 Vine St Ste 1400
Cincinnati OH 45202
513 241-2200

(G-3620)
FIRST STUDENT INC
1801 Transpark Dr (45229-1239)
PHONE 513 531-6888
Karla Hunter, *General Mgr*
John Nardini, *Branch Mgr*
EMP: 100

SALES (corp-wide): 7B **Privately Held**
WEB: www.firststudentinc.com
SIC: 4151 School buses
HQ: First Student, Inc.
600 Vine St Ste 1400
Cincinnati OH 45202

(G-3621)
FIRST STUDENT INC
Also Called: Laidlaw Education Services
100 Hamilton Blvd (45215-5471)
PHONE 513 761-6100
Lisa Jajowka, *Manager*
EMP: 66
SALES (corp-wide): 7B **Privately Held**
WEB: www.leag.com
SIC: 4151 School buses
HQ: First Student, Inc.
600 Vine St Ste 1400
Cincinnati OH 45202

(G-3622)
FIRST STUDENT INC
Also Called: First Group America
100 Hamilton Blvd (45215-5471)
PHONE 513 761-5136
B Echelbarger, *Branch Mgr*
Thad Cord, *Executive*
Richelle Gibson, *Executive*
EMP: 400
SALES (corp-wide): 7B **Privately Held**
WEB: www.firststudentinc.com
SIC: 4151 School buses
HQ: First Student, Inc.
600 Vine St Ste 1400
Cincinnati OH 45202

(G-3623)
FIRST STUDENT INC (DH)
600 Vine St Ste 1400 (45202-2426)
PHONE 513 241-2200
Dennis Maple, *President*
Christian Gartner, *Senior VP*
Bruce Rasch, *Senior VP*
Robert Lindsey, *Vice Pres*
Beth Wilson, *Project Mgr*
EMP: 50
SQ FT: 12,500
SALES (est): 7.4B
SALES (corp-wide): 7B **Privately Held**
WEB: www.firststudentinc.com
SIC: 4151 School buses
HQ: Firstgroup America, Inc.
600 Vine St Ste 1400
Cincinnati OH 45202
513 241-2200

(G-3624)
FIRST TRANSIT INC (DH)
600 Vine St Ste 1400 (45202-2426)
PHONE 513 241-2200
Brad Thomas, *President*
Ric Dunning, *Senior VP*
Jarod Varner, *Vice Pres*
Todd Hawkins, *VP Mfg*
Jim Tippen, *CFO*
EMP: 300 EST: 1969
SQ FT: 15,000
SALES (est): 1.1B
SALES (corp-wide): 7B **Privately Held**
WEB: www.firsttransit.com
SIC: 8741 7539 8742 Management services; automotive repair shops; transportation consultant
HQ: Firstgroup America, Inc.
600 Vine St Ste 1400
Cincinnati OH 45202
513 241-2200

(G-3625)
FIRST VEHICLE SERVICES INC (DH)
600 Vine St Ste 1400 (45202-2426)
PHONE 513 241-2200
Brad Thomas, *President*
Dale Domish, *Senior VP*
Casey Dunn, *Manager*
Adam Silber, *Info Tech Mgr*
Tony Bezilla, *Director*
EMP: 200
SALES (est): 81.2MM
SALES (corp-wide): 7B **Privately Held**
SIC: 7549 Automotive maintenance services

GEOGRAPHIC SECTION

Cincinnati - Hamilton County (G-3647)

HQ: First Transit, Inc.
600 Vine St Ste 1400
Cincinnati OH 45202
513 241-2200

(G-3626)
FIRSTGROUP AMERICA INC (DH)
Also Called: First Group of America
600 Vine St Ste 1400 (45202-2426)
PHONE.................513 241-2200
Fax: 513 684-8852
Dennis Maple, *President*
Brad Thomas, *President*
Robert Timilty, *General Mgr*
Christian Gartner, *Senior VP*
Steve Hemmerlein, *Senior VP*
EMP: 58
SQ FT: 350,000
SALES (est): 8.7B
SALES (corp-wide): 7B **Privately Held**
WEB: www.firstgroupamerica.com
SIC: 4151 4111 4119 4131 School buses; local & suburban transit; local passenger transportation; intercity & rural bus transportation; local bus charter service; facilities support services; base maintenance (providing personnel on continuing basis);
HQ: Firstgroup Usa, Inc.
600 Vine St Ste 1400
Cincinnati OH 45202
513 241-2200

(G-3627)
FIRSTGROUP AMERICA INC
Also Called: Laidlaw Educational Services
600 Vine St Ste 1400 (45202-2426)
PHONE.................513 419-8611
Martin Gilbert, *Chairman*
John Sebastian, *Manager*
Regina Snow, *Manager*
David Butts, *Supervisor*
Keith Tyrka, *Supervisor*
EMP: 400
SALES (corp-wide): 7B **Privately Held**
WEB: www.firstgroup.com
SIC: 4151 School buses
HQ: Firstgroup America, Inc.
600 Vine St Ste 1400
Cincinnati OH 45202
513 241-2200

(G-3628)
FIRSTGROUP AMERICA INC
705 Central Ave (45202-1967)
PHONE.................513 241-2200
David Liston, *Vice Pres*
Venyke Payton, *Marketing Mgr*
Tonya Knott, *Office Mgr*
Bruce Ballard, *Manager*
Gary Fredenborg, *MIS Dir*
EMP: 75
SALES (corp-wide): 7B **Privately Held**
SIC: 4151 4111 4119 School buses; local & suburban transit; local passenger transportation
HQ: Firstgroup America, Inc.
600 Vine St Ste 1400
Cincinnati OH 45202
513 241-2200

(G-3629)
FIRSTGROUP USA INC (HQ)
Also Called: First Transit
600 Vine St Ste 1400 (45202-2426)
PHONE.................513 241-2200
Bruce Ballard, *CEO*
Tim O'Toole, *Chairman*
Kristi Keyes, *Human Res Dir*
Christian Gartner, *Marketing Mgr*
Kevin Mulcahy, *Director*
EMP: 425
SALES: 2.3MM
SALES (corp-wide): 7B **Privately Held**
SIC: 7513 4212 4213 4225 Truck leasing, without drivers; truck rental, without drivers; local trucking, without storage; trucking, except local; general warehousing; school buses; local & suburban transit
PA: Firstgroup Plc
395 King Street
Aberdeen AB24
122 465-0100

(G-3630)
FISHER DESIGN INC (PA)
4101 Spring Grove Ave B (45223-1180)
PHONE.................513 417-8235
Bryan Librandi, *CEO*
William Fisher, *Chairman*
Mary Frazier, *Business Mgr*
Thomas Schmidt, *Exec VP*
Alex Mavridoglou, *Prdtn Mgr*
EMP: 40
SQ FT: 20,000
SALES (est): 5MM **Privately Held**
WEB: www.fisherdesign.com
SIC: 7336 Commercial art & illustration; graphic arts & related design; package design

(G-3631)
FITWORKS HOLDING LLC
5840 Cheviot Rd (45247-6225)
PHONE.................513 923-9931
Fax: 513 923-9942
Mike Korn, *Branch Mgr*
Parker John, *Manager*
EMP: 362 **Privately Held**
WEB: www.fitworks.com
SIC: 8742 Training & development consultant
PA: Fitworks Holding, Llc
849 Brainard Rd
Cleveland OH 44143

(G-3632)
FITWORKS HOLDING LLC
Also Called: Fitworks Fitness & Spt Therapy
4600 Smith Rd Ste G (45212-2784)
PHONE.................513 531-1500
Andrew Bradley, *General Mgr*
EMP: 36 **Privately Held**
SIC: 7991 Health club
PA: Fitworks Holding, Llc
849 Brainard Rd
Cleveland OH 44143

(G-3633)
FIVE SEASONS SPT CNTRY CLB INC
11790 Snider Rd (45249-1223)
PHONE.................513 842-1188
Fax: 513 469-1422
Ben Goodyear, *Manager*
Dehaven Brian, *Director*
Greg Edmonds, *Athletic Dir*
EMP: 100 **Privately Held**
WEB: www.fiveseasonsday.com
SIC: 7997 Country club, membership
HQ: Five Seasons Sports Country Club, Inc.
100 E Rivercenter Blvd # 1100
Covington KY 41011

(G-3634)
FLYPAPER STUDIO INC
311 Elm St Ste 200 (45202-2743)
PHONE.................602 801-2208
Patrick Sullivan, *CEO*
Greg Head, *President*
Pat Stoner, *Treasurer*
Sunil Padiyar, *CTO*
Don Perison, *Admin Sec*
EMP: 30
SQ FT: 16,778
SALES: 1.9MM **Privately Held**
WEB: www.interactivealchemy.com
SIC: 7372 Educational computer software

(G-3635)
FOCUS SOLUTIONS INC
Also Called: Focus Staffing
1821 Summit Rd Ste 103 (45237-2818)
PHONE.................513 376-8349
Zola Stewart, *President*
Barbara Johnson, *COO*
EMP: 101
SALES (est): 3.6MM **Privately Held**
SIC: 7363 8742 8741 Labor resource services; management consulting services; management services

(G-3636)
FOLKERS MANAGEMENT CORPORATION (PA)
7741 Thompson Rd (45247-2252)
P.O. Box 54947 (45254-0947)
PHONE.................513 421-0230
David Folkers, *President*
Winston Folkers, *Vice Pres*
Marilyn Compton, *Treasurer*
EMP: 25
SQ FT: 150,000
SALES (est): 2.7MM **Privately Held**
SIC: 8741 Management services

(G-3637)
FORD DEVELOPMENT CORP
Also Called: Trend Construction
11148 Woodward Ln (45241-1876)
PHONE.................513 772-1521
Fax: 513 772-0324
Robert J Henderson, *CEO*
Robert F Henderson, *President*
Andrew Kloenne, *Vice Pres*
Mike Frey, *Project Mgr*
Barbara Marzullo, *Treasurer*
EMP: 100
SQ FT: 22,000
SALES (est): 34.9MM **Privately Held**
WEB: www.forddevelopment.com
SIC: 1542 1623 1794 Commercial & office building, new construction; water, sewer & utility lines; excavation work

(G-3638)
FORSYTHE SOLUTIONS GROUP INC
8845 Governors Hill Dr # 201 (45249-3316)
PHONE.................513 697-5100
Andrew Anderson, *Branch Mgr*
EMP: 58
SALES (corp-wide): 3.3B **Privately Held**
SIC: 7379 Computer related consulting services
HQ: Forsythe Solutions Group, Inc.
7770 Frontage Rd
Skokie IL 60077

(G-3639)
FORT WASH INV ADVISORS INC (DH)
303 Broadway St Ste 1100 (45202-4220)
P.O. Box 2388 (45201-2388)
PHONE.................513 361-7600
Fax: 513 361-7689
Maribeth S Rahe, *President*
Larry Carone, *President*
Bunn William, *President*
Stephen A Baker, *Managing Dir*
Margaret C Bell, *Managing Dir*
EMP: 76
SALES (est): 126.8MM **Privately Held**
WEB: www.fortwashington.com
SIC: 6282 Investment advisory service
HQ: The Western & Southern Life Insurance Company
400 Broadway St
Cincinnati OH 45202
513 629-1800

(G-3640)
FORTEC MEDICAL INC
2050 Northwest Dr (45231-1700)
PHONE.................513 742-9100
Fax: 513 742-9104
Paul Dierks, *Manager*
EMP: 25
SALES (corp-wide): 16.3MM **Privately Held**
SIC: 7352 Medical equipment rental
PA: Fortec Medical, Inc.
6245 Hudson Crossing Pkwy
Hudson OH 44236
330 463-1265

(G-3641)
FOSDICK & HILMER INC
525 Vine St Ste 1100 (45202-3141)
PHONE.................513 241-5640
Fax: 513 241-3659
Jim Pretz, *Ch of Bd*
Joel Grubbs, *Senior VP*
Richard M Saunders, *Vice Pres*
John Kuhr, *Engineer*
Steven Tate, *Engineer*
EMP: 56
SQ FT: 16,000
SALES: 9.1MM **Privately Held**
WEB: www.fosdickandhilmer.com
SIC: 8711 Consulting engineer

(G-3642)
FOUNTAIN SQUARE MGT GROUP LLC
Also Called: Fsmg
1203 Walnut St Fl 4 (45202-7153)
PHONE.................513 621-4400
Fax: 513 621-5900
Heather Saupe, *Vice Pres*
Timothy Szilasi, *CFO*
Bill Donabedian, *Manager*
EMP: 50
SQ FT: 12,000
SALES (est): 142.1K **Privately Held**
SIC: 7929 Entertainment service

(G-3643)
FOXX & COMPANY
324 W 9th St Fl 5 (45202-2043)
PHONE.................513 241-1616
Patricia Foxx, *President*
Martin O'Neill, *Vice Pres*
Monica Foxx, *Marketing Mgr*
Allen Burke, *Marketing Staff*
EMP: 30
SQ FT: 5,000
SALES (est): 2.3MM **Privately Held**
SIC: 8721 Certified public accountant

(G-3644)
FRCH DESIGN WORLDWIDE - CINCIN
311 Elm St Ste 600 (45202-2774)
PHONE.................513 241-3000
James R Tippmann, *CEO*
James R Lazzari, *President*
Brandon Avery, *Managing Dir*
Phillip Freer, *Managing Dir*
Thomas E Horwitz, *Senior VP*
EMP: 275
SQ FT: 22,000
SALES (est): 47.4MM
SALES (corp-wide): 96.4MM **Privately Held**
SIC: 8712 House designer
PA: Nelson Worldwide, Inc.
222-230 Walnut St
Philadelphia PA 19106
215 925-6562

(G-3645)
FRED A NEMANN CO
6480 Bender Rd (45233-1552)
PHONE.................513 467-9400
Fax: 513 467-0510
Fred Nemann, *President*
Fred Nemann III, *Vice Pres*
Sandra Timler, *Vice Pres*
Tim Nemann, *Treasurer*
Margie Pandeca, *Manager*
EMP: 40
SQ FT: 3,000
SALES: 9.7MM **Privately Held**
SIC: 1611 Highway & street construction

(G-3646)
FREDERICK STEEL COMPANY LLC
Also Called: Bfs Supply
630 Glendale Milford Rd (45215-1105)
PHONE.................513 821-6400
Burke Byer, *Principal*
Timothy Nagy, *Asst Sec*
EMP: 60 **EST:** 2013
SALES (est): 8.5MM
SALES (corp-wide): 86.5MM **Privately Held**
SIC: 1791 3441 Structural steel erection; building components, structural steel
PA: Benjamin Steel Company, Inc.
777 Benjamin Dr
Springfield OH 45502
937 322-8600

(G-3647)
FREDERICKS LANDSCAPING INC
301 S Cooper Ave (45215-4519)
PHONE.................513 821-9407
Fax: 513 679-4141
Frederick Hollmann, *President*
Mike Clark, *Accounts Mgr*
Allan Frankel, *Manager*
Lisa Wong, *Manager*
EMP: 50
SQ FT: 9,000

Cincinnati - Hamilton County (G-3648)

SALES: 2MM **Privately Held**
WEB: www.frederickslandscaping.com
SIC: 0782 Lawn care services; landscape contractors

(G-3648)
FREE STORE/FOOD BANK INC (PA)
1250 Tennessee Ave (45229-1012)
PHONE.................513 482-4526
Fax: 513 482-4504
John Young, *President*
Tim Weidner, *VP Finance*
Bill Kolb, *Manager*
Sarah Humphries, *Supervisor*
Mick Clay, *Director*
EMP: 45 EST: 1971
SQ FT: 100,000
SALES (est): 5.8MM **Privately Held**
SIC: 8322 Social service center; emergency social services

(G-3649)
FREE STORE/FOOD BANK INC
Meyerson Food Distribution
1250 Tennessee Ave (45229-1012)
PHONE.................513 241-1064
Fax: 513 357-4683
Steve Gibbs, *Manager*
Jennifer Ebelhar, *Director*
EMP: 30
SALES (corp-wide): 5.8MM **Privately Held**
SIC: 8322 Social services for the handicapped; public welfare center
PA: Free Store/Food Bank, Inc
1250 Tennessee Ave
Cincinnati OH 45229
513 482-4526

(G-3650)
FREESTORE/FOODBANK
Central Pkwy (45229)
PHONE.................513 482-4500
Tammy Reasoner, *Principal*
Julie Morrow, *Vice Pres*
Timothy Weidner, *Controller*
Jennifer Morrison, *Accountant*
Stephanie Togneri, *Volunteer Dir*
EMP: 42
SALES: 61.1MM **Privately Held**
SIC: 8322 Social services for the handicapped

(G-3651)
FREIGHTLNER TRCKS OF CNCINNATI
1 Freightliner Dr (45241-6418)
PHONE.................513 772-7171
Fax: 513 772-7172
Gary Gibson, *President*
Brent Billet, *Sales Staff*
EMP: 40
SALES (est): 10MM **Privately Held**
SIC: 5511 5012 Trucks, tractors & trailers: new & used; trucks, commercial

(G-3652)
FREKING BETZ
525 Vine St Fl 6 (45202-3151)
PHONE.................513 721-1975
Fax: 513 651-2570
Randolph H Freking, *Partner*
Carrie Myers, *Partner*
Sheila Smith, *Partner*
Katherine Neff, *Editor*
George Reul, *Personal Injury*
EMP: 30
SQ FT: 5,360
SALES (est): 3.9MM **Privately Held**
WEB: www.frekingandbetz.com
SIC: 8111 Labor & employment law

(G-3653)
FREY ELECTRIC INC
5700 Cheviot Rd Ste A (45247-7101)
P.O. Box 53785 (45253-0785)
PHONE.................513 385-0700
Fax: 513 385-0703
David Frey, *President*
Mark Frey, *Marketing Staff*
EMP: 60
SQ FT: 16,000
SALES (est): 9.2MM **Privately Held**
WEB: www.freyelectric.com
SIC: 1731 General electrical contractor

(G-3654)
FRIARS CLUB INC
Also Called: ST FRANCIS FRIARY
4300 Vine St (45217-1542)
PHONE.................513 488-8777
Fax: 513 381-7909
Mike Besl, *Ch of Bd*
Beth Bowsky, *Director*
EMP: 71
SQ FT: 20,000
SALES: 548.1K
SALES (corp-wide): 12MM **Privately Held**
WEB: www.rogerbacon.org
SIC: 8361 7032 7991 Boys' Towns; summer camp, except day & sports instructional; athletic club & gymnasiums, membership
PA: The Province Of St John Baptist Order Friars Minor
1615 Vine St
Cincinnati OH 45202
513 721-4700

(G-3655)
FRIEDMAN-SWIFT ASSOCIATES INC
110 Boggs Ln Ste 200 (45246-3147)
P.O. Box 9185 (45209-0185)
PHONE.................513 772-9200
Fax: 513 772-9207
Jeffrey Friedman, *President*
Judith George, *Senior VP*
Dolly Tekulde, *Controller*
Steve Barbash, *Natl Sales Mgr*
EMP: 100
SQ FT: 5,500
SALES (est): 6.8MM **Privately Held**
WEB: www.friedmanswift.com
SIC: 8732 Market analysis or research

(G-3656)
FROST BROWN TODD LLC (PA)
3300 Grt Amrcn Towe 301e (45202)
PHONE.................513 651-6800
George Yund, *Managing Prtnr*
Bernard L McKay, *Partner*
Ronald Gold, *Editor*
Bart Greenwald, *Vice Chairman*
Michael Yarbrough, *Vice Chairman*
EMP: 294
SALES (est): 153.4MM **Privately Held**
WEB: www.fbtextra.com
SIC: 8111 General practice attorney, lawyer; labor & employment law; environmental law; patent, trademark & copyright law

(G-3657)
FTE NETWORKS INC
11260 Chester Rd Ste 350 (45246-6201)
PHONE.................502 657-3500
Tom Bell, *Manager*
EMP: 72
SALES (corp-wide): 12.2MM **Publicly Held**
SIC: 4813 Telephone communication, except radio; data telephone communications
PA: Fte Networks, Inc.
999 Vanderbilt Beach Rd # 601
Naples FL 34108
877 878-8136

(G-3658)
FUND EVALUATION GROUP LLC (PA)
201 E 5th St Ste 1600 (45202-4156)
PHONE.................513 977-4400
Fax: 513 977-4430
John Labmeier, *Counsel*
Rebecca Wood, *Sr Corp Ofcr*
Tim O'Donnell, *Senior VP*
Christian Busken, *Vice Pres*
Emily Crail, *Vice Pres*
EMP: 50
SQ FT: 12,000
SALES (est): 11MM **Privately Held**
WEB: www.feg.com
SIC: 6282 7371 Investment advisory service; computer software development & applications

(G-3659)
G4S SECURE SOLUTIONS (USA)
625 Eden Park Dr Ste 700 (45202-6016)
PHONE.................513 874-0941
Ryan Krause, *Manager*
EMP: 250
SALES (corp-wide): 9.3B **Privately Held**
SIC: 7381 Security guard service
HQ: G4s Secure Solutions (Usa) Inc.
1395 University Blvd
Jupiter FL 33458
561 622-5656

(G-3660)
GALAXY ASSOCIATES INC (HQ)
3630 E Kemper Rd (45241-2011)
PHONE.................513 731-6350
William D Oeters, *President*
Philip P Dober, *CFO*
Shawn Garver, *CFO*
Thomas Miller, *Controller*
Timothy Scarbrough, *VP Sales*
EMP: 34
SQ FT: 12,300
SALES (est): 17MM **Privately Held**
SIC: 5169 Industrial chemicals

(G-3661)
GANNETT MEDIA TECH INTL (HQ)
Also Called: Gmti
312 Elm St Ste 2g (45202-2763)
PHONE.................513 665-3777
Fax: 513 241-7219
Daniel D Zito, *CEO*
Kent Chisler, *Engineer*
Natalie Dennis, *Accountant*
Mike Creedon, *Manager*
Alan Dawkins, *Manager*
EMP: 44
SALES (est): 8MM
SALES (corp-wide): 3.1B **Publicly Held**
WEB: www.gmti.com
SIC: 7371 Computer software development
PA: Gannett Co., Inc.
7950 Jones Branch Dr
Mc Lean VA 22102
703 854-6000

(G-3662)
GARDEN STREET IRON & METAL (PA)
2885 Spring Grove Ave (45225-2222)
PHONE.................513 853-3700
Fax: 513 977-4264
Earl J Weber Jr, *President*
Dave Hollbroke, *General Mgr*
Margaret Weber, *Vice Pres*
Sarah Weber, *Office Mgr*
Mike Chard, *Supervisor*
▲ EMP: 40
SQ FT: 43,000
SALES (est): 7.2MM **Privately Held**
SIC: 4953 3341 3312 Recycling, waste materials; secondary nonferrous metals; blast furnaces & steel mills

(G-3663)
GARDENS HOCKEY INC
Also Called: Cincinnati Mighty Ducks
2250 Seymour Ave (45212-1106)
PHONE.................513 351-3999
Fax: 513 351-5898
Peter Robinson, *CEO*
Judy Lienemann, *Controller*
EMP: 25
SALES (est): 422.1K **Privately Held**
WEB: www.cincinnatimightyducks.com
SIC: 7997 Hockey club, except professional & semi-professional

(G-3664)
GATEWAY DISTRIBUTION INC (PA)
11755 Lebanon Rd (45241-2038)
PHONE.................513 891-4477
Wayne Carucci, *CEO*
Dave Neely, *President*
Benjamin P Kenner, *Vice Pres*
Greg Atwood, *Maint Mgr*
Dominic Carucci, *Terminal Mgr*
EMP: 40
SQ FT: 100,000
SALES: 17MM **Privately Held**
WEB: www.gatewaydistribution.com
SIC: 4731 7389 Freight forwarding; brokers' services

(G-3665)
GEARS GARDEN CENTER INC (PA)
Also Called: Gear's Florists & Garden Ctrs
1579 Goodman Ave (45224-1004)
PHONE.................513 931-3800
William H Gear IV, *President*
William H Gear III, *Vice Pres*
David W Gear, *Admin Sec*
EMP: 30
SQ FT: 25,000
SALES (est): 3.5MM **Privately Held**
WEB: www.busseborgmann.com
SIC: 5992 5261 0782 Flowers, fresh; lawn & garden supplies; landscape contractors

(G-3666)
GEICO GENERAL INSURANCE CO
5050 Section Ave Ste 420 (45212-2057)
PHONE.................513 794-3426
Sidney Taghiof, *Manager*
EMP: 384
SALES (corp-wide): 242.1B **Publicly Held**
SIC: 6331 Automobile insurance
HQ: Geico General Insurance Company
1 Geico Plz
Washington DC 20076

(G-3667)
GENERAL ELECTRIC COMPANY
201 W Crescentville Rd (45246-1733)
PHONE.................513 977-1500
Thomas Cooper, *Vice Pres*
Brad Mottier, *Vice Pres*
Russell Sparks, *Vice Pres*
Roy Flores, *Purch Agent*
Bruce Haverkamp, *Buyer*
EMP: 500
SALES (corp-wide): 122B **Publicly Held**
SIC: 7629 3769 3728 3537 Aircraft electrical equipment repair; electrical equipment repair, high voltage; guided missile & space vehicle parts & auxiliary equipment; aircraft parts & equipment; industrial trucks & tractors
PA: General Electric Company
41 Farnsworth St
Boston MA 02210
617 443-3000

(G-3668)
GENERAL ELECTRIC COMPANY
1 Neumann Way (45215-1988)
PHONE.................513 552-2000
Denise Beach, *Buyer*
Partha Sreenivasan, *Program Mgr*
Randy Bates, *Manager*
Robert Doyon, *Manager*
Diane Orr, *Senior Mgr*
EMP: 1000
SQ FT: 84,308
SALES (corp-wide): 122B **Publicly Held**
SIC: 4581 3724 Hangar operation; aircraft engines & engine parts
PA: General Electric Company
41 Farnsworth St
Boston MA 02210
617 443-3000

(G-3669)
GENERAL ELECTRIC COMPANY
8700 Governors Hill Dr (45249-1363)
PHONE.................513 583-3500
Steve Doublett, *Managing Dir*
Robert Gatch Jr, *Business Mgr*
Jeff Diesel, *Traffic Mgr*
Debbie Beke, *Buyer*
Michael Andersen, *Engineer*
EMP: 150
SQ FT: 7,273
SALES (corp-wide): 122B **Publicly Held**
SIC: 1731 7376 Electrical work; computer facilities management
PA: General Electric Company
41 Farnsworth St
Boston MA 02210
617 443-3000

GEOGRAPHIC SECTION

(G-3670)
GENERAL ELECTRIC COMPANY
2411 Glendale Milford Rd (45241-3120)
PHONE................513 243-9404
Robert Pawlowski, *Manager*
Lynne Haag, *Supervisor*
Duwayne Scott, *Supervisor*
EMP: 30
SALES (corp-wide): 122B **Publicly Held**
SIC: 7991 Physical fitness facilities
PA: General Electric Company
41 Farnsworth St
Boston MA 02210
617 443-3000

(G-3671)
GENERAL ELECTRIC CREDIT UNION (PA)
Also Called: GECU
10485 Reading Rd (45241-2580)
PHONE................513 243-4328
Fax: 513 243-0839
Timothy D Ballinger, *CEO*
Joan Moore, *CFO*
Tyrina Smith, *Accountant*
Sherry Vearil, *Manager*
Kevin Reedy, *Director*
EMP: 90
SQ FT: 23,000
SALES: 72.5MM **Privately Held**
WEB: www.gecreditunion.org
SIC: 6062 State credit unions, not federally chartered

(G-3672)
GENERAL ELECTRIC EMPLOYEES
Also Called: Geeaa Park Golf Course
12110 Princeton Pike (45246-1726)
PHONE................513 243-2129
Gene Neff, *Manager*
EMP: 45
SQ FT: 10,000
SALES: 399.1K **Privately Held**
WEB: www.geeaa.org
SIC: 7997 Membership sports & recreation clubs

(G-3673)
GENERAL ELECTRIC INTL INC (HQ)
191 Rosa Parks St (45202-2573)
P.O. Box 861, Shelton CT (06484)
PHONE................203 944-3019
Fax: 203 944-3019
Giuseppe Recchi, *President*
Chuck Elias, *General Mgr*
Brian Fitzgerald, *District Mgr*
Candace F Carson, *Vice Pres*
Brad Greene, *Vice Pres*
EMP: 125
SQ FT: 11,390
SALES: 13.3B
SALES (corp-wide): 122B **Publicly Held**
SIC: 8711 Engineering services
PA: General Electric Company
41 Farnsworth St
Boston MA 02210
617 443-3000

(G-3674)
GENERAL FACTORY SUPS CO INC
Also Called: Gfwd Supply
4811 Winton Rd (45232-1502)
PHONE................513 864-6007
Fax: 513 681-0935
Teri Stautberg, *Principal*
Jeff Stautberg, *CFO*
DOT Haarmeyer, *Admin Sec*
EMP: 40 **EST:** 1946
SQ FT: 33,000
SALES: 50MM **Privately Held**
SIC: 5085 Industrial supplies

(G-3675)
GENERAL TOOL COMPANY (PA)
101 Landy Ln (45215-3495)
PHONE................513 733-5500
Fax: 513 733-5604
William J Kramer Jr, *CEO*
John Cozad, *COO*
Elliot Adams, *Exec VP*
Bruce Horton, *Project Mgr*
William Watkins, *Engineer*

▲ **EMP:** 250 **EST:** 1947
SQ FT: 150,000
SALES: 39.8MM **Privately Held**
WEB: www.gentool.com
SIC: 3599 3443 3444 3544 Machine shop, jobbing & repair; fabricated plate work (boiler shop); sheet metalwork; special dies & tools; welding repair

(G-3676)
GENESIS TECHNOLOGY PARTNERS
Also Called: Masterplan
3200 Burnet Ave (45229-3019)
PHONE................513 585-5800
Joe Happ, *Manager*
EMP: 50
SALES (est): 1.8MM **Privately Held**
WEB: www.genesispartners.net
SIC: 8741 Management services

(G-3677)
GEOFF ANSWINI
10506 Montgomery Rd (45242-4487)
PHONE................513 792-7800
Geoff Answini, *Principal*
EMP: 50
SALES (est): 451.7K **Privately Held**
SIC: 8011 Physical medicine, physician/surgeon

(G-3678)
GLENDALE PLACE CARE CENTER LLC
779 Glendale Milford Rd (45215-1161)
PHONE................513 771-1779
Fax: 513 771-4799
Barry Kohn, *Mng Member*
EMP: 39
SALES (est): 3.6MM **Privately Held**
SIC: 8051 Convalescent home with continuous nursing care

(G-3679)
GLENWAY AUTOMOTIVE SERVICE
Also Called: Sanfillipos Automotive Service
4033 Glenway Ave (45205-1444)
PHONE................513 921-2117
Fax: 513 921-6928
Joseph Sanfillipo Jr, *President*
Marty Sanfillipo, *Vice Pres*
Maria Sanfillipo, *Treasurer*
Joseph Sanfillipo III, *Admin Sec*
EMP: 28 **EST:** 1971
SQ FT: 25,000
SALES (est): 2.8MM **Privately Held**
SIC: 7538 General automotive repair shops

(G-3680)
GLOBAL SPECTRUM
Also Called: Duke Energy Convention Center
525 Elm St (45202-2316)
PHONE................513 419-7300
Fax: 513 419-7327
Ric Booth, *General Mgr*
Rebecca Dossett, *Opers Spvr*
Matt Deaton, *Opers Staff*
Michael Scott, *Chief Engr*
Carla Ballard, *Natl Sales Mgr*
EMP: 65
SALES (est): 6.1MM **Privately Held**
SIC: 7389 Convention & show services

(G-3681)
GODDARD SCHOOL
Also Called: Goddard School, The
4430 Red Bank Rd (45227-2116)
PHONE................513 271-6311
Kate Joseph, *Owner*
EMP: 25
SALES (est): 335.3K **Privately Held**
SIC: 8351 Child day care services; nursery school; preschool center

(G-3682)
GOETTLE CO
12071 Hamilton Ave (45231-1032)
PHONE................513 825-8100
Jon Huff, *Project Mgr*
Kris King, *Project Mgr*
Tony Eckert, *Opers Mgr*
Chad Linz, *Project Engr*
Dan Baker, *CFO*

EMP: 75
SALES (est): 10.1MM **Privately Held**
SIC: 1521 Single-family housing construction

(G-3683)
GOETTLE HOLDING COMPANY INC (PA)
Also Called: Goettle Construction
12071 Hamilton Ave (45231-1032)
PHONE................513 825-8100
Larry P Rayburn, *Ch of Bd*
Terrence Tucker, *President*
Roger W Healey, *Principal*
Janet E Goettle, *Principal*
Richard J Goettle III, *Principal*
▲ **EMP:** 129
SQ FT: 15,000
SALES (est): 75.2MM **Privately Held**
WEB: www.goettle.com
SIC: 1799 1629 1771 1794 Shoring & underpinning work; pile driving contractor; foundation & footing contractor; excavation work

(G-3684)
GOLD STAR CHILI INC (PA)
650 Lunken Park Dr (45226-1800)
PHONE................513 231-4541
Fax: 513 624-4415
Roger David, *President*
Ali Abusway, *Business Mgr*
Faris Naser, *Business Mgr*
James Conover, *CFO*
Kim Olden, *Controller*
EMP: 33 **EST:** 1965
SQ FT: 5,000
SALES (est): 47.9MM **Privately Held**
SIC: 2032 2099 6794 5499 Chili with or without meat: packaged in cans, jars, etc.; food preparations; franchises, selling or licensing; spices & herbs

(G-3685)
GOOD SAMARITAN HOSP CINCINNATI (HQ)
Also Called: CHI
375 Dixmyth Ave (45220-2489)
P.O. Box 636000, Littleton CO (80163-6000)
PHONE................513 569-6251
Fax: 513 861-6831
John S Prout, *President*
Robert L Walker, *Chairman*
Linda Hayes, *Dean*
Gerald Oliphant, *COO*
John R Robinson, *Senior VP*
EMP: 50
SALES: 578.9MM **Privately Held**
SIC: 8062 8082 8011 General medical & surgical hospitals; home health care services; offices & clinics of medical doctors

(G-3686)
GOODALL PROPERTIES LTD
Also Called: Goodall Complex
324 W 9th St Ste 500 (45202-2043)
PHONE................513 621-5522
David E Foxx, *President*
Levon Thompson Jr, *COO*
EMP: 40
SALES (est): 1.6MM **Privately Held**
SIC: 6512 Commercial & industrial building operation

(G-3687)
GOODWILL SERVICE GUILD
Also Called: Treasure Island Gift Shop
10600 Springfield Rd (45215-1184)
PHONE................513 771-4800
Mike Speed, *Financial Exec*
Jane Kreps, *Manager*
Gail Hana, *Manager*
EMP: 30
SQ FT: 1,500
SALES (est): 362.7K **Privately Held**
SIC: 8641 Social associations

(G-3688)
GORILLA GLUE COMPANY
2101 E Kemper Rd (45241-1805)
PHONE................513 271-3300
Howard N Ragland III, *President*
William J Keating Jr, *Principal*
Joseph P Rouse, *Principal*
S K Von Hoene, *Principal*

Joe Ragland, *COO*
◆ **EMP:** 49 **EST:** 1904
SQ FT: 44,000
SALES (est): 86.4MM **Privately Held**
WEB: www.gorillaglue.com
SIC: 5169 5085 Glue; adhesives, tape & plasters

(G-3689)
GOVERNMENT ACQUISITIONS INC
720 E Pete Rose Way # 360 (45202-3576)
PHONE................513 721-8700
Fax: 513 721-3999
Roger Brown, *Owner*
Kathy Meece, *Project Mgr*
Javier Pardo, *Engineer*
Bobby Brown, *CFO*
Stan Jones, *CFO*
EMP: 35
SQ FT: 20,000
SALES (est): 68.6MM **Privately Held**
WEB: www.gov-acq.com
SIC: 5045 7378 3577 Computers, peripherals & software; computer software; computer maintenance & repair; computer peripheral equipment

(G-3690)
GRACE HOSPICE LLC
2100 Sherman Ave Ste 103 (45212-2775)
PHONE................513 458-5545
Mark Mitchell, *Branch Mgr*
EMP: 104 **Privately Held**
SIC: 8052 Personal care facility
PA: Grace Hospice, Llc
500 Kirts Blvd Ste 250
Troy MI 48084

(G-3691)
GRADY VETERINARY HOSPITAL INC
9255 Winton Rd (45231-3935)
PHONE................513 931-8675
Fax: 513 931-4109
Jeff Grady, *President*
Marsha Weiss, *Office Mgr*
James Auvil,
Jessica Brownfield,
Karl S Grady Jr,
EMP: 50 **EST:** 1957
SQ FT: 5,000
SALES (est): 3MM **Privately Held**
WEB: www.gradyvet.com
SIC: 0742 Animal hospital services, pets & other animal specialties

(G-3692)
GRANGE MUTUAL CASUALTY COMPANY
Also Called: Grange Mutual Casualty Co 721
12021 Sheraton Ln (45246-1611)
P.O. Box 46645 (45246-0645)
PHONE................513 671-3722
Fax: 513 671-6151
George Carol, *Manager*
EMP: 30
SALES (corp-wide): 1.2B **Privately Held**
SIC: 6331 Fire, marine & casualty insurance
PA: Grange Mutual Casualty Company
671 S High St
Columbus OH 43206
614 445-2900

(G-3693)
GRANT THORNTON LLP
4000 Smith Rd Ste 500 (45209-1967)
PHONE................513 762-5000
Steve Albert, *Partner*
Sean V McGrory, *Partner*
Kevin Deters, *Auditing Mgr*
Bob Taylor, *Branch Mgr*
Matthew Jessup, *Senior Mgr*
EMP: 95
SALES (corp-wide): 75.8MM **Privately Held**
WEB: www.gt.com
SIC: 8721 Certified public accountant
HQ: Grant Thornton Llp
171 N Clark St Ste 200
Chicago IL 60601
312 856-0200

Cincinnati - Hamilton County (G-3694) GEOGRAPHIC SECTION

(G-3694)
GRAY & PAPE INC (PA)
1318 Main St Fl 1 (45202-6619)
PHONE.................513 287-7700
Fax: 513 287-7703
W Kevin Pape, *President*
Mirna Colon, *General Mgr*
Cinder Miller, *VP Opers*
Christina Inman, *Financial Exec*
Beth McCord, *Branch Mgr*
EMP: 33
SQ FT: 16,000
SALES: 7.7MM **Privately Held**
WEB: www.graypape.com
SIC: 8742 Management consulting services

(G-3695)
GRAYBAR ELECTRIC COMPANY INC
1022 W 8th St (45203-1269)
PHONE.................513 719-7400
Jon Dimichele, *Finance*
Bob Wissel, *Sales Staff*
Phil Grimes, *Branch Mgr*
Justin Bass, *Manager*
Mark Hirst, *Manager*
EMP: 56
SQ FT: 60,000
SALES (corp-wide): 6.6B **Privately Held**
WEB: www.graybar.com
SIC: 5063 Electrical supplies
PA: Graybar Electric Company, Inc.
 34 N Meramec Ave
 Saint Louis MO 63105
 314 573-9200

(G-3696)
GREAT AMERICAN ADVISORS INC (DH)
301 E 4th St Fl 8 (45202-4257)
P.O. Box 357 (45201-0357)
PHONE.................513 357-3300
Fax: 513 412-5109
Jim Henderson, *President*
Bill Bair, *Vice Pres*
James Mc Vey, *Vice Pres*
Laronda Eliopulos, *Financial Exec*
John Lawrence III, *Director*
EMP: 30
SQ FT: 9,000
SALES (est): 4.3MM **Publicly Held**
SIC: 6411 Insurance agents, brokers & service
HQ: Great American Financial Resources, Inc.
 250 E 5th St Ste 1000
 Cincinnati OH 45202
 513 333-5300

(G-3697)
GREAT AMERICAN INSURANCE CO (HQ)
301 E 4th St Fl 8 (45202-4257)
P.O. Box 5420 (45201-5420)
PHONE.................513 369-5000
Fax: 513 369-3658
Carl H Lindner III, *CEO*
Michael E Chevrette, *President*
Freeman Durham, *President*
Julie F Kadnar, *President*
Jane Kornesczuk, *President*
EMP: 3000
SQ FT: 250,000
SALES (est): 1.7B **Publicly Held**
SIC: 6331 Fire, marine & casualty insurance; automobile insurance; property damage insurance; agricultural insurance

(G-3698)
GREAT AMERICAN INSURANCE CO
49 E 4th St Bsmt (45202-3803)
P.O. Box 5425 (45201-5425)
PHONE.................513 763-7035
Robert Burkholder, *Senior VP*
Stephanie Hoboth, *Vice Pres*
Doug Svenkerud, *Vice Pres*
Paul Morande, *Manager*
Thomas Cappel, *Info Tech Mgr*
EMP: 100 **Publicly Held**
SIC: 6331 Fire, marine & casualty insurance

HQ: Great American Insurance Company
 301 E 4th St Fl 8
 Cincinnati OH 45202
 513 369-5000

(G-3699)
GREAT AMERICAN LIFE INSUR CO (HQ)
250 E 5th St Ste 1000 (45202-4127)
P.O. Box 5420 (45201-5420)
PHONE.................513 357-3300
Fax: 513 357-3397
Charles Scheper, *President*
Elizabeth Fryman, *Vice Pres*
Chris Miliano, *Asst Treas*
Cari Potts, *Human Res Mgr*
Robert Hodder, *Sales Mgr*
EMP: 27
SALES (est): 16.3MM **Publicly Held**
WEB: www.galic.com
SIC: 6311 Life insurance carriers

(G-3700)
GREAT AMRCN FNCL RESOURCES INC (HQ)
250 E 5th St Ste 1000 (45202-4127)
PHONE.................513 333-5300
Carl H Lindner, *Ch of Bd*
S Craig Lindner, *President*
Charles R Scheper, *COO*
Sarah Patton, *Counsel*
Ernest T Giambra, *Exec VP*
EMP: 150
SQ FT: 140,000
SALES (est): 608.9MM **Publicly Held**
WEB: www.aagcorp.com
SIC: 6371 Pension, health & welfare funds; union welfare, benefit & health funds

(G-3701)
GREAT AMRCN PLAN ADMIN INC
525 Vine St Fl 7 (45202-3169)
PHONE.................513 412-2316
Fax: 513 357-3199
Mark Muething, *President*
Wendy Wilson, *Assistant VP*
Kevin Kelley, *Vice Pres*
Peter Nerone, *Vice Pres*
Thomas Coleman, *VP Mktg*
EMP: 55
SALES (est): 15MM **Privately Held**
SIC: 6371 Pension, health & welfare funds

(G-3702)
GREAT LAKES COMPANIES INC
925 Laidlaw Ave (45237-5003)
PHONE.................513 554-0720
Eric Reed, *Superintendent*
Mark Grdina, *Vice Pres*
Kurtis Knapp, *Vice Pres*
Albert Leonard, *Vice Pres*
Sean Moloney, *Engineer*
EMP: 125
SALES (corp-wide): 63.3MM **Privately Held**
SIC: 1521 Single-family housing construction
PA: Great Lakes Companies Inc
 2608 Great Lakes Way
 Hinckley OH
 330 220-3900

(G-3703)
GREAT OAKS INST TECH CREER DEV (PA)
3254 E Kemper Rd (45241-6421)
P.O. Box 62627 (45262-0627)
PHONE.................513 771-8840
Harry Snyder, *President*
Jon Quatman, *Vice Pres*
Michelle Means Walker, *Vice Pres*
Jeff Johnson, *Facilities Dir*
Ben Vanhorn, *Purch Dir*
EMP: 98 **EST:** 1971
SQ FT: 10,000
SALES: 67.1MM **Privately Held**
SIC: 8211 8299 8331 8249 Public vocational/technical school; educational service, nondegree granting; continuing educ.; job training & vocational rehabilitation services; vocational schools

(G-3704)
GREAT OAKS INST TECH CREER DEV
Also Called: Center For Employment Resource
3254 E Kemper Rd (45241-6421)
PHONE.................513 771-8840
Fax: 513 771-4932
Robert Giuffre, *CFO*
Gary Gebhert, *Director*
EMP: 50
SALES (corp-wide): 67.1MM **Privately Held**
SIC: 8211 8299 8331 8249 Public adult education school; educational service, nondegree granting: continuing educ.; job training & vocational rehabilitation services; vocational schools
PA: Great Oaks Institute Of Technology & Career Development
 3254 E Kemper Rd
 Cincinnati OH 45241
 513 771-8840

(G-3705)
GREATER ANDRSON PREMOTES PEACE
7642 Athenia Dr (45244-2900)
PHONE.................513 588-8391
Luise Lawarre, *CEO*
EMP: 35
SALES (est): 299.1K **Privately Held**
WEB: www.gappeace.org
SIC: 8412 Museums & art galleries

(G-3706)
GREATER CIN CARDI CONSULTS IN
Also Called: Greater Cnti Crdovascular Cons
2123 Auburn Ave (45219-2906)
PHONE.................513 751-4222
Fax: 513 751-4353
F Thomas Jenike, *President*
David G Babbitt, *Vice Pres*
John S Held, *Vice Pres*
Lester E Suna, *Vice Pres*
Byron W Gustin, *Treasurer*
EMP: 50
SQ FT: 7,000
SALES (est): 3.4MM **Privately Held**
SIC: 8011 Cardiologist & cardio-vascular specialist

(G-3707)
GREATER CINCINNATI CNVNTN/VSTR
525 Vine St Ste 1200 (45202-3174)
PHONE.................513 621-2142
Fax: 513 621-5020
Ben Lincoln, *President*
Cindi Flick, *Vice Pres*
Barrie Perks, *Vice Pres*
Stephen Stickford, *VP Sales*
Mary Baluta, *Sales Staff*
EMP: 32
SQ FT: 10,000
SALES: 9.4MM **Privately Held**
WEB: www.cincyusa.com
SIC: 8641 Civic associations

(G-3708)
GREATER CINCINNATI DENTAL LABS
3719 Struble Rd (45251-4951)
P.O. Box 53070 (45253-0070)
PHONE.................513 385-4222
Fax: 513 385-4291
Ken Blaylock, *President*
Robert Blaylock, *Treasurer*
Darlene Rogg, *Admin Sec*
EMP: 49
SALES (est): 4MM **Privately Held**
WEB: www.gcapmd.com
SIC: 8072 Denture production

(G-3709)
GREATER CINCINNATI GASTRO ASSC (PA)
2925 Vernon Pl Ste 100 (45219-2425)
PHONE.................513 336-8636
Fax: 513 872-4553
Ronald Schneider, *President*
Randall Edwards, *Vice Chairman*
George Waissbluth, *Vice Pres*

Alan Safdi, *Treasurer*
Lori G Stotz, *Director*
EMP: 60
SQ FT: 6,000
SALES (est): 9.9MM **Privately Held**
WEB: www.cincygastro.com
SIC: 8011 Gastronomist

(G-3710)
GREATER CINCINNATI OB/GYN INC (PA)
2830 Victory Pkwy Ste 140 (45206-1786)
PHONE.................513 245-3103
Baha Sivai, *President*
Thomas Frerick, *Treasurer*
Clarence R McLaine, *Admin Sec*
EMP: 60
SALES: 12.9MM **Privately Held**
SIC: 8011 Obstetrician

(G-3711)
GREATER CINCINNATI TV EDUC FND
Also Called: CHANNEL 48
1223 Central Pkwy (45214-2834)
PHONE.................513 381-4033
Susan Howarth, *CEO*
Ted Hillburg, *Financial Exec*
Jason Dennison, *Manager*
Lauren Hess, *Manager*
Kellie May, *Manager*
EMP: 70
SQ FT: 84,210
SALES: 4.8MM **Privately Held**
WEB: www.ohiomathworks.net
SIC: 4833 7812 Television broadcasting stations; television film production

(G-3712)
GREEN TOWNSHIP HOSPITALITY LLC (PA)
Also Called: Holiday Inn
5505 Rybolt Rd (45248-1029)
PHONE.................513 574-6000
Fax: 513 574-6566
Katen Patel, *Mng Member*
Joanie Haskell, *Manager*
Sanjiv Mehrotra,
Sejal Patel,
EMP: 294
SQ FT: 100,000
SALES (est): 9.3MM **Privately Held**
SIC: 7011 5812 Hotels; eating places

(G-3713)
GREYHOUND LINES INC
1005 Gilbert Ave (45202-1425)
PHONE.................513 421-7442
Fax: 513 352-6069
Virginia Purdy, *Manager*
EMP: 50
SALES (corp-wide): 7B **Privately Held**
WEB: www.greyhound.com
SIC: 4131 Interstate bus line
HQ: Greyhound Lines, Inc.
 350 N Saint Paul St # 300
 Dallas TX 75201
 214 849-8000

(G-3714)
GRIPPO FOODS INC
6750 Colerain Ave (45239-5542)
PHONE.................513 923-1900
Ralph W Pagel II, *President*
Linda Foster, *Vice Pres*
James Pagel, *Vice Pres*
Nancy Schreiber, *Vice Pres*
Teri Baker, *VP Mfg*
EMP: 50 **EST:** 1919
SQ FT: 27,000
SALES (est): 8.1MM **Privately Held**
SIC: 5145 Snack foods; potato chips

(G-3715)
GROTE ENTERPRISES LLC (PA)
5240 Lester Rd (45213-2522)
PHONE.................513 731-5700
Fax: 513 731-4277
Tom Grote Jr, *Principal*
Toni Clever, *Controller*
Shannon Kemme, *Human Resources*
James Potts, *Sales Dir*
Resa Young, *Office Mgr*
EMP: 85

GEOGRAPHIC SECTION

Cincinnati - Hamilton County (G-3739)

SALES (est): 11.4MM Privately Held
SIC: 8741 Management services

(G-3716)
GUARDIAN LIFE INSUR CO OF AMER
419 Plum St (45202-2632)
PHONE 513 579-1114
Fax: 513 723-0298
Patrick Wilson, *Branch Mgr*
Parker Bailey, *Property Mgr*
Richard Shurmer, *Agent*
Jared Wolever, *Advisor*
EMP: 30
SALES (corp-wide): 9.7B Privately Held
WEB: www.glic.net
SIC: 6311 Life insurance
PA: The Guardian Life Insurance Company Of America
    7 Hanover Sq Fl 14
    New York NY 10004
    212 598-8000

(G-3717)
GUARDIAN SAVINGS BANK
560 Ohio Pike (45255-3315)
PHONE 513 528-8787
Fax: 513 528-8788
Brian Neuhaus, *Loan Officer*
Tom Powers, *Broker*
Justin Theilman, *Broker*
Tracy Royse, *Manager*
EMP: 30
SALES (corp-wide): 42.4MM Privately Held
SIC: 6163 6035 Loan brokers; savings institutions, federally chartered
PA: Guardian Savings Bank
    6100 W Chester Rd
    West Chester OH 45069
    513 942-3535

(G-3718)
GUARDSMARK LLC
4050 Executive Park Dr # 350 (45241-2077)
PHONE 513 851-5523
Fax: 513 851-5911
Mark Morrissey, *Manager*
EMP: 250
SALES (corp-wide): 746.3MM Privately Held
WEB: www.guardsmark.com
SIC: 7381 Security guard service
HQ: Guardsmark, Llc
    1551 N Tustin Ave Ste 650
    Santa Ana CA 92705
    714 619-9700

(G-3719)
GUNNING & ASSOCIATES MKTG INC
Also Called: G&A Marketing Inc
1001 Ford Cir (45202)
PHONE 513 688-1370
Fax: 513 688-1570
Patrick Gunning, *President*
Todd Sprouse, *Mktg Dir*
Robyn Terrell, *Marketing Staff*
EMP: 40
SQ FT: 3,700
SALES (est): 2.8MM Privately Held
SIC: 8748 Business consulting

(G-3720)
GUS HOLTHAUS SIGNS INC
Also Called: Holthaus Lackner Signs
817 Ridgeway Ave (45229-3222)
P.O. Box 29373 (45229-0373)
PHONE 513 861-0060
Fax: 513 559-0975
Kevin Holthaus, *President*
Scott Holthaus, *Vice Pres*
Rick Souder, *Prdtn Mgr*
Charlie Holthaus, *Purch Mgr*
Jon Holthaus, *Sales Staff*
EMP: 40
SQ FT: 38,600
SALES (est): 6.5MM Privately Held
WEB: www.holthaussigns.com
SIC: 3993 1799 Electric signs; sign installation & maintenance

(G-3721)
GUS PERDIKAKIS ASSOCIATES
Also Called: GPA
9155 Governors Way Unit A (45249-4005)
P.O. Box 498612 (45249-8612)
PHONE 513 583-0900
Fax: 513 583-9193
Gus G Perdikakis, *President*
Joann L Perdikakis, *Treasurer*
Steve Saunders, *Marketing Staff*
Steve Hatke, *Manager*
Lynn Perdikakis, *Admin Sec*
EMP: 70
SQ FT: 1,600
SALES (est): 9.7MM Privately Held
WEB: www.gpainc.net
SIC: 8711 7361 Engineering services; employment agencies

(G-3722)
H DENNERT DISTRIBUTING CORP
351 Wilmer Ave (45226-1831)
P.O. Box 721768, Newport KY (41072-1768)
PHONE 513 871-7272
Fax: 513 871-4432
Ronald J Plattner, *President*
Greg Kuntz, *Personnel Exec*
Ronald Jplattner,
▲ EMP: 110
SALES (est): 10.1MM Privately Held
SIC: 5182 Wine

(G-3723)
H P PRODUCTS CORPORATION
7135 E Kemper Rd (45249-1028)
PHONE 513 683-8553
Mike Brown, *Branch Mgr*
EMP: 75
SALES (corp-wide): 19.2B Privately Held
SIC: 5087 Janitors' supplies
HQ: H P Products Corporation
    4220 Saguaro Trl
    Indianapolis IN 46268
    317 298-9957

(G-3724)
HABEGGER CORPORATION (PA)
Also Called: Johnson Contrls Authorized Dlr
4995 Winton Rd (45232-1504)
PHONE 513 853-6644
Fax: 513 853-6642
Fred Habegger III, *Ch of Bd*
John Dor, *President*
Rick Travis, *Regional Mgr*
Susan Brickweg, *Business Mgr*
Jeff Gilley, *COO*
▲ EMP: 49
SQ FT: 20,000
SALES (est): 91.9MM Privately Held
WEB: www.habeggercorp.com
SIC: 5075 Warm air heating equipment & supplies; air conditioning & ventilation equipment & supplies

(G-3725)
HABEGGER CORPORATION
Also Called: C A C Distributing
11413 Enterprise Park Dr (45241-1561)
PHONE 513 612-4700
Fax: 513 612-4701
Tom Lovich, *Division Mgr*
Butch West, *Division Mgr*
Ken Kellogg, *Opers Mgr*
John Karasarides, *Prdtn Mgr*
Scott Anderson, *Parts Mgr*
EMP: 60
SQ FT: 29,320
SALES (corp-wide): 91.9MM Privately Held
WEB: www.habeggercorp.com
SIC: 5074 5075 Heating equipment (hydronic); air conditioning equipment, except room units
PA: The Habegger Corporation
    4995 Winton Rd
    Cincinnati OH 45232
    513 853-6644

(G-3726)
HABITAT FOR HUMANITY INTL
4910 Para Dr (45237-5012)
PHONE 513 721-4483
Fax: 513 621-6869
Jonathan Reckford, *CEO*
Renee Glover, *Chairman*
Joe Price, *Treasurer*
Marissa Woodly, *Director*
Bradford L Hewitt, *Admin Sec*
EMP: 27 EST: 1977
SALES: 6.9MM Privately Held
SIC: 8399 Community development groups

(G-3727)
HACKENSACK MERIDIAN HEALTH INC
Also Called: Carriage Court of Kenwood
4650 E Galbraith Rd (45236-2792)
PHONE 513 792-9697
K Pfeifer, *Finance*
EMP: 80
SALES (corp-wide): 4.4B Privately Held
SIC: 8361 Home for the aged
PA: Hackensack Meridian Health, Inc.
    343 Thornall St
    Edison NJ 08837
    732 751-7500

(G-3728)
HAID ACQUISITIONS LLC
1053 Ebenezer Rd (45233-4820)
PHONE 513 941-8700
Aaron Haid, *Mng Member*
EMP: 75 EST: 2015
SALES (est): 3.2MM Privately Held
SIC: 4731 Transportation agents & brokers

(G-3729)
HAIR FORUM
5801 Cheviot Rd Unit 1 (45247-6206)
PHONE 513 245-0800
Don Feldmann, *Owner*
EMP: 25
SALES (est): 417.7K Privately Held
WEB: www.hairforum.com
SIC: 7231 Hairdressers

(G-3730)
HAMILTON CNTY AUDITOR OFFICE
138 E Court St Rm 501 (45202-1226)
PHONE 513 946-4000
Fax: 513 632-8722
Dusty Rhodes, *Auditor*
Terry Munz, *Director*
Sharon Booker, *Admin Asst*
Susan Silver, *Administration*
Bradley A Bookheimer, *Real Est Agnt*
EMP: 142
SALES (est): 6.4MM Privately Held
WEB: www.auditor.hamilton-co.org
SIC: 7389 Personal service agents, brokers & bureaus

(G-3731)
HAMILTON COUNTY EDUCTL SVC CTR
924 Waycross Rd (45240-3022)
PHONE 513 674-4200
Kathy Tirey, *Exec Dir*
EMP: 100
SALES (corp-wide): 75MM Privately Held
SIC: 8351 Head start center, except in conjunction with school
PA: Hamilton County Educational Service Center
    11083 Hamilton Ave
    Cincinnati OH 45231
    513 674-4200

(G-3732)
HAMILTON COUNTY PARKS DISTRICT
10999 Mill Rd (45240-3515)
PHONE 513 825-3701
Andi Lanz, *Office Mgr*
Matt Starr, *Director*
Andrew Horner, *Director*
Doug Stulz, *Director*
EMP: 50
SALES (est): 804K Privately Held
SIC: 7999 Golf driving range

(G-3733)
HAMILTON COUNTY SOCIETY (PA)
Also Called: S P C A Cincinnati
3949 Colerain Ave (45223-2518)
PHONE 513 541-6100
Fax: 513 542-7722
Harold Dates, *Director*
EMP: 36
SQ FT: 15,255
SALES: 4.2MM Privately Held
SIC: 8699 Animal humane society

(G-3734)
HAMMOND LAW GROUP LLC
441 Vine St Ste 3200 (45202-2800)
PHONE 513 381-2011
Fax: 513 381-2227
Michael F Hammond,
Jonathan A Hammond, *Legal Staff*
Jonathan Hammond, *Legal Staff*
Colleen Sullivan, *Legal Staff*
Christopher Pogue, *Associate*
EMP: 30
SALES (est): 4.1MM Privately Held
WEB: www.hammondlawfirm.com
SIC: 8111 General practice attorney, lawyer

(G-3735)
HANEY INC
Also Called: Haney PRC
5657 Wooster Pike (45227-4120)
PHONE 513 561-1441
Fax: 513 561-1442
Matthew J Haney, *CEO*
Daniel E Haney, *President*
Jeff Milinovich, *Vice Pres*
Damon Alford, *Opers Staff*
Mike Sewak, *QC Mgr*
EMP: 52
SQ FT: 4,000
SALES (est): 10.1MM Privately Held
SIC: 7336 Graphic arts & related design

(G-3736)
HARBOR FREIGHT TOOLS USA INC
5710 Harrison Ave (45248-1602)
PHONE 513 598-4897
Fax: 513 598-6807
Jeff Raymond, *Principal*
EMP: 77
SALES (corp-wide): 2.3B Privately Held
SIC: 4213 Trucking, except local
PA: Harbor Freight Tools Usa, Inc.
    26541 Agoura Rd
    Calabasas CA 91302
    818 836-5001

(G-3737)
HARRIS DISTRIBUTING CO
4261 Crawford Ave (45223-1857)
PHONE 513 541-4222
Irma Harris, *President*
Carl Harris Jr, *Vice Pres*
Dennis A Harris, *Vice Pres*
Patricia Junker, *Treasurer*
EMP: 30
SALES (est): 3.6MM Privately Held
SIC: 4213 Contract haulers

(G-3738)
HARRISON PAVILION
2171 Harrison Ave (45211-8159)
PHONE 513 662-5800
Fax: 513 389-4584
Skip Roos, *Principal*
EMP: 35
SALES (est): 2.5MM Privately Held
SIC: 8322 8059 Rehabilitation services; nursing home, except skilled & intermediate care facility

(G-3739)
HARTE-HANKS TRNSP SVCS
2950 Robinson Ave (45209)
PHONE 513 458-7600
Fax: 513 458-7644
Paul Lampone, *Manager*
EMP: 55
SALES (corp-wide): 9.3MM Privately Held
SIC: 4213 Trucking, except local
PA: Harte-Hanks Transportation Services
    1400 E Nwport Ctr Dr 21
    Deerfield Beach FL 33442
    954 429-3771

Cincinnati - Hamilton County (G-3740)

GEOGRAPHIC SECTION

(G-3740)
HARTWIG TRANSIT INC
11971 Reading Rd (45241-1543)
PHONE..................513 563-1765
Fax: 513 563-1806
Caleb France, *Manager*
EMP: 40
SQ FT: 3,648
SALES (corp-wide): 32.9MM **Privately Held**
WEB: www.hartwigtransit.com
SIC: 7538 Truck engine repair, except industrial
PA: Hartwig Transit, Inc.
3833 Industrial Ave
Rolling Meadows IL 60008
847 749-1101

(G-3741)
HAUCK HOSPITALITY LLC
Also Called: Holiday Inn
3855 Hauck Rd (45241-1609)
PHONE..................513 563-8330
Fax: 513 563-9679
Robin Rankin, *Sales Dir*
Susan Grodecki, *Sales Mgr*
Becky Hayes, *Sales Mgr*
Katie O'Connor, *Asst Mgr*
John Gieseke, *Director*
EMP: 80
SQ FT: 24,311
SALES (est): 4.3MM **Privately Held**
WEB: www.hicincy.com
SIC: 7011 5812 Hotels; eating places

(G-3742)
HAYES CONCRETE CONSTRUCTION
2120 Waycross Rd (45240-2719)
PHONE..................513 648-9400
Fax: 513 648-9777
Ed Hayes, *President*
EMP: 35
SALES (est): 4.3MM **Privately Held**
SIC: 1771 Foundation & footing contractor

(G-3743)
HAYS & SONS CONSTRUCTION INC
190 Container Pl (45246-1709)
PHONE..................513 671-9110
Grant Saunders, *President*
EMP: 27
SALES (corp-wide): 40.9MM **Privately Held**
SIC: 1521 Single-family home remodeling, additions & repairs
PA: Hays & Sons Construction, Inc.
757 E Murry St
Indianapolis IN 46227
317 788-0911

(G-3744)
HC TRANSPORT INC
Also Called: For Hire Carrier
6045 Bridgetown Rd (45248-3049)
P.O. Box 111116 (45211-1116)
PHONE..................513 574-1800
Edward Sedler, *President*
Rob Gillun, *Opers Staff*
Clifford Riegler, *Director*
EMP: 30
SQ FT: 16,000
SALES (est): 7MM **Privately Held**
SIC: 4212 Delivery service, vehicular

(G-3745)
HCESC EARLY LEARNING PROGRAM
924 Waycross Rd (45240-3022)
PHONE..................513 589-3021
Fax: 513 851-5747
Dorothy Echoles, *Personnel Exec*
Zena Vaughn, *Manager*
Kathleen Tirey, *Director*
Dorothy Jones, *Executive*
EMP: 150
SALES (est): 3MM **Privately Held**
WEB: www.hcheadstart.org
SIC: 8351 8741 Head start center, except in conjunction with school; management services

(G-3746)
HCR MANORCARE MED SVCS FLA LLC
Also Called: Manor Care
4580 E Galbraith Rd (45236-2799)
PHONE..................513 745-9600
Fax: 513 745-9777
Jana Longbons-Saab, *Manager*
Jana Longbons, *Exec Dir*
EMP: 50
SALES (corp-wide): 3.6B **Publicly Held**
WEB: www.manorcare.com
SIC: 8051 Extended care facility
HQ: Hcr Manorcare Medical Services Of Florida, Llc
333 N Summit St Ste 100
Toledo OH 43604
419 252-5500

(G-3747)
HCR MANORCARE MED SVCS FLA LLC
Also Called: Arden Courts of Anderson Twp.
6870 Clough Pike (45244-4161)
PHONE..................513 233-0831
Fax: 513 233-0832
Jay Boyce, *Exec Dir*
EMP: 60
SQ FT: 1,220
SALES (corp-wide): 3.6B **Publicly Held**
WEB: www.manorcare.com
SIC: 8051 8082 Convalescent home with continuous nursing care; home health care services
HQ: Hcr Manorcare Medical Services Of Florida, Llc
333 N Summit St Ste 100
Toledo OH 43604
419 252-5500

(G-3748)
HCR MANORCARE MED SVCS FLA LLC
Also Called: Manor Care
4900 Cooper Rd (45242-6915)
PHONE..................513 561-4111
Fax: 513 561-1496
Pat Cunningham, *CFO*
Michael Smith, *CFO*
Cindy Tipton, *Manager*
Amy McFerron, *Manager*
Aman Ahmed, *Director*
EMP: 170
SALES (corp-wide): 3.6B **Publicly Held**
WEB: www.manorcare.com
SIC: 8051 Convalescent home with continuous nursing care
HQ: Hcr Manorcare Medical Services Of Florida, Llc
333 N Summit St Ste 100
Toledo OH 43604
419 252-5500

(G-3749)
HCR MANORCARE MED SVCS FLA LLC
2250 Banning Rd (45239-6608)
PHONE..................513 591-0400
Brett Kirkpatrick, *Administration*
EMP: 105
SALES (corp-wide): 3.6B **Publicly Held**
WEB: www.manorcare.com
SIC: 8051 Convalescent home with continuous nursing care
HQ: Hcr Manorcare Medical Services Of Florida, Llc
333 N Summit St Ste 100
Toledo OH 43604
419 252-5500

(G-3750)
HCTEC PARTNERS LLC
4605 E Galbraith Rd # 200 (45236-2888)
PHONE..................513 985-6400
Laura Cottingham, *CFO*
Jordan Leach, *Human Resources*
Jon Heid, *Marketing Staff*
William Bartholomew, *Branch Mgr*
Chris Chisholm, *Consultant*
EMP: 60
SALES (corp-wide): 120MM **Privately Held**
SIC: 8742 General management consultant

PA: Hctec Partners, Llc
5106 Maryland Way
Brentwood TN 37027
615 577-4030

(G-3751)
HEALTH CARE RTREMENT CORP AMER
Also Called: Oak Pavilion Nursing & Rehabil
510 Oak St (45219-2507)
PHONE..................513 751-0880
Fax: 513 751-0882
Dorothy Dew, *Chf Purch Ofc*
Vanessa Farmer, *Corp Comm Staff*
Kimberly Jewell, *Office Mgr*
Shelley Owens, *Branch Mgr*
EMP: 113
SALES (corp-wide): 3.6B **Publicly Held**
WEB: www.hrc-manorcare.com
SIC: 8051 Skilled nursing care facilities
HQ: Health Care And Retirement Corporation Of America
333 N Summit St Ste 103
Toledo OH 43604
419 252-5500

(G-3752)
HEALTH CAROUSEL LLC (PA)
Also Called: Tailored Healthcare Staffing
3805 Edwards Rd Ste 700 (45209-1955)
PHONE..................866 665-4544
Fax: 513 797-3341
William Deville, *CEO*
Robert Gammill, *Senior VP*
Lair Kennedy, *CFO*
Sadie Wonders, *Accountant*
Andrew Lingo, *Mktg Dir*
EMP: 111
SALES (est): 14.5MM **Privately Held**
WEB: www.globalscholarship.net
SIC: 7363 Temporary help service

(G-3753)
HEALTH COLLABORATIVE
615 Elsinore Pl Bldg B (45202-1459)
PHONE..................513 618-3600
Craig Brammer, *CEO*
Jason Buckner, *Senior VP*
Pat O'Callaghan, *Vice Pres*
Ron Reblando, *Vice Pres*
Keith Hepp, *CFO*
EMP: 97
SQ FT: 18,300
SALES: 3.1MM **Privately Held**
SIC: 8621 8011 Professional membership organizations; health maintenance organization

(G-3754)
HEALTHLINX INC
Also Called: ARA Staffing Services
602 Main St Ste 300 (45202-2554)
PHONE..................513 402-2018
Brian Hubbard, *President*
EMP: 50
SALES (est): 493.1K **Privately Held**
SIC: 8082 Home health care services

(G-3755)
HEARING SPCH DEAF CTR GRTR CNC
2825 Burnet Ave Ste 401 (45219-2426)
PHONE..................513 221-0527
Brigid Mercer, *Sales Mgr*
Robert Thoroughman, *Director*
EMP: 35
SALES: 2.5MM **Privately Held**
SIC: 8322 Rehabilitation services

(G-3756)
HEITS BUILDING SVCS CNKD LLC
Also Called: Heits Building Services Cincin
52 E Crescentville Rd (45246-1344)
PHONE..................855 464-3487
Joseph Okum, *CEO*
Robert Okum, *CFO*
David Okum,
Elizabeth Okum,
EMP: 75
SQ FT: 2,900
SALES: 750K **Privately Held**
SIC: 7349 Janitorial service, contract basis

(G-3757)
HENSLEY INDUSTRIES INC (PA)
2150 Langdon Farm Rd (45237-4711)
PHONE..................513 769-6666
Fax: 513 769-9666
Trina Ewald, *President*
Linda Hensley, *President*
David Metzcar, *COO*
Thomas Young, *COO*
Dalaina Fancher, *Vice Pres*
EMP: 50
SQ FT: 182,000
SALES (est): 6.4MM **Privately Held**
WEB: www.hensleyindustries.com
SIC: 1796 Machine moving & rigging

(G-3758)
HERTZ CORPORATION
Cincinnati N Kentucky A P (45275)
P.O. Box 75016 (45275-0016)
PHONE..................513 533-3161
Art Gunpher, *Branch Mgr*
EMP: 30
SALES (corp-wide): 8.8B **Publicly Held**
WEB: www.hertz.com
SIC: 7514 Rent-a-car service
HQ: The Hertz Corporation
8501 Williams Rd
Estero FL 33928
239 301-7000

(G-3759)
HGC CONSTRUCTION CO (PA)
Also Called: H G C
2814 Stanton Ave (45206-1123)
PHONE..................513 861-8866
Fax: 513 861-7878
Mike Huseman, *President*
Sara Jones, *Manager*
EMP: 76
SQ FT: 22,000
SALES (est): 25.5MM **Privately Held**
WEB: www.hgc1040.com
SIC: 1751 1796 Carpentry work; millwright

(G-3760)
HICON INC
93 Caldwell Dr A (45216-1541)
PHONE..................513 242-3612
Fax: 513 242-3126
Wayne Moratschek, *President*
Sherree Turner, *Dean*
Daniel Verst, *Exec VP*
Steve Sprengard, *Vice Pres*
Steve P Paving, *Project Mgr*
EMP: 60
SQ FT: 6,000
SALES (est): 6.6MM **Privately Held**
WEB: www.hiconinc.com
SIC: 1741 1611 Masonry & other stonework; highway & street paving contractor

(G-3761)
HILLEBRAND HOME HEALTH INC
4343 Bridgetown Rd (45211-4427)
PHONE..................513 598-6648
Fax: 513 598-3942
Michelle Schneider, *President*
DOT Kemper, *Vice Pres*
Vicki Dirr, *Administration*
Bobbie Knue, *Administration*
EMP: 50
SALES (est): 1.6MM **Privately Held**
WEB: www.hillebrandhomehealth.com
SIC: 8082 Visiting nurse service

(G-3762)
HILLMAN COMPANIES INC
Also Called: Hillman Group Anchor Wire
10590 Hamilton Ave (45231-1764)
PHONE..................513 851-4900
Dawn Jones, *Purch Agent*
Steve Seaford, *Branch Mgr*
EMP: 57
SALES (corp-wide): 838.3MM **Privately Held**
WEB: www.quicktag.com
SIC: 5072 Hardware
HQ: The Hillman Companies Inc
10590 Hamilton Ave
Cincinnati OH 45231
513 851-4900

Cincinnati - Hamilton County

(G-3763)
HILLMAN COMPANIES INC
1700 Carillion Blvd (45240-2795)
PHONE....................513 851-4900
Rick Bore, *Branch Mgr*
EMP: 300
SALES (corp-wide): 838.3MM **Privately Held**
WEB: www.quicktag.com
SIC: 5072 Hardware
HQ: The Hillman Companies Inc
  10590 Hamilton Ave
  Cincinnati OH 45231
  513 851-4900

(G-3764)
HILLMAN COMPANIES INC (HQ)
10590 Hamilton Ave (45231-1764)
PHONE....................513 851-4900
Douglas J Cahill, *Ch of Bd*
Gail Grout, *District Mgr*
Lee Williams, *Business Mgr*
Terry R Owe, *Senior VP*
Dianne Lowry, *Vice Pres*
◆ EMP: 400
SQ FT: 270,000
SALES: 838.3MM **Privately Held**
SIC: 5072 7699 Hardware; miscellaneous fasteners; bolts, nuts & screws; key duplicating shop
PA: Hman Intermediate Ii Holdings Corp.
  10590 Hamilton Ave
  Cincinnati OH 45231
  513 851-4900

(G-3765)
HILLMAN GROUP INC (DH)
10590 Hamilton Ave (45231-1764)
PHONE....................513 851-4900
Gregory J Gluchowski Jr, *CEO*
Douglas J Cahill, *Chairman*
Ali Fartaj, *Senior VP*
John Glass, *Senior VP*
Gary L Seeds, *Vice Pres*
◆ EMP: 153
SALES (est): 783.3MM
SALES (corp-wide): 838.3MM **Privately Held**
WEB: www.quicktag.com
SIC: 5072 Hardware
HQ: The Hillman Companies Inc
  10590 Hamilton Ave
  Cincinnati OH 45231
  513 851-4900

(G-3766)
HILLSBORO TRANSPORTATION CO
2889 E Crescentville Rd (45246)
P.O. Box 62595 (45262-0595)
PHONE....................513 772-9223
Fax: 513 672-7566
Jeff Duckwall, *Vice Pres*
Michael Duckwall, *Office Mgr*
EMP: 35
SQ FT: 4,800
SALES (corp-wide): 4.9MM **Privately Held**
WEB: www.hillsborotransportation.com
SIC: 4213 Contract haulers
PA: Hillsboro Transportation Co.
  6256 Us Route 50
  Hillsboro OH 45133

(G-3767)
HILLSIDE MAINT SUP CO INC
3300 Spring Grove Ave (45225-1327)
PHONE....................513 751-4100
Fax: 513 559-4161
Thomas R Glueck, *President*
James Glueck, *Vice Pres*
Danielle Baer, *Controller*
Trish Butram, *Manager*
Beth Probst, *Info Tech Mgr*
EMP: 25
SQ FT: 100,000
SALES (est): 8.6MM **Privately Held**
WEB: www.hillsideonline.com
SIC: 5087 5169 Janitors' supplies; chemicals & allied products

(G-3768)
HILLTOP BASIC RESOURCES INC
Also Called: Hilltop Concrete
511 W Water St (45202-3400)
PHONE....................513 621-1500
Fax: 513 684-8290
Mike Marchioni, *Manager*
EMP: 45
SQ FT: 1,758
SALES (corp-wide): 116.7MM **Privately Held**
WEB: www.hilltopbasicresources.com
SIC: 3273 3272 1442 Ready-mixed concrete; concrete products; construction sand & gravel
PA: Hilltop Basic Resources, Inc.
  1 W 4th St Ste 1100
  Cincinnati OH 45202
  513 651-5000

(G-3769)
HIRSCH INTERNATIONAL HOLDINGS
4 Kovach Dr Ste 470a (45215-1061)
PHONE....................513 733-4111
Leo Stenger, *Branch Mgr*
EMP: 70 **Privately Held**
SIC: 5084 Printing trades machinery, equipment & supplies
PA: Hirsch International Holdings
  490 Wheeler Rd Ste 285
  Hauppauge NY 11788

(G-3770)
HIT PORTFOLIO I MISC TRS LLC
Also Called: Hyatt Hotel
151 W 5th St (45202-2703)
PHONE....................513 241-3575
Fax: 773 579-0107
Herb Rackliff, *General Mgr*
Debbie Reneman, *Purch Dir*
Janis L Jones, *Controller*
Casey Burnett, *Human Res Dir*
Michelle Logel, *Sales Mgr*
EMP: 225
SALES (corp-wide): 4.6B **Publicly Held**
WEB: www.hyatt.com
SIC: 7011 Hotels & motels
HQ: Hit Portfolio I Misc Trs, Llc
  150 N Riverside Plz
  Chicago IL 60606
  312 750-1234

(G-3771)
HIXSON INCORPORATED
Also Called: Hixson Archtcts/Ngnrs/Nteriors
659 Van Meter St Ste 300 (45202-1568)
PHONE....................513 241-1230
Fax: 513 241-1287
J Wickliffe Ach, *President*
Scott Schroeder, *Business Mgr*
Mitch Vanover, *Business Mgr*
Bruce Mirrielees, *Senior VP*
Bill Sander, *Senior VP*
EMP: 125 EST: 1948
SQ FT: 125,000
SALES (est): 26.1MM **Privately Held**
WEB: www.hixson-inc.com
SIC: 8712 Architectural engineering

(G-3772)
HJ BENKEN FLOR & GREENHOUSES
6000 Plainfield Rd (45213-2335)
PHONE....................513 891-1040
Fax: 513 792-7504
Michael Benken, *President*
Timothy Clark, *General Mgr*
Kathleen A Benken, *Vice Pres*
John Clark, *Manager*
Doug Young, *Manager*
EMP: 75 EST: 1938
SQ FT: 6,500
SALES (est): 5.4MM **Privately Held**
WEB: www.benkens.com
SIC: 5992 0181 5261 Flowers, fresh; plants, potted; nursery stock, growing of; nurseries & garden centers

(G-3773)
HMAN GROUP HOLDINGS INC
10590 Hamilton Ave (45231-1764)
PHONE....................513 851-4900
Steve Murray, *President*
EMP: 3405
SALES (est): 531.3MM **Privately Held**
SIC: 6719 5072 7699 Investment holding companies, except banks; hardware; miscellaneous fasteners; bolts, nuts & screws; key duplicating shop

(G-3774)
HOBSONS INC (DH)
50 E-Business Way Ste 300 (45241-2398)
PHONE....................513 891-5444
Craig Heldman, *President*
Todd Jibby, *President*
Howard Bell, *Senior VP*
Kathy Ovans, *Vice Pres*
Dave Braud, *QC Mgr*
EMP: 200
SALES (est): 73MM **Privately Held**
WEB: www.hobsons.com
SIC: 8748 Educational consultant
HQ: Daily Mail And General Trust P L C
  Northcliffe House
  London W8 5T
  207 938-6000

(G-3775)
HOETING INC (PA)
Also Called: Hoeting Realtors
6048 Bridgetown Rd (45248-3021)
PHONE....................513 451-4800
Fax: 513 451-4555
Robert Bartholomew, *President*
Steven Florian, *Vice Pres*
Dan Grote, *Vice Pres*
Jack Hoeting, *Vice Pres*
Mike Rolfes, *Controller*
EMP: 52
SALES (est): 3.8MM **Privately Held**
WEB: www.hoeting.com
SIC: 6531 Real estate agent, residential

(G-3776)
HOLT RENTAL SERVICES (PA)
Also Called: Cat The Rental Store
11330 Mosteller Rd (45241-1828)
PHONE....................513 771-0515
Toll Free:....................888 -
Fax: 513 612-5601
Peter Holt, *Owner*
Paul Lorenze, *Sales Executive*
Chris Kirk, *Marketing Staff*
Tom Moore, *Branch Mgr*
Robert Beck, *Manager*
EMP: 45 EST: 1997
SQ FT: 20,000
SALES (est): 7.9MM **Privately Held**
WEB: www.cattherentalstore.com
SIC: 7353 Heavy construction equipment rental

(G-3777)
HOME BLDRS ASSN GRTER CNCNNATI
11260 Chester Rd Ste 800 (45246-4007)
PHONE....................513 851-6300
Fax: 513 589-3211
Valerie Fee, *Vice Pres*
Dan Dressman, *Exec Dir*
EMP: 60
SQ FT: 3,000
SALES: 19.7K **Privately Held**
WEB: www.cincybuilders.com
SIC: 8611 Contractors' association

(G-3778)
HOME DEPOT USA INC
Also Called: Home Depot, The
520 Ohio Pike (45255-3728)
PHONE....................513 688-1654
Fax: 513 688-2517
Matt Hingle, *Manager*
Steve Holt, *Manager*
EMP: 150
SALES (corp-wide): 100.9B **Publicly Held**
WEB: www.homerentalsdepot.com
SIC: 5211 7359 Home centers; tool rental
HQ: Home Depot U.S.A., Inc.
  2455 Paces Ferry Rd Se
  Atlanta GA 30339

(G-3779)
HOME DEPOT USA INC
Also Called: Home Depot, The
6300 Glenway Ave (45211-6303)
PHONE....................513 661-2413
Fax: 513 389-4716
Ken Hedges, *Principal*
EMP: 200
SALES (corp-wide): 100.9B **Publicly Held**
WEB: www.homerentalsdepot.com
SIC: 5211 7359 Home centers; tool rental
HQ: Home Depot U.S.A., Inc.
  2455 Paces Ferry Rd Se
  Atlanta GA 30339

(G-3780)
HOME DEPOT USA INC
Also Called: Home Depot, The
3400 Highland Ave (45213-2612)
PHONE....................513 631-1705
Fax: 513 458-4416
Brenda Brown, *Manager*
EMP: 150
SALES (corp-wide): 100.9B **Publicly Held**
WEB: www.homerentalsdepot.com
SIC: 5211 7359 Home centers; tool rental
HQ: Home Depot U.S.A., Inc.
  2455 Paces Ferry Rd Se
  Atlanta GA 30339

(G-3781)
HOMELAND DEFENSE SOLUTIONS
128 E 6th St (45202-3211)
PHONE....................513 333-7800
James Noe, *Principal*
EMP: 40
SALES (est): 1.2MM **Privately Held**
SIC: 8748 Business consulting

(G-3782)
HONEYWELL INTERNATIONAL INC
1280 Kemper Meadow Dr (45240-1632)
PHONE....................513 745-7200
Naresh Subramanian, *Business Mgr*
Carlos Nazario, *Senior Engr*
Thomas Tike, *Human Res Mgr*
Steve Sena, *Marketing Mgr*
Tracy Glendy, *Branch Mgr*
EMP: 100
SALES (corp-wide): 40.5B **Publicly Held**
SIC: 7373 7372 Computer systems analysis & design; prepackaged software
PA: Honeywell International Inc.
  115 Tabor Rd
  Morris Plains NJ 07950
  973 455-2000

(G-3783)
HORIZON HEALTH MANAGEMENT LLC
3889 E Galbraith Rd (45236-1514)
PHONE....................513 793-5220
Raymond Schneider, *Principal*
EMP: 100 EST: 2013
SALES (est): 3.7MM **Privately Held**
SIC: 8051 Skilled nursing care facilities

(G-3784)
HORTER INVESTMENT MGT LLC
11726 7 Gables Rd (45249-1735)
PHONE....................513 984-9933
Fax: 513 984-5219
Jack Peters, *Senior VP*
Tim Becker, *Vice Pres*
Kirk Horter, *Opers Staff*
Leigh Fisher, *Marketing Staff*
Drew Horter, *Mng Member*
EMP: 40
SALES (est): 746.6K **Privately Held**
SIC: 7389 Financial services

(G-3785)
HOSPICE CINCINNATI INC
Also Called: Trihealth Work Capacity Center
2800 Winslow Ave (45206-1144)
PHONE....................513 862-1100
Katrina Trimble, *Counsel*
Dave Bertke, *Vice Pres*
Barbara Pasztor, *Vice Pres*
Tom Arnold, *Opers Spvr*
Kenneth Stone, *Engineer*
EMP: 29 **Privately Held**
SIC: 8082 8051 Home health care services; skilled nursing care facilities

Cincinnati - Hamilton County (G-3786)   GEOGRAPHIC SECTION

HQ: Hospice Of Cincinnati, Incorporated
4360 Cooper Rd Ste 300
Cincinnati OH 45242
513 891-7700

(G-3786)
HOSPICE CINCINNATI INC (DH)
4360 Cooper Rd Ste 300 (45242-5636)
PHONE.................................513 891-7700
Fax: 513 792-6980
Sandra Lobert, *President*
Cheryl Campbell, *Vice Pres*
Brendan Reidy, *Vice Pres*
Deborah Novak, *Treasurer*
Adhrain Griffith, *Finance*
EMP: 100
SALES (est): 48.7MM **Privately Held**
SIC: 8082 8051 Home health care services; skilled nursing care facilities
HQ: Trihealth, Inc.
619 Oak St
Cincinnati OH 45206
513 569-6111

(G-3787)
HOSPICE SOUTHWEST OHIO INC
7625 Camargo Rd (45243-3107)
PHONE.................................513 770-0820
Joseph Killian, *CEO*
Steven Boymel, *Ch of Bd*
Michael Doddy, *Principal*
Jane Vetorino, *Business Mgr*
Betty Barnett, *COO*
EMP: 100
SALES (est): 47.8K **Privately Held**
WEB: www.hswo.org
SIC: 8052 Personal care facility

(G-3788)
HOST CINCINNATI HOTEL LLC
Also Called: Starwood Hotels & Resorts
21 E 5th St Ste A (45202-3120)
PHONE.................................513 621-7700
Wayne Bodington, *General Mgr*
Jon Coleman, *General Mgr*
Ted Vondenbenken, *General Mgr*
Kris Brannock, *Vice Pres*
Chris Groseclose, *Facilities Mgr*
EMP: 200
SALES (est): 10.7MM
SALES (corp-wide): 5.3B **Publicly Held**
WEB: www.hostmarriott.com
SIC: 7011 Hotels & motels
PA: Host Hotels & Resorts, Inc.
6903 Rockledge Dr # 1500
Bethesda MD 20817
240 744-1000

(G-3789)
HOUSE CALLS LLC
1936 Elm Ave (45212-2536)
PHONE.................................513 841-9800
Fax: 513 841-0306
Stephanie Harden,
Darrell Harden,
EMP: 25
SQ FT: 1,200
SALES (est): 680.3K **Privately Held**
WEB: www.housecallsllc.com
SIC: 7349 Janitorial service, contract basis

(G-3790)
HOWARD JOHNSON
400 Glensprin Dr L 275 Sr (45246)
PHONE.................................513 825-3129
Howard Johnson, *Principal*
EMP: 88
SALES (est): 1.2MM **Publicly Held**
SIC: 7011 Hotels & motels
HQ: Howard Johnson International Inc
1 Sylvan Way
Parsippany NJ 07054

(G-3791)
HP INC
300 E 6th St (45202-3308)
PHONE.................................513 983-2817
April Chapman, *VP Mktg*
Bud Osborne, *Manager*
Richard Jenny, *Manager*
EMP: 50
SALES (corp-wide): 52B **Publicly Held**
SIC: 5045 7378 8711 Computers; computer peripheral equipment; computer maintenance & repair; engineering services
PA: Hp Inc.
1501 Page Mill Rd
Palo Alto CA 94304
650 857-1501

(G-3792)
HSR MARKETING COMMUNICATIONS
Also Called: Hsr Business To Business
300 E Bus Way Ste 500 (45241)
PHONE.................................513 671-3811
Richard A Segal Jr, *CEO*
Michael Hensley, *Exec VP*
Thomas B Rentschler Jr, *Exec VP*
Judith R Begehr, *Vice Pres*
John R Dobbs, *Vice Pres*
EMP: 75
SQ FT: 30,000
SALES (est): 6.6MM
SALES (corp-wide): 8.2B **Privately Held**
WEB: www.hsrb2b.com
SIC: 7311 Advertising agencies
HQ: Gyro, Llc
7755 Montgomery Rd # 300
Cincinnati OH 45236

(G-3793)
HST LESSEE CINCINNATI LLC
Also Called: Westin Cincinnati, The
21 E 5th St (45202-3114)
PHONE.................................513 852-2702
Gary Tarpinian, *Sales Dir*
Monique Taylor, *Manager*
EMP: 160
SALES (est): 500K
SALES (corp-wide): 5.3B **Publicly Held**
SIC: 7011 Hotels & motels
HQ: Host Hotels & Resorts, L.P.
6903 Rockledge Dr # 1500
Bethesda MD 20817
240 744-1000

(G-3794)
HUBBARD RADIO CINCINNATI LLC
Also Called: Queen City Jobs
2060 Reading Rd Ste 400 (45202-1456)
PHONE.................................513 699-5102
Michael Frederick, *President*
James Bryant, *Partner*
Lisa Thal, *Sales Mgr*
David Bethel, *Accounts Exec*
Julie Hengehold, *Accounts Exec*
EMP: 99
SALES (est): 5.4MM **Privately Held**
SIC: 4832 Radio broadcasting stations

(G-3795)
HUMAN RESOURCE PROFILE INC
Also Called: Hr Profile
8506 Beechmont Ave (45255-4708)
PHONE.................................513 388-4300
Fax: 513 388-4320
Mark Owens, *President*
Diana Schowalter, *Controller*
Robin Paraska, *Natl Sales Mgr*
Jennifer Holt, *Mktg Dir*
Melinda Smith, *Mktg Coord*
EMP: 34
SQ FT: 4,500
SALES (est): 3.1MM **Privately Held**
WEB: www.hrprofile.com
SIC: 7389 Personal investigation service

(G-3796)
HUMANA HEALTH PLAN OHIO INC
111 Merchant St (45246-3730)
PHONE.................................513 784-5200
Fax: 513 784-5310
Wayne Thomas Smith, *President*
Steve Ringel, *Vice Pres*
Amber Flynn, *Production*
Frank Armstrong, *VP Sls/Mktg*
Bill Banks, *Finance Mgr*
EMP: 100
SALES (est): 48.8MM
SALES (corp-wide): 53.7B **Publicly Held**
WEB: www.humanahealth.com
SIC: 6324 Health maintenance organization (HMO), insurance only
PA: Humana Inc.
500 W Main St Ste 300
Louisville KY 40202
502 580-1000

(G-3797)
HUMASERVE HR LLC
9435 Waterstone Blvd (45249-8226)
PHONE.................................513 605-3522
Billy Southerland, *President*
EMP: 30
SALES (est): 347.8K **Privately Held**
SIC: 8631 8721 Employees' association; payroll accounting service

(G-3798)
HUMMEL INDUSTRIES INCORPORATED
Also Called: David Hummel Building
93 Caldwell Dr B (45216-1541)
PHONE.................................513 242-1321
Greg Moratschek, *President*
Carl Kappes III, *Vice Pres*
Scott Whittle, *Vice Pres*
Frank Brown, *Controller*
Shanda Bush, *Office Mgr*
EMP: 30
SQ FT: 6,000
SALES (est): 3.5MM **Privately Held**
WEB: www.hummelindustries.com
SIC: 1799 1741 Caulking (construction); waterproofing; masonry & other stonework

(G-3799)
HUNTINGTON NATIONAL BANK
525 Vine St Ste 14 (45202-3133)
PHONE.................................513 762-1860
Fax: 513 762-1876
Jan Siotkowski, *Facilities Mgr*
Chad Todd, *Branch Mgr*
EMP: 120
SALES (corp-wide): 4.7B **Publicly Held**
WEB: www.huntingtonnationalbank.com
SIC: 6029 6162 6021 Commercial banks; mortgage bankers; national commercial banks
HQ: The Huntington National Bank
17 S High St Fl 1
Columbus OH 43215
614 480-4293

(G-3800)
HWZ DISTRIBUTION GROUP LLC
Also Called: Nexgen Building Supply
3274 Spring Grove Ave (45225-1338)
PHONE.................................513 723-1150
Jeff Worthington, *Manager*
EMP: 35
SALES (corp-wide): 160.7MM **Privately Held**
WEB: www.nexgenbuildingsupply.com
SIC: 5211 5032 Lumber products; drywall materials
HQ: Hwz Distribution Group, Llc
40 W Crescentville Rd
West Chester OH 45246
513 618-0300

(G-3801)
HYDE PARK GOLF & COUNTRY CLUB
3740 Erie Ave (45208-1923)
PHONE.................................513 321-3721
Fax: 513 871-3274
Jeff McGrath, *President*
Eric O'Bryan, *General Mgr*
Sandy Wassendorf, *Business Mgr*
Marshall Maynard, *Assistant*
EMP: 75
SALES (est): 2.1MM **Privately Held**
WEB: www.hydeparkcc.com
SIC: 7997 Country club, membership

(G-3802)
HYDE PARK HEALTH CENTER
3763 Hopper Hill Rd (45255-5051)
PHONE.................................513 272-0600
Aileen Jones, *Principal*
Lisa Koch, *Purchasing*
Becky Eichler, *Office Mgr*
Aman Ahmed, *Director*
Booker Betts, *Director*
EMP: 38 EST: 2008
SALES (est): 3MM **Privately Held**
SIC: 8099 Health & allied services

(G-3803)
HYDE PARK LDSCP & TREE SVC INC
Also Called: Hyde Park Landscaping
5055 Wooster Rd (45226-2326)
P.O. Box 8100 (45208-0100)
PHONE.................................513 731-1334
Fax: 513 366-4612
Michael Shumrick, *President*
Vicki Seiter, *Admin Sec*
EMP: 49
SQ FT: 9,622
SALES (est): 5MM **Privately Held**
WEB: www.hydeparklandscaping.com
SIC: 0782 0783 Lawn & garden services; planting, pruning & trimming services

(G-3804)
HYDE PARK PLAY SCHOOL
3846 Drake Ave (45209-2124)
PHONE.................................513 631-2095
Fax: 513 631-2755
Nancy Philpott, *Owner*
EMP: 35
SQ FT: 2,768
SALES (est): 788K **Privately Held**
WEB: www.thehydeparkplayschool.com
SIC: 8351 Preschool center

(G-3805)
HYLANT GROUP INC
Also Called: Hylant Group of Cincinnati
50 E-Business Way Ste 420 (45241-2398)
PHONE.................................513 985-2400
Fax: 513 985-2404
Craig Markos, *Branch Mgr*
Crystal Goodwin, *Manager*
EMP: 29
SALES (corp-wide): 122MM **Privately Held**
WEB: www.hylant.com
SIC: 6411 Insurance agents
PA: Hylant Group, Inc.
811 Madison Ave Fl 11
Toledo OH 43604
419 255-1020

(G-3806)
HYPERQUAKE LLC
205 W 4th St Ste 1010 (45202-2628)
PHONE.................................513 563-6555
Fax: 513 563-6080
Steve Bruce, *CEO*
Colin Crotty, *President*
Jeanne Bruce, *CFO*
Molly Danks, *Human Res Mgr*
Lauren McKenna, *Project Leader*
EMP: 40
SALES (est): 4.8MM **Privately Held**
SIC: 7374 Computer graphics service

(G-3807)
IHEARTCOMMUNICATIONS INC
Also Called: Wkrc-Tv/Cbs
1906 Highland Ave (45219-3104)
PHONE.................................513 763-5500
Fax: 513 763-5474
John Lawhead, *General Mgr*
Tim Fair, *Editor*
Marc Juszak, *Editor*
Darren McCullah, *Traffic Mgr*
Lisa M Freeman, *Accounts Exec*
EMP: 290 **Publicly Held**
SIC: 4833 Television broadcasting stations
HQ: Iheartcommunications, Inc.
20880 Stone Oak Pkwy
San Antonio TX 78258
210 822-2828

(G-3808)
IMAGE ENGINEERING INC
Also Called: Great Clips
7038 Golfway Dr (45239-5632)
PHONE.................................513 541-8544
Alfred Scheide, *President*
Sally Sheide, *Vice Pres*
EMP: 25

GEOGRAPHIC SECTION

Cincinnati - Hamilton County (G-3832)

SALES (est): 488K **Privately Held**
WEB: www.imageengineering.com
SIC: 7231 Unisex hair salons

(G-3809)
IMAGEPACE LLC
5375 Medpace Way (45227-1543)
PHONE...................513 579-9911
Mike Brown, *Director*
EMP: 382
SALES (est): 64.4MM
SALES (corp-wide): 436.1MM **Publicly Held**
SIC: 5122 Biotherapeutics
PA: Medpace Holdings, Inc.
5375 Medpace Way
Cincinnati OH 45227
513 579-9911

(G-3810)
IN HOME HEALTH LLC
Also Called: Heartland Hospice Services
3960 Red Bank Rd Ste 140 (45227-3421)
PHONE...................513 831-5800
Fax: 513 831-5159
EMP: 38
SALES (corp-wide): 3.6B **Publicly Held**
SIC: 8082 Home health care services
HQ: In Home Health, Llc
333 N Summit St
Toledo OH 43604

(G-3811)
IN-PLAS RECYCLING INC
4211 Crawford Ave (45223-1838)
PHONE...................513 541-9800
Dennis Boyer, *President*
Richard Smith, *Vice Pres*
Rick Smith, *VP Opers*
Mary Rose, *Traffic Mgr*
EMP: 30
SALES (est): 6.5MM **Privately Held**
SIC: 4953 Recycling, waste materials

(G-3812)
INC RESEARCH LLC
441 Vine St Ste 1200 (45202-2902)
PHONE...................513 381-5550
J M Sprafka, *Vice Pres*
Julie Arnold, *Project Mgr*
Laetitia Branco, *Project Mgr*
Naomi Croll, *Project Mgr*
Stephanie Davison, *Project Mgr*
EMP: 215
SALES (corp-wide): 2.6B **Publicly Held**
SIC: 8731 Medical research, commercial
HQ: Inc Research, Llc
3201 Beechleaf Ct Ste 600
Raleigh NC 27604

(G-3813)
INDIANA & OHIO RAIL CORP (DH)
Also Called: Central Railroad of Indiana
2856 Cypress Way (45212-2446)
PHONE...................513 860-1000
Fax: 513 538-4803
Bill Hudran, *CEO*
Gary Mareno, *Ch of Bd*
EMP: 30
SQ FT: 5,700
SALES (est): 16.8MM
SALES (corp-wide): 2.2B **Publicly Held**
SIC: 4011 Railroads, line-haul operating
HQ: Railtex, Inc.
1355 Central Pkwy S # 700
San Antonio TX 78292
210 301-7600

(G-3814)
INDIANA & OHIO RAILWAY COMPANY
2856 Cypress Way (45212-2446)
PHONE...................513 860-1000
Ryan Ratledge, *President*
Mick Burkart, *Senior VP*
EMP: 90
SALES (est): 950K **Privately Held**
SIC: 4011 Railroads, line-haul operating

(G-3815)
INDROLECT CO
630 W Wyoming Ave (45215-4527)
P.O. Box 15492 (45215-0492)
PHONE...................513 821-4788
Fax: 513 679-6243

Dave Schlager, *President*
Joseph Schlager, *President*
Greg Finn, *Manager*
EMP: 30
SQ FT: 11,000
SALES (est): 3.7MM **Privately Held**
WEB: www.indrolect.com
SIC: 1731 General electrical contractor

(G-3816)
INDUSTRIAL COMM & SOUND INC
Also Called: I C S
2105 Schappelle Ln (45240-2724)
PHONE...................614 276-8123
Fax: 513 834-6650
C K Satyapriya, *President*
Thomas A Volz, *President*
Allen Volz, *Vice Pres*
Mary Volz, *Vice Pres*
John Trammel, *Engineer*
EMP: 28 EST: 1948
SQ FT: 11,000
SALES (est): 5.2MM
SALES (corp-wide): 36.1MM **Privately Held**
WEB: www.icands.com
SIC: 1731 Electronic controls installation; sound equipment specialization
PA: Ctl Engineering, Inc.
2860 Fisher Rd
Columbus OH 43204
614 276-8123

(G-3817)
INDUSTRIAL SORTING SVCS INC
2599 Commerce Blvd (45241-1536)
PHONE...................513 772-6501
Joe Walden, *President*
Paul Pahl, *Opers Mgr*
Dan Grammer, *Opers Staff*
Angela Walden, *CFO*
Mary Tabor, *Accounting Mgr*
EMP: 35
SQ FT: 10,000
SALES (est): 4.7MM **Privately Held**
SIC: 7549 Automotive maintenance services; inspection & diagnostic service, automotive

(G-3818)
INFUSION PARTNERS INC (HQ)
Also Called: Texas Infusion Partners
4623 Wesley Ave Ste H (45212-2272)
PHONE...................513 396-6060
Dana Soper, *Vice Pres*
Ray Di Saldo, *Vice Pres*
Pat Humphrey, *Controller*
Tonya Osborne, *Accounts Exec*
▲ EMP: 27
SQ FT: 12,000
SALES (est): 12.6MM
SALES (corp-wide): 23.6MM **Privately Held**
SIC: 8082 Home health care services
PA: The Deaconess Associations Inc
615 Elsinore Pl Bldg B
Cincinnati OH 45202
513 559-2100

(G-3819)
INNERWORKINGS INC
7141 E Kemper Rd (45249-1028)
PHONE...................513 984-9500
Danny Roundtree, *Opers Staff*
EMP: 32
SALES (corp-wide): 1.1B **Publicly Held**
SIC: 8742 Marketing consulting services
PA: Innerworkings, Inc.
600 W Chicago Ave Ste 850
Chicago IL 60654
312 642-3700

(G-3820)
INREALITY LLC
403 Vine St Ste 200 (45202-2830)
PHONE...................513 218-9603
John Decaprio, *CEO*
Michelle Murcia, *CFO*
Shaun Yeu, *Controller*
EMP: 27
SALES: 5MM **Privately Held**
SIC: 7371 Computer software development & applications

(G-3821)
INSTITUTE/REPRODUCTIVE HEALTH
2123 Auburn Ave Ste A44 (45219-2906)
PHONE...................513 585-2355
Michael D Scheiber MD, *Partner*
Sheris Awadalla MD, *Partner*
Michael Thomas, *Endocrinology*
EMP: 25
SALES (est): 1.2MM **Privately Held**
SIC: 8011 General & family practice, physician/surgeon

(G-3822)
INSTRMNTATION CTRL SYSTEMS INC
Also Called: Ics Electrical Services
11355 Sebring Dr (45240-2796)
PHONE...................513 662-2600
Fax: 513 662-2011
John Guenther, *President*
Cristein French, *Office Mgr*
▲ EMP: 43
SQ FT: 15,500
SALES (est): 7.6MM **Privately Held**
WEB: www.icselectricalservices.com
SIC: 1731 7629 3613 General electrical contractor; electric power systems contractors; electronic controls installation; fiber optic cable installation; electrical measuring instrument repair & calibration; control panels, electric

(G-3823)
INSULATING SALES CO INC
11430 Sebring Dr (45240-2791)
PHONE...................513 742-2600
Fax: 513 742-2661
Steve Adam, *President*
Josh Adam, *Vice Pres*
Rebbeca Adam, *Vice Pres*
Thomas E Meckstroth, *Treasurer*
Becky Adam, *Info Tech Mgr*
EMP: 30
SQ FT: 8,000
SALES (est): 3MM **Privately Held**
SIC: 1742 Insulation, buildings

(G-3824)
INTEGRA GROUP INC
Also Called: Health Service Preferred
16 Triangle Park Dr # 1600 (45246-3411)
PHONE...................513 326-5600
Fax: 513 326-5610
Kathleen Lutz, *President*
Rose Longworth, *Financial Exec*
Sarah Rice, *Med Doctor*
Mark Warner, *CIO*
Karen Cassidy, *Admin Asst*
EMP: 28
SALES (est): 2.5MM **Privately Held**
WEB: www.integragrp.com
SIC: 8742 Hospital & health services consultant

(G-3825)
INTEGRA OHIO INC
4900 Charlemar Dr Bldg A (45227-1595)
PHONE...................513 378-5214
Chuck Gomien, *Principal*
Chuk Gomein, *Controller*
Ted Melton, *Sales Dir*
Debra Rich, *Administration*
EMP: 343
SALES (est): 1.8MM **Publicly Held**
WEB: www.integra-ls.com
SIC: 8741 Business management
PA: Integra Lifesciences Holdings Corporation
311 Enterprise Dr
Plainsboro NJ 08536

(G-3826)
INTEGRA REALTY RESOURCES - CIN
8241 Cornell Rd Ste 210 (45249-2285)
PHONE...................513 561-2305
Gary Wright, *Principal*
EMP: 277
SALES (est): 7.2MM
SALES (corp-wide): 164.9MM **Privately Held**
SIC: 8742 Management consulting services

PA: Integra Realty Resources, Inc.
7800 E Union Ave Ste 400
Denver CO 80237
212 255-7858

(G-3827)
INTEGRATED PROTECTION SVCS INC (PA)
Also Called: I P S
5303 Lester Rd (45213-2523)
PHONE...................513 631-5505
Fax: 513 631-4140
Garfield Hartman, *President*
Richard Keller, *COO*
Andy Boyd, *Vice Pres*
Adam Kalemba, *Project Mgr*
Tim Bauer, *Opers Staff*
EMP: 55
SQ FT: 15,000
SALES (est): 14.2MM **Privately Held**
WEB: www.integratedprotection.com
SIC: 7382 Burglar alarm maintenance & monitoring

(G-3828)
INTEGRITY EX LOGISTICS LLC
4420 Cooper Rd (45242-5615)
P.O. Box 42275 (45242-0275)
PHONE...................888 374-5138
James Steger, *President*
Matt Darrah, *Accounts Exec*
Alyssa Marlin, *Accounts Exec*
Kristen Rossi, *Accounts Exec*
Amanda Pynappel, *Admin Asst*
EMP: 116
SQ FT: 6,000
SALES (est): 55.9MM **Privately Held**
SIC: 4212 4731 Local trucking, without storage; truck transportation brokers

(G-3829)
INTELLIQ HEALTH
5050 Section Ave Ste 320 (45212-2052)
PHONE...................513 489-8838
Fax: 513 489-3691
Robert V Miller, *President*
Ronald L Garner, *Vice Pres*
Lyn Kummer, *Vice Pres*
Alexander Carol, *Executive*
EMP: 60
SQ FT: 8,500
SALES (est): 3.7MM **Privately Held**
WEB: www.cooper-research.com
SIC: 8732 Market analysis or research

(G-3830)
INTER HEALT CARE OF CAMBR ZANE
Also Called: Interim Services
8050 Hosbrook Rd Ste 406 (45236-2907)
PHONE...................513 984-1110
Fax: 513 984-1442
Tom Kirker, *Branch Mgr*
EMP: 39 **Privately Held**
SIC: 8049 8082 Nurses & other medical assistants; home health care services
PA: Interim Health Care Of Cambridge-Zanesville, Inc
960 Checkrein Ave Ste A
Columbus OH 43229

(G-3831)
INTERACT FOR HEALTH
Also Called: HEALTH FOUNDATION OF GREATER C
3805 Edwards Rd Ste 500 (45209-1948)
PHONE...................513 458-6600
Fax: 513 458-6610
Donald E Hoffman, *CEO*
Jennifer Chubinski, *Vice Pres*
Patricia O'Connor, *Vice Pres*
Daniel Geeding, *CFO*
Patricia Ruwe, *Accounting Dir*
EMP: 30 EST: 1978
SQ FT: 27,490
SALES: 5.7MM **Privately Held**
SIC: 8399 Fund raising organization, non-fee basis

(G-3832)
INTERACTIVE BUS SYSTEMS INC
130 Tri County Pkwy # 208 (45246-3289)
PHONE...................513 984-2205
Fax: 513 984-2274

Cincinnati - Hamilton County (G-3833)   GEOGRAPHIC SECTION

Jeff Jorgensen, *General Mgr*
EMP: 40
SALES (corp-wide): 64.2MM **Privately Held**
WEB: www.ibs.com
SIC: 7379 Data processing consultant
PA: Interactive Business Systems, Inc.
2625 Bttrfeld Rd Ste 114w
Oak Brook IL 60523
630 571-9100

(G-3833)
INTERACTIVE SOLUTIONS INTL LLC
155 Tri County Pkwy 111 (45246-3238)
PHONE 513 619-5100
Rodney Sizemore, *Mng Member*
EMP: 26 **EST:** 2000
SQ FT: 9,600
SALES (est): 978.6K
SALES (corp-wide): 42.4MM **Privately Held**
WEB: www.citywatch.com
SIC: 8748 Communications consulting
PA: Avtex Solutions, Llc
3500 Amrcn Blvd W Ste 300
Minneapolis MN 55431
952 831-0888

(G-3834)
INTERBRAND DESIGN FORUM INC
700 W Pete Rose Way # 460 (45203-1870)
PHONE 937 439-4400
Fax: 937 439-4340
D Lee Carpenter, *CEO*
Scott Smith, *Vice Pres*
Mandy Napier, *Marketing Staff*
Joseph Poulous, *Manager*
Peter Acimovic, *Senior Mgr*
EMP: 225
SQ FT: 35,000
SALES (est): 25.8MM
SALES (corp-wide): 15.2B **Publicly Held**
WEB: www.designforum.com
SIC: 8742 7389 Planning consultant; merchandising consultant; interior design services
HQ: Interbrand Corporation
130 5th Ave Fl 4
New York NY 10011
212 798-7500

(G-3835)
INTERBRAND HULEFELD INC
700 W Pete Rose Way (45203-1892)
PHONE 513 421-2210
Bruce Dyvbad, *President*
Jill Verkamp, *Senior Mgr*
Kathy Hoopes, *Account Dir*
EMP: 80
SQ FT: 23,000
SALES: 16MM
SALES (corp-wide): 15.2B **Publicly Held**
WEB: www.interbrandcinti.com
SIC: 7336 Graphic arts & related design
HQ: Interbrand Corporation
130 5th Ave Fl 4
New York NY 10011
212 798-7500

(G-3836)
INTERNATIONAL HEALTHCARE CORP
2837 Burnet Ave (45219-2401)
PHONE 513 731-3338
Fax: 513 731-3777
EMP: 85
SQ FT: 2,288 **Privately Held**
SIC: 8082 6411 Home health care services; insurance agents, brokers & service
PA: International Healthcare Corporation
6937 N Main St
Dayton OH 45415

(G-3837)
INTERNATIONAL UNION UNITED AU
Also Called: Uaw Local 863
10708 Reading Rd (45241-2529)
PHONE 513 563-1252
Fax: 513 563-2903
Tom Klein, *Branch Mgr*
EMP: 82
SALES (corp-wide): 207.4MM **Privately Held**
SIC: 8631 Labor union
PA: International Union, United Automobile, Aerospace And Agricultural Implement Workers Of Am
8000 E Jefferson Ave
Detroit MI 48214
313 926-5000

(G-3838)
INTERSTATE TRUCKWAY INC (PA)
Also Called: Truckway Leasing
1755 Dreman Ave (45223-2445)
PHONE 513 542-5500
Fax: 513 542-5572
Ron Horstman, *President*
Jeff Barber, *Vice Pres*
Robert Jones, *Vice Pres*
Shawn Watson, *Vice Pres*
Howard Elmore, *Opers Staff*
EMP: 70
SALES: 68.6MM **Privately Held**
WEB: www.itdsdedicated.com
SIC: 7513 5012 Truck rental & leasing, no drivers; commercial vehicles

(G-3839)
INTGRTED BRIDGE COMMUNICATIONS
302 W 3rd St Ste 900 (45202-3424)
PHONE 513 381-1380
Jay Woffington, *President*
Steve Fader, *Principal*
Jason Brush, *Exec VP*
Tony Ip, *Director*
Chester Tan, *Director*
EMP: 35
SALES (est): 2MM **Privately Held**
WEB: www.bridgeagency.com
SIC: 4813 7812 ; audio-visual program production

(G-3840)
INTITLE AGENCY INC
120 E 4th St Ste 400 (45202-4010)
PHONE 513 241-4094
Fax: 513 241-4094
Richard Rothfuss, *CFO*
Jan Dorgan, *Treasurer*
EMP: 100
SALES (est): 3.3MM **Privately Held**
SIC: 6541 Title & trust companies

(G-3841)
INTREN INC
Also Called: Midwest East Division
1267 Tennessee Ave (45229-1011)
PHONE 815 482-0651
Brian Carlin, *Manager*
EMP: 82
SALES (corp-wide): 158.5MM **Privately Held**
SIC: 8711 Construction & civil engineering; consulting engineer
PA: Intren, Llc
18202 W Union Rd
Union IL 60180
815 923-2300

(G-3842)
IPSOS-ASI LLC
Also Called: Ipsos-Asi, Inc.
3505 Columbia Pkwy # 300 (45226-2181)
PHONE 513 872-4300
Fax: 513 871-2292
Denice Patton, *Principal*
Marilyn O'Brien, *Co-Owner*
Chad Seibert, *Manager*
Samantha Centers, *Director*
Felipe Hernandez, *Director*
EMP: 60
SQ FT: 1,000
SALES (est): 4.8MM
SALES (corp-wide): 475.9K **Privately Held**
WEB: www.understandingunlimited.com
SIC: 8742 8732 Marketing consulting services; commercial nonphysical research
HQ: Ipsos America, Inc
360 Park Ave S Fl 17
New York NY 10010
212 265-3200

(G-3843)
IPSOS-INSIGHT LLC
11499 Chester Rd Ste 401 (45246-4012)
PHONE 513 552-1100
Fax: 513 552-1112
Lisa Lanier, *Principal*
Lindsay Holbrook, *Senior VP*
Jason McGrath, *Senior VP*
Alyson Scanlon, *Senior VP*
Anna Frano, *Vice Pres*
EMP: 120
SALES (corp-wide): 475.9K **Privately Held**
WEB: www.ipsos-asi.com
SIC: 8732 Market analysis or research
HQ: Ipsos-Insight, Llc
1600 Stewart Ave Ste 500
Westbury NY 11590
516 507-3000

(G-3844)
IRON MOUNTAIN INFO MGT LLC
5845 Highland Ridge Dr (45232-1441)
PHONE 513 297-3268
Fax: 513 242-0714
Brian Burnhard, *Manager*
EMP: 38
SALES (corp-wide): 3.8B **Publicly Held**
SIC: 4226 Special warehousing & storage
HQ: Iron Mountain Information Management, Llc
1 Federal St
Boston MA 02110
800 899-4766

(G-3845)
ISQFT INC (HQ)
Also Called: Constructconnect
3825 Edwards Rd Ste 800 (45209-1289)
PHONE 513 645-8004
Fax: 513 645-8005
Dave Conway, *President*
Rose Wilkerson, *Regional Mgr*
Fred Pugh, *COO*
Scott Waterbury, *COO*
Karen Herdina, *Vice Pres*
EMP: 132
SQ FT: 30,000
SALES (est): 77.7MM
SALES (corp-wide): 4.6B **Publicly Held**
WEB: www.isqft.com
SIC: 7371 5045 Computer software development; computer software
PA: Roper Technologies, Inc.
6901 Prof Pkwy E Ste 200
Sarasota FL 34240
941 556-2601

(G-3846)
ISRAEL ADATH (PA)
3201 E Galbraith Rd (45236-1307)
PHONE 513 793-1800
Fax: 513 792-5085
Irvin Wise, *President*
Debbie Lempert, *Vice Pres*
Barbara Bresler, *Librarian*
Ralph Davis, *Manager*
Sharon Wasserberg, *Exec Dir*
EMP: 25
SALES (est): 1.3MM **Privately Held**
SIC: 8351 8661 Child day care services; synagogue

(G-3847)
ITELLIGENCE INC (DH)
10856 Reed Hartman Hwy (45242-2820)
PHONE 513 956-2000
Herbert Vogel, *CEO*
Steven Niesman, *President*
Rob Clifton, *Business Mgr*
Ken Golisch, *COO*
Uwe Bohnhorst, *Exec VP*
EMP: 85
SALES (est): 93.9MM
SALES (corp-wide): 100.2B **Privately Held**
SIC: 7379 Computer related consulting services
HQ: Itelligence Ag
Konigsbreede 1
Bielefeld 33605
521 914-480

(G-3848)
ITELLIGENCE OUTSOURCING INC (DH)
Also Called: Schmidt-Vogel Consulting
10856 Reed Hartman Hwy (45242-2820)
PHONE 513 956-2000
Steven Niesman, *President*
Ken Golisch, *CFO*
Ryan Schisler, *Sr Software Eng*
Justin Brading, *Director*
EMP: 80
SQ FT: 4,000
SALES (est): 9.7MM
SALES (corp-wide): 100.2B **Privately Held**
WEB: www.itelligencegroup.com
SIC: 7379

(G-3849)
IVY HEALTH CARE INC (PA)
Also Called: Ivy Woods Care Center
2025 Wyoming Ave (45205-1112)
PHONE 513 251-2557
Harold Sosna, *President*
Kris Rolfsen, *Director*
EMP: 105
SALES: 7.5MM **Privately Held**
WEB: www.ivywoodscare.com
SIC: 8051 Convalescent home with continuous nursing care

(G-3850)
J & E LLC
Also Called: Chavez Properties
250 W Court St Ste 200e (45202-1064)
PHONE 513 241-0429
Robert Chavez, *Partner*
Manuel Chavez Sr, *Partner*
Carl Fisher, *Finance*
Pete Guggenheim, *Mktg Dir*
Beth Freemal, *General Counsel*
EMP: 30
SQ FT: 8,100
SALES (est): 3.3MM **Privately Held**
SIC: 6519 Real property lessors

(G-3851)
J E F INC
Also Called: Westside Health Care
1857 Grand Ave (45214-1503)
PHONE 513 921-4130
Fax: 513 921-5331
Jacob Fischer, *President*
Eta Fischer, *Vice Pres*
Abe Fischer, *Treasurer*
Beryl Barmore, *Bd of Directors*
EMP: 55
SQ FT: 20,000
SALES (est): 1.6MM **Privately Held**
WEB: www.jef.com
SIC: 8059 Convalescent home, rest home, with health care

(G-3852)
J RUTLEDGE ENTERPRISES INC
Also Called: Rutledge Environmental Svcs
3512 Spring Grove Ave (45223-2448)
PHONE 502 241-4100
H Jack Rutledge, *President*
Anne Evans, *Office Mgr*
EMP: 35
SQ FT: 15,000
SALES (est): 1.3MM **Privately Held**
WEB: www.rutledgeenvironmental.com
SIC: 7349 Building maintenance services

(G-3853)
JACK & JILL BABYSITTING SVC
Also Called: Jack & Jill Babysitter Serv
6252 Beechmont Ave Apt 11 (45230-1930)
PHONE 513 731-5261
Nancy Yeatts, *Owner*
N Yates, *Owner*
EMP: 28
SALES (est): 290.3K **Privately Held**
SIC: 7299 Babysitting bureau

(G-3854)
JACOBS CONSTRUCTORS INC
1880 Waycross Rd (45240-2825)
PHONE 513 595-7900
John Kadkah, *Manager*
EMP: 35

GEOGRAPHIC SECTION

Cincinnati - Hamilton County (G-3878)

SALES (corp-wide): 10B **Publicly Held**
SIC: 1629 Land preparation construction
HQ: Jacobs Constructors, Inc.
4949 Essen Ln
Baton Rouge LA 70809
225 769-7700

(G-3855)
JACOBS ENGINEERING GROUP INC
1880 Waycross Rd (45240-2825)
PHONE...................513 595-7500
Fax: 513 595-7860
Craig Martin, *President*
Thomas Bogel, *Project Mgr*
Greg Chrzanawski, *Project Mgr*
Mark Kile, *Project Mgr*
Pat Sanders, *Project Mgr*
EMP: 40
SALES (corp-wide): 10B **Publicly Held**
WEB: www.jacobs.com
SIC: 8711 Consulting engineer
PA: Jacobs Engineering Group Inc.
1999 Bryan St Ste 1200
Dallas TX 75201
214 583-8500

(G-3856)
JACOBS ENGINEERING GROUP INC
1880 Waycross Rd (45240-2825)
PHONE...................513 595-7500
John Lachlan, *Vice Pres*
J Thiesing, *Vice Pres*
Wheeler Anderson, *Engineer*
Donald Barici, *Engineer*
Ralph Norman, *Engineer*
EMP: 88
SALES (corp-wide): 10B **Publicly Held**
WEB: www.jacobs.com
SIC: 8711 Consulting engineer
PA: Jacobs Engineering Group Inc.
1999 Bryan St Ste 1200
Dallas TX 75201
214 583-8500

(G-3857)
JACOBS MECHANICAL CO
4500 W Mitchell Ave (45232-1912)
PHONE...................513 681-6800
Fax: 513 681-6855
John E Mc Donald, *President*
EMP: 125
SQ FT: 20,000
SALES (est): 24.4MM **Privately Held**
WEB: www.jacobsmech.com
SIC: 1711 3444 Ventilation & duct work contractor; sheet metalwork

(G-3858)
JAGI JUNO LLC (PA)
Also Called: Holiday Inn
8534 E Kemper Rd (45249-3701)
PHONE...................513 489-1955
Barb Soete,
EMP: 40
SALES (est): 1.5MM **Privately Held**
SIC: 7011 Hotels & motels

(G-3859)
JAKE SWEENEY AUTOMOTIVE INC
33 W Kemper Rd (45246-2509)
PHONE...................513 782-2800
Fax: 513 346-7213
Jake Sweeney Jr, *President*
Jim Daniel, *General Mgr*
Mark Postallian, *Business Mgr*
Gregory D Sweeney, *Vice Pres*
Mike Thom, *Sales Mgr*
EMP: 200
SQ FT: 60,000
SALES (est): 19.8MM **Privately Held**
WEB: www.jakesweeney.com
SIC: 8741 7538 7532 7515 Management services; general automotive repair shops; top & body repair & paint shops; passenger car leasing; used car dealers; new & used car dealers

(G-3860)
JAKE SWEENEY BODY SHOP
Also Called: Jake Sweeney Chevrolet Imports
169 Northland Blvd Ste 1 (45246-3154)
PHONE...................513 782-1100
Fax: 513 771-0307
Jake Sweeney, *Owner*
Fred Mangold, *General Mgr*
Jim Pulskamp, *Sales Mgr*
Scotty Rienschield, *Sales Mgr*
Skip Jones, *Sales Staff*
EMP: 30
SQ FT: 21,892
SALES (est): 1.9MM **Privately Held**
SIC: 7532 Body shop, automotive

(G-3861)
JAMES HUNT CONSTRUCTION CO
1865 Summit Rd (45237-2803)
PHONE...................513 721-0559
Fax: 513 721-6888
Veronica Davis, *President*
David Thierry, *Superintendent*
Chris Davis, *Vice Pres*
Rich Hinton, *Project Mgr*
Danny Rusconi, *Project Mgr*
EMP: 30
SQ FT: 5,000
SALES (est): 20.2MM **Privately Held**
SIC: 1542 Commercial & office buildings, renovation & repair; commercial & office building, new construction

(G-3862)
JANCOA JANITORIAL SERVICES INC
5235 Montgomery Rd (45212-1655)
PHONE...................513 351-7200
Fax: 513 458-3785
Mary Miller, *CEO*
Anthony Miller, *President*
Clint Bard, *COO*
Soraya Bass, *Human Res Mgr*
Amy Miller, *Accounts Mgr*
EMP: 275
SALES (est): 10.2MM **Privately Held**
WEB: www.jancoa.com
SIC: 7349 Janitorial service, contract basis

(G-3863)
JAVITCH BLOCK LLC
Also Called: Mapother & Mapother Attorneys
700 Walnut St Ste 300 (45202-2011)
PHONE...................513 381-3051
Fax: 513 744-9602
Robert K Hogan, *Manager*
K Hogan, *Manager*
EMP: 31
SALES (corp-wide): 58.1MM **Privately Held**
WEB: www.jber.com
SIC: 8111 General practice law office
PA: Javitch Block Llc
1100 Superior Ave E Fl 19
Cleveland OH 44114
216 623-0000

(G-3864)
JBJS ACQUISITIONS LLC
Also Called: Alleen Company, The
11939 Tramway Dr (45241-1666)
PHONE...................513 769-0393
Fax: 513 554-3143
Kenny Kaeser, *Warehouse Mgr*
Jeanne Trows, *Accountant*
Anne Sheehan, *Sales Mgr*
Dana McConnaughey, *Marketing Staff*
Dana Wilson, *Marketing Staff*
EMP: 35
SQ FT: 36,000
SALES (est): 5.2MM **Privately Held**
SIC: 7359 7389 Party supplies rental services; convention & show services

(G-3865)
JEDSON ENGINEERING INC (PA)
705 Central Ave Ste 300 (45202-1900)
PHONE...................513 965-5999
Fax: 513 965-5998
Rachid Abdallah, *CEO*
John Vignale, *President*
Carl Bergsten, *General Mgr*
Mark Engelmeyer, *Project Mgr*
Angela Carroll, *CFO*
EMP: 90
SQ FT: 20,000
SALES (est): 45.3MM **Privately Held**
WEB: www.jedson.com
SIC: 8711 Industrial engineers

(G-3866)
JESS HAUER MASONRY INC
7430 Roettele Pl (45231-4219)
PHONE...................513 521-2178
Fax: 513 521-2179
Michael Hauer, *President*
Jason Hauer, *Superintendent*
Jess Hauer, *Vice Pres*
Jess Masonry, *Vice Pres*
Denise Dunn, *Treasurer*
EMP: 40
SQ FT: 2,450
SALES: 4MM **Privately Held**
SIC: 1741 Bricklaying; concrete block masonry laying

(G-3867)
JETSON ENGINEERING
705 Central Ave (45202-1967)
PHONE...................513 965-5999
Judson Tammy, *Principal*
EMP: 69
SALES (est): 13.4MM **Privately Held**
SIC: 8711 Consulting engineer

(G-3868)
JEWISH COMMUNITY CENTER INC
8485 Ridge Rd (45236-1300)
PHONE...................513 761-7500
Fax: 513 761-0084
Debbie Brant, *Vice Pres*
Dedra Perlmutter, *Manager*
Matt Multer, *Supervisor*
Roz Kaplan, *Exec Dir*
Debra Gass, *Director*
EMP: 90 **EST:** 1935
SQ FT: 150,000
SALES (est): 7.9MM **Privately Held**
WEB: www.jcc-cinci.com
SIC: 8641 Community membership club

(G-3869)
JEWISH FAMILY SERVICE OF THE C
8487 Ridge Rd (45236-1300)
PHONE...................513 469-1188
John Youkilif, *President*
Doug Sandor, *CFO*
Sherry Kaplan, *Finance Asst*
Stephanie Aronhalt, *Manager*
Amanda Huecker, *Manager*
EMP: 40
SALES: 5.5MM **Privately Held**
WEB: www.jfscinti.org
SIC: 8322 Family service agency

(G-3870)
JEWISH FDERATION OF CINCINNATI
8499 Ridge Rd (45236-1300)
PHONE...................513 985-1500
Shepard Englander, *CEO*
Bret Caller, *President*
Val Krueckeberg, *Managing Dir*
Michael Sarason, *Editor*
Dan Fagin, *COO*
EMP: 35
SALES: 22.4MM **Privately Held**
SIC: 8322 Social service center

(G-3871)
JEWISH HOSPITAL LLC
4777 E Galbraith Rd (45236-2814)
P.O. Box 636641 (45263-6641)
PHONE...................513 686-3000
Fax: 513 686-5443
Aurora M Lambert, *Exec VP*
Janice Falstrom, *VP Admin*
Julie Clark, *Vice Pres*
Pam Vansant, *Vice Pres*
Stephanie Sivicki, *Mktg Dir*
▲ **EMP:** 1700
SALES (est): 185.5MM **Privately Held**
SIC: 8062 General medical & surgical hospitals

(G-3872)
JEWISH HOSPITAL CINCINNATI INC
4777 E Galbraith Rd (45236-2814)
PHONE...................513 686-3303
Patricia Davis-Hagens, *President*
Craig Schmidt, *COO*
Julie McGregor, *VP Human Res*
Laura S Lynn, *Human Resources*
Janet Mudd, *Nursing Mgr*
▲ **EMP:** 2500
SQ FT: 1,000,000
SALES (est): 144.4MM
SALES (corp-wide): 4.2B **Privately Held**
SIC: 8062 General medical & surgical hospitals
HQ: Mercy Health Cincinnati Llc
1701 Mercy Health Pl
Cincinnati OH 45237
513 952-5000

(G-3873)
JIM HAYDEN INC
3154 Exon Ave (45241-2548)
PHONE...................513 563-8828
Jim Hayden, *President*
Ruth Hayden, *Treasurer*
Ken Rehling, *Controller*
Lida Hayden, *Admin Sec*
Lisa Hayden, *Admin Sec*
EMP: 86
SQ FT: 24,000
SALES: 9.1MM **Privately Held**
SIC: 5013 5531 5731 Seat covers; automotive supplies & parts; automotive accessories; sound equipment, automotive

(G-3874)
JLW MARKETING LLC
4240 Airport Rd Ste 106 (45226-1629)
PHONE...................513 260-8418
Jerry Jenkins, *Principal*
Daniel Listo, *Principal*
EMP: 80
SQ FT: 2,500
SALES (est): 3MM **Privately Held**
SIC: 7389

(G-3875)
JOE LASITA & SONS INC
940 W 5th St (45203-1848)
PHONE...................513 241-5288
Fax: 513 241-6660
Dan Lasita, *President*
Joe Lasita, *Principal*
John M Lasita, *Principal*
Vincent C Lasita, *Principal*
Jerry Lasita, *CFO*
EMP: 35
SQ FT: 30,000
SALES (est): 19.8MM **Privately Held**
WEB: www.lasitaproduce.com
SIC: 5148 Fruits, fresh; vegetables, fresh

(G-3876)
JOHN A BECKER CO
Also Called: Becker Electric Supply
11310 Mosteller Rd (45241-1828)
PHONE...................513 771-2550
Fax: 513 771-6527
Jim Dichito, *Sales/Mktg Mgr*
EMP: 65
SQ FT: 18,880
SALES (corp-wide): 239.6MM **Privately Held**
WEB: www.beckerelectric.com
SIC: 5063 Electrical supplies
PA: The John A Becker Co
1341 E 4th St
Dayton OH 45402
937 226-1341

(G-3877)
JOHN H COOPER ELEC CONTG CO
1769 Elmore St (45223-2482)
PHONE...................513 271-5000
Fax: 513 527-3246
Gregory T Hyland, *President*
Doug Taulbee, *Engineer*
Steve Sekellick, *Sales Executive*
Martha A Hyland, *Admin Sec*
EMP: 26
SQ FT: 3,200
SALES (est): 4.4MM **Privately Held**
WEB: www.cooper-electric.net
SIC: 1731 General electrical contractor

(G-3878)
JOHN STEWART COMPANY
6819 Montgomery Rd (45236-3818)
PHONE...................513 703-5412
John Stewart, *Branch Mgr*
EMP: 63

Cincinnati - Hamilton County (G-3879)

SALES (corp-wide): 131.4MM **Privately Held**
SIC: 7389
PA: John Stewart Company
1388 Sutter St Ste 1100
San Francisco CA 94109
213 833-1860

(G-3879)
JOHNNYS CARWASH
7901 Beechmont Ave (45255-4212)
PHONE.....................513 474-6603
Fax: 513 474-6604
Kevin Mc Clurley, *Owner*
EMP: 55
SALES (est): 830.4K **Privately Held**
SIC: 7542 Washing & polishing, automotive

(G-3880)
JOHNSON CNTRLS SEC SLTIONS LLC
4750 Wesley Ave Ste Q (45212-2273)
PHONE.....................513 277-4966
Fax: 513 924-2399
Tereasa Schott, *Manager*
EMP: 25 **Privately Held**
WEB: www.adt.com
SIC: 7382 Protective devices, security
HQ: Johnson Controls Security Solutions Llc
4700 Exchange Ct Ste 300
Boca Raton FL 33431
561 264-2071

(G-3881)
JOHNSON CONTROLS INC
7863 Palace Dr (45249-1635)
PHONE.....................513 489-0950
Brian Ballitch, *Branch Mgr*
EMP: 52 **Privately Held**
SIC: 1711 Plumbing, heating, air-conditioning contractors
HQ: Johnson Controls, Inc.
5757 N Green Bay Ave
Milwaukee WI 53209
414 524-1200

(G-3882)
JOHNSON ELECTRIC SUPPLY CO (PA)
1841 Riverside Dr (45202-1738)
PHONE.....................513 421-3700
Fax: 513 421-2469
Douglas Johnson, *President*
W M Beinhart, *Principal*
A B Horton, *Principal*
Wm J McCauley, *Principal*
Robert White, *Corp Secy*
EMP: 34 EST: 1907
SQ FT: 48,000
SALES: 15MM **Privately Held**
WEB: www.johnson-electric.com
SIC: 5063 Electrical construction materials; lighting fixtures

(G-3883)
JOHNSON HOWARD INTERNATIONAL
Also Called: Howard Johnson
400 Glensprings Dr (45246-2306)
PHONE.....................513 825-3129
Robert Eckley, *Branch Mgr*
EMP: 30 **Publicly Held**
SIC: 7011 Hotels & motels
HQ: Howard Johnson International Inc
1 Sylvan Way
Parsippany NJ 07054

(G-3884)
JOHNSON TRUST CO
Also Called: Johnson Institutional MGT
3777 W Fork Rd Fl 2 (45247-7575)
PHONE.....................513 598-8859
Timothy E Johnson, *CEO*
Ryan W Easter, *Project Mgr*
Jeff Dwyer, *Opers Mgr*
Lisa Oliverio, *Controller*
Sandy Appel, *Portfolio Mgr*
EMP: 120
SALES (est): 10.3MM **Privately Held**
SIC: 6282 Investment counselors

(G-3885)
JONLE CO INC
Also Called: Jonle Heating & Cooling
4117 Bridgetown Rd (45211-4503)
PHONE.....................513 662-2282
Fax: 513 389-7737
Gregory Leisgang, *President*
Julie Gerhardt, *Treasurer*
Mike Breiner, *Sales Staff*
Ray Huber, *Manager*
Frank Boeckermann, *Consultant*
EMP: 38
SQ FT: 9,000
SALES (est): 5.2MM **Privately Held**
SIC: 1711 Warm air heating & air conditioning contractor

(G-3886)
JORDAN REALTORS INC
7658 Montgomery Rd (45236-4204)
PHONE.....................513 791-0281
Fax: 513 791-0286
Kenneth G Jordan, *President*
Jeffrey L Jordan, *Exec VP*
Michael W Jordan, *Exec VP*
Shannon Goodman, *Assistant*
EMP: 44
SQ FT: 4,000
SALES (est): 2.2MM **Privately Held**
WEB: www.jordan-realtors.com
SIC: 6531 Real estate agent, residential

(G-3887)
JOSEPH CHEVROLET OLDSMOBILE CO
8733 Colerain Ave (45251-2992)
PHONE.....................513 741-6700
Fax: 513 741-6700
Ronald Joseph, *Ch of Bd*
Louis Rouse, *Corp Secy*
Ben Bishop, *Exec VP*
Tibi Kelemen, *Manager*
EMP: 110 EST: 1965
SQ FT: 50,000
SALES (est): 38MM **Privately Held**
WEB: www.josephchevrolet.com
SIC: 5511 5521 7538 7532 Automobiles, new & used; trucks, tractors & trailers: new & used; used car dealers; general automotive repair shops; top & body repair & paint shops

(G-3888)
JOSEPH S MISCHELL
5109 Winton Rd (45232-1508)
PHONE.....................513 542-9800
Joseph S Mischell, *Principal*
EMP: 30 EST: 2012
SALES (est): 267.4K **Privately Held**
SIC: 7215 Laundry machine routes, coin-operated

(G-3889)
JOSTIN CONSTRUCTION INC
2335 Florence Ave (45206-2430)
PHONE.....................513 559-9390
Fax: 513 559-1997
Albert C Smitherman, *President*
Chris Gray, *Vice Pres*
Liza Smitherman, *Vice Pres*
Michael Mattis, *VP Opers*
Andrew Brueggen, *Project Mgr*
EMP: 50
SQ FT: 16,000
SALES (est): 8.1MM **Privately Held**
WEB: www.jostinconcrete.com
SIC: 1771 Concrete work

(G-3890)
JPMORGAN CHASE BANK NAT ASSN
4805 Montgomery Rd (45212-2198)
PHONE.....................513 221-1040
EMP: 26
SALES (corp-wide): 99.6B **Publicly Held**
SIC: 6021 National commercial banks
HQ: Jpmorgan Chase Bank, National Association
1111 Polaris Pkwy
Columbus OH 43240
614 436-3055

(G-3891)
JPMORGAN CHASE BANK NAT ASSN
822 Delta Ave (45226-1256)
PHONE.....................513 985-5120
Sheree Rosfeld, *Principal*
EMP: 26
SALES (corp-wide): 99.6B **Publicly Held**
SIC: 6021 National commercial banks
HQ: Jpmorgan Chase Bank, National Association
1111 Polaris Pkwy
Columbus OH 43240
614 436-3055

(G-3892)
JPMORGAN CHASE BANK NAT ASSN
45 E 4th St (45202-3731)
PHONE.....................513 784-0770
Erik P Hoffman, *Principal*
EMP: 26
SALES (corp-wide): 99.6B **Publicly Held**
SIC: 6021 National commercial banks
HQ: Jpmorgan Chase Bank, National Association
1111 Polaris Pkwy
Columbus OH 43240
614 436-3055

(G-3893)
JPMORGAN CHASE BANK NAT ASSN
11745 Princeton Pike (45246-2521)
PHONE.....................513 595-6450
Diane Draman, *Principal*
EMP: 26
SALES (corp-wide): 99.6B **Publicly Held**
SIC: 6021 National commercial banks
HQ: Jpmorgan Chase Bank, National Association
1111 Polaris Pkwy
Columbus OH 43240
614 436-3055

(G-3894)
JUDSON CARE CENTER INC
2373 Harrison Ave (45211-7927)
PHONE.....................216 292-5706
James Piepenbrink, *CEO*
EMP: 40
SQ FT: 59,607
SALES: 8.5MM
SALES (corp-wide): 68.5MM **Privately Held**
SIC: 8051 8052 Skilled nursing care facilities; personal care facility
PA: Saber Healthcare Group, L.L.C.
26691 Richmond Rd Frnt
Bedford OH 44146
216 292-5706

(G-3895)
JUDY MILLS COMPANY INC (PA)
3360 Red Bank Rd (45227-4107)
PHONE.....................513 271-4241
Mike Judy, *President*
EMP: 36 EST: 1922
SALES (est): 6.9MM **Privately Held**
SIC: 6512 5211 2431 Commercial & industrial building operation; lumber & other building materials; millwork

(G-3896)
K - O - I WAREHOUSE INC (DH)
Also Called: K O I Auto Parts
2701 Spring Grove Ave (45225-2221)
P.O. Box 14240 (45250-0240)
PHONE.....................513 357-2400
David Wesselman, *President*
Mary Riesenbeck, *Corp Secy*
Tom Frank, *CFO*
Larry Bowling, *Sales Associate*
Anthony Neltner, *Administration*
▲ EMP: 50
SQ FT: 9,000
SALES: 69.7MM
SALES (corp-wide): 626MM **Privately Held**
WEB: www.koiwarehouse.com
SIC: 5013 Automotive supplies & parts
HQ: K.O.I. Enterprises, Inc.
2701 Spring Grove Ave
Cincinnati OH 45225
513 357-2400

(G-3897)
K F T INC
726 Mehring Way (45203-1809)
PHONE.....................513 241-5910
Ronald Eubanks, *President*
EMP: 60
SQ FT: 45,000
SALES (est): 13.7MM **Privately Held**
WEB: www.tkf.com
SIC: 3535 1796 Conveyors & conveying equipment; overhead conveyor systems; millwright; machinery installation

(G-3898)
K R DRENTH TRUCKING INC
119 E Court St (45202-1203)
PHONE.....................708 983-6340
Kristine Roy, *Principal*
EMP: 67 **Privately Held**
SIC: 4212 Dump truck haulage
PA: K. R. Drenth Trucking, Inc.
20340 Stoney Island Ave
Chicago Heights IL 60411

(G-3899)
K4 ARCHITECTURE LLC
555 Gest St (45203-1716)
PHONE.....................513 455-5005
Fax: 513 455-5008
Larry Hatfield, *Vice Pres*
David Noell, *Vice Pres*
John A Schaefer, *Vice Pres*
Mike Christensen, *Project Mgr*
Sandy Tenhundfeld, *Project Mgr*
EMP: 60 EST: 1998
SQ FT: 25,000
SALES (est): 10MM **Privately Held**
WEB: www.k4arch.com
SIC: 8712 Architectural engineering

(G-3900)
KAFFENBARGER TRUCK EQP CO
3260 E Kemper Rd (45241-1519)
PHONE.....................513 772-6800
Fax: 513 772-7609
Rodney Swigert, *Manager*
Herbert Lam, *Manager*
EMP: 35
SQ FT: 18,280
SALES (est): 2MM
SALES (corp-wide): 68MM **Privately Held**
WEB: www.kaffenbarger.com
SIC: 7538 5531 3713 3532 Truck engine repair, except industrial; truck equipment & parts; truck bodies & parts; mining machinery; construction machinery
PA: Kaffenbarger Truck Equipment Co Inc
10100 Ballentine Pike
New Carlisle OH 45344
937 845-3804

(G-3901)
KAO COLLINS INC (PA)
1201 Edison Dr (45216-2277)
PHONE.....................513 948-9000
Lawrence Gamblin, *President*
Chris Rogers, *Vice Pres*
Stephen Sung, *Production*
Lisa Gamblin, *Treasurer*
Patty Hellmann, *Administration*
▲ EMP: 53
SQ FT: 8,700
SALES (est): 78.7MM **Privately Held**
WEB: www.collinsink.com
SIC: 5043 5946 Photographic equipment & supplies; camera & photographic supply stores

(G-3902)
KATZ TELLER BRANT HILD CO LPA
Also Called: Katz Teller
255 E 5th St Fl 24 (45202-4724)
PHONE.....................513 721-4532
Fax: 513 721-7120
Katz Teller, *President*
Mark Jahnke, *President*
Ronald Goret, *Counsel*
Jerome S Teller, *Vice Pres*
Guy Hild, *Treasurer*
EMP: 65 EST: 1967

Cincinnati - Hamilton County (G-3927)

SALES (est): 9.2MM Privately Held
WEB: www.katzteller.com
SIC: 8111 General practice attorney, lawyer

(G-3903)
KCBS LLC
7800 E Kemper Rd Ste 160 (45249-1665)
PHONE 513 421-9422
Christie Burnette, *Finance*
Robert Lynn Sarsgard, *Finance*
EMP: 35
SQ FT: 1,500
SALES (est): 3.8MM Privately Held
SIC: 5141 Food brokers

(G-3904)
KEATING MUETHING & KLEKAMP PLL (PA)
Also Called: Kmk
1 E 4th St Ste 1400 (45202-3752)
PHONE 513 579-6400
Fax: 513 579-6578
Donald P Klekamp, *Senior Partner*
J Rosenberg, *Senior Partner*
Jody T Klekamp, *Partner*
Mary Ellen Malas, *Partner*
Paul V Muething, *Partner*
EMP: 350 EST: 1955
SQ FT: 60,000
SALES (est): 50.6MM Privately Held
WEB: www.kmklaw.com
SIC: 8111 General practice law office

(G-3905)
KEEN & CROSS ENVMTL SVCS INC
504 Northland Blvd (45240-3213)
PHONE 513 674-1700
Fax: 513 674-2230
Edwin Keen, *President*
Don Cross, *Vice Pres*
EMP: 30
SQ FT: 6,500
SALES (est): 3.4MM Privately Held
SIC: 1799 Asbestos removal & encapsulation

(G-3906)
KEIDEL SUPPLY COMPANY INC (PA)
1150 Tennessee Ave (45229-1010)
PHONE 513 351-1600
Fax: 513 351-9649
Michael Barton, *Ch of Bd*
Barry Keidel, *President*
John Haynes, *Opers Mgr*
Gordon Hemsink, *Store Mgr*
Andy Hemsath, *Purch Mgr*
EMP: 49 EST: 1954
SQ FT: 20,000
SALES (est): 50.8MM Privately Held
WEB: www.keidel.com
SIC: 5074 5031 5099 Plumbing fittings & supplies; kitchen cabinets; firearms & ammunition, except sporting

(G-3907)
KELLER WILLIAMS ADVISORS LLC
3505 Columbia Pkwy # 125 (45226-2188)
PHONE 513 766-9200
Sarah Benza, *Mng Member*
EMP: 40
SALES (est): 1.9MM Privately Held
SIC: 6531 Real estate agent, residential

(G-3908)
KELLER WILLIAMS ADVISORY RLTY
8276 Beechmont Ave (45255-3153)
PHONE 513 372-6500
Monica Weakley, *Principal*
Julie E Evans, *COO*
EMP: 25 EST: 2012
SALES (est): 677.1K Privately Held
SIC: 6531 Real estate agent, residential

(G-3909)
KELLY FARRISH LPA
Also Called: Farrish & Farrish Lpa
810 Sycamore St Fl 6 (45202-2182)
PHONE 513 621-8700
Kelly Farrish, *Owner*
Stephan D Madden,
Walter C Wurster,
Robert Dziech, *Legal Staff*
EMP: 30
SALES (est): 2.6MM Privately Held
SIC: 8111 General practice law office

(G-3910)
KELLY YOUTH SERVICES INC
800 Compton Rd Unit 11 (45231-3846)
PHONE 513 761-0700
Fax: 513 761-3173
Joe Kelly, *President*
Bob Kelly, *Administration*
EMP: 25 EST: 1997
SALES (est): 1.4MM Privately Held
SIC: 8322 Youth center

(G-3911)
KENCOR PROPERTIES INC
7565 Kenwood Rd Ste 100 (45236-2835)
PHONE 513 984-3870
Greg Pancero, *President*
EMP: 50
SALES (est): 1.1MM Privately Held
SIC: 6531 Real estate managers

(G-3912)
KENDLE INTERNATIONAL INC
441 Vine St Ste 500 (45202-2858)
PHONE 513 763-1414
Fax: 513 381-5870
Thomas Stilgenbauer, *Vice Pres*
Lisa Sawyer, *VP Mktg*
EMP: 31 EST: 2014
SALES (est): 2.8MM Privately Held
SIC: 8733 Medical research

(G-3913)
KENMARC INC
Also Called: Kenmarc Electrical Contractors
1055 Heywood St (45225-2209)
PHONE 513 541-2791
Fax: 513 541-0009
Ken Stenger, *President*
Mark Baverman, *Treasurer*
William Seitz III, *Admin Sec*
EMP: 25
SQ FT: 5,000
SALES (est): 3MM Privately Held
WEB: www.kenmarcelectric.com
SIC: 1731 General electrical contractor

(G-3914)
KENWOOD COUNTRY CLUB INC
6501 Kenwood Rd (45243-2315)
PHONE 513 527-3590
Fax: 513 272-4277
Fred Habegger, *President*
Chuck Deidesheimer, *Vice Pres*
Bob Schottelkotte, *Facilities Dir*
Chuck Deisesheimer, *Controller*
Carolyn Brockman, *Human Res Mgr*
EMP: 200
SQ FT: 40,000
SALES (est): 8.6MM Privately Held
SIC: 7997 Country club, membership

(G-3915)
KENWOOD TER HLTH CARE CTR INC
Also Called: Kenwood Terrace Care Center
7450 Keller Rd (45243-1028)
PHONE 513 793-2255
Fax: 513 745-8743
Harold Sosna, *President*
Kris Rolfsen, *Director*
EMP: 145
SALES (est): 9.2MM Privately Held
SIC: 8051 Convalescent home with continuous nursing care

(G-3916)
KENWORTH OF CINCINNATI INC
Also Called: PacLease
65 Partnership Way (45241-1570)
P.O. Box 62477 (45262-0477)
PHONE 513 771-5831
Fax: 513 771-1537
John Nichols, *President*
Eldon Palmer, *Chairman*
Jeffrey Curry, *Vice Pres*
Steve Hedger, *Store Mgr*
Jeffrey Gauger, *Treasurer*
EMP: 90
SQ FT: 32,000
SALES (est): 33.1MM Privately Held
SIC: 5012 5013 7538 7513 Trucks, commercial; truck parts & accessories; general automotive repair shops; truck leasing, without drivers

(G-3917)
KERKAN ROOFING INC
721 W Wyoming Ave (45215-4528)
PHONE 513 821-0556
Fax: 513 821-2279
Dave Kern, *President*
Ken Hunt, *General Mgr*
Paul Snarski, *Project Mgr*
Dave Reinhart, *Treasurer*
Mary Sparks, *Human Res Dir*
EMP: 72
SQ FT: 20,000
SALES (est): 13.6MM Privately Held
WEB: www.kerkan.com
SIC: 1761 Roofing contractor

(G-3918)
KERRY FORD INC (PA)
Also Called: Kerry Mitsubishi
155 W Kemper Rd (45246-2590)
PHONE 513 671-6400
Fax: 513 671-6608
Patrick De Castro, *President*
Jim Bloebaum, *General Mgr*
Paul W Krone, *Principal*
Daniel J Brady, *Corp Secy*
Mark Chaney, *Parts Mgr*
EMP: 100
SQ FT: 50,000
SALES (est): 46MM Privately Held
SIC: 5511 7538 7532 7515 Automobiles, new & used; pickups, new & used; vans, new & used; general automotive repair shops; top & body repair & paint shops; passenger car leasing; automotive & home supply stores

(G-3919)
KEYSOURCE ACQUISITION LLC
Also Called: Keysource Medical
7820 Palace Dr (45249-1631)
PHONE 513 469-7881
Fax: 513 469-7885
Dave Hoffman, *VP Opers*
Dave Houston, *Accounting Dir*
Dyann Harris, *Human Resources*
Corey Ziehm, *Natl Sales Mgr*
Alexa Newberry, *Sales Mgr*
EMP: 45
SQ FT: 22,000
SALES (est): 17.3MM Privately Held
WEB: www.keysourcemedical.com
SIC: 5122 5047 Pharmaceuticals; medical equipment & supplies

(G-3920)
KEYSTONE AUTOMOTIVE INDS INC
2831 Stanton Ave (45206-1122)
PHONE 513 961-5500
Paul Howell, *Manager*
Crystal Garrett, *Manager*
EMP: 58
SALES (corp-wide): 9.7B Publicly Held
WEB: www.kool-vue.com
SIC: 5013 Automotive supplies & parts
HQ: Keystone Automotive Industries, Inc.
655 Grassmere Park
Nashville TN 37211
615 781-5200

(G-3921)
KIDNEY & HYPERTENSION CENTER (PA)
Also Called: Good Samaritan Hospital Med
3219 Clifton Ave Ste 325 (45220-3046)
PHONE 513 861-0800
Kenneth Newmark, *President*
Bobbi Falon, *Project Mgr*
Frank J Albers, *Nephrology*
Danny Fisher, *Nephrology*
Kenneth J Newmark, *Nephrology*
EMP: 25
SALES (est): 6.8MM Privately Held
WEB: www.khc.cc
SIC: 8011 Nephrologist

(G-3922)
KILGORE GROUP INC
Also Called: Columbia Staffing
201 E 4th St (45202-4248)
PHONE 513 684-3721
Suzanne Perry, *Director*
EMP: 35
SALES (corp-wide): 16.1B Privately Held
SIC: 7363 7361 Temporary help service; employment agencies
HQ: Kilgore Group, Inc.
4700 Forest Dr Ste 200
Columbia SC 29206
803 782-2000

(G-3923)
KILLER SPOTSCOM INC
Also Called: Killer Creative Media
463 Ohio Pike Ste 301 (45255-3722)
PHONE 513 201-1380
Storm Bennett, *CEO*
James H Bennett III, *Vice Pres*
Tony Frabes, *Manager*
Ray Brown, *Director*
EMP: 75
SQ FT: 4,000
SALES (est): 5.9MM Privately Held
WEB: www.killerspots.com
SIC: 7313 Radio advertising representative

(G-3924)
KINDER MRGAN LQDS TRMINALS LLC
5297 River Rd (45233-1642)
P.O. Box 33041 (45233-0041)
PHONE 513 841-0500
Don Alexander, *Sr Corp Ofcr*
Timothy E Roddy, *Sales/Mktg Mgr*
Connie Santa Vicca,
EMP: 48 Publicly Held
SIC: 4491 Marine cargo handling
HQ: Kinder Morgan Liquids Terminals Llc
1001 La St Ste 1000
Houston TX 77002
713 369-9000

(G-3925)
KINDERCARE LEARNING CTRS LLC
Also Called: Kindercare Child Care Network
1459 E Kemper Rd (45246-3905)
PHONE 513 771-8787
Fax: 513 771-3750
Lynnette Dowers, *Director*
Lynette M Dowers, *Director*
EMP: 30
SALES (corp-wide): 1.2B Privately Held
WEB: www.kindercare.com
SIC: 8351 Nursery school
HQ: Kindercare Learning Centers, Llc
650 Ne Holladay St # 1400
Portland OR 97232
503 872-1300

(G-3926)
KINDERCARE LEARNING CTRS LLC
Also Called: Kindercare Child Care Network
2850 Winslow Ave (45206-1169)
PHONE 513 961-3164
Fax: 513 569-4001
Pam Daudistel, *Director*
EMP: 26
SALES (corp-wide): 1.2B Privately Held
WEB: www.kindercare.com
SIC: 8351 Child day care services
HQ: Kindercare Learning Centers, Llc
650 Ne Holladay St # 1400
Portland OR 97232
503 872-1300

(G-3927)
KINDERCARE LEARNING CTRS LLC
Also Called: Kindercare Child Care Network
10580 Montgomery Rd (45242-4469)
P.O. Box 6760 (45206-0760)
PHONE 513 791-4712
Fax: 513 745-1501
Ruby Kalyani, *Director*
EMP: 25
SALES (corp-wide): 1.2B Privately Held
WEB: www.kindercare.com
SIC: 8351 Group day care center

HQ: Kindercare Learning Centers, Llc
650 Ne Holladay St # 1400
Portland OR 97232
503 872-1300

(G-3928)
KINGS TOYOTA INC
Also Called: Kings Toyota Scion
4700 Fields Ertel Rd (45249-8200)
PHONE.....................513 583-4333
Fax: 513 683-3671
Gerald Carmichael, President
Darren Fay, Business Mgr
Dan Precht, Business Mgr
Dennis Collins, Sales Mgr
Mike Rutherford, Sales Mgr
EMP: 95
SALES (est): 34.1MM Privately Held
SIC: 5511 7515 7538 Automobiles, new & used; passenger car leasing; general automotive repair shops

(G-3929)
KIRK & BLUM MANUFACTURING CO (DH)
4625 Red Bank Rd Ste 200 (45227-1552)
PHONE.....................513 458-2600
Fax: 513 351-5475
L Bertoli, Vice Pres
D W Blazer, CFO
Jeanie Cook, Office Mgr
Wilma Girdner, Manager
Tom Young, Manager
◆ EMP: 200 EST: 1907
SQ FT: 250,000
SALES (est): 78.7MM
SALES (corp-wide): 345MM Publicly Held
SIC: 1761 3444 3443 Sheet metalwork; sheet metal specialties, not stamped; fabricated plate work (boiler shop)
HQ: Ceco Group, Inc.
4625 Red Bank Rd Ste 200
Cincinnati OH 45227
513 458-2600

(G-3930)
KISSEL BROS SHOWS INC
6104 Rose Petal Dr (45247-5864)
PHONE.....................513 741-1080
Fax: 513 741-1081
Barbara Kissel, President
Dwayne Masek, Admin Sec
EMP: 50
SALES (est): 1.5MM Privately Held
WEB: www.kisselbros.com
SIC: 7999 Amusement ride; amusement concession

(G-3931)
KIWIPLAN INC
7870 E Kemper Rd Ste 200 (45249-1675)
PHONE.....................513 554-1500
Rodney McGee, President
Mark W Croll, Vice Pres
Felix L Rodriguez, Vice Pres
Allan C Sutherland, Vice Pres
Ronda Asher, Accounts Mgr
EMP: 45
SQ FT: 17,000
SALES (est): 6.5MM Privately Held
SIC: 7371 5045 Computer software development; computer software
HQ: Signode Packaging Group Nz
Level 7
Wellington
927 276-22

(G-3932)
KLOECKNER METALS CORPORATION
11501 Reading Rd (45241-2240)
PHONE.....................513 769-4000
Darryle Grinstead, General Mgr
Darryl Grinstead, Branch Mgr
EMP: 76
SALES (corp-wide): 7.4B Privately Held
WEB: www.macsteelusa.com
SIC: 5051 Steel
HQ: Kloeckner Metals Corporation
500 Colonial Center Pkwy # 500
Roswell GA 30076

(G-3933)
KLOSTERMAN BAKING CO
1000 E Ross Ave (45217-1191)
PHONE.....................513 242-1004
Fax: 513 242-3703
Diane Bullock, Human Res Dir
Larry Moore, Manager
EMP: 85
SALES (corp-wide): 212.9MM Privately Held
SIC: 5149 2051 Bakery products; bread, cake & related products
PA: Klosterman Baking Co.
4760 Paddock Rd
Cincinnati OH 45229
513 242-5667

(G-3934)
KMH SYSTEMS INC
675 Redna Ter (45215-1108)
PHONE.....................513 469-9400
Phil Thomas, Branch Mgr
EMP: 30
SALES (corp-wide): 57.2MM Privately Held
SIC: 5084 Materials handling machinery
PA: Kmh Systems, Inc.
6900 Poe Ave
Dayton OH 45414
800 962-3178

(G-3935)
KNEISEL CONTRACTING CORP
3461 Mustafa Dr (45241-1668)
P.O. Box 158, West Chester (45071-0158)
PHONE.....................513 615-8816
Fax: 513 554-1303
Francis P Kneisel, President
Dennis Bustle, General Mgr
Richard Kneisel, Vice Pres
EMP: 30
SQ FT: 8,000
SALES (est): 1.5MM Privately Held
SIC: 1721 Pavement marking contractor

(G-3936)
KNOW THEATRE OF CINCINNATI
1120 Jackson St (45202-7215)
PHONE.....................513 300-5669
Alexandra Kesman, Marketing Staff
Jay Kalagayan, Exec Dir
Jason Ballweber, Director
Maggie Rader, Director
Lissa Gapultos, Bd of Directors
EMP: 25
SALES: 615K Privately Held
SIC: 7999 Amusement ride

(G-3937)
KNOWLEDGEWORKS FOUNDATION (PA)
1 W 4th St Ste 200 (45202-3624)
PHONE.....................513 241-1422
Tim Tuff, CEO
Brian Ross, President
William E McNeese, Senior VP
Andrew Benson, Vice Pres
Holly A Brinkman, Vice Pres
EMP: 93
SQ FT: 8,000
SALES: 8.8MM Privately Held
WEB: www.kwfdn.org
SIC: 8299 8742 Educational services; management consulting services

(G-3938)
KOHNEN & PATTON
201 E 5th St Ste 800 (45202-4190)
PHONE.....................513 381-0656
Malinda L Langston, Partner
EMP: 50
SALES (est): 1.2MM Privately Held
SIC: 8111 General practice attorney, lawyer

(G-3939)
KOI ENTERPRISES INC (HQ)
Also Called: K O I
2701 Spring Grove Ave (45225-2221)
P.O. Box 14240 (45250-0240)
PHONE.....................513 357-2400
Fax: 513 723-9204
David Wesselman, President
Bill Beckman, General Mgr
Joe Eagan, Regional Mgr
Marty Spegal, Regional Mgr
Michael Wesselman, VP Opers
▲ EMP: 100
SALES (est): 495.8MM
SALES (corp-wide): 626MM Privately Held
SIC: 5013 5531 Automotive supplies & parts; automotive & home supply stores
PA: Fisher Auto Parts, Inc.
512 Greenville Ave
Staunton VA 24401
540 885-8901

(G-3940)
KPMG LLP
312 Walnut Strste 3400 (45202)
PHONE.....................513 421-6430
Rick Siebert, Branch Mgr
Sean Morrison, Senior Mgr
Kari Palmer, Senior Mgr
Bill Sutherland, Contractor
EMP: 120
SALES (corp-wide): 5.3B Privately Held
SIC: 8721 Certified public accountant
PA: Kpmg Llp
345 Park Ave Lowr Ll4
New York NY 10154
212 758-9700

(G-3941)
KRAFT ELECTRICAL CONTG INC (PA)
Also Called: Kraft Electrical & Telecom Svs
5710 Hillside Ave (45233-1508)
PHONE.....................513 467-0500
Fax: 513 467-0200
Kelly Degregorio, President
Mike Jungkunz, Vice Pres
John Kraft, Vice Pres
Dave Joesting, Draft/Design
Craig Adams, Manager
EMP: 39
SALES (est): 13.4MM Privately Held
WEB: www.kecc.com
SIC: 1731 General electrical contractor

(G-3942)
KRAMER & FELDMAN INC
7636 Production Dr (45237-3209)
PHONE.....................513 821-7444
Fax: 513 821-2271
Daniel Kramer, President
Lori Feldman, Corp Secy
Michael Feldman, Vice Pres
Joshua Smallwood, Project Mgr
Renee Kraus, Office Mgr
EMP: 27
SQ FT: 8,000
SALES: 10.8MM Privately Held
WEB: www.kfigeneralcontractor.com
SIC: 1542 1541 Commercial & office building contractors; industrial buildings & warehouses

(G-3943)
KRAMIG CO
323 S Wayne Ave (45215-4522)
P.O. Box 9909 (45209-0909)
PHONE.....................513 761-4010
Andrew Kulesza, President
David Pierce Jr, COO
Sean Murphy, Project Mgr
Jeff Wilkening, Project Mgr
Brian Dietz, Safety Mgr
EMP: 40 EST: 1987
SALES (est): 951.3K Privately Held
SIC: 1742 1799 Plastering, drywall & insulation; scaffolding construction; asbestos removal & encapsulation

(G-3944)
KREBS STEVE BP OIL CO
930 Tennessee Ave (45229-1006)
P.O. Box 17108 (45217-0108)
PHONE.....................513 641-0150
Steven Krebs, Owner
Kristen Krebbs, Co-Owner
Bill Chapman, Maintence Staff
EMP: 40 EST: 1967
SALES (est): 5.2MM Privately Held
SIC: 5172 Gasoline

(G-3945)
KRELLER BUS INFO GROUP INC
Also Called: Kreller Group
817 Main St Ste 300 (45202-2153)
PHONE.....................513 723-8900
Fax: 513 723-8907
Joe Davidoski, President
Harvey Rosen, COO
Scott Shaffer, Vice Pres
Christy Temple, Sales Staff
Bonnie Keller, Administration
EMP: 30
SQ FT: 5,000
SALES (est): 8.1MM Privately Held
WEB: www.kreller.com
SIC: 7323 7381 Credit reporting services; private investigator

(G-3946)
KROGER CO
150 Tri County Pkwy (45246-3246)
P.O. Box 46234 0234 (45246)
PHONE.....................513 782-3300
Fax: 513 782-3359
Jeff Covert, President
Tim Purdon, District Mgr
Tod Foley, Controller
Sean Powerly, Controller
Cathy Hendrix, Human Res Dir
EMP: 200
SALES (corp-wide): 122.6B Publicly Held
SIC: 5411 8741 Supermarkets, chain; management services
PA: The Kroger Co
1014 Vine St Ste 1000
Cincinnati OH 45202
513 762-4000

(G-3947)
KROGER CO FOUNDATION
1014 Vine St Ste 1000 (45202-1119)
P.O. Box 305261, Nashville TN (37230-5261)
PHONE.....................513 762-4000
Donald Becker, Exec VP
Kathleen Barclay, Senior VP
Christopher Hjelm, Senior VP
J M Schlotman, Senior VP
R P Williams, Senior VP
EMP: 44
SALES (est): 3.3MM Privately Held
SIC: 8699 Charitable organization

(G-3948)
KUEMPEL SERVICE INC
3976 Southern Ave (45227-3562)
PHONE.....................513 271-6500
Fax: 513 271-4676
Joseph Clark, CEO
John L Kuempel Jr, Vice Pres
Dave Gleason, Project Mgr
Thomas Sucher, Project Mgr
Mike Harris, Safety Mgr
EMP: 30 EST: 1981
SQ FT: 35,000
SALES (est): 5MM
SALES (corp-wide): 7.6B Publicly Held
WEB: www.emcorgroup.com
SIC: 1711 Heating & air conditioning contractors; mechanical contractor; warm air heating & air conditioning contractor; refrigeration contractor
PA: Emcor Group, Inc.
301 Merritt 7 Fl 6
Norwalk CT 06851
203 849-7800

(G-3949)
KUNKEL PHARMACEUTICALS INC
Also Called: Kunkel Apothecary
7717 Beechmont Ave (45255-4203)
PHONE.....................513 231-1943
Fax: 513 231-1442
John Dinkelaker, President
Donna Dinkelaker, Vice Pres
David Barbaric, Manager
Rich Broderick, Manager
Lynn Lewis, Admin Sec
EMP: 35
SQ FT: 10,600
SALES (est): 5.4MM Privately Held
WEB: www.kunkelrx.com
SIC: 5912 5047 Drug stores; surgical equipment & supplies

(G-3950)
KURZHALS INC
6847 Menz Ln (45233-4312)
PHONE.....................513 941-4624

Cincinnati - Hamilton County (G-3973)

Fax: 513 661-3587
John Kurzhals, *President*
Ed Kurzhals, *Vice Pres*
Rick Kurzhals, *Vice Pres*
Margaret Kurzhals, *Admin Sec*
EMP: 35
SALES (est): 3.2MM **Privately Held**
SIC: 1741 Bricklaying

(G-3951) KZF BWSC JOINT VENTURE
700 Broadway St (45202-2237)
PHONE.................513 621-6211
Bill Wilson, *President*
EMP: 50
SALES (est): 1.6MM **Privately Held**
SIC: 8712 8711 Architectural services; engineering services

(G-3952) KZF DESIGN INC
700 Broadway St (45202-6010)
PHONE.................513 621-6211
Fax: 513 621-6530
Robert B Steele, *CEO*
William H Wilson III, *President*
Joe Morgan, *Exec VP*
Greg Otis, *Exec VP*
Gregory Otis, *Exec VP*
EMP: 74 **EST:** 1956
SQ FT: 36,000
SALES (est): 11.6MM **Privately Held**
SIC: 8712 8711 Architectural engineering; engineering services

(G-3953) L M BERRY AND COMPANY
312 Plum St Ste 600 (45202-4809)
PHONE.................513 768-7700
Michele Emmert, *Manager*
Sam Crowley, *Manager*
Kevin Payne, *Manager*
EMP: 100
SALES (corp-wide): 71MM **Privately Held**
SIC: 5199 Advertising specialties
PA: L. M. Berry And Company
  3170 Kettering Blvd
  Moraine OH 45439
  937 296-2121

(G-3954) LA FORCE INC
2851 E Kemper Rd (45241-1819)
P.O. Box 10068, Green Bay WI (54307-0068)
PHONE.................513 772-0783
Brian Vogeltanz, *Credit Mgr*
Mark Laforce, *Sales Staff*
Jodie Gilroy, *Marketing Staff*
Tom Gaible, *Branch Mgr*
EMP: 30
SALES (corp-wide): 156.3MM **Privately Held**
WEB: www.laforceinc.com
SIC: 5031 Doors; metal doors, sash & trim; building materials, interior
PA: La Force, Inc.
  1060 W Mason St
  Green Bay WI 54303
  920 497-7100

(G-3955) LABONE INC
3200 Burnet Ave (45229-3019)
PHONE.................513 585-9000
Dr Wendell O'Neal, *VP Opers*
Lorene Altenbernd, *Purchasing*
EMP: 600
SALES (corp-wide): 7.7B **Publicly Held**
SIC: 8071 Medical laboratories
HQ: Labone, Inc.
  10101 Renner Blvd
  Lenexa KS 66219
  913 888-1770

(G-3956) LABORATORY CORPORATION AMERICA
Also Called: Genetica Dna Laboratories
1737 Tennessee Ave (45229-1201)
PHONE.................513 242-6800
Fax: 513 482-4877
Erin Hall, *Senior Mgr*
EMP: 25 **Publicly Held**
SIC: 8071 Testing laboratories

HQ: Laboratory Corporation Of America
  358 S Main St Ste 458
  Burlington NC 27215
  336 229-1127

(G-3957) LACAISSE INC
700 Broadway St (45202-2237)
PHONE.................513 621-6211
Bill Wilson, *President*
Robert Steele, *CFO*
EMP: 80
SALES (est): 3.8MM **Privately Held**
SIC: 8712 Architectural engineering

(G-3958) LAFAYETTE LIFE INSURANCE CO (DH)
400 Broadway St (45202-3312)
P.O. Box 5740 (45201-5740)
PHONE.................800 443-8793
Fax: 765 477-3349
Larry Griypp, *President*
Vincent Serpe, *President*
William Olds, *COO*
Jeffrey A Poxon, *Senior VP*
G Allhands, *Assistant VP*
EMP: 185
SQ FT: 102,000
SALES (est): 35.3MM **Privately Held**
WEB: www.llic.com
SIC: 6311 Life insurance
HQ: Western & Southern Financial Group, Inc.
  400 Broadway St
  Cincinnati OH 45202
  866 832-7719

(G-3959) LAIDLAW TRANSIT SERVICES INC (DH)
600 Vine St Ste 1400 (45202-2426)
PHONE.................513 241-2200
Mike Rushin, *President*
Jeff C Baker, *Vice Pres*
Josh Herr, *Engineer*
Larry Sisel, *CFO*
Michel Churchil, *Manager*
EMP: 45
SQ FT: 23,000
SALES (est): 104MM
SALES (corp-wide): 7B **Privately Held**
SIC: 4131 Intercity & rural bus transportation
HQ: Firstgroup America, Inc.
  600 Vine St Ste 1400
  Cincinnati OH 45202
  513 241-2200

(G-3960) LANGDON INC
9865 Wayne Ave (45215-1403)
P.O. Box 15308 (45215-0308)
PHONE.................513 733-5955
Fax: 513 733-8050
David Sandman, *President*
Michael Sandman, *Vice Pres*
▲ **EMP:** 40
SQ FT: 42,000
SALES (est): 11.6MM **Privately Held**
WEB: www.langdonsheetmetal.com
SIC: 3444 1711 3564 3446 Ducts, sheet metal; warm air heating & air conditioning contractor; ventilation & duct work contractor; blowers & fans; architectural metalwork; fabricated plate work (boiler shop); fabricated structural metal

(G-3961) LANGUAGE LOGIC
600 Vine St Ste 2020 (45202-2430)
PHONE.................513 241-9112
Richard Thoman, *Partner*
Charles Baylis, *Partner*
Dean Kotchka, *Software Dev*
EMP: 30
SQ FT: 1,500
SALES: 428K **Privately Held**
WEB: www.languagelogic.net
SIC: 8742 Marketing consulting services

(G-3962) LAROSAS INC (PA)
2334 Boudinot Ave (45238-3492)
PHONE.................513 347-5660
Fax: 513 922-2710

Denise Gemmer, *General Mgr*
Rob Kurre, *General Mgr*
Joe Mieners, *General Mgr*
Donald S Larosa, *Principal*
Mark Larosa, *Corp Secy*
EMP: 515
SQ FT: 10,000
SALES (est): 71.8MM **Privately Held**
WEB: www.larosas.com
SIC: 5812 6794 5141 5921 Pizzeria, chain; franchises, selling or licensing; groceries, general line; wine

(G-3963) LASIK PLUS VISION CENTER
7840 Montgomery Rd (45236-4301)
PHONE.................513 794-9964
Steven Jeoffe, *Principal*
EMP: 65
SALES (est): 4MM **Privately Held**
SIC: 8011 Physical medicine, physician/surgeon

(G-3964) LAWN MANAGEMENT SPRINKLER CO
3828 Round Bottom Rd F (45244-2456)
PHONE.................513 272-3808
Fax: 513 272-3820
Steven J Blauwkamp, *President*
Jill Blauwkamp, *Vice Pres*
EMP: 30
SALES (est): 2.6MM **Privately Held**
SIC: 1711 1731 1799 Irrigation sprinkler system installation; lighting contractor; fountain installation

(G-3965) LAWYERS TITLE CINCINNATI INC (HQ)
3500 Red Bank Rd (45227-4111)
PHONE.................513 421-1313
Fax: 513 421-7828
Timothy Griffin, *President*
Michael Fletcher, *Exec VP*
Ernie Overstreet, *Manager*
EMP: 60
SQ FT: 10,000
SALES (est): 10.8MM
SALES (corp-wide): 7.6B **Publicly Held**
SIC: 6361 Real estate title insurance
PA: Fidelity National Financial, Inc.
  601 Riverside Ave Fl 4
  Jacksonville FL 32204
  904 854-8100

(G-3966) LCA-VISION INC (HQ)
7840 Montgomery Rd (45236-4348)
PHONE.................513 792-9292
Fax: 513 792-5620
Craig Joffe, *CEO*
Marcello J Celentano, *Senior VP*
David Thomas, *Vice Pres*
Ronald Allen MD, *Med Doctor*
Sally Thompson MD, *Med Doctor*
EMP: 107
SQ FT: 30,000
SALES (est): 32.6MM
SALES (corp-wide): 33.8MM **Privately Held**
WEB: www.lca-vision.com
SIC: 8011 Eyes, ears, nose & throat specialist: physician/surgeon
PA: Vision Acquisition, Llc
  7840 Montgomery Rd
  Cincinnati OH 45236
  513 792-9292

(G-3967) LEE PERSONNEL INC
621 E Mehring Way # 807 (45202-3528)
P.O. Box 1175 (45201-1175)
PHONE.................513 744-6780
Gloria Sustor, *President*
EMP: 30
SALES (est): 709.6K **Privately Held**
SIC: 7363 Temporary help service

(G-3968) LEGAL AID SOCIETY CINCINNATI (PA)
Also Called: LEGAL AID SOCIETY OF GREATER C
215 E 9th St Ste 200 (45202-1084)
PHONE.................513 241-9400
Fax: 513 241-6061
Phil Harmon, *Opers Staff*
Mary Asbury, *Exec Dir*
Gayle Bogardus, *Director*
Kristi Miller, *Admin Sec*
Phillip Hagan, *Admin Asst*
EMP: 75
SQ FT: 21,000
SALES (est): 8.1MM **Privately Held**
WEB: www.lascinti.org
SIC: 8111 Legal aid service

(G-3969) LERNER SAMPSON & ROTHFUSS (PA)
Also Called: L S R
120 E 4th St (45202-4070)
PHONE.................513 241-3100
Richard M Rothfuss, *President*
Donald M Lerner, *Principal*
Teresa Miller, *COO*
Ryan Gilene, *Purch Mgr*
Janis Dorgan, *CFO*
EMP: 351
SALES (est): 39.8MM **Privately Held**
SIC: 8111 General practice law office

(G-3970) LEVEL 3 TELECOM LLC
Also Called: Time Warner Cable
3268 Highland Ave (45213-2508)
PHONE.................513 841-0000
Jeffrey Bewkes, *Branch Mgr*
EMP: 29
SALES (corp-wide): 17.6B **Publicly Held**
SIC: 4813
HQ: Level 3 Telecom, Llc
  10475 Park Meadows Dr
  Lone Tree CO 80124
  303 566-1000

(G-3971) LEVEL 3 TELECOM LLC
Also Called: Time Warner Cable
3268 Highland Ave (45213-2508)
PHONE.................513 841-0000
EMP: 29
SALES (corp-wide): 17.6B **Publicly Held**
SIC: 4813 Telephone communication, except radio
HQ: Level 3 Telecom, Llc
  10475 Park Meadows Dr
  Lone Tree CO 80124
  303 566-1000

(G-3972) LEVEL 3 TELECOM LLC
Also Called: Time Warner Cable
3268 Highland Ave (45213-2508)
PHONE.................513 841-0000
EMP: 29
SALES (corp-wide): 17.6B **Publicly Held**
SIC: 4813 Telephone communication, except radio
HQ: Level 3 Telecom, Llc
  10475 Park Meadows Dr
  Lone Tree CO 80124
  303 566-1000

(G-3973) LEVINE ARNOLD S LAW OFFICES
324 Reading Rd (45202-1316)
PHONE.................513 241-6748
Fax: 513 241-1615
Arnold Levine, *President*
Michael A Lanzillotta,
Andrew Macfarland,
EMP: 25
SQ FT: 2,000
SALES (est): 2.4MM **Privately Held**
WEB: www.cincinnatiinjurylaw.com
SIC: 8111 General practice attorney, lawyer

Cincinnati - Hamilton County (G-3974)

(G-3974)
LIBBY PRSZYK KTHMAN HLDNGS INC (PA)
Also Called: L P K
19 Garfield Pl Fl 5 (45202-4391)
PHONE.................513 241-6330
Fax: 513 241-1423
Jerome Kathman, *President*
John Recker, *President*
Phil Best, *COO*
Valerie Jacobs, *Vice Pres*
Bob Remley, *Vice Pres*
EMP: 120
SQ FT: 125,000
SALES (est): 29.8MM **Privately Held**
WEB: www.lpklive.com
SIC: 7336 Package design

(G-3975)
LIBERTY NRSING CTR RVRSIDE LLC
315 Lilienthal St (45204-1170)
P.O. Box 11499 (45211-0499)
PHONE.................513 557-3621
Tina Crouch, *Director*
Pat Schmidt, *Executive*
Linda B Kurek,
EMP: 100
SALES (est): 5MM **Privately Held**
SIC: 8051 8069 Convalescent home with continuous nursing care; specialty hospitals, except psychiatric

(G-3976)
LIBERTY NURSING CENTER OF THRE
7800 Jandaracres Dr (45248-2032)
PHONE.................513 941-0787
Fax: 513 467-3389
Linda Black-Kurek, *President*
Krystal Ellis, *Office Mgr*
Paul Haislip,
EMP: 150
SQ FT: 20,000
SALES (est): 6.8MM **Privately Held**
SIC: 8052 8322 Intermediate care facilities; rehabilitation services

(G-3977)
LIEBEL-FLARSHEIM COMPANY LLC
Also Called: Guerbet
2111 E Galbraith Rd (45237-1624)
P.O. Box 152760567 (45237)
PHONE.................513 761-2700
Fax: 513 761-2388
Cliff Brown, *Purch Mgr*
Jerry Kuemmel, *Accounting Dir*
Joseph Rhorer, *CIO*
EMP: 186
SALES (corp-wide): 392.7MM **Privately Held**
SIC: 1541 Pharmaceutical manufacturing plant construction
HQ: Liebel-Flarsheim Company Llc
1034 S Brentwood Blvd
Saint Louis MO 63117
314 654-8625

(G-3978)
LIFECENTER ORGAN DONOR NETWORK (PA)
615 Elsinore Pl Ste 400 (45202-1475)
PHONE.................513 558-5555
Jeff Matthews MD, *Chairman*
Barry Massa, *CFO*
Barry Sanders, *Finance Mgr*
Gene Scholes, *Web Proj Mgr*
David D Lewis, *Director*
EMP: 47
SQ FT: 4,500
SALES (est): 9.6MM **Privately Held**
WEB: www.lifecnt.org
SIC: 8099 Medical services organization

(G-3979)
LIFETOUCH NAT SCHL STUDIOS INC
11815 Highway Dr Ste 100 (45241-2064)
PHONE.................513 772-2110
Fax: 513 326-8522
Jody Mello, *Manager*
EMP: 50
SALES (corp-wide): 856.2MM **Privately Held**
SIC: 7221 School photographer
HQ: Lifetouch National School Studios Inc.
11000 Viking Dr Ste 300
Eden Prairie MN 55344
952 826-4000

(G-3980)
LIGHTHOUSE YOUTH SERVICES INC
Also Called: Youth Development Center
3603 Washington Ave (45229-2009)
PHONE.................513 221-1017
Karen Doggett, *Exec Dir*
EMP: 81
SALES (corp-wide): 25.2MM **Privately Held**
SIC: 8322 Youth center
PA: Lighthouse Youth Services, Inc.
401 E Mcmillan St
Cincinnati OH 45206
513 221-3350

(G-3981)
LIGHTHOUSE YOUTH SERVICES INC
2522 Highland Ave (45219-2649)
PHONE.................513 861-1111
Fax: 513 861-8803
Debbie Latter, *Branch Mgr*
EMP: 57
SALES (corp-wide): 25.2MM **Privately Held**
SIC: 8999 7389 Artists & artists' studios; fund raising organizations
PA: Lighthouse Youth Services, Inc.
401 E Mcmillan St
Cincinnati OH 45206
513 221-3350

(G-3982)
LIGHTHOUSE YOUTH SERVICES INC (PA)
401 E Mcmillan St (45206-1922)
PHONE.................513 221-3350
Fax: 513 891-3353
Robert C Mecum, *President*
Jean Sepate, *Vice Pres*
Judy Oakman, *CFO*
EMP: 65
SQ FT: 13,710
SALES: 25.2MM **Privately Held**
SIC: 8322 Child related social services

(G-3983)
LINCOLN CRAWFORD NRSG/REHAB CT
1346 Lincoln Ave (45206-1341)
PHONE.................513 861-2044
Fax: 513 487-6453
Richard Binenfeld, *Principal*
Donna Harriss, *Executive*
EMP: 41
SALES (est): 2.9MM **Privately Held**
SIC: 8051 Convalescent home with continuous nursing care

(G-3984)
LINCOLN MRCURY KINGS AUTO MALL (PA)
Also Called: Montgomery Jeep Eagle
9600 Kings Auto Mall Rd (45249-8240)
PHONE.................513 683-3800
Fax: 513 683-3262
Robert C Reichert, *President*
Lou Galbraith, *Corp Secy*
Gerald M Car Michael, *Vice Pres*
Mark Pittman, *Vice Pres*
EMP: 163 **EST:** 1954
SQ FT: 23,000
SALES (est): 42.4MM **Privately Held**
WEB: www.kingslincolnmercury.com
SIC: 5511 7514 7538 7515 Automobiles, new & used; passenger car rental; general automotive repair shops; passenger car leasing; used car dealers

(G-3985)
LINDA CPERS IDNTITY HAIR DSIGN
7800 Montgomery Rd (45236-4388)
P.O. Box 54384 (45254-0384)
PHONE.................513 791-2555
Linda Cooper-Keller, *President*
Gary Keller, *Corp Secy*
EMP: 80
SALES (est): 1.6MM **Privately Held**
SIC: 7231 Beauty shops

(G-3986)
LINDHORST & DREIDAME CO LPA
312 Walnut St Ste 3100 (45202-4091)
PHONE.................513 421-6630
Fax: 513 421-0212
William Kirkham, *President*
Michelle Korb, *Human Resources*
Paula Graszus, *Legal Staff*
Brian M Kneafsey Jr, *Associate*
Bradley McPeek, *Associate*
EMP: 51
SQ FT: 20,000
SALES (est): 5.6MM **Privately Held**
SIC: 8111 General practice law office

(G-3987)
LINDNER CLINICAL TRIAL CENTER
Also Called: Research and Education The
2123 Auburn Ave Ste 424 (45219-2906)
PHONE.................513 585-1777
Linda Martin, *Exec Dir*
EMP: 25
SALES (est): 2.4MM **Privately Held**
SIC: 8732 8731 Business research service; commercial physical research

(G-3988)
LINN STREET HOLDINGS LLC
2135 Dana Ave Ste 200 (45207-1327)
PHONE.................513 699-8825
Colleen Kroell, *Controller*
EMP: 25 **EST:** 2013
SALES (est): 1.3MM **Privately Held**
SIC: 6531 Real estate agents & managers

(G-3989)
LIQUID TRANSPORT CORP
10711 Evendale Dr (45241-2535)
PHONE.................513 769-4777
Fax: 513 554-6226
Greg Blair, *Manager*
EMP: 28
SALES (corp-wide): 285.6MM **Privately Held**
WEB: www.liquidtransport.com
SIC: 4213 Contract haulers
HQ: Liquid Transport Corp.
8470 Allison Pointe Blvd # 400
Indianapolis IN 46250
317 841-4200

(G-3990)
LISNR INC
920 Race St Ste 4 (45202-1040)
PHONE.................513 322-8400
Rodney Williams, *CEO*
Eric Allen, *President*
Vicky Sagehorn, *Vice Pres*
Jillian Zatta, *Marketing Staff*
Mick Suh, *Officer*
EMP: 31
SALES (est): 641.3K **Privately Held**
SIC: 7371 Computer software development

(G-3991)
LITHUANIAN WORLD COMMUNITY
5927 Monticello Ave (45224-2319)
PHONE.................513 542-0076
Horace Zibas, *Director*
EMP: 30
SALES (est): 1MM **Privately Held**
SIC: 8641 Civic social & fraternal associations

(G-3992)
LITIGATION SUPPORT SVCS INC
817 Main St Ste 400 (45202-2153)
PHONE.................513 241-5605
Fax: 513 361-8646
Kirk McCracken, *President*
Jo Sabrowsky, *Manager*
Paul Jahn, *Info Tech Dir*
EMP: 25 **EST:** 1981
SALES (est): 1.5MM **Privately Held**
WEB: www.litsup.com
SIC: 7819 8111 Video tape or disk reproduction; legal services

(G-3993)
LOGIKOR LLC
463 Ohio Pike Ste 105 (45255-3722)
PHONE.................513 762-7678
Chris Painter, *President*
Paul Silk, *CFO*
Abe Adams, *Representative*
EMP: 70
SQ FT: 46,000
SALES: 5.5MM **Privately Held**
SIC: 4731 Freight transportation arrangement

(G-3994)
LOSANTIVILLE COUNTRY CLUB
3097 Losantiville Ave (45213-1398)
PHONE.................513 631-4133
Fax: 513 631-3442
Steve Vanburen, *General Mgr*
Marilyn Sferra, *Asst Mgr*
EMP: 70
SQ FT: 36,000
SALES: 2.1MM **Privately Held**
SIC: 7997 Country club, membership

(G-3995)
LOTH INC (PA)
Also Called: Asset Solutions
3574 E Kemper Rd (45241-2009)
PHONE.................513 554-4900
Fax: 513 554-8700
JB Buse Jr, *CEO*
Rick Naber, *President*
Dave Gerding, *VP Opers*
Haley Dodds, *Project Mgr*
Erik Ward, *Project Mgr*
EMP: 141 **EST:** 1994
SQ FT: 212,000
SALES (est): 62.3MM **Privately Held**
WEB: www.lothmbi.com
SIC: 7389 8712 Design services; architectural services

(G-3996)
LOWES HOME CENTERS LLC
10235 Colerain Ave (45251-4903)
PHONE.................513 741-0585
Fax: 513 741-1365
Bob Czerniak, *Manager*
EMP: 150
SQ FT: 1,476
SALES (corp-wide): 68.6B **Publicly Held**
SIC: 5211 5031 5722 5064 Home centers; building materials, exterior; building materials, interior; household appliance stores; electrical appliances, television & radio
HQ: Lowe's Home Centers, Llc
1605 Curtis Bridge Rd
Wilkesboro NC 28697
336 658-4000

(G-3997)
LOWES HOME CENTERS LLC
6150 Harrison Ave (45247-7848)
PHONE.................513 598-7050
Fax: 513 598-7053
Fausto Fuentes, *Branch Mgr*
EMP: 150
SALES (corp-wide): 68.6B **Publicly Held**
SIC: 5211 5031 5722 5064 Home centers; building materials, exterior; building materials, interior; household appliance stores; electrical appliances, television & radio
HQ: Lowe's Home Centers, Llc
1605 Curtis Bridge Rd
Wilkesboro NC 28697
336 658-4000

(G-3998)
LOWES HOME CENTERS LLC
5385 Ridge Ave (45213-2543)
PHONE.................513 731-6127
Fax: 513 731-6179
Rob Harbaum, *Manager*
EMP: 150

GEOGRAPHIC SECTION
Cincinnati - Hamilton County (G-4022)

SALES (corp-wide): 68.6B **Publicly Held**
SIC: **5211** 5031 5722 5064 Home centers; building materials, exterior; building materials, interior; household appliance stores; electrical appliances, television & radio
HQ: Lowe's Home Centers, Llc
1605 Curtis Bridge Rd
Wilkesboro NC 28697
336 658-4000

(G-3999)
LOWES HOME CENTERS LLC
505 E Kemper Rd (45246-3230)
PHONE.................513 671-2093
Fax: 513 671-2187
Joe Madrigal, *Manager*
EMP: 150
SALES (corp-wide): 68.6B **Publicly Held**
SIC: **5211** 5031 5722 5064 Home centers; building materials, exterior; building materials, interior; household appliance stores; electrical appliances, television & radio
HQ: Lowe's Home Centers, Llc
1605 Curtis Bridge Rd
Wilkesboro NC 28697
336 658-4000

(G-4000)
LOYAL AMERICAN LIFE INSUR CO (DH)
250 E 5th St Fl 8 (45202-4119)
PHONE.................800 633-6752
Fax: 937 470-6424
Robert A Adams, *Ch of Bd*
Charles Scheper, *President*
Jane Rollinson, *COO*
Mark Muething, *Exec VP*
Edward C Dahmer Jr, *Senior VP*
EMP: 180
SALES: 125.4MM
SALES (corp-wide): 41.6B **Publicly Held**
SIC: **6311** Life insurance

(G-4001)
LPL FINANCIAL HOLDINGS INC
11260 Chester Rd Ste 250 (45246-0002)
PHONE.................513 772-2592
Gary Mathews, *Branch Mgr*
Edwin G Garvin, *Agent*
EMP: 287 **Publicly Held**
SIC: **8742** Financial consultant
PA: Lpl Financial Holdings Inc.
75 State St Ste 2401
Boston MA 02109

(G-4002)
LQ MANAGEMENT LLC
Also Called: La Quinta Inn
11029 Dowlin Dr (45241-1833)
PHONE.................513 771-0300
William Goetz, *Branch Mgr*
EMP: 80
SALES (corp-wide): 980.6MM **Publicly Held**
WEB: www.neubayern.net
SIC: **7011** Hotels
HQ: Lq Management L.L.C.
909 Hidden Rdg Ste 600
Irving TX 75038
214 492-6600

(G-4003)
LUXFER MAGTECH INC (HQ)
Also Called: Heatermeals
2940 Highland Ave Ste 210 (45212-2402)
PHONE.................513 772-3000
Brian Purves, *CEO*
Marc Lamensdorf, *President*
Deborah Simsen, *Treasurer*
Cindy Reinhardt, *Accountant*
Deepak Madan, *Admin Sec*
EMP: 38
SALES (est): 8.5MM
SALES (corp-wide): 414.8MM **Privately Held**
SIC: **2899** 5149 Desalter kits, sea water; groceries & related products; beverages, except coffee & tea
PA: Luxfer Holdings Plc
Ancorage Gateway
Salford LANCS M50 3
161 300-0611

(G-4004)
LYONDELL CHEMICAL COMPANY
11530 Northlake Dr (45249-1642)
PHONE.................513 530-4000
Michael Bridges, *Research*
Norma Maraschin, *Manager*
Richard Purgason, *Manager*
Sarosh Hussain, *Network Tech*
Jim Newgard, *Director*
EMP: 79
SALES (corp-wide): 29.2B **Privately Held**
WEB: www.lyondell.com
SIC: **2869** 2822 8731 Olefins; ethylene; polyethylene, chlorosulfonated (hypalon); commercial physical research
HQ: Lyondell Chemical Company
1221 Mckinney St Ste 300
Houston TX 77010
713 309-7200

(G-4005)
M & M METALS INTERNATIONAL INC
840 Dellway St (45229-3396)
PHONE.................513 221-4411
Fax: 513 221-2034
Beatrice Brunner, *President*
Steve Schuler, *Principal*
Beryl Merritt, *Vice Pres*
EMP: 25
SQ FT: 50,000
SALES (est): 11.1MM **Privately Held**
SIC: **5093** Nonferrous metals scrap

(G-4006)
M T GOLF COURSE MANAGMENT INC (PA)
Also Called: Pebble Creek Golf Course
9799 Prechtel Rd (45252-2117)
PHONE.................513 923-1188
Fax: 513 923-3297
Michael R Macke, *CEO*
Carl F Tuke Jr, *Principal*
Mary J Padro, *Vice Pres*
Mike Faillece, *Manager*
EMP: 50
SQ FT: 15,000
SALES (est): 8MM **Privately Held**
WEB: www.pebblecreekgc.com
SIC: **1799** 1629 Coating, caulking & weather, water & fireproofing; golf course construction

(G-4007)
M-E COMPANIES INC
23 Triangle Park Dr # 2300 (45246-3411)
PHONE.................513 942-3141
Dick Longenecker, *Principal*
Jeff Koehn, *Manager*
Rodney Saylor, *Info Tech Mgr*
EMP: 30
SALES (corp-wide): 261.9MM **Privately Held**
SIC: **8711** Consulting engineer
HQ: M-E Companies, Inc.
635 Brooksedge Blvd
Westerville OH 43081
614 818-4900

(G-4008)
MACKE BROTHERS INC
10355 Spartan Dr (45215-1220)
PHONE.................513 771-7500
Fax: 513 771-3830
Joseph D Macke Sr, *President*
Joseph D Macke Jr, *Vice Pres*
Bill Macke, *Treasurer*
Nick Macke, *Admin Sec*
EMP: 85 **EST**: 1908
SQ FT: 43,000
SALES (est): 8.4MM **Privately Held**
SIC: **2789** 7331 Pamphlets, binding; bookbinding & repairing: trade, edition, library, etc.; mailing service

(G-4009)
MADEIRA HEALTH CARE CENTER
6940 Stiegler Ln (45243-2635)
PHONE.................513 561-4105
Fax: 513 561-2450
EMP: 110
SALES (est): 4.7MM **Privately Held**
SIC: **8051** Skilled Nursing Facility

(G-4010)
MADISON BOWL INC
4761 Madison Rd (45227-1425)
PHONE.................513 271-2700
Fax: 513 271-2704
Harry S Osgood, *President*
Linda Osgood, *Admin Sec*
EMP: 35 **EST**: 1956
SQ FT: 15,000
SALES (est): 1.3MM **Privately Held**
WEB: www.madisonbowl.com
SIC: **7933** Ten pin center

(G-4011)
MAE HOLDING COMPANY (PA)
7290 Deaconsbench Ct (45244-3708)
PHONE.................513 751-2424
George Thurner III, *President*
EMP: 32
SQ FT: 80,000
SALES (est): 20.5MM **Privately Held**
SIC: **5031** 5072 Door frames, all materials; hardware

(G-4012)
MAGNUM MEDICAL OVERSEAS JV LLC
2936 Vernon Pl 3 (45219-2433)
PHONE.................979 848-8169
Richard Blatt, *CEO*
Kevin Korb, *CFO*
EMP: 99
SALES (est): 1.2MM **Privately Held**
SIC: **8011** Offices & clinics of medical doctors

(G-4013)
MAIDS HOME SERVICE OF CINCY
1830 Sherman Ave (45212-2516)
PHONE.................513 396-6900
Margie Hall, *President*
EMP: 25
SQ FT: 2,174
SALES (est): 687.2K **Privately Held**
SIC: **7363** Domestic help service

(G-4014)
MAIL CONTRACTORS AMERICA INC
3065 Crescentville Rd (45262)
PHONE.................513 769-5967
Sue Deserisy, *Manager*
EMP: 225
SALES (corp-wide): 321.6MM **Privately Held**
WEB: www.mailcontractors.com
SIC: **4212** Local trucking, without storage
HQ: Mail Contractors Of America, Inc.
3809 Roundtop Dr
North Little Rock AR 72117
501 280-0500

(G-4015)
MAKETEWAH COUNTRY CLUB COMPANY
5401 Reading Rd (45237-5398)
PHONE.................513 242-9333
Fax: 513 242-7024
Charles Carpenter, *President*
EMP: 75
SQ FT: 59,007
SALES (est): 3.7MM **Privately Held**
WEB: www.maketewah.com
SIC: **7997** Country club, membership

(G-4016)
MAKING EVRLASTING MEMORIES LLC
11475 Northlake Dr (45249-1641)
PHONE.................513 864-0100
Scott Mindrum, *President*
Steven Sefton, *COO*
Mike Piehler, *Engineer*
Tony Hume, *Software Dev*
Lorien Rensing, *Software Dev*
EMP: 30
SQ FT: 2,000
SALES (est): 3MM **Privately Held**
WEB: www.familyheritageregistry.com
SIC: **4813**

(G-4017)
MALIK PUNAM
3333 Burnet Ave (45229-3026)
PHONE.................513 636-1333
Dr Punam Malik, *Owner*
EMP: 99
SALES: 12K **Privately Held**
SIC: **8742** Hospital & health services consultant

(G-4018)
MALLARD COVE SENIOR DEV LLC
Also Called: Mallard Cove Senior Living
1410 Mallard Cove Dr Ofc (45246-3930)
PHONE.................513 772-6655
Fax: 513 772-7908
Shamela Limbaugh, *Owner*
Alison Asbury, *Marketing Staff*
Jonathan Levey, *Mng Member*
David A Smith, *Mng Member*
Lisa Jones, *Director*
EMP: 105 **EST**: 2008
SALES (est): 10.5MM **Privately Held**
SIC: **8051** Skilled nursing care facilities

(G-4019)
MAPLE KNOLL COMMUNITIES INC (PA)
Also Called: Maple Knoll Village
11100 Springfield Pike (45246-4165)
PHONE.................513 782-2400
Fax: 513 772-1056
Nancy Vilaboy, *Pastor*
Rose Denman, *Vice Pres*
Kenneth Huff, *CFO*
Nancy Hendricks, *Controller*
Beth Bolin, *VP Human Res*
EMP: 400
SQ FT: 323,000
SALES: 44.7MM **Privately Held**
SIC: **8051** 8052 8082 Convalescent home with continuous nursing care; intermediate care facilities; home health care services

(G-4020)
MARCUMS DON POOL CARE INC
6841 Main St Ste 1 (45244-3475)
PHONE.................513 561-7050
Fax: 513 561-6870
Donald Marcum, *President*
Darlene Marcum, *Corp Secy*
Dave Bachman, *Vice Pres*
Gene Pollack, *Technician*
EMP: 25 **EST**: 1981
SQ FT: 5,000
SALES (est): 4.2MM **Privately Held**
SIC: **5999** 7389 Swimming pool chemicals, equipment & supplies; swimming pool & hot tub service & maintenance

(G-4021)
MARFRE INC
Also Called: Riggs School Buses
4785 Morse St (45226-2316)
PHONE.................513 321-3377
Fax: 513 533-8743
Dennis Riggs, *CEO*
Rebecca Campbell, *President*
Terry Howard, *Vice Pres*
EMP: 103
SQ FT: 4,000
SALES (est): 3.2MM **Privately Held**
WEB: www.marfre.com
SIC: **4151** 4141 School buses; local bus charter service

(G-4022)
MARKETING RESEARCH SVCS INC
110 Boggs Ln Ste 380 (45246-3150)
PHONE.................513 772-7580
Valerie Enderle, *Manager*
EMP: 100 **Privately Held**
SIC: **8732** Commercial nonphysical research
HQ: Marketing Research Services, Inc.
310 Culvert St Fl 2
Cincinnati OH 45202
513 579-1555

Cincinnati - Hamilton County (G-4023)   GEOGRAPHIC SECTION

(G-4023)
MARKETING RESEARCH SVCS INC (DH)
Also Called: M R S I
310 Culvert St Fl 2 (45202-2229)
PHONE 513 579-1555
Fax: 513 562-8819
Todd Earhart, *President*
William Eder, *Senior Partner*
Linda Maichl, *Senior Partner*
Frank Forney, *General Mgr*
John Barth, *Exec VP*
EMP: 95
SQ FT: 30,000
SALES (est): 13.7MM **Privately Held**
SIC: 8732 Market analysis or research
HQ: Orc International, Inc
    902 Carnegie Ctr Ste 220
    Princeton NJ 08540
    609 452-5400

(G-4024)
MARKETING SUPPORT SERVICES INC (PA)
4921 Para Dr (45237-5011)
PHONE 513 752-1200
Fax: 513 752-9800
Greg Fischer, *President*
Pam Fischer, *Corp Secy*
Dan Robinett, *Controller*
Angie Martin, *Human Res Dir*
Mark Goodwin, *Natl Sales Mgr*
EMP: 51
SQ FT: 100,000
SALES (est): 9.3MM **Privately Held**
WEB: www.m-s-s.com
SIC: 7311 Advertising agencies

(G-4025)
MARRIOTT INTERNATIONAL INC
151 Goodman St (45219-2105)
PHONE 513 487-3800
Fax: 513 487-3810
EMP: 167
SALES (corp-wide): 14.4B **Publicly Held**
SIC: 7011 Hotels And Motels
PA: Marriott International, Inc.
    10400 Fernwood Rd
    Bethesda MD 20817
    301 380-3000

(G-4026)
MARSH INC (PA)
333 E 8th St (45202-2205)
PHONE 513 421-1344
Fax: 513 421-2172
Edward E Betz, *Ch of Bd*
Ken Neiheisel, *President*
Peter Costanzo, *Vice Pres*
Brandi Hall, *Production*
Janet Luebbert, *Production*
EMP: 27 EST: 1937
SQ FT: 12,000
SALES (est): 11.4MM **Privately Held**
WEB: www.marshinc.com
SIC: 7336 8743 7335 Package design; promotion service; commercial photography

(G-4027)
MARSH USA INC
525 Vine St Ste 1600 (45202-3132)
PHONE 513 287-1600
Wren Schnelle, *Assistant VP*
Julie Reinhardt, *Vice Pres*
Bernie Calonge, *Manager*
Mary Calonge, *Agent*
EMP: 70
SALES (corp-wide): 14B **Publicly Held**
WEB: www.marsh.com
SIC: 6411 Insurance brokers
HQ: Marsh Usa Inc.
    1166 Ave Of The Americas
    New York NY 10036
    212 345-6000

(G-4028)
MASSACHUSETTS MUTL LF INSUR CO
1 W 4th St Ste 1000 (45202-3632)
PHONE 513 579-8555
Clair Greenwell, *Manager*
EMP: 48

SALES (corp-wide): 19.7B **Privately Held**
WEB: www.massmutual.com
SIC: 6311 Life insurance
PA: Massachusetts Mutual Life Insurance Company
    1295 State St
    Springfield MA 01111
    413 788-8411

(G-4029)
MASUR TRUCKING INC
11825 Reading Rd Ste 1 (45241-5515)
PHONE 513 860-9600
Fax: 513 771-1646
Joseph N Masur, *President*
Paul J Masur, *Treasurer*
Charles Masur, *Admin Sec*
EMP: 30 EST: 1932
SQ FT: 520
SALES (est): 5.1MM **Privately Held**
WEB: www.masurtrucking.com
SIC: 4212 Delivery service, vehicular

(G-4030)
MATLOCK ELECTRIC CO INC (PA)
2780 Highland Ave (45212-2494)
PHONE 513 731-9600
Fax: 513 731-9646
Joseph P Geoppinger, *President*
Thomas J Geoppinger, *Chairman*
Rick Mullaney, *Controller*
Eric Weber, *Accounts Mgr*
Casey McKenna, *Manager*
EMP: 38
SQ FT: 25,000
SALES (est): 9.2MM **Privately Held**
WEB: www.matlockelectric.com
SIC: 7694 5063 3699 3612 Electric motor repair; motors, electric; electrical equipment & supplies; transformers, except electric; speed changers, drives & gears

(G-4031)
MAXIMUM COMMUNICATIONS INC
Also Called: Maximum Call Center
117 Williams St (45215-4601)
PHONE 513 489-3414
Fax: 513 489-3432
Clark Sarver, *President*
Joe Konrardy, *COO*
Carol Sarver,
EMP: 30
SQ FT: 3,500
SALES (est): 2.3MM **Privately Held**
WEB: www.maximumcallcenter.com
SIC: 4812 4822 7389 5999 Paging services; electronic mail; telephone answering service; telephone & communication equipment

(G-4032)
MAYERS ELECTRIC CO INC
4004 Erie Ct Ste B (45227-2167)
PHONE 513 272-2900
Howard Mayers, *President*
Jim Hopper, *Vice Pres*
Jim Amend, *Project Mgr*
Patrick Bates, *Project Mgr*
Bill Puthoff, *Project Mgr*
▲ EMP: 150 EST: 1948
SQ FT: 22,250
SALES: 22.1MM **Privately Held**
WEB: www.mayerselectric.com
SIC: 1731 General electrical contractor

(G-4033)
MAYFIELD CLINIC INC (PA)
3825 Edwards Rd Ste 300 (45209-1288)
PHONE 513 221-1100
Fax: 513 872-7360
Michael J Gilligan, *President*
Thomas Van Rosenberger, *President*
Bradley Mullin, *Principal*
Hwa Shain Yeh, *Principal*
Mary Kemper, *Editor*
EMP: 82
SQ FT: 25,000
SALES (est): 14.4MM **Privately Held**
WEB: www.mayfieldspine.com
SIC: 8011 Neurologist; neurosurgeon

(G-4034)
MC GREGOR FAMILY ENTERPRISES (PA)
Also Called: Play It Again Sports
9990 Kings Auto Mall Rd (45249-8234)
PHONE 513 583-0040
Fax: 513 583-0045
John Mc Gregor, *President*
Mary Mc Gregor, *Vice Pres*
EMP: 30
SQ FT: 4,200
SALES (est): 3.3MM **Privately Held**
SIC: 5941 5091 5932 Sporting goods & bicycle shops; sporting & recreation goods; used merchandise stores

(G-4035)
MCCLUSKEY CHEVROLET INC (PA)
Also Called: McCluskey Automotive
8525 Reading Rd (45215-5598)
P.O. Box 15309 (45215-0309)
PHONE 513 761-1111
Fax: 513 679-9440
Daniel McCluskey, *CEO*
Keith P McCluskey, *President*
Gina Owens, *Corp Secy*
Brent Martin, *Buyer*
James Gamble, *Finance Mgr*
EMP: 140 EST: 1927
SQ FT: 100,000
SALES (est): 56.5MM **Privately Held**
WEB: www.7611111.com
SIC: 5511 7515 7513 5521 Automobiles, new & used; pickups, new & used; vans, new & used; passenger car leasing; truck rental & leasing, no drivers; used car dealers; automobiles & other motor vehicles

(G-4036)
MCGILL SMITH PUNSHON INC
3700 Park 42 Dr Ste 190b (45241-2081)
PHONE 513 759-0004
Fax: 513 563-7099
Stephen C Roat, *President*
J Craig Rambo, *Chairman*
Stephanie Kirschner, *Corp Secy*
Richard Arnold II, *Vice Pres*
Jim Watson, *Vice Pres*
EMP: 28
SQ FT: 17,000
SALES (est): 4.3MM **Privately Held**
WEB: www.mcgillsmithpunshon.com
SIC: 8711 8712 8713 0781 Consulting engineer; architectural engineering; surveying services; landscape architects

(G-4037)
MCGINNIS INC
5525 River Rd (45233-1511)
P.O. Box 33177 (45233-0177)
PHONE 513 941-8070
Fax: 513 941-0229
Chris Mc Ginnis, *Manager*
EMP: 35
SALES (corp-wide): 152.4MM **Privately Held**
WEB: www.mcginnisinc.com
SIC: 4491 Marine cargo handling
HQ: Mcginnis, Inc.
    502 2nd St E
    South Point OH 45680
    740 377-4391

(G-4038)
MCKESSON MEDICAL-SURGICAL TOP
Also Called: Physician Sales & Service
12074 Champion Way (45241-6406)
PHONE 513 985-0525
Fax: 513 985-0236
Kelly Guerin-Lower, *Manager*
EMP: 40
SALES (corp-wide): 198.5B **Publicly Held**
WEB: www.pssworldmedical.com
SIC: 5047 Medical equipment & supplies
HQ: Mckesson Medical-Surgical Top Holdings Inc.
    4345 Southpoint Blvd
    Jacksonville FL 32216
    904 332-3000

(G-4039)
MCNERNEY & ASSOCIATES LLC (PA)
Also Called: P J McNerney & Associates
440 Northland Blvd (45240-3211)
PHONE 513 241-9951
Fax: 513 825-5601
Patrick J McNerney, *President*
Jan McNerney, *Vice Pres*
Tim Egan, *Sales Executive*
Bryan Morton, *Maintence Staff*
◆ EMP: 26
SQ FT: 70,000
SALES (est): 4.8MM **Privately Held**
WEB: www.pjmcnerney.com
SIC: 2752 4783 Commercial printing, lithographic; packing goods for shipping

(G-4040)
MECHANCAL/INDUSTRIAL CONTG INC
Also Called: Honeywell Authorized Dealer
11863 Solzman Rd (45249-1236)
PHONE 513 489-8282
Fax: 513 489-8482
Clay Craig, *President*
Bill Sempsrott, *Vice Pres*
Alisa Hipple, *Accountant*
EMP: 29
SQ FT: 20,000
SALES: 6.5MM **Privately Held**
SIC: 1711 Mechanical contractor

(G-4041)
MEDA-CARE TRANSPORTATION INC
270 Northland Blvd # 227 (45246-3660)
PHONE 513 521-4799
Fax: 513 771-4822
RAD Galitsky, *President*
Boris Galitsky, *Principal*
EMP: 30
SALES (est): 187.8K **Privately Held**
SIC: 4789 Cargo loading & unloading services

(G-4042)
MEDICAL CARE PSC INC
Also Called: Medical Reimbursment
2950 Robertson Ave Fl 2 (45209-1267)
PHONE 513 281-4400
Richard C Levy MD, *President*
EMP: 27
SALES (est): 1.1MM **Privately Held**
SIC: 8721 7322 Billing & bookkeeping service; collection agency, except real estate

(G-4043)
MEDICAL CARE REIMBURSEMENT
Also Called: Medical Reimbursment
2950 Robertson Ave Fl 2 (45209-1267)
PHONE 513 281-4400
Fax: 513 281-4545
Michael Jeffery, *CEO*
Jay Ripa, *Exec VP*
Bonnie Collins, *Accounts Mgr*
Monica Fussinger, *Director*
Tabka Coomer, *Admin Asst*
EMP: 50
SALES (est): 2MM **Privately Held**
SIC: 8721 Billing & bookkeeping service

(G-4044)
MEDICAL RECOVERY SYSTEMS INC
Also Called: Mrsi
3372 Central Pkwy (45225-2307)
PHONE 513 872-7000
Fax: 513 872-7011
Stephen I Caroll, *President*
Jean Even, *General Mgr*
Clyde Findley, *Manager*
EMP: 100
SALES (est): 9MM **Privately Held**
SIC: 8742 Hospital & health services consultant

(G-4045)
MEDICINE MIDWEST LLC (PA)
4700 Smith Rd Ste A (45212-2777)
PHONE 513 533-1199
Bill Scholl, *Facilities Mgr*

Robert Roettker,
EMP: 25 EST: 1998
SALES (est): 3.6MM **Privately Held**
SIC: **8011** Offices & clinics of medical doctors

(G-4046)
MEDICOUNT MANAGEMENT INC
10361 Spartan Dr (45215-1220)
P.O. Box 621005 (45262-1005)
PHONE..................................513 772-4465
Fax: 513 772-4464
Joseph D Newcomb, *Ch of Bd*
Joseph A Newcomb, *President*
Tim Newcomb, *Vice Pres*
Arnold Mann, *Controller*
Brenda Hall, *Financial Exec*
EMP: 40
SQ FT: 7,500
SALES (est): 4.8MM **Privately Held**
WEB: www.medicount.com
SIC: **8741** Business management

(G-4047)
MEDISYNC MIDWEST LTD LBLTY CO
25 Merchant St Ste 220 (45246-3740)
PHONE..................................513 533-1199
Fax: 513 533-6001
Robert E Matthews, *CEO*
Bob Roettker, *CFO*
Robert E Roettker, *CFO*
Sharon Earl, *Accounting Mgr*
Shelly Spohn, *HR Admin*
EMP: 85
SQ FT: 12,000
SALES (est): 13.7MM **Privately Held**
WEB: www.medisync.com
SIC: **8742** Hospital & health services consultant

(G-4048)
MEDPACE INC
5355 Medpace Way (45227-1543)
PHONE..................................513 366-3220
August J Troendle, *Branch Mgr*
EMP: 1200
SALES (corp-wide): 436.1MM **Publicly Held**
SIC: **8071** Biological laboratory
HQ: Medpace, Inc.
   5375 Medpace Way
   Cincinnati OH 45227

(G-4049)
MEDPACE INC (DH)
5375 Medpace Way (45227-1543)
PHONE..................................513 579-9911
Fax: 513 579-0444
August Troendle, *President*
Kurt Brykman, *COO*
Richard D Scheyer, *Vice Pres*
Franklin O Smith, *Vice Pres*
Dan Weng, *Vice Pres*
EMP: 700
SQ FT: 30,000
SALES (est): 434.7MM
SALES (corp-wide): 436.1MM **Publicly Held**
WEB: www.medpace.com
SIC: **8731** 5122 5047 Biotechnical research, commercial; pharmaceuticals; medical equipment & supplies
HQ: Medpace Intermediateco, Inc.
   5375 Medpace Way
   Cincinnati OH 45227
   513 579-9911

(G-4050)
MEDPACE BIOANALYTICAL LABS LLC
5365 Medpace Way (45227-1543)
PHONE..................................513 366-3260
August Troendle, *President*
Jesse Geiger, *CFO*
Stephen Ewald, *Admin Sec*
EMP: 27
SQ FT: 140,000
SALES (est): 433.2K
SALES (corp-wide): 436.1MM **Publicly Held**
SIC: **8071** Testing laboratories
HQ: Medpace, Inc.
   5375 Medpace Way
   Cincinnati OH 45227

(G-4051)
MEES DISTRIBUTORS INC (PA)
1541 W Fork Rd (45223-1203)
PHONE..................................513 541-2311
Fax: 513 541-4831
Howard L Mees, *President*
Chris Buchler, *Opers Mgr*
Dan Sanders, *Controller*
Michelle Connor, *Accounting Dir*
Larry Bugler, *Human Res Dir*
▲ EMP: 50 EST: 1954
SQ FT: 58,000
SALES (est): 21.1MM **Privately Held**
WEB: www.meesdistributors.com
SIC: **5032** Ceramic construction materials, excluding refractory

(G-4052)
MEGEN CONSTRUCTION COMPANY INC (PA)
11130 Ashburn Rd (45240-3813)
PHONE..................................513 742-9191
Fax: 513 742-9393
Evans N Nwankwo, *President*
Timothy Sharp, *General Mgr*
Fleet P Fangman, *Vice Pres*
Frank A Regueyra, *Vice Pres*
Benjamin Nwankwo, *VP Opers*
EMP: 40
SQ FT: 4,000
SALES (est): 36.8MM **Privately Held**
SIC: **8741** Construction management

(G-4053)
MELLOTT & MELLOTT PLL
12 Walnut St Ste 2500 (45216-2453)
PHONE..................................513 241-2940
Fax: 513 241-0712
Donald Mellott Jr, *Partner*
Donald Mellott Sr, *Partner*
John Mellot, *Partner*
Rick Rumper, *Partner*
EMP: 40
SALES (est): 3.3MM **Privately Held**
WEB: www.mellottcpa.com
SIC: **8721** Certified public accountant

(G-4054)
MELS AUTO GLASS INC
11775 Reading Rd (45241-1548)
PHONE..................................513 563-7771
Lisa M Gabrielle, *President*
Melvin W Wolf, *Principal*
Amanda Cassinelli, *Admin Asst*
EMP: 30
SQ FT: 8,000
SALES (est): 5.3MM **Privately Held**
WEB: www.melsautoglass.com
SIC: **7536** Automotive glass replacement shops

(G-4055)
MENTAL HEALTH AND ADDI SERV
Also Called: Summit Bhvioral Healthcare Ctr
1101 Summit Rd (45237-2621)
PHONE..................................513 948-3600
Dan Moles, *COO*
Bailey Bryant, *Psychologist*
Rachel Thompson, *Psychologist*
Todd Holmes, *Librarian*
Eric Bradley, *CIO*
EMP: 400 **Privately Held**
SIC: **8063** 9431 Psychiatric hospitals; mental health agency administration, government;
HQ: Ohio Department Of Mental Health And Addiction Services
   30 E Broad St Fl 8
   Columbus OH 43215

(G-4056)
MERCER (US) INC
525 Vine St Ste 1600 (45202-3132)
PHONE..................................513 632-2600
Fax: 513 632-2650
James Jackson, *Principal*
Miriam R Leonard, *Principal*
William Burnette, *Branch Mgr*
Paul Barbick, *Consultant*
Mark Woomer, *Info Tech Mgr*
EMP: 40
SALES (corp-wide): 14B **Publicly Held**
SIC: **8742** Compensation & benefits planning consultant
HQ: Mercer (Us) Inc.
   1166 Ave Of The Americ
   New York NY 10036
   212 345-7000

(G-4057)
MERCY FRANCISCAN HOSP MT AIRY (PA)
2446 Kipling Ave (45239-6650)
PHONE..................................513 853-5101
Fax: 513 853-5920
Rodney Reider, *President*
Ruby Hemphil Crowford, *Vice Pres*
Judy Daleiden, *Vice Pres*
Mark Johnson, *Pharmacist*
Mark Zoellner, *Med Doctor*
EMP: 1000
SQ FT: 10,500
SALES (est): 105.6MM **Privately Held**
SIC: **8741** 8062 Hospital management; nursing & personal care facility management; general medical & surgical hospitals

(G-4058)
MERCY FRNCSCAN HOSP WSTN HILLS
3131 Queen City Ave (45238-2316)
PHONE..................................513 389-5000
Fax: 513 389-5877
Michael Stephen, *President*
Joyce Keegan, *Vice Pres*
Donald Stinnett, *VP Finance*
Gail Presutto, *Persnl Dir*
Aaron A Biley, *Adv Dir*
EMP: 886
SQ FT: 100,000
SALES: 81MM **Privately Held**
SIC: **8062** General medical & surgical hospitals

(G-4059)
MERCY HEALTH
4750 E Galbraith Rd # 207 (45236-6706)
PHONE..................................513 686-5392
Neilendu Kundu, *Surgeon*
EMP: 35
SALES (corp-wide): 4.2B **Privately Held**
SIC: **8011** Surgeon
PA: Mercy Health
   1701 Mercy Health Pl
   Cincinnati OH 45237
   513 639-2800

(G-4060)
MERCY HEALTH
P.O. Box 5203 (45201-5203)
PHONE..................................513 639-0250
EMP: 97
SALES (corp-wide): 4.2B **Privately Held**
SIC: **8062** General medical & surgical hospitals
PA: Mercy Health
   1701 Mercy Health Pl
   Cincinnati OH 45237
   513 639-2800

(G-4061)
MERCY HEALTH
3301 Mercy Health Blvd (45211-1105)
PHONE..................................513 981-5750
EMP: 145
SALES (corp-wide): 4.2B **Privately Held**
SIC: **8099** Childbirth preparation clinic
PA: Mercy Health
   1701 Mercy Health Pl
   Cincinnati OH 45237
   513 639-2800

(G-4062)
MERCY HEALTH (PA)
1701 Mercy Health Pl (45237-6147)
PHONE..................................513 639-2800
Fax: 513 639-2700
Michael D Connelly, *President*
Randy Curnow, *President*
Brian Smith, *COO*
David A Catalano, *Exec VP*
Brent Asplin, *Senior VP*
EMP: 125
SALES (est): 4.2B **Privately Held**
SIC: **8062** General medical & surgical hospitals

(G-4063)
MERCY HEALTH
8094 Beechmont Ave (45255-3145)
PHONE..................................513 232-7100
Fax: 513 232-6975
EMP: 62
SALES (corp-wide): 4.2B **Privately Held**
SIC: **8011** General & family practice, physician/surgeon
PA: Mercy Health
   1701 Mercy Health Pl
   Cincinnati OH 45237
   513 639-2800

(G-4064)
MERCY HEALTH
Also Called: Accounts Payable Sso
P.O. Box 5203 (45201-5203)
PHONE..................................513 639-2800
EMP: 48
SALES (corp-wide): 4.2B **Privately Held**
SIC: **8062** General medical & surgical hospitals
PA: Mercy Health
   1701 Mercy Health Pl
   Cincinnati OH 45237
   513 639-2800

(G-4065)
MERCY HEALTH
Also Called: Catholic Healthcare Par
7500 State Rd (45255-2439)
PHONE..................................513 233-6736
EMP: 83
SALES (corp-wide): 4.2B **Privately Held**
SIC: **8011** Offices & clinics of medical doctors
PA: Mercy Health
   1701 Mercy Health Pl
   Cincinnati OH 45237
   513 639-2800

(G-4066)
MERCY HEALTH
10475 Reading Rd Ste 209 (45241-2500)
PHONE..................................513 585-9600
Nancy Riley, *Med Doctor*
Christopher Sweeney, *Med Doctor*
Elizabeth Ruchhoft, *Obstetrician*
EMP: 55
SALES (corp-wide): 4.2B **Privately Held**
SIC: **8011** Offices & clinics of medical doctors
PA: Mercy Health
   1701 Mercy Health Pl
   Cincinnati OH 45237
   513 639-2800

(G-4067)
MERCY HEALTH ANDERSON HOSPITAL (DH)
Also Called: Mercy Hospital Anderson
7500 State Rd (45255-2439)
PHONE..................................513 624-4500
Fax: 513 624-3299
Patrica Shroer, *President*
Julie Holt, *Vice Pres*
Marlynn Huelsman, *Purch Agent*
Maggie Lund, *VP Human Res*
Sandy Ferrigno, *Human Res Dir*
EMP: 728
SQ FT: 115,000
SALES: 231.5MM
SALES (corp-wide): 4.2B **Privately Held**
WEB: www.mercy.health-partners.org
SIC: **8062** General medical & surgical hospitals
HQ: Mercy Health Cincinnati Llc
   1701 Mercy Health Pl
   Cincinnati OH 45237
   513 952-5000

(G-4068)
MERCY HEALTH ANDERSON HOSPITAL
Also Called: Mercy Anderson Ambulatory Ctr
7520 State Rd (45255-2439)
PHONE..................................513 624-1950
Fax: 513 624-1952
Julie Hanser, *Principal*
EMP: 35
SALES (corp-wide): 4.2B **Privately Held**
WEB: www.mercy.health-partners.org
SIC: **8062** General medical & surgical hospitals

Cincinnati - Hamilton County (G-4069)

HQ: Mercy Health Anderson Hospital
7500 State Rd
Cincinnati OH 45255
513 624-4500

(G-4069)
MERCY HEALTH ANDERSON HOSPITAL
Also Called: Mercy Anderson Cancer Center
8000 5 Mile Rd Ste 105 (45230-2187)
PHONE.................513 624-4025
Fax: 513 231-1971
Terry Beckman, *Director*
EMP: 25
SALES (corp-wide): 4.2B **Privately Held**
WEB: www.mercy.health-partners.org
SIC: 8062 8069 General medical & surgical hospitals; cancer hospital
HQ: Mercy Health Anderson Hospital
7500 State Rd
Cincinnati OH 45255
513 624-4500

(G-4070)
MERCY HEALTH CINCINNATI LLC (HQ)
1701 Mercy Health Pl (45237-6147)
PHONE.................513 952-5000
Tom Urban, *CEO*
Michael W Garfield, *Principal*
Scott T Welton, *Ch Radiology*
Loretta L Lee, *Senior VP*
Kenneth C Page, *Senior VP*
EMP: 100
SALES (est): 526.3MM
SALES (corp-wide): 4.2B **Privately Held**
WEB: www.mercyweb.org
SIC: 8062 General medical & surgical hospitals
PA: Mercy Health
1701 Mercy Health Pl
Cincinnati OH 45237
513 639-2800

(G-4071)
MERCY HEALTH PARTNERS
Also Called: MERCY HEALTH PARTNERS OF SOUTHWEST OHIO
8000 5 Mile Rd Ste 350 (45230-2192)
PHONE.................513 233-2444
Fax: 513 232-8483
Kelly Franer, *Principal*
Monica Hunter, *Director*
Ted W Gossard, *Gnrl Med Prac*
James S Kleinfelder, *Gnrl Med Prac*
Paula L Peake, *Gnrl Med Prac*
EMP: 58
SALES (corp-wide): 4.2B **Privately Held**
SIC: 8062 General medical & surgical hospitals
HQ: Mercy Health Cincinnati Llc
1701 Mercy Health Pl
Cincinnati OH 45237
513 952-5000

(G-4072)
MERCY HEALTH PARTNERS
Also Called: Mercy Franciscan Hospital
3301 Mercy Health Blvd # 100 (45211-1105)
P.O. Box 587101 (45258-7101)
PHONE.................513 389-5000
Fax: 513 389-9207
Rodney Ryder, *CEO*
Randy Schroeder, *Marketing Mgr*
Susan Bonelli, *Office Mgr*
Jay J Jiang, *Pathologist*
Garry Faja, *CTO*
EMP: 58
SALES (corp-wide): 4.2B **Privately Held**
WEB: www.mercyweb.org
SIC: 8062 General medical & surgical hospitals
HQ: Mercy Health Cincinnati Llc
1701 Mercy Health Pl
Cincinnati OH 45237
513 952-5000

(G-4073)
MERCY HEALTH PARTNERS
Also Called: Mercy Franciscan Hosp Mt Airy
2446 Kipling Ave (45239-6650)
PHONE.................513 853-5101
Paul Hiltv, *President*
Charles Lobeck, *Manager*
EMP: 130
SQ FT: 2,298
SALES (corp-wide): 4.2B **Privately Held**
WEB: www.mercyweb.org
SIC: 8062 General medical & surgical hospitals
HQ: Mercy Health Cincinnati Llc
1701 Mercy Health Pl
Cincinnati OH 45237
513 952-5000

(G-4074)
MERCY HEALTH PARTNERS
Also Called: Mercy Franciscan Senior Netwrk
2950 West Park Dr Ofc (45238-3542)
PHONE.................513 451-8900
Fax: 513 451-3728
Victor Lee, *Director*
Kendra Couch, *Administration*
EMP: 300
SALES (corp-wide): 4.2B **Privately Held**
WEB: www.mercyweb.org
SIC: 8322 Senior citizens' center or association
HQ: Mercy Health Cincinnati Llc
1701 Mercy Health Pl
Cincinnati OH 45237
513 952-5000

(G-4075)
MERCY HEALTH PARTNERS
4750 E Galbraith Rd # 207 (45236-6706)
PHONE.................513 686-4800
Dr Cari Ogg, *Principal*
EMP: 58
SALES (corp-wide): 4.2B **Privately Held**
SIC: 8062 General medical & surgical hospitals
HQ: Mercy Health Cincinnati Llc
1701 Mercy Health Pl
Cincinnati OH 45237
513 952-5000

(G-4076)
MERCY HEALTH WEST PARK
Also Called: West Park Retirement Community
2950 West Park Dr (45238-3599)
PHONE.................513 451-8900
Rachel Wirth, *President*
Tim Dressman, *Administration*
EMP: 250
SQ FT: 88,000
SALES (est): 4.7MM **Privately Held**
SIC: 6513 8059 8051 Apartment building operators; nursing home, except skilled & intermediate care facility; skilled nursing care facilities

(G-4077)
MERCY MEDICAL ASSOCIATES
4750 E Galbraith Rd # 207 (45236-6705)
PHONE.................513 686-4840
Jim May, *CEO*
EMP: 30
SALES (est): 1.5MM **Privately Held**
SIC: 8011 Internal medicine, physician/surgeon

(G-4078)
MERCY ST THERESA CENTER INC
7010 Rowan Hill Dr # 200 (45227-3380)
PHONE.................513 271-7010
Fax: 513 527-0181
Brian Forschner, *President*
EMP: 180
SALES (est): 6.6MM **Privately Held**
SIC: 8051 Skilled nursing care facilities

(G-4079)
MERRILL LYNCH PIERCE FENNER
425 Walnut St Ste 2500 (45202-3930)
PHONE.................513 579-3600
Fax: 513 579-3677
Harvey Knowles, *Senior VP*
John Nicholson, *Branch Mgr*
Carol Eyink, *Manager*
Sergey Alexandrov, *Assistant*
Christopher Eaton, *Advisor*
EMP: 130
SALES (corp-wide): 100.2B **Publicly Held**
WEB: www.merlyn.com
SIC: 8742 Financial consultant
HQ: Merrill Lynch, Pierce, Fenner & Smith Incorporated
111 8th Ave
New York NY 10011
800 637-7455

(G-4080)
MERRILL LYNCH PIERCE FENNER
312 Walnut St Ste 2400 (45202-4060)
PHONE.................513 562-2100
Fax: 513 579-3899
Paul Hansen, *Assistant VP*
Chris Sprenkle, *Manager*
Anthony Duggan, *Agent*
Gregory A Hopkins, *Agent*
Matthew Palmer, *Agent*
EMP: 30
SALES (corp-wide): 100.2B **Publicly Held**
WEB: www.merlyn.com
SIC: 6211 Brokers, security
HQ: Merrill Lynch, Pierce, Fenner & Smith Incorporated
111 8th Ave
New York NY 10011
800 637-7455

(G-4081)
MESA INDUSTRIES INC (PA)
Also Called: Airplaco Equipment Company
4027 Eastern Ave (45226-1747)
PHONE.................513 321-2950
Fax: 513 321-8178
Terry Segerberg, *CEO*
Kent Sexton, *President*
Ken Segerberg, *Vice Pres*
James R Sexton, *Vice Pres*
Todd Ferguson, *Sls & Mktg Exec*
◆ **EMP:** 82
SQ FT: 100,000
SALES (est): 27.3MM **Privately Held**
WEB: www.mesa-ind.net
SIC: 3531 5082 5085 Bituminous, cement & concrete related products & equipment; construction & mining machinery; hose, belting & packing

(G-4082)
MESSER CONSTRUCTION CO
2495 Langdon Farm Rd (45237-4950)
PHONE.................513 672-5000
Mark Leugering, *Principal*
Justin Angrick, *Project Mgr*
Adam M Laker, *Project Mgr*
Boyd Pollard, *Project Mgr*
Jerry Williams, *Safety Mgr*
EMP: 25
SALES (corp-wide): 1B **Privately Held**
SIC: 1542 Hospital construction
PA: Messer Construction Co.
643 W Court St
Cincinnati OH 45203
513 242-1541

(G-4083)
MESSER CONSTRUCTION CO (PA)
Also Called: FRANK MESSER & SONS CONSTRUCTI
643 W Court St (45203-1511)
PHONE.................513 242-1541
Fax: 513 672-5001
Thomas M Keckeis, *President*
Matt Monnin, *President*
Ryan Wise, *Superintendent*
M W King, *Principal*
C Allen Begley, *Senior VP*
EMP: 100
SQ FT: 26,000
SALES: 1B **Privately Held**
WEB: www.messer.com
SIC: 1542 1522 1541 Hospital construction; commercial & office building, new construction; commercial & office buildings, renovation & repair; school building construction; hotel/motel, new construction; multi-family dwellings, new construction; industrial buildings & warehouses; renovation, remodeling & repairs; industrial buildings; warehouse construction

(G-4084)
METCUT RESEARCH ASSOCIATES INC (PA)
3980 Rosslyn Ave (45209-1110)
PHONE.................513 271-5100
Fax: 513 271-9511
William P Koster, *Ch of Bd*
John P Kahles, *President*
John H Clippinger, *Principal*
Robert T Keeler, *Principal*
John H More, *Principal*
EMP: 85
SQ FT: 25,000
SALES: 12.6MM **Privately Held**
WEB: www.metcut.com
SIC: 8734 3599 Metallurgical testing laboratory; machine & other job shop work

(G-4085)
MH EQUIPMENT COMPANY
2650 Spring Grove Ave (45214-1732)
PHONE.................513 681-2200
Bob Risheill, *Vice Pres*
Pat McCucheon, *Sales Mgr*
EMP: 55
SALES (corp-wide): 237.2MM **Privately Held**
SIC: 5084 Materials handling machinery
HQ: Mh Equipment Company
8901 N Industrial Rd
Peoria IL 61615
309 579-8020

(G-4086)
MIAMI CORPORATION (PA)
720 Anderson Ferry Rd (45238-4742)
PHONE.................513 451-6700
Fax: 513 451-7998
Timothy J Niehaus, *President*
Mike Maisonet, *General Mgr*
Edward Cappel, *Principal*
Brian Oeder, *Principal*
Robert Tomlinson, *Principal*
▲ **EMP:** 45 **EST:** 1923
SQ FT: 40,000
SALES: 22.7MM **Privately Held**
WEB: www.miamicorp.com
SIC: 5131 5091 Upholstery fabrics, woven; boat accessories & parts

(G-4087)
MIAMI VALLEY INTL TRCKS INC
Also Called: Idealease Miami Valley Intl
11775 Highway Dr Ste D (45241-2005)
PHONE.................513 733-8500
Chuck Siebert, *Manager*
Mike Houston, *Manager*
EMP: 100
SALES (corp-wide): 41.6MM **Privately Held**
WEB: www.mvi.com
SIC: 7513 Truck rental & leasing, no drivers
PA: Miami Valley International Trucks, Inc.
7655 Poe Ave
Dayton OH 45414
937 898-3660

(G-4088)
MICHAEL G LAWLEY
8099 Cornell Rd (45249-2231)
PHONE.................513 793-3933
Michael G Lawley, *Principal*
EMP: 30 **EST:** 2001
SALES (est): 863.5K **Privately Held**
SIC: 8031 Offices & clinics of osteopathic physicians

(G-4089)
MICHAEL SCHUSTER ASSOCIATES
Also Called: MSA Architects
316 W 4th St Ste 600 (45202-2677)
PHONE.................513 241-5666
Fax: 513 241-0978
Michael Schuster, *Principal*
Richard Tripp, *Principal*
Sharon Voegeli, *Office Mgr*
Andrew Rowekamp, *Architect*
Dwayne Boso, *Info Tech Mgr*
EMP: 39
SQ FT: 10,000

▲ = Import ▼=Export
◆ =Import/Export

GEOGRAPHIC SECTION
Cincinnati - Hamilton County (G-4112)

SALES (est): 7.5MM **Privately Held**
WEB: www.msaarch.com
SIC: **8712** 7389 Architectural engineering; interior designer

(G-4090)
MICRO ELECTRONICS INC
Also Called: Micro Center
11755 Mosteller Rd Rear (45241-5505)
PHONE..................513 782-8500
Fax: 513 782-8501
Chuck Gammello, *Manager*
EMP: 125
SALES (corp-wide): 3.3B **Privately Held**
WEB: www.microcenter.com
SIC: **5734** 5045 Personal computers; computer peripheral equipment
PA: Micro Electronics, Inc.
4119 Leap Rd
Hilliard OH 43026
614 850-3000

(G-4091)
MIDLAND ATLANTIC PRPTS LLC (PA)
8044 Montgomery Rd # 710 (45236-2919)
PHONE..................513 792-5000
Fax: 513 891-5131
Scott Catz, *Principal*
John Silverman, *Principal*
Daniel Shick, *Senior VP*
Julie Krause, *Property Mgr*
William Mees, *Manager*
EMP: 25
SQ FT: 3,600
SALES (est): 2.8MM **Privately Held**
SIC: **6531** Real estate agent, commercial

(G-4092)
MIDWEST LAUNDRY INC
10110 Cncnnati Dyton Pike (45241-1006)
PHONE..................513 563-5560
Fax: 513 577-7460
Tom Jaynes, *General Mgr*
EMP: 70
SQ FT: 32,000
SALES: 1.9MM **Privately Held**
WEB: www.midwestlaundryinc.com
SIC: **7211** 7218 7216 7213 Power laundries, family & commercial; industrial launderers; drycleaning plants, except rugs; linen supply

(G-4093)
MIDWEST ULTRASOUND INC
237 Wlliam Howard Taft Rd (45219-2610)
PHONE..................513 936-0444
Fax: 513 936-0426
Michael Schwebler, *Branch Mgr*
Jennifer Schaff, *Manager*
Joni Wainwright, *Manager*
EMP: 32
SALES (corp-wide): 1.2MM **Privately Held**
SIC: **8071** Medical laboratories
PA: Midwest Ultrasound, Inc
50 W Techne Center Dr D
Milford OH 45150
513 248-8885

(G-4094)
MIDWESTERN PLUMBING SERVICE
3984 Bach Buxton Rd (45202)
PHONE..................513 753-0050
Gene Hehemann, *President*
Eugene Heheman, *President*
Archie Wilson, *Vice Pres*
Chris Wilson, *Vice Pres*
Mike Bradford, *Project Mgr*
EMP: 40 EST: 1978
SQ FT: 4,700
SALES (est): 8.6MM **Privately Held**
WEB: www.midwestern-plumbing.com
SIC: **1711** 6552 Plumbing contractors; subdividers & developers

(G-4095)
MILLER BROS WALLPAPER COMPANY
Also Called: Miller Bros Paint & Decorating
8460 Beechmont Ave Ste A (45255-4782)
PHONE..................513 231-4470
Fax: 513 231-4471
Eddy Mills, *Manager*
EMP: 35
SALES (corp-wide): 6.8MM **Privately Held**
SIC: **5198** 5231 Paints; paint
PA: Miller Bros. Wallpaper Company
4343 Montgomery Rd
Cincinnati OH 45212
513 531-1517

(G-4096)
MILLER CNFELD PDDOCK STONE PLC
511 Walnut St (45202-3115)
PHONE..................513 394-5252
Linda K Wells, *Branch Mgr*
EMP: 55
SALES (corp-wide): 115.1MM **Privately Held**
SIC: **8111** General practice attorney, lawyer
PA: Miller, Canfield, Paddock And Stone, P.L.C.
150 W Jefferson Ave # 2500
Detroit MI 48226
313 963-6420

(G-4097)
MILLER-VALENTINE PARTNERS LTD
Also Called: M-V Rlty Mller Valentine Group
9349 Waterstone Blvd # 200 (45249-8320)
PHONE..................513 588-1000
Fax: 513 683-6165
Tom Adams, *Partner*
Jack Goodwin, *Manager*
Joyce E Bogan, *Manager*
Don Bolton, *Manager*
Laura Webb, *Manager*
EMP: 30
SALES (corp-wide): 14.2MM **Privately Held**
SIC: **6531** Real estate agents & managers
PA: Miller-Valentine Partners Ltd.
137 N Main St Ste 900
Dayton OH 45402
937 293-0900

(G-4098)
MILLER-VLNTINE PARTNERS LTD LC
Also Called: Mv Communities
9349 Waterstone Blvd # 200 (45249-8320)
PHONE..................513 588-1000
John Rosenberg, *Manager*
Jeff Ramsey, *Asst Controller*
Gregg Susaro, *Manager*
EMP: 28
SALES (corp-wide): 14.2MM **Privately Held**
SIC: **6531** Real estate agent, residential
PA: Miller-Valentine Partners Ltd.
137 N Main St Ste 900
Dayton OH 45402
937 293-0900

(G-4099)
MILLS CORPORATION
Also Called: Forest Fair Mall
600 Cincinnati Mills Dr (45240-1260)
PHONE..................513 671-2882
Gene Condon, *Vice Pres*
John Dahl, *Vice Pres*
Laurel Sibert, *Vice Pres*
Jim Childress, *Manager*
EMP: 31 **Privately Held**
WEB: www.millscorp.com
SIC: **6512** Shopping center, property operation only
HQ: The Mills Corporation
5425 Wisconsin Ave # 300
Chevy Chase MD 20815
301 968-6000

(G-4100)
MILLS FENCE CO INC (PA)
6315 Wiehe Rd (45237-4213)
PHONE..................513 631-0333
Fax: 513 631-2703
Kenneth Mills, *President*
John Lyttle, *Vice Pres*
Kimberly Willims, *Accounts Mgr*
▲ EMP: 50
SQ FT: 100,000
SALES: 16.8MM **Privately Held**
WEB: www.millsfence.com
SIC: **5039** 1799 5211 Wire fence, gates & accessories; fence construction; fencing

(G-4101)
MILLS SECURITY ALARM SYSTEMS
490 Mount Hope Ave (45204-1394)
PHONE..................513 921-4600
Fax: 513 557-3247
Michael J Mills, *President*
Katie Mills, *Executive Asst*
EMP: 25
SQ FT: 7,500
SALES (est): 1.5MM **Privately Held**
WEB: www.mills-security.com
SIC: **7382** 1731 Burglar alarm maintenance & monitoring; safety & security specialization

(G-4102)
MINATURE SOCIETY CINCINNATI
6718 Siebern Ave (45236-3832)
PHONE..................513 931-9708
Gail Palmer, *President*
EMP: 58 EST: 1975
SALES (est): 331.7K **Privately Held**
SIC: **8641** Social club, membership

(G-4103)
MIRACLE RENOVATIONS
2786 Shaffer Ave (45211-7113)
PHONE..................513 371-0750
Merrick Collins, *Owner*
EMP: 25
SALES: 950K **Privately Held**
SIC: **1521** Single-family housing construction

(G-4104)
MITCHELLS SALON & DAY SPA (PA)
5901 E Galbraith Rd # 230 (45236-2230)
PHONE..................513 793-0900
Deborah M Schmidt, *President*
Jeanine Kreimer, *Managing Dir*
Mindy Wilson, *Managing Dir*
Vivian Moore, *Vice Pres*
Logan Schmidt, *Mktg Dir*
EMP: 397 EST: 1983
SQ FT: 11,000
SALES (est): 5.3MM **Privately Held**
WEB: www.mitchellssalon.com
SIC: **7231** 7991 Hairdressers; spas

(G-4105)
MITCHELLS SALON & DAY SPA
11330 Princeton Pike (45246-3202)
PHONE..................513 772-3200
Fax: 513 772-3919
Susie Thorpe, *Manager*
EMP: 50
SALES (est): 430.4K
SALES (corp-wide): 5.3MM **Privately Held**
WEB: www.mitchellssalon.com
SIC: **7231** Unisex hair salons
PA: Mitchell's Salon & Day Spa Inc
5901 E Galbraith Rd # 230
Cincinnati OH 45236
513 793-0900

(G-4106)
MITCHELLS SALON & DAY SPA
2692 Madison Rd (45208-1321)
PHONE..................513 731-0600
Fax: 513 731-9315
Kim Socha, *Branch Mgr*
EMP: 60
SALES (est): 436.8K
SALES (corp-wide): 5.3MM **Privately Held**
WEB: www.mitchellssalon.com
SIC: **7231** 7991 Unisex hair salons; spas
PA: Mitchell's Salon & Day Spa Inc
5901 E Galbraith Rd # 230
Cincinnati OH 45236
513 793-0900

(G-4107)
MK CHILDCARE WARSAW AVE LLC
3711 Warsaw Ave (45205-1773)
PHONE..................513 922-6279
Mary B Walker,
EMP: 40
SALES (est): 143K **Privately Held**
SIC: **8351** Child day care services

(G-4108)
MKJB INC
Also Called: Meadows Healthcare
11760 Pellston Ct (45240-4122)
PHONE..................513 851-8400
Fax: 513 674-3210
Karen Jamison, *CEO*
EMP: 130
SALES (corp-wide): 4.6MM **Privately Held**
WEB: www.mkjb.com
SIC: **8059** 8051 Nursing home, except skilled & intermediate care facility; skilled nursing care facilities
PA: Mkjb Inc
3536 Washington Ave
Cincinnati OH 45229
513 751-4900

(G-4109)
MLM CHILDCARE LLC
16 Beaufort Hunt Ln (45242-4672)
PHONE..................513 623-8243
Courtney Berling,
EMP: 35
SALES (est): 120.4K **Privately Held**
SIC: **8351** Child day care services

(G-4110)
MOBILCOMM INC
1211 W Sharon Rd (45240-2916)
PHONE..................513 742-5555
Fax: 513 595-5919
Greg Conrad, *President*
Steve Munsey, *Vice Pres*
Chip Donaldson, *Project Mgr*
Larry Vandruten, *Project Mgr*
Cindy King, *Controller*
EMP: 97
SALES (est): 14.2MM
SALES (corp-wide): 14.9MM **Privately Held**
WEB: www.mobilcomm.com
SIC: **7622** 7359 5999 5065 Communication equipment repair; mobile communication equipment rental; communication equipment; electronic parts & equipment; electrical appliances, television & radio
PA: Combined Tecnologies, Inc.
1211 W Sharon Rd
Cincinnati OH 45240
513 595-5900

(G-4111)
MODAL SHOP INC
Also Called: T M S
3149 E Kemper Rd (45241-1516)
PHONE..................513 351-9919
Fax: 513 458-2172
Michael J Lally, *President*
Emily T O'Dell, *President*
Kevin McCluskey, *Opers Mgr*
Tom Clary, *Engineer*
Aaron Goosman, *Engineer*
EMP: 70
SQ FT: 17,000
SALES (est): 37.8MM
SALES (corp-wide): 787.9MM **Publicly Held**
WEB: www.modalshop.com
SIC: **5084** 7359 8711 Controlling instruments & accessories; electronic equipment rental, except computers; engineering services
HQ: Pcb Group, Inc.
3425 Walden Ave
Depew NY 14043
716 684-0001

(G-4112)
MODEL GROUP INC
2170 Gilbert Ave Ste 100 (45206-2577)
PHONE..................513 559-0048
Arthur Reckman, *President*
Stephen Smith, *Vice Pres*
Andy Bacca, *Project Mgr*
Shirley Poe, *Treasurer*
Gregory Kuertz, *Controller*
EMP: 50 EST: 1978
SQ FT: 3,540

Cincinnati - Hamilton County (G-4113)

GEOGRAPHIC SECTION

SALES: 7.1MM **Privately Held**
WEB: www.modelmgt.com
SIC: 6531 Real estate managers

(G-4113)
MODERN BUILDERS SUPPLY INC
6225 Wiehe Rd (45237-4211)
PHONE...................................513 531-1000
Fax: 513 531-3004
Dave Thiem, *General Mgr*
David Phiem, *Manager*
EMP: 25
SQ FT: 26,000
SALES (corp-wide): 437.3MM **Privately Held**
WEB: www.polaristechnologies.com
SIC: 5033 5031 Roofing, siding & insulation; doors & windows
PA: Modern Builders Supply, Inc.
   302 Mcclurg Rd
   Youngstown OH 44512
   330 729-2690

(G-4114)
MONARCH CONSTRUCTION COMPANY
1654 Sherman Ave (45212-2598)
P.O. Box 12249 (45212-0249)
PHONE...................................513 351-6900
Fax: 513 351-0979
Ronald A Koetters, *CEO*
Thomas P Butler, *President*
Jerome J Corbett Jr, *CFO*
William C Otte, *Treasurer*
Dave Rieger, *Manager*
EMP: 200
SQ FT: 21,500
SALES (est): 73MM **Privately Held**
SIC: 1542 1541 Commercial & office building, new construction; commercial & office buildings, renovation & repair; institutional building construction; school building construction; industrial buildings & warehouses

(G-4115)
MONSTER WORLDWIDE INC
10296 Springfield Pike # 500 (45215-1194)
PHONE...................................513 719-3331
Andy Meng, *Engineer*
Pat Obrien, *Branch Mgr*
EMP: 68
SALES (corp-wide): 27.4B **Privately Held**
SIC: 7311 Advertising agencies
HQ: Monster Worldwide, Inc.
   133 Boston Post Rd
   Weston MA 02493
   978 461-8000

(G-4116)
MORELIA CONSULTANTS LLC
11210 Montgomery Rd (45249-2311)
PHONE...................................513 469-1500
Christopher Hildebrant,
EMP: 75
SQ FT: 10,200
SALES (est): 6.8MM **Privately Held**
SIC: 6798 6531 Real estate investment trusts; real estate managers

(G-4117)
MORELIA GROUP LLC
8600 Governors Hill Dr # 160 (45249-1360)
PHONE...................................513 469-1500
Christopher Hildebrant, *CEO*
EMP: 35
SALES (est): 482.8K **Privately Held**
SIC: 4813 Telephone communication, except radio

(G-4118)
MORGAN STANLEY
221 E 4th St Ste 2200 (45202-4147)
PHONE...................................513 721-2000
Matt Maloney, *Branch Mgr*
EMP: 50
SALES (corp-wide): 43.6B **Publicly Held**
SIC: 6211 6282 Brokers, security; investment advice
PA: Morgan Stanley
   1585 Broadway
   New York NY 10036
   212 761-4000

(G-4119)
MORRIS TECHNOLOGIES INC
11988 Tramway Dr (45241-1664)
PHONE...................................513 733-1611
Gregory M Morris, *CEO*
William G Noack, *President*
Mike Bauer, *Purchasing*
Ping Wang, *Engineer*
Wendell H Morris, *Treasurer*
EMP: 105
SQ FT: 25,000
SALES (est): 11.5MM **Privately Held**
WEB: www.morristech.com
SIC: 8711 3999 3313 8731 Mechanical engineering; models, except toy; alloys, additive, except copper: not made in blast furnaces; engineering laboratory, except testing; electrical discharge machining (EDM); surgical & medical instruments

(G-4120)
MORROW GRAVEL COMPANY INC (PA)
11641 Mosteller Rd Ste 2 (45241-1520)
PHONE...................................513 771-0820
James P Jurgensen, *President*
Tim St Clair, *CFO*
Dave Patterson, *Manager*
EMP: 120 EST: 1958
SQ FT: 15,000
SALES (est): 16.7MM **Privately Held**
SIC: 1442 1771 2951 Construction sand mining; gravel mining; blacktop (asphalt) work; asphalt & asphaltic paving mixtures (not from refineries)

(G-4121)
MOSKOWITZ BROS INC
5300 Vine St (45217-1030)
PHONE...................................513 242-2100
Fax: 513 242-2107
Robert Moskowitz, *President*
Ira Moskowitz, *Principal*
Mark Moskowitz, *Vice Pres*
Linda Curtis, *VP Human Res*
EMP: 35 EST: 1901
SQ FT: 70,000
SALES (est): 14.5MM **Privately Held**
WEB: www.moskowitzbros.com
SIC: 5093 3341 Ferrous metal scrap & waste; nonferrous metals scrap; secondary nonferrous metals

(G-4122)
MOSKOWITZ FAMILY LTD
Also Called: Moskowitz Family Trust
7220 Pippin Rd (45239-4607)
PHONE...................................513 729-2300
EMP: 115
SQ FT: 40,000
SALES (est): 8.4MM **Privately Held**
SIC: 6798 Real Estate Investment Trust

(G-4123)
MOTZ GROUP INC (PA)
3607 Church St Ste 300 (45244-3097)
PHONE...................................513 533-6452
Joseph Motz, *President*
Robert Elliott, *Asst Supt*
Mark Heinlein, *Senior VP*
Matt Rinas, *Project Mgr*
Allen Verdin, *Project Mgr*
▲ EMP: 50
SQ FT: 1,600
SALES (est): 12.6MM **Privately Held**
WEB: www.themotzgroup.com
SIC: 1799 0782 Artificial turf installation; turf installation services, except artificial

(G-4124)
MOUNT AUBURN COMMUNITY HDO
2236 Burnet Ave (45219-3114)
PHONE...................................513 659-4514
Charles McNeal, *Exec Dir*
EMP: 51 EST: 2016 **Privately Held**
SIC: 9531 7389 Housing programs; housing programs, planning & development: government;

(G-4125)
MPLX TERMINALS LLC
4015 River Rd (45204-1035)
PHONE...................................513 451-0485
Sam O'Koon, *Manager*

EMP: 30
SALES (corp-wide): 3.8B **Publicly Held**
WEB: www.mapllc.com
SIC: 5172 Petroleum products
HQ: Mplx Terminals Llc
   200 E Hardin St
   Findlay OH

(G-4126)
MRC GLOBAL (US) INC
Also Called: M R C
7275 Edington Dr (45249-1064)
PHONE...................................513 489-6922
Dawn Stepp, *District Mgr*
EMP: 25 **Publicly Held**
SIC: 5085 Industrial supplies
HQ: Mrc Global (Us) Inc.
   1301 Mckinney St Ste 2300
   Houston TX 77010
   877 294-7574

(G-4127)
MSK HOSPITALITY INC
Also Called: Econo Lodge
11620 Chester Rd (45246-2804)
PHONE...................................513 771-0370
Fax: 513 771-1104
Sanmukh Patel, *President*
EMP: 25
SALES (est): 1.3MM **Privately Held**
SIC: 7011 Hotel, franchised

(G-4128)
MT HEALTHY CHRISTIAN HOME INC
Also Called: CHRISTIAN BENEVOLENT ASSOCIATI
8097 Hamilton Ave (45231-2395)
PHONE...................................513 931-5000
Fax: 513 931-0261
Rod Huron, *Ch of Bd*
Lizz Stephens, *President*
Julie Price, *Sls & Mktg Exec*
Vickie Brashear, *CFO*
Kitty Garner, *Treasurer*
EMP: 175 EST: 1964
SQ FT: 300,000
SALES: 7.3MM
SALES (corp-wide): 1.7MM **Privately Held**
SIC: 8059 Rest home, with health care
PA: The Christian Benevolent Association Of Greater Cincinnati Inc
   8097 Hamilton Ave
   Cincinnati OH 45231
   513 931-5000

(G-4129)
MT TEXAS LLC
3055 Colerain Ave (45225-1827)
PHONE...................................513 853-4400
Michael Gonzales, *Engineer*
Doug Lang, *Mng Member*
EMP: 35
SALES (est): 1.7MM **Privately Held**
SIC: 7699 Aircraft & heavy equipment repair services

(G-4130)
MT WASHINGTON CARE CENTER INC
6900 Beechmont Ave (45230-2910)
PHONE...................................513 231-4561
Fax: 513 624-3725
James Farley, *President*
Michael Scharfenberger, *Exec VP*
Sylvia Wells, *Vice Pres*
Estate of Robert Wynne, *Treasurer*
EMP: 215
SALES (est): 11.6MM **Privately Held**
WEB: www.mtwcc.com
SIC: 8051 8322 6282 7389 Convalescent home with continuous nursing care; individual & family services; investment advice;

(G-4131)
MUNICPAL CNTRS SALING PDTS INC
Also Called: Sewer Savors
7740 Reinhold Dr (45237-2806)
PHONE...................................513 482-3300
Robert O'Connor, *President*
EMP: 25 EST: 2000
SQ FT: 10,000

SALES (est): 3MM **Privately Held**
SIC: 1623 Sewer line construction

(G-4132)
MURPHY TRACTOR & EQP CO INC
Also Called: John Deere Authorized Dealer
11441 Mosteller Rd (45241-1829)
PHONE...................................513 772-3232
Thomas Udland, *President*
Savannah Sterbens, *Accountant*
Mike Skiles, *Branch Mgr*
EMP: 40 **Privately Held**
SIC: 5082 General construction machinery & equipment
HQ: Murphy Tractor & Equipment Co., Inc.
   5375 N Deere Rd
   Park City KS 67219
   855 246-9124

(G-4133)
MV RESIDENTIAL CNSTR INC
9349 Waterstone Blvd # 200 (45249-8325)
PHONE...................................513 588-1000
Mike Green, *CEO*
Randy Humbert, *President*
Gerry Smith, *Indstl Engineer*
Jane E Marx, *Controller*
Sior Peters, *Sales Staff*
EMP: 750
SQ FT: 23,000
SALES (est): 106.8MM **Privately Held**
SIC: 1522 Residential construction

(G-4134)
MV TRANSPORTATION INC
Also Called: Lancaster Transportation
1801 Transpark Dr (45229-1239)
P.O. Box 2583, Lancaster (43130-5583)
PHONE...................................740 681-5086
Fax: 740 681-5088
Chad Hockmay, *Manager*
EMP: 78
SALES (corp-wide): 2.1B **Privately Held**
WEB: www.mvtransit.com
SIC: 4111 Bus transportation
PA: Mv Transportation, Inc.
   2711 N Haskell Ave
   Dallas TX 75204
   214 265-3400

(G-4135)
N COOK INC
5762 Argus Rd (45224-3204)
PHONE...................................513 275-9872
Nathan Cook, *Principal*
EMP: 33
SALES (est): 1.2MM **Privately Held**
SIC: 1542 Commercial & office building contractors

(G-4136)
NATIONAL AMUSEMENTS INC
760 Cincinnati Mills Dr (45240-1261)
PHONE...................................513 699-1500
John Beinke, *Branch Mgr*
EMP: 41
SALES (corp-wide): 13.7B **Publicly Held**
WEB: www.nationalamusements.com
SIC: 7832 Motion picture theaters, except drive-in
PA: National Amusements, Inc.
   846 University Ave
   Norwood MA 02062
   781 461-1600

(G-4137)
NATIONAL EXPRESS TRANSIT CORP
8041 Hosbrook Rd Ste 330 (45236-2909)
PHONE...................................513 322-6214
Gary Waits, *CEO*
Mark Foster, *Vice Pres*
Thomas M Greufe, *Vice Pres*
Greg Harrington, *Vice Pres*
Mike Rushin, *CFO*
EMP: 99
SALES (est): 2.4MM **Privately Held**
SIC: 4119 Local passenger transportation

GEOGRAPHIC SECTION

Cincinnati - Hamilton County (G-4163)

(G-4138)
NATIONAL HERITG ACADEMIES INC
Also Called: Orion Academy
1798 Queen City Ave (45214-1427)
PHONE.................513 251-6000
Terrez Thomas, *Branch Mgr*
EMP: 54 **Privately Held**
SIC: 8741 Management services
PA: National Heritage Academies, Inc.
3850 Broadmoor Ave Se # 201
Grand Rapids MI 49512

(G-4139)
NATIONAL HERITG ACADEMIES INC
Also Called: Alliance Academy of Cincinnati
1712 Duck Creek Rd (45207-1644)
PHONE.................513 751-5555
Juanita Preston, *Principal*
EMP: 54 **Privately Held**
SIC: 8741 Management services
PA: National Heritage Academies, Inc.
3850 Broadmoor Ave Se # 201
Grand Rapids MI 49512

(G-4140)
NATIONAL MARKETSHARE GROUP (PA)
2155 W 8th St (45204-2051)
PHONE.................513 921-0800
William Burwinkel, *President*
Beth A Burwinkel, *Treasurer*
Jerrick Taber, *Sales Associate*
Scott Ruth, *Director*
Kristi Codling, *Executive Asst*
EMP: 37
SQ FT: 18,000
SALES (est): 6.2MM **Privately Held**
SIC: 5023 5092 5013 5087 Home furnishings; toys; automotive supplies & parts; janitors' supplies; specialty food items

(G-4141)
NATIONAL MENTOR HOLDINGS INC
2245 Gilbert Ave (45206-3040)
PHONE.................513 221-0175
EMP: 639
SALES (corp-wide): 741.5MM **Privately Held**
SIC: 8322 Community center
PA: National Mentor Holdings, Inc.
313 Congress St Fl 5
Boston MA 02210
617 790-4800

(G-4142)
NATIONAL UNDERGROUND RAILROAD
250 W Court St Ste 300e (45202-1095)
PHONE.................513 333-7500
Kim Robinson, *CEO*
Edwin Rigaud, *Ch of Bd*
Spencer Crew, *President*
Daniel Hoffheimer, *Chairman*
Love Collins, *Vice Pres*
EMP: 85 EST: 1995
SQ FT: 158,000
SALES: 4.4MM **Privately Held**
WEB: www.nurfc.org
SIC: 8412 Historical society

(G-4143)
NATIONAL VALUATION CONSULTANTS
441 Vine St (45202-2821)
PHONE.................513 929-4100
Jim Moher, *Branch Mgr*
EMP: 34 **Privately Held**
SIC: 8999 Scientific consulting
PA: National Valuation Consultants
7807 E Pkview Ave Ste 200
Centennial CO 80111

(G-4144)
NATIONWIDE TRANSPORT LLC
4445 Lk Frest Dr Ste 475 (45242)
PHONE.................513 554-0203
Alan Hiatt,
EMP: 33
SQ FT: 15,000
SALES (est): 7MM **Privately Held**
WEB: www.nationwidetransport.net
SIC: 4731 Truck transportation brokers

(G-4145)
NATL CITY COML CAPITOL LLC
995 Dalton Ave (45203-1100)
PHONE.................513 455-9746
Vince Rinaldi, *Principal*
EMP: 31
SALES (est): 6.2MM **Privately Held**
SIC: 6799 Investors

(G-4146)
NATROP INC
4400 Reading Rd (45229-1254)
PHONE.................513 242-1375
Fax: 513 242-1531
William Kenneth Natorp, *CEO*
John Schmidt, *President*
Marian Brush, *Admin Sec*
EMP: 80
SQ FT: 15,000
SALES (est): 3.1MM **Privately Held**
SIC: 0782 Landscape contractors

(G-4147)
NBDC II LLC
2127 W North Bend Rd (45224-2371)
PHONE.................513 681-5439
Christopher Hildebrant, *President*
EMP: 40
SQ FT: 11,500
SALES (est): 480.2K **Privately Held**
SIC: 8351 Child day care services

(G-4148)
NCS HEALTHCARE OF OHIO LLC (DH)
201 E 4th St Ste 900 (45202-4160)
PHONE.................513 719-2600
James Cialdini, *President*
EMP: 56
SALES: 46.7MM
SALES (corp-wide): 184.7B **Publicly Held**
SIC: 5122 Drugs, proprietaries & sundries

(G-4149)
NEALS CONSTRUCTION COMPANY
Also Called: Neals Design Remodel
7770 E Kemper Rd (45249-1612)
PHONE.................513 489-7700
Fax: 513 489-7007
Neal P Hendy, *CEO*
Allan Hendy, *Vice Pres*
Allen Hendy, *Vice Pres*
Neal Hendy Jr, *Vice Pres*
Steve Hendy, *Vice Pres*
EMP: 29 EST: 1972
SQ FT: 3,000
SALES (est): 4.8MM **Privately Held**
WEB: www.neals.com
SIC: 1521 General remodeling, single-family houses

(G-4150)
NEHEMIAH MANUFACTURING CO LLC
1130 Findlay St (45214-2052)
PHONE.................513 351-5700
Daniel Meyer, *CEO*
Richard T Palmer, *President*
Mike Pachko, *COO*
Rich Halsey, *Vice Pres*
Dan Wall, *Vice Pres*
▲ EMP: 50
SQ FT: 33,706
SALES (est): 31.5MM **Privately Held**
SIC: 5122 2844 Toiletries; toilet preparations

(G-4151)
NEIGHBORCARE INC (DH)
201 E 4th St Ste 900 (45202-4160)
PHONE.................513 719-2600
Elizabeth A Haley, *President*
Robert A Smith, *COO*
John L Kordash, *Exec VP*
John F Gaither Jr, *Senior VP*
Kirk Popeo, *Senior VP*
EMP: 600
SQ FT: 90,000
SALES (est): 500.8MM
SALES (corp-wide): 184.7B **Publicly Held**
WEB: www.ghv.com
SIC: 5122 5912 5047 7389 Pharmaceuticals; drug stores & proprietary stores; medical equipment & supplies; purchasing service
HQ: Omnicare Holding Company
1105 Market St Ste 1300
Cincinnati OH 45215
513 719-2600

(G-4152)
NEIGHBORHOOD HEALTH CARE INC (PA)
2415 Auburn Ave (45219-2701)
PHONE.................513 221-4949
Fax: 513 221-4954
Johnny B Daniels, *President*
Shayla Toombs-Withers, *Family Practiti*
Monica Hampton, *Exec Sec*
EMP: 37
SALES: 6.5MM **Privately Held**
SIC: 8399 Social services

(G-4153)
NEIL KRAVITZ GROUP SALES INC
412 S Cooper Ave (45215-4555)
PHONE.................513 961-8697
Fax: 513 961-0888
Neil Kravitz, *President*
Daniel Conwell, *Vice Pres*
Jason Ernst, *Vice Pres*
Mike Paniccia, *Vice Pres*
Judy Nevans, *Office Mgr*
◆ EMP: 29
SQ FT: 370,000
SALES: 22.4MM **Privately Held**
WEB: www.groupsalesinc.com
SIC: 5092 Toys & hobby goods & supplies

(G-4154)
NELSON STARK COMPANY
7685 Fields Ertel Rd D2 (45241-6084)
PHONE.................513 489-0866
Jeff Read, *President*
Mark Stark, *President*
Ken Adkins, *General Mgr*
Charles Nelson, *Senior VP*
H Joseph Iori, *Vice Pres*
EMP: 170
SQ FT: 45,000
SALES: 46.1MM **Privately Held**
WEB: www.nelsonstark.com
SIC: 1711 1623 1794 Plumbing contractors; water, sewer & utility lines; underground utilities contractor; excavation work

(G-4155)
NEW ENGLAND MOTOR FREIGHT INC
11101 Mosteller Rd Ste 1 (45241-1882)
PHONE.................513 782-0017
Brian Chante, *Manager*
Tom Arnold, *Manager*
EMP: 51
SALES (corp-wide): 882.8MM **Privately Held**
WEB: www.nemf.com
SIC: 4213 Automobiles, transport & delivery
PA: New England Motor Freight, Inc.
1-71 North Ave E
Elizabeth NJ 07201
908 965-0100

(G-4156)
NEW HOPE & HORIZONS
4055 Executive Park Dr # 100 (45241-2095)
PHONE.................513 761-7999
Fax: 513 761-4597
Marvin W Sims, *Owner*
EMP: 40
SQ FT: 428
SALES (est): 4MM **Privately Held**
SIC: 8052 Intermediate care facilities

(G-4157)
NEW SCHOOL INC
3 Burton Woods Ln (45229-1399)
PHONE.................513 281-7999
Fax: 513 281-7996
Eric Dustman, *Director*
Nancy Fraser, *Professor*
Jennifer Wilson, *Assoc Prof*
Jen Doerr, *Exec Sec*
EMP: 30
SQ FT: 10,000
SALES: 1.9MM **Privately Held**
WEB: www.thenewschool.cc
SIC: 8211 8351 Private elementary school; child day care services

(G-4158)
NEW VULCO MFG & SALES CO LLC
Also Called: Vulcan Oil Company
5353 Spring Grove Ave (45217-1026)
PHONE.................513 242-2672
Garry Ferraris,
Larry Schirmann,
EMP: 60
SALES (est): 14.6MM **Privately Held**
SIC: 5983 2992 5171 2899 Fuel oil dealers; oils & greases, blending & compounding; petroleum bulk stations; petroleum terminals; chemical preparations; specialty cleaning, polishes & sanitation goods; soap & other detergents

(G-4159)
NEW YORK LIFE INSURANCE CO
5905 E Galbraith Rd # 4000 (45236-2972)
PHONE.................513 621-9999
Brian Burger, *Sales Executive*
Jeffrey Slattery, *Manager*
Andrew Magenheim, *Advisor*
EMP: 58
SALES (corp-wide): 27.9B **Privately Held**
WEB: www.newyorklife.com
SIC: 6411 Insurance agents & brokers
PA: New York Life Insurance Company
51 Madison Ave Bsmt 1b
New York NY 10010
212 576-7000

(G-4160)
NEWCOMER FUNERAL SVC GROUP INC
7830 Hamilton Ave (45231-3106)
PHONE.................513 521-1971
John Fish, *Director*
EMP: 379
SALES (corp-wide): 22.8MM **Privately Held**
SIC: 7261 Funeral home
PA: Newcomer Funeral Service Group, Inc.
520 Sw 27th St
Topeka KS 66611
785 233-6655

(G-4161)
NEWPORT WALKING TOURS LLC
Also Called: American Legacy Tours
6292 Eagles Lake Dr (45248-6857)
PHONE.................859 951-8560
Brad Hill, *Mng Member*
EMP: 36
SALES (est): 805.2K **Privately Held**
SIC: 4725 Tours, conducted

(G-4162)
NEXGEN ENTERPRISES INC (PA)
Also Called: Nexgen Building Supply
3274 Spring Grove Ave (45225-1338)
PHONE.................513 618-0300
Robert Hoge, *CEO*
Richard C Wolgemuth, *President*
Bruce Kirchhofer, *Senior VP*
Richard J Hoge, *Vice Pres*
Bruce J Fahey, *CFO*
EMP: 225 EST: 1920
SALES (est): 160.7MM **Privately Held**
WEB: www.hwzco.com
SIC: 5032 Brick, stone & related material

(G-4163)
NEXTEL COMMUNICATIONS INC
7878 Montgomery Rd (45236-4301)
PHONE.................513 891-9200
Fax: 513 745-0492
Kat Williams, *Principal*
EMP: 60

Cincinnati - Hamilton County (G-4164)   GEOGRAPHIC SECTION

SALES (corp-wide): 78.3B **Publicly Held**
SIC: 4812 Cellular telephone services
HQ: Nextel Communications, Inc.
12502 Sunrise Valley Dr
Reston VA 20191
703 433-4000

(G-4164)
NEXTMED SYSTEMS INC (PA)
16 Triangle Park Dr (45246-3411)
PHONE.................................216 674-0511
David Shute, *CEO*
James Bennett, *Ch of Bd*
Tony Paparella, *COO*
Wolfgang Sprie, *Finance*
Ronald Amrich, *Senior Mgr*
EMP: 44
SQ FT: 3,000
SALES (est): 3.6MM **Privately Held**
SIC: 7372 Business oriented computer software

(G-4165)
NEXTT CORP
106 Koehler Ave Apt 4 (45215-4844)
PHONE.................................513 813-6398
Travis Bea, *Principal*
EMP: 25
SALES (est): 807K **Privately Held**
SIC: 1521 General remodeling, single-family houses; repairing fire damage, single-family houses

(G-4166)
NEXXTSHOW EXPOSITION SVCS LLC
645 Linn St (45203-1722)
PHONE.................................877 836-3131
Aaron Bludworth, *CEO*
John Brown, *Opers Mgr*
Tim Fox, *Opers Mgr*
Patrick McCracken, *Opers Staff*
Jt Barclay, *CFO*
EMP: 50
SALES (est): 2.5MM
SALES (corp-wide): 44.5MM **Privately Held**
SIC: 7389 Convention & show services
PA: Fern Exposition Services Llc
645 Linn St
Cincinnati OH 45203
513 621-6111

(G-4167)
NEYER REAL ESTATE MGT LLC
Also Called: Neyer Management
3927 Brotherton Rd # 200 (45209-1100)
PHONE.................................513 618-6000
Fax: 513 618-6010
Anita Massarella, *Marketing Mgr*
Kathy Macke, *Property Mgr*
John E Neyer,
EMP: 30
SALES (est): 5.6MM **Privately Held**
WEB: www.neyermanagement.com
SIC: 6531 Rental agent, real estate

(G-4168)
NGM INC
Also Called: Custom Mail Services
7676 Reinhold Dr (45237-3312)
P.O. Box 37387 (45222-0387)
PHONE.................................513 821-7363
Fax: 513 821-7370
Gene Magers, *President*
Deborah Magers, *Vice Pres*
David Cutlip, *Controller*
Jim Conley, *Accounts Exec*
Kristyn Kleinhenz, *Marketing Staff*
EMP: 25
SQ FT: 30,000
SALES (est): 2.6MM **Privately Held**
WEB: www.custommailservices.com
SIC: 7389 Mailbox rental & related service

(G-4169)
NIEMAN PLUMBING INC
2030 Stapleton Ct (45240-2778)
PHONE.................................513 851-5588
Fax: 513 851-5588
Drew Nieman, *President*
Jo Ellen Nieman, *Corp Secy*
A J Nieman, *Mktg Dir*
EMP: 95
SQ FT: 20,000

SALES (est): 13MM **Privately Held**
WEB: www.niemanplumbing.com
SIC: 1711 Septic system construction

(G-4170)
NISBET CORPORATION
Also Called: West Shell Coml Encore Intl
11575 Reading Rd (45241-2240)
PHONE.................................513 563-1111
Mark Rippe, *President*
EMP: 150
SALES (est): 3.9MM **Privately Held**
SIC: 6531 Real estate agents & managers

(G-4171)
NOGGINS HAIR DESIGN INC
8556 Beechmont Ave # 450 (45255-4787)
PHONE.................................513 474-4405
Jeff Anderson, *President*
EMP: 26
SALES (est): 439.1K **Privately Held**
SIC: 7231 7299 Hairdressers; tanning salon

(G-4172)
NORAMCO TRANSPORT CORP (PA)
9252 Colerain Ave Ste 4 (45251-2447)
PHONE.................................513 245-9050
Michael A Wetterich, *President*
Mark Wetterich, *Vice Pres*
Josh Cahill, *Controller*
EMP: 25
SQ FT: 50,000
SALES (est): 8MM **Privately Held**
SIC: 4731 4213 Freight forwarding; trucking, except local

(G-4173)
NORFOLK SOUTHERN CORPORATION
5555 Wooster Pike (45227-4119)
PHONE.................................513 271-0972
Kenneth Weatherspoon, *Branch Mgr*
EMP: 43
SALES (corp-wide): 10.5B **Publicly Held**
SIC: 4011 Railroads, line-haul operating
PA: Norfolk Southern Corporation
3 Commercial Pl Ste 1a
Norfolk VA 23510
757 629-2680

(G-4174)
NORFOLK SOUTHERN CORPORATION
1410 Gest St Fl 2 (45203-1019)
PHONE.................................513 977-3246
Fax: 513 977-3372
BJ Mackey, *Manager*
Kerry McIntyre, *Manager*
EMP: 70
SALES (corp-wide): 10.5B **Publicly Held**
WEB: www.nscorp.com
SIC: 4011 Railroads, line-haul operating
PA: Norfolk Southern Corporation
3 Commercial Pl Ste 1a
Norfolk VA 23510
757 629-2680

(G-4175)
NORMANDY OFFICE ASSOCIATES
Also Called: Normanity Town
1055 Saint Paul Pl (45202-6042)
PHONE.................................513 381-8696
Neil K Bortz, *General Ptnr*
Marvin Rosenberg, *General Ptnr*
EMP: 75
SQ FT: 10,000
SALES (est): 1.7MM **Privately Held**
SIC: 6531 Real estate agents & managers

(G-4176)
NORTH AMERICAN PROPERTIES INC
212 E 3rd St Ste 300 (45202-5500)
PHONE.................................513 721-2744
Fax: 513 721-0332
Thomas L Williams, *President*
Dale Hafele, *Principal*
Anthony Hobson, *Principal*
William J Williams Jr, *Chairman*
Jennifer Lamm, *Regional Mgr*
EMP: 40
SQ FT: 5,500

SALES (est): 9.5MM **Privately Held**
SIC: 6531 6552 Real estate managers; subdividers & developers

(G-4177)
NORTH SIDE BANK AND TRUST CO (PA)
4125 Hamilton Ave (45223-2246)
P.O. Box 23128 (45223-0128)
PHONE.................................513 542-7800
Clifford Coors, *Ch of Bd*
John A Coors, *President*
Donald Beimesche, *Vice Pres*
Linda Boiman, *Vice Pres*
Mary Weigel, *Vice Pres*
EMP: 100 **EST:** 1891
SQ FT: 19,348
SALES (est): 23.3MM **Privately Held**
WEB: www.nsbt.net
SIC: 6022 State trust companies accepting deposits, commercial

(G-4178)
NORTH SIDE BANK AND TRUST CO
2739 Madison Rd (45209-2208)
PHONE.................................513 533-8000
Clifford Coors, *CEO*
EMP: 99
SALES (corp-wide): 23.3MM **Privately Held**
SIC: 6022 State trust companies accepting deposits, commercial
PA: The North Side Bank And Trust Company
4125 Hamilton Ave
Cincinnati OH 45223
513 542-7800

(G-4179)
NORTHBEND ARCHTCTURAL PDTS INC
2080 Waycross Rd (45240-2717)
PHONE.................................513 577-7988
Fax: 513 825-0582
Mark Smith, *President*
Dave Hensley, *Plant Mgr*
Richard Perkins, *CFO*
▲ **EMP:** 38
SQ FT: 3,000
SALES (est): 5.4MM **Privately Held**
WEB: www.walteklld.com
SIC: 1791 Structural steel erection

(G-4180)
NORTHGATE CHRYSLER JEEP INC
8536 Colerain Ave (45251-2914)
PHONE.................................513 385-3900
Fax: 513 385-0625
Peter Pannier, *President*
Kathy Hettesheimer, *Treasurer*
EMP: 60
SQ FT: 40,000
SALES (est): 24.9MM **Privately Held**
WEB: www.northgatechrysler.com
SIC: 5511 7538 7515 5531 Automobiles, new & used; general automotive repair shops; passenger car leasing; body shop, automotive

(G-4181)
NORTHGATE PK RETIREMENT CMNTY
9191 Round Top Rd Ofc (45251-2465)
PHONE.................................513 923-3711
Fax: 513 245-5841
Kris Schulze, *Marketing Staff*
Patricia Jett, *Director*
EMP: 60
SQ FT: 50,000
SALES (est): 2MM
SALES (corp-wide): 17.7MM **Privately Held**
SIC: 8322 Senior citizens' center or association
PA: American Retirement Villas Properties Ii Lp
245 Fischer Ave Ste D1
Costa Mesa CA

(G-4182)
NORTHWEST LOCAL SCHOOL DST
3308 Compton Rd (45251-2508)
PHONE.................................513 923-1000
EMP: 73
SALES (corp-wide): 114.6MM **Privately Held**
SIC: 8211 8351 Public elementary & secondary schools; preschool center
PA: Northwest Local School District
3240 Banning Rd
Cincinnati OH 45239
513 923-1000

(G-4183)
NORTHWESTERN MUTL LF INSUR CO
3805 Edwards Rd Ste 200 (45209-1939)
PHONE.................................513 366-3600
Charles Leadingham, *Facilities Mgr*
Shawn Kelley, *Manager*
EMP: 100
SALES (corp-wide): 28.1B **Privately Held**
WEB: www.nmfn.com
SIC: 6411 Insurance agents, brokers & service
PA: The Northwestern Mutual Life Insurance Company
720 E Wisconsin Ave
Milwaukee WI 53202
414 271-1444

(G-4184)
NORWOOD ENDOSCOPY CENTER
4746 Montgomery Rd # 100 (45212-2626)
PHONE.................................513 731-5600
Daniel G Walker, *Principal*
EMP: 25
SALES (est): 1.1MM **Privately Held**
SIC: 8011 Gastronomist; endocrinologist

(G-4185)
NORWOOD HARDWARE & SUPPLY CO (PA)
2906 Glendale Milford Rd (45241-3131)
PHONE.................................513 733-1175
Fax: 513 733-8667
Matt Chabot, *CEO*
Matthew Chabot, *Vice Pres*
Dan Brinkman, *VP Opers*
Silvano Quintaba, *Project Mgr*
Alex Fibbe, *Mfg Staff*
▲ **EMP:** 50
SQ FT: 58,000
SALES (est): 22.2MM **Privately Held**
WEB: www.norwoodhardware.com
SIC: 5072 5031 5023 Hardware; metal doors, sash & trim; doors; home furnishings

(G-4186)
NORWOOD HEALTH CARE CENTER LLC
1578 Sherman Ave (45212-2510)
PHONE.................................513 351-0153
Lorie Keeney, *Office Mgr*
Herbert Seidner, *Mng Member*
Missy McClellan, *Executive*
Jennifer Gardner, *Administration*
EMP: 85
SQ FT: 23,000
SALES (est): 1.5MM **Privately Held**
SIC: 8051 8052 8059 Skilled nursing care facilities; intermediate care facilities; nursing home, except skilled & intermediate care facility

(G-4187)
NOVELART MANUFACTURING COMPANY (PA)
Also Called: TOPICZ
2121 Section Rd (45237-3509)
P.O. Box 37289 (45222-0289)
PHONE.................................513 351-7700
Fax: 513 351-9604
Marvin H Schwartz, *President*
Dan Sunderhaus, *General Mgr*
Darlene Miller, *Buyer*
Mike Fields, *Controller*
Nancy Madden, *Human Res Dir*
EMP: 160 **EST:** 1903
SQ FT: 90,000

GEOGRAPHIC SECTION

Cincinnati - Hamilton County (G-4213)

SALES: 343.8MM **Privately Held**
SIC: 5141 5145 5194 Groceries, general line; confectionery; tobacco & tobacco products

(G-4188)
NTT DATA INC
3284 North Bend Rd # 107 (45239-7688)
PHONE..................513 794-1400
Fax: 513 794-1040
EMP: 58
SALES (corp-wide): 93.3B **Privately Held**
SIC: 7371 Custom Computer Programing
HQ: Ntt Data, Inc.
 5601 Gran Pkwy Ste 1000
 Plano TX 75024
 800 745-3263

(G-4189)
NUCOR CORPORATION
P.O. Box 5810 (45201-5810)
PHONE..................407 855-2990
EMP: 46
SALES (corp-wide): 20.2B **Publicly Held**
SIC: 4953 Recycling, waste materials
PA: Nucor Corporation
 1915 Rexford Rd Ste 400
 Charlotte NC 28211
 704 366-7000

(G-4190)
NUEROLOGICAL & SLEEP DISORDERS
Also Called: Fleet Management Institute
8250 Kenwood Crossing Way # 225 (45236-3668)
PHONE..................513 721-7533
James Armitage, *CEO*
Bruce Corser, *CEO*
John Stigler, *Financial Exec*
Barbara McDonald, *Office Mgr*
EMP: 35
SALES (est): 3.4MM **Privately Held**
SIC: 8011 Neurologist

(G-4191)
NURAY RADIOLOGISTS INC
8160 Corp Pk Dr Ste 330 (45242)
P.O. Box 42417 (45242-0417)
PHONE..................513 965-8059
Beverly Shilton, *Manager*
EMP: 50
SALES (est): 2.6MM **Privately Held**
SIC: 8011 Radiologist

(G-4192)
NUROTOCO MASSACHUSETTS INC
Also Called: Roto-Rooter
255 E 5th St (45202-4700)
PHONE..................513 762-6690
Spencer Lee, *CEO*
EMP: 110
SALES (est): 2.6MM
SALES (corp-wide): 1.6B **Publicly Held**
SIC: 7699 Sewer cleaning & rodding
HQ: Roto-Rooter Services Company
 255 E 5th St Ste 2500
 Cincinnati OH 45202
 513 762-6690

(G-4193)
NURSES CARE INC
9200 Montgomery Rd 13b (45242-7792)
PHONE..................513 791-0233
Fax: 513 791-0233
Tammy Stover, *Branch Mgr*
EMP: 45
SALES (corp-wide): 3.9MM **Privately Held**
WEB: www.nursescareinc.com
SIC: 7361 Employment agencies
PA: Nurses Care, Inc
 9009 Springboro Pike
 Miamisburg OH 45342
 513 424-1141

(G-4194)
NURSING CARE MGT AMER INC
Also Called: Montgomery Care Center
7777 Cooper Rd (45242-7703)
PHONE..................513 793-5092
Kevin Faus, *Maint Spvr*
Mark Osendorf, *Manager*
Robyn Herzfeld, *Hlthcr Dir*
EMP: 95

SALES (corp-wide): 26.1MM **Privately Held**
WEB: www.nursinghomeinfo.org
SIC: 8741 8051 8059 Nursing & personal care facility management; skilled nursing care facilities; nursing home, except skilled & intermediate care facility
PA: Nursing Care Management Of America, Inc.
 7265 Kenwood Rd Ste 300
 Cincinnati OH 45236
 513 793-8804

(G-4195)
OAK HILLS SWIM & RACQUET
5850 Muddy Creek Rd (45233-1808)
P.O. Box 58202 (45258-0202)
PHONE..................513 922-1827
Brian Galliger, *Principal*
EMP: 40
SALES: 186.2K **Privately Held**
SIC: 7997 Swimming club, membership

(G-4196)
OAKTREE LLC
Also Called: Oak Hlls Nrsing Rehabilitation
4307 Bridgetown Rd (45211-4427)
PHONE..................513 598-8000
Aharon Kibel,
EMP: 70 **EST:** 2010
SQ FT: 72,000
SALES: 6.7MM **Privately Held**
SIC: 8051 Skilled nursing care facilities

(G-4197)
OCEAN WIDE SEAFOOD COMPANY
2601 W 8th St Apt 10 (45204-1425)
PHONE..................937 610-5740
Dale Hartlage, *President*
Eileen Hartlege, *Controller*
Emy Luges, *Office Mgr*
EMP: 35
SALES (est): 8.8MM **Privately Held**
WEB: www.owseafood.com
SIC: 5146 Seafoods

(G-4198)
OCONNOR ACCIANI & LEVY LLC (PA)
600 Vine St Ste 1600 (45202-1133)
PHONE..................513 241-7111
Michael O'Connor, *Partner*
Henry Acciani, *Partner*
Barry D Levy, *Partner*
Eric Rowe, *Technology*
Carrie L Budinger,
EMP: 31
SALES (est): 7.6MM **Privately Held**
WEB: www.oal-law.com
SIC: 8111 General practice law office

(G-4199)
OCR SERVICES CORPORATION
201 E 4th St Ste 900 (45202-4160)
PHONE..................513 719-2600
Joel F Dumunder, *President*
Kenneth Chesterman, *Vice Pres*
Patrick E Keefe, *Vice Pres*
Cheryl Hodge, *Admin Sec*
EMP: 180
SALES (corp-wide): 184.7B **Publicly Held**
WEB: www.omnicare.com
SIC: 6719 Investment holding companies, except banks
HQ: Omnicare Holding Company
 1105 Market St Ste 1300
 Cincinnati OH 45215
 513 719-2600

(G-4200)
OFFICIAL INVESTIGATIONS INC
Also Called: Tri-State Mobile Notaries
3284 North Bend Rd # 310 (45239-7688)
PHONE..................844 263-3424
Michael P Rolfes, *President*
EMP: 63
SQ FT: 900
SALES (est): 1.4MM **Privately Held**
WEB: www.officialinvestigations.com
SIC: 7381 7389 Guard services; private investigator; notary publics

(G-4201)
OGARA GROUP INC (PA)
9113 Le Street Dr (45249)
PHONE..................513 338-0660
Fax: 513 338-0692
Bill T O'Gara, *CEO*
Thomas M O'Gara, *Ch of Bd*
Jeff Bozworth, *President*
Tony Russell, *President*
Ritchie Allen, *Business Mgr*
EMP: 57
SALES (est): 31.7MM **Privately Held**
SIC: 7382 Security systems services

(G-4202)
OHIO BUILDING SERVICE INC
2212 Losantiville Ave (45237-4206)
PHONE..................513 761-0268
Fax: 513 761-1098
Lina Orr, *President*
Steven Statman, *Vice Pres*
EMP: 30
SQ FT: 2,500
SALES: 600K **Privately Held**
WEB: www.ohiobuildingservices.com
SIC: 7349 7217 Janitorial service, contract basis; building cleaning service; carpet & upholstery cleaning

(G-4203)
OHIO CHECK CASHERS INC
3513 Reading Rd (45229-2603)
PHONE..................513 559-0220
Fax: 513 487-6161
Tim Erwin, *General Mgr*
Bridget Williams, *Manager*
EMP: 30
SALES (est): 2.7MM **Privately Held**
SIC: 6099 Check cashing agencies

(G-4204)
OHIO HEART
7545 Beechmont Ave Ste E (45255-4238)
PHONE..................513 206-1320
John F Schneider, *President*
EMP: 25
SALES (est): 477.5K **Privately Held**
SIC: 8011 Cardiologist & cardio-vascular specialist

(G-4205)
OHIO HEART AND VASCULAR
5885 Harrison Ave # 1900 (45248-1721)
PHONE..................513 206-1800
A Daniel Glassman, *Principal*
Andrew Daniel Glassman, *Principal*
EMP: 25
SALES (est): 887.3K **Privately Held**
SIC: 8011 Offices & clinics of medical doctors

(G-4206)
OHIO HEART HEALTH CENTER INC (PA)
237 Wlliam Howard Taft Rd (45219-2610)
PHONE..................513 351-9900
Dean Kereiakes, *President*
Pete L Caples MD, *Principal*
Steven Ware, *CFO*
EMP: 200
SALES (est): 9.8MM **Privately Held**
WEB: www.ohioheart.com
SIC: 8011 Cardiologist & cardio-vascular specialist

(G-4207)
OHIO HYDRAULICS INC
2510 E Sharon Rd Ste 1 (45241-1891)
PHONE..................513 771-2590
Fax: 513 771-1447
John Davis, *Ch of Bd*
Kathleen Hilliard, *President*
Tamera Fair, *Corp Secy*
Dave Davis, *Vice Pres*
Robert Farwick, *Vice Pres*
EMP: 25 **EST:** 1971
SQ FT: 13,500
SALES (est): 6.5MM **Privately Held**
WEB: www.ohiohydraulics.com
SIC: 3492 3599 5084 7699 Hose & tube fittings & assemblies, hydraulic/pneumatic; flexible metal hose, tubing & bellows; hydraulic systems equipment & supplies; tank repair & cleaning services; welding repair; manufactured hardware (general)

(G-4208)
OHIO LIVING
Also Called: Llanfair Retirement Community
1701 Llanfair Ave (45224-2972)
PHONE..................513 681-4230
Fax: 513 681-0417
Cassandra Bray, *Purchasing*
Gary Huber, *Envir Svcs Dir*
Judy Sweeney, *Human Res Dir*
Sheena Parton, *Branch Mgr*
Ryan Carneson, *Manager*
EMP: 220 **Privately Held**
WEB: www.nwo.oprs.org
SIC: 8361 8052 8051 Home for the aged; intermediate care facilities; skilled nursing care facilities
PA: Ohio Living
 1001 Kingsmill Pkwy
 Columbus OH 43229

(G-4209)
OHIO MACHINERY CO
Also Called: Caterpillar Authorized Dealer
11330 Mosteller Rd (45241-1828)
PHONE..................513 771-0515
Jeffrey Whaley, *Manager*
Greg Sanker,
EMP: 125
SALES (corp-wide): 222.7MM **Privately Held**
WEB: www.enginesnow.com
SIC: 5082 General construction machinery & equipment
PA: Ohio Machinery Co.
 3993 E Royalton Rd
 Broadview Heights OH 44147
 440 526-6200

(G-4210)
OHIO RVER VLY WTR SNTTION COMM
Also Called: Orsanco
5735 Kellogg Ave (45230-7112)
PHONE..................513 231-7719
Fax: 513 231-7761
Douglas Conrow, *Ch of Bd*
Jay Patel, *MIS Staff*
Alan Vicory Jr, *Exec Dir*
David Paylor, *Director*
David Bailey, *Administration*
EMP: 26 **EST:** 1948
SQ FT: 15,000
SALES: 202.8K **Privately Held**
WEB: www.orsanco.org
SIC: 8734 8641 Pollution testing; civic social & fraternal associations

(G-4211)
OHIO VALLEY ACQUISITION INC
Also Called: Ameristop Food Marts
250 E 5th St Ste 1200 (45202-4139)
PHONE..................513 553-0768
Don Bloom, *President*
Tony Parnigoni, *COO*
William Zembrodt, *CFO*
EMP: 415
SQ FT: 13,500
SALES (est): 63MM **Privately Held**
SIC: 6794 Franchises, selling or licensing

(G-4212)
OHIO VALLEY FLOORING INC (PA)
5555 Murray Ave (45227-2707)
PHONE..................513 271-3434
Fax: 513 527-9595
Al Hurt, *President*
Randy Flowers, *President*
Pat Seibert, *President*
Mike Spivey, *President*
Luann Doyle, *Opers Mgr*
▲ **EMP:** 70
SQ FT: 300,000
SALES: 119.6MM **Privately Held**
WEB: www.ovf.com
SIC: 5023 Carpets

(G-4213)
OHIO VALLEY WINE COMPANY (PA)
Also Called: Ohio Valley Wine & Beer
10975 Medallion Dr (45241-4830)
PHONE..................513 771-9370
Fax: 513 771-5130
Steve Lowrey, *President*

Cincinnati - Hamilton County (G-4214)

Greg Swartz, *District Mgr*
Greg Maurer, *Exec VP*
Mike Earn, *Vice Pres*
Joe Noll, *Vice Pres*
▲ **EMP:** 100
SQ FT: 86,000
SALES (est): 41.4MM **Privately Held**
SIC: 5182 5181 Wine; beer & other fermented malt liquors

(G-4214)
OHIO-KENTUCKY-INDIANA REGIONAL
720 E Pete Rose Way # 420 (45202-3576)
PHONE..................513 621-6300
Mark Polinski, *Director*
Robert Koeler, *Director*
Mark Poticentski, *Director*
Mark McCormack, *Planning*
EMP: 40
SQ FT: 15,400
SALES (est): 3.8MM **Privately Held**
SIC: 8742 Planning consultant

(G-4215)
OHIO/OKLAHOMA HEARST TV INC
1700 Young St (45202-6821)
PHONE..................513 412-5000
Fax: 405 475-5219
Brent Hensely, *President*
David Evans, *Purch Agent*
Pat Ronne, *Controller*
Tom Comersford, *Sales Mgr*
EMP: 110
SQ FT: 37,285
SALES (est): 8.5MM
SALES (corp-wide): 6.7B **Privately Held**
WEB: www.kocotv.com
SIC: 4833 Television broadcasting stations
HQ: Hearst Television, Inc.
  300 W 57th St
  New York NY 10019

(G-4216)
OHIO/OKLAHOMA HEARST TV INC
Also Called: Wlwt
1700 Young St (45202-6821)
PHONE..................513 412-5000
Richard Dyer, *President*
Lisa Snell, *Human Res Mgr*
Mark Diangelo, *Sales Mgr*
Janet Henderson, *Accounts Exec*
Bob Sommerkamp, *Accounts Exec*
EMP: 160
SALES (est): 6MM
SALES (corp-wide): 6.7B **Privately Held**
WEB: www.wbal.com
SIC: 4833 6794 Television broadcasting stations; patent owners & lessors
HQ: Hearst Television, Inc.
  300 W 57th St
  New York NY 10019

(G-4217)
OK INTERIORS CORP
11100 Ashburn Rd (45240-3813)
PHONE..................513 742-3278
Fax: 513 595-8493
Todd Prewitt, *President*
Loren Schramm, *President*
Mark Konradi, *Superintendent*
Derrick Stacy, *Superintendent*
Gregory J Meurer, *Principal*
EMP: 150
SQ FT: 18,500
SALES: 27MM **Privately Held**
WEB: www.okinteriors.com
SIC: 1742 5031 1751 1752 Acoustical & ceiling work; doors; window & door (prefabricated) installation; access flooring system installation; partitions

(G-4218)
OKL CAN LINE INC
11235 Sebring Dr (45240-2714)
PHONE..................513 825-1655
Fax: 513 825-1948
Anthony Lacey, *CEO*
Paul Henderson, *Vice Pres*
Douglas Stewart, *Vice Pres*
Scott Feldmann, *Prdtn Mgr*
Peter Farwick, *Engineer*
◆ **EMP:** 47
SQ FT: 50,000
SALES (est): 11.7MM
SALES (corp-wide): 3MM **Privately Held**
WEB: www.oklcan.com
SIC: 3565 7699 Bottling & canning machinery; industrial machinery & equipment repair
PA: Allcan Global Services, Inc
  11235 Sebring Dr
  Cincinnati OH 45240
  513 825-1655

(G-4219)
OLD TIME POTTERY INC
1191 Smiley Ave (45240-1832)
PHONE..................513 825-5211
Fax: 513 825-5517
Ron Gribbins, *Branch Mgr*
EMP: 70
SALES (corp-wide): 799.3MM **Privately Held**
WEB: www.oldtimepottery.com
SIC: 5999 5023 Art, picture frames & decorations; home furnishings
PA: Old Time Pottery, Llc
  480 River Rock Blvd
  Murfreesboro TN 37128
  615 890-6060

(G-4220)
OMNICARE INC (DH)
900 Omnicare Ctr 201e4t (45202-2520)
PHONE..................513 719-2600
Nitin Sahney, *President*
David Rombro, *General Mgr*
David Hileman, *Senior VP*
Amit Jain, *Senior VP*
Alexander M Kayne, *Senior VP*
EMP: 250
SALES (est): 4.7B
SALES (corp-wide): 184.7B **Publicly Held**
WEB: www.omnicare.com
SIC: 5122 5047 8082 8741 Pharmaceuticals; medical & hospital equipment; home health care services; nursing & personal care facility management
HQ: Cvs Pharmacy, Inc.
  1 Cvs Dr
  Woonsocket RI 02895
  401 765-1500

(G-4221)
OMNICARE DISTRIBUTION CTR LLC
201 E 4th St Ste 1 (45202-4248)
PHONE..................419 720-8200
Carl Schleuter, *Controller*
Dwayne Gustwsky, *Supervisor*
Dennis Holmes,
EMP: 100
SALES (est): 18.7MM
SALES (corp-wide): 184.7B **Publicly Held**
WEB: www.omnicare.com
SIC: 5122 Pharmaceuticals
HQ: Omnicare, Inc.
  900 Omnicare Ctr 201e4t
  Cincinnati OH 45202
  513 719-2600

(G-4222)
OMNICARE MANAGEMENT COMPANY
201 E 4th St Ste 900 (45202-1513)
PHONE..................513 719-1535
David Hileman, *President*
Cheryl Hodges, *Vice Pres*
Amkur Bhandari, *Treasurer*
Cecilia Temple, *Manager*
Jody Drier, *Executive Asst*
EMP: 3000
SALES (est): 65.6MM
SALES (corp-wide): 184.7B **Publicly Held**
SIC: 8741 Management services
HQ: Omnicare Holding Company
  1105 Market St Ste 1300
  Cincinnati OH 45215
  513 719-2600

(G-4223)
OMNICARE PHRM OF MIDWEST LLC (DH)
201 E 4th St Ste 900 (45202-1513)
PHONE..................513 719-2600
Joel Gemunder, *Principal*

Kathy Kopp, *COO*
Lisa Morgenthaler, *Controller*
Charlene Francis, *Marketing Staff*
Victoria Kasten, *Manager*
EMP: 100
SALES (est): 33.5MM
SALES (corp-wide): 184.7B **Publicly Held**
SIC: 5122 5912 2834 Drugs & drug proprietaries; drug stores; pharmaceutical preparations

(G-4224)
OMNICARE PURCH LTD PARTNER INC
201 E 4th St Ste 900 (45202-1513)
PHONE..................800 990-6664
Janice Rice, *Principal*
EMP: 121
SALES (est): 161.6K
SALES (corp-wide): 184.7B **Publicly Held**
SIC: 8741 Business management
HQ: Omnicare, Inc.
  900 Omnicare Ctr 201e4t
  Cincinnati OH 45202
  513 719-2600

(G-4225)
ONCALL LLC
8044 Montgomery Rd # 420 (45236-2919)
PHONE..................513 381-4320
Rolando Collado, *Managing Dir*
James Tenhundfeld, *Human Resources*
Martha Starkey, *Office Mgr*
Julie Stearns, *Supervisor*
James Erion, *Technology*
EMP: 92 EST: 1996
SQ FT: 2,900
SALES (est): 9.8MM
SALES (corp-wide): 17.7B **Privately Held**
WEB: www.oncall-llc.com
SIC: 8742 General management consultant
HQ: Grey Healthcare Group Inc.
  200 5th Ave Ste 500
  New York NY 10010
  212 886-3000

(G-4226)
ONCOLGY/HMATOLOGY CARE INC PSC (PA)
Also Called: O C I
5053 Wooster Rd (45226-2326)
PHONE..................513 751-2145
Fax: 513 751-2138
E Randolph Broun, *CEO*
Missy Brauckmann, *Manager*
Kelly Donohue, *Manager*
Charlie Walls, *Manager*
Joanie Manzo, *Director*
EMP: 70
SALES (est): 21.8MM **Privately Held**
SIC: 8011 Oncologist

(G-4227)
ONESTAFF INC
2358 Harrison Ave Apt 20 (45211-7929)
PHONE..................859 815-1345
George Thomas, *President*
Mark Ryan, *Principal*
Mary Longbottom, *Human Resources*
Mark M Ryan, *Manager*
EMP: 40
SALES: 500K **Privately Held**
SIC: 7361 Employment agencies

(G-4228)
OPPENHEIMER & CO INC
5905 E Galbraith Rd # 6200 (45236-2376)
PHONE..................513 723-9200
Laurence Wulker, *Agent*
Carlina Mattos, *Advisor*
EMP: 27 **Publicly Held**
SIC: 8742 Financial consultant
HQ: Oppenheimer & Co. Inc.
  85 Broad St Fl 3
  New York NY 10004
  212 668-8000

(G-4229)
OPPORTUNITIES FOR OHIOANS
Also Called: Vocational Rehabilitation
895 Central Ave Fl 7 (45202-1989)
PHONE..................513 852-3260
Fax: 513 651-3309

Mark Fay, *Manager*
EMP: 40 **Privately Held**
WEB: www.rsc.ohio.gov
SIC: 9431 8093 Administration of public health programs; ; rehabilitation center, outpatient treatment
HQ: Opportunities For Ohioans With Disabilities Agency
  400 E Campus View Blvd
  Columbus OH 43235
  614 438-1200

(G-4230)
OPTIS SOLUTIONS
6705 Steger Dr (45237-3097)
PHONE..................513 948-2070
Jon Iverson, *CEO*
Sven Thiesen, *COO*
EMP: 45
SALES: 605.6K **Privately Held**
SIC: 8711 Aviation &/or aeronautical engineering

(G-4231)
ORC INTERNATIONAL INC
310 Culvert St Fl 2 (45202-2229)
PHONE..................513 579-1555
Simon Kooyman, *Branch Mgr*
Donna Tabb, *Director*
EMP: 99 **Privately Held**
SIC: 8732 Market analysis or research
HQ: Orc International, Inc
  902 Carnegie Ctr Ste 220
  Princeton NJ 08540
  609 452-5400

(G-4232)
ORCHARD HILL SWIM CLUB
8601 Cheviot Rd (45251-5903)
P.O. Box 53114 (45253-0114)
PHONE..................513 385-0211
Paul Jeanmougin, *Administration*
Linda Templin, *Administration*
EMP: 75
SQ FT: 1,568
SALES: 135.8K **Privately Held**
WEB: www.orchardhillsswimclub.com
SIC: 7997 Swimming club, membership

(G-4233)
OREILLY AUTOMOTIVE INC
4630 Ridge Ave (45209-1029)
PHONE..................513 731-7700
Richard Eisen, *Branch Mgr*
EMP: 46 **Publicly Held**
SIC: 7538 General automotive repair shops
PA: O'reilly Automotive, Inc.
  233 S Patterson Ave
  Springfield MO 65802

(G-4234)
ORIGINAL PARTNERS LTD PARTNR (PA)
Also Called: Towne Properties
1055 Saint Paul Pl (45202-6042)
PHONE..................513 381-8696
Fax: 513 345-6974
Benita Guadian, *President*
Marvin Rosenberg, *Partner*
Linda Eckersley, *General Mgr*
Neil K Bortz, *General Ptnr*
Kim Brown, *District Mgr*
EMP: 150
SQ FT: 5,000
SALES: 16.7MM **Privately Held**
SIC: 6514 6513 Dwelling operators, except apartments; apartment building operators

(G-4235)
OROURKE WRECKING COMPANY
660 Lunken Park Dr (45226-1800)
PHONE..................513 871-1400
Fax: 513 871-1313
Michael Orourke, *President*
EMP: 75
SQ FT: 20,000
SALES: 24.7MM **Privately Held**
WEB: www.orourkewrecking.com
SIC: 1795 Demolition, buildings & other structures

GEOGRAPHIC SECTION
Cincinnati - Hamilton County (G-4259)

(G-4236)
ORTHOPEDIC CONS CINCINNATI
Also Called: Wellington Orthopedics
7575 5 Mile Rd (45230-4346)
PHONE.................513 232-6677
Fax: 513 721-8688
Julie Moore, *Manager*
Sonya Hughes, *Manager*
EMP: 31
SALES (corp-wide): 18MM **Privately Held**
SIC: 8011 Orthopedic physician; sports medicine specialist, physician
PA: Orthopedic Consultants Of Cincinnati
   4701 Creek Rd Ste 110
   Blue Ash OH 45242
   513 733-8894

(G-4237)
ORTHOPEDIC CONS CINCINNATI
Also Called: Wellington Orthpd Spt Medicine
7663 5 Mile Rd (45230-4340)
PHONE.................513 245-2500
Sonya Hughes, *General Mgr*
S M Lawhon, *Principal*
Stephen W Daily, *Med Doctor*
EMP: 32
SALES (corp-wide): 18MM **Privately Held**
SIC: 8011 Orthopedic physician
PA: Orthopedic Consultants Of Cincinnati
   4701 Creek Rd Ste 110
   Blue Ash OH 45242
   513 733-8894

(G-4238)
ORTHOPEDIC CONS CINCINNATI
Also Called: Wellington Orthpd Spt Medicine
6909 Good Samaritan Dr (45247-5208)
PHONE.................513 347-9999
Sonya Hughes, *Manager*
Brad R Wenstrup, *Podiatrist*
Gordon H Yun, *Podiatrist*
Paul J Favorito, *Surgeon*
Warren G Harding III, *Surgeon*
EMP: 30
SALES (corp-wide): 18MM **Privately Held**
SIC: 8011 Orthopedic physician
PA: Orthopedic Consultants Of Cincinnati
   4701 Creek Rd Ste 110
   Blue Ash OH 45242
   513 733-8894

(G-4239)
ORTHOPEDIC DIAGNSTC TRTMNT CTR
4600 Smith Rd Ste B (45212-2784)
PHONE.................513 221-4848
Thomas Shockley, *Med Doctor*
Errol Stern, *Med Doctor*
Rose Meyer, *Nursing Dir*
Valerie Berry, *Administration*
EMP: 30
SALES (corp-wide): 3MM **Privately Held**
SIC: 8011 Orthopedic physician
PA: Orthopedic Diagnostic & Treatment Center Inc
   4600 Smith Rd Ste B
   Cincinnati OH 45212
   513 221-4848

(G-4240)
OSTERWISCH COMPANY INC
6755 Highland Ave (45236-3968)
PHONE.................513 791-3282
Fax: 513 791-3288
James W Osterwisch, *President*
Donald Osterwisch, *Vice Pres*
George Lucas, *Manager*
EMP: 80
SQ FT: 30,000
SALES (est): 19.6MM **Privately Held**
WEB: www.osterwisch.com
SIC: 1731 1711 General electrical contractor; warm air heating & air conditioning contractor; refrigeration contractor; plumbing contractors

(G-4241)
OSWALD COMPANY INC (PA)
308 E 8th St Ste 500 (45202-2204)
PHONE.................513 745-4424
Fax: 513 793-8313
Ken C Oswald, *CEO*
Neil Quinn, *President*
Todd Haidet, *Corp Secy*
John Bumgarner, *Vice Pres*
Jim Laber, *Vice Pres*
EMP: 35
SQ FT: 5,000
SALES: 45.2MM **Privately Held**
WEB: www.oswaldco.com
SIC: 1542 1541 Commercial & office building contractors; industrial buildings & warehouses

(G-4242)
OTIS ELEVATOR COMPANY
2463 Crowne Point Dr (45241-5407)
PHONE.................513 531-7888
Fax: 513 458-5399
David Holland, *Sales Staff*
Dave Rettenmaier, *Manager*
EMP: 65
SALES (corp-wide): 59.8B **Publicly Held**
WEB: www.otis.com
SIC: 1796 7699 Elevator installation & conversion; elevators: inspection, service & repair
HQ: Otis Elevator Company
   1 Carrier Pl
   Farmington CT 06032
   860 674-3000

(G-4243)
OUR LADY PRPTUL HLP CNMTY BNGO
9908 Shellbark Ln (45231-2328)
P.O. Box 31271 (45231-0271)
PHONE.................513 742-3200
Celsus Griese, *Pastor*
EMP: 50
SALES (est): 392.9K **Privately Held**
SIC: 7999 Bingo hall

(G-4244)
OVATIONS FOOD SERVICES LP
525 Elm St (45202-2316)
PHONE.................513 419-7254
Ian Saroyan, *General Mgr*
EMP: 85
SALES (corp-wide): 84.5B **Publicly Held**
SIC: 5141 Groceries, general line
HQ: Ovations Food Services, L.P.
   18228 N Us Highway 41
   Lutz FL 33549
   813 948-6900

(G-4245)
OVERLAND XPRESS LLC (PA)
431 Ohio Pike Ste 311 (45255-3629)
PHONE.................513 528-1158
Jonathan Rodriguez, *General Mgr*
Terese Brown, *VP Opers*
Amanda Walters, *HR Admin*
Edvin Tomini, *Accounts Mgr*
Matthew Best, *Accounts Exec*
EMP: 40
SQ FT: 1,600
SALES (est): 15.9MM **Privately Held**
SIC: 4731 Freight forwarding

(G-4246)
P & D REMOVAL SERVICE
400 N Wayne Ave (45215-2845)
PHONE.................513 226-7687
Dwayne Jordan, *Owner*
EMP: 25
SALES: 200K **Privately Held**
SIC: 8999 Services

(G-4247)
P & M EXHAUST SYSTEMS WHSE
Also Called: Car-X Muffler & Brake
11843 Kemper Springs Dr (45240-1641)
PHONE.................513 825-2660
Ranga Gorrepati, *President*
Sumeeta Chalasani, *Vice Pres*
Ajay Gorrepati, *Vice Pres*
Madhavi Gorrepati, *Vice Pres*
Pallavi Gorrepati, *Vice Pres*
EMP: 25
SQ FT: 15,000
SALES (est): 6MM **Privately Held**
SIC: 5013 Exhaust systems (mufflers, tail pipes, etc.)

(G-4248)
PAKTEEM TECHNICAL SERVICES
1201 Glendale Milford Rd (45215-1247)
PHONE.................513 772-1515
Denise Demoss, *President*
Kevin Haspings, *Manager*
Laura Bryant, *Admin Asst*
Paul Hartman, *Sr Consultant*
EMP: 51
SALES (est): 3.7MM **Privately Held**
WEB: www.pakteem.com
SIC: 8711 Consulting engineer

(G-4249)
PARAGON SALONS INC (PA)
6775 Harrison Ave (45247-3239)
PHONE.................513 574-7610
Fax: 513 598-2812
Deborah Celek, *President*
Steven Celek, *Corp Secy*
EMP: 40
SQ FT: 2,600
SALES (est): 2.3MM **Privately Held**
WEB: www.paragonsalon.com
SIC: 7991 Spas

(G-4250)
PARAGON SALONS INC
441 Race St (45202-2804)
PHONE.................513 651-4600
Fax: 513 333-4883
Toni Maurer, *General Mgr*
EMP: 35
SALES (corp-wide): 2.3MM **Privately Held**
WEB: www.paragonsalon.com
SIC: 7231 Beauty shops; manicurist, pedicurist
PA: Paragon Salons, Inc
   6775 Harrison Ave
   Cincinnati OH 45247
   513 574-7610

(G-4251)
PARAGON SALONS INC
12064 Montgomery Rd (45249-1729)
PHONE.................513 683-6700
Fax: 513 333-4961
Tanya Garnica, *Manager*
EMP: 40
SALES (corp-wide): 2.3MM **Privately Held**
WEB: www.paragonsalon.com
SIC: 7231 Hairdressers
PA: Paragon Salons, Inc
   6775 Harrison Ave
   Cincinnati OH 45247
   513 574-7610

(G-4252)
PARK CINCINNATI BOARD
Also Called: Krohn Conservatory Gift Shop
1501 Eden Park Dr (45202-6030)
PHONE.................513 421-4086
Fax: 513 421-6007
Betty Moscofe, *Vice Pres*
Sue Kellogg, *Treasurer*
Andrea L Schepmann, *Manager*
Willy Carden, *Director*
Ellen Geohegan, *Admin Sec*
EMP: 100 EST: 1975
SQ FT: 150
SALES (est): 4.1MM **Privately Held**
SIC: 5992 5947 8422 6512 Plants, potted; flowers, fresh; gift shop; arboreta & botanical or zoological gardens; nonresidential building operators

(G-4253)
PARK INTERNATIONAL THEME SVCS
2195 Victory Pkwy (45206-2812)
PHONE.................513 381-6131
Fax: 513 381-2756
Dennis Speigel, *President*
Shawn Haas, *Vice Pres*
Pam Westerman, *Vice Pres*
Lisa Cooke, *Opers Mgr*
Linda Minton, *Accounting Mgr*
EMP: 25
SALES (est): 1.8MM **Privately Held**
WEB: www.interthemepark.com
SIC: 8742 Management consulting services

(G-4254)
PARKING COMPANY AMERICA INC
Also Called: Hartsfield Atlanta Intl Arprt
250 W Court St Ste 200e (45202-1078)
PHONE.................513 241-0415
William Miller, *Branch Mgr*
Sandeep Sivadas, *Software Dev*
EMP: 350
SALES (corp-wide): 94.4MM **Privately Held**
WEB: www.airportfastparkandshuttle.com
SIC: 7521 Parking lots
PA: Parking Company Of America, Inc.
   250 W Court St Ste 200e
   Cincinnati OH 45202
   513 241-0415

(G-4255)
PARKING COMPANY AMERICA INC
Also Called: Downtown Fast Park
250 W Court St Ste 100e (45202-1046)
P.O. Box 6187 (45206-0187)
PHONE.................513 381-2179
Fax: 513 381-3734
Ayo Owoeye, *Manager*
EMP: 40
SALES (corp-wide): 94.4MM **Privately Held**
WEB: www.airportfastparkandshuttle.com
SIC: 7521 Parking garage
PA: Parking Company Of America, Inc.
   250 W Court St Ste 200e
   Cincinnati OH 45202
   513 241-0415

(G-4256)
PARSEC INC (PA)
Also Called: Parsec Intermodal Cannada
1100 Gest St (45203-1114)
PHONE.................513 621-6111
Otto Budig Jr, *President*
David H Budig, *COO*
Don Allan, *Vice Pres*
George J Budig, *Vice Pres*
Jamie Hribar, *Opers Mgr*
EMP: 26
SQ FT: 55,000
SALES (est): 174.9MM **Privately Held**
WEB: www.parsecinc.com
SIC: 4789 Cargo loading & unloading services

(G-4257)
PASTORAL CARE MANAGEMENT SVCS
1240 Rosemont Ave (45205-1424)
PHONE.................513 205-1398
Ruben D Brazzile, *Exec Dir*
Alex Brandon, *Bd of Directors*
Christina Adams, *Administration*
James Stanford, *Administration*
Robin Webb, *Administration*
EMP: 26
SALES (est): 397.1K **Privately Held**
SIC: 8661 8322 Religious organizations; individual & family services; substance abuse counseling

(G-4258)
PATHWAY 2 HOPE INC
3036 Gilbert Ave (45206-1021)
PHONE.................866 491-3040
Tyler P Powell, *Exec Dir*
EMP: 25
SALES (est): 183.3K **Privately Held**
SIC: 8322 Individual & family services

(G-4259)
PATIENTPINT HOSP SOLUTIONS LLC
8230 Montgomery Rd # 300 (45236-2200)
PHONE.................513 936-6800
EMP: 184 EST: 2009
SALES (est): 4.3MM
SALES (corp-wide): 37.3MM **Privately Held**
SIC: 8742 Marketing consulting services
HQ: Patientpoint Holdings, Inc.
   8230 Montgomery Rd # 300
   Cincinnati OH 45236
   513 936-6800

Cincinnati - Hamilton County (G-4260)

(G-4260)
PATIENTPINT NTWRK SLUTIONS LLC (DH)
Also Called: Healthy Advice Networks
5901 E Galbraith Rd (45236-2230)
PHONE..................................513 936-6800
Sara Slater, *Accountant*
Mike Collette, *Mng Member*
Patricia Henze, *Exec Dir*
EMP: 63
SQ FT: 15,000
SALES (est): 18.8MM
SALES (corp-wide): 37.3MM **Privately Held**
WEB: www.ontargetmedia.com
SIC: 8742 Marketing consulting services
HQ: Patientpoint Holdings, Inc.
 8230 Montgomery Rd # 300
 Cincinnati OH 45236
 513 936-6800

(G-4261)
PATIENTPOINT LLC (PA)
5901 E Galbraith Rd (45236-2230)
PHONE..................................513 936-6800
Mike Colette, *CEO*
George Batsakes, *Director*
Estefania Campo, *Director*
Toni Thomas, *Director*
EMP: 40
SALES (est): 37.3MM **Privately Held**
SIC: 8742 Marketing consulting services

(G-4262)
PATRICK J BURKE & CO
Also Called: Burke & Company
901 Adams Crossing Fl 1 (45202-1693)
PHONE..................................513 455-8200
Fax: 513 455-8212
Patrick Burke, *Owner*
Mark Miller, *Managing Dir*
Eugene Schindler, *Co-Owner*
Jamie Baker-Prewitt, *Senior VP*
Dianne Marschman, *Vice Pres*
EMP: 25
SALES (est): 2.9MM **Privately Held**
SIC: 8721 7372 Certified public accountant; prepackaged software

(G-4263)
PATTERSON POPE INC
10321 S Medallion Dr (45241-4825)
PHONE..................................513 891-4430
Jeff Pfohl, *Manager*
EMP: 80
SALES (corp-wide): 100.4MM **Privately Held**
SIC: 5021 7371 5712 Filing units; computer software development; furniture stores
PA: Patterson Pope, Inc.
 3001 N Graham St
 Charlotte NC 28206
 704 523-4400

(G-4264)
PAUL R YOUNG FUNERAL HOMES (PA)
7345 Hamilton Ave (45231-4321)
PHONE..................................513 521-9303
Fax: 513 728-4593
Paul R Young, *President*
Paul R Young Jr, *Office Mgr*
Paul Young III, *Manager*
Walter Mc Kay, *Admin Sec*
EMP: 30
SQ FT: 8,000
SALES (est): 3.6MM **Privately Held**
WEB: www.paulyoungfuneralhome.com
SIC: 7261 Funeral home

(G-4265)
PAULS BUS SERVICE INC
3561 W Kemper Rd (45251-4236)
PHONE..................................513 851-5089
Fax: 513 851-4081
Dennis P Wurzelbacher, *President*
Cynthia Wurzelbacher, *Vice Pres*
Rick Hust, *Manager*
EMP: 40 EST: 1952
SQ FT: 4,650
SALES: 1.5MM **Privately Held**
SIC: 4151 School buses

(G-4266)
PAXTON HARDWOODS LLC
Also Called: Frank Paxton Lumber Company
7455 Dawson Rd (45243-2537)
P.O. Box 16343, Denver CO (80216-0343)
PHONE..................................513 984-8200
Fax: 513 984-5060
Tom Varley, *General Mgr*
Joel Delgado, *Opers Mgr*
Jared Ory, *Opers Mgr*
Mike Slates, *Opers Mgr*
Hector Gamez, *Credit Mgr*
EMP: 30
SALES (corp-wide): 583.8MM **Privately Held**
SIC: 5031 Lumber: rough, dressed & finished
HQ: Paxton Hardwoods Llc
 4837 Jackson St
 Denver CO 80216
 303 399-6810

(G-4267)
PAYCOM SOFTWARE INC
255 E 5th St (45202-4700)
PHONE..................................888 678-0796
Fax: 513 455-5875
EMP: 505
SALES (corp-wide): 433MM **Publicly Held**
SIC: 8721 Payroll accounting service
PA: Paycom Software, Inc.
 7501 W Memorial Rd
 Oklahoma City OK 73142
 405 722-6900

(G-4268)
PAYCOR INC (PA)
4811 Montgomery Rd (45212-2163)
PHONE..................................513 381-0505
Stacey Browning, *President*
Robert J Coughlin, *Chairman*
Rick Chouteau, *Senior VP*
Jennifer Langer, *Senior VP*
Don Chun, *Vice Pres*
EMP: 200
SQ FT: 33,000
SALES (est): 105.2MM **Privately Held**
SIC: 8721 Payroll accounting service

(G-4269)
PCMS DATAFIT INC
25 Merchant St Ste 135 (45246-3740)
PHONE..................................513 587-3100
Fax: 513 587-3111
Richard Smith, *President*
Bill White, *Project Mgr*
Adam Dunlop, *Production*
Laura Alanis, *QA Dir*
Madhuri Chenepalli, *QA Dir*
EMP: 68
SALES (est): 11.5MM
SALES (corp-wide): 67MM **Privately Held**
WEB: www.pcmsdatafit.com
SIC: 7371 7373 Computer software writing services; computer integrated systems design
HQ: The Pcms Group Limited
 P C M S House, Torwood Close
 Coventry W MIDLANDS CV4 8
 247 669-4455

(G-4270)
PCY ENTERPRISES INC
Also Called: Young & Bertke Air Systems
3111 Spring Grove Ave (45225-1821)
PHONE..................................513 241-5566
Roger Young, *President*
Lori Morgan, *Vice Pres*
Michael Munafo, *Vice Pres*
Tim Rohrer, *Vice Pres*
Phillip C Young, *Shareholder*
EMP: 28
SQ FT: 51,000
SALES: 4MM **Privately Held**
WEB: www.youngbertke.com
SIC: 1761 3441 3564 3444 Sheet metalwork; fabricated structural metal; blowers & fans; sheet metalwork; fabricated plate work (boiler shop)

(G-4271)
PECK-HANNAFORD BRIGGS SVC CORP
Also Called: Peck Hannaford Briggs Service
4673 Spring Grove Ave (45232-1952)
PHONE..................................513 681-1200
Fax: 513 681-0311
James G Briggs Jr, *President*
Gerald Lindsay, *General Mgr*
Jerry Govert, *Vice Pres*
Tracy Reuss, *Human Res Dir*
Tony Caminiti, *Marketing Staff*
EMP: 57
SQ FT: 4,000
SALES (est): 12.9MM
SALES (corp-wide): 52.9MM **Privately Held**
SIC: 1711 Warm air heating & air conditioning contractor; refrigeration contractor
PA: Peck-Hannaford & Briggs Co, The (Inc)
 4670 Chester Ave
 Cincinnati OH 45232
 513 681-4600

(G-4272)
PEDIATRIC ASSOC CINCINNATI
4360 Cooper Rd Ste 201 (45242-5636)
PHONE..................................513 791-1222
Fax: 513 791-2561
Joe Heitker, *General Mgr*
Robert C Schiff Jr, *Corp Secy*
Sharon C Miller, *Med Doctor*
Sandi Nardini, *Practice Mgr*
Ann Lichtenberg, *Director*
EMP: 28
SQ FT: 2,000
SALES (est): 2.8MM **Privately Held**
SIC: 8011 Pediatrician

(G-4273)
PEDIATRIC CARE INC (PA)
800 Compton Rd Unit 25 (45231-5959)
PHONE..................................513 931-6357
Fax: 513 728-4762
Mark S Dine, *President*
Daniel L Friedberg, *Vice Pres*
EMP: 32
SALES (est): 3.7MM **Privately Held**
SIC: 8011 Pediatrician

(G-4274)
PEGASUS TECHNICAL SERVICES INC
46 E Hollister St (45219-1704)
PHONE..................................513 793-0094
Asit B Saha, *President*
Bijoli Saha, *Vice Pres*
John Zoller, *Manager*
EMP: 50
SQ FT: 200
SALES: 6.3MM **Privately Held**
WEB: www.ptsied.com
SIC: 8711 7371 7373 Consulting engineer; custom computer programming services; computer-aided design (CAD) systems service

(G-4275)
PELLA CORPORATION
145 B Colwell Dr (45216)
PHONE..................................513 948-8480
James M Frey, *President*
Tom Frey, *Sales Executive*
EMP: 60
SALES (corp-wide): 1.9B **Privately Held**
SIC: 5031 Windows
PA: Pella Corporation
 102 Main St
 Pella IA 50219
 641 621-1000

(G-4276)
PENNINGTON INTERNATIONAL INC
1977 Section Rd Ste 1 (45237-3333)
PHONE..................................513 631-2130
Fax: 513 631-2174
Gladys Pennington, *President*
L Paulette Kihm, *Exec VP*
Sheila Pennington, *Asst Treas*
EMP: 36
SQ FT: 3,200
SALES (est): 594.2K **Privately Held**
WEB: www.penningtoninternational.com
SIC: 7381 Detective & armored car services; security guard service; detective agency

(G-4277)
PENSION CORPORATION AMERICA
Also Called: ABG Advisors
2133 Luray Ave (45206-2604)
PHONE..................................513 281-3366
Fax: 513 281-3389
Tom Seitz, *President*
Jim Eckeroe, *Vice Pres*
JM Ries, *Opers Mgr*
Gina Stebbins, *Opers Staff*
Megan Haynes, *Accounts Exec*
EMP: 35
SQ FT: 3,500
SALES (est): 4.1MM **Privately Held**
WEB: www.pencorp.com
SIC: 8742 Financial consultant

(G-4278)
PENSKE TRUCK LEASING CO LP
2528 Commodity Cir (45241-1550)
PHONE..................................513 771-7701
Fax: 513 771-5840
Brad Brockhoff, *Accounts Mgr*
Chad Powell, *Manager*
EMP: 30
SQ FT: 2,000
SALES (corp-wide): 2.9B **Privately Held**
WEB: www.pensketruckleasing.com
SIC: 7513 Truck rental & leasing, no drivers
PA: Penske Truck Leasing Co., L.P.
 2675 Morgantown Rd
 Reading PA 19607
 610 775-6000

(G-4279)
PERFECTION GROUP INC (PA)
Also Called: Honeywell Authorized Dealer
2649 Commerce Blvd (45241-1553)
PHONE..................................513 772-7545
William J Albrecht, *CEO*
Anthony Apro, *President*
John Shaw, *Vice Pres*
Mike Smith, *Project Mgr*
Andy Stegman, *Project Mgr*
EMP: 151
SQ FT: 10,000
SALES: 34.5MM **Privately Held**
WEB: www.perfectionservices.com
SIC: 1711 Warm air heating & air conditioning contractor

(G-4280)
PERFECTION MECHANICAL SVCS INC
2649 Commerce Blvd (45241-1553)
PHONE..................................513 772-7545
William Albrecht, *President*
John E Shaw, *Vice Pres*
Mary A Straley, *VP Finance*
EMP: 90
SQ FT: 10,000
SALES (est): 9.6MM
SALES (corp-wide): 34.5MM **Privately Held**
WEB: www.perfectionservices.com
SIC: 1711 Mechanical contractor
PA: Perfection Group, Inc.
 2649 Commerce Blvd
 Cincinnati OH 45241
 513 772-7545

(G-4281)
PERFECTION SERVICES INC
2649 Commerce Blvd (45241-1553)
PHONE..................................513 772-7545
Fax: 513 326-2383
William Albrecht, *President*
John E Shaw, *Vice Pres*
EMP: 50 EST: 1972
SQ FT: 10,000
SALES: 4MM
SALES (corp-wide): 34.5MM **Privately Held**
SIC: 1711 Warm air heating & air conditioning contractor

GEOGRAPHIC SECTION

Cincinnati - Hamilton County (G-4307)

PA: Perfection Group, Inc.
2649 Commerce Blvd
Cincinnati OH 45241
513 772-7545

(G-4282)
PERRY KELLY PLUMBING INC
4498 Mt Carmel Tobasco Rd (45244-2222)
PHONE..................513 528-6554
Fax: 513 528-7032
Perry Kelly, *President*
Mary Jo Kelly, *Corp Secy*
EMP: 27
SQ FT: 1,000
SALES: 3.5MM **Privately Held**
WEB: www.perrykelly.com
SIC: 1711 Plumbing contractors

(G-4283)
PERSONAL TOUCH HM CARE IPA INC
8260 Northcreek Dr # 140 (45236-2293)
PHONE..................513 984-9600
Fax: 513 984-9609
Barbie Wenman, *Manager*
Terri Carpenter, *Administration*
EMP: 60
SALES (corp-wide): 363MM **Privately Held**
WEB: www.pthomecare.com
SIC: 8082 Home health care services
PA: Personal Touch Home Care Ipa, Inc.
1985 Marcus Ave Ste 202
New Hyde Park NY 11042
718 468-4747

(G-4284)
PETER A WIMBERG COMPANY INC
Also Called: Wimberg Lansdscaping
5401 Hetzell St (45227-1515)
PHONE..................513 271-2332
Fax: 513 271-2360
Peter A Wimberg, *President*
John Wimberg, *Vice Pres*
Connie Brasington, *Office Mgr*
EMP: 40
SALES (est): 3.1MM **Privately Held**
WEB: www.wimberglandscaping.com
SIC: 0782 Landscape contractors

(G-4285)
PETERBILT OF CINCINNATI
2550 Annuity Dr (45241-1502)
PHONE..................513 772-1740
Fax: 513 554-2237
Taylor Edwards, *President*
Melissa Larson, *General Mgr*
Taylor Edward, *Manager*
EMP: 30
SQ FT: 50,000
SALES (est): 10.4MM
SALES (corp-wide): 120.5MM **Privately Held**
WEB: www.peterbiltofcincinnati.com
SIC: 5012 5013 7538 Truck tractors; trailers for trucks, new & used; truck parts & accessories; trailer parts & accessories; general truck repair
PA: W. D. Larson Companies Ltd., Inc.
500 Ford Rd
St Louis Park MN 55426
952 888-4934

(G-4286)
PETERMANN NORTHEAST LLC
8041 Hosbrook Rd Ste 330 (45236-2909)
PHONE..................513 351-7383
Michael J Settle, *COO*
EMP: 1676
SALES (est): 6.9MM **Privately Held**
SIC: 4151 School buses
HQ: National Express Llc
2601 Navistar Dr
Lisle IL 60532

(G-4287)
PETRO ENVIRONMENTAL TECH (PA)
Also Called: Petro Cells
8160 Corp Pk Dr Ste 300 (45242)
PHONE..................513 489-6789
Pete Mather, *President*
Peter Mather, *President*
Mark Mather, *Corp Secy*

Cliff Poppel, *Project Mgr*
EMP: 40
SQ FT: 7,500
SALES (est): 8MM **Privately Held**
SIC: 1629 4959 Land preparation construction; toxic or hazardous waste cleanup

(G-4288)
PETSUITES OF AMERICA INC
3701 Hauck Rd (45241-1607)
PHONE..................513 554-4408
Fax: 513 554-4409
Joseph G Mason III, *Manager*
EMP: 25
SALES (corp-wide): 1.2MM **Privately Held**
SIC: 0752 Boarding services, kennels
PA: Petsuites Of America, Inc.
620 Holly Ln
Erlanger KY 41018
859 727-7880

(G-4289)
PFH PARTNERS LLC
Also Called: Jefferey Anderson Real Estate
3805 Edwards Rd Ste 700 (45209-1955)
PHONE..................513 241-5800
Jefferey Anderson, *President*
EMP: 25
SALES (est): 823.2K **Privately Held**
SIC: 6531 Real estate leasing & rentals

(G-4290)
PFPC ENTERPRISES INC
5750 Hillside Ave (45233-1508)
PHONE..................513 941-6200
Peter F Coffaro, *Ch of Bd*
James Coffaro, *President*
Gina Antrim, *Purch Agent*
Stephen Stout, *CFO*
Art Schutte, *Controller*
EMP: 300 EST: 1963
SQ FT: 52,000
SALES (est): 18.7MM **Privately Held**
WEB: www.pabcofluidpower.com
SIC: 5023 5084 3594 3535 Floor coverings; industrial machinery & equipment; pumps & pumping equipment; water pumps (industrial); hydraulic systems equipment & supplies; fluid power pumps & motors; conveyors & conveying equipment; turbines & turbine generator sets

(G-4291)
PHILLIPS EDISON & COMPANY LLC (HQ)
11501 Northlake Dr Fl 1 (45249-1667)
PHONE..................513 554-1110
Jeffrey S Edison, *CEO*
Bob Myers, *President*
Robert F Myers, *President*
Eric Richer, *Owner*
Dj Belock, *Senior VP*
EMP: 27
SQ FT: 5,000
SALES (est): 27.4MM **Privately Held**
WEB: www.phillipsedison.com
SIC: 6531 6552 Real estate brokers & agents; real estate managers; land subdividers & developers, commercial

(G-4292)
PHILLIPS SUPPLY COMPANY (PA)
1230 Findlay St (45214-2096)
PHONE..................513 579-1762
Pamela Rossmann, *President*
Eleanor Roth, *Principal*
Claire B Phillips, *Treasurer*
Steven Cramer, *Controller*
Donna Ashley, *Sales Staff*
▲ EMP: 55 EST: 1965
SQ FT: 40,000
SALES (est): 29.9MM **Privately Held**
WEB: www.phillipssupply.com
SIC: 5087 Janitors' supplies

(G-4293)
PHOENIX
812 Race St (45202-2006)
PHONE..................513 721-8901
Justin Kittle, *General Mgr*
Watch M Corp, *General Ptnr*
Amy Flaherty, *Executive*
EMP: 60

SQ FT: 40,000
SALES (est): 3.3MM **Privately Held**
WEB: www.thephx.com
SIC: 7941 Stadium event operator services

(G-4294)
PHOENIX RESOURCE NETWORK LLC
602 Main St Ste 202 (45202-2521)
PHONE..................800 990-4948
Thomas L Jordan,
Roger C Noble,
EMP: 26
SQ FT: 1,400
SALES: 250K **Privately Held**
SIC: 8742 5047 Business consultant; financial consultant; hospital equipment & supplies

(G-4295)
PHYLLIS AT MADISON
2324 Madison Rd Ste 1 (45208-2693)
PHONE..................513 321-1300
Fax: 513 533-6406
Phyllis Rinaldi, *President*
EMP: 30
SQ FT: 2,200
SALES (est): 772.8K **Privately Held**
WEB: www.phyllisatthemadison.com
SIC: 7231 Facial salons

(G-4296)
PIATT PARK LTD PARTNERSHIP
1055 Saint Paul Pl # 300 (45202-6042)
PHONE..................513 381-8696
Arn Bortz, *Partner*
Dan Bayer, *Partner*
Fred Casper, *Partner*
William Curran, *Partner*
Ralph Heyman, *Partner*
EMP: 70
SALES (est): 4.4MM **Privately Held**
SIC: 6552 Subdividers & developers

(G-4297)
PICS PRODUCE INC
4756 Paddock Rd (45229-1004)
PHONE..................513 381-1239
Fax: 513 632-5412
Joe Ellis, *Exec VP*
Beverly Williams, *Manager*
Jeff Pichichero, *Admin Sec*
EMP: 27 EST: 1945
SQ FT: 2,000
SALES (est): 8.5MM **Privately Held**
WEB: www.picsproduce.com
SIC: 5148 Fruits, fresh

(G-4298)
PIER N PORT TRAVEL INC
Also Called: Virtuoso
2692 Madison Rd Ste H1 (45208-1350)
PHONE..................513 841-9900
Fax: 513 841-5938
Richard Cronenberg, *Ch of Bd*
Kristin Tatman, *President*
Patricia J Cronenberg, *Principal*
Beverly Hardiman, *Exec VP*
Michele Uckotter, *Exec VP*
EMP: 34
SQ FT: 2,400
SALES (est): 3.6MM **Privately Held**
WEB: www.virtuoso.com
SIC: 4724 Travel agencies

(G-4299)
PILGRIM UNITED CHURCH CHRIST
4418 Bridgetown Rd (45211-4493)
PHONE..................513 574-4208
Dave Bucey, *Pastor*
EMP: 25
SALES (est): 860K **Privately Held**
SIC: 8661 8351 Church of Christ; preschool center

(G-4300)
PILLAR OF FIRE
Also Called: Star 93.3 FM
6275 Collegevue Pl (45224-1959)
PHONE..................513 542-1212
Fax: 513 542-9333
Joseph W Gross, *President*
Christopher M Stanko, *Corp Secy*
Hunter T Barnes, *Trustee*
Robert B Dallenbach, *Trustee*

Larry W Dinkins Sr, *Vice Pres*
EMP: 40
SQ FT: 8,694
SALES (est): 4.6MM **Privately Held**
WEB: www.mystar933.com
SIC: 8211 4832 8661 Private elementary school; radio broadcasting stations; religious organizations

(G-4301)
PIQUA MATERIALS INC (PA)
11641 Mosteller Rd Ste 1 (45241-1520)
PHONE..................513 771-0820
James Jurgensen, *President*
Tim Saintclair, *Corp Secy*
James Jurgenson II, *Vice Pres*
Kate Holden, *Project Mgr*
Beth Baker, *Controller*
EMP: 31
SALES (est): 16.3MM **Privately Held**
SIC: 1422 Limestones, ground

(G-4302)
PLANNED PARENTHOOD OF SW OH (PA)
2314 Auburn Ave (45219-2802)
PHONE..................513 721-7635
Fax: 513 287-6580
Jerry Lawson, *CEO*
Lee Bower, *COO*
Danielle Craig, *Vice Pres*
Kelli Halter, *Vice Pres*
Leslie Mitchell, *Vice Pres*
EMP: 35
SQ FT: 35,000
SALES: 9.4MM **Privately Held**
SIC: 8093 Family planning clinic; birth control clinic; abortion clinic

(G-4303)
PLASTIC SURGERY GROUP INC (PA)
4050 Red Bank Rd Ste 42 (45227-3416)
PHONE..................513 791-4440
Fax: 513 985-6615
Richard Williams, *President*
Gene Ireland, *Vice Pres*
Michael Leadbetter, *Treasurer*
Joyce Dickman, *Office Mgr*
Debbie Thacker, *Office Mgr*
EMP: 25
SALES (est): 2.3MM **Privately Held**
WEB: www.tpsg.net
SIC: 8093 8011 Specialty outpatient clinics; plastic surgeon

(G-4304)
PLAY TIME DAY NURSERY INC
9550 Colerain Ave (45251-2004)
PHONE..................513 385-8281
Fax: 513 385-8282
Larry W Napier, *President*
Nancy Jo Napier, *Vice Pres*
EMP: 25
SQ FT: 8,000
SALES (est): 667.9K **Privately Held**
SIC: 8351 Nursery school; group day care center

(G-4305)
PLEASANT RIDGE CARE CENTER INC (PA)
5501 Verulam Ave (45213-2417)
PHONE..................513 631-1310
Harold Sosna, *President*
Kris Rolfsen, *Director*
EMP: 103
SALES: 6.5MM **Privately Held**
SIC: 8051 Skilled nursing care facilities

(G-4306)
PLS PROTECTIVE SERVICES
8263 Clara Ave (45239-4214)
PHONE..................513 521-3581
Paul Smith, *President*
EMP: 30
SALES (est): 649K **Privately Held**
SIC: 7381 Security guard service

(G-4307)
PNC BANC CORP OHIO (HQ)
Also Called: PNC Bank
201 E 5th St (45202-4152)
PHONE..................513 651-8738
Fax: 513 651-8884

Cincinnati - Hamilton County (G-4308) GEOGRAPHIC SECTION

Keith K Johnson, *Area Mgr*
Ed Arbaugh, *Exec VP*
Barry Friedman, *Vice Pres*
Michael N Harrison, *Vice Pres*
Jean Strickerton, *Vice Pres*
EMP: 26 **EST:** 1968
SQ FT: 10,000
SALES (est): 13.1MM
SALES (corp-wide): 18B **Publicly Held**
SIC: 6512 6021 Commercial & industrial building operation; national commercial banks
PA: The Pnc Financial Services Group Inc
300 5th Ave
Pittsburgh PA 15222
412 762-2000

(G-4308)
PNC BANK NATIONAL ASSOCIATION
5 Main Dr (45231-2300)
PHONE..................513 721-2500
Edward Korfhagen, *Branch Mgr*
EMP: 400
SALES (corp-wide): 18B **Publicly Held**
WEB: www.pncfunds.com
SIC: 6021 National trust companies with deposits, commercial
HQ: Pnc Bank, National Association
222 Delaware Ave
Wilmington DE 19801
877 762-2000

(G-4309)
PNC BANK NATIONAL ASSOCIATION
995 Dalton Ave (45203-1100)
PHONE..................513 455-9522
Jeff Wiener, *Senior VP*
Chris Kelley, *Vice Pres*
Terry Karageorges, *Vice Pres*
Dana Pace, *Vice Pres*
James Bissantz, *VP Finance*
EMP: 26
SALES (corp-wide): 18B **Publicly Held**
SIC: 6021 National trust companies with deposits, commercial
HQ: Pnc Bank, National Association
222 Delaware Ave
Wilmington DE 19801
877 762-2000

(G-4310)
PNC EQUIPMENT FINANCE LLC
995 Dalton Ave (45203-1100)
PHONE..................513 421-9191
Scott Ackerman, *Vice Pres*
Douglas Shaffer, *Branch Mgr*
EMP: 91
SALES (corp-wide): 18B **Publicly Held**
SIC: 6159 Equipment & vehicle finance leasing companies; machinery & equipment finance leasing
HQ: Pnc Equipment Finance, Llc
620 Liberty Ave
Pittsburgh PA 15222

(G-4311)
PNG TELECOMMUNICATIONS INC (PA)
Also Called: Powernet Global Communications
8805 Governors Hill Dr # 250 (45249-3314)
PHONE..................513 942-7900
Allison Stevens, *CEO*
Bernie Stevens, *President*
John Putnam, *Vice Pres*
Martha Shirley, *Project Mgr*
Michael Macke, *Opers Staff*
EMP: 99
SQ FT: 55,000
SALES (est): 40.8MM **Privately Held**
WEB: www.pngnet.com
SIC: 4813 7375 Long distance telephone communications; information retrieval services

(G-4312)
PNK (OHIO) LLC
Also Called: River Downs
6301 Kellogg Rd (45230-5237)
PHONE..................513 232-8000
Fax: 513 232-1412
Anthony San Filippo, *CEO*
Kevin Hollt, *Human Res Mgr*
Lauren Corbitt, *Sales Staff*
John Engelhardt, *Mktg Dir*
Karen Mollaun, *Manager*
EMP: 700
SALES (est): 2.1MM
SALES (corp-wide): 971.3MM **Publicly Held**
SIC: 7948 7993 Horse race track operation; coin-operated amusement devices
HQ: Gold Merger Sub, Llc
845 Berkshire Blvd # 200
Wyomissing PA 19610
610 401-2900

(G-4313)
POISON INFORMATION CENTER
Also Called: Drug & Poison Information Ctr
3333 Burnet Ave Fl 3 (45229-3026)
PHONE..................513 636-5111
Earl Siegel, *Director*
Timothy Cripe, *Oncology*
EMP: 35
SALES (est): 2.1MM **Privately Held**
SIC: 7363 Medical help service

(G-4314)
POPE & ASSOCIATES INC
Also Called: Pope Consulting
11800 Conrey Rd Ste 240 (45249-1067)
PHONE..................513 671-1277
Fax: 513 671-1815
Patricia Pope, *President*
Sara Mettler, *Comms Dir*
Lea Ann Hilboldt, *Manager*
Bobby Childers, *Director*
EMP: 27
SQ FT: 1,650
SALES (est): 3MM **Privately Held**
WEB: www.popeandassociates.com
SIC: 8742 General management consultant; personnel management consultant

(G-4315)
PORT GRTER CINCINNATI DEV AUTH
Also Called: Greater Cincinnati Redevelopme
3 E 4th St Ste 300 (45202-3745)
PHONE..................513 621-3000
Fax: 513 621-1080
Laura Brunner, *President*
Charlie Luken, *Chairman*
Richard Hudson, *Director*
Susan Thomas, *Director*
Joseph Hall, *Executive Asst*
EMP: 25
SALES (est): 6.3MM **Privately Held**
SIC: 8748 Economic consultant

(G-4316)
PORTER WRGHT MORRIS ARTHUR LLP
250 E 5th St Ste 2200 (45202-5118)
PHONE..................513 381-4700
Fax: 513 421-0991
Donna Wihl, *President*
David Croall, *Branch Mgr*
Jerome J Metz Jr,
Chris Dutton, *Sr Associate*
EMP: 40
SALES (corp-wide): 90.5MM **Privately Held**
SIC: 8111 Legal services
PA: Porter, Wright, Morris & Arthur Llp
41 S High St Ste 2900
Columbus OH 43215
614 227-2000

(G-4317)
POSITIVE BUS SOLUTIONS INC
Also Called: Pbsi
200 Northland Blvd 100 (45246-3604)
PHONE..................513 772-2255
Fax: 513 772-0827
Ray Cool, *President*
Garrett Grover, *General Mgr*
Teresa Aldrich, *Vice Pres*
Graydon Gorby, *Vice Pres*
Garrett Gover, *Vice Pres*
EMP: 56
SQ FT: 15,000
SALES (est): 7.3MM **Privately Held**
WEB: www.pbsinet.com
SIC: 7378 5045 7371 Computer & data processing equipment repair/maintenance; computer software; computer software development

(G-4318)
POWER ENGINEERS INCORPORATED
Also Called: Environmental Division
11733 Chesterdale Rd (45246-3405)
PHONE..................513 326-1500
Tim Gessner, *Branch Mgr*
EMP: 35
SALES (corp-wide): 398.7MM **Privately Held**
WEB: www.bheenv.com
SIC: 8711 Consulting engineer
PA: Power Engineers, Incorporated
3940 Glenbrook Dr
Hailey ID 83333
208 788-3456

(G-4319)
PPS HOLDING LLC
4605 E Galbraith Rd # 200 (45236-2887)
PHONE..................513 985-6400
Nicole Wiwi, *Manager*
Lisa Kahle, *Info Tech Mgr*
Lisa Hack, *Director*
Terry Correll, *Executive*
Greg Hopkins,
EMP: 67
SALES (est): 34.7MM **Privately Held**
WEB: www.partnerps.com
SIC: 7361 Executive placement

(G-4320)
PRECISION VHCL SOLUTIONS LLC
559 Liberty Hl (45202-6869)
PHONE..................513 651-9444
Bret Griffin, *Principal*
Darrin McElroy, *Principal*
EMP: 35
SQ FT: 2,000
SALES (est): 354.9K **Privately Held**
SIC: 4789 Freight car loading & unloading

(G-4321)
PREGNANCY CARE OF CINCINNATI
2415 Auburn Ave (45219-2701)
PHONE..................513 487-7777
Fax: 513 487-7778
Mary Beth Lacy, *Principal*
EMP: 25
SALES (est): 557.3K **Privately Held**
WEB: www.pregnancycareofcincinnati.com
SIC: 8322 8093 Referral service for personal & social problems; specialty outpatient clinics

(G-4322)
PREMIER ESTATES 521 LLC
Also Called: Premier Estate of Three Rivers
7800 Jandacres Dr (45248)
PHONE..................765 288-2488
Shari Bench,
EMP: 99
SQ FT: 46,878
SALES (est): 431.6K **Privately Held**
SIC: 8051 Skilled nursing care facilities

(G-4323)
PREMIER ESTATES 525 LLC ✪
Also Called: Pristine Senior Living
1578 Sherman Ave (45212-2510)
PHONE..................513 631-6800
Shari Bench, *Manager*
EMP: 63 **EST:** 2017
SALES (est): 671.9K
SALES (corp-wide): 6.3MM **Privately Held**
SIC: 8361 Home for the aged
PA: Trillium Healthcare Group, Llc
5115 E State Road 64
Bradenton FL 34208
941 758-4745

(G-4324)
PREMIER ESTATES 526 LLC
Also Called: Premier Esttes Cncnnt-Rverview
5999 Bender Rd (45233-1601)
PHONE..................513 922-1440
Brian McCoy, *COO*
EMP: 80
SALES (est): 1MM
SALES (corp-wide): 6.3MM **Privately Held**
SIC: 8361 Home for the aged
PA: Trillium Healthcare Group, Llc
5115 E State Road 64
Bradenton FL 34208
941 758-4745

(G-4325)
PRESSLEY RIDGE PRYDE
7162 Reading Rd Ste 300 (45237-3899)
PHONE..................513 559-1402
Fax: 513 559-5475
Jane Wintz, *Manager*
Jane Wingz, *Director*
EMP: 28
SALES (est): 1MM **Privately Held**
SIC: 8322 General counseling services

(G-4326)
PRESTIGE AUDIO VISUAL INC
Also Called: Prestige AV & Creative Svcs
4835 Para Dr (45237-5009)
PHONE..................513 641-1600
Fax: 513 731-9219
Tony Ramstetter, *President*
Roy King, *Editor*
Terry Ramstetter, *Vice Pres*
Tom Bell, *Project Mgr*
Ryan Fielding, *Project Mgr*
EMP: 58
SQ FT: 57,000
SALES (est): 9.2MM **Privately Held**
WEB: www.prestigeaudiovisual.com
SIC: 7359 Audio-visual equipment & supply rental

(G-4327)
PRESTIGE VALET INC
4220 Appleton St (45209-1204)
PHONE..................513 871-4220
Fax: 513 871-1056
Jeff Blevins, *President*
Mark Nartker, *Manager*
EMP: 60
SALES (est): 924.9K **Privately Held**
SIC: 7521 Parking lots

(G-4328)
PRICEWATERHOUSECOOPERS LLP
201 E 5th St Ste 2300 (45202-4174)
PHONE..................513 723-4700
Dennis Bartolucci, *Partner*
Don Bush, *Manager*
Julie Peters, *Manager*
Vincent Scott, *Manager*
Sherri Creighton, *Sr Associate*
EMP: 100
SALES (corp-wide): 5.6B **Privately Held**
WEB: www.pwcglobal.com
SIC: 8721 Certified public accountant
PA: Pricewaterhousecoopers Llp
300 Madison Ave Fl 24
New York NY 10017
646 471-4000

(G-4329)
PRIMAX MARKETING GROUP
2300 Montana Ave Ste 102 (45211-3888)
PHONE..................513 443-2797
Steve P Miklavic, *President*
EMP: 40
SQ FT: 2,400
SALES: 3.5MM **Privately Held**
WEB: www.primax.com
SIC: 4813 7371 ; computer software development

(G-4330)
PRIMROSE SCHOOL OF SYMMES
Also Called: Geier School Company
9175 Governors Way (45249-2037)
PHONE..................513 697-6970
Fax: 513 697-7021
Richard Geier, *President*
Karen Rice, *Director*
Stephanie Adams,
EMP: 35
SQ FT: 4,651
SALES (est): 1MM **Privately Held**
SIC: 8351 Preschool center

(G-4331)
PRINTPACK INC
8044 Montgomery Rd # 600 (45236-2976)
PHONE..................513 891-7886
Fax: 513 891-9248

GEOGRAPHIC SECTION
Cincinnati - Hamilton County (G-4355)

J Erskine Love, *Owner*
EMP: 200
SALES (corp-wide): 1.3B **Privately Held**
SIC: 7389 Packaging & labeling services
HQ: Printpack, Inc.
2800 Overlook Pkwy Ne
Atlanta GA 30339
404 460-7000

(G-4332)
PRIORITY 1 CONSTRUCTION SVCS
5178 Crookshank Rd (45238-3304)
PHONE....................513 922-0203
Barry Kirby, *President*
EMP: 34
SALES (est): 3.3MM **Privately Held**
SIC: 1742 1799 Insulation, buildings; asbestos removal & encapsulation

(G-4333)
PRIORITY III CONTRACTING INC
5178 Crookshank Rd (45238-3304)
PHONE....................513 922-0203
Brian Kirby, *President*
EMP: 35
SQ FT: 33,000
SALES (est): 3.6MM **Privately Held**
WEB: www.priorityinsulation.com
SIC: 1799 Insulation of pipes & boilers; asbestos removal & encapsulation

(G-4334)
PRISTINE SENIOR LIVING ✪
Also Called: Premier Esttes Cncnnt-Rverside
315 Lilienthal St (45204-1170)
PHONE....................513 471-8667
Jensen Glaze,
EMP: 60 **EST:** 2017
SALES (est): 653.5K
SALES (corp-wide): 6.3MM **Privately Held**
SIC: 8361 Home for the aged
PA: Trillium Healthcare Group, Llc
5115 E State Road 64
Bradenton FL 34208
941 758-4745

(G-4335)
PRIVATE HM CARE FOUNDATION INC
Also Called: PHC Foundation
3808 Applegate Ave (45211-6503)
PHONE....................513 662-8999
Fax: 513 662-7640
Linda Puthoff, *President*
Tracy Beiting, *Director*
EMP: 60
SALES (est): 2.5MM **Privately Held**
WEB: www.privatehcfoundation.org
SIC: 8082 Home health care services

(G-4336)
PRN HEALTH SERVICES INC
8044 Montgomery Rd # 700 (45236-2919)
PHONE....................513 792-2217
Fax: 513 792-2218
Anne Dejewski, *Branch Mgr*
EMP: 68
SALES (est): 1.1MM **Privately Held**
SIC: 7361 Nurses' registry
PA: Prn Health Services, Inc.
1101 E South River St
Appleton WI 54915

(G-4337)
PRO ONCALL TECHNOLOGIES LLC (PA)
6902 E Kemper Rd (45249-1025)
P.O. Box 498337 (45249-7337)
PHONE....................513 489-7660
John O Brian, *President*
Don Walter, *Vice Pres*
Judith Evans, *Controller*
Brendan Caine, *Accounts Mgr*
Tiffany Licot, *Manager*
▲ **EMP:** 80
SQ FT: 10,000
SALES (est): 34.8MM **Privately Held**
SIC: 5065 Telephone equipment; communication equipment

(G-4338)
PRO SENIORS INC
7162 Reading Rd Ste 1150 (45237-3849)
PHONE....................513 345-4160
Laurie Crothers, *Controller*
Rhonda Moore, *Exec Dir*
Katie Chisholm, *Admin Asst*
EMP: 30
SALES: 2.3MM **Privately Held**
SIC: 8322 Senior citizens' center or association

(G-4339)
PROCESS CONSTRUCTION INC
2128 State Ave (45214-1614)
PHONE....................513 251-2211
Klem Fennell, *President*
David M Spaulding, *COO*
Joe Doxsey, *Project Mgr*
Mike Schmidt, *Project Mgr*
Tim Young, *Project Mgr*
EMP: 55
SALES (corp-wide): 17.5MM **Privately Held**
SIC: 1711 Mechanical contractor
PA: Process Construction, Inc.
1421 Queen City Ave
Cincinnati OH 45214
513 251-2211

(G-4340)
PROCESS PLUS LLC (PA)
135 Merchant St Ste 300 (45246-3759)
PHONE....................513 742-7590
Fax: 513 742-7593
Grant Mitchell P E, *President*
Ken Popham R A, *Principal*
Larry Greis, *Principal*
Roy Spreng, *Vice Pres*
Roger Benjamin, *Project Mgr*
EMP: 107
SQ FT: 32,000
SALES (est): 24.2MM **Privately Held**
WEB: www.processplus.com
SIC: 8711 Consulting engineer

(G-4341)
PROCTER & GAMBLE DISTRG LLC
2 P&G Plz Tn8 235 (45202)
PHONE....................513 945-7960
Mark Jarvis, *Associate Dir*
EMP: 272
SALES (corp-wide): 65B **Publicly Held**
SIC: 5169 Detergents
HQ: Procter & Gamble Distributing Llc
1 Procter And Gamble Plz
Cincinnati OH 45202
513 983-1100

(G-4342)
PROFESSIONAL CONTRACT SYSTEMS
11804 Conrey Rd Ste 100 (45249-1076)
PHONE....................513 469-8800
Fax: 513 469-5700
Larry Bayer, *President*
Mike Cariappa, *Vice Pres*
Joel Heckart, *Vice Pres*
Kim Owens, *Accounts Mgr*
Chuck Clevenger, *Manager*
EMP: 120
SQ FT: 4,800
SALES (est): 6.5MM **Privately Held**
WEB: www.pcsts.com
SIC: 7361 Placement agencies

(G-4343)
PROFESSIONAL MAINT OF COLUMBUS
Also Called: Professnal Mnt Lttle Ohio Div
1 Crosley Field Ln (45214-2004)
PHONE....................513 579-1762
Eldon Hall, *Ch of Bd*
Dale Barnett, *President*
EMP: 290
SALES (est): 1.7MM **Privately Held**
SIC: 8351 7349 Child day care services; janitorial service, contract basis

(G-4344)
PROFESSIONAL TELECOM SVCS
2119 Beechmont Ave (45230-5414)
PHONE....................513 232-7700
Fax: 513 624-2144
Joey Hazenfield, *President*
Jamie Hazenfield, *Vice Pres*
Sandy Wamsley, *Admin Sec*
EMP: 27
SQ FT: 3,665
SALES (est): 4MM **Privately Held**
WEB: www.ptscinti.com
SIC: 5999 1731 7622 7629 Communication equipment; communications specialization; communication equipment repair; telephone set repair; long distance telephone communications

(G-4345)
PROFESSNAL MINT CINCINNATI INC
1230 Findlay St (45214-2050)
PHONE....................513 579-1161
Fax: 513 579-0330
James L Miller, *President*
Mike Durbin, *General Mgr*
Annie Baucom, *Maint Spvr*
EMP: 700
SALES (est): 9.9MM **Privately Held**
WEB: www.pmcincinnati.com
SIC: 7349 8742 Janitorial service, contract basis; management consulting services

(G-4346)
PROJETECH INC
3815 Harrison Ave (45211-4725)
PHONE....................513 481-4900
Fax: 513 481-3006
Steven K Richmond, *President*
Darrell Tucker, *Business Mgr*
Mack Parrott, *Project Mgr*
Jacquie Chischillie, *Sales Staff*
Bill Brown, *Manager*
EMP: 28
SALES (est): 3.7MM **Privately Held**
WEB: www.emaintenance.com
SIC: 8742 Business consultant

(G-4347)
PROKIDS INC
2605 Burnet Ave (45219-2502)
PHONE....................513 281-2000
Fax: 513 487-6444
Candy Stemple, *Manager*
Tracy Cook, *Exec Dir*
Paul Hunt, *Director*
Carol Igoe, *Director*
Jennifer McKettrick, *Director*
EMP: 27
SALES (est): 1.9MM **Privately Held**
WEB: www.prokidscasa.com
SIC: 8322 Children's aid society

(G-4348)
PROPERTY ESTATE MANAGEMENT LLC
1526 Elm St Ste 1 (45202-6907)
PHONE....................513 684-0418
EMP: 25
SALES (est): 1.7MM **Privately Held**
SIC: 1522 1542 Residential Construction Nonresidential Construction

(G-4349)
PROSCAN IMAGING LLC (PA)
5400 Kennedy Ave Ste 1 (45213-2668)
PHONE....................513 281-3400
Fax: 513 351-3800
Judith Turner, *General Mgr*
Mark Grossman, *COO*
Michael Obrien, *Controller*
Jennifer Broge, *Facilities Mgr*
Tammy Lunsford, *QA Dir*
EMP: 100 **EST:** 1996
SALES (est): 37.6MM **Privately Held**
SIC: 8071 Ultrasound laboratory

(G-4350)
PROVIDENCE HOSPITAL (PA)
2446 Kipling Ave (45239-6650)
PHONE....................513 853-5000
Fax: 513 853-5758
Paul Hiltz, *President*
Edward Roeber, *Vice Pres*
Brandie Schroeder, *Marketing Mgr*
Pat Conlon, *Admin Sec*
EMP: 1178
SALES (est): 11.3MM **Privately Held**
SIC: 8062 General medical & surgical hospitals

(G-4351)
PROVIDENT TRAVEL CORPORATION
11309 Montgomery Rd Ste B (45249-2379)
PHONE....................513 247-1100
Fax: 513 247-1121
Jane Jones, *General Mgr*
Michele Uckotter, *Vice Pres*
Jane Riesen, *Opers Staff*
Anne Linnemann, *Accounts Exec*
Paula Murphy, *Accounts Exec*
EMP: 95
SALES (est): 12.3MM
SALES (corp-wide): 143.9MM **Privately Held**
WEB: www.providenttravel.com
SIC: 4724 Tourist agency arranging transport, lodging & car rental
PA: Aaa Allied Group, Inc.
15 W Central Pkwy
Cincinnati OH 45202
513 762-3100

(G-4352)
PROVINCE OF ST JOHN THE BAPTIS
Also Called: St Anthony Messenger Press
28 W Liberty St (45202-6442)
PHONE....................513 241-5615
Fax: 513 241-1197
Jeremy Harrington, *Principal*
John Koize, *Sales Dir*
Tom Bruce, *Marketing Staff*
John Feister, *CIO*
Sandy Digman, *Art Dir*
EMP: 100
SQ FT: 30,514
SALES (corp-wide): 12MM **Privately Held**
WEB: www.rogerbacon.org
SIC: 2721 5942 7812 2752 Magazines: publishing only, not printed on site; book stores; motion picture & video production; commercial printing, lithographic; miscellaneous publishing; book publishing
PA: The Province Of St John Baptist Order Friars Minor
1615 Vine St
Cincinnati OH 45202
513 721-4700

(G-4353)
PRUDENTIAL INSUR CO OF AMER
3 Crowne Point Ct Ste 100 (45241-5430)
PHONE....................513 612-6400
Fax: 513 612-6419
Jackie Charles, *Branch Mgr*
Michael Lee, *Agent*
Sherry Sicking, *Agent*
Anthony Fehring, *Officer*
John Hakemoller, *Administration*
EMP: 30
SALES (corp-wide): 59.6B **Publicly Held**
SIC: 6411 Insurance agents, brokers & service
HQ: The Prudential Insurance Company Of America
751 Broad St
Newark NJ 07102
973 802-6000

(G-4354)
PRUS CONSTRUCTION COMPANY
5325 Wooster Piko (45226-2224)
PHONE....................513 321-7774
Joseph M Prus, *President*
William J Prus, *Vice Pres*
EMP: 130
SALES (est): 20.6MM **Privately Held**
WEB: www.prusconstruction.com
SIC: 1771 1622 Blacktop (asphalt) work; bridge construction

(G-4355)
PSYCHPROS INC
2404 Auburn Ave (45219-2735)
PHONE....................513 651-9500
Holly Dorna, *CEO*
Dianne Osten, *Accounts Mgr*
Imar Edgardo, *Manager*
EMP: 30
SQ FT: 3,240

Cincinnati - Hamilton County (G-4356)   GEOGRAPHIC SECTION

SALES: 3.3MM **Privately Held**
WEB: www.psychpros.com
SIC: **7361** Executive placement

(G-4356)
PURE ROMANCE LLC (PA)
655 Plum St Ste 3 (45202-2367)
PHONE...................513 248-8656
Chris Cicchinelli, *CEO*
Brian Parsley, *Senior VP*
Victoria Chester, *CFO*
Sandy Neff, *Controller*
Sandy Neft, *Controller*
EMP: 68
SALES (est): 9MM **Privately Held**
WEB: www.pureromance.com
SIC: **7299** 5961 5632 Party planning service; books, mail order (except book clubs); toys & games (including dolls & models); mail order; lingerie & corsets (underwear)

(G-4357)
PYRAMID CONTROL SYSTEMS INC
Also Called: Pyramid Controls
5546 Fair Ln (45227-3402)
PHONE...................513 679-7400
Fax: 513 679-7415
Mukesh Ram, *President*
Thomas E Martin, *Principal*
Kevin Storn, *Project Mgr*
Terry Hardwick, *Warehouse Mgr*
Joyce Gundling, *Accountant*
EMP: 31
SALES (est): 6.6MM **Privately Held**
WEB: www.pyramidcontrols.com
SIC: **8711** Electrical or electronic engineering

(G-4358)
Q FACT MARKETING RESEARCH INC (PA)
11767 Thayer Ln (45249-1573)
PHONE...................513 891-2271
Fax: 513 791-7356
Joann Monroe, *President*
Yolonda Norman, *Project Dir*
Susan Boudreau, *Admin Asst*
EMP: 104
SQ FT: 20,400
SALES (est): 5.4MM **Privately Held**
WEB: www.qfact.com
SIC: **8732** Market analysis or research

(G-4359)
Q LABS LLC (PA)
Also Called: Q Laboratories
1400 Harrison Ave (45214-1606)
PHONE...................513 471-1300
Fax: 513 471-5600
Jeffrey Rowe, *President*
Michelle Kelly, *Vice Pres*
Megan Boyle, *Research*
Holly Graves, *Research*
Sarah Stolze, *Office Mgr*
EMP: 143
SQ FT: 24,000
SALES (est): 5.9MM **Privately Held**
WEB: www.qlaboratories.com
SIC: **8734** 8731 Testing laboratories; commercial physical research

(G-4360)
QUALITY SUPPLY CO (PA)
Also Called: Quality Restaurant Supply
4020 Rev Dr (45232-1914)
PHONE...................937 890-6114
Fax: 513 542-4505
Bruce Feldman, *Ch of Bd*
Leland D Manders, *President*
Alan Moscowitz, *Vice Pres*
Mark Foster, *Treasurer*
Irvin Moscowitz, *Admin Sec*
EMP: 35
SALES (est): 6.7MM **Privately Held**
SIC: **5046** Commercial cooking & food service equipment

(G-4361)
QUANTUM CONSTRUCTION COMPANY
1654 Sherman Ave (45212-2544)
P.O. Box 12249 (45212-0249)
PHONE...................513 351-6903
Fax: 513 351-5193
Ronald A Koetters, *Ch of Bd*
H Timothy Kemme, *President*
EMP: 25
SQ FT: 1,400
SALES (est): 3.2MM **Privately Held**
SIC: **1542** 1541 Commercial & office building, new construction; institutional building construction; industrial buildings & warehouses

(G-4362)
QUEEN CITY BLACKTOP COMPANY
2130 Osterfeld St (45214-1590)
PHONE...................513 251-8400
Fax: 513 557-4132
Martin Steinbach, *President*
Nancy S Kuley, *Vice Pres*
Nathan Steinbach, *VP Opers*
Andrew Steinbach, *Info Tech Mgr*
EMP: 26 EST: 1978
SQ FT: 3,000
SALES (est): 3.4MM **Privately Held**
WEB: www.qcbpave.com
SIC: **1771** 1611 Blacktop (asphalt) work; highway & street construction

(G-4363)
QUEEN CITY ELECTRIC INC
4015 Cherry St Ste 2 (45223-2587)
PHONE...................513 591-2600
Fax: 513 591-1300
Mike J Cavanaugh, *President*
John Coffield, *Project Mgr*
EMP: 25
SALES: 1,000K **Privately Held**
WEB: www.queencityelectric.net
SIC: **1731** General electrical contractor

(G-4364)
QUEEN CITY GENERAL & VASCULAR (PA)
Also Called: Queen City Generl Consultants
10506 Montgomery Rd # 101 (45242-4487)
PHONE...................513 232-8181
Fax: 513 624-2964
Bradley Osborne, *Principal*
Richard Welling, *Program Dir*
Stuart Donovan,
EMP: 25
SALES (est): 3.4MM **Privately Held**
SIC: **8011** Surgeon

(G-4365)
QUEEN CITY HOSPICE LLC
Also Called: Queen Cy Hspice Plliative Care
8250 Kenwood Crossing Way # 200 (45236-3669)
PHONE...................513 510-4406
Tony Izquierdo, *Principal*
EMP: 25
SALES (est): 1.5MM **Privately Held**
SIC: **8052** Personal care facility

(G-4366)
QUEEN CITY MECHANICALS INC
1950 Waycross Rd (45240-2827)
PHONE...................513 353-1430
Fax: 513 353-1460
Gary W Gilbert, *President*
Bradley Gilbert, *Vice Pres*
Bryan Gilbert, *Vice Pres*
Beverly Gilbert, *Treasurer*
Kathy Ward, *Administration*
EMP: 29
SALES (est): 5.8MM **Privately Held**
WEB: www.queencitymech.com
SIC: **1711** Plumbing contractors

(G-4367)
QUEEN CITY MEDICAL GROUP
7991 Beechmont Ave (45255-3189)
PHONE...................513 528-5600
Fax: 513 528-9716
Diane Dolensky, *Managing Prtnr*
Dr Georges M Feghali, *Partner*
EMP: 30
SALES (est): 2.8MM **Privately Held**
SIC: **8011** Internal medicine, physician/surgeon; pediatrician

(G-4368)
QUEEN CITY PHYSICIANS
Also Called: Queen City of Physicians
2475 W Galbraith Rd Ste 3 (45239-4369)
PHONE...................513 872-2061
Fax: 513 931-0132
Neil Deithsel, *President*
Dr Charles Dietschel, *Partner*
Dr Susan N Finney, *Partner*
Dr Kathleen Lamping-Arar, *Partner*
Dr Ellen H Norby, *Partner*
EMP: 54
SQ FT: 1,800
SALES (est): 4.6MM **Privately Held**
SIC: **8011** Pediatrician

(G-4369)
QUEEN CITY PHYSICIANS LTD
7825 Laurel Ave (45243-2608)
P.O. Box 43192 (45243-0192)
PHONE...................513 791-6992
Nan Matteson, *Branch Mgr*
EMP: 40
SALES (corp-wide): 4.7MM **Privately Held**
SIC: **8011** Offices & clinics of medical doctors
PA: Queen City Physicians, Ltd.
    619 Oak St
    Cincinnati OH 45206
    513 246-8000

(G-4370)
QUEEN CITY RACQUET CLUB LLC
11275 Chester Rd (45246-4014)
PHONE...................513 771-2835
Fax: 513 672-6667
Keven Shell, *President*
Doranne James, *General Mgr*
Carl Myers, *Treasurer*
Nick Lockman, *Office Mgr*
William P Martin, *Admin Sec*
EMP: 60
SQ FT: 100,000
SALES (est): 1.7MM **Privately Held**
WEB: www.queencityfitness.com
SIC: **7991** Physical fitness facilities
PA: Central Investment Llc
    7265 Kenwood Rd Ste 240
    Cincinnati OH 45236

(G-4371)
QUEEN CITY REPROGRAPHICS
2863 E Sharon Rd (45241-1923)
PHONE...................513 326-2300
Fax: 513 326-2312
Joe Herbst, *CEO*
Chris Chalifoux, *President*
Kevin Cartener, *Controller*
Dawn Hail, *Controller*
Craig Edmonston, *Sales Staff*
EMP: 105
SQ FT: 30,000
SALES (est): 15.9MM
SALES (corp-wide): 394.5MM **Publicly Held**
WEB: www.ohioblue.com
SIC: **5049** 7334 7335 2752 Drafting supplies; blueprinting service; commercial photography; lithographing on metal
PA: Arc Document Solutions, Inc.
    1981 N Broadway Ste 385
    Walnut Creek CA 94596
    925 949-5100

(G-4372)
QUEEN CITY TRANSPORTATION LLC
Also Called: Charter Bus Service
211 Township Ave Ste 2 (45216-2501)
PHONE...................513 941-8700
Jeff Klug, *Manager*
Greg Schroer, *Manager*
Arron Haid,
EMP: 300
SALES (est): 9MM **Privately Held**
WEB: www.charterbusservice.com
SIC: **4141** 4142 4151 Local bus charter service; bus charter service, except local; school buses

(G-4373)
QUEEN CY SPT MDCINE RHBLTATION
3950 Red Bank Rd (45227-3429)
PHONE...................513 561-1111
Fax: 513 561-1241
John E Turba MD, *President*
EMP: 26
SQ FT: 12,000
SALES (est): 605.7K **Privately Held**
SIC: **8011** Orthopedic physician; sports medicine specialist, physician

(G-4374)
QUEENSGATE FOOD GROUP LLC
Also Called: Queensgate Food Service
619 Linn St (45203-1794)
P.O. Box 14120 (45250-0120)
PHONE...................513 721-5503
Mark Mullen, *CFO*
Joe Hurst, *Sales Mgr*
Matt Mazza, *Sales Mgr*
Bill Hills, *Mktg Dir*
Bill Hills, *Mktg Dir*
EMP: 75
SQ FT: 55,000
SALES (est): 36.5MM **Publicly Held**
WEB: www.queensgatefoods.com
SIC: **5141** Food brokers
PA: The Chefs' Warehouse Inc
    100 E Ridge Rd
    Ridgefield CT 06877

(G-4375)
QUEST GLOBAL SERVICES-NA INC
11499 Chester Rd Ste 600 (45246-4000)
PHONE...................513 563-8855
EMP: 59
SALES (corp-wide): 107.7MM **Privately Held**
SIC: **8731** Engineering laboratory, except testing
HQ: Quest Global Services-Na, Inc.
    11499 Chester Rd Ste 600
    Cincinnati OH 45246

(G-4376)
QUEST GLOBAL SERVICES-NA INC (HQ)
Also Called: Quest Ase
11499 Chester Rd Ste 600 (45246-4000)
PHONE...................513 648-4900
Fax: 513 563-8865
Ajit Prabhu, *CEO*
Bob Harvey, *President*
Ajay Prabhu, *COO*
Raman Subramanian, *Senior VP*
Andrew Lewis, *Vice Pres*
EMP: 65
SALES (est): 63.2MM
SALES (corp-wide): 107.7MM **Privately Held**
WEB: www.asetech.com
SIC: **8731** 8711 Engineering laboratory, except testing; aviation &/or aeronautical engineering; electrical or electronic engineering; mechanical engineering
PA: Quest Global Engineering Services Private Limited
    Quest Tower, Plot No. 73 And 74
    Thiruvananthapuram KL 69558
    471 309-5000

(G-4377)
R A HERMES INC
4015 Cherry St Ste 27 (45223-2587)
PHONE...................513 251-5200
Fax: 513 251-5208
Rudolph Hermes, *President*
Carole Hermes, *Treasurer*
EMP: 28
SQ FT: 1,500
SALES (est): 4.5MM **Privately Held**
SIC: **1542** 1521 6531 Commercial & office building, new construction; commercial & office buildings, renovation & repair; new construction, single-family houses; general remodeling, single-family houses; real estate agents & managers

Cincinnati - Hamilton County (G-4403)

(G-4378)
R E KRAMIG & CO INC
323 S Wayne Ave (45215-4594)
P.O. Box 9909 (45209-0909)
PHONE.................513 761-4010
Fax: 513 761-0362
George Kulesza, *President*
Howard H Horne, *Exec VP*
Sean Murphy, *Project Mgr*
Roger Ripperger, *Project Mgr*
Nick Welter, *Purchasing*
EMP: 200
SQ FT: 65,000
SALES (est): 20.2MM **Privately Held**
SIC: **1799** 5033 1742 Insulation of pipes & boilers; insulation materials; acoustical & insulation work

(G-4379)
R KELLY INC
7645 Production Dr (45237-3208)
PHONE.................513 631-8488
Fax: 513 631-0475
Raymond Kelly, *President*
EMP: 35
SQ FT: 7,800
SALES: 6MM **Privately Held**
WEB: www.rkelly.com
SIC: **1711** Mechanical contractor

(G-4380)
R W GODBEY RAILROAD SERVICES
Also Called: B & R Railroad Services
2815 Spring Grove Ave (45225-2222)
PHONE.................513 651-3800
Fax: 513 651-4478
Richard W Godbey, *CEO*
Ric Godbey, *President*
EMP: 25
SALES (est): 1.1MM **Privately Held**
SIC: **4789** Railroad car repair

(G-4381)
R&F ERECTORS INC
Also Called: South Eastern Erectors
5763 Snyder Rd (45247-5723)
PHONE.................513 574-8273
Steve Rigney, *President*
Jerry Freidman, *Admin Sec*
EMP: 25
SALES (est): 2.3MM **Privately Held**
SIC: **1791** Structural steel erection

(G-4382)
RACK SEVEN PAVING CO INC
7208 Main St (45244-3014)
PHONE.................513 271-4863
Fax: 513 271-5863
Tim Rack, *President*
Kim Rack, *President*
EMP: 28
SQ FT: 700
SALES (est): 3.3MM **Privately Held**
SIC: **1611** Surfacing & paving; highway & street paving contractor

(G-4383)
RADIO PROMOTIONS
2518 Spring Grove Ave (45214-1730)
P.O. Box 14928 (45250-0928)
PHONE.................513 381-5000
Fax: 513 684-9276
Thomas O'Toole, *President*
Thomas Ludlow, *Vice Pres*
EMP: 150
SALES (est): 3.1MM **Privately Held**
SIC: **4832** Radio broadcasting stations

(G-4384)
RAITZ INC
Also Called: Alliance Calibration
11402 Reading Rd (45241-2247)
PHONE.................513 769-1200
Charles Goodall, *CEO*
Bradley Combs, *President*
Richard Barrett, *Principal*
Phil Wiseman, *COO*
Carissa Goodall, *Vice Pres*
EMP: 25
SQ FT: 5,400
SALES (est): 4.6MM **Privately Held**
SIC: **8734** Calibration & certification

(G-4385)
RAPID DELIVERY SERVICE CO INC
529 N Wayne Ave (45215-2800)
P.O. Box 15819 (45215-0819)
PHONE.................513 733-0500
Fax: 513 956-5237
Jerry Delp, *President*
Tina Delp, *President*
Mike Curd, *VP Sls/Mktg*
EMP: 40
SQ FT: 13,600
SALES: 3MM **Privately Held**
SIC: **4212** Delivery service, vehicular

(G-4386)
RASSAK LLC
Also Called: Benchmark Outfitters
7680 Demar Rd (45243-3504)
PHONE.................513 791-9453
Fax: 513 793-9569
Makr A Denney,
Richard Casser,
EMP: 25
SALES (est): 8.9MM **Privately Held**
SIC: **5136** 5137 Men's & boys' clothing; women's & children's clothing

(G-4387)
RAYCOM MEDIA INC
Also Called: W X I X
635 W 7th St Ste 200 (45203-1549)
PHONE.................513 421-1919
Fax: 513 421-3105
Bill Lansey, *General Mgr*
Jon Lawhead, *Info Tech Mgr*
EMP: 144 **Privately Held**
WEB: www.kwwl.com
SIC: **4833** Television broadcasting stations
PA: Raycom Media, Inc.
  201 Monroe St Fl 20
  Montgomery AL 36104

(G-4388)
RAYMOND JAMES FINCL SVCS INC
255 E 5th St Ste 2210 (45202-4701)
PHONE.................513 287-6777
Robert W Niehaus, *Senior VP*
Michael D Reagan, *Senior VP*
Benjamin Blemker, *Assoc VP*
Samuel Bortz, *Sales Mgr*
Raymond Schlinkert, *Sales Associate*
EMP: 25
SALES (corp-wide): 6.5B **Publicly Held**
WEB: www.raymondjames.com
SIC: **6211** Brokers, security
HQ: Raymond James Financial Services, Inc.
  880 Carillon Pkwy
  Saint Petersburg FL 33716
  727 567-1000

(G-4389)
RCR EAST INC (PA)
Also Called: Residence At Garden Gate
6922 Ohio Ave (45236-3506)
PHONE.................513 793-2090
Rodger King, *President*
Jerry Moore, *Facilities Dir*
Tracey Applebee, *Director*
Beth Ann Dailey, *Director*
Gayle Hollander, *Executive*
EMP: 150
SALES (est): 6.6MM **Privately Held**
SIC: **8051** Convalescent home with continuous nursing care

(G-4390)
RCR EAST INC
Also Called: Residence At Salem Woods
6164 Salem Rd (45230-2743)
PHONE.................513 231-8292
Rodger King, *Principal*
EMP: 150
SALES (est): 2.6MM
SALES (corp-wide): 6.6MM **Privately Held**
SIC: **8051** Convalescent home with continuous nursing care
PA: Rcr East Inc
  6922 Ohio Ave
  Cincinnati OH 45236
  513 793-2090

(G-4391)
READING FAMILY PRACTICE
Also Called: Rivera, Mary
9400 Reading Rd Ste 2 (45215-3401)
PHONE.................513 563-6934
Fax: 513 769-2622
John Nolan MD, *Owner*
EMP: 25
SQ FT: 7,960
SALES (est): 1.8MM **Privately Held**
SIC: **8011** General & family practice, physician/surgeon

(G-4392)
RECARO CHILD SAFETY LLC
4921 Para Dr (45237-5011)
PHONE.................248 904-1570
Angela Tenaglia, *Accountant*
Julie Laird, *Marketing Mgr*
Brady Lanter, *Technology*
Kai Weisskopf,
Bill Pierchala,
▲ EMP: 38
SQ FT: 40,000
SALES (est): 9.3MM **Privately Held**
SIC: **3944** 5099 Child restraint seats, automotive; child restraint seats, automotive

(G-4393)
RECKER CONSULTING LLC
Also Called: Path Forward It
6900 Steger Dr (45237-3096)
PHONE.................513 924-5500
Clint Holliday, *President*
Joe Anderson, *Engineer*
Tami Forman, *Exec Dir*
Marshall Taylor, *Exec Dir*
Heather Recker, *Director*
EMP: 60
SALES (est): 11MM **Privately Held**
SIC: **7379**

(G-4394)
RECONSTRUCTIVE ORTHOPEDICS (PA)
Also Called: Reconstructive Ortho Sports
10615 Montgomery Rd # 200 (45242-4461)
PHONE.................513 793-3933
Jonathan W Bell, *President*
George Nuktas, *Exec Dir*
EMP: 60
SQ FT: 8,500
SALES (est): 6.7MM **Privately Held**
WEB: www.reconstructiveorthopedics.com
SIC: **8011** Orthopedic physician

(G-4395)
RED CARPET JANITORIAL SERVICE (PA)
3478 Hauck Rd Ste D (45241-4604)
PHONE.................513 242-7575
Fax: 513 242-0856
Dale E Euller, *President*
EMP: 300
SQ FT: 2,000
SALES (est): 10.2MM **Privately Held**
WEB: www.redcarpetjanitorial.com
SIC: **7349** Janitorial service, contract basis

(G-4396)
RED DOG PET RESORT & SPA
4975 Babson Pl (45227-2683)
PHONE.................513 733-3647
Grant Johnson, *Managing Dir*
Brittany Hedberg, *Business Mgr*
Raymond Schneider, *Mng Member*
Stacey Zeschin, *Manager*
Sherry Agar, *Director*
EMP: 30
SQ FT: 28,000
SALES (est): 760.6K **Privately Held**
SIC: **0752** 5999 Shelters, animal; grooming services, pet & animal specialties; pets & pet supplies

(G-4397)
REECE-CAMPBELL INC
10839 Chester Rd (45246-4707)
PHONE.................513 542-4600
Fax: 513 542-4753
Peter W Chronis, *CEO*
Mike Olding, *Superintendent*
Rob Hekler, *Vice Pres*
James Kohne, *Vice Pres*
Elio Zerbini, *Vice Pres*
EMP: 60
SQ FT: 10,000
SALES (est): 17.4MM **Privately Held**
SIC: **1542** Commercial & office building contractors

(G-4398)
REHAB MEDICAL INC
1150 W 8th St Ste 110 (45203-1245)
PHONE.................513 381-3740
Patrick McGinley, *Principal*
EMP: 104
SALES (corp-wide): 10.6MM **Privately Held**
SIC: **8093** Rehabilitation center, outpatient treatment
PA: Rehab Medical, Inc.
  6365 Castleplace Dr
  Indianapolis IN 46250
  877 813-0205

(G-4399)
REHAB RESOURCES
8595 Beechmont Ave # 204 (45255-4740)
P.O. Box 541127 (45254-1127)
PHONE.................513 474-4123
Teresa Hollenkany, *Owner*
EMP: 25
SALES (est): 927.7K **Privately Held**
SIC: **8322** Rehabilitation services

(G-4400)
REINHART FOODSERVICE LLC
535 Shepherd Ave (45215-3115)
PHONE.................513 421-9184
Neil Hoover, *General Mgr*
Tricia Catanzaro, *Purchasing*
Denny Lundy, *Sales Staff*
Bill Devine, *Branch Mgr*
Toni Kuhlman, *Manager*
EMP: 175 **Privately Held**
WEB: www.reinhartfoodservice.com
SIC: **5148** Fruits, fresh
HQ: Reinhart Foodservice, L.L.C.
  6250 N River Rd Ste 9000
  Rosemont IL 60018
  608 782-2660

(G-4401)
REISENFELD & ASSOC LPA LLC (PA)
Also Called: Fojournerf Title Agency
3962 Red Bank Rd (45227-3408)
PHONE.................513 322-7000
Joyce Nocton, *CFO*
Janice Oelker, *Human Res Mgr*
Bradley A Reisenfeld, *Mng Member*
Michael Hoehn, *Info Tech Dir*
Steven Giordullo, *Director*
EMP: 170
SQ FT: 38,000
SALES (est): 24.4MM **Privately Held**
WEB: www.rslegal.com
SIC: **8111** General practice law office

(G-4402)
RELADYNE LLC (DH)
8280 Montgomery Rd # 101 (45236-6101)
PHONE.................513 489-6000
Larry J Stoddard, *CEO*
Jeff Hart, *Exec VP*
Jay Hurt, *Exec VP*
Doug Oehler, *Exec VP*
Glenn Pumpelly, *Exec VP*
EMP: 31
SALES (est): 4.6MM **Privately Held**
SIC: **7699** 7549 Industrial equipment services; lubrication service, automotive
HQ: Rel Ii Llc
  9395 Kenwood Rd Ste 104
  Blue Ash OH 45242
  513 489-6000

(G-4403)
REMINGER CO LPA
525 Vine St Ste 1700 (45202-3123)
PHONE.................513 721-1311
Fax: 513 891-6926
Stephanie Cook, *Manager*
EMP: 28
SALES (corp-wide): 59.8MM **Privately Held**
WEB: www.reminger.com
SIC: **8111** General practice law office

Cincinnati - Hamilton County (G-4404)

PA: Reminger Co., L.P.A.
101 W Prospect Ave # 1400
Cleveland OH 44115
216 687-1311

(G-4404)
RENDIGS FRY KIELY & DENNIS LLP (PA)
600 Vine St Ste 2602 (45202-2491)
PHONE 513 381-9200
Fax: 513 381-9200
Donald C Adams, *Partner*
Lawrence E Barbiere, *Partner*
W Roger Fry, *Partner*
J W Gelwicks, *Partner*
Edward R Goldman, *Partner*
EMP: 76 EST: 1940
SQ FT: 33,000
SALES (est): 13.3MM **Privately Held**
WEB: www.rendigs.com
SIC: 8111 General practice law office

(G-4405)
RENNIE & JONSON MONTGOMERY
36 E 7th St Ste 2100 (45202-4452)
PHONE 513 241-4722
Fax: 513 241-8775
James Montgomery, *President*
George Jonson, *Principal*
Douglas Rennie, *Principal*
Lance Dickinson, *Financial Exec*
Sarah Palmer, *Corp Counsel*
EMP: 30
SQ FT: 1,400
SALES (est): 3.9MM **Privately Held**
WEB: www.mrj.cc
SIC: 8111 General practice attorney, lawyer

(G-4406)
RENT-N-ROLL
7841 Laurel Ave (45243-2608)
PHONE 513 528-6929
Gre Lewalle, *President*
EMP: 60
SALES (est): 2.2MM **Privately Held**
SIC: 7359 Equipment rental & leasing

(G-4407)
REPUBLIC SERVICES INC
10751 Evendale Dr (45241-2535)
PHONE 513 554-0237
EMP: 34
SALES (corp-wide): 10B **Publicly Held**
SIC: 4953 Refuse collection & disposal services
PA: Republic Services, Inc.
18500 N Allied Way # 100
Phoenix AZ 85054
480 627-2700

(G-4408)
REPUBLIC SERVICES INC
11563 Mosteller Rd (45241-1831)
PHONE 513 771-4200
Charles Johnson, *General Mgr*
Delores Taylor, *Financial Exec*
William Weber, *Human Res Mgr*
Carolyn Smith, *Accounts Mgr*
Tim Trost, *Manager*
EMP: 100
SQ FT: 27,862
SALES (corp-wide): 10B **Publicly Held**
WEB: www.republicservices.com
SIC: 4953 4212 Garbage: collecting, destroying & processing; local trucking, without storage
PA: Republic Services, Inc.
18500 N Allied Way # 100
Phoenix AZ 85054
480 627-2700

(G-4409)
RESOLVIT RESOURCES LLC
895 Central Ave Ste 350 (45202-1975)
PHONE 513 619-5900
Fax: 513 619-5904
Iain Murray, *Accounts Mgr*
Lowell Lehmann, *Branch Mgr*
EMP: 42
SALES (corp-wide): 27MM **Privately Held**
SIC: 8748 Business consulting

PA: Resolvit Resources, Llc
8000 Twrs Crscnt Dr 110
Vienna VA 22182
703 734-3330

(G-4410)
REUPERT HEATING AND AC CO INC
5137 Crookshank Rd (45238-3386)
PHONE 513 922-5050
Fax: 513 922-5176
Kenneth Reupert, *President*
Donald Reupert, *Corp Secy*
Richard Reupert, *Vice Pres*
EMP: 27
SQ FT: 3,200
SALES (est): 4.7MM **Privately Held**
SIC: 1711 Warm air heating & air conditioning contractor

(G-4411)
RGI INC
2245 Gilbert Ave Ste 103 (45206-3000)
PHONE 513 221-2121
Richard McGraw, *CEO*
Kelly R Smith, *CEO*
Richard L McGraw, *President*
Barbara R McGraw, *Corp Secy*
Larry McGraw, *Exec VP*
EMP: 40
SQ FT: 8,000
SALES (est): 10.4MM **Privately Held**
SIC: 7336 Graphic arts & related design

(G-4412)
RGIS LLC
4000 Executive Park Dr # 105 (45241-2023)
PHONE 513 772-5990
Fax: 513 772-5993
Debbie Cappel, *General Mgr*
Steve Lighner, *Manager*
EMP: 110
SALES (corp-wide): 7.1B **Publicly Held**
WEB: www.rgisinv.com
SIC: 7389 Inventory computing service
HQ: Rgis, Llc
2000 Taylor Rd
Auburn Hills MI 48326
248 651-2511

(G-4413)
RHC INC (PA)
Also Called: RESIDENT HOME, THE
3030 W Fork Rd (45211-1944)
PHONE 513 389-7501
Fax: 513 661-5804
Peter Keiser, *President*
Robert South, *Chairman*
Susan Pahner, *Vice Pres*
Michael Nolan, *VP Opers*
David Levine, *QC Mgr*
EMP: 150
SQ FT: 11,077
SALES (est): 8.7MM **Privately Held**
WEB: www.rhcorp.org
SIC: 8361 Home for the mentally handicapped

(G-4414)
RHINEGEIST LLC
Also Called: Rhinegeist Brewery
1910 Elm St (45202-7751)
PHONE 513 381-1367
Nick Vitalo, *Sales Dir*
Omar Elayan, *Sales Mgr*
Dan Klemmer, *Sales Mgr*
Patrick Lang, *Sales Mgr*
Will Parker, *Sales Mgr*
▲ EMP: 71
SQ FT: 120,000
SALES (est): 10MM **Privately Held**
SIC: 5181 5813 Beer & other fermented malt liquors; bars & lounges

(G-4415)
RICHARD GOETTLE INC
12071 Hamilton Ave (45231-1032)
PHONE 513 825-8100
Fax: 513 825-8107
Douglas Keller, *CEO*
John Conety, *Superintendent*
Cordale Francis, *Superintendent*
Kelly Hedger, *Superintendent*
Chris Herth, *Superintendent*
◆ EMP: 99

SALES (est): 75.2MM **Privately Held**
SIC: 5082 Contractors' materials
PA: Goettle Holding Company, Inc.
12071 Hamilton Ave
Cincinnati OH 45231
513 825-8100

(G-4416)
RICHARDS ELECTRIC SUP CO INC (PA)
4620 Reading Rd (45229-1297)
P.O. Box 29860 (45229-0860)
PHONE 513 242-8800
Fax: 513 242-8509
Ivan S Misrach, *President*
Richard Misrach, *Principal*
Joseph Schwartz, *Principal*
Norma Strelow, *Principal*
Mark Schmidlin, *Vice Pres*
▲ EMP: 150
SQ FT: 62,500
SALES (est): 174.2MM **Privately Held**
WEB: www.richardselectric.com
SIC: 5063 Electrical supplies; electrical construction materials; lighting fixtures

(G-4417)
RICK BLAZING INSURANCE AGENCY
Also Called: Nationwide
300 E Bus Way Ste 200 (45241)
PHONE 513 677-8300
Rick Blazing, *Owner*
Jamon Sellman, *Manager*
EMP: 30
SALES (est): 2.6MM **Privately Held**
SIC: 6411 Insurance agents

(G-4418)
RICKING PAPER AND SPECIALTY CO
525 Northland Blvd (45240-3233)
PHONE 513 825-3551
Fax: 513 825-3738
Carl Ricking Jr, *President*
Preston M Simpson, *Principal*
Carla Droll, *Vice Pres*
Karla Droll, *Vice Pres*
Julie Ricking, *Vice Pres*
EMP: 50
SQ FT: 84,000
SALES (est): 14.9MM **Privately Held**
WEB: www.ricking.com
SIC: 5113 5141 2656 Industrial & personal service paper; bags, paper & disposable plastic; towels, paper; napkins, paper; groceries, general line; cups, paper; made from purchased material

(G-4419)
RIDE SHARE INFORMATION
Also Called: Oki Rgonal Council Governments
720 E Pete Rose Way # 420 (45202-3579)
PHONE 513 621-6300
Fax: 513 621-9325
Katie Hannum, *Accountant*
Nicole Hartman, *Human Resources*
Lorrie Platt, *Comms Dir*
Summer Jones, *Corp Comm Staff*
Mark Policinski, *Exec Dir*
EMP: 32
SALES (est): 3.8MM **Privately Held**
WEB: www.oki.org
SIC: 8742 Administrative services consultant

(G-4420)
RILCO INDUSTRIAL CONTROLS INC (HQ)
5012 Calvert St (45209-1076)
PHONE 513 530-0055
Fax: 513 530-5448
Chris Cowell, *President*
Diane Ellison, *Manager*
EMP: 27
SQ FT: 1,250
SALES (est): 5.5MM
SALES (corp-wide): 43.6MM **Privately Held**
WEB: www.cincinnaticontrols.com
SIC: 5084 Controlling instruments & accessories

PA: Triad Technologies, Llc
985 Falls Creek Dr
Vandalia OH 45377
937 832-2861

(G-4421)
RIPPE & KINGSTON SYSTEMS INC (PA)
Also Called: Broughton International
1077 Celestial St Ste 124 (45202-1628)
PHONE 513 241-1375
Fax: 513 241-7843
George Kingston, *President*
Joyce Tabar, *General Mgr*
John Fink, *District Mgr*
Mike Albers, *Vice Pres*
Thomas Davidson, *Vice Pres*
EMP: 60
SQ FT: 15,000
SALES (est): 11.5MM **Privately Held**
WEB: www.rippe.com
SIC: 7379 7371 Computer related consulting services; computer software development

(G-4422)
RITTER & RANDOLPH LLC
1 E 4th St Ste 700 (45202-3705)
PHONE 513 381-5700
Daniel P Randolph, *Partner*
Maryann Jacobs, *Partner*
Dara Neer, *Admin Asst*
Marcia Beasley, *Legal Staff*
Beth Klosterman, *Legal Staff*
EMP: 32
SALES (est): 3.7MM **Privately Held**
WEB: www.ritterandrandolph.com
SIC: 8111 General practice attorney, lawyer

(G-4423)
RIVER DOWNS TURF CLUB INC
Also Called: River Downs Race Course
6301 Kellogg Rd (45230-5237)
P.O. Box 30286 (45230-0286)
PHONE 513 232-8000
EMP: 50
SQ FT: 2,000
SALES (est): 2MM **Privately Held**
SIC: 7948 Horse Race Track

(G-4424)
RIVERFRONT STEEL INC
10310 S Medallion Dr (45241-4836)
P.O. Box 62718 (45262-0718)
PHONE 513 769-9999
Fax: 513 769-9600
Bradley Kuhr, *Owner*
Rick Tenenholtz, *Vice Pres*
Scott Heuser, *Transptn Dir*
Kurt Enneking, *Opers Mgr*
Dave Decker, *Purch Mgr*
▲ EMP: 95
SQ FT: 120,000
SALES (est): 124.8MM **Privately Held**
WEB: www.riverfrontsteel.com
SIC: 5051 Steel

(G-4425)
RIVERHILLS HEALTHCARE INC (PA)
111 Wellington Pl Lowr (45219-2082)
PHONE 513 241-2370
Fax: 513 961-1912
P Robert Schwetschenau, *President*
Linda Burnhardt, *Principal*
Thomas Frerick, *COO*
Peter Vicente, *Vice Pres*
Colin Zadikoff MD, *Treasurer*
EMP: 38
SQ FT: 22,224
SALES (est): 11.7MM **Privately Held**
SIC: 8011 Neurologist

(G-4426)
RIVERHILLS HEALTHCARE INC
4805 Montgomery Rd # 150 (45212-2280)
PHONE 513 791-6400
Fax: 513 984-5447
Barbara Mitchell, *Office Mgr*
James Farrell MD, *Director*
John Feibel MD, *Director*
Maureen LI MD, *Director*
Robert Reed MD, *Director*
EMP: 45

GEOGRAPHIC SECTION
Cincinnati - Hamilton County (G-4450)

SALES (corp-wide): 11.7MM **Privately Held**
SIC: 8011 Surgeon
PA: Riverhills Healthcare Inc
111 Wellington Pl Lowr
Cincinnati OH 45219
513 241-2370

(G-4427)
RIVERSIDE CNSTR SVCS INC
218 W Mcmicken Ave (45214-2314)
PHONE 513 723-0900
Fax: 513 723-0990
Robert S Krejci, *President*
Timothy L Pierce, *Vice Pres*
Karen Lampson, *Senior Mgr*
EMP: 32
SQ FT: 21,000
SALES (est): 5.5MM **Privately Held**
WEB: www.riversidearchitectural.com
SIC: 2431 1751 2434 Millwork; carpentry work; wood kitchen cabinets

(G-4428)
RIVERSIDE MEDICAL INC
111 Wellington Pl (45219-1758)
PHONE 513 936-5360
Peggy Stanford, *President*
Thomas Young, *General Mgr*
Luis Pagani, *Treasurer*
Colin Zadikoff, *Admin Sec*
EMP: 35
SALES (est): 1.6MM **Privately Held**
WEB: www.rhihealth.com
SIC: 7389 Personal service agents, brokers & bureaus

(G-4429)
RK EXPRESS INTERNATIONAL LLC
5474 Sanrio Ct (45247-7408)
P.O. Box 531106 (45253-1106)
PHONE 513 574-2400
Randy Lee, *Principal*
EMP: 55
SQ FT: 30,000
SALES (est): 4.7MM **Privately Held**
SIC: 4731 Freight transportation arrangement

(G-4430)
RLA INVESTMENTS INC
389 Wade St (45214)
PHONE 513 554-1470
Robert L Adleta II, *President*
Ron Hill, *Foreman/Supr*
Carol Smith, *Office Mgr*
EMP: 45
SALES (est): 9.9MM **Privately Held**
SIC: 1623 Sewer line construction

(G-4431)
RMS OF OHIO INC
7162 Reading Rd Ste 1010 (45237-3849)
PHONE 513 841-0990
Fax: 513 841-9880
Harriett Doyle, *Manager*
Gwen Lee, *Director*
EMP: 30
SALES (corp-wide): 11.8MM **Privately Held**
SIC: 8059 Convalescent home
PA: Rms Of Ohio, Inc
733 E Dublin Granville Rd # 100
Columbus OH 43229
614 844-6767

(G-4432)
ROADTRIPPERS INC
131 E Mcmicken Ave (45202-6520)
PHONE 917 688-9887
James Fischer, *CEO*
Joshua Smibert, *COO*
Jonathan Richman, *Vice Pres*
Jill Dillingham, *Sales Dir*
Tim Balzer, *Manager*
EMP: 25
SALES: 2MM **Privately Held**
SIC: 7371 Custom computer programming services

(G-4433)
ROBBINS KELLY PATTERSON TUCKER
7 W 7th St Ste 1400 (45202-2451)
PHONE 513 721-3330
Fredric J Robbins, *President*
James M Kelly, *Vice Pres*
Debra Staggs, *Bookkeeper*
Randy J Blankenship, *Shareholder*
Thomas M Gaier, *Shareholder*
EMP: 45 **EST:** 1965
SALES (est): 5.2MM **Privately Held**
SIC: 8111 General practice law office

(G-4434)
ROBERT E LUBOW MD
3001 Highland Ave (45219-2315)
PHONE 513 961-8861
Robedrt Lubow, *Owner*
EMP: 37
SALES (est): 511.6K **Privately Held**
SIC: 8011 Offices & clinics of medical doctors

(G-4435)
ROBERT ELLIS
305 Crescent Ave (45215-4406)
PHONE 513 821-0275
Jennifer Schneider, *Office Mgr*
Robert Ellis, *Med Doctor*
Norman Gilinsky, *Med Doctor*
EMP: 25
SALES (est): 130.5K **Privately Held**
SIC: 8011 General & family practice, physician/surgeon

(G-4436)
ROBERT HALF INTERNATIONAL INC
201 E 5th St Ste 2000a (45202-4162)
PHONE 513 621-8367
Fax: 513 621-3070
Danielle Skelton, *Branch Mgr*
Jill Turski, *Manager*
EMP: 92
SALES (corp-wide): 5.2B **Publicly Held**
SIC: 7361 Placement agencies
PA: Robert Half International Inc.
2884 Sand Hill Rd Ste 200
Menlo Park CA 94025
650 234-6000

(G-4437)
ROBERT LUCKE HOMES INC
8825 Chapelsquare Ln B (45249-4702)
PHONE 513 683-3300
Fax: 513 683-3315
Robert Lucke, *President*
Andrea Lucke, *VP Mktg*
Tyler Lamar, *Mktg Dir*
EMP: 20
SALES (est): 5MM **Privately Held**
SIC: 1521 New construction, single-family houses

(G-4438)
ROCKFISH INTERACTIVE CORP
659 Van Meter St Ste 520 (45202-1585)
PHONE 513 381-1583
Kenny Tomlin, *CEO*
EMP: 63
SALES (corp-wide): 17.7B **Privately Held**
SIC: 7311 Advertising agencies
HQ: Rockfish Interactive Llc
3100 S Market St Ste 100
Rogers AR 72758

(G-4439)
RODEM INC (PA)
Also Called: Rodem Process Equipment
5095 Crookshank Rd (45238-3366)
PHONE 513 922-0140
Fax: 513 922-1680
Christopher Diener, *President*
Christopher D Diener, *President*
Jeffrey L Diener, *Vice Pres*
Susan D Kerr, *Treasurer*
Stan Pritchard, *Sales Dir*
▲ **EMP:** 40
SQ FT: 15,000
SALES (est): 61.5MM **Privately Held**
WEB: www.rodem.com
SIC: 5084 Dairy products manufacturing machinery; food product manufacturing machinery

(G-4440)
RONALD MCDONALD HSE GRTR CINCI
350 Erkenbrecher Ave (45229-2806)
PHONE 513 636-5591
Fax: 513 636-4887
David Anderson, *President*
Carine Lange, *Opers Staff*
EMP: 27
SQ FT: 56,000
SALES: 6.1MM **Privately Held**
SIC: 8699 Charitable organization

(G-4441)
ROSS SINCLAIRE & ASSOC LLC (PA)
700 Walnut St Ste 600 (45202-2027)
PHONE 513 381-3939
Fax: 513 381-0124
David Banta, *Managing Dir*
Daniel Blank, *Managing Dir*
Omar Ganoom, *Managing Dir*
Andy Warning, *Managing Dir*
Drew Conti, *Vice Pres*
EMP: 40
SQ FT: 6,000
SALES (est): 14.9MM **Privately Held**
WEB: www.rsanet.com
SIC: 6211 Stock brokers & dealers; investment bankers

(G-4442)
ROTO-ROOTER DEVELOPMENT CO (HQ)
255 E 5th St Ste 2500 (45202-4793)
PHONE 513 762-6690
Spencer S Lee, *CEO*
Edward L Hutton, *Ch of Bd*
Kevin J McNamara, *Vice Ch Bd*
Rick Arquilla, *President*
Mark A Conners, *Senior VP*
EMP: 95
SQ FT: 20,000
SALES (est): 240.5MM
SALES (corp-wide): 1.6B **Publicly Held**
SIC: 7699 1711 Sewer cleaning & rodding; gas appliance repair service; plumbing contractors; septic system construction
PA: Chemed Corporation
255 E 5th St Ste 2600
Cincinnati OH 45202
513 762-6690

(G-4443)
ROTO-ROOTER GROUP INC (HQ)
2500 Chemed Ctr (45202-4725)
PHONE 513 762-6690
Spencer Lee, *CEO*
Rick Arquilla, *President*
Frank Castillo, *President*
Robert Goldschmidt, *Exec VP*
Gary H Sander, *Exec VP*
EMP: 140
SALES (est): 3.6MM
SALES (corp-wide): 1.6B **Publicly Held**
WEB: www.chemed.com
SIC: 7699 Sewer cleaning & rodding
PA: Chemed Corporation
255 E 5th St Ste 2600
Cincinnati OH 45202
513 762-6690

(G-4444)
ROTO-ROOTER SERVICES COMPANY (DH)
255 E 5th St Ste 2500 (45202-4793)
PHONE 513 762-6690
Fax: 513 762-6590
Spencer S Lee, *CEO*
Rick L Arquilla, *President*
David Williams, *CFO*
Sharon Talladira, *Accountant*
EMP: 100
SALES (est): 232MM
SALES (corp-wide): 1.6B **Publicly Held**
SIC: 7699 1711 Sewer cleaning & rodding; plumbing contractors
HQ: Roto-Rooter Development Company
255 E 5th St Ste 2500
Cincinnati OH 45202
513 762-6690

(G-4445)
ROTO-ROOTER SERVICES COMPANY
2125 Montana Ave (45211-2741)
PHONE 513 541-3840
Mike Walker, *Manager*
EMP: 70
SQ FT: 13,761
SALES (corp-wide): 1.6B **Publicly Held**
SIC: 7699 1711 7623 Sewer cleaning & rodding; plumbing, heating, air-conditioning contractors; heating systems repair & maintenance; refrigeration repair service
HQ: Roto-Rooter Services Company
255 E 5th St Ste 2500
Cincinnati OH 45202
513 762-6690

(G-4446)
ROUGH BROTHERS MFG INC
5513 Vine St Ste 1 (45217-1022)
PHONE 513 242-0310
Fax: 513 242-0816
Richard Reilly, *President*
James Parris, *General Mgr*
Nick Workman, *Superintendent*
Kevin Caron, *Vice Pres*
Brad Hull, *Project Mgr*
◆ **EMP:** 90
SQ FT: 100,000
SALES (est): 96.7MM
SALES (corp-wide): 986.9MM **Publicly Held**
SIC: 1542 3448 Greenhouse construction; greenhouses: prefabricated metal
HQ: Rough Brothers Holding Co., Inc
3556 Lake Shore Rd # 100
Buffalo NY 14219
716 826-6500

(G-4447)
ROUNDTOWER TECHNOLOGIES LLC (PA)
5905 E Galbraith Rd # 3000 (45236-0702)
PHONE 513 247-7900
Stephen West, *President*
Andy Stein, *President*
Stephen Power, *Managing Prtnr*
Jim Armentrout, *District Mgr*
Pat Haller, *District Mgr*
EMP: 62
SQ FT: 5,000
SALES (est): 62.9MM **Privately Held**
SIC: 7379 Computer related consulting services

(G-4448)
ROYAL CAR WASH INC
6925 Colerain Ave (45239-5545)
PHONE 513 385-2777
Rick Ennis, *President*
EMP: 34
SQ FT: 1,000
SALES (est): 873.9K **Privately Held**
SIC: 7542 Carwash, automatic

(G-4449)
RPC MECHANICAL SERVICES (HQ)
5301 Lester Rd (45213-2523)
PHONE 513 733-1641
John Lowe, *President*
Becky Keeble, *Human Res Mgr*
EMP: 164 **EST:** 1937
SQ FT: 40,000
SALES (est): 15.3MM
SALES (corp-wide): 76.6MM **Privately Held**
SIC: 1711 Mechanical contractor
PA: The Thomas J Dyer Company
5240 Lester Rd
Cincinnati OH 45213
513 321-8100

(G-4450)
RPF CONSULTING LLC
7870 E Kemper Rd Ste 300 (45249-1675)
PHONE 678 494-8030
Carol Whitten, *Office Mgr*
Tom Gaster, *Manager*
Robert Fiorillo,
Mary Katherine Fiorillo,
EMP: 28
SQ FT: 500
SALES (est): 979.9K
SALES (corp-wide): 100.2B **Privately Held**
SIC: 8742 Management consulting services
HQ: Itelligence Ag
Konigsbreede 1
Bielefeld 33605
521 914-480

Cincinnati - Hamilton County (G-4451)

GEOGRAPHIC SECTION

(G-4451)
RPM MIDWEST LLC
352 Gest St (45203-1822)
PHONE................513 762-9000
Brian Boland, *Controller*
Sam Thompson,
EMP: 26
SALES: 3.4MM **Privately Held**
SIC: 6531 Real estate managers

(G-4452)
RUMPKE AMUSEMENTS INC
Also Called: Rumpke Softball Park
10795 Hughes Rd (45251-4598)
PHONE................513 738-2646
William Rumpke, *Branch Mgr*
EMP: 26
SALES (corp-wide): 783.2K **Privately Held**
SIC: 7996 Amusement parks
PA: Rumpke Amusements Inc
  10795 Hughes Rd
  Cincinnati OH 45251
  513 742-2900

(G-4453)
RUMPKE SANITARY LANDFILL INC
10795 Hughes Rd (45251-4598)
PHONE................513 851-0122
William J Rumpke, *President*
Philip Wehrman, *CFO*
EMP: 150
SQ FT: 25,000
SALES (est): 14.7MM **Privately Held**
SIC: 4953 Sanitary landfill operation
PA: Rumpke Consolidated Companies, Inc.
  3963 Kraus Ln
  Hamilton OH 45014

(G-4454)
RUMPKE TRANSPORTATION CO LLC
Also Called: Rumpke Container Service
553 Vine St (45202-3105)
PHONE................513 242-4600
Jeff Rumpke, *Manager*
Bruce R Ullrey, *CIO*
EMP: 150 **Privately Held**
SIC: 4953 3341 3231 2611 Recycling, waste materials; secondary nonferrous metals; products of purchased glass; pulp mills
HQ: Rumpke Transportation Company, Llc
  10795 Hughes Rd
  Cincinnati OH 45251
  513 851-0122

(G-4455)
RUMPKE WASTE INC (HQ)
10795 Hughes Rd (45251-4598)
PHONE................513 851-0122
Fax: 513 741-2635
Bill Rumpke Jr, *President*
William J Rumpke, *President*
Downard Bruce, *General Mgr*
Todd Wielinski, *Opers Mgr*
Bruce Wilcox, *Sls & Mktg Exec*
EMP: 60
SQ FT: 25,000
SALES (est): 949.5MM **Privately Held**
SIC: 4953 Garbage: collecting, destroying & processing

(G-4456)
RUMPKE WASTE INC
Also Called: Rumpke Recycling
5535 Vine St (45217-1003)
PHONE................513 242-4401
Fax: 513 242-4459
Brad Dunn, *District Mgr*
Larry Ochs, *Manager*
Brian Huffman, *Manager*
Sue Tatman, *Info Tech Mgr*
Ann Powers, *Director*
EMP: 100
SQ FT: 51,870 **Privately Held**
SIC: 4953 4212 Recycling, waste materials; local trucking, without storage
HQ: Rumpke Waste, Inc.
  10795 Hughes Rd
  Cincinnati OH 45251
  513 851-0122

(G-4457)
RUSH PACKAGE DELIVERY INC
Also Called: Rush Trans
10091 Moteller Ln (45201)
PHONE................513 771-7874
Fax: 513 672-8164
Brian Kressin, *Branch Mgr*
EMP: 40
SALES (corp-wide): 14.6MM **Privately Held**
WEB: www.rush-delivery.com
SIC: 7389 Courier or messenger service
PA: Rush Package Delivery, Inc.
  2619 Needmore Rd
  Dayton OH 45414
  937 224-7874

(G-4458)
RUSH TRUCK CENTERS OHIO INC (HQ)
Also Called: Rush Truck Center, Cincinnati
11775 Highway Dr (45241-2005)
PHONE................513 733-8500
EMP: 73
SALES: 56.7MM
SALES (corp-wide): 4.7B **Publicly Held**
SIC: 5012 7538 5531 5014 Automobiles & other motor vehicles; general automotive repair shops; automotive & home supply stores; tires & tubes; truck rental & leasing, no drivers
PA: Rush Enterprises, Inc.
  555 S Ih 35 Ste 500
  New Braunfels TX 78130
  830 302-5200

(G-4459)
RWB PROPERTIES AND CNSTR LLC
611 Shepherd Dr Unit 6 (45215-2172)
PHONE................513 541-0900
Fax: 513 672-9330
Rodrigo M Williams, *CEO*
Jimmy Hill,
EMP: 60
SQ FT: 40,000
SALES (est): 6.2MM **Privately Held**
SIC: 1622 Bridge, tunnel & elevated highway

(G-4460)
RWS ENTERPRISES LLC
Also Called: Visiting Angels
9019 Colerain Ave (45251-2401)
PHONE................513 598-6770
Michael Schroth, *Owner*
EMP: 60
SALES: 1.2MM **Privately Held**
SIC: 8082 Home health care services

(G-4461)
RYANS ALL-GLASS INCORPORATED (PA)
9884 Springfield Pike (45215-1441)
PHONE................513 771-4440
Fax: 513 771-4153
Bruce Ryan, *President*
Ken Ryan, *Vice Pres*
Rich Hagedorn, *Manager*
Kathi McKenzie, *Manager*
Anita Salyers, *Manager*
EMP: 30
SQ FT: 22,000
SALES (est): 8MM **Privately Held**
WEB: www.ryansallglass.com
SIC: 1793 7536 1751 Glass & glazing work; automotive glass replacement shops; window & door (prefabricated) installation

(G-4462)
RYDER TRUCK RENTAL INC
1190 Gest St (45203-1114)
PHONE................513 241-7736
Fax: 513 241-6172
Pat Murphy, *Branch Mgr*
EMP: 40
SALES (corp-wide): 7.3B **Publicly Held**
SIC: 7513 Truck rental, without drivers
HQ: Ryder Truck Rental, Inc.
  11690 Nw 105th St
  Medley FL 33178
  305 500-3726

(G-4463)
RYDER TRUCK RENTAL INC
2575 Commodity Cir (45241-1563)
PHONE................513 772-0223
Fax: 513 772-6109
Joe Florhe, *Safety Mgr*
Steve Lennon, *CPA*
Bob Anks, *Manager*
Matthew Copeland, *Manager*
EMP: 30
SQ FT: 9,870
SALES (corp-wide): 7.3B **Publicly Held**
SIC: 7513 7519 Truck rental, without drivers; trailer rental
HQ: Ryder Truck Rental, Inc.
  11690 Nw 105th St
  Medley FL 33178
  305 500-3726

(G-4464)
S & S HALTHCARE STRATEGIES LTD
1385 Kemper Meadow Dr (45240-1635)
PHONE................513 772-8866
Gail Scheitzer, *President*
Gail Schweitzer, *President*
Richard Rostowsky, *Vice Pres*
Debra Beckett, *Project Mgr*
Deborah Meek, *Opers Staff*
EMP: 120
SQ FT: 60,000
SALES (est): 36.3MM **Privately Held**
SIC: 6411 Insurance adjusters

(G-4465)
SABER HEALTHCARE GROUP LLC
Also Called: Victoria Retirement Community
1500 Sherman Ave (45212-2510)
PHONE................513 631-6800
Fax: 513 631-5677
Jennifer Gardner, *Administration*
EMP: 36
SALES (corp-wide): 68.5MM **Privately Held**
SIC: 8051 Skilled nursing care facilities
PA: Saber Healthcare Group, L.L.C.
  26691 Richmond Rd Frnt
  Bedford OH 44146
  216 292-5706

(G-4466)
SADLER-NECAMP FINANCIAL SVCS
Also Called: Proware
7621 E Kemper Rd (45249-1609)
PHONE................513 489-5477
Fax: 513 489-0571
Randal R Sadler, *CEO*
Don Flischel, *Vice Pres*
Bret Sadler, *Vice Pres*
Deanne Ormes, *Consultant*
Wane Yarborough, *Consultant*
EMP: 40
SQ FT: 7,400
SALES: 6.2MM **Privately Held**
WEB: www.proware.com
SIC: 7371 8748 5045 Computer software development; systems engineering consultant, ex. computer or professional; computers, peripherals & software; computer software

(G-4467)
SAEC/KINETIC VISION INC
10255 Evendale Commons Dr (45241-3250)
PHONE................513 793-4959
Fax: 513 793-5197
Richard Schweet, *President*
Catherine Bennett, *Opers Mgr*
Brian C Carovillano, *Purch Mgr*
Jim Topich, *Engineer*
Nicholas Trevethan, *Engineer*
EMP: 130
SQ FT: 28,000
SALES (est): 3.7MM **Privately Held**
WEB: www.saec-kv.com
SIC: 8711 7371 Mechanical engineering; computer software development & applications

(G-4468)
SAFRAN HUMN RSRCES SUPPORT INC (HQ)
111 Merchant St (45246-3730)
P.O. Box 15514 (45215-0514)
PHONE................513 552-3230
Jacques Riboni, *Exec VP*
Luc Bramy, *Vice Pres*
EMP: 72
SQ FT: 5,000
SALES (est): 4.3MM
SALES (corp-wide): 555.1MM **Privately Held**
SIC: 8711 Consulting engineer
PA: Safran
  2 Bd Du General Martial Valin
  Paris 75015
  140 608-080

(G-4469)
SAGE HOSPITALITY RESOURCES LLC
Also Called: Crowne Plaza Ci
11320 Chester Rd (45246-4003)
PHONE................513 771-2080
Matthew Bryant, *Branch Mgr*
EMP: 67
SALES (corp-wide): 407.4MM **Privately Held**
WEB: www.21chotel.com
SIC: 7011 Hotel, franchised
PA: Sage Hospitality Resources L.L.C.
  1575 Welton St Ste 300
  Denver CO 80202
  303 595-7200

(G-4470)
SAINT JAMES DAY CARE CENTER
3929 Boudinot Ave (45211-3603)
PHONE................513 662-2287
Fax: 513 662-3563
Joan Chouteau, *Director*
EMP: 25
SALES: 837.5K **Privately Held**
SIC: 8351 Child day care services

(G-4471)
SAINT JOSEPH ORPHANAGE
274 Sutton Rd (45230-3521)
PHONE................513 231-5010
Tom Uhl, *Branch Mgr*
EMP: 95
SALES (corp-wide): 16.2MM **Privately Held**
SIC: 8361 Orphanage
PA: Saint Joseph Orphanage
  5400 Edalbert Dr
  Cincinnati OH 45239
  513 741-3100

(G-4472)
SAINT JOSEPH ORPHANAGE (PA)
5400 Edalbert Dr (45239-7695)
PHONE................513 741-3100
Fax: 513 245-9401
Eric Cummins, *CEO*
Jim Jenkins, *Sls & Mktg Exec*
John Colegrove, *CFO*
Deb Kelly, *Human Res Dir*
Tawana Leary, *Human Resources*
EMP: 66
SALES: 16.2MM **Privately Held**
WEB: www.stjosephorphanage.org
SIC: 8361 Children's home

(G-4473)
SALON LA
2711 Edmondson Rd (45209-1912)
PHONE................513 784-1700
Fax: 513 784-1950
Linda August, *Owner*
EMP: 30
SQ FT: 2,700
SALES (est): 493.1K **Privately Held**
WEB: www.salonla.com
SIC: 7231 Hairdressers

(G-4474)
SALVATION ARMY
2250 Park Ave (45212-3200)
P.O. Box 12546 (45212-0546)
PHONE................859 255-5791
Fax: 513 351-8084

Cincinnati - Hamilton County

EMP: 82
SALES (corp-wide): 4.3B **Privately Held**
SIC: 8322 Individual/Family Services
HQ: The Salvation Army
440 W Nyack Rd Ofc
West Nyack NY 10994
845 620-7200

(G-4475)
SALVATION ARMY
114 East Central Pkwy (45202-7234)
P.O. Box 596 (45201-0596)
PHONE.................513 762-5600
Fax: 513 762-5605
Maj Kenneth Maynor, *Manager*
Ruth Clinton, *Manager*
Rodney Fudge, *Manager*
Vernon Venter, *Info Tech Mgr*
EMP: 100
SALES (corp-wide): 4.3B **Privately Held**
WEB: www.salvationarmyusa.org
SIC: 8399 8322 Advocacy group; individual & family services
HQ: The Salvation Army
440 W Nyack Rd Ofc
West Nyack NY 10994
845 620-7200

(G-4476)
SANDER WOODY FORD (PA)
235 W Mitchell Ave (45232-1907)
PHONE.................513 541-5586
Fax: 513 699-4827
William G Sander, *President*
James Mullen, *Vice Pres*
Thomas Paul Sander, *Treasurer*
Marlene Schum, *Manager*
EMP: 60 EST: 1962
SQ FT: 30,000
SALES (est): 7.4MM **Privately Held**
SIC: 7389 Personal service agents, brokers & bureaus; balloons, novelty & toy; building scale models

(G-4477)
SANTA MARIA COMMUNITY SVCS INC (PA)
617 Steiner St (45204-1327)
PHONE.................513 557-2720
Fax: 513 557-5375
H A Musser Jr, *President*
Blair Schoen, *Vice Pres*
Shari Patrick, *Controller*
Gladys Bell, *Volunteer Dir*
EMP: 40
SQ FT: 4,608
SALES: 4.3MM **Privately Held**
WEB: www.santamaria-cincy.org
SIC: 8322 Social service center

(G-4478)
SAP AMERICA INC
312 Walnut St Ste 1600 (45202-4038)
PHONE.................513 762-7630
Fax: 513 762-7602
Tim Mc Larkey, *Principal*
Ryan Carroll, *Sales Staff*
John Goetz, *Director*
EMP: 38
SALES (corp-wide): 27.6B **Privately Held**
WEB: www.sap.com
SIC: 7371 Computer software development
HQ: Sap America, Inc.
3999 West Chester Pike
Newtown Square PA 19073
610 661-1000

(G-4479)
SCARLET & GRAY CLEANING SVC
3247 Glenmore Ave Apt 1 (45211-6628)
PHONE.................513 661-4483
Fax: 513 389-3882
Mark Cappel, *President*
Chris Cappel, *District Mgr*
Perry Como, *CFO*
David Schell, *Manager*
EMP: 135
SQ FT: 1,800
SALES (est): 2.7MM **Privately Held**
SIC: 7349 Office cleaning or charring

(G-4480)
SCHERZINGER CORP
Also Called: Scherzinger Trmt & Pest Ctrl
10557 Medallion Dr (45241-3193)
PHONE.................513 531-7848
Steven Scherzinger, *President*
Hank Althaus, *E-Business*
EMP: 75
SQ FT: 13,500
SALES (est): 7.3MM **Privately Held**
WEB: www.stopzbugs.com
SIC: 7342 0782 Termite control; pest control in structures; lawn care services

(G-4481)
SCHIBI HEATING & COOLING CORP
Also Called: Comfort Distributors
5025 Hubble Rd (45247-3660)
PHONE.................513 385-3344
Fax: 513 385-5399
Kenneth A Schibi, *CEO*
Norb Kinross, *President*
Dale M Schibi, *Vice Pres*
Craig Hines, *Treasurer*
Mary Alexzander, *Admin Sec*
EMP: 25
SQ FT: 561
SALES (est): 4.8MM **Privately Held**
SIC: 1711 Heating & air conditioning contractors

(G-4482)
SCHIMPF GINOCCHIO MULLINS LPA
36 E 7th St Ste 2600 (45202-4452)
PHONE.................513 977-5570
Richard Schimpf, *President*
EMP: 25 EST: 1971
SALES (est): 1.9MM **Privately Held**
SIC: 8111 General practice attorney, lawyer

(G-4483)
SCHNEIDER HOME EQUIPMENT CO (PA)
7948 Pippin Rd (45239-4696)
PHONE.................513 522-1200
Fax: 513 728-3482
Michael Schneider, *President*
Stanley C Schneider, *Vice Pres*
Steven Scheider, *Treasurer*
Annette Littrell, *Controller*
EMP: 30 EST: 1936
SQ FT: 10,000
SALES (est): 5.4MM **Privately Held**
WEB: www.schneiderhomeequipment.com
SIC: 5211 5039 5031 Lumber & other building materials; door & window products; awnings; building materials, exterior; building materials, interior; doors & windows

(G-4484)
SCHOCH TILE & CARPET INC
5282 Crookshank Rd (45238-3376)
PHONE.................513 922-3466
Fax: 513 347-2315
Dennis Bley, *President*
Ruth Bley, *Corp Secy*
EMP: 40 EST: 1927
SQ FT: 5,000
SALES: 4.5MM **Privately Held**
WEB: www.schochtile.com
SIC: 1752 5713 Carpet laying; floor covering stores

(G-4485)
SCHWEITZER CONSTRUCTION CO
325 Clark Rd Ste 1 (45215-5549)
P.O. Box 15426 (45215-0426)
PHONE.................513 761-4980
Fax: 513 761-0418
Roy B Schweitzer, *President*
Marian Webbring, *Controller*
EMP: 25 EST: 1955
SQ FT: 10,000
SALES: 3.5MM **Privately Held**
SIC: 1629 1623 1611 Land preparation construction; trenching contractor; water main construction; sewer line construction; general contractor, highway & street construction

(G-4486)
SCROGGINSGREAR INC
Also Called: William X Greene Bus Advisor
200 Northland Blvd (45246-3604)
PHONE.................513 672-4281
Fax: 513 326-7640
Terry Grear, *President*
Mark D Scroggins, *Principal*
Robert C Scroggins, *Principal*
Luke R Trenz, *Principal*
Paul R Trenz, *Principal*
EMP: 105 EST: 1946
SQ FT: 36,000
SALES (est): 15.8MM **Privately Held**
WEB: www.scroggins.com
SIC: 8742 Business consultant

(G-4487)
SCS CONSTRUCTION SERVICES INC
2130 Western Ave (45214-1744)
PHONE.................513 929-0260
Jerry Back, *President*
Larry Back, *Vice Pres*
Charlie Hull, *CFO*
EMP: 45 EST: 2000
SQ FT: 8,000
SALES (est): 8.7MM **Privately Held**
SIC: 1542 3231 1761 3449 Commercial & office building, new construction; doors, glass; made from purchased glass; skylight installation; curtain walls for buildings, steel; metalware

(G-4488)
SECURITAS SEC SVCS USA INC
Automotive Services Division
655 Plum St 150 (45202-2339)
PHONE.................513 639-7615
Fax: 513 684-0635
Jason Bricking, *Business Mgr*
James Coleman, *Persnl Dir*
Chuck Baker, *Branch Mgr*
Joe Donaldson, *Manager*
Angel M Poynter, *Manager*
EMP: 100
SALES (corp-wide): 9.5B **Privately Held**
WEB: www.securitasinc.com
SIC: 7381 Detective services
HQ: Securitas Security Services Usa, Inc.
9 Campus Dr
Parsippany NJ 07054
973 267-5300

(G-4489)
SECURITY FENCE GROUP INC (PA)
4260 Dane Ave (45223-1855)
PHONE.................513 681-3700
Fax: 513 681-5487
Christine Frankenstein, *President*
Angela Case, *Corp Secy*
George Frankenstein, *Vice Pres*
EMP: 37
SQ FT: 140,000
SALES (est): 11.3MM **Privately Held**
SIC: 1611 1799 3446 5039 Guardrail construction, highways; highway & street sign installation; fence construction; architectural metalwork; wire fence, gates & accessories; general electrical contractor; traffic signals, electric

(G-4490)
SECURITY STORAGE CO INC
Also Called: Lewis and Michael SEC Stor
706 Oak St (45206-1616)
P.O. Box 6417 (45206-0417)
PHONE.................513 961-2700
Fax: 513 961-1298
Dave Lewis, *President*
David M Lewis, *President*
Seth Jaeger, *Sales Mgr*
Gordon Massey, *Sales Mgr*
EMP: 60
SALES (est): 4.3MM
SALES (corp-wide): 8MM **Privately Held**
SIC: 4214 4213 Household goods moving & storage, local; trucking, except local
PA: Lewis & Michael, Inc.
1827 Woodman Dr
Dayton OH 45420
937 252-6683

(G-4491)
SECURITY TITLE GUARANTEE AGCY
150 E 4th St Fl 4 (45202-4186)
PHONE.................513 651-3393
Fax: 513 241-8259
William Strausse, *CEO*
William V Strauss, *President*
EMP: 110
SALES (est): 2.3MM **Privately Held**
SIC: 6541 Title & trust companies

(G-4492)
SEILKOP INDUSTRIES INC (PA)
Also Called: Epcor Foundries
425 W North Bend Rd (45216-1731)
PHONE.................513 761-1035
Fax: 513 761-0368
Ken Seilkop, *President*
Dave Seilkop, *Vice Pres*
Paul Kiefer, *Plant Mgr*
Marilyn Seilkop, *Production*
Robin Vogel, *CFO*
EMP: 50
SQ FT: 35,000
SALES (est): 24.1MM **Privately Held**
WEB: www.epcorfoundry.com
SIC: 3363 3544 3553 3469 Aluminum die-castings; special dies & tools; pattern makers' machinery, woodworking; patterns on metal; industrial tool grinding

(G-4493)
SELECT SPECIALTY HOSPITAL
375 Dixmyth Ave Fl 15 (45220-2475)
PHONE.................513 862-4700
John Baird, *Branch Mgr*
Bonnie Eckart, *Director*
Joyce Benter, *Nursing Dir*
Bobbi Schmidt, *Nursing Dir*
Patty Grob, *Hlthcr Dir*
EMP: 100
SALES (corp-wide): 3.7B **Publicly Held**
SIC: 8062 General medical & surgical hospitals
HQ: Select Specialty Hospital-North Knoxville, Inc.
1901 W Clinch Ave Ste 602
Knoxville TN 37916
865 541-2615

(G-4494)
SELECTION MGT SYSTEMS INC
Also Called: Selection.com
155 Tri County Pkwy # 150 (45246-3240)
PHONE.................513 522-8764
Fax: 513 728-4420
John Hart II, *CEO*
James Boeddeker, *President*
Thomas A Coz, *Vice Pres*
Don Mayer, *Engineer*
Diana Nelson, *CFO*
EMP: 65
SQ FT: 3,500
SALES (est): 7.2MM **Privately Held**
WEB: www.selection.com
SIC: 8742 Personnel management consultant

(G-4495)
SENA WELLER ROHS WILLIAMS
Also Called: Reynolds, De Witt Securities
300 Main St Fl 4 (45202-4185)
PHONE.................513 241-6443
Fax: 513 241-9448
William T Sena, *Ch of Bd*
Edward Donohoe, *President*
Mercer Reynolds, *President*
J Grant Troja, *Exec VP*
William M Higgins, *Senior VP*
EMP: 35
SQ FT: 4,500
SALES (est): 7.2MM **Privately Held**
SIC: 6282 Investment counselors

(G-4496)
SENIOR LIFESTYLE EVERGREEN LTD
230 W Galbraith Rd (45215-5223)
PHONE.................513 948-2308
Sharon Cranston, *Marketing Staff*
Martha Ingram, *Administration*
Dan Suer, *Admin Sec*
EMP: 150

Cincinnati - Hamilton County (G-4497)   GEOGRAPHIC SECTION

SALES (est): 4.1MM **Privately Held**
SIC: 6513 Retirement hotel operation

(G-4497)
SENIOR STAR MANAGEMENT COMPANY
5435 Kenwood Rd (45227-1328)
PHONE..................513 271-1747
Terry Bigger, *Branch Mgr*
EMP: 323
SALES (corp-wide): 51.2MM **Privately Held**
SIC: 8322 Senior citizens' center or association
PA: Senior Star Management Company
1516 S Boston Ave Ste 301
Tulsa OK 74119
918 592-4400

(G-4498)
SERV-A-LITE PRODUCTS INC (DH)
Also Called: A-1 Best Locksmith
10590 Hamilton Ave (45231-1764)
PHONE..................309 762-7741
Thomas L Rowe, *President*
Mary J Rowe, *Treasurer*
William Perry, *Sales Executive*
▲ EMP: 216
SQ FT: 115,000
SALES (est): 89.8MM
SALES (corp-wide): 838.3MM **Privately Held**
WEB: www.servalite.com
SIC: 5072 Hardware
HQ: The Hillman Companies Inc
10590 Hamilton Ave
Cincinnati OH 45231
513 851-4900

(G-4499)
SERVALL ELECTRIC COMPANY INC
11697 Lebanon Rd (45241-2012)
P.O. Box 621078 (45262-1078)
PHONE..................513 771-5584
Ryan Pogozalski, *CEO*
Julianne Pogozalski, *Director*
EMP: 45 EST: 1954
SQ FT: 4,000
SALES (est): 5.4MM **Privately Held**
SIC: 1731 General electrical contractor

(G-4500)
SERVATII INC (PA)
Also Called: Servatii Pastry and Dealey
3888 Virginia Ave (45227-3410)
PHONE..................513 271-5040
Fax: 513 271-1521
Gregory Gottenbusch, *President*
Gary Gottenbusch, *Vice Pres*
Jeff Knight, *Manager*
EMP: 75 EST: 1963
SQ FT: 15,000
SALES (est): 35.4MM **Privately Held**
WEB: www.servati.com
SIC: 5461 5149 Bakeries; groceries & related products

(G-4501)
SERVICE SOLUTIONS GROUP LLC
Also Called: Certified Service Center
890 Redna Ter (45215-1111)
P.O. Box 640881 (45264-0881)
PHONE..................513 772-6600
Fax: 513 612-6600
Don Adams, *Manager*
Ben Tate, *Manager*
David Filson, *Supervisor*
Randy Perkins, *Supervisor*
EMP: 27
SALES (corp-wide): 2.9B **Privately Held**
WEB: www.servicesolutionsgroup.com
SIC: 7629 5046 Electronic equipment repair; commercial cooking & food service equipment
HQ: Service Solutions Group, Llc
800 Aviation Pkwy
Smyrna TN 37167
615 462-4000

(G-4502)
SETCO SALES COMPANY (HQ)
5880 Hillside Ave (45233-1599)
PHONE..................513 941-5110
Fax: 513 941-6913
Jeffrey J Clark, *President*
Jim Broz, *Vice Pres*
Joseph S Haas, *Vice Pres*
Scott Bubenhofer, *Plant Mgr*
George Rosen, *Senior Buyer*
▲ EMP: 80 EST: 1986
SQ FT: 55,000
SALES: 30MM
SALES (corp-wide): 302.2MM **Privately Held**
SIC: 3545 7694 Machine tool accessories; armature rewinding shops
PA: Holden Industries, Inc.
500 Lake Cook Rd Ste 400
Deerfield IL 60015
847 940-1500

(G-4503)
SEVEN HILLS OBGYN ASSOCIATES
6350 Glenway Ave Ste 205 (45211-6375)
PHONE..................513 922-6666
Robert Stephens, *President*
Eric Stamler, *Vice Pres*
Mabkaran Singh, *Treasurer*
EMP: 30
SALES (est): 1.1MM **Privately Held**
SIC: 8011 Obstetrician

(G-4504)
SEVEN HILLS WOMENS HEALTH CTRS (PA)
2060 Reading Rd Ste 150 (45202-1488)
PHONE..................513 721-3200
Joseph Sclafani, *President*
Jennifer Dunaway, *Principal*
Ambrose Puttmann, *Vice Pres*
Michael Karram, *Treasurer*
Holly Lasiter, *Med Doctor*
EMP: 120
SQ FT: 2,900
SALES (est): 13.6MM **Privately Held**
WEB: www.womenshealthcenters.com
SIC: 8011 Obstetrician; gynecologist

(G-4505)
SEVEN HLLS NEIGHBORHOOD HOUSES (PA)
Also Called: FRIENDLY STREET NEIGHBORHOOD
901 Findlay St (45214-2135)
PHONE..................513 407-5362
Fax: 513 632-7130
Leonard Small, *President*
EMP: 60
SQ FT: 7,500
SALES (est): 380.9K **Privately Held**
SIC: 8322 Neighborhood center

(G-4506)
SGK LLC
Also Called: Schawk
537 E Pete Rose Way # 100 (45202-3578)
PHONE..................513 569-9900
Fax: 513 487-5234
Rhett Warner, *Opers Mgr*
EMP: 65
SALES (corp-wide): 1.5B **Publicly Held**
WEB: www.schawk.com
SIC: 7311 Advertising agencies
HQ: Sgk, Llc
1600 Sherwin Ave
Des Plaines IL 60018
847 827-9494

(G-4507)
SGS NORTH AMERICA INC
Also Called: Automotive Div Of,
650 Northland Blvd # 600 (45240-3242)
PHONE..................513 674-7048
Mark Van Horck Vp, *Principal*
Robert Gapinski, *VP Sales*
EMP: 50
SALES (est): 1.7MM
SALES (corp-wide): 6.4B **Privately Held**
SIC: 7549 Inspection & diagnostic service, automotive
HQ: Sgs North America Inc.
201 Route 17
Rutherford NJ 07070
201 508-3000

(G-4508)
SHARED SERVICES LLC
5905 E Galbraith Rd # 8000 (45236-2378)
PHONE..................513 821-4278
Matthew Gockerman, *CFO*
EMP: 80 EST: 2014
SQ FT: 20,000
SALES: 3MM **Privately Held**
SIC: 8111 Legal services

(G-4509)
SHARONVILLE CAR WASH
11727 Lebanon Rd (45241-2038)
PHONE..................513 769-4219
Fax: 513 769-0439
O Doyle Barnett, *Owner*
Judith Barnett, *Co-Owner*
EMP: 37
SALES (est): 861.2K **Privately Held**
SIC: 7542 7532 Washing & polishing, automotive; lettering & painting services

(G-4510)
SHARONVILLE MTHDIST WKDAYS NRS
3751 Creek Rd (45241-2707)
PHONE..................513 563-8278
Barbara Pendelton, *Director*
EMP: 32
SALES (est): 372.7K **Privately Held**
WEB: www.pendleton.net
SIC: 8351 8661 Child day care services; Methodist Church

(G-4511)
SHEAKLEY CENTE
401 E Mcmillan St (45206-1922)
PHONE..................513 487-7106
Robert Mecum, *CEO*
Judith Oakman, *CFO*
EMP: 30 EST: 2015
SALES (est): 137.5K **Privately Held**
SIC: 8322 Youth center

(G-4512)
SHEAKLEY MED MGT RESOURCES LLC
Also Called: Plettner Hart Management
8212 Blue Ash Rd (45236-1942)
P.O. Box 465602 (45246)
PHONE..................513 891-1006
Fax: 513 793-1032
Ruth Hart, *Principal*
EMP: 60
SALES (est): 1.7MM **Privately Held**
SIC: 8721 8748 Billing & bookkeeping service; business consulting

(G-4513)
SHEAKLEY UNICOMP INC
1 Sheakley Way Ste 100 (45246-3774)
PHONE..................513 771-2277
Larry Sheakley, *CEO*
EMP: 175 EST: 1996
SQ FT: 23,000
SALES (est): 7.3MM **Privately Held**
SIC: 8742 Human resource consulting services

(G-4514)
SHEAKLEY-UNISERVICE INC
1 Sheakley Way Ste 100 (45246-3774)
PHONE..................513 771-2277
Fax: 513 326-4681
Larry A Sheakley, *CEO*
Thomas E Pappas Jr, *CFO*
John Tekulve, *Controller*
Marsh Godwin, *Accountant*
EMP: 120
SALES (est): 11.6MM **Privately Held**
SIC: 8742 8721 Human resource consulting services; payroll accounting service

(G-4515)
SHELTER HOUSE VOLUNTEER GROUP (PA)
Also Called: ALCOHOLIC DROP-IN CENTER
411 Gest St (45203-1730)
PHONE..................513 721-0643
Fax: 513 455-5045
Arlene Nolan, *CEO*
Don Gardner, *President*
John Wagers, *COO*
Melissa Merritt, *Treasurer*
Gail Holtmeier, *Director*
EMP: 45
SQ FT: 2,000
SALES: 6.3MM **Privately Held**
WEB: www.dropinn.org
SIC: 8322 Aid to families with dependent children (AFDC)

(G-4516)
SHERMAN FINANCIAL GROUP LLC
8600 Governors Hill Dr # 201 (45249-2515)
PHONE..................513 707-3000
Alison Wood, *Project Mgr*
Brian Gardner, *Branch Mgr*
Earl Combs, *Sr Project Mgr*
Jody Geier, *Manager*
Tim West, *Manager*
EMP: 30
SALES (est): 6.5MM
SALES (corp-wide): 152.4MM **Privately Held**
WEB: www.sfg.com
SIC: 6153 Buying of installment notes
PA: Sherman Financial Group Llc
200 Meeting St Ste 206
Charleston SC 29401
212 922-1616

(G-4517)
SHOPTECH INDUSTRIAL SFTWR
400 E Bus Way Ste 300 (45241)
PHONE..................513 985-9900
Paul Ventura, *VP Mktg*
EMP: 55
SALES (corp-wide): 30MM **Privately Held**
WEB: www.shoptech.com
SIC: 7371 Computer software development
PA: Shoptech Industrial Software Corp.
180 Glastonbury Blvd # 303
Glastonbury CT 06033
860 633-0740

(G-4518)
SHP LEADING DESIGN (PA)
312 Plum St Ste 700 (45202-2618)
PHONE..................513 381-2112
Gerald S Hammond, *President*
Kirk McMahon, *Business Mgr*
Lauren Dellabella, *Vice Pres*
Cindy Dingeldein, *Vice Pres*
Michael Dingeldein, *Vice Pres*
EMP: 80
SQ FT: 6,160
SALES (est): 11.5MM **Privately Held**
WEB: www.shp.com
SIC: 8742 8712 Planning consultant; architectural services

(G-4519)
SHRINERS HSPITALS FOR CHILDREN
3229 Burnet Ave (45229-3018)
PHONE..................513 872-6000
Mashayla Colwell, *Mktg Dir*
Ralph Lewkowicz, *Director*
Joellen McCarthy, *Director*
Vanessa Nicely, *Director*
Robert Kopcha, *Pharmacy Dir*
EMP: 320 **Privately Held**
SIC: 8069 Children's hospital
HQ: Shriners Hospitals For Children
12502 Usf Pine Dr
Tampa FL 33612
813 972-2250

(G-4520)
SIBCY CLINE INC
Also Called: Kenwood Office
8040 Montgomery Rd (45236-2903)
PHONE..................513 793-2121
Fax: 513 793-1826
Stephanie Busam, *Manager*
Pat Oneil, *Info Tech Dir*
EMP: 100
SALES (corp-wide): 2.1B **Privately Held**
WEB: www.sibcycline.com
SIC: 6531 Real estate agent, residential

▲ = Import ▼=Export
◆ =Import/Export

GEOGRAPHIC SECTION
Cincinnati - Hamilton County (G-4543)

PA: Sibcy Cline, Inc.
8044 Montgomery Rd # 300
Cincinnati OH 45236
513 984-4100

(G-4521)
SIBCY CLINE INC (PA)
Also Called: Sibcy Cline Realtors
8044 Montgomery Rd # 300 (45236-2922)
PHONE..................513 984-4100
Fax: 513 984-3733
Robert N Sibcy, *President*
Rob Fix, *General Mgr*
James Stosko, *General Mgr*
William D Borek, *Corp Secy*
Bill Borek, *COO*
EMP: 82 **EST:** 1952
SQ FT: 30,000
SALES: 2.1B **Privately Held**
WEB: www.sibcycline.com
SIC: 6531 Real estate agent, residential

(G-4522)
SIBCY CLINE INC
9979 Montgomery Rd (45242-5311)
PHONE..................513 793-2700
Fax: 513 793-0915
Sharon Watson, *VP Sales*
Tim Mahoney, *Manager*
EMP: 90
SALES (corp-wide): 2.1B **Privately Held**
WEB: www.sibcycline.com
SIC: 6531 Real estate brokers & agents
PA: Sibcy Cline, Inc.
8044 Montgomery Rd # 300
Cincinnati OH 45236
513 984-4100

(G-4523)
SIBCY CLINE INC
Also Called: Sibcy Cline Realtors
9250 Winton Rd (45231-3936)
PHONE..................513 931-7700
Fax: 513 931-5014
Beth Sehling, *Manager*
EMP: 50
SALES (corp-wide): 2.1B **Privately Held**
WEB: www.sibcycline.com
SIC: 6531 Real estate brokers & agents
PA: Sibcy Cline, Inc.
8044 Montgomery Rd # 300
Cincinnati OH 45236
513 984-4100

(G-4524)
SIBCY CLINE MORTGAGE SERVICES
8044 Montgomery Rd # 301 (45236-2922)
PHONE..................513 984-6776
Fax: 513 984-6863
Patricia Kuether, *President*
William Borek, *Corp Secy*
Tim Feller, *Loan Officer*
EMP: 30
SQ FT: 4,182
SALES (est): 1.9MM **Privately Held**
WEB: www.foxchapelneighborhoods.com
SIC: 6163 Mortgage brokers arranging for loans, using money of others

(G-4525)
SICKLE CELL AWAREMESS GRP
3458 Reading Rd (45229-3128)
PHONE..................513 281-4450
Fax: 513 872-8812
Donna Jones Stanley, *CEO*
Kenctra Mathio, *Technology*
EMP: 43
SQ FT: 2,736
SALES: 67.7K **Privately Held**
WEB: www.gcul.org
SIC: 8322 Individual & family services

(G-4526)
SIEMENS INDUSTRY INC
1310 Kemper Meadow Dr # 500 (45240-4127)
PHONE..................513 742-5590
A Riccella, *General Mgr*
Tony Riccella, *Sales/Mktg Mgr*
Bilel Bourkhis, *Financial Analy*
David Smith, *Accounts Exec*
Nacole Schmitz, *Mktg Coord*
EMP: 70

SALES (corp-wide): 97.7B **Privately Held**
WEB: www.sibt.com
SIC: 5063 Electrical apparatus & equipment
HQ: Siemens Industry, Inc.
100 Technology Dr
Alpharetta GA 30005
770 740-3000

(G-4527)
SIGMATEK SYSTEMS LLC (PA)
Also Called: Sigma T E K
1445 Kemper Meadow Dr (45240-1637)
PHONE..................513 674-0005
Fax: 513 674-0009
Ben Terreblanche, *CEO*
John Salisbury, *President*
Chris Cooper, *Principal*
Jandre Terreblanche, *Principal*
Jim Elmore, *Regional Mgr*
EMP: 65
SQ FT: 23,000
SALES (est): 22MM **Privately Held**
WEB: www.sigmanest.com
SIC: 7372 Prepackaged software

(G-4528)
SIGNAL OFFICE SUPPLY INC
Also Called: Sos2000
415 W Benson St (45215-3193)
PHONE..................513 821-2280
Fax: 513 821-2242
C G Thiergartner, *President*
Chris Thiergartner, *President*
Matt Thiergartner, *Vice Pres*
Tracey Bradley, *Accountant*
EMP: 40
SQ FT: 17,000
SALES (est): 18.7MM **Privately Held**
WEB: www.everybodysb2b.com
SIC: 5112 5021 Stationery & office supplies; office & public building furniture

(G-4529)
SIMS-LOHMAN INC (PA)
Also Called: Sims-Lohman Fine Kitchens Gran
6325 Este Ave (45232-1458)
PHONE..................513 651-3510
Steve Steinman, *CEO*
John Beiersdorfer, *President*
James Mitchell, *Opers Mgr*
Roger Llila, *Controller*
Julie Conners, *Accountant*
▲ **EMP:** 50
SQ FT: 153,000
SALES (est): 105.2MM **Privately Held**
WEB: www.moelleringindustries.com
SIC: 5031 2435 Kitchen cabinets; hardwood veneer & plywood

(G-4530)
SINCLAIR BROADCAST GROUP INC
Also Called: W S T R
1906 Highland Ave (45219-3104)
PHONE..................513 641-4400
Fax: 513 651-0704
Dale Thomas, *Accounts Exec*
Jon Lawhead, *Manager*
Mike Horsley, *Manager*
EMP: 40
SQ FT: 8,658
SALES (corp-wide): 2.7B **Publicly Held**
SIC: 4833 Television broadcasting stations
PA: Sinclair Broadcast Group, Inc.
10706 Beaver Dam Rd
Hunt Valley MD 21030
410 568-1500

(G-4531)
SINCLAIR BROADCAST GROUP INC
Also Called: Star 64
1906 Highland Ave (45219-3104)
PHONE..................513 641-4400
Jeannetta Gaunt, *Accountant*
Mark Dillon, *Manager*
EMP: 55
SALES (corp-wide): 2.7B **Publicly Held**
SIC: 4833 Television broadcasting stations
PA: Sinclair Broadcast Group, Inc.
10706 Beaver Dam Rd
Hunt Valley MD 21030
410 568-1500

(G-4532)
SISTERS OF LITTLE
Also Called: Archbishop Leibold Home
476 Riddle Rd (45220-2411)
PHONE..................513 281-8001
Fax: 513 281-4943
Motherjoseph Grenon, *Manager*
Neal Hafertepe, *Telecom Exec*
EMP: 125
SQ FT: 13,932
SALES (corp-wide): 3.5MM **Privately Held**
SIC: 8361 8052 Home for the aged; intermediate care facilities
PA: Little Sisters Of The Poor, Baltimore, Inc.
601 Maiden Choice Ln
Baltimore MD 21228
410 744-9367

(G-4533)
SIX CONTINENTS HOTELS INC
Also Called: Holiday Inn
3855 Hauck Rd (45241-1609)
PHONE..................513 563-8330
Ted Von Den Benken, *Branch Mgr*
EMP: 110
SALES (corp-wide): 1.7B **Privately Held**
WEB: www.sixcontinenthotels.com
SIC: 7011 5812 Hotels; eating places
HQ: Six Continents Hotels, Inc.
3 Ravinia Dr Ste 100
Atlanta GA 30346
770 604-2000

(G-4534)
SJN DATA CENTER LLC (PA)
Also Called: Encore Technologies
4620 Wesley Ave (45212-2234)
PHONE..................513 386-7871
Fax: 513 672-0050
John Burns, *President*
Jay Vollmer, *General Mgr*
Clay Stevens, *Vice Pres*
Suraj Dhungana, *Opers Mgr*
Laura Maynard, *Admin Asst*
EMP: 50
SQ FT: 90,000
SALES: 2.5MM **Privately Held**
WEB: www.elantech.net
SIC: 8748 7378 7379 Systems engineering consultant, ex. computer or professional; computer maintenance & repair;

(G-4535)
SJS PACKAGING GROUP INC
Also Called: EZ Pack
6545 Wiehe Rd (45237-4217)
PHONE..................513 841-1351
Barry Schwartz, *President*
Terry Junker, *Vice Pres*
Kim Sherman, *Accountant*
EMP: 26
SALES: 4MM **Privately Held**
SIC: 5199 Packaging materials

(G-4536)
SK RIGGING CO INC
11515 Rockfield Ct (45241-1918)
P.O. Box 62092 (45262-0092)
PHONE..................513 771-7766
Fax: 513 782-3666
Alan Schneider, *President*
Mike Schneider, *Vice Pres*
Bradley Schneider, *Info Tech Mgr*
▲ **EMP:** 25
SQ FT: 50,000
SALES (est): 3.8MM **Privately Held**
WEB: www.skrigging.com
SIC: 1796 Machine moving & rigging

(G-4537)
SKALLYS OLD WORLD BAKERY INC
Also Called: Skally's Restaurant
1933 W Galbraith Rd (45239-4767)
PHONE..................513 931-1411
Fax: 513 931-3560
Odette Skally, *President*
Drew Skally, *Vice Pres*
Jennifer Skally, *Vice Pres*
EMP: 45 **EST:** 1977
SQ FT: 40,000
SALES (est): 13.9MM **Privately Held**
SIC: 5149 5812 Bakery products; eating places

(G-4538)
SKANSKA USA BUILDING INC
201 E 5th St Ste 2020 (45202-4164)
PHONE..................513 421-0083
Craig Eckert, *Branch Mgr*
EMP: 29
SALES (corp-wide): 15.6B **Privately Held**
SIC: 1541 1542 8741 Industrial buildings & warehouses; nonresidential construction; management services
HQ: Skanska Usa Building Inc.
389 Interpace Pkwy Ste 5
Parsippany NJ 07054
973 753-3500

(G-4539)
SKY ZONE INDOOR TRAMPOLINE PK
Also Called: Sky Zone Indoor Trampoline Pk
11745 Commons Dr (45246-2551)
PHONE..................614 302-6093
EMP: 75
SALES (est): 963.6K **Privately Held**
SIC: 7999 Trampoline operation

(G-4540)
SL WELLSPRING LLC
Also Called: Wellspring Health Care
8000 Evergreen Ridge Dr (45215-5750)
PHONE..................513 948-2339
Peggy Macgregor, *Human Res Dir*
Janet Fairclough, *Office Mgr*
Lory J Ward, *President*
EMP: 80
SQ FT: 70,000
SALES (est): 11.5MM
SALES (corp-wide): 342.7MM **Privately Held**
SIC: 5051 Metals service centers & offices
PA: Senior Lifestyle Corporation
303 E Wacker Dr Ste 2400
Chicago IL 60601
312 673-4333

(G-4541)
SMITH ROLFES & SKAZDAHL LPA (PA)
Also Called: Smith, Matthew J Co Lpa
600 Vine St Ste 2600 (45202-1170)
PHONE..................513 579-0080
Fax: 513 579-0222
Matthew J Smith, *President*
Diana Reynard, *President*
Bret Dubbert, *Managing Prtnr*
Rebecca Johnson, *Counsel*
Tracy Cavender, *Legal Staff*
EMP: 43
SQ FT: 2,000
SALES (est): 6.6MM **Privately Held**
SIC: 8111 General practice attorney, lawyer

(G-4542)
SMITHFIELD PACKAGED MEATS CORP
801 E Kemper Rd (45246-2515)
PHONE..................513 782-3805
Steve Shannon, *Mfg Staff*
Jerry McAleece, *CFO*
Amy Dykstra, *Human Res Dir*
Bill McGaffee, *Human Res Dir*
Tarissa Morgan, *HR Admin*
EMP: 350 **Privately Held**
WEB: www.johnmorrell.com
SIC: 5147 Meats, cured or smoked
HQ: Smithfield Packaged Meats Corp
805 E Kemper Rd
Cincinnati OH 45246
513 782-3800

(G-4543)
SMYTH AUTOMOTIVE INC (PA)
4275 Mt Carmel Tobasco Rd (45244-2319)
PHONE..................513 528-2800
Fax: 513 528-6057
Joseph M Smyth, *President*
Lynette Smithson, *Corp Secy*
Jim Smyth, *Vice Pres*
Holly Leitz, *Human Res Dir*
Natalie Hansman, *Mktg Dir*
EMP: 87 **EST:** 1963
SQ FT: 23,000

Cincinnati - Hamilton County (G-4544)   GEOGRAPHIC SECTION

SALES (est): 160.2MM Privately Held
WEB: www.smythautomotive.com
SIC: 5013 5531 Automotive supplies & parts; automotive parts

(G-4544)
SMYTH AUTOMOTIVE INC
4271 Mt Carmel Tobasco Rd (45244-2319)
PHONE.................513 528-0061
Fax: 513 528-4561
Lisa Gallimore, *Human Res Mgr*
Rita Summers, *Manager*
EMP: 77
SALES (corp-wide): 160.2MM Privately Held
WEB: www.smythautomotive.com
SIC: 5013 5531 Automotive supplies & parts; automotive parts
PA: Smyth Automotive, Inc.
    4275 Mt Carmel Tobasco Rd
    Cincinnati OH 45244
    513 528-2800

(G-4545)
SNAPBLOX HOSTED SOLUTIONS LLC
131 Eight Mile Rd (45255-4612)
PHONE.................866 524-7707
Michael Earls, *Mng Member*
EMP: 30
SALES: 300K Privately Held
SIC: 7379 7389 Computer related consulting services;

(G-4546)
SNOWS LAKESIDE TAVERN
4344 Dry Ridge Rd (45252-1918)
PHONE.................513 954-5626
Mark Fehring, *Owner*
EMP: 35
SQ FT: 1,000
SALES (est): 200.8K Privately Held
SIC: 5813 7999 Tavern (drinking places); fishing lakes & piers, operation

(G-4547)
SOCIETY OF ST VINCENT DE PAUL
1125 Bank St (45214-2130)
PHONE.................513 421-2273
Tim Heile, *Manager*
Tim Hiele, *Director*
EMP: 50
SALES (corp-wide): 13.9MM Privately Held
SIC: 8322 Individual & family services
PA: Society Of St. Vincent De Paul Archdiocesan Council Of St. Louis
    1310 Papin St Ste 104
    Saint Louis MO 63103
    314 881-6000

(G-4548)
SOCIETY OF THE TRANSFIGURATION (PA)
Also Called: Sisters of The Transfiguration
555 Albion Ave (45246-4649)
PHONE.................513 771-7462
Fax: 513 771-2292
Sister Ann, *Principal*
Kimberly Knight, *Pastor*
Sharon Snavely, *Director*
Donna Day, *Tech/Comp Coord*
Angela Bell, *Teacher*
EMP: 48
SALES (est): 4.6MM Privately Held
SIC: 8661 8211 8059 7999 Religious organizations; boarding school; nursing home, except skilled & intermediate care facility; recreation center

(G-4549)
SOFCO ERECTORS INC (PA)
10360 Wayne Ave (45215-1129)
PHONE.................513 771-1600
John Hesford, *President*
John C Hesford, *President*
Daniel Powell, *Vice Pres*
Jim Frondorf, *Manager*
Caroline Perkins, *Info Tech Mgr*
EMP: 218
SQ FT: 5,000
SALES (est): 22.4MM Privately Held
SIC: 1791 Iron work, structural

(G-4550)
SOFTWARE INFO SYSTEMS LLC
8805 Governors Hill Dr # 210 (45249-3314)
PHONE.................513 791-7777
Steve Sigg, *Branch Mgr*
Jarrod Bradford, *Technology*
EMP: 26
SALES (corp-wide): 173.1MM Privately Held
SIC: 5045 Computer software
PA: Software Information Systems, Llc
    165 Barr St
    Lexington KY 40507
    859 977-4747

(G-4551)
SOFTWARE MANAGEMENT GROUP
1128 Main St Fl 6 (45202-7276)
PHONE.................513 618-2165
Dave Nolnan, *President*
EMP: 25
SALES (est): 878.2K Privately Held
SIC: 7372 Prepackaged software

(G-4552)
SOUTHWEST FINANCIAL SVCS LTD
537 E Pete Rose Way Ste 3 (45202-3567)
PHONE.................513 621-6699
Fax: 513 621-2065
Gregory Schroeder, *President*
Barbara Schroeder, *Vice Pres*
Diane Sweeney, *Human Res Dir*
Nina Bedel, *Sales Mgr*
Benita Dottery, *Accounts Mgr*
EMP: 160
SQ FT: 35,000
SALES (est): 46.1MM Privately Held
WEB: www.sfsltd.com
SIC: 6211 Mortgages, buying & selling

(G-4553)
SOUTHWEST OH TRANS AUTH (PA)
Also Called: S O R T A
602 Main St Ste 1100 (45202-2549)
PHONE.................513 621-4455
Terry Garcia Cruz, *CEO*
Dwight Ferrell, *General Mgr*
William L Mallory Sr, *Vice Chairman*
Mike Davenport, *Foreman/Supr*
Philip Lind, *Opers Staff*
EMP: 865 EST: 1880
SQ FT: 18,000
SALES (est): 66.4MM Privately Held
WEB: www.go-metro.com
SIC: 4111 Bus line operations

(G-4554)
SOUTHWEST OH TRANS AUTH
Also Called: Mreto
1401 Bank St (45214-1737)
PHONE.................513 632-7511
Bill Speraul, *Manager*
EMP: 700
SALES (est): 17.2MM
SALES (corp-wide): 66.4MM Privately Held
SIC: 4111 Bus line operations
PA: Southwest Ohio Regional Transit Authority
    602 Main St Ste 1100
    Cincinnati OH 45202
    513 621-4455

(G-4555)
SOUTHWESTERN PCF SPCLTY FIN INC (HQ)
7755 Montgomery Rd # 400 (45236-4291)
P.O. Box 36382 (45236-0382)
PHONE.................513 336-7735
A David Davis, *President*
EMP: 25
SALES (est): 22.8MM
SALES (corp-wide): 664.6MM Privately Held
SIC: 6099 Check cashing agencies
PA: Cng Financial Corporation
    7755 Montgomery Rd # 400
    Cincinnati OH 45236
    513 336-7735

(G-4556)
SPARTANNASH COMPANY
1 Sheakley Way Ste 160 (45246-3779)
PHONE.................513 793-6300
Steve Waliga, *Purch Agent*
John Dietrich, *Branch Mgr*
Greg Neff, *Manager*
Jim Zedeker, *Manager*
EMP: 94
SALES (corp-wide): 8.1B Publicly Held
SIC: 5141 5148 5142 5147 Food brokers; fruits, fresh; vegetables, fresh; packaged frozen goods; meats, fresh; meats, cured or smoked; supermarkets, chain
PA: Spartannash Company
    850 76th St Sw
    Byron Center MI 49315
    616 878-2000

(G-4557)
SPECIALIZED PHARMACY SVCS LLC (DH)
Also Called: Specialized Pharmacy Svcs - N
201 E 4th St Ste 900 (45202-4160)
PHONE.................513 719-2600
John Workman, *CEO*
Anita Holland, *General Mgr*
Gary W Kadlec, *Vice Pres*
Cecilia Temple, *Project Mgr*
David W Froesel Jr, *CFO*
EMP: 29 EST: 1977
SQ FT: 28,000
SALES (est): 29.7MM
SALES (corp-wide): 184.7B Publicly Held
WEB: www.spsomnicare.com
SIC: 5122 Pharmaceuticals; druggists' sundries

(G-4558)
SPECIALTY LOGISTICS INC (PA)
Also Called: Vogt Warehouse
1440 W 8th St (45203-1009)
PHONE.................513 421-2041
Fax: 513 421-2507
Stephen P Hayward, *President*
Thomas Hayward, *Warehouse Mgr*
EMP: 33
SALES (est): 6.5MM Privately Held
SIC: 4789 Freight car loading & unloading

(G-4559)
SPECTRUM MGT HOLDG CO LLC
3290 Westbourne Dr (45248-5107)
PHONE.................513 469-1112
Fax: 513 451-1547
EMP: 87
SALES (corp-wide): 41.5B Publicly Held
SIC: 4841 Cable television services
HQ: Spectrum Management Holding Company, Llc
    400 Atlantic St
    Stamford CT 06901
    203 905-7801

(G-4560)
SPECTRUM NETWORKS INC
9145 Governors Way (45249-2037)
PHONE.................513 697-2000
Fax: 513 697-2001
Troy McCracken, *CEO*
EMP: 29
SALES (est): 4.3MM Privately Held
SIC: 4813 5999 7389 Telephone communication, except radio; telephone equipment & systems; telephone services

(G-4561)
SPORTS THERAPY INC
11729 Springfield Pike (45246-2311)
PHONE.................513 671-5841
Kathleen Novicki, *President*
Eric Novicki, *Director*
EMP: 40
SALES (est): 1.7MM Privately Held
SIC: 8049 Physical therapist

(G-4562)
SPORTS THERAPY INC
4600 Smith Rd Rear Rear (45212-2784)
PHONE.................513 531-1698
Fax: 513 531-4645
Eric Novici, *President*
EMP: 45
SALES (est): 485.3K Privately Held
WEB: www.sportstherapyinc.com
SIC: 8049 Physical therapist

(G-4563)
SPRING GROVE CMTRY & ARBORETUM (PA)
4521 Spring Grove Ave (45232-1954)
PHONE.................513 681-7526
Fax: 513 853-6802
Gary M Freytag, *President*
Jeannette Humphries, *Purch Agent*
David Kelly, *CFO*
David P Kelley, *Financial Exec*
Tracey Brumley, *Manager*
EMP: 75
SALES: 16.3MM Privately Held
WEB: www.springgrove.com
SIC: 6553 Cemetery association; mausoleum operation

(G-4564)
SPRING GROVE FUNERAL HOMES INC
4389 Spring Grove Ave (45223-1862)
PHONE.................513 681-7526
Gary Freytag, *CEO*
Jerry Wantz, *VP Opers*
Samantha Brown, *Director*
EMP: 120 EST: 1999
SQ FT: 40,000
SALES (est): 4.8MM Privately Held
SIC: 7261 Funeral home

(G-4565)
SPRING GROVE RSRCE RCOVERY INC
4879 Spring Grove Ave (45232-1938)
PHONE.................513 681-6242
Alan McKin, *CEO*
Mike Jana, *General Mgr*
John P Lawton, *Senior VP*
Eugene Cookson, *Vice Pres*
Stephen E Dovell, *Vice Pres*
EMP: 70
SQ FT: 50,000
SALES (est): 16.5MM
SALES (corp-wide): 2.9B Publicly Held
SIC: 4953 4212 Sanitary landfill operation; local trucking, without storage
PA: Clean Harbors, Inc.
    42 Longwater Dr
    Norwell MA 02061
    781 792-5000

(G-4566)
SPRINGDALE FAMILY MEDICINE PC
Also Called: Webb, Barry W
212 W Sharon Rd (45246-4137)
PHONE.................513 771-7213
Fax: 513 771-4356
Thomas Todd, *President*
Dr Douglas L Hancher, *Corp Secy*
Dr Barry Webb, *Vice Pres*
Michael Todd, *Med Doctor*
EMP: 30
SALES (est): 1.7MM Privately Held
SIC: 8011 General & family practice, physician/surgeon

(G-4567)
SPRINGDALE ICE CREAM BEVERAGE
11801 Chesterdale Rd (45246-3407)
PHONE.................513 699-4984
Fax: 513 671-2864
EMP: 35
SALES (est): 5.8MM Privately Held
SIC: 2024 0241 Mfg Ice Cream/Frozen Desert Dairy Farm

(G-4568)
SPRINGDOT INC
2611 Colerain Ave (45214-1711)
PHONE.................513 542-4000
Jeff Deutsch, *Ch of Bd*
Josh Deutsch, *President*
John Brenner, *Vice Pres*
Craig Miller, *Vice Pres*
Bill Fultz, *Traffic Mgr*
EMP: 65 EST: 1904
SQ FT: 70,000

SALES (est): 15MM **Privately Held**
WEB: www.springdot.com
SIC: 2752 4899 2759 2675 Commercial printing, offset; color lithography; data communication services; commercial printing; die-cut paper & board; packaging paper & plastics film, coated & laminated

(G-4569)
SQUIRE PATTON BOGGS (US) LLP
221 E 4th St Ste 2900 (45202-4095)
PHONE...................513 361-1200
Scott Kane, *Managing Prtnr*
Colter Paulson, *Sr Associate*
Elliot M Smith, *Sr Associate*
Andrew M Simon, *Associate*
EMP: 30
SALES (corp-wide): 365MM **Privately Held**
WEB: www.squiresandersdempsey.com
SIC: 8111 Legal services
PA: Squire Patton Boggs (Us) Llp
4900 Key Tower 127 Pub Sq
Cleveland OH 44114
216 479-8500

(G-4570)
SREE HOTELS LLC
Also Called: Hampton Inn
617 Vine St Ste A (45202-2418)
PHONE...................513 354-2430
Ted Vondenbenken, *General Mgr*
EMP: 50
SALES (corp-wide): 7.8MM **Privately Held**
SIC: 7011 Hotels
PA: Sree Hotels, L.L.C.
5113 Piper Station Dr # 300
Charlotte NC 28277
704 364-6008

(G-4571)
ST ALOYSIUS SERVICES INC
4721 Reading Rd (45237-6107)
PHONE...................513 482-1745
Joan Pumbelison, *COO*
Rosemary Oglesby-Henry, *Supervisor*
EMP: 35
SALES: 41.5K **Privately Held**
SIC: 8093 Mental health clinic, outpatient

(G-4572)
ST JOSEPH INFANT MATERNITY HM
Also Called: ST JOSEPH'S HOME
10722 Wyscarver Rd (45241-3061)
PHONE...................513 563-2520
Fax: 513 563-1958
Lynn Heper, *Vice Pres*
Patricia Vonderahe, *Vice Pres*
Daniel Connors, *VP Opers*
Debbie Kaegi, *Safety Dir*
Drew Curtis, *Manager*
EMP: 136
SALES: 9.4MM **Privately Held**
WEB: www.stjosephshome.com
SIC: 8052 8322 Home for the mentally retarded, with health care; individual & family services

(G-4573)
STAFFMARK HOLDINGS INC (HQ)
201 E 4th St Ste 800 (45202-4248)
PHONE...................513 651-1111
Geno A Cutolo, *CEO*
Anthony Fanzo, *Managing Dir*
Hitoshi Motohara, *Chairman*
Patricia Cochran, *Business Mgr*
Yuichiro Miura, *COO*
EMP: 75
SALES (est): 175.3MM
SALES (corp-wide): 16.1B **Privately Held**
WEB: www.cbscompanies.com
SIC: 7361 7363 Placement agencies; executive placement; labor resource services; temporary help service
PA: Recruit Holdings Co.,Ltd.
1-9-2, Marunouchi
Chiyoda-Ku TKY 100-0
368 351-111

(G-4574)
STAFFMARK INVESTMENT LLC (DH)
201 E 4th St Ste 800 (45202-4248)
PHONE...................513 651-3600
W David Bartholomew, *CEO*
Clay Bullock, *President*
Hitoshi Motohara, *Principal*
Heather Healy, *Area Mgr*
Kenny Berkemeyer, *Vice Pres*
EMP: 120
SALES (est): 175.2MM
SALES (corp-wide): 16.1B **Privately Held**
WEB: www.staffmark.com
SIC: 7361 Labor contractors (employment agency)
HQ: Staffmark Holdings, Inc.
201 E 4th St Ste 800
Cincinnati OH 45202
513 651-1111

(G-4575)
STAGE WORKS
7800 Perry St (45231-3426)
P.O. Box 31227 (45231-0227)
PHONE...................513 522-3118
Tony Peters, *Partner*
Kevin Prows, *Partner*
EMP: 25 **EST:** 1994
SALES (est): 1.2MM **Privately Held**
SIC: 7363 Labor resource services

(G-4576)
STAGNARO SABA PATTERSON CO LPA (PA)
2623 Erie Ave (45208-2001)
PHONE...................513 533-2700
Fax: 513 533-2999
Paul Saba, *Managing Prtnr*
Christopher P Finney, *Mng Member*
William J Patterson,
Paul T Saba,
Peter A Saba,
EMP: 39
SALES (est): 3.9MM **Privately Held**
SIC: 8111 8742 General practice law office; real estate law; compensation & benefits planning consultant

(G-4577)
STAGNARO SABA PATTERSON CO LPA
7373 Beechmont Ave (45230-4100)
PHONE...................513 533-2700
William Patterson, *Branch Mgr*
EMP: 30 **Privately Held**
SIC: 8111 General practice law office
PA: Stagnaro, Saba & Patterson Co., L.P.A
2623 Erie Ave
Cincinnati OH 45208

(G-4578)
STAND ENERGY CORPORATION
1077 Celestial St Ste 110 (45202-1629)
PHONE...................513 621-1113
Fax: 513 621-3773
Judith Phillips, *President*
Matth Toebben, *Chairman*
Lawrence Freeman, *Exec VP*
Carla Piening, *Vice Pres*
Robert Embry, *CFO*
EMP: 34
SQ FT: 4,580
SALES: 110.3MM **Privately Held**
SIC: 4924 Natural gas distribution

(G-4579)
STANDARD TEXTILE CO INC (PA)
Also Called: Pridecraft Enterprises
1 Knollcrest Dr (45237-1608)
P.O. Box 371805 (45222-1805)
PHONE...................513 761-9255
Fax: 513 761-0467
Gary Heiman, *President*
Santa J Ono Lauds Gov John Kas, *President*
Norman Frankel, *Senior VP*
Kim Heiman, *Senior VP*
Steve Tracey, *Senior VP*
◆ **EMP:** 300
SQ FT: 150,000

SALES (est): 912.3MM **Privately Held**
WEB: www.standardtextile.com
SIC: 2389 2326 2337 2211 Hospital gowns; medical & hospital uniforms, men's; uniforms, except athletic: women's, misses' & juniors'; bandages, gauzes & surgical fabrics, cotton; surgical fabrics, cotton; draperies, plastic & textile: from purchased materials; uniforms, men's & boys'

(G-4580)
STANDEX INTERNATIONAL CORP
Also Called: Standex Electronics
4538 Camberwell Rd (45209-1155)
PHONE...................513 871-3777
Matt Crost, *Plant Mgr*
Stacy Shinkle, *Buyer*
Mark Faulhaber, *Engineer*
Kehinde Omolayo, *Engineer*
Tom Pierce, *Engineer*
EMP: 28
SALES (corp-wide): 755.2MM **Publicly Held**
SIC: 1446 Molding sand mining
PA: Standex International Corporation
11 Keewaydin Dr Ste 300
Salem NH 03079
603 893-9701

(G-4581)
STANDRDAERO COMPONENT SVCS INC
11550 Mosteller Rd (45241-1832)
PHONE...................513 618-9588
Fax: 513 878-2600
Russell Ford, *CEO*
Kim Olson, *Senior VP*
Rick Stine, *Senior VP*
Brent Fawkes, *Vice Pres*
Clinton Kent, *Vice Pres*
EMP: 700
SQ FT: 236,000
SALES (est): 48.9MM **Privately Held**
WEB: www.tssaviation.com
SIC: 7699 Aviation propeller & blade repair
HQ: Standard Aero, Inc.
3523 General Hudnell Dr
San Antonio TX 78226
210 704-1100

(G-4582)
STANLEY STEEMER INTL INC
Also Called: Stanley Steemer Carpet Clr 07
637 Redna Ter (45215-1108)
PHONE...................513 771-0213
Fax: 513 755-6265
Aaron Huffman, *Opers-Prdtn-Mfg*
EMP: 30
SALES (corp-wide): 241.9MM **Privately Held**
WEB: www.stanley-steemer.com
SIC: 7217 Carpet & furniture cleaning on location
PA: Stanley Steemer International, Inc.
5800 Innovation Dr
Dublin OH 43016
614 764-2007

(G-4583)
STANTEC CONSULTING SVCS INC
11687 Lebanon Rd (45241-2012)
PHONE...................513 842-8200
David Hayson, *Project Engr*
Christina Han, *Marketing Staff*
Lori Van Dermark, *Marketing Staff*
John Montgomery, *Branch Mgr*
Reshma Panjanani, *Information Mgr*
EMP: 73
SALES (corp-wide): 3.1B **Privately Held**
WEB: www.fmsm.com
SIC: 8712 8711 Architectural services; engineering services
HQ: Stantec Consulting Services Inc.
475 5th Ave Fl 12
New York NY 10017
212 352-5160

(G-4584)
STAR ONE HOLDINGS INC
8118 Beechmont Ave (45255-5112)
PHONE...................513 474-9100
Fax: 513 388-4543
Sandi Cornett, *Sales Associate*

Karen Meyer, *Manager*
Kathy Buckley, *Real Est Agnt*
C C Dacey, *Real Est Agnt*
Sara Goldsmith, *Real Est Agnt*
EMP: 40
SALES (corp-wide): 8.8MM **Privately Held**
WEB: www.nkybuilders.com
SIC: 6531 Real estate agent, residential
PA: Star One Holdings, Inc.
3895 Woodridge Blvd
Fairfield OH 45014
513 870-9100

(G-4585)
STAR ONE HOLDINGS INC
9722 Montgomery Rd (45242-7208)
PHONE...................513 300-6663
Fax: 513 791-2923
Stephen R Fisk, *Sales Associate*
Tom Richardson, *Sales Executive*
Karen Weber, *Manager*
David Horwitz, *Manager*
Tina M Lay, *Real Est Agnt*
EMP: 30
SQ FT: 9,402
SALES (corp-wide): 8.8MM **Privately Held**
WEB: www.nkybuilders.com
SIC: 6531 Real estate brokers & agents
PA: Star One Holdings, Inc.
3895 Woodridge Blvd
Fairfield OH 45014
513 870-9100

(G-4586)
STARFORCE NATIONAL CORPORATION
455 Delta Ave Ste 410 (45226-1178)
P.O. Box 21600, Georgetown (45121-0600)
PHONE...................513 979-3600
Frank Mayfield Jr, *Ch of Bd*
Judith Mc Cullough, *Corp Secy*
Lauren Gibson, *Vice Pres*
EMP: 110 **EST:** 2001
SQ FT: 2,000
SALES (est): 6MM **Privately Held**
SIC: 4142 Bus charter service, except local

(G-4587)
STAUTBERG FAMILY LLC
3871 Deerpath Ln (45248-1343)
PHONE...................513 941-5070
Timothy Stautberg, *Mng Member*
EMP: 40
SALES (est): 1.3MM **Privately Held**
SIC: 6513 Apartment building operators

(G-4588)
STEELSUMMIT HOLDINGS INC
Steelsummit Ohio
11150 Southland Rd (45240-3202)
PHONE...................513 825-8550
Arnie Killberw, *Principal*
Todd Rollins, *COO*
Amy Alvarez, *Marketing Staff*
EMP: 38
SALES (corp-wide): 35.1B **Privately Held**
SIC: 5051 Steel
HQ: Steelsummit Holdings, Inc.
1718 Jp Hennessy Dr
La Vergne TN 37086
615 641-3300

(G-4589)
STERLING BUYING GROUP LLC
3802 Ford Cir (45227-3403)
PHONE...................513 564-9000
Paul L Hunter, *President*
Jill Barnett, *Vice Pres*
George Mahowald, *Vice Pres*
Howard Cooper, *Mng Member*
Kevin Schifrin,
EMP: 36
SALES (est): 3.2MM
SALES (corp-wide): 115.7MM **Privately Held**
SIC: 7389 7373 Financial services; systems integration services
HQ: Sterling Payment Technologies, Llc
1111 N West Shore Blvd # 500
Tampa FL 33607
813 637-9696

Cincinnati - Hamilton County (G-4590)

(G-4590)
STERLING MEDICAL ASSOCIATES
411 Oak St (45219-2504)
PHONE.................513 984-1800
Richard Blatt, *CEO*
Edwin Blatt, *President*
Brandon Blatt, *Treasurer*
Tammy Hinkle, *Manager*
Dr Ethel Blatt, *Admin Sec*
EMP: 70 **EST:** 1963
SQ FT: 15,000
SALES (est): 220.3K
SALES (corp-wide): 3.7MM **Privately Held**
SIC: 8099 Medical services organization
PA: Sterling Medical Corporation
411 Oak St
Cincinnati OH 45219
513 984-1800

(G-4591)
STERLING MEDICAL CORPORATION
411 Oak St (45219-2504)
PHONE.................513 984-1800
Kevin Korb, *Branch Mgr*
EMP: 99
SALES (corp-wide): 3.7MM **Privately Held**
SIC: 8741 Hospital management; nursing & personal care facility management
PA: Sterling Medical Corporation
411 Oak St
Cincinnati OH 45219
513 984-1800

(G-4592)
STERLING MEDICAL CORPORATION (PA)
Also Called: Sterling Med Staffing Group
411 Oak St (45219-2504)
PHONE.................513 984-1800
Fax: 513 984-4909
Richard Blatt, *CEO*
Edwin Blatt, *President*
Brandon Blatt, *Vice Pres*
Deborah Aldridge, *Site Mgr*
Renee Seiler, *Site Mgr*
EMP: 119
SQ FT: 15,000
SALES: 3.7MM **Privately Held**
SIC: 8741 Management services; administrative management

(G-4593)
STEVEN SCHAEFER ASSOCIATES INC (PA)
10411 Medallion Dr # 121 (45241-4817)
PHONE.................513 542-3300
Steven E Schaefer, *Ch of Bd*
James Miller, *President*
Howard Harrison, *Vice Pres*
Ryan Konst, *Vice Pres*
Ed Schwieter, *Vice Pres*
EMP: 56
SQ FT: 13,000
SALES (est): 9.7MM **Privately Held**
WEB: www.ssastructural.com
SIC: 8711 Structural engineering

(G-4594)
STRAND ASSOCIATES INC
615 Elsinore Pl Ste 320 (45202-1475)
PHONE.................513 861-5600
Fax: 513 861-5601
Ted Richards, *CEO*
EMP: 36
SALES (corp-wide): 55.2MM **Privately Held**
SIC: 8711 Professional engineer
PA: Strand Associates, Inc.
910 W Wingra Dr
Madison WI 53715
608 251-4843

(G-4595)
STRATEGIC DATA SYSTEMS INC
11260 Chester Rd Ste 425 (45246-4040)
PHONE.................513 772-3374
Fax: 937 886-9407
David Pledger, *President*
Keith Stafford, *Managing Prtnr*
John Barrow, *Sr Consultant*

Keith Callis, *Sr Consultant*
EMP: 25
SQ FT: 1,500
SALES (est): 2.4MM **Privately Held**
WEB: www.sds-consulting.com
SIC: 7371 Custom computer programming services

(G-4596)
STS OPERATING INC
Also Called: Sunsource Pabco
5750 Hillside Ave (45233-1508)
PHONE.................513 941-6200
Fax: 513 941-1630
Mark Jira, *Manager*
Mark Dreifke, *Director*
EMP: 25
SALES (corp-wide): 740.9MM **Privately Held**
WEB: www.sun-source.com
SIC: 5084 Hydraulic systems equipment & supplies
PA: Sts Operating, Inc.
2301 W Windsor Ct
Addison IL 60101
630 317-2700

(G-4597)
STUDENT LOAN STRATEGIES LLC
Also Called: Innovative Studnt Ln Solutions
151 W 4th St Frnt (45202-0026)
PHONE.................513 645-5400
Stuart Smylie, *CEO*
Karen Fessler, *Corp Comm Staff*
Meghan Davis, *Manager*
Melissa Bedwell, *Advisor*
Marc Darby, *Advisor*
EMP: 30
SALES (est): 1.5MM **Privately Held**
SIC: 6141 Personal credit institutions

(G-4598)
SUMMITHOTEL ◯
5345 Medpace Way (45227-1543)
PHONE.................513 527-9900
Bruce Flyer, *General Mgr*
EMP: 100 **EST:** 2017
SALES (est): 630.8K **Privately Held**
SIC: 7011 Hotels

(G-4599)
SUMNER SOLUTIONS INC
3610 Sherbrooke Dr (45241-3286)
PHONE.................513 531-6382
Mark Lacker, *President*
EMP: 26
SALES (est): 1.1MM **Privately Held**
WEB: www.sumnersolutions.com
SIC: 8742 Marketing consulting services

(G-4600)
SUNRISE SENIOR LIVING LLC
Also Called: Sunrise At Finneytown
9101 Winton Rd (45231-3829)
PHONE.................513 729-5233
Fax: 513 729-5234
Valerie Heine, *Exec Dir*
Nancy Phillips, *Exec Dir*
EMP: 40
SALES (corp-wide): 4.3B **Publicly Held**
WEB: www.sunrise.com
SIC: 8051 Skilled nursing care facilities
HQ: Sunrise Senior Living, Llc
7902 Westpark Dr
Mc Lean VA 22102

(G-4601)
SUNSOURCE INC
5750 Hillside Ave (45233-1508)
PHONE.................513 941-6200
Fax: 513 941-0583
Rose Samay, *Principal*
Mark Jira, *District Mgr*
David Sacher, *COO*
▲ **EMP:** 40
SALES (est): 13.7MM **Privately Held**
SIC: 5169 Chemicals & allied products

(G-4602)
SUPER SYSTEMS INC (PA)
7205 Edington Dr (45249-1064)
PHONE.................513 772-0060
Stephen Thompson, *President*
Scott Johnstone, *President*
Jim Oakes, *President*

Velvet Twist, *Business Mgr*
Bill Heckman, *Project Mgr*
EMP: 45
SQ FT: 5,000
SALES (est): 6.9MM **Privately Held**
SIC: 3829 5084 Measuring & controlling devices; industrial machinery & equipment

(G-4603)
SUPERIOR CARE PHARMACY INC
Also Called: Omnicare of St. George
201 E 4th St Ste 900 (45202-4160)
PHONE.................513 719-2600
Owen E Wood, *President*
Janet Wood, *Vice Pres*
Bradley S Abbott, *Treasurer*
Catherine I Geary, *Admin Sec*
EMP: 150
SALES (est): 18.9MM
SALES (corp-wide): 184.7B **Publicly Held**
WEB: www.omnicare.com
SIC: 5122 Pharmaceuticals
HQ: Omnicare Holding Company
1105 Market St Ste 1300
Cincinnati OH 45215
513 719-2600

(G-4604)
SUPERIOR LINEN & AP SVCS INC
Also Called: Superior Linen & Apparel Svcs
481 Wayne St (45206-2392)
PHONE.................513 751-1345
Fax: 513 751-1515
G Jerry Ruwe, *President*
Rick Herbers, *Sales Executive*
Jerry Focke, *Maintence Staff*
EMP: 60
SALES (est): 4.8MM **Privately Held**
WEB: www.superior-linen.com
SIC: 7213 Towel supply; coat supply; uniform supply

(G-4605)
SUPREME COURT UNITED STATES
Also Called: US Probation & Parole Svc.
100 E 5th St Rm 110 (45202-3911)
PHONE.................513 564-7575
Fax: 513 564-7587
John Dierna, *Chief*
EMP: 27 **Publicly Held**
SIC: 8322 9211 Probation office; courts;
HQ: Supreme Court, United States
1 1st St Ne
Washington DC 20543
202 479-3000

(G-4606)
SWEENEY TEAM INC (PA)
Also Called: Comey Shepherd Realtors Cy Off
1440 Main St (45202-7642)
PHONE.................513 241-3400
Fax: 513 333-4801
Michael Sweeney, *President*
Shaun Daley, *Real Est Agnt*
Thomas Porter, *Real Est Agnt*
EMP: 46
SQ FT: 10,000
SALES (est): 2.7MM **Privately Held**
SIC: 6531 Multiple listing service, real estate

(G-4607)
SWEENY WALT PNTC GMC TRCK SLES
Also Called: Mark Sweeney Burick
3365 Highland Ave (45213-2609)
PHONE.................513 621-4888
Fax: 513 621-3505
Mark Sweeney, *President*
Joe Dezarn, *Manager*
Joanne Sweeney, *Admin Sec*
EMP: 50
SQ FT: 21,600
SALES (est): 18MM **Privately Held**
WEB: www.marksweeneyauto.com
SIC: 5511 7514 Automobiles, new & used; pickups, new & used; passenger car rental

(G-4608)
SYCAMORE BOARD OF EDUCATION
YMCA Child Care-Montgomery
9609 Montgomery Rd (45242-7205)
PHONE.................513 489-3937
Charles Day, *Director*
EMP: 60
SALES (corp-wide): 82.7MM **Privately Held**
SIC: 8211 7991 8351 7032 Public elementary & secondary schools; physical fitness facilities; child day care services; youth camps; individual & family services; youth organizations
PA: Sycamore Board Of Education
5959 Hagewa Dr
Blue Ash OH 45242
513 686-1700

(G-4609)
SYSCO CINCINNATI LLC
10510 Evendale Dr (45241-2516)
PHONE.................513 563-6300
Fax: 513 483-6717
Michael Haunert, *President*
Dwuan Hamond, *President*
Jim Norris, *Regional Mgr*
Daniel Pinsel, *Vice Pres*
Tom Moyer, *Purch Dir*
EMP: 483
SALES (est): 180.3MM
SALES (corp-wide): 55.3B **Publicly Held**
SIC: 5144 5149 5143 5113 Poultry & poultry products; groceries & related products; dairy products, except dried or canned; industrial & personal service paper
PA: Sysco Corporation
1390 Enclave Pkwy
Houston TX 77077
281 584-1390

(G-4610)
SYSTEMS EVOLUTION INC
Also Called: SEI Cincinnati
7870 E Kemper Rd Ste 400 (45249-1675)
PHONE.................513 459-1992
Paul Ratkovich, *Branch Mgr*
Cheryl Brankamp, *Consultant*
EMP: 70 **Privately Held**
SIC: 8748 Business consulting
PA: Systems Evolution, Inc.
7870 E Kemper Rd Ste 400
Cincinnati OH 45249

(G-4611)
SYSTEMS EVOLUTION INC (PA)
7870 E Kemper Rd Ste 400 (45249-1675)
PHONE.................513 459-1992
Fax: 513 459-1911
Daniel J Pierce, *President*
Erin Sullivan, *Managing Dir*
Maria Korengel, *Corp Secy*
Rob Seichter, *COO*
Lynn Pierce, *Human Resources*
EMP: 71
SQ FT: 6,000
SALES (est): 13.9MM **Privately Held**
SIC: 7371 Computer software development

(G-4612)
T C RUMPKE WASTE COLLECTION
Also Called: Theodore C Rumpke
5665 Dunlap Rd (45252-1013)
PHONE.................513 385-7627
Theodore C Rumpke, *President*
Alan Rumpke, *Vice Pres*
EMP: 29
SALES (est): 1.3MM **Privately Held**
SIC: 4953 Refuse systems

(G-4613)
T H WINSTON COMPANY
4817 Glenshade Ave (45227-2419)
PHONE.................513 271-2123
Fax: 513 271-5573
William Underwood, *President*
Terry Rusche, *Vice Pres*
▲ **EMP:** 25
SQ FT: 1,500

GEOGRAPHIC SECTION
Cincinnati - Hamilton County (G-4637)

SALES: 1.9MM Privately Held
WEB: www.thwinston.com
SIC: 1743 Marble installation, interior; tile installation, ceramic; terrazzo work

(G-4614)
TAFARO JOHN
1 W 4th St Ste 800 (45202-3609)
PHONE.....................513 381-0656
N Cougherty, *General Mgr*
Natalie Cougherty, *General Mgr*
EMP: 60
SALES (est): 1.4MM Privately Held
SIC: 8111 General practice attorney, lawyer

(G-4615)
TAFT MUSEUM OF ART
316 Pike St (45202-4293)
P.O. Box 631419 (45263-1419)
PHONE.....................513 241-0343
Beth Siler, *Finance Dir*
Anne Sunyak, *Manager*
EMP: 41
SALES: 5.4MM Privately Held
SIC: 8412 Museum

(G-4616)
TAFT STETTINIUS HOLLISTER LLP (PA)
425 Walnut St Ste 1800 (45202-3920)
PHONE.....................513 381-2838
Fax: 513 381-0205
Kimberlie Huff, *Editor*
Paul Kortepeter, *Counsel*
Roderick Willcox, *Counsel*
Luke Scott, *Engineer*
Brain Schofield, *Controller*
EMP: 278
SQ FT: 114,000
SALES (est): 104.2MM Privately Held
SIC: 8111 General practice law office

(G-4617)
TALBERT HOUSE
Also Called: Spring Grove Center
3129 Spring Grove Ave (45225-1821)
PHONE.....................513 541-0127
Fax: 513 853-6934
William Marshall, *Branch Mgr*
Fred Willis, *Manager*
Alexander A Weech Jr, *Psychiatry*
EMP: 25
SALES (corp-wide): 58.6MM Privately Held
WEB: www.talberthouse.org
SIC: 8322 Rehabilitation services
PA: Talbert House
    2600 Victory Pkwy
    Cincinnati OH 45206
    513 872-5863

(G-4618)
TALBERT HOUSE
5837 Hamilton Ave (45224-2923)
PHONE.....................513 751-7747
Talbert House, *Senior Buyer*
Suzanne Lukacs, *Branch Mgr*
EMP: 195
SALES (corp-wide): 58.6MM Privately Held
SIC: 8069 Drug addiction rehabilitation hospital
PA: Talbert House
    2600 Victory Pkwy
    Cincinnati OH 45206
    513 872-5863

(G-4619)
TALBERT HOUSE
1611 Emerson Ave (45239-4932)
PHONE.....................513 541-1184
Neil F Tilow, *Branch Mgr*
EMP: 32
SALES (corp-wide): 58.6MM Privately Held
SIC: 8322 Substance abuse counseling
PA: Talbert House
    2600 Victory Pkwy
    Cincinnati OH 45206
    513 872-5863

(G-4620)
TALBERT HOUSE (PA)
2600 Victory Pkwy (45206-1395)
PHONE.....................513 872-5863
Fax: 513 751-8107
Neil F Tilow, *President*
Josh Arnold, *Vice Pres*
Brad McMonigle, *Vice Pres*
Kevin Corey, *Opers Spvr*
Brenda Harris, *Opers Spvr*
EMP: 70
SQ FT: 40,000
SALES: 58.6MM Privately Held
WEB: www.talberthouse.org
SIC: 8322 Rehabilitation services; substance abuse counseling; family counseling services

(G-4621)
TALBERT HOUSE
328 Mcgregor Ave Ste 106 (45219-3135)
PHONE.....................513 684-7968
Fax: 513 684-7953
Victor Gray, *Manager*
EMP: 89
SALES (corp-wide): 58.6MM Privately Held
WEB: www.talberthouse.org
SIC: 8069 Alcoholism rehabilitation hospital

(G-4622)
TALBERT HOUSE HEALTH (HQ)
Also Called: Centerpoint Health Inc
5837 Hamilton Ave Unit 3 (45224-2923)
PHONE.....................513 541-7577
Cordilia Schaber, *Opers Staff*
Paul Guggenheim, *Director*
John Francis, *Director*
EMP: 35 EST: 1972
SQ FT: 13,000
SALES (est): 2.6MM
SALES (corp-wide): 58.6MM Privately Held
SIC: 8322 General counseling services
PA: Talbert House
    2600 Victory Pkwy
    Cincinnati OH 45206
    513 872-5863

(G-4623)
TANYAS IMAGE LLC (PA)
Also Called: Tanyas Image & Wellness Salon
2716 Erie Ave Ste 3 (45208-2135)
PHONE.....................513 386-9981
Fax: 513 533-7354
Kelly Brinkman, *Manager*
Thomas L Cuni,
EMP: 40
SALES (est): 955.1K Privately Held
SIC: 7231 Hairdressers

(G-4624)
TAPE PRODUCTS COMPANY (PA)
11630 Deerfield Rd (45242-1499)
P.O. Box 42413 (45242-0413)
PHONE.....................513 489-8840
Fax: 513 489-4616
John Fette, *CEO*
Janet F Fette, *Chairman*
Gail B Frazier, *Vice Pres*
Carlos Jimenez, *Vice Pres*
Cynthia L Kagrise, *Vice Pres*
▲ EMP: 80
SQ FT: 62,500
SALES (est): 60.4MM Privately Held
WEB: www.tapeproducts.com
SIC: 5113 5084 Pressure sensitive tape; packaging machinery & equipment

(G-4625)
TARGET CORPORATION
900 E Kemper Rd (45246-2518)
PHONE.....................513 671-8603
Fax: 513 322-3647
Rick Barnette, *Branch Mgr*
EMP: 116
SALES (corp-wide): 71.8B Publicly Held
WEB: www.target.com
SIC: 4226 Special warehousing & storage
PA: Target Corporation
    1000 Nicollet Mall
    Minneapolis MN 55403
    612 304-6073

(G-4626)
TAYLOR DISTRIBUTING COMPANY
2875 E Sharon Rd (45241-1923)
PHONE.....................513 771-1850
Fax: 513 672-8549
Rex Taylor, *President*
Drew Taylor, *Vice Pres*
James B Taylor, *Vice Pres*
John A Taylor, *Vice Pres*
Keith Swensen, *Human Res Dir*
EMP: 80
SQ FT: 300,000
SALES (est): 15.2MM Privately Held
WEB: www.taylorwarehouse.com
SIC: 4214 Local trucking with storage

(G-4627)
TAYLOR WAREHOUSE CORPORATION
2875 E Sharon Rd (45241-1976)
PHONE.....................513 771-2956
Rex C Taylor, *President*
James B Taylor, *Vice Pres*
John A Taylor, *Vice Pres*
EMP: 25 EST: 1972
SALES (est): 2.4MM Privately Held
WEB: www.taylorwarehouse.com
SIC: 4225 General warehousing

(G-4628)
TEASDALE FENTON CARPET CLEANIN
12145 Centron Pl (45246-1704)
PHONE.....................513 797-0900
Fax: 513 797-0400
James Olmstead, *President*
Bill Otte, *Controller*
Leah Olmstead, *Office Mgr*
EMP: 75
SQ FT: 20,000
SALES: 9.6MM Privately Held
SIC: 7217 7299 Pipeline construction; carpet & upholstery cleaning; home improvement & renovation contractor agency

(G-4629)
TECHNICAL CONSULTANTS INC
Also Called: TCI
8228 Winton Rd Ste 200a (45231)
PHONE.....................513 521-2696
Fax: 513 521-2699
Horst Steigerwald, *President*
EMP: 43
SQ FT: 5,000
SALES: 5MM Privately Held
SIC: 8711 8741 Engineering services; construction management

(G-4630)
TECHSOFT SYSTEMS INC
10296 Springfield Pike (45215-1193)
PHONE.....................513 772-5010
Clifford A Bailey, *President*
Chad Hall, *Engineer*
Jim Williams, *Finance Mgr*
Karen Eatmon, *Office Mgr*
Danielle Prewitt, *Info Tech Mgr*
EMP: 25
SQ FT: 5,000
SALES: 3MM Privately Held
WEB: www.techsoftsystems.com
SIC: 7379 Computer related consulting services

(G-4631)
TECHSOLVE INC
6705 Steger Dr (45237-3097)
PHONE.....................513 948-2000
Fax: 513 948-2019
David R Linger, *President*
Rick Henkel, *Exec VP*
Dave Levine, *Exec VP*
Kara Valz, *Exec VP*
Jon Iverson, *Vice Pres*
EMP: 51
SQ FT: 22,000
SALES: 9MM Privately Held
WEB: www.techsolve.org
SIC: 8742 8748 8711 Manufacturing management consultant; business consulting; mechanical engineering

(G-4632)
TECTA AMERICA ZERO COMPANY LLC (HQ)
6225 Wiehe Rd (45237-4211)
PHONE.....................513 541-1848
Jonathan Wolf, *President*
Jim Stark, *Senior VP*
Thomas M Miller, *Vice Pres*
Edward Phillip, *Vice Pres*
Jim Haitz, *Safety Dir*
EMP: 100
SQ FT: 30,000
SALES: 24.5MM
SALES (corp-wide): 922.9MM Privately Held
SIC: 1761 Roofing contractor; sheet metalwork
PA: Tecta America Corp.
    9450 Bryn Mawr Ave
    Rosemont IL 60018
    847 581-3888

(G-4633)
TEKSYSTEMS INC
Also Called: Teksystems 611
3825 Edwards Rd Ste 500 (45209-1288)
PHONE.....................513 719-3950
Sarah Downs, *Manager*
Lori Jerome, *Manager*
Allison Lambert, *Manager*
EMP: 40
SALES (corp-wide): 4.1B Privately Held
WEB: www.teksystems.com
SIC: 7379 Computer related consulting services
HQ: Teksystems, Inc.
    7437 Race Rd
    Hanover MD 21076

(G-4634)
TENABLE PROTECTIVE SVCS INC
5643 Cheviot Rd Ste 5 (45247-7080)
PHONE.....................513 741-3560
Karl Angelo, *Branch Mgr*
EMP: 950
SALES (est): 6.2MM
SALES (corp-wide): 85.3MM Privately Held
WEB: www.ac-products.com
SIC: 7381 Security guard service
PA: Tenable Protective Services, Inc.
    2423 Payne Ave
    Cleveland OH 44114
    216 361-0002

(G-4635)
TENDER MERCIES INC (PA)
27 W 12th St (45202-7205)
P.O. Box 14465 (45250-0465)
PHONE.....................513 721-8666
Fax: 513 639-7037
Marsha Spaeth, *CEO*
Kirsch Mary, *COO*
Latricia Hibbitt, *Hum Res Coord*
Jackie Baumgartner, *Director*
Crystal Wimzie, *Admin Asst*
EMP: 49
SQ FT: 40,000
SALES: 3MM Privately Held
SIC: 8322 Emergency shelters

(G-4636)
TERRACON CONSULTANTS INC
Also Called: Terracon Consultants N1
611 Lunken Park Dr (45226-1813)
PHONE.....................513 321-5816
Jason Sander, *Branch Mgr*
EMP: 130
SALES (corp-wide): 654.9MM Privately Held
SIC: 8711 Consulting engineer
PA: Terracon Consultants, Inc.
    18001 W 106th St Ste 300
    Olathe KS 66061
    913 599-6886

(G-4637)
TESTAMERICA LABORATORIES INC
11416 Reading Rd (45241-2247)
PHONE.....................513 733-5700
Steve West, *Manager*
EMP: 48

Cincinnati - Hamilton County (G-4638)   GEOGRAPHIC SECTION

SALES (corp-wide): 609.6MM **Privately Held**
SIC: 8734 Soil analysis
HQ: Testamerica Laboratories, Inc.
4101 Shuffel St Nw
North Canton OH 44720
800 456-9396

(G-4638)
TETRA TECH INC
250 W Court St Ste 200w (45202-1072)
PHONE....................513 251-2730
Rust Murphy, *Principal*
Michael Gibbons, *Manager*
EMP: 30
SALES (corp-wide): 2.7B **Publicly Held**
WEB: www.ttnus.com
SIC: 8748 Environmental consultant
PA: Tetra Tech, Inc.
3475 E Foothill Blvd
Pasadena CA 91107
626 351-4664

(G-4639)
TEVA WOMENS HEALTH INC (DH)
5040 Duramed Rd (45213-2520)
PHONE....................513 731-9900
Fax: 513 731-5270
Bruce L Downey, *Principal*
Timothy J Holt, *Principal*
David J Furniss, *Senior VP*
Lawrence A Glassman, *Senior VP*
Lawrence Glassmann, *Senior VP*
EMP: 250 **EST:** 1982
SQ FT: 28,200
SALES (est): 125.7MM
SALES (corp-wide): 23.8B **Privately Held**
WEB: www.barrlabs.com
SIC: 5122 2834 7389 Patent medicines; pharmaceutical preparations; packaging & labeling services
HQ: Teva Pharmaceuticals Usa, Inc.
1090 Horsham Rd
North Wales PA 19454
215 591-3000

(G-4640)
THE CINCINNATI CORDAGE PPR CO
Also Called: Cincinnati Division
800 E Ross Ave (45217-1177)
PHONE....................513 242-3600
John F Church Jr, *Ch of Bd*
Lawrence Bresko, *President*
Charles Johansen, *VP Opers*
Frederick Beck, *Treasurer*
Lee R Thompkins, *Credit Staff*
EMP: 45 **EST:** 1892
SQ FT: 60,000
SALES (est): 7.1MM **Privately Held**
SIC: 5111 5113 Printing paper; industrial & personal service paper

(G-4641)
THE FOR CINCINNATI ASSOCIATION (PA)
650 Walnut St (45202-2517)
PHONE....................513 744-3344
Steve Loftin, *President*
Dudly S Taft, *Chairman*
Kim Watling, *Manager*
Van Ackerman, *Director*
Scott Santangelo, *Director*
EMP: 75
SQ FT: 200,000
SALES: 14.2MM **Privately Held**
WEB: www.cincinnatiarts.org
SIC: 8641 Dwelling-related associations

(G-4642)
THE HEALTHCARE CONNECTION INC (PA)
Also Called: Lincoln Hts Hlth Connection
1401 Steffen Ave (45215-2338)
PHONE....................513 588-3623
Fax: 513 554-4115
Dolores Lindsay, *Principal*
Joseph Stickle, *Facilities Dir*
Diane Becker, *Opers Mgr*
Joanne Dwyer, *CFO*
Charles H Woode, *Treasurer*
EMP: 33
SQ FT: 42,000

SALES: 8MM **Privately Held**
SIC: 8011 Ambulatory surgical center; clinic, operated by physicians

(G-4643)
THE HUNTINGTON INVESTMENT CO
Also Called: Huntington Wealth Advisors
525 Vine St Ste 2100 (45202-3121)
PHONE....................513 351-2555
Fax: 513 366-3089
Bruce Ross, *Exec VP*
Mark Reitzes, *Manager*
EMP: 45
SALES (corp-wide): 4.7B **Publicly Held**
SIC: 6211 6799 Brokers, security; investors
HQ: The Huntington Investment Company
41 S High St Fl 7
Columbus OH 43215
614 480-3600

(G-4644)
THE IN CINCINNATI PLAYHOUSE
962 Mount Adams Cir (45202-6023)
PHONE....................513 421-3888
Jule Horton, *Sales Mgr*
Timothy Keeler, *Technical Staff*
Edward Stern, *Director*
Phil Rundle, *Director*
EMP: 100
SALES (corp-wide): 12.4MM **Privately Held**
WEB: www.cincyplay.com
SIC: 7922 Community theater production
PA: The Cincinnati Playhouse In The Park Inc
962 Mount Adams Cir
Cincinnati OH 45202
513 345-2242

(G-4645)
THE PECK-HANNAFORD BRIGGS CO (PA)
Also Called: PH B
4670 Chester Ave (45232-1851)
PHONE....................513 681-4600
Fax: 513 681-4708
James G Briggs Jr, *President*
Jerry A Govert, *Vice Pres*
Bill Reis, *Safety Dir*
Mark Heyl, *Project Mgr*
Ed Metzger, *Project Mgr*
EMP: 90 **EST:** 1899
SQ FT: 40,000
SALES (est): 52.9MM **Privately Held**
SIC: 1711 Mechanical contractor; warm air heating & air conditioning contractor; refrigeration contractor

(G-4646)
THE SHEAKLEY GROUP INC (PA)
Also Called: S G I
1 Sheakley Way Ste 100 (45246-3774)
PHONE....................513 771-2277
Larry Sheakley, *CEO*
Guy Zimmerman, *Top Exec*
Shari Herper, *VP Opers*
Shelli Hensley, *Opers Mgr*
Anita Miracle, *Opers Mgr*
EMP: 30
SQ FT: 5,500
SALES (est): 32.1MM **Privately Held**
WEB: www.sheakley.com
SIC: 8742 8741 6411 8721 Compensation & benefits planning consultant; administrative management; pension & retirement plan consultants; accounting, auditing & bookkeeping

(G-4647)
THEATRE MANAGEMENT CORPORATION
125 E Court St Ste 1000 (45202-1227)
PHONE....................513 723-1180
Gary Goldman, *President*
EMP: 50
SALES (est): 1.9MM **Privately Held**
SIC: 7922 Entertainment promotion

(G-4648)
THELEN ASSOCIATES INC
1780 Carillion Blvd (45240-2795)
PHONE....................513 825-4350

Fax: 513 825-4756
Nancy Niemeyer, *Sales Executive*
Steven Proffitt, *Marketing Staff*
Dale Proffitt, *Manager*
Burcin Inanli, *Technology*
EMP: 30
SALES (corp-wide): 15.9MM **Privately Held**
WEB: www.thelenassoc.com
SIC: 8711 Civil engineering
PA: Thelen Associates, Inc.
1398 Cox Ave
Erlanger KY 41018
859 746-9400

(G-4649)
THERMALTECH ENGINEERING INC (PA)
3960 Red Bank Rd Ste 250 (45227-3437)
PHONE....................513 561-2271
Jeff Celuch, *President*
Bill W Widman, *Managing Dir*
Stephen D Williams, *Project Mgr*
David Bol, *Engineer*
Shane Bowser, *Engineer*
EMP: 33
SQ FT: 8,000
SALES: 25MM **Privately Held**
WEB: www.thermaltech.com
SIC: 8711 Electrical or electronic engineering

(G-4650)
THINKWARE INCORPORATED
7611 Cheviot Rd Ste 2 (45247-4015)
PHONE....................513 598-3300
Fax: 513 598-3315
Kevin Eickmann, *President*
Chris Bross, *Office Mgr*
Jack Dossou, *Software Engr*
Melissa Overberg, *Assistant*
EMP: 28
SQ FT: 7,500
SALES: 5.4MM **Privately Held**
WEB: www.thinkwareinc.com
SIC: 7371 7374 7372 Computer software development; data processing & preparation; prepackaged software

(G-4651)
THOMAN WEIL MOVING & STOR CO
Also Called: Bekins Van Lines
5151 Fischer Ave (45217-1157)
P.O. Box 17105 (45217-0105)
PHONE....................513 251-5000
Fax: 513 251-0291
Joseph C Thoman, *President*
James B Thoman, *VP Sales*
EMP: 50 **EST:** 1900
SQ FT: 9,000
SALES (est): 4.9MM **Privately Held**
SIC: 4213 4214 Trucking, except local; local trucking with storage

(G-4652)
THOMAS GENTZ
Also Called: AFLAC
10284 Falling Waters Ln (45241-3843)
PHONE....................513 247-7300
Fax: 513 247-7308
Thomas Gentz, *Owner*
Kimberley Donovan, *Admin Sec*
EMP: 30
SALES: 3.4MM **Privately Held**
SIC: 6411 Insurance agents, brokers & service

(G-4653)
THOMAS J DYER COMPANY (PA)
5240 Lester Rd (45213-2522)
PHONE....................513 321-8100
Fax: 513 979-8120
Thomas D Grote Sr, *CEO*
Joe Mirlisena, *COO*
Ken Adkins, *Manager*
Tim Rechel, *Director*
EMP: 164 **EST:** 1908
SQ FT: 29,600
SALES (est): 76.6MM **Privately Held**
WEB: www.tjdyer.com
SIC: 1711 Plumbing contractors; ventilation & duct work contractor; warm air heating & air conditioning contractor

(G-4654)
THOMAS TRUCKING INC
2558 Apple Ridge Ln (45236-1331)
PHONE....................513 731-8411
Fax: 513 731-0284
Callis A Thomas, *President*
Mark Thomas, *Vice Pres*
Christine Thomas, *Treasurer*
Kathy Thomas-Dawson, *Admin Sec*
EMP: 40
SQ FT: 2,000
SALES (est): 6.6MM **Privately Held**
SIC: 4213 Contract haulers

(G-4655)
THOMPSON HALL & JORDAN FNRL HM
400 N Wayne Ave (45215-2845)
PHONE....................513 761-8881
Katherine Jordan, *President*
Donald Jordan, *Vice Pres*
EMP: 50
SALES (est): 1.6MM **Privately Held**
SIC: 6512 Commercial & industrial building operation

(G-4656)
THOMPSON HEATING & COOLING
800 E Ross Ave (45217-1177)
PHONE....................513 242-4450
Wesley Holm, *President*
EMP: 40
SALES (est): 2.6MM **Privately Held**
SIC: 1711 Heating systems repair & maintenance

(G-4657)
THOMPSON HEATING CORPORATION
Also Called: Thompson Plumbing Htg Coolg
6 N Commerce Park Dr (45215-3174)
PHONE....................513 769-7696
Wesley R Holm, *CEO*
Cheryl Holm, *Admin Sec*
EMP: 75
SQ FT: 9,000
SALES (est): 12.1MM **Privately Held**
WEB: www.thompsonheatingcooling.com
SIC: 1711 5075 5722 Heating systems repair & maintenance; air conditioning & ventilation equipment & supplies; electric household appliances

(G-4658)
THP LIMITED INC
100 E 8th St Ste 3 (45202-2133)
PHONE....................513 241-3222
Fax: 513 241-2981
James Millar, *President*
E James Millar, *President*
Julie C Cromwell, *Managing Dir*
Frank J Ellert, *Principal*
Mark H Hoffman, *Principal*
EMP: 55
SQ FT: 20,000
SALES: 8.8MM **Privately Held**
WEB: www.thpltd.com
SIC: 8711 Structural engineering; civil engineering

(G-4659)
THYSSENKRUPP ELEVATOR CORP
934 Dalton Ave (45203-1102)
PHONE....................513 241-6000
Toll Free:....................888 -
Fax: 513 719-5001
Dave Forthuber, *Superintendent*
Luke Mathis, *Engineer*
Tom Zwick, *Branch Mgr*
EMP: 50
SALES (corp-wide): 48.7B **Privately Held**
WEB: www.tyssenkrupp.com
SIC: 1796 7699 Elevator installation & conversion; elevators: inspection, service & repair
HQ: Thyssenkrupp Elevator Corporation
11605 Haynes Bridge Rd # 650
Alpharetta GA 30009
678 319-3240

GEOGRAPHIC SECTION
Cincinnati - Hamilton County (G-4683)

(G-4660)
TKF CONVEYOR SYSTEMS LLC
5298 River Rd (45233-1643)
PHONE..................513 621-5260
Ron Eubanks,
EMP: 110
SALES (est): 285.1K **Privately Held**
SIC: 5084 Conveyor systems

(G-4661)
TNS NORTH AMERICA INC
Also Called: Tns Global
600 Vine St Ste 300 (45202-2413)
PHONE..................513 621-7887
John Packer, *Vice Pres*
Michelle Johnson, *Manager*
EMP: 67
SALES (corp-wide): 17.7B **Privately Held**
SIC: 8732 Market analysis or research
HQ: Tns North America, Inc.
   11 Madison Ave Fl 12
   New York NY 10010
   212 991-6100

(G-4662)
TOTAL PACKAGE EXPRESS INC (PA)
5871 Cheviot Rd Ste 1 (45247-6200)
P.O. Box 53435 (45253-0435)
PHONE..................513 741-5500
Fax: 513 741-5505
Joseph Amareno, *President*
Dave Wilkins, *General Mgr*
Russ Hoffman, *Safety Dir*
Doug Simonson, *Accounting Mgr*
Joseph S Amareno, *Shareholder*
EMP: 25
SQ FT: 900
SALES (est): 6.9MM **Privately Held**
SIC: 4212 4213 4731 Delivery service, vehicular; trucking, except local; truck transportation brokers

(G-4663)
TOTAL QUALITY LOGISTICS LLC
5130 Glncrssing Way Ste 3 (45238)
PHONE..................513 831-2600
Joe Myers, *Branch Mgr*
EMP: 74
SALES (corp-wide): 2.3B **Privately Held**
SIC: 4731 Freight transportation arrangement
HQ: Total Quality Logistics, Llc
   4289 Ivy Pointe Blvd
   Cincinnati OH 45245

(G-4664)
TOUCHSTONE GROUP ASSOC LLC
9675 Montgomery Rd # 201 (45242-7263)
PHONE..................513 791-1717
Tracy Queen, *Manager*
Melissa Smith, *Manager*
Larry Sowders, *Manager*
Karen Werling, *Manager*
William Willis, *Manager*
EMP: 35
SALES (est): 20.2MM **Privately Held**
WEB: www.findthevine.com
SIC: 8742 Hospital & health services consultant

(G-4665)
TOWERS WATSON PENNSYLVANIA INC
Also Called: Towers Perrin
255 E 5th St Ste 2120 (45202-4720)
PHONE..................513 345-4200
Fax: 513 345-4240
Barbara Impens, *Human Resources*
Jennifer Webber, *Manager*
Cheryl Ross, *Office Admin*
Mary E Laird, *Consultant*
Edward McMahon, *Director*
EMP: 40 **Privately Held**
WEB: www.towers.com
SIC: 8742 Management consulting services
HQ: Towers Watson Pennsylvania Inc.
   263 Tresser Blvd Ste 700
   Stamford CT 06901
   203 326-5400

(G-4666)
TOWNE BUILDING GROUP INC (PA)
1055 Saint Paul Pl (45202-6042)
PHONE..................513 381-8696
Neil K Bortz, *President*
Philip T Montanus, *Principal*
Marvin Rosenberg, *Principal*
Derek Wehman, *Vice Pres*
Max L Wiseman, *Vice Pres*
EMP: 90
SQ FT: 2,000
SALES (est): 4.5MM **Privately Held**
SIC: 1522 Apartment building construction; multi-family dwellings, new construction

(G-4667)
TOWNE DEVELOPMENT GROUP LTD
1055 Saint Paul Pl # 300 (45202-6042)
PHONE..................513 381-8696
Jim Jagers, *COO*
Joseph Roda, *Vice Pres*
Neil K Bortz,
Marvin Rosenberg,
EMP: 32
SQ FT: 1,200
SALES (est): 5.6MM **Privately Held**
WEB: www.townedevelopmentgroup.com
SIC: 6552 1521 Land subdividers & developers, residential; new construction, single-family houses

(G-4668)
TOWNE INVESTMENT COMPANY LP
1055 Saint Paul Pl (45202-6042)
PHONE..................513 381-8696
Marvin Rosenberg, *Partner*
Neil Bortz, *General Ptnr*
Adam Bortz, *Manager*
EMP: 70 **Privately Held**
SIC: 6719 Investment holding companies, except banks

(G-4669)
TOWNE PROPERTIES ASSET MGT (PA)
Also Called: Towne Properties Asset MGT
1055 Saint Paul Pl # 100 (45202-1687)
PHONE..................513 381-8696
Bob Wahlke, *President*
Robert Wahlke, *President*
Neil Bortz, *Partner*
Phil Montanus, *Partner*
Judd Oscherwitz, *Property Mgr*
EMP: 600
SQ FT: 5,000
SALES (est): 28.6MM **Privately Held**
SIC: 6513 Apartment building operators

(G-4670)
TOWNE PROPERTIES ASSOC INC
Also Called: Racquet Club At Harper's Point
8675 E Kemper Rd (45249-2503)
PHONE..................513 489-9700
Fax: 513 489-5244
Laura Wagner, *Principal*
EMP: 25
SALES (corp-wide): 33.3MM **Privately Held**
WEB: www.towneprop.com
SIC: 7941 Sports field or stadium operator, promoting sports events
PA: Towne Properties Associates, Inc.
   1055 Saint Paul Pl # 100
   Cincinnati OH 45202
   513 381-8696

(G-4671)
TOWNE PROPERTIES ASSOC INC
Also Called: Towne Management Realty
11340 Montgomery Rd # 202 (45249-2377)
P.O. Box 691650 (45269-0001)
PHONE..................513 489-4059
Fax: 513 489-3941
Char Ostholthoff, *Manager*
Rich Wegelin, *Manager*
EMP: 27

SALES (corp-wide): 33.3MM **Privately Held**
WEB: www.towneprop.com
SIC: 6531 Real estate managers
PA: Towne Properties Associates, Inc.
   1055 Saint Paul Pl # 100
   Cincinnati OH 45202
   513 381-8696

(G-4672)
TOWNE PROPERTIES ASSOC INC
11840 Kemper Springs Dr C (45240-4130)
PHONE..................513 874-3737
Wil Browning, *Manager*
EMP: 50
SALES (corp-wide): 33.3MM **Privately Held**
WEB: www.towneprop.com
SIC: 6513 6514 6531 Apartment building operators; dwelling operators, except apartments; real estate agents & managers
PA: Towne Properties Associates, Inc.
   1055 Saint Paul Pl # 100
   Cincinnati OH 45202
   513 381-8696

(G-4673)
TOWNEPLACE SUITES BY MARRIOTT
9369 Waterstone Blvd (45249-8218)
PHONE..................513 774-0610
Fax: 513 774-0710
Pete Pordash, *Principal*
EMP: 25
SALES (est): 1.2MM **Privately Held**
SIC: 7011 Hotel, franchised

(G-4674)
TOWNSHIP OF COLERAIN
Also Called: Fire Dept
3360 W Galbraith Rd (45239-3969)
PHONE..................513 741-7551
Frank W Cook, *Director*
EMP: 173 **Privately Held**
WEB: www.coleraintwp.org
SIC: 9224 8011 Fire department, not including volunteer; freestanding emergency medical center
PA: Township Of Colerain
   4200 Springdale Rd
   Cincinnati OH 45251
   513 923-5000

(G-4675)
TP MECHANICAL CONTRACTORS INC (PA)
Also Called: Honeywell Authorized Dealer
1500 Kemper Meadow Dr (45240-1638)
PHONE..................513 851-8881
Scott Teepe Sr, *President*
Bill Riddle, *President*
Robert J Mauntel, *Managing Prtnr*
Mike Meinking, *Superintendent*
Keith Miller, *Superintendent*
EMP: 525
SQ FT: 3,200
SALES (est): 54.5MM **Privately Held**
SIC: 6552 Subdividers & developers

(G-4676)
TPG NORAMCO LLC
9252 Colerain Ave Ste 4 (45251-2447)
PHONE..................513 245-9050
Josh Cahill, *Controller*
Mark Wetterich,
EMP: 30
SQ FT: 104,000
SALES (est): 3.8MM **Privately Held**
SIC: 4213 4731 Trucking, except local; freight forwarding

(G-4677)
TRAK STAFFING SERVICES INC (PA)
625 Eden Park Dr Ste 300 (45202-6006)
PHONE..................513 333-4199
Joseph McCullough, *President*
John Murley, *Vice Pres*
Jennifer Spaulding-Marsh, *Vice Pres*
Jennifer Daly, *Accounts Mgr*
Heather Gabbard, *Accounts Mgr*
EMP: 25
SQ FT: 11,000

SALES (est): 2MM **Privately Held**
WEB: www.trakcincy.com
SIC: 7361 Executive placement

(G-4678)
TRANS-CONTINENTAL SYSTEMS INC (PA)
Also Called: TCS
10801 Evendale Dr Ste 105 (45241-7509)
PHONE..................513 769-4774
Fax: 513 769-3215
Gary W Stone, *Principal*
Robin Wright, *Safety Dir*
William Danford, *Controller*
Gayle Hoyda, *Manager*
Diana Stone, *Admin Sec*
EMP: 30
SQ FT: 6,000
SALES (est): 8.1MM **Privately Held**
WEB: www.tcsohio.com
SIC: 4011 Railroads, line-haul operating

(G-4679)
TRANS-STATES EXPRESS INC
7750 Reinhold Dr (45237-2806)
PHONE..................513 679-7100
William Edmund, *President*
Herb Glischinski, *Director*
Mary Edmund, *Admin Sec*
EMP: 70
SQ FT: 23,000
SALES (est): 5.8MM **Privately Held**
WEB: www.onecalldoesall.com
SIC: 4213 4212 Contract haulers; local trucking, without storage

(G-4680)
TRANSPORT SPECIALISTS INC (PA)
Also Called: Thermo King
12130 Best Pl (45241-1569)
PHONE..................513 771-2220
Fax: 513 771-6520
Jake Jennings, *President*
Dan Jennings, *Parts Mgr*
Ryan Sines, *Parts Mgr*
Glenn Martin, *Controller*
Beverly Jennings, *Accountant*
▲ **EMP:** 25
SQ FT: 24,000
SALES (est): 31.9MM **Privately Held**
SIC: 5531 7623 Truck equipment & parts; refrigeration repair service

(G-4681)
TRAVEL AUTHORITY (PA)
6800 Wooster Pike (45227-4324)
PHONE..................513 272-2887
Denise Daum, *President*
Joyce Dill, *President*
Thomas Fucito, *Corp Secy*
Thomas Herbert, *Vice Pres*
John Stump, *Vice Pres*
EMP: 27
SQ FT: 2,500
SALES (est): 3.6MM **Privately Held**
SIC: 4724 Travel agencies

(G-4682)
TRAVELERS PROPERTY CSLTY CORP
Also Called: Travelers Insurance
615 Elsinore Pl Bldg B (45202-1459)
PHONE..................513 639-5300
Bruce Brizzi, *Manager*
Tina Kramer, *Manager*
Brian Barnes, *Info Tech Mgr*
EMP: 35
SALES (corp-wide): 28.9B **Publicly Held**
WEB: www.travelerspc.com
SIC: 6411 Insurance agents
HQ: Travelers Property Casualty Corp.
   1 Tower Sq 8ms
   Hartford CT 06183

(G-4683)
TRI STATE CORPORATION
923 Glenwood Ave (45229-2713)
PHONE..................513 763-0215
Joseph Lentine, *Branch Mgr*
EMP: 46

Cincinnati - Hamilton County (G-4684) GEOGRAPHIC SECTION

SALES (est): 2.8MM
SALES (corp-wide): 7MM **Privately Held**
SIC: 1611 1622 1541 1542 Highway & street construction; bridge, tunnel & elevated highway; industrial buildings & warehouses; nonresidential construction
PA: Tri State Corporation
1633 Main St
Bridgeport CT 06604
513 763-0215

(G-4684)
TRI STATE URLOGIC SVCS PSC INC (PA)
Also Called: Urology Group
2000 Joseph E Sanker Blvd (45212-1979)
PHONE..................513 841-7400
Fax: 513 366-4001
Earl L Walz, *CEO*
William Corbett, *Research*
Robin Brinck, *Corp Comm Staff*
Vicky Turner, *Office Mgr*
Kevin Shepherd, *Info Tech Mgr*
EMP: 100
SALES (est): 21.7MM **Privately Held**
SIC: 8011 Medical centers

(G-4685)
TRI-STATE BEEF CO INC
2124 Baymiller St (45214-2208)
PHONE..................513 579-1722
Yong Woo Koo, *President*
EMP: 30
SALES (est): 6MM **Privately Held**
SIC: 2011 2013 5147 Meat packing plants; sausages & other prepared meats; meats & meat products

(G-4686)
TRIANGLE OFFICE PARK LLC
2135 Dana Ave Ste 200 (45207-1327)
PHONE..................513 563-7555
Dan Neyer, *Principal*
Colleen Kroell, *Controller*
EMP: 25
SALES (est): 860K **Privately Held**
SIC: 6531 Real estate leasing & rentals

(G-4687)
TRIHEALTH INC
415 W Court St Ste 100 (45203-1552)
PHONE..................513 929-0020
EMP: 50 **Privately Held**
SIC: 8741 Management Services
HQ: Trihealth, Inc.
619 Oak St
Cincinnati OH 45206
513 569-6111

(G-4688)
TRIHEALTH INC
Also Called: Bethesda North Hospital
10506 Montgomery Rd (45242-4487)
PHONE..................513 865-1111
Jason Niehaus, *Senior VP*
Lisa Drake, *Opers Staff*
Chris Hamant, *Accounts Mgr*
Walter Krimmer, *Manager*
Jeff Wiesemann, *Consultant*
EMP: 50 **Privately Held**
SIC: 8741 Hospital management
HQ: Trihealth, Inc.
619 Oak St
Cincinnati OH 45206
513 569-6111

(G-4689)
TRIHEALTH INC
Also Called: Senior Behaviroal Health
375 Dixmyth Ave (45220-2475)
PHONE..................513 569-6777
Fax: 513 872-2205
Robert Cercek, *Senior VP*
Jason Niehaus, *Senior VP*
Katie McGee, *Vice Pres*
Larry Johnstal, *QA Dir*
Greg Green, *Human Resources*
EMP: 50 **Privately Held**
WEB: www.trihealth.com
SIC: 8741 8093 Hospital management; mental health clinic, outpatient
HQ: Trihealth, Inc.
619 Oak St
Cincinnati OH 45206
513 569-6111

(G-4690)
TRIHEALTH INC (HQ)
619 Oak St (45206-1613)
PHONE..................513 569-6111
Fax: 513 569-5409
John Prout, *President*
Myra James Bradley, *Principal*
L Thomas Wilburn Jr, *Principal*
Pat McMahon, *Dean*
Will Groneman, *Exec VP*
EMP: 50
SALES: 184MM **Privately Held**
WEB: www.trihealth.com
SIC: 8741 Hospital management

(G-4691)
TRIHEALTH INC
2753 Erie Ave (45208-2204)
PHONE..................513 871-2340
Raejean Hardig, *Branch Mgr*
EMP: 50 **Privately Held**
WEB: www.trihealth.com
SIC: 8741 Hospital management
HQ: Trihealth, Inc.
619 Oak St
Cincinnati OH 45206
513 569-6111

(G-4692)
TRIHEALTH EVENDALE HOSPITAL (DH)
3155 Glendale Milford Rd (45241-3134)
PHONE..................513 454-2222
Fax: 513 454-2500
Ajay Mangal, *President*
Rhonda Bunch, *Materials Mgr*
Chris Denning, *QA Dir*
Michael Griffin, *CFO*
Donna Ertel, *Manager*
EMP: 166
SALES: 0 **Privately Held**
SIC: 8062 General medical & surgical hospitals
HQ: Trihealth, Inc.
619 Oak St
Cincinnati OH 45206
513 569-6111

(G-4693)
TRIHEALTH G LLC (DH)
Also Called: Cincinnati Group Health
4600 Wesley Ave Ste N (45212-2274)
PHONE..................513 732-0700
Fax: 513 841-1580
Vesta Johns, *COO*
Donna Nienaber, *Senior VP*
Thomas Duc, *Vice Pres*
Gregory Delorenzo, *Med Doctor*
Joseph Hellmann, *Med Doctor*
EMP: 75
SQ FT: 50,000
SALES (est): 60.5MM **Privately Held**
WEB: www.cgha.com
SIC: 8011 Physicians' office, including specialists
HQ: Trihealth, Inc.
619 Oak St
Cincinnati OH 45206
513 569-6111

(G-4694)
TRIHEALTH G LLC
Also Called: Blumenthal, Barry
55 Progress Pl (45246-1715)
PHONE..................513 346-5000
Diana Hendry, *Manager*
EMP: 45 **Privately Held**
WEB: www.cgha.com
SIC: 8093 8011 Rehabilitation center, outpatient treatment; offices & clinics of medical doctors
HQ: Trihealth, Llc
4600 Wesley Ave Ste N
Cincinnati OH 45212
513 732-0700

(G-4695)
TRIHEALTH G LLC
7691 5 Mile Rd Ste 214 (45230-4348)
PHONE..................513 624-5535
Raymond Dasenbrock, *Med Doctor*
Jo Ann Vill, *Manager*
EMP: 100 **Privately Held**
WEB: www.cgha.com
SIC: 8011 Pediatrician
HQ: Trihealth G, Llc
4600 Wesley Ave Ste N
Cincinnati OH 45212
513 732-0700

(G-4696)
TRIHEALTH G LLC
Also Called: Group Health Associates
2001 Anderson Ferry Rd (45238-3325)
PHONE..................513 922-1200
Fax: 513 922-2103
Gregory Dlorenzo, *Med Doctor*
Robert E Gregory MD, *Med Doctor*
Robert Gregory, *Med Doctor*
Lee Moeller, *Manager*
Ida Combs, *Manager*
EMP: 100 **Privately Held**
WEB: www.cgha.com
SIC: 8049 8011 Physical therapist; offices & clinics of medical doctors
HQ: Trihealth G, Llc
4600 Wesley Ave Ste N
Cincinnati OH 45212
513 732-0700

(G-4697)
TRIHEALTH ONCOLOGY INST LLC
Also Called: Oncology Partners Network
5520 Cheviot Rd (45247-7069)
PHONE..................513 451-4033
Daniel White, *Med Doctor*
Richard Louis Meyer, *Mng Member*
Sheena Gaeke, *Nursing Dir*
Sue Powers, *Admin Asst*
Thomas Coyle, *Hematology*
EMP: 35 EST: 1963
SQ FT: 1,900
SALES (est): 5.7MM **Privately Held**
SIC: 8011 Oncologist; hematologist

(G-4698)
TRIHEALTH REHABILITATION HOSP
2155 Dana Ave (45207-1340)
PHONE..................513 601-0600
Mark Asmen, *CEO*
Kimberly Brown, *Director*
Tom Fazio, *Director*
Steve Hartong, *Director*
Jerri Kussman, *Director*
EMP: 160
SALES (est): 48.6K
SALES (corp-wide): 3.7B **Publicly Held**
SIC: 8322 Rehabilitation services
HQ: Select Medical Corporation
4714 Gettysburg Rd
Mechanicsburg PA 17055
717 972-1100

(G-4699)
TRINITY CREDIT COUNSELING INC
Also Called: TRINITY DEBT MANAGEMENT
11229 Reading Rd Ste 1 (45241-2238)
PHONE..................513 769-0621
Gary Vosick, *President*
Jade Durham, *Director*
EMP: 28
SQ FT: 10,000
SALES: 3.9MM **Privately Held**
WEB: www.trinitycredit.org
SIC: 8742 Banking & finance consultant

(G-4700)
TRINITY HEALTHCARE CORPORATION
Also Called: Meadbrook Care Center
8211 Weller Rd (45242-3208)
PHONE..................513 489-2444
Fax: 513 247-2943
Enrico Galante, *Director*
Karen Hunt, *Executive*
Mitch Stewart, *Telecom Exec*
Kathy Brown, *Administration*
EMP: 125
SALES (corp-wide): 10.6MM **Privately Held**
WEB: www.trinityusa.org
SIC: 8051 Convalescent home with continuous nursing care
PA: Trinity Healthcare Corporation
2640 Peerless Rd Nw
Cleveland TN 37312
423 476-3035

(G-4701)
TRIO TRUCKING INC
7750 Reinhold Dr (45237-2806)
PHONE..................513 679-7100
Bill Edmond, *Branch Mgr*
EMP: 45
SALES (corp-wide): 6.9MM **Privately Held**
SIC: 4213 4212 Trucking, except local; local trucking, without storage
PA: Trio Trucking, Inc.
7750 Reinhold Dr
Cincinnati OH 45237
513 679-7100

(G-4702)
TRIVERSITY CONSTRUCTION CO LLC
5050 Section Ave Ste 330 (45212-2052)
PHONE..................513 733-0046
Arlene Koth, *Human Res Dir*
Melvin J Gravely II, *Mng Member*
EMP: 32 EST: 2005
SQ FT: 2,585
SALES (est): 7.1MM **Privately Held**
SIC: 8741 Construction management

(G-4703)
TSC APPAREL LLC (PA)
Also Called: T-Shirt City
Centennial Plaza Iii 895 (45202)
PHONE..................513 771-1138
Fax: 513 771-6865
Rick Mouty, *CEO*
Bob Winget, *President*
Michelle Technow, *Vice Pres*
Vince Bankett, *Opers Mgr*
Pete Tuff, *Purch Dir*
▲ EMP: 55
SQ FT: 170,000
SALES (est): 18.1MM **Privately Held**
WEB: www.tscapparel.com
SIC: 5699 5137 T-shirts, custom printed; shirts, custom made; sportswear, women's & children's

(G-4704)
TSS REAL ESTATE LTD
1201 Hill Smith Dr (45215-1228)
PHONE..................513 772-7000
Charles B Nichols Jr, *Managing Prtnr*
Nicholas Brasset, *Accountant*
EMP: 114
SALES (est): 2.3MM
SALES (corp-wide): 104.6MM **Privately Held**
SIC: 6531 Real estate brokers & agents
PA: Tss Technologies, Inc.
8800 Global Way
West Chester OH 45069
513 772-7000

(G-4705)
TURNER CONSTRUCTION COMPANY
250 W Court St Ste 300w (45202-1071)
PHONE..................513 721-4224
Fax: 513 721-4231
Doug Rack, *Superintendent*
Ken Wilson, *Vice Pres*
Kenneth Butler, *Branch Mgr*
Roy Boyen, *Manager*
Jason Spaulding, *Manager*
EMP: 200
SQ FT: 7,000
SALES (corp-wide): 1.5B **Privately Held**
WEB: www.tcco.com
SIC: 1541 1542 1522 Industrial buildings, new construction; commercial & office building, new construction; multi-family dwellings, new construction
HQ: Turner Construction Company Inc
375 Hudson St Fl 6
New York NY 10014
212 229-6000

(G-4706)
TURNER CONSTRUCTION COMPANY
2315 Iowa Ave (45206-2312)
PHONE..................513 363-0883
EMP: 60
SALES (corp-wide): 1.5B **Privately Held**
SIC: 1542 Commercial & office building, new construction

▲ = Import ▼=Export
♦ =Import/Export

GEOGRAPHIC SECTION

Cincinnati - Hamilton County (G-4730)

HQ: Turner Construction Company Inc
375 Hudson St Fl 6
New York NY 10014
212 229-6000

(G-4707)
TURPIN HILLS SWIM RACQUET CLB
3814 West St Ste 311 (45227-3743)
PHONE.................513 231-3242
Jane Tillinghast, President
EMP: 25
SQ FT: 2,870
SALES: 376K Privately Held
WEB: www.turpinswimclub.org
SIC: 7997 Swimming club, membership

(G-4708)
TUSCANY SPA SALON
11355 Montgomery Rd (45249-2312)
PHONE.................513 489-8872
Fax: 513 489-8801
Amy Kobs, Owner
EMP: 30
SQ FT: 5,600
SALES (est): 668.1K Privately Held
WEB: www.tuscanyspaandsalon.com
SIC: 7991 Spas

(G-4709)
TWC CONCRETE SERVICES LLC
10737 Medallion Dr (45241-4837)
PHONE.................513 771-8192
Anthony R Decarlo, CEO
Donald J Wagner, President
Anthony Decarlo Jr, Exec VP
James J Skillman, Vice Pres
Rick Barton, Foreman/Supr
EMP: 70
SALES (est): 19.9MM Privately Held
SIC: 1541 Industrial buildings, new construction

(G-4710)
TWIN TOWERS
5343 Hamilton Ave Apt 513 (45224-3174)
PHONE.................513 853-2000
Fax: 513 853-2044
Scott McQuinn, CEO
Connie Schmitt, Vice Pres
Josh Blackmore, Purch Mgr
James Bowersox, CFO
Ken Mc Donald, Finance
EMP: 400
SQ FT: 535,000
SALES: 9.6MM Privately Held
SIC: 8052 6513 Intermediate care facilities; retirement hotel operation

(G-4711)
TWISM ENTERPRISES LLC
Also Called: Valucadd Solutions
12110 Regency Run Ct # 9 (45240-1090)
PHONE.................513 800-1098
Shawn Alexander,
EMP: 50
SALES (est): 876.1K Privately Held
SIC: 8712 8711 7373 8748 Architectural engineering; mechanical engineering; electrical or electronic engineering; computer-aided engineering (CAE) systems service; telecommunications consultant

(G-4712)
TYCO INTERNATIONAL MGT CO LLC
Also Called: Real Time Systems
2884 E Kemper Rd (45241-1820)
PHONE.................888 787-8324
Ron Hartmann, Branch Mgr
EMP: 50 Privately Held
SIC: 7373 7371 Systems integration services; custom computer programming services
HQ: Tyco International Management Company, Llc
9 Roszel Rd Ste 2
Princeton NJ 08540
609 720-4200

(G-4713)
U C CHILD CARE CENTER INC
3310 Ruther Ave (45220-2111)
PHONE.................513 961-2825

Fax: 513 281-7676
Sally Wehby, Director
Bruce Ault, Director
Jonathan Kamholtz, Director
Daniel Langmeyer, Director
Ricardo Moena, Director
EMP: 30
SALES: 1.6MM Privately Held
SIC: 8351 Child day care services

(G-4714)
U S ARMY CORPS OF ENGINEERS
Regional Acquisition
550 Main St Ste 10022 (45202-3222)
PHONE.................513 684-3048
Bruce Berwick, Commissioner
EMP: 100 Publicly Held
WEB: www.sac.usace.army.mil
SIC: 8711 9711 Engineering services; Army
HQ: U S Army Corps Of Engineers
441 G St Nw
Washington DC 20314
202 761-0001

(G-4715)
UBS FINANCIAL SERVICES INC
312 Walnut St Ste 3300 (45202-4045)
PHONE.................513 576-5000
Jeff Greenwald, Exec VP
Richard Baylis, Senior VP
Kevin Shepherd, Senior VP
Daniel Driscoll, Manager
Robert Unger, Advisor
EMP: 100
SQ FT: 3,500
SALES (corp-wide): 28B Privately Held
SIC: 6211 Stock brokers & dealers; bond dealers & brokers
HQ: Ubs Financial Services Inc.
1285 Ave Of The Americas
New York NY 10019
212 713-2000

(G-4716)
UBS FINANCIAL SERVICES INC
8044 Montgomery Rd # 200 (45236-2926)
PHONE.................513 792-2146
Thomas Frank, Manager
EMP: 48
SALES (corp-wide): 28B Privately Held
SIC: 6211 Security brokers & dealers
HQ: Ubs Financial Services Inc.
1285 Ave Of The Americas
New York NY 10019
212 713-2000

(G-4717)
UBS FINANCIAL SERVICES INC
8044 Montgomery Rd # 200 (45236-2926)
PHONE.................513 792-2100
Scott L Carter, Vice Pres
Tricia Mercalde, Vice Pres
Troy Debord, Branch Mgr
Thomas Frank, Manager
David Hoffmann, Manager
EMP: 50
SALES (corp-wide): 28B Privately Held
SIC: 6211 Security brokers & dealers
HQ: Ubs Financial Services Inc.
1285 Ave Of The Americas
New York NY 10019
212 713-2000

(G-4718)
UC HEALTH LLC
222 Piedmont Ave Ste 0000 (45219-4223)
PHONE.................513 475-7880
Fax: 513 558-4706
Karl Braun, Med Doctor
John Galla, Med Doctor
Stephen M Strakowski, Director
EMP: 568 Privately Held
SIC: 8011 Internal medicine, physician/surgeon
PA: Uc Health, Llc.
3200 Burnet Ave
Cincinnati OH 45229

(G-4719)
UC HEALTH LLC
3200 Burnet Ave (45229-3019)
PHONE.................513 585-7600
Donald Kegg, CEO
Beth Hoff, Accountant

Melissa Slater, Human Res Mgr
Nicole Proffitt, HR Admin
Laura Allerding, Mktg Dir
EMP: 252 Privately Held
SIC: 6324 Health maintenance organization (HMO), insurance only
PA: Uc Health, Llc.
3200 Burnet Ave
Cincinnati OH 45229

(G-4720)
UC HEALTH LLC
11590 Century Blvd # 102 (45246-3317)
PHONE.................513 648-9077
Amy Mechley MD, Med Doctor
Harry J Stagaman MD, Med Doctor
Philip M Diller, Director
Michael B Holliday, Director
Lawson Wulsin, Psychiatry
EMP: 505 Privately Held
SIC: 8011 General & family practice, physician/surgeon
PA: Uc Health, Llc.
3200 Burnet Ave
Cincinnati OH 45229

(G-4721)
UC HEALTH LLC
Also Called: Alliance Health
3120 Burnet Ave Ste 203 (45229-3091)
PHONE.................513 584-8600
James Peters, Exec Dir
Bob Helferich, Administration
Timothy D Freeman, Family Practiti
Christopher Edwards, Nurse Practr
Christine Gilliam, Nurse Practr
EMP: 30 Privately Held
SIC: 8741 8062 Management services; general medical & surgical hospitals
PA: Uc Health, Llc.
3200 Burnet Ave
Cincinnati OH 45229

(G-4722)
UC HEALTH LLC (PA)
3200 Burnet Ave (45229-3019)
PHONE.................513 585-6000
James Kingsbury, CEO
Myles Pensak, Chief
Peter N Gilbert, COO
Jay Brown, Vice Pres
Craig Cain, Vice Pres
EMP: 800
SALES: 1.5B Privately Held
SIC: 8741 Management services; hospital management

(G-4723)
ULMER & BERNE LLP
600 Vine St Ste 2800 (45202-2448)
PHONE.................513 698-5000
Scott Kadish, Manager
EMP: 100
SALES (corp-wide): 85.9MM Privately Held
SIC: 8111 General practice law office
PA: Ulmer & Berne Llp
1660 W 2nd St Ste 1100
Cleveland OH 44113
216 583-7000

(G-4724)
ULMER & BERNE LLP
600 Vine St Ste 2800 (45202-2448)
PHONE.................513 698-5058
Jennifer Snyder, Branch Mgr
Scott Kadish, Manager
EMP: 104
SALES (corp-wide): 85.9MM Privately Held
SIC: 8111 General practice attorney, lawyer
PA: Ulmer & Berne Llp
1660 W 2nd St Ste 1100
Cleveland OH 44113
216 583-7000

(G-4725)
ULTIMUS FUND SOLUTIONS LLC (PA)
225 Pictoria Dr Ste 450 (45246-1617)
PHONE.................513 587-3400
Fax: 513 587-3437
Robert G Dorsey, President
Gary Tenkman, President
Mark J Seger, Co-CEO

Dina Tantra, Exec VP
Bill Tomko, Exec VP
EMP: 36
SQ FT: 21,900
SALES: 10.8MM Privately Held
WEB: www.ultimusfundsolutions.com
SIC: 6211 Mutual funds, selling by independent salesperson

(G-4726)
UNION CENTRAL LIFE INSUR CO (DH)
1876 Waycross Rd (45240-2899)
P.O. Box 40888 (45240-0888)
PHONE.................866 696-7478
Fax: 513 595-2888
Joann Martin, CEO
John Lucas, Counsel
David F Westerbeck, Exec VP
Dale Donald Johnson, Senior VP
Kurt Allen, Vice Pres
EMP: 600
SQ FT: 165,000
SALES (est): 240.2MM
SALES (corp-wide): 2.2B Privately Held
WEB: www.uclfinancial.com
SIC: 6311 6321 Mutual association life insurance; mutual accident & health associations
HQ: Ameritas Holding Company
5900 O St
Lincoln NE 68510
402 467-1122

(G-4727)
UNION SECURITY INSURANCE CO
Also Called: Assurant Employee Benefits
312 Elm St Ste 1500 (45202-2769)
PHONE.................513 621-1924
EMP: 25
SALES (corp-wide): 7.5B Publicly Held
SIC: 6411 Insurance Agent/Broker
HQ: Union Security Insurance Company
6941 Vista Dr
West Des Moines IA 50266
651 361-4000

(G-4728)
UNITED AUDIT SYSTEMS INC
Also Called: Uasi
1924 Dana Ave (45207-1212)
PHONE.................513 723-1122
Fax: 513 535-5165
Ty C Hare, President
Frank Kerley, Exec VP
Beverly J Bredenfoerder, Vice Pres
John De Fraites, Vice Pres
John A Defraites, Vice Pres
EMP: 206
SQ FT: 16,000
SALES (est): 27.1MM Privately Held
WEB: www.uasi-qc.com
SIC: 8742 Hospital & health services consultant

(G-4729)
UNITED CEREBRAL PALSY GR CINC
Also Called: CEREBRAL PALSY SERVICES CENTER
2300 Drex Ave (45212-1216)
PHONE.................513 221-4606
Fax: 513 872-5262
Leonard Wagers, Treasurer
Susan Schiller, Director
Melissa Tally,
EMP: 42
SALES: 3.5K Privately Held
WEB: www.ucp-cincinnati.org
SIC: 8361 Rehabilitation center, residential: health care incidental

(G-4730)
UNITED CHURCH HOMES INC
Also Called: Riverview Community
5999 Bender Rd (45233-1601)
PHONE.................513 922-1440
Fax: 513 922-2927
Leigh Deaton, Principal
Edwin Allen, Vice Pres
Robert Weisbrodt, Vice Pres
Rick Williams, Vice Pres
Daniel Barnes, Director
EMP: 200
SQ FT: 2,125

Cincinnati - Hamilton County (G-4731)   GEOGRAPHIC SECTION

SALES (corp-wide): 78.1MM Privately Held
WEB: www.altenheimcommunity.org
SIC: 8051 8052 8361 Convalescent home with continuous nursing care; intermediate care facilities; home for the aged; rest home, with health care incidental
PA: United Church Homes Inc
170 E Center St
Marion OH 43302
740 382-4885

(G-4731)
UNITED DAIRY FARMERS INC (PA)
Also Called: U D F
3955 Montgomery Rd (45212-3798)
PHONE.................513 396-8700
Fax: 513 396-8736
Brad Lindner, *President*
Frank Cogliano, *Vice Pres*
My-Linh Hartsgrove, *Plant Mgr*
Tom Ball, *Project Mgr*
Ronald Anderson, *Opers Mgr*
EMP: 200
SALES (est): 614.2MM Privately Held
SIC: 5411 5143 2026 2024 Convenience stores, chain; ice cream & ices; frozen dairy desserts; milk processing (pasteurizing, homogenizing, bottling); ice cream & ice milk; filling stations, gasoline; dairy products stores

(G-4732)
UNITED ELECTRIC COMPANY INC
1309 Ethan Ave (45225-1809)
PHONE.................502 459-5242
Fax: 513 542-2213
Larry Farrell, *General Mgr*
Tom Schroth, *Project Mgr*
Tom Murray, *Office Mgr*
Denny Murray, *Branch Mgr*
EMP: 50
SQ FT: 10,000
SALES (est): 5.3MM
SALES (corp-wide): 28.5MM Privately Held
WEB: www.unitedelec.com
SIC: 1731 General electrical contractor
PA: United Electric Company, Inc.
4333 Robards Ln
Louisville KY 40218
502 459-5242

(G-4733)
UNITED INSURANCE COMPANY AMER
135 Merchant St Ste 120 (45246-3773)
PHONE.................513 771-6771
Fax: 513 771-8588
Randy Chasteen, *District Mgr*
EMP: 25
SALES (corp-wide): 2.7B Publicly Held
SIC: 6411 Insurance agents, brokers & service
HQ: United Insurance Company Of America
12115 Lackland Rd
Saint Louis MO 63146
314 819-4300

(G-4734)
UNITED MAIL LLC
1221 Harrison Ave (45214-1719)
PHONE.................513 482-7429
Lee Kirkwood, *Mng Member*
Chase Kirkwood,
Anna Knue,
Diane Moore,
EMP: 80
SALES (est): 10.1MM
SALES (corp-wide): 24.8MM Privately Held
WEB: www.unitedmail.com
SIC: 7331 Mailing service
PA: United Mail Sorting, Inc.
4410 Bishop Ln
Louisville KY 40218
502 485-1400

(G-4735)
UNITED MANAGEMENT INC
8280 Montgomery Rd # 303 (45236-6101)
PHONE.................513 936-8568
Fax: 513 936-8569
Greg Malone, *Officer*

EMP: 30
SALES (corp-wide): 70.2MM Privately Held
SIC: 6531 Real estate agents & managers
PA: United Management, Inc.
250 Civic Center Dr
Columbus OH 43215
614 228-5331

(G-4736)
UNITED PARCEL SERVICE INC OH
Also Called: UPS
500 Gest St (45203-1717)
PHONE.................513 852-6135
Fax: 513 852-3614
Tom Langenkamp, *Accounts Mgr*
EMP: 158
SALES (corp-wide): 65.8B Publicly Held
WEB: www.upsscs.com
SIC: 4215 Parcel delivery, vehicular
HQ: United Parcel Service, Inc. (Oh)
55 Glenlake Pkwy
Atlanta GA 30328
404 828-6000

(G-4737)
UNITED PARCEL SERVICE INC OH
Also Called: UPS
640 W 3rd St (45202-3483)
PHONE.................513 241-5289
EMP: 158
SALES (corp-wide): 65.8B Publicly Held
WEB: www.upsscs.com
SIC: 4215 Parcel delivery, vehicular
HQ: United Parcel Service, Inc. (Oh)
55 Glenlake Pkwy
Atlanta GA 30328
404 828-6000

(G-4738)
UNITED PARCEL SERVICE INC OH
Also Called: UPS
11141 Canal Rd (45241-1861)
PHONE.................513 782-4000
Fax: 513 782-4003
Judy Henry, *District Mgr*
Jason Reynolds, *Opers Mgr*
Curtis Costello, *Technical Mgr*
Francis Ngumbi, *Plant Engr Mgr*
Bryan Schweinefus, *Human Res Mgr*
EMP: 158
SALES (corp-wide): 65.8B Publicly Held
WEB: www.upsscs.com
SIC: 4215 Parcel delivery, vehicular
HQ: United Parcel Service, Inc. (Oh)
55 Glenlake Pkwy
Atlanta GA 30328
404 828-6000

(G-4739)
UNITED PARCEL SERVICE INC OH
Also Called: UPS
644 Linn St Ste 325 (45203-1734)
PHONE.................513 241-5316
Fax: 513 352-1330
Karma Hopper, *Branch Mgr*
EMP: 55
SALES (corp-wide): 65.8B Publicly Held
WEB: www.upsscs.com
SIC: 4215 Parcel delivery, vehicular
HQ: United Parcel Service, Inc. (Oh)
55 Glenlake Pkwy
Atlanta GA 30328
404 828-6000

(G-4740)
UNITED STEELWORKERS
Also Called: Uswa
8968 Blue Ash Rd (45242-7810)
PHONE.................513 793-0272
Fax: 513 793-4664
Don Brammer, *Branch Mgr*
EMP: 44
SALES (corp-wide): 61.5K Privately Held
WEB: www.uswa.org
SIC: 8631 Trade union
PA: United Steelworkers
60 Bolevard Of The Allies
Pittsburgh PA 15222
412 562-2400

(G-4741)
UNITED STTES BOWL CONGRESS INC
520 W Wyoming Ave (45215-4525)
PHONE.................513 761-3338
Willie Dean, *Vice Pres*
EMP: 51
SALES (corp-wide): 32.9MM Privately Held
SIC: 8699 Bowling club
PA: United States Bowling Congress, Inc.
621 Six Flags Dr
Arlington TX 76011
817 385-8200

(G-4742)
UNITED WAY GREATER CINCINNATI (PA)
2400 Reading Rd (45202-1458)
PHONE.................513 762-7100
Fax: 513 762-7203
Robert C Reifsnyder, *President*
Yvonne L Gray, *COO*
Ross Meyer, *Senior VP*
Sheri Vogel, *Senior VP*
Margaret Hulbert, *Vice Pres*
EMP: 100
SQ FT: 70,000
SALES: 57.7MM Privately Held
WEB: www.uwgc.org
SIC: 8322 Individual & family services

(G-4743)
UNITED-MAIER SIGNS INC
1030 Straight St (45214-1734)
PHONE.................513 681-6600
Fax: 513 681-0818
Antony E Maier, *President*
Elvera Maier, *Vice Pres*
Michele Wocher, *Human Resources*
Gene Bare, *VP Sales*
Sally Land, *Sales Mgr*
EMP: 54 EST: 1964
SQ FT: 18,000
SALES (est): 7.9MM Privately Held
WEB: www.united-maier.com
SIC: 3993 1799 Electric signs; sign installation & maintenance

(G-4744)
UNITEDHEALTH GROUP INC
Also Called: United Healthcare
400 E Bus Way Ste 100 (45241)
PHONE.................513 603-6200
Fax: 513 603-6271
Dorothy Coleman, *CEO*
Renee Cassella, *Facilities Mgr*
Patricia Bosch, *Human Resources*
Natalie Correa, *Accounts Mgr*
Lucy Carr, *Accounts Exec*
EMP: 270
SALES (corp-wide): 201.1B Publicly Held
WEB: www.unitedhealthgroup.com
SIC: 6324 Health maintenance organization (HMO), insurance only
PA: Unitedhealth Group Incorporated
9900 Bren Rd E Ste 300w
Minnetonka MN 55343
952 936-1300

(G-4745)
UNIV DERMATOLOGY
Also Called: Uc Health Dermatology
3012 Glenmore Ave Ste 307 (45238-2258)
PHONE.................513 475-7630
Fax: 513 481-6524
Dr Raymond Ringenbach, *President*
BR Brian Adams, *President*
EMP: 100
SALES (est): 4.9MM Privately Held
SIC: 8011 8093 Dermatologist; specialty outpatient clinics

(G-4746)
UNIVERSAL ADVERTISING ASSOC
Also Called: Business Community Section
2530 Civic Center Dr (45231-1310)
P.O. Box 31132 (45231-0132)
PHONE.................513 522-5000
Fax: 513 522-5530
Larry Vonderhaar, *President*
Matt Vonderhaar, *Executive*
EMP: 49

SQ FT: 7,500
SALES (est): 7.2MM Privately Held
WEB: www.uaai.com
SIC: 7311 8611 Advertising consultant; business associations

(G-4747)
UNIVERSAL CONTRACTING CORP
5151 Fishwick Dr (45216-2215)
PHONE.................513 482-2700
Phillip J Neumann, *President*
Glenn Chapman, *Controller*
EMP: 30 EST: 1957
SQ FT: 7,500
SALES (est): 7.5MM Privately Held
SIC: 1541 1542 Industrial buildings, new construction; commercial & office building, new construction

(G-4748)
UNIVERSAL PACKG SYSTEMS INC
Also Called: Paklab
470 Northland Blvd (45240-3211)
PHONE.................513 674-9400
Jeff Topits, *Branch Mgr*
EMP: 388
SALES (corp-wide): 423.8MM Privately Held
SIC: 2844 3565 7389 2671 Cosmetic preparations; bottling machinery: filling, capping, labeling; packaging & labeling services; plastic film, coated or laminated for packaging
PA: Universal Packaging Systems, Inc.
380 Townline Rd Ste 130
Hauppauge NY 11788
631 543-2277

(G-4749)
UNIVERSITY CLUB INC
401 E 4th St (45202-3373)
PHONE.................513 721-2600
Fax: 513 721-2850
Ron Koetters, *President*
Debbie Kramer, *Business Mgr*
Paul Satoril, *Treasurer*
Kelly Wertz, *Marketing Staff*
EMP: 35
SQ FT: 35,000
SALES: 1.1MM Privately Held
SIC: 8641 Social club, membership

(G-4750)
UNIVERSITY DERMATOLOGY CONS
234 Goodman St A3 (45219-2364)
PHONE.................513 584-4775
Fax: 513 558-6636
Diya Mutsin, *President*
David Astles, *Treasurer*
EMP: 40
SQ FT: 5,000
SALES (est): 1.6MM Privately Held
SIC: 8011 Dermatologist

(G-4751)
UNIVERSITY DERMATOLOGY CONS
222 Piedmont Ave Ste 5300 (45219-4215)
PHONE.................513 475-7630
Fax: 513 475-7636
Diya F Mutasim, *President*
Brian Adams, *Med Doctor*
Teri Hanlon, *Manager*
Mirza Alikhan, *Dermatology*
Bobbie Lambert, *Receptionist Se*
EMP: 50
SALES: 10.3MM Privately Held
SIC: 8011 Dermatologist

(G-4752)
UNIVERSITY FAMILY PHYSICIANS
2123 Auburn Ave (45219-2906)
PHONE.................513 929-0104
Laura J Ranz, *Branch Mgr*
EMP: 43
SALES (corp-wide): 3.6MM Privately Held
SIC: 8011 General & family practice, physician/surgeon

GEOGRAPHIC SECTION

Cincinnati - Hamilton County (G-4773)

PA: University Family Physicians Inc
3235 Eden Ave
Cincinnati OH 45267
513 558-4022

(G-4753)
UNIVERSITY FAMILY PHYSICIANS
Also Called: Wyoming Family Practice Center
305 Crescent Ave (45215-4406)
PHONE.................513 475-7505
Fax: 513 821-3621
Elouise Clark, *Manager*
Nicole Gulley, *Assistant*
EMP: 80
SQ FT: 11,081
SALES (corp-wide): 3.6MM **Privately Held**
SIC: 8011 General & family practice, physician/surgeon
PA: University Family Physicians Inc
3235 Eden Ave
Cincinnati OH 45267
513 558-4022

(G-4754)
UNIVERSITY NEUROLOGY INC
222 Piedmont Ave Ste 3200 (45219-4217)
PHONE.................513 475-8730
Joseph Broderick, *President*
Bratt Kissela, *Vice Pres*
Brett Kissela, *Vice Pres*
Neil Holsing, *Treasurer*
Alberto Espay, *Med Doctor*
EMP: 66
SALES: 7.7MM **Privately Held**
SIC: 8011 Neurologist

(G-4755)
UNIVERSITY OF CINCINNATI
Also Called: Department of Anesthetia
231 Albert Sabin Way (45267-2827)
PHONE.................513 558-4194
Fax: 513 558-2289
Mary Schaefer, *Business Mgr*
Laura Hildreth, *Dean*
Arnold Miller, *Vice Pres*
Mary McGrew, *Assoc VP*
Cheryl Johnson, *Project Mgr*
EMP: 35
SALES (corp-wide): 1.3B **Privately Held**
SIC: 8011 8221 Offices & clinics of medical doctors; university
PA: University Of Cincinnati
2600 Clifton Ave
Cincinnati OH 45220
513 556-6000

(G-4756)
UNIVERSITY OF CINCINNATI
Also Called: University Hosp A & MBL Care
3200 Burnet Ave (45229-3019)
PHONE.................513 584-7522
Dudley Smith, *Principal*
Jeanette Jones, *Manager*
Debbie Rauh, *Manager*
Jasmine Burno, *Nurse Practr*
Emanuel Lewis, *Nurse Practr*
EMP: 30
SALES (corp-wide): 1.3B **Privately Held**
SIC: 8062 8221 Hospital, medical school affiliation; university
PA: University Of Cincinnati
2600 Clifton Ave
Cincinnati OH 45220
513 556-6000

(G-4757)
UNIVERSITY OF CINCINNATI
231 Albert Sabin Way (45267-2827)
PHONE.................513 558-4516
Wendy Ramalingam, *Branch Mgr*
Stacey Grippa, *Director*
Maryann Cook, *Professor*
Glenn Talaska, *Professor*
EMP: 65
SALES (corp-wide): 1.3B **Privately Held**
SIC: 8011 Orthopedic physician
PA: University Of Cincinnati
2600 Clifton Ave
Cincinnati OH 45220
513 556-6000

(G-4758)
UNIVERSITY OF CINCINNATI
Also Called: Department of Psychiatry
260 Stetson St Ste 3200 (45219-2472)
P.O. Box 670559 (45269-0001)
PHONE.................513 558-7700
Stephen M Strakowski, *Branch Mgr*
Susan McElroy, *Director*
Cindy Starr, *Education*
Andrew Massey, *Neurology*
Aristide Merola, *Neurology*
EMP: 67
SALES (corp-wide): 1.3B **Privately Held**
SIC: 8011 Psychiatrist
PA: University Of Cincinnati
2600 Clifton Ave
Cincinnati OH 45220
513 556-6000

(G-4759)
UNIVERSITY OF CINCINNATI
Also Called: University Hsptl-Uc Physicians
222 Piedmont Ave Ste 7000 (45219-4224)
PHONE.................513 475-8771
Michael Nussbaum, *CEO*
Rosemary Keiser, *Vice Pres*
Cathy Maltbie, *Research*
Sue Hoblitvell, *CFO*
Michael Hanaway, *Med Doctor*
EMP: 40
SALES (corp-wide): 1.3B **Privately Held**
SIC: 8011 8221 General & family practice, physician/surgeon; university
PA: University Of Cincinnati
2600 Clifton Ave
Cincinnati OH 45220
513 556-6000

(G-4760)
UNIVERSITY OF CINCINNATI
Also Called: Blood Center
3130 Highland Ave Fl 3 (45219-2399)
P.O. Box 670055 (45267-0001)
PHONE.................513 558-1200
Michael Lieberman, *Dean*
Howard Jackson, *Vice Pres*
Caroline Miller, *Assoc VP*
Angela Smith, *Research*
Helen Williams, *Med Doctor*
EMP: 300
SALES (corp-wide): 1.3B **Privately Held**
SIC: 8011 8221 Offices & clinics of medical doctors; university
PA: University Of Cincinnati
2600 Clifton Ave
Cincinnati OH 45220
513 556-6000

(G-4761)
UNIVERSITY OF CINCINNATI
Also Called: Administration Services Dept
51 Goodman St (45219-2477)
P.O. Box 210080 (45221-0080)
PHONE.................513 556-6381
James Tucker, *Director*
John Combs, *Asst Director*
EMP: 1600
SALES (corp-wide): 1.3B **Privately Held**
SIC: 8221 7349 5812 0782 University; building maintenance services; eating places; lawn & garden services
PA: University Of Cincinnati
2600 Clifton Ave
Cincinnati OH 45220
513 556-6000

(G-4762)
UNIVERSITY OF CINCINNATI
Also Called: Endocrine Lab
3125 Eden Ave (45219-2293)
P.O. Box 670547 (45267-0001)
PHONE.................513 558-4444
David A'Lessio, *Manager*
Thomas Ridgeway, *Director*
Fred Finkelman, *Professor*
Wallace Ip, *Professor*
EMP: 30
SQ FT: 1,203
SALES (corp-wide): 1.3B **Privately Held**
SIC: 8071 8221 Medical laboratories; university
PA: University Of Cincinnati
2600 Clifton Ave
Cincinnati OH 45220
513 556-6000

(G-4763)
UNIVERSITY OF CINCINNATI
Also Called: University Hosp Rdilology Dept
234 Goodman St 761 (45219-2364)
PHONE.................513 584-4396
Robert Lukin MD, *Chairman*
Sean Gallagher, *CFO*
Jeffery Sussman, *Med Doctor*
Mark Thomas, *Med Doctor*
Mary Bakis, *Anesthesiology*
EMP: 30
SALES (corp-wide): 1.3B **Privately Held**
SIC: 8062 8221 General medical & surgical hospitals; university
PA: University Of Cincinnati
2600 Clifton Ave
Cincinnati OH 45220
513 556-6000

(G-4764)
UNIVERSITY OF CINCINNATI
Also Called: McMicken College of Asa
146 Mcmicken Hall (45221-0001)
PHONE.................513 556-5087
Peg Ellensworth, *Principal*
Stewart Wright, *Assoc Prof*
EMP: 2000
SALES (corp-wide): 1.3B **Privately Held**
SIC: 8999 8221 Communication services; university
PA: University Of Cincinnati
2600 Clifton Ave
Cincinnati OH 45220
513 556-6000

(G-4765)
UNIVERSITY OF CINCINNATI
Also Called: Ucvp For Research
2614 Mecken Cir (45221-0001)
PHONE.................513 556-4054
Nedille Pinto, *Principal*
EMP: 28
SALES (corp-wide): 1.3B **Privately Held**
SIC: 8221 8732 University; educational research
PA: University Of Cincinnati
2600 Clifton Ave
Cincinnati OH 45220
513 556-6000

(G-4766)
UNIVERSITY OF CINCINNATI
Also Called: Institute Environmental Health
3223 Eden Avenue (45267-0001)
P.O. Box 6756 (45206-0756)
PHONE.................513 558-5439
Fax: 513 558-4397
Neville Tam, *Research*
Joseph Broderick, *Med Doctor*
Sunila Nair, *Manager*
Thomas Ridgeway, *Network Mgr*
Marshall W Anderson, *Director*
EMP: 200
SALES (corp-wide): 1.3B **Privately Held**
SIC: 8071 8221 Medical laboratories; university
PA: University Of Cincinnati
2600 Clifton Ave
Cincinnati OH 45220
513 556-6000

(G-4767)
UNIVERSITY OF CINCINNATI
Also Called: University Cincinnati Book Str
51 W Goodman Dr (45221-0001)
PHONE.................513 556-4200
Gerald Siegert, *Assoc VP*
Joseph Treinen, *Engineer*
Mike Zimmerman, *Branch Mgr*
James Dusing, *Manager*
Brenda Frankenhoff, *Manager*
EMP: 50
SALES (corp-wide): 1.3B **Privately Held**
SIC: 8741 5942 Administrative management; book stores
PA: University Of Cincinnati
2600 Clifton Ave
Cincinnati OH 45220
513 556-6000

(G-4768)
UNIVERSITY OF CINCINNATI
Also Called: Uima
231 Albert Sabin Way (45267-2827)
PHONE.................513 558-4231
Andrew T Filak Jr, *Vice Pres*
Kathy Qualls, *CFO*
B E Martin, *Treasurer*
Bradley Britigan, *Branch Mgr*
Robert Baughman, *Professor*
EMP: 150
SALES (corp-wide): 1.3B **Privately Held**
SIC: 8741 8221 Administrative management; university
PA: University Of Cincinnati
2600 Clifton Ave
Cincinnati OH 45220
513 556-6000

(G-4769)
UNIVERSITY OF CINCINNATI
Also Called: Breast Consultation Center
234 Goodman St (45219-2364)
PHONE.................513 584-5331
Fax: 513 558-4391
Carolyn Thomas, *Director*
EMP: 55
SALES (corp-wide): 1.3B **Privately Held**
SIC: 8071 8221 Testing laboratories; university
PA: University Of Cincinnati
2600 Clifton Ave
Cincinnati OH 45220
513 556-6000

(G-4770)
UNIVERSITY OF CINCINNATI
Also Called: Geological Department
500 Geo Physics Bldg 5f (45221-0001)
P.O. Box 2210030
PHONE.................513 556-3732
Arnold Miller, *Principal*
EMP: 40
SALES (corp-wide): 1.3B **Privately Held**
SIC: 8221 8711 University; engineering services
PA: University Of Cincinnati
2600 Clifton Ave
Cincinnati OH 45220
513 556-6000

(G-4771)
UNIVERSITY OF CINCINNATI
Also Called: Athletics Dept
2751 O'vrsity Way Ste 880 (45221-0001)
P.O. Box 210021 (45221-0021)
PHONE.................513 556-4603
Fax: 513 556-0619
Mike Bohn, *Director*
Isidro Risma, *Family Practiti*
EMP: 140
SALES (corp-wide): 1.3B **Privately Held**
SIC: 8699 8221 Athletic organizations; university
PA: University Of Cincinnati
2600 Clifton Ave
Cincinnati OH 45220
513 556-6000

(G-4772)
UNIVERSITY OF CINCINNATI
Also Called: Consolidated Utilities
3001 Short Vine St (45219-2024)
PHONE.................513 558-1799
Sallie Troutman, *Director*
EMP: 60
SALES (corp-wide): 1.3B **Privately Held**
SIC: 4939 8221 Combination utilities; university
PA: University Of Cincinnati
2600 Clifton Ave
Cincinnati OH 45220
513 556-6000

(G-4773)
UNIVERSITY OF CINCINNATI
Also Called: Cancer Center
234 Goodman St (45219-2364)
PHONE.................513 584-3200
Dawn Harper-Smith, *Human Resources*
Elizabeth Shaughnessy, *Med Doctor*
Barbara Stumps, *Manager*
Alison Kastl, *Director*
EMP: 150
SALES (corp-wide): 1.3B **Privately Held**
SIC: 8093 8221 Specialty outpatient clinics; university
PA: University Of Cincinnati
2600 Clifton Ave
Cincinnati OH 45220
513 556-6000

Cincinnati - Hamilton County (G-4774) GEOGRAPHIC SECTION

(G-4774)
UNIVERSITY OF CINCINNATI
Also Called: Nephrology Department
231 Albert Sabin Way G258 (45267-2827)
P.O. Box 670585 (45267-0001)
PHONE.....................513 558-5471
Heather Koman, *Manager*
Manoocher Soleimani, *Professor*
Doug S Kennedy, *Assistant*
EMP: 50
SALES (corp-wide): 1.3B Privately Held
SIC: 8011 8221 Nephrologist; university
PA: University Of Cincinnati
  2600 Clifton Ave
  Cincinnati OH 45220
  513 556-6000

(G-4775)
UNIVERSITY OF CINCINNATI
222 Piedmont Ave Ste 6000 (45219-4223)
PHONE.....................513 475-8524
Fax: 513 475-7355
Abhinav Diwan MD, *Med Doctor*
Norman H Gilinsky, *Med Doctor*
James Knepler, *Med Doctor*
Jonathan P Kushner, *Med Doctor*
Kenneth E Shrman, *Med Doctor*
EMP: 67
SALES (corp-wide): 1.3B Privately Held
SIC: 8011 Internal medicine, physician/surgeon
PA: University Of Cincinnati
  2600 Clifton Ave
  Cincinnati OH 45220
  513 556-6000

(G-4776)
UNIVERSITY OF CINCINNATI
Also Called: Univ Hospital, The
331 Albert Sabin Way (45229-2838)
PHONE.....................513 584-1000
Mark Slye, *Branch Mgr*
Lisa Ann, *Director*
Thomas F Boat, *Pediatrics*
EMP: 30
SALES (corp-wide): 1.3B Privately Held
SIC: 8062 8221 Hospital, medical school affiliation; university
PA: University Of Cincinnati
  2600 Clifton Ave
  Cincinnati OH 45220
  513 556-6000

(G-4777)
UNIVERSITY OF CINCINNATI
Also Called: Pulmonary Division
231 Albert Sabin Way (45267-2827)
PHONE.....................513 558-4831
Melanie Maughlin, *Med Doctor*
Michael Newton, *Med Doctor*
Dee Douglas, *Manager*
EMP: 25
SALES (corp-wide): 1.3B Privately Held
SIC: 8011 8221 Pulmonary specialist, physician/surgeon; university
PA: University Of Cincinnati
  2600 Clifton Ave
  Cincinnati OH 45220
  513 556-6000

(G-4778)
UNIVERSITY OF CINCINNATI
Also Called: University Hospital
234 Goodman St (45219-2364)
PHONE.....................513 584-1000
Sarah Fenske, *Managing Dir*
William Slater, *COO*
Rick Hinds, *Exec VP*
Paul Uhlig, *Vice Pres*
Andrew Burger, *Research*
EMP: 30
SALES (corp-wide): 1.3B Privately Held
SIC: 8062 8221 General medical & surgical hospitals; university
PA: University Of Cincinnati
  2600 Clifton Ave
  Cincinnati OH 45220
  513 556-6000

(G-4779)
UNIVERSITY OF CINCINNATI
Also Called: Arlette Child Family Rese
Edwards 1 Bldg (45221-0001)
P.O. Box 210105 (45221-0105)
PHONE.....................513 556-3803
Vicky Carr, *Director*
EMP: 60
SALES (corp-wide): 1.3B Privately Held
SIC: 8322 8221 Child related social services; university
PA: University Of Cincinnati
  2600 Clifton Ave
  Cincinnati OH 45220
  513 556-6000

(G-4780)
UNIVERSITY OF CINCINNATI PHYS (PA)
Also Called: Uc Physicians
222 Piedmont Ave Ste 2200 (45219-4238)
PHONE.....................513 475-8521
Myles Pensak, *CEO*
Thomas Boat, *President*
David J Fine, *Principal*
Randall Sakai, *Editor*
Lori A Mackey, *COO*
EMP: 40
SQ FT: 2,800
SALES (est): 55.3MM Privately Held
SIC: 8742 Hospital & health services consultant

(G-4781)
UNIVERSITY OF CINCINNATI PHYS
2830 Victory Pkwy Ste 320 (45206-3700)
PHONE.....................513 475-7934
Keith Luken, *General Mgr*
Daniel Schneider, *Project Dir*
Tom Ducro, *Controller*
Susann Schulte, *Branch Mgr*
Mark Sauer, *Technology*
EMP: 220 Privately Held
SIC: 8011 Offices & clinics of medical doctors
PA: University Of Cincinnati Physicians, Inc.
  222 Piedmont Ave Ste 2200
  Cincinnati OH 45219

(G-4782)
UNIVERSITY OF CNCNNATI SRGEONS (PA)
2830 Victory Pkwy Ste 320 (45206-3700)
P.O. Box 630251 (45263-0251)
PHONE.....................513 245-3300
Tal Richards, *President*
Mary Rich, *Program Mgr*
EMP: 50
SALES (est): 11.9MM Privately Held
SIC: 8011 Surgeon

(G-4783)
UNIVERSITY ORTHOPAEDIC CNSLTNT
Also Called: Angelo J Colosimo MD
222 Piedmont Ave Ste 2200 (45219-4238)
P.O. Box 670212 (45267-0001)
PHONE.....................513 475-8690
Fax: 513 475-7243
Peter Stern, *President*
Angelo Colosimo, *Med Doctor*
EMP: 50
SALES (est): 2.3MM Privately Held
SIC: 8011 Orthopedic physician

(G-4784)
UNIVERSITY RADIOLOGY ASSOC
Also Called: Uc Health
222 Piedmont Ave Ste 2100 (45219-4238)
PHONE.....................513 475-8760
Fax: 513 618-2911
Karen Krebs, *Branch Mgr*
Lisa Renner, *Business Mgr*
Rena Alex, *Marketing Staff*
EMP: 100
SALES (est): 2MM Privately Held
SIC: 8011 8093 Radiologist; specialty outpatient clinics

(G-4785)
UNIVERSTY OF CINCINNTI MEDCL C (PA)
234 Goodman St (45219-2364)
PHONE.....................513 584-1000
Bryan Gibler, *President*
George L Strike, *Chairman*
Nancy Barone, *COO*
Peter D Gosmak, *Trustee*
Arthur T Evans II, *Ch OB/GYN*
▲ EMP: 35
SALES: 913.1MM Privately Held
SIC: 8062 General medical & surgical hospitals

(G-4786)
UNIVERSTY OF CINCINNTI MEDCL C
222 Piedmont Ave (45219-4231)
PHONE.....................513 475-8000
David Megee, *Plastic Surgeon*
Kathleen Ballman, *Assoc Prof*
Lilia Lovera, *Neurology*
Walter McFarland, *Neurology*
EMP: 3724
SALES (corp-wide): 913.1MM Privately Held
SIC: 8011 Offices & clinics of medical doctors
PA: University Of Cincinnati Medical Center, Llc
  234 Goodman St
  Cincinnati OH 45219
  513 584-1000

(G-4787)
URBAN LEAGUE OF GREATER SOUTHW
3458 Reading Rd (45229-3128)
PHONE.....................513 281-9955
Fax: 513 281-0455
Donna Jones Baker, *President*
Jeanette Shoecraft, *General Mgr*
Levon Thompson Jr, *COO*
Tom Hanrahan, *Vice Pres*
Cato Mayberry, *Vice Pres*
EMP: 54
SQ FT: 27,000
SALES: 4.4MM Privately Held
SIC: 8399 Community development groups

(G-4788)
URBAN ONE INC
Also Called: Wizf-FM
1821 Summit Rd Ste 400 (45237-2822)
PHONE.....................513 749-1009
Alfred Leggins, *Owner*
Jim Wood, *Manager*
EMP: 50
SALES (corp-wide): 440MM Publicly Held
WEB: www.radio-one.com
SIC: 4832 Radio broadcasting stations
PA: Urban One, Inc.
  1010 Wayne Ave Fl 14
  Silver Spring MD 20910
  301 429-3200

(G-4789)
URBAN ONE INC
Also Called: Blue Chip Broadcasting
705 Central Ave Ste 200 (45202-1900)
PHONE.....................513 679-6000
Jeri Tolliver, *Branch Mgr*
EMP: 40
SALES (corp-wide): 440MM Publicly Held
WEB: www.radio-one.com
SIC: 4832 Radio broadcasting stations
PA: Urban One, Inc.
  1010 Wayne Ave Fl 14
  Silver Spring MD 20910
  301 429-3200

(G-4790)
URBAN RETAIL PROPERTIES LLC
Also Called: Kenwood Management
7875 Montgomery Rd (45236-4344)
PHONE.....................513 346-4482
Wanda Wagner, *General Mgr*
EMP: 25
SALES (corp-wide): 99.7MM Privately Held
WEB: www.kaanapali-golf.com
SIC: 6552 Subdividers & developers
HQ: Urban Retail Properties, Llc
  111 E Wacker Dr Ste 2400
  Chicago IL 60601

(G-4791)
URS GROUP INC
525 Vine St Ste 1900 (45202-3124)
PHONE.....................513 651-3440
Fax: 513 651-6452
J Suhre, *Vice Pres*
Glenn Armstrong, *Branch Mgr*
EMP: 69
SALES (corp-wide): 18.2B Publicly Held
SIC: 8711 Engineering services
HQ: Urs Group, Inc.
  300 S Grand Ave Ste 1100
  Los Angeles CA 90071
  213 593-8000

(G-4792)
US BANK NATIONAL ASSOCIATION (HQ)
Also Called: US Bank
425 Walnut St Fl 1 (45202-3989)
PHONE.....................513 632-4234
Richard K Davis, *Ch of Bd*
Steven Bennett, *President*
Marsha Cruzan, *President*
Phyllis D Slusher, *President*
Terrance R Dolan, *Vice Chairman*
EMP: 1150
SQ FT: 244,000
SALES: 22.2B
SALES (corp-wide): 22.7B Publicly Held
WEB: www.firstar.com
SIC: 6021 National commercial banks
PA: U.S. Bancorp
  800 Nicollet Mall # 1500
  Minneapolis MN 55402
  612 303-4770

(G-4793)
US BANK NATIONAL ASSOCIATION
Also Called: US Bank
5065 Wooster Rd (45226-2326)
PHONE.....................513 979-1000
Diane Johnson, *Branch Mgr*
EMP: 800
SALES (corp-wide): 22.7B Publicly Held
SIC: 6021 National commercial banks
HQ: U.S. Bank National Association
  425 Walnut St Fl 1
  Cincinnati OH 45202
  513 632-4234

(G-4794)
US BANK NATIONAL ASSOCIATION
Also Called: US Bank
2300 Wall St Ste A (45212-2742)
PHONE.....................513 458-2844
Sandy Metcalf, *Branch Mgr*
EMP: 50
SALES (corp-wide): 22.7B Publicly Held
SIC: 6021 National commercial banks
HQ: U.S. Bank National Association
  425 Walnut St Fl 1
  Cincinnati OH 45202
  513 632-4234

(G-4795)
US INSPECTION SERVICES INC
502 W Crescentville Rd (45246-1222)
PHONE.....................513 671-7073
Fax: 513 671-7084
Ed Graham, *Branch Mgr*
EMP: 35
SALES (corp-wide): 1.6B Privately Held
SIC: 8734 Testing laboratories
HQ: U.S. Inspection Services, Inc.
  7333 Paragon Rd Ste 240
  Dayton OH 45459

(G-4796)
US PROTECTION SERVICE LLC
Also Called: Now Security Group
1850 W Galbraith Rd (45239-4851)
PHONE.....................513 422-7910
Michael Pendleton, *Branch Mgr*
EMP: 55
SALES (corp-wide): 4.5MM Privately Held
SIC: 7381 7389 Security guard service; private investigator; commodities sampling
PA: U.S. Protection Service Llc
  5785 Emporium Sq
  Columbus OH 43231
  614 794-4950

Cincinnati - Hamilton County (G-4820)

(G-4797)
US SECURITY ASSOCIATES INC
230 Northland Blvd # 307 (45246-0016)
PHONE..................513 381-7033
Lisa K Crawford, *Owner*
EMP: 108 **Privately Held**
SIC: 7381 Security guard service
PA: U.S. Security Associates, Inc.
200 Mansell Ct E Ste 500
Roswell GA 30076

(G-4798)
USI MIDWEST LLC (DH)
312 Elm St Ste 24 (45202-2992)
PHONE..................513 852-6300
Thomas Cassady, *CEO*
Tom Cassady, *President*
Candy Schoeps, *Senior VP*
Paul J Cook, *Vice Pres*
Stephen Diienno, *Vice Pres*
EMP: 111
SQ FT: 24,000
SALES (est): 34MM **Privately Held**
SIC: 6411 Insurance agents, brokers & service

(G-4799)
USIC LOCATING SERVICES LLC
3478 Hauck Rd Ste D (45241-4604)
PHONE..................513 554-0456
Bekah Samad, *Financial Exec*
Tom Mox, *Director*
EMP: 100 **Privately Held**
SIC: 1623 Underground utilities contractor
HQ: Usic Locating Services, Llc
9045 River Rd Ste 300
Indianapolis IN 46240
317 575-7800

(G-4800)
UTS INC
P.O. Box 36342 (45236-0342)
PHONE..................513 332-9000
John Broke, *Principal*
EMP: 25
SALES (est): 431.8K **Privately Held**
SIC: 8748 Telecommunications consultant

(G-4801)
VALLEY INTERIOR SYSTEMS INC (PA)
2203 Fowler St (45206-2307)
P.O. Box 68109 (45206-8109)
PHONE..................513 961-0400
Fax: 513 961-1717
Mike Strawser, *CEO*
Jeff Hudepohl, *President*
Todd Brandenburg, *Superintendent*
Steve Erhart, *Superintendent*
Scott Hardman, *Superintendent*
EMP: 350
SQ FT: 9,000
SALES (est): 70.7MM **Privately Held**
SIC: 1742 Drywall; acoustical & ceiling work; plastering, plain or ornamental

(G-4802)
VALVOLINE LLC
3901 River Rd (45204-1033)
PHONE..................513 557-3100
Fax: 513 557-3109
Patrick Nelson, *General Mgr*
Missy Voges, *Cust Svc Dir*
James Jones, *Branch Mgr*
EMP: 100
SALES (corp-wide): 2B **Publicly Held**
SIC: 7549 Automotive maintenance services
HQ: Valvoline Llc
100 Valvoline Way
Lexington KY 40509
859 357-7777

(G-4803)
VAN PELT CORPORATION
Also Called: Service Steel Div
5170 Broerman Ave (45217-1140)
PHONE..................513 242-6000
Fax: 513 242-7281
Ron Wood, *Branch Mgr*
Todd McEntyre, *Manager*
EMP: 25
SQ FT: 55,000
SALES (corp-wide): 31.6MM **Privately Held**
WEB: www.servicesteel.com
SIC: 5051 Steel
PA: Van Pelt Corporation
13700 Sherwood St Ste 2
Detroit MI 48212
313 365-3600

(G-4804)
VARNEY DISPATCH INC
4 Triangle Park Dr # 404 (45246-3401)
PHONE..................513 682-4200
EMP: 40
SQ FT: 22,000
SALES (est): 3.7MM **Privately Held**
SIC: 4212 Local Trucking Operator

(G-4805)
VELCO INC
Also Called: Coit
10280 Chester Rd (45215-1200)
PHONE..................513 772-4226
Dennis Desserich, *President*
Keith Desserich, *Vice Pres*
Douglas Desserich, *Treasurer*
Brooke Desserich, *Accountant*
EMP: 38
SQ FT: 27,000
SALES (est): 2.9MM **Privately Held**
WEB: www.restoraid.net
SIC: 7217 7216 Carpet & furniture cleaning on location; upholstery cleaning on customer premises; curtain cleaning & repair

(G-4806)
VENCO VENTURO INDUSTRIES LLC (PA)
Also Called: Venco/Venturo Div
12110 Best Pl (45241-1569)
PHONE..................513 772-8448
Brett Collins, *President*
Dave Foster, *Vice Pres*
Terry Woosley, *VP Opers*
Mike Strittholt, *CFO*
Larry Jones, *Sales Staff*
▲ **EMP:** 41
SQ FT: 100,000
SALES (est): 18.3MM **Privately Held**
WEB: www.venturo.com
SIC: 3713 5012 3714 5084 Truck bodies (motor vehicles); truck bodies; motor vehicle parts & accessories; cranes, industrial

(G-4807)
VENTURO MANUFACTURING INC
12110 Best Pl (45241-1569)
PHONE..................513 772-8448
Larry Collins, *President*
Ronald A Collins, *Vice Pres*
Sandy Riley, *Vice Pres*
Charlie Klein, *Prdtn Mgr*
Brad Clarkson, *Purch Agent*
EMP: 32
SQ FT: 5,000
SALES (est): 9MM
SALES (corp-wide): 18.3MM **Privately Held**
WEB: www.venturo.com
SIC: 3537 5084 Cranes, industrial truck; industrial machinery & equipment
PA: Venco Venturo Industries Llc
12110 Best Pl
Cincinnati OH 45241
513 772-8448

(G-4808)
VERSATEX LLC
324 W 9th St (45202-2043)
PHONE..................513 639-3119
Gerald Sparkman, *President*
Melinda Lowe, *Regional Mgr*
Tracy Wells, *Regional Mgr*
Tom Booher, *Accountant*
Constance A Hill, *Legal Staff*
EMP: 40
SQ FT: 4,000
SALES (est): 6.5MM
SALES (corp-wide): 124.9MM **Privately Held**
SIC: 8742 Business consultant
PA: D.E. Foxx & Associates, Inc.
324 W 9th St Fl 5
Cincinnati OH 45202
513 621-5522

(G-4809)
VERST GROUP LOGISTICS INC
Zenith Logistics
98 Glendale Milford Rd (45215-1101)
PHONE..................513 782-1725
Rich Grau, *Vice Pres*
EMP: 240
SALES (corp-wide): 59.2MM **Privately Held**
SIC: 4225 General warehousing & storage
PA: Verst Group Logistics, Inc.
300 Shorland Dr
Walton KY 41094
859 485-1212

(G-4810)
VERST GROUP LOGISTICS INC
11880 Enterprise Dr (45241-1512)
PHONE..................513 772-2494
Fax: 513 782-4485
Keith Berry, *Opers Mgr*
Jonathan O Carroll, *Opers Mgr*
Dan Meyer, *Opers Mgr*
Lori Ollier, *Human Resources*
Jeff Antrobus, *Branch Mgr*
EMP: 30
SALES (corp-wide): 59.2MM **Privately Held**
WEB: www.verstgroup.com
SIC: 4225 4731 8741 General warehousing & storage; freight transportation arrangement; management services
PA: Verst Group Logistics, Inc.
300 Shorland Dr
Walton KY 41094
859 485-1212

(G-4811)
VETERAN SECURITY PATROL CO
36 E 7th St Ste 2201 (45202-4453)
PHONE..................513 381-4482
Fax: 513 381-6682
Lawrence Rogg, *General Mgr*
Scott Curry, *Marketing Staff*
Pat Navin, *Branch Mgr*
EMP: 225 **Privately Held**
WEB: www.veteransecurity.com
SIC: 7381 Guard services
PA: Veteran Security Patrol Co.
215 Taylor Ave
Bellevue KY 41073

(G-4812)
VETERANS HEALTH ADMINISTRATION
Also Called: Cincinnati V A Medical Center
3200 Vine St (45220-2213)
PHONE..................513 861-3100
Fax: 513 475-6454
Heidi Barta, *Pharmacist*
Jasmina Jovic, *Med Doctor*
Linda Klein, *Med Doctor*
Peter Kotcher, *Med Doctor*
Kendra Unterbrink, *Med Doctor*
EMP: 1200 **Publicly Held**
WEB: www.veterans-ru.org
SIC: 8011 9451 Medical centers; administration of veterans' affairs;
HQ: Veterans Health Administration
810 Vermont Ave Nw
Washington DC 20420

(G-4813)
VETERANS HEALTH ADMINISTRATION
Also Called: Clermont County Community
4600 Beechwood Rd (45244-1809)
PHONE..................513 943-3680
Donna Witt, *Branch Mgr*
EMP: 263 **Publicly Held**
WEB: www.veterans-ru.org
SIC: 8011 9451 Clinic, operated by physicians; psychiatric clinic;
HQ: Veterans Health Administration
810 Vermont Ave Nw
Washington DC 20420

(G-4814)
VIG PROPERTY DEVELOPMENT LLC
201 E 5th St 19001065 (45202-4152)
PHONE..................888 384-5970
Alexander Vaughn, *CEO*
EMP: 31
SQ FT: 1,500
SALES (est): 1.4MM **Privately Held**
SIC: 1542 Commercial & office building, new construction

(G-4815)
VISITING NURSE ASSOCIAT (PA)
2400 Reading Rd Ste 207 (45202-1468)
PHONE..................513 345-8000
Fax: 513 345-8082
Valerie Landell, *CEO*
Trudy Schwab, *Exec VP*
Ted Clingner, *Vice Pres*
Don Turner, *Vice Pres*
Ernie Cook, *Controller*
EMP: 202
SQ FT: 11,492
SALES: 8.3MM **Privately Held**
SIC: 8082 Home health care services

(G-4816)
VITAS HEALTHCARE CORPORATION
11500 Northlake Dr # 400 (45249-1658)
PHONE..................513 742-6310
Joe Killian, *General Mgr*
EMP: 95
SALES (corp-wide): 1.6B **Publicly Held**
WEB: www.vitasinnovativehospicecare.com
SIC: 8082 Home health care services
HQ: Vitas Healthcare Corporation
100 S Biscayne Blvd # 1600
Miami FL 33131
305 374-4143

(G-4817)
VIVIAL MEDIA LLC
720 E Pete Rose Way # 350 (45202-3576)
PHONE..................513 768-7800
EMP: 37
SALES (corp-wide): 31.3MM **Privately Held**
SIC: 8721 Accounting, auditing & bookkeeping
PA: Vivial Media Llc
160 Inverness Dr W # 250
Englewood CO 80112
303 867-1600

(G-4818)
VOLT MANAGEMENT CORP
Also Called: Volt Workforce Solutions
8044 Montgomery Rd # 630 (45236-2919)
PHONE..................513 791-2600
Ed Coleman, *Branch Mgr*
EMP: 56
SALES (corp-wide): 1.1B **Publicly Held**
SIC: 7363 Help supply services
HQ: Volt Management Corp.
1133 Ave Of The Americas
New York NY 10036

(G-4819)
VORYS SATER SEYMOUR PEASE LLP
301 E 4th St Ste 3410 (45202-4257)
P.O. Box 236 (45201-0236)
PHONE..................513 723-4000
Fax: 513 723-4056
Thomas Gabelman, *Partner*
Roger Lautenhiser, *Principal*
Weigel W Breck,
Sheilah Duncan,
Eugene P Ruehlman,
EMP: 125
SALES (corp-wide): 133.4MM **Privately Held**
SIC: 8111 Corporate, partnership & business law
PA: Vorys, Sater, Seymour And Pease Llp
52 E Gay St
Columbus OH 43215
614 464-6400

(G-4820)
W L W TT V 5
1700 Young St (45202-6821)
PHONE..................513 412-5000

Cincinnati - Hamilton County (G-4821)

GEOGRAPHIC SECTION

Fax: 513 412-6121
EMP: 150
SALES (est): 415.4K Privately Held
SIC: 4833 Television Station

(G-4821)
W P DOLLE LLC
201 E 5th St Ste 1000 (45202-4188)
PHONE..................513 421-6515
Mark Rummler, *Vice Pres*
Robert Lang, *CFO*
Marcie Carey, *Accounts Exec*
Gerry Stricker, *Accounts Exec*
David Poignard, *Sales Associate*
EMP: 25
SQ FT: 18,000
SALES (est): 4.4MM Privately Held
SIC: 6411 Insurance agents

(G-4822)
WALNUT HILLS PRESERVATION LP
Also Called: Walnut Hills Apartments
861 Beecher St Ofc Ofc (45206-1571)
PHONE..................513 281-1288
George Buchanan, *Partner*
Leeann Morein, *Principal*
EMP: 99
SALES: 950K Privately Held
SIC: 6513 Apartment building operators

(G-4823)
WALTER ALEXANDER ENTPS INC
Also Called: Cincinnati Vending Company
1940 Losantiville Ave (45237-4106)
PHONE..................513 841-1100
Richard Walter, *President*
Norman Alexander, *COO*
EMP: 27
SQ FT: 8,000
SALES (est): 2.7MM Privately Held
WEB: www.cincinnativending.com
SIC: 5962 7389 Food vending machines; coffee service

(G-4824)
WATERFRONT & ASSOCIATES INC
Also Called: South Beach Grille
700 Walnut St Ste 200 (45202-2015)
PHONE..................859 581-1414
Jeff Ruby, *President*
EMP: 400
SQ FT: 30,000
SALES (est): 6.3MM Privately Held
SIC: 5812 5813 6512 Grills (eating places); bar (drinking places); auditorium & hall operation

(G-4825)
WAYPOINT AVIATION LLC
4765 Airport Rd (45226-1613)
PHONE..................800 769-4765
Mark Davis, *President*
EMP: 25
SQ FT: 50,000
SALES: 10K Privately Held
SIC: 7363 Pilot service, aviation

(G-4826)
WCM HOLDINGS INC (PA)
11500 Canal Rd (45241-1862)
PHONE..................513 705-2100
Fax: 513 705-2138
David Herche, *CEO*
Tim Fogarty, *President*
Melvyn Fisher, *Chairman*
Cindy Schoch, *Sales Mgr*
▲ EMP: 120
SALES (est): 25.3MM Privately Held
SIC: 5099 2381 3842 Safety equipment & supplies; gloves, work: woven or knit, made from purchased materials; clothing, fire resistant & protective

(G-4827)
WEED MAN LAWNCARE LLC
12100 Phanpion Way (45241)
PHONE..................513 683-6310
Fax: 513 771-6315
Mike Ward, *Mng Member*
EMP: 40
SALES (est): 646.8K Privately Held
SIC: 0782 Lawn services

(G-4828)
WEGMAN CONSTRUCTION COMPANY
Also Called: Wegman Company
1101 York St Ste 500 (45214-2131)
PHONE..................513 381-1111
Fax: 513 345-4100
Joseph Wegman, *Ch of Bd*
Scott Wegman, *President*
Melissa Wegman, *Vice Pres*
Steve Stoecklin, *Project Mgr*
Jake Lammers, *Opers Mgr*
EMP: 50
SQ FT: 175,000
SALES (est): 9.2MM Privately Held
WEB: www.wegmancompany.com
SIC: 1799 7389 Office furniture installation; relocation service

(G-4829)
WELCH HOLDINGS INC
8953 E Miami River Rd (45247-2232)
PHONE..................513 353-3220
James R Welch, *President*
Ronnie L Welch, *Corp Secy*
Connie Tolson, *Human Resources*
Michael Judd, *Marketing Staff*
EMP: 45
SQ FT: 3,400
SALES (est): 4.4MM Privately Held
WEB: www.welchsand.com
SIC: 1442 Common sand mining; gravel mining

(G-4830)
WELD PLUS INC
4790 River Rd (45233-1633)
PHONE..................513 941-4411
Fax: 513 941-0044
Laurie Rensing, *Ch of Bd*
Paul Rensing, *President*
Pete Behymer, *General Mgr*
Elizabeth Byrum, *General Mgr*
Daniel Hughes, *Opers Mgr*
EMP: 30
SQ FT: 42,000
SALES: 10.3MM Privately Held
WEB: www.weldplus.com
SIC: 5084 Welding machinery & equipment

(G-4831)
WELLS FARGO CLEARING SVCS LLC
Also Called: Wells Fargo Advisors
255 E 5th St Ste 1400 (45202-4184)
PHONE..................513 241-9900
Fax: 513 241-7831
Steven Wellins, *Vice Pres*
Art Fischer, *Manager*
Adam Boerger, *Agent*
Eric Greenwell, *Advisor*
Mark Mechley, *Advisor*
EMP: 40
SALES (corp-wide): 97.7B Publicly Held
SIC: 6211 Brokers, security
HQ: Wells Fargo Clearing Services, Llc
1 N Jefferson Ave
Saint Louis MO 63103
314 955-3000

(G-4832)
WELTMAN WEINBERG & REIS CO LPA
525 Vine St Ste 800 (45202-3171)
PHONE..................513 723-2200
Fax: 513 723-2239
Nicole Smith, *Chief Mktg Ofcr*
Heather Bell, *Marketing Staff*
Frank Veneziano, *Manager*
EMP: 151
SALES (est): 11.9MM
SALES (corp-wide): 98.4MM Privately Held
SIC: 8111 General practice attorney, lawyer
PA: Weltman, Weinberg & Reis Co., L.P.A.
323 W Lkeside Ave Ste 200
Cleveland OH 44113
216 685-1000

(G-4833)
WESBANCO BANK INC
5511 Cheviot Rd (45247-7003)
PHONE..................513 741-5766
Kathleen Nunlist, *Broker*
Susan Osterhage, *Manager*
Paul K Bricner, *Info Tech Mgr*
EMP: 45
SQ FT: 4,670
SALES (corp-wide): 421.2MM Publicly Held
WEB: www.realtydoneright.net
SIC: 6036 Savings & loan associations, not federally chartered
HQ: Wesbanco Bank, Inc.
1 Bank Plz
Wheeling WV 26003
304 234-9000

(G-4834)
WESLEY EDUC CNTR FOR CHLDRN
525 Hale Ave (45229-3105)
PHONE..................513 569-1840
Fax: 513 861-4268
Rita Bryant, *CEO*
Carla Butler, *Principal*
Rick Wagner, *Chairman*
Rose Palmieri, *Admin Sec*
EMP: 45
SALES (est): 791.7K Privately Held
SIC: 8351 Group day care center

(G-4835)
WEST END HEALTH CENTER INC
1413 Linn St (45214-2605)
PHONE..................513 621-2726
Fax: 513 621-0720
Wendell Walker, *Exec Dir*
EMP: 28
SQ FT: 4,500
SALES (est): 212.2K Privately Held
SIC: 8093 Specialty outpatient clinics

(G-4836)
WEST PARK RETIREMENT COMMUNITY
Also Called: Mercy House Partners
2950 West Park Dr Ofc (45238-3542)
PHONE..................513 451-8900
Kendra Couch, *President*
Donald Stinnett, *Treasurer*
EMP: 200
SQ FT: 206,000
SALES (est): 1.5MM Privately Held
SIC: 8052 8051 Personal care facility; extended care facility

(G-4837)
WEST SHELL COMMERCIAL INC
Also Called: Colliers International
425 Walnut St Ste 1200 (45202-3993)
PHONE..................513 721-4200
Fax: 513 721-0630
Shenan Murphy, *President*
Mark Rippe, *Exec VP*
Michael Daly, *Vice Pres*
Mike Finke, *Vice Pres*
Jerry Stanislaw, *Vice Pres*
EMP: 55 EST: 2000
SQ FT: 11,000
SALES (est): 6.7MM Privately Held
WEB: www.westshell.com
SIC: 6531 Real estate agent, commercial

(G-4838)
WEST SIDE PEDIATRICS INC (PA)
663 Anderson Ferry Rd # 1 (45238-4798)
PHONE..................513 922-8200
Fax: 513 347-2407
Lee Burroughs MD, *President*
R Scott Hunter, *Vice Pres*
Pamela Holmes, *Pediatrics*
EMP: 44
SALES (est): 7.8MM Privately Held
SIC: 8011 Pediatrician

(G-4839)
WESTERN & SOUTHERN LF INSUR CO (DH)
Also Called: Western-Southern Life
400 Broadway St (45202-3341)
P.O. Box 1119 (45201-1119)
PHONE..................513 629-1800
Fax: 513 629-1212
John F Barrett, *President*
David Dimartino, *President*
Donna Parobek, *President*
Mark Pfefferman, *President*
Elaine Reuss, *President*
EMP: 982 EST: 1888
SQ FT: 600,000
SALES (est): 1.7B Privately Held
SIC: 6211 6311 2511 Investment firm, general brokerage; life insurance; play pens, children's: wood
HQ: Western & Southern Financial Group, Inc.
400 Broadway St
Cincinnati OH 45202
866 832-7719

(G-4840)
WESTERN FAMILY PHYSICIANS
3425 North Bend Rd Ste A (45239-7660)
PHONE..................513 853-4900
R Stephen EBY, *President*
Lisbeth Lazaron, *Vice Pres*
William Schulter, *Office Mgr*
Sherry Carle, *Manager*
Lisa Cantor, *Officer*
EMP: 31
SQ FT: 2,000
SALES (est): 3.6MM Privately Held
WEB: www.westernfamilyphysicians.com
SIC: 8011 General & family practice, physician/surgeon

(G-4841)
WESTERN HILLS CARE CENTER
6210 Cleves Warsaw Pike (45233-4510)
PHONE..................513 941-0099
Fax: 513 467-3563
Barry A Kohn, *President*
Sam Boymel, *Chairman*
Rick Friedman, *Vice Pres*
EMP: 200
SQ FT: 150,000
SALES (est): 4.8MM Privately Held
WEB: www.whrv.org
SIC: 8051 Skilled nursing care facilities

(G-4842)
WESTERN HILLS COUNTRY CLUB
5780 Cleves Warsaw Pike (45233-4900)
P.O. Box 58644 (45258-0644)
PHONE..................513 922-0011
Fax: 513 922-6935
Paul Garrett, *General Mgr*
Dana Cinorell, *COO*
EMP: 75
SQ FT: 20,000
SALES (est): 2.8MM Privately Held
SIC: 7997 Country club, membership

(G-4843)
WESTERN HILLS SPORTSPLEX INC (PA)
Also Called: Western Sports Mall
2323 Ferguson Rd Ste 1 (45238-3500)
PHONE..................513 451-4900
Fax: 513 451-8956
John P Torbeck, *President*
Bobby Farley, *Owner*
Robert Czerwinski, *Vice Pres*
John L Torbeck, *Treasurer*
EMP: 75 EST: 1972
SQ FT: 40,000
SALES (est): 2.4MM Privately Held
WEB: www.westernsportsmall.net
SIC: 7997 7999 Tennis club, membership; racquetball club, membership; swimming club, membership; indoor court clubs; baseball batting cage

(G-4844)
WESTERN SOUTHERN MUTL HOLDG CO (PA)
400 Broadway St (45202-3341)
PHONE..................866 832-7719
John F Barrett, *President*
Jonathan Niemeyer, *Senior VP*
Todd Henderson, *Vice Pres*
Terry Sizemore, *Sales Mgr*
EMP: 1450
SALES (est): 3.3B Privately Held
SIC: 6211 Investment firm, general brokerage

▲ = Import ▼=Export
◆ =Import/Export

GEOGRAPHIC SECTION

Cincinnati - Hamilton County (G-4866)

(G-4845)
WESTERN STHERN FINCL GROUP INC (HQ)
400 Broadway St (45202-3312)
P.O. Box 1119 (45201-1119)
PHONE..................866 832-7719
John F Barrett, *President*
Gary Enzweiler, *President*
Lisa Fangman, *President*
Donna Parobek, *President*
Eric Walzer, *President*
EMP: 1800
SALES: 3.3B **Privately Held**
WEB: www.westernsouthern.com
SIC: 6211 Investment firm, general brokerage

(G-4846)
WESTWAY TRML CINCINNATI LLC
3500 Southside Ave (45204-1138)
PHONE..................513 921-8441
Eric Thomas, *General Mgr*
William Lindsey, *Mng Member*
Shawn Wolfe, *Manger*
Gwen Dukes, *Admin Sec*
EMP: 30
SQ FT: 12,000
SALES (est): 3.2MM
SALES (corp-wide): 104.2MM **Privately Held**
WEB: www.ssrrt.com
SIC: 4225 General warehousing & storage
PA: Contanda Llc
 1111 Bagby St Ste 1800
 Houston TX 77002
 832 699-4001

(G-4847)
WFTS
Also Called: W C P O - T V
1720 Gilbert Ave (45202-1401)
PHONE..................513 721-9900
Fax: 513 852-4914
Bill Fee, *General Mgr*
J B Chase, *Sales Mgr*
Deborah Cook, *Sales Executive*
Brian Wagner, *Manager*
EMP: 172
SALES (corp-wide): 3.1B **Publicly Held**
WEB: www.diytv.com
SIC: 4833 Television broadcasting stations
HQ: Wfts
 4045 N Himes Ave
 Tampa FL 33607
 813 354-2800

(G-4848)
WIDMERS LLC (HQ)
Also Called: Widmer's Drycleaners
2016 Madison Rd (45208-3238)
PHONE..................513 321-5100
Steve Carico, *Sr Corp Ofcr*
Chris Vanada, *Controller*
Tod Krasnow,
EMP: 200
SQ FT: 33,000
SALES (est): 8.7MM
SALES (corp-wide): 67.7MM **Privately Held**
WEB: www.widmerscleaners.com
SIC: 7216 7217 Cleaning & dyeing, except rugs; carpet & upholstery cleaning
PA: Zoots Holding Corporation
 153 Needham St Bldg 1
 Newton MA
 617 558-9666

(G-4849)
WILLIAM HAFER DRAYAGE INC
11320 Mosteller Rd Ste 1 (45241-5808)
PHONE..................513 771-5000
Fax: 513 771-3022
Michael Fitzgibbons, *President*
Amy Marie Fitzgibbons, *Vice Pres*
Ken Smith, *Manager*
EMP: 30
SQ FT: 4,800
SALES: 6.2MM **Privately Held**
SIC: 4212 Light haulage & cartage, local

(G-4850)
WILLIAM ROYCE INC
Also Called: Riley's Restaurant
11568 Springfield Pike (45246-3527)
PHONE..................513 771-3361
Ken Riley, *President*
Gloria Riley, *Admin Sec*
EMP: 80
SQ FT: 6,500
SALES (est): 2.1MM **Privately Held**
WEB: www.rileysfamilydining.com
SIC: 7299 5812 8741 Banquet hall facilities; eating places; restaurant management

(G-4851)
WILLIAM THOMAS GROUP INC
10795 Hughes Rd (45251-4523)
P.O. Box 538703 (45253-8703)
PHONE..................800 582-3107
William Rumpke Jr, *President*
Bradley Warrma, *Division Mgr*
Shawn Meadows, *Natl Sales Mgr*
Kevin Luther, *Manager*
EMP: 85
SALES (est): 10.2MM **Privately Held**
SIC: 8742 Management consulting services
PA: Rumpke Consolidated Companies, Inc.
 3963 Kraus Ln
 Hamilton OH 45014

(G-4852)
WILLIAMSBURG OF CINCINNATI MGT
Also Called: Evergreen Kindervelt Gift Shop
230 W Galbraith Rd (45215-5223)
PHONE..................513 948-2308
Fax: 513 948-0063
Peggy M Gregor, *Personnel Exec*
Lynn Saul, *Exec Dir*
Jeremy Yates, *Director*
EMP: 250
SALES (est): 8.1MM
SALES (corp-wide): 342.7MM **Privately Held**
SIC: 8059 5947 Rest home, with health care; gift, novelty & souvenir shop
PA: Senior Lifestyle Corporation
 303 E Wacker Dr Ste 2400
 Chicago IL 60601
 312 673-4333

(G-4853)
WINGS INVESTORS COMPANY LTD
3805 Edwards Rd Ste 200 (45209-1939)
PHONE..................513 241-5800
Jeffrey R Anderson, *President*
Britney Bouldin, *Admin Asst*
EMP: 25
SALES (est): 1.4MM **Privately Held**
SIC: 6799 8741 Investors; management services

(G-4854)
WITT GLVNZING - CINCINNATI INC
Also Called: Aaz Galvanizing Cincinnati
4454 Steel Pl (45209-1135)
PHONE..................513 871-5700
Tom Ferguson, *President*
Michelle Scott, *Executive Asst*
EMP: 45
SALES (est): 7.6MM
SALES (corp-wide): 858.9MM **Publicly Held**
SIC: 5051 Sheets, galvanized or other coated
PA: Azz Inc.
 3100 W 7th St Ste 500
 Fort Worth TX 76107
 817 810-0095

(G-4855)
WNB GROUP LLC
Also Called: Ray Hamilton Company
4817 Section Ave (45212-2118)
P.O. Box 12370 (45212-0370)
PHONE..................513 641-5400
Fax: 513 641-1656
James Wallis, *President*
Don Hinkley, *Sls & Mktg Exec*
Rod Burton, *Accounts Exec*
EMP: 49 **EST:** 1892
SALES: 12.1MM **Privately Held**
SIC: 4212 4214 4731 Moving services; local trucking with storage; freight transportation arrangement

(G-4856)
WOOD HERRON & EVANS LLP (PA)
441 Vine St Ste 2700 (45202-2814)
PHONE..................513 241-2324
Bruce Tittel, *President*
J Robert Chambers, *Principal*
Donald F Frei, *Principal*
Kurt Grossman, *Principal*
David J Josephic, *Principal*
EMP: 57
SQ FT: 15,000
SALES (est): 18.4MM **Privately Held**
WEB: www.whepatent.com
SIC: 8111 General practice law office

(G-4857)
WOOD & LAMPING LLP
600 Vine St Ste 2500 (45202-2491)
PHONE..................513 852-6000
Fax: 513 852-6087
Diane Werner, *President*
Mark R Fitch, *Partner*
William Price, *Partner*
Mark Reckman, *Partner*
Thomas M Woebkenberg, *Partner*
EMP: 60
SALES (est): 9.4MM **Privately Held**
SIC: 8111 General practice attorney, lawyer

(G-4858)
WOOD GRAPHICS INC (HQ)
Also Called: United Engraving
8075 Reading Rd Ste 301 (45237-1416)
PHONE..................513 771-6300
Fax: 513 771-3112
Mark Richler, *President*
Gaylord H Fill, *Corp Secy*
◆ **EMP:** 30
SQ FT: 21,500
SALES (est): 2.7MM
SALES (corp-wide): 164.4MM **Privately Held**
SIC: 3555 7699 2796 Printing trades machinery; industrial machinery & equipment repair; platemaking services
PA: Rotation Dynamics Corporation
 1101 Windham Pkwy
 Romeoville IL 60446
 630 769-9255

(G-4859)
WOODCRAFT SUPPLY LLC
11711 Princeton Pike # 251 (45246-2534)
PHONE..................513 407-8371
Fax: 513 407-8606
Mark Miller, *Owner*
EMP: 76
SALES (corp-wide): 226.7MM **Privately Held**
SIC: 5099 Firearms & ammunition, except sporting
PA: Woodcraft Supply, Llc
 1177 Rosemar Rd
 Parkersburg WV 26105
 304 422-5412

(G-4860)
WORLDWIDE EQUIPMENT INC
Also Called: Worldwide of Cincinnati
10649 Evendale Dr (45241-2517)
PHONE..................513 563-6363
Fax: 513 563-8205
Betty Blake, *Office Mgr*
Sam Huffman, *Manager*
Steve Harris, *Director*
EMP: 80
SALES (corp-wide): 245.8MM **Privately Held**
SIC: 5012 Trailers for trucks, new & used
HQ: Worldwide Equipment, Inc.
 73 We Dr
 Prestonsburg KY 41653
 606 874-2172

(G-4861)
WPH CINCINNATI LLC
Also Called: Crown Plaza
11320 Chester Rd (45246-4003)
PHONE..................513 771-2080
Ted Hyle, *General Mgr*
Connie Putteet, *Accountant*
Wilbert Schwartz,
EMP: 110
SQ FT: 150,000
SALES: 7MM **Privately Held**
SIC: 7011 Hotels

(G-4862)
WULCO INC (PA)
Also Called: Jet Machine & Manufacturing
6899 Steger Dr Ste A (45237-3059)
PHONE..................513 679-2600
Fax: 513 679-2653
Richard G Wulfeck, *President*
Chris Wulfeck, *Safety Dir*
Brad Wulfeck, *Safety Mgr*
Ken Smith, *Purch Agent*
Ken Wulfeck, *Treasurer*
▲ **EMP:** 100
SQ FT: 100,000
SALES (est): 145.3MM **Privately Held**
WEB: www.wulco.com
SIC: 5085 3599 Industrial supplies; machine shop, jobbing & repair

(G-4863)
XAVIER UNIVERSITY
Also Called: Wvxu Radio
3800 Victory Pkwy Unit 1 (45207-1092)
PHONE..................513 745-3335
Fax: 513 745-1004
James King, *Manager*
EMP: 25
SALES (corp-wide): 166.6MM **Privately Held**
WEB: www.xu.edu
SIC: 4832 8221 Radio broadcasting stations; university
PA: Xavier University
 3800 Victory Pkwy Unit 1
 Cincinnati OH 45207
 513 961-0133

(G-4864)
YOUNG & RUBICAM INC
Landor Associates
110 Shillito Pl (45202-2361)
PHONE..................513 419-2300
Trent Miller, *Finance*
Karen Floyd, *Human Res Dir*
Heather Mulvaney, *Human Resources*
Marie Zalla, *Manager*
Scott Hosa, *Manager*
EMP: 150
SALES (corp-wide): 17.7B **Privately Held**
SIC: 7336 Commercial art & illustration
HQ: Young & Rubicam Inc.
 3 Columbus Cir Fl 8
 New York NY 10019
 212 210-3000

(G-4865)
YOUNG MENS CHRISTIAN ASSOCIAT
Also Called: Powel Crosley Jr Branch
9601 Winton Rd (45231-2637)
PHONE..................513 521-7112
Fax: 513 728-2192
Allen Magane, *Facilities Mgr*
Cindy Tomaszewski, *Manager*
Amber Long, *Manager*
Pam Butler, *Director*
EMP: 60
SALES (corp-wide): 33.6MM **Privately Held**
WEB: www.cincinnatiymca.org
SIC: 8641 7997 Youth organizations; membership sports & recreation clubs
PA: Young Mens Christian Association Of Greater Cincinnati
 1105 Elm St
 Cincinnati OH 45202
 513 651-2100

(G-4866)
YOUNG MENS CHRISTIAN ASSOCIAT
Also Called: Y M C A
2039 Sherman Ave (45212-2634)
PHONE..................513 731-0115
Alan Geans, *Director*
EMP: 40
SQ FT: 14,869

Cincinnati - Hamilton County (G-4867)

SALES (corp-wide): 33.6MM **Privately Held**
WEB: www.cincinnatiymca.org
SIC: **8641** 8351 7997 7991 Youth organizations; child day care services; membership sports & recreation clubs; athletic club & gymnasiums, membership
PA: Young Mens Christian Association Of Greater Cincinnati
1105 Elm St
Cincinnati OH 45202
513 651-2100

(G-4867)
YOUNG MENS CHRISTIAN ASSOCIAT
Also Called: Ymca/M.e.lions
8108 Clough Pike Fl 1 (45244-2745)
PHONE.....................513 474-1400
Fax: 513 388-4154
Myrita Craig, *COO*
Jennifer Snyder, *Director*
Lynn McAlpin, *Admin Asst*
EMP: 180
SQ FT: 5,320
SALES (corp-wide): 33.6MM **Privately Held**
WEB: www.cincinnatiymca.org
SIC: **8641** 8351 7997 7991 Youth organizations; child day care services; membership sports & recreation clubs; physical fitness facilities
PA: Young Mens Christian Association Of Greater Cincinnati
1105 Elm St
Cincinnati OH 45202
513 651-2100

(G-4868)
YOUNG MENS CHRISTIAN ASSOCIAT
Also Called: West End YMCA
1425b Linn St (45214-2605)
PHONE.....................513 241-9622
Fax: 513 241-9895
Mick Ellsworth, *Facilities Mgr*
Christopher Lowe, *Site Mgr*
Paris Hodgson, *Asst Controller*
Joseph C Calloway, *Branch Mgr*
Seth Borin, *Property Mgr*
EMP: 60
SALES (corp-wide): 33.6MM **Privately Held**
WEB: www.cincinnatiymca.org
SIC: **8641** 7991 8351 7032 Youth organizations; physical fitness facilities; child day care services; youth camps; individual & family services
PA: Young Mens Christian Association Of Greater Cincinnati
1105 Elm St
Cincinnati OH 45202
513 651-2100

(G-4869)
YOUNG MENS CHRISTIAN ASSOCIAT
Also Called: William & Clippard YMCA
8920 Cheviot Rd (45251-5910)
PHONE.....................513 923-4466
Fax: 513 923-3796
Dirk Langfoss, *Director*
EMP: 75
SQ FT: 29,230
SALES (corp-wide): 33.6MM **Privately Held**
WEB: www.cincinnatiymca.org
SIC: **8641** 7991 8351 7032 Youth organizations; physical fitness facilities; child day care services; youth camps; individual & family services
PA: Young Mens Christian Association Of Greater Cincinnati
1105 Elm St
Cincinnati OH 45202
513 651-2100

(G-4870)
YWCA OF GREATER CINCINNATI (PA)
898 Walnut St Fl 1 (45202-2088)
PHONE.....................513 241-7090
Fax: 513 361-2153
Charlene Ventura, *President*
Debbie Brook, *Vice Pres*
Sandra Genco, *VP Finance*
EMP: 65
SALES: 6.2MM **Privately Held**
SIC: **8641** 7991 8351 7032 Youth organizations; physical fitness facilities; child day care services; youth camps; individual & family services

(G-4871)
ZICKA WALKER BUILDERS LTD
Also Called: Zicka Development
7861 E Kemper Rd (45249-1622)
PHONE.....................513 247-3500
E Michael Zicka, *President*
William L Martin Jr, *Principal*
Dennis Walker, *Vice Pres*
EMP: 40
SQ FT: 6,500
SALES (est): 4.1MM **Privately Held**
WEB: www.zickahomes.com
SIC: **1531** Speculative builder, single-family houses

(G-4872)
ZIPSCENE LLC
615 Main St Fl 5 (45202-2538)
PHONE.....................513 201-5174
Sameer Mungur, *CEO*
Mike Grosser, *President*
Colin Klayer, *Vice Pres*
Jonathan Richman, *Vice Pres*
Jen Sanning, *Vice Pres*
EMP: 62
SQ FT: 2,000
SALES (est): 10.8MM **Privately Held**
SIC: **7372** Business oriented computer software

(G-4873)
ZOO CINCINNATI
3400 Vine St (45220-1333)
PHONE.....................513 961-0041
Fax: 513 475-6131
Jenny Gainer, *Principal*
David Jenike, *COO*
Mark Fisher, *Vice Pres*
Terri Roth, *Vice Pres*
Lori Voss, *Vice Pres*
EMP: 63 EST: 2009
SALES (est): 3.9MM **Privately Held**
SIC: **8699** Charitable organization

(G-4874)
ZOOLOGICAL SOCIETY CINCINNATI
Also Called: CINCINNATI ZOO & BOTANICAL GAR
3400 Vine St (45220-1333)
PHONE.....................513 281-4700
Fax: 513 487-3336
Craig Maier, *Vice Chairman*
Lori Voss, *Vice Pres*
Damon Mounce, *Maint Spvr*
Steve Combs, *Controller*
Jeff Walton, *Human Resources*
▲ EMP: 320 EST: 1875
SALES: 47.1MM **Privately Held**
WEB: www.cincinnatizoo.org
SIC: **8422** Zoological garden, noncommercial

Circleville
Pickaway County

(G-4875)
1ST CARRIER CORP
177 Neville St (43113-9129)
PHONE.....................740 477-2587
Jeffrey Lanman, *President*
Jeffrey Beaver, *Vice Pres*
Tom Taylor, *Personnel Exec*
Steve Williams, *Marketing Staff*
EMP: 80
SALES (est): 9.7MM **Privately Held**
WEB: www.1stcarrier.com
SIC: **4213** 4212 Trucking, except local; local trucking, without storage

(G-4876)
ACCENTCARE HOME HEALTH CAL INC
Also Called: Sunplus HM Care - Circleville
119 S Court St Ste A (43113-1658)
PHONE.....................740 474-7826
Jenny Clark, *President*
EMP: 150
SALES (corp-wide): 379.9MM **Privately Held**
WEB: www.dhsi.com
SIC: **8082** Visiting nurse service
HQ: Accentcare Home Health Of California, Inc.
17855 Dallas Pkwy
Dallas TX 75287

(G-4877)
ADENA HEALTH SYSTEM
798 N Court St (43113-1262)
PHONE.....................740 420-3000
Christa Lagard, *Auditor*
Tony Dial, *Sales Staff*
Richard Ash, *Pharmacist*
Paul Smallwood, *Network Analyst*
Lisa Lloyd, *Nurse*
EMP: 213
SALES (corp-wide): 111.9MM **Privately Held**
SIC: **8062** Hospital, medical school affiliated with nursing & residency
PA: Adena Health System
272 Hospital Rd
Chillicothe OH 45601
740 779-7360

(G-4878)
BHM CPA GROUP INC (PA)
129 Pinckney St (43113-1627)
P.O. Box 875 (43113-0875)
PHONE.....................740 474-5210
Jeffrey Harr, *President*
Michael Balestra, *Vice Pres*
Alan Schmandt, *Auditing Mgr*
Dawn Knaub, *Accountant*
Amanda Pridemore, *CPA*
EMP: 60
SQ FT: 4,000
SALES (est): 5.2MM **Privately Held**
SIC: **8721** Certified public accountant

(G-4879)
BLB TRANSPORT INC
20615 Us Highway 23 N (43113-8971)
PHONE.....................740 474-1341
William Fletcher, *President*
EMP: 40
SALES (est): 3.1MM **Privately Held**
SIC: **4212** 4213 Local trucking, without storage; trucking, except local

(G-4880)
BROWN MEMORIAL HOME INC
158 E Mound St (43113-1702)
PHONE.....................740 474-6238
Fax: 740 474-6065
Charles Gerhart, *Treasurer*
Yadwinder Singh, *Director*
Luke Conley, *Administration*
EMP: 72
SALES: 3.6MM **Privately Held**
SIC: **8052** Personal care facility

(G-4881)
CAMCO INC
Also Called: Clean Image
24685 Us Highway 23 S (43113-9191)
P.O. Box 363 (43113-0363)
PHONE.....................740 477-3682
Fax: 740 420-9941
Clark Moats, *President*
Mary Moats, *Vice Pres*
EMP: 30
SALES: 3.4MM **Privately Held**
WEB: www.cleanimage.net
SIC: **1799** 7349 0782 Parking lot maintenance; building maintenance services; lawn & garden services

(G-4882)
CIRCLEVILLE OIL CO
315 Town St (43113-2220)
P.O. Box 189 (43113-0189)
PHONE.....................740 474-7568
Fax: 740 474-5766
Gary Scherer, *Branch Mgr*
EMP: 60
SALES (corp-wide): 43.7MM **Privately Held**
WEB: www.circlevilleoil.com
SIC: **5983** 5172 Fuel oil dealers; petroleum products
PA: Circleville Oil Co (Inc)
315 Town St
Circleville OH 43113
740 474-7544

(G-4883)
CITY OF CIRCLEVILLE
Also Called: Department of Public Utilities
108 E Franklin St (43113-1718)
PHONE.....................740 477-8255
Nathan Anderson, *Director*
EMP: 30 **Privately Held**
WEB: www.circlevillecourt.com
SIC: **8611** Public utility association
PA: City Of Circleville
133 S Court St
Circleville OH 43113
740 477-2551

(G-4884)
CONSTANCE CARE HOME HLTH CARE
774 N Court St (43113-1262)
PHONE.....................740 477-6360
Fax: 740 477-8693
Charles Bradley, *Owner*
Lisa Kim, *Human Res Mgr*
Don Bradley, *Manager*
EMP: 70
SALES (est): 1.6MM **Privately Held**
WEB: www.constancecare.com
SIC: **8082** Visiting nurse service

(G-4885)
COUNTY OF PICKAWAY
Also Called: Dept of Human Service
110 Island Rd Ste E (43113-9197)
P.O. Box 610 (43113-0610)
PHONE.....................740 474-7588
Rojanne Woodward, *Branch Mgr*
EMP: 80 **Privately Held**
SIC: **8322** 9111 Individual & family services; county supervisors' & executives' offices
PA: County Of Pickaway
139 W Franklin St
Circleville OH 43113
740 474-6093

(G-4886)
DARBY CREEK EXCAVATING INC
19524 London Rd (43113-9614)
PHONE.....................740 477-8600
Fax: 740 477-9865
Kevin Steward, *President*
Mary Steward, *Corp Secy*
Cary Purcell, *Vice Pres*
Amy Gressierer, *Controller*
Sue Ehmann, *Manager*
EMP: 90
SQ FT: 7,000
SALES (est): 15.8MM **Privately Held**
SIC: **1794** 1623 Excavation & grading, building construction; sewer line construction

(G-4887)
EATON CONSTRUCTION CO INC
653 Island Rd (43113-9594)
P.O. Box 684 (43113-0684)
PHONE.....................740 474-3414
Fax: 740 474-9616
Debbie Manson, *CEO*
EMP: 60
SALES: 2MM **Privately Held**
SIC: **1611** Highway & street maintenance

(G-4888)
ELECT GENERAL CONTRACTORS INC
27634 Jackson Rd (43113-9039)
P.O. Box 1135 (43113-5135)
PHONE.....................740 420-3437
Fax: 740 474-1037
Timothy R Covell, *President*
Gary Smith, *Project Mgr*
Scott Josephson, *Controller*
David Covell, *Manager*

Joyce Skaggs, *Manager*
EMP: 30
SALES (est): 5MM **Privately Held**
WEB: www.electgeneralcontractors.com
SIC: 1731 Fiber optic cable installation

(G-4889)
HATZEL & BUEHLER INC
3381 Congo Dr (43113-9087)
P.O. Box 848 (43113-0848)
PHONE.................................740 420-3088
Fax: 740 420-9048
James Ivey, *Manager*
EMP: 50
SALES (corp-wide): 256.4MM **Privately Held**
WEB: www.hatzelandbuehler.com
SIC: 1731 General electrical contractor
HQ: Hatzel & Buehler, Inc.
3600 Silverside Rd Ste A
Wilmington DE 19810
302 478-4200

(G-4890)
HILLS SUPPLY INC
8476 Us Highway 22 E (43113-9260)
PHONE.................................740 477-8994
David Hill, *CEO*
Dolores Hill, *President*
EMP: 40
SALES (est): 2.1MM **Privately Held**
SIC: 5159 Farm animals

(G-4891)
JAMES LAFONTAINE
Also Called: Captain D's
25050 Us Highway 23 S (43113-9131)
PHONE.................................740 474-5052
James Lafontaine, *Partner*
Steve Kay, *Partner*
George Sanson, *Partner*
Isaac Crabtree, *Facilities Mgr*
EMP: 30
SQ FT: 2,800
SALES (est): 763K **Privately Held**
SIC: 5812 6519 Seafood restaurants; landholding office

(G-4892)
JD MUSIC TILE CO
105 E Ohio St (43113-1917)
PHONE.................................740 420-9611
Joe Music, *President*
Deana Music, *Vice Pres*
EMP: 30
SALES (est): 3.2MM **Privately Held**
SIC: 1752 Floor laying & floor work; ceramic floor tile installation; vinyl floor tile & sheet installation; carpet laying

(G-4893)
NEW HOPE CHRISTIAN ACADEMY
2264 Walnut Creek Pike (43113-8938)
PHONE.................................740 477-6427
Fax: 740 420-3910
Julie Baumgardner, *Principal*
Tami McCallister, *CFO*
Dr Frank Martin III, *Director*
EMP: 35
SALES (est): 700K **Privately Held**
WEB: www.newhopechristianschool.org
SIC: 8351 8211 Preschool center; private elementary & secondary schools

(G-4894)
PICKAWAY COUNTY COMMUNITY ACTI (PA)
Also Called: P I C C A
469 E Ohio St (43113-2034)
PHONE.................................740 477-1655
Fax: 740 477-5735
Dave Kline, *CFO*
Dave Hannahs, *Exec Dir*
Michael Logan, *Exec Dir*
Paul Kidwell, *Director*
EMP: 65
SQ FT: 6,000
SALES: 5.9MM **Privately Held**
SIC: 8322 6513 4121 4119 Social service center; apartment building operators; taxicabs; local passenger transportation; local & suburban transit

(G-4895)
PICKAWAY COUNTY COMMUNITY ACTI
Also Called: Headstart Program
145 E Corwin St (43113-1904)
PHONE.................................740 474-7411
Fax: 740 477-3319
Donna Solovey, *Director*
EMP: 40
SALES (est): 1.4MM
SALES (corp-wide): 5.9MM **Privately Held**
SIC: 8322 8351 Social service center; head start center, except in conjunction with school
PA: Pickaway County Community Action Organization
469 E Ohio St
Circleville OH 43113
740 477-1655

(G-4896)
PICKAWAY COUNTY COMMUNITY ACTI
Also Called: Pickaway Senior Citizen Center
590 E Ohio St (43113-2000)
PHONE.................................740 477-1655
Sue Frey, *Manager*
Robert Hartinger, *Bd of Directors*
Andi Humphries, *Admin Sec*
EMP: 25
SALES (est): 323.9K
SALES (corp-wide): 5.9MM **Privately Held**
SIC: 8322 Senior citizens' center or association
PA: Pickaway County Community Action Organization
469 E Ohio St
Circleville OH 43113
740 477-1655

(G-4897)
PICKAWAY DIVERSFIED INDUSTRIES
548 Lancaster Pike (43113-9026)
PHONE.................................740 474-1522
Fax: 740 474-1133
Kim McPeek, *Director*
EMP: 93
SALES (est): 3.4MM **Privately Held**
SIC: 8331 7331 Job training & vocational rehabilitation services; direct mail advertising services

(G-4898)
PICKAWAY DIVERSIFIED
548 Lancaster Pike (43113-9026)
PHONE.................................740 474-1522
Robert Hhuffer, *Principal*
Tammy Alvoid, *Director*
EMP: 25
SALES (est): 702K **Privately Held**
SIC: 8322 Social services for the handicapped

(G-4899)
PICKAWAY MANOR INC
391 Clark Dr (43113-1598)
PHONE.................................740 474-5400
Robert Kenworthy, *President*
Ned Hardin, *Treasurer*
EMP: 150 EST: 1969
SQ FT: 10,000
SALES (est): 3.2MM **Privately Held**
SIC: 8051 8052 Convalescent home with continuous nursing care; intermediate care facilities

(G-4900)
PICKAWAY PLAINS AMBULANCE SVC (PA)
Also Called: Pro Care Medical Trnsp Svc
1950 Stoneridge Dr (43113-8955)
PHONE.................................740 474-4180
Fax: 740 474-8172
Clyde Cook, *CEO*
Gary Cook, *President*
Jarrod Strouth, *General Mgr*
Elaine Cook, *Corp Secy*
EMP: 190
SALES (est): 7.5MM **Privately Held**
SIC: 4119 Ambulance service

(G-4901)
PRECISION ELECTRICAL SERVICES
201 W Main St (43113-1621)
PHONE.................................740 474-4490
Fax: 740 474-5028
John Seyfang II, *President*
Kelly Seyfang, *Treasurer*
EMP: 35
SQ FT: 12,000
SALES (est): 3.1MM **Privately Held**
WEB: www.precisionelectricalservices.com
SIC: 1731 General electrical contractor

(G-4902)
RUMPKE WASTE INC
Also Called: Rumpke Recycling
819 Island Rd (43113-9594)
PHONE.................................740 474-9790
Fax: 740 477-6020
Bill Rumpke, *President*
Shawn Meadows, *Marketing Staff*
EMP: 55 **Privately Held**
SIC: 4953 Recycling, waste materials
HQ: Rumpke Waste, Inc.
10795 Hughes Rd
Cincinnati OH 45251
513 851-0122

(G-4903)
SAVINGS BANK (PA)
118 N Court St 120 (43113-1606)
P.O. Box 310 (43113-0310)
PHONE.................................740 474-3191
Fax: 740 474-3077
Steven Gary, *President*
Connie Campbell, *Exec VP*
Jeff Farthing, *Exec VP*
Dale Davis, *Human Resources*
James Stevens, *CTO*
EMP: 35 **EST:** 1912
SQ FT: 8,000
SALES: 14MM **Privately Held**
WEB: www.thesavingsbank.com
SIC: 6022 State commercial banks

(G-4904)
SHELLY COMPANY
24537 Canal Rd (43113-9691)
P.O. Box 600, Thornville (43076-0600)
PHONE.................................740 441-1714
EMP: 30
SALES (corp-wide): 29.7B **Privately Held**
SIC: 1611 Surfacing & paving
HQ: Shelly Company
80 Park Dr
Thornville OH 43076
740 246-6315

(G-4905)
SOUTH CENTRAL POWER COMPANY
2100 Chickasaw Dr (43113-9199)
PHONE.................................740 474-6045
Fax: 740 477-2219
Ron Bussard, *Opers Staff*
Jan Bussert, *Branch Mgr*
EMP: 26
SALES (est): 2.8MM
SALES (corp-wide): 282.1MM **Privately Held**
WEB: www.southcentralpower.com
SIC: 4911 Distribution, electric power
PA: South Central Power Company Inc
2780 Coonpath Rd Ne
Lancaster OH 43130
740 653-4422

(G-4906)
SUNBRIDGE CIRCLEVILLE
Also Called: Circlvlle Care Rhblitation Ctr
1155 Atwater Ave (43113-1301)
PHONE.................................740 477-1695
Fax: 614 477-2690
Sherry Cook, *Chf Purch Ofc*
Michelle Unger, *Personnel Exec*
Vernon Bolender, *Director*
Debbie Blair, *Nursing Dir*
Debi Blair, *Nursing Dir*
EMP: 50 **Publicly Held**
SIC: 8051 Convalescent home with continuous nursing care
HQ: Sunbridge Circleville Health Care Corp.
101 Sun Ave Ne
Albuquerque NM

(G-4907)
WESTFALL AGGREGATE & MTLS INC
19522 London Rd (43113-9614)
PHONE.................................740 420-9090
Kenneth Stewart, *President*
Sue Ehmann, *Office Mgr*
Tim Miller, *Manager*
EMP: 80
SALES (est): 9.2MM **Privately Held**
SIC: 5032 Gravel

(G-4908)
WHETSTONE CARE CENTER LLC
Also Called: Pickaway Manor Care Center
391 Clark Dr (43113-1561)
PHONE.................................740 474-6036
Fax: 740 420-3342
Ned Hardin, *Treasurer*
Noah Moore, *Branch Mgr*
Elizabeth Vogt, *Administration*
EMP: 130
SALES (corp-wide): 22.4MM **Privately Held**
WEB: www.macintoshcompany.com
SIC: 8051 8059 Convalescent home with continuous nursing care; convalescent home
PA: Whetstone Care Center Llc
3863 Trueman Ct
Hilliard OH 43026
614 345-9500

(G-4909)
YOUNG MENS CHRISTIAN ASSOC
Also Called: Y M C A
440 Nichalas Dr (43113-1535)
PHONE.................................740 477-1661
Fax: 740 477-1662
Jan Fetters Sr, *COO*
Jean Tom Sr, *Vice Pres*
Hollie Queen, *Director*
EMP: 100
SALES (corp-wide): 44.9MM **Privately Held**
WEB: www.ymca-columbus.com
SIC: 8641 7997 7991 7999 Youth organizations; membership sports & recreation clubs; physical fitness facilities; recreation center
PA: Young Men's Christian Association Of Central Ohio
40 W Long St
Columbus OH 43215
614 389-4409

Clay Center
Ottawa County

(G-4910)
WHITE ROCK QUARRY L P
3800 N Bolander Rd (43408)
PHONE.................................419 855-8388
Ray Advnia, *Principal*
U S Aggregates, *General Ptnr*
Robert Simpson, *General Ptnr*
Jim Fohoenocld, *Ltd Ptnr*
Heritage Group, *Ltd Ptnr*
EMP: 590
SALES (est): 13.6MM
SALES (corp-wide): 251.8MM **Privately Held**
SIC: 1422 Crushed & broken limestone
PA: Asphalt Materials, Inc.
5400 W 86th St
Indianapolis IN 46268
317 872-6010

Clayton
Montgomery County

(G-4911)
IDEAL COMPANY INC (PA)
Also Called: F & M Contractors
8313 Kimmel Rd Ste A (45315-8905)
P.O. Box 149 (45315-0149)
PHONE..............................937 836-8683
Fax: 937 832-2133
Fred A Sink, *President*
Kent Filbrun, *Principal*
Kevin G Filbrun, *Vice Pres*
Bruce Neador, *Vice Pres*
Margaret Matchen, *Opers Mgr*
EMP: 40 EST: 1960
SQ FT: 2,400
SALES (est): 19.2MM **Privately Held**
SIC: 1542 Commercial & office building, new construction

(G-4912)
LANDES FRESH MEATS INC
Also Called: Ol' Smokehaus
9476 Haber Rd (45315-9711)
PHONE..............................937 836-3613
Fax: 937 836-9352
Keith Landes, *President*
Mark Landes, *Vice Pres*
EMP: 50
SQ FT: 16,000
SALES (est): 3.9MM **Privately Held**
WEB: www.landesfreshmeats.com
SIC: 5421 0751 5147 Meat markets, including freezer provisioners; slaughtering; custom livestock services; meats, fresh

(G-4913)
MEADOWBROOK COUNTRY CLUB
6001 Salem Ave (45315-9736)
PHONE..............................937 836-5186
Bill Williams, *Manager*
Steve Taylor, *Manager*
EMP: 75
SALES: 1.9MM **Privately Held**
SIC: 7999 5941 7997 7991 Golf professionals; golf, tennis & ski shops; membership sports & recreation clubs; physical fitness facilities; eating places

(G-4914)
MEADOWBROOK COUNTRY CLUB
6001 Salem Ave (45315-9736)
PHONE..............................937 836-5186
Fax: 937 836-3185
Brian Early, *General Mgr*
EMP: 100
SQ FT: 35,000
SALES (est): 2.3MM **Privately Held**
SIC: 7997 Country club, membership

(G-4915)
MOYER INDUSTRIES INC
7555 Jacks Ln (45315-8778)
PHONE..............................937 832-7283
John Moyer, *President*
Jane Moyer, *Exec VP*
Crystal Walker, *Manager*
EMP: 50
SQ FT: 13,000
SALES (est): 9.7MM **Privately Held**
SIC: 1521 1611 Single-family housing construction; surfacing & paving

(G-4916)
SALEM CHURCH OF GOD INC
6500 Southway Rd Unit 2 (45315-7938)
P.O. Box 39 (45315-0039)
PHONE..............................937 836-6500
Fax: 937 832-2513
Rolland Daniels, *Pastor*
EMP: 27
SQ FT: 1,470
SALES (est): 1.8MM **Privately Held**
WEB: www.salemchurch.org
SIC: 8661 8351 Church of God; preschool center

Cleveland
Cuyahoga County

(G-4917)
1 COMMUNITY
1375 Euclid Ave (44115-1826)
PHONE..............................216 923-2272
Charles Berry, *COO*
EMP: 37 EST: 2011
SALES (est): 1.8MM **Privately Held**
SIC: 4813

(G-4918)
1-888 OHIO COMP LLC
2900 Carnegie Ave (44115-2649)
PHONE..............................216 426-0646
Dave Neubert, *Exec Dir*
Jay Lucarelli,
EMP: 80
SALES (est): 23.7MM **Privately Held**
WEB: www.1-888-ohiocomp.com
SIC: 6321 6324 Accident & health insurance; health maintenance organization (HMO), insurance only

(G-4919)
1100 CARNEGIE LP
Also Called: Hilton
1100 Carnegie Ave (44115-2806)
P.O. Box 91126 (44101-3126)
PHONE..............................216 658-6400
Fax: 216 658-6405
Harvey Schach, *General Ptnr*
Beth Noll, *Sales Dir*
Jeff Glover, *Sales Mgr*
Tom Dinardo, *Executive*
EMP: 66
SALES (est): 7.5MM **Privately Held**
SIC: 7011 Hotels

(G-4920)
127 PS FEE OWNER LLC
1300 Key Tower 127 Pub Sq (44114)
PHONE..............................216 520-1250
Frank Sinito,
EMP: 99
SALES (est): 1.1MM **Privately Held**
SIC: 6512 Commercial & industrial building operation

(G-4921)
1460 NINTH ST ASSOC LTD PARTNR
Also Called: Brampton Inn
1460 E 9th St (44114-1708)
PHONE..............................216 241-6600
Ray Valle, *General Mgr*
Jeff Charo, *General Mgr*
Shannon Ambler, *Sales Mgr*
EMP: 40
SQ FT: 18,836
SALES (est): 855.2K **Privately Held**
SIC: 7011 Hotels & motels

(G-4922)
1ST CHOICE LLC
600 Superior Ave E # 1300 (44114-2614)
PHONE..............................877 564-6658
Sartara Williams, *Manager*
EMP: 60 **Privately Held**
SIC: 7353 Heavy construction equipment rental
PA: 1st Choice, Llc
400 E Pratt St
Baltimore MD 21202

(G-4923)
1ST CHOICE ROOFING COMPANY
10311 Berea Rd (44102-2503)
PHONE..............................216 227-7755
Ian Fess, *President*
EMP: 37
SQ FT: 33,000
SALES (est): 1.2MM **Privately Held**
WEB: www.1stchoiceroofing.com
SIC: 1761 Roofing contractor

(G-4924)
2100 LAKESIDE SHELTER FOR MEN
2100 Lakeside Ave E (44114-1126)
PHONE..............................216 566-0047
Megan Billow, *Comms Dir*
Jessica Rocha, *Comms Mgr*
Dewayne Drotar, *Director*
EMP: 30
SALES (est): 300.7K **Privately Held**
SIC: 8322 Adult day care center

(G-4925)
21ST CENTURY CON CNSTR INC
13925 Enterprise Ave (44135-5117)
PHONE..............................216 362-0900
Patrick Butler, *President*
Carol Lanese, *Office Mgr*
EMP: 50
SQ FT: 28,000
SALES (est): 9.3MM **Privately Held**
WEB: www.21stcenturyconcrete.com
SIC: 1771 Concrete work

(G-4926)
3B HOLDINGS INC (PA)
Also Called: 3b Supply
11470 Euclid Ave Ste 407 (44106-3934)
PHONE..............................800 791-7124
Leonard Dashkin, *President*
David L Porter, *President*
Robert Dashkin, *VP Opers*
Fonda Hudson, *Program Mgr*
Nathan Keen, *Program Mgr*
EMP: 61
SQ FT: 250,000
SALES (est): 25MM **Privately Held**
SIC: 5085 Industrial supplies

(G-4927)
6200 ROCKSIDE LLC
Also Called: Vantage Financial Group
6200 Rockside Rd Ste 100 (44131-2214)
PHONE..............................216 642-8004
Manish Bhatt, *Partner*
William McCormick, *Vice Pres*
Anthony McDonald, *Accounts Mgr*
Kemper Arnold, *Director*
Michael Cleary, *Director*
EMP: 80
SALES (est): 3.7MM **Privately Held**
SIC: 7389 Financial services

(G-4928)
A A ASTRO SERVICE INC
5283 Pearl Rd (44129-1550)
PHONE..............................216 459-0363
Philip Tromba, *President*
EMP: 56
SALES (est): 4.3MM **Privately Held**
SIC: 1711 Warm air heating & air conditioning contractor

(G-4929)
A B C RENTAL CENTER EAST INC
5204 Warrensville Ctr Rd (44137-1902)
PHONE..............................216 475-8240
Howard R Kelley, *President*
Molly Kelley, *Corp Secy*
EMP: 25
SQ FT: 9,400
SALES (est): 2.4MM **Privately Held**
SIC: 7359 Party supplies rental services; tool rental

(G-4930)
A BEE C SERVICE INC (PA)
Also Called: Service-Tech
7589 First Pl Ste 1 (44146-6727)
PHONE..............................440 735-1505
Fax: 440 735-1433
Alan Sutton, *President*
Todd Kline, *Project Mgr*
Barbara Sutton, *Treasurer*
Doug Stastny, *Regl Sales Mgr*
Kathy Bane, *Manager*
EMP: 28
SQ FT: 22,000
SALES (est): 7MM **Privately Held**
WEB: www.service-techcorp.com
SIC: 7349 Air duct cleaning

(G-4931)
A C MANAGEMENT INC
Also Called: Holiday Inn
780 Beta Dr (44143-2328)
PHONE..............................440 461-9200
Fax: 440 461-7564
Alfred Quagliata, *President*
Kathy Quagliata, *Vice Pres*
EMP: 40
SALES (est): 2.6MM **Privately Held**
SIC: 7011 5813 5812 Hotels & motels; drinking places; eating places

(G-4932)
A D A ARCHITECTS INC
17710 Detroit Ave (44107-3451)
PHONE..............................216 521-5134
Robert Acciarri, *President*
EMP: 35
SQ FT: 1,000
SALES (est): 5.1MM **Privately Held**
WEB: www.adaarchitects.cc
SIC: 8712 Architectural engineering

(G-4933)
A M MC GREGOR HOME
14900 Private Dr Ofc (44112-3495)
PHONE..............................216 851-8200
Fax: 216 851-6634
Rob Hilton, *CEO*
Robertson Hilton, *CEO*
Ann Conn, *CFO*
Barry Koster, *CFO*
Sue W Neff, *Exec Dir*
EMP: 275
SALES: 21.1MM **Privately Held**
SIC: 8052 Intermediate care facilities

(G-4934)
A NEW BEGINNING PRESCHOOL
18403 Euclid Ave (44112-1016)
PHONE..............................216 531-7465
Fax: 216 531-0832
Monee Kidd, *Director*
EMP: 62
SALES (est): 49.7K **Privately Held**
SIC: 8351 Preschool center

(G-4935)
A RESSLER INC
Also Called: Down To Earth Landscaping
12750 Broadway Ave (44125-1855)
PHONE..............................216 518-1804
Adam Ressler, *President*
EMP: 25
SQ FT: 6,000
SALES (est): 1.4MM **Privately Held**
SIC: 0782 Landscape contractors

(G-4936)
A TEAM LLC
Also Called: Service Master By Ameri Steam
5280 W 161st St Frnt Ste (44142-1607)
PHONE..............................216 271-7223
Fax: 216 362-6969
Jessica Pollard, *Manager*
Enzo Maddalena,
EMP: 30
SALES: 2MM **Privately Held**
WEB: www.a-team.com
SIC: 8322 1711 Disaster service; plumbing contractors

(G-4937)
A W S INC
Also Called: S A W Adult Training Center
4720 Hinckley Indus Pkwy (44109-6003)
PHONE..............................216 749-0356
Fax: 216 398-8746
William Oliverio, *Manager*
Karen Fiselski, *Manager*
Joan McFaul, *Info Tech Mgr*
EMP: 350
SALES (corp-wide): 7.8MM **Privately Held**
SIC: 8331 7331 Vocational training agency; direct mail advertising services
PA: A W S Inc
1275 Lakeside Ave E
Cleveland OH 44114
216 861-0250

Cleveland - Cuyahoga County (G-4961)

(G-4938)
A W S INC
Also Called: Brooklyn Adult Activity Center
10991 Memphis Ave (44144-2055)
PHONE.................216 941-8800
David Nodge, *Manager*
EMP: 77
SALES (corp-wide): 7.8MM Privately Held
SIC: 8093 8331 Mental health clinic, outpatient; job training & vocational rehabilitation services
PA: A W S Inc
1275 Lakeside Ave E
Cleveland OH 44114
216 861-0250

(G-4939)
A-1 GENERAL INSURANCE AGENCY (DH)
9700 Rockside Rd Ste 250 (44125-6264)
PHONE.................216 986-3000
Steven Mason, *Ch of Bd*
Randy Parker, *President*
Randy P Parker, *President*
Dick Muma, *Principal*
EMP: 80
SQ FT: 24,000
SALES (est): 2.9MM
SALES (corp-wide): 9.3B Privately Held
WEB: www.thegeneral.com
SIC: 6411 Insurance agents
HQ: Pga Service Corporation
2636 Elm Hill Pike # 510
Nashville TN 37214
615 242-1961

(G-4940)
AAA AMRICAN ABATEMENT ASB CORP
15401 Chatfield Ave (44111-4309)
PHONE.................216 281-9400
Fax: 216 281-9438
John P Donalon, *President*
Robert E Donalon, *Vice Pres*
Terry Donelon, *Vice Pres*
EMP: 75
SQ FT: 4,000
SALES: 2.5MM Privately Held
WEB: www.americanabatement.com
SIC: 1799 Asbestos removal & encapsulation

(G-4941)
AAA FLEXIBLE PIPE CLEANING
7277 Bessemer Ave (44127-1815)
P.O. Box 16692, Rocky River (44116-0692)
PHONE.................216 341-2900
Margaret Ziegenruecker, *President*
Carol Ann Fisco, *Treasurer*
Karol Taylor, *Manager*
Susan Kubach, *Director*
EMP: 45
SALES (est): 5.7MM Privately Held
SIC: 1623 Pipeline construction

(G-4942)
AAA PIPE CLEANING CORPORATION (PA)
Also Called: AAA Flexible Pipe
7277 Bessemer Ave (44127-1815)
PHONE.................216 341-2900
Fax: 216 341-6681
Ernest Fisco Jr, *President*
Benjamin Fisco III, *Vice Pres*
Brian Nix, *Controller*
EMP: 103 **EST:** 1935
SQ FT: 90,000
SALES (est): 9.5MM Privately Held
WEB: www.aaapipecleaning.com
SIC: 7699 1711 Sewer cleaning & rodding; plumbing, heating, air-conditioning contractors

(G-4943)
AARONS INC
11629 Lorain Ave (44111-5404)
PHONE.................216 251-4500
Fax: 216 251-2005
Pat Cassidy, *Manager*
EMP: 25
SALES (corp-wide): 3.3B Publicly Held
WEB: www.aaronrents.com
SIC: 7359 Furniture rental

PA: Aaron's, Inc.
400 Galleria Pkwy Se # 300
Atlanta GA 30339
678 402-3000

(G-4944)
ABB INC
23000 Harvard Rd (44122-7234)
PHONE.................440 585-8500
Fax: 440 585-5101
William Sulivan, *Branch Mgr*
EMP: 250
SALES (corp-wide): 33.8B Privately Held
WEB: www.elsterelectricity.com
SIC: 3823 5084 Industrial instrmnts msrmnt display/control process variable; controllers for process variables, all types; instruments & control equipment; controlling instruments & accessories; indicating instruments & accessories
HQ: Abb Inc.
305 Gregson Dr
Cary NC 27511

(G-4945)
ABCO FIRE LLC (HQ)
4545 W 160th St (44135-2647)
PHONE.................216 433-7200
Steve Dejohn, *President*
Heather Almendinger, *Administration*
EMP: 68
SALES (est): 3.2MM
SALES (corp-wide): 14.2MM Privately Held
SIC: 7389 Fire protection service other than forestry or public
PA: Abco Holdings, Llc
4545 W 160th St
Cleveland OH 44135
216 433-7200

(G-4946)
ABCO HOLDINGS LLC (PA)
Also Called: Abco Fire Protection
4545 W 160th St (44135-2647)
PHONE.................216 433-7200
Fax: 216 433-7209
Robert J Titmas Jr, *President*
Mary Kraft, *General Mgr*
Jarret Ryan, *General Mgr*
Merrick E Murphy, *Vice Pres*
Tony Duncan, *Opers Mgr*
▼ **EMP:** 90
SQ FT: 12,000
SALES: 14.2MM Privately Held
WEB: www.abcofire.net
SIC: 5099 7389 Safety equipment & supplies; fire extinguisher servicing

(G-4947)
ABF FREIGHT SYSTEM INC
5630 Chevrolet Blvd (44130-1404)
PHONE.................440 843-4600
Fax: 440 843-4620
Richard De Santos, *Manager*
EMP: 70
SQ FT: 15,000
SALES (corp-wide): 2.8B Publicly Held
WEB: www.abfs.com
SIC: 4213 Contract haulers
HQ: Abf Freight System, Inc.
3801 Old Greenwood Rd
Fort Smith AR 72903
479 785-8700

(G-4948)
ABM JANITORIAL SERVICES INC
1501 Euclid Ave Ste 320 (44115-2108)
PHONE.................216 861-1199
Fax: 216 861-3246
Robert J Pfahl, *Manager*
Robert Castle, *Manager*
Patrick Oconnell, *Manager*
EMP: 105
SALES (corp-wide): 5.4B Publicly Held
SIC: 7349 Janitorial service, contract basis
HQ: Abm Janitorial Services, Inc.
1111 Fannin St Ste 1500
Houston TX 77002
713 654-8924

(G-4949)
ABM PARKING SERVICES INC
Also Called: Ampco System Parking
1459 Hamilton Ave (44114-1105)
PHONE.................216 621-6600
John Leaf, *Regional Mgr*
Steve Brown, *Manager*
EMP: 50
SALES (corp-wide): 5.4B Publicly Held
WEB: www.meyers.net
SIC: 7521 Parking lots
HQ: Abm Parking Services, Inc.
1150 S Olive St Fl 19
Los Angeles CA 90015
213 284-7600

(G-4950)
ACADEMY ANSWERING SERVICE INC
Also Called: Academy Communications
1446 Som Center Rd Ste 7 (44124-2121)
PHONE.................440 442-8500
Fax: 440 442-8500
Daniel J Day, *President*
David Priest, *Sales Executive*
EMP: 50
SQ FT: 3,500
SALES (est): 2.6MM Privately Held
WEB: www.academycom.com
SIC: 7389 Telephone answering service

(G-4951)
ACADEMY COURT REPORTING INC
2044 Euclid Ave Lbby Lbby (44115-2273)
PHONE.................216 861-3222
Christen Chester, *Manager*
Chester Christen, *Director*
EMP: 25 Privately Held
SIC: 8244 7338 Business & secretarial schools; court reporting service
HQ: Academy Of Court Reporting, Inc.
6400 Rockside Rd
Independence OH 44131
216 834-1301

(G-4952)
ACADEMY GRAPHIC COMM INC
1000 Brookpark Rd (44109-5824)
PHONE.................216 661-2550
Fax: 216 661-7169
James M Champion, *President*
Erik Eichenberger, *General Mgr*
Elaine Champion, *Vice Pres*
Jeffrey Parsons, *Accounts Exec*
Courtney Champion, *Mktg Dir*
EMP: 27
SQ FT: 1,400
SALES (est): 4.7MM Privately Held
WEB: www.visitagc.com
SIC: 2752 7336 Commercial printing, offset; graphic arts & related design

(G-4953)
ACCENTURE LLP
1400 W 10th St (44113-1215)
PHONE.................216 685-1435
Fax: 216 535-5350
Tammy Crosby, *Vice Pres*
Howard Schreiber, *Vice Pres*
Craig Larkins, *VP Opers*
Mike Skaggs, *Human Res Mgr*
Angela Card, *Human Resources*
EMP: 180 Privately Held
WEB: www.wavesecurities.com
SIC: 8742 8748 Business consultant; business consulting
HQ: Accenture Llp
161 N Clark St Ste 1100
Chicago IL 60601
312 693-0161

(G-4954)
ACHIEVEMENT CTRS FOR CHILDREN (PA)
4255 Northfield Rd (44128-2811)
PHONE.................216 292-9700
Fax: 216 292-9721
Patricia Nobili, *President*
Sally Farwell, *Vice Pres*
Deborah Osgood, *Vice Pres*
Scott Peplin, *CFO*
Betsey Saffar, *Controller*
EMP: 70 **EST:** 1940
SQ FT: 38,000

SALES: 8.2MM Privately Held
WEB: www.achievementcenters.org
SIC: 8322 Social services for the handicapped

(G-4955)
ADCOM GROUP INC
1370 W 6th St Fl 3 (44113-1315)
PHONE.................216 574-9100
Fax: 216 574-6131
Joe Kubic, *CEO*
Tara Stultz, *Editor*
Patricia Ross, *Business Mgr*
Tim Sieple, *COO*
Loren Chylla, *Exec VP*
EMP: 32
SQ FT: 15,000
SALES (est): 7.9MM Privately Held
SIC: 7336 Graphic arts & related design

(G-4956)
ADRIAN M SCHNALL MD
1611 S Green Rd Lbby A (44121-4121)
PHONE.................216 291-4300
Philip Junglas MD, *President*
Adrian M Schnall MD, *Owner*
Dr Debra Dejoseph, *Vice Pres*
Dr James Cobiello, *Treasurer*
Dr Steven Turocvi, *Admin Sec*
EMP: 62
SALES (est): 968.5K Privately Held
SIC: 8011 Offices & clinics of medical doctors

(G-4957)
ADVANCE DOOR COMPANY
4555 Willow Pkwy (44125-1081)
PHONE.................216 883-2424
Fax: 216 883-8952
Bill Giordano, *President*
EMP: 30
SQ FT: 15,000
SALES (est): 6.5MM Privately Held
SIC: 7699 5031 1751 Door & window repair; doors; window & door (prefabricated) installation

(G-4958)
ADVANCE VENDING CORP
14600 Industrial Ave S D (44137-3268)
PHONE.................216 587-9500
Fax: 216 587-9596
Allan Kleinman, *President*
Reed Kleinman, *Corp Secy*
EMP: 25
SQ FT: 12,000
SALES: 2.5MM Privately Held
WEB: www.advancevending.com
SIC: 7359 Vending machine rental

(G-4959)
ADVANCED GROUP CORP (PA)
Also Called: Advanced Benefit Cons Agcy
3800 Lkside Ave E Ste 400 (44114)
PHONE.................216 431-8800
Philip Galaska, *Ch of Bd*
James Kretzschmar, *President*
Bob Lucas, *Senior VP*
Ruth Hirsch, *Executive Asst*
EMP: 40
SQ FT: 7,700
SALES (est): 5.1MM Privately Held
WEB: www.advanced-on-line.com
SIC: 6411 Insurance agents, brokers & service

(G-4960)
ADVOCARE INC
25001 Emery Rd (44128-5626)
PHONE.................216 514-1451
Fax: 216 514-1227
Joseph M Cannelongo, *CEO*
Karen Agnich, *President*
Dustin Napier, *Vice Pres*
Ted Cannelongo, *Technology*
George W Cyphers, *Director*
EMP: 75
SALES (est): 6MM Privately Held
WEB: www.advocare-inc.com
SIC: 8741 Management services

(G-4961)
AECOM
1300 E 9th St Ste 500 (44114-1503)
PHONE.................330 253-9741
Daniel Deighan, *Project Mgr*

Cleveland - Cuyahoga County (G-4962)

Michael Krosky, *Electrical Engi*
EMP: 66
SALES (corp-wide): 18.2B **Publicly Held**
SIC: 8711 Consulting engineer
PA: Aecom
1999 Avenue Of The Stars # 2600
Los Angeles CA 90067
213 593-8000

(G-4962)
AECOM ENERGY & CNSTR INC
Also Called: Washington Group
1300 E 9th St Ste 500 (44114-1503)
PHONE 216 622-2300
James Bickford, *Manager*
EMP: 400
SALES (corp-wide): 18.2B **Publicly Held**
WEB: www.wgint.com
SIC: 1622 1611 1629 1623 Bridge construction; tunnel construction; highway construction, elevated; general contractor, highway & street construction; dams, waterways, docks & other marine construction; industrial plant construction; power plant construction; pipeline construction; industrial buildings, new construction; institutional building construction; commercial & office building, new construction
HQ: Aecom Energy & Construction, Inc.
1999 Avenue Of The Stars
Los Angeles CA 90067
213 593-8100

(G-4963)
AECOM ENERGY & CNSTR INC
Also Called: URS
1500 W 3rd St Ste 200 (44113-1453)
P.O. Box 73, Boise ID (83729-0073)
PHONE 216 523-5600
Jim Bickford, *Opers Staff*
Mark Foster, *Engineer*
Dan Kascak, *Engineer*
Cliff Mueller, *Engineer*
Larry Beers, *Manager*
EMP: 700
SALES (corp-wide): 18.2B **Publicly Held**
WEB: www.wgint.com
SIC: 7389 Personal service agents, brokers & bureaus
HQ: Aecom Energy & Construction, Inc.
1999 Avenue Of The Stars
Los Angeles CA 90067
213 593-8100

(G-4964)
AECOM ENERGY & CNSTR INC
Also Called: URS
1500 W 3rd St Ste 200 (44113-1453)
PHONE 216 523-5600
EMP: 600
SALES (corp-wide): 18.2B **Publicly Held**
WEB: www.wgint.com
SIC: 7389 Personal service agents, brokers & bureaus
HQ: Aecom Energy & Construction, Inc.
1999 Avenue Of The Stars
Los Angeles CA 90067
213 593-8100

(G-4965)
AECOM ENERGY & CNSTR INC
Also Called: URS
1500 W 3rd St Ste 470 (44113-1440)
PHONE 216 523-5600
Steve Hanks, *Branch Mgr*
EMP: 99
SALES (corp-wide): 18.2B **Publicly Held**
WEB: www.wgint.com
SIC: 8711 Engineering services
HQ: Aecom Energy & Construction, Inc.
1999 Avenue Of The Stars
Los Angeles CA 90067
213 593-8100

(G-4966)
AECOM GLOBAL II LLC
1500 W 3rd St Fl 2 (44113-1467)
PHONE 216 523-5600
Diane Roth, *Manager*
EMP: 84
SALES (corp-wide): 18.2B **Publicly Held**
SIC: 8711 8712 8741 Engineering services; consulting engineer; architectural engineering; construction management
HQ: Aecom Global Ii, Llc
1999 Avenue Of The Stars
Los Angeles CA 90067
213 593-8100

(G-4967)
AG INTERACTIVE INC (DH)
Also Called: American Greetings
1 American Rd (44144-2301)
PHONE 216 889-5000
Fax: 216 252-6778
David Ricanati, *President*
Josef Mandelbaum, *Chairman*
Sally Babcock, *Senior VP*
Kathy Hecht, *Senior VP*
Rajiv Jain, *Senior VP*
EMP: 120
SQ FT: 34,000
SALES (est): 32.1MM
SALES (corp-wide): 1.9B **Privately Held**
WEB: www.aginteractive.com
SIC: 5947 7335 Greeting cards; commercial photography
HQ: American Greetings Corporation
1 American Blvd
Cleveland OH 44145
216 252-7300

(G-4968)
AGE LINE INC
4350 Rocky River Dr (44135-2504)
PHONE 216 941-9990
Fax: 216 941-6127
June Pearce Novatney, *President*
Norma Robinette, *COO*
EMP: 30
SALES (est): 984.9K **Privately Held**
WEB: www.age-line.com
SIC: 8059 4789 Personal care home, with health care; cabs, horse drawn: for hire

(G-4969)
AGMET LLC (PA)
7800 Medusa Rd (44146-5549)
PHONE 440 439-7400
Fax: 440 439-7446
Dana Cassidy, *President*
Timothy Andel, *CFO*
Rajesh Shah, *CTO*
▲ **EMP:** 35
SQ FT: 78,000
SALES (est): 21.8MM **Privately Held**
SIC: 5093 Ferrous metal scrap & waste; nonferrous metals scrap

(G-4970)
AIDS TSKFRCE GRTER CLVLAND INC
2829 Euclid Ave (44115-2413)
PHONE 216 357-3131
Fax: 216 622-7785
David Postero, *President*
Kent Holmes, *Opers Staff*
Gail Anderson, *Case Mgr*
Laraun Clayton, *Director*
Garith Fulham, *Director*
EMP: 80
SALES: 1.6MM **Privately Held**
SIC: 8322 Social service center; self-help organization

(G-4971)
AIR COMFORT SYSTEMS INC
Also Called: Comfort Air
5108 Richmond Rd (44146-1331)
PHONE 216 587-4125
Frank Demarco, *President*
Steven Smylie, *Shareholder*
William Smylie, *Shareholder*
Elaine Weinberg, *Shareholder*
EMP: 50
SQ FT: 3,000
SALES (est): 2.8MM **Privately Held**
SIC: 1711 Warm air heating & air conditioning contractor

(G-4972)
AIR COMPLIANCE TESTING INC (PA)
5525 Canal Rd Ste 1 (44125-4866)
P.O. Box 41156 (44141-0156)
PHONE 216 525-0900
Fax: 216 525-0901
Philip J Billick, *President*
Alan Schreiner, *Exec VP*
Philip Lynch, *Human Res Dir*
Robert J Lisy Jr, *Director*
EMP: 26
SQ FT: 15,000
SALES (est): 2.6MM **Privately Held**
WEB: www.aircomp.com
SIC: 7549 Emissions testing without repairs, automotive

(G-4973)
AIR CONDITIONING ENTPS INC
1370 Ontario St Ste 450 (44113-1812)
PHONE 440 729-0900
Ron Willner, *President*
John Koran, *Exec VP*
Martin Radesic, *Vice Pres*
EMP: 25 **EST:** 1970
SQ FT: 2,000
SALES (est): 2.3MM **Privately Held**
SIC: 1711 Warm air heating & air conditioning contractor

(G-4974)
AIR-TEMP CLIMATE CONTROL INC
Also Called: Air-Temp Mechanical
3013 Payne Ave (44114-4594)
PHONE 216 579-1552
Fax: 216 579-0413
Allen J Krupar, *President*
Timothy Holmes, *Vice Pres*
EMP: 40
SQ FT: 11,000
SALES (est): 7MM **Privately Held**
WEB: www.air-tempmech.com
SIC: 1711 Warm air heating & air conditioning contractor; refrigeration contractor

(G-4975)
AIRGAS INC
2020 Train Ave (44113-4205)
PHONE 866 935-3370
Tom Kall, *Manager*
EMP: 269
SALES (corp-wide): 163.9MM **Privately Held**
SIC: 5169 Industrial gases
HQ: Airgas, Inc.
259 N Radnor Chester Rd # 100
Radnor PA 19087
610 687-5253

(G-4976)
AIRGAS MERCHANT GASES LLC
6055 Rckside Woods Blvd N (44131-2301)
PHONE 800 242-0105
Thomas Smyth, *Vice Pres*
Carrie Pini, *Controller*
Tom Thoman,
Chris Plitnick,
▲ **EMP:** 335
SALES (est): 104.7MM
SALES (corp-wide): 163.9MM **Privately Held**
WEB: www.airgas.com
SIC: 5169 Industrial gases
HQ: Airgas, Inc.
259 N Radnor Chester Rd # 100
Radnor PA 19087
610 687-5253

(G-4977)
AIRGAS USA LLC
6055 Rocksd Woods Blv 400 (44131)
PHONE 440 232-1590
Fax: 440 232-7799
Kevin McBride, *Branch Mgr*
EMP: 148
SALES (corp-wide): 163.9MM **Privately Held**
SIC: 8711 Engineering services
HQ: Airgas Usa, Llc
259 N Radnor Chester Rd # 100
Radnor PA 19087
610 687-5253

(G-4978)
AIRKO INC
20160 Center Ridge Rd # 101 (44116-3507)
PHONE 440 333-0133
James Gilbert, *President*
Raymond Gilbert, *Senior VP*
Andy Zarlinski, *Vice Pres*
Barb Gilbert, *Office Admin*
Craig Makar, *Applctn Conslt*
EMP: 35
SQ FT: 1,500
SALES: 2MM **Privately Held**
WEB: www.airkoinc.com
SIC: 1761 1751 1542 1521 Siding contractor; carpentry work; window & door installation & erection; commercial & office buildings, renovation & repair; general remodeling, single-family houses

(G-4979)
AITHERAS AVIATION GROUP LLC (PA)
2301 N Marginal Rd (44114-3708)
PHONE 216 298-9060
George Katsikas, *CEO*
Kevin Weir, *COO*
EMP: 29
SALES (est): 9.4MM **Privately Held**
WEB: www.aitherasaviationgroup.com
SIC: 4581 Aircraft maintenance & repair services

(G-4980)
AJAX CLEANING CONTRACTORS CO
1561 E 40th St (44103-2301)
P.O. Box 603126 (44103-0126)
PHONE 216 881-8484
Martin Presser, *President*
EMP: 100
SQ FT: 3,375
SALES (est): 1MM **Privately Held**
SIC: 7349 Window cleaning; janitorial service, contract basis

(G-4981)
ALADDINS BAKING COMPANY INC
1301 Carnegie Ave (44115-2809)
PHONE 216 861-0317
Fax: 216 861-5536
Carl E Nahra, *President*
Carl Nahra, *President*
Maurice Abood, *Vice Pres*
Rick Nahra, *Vice Pres*
Constance Nahra, *Finance*
EMP: 48
SQ FT: 10,000
SALES (est): 8.7MM **Privately Held**
WEB: www.aladdinbaking.com
SIC: 5149 5461 Bakery products; bakeries

(G-4982)
ALBERT M HIGLEY COMPANY (PA)
2926 Chester Ave (44114-4414)
PHONE 216 404-5783
Fax: 216 861-0038
Albert M Higley Jr, *Ch of Bd*
Charles Stephenson, *President*
Kurt Heinicke, *Vice Pres*
Rex Lewers, *Vice Pres*
Thomas Lippert, *Vice Pres*
EMP: 180
SQ FT: 14,000
SALES: 159MM **Privately Held**
WEB: www.amhigley.com
SIC: 1542 1541 Commercial & office building, new construction; industrial buildings, new construction

(G-4983)
ALEPH HOME & SENIOR CARE INC
Also Called: Infinity
2448 Beachwood Blvd (44122-1547)
PHONE 216 382-7689
William Bein, *President*
EMP: 60 **EST:** 2001
SALES (est): 820.1K **Privately Held**
SIC: 8361 Home for the aged

(G-4984)
ALEXANDER MANN SOLUTIONS CORP
1301 E 9th St Ste 1200 (44114-1823)
PHONE 216 336-6756
Rosaleen M Blair, *President*
Mark Jones, *COO*
Penny Queller, *Senior VP*
Richard Timmins, *CFO*
Lisa REA, *Asst Treas*
EMP: 425
SQ FT: 13,000

GEOGRAPHIC SECTION
Cleveland - Cuyahoga County (G-5008)

SALES: 48.5MM
SALES (corp-wide): 249.2MM **Privately Held**
SIC: **7361** Executive placement
HQ: Alexander Mann Solutions Limited
7-11 Bishopsgate
London EC2N
207 832-2700

(G-4985)
ALGART HEALTH CARE INC
8902 Detroit Ave (44102-1840)
PHONE..................................216 631-1550
Fax: 216 631-2343
Gary Klein, *President*
Tom Jacobs, *Treasurer*
Karl Fotinos, *Director*
Garth Ireland, *Admin Sec*
EMP: 85 EST: 1979
SQ FT: 29,000
SALES (est): 5.4MM **Privately Held**
WEB: www.algart.com
SIC: **8052** Intermediate care facilities

(G-4986)
ALL ERECTION & CRANE RENTAL (PA)
4700 Acorn Dr (44131-6940)
P.O. Box 318047 (44131-8047)
PHONE..................................216 524-6550
Michael C Liptak Jr, *President*
John Sivak, *CFO*
Lawrence Liptak, *Treasurer*
Wayne C Linson, *Credit Mgr*
Katie Spahnie, *Human Res Mgr*
EMP: 225
SQ FT: 50,000
SALES (est): 100.5MM **Privately Held**
WEB: www.allcrane.com
SIC: **7353** 7359 Heavy construction equipment rental; equipment rental & leasing

(G-4987)
ALL ERECTION & CRANE RENTAL
7809 Old Rockside Rd (44131-2384)
PHONE..................................216 524-6550
Fax: 216 524-6290
Daniel Shop, *Engineer*
John Sivak, *CFO*
Sharon Voyten, *Accounting Mgr*
Steve Stefancic, *Branch Mgr*
Matt Barry, *Manager*
EMP: 69
SALES (corp-wide): 100.5MM **Privately Held**
SIC: **7353** 7359 Heavy construction equipment rental; equipment rental & leasing
PA: All Erection' & Crane Rental Corp
4700 Acorn Dr
Cleveland OH 44131
216 524-6550

(G-4988)
ALL HEARTS HOME HEALTH CARE
6009 Landerhaven Dr Ste D (44124-4192)
PHONE..................................440 342-2026
Kelli Goodrick, *President*
EMP: 50
SALES (est): 659.4K **Privately Held**
SIC: **8082** Home health care services

(G-4989)
ALL MY SONS BUSINESS DEV CORP
15224 Neo Pkwy (44120-3153)
PHONE..................................469 461-5000
EMP: 50 **Privately Held**
SIC: **8351** Child day care services
PA: All My Sons Business Development Corporation
2400 Old Mill Rd
Carrollton TX 75007

(G-4990)
ALL OHIO THREADED ROD CO INC
5349 Saint Clair Ave (44103-1311)
PHONE..................................216 426-1800
Fax: 216 426-1802
James Wolford, *CEO*
Rick Fien, *President*
Brian Wolford, *VP Sales*
Raechel Sanichar, *Office Mgr*

▲ EMP: 28
SQ FT: 40,000
SALES (est): 7.6MM **Privately Held**
SIC: **3312** 5085 3316 Bar, rod & wire products; industrial supplies; cold finishing of steel shapes

(G-4991)
ALL-TYPE WELDING & FABRICATION
7690 Bond St (44139-5351)
PHONE..................................440 439-3990
Fax: 440 439-3990
Mike Distaulo, *President*
William Jones, *Vice Pres*
Dennis Whitaker, *Vice Pres*
Jennifer Mangello, *Buyer*
EMP: 40
SQ FT: 34,000
SALES (est): 8.1MM **Privately Held**
WEB: www.atwf-inc.com
SIC: **3599** 7692 1761 Machine & other job shop work; welding repair; sheet metalwork

(G-4992)
ALLEGA RECYCLED MTLS & SUP CO
5585 Canal Rd (44125-4874)
PHONE..................................216 447-0814
Joe Allega, *President*
Jeffrey F Wallis, *Treasurer*
EMP: 25
SQ FT: 30,000
SALES (est): 4MM **Privately Held**
SIC: **5211** 5032 Concrete & cinder block; concrete & cinder block

(G-4993)
ALLIED BUILDING PRODUCTS CORP
12800 Brookpark Rd (44130-1158)
PHONE..................................216 362-1764
Fax: 216 362-1758
Denis Edixon, *Sales Mgr*
George Botoulis, *Manager*
EMP: 30
SALES (corp-wide): 4.3B **Publicly Held**
WEB: www.alliedbuilding.com
SIC: **5033** Roofing & siding materials
HQ: Allied Building Products Corp.
15 E Union Ave
East Rutherford NJ 07073
201 507-8400

(G-4994)
ALMOST FAMILY INC
23611 Chagrin Blvd # 130 (44122-5540)
PHONE..................................216 464-0443
Fax: 216 283-0365
EMP: 30
SALES (corp-wide): 796.9MM **Publicly Held**
SIC: **8082** Home health care services
PA: Almost Family, Inc.
9510 Ormsby Station Rd
Louisville KY 40223
502 891-1000

(G-4995)
ALORICA CUSTOMER CARE INC
9525 Sweet Valley Dr (44125-4237)
PHONE..................................216 525-3311
EMP: 563
SALES (corp-wide): 7.7B **Privately Held**
SIC: **7389** Telemarketing services
HQ: Alorica Customer Care, Inc.
5085 W Park Blvd Ste 300
Plano TX

(G-4996)
ALPHA GROUP AGENCY INC (PA)
4200 Rockside Rd Ste 300 (44131-2530)
PHONE..................................216 520-0440
Kevin Mackay, *President*
Jim Schade, *Vice Pres*
Adrienne Vichill, *Vice Pres*
John Wain, *Vice Pres*
Stephanie Stadler, *Broker*
EMP: 25
SQ FT: 8,000

SALES (est): 13MM **Privately Held**
WEB: www.thealphaga.com
SIC: **6411** Pension & retirement plan consultants

(G-4997)
ALPHAPORT INC
18013 Cleveland Ste 170 (44135)
PHONE..................................216 619-2400
Fax: 216 441-2013
Rosella Miranda, *CEO*
Anthony Miranda, *COO*
Jennifer Jones, *Vice Pres*
Grant Illenberger, *CFO*
James May, *Program Mgr*
EMP: 50
SQ FT: 5,500
SALES (est): 6MM **Privately Held**
WEB: www.alpha-port.com
SIC: **8711** Consulting engineer

(G-4998)
ALPINE NURSING CARE
5555 Brecksville Rd (44131-1524)
PHONE..................................216 650-6295
Divyech Patel, *CEO*
Dermesh Patel, *President*
Mili Patel, *Vice Pres*
John Herman, *CFO*
Belita Bush, *Human Resources*
EMP: 32
SALES (est): 1.4MM **Privately Held**
WEB: www.alpinehhc.com
SIC: **8082** Home health care services

(G-4999)
ALS SERVICES USA CORP
Also Called: Als Laboratory Group
6180 Halle Dr Ste D (44125-4636)
PHONE..................................604 998-5311
Mike Scruggs, *General Mgr*
EMP: 40
SALES (corp-wide): 975.4MM **Privately Held**
SIC: **8734** Testing laboratories
HQ: Als Services Usa, Corp.
10450 Stncliff Rd Ste 210
Houston TX 77099
281 530-5656

(G-5000)
AM INDUSTRIAL GROUP LLC
4680 Grayton Rd (44135-2357)
PHONE..................................216 267-6783
Reginald Wyman, *Owner*
EMP: 35 **Privately Held**
WEB: www.amindustrial.com
SIC: **4225** General warehousing & storage
PA: Am Industrial Group, Llc
16000 Commerce Park Dr
Brookpark OH 44142

(G-5001)
AMALGAMATED TRANSIT UNION
Also Called: Local 268
2428 Saint Clair Ave Ne (44114-4011)
PHONE..................................216 861-3350
Fax: 216 861-4542
Gary Johnson, *President*
EMP: 27
SQ FT: 4,620
SALES (corp-wide): 28.8MM **Privately Held**
WEB: www.atu1005.com
SIC: **8631** Trade union
PA: Amalgamated Transit Union
10000 New Hampshire Ave
Silver Spring MD 20903
202 537-1645

(G-5002)
AMERICAB INC
3380 W 137th St (44111-2412)
PHONE..................................216 429-1134
Fax: 216 429-1103
Jonathan Schwartz, *President*
Robert Zarin, *President*
Robert Roesch, *General Mgr*
Robin Sue Lansburg, *Corp Secy*
Samuel Schwartz, *Vice Pres*
EMP: 40
SQ FT: 3,500
SALES (est): 1.8MM **Privately Held**
SIC: **4121** Taxicabs

(G-5003)
AMERICAN AIRLINES INC
Also Called: US Airways
5300 Riverside Dr Ste 8a (44135-3147)
PHONE..................................216 706-0702
Robert Mitchell, *Manager*
EMP: 48
SALES (corp-wide): 42.2B **Publicly Held**
WEB: www.usair.com
SIC: **4581** Airport terminal services
HQ: American Airlines, Inc.
4333 Amon Carter Blvd
Fort Worth TX 76155
817 963-1234

(G-5004)
AMERICAN AIRLINES INC
5300 Riverside Dr Ste 1a (44135-3145)
PHONE..................................216 898-1347
Mike Costello, *Vice Pres*
Bob Mitchell, *Manager*
Bob Arkangel, *Manager*
EMP: 50
SALES (corp-wide): 42.2B **Publicly Held**
WEB: www.aa.com
SIC: **4581** 4512 Airport terminal services; air transportation, scheduled
HQ: American Airlines, Inc.
4333 Amon Carter Blvd
Fort Worth TX 76155
817 963-1234

(G-5005)
AMERICAN CANCER SOCIETY EAST
10501 Euclid Ave (44106-2204)
PHONE..................................800 227-2345
Fax: 216 844-2959
Rimas Jasin, *Exec Dir*
EMP: 25
SALES (corp-wide): 91.7MM **Privately Held**
SIC: **8322** Social service center
PA: American Cancer Society, East Central Division, Inc.
Sipe Ave Rr 422
Hershey PA 17033
717 533-6144

(G-5006)
AMERICAN COMMODORE TU (PA)
4130 Mayfield Rd (44121-3033)
PHONE..................................216 291-4601
Fax: 216 291-5661
Frank Simoni Jr, *President*
Joe N Simoni, *Principal*
Mary Simoni, *Principal*
Toni Wick, *Corp Secy*
Raymond Caporale, *Vice Pres*
EMP: 60 EST: 1947
SQ FT: 35,000
SALES (est): 6.1MM **Privately Held**
WEB: www.actux.com
SIC: **7299** 5699 Dress suit rental; tuxedo rental; formal wear

(G-5007)
AMERICAN CONSOLIDATED INDS INC (PA)
4650 Johnston Pkwy (44128-3219)
PHONE..................................216 587-8000
Joyce Kaufman, *Ch of Bd*
Josh Kaufman, *President*
Steve Lefkowitz, *CFO*
Larry Kerr, *Controller*
◆ EMP: 40
SQ FT: 118,000
SALES (est): 80.8MM **Privately Held**
SIC: **5051** Metals service centers & offices

(G-5008)
AMERICAN COPY EQUIPMENT INC
Also Called: Online Imaging Solutions
6599 Granger Rd (44131-1415)
PHONE..................................330 722-9555
Fax: 216 642-9080
John Baron, *President*
Katherine L Huff, *Principal*
Marilyn Podracky, *CFO*
EMP: 195
SQ FT: 30,000

Cleveland - Cuyahoga County (G-5009)

SALES (est): 73.1MM **Privately Held**
WEB: www.acecleveland.com
SIC: 5044 Office equipment

(G-5009)
AMERICAN HEART ASSN OHIO VLY
Also Called: Great Rivers
1375 E 9th St Ste 600 (44114-1785)
PHONE..................216 791-7500
Valerie Hillow, *Manager*
Dawn Clark, *Director*
EMP: 25
SQ FT: 36,000
SALES (est): 1.8MM **Privately Held**
SIC: 8733 Research institute

(G-5010)
AMERICAN INCOME LIFE INSUR CO
12301 Ridge Rd (44133-3744)
P.O. Box 33160, North Royalton (44133-0160)
PHONE..................440 582-0040
Fax: 440 582-1312
James M Surace, *Principal*
EMP: 60
SQ FT: 750
SALES (corp-wide): 4.1B **Publicly Held**
WEB: www.ailfl.com
SIC: 6311 6411 Life insurance carriers; insurance agents
HQ: American Income Life Insurance Company Inc
  1200 Wooded Acres Dr
  Waco TX 76710
  254 741-5701

(G-5011)
AMERICAN LIVERY SERVICE INC
Also Called: American Limousine Service
11723 Detroit Ave (44107-3001)
PHONE..................216 221-9330
Fax: 216 221-2005
Robert Mazzarella, *President*
Joanne Mazzarella, *Corp Secy*
EMP: 45
SQ FT: 2,500
SALES (est): 2.4MM **Privately Held**
WEB: www.americanlimousineservice.com
SIC: 4119 Limousine rental, with driver; hearse rental, with driver

(G-5012)
AMERICAN MARINE EXPRESS INC
Also Called: Amx
765 E 140th St Ste A (44110-2181)
P.O. Box 32487 (44132-0487)
PHONE..................216 268-3005
Harjit S Dhillon, *President*
Dan Cain, *General Mgr*
Julie Boothe-Rhodes, *Business Mgr*
Cathy Behringer, *Manager*
EMP: 30
SALES: 10.4MM **Privately Held**
SIC: 4731 Truck transportation brokers

(G-5013)
AMERICAN MED
13929 W Parkway Rd (44135-4511)
PHONE..................216 251-5319
EMP: 106
SALES (corp-wide): 7.8B **Publicly Held**
SIC: 4119 Ambulance service
HQ: American Medical Response, Inc.
  6363 S Fiddlers Green Cir # 1400
  Greenwood Village CO 80111

(G-5014)
AMERICAN MIDWEST MORTGAGE CORP (PA)
6363 York Rd Ste 300 (44130-3031)
PHONE..................440 882-5210
Fax: 440 884-5034
John Paulozzi, *President*
Randee Estep, *Vice Pres*
Scott Dillen, *Loan Officer*
Robert Dollinger, *Loan Officer*
Dan Lease, *Broker*
EMP: 50
SALES (est): 10.9MM **Privately Held**
SIC: 6162 Mortgage bankers

(G-5015)
AMERICAN MULTI-CINEMA INC
Also Called: AMC
4788 Ridge Rd (44144-3327)
PHONE..................216 749-0260
Paul Gellott, *Branch Mgr*
EMP: 50 **Publicly Held**
WEB: www.arrowheadtownecenter.com
SIC: 7832 Motion picture theaters, except drive-in
HQ: American Multi-Cinema, Inc.
  1 Amc Way
  Leawood KS 66211
  913 213-2000

(G-5016)
AMERICAN MUTUAL LIFE ASSN (PA)
Also Called: AMLA
19424 S Waterloo Rd (44119-3250)
PHONE..................216 531-1900
Fax: 216 531-8123
Stanley Ziherl, *President*
Joseph Petric Jr, *Corp Secy*
Tereasa Aveni, *Exec VP*
Albert Amigoni, *Vice Pres*
Anna Mae Mannian, *Vice Pres*
EMP: 25
SQ FT: 1,500
SALES: 3.5MM **Privately Held**
WEB: www.americanmutual.org
SIC: 6311 Fraternal life insurance organizations

(G-5017)
AMERICAN NAT FLEET SVC INC
Also Called: American Fleet Services
7714 Commerce Park Oval (44131-2306)
PHONE..................216 447-6060
Fax: 216 447-9132
Joe Schuerger, *CEO*
Macon Sylvia, *Human Res Dir*
Sandra Schuerger, *Accounts Mgr*
EMP: 65
SQ FT: 40,000
SALES (est): 10.8MM **Privately Held**
WEB: www.fleetme.com
SIC: 7538 7532 General truck repair; body shop, automotive; body shop, trucks

(G-5018)
AMERICAN NATIONAL RED CROSS
3747 Euclid Ave (44115-2501)
PHONE..................216 431-3152
David Plate, *CEO*
EMP: 71
SALES (corp-wide): 2.5B **Privately Held**
SIC: 8999 Artists & artists' studios
PA: The American National Red Cross
  430 17th St Nw
  Washington DC 20006
  202 737-8300

(G-5019)
AMERICAN PRSERVATION BLDRS LLC
127 Public Sq Ste 1300 (44114-1310)
PHONE..................216 236-2007
Michael Kucera, *President*
Dennis Arian, *Vice Pres*
Harry Lee, *Vice Pres*
Todd Wallace, *Vice Pres*
Gregg Burke, *Project Mgr*
EMP: 68
SALES: 45.6MM **Privately Held**
SIC: 1531 Operative builders

(G-5020)
AMERICAN RESIDENTIAL SVCS LLC
4547 Hinckley Industrial (44109-6018)
PHONE..................216 561-8880
Bill Linn, *General Mgr*
Divyesh Patel, *Branch Mgr*
EMP: 59
SALES (corp-wide): 2.6B **Privately Held**
SIC: 1711 Plumbing contractors
PA: American Residential Services Llc
  965 Ridge Lake Blvd # 201
  Memphis TN 38120
  901 271-9700

(G-5021)
AMERICAN RETIREMENT CORP
Also Called: Homewood Rsdnce At Richmond Hts
3 Homewood Way (44143-2955)
PHONE..................216 291-6140
Fax: 216 291-6149
Minnie Cleaves, *Office Mgr*
Kim Hutter, *Branch Mgr*
Mea Layman, *Director*
EMP: 55
SALES (corp-wide): 4.7B **Publicly Held**
WEB: www.arclp.com
SIC: 8059 8052 Rest home, with health care; intermediate care facilities
HQ: American Retirement Corporation
  111 Westwood Pl Ste 200
  Brentwood TN 37027
  615 221-2250

(G-5022)
AMERICAN RETIREMENT CORP
Also Called: Homewood Residence At Rockefel
3151 Mayfield Rd Apt 1105 (44118-1756)
PHONE..................216 321-6331
Fax: 216 321-6651
Toni Colon, *Manager*
EMP: 60
SQ FT: 2,726
SALES (corp-wide): 4.7B **Publicly Held**
WEB: www.arclp.com
SIC: 8361 Residential care
HQ: American Retirement Corporation
  111 Westwood Pl Ste 200
  Brentwood TN 37027
  615 221-2250

(G-5023)
AMERICAN TANK & FABRICATING CO (PA)
Also Called: A T & F Co
12314 Elmwood Ave (44111-5991)
PHONE..................216 252-1500
Fax: 216 251-4963
Terry Ripich, *Ch of Bd*
Bob Ripich, *President*
Michael Ripich, *President*
Kevin Cantrell, *Vice Pres*
Michael Puleo, *Vice Pres*
▲ EMP: 100 EST: 1940
SQ FT: 300,000
SALES (est): 43MM **Privately Held**
WEB: www.amtank.com
SIC: 3443 5051 Fabricated plate work (boiler shop); weldments; metals service centers & offices; iron & steel (ferrous) products

(G-5024)
AMERICAN TITLE OF OHIO LLC
600 Superior Ave E # 1300 (44114-2654)
PHONE..................303 868-2250
Richard Talley,
EMP: 25
SALES: 950K **Privately Held**
SIC: 6411 Insurance agents, brokers & service

(G-5025)
AMERIMARK HOLDINGS LLC (PA)
Also Called: Complements
6864 Engle Rd (44130-7910)
PHONE..................440 325-2000
Mark Ethier, *CEO*
Linda Dulcie, *Vice Pres*
Jill Friedman, *Vice Pres*
John Buzby, *Purch Mgr*
Joanne Cammett, *Buyer*
EMP: 425
SALES (est): 639.3MM **Privately Held**
SIC: 7331 5961 Direct mail advertising services; catalog sales; mail order house

(G-5026)
AMIN TUROCY & WATSON LLP (PA)
127 Public Sq Fl 57 (44114-1233)
PHONE..................216 696-8730
Fax: 216 696-8731
Gregory Turocy, *Partner*
Himanshu S Amin, *General Ptnr*
Daniel Bedell, *Counsel*
Bernard Berman, *Counsel*
Gerardo Orlando, *Counsel*
EMP: 49
SALES (est): 5.4MM **Privately Held**
WEB: www.thepatentattorneys.com
SIC: 8111 Corporate, partnership & business law

(G-5027)
AMITEL BEACHWOOD LTD PARTNR
Also Called: Residence Inn By Marriott
3628 Park Dr (44134-4651)
PHONE..................216 831-3030
Fax: 216 831-3232
Terry Knowlan, *General Mgr*
EMP: 25
SALES (est): 1MM
SALES (corp-wide): 2.4MM **Privately Held**
SIC: 7011 Hotels
PA: Amitel Beachwood Limited Partnership
  6000 Rckside Woods Blvd N
  Cleveland OH 44131
  216 707-9839

(G-5028)
AMITEL LIMITED PARTNERSHIP
Also Called: Residence Inn By Marriott
17525 Rosbough Blvd (44130-2580)
PHONE..................440 234-6688
Colleen Murphy, *Opers-Prdtn-Mfg*
Colleen Davis, *Manager*
EMP: 50
SALES (est): 1.1MM
SALES (corp-wide): 2.7MM **Privately Held**
SIC: 7011 7991 Hotels; physical fitness facilities
PA: Amitel Limited Partnership
  6000 Rckside Woods Blvd N
  Cleveland OH

(G-5029)
AMITEL ROCKSIDE LTD PARTNR
Also Called: Residence Inn By Marriott
5101 Independence (44131)
PHONE..................216 520-1450
Fax: 216 642-9830
Darrell Glenn, *General Mgr*
Brad Huwar, *Vice Pres*
Carl Trakofler, *Treasurer*
Sigrid Bennett, *Sales Dir*
Melissa Garten, *Manager*
EMP: 49
SQ FT: 41,267
SALES (est): 1.2MM
SALES (corp-wide): 2.8MM **Privately Held**
SIC: 7011 Hotels
PA: Amitel Rockside Limited Partnership
  6000 Rockside Woods Blvd
  Cleveland OH

(G-5030)
AMOTEC INC (PA)
1701 E 12th St Apt 10b (44114-3271)
PHONE..................440 250-4600
Carmine Izzo, *President*
Steve Melfi, *Managing Dir*
Jay Young, *Business Mgr*
Lisa Peters, *Vice Pres*
Amy Holland, *Human Resources*
EMP: 31
SQ FT: 5,000
SALES: 3.5MM **Privately Held**
WEB: www.amotecinc.com
SIC: 8742 Human resource consulting services

(G-5031)
AMSDELL CONSTRUCTION INC (PA)
20445 Emerald Pkwy # 220 (44135-6009)
PHONE..................216 458-0670
Fax: 440 234-5899
Berry Amsdell, *President*
Robert J Amsdell, *Vice Pres*
John Black, *CFO*
EMP: 180
SQ FT: 8,000

GEOGRAPHIC SECTION

Cleveland - Cuyahoga County (G-5055)

SALES (est): 17.4MM Privately Held
SIC: 1522 1541 1542 6531 Hotel/motel, new construction; warehouse construction; industrial buildings, new construction; commercial & office building, new construction; shopping center construction; real estate agents & managers

(G-5032)
AMTRUST NORTH AMERICA INC (HQ)
Also Called: Amtrust Financial Services
800 Superior Ave E # 2100 (44114-2613)
PHONE.................................216 328-6100
Barry D Zyskind, *CEO*
Michael M Saxon, *Exec VP*
Robert Eisendrath, *Senior VP*
Joey Andrews, *Assistant VP*
Matt Gillespie, *Assistant VP*
EMP: 230
SQ FT: 60,000
SALES (est): 1.1B Publicly Held
SIC: 6331 6411 Workers' compensation insurance; insurance claim processing, except medical

(G-5033)
ANCHOR BRONZE AND METALS INC
11470 Euclid Ave Ste 509 (44106-3934)
PHONE.................................440 549-5653
Roger Moore, *President*
Tim Nielsen, *Sales Mgr*
EMP: 32
SQ FT: 42,000
SALES (est): 7MM Privately Held
SIC: 3366 5051 Copper foundries; brass foundry; bronze foundry; castings (except die): copper & copper-base alloy; copper; copper products; miscellaneous nonferrous products; castings, rough: iron or steel

(G-5034)
ANCHOR CLEANING CONTRACTORS
1966 W 52nd St (44102-3367)
P.O. Box 602160 (44102-0160)
PHONE.................................216 961-7343
Fax: 216 961-8339
Paul Gwinn, *President*
EMP: 25
SQ FT: 750
SALES (est): 650K Privately Held
SIC: 7349 Janitorial service, contract basis; window cleaning

(G-5035)
ANCHOR METAL PROCESSING INC (PA)
11830 Brookpark Rd (44130-1103)
PHONE.................................216 362-1850
Fax: 216 362-1839
Edward Pfaff, *Ch of Bd*
Frederick Pfaff, *President*
Jeff Pfaff, *Vice Pres*
Dave Pippert, *Purchasing*
Judy Quayle, *Executive Asst*
EMP: 30
SQ FT: 46,000
SALES (est): 9MM Privately Held
SIC: 3599 1761 3444 Machine shop, jobbing & repair; sheet metalwork; sheet metalwork

(G-5036)
ANGELS ON EARTH CHILD CARE CO
13439 Lorain Ave (44111-3283)
PHONE.................................216 476-8100
Fax: 216 476-1212
Robert Gonzalez, *President*
Marilyn Gonzalez, *Vice Pres*
EMP: 40
SQ FT: 7,500
SALES (est): 1.1MM Privately Held
SIC: 8351 Child day care services

(G-5037)
ANGSTROM GRAPHICS INC MIDWEST (HQ)
4437 E 49th St (44125-1005)
PHONE.................................216 271-5300
Wayne R Angstrom, *Ch of Bd*
Rachel Malakoff, *CFO*
Tim Gailey, *Accounting Mgr*
Rhonda Perry, *VP Sales*
Bruce Macdonald, *Marketing Staff*
EMP: 295
SQ FT: 230,000
SALES (est): 56.9MM
SALES (corp-wide): 288.8MM Privately Held
SIC: 2752 7331 Commercial printing, offset; direct mail advertising services
PA: Angstrom Graphics Inc
4437 E 49th St
Cleveland OH 44125
216 271-5300

(G-5038)
ANGSTROM GRAPHICS INC MIDWEST
Also Called: New Channel Direct
4437 E 49th St (44125-1005)
PHONE.................................330 225-8950
Carol Swearingen, *Manager*
EMP: 45
SALES (corp-wide): 288.8MM Privately Held
SIC: 7331 Mailing service
HQ: Angstrom Graphics Inc Midwest
4437 E 49th St
Cleveland OH 44125
216 271-5300

(G-5039)
ANIMAL PROTECTIVE LEAGUE
1729 Willey Ave (44113-4391)
PHONE.................................216 771-4616
Fax: 216 771-2810
Jeffrey L Kocian, *President*
Dan Storer, *Exec VP*
Laura Koballa, *Vice Pres*
EMP: 35
SQ FT: 22,400
SALES: 4MM Privately Held
SIC: 8699 0742 Animal humane society; veterinary services, specialties

(G-5040)
ANSELMO RSSIS PREMIER PROD LTD
Also Called: Premiere Produce
4500 Willow Pkwy (44125-1042)
PHONE.................................800 229-5517
Fax: 216 391-3068
Anthony Anselmo, *President*
Anthony Rossi, *Partner*
Joe Harvey, *General Mgr*
EMP: 43
SALES (est): 22.2MM Privately Held
SIC: 5148 Fruits, fresh

(G-5041)
ANSWERING SERVICE INC
Also Called: Radio Page Leasing
5767 Mayfield Rd Rear 1 (44124-2991)
PHONE.................................440 473-1200
Fax: 440 449-4868
William Smylie, *Ch of Bd*
Shari Rosen, *President*
EMP: 30
SQ FT: 800
SALES (est): 2.1MM Privately Held
SIC: 7389 4812 Telephone answering service; paging services

(G-5042)
ANTHONY ALLEGA CEMENT CONTR
5585 Canal Rd (44125-4874)
PHONE.................................216 447-0814
Fax: 216 447-5016
John Allega, *President*
James Allega, *Vice Pres*
Joseph Allega, *Vice Pres*
Jeff Repenning, *Manager*
Jeffrey F Wallis, *Admin Sec*
EMP: 50 EST: 1946
SQ FT: 5,000
SALES (est): 19.8MM Privately Held
WEB: www.allega.com
SIC: 1611 Highway & street construction

(G-5043)
ANTHONY OMALLEY ATTY
1375 E 9th St (44114-1739)
PHONE.................................216 479-6100
Anthony Omalley, *Managing Prtnr*
F D Balmert, *Principal*
EMP: 50 EST: 2010
SALES (est): 1.5MM Privately Held
SIC: 8111 General practice attorney, lawyer

(G-5044)
ANTHONY ROCCOS HAIR DESIGN
6255 Highland Rd (44143-2110)
PHONE.................................440 646-1925
Mark Rassy, *Owner*
EMP: 25
SALES (est): 404.5K Privately Held
WEB: www.anthonyroccos.com
SIC: 7231 Hairdressers

(G-5045)
ANY DOMEST WORK INC
Also Called: Adw
5735 Pearl Rd (44129-2849)
PHONE.................................440 845-9911
Fax: 440 845-8889
Joseph Sokolowski, *President*
EMP: 80
SALES (est): 2.3MM Privately Held
SIC: 7349 Cleaning service, industrial or commercial

(G-5046)
AON CONSULTING INC
1660 W 2nd St Ste 650 (44113-1419)
PHONE.................................216 621-8100
Fax: 216 623-4171
Jerry Kysela, *Manager*
EMP: 40
SALES (corp-wide): 11.6B Privately Held
SIC: 6411 Insurance brokers
HQ: Aon Consulting, Inc.
200 E Randolph St Ll3
Chicago IL 60601
312 381-1000

(G-5047)
AON RISK SVCS NORTHEAST INC (HQ)
Also Called: A O N
1660 W 2nd St (44113-1454)
PHONE.................................216 621-8100
Richard Longyhore, *Principal*
Jerry G Kysela, *Director*
EMP: 1100
SALES (est): 335.3MM
SALES (corp-wide): 11.6B Privately Held
SIC: 6411 Insurance brokers
PA: Aon Plc
The Aon Centre
London EC3V
207 623-5500

(G-5048)
APG OFFICE FURNISHINGS INC
3615 Superior Ave E 4407a (44114-4139)
PHONE.................................216 621-4590
Dia Novotney, *Project Mgr*
Paul Johanni, *VP Sales*
Sean Regan, *Branch Mgr*
EMP: 45
SALES (corp-wide): 28.9MM Privately Held
WEB: www.apgof.com
SIC: 5021 5044 Office furniture; office equipment
PA: Apg Office Furnishings, Inc.
12075 Northwest Blvd # 100
Cincinnati OH 45246
513 621-9111

(G-5049)
APPALACHIAN HARDWOOD LUMBER CO
5433 Perkins Rd (44146-1856)
PHONE.................................440 232-6767
Fax: 440 232-6795
Gary S Kaufman, *President*
Stephen Kaufman, *Vice Pres*
Sherri Walsh, *Manager*
▲ EMP: 30
SQ FT: 100,000
SALES (est): 16.3MM Privately Held
WEB: www.appalachianlumber.com
SIC: 5031 Lumber: rough, dressed & finished; millwork; hardboard

(G-5050)
APPLEWOOD CENTERS INC (PA)
10427 Detroit Ave (44102-1645)
PHONE.................................216 696-6815
Tom Browne, *CFO*
Christine Evangelista, *CFO*
Vernessa Bowles, *Psychologist*
Christina Chin, *Psychologist*
Lucy Ddungu, *Psychologist*
EMP: 325
SQ FT: 17,000
SALES (est): 19.6MM Privately Held
SIC: 8322 Child related social services

(G-5051)
APPLEWOOD CENTERS INC
Also Called: Children's Aide Society Campus
10427 Detroit Ave (44102-1645)
PHONE.................................216 521-6511
Roberta King, *Manager*
EMP: 90
SALES (est): 389K
SALES (corp-wide): 19.6MM Privately Held
SIC: 8322 Child related social services
PA: Applewood Centers, Inc.
10427 Detroit Ave
Cleveland OH 44102
216 696-6815

(G-5052)
APPLEWOOD CENTERS INC
3518 W 25th St (44109-1951)
PHONE.................................216 741-2241
J Blumhagen, *Branch Mgr*
Elizabeth Frantz, *Psychologist*
EMP: 143
SALES (corp-wide): 19.6MM Privately Held
SIC: 8322 Child related social services
PA: Applewood Centers, Inc.
10427 Detroit Ave
Cleveland OH 44102
216 696-6815

(G-5053)
APPLIED INDUS TECH - CA LLC (HQ)
1 Applied Plz (44115-2511)
PHONE.................................216 426-4000
David L Pugh, *CEO*
▲ EMP: 307
SALES (est): 184.3MM
SALES (corp-wide): 2.5B Publicly Held
WEB: www.ait-applied.com
SIC: 5063 Power transmission equipment, electric
PA: Applied Industrial Technologies, Inc.
1 Applied Plz
Cleveland OH 44115
216 426-4000

(G-5054)
APPLIED INDUS TECH - DIXIE INC (HQ)
1 Applied Plz (44115-2511)
P.O. Box 6925 (44101-2193)
PHONE.................................216 426-4000
Fax: 216 426-4884
David L Pugh, *Ch of Bd*
Robert Christensen, *President*
Michael Coticchia, *President*
Krysta Dodd, *General Mgr*
Tom Jindra, *General Mgr*
▲ EMP: 153 EST: 1923
SQ FT: 146,000
SALES (est): 409.4MM
SALES (corp-wide): 2.5B Publicly Held
SIC: 5172 5169 Lubricating oils & greases; sealants
PA: Applied Industrial Technologies, Inc.
1 Applied Plz
Cleveland OH 44115
216 426-4000

(G-5055)
APPLIED INDUSTRIAL TECH INC (PA)
1 Applied Plz (44115-2511)
PHONE.................................216 426-4000
Fax: 216 426-4845
Peter C Wallace, *Ch of Bd*
Neil A Schrimsher, *President*
Todd A Barlett, *Vice Pres*

(PA)=Parent Co (HQ)=Headquarters (DH)=Div Headquarters
✪ = New Business established in last 2 years

2018 Harris Ohio
Services Directory

Cleveland - Cuyahoga County (G-5056)

GEOGRAPHIC SECTION

Fred D Bauer, *Vice Pres*
Warren E Hoffner, *Vice Pres*
▲ **EMP:** 296 **EST:** 1923
SALES: 2.5B **Publicly Held**
WEB: www.appliedindustrial.com
SIC: 5085 5169 7699 Industrial supplies; bearings; power transmission equipment & apparatus; seals, industrial; sealants; industrial machinery & equipment repair

(G-5056)
APRIA HEALTHCARE LLC
5480 Cloverleaf Pkwy # 4 (44125-4867)
PHONE..................................216 485-1180
Fax: 216 485-1093
Lynn Rampley, *Manager*
Patricia Mahon, *Manager*
EMP: 37 **Privately Held**
WEB: www.apria.com
SIC: 7352 5999 Medical equipment rental; medical apparatus & supplies
HQ: Apria Healthcare Llc
26220 Enterprise Ct
Lake Forest CA 92630
949 616-2606

(G-5057)
ARAMARK FACILITY SERVICES LLC
2121 Euclid Ave (44115-2214)
PHONE..................................216 687-5000
Fax: 216 687-5001
Pat Underwood, *Manager*
EMP: 50 **Publicly Held**
SIC: 7349 8744 Janitorial service, contract basis; facilities support services
HQ: Aramark Facility Services, Llc
1101 Market St
Philadelphia PA 19107
215 238-3000

(G-5058)
ARAMARK UNF & CAREER AP LLC
3600 E 93rd St (44105-1686)
PHONE..................................216 341-7400
Douglas Johnson, *General Mgr*
Joe Alexander, *General Mgr*
Jason Haury, *General Mgr*
Casey Hewitt, *General Mgr*
Ty Hoffman, *General Mgr*
EMP: 140
SQ FT: 85,000 **Publicly Held**
WEB: www.aramark-uniform.com
SIC: 7218 7213 Industrial launderers; linen supply
HQ: Aramark Uniform & Career Apparel, Llc
115 N First St Ste 203
Burbank CA 91502
818 973-3700

(G-5059)
ARBOR CONSTRUCTION CO
1350 W 3rd St (44113-1806)
PHONE..................................216 360-8989
Robert Stark, *President*
Howard Beder, *Vice Pres*
Cyndie O'Bryon, *Vice Pres*
Sue Frankel, *Human Res Mgr*
EMP: 30 **EST:** 1980
SQ FT: 3,400
SALES (est): 5.5MM **Privately Held**
SIC: 1542 Shopping center construction

(G-5060)
ARBOR PARK PHASE TWO ASSOC
Also Called: Arbor Park Village
3750 Fleming Ave (44115-3741)
PHONE..................................561 998-0700
Dennis Blackinton, *Partner*
EMP: 30
SALES: 950K **Privately Held**
SIC: 6513 Apartment building operators

(G-5061)
ARBOR PK PHASE THREE ASSOC LP
Also Called: ARBOR PARK VILLAGE
3750 Fleming Ave (44115-3741)
PHONE..................................561 998-0700
Dennis Blackinton, *Treasurer*
EMP: 30
SALES: 1.7MM **Privately Held**
SIC: 6513 Apartment building operators

(G-5062)
ARC DOCUMENT SOLUTIONS INC
Also Called: A R C
3666 Carnegie Ave (44115-2714)
PHONE..................................216 281-1234
Tina Lemanomcz, *Branch Mgr*
EMP: 92
SALES (corp-wide): 394.5MM **Publicly Held**
SIC: 7334 Photocopying & duplicating services; blueprinting service
PA: Arc Document Solutions, Inc.
1981 N Broadway Ste 385
Walnut Creek CA 94596
925 949-5100

(G-5063)
ARC GAS & SUPPLY LLC
4560 Nicky Blvd Ste D (44125-1058)
PHONE..................................216 341-5882
Sam Strazzanti, *President*
Jim Kinser, *Vice Pres*
Danny Strazzanti, *Opers Mgr*
Dan Trappe, *Store Mgr*
Don Wisniewski, *Sales Staff*
EMP: 29
SALES (est): 4.4MM **Privately Held**
SIC: 4923 Gas transmission & distribution

(G-5064)
ARCADIS US INC
1111 Superior Ave E # 1300 (44114-2577)
PHONE..................................216 781-6177
Ben Webster, *Branch Mgr*
Dale Swearingen, *Manager*
EMP: 35
SALES (corp-wide): 2.6B **Privately Held**
SIC: 8712 Architectural services
HQ: Arcadis U.S., Inc.
630 Plaza Dr Ste 200
Highlands Ranch CO 80129
720 344-3500

(G-5065)
ARCHITECTURAL INTR RESTORATION
2401 Train Ave (44113-4207)
PHONE..................................216 241-2255
John L Textoris Jr, *President*
Corey Stone, *Foreman/Supr*
EMP: 45
SQ FT: 11,000
SALES (est): 3.3MM **Privately Held**
SIC: 1742 Drywall; acoustical & ceiling work

(G-5066)
ARISTOCRAT W NURSING HM CORP
Also Called: Call Traditions
4401 W 150th St (44135-1311)
PHONE..................................216 252-7730
Fax: 216 252-6826
Anthony M Coury, *President*
John McNea, *Financial Exec*
Beth Fallen, *Manager*
EMP: 105
SALES (corp-wide): 3.2MM **Privately Held**
SIC: 8051 Skilled nursing care facilities
PA: Aristocrat West Nursing Home Corporation
24340 Sperry Dr
Cleveland OH 44145
440 835-0660

(G-5067)
ARRAS GROUP INC
1151 N Marginal Rd (44114-3730)
PHONE..................................216 621-1601
Fax: 216 377-1919
Jim Hickey, *President*
Scott Keglovic, *Exec VP*
Michael Zimmerman, *Senior VP*
Mark Bouffard, *Vice Pres*
Sharon Petrowiski, *Vice Pres*
EMP: 31
SQ FT: 24,000
SALES (est): 3.4MM **Privately Held**
WEB: www.arrasgroup.com
SIC: 8742 7311 Distribution channels consultant; advertising agencies

(G-5068)
ARS RESCUE ROOTER INC
4547 Hinckley Industrial (44109-6018)
PHONE..................................440 842-8494
Bill Linn, *Manager*
EMP: 30
SALES (est): 1MM **Privately Held**
SIC: 1711 Plumbing contractors

(G-5069)
ART-AMERICAN PRINTING PLATES
1138 W 9th St Fl 4 (44113-1007)
PHONE..................................216 241-4420
Fax: 216 241-4420
John T Mc Sweeney, *President*
Lawrence Mc Sweeney, *Vice Pres*
EMP: 25
SQ FT: 11,000
SALES (est): 3.5MM **Privately Held**
WEB: www.art-american.com
SIC: 2796 7336 Platemaking services; graphic arts & related design

(G-5070)
ASHLAND LLC
Also Called: Ashland Distribution
2191 W 110th St (44102-3509)
PHONE..................................216 961-4690
Fax: 216 961-5976
Sam Mitchell, *Exec VP*
Kenneth Aulen, *Vice Pres*
Joe Jenko, *Engineer*
Don Matson, *Branch Mgr*
Andrea Catalano, *Manager*
EMP: 60
SALES (corp-wide): 3.2B **Publicly Held**
WEB: www.ashland.com
SIC: 5169 Alkalines & chlorine
HQ: Ashland Llc
50 E Rivercenter Blvd # 1600
Covington KY 41011
859 815-3333

(G-5071)
ASHLAND LLC
Ashland Distribution
4600 E 71st St (44125-1051)
PHONE..................................216 883-8200
Fax: 216 883-9840
Dana Cooper, *Manager*
EMP: 32
SQ FT: 95,730
SALES (corp-wide): 3.2B **Publicly Held**
WEB: www.ashland.com
SIC: 5169 Alkalines & chlorine
HQ: Ashland Llc
50 E Rivercenter Blvd # 1600
Covington KY 41011
859 815-3333

(G-5072)
ASPEN WOODSIDE VILLAGE
19455 Rockside Rd Ofc (44146-2056)
PHONE..................................440 439-8666
Renee Owens, *Exec VP*
Linda Cichon, *Facilities Dir*
Sanjay Kansupada, *Exec Dir*
John Robison, *Exec Dir*
Bill Way, *Exec Dir*
EMP: 80
SALES (est): 3.3MM **Privately Held**
SIC: 8361 Home for the aged

(G-5073)
ASSOCIATED STEEL COMPANY INC
Also Called: N-T Steel
18200 Miles Rd (44128-3484)
PHONE..................................216 475-8000
Ron Dekamp, *Manager*
EMP: 25
SALES (corp-wide): 9.4MM **Privately Held**
SIC: 5051 Steel
PA: Associated Steel Company, Inc.
18200 Miles Rd
Cleveland OH 44128
216 475-8200

(G-5074)
AT&T CORP
45 Erieview Plz Ste 1360 (44114-1801)
PHONE..................................216 298-1513
Fred Yount, *Accounts Mgr*
Patrick Beasley, *Accounts Mgr*
Susan Davidson, *Accounts Exec*
Ron Decapite, *Manager*
Karl Kressler, *Manager*
EMP: 3000
SALES (corp-wide): 160.5B **Publicly Held**
WEB: www.swbell.com
SIC: 8748 Telecommunications consultant
HQ: At&T Corp.
1 At&T Way
Bedminster NJ 07921
800 403-3302

(G-5075)
AT&T CORP
Also Called: ATT
3530 Ridge Rd (44102-5462)
PHONE..................................216 672-0809
EMP: 118
SALES (corp-wide): 160.5B **Publicly Held**
SIC: 4813 Local & long distance telephone communications
HQ: At&T Corp.
1 At&T Way
Bedminster NJ 07921
800 403-3302

(G-5076)
AT&T MOBILITY LLC
25309 Cedar Rd (44124-3785)
PHONE..................................216 382-0825
EMP: 26
SALES (corp-wide): 160.5B **Publicly Held**
SIC: 4812 Radio telephone communication
HQ: At&T Mobility Llc
1025 Lenox Park Blvd Ne
Brookhaven GA 30319
800 331-0500

(G-5077)
ATI AVIATION SERVICES LLC
12401 Taft Ave (44108-1627)
PHONE..................................216 268-4888
Fax: 216 268-4889
Jim Lufrano, *Vice Pres*
Roman Liscynesky, *Controller*
Pablo Prieto,
Chris Di Lillo,
Thomas Shumay,
EMP: 25 **EST:** 2001
SQ FT: 55,000
SALES: 2.5MM **Privately Held**
SIC: 4581 Aircraft maintenance & repair services; aircraft servicing & repairing

(G-5078)
ATLANTIS CO INC (PA)
Also Called: Atlantis Company, The
105 Ken Mar Indus Pkwy (44147-2950)
PHONE..................................888 807-3272
Fax: 440 717-7055
Brian Whitaker, *President*
Alphonzo Moore, *Opers Mgr*
Chris Matejka, *Director*
EMP: 70
SALES (est): 13.3MM **Privately Held**
WEB: www.atlantissecurity.com
SIC: 7349 7381 Building maintenance services; detective services

(G-5079)
ATLAS ROOFING COMPANY
4190 E 71st St (44105-5831)
PHONE..................................330 467-7683
Anthony J Hadala, *President*
Nick Rolfsen, *Sales Staff*
Dan Whitford, *Sales Staff*
EMP: 25
SALES (est): 2.3MM **Privately Held**
SIC: 1761 Roofing contractor

(G-5080)
ATOTECH USA INC
1000 Harvard Ave (44109-3048)
PHONE..................................216 398-0550
Stephen TSE, *Engineer*
Steve Bellavita, *Branch Mgr*
EMP: 80
SALES (corp-wide): 7.3B **Publicly Held**
SIC: 2899 4225 Chemical supplies for foundries; general warehousing & storage

GEOGRAPHIC SECTION

Cleveland - Cuyahoga County (G-5102)

HQ: Atotech Usa, Llc
1750 Overview Dr
Rock Hill SC 29730

(G-5081)
AUSTIN BUILDING AND DESIGN INC (DH)
Also Called: Austin Company, The
6095 Parkland Blvd # 100 (44124-6139)
PHONE..................440 544-2600
Fax: 216 544-2684
Michael G Pierce, *President*
Charlie Stevens, *Division Mgr*
Brandon Davis, *General Mgr*
Noriaki Ohashi, *Chairman*
Greg Carr, *Business Mgr*
EMP: 121
SQ FT: 21,869
SALES (est): 103.7MM
SALES (corp-wide): 16B **Privately Held**
WEB: www.kajimausa.com
SIC: 1541 1542 8742 8711 Industrial buildings, new construction; commercial & office building, new construction; institutional building construction; management consulting services; engineering services; architectural engineering
HQ: Kajima International Inc.
6095 Parkland Blvd
Cleveland OH 44124
440 544-2600

(G-5082)
AUTOMATIC DATA PROCESSING INC
Also Called: ADP
7007 E Pleasant Valley Rd (44131-5543)
PHONE..................216 447-1980
Fax: 216 643-5308
Brian David, *District Mgr*
Jon Delvecchio, *District Mgr*
Meredith Parrilla, *District Mgr*
Don Hill, *Opers Staff*
Carlo Giaimo, *Purch Dir*
EMP: 250
SQ FT: 20,000
SALES (corp-wide): 12.3B **Publicly Held**
SIC: 7374 Data processing service; computer processing services; data entry service
PA: Automatic Data Processing, Inc.
1 Adp Blvd Ste 1 # 1
Roseland NJ 07068
973 974-5000

(G-5083)
AUTOMOTIVE DISTRIBUTORS CO INC
990 Valley Belt Dr (44109)
PHONE..................216 398-2014
Fax: 216 398-2088
Randy Primer, *Branch Mgr*
EMP: 30
SALES (corp-wide): 132.8MM **Privately Held**
WEB: www.adw1.com
SIC: 5013 Automotive supplies & parts
PA: Automotive Distributors Co., Inc.
2981 Morse Rd
Columbus OH 43231
614 476-1315

(G-5084)
AUXILIARY BD FAIRVIEW GEN HOSP
Also Called: FAIRVIEW WEST PHYSICIAN CENTER
18101 Lorain Ave (44111-5612)
PHONE..................216 476-7000
EMP: 1187
SALES: 44.4K
SALES (corp-wide): 8B **Privately Held**
SIC: 8062 General medical & surgical hospitals
HQ: Fairview Hospital
18101 Lorain Ave
Cleveland OH 44111
216 476-7000

(G-5085)
AVANTIA INC
9655 Sweet Valley Dr # 1 (44125-4271)
PHONE..................216 901-9366
Jennie Zamberlan, *President*
Michael Canterbury, *Managing Dir*
Joe Banar, *QA Dir*
Tracy Trivisonno, *QA Dir*
Michael Knoll, *Business Anlyst*
EMP: 35
SQ FT: 4,500
SALES (est): 2.8MM **Privately Held**
WEB: www.avantia-inc.com
SIC: 8748 Business consulting

(G-5086)
AW FABER-CASTELL USA INC
Also Called: Creativity For Kids
9450 Allen Dr Ste B (44125-4602)
PHONE..................216 643-4660
Fax: 216 643-4663
Jamie Gallagher, *CEO*
Phyllis Brody, *Vice Pres*
Sara McDonald, *Vice Pres*
Tom Biddel, *Safety Mgr*
Susan Mintmire, *Design Engr*
▲ EMP: 100
SQ FT: 85,000
SALES (est): 37MM
SALES (corp-wide): 712.9MM **Privately Held**
WEB: www.faber-castell.com
SIC: 5092 5112 3944 Arts & crafts equipment & supplies; stationery & office supplies; writing instruments & supplies; games, toys & children's vehicles; craft & hobby kits & sets
HQ: Faber-Castell Ag
Nurnberger Str. 2
Stein 90547
911 996-50

(G-5087)
AXA ADVISORS LLC
1001 Lakeside Ave E # 1650 (44114-1158)
PHONE..................216 621-7715
Ryan Radonich, *Human Resources*
Melissa Looney, *Marketing Staff*
Tom Marinic, *Branch Mgr*
Mary Krejsa, *Manager*
Arun Lai, *Agent*
EMP: 60
SALES (corp-wide): 3.8B **Publicly Held**
WEB: www.axacs.com
SIC: 6411 Insurance agents, brokers & service
HQ: Axa Advisors, Llc
1290 Ave Of Amrcs Fl Cnc1
New York NY 10104
212 554-1234

(G-5088)
AZALEA ALABAMA INVESTMENT LLC
8111 Rockside Rd Ste 200 (44125-6135)
PHONE..................216 520-1250
Frank Sinito,
EMP: 99
SALES (est): 789.1K **Privately Held**
SIC: 6513 Apartment building operators

(G-5089)
B & B WRECKING & EXCVTG INC
4510 E 71st St Ste 6 (44105-5638)
PHONE..................216 429-1700
Pete Boyas, *Principal*
Robert Baumann, *Vice Pres*
William A Baumann, *Vice Pres*
Nik Filippi, *Project Mgr*
Chris Jaskolka, *Project Mgr*
EMP: 40 EST: 1957
SQ FT: 50,000
SALES (est): 10.8MM **Privately Held**
SIC: 1795 1794 Demolition, buildings & other structures; excavation & grading, building construction

(G-5090)
B&F CAPITAL MARKETS INC
635 W Lkeside Ave Apt 201 (44113)
PHONE..................216 472-2700
Craig Deering, *Managing Dir*
Bracton Thoma, *Managing Dir*
Saira Rahman, *Vice Pres*
Greg Marston, *Info Tech Dir*
Dolf Roell, *Exec Dir*
EMP: 25
SQ FT: 4,000
SALES (est): 1.8MM **Privately Held**
WEB: www.bfcmi.com
SIC: 8742 Financial consultant

(G-5091)
BAKER & HOSTETLER LLP
127 Public Sq Ste 2000 (44114-1214)
PHONE..................216 861-7587
Fax: 216 861-7904
Hewitt Shaw, *Managing Prtnr*
Stacey Hutton, *Project Mgr*
Tracy Hager, *Pub Rel Mgr*
Aileen Reilly, *Human Res Mgr*
David Hintz, *Comms Mgr*
EMP: 274
SALES (corp-wide): 313.3MM **Privately Held**
SIC: 8111 General practice attorney, lawyer; bankruptcy law; labor & employment law; taxation law
PA: Baker & Hostetler Llp
127 Public Sq Ste 2000
Cleveland OH 44114
216 621-0200

(G-5092)
BAKER & HOSTETLER LLP (PA)
127 Public Sq Ste 2000 (44114-1214)
PHONE..................216 621-0200
Fax: 216 696-0740
John M Gherlein, *Ch of Bd*
John H Weber, *Ch of Bd*
W Ray Whitman, *Ch of Bd*
Ronald G Linville, *Managing Prtnr*
Christopher M Arena, *Managing Prtnr*
EMP: 274 EST: 1916
SQ FT: 160,000
SALES (est): 313.3MM **Privately Held**
WEB: www.bakerlaw.com
SIC: 8111 General practice attorney, lawyer; bankruptcy law; labor & employment law; real estate law

(G-5093)
BARBS GRAFFITI INC
3111 Carnegie Ave (44115-2632)
PHONE..................216 881-5550
Abe Miller, *Manager*
EMP: 65
SALES (corp-wide): 6.3MM **Privately Held**
WEB: www.graffiticaps.com
SIC: 5136 5137 Sportswear, men's & boys'; sportswear, women's & children's
PA: Barb's Graffiti, Inc.
3111 Carnegie Ave
Cleveland OH 44115
216 881-5550

(G-5094)
BARBS GRAFFITI INC (PA)
Also Called: Graffiti Co
3111 Carnegie Ave (44115-2632)
PHONE..................216 881-5550
Fax: 216 881-4043
Abe Miller, *President*
Barbara Miller, *Corp Secy*
Monica McKinley, *Controller*
▲ EMP: 40
SQ FT: 18,000
SALES (est): 6.3MM **Privately Held**
WEB: www.graffiticaps.com
SIC: 2353 2395 5136 5137 Baseball caps; pleating & stitching; sportswear, men's & boys'; sportswear, women's & children's

(G-5095)
BARNES WENDLING CPAS INC (PA)
1350 Euclid Ave Ste 1400 (44115 1830)
PHONE..................216 566-9000
Fax: 216 566-9321
Jeffrey Neuman, *President*
Janine Iacobelli, *Treasurer*
Wade Gray, *Tax Mgr*
Sondra Sofranko, *Tax Mgr*
Jeremy Banchek, *Accountant*
EMP: 45
SQ FT: 18,500
SALES (est): 10.2MM **Privately Held**
SIC: 8721 7291 Certified public accountant; tax return preparation services

(G-5096)
BASELINE CONSULTING LLC
21298 Endsley Ave (44116-2231)
PHONE..................440 336-5382
David A Hein,
Douglas Drier,
EMP: 54
SALES (est): 2.2MM **Privately Held**
SIC: 7379 Computer related consulting services

(G-5097)
BASF CATALYSTS LLC
23800 Mercantile Rd (44122-5908)
P.O. Box 22126 (44122-0126)
PHONE..................216 360-5005
David Disantis, *Engineer*
John Ferek, *Branch Mgr*
EMP: 83
SALES (corp-wide): 76B **Privately Held**
SIC: 2819 8731 Industrial inorganic chemicals; commercial physical research
HQ: Basf Catalysts Llc
25 Middlesex Tpke
Iselin NJ 08830
732 205-5000

(G-5098)
BASF CONSTRUCTION CHEM LLC (DH)
Also Called: Degussa Construction
23700 Chagrin Blvd (44122-5506)
PHONE..................216 831-5500
John Salvatore, *President*
Frank Apicella, *Research*
Michael Pelsozy, *Research*
Donald Kehr, *Treasurer*
Sandy Sanson, *Credit Staff*
◆ EMP: 50
SALES (est): 316.6MM
SALES (corp-wide): 76B **Privately Held**
WEB: www.basf-admixtures.com
SIC: 2899 2851 1799 Concrete curing & hardening compounds; epoxy coatings; vinyl coatings, strippable; caulking (construction); waterproofing
HQ: Basf Corporation
100 Park Ave
Florham Park NJ 07932
973 245-6000

(G-5099)
BASISTA FURNITURE INC
Also Called: Warehouse
5340 Brookpark Rd (44134-1044)
PHONE..................216 398-5900
Stanley Basista, *Branch Mgr*
EMP: 30
SALES (corp-wide): 8.9MM **Privately Held**
WEB: www.basista.com
SIC: 4225 General warehousing & storage
PA: Basista Furniture, Inc.
5277 State Rd
Cleveland OH 44134
216 635-1200

(G-5100)
BATCH LABS INC
9655 Sweet Valley Dr # 1 (44125-4270)
PHONE..................216 901-9366
Jennie Zamberlan, *CEO*
Martin Hlavaty, *Human Resources*
EMP: 54
SALES (est): 992.5K **Privately Held**
SIC: 7371 Computer software development & applications

(G-5101)
BATTLE BULLYING HOTLINE INC
3185 Warren Rd (44111-1153)
PHONE..................216 731-1976
Michael Prandich, *President*
EMP: 75
SALES (est): 233K **Privately Held**
SIC: 8322 Hotline

(G-5102)
BAY VILLAGE CITY SCHOOL DST
Also Called: Glenview Cntr For Chld Cr & Lr
28727 Wolf Rd (44140-1351)
PHONE..................440 617-7330
Fax: 440 617-7331
Barbara Manning, *Director*
EMP: 35
SALES (corp-wide): 37.1MM **Privately Held**
SIC: 8211 8351 Public elementary school; child day care services

---

(PA)=Parent Co (HQ)=Headquarters (DH)=Div Headquarters
✪ = New Business established in last 2 years

2018 Harris Ohio
Services Directory

Cleveland - Cuyahoga County (G-5103)

PA: Bay Village City School District
377 Dover Center Rd
Cleveland OH 44140
440 617-7300

(G-5103)
BAYLESS PATHMARK INC
19250 Bagley Rd Ste 101 (44130-3348)
PHONE..................440 274-2494
Fax: 330 829-4279
Benjamin Tanseco, *CEO*
Joseph Huffman, *Human Resources*
EMP: 34
SALES (est): 3MM Privately Held
SIC: 8071 8734 Pathological laboratory; testing laboratories

(G-5104)
BDI INC (PA)
Also Called: Baring Distributors
8000 Hub Pkwy (44125-5731)
PHONE..................216 642-9100
Frank L Bystricky, *CEO*
Mike Fryz, *Principal*
Chris Hawkins, *COO*
Kenneth Miko, *Vice Pres*
Bud Thayer, *Vice Pres*
▲ EMP: 500
SALES (est): 57.6MM Privately Held
WEB: www.bdi.com
SIC: 1389 Oil sampling service for oil companies

(G-5105)
BDO USA LLP
1422 Euclid Ave Ste 1500 (44115-2068)
PHONE..................216 325-1700
Ross Vozar, *Director*
EMP: 52
SALES (corp-wide): 1.2B Privately Held
SIC: 8721 Accounting, auditing & bookkeeping
PA: Bdo Usa, Llp
330 N Wabash Ave Ste 3200
Chicago IL 60611
312 240-1236

(G-5106)
BEACHWOOD CITY SCHOOLS
23757 Commerce Park (44122-5825)
PHONE..................216 464-6609
Fax: 216 763-0061
Paul Williams, *Superintendent*
Windella Williford, *Manager*
EMP: 40
SQ FT: 13,600
SALES (corp-wide): 40MM Privately Held
SIC: 4151 School buses
PA: Beachwood City Schools
24601 Fairmount Blvd
Cleveland OH 44122
216 464-2600

(G-5107)
BEARING DISTRIBUTORS INC (HQ)
Also Called: B D I
8000 Hub Pkwy (44125-5788)
P.O. Box 5931, Troy MI (48007-5931)
PHONE..................216 642-9100
Carl G James, *President*
John Ruth, *President*
Steve Kieffer, *Vice Pres*
Bud Thayer, *Vice Pres*
Darren W Robinson, *Opers Mgr*
◆ EMP: 200 EST: 1935
SQ FT: 150,000
SALES (est): 488.5MM
SALES (corp-wide): 493.6MM Privately Held
WEB: www.bdi-usa.com
SIC: 5085 Bearings; gears; power transmission equipment & apparatus
PA: Forge Industries, Inc.
4450 Market St
Youngstown OH 44512
330 782-8301

(G-5108)
BECK ALUMINUM INTL LLC
6150 Parkland Blvd # 260 (44124-6147)
PHONE..................440 684-4848
Scott W Beck, *President*
Bryan C Beck, *Exec VP*
Tom Kish, *CFO*
Michael Poling, *CFO*
Jean Robertson, *General Counsel*
◆ EMP: 68
SALES (est): 5MM Privately Held
SIC: 5051 Aluminum bars, rods, ingots, sheets, pipes, plates, etc.

(G-5109)
BECK CENTER FOR ARTS
17801 Detroit Ave (44107-3499)
PHONE..................216 521-2540
Lucinda Einhouse, *CEO*
Frederick B Unger, *Chairman*
William J Backus Jr, *Treasurer*
Jerry McThersom, *Finance*
Donald G Bain Jr,
EMP: 127
SQ FT: 60,000
SALES: 3.3MM Privately Held
WEB: www.beckcenter.org
SIC: 7922 Performing arts center production

(G-5110)
BECK COMPANY
10701 Broadway Ave (44125-1650)
P.O. Box 25469 (44125-0469)
PHONE..................216 883-0909
Fax: 216 883-0970
Mark Beck, *President*
EMP: 35 EST: 1983
SQ FT: 20,000
SALES (est): 4.3MM Privately Held
WEB: www.engineeredroofing.com
SIC: 1761 Roofing contractor; sheet metalwork

(G-5111)
BEECHMONT INC
Also Called: BEECHMONT COUNTRY CLUB
29600 Chagrin Blvd (44122-4620)
PHONE..................216 831-9100
Fax: 216 831-6430
Doug Foote, *Principal*
Jake Houston, *Assistant*
EMP: 100
SQ FT: 40,000
SALES: 5.2MM Privately Held
WEB: www.beechmontcc.com
SIC: 7997 Country club, membership

(G-5112)
BELLWETHER ENTP RE CAPITL LLC (PA)
1360 E 9th St Ste 300 (44114-1730)
PHONE..................216 820-4500
Ned Huffman, *CEO*
Trent Brooks, *Exec VP*
Todd Harrop, *Exec VP*
Debbie Rogan, *Exec VP*
Deborah Rogan, *Exec VP*
EMP: 34 EST: 2008
SQ FT: 7,000
SALES (est): 15.2MM Privately Held
SIC: 6531 Real estate agent, commercial

(G-5113)
BELMORE LEASING CO LLC
Also Called: Candlewood Park Healthcare Ctr
1835 Belmore Rd (44112-4301)
PHONE..................216 268-3600
Fax: 216 761-1322
David W Trimble, *CPA*
Stephen L Rosedale, *Mng Member*
Charles R Stoltz,
Ronald S Wilheim,
EMP: 156
SQ FT: 28,000
SALES (est): 4.4MM Privately Held
SIC: 8051 Skilled nursing care facilities

(G-5114)
BENEVENTO ENTERPRISES INC
Also Called: Herbst Electric Company
1384 E 26th St (44114-4039)
PHONE..................216 621-5890
Fax: 216 621-5893
John R Benevento, *President*
Duke Benevento, *President*
Kenneth Maher, *President*
Deborah Benevento, *Corp Secy*
Cody Roswell, *Project Mgr*
EMP: 65 EST: 1946
SQ FT: 6,000
SALES (est): 12.8MM Privately Held
WEB: www.herbstelectric.com
SIC: 1731 General electrical contractor

(G-5115)
BENJAMIN ROSE INSTITUTE
850 Euclid Ave Ste 1100 (44113-3313)
PHONE..................216 791-8000
Fax: 216 621-7521
Carole Johnson, *Principal*
EMP: 88
SALES (corp-wide): 27.9MM Privately Held
SIC: 8733 Noncommercial research organizations
PA: Benjamin Rose Institute
11890 Fairhill Rd
Cleveland OH 44120
216 791-8000

(G-5116)
BENJAMIN ROSE INSTITUTE
Also Called: Margret Wagner House
2373 Euclid Heights Blvd 2f (44106-2716)
PHONE..................216 791-3580
Fax: 216 791-8030
Richard Browdie, *CEO*
Anne Marie, *Vice Pres*
Semanthie Brooks, *Director*
Crystal Wallace, *Asst Director*
Carol Whitlatch, *Asst Director*
EMP: 53
SQ FT: 27,326
SALES (corp-wide): 27.9MM Privately Held
SIC: 8361 8741 8322 Rest home, with health care incidental; management services; individual & family services
PA: Benjamin Rose Institute
11890 Fairhill Rd
Cleveland OH 44120
216 791-8000

(G-5117)
BENJAMIN ROSE INSTITUTE (PA)
11890 Fairhill Rd (44120-1000)
PHONE..................216 791-8000
Fax: 216 373-1816
Richard Browdie, *President*
Mary Marita, *COO*
Shelley Rivera, *Purch Mgr*
Frank Cardinale, *CFO*
Yvette Ittu, *Treasurer*
EMP: 80
SQ FT: 31,000
SALES (est): 27.9MM Privately Held
SIC: 8082 8322 Home health care services; individual & family services

(G-5118)
BEST CUTS INC
Also Called: Signature Salon
7541 W Ridgewood Dr (44129-5536)
PHONE..................440 884-6300
Andre Duval, *Manager*
EMP: 30
SALES (corp-wide): 11.2MM Privately Held
SIC: 7231 Unisex hair salons
PA: Best Cuts, Inc.
3626 Mayfield Rd
Cleveland OH 44118
216 382-2600

(G-5119)
BEST REWARD CREDIT UNION
Also Called: PARMAUTO FEDERAL CREDIT UNION
5681 Smith Rd (44142-2030)
PHONE..................216 367-8000
Fax: 216 367-8002
Susan Madden, *President*
Stephen Halas, *Exec VP*
Pam Akers, *Assistant VP*
Sandy Sauvey, *Vice Pres*
Jennifer Cole, *Marketing Staff*
EMP: 32
SQ FT: 2,800
SALES: 3.5MM Privately Held
WEB: www.vantagefcu.com
SIC: 6061 6163 Federal credit unions; loan brokers

(G-5120)
BETHLEHEM LUTHERAN CH PARMA
7500 State Rd (44134-6199)
PHONE..................440 845-2230
Robert Green, *Pastor*
EMP: 30
SQ FT: 8,579
SALES (est): 949.6K Privately Held
SIC: 8661 8351 Lutheran Church; child day care services

(G-5121)
BEVERAGE DISTRIBUTORS INC
3800 King Ave (44114-3703)
PHONE..................216 431-1600
Fax: 216 431-0961
James V Conway, *President*
Greg Findura, *District Mgr*
Bruce Leach, *District Mgr*
Ronald Natola, *District Mgr*
Jeff Ryckman, *Vice Pres*
▲ EMP: 150 EST: 1933
SQ FT: 125,000
SALES (est): 72.9MM Privately Held
WEB: www.beveragedist.com
SIC: 5181 Beer & other fermented malt liquors

(G-5122)
BEYOND 2000 REALTY INC
18332 Bagley Rd (44130-3411)
PHONE..................440 842-7200
Mark Snyder, *President*
EMP: 50
SALES (est): 2.7MM Privately Held
WEB: www.beyond2000realty.com
SIC: 6531 Real estate agent, residential

(G-5123)
BLOOD COURIER INC
3965 W 130th St (44111-5103)
P.O. Box 110634 (44111-0634)
PHONE..................216 251-3050
Fax: 216 941-4055
James T Mahony Jr, *President*
Mary Mahony, *Corp Secy*
Ken Kerns, *Manager*
EMP: 38
SQ FT: 5,000
SALES (est): 2.9MM Privately Held
WEB: www.bloodcourier.com
SIC: 4212 4731 Delivery service, vehicular; freight forwarding

(G-5124)
BLUE RIBBON MEATS INC
3316 W 67th Pl (44102-5243)
PHONE..................216 631-8850
Fax: 216 631-8934
Albert J Radis, *President*
June Altschuld, *Principal*
Mary Cain, *Principal*
John Forrester, *Principal*
Paul Radis, *Corp Secy*
EMP: 100 EST: 1952
SQ FT: 8,400
SALES (est): 57.6MM Privately Held
SIC: 5147 5142 Meats, fresh; meat, frozen; packaged

(G-5125)
BLUE TECH SMART SOLUTIONS LLC
5885 Grant Ave (44105-5607)
PHONE..................216 271-4800
Paul Hanna, *President*
EMP: 47 EST: 2013
SALES (est): 7.6MM Privately Held
SIC: 5045 Computers, peripherals & software
PA: Blue Technologies, Inc.
5885 Grant Ave
Cleveland OH 44105

(G-5126)
BLUE TECHNOLOGIES INC (PA)
5885 Grant Ave (44105-5607)
P.O. Box 31475 (44131-0475)
PHONE..................216 271-4800
Fax: 216 271-0084
Paul Hanna, *President*
David Morrell, *Vice Pres*
William Nelson, *Vice Pres*
David Vitaz, *CFO*

Keith Stump, *Treasurer*
EMP: 107
SQ FT: 36,000
SALES: 26.5MM Privately Held
WEB: www.btohio.com
SIC: 5044 Copying equipment

(G-5127)
BLUE WATER CHAMBER ORCHESTRA ✪
3631 Perkins Ave Apt 4cn (44114-4707)
PHONE....................440 781-6215
Carlton R Woods, *Administration*
Nancy Patterson, *Admin Asst*
EMP: 44 **EST:** 2017
SALES (est): 229.4K Privately Held
SIC: 7929 Orchestras or bands

(G-5128)
BONEZZI SWTZER MRPHY PLITO LPA (PA)
1300 E 9th St Ste 1950 (44114-1503)
PHONE....................216 875-2767
Fax: 216 875-1570
William Bonezzi, *President*
John Polito, *Vice Pres*
Donald Switzer, *Vice Pres*
Ann Medwetz, *Sls & Mktg Exec*
Patrick Murphy, *Treasurer*
EMP: 46
SQ FT: 11,000
SALES (est): 6.7MM Privately Held
WEB: www.bsmplaw.com
SIC: 8111 Criminal law

(G-5129)
BOSTWICK DESIGN PARTNR INC
2729 Prospect Ave E (44115-2605)
PHONE....................216 621-7900
Robert Bostwick, *President*
Michael Zambo, *Project Mgr*
Pam Neckar, *CFO*
Alyssa Delvecchio, *Asst Controller*
Apostolos Nacopoulos, *Manager*
EMP: 32
SQ FT: 12,500
SALES (est): 5.1MM Privately Held
WEB: www.cgbarch.com
SIC: 8712 Architectural engineering

(G-5130)
BOULEVARD MOTEL CORP
Also Called: Comfort Inn
17550 Rosbough Blvd (44130-2580)
PHONE....................440 234-3131
Lindsey Stoneman, *Branch Mgr*
EMP: 30
SQ FT: 21,973
SALES (corp-wide): 198.1MM Privately Held
WEB: www.hotspringsclarion.com
SIC: 7011 Hotel, franchised
HQ: Boulevard Motel Corp
10750 Columbia Pike # 300
Silver Spring MD 20901

(G-5131)
BOYAS EXCAVATING INC (PA)
11311 Rockside Rd (44125-6208)
PHONE....................216 524-3620
Fax: 216 642-8836
Lea Boyas Morabito, *President*
Michael Boyas, *President*
Joseph J Berdis, *Owner*
Stacey Asimou, *Treasurer*
Jay Johnson, *Accounts Mgr*
EMP: 37
SQ FT: 6,000
SALES (est): 8.6MM Privately Held
WEB: www.boyas.com
SIC: 1795 1542 1794 1799 Wrecking & demolition work; commercial & office building contractors; excavation work; shoring & underpinning work

(G-5132)
BRAEVIEW MANOR INC
20611 Euclid Ave (44117-1592)
PHONE....................216 486-9300
Fax: 216 486-2603
A John Bartholemew, *President*
Kimberly Armstrong, *Principal*
Ray Lin Walsh, *Accounting Mgr*
Natalya Myaskovsky, *Office Mgr*
Stephanie Mills, *Nursing Dir*
EMP: 190 **EST:** 1964
SQ FT: 160,000
SALES (est): 4.4MM Privately Held
SIC: 8051 8052 Convalescent home with continuous nursing care; intermediate care facilities

(G-5133)
BRANDMUSCLE INC (HQ)
1100 Superior Ave E # 500 (44114-2530)
PHONE....................216 464-4342
Philip Alexander, *CEO*
Dan Hickox, *President*
Dave Wilson, *President*
Robert Bernstein, *Exec VP*
Mike Marchetti, *Exec VP*
EMP: 150
SQ FT: 24,000
SALES (est): 40.9MM
SALES (corp-wide): 3.7B Privately Held
WEB: www.brandmuscle.com
SIC: 7373 8742 Systems software development services; marketing consulting services
PA: Riverside Partners L.L.C.
45 Rockefeller Plz # 400
New York NY 10111
212 265-6575

(G-5134)
BRAVO WELLNESS LLC (PA)
20445 Emerald Pkwy # 400 (44135-6010)
PHONE....................216 658-9500
Jim Pshock, *CEO*
Chris Yessayan, *President*
Cheryl Tidwell, *Exec VP*
Rick Kjerstad, *Senior VP*
Mikhail Koumoundouros, *Senior VP*
EMP: 35
SQ FT: 7,000
SALES: 22.5MM Privately Held
SIC: 8748 8741 Employee programs administration; administrative management

(G-5135)
BRENNAN & ASSOCIATES INC
1550 E 33rd St (44114-4322)
PHONE....................216 391-4822
David J Masciarelli, *President*
William D Call Jr, *Corp Secy*
Frederick Johnston, *Vice Pres*
EMP: 28
SQ FT: 6,000
SALES (est): 4.5MM Privately Held
WEB: www.brennanhvac.com
SIC: 1711 Warm air heating & air conditioning contractor

(G-5136)
BRENNAN INDUSTRIES INC (PA)
Also Called: B I
6701 Cochran Rd (44139-3997)
PHONE....................440 248-1880
Fax: 440 248-1880
David D Carr, *CEO*
Butch Atkinson, *President*
David M Carr, *President*
Dennis Brennan, *General Mgr*
Michael Donahoe, *General Mgr*
▲ **EMP:** 26
SQ FT: 24,000
SALES (est): 40.1MM Privately Held
WEB: www.brennaninc.com
SIC: 5085 Valves, pistons & fittings

(G-5137)
BRENTLEY INSTITUTE INC
3143 W 33rd St Ste 2 (44109-1552)
P.O. Box 20724 (44120-7724)
PHONE....................216 225-0087
Fax: 216 229-3001
Toney Foreman, *President*
EMP: 34
SALES (est): 350K Privately Held
WEB: www.brentleyonline.com
SIC: 7382 8742 Security systems services; industry specialist consultants

(G-5138)
BRIDGEWAY INC (PA)
2202 Prame Ave (44109-1626)
PHONE....................216 688-4114
Lisa Bates, *Managing Prtnr*
Deborah Barris, *COO*
Mike Lovejoy, *CFO*
Elisa Smith, *Marketing Staff*
Ralph Fee, *Director*
EMP: 278
SQ FT: 50,000
SALES (est): 2.9MM Privately Held
WEB: www.employmentalliance.org
SIC: 8322 8093 Social service center; general counseling services; alcoholism counseling, nontreatment; offender rehabilitation agency; specialty outpatient clinics

(G-5139)
BRINKS INCORPORATED
1422 Superior Ave E (44114-2904)
PHONE....................216 621-7493
Fax: 216 696-0958
Jerry Hallman, *Persnl Dir*
Dennis Baker, *Branch Mgr*
Justo Rodriguez, *Manager*
Ron Ciora, *Manager*
EMP: 85
SQ FT: 18,105
SALES (corp-wide): 3.3B Publicly Held
WEB: www.brinksinc.com
SIC: 7381 Armored car services
HQ: Brink's, Incorporated
1801 Bayberry Ct Ste 400
Richmond VA 23226
804 289-9600

(G-5140)
BRITESKIES LLC
2306 W 17th St Ste 1 (44113-4373)
PHONE....................216 369-3600
Hannah Gierosky, *Marketing Staff*
Michael Berlin, *Mng Member*
Lee Jayne, *Consultant*
William Onion,
EMP: 25
SALES (est): 1.3MM Privately Held
SIC: 7371 Computer software development

(G-5141)
BRITTON-GALLAGHER & ASSOC INC
1375 E 9th St Fl 30 (44114-1797)
PHONE....................216 658-7100
Fax: 440 248-4711
Bruce H Ball, *Ch of Bd*
Jeremy Bryant, *President*
John L Hazen, *President*
Terry Dragan, *Principal*
Jeremy A Bryant, *Senior VP*
EMP: 60
SQ FT: 15,000
SALES (est): 21.6MM Privately Held
WEB: www.britton-gallagher.com
SIC: 6411 Insurance agents

(G-5142)
BROADVOX LLC (HQ)
75 Erieview Plz Fl 4 (44114-1839)
PHONE....................216 373-4600
Fritz Hendricks, *President*
Gary Kosin, *Engineer*
Brandon Robinson, *Engineer*
Jason Shuster, *Engineer*
Teri Asiala, *VP Sls/Mktg*
EMP: 45
SALES (est): 41.3MM
SALES (corp-wide): 290.4MM Privately Held
WEB: www.broadvox.net
SIC: 4813 ;
PA: Onvoy, Llc
10300 6th Ave N
Plymouth MN 55441
763 230-2036

(G-5143)
BROKAW INC
1213 W 6th St (44113-1339)
PHONE....................216 241-8003
Fax: 216 241-8033
Bill Brokaw, *Principal*
Bart Slak, *Vice Pres*
Mike Bratton, *Financial Exec*
Kelly Gentile, *Comms Mgr*
Mike Bratten, *Manager*
EMP: 35
SQ FT: 11,300
SALES (est): 8.9MM Privately Held
WEB: www.brokaw.com
SIC: 7311 Advertising consultant

(G-5144)
BROOK BEECH
3737 Lander Rd (44124-5712)
PHONE....................216 831-2255
Fax: 216 831-0436
Mario Tonti, *President*
Bari E Goggins, *Chairman*
Laura McMullen, *Business Mgr*
Dale Winsberg, *COO*
Lynn Avery, *Assistant VP*
EMP: 200 **EST:** 1852
SQ FT: 30,000
SALES (est): 21.2MM Privately Held
WEB: www.beechbrook.org
SIC: 8322 Child related social services; adoption services; outreach program; family counseling services

(G-5145)
BROOKDALE SENIOR LIVING INC
3151 Mayfield Rd (44118-1757)
PHONE....................216 321-6331
Linda Delozier, *Branch Mgr*
EMP: 36
SALES (corp-wide): 4.7B Publicly Held
SIC: 6513 Retirement hotel operation
PA: Brookdale Senior Living
111 Westwood Pl Ste 400
Brentwood TN 37027
615 221-2250

(G-5146)
BROOKPARK FREEWAY LANES LLC
12859 Brookpark Rd (44130-1159)
PHONE....................216 267-2150
Glen Gable,
Dave Patz,
EMP: 30
SALES (est): 1.5MM Privately Held
SIC: 7933 Ten pin center

(G-5147)
BROOKS & STAFFORD CO
55 Public Sq Ste 1650 (44113-1972)
PHONE....................216 696-3000
Fax: 216 621-7336
Neil Corrigan, *President*
Mike Bentley, *Vice Pres*
John Kunze, *Vice Pres*
EMP: 39
SQ FT: 11,000
SALES (est): 6.8MM Privately Held
WEB: www.brooks-stafford.com
SIC: 6411 Insurance agents

(G-5148)
BROUSE MCDOWELL LPA
600 Superior Ave E # 1600 (44114-2604)
PHONE....................216 830-6830
Fax: 216 830-6807
Craig Marvinney, *Partner*
Richard Cunningham, *Counsel*
Linda L Bluso, *Branch Mgr*
Rebecca Haupt, *Legal Staff*
EMP: 29
SALES (corp-wide): 10.1MM Privately Held
SIC: 8111 General practice law office
PA: Brouse Mcdowell, Lpa
388 S Main St Ste 500
Akron OH
330 535-5711

(G-5149)
BROWN AND MARGOLIUS CO LPA
55 Public Sq Ste 1100 (44113-1901)
PHONE....................216 621-2034
Fax: 330 621-1908
Marsha Margolius, *President*
EMP: 50
SALES (est): 3.2MM Privately Held
SIC: 8111 General practice law office

(G-5150)
BROWN GIBBONS LANG & CO LLC (PA)
1 Cleveland C (44114)
PHONE....................216 241-2800

Cleveland - Cuyahoga County (G-5151)

Fax: 216 241-7417
Anthony Delfre, *Managing Dir*
William Montana, *Managing Dir*
Vince Pappalardo, *Managing Dir*
Clint Parker, *Managing Dir*
Andrew K Petry, *Managing Dir*
EMP: 40
SQ FT: 13,000
SALES (est): 16.9MM **Privately Held**
WEB: www.bglco.com
SIC: 6211 Investment bankers

(G-5151)
BROWN GIBBONS LANG LTD PTRSHIP
1111 Superior Ave E # 900 (44114-2522)
PHONE.................216 241-2800
Michael Gibbons, *President*
EMP: 30
SALES (est): 2MM **Privately Held**
SIC: 7519 Utility trailer rental

(G-5152)
BROWN WD GENERAL AGENCY INC
Also Called: Northwestern Mutl Fincl Netwrk
950 Main Ave Ste 600 (44113-7207)
PHONE.................216 241-5840
Fax: 216 566-9489
William D Brown, *President*
EMP: 75
SALES (est): 12.5MM **Privately Held**
SIC: 6411 6282 Life insurance agents; investment advice

(G-5153)
BRYANT ELIZA VILLAGE
7201 Wade Park Ave (44103-2765)
PHONE.................216 361-6141
Harvey Shankman, *President*
Odessa Fields, *Accountant*
Shelia Norman, *Nursing Mgr*
Rhonda Roberts, *Nursing Mgr*
David Siegel, *Exec Dir*
EMP: 255
SQ FT: 50,450
SALES: 14.6MM **Privately Held**
SIC: 8322 8051 Outreach program; skilled nursing care facilities

(G-5154)
BSL - APPLIED LASER TECH LLC (PA)
Also Called: A L T
4560 Johnston Pkwy (44128-2953)
PHONE.................216 663-8181
Fax: 216 663-8445
Judy Harshman, *President*
Dov Nisman, *General Mgr*
Judith Sniderman, *Business Mgr*
Gary Rosewell, *Accountant*
Debra Parker, *Marketing Staff*
EMP: 50
SQ FT: 20,000
SALES (est): 22.3MM **Privately Held**
WEB: www.altconnect.com
SIC: 5045 7378 Printers, computer; computer maintenance & repair

(G-5155)
BUCKINGHAM DLTTLE BRROUGHS LLC
Also Called: Buckingham Doolittle Burroughs
1375 E 9th St Ste 1700 (44114-1790)
PHONE.................216 621-5300
Fax: 216 621-5440
David M Abromowitz, *Partner*
Joseph L Ackerman, *Partner*
Ronald C Allan, *Partner*
Ralph D Amiet, *Partner*
Steven A Armatas, *Partner*
EMP: 62
SALES (corp-wide): 40.6MM **Privately Held**
SIC: 8111 General practice law office
PA: Buckingham, Doolittle & Burroughs, Llc
3800 Embassy Pkwy
Akron OH 44333
330 376-5300

(G-5156)
BUDDIES INC (PA)
Also Called: A J'S Body Shop
3888 Pearl Rd (44109-3159)
P.O. Box 33022 (44133-0022)
PHONE.................216 642-3362
James Dillinger, *President*
Alvin J Alvarez, *Admin Sec*
EMP: 30
SQ FT: 4,800
SALES (est): 1.2MM **Privately Held**
WEB: www.buddies.com
SIC: 7532 7549 Body shop, automotive; interior repair services; undercoating/rust-proofing cars

(G-5157)
BUDGET RENT A CAR SYSTEM INC
Also Called: Budget Rent-A-Car
19719 Maplewood Ave (44135-2459)
PHONE.................216 267-2080
Fax: 216 362-2962
Harry Baker, *Manager*
EMP: 80
SALES (corp-wide): 8.8B **Publicly Held**
WEB: www.blackdogventures.com
SIC: 7514 Rent-a-car service
HQ: Budget Rent A Car System, Inc.
6 Sylvan Way Ste 1
Parsippany NJ 07054
973 496-3500

(G-5158)
BUILDERS EXCHANGE INC (PA)
Also Called: Bx Ohio
9555 Rockside Rd Ste 300 (44125-6282)
PHONE.................216 393-6300
Jack Speer, *Project Mgr*
Ashley Grandetti, *Branch Mgr*
Gregg Mazurek, *Exec Dir*
Jim Chevraux, *Director*
Laurel Screptock, *Admin Sec*
EMP: 36
SQ FT: 10,000
SALES (est): 3.8MM **Privately Held**
WEB: www.bxcleve.com
SIC: 8611 Contractors' association

(G-5159)
BURKSHIRE CONSTRUCTION COMPANY
6033 State Rd (44134-2869)
P.O. Box 347248 (44134-7248)
PHONE.................440 885-9700
Anne M Burkey, *President*
EMP: 30
SALES (est): 3MM **Privately Held**
SIC: 1521 Single-family housing construction

(G-5160)
BURTON CAROL MANAGEMENT (PA)
Also Called: B C M
4832 Richmond Rd Ste 200 (44128-5993)
PHONE.................216 464-5130
Robert G Risman, *CEO*
Joy Anzalone, *COO*
Joseph W Kincaid, *Vice Pres*
John Petryshin, *Vice Pres*
Marcia Hayward, *Opers Staff*
EMP: 40
SALES (est): 7.6MM **Privately Held**
SIC: 6513 Apartment building operators

(G-5161)
BUSCH DEVELOPMENT CORPORATION
Also Called: Busch Family Chapels
7501 Ridge Rd (44129-6628)
PHONE.................440 842-7800
Fax: 440 885-5139
James H Busch, *President*
EMP: 50
SALES (est): 2.5MM **Privately Held**
WEB: www.buschfuneral.com
SIC: 7261 Funeral director

(G-5162)
BUSINESS AIRCRAFT GROUP INC (PA)
Also Called: Bussines Air Craft Center
2301 N Marginal Rd (44114-3708)
PHONE.................216 348-1415
Fax: 216 781-1018
Mike Hoyle, *President*
Dave Lucas, *CFO*
Taushine Frolick, *Accounting Mgr*
Beth Lozey, *Accounting Mgr*
EMP: 60
SQ FT: 25,000
SALES (est): 8.2MM **Privately Held**
WEB: www.businessaircraftgroup.com
SIC: 4522 Nonscheduled charter services

(G-5163)
BUSINESS RESEARCH SERVICES
26600 Renaissance Pkwy (44128-5795)
PHONE.................216 831-5200
Ronald J Mayher, *President*
Trudy M Mayher, *Corp Secy*
EMP: 25
SALES (est): 1.9MM **Privately Held**
SIC: 8732 Business research service; market analysis or research

(G-5164)
BUSINESS STATIONERY LLC
4944 Commerce Pkwy (44128-5908)
PHONE.................216 514-1192
Fax: 216 514-1280
Brad Wolf, *President*
Lee Brantley, *Vice Pres*
Patrick Cowan, *Plant Mgr*
John Baur, *Purch Mgr*
Mark Cupach, *Sls & Mktg Exec*
EMP: 85
SALES: 35.7MM
SALES (corp-wide): 259.3MM **Privately Held**
WEB: www.bsiprint.com
SIC: 5112 Stationery
HQ: Identity Group Holdings Llc
1480 Gould Dr
Cookeville TN 38506
931 432-4000

(G-5165)
BUY BELOW RETAIL INC
23600 Mercantile Rd Ste G (44122-5949)
PHONE.................216 292-7805
Benjamin Woomer, *President*
EMP: 45 **EST:** 2000
SALES (est): 3.4MM **Privately Held**
WEB: www.factorydirectltd.com
SIC: 5199 General merchandise, nondurable

(G-5166)
BWXT NCLEAR OPRTIONS GROUP INC
24703 Euclid Ave (44117-1714)
PHONE.................216 912-3000
Pete Goumas, *General Mgr*
Alex Dimoff, *Engineer*
Mary Salomone, *Branch Mgr*
Bruce Buffie, *Manager*
Dave Roth, *Manager*
EMP: 34 **Publicly Held**
SIC: 1799 Nuclear power refueling
HQ: Bwxt Nuclear Operations Group, Inc.
2016 Mount Athos Rd
Lynchburg VA 24504

(G-5167)
C & J CONTRACTORS INC
866 Addison Rd (44103-1608)
P.O. Box 874, Willoughby (44096-0874)
PHONE.................216 391-5700
Fax: 216 391-7825
James Crawford, *President*
Craig Crawford, *Vice Pres*
Robert Crawford, *VP Sales*
Alicia R Wigand, *Admin Sec*
EMP: 25
SQ FT: 3,500
SALES (est): 2.8MM **Privately Held**
WEB: www.cjcontractorsinc.com
SIC: 1795 1794 Demolition, buildings & other structures; excavation work

(G-5168)
C C MITCHELL SUPPLY COMPANY
3001 E Royalton Rd (44147-2894)
PHONE.................440 526-2040
Fax: 440 526-6034
Jerome Mitchell, *Ch of Bd*
Stu Kaine, *Sales Staff*
Eric Schniegenberg, *Marketing Staff*
EMP: 35
SQ FT: 48,000
SALES (est): 10.5MM **Privately Held**
WEB: www.mtndew.com
SIC: 5064 Electrical appliances, major

(G-5169)
C-AUTO GLASS INC
Also Called: Pure Led Solutions
2500 Brookpark Rd # 111 (44134-1400)
PHONE.................216 351-2193
Joeseph Tieber, *President*
Pam Houdeshell, *Office Mgr*
Tim Szakal, *Manager*
Eileen Joyce, *Admin Sec*
▲ **EMP:** 29
SALES (est): 4.7MM **Privately Held**
SIC: 7536 Automotive glass replacement shops

(G-5170)
CABLE TV SERVICES INC
6400 Kolthoff Dr (44142-1313)
PHONE.................440 816-0033
Jay Geib, *President*
Dan Geib, *Corp Secy*
Chris Yeager, *Project Mgr*
EMP: 50
SALES (est): 5MM **Privately Held**
SIC: 1731 Cable television installation

(G-5171)
CALABRESEM RACEK & MARKOS INC
1110 Euclid Ave Ste 300 (44115-1626)
PHONE.................216 696-5442
Fax: 216 696-5499
Richard G Racek, *President*
Steve Calabrese, *Exec VP*
Eric Calabrese, *Treasurer*
Marcie Gilmore, *Marketing Staff*
David S Calabrese, *Property Mgr*
EMP: 25
SQ FT: 10,000
SALES (est): 3.3MM **Privately Held**
WEB: www.crmonline.com
SIC: 6531 8748 Appraiser, real estate; real estate brokers & agents; real estate managers; business consulting

(G-5172)
CALFEE HALTER & GRISWOLD LLP (PA)
1405 E 6th St Ste 1 (44114-1601)
PHONE.................216 831-2732
Amy Flanigan, *President*
Debra Hale, *President*
Judi Krahn, *President*
Kathleen Kunes, *President*
Nancy Malinowski, *President*
EMP: 358
SALES (est): 49.3MM **Privately Held**
SIC: 8111 General practice attorney, lawyer

(G-5173)
CALVERT WIRE & CABLE CORP (DH)
17909 Cleve Pkwy Ste 180 (44142)
PHONE.................216 433-7600
Fax: 216 433-7614
Lorraine Nunez, *President*
Allen Layman, *General Mgr*
Lee Ferguson, *Vice Pres*
Kim Cushing, *Sales Mgr*
Mark Brown, *Sales Staff*
◆ **EMP:** 38
SQ FT: 12,000
SALES (est): 42.9MM **Publicly Held**
WEB: www.calvert-wire.com
SIC: 5063 4899 Electrical apparatus & equipment; wire & cable; data communication services

GEOGRAPHIC SECTION
Cleveland - Cuyahoga County (G-5198)

HQ: Communications Supply Corp
200 E Lies Rd
Carol Stream IL 60188
630 221-6400

(G-5174)
CAMGEN LTD
1621 Euclid Ave Ste 220-3 (44115-2114)
P.O. Box 13141, Akron (44334-8541)
PHONE..................................330 204-8636
William Genkin,
EMP: 55
SALES (est): 1.2MM Privately Held
SIC: 7371 Computer software development & applications

(G-5175)
CAMPUSEAI INC
1111 Superior Ave E # 310 (44114-2540)
PHONE..................................216 589-9626
Divye Chugh, *Counsel*
Rich Griffin, *Exec VP*
Arun K Chopra, *CFO*
Carol Arroyo, *Controller*
Chris Aurora, *Manager*
EMP: 120
SALES (est): 16.7MM Privately Held
SIC: 7371 Software programming applications

(G-5176)
CANAL ROAD PARTNERS
5585 Canal Rd (44125-4874)
PHONE..................................216 447-0814
Jeffrey Wallis, *Partner*
Jim Allega, *Partner*
John Allega, *Partner*
EMP: 30
SALES (est): 1.7MM Privately Held
SIC: 6512 Nonresidential building operators

(G-5177)
CANTERBURY GOLF CLUB INC
22000 S Woodland Rd (44122-3061)
PHONE..................................216 561-1914
Fax: 216 561-6566
Dan Denihan, *Sales/Mktg Mgr*
Edward Kloboves, *Controller*
EMP: 80
SQ FT: 50,000
SALES: 4.7MM Privately Held
SIC: 7997 5812 Golf club, membership; eating places

(G-5178)
CAPITAL PROPERTIES MGT LTD
12929 Shaker Blvd (44120-2034)
PHONE..................................216 991-3057
David J Goodman, *Partner*
EMP: 30
SALES (est): 3.7MM Privately Held
WEB: www.cpm-ltd.com
SIC: 6531 Real estate managers

(G-5179)
CAR WASH
5195 Northfield Rd (44146-1130)
PHONE..................................216 662-6289
Fax: 216 662-6344
Russell Patel, *President*
Rusell Patel, *President*
EMP: 25
SQ FT: 5,700
SALES (est): 780.5K Privately Held
SIC: 7542 Washing & polishing, automotive

(G-5180)
CARDINAL HEALTH 200 LLC
Also Called: Cardinal Health Medical
5260 Naiman Pkwy (44139-1006)
PHONE..................................440 349-1247
Debbie Vargo, *Vice Pres*
Mark Howard, *Branch Mgr*
Audrey Hurley, *Analyst*
EMP: 35
SQ FT: 5,000
SALES (corp-wide): 129.9B Publicly Held
WEB: www.allegiancehealth.com
SIC: 5047 Medical & hospital equipment
HQ: Cardinal Health 200, Llc
3651 Birchwood Dr
Waukegan IL 60085

(G-5181)
CARDIOLOGIST
6525 Powers Blvd 301 (44129-5461)
PHONE..................................440 882-0075
Richard Ader, *Principal*
Connie Klein, *Practice Mgr*
EMP: 75
SALES (est): 1.1MM Privately Held
SIC: 8011 Offices & clinics of medical doctors

(G-5182)
CARDIOVASCULAR CLINIC INC
6525 Powers Blvd Rm 301 (44129-5461)
PHONE..................................440 882-0075
Fax: 440 884-8009
Richard S Ader MD, *President*
Christine Zirafi MD, *Corp Secy*
Neelesh Desai, *Vice Pres*
Connie Klein, *Office Mgr*
Raju Modi, *Cardiovascular*
EMP: 70
SALES (est): 8.9MM Privately Held
SIC: 8011 Cardiologist & cardio-vascular specialist

(G-5183)
CARDIOVASCULAR MEDICINE ASSOC
7255 Old Oak Blvd C208 (44130-3329)
PHONE..................................440 816-2708
Fax: 440 243-8480
Trilok C Sharma MD, *President*
Sabino Velloze MD, *Vice Pres*
EMP: 30
SALES (est): 4.1MM Privately Held
SIC: 8011 Cardiologist & cardio-vascular specialist

(G-5184)
CARGILL INCORPORATED
2400 Ships Channel (44113-2673)
P.O. Box 6920 (44101-1920)
PHONE..................................216 651-7200
Wayne L Streble, *Buyer*
Luba Varous, *Controller*
Bob Soupko, *Branch Mgr*
EMP: 205
SALES (corp-wide): 109.7B Privately Held
WEB: www.cargill.com
SIC: 1479 2899 Salt (common) mining; chemical preparations
PA: Cargill, Incorporated
15407 Mcginty Rd W
Wayzata MN 55391
952 742-7575

(G-5185)
CARNEGIE CAPITAL ASSET MGT LLC
Also Called: Carnegie Investment Counsel
30300 Chagrin Blvd (44124-5725)
PHONE..................................216 595-1349
Richard Alt, *President*
EMP: 44
SALES (est): 138.1K Privately Held
SIC: 6282 Investment advice

(G-5186)
CARRIE CERINO RESTAURANTS INC
8922 Ridge Rd (44133-1869)
PHONE..................................440 237-3434
Fax: 440 237-7434
Carmen Cerino, *President*
Michael Cerino, *Corp Secy*
Dominic Cerino III, *Vice Pres*
EMP: 115
SQ FT: 30,000
SALES (est): 4.6MM Privately Held
WEB: www.carriecerinos.com
SIC: 5812 5813 7299 Italian restaurant; American restaurant; cocktail lounge; banquet hall facilities

(G-5187)
CASE WESTERN RESERVE UNIV
Also Called: Shipping & Receiving Dept
2232 Circle Dr (44106-2629)
PHONE..................................216 368-2560
Jordan Genovese, *Research*
Kanokwan Limnuson, *Research*
Art Hardee, *Branch Mgr*
Rachel Begley, *Director*
Elisse Cortez, *Asst Director*
EMP: 25
SALES (corp-wide): 1B Privately Held
WEB: www.cwru.edu
SIC: 7331 8221 Mailing service; university
PA: Case Western Reserve University
10900 Euclid Ave
Cleveland OH 44106
216 368-2000

(G-5188)
CATHOLIC ASSOCIATION OF THE DI (PA)
10000 Miles Ave (44105-6130)
P.O. Box 605310 (44105-0310)
PHONE..................................216 641-7575
Fax: 216 441-2910
Robert Winnicki, *CFO*
Andrej Lah, *Director*
EMP: 117
SALES (est): 7.1MM Privately Held
SIC: 8641 Dwelling-related associations

(G-5189)
CATHOLIC CHARITIES CORPORATION
Also Called: Catholic Charities Svc Cuyah
7800 Detroit Ave (44102-2814)
PHONE..................................216 939-3713
Fax: 216 881-8029
Edward Carter, *Director*
Evelyn Santos, *Director*
EMP: 30 Privately Held
WEB: www.catholic-action.org
SIC: 8399 8322 Fund raising organization, non-fee basis; general counseling services
PA: Catholic Charities Corporation
7911 Detroit Ave
Cleveland OH 44102

(G-5190)
CATHOLIC CHARITIES CORPORATION
Also Called: Deporres, Martin Emrgncy Asst
1264 E 123rd St (44108-4002)
PHONE..................................216 268-4006
Marsha Blanks, *Principal*
M Miller, *Manager*
EMP: 35 Privately Held
WEB: www.catholic-action.org
SIC: 8399 8322 Fund raising organization, non-fee basis; individual & family services
PA: Catholic Charities Corporation
7911 Detroit Ave
Cleveland OH 44102

(G-5191)
CATHOLIC CHARITIES CORPORATION (PA)
Also Called: Catholic Chrties Dcese Clvland
7911 Detroit Ave (44102-2815)
PHONE..................................216 334-2900
Fax: 216 391-8946
Patrick Gareau, *President*
Patricia Holian, *COO*
Wayne Peel, *CFO*
Keith Johnson, *Finance*
Samantha Mealy, *Mktg Dir*
EMP: 50
SALES: 48.7MM Privately Held
WEB: www.catholic-action.org
SIC: 8399 Fund raising organization, non-fee basis

(G-5192)
CATHOLIC DIOCESE OF CLEVELAND
Also Called: Holy Cross Cemetary
14609 Brookpark Rd (44142-1709)
PHONE..................................216 267-2850
Fax: 216 267-3031
Sharon Merzina, *Manager*
Len Martz, *Manager*
EMP: 40
SALES (corp-wide): 79.9MM Privately Held
WEB: www.oce-ocs.org
SIC: 6553 Cemetery subdividers & developers
PA: Catholic Diocese Of Cleveland
1404 E 9th St Ste 201
Cleveland OH 44114
216 696-6525

(G-5193)
CAVALIERS HOLDINGS LLC (PA)
Also Called: Quicken Loans Arena
1 Center Ct (44115-4001)
PHONE..................................216 420-2000
Fax: 216 420-2298
Damy Farry, *General Mgr*
Kevin Libal, *Editor*
Tracy Marek, *Senior VP*
Gayle Bibby-Creme, *Vice Pres*
Antony Bonavita, *Vice Pres*
EMP: 134
SALES (est): 87.3MM Privately Held
WEB: www.theqarena.com
SIC: 7941 6512 Basketball club; nonresidential building operators

(G-5194)
CAVALIERS OPERATING CO LLC
Also Called: Q, The
1 Center Ct (44115-4001)
PHONE..................................216 420-2000
Len Komorski, *CEO*
Scott Woodruff, *COO*
Alberta Lee, *Vice Pres*
Chris Poole, *Vice Pres*
Bob Pollard, *Facilities Dir*
EMP: 1300
SALES (est): 48.6MM
SALES (corp-wide): 87.3MM Privately Held
SIC: 7941 Sports field or stadium operator, promoting sports events
PA: Cavaliers Holdings, Llc
1 Center Ct
Cleveland OH 44115
216 420-2000

(G-5195)
CAVITCH FAMILO & DURKIN CO LPA
1300 E 9th St (44114-1501)
PHONE..................................216 621-7860
Fax: 216 621-3415
Harvey L Furtkin, *Partner*
Michael C Cohen, *Partner*
Howard P Kasdan, *Counsel*
Alex Goetsch,
Thomas G Belden,
EMP: 40
SQ FT: 16,500
SALES (est): 5.3MM Privately Held
WEB: www.cfdf.com
SIC: 8111 General practice law office

(G-5196)
CBIZ INC (PA)
6050 Oak Tree Blvd # 500 (44131-6951)
PHONE..................................216 447-9000
Steven L Gerard, *Ch of Bd*
Rick L Burdick, *Vice Ch Bd*
Jerome P Grisko Jr, *President*
Michael P Kouzelos, *President*
Chris Spurio, *President*
EMP: 148
SALES: 855.3MM Publicly Held
WEB: www.cbizinc.com
SIC: 8742 7389 7363 Management consulting services; financial services; employee leasing service

(G-5197)
CBIZ MHM LLC (HQ)
6050 Oak Tree Blvd (44131-6927)
PHONE..................................216 447-9000
Fax: 216 574-5264
Jerry Grisko, *CEO*
Jerome P Grisko, *CEO*
Lawrence J Berland, *Partner*
Stephen Danner, *Partner*
Chuck Sockett, *Partner*
EMP: 148
SQ FT: 30,000
SALES (est): 47.6MM Publicly Held
WEB: www.mahoneycohen.com
SIC: 8721 Accounting, auditing & bookkeeping

(G-5198)
CBRE INC
950 Main Ave Ste 200 (44113-7203)
PHONE..................................216 687-1800
Fax: 216 363-6466
Kevin Malinowski, *Vice Pres*

Cleveland - Cuyahoga County (G-5199)

GEOGRAPHIC SECTION

Chris Corfias, *Project Mgr*
Jennifer Priest, *Marketing Staff*
David Browning, *Manager*
Terry D Kaufman, *Manager*
EMP: 45
SALES (corp-wide): 14.2B **Publicly Held**
SIC: 6531 Real estate agent, commercial
HQ: Cbre, Inc.
400 S Hope St Ste 25
Los Angeles CA 90071
310 477-5876

(G-5199)
CBS RADIO INC
1041 Huron Rd E (44115-1706)
PHONE 216 861-0100
Fax: 216 241-0449
Linda Rodriguez, *Sales Mgr*
Jeff Miller, *Adv Mgr*
Walter Tiburski, *Branch Mgr*
Bill Louis, *Program Dir*
EMP: 25
SALES (corp-wide): 592.8MM **Publicly Held**
WEB: www.infinityradio.com
SIC: 4832 Radio broadcasting stations
HQ: Cbs Radio Inc.
345 Hudson St Fl 10
New York NY 10014
212 314-9200

(G-5200)
CDC OF SHAKER HEIGHTS
Also Called: Center For Dialysis Care
11717 Euclid Ave (44106-4350)
PHONE 216 295-7000
Dave Long, *Office Mgr*
Diane Wish, *Branch Mgr*
EMP: 30 **Privately Held**
WEB: www.curvesohio.com
SIC: 8092 Kidney dialysis centers
PA: Cdc Of Shaker Heights
18720 Chagrin Blvd
Shaker Heights OH 44122

(G-5201)
CEFARATTI INVESTIGATION & PRCS
Also Called: Cefaratti Group
4608 Saint Clair Ave (44103-1206)
PHONE 216 696-1161
Fax: 216 687-0973
Arther Cefaratti, *President*
Robert Adelman, *Managing Prtnr*
Paul Cefaratti, *Vice Pres*
Kim Fleming, *Financial Exec*
Carmen Cefaratti, *Human Resources*
EMP: 25
SALES (est): 710.6K **Privately Held**
WEB: www.cefgroup.com
SIC: 7381 Detective agency

(G-5202)
CELEBRITY SECURITY INC
3408 West Blvd (44111-1232)
PHONE 216 671-6425
Paul Jurcisin, *President*
Jim Morrison, *Vice Pres*
EMP: 50
SALES (est): 920K **Privately Held**
SIC: 7381 8748 Private investigator; traffic consultant

(G-5203)
CELLCO PARTNERSHIP
Also Called: Verizon
5945 Mayfield Rd (44124-2902)
PHONE 440 646-9625
Jim Sankey, *Branch Mgr*
EMP: 25
SALES (corp-wide): 126B **Publicly Held**
SIC: 4812 5999 Cellular telephone services; mobile telephones & equipment
HQ: Cellco Partnership
1 Verizon Way
Basking Ridge NJ 07920

(G-5204)
CENTER FOR COMMUNITY SOLUTIONS
1501 Euclid Ave Ste 311 (44115-2108)
PHONE 216 781-2944
Cheryl Brewington, *Finance Dir*
Roslyn Kaleal, *Office Admin*
Gregory L Brown, *Exec Dir*
Tara Britton, *Director*

Sheila Lettsome, *Executive Asst*
EMP: 30
SQ FT: 17,500
SALES: 2.3MM **Privately Held**
SIC: 8399 Advocacy group

(G-5205)
CENTER FOR FAMILIES & CHILDREN
5955 Ridge Rd (44129-3936)
PHONE 440 888-0300
Fax: 440 888-1686
Betty Rossi, *Director*
EMP: 25
SALES (corp-wide): 26MM **Privately Held**
SIC: 8322 General counseling services
PA: Center For Families & Children, Inc
4500 Euclid Ave
Cleveland OH 44103
216 432-7200

(G-5206)
CENTER FOR FAMILIES & CHILDREN (PA)
4500 Euclid Ave (44103-3736)
PHONE 216 432-7200
Fax: 216 426-2749
Lee Fisher, *President*
Melanie Nigro, *General Mgr*
Sara Sullivan, *Managing Dir*
Sharon Sobol Jordan, *Principal*
Elizabeth Newman, *COO*
EMP: 65
SQ FT: 23,000
SALES (est): 26MM **Privately Held**
SIC: 8322 Child related social services

(G-5207)
CENTER FOR FAMILIES & CHILDREN
3929 Rocky River Dr (44111-4153)
PHONE 216 252-5800
Fax: 216 252-1106
Mary McCaffery-Hull, *Vice Pres*
Nathan Rhea, *Opers Spvr*
Bob Bengele, *Engineer*
Charlie Bango, *Manager*
Josephine Orlowski, *Manager*
EMP: 25
SALES (corp-wide): 26MM **Privately Held**
SIC: 8322 8093 Family counseling services; mental health clinic, outpatient
PA: Center For Families & Children, Inc
4500 Euclid Ave
Cleveland OH 44103
216 432-7200

(G-5208)
CENTER FOR HEALTH AFFAIRS
Also Called: Greater Cleveland Hosp Assn
1226 Huron Rd E (44115-1789)
PHONE 800 362-2628
Fax: 216 696-1837
William T Ryan, *President*
Toni Hare, *Vice Pres*
Betty Goodman, *Human Res Mgr*
Rick Lakatos, *Manager*
Janet Nelson, *Manager*
EMP: 78 **EST:** 1997
SALES: 1MM **Privately Held**
SIC: 8062 8699 8742 General medical & surgical hospitals; athletic organizations; management consulting services

(G-5209)
CENTRAL CADILLAC LIMITED
Also Called: Central Cadillac-Hummer
2801 Carnegie Ave (44115-2628)
PHONE 216 861-5800
Fax: 216 861-5857
Frank H Porter Jr, *President*
Michael Hamilton, *Sales Mgr*
Angelo Ezzo, *Sales Associate*
Mike Wonder, *Manager*
EMP: 83
SQ FT: 40,000
SALES (est): 8.4MM **Privately Held**
WEB: www.centralcadillac.com
SIC: 7538 5521 5511 General automotive repair shops; used car dealers; automobiles, new & used

(G-5210)
CENTRAL EXTERMINATING COMPANY (PA)
3202 Saint Clair Ave Ne (44114-4008)
PHONE 216 771-0555
Fax: 216 771-1350
Vanessa Phillips, *Principal*
Charles Kettler, *Vice Pres*
Kathleen Roark, *Manager*
Dave Thompson, *Manager*
EMP: 50 **EST:** 1940
SQ FT: 5,000
SALES (est): 4.1MM **Privately Held**
WEB: www.centralexterminating.com
SIC: 7342 Pest control in structures

(G-5211)
CENTRAL HOSPITAL SERVICES INC
Also Called: CHAMPS MANAGEMENT SERVICES
1226 Huron Rd E Ste 2 (44115-1702)
PHONE 216 696-6900
Fax: 216 696-6318
Bill Ryan, *President*
Phil Mazanec, *COO*
Laura Gronowski, *Vice Pres*
John Piazza, *Vice Pres*
EMP: 55
SQ FT: 18,000
SALES: 7MM **Privately Held**
SIC: 8621 Medical field-related associations

(G-5212)
CENTRAL HUMMR EAST
25975 Central Pkwy (44122-7308)
PHONE 216 514-2700
Philip Marotta, *Sales Staff*
Anna Masterson, *Sales Staff*
Dave Mooney, *Sales Staff*
Scott Newman, *Manager*
EMP: 30
SALES: 1MM **Privately Held**
SIC: 5012 Automobiles

(G-5213)
CENTURA INC
Also Called: Centura X-Ray
4381 Renaissance Pkwy (44128-5759)
PHONE 216 593-0226
Fax: 216 831-6959
Douglas Brook, *President*
Mary Luzi, *Principal*
John T Mulligan, *Principal*
Mark Hale, *CFO*
Harris Ron, *Sales Mgr*
EMP: 40
SQ FT: 16,500
SALES (est): 10.2MM **Privately Held**
WEB: www.centuraxray.com
SIC: 5047 Medical equipment & supplies; X-ray machines & tubes

(G-5214)
CENTURY 21 TRAMMELL ODONNELL
7087 Pearl Rd (44130-4940)
PHONE 440 888-6800
Fax: 440 888-7551
Bruce Trammell, *Partner*
Janet O Donnell, *Partner*
EMP: 70
SQ FT: 4,700
SALES (est): 3MM **Privately Held**
SIC: 6531 Real estate agent, residential

(G-5215)
CENTURY CONTRACTORS INC
26100 Broadway Ave Ste B (44146-6532)
PHONE 440 232-2626
Fax: 440 232-0342
Lou Occhionero, *President*
Linda Occhionero, *Vice Pres*
EMP: 30 **EST:** 1978
SQ FT: 2,400
SALES (est): 2.8MM **Privately Held**
SIC: 1742 Acoustical & ceiling work; drywall

(G-5216)
CENTURY EQUIPMENT INC
26565 Miles Rd Ste 200 (44128-5998)
PHONE 216 292-6911
Ron Smallwick, *Branch Mgr*

EMP: 37
SALES (corp-wide): 41.7MM **Privately Held**
WEB: www.centuryequip.com
SIC: 5083 5088 Mowers, power; lawn machinery & equipment; garden machinery & equipment; irrigation equipment; golf carts
PA: Century Equipment, Inc.
5959 Angola Rd
Toledo OH 43615
419 865-7400

(G-5217)
CENTURY FEDERAL CREDIT UNION
10701 East Blvd (44106-1702)
PHONE 216 535-3600
Fax: 216 535-3609
Adrew Dickson, *Manager*
EMP: 30
SALES (corp-wide): 10.5MM **Privately Held**
WEB: www.centuryfederalcreditunion.com
SIC: 6061 Federal credit unions
PA: Century Federal Credit Union Inc
1240 E 9th St Ste 719
Cleveland OH
216 535-3200

(G-5218)
CENTURY GLASS CO
6211 Cedar Ave (44103-4797)
PHONE 216 361-7700
Fax: 216 361-7702
Charles Kehres, *President*
James Kehres, *Vice Pres*
EMP: 25
SQ FT: 22,000
SALES: 3MM **Privately Held**
SIC: 5039 5023 Exterior flat glass: plate or window; interior flat glass: plate or window; mirrors & pictures, framed & unframed

(G-5219)
CENTURY LINES INC
3184 E 79th St (44104-4325)
P.O. Box 27469 (44127-0469)
PHONE 216 271-0700
Fax: 216 271-0484
Robert O Rucker, *President*
Mike Trent, *Vice Pres*
Marilyn Rucker, *Admin Sec*
EMP: 50 **EST:** 1973
SQ FT: 150,000
SALES (est): 6.7MM **Privately Held**
SIC: 4212 4213 Local trucking, without storage; trucking, except local

(G-5220)
CETEK LTD
6779 Engle Rd Ste A (44130-7926)
PHONE 216 362-3900
Derek Scott, *CEO*
John Bacon, *Vice Pres*
EMP: 30
SALES (est): 2.1MM **Privately Held**
SIC: 2851 8711 Lacquers, varnishes, enamels & other coatings; heating & ventilation engineering
PA: Integrated Global Services, Inc.
7600 Whitepine Rd
North Chesterfield VA 23237

(G-5221)
CEVA FREIGHT LLC
Also Called: Ceva Ocean Line
18601 Cleveland Pkwy Dr (44135-3231)
PHONE 216 898-6765
Ken Towers, *Manager*
EMP: 45 **Publicly Held**
WEB: www.tntlogistics.com
SIC: 4731 Freight forwarding
HQ: Ceva Freight, Llc
15350 Vickery Dr
Houston TX 77032

(G-5222)
CGI TECHNOLOGIES SOLUTIONS INC
1001 Lakeside Ave E # 800 (44114-1158)
PHONE 216 687-1480
Jeff Lawson, *President*
Renee Jones, *Facilities Mgr*
Sophia Youngbauer, *HR Admin*
Paula Stacey, *Human Resources*

Don Canzonetta, *Business Anlyst*
EMP: 150
SALES (corp-wide): 8.6B **Privately Held**
SIC: 7379
HQ: Cgi Technologies And Solutions Inc.
11325 Random Hills Rd
Fairfax VA 22030
703 267-8000

(G-5223)
CH ROBINSON FREIGHT SVCS LTD
Also Called: Phoenix International Frt Svcs
7261 Engle Rd Ste 400 (44130-3479)
PHONE.....................440 234-7811
Michelle Yancy, *Principal*
Matthew Hopkins, *Sales Mgr*
Katey Brennan, *Sales Staff*
Michelle Yancey, *Branch Mgr*
EMP: 50
SALES (corp-wide): 14.8B **Publicly Held**
WEB: www.phoenixintl.com
SIC: 4731 Freight forwarding
HQ: C.H. Robinson Freight Services, Ltd.
1501 N Mittel Blvd Ste A
Wood Dale IL 60191
630 766-4445

(G-5224)
CHA CONSULTING INC
1501 N Marginal Rd # 200 (44114-3760)
PHONE.....................216 443-1700
Fax: 216 443-1780
William Barley, *Vice Pres*
Bill Barley, *Vice Pres*
EMP: 115 **Privately Held**
SIC: 8711 8712 Consulting engineer; architectural services
HQ: Cha Consulting, Inc.
3 Winners Cir Ste 301
Albany NY 12205
518 453-4500

(G-5225)
CHAL-RON LLC
Also Called: Jubilee Academy
15751 Lake Shore Blvd (44110-1020)
P.O. Box 37214, Maple Heights (44137-0214)
PHONE.....................216 383-9050
Chalfonte Smith,
Arrian Smith,
Marche Smith,
EMP: 25
SALES (est): 1.1MM **Privately Held**
SIC: 8351 Child day care services

(G-5226)
CHANDLER PRODUCTS LLC
1491 Chardon Rd (44117-1598)
PHONE.....................216 481-4400
Fax: 216 481-4427
Ron Kiter, *Manager*
Chris Grote, *Info Tech Dir*
EMP: 31
SALES (est): 4.8MM
SALES (corp-wide): 70MM **Privately Held**
SIC: 5085 Fasteners, industrial: nuts, bolts, screws, etc.
HQ: Elgin Fastener Group, Llc
10217 Brecksville Rd # 101
Brecksville OH 44141

(G-5227)
CHANGE HEALTHCARE HOLDINGS INC
2060 E 9th St (44115-1313)
PHONE.....................216 589-5878
Pete Titas, *Sales Staff*
Aji Fabi, *Branch Mgr*
EMP: 37
SALES (corp-wide): 1.9B **Privately Held**
SIC: 7374 Data processing service
HQ: Change Healthcare Holdings, Inc.
3055 Lebanon Pike # 1000
Nashville TN 37214
615 932-3000

(G-5228)
CHARLES RVER LABS CLVELAND INC
Also Called: Chantest Corporation
14656 Neo Pkwy (44128-3156)
PHONE.....................216 332-1665
Fax: 216 332-1706
Emily Hickey, *President*
David Smith, *Treasurer*
Andrea Smith, *Sales Mgr*
Brian Little, *Supervisor*
Luke Armstrong, *Director*
EMP: 55
SQ FT: 27,000
SALES (est): 8.1MM
SALES (corp-wide): 1.8B **Publicly Held**
WEB: www.chantest.com
SIC: 8731 Commercial physical research
HQ: Charles River Laboratories, Inc.
251 Ballardvale St
Wilmington MA 01887
978 658-6000

(G-5229)
CHARLES SCHWAB CORPORATION
24737 Cedar Rd (44124-3786)
PHONE.....................216 291-9333
Jeffrey L Hurst, *Principal*
Mike Peterson, *Pub Rel Dir*
Mike Myers, *Manager*
Gerry Weil, *Manager*
EMP: 26
SALES (corp-wide): 8.6B **Publicly Held**
SIC: 6211 Brokers, security
PA: The Charles Schwab Corporation
211 Main St Fl 17
San Francisco CA 94105
415 667-7000

(G-5230)
CHARTWELL GROUP LLC (PA)
1350 Euclid Ave Ste 700 (44115-1889)
PHONE.....................216 360-0009
Fax: 216 360-0395
Robert Biggar, *Mng Member*
William Nice,
David Wagner,
EMP: 25
SQ FT: 4,500
SALES: 3.5MM **Privately Held**
SIC: 6531 8742 Real estate brokers & agents; real estate consultant

(G-5231)
CHATTREE AND ASSOCIATES INC
Also Called: Community Behavioral Hlth Ctr
3355 Richmond Rd Ste 225 (44122-4180)
PHONE.....................216 831-1494
Arun Chattree, *President*
Luan Hutchinson, *Vice Pres*
EMP: 87
SALES: 3.5MM **Privately Held**
SIC: 8742 Hospital & health services consultant

(G-5232)
CHEMICAL SOLVENTS INC (PA)
3751 Jennings Rd (44109-2889)
PHONE.....................216 741-9310
Fax: 216 741-4080
Edward Pavlish, *Ch of Bd*
Thos A Mason, *Principal*
E H Pavlish, *Principal*
Patricia Pavlish, *Corp Secy*
Blaine Davidson, *Vice Pres*
▲ **EMP:** 45 **EST:** 1970
SQ FT: 30,000
SALES (est): 112.5MM **Privately Held**
WEB: www.chemicalsolvents.com
SIC: 5169 7349 3471 2992 Detergents & soaps, except specialty cleaning: specialty cleaning & sanitation preparations; chemical cleaning services; cleaning & descaling metal products; oils & greases, blending & compounding

(G-5233)
CHEMICAL SOLVENTS INC
1010 Denison Ave (44109-2853)
P.O. Box 931705 (44193-1813)
PHONE.....................216 741-9310
Dan Reynolds, *Manager*
EMP: 65
SALES (est): 6.4MM
SALES (corp-wide): 112.5MM **Privately Held**
WEB: www.chemicalsolvents.com
SIC: 5169 Industrial chemicals; specialty cleaning & sanitation preparations
PA: Chemical Solvents, Inc.
3751 Jennings Rd
Cleveland OH 44109
216 741-9310

(G-5234)
CHICAGO TITLE INSURANCE CO
1111 Superior Ave E # 600 (44114-2541)
PHONE.....................216 241-6045
Deborah Zielinski, *Underwriter*
Shelley Maggard, *Manager*
Mark Cook, *Manager*
Paulina Thorpe, *Manager*
Barbara Ryback, *Administration*
EMP: 50
SALES (corp-wide): 7.6B **Publicly Held**
SIC: 6541 Title & trust companies
HQ: Chicago Title Insurance Company
601 Riverside Ave
Jacksonville FL 32204

(G-5235)
CHIEFTAIN TRUCKING & EXCAV INC
3926 Valley Rd Ste 300 (44109-3058)
PHONE.....................216 485-8034
Eileen Martin, *President*
Betty Martin, *President*
Brian Murphy, *Project Mgr*
Colton Rock, *Engineer*
Patrick Tomazic, *Controller*
EMP: 35
SQ FT: 17,500
SALES: 8MM **Privately Held**
SIC: 1794 4231 Excavation & grading, building construction; trucking terminal facilities

(G-5236)
CHILD CARE RESOURCE CENTER (PA)
Also Called: Starting Point
4600 Euclid Ave Ste 500 (44103-3761)
PHONE.....................216 575-0061
Fax: 216 575-0102
Bilie Osbourne, *Director*
EMP: 33
SALES (est): 9.9MM **Privately Held**
SIC: 8351 Child day care services

(G-5237)
CHILDRENS AID SOCIETY
10427 Detroit Ave (44102-1694)
PHONE.....................216 521-6511
Lawrence S Waldman, *Owner*
Roberta King, *Branch Mgr*
EMP: 50
SALES (est): 1.5MM **Privately Held**
SIC: 8049 Clinical psychologist

(G-5238)
CHOICES BEHAVIORAL HEALTHCARE
3414 Prospect Ave E (44115-2618)
PHONE.....................216 881-4060
EMP: 38
SALES (corp-wide): 1.5MM **Privately Held**
SIC: 8093 Detoxification center, outpatient
PA: Choices Behavioral Healthcare
5726 Southwyck Blvd
Toledo OH 43614
419 865-5690

(G-5239)
CINEMARK USA INC
Also Called: Cinemark At Valley View
6001 Canal Rd (44125-4232)
PHONE.....................216 447-8820
Melissa Truhn, *Manager*
EMP: 110 **Publicly Held**
SIC: 7832 Motion picture theaters, except drive-in
HQ: Cinemark Usa, Inc.
3900 Dallas Pkwy Ste 500
Plano TX 75093
972 665-1000

(G-5240)
CINTAS CORPORATION NO 2
1 Andrews Cir (44141-3250)
PHONE.....................440 838-8611
Robert Heyd, *Sales Executive*
Lisa Coone, *Manager*
EMP: 57
SQ FT: 110,970
SALES (corp-wide): 5.3B **Publicly Held**
WEB: www.cintas-corp.com
SIC: 7389 Document storage service
HQ: Cintas Corporation No. 2
6800 Cintas Blvd
Mason OH 45040

(G-5241)
CIPRIANO PAINTING
27387 Hollywood Dr (44145-5356)
PHONE.....................440 892-1827
Mike Cipriano, *Owner*
EMP: 25
SALES (est): 731.1K **Privately Held**
SIC: 1721 Residential painting

(G-5242)
CIRCLE HEALTH SERVICES
12201 Euclid Ave (44106-4310)
PHONE.....................216 721-4010
Fax: 216 721-2431
Jim Young, *Purch Mgr*
Reza Khoramshahi, *Development*
Tod Welki, *Finance*
Jolynda Gibbs, *Human Res Mgr*
Cheryl Farine, *Pharmacist*
EMP: 44
SQ FT: 28,000
SALES: 3.8MM **Privately Held**
WEB: www.thefreeclinic.org
SIC: 8322 Individual & family services

(G-5243)
CITIGROUP GLOBAL MARKETS INC
Also Called: Smith Barney
2035 Crocker Rd Ste 201 (44145-2194)
PHONE.....................440 617-2000
EMP: 25
SALES (corp-wide): 92.5B **Publicly Held**
SIC: 6211 Securities Brokers/Dealers
HQ: Citigroup Global Markets Inc.
388 Greenwich St Fl 18
New York NY 10013
212 816-6000

(G-5244)
CITIZENS CAPITAL MARKETS INC
200 Public Sq Ste 3750 (44114-2321)
PHONE.....................216 589-0900
Ralph M Della Ratta, *General Mgr*
EMP: 28
SALES (corp-wide): 6.4B **Publicly Held**
SIC: 6141 Personal credit institutions
HQ: Citizens Capital Markets, Inc.
28 State St Fl 13
Boston MA 02109
617 725-5636

(G-5245)
CITY ARCHITECTURE INC
3636 Euclid Ave Fl 3 (44115-2539)
PHONE.....................216 881-2444
Fax: 216 881-6713
Paul Volpe, *President*
Charles C Miller, *Vice Chairman*
Mark Dodds, *Corp Secy*
Ryan Grass, *Project Mgr*
Christophe Auvil, *Architect*
EMP: 30
SQ FT: 9,000
SALES (est): 3.7MM **Privately Held**
WEB: www.cityarch.com
SIC: 8712 Architectural services

(G-5246)
CITY LIFE INC (PA)
Also Called: Sammy's
1382 W 9th St Ste 310 (44113-1231)
PHONE.....................216 523-5899
Fax: 216 523-1873
Denise M Fugo, *President*
Ralph Diorio, *COO*
Jim Harris, *Sls & Mktg Exec*
Jeanne Scalley, *Financial Exec*
Patty Custer, *Personnel Exec*
EMP: 40
SQ FT: 14,550
SALES (est): 12.1MM **Privately Held**
WEB: www.sammys.com
SIC: 5812 5813 7299 American restaurant; caterers; cocktail lounge; banquet hall facilities

Cleveland - Cuyahoga County (G-5247)   GEOGRAPHIC SECTION

(G-5247)
CITY MISSION (PA)
5310 Carnegie Ave (44103-4360)
PHONE..................................216 431-3510
Fax: 216 431-3513
Mark Charvat, *Finance Dir*
Michaela Kekedy, *Marketing Staff*
Deborah Phillips, *Manager*
Leah Uveges, *Supervisor*
Johnny Braden, *Info Tech Mgr*
EMP: 42 **EST:** 1910
SALES (est): 6.8MM **Privately Held**
WEB: www.thecitymission.org
SIC: 8322 8361 Rehabilitation services; rehabilitation center, residential: health care incidental

(G-5248)
CITY OF BROOK PARK
Also Called: Brook Park Recreation Center
17400 Holland Rd (44142-3524)
PHONE..................................216 433-1545
Gary Marken, *Director*
EMP: 35 **Privately Held**
WEB: www.cityofbrookpark.com
SIC: 7999 Recreation center
PA: City Of Brook Park
    6161 Engle Rd
    Cleveland OH 44142
    216 433-1533

(G-5249)
CITY OF CLEVELAND
Also Called: Public Safety
1701 Lakeside Ave E (44114-1118)
PHONE..................................216 664-2555
George Chaloupka, *Commander*
Edward Eckart, *Mfg Staff*
EMP: 325 **Privately Held**
SIC: 4119 9229 Ambulance service; emergency management office, government;
PA: City Of Cleveland
    601 Lakeside Ave E Rm 210
    Cleveland OH 44114
    216 664-2000

(G-5250)
CITY OF CLEVELAND
Also Called: Cleveland Emergency Med Svc
1701 Lakeside Ave E (44114-1118)
PHONE..................................216 664-2555
Fax: 216 623-4599
Edward Eckart, *Commissioner*
EMP: 325 **Privately Held**
SIC: 4119 Ambulance service
PA: City Of Cleveland
    601 Lakeside Ave E Rm 210
    Cleveland OH 44114
    216 664-2000

(G-5251)
CITY OF CLEVELAND
Public Services Dept
955 Clague Rd (44145-1504)
PHONE..................................216 664-3121
Alex Malkin, *Manager*
Mark Petre, *Manager*
Rich Patt, *Exec Dir*
EMP: 42 **Privately Held**
SIC: 4941 9511 Water supply; air, water & solid waste management;
PA: City Of Cleveland
    601 Lakeside Ave E Rm 210
    Cleveland OH 44114
    216 664-2000

(G-5252)
CITY OF CLEVELAND
Division Information Tech Svcs
205 W Saint Clair Ave # 4 (44113-1503)
PHONE..................................216 664-2941
Doug Davis, *Branch Mgr*
EMP: 40 **Privately Held**
SIC: 7376 Computer facilities management
PA: City Of Cleveland
    601 Lakeside Ave E Rm 210
    Cleveland OH 44114
    216 664-2000

(G-5253)
CITY OF CLEVELAND
Public Works, Dept of
500 Lkeside Ave Ground Fl (44114)
PHONE..................................216 621-4231
Fax: 216 348-2262
Suzi Claytor, *Commissioner*
EMP: 47 **Privately Held**
SIC: 6512 9512 Nonresidential building operators; recreational program administration, government;
PA: City Of Cleveland
    601 Lakeside Ave E Rm 210
    Cleveland OH 44114
    216 664-2000

(G-5254)
CITY OF CLEVELAND
Also Called: Finance Dept
205 W Saint Clair Ave # 4 (44113-1503)
PHONE..................................216 664-2430
Doug Divish, *Commissioner*
EMP: 60 **Privately Held**
SIC: 7374 9199 Data processing & preparation; general government administration;
PA: City Of Cleveland
    601 Lakeside Ave E Rm 210
    Cleveland OH 44114
    216 664-2000

(G-5255)
CITY OF CLEVELAND
Also Called: Finance Dept
601 Lakeside Ave E Rm 128 (44114-1065)
PHONE..................................216 664-2620
Lisha Strickland, *Buyer*
Tiffany White Johnson, *Manager*
EMP: 25 **Privately Held**
SIC: 7389 9311 Purchasing service; finance, taxation & monetary policy;
PA: City Of Cleveland
    601 Lakeside Ave E Rm 210
    Cleveland OH 44114
    216 664-2000

(G-5256)
CITY OF CLEVELAND
Also Called: Parks Recreation & Prpts Dept
21400 Chagrin Blvd (44122-5308)
PHONE..................................216 348-7210
Fax: 216 348-7209
David R Mitchell, *Manager*
EMP: 35
SQ FT: 856 **Privately Held**
SIC: 6553 9512 Cemetery subdividers & developers; land, mineral & wildlife conservation;
PA: City Of Cleveland
    601 Lakeside Ave E Rm 210
    Cleveland OH 44114
    216 664-2000

(G-5257)
CITY OF CLEVELAND
Also Called: Fire Station
3765 Pearl Rd (44109-2752)
PHONE..................................216 664-6800
Kevin Gerrity, *Principal*
EMP: 72 **Privately Held**
SIC: 9224 7922 Fire department, not including volunteer; ; theatrical producers & services
PA: City Of Cleveland
    601 Lakeside Ave E Rm 210
    Cleveland OH 44114
    216 664-2000

(G-5258)
CITY OF CLEVELAND
Also Called: Department of Public Utilities
1300 Lakeside Ave E (44114-1135)
PHONE..................................216 664-3922
Jim Mager, *Branch Mgr*
Robert Bonner, *Manager*
Marcia Hines, *Manager*
James McDonnell, *Manager*
Christopher Lielson, *Commissioner*
EMP: 32 **Privately Held**
SIC: 7389 Patrol of electric transmission or gas lines
PA: City Of Cleveland
    601 Lakeside Ave E Rm 210
    Cleveland OH 44114
    216 664-2000

(G-5259)
CITY OF CLEVELAND HEIGHTS
Recycling Department
14200 Superior Rd (44118-1748)
PHONE..................................216 691-7300
Tony Torres, *Manager*
EMP: 35 **Privately Held**
WEB: www.clevelandheights.com
SIC: 4953 Recycling, waste materials
PA: City Of Cleveland Heights
    40 Severance Cir
    Cleveland Heights OH 44118
    216 291-4444

(G-5260)
CITY OF EUCLID
Also Called: Streets & Sewer Departments
25500 Lakeland Blvd (44132-2633)
PHONE..................................216 289-2800
Fax: 216 289-2867
Steve Marco, *Manager*
EMP: 40 **Privately Held**
WEB: www.cityofeuclid.com
SIC: 1611 9111 Highway & street maintenance; executive offices
PA: City Of Euclid
    585 E 222nd St
    Cleveland OH 44123
    216 289-2700

(G-5261)
CITY OF GARFIELD HEIGHTS
Also Called: Service Garage
13600 Mccracken Rd (44125-1976)
PHONE..................................216 475-1107
Fax: 216 475-5776
Mark Sikon, *Manager*
EMP: 35 **Privately Held**
WEB: www.garfieldhts.org
SIC: 7521 Parking garage
PA: City Of Garfield Heights
    5407 Turney Rd
    Cleveland OH 44125
    216 475-1100

(G-5262)
CITY OF HIGHLAND HEIGHTS
Senior Assistance
5827 Highland Rd (44143-2017)
PHONE..................................440 461-2441
Mary Velota, *Director*
EMP: 55 **Privately Held**
SIC: 8322 Geriatric social service
PA: City Of Highland Heights
    5827 Highland Rd
    Cleveland OH 44143
    440 461-2440

(G-5263)
CITY OF INDEPENDENCE
Also Called: Recreation Dept
6363 Selig Blvd (44131-4926)
PHONE..................................216 524-3262
Fax: 216 524-8704
Tonya Cady, *Manager*
Tom Walchanowicz, *Director*
EMP: 37 **Privately Held**
SIC: 7999 Recreation services
PA: City Of Independence
    6800 Brecksville Rd
    Independence OH 44131
    216 524-4131

(G-5264)
CITY OF INDEPENDENCE
Also Called: Civic Center
6363 Selig Blvd (44131-4926)
PHONE..................................216 524-7373
Fax: 216 524-6060
Natalie Buc, *Director*
EMP: 40
SQ FT: 8,463 **Privately Held**
WEB: www.independenceohio.org
SIC: 8322 Community center
PA: City Of Independence
    6800 Brecksville Rd
    Independence OH 44131
    216 524-4131

(G-5265)
CITY OF LAKEWOOD
Also Called: Div of Refuse and Recycling
12920 Berea Rd (44111-1626)
PHONE..................................216 252-4322
Fax: 216 251-3870
Chris Perry, *General Mgr*
EMP: 30
SQ FT: 28,810 **Privately Held**
SIC: 4953 9511 Refuse systems; water control & quality agency, government

PA: City Of Lakewood
    12650 Detroit Ave
    Lakewood OH 44107
    216 521-7580

(G-5266)
CITY OF LAKEWOOD
Also Called: Lakewood Community Care Center
2019 Woodward Ave (44107-5635)
PHONE..................................216 226-0080
Stephanie McMahan, *Principal*
Jeanne E Halladay, *Branch Mgr*
EMP: 37 **Privately Held**
SIC: 8351 Child day care services
PA: City Of Lakewood
    12650 Detroit Ave
    Lakewood OH 44107
    216 521-7580

(G-5267)
CITY OF LAKEWOOD
Also Called: Lakewood Police Dept
12650 Detroit Ave (44107-2832)
PHONE..................................216 529-6170
Fax: 216 521-7727
Daniel Clark, *Chief*
Timothy J Malley, *Chief*
Jennifer Pae, *Financial Exec*
Kevin Chisar, *Manager*
Kenneth Warren, *Director*
EMP: 110 **Privately Held**
SIC: 9221 8111 ; legal services
PA: City Of Lakewood
    12650 Detroit Ave
    Lakewood OH 44107
    216 521-7580

(G-5268)
CITY OF LAKEWOOD
Also Called: Municipal Garage
12920 Berea Rd (44111-1626)
PHONE..................................216 941-1116
Larry Slanick, *Manager*
EMP: 55 **Privately Held**
SIC: 7521 Automobile parking
PA: City Of Lakewood
    12650 Detroit Ave
    Lakewood OH 44107
    216 521-7580

(G-5269)
CITY OF LAKEWOOD
16024 Madison Ave (44107-5616)
PHONE..................................216 521-1288
Paulette McMoneguel, *Director*
EMP: 31 **Privately Held**
SIC: 4119 Local passenger transportation
PA: City Of Lakewood
    12650 Detroit Ave
    Lakewood OH 44107
    216 521-7580

(G-5270)
CITY OF NORTH ROYALTON
Also Called: Street and Service Department
11545 Royalton Rd (44133-4458)
PHONE..................................440 582-3002
Fax: 440 582-3089
Skip Mayor, *Branch Mgr*
Kris Kamps, *Director*
EMP: 40 **Privately Held**
WEB: www.northroyalton.org
SIC: 1611 Highway & street maintenance
PA: City Of North Royalton
    14600 State Rd
    North Royalton OH 44133
    440 237-5686

(G-5271)
CITY OF PARMA
Also Called: Parma Service Garage
5680 Chevrolet Blvd (44130-1404)
PHONE..................................440 885-8983
Fax: 440 885-8988
Jack Sparks, *General Mgr*
EMP: 100
SQ FT: 41,762 **Privately Held**
WEB: www.parmajustice.net
SIC: 7521 Parking garage
PA: Parma City Of (Inc)
    6611 Ridge Rd
    Cleveland OH 44129
    440 885-8000

GEOGRAPHIC SECTION

Cleveland - Cuyahoga County (G-5295)

(G-5272)
CITY OF PARMA
Also Called: Ridgewood Golf Course
6505 Ridge Rd (44129-5528)
PHONE.................................440 885-8876
Fax: 440 885-8877
Tyler Good, *Superintendent*
Sarah Tilton, *Editor*
Howard Murphy, *Manager*
EMP: 50
SQ FT: 9,468 **Privately Held**
WEB: www.parmajustice.net
SIC: 7992 7997 Public golf courses; golf club, membership
PA: Parma City Of (Inc)
6611 Ridge Rd
Cleveland OH 44129
440 885-8000

(G-5273)
CITY OF PARMA
Senior Center
7001 W Ridgewood Dr (44129-6922)
PHONE.................................440 888-4514
Fax: 440 885-8817
Deborah Kelley, *VP Finance*
EMP: 28 **Privately Held**
WEB: www.parmajustice.net
SIC: 8322 Senior citizens' center or association
PA: Parma City Of (Inc)
6611 Ridge Rd
Cleveland OH 44129
440 885-8000

(G-5274)
CITY OF ROCKY RIVER
Also Called: Hamilton Ice Arena
21018 Hilliard Blvd (44116-3312)
PHONE.................................440 356-5656
Fax: 440 895-2624
Mike Patterson, *Manager*
EMP: 26 **Privately Held**
WEB: www.rrcity.com
SIC: 7999 Recreation center
PA: City Of Rocky River
21012 Hilliard Blvd
Rocky River OH 44116
440 331-0600

(G-5275)
CITY OF ROCKY RIVER
21012 Hilliard Blvd (44116-3312)
PHONE.................................440 356-5630
Fax: 440 895-0042
Dave Winterich, *Commissioner*
EMP: 50 **Privately Held**
WEB: www.rrcity.com
SIC: 8999 Personal services
PA: City Of Rocky River
21012 Hilliard Blvd
Rocky River OH 44116
440 331-0600

(G-5276)
CITY OF SOUTH EUCLID
Also Called: Victory Pool
1352 Victory Dr (44121-3629)
PHONE.................................216 291-3902
Peter Titas, *Manager*
EMP: 31 **Privately Held**
WEB: www.cityofsoutheuclid.com
SIC: 7999 Swimming pool, non-membership
PA: City Of South Euclid
1349 S Green Rd
South Euclid OH 44121
216 381-1214

(G-5277)
CITY OF WARRENSVILLE HEIGHTS
Also Called: Service Dept
19700 Miles Rd (44128-4116)
PHONE.................................216 587-1230
Albert C Williams, *Manager*
EMP: 30
SALES (est): 1.1MM **Privately Held**
SIC: 8399 Social service information exchange
PA: City Of Warrensville Heights
4301 Warrensville Ctr Rd
Warrensville Heights OH 44128
216 587-6500

(G-5278)
CITY OF WESTLAKE
Also Called: Westlake Fire Dept
3200 Crocker Rd (44145-6706)
PHONE.................................440 871-3441
Fax: 440 835-6463
Ronald Janicek, *Chief*
EMP: 45 **Privately Held**
SIC: 4119 Ambulance service
PA: City Of Westlake
27700 Hilliard Blvd
Cleveland OH 44145
440 871-3300

(G-5279)
CITY VIEW NURSING & REHAB LLC
Also Called: Cityview Nrsing Rhbltation Ctr
6606 Carnegie Ave (44103-4622)
PHONE.................................216 361-1414
Fax: 216 361-2822
Stephen L Rosedale, *President*
Charles R Stoltz, *Exec VP*
Ronald S Wilheim, *Exec VP*
Bill Glaspy, *Envir Svcs Dir*
David W Trimble, *CPA*
EMP: 225
SQ FT: 41,000
SALES: 9.1MM **Privately Held**
SIC: 8051 Convalescent home with continuous nursing care

(G-5280)
CIULLA SMITH & DALE LLP (PA)
6364 Pearl Rd Ste 4 (44130-3063)
PHONE.................................440 884-2036
Fax: 440 884-2048
Joseph Ciulla, *Partner*
Ted L Hlavka, *Partner*
Dennis R Horan, *Partner*
Robert A Huttner, *Partner*
Robert Mc Minn, *Partner*
EMP: 28
SQ FT: 5,500
SALES (est): 4.1MM **Privately Held**
SIC: 8721 Certified public accountant

(G-5281)
CIUNI & PANICHI INC
25201 Chagrin Blvd # 200 (44122-5683)
PHONE.................................216 831-7171
Fax: 216 631-3020
Charles Ciuni, *Managing Prtnr*
Charles Ciunini, *Managing Prtnr*
Vincent Panichi, *Senior Partner*
Jay A Bagdasarian, *Partner*
David A Linscott, *Partner*
EMP: 60
SQ FT: 20,000
SALES (est): 5.7MM **Privately Held**
WEB: www.cp-advisors.com
SIC: 8721 Certified public accountant

(G-5282)
CLARK SCHAEFER HACKETT & CO
600 Superior Ave E # 1300 (44114-2614)
PHONE.................................216 672-5252
Carl Coburn, *President*
EMP: 50
SALES (corp-wide): 40.4MM **Privately Held**
SIC: 8721 Certified public accountant
PA: Clark, Schaefer, Hackett & Co.
1 E 4th St Ste 1200
Cincinnati OH 45202
513 241-3111

(G-5283)
CLEAN HARBORS ENVMTL SVCS INC
Also Called: Milestone
2900 Broadway Ave (44115-3606)
PHONE.................................216 429-2402
Fax: 216 429-2713
Clayton Burtif, *Manager*
Laura Kravitz, *Associate*
EMP: 80
SQ FT: 14,616
SALES (corp-wide): 2.9B **Publicly Held**
SIC: 4953 Hazardous waste collection & disposal
HQ: Clean Harbors Environmental Services, Inc.
42 Longwater Dr
Norwell MA 02061
781 792-5000

(G-5284)
CLEAN HARBORS ENVMTL SVCS INC
2930 Independence Rd (44115-3616)
PHONE.................................216 429-2401
Michael Petkozich, *General Mgr*
Brian Overmyer, *Manager*
EMP: 78
SALES (corp-wide): 2.9B **Publicly Held**
SIC: 4953 Hazardous waste collection & disposal
HQ: Clean Harbors Environmental Services, Inc.
42 Longwater Dr
Norwell MA 02061
781 792-5000

(G-5285)
CLEARVIEW CLEANING CONTRACTORS
2140 Hamilton Ave (44114-1144)
P.O. Box 93631 (44101-5631)
PHONE.................................216 621-6688
Fax: 216 621-9676
Richard Matonis, *President*
EMP: 40
SALES (est): 1.4MM **Privately Held**
SIC: 7349 Window cleaning

(G-5286)
CLEVELAN CLINIC HLTH SYS W REG
5555 Transportation Blvd (44125-5371)
PHONE.................................216 518-3444
William Wick, *Branch Mgr*
EMP: 411
SALES (corp-wide): 8B **Privately Held**
SIC: 8741 Hospital management
HQ: Cleveland Clinic Health System-Western Region
18101 Lorain Ave
Cleveland OH 44111
216 476-7000

(G-5287)
CLEVELAN CLINIC HLTH SYS W REG (HQ)
18101 Lorain Ave (44111-5612)
PHONE.................................216 476-7000
Fred M Degrandis, *CEO*
Molly Mooney, *Editor*
Johanna Goldfarb, *Top Exec*
John Olach, *Project Mgr*
Nancy Karabinus, *Auditing Mgr*
EMP: 2800
SQ FT: 327,000
SALES (est): 108.1MM
SALES (corp-wide): 8B **Privately Held**
SIC: 8741 Hospital management
PA: The Cleveland Clinic Foundation
9500 Euclid Ave
Cleveland OH 44195
216 636-8335

(G-5288)
CLEVELAN CLINIC HLTH SYS W REG
Also Called: Hassler Medical Center
18200 Lorain Ave (44111-5605)
PHONE.................................216 476-7606
Fax: 216 476-7604
Stevens Flynn, *Director*
Fred J Orgensen, *Director*
Richard D Drake, *Oncology*
EMP: 40
SALES (corp-wide): 8B **Privately Held**
SIC: 8741 8011 Hospital management; general & family practice, physician/surgeon
HQ: Cleveland Clinic Health System-Western Region
18101 Lorain Ave
Cleveland OH 44111
216 476-7000

(G-5289)
CLEVELAN CLINIC HLTH SYS W REG
15531 Lorain Ave (44111-5539)
PHONE.................................216 476-7007
EMP: 63
SALES (corp-wide): 6.4B **Privately Held**
SIC: 8741 8011 Management Services Medical Doctor's Office
HQ: Cleveland Clinic Health System-Western Region
18101 Lorain Ave
Cleveland OH 44111
216 476-7000

(G-5290)
CLEVELAND ALL BREED TRNING CLB
210 Hayes Dr Ste B (44131-1094)
PHONE.................................216 398-1118
Debbie Sacerich, *Principal*
EMP: 100
SALES (est): 1MM **Privately Held**
WEB: www.cabtc.org
SIC: 0752 Training services, pet & animal specialties (not horses)

(G-5291)
CLEVELAND AUTO LIVERY INC
Also Called: A A Angelone
10802 Cedar Ave (44106-3032)
PHONE.................................216 421-1101
Fax: 216 421-1108
Peter T Angelone, *President*
EMP: 25
SQ FT: 7,200
SALES: 500K **Privately Held**
SIC: 4119 Limousine rental, with driver

(G-5292)
CLEVELAND BOTANICAL GARDEN (PA)
11030 East Blvd (44106-1706)
PHONE.................................216 721-1600
Fax: 216 721-2056
Natalie A Ronayne, *President*
Bisi Mikleus, *General Mgr*
Patricia Roberts, *Opers Staff*
Robert Rensel, *CFO*
Robert A Rensel, *CFO*
EMP: 30
SQ FT: 125,000
SALES: 4.8MM **Privately Held**
WEB: www.cbgarden.org
SIC: 8641 Civic associations

(G-5293)
CLEVELAND CHILD CARE INC (PA)
3274 W 58th St Fl 1 (44102-5681)
PHONE.................................216 631-3211
Fax: 216 631-3211
Gil Janke, *President*
William Mldasi, *Treasurer*
Patty Skiba, *Director*
EMP: 38
SQ FT: 5,000
SALES: 447.4K **Privately Held**
SIC: 8351 Child day care services

(G-5294)
CLEVELAND CHRISTIAN HOME INC
4614 Prospect Ave Ste 240 (44103-4365)
PHONE.................................216 671-0977
Fax: 216 688-4187
James M McCafferty, *CEO*
Katharine Johnson Vinciquerra, *Development*
Steve Letsky, *CFO*
Christopher Cassidy, *Financial Exec*
Mike Schere, *Hum Res Coord*
EMP: 112
SALES: 7.9MM **Privately Held**
SIC: 8322 8331 8361 Social service center; job training & vocational rehabilitation services; residential care

(G-5295)
CLEVELAND CLINIC COLE EYE INST
9500 Euclid Ave (44195-0001)
PHONE.................................216 444-4508
Toby Cosgrove, *CEO*

Cleveland - Cuyahoga County (G-5296)

Courtenay Moore, *Urology*
EMP: 26
SALES (est): 5.6MM **Privately Held**
SIC: 8011 Clinic, operated by physicians

(G-5296)
CLEVELAND CLINIC FOUNDATION (PA)
Also Called: Cleveland Clinic Health System
9500 Euclid Ave (44195-0002)
PHONE..................216 636-8335
Fax: 216 444-5331
Delos M Cosgrove, *CEO*
Janet Gulley, *President*
Ray Borazanian, *Editor*
Wiliams Peacock, *COO*
Tim Gibbons, *Vice Pres*
▲ **EMP:** 13500
SALES: 8B **Privately Held**
SIC: 8062 8011 8741 General medical & surgical hospitals; medical centers; management services

(G-5297)
CLEVELAND CLINIC FOUNDATION
Also Called: Council of Child & Adoles
9500 Euclid Ave Ste P57 (44195-0002)
PHONE..................216 444-2820
Tom Schiltz, *Branch Mgr*
Georgina Rodgers,
EMP: 82
SALES (corp-wide): 8B **Privately Held**
SIC: 6733 8062 Trusts; general medical & surgical hospitals
PA: The Cleveland Clinic Foundation
9500 Euclid Ave
Cleveland OH 44195
216 636-8335

(G-5298)
CLEVELAND CLINIC FOUNDATION
Also Called: Alcohol and Drug Recovery Ctr
9500 Euclid Ave P-47 (44195-0002)
PHONE..................216 445-8585
Fax: 216 445-5747
Bruce Marich, *Prdtn Mgr*
Rita Hanuschock, *Manager*
EMP: 30
SALES (corp-wide): 8B **Privately Held**
SIC: 6733 Trusts
PA: The Cleveland Clinic Foundation
9500 Euclid Ave
Cleveland OH 44195
216 636-8335

(G-5299)
CLEVELAND CLINIC FOUNDATION
Also Called: Cleveland Clnic HSP Fincl Dept
9500 Euclid Ave (44195-0002)
P.O. Box 931058 (44193-1384)
PHONE..................216 444-5000
Nancy S Foldvary, *Director*
Jackie Puntel, *Director*
Frank Lauderman, *Administration*
Viktoria Luppa, *Nurse Practr*
EMP: 300
SALES (corp-wide): 8B **Privately Held**
SIC: 6733 7389 Trusts; financial services
PA: The Cleveland Clinic Foundation
9500 Euclid Ave
Cleveland OH 44195
216 636-8335

(G-5300)
CLEVELAND CLINIC FOUNDATION
2111 E 96th St (44106-2917)
PHONE..................800 223-2273
EMP: 2554
SALES (corp-wide): 8B **Privately Held**
SIC: 8062 General medical & surgical hospitals
PA: The Cleveland Clinic Foundation
9500 Euclid Ave
Cleveland OH 44195
216 636-8335

(G-5301)
CLEVELAND CLINIC FOUNDATION
10300 Carnegie Ave (44106-2132)
PHONE..................216 444-5755

Darryl East, *Marketing Staff*
Nancy Paxton, *Manager*
Florence Stone, *Manager*
Roseanna Moore, *Supervisor*
Richard Johnson, *Programmer Anys*
EMP: 2554
SALES (corp-wide): 8B **Privately Held**
SIC: 8062 General medical & surgical hospitals
PA: The Cleveland Clinic Foundation
9500 Euclid Ave
Cleveland OH 44195
216 636-8335

(G-5302)
CLEVELAND CLINIC FOUNDATION
Also Called: Cleveland Clnic Lyndhrst Cmpus
1950 Richmond Rd (44124-3719)
PHONE..................216 448-4325
Scarlet Soriano, *Director*
Charlie Colosky, *Director*
Brian Jones, *Analyst*
EMP: 300
SALES (corp-wide): 8B **Privately Held**
SIC: 8011 Medical centers; primary care medical clinic
PA: The Cleveland Clinic Foundation
9500 Euclid Ave
Cleveland OH 44195
216 636-8335

(G-5303)
CLEVELAND CLINIC FOUNDATION
6801 Brecksville Rd # 10 (44131-5058)
PHONE..................216 444-2200
Mike Berk, *Manager*
Ruth Farrell, *Director*
Aaron Fleischman, *Co-Director*
Joan Vinski,
EMP: 85
SALES (corp-wide): 8B **Privately Held**
SIC: 6733 Trusts
PA: The Cleveland Clinic Foundation
9500 Euclid Ave
Cleveland OH 44195
216 636-8335

(G-5304)
CLEVELAND CLINIC FOUNDATION
Also Called: Cleveland Clinic Coordinating
9500 Euclid Ave (44195-0002)
PHONE..................216 445-6439
EMP: 85
SALES (corp-wide): 6.4B **Privately Held**
SIC: 6733 Trust Management
PA: The Cleveland Clinic Foundation
9500 Euclid Ave
Cleveland OH 44195
216 636-8335

(G-5305)
CLEVELAND CLINIC FOUNDATION
Also Called: Cleveland Clinic Innovations
10000 Cedar Ave Ste 6 (44106-2119)
PHONE..................216 444-5757
Austriaco Michael, *Manager*
Gary Fingerhut, *Exec Dir*
EMP: 85
SALES (corp-wide): 8B **Privately Held**
SIC: 8062 General medical & surgical hospitals
PA: The Cleveland Clinic Foundation
9500 Euclid Ave
Cleveland OH 44195
216 636-8335

(G-5306)
CLEVELAND CLINIC FOUNDATION
9500 Euclid Ave (44195-0002)
PHONE..................216 444-2200
Fax: 216 444-7360
Gary Fingerhut, *General Mgr*
Britten King, *Senior VP*
Colleen Rouse, *QA Dir*
John Peterson, *Research*
Steve Glass, *CFO*
EMP: 3544
SALES (corp-wide): 8B **Privately Held**
SIC: 8062 General medical & surgical hospitals

PA: The Cleveland Clinic Foundation
9500 Euclid Ave
Cleveland OH 44195
216 636-8335

(G-5307)
CLEVELAND CLINIC HEALTH SYSTEM
Also Called: Hillcrest Hospital
6780 Mayfield Rd (44124-2203)
PHONE..................440 449-4500
Marilyn Jaksic, *Purchasing*
Ross Federico, *Human Res Dir*
Tyler Katz, *Obstetrician*
Dennis L Laffay, *Pathologist*
Samuel V Calabrese, *Director*
EMP: 45
SALES (corp-wide): 8B **Privately Held**
SIC: 8062 General medical & surgical hospitals
HQ: Cleveland Clinic Health System-East Region
6803 Mayfield Rd Ste 500
Cleveland OH 44124
440 312-6010

(G-5308)
CLEVELAND CLINIC HEALTH SYSTEM
Also Called: Euclid Hospital
18901 Lake Shore Blvd (44119-1078)
PHONE..................216 692-7555
Fax: 216 692-7555
Del Stanback, *Office Mgr*
Timothy Rhudy, *Acupuncture*
William R Welches, *Manager*
Pasha Saeed, *Anesthesiology*
Warren Rock, *Mng Officer*
EMP: 25
SALES (corp-wide): 8B **Privately Held**
SIC: 8062 General medical & surgical hospitals
HQ: Cleveland Clinic Health System-East Region
6803 Mayfield Rd Ste 500
Cleveland OH 44124
440 312-6010

(G-5309)
CLEVELAND CLINIC LERNER COLLEG
9500 Euclid Ave (44195-0001)
PHONE..................216 445-3853
Jacqueline Whatley, *Principal*
Peter Imrey, *Research*
Penny Houghtaling, *Manager*
Moses Anabila, *Programmer Anys*
Wu Daniel, *Programmer Anys*
EMP: 99
SALES: 500K **Privately Held**
SIC: 8062 8221 Hospital, medical school affiliation; colleges universities & professional schools

(G-5310)
CLEVELAND CORPORATE SVCS INC
Also Called: Smart Ed Services
2929 Clarkson Rd (44118-2810)
PHONE..................216 397-1492
Fax: 216 432-0044
Gregory Peck, *President*
Chris Sliwinski, *Opers Mgr*
Pamela Fioritto, *Marketing Staff*
Tiffany Garzon, *Manager*
Kristi Peters, *Director*
EMP: 106
SQ FT: 32,000
SALES: 41.3MM **Privately Held**
WEB: www.teachsmart.com
SIC: 5999 7359 Audio-visual equipment & supplies; audio-visual equipment & supply rental

(G-5311)
CLEVELAND CROWNE PLAZA AIRPORT
7230 Engle Rd (44130-3427)
PHONE..................440 243-4040
Fax: 440 243-3178
Scott Klukas, *Manager*
EMP: 41
SALES (est): 995.1K **Privately Held**
SIC: 7011 5812 Hotels; eating places

(G-5312)
CLEVELAND EAST HOTEL LLC
Also Called: Marriott
26300 Harvard Rd (44122-6146)
PHONE..................216 378-9191
Fax: 216 378-9292
Rachel Oliver, *Office Mgr*
Kenny Didier, *Manager*
EMP: 99
SQ FT: 64,509
SALES (est): 8.6MM **Privately Held**
SIC: 7011 Hotels & motels

(G-5313)
CLEVELAND EXPRESS TRCKG CO INC
3091 Rockefeller Ave (44115-3611)
PHONE..................216 348-0922
Fax: 216 348-0999
John Lamb, *Ch of Bd*
Jeb Black, *Vice Pres*
Jeff Darkow, *Treasurer*
Nick Loparo, *Marketing Staff*
Mike Marino, *Manager*
EMP: 75
SQ FT: 20,000
SALES: 4.8MM **Privately Held**
WEB: www.cetruck.com
SIC: 4214 4213 Local trucking with storage; trucking, except local

(G-5314)
CLEVELAND F E S CENTER
10701 East Blvd (44106-1702)
PHONE..................216 231-3257
Paul P Pechkan, *CEO*
Merien Washington, *Purch Agent*
Kevin Kilgore, *Research*
Dennis Johnson, *Engineer*
Mary Buckett, *Corp Comm Staff*
EMP: 75
SALES (est): 3.7MM **Privately Held**
SIC: 8731 Commercial physical research

(G-5315)
CLEVELAND FOUNDATION
1422 Euclid Ave Ste 1300 (44115-2063)
PHONE..................216 861-3810
Fax: 216 861-1729
Ronald B Richard, *CEO*
James A Ratner, *Principal*
Charles P Bolton, *Chairman*
Sue Krey, *COO*
Robert E Eckardt, *Exec VP*
EMP: 75
SQ FT: 26,000
SALES: 87.1MM **Privately Held**
SIC: 6732 Charitable trust management; educational trust management

(G-5316)
CLEVELAND GLASS BLOCK INC (PA)
Also Called: Mid America Glass Block
4566 E 71st St (44105-5604)
PHONE..................216 531-6363
Michael Foti, *President*
Frank Foti, *Corp Secy*
Ryan Temple, *Property Mgr*
C Foti, *Manager*
Rosaleen P Rose, *Info Tech Mgr*
▼ **EMP:** 46
SQ FT: 15,500
SALES (est): 11.7MM **Privately Held**
WEB: www.clevelandglassblock.com
SIC: 5231 5039 Glass; glass construction materials

(G-5317)
CLEVELAND HEARTLAB INC
6701 Carnegie Ave Ste 500 (44103-4623)
PHONE..................866 358-9828
Jake Orville, *President*
Darren Hudach, *COO*
Paul Haber, *Vice Pres*
Scott Purvis, *Vice Pres*
Deborah H Sun, *Vice Pres*
▼ **EMP:** 100
SQ FT: 38,000
SALES (est): 13.3MM
SALES (corp-wide): 7.7B **Publicly Held**
SIC: 8071 Medical laboratories

PA: Quest Diagnostics Incorporated
500 Plaza Dr Ste G
Secaucus NJ 07094
973 520-2700

(G-5318)
CLEVELAND HEIGHTS HIGHSCHOOL
Also Called: Cleveland Heights Gospel Choir
3638 Mount Laurel Rd (44121-1329)
PHONE..........................216 691-5452
Sandra Dixon, Director
EMP: 25 EST: 2010
SALES (est): 130.5K Privately Held
SIC: 8641 Singing society

(G-5319)
CLEVELAND HTS TIGERS YOUTH SPO
3686 Berkeley Rd (44118-1970)
PHONE..........................216 906-4168
Michael Payne, President
Branella Basit, Vice Pres
Cedric Marshall, Vice Pres
Lakesha Farrow, Bd of Directors
Charnita Hairston, Bd of Directors
EMP: 40 EST: 2014
SALES (est): 489.6K Privately Held
SIC: 7997 Membership sports & recreation clubs

(G-5320)
CLEVELAND HUNGARIAN HERITG SOC
Also Called: CLEVELAND HUNGARIAN HERITAGE M
1301 E 9th St Ste 2400 (44114-1888)
P.O. Box 24134 (44124-0134)
PHONE..........................216 523-3900
Andrea Meszaros, President
Otto Friedrich, Exec Dir
EMP: 50
SALES: 69.3K Privately Held
SIC: 8412 Museum

(G-5321)
CLEVELAND INDIANS BASEBALL COM (PA)
2401 Ontario St (44115-4003)
PHONE..........................216 420-4487
Fax: 216 420-4358
Paul J Dolan, CEO
Mark Shapiro, President
Lawrence J Dolan, Owner
Chris Antonetti, Exec VP
Valerie Arcuri, Vice Pres
EMP: 100
SQ FT: 4,000
SALES (est): 17.8MM Privately Held
SIC: 7941 Baseball club, professional & semi-professional

(G-5322)
CLEVELAND JEWISH FEDERATION
25701 Science Park Dr (44122-7302)
PHONE..........................216 593-2900
Fax: 216 861-1230
Steve Hoffman, President
Jennifer Schwarz, General Mgr
E Joseph, Principal
Howard Wolf, Business Mgr
Paul Feinberg, Counsel
EMP: 130
SQ FT: 20,000
SALES: 93.2MM Privately Held
WEB: www.jctcleve.net
SIC: 8399 Fund raising organization, non-fee basis

(G-5323)
CLEVELAND JOB CORPS CENTER
13421 Coit Rd (44110-2269)
PHONE..........................216 541-2500
Ramon Serrato, President
Tom Fitzwater, Principal
Ace Thomas, Supervisor
EMP: 160
SALES (est): 13MM Privately Held
SIC: 7361 Employment agencies

(G-5324)
CLEVELAND MARBLE MOSAIC CO (PA)
4595 Hinckley Indus Pkwy (44109-6099)
PHONE..........................216 749-2840
Fax: 216 749-2226
Robert J Zavagno Jr, President
Jim Small, Regional Mgr
Raymond L Zavagno, Vice Pres
Edward Drobnick, Project Mgr
Matt Kelly, Project Mgr
▲ EMP: 246
SQ FT: 26,800
SALES (est): 31.7MM Privately Held
WEB: www.clevelandmarble.com
SIC: 1743 1741 Marble installation, interior; tile installation, ceramic; terrazzo work; marble masonry, exterior construction; stone masonry

(G-5325)
CLEVELAND METRO BAR ASSN
1301 E 9th St (44114-1804)
PHONE..........................216 696-3525
Fax: 216 696-2129
Larkin Chenault, President
Alla Leydiker, CFO
L Chenault, Exec Dir
EMP: 30
SALES: 3.1MM Privately Held
SIC: 8111 Legal services

(G-5326)
CLEVELAND METROPARKS
Also Called: Cleveland Metroparks Zoo
3900 Wildlife Way (44109-3132)
PHONE..........................216 661-6500
Fax: 216 661-3312
Greg Headley, Safety Mgr
B Shawhan, Park Mgr
Gayle Albers, Manager
Trisha Vaughn, Manager
Steve Taylor, Director
EMP: 110
SALES (corp-wide): 57.3MM Privately Held
WEB: www.clemetparks.com
SIC: 8422 7299 Botanical garden; banquet hall facilities
PA: Cleveland Metroparks
4101 Fulton Pkwy
Cleveland OH 44144
216 635-3200

(G-5327)
CLEVELAND METROPARKS
4600 Valley Pkwy (44126-2853)
PHONE..........................440 331-5530
EMP: 60
SALES (corp-wide): 57.3MM Privately Held
SIC: 7999 Recreation services
PA: Cleveland Metroparks
4101 Fulton Pkwy
Cleveland OH 44144
216 635-3200

(G-5328)
CLEVELAND METROPARKS (PA)
4101 Fulton Pkwy (44144-1923)
PHONE..........................216 635-3200
Fax: 216 351-2584
Brian Zimmerman, CEO
Debra K Berry, Vice Pres
David Whitehead, Vice Pres
Steven Dice, Opers Staff
Becky Eicher, Purch Agent
EMP: 292
SQ FT: 9,000
SALES (est): 57.3MM Privately Held
WEB: www.clemetparks.com
SIC: 7999 Recreation services

(G-5329)
CLEVELAND METROPARKS
Also Called: Rainforest At Zoo
3900 Wildlife Way (44109-3132)
PHONE..........................216 661-6500
Steve Taylor, Director
EMP: 110
SALES (corp-wide): 57.3MM Privately Held
WEB: www.clemetparks.com
SIC: 8422 Arboreta & botanical or zoological gardens

(G-5330)
CLEVELAND METROPARKS
Also Called: Shawnee Hills Golf Course
18753 Egbert Rd (44146-4239)
PHONE..........................440 232-7184
Fax: 440 232-7250
Linda Janson, Manager
EMP: 60
SQ FT: 5,488
SALES (corp-wide): 57.3MM Privately Held
WEB: www.clemetparks.com
SIC: 7992 Public golf courses
PA: Cleveland Metroparks
4101 Fulton Pkwy
Cleveland OH 44144
216 635-3200

(G-5331)
CLEVELAND METROPARKS
Also Called: Big Mat Golf Course
4811 Valley Pkwy (44126-2846)
PHONE..........................440 331-1070
Fax: 440 356-4593
Mike Raby, Principal
EMP: 38
SALES (corp-wide): 57.3MM Privately Held
SIC: 7992 Public golf courses
PA: Cleveland Metroparks
4101 Fulton Pkwy
Cleveland OH 44144
216 635-3200

(G-5332)
CLEVELAND MUNICIPAL SCHOOL DST
Also Called: Ridge Road Depot
3832 Ridge Rd (44144-1112)
PHONE..........................216 634-7005
Mark Cegelski, Branch Mgr
Martha Verde, Teacher
EMP: 300
SALES (corp-wide): 854.1MM Privately Held
WEB: www.cmsdnet.net
SIC: 4151 School buses
PA: Cleveland Municipal School District
1111 Superior Ave E # 1800
Cleveland OH 44114
216 838-0000

(G-5333)
CLEVELAND MUNICIPAL SCHOOL DST
Also Called: Lake Center Depot
870 E 79th St (44103-1820)
PHONE..........................216 432-4600
Mark Cegelski, Branch Mgr
Carlotta Cummings, Assistant
EMP: 360
SALES (corp-wide): 854.1MM Privately Held
WEB: www.cmsdnet.net
SIC: 4151 School buses
PA: Cleveland Municipal School District
1111 Superior Ave E # 1800
Cleveland OH 44114
216 838-0000

(G-5334)
CLEVELAND MUNICIPAL SCHOOL DST
Also Called: Rhodes Hs-Sch of Leadership
5100 Biddulph Ave (44144-3802)
PHONE..........................216 459-4200
Fax: 216 459-3133
Charlene Hilliard, Principal
Kathleen Freilino, Principal
Cynthia Anzalone-Fox, Librarian
Brian K Evans, Assistant
Elaine Gollate, Assistant
EMP: 85
SALES (corp-wide): 854.1MM Privately Held
WEB: www.cmsdnet.net
SIC: 8641 8222 8221 8211 Environmental protection organization; technical institute; professional schools; public adult education school

(G-5335)
CLEVELAND MUNICIPAL SCHOOL DST (PA)
Also Called: CLEVELAND METROPOLITAN SCHOOL
1111 Superior Ave E # 1800 (44114-2500)
PHONE..........................216 838-0000
Fax: 216 574-8168
Eric Gordon, CEO
Denise W Link, Ch of Bd
Eric S Gordon, Superintendent
Patrick Zohn, COO
Angie Hartzell, Counsel
EMP: 350 EST: 2012
SQ FT: 70,000
SALES: 854.1MM Privately Held
WEB: www.cmsdnet.net
SIC: 8211 8399 Public elementary & secondary schools; advocacy group

(G-5336)
CLEVELAND MUNICIPAL SCHOOL DST
Also Called: New Tech West High School
11801 Worthington Ave (44111-5064)
PHONE..........................216 838-8700
Shaunamichelle Leonard, Principal
EMP: 32
SALES (corp-wide): 854.1MM Privately Held
SIC: 8211 8399 Public elementary & secondary schools; advocacy group
PA: Cleveland Municipal School District
1111 Superior Ave E # 1800
Cleveland OH 44114
216 838-0000

(G-5337)
CLEVELAND MUNICIPAL SCHOOL DST
Also Called: Children's Aid Society
10427 Detroit Ave (44102-1645)
PHONE..........................216 521-6511
Fax: 216 521-6006
Jennifer Blumhagen, CEO
EMP: 75
SQ FT: 44,926
SALES (corp-wide): 854.1MM Privately Held
WEB: www.cmsdnet.net
SIC: 8322 Children's aid society
PA: Cleveland Municipal School District
1111 Superior Ave E # 1800
Cleveland OH 44114
216 838-0000

(G-5338)
CLEVELAND MUNICIPAL SCHOOL DST
Also Called: Jones Home, The
3518 W 25th St (44109-1951)
PHONE..........................216 459-9818
Fax: 216 459-9821
Harriet Freeman, Branch Mgr
EMP: 150
SALES (corp-wide): 854.1MM Privately Held
WEB: www.cmsdnet.net
SIC: 8361 Residential care
PA: Cleveland Municipal School District
1111 Superior Ave E # 1800
Cleveland OH 44114
216 838-0000

(G-5339)
CLEVELAND MUS SCHL SETTLEMENT
11125 Magnolia Dr (44106-1813)
PHONE..........................216 421-5806
Fax: 216 421-5813
Charles D Lawrence, President
Rachel Bernstein, Sales Mgr
M Kheitlinger, Chief Mktg Ofcr
Lynn B Johnson, Mktg Dir
Ella Karasik, Marketing Mgr
EMP: 220
SQ FT: 800,000

Cleveland - Cuyahoga County (G-5340)

GEOGRAPHIC SECTION

SALES: 5MM **Privately Held**
WEB: www.thecmss.org
SIC: 8299 8351 7911 Art school, except commercial; child day care services; dance studios, schools & halls

(G-5340)
CLEVELAND PRETERM
12000 Shaker Blvd (44120-1922)
PHONE 216 991-4577
Chrisse France, *Exec Dir*
EMP: 40
SQ FT: 15,000
SALES: 3.9MM **Privately Held**
WEB: www.preterm.org
SIC: 8093 8011 Abortion clinic; birth control clinic; offices & clinics of medical doctors

(G-5341)
CLEVELAND RACQUET CLUB INC
29825 Chagrin Blvd (44124-5797)
PHONE 216 831-2155
Fax: 216 831-2155
Michael Schumann, *President*
George Champman, *Vice Pres*
Oliver Emerson, *Treasurer*
Julie Konrad, *Sales Staff*
Wendi Crites, *Manager*
EMP: 75 **EST:** 1968
SQ FT: 50,000
SALES: 4.9MM **Privately Held**
WEB: www.clevelandracquet.com
SIC: 7997 5812 Tennis club, membership; swimming club, membership; squash club, membership; racquetball club, membership; eating places

(G-5342)
CLEVELAND REAL ESTATE PARTNERS
1801 E 9th St Ste 1700 (44114-3187)
PHONE 216 623-1600
Fax: 216 696-8590
Thomas W Adler, *Ch of Bd*
Eric Friedman, *Principal*
Adam Fishman, *Vice Pres*
George Hutchinson, *Vice Pres*
Steven Joseph, *Vice Pres*
EMP: 30
SQ FT: 3,000
SALES (est): 1.2MM **Privately Held**
SIC: 6531 Real estate agents & managers; real estate managers; rental agent, real estate

(G-5343)
CLEVELAND RESEARCH COMPANY LLC
1375 E 9th St Ste 2700 (44114-1795)
PHONE 216 649-7250
Corey Paquette, *Senior VP*
Scott Cielinski, *Research*
Rob Cottrell, *Research*
Sean Muir, *Research*
Rob Stuyck, *Research*
EMP: 34
SALES (est): 9.7MM **Privately Held**
SIC: 6282 Investment research

(G-5344)
CLEVELAND REST OPER LTD PARTNR
6000 Fredom Sq Dr Ste 280 (44131)
PHONE 216 328-1121
John Climaco, *Partner*
Mike Climaco, *Partner*
Ross Farro, *General Ptnr*
EMP: 180
SALES (est): 2.1MM **Privately Held**
SIC: 5812 6794 Eating places; patent owners & lessors

(G-5345)
CLEVELAND S HOSPITALITY LLC
Also Called: Doubletree Hotel
6200 Quarry Ln (44131-2218)
PHONE 216 447-1300
Jock Litras, *General Mgr*
EMP: 49
SQ FT: 59,489
SALES (est): 4MM **Privately Held**
SIC: 7011 Hotels & motels

(G-5346)
CLEVELAND SKATING CLUB
2500 Kemper Rd (44120-1299)
PHONE 216 791-2800
Fax: 216 791-9501
Bryan Johnson, *General Mgr*
Fred Barr, *Controller*
Eric Toth, *Controller*
Sheila Henry, *Bookkeeper*
Mike Sullivan,
EMP: 125
SQ FT: 60,000
SALES (est): 5.6MM **Privately Held**
WEB: www.clevelandskatingclub.org
SIC: 7997 Country club, membership

(G-5347)
CLEVELAND SOC FOR THE BLIND
Also Called: Cleveland Sight Center
1909 E 101st St (44106-4110)
P.O. Box 1988 (44106-0188)
PHONE 216 791-8118
Fax: 216 791-1101
Andrew L Sikorovsky, *Chairman*
Karen Assink, *Vice Chairman*
Christopher Gruber, *Facilities Mgr*
Bobbie Christopher, *Purch Agent*
Kevin Krencisz, *CFO*
EMP: 140
SQ FT: 100,000
SALES: 9.9MM **Privately Held**
SIC: 8322 5441 Association for the handicapped; rehabilitation services; confectionery produced for direct sale on the premises

(G-5348)
CLEVELAND STATE UNIVERSITY
Computer Science Information
1860 E 18th St Rm 344 (44114-3602)
PHONE 216 687-3786
Fax: 216 687-9354
Steven Adams, *Technology*
Santos Misra, *Director*
Toshinori Munakata, *Professor*
EMP: 25
SALES (corp-wide): 204.4MM **Privately Held**
WEB: www.csuohio.edu
SIC: 7374 8221 Data processing & preparation; university
PA: Cleveland State University
2121 Euclid Ave
Cleveland OH 44115
216 687-2000

(G-5349)
CLEVELAND SYSCO INC (HQ)
4747 Grayton Rd (44135-2300)
P.O. Box 94570 (44101-4570)
PHONE 216 201-3000
Fax: 216 201-3511
Bill Delaney, *CEO*
Bill Day, *Exec VP*
Chuck Staes, *Senior VP*
Mark Kleiman, *VP Sls/Mktg*
Roger Wioder, *Controller*
EMP: 640
SQ FT: 990
SALES (est): 232.4MM
SALES (corp-wide): 55.3B **Publicly Held**
WEB: www.syscocleveland.com
SIC: 5149 Specialty food items
PA: Sysco Corporation
1390 Enclave Pkwy
Houston TX 77077
281 584-1390

(G-5350)
CLEVELAND TANK & SUPPLY INC
6560 Juniata Ave (44103-1614)
PHONE 216 771-8265
Fax: 216 771-8239
Jack Sattler, *President*
EMP: 28
SQ FT: 10,000
SALES (est): 12.3MM **Privately Held**
WEB: www.clevelandtank.com
SIC: 5084 Tanks, storage

(G-5351)
CLEVELAND TEACHERS UNION INC
1228 Euclid Ave Ste 1100 (44115-1846)
PHONE 216 861-7676
Fax: 216 861-4113
Richard Decolibus, *President*
Robert J Martin, *CPA*
EMP: 40
SQ FT: 20,000
SALES: 3.3MM **Privately Held**
SIC: 8631 8111 Labor union; legal services

(G-5352)
CLEVELAND THERMAL LLC
1921 Hamilton Ave (44114-1112)
PHONE 216 241-3636
Marc G Divis, *President*
Donald J Hoffman, *Chairman*
James R Kavalec, *Vice Pres*
Linda S Atkins, *CFO*
Linda Atkins, *CFO*
EMP: 46
SQ FT: 4,000
SALES (est): 10.3MM **Privately Held**
WEB: www.clevelandthermal.com
SIC: 4961 Steam supply systems, including geothermal

(G-5353)
CLEVELAND VA MEDICAL RESEARCH
10701 East Blvd (44106-1702)
PHONE 216 791-2300
Magdalena Taracila, *Manager*
Medhat O Hassan, *Pathologist*
Susan Fuehrer, *CIO*
Gail Burns, *Exec Dir*
Eric Konicki, *Director*
EMP: 25
SALES: 1.7MM **Privately Held**
SIC: 8733 Medical research

(G-5354)
CLEVELAND WATER DEPARTMENT
5953 Deering Ave (44130-2306)
PHONE 216 664-3168
Dick Kmetz, *Principal*
Rich Papp, *Plant Mgr*
Brian Finks, *Manager*
Bernardo Garcia, *Commissioner*
Kenitha Sturdivant, *Info Tech Dir*
EMP: 1200
SALES (est): 76.7MM **Privately Held**
SIC: 4941 Water supply

(G-5355)
CLEVELAND WORKS RAILWAY CO
3175 Independence Rd (44105-1045)
PHONE 216 429-7267
Ted Shank, *Manager*
Lonnie Short, *Supervisor*
EMP: 78
SALES (est): 3.2MM **Privately Held**
SIC: 4011 Railroads, line-haul operating

(G-5356)
CLEVELAND YACHTING CLUB INC
200 Yacht Club Dr (44116-1736)
PHONE 440 333-1155
Fax: 440 333-3136
John Spies, *General Mgr*
Diane May, *Controller*
Clark Gill, *Controller*
Brian O"malley, *Manager*
Joe Rondini, *Manager*
EMP: 60
SQ FT: 25,000
SALES: 2.8MM **Privately Held**
WEB: www.cycrr.org
SIC: 7997 Yacht club, membership

(G-5357)
CLEVELAND-CLIFFS INC (PA)
200 Public Sq Ste 3300 (44114-2315)
PHONE 216 694-5700
Lourenco Goncalves, *Ch of Bd*
Kristy Dubitsky, *General Mgr*
Jon Lester, *General Mgr*
Stormy McCoy, *Superintendent*
P Kelly Tompkins, *COO*
◆ **EMP:** 76
SALES: 2.3B **Publicly Held**
WEB: www.cliffsnaturalresources.com
SIC: 1011 Iron ore mining; iron ore pelletizing

(G-5358)
CLEVELND CLNC HLTH SYSTM EAST
Also Called: Huron School of Nursing
13951 Terrace Rd (44112-4308)
PHONE 216 761-3300
Fax: 216 761-7541
Kathleen Mitchell, *President*
Michael Oconnell, *COO*
Pasha Saeed, *Med Doctor*
Carol Peltz, *Manager*
Pat Dickinson, *Telecom Exec*
EMP: 25
SALES (corp-wide): 8B **Privately Held**
SIC: 8062 General medical & surgical hospitals
HQ: Cleveland Clinic Health System-East Region
6803 Mayfield Rd Ste 500
Cleveland OH 44124
440 312-6010

(G-5359)
CLEVELND MUSEUM OF NATURAL HIS
1 Wade Oval Dr (44106-1701)
PHONE 216 231-4600
Fax: 216 231-5919
Douglass Stelzer, *CFO*
Dawn Shaffer, *Human Res Mgr*
Robert Bartolotta, *Manager*
Joe Dellanno, *Co-Mgr*
Bonnie Cummings, *Director*
▲ **EMP:** 90
SQ FT: 225,000
SALES: 25.8MM **Privately Held**
WEB: www.cmnh.org
SIC: 8412 Museum

(G-5360)
CLIFFS CLEVELAND FOUNDATION
1100 Superior Ave E # 1500 (44114-2530)
PHONE 216 694-5700
John Brinzo, *Principal*
E C Dowling, *Senior VP*
Steven A Elmquist, *Vice Pres*
Gerald P Kohanski, *Purch Agent*
William C Boor, *Marketing Staff*
EMP: 42
SALES: 3MM **Privately Held**
SIC: 8699 Charitable organization

(G-5361)
CLIFFS MINNESOTA MINERALS CO
1100 Superior Ave E (44114-2530)
PHONE 216 694-5700
W R Calfee, *President*
EMP: 511
SQ FT: 65,000
SALES (est): 9.1MM
SALES (corp-wide): 2.3B **Publicly Held**
SIC: 1011 4931 Iron ore mining; electric & other services combined
PA: Cleveland-Cliffs Inc.
200 Public Sq Ste 3300
Cleveland OH 44114
216 694-5700

(G-5362)
CLIFFS RESOURCES INC (HQ)
200 Public Sq Ste 200 (44114-2301)
PHONE 216 694-5700
J S Brinzo, *CEO*
James A Trethewey, *President*
Clifford T Smith, *Senior VP*
Cynthia B Bezik, *CFO*
Ronald C Cambre, *Director*
EMP: 160
SQ FT: 65,000
SALES (est): 21.3MM
SALES (corp-wide): 2.3B **Publicly Held**
SIC: 4011 Railroads, line-haul operating
PA: Cleveland-Cliffs Inc.
200 Public Sq Ste 3300
Cleveland OH 44114
216 694-5700

GEOGRAPHIC SECTION
Cleveland - Cuyahoga County (G-5384)

(G-5363)
CLIMACO LEFKWTZ PECA WLCOX & (PA)
55 Public Sq Ste 1950 (44113-1972)
PHONE..................216 621-8484
John R Climaco, *Partner*
EMP: 100
SQ FT: 40,000
SALES (est): 8.7MM **Privately Held**
WEB: www.climacolaw.com
SIC: 8111 General practice law office

(G-5364)
CLINIC CARE INC
Also Called: Cleveland Clinic Guesthouse
9601 Euclid Ave (44106-4700)
PHONE..................216 707-4200
Fax: 216 707-4221
Kathy Gransford, *Manager*
EMP: 52
SALES (corp-wide): 19.4MM **Privately Held**
SIC: 7011 Hotels & motels
PA: Clinic Care Inc.
    6100 W Creek Rd Ste 25
    Cleveland OH 44131
    216 986-2680

(G-5365)
CLOUDROUTE LLC
59 Alpha Park (44143-2202)
PHONE..................216 373-4601
Andre Temnorod, *President*
Eugene Blumin, *CFO*
Douglas Dilillo, *Manager*
Matthew Sharp, *Manager*
EMP: 25
SALES (est): 1MM **Privately Held**
SIC: 7371 Computer software development

(G-5366)
CLOVERLEAF BOWLING CENTER INC
Also Called: Cloverleaf Lanes
5619 Brecksville Rd (44131-1510)
PHONE..................216 524-4833
Fax: 216 524-4833
Joan Spehar, *President*
Michael Copalian, *Corp Secy*
EMP: 34
SQ FT: 45,000
SALES (est): 1.1MM **Privately Held**
WEB: www.bowlcloverleaflanes.com
SIC: 7933 7999 Ten pin center; billiard parlor

(G-5367)
CLUBCORP USA INC
Also Called: Shoreby Club
40 Shoreby Dr (44108-1191)
PHONE..................216 851-2582
Randy Owoc, *Manager*
EMP: 30
SQ FT: 10,368
SALES (corp-wide): 433.7MM **Privately Held**
WEB: www.remington-gc.com
SIC: 7997 Country club, membership
HQ: Clubcorp Usa, Inc.
    3030 Lyndon B Johnson Fwy
    Dallas TX 75234
    972 243-6191

(G-5368)
CLUBHOUSE PUB N GRUB
Also Called: Clubhouse, The
6365 Pearl Rd (44130-3077)
PHONE..................440 884-2582
Roberta House Peschock, *President*
Charles Belsito, *Corp Secy*
EMP: 25
SALES (est): 900K **Privately Held**
WEB: www.cbdecorating.com
SIC: 1721 1742 5812 5813 Wallcovering contractors; drywall; eating places; drinking places

(G-5369)
COIT SERVICES OF OHIO INC
23580 Miles Rd (44128-5433)
PHONE..................216 626-0040
Fax: 440 626-0080
Harvey Siegel, *President*
Teresa Fryer, *General Mgr*
Adrian Siegal, *Corp Secy*
Ralph Mosco, *Sales Executive*
Sandra Gannon, *Office Mgr*
EMP: 55 EST: 1934
SQ FT: 22,000
SALES: 6MM **Privately Held**
WEB: www.cleveland.coit.com
SIC: 7216 7217 Cleaning & dyeing, except rugs; curtain cleaning & repair; carpet & furniture cleaning on location; upholstery cleaning on customer premises

(G-5370)
COLEMAN SPOHN CORPORATION (PA)
1775 E 45th St (44103-2318)
PHONE..................216 431-8070
Fax: 216 431-6924
Lonzo Coleman, *President*
David Cause, *Vice Pres*
David Kause, *Vice Pres*
Tom Campbell, *Project Mgr*
Charlie Coleman, *Project Mgr*
EMP: 30
SQ FT: 12,000
SALES (est): 8.8MM **Privately Held**
WEB: www.colemanspohn.com
SIC: 1711 Mechanical contractor

(G-5371)
COLORTONE AUDIO VISUAL (PA)
Also Called: Colortone Staging & Rentals
5401 Naiman Pkwy Ste A (44139-1023)
PHONE..................216 928-1530
Fax: 440 615-8065
Robert E Leon, *President*
Karen N Leon, *Vice Pres*
Edward Rezny, *Opers Staff*
Matt Rowe, *Manager*
Carla Sims, *Social Dir*
EMP: 32
SQ FT: 7,900
SALES (est): 5.1MM **Privately Held**
SIC: 7359 Audio-visual equipment & supply rental

(G-5372)
COLUMBIA GAS OF OHIO INC
7080 Fry Rd (44130-2513)
PHONE..................440 891-2458
Fax: 440 826-3485
Paul Fackler, *Area Mgr*
Doug Nusbaum, *Sales Dir*
EMP: 100
SALES (corp-wide): 4.8B **Publicly Held**
WEB: www.meterrepairshop.com
SIC: 4924 Natural gas distribution
HQ: Columbia Gas Of Ohio, Inc.
    290 W Nationwide Blvd # 114
    Columbus OH 43215
    614 460-6000

(G-5373)
COMCAST SPOTLIGHT INC
Also Called: Adelphia
3300 Lakeside Ave E (44114-3751)
PHONE..................216 575-8016
Larry Drake, *Branch Mgr*
EMP: 300
SALES (corp-wide): 84.5B **Publicly Held**
WEB: www.cablecomcast.com
SIC: 4841 Cable television services
HQ: Comcast Spotlight
    55 W 46th St Fl 33
    New York NY 10036
    212 907-8641

(G-5374)
COMEX NORTH AMERICA INC (HQ)
Also Called: Comex Group
101 W Prospect Ave # 1020 (44115-1093)
PHONE..................303 307-2100
Christopher Connor, *CEO*
Leon Cohen, *President*
Cathy Pereira, *Controller*
◆ EMP: 90
SQ FT: 2,900
SALES (est): 204.4MM
SALES (corp-wide): 14.9B **Publicly Held**
WEB: www.professionalpaintinc.com
SIC: 2851 8742 5198 5231 Paints & paint additives; paints, waterproof; paints: oil or alkyd vehicle or water thinned; corporation organizing; paints; paint brushes, rollers, sprayers; wallcoverings; paint; paint brushes, rollers, sprayers & other supplies; wallcoverings
PA: The Sherwin-Williams Company
    101 W Prospect Ave # 1020
    Cleveland OH 44115
    216 566-2000

(G-5375)
COMFORT HEALTHCARE
8310 Detroit Ave (44102-1806)
PHONE..................216 281-9999
Kirill Simakovsky, *Owner*
Vavitaly Kucsay, *Co-Owner*
EMP: 50
SALES (est): 870.3K **Privately Held**
SIC: 8082 Home health care services

(G-5376)
COMMERCIAL ELECTRIC PDTS CORP (PA)
1821 E 40th St (44103-3503)
PHONE..................216 241-2886
Fax: 216 241-1734
Roger Meyer, *President*
Russ Arslanian, *General Mgr*
Kenneth Culp, *Vice Pres*
Char Page, *Sales Mgr*
David St George, *Sales Staff*
EMP: 44 EST: 1927
SQ FT: 15,000
SALES (est): 25.7MM **Privately Held**
WEB: www.commercialelectric.com
SIC: 5085 3661 3824 1731 Power transmission equipment & apparatus; telephones & telephone apparatus; telegraph & related apparatus; mechanical & electromechanical counters & devices; general electrical contractor; industrial equipment services; electrical equipment & supplies

(G-5377)
COMMERCIAL TRAFFIC COMPANY (PA)
Also Called: C T Logistics
12487 Plaza Dr (44130-1084)
PHONE..................216 267-2000
Fax: 216 267-5945
Jack Miner, *CEO*
Allan J Miner, *President*
Debra Rose, *Purch Dir*
Bill Wasney, *Accountant*
Patrick Cahill, *Finance*
EMP: 170
SQ FT: 16,000
SALES (est): 38MM **Privately Held**
WEB: www.freitrater.com
SIC: 4731 Transportation agents & brokers

(G-5378)
COMMERCIAL TRAFFIC COMPANY
Also Called: C T Logistics
12487 Plaza Dr (44130-1084)
PHONE..................216 267-2000
Robert Dibello, *General Mgr*
EMP: 70
SALES (corp-wide): 38MM **Privately Held**
WEB: www.freitrater.com
SIC: 4731 Transportation agents & brokers
PA: The Commercial Traffic Company
    12487 Plaza Dr
    Cleveland OH 44130
    216 267-2000

(G-5379)
COMMONWEALTH FINANCIAL SVCS (PA)
26451 Curtiss Wright Pkwy (44143-4410)
PHONE..................440 449-7709
Fax: 216 261-0919
Frank Kolbe, *President*
Armand Cosenza Jr, *Corp Secy*
Caitlyn Feeney, *Accountant*
Ashley Graham, *Practice Mgr*
John Bednarski, *Manager*
EMP: 25
SQ FT: 6,000
SALES (est): 4.3MM **Privately Held**
SIC: 6163 Mortgage brokers arranging for loans, using money of others

(G-5380)
COMMONWEALTH HOTELS LLC
Also Called: Embassy Suites
5800 Rockside Woods Blvd (44131-2346)
PHONE..................216 524-5814
Fax: 216 986-9901
Bob Grossman, *Branch Mgr*
EMP: 66
SALES (corp-wide): 91.6MM **Privately Held**
WEB: www.commonwealth-hotels.com
SIC: 7011 Hotels & motels
PA: Commonwealth Hotels, Llc
    100 E Rivercenter Blvd # 1050
    Covington KY 41011
    859 392-2264

(G-5381)
COMMUNICATIONS SUPPLY CORP
Also Called: CSC
4741 Hinckley Indus Pkwy (44109-6004)
PHONE..................330 208-1900
Fax: 330 376-4283
Brian Singer, *Opers Mgr*
Annette Davidson, *Purch Mgr*
Wendy Ovian, *Sales Staff*
Annette McCutcheon, *Sales Associate*
Christine Longville, *Manager*
EMP: 25
SQ FT: 35,906 **Publicly Held**
WEB: www.calvert-wire.com
SIC: 5063 Electrical apparatus & equipment
HQ: Communications Supply Corp
    200 E Lies Rd
    Carol Stream IL 60188
    630 221-6400

(G-5382)
COMMUNITY ACTION AGAINST ADDIC
5209 Euclid Ave (44103-3703)
PHONE..................216 881-0765
Fax: 216 431-2190
Dave Jackson, *Supervisor*
Ronald Winbush, *Director*
EMP: 35
SQ FT: 24,000
SALES: 5.7MM **Privately Held**
SIC: 8093 Drug clinic, outpatient

(G-5383)
COMMUNITY ASSESMENT AND TREATM (PA)
8411 Broadway Ave (44105-3932)
PHONE..................216 441-0200
Fax: 216 441-3176
Albertina Douglas, *Trustee*
Amos Mahsua, *Trustee*
Kevin Clancy, *Vice Pres*
Paul M Gerace, *Project Mgr*
Darla Ginter, *Project Mgr*
EMP: 64
SQ FT: 19,000
SALES: 7.1MM **Privately Held**
WEB: www.communityassessment.com
SIC: 8093 Specialty outpatient clinics

(G-5384)
COMMUNITY DIALYSIS CENTER
Also Called: Center For Dialysis Care
11717 Euclid Ave (44106-4350)
P.O. Box 12220 (44112-0220)
PHONE..................216 229-6170
Fax: 216 229-2145
Dave Hlavac, *Controller*
Dee Conway, *Accounting Mgr*
Mark Horste, *Manager*
Jeffrey J Maursic, *Manager*
Jeffrey Maursic, *Manager*
EMP: 125 EST: 1974
SQ FT: 25,000
SALES (est): 9.2MM **Privately Held**
SIC: 8092 Kidney dialysis centers

(PA)=Parent Co (HQ)=Headquarters (DH)=Div Headquarters
✪ = New Business established in last 2 years

Cleveland - Cuyahoga County (G-5385)

(G-5385)
COMMUNITY RE-ENTRY INC
4515 Superior Ave (44103-1215)
PHONE.................216 696-2717
Charles See, *Director*
EMP: 40
SALES: 919.1K **Privately Held**
WEB: www.reentrymediaoutreach.org
SIC: 8399 Social change association

(G-5386)
COMMUNITY SRGL SPLY TOMS RVR
14500 Broadway Ave (44125-1960)
PHONE.................216 475-8440
Michael Fried, *Branch Mgr*
EMP: 126
SALES (corp-wide): 176.7MM **Privately Held**
SIC: 5047 Surgical equipment & supplies
PA: Community Surgical Supply Of Toms River Inc
1390 Rte 37 W
Toms River NJ 08755
732 349-2990

(G-5387)
COMPANY INC
4125 Payne Ave (44103-2324)
PHONE.................216 431-2334
Fax: 216 431-9453
James Zadd, *President*
Steven Vitas, *Vice Pres*
EMP: 25
SQ FT: 4,000
SALES (est): 3.3MM **Privately Held**
SIC: 1752 Floor laying & floor work

(G-5388)
COMPASS SELF STORAGE LLC (PA)
Also Called: Moore Self Storage
20445 Emerald Pkwy (44135-6009)
PHONE.................216 458-0670
Todd Amsdell, *President*
Michelle Conway, *District Mgr*
Shawn Madison, *District Mgr*
Hal Wallace, *District Mgr*
Amanda Levers, *Office Mgr*
EMP: 36
SQ FT: 784
SALES (est): 6.1MM **Privately Held**
SIC: 4225 Warehousing, self-storage

(G-5389)
COMPLIANT HEALTHCARE TECH LLC (PA)
Also Called: C H T
7123 Pearl Rd Ste 305 (44130-4944)
PHONE.................216 255-9607
Keith Kassouf, *Sales Staff*
Jason Di Marco, *Mng Member*
Patrick Dimarco, *Administration*
Scot Wederquist,
EMP: 25
SQ FT: 8,200
SALES: 7.5MM **Privately Held**
SIC: 7389 3826 Gas system conversion; gas testing apparatus

(G-5390)
COMPOSITE TECH AMER INC
25201 Chagrin Blvd # 360 (44122-5600)
PHONE.................330 562-5201
Fax: 216 591-0255
Bassem A Mansour, *Principal*
Jeff Schiopota, *VP Opers*
Tracy Roskey, *Materials Mgr*
Ronald Smith, *Opers Staff*
Dan Mormile, *Controller*
EMP: 41
SALES (est): 1.2MM
SALES (corp-wide): 2.9B **Privately Held**
SIC: 8748 Business consulting
HQ: Custom Pultrusions, Inc.
1331 S Chillicothe Rd
Aurora OH 44202

(G-5391)
CONCORDIA CARE
2373 Euclid Heights Blvd (44106-2776)
PHONE.................216 791-3580
Fax: 216 791-3281
Janis Fraehnrich, *President*
Bridget O'Callahan, *Director*
EMP: 62
SQ FT: 17,000
SALES (est): 12.5MM **Privately Held**
SIC: 8322 Geriatric social service

(G-5392)
CONRADS TIRE SERVICE INC (PA)
Also Called: Conrad's Total Car Care
14577 Lorain Ave (44111-3156)
P.O. Box 110584 (44111-0584)
PHONE.................216 941-3333
Fax: 216 941-2064
John Turk, *President*
Ron Mendak, *Business Mgr*
EMP: 35
SQ FT: 10,000
SALES (est): 43.6MM **Privately Held**
WEB: www.econrads.com
SIC: 7538 5531 5014 General automotive repair shops; automotive tires; automobile tires & tubes

(G-5393)
CONSOLDATED GRAPHICS GROUP INC
Also Called: Consolidated Solutions
1614 E 40th St (44103-2319)
PHONE.................216 881-9191
Kenneth A Lanci, *CEO*
Len Vargo, *President*
Matt Reville, *COO*
Joseph Turi, *Vice Pres*
Neil Gallagher, *VP Opers*
▲ EMP: 140
SQ FT: 75,000
SALES: 25MM **Privately Held**
SIC: 2752 2759 7331 2791 Commercial printing, offset; commercial printing; direct mail advertising services; typesetting; bookbinding & related work

(G-5394)
CONSORTIUM FOR HLTHY & IMMUNZD
Also Called: CHIC
10840 Barrington Blvd (44130-4407)
PHONE.................216 201-2001
Adrianne Addison, *Comms Mgr*
Cindy Modie, *Director*
EMP: 99
SALES: 24.8K **Privately Held**
SIC: 8621 Health association

(G-5395)
CONSTANT AVIATION LLC
355 Richmond Rd (44143-4405)
PHONE.................216 261-7119
Derek Morris, *Manager*
Mike Rossi,
EMP: 50 **Privately Held**
SIC: 7699 Aircraft & heavy equipment repair services
PA: Constant Aviation, Llc
18601 Cleveland Pkwy Dr 1b
Cleveland OH 44135

(G-5396)
CONSTANT AVIATION LLC (PA)
18601 Cleveland Pkwy Dr 1b (44135-3267)
PHONE.................800 440-9004
Stephen Maiden, *President*
Dave Bowman, *Vice Pres*
Kevin Dillon, *Vice Pres*
Dan Podojil, *Maintenance Dir*
Collin Stannard, *Opers Mgr*
EMP: 200
SALES (est): 41.3MM **Privately Held**
SIC: 7363 4581 Pilot service, aviation; aircraft maintenance & repair services

(G-5397)
CONSTRUCTION RESOURCES INC
33900 Station St (44139-2938)
PHONE.................440 248-9800
Fax: 440 248-9939
Bud Griffith, *President*
Mark Rubins, *Project Mgr*
EMP: 36
SALES (est): 2.8MM **Privately Held**
WEB: www.constres.com
SIC: 8748 Systems engineering consultant, ex. computer or professional

(G-5398)
CONSULATE MANAGEMENT CO LLC
Also Called: Mt Royal Villa Care Center
13900 Bennett Rd (44133-3808)
PHONE.................440 237-7966
Fax: 216 524-2558
Doug Pearson, *Manager*
Michael Debs, *Director*
EMP: 60
SALES (corp-wide): 581.9MM **Privately Held**
WEB: www.tandemhealthcare.com
SIC: 8051 8052 Skilled nursing care facilities; intermediate care facilities
PA: Consulate Management Company, Llc
800 Concourse Pkwy S
Maitland FL 32751
407 571-1550

(G-5399)
CONSUMER CREDIT COUNSELING (PA)
1228 Euclid Ave Ste 390 (44115-1800)
PHONE.................800 254-4100
Jay Seaton, *President*
EMP: 50
SQ FT: 1,700
SALES: 2.1MM **Privately Held**
SIC: 8742 Financial consultant

(G-5400)
CONTAINERPORT GROUP INC (HQ)
1340 Depot St Fl 2 (44116-1741)
PHONE.................440 333-1330
Fax: 440 333-1520
Frederick Hunger, *CEO*
Richard C Coleman, *President*
Russell A Graef, *President*
John Morrow, *General Mgr*
Rob Movshin, *General Mgr*
EMP: 57
SQ FT: 14,000
SALES (est): 175.2MM
SALES (corp-wide): 241.2MM **Privately Held**
WEB: www.containerport.com
SIC: 4731 Brokers, shipping
PA: World Shipping, Inc.
1340 Depot St Ste 200
Cleveland OH 44116
440 356-7676

(G-5401)
CONTAINERPORT GROUP INC
5155 Warner Rd (44125-1124)
PHONE.................216 341-4800
Fax: 216 341-0161
Stan Jurcevic, *Vice Pres*
Brian Barry, *Manager*
Karen Wanosky, *Manager*
EMP: 30
SALES (corp-wide): 241.2MM **Privately Held**
WEB: www.containerport.com
SIC: 4225 4214 4213 General warehousing; local trucking with storage; trucking, except local
HQ: Containerport Group, Inc.
1340 Depot St Fl 2
Cleveland OH 44116
440 333-1330

(G-5402)
CONTINENTAL PRODUCTS COMPANY
1150 E 222nd St (44117-1103)
PHONE.................216 531-0710
Mary Ann Strebeck, *CEO*
EMP: 26
SALES (corp-wide): 3.9MM **Privately Held**
WEB: www.paintdoc.com
SIC: 2851 5198 2891 Paints & paint additives; stains; varnish, oil or wax; putty; paints, varnishes & supplies; adhesives & sealants
PA: The Continental Products Company
1150 E 222nd St
Euclid OH 44117
216 383-3932

(G-5403)
CONTRACT TRANSPORT SERVICES
3223 Perkins Ave (44114-4629)
PHONE.................216 524-8435
Fax: 216 524-5435
William Madachik, *President*
EMP: 26
SALES (est): 1.4MM **Privately Held**
SIC: 4119 Limousine rental, with driver

(G-5404)
CONTROLSOFT INC
5387 Avion Park Dr (44143-1916)
PHONE.................440 443-3900
Tien LI Chia, *President*
Eric Beiler, *Engineer*
Matt Petras, *Project Engr*
Paul Botzman, *Sales Staff*
Karen Ledasil, *Sales Staff*
EMP: 50
SALES (est): 4.7MM **Privately Held**
WEB: www.controlsoftinc.com
SIC: 8748 Systems engineering consultant, ex. computer or professional

(G-5405)
CONVENTION & VISTORS BUREAU OF (PA)
Also Called: Convention & Visitors Bureau
50 Public Sq Ste 3100 (44113-2242)
PHONE.................216 875-6603
Fax: 216 621-5967
Dennis Roche, *President*
Grace Nicholas, *Controller*
Kelly Brewer, *VP Sales*
Tami Brown, *VP Mktg*
Tamara Dyers, *Manager*
EMP: 33
SQ FT: 7,200
SALES (est): 8MM **Privately Held**
WEB: www.travelcleveland.com
SIC: 7389 Convention & show services; tourist information bureau

(G-5406)
CONVIVO NETWORK LLC
1999 W 58th St (44102-3263)
PHONE.................216 631-9000
Roland Straubs, *Mng Member*
EMP: 50
SALES: 500K **Privately Held**
SIC: 7389 Decoration service for special events

(G-5407)
COOPERATE SCREENING SERVICES
16530 Commerce Ct Ste 1 (44130-6316)
PHONE.................440 816-0500
Dennis E Drellishak, *President*
Sandra Drellishak, *Corp Secy*
Greg Dubecky, *Vice Pres*
Todd Feher, *Manager*
EMP: 30
SALES (est): 330.3K **Privately Held**
SIC: 7381 Private investigator

(G-5408)
CORAL COMPANY (PA)
13219 Shaker Sq (44120-2314)
PHONE.................216 932-8822
Peter Rubin, *President*
Jeffrey Epstein, *Vice Pres*
Corey Rubin, *Project Mgr*
Alexis Boothe, *Development*
Vera Rebrovich, *Controller*
EMP: 37
SQ FT: 4,000
SALES (est): 23.3MM **Privately Held**
SIC: 6552 Land subdividers & developers, commercial

(G-5409)
CORPORATE FLOORS INC
15901 Mccracken Rd (44128-3224)
PHONE.................216 475-3232
Scott Reese, *President*
Mary Bennet, *Manager*
Kimberly Reese, *Admin Sec*
EMP: 40
SALES (est): 5.5MM **Privately Held**
SIC: 1752 Access flooring system installation

Cleveland - Cuyahoga County

(G-5410)
CORPORATE SCREENING SVCS INC (PA)
16530 Commerce Ct Ste 3 (44130-6316)
P.O. Box 361219 (44136-0021)
PHONE..................440 816-0500
Fax: 440 243-7275
Dennis E Drellishak, *CEO*
Greg Dubecky, *President*
Sandra Drellishak, *Corp Secy*
Todd Feher, *Vice Pres*
Kathi Smith, *Vice Pres*
EMP: 63
SQ FT: 12,900
SALES (est): 8.9MM **Privately Held**
WEB: www.corporatescreening.com
SIC: 7381 Private investigator

(G-5411)
CORPORATE WNGS - CLEVELAND LLC
355 Richmond Rd Ste 8 (44143-4404)
PHONE..................216 261-9000
Fax: 216 261-4260
Chris J Herzberg, *COO*
Joseph Salate, *Vice Pres*
Mark Gully, *VP Opers*
Beth Lovey, *Opers Mgr*
Robert Ward, *Opers Staff*
EMP: 30
SALES (est): 4MM **Privately Held**
SIC: 4581 Airport control tower operation, except government

(G-5412)
COUNCIL FOR ECONOMIC OPPORT
14209 Euclid Ave (44112-3809)
PHONE..................216 541-7878
EMP: 63
SALES (corp-wide): 36.6MM **Privately Held**
SIC: 8399 Antipoverty board
PA: Council For Economic Opportunities In Greater Cleveland
1801 Superior Ave E Fl 4
Cleveland OH 44114
216 696-9077

(G-5413)
COUNCIL FOR ECONOMIC OPPORT
14402 Puritas Ave (44135-2800)
PHONE..................216 476-3201
Fax: 216 476-3205
Kelly Demarco, *Branch Mgr*
EMP: 94
SALES (corp-wide): 36.6MM **Privately Held**
SIC: 8699 Charitable organization
PA: Council For Economic Opportunities In Greater Cleveland
1801 Superior Ave E Fl 4
Cleveland OH 44114
216 696-9077

(G-5414)
COUNCIL FOR ECONOMIC OPPORT (PA)
Also Called: Ceogc
1801 Superior Ave E Fl 4 (44114-2135)
PHONE..................216 696-9077
Fax: 216 696-0770
Jacklyn Chisholm, *President*
Bryan Glyesser, *COO*
Deborah Armstrong, *CFO*
Abdul Shahid, *Manager*
Arlene Houston, *IT/INT Sup*
EMP: 100
SQ FT: 26,000
SALES: 36.6MM **Privately Held**
WEB: www.ceogc.org
SIC: 8399 8322 8351 Antipoverty board; individual & family services; child day care services

(G-5415)
COUNCIL FOR ECONOMIC OPPORT
Also Called: Carl B Stokes Head Start Ctr
1883 Torbenson Dr (44112-1308)
PHONE..................216 692-4010
Sonya Dean, *Supervisor*
EMP: 35
SQ FT: 67,962
SALES (corp-wide): 36.6MM **Privately Held**
WEB: www.ceogc.org
SIC: 8399 Antipoverty board
PA: Council For Economic Opportunities In Greater Cleveland
1801 Superior Ave E Fl 4
Cleveland OH 44114
216 696-9077

(G-5416)
COUNCIL OF ECNMC OPPRTNTS OF G
Also Called: Willard Head Start Day Care
2220 W 95th St (44102-3762)
PHONE..................216 651-5154
Fax: 216 651-0981
Leynnore Walker, *Administration*
EMP: 36
SALES (est): 679.3K **Privately Held**
SIC: 8351 Head start center, except in conjunction with school

(G-5417)
COUNTRY CLUB INC
2825 Lander Rd (44124-4899)
PHONE..................216 831-9200
Fax: 216 831-3120
Robert C Josey, *CEO*
EMP: 110
SQ FT: 112,000
SALES: 10.2MM **Privately Held**
WEB: www.thecountryclub.com
SIC: 7997 Country club, membership

(G-5418)
COUNTY OF CUYAHOGA
Also Called: Alcohol/Drug Outpatient T
1276 W 3rd St Ste 210 (44113-1512)
PHONE..................216 443-7035
Fax: 216 443-5625
Maria Nemec, *Manager*
Steven Terry, *Director*
EMP: 25 **Privately Held**
SIC: 8093 9431 Substance abuse clinics (outpatient); public health agency administration, government
PA: County Of Cuyahoga
1215 W 3rd St
Cleveland OH 44113
216 443-7022

(G-5419)
COUNTY OF CUYAHOGA
Also Called: Maple Heights Atc
14775 Broadway Ave (44137-1103)
PHONE..................216 475-7066
Fax: 216 587-6853
David Gillespie, *Manager*
EMP: 70
SQ FT: 42,389 **Privately Held**
SIC: 8331 9229 Vocational rehabilitation agency;
PA: County Of Cuyahoga
1215 W 3rd St
Cleveland OH 44113
216 443-7022

(G-5420)
COUNTY OF CUYAHOGA
Also Called: Coroner's Office
11001 Cedar Ave Ste 400 (44106-3043)
PHONE..................216 721-5610
Fax: 216 721-2559
Elizabeth Balraj, *Manager*
Paul Boggs, *Supervisor*
Nasir Butt, *Comp Lab Dir*
EMP: 80
SQ FT: 720 **Privately Held**
SIC: 8049 9431 ;
PA: County Of Cuyahoga
1215 W 3rd St
Cleveland OH 44113
216 443-7022

(G-5421)
COUNTY OF CUYAHOGA
Also Called: Department Information Tech
2079 E 9th St Fl 6 (44115-1302)
PHONE..................216 443-8011
Fax: 216 443-7363
Debbie Davtovich, *Human Res Mgr*
Scot Rourke, *Branch Mgr*
Gerry Mc Clamy, *Manager*
Gerry M Clay, *Info Tech Mgr*
Joyce Coffman, *Admin Asst*
EMP: 142
SQ FT: 2,332 **Privately Held**
SIC: 7374 9431 Data processing service; health statistics center, government
PA: County Of Cuyahoga
1215 W 3rd St
Cleveland OH 44113
216 443-7022

(G-5422)
COUNTY OF CUYAHOGA
Also Called: Child Support Enforcement Agcy
1640 Superior Ave E (44114-2908)
P.O. Box 93318 (44101-5318)
PHONE..................216 443-5100
Cassondra McArthuour, *Manager*
EMP: 50
SQ FT: 44,726 **Privately Held**
SIC: 9441 8322 ; child guidance agency
PA: County Of Cuyahoga
1215 W 3rd St
Cleveland OH 44113
216 443-7022

(G-5423)
COUNTY OF CUYAHOGA
Also Called: Central Services Department
2079 E 9th St (44115-1302)
PHONE..................216 443-6954
Jay Ross, *Manager*
Lisa C Averyhart, *Asst Director*
Karen Greene, *Legal Staff*
EMP: 650
SQ FT: 35,640 **Privately Held**
SIC: 7349 9431 Building maintenance services; health statistics center, government
PA: County Of Cuyahoga
1215 W 3rd St
Cleveland OH 44113
216 443-7022

(G-5424)
COUNTY OF CUYAHOGA
Also Called: Cuyahoga County Board of Menta
1275 Lakeside Ave E (44114-1129)
PHONE..................216 241-8230
Maggie Jackson, *Vice Pres*
L Stevens, *VP Finance*
John McLaughlin, *Human Res Dir*
John Moreland, *Human Res Mgr*
Valerie Funtik, *HR Admin*
EMP: 200 **Privately Held**
SIC: 8361 9431 Home for the mentally retarded; mental health agency administration, government
PA: County Of Cuyahoga
1215 W 3rd St
Cleveland OH 44113
216 443-7022

(G-5425)
COUNTY OF CUYAHOGA
Also Called: Activity Training
13231 Euclid Ave (44112-4523)
PHONE..................216 681-4433
Fax: 216 249-6926
Gary Shy, *Prdtn Mgr*
Albert Trefeny, *Manager*
EMP: 75 **Privately Held**
SIC: 9441 8322 ; individual & family services
PA: County Of Cuyahoga
1215 W 3rd St
Cleveland OH 44113
216 443-7022

(G-5426)
COUNTY OF CUYAHOGA
Also Called: County Administrator's Office
1219 Ontario St Rm 304 (44113-1601)
PHONE..................216 443-7181
Joyce Burke-Jones, *Exec Officer*
Lee A Trotter, *Administration*
Laura Roche, *Admin Asst*
EMP: 300 **Privately Held**
SIC: 8741 Administrative management
PA: County Of Cuyahoga
1215 W 3rd St
Cleveland OH 44113
216 443-7022

(G-5427)
COUNTY OF CUYAHOGA
Also Called: Department Children Services
3955 Euclid Ave Rm 344e (44115-2505)
PHONE..................216 432-2621
James Mc Cafferty, *Manager*
James McCafferty, *Manager*
EMP: 650 **Privately Held**
SIC: 8322 9431 Child related social services; child health program administration, government
PA: County Of Cuyahoga
1215 W 3rd St
Cleveland OH 44113
216 443-7022

(G-5428)
COUNTY OF CUYAHOGA
Also Called: Youth Services
1276 W 3rd St Ste 319 (44113-1512)
PHONE..................216 443-7265
Steven Terry, *Branch Mgr*
Marty Murphy, *Director*
EMP: 65 **Privately Held**
SIC: 9441 8641 Administration of social & human resources; youth organizations
PA: County Of Cuyahoga
1215 W 3rd St
Cleveland OH 44113
216 443-7022

(G-5429)
COURTYARD BY MARRIOTT
3695 Orange Pl (44122-4401)
PHONE..................216 765-1900
Fax: 216 765-1841
Graham Herscham, *President*
Rich Somsak, *General Mgr*
EMP: 30 EST: 2008
SALES (est): 1.4MM **Privately Held**
SIC: 7011 Hotels & motels

(G-5430)
COURTYARD MANAGEMENT CORP
5051 W Creek Rd (44131-2165)
PHONE..................216 901-9988
Fax: 216 901-9989
Scott Arra, *Branch Mgr*
EMP: 50
SALES (corp-wide): 22.8B **Publicly Held**
SIC: 7011 Hotels
HQ: Courtyard Management Corporation
10400 Fernwood Rd
Bethesda MD 20817

(G-5431)
COX CABLE CLEVELAND AREA INC
12221 Plaza Dr (44130-1072)
PHONE..................216 676-8300
Fax: 216 676-8689
Ron Hammaker, *President*
Jeannie Becka, *Marketing Mgr*
EMP: 121
SALES (est): 6.6MM
SALES (corp-wide): 33B **Privately Held**
WEB: www.coxenterprises.com
SIC: 4841 Cable television services
PA: Cox Enterprises, Inc.
6205 Pachtree Dunwoody Rd
Atlanta GA 30328
678 645-0000

(G-5432)
CRAWFORD & COMPANY
7271 Engle Rd Ste 303 (44130-8404)
PHONE..................440 243-8710
Fax: 440 243-1171
Joseph M Weber, *Branch Mgr*
Steve Blakemore, *Manager*
EMP: 36
SQ FT: 2,700
SALES (corp-wide): 1.1B **Privately Held**
WEB: www.crawfordandcompany.com
SIC: 6411 Insurance adjusters
PA: Crawford & Company
5335 Triangle Pkwy Ofc C
Peachtree Corners GA 30092
404 300-1000

Cleveland - Cuyahoga County (G-5433)

(G-5433)
CREATIVE PLAYROOM (PA)
Also Called: Solon Crtive Plyroom Mntessori
16574 Broadway Ave (44137-2602)
PHONE..................216 475-6464
Joan Wenk, *President*
EMP: 60
SQ FT: 12,000
SALES (est): 1.8MM **Privately Held**
SIC: 8351 Child day care services;
Montessori child development center

(G-5434)
CREDIT FIRST NATIONAL ASSN
Also Called: C F N A
6275 Eastland Rd (44142-1301)
P.O. Box 81315 (44181-0315)
PHONE..................216 362-5300
Dean S Miller, *President*
Alan K Meier, *Finance Dir*
Donald Wolf, *Accountant*
EMP: 300
SALES: 35MM
SALES (corp-wide): 32.5B **Privately Held**
SIC: 7389 Financial services
HQ: Bridgestone Americas Tire Operations, Llc
200 4th Ave S Ste 100
Nashville TN 37201
615 937-1000

(G-5435)
CREMATION SERVICE INC (PA)
1612 Leonard St (44113-2418)
PHONE..................216 861-2334
Fax: 216 621-1762
Robert J Inman, *President*
Marilyn Nixon, *Vice Pres*
EMP: 46
SQ FT: 600
SALES (est): 2.2MM **Privately Held**
SIC: 7261 4119 Crematory; local passenger transportation

(G-5436)
CREMATION SERVICE INC
Also Called: Inman Nationwide Shipping
1605 Merwin Ave (44113-2421)
PHONE..................216 621-6222
Fax: 216 771-8588
Robert J Inman, *Branch Mgr*
EMP: 26
SALES (corp-wide): 2.2MM **Privately Held**
SIC: 7261 Funeral service & crematories
PA: Cremation Service Inc
1612 Leonard St
Cleveland OH 44113
216 861-2334

(G-5437)
CRESTMONT CADILLAC CORPORATION (PA)
26000 Chagrin Blvd (44122-4298)
PHONE..................216 831-5300
Fax: 216 831-6433
Jay Park, *President*
Tom Schrader, *Business Mgr*
Mario Bennici, *Parts Mgr*
Dan Artino, *Sales Mgr*
Michael Gutowitz, *Sales Mgr*
EMP: 44
SQ FT: 45,000
SALES (est): 31.1MM **Privately Held**
WEB: www.crestmontcadillac.com
SIC: 5511 7538 Automobiles, new & used; general automotive repair shops

(G-5438)
CRESTWOOD MGMT LLC
23550 Commerce Park # 5000 (44122-5862)
PHONE..................440 484-2400
Marcel Dovier,
EMP: 75
SALES (est): 5.5MM **Privately Held**
SIC: 8741 Management services

(G-5439)
CROWE HORWATH LLP
600 Superior Ave E # 902 (44114-2619)
PHONE..................216 623-7500
Fax: 216 623-7502
Tina Berdan, *Project Mgr*
Fred Bauters, *Accounts Exec*
Greg McClure, *Branch Mgr*

Bill Brewer, *Manager*
Curtis Shelton, *Web Dvlpr*
EMP: 37
SALES (corp-wide): 809.4MM **Privately Held**
SIC: 8721 Certified public accountant
PA: Crowe Horwath Llp
225 W Wacker Dr Ste 2600
Chicago IL 60606
312 899-7000

(G-5440)
CROWNE GROUP LLC (PA)
127 Public Sq Ste 5110 (44114-1313)
PHONE..................216 589-0198
Robert Henderson, *Mng Member*
EMP: 57
SALES (est): 824.3MM **Privately Held**
SIC: 3559 8711 Degreasing machines, automotive & industrial; industrial engineers

(G-5441)
CSA AMERICA INC (HQ)
Also Called: Csa Group
8501 E Pleasant Valley Rd (44131-5516)
PHONE..................216 524-4990
Fax: 216 520-8979
Rich Weiser, *President*
Raymond Varcho, *Principal*
Richard McNitt, *Business Mgr*
Richard Papa, *Vice Pres*
Shannon Corcoran, *Project Mgr*
EMP: 150 **EST:** 1997
SQ FT: 140,000
SALES: 37.2MM
SALES (corp-wide): 253.6MM **Privately Held**
SIC: 8734 Testing laboratories
PA: Canadian Standards Association
178 Rexdale Blvd
Etobicoke ON M9W 1
416 747-4000

(G-5442)
CSA AMERICA INC
Also Called: Csa International Services
8501 E Pleasant Valley Rd (44131-5516)
PHONE..................216 524-4990
Jeanette Preston, *Business Mgr*
Randall Luecke, *Vice Pres*
Terry Nagy, *Opers Mgr*
Steve Kazubski, *Project Engr*
Milton Ondrusko, *Project Engr*
EMP: 100
SALES (corp-wide): 253.6MM **Privately Held**
SIC: 8734 Testing laboratories
HQ: Csa America, Inc.
8501 E Pleasant Valley Rd
Cleveland OH 44131
216 524-4990

(G-5443)
CSL PLASMA INC
Also Called: Z L B
3204 W 25th St (44109-1641)
PHONE..................216 398-0440
Doug Pearbeck, *Manager*
Jada Burt, *Manager*
EMP: 60
SALES (corp-wide): 6.9B **Privately Held**
WEB: www.zlbplasma.com
SIC: 8099 Plasmapherous center
HQ: Csl Plasma Inc.
900 Broken Sound Pkwy # 4
Boca Raton FL 33487
561 981-3700

(G-5444)
CSR COLORTONE STAGING RENTALS
5401 Naiman Pkwy Ste A (44139-1023)
PHONE..................440 914-9500
Bob Leon, *President*
Karen Leon, *Vice Pres*
EMP: 25
SALES (est): 1.1MM **Privately Held**
SIC: 7359 Audio-visual equipment & supply rental

(G-5445)
CSU/CAREER SERVICES CENTER
2121 Euclid Ave (44115-2214)
PHONE..................216 687-2233
Paul Klein, *Director*

EMP: 30
SALES (est): 1.6MM **Privately Held**
WEB: www.nhlink.net
SIC: 7361 Employment agencies

(G-5446)
CT LOGISTICS INC
12487 Plaza Dr (44130-1056)
PHONE..................216 267-1636
Allan Miner, *President*
Patrick Cahill, *CFO*
Pat Cahill, *Finance Dir*
EMP: 150
SQ FT: 1,000
SALES (est): 6.2MM **Privately Held**
SIC: 4789 7371 Pipeline terminal facilities, independently operated; computer software development

(G-5447)
CTRAC INC
2222 W 110th St (44102-3512)
PHONE..................440 572-1000
Susan Williamson, *President*
Gary A Seitz, *Exec VP*
Cindy Miklosko, *Vice Pres*
Gina Greco, *Research*
Matt Wisniewski, *Accounting Mgr*
EMP: 50 **EST:** 1972
SQ FT: 15,000
SALES (est): 7.2MM
SALES (corp-wide): 7.7MM **Privately Held**
WEB: www.ctrac.com
SIC: 7331 7374 Mailing service; data processing service; data entry service
PA: Pierry, Inc.
785 Broadway St
Redwood City CA 94063
800 860-7953

(G-5448)
CUMMINGS AND DAVIS FNRL HM INC
Also Called: Service Corporation Intl
13201 Euclid Ave (44112-4523)
PHONE..................216 541-1111
Fax: 216 541-1908
Wallace D Davis, *President*
Evelyn B Davis, *Corp Secy*
EMP: 25
SQ FT: 45,000
SALES (est): 1.7MM **Privately Held**
SIC: 7261 Funeral home

(G-5449)
CUSTOM HALTHCARE PROFFESSIONAL
5001 Mayfield Rd Ste 210 (44124-2609)
PHONE..................216 381-1010
Paul Kloppman, *President*
EMP: 30
SALES (est): 1.6MM **Privately Held**
SIC: 7361 Placement agencies

(G-5450)
CUYAHOGA COUNTY
Also Called: Department Senior Adult S
1701 E 12th St Ste 11 (44114-3237)
PHONE..................216 420-6750
Fax: 216 420-6742
Susan E Axelrod, *Manager*
EMP: 62 **Privately Held**
SIC: 9441 8322 Administration of social & human resources; senior citizens' center or association
PA: County Of Cuyahoga
1215 W 3rd St
Cleveland OH 44113
216 443-7022

(G-5451)
CUYAHOGA COUNTY
Also Called: Parma Adult Training Center
12660 Plaza Dr (44130-1046)
PHONE..................216 265-3030
Fax: 216 265-3068
Karen Fifelski, *Manager*
EMP: 60 **Privately Held**
SIC: 8331 9411 Sheltered workshop;
PA: County Of Cuyahoga
1215 W 3rd St
Cleveland OH 44113
216 443-7022

(G-5452)
CUYAHOGA COUNTY
Also Called: Children and Family Services
3955 Euclid Ave (44115-2505)
PHONE..................216 431-4500
Fax: 216 432-3512
William Denihan, *Branch Mgr*
EMP: 650 **Privately Held**
SIC: 8322 9441 Individual & family services;
PA: County Of Cuyahoga
1215 W 3rd St
Cleveland OH 44113
216 443-7022

(G-5453)
CUYAHOGA COUNTY
Also Called: Cuyahoga County Dept Pub Works
2079 E 9th St (44115-1302)
PHONE..................216 348-3800
Fax: 216 348-3896
Robert C Klaiber, *Principal*
Dottie Sievers, *Technology*
Michael Dever, *Deputy Dir*
EMP: 640 **Privately Held**
SIC: 8711 9532 Engineering services;
PA: County Of Cuyahoga
1215 W 3rd St
Cleveland OH 44113
216 443-7022

(G-5454)
CUYAHOGA COUNTY
Also Called: Marriage License Bureau
1 W Lakeside Ave Ste 146 (44113-1023)
PHONE..................216 443-8920
EMP: 62 **Privately Held**
SIC: 9441 7299 Administration of social & human resources; marriage bureau
PA: County Of Cuyahoga
1215 W 3rd St
Cleveland OH 44113
216 443-7022

(G-5455)
CUYAHOGA COUNTY CONVENTION FAC
Also Called: SMG AGENT FOR CLEVELAND CONVEN
1 Saint Clair Ave Ne (44114-1251)
PHONE..................216 928-1600
Matt Carroll, *President*
Mark Leahy, *General Mgr*
Steve Wells, *Finance*
EMP: 75
SALES (est): 6MM **Privately Held**
SIC: 8744 Facilities support services

(G-5456)
CUYAHOGA COUNTY SANI ENGRG SVC
6100 W Canal Rd (44125-3330)
PHONE..................216 443-8211
Fax: 216 443-8236
William Applegarth, *Foreman/Supr*
David Reines, *Director*
EMP: 105
SALES (est): 6.9MM **Privately Held**
SIC: 4959 Sanitary services

(G-5457)
CUYAHOGA MARKETING SERVICE
Also Called: Great Day Tours Chrtr Bus Svc
375 Treeworth Blvd (44147-2985)
PHONE..................440 526-5350
Allen Kinney, *President*
Phyllis Ann Kinney, *Treasurer*
Jill Smialek, *Manager*
Doris Kinney, *Admin Sec*
EMP: 40
SQ FT: 3,000
SALES (est): 2.3MM **Privately Held**
WEB: www.greatdaytours.com
SIC: 4141 4142 Local bus charter service; bus charter service, except local

(G-5458)
CWM ENVRONMENTAL CLEVELAND LLC
4450 Johnston Pkwy Ste B (44128-2956)
PHONE..................216 663-0808
Tanya Hooks, *Controller*
David Kohl, *Mng Member*

GEOGRAPHIC SECTION

Cleveland - Cuyahoga County (G-5481)

EMP: 30
SQ FT: 15,000
SALES (est): 4MM
SALES (corp-wide): 8.3MM **Privately Held**
WEB: www.precisionanalytical.com
SIC: 7389 Water softener service
PA: Cwm Environmental, Inc.
101 Parkview Drive Ext
Kittanning PA 16201
724 545-2827

(G-5459)
CYPRESS COMMUNICATIONS INC (DH)
75 Erieview Plz Fl 4 (44114-1839)
PHONE 404 965-7248
Stephen L Schilling, *President*
Ray Johnson, *President*
Frank M Grillo, *Exec VP*
Jorge L Rosado, *Exec VP*
John A Harwood, *Vice Pres*
EMP: 125
SQ FT: 64,952
SALES (est): 41.3MM
SALES (corp-wide): 290.4MM **Privately Held**
WEB: www.cypresscom.net
SIC: 8741 4813 Management services; telephone communication, except radio; local & long distance telephone communications
HQ: Broadvox, Llc
75 Erieview Plz Fl 4
Cleveland OH 44114
216 373-4600

(G-5460)
CYXTERA DATA CENTERS INC
6100 Oak Tree Blvd # 200 (44131-2544)
PHONE 216 986-2742
EMP: 354
SALES (corp-wide): 729.1MM **Privately Held**
WEB: www.savvis.net
SIC: 7375 Information retrieval services
HQ: Cyxtera Data Centers, Inc.
2333 Ponce De Leon Blvd
Coral Gables FL 33134
305 537-9500

(G-5461)
DAKOTA SOFTWARE CORPORATION (PA)
1375 Euclid Ave Ste 500 (44115-1808)
PHONE 216 765-7100
Fax: 585 244-3301
Reginald C Shiverick, *President*
Susan Bloom, *Business Mgr*
Erin Scott, *Manager*
Brooks Pollock, *Info Tech Dir*
Christopher Brown, *Director*
EMP: 61
SALES (est): 7.7MM **Privately Held**
WEB: www.dakotasoft.com
SIC: 7372 Prepackaged software

(G-5462)
DAN-RAY CONSTRUCTION LLC
4500 Lee Rd Ste 207 (44128-2959)
P.O. Box 221095, Beachwood (44122-0993)
PHONE 216 518-8484
Paul R Jenkins, *Principal*
Ralph Birdsong, *Principal*
Clem Jackson, *Principal*
Tim Jenkins, *Principal*
Steve Rogers, *Principal*
EMP: 25
SQ FT: 1,000
SALES (est): 2MM **Privately Held**
SIC: 8748 Business consulting

(G-5463)
DATA DIRECTION INC
6675 Eastland Rd Ste Bk (44130-2423)
PHONE 216 362-5900
Fax: 216 362-0003
Mary McIntyre, *Vice Pres*
Rita Cianciola, *Sales Mgr*
EMP: 40
SALES (corp-wide): 5.7MM **Privately Held**
WEB: www.datadirection.com
SIC: 7374 Data processing service

PA: Data Direction Inc
26877 Nrthwstrn Hwy 420
Southfield MI 48033
248 552-0110

(G-5464)
DATAVANTAGE CORPORATION (DH)
Also Called: Micros Retail
30500 Bruce Industrial Pk (44139-3970)
PHONE 440 498-4414
Fax: 440 542-3043
Marvin Lader, *CEO*
John E Gularson, *President*
Jeremy Grunzweig, *COO*
Bob Walters, *Senior VP*
Clint Cook, *Vice Pres*
EMP: 270
SQ FT: 56,400
SALES (est): 32MM
SALES (corp-wide): 37.7B **Publicly Held**
SIC: 5734 5045 8748 7371 Computer & software stores; computers, peripherals & software; business consulting; custom computer programming services
HQ: Micros Systems, Inc.
7031 Columbia Gateway Dr # 1
Columbia MD 21046
443 285-6000

(G-5465)
DAVEY TREE EXPERT COMPANY
Also Called: Davey Tree & Lawn Care
7625 Bond St (44139-5350)
PHONE 440 439-4770
Fax: 440 439-4425
Ken Cloutier, *Manager*
EMP: 25
SALES (corp-wide): 915.9MM **Privately Held**
SIC: 0782 0783 Lawn services; ornamental shrub & tree services
PA: The Davey Tree Expert Company
1500 N Mantua St
Kent OH 44240
330 673-9511

(G-5466)
DAVID FRANCIS CORPORATION (PA)
Also Called: Electronic Merchant Systems
5005 Rockside Rd Ste 100 (44131-6808)
PHONE 216 524-0900
Fax: 216 524-0900
James Weiland, *Ch of Bd*
Dan Neistadt, *President*
Jayne Overturf, *General Mgr*
Heidi Shotts, *General Mgr*
Ed Graham, *Exec VP*
EMP: 110
SQ FT: 23,400
SALES (est): 33.5MM **Privately Held**
WEB: www.emscorporate.com
SIC: 7359 5044 Business machine & electronic equipment rental services; office equipment

(G-5467)
DAVID GROUP (PA)
1360 E 9th St Ste 830 (44114-1741)
PHONE 216 685-4400
Fax: 216 696-5543
Louis Schaul, *President*
Michael Busta, *Financial Exec*
Courtney Chen, *Accounts Mgr*
Jessica Dube, *Accounts Exec*
Suzanne Torres, *Accounts Exec*
EMP: 25
SQ FT: 2,200
SALES (est): 4.1MM **Privately Held**
SIC: 7311 Advertising consultant

(G-5468)
DAVIS YOUNG A LEGAL PROF ASSN (PA)
600 Superior Ave E # 1200 (44114-2614)
PHONE 216 348-1700
Gregory H Collins, *Managing Prtnr*
Richard C McDonald, *General Mgr*
Suzanne Pettit, *Counsel*
Martin J Murphy, *Vice Pres*
Ralph Trepal, *Vice Pres*
EMP: 50
SQ FT: 12,000

SALES (est): 4.1MM **Privately Held**
WEB: www.dyyoungstown.com
SIC: 8111 General practice law office

(G-5469)
DAVITA HEALTHCARE PARTNERS INC
7901 Detroit Ave (44102-2828)
PHONE 216 961-6498
Gayle Nemecek, *Branch Mgr*
EMP: 27 **Publicly Held**
SIC: 8092 Kidney dialysis centers
PA: Davita Inc.
2000 16th St
Denver CO 80202

(G-5470)
DAVITA INC
Also Called: Davita 1620
7360 Engle Rd (44130-3429)
PHONE 440 891-5645
Anthony Marflak, *Project Mgr*
Davita Smith, *Branch Mgr*
EMP: 27 **Publicly Held**
SIC: 8092 Kidney dialysis centers
PA: Davita Inc.
2000 16th St
Denver CO 80202

(G-5471)
DAYTON HEIDELBERG DISTRG CO
9101 E Pleasant Vly (44131-5504)
PHONE 216 520-2626
Fax: 216 520-2620
Kevin Fair, *Marketing Staff*
Daniel Greathouse, *Branch Mgr*
Ian McDonald, *Manager*
EMP: 170
SALES (corp-wide): 369.4MM **Privately Held**
SIC: 5182 Wine
PA: Dayton Heidelberg Distributing Co.
3601 Dryden Rd
Moraine OH 45439
937 222-8692

(G-5472)
DEALER TIRE LLC (PA)
7012 Euclid Ave (44103-4014)
PHONE 216 432-0088
Fax: 216 881-7923
Scott Mueller, *CEO*
Dean T Mueller, *President*
Jim Kutscher, *General Mgr*
Michelle Francz, *Editor*
Andes Candies, *Vice Pres*
◆ **EMP:** 450 **EST:** 2000
SQ FT: 50,000
SALES (est): 2.1B **Privately Held**
SIC: 5014 Tires & tubes

(G-5473)
DECKER EQUIPMENT COMPANY INC
Also Called: Decker Forklifts
9601 Granger Rd (44125-5350)
PHONE 866 252-4395
Andrew C Decker, *President*
▼ **EMP:** 28
SALES (est): 8.4MM **Privately Held**
SIC: 5084 Materials handling machinery

(G-5474)
DELOITTE & TOUCHE LLP
127 Public Sq Ste 3300 (44114-1303)
PHONE 216 589-1300
Fax: 216 589-1369
Patrick Mullen, *Partner*
Jeffrey A Aukerman, *Partner*
Michael J O Brien, *Partner*
Joseph A Buccilli, *Partner*
Michael J Deering, *Partner*
EMP: 250
SALES (corp-wide): 5.9B **Privately Held**
WEB: www.deloitte.com
SIC: 8721 8742 Accounting, auditing & bookkeeping; management consulting services
HQ: Deloitte & Touche Llp
30 Rockefeller Plz # 4350
New York NY 10112
212 492-4000

(G-5475)
DELTA AIR LINES INC
Also Called: Delta Airlines
5300 Riverside Dr Ste 11 (44135-3146)
PHONE 216 265-2400
Pat Jones, *Manager*
Scott Wetmore, *Technology*
EMP: 30
SALES (corp-wide): 41.2B **Publicly Held**
WEB: www.delta.com
SIC: 4729 Transportation ticket offices
PA: Delta Air Lines, Inc.
1030 Delta Blvd
Atlanta GA 30354
404 715-2600

(G-5476)
DEPENDABLE PAINTING CO
4403 Superior Ave (44103-1135)
PHONE 216 431-4470
Fax: 216 431-6670
Cindy Friedmann, *President*
Donald K Hansen, *Exec VP*
Martha Shearman, *Admin Asst*
EMP: 50 **EST:** 1928
SQ FT: 20,000
SALES (est): 4.7MM **Privately Held**
WEB: www.dependableptg.com
SIC: 1721 Exterior commercial painting contractor; commercial wallcovering contractor

(G-5477)
DEPT OF PUBLIC WORKS R B
4000 Brookpark Rd (44134-1132)
PHONE 216 661-2800
John Pinter, *Office Mgr*
EMP: 25
SALES (est): 1.1MM **Privately Held**
SIC: 1611 Concrete construction: roads, highways, sidewalks, etc.

(G-5478)
DETROIT DOVER ANIMALS HOSPITAL
27366 Detroit Rd (44145-2298)
PHONE 440 871-5220
Fax: 440 871-5497
David Snavely, *President*
Loretta Dennis MD, *President*
Don Grath, *Treasurer*
Clyde Rhein, *Admin Sec*
EMP: 30
SQ FT: 10,000
SALES (est): 1MM **Privately Held**
SIC: 0742 Animal hospital services, pets & other animal specialties

(G-5479)
DETROIT ROYALTY INCORPORATED
1100 Superior Ave E Fl 10 (44114-2530)
PHONE 216 771-5700
Fax: 216 771-1308
Andrew Norton, *Vice Pres*
Brandi Domingo, *Accounts Exec*
David Demuth, *Branch Mgr*
Jon Vokish, *Senior Mgr*
EMP: 65
SALES (corp-wide): 75.6MM **Privately Held**
WEB: www.donerus.com
SIC: 7311 Advertising agencies
PA: Detroit Royalty, Incorporated
25900 Northwestern Hwy
Southfield MI 48075
248 354-9700

(G-5480)
DHL EXPRESS (USA) INC
19987 Commerce Pkwy (44130-2405)
PHONE 440 239-0670
Steven Mikan, *Project Mgr*
EMP: 31
SALES (corp-wide): 71.2B **Privately Held**
SIC: 4513 Air courier services
HQ: Dhl Express (Usa), Inc.
1210 S Pine Island Rd
Plantation FL 33324
954 888-7000

(G-5481)
DIALAMERICA MARKETING INC
7271 Engle Rd Ste 400 (44130-8404)
PHONE 440 234-4410

Cleveland - Cuyahoga County (G-5482)   GEOGRAPHIC SECTION

Fax: 440 891-7846
Jerry Banchek, *Director*
Steiner Karen, *Executive*
EMP: 125
SALES (corp-wide): 395.1MM **Privately Held**
WEB: www.dialupamerica.net
SIC: 7389 Telemarketing services
PA: Dialamerica Marketing, Inc.
 960 Macarthur Blvd
 Mahwah NJ 07430
 201 327-0200

(G-5482)
DIAMONDS PEARLS HLTH SVCS LLC
Also Called: DIAMONDS & PEARLS RCH
3570 Warrensville Ctr Rd (44122-5288)
PHONE.................................216 752-8500
Fax: 216 752-8670
Jason D Price,
Terrence Hobson,
Marry Willis,
EMP: 90
SQ FT: 2,680
SALES: 808.4K **Privately Held**
SIC: 8082 Home health care services

(G-5483)
DIGIKNOW INC
3615 Superior Ave E 4404a (44114-4139)
PHONE.................................888 482-4455
Fax: 216 325-1801
King Hill, *President*
Mariann Janosko, *Vice Pres*
John Katila, *Vice Pres*
Harvey Scholnick, *Vice Pres*
Ian Verschuren, *Vice Pres*
EMP: 43
SQ FT: 22,500
SALES (est): 3MM
SALES (corp-wide): 20.7MM **Privately Held**
WEB: www.digiknow.com
SIC: 7371 Custom computer programming services
PA: Marcus Thomas, Llc.
 4781 Richmond Rd
 Cleveland OH 44128
 216 292-4700

(G-5484)
DINN HOCHMAN AND POTTER LLC
5910 Landerbrook Dr # 200 (44124-6500)
PHONE.................................440 446-1100
Fax: 440 446-1240
David B Hochman, *Managing Prtnr*
Aaron Minc, *Counsel*
Leslie L Edelsburg, *Mktg Dir*
Irwin Dinn,
Tracey Stockton,
EMP: 25
SALES (est): 2.8MM **Privately Held**
WEB: www.dhplaw.com
SIC: 8111 General practice law office

(G-5485)
DIRECT IMPORT HOME DECOR INC (PA)
Also Called: Cabinet and Granite Direct
4979 W 130th St (44135-5139)
PHONE.................................216 898-9758
Eddie Ni, *President*
Fannie Chen, *General Mgr*
Eric Cheung, *Vice Pres*
Samantha Wolske, *Sales Mgr*
Stephanie Walkos, *Office Admin*
▲ EMP: 35
SQ FT: 50,000
SALES (est): 10.4MM **Privately Held**
SIC: 5032 5031 Granite building stone; kitchen cabinets

(G-5486)
DIRECTCONNECTGROUP LTD
Also Called: D C G
5501 Cass Ave (44102-2121)
PHONE.................................216 281-2866
Robert A Durham, *Partner*
Brad Clarke, *Partner*
Scott L Durham, *Partner*
Tammy Peniston, *Partner*
James E Pinkin, *Partner*
EMP: 525

SALES (est): 23.1MM **Privately Held**
WEB: www.dcgrp.net
SIC: 7331 2752 Direct mail advertising services; mailing service; mailing list management; commercial printing, lithographic

(G-5487)
DISANTO COMPANIES
1960 Caronia Dr (44124-3919)
PHONE.................................440 442-0600
Carolyn Disanto, *Treasurer*
EMP: 30
SALES: 150K **Privately Held**
SIC: 0782 Landscape contractors

(G-5488)
DISKCOPY DUPLICATION SERVICES
107 Alpha Park (44143-2224)
PHONE.................................440 460-0800
Fax: 440 460-0801
Sheldon Rubin, *President*
Pam Lewis, *General Mgr*
Shannon Klee, *Vice Pres*
Darrel Rubin, *Vice Pres*
EMP: 26
SQ FT: 10,500
SALES: 4.1MM **Privately Held**
SIC: 7371 Computer software development

(G-5489)
DISTILLATA COMPANY (PA)
1608 E 24th St (44114-4212)
P.O. Box 93845 (44101-5845)
PHONE.................................216 771-2900
Fax: 216 771-1672
William E Schroeder, *President*
Dalphne Axline, *Principal*
R M Egan, *Principal*
J C Little, *Principal*
Herbert Buckman, *Corp Secy*
EMP: 70 EST: 1897
SQ FT: 100,000
SALES (est): 15.9MM **Privately Held**
WEB: www.distillata.com
SIC: 2899 5149 Distilled water; mineral or spring water bottling

(G-5490)
DISTTECH LLC
8101 Union Ave (44105-1560)
PHONE.................................800 321-3143
John Manfredi, *Manager*
EMP: 100
SQ FT: 1,749
SALES (corp-wide): 2.7B **Privately Held**
WEB: www.disttech.com
SIC: 4231 4213 4212 Trucking terminal facilities; trucking, except local; local trucking, without storage
HQ: Disttech, Llc
 4366 Mount Pleasant St Nw
 North Canton OH 44720
 330 491-0474

(G-5491)
DIVERSICARE OF AVON LLC
Also Called: Good Samaritan Nursing Home
4110 Rocky River Dr (44135-1175)
PHONE.................................440 937-6201
Kelly Gill, *President*
EMP: 137
SALES (est): 7.1MM
SALES (corp-wide): 574.7MM **Publicly Held**
SIC: 8051 Skilled nursing care facilities
PA: Diversicare Healthcare Services, Inc.
 1621 Galleria Blvd
 Brentwood TN 37027
 615 771-7575

(G-5492)
DIVERSIFIED LABOR SUPPORT LLC
7050 Engle Rd Ste 101 (44130-8406)
P.O. Box 42242, Brookpark (44142-0242)
PHONE.................................440 234-3090
EMP: 482
SQ FT: 2,769
SALES: 4.4MM **Privately Held**
SIC: 7363 Help Supply Services

(G-5493)
DIX & EATON INCORPORATED
200 Public Sq Ste 3900 (44114-2322)
PHONE.................................216 241-0405
Fax: 216 241-3070
Chas Withers, *CEO*
Angela Rodenhauser, *President*
Lisa Rose, *President*
David Hertz, *Managing Dir*
Jeffrey Linton, *Managing Dir*
EMP: 50
SQ FT: 23,000
SALES (est): 12MM **Privately Held**
WEB: www.dix-eaton.com
SIC: 8743 7311 Public relations & publicity; advertising agencies

(G-5494)
DJ NEFF ENTERPEISES INC
Also Called: Neff and Associates
6405 York Rd (44130-3033)
PHONE.................................440 884-3100
Dan Neff, *President*
Elaine O'Connor, *Admin Sec*
EMP: 35
SALES: 2.5MM **Privately Held**
WEB: www.neff-assoc.com
SIC: 8711 8713 Civil engineering; surveying services

(G-5495)
DLR GROUP INC
Also Called: Dlr Group Wstlake Reed Lskosky
1422 Euclid Ave Ste 300 (44115-1912)
PHONE.................................216 522-1350
Stanley Meradith, *President*
O H Martin Berglund, *Vice Pres*
Robert Carlson, *Vice Pres*
Shawn Carr, *Vice Pres*
Monica Green, *Vice Pres*
EMP: 60
SQ FT: 24,000
SALES (est): 1.1MM **Privately Held**
SIC: 8712 8711 7389 Architectural services; engineering services; interior design services

(G-5496)
DMD MANAGEMENT INC (PA)
Also Called: Legacy Health Services
12380 Plaza Dr (44130-1043)
PHONE.................................216 898-8399
Bruce Daskal, *CEO*
Jim Taylor, *COO*
Jim Wilson, *COO*
Harold Shachter, *Vice Pres*
Barbara Thomas, *Safety Mgr*
EMP: 50
SQ FT: 28,360
SALES (est): 106.8MM **Privately Held**
SIC: 8741 Nursing & personal care facility management

(G-5497)
DMD MANAGEMENT INC
12504 Cedar Rd (44106-3217)
PHONE.................................216 371-3600
Bruce Daskal, *Branch Mgr*
Larry White, *Officer*
EMP: 590 **Privately Held**
SIC: 8322 8051 Adult day care center; skilled nursing care facilities
PA: Dmd Management, Inc.
 12380 Plaza Dr
 Cleveland OH 44130

(G-5498)
DOLLAR PARADISE (PA)
Also Called: United Discount
1240 E 55th St (44103-1029)
PHONE.................................216 432-0421
Amin Alsoussou, *President*
EMP: 27
SALES (est): 8.6MM **Privately Held**
SIC: 5199 5331 Gifts & novelties; variety stores

(G-5499)
DOMINO FOODS INC
Also Called: Domino Sugar
2075 E 65th St (44103-4630)
PHONE.................................216 432-3222
Dan Macone, *Vice Pres*
Robert Ruppe, *QA Dir*
Aranka Vitarius, *Accountant*
Darrell Lubinsky, *VP Sales*

Jeffrey Bender, *Branch Mgr*
EMP: 70
SALES (corp-wide): 1.7B **Privately Held**
WEB: www.dominospecialtyingredients.com
SIC: 2099 7389 Sugar; packaging & labeling services
HQ: Domino Foods Inc.
 99 Wood Ave S Ste 901
 Iselin NJ 08830
 732 590-1173

(G-5500)
DON BOSCO COMMUNITY CENTER INC (PA)
Also Called: Don Bosco Centers
1763 Wickford Rd (44112-1207)
PHONE.................................816 421-3160
Nicholas Scielzo, *President*
Sheila Dann, *Vice Chairman*
Robert Metzler, *Vice Chairman*
Christine Hollis, *Accounting Mgr*
MO Orpin, *Exec Dir*
EMP: 92
SQ FT: 75,000
SALES: 1.9MM **Privately Held**
SIC: 8322 8211 8331 Individual & family services; community center; refugee service; high school, junior or senior; job training & vocational rehabilitation services; job counseling

(G-5501)
DON BOSCO COMMUNITY CENTER INC
Also Called: Bosco Centre For Senior
1763 Wickford Rd (44112-1207)
PHONE.................................816 421-3160
Brad Mullins, *Technology*
Nick Fcielzo, *Director*
EMP: 25
SALES (est): 216.5K
SALES (corp-wide): 1.9MM **Privately Held**
SIC: 8322 Community center
PA: The Don Bosco Community Center Inc
 1763 Wickford Rd
 Cleveland OH 44112
 816 421-3160

(G-5502)
DONLEN INC (HQ)
8905 Lake Ave (44102-6315)
PHONE.................................216 961-6767
Donald Strang, *President*
EMP: 75
SALES (est): 2.1MM
SALES (corp-wide): 17.3MM **Privately Held**
SIC: 7011 Hotels & motels
PA: Strang Corporation
 8905 Lake Ave Fl 1
 Cleveland OH 44102
 216 961-6767

(G-5503)
DONLEYS INC (PA)
5430 Warner Rd (44125-1140)
PHONE.................................216 524-6800
Fax: 216 642-3216
Terrance K Donley, *Ch of Bd*
Malcolm M Donley, *President*
Drew Holtzman, *President*
Kevin Beat, *Superintendent*
Joshua Brown, *Superintendent*
EMP: 148 EST: 1941
SQ FT: 44,000
SALES (est): 155.8MM **Privately Held**
WEB: www.donleyinc.com
SIC: 1542 Commercial & office building, new construction

(G-5504)
DONS BROOKLYN CHEVROLET INC
4941 Pearl Rd (44109-5184)
PHONE.................................216 741-1500
Fax: 216 674-1517
Donald Petruzzi, *President*
EMP: 45
SQ FT: 31,920
SALES: 13.3MM **Privately Held**
WEB: www.donsbrooklyn.com
SIC: 5511 5012 Automobiles, new & used; automobiles & other motor vehicles

GEOGRAPHIC SECTION
Cleveland - Cuyahoga County (G-5528)

(G-5505)
DORSKY HODGSON + PARTNERS INC (PA)
Also Called: Dorsky Hodgson Parrish Yue
23240 Chagrin Blvd # 300 (44122-5405)
PHONE..................216 464-8600
Fax: 216 464-8608
William Dorsky, *Ch of Bd*
Corneila Hodgeson, *President*
Charles A Cohen, *Principal*
James M Friedman, *Principal*
Geoffrey J Porter, *Principal*
EMP: 60
SALES (est): 10.3MM **Privately Held**
WEB: www.dorskyhodgson.com
SIC: 8712 Architectural engineering

(G-5506)
DORTRONIC SERVICE INC (PA)
Also Called: Action Door
201 E Granger Rd (44131-6728)
PHONE..................216 739-3667
Fax: 216 739-3680
Michelle Lorello-Zoocki, *CEO*
Michael Wittwer, *President*
Jeff Haines, *General Mgr*
Dino Mastanuono, *Vice Pres*
Dave Cavasini, *Treasurer*
EMP: 50
SQ FT: 25,000
SALES (est): 18.9MM **Privately Held**
SIC: 1751 7699 5031 Garage door, installation or erection; door & window repair; doors

(G-5507)
DOUGLASS & ASSOCIATES CO LPA
4725 Grayton Rd (44135-2307)
PHONE..................216 362-7777
David Douglass, *Managing Prtnr*
Sean Berney, *Vice Pres*
EMP: 28 EST: 1983
SALES (est): 1.9MM **Privately Held**
WEB: www.douglasslaw.com
SIC: 8111 General practice attorney, lawyer

(G-5508)
DOVETAIL CONSTRUCTION CO INC (PA)
Also Called: Dovetail Solar and Wind
26055 Emery Rd Ste G (44128-6211)
PHONE..................740 592-1800
Fax: 740 448-8022
Alan R Frasz, *President*
Matthew Bennett, *Vice Pres*
Rick Coan, *Finance*
Tom Taylor, *Manager*
Dave Leahy, *Director*
EMP: 25
SQ FT: 7,200
SALES (est): 6MM **Privately Held**
WEB: www.dovetailsolar.com
SIC: 1731 1711 Electric power systems contractors; solar energy contractor

(G-5509)
DRS HILL & THOMAS CO
Also Called: Eastside Mri
2785 Som Center Rd (44194-0001)
PHONE..................440 944-8887
EMP: 25
SALES (corp-wide): 11.4MM **Privately Held**
SIC: 8011 8071 Medical Doctor's Office Medical Laboratory
PA: Drs Hill & Thomas Co
  4853 Galaxy Pkwy Ste I
  Cleveland OH 44128
  216 831-9786

(G-5510)
DUANE MORRIS LLP
1614 E 40th St Fl 3 (44103-2319)
PHONE..................202 577-3075
Duane Morris, *Branch Mgr*
EMP: 36
SALES (corp-wide): 300MM **Privately Held**
SIC: 8111 General practice attorney, lawyer
PA: Duane Morris Llp
  30 S 17th St Fl 5
  Philadelphia PA 19103
  215 979-1000

(G-5511)
DUCTS INC
883 Addison Rd (44103-1607)
PHONE..................216 391-2400
Patricia Sickle Mc Elroy, *CEO*
John E Sickle Jr, *President*
John Haggerty, *Division Mgr*
Charlotte Sickle, *Chairman*
James Sickle, *Vice Pres*
EMP: 50
SQ FT: 30,000
SALES (est): 3.1MM **Privately Held**
SIC: 1761 3444 Sheet metalwork; sheet metalwork

(G-5512)
DUNBAR ARMORED INC
5505 Cloverleaf Pkwy (44125-4814)
PHONE..................216 642-5700
Fax: 216 642-9323
Jeff Johansen, *President*
Chad Tylicki, *Senior VP*
Art Schossow, *Vice Pres*
Lynne Cassell, *Human Resources*
David Spring, *Manager*
EMP: 50
SALES (corp-wide): 700.1MM **Privately Held**
WEB: www.dunbararmored.com
SIC: 7381 Armored car services
PA: Dunbar Armored, Inc.
  50 Schilling Rd
  Hunt Valley MD 21031
  410 584-9800

(G-5513)
DWELLWORKS LLC (PA)
Also Called: Rss
1317 Euclid Ave (44115-1819)
PHONE..................216 682-4200
Bob Rosing, *CEO*
Jessica Pike, *HR Admin*
Dori Condo, *Sales Staff*
Gene Novak, *Mng Member*
Robert Fela, *Manager*
EMP: 97
SQ FT: 11,000
SALES (est): 27.1MM **Privately Held**
SIC: 7389 Relocation service

(G-5514)
DWORKEN & BERNSTEIN CO LPA (PA)
Also Called: Dworken and Bernstein
1468 W 9th St Ste 135 (44113-1220)
PHONE..................216 861-4211
Fax: 216 861-1403
David M Dworken, *President*
Howard W Bernstein, *Vice Pres*
Marvin F Dworken, *Treasurer*
EMP: 43
SQ FT: 2,000
SALES (est): 4.6MM **Privately Held**
WEB: www.dworken-bernstein.com
SIC: 8111 General practice attorney, lawyer

(G-5515)
DWORKIN INC (PA)
Also Called: Dworkin Trucking
5400 Harvard Ave (44105-4899)
PHONE..................216 271-5318
Fax: 216 883-9103
Jack E Hankison, *Principal*
Jake Dworkin, *Principal*
Otto L Hankison, *Principal*
Patrick Perriello, *Plant Mgr*
Lewis Battaglia, *CFO*
EMP: 50 EST: 1939
SQ FT: 15,000
SALES (est): 8MM **Privately Held**
WEB: www.dworkin.com
SIC: 4213 Contract haulers

(G-5516)
E F BOYD & SON INC (PA)
Also Called: Boyd Funeral Home
2165 E 89th St (44106-3420)
PHONE..................216 791-0770
Fax: 216 421-2776
William F Boyd II, *President*
Marcella Boydcox, *Vice Pres*
Marcella Cox, *Vice Pres*
Marina Grant, *Vice Pres*
Mark Katzbach, *Bookkeeper*
EMP: 34
SQ FT: 20,000
SALES (est): 3.6MM **Privately Held**
SIC: 7261 Funeral home

(G-5517)
EAB TRUCK SERVICE
7951 Granger Rd (44125-4826)
PHONE..................216 525-0020
Fax: 216 447-1105
Darryl Fife, *CEO*
Ed Woods, *General Mgr*
Don Jones, *Vice Pres*
Dennis Myers, *Vice Pres*
Ed Adair, *Manager*
EMP: 64
SALES (est): 5MM **Privately Held**
WEB: www.trksvc.com
SIC: 4231 Trucking terminal facilities

(G-5518)
EARLY CHILDHOOD ENRICHMENT CTR
19824 Sussex Rd Rm 178 (44122-4917)
PHONE..................216 991-9761
Fax: 216 283-3585
Lynne Prange, *Director*
Michelle Block, *Asst Director*
EMP: 25
SALES (est): 2.4MM **Privately Held**
SIC: 8351 Preschool center

(G-5519)
EAST END NEIGHBORHOOD HSE ASSN
2749 Woodhill Rd (44104-3660)
PHONE..................216 791-9378
Fax: 216 791-9106
Connie Chrosniak, *Sales Executive*
Paul Hill Jr, *Director*
Denise Draper, *Program Dir*
EMP: 43
SQ FT: 50,000
SALES (est): 2.4MM **Privately Held**
WEB: www.ritesofpassage.org
SIC: 8322 8351 Social service center; youth center; senior citizens' center or association; child day care services

(G-5520)
EAST OHIO GAS COMPANY
Also Called: Dominion Energy Ohio
21200 Miles Rd (44128-4502)
PHONE..................216 736-6959
Bill Armstrong, *Manager*
EMP: 50
SQ FT: 37,452
SALES (corp-wide): 12.5B **Publicly Held**
SIC: 4924 Natural gas distribution
HQ: The East Ohio Gas Company
  19701 Libby Rd
  Maple Heights OH 44137
  800 362-7557

(G-5521)
EASTERN STAR HM OF CYHOGA CNTY
2114 Noble Rd (44112-1725)
PHONE..................216 761-0170
Fax: 216 681-0961
Jim Eckerle, *Administration*
EMP: 100
SQ FT: 15,000
SALES: 196.1K **Privately Held**
SIC: 8052 8051 Intermediate care facilities; skilled nursing care facilities

(G-5522)
EASTSIDE LANDSCAPING INC
572 Trebisky Rd (44143-2862)
P.O. Box 21801 (44121-0801)
PHONE..................216 381-0070
Fax: 216 381-9112
Ned Cultrona, *President*
Jim Freireich, *Vice Pres*
Gary Henry, *Manager*
EMP: 25
SALES (est): 1.7MM **Privately Held**
WEB: www.eastsidelandscaping.com
SIC: 0781 Landscape services

(G-5523)
EASY2 TECHNOLOGIES INC
Also Called: Easy 2 Technologies
1111 Chester Ave (44114-3545)
PHONE..................216 479-0482
Ethan Cohen, *CEO*
Matt Walsh, *President*
Carl Persson, *Vice Pres*
Michael Zurbuch, *QA Dir*
George Koenig, *VP Sales*
EMP: 30
SQ FT: 9,400
SALES (est): 2.6MM
SALES (corp-wide): 8.2MM **Privately Held**
WEB: www.easy2.com
SIC: 7373 Systems software development services
HQ: Answers Corporation
  6665 Delmar Blvd Ste 3000
  Saint Louis MO 63130

(G-5524)
EATON CORPORATION
Eaton Family Credit Union
333 Babbitt Rd Ste 100 (44123-1636)
PHONE..................216 920-2000
Michael Losneck, *Branch Mgr*
EMP: 260 **Privately Held**
WEB: www.eaton.com
SIC: 3714 5084 Hydraulic fluid power pumps for auto steering mechanism; hydraulic systems equipment & supplies
HQ: Eaton Corporation
  1000 Eaton Blvd
  Cleveland OH 44122
  216 523-5000

(G-5525)
EBSO INC
Also Called: Administrative Service Cons
3301 E Royalton Rd Ste 1 (44147-2835)
PHONE..................440 262-1133
Fax: 440 526-1608
Lisa Messer, *Branch Mgr*
Lynn Bletsh, *Info Tech Dir*
EMP: 30
SALES (corp-wide): 9.2MM **Privately Held**
SIC: 6324 Hospital & medical service plans
PA: Ebso Inc.
  7020 N Pt Wshngton Rd 2
  Glendale WI 53217
  414 410-1802

(G-5526)
ECLIPSE CO LLC
23209 Miles Rd (44128-5465)
PHONE..................440 552-9400
Yvette Jones, *Mng Member*
Jennifer Agresta,
Tom Agresta,
EMP: 50
SQ FT: 700
SALES (est): 4.1MM **Privately Held**
SIC: 8741 Construction management

(G-5527)
EDUCATION LOAN SERVICING CORP
Also Called: Xpress Loan Servicing
1500 W 3rd St Ste 125 (44113-1422)
PHONE..................216 706-8130
David H Harmon, *President*
Douglas L Feist, *Exec VP*
Perry D Moore, *Exec VP*
James G Clark, *CFO*
Jerry McFadden, *CFO*
EMP: 99
SQ FT: 20,000
SALES (est): 11.9MM **Privately Held**
WEB: www.educationloanservicingcorporation.com
SIC: 6141 Personal credit institutions

(G-5528)
EDWARD HOWARD & CO (PA)
1100 Superior Ave E # 1600 (44114-2530)
PHONE..................216 781-2400
Fax: 216 781-8810
Kathleen A Obert, *Ch of Bd*
Wayne R Hill, *President*
Mark Grieves, *Exec VP*
Nora C Jacobs, *Exec VP*
Marilyn Tomasi, *Exec VP*
EMP: 43

Cleveland - Cuyahoga County (G-5529)

SALES (est): 3.3MM Privately Held
SIC: 8743 7336 Public relations & publicity; graphic arts & related design

(G-5529)
EIGHTH DAY SOUND SYSTEMS INC
5450 Avion Park Dr (44143-1919)
PHONE..................440 995-2647
Fax: 440 995-2828
Tom Arko, *President*
Jack Boessneck, *Exec VP*
Alan Herschman, *Senior VP*
Cw Alkire, *Project Mgr*
Catherine Bellante, *CFO*
▲ **EMP:** 27
SQ FT: 27,500
SALES (est): 7.7MM Privately Held
WEB: www.8thdaysound.com
SIC: 1731 Sound equipment specialization

(G-5530)
ELDERCARE SERVICES INST LLC
11890 Fairhill Rd (44120-1053)
PHONE..................216 791-8000
Frank Cardinale, *CFO*
EMP: 85 **EST:** 2006
SALES (est): 752.5K Privately Held
SIC: 8082 Home health care services

(G-5531)
ELECTRA SOUND INC
10779 Brookpark Rd Ste A (44130-1164)
PHONE..................216 433-1050
Fax: 216 433-9425
Charles Masa, *President*
Greg Schwartz, *Parts Mgr*
Ray Grospitch, *Sales Mgr*
Charles Mesa, *Sales Executive*
EMP: 125
SALES (est): 3.2MM
SALES (corp-wide): 31MM Privately Held
WEB: www.electrasound.com
SIC: 7622 7382 Television repair shop; security systems services
PA: Electra Sound, Inc.
5260 Commerce Pkwy W
Parma OH 44130
216 433-9600

(G-5532)
ELEMENT MTRLS TCHNLGY HNTNGTN
Also Called: Stork Herron Cleveland
5405 E Schaaf Rd (44131-1337)
PHONE..................216 643-1208
EMP: 50
SALES (corp-wide): 135.5MM Privately Held
SIC: 8734 Testing Laboratory
HQ: Element Materials Technology Huntington Beach Inc.
15062 Bolsa Chica St
Huntington Beach CA 92649
714 933-2070

(G-5533)
EMERALD DEV ECNOMIC NETWRK INC
Also Called: Eden
7812 Madison Ave (44102-4056)
PHONE..................216 961-9690
Fax: 216 651-4066
Elaine Gimme, *COO*
Irene Collins, *CFO*
Timothy Wilber, *Accountant*
Christopher West, *Finance*
Linda Erb, *Human Res Mgr*
EMP: 51
SQ FT: 17,000
SALES: 27.6MM Privately Held
WEB: www.edeninc.org
SIC: 6513 Apartment building operators

(G-5534)
EMERGENCY MEDICAL SVCS BILLING
1701 Lakeside Ave E (44114-1118)
PHONE..................216 664-2598
Fax: 216 664-4592
Nicole Carlton, *Principal*
EMP: 40 **EST:** 2010

SALES (est): 71.2K Privately Held
SIC: 8721 9199 Billing & bookkeeping service; supply agency, government

(G-5535)
EMERITUS CORPORATION
Also Called: Emeritus At Brookside Estates
15435 Bagley Rd Ste 1 (44130-4827)
PHONE..................440 201-9200
Fax: 440 887-1126
Chris Belford, *Principal*
EMP: 60
SALES (corp-wide): 4.7B Publicly Held
WEB: www.emeraldestatesslc.com
SIC: 8361 Residential care
HQ: Emeritus Corporation
3131 Elliott Ave Ste 500
Milwaukee WI 53214

(G-5536)
EMERY LEASING CO LLC
Also Called: SUBURBAN PAVILION NURSING AND
20265 Emery Rd (44128-4122)
PHONE..................216 475-8880
David W Trimble, *CPA*
Stephen L Rosedale, *Mng Member*
EMP: 270
SALES: 11.4MM Privately Held
SIC: 8051 Convalescent home with continuous nursing care

(G-5537)
EMPIRE BRASS CO
Also Called: American Brass
5000 Superior Ave (44103-1238)
PHONE..................216 431-6565
Robert Mc Connville, *President*
▲ **EMP:** 50
SALES (est): 6.8MM Privately Held
WEB: www.empirebrassfaucets.com
SIC: 5074 3432 3364 Plumbing fittings & supplies; plumbing fixture fittings & trim; nonferrous die-castings except aluminum

(G-5538)
EMS RAMS YOUTH DEV GROUP INC
Also Called: E.M.s Rams Youth Football Team
1536 E 85th St (44106-3706)
PHONE..................216 282-4688
Heyward R Prude III, *CEO*
Latif Ali, *COO*
EMP: 30
SALES: 70.7K Privately Held
WEB: www.emsrams.org
SIC: 8641 Civic social & fraternal associations

(G-5539)
ENERGY MGT SPECIALISTS INC
Also Called: Ems
15800 Industrial Pkwy (44135-3320)
PHONE..................216 676-9045
Fax: 216 676-5948
Alan J Guzik, *President*
Kristine Guzik, *VP Sales*
EMP: 30
SQ FT: 8,800
SALES (est): 5.3MM Privately Held
WEB: www.energyman.com
SIC: 1711 Mechanical contractor

(G-5540)
ENGINEERED CON STRUCTURES CORP
14510 Broadway Ave (44125-1960)
PHONE..................216 520-2000
Fax: 216 520-2001
Donald J Mayer, *President*
Richard M Mayer, *Vice Pres*
EMP: 30
SALES (est): 4.2MM Privately Held
WEB: www.lakesideconstruction.com
SIC: 1771 Concrete work

(G-5541)
ENGINEERING DESIGN AND TESTING
Also Called: Ebnt
P.O. Box 30160 (44130-0160)
PHONE..................440 239-0362
Kim A Jur PHD, *President*
Mark Rusell, *Chief Engr*

Laurie Bartels, *Manager*
EMP: 100
SALES (est): 301.6K Privately Held
SIC: 8711 Consulting engineer

(G-5542)
ENPROTECH INDUSTRIAL TECH LLC (DH)
4259 E 49th St (44125-1001)
PHONE..................216 883-3220
Judy Collins, *Credit Mgr*
Pedro Garcia, *Mng Member*
Ben Handshue, *Sr Project Mgr*
David Kaminowski, *Manager*
▲ **EMP:** 210
SQ FT: 96,000
SALES: 75MM
SALES (corp-wide): 42.5B Privately Held
WEB: www.itochu.com
SIC: 3547 3365 3599 8711 Rolling mill machinery; machinery castings, aluminum; custom machinery; engineering services; electrical repair shops
HQ: Enprotech Corp.
4259 E 49th St
Cleveland OH 44125
216 206-0080

(G-5543)
ENRICHMENT CENTER OF WISHING W (PA)
14574 Ridge Rd (44133-4940)
PHONE..................440 237-5000
Fax: 440 237-5000
Johanne Wigton, *President*
EMP: 80
SQ FT: 11,000
SALES (est): 1.9MM Privately Held
SIC: 8351 Child day care services; preschool center

(G-5544)
ENTRYPOINT CONSULTING LLC
600 Superior Ave E # 1300 (44114-2654)
PHONE..................216 674-9070
Fax: 216 674-9069
Peter Martin, *President*
Robert Waldrop, *Vice Pres*
Diane Schloffer, *Manager*
Mario Mancini, *Director*
Nichalas A Canitano,
EMP: 55
SQ FT: 1,500
SALES (est): 5.9MM Privately Held
WEB: www.entrypointconsulting.com
SIC: 7379

(G-5545)
ENVIROTEST SYSTEMS CORP
13000 York Delta Dr (44133-3521)
PHONE..................330 963-4464
F Miller, *Branch Mgr*
EMP: 34
SQ FT: 7,672 Privately Held
WEB: www.il.etest.com
SIC: 7549 Emissions testing without repairs, automotive
HQ: Envirotest Systems Corp.
7 Kripes Rd
East Granby CT 06026

(G-5546)
ENVIROTEST SYSTEMS CORP
Also Called: Ohio E-Check
24770 Sperry Dr (44145-1531)
PHONE..................330 963-4464
EMP: 34
SQ FT: 7,651 Privately Held
WEB: www.il.etest.com
SIC: 7549 Emissions testing without repairs, automotive
HQ: Envirotest Systems Corp.
7 Kripes Rd
East Granby CT 06026

(G-5547)
ENVISION WASTE SERVICES LLC
4451 Renaissance Pkwy (44128-5754)
PHONE..................216 831-1818
Steven M Viny, *CEO*
Gary Kaufman, *Plant Mgr*
Clayton A Minder, *CFO*
Debbie Sideris, *Administration*
EMP: 93

SQ FT: 4,000
SALES (est): 13.1MM Privately Held
SIC: 4953 Recycling, waste materials

(G-5548)
EQUIPMENT MANUFACTURERS INTL
Also Called: E M I
16151 Puritas Ave (44135-2617)
P.O. Box 94725 (44101-4725)
PHONE..................216 651-6700
Fax: 216 524-3660
Scott Shaver, *President*
Jerry Senk, *Principal*
John Zelli, *Engineer*
R T Mackin, *Treasurer*
Bob Armstrong, *Controller*
▲ **EMP:** 30
SQ FT: 65,000
SALES: 10MM Privately Held
WEB: www.emi-inc.com
SIC: 3559 5084 Foundry machinery & equipment; industrial machinery & equipment

(G-5549)
EQUITY RESIDENTIAL PROPERTIES
Also Called: Reserve Square Apts
1701 E 12th St Ste 35 (44114-3237)
PHONE..................216 861-2700
Sandy Gorie, *General Mgr*
Greg Turvey, *Engineer*
Trisha Curiale, *Manager*
Kenric Hall, *Manager*
Ray Ratermann, *Manager*
EMP: 50
SQ FT: 1,709,000
SALES (est): 3.1MM Privately Held
WEB: www.thekanddgroup.com
SIC: 6513 6512 Apartment building operators; commercial & industrial building operation

(G-5550)
ERNST & YOUNG LLP
Also Called: Ey
950 Main Ave Ste 1800 (44113-7214)
PHONE..................216 861-5000
Fax: 216 861-8157
Michael Frederick, *Vice Pres*
Mary Dalic, *Human Resources*
Jeremy D Moe, *Human Resources*
Christopher W Smith, *Manager*
Kelsey Anthony, *Manager*
EMP: 65
SALES (corp-wide): 5.3B Privately Held
WEB: www.ey.com
SIC: 8721 Certified public accountant
PA: Ernst & Young Llp
5 Times Sq Fl Conlv1
New York NY 10036
212 773-3000

(G-5551)
ERNST & YOUNG LLP
Also Called: Ey
1660 W 2nd St Ste 200 (44113-1446)
PHONE..................216 583-1823
Fax: 216 861-2162
Michelle Settecase, *Principal*
EMP: 228
SALES (corp-wide): 5.3B Privately Held
SIC: 8721 Certified public accountant
PA: Ernst & Young Llp
5 Times Sq Fl Conlv1
New York NY 10036
212 773-3000

(G-5552)
ETHNIC VOICE OF AMERICA
4606 Bruening Dr (44134-4640)
PHONE..................440 845-0922
Irene K Smirnov, *President*
EMP: 30
SALES: 0 Privately Held
WEB: www.ethnic-voice.com
SIC: 8699 Personal interest organization

(G-5553)
EUCLID INDUS MAINT CLG CONTRS
1561 E 40th St (44103-2301)
PHONE..................216 361-0288
Fax: 216 361-0290

GEOGRAPHIC SECTION

Cleveland - Cuyahoga County (G-5577)

Carol Presser, *President*
EMP: 150
SQ FT: 5,000
SALES (est): 4.1MM **Privately Held**
SIC: 7349 1799 Janitorial service, contract basis; window cleaning; sandblasting of building exteriors

(G-5554)
EUCLID SC TRANSPORTATION
393 Babbitt Rd (44123-1645)
PHONE.................................216 797-7600
Fax: 216 797-7606
Dan Dodson, *Principal*
Kimberly Allen, *Asst Supt*
Rod Mazzaro, *Foreman/Supr*
Lisa Rastatter, *Manager*
Glenn Blade, *Maintence Staff*
EMP: 65
SALES (est): 1.7MM **Privately Held**
SIC: 4789 Transportation services

(G-5555)
EURO USA INC (PA)
4481 Johnston Pkwy (44128-2952)
PHONE.................................216 714-0500
Fax: 216 663-3759
Joseph D O'Donnell, *President*
Nancy A Farmer, *President*
Jerry L Marshaw Jr, *Principal*
Terry Comer, *Vice Pres*
Frank Fox, *Opers Mgr*
▲ **EMP:** 100
SQ FT: 75,000
SALES (est): 67.3MM **Privately Held**
SIC: 5149 Specialty food items

(G-5556)
EVENTIONS LTD
14925 Shaker Blvd (44120-1647)
PHONE.................................216 952-9898
Randy Dauchot, *Managing Prtnr*
Stephanie Eisele, *Partner*
EMP: 32
SALES: 70K **Privately Held**
WEB: www.eventions.net
SIC: 7299 7389 Party planning service; business services

(G-5557)
EVERFAST INC
Also Called: Calico Corners
24651 Cedar Rd (44124-3781)
PHONE.................................216 360-9176
Christine Walker, *Principal*
EMP: 288
SALES (corp-wide): 374.2MM **Privately Held**
SIC: 5023 Decorative home furnishings & supplies
PA: Everfast, Inc.
   203 Gale Ln
   Kennett Square PA 19348
   610 444-9700

(G-5558)
EVERGREEN COOPERATIVE LDRY INC
540 E 105th St Ste 206 (44108-4310)
PHONE.................................216 268-3548
Cecil Lee, *CEO*
EMP: 40
SQ FT: 15,000
SALES (est): 1.1MM **Privately Held**
SIC: 7211 Power laundries, family & commercial

(G-5559)
EVERSTAFF LLC (PA)
6500 Rockside Rd Ste 385 (44131-2353)
PHONE.................................877 392-6151
Fax: 216 369-2565
Harold E Dahringer, *CFO*
Rebecca Hannan, *Accounting Mgr*
Jon Gilbow, *Branch Mgr*
Luanne Eddy, *Program Mgr*
Gabrielle Howell, *Program Mgr*
EMP: 50
SALES (est): 4.1MM **Privately Held**
SIC: 7361 Executive placement

(G-5560)
EXCELAS LLC
387 Golfview Ln Ste 200 (44143-4417)
PHONE.................................440 442-7310
Jean C Bourgeois, *Principal*

Linda Rausch, *Director*
Kim Henchar, *Officer*
EMP: 40
SALES (est): 2.2MM **Privately Held**
SIC: 8099 Medical services organization

(G-5561)
EXEL GLOBAL LOGISTICS INC
21500 Aerospace Pkwy (44142-1071)
PHONE.................................440 243-5900
Liz McBride, *Finance Mgr*
Bill Krabec, *Branch Mgr*
James Sobota, *Manager*
EMP: 70
SALES (corp-wide): 71.2B **Privately Held**
WEB: www.exelgloballogistics.com
SIC: 4731 Freight forwarding
HQ: Exel Global Logistics Inc.
   22879 Glenn Dr Ste 100
   Sterling VA 20164
   703 350-1298

(G-5562)
EXPEDITORS INTL WASH INC
18029 Cleveland Pkwy Dr (44135-3247)
PHONE.................................440 243-9900
Fax: 440 243-9037
Rick Rostan, *Senior VP*
Robert Gierszal, *Manager*
EMP: 80
SALES (corp-wide): 6.9B **Publicly Held**
WEB: www.expd.com
SIC: 4731 Foreign freight forwarding
PA: Expeditors International Of Washington, Inc.
   1015 3rd Ave Fl 12
   Seattle WA 98104
   206 674-3400

(G-5563)
EXPLORYS INC
1111 Superior Ave E (44114-2522)
PHONE.................................216 767-4700
Stephen McHale, *CEO*
Charles Lougheed, *President*
Thomas Chickerella, *COO*
Anil Jain, *Senior VP*
Dave Diamond, *Vice Pres*
EMP: 54
SALES (est): 12.7MM
SALES (corp-wide): 79.1B **Publicly Held**
SIC: 7372 Prepackaged software
PA: International Business Machines Corporation
   1 New Orchard Rd Ste 1 # 1
   Armonk NY 10504
   914 499-1900

(G-5564)
FABRIZI TRUCKING & PAV CO INC (PA)
20389 1st Ave (44130-2433)
PHONE.................................330 483-3291
Fax: 330 483-3841
Emilio Fabrizi Jr, *President*
Maria Fearer, *Exec VP*
Alex Denigris, *Project Mgr*
Maria Fabrizi, *CFO*
Patricia A Fabrizi, *Treasurer*
EMP: 160 **EST:** 1949
SQ FT: 5,000
SALES (est): 33.8MM **Privately Held**
SIC: 1623 1611 Water & sewer line construction; highway & street paving contractor

(G-5565)
FAIRMOUNT MONTESSORI ASSN
Also Called: RUFFING MONTESSORI SCHOOL
3380 Fairmount Blvd (44118-4214)
PHONE.................................216 321-7571
Fax: 216 321-7568
Gordon Maas, *Director*
Julia Sheehan, *Director*
Beth Ambrose, *Teacher*
EMP: 44
SQ FT: 22,250
SALES (est): 5.4MM **Privately Held**
WEB: www.ruffingeast.org
SIC: 8351 8211 Montessori child development center; private elementary & secondary schools

(G-5566)
FAIRVIEW EYE CENTER INC
21375 Lorain Rd (44126-2122)
PHONE.................................440 333-3060
Fax: 440 333-0273
Dr Louis P Caravella, *President*
Jeff Terbeck, *Vice Pres*
Mary Becka, *Practice Mgr*
Theresa G Dillehay, *Administration*
EMP: 45
SQ FT: 5,000
SALES (est): 5.2MM **Privately Held**
WEB: www.fairvieweyecenter.com
SIC: 8011 Ophthalmologist

(G-5567)
FAIRVIEW HLTH SYS FDERAL CR UN
18101 Lorain Ave (44111-5612)
PHONE.................................216 476-7000
Fax: 216 476-2944
K Gopal, *Owner*
EMP: 1038
SALES (est): 1.1MM
SALES (corp-wide): 8B **Privately Held**
SIC: 6061 Federal credit unions
HQ: Fairview Hospital
   18101 Lorain Ave
   Cleveland OH 44111
   216 476-7000

(G-5568)
FAIRVIEW HOSPITAL (HQ)
Also Called: CLEVELAND CLINIC HEALTH SYSTEM
18101 Lorain Ave (44111-5612)
PHONE.................................216 476-7000
Fax: 216 476-7017
Toby Cosgrove, *CEO*
Louis Caravella MD, *President*
Delos Cosgrove, *President*
Adam Miller, *Business Mgr*
John Mills, *COO*
EMP: 39
SQ FT: 327,000
SALES: 474.3MM
SALES (corp-wide): 8B **Privately Held**
SIC: 8062 8011 General medical & surgical hospitals; offices & clinics of medical doctors
PA: The Cleveland Clinic Foundation
   9500 Euclid Ave
   Cleveland OH 44195
   216 636-8335

(G-5569)
FAMICOS FOUNDATION
1325 Ansel Rd (44106-1079)
PHONE.................................216 791-6476
Fax: 216 791-6485
Richard Weaver, *Ch of Bd*
Peter Lee, *Vice Ch Bd*
Michael Griffen, *Treasurer*
Don Woodruff, *Manager*
John Anoliefo, *Exec Dir*
EMP: 29
SALES: 7.4MM **Privately Held**
WEB: www.famicos.org
SIC: 8399 Community development groups

(G-5570)
FAMILY PHYSICIANS ASSOCIATES (PA)
5187 Mayfield Rd Ste 102 (44124-2467)
PHONE.................................440 442-3866
Fax: 440 449-8157
Terrence Isakov, *President*
Patti Hines, *Supervisor*
EMP: 50
SQ FT: 14,179
SALES (est): 5.4MM **Privately Held**
WEB: www.southernrain.net
SIC: 8011 General & family practice, physician/surgeon

(G-5571)
FAMOUS ENTERPRISES INC
11200 Madison Ave (44102-2323)
PHONE.................................216 529-1010
Steve Wisman, *Manager*
EMP: 50 **Privately Held**
WEB: www.jfgood.com
SIC: 5251 5075 Hardware; warm air heating equipment & supplies

PA: Famous Enterprises, Inc.
   2620 Ridgewood Rd Ste 200
   Akron OH 44313

(G-5572)
FANTON LOGISTICS INC (PA)
10801 Broadway Ave (44125-1653)
PHONE.................................216 341-2400
Mycola Kachaluba, *President*
EMP: 52
SQ FT: 3,700
SALES: 7.6MM **Privately Held**
SIC: 4213 Trucking, except local

(G-5573)
FARM HOUSE FOOD DISTRS INC
9000 Woodland Ave (44104-3225)
PHONE.................................216 791-6948
Fax: 216 791-3474
Daniel Simon, *President*
Meryl Simon, *Corp Secy*
Matt Armstrong, *Controller*
EMP: 25
SQ FT: 10,000
SALES (est): 3.4MM **Privately Held**
WEB: www.farmhousefish.com
SIC: 5411 5146 Supermarkets, independent; fish & seafoods

(G-5574)
FARROW CLEANERS CO (PA)
Also Called: Guild Custom Drapery
3788 Lee Rd (44128-1464)
PHONE.................................216 561-2355
Jack Grimaldi, *President*
Salvatore P Grimaldi, *Vice Pres*
Laura Healy, *Manager*
EMP: 39 **EST:** 1948
SQ FT: 8,000
SALES (est): 2.8MM **Privately Held**
SIC: 7217 5714 5713 7216 Carpet & rug cleaning plant; draperies; carpets; drycleaning plants, except rugs; curtain cleaning & repair; repairing fire damage, single-family houses; renovation, remodeling & repairs: industrial buildings

(G-5575)
FASHION WALLCOVERINGS INC
4005 Carnegie Ave (44103-4334)
PHONE.................................216 432-1600
Fax: 216 432-0800
Louis Roesch, *Ch of Bd*
Joseph Olivier, *President*
Dorothy Roesch, *Corp Secy*
EMP: 90 **EST:** 1959
SQ FT: 92,500
SALES (est): 12.4MM **Privately Held**
WEB: www.fashionwallcoverings.com
SIC: 5198 Wallcoverings

(G-5576)
FASTBALL SPT PRODUCTIONS LLC
Also Called: Sportstime Ohio
1333 Lakeside Ave E (44114-1134)
PHONE.................................440 746-8000
F McGillicuedy, *General Mgr*
Francois McGillicuedy, *General Mgr*
Mark Conzelomann, *Manager*
EMP: 35
SALES (est): 1.3MM
SALES (corp-wide): 28.5B **Publicly Held**
SIC: 7812 Motion picture & video production
PA: Twenty-First Century Fox, Inc.
   1211 Ave Of The Americas
   New York NY 10036
   212 852-7000

(G-5577)
FATHOM SEO LLC (PA)
Also Called: Fathom Online Marketing
8200 Sweet Valley Dr (44125-4267)
PHONE.................................216 525-0510
Fax: 216 369-2227
Evan Horomanski, *Business Mgr*
Beth Ainslie, *Vice Pres*
Elizabeth Ainslie, *Vice Pres*
Steve Kozak, *Vice Pres*
Elizabeth Lynch, *Vice Pres*
EMP: 68
SALES (est): 24.5MM **Privately Held**
WEB: www.fathomseo.com
SIC: 8742 Marketing consulting services

Cleveland - Cuyahoga County (G-5578)

(G-5578)
FAY SHARPE LLP
The Halle Bldg 1228e (44115)
PHONE..................216 363-9000
Roseanne Giuliani, *President*
Patrick Roche, *Managing Prtnr*
Joseph D Dreher, *Partner*
Steven Haas, *Partner*
Richard M Klein, *Partner*
EMP: 94
SQ FT: 40,000
SALES (est): 13.2MM **Privately Held**
WEB: www.faysharpe.com
SIC: 8111 General practice law office

(G-5579)
FC CONTINENTAL LANDLORD LLC
50 Public Sq Ste 1360 (44113-2233)
PHONE..................216 621-6060
Forest City Residential Group, *Mng Member*
Fc Continental Master Tenant L,
EMP: 2917
SQ FT: 2,500
SALES: 5MM
SALES (corp-wide): 911.9MM **Privately Held**
SIC: 6531 Real estate agents & managers
HQ: Forest City Enterprises, L.P.
  50 Public Sq Ste 1100
  Cleveland OH 44113
  216 621-6060

(G-5580)
FEDELI GROUP INC
5005 Rockside Rd Ste 500 (44131-2184)
P.O. Box 318003 (44131-8003)
PHONE..................216 328-8080
Fax: 216 328-8081
Umberto Fedeli, *CEO*
Harry Brownfield Jr, *Senior VP*
Edward M Draine, *Vice Pres*
David Graf, *Controller*
Lori Daley, *Manager*
EMP: 90 **EST:** 1975
SQ FT: 25,000
SALES (est): 35.8MM **Privately Held**
WEB: www.thefedeligroup.com
SIC: 6411 Insurance agents; property & casualty insurance agent

(G-5581)
FEDERAL INSURANCE COMPANY
Also Called: Chubb
1375 E 9th St Ste 1960 (44114-1724)
PHONE..................216 687-1700
Fax: 216 987-8601
Jessica M Jung, *Manager*
EMP: 35
SALES (corp-wide): 28.7B **Privately Held**
WEB: www.federalinsurancecompany.com
SIC: 6411 Insurance agents, brokers & service
HQ: Federal Insurance Company
  15 Mountainview Rd
  Warren NJ 07059
  908 903-2000

(G-5582)
FEDERAL MACHINERY & EQP CO (PA)
Also Called: Federal Equipment Company
8200 Bessemer Ave (44127-1837)
PHONE..................800 652-2466
Fax: 216 271-5210
Larry Kadis, *CEO*
Michael Kadis, *President*
Morris I Goldsmithn, *Principal*
Matt Hicks, *COO*
Adam Covitt, *Vice Pres*
◆ **EMP:** 33 **EST:** 1957
SQ FT: 350,000
SALES (est): 15MM **Privately Held**
WEB: www.fedequip.com
SIC: 5084 Materials handling machinery

(G-5583)
FEDERAL RSRVE BNK OF CLEVELAND (HQ)
1455 E 6th St (44114-2517)
P.O. Box 6387 (44101-1387)
PHONE..................216 579-2000
Fax: 216 579-3198
Sandra Pianalto, *CEO*
Alfred M Rankin Jr, *Ch of Bd*
John P Surma, *Ch of Bd*
John Lytell, *President*
Anthony Powell, *President*
EMP: 760 **EST:** 1914
SALES (est): 4.3MM **Privately Held**
WEB: www.clevelandfed.org
SIC: 6011 Federal reserve banks
PA: Board Of Governors Of The Federal Reserve System
  20th St Cnsttution Ave Nw
  Washington DC 20551
  202 452-3000

(G-5584)
FEDEX CORPORATION
17831 Englewood Dr (44130-3452)
PHONE..................440 234-0315
EMP: 34
SALES (corp-wide): 47.4B **Publicly Held**
SIC: 4513 Air Courier Services
PA: Fedex Corporation
  942 Shady Grove Rd S
  Memphis TN 38120
  901 818-7500

(G-5585)
FERRALLOY INC
28001 Ranney Pkwy (44145-1159)
PHONE..................440 250-1900
William Habansky Jr, *President*
Sherri Habansky, *Corp Secy*
▲ **EMP:** 27
SQ FT: 15,000
SALES (est): 10.3MM **Privately Held**
WEB: www.ferralloy.com
SIC: 5051 3599 Castings, rough: iron or steel; machine shop, jobbing & repair

(G-5586)
FINANCIAL PLNNERS OF CLEVELAND
Also Called: Nca Financial Planners
6095 Parkland Blvd # 210 (44124-6139)
PHONE..................440 473-1115
Kevin Myeroff, *President*
Les Globits, *Ch Invest Ofcr*
Amanda Ballantyne, *Financial Analy*
Jeannette Fabian, *Technology*
Amy Smith, *Assistant*
EMP: 28
SQ FT: 3,000
SALES (est): 4.8MM **Privately Held**
WEB: www.ncafinancial.com
SIC: 6282 6411 Investment advisory service; pension & retirement plan consultants

(G-5587)
FIREFIGHTERS CMNTY CR UN INC
2300 Saint Clair Ave Ne (44114-4049)
PHONE..................216 621-4644
William Deighton, *Ch of Bd*
Lyn Ruggeri, *COO*
Barbara Starynchak, *Opers Mgr*
John Carrick, *CFO*
Ron Froelich, *Auditing Mgr*
EMP: 28
SALES (est): 3.7MM
SALES (corp-wide): 9.5MM **Privately Held**
SIC: 6062 6163 State credit unions, not federally chartered; loan brokers
PA: Firefighters Community Credit Union, Inc.
  4664 E 71st St
  Cleveland OH 44125
  216 621-4644

(G-5588)
FIRST AMERICAN EQUITY LN SVCS (DH)
1100 Superior Ave E # 3 (44114-2530)
PHONE..................800 221-8683
Michael B Hopkins, *President*
John Baumbick, *Counsel*
Michael Cullen, *Senior VP*
Alyse Butts, *Vice Pres*
Sean Conway, *CFO*
EMP: 200
SQ FT: 37,736
SALES (est): 70MM **Publicly Held**
WEB: www.faequity.com
SIC: 6361 Real estate title insurance
HQ: First American Title Insurance Company
  1 First American Way
  Santa Ana CA 92707
  800 854-3643

(G-5589)
FIRST AMERICAN TITLE INSUR CO
1100 Superior Ave E # 200 (44114-2518)
PHONE..................216 241-1278
Stephen Vogt, *Branch Mgr*
EMP: 27 **Publicly Held**
SIC: 6361 Real estate title insurance
HQ: First American Title Insurance Company
  1 First American Way
  Santa Ana CA 92707
  800 854-3643

(G-5590)
FIRST BAPTIST DAY CARE CENTER
Also Called: Childrens Ctr of Frst Bptst Ch
3630 Fairmount Blvd (44118-4341)
PHONE..................216 371-9394
Fax: 216 932-8554
Jane Pernicone, *Director*
EMP: 31
SALES (est): 951.5K **Privately Held**
SIC: 8351 Child day care services

(G-5591)
FIRST BUSINESS FINCL SVCS INC
5005 Rockside Rd Ste 600 (44131-6827)
PHONE..................216 573-3792
Lisa Allen, *Branch Mgr*
EMP: 30
SALES (corp-wide): 92.4MM **Publicly Held**
SIC: 6799 Investors
PA: First Business Financial Services, Inc.
  401 Charmany Dr
  Madison WI 53719
  608 238-8008

(G-5592)
FIRST CHOICE MEDICAL STAFFING
1457 W 117th St (44107-5101)
PHONE..................216 521-2222
Fax: 216 521-2220
Ed Newton, *Principal*
EMP: 152
SALES (corp-wide): 4.6MM **Privately Held**
SIC: 8059 Nursing home, except skilled & intermediate care facility
PA: First Choice Medical Staffing Of Ohio, Inc.
  1457 W 117th St
  Cleveland OH 44107
  216 521-2222

(G-5593)
FIRST CHOICE MEDICAL STAFFING (PA)
1457 W 117th St (44107-5101)
PHONE..................216 521-2222
Charles Slone, *President*
Terry Mathews, *Controller*
Charles Sloan, *Financial Exec*
Karen V D, *Medical Dir*
EMP: 425
SALES (est): 4.6MM **Privately Held**
SIC: 7361 Employment agencies

(G-5594)
FIRST CLASS LIMOS INC
31525 Aurora Rd Ste 5 (44139-2763)
PHONE..................440 248-1114
Jimmy Michalek, *President*
EMP: 25
SALES (est): 636K **Privately Held**
WEB: www.firstclasslimos.net
SIC: 4119 Limousine rental, with driver

(G-5595)
FIRST ENERGY NUCLEAR OPER CO
Also Called: Beta Lab & Technical Svcs
6670 Beta Dr (44143-2352)
PHONE..................440 604-9836
Fax: 440 604-9800
Pete Cena, *President*
Michael J Yeager, *Technical Staff*
Steve Braunfield, *Director*
EMP: 75
SQ FT: 66,000
SALES (est): 10MM **Privately Held**
SIC: 8734 8731 Testing laboratories; commercial research laboratory

(G-5596)
FIRST FEDERAL CREDIT CONTROL
Also Called: Interntnl Spcial Adit Systems
24700 Chagrin Blvd # 205 (44122-5630)
PHONE..................216 360-2000
Fax: 216 360-2005
Norm Shafran, *President*
Brian Himmel, *Vice Pres*
Leah Mandel, *Vice Pres*
Jill Joseph, *Manager*
EMP: 40
SQ FT: 6,300
SALES (est): 2.8MM **Privately Held**
SIC: 7322 Collection agency, except real estate

(G-5597)
FIRST FINCL TITLE AGCY OF OHIO
1500 W 3rd St Ste 400 (44113-1438)
PHONE..................216 664-1920
David Kreisman, *President*
Kriss Felty, *Manager*
EMP: 28
SALES (est): 1.1MM **Privately Held**
SIC: 6541 Title & trust companies

(G-5598)
FIRST INTERSTATE PROPERTIES
25333 Cedar Rd Ste 300 (44124-3763)
PHONE..................216 381-2900
Fax: 216 381-2901
Mitchell Schneider, *President*
Kelly Hoy, *Counsel*
Daniel Hoy, *Opers Staff*
Emily Christyson, *Marketing Staff*
John Grafton, *Manager*
EMP: 40
SQ FT: 2,400
SALES (est): 5.5MM **Privately Held**
WEB: www.first-interstate.com
SIC: 6512 Shopping center, property operation only

(G-5599)
FIRST OHIO BANC & LENDING INC
6100 Rckside Woods Blvd N (44131-2366)
PHONE..................216 642-8900
Fax: 216 642-9110
Kirk Doskocil, *President*
Tim Boyle, *Manager*
Jason Lukasik, *Manager*
EMP: 280
SALES (est): 32.8MM **Privately Held**
SIC: 6162 Mortgage bankers & correspondents

(G-5600)
FIRSTAT NURSING SERVICES
21825 Chagrin Blvd # 300 (44122-5359)
PHONE..................216 295-1500
Fax: 216 295-0750
David Skoglunb, *Owner*
Rene Hollon, *Financial Exec*
EMP: 100
SALES (est): 2.6MM **Privately Held**
WEB: www.firstat.cc
SIC: 7361 7363 Nurses' registry; help supply services

(G-5601)
FIT TECHNOLOGIES LLC
1375 Euclid Ave Ste 310 (44115-1808)
PHONE..................216 583-0733
Micki Tubbs, *CEO*
Michelle Tomallo, *President*
Jay Ford, *Opers Staff*
Ruth Cruzadl, *Office Mgr*
Fred Franks, *CIO*
EMP: 48

GEOGRAPHIC SECTION

Cleveland - Cuyahoga County (G-5623)

SALES (est): 11.2MM **Privately Held**
WEB: www.schoolone.com
SIC: 7379

(G-5602)
FIVE SEASONS SPT CNTRY CLB INC
28105 Clemens Rd (44145-1100)
PHONE..................440 899-4555
Fax: 440 892-3376
John Sherwood, *Chief*
EMP: 100 **Privately Held**
WEB: www.fiveseasonsday.com
SIC: 7997 Country club, membership
HQ: Five Seasons Sports Country Club, Inc.
100 E Rivercenter Blvd # 1100
Covington KY 41011

(G-5603)
FLACK STEEL LLC (PA)
Also Called: Flack Global Metals
425 W Lkeside Ave Ste 200 (44113)
PHONE..................216 456-0700
Jeremy Flack, *President*
Ben Bucci, *President*
Greg Underwood, *Exec VP*
John Lascola, *Vice Pres*
Brittany Damico, *Project Mgr*
▲ EMP: 25
SALES (est): 94.6MM **Privately Held**
SIC: 5051 Steel

(G-5604)
FLASH SEATS LLC (PA)
1 Center Ct (44115-4001)
PHONE..................216 420-2000
Samuel Gerace,
EMP: 31
SALES (est): 3.5MM **Privately Held**
SIC: 7999 Concession operator

(G-5605)
FLAVIK VILLAGE DEVELOPMENT
5620 Broadway Ave Rm 200 (44127-1754)
PHONE..................216 429-1182
Peter Gentile, *President*
William Woods, *Vice Pres*
Christine Smetna, *Treasurer*
Anthony Brancatelli, *Exec Dir*
Sr Ann Solma, *Admin Sec*
EMP: 30 EST: 1981
SQ FT: 4,500
SALES: 2MM **Privately Held**
WEB: www.slavicvillage.org
SIC: 8748 Urban planning & consulting services

(G-5606)
FLEXECO INCORPORATED
Also Called: Flex Spas Cleveland
2600 Hamilton Ave (44114-3756)
PHONE..................216 812-3304
Cleve Rudolph, *Branch Mgr*
EMP: 35
SALES (corp-wide): 5.1MM **Privately Held**
WEB: www.flexbaths.com
SIC: 7991 Health club; exercise facilities; spas
PA: Flexeco Incorporated
2600 Hamilton Ave
Cleveland OH 44114
216 812-3371

(G-5607)
FLEXNOVA INC
6100 Oak Tree Blvd (44131-2544)
PHONE..................216 288-6961
Steve Rossi, *President*
EMP: 30
SQ FT: 1,000
SALES (est): 2MM **Privately Held**
SIC: 7372 Prepackaged software

(G-5608)
FLIGHT OPTIONS LLC (HQ)
26180 Curtiss Wright Pkwy (44143-1453)
PHONE..................216 261-3500
Kenn Ricci, *CEO*
Doug Lightcap, *General Mgr*
Ernest Royal, *General Mgr*
Christian McCracken, *Area Mgr*
Aaron Misko, *Area Mgr*
EMP: 240

SQ FT: 119,000
SALES (est): 54.8MM
SALES (corp-wide): 82MM **Privately Held**
WEB: www.flightoptions.com
SIC: 7359 Aircraft rental
PA: Directional Capital Llc
355 Richmond Rd Ste 8
Richmond Heights OH 44143
216 261-3000

(G-5609)
FLIGHT SERVICES & SYSTEMS INC (PA)
5005 Rockside Rd Ste 940 (44131-6829)
PHONE..................216 328-0090
Robert Weitzel, *CEO*
Brett West, *General Mgr*
Phil Armstrong, *Exec VP*
Christopher Kubala, *Info Tech Dir*
Sarah Collier, *Director*
EMP: 104
SALES (est): 94MM **Privately Held**
SIC: 7389 Safety inspection service

(G-5610)
FNB CORPORATION
413 Northfield Rd (44146-2202)
PHONE..................440 439-2200
Robert Toth, *Branch Mgr*
EMP: 29
SALES (corp-wide): 1.2B **Publicly Held**
SIC: 6021 National commercial banks
PA: F.N.B. Corporation
1 N Shore Ctr
Pittsburgh PA 15212
800 555-5455

(G-5611)
FOR WOMEN LIKE ME INC
8800 Woodland Ave (44104-3221)
PHONE..................407 848-7339
Arline Burks, *CEO*
EMP: 42
SALES (corp-wide): 53MM **Privately Held**
SIC: 7812 Television film production
PA: For Women Like Me, Inc.
46 Shopping Plz Ste 155
Chagrin Falls OH 44022
407 848-7339

(G-5612)
FOREST CITY COMMERCIAL MGT INC (DH)
50 Public Sq Ste 1410 (44113-2202)
PHONE..................216 621-6060
Fax: 216 263-6208
Samuel Miller, *Ch of Bd*
Albert Ratner, *Ch of Bd*
Charles Ratner, *President*
Robert Prien, *CFO*
Linda Kane, *Controller*
EMP: 250
SALES (est): 36.4MM
SALES (corp-wide): 911.9MM **Privately Held**
SIC: 6531 Real estate managers
HQ: Forest City Properties, Llc
50 Public Sq Ste 1360
Cleveland OH 44113
216 621-6060

(G-5613)
FOREST CITY ENTERPRISES INC
50 Public Sq Ste 750 (44113-2200)
PHONE..................216 621-6060
Ron Ratner, *Manager*
EMP: 70
SALES (corp-wide): 911.9MM **Privately Held**
WEB: www.fceinc.com
SIC: 8742 Management consulting services
HQ: Forest City Enterprises, L.P.
50 Public Sq Ste 1100
Cleveland OH 44113
216 621-6060

(G-5614)
FOREST CITY ENTERPRISES LP (HQ)
50 Public Sq Ste 1100 (44113-2267)
PHONE..................216 621-6060

David J Larue, *President*
James A Ratner, *Chairman*
Duane F Bishop Jr, *COO*
Charles D Obert, *Exec VP*
Brian J Ratner, *Exec VP*
EMP: 350
SALES: 966MM
SALES (corp-wide): 911.9MM **Privately Held**
WEB: www.fceinc.com
SIC: 6512 6513 6552 Nonresidential building operators; apartment building operators; subdividers & developers
PA: Forest City Realty Trust, Inc.
127 Public Sq Ste 3100
Cleveland OH 44114
216 621-6060

(G-5615)
FOREST CITY ENTERPRISES LP
Also Called: Cascade Crossing
3454 Main St (44113)
PHONE..................216 416-3756
John Neely, *Manager*
EMP: 28
SALES (corp-wide): 911.9MM **Privately Held**
WEB: www.fceinc.com
SIC: 6512 Nonresidential building operators
HQ: Forest City Enterprises, L.P.
50 Public Sq Ste 1100
Cleveland OH 44113
216 621-6060

(G-5616)
FOREST CITY ENTERPRISES LP
Also Called: Independence Place II
9233 Independence Blvd # 114 (44130-4781)
PHONE..................440 888-8664
George Gorman, *Branch Mgr*
EMP: 28
SALES (corp-wide): 911.9MM **Privately Held**
SIC: 6512 Nonresidential building operators
HQ: Forest City Enterprises, L.P.
50 Public Sq Ste 1100
Cleveland OH 44113
216 621-6060

(G-5617)
FOREST CITY ENTERPRISES LP
Also Called: Parmatown South
6880 Ridge Rd (44129-5627)
PHONE..................216 416-3780
John Neely, *Branch Mgr*
EMP: 28
SQ FT: 3,998
SALES (corp-wide): 911.9MM **Privately Held**
WEB: www.fceinc.com
SIC: 6512 Nonresidential building operators
HQ: Forest City Enterprises, L.P.
50 Public Sq Ste 1100
Cleveland OH 44113
216 621-6060

(G-5618)
FOREST CITY ENTERPRISES LP
Also Called: Aberdeen Business Park
50 Public Sq Ste 1050 (44113-2269)
PHONE..................216 416-3766
Samuel Miller, *Manager*
Michael Smith, *Director*
Julie Anderson, *Admin Asst*
EMP: 100
SALES (corp-wide): 911.9MM **Privately Held**
WEB: www.fceinc.com
SIC: 6512 Nonresidential building operators
HQ: Forest City Enterprises, L.P.
50 Public Sq Ste 1100
Cleveland OH 44113
216 621-6060

(G-5619)
FOREST CITY PROPERTIES LLC (DH)
50 Public Sq Ste 1360 (44113-2233)
PHONE..................216 621-6060
Fax: 216 263-4808
David La Rue, *CEO*

Charles Ratner, *Ch of Bd*
James Ratner, *Exec VP*
Michael R Finnegan, *Senior VP*
Thomas L Ballman, *Vice Pres*
EMP: 130
SALES (est): 92.1MM
SALES (corp-wide): 911.9MM **Privately Held**
SIC: 6512 6513 Shopping center, property operation only; commercial & industrial building operation; apartment hotel operation
HQ: Forest City Enterprises, L.P.
50 Public Sq Ste 1100
Cleveland OH 44113
216 621-6060

(G-5620)
FOREST CITY REALTY TRUST INC (PA)
127 Public Sq Ste 3100 (44114-1228)
PHONE..................216 621-6060
Charles A Ratner, *Ch of Bd*
David J Larue, *President*
Duane F Bishop, *COO*
James A Ratner, *Exec VP*
Mark Gerteis, *Senior VP*
EMP: 39
SALES: 911.9MM **Privately Held**
SIC: 6798 Real estate investment trusts

(G-5621)
FOREST CITY RESIDENTIAL DEV (DH)
1170 Trml Twr 50 Pub Sq 1170 Terminal Tower (44113)
PHONE..................216 621-6060
Ronald A Ratner, *Ch of Bd*
Edward Pelavin, *Vice Pres*
Albert B Ratner, *Vice Pres*
Samuel H Miller, *Treasurer*
Thomas T Kmiecik, *Asst Treas*
EMP: 50 EST: 1955
SALES (est): 13.8MM
SALES (corp-wide): 911.9MM **Privately Held**
SIC: 1522 1542 6163 Apartment building construction; condominium construction; specialized public building contractors; mortgage brokers arranging for loans, using money of others
HQ: Forest City Enterprises, L.P.
50 Public Sq Ste 1100
Cleveland OH 44113
216 621-6060

(G-5622)
FOREST CITY WASHINGTON LLC (DH)
Also Called: Forest City Washington, Inc.
50 Public Sq Ste 1360 (44113-2233)
PHONE..................202 496-6600
David J Larue, *President*
Duane F Bishop, *Vice Pres*
Peter Calkins, *Vice Pres*
James W Finnerty, *Vice Pres*
Mark Gerteis, *Vice Pres*
EMP: 42
SALES (est): 6.8MM
SALES (corp-wide): 911.9MM **Privately Held**
SIC: 6552 Land subdividers & developers, commercial; land subdividers & developers, residential
HQ: Forest City Properties, Llc
50 Public Sq Ste 1360
Cleveland OH 44113
216 621-6060

(G-5623)
FOREST CY RESIDENTIAL MGT INC (DH)
50 Public Sq Ste 1200 (44113-2204)
PHONE..................216 621-6060
Ron Ratner, *CEO*
Charles A Ratner, *CEO*
James J Prohaska, *Exec VP*
Doug Bardwell, *Vice Pres*
John D Brocklehurst, *Vice Pres*
EMP: 120
SQ FT: 25,000

Cleveland - Cuyahoga County (G-5624)

SALES (est): 55.1MM
SALES (corp-wide): 911.9MM **Privately Held**
SIC: **6531** 6552 Real estate managers; subdividers & developers
HQ: Forest City Enterprises, L.P.
50 Public Sq Ste 1100
Cleveland OH 44113
216 621-6060

(G-5624)
FORT AUSTIN LTD PARTNERSHIP
Also Called: Westlake Village
28550 Westlake Village Dr (44145-7608)
PHONE..................440 892-4200
Jeanne Barnard, *Director*
EMP: 240 **Privately Held**
SIC: **6513** 8052 Retirement hotel operation; intermediate care facilities
PA: Fort Austin Limited Partnership
111 Westwood Pl Ste 200
Brentwood TN 37027

(G-5625)
FOSBEL HOLDING INC (PA)
20600 Sheldon Rd (44142-1319)
PHONE..................216 362-3900
Derek Scott, *President*
Kathleen Stevens, *CFO*
Ritch Serowski, *Controller*
EMP: 30
SALES (est): 27MM **Privately Held**
SIC: **7692** Welding repair

(G-5626)
FOSECO MANAGEMENT INC
20200 Sheldon Rd (44142-1315)
PHONE..................440 826-4548
EMP: 300
SALES (est): 4.9MM **Privately Held**
SIC: **8741** Mgt Services

(G-5627)
FOX TELEVISION STATIONS INC
Also Called: Fox 8
5800 S Marginal Rd (44103-1040)
PHONE..................216 432-4278
Mike Renda, *General Mgr*
Greg Easterly, *Manager*
EMP: 250
SALES (corp-wide): 28.5B **Publicly Held**
WEB: www.foxtv.com
SIC: **7812** 4833 Motion picture production & distribution, television; television broadcasting stations
HQ: Fox Television Stations, Llc
1999 S Bundy Dr
Los Angeles CA 90025
310 584-2000

(G-5628)
FPT CLEVELAND LLC (DH)
Also Called: Ferrous Processing and Trading
8550 Aetna Rd (44105-1607)
PHONE..................216 441-3800
Fax: 216 441-1079
Andrew M Luntz, *President*
Jan Hemme, *Vice Pres*
Tim Pucky, *CFO*
Yale Levin,
▲ EMP: 115
SALES (est): 31.1MM
SALES (corp-wide): 1.8B **Privately Held**
SIC: **4953** 5051 5093 3341 Recycling, waste materials; iron & steel (ferrous) products; ferrous metal scrap & waste; secondary nonferrous metals
HQ: Ferrous Processing And Trading Company
3400 E Lafayette St
Detroit MI 48207
313 582-2910

(G-5629)
FRAMECO INC
9005 Bank St (44125-3425)
PHONE..................216 433-7080
Kevin Wyman, *President*
Jean Wyman, *President*
Reginald Wyman, *CFO*
Lynn Wyman, *Finance Mgr*
Margie Wyman, *Manager*
EMP: 35

SALES: 4.5MM **Privately Held**
SIC: **1791** Precast concrete structural framing or panels, placing of

(G-5630)
FRANCISCAN SISTERS OF CHICAGO
Also Called: Mount Alverna Home
6765 State Rd (44134-4581)
PHONE..................440 843-7800
Patrick Walsh, *Manager*
Patrick Welsh, *Exec Dir*
Emily Keeran, *Director*
EMP: 250
SALES (corp-wide): 56.7MM **Privately Held**
SIC: **8051** Skilled nursing care facilities
PA: Franciscan Sisters Of Chicago
11500 Theresa Dr
Lemont IL 60439
708 647-6500

(G-5631)
FRANCK AND FRIC INCORPORATED
7919 Old Rockside Rd (44131-2300)
P.O. Box 31148 (44131-0148)
PHONE..................216 524-4451
Fax: 216 524-5865
Donald R Skala Sr, *President*
Stacey Carson, *Assistant VP*
David R Skala, *Vice Pres*
Donald C Skala Jr, *Treasurer*
EMP: 51
SQ FT: 20,000
SALES (est): 7.2MM **Privately Held**
SIC: **1711** 1761 3441 3444 Ventilation & duct work contractor; warm air heating & air conditioning contractor; sheet metalwork; fabricated structural metal; sheet metalwork

(G-5632)
FRANK NOVAK & SONS INC
Also Called: Flooring Specialties Div
23940 Miles Rd (44128-5425)
PHONE..................216 475-2495
Fax: 216 475-2802
Gayle Pinchot, *President*
Allen J Pinchot, *Vice Pres*
Brad Pinchot, *Vice Pres*
Mark Pinchot, *Vice Pres*
Pamela Bozsvai Pinchot, *Vice Pres*
EMP: 100
SQ FT: 12,000
SALES (est): 12.9MM **Privately Held**
WEB: www.franknovak.com
SIC: **1721** 1752 1742 Interior commercial painting contractor; exterior commercial painting contractor; wood floor installation & refinishing; acoustical & ceiling work

(G-5633)
FRANKLIN BOULEVARD NURSING HM
Also Called: Franklin Plaza
3600 Franklin Blvd (44113-2831)
PHONE..................216 651-1600
Fax: 216 651-8330
Bruce Daskal, *President*
David Farkas, *Vice Pres*
Larry Dancziger, *Treasurer*
Laura Roth, *Human Res Mgr*
Harold Schachter, *Admin Sec*
EMP: 220 EST: 1948
SQ FT: 26,000
SALES (est): 10.3MM **Privately Held**
WEB: www.hueyproductions.com
SIC: **8051** Extended care facility

(G-5634)
FRANTZ WARD LLP
200 Public Sq Ste 3020 (44114-1230)
PHONE..................216 515-1660
Fax: 216 515-1650
Gina Gennaro, *President*
Carrie Grieco, *President*
Lisa Lindhurst, *President*
Sue Ritter, *President*
Eve Stratton, *President*
EMP: 115
SQ FT: 27,000
SALES (est): 21.2MM **Privately Held**
WEB: www.franzward.com
SIC: **8111** Specialized law offices, attorneys

(G-5635)
FREDERICKS WINE & DINE
22005 Emery Rd (44128-4609)
PHONE..................216 581-5299
Frederick Parks, *Principal*
EMP: 43 EST: 2010
SALES (est): 1.2MM **Privately Held**
SIC: **5182** 5812 Brandy & brandy spirits; caterers

(G-5636)
FREEDONIA PUBLISHING LLC
767 Beta Dr (44143-2379)
PHONE..................440 684-9600
Fax: 440 646-0484
Jeffrey Weiss, *CEO*
Katherine Brink, *Editor*
Jean Nadeau, *Editor*
Matthew Trammell, *Editor*
Chris Staneluis, *Business Mgr*
EMP: 100
SQ FT: 11,000
SALES (est): 8.9MM
SALES (corp-wide): 31.9MM **Privately Held**
WEB: www.freedoniagroup.com
SIC: **8732** Market analysis or research
PA: Marketresearch.Com, Inc.
11200 Rockville Pike # 504
Rockville MD 20852
240 747-3093

(G-5637)
FRESENIUS MED CARE HLDINGS INC
14670 Snow Rd (44142-2461)
PHONE..................216 267-1451
Lori Shelby, *Manager*
EMP: 30
SALES (corp-wide): 20.9B **Privately Held**
SIC: **8011** Clinic, operated by physicians
HQ: Fresenius Medical Care Holdings, Inc.
920 Winter St
Waltham MA 02451

(G-5638)
FRIEDBERG MEYERS ROMAN
28601 Chagrin Blvd # 500 (44122-4556)
PHONE..................216 831-0042
Fax: 216 831-0542
Anne L Meyers, *Owner*
Gerald Goldberg, *Counsel*
Janice Isakoff, *Counsel*
Anne Houdek, *Corp Counsel*
M Reed, *Office Admin*
EMP: 41
SQ FT: 7,700
SALES: 6MM **Privately Held**
SIC: **8111** General practice attorney, lawyer

(G-5639)
FRIEDMAN DOMIANO SMITH CO LPA
55 Public Sq Ste 1055 (44113-1901)
PHONE..................216 621-0070
Fax: 216 621-4008
Jeffrey Friedman, *President*
Joseph Domiano, *Treasurer*
Stephen Vanek, *Financial Exec*
Friedman D Smith, *Personnel*
David Smith, *Admin Sec*
EMP: 30
SQ FT: 12,500
SALES (est): 3.4MM **Privately Held**
SIC: **8111** General practice attorney, lawyer

(G-5640)
FRIEND TO FRIEND PROGRAM
4515 Superior Ave (44103-1215)
PHONE..................216 861-1838
Stephen Messner, *Manager*
EMP: 33
SALES (est): 388.3K **Privately Held**
SIC: **8322** General counseling services

(G-5641)
FRIENDLY INN SETTLEMENT HOUSE
2386 Unwin Rd (44104-1099)
PHONE..................216 431-7656
Fax: 216 431-8189
Che Johnson, *Business Mgr*
Richgina Jeff, *Exec Dir*

Richgina Jeff-Carter, *Director*
EMP: 39
SALES: 1.8MM **Privately Held**
SIC: **8322** Neighborhood center

(G-5642)
FRITO-LAY NORTH AMERICA INC
4580 Hinckley Indus Pkwy (44109-6010)
PHONE..................216 491-4000
Chris Patterson, *Manager*
Janet Waller, *Manager*
Michelle Dematteis, *Assistant*
EMP: 150
SQ FT: 65,936
SALES (corp-wide): 63.5B **Publicly Held**
WEB: www.fritolay.com
SIC: **5145** 5149 Snack foods; groceries & related products
HQ: Frito-Lay North America, Inc.
7701 Legacy Dr
Plano TX 75024

(G-5643)
FX DIGITAL MEDIA INC (PA)
1600 E 23rs St Rs (44114)
PHONE..................216 241-4040
John Gadd, *CEO*
Columbus Woodruff, *President*
Karl Singleton, *COO*
Greg Schwartz, *Sales Staff*
Nora Lane, *Mktg Dir*
EMP: 35
SQ FT: 15,000
SALES (est): 4MM **Privately Held**
WEB: www.hotcards.com
SIC: **7336** 2754 Commercial art & graphic design; color printing, gravure

(G-5644)
G & S METAL PRODUCTS CO INC
26840 Fargo Ave (44146-1339)
PHONE..................216 831-2388
David Persichitti, *Finance*
Mark Schwartz, *Branch Mgr*
EMP: 135
SQ FT: 145,964
SALES (corp-wide): 90.9MM **Privately Held**
WEB: www.gsmetal.com
SIC: **4225** General warehousing & storage
PA: G & S Metal Products Co., Inc.
3330 E 79th St
Cleveland OH 44127
216 441-0700

(G-5645)
G HERSCHMAN ARCHITECTS INC (PA)
25001 Emery Rd Ste 400 (44128-5627)
PHONE..................216 223-3200
Fax: 216 223-3210
Mike Crislip, *President*
Jerry Herschman, *Chairman*
Carole Sanderson, *Corp Secy*
Patrick Fox, *Project Mgr*
Roman Gumieniak, *Project Mgr*
EMP: 60
SQ FT: 20,000
SALES: 13.2MM **Privately Held**
SIC: **8712** 8711 7389 Architectural engineering; engineering services; interior design services

(G-5646)
G J GOUDREAU & CO (PA)
Also Called: Goudreau Management
9701 Brookpark Rd Ste 200 (44129-6824)
PHONE..................216 351-5233
Fax: 216 351-5551
George J Goudreau Jr, *President*
Kathy Goudreau, *Manager*
EMP: 28
SQ FT: 12,500
SALES (est): 6.3MM **Privately Held**
SIC: **1522** 1542 6531 7349 Apartment building construction; commercial & office building, new construction; real estate managers; building maintenance, except repairs

GEOGRAPHIC SECTION

Cleveland - Cuyahoga County (G-5670)

(G-5647)
G J GOUDREAU OPERATING CO
9701 Brookpark Rd Ste 200 (44129-6824)
PHONE..................................216 741-7524
G J Goudreau Jr, *Partner*
A G Homza, *CFO*
EMP: 30
SQ FT: 10,000
SALES (est): 1.4MM **Privately Held**
SIC: 6513 Apartment building operators

(G-5648)
G ROBERT TONEY & ASSOC INC (PA)
Also Called: National Liquidators
5401 N Marginal Rd (44114-3925)
PHONE..................................954 791-9600
Fax: 954 990-1288
Matthew J Amata, *President*
Robert McKee, *General Mgr*
Michael Bacchiocchi, *Vice Pres*
Shane Hunt, *Vice Pres*
Frank Kups, *Vice Pres*
EMP: 50
SQ FT: 6,500
SALES (est): 6MM **Privately Held**
WEB: www.nationalyachtsales.com
SIC: 7389 Repossession service; auctioneers, fee basis; yacht brokers

(G-5649)
G&M TOWING AND RECOVERY LLC
3030 E 55th St (44127-1209)
PHONE..................................216 271-0581
Craig Stacy,
EMP: 30
SALES (est): 2.5MM **Privately Held**
SIC: 7549 Towing services

(G-5650)
GABRIEL PARTNERS LLC
200 Public Sq Ste 3100 (44114-2311)
PHONE..................................216 771-1250
Sam Rosenfeld, *Mng Member*
Elizabeth Albano, *Manager*
EMP: 50
SALES (est): 3.2MM **Privately Held**
SIC: 7389 Financial services

(G-5651)
GALAXY BALLOONS INCORPORATED
11750 Berea Rd Ste 3 (44111-1603)
P.O. Box 698, Lakewood (44107-0998)
PHONE..................................216 476-3360
Fax: 216 476-3320
Terry Brizz, *President*
Nellie Elwell, *General Mgr*
Gary Fickles, *Purchasing*
Kaitlyn Kelly, *Mktg Coord*
Carol Goebelt, *Manager*
▲ **EMP:** 130
SQ FT: 50,000
SALES (est): 21.1MM **Privately Held**
WEB: www.galaxyballoon.com
SIC: 2752 7336 5092 5199 Commercial printing, offset; silk screen design; balloons, novelty; advertising specialties; signs & advertising specialties; sporting & athletic goods

(G-5652)
GALLAGHER BENEFIT SERVICES INC
1100 Superior Ave E # 1700 (44114-2521)
PHONE..................................216 623-2600
Fax: 216 623-2621
Mark Alder, *President*
Pam Breeden, *Vice Pres*
Glenn Szana, *Empl Benefits*
Thomas B Herruck, *Accounts Exec*
Dana Lesniak, *Accounts Exec*
EMP: 30
SALES (est): 5.8MM **Privately Held**
WEB: www.herbruckalder.com
SIC: 6411 Insurance information & consulting services

(G-5653)
GALLAGHER SHARP
1501 Euclid Ave Fl 7 (44115-2131)
PHONE..................................216 241-5310
Fax: 216 241-1608
Todd Haemmerle, *Partner*
Thomas E Dover, *Partner*
Robert H Eddy, *Partner*
Patrick Foy, *Partner*
Forrest A Norman, *Partner*
EMP: 110
SALES (est): 18.4MM **Privately Held**
SIC: 8111 General practice law office

(G-5654)
GARDNER CONTRACTING COMPANY
2662 E 69th St (44104-2955)
PHONE..................................216 881-3800
Fax: 216 881-8021
Joseph E Gardner, *President*
Thomas Victory, *Bd of Directors*
EMP: 30
SQ FT: 85,000
SALES (est): 2.4MM **Privately Held**
SIC: 1796 4213 Machine moving & rigging; millwright; heavy machinery transport

(G-5655)
GARLAND/DBS INC
3800 E 91st St (44105-2103)
PHONE..................................216 641-7500
Dave Sokol, *President*
Melvin Chrostowski, *Vice Pres*
Richard Debacco, *Vice Pres*
Dan Healy, *Plant Mgr*
Chuck Ripepi, *CFO*
EMP: 250
SALES: 59.6MM
SALES (corp-wide): 257.8MM **Privately Held**
WEB: www.garlandco.com
SIC: 2952 6512 8712 Roofing materials; roofing felts, cements or coatings; coating compounds, tar; commercial & industrial building operation; architectural services
HQ: The Garland Company Inc
3800 E 91st St
Cleveland OH 44105
216 641-7500

(G-5656)
GASTRNTRLOGY ASSOC CLVLAND INC (PA)
3700 Park East Dr Ste 100 (44122-4339)
PHONE..................................216 593-7700
James Andrassy, *CEO*
Mario D Kamionkowski, *President*
Michael H Frankel, *Vice Pres*
Jack S Lissauer, *Treasurer*
Sue Andrassy, *Manager*
EMP: 44
SQ FT: 1,500
SALES (est): 7.6MM **Privately Held**
SIC: 8011 Gastronomist

(G-5657)
GATEWAY ELECTRIC INCORPORATED
4450 Johnston Pkwy Ste A (44128-2956)
PHONE..................................216 518-5500
Rajinder Singh, *President*
Vernon Krieger, *Superintendent*
Satwant Singh, *Corp Secy*
Brenda Smith, *Controller*
Humberto Gonzales, *Manager*
EMP: 110
SQ FT: 5,000
SALES (est): 16.2MM **Privately Held**
SIC: 1731 General electrical contractor

(G-5658)
GATEWAY HEALTH CARE CENTER
3 Gateway (44119-2447)
PHONE..................................216 486-4949
Fax: 216 481-5155
Michelle Betkoski, *Marketing Staff*
Joseph Karimpil, *Director*
Teawnna Cooper, *Records Dir*
Nancy Sugarman, *Administration*
EMP: 140
SQ FT: 42,177
SALES (est): 8.6MM **Privately Held**
SIC: 8051 8052 Skilled nursing care facilities; intermediate care facilities

(G-5659)
GATEWAY PRODUCTS RECYCLING INC (PA)
Also Called: Gateway Recycling
4223 E 49th St (44125-1001)
PHONE..................................216 341-8777
Fax: 216 341-8785
Tom Sustersic, *President*
Ryan Palmier, *General Mgr*
Cindy Sustersic, *Treasurer*
EMP: 44
SQ FT: 24,000
SALES (est): 20MM **Privately Held**
WEB: www.gatewayrecycle.com
SIC: 4953 5084 Recycling, waste materials; recycling machinery & equipment

(G-5660)
GC NEIGHBORHOOD CTRS ASSOC INC
Also Called: NEIGHBORHOOD CENTERS
3311 Perkins Ave Ste 200 (44114-4642)
PHONE..................................216 298-4440
Fax: 216 298-4421
Kimberley Spates, *Accountant*
Allison L Wallace, *Exec Dir*
Stanley Miller, *Director*
Peggy B Szpatura, *Director*
EMP: 247
SALES (est): 1.3MM **Privately Held**
SIC: 8399 Neighborhood development group

(G-5661)
GCA SERVICES GROUP INC (HQ)
1350 Euclid Ave Ste 1500 (44115-1832)
PHONE..................................800 422-8760
Robert Norton, *President*
Eric Hudgens, *President*
Hector Aguilar, *Regional Mgr*
Robert Fuente, *Regional Mgr*
Carl Kreighbaum, *Regional Mgr*
EMP: 60
SQ FT: 17,000
SALES (est): 800MM
SALES (corp-wide): 5.4B **Publicly Held**
WEB: www.gcaservices.com
SIC: 7349 Janitorial service, contract basis
PA: Abm Industries Incorporated
1 Liberty Plz Fl 7
New York NY 10006
212 297-0200

(G-5662)
GCHA
1226 Huron Rd E (44115-1702)
PHONE..................................216 696-6900
Bill Ryan, *CEO*
EMP: 70
SALES (est): 10MM **Privately Held**
SIC: 8741 Hospital management

(G-5663)
GE LIGHTING SOLUTIONS LLC (HQ)
1975 Noble Rd Ste 338e (44112-1719)
P.O. Box 5000, Schenectady NY (12301-5000)
PHONE..................................216 266-4800
Maryrose Sylvester, *President*
Agostino Renna, *President*
Shin Kimura, *Vice Pres*
Steve Germain, *Engineer*
James Kostka, *Engineer*
◆ **EMP:** 42
SQ FT: 20,890
SALES (est): 21.8MM
SALES (corp-wide): 122B **Publicly Held**
WEB: www.gelcore.com
SIC: 3648 5063 Lighting equipment; lighting fixtures
PA: General Electric Company
41 Farnsworth St
Boston MA 02210
617 443-3000

(G-5664)
GE REUTER STOKES
4710 Elizabeth Ln (44144-3244)
PHONE..................................216 749-6332
Al Lada, *Owner*
EMP: 100
SALES (est): 90.3K **Privately Held**
SIC: 8399 Social services

(G-5665)
GEARITY EARLY CHILD CARE CTR
Also Called: Stepping Stones Child Care
2323 Wrenford Rd (44118-3902)
PHONE..................................216 371-7356
Sherry Miller, *Principal*
Lisa Goodell, *Admin Sec*
EMP: 45
SALES (est): 868.6K **Privately Held**
SIC: 8351 Child day care services

(G-5666)
GENE PTACEK SON FIRE EQP INC (PA)
Also Called: G P S Fire Equipment
7310 Associate Ave (44144-1101)
PHONE..................................216 651-8300
Fax: 216 651-2435
Mary Jane Ptacek, *President*
Gene Ptacek Jr, *Vice Pres*
Ken May, *VP Opers*
Wade Watts, *Sales Staff*
Jim Davis, *Manager*
EMP: 35
SQ FT: 15,000
SALES (est): 10.2MM **Privately Held**
WEB: www.gpsfire.com
SIC: 5099 5999 5063 1731 Fire extinguishers; alcoholic beverage making equipment & supplies; fire alarm systems; fire detection & burglar alarm systems specialization; fire alarm maintenance & monitoring

(G-5667)
GENERAL ELECTRIC COMPANY
4477 E 49th St (44125-1097)
PHONE..................................216 883-1000
Fax: 216 429-3350
Pat Schaldenbrand, *Area Mgr*
John Schneider, *Purch Mgr*
Donald Mysliwiec, *Enginr/R&D Mgr*
Osvaldo Alers, *Manager*
Pat Baranack, *Manager*
EMP: 100
SQ FT: 12,000
SALES (corp-wide): 122B **Publicly Held**
SIC: 7629 3621 3613 3612 Electrical repair shops; motors & generators; switchgear & switchboard apparatus; transformers, except electric; power transmission equipment; pumps & pumping equipment
PA: General Electric Company
41 Farnsworth St
Boston MA 02210
617 443-3000

(G-5668)
GENERAL PEST CONTROL COMPANY
3561 W 105th St (44111-3897)
PHONE..................................216 252-7140
Fax: 216 252-7144
John H Gedeon Jr, *President*
Ruth Gedeon, *Corp Secy*
EMP: 35 **EST:** 1949
SQ FT: 5,000
SALES (est): 2.7MM **Privately Held**
SIC: 7342 Pest control in structures

(G-5669)
GENOMONCOLOGY LLC
1375 E 9th St Ste 1120 (44114-1753)
PHONE..................................216 496-4216
Manuel J Glynias, *CEO*
Ian Maurer, *Vice Pres*
Baiju Parikh, *Vice Pres*
Victor Peroni, *CFO*
David Lasecki, *Ch Credit Ofcr*
EMP: 30
SALES (est): 2.3MM **Privately Held**
SIC: 7371 Computer software systems analysis & design, custom

(G-5670)
GIA USA INC
4701 Richmond Rd (44128-5949)
PHONE..................................216 831-8678
Fax: 216 831-8692
Gino Zavarrella Jr, *CEO*
Joseph Fabetese, *President*
Karen Miller, *Principal*
Lorri Parenti, *Exec VP*

Cleveland - Cuyahoga County (G-5671)

EMP: 38
SALES (est): 2.8MM **Privately Held**
SIC: 5099 Crystal goods

(G-5671)
GIDEON ○
4122 Superior Ave (44103-1130)
PHONE..................800 395-6014
Osmon Wright, *Principal*
EMP: 58 EST: 2017
SALES (est): 619.4K **Privately Held**
SIC: 6531 Real estate agents & managers

(G-5672)
GILLMORE SECURITY SYSTEMS INC
Also Called: Honeywell Authorized Dealer
26165 Broadway Ave (44146-6512)
PHONE..................440 232-1000
Fax: 440 232-3040
Alan H Gillmore III, *President*
Connie Pederi, *Sales Mgr*
Jim Bartholomew, *Sales Staff*
Alan Kurek, *Consultant*
EMP: 40
SQ FT: 6,000
SALES (est): 8.4MM **Privately Held**
SIC: 1731 7382 Fire detection & burglar alarm systems specialization; fire alarm maintenance & monitoring; burglar alarm maintenance & monitoring

(G-5673)
GIRL SCOUTS NORTH EAST OHIO
4019 Prospect Ave (44103-4317)
PHONE..................216 481-1313
Fax: 216 692-4060
Kim Klima, *Branch Mgr*
EMP: 70 **Privately Held**
SIC: 8641 Girl Scout organization
PA: Girl Scouts Of North East Ohio
1 Girl Scout Way
Macedonia OH 44056

(G-5674)
GLIDDEN HOUSE ASSOCIATES LTD
Also Called: Glidden House Inn
1901 Ford Dr (44106-3923)
PHONE..................216 231-8900
Fax: 216 231-2130
Joseph Shafran, *Managing Prtnr*
Thomas Farinacci, *General Mgr*
Lee Dorrance, *Financial Exec*
Amanda Kane, *Sales Dir*
Karol Germany, *Marketing Staff*
EMP: 30
SALES (est): 2.5MM **Privately Held**
WEB: www.gliddenhouse.com
SIC: 7011 Hotels

(G-5675)
GLORIA GADMACK DO
Also Called: Premier Physicians
1730 W 25th St (44113-3108)
PHONE..................216 363-2353
Gloria Gadmack, *Partner*
Beth Rehor, *Project Mgr*
Joyce Cox, *Office Mgr*
Mark Berkowitz, *Med Doctor*
Bryan Loos, *Med Doctor*
EMP: 150
SALES (est): 2.7MM **Privately Held**
SIC: 8071 Medical laboratories

(G-5676)
GMS MANAGEMENT CO INC IOWA (PA)
Also Called: Gms Realty
4645 Richmond Rd Ste 101 (44128-5917)
PHONE..................216 766-6000
Fax: 216 766-6010
Susan Graines, *President*
EMP: 45
SQ FT: 12,000
SALES (est): 3.7MM **Privately Held**
SIC: 6513 6512 Apartment building operators; commercial & industrial building operation

(G-5677)
GOLDBERG COMPANIES INC
Also Called: Clarkwood Granada Apartments
4440 Granada Blvd Apt 1 (44128-6018)
PHONE..................216 475-2600
Melvin Tucker, *Manager*
EMP: 25
SALES (est): 1MM
SALES (corp-wide): 17.5MM **Privately Held**
WEB: www.goldbergcompanies.com
SIC: 6512 6513 Commercial & industrial building operation; apartment building operators
PA: Goldberg Companies, Inc.
25101 Chagrin Blvd # 300
Beachwood OH 44122
216 831-6100

(G-5678)
GOODRICH GNNETT NGHBORHOOD CTR
Also Called: Goodrich Gannett Headstart
1400 E 55th St (44103-1304)
PHONE..................216 432-1717
Fax: 216 432-0770
Dave Gunning, *President*
Stuart Bryan, *Vice Pres*
William D Pattie, *Treasurer*
Allison Wallace, *Director*
Kristi Andrasik, *Associate Dir*
EMP: 48
SALES (est): 1MM **Privately Held**
WEB: www.ggnc.org
SIC: 8322 7999 Family service agency; social service center; recreation services

(G-5679)
GOODWILL IDSTRS GRTR CLVLND L
12650 Rockside Rd (44125-4525)
PHONE..................216 581-6320
John Mitchell, *Exec Dir*
EMP: 27
SALES (corp-wide): 27.6MM **Privately Held**
SIC: 8331 Vocational rehabilitation agency
PA: Goodwill Industries Of Greater Cleveland And East Central Ohio, Inc.
408 9th St Sw
Canton OH 44707
330 454-9461

(G-5680)
GORDON FOOD SERVICE INC
Also Called: G F S Marketplace
7575 Granger Rd (44125-4818)
PHONE..................216 573-4900
Fax: 216 573-4904
Zscoot Schnieter, *Manager*
EMP: 50
SALES (corp-wide): 88.9MM **Privately Held**
WEB: www.gfs.com
SIC: 5149 5142 Groceries & related products; packaged frozen goods
PA: Gordon Food Service, Inc.
1300 Gezon Pkwy Sw
Wyoming MI 49509
888 437-3663

(G-5681)
GORJANC COMFORT SERVICES INC
Also Called: Gorjanc Mechanical
42 Alpha Park (44143-2208)
PHONE..................440 449-4411
Fax: 440 449-1077
John Gorjanc, *President*
Phillip Gorjanc, *Vice Pres*
Gregory Gorjanc, *Treasurer*
Paul Hamilton, *Controller*
Phil Gorjanc, *Marketing Mgr*
EMP: 34
SQ FT: 3,400
SALES (est): 4.7MM **Privately Held**
SIC: 1711 1731 Heating & air conditioning contractors; general electrical contractor

(G-5682)
GOVERNORS VILLAGE LLC
Also Called: Governor's Village Assisted LI
280 N Cmmons Blvd Apt 101 (44143)
PHONE..................440 449-8788
Fax: 440 442-8648

Christopher Randall, *Mng Member*
Alice Channell, *Exec Dir*
Michelle Gorman, *Exec Dir*
Lloyd R Chapman,
Charles E Randall,
EMP: 45
SQ FT: 33,800
SALES (est): 2.3MM **Privately Held**
SIC: 8051 Extended care facility

(G-5683)
GRACE HOSPICE LLC
Also Called: Grace Hospice of Middleburg
16600 W Sprague Rd Ste 35 (44130-6318)
PHONE..................440 826-0350
Michael E Smith, *CEO*
EMP: 140 **Privately Held**
SIC: 8361 Geriatric residential care
PA: Grace Hospice, Llc
500 Kirts Blvd Ste 250
Troy MI 48084

(G-5684)
GRACE HOSPITAL
18101 Lorain Ave (44111-5612)
PHONE..................216 476-2704
Fax: 216 476-2706
David Pelini, *Principal*
Mary Chentnik, *VP Human Res*
EMP: 60
SALES (corp-wide): 17.4MM **Privately Held**
SIC: 8062 General medical & surgical hospitals
PA: Grace Hospital
2307 W 14th St
Cleveland OH 44113
216 687-1500

(G-5685)
GRAFFITI INC
3200 Carnegie Ave (44115-2635)
PHONE..................216 881-5550
Russ Beller, *Controller*
EMP: 70
SALES (est): 2.2MM **Privately Held**
SIC: 7336 Commercial art & graphic design

(G-5686)
GRANGE MUTUAL CASUALTY COMPANY
Also Called: Grange Mutual Casualty Co 601
7271 Engle Rd Ste 400 (44130-8404)
P.O. Box 182087, Columbus (43218-2087)
PHONE..................614 337-4400
Brian Crisp, *Manager*
Rob Hallier, *Manager*
Kenneth M Zolac, *Manager*
EMP: 30
SALES (corp-wide): 1.2B **Privately Held**
SIC: 6411 Insurance claim processing, except medical
PA: Grange Mutual Casualty Company
671 S High St
Columbus OH 43206
614 445-2900

(G-5687)
GRANT THORNTON LLP
1375 E 9th St Ste 1500 (44114-1718)
PHONE..................216 771-1400
Fax: 216 771-1409
Patricia Clute, *Auditing Mgr*
Eric Floriani, *Auditing Mgr*
Karolyn Ladas, *Auditing Mgr*
Jeff French, *Auditor*
Pat Gable, *Auditor*
EMP: 110
SALES (corp-wide): 75.8MM **Privately Held**
WEB: www.gt.com
SIC: 8721 Certified public accountant
HQ: Grant Thornton Llp
171 N Clark St Ste 200
Chicago IL 60601
312 856-0200

(G-5688)
GRAYBAR ELECTRIC COMPANY INC
6161 Halle Dr (44125-4613)
PHONE..................216 573-6144
Gerard Musbach, *Sales/Mktg Mgr*
EMP: 45
SQ FT: 41,949

SALES (corp-wide): 6.6B **Privately Held**
WEB: www.graybar.com
SIC: 5063 5065 Electrical supplies; electronic parts & equipment
PA: Graybar Electric Company, Inc.
34 N Meramec Ave
Saint Louis MO 63105
314 573-9200

(G-5689)
GREAT LAKES GROUP
Also Called: Great Lakes Towing
4500 Division Ave (44102-2228)
PHONE..................216 621-4854
Sheldon Guren, *Ch of Bd*
Ronald Rasmus, *President*
George Sogar, *Vice Pres*
Joseph Craine, *Manager*
EMP: 120
SQ FT: 6,000
SALES (est): 21.3MM **Privately Held**
SIC: 3731 4492 Shipbuilding & repairing; marine towing services

(G-5690)
GREAT LAKES MSEUM OF SCNCE ENV
Also Called: GREAT LAKES SCIENCE CENTER
601 Erieside Ave (44114-1021)
PHONE..................216 694-2000
Fax: 216 696-2140
Kirsten M Ellenbogen, *CEO*
Linda Abrams-Silver, *President*
Richard Coyne, *President*
Cindy Flores, *General Mgr*
Gary Oatey, *Chairman*
▲ EMP: 145
SALES: 7.4MM **Privately Held**
WEB: www.glsc.org
SIC: 8412 Museum

(G-5691)
GREAT LAKES PUBLISHING COMPANY (PA)
Also Called: Cleveland Magazine
1422 Euclid Ave Ste 730 (44115-2001)
PHONE..................216 771-2833
Fax: 216 781-6318
Lute Harmon Jr, *Ch of Bd*
Steve Gleydura, *Vice Pres*
Susan Harmon, *Vice Pres*
George Sedlak, *CFO*
Sarah Desmond, *Director*
EMP: 75
SQ FT: 19,000
SALES (est): 9.2MM **Privately Held**
WEB: www.clevelandmagazine.com
SIC: 2721 7374 Magazines: publishing only, not printed on site; computer graphics service

(G-5692)
GREAT LAKES WATER TREATMENT
4949 Galaxy Pkwy Ste Q (44128-5959)
PHONE..................216 464-8292
Fax: 216 464-0531
Abe Bahhage, *President*
Jim McGreal, *Vice Pres*
EMP: 32
SQ FT: 3,000
SALES (est): 3.6MM **Privately Held**
SIC: 5999 5084 Water purification equipment; industrial machinery & equipment

(G-5693)
GREAT SOUTHERN VIDEO INC
Also Called: Great Expectations
4511 Rockside Rd Ste 210 (44131-2157)
PHONE..................216 642-8855
John Mereggi, *Owner*
EMP: 30 **Privately Held**
WEB: www.greatexpectationsdfw.com
SIC: 7299 Dating service
PA: Great Southern Video, Inc
14180 Dallas Pkwy Ste 100
Dallas TX 75254

(G-5694)
GREATER CLEVELAND
Also Called: E & C Div
1240 W 6th St Fl 6 (44113-1302)
PHONE..................216 566-5107
Sheryl King Benford, *Manager*

GEOGRAPHIC SECTION

Cleveland - Cuyahoga County (G-5718)

Jon Fedak, *Comp Spec*
Rita Hewitt, *Admin Asst*
EMP: 2200
SQ FT: 17,000
SALES (corp-wide): 48.5MM **Privately Held**
WEB: www.riderta.com
SIC: 4111 Passenger rail transportation; local railway passenger operation
PA: Greater Cleveland Regional Transit Authority
1240 W 6th St
Cleveland OH 44113
216 566-5100

(G-5695)
GREATER CLEVELAND AUTO AUCTION
5801 Engle Rd (44142-1598)
PHONE..................................216 433-7777
Patrick A Morsillo, *President*
Thomas Coury, *Corp Secy*
Michael Morsillo, *Vice Pres*
Kathleen Gallagher, *Manager*
EMP: 55
SQ FT: 22,500
SALES (est): 6.7MM **Privately Held**
WEB: www.gcaacars.com
SIC: 5012 Automobile auction

(G-5696)
GREATER CLEVELAND FOOD BNK INC
15500 S Waterloo Rd (44110-3800)
PHONE..................................216 738-2265
Kristin Warzocha, *President*
Anthony Rego, *Vice Chairman*
John Corlett, *Trustee*
John Cymanski, *Trustee*
Anita Gray, *Trustee*
EMP: 130
SQ FT: 125,000
SALES: 92.2MM **Privately Held**
WEB: www.clevelandfoodbank.com
SIC: 8399 8322 Community development groups; individual & family services

(G-5697)
GREATER CLEVELAND HOSP ASSN
1226 Huron Rd E Ste 2 (44115-1702)
PHONE..................................216 696-6900
C Wayne Rice, *President*
Richard Fox, *CFO*
EMP: 83
SQ FT: 30,000
SALES (est): 941.1K **Privately Held**
SIC: 8621 Medical field-related associations

(G-5698)
GREATER CLEVELAND PARTNERSHIP (PA)
Also Called: CLEVELAND DEVELOPMENT FOUNDATI
1240 Huron Rd E Ste 300 (44115-1722)
PHONE..................................216 621-3300
William Christopher, *Ch of Bd*
Joe Roman, *President*
John Kropf, *Principal*
Jennifer Frimel, *Editor*
Steve Millard, *COO*
EMP: 95
SQ FT: 45,000
SALES: 10MM **Privately Held**
WEB: www.cose.com
SIC: 8611 Chamber of Commerce

(G-5699)
GREATER CLEVELAND REGIONAL
1240 W 6th St (44113-1302)
PHONE..................................216 575-3932
Joseph A Calabrese, *Branch Mgr*
Charles Brown, *Manager*
EMP: 88
SALES (corp-wide): 48.5MM **Privately Held**
SIC: 4111 Local & suburban transit
PA: Greater Cleveland Regional Transit Authority
1240 W 6th St
Cleveland OH 44113
216 566-5100

(G-5700)
GREATER CLEVELAND REGIONAL
Paratransit
4601 Euclid Ave (44103-3737)
PHONE..................................216 781-1110
Sylvester Williams, *Principal*
Loretta Jordan, *Asst Mgr*
EMP: 110
SALES (corp-wide): 48.5MM **Privately Held**
WEB: www.riderta.com
SIC: 4119 Local passenger transportation
PA: Greater Cleveland Regional Transit Authority
1240 W 6th St
Cleveland OH 44113
216 566-5100

(G-5701)
GREATER CLVLAND HALTHCARE ASSN
Also Called: GCHA
1226 Huron Rd E (44115-1702)
PHONE..................................216 696-6900
William Ryan, *President*
Mark Melvin, *CFO*
EMP: 99
SALES (est): 2.4MM **Privately Held**
SIC: 8611 8099 Trade associations; health & allied services

(G-5702)
GREENBRIER SENIOR LIVING CMNTY
Also Called: Greenbriar Retirement Center
6455 Pearl Rd (44130-2984)
PHONE..................................440 888-5900
Terri Plush, *Manager*
Katherine Myers, *Nursing Dir*
EMP: 240
SALES (est): 2.1MM
SALES (corp-wide): 5MM **Privately Held**
SIC: 8051 8069 Convalescent home with continuous nursing care; specialty hospitals, except psychiatric
PA: Senior Greenbrier Living Community
2 Berea Commons Ste 1
Berea OH 44017
440 888-5900

(G-5703)
GREENBRIER SENIOR LIVING CMNTY
Also Called: Greenbrier Retirement Cmnty
6457 Pearl Rd (44130-2936)
PHONE..................................440 888-0400
Fax: 440 842-0911
Debbie Smith, *Manager*
EMP: 68
SALES (corp-wide): 5MM **Privately Held**
SIC: 8361 8051 Residential care; skilled nursing care facilities
PA: Senior Greenbrier Living Community
2 Berea Commons Ste 1
Berea OH 44017
440 888-5900

(G-5704)
GREENS OF LYNDHURST THE INC
Also Called: The Fountain On The Greens
1555 Brainard Rd Apt 305 (44124-6201)
PHONE..................................440 460-1000
Fax: 440 460-1414
Linda Curran, *Info Tech Mgr*
Liz Gay, *Administration*
EMP: 120
SALES (est): 3.5MM **Privately Held**
WEB: www.greenscommunities.com
SIC: 8051 8052 Skilled nursing care facilities; intermediate care facilities

(G-5705)
GREYSTONE GROUP-AVERY LTD
30050 Chagrin Blvd # 360 (44124-5716)
PHONE..................................216 464-3580
Anthony Visconsi,
William M Phillips,
Dominic Visconsi,
EMP: 32
SALES (est): 1.7MM **Privately Held**
SIC: 6531 6552 1542 Real estate agents & managers; subdividers & developers; nonresidential construction

(G-5706)
GROOVERYDE CLE
1120 Chester Ave (44114-3546)
PHONE..................................323 595-1701
Zosimo Maximo,
EMP: 25
SALES (est): 97K **Privately Held**
SIC: 7991 Physical fitness facilities

(G-5707)
GROUPCLE LLC
12500 Berea Rd (44111-1618)
PHONE..................................216 251-9641
David Ticchione, *Mng Member*
Robert Fujita, *Manager*
Andrew Bacher,
David Gabe,
EMP: 30
SQ FT: 90,000
SALES (est): 6MM **Privately Held**
SIC: 7319 Display advertising service

(G-5708)
GROVER MUSICAL PRODUCTS INC (PA)
Also Called: Grover Trophy Musical Products
9287 Midwest Ave (44125-2415)
PHONE..................................216 391-1188
Fax: 216 391-8999
Richard I Berger, *President*
Dann Skutt, *Vice Pres*
Rich Szabo, *Prdtn Mgr*
Olga Jereb, *Opers Staff*
Vella Dennis, *Purchasing*
▲ **EMP:** 25
SQ FT: 60,000
SALES (est): 6.7MM **Privately Held**
SIC: 5099 Musical instruments parts & accessories

(G-5709)
GUND SPORTS MARKETING LLC
100 Gateway Plz (44115-4002)
PHONE..................................216 420-2000
Gordon Gund, *Ch of Bd*
EMP: 25
SALES: 2.4MM **Privately Held**
SIC: 8742 Marketing consulting services

(G-5710)
GUNTON CORPORATION (PA)
Also Called: Pella Window & Door
26150 Richmond Rd (44146-1438)
PHONE..................................216 831-2420
Fax: 216 831-2941
Mark Mead, *President*
Robert J Gunton, *Co-COB*
William E Gunton, *Co-COB*
Reggie Stacy, *Treasurer*
Soc Colovas, *Controller*
EMP: 180
SQ FT: 90,000
SALES (est): 90.2MM **Privately Held**
WEB: www.guntonpella.com
SIC: 5031 Windows; doors; metal doors, sash & trim

(G-5711)
GUST GALLUCCI CO
Also Called: Imperial Foods
6610 Euclid Ave (44103-3912)
PHONE..................................216 881-0045
Fax: 216 881-4838
Ray Gallucci Jr, *President*
Joan A Skok, *Corp Secy*
Kevin Balaban, *Vice Pres*
Carol Kotora, *Vice Pres*
Marc Kotora, *Vice Pres*
▲ **EMP:** 25
SQ FT: 42,000
SALES (est): 4.5MM **Privately Held**
WEB: www.gustgallucci.com
SIC: 5149 5499 Groceries & related products; gourmet food stores

(G-5712)
GYMNASTIC WORLD INC
6630 Harris Rd (44147-2960)
PHONE..................................440 526-2970
Fax: 440 526-0381
Ron Ganim, *President*
Greg Ganim, *Vice Pres*
Joan Ganim, *Admin Sec*
EMP: 36 **EST:** 1976
SALES (est): 1.8MM **Privately Held**
WEB: www.gymworldohio.com
SIC: 7999 5699 5136 5137 Gymnastic instruction, non-membership; sports apparel; sportswear, men's & boys'; sportswear, women's & children's

(G-5713)
H & R BLOCK INC
5488 Broadway Ave (44127-1509)
PHONE..................................216 271-7108
Lamar Peters, *Manager*
EMP: 32
SALES (corp-wide): 3B **Publicly Held**
WEB: www.hrblock.com
SIC: 7291 Tax return preparation services
PA: H&R Block, Inc.
1 H&R Block Way
Kansas City MO 64105
816 854-3000

(G-5714)
H A M LANDSCAPING INC
4667 Northfield Rd (44128-4508)
PHONE..................................216 663-6666
Herrick Mann, *President*
Lisa Mann, *Vice Pres*
EMP: 25 **EST:** 1971
SQ FT: 5,000
SALES: 1MM **Privately Held**
WEB: www.hamlandscaping.com
SIC: 0781 4959 0782 Landscape services; snowplowing; lawn & garden services

(G-5715)
H LEFF ELECTRIC COMPANY (PA)
4700 Spring Rd (44131-1027)
PHONE..................................216 325-0941
Fax: 216 432-0051
Jim Bracken, *CEO*
Bruce E Leff, *President*
Tom Koberna, *General Mgr*
Sanford Leff Jr, *Exec VP*
Mitch Edmonson, *Opers Mgr*
EMP: 107
SQ FT: 60,000
SALES (est): 107.5MM **Privately Held**
WEB: www.leffelectric.com
SIC: 5063 Electrical supplies

(G-5716)
H T V INDUSTRIES INC
30195 Chagrin Blvd 310n (44124-5763)
PHONE..................................216 514-0060
Fax: 216 514-0064
Daniel Harrington, *Ch of Bd*
Pat Johnson, *Controller*
EMP: 100
SALES (est): 7.3MM **Privately Held**
SIC: 8742 Management consulting services

(G-5717)
H&R BLOCK INC
Also Called: H & R Block
2068 W 25th St (44113-4114)
PHONE..................................216 861-1185
Marion Gross, *Manager*
EMP: 25
SALES (corp-wide): 3B **Publicly Held**
WEB: www.hrblock.com
SIC: 7291 Tax return preparation services
PA: H&R Block, Inc.
1 H&R Block Way
Kansas City MO 64105
816 854-3000

(G-5718)
HABITAT FOR HUMANITY
2110 W 110th St (44102-3510)
PHONE..................................216 429-1299
Fax: 216 429-3629
Jeffrey Bowen, *Principal*
Rebecca Smiddy, *Volunteer Dir*
EMP: 42
SALES: 2.9MM **Privately Held**
SIC: 8399 Community development groups

(PA)=Parent Co (HQ)=Headquarters (DH)=Div Headquarters
✪ = New Business established in last 2 years

2018 Harris Ohio Services Directory

Cleveland - Cuyahoga County (G-5719)

GEOGRAPHIC SECTION

(G-5719)
HAHMOOESER & PARKS
200 Public Sq Ste 2000 (44114-2316)
PHONE.................................330 864-5550
Mark Watkins, *Partner*
Erik Gum, *Partner*
Scott Oldham, *Partner*
EMP: 30
SQ FT: 7,600
SALES (est): 1.8MM **Privately Held**
SIC: 8111 General practice law office

(G-5720)
HAHN LOESER & PARKS LLP (PA)
200 Public Sq Ste 2800 (44114-2303)
PHONE.................................216 621-0150
Fax: 216 271-2824
Stephen J Knerly Jr, *Partner*
N Herschel Koblenz, *Partner*
Lawrence E Oscar, *Partner*
John D Rockefeller, *Principal*
Neil Evans, *Counsel*
EMP: 172
SQ FT: 83,400
SALES (est): 33.7MM **Privately Held**
WEB: www.hahnloeser.com
SIC: 8111 General practice law office

(G-5721)
HAJOCA CORPORATION
Also Called: Welker-Mckee Div
6606 Granger Rd (44131-1429)
PHONE.................................216 447-0050
Bill Irwin, *Sales Associate*
Gene Strine, *Manager*
Richard Garber, *Manager*
EMP: 50
SALES (corp-wide): 2.6B **Privately Held**
WEB: www.hajoca.com
SIC: 5074 Plumbing fittings & supplies
PA: Hajoca Corporation
2001 Joshua Rd
Lafayette Hill PA 19444
610 649-1430

(G-5722)
HALLMARK MANAGEMENT ASSOCIATES (PA)
1821 Noble Rd Ofc C (44112-1670)
PHONE.................................216 681-0080
Leon R Hogg, *President*
Wilmer Cooks, *Vice Pres*
Roger Saffold, *Treasurer*
Linda Thompson, *Accountant*
EMP: 39
SQ FT: 4,500
SALES (est): 3.4MM **Privately Held**
SIC: 6531 Real estate managers

(G-5723)
HANNA COMMERCIAL LLC
Also Called: Hanna Commercial Real Estate
1350 Euclid Ave Ste 700 (44115-1889)
PHONE.................................216 861-7200
Mac Biggar Jr, *President*
Diana Whisenant, *Managing Dir*
Larry Collins, *Sales Associate*
Tom Conroy, *Sales Associate*
Jonny Prell, *Executive Asst*
EMP: 65 EST: 2016
SALES (est): 2.7MM **Privately Held**
SIC: 8742 Real estate consultant

(G-5724)
HANS TRUCK AND TRLR REPR INC
Also Called: Hans' Freightliner Cleveland
14520 Broadway Ave (44125-1960)
PHONE.................................216 581-0046
Fax: 216 581-8610
Hans Dabernig, *President*
Ilse Dabernig, *Treasurer*
Dawn Dabernig, *Manager*
Cheryl Lee, *Manager*
Chris Tench, *Admin Sec*
EMP: 45
SQ FT: 20,000
SALES (est): 8.6MM **Privately Held**
WEB: www.hansfreightliner.com
SIC: 7539 4173 7699 5511 Trailer repair; maintenance facilities, buses; construction equipment repair; trucks, tractors & trailers: new & used

(G-5725)
HANSON-FASO SALES & MARKETING
372 Ridgeview Dr (44131-5618)
PHONE.................................216 642-4500
John Bacha, *Branch Mgr*
EMP: 25
SALES (corp-wide): 5.3MM **Privately Held**
SIC: 5149 Natural & organic foods
PA: Hanson-Faso Sales & Marketing Inc
1919 S Highland Ave 204c
Lombard IL 60148
630 953-9800

(G-5726)
HARLEY-DVIDSON DLR SYSTEMS INC
9885 Rockside Rd Ste 100 (44125-6200)
PHONE.................................216 573-1393
Dennis Stapleton, *President*
Robert Maurer, *Vice Pres*
EMP: 78
SQ FT: 20,000
SALES (est): 12.1MM
SALES (corp-wide): 5.6B **Publicly Held**
WEB: www.harley-davidson.com
SIC: 5734 7371 Computer & software stores; custom computer programming services
PA: Harley-Davidson, Inc.
3700 W Juneau Ave
Milwaukee WI 53208
414 342-4680

(G-5727)
HARRINGTON ELECTRIC COMPANY
3800 Perkins Ave (44114-4635)
PHONE.................................216 361-5101
Fax: 216 361-0582
Thomas A Morgan, *President*
Jerry Yeamans, *President*
James B Morgan Jr, *Exec VP*
Dale Rogers, *Vice Pres*
Gary Laidman, *VP Opers*
EMP: 70
SQ FT: 18,500
SALES (est): 14.3MM **Privately Held**
WEB: www.harringtonelectric.com
SIC: 1731 General electrical contractor; communications specialization

(G-5728)
HARRY ROCK & COMPANY
8550 Aetna Rd (44105-1607)
PHONE.................................330 644-3748
James Eubank, *General Mgr*
EMP: 30
SQ FT: 5,000
SALES (est): 3.4MM **Privately Held**
SIC: 5093 Ferrous metal scrap & waste; nonferrous metals scrap

(G-5729)
HARTFORD FIRE INSURANCE CO
7100 E Pleasant Valley Rd # 200 (44131-5544)
PHONE.................................216 447-1000
Fax: 216 986-6258
Fred Hammond, *Branch Mgr*
Barbara Gaglione, *Agent*
Clint Apkinson, *Administration*
Baker E Niles,
EMP: 135 **Publicly Held**
WEB: www.hartfordinvestmentscanada.com
SIC: 6411 Insurance agents
HQ: Hartford Fire Insurance Company
1 Hartford Plz
Hartford CT 06115
860 547-5000

(G-5730)
HARVEST FACILITY HOLDINGS LP
Also Called: Pearl Crossing
19205 Pearl Rd Ofc (44136-6902)
PHONE.................................440 268-9555
Fax: 440 238-5869
Robert Kobak, *Branch Mgr*
EMP: 30

SALES (corp-wide): 1.1B **Privately Held**
WEB: www.holidaytouch.com
SIC: 6513 Retirement hotel operation
HQ: Harvest Facility Holdings Lp
5885 Meadows Rd Ste 500
Lake Oswego OR 97035
503 370-7070

(G-5731)
HATTENBACH COMPANY (PA)
5309 Hamilton Ave (44114-3909)
PHONE.................................216 881-5200
Fax: 216 881-5425
Cathy Hattenbach, *President*
Joseph G Berick, *Principal*
Dennis Bruckman, *Vice Pres*
John Heinert, *CFO*
EMP: 65 EST: 1944
SQ FT: 50,000
SALES (est): 15MM **Privately Held**
WEB: www.hattenbach.com
SIC: 1711 5078 2541 2434 Refrigeration contractor; commercial refrigeration equipment; cabinets, except refrigerated: show, display, etc.: wood; wood kitchen cabinets

(G-5732)
HAVEN FINANCIAL ENTERPRISE
675 Alpha Dr Ste E (44143-2139)
PHONE.................................800 265-2401
EMP: 27
SALES (est): 176.5K **Privately Held**
SIC: 6211 7389 Security Broker/Dealer Business Services At Non-Commercial Site

(G-5733)
HAWKINS & CO LPA LTD
Also Called: Edward C Hawkins & Co Limited
1267 W 9th St Ste 500 (44113-1064)
PHONE.................................216 861-1365
Fax: 216 861-0714
Ann Hawkins, *President*
EMP: 25 EST: 1976
SALES (est): 2.7MM **Privately Held**
SIC: 8111 General practice attorney, lawyer

(G-5734)
HCA HOLDINGS INC
Also Called: The Surgery Center
19250 Bagley Rd Ste 100 (44130-3348)
PHONE.................................440 826-3240
Al Tracy, *CFO*
Barbara Paris Draves, *Manager*
Linda McCall, *Manager*
EMP: 82
SQ FT: 13,000 **Publicly Held**
SIC: 8093 Specialty outpatient clinics
HQ: Hca Inc.
1 Park Plz
Nashville TN 37203
615 344-9551

(G-5735)
HCR MANORCARE MED SVCS FLA LLC
Also Called: Manorcare Hlth Svcs Rcky River
4102 Rocky River Dr (44135-1139)
PHONE.................................216 251-3300
Brian Karstetter, *Administration*
EMP: 220
SQ FT: 22,000
SALES (corp-wide): 3.6B **Publicly Held**
WEB: www.manorcare.com
SIC: 8051 Convalescent home with continuous nursing care
HQ: Hcr Manorcare Medical Services Of Florida, Llc
333 N Summit St Ste 100
Toledo OH 43604
419 252-5500

(G-5736)
HCR MANORCARE MED SVCS FLA LLC
Also Called: Manorcare Hlth Svcs-Mayfield H
6757 Mayfield Rd (44124-2236)
PHONE.................................440 473-0090
Fax: 440 473-1170
Marge Hartman, *Director*
Yumiko Nutt, *Director*
Miodrag Zivic, *Director*
Jennifer Mann, *Administration*
EMP: 100

SQ FT: 27,730
SALES (corp-wide): 3.6B **Publicly Held**
WEB: www.manorcare.com
SIC: 8051 Convalescent home with continuous nursing care
HQ: Hcr Manorcare Medical Services Of Florida, Llc
333 N Summit St Ste 100
Toledo OH 43604
419 252-5500

(G-5737)
HCR MANORCARE MED SVCS FLA LLC
Also Called: Manorcare Hlth Svcs Lakeshore
16101 Euclid Beach Blvd (44110-1175)
PHONE.................................216 486-2300
Fax: 216 486-6338
Melissa Campbell, *Branch Mgr*
EMP: 135
SQ FT: 30,000
SALES (corp-wide): 3.6B **Publicly Held**
WEB: www.manorcare.com
SIC: 8051 Convalescent home with continuous nursing care
HQ: Hcr Manorcare Medical Services Of Florida, Llc
333 N Summit St Ste 100
Toledo OH 43604
419 252-5500

(G-5738)
HEALTHCOMP INC
Also Called: Champs
1226 Huron Rd E Ste 2 (44115-1702)
PHONE.................................216 696-6900
Bill Ryan, *President*
Philip C Mazanec, *COO*
Valerie Vanzandt, *Manager*
Debora Curtis, *Director*
Amy Witzigreuter, *Director*
EMP: 55
SALES (est): 5.2MM **Privately Held**
SIC: 8742 Hospital & health services consultant

(G-5739)
HEALTHSPAN INTEGRATED CARE
Also Called: Kaiser Foundation Health Plan
12301 Snow Rd (44130-1002)
PHONE.................................216 362-2000
Fax: 216 265-4440
Geoffrey Moebius, *Branch Mgr*
Amy Kramer, *Pharmacist*
Kay E Frank, *Ophthalmology*
Carol Dsouza, *Med Doctor*
Shih-Mou Hsu, *Med Doctor*
EMP: 60
SALES (corp-wide): 4.2B **Privately Held**
SIC: 8062 General medical & surgical hospitals
HQ: Healthspan Integrated Care
1001 Lakeside Ave E # 1200
Cleveland OH 44114
216 621-5600

(G-5740)
HEALTHSPAN INTEGRATED CARE
Also Called: Kaiser Foundation Health Plan
11203 Stokes Blvd (44104-2525)
PHONE.................................216 621-5600
Fax: 216 621-7354
Avtar Saran, *Chief*
EMP: 45
SALES (corp-wide): 4.2B **Privately Held**
SIC: 6324 Hospital & medical service plans
HQ: Healthspan Integrated Care
1001 Lakeside Ave E # 1200
Cleveland OH 44114
216 621-5600

(G-5741)
HEALTHSPAN INTEGRATED CARE
Also Called: Kaiser Foundation Health Plan
3733 Park East Dr (44122-4338)
PHONE.................................216 524-7377
Fax: 216 529-4557
Lil Charlotte, *General Mgr*
Willl Charlotte, *General Mgr*
Dr Mark Binstock, *Director*
Howard S Nathan, *Director*
EMP: 45

SALES (corp-wide): 4.2B **Privately Held**
SIC: 6324 Hospital & medical service plans
HQ: Healthspan Integrated Care
1001 Lakeside Ave E # 1200
Cleveland OH 44114
216 621-5600

(G-5742)
HEALTHSPAN INTEGRATED CARE (HQ)
1001 Lakeside Ave E # 1200 (44114-1158)
P.O. Box 5316 (44101-0316)
PHONE..................................216 621-5600
Kenneth Page, *CEO*
George Halverson, *CEO*
Patricia D Kennedy-Scott, *President*
Paula Ohliger, *Counsel*
Thomas Revis, *CFO*
EMP: 250
SALES: 435MM
SALES (corp-wide): 4.2B **Privately Held**
SIC: 8011 Health maintenance organization
PA: Mercy Health
1701 Mercy Health Pl
Cincinnati OH 45237
513 639-2800

(G-5743)
HEALTHSPAN INTEGRATED CARE
Also Called: Kaiser Foundation Health Plan
17406 Royalton Rd (44136-5151)
PHONE..................................440 572-1000
Fax: 440 846-2808
Patricia A Fuller, *Manager*
EMP: 32
SALES (corp-wide): 4.2B **Privately Held**
SIC: 6324 Health maintenance organization (HMO), insurance only
HQ: Healthspan Integrated Care
1001 Lakeside Ave E # 1200
Cleveland OH 44114
216 621-5600

(G-5744)
HEARTHSTONE UTILITIES INC (HQ)
Also Called: Gas Natural Inc.
1375 E 9th St Ste 3100 (44114-1797)
PHONE..................................440 974-3770
Gregory J Osborne, *President*
Kevin J Degenstein, *COO*
James Sprague, *CFO*
Sanjay Sauldie, *Corp Comm Staff*
Kim Woodman, *Executive Asst*
EMP: 65 EST: 1909
SQ FT: 5,300
SALES: 99.4MM **Privately Held**
WEB: www.ewst.com
SIC: 4924 4911 5172 5984 Natural gas distribution; distribution, electric power; gases, liquefied petroleum (propane); propane gas, bottled
PA: Fr Bison Holdings, Inc.
1375 E 9th St Ste 3100
Cleveland OH 44114
440 974-3770

(G-5745)
HEERY INTERNATIONAL INC
5445 West Blvd (44137-2656)
PHONE..................................216 510-4701
EMP: 31
SALES (corp-wide): 15B **Privately Held**
SIC: 8712 Architectural Services
HQ: Heery International, Inc.
999 Peachtree St Ne # 300
Atlanta GA 30309
404 881-9880

(G-5746)
HEERY INTERNATIONAL INC
1660 W 2nd St (44113-1454)
PHONE..................................216 781-1313
John R May, *Manager*
Steve Ludwinski, *Manager*
Mark Myers, *Manager*
EMP: 25
SALES (corp-wide): 14.2B **Publicly Held**
WEB: www.hlm-heery.com
SIC: 8711 8712 8741 Engineering services; architectural services; management services

HQ: Heery International, Inc.
999 Peachtree St Ne # 300
Atlanta GA 30309
404 881-9880

(G-5747)
HEIGHTS EMERGENCY FOOD CENTER
3663 Mayfield Rd (44121-1733)
PHONE..................................216 381-0707
Hazel Haffner, *Director*
EMP: 80
SALES: 81.4K **Privately Held**
SIC: 8699 5411 Food co-operative; grocery stores

(G-5748)
HELP FOUNDATION INC
Also Called: Nottingham Home
17702 Nottingham Rd (44119-2946)
PHONE..................................216 486-5258
Fax: 216 486-5259
Peggy Congdon, *Director*
EMP: 37
SALES (corp-wide): 8.3MM **Privately Held**
SIC: 8361 Group foster home
PA: Help Foundation, Inc
26900 Euclid Ave
Euclid OH 44132
216 432-4810

(G-5749)
HENRY CALL INC
308 Pines St Ste 100 (44135)
PHONE..................................216 433-5609
Clarence Sneed, *Manager*
Flowe Barry, *Manager*
Debbie Phenicie, *Info Tech Dir*
Leonard Bunten, *Admin Asst*
EMP: 125 **Privately Held**
SIC: 8744 7371 8742 Base maintenance (providing personnel on continuing basis); computer software development; management consulting services
PA: Call Henry Inc
1425 Chaffee Dr Ste 4
Titusville FL 32780

(G-5750)
HENRY SCHEIN INC
30600 Aurora Rd Ste 110 (44139-2761)
PHONE..................................440 349-0891
Fax: 440 349-1398
Henry Schein, *President*
Bob Lavigna, *Marketing Staff*
Richard Schwarz, *Technical Staff*
EMP: 37
SALES (corp-wide): 12.4B **Publicly Held**
SIC: 5047 Dental equipment & supplies
PA: Henry Schein, Inc.
135 Duryea Rd
Melville NY 11747
631 843-5500

(G-5751)
HERMANN CAHN & SCHNEIDER LLP
1375 E 9th St Ste 3150 (44114-1789)
PHONE..................................216 781-5515
Fax: 216 781-1030
Gary Hermann, *Managing Prtnr*
James S Cahn, *Partner*
Bradford R Carver, *Partner*
Anthony J Hartman, *Partner*
Peter J Krembs, *Partner*
EMP: 35
SALES (est): 4.6MM **Privately Held**
WEB: www.hcsattys.com
SIC: 8111 General practice law office

(G-5752)
HERMENIA INC
Also Called: Sunset Nursing Home
1802 Crawford Rd (44106-2030)
PHONE..................................216 795-5710
Fax: 216 795-1105
Hermenia Alford, *President*
Deanna Dothard, *Administration*
EMP: 75
SALES (est): 1.3MM **Privately Held**
SIC: 8051 Skilled nursing care facilities

(G-5753)
HERNANDO ZEGARRA
3401 Entp Pkwy Ste 300 (44122)
PHONE..................................216 831-5700
Hernando Zegarra, *Owner*
EMP: 50
SALES (est): 1.2MM **Privately Held**
SIC: 8011 Physical medicine, physician/surgeon

(G-5754)
HERTZ CLVLAND 600 SUPERIOR LLC
600 Superior Ave E # 100 (44114-2614)
PHONE..................................310 584-8108
Gary Horwitz, *President*
Dana Galindo, *Admin Asst*
EMP: 50 EST: 2015
SALES (est): 2.4MM **Privately Held**
SIC: 6519 Real property lessors

(G-5755)
HERTZ CORPORATION
19025 Maplewood Ave (44135-2445)
PHONE..................................216 267-8900
Fax: 216 265-1239
Steve McCraw, *Manager*
EMP: 88
SALES (corp-wide): 8.8B **Publicly Held**
WEB: www.hertz.com
SIC: 7514 Rent-a-car service
HQ: The Hertz Corporation
8501 Williams Rd
Estero FL 33928
239 301-7000

(G-5756)
HILL SIDE PLAZA
Also Called: Hillside Plaza
18220 Euclid Ave (44112-1013)
PHONE..................................216 486-6300
Fax: 216 486-6560
David Farkas, *Vice Pres*
Kelly Foor, *Corp Comm Staff*
Sharon Edwards, *Manager*
Teah Abashidze, *Director*
Linette Bland, *Hlthcr Dir*
EMP: 55
SQ FT: 14,000
SALES (est): 1.9MM **Privately Held**
SIC: 8051 8052 Convalescent home with continuous nursing care; intermediate care facilities

(G-5757)
HILLCREST EGG & CHEESE CO (PA)
Also Called: Hillcrest Foodservice
2735 E 40th St (44115-3510)
PHONE..................................216 361-4625
Fax: 216 361-0764
Armin Abraham, *President*
Mark Kobak, *President*
David Abraham, *Vice Pres*
Joe Abraham, *Vice Pres*
David Ross, *Vice Pres*
EMP: 90 EST: 1974
SQ FT: 95,000
SALES (est): 110.2MM **Privately Held**
SIC: 5143 5142 5147 5144 Dairy products, except dried or canned; packaged frozen goods; meats, fresh; eggs; canned goods: fruit, vegetables, seafood, meats, etc.; fruits, fresh; vegetables, fresh

(G-5758)
HILLTOP VILLAGE
25900 Euclid Ave Ofc (44132-2751)
PHONE..................................216 261-8383
Fax: 216 261-6816
Dale Giffin, *Business Mgr*
Audrey Keppler, *Director*
EMP: 50
SALES (est): 3MM **Privately Held**
WEB: www.hilltopvillage.com
SIC: 6513 Retirement hotel operation

(G-5759)
HISPANC URBN MNRTY ALCHLSM DRG
Also Called: HISPANIC UMADAOP
3305 W 25th St (44109-1613)
PHONE..................................216 398-2333
Francisco Alfonzo, *Exec Dir*
Ivan Rosas, *Exec Dir*
EMP: 30
SQ FT: 2,564
SALES: 1.2MM **Privately Held**
WEB: www.hispanicumadaop.com
SIC: 8322 Substance abuse counseling

(G-5760)
HIT PORTFOLIO I MISC TRS LLC
Also Called: Hyatt Hotel
420 Superior Ave E (44114-1208)
PHONE..................................216 575-1234
Fax: 216 776-4468
Tim Meyer, *General Mgr*
Tara Armer, *Asst Director*
EMP: 200
SALES (corp-wide): 4.6B **Publicly Held**
WEB: www.hyatt.com
SIC: 7011 5812 Hotels; eating places
HQ: Hit Portfolio I Misc Trs, Llc
150 N Riverside Plz
Chicago IL 60606
312 750-1234

(G-5761)
HITCHCOCK CENTER FOR WOMEN INC
Also Called: HCFW
1227 Ansel Rd (44108-3323)
PHONE..................................216 421-0662
Fax: 216 421-0911
Stephen Monto, *President*
Sharon Brettas, *Vice Pres*
Tony Kuhel, *Treasurer*
Melvin Haynes, *Info Tech Dir*
Rochena Hall, *Info Tech Mgr*
EMP: 45
SQ FT: 20,000
SALES: 1.9MM **Privately Held**
WEB: www.hcfw.org
SIC: 8361 8093 Rehabilitation center, residential; health care incidental; alcohol clinic, outpatient; drug clinic, outpatient

(G-5762)
HKM DRECT MKT CMMNICATIONS INC (PA)
Also Called: H K M
5501 Cass Ave (44102-2121)
PHONE..................................216 651-9500
Fax: 216 961-6330
Rob Durham, *President*
Scott Durham, *COO*
Robert Solevenec, *Vice Pres*
Patricia Stealey, *Manager*
EMP: 135 EST: 1922
SQ FT: 86,000
SALES (est): 18MM **Privately Held**
WEB: www.hkmdirectmarket.com
SIC: 7331 2752 7375 2791 Direct mail advertising services; mailing service; mailing list management; commercial printing, lithographic; information retrieval services; typesetting; commercial printing

(G-5763)
HNTB CORPORATION
1100 Superior Ave E # 1701 (44114-2518)
PHONE..................................216 522-1140
Anthony Yacobucci, *Branch Mgr*
EMP: 41
SALES (corp-wide): 48.1MM **Privately Held**
WEB: www.hntb.com
SIC: 8711 Consulting engineer
HQ: Hntb Corporation
715 Kirk Dr
Kansas City MO 64105
816 472-1201

(G-5764)
HOBE LCAS CRTIF PUB ACCNTANTS
4807 Rockside Rd Ste 510 (44131-2161)
PHONE..................................216 524-7167
Fax: 216 524-8777
David Hobe, *Principal*
Francis G Bonning Jr, *Principal*
Jerry Lucas, *Principal*
Floyd Trouten, *Principal*
EMP: 31
SALES (est): 2.2MM **Privately Held**
WEB: www.hobe.com
SIC: 8721 Certified public accountant

Cleveland - Cuyahoga County (G-5765)

(G-5765)
HODELL-NATCO INDUSTRIES INC (PA)
Also Called: Locktooth Division
7825 Hub Pkwy (44125-5710)
PHONE.................................773 472-2305
Otto Reidl, *CEO*
Kevin Reidl, *President*
Dave Crowl, *General Mgr*
Ken Lyman, *General Mgr*
Brandon Liebhard, *Vice Pres*
▲ **EMP:** 40
SQ FT: 101,000
SALES (est): 34.7MM **Privately Held**
WEB: www.hodell-natco.com
SIC: 5072 Bolts; nuts (hardware); screws

(G-5766)
HOLLAND ENTERPRISES INC
Also Called: Holland Paving & Seal Coating
4538 W 130th St Ste 3 (44135-3576)
PHONE.................................216 671-9333
Fax: 216 671-9399
Tom Holland, *President*
EMP: 40
SQ FT: 5,000
SALES (est): 5MM **Privately Held**
SIC: 1771 Driveway, parking lot & blacktop contractors; blacktop (asphalt) work; driveway contractor; parking lot construction

(G-5767)
HOME DEPOT USA INC
Also Called: Home Depot, The
10800 Brookpark Rd (44130-1119)
PHONE.................................216 676-9969
Fax: 216 898-0416
Louis Zager, *Manager*
EMP: 200
SALES (corp-wide): 100.9B **Publicly Held**
WEB: www.homerentalsdepot.com
SIC: 5211 7359 Home centers; tool rental
HQ: Home Depot U.S.A., Inc.
2455 Paces Ferry Rd Se
Atlanta GA 30339

(G-5768)
HOME DEPOT USA INC
Also Called: Home Depot, The
11901 Berea Rd (44111-1606)
PHONE.................................216 251-3091
Fax: 216 688-4016
Kennett Johansson, *Manager*
Bob Bailey, *Executive*
EMP: 150
SALES (corp-wide): 100.9B **Publicly Held**
WEB: www.homerentalsdepot.com
SIC: 5211 7359 Home centers; tool rental
HQ: Home Depot U.S.A., Inc.
2455 Paces Ferry Rd Se
Atlanta GA 30339

(G-5769)
HOMETECH HEALTHCARE SVCS LLC
Also Called: Hometech Transportation Svcs
17325 Euclid Ave Ste 3024 (44112-1255)
PHONE.................................216 295-9120
Edward E Long,
EMP: 26
SALES (est): 1MM **Privately Held**
SIC: 8082 8249 4789 Home health care services; medical training services; cargo loading & unloading services

(G-5770)
HONEYWELL INTERNATIONAL INC
925 Keynote Cir Ste 100 (44131-1869)
PHONE.................................216 459-6053
Fax: 216 459-6282
George Daulerio, *CFO*
Mark Gilger, *Branch Mgr*
Molly Hooper, *Executive*
EMP: 80
SALES (corp-wide): 40.5B **Publicly Held**
WEB: www.honeywell.com
SIC: 5075 7623 7699 4961 Warm air heating & air conditioning; refrigeration service & repair; boiler & heating repair services; steam & air-conditioning supply
PA: Honeywell International Inc.
115 Tabor Rd
Morris Plains NJ 07950
973 455-2000

(G-5771)
HOPKINS AIRPORT LIMOUSINE SVC (PA)
Also Called: Hopkins Transportation Svcs
13315 Brookpark Rd (44142-1822)
PHONE.................................216 267-8810
Fax: 216 362-3796
Tom Goebel, *President*
Mike Goebel, *Corp Secy*
Chris Goebel, *Vice Pres*
Jack Goebel, *Vice Pres*
James Goebel, *Vice Pres*
EMP: 200
SQ FT: 1,000
SALES: 4.5MM **Privately Held**
WEB: www.gohopkins.com
SIC: 4111 Airport limousine, scheduled service

(G-5772)
HOPKINS PARTNERS
Also Called: Sheraton Airport Hotel
5300 Riverside Dr Ste 30 (44135-3145)
PHONE.................................216 267-1500
Fax: 216 267-3177
David McArdle, *Partner*
Kerry Chelm, *Partner*
Richard Watson, *Partner*
Mark Williams, *General Mgr*
Tom Curry, *Finance*
EMP: 180
SALES (est): 9.4MM **Privately Held**
WEB: www.hopkinspartners.com
SIC: 7011 Resort hotel

(G-5773)
HORIZON FREIGHT SYSTEM INC
Horizon Mid Atlantic
6600 Bessemer Ave (44127-1804)
PHONE.................................216 341-3322
David Ferrante, *Branch Mgr*
EMP: 50
SALES (corp-wide): 45.8MM **Privately Held**
SIC: 4213 Trucking, except local
PA: Horizon Freight System, Inc.
6600 Bessemer Ave
Cleveland OH 44127
216 341-7410

(G-5774)
HORIZON FREIGHT SYSTEM INC (PA)
6600 Bessemer Ave (44127-1804)
PHONE.................................216 341-7410
David Ferrante, *President*
Keith Harris, *Business Mgr*
Tracy Green, *Safety Dir*
Janet Fraley, *Safety Mgr*
Michael Banach, *Terminal Mgr*
EMP: 50
SQ FT: 3,000
SALES (est): 45.8MM **Privately Held**
WEB: www.horizonfreightsyste.com
SIC: 4213 Trucking, except local

(G-5775)
HORIZON SOUTH INC
Also Called: Horizon Freight
6600 Bessemer Ave (44127-1804)
PHONE.................................800 480-6829
Dave Ferrante, *CEO*
EMP: 78 **EST:** 2012
SALES (est): 5.4MM
SALES (corp-wide): 45.8MM **Privately Held**
SIC: 4731 Domestic freight forwarding
PA: Horizon Freight System, Inc.
6600 Bessemer Ave
Cleveland OH 44127
216 341-7410

(G-5776)
HORSESHOE CLEVELAND MGT LLC
Also Called: Jack Entertainment
100 Public Sq Ste 100 (44113-2208)
PHONE.................................216 297-4777
Joe Childs, *Supervisor*
Jim Hindman, *Director*
Maila Aganon,
EMP: 45 **EST:** 2010
SALES (est): 2.7MM **Privately Held**
SIC: 7011 Casino hotel

(G-5777)
HOSPICE OF OHIO LLC (PA)
Also Called: Harbor Light Hospice
677 Alpha Dr Ste H (44143-2165)
PHONE.................................440 286-2500
Brian Crum, *Sales Executive*
Lisa Owens, *Manager*
Gina Covelli,
Frank Rosenbaum,
EMP: 90
SALES (est): 6.7MM **Privately Held**
WEB: www.hospiceofohio.com
SIC: 8082 Home health care services

(G-5778)
HOSPICE OF THE WESTERN RESERVE
4670 Richmond Rd Ste 200 (44128-6411)
PHONE.................................800 707-8921
Fax: 216 283-3181
Angie Conyards, *Principal*
Rosemary Messner, *Vice Pres*
Scott Webb, *Project Dir*
Patricia Kilfoyle, *Director*
EMP: 60
SALES (corp-wide): 89.8MM **Privately Held**
SIC: 8082 Visiting nurse service
PA: Hospice Of The Western Reserve, Inc
17876 Saint Clair Ave
Cleveland OH 44110
216 383-2222

(G-5779)
HOSPICE OF THE WESTERN RESERVE (PA)
17876 Saint Clair Ave (44110-2602)
PHONE.................................216 383-2222
Fax: 216 383-3750
William E Finn, *CEO*
James L Hambrick, *Vice Chairman*
Kimberly Tutolo, *Pub Rel Mgr*
Jane Van Bergen, *Sls & Mktg Exec*
John E Harvan Jr, *CFO*
EMP: 130
SQ FT: 60,000
SALES: 89.8MM **Privately Held**
SIC: 8059 Personal care home, with health care

(G-5780)
HOSPICE OF THE WESTERN RESERVE
17876 Saint Clair Ave (44110-2602)
PHONE.................................800 707-8922
Fax: 216 231-8291
Mary Kay Tyler, *Manager*
Amanda James, *Supervisor*
Susan Fontaine, *Admin Asst*
Glenna Schultz, *Admin Asst*
Mary Trivisonno, *Admin Asst*
EMP: 60
SALES (corp-wide): 89.8MM **Privately Held**
SIC: 8082 Home health care services
PA: Hospice Of The Western Reserve, Inc
17876 Saint Clair Ave
Cleveland OH 44110
216 383-2222

(G-5781)
HOSPICE OF THE WESTERN RESERVE
22730 Fairview Center Dr # 100 (44126-3614)
PHONE.................................216 227-9048
Nancy Miller, *Branch Mgr*
EMP: 115
SALES (corp-wide): 89.8MM **Privately Held**
SIC: 8059 Convalescent home
PA: Hospice Of The Western Reserve, Inc
17876 Saint Clair Ave
Cleveland OH 44110
216 383-2222

(G-5782)
HOWARD HANNA SMYTHE CRAMER (HQ)
6000 Parkland Blvd (44124-6120)
PHONE.................................216 447-4477
Lucius B Mc Kelvey, *Ch of Bd*
David C Paul, *President*
Alan C Chandler, *Senior VP*
Catherine Andre, *Broker*
Elaine Beck, *Broker*
EMP: 250 **EST:** 1972
SQ FT: 16,500
SALES (est): 17.3MM
SALES (corp-wide): 76.4MM **Privately Held**
WEB: www.smythecramer.com
SIC: 6531 Real estate agent, residential
PA: Hanna Holdings, Inc.
1090 Freeport Rd Ste 1a
Pittsburgh PA 15238
412 967-9000

(G-5783)
HOWARD HANNA SMYTHE CRAMER
Also Called: Howard Hannah Smythe Cramer
27115 Knickerbocker Rd (44140-2345)
PHONE.................................440 835-2800
Fax: 440 835-8276
Kathy Miller, *Manager*
Kristen Eiermann, *Real Est Agnt*
Susan Haley, *Real Est Agnt*
Mary Whitaker, *Real Est Agnt*
EMP: 45
SQ FT: 2,975
SALES (corp-wide): 76.4MM **Privately Held**
WEB: www.smythecramer.com
SIC: 6531 Real estate brokers & agents
HQ: Howard Hanna Smythe Cramer
6000 Parkland Blvd
Cleveland OH 44124
216 447-4477

(G-5784)
HOWARD HANNA SMYTHE CRAMER
Also Called: Smythe Cramer Reltrs
6240 Som Center Rd # 100 (44139-2950)
PHONE.................................440 248-3380
Barbara Jayme, *Manager*
Gale L Grau, *Real Est Agnt*
EMP: 35
SALES (corp-wide): 76.4MM **Privately Held**
WEB: www.smythecramer.com
SIC: 6531 Real estate agents & managers
HQ: Howard Hanna Smythe Cramer
6000 Parkland Blvd
Cleveland OH 44124
216 447-4477

(G-5785)
HOWARD HANNA SMYTHE CRAMER
8949 Brecksville Rd (44141-2301)
PHONE.................................440 526-1800
Fax: 440 526-0946
Shannon Gallagher, *Broker*
Shelly Good, *Broker*
Mary E Hubach, *Broker*
Tammy Manjerovic, *Broker*
Sharon Polanco, *Broker*
EMP: 35
SALES (corp-wide): 76.4MM **Privately Held**
WEB: www.smythecramer.com
SIC: 6531 Real estate agents & managers
HQ: Howard Hanna Smythe Cramer
6000 Parkland Blvd
Cleveland OH 44124
216 447-4477

(G-5786)
HOWARD WERSHBALE & CO (PA)
23240 Chagrin Blvd # 700 (44122-5450)
PHONE.................................216 831-1200
Fax: 216 831-1842
Harvey Wershbale, *CEO*
Stanley J Olejarski, *President*
Kristine Kalinic, *Asst Controller*
Adam Wright, *Accountant*
Ryan Kramer, *Senior Mgr*
EMP: 75

SQ FT: 3,374
SALES (est): 12.3MM **Privately Held**
SIC: 8721 Certified public accountant

(G-5787)
HP INC
5005 Rockside Rd Ste 600 (44131-6827)
PHONE..................................440 234-7022
EMP: 42
SALES (corp-wide): 52B **Publicly Held**
WEB: www.3com.com
SIC: 7373 Local area network (LAN) systems integrator
PA: Hp Inc.
 1501 Page Mill Rd
 Palo Alto CA 94304
 650 857-1501

(G-5788)
HP MANUFACTURING COMPANY INC (PA)
Also Called: House of Plastics
3705 Carnegie Ave (44115-2750)
PHONE..................................216 361-6500
Fax: 216 361-6508
John R Melchiorre, *President*
Elmer Krizek, *Principal*
Paul Glozer, *QC Mgr*
Cathy Lamb, *Accounts Mgr*
Robert J Ryan, *Accounts Mgr*
EMP: 63
SQ FT: 110,000
SALES (est): 10.2MM **Privately Held**
WEB: www.hpmanufacturing.com
SIC: 3089 5162 3993 3082 Plastic processing; plastics sheets & rods; signs & advertising specialties; unsupported plastics profile shapes; partitions & fixtures, except wood

(G-5789)
HUNTER REALTY INC
Also Called: Coldwell Banker
25101 Chagrin Blvd # 170 (44122-5688)
PHONE..................................216 831-2911
Fax: 216 831-2911
Edwin Dolinski, *President*
Robert Haseley, *Buyer*
Dave Boccheri, *Manager*
Louis Golden, *Agent*
Angela Chiu, *Real Est Agnt*
EMP: 30
SALES (corp-wide): 2.6MM **Privately Held**
WEB: www.cbhunter.com
SIC: 6531 Real estate agent, residential
PA: Hunter Realty Inc
 24600 Detroit Rd Ste 240
 Westlake OH 44145
 440 892-7040

(G-5790)
HUNTINGTON INSURANCE INC
925 Euclid Ave Ste 550 (44115-1405)
PHONE..................................216 206-1787
Biagio Impala, *Vice Pres*
EMP: 37
SALES (corp-wide): 4.7B **Publicly Held**
WEB: www.skyinsure.com
SIC: 6411 Insurance agents, brokers & service
HQ: Huntington Insurance, Inc.
 519 Madison Ave
 Toledo OH 43604
 419 720-7900

(G-5791)
HUNTINGTON NATIONAL BANK
101 W Prospect Ave (44115-1093)
PHONE..................................216 621-1717
Fax: 216 621-3201
David Janus, *CEO*
EMP: 50
SQ FT: 800
SALES (corp-wide): 4.7B **Publicly Held**
SIC: 6021 National commercial banks
HQ: The Huntington National Bank
 17 S High St Fl 1
 Columbus OH 43215
 614 480-4293

(G-5792)
HUNTINGTON NATIONAL BANK
Also Called: Home Mortgage
905 Euclid Ave (44115-1401)
P.O. Box 5065 (44101-0065)
PHONE..................................216 515-6401
Eddie Strattonbey, *Manager*
EMP: 38
SALES (corp-wide): 4.7B **Publicly Held**
WEB: www.huntingtonnationalbank.com
SIC: 6029 6021 Commercial banks; national trust companies with deposits, commercial
HQ: The Huntington National Bank
 17 S High St Fl 1
 Columbus OH 43215
 614 480-4293

(G-5793)
HUNTLEIGH USA CORPORATION
11147 Barrington Blvd (44130-4414)
P.O. Box 81333 (44181-0333)
PHONE..................................216 265-3707
Greg Conwell, *Manager*
EMP: 300
SALES (corp-wide): 255.5MM **Privately Held**
WEB: www.huntleighusa.com
SIC: 4581 Aircraft servicing & repairing
HQ: Huntleigh Usa Corporation
 545 E John Carpenter Fwy
 Irving TX

(G-5794)
HWH ARCHTCTS-NGNRS-PLNNERS INC
600 Superior Ave E # 1100 (44114-2614)
PHONE..................................216 875-4000
Fax: 216 875-4125
Joseph J Matts, *President*
Peter P Jancar, *Chairman*
David Lehmer, *Exec VP*
Robert McCullough, *Exec VP*
Terry Angle, *Vice Pres*
EMP: 80
SQ FT: 20,000
SALES (est): 9.6MM **Privately Held**
WEB: www.hwhaep.com
SIC: 8711 8712 0781 Consulting engineer; architectural services; landscape counseling & planning

(G-5795)
HY-GRADE CORPORATION (PA)
3993 E 93rd St (44105-4052)
PHONE..................................216 341-7711
Fax: 216 341-8514
Michael Pemberton, *President*
Kim Gabele, *Purch Mgr*
EMP: 35
SQ FT: 25,000
SALES (est): 9.1MM **Privately Held**
WEB: www.upm.com
SIC: 5032 2952 2951 Asphalt mixture; asphalt felts & coatings; asphalt paving mixtures & blocks

(G-5796)
HYATT LEGAL PLANS INC
1111 Superior Ave E # 800 (44114-2541)
PHONE..................................216 241-0022
William H Brooks, *President*
Brett Fisher, *Regional Mgr*
David Seed, *Business Mgr*
Andrew Kohn, *Vice Pres*
Mike Penzner, *CFO*
EMP: 96
SQ FT: 20,000
SALES (est): 25.5MM
SALES (corp-wide): 63.4B **Publicly Held**
WEB: www.legalplans.com
SIC: 6411 Insurance brokers; advisory services, insurance; information bureaus, insurance; policyholders' consulting service
HQ: Metropolitan Life Insurance Company (Inc)
 501 Us Highway 22
 Bridgewater NJ 08807
 212 578-2211

(G-5797)
HYLANT GROUP INC
Also Called: Hylant Group of Cleveland
6000 Fredom Sq Dr Ste 400 (44131)
P.O. Box 31807 (44131-0807)
PHONE..................................216 447-1050
Fax: 216 447-4088
William Gahr, *Vice Pres*
Nick Milanich, *Vice Pres*
Larry E Pierce, *Vice Pres*
Cally Fleming, *Office Mgr*
John Gallagher, *Branch Mgr*
EMP: 82
SALES (corp-wide): 122MM **Privately Held**
WEB: www.hylant.com
SIC: 6411 Insurance agents
PA: Hylant Group, Inc.
 811 Madison Ave Fl 11
 Toledo OH 43604
 419 255-1020

(G-5798)
I & M J GROSS COMPANY (PA)
Also Called: Gross Builders
14300 Ridge Rd Ste 100 (44133-4936)
PHONE..................................440 237-1681
Gary Gross, *President*
Eric Clements, *Superintendent*
Brian Kelley, *Superintendent*
Jeff Piascik, *Superintendent*
Harley Gross, *Vice Pres*
EMP: 35 EST: 1916
SQ FT: 9,425
SALES (est): 94MM **Privately Held**
WEB: www.grossbuilders.com
SIC: 1522 Multi-family dwellings, new construction

(G-5799)
I-X CENTER CORPORATION
Also Called: International Exposition Ctr
6200 Riverside Dr (44135-3189)
PHONE..................................216 265-2675
Fax: 216 267-7876
Brad Gentille, *President*
Robert Peterson, *President*
Jerald Krueger, *Manager*
EMP: 125
SQ FT: 2,000,000
SALES (est): 20.7MM
SALES (corp-wide): 516.4MM **Privately Held**
WEB: www.ixcenter.com
SIC: 7389 5812 6512 Convention & show services; eating places; nonresidential building operators
PA: Park Corporation
 6200 Riverside Dr
 Cleveland OH 44135
 216 267-4870

(G-5800)
ICX CORPORATION (DH)
2 Summit Park Dr Ste 105 (44131-2558)
PHONE..................................330 656-3611
Fax: 216 328-8710
Mark Marinik, *President*
Michael Babbitt, *Senior VP*
Gerald F Bender, *Senior VP*
Robert Rowland, *Senior VP*
James T Lovins, *CFO*
EMP: 50
SQ FT: 14,270
SALES (est): 9.6MM
SALES (corp-wide): 6.4B **Publicly Held**
WEB: www.icxcorp.com
SIC: 6021 National commercial banks
HQ: Citizens Bank, National Association
 1 Citizens Plz Ste 1 # 1
 Providence RI 02903
 401 282-7000

(G-5801)
IDEASTREAM (PA)
Also Called: Wviz/Pbs Hd
1375 Euclid Ave (44115-1826)
PHONE..................................216 916-6100
Jerry F Wareham, *CEO*
Larry Pollock, *Managing Prtnr*
Sylvia Strobel, *COO*
Earl Carlton, *Sr Corp Ofcr*
Mike Vendeland, *Prdtn Mgr*
▲ EMP: 130
SQ FT: 70,000
SALES: 24.3MM **Privately Held**
WEB: www.ideastream.com
SIC: 4833 Television broadcasting stations

(G-5802)
IEH AUTO PARTS LLC
Also Called: Kovachy Auto Parts
4565 Hinckley Indus Pkwy (44109-6009)
PHONE..................................216 351-2560
Chuck Reimel, *Manager*
Darryl Brown, *Manager*
John Habermannr, *Manager*
EMP: 30
SALES (corp-wide): 21.7B **Publicly Held**
SIC: 4225 General warehousing & storage
HQ: Ieh Auto Parts Llc
 108 Townpark Dr Nw
 Kennesaw GA 30144
 770 701-5000

(G-5803)
IHEARTCOMMUNICATIONS INC
Also Called: Wmvx Radio
6200 Oak Tree Blvd Fl 4 (44131-6933)
PHONE..................................216 520-2600
Allen Colon, *Managing Dir*
Mike Kenney, *Principal*
Jim Meltzer, *Vice Pres*
Rachel Oettinger, *Project Mgr*
Mark Manolio, *Engineer*
EMP: 200 **Publicly Held**
SIC: 4832 4833 Radio broadcasting stations; television broadcasting stations
HQ: Iheartcommunications, Inc.
 20880 Stone Oak Pkwy
 San Antonio TX 78258
 210 822-2828

(G-5804)
IHEARTCOMMUNICATIONS INC
Also Called: Wmji-FM
310 W Lakeside Ave Fl 6 (44113-1021)
PHONE..................................216 409-9673
Fax: 216 696-9654
Rick Weinkauf, *Manager*
EMP: 43 **Publicly Held**
SIC: 4832 Radio broadcasting stations
HQ: Iheartcommunications, Inc.
 20880 Stone Oak Pkwy
 San Antonio TX 78258
 210 822-2828

(G-5805)
ILS TECHNOLOGY LLC
6065 Parkland Blvd (44124-6119)
PHONE..................................800 695-8650
Fred Yentz, *President*
Ann Carrick, *Accountant*
EMP: 30
SQ FT: 41,000
SALES (est): 2.6MM
SALES (corp-wide): 1.4B **Publicly Held**
WEB: www.pkoh.com.cn
SIC: 7371 Computer software development
HQ: Park-Ohio Industries, Inc.
 6065 Parkland Blvd Ste 1
 Cleveland OH 44124
 440 947-2000

(G-5806)
IMAGE CONSULTING SERVICES INC (PA)
1775 Donwell Dr (44121-3780)
PHONE..................................440 951-9919
Amy G O'Dea, *President*
Amy O'Dea, *President*
Patrick W O'Dea, *Vice Pres*
Charles Caplan, *Project Mgr*
Cindi Sullivan, *Office Mgr*
EMP: 25
SALES (est): 3.8MM **Privately Held**
SIC: 8748 Business consulting

(G-5807)
IMPACT CERAMICS LLC
17000 Saint Clair Ave # 3 (44110-2535)
PHONE..................................440 554-3624
Matthew Mullarkey,
EMP: 50
SALES (est): 2.6MM **Privately Held**
SIC: 8742 Manufacturing management consultant

Cleveland - Cuyahoga County (G-5808)	GEOGRAPHIC SECTION

(G-5808)
INCENTISOFT SOLUTIONS LLC
20445 Emerald Pkwy # 400 (44135-6010)
PHONE...................................877 562-4461
James Pshock, CEO
EMP: 69
SALES (est): 2.9MM
SALES (corp-wide): 22.5MM Privately Held
SIC: 8742 8748 Administrative services consultant; employee programs administration
PA: Bravo Wellness, Llc
   20445 Emerald Pkwy # 400
   Cleveland OH 44135
   216 658-9500

(G-5809)
INDEPENDENCE BANK
4401 Rockside Rd (44131-2146)
P.O. Box 318048 (44131-8048)
PHONE...................................216 447-1444
Fax: 216 447-1337
Christopher W Mack, Ch of Bd
Jeffrey Imka, Senior VP
Russell G Fortlage, Vice Pres
Albert E Wainio, Vice Pres
Dennis A Williams, Vice Pres
EMP: 30
SALES: 6.4MM
SALES (corp-wide): 7.1MM Privately Held
SIC: 6022 State commercial banks
PA: Independence Bancorp
   4401 Rockside Rd
   Cleveland OH 44131
   216 447-1444

(G-5810)
INDEPENDENCE CAPITAL CORP
5579 Pearl Rd Ste 100 (44129-2555)
PHONE...................................440 888-7000
Tom Scheiman, President
Kurt Heinicke, Vice Pres
Bruce Higley, Vice Pres
Keith Johnson, Vice Pres
Gareth Vaughan, Manager
EMP: 30
SALES (est): 3.4MM Privately Held
SIC: 6211 Security brokers & dealers

(G-5811)
INDEPENDENCE EQUIPMENT LSG CO
4401 Rockside Rd (44131-2146)
PHONE...................................216 642-3408
Christopher W Mack, President
Russell G Fortlage, Vice Pres
EMP: 29
SALES (est): 1.8MM
SALES (corp-wide): 7.1MM Privately Held
SIC: 7359 Equipment rental & leasing; business machine & electronic equipment rental services
PA: Independence Bancorp
   4401 Rockside Rd
   Cleveland OH 44131
   216 447-1444

(G-5812)
INDEPENDENCE ONCOLOGY
6100 W Creek Rd Ste 16 (44131-2133)
PHONE...................................216 524-7979
Fax: 216 447-9746
Nanat Rock, Owner
EMP: 30
SALES (est): 818.4K Privately Held
WEB: www.independence-ohio.com
SIC: 8011 Oncologist

(G-5813)
INDEPENDENCE TRAVEL
5000 Rockside Rd Ste 240 (44131-2141)
PHONE...................................216 447-9950
Fax: 216 447-0090
Corinne Smith, Owner
EMP: 25
SALES (est): 2.2MM Privately Held
SIC: 4724 Tourist agency arranging transport, lodging & car rental

(G-5814)
INDEPENDENT HOTEL PARTNERS LLC
Also Called: Shereton Hotel Independance
5300 Rockside Rd (44131-2118)
PHONE...................................216 524-0700
Lee Jackson, General Mgr
Scott Schmelzer, General Mgr
Ernie Malas, Mng Member
EMP: 75
SQ FT: 300,000
SALES (est): 4.6MM Privately Held
SIC: 7011 Hotels

(G-5815)
INDEPNDENCE OFFICE BUS SUP INC
Also Called: Independence Business Supply
4550 Hinckley Indus Pkwy (44109-6010)
PHONE...................................216 398-8880
Fax: 216 398-6327
Steven Gordon, President
Tony Angelo, Vice Pres
Pat Bova, Vice Pres
James Connelly, Vice Pres
Ken Cramer, Vice Pres
EMP: 55
SQ FT: 10,250
SALES (est): 42.7MM Privately Held
WEB: www.ibuyibs.com
SIC: 5112 5021 Stationery & office supplies; office supplies; furniture

(G-5816)
INDUSTRIAL ENERGY SYSTEMS INC
15828 Industrial Pkwy # 3 (44135-3349)
PHONE...................................216 267-9590
Fax: 216 267-9593
Michael Dragics, President
Wenda Cline, Admin Asst
EMP: 45
SQ FT: 9,500
SALES (est): 6.2MM Privately Held
SIC: 1761 Roofing contractor; sheet metalwork

(G-5817)
INDUSTRIAL ORIGAMI INC
6755 Engle Rd Ste A (44130-7947)
PHONE...................................440 260-0000
V Gerry Corrigan, President
Zach Koekemoer, CFO
Max Durney, CTO
EMP: 29
SALES (est): 3.2MM Privately Held
SIC: 8711 Industrial engineers

(G-5818)
INERTIAL AIRLINE SERVICES INC
Also Called: Inertial Aerospace Services
375 Alpha Park (44143-2237)
PHONE...................................440 995-6555
Fax: 440 995-9559
Eric Mendelson, President
C Jeff Willams, Vice Pres
Kyle Fardink, Prdtn Mgr
Blaine Lewis, QC Mgr
Joseph Mastromonaco, Accountant
EMP: 33
SALES (est): 5.8MM Publicly Held
SIC: 7699 Nautical & navigational instrument repair
HQ: Heico Aerospace Holdings Corp.
   3000 Taft St
   Hollywood FL 33021
   954 987-4000

(G-5819)
INFOACCESSNET LLC
8801 E Pleasant Valley Rd (44131-5510)
PHONE...................................216 328-0100
Dan Rife, VP Opers
Ann McCauley, Project Mgr
Sierra Patterson, Project Mgr
Sue Rife, Project Mgr
Michael Minch, CFO
EMP: 31
SQ FT: 25,000
SALES (est): 3.3MM
SALES (corp-wide): 541.4MM Privately Held
WEB: www.infoaccess.net
SIC: 7372 Business oriented computer software
HQ: Corcentric Collective Business System Corp.
   7927 Jones Branch Dr # 3200
   Mc Lean VA 22102
   703 790-7272

(G-5820)
INFOSTORE LLC
1200 E Granger Rd (44131-1234)
P.O. Box 1150, Grove City (43123-6150)
PHONE...................................216 749-4636
Mark Riggs, Accounting Mgr
Ted Pinnick, Sales Associate
Bill Berry, Manager
Toby O'Brian,
Mike James,
EMP: 30
SALES (est): 5MM Privately Held
SIC: 4226 Document & office records storage

(G-5821)
INFOTELECOM HOLDINGS LLC (PA)
Also Called: Broadvox
75 Erieview Plz Fl 4 (44114-1839)
PHONE...................................216 373-4811
Patrick Cook, Senior Engr
Richard Enriquez, Controller
Eugene Blumin,
Alex Bederman,
Andre Temnorod,
EMP: 400
SALES (est): 23.1MM Privately Held
SIC: 4813 7373 ; ; computer system selling services

(G-5822)
INNER CITY NURSING HOME
Also Called: Fairfax Health Care Center
9014 Cedar Ave (44106-2932)
PHONE...................................216 795-1363
Fax: 216 795-1573
Melvin Pye Jr, President
Ethel Pye, Vice Pres
John Dugard, Manager
Victoria Gurdy, MIS Dir
Barbara Messinger-Rappo, Director
EMP: 130
SQ FT: 10,000
SALES (est): 5.6MM Privately Held
WEB: www.fairfaxplace.com
SIC: 8052 Personal care facility

(G-5823)
INNER-SPACE CLEANING CORP
6151 Wilson Mills Rd # 240 (44143-2134)
PHONE...................................440 646-0701
Fax: 440 646-0277
Bill Spigoutz, President
EMP: 125
SALES (est): 2.9MM Privately Held
SIC: 7349 Building maintenance services

(G-5824)
INTEGER HOLDINGS CORPORATION
1771 E 30th St (44114-4407)
PHONE...................................216 937-2800
EMP: 50
SALES (corp-wide): 1.3B Publicly Held
SIC: 8732 Commercial Nonphysical Research
PA: Integer Holdings Corporation
   2595 Dallas Pkwy Ste 310
   Frisco TX 75034
   214 618-5243

(G-5825)
INTEGRATED CC LLC
Also Called: Holiday Inn
8650 Euclid Ave (44106-2034)
PHONE...................................216 707-4132
John T Murphy, Mng Member
Michael Ciuni, Director
EMP: 50 EST: 2014
SALES (est): 898.6K Privately Held
SIC: 7011 Hotels

(G-5826)
INTEGRATED POWER SERVICES LLC
Also Called: Monarch
5325 W 130th St (44130-1034)
PHONE...................................216 433-7808
Bridgette Gullatta, President
EMP: 27
SALES (corp-wide): 1.3B Privately Held
SIC: 7694 Armature rewinding shops
HQ: Integrated Power Services Llc
   3 Independence Pt Ste 100
   Greenville SC 29615

(G-5827)
INTELLINET CORPORATION (PA)
1111 Chester Ave Ste 200 (44114-3516)
PHONE...................................216 289-4100
Fax: 216 732-3631
Richard E Taton, CEO
Ronald J Taton, President
John O'Donnell, Vice Pres
John Odonnell, Vice Pres
Kenneth Maurer, Engineer
EMP: 29
SQ FT: 4,000
SALES (est): 15.1MM Privately Held
WEB: www.intellinetcorp.com
SIC: 4813

(G-5828)
INTERCNTNNTAL HT GROUP RSRUCES
8800 Euclid Ave (44106-2038)
PHONE...................................216 707-4300
Fax: 216 707-4129
Pablo Criado, Manager
Campbell Black, Manager
EMP: 74
SALES (corp-wide): 1.7B Privately Held
WEB: www.intercontinentalhotel.com
SIC: 7011 Hotels
HQ: Intercontinental Hotels Group Resources, Inc.
   3 Ravinia Dr Ste 100
   Atlanta GA 30346
   770 604-5000

(G-5829)
INTERCONTINENTAL HOTELS GROUP
9801 Carnegie Ave (44106-2100)
PHONE...................................216 707-4100
Fax: 216 707-4101
Lucas Barlow, General Mgr
Candace Palec, General Mgr
Flo M Hunt, Human Res Dir
Rob Austin, Manager
Leeland Lewis, Manager
EMP: 50
SALES (corp-wide): 1.7B Privately Held
SIC: 7011 Hotel, franchised
HQ: Intercontinental Hotels Group Resources, Inc.
   3 Ravinia Dr Ste 100
   Atlanta GA 30346
   770 604-5000

(G-5830)
INTERNATIONAL MANAGEMENT GROUP (PA)
1360 E 9th St Ste 100 (44114-1782)
PHONE...................................216 522-1200
Ian Todd, President
Donald Berardini, General Mgr
Russell Dean, General Mgr
George Smalley, General Mgr
Shane Warden, General Mgr
◆ EMP: 289
SALES: 435.9K Privately Held
WEB: www.imgworld.com
SIC: 7941 7999 7922 Manager of individual professional athletes; sports instruction, schools & camps; theatrical producers & services

(G-5831)
INTERNATIONAL MDSG CORP (HQ)
1360 E 9th St Ste 100 (44114-1730)
PHONE...................................216 522-1200
Mark H Mc Cormack, President
Peter Kuhn, CFO
Arthur J La Fave Jr, CFO
EMP: 325 EST: 1967

GEOGRAPHIC SECTION

Cleveland - Cuyahoga County (G-5857)

SQ FT: 15,000
SALES (est): 3.8MM
SALES (corp-wide): 435.9K Privately Held
SIC: 7941 7999 Manager of individual professional athletes; sports instruction, schools & camps
PA: International Management Group (Overseas), Llc
1360 E 9th St Ste 100
Cleveland OH 44114
216 522-1200

(G-5832)
INTERNATIONAL UNION UNITED AU
Also Called: U A W Region 2 Headquarters
5000 Rockside Rd Ste 300 (44131-2178)
PHONE..................216 447-6080
Fax: 216 447-1719
Warren Davis, Director
EMP: 30
SALES (corp-wide): 207.4MM Privately Held
SIC: 8631 Labor union
PA: International Union, United Automobile, Aerospace And Agricultural Implement Workers Of Am
8000 E Jefferson Ave
Detroit MI 48214
313 926-5000

(G-5833)
INTERNATL UN OPER ENG 18 (PA)
Also Called: LOCAL 18 I.U.O.E.
3515 Prospect Ave E Fl 1 (44115-2661)
PHONE..................216 432-3131
Fax: 216 432-0370
Joe Casto, Treasurer
Patrick L Sink, Manager
EMP: 25
SALES: 20.6MM Privately Held
SIC: 8631 Labor unions & similar labor organizations

(G-5834)
INTERSTATE DIESEL SERVICE INC (PA)
Also Called: Interstate-Mcbee
5300 Lakeside Ave E (44114-3916)
PHONE..................216 881-0015
Fax: 216 881-0805
Alfred J Buescher, CEO
Ann Buescher, President
Brad Buescher, COO
▲ EMP: 125 EST: 1947
SQ FT: 70,000
SALES (est): 75.6MM Privately Held
WEB: www.interstate-mcbee.com
SIC: 5013 3714 Automotive engines & engine parts; fuel systems & parts, motor vehicle; fuel pumps, motor vehicle

(G-5835)
INTERSTATE LIFT TRUCKS INC
Also Called: Ilt Toyota-Lift
5667 E Schaaf Rd (44131-1395)
PHONE..................216 328-0970
Fax: 216 328-0970
Philip J Graffy, President
Robert Graffy, Chairman
Ed Borowy, Project Mgr
Daniel J Hegler, CFO
EMP: 45
SQ FT: 25,000
SALES (est): 15.9MM Privately Held
SIC: 5084 7353 7699 Lift trucks & parts; cranes & aerial lift equipment, rental or leasing; industrial equipment services

(G-5836)
INTL EUROPA SALON & SPA
24700 Chagrin Blvd # 101 (44122-5630)
PHONE..................216 292-6969
Tanya Sigal, Owner
EMP: 30
SALES (est): 440K Privately Held
SIC: 7231 Beauty shops

(G-5837)
ISLANDER COMPANY
Also Called: Islander Apartments
7711 Normandie Blvd (44130-6522)
PHONE..................440 243-0593
Fax: 440 243-8896
Moses Krislov, Partner
EMP: 40
SQ FT: 13,448
SALES (est): 2.6MM Privately Held
SIC: 6513 6512 Apartment hotel operation; commercial & industrial building operation

(G-5838)
IVORY SERVICES INC
2122 Saint Clair Ave Ne (44114-4047)
P.O. Box 181082 (44118-7082)
PHONE..................216 344-3094
Ivory Brooks, President
EMP: 27
SALES: 700K Privately Held
SIC: 7349 Janitorial service, contract basis

(G-5839)
J A A INTERIOR & COML CNSTR
3615 Superior Ave E 3103h (44114-4138)
PHONE..................216 431-7633
John Berry, Owner
EMP: 36
SALES: 900K Privately Held
SIC: 1521 Single-family housing construction

(G-5840)
J AND S TOOL INCORPORATED
15330 Brookpark Rd (44135-3332)
PHONE..................216 676-8330
Fax: 216 676-8383
Vernon Justice, President
Donald Justice, Vice Pres
Carol Winchester, Manager
EMP: 36
SQ FT: 10,000
SALES: 2MM Privately Held
SIC: 3542 5084 3544 3541 Machine tools, metal forming type; machine tools & accessories; special dies, tools, jigs & fixtures; machine tools, metal cutting type; saw blades & handsaws; hand & edge tools

(G-5841)
J G MARTIN INC
4159 Lee Rd (44128-2462)
PHONE..................216 491-1584
John Martin, Principal
EMP: 66
SALES (est): 4.1MM Privately Held
WEB: www.jgmartin.com
SIC: 8742 Management consulting services

(G-5842)
J R JOHNSON ENGINEERING INC
6673 Eastland Rd (44130-2423)
PHONE..................440 234-9972
Fax: 440 234-9982
James R Johnson, President
Ken Lewis, Vice Pres
Raymond Esser, Project Mgr
Drew Conant, Engineer
Joe Mandic, Engineer
EMP: 40
SQ FT: 10,000
SALES (est): 2.7MM Privately Held
WEB: www.jrjohnsonengr.com
SIC: 8711 Consulting engineer

(G-5843)
J S N HOLDINGS
6055 Rockside Woods Blvd # 100 (44131-2317)
PHONE..................216 447-0070
Neil D Viny, Principal
Wynn Gerber, Officer
Charlene Sufka, Administration
EMP: 40
SALES: 106K Privately Held
WEB: www.daladgroup.com
SIC: 6531 Real estate agent, commercial

(G-5844)
J T ADAMS CO INC
Also Called: Tensile Testing
4520 Willow Pkwy (44125-1042)
PHONE..................216 641-3290
Fax: 216 641-1223
Tim Adams, President
Clark Lander, Project Mgr
James Rauckhorst, QC Mgr
Tracey Waugaman, Treasurer
Bree Movens, Marketing Staff
EMP: 30
SQ FT: 30,000
SALES (est): 5.5MM Privately Held
WEB: www.tensile.com
SIC: 8734 Metallurgical testing laboratory

(G-5845)
J V JANITORIAL SERVICES INC
1230 E Schaaf Rd Ste 1 (44131-1399)
PHONE..................216 749-1150
Fax: 216 749-1153
Joseph N Vocaire Sr, President
EMP: 25
SQ FT: 6,600
SALES (est): 1.3MM Privately Held
WEB: www.jvjanitorial.com
SIC: 7349 Janitorial service, contract basis

(G-5846)
JACK THISTLEDOWN RACINO LLC (PA)
21501 Emery Rd (44128-4513)
PHONE..................216 662-8600
Mark Miller, President
Glen Tomaszewski, Senior VP
Van Baltz, Vice Pres
Bill Hyde, Vice Pres
Shawn Hollander, Facilities Mgr
EMP: 44
SALES (est): 3.8MM Privately Held
SIC: 7993 Gambling establishments operating coin-operated machines

(G-5847)
JACKSON KOHRMAN & PLL KRANTZ
1375 E 9th St Fl 29 (44114-1797)
PHONE..................216 696-8700
Fax: 216 621-6536
Jessica B Rescina, President
Rachel Stewart, President
Lori Walter, President
Marc C Krantz, Partner
Steven Berstricker, Partner
EMP: 60
SQ FT: 20,000
SALES (est): 9.1MM Privately Held
WEB: www.kjk.com
SIC: 8111 General practice law office

(G-5848)
JAGI CLVELAND INDEPENDENCE LLC
Also Called: Holiday Inn
6001 Rockside Rd (44131-2209)
PHONE..................216 524-8050
Fax: 216 524-9280
Tom Hibsman, General Mgr
Shannon Besenfelder, Manager
Lynette Slama, Manager
Laura Surace, Director
EMP: 180
SQ FT: 81,713
SALES (est): 8.6MM Privately Held
SIC: 7011 Hotels & motels

(G-5849)
JAMES AIR CARGO INC
6519 Eastland Rd Ste 6 (44142-1347)
P.O. Box 81852 (44181-0852)
PHONE..................440 243-9095
Fax: 440 243-9288
James T Goff, President
EMP: 26
SQ FT: 10,000
SALES: 2MM Privately Held
WEB: www.jamesaircargo.com
SIC: 4212 4581 Delivery service, vehicular; air freight handling at airports

(G-5850)
JANIK LLP (PA)
9200 S Hills Blvd Ste 300 (44147-3524)
PHONE..................440 838-7600
Fax: 440 838-7601
Brian Gambrell, Counsel
Christopher Pitet, Counsel
Timothy Puin, Counsel
Scott Berney, Office Mgr
Steven Janik, Mng Member
EMP: 52
SQ FT: 8,000
SALES (est): 8.9MM Privately Held
WEB: www.janiklaw.com
SIC: 8111 General practice law office

(G-5851)
JANITORIAL SERVICES INC
8555 Sweet Valley Dr H (44125-4254)
PHONE..................216 341-8601
Ronald J Martinez Sr, President
Ronald J Martinez Jr, Vice Pres
Tyara Webb, Manager
Denise Thompson, Asst Director
Kristin Bennie, Admin Sec
EMP: 325
SQ FT: 6,000
SALES (est): 12.1MM Privately Held
WEB: www.jsijanitorial.com
SIC: 7349 Janitorial service, contract basis

(G-5852)
JAVITCH BLOCK LLC (PA)
1100 Superior Ave E Fl 19 (44114-2521)
PHONE..................216 623-0000
Fax: 216 623-0190
Mark Cashmere, Technical Mgr
Gene Karlen, Controller
William McGrew, Controller
Kelly Volckening, Accountant
Bruce A Block, Mng Member
EMP: 220
SQ FT: 54,000
SALES (est): 58.1MM Privately Held
WEB: www.jber.com
SIC: 8111 General practice law office

(G-5853)
JAY BLUE COMMUNICATIONS
7500 Associate Ave (44144-1105)
PHONE..................216 661-2828
John Houlihan, Owner
Wayne Davis, Project Mgr
Donald Schwark, Project Mgr
EMP: 25
SALES (est): 3.4MM Privately Held
SIC: 4899 Data communication services

(G-5854)
JBK GROUP INC (PA)
Also Called: Event Source
6001 Towpath Dr (44125-4221)
PHONE..................216 901-0000
Fax: 216 901-6200
John Bibbo, President
Lisa Lawlor, Publisher
Kevin Bibbo, General Mgr
Bill Furguson, General Mgr
Bryan Bibbo, Vice Pres
EMP: 45
SQ FT: 57,530
SALES (est): 12.3MM Privately Held
WEB: www.eventsource.com
SIC: 7353 7359 Heavy construction equipment rental; equipment rental & leasing

(G-5855)
JBO HOLDING COMPANY
Also Called: Oswald Companies
1100 Superior Ave E # 1500 (44114-2530)
PHONE..................216 367-8787
Marc S Byrnes, Ch of Bd
Todd Miller, Vice Pres
Jeffery Phillips, Vice Pres
Denise Tapp, Controller
Bill Fisher, Marketing Staff
EMP: 180
SQ FT: 30,000 Privately Held
SIC: 6719 Personal holding companies, except banks

(G-5856)
JEFFERSON MEDICAL CO
950 Main Ave Ste 500 (44113-7206)
PHONE..................216 443-9000
L Erb, Principal
EMP: 40
SALES (est): 894.8K Privately Held
SIC: 8111 Legal services

(G-5857)
JENNINGS ELIZA HOME INC (HQ)
10603 Detroit Ave (44102-1647)
PHONE..................216 226-0282
Fax: 216 226-8905
Deborah Hiller, CEO
Jim Rogerson, COO

Cleveland - Cuyahoga County (G-5858)

Joan Lampe, *CFO*
Nancy Young, *Personnel*
EMP: 210
SQ FT: 60,000
SALES (est): 8.6MM **Privately Held**
WEB: www.elizajen.org
SIC: 8051 8052 Convalescent home with continuous nursing care; intermediate care facilities

(G-5858)
JENNINGS CTR FOR OLDER ADULTS
Also Called: Jennings Hall Nursing Facility
10204 Granger Rd 232 (44125-3106)
PHONE 216 581-2900
Fax: 216 581-1517
Martha M Kutik, *President*
Don Posner, *COO*
Allison Salopeck, *COO*
Matthew Bollin, *CFO*
Richard Zak, *CFO*
EMP: 375
SQ FT: 120,000
SALES: 19.2MM **Privately Held**
WEB: www.jenningscenter.org
SIC: 8059 8051 8052 Nursing home, except skilled & intermediate care facility; skilled nursing care facilities; intermediate care facilities

(G-5859)
JERGENS INC (PA)
Also Called: Tooling Components Division
15700 S Waterloo Rd (44110-3898)
PHONE 216 486-5540
Jack H Schron Jr, *President*
Avis Kanocz, *President*
Bob Rubenstahl, *General Mgr*
Matt Schron, *General Mgr*
Cheryl Vyskol, *General Mgr*
▲ **EMP:** 307 **EST:** 1942
SQ FT: 104,000
SALES (est): 81.3MM **Privately Held**
WEB: www.jergensinc.com
SIC: 3544 3443 3452 5084 Special dies, tools, jigs & fixtures; jigs & fixtures; fabricated plate work (boiler shop); bolts, nuts, rivets & washers; machine tools & accessories; drill bushings (drilling jig); precision measuring tools

(G-5860)
JERSEY CENTRAL PWR & LIGHT CO
Also Called: Firstenergy
6800 S Marginal Rd (44103-1047)
PHONE 216 432-6330
EMP: 65
SALES (corp-wide): 15B **Publicly Held**
SIC: 4911 Electric Services
HQ: Jersey Central Power & Light Company
76 S Main St
Akron OH 44308
800 736-3402

(G-5861)
JERSEY CENTRAL PWR & LIGHT CO
Also Called: Firstenergy
2423 Payne Ave (44114-4428)
PHONE 216 479-1132
Rick Louse, *Branch Mgr*
EMP: 67 **Publicly Held**
WEB: www.jersey-central-power-light.monmouth.n
SIC: 4911 Distribution, electric power
HQ: Jersey Central Power & Light Company
76 S Main St
Akron OH 44308
800 736-3402

(G-5862)
JETRO CASH AND CARRY ENTPS LLC
Also Called: Restaurant Depot
6150 Halle Dr (44125-4614)
PHONE 216 525-0101
Dan Nicholas, *Manager*
EMP: 100 **Privately Held**
WEB: www.jetro.com
SIC: 5147 5194 5141 5181 Meats, fresh; tobacco & tobacco products; groceries, general line; beer & other fermented malt liquors; packaged frozen goods
HQ: Jetro Cash And Carry Enterprises, Llc
1524 132nd St
College Point NY 11356
718 939-6400

(G-5863)
JEWISH FAMILY SERVICES ASSOCIA (PA)
Also Called: Jewish Community Care At Home
3659 Green Rd Ste 322 (44122-5715)
PHONE 216 292-3999
Robert Shakno, *President*
Patrick Sidley, *CFO*
Dave Lavac, *Finance*
Sara Kroloff, *Case Mgr*
Veronica Bellay, *Program Mgr*
EMP: 50
SQ FT: 16,000
SALES: 25.8MM **Privately Held**
WEB: www.jfsa-cleveland.org
SIC: 8322 Family service agency

(G-5864)
JEWISH FAMILY SERVICES ASSOCIA
Also Called: Professional Services
24075 Commerce Park # 105 (44122-5846)
PHONE 216 292-3999
Fax: 216 378-2783
Jessica Rosenblitt, *Manager*
Stephen Schwartz, *Exec Dir*
Kathy Levine, *Director*
Michael Schultz, *Director*
Jaime Lowy, *Associate Dir*
EMP: 40
SQ FT: 9,900
SALES (corp-wide): 25.8MM **Privately Held**
WEB: www.jfsa-cleveland.org
SIC: 8322 Social service center
PA: Jewish Family Service Association Of Cleveland, Ohio
3659 Green Rd Ste 322
Cleveland OH 44122
216 292-3999

(G-5865)
JMA HEALTHCARE LLC
Also Called: Oak Park Health Care Center
24579 Broadway Ave (44146-6338)
PHONE 440 439-7976
Fax: 440 232-7113
Lisa Berkowitz, *Principal*
Linda Maynard, *Facilities Dir*
Damon Chapman, *Purch Mgr*
Eric Saylek, *Personnel*
Elizabeth Treadwell, *Manager*
EMP: 125 **EST:** 1990
SQ FT: 33,000
SALES (est): 2.2MM **Privately Held**
SIC: 8051 Convalescent home with continuous nursing care

(G-5866)
JOBAR ENTERPRISE INC
3361 E 147th St (44120-4133)
P.O. Box 20264 (44120-0264)
PHONE 216 561-5184
Barbara McMahn, *President*
EMP: 25
SALES: 110K **Privately Held**
SIC: 6531 Real estate agents & managers

(G-5867)
JOHN H KAPPUS CO (PA)
Also Called: Kappus Company
4755 W 150th St (44135-3329)
PHONE 216 367-6677
Fred Kappus, *CEO*
John Kappus, *President*
John Zalenka, *COO*
Michael J Marcis, *CFO*
Ryan Huffman, *Mng Member*
EMP: 49
SALES (est): 21.1MM **Privately Held**
WEB: www.kappuscompany.com
SIC: 5046 Restaurant equipment & supplies

(G-5868)
JOHN RBRTS HAIR STUDIO SPA INC (PA)
673 Alpha Dr Ste F (44143-2140)
PHONE 216 839-1430
John R Di Julius III, *President*
Eric Hammond, *Exec Dir*
EMP: 73
SQ FT: 7,000
SALES (est): 3.8MM **Privately Held**
SIC: 7231 Hairdressers

(G-5869)
JOHNSON MIRMIRAN THOMPSON INC
959 W Saint Clair Ave # 300 (44113-1298)
PHONE 614 714-0270
James Prevost, *Vice Pres*
EMP: 70
SALES (corp-wide): 224.9MM **Privately Held**
SIC: 8711 Civil engineering
PA: Johnson, Mirmiran & Thompson, Inc.
40 Wight Ave
Hunt Valley MD 21030
410 329-3100

(G-5870)
JONATHON R JOHNSON & ASSOC
1489 Rydalmount Rd (44118-1347)
PHONE 216 932-6529
Johnathon R Johnson, *Principal*
EMP: 25
SALES (est): 1.1MM **Privately Held**
SIC: 8742 Management consulting services

(G-5871)
JONES DAY LIMITED PARTNERSHIP (PA)
901 Lakeside Ave E Ste 2 (44114-1190)
PHONE 216 586-3939
Jones Day, *Partner*
Brett P Barragate, *Partner*
Dennis Barsky, *Partner*
Patrick Belville, *Partner*
Erin L Burke, *Partner*
EMP: 900
SQ FT: 300,000
SALES (est): 926MM **Privately Held**
SIC: 8111 General practice law office

(G-5872)
JOSHEN PAPER & PACKAGING CO (PA)
5800 Grant Ave (44105-5608)
PHONE 216 441-5600
Fax: 216 441-7647
Michelle Reiner, *CEO*
Bob Reiner, *President*
Elliot M Kaufman, *Principal*
John Caldwell, *Vice Pres*
Don Morgenroth, *Vice Pres*
◆ **EMP:** 140
SQ FT: 180,000
SALES (est): 295.4MM **Privately Held**
WEB: www.joshen.com
SIC: 5113 5169 Bags, paper & disposable plastic; cups, disposable plastic & paper; boxes & containers; sanitation preparations

(G-5873)
JPMORGAN CHASE BANK NAT ASSN
5332 Mayfield Rd (44124-2452)
PHONE 440 442-7800
Fax: 440 442-3824
Jonathan Willie, *Branch Mgr*
EMP: 26
SALES (corp-wide): 99.6B **Publicly Held**
SIC: 6021 National commercial banks
HQ: Jpmorgan Chase Bank, National Association
1111 Polaris Pkwy
Columbus OH 43240
614 436-3055

(G-5874)
JPMORGAN CHASE BANK NAT ASSN
1300 E 9th St Fl 13 (44114-1501)
PHONE 216 781-4437
Pete Van Allsburg, *Assistant VP*
Richard Landel, *Manager*
Frances Vukovic, *Manager*
EMP: 32
SALES (corp-wide): 99.6B **Publicly Held**
WEB: www.chase.com
SIC: 6021 National commercial banks
HQ: Jpmorgan Chase Bank, National Association
1111 Polaris Pkwy
Columbus OH 43240
614 436-3055

(G-5875)
JTC CONTRACTING INC
Also Called: Jtc Office Services
7635 Hub Pkwy Ste C (44125-5741)
PHONE 216 635-0745
Kathleen Morris, *President*
Ty Morris, *Opers Mgr*
Ken Morris, *Treasurer*
EMP: 40
SALES (est): 4.8MM **Privately Held**
WEB: www.jtcinstall.com
SIC: 1799 Office furniture installation

(G-5876)
JUDSON (PA)
Also Called: JUDSON UNIVERSITY CIRCLE
2181 Ambleside Dr Apt 411 (44106-7604)
PHONE 216 791-2004
Fax: 216 721-2607
Hong Chae, *CEO*
Cynthia Dunn, *President*
James Carnovale, *Senior VP*
Roy Call, *Vice Pres*
Bill Fehrenbach, *Vice Pres*
EMP: 80
SQ FT: 800,000
SALES: 23.7MM **Privately Held**
WEB: www.judsonretirement.com
SIC: 8059 6513 8052 Domiciliary care; personal care home, with health care; retirement hotel operation; intermediate care facilities

(G-5877)
JUDSON
Also Called: Judson Manor
1890 E 107th St (44106-2235)
PHONE 216 791-2555
Fax: 216 795-0449
Julie Anderson, *Vice Pres*
Heather Freemont, *Vice Pres*
Mary Schellhammer, *Nutritionist*
Cynthia Dunn, *Manager*
Joan Riede, *Director*
EMP: 80
SALES (est): 4.8MM
SALES (corp-wide): 23.7MM **Privately Held**
WEB: www.judsonretirement.com
SIC: 8361 Residential care
PA: Judson
2181 Ambleside Dr Apt 411
Cleveland OH 44106
216 791-2004

(G-5878)
JZE ELECTRIC INC (PA)
Also Called: Hilliard Electric
6800 Eastland Rd (44130-2426)
PHONE 440 243-7600
Mike O'Hara, *President*
Craig Rydalch, *Sales Executive*
EMP: 175
SALES (est): 9.9MM **Privately Held**
WEB: www.hilliardelectric.com
SIC: 1731 General electrical contractor

(G-5879)
K M & M
9715 Clinton Rd (44144-1031)
P.O. Box 360379, Strongsville (44136-0036)
PHONE 216 651-3333
Robert Kassouf, *Managing Prtnr*
Mike Martin, *Controller*
EMP: 150
SQ FT: 10,000
SALES (est): 6.2MM **Privately Held**
SIC: 1622 Tunnel construction

(G-5880)
KAJIMA INTERNATIONAL INC (DH)
6095 Parkland Blvd (44124-6139)
PHONE....................440 544-2600
Shinya Urano, *CEO*
Katsushi Norihama, *Treasurer*
▲ **EMP:** 174
SQ FT: 50,000
SALES (est): 676.9MM
SALES (corp-wide): 16B **Privately Held**
SIC: 1541 3446 1542 Industrial buildings & warehouses; architectural metalwork; nonresidential construction
HQ: Kajima U.S.A. Inc.
3475 Piedmont Rd Ne
Atlanta GA 30305
404 564-3900

(G-5881)
KANGAROO POUCH DAYCARE INC
488 Leverett Ln (44143-3722)
PHONE....................440 473-4725
Teresa Fragomeni, *President*
EMP: 25
SALES (est): 397.3K **Privately Held**
SIC: 8351 Child day care services

(G-5882)
KAPLAN TRUCKING COMPANY (PA)
6600 Bessemer Ave (44127-1897)
PHONE....................216 341-3322
Fax: 216 341-3348
David Ferrante, *President*
Anthony Ferrante, *Chairman*
Dave Feronite, *Vice Pres*
James B Gifford, *Vice Pres*
John Wynne, *Vice Pres*
EMP: 73 **EST:** 1934
SQ FT: 70,000
SALES (est): 56.9MM **Privately Held**
SIC: 4213 Contract haulers

(G-5883)
KAPTON CAULKING & BUILDING
6500 Harris Rd (44147-2978)
PHONE....................440 526-0670
Fax: 440 526-2408
Joseph H Anton, *President*
Mildred B Anton, *Corp Secy*
John S Anton, *Vice Pres*
Debbie Ziebret, *Admin Asst*
EMP: 38
SQ FT: 4,000
SALES: 2MM **Privately Held**
SIC: 1741 1799 Tuckpointing or restoration; waterproofing; caulking (construction)

(G-5884)
KAR PRODUCTS
1301 E 9th St Ste 700 (44114-1800)
PHONE....................216 416-7200
Ronald Koskela, *Principal*
EMP: 1200
SALES (est): 82.7MM
SALES (corp-wide): 1.4B **Publicly Held**
WEB: www.barnesgroupinc.com
SIC: 5013 5084 5072 Automotive supplies & parts; automobile glass; hydraulic systems equipment & supplies; pneumatic tools & equipment; screws; nuts (hardware); bolts; washers (hardware)
PA: Barnes Group Inc.
123 Main St
Bristol CT 06010
860 583-7070

(G-5885)
KARAMU HOUSE INC (PA)
Also Called: KARAMU THEATRE
2355 E 89th St (44106-3403)
PHONE....................216 795-7070
Gerry McClamy, *Director*
EMP: 31 **EST:** 1919
SQ FT: 50,000
SALES: 945.7K **Privately Held**
SIC: 8399 Community development groups

(G-5886)
KARPINSKI ENGINEERING INC (PA)
3135 Euclid Ave Ste 200 (44115-2524)
PHONE....................216 391-3700
Fax: 216 391-0108
Jim Cicero, *President*
James T Cicero, *Principal*
Rocco Gallo, *Vice Pres*
Henry Barker, *Engineer*
Doug Barnes, *Engineer*
EMP: 60
SQ FT: 14,000
SALES (est): 10.4MM **Privately Held**
SIC: 8711 Electrical or electronic engineering; mechanical engineering

(G-5887)
KAUFMAN CONTAINER COMPANY (PA)
1000 Keystone Pkwy # 100 (44135-5119)
P.O. Box 35902 (44135-0902)
PHONE....................216 898-2000
Fax: 216 898-8940
Roger Seid, *CEO*
Ken Slater, *President*
Dave Wiktorowski, *COO*
Charles Borowiak, *Vice Pres*
Roderick Cywinski, *Vice Pres*
▲ **EMP:** 128 **EST:** 1910
SQ FT: 180,000
SALES (est): 74.5MM **Privately Held**
SIC: 5085 2759 Commercial containers; plastic bottles; glass bottles; screen printing; labels & seals; printing

(G-5888)
KEGLER BROWN HL RITTER CO LPA
600 Superior Ave E # 2500 (44114-2600)
PHONE....................216 586-6650
Jim Sammon, *President*
EMP: 70
SALES (est): 2.4MM
SALES (corp-wide): 30.5MM **Privately Held**
SIC: 8111 General practice attorney, lawyer
PA: Kegler, Brown, Hill & Ritter Co Lpa
65 E State St Ste 1800
Columbus OH 43215
614 462-5400

(G-5889)
KEITHLEY INSTRUMENTS INTL CORP
28775 Aurora Rd (44139-1891)
PHONE....................440 248-0400
Joseph P Keithley, *President*
Ron Molder, *Treasurer*
Sharon Fernandize, *Credit Mgr*
Marla Mock, *Manager*
EMP: 450
SQ FT: 200,000
SALES (est): 38.8MM
SALES (corp-wide): 6.6B **Publicly Held**
WEB: www.keithley.com
SIC: 5065 3825 Electronic parts & equipment; test equipment for electronic & electric measurement
HQ: Keithley Instruments, Llc
28775 Aurora Rd
Solon OH 44139
440 248-0400

(G-5890)
KELLEY & FERRARO LLP
950 Main Ave Ste 1300 (44113-7210)
PHONE....................216 575-0777
Fax: 216 575-0799
James L Ferraro, *Partner*
Anthony Gallucci, *Partner*
John M Murphy, *Partner*
Thomas M Wilson, *Partner*
Jack Ruddy, *Marketing Staff*
EMP: 60
SALES (est): 7.7MM **Privately Held**
WEB: www.kelley-ferraro.com
SIC: 8111 General practice attorney, lawyer

(G-5891)
KELLEY STEEL ERECTORS INC (PA)
7220 Division St (44146-5406)
PHONE....................440 232-1573
Fax: 440 232-9506
Dan Gold, *CEO*
Michael Kelley, *President*
Bob Hurley, *COO*
Jim Diver, *VP Opers*
Nancy Thompson, *Safety Dir*
EMP: 58
SQ FT: 150,000
SALES (est): 42.6MM **Privately Held**
SIC: 1791 7353 Structural steel erection; cranes & aerial lift equipment, rental or leasing

(G-5892)
KELLISON & CO (PA)
4925 Galaxy Pkwy Ste U (44128-5961)
PHONE....................216 464-5160
Fax: 216 464-5176
Kevin Ellison, *Owner*
Mark Edwards, *Vice Pres*
EMP: 59
SALES (est): 12.5MM **Privately Held**
WEB: www.kellison.com
SIC: 6411 Insurance brokers

(G-5893)
KENDIS & ASSOCIATES CO LPA
614 W Superior Ave # 1500 (44113-1334)
PHONE....................216 579-1818
Toll Free:....................888 -
Fax: 216 621-3672
James D Kendis, *President*
Robert D Kendis, *Corp Secy*
Mary Herbert, *Accountant*
Carl J Stanek,
EMP: 25
SALES (est): 2.5MM **Privately Held**
SIC: 8111 General practice law office

(G-5894)
KENNAMETAL INC
18105 Cleveland Pkwy Dr (44135-3251)
PHONE....................216 898-6120
Fax: 216 898-6123
Tom McNamara, *Manager*
Andy Moler, *Executive*
EMP: 80
SALES (corp-wide): 2B **Publicly Held**
WEB: www.kennametal.com
SIC: 5084 Industrial machinery & equipment
PA: Kennametal Inc.
600 Grant St Ste 5100
Pittsburgh PA 15219
412 248-8000

(G-5895)
KENNEDY MINT INC
Also Called: Kennedy Graphics
12102 Pearl Rd Rear (44136-3398)
PHONE....................440 572-3222
Fax: 440 572-3692
Renato Montorsi, *President*
Theresa Montorsi, *Vice Pres*
EMP: 55
SQ FT: 60,000
SALES (est): 8.4MM **Privately Held**
WEB: www.kennedysg.com
SIC: 2653 2752 7538 Corrugated boxes, partitions, display items, sheets & pad; offset & photolithographic printing; general automotive repair shops

(G-5896)
KEY CAREER PLACE
2415 Woodland Ave (44115-3239)
PHONE....................216 987-3029
Fax: 216 987-3198
Jeri Sue Thorton, *President*
EMP: 100 **EST:** 2001
SALES (est): 1MM **Privately Held**
WEB: www.keycareerplace.com
SIC: 8222 7361 8299 Community college; employment agencies; schools & educational service

(G-5897)
KEY CENTER PROPERTIES LP
127 Public Sq Ste 2727 (44114-1216)
PHONE....................216 687-0500
Tom Kroth, *Partner*

EMP: 30
SALES (est): 2.2MM **Privately Held**
SIC: 7349 Building maintenance services

(G-5898)
KEYBANC CAPITAL MARKETS INC (HQ)
Also Called: McDonald Finanacial Group
127 Public Sq (44114-1217)
PHONE....................800 553-2240
Fax: 216 443-2343
Douglas Preiser, *CEO*
Randy Paine, *President*
Matt Bevenour, *Managing Dir*
Doug Fitzgerald, *Managing Dir*
Ken Hirsch, *Managing Dir*
EMP: 400
SQ FT: 70,000
SALES (est): 278.7MM
SALES (corp-wide): 6.8B **Publicly Held**
WEB: www.keybanccm.com
SIC: 6021 6211 National commercial banks; security brokers & dealers
PA: Keycorp
127 Public Sq
Cleveland OH 44114
216 689-3000

(G-5899)
KEYBANK NATIONAL ASSOCIATION (HQ)
127 Public Sq Ste 5600 (44114-1226)
P.O. Box 92986 (44194-2986)
PHONE....................800 539-2968
R B Heisler, *CEO*
Patrick Auletta, *President*
Mark R Danahy, *President*
Eric Girard, *President*
Jeffrey Lang, *General Mgr*
EMP: 500
SALES: 5B
SALES (corp-wide): 6.8B **Publicly Held**
WEB: www.keybank.com
SIC: 6021 6022 6159 National commercial banks; state commercial banks; automobile finance leasing
PA: Keycorp
127 Public Sq
Cleveland OH 44114
216 689-3000

(G-5900)
KEYBANK NATIONAL ASSOCIATION
100 Public Sq Ste 600 (44113-2207)
P.O. Box 94768 (44101-4768)
PHONE....................216 689-8481
Fax: 216 722-7092
Eric Brown, *Senior VP*
Lara Deleone, *Senior VP*
Judy Jablonski, *Vice Pres*
Sean Flinn, *Engineer*
Drew Garceau, *Engineer*
EMP: 35
SALES (corp-wide): 6.8B **Publicly Held**
SIC: 6512 Bank building operation
HQ: Keybank National Association
127 Public Sq Ste 5600
Cleveland OH 44114
800 539-2968

(G-5901)
KEYBANK NATIONAL ASSOCIATION
Key Education Resources
4910 Tiedeman Rd (44144-2338)
PHONE....................216 813-0000
EMP: 130
SALES (corp-wide): 4.5B **Publicly Held**
SIC: 6411 Insurance Educational Services
HQ: Keybank National Association
127 Public Sq Ste 5600
Cleveland OH 44114
800 539-2968

(G-5902)
KINDERCARE EDUCATION LLC
Also Called: Children's World Learning Cent
679 Alpha Dr (44143-2152)
PHONE....................440 442-3360
Fax: 440 442-6989
Sherri Wallace, *Director*
Erin Porter, *Director*
EMP: 30

Cleveland - Cuyahoga County (G-5903)   GEOGRAPHIC SECTION

SALES (corp-wide): 1.2B Privately Held
WEB: www.knowledgelearning.com
SIC: 8351 Group day care center
PA: Kindercare Education Llc
650 Ne Holladay St # 1400
Portland OR 97232
503 872-1300

(G-5903)
KINDERCARE LEARNING CTRS LLC
Also Called: Kindercare Child Care Network
5684 Mayfield Rd (44124-2916)
PHONE...................................440 442-8067
Fax: 440 446-1284
Melanie Baisden, Director
EMP: 26
SALES (corp-wide): 1.2B Privately Held
WEB: www.kindercare.com
SIC: 8351 Group day care center
HQ: Kindercare Learning Centers, Llc
650 Ne Holladay St # 1400
Portland OR 97232
503 872-1300

(G-5904)
KINGSBURY TOWER I LTD
8925 Hough Ave (44106-5700)
PHONE...................................216 795-3950
EMP: 99 EST: 2012
SALES (est): 2.7MM Privately Held
SIC: 6513 Apartment Building Operator

(G-5905)
KNALL BEVERAGE INC
4550 Tiedeman Rd Ste 1 (44144-2394)
PHONE...................................216 252-2500
Fax: 216 252-2512
Robert Knall, CEO
Michael A Knall, Vice Pres
Greg Kelley, Director
▲ EMP: 65
SQ FT: 65,000
SALES (est): 9.8MM Privately Held
WEB: www.knallbev.com
SIC: 5181 5149 Beer & other fermented malt liquors; ale; beverages, except coffee & tea; mineral or spring water bottling

(G-5906)
KOINONIA HOMES INC
6161 Oak Tree Blvd # 400 (44131-2516)
PHONE...................................216 588-8777
William E Tumney, Principal
James C Maher, Principal
Dineen B Terstage, Principal
Candy Kelly, Director
EMP: 500
SALES: 25.2MM Privately Held
SIC: 8699 Charitable organization

(G-5907)
KOINONIA HOMES INC
Also Called: Brooklyn House
4248 W 35th St (44109-3108)
PHONE...................................216 351-5361
Dave Baund, Branch Mgr
EMP: 63
SALES (corp-wide): 5.5MM Privately Held
SIC: 8059 Rest home, with health care
PA: Koinonia Homes Inc
6797 Stearns Rd
North Olmsted OH 44070
216 588-8777

(G-5908)
KOLBUS AMERICA INC (HQ)
812 Huron Rd E Ste 750 (44115-1126)
PHONE...................................216 931-5100
Robert Shafer, President
Kelly Adams, Area Mgr
Kenneth Carlile, Engineer
Charlie Carlevarini, VP Finance
Ruth Wilson, Human Res Mgr
▲ EMP: 31 EST: 1980
SQ FT: 22,000
SALES (est): 11.1MM
SALES (corp-wide): 136MM Privately Held
SIC: 5084 Industrial machinery & equipment
PA: Kolbus Gmbh & Co. Kg
Osnabrucker Str. 77
Rahden 32369
577 171-0

(G-5909)
KOLLANDER WORLD TRAVEL INC
761 E 200th St (44119-3082)
PHONE...................................216 692-1000
Fax: 216 692-1831
Maya Kollander, CEO
August Kollander, Ch of Bd
Michael Benz, President
Tony Petkovsek, Vice Pres
Joseph Tomsick, Vice Pres
EMP: 30
SQ FT: 4,200
SALES (est): 4.2MM Privately Held
WEB: www.kollander-travel.com
SIC: 4724 Tourist agency arranging transport, lodging & car rental

(G-5910)
KONE INC
6670 W Snowville Rd Ste 7 (44141-4300)
PHONE...................................330 762-8886
David Lytle, President
Jeffery Howe, Superintendent
EMP: 25
SALES (corp-wide): 650.6MM Privately Held
WEB: www.us.kone.com
SIC: 7699 Elevators: inspection, service & repair
HQ: Kone Inc.
4225 Naperville Rd # 400
Lisle IL 60532
630 577-1650

(G-5911)
KONICA MINOLTA BUSINESS SOLUTI
2 Summit Park Dr Ste 450 (44131-2586)
PHONE...................................910 990-5837
John Fabinak, Branch Mgr
EMP: 35
SQ FT: 12,000
SALES (corp-wide): 8.4B Privately Held
WEB: www.konicabt.com
SIC: 5044 Duplicating machines
HQ: Konica Minolta Business Solutions U.S.A., Inc.
100 Williams Dr
Ramsey NJ 07446
201 825-4000

(G-5912)
KPMG LLP
1375 E 9th St Ste 2600 (44114-1796)
PHONE...................................216 696-9100
John Switzer, Managing Prtnr
Jane Peer, Comms Mgr
Robert Raaf, Manager
Sphr K Koutris, Manager
Doug Logozar, Manager
EMP: 168
SALES (corp-wide): 5.3B Privately Held
SIC: 8721 Certified public accountant
PA: Kpmg Llp
345 Park Ave Lowr Ll4
New York NY 10154
212 758-9700

(G-5913)
L B & B ASSOCIATES INC
555 E 88th St (44108-1068)
PHONE...................................216 451-2672
Rachel M Rakes, Branch Mgr
EMP: 42 Privately Held
SIC: 8744 Facilities support services
PA: L B & B Associates Inc.
9891 Broken Land Pkwy # 400
Columbia MD 21046

(G-5914)
L O M INC
1370 Ontario St Ste 2000 (44113-1812)
PHONE...................................216 363-6009
Charles R Laurie, President
William T Doyle, Vice Pres
Patrick J Gannon, Vice Pres
Daniel J Ryan, Treasurer
Michael Flament, Admin Sec
EMP: 35
SQ FT: 20,000
SALES (est): 2.3MM Privately Held
SIC: 6531 Real estate managers

(G-5915)
LA VILLA CNFERENCE BANQUET CTR
11500 Brookpark Rd (44130-1133)
PHONE...................................216 265-9305
Ali Faraj, President
EMP: 25
SALES (est): 565.2K Privately Held
SIC: 7299 Banquet hall facilities

(G-5916)
LABELLE HMHEALTH CARE SVCS LLC
5500 Ridge Rd Ste 138 (44129-2367)
PHONE...................................440 842-3005
Sally Njume-Tatsing, President
EMP: 64
SALES (corp-wide): 2.4MM Privately Held
SIC: 8082 Home health care services
PA: Labelle Homehealth Care Services Llc
1653 Brice Rd
Reynoldsburg OH 43068
614 367-0881

(G-5917)
LABORATORY CORPORATION AMERICA
6789 Ridge Rd Ste 210 (44129-5635)
PHONE...................................440 884-1591
Fax: 440 842-4549
Tammy Rose, Branch Mgr
EMP: 25 Publicly Held
WEB: www.labcorp.com
SIC: 8071 Testing laboratories
HQ: Laboratory Corporation Of America
358 S Main St Ste 458
Burlington NC 27215
336 229-1127

(G-5918)
LABORATORY CORPORATION AMERICA
2525 E Royalton Rd Ste 3 (44147-2842)
PHONE...................................440 838-0404
Fax: 440 838-1633
Barbara Stone, General Mgr
Tonya Rhodes, Manager
EMP: 43 Publicly Held
WEB: www.labcorp.com
SIC: 8071 Blood analysis laboratory
HQ: Laboratory Corporation Of America
358 S Main St Ste 458
Burlington NC 27215
336 229-1127

(G-5919)
LAKE SIDE BUILDING MAINTENANCE
200 Public Sq (44114-2316)
PHONE...................................216 589-9900
Fax: 216 589-9900
Palmer Roy, Manager
EMP: 30
SALES (est): 304K Privately Held
SIC: 7349 Building maintenance services

(G-5920)
LAKESIDE SUPPLY CO
3000 W 117th St (44111-1667)
PHONE...................................216 941-6800
Fax: 216 941-8408
Ken Mathews, President
Brian Driscoll, Vice Pres
John Joseph Mathews, Vice Pres
Mike Kenney, Purch Agent
Mark Maki, Buyer
EMP: 39 EST: 1932
SQ FT: 35,000
SALES (est): 32MM Privately Held
WEB: www.lakesidesupply.com
SIC: 5085 5074 5075 Industrial supplies; valves & fittings; plumbing fittings & supplies; warm air heating equipment & supplies

(G-5921)
LAKEWOOD ACCEPTANCE CORP
15200 Lorain Ave (44111-5531)
PHONE...................................216 658-1234
Robert M Fairchild, President
Derre Buike, Vice Pres
EMP: 25

SALES (est): 3.8MM Privately Held
SIC: 6153 Financing of dealers by motor vehicle manufacturers organ.

(G-5922)
LAKEWOOD COUNTRY CLUB COMPANY
2613 Bradley Rd (44145-1799)
PHONE...................................440 871-0400
Fax: 440 871-7524
Brian Pizzimenti, General Mgr
Dan Draeger, Manager
Alfredo Hildebrandt, Manager
Clint Miller, Manager
EMP: 75
SQ FT: 24,952
SALES: 5.9MM Privately Held
SIC: 7997 Country club, membership

(G-5923)
LAKEWOOD HOSPITAL ASSOCIATION
1450 Belle Ave (44107-4211)
PHONE...................................216 228-5437
Fax: 216 227-2577
Mary Jo Schwartz, Personnel
Mary Jo Swartz, Manager
EMP: 25
SALES (corp-wide): 8B Privately Held
SIC: 8062 8011 General medical & surgical hospitals; offices & clinics of medical doctors
HQ: Lakewood Hospital Association
14519 Detroit Ave
Lakewood OH 44107
216 529-7160

(G-5924)
LAMAR ADVERTISING COMPANY
12222 Plaza Dr (44130-1058)
PHONE...................................216 676-4321
Fax: 216 676-5238
Megan Waite, Area Mgr
Rick Riefenstahl, Opers Staff
Brian Callahan, Financial Exec
Joanne Alesi, Accounts Exec
Sean G Grevy, Accounts Exec
EMP: 40
SQ FT: 4,879 Publicly Held
WEB: www.clearchanneloutdoor.com
SIC: 7312 Outdoor advertising services
PA: Lamar Advertising Company
5321 Corporate Blvd
Baton Rouge LA 70808

(G-5925)
LANCER INSURANCE COMPANY
734 Alfa Dr Ste L (44143)
PHONE...................................440 473-1634
Fax: 440 473-1650
Paul Burn, Vice Pres
Pier Langmack, Office Admin
EMP: 50 Privately Held
WEB: www.mopslicenseins.com
SIC: 6331 Fire, marine & casualty insurance
HQ: Lancer Insurance Company
370 W Park Ave
Long Beach NY 11561

(G-5926)
LARCHWOOD HEALTH GROUP LLC
Also Called: Larchwood Village Independent
4110 Rcky Rver Dr Ste 251 (44135)
PHONE...................................216 941-6100
Fax: 216 941-6102
Paul Dennis, Partner
Associated Estates, General Ptnr
Estate of Morris Fine, General Ptnr
Jeffrey Friedman, General Ptnr
Mark Milstein, General Ptnr
EMP: 35
SQ FT: 24,784
SALES (est): 2.4MM Privately Held
SIC: 8361 8051 Residential care; skilled nursing care facilities

(G-5927)
LASSITER CORPORATION
Also Called: Financial Bookkeeping Service
3700 Kelley Ave (44114-4533)
PHONE...................................216 391-4800
Fax: 216 391-9929

Frank Arstone, *President*
EMP: 50
SQ FT: 4,000
SALES (est): 1.9MM **Privately Held**
SIC: 8721 6282 Accounting, auditing & bookkeeping; investment advice

(G-5928)
LAUREL SCHOOL (PA)
1 Lyman Cir (44122-2199)
PHONE..................216 464-1441
Fax: 216 464-8996
Heather Ettinger, *President*
Ann Klotz, *Principal*
Mary Pellerano, *Facilities Dir*
Yvette White-Baker, *Facilities Mgr*
Monica Cowans, *Finance Mgr*
EMP: 165
SQ FT: 70,000
SALES: 19.9MM **Privately Held**
SIC: 8351 8211 Preschool center; private combined elementary & secondary school

(G-5929)
LAWRENCE INDUSTRIES INC (PA)
4500 Lee Rd Ste 120 (44128-2959)
PHONE..................216 518-7000
Lawrence A Kopittke Sr, *President*
Arthur Kopittke, *Vice Pres*
Richard L Kopittke, *Vice Pres*
◆ EMP: 151
SQ FT: 160,000
SALES (est): 17.2MM **Privately Held**
WEB: www.hudsonsupply.com
SIC: 3599 3541 7699 5084 Machine shop, jobbing & repair; sawing & cutoff machines (metalworking machinery); tool repair services; metalworking tools (such as drills, taps, dies, files); machine tools & metalworking machinery; industrial supplies; abrasive products

(G-5930)
LE NAILS (PA)
1144 Southpark Ctr (44136-9326)
PHONE..................440 846-1866
Luu Tran, *Owner*
Jackie Volfe, *Owner*
EMP: 46
SALES (est): 601.9K **Privately Held**
SIC: 7231 Manicurist, pedicurist

(G-5931)
LEFCO WORTHINGTON LLC
18451 Euclid Ave (44112-1016)
PHONE..................216 432-4422
Fax: 216 432-4424
Jennifer Vianvourt, *Office Mgr*
Larry E Fulton,
EMP: 31
SQ FT: 30,000
SALES: 6.2MM **Privately Held**
WEB: www.lefcoindustries.com
SIC: 4783 2441 4226 Packing & crating; boxes, wood; special warehousing & storage

(G-5932)
LEGACY VILLAGE HOSPITALITY LLC
Also Called: Hyatt Place Cleveland/
24665 Cedar Rd (44124-3789)
PHONE..................216 382-3350
Dena St Clair, *General Mgr*
EMP: 99
SALES (est): 301.3K **Privately Held**
SIC: 7011 Hotels

(G-5933)
LEGACY VILLAGE MANAGEMENT OFF
25333 Cedar Rd Ste 303 (44124-3788)
PHONE..................216 382-3871
Fax: 216 382-6206
Diane Kotowski, *Owner*
EMP: 30
SALES (est): 3.1MM **Privately Held**
SIC: 8741 Management services

(G-5934)
LEGAL AID SOCIETY OF CLEVELAND (PA)
1223 W 6th St Fl 4 (44113-1354)
PHONE..................216 861-5500

Ilah Adkins, *Vice Pres*
Tom Mlakar, *Vice Pres*
Bettina Kaplan, *Finance*
Colleen Cotter, *Exec Dir*
Peter Iskin, *Director*
EMP: 60
SQ FT: 25,200
SALES (est): 7.3MM **Privately Held**
SIC: 8111 Legal aid service

(G-5935)
LEGNDARY CLEANERS LLC
1215 W 10th St Apt 1003 (44113-1285)
PHONE..................216 374-1205
Donnie Burton, *Director*
EMP: 35 EST: 2011
SALES (est): 1.5MM **Privately Held**
SIC: 4581 Aircraft cleaning & janitorial service

(G-5936)
LESCO INC (HQ)
1385 E 36th St (44114-4114)
PHONE..................216 706-9250
Fax: 216 706-5240
J Martin Erbaugh, *Ch of Bd*
Jeffrey L Rutherford, *President*
Henry Attard, *Managing Dir*
Crisis Donahue, *Managing Dir*
Lauren Fine, *Managing Dir*
▼ EMP: 220 EST: 1962
SQ FT: 38,643
SALES (est): 193.7MM
SALES (corp-wide): 29.7B **Publicly Held**
WEB: www.lesco.com
SIC: 5191 5083 5261 Grass seed; lawn machinery & equipment; mowers, power; nurseries; lawn & garden equipment; lawn & garden supplies
PA: Deere & Company
1 John Deere Pl
Moline IL 61265
309 765-8000

(G-5937)
LEWIS ADKINS W JR
1375 E 9th St Ste 900 (44114-1724)
PHONE..................216 623-0501
Lewis Adkins, *Partner*
EMP: 55
SALES (est): 1.8MM **Privately Held**
SIC: 8111 Legal services

(G-5938)
LIBERTY EMS SERVICES LLC
1294 W 70th St (44102-2018)
PHONE..................216 630-6626
Heinrich Kitiss, *Partner*
Susan Rushworth,
EMP: 50
SALES (est): 574.5K **Privately Held**
SIC: 4119 Local passenger transportation; ambulance service

(G-5939)
LIBERTY FORD SOUTHWEST INC
6600 Pearl Rd (44130-3808)
PHONE..................440 888-2600
James Herrick, *President*
Kim Keegler, *Manager*
EMP: 60
SALES (est): 18.7MM **Privately Held**
SIC: 5511 5012 Automobiles, new & used; trucks, commercial

(G-5940)
LIFEBANC
4775 Richmond Rd (44128-5919)
PHONE..................216 752-5433
Valerie Horvath, *QA Dir*
Barbara Welker, *Finance*
James Bartlebaugh, *Human Res Dir*
Jillian Frazier, *Supervisor*
Tom Krempa, *Info Tech Dir*
EMP: 81
SQ FT: 2,100
SALES (est): 31.8MM **Privately Held**
WEB: www.lifebanc.org
SIC: 8099 Organ bank

(G-5941)
LIGHT OF HEARTS VILLA
283 Union St Ofc (44146-4500)
PHONE..................440 232-1991
Fax: 440 232-1782

Sister Christine Rody, *Principal*
Lynn Veres, *CFO*
Justin Fegan, *Accountant*
Ida Stanley, *Mktg Dir*
Nancy Ilg, *Manager*
EMP: 70
SALES: 3.9MM **Privately Held**
SIC: 8322 8052 Emergency shelters; intermediate care facilities

(G-5942)
LILLIAN AND BETTY RATNER SCHL
27575 Shaker Blvd (44124-5002)
PHONE..................216 464-0033
Fax: 216 464-0031
Marina Leydiker, *Business Mgr*
Sam Chestnut, *Headmaster*
Andy Persanyi, *Comp Lab Dir*
Jacqueline Chapnick, *Assistant*
EMP: 40
SQ FT: 32,248
SALES (est): 2.5MM **Privately Held**
SIC: 8351 8211 Child day care services; Montessori child development center; private elementary school

(G-5943)
LINCOLN MOVING & STORAGE CO
8686 Brookpark Rd (44129-6808)
PHONE..................216 741-5500
Toll Free:..................888 -
Fax: 216 741-1818
Lawrence H Roush, *President*
Jim Morris, *General Mgr*
Eugene Dietrich, *Vice Pres*
Edith Roush, *Treasurer*
Judy Carcioppolo, *Human Res Mgr*
EMP: 70 EST: 1976
SQ FT: 60,000
SALES (est): 7.8MM **Privately Held**
WEB: www.lincolnstorage.com
SIC: 1799 4213 4214 Office furniture installation; trucking, except local; local trucking with storage

(G-5944)
LINKING EMPLOYMENT ABILITIES (PA)
Also Called: LEAP
2545 Lorain Ave (44113-3412)
PHONE..................216 696-2716
Fax: 216 678-1453
Michael Sering, *Vice Pres*
George Hill, *Treasurer*
Megan Billow, *Comms Dir*
Melanie Hogan, *Exec Dir*
David Reichert, *Exec Dir*
EMP: 36
SQ FT: 9,000
SALES (est): 2.3MM **Privately Held**
WEB: www.leapinfo.org
SIC: 8331 Job counseling

(G-5945)
LINSALATA CAPITAL PARTNERS FUN
5900 Landerbrook Dr # 280 (44124-4020)
PHONE..................440 684-1400
Frank Linsalata, *Partner*
Steve Perry, *CFO*
Kurtis Zabaell, *Finance*
EMP: 204
SALES (est): 13.1MM **Privately Held**
SIC: 6211 Brokers, security; dealers, security

(G-5946)
LITTLE BARK VIEW LIMITED (PA)
8111 Rockside Rd Ste 200 (44125-6135)
PHONE..................216 520-1250
Terry A Gardner, *Partner*
Linda McConnell, *Regional Mgr*
Andrew R Bailey, *Exec VP*
Domenic Vitanza, *Purch Mgr*
Richard Mays, *Controller*
EMP: 30
SQ FT: 5,480
SALES (est): 9.7MM **Privately Held**
SIC: 6513 Apartment building operators

(G-5947)
LITTLER MENDELSON PC
1100 Superior Ave E Fl 20 (44114-2518)
PHONE..................216 696-7600
Richard Kessler, *Treasurer*
Bradley Scherman, *Branch Mgr*
Lisa Darden, *Assistant*
Alex R Frondorf, *Associate*
EMP: 80
SALES (corp-wide): 423.3MM **Privately Held**
SIC: 8111 General practice law office
PA: Littler Mendelson, P.C.
333 Bush St Fl 34
San Francisco CA 94104
415 433-1940

(G-5948)
LIVING MATTERS LLC
13613 Caine Ave (44105-6335)
P.O. Box 25771 (44125-0771)
PHONE..................866 587-8074
Charlea Brown, *CEO*
EMP: 35
SALES (est): 401.4K **Privately Held**
SIC: 7349 7342 Building & office cleaning services; building cleaning service; office cleaning or charring; rest room cleaning service

(G-5949)
LLP ZIEGLER METZGER
1111 Superior Ave E # 1000 (44114-2568)
PHONE..................216 781-5470
Robert Metzger, *Managing Prtnr*
Stephen M Darlington, *Partner*
Paul Klaug, *Partner*
Richard Spotz Jr, *Partner*
William L Spring, *Partner*
EMP: 40
SALES (est): 4.6MM **Privately Held**
SIC: 8111 General practice law office

(G-5950)
LOGAN CLUTCH CORPORATION
Also Called: Lc
28855 Ranney Pkwy (44145-1173)
PHONE..................440 808-4258
Fax: 440 431-4949
Madelon Logan, *CEO*
William A Logan, *President*
Elyse Logan, *Vice Pres*
Christina Seichko, *Accounts Mgr*
Cindy Sheferstine, *Manager*
▲ EMP: 30
SQ FT: 33,000
SALES (est): 8.1MM **Privately Held**
WEB: www.loganclutch.com
SIC: 3568 5085 Clutches, except vehicular; industrial supplies

(G-5951)
LONGWOOD PHASE ONE ASSOC LP
Also Called: Arbor Park Village
3750 Fleming Ave (44115-3741)
PHONE..................561 998-0700
Dennis H Blackinton, *Partner*
EMP: 30
SALES (est): 1MM **Privately Held**
SIC: 6531 Real estate agents & managers

(G-5952)
LOUIS STOKES HEAD START
4075 E 173rd St (44128-1700)
PHONE..................216 295-0854
Fax: 216 295-2285
Brenda Vann, *Manager*
EMP: 30
SALES (est): 686.9K **Privately Held**
SIC: 8351 Head start center, except in conjunction with school

(G-5953)
LOWES HOME CENTERS LLC
7327 Northcliff Ave (44144-3249)
PHONE..................216 351-4723
Fax: 216 351-5363
Mike Hoffmeier, *Branch Mgr*
Patrick Grant, *Manager*
EMP: 150

Cleveland - Cuyahoga County (G-5954)

SALES (corp-wide): 68.6B **Publicly Held**
SIC: **5211** 5031 5722 5064 Lumber & other building materials; building materials, exterior; building materials, interior; household appliance stores; electrical appliances, television & radio
HQ: Lowe's Home Centers, Llc
1605 Curtis Bridge Rd
Wilkesboro NC 28697
336 658-4000

(G-5954)
LQ MANAGEMENT LLC
Also Called: La Quinta Inn
6161 Quarry Ln (44131-2203)
PHONE..................216 447-1133
Virginia Klamut, *Branch Mgr*
EMP: 25
SALES (corp-wide): 980.6MM **Publicly Held**
WEB: www.neubayern.net
SIC: **7011** Hotels
HQ: Lq Management L.L.C.
909 Hidden Rdg Ste 600
Irving TX 75038
214 492-6600

(G-5955)
LQ MANAGEMENT LLC
Also Called: La Quinta Inn
4222 W 150th St (44135-1308)
PHONE..................216 251-8500
Greg Shields, *Manager*
EMP: 30
SALES (corp-wide): 980.6MM **Publicly Held**
WEB: www.neubayern.net
SIC: **7011** Hotels
HQ: Lq Management L.L.C.
909 Hidden Rdg Ste 600
Irving TX 75038
214 492-6600

(G-5956)
LU-JEAN FENG CLINIC LLC
31200 Pinetree Rd (44124-5928)
PHONE..................216 831-7007
Lu Jean Feng, *Ltd Ptnr*
Quinn Walko, *Opers Staff*
Gary Williams, *Controller*
Alyx Cyr, *Marketing Mgr*
Jamie Francis, *Manager*
EMP: 30
SALES (est): 4.4MM **Privately Held**
SIC: **8011** Plastic surgeon

(G-5957)
LUCAS PRECISION LLC
13020 Saint Clair Ave (44108-2033)
PHONE..................216 451-5588
Fax: 216 451-5174
Jiri Ferenc, *President*
Paul Mandelbaum, *Vice Pres*
Zdena Urbanova, *Export Mgr*
JD Correa, *Accounts Mgr*
Jim Gray, *Accounts Mgr*
▲ EMP: 25 EST: 2014
SALES (est): 4.3MM **Privately Held**
SIC: **7699** Industrial machinery & equipment repair

(G-5958)
LUCIEN REALTY
18630 Detroit Ave (44107-3202)
PHONE..................440 331-8500
Fax: 440 331-9504
Ron Lucien, *Owner*
John Lucien, *Co-Owner*
EMP: 60
SALES (est): 1.6MM **Privately Held**
SIC: **6531** Real estate agent, residential

(G-5959)
LUTHERAN HOME
2116 Dover Center Rd (44145-3154)
PHONE..................440 871-0090
Fax: 440 871-7289
Charles H Rinne, *CEO*
Greg Wiechert, *COO*
Carolyn Nyikes, *CFO*
Nancy Marks, *Asst Controller*
Brent Berrett, *Cust Mgr*
EMP: 280
SQ FT: 120,000
SALES: 16.8K **Privately Held**
WEB: www.lutheran-home.org
SIC: **8052** 8051 Intermediate care facilities; skilled nursing care facilities

(G-5960)
LUTHERAN METROPOLITAN MINISTRY
Also Called: Homeless Center
2100 Lakeside Ave E (44114-1126)
P.O. Box 201443 (44120-8107)
PHONE..................216 658-4638
Sue Cynatus, *CFO*
Michael Sering, *Director*
EMP: 180
SALES: 950K **Privately Held**
SIC: **8399** Community development groups

(G-5961)
M & M WINTERGREENS INC
3728 Fulton Rd (44109-2379)
P.O. Box 34179 (44134-0879)
PHONE..................216 398-1288
Fax: 216 398-0798
Michael Boost, *President*
Mary L Boost, *Vice Pres*
Shannon M Kurt, *Vice Pres*
EMP: 53
SQ FT: 48,000
SALES: 1.6MM **Privately Held**
WEB: www.wintergreens.com
SIC: **5199** Gifts & novelties

(G-5962)
MAC MECHANICAL CORPORATION
1441 Dille Rd (44117-1405)
PHONE..................216 531-0444
Fax: 216 531-9444
Delores Mc Kinley, *President*
James Mc Kinley, *Vice Pres*
EMP: 30
SQ FT: 23,000
SALES (est): 3.4MM **Privately Held**
SIC: **1711** Fire sprinkler system installation

(G-5963)
MACDONALD MOTT LLC
18013 Cleveland Pkwy Dr # 200 (44135-3235)
PHONE..................216 535-3640
Fax: 216 243-8021
Michael Vitale, *Vice Pres*
Zachary Cline, *Project Mgr*
Frank Frandina, *Project Mgr*
Donald Wotring, *Engineer*
Mike McCarthy, *Office Mgr*
EMP: 25
SALES (corp-wide): 507.4MM **Privately Held**
SIC: **8711** Sanitary engineers; consulting engineer
HQ: Macdonald Mott Llc
4301 Hacienda Dr Ste 300
Pleasanton CA 94588

(G-5964)
MACE PERSONAL DEF & SEC INC (HQ)
4400 Carnegie Ave (44103-4342)
PHONE..................440 424-5321
John J McCann, *President*
Ron Carlson, *General Mgr*
Phil Coutts, *Managing Dir*
Garnett Meador, *Senior VP*
John Campbell, *Project Dir*
◆ EMP: 30
SQ FT: 30,000
SALES (est): 4.9MM
SALES (corp-wide): 32.1MM **Publicly Held**
SIC: **3999** 5065 Self-defense sprays; security control equipment & systems
PA: Mace Security International, Inc.
4400 Carnegie Ave
Cleveland OH 44103
440 424-5321

(G-5965)
MAGOLIUS MARGOLIUS & ASSOC LPA
55 Public Sq Ste 1100 (44113-1901)
PHONE..................216 621-2034
Fax: 216 621-1908
Andrew Margolius, *Owner*
EMP: 60
SALES (est): 5.8MM **Privately Held**
SIC: **8111** General practice attorney, lawyer

(G-5966)
MAHALLS 20 LANES
13200 Madison Ave (44107-4813)
PHONE..................216 521-3280
Fax: 216 226-9038
Thomas J Mahall, *President*
Kurt Breudigam, *Manager*
EMP: 45
SQ FT: 16,000
SALES (est): 1.8MM **Privately Held**
WEB: www.mahalls.com
SIC: **7933** 5813 Ten pin center; tavern (drinking places)

(G-5967)
MAI CAPITAL MANAGEMENT LLC
1360 E 9th St Ste 1100 (44114-1717)
PHONE..................216 920-4800
Martin Christ, *Managing Dir*
John Ciancibello, *Managing Dir*
Roberta Lemmo, *Managing Dir*
John Palguta, *Managing Dir*
Scott Roulston, *Managing Dir*
EMP: 95
SQ FT: 25,500
SALES: 22.5MM **Privately Held**
SIC: **6282** Investment advisory service

(G-5968)
MAI CAPITAL MANAGEMENT LLC
1360 E 9th St Ste 1100 (44114-1717)
PHONE..................216 920-4913
Scott Roulston, *Principal*
Erica Dobie, *Associate*
EMP: 42
SALES (est): 6.7MM **Privately Held**
SIC: **6211** Security brokers & dealers

(G-5969)
MAIN SAIL LLC
20820 Chagrin Blvd # 102 (44122-5323)
PHONE..................216 472-5100
D Brian Conley, *Managing Prtnr*
Ken Conley, *Partner*
Scott Harris, *Partner*
Robert Mackinley, *Partner*
Jack Schikowski, *Vice Pres*
EMP: 70
SQ FT: 5,000
SALES (est): 11.7MM **Privately Held**
SIC: **7379**

(G-5970)
MAINTHIA TECHNOLOGIES INC
Also Called: MTI
21000 Brookpark Rd (44135-3127)
PHONE..................216 433-2198
Hemant Mainthia, *President*
EMP: 80
SALES (est): 6.5MM **Privately Held**
SIC: **1531** Operative builders
PA: Mainthia Technologies, Inc.
7055 Engle Rd Ste 502
Cleveland OH 44130

(G-5971)
MAJASTAN GROUP LLC
Also Called: Visiting Angels
12200 Fairhill Rd B201 (44120-1058)
PHONE..................216 231-6400
Kevin Johnson, *CEO*
Connie Johnson, *Director*
EMP: 80
SALES (est): 1.8MM **Privately Held**
SIC: **8082** Home health care services

(G-5972)
MAJESTIC STEEL PROPERTIES INC
31099 Chagrin Blvd # 150 (44124-5930)
PHONE..................440 786-2666
Todd Leebow, *President*
Matthew Leebow, *Principal*
George Reider, *Vice Pres*
Susan Suvak, *Treasurer*
Christopher Meyer, *Admin Sec*
EMP: 100 EST: 2012

SALES (est): 2.4MM **Privately Held**
SIC: **6512** Commercial & industrial building operation

(G-5973)
MAJESTIC STEEL USA INC (PA)
Also Called: Majestic Steel Service
31099 Chagrin Blvd # 150 (44124-5930)
PHONE..................440 786-2666
Fax: 440 786-0576
Dennis Leebow, *CEO*
Todd Leebow, *President*
Jonathan Leebow, *Exec VP*
Matthew Leebow, *Exec VP*
Kyle Boomsma, *Transptn Dir*
▲ EMP: 186
SQ FT: 450,000
SALES (est): 207.2MM **Privately Held**
WEB: www.majesticsteel.com
SIC: **5051** Sheets, metal; structural shapes, iron or steel

(G-5974)
MALLEYS CANDIES INC
Also Called: Malley's Chocolates
13400 Brookpark Rd (44135-5145)
PHONE..................216 529-6262
Fax: 216 529-6264
Patrick Malley, *Manager*
EMP: 25
SQ FT: 1,960
SALES (corp-wide): 51.2MM **Privately Held**
WEB: www.malleys.com
SIC: **2066** 4225 5441 2064 Chocolate & cocoa products; general warehousing & storage; candy, nut & confectionery stores; candy & other confectionery products
PA: Malley's Candies
1685 Victoria Ave
Lakewood OH 44107
216 362-8700

(G-5975)
MALONEY + NOVOTNY LLC (PA)
1111 Superior Ave E # 700 (44114-2540)
PHONE..................216 363-0100
Thomas J Marinic, *Controller*
Matthew Maloney, *Mng Member*
Pam Lebold, *Shareholder*
Peter J Chudyk,
Chris Felice,
EMP: 82 EST: 1930
SQ FT: 33,241
SALES (est): 18.3MM **Privately Held**
SIC: **8721** Certified public accountant

(G-5976)
MANNION & GRAY CO LPA
1375 E 9th St Ste 1600 (44114-1752)
PHONE..................216 344-9422
Thomas P Mannion, *Principal*
Mark McGhee, *Associate*
EMP: 29
SALES (est): 4.5MM **Privately Held**
SIC: **8111** General practice law office

(G-5977)
MARC GLASSMAN INC
Also Called: Marc's Distribution Center
19101 Snow Rd (44142-1416)
PHONE..................216 265-7700
Bob Guddy, *Vice Pres*
Jim How, *Manager*
EMP: 200
SALES (corp-wide): 1.3B **Privately Held**
WEB: www.marcs.com
SIC: **4225** General warehousing & storage
PA: Marc Glassman, Inc.
5841 W 130th St
Cleveland OH 44130
216 265-7700

(G-5978)
MARCUS THOMAS LLC (PA)
4781 Richmond Rd (44128-5919)
PHONE..................216 292-4700
Jim Nash, *President*
Kara Gildone, *Vice Pres*
Michelle Vocaire, *Accountant*
Timothy M Scenna, *Manager*
Ryan R Unge, *Director*
EMP: 94
SQ FT: 26,000

GEOGRAPHIC SECTION
Cleveland - Cuyahoga County (G-6000)

SALES (est): 20.7MM **Privately Held**
WEB: www.marcusthomasad.com
SIC: 7311 Advertising consultant

(G-5979)
MARIOS INTERNATIONAL SPA & HT
7155 W Pleasant Valley Rd (44129-6747)
PHONE.................................440 845-7373
Fax: 440 845-3881
Bonnie Kadelski, *Branch Mgr*
EMP: 25
SQ FT: 2,842
SALES (est): 234.7K
SALES (corp-wide): 2.2MM **Privately Held**
SIC: 7231 Hairdressers
PA: Mario's International Spa & Hotel, Inc
  34 N Chillicothe Rd
  Aurora OH 44202
  330 562-5141

(G-5980)
MARKOWITZ ROSENBERG ASSOC DRS
5850 Landerbrook Dr # 100 (44124-4067)
PHONE.................................440 646-2200
Fax: 440 646-2209
Stuart Markowitz, *President*
EMP: 26
SALES (est): 2.1MM **Privately Held**
SIC: 8011 Internal medicine, physician/surgeon

(G-5981)
MARLIN MECHANICAL LLC
6600 Grant Ave (44105-5624)
PHONE.................................800 669-2645
Fax: 216 881-2924
Robert M Ambrose,
EMP: 25
SQ FT: 12,500
SALES (est): 3.1MM
SALES (corp-wide): 107.5MM **Privately Held**
WEB: www.marlinmech.com
SIC: 1711 Mechanical contractor
PA: Columbia National Group, Inc.
  6600 Grant Ave
  Cleveland OH 44105
  216 883-4972

(G-5982)
MARRIOTT HOTEL SERVICES INC
4277 W 150th St (44135-1310)
PHONE.................................216 252-5333
Fax: 216 251-1508
Greg Huber, *General Mgr*
Angela Horwedel, *Human Res Dir*
Andi Needham, *Sales Dir*
Sean Grandage, *Manager*
EMP: 150
SALES (corp-wide): 22.8B **Publicly Held**
SIC: 7011 5812 5947 5813 Hotels; eating places; gift, novelty & souvenir shop; drinking places
HQ: Marriott Hotel Services, Inc.
  10400 Fernwood Rd
  Bethesda MD 20817

(G-5983)
MARRIOTT INTERNATIONAL INC
127 Public Sq Fl 1 (44114-1216)
PHONE.................................216 696-9200
Fax: 216 696-8615
Dean Overholtz, *Purch Agent*
Mike Lester, *Engineer*
Julie Lutz, *Human Resources*
John Zangas, *Sales Dir*
Renee Domaratz, *Sales Mgr*
EMP: 300
SALES (corp-wide): 22.8B **Publicly Held**
SIC: 7011 Hotels & motels
PA: Marriott International, Inc.
  10400 Fernwood Rd
  Bethesda MD 20817
  301 380-3000

(G-5984)
MARS ELECTRIC COMPANY (PA)
6655 Beta Dr Ste 200 (44143-2380)
PHONE.................................440 946-2250
Fax: 440 946-3214
Mark Doris, *President*
Steve Funk, *Business Mgr*
John Kisley, *COO*
Dan Nitowsky, *Vice Pres*
David Rathbun, *Project Mgr*
EMP: 60
SQ FT: 43,000
SALES: 52.6MM **Privately Held**
WEB: www.mars-electric.com
SIC: 5063 5719 Electrical supplies; lighting fixtures; lighting fixtures

(G-5985)
MARSH USA INC
200 Public Sq Ste 3760 (44114-2321)
PHONE.................................216 937-1700
Fax: 216 937-1710
Matt J Wey, *Managing Dir*
Leonard Gray, *Principal*
Michael Jackisch, *Vice Pres*
Charles Becker, *Sales/Mktg Mgr*
John Moroscak, *Sales Mgr*
EMP: 300
SALES (corp-wide): 14B **Publicly Held**
WEB: www.marsh.com
SIC: 6411 Insurance brokers
HQ: Marsh Usa Inc.
  1166 Ave Of The Americas
  New York NY 10036
  212 345-6000

(G-5986)
MARSH USA INC
200 Public Sq Ste 900 (44114-2312)
PHONE.................................216 830-8000
Craig Delano, *Principal*
Les B Artman, *Manager*
EMP: 64
SALES (corp-wide): 14B **Publicly Held**
WEB: www.marsh.com
SIC: 6411 Insurance brokers
HQ: Marsh Usa Inc.
  1166 Ave Of The Americas
  New York NY 10036
  212 345-6000

(G-5987)
MARSOL APARTMENTS
6503 1/2 Marsol Rd (44124-3599)
PHONE.................................440 449-5800
Alvin Krenzler, *Partner*
Aron Drost, *Partner*
Charles Lawrence, *Partner*
Michael Link, *Partner*
Andrew Rosenfeld, *Partner*
EMP: 40
SQ FT: 12,000
SALES: 5.9MM **Privately Held**
SIC: 6513 Apartment building operators

(G-5988)
MARTENS DONALD & SONS (PA)
Also Called: Donald Martens Sons
10830 Brookpark Rd (44130-1119)
PHONE.................................216 265-4211
Dean Martens, *Owner*
Donald A Martens Jr, *Vice Pres*
Maureen Mino, *Human Res Dir*
Michael Rodriguez,
EMP: 70
SQ FT: 7,410
SALES (est): 19.5MM **Privately Held**
SIC: 4119 Ambulance service

(G-5989)
MARVEL CONSULTANTS (PA)
28601 Chagrin Blvd # 210 (44122-4546)
PHONE.................................216 292-2855
Fax: 216 292-2855
John M Sowers, *President*
Amy Bluso, *Opers Staff*
Peter Dobrowski, *Consultant*
David Goldie, *Director*
Linda L Sowers, *Admin Sec*
EMP: 32
SQ FT: 5,000
SALES (est): 2.1MM **Privately Held**
SIC: 7361 Executive placement

(G-5990)
MARYMOUNT HEALTH CARE SYSTEMS
Also Called: CLEVELAND CLINIC HEALTH SYSTEM
13900 Mccracken Rd (44125-1902)
PHONE.................................216 332-1100
Fax: 216 587-8896
Peggy Mathews, *VP Mktg*
Brenda Milanczuk, *Manager*
Peggy Matthews, *Administration*
EMP: 30
SQ FT: 411,000
SALES: 2.4MM
SALES (corp-wide): 8B **Privately Held**
WEB: www.marymountplace.com
SIC: 8059 8741 Convalescent home; hospital management
PA: The Cleveland Clinic Foundation
  9500 Euclid Ave
  Cleveland OH 44195
  216 636-8335

(G-5991)
MARYMOUNT HOSPITAL INC (HQ)
9500 Euclid Ave (44195-0001)
PHONE.................................216 581-0500
Fax: 216 587-8298
David Kilarski, *CEO*
Bi Welch, *Office Mgr*
Mary Ghaly, *Anesthesiology*
John Pineda, *Anesthesiology*
Gurdev Garewal, *Pathologist*
▲ EMP: 445
SQ FT: 411,000
SALES: 149.5MM
SALES (corp-wide): 8B **Privately Held**
SIC: 8062 8063 8051 8082 General medical & surgical hospitals; psychiatric hospitals; skilled nursing care facilities; home health care services
PA: The Cleveland Clinic Foundation
  9500 Euclid Ave
  Cleveland OH 44195
  216 636-8335

(G-5992)
MASON STEEL ERECTING INC
7500 Northfield Rd (44146-6110)
PHONE.................................440 439-1040
Leonard N Polster, *Partner*
Keith Polster, *Partner*
Daryl Rophenfeld, *Sls & Mktg Exec*
EMP: 40
SQ FT: 40,000
SALES (est): 2.3MM **Privately Held**
SIC: 1791 Structural steel erection

(G-5993)
MASSACHUSETTS MUTL LF INSUR CO
Also Called: Blue Chip, The
1660 W 2nd St Ste 850 (44113-1419)
PHONE.................................216 592-7359
Fax: 216 621-1096
Robert Fichter, *Sales Mgr*
Jeffrey Gale, *Branch Mgr*
Brenda James, *Case Mgr*
Timothy Finster, *Manager*
Erin Stidham, *Manager*
EMP: 45
SALES (corp-wide): 19.7B **Privately Held**
WEB: www.massmutual.com
SIC: 6311 Life insurance
PA: Massachusetts Mutual Life Insurance Company
  1295 State St
  Springfield MA 01111
  413 788-8411

(G-5994)
MATT CONSTRUCTION SERVICES
6600 Grant Ave (44105-5624)
PHONE.................................216 641-0030
Fax: 216 641-5221
David Miller, *Ch of Bd*
George Giallovrakis, *Division Mgr*
Stephen F Ruscher, *Vice Pres*
EMP: 75
SQ FT: 13,000
SALES: 7MM
SALES (corp-wide): 107.5MM **Privately Held**
SIC: 1541 Renovation, remodeling & repairs: industrial buildings
PA: Columbia National Group, Inc.
  6600 Grant Ave
  Cleveland OH 44105
  216 883-4972

(G-5995)
MAYFIELD SAND RIDGE CLUB
1545 Sheridan Rd (44121-4023)
PHONE.................................216 381-0826
Robert McCreary III, *President*
Ned Welc, *COO*
Bonnie Milo, *Accountant*
Randy Owoc, *Asst Mgr*
Sterrin Kraska, *Director*
EMP: 90
SQ FT: 50,000
SALES: 8.4MM **Privately Held**
SIC: 7997 5941 5813 5812 Country club, membership; sporting goods & bicycle shops; drinking places; eating places

(G-5996)
MAZANEC RASKIN & RYDER CO LPA (PA)
Also Called: Mazanec Raskin & Ryder
34305 Solon Rd Ste 100 (44139-2660)
PHONE.................................440 248-7906
Todd M Raskin, *President*
Carrie Lunder, *President*
Joseph Nicholas Jr, *Managing Prtnr*
Stanley S Keller, *Partner*
Walter H Krohngold, *Partner*
EMP: 70
SALES (est): 10.8MM **Privately Held**
WEB: www.mrrlaw.com
SIC: 8111 General practice attorney, lawyer

(G-5997)
MAZZELLA HOLDING COMPANY INC (PA)
Also Called: Mazella Companies
21000 Aerospace Pkwy (44142-1072)
PHONE.................................513 772-4466
Tony Mazzella, *CEO*
Kenneth Wright, *General Mgr*
James J Mazzella, *Vice Pres*
Mark Shubel, *Vice Pres*
Kevin Paul, *Safety Dir*
EMP: 56
SALES (est): 121.5MM **Privately Held**
SIC: 5051 5085 5088 5072 Rope, wire (not insulated); industrial supplies; marine supplies; builders' hardware

(G-5998)
MC CORMACK ADVISORS INTL
1360 E 9th St Ste 100 (44114-1730)
PHONE.................................216 522-1200
Rodney I Woods, *CEO*
Raymond G Banta, *CFO*
Gerald Gray, *Administration*
EMP: 47
SALES (est): 3.6MM **Privately Held**
SIC: 6282 Investment counselors

(G-5999)
MC MEECHAN CONSTRUCTION CO
17633 S Miles Rd (44128-3900)
PHONE.................................216 581-9373
Fax: 216 581-1579
Richard Mc Meechan, *President*
John Mc Meechan, *Vice Pres*
Gary Fetsko, *Manager*
EMP: 40
SQ FT: 5,000
SALES (est): 2.8MM **Privately Held**
WEB: www.mcmeechan.com
SIC: 1542 1541 Commercial & office buildings, renovation & repair; renovation, remodeling & repairs: industrial buildings

(G-6000)
MC PHILLIPS PLBG HTG & AC CO
Also Called: Honeywell Authorized Dealer
16115 Waterloo Rd (44110-1665)
PHONE.................................216 481-1400
Fax: 216 481-5481

Cleveland - Cuyahoga County (G-6001)

Thomas P Mc Phillips III, *President*
Erika Pankevich, *Corp Secy*
EMP: 35
SQ FT: 8,000
SALES (est): 4.5MM **Privately Held**
SIC: 1711 1731 Plumbing contractors; mechanical contractor; warm air heating & air conditioning contractor; boiler maintenance contractor; energy management controls

(G-6001)
MCBEE SUPPLY CORPORATION
Also Called: Interstate McBee
5300 Lakeside Ave E (44114-3916)
PHONE..................216 881-0015
Ann Buescher, *President*
Brad Buescher, *Principal*
Catherine McDonnell, *Vice Pres*
Alma Solice, *Purchasing*
Lawrence Graham, *CFO*
▲ **EMP:** 100 **EST:** 1958
SQ FT: 65,000
SALES (est): 32.5MM **Privately Held**
SIC: 5013 Automotive supplies & parts

(G-6002)
MCDONALD HOPKINS LLC (PA)
600 Superior Ave E # 2100 (44114-2690)
PHONE..................216 348-5400
Fax: 216 348-5474
Todd Benni, *Ch of Bd*
James Dimitrijevs, *Ch of Bd*
David Movius, *Ch of Bd*
Edward G Quinlisk, *Ch of Bd*
Michael P Witzke, *Ch of Bd*
EMP: 175 **EST:** 1933
SQ FT: 80,000
SALES (est): 44.6MM **Privately Held**
WEB: www.mcdonaldhopkins.com
SIC: 8111 General practice law office

(G-6003)
MCGOWAN & COMPANY INC (PA)
Also Called: McGowan Program Administrators
20595 Lorain Rd Ste 300 (44126-2062)
PHONE..................800 545-1538
Thomas B Mc Gowan IV, *President*
Edward J Maher, *Director*
Thomas B McGowan III, *Director*
EMP: 89 **EST:** 1954
SQ FT: 48,000
SALES (est): 45.5MM **Privately Held**
WEB: www.mcgowanpersonal.com
SIC: 6411 Property & casualty insurance agent

(G-6004)
MCGREGOR SENIOR IND HSING
14900 Private Dr (44112-3470)
PHONE..................216 851-8200
Robertson Hilton, *Principal*
EMP: 99
SQ FT: 96,040
SALES: 203.1K **Privately Held**
SIC: 8051 Skilled nursing care facilities

(G-6005)
MCI COMMUNICATIONS SVCS INC
Also Called: Verizon Business
21000 Brookpark Rd (44135-3127)
PHONE..................216 265-9953
David Fleming, *Branch Mgr*
David Robinson, *Technical Staff*
EMP: 450
SALES (corp-wide): 126B **Publicly Held**
SIC: 4813 Long distance telephone communications
HQ: Mci Communications Services, Inc.
22001 Loudoun County Pkwy
Ashburn VA 20147
703 886-5600

(G-6006)
MCKINSEY & COMPANY INC
950 Main Ave Ste 1200 (44113-7209)
PHONE..................216 274-4000
Steve Schwarzwaelder, *Manager*
Michael Litt, *IT/INT Sup*
EMP: 45
SQ FT: 3,000
SALES (corp-wide): 2.3B **Privately Held**
WEB: www.mckinsey.com
SIC: 8742 Business consultant
PA: Mckinsey & Company, Inc.
55 E 52nd St Fl 16
New York NY 10055
212 446-7000

(G-6007)
MCKINSEY & COMPANY INC
950 Main Ave Ste 1200 (44113-7209)
PHONE..................216 274-4000
Stefan Knupfer, *Manager*
EMP: 55
SALES (corp-wide): 2.3B **Privately Held**
WEB: www.mckinsey.com
SIC: 8742 Management consulting services
PA: Mckinsey & Company, Inc.
55 E 52nd St Fl 16
New York NY 10055
212 446-7000

(G-6008)
MCM GENERAL PROPERTIES LTD
13829 Euclid Ave (44112-4203)
PHONE..................216 851-8000
T Lichko, *Owner*
EMP: 25
SALES (est): 1.4MM **Privately Held**
SIC: 6512 Nonresidential building operators

(G-6009)
MCTECH CORP (PA)
8100 Grand Ave Ste 100 (44104-3164)
P.O. Box 5270 (44101-0270)
PHONE..................216 391-7700
Fax: 216 391-6951
Mark F Perkins, *President*
Lisa Cifani, *Corp Secy*
David Zupanic, *Plant Mgr*
Jan Knight, *Administration*
Tina S Milczewski, *Administration*
EMP: 40
SALES: 32.7MM **Privately Held**
WEB: www.mctech360.com
SIC: 1541 Industrial buildings & warehouses

(G-6010)
MEADEN & MOORE LLP (PA)
1375 E 9th St Ste 1800 (44114-1790)
PHONE..................216 241-3272
Fax: 216 771-4511
James P Carulas, *President*
Larry J Holland, *President*
Karen Cooney, *Vice Pres*
David E Daywalt, *Vice Pres*
Peter A Demarco, *Vice Pres*
EMP: 90
SQ FT: 27,000
SALES (est): 36.2MM **Privately Held**
WEB: www.meadenmoore.com
SIC: 8721 Certified public accountant

(G-6011)
MED -CENTER/MED PARTNERS
Also Called: Med Center
34055 Solon Rd Ste 106 (44139-2600)
PHONE..................440 349-6400
Walter Offenhartz MD, *President*
Mariam Offenhartz, *Corp Secy*
Jeffery Folkman, *Vice Pres*
Susan Gerard, *Systems Staff*
EMP: 25
SQ FT: 2,525
SALES (est): 1.3MM **Privately Held**
SIC: 8011 Freestanding emergency medical center; general & family practice, physician/surgeon; occupational & industrial specialist, physician/surgeon; allergist

(G-6012)
MEDIC HOME HEALTH CARE LLC
701 Beta Dr Ste 7 (44143-2330)
PHONE..................440 449-7727
Fax: 440 449-7725
Alan Lipsyc, *Exec Dir*
Nathan Lipsyc,
EMP: 25
SALES (est): 7.2MM **Privately Held**
SIC: 7352 Medical equipment rental

(G-6013)
MEDICAL ARTS PHYSICIAN CENTER
Also Called: St Vincent Medical Group
2475 E 22nd St Ste 120 (44115-3221)
PHONE..................216 431-1500
Fax: 216 229-1088
Stephanie Houston, *Principal*
Lloyd Cook MD, *Med Doctor*
Elueze Emmanuel I, *Med Doctor*
Robert Needlman, *Director*
Suzanne K Scharfstein, *Director*
EMP: 60
SALES (est): 123.3K **Privately Held**
SIC: 8099 8011 Health & allied services; physicians' office, including specialists

(G-6014)
MEDICAL CENTER CO (INC)
Also Called: MCCO
2250 Circle Dr (44106-2664)
PHONE..................216 368-4256
Michael B Heise, *President*
Anne Roberts, *Business Mgr*
Todd Gadawski, *Vice Pres*
Gary Pekarcsik, *Chief Engr*
Scott Wilson, *Asst Treas*
EMP: 31
SQ FT: 112,000
SALES: 40.4MM **Privately Held**
SIC: 4961 4931 4941 Steam & air-conditioning supply; electric & other services combined; water supply

(G-6015)
MEDICAL MUTUAL OF OHIO (PA)
Also Called: Consumers Life Insurance Co
2060 E 9th St Frnt Ste (44115-1355)
PHONE..................216 687-7000
Fax: 216 687-1772
Rick A Chiricosta, *CEO*
Gardner Abbott, *Principal*
Et Al, *Principal*
John S Garber, *Principal*
Carter Kissell, *Principal*
EMP: 1400
SQ FT: 381,000
SALES (est): 1.4B **Privately Held**
WEB: www.medmutual.com
SIC: 6324 Hospital & medical service plans; dental insurance; group hospitalization plans

(G-6016)
MEDLINK OF OHIO INC (HQ)
20600 Chagrin Blvd # 290 (44122-5327)
PHONE..................216 751-5900
Stuart R Russell, *President*
Donald G Foster, *Admin Sec*
Robert Louche, *Administration*
Mary Willis, *Administration*
EMP: 400
SQ FT: 1,200
SALES (est): 9.7MM
SALES (corp-wide): 796.9MM **Publicly Held**
SIC: 8049 8082 Nurses, registered & practical; home health care services
PA: Almost Family, Inc.
9510 Ormsby Station Rd
Louisville KY 40223
502 891-1000

(G-6017)
MEDPORT INC
8104 Madison Ave (44102-2725)
P.O. Box 25277 (44125-0277)
PHONE..................216 244-6832
Jay Reinholz, *President*
EMP: 54
SQ FT: 12,000
SALES (est): 4.6MM **Privately Held**
SIC: 7363 Medical help service

(G-6018)
MEDSEARCH STAFFING SERVICE (PA)
7530 Lucerne Dr Ste 208 (44130-6557)
PHONE..................440 243-6363
Fax: 440 243-9117
Ralph E Steeber, *CEO*
Judith Steeber, *President*
Lorri Chuma, *Managing Dir*
EMP: 30
SQ FT: 2,400
SALES (est): 1.6MM **Privately Held**
WEB: www.medsearchonline.com
SIC: 7363 Help supply services; labor resource services; medical help service; temporary help service

(G-6019)
MEGA TECHWAY INC
760 Beta Dr Ste F (44143-2334)
PHONE..................440 605-0700
Richard Sadler, *President*
Paul Burkholder, *Vice Pres*
Teodoro Fragoso, *Vice Pres*
Steven Turchik, *Project Mgr*
Karl Weinfurtner, *CFO*
EMP: 125
SQ FT: 3,500
SALES (est): 80.6MM **Privately Held**
WEB: www.megatechway.com
SIC: 5065 Electronic parts & equipment

(G-6020)
MEHLER AND HAGESTROM INC (PA)
Also Called: Mehler & Hagestrom
1660 W 2nd St Ste 780 (44113-1455)
PHONE..................216 621-4984
Fax: 216 621-0050
Edward Mehler, *President*
Pamela Greenfield, *Vice Pres*
EMP: 40
SQ FT: 6,000
SALES (est): 3.8MM **Privately Held**
WEB: www.mandh.com
SIC: 7338 Court reporting service

(G-6021)
MEI HOTELS INCORPORATED
1375 E 9th St Ste 2800 (44114-1795)
PHONE..................216 589-0441
David Moyar, *CEO*
Leandra James, *General Mgr*
Bert Moyar, *Chairman*
Gretchen Roberts, *Director*
Tracey Nixon, *Admin Asst*
EMP: 250 **EST:** 1998
SALES (est): 18.1MM **Privately Held**
WEB: www.meihotels.com
SIC: 8741 6512 Hotel or motel management; commercial & industrial building operation

(G-6022)
MELAMED RILEY ADVERTISING LLC
1375 Euclid Ave Ste 410 (44115-1838)
PHONE..................216 241-2141
Fax: 216 479-2438
Sarah Melamed,
Chuck Hurley,
Rick Riley,
EMP: 25
SQ FT: 8,000
SALES (est): 5.6MM **Privately Held**
WEB: www.mradvertising.com
SIC: 7311 Advertising agencies

(G-6023)
MELO INTERNATIONAL INC
3700 Kelley Ave (44114-4533)
PHONE..................440 519-0526
Rondee Kamins, *CEO*
Chad Thompson, *Director*
EMP: 350
SALES (est): 9.8MM **Privately Held**
SIC: 8742 Retail trade consultant

(G-6024)
MENORAH PARK CENTER FOR SENIO (PA)
27100 Cedar Rd (44122-1156)
PHONE..................216 831-6500
Fax: 216 595-7321
Ira Kaplan, *President*
Enid Roseinberg, *President*
Robert S Matitia, *CFO*
Bob Schaefer, *CFO*
David Tien, *Controller*
EMP: 920
SQ FT: 242,000
SALES: 71.1MM **Privately Held**
WEB: www.menorahpark.org
SIC: 8051 6513 8322 Skilled nursing care facilities; apartment building operators; outreach program

GEOGRAPHIC SECTION
Cleveland - Cuyahoga County (G-6047)

(G-6025)
MENTAL HEALTH SERVICES (PA)
Also Called: Frontline Service
1744 Payne Ave (44114-2910)
PHONE...........................216 623-6555
Meredith Black, *Human Res Dir*
Kerry Bohac, *Human Res Dir*
Steve Friedman, *Exec Dir*
Katie Ward, *Executive Asst*
Aimee Wade, *Training Spec*
EMP: 40
SQ FT: 7,500
SALES: 24.4MM **Privately Held**
SIC: 8322 General counseling services

(G-6026)
MENZIES AVIATION (TEXAS) INC
5921 Cargo Rd (44135-3111)
P.O. Box 81145 (44181-0145)
PHONE...........................216 362-6565
Fax: 216 362-6566
Paul Yagel, *Branch Mgr*
EMP: 50
SALES (corp-wide): 2.4B **Privately Held**
WEB: www.asig.com
SIC: 4512 Air passenger carrier, scheduled
HQ: Menzies Aviation (Texas), Inc.
4900 Diplomacy Rd
Fort Worth TX 76155
469 281-8200

(G-6027)
MERIT LEASING CO LLC
Also Called: Grande Pointe Healthcare Cmnty
3 Merit Dr (44143-1457)
PHONE...........................216 261-9592
Stephen L Rosedale, *Chairman*
David W Trimble, *Vice Pres*
Tim Barnes, *Sales/Mktg Mgr*
Charles R Stoltz, *CPA*
Bob Carruth, *Executive*
EMP: 180
SQ FT: 62,000
SALES (est): 4.9MM **Privately Held**
SIC: 8051 Skilled nursing care facilities

(G-6028)
MERITECH INC
4577 Hinckley Indus Pkwy (44109-6009)
PHONE...........................216 459-8333
Fax: 216 741-4581
Dennis Bednar, *President*
Terry Goostree, *General Mgr*
Mary Ann Bednar, *Vice Pres*
Greg Pitner, *Purch Dir*
Greg Pittman, *Purch Mgr*
EMP: 98 EST: 1983
SQ FT: 30,000
SALES (est): 55.1MM **Privately Held**
SIC: 5044 Copying equipment

(G-6029)
MERLE-HOLDEN ENTERPRISES INC (PA)
Also Called: Illusion Unlimited
5715 Broadview Rd (44134-1601)
PHONE...........................216 661-6887
Dennis Millard, *President*
Tom Reid, *Vice Pres*
EMP: 25
SQ FT: 3,000
SALES: 1.2MM **Privately Held**
WEB: www.illusionunlimited.com
SIC: 7231 Unisex hair salons

(G-6030)
MERRILL LYNCH PIERCE FENNER
1375 E 9th St Ste 1400 (44114-1747)
PHONE...........................216 363-6500
Fax: 216 363-6781
Dan Bragg, *Investment Ofcr*
Patrick Denitto, *Investment Ofcr*
Dean Ducato, *Investment Ofcr*
Paul Katz, *Investment Ofcr*
Paul Lehrman, *Investment Ofcr*
EMP: 165
SALES (corp-wide): 100.2B **Publicly Held**
WEB: www.merlyn.com
SIC: 6211 6282 Security brokers & dealers; investment advice
HQ: Merrill Lynch, Pierce, Fenner & Smith Incorporated
111 8th Ave
New York NY 10011
800 637-7455

(G-6031)
MERRILL LYNCH PIERCE FENNER
30195 Chagrin Blvd # 120 (44124-5776)
PHONE...........................216 292-8000
Fax: 216 292-8076
Edward Grimpe, *Manager*
Kenneth Otstot, *Manager*
Martin R Berwitt, *Agent*
Jeffrey Danzinger, *Agent*
EMP: 40
SALES (corp-wide): 100.2B **Publicly Held**
WEB: www.merlyn.com
SIC: 6211 Security brokers & dealers
HQ: Merrill Lynch, Pierce, Fenner & Smith Incorporated
111 8th Ave
New York NY 10011
800 637-7455

(G-6032)
METAL FRAMING ENTERPRISES LLC
Also Called: Frameco
9005 Bank St (44125-3425)
PHONE...........................216 433-7080
Neville McAlman, *President*
Kevin Wyman, *Engineer*
Margie Wyman, *Office Mgr*
Wyman Tracy, *Manager*
Tracy Wyman, *Manager*
EMP: 29
SQ FT: 3,300
SALES: 6MM **Privately Held**
WEB: www.framecoframing.com
SIC: 1751 Framing contractor

(G-6033)
METCALF & EDDY INC
1375 E 9th St Ste 2801 (44114-1739)
PHONE...........................216 910-2000
Fax: 216 910-2010
Debra Gay, *Manager*
EMP: 27
SALES (corp-wide): 18.2B **Publicly Held**
WEB: www.m-e.aecom.com
SIC: 8711 Engineering services
HQ: Metcalf & Eddy, Inc.
1 Federal St Ste 800
Boston MA 02110
781 246-5200

(G-6034)
METRO HEALTH DENTAL ASSOCIATES
2500 Metrohealth Dr (44109-1900)
PHONE...........................216 778-4982
Fax: 216 778-8227
Terry White, *CEO*
Kathy Blessinger, *General Mgr*
Walter Jones, *Senior VP*
Rita Andolsen, *Comms Dir*
Mary Jarachovic, *Nursing Mgr*
EMP: 40
SALES (est): 4.5MM **Privately Held**
SIC: 8021 Offices & clinics of dentists

(G-6035)
METROHEALTH DEPT OF DENTISTRY
2500 Metrohealth Dr (44109-1900)
PHONE...........................216 778-4739
John Sideris, *President*
Zahid Shah, *Med Doctor*
EMP: 25
SALES (est): 501.7K **Privately Held**
SIC: 8021 Dental clinic

(G-6036)
METROHEALTH MEDICAL CENTER (PA)
Also Called: Metrohealth System The
2500 Metrohealth Dr (44109-1900)
PHONE...........................216 778-7800
Fax: 216 459-4543
Ekran Boutros, *CEO*
Akram Boutros, *President*
Sharon Sobol Jordan, *Principal*
J B Silvers PHD, *Principal*
Wendy Lachowski, *Business Mgr*
EMP: 6000
SALES: 883.9MM **Privately Held**
SIC: 8062 General medical & surgical hospitals

(G-6037)
METROHEALTH SYSTEM
Also Called: Metrohealth West Park Hlth Ctr
3838 W 150th St (44111-5805)
PHONE...........................216 957-5000
Thomas Ginley, *Principal*
Ann Marie Slice, *Nutritionist*
Jeffrey Galvin, *Med Doctor*
EMP: 26
SALES (corp-wide): 888.4MM **Privately Held**
SIC: 8093 8099 9221 Specialty outpatient clinics; medical rescue squad; police protection
PA: The Metrohealth System
2500 Metrohealth Dr
Cleveland OH 44109
216 398-6000

(G-6038)
METROHEALTH SYSTEM (PA)
2500 Metrohealth Dr (44109-1900)
PHONE...........................216 398-6000
Fax: 216 459-7777
Thomas McDonald, *Ch of Bd*
Barbara Riley, *General Mgr*
Thomas M McDonald, *Chairman*
Linda Lavelle, *Business Mgr*
Daniel K Lewis, *COO*
EMP: 4000
SQ FT: 1,860,000
SALES: 888.4MM **Privately Held**
SIC: 8062 Hospital, affiliated with AMA residency

(G-6039)
METROHEALTH SYSTEM
Also Called: Metrohealth Buckeye Health Ctr
2816 E 116th St (44120-2111)
PHONE...........................216 957-4000
E Harry Walker, *Director*
Harry E Walker, *Director*
EMP: 150
SALES (corp-wide): 888.4MM **Privately Held**
SIC: 8062 4119 Hospital, affiliated with AMA residency; ambulance service
PA: The Metrohealth System
2500 Metrohealth Dr
Cleveland OH 44109
216 398-6000

(G-6040)
METROHEALTH SYSTEM
Also Called: Department of Ob/Gyn
2500 Metrohealth Dr (44109-1900)
PHONE...........................216 778-8446
Brian Mercer, *Med Doctor*
EMP: 100
SALES (corp-wide): 888.4MM **Privately Held**
SIC: 8011 8093 Obstetrician; gynecologist; rehabilitation center, outpatient treatment
PA: The Metrohealth System
2500 Metrohealth Dr
Cleveland OH 44109
216 398-6000

(G-6041)
METROHEALTH SYSTEM
Also Called: Metrohealth Broadway Hlth Ctr
6835 Broadway Ave (44105-1313)
PHONE...........................216 957-1500
Anne C Sowell, *Branch Mgr*
Mary Massie-Story, *Med Doctor*
Elizabeth Jones, *Administration*
EMP: 26
SALES (corp-wide): 888.4MM **Privately Held**
SIC: 8062 8021 General medical & surgical hospitals; offices & clinics of dentists
PA: The Metrohealth System
2500 Metrohealth Dr
Cleveland OH 44109
216 398-6000

(G-6042)
METROHEALTH SYSTEM
2500 Metrohealth Dr (44109-1900)
PHONE...........................216 778-3867
Fax: 216 778-4499
Arthur M Brown, *Vice Pres*
EMP: 26
SALES (corp-wide): 888.4MM **Privately Held**
SIC: 4119 6324 8069 Ambulance service; hospital & medical service plans; children's hospital
PA: The Metrohealth System
2500 Metrohealth Dr
Cleveland OH 44109
216 398-6000

(G-6043)
METROHEALTH SYSTEM
4229 Pearl Rd (44109-4218)
PHONE...........................216 957-2100
Jerome Klue, *Safety Dir*
Amy Delp, *QA Dir*
Rob Kubasak, *Branch Mgr*
Ronda Heitz, *Supervisor*
Ashoke Talukdar, *Info Tech Dir*
EMP: 210
SALES (corp-wide): 888.4MM **Privately Held**
SIC: 9221 8069 0783 Police protection; cancer hospital; surgery services, ornamental tree
PA: The Metrohealth System
2500 Metrohealth Dr
Cleveland OH 44109
216 398-6000

(G-6044)
METROPOLITAN SECURITY SVCS INC
Also Called: Walden Security
801 W Superior Ave (44113-1829)
PHONE...........................216 298-4076
EMP: 877 **Privately Held**
SIC: 7381 Guard services
PA: Metropolitan Security Services, Inc.
100 E 10th St Ste 400
Chattanooga TN 37402

(G-6045)
MICELI DAIRY PRODUCTS CO (PA)
2721 E 90th St (44104-3396)
PHONE...........................216 791-6222
Fax: 216 231-2504
Joseph D Miceli, *CEO*
John J Miceli Jr, *Exec VP*
Joseph Lograsso, *Vice Pres*
Charles Surace, *Vice Pres*
Adam Csanyi, *Prdtn Mgr*
▲**EMP:** 90
SQ FT: 25,000
SALES (est): 74.4MM **Privately Held**
SIC: 2022 0241 Natural cheese; milk production

(G-6046)
MICHAEL BAKER INTL INC
1111 Superior Ave E # 2300 (44114-2568)
PHONE...........................412 269-6300
Fax: 216 664-6532
Aron Krish, *Project Engr*
Steven Collar, *Manager*
B Parker, *Manager*
Robert P Pe, *Manager*
Amilyn Cedergreen, *Training Spec*
EMP: 30
SALES (corp-wide): 592.9MM **Privately Held**
WEB: www.reedfarmstead.com
SIC: 8711 8741 Civil engineering; management services
HQ: Baker Michael International Inc
500 Grant St Ste 5400
Pittsburgh PA 15219
412 269-6300

(G-6047)
MICHAEL CHRISTOPHER SALON INC
6255 Wilson Mills Rd (44143-2106)
PHONE...........................440 449-0999
Fax: 440 449-2544
Marianne Nicolli, *President*
Darren Nicolli, *Vice Pres*

Cleveland - Cuyahoga County (G-6048)   GEOGRAPHIC SECTION

EMP: 25
SALES (est): 861.6K Privately Held
WEB: www.michaelchristophersalon.com
SIC: 7231 Beauty shops

(G-6048)
MICHAELS BAKERY INC
Also Called: Michael's Bakery & Deli
4478 Broadview Rd (44109-4372)
PHONE.................................216 351-7530
Fax: 216 661-6717
Michael Mitterholzer, *President*
Becky Mitterholzer, *Corp Secy*
EMP: 27
SQ FT: 4,800
SALES (est): 1MM Privately Held
SIC: 5461 5149 5411 Bakeries; bakery products; delicatessens

(G-6049)
MICRO ELECTRONICS INC
1349 Som Center Rd (44124-2103)
PHONE.................................440 449-7000
Fax: 440 449-7013
Chris Tripodo, *Manager*
EMP: 150
SALES (corp-wide): 3.3B Privately Held
WEB: www.microcenter.com
SIC: 5734 5045 Personal computers; computer peripheral equipment
PA: Micro Electronics, Inc.
   4119 Leap Rd
   Hilliard OH 43026
   614 850-3000

(G-6050)
MICROSOFT CORPORATION
6050 Oak Tree Blvd # 300 (44131-6929)
PHONE.................................216 986-1440
Fax: 216 986-1445
Kerry Duncan, *Accounts Mgr*
Chris Caster, *Manager*
Eric Daigle, *Manager*
Deedee Parker, *Manager*
Bruce Szabo, *Technical Staff*
EMP: 50
SALES (corp-wide): 89.9B Publicly Held
WEB: www.microsoft.com
SIC: 7372 Application computer software
PA: Microsoft Corporation
   1 Microsoft Way
   Redmond WA 98052
   425 882-8080

(G-6051)
MID AMERICA TRUCKING COMPANY
Also Called: Anthony Allega
5585 Canal Rd (44125-4874)
PHONE.................................216 447-0814
John Allega, *President*
James Allega, *Vice Pres*
Joseph Allega, *Vice Pres*
EMP: 25 EST: 1979
SQ FT: 15,000
SALES (est): 3.4MM Privately Held
SIC: 4212 Local trucking, without storage

(G-6052)
MID-AMERICA STEEL CORP
Also Called: Mid-America Stainless
20900 Saint Clair Ave (44117-1020)
PHONE.................................800 282-3466
Fax: 216 692-3803
Jonathan Kaufman, *Vice Pres*
Don Snyder, *Accountant*
Katherine Denner, *Sales Staff*
John Ratica, *Sales Staff*
Jim Cash, *Pub Rel Dir*
EMP: 50
SQ FT: 120,000
SALES (est): 58.4MM Privately Held
SIC: 5051 3469 3316 3312 Steel; sheets, metal; metal stampings; cold finishing of steel shapes; blast furnaces & steel mills

(G-6053)
MID-AMRICA CNSULTING GROUP INC
3700 Euclid Ave 2 (44115-2502)
PHONE.................................216 432-6925
Andrew Banks, *President*
Ademola O Solaru, *Vice Pres*
Joe Casamento, *Controller*
Al Struck, *Business Anlyst*
Carl Anderson, *Admin Sec*

EMP: 85
SQ FT: 3,500
SALES (est): 8.2MM Privately Held
SIC: 7373 8742 Systems software development services; systems integration services; management consulting services; planning consultant; management information systems consultant

(G-6054)
MIDDOUGH INC (PA)
1901 E 13th St Ste 400 (44114-3542)
PHONE.................................216 367-6000
Fax: 216 367-6020
Ronald Ledin, *President*
Joseph S Cardile, *Senior VP*
Charles Dietz, *Senior VP*
George Hlavacs, *Vice Pres*
Charles L Krzysiak, *Vice Pres*
EMP: 390
SQ FT: 120,000
SALES (est): 141.5MM Privately Held
SIC: 8711 8712 Consulting engineer; architectural engineering

(G-6055)
MIDFITZ INC
23800 Corbin Dr (44128-5454)
PHONE.................................216 663-8816
Brad Robbins, *CEO*
Marcy Robbins, *President*
Doug Phillips, *Controller*
Bob Jacobs, *Consultant*
EMP: 25 EST: 1912
SQ FT: 40,000
SALES (est): 7.2MM Privately Held
WEB: www.bermanmovers.com
SIC: 4213 4214 Household goods transport; household goods moving & storage, local

(G-6056)
MIDLAND HARDWARE COMPANY (PA)
1521 W 117th St (44107-5100)
PHONE.................................216 228-7721
Richard H Geissenhainer, *President*
Gino Milovan, *Vice Pres*
Elizabeth Milovan, *Treasurer*
Marjorie Czekalinski, *Admin Sec*
EMP: 30 EST: 1924
SQ FT: 8,000
SALES (est): 7.9MM Privately Held
SIC: 5072 Builders' hardware

(G-6057)
MIDLAND TITLE SECURITY INC (DH)
Also Called: First Amrcn Ttle Midland Title
1111 Superior Ave E # 700 (44114-2540)
PHONE.................................216 241-6045
Fax: 216 241-4183
James Stipanovich, *President*
Michael Koors, *Vice Pres*
Jeff Myers, *Vice Pres*
Norman Romansky, *CFO*
Diane Davies, *Manager*
EMP: 100
SALES (est): 72.9MM Publicly Held
WEB: www.lancotitle.com
SIC: 6361 Real estate title insurance
HQ: First American Title Insurance Company
   1 First American Way
   Santa Ana CA 92707
   800 854-3643

(G-6058)
MIDPARK ANIMAL HOSPITAL
6611 Smith Rd (44130-2699)
PHONE.................................216 362-6622
Fax: 216 362-0311
Art Anton, *President*
EMP: 25
SQ FT: 3,000
SALES (est): 746.8K
SALES (corp-wide): 1.1MM Privately Held
WEB: www.vcawoodlands.com
SIC: 0742 Animal hospital services, pets & other animal specialties
HQ: Vca Inc.
   12401 W Olympic Blvd
   Los Angeles CA 90064
   310 571-6500

(G-6059)
MIDWAY DELIVERY SERVICE
4699 Commerce Ave (44103-3517)
PHONE.................................216 391-0700
Fax: 216 391-0014
Moses Groves, *Owner*
EMP: 33
SQ FT: 3,000
SALES (est): 2MM Privately Held
SIC: 4212 Delivery service, vehicular

(G-6060)
MIDWEST CURTAINWALLS INC
5171 Grant Ave (44125-1031)
PHONE.................................216 641-7900
Fax: 216 641-5041
Donald F Kelly Jr, *President*
Lisa Smith, *Mktg Dir*
EMP: 80
SQ FT: 55,000
SALES (est): 22.5MM Privately Held
WEB: www.midwestcurtainwalls.com
SIC: 3449 3442 1751 Curtain wall, metal; curtain walls for buildings, steel; window & door frames; window & door (prefabricated) installation

(G-6061)
MIDWEST EQUIPMENT CO
9800 Broadway Ave (44125-1639)
PHONE.................................216 441-1400
Fax: 216 441-1091
Joseph Manos, *Ch of Bd*
Mike Ricchino, *President*
EMP: 25
SQ FT: 26,000
SALES (est): 4.4MM Privately Held
WEB: www.midwestcranerental.com
SIC: 7353 Heavy construction equipment rental; cranes & aerial lift equipment, rental or leasing

(G-6062)
MILES ALLOY INC
13800 Miles Ave (44105-5594)
PHONE.................................216 245-8893
Michael Shubert, *President*
EMP: 30
SQ FT: 30,000
SALES (est): 7.9MM Privately Held
SIC: 5093 Nonferrous metals scrap

(G-6063)
MILLCRAFT GROUP LLC (PA)
Also Called: Deltacraft
6800 Grant Ave (44105-5628)
PHONE.................................216 441-5500
Fax: 216 641-2610
Kay Mlakar, *Ch of Bd*
Katherine Mlakar, *Ch of Bd*
Travis Mlakar, *President*
Mark Hephner, *Division Mgr*
Jack Oldiges, *Division Mgr*
▲ EMP: 75
SQ FT: 90,000
SALES (est): 433.7MM Privately Held
WEB: www.deltacraft.com
SIC: 5111 5113 2679 Printing & writing paper; industrial & personal service paper; paper products, converted

(G-6064)
MILLCRAFT PAPER COMPANY (HQ)
6800 Grant Ave (44105-5628)
PHONE.................................216 441-5505
Fax: 216 441-0760
Travis Mlakar, *President*
Charles Mlakar, *President*
John Orlando, *Exec VP*
Peter Vogel Jr, *Exec VP*
Mike Davoran, *Vice Pres*
▲ EMP: 138
SQ FT: 90,000
SALES (est): 430.1MM Privately Held
WEB: www.millcraft.com
SIC: 5111 5113 Printing paper; industrial & personal service paper

(G-6065)
MILLCRAFT PAPER COMPANY
Also Called: Cleveland Division
6800 Grant Ave (44105-5628)
PHONE.................................216 441-5500
Sid Greenwood, *Branch Mgr*
EMP: 45 Privately Held

WEB: www.millcraft.com
SIC: 5111 5113 Printing paper; industrial & personal service paper
HQ: The Millcraft Paper Company
   6800 Grant Ave
   Cleveland OH 44105
   216 441-5505

(G-6066)
MILLENNIA HOUSING MGT LTD (PA)
127 Public Sq Ste 1300 (44114-1310)
PHONE.................................216 520-1250
Frank T Sinito, *CEO*
Malisse Sinito, *President*
Gloria Lankin, *Regional Mgr*
Linda McConnell, *Regional Mgr*
Rita Mooney, *Vice Pres*
EMP: 43
SALES (est): 8.2MM Privately Held
SIC: 6513 Apartment building operators

(G-6067)
MILLERS RENTAL AND SLS CO INC
5410 Warner Rd (44125-1100)
PHONE.................................216 642-1447
Fax: 216 642-9795
Bittel Steve, *CFO*
Ric Miller, *Branch Mgr*
Chuck Lewis, *Manager*
EMP: 30
SALES (est): 1.5MM
SALES (corp-wide): 20.5MM Privately Held
SIC: 7359 Equipment rental & leasing
PA: Miller's Rental And Sales Company Incorporated
   2023 Romig Rd
   Akron OH 44320
   330 753-8600

(G-6068)
MINISTERIAL DAY CARE-HEADSTART (PA)
Also Called: Ministerial Dare Care
7020 Superior Ave (44103-2638)
PHONE.................................216 541-7400
Fax: 216 685-0792
Verneda Bentley, *Exec Dir*
Berkley Dickson, *Asst Director*
EMP: 30 EST: 1970
SQ FT: 15,000
SALES (est): 6.3MM Privately Held
SIC: 8351 8741 Group day care center; management services

(G-6069)
MINUTE MEN INC (PA)
Also Called: Minute Men of FL
3740 Carnegie Ave Ste 201 (44115-2756)
PHONE.................................216 426-2225
Fax: 216 621-9630
Samuel Lucarelli, *President*
Sam Lucarelli, *Principal*
Jason Lucarelli, *Vice Pres*
Dan Wilkins, *VP Finance*
Brent Ponstingle, *Regl Sales Mgr*
EMP: 60
SQ FT: 5,000
SALES (est): 26.4MM Privately Held
WEB: www.minutemeninc.com
SIC: 7363 Temporary help service

(G-6070)
MIRACLE SPIRTL RETRST ORGNSIZN
11609 Wade Park Ave (44106-4403)
PHONE.................................216 324-4287
Delilah Bell Fowler, *Director*
EMP: 25
SALES: 5K Privately Held
SIC: 8322 Individual & family services

(G-6071)
MJR-CONSTRUCTION CO
Also Called: Mrivera Construction
3101 W 25th St Ste 100 (44109-1646)
PHONE.................................216 523-8050
Mark Rivera, *President*
EMP: 25
SQ FT: 3,000
SALES (est): 3MM Privately Held
SIC: 1751 Carpentry work

(G-6072)
MODULAR SYSTEMS TECHNICIANS
15708 Industrial Pkwy (44135-3318)
PHONE.....................216 459-2630
Kirk Meurer, *President*
Francesca Meurer, *Vice Pres*
Angela Easa, *Admin Sec*
EMP: 30
SQ FT: 2,500
SALES: 460.9K **Privately Held**
WEB: www.modsystech.com
SIC: 1799 Office furniture installation

(G-6073)
MONARCH ELECTRIC SERVICE CO (DH)
5325 W 130th St (44130-1034)
PHONE.....................216 433-7800
John Zuleger, *CEO*
George E Roller, *CEO*
Don Dolence, *President*
Tim Jeans, *Chairman*
Neil Gurney, *Corp Secy*
◆ EMP: 80 EST: 1958
SQ FT: 55,000
SALES (est): 18.1MM
SALES (corp-wide): 1.3B **Privately Held**
WEB: www.monarch-electric.com
SIC: 7699 5063 Industrial machinery & equipment repair; electrical apparatus & equipment

(G-6074)
MONARCH STEEL COMPANY INC
4650 Johnston Pkwy (44128-3219)
PHONE.....................216 587-8000
Josh Kaufman, *CEO*
Robert L Meyer, *President*
James McCracken, *Regional Mgr*
Garry Engle, *Plant Mgr*
Phil Stidham, *Plant Mgr*
▲ EMP: 40 EST: 1934
SQ FT: 118,000
SALES (est): 43.6MM
SALES (corp-wide): 80.8MM **Privately Held**
WEB: www.monarchsteel.com
SIC: 5051 5049 3353 Steel; precision tools; coils, sheet aluminum
PA: American Consolidated Industries, Inc.
    4650 Johnston Pkwy
    Cleveland OH 44128
    216 587-8000

(G-6075)
MORGAN SERVICES INC
Also Called: Morgan Uniforms & Linen Rental
2013 Columbus Rd (44113-3553)
PHONE.....................216 241-3107
Fax: 216 241-0208
Larry Cooper, *General Mgr*
Curtis Smith, *Maint Spvr*
Mark Kinzel, *Controller*
Shawn Dean, *Sales Associate*
Chris Radford, *Manager*
EMP: 150
SQ FT: 15,000
SALES (corp-wide): 38.6MM **Privately Held**
WEB: www.morganservices.com
SIC: 7213 7218 Linen supply; industrial uniform supply
PA: Morgan Services, Inc.
    323 N Michigan Ave
    Chicago IL 60601
    312 346-3181

(G-6076)
MORGAN STANLEY
1301 E 9th St Ste 3100 (44114-1831)
PHONE.....................216 523-3000
Kathy Ohara, *Opers Mgr*
Richard Radke, *Manager*
Stephen Mihalek, *Advisor*
George Mohan, *Advisor*
Chris Naso, *Advisor*
EMP: 50
SQ FT: 1,500
SALES (corp-wide): 43.6B **Publicly Held**
SIC: 6211 Stock brokers & dealers
PA: Morgan Stanley
    1585 Broadway
    New York NY 10036
    212 761-4000

(G-6077)
MORGAN STNLEY SMITH BARNEY LLC
31099 Chagrin Blvd Fl 3 (44124-5959)
PHONE.....................216 360-4900
Tom Russ, *Branch Mgr*
EMP: 50
SALES (corp-wide): 43.6B **Publicly Held**
SIC: 6211 Stock brokers & dealers
HQ: Morgan Stanley Smith Barney, Llc
    2000 Westchester Ave
    Purchase NY 10577

(G-6078)
MORTGAGE INFORMATION SERVICES (PA)
4877 Galaxy Pkwy Ste I (44128-5952)
PHONE.....................216 514-7480
Fax: 216 514-7480
Leonard R Stein-Sapir, *Ch of Bd*
Dawn Podobnik, *Vice Pres*
Brian Schorr, *Vice Pres*
Dawn Wolf, *Vice Pres*
Ramesh J Gursahaney, *Plant Mgr*
EMP: 60
SALES (est): 134.5MM **Privately Held**
SIC: 6361 6531 Title insurance; appraiser, real estate

(G-6079)
MORTGAGE NOW INC (PA)
9700 Rockside Rd Ste 295 (44125-6267)
PHONE.....................800 245-1050
Fax: 216 635-1111
James Marchese, *President*
Michael Perry, *Vice Pres*
Scott Marinelli, *Director*
EMP: 38 EST: 1997
SQ FT: 6,800
SALES (est): 26.2MM **Privately Held**
WEB: www.mtgnow.com
SIC: 6162 Mortgage bankers

(G-6080)
MOTI CORPORATION
Also Called: Ramada Inn
22115 Brookpark Rd (44126-3121)
P.O. Box 688, New York NY (10150-0688)
PHONE.....................440 734-4500
Soheila Spaeth, *President*
Sandip Thakkar, *Manager*
EMP: 45
SQ FT: 85,000
SALES (est): 2.3MM **Privately Held**
SIC: 7011 Hotels & motels

(G-6081)
MOYAL AND PETROFF MD
730 Som Center Rd Ste 230 (44143-2362)
PHONE.....................440 461-6477
Roman Petroff MD, *Owner*
EMP: 25
SALES (est): 1.5MM **Privately Held**
SIC: 8011 Internal medicine, physician/surgeon

(G-6082)
MPLX TERMINALS LLC
10439 Brecksville Rd (44141-3339)
PHONE.....................440 526-4653
Fax: 440 526-2598
Keith Gigliotti, *Manager*
EMP: 50
SALES (corp-wide): 3.8B **Publicly Held**
WEB: www.mapllc.com
SIC: 5172 Gasoline
HQ: Mplx Terminals Llc
    200 E Hardin St
    Findlay OH

(G-6083)
MPW CONTAINER MANAGEMENT CORP
4848 W 130th St (44135-5163)
PHONE.....................216 362-8400
Monte R Black, *CEO*
EMP: 66
SALES (est): 3.7MM
SALES (corp-wide): 257.9MM **Privately Held**
SIC: 7699 Industrial equipment cleaning
HQ: Mpw Industrial Services, Inc.
    9711 Lancaster Rd
    Hebron OH 43025
    800 827-8790

(G-6084)
MRN LIMITED PARTNERSHIP
629 Euclid Ave (44114-3007)
P.O. Box 14100 (44114-0100)
PHONE.....................216 589-5631
Richard Maron, *Partner*
Judith Eigenfeld, *Partner*
Alan Hazzard, *Opers Mgr*
Jonathan Seeholzer, *Opers Mgr*
Rebecca Harper, *Hum Res Coord*
EMP: 29
SALES (est): 4MM **Privately Held**
WEB: www.east4thstreet.com
SIC: 6513 Apartment building operators

(G-6085)
MRN-NEWGAR HOTEL LTD
Also Called: Holiday Inn
629 Euclid Ave Lbby 1 (44114-3008)
PHONE.....................216 443-1000
Fax: 216 443-1722
Thomas W Adler, *CEO*
Chris Bitikofer, *General Mgr*
Pranitha Peesari, *Manager*
EMP: 48
SALES: 3.3MM **Privately Held**
SIC: 7011 Hotels & motels

(G-6086)
MS CONSULTANTS INC
600 Superior Ave E # 1300 (44114-2654)
PHONE.....................216 522-1926
Fax: 216 475-9655
Alex Beres, *Finance*
Denis Yurkovich, *Branch Mgr*
EMP: 39
SALES (est): 1.2MM
SALES (corp-wide): 39.8MM **Privately Held**
SIC: 8711 Professional engineer
PA: Ms Consultants, Inc
    333 E Federal St
    Youngstown OH 44503
    330 744-5321

(G-6087)
MSI INTERNATIONAL LLC
6100 Oak Tree Blvd # 200 (44131-2544)
PHONE.....................330 869-6459
Patricia Steel, *Vice Pres*
William C Allio,
EMP: 32
SQ FT: 4,000
SALES (est): 1.8MM **Privately Held**
SIC: 7371 Computer software development

(G-6088)
MULTI BUILDERS INC
27800 Cedar Rd (44122-1186)
PHONE.....................216 831-1400
Norman Millsteen, *President*
EMP: 25
SALES (est): 1.4MM **Privately Held**
SIC: 6531 Real estate managers

(G-6089)
MULTI CNTRY SEC SLUTIONS GROUP
3459 W 117th St (44111-3580)
PHONE.....................216 973-0291
Timothy Williams, *Owner*
EMP: 35
SALES: 950K **Privately Held**
SIC: 1799 Special trade contractors

(G-6090)
MURAL & SON INC
11340 Brookpark Rd (44130-1129)
PHONE.....................216 267-3322
Fax: 216 267-0747
Robert W Mural, *President*
Sandra Simon, *Corp Secy*
David Simon, *Vice Pres*
EMP: 25
SQ FT: 5,000
SALES (est): 2.1MM **Privately Held**
SIC: 1741 1799 1541 1542 Foundation building; waterproofing; renovation, remodeling & repairs: industrial buildings; commercial & office buildings, renovation & repair; general remodeling, single-family houses

(G-6091)
MURTECH CONSULTING LLC
4700 Rockside Rd Ste 310 (44131-2171)
PHONE.....................216 328-8580
Remo Difranco, *CFO*
Bill Bozak, *Accounts Mgr*
Kristin A Kellerman, *Accounts Mgr*
Ailish Murphy, *Mng Member*
Andy Ringer, *Manager*
EMP: 95 EST: 2000
SQ FT: 1,600
SALES (est): 11.9MM **Privately Held**
WEB: www.murtechconsulting.com
SIC: 8742 7361 General management consultant; employment agencies

(G-6092)
MUSEUM CNTMPRARY ART CLEVELAND
Also Called: Moca Cleveland
11400 Euclid Ave (44106-3926)
PHONE.....................216 421-8671
Fax: 216 421-0737
Trina Hines, *Development*
Grace Garver, *CFO*
Reese Shebel, *Marketing Staff*
Ray Juaire, *Manager*
Jill Snyder, *Director*
▲ EMP: 27 EST: 1968
SQ FT: 34,000
SALES: 3.4MM **Privately Held**
SIC: 8412 Museum

(G-6093)
MUSICAL ARTS ASSOCIATION (PA)
Also Called: Cleveland Orchestra, The
11001 Euclid Ave (44106-1796)
PHONE.....................216 231-7300
Fax: 216 231-4038
Cleveland Miami, *Managing Dir*
Alfred Rankin, *Vice Pres*
Bryan Read, *Research*
James E Menger, *Finance*
Sandra Sprenger, *Sales Associate*
▲ EMP: 205 EST: 1925
SQ FT: 125,000
SALES: 66MM **Privately Held**
WEB: www.clevelandorchestra.com
SIC: 7929 6512 Musical entertainers; orchestras or bands; auditorium & hall operation

(G-6094)
MUTUAL HEALTH SERVICES COMPANY
Also Called: Mutual Holding Company
2060 E 9th St (44115-1313)
PHONE.....................216 687-7000
John Burry Jr, *CEO*
James W Harless, *President*
Belinda Cox, *Vice Pres*
Kent Clapp, *Treasurer*
Chuck Ledger, *Manager*
EMP: 85
SQ FT: 18,600
SALES (est): 10MM
SALES (corp-wide): 1.4B **Privately Held**
SIC: 8099 Medical services organization
HQ: Medical Mutual Services, Llc
    17800 Royalton Rd
    Strongsville OH 44136
    440 878-4800

(G-6095)
MYOCARE NURSING HOME INC
Also Called: West Park Healthcare
24340 Sperry Dr (44145-1565)
PHONE.....................216 252-7555
Elias J Coury, *President*
Norman A Fox Jr, *Corp Secy*
Steve Demeter, *CFO*
EMP: 135
SQ FT: 44,000
SALES (est): 5MM **Privately Held**
SIC: 8051 Skilled nursing care facilities

Cleveland - Cuyahoga County (G-6096)

(G-6096)
MZF INC
Also Called: Studio Mz Hair Design
27629 Chagrin Blvd 101b (44122-4477)
PHONE..................216 464-3910
Tracy Fish, *President*
Susan Bell, *Vice Pres*
EMP: 35
SQ FT: 3,000
SALES (est): 1.1MM **Privately Held**
SIC: 7231 Beauty shops

(G-6097)
N C B INTERNATIONAL DEPARTMENT
23000 Millcreek Blvd # 7350 (44122-5720)
PHONE..................216 488-7990
Laraine Sharp, *Administration*
EMP: 60
SALES (est): 4.4MM **Privately Held**
SIC: 6159 Intermediate investment banks

(G-6098)
NACCO INDUSTRIES INC (PA)
5875 Landerbrook Dr # 220 (44124-6511)
PHONE..................440 229-5151
Fax: 440 449-9607
JC Butler Jr, *President*
Miles B Haberer, *Counsel*
Mary D Maloney, *Counsel*
David Ladue, *Vice Pres*
Bob McGowan, *Vice Pres*
EMP: 39
SALES: 104.7MM **Publicly Held**
SIC: 3634 1221 5719 3631 Electric household cooking appliances; toasters, electric; household; irons, electric: household; coffee makers, electric: household; surface mining, lignite; kitchenware; cookware, except aluminum; household cooking equipment; microwave ovens, including portable: household

(G-6099)
NANAELES DAY CARE INC
3685 Lee Rd (44120-5108)
PHONE..................216 991-6139
Fax: 216 991-6496
Denise Zama, *President*
Ella Witherspoon, *Principal*
EMP: 50
SALES (est): 588.3K **Privately Held**
SIC: 8351 Child day care services

(G-6100)
NAS RCRTMENT CMMUNICATIONS LLC (HQ)
Also Called: N A S
9700 Rockside Rd Ste 170 (44125-6267)
PHONE..................216 478-0300
Fax: 216 468-8280
Philip Ridolfi, *CEO*
Matthew Adam, *President*
Patrick Montesanto, *Regional Mgr*
Matt Adam, *Exec VP*
Patty Van Leer, *Exec VP*
EMP: 102
SALES: 16.9MM
SALES (corp-wide): 35MM **Privately Held**
WEB: www.nasrecruitment.com
SIC: 7311 8748 Advertising consultant; communications consulting
PA: Stone-Goff Partners, Llc
900 3rd Ave
New York NY 10022
212 308-2058

(G-6101)
NATIONAL BENEVOLENT ASSOCIATIO
Also Called: Cleveland Christian Home
4614 Prospect Ave Ste 240 (44103-4365)
PHONE..................216 476-0333
David Lundeen, *CEO*
EMP: 60
SQ FT: 36,548
SALES (corp-wide): 17.4MM **Privately Held**
WEB: www.cchome.org
SIC: 8351 8361 Child day care services; residential care
PA: The National Benevolent Association Of The Christian Church
733 Union Blvd 300
Saint Louis MO 63108
314 993-9000

(G-6102)
NATIONAL CAR MART III INC
9255 Brookpark Rd (44129-6822)
PHONE..................216 398-2228
Fax: 216 398-7046
William Wise, *President*
David Venable, *Vice Pres*
Marge Eger, *Manager*
▼ EMP: 35
SQ FT: 30,000
SALES (est): 8.1MM **Privately Held**
WEB: www.nationalcarmart.com
SIC: 5012 Automobiles & other motor vehicles

(G-6103)
NATIONAL CITY CMNTY DEV CORP
1900 E 9th St (44114-3404)
PHONE..................216 575-2000
Fax: 216 222-2670
Danny Cameran, *President*
Atwiine Bernard, *Vice Pres*
Jason Birky, *Vice Pres*
Cathy Graham, *Vice Pres*
Joe McCarthy, *Vice Pres*
EMP: 250
SALES (est): 12.3MM
SALES (corp-wide): 18B **Publicly Held**
WEB: www.pnc.com
SIC: 8742 Planning consultant
PA: The Pnc Financial Services Group Inc
300 5th Ave
Pittsburgh PA 15222
412 762-2000

(G-6104)
NATIONAL CONCESSION COMPANY
4582 Willow Pkwy (44125-1046)
PHONE..................216 881-9911
Fax: 216 881-9535
Tuck Axelrod, *President*
Christopher Axelrod, *Vice Pres*
EMP: 35
SQ FT: 7,500
SALES (est): 3MM **Privately Held**
WEB: www.nationalconcession.com
SIC: 7999 Concession operator; amusement concession

(G-6105)
NATIONAL DENTEX LLC
Also Called: Salem Dental Laboratory
3873 Rocky River Dr (44111-4112)
PHONE..................216 671-0577
Fax: 216 671-4347
George Salem, *Vice Pres*
David Brown, *Manager*
Nancy George, *Exec Sec*
EMP: 39
SALES (corp-wide): 147.8MM **Privately Held**
WEB: www.nationaldentex.com
SIC: 8072 Crown & bridge production
HQ: National Dentex Llc
11601 Kew Gardens Ave # 200
Palm Beach Gardens FL 33410
877 942-5871

(G-6106)
NATIONAL ELECTRO-COATINGS INC
Also Called: National Office
15655 Brookpark Rd (44142-1619)
PHONE..................216 898-0080
Fax: 216 898-8388
Gregory R Schneider, *CEO*
Richard Corl, *President*
Robert W Schneider, *Chairman*
Teresa Corl, *Safety Dir*
Michael Schneider, *Safety Dir*
▲ EMP: 90
SQ FT: 175,000
SALES (est): 20MM **Privately Held**
WEB: www.natoffice.com
SIC: 2522 2521 1721 Office furniture, except wood; wood office furniture; painting & paper hanging

(G-6107)
NATIONAL ENGRG & CONTG CO
Also Called: Netco
50 Public Sq Ste 2175 (44113-2252)
PHONE..................440 238-3331
Walter Gratz, *CEO*
Bob Mancuso, *Exec VP*
Clarke Wilson, *Vice Pres*
Anthony Martin, *Treasurer*
EMP: 700 EST: 1933
SQ FT: 50,000
SALES (est): 88MM
SALES (corp-wide): 8.5B **Privately Held**
SIC: 1622 1623 Bridge construction; sewer line construction
HQ: Balfour Beatty, Llc
1011 Centre Rd Ste 322
Wilmington DE 19805
302 573-3873

(G-6108)
NATIONAL GENERAL INSURANCE
Also Called: Ngic
800 Superior Ave E (44114-2613)
PHONE..................212 380-9462
Kevin Bailey, *Principal*
Cory Jacobs, *Sales Associate*
Kathy McCall, *Manager*
Jimmy Hernandez, *Agent*
EMP: 500
SALES (corp-wide): 135.5MM **Privately Held**
SIC: 6411 Insurance agents; insurance agents & brokers
PA: National General Insurance
59 Maiden Ln Fl 38
New York NY 10038
212 380-9477

(G-6109)
NATIONAL HERITG ACADEMIES INC
Also Called: Apex Academy
16005 Terrace Rd (44112-2001)
PHONE..................216 451-1725
Michael Bean, *Branch Mgr*
EMP: 54 **Privately Held**
SIC: 8741 Management services
PA: National Heritage Academies, In.
3850 Broadmoor Ave Se # 201
Grand Rapids MI 49512

(G-6110)
NATIONAL LABOR RELATIONS BOARD
Also Called: Region 8
1240 E 9th St Rm 1695 (44199-2001)
PHONE..................216 522-3716
Fax: 216 522-2418
Frederick Calatrello, *Director*
EMP: 46 **Publicly Held**
SIC: 8111 Labor & employment law
HQ: National Labor Relations Board
1015 Half St Se
Washington DC 20003
202 273-3884

(G-6111)
NATIONAL MENTOR INC
9800 Rockside Rd Ste 800 (44125-6265)
PHONE..................216 525-1885
Lisa Clark, *Manager*
EMP: 25
SALES (corp-wide): 741.5MM **Privately Held**
SIC: 8361 Residential care
HQ: National Mentor, Inc.
313 Congress St Fl 5
Boston MA 02210
617 790-4800

(G-6112)
NATIONAL TESTING LABORATORIES (PA)
6571 Wilson Mills Rd # 3 (44143-3439)
PHONE..................440 449-2525
Fax: 440 449-8585
Robert Gelbach, *President*
Thomas Zimmerman, *VP Finance*
Steve Tischler, *Director*
EMP: 37
SQ FT: 3,500
SALES (est): 5.8MM **Privately Held**
WEB: www.quasintl.com
SIC: 8734 Water testing laboratory

(G-6113)
NATIONAL WEATHER SERVICE
5301 W Hngr Fdral Fclties (44135)
PHONE..................216 265-2370
William Comeaux, *Principal*
EMP: 28 **Publicly Held**
SIC: 8999 9611 Weather forecasting; administration of general economic programs;
HQ: National Weather Service
1325 E West Hwy
Silver Spring MD 20910

(G-6114)
NBW INC
4556 Industrial Pkwy (44135-4542)
PHONE..................216 377-1700
Fax: 216 377-1711
Burgess J Holt, *Chairman*
Thomas Graves, *Vice Pres*
Buck L Holt, *Treasurer*
Cherie Patton, *Accountant*
Todd Holt, *Admin Sec*
EMP: 48
SQ FT: 25,000
SALES (est): 15MM **Privately Held**
WEB: www.nbwinc.com
SIC: 1711 1796 7699 3443 Boiler setting contractor; installing building equipment; boiler & heating repair services; fabricated plate work (boiler shop)

(G-6115)
NCS INCORPORATED
729 Miner Rd (44143-2117)
PHONE..................440 684-9455
Mary B Cowan, *President*
Deloras Cowan, *Vice Pres*
Jeremy Fahl, *Officer*
Jay Prots, *Associate*
EMP: 68
SALES (est): 7.6MM **Privately Held**
SIC: 7322 Collection agency, except real estate

(G-6116)
NEIGHBORHOOD HEALTH CARE INC (PA)
Also Called: Neighborhood Family Practice
4115 Bridge Ave 300 (44113-3304)
PHONE..................216 281-8945
Fax: 216 281-9565
Jean Polster, *CEO*
Laurel Domanski, *Vice Pres*
Peggy Keating, *Vice Pres*
Daniel Gauntner, *CFO*
Jim Massey, *CFO*
EMP: 36
SALES: 11.4MM **Privately Held**
WEB: www.neighborhoodfamilypractice.com
SIC: 8011 General & family practice, physician/surgeon

(G-6117)
NEIGHBORHOOD PROGRESS INC (PA)
Also Called: N P I
11327 Shaker Blvd Ste 500 (44104-3863)
PHONE..................216 830-2770
Joe Ratner, *President*
Steve Strnisha, *Principal*
Mark McDermott, *Vice Pres*
Jeanine Ornt, *Vice Pres*
Jenny Swanson, *Accountant*
EMP: 26
SALES: 14.5MM **Privately Held**
SIC: 8399 Community action agency

(G-6118)
NEO-PET LLC
1894 E 123rd St Apt 1 (44106-1942)
PHONE..................440 893-9949
Fax: 440 893-9219
Carla Miraldi, *Mng Member*
Vito Salvo, *Mng Member*
Floro Miraldi,
Lee Adler,
Audry Schmidt, *Exec Sec*
EMP: 30

GEOGRAPHIC SECTION
Cleveland - Cuyahoga County (G-6143)

SALES (est): 2.6MM **Privately Held**
WEB: www.neopet.com
SIC: 7363 Medical help service

(G-6119)
NEPTUNE PLUMBING & HEATING CO
23860 Miles Rd Ste G (44128-5464)
PHONE..................216 475-9100
Fax: 216 475-2996
Scott Wallenstein, *President*
Mark Novak, *Vice Pres*
Pat Looby, *Project Mgr*
Keith Krentz, *Purch Agent*
Michael Wallenstein, *Senior Engr*
EMP: 80
SQ FT: 8,000
SALES (est): 14MM **Privately Held**
WEB: www.neptuneplumbing.net
SIC: 1711 Plumbing contractors

(G-6120)
NERONE & SONS INC
19501 S Miles Rd Ste 1 (44128-4261)
PHONE..................216 662-2235
Fax: 216 662-5522
Ton Nerone, *President*
Rick Nerone Sr, *President*
Tom Nerone, *President*
Richard Nerone, *Corp Secy*
Rick Nerone Jr, *Corp Secy*
EMP: 50 EST: 1955
SQ FT: 28,500
SALES: 17MM **Privately Held**
WEB: www.nerone.biz
SIC: 1623 1611 Sewer line construction; general contractor, highway & street construction

(G-6121)
NETEAM SYSTEMS LLC
1111 Superior Ave E # 1111 (44114-2522)
PHONE..................330 523-5100
Michael Wyss, *Ch of Bd*
Patrick Aulizia, *President*
William Cannon, *COO*
John Kish, *Vice Pres*
James Portaro, *Vice Pres*
EMP: 40
SQ FT: 10,000
SALES: 12.3MM **Privately Held**
SIC: 5065 8711 Telephone equipment; engineering services

(G-6122)
NEW AVENUES TO INDEPENDENCE (PA)
17608 Euclid Ave (44112-1216)
PHONE..................216 481-1907
Tom Lewins, *President*
Donnamarie Berardinelli, *Project Mgr*
Marc Rubinstein, *CFO*
Lou Baga, *Controller*
Jane Rinaldi, *Human Res Mgr*
EMP: 100
SQ FT: 30,000
SALES: 14.5MM **Privately Held**
WEB: www.newavenues.net
SIC: 8361 Home for the mentally retarded; home for the physically handicapped

(G-6123)
NEW AVENUES TO INDEPENDENCE
12131 Bennington Ave (44135-3729)
PHONE..................216 671-8224
EMP: 26
SALES (corp-wide): 14.5MM **Privately Held**
SIC: 8361 Home for the mentally retarded; home for the physically handicapped
PA: New Avenues To Independence Inc
17608 Euclid Ave
Cleveland OH 44112
216 481-1907

(G-6124)
NEW DIRECTIONS INC
30800 Chagrin Blvd (44124-5925)
PHONE..................216 591-0324
Fax: 216 591-0324
Michael Matoney, *CEO*
Laura Gest, *Controller*
Kathleen N Gustafson, *Controller*
Duane Byrdsong, *Supervisor*
Dee Duncan, *Exec Dir*
EMP: 55
SQ FT: 19,000
SALES: 3.7MM **Privately Held**
WEB: www.newdirect.org
SIC: 8361 Rehabilitation center, residential: health care incidental

(G-6125)
NEW WRLD CMMUNICATIONS OF OHIO
Also Called: Wjw TV
5800 S Marginal Rd (44103-1040)
PHONE..................216 432-4041
Fax: 216 391-9559
Michael Renda, *General Mgr*
Greg Easterly, *General Mgr*
Toni Garbo, *Editor*
Scott Johnson, *Editor*
Kevin Salyer, *Vice Pres*
EMP: 200
SQ FT: 75,000
SALES (est): 15.6MM **Privately Held**
SIC: 4833 Television broadcasting stations

(G-6126)
NEW YORK COMMUNITY BANK
5767 Broadview Rd (44134-1681)
PHONE..................216 741-7333
Kelly Rusthn, *Manager*
EMP: 31 **Publicly Held**
WEB: www.amtrustinvest.com
SIC: 6035 Federal savings & loan associations
HQ: New York Community Bank
615 Merrick Ave
Westbury NY 11590
516 203-0010

(G-6127)
NEWMARK & COMPANY RE INC
Also Called: Newmark Grubb Knight Frank
1350 Euclid Ave Ste 300 (44115-1833)
PHONE..................216 453-3000
D Green, *Vice Pres*
David Hooper, *Manager*
EMP: 35
SALES (corp-wide): 3.3B **Publicly Held**
SIC: 6531 6799 Real estate agents & managers; investors
HQ: Newmark & Company Real Estate, Inc.
125 Park Ave
New York NY 10017
212 372-2000

(G-6128)
NEXSTEP HEALTHCARE LLC
673 Alpha Dr Ste G (44143-2140)
PHONE..................216 797-4040
Michelle Haines, *COO*
David Michaels, *VP Opers*
Gary Knouff, *CFO*
Jerry Cangelosi, *Mng Member*
EMP: 150
SQ FT: 4,200
SALES (est): 6.8MM **Privately Held**
WEB: www.nexstephc.com
SIC: 8049 8741 Physical therapist; management services

(G-6129)
NEXUS ENGINEERING GROUP LLC (PA)
1422 Euclid Ave Ste 1400 (44115-2015)
PHONE..................216 404-7867
Jeffrey O Herzog, *Principal*
Neal Curran, *COO*
Dave Schiele, *Project Dir*
Elliott Joyce, *Engineer*
Sean Stroshine, *Engineer*
EMP: 90
SALES (est): 15.1MM **Privately Held**
SIC: 8711 Consulting engineer

(G-6130)
NF II CLEVELAND OP CO LLC
Also Called: Residence Inn Cleveland Dwntwn
527 Prospect Ave E (44115-1113)
PHONE..................216 443-9043
Fax: 216 443-9843
Steven Rudolph, *General Mgr*
Laura Metzo, *Managing Dir*
EMP: 40
SQ FT: 700,000
SALES: 7MM **Privately Held**
SIC: 7011 Hotel, franchised

(G-6131)
NICOLA GUDBRANSON & COOPER LLC
25 W Prospect Ave # 1400 (44115-1048)
PHONE..................216 621-7227
Fax: 216 621-3999
James L Juliano Jr, *Partner*
Megan Mehalko, *Partner*
Vincent A Feudo, *Counsel*
Bruce Waterhouse, *Counsel*
Kevin Calhoun, *Office Mgr*
EMP: 34
SQ FT: 6,000
SALES: 2.5MM **Privately Held**
WEB: www.nicola.com
SIC: 8111 General practice attorney, lawyer

(G-6132)
NICOLES CHILD CARE CENTER (PA)
4035 E 141st St (44128-1803)
P.O. Box 39395, Solon (44139-0395)
PHONE..................216 751-6668
Fax: 216 751-3798
Reginald Fields, *Facilities Mgr*
C Gail Fields, *Exec Dir*
EMP: 64
SALES: 1.1MM **Privately Held**
SIC: 8351 Child day care services

(G-6133)
NIEDERST MANAGEMENT LTD (PA)
21400 Lorain Rd (44126-2125)
PHONE..................440 331-8800
Michael Niederst,
EMP: 53
SQ FT: 4,600
SALES: 32.2MM **Privately Held**
WEB: www.niederstmanagement.com
SIC: 8741 Management services

(G-6134)
NORFOLK SOUTHERN CORPORATION
6409 Clark Ave (44102-5301)
PHONE..................216 362-6087
EMP: 43
SALES (corp-wide): 10.5B **Publicly Held**
SIC: 4011 Railroads, line-haul operating
PA: Norfolk Southern Corporation
3 Commercial Pl Ste 1a
Norfolk VA 23510
757 629-2680

(G-6135)
NORFOLK SOUTHERN CORPORATION
4860 W 150th St (44135-3302)
PHONE..................216 362-6087
Brent Toth, *Foreman/Supr*
Joseph Giuliano, *Manager*
Michael Bradley, *Manager*
Chester Hogston, *Supervisor*
EMP: 43
SALES (corp-wide): 10.5B **Publicly Held**
WEB: www.nscorp.com
SIC: 4011 Railroads, line-haul operating
PA: Norfolk Southern Corporation
3 Commercial Pl Ste 1a
Norfolk VA 23510
757 629-2680

(G-6136)
NORMAN NOBLE INC
6120 Parkland Blvd # 306 (44124-6129)
PHONE..................216 761-2133
Daniel Haddock, *Branch Mgr*
EMP: 190
SALES (corp-wide): 125.3MM **Privately Held**
WEB: www.nnoble.com
SIC: 3599 7692 Machine shop, jobbing & repair; welding repair
PA: Norman Noble, Inc.
5507 Avion Park Dr
Highland Heights OH 44143
216 761-5387

(G-6137)
NORRIS BROTHERS CO INC
2138 Davenport Ave (44114-3724)
PHONE..................216 771-2233
Fax: 216 771-2241
Bernard E Weir Jr, *President*
Kenneth McBride, *President*
Catherine McBride, *Corp Secy*
Richard S Thomas, *Vice Pres*
Bernard E Wir, *Manager*
EMP: 120 EST: 1867
SQ FT: 60,000
SALES (est): 16.5MM **Privately Held**
WEB: www.norrisbr.com
SIC: 1796 1541 7699 1771 Machinery installation; industrial buildings, new construction; boiler repair shop; concrete work

(G-6138)
NORTH CENTRAL SALES INC
528 E 200th St (44119-1569)
PHONE..................216 481-2418
Fax: 216 481-3660
Thomas R Shankal, *President*
Karen Shenkal, *Vice Pres*
EMP: 26
SALES (est): 4.2MM **Privately Held**
WEB: www.northcentralsales.com
SIC: 5087 Beauty parlor equipment & supplies

(G-6139)
NORTH COAST CONCRETE INC
6061 Carey Dr (44125-4259)
PHONE..................216 642-1114
Fax: 216 642-3346
Robert Dalrymple, *President*
Linda A Dalrymple, *Admin Sec*
EMP: 30
SQ FT: 5,000
SALES (est): 3.6MM **Privately Held**
WEB: www.northcoastconcrete.com
SIC: 1771 Concrete pumping

(G-6140)
NORTH ELECTRIC INC
12117 Bennington Ave # 200 (44135-3729)
PHONE..................216 331-4141
Jose Rivera, *President*
EMP: 40 EST: 1996
SALES (est): 4.4MM **Privately Held**
SIC: 1731 Electrical work

(G-6141)
NORTH OHIO HEART CENTER INC
Also Called: Ohio Medical Group
7255 Old Oak Blvd C408 (44130-3331)
PHONE..................440 414-9500
Qarab Syed MD, *Director*
EMP: 47
SALES (corp-wide): 13.5MM **Privately Held**
SIC: 8011 Cardiologist & cardio-vascular specialist
PA: North Ohio Heart Center, Inc
3600 Kolbe Rd Ste 127
Lorain OH 44053
440 204-4000

(G-6142)
NORTH PARK RETIREMENT CMNTY (PA)
Also Called: Sovereign Healthcare
14801 Holland Rd Lbby (44142-3080)
PHONE..................216 267-0555
Fax: 216 267-0883
John Coury Jr, *President*
Eileen Harrison, *Human Res Dir*
EMP: 50
SALES (est): 3.8MM **Privately Held**
SIC: 8059 Rest home, with health care

(G-6143)
NORTH RANDALL VILLAGE (PA)
21937 Miles Rd Side (44128-4775)
PHONE..................216 663-1112
Fax: 216 587-9280
David Smith, *Mayor*
Janda Singleton, *Finance*
EMP: 82
SQ FT: 6,000

Cleveland - Cuyahoga County (G-6144)

SALES (est): 8.9MM **Privately Held**
WEB: www.northrandall.com
SIC: 8741 Office management

(G-6144)
NORTHAST OHIO RGONAL SEWER DST (PA)
3900 Euclid Ave (44115-2506)
PHONE..................216 881-6600
Fax: 216 881-7644
Darnell Brown, *President*
Robert Bonnett, *Superintendent*
Scott Broski, *Superintendent*
Tamar Gontovnik, *Counsel*
Ronald D Sulik, *Vice Pres*
EMP: 120
SQ FT: 85,000
SALES: 313MM **Privately Held**
SIC: 4959 Sanitary services

(G-6145)
NORTHAST OHIO RGONAL SEWER DST
Also Called: Southrly Wstwater Trtmnt Plant
6000 Canal Rd (44125-1026)
PHONE..................216 641-3200
Fax: 216 641-1730
Lowell Eisnaugle, *Manager*
Thomas Seiter, *Manager*
Charles Stennis, *Supervisor*
EMP: 151
SQ FT: 9,916
SALES (corp-wide): 313MM **Privately Held**
SIC: 4959 4952 Sanitary services; sewerage systems
PA: Northeast Ohio Regional Sewer District
3900 Euclid Ave
Cleveland OH 44115
216 881-6600

(G-6146)
NORTHAST OHIO RGONAL SEWER DST
Also Called: Westerly Wstwater Trtmnt Plant
5800 Cleveland Mem Shr (44102-2122)
PHONE..................216 961-2187
Fax: 216 961-0155
Andrew Rossiter, *Superintendent*
Kevin Zebrowski, *Asst Supt*
Carol Turner, *QA Dir*
Alexander Render, *Engineer*
Douglas Gabriel, *Manager*
EMP: 59
SALES (corp-wide): 313MM **Privately Held**
SIC: 8711 Civil engineering
PA: Northeast Ohio Regional Sewer District
3900 Euclid Ave
Cleveland OH 44115
216 881-6600

(G-6147)
NORTHAST OHIO RGONAL SEWER DST
Also Called: Amsc
4747 E 49th St (44125-1011)
PHONE..................216 641-6000
Fax: 216 641-8118
Frank Foley, *Superintendent*
Tom Madej, *Superintendent*
Tim Weber, *Principal*
Jacqueline Williams, *Purchasing*
John Graves, *Engineer*
EMP: 122
SALES (corp-wide): 313MM **Privately Held**
SIC: 4952 8734 Sewerage systems; testing laboratories
PA: Northeast Ohio Regional Sewer District
3900 Euclid Ave
Cleveland OH 44115
216 881-6600

(G-6148)
NORTHAST OHIO RGONAL SEWER DST
Also Called: Southerly Waste Water Plant
14021 Lake Shore Blvd (44110-1932)
PHONE..................216 531-4892
Fax: 216 692-1442
Bob Bonnett, *Superintendent*
Reena Jinde, *Engineer*
Raymond Weeden, *Branch Mgr*
James Cassese, *Manager*

Jay Harris, *Manager*
EMP: 53
SQ FT: 3,383
SALES (corp-wide): 313MM **Privately Held**
SIC: 4952 Sewerage systems
PA: Northeast Ohio Regional Sewer District
3900 Euclid Ave
Cleveland OH 44115
216 881-6600

(G-6149)
NORTHAST OHIO TRNCHING SVC INC
17900 Miles Rd (44128-3400)
PHONE..................216 663-6006
Fax: 216 663-9250
George J Gorup, *President*
Kim Heiman, *Controller*
EMP: 35
SQ FT: 14,422
SALES (est): 5MM **Privately Held**
SIC: 1794 Excavation & grading, building construction

(G-6150)
NORTHCOAST DUPLICATING INC
7850 Hub Pkwy (44125-5711)
PHONE..................216 573-6681
Fax: 216 901-4876
Sunantan Kumar, *President*
Ineka Kumar, *Vice Pres*
EMP: 130
SQ FT: 7,500
SALES (est): 8.3MM
SALES (corp-wide): 42.8B **Privately Held**
WEB: www.northcoastduplicating.com
SIC: 5044 7378 Duplicating machines; computer maintenance & repair
HQ: Topac U.S.A., Inc.
25530 Commercentre Dr
Lake Forest CA 92630

(G-6151)
NORTHEAST LUBRICANTS LTD (PA)
4500 Renaissance Pkwy (44128-5702)
PHONE..................216 478-0507
Dan McCollum, *Controller*
Ken Koliha, *Credit Mgr*
Thomas Arcoria, *Mng Member*
EMP: 143
SALES: 25MM **Privately Held**
SIC: 5172 Lubricating oils & greases

(G-6152)
NORTHEAST OH NEIGHBORHOOD HEAL (PA)
8300 Hough Ave (44103-4247)
PHONE..................216 231-2323
Fax: 216 231-7920
Willie S Austin, *President*
Karen Butler, *COO*
Cong Lu, *Engineer*
Perry Murdock, *Human Res Dir*
Robert Lukens, *Manager*
EMP: 125
SQ FT: 67,000
SALES: 23.2MM **Privately Held**
SIC: 8099 8071 8011 5912 Medical services organization; medical laboratories; offices & clinics of medical doctors; drug stores & proprietary stores

(G-6153)
NORTHEAST OHIO AREAWIDE
Also Called: Noaca
1299 Superior Ave E (44114-3204)
PHONE..................216 621-3055
Fax: 216 621-3024
William M Grace, *Chairman*
Robert Stefanik, *Mayor*
Mark Tyler, *Mayor*
Paul Bican, *Chief*
Cheryl Kurkowski, *Finance Dir*
EMP: 45
SALES: 5.8MM **Privately Held**
WEB: www.mpo.noaca.org
SIC: 8748 Urban planning & consulting services

(G-6154)
NORTHEAST OHIO CHAPTER NATNL (PA)
6155 Rockside Rd Ste 202 (44131-2217)
PHONE..................216 696-8220
Janet L Kramer, *President*
Beth Robertson, *Vice Pres*
Lois Walter, *Vice Pres*
EMP: 25 EST: 1953
SALES (est): 928.7K **Privately Held**
SIC: 8322 Association for the handicapped

(G-6155)
NORTHEAST OHIO ELECTRIC LLC (PA)
Also Called: Doan Pyramid Electric
5069 Corbin Dr (44128-5413)
PHONE..................216 587-9510
Fax: 216 578-3711
Bob Gubana, *Purchasing*
Mike Forlani, *Mng Member*
Lenny Heisler,
Douglas K Sesnowitz,
▼ EMP: 440
SALES (est): 55.1MM **Privately Held**
SIC: 1731 General electrical contractor

(G-6156)
NORTHEAST PROJECTIONS INC
Also Called: N P I Audio Video Solutions
8600 Sweet Valley Dr (44125-4212)
PHONE..................330 375-9444
Fax: 330 514-6059
Joe Thompson, *President*
Ted Van Hyning, *Principal*
Alex Kay, *Project Mgr*
Gary Heinrich, *Manager*
Trina Summerlin, *Director*
EMP: 25
SQ FT: 4,400
SALES (est): 4.8MM **Privately Held**
WEB: www.npiav.com
SIC: 7359 Audio-visual equipment & supply rental

(G-6157)
NORTHEAST SCENE INC
Also Called: Scene Magazine
737 Bolivar Rd (44115-1246)
PHONE..................216 241-7550
Fax: 216 241-6275
Richard Kabat, *President*
Desiree Bourgeois, *Publisher*
Keith Rathbun, *Corp Secy*
EMP: 48
SQ FT: 5,300
SALES (est): 4.1MM **Privately Held**
SIC: 2721 7336 2711 Periodicals: publishing only; graphic arts & related design; newspapers

(G-6158)
NORTHERN FROZEN FOODS INC
Also Called: Northern Haserot
21500 Alexander Rd (44146-5511)
PHONE..................440 439-0600
Fax: 440 439-1990
Douglas Kern, *President*
Bruce Kern, *Corp Secy*
Richard C Speicher, *Vice Pres*
Alan Stofcho, *Purchasing*
Andrea Anselmo, *Sales Staff*
EMP: 200
SQ FT: 105,000
SALES (est): 209.7MM **Privately Held**
WEB: www.northernhaserot.com
SIC: 5142 5149 5147 Packaged frozen goods; canned goods: fruit, vegetables, seafood, meats, etc.; meats, fresh

(G-6159)
NORTHERN MANAGEMENT & LEASING
5231 Engle Rd (44142-1531)
PHONE..................216 676-4600
Todd Armanini, *President*
Marlene Sutowski, *Treasurer*
EMP: 70
SALES (est): 2MM **Privately Held**
SIC: 7513 Truck rental & leasing, no drivers

(G-6160)
NORTHERN OHIO PRINTING INC
4721 Hinckley Indus Pkwy (44109-6004)
PHONE..................216 398-0000
Gary Chmielewski, *President*
Joann Luecke, *Business Mgr*
Mark Merlihan, *Accounts Exec*
John Loprich, *Sales Staff*
Mark Massey, *Sales Staff*
EMP: 35
SQ FT: 5,000
SALES (est): 7.1MM **Privately Held**
WEB: www.nohioprint.com
SIC: 7336 Commercial art & graphic design

(G-6161)
NORTHERN OHIO RECOVERY ASSN (PA)
3746 Prospect Ave E (44115-2706)
PHONE..................216 391-6672
Carolyn Cleveland, *President*
Eugene Dawson, *Vice Pres*
Anita Bertrend, *Exec Dir*
Courtney Freeman, *Executive Asst*
Tammie Robinson, *Admin Sec*
EMP: 35
SALES: 2.5MM **Privately Held**
WEB: www.norainc.org
SIC: 8322 Alcoholism counseling, nontreatment

(G-6162)
NORTHWESTERLY LTD
Also Called: Northwesterly Assisted Living
1341 Marlowe Ave (44107-2654)
PHONE..................216 228-2266
Mike Saunders, *Director*
Sue Bollin, *Food Svc Dir*
Jean Rosenthal, *Administration*
Kristen Montauge, *Administration*
EMP: 30
SQ FT: 200
SALES (est): 1.5MM
SALES (corp-wide): 6MM **Privately Held**
WEB: www.northwesterly.com
SIC: 6513 Retirement hotel operation
PA: Kandu Capital, Llc
260 E Brown St Ste 315
Birmingham MI 48009
248 642-2914

(G-6163)
NORTHWIND INDUSTRIES INC
15500 Commerce Park Dr (44142-2013)
PHONE..................216 433-0666
Fax: 216 433-1189
Garry Patla, *President*
Christine Klukan, *Vice Pres*
EMP: 27
SQ FT: 2,000
SALES (est): 3.4MM **Privately Held**
SIC: 3599 7692 3469 3444 Machine shop, jobbing & repair; grinding castings for the trade; welding repair; metal stampings; sheet metalwork; fabricated structural metal; metal heat treating

(G-6164)
NOTRE DAME ACADEMY APARTMENTS
1325 Ansel Rd (44106-1079)
PHONE..................216 707-1590
Joseph Weiss Jr, *President*
EMP: 30
SALES: 430.3K **Privately Held**
SIC: 6513 Apartment building operators

(G-6165)
NOTTINGHAM-SPIRK DES
2200 Overlook Rd (44106-2326)
PHONE..................216 800-5782
Fax: 216 231-6275
John Nottingham, *President*
John Spirk, *President*
Pat Coyne, *COO*
Nancy Silfer, *Manager*
Jeffrey Taggart, *Program Dir*
EMP: 50
SQ FT: 8,000
SALES (est): 8.7MM **Privately Held**
WEB: www.ns-design.com
SIC: 7336 8711 Package design; designing: ship, boat, machine & product

GEOGRAPHIC SECTION
Cleveland - Cuyahoga County (G-6188)

(G-6166)
NRP CONTRACTORS LLC (PA)
5309 Transportation Blvd (44125-5333)
PHONE..................216 475-8900
Andrew Tanner, *CFO*
Erika Arslanian, *Controller*
J David Heller, *Mng Member*
T R Bailey,
Alan Scott,
EMP: 40
SQ FT: 15,000
SALES (est): 86.2MM **Privately Held**
SIC: 1521 1522 Single-family housing construction; hotel/motel & multi-family home construction

(G-6167)
NRP GROUP LLC (PA)
5309 Transportation Blvd (44125-5333)
PHONE..................216 475-8900
Fax: 216 584-2558
JD Crow, *Asst Supt*
Tony Perry, *Asst Supt*
Ken Outcall, *Exec VP*
Alastair Jenkin, *Vice Pres*
Kurt Kehoe, *Vice Pres*
EMP: 60
SALES (est): 36.2MM **Privately Held**
SIC: 1521 General remodeling, single-family houses

(G-6168)
NRP HOLDINGS LLC
5309 Transportation Blvd (44125-5333)
PHONE..................216 475-8900
Erika Arslanian, *Controller*
J David Heller, *Mng Member*
Shannon Cathers, *Manager*
T R Bailey,
Alan Scott,
EMP: 150
SALES: 100MM **Privately Held**
SIC: 1531 Townhouse developers

(G-6169)
NSL ANALYTICAL SERVICES INC (PA)
4450 Cranwood Pkwy (44128-4004)
PHONE..................216 438-5200
Fax: 216 438-5050
Lawrence Somrack, *President*
Jennifer Villa, *Human Res Dir*
Melissa Gorris, *Marketing Staff*
Bridgett Pavlish, *Office Mgr*
Katie Douglas, *Supervisor*
EMP: 55
SQ FT: 30,877
SALES (est): 21MM **Privately Held**
WEB: www.nslanalytical.com
SIC: 8734 Testing laboratories

(G-6170)
NU-DI PRODUCTS CO INC
Also Called: Nu-Di Corporation
12730 Triskett Rd (44111-2529)
PHONE..................216 251-9070
Fax: 216 251-9089
Kenneth Bihn, *President*
Tim Bihn, *Vice Pres*
Sumant Kapoor, *Vice Pres*
David Novicky, *Vice Pres*
Joseph Sikora, *Vice Pres*
EMP: 85
SQ FT: 38,000
SALES (est): 17.4MM **Privately Held**
WEB: www.nu-di.com
SIC: 3825 5013 Engine electrical test equipment; testing equipment, electrical; automotive

(G-6171)
NULIFE MUSIC GROUP
16781 Chagrin Blvd # 174 (44120-3721)
PHONE..................216 870-3720
James Abramsm, *Principal*
EMP: 25
SALES (est): 163.8K **Privately Held**
SIC: 7929 Entertainers & entertainment groups

(G-6172)
NURENBERG PLEVIN HELLER
600 Superior Ave E # 1200 (44114-2654)
PHONE..................440 423-0750
Fax: 216 771-2242
Leon M Plevin, *President*
Marshall I Nurenberg, *Vice Pres*
Maurice L Heller, *Treasurer*
John J McCarthy, *Admin Sec*
Andrew P Krembs,
EMP: 64 **EST:** 1926
SQ FT: 20,000
SALES (est): 8.2MM **Privately Held**
WEB: www.nphm.com
SIC: 8111 General practice law office

(G-6173)
NYMAN CONSTRUCTION CO
23209 Miles Rd Fl 2 (44128-5467)
PHONE..................216 475-7800
Michael Nyman, *President*
Ken Murphy, *Vice Pres*
EMP: 30
SQ FT: 16,000
SALES (est): 10.7MM **Privately Held**
SIC: 1541 1542 Industrial buildings & warehouses; nonresidential construction

(G-6174)
OAKWOOD CLUB INC
1545 Sheridan Rd (44121-4023)
PHONE..................216 381-7755
Fax: 216 381-0749
Claudio Caviglia, *Manager*
EMP: 55 **EST:** 1905
SQ FT: 200,000
SALES (est): 56.4K **Privately Held**
WEB: www.oakwoodclub.org
SIC: 7997 Country club, membership

(G-6175)
OAKWOOD HEALTH CARE SVCS INC
Also Called: Grande Oaks & Grande Pavillion
24579 Broadway Ave (44146-6338)
PHONE..................440 439-7976
Aaron Handler, *President*
EMP: 99
SQ FT: 5,000
SALES (est): 5.8MM **Privately Held**
SIC: 8059 Nursing home, except skilled & intermediate care facility

(G-6176)
OATEY SUPPLY CHAIN SVCS INC (HQ)
Also Called: Oatey Company
20600 Emerald Pkwy (44135-6022)
PHONE..................216 267-7100
John H McMillan, *CEO*
Gary Oatey, *Ch of Bd*
Barbara Philibert, *Vice Pres*
Lennon Taylor, *Controller*
Matt Foraker, *Sales Staff*
▲ **EMP:** 200
SQ FT: 165,000
SALES (est): 83MM
SALES (corp-wide): 470MM **Privately Held**
WEB: www.oateyscs.com
SIC: 3444 5074 Metal roofing & roof drainage equipment; plumbing & hydronic heating supplies
PA: Oatey Co.
  20600 Emerald Pkwy
  Cleveland OH 44135
  800 203-1155

(G-6177)
OATEY SUPPLY CHAIN SVCS INC
Also Called: Oatey Distribution Center
4565 Industrial Pkwy (44135-4541)
PHONE..................216 267-7100
John Dettorre, *Manager*
EMP: 50
SALES (corp-wide): 470MM **Privately Held**
WEB: www.oateyscs.com
SIC: 4225 Warehousing, self-storage
HQ: Oatey Supply Chain Services, Inc.
  20600 Emerald Pkwy
  Cleveland OH 44135
  216 267-7100

(G-6178)
OBRIEN CUT STONE COMPANY (PA)
19100 Miles Rd (44128-4104)
PHONE..................216 663-7800
Fax: 216 663-8909
John O'Brien, *President*
Margaret Kingsmill, *Corp Secy*
Robert O'Brien, *Vice Pres*
Kim Szymanski, *Manager*
▲ **EMP:** 29
SQ FT: 20,000
SALES (est): 4.3MM **Privately Held**
WEB: www.obriencutstone.net
SIC: 1741 Masonry & other stonework

(G-6179)
OFFICE DEPOT INC
9880 Sweet Valley Dr # 2 (44125-4268)
PHONE..................800 463-3768
Amy Hannum, *Sales Associate*
Rannigan Walsh, *Branch Mgr*
EMP: 29
SALES (corp-wide): 10.2B **Publicly Held**
WEB: www.officedepot.com
SIC: 5943 5044 5045 Office forms & supplies; office equipment; computers, peripherals & software; computers
PA: Office Depot, Inc.
  6600 N Military Trl
  Boca Raton FL 33496
  561 438-4800

(G-6180)
OFFICE FURNITURE RESOURCES INC
Also Called: S. Rose Company
1213 Prospect Ave E (44115-1258)
PHONE..................216 781-8200
Fax: 216 781-8206
Richard Rose, *Ch of Bd*
Clark Rose, *President*
Paul Johanni, *COO*
Gary Herwald, *Vice Pres*
Greg Strimple, *Opers Staff*
EMP: 36
SQ FT: 30,000
SALES (est): 15.1MM
SALES (corp-wide): 68.9MM **Privately Held**
WEB: www.srose.com
SIC: 5021 Office furniture
PA: River City Furniture, Llc
  6454 Centre Park Dr
  West Chester OH 45069
  513 612-7303

(G-6181)
OFFICE PRODUCTS INC/CLEVELAND
Also Called: Mt Business Technologies
1239 W 6th St (44113-1339)
PHONE..................919 754-3700
Fax: 216 237-4363
John C Fetnyak, *President*
Ray Myers, *Area Mgr*
Karen Patterson, *Purchasing*
Daniel Camille, *Accountant*
Joe Esposito, *Sales Mgr*
EMP: 36
SALES (est): 5.1MM **Privately Held**
SIC: 5044 Office equipment

(G-6182)
OFFICEMAX CONTRACT INC
18673 Sheldon Rd B (44130-2471)
PHONE..................216 898-2400
Fax: 216 898-2425
Josh Longdon, *Sales Executive*
Dan Zettle, *Manager*
EMP: 90
SALES (corp-wide): 10.2B **Publicly Held**
WEB: www.bcop.com
SIC: 5111 Printing & writing paper
HQ: Officemax Contract, Inc.
  263 Shuman Blvd
  Naperville IL 60563
  630 438-7800

(G-6183)
OGRINC MECHANICAL CORPORATION
26650 Rnohance Pkwy Ste 1 (44128)
PHONE..................216 765-8010
Dan Ogrinc, *President*
Andrea Ogrinc, *Corp Secy*
EMP: 25
SQ FT: 6,000
SALES (est): 1.7MM **Privately Held**
SIC: 1711 Warm air heating & air conditioning contractor

(G-6184)
OHIO AEROSPACE INSTITUTE (PA)
Also Called: O A I
22800 Cedar Point Rd (44142-1012)
PHONE..................440 962-3000
Fax: 440 962-3120
Salvatore Miraglia, *Ch of Bd*
Michael Heil, *President*
Jake Breland, *Vice Pres*
Nick Gattozzi, *Vice Pres*
Tony H Smith, *Vice Pres*
EMP: 57
SQ FT: 70,000
SALES: 13.7MM **Privately Held**
SIC: 8733 Noncommercial research organizations

(G-6185)
OHIO BELL TELEPHONE COMPANY (DH)
Also Called: AT&T Ohio
45 Erieview Plz (44114-1801)
PHONE..................216 822-3439
Fax: 216 822-5522
Jolie Lagrange-Johnson, *Manager*
EMP: 869
SQ FT: 100,000
SALES (est): 651.9MM
SALES (corp-wide): 160.5B **Publicly Held**
SIC: 4813 8721 Local & long distance telephone communications; local telephone communications; voice telephone communications; data telephone communications; billing & bookkeeping service
HQ: At&T Teleholdings, Inc.
  30 S Wacker Dr Fl 34
  Chicago IL 60606
  800 288-2020

(G-6186)
OHIO BLOW PIPE COMPANY (PA)
446 E 131st St (44108-1684)
PHONE..................216 681-7379
Fax: 216 681-7713
Edward Fakeris, *President*
William Roberts, *Vice Pres*
David Anderson, *Purch Dir*
John McNally, *Engineer*
Lisa Kern, *CFO*
EMP: 33
SQ FT: 45,000
SALES (est): 23.9MM **Privately Held**
WEB: www.obpairsystems.com
SIC: 8711 3564 3444 Engineering services; blowers & fans; sheet metalwork

(G-6187)
OHIO BUSINESS MACHINES LLC (PA)
Also Called: O B M
1111 Superior Ave E # 105 (44114-2522)
PHONE..................216 485-2000
Fax: 419 861-8228
Richard Backman, *Controller*
Danielle Spoerl, *Marketing Staff*
Esther Graves, *Manager*
Dick Nowak, *Manager*
Sal Spagnola, *Manager*
EMP: 25
SALES (est): 46.5MM **Privately Held**
SIC: 5044 7629 5734 Office equipment; business machine repair, electric; computer & software stores

(G-6188)
OHIO CATHOLIC FEDERAL CR UN (PA)
13623 Rockside Rd (44125-5173)
PHONE..................216 663-6800
Stephen Halas, *CEO*
Joseph Zaite, *President*
Stephanie Thomas, *Opers Mgr*
George Paul, *Purch Agent*
John Hartman, *Treasurer*
EMP: 43 **EST:** 1945
SALES: 6.3MM **Privately Held**
WEB: www.ohiocatholicfederalcreditunion.com
SIC: 6061 Federal credit unions

Cleveland - Cuyahoga County (G-6189)

(G-6189)
OHIO CITIZEN ACTION (PA)
614 W Superior Ave # 1200 (44113-1386)
PHONE.................................216 861-5200
Fax: 216 694-6904
Alexandra Buchanan, *Exec Dir*
EMP: 50
SALES: 1MM **Privately Held**
WEB: www.ohiocitizenaction.org
SIC: 8399 Community action agency

(G-6190)
OHIO FABRICATORS INC (PA)
883 Addison Rd (44103-1607)
PHONE.................................216 391-2400
Patricia McElroy, *Ch of Bd*
John Sickle Jr, *President*
James Sickle, *Vice Pres*
Todd Windhorst, *Purchasing*
EMP: 25 EST: 1970
SQ FT: 25,000
SALES: 4MM **Privately Held**
WEB: www.tinshops.com
SIC: 1761 1711 7389 Sheet metalwork; heating & air conditioning contractors; industrial & commercial equipment inspection service

(G-6191)
OHIO HEALTH CHOICE INC (DH)
6000 Parkland Blvd # 100 (44124-6120)
P.O. Box 2090, Akron (44309-2090)
PHONE.................................800 554-0027
Fax: 440 363-1769
Bryan Kennedy, *President*
Michael Rutherford, *Exec VP*
Diana Jacobs, *Engineer*
Peter Craig, *Sales Associate*
Michele Bartko, *Manager*
EMP: 58
SQ FT: 8,100
SALES (est): 10.4MM
SALES (corp-wide): 1B **Privately Held**
SIC: 6324 Group hospitalization plans

(G-6192)
OHIO NEWS NETWORK
3001 Euclid Ave (44115-2516)
PHONE.................................216 367-7493
Michael Fiorello, *Vice Pres*
Harry Wilkins, *Engineer*
Dessa Augsburger, *Asst Director*
EMP: 70
SALES (est): 925.5K **Privately Held**
WEB: www.ohionewsnetwork.com
SIC: 4833 Television broadcasting stations

(G-6193)
OHIO PAVING GROUP LLC
4873 Osborn Rd (44128-3139)
PHONE.................................216 475-1700
Brock Evans, *Mng Member*
EMP: 25
SALES (est): 1.7MM **Privately Held**
SIC: 1771 Concrete work

(G-6194)
OHIO REAL TITLE AGENCY LLC (PA)
1213 Prospect Ave E # 200 (44115-1260)
PHONE.................................216 373-9900
Ryan Marrie, *General Mgr*
Donald McFadden, *Principal*
Donald P McFadden, *Vice Pres*
Dean Talaganis, *Opers Mgr*
Robert Heckman, *Accountant*
EMP: 30
SALES (est): 7.4MM **Privately Held**
SIC: 6361 Real estate title insurance

(G-6195)
OHIO TECHNICAL COLLEGE INC
Powersport Institute PSI
1374 E 51st St (44103-1269)
PHONE.................................216 881-1700
Bernie Thompson, *Principal*
EMP: 195
SALES (corp-wide): 20.7MM **Privately Held**
SIC: 8733 Noncommercial research organizations
PA: Ohio Technical College, Inc.
  1374 E 51st St
  Cleveland OH 44103
  216 361-0983

(G-6196)
OHIO TRANSPORT INC
Also Called: Cincinnati
3750 Valley Rd Ste A (44109-3095)
PHONE.................................216 741-8000
Fax: 216 398-3986
Gregory F Tavrell, *President*
William Hill, *Vice Pres*
Kurt Hilgefort, *Opers Staff*
Ken Harbert, *Credit Mgr*
EMP: 25
SQ FT: 21,000
SALES (est): 3MM **Privately Held**
SIC: 4731 Truck transportation brokers

(G-6197)
OHIOGUIDESTONE
Also Called: Pro Kids & Families Program
3500 Carnegie Ave (44115-2641)
PHONE.................................440 260-8900
Fax: 216 441-5583
Thomas Copper, *Vice Pres*
EMP: 200
SALES (corp-wide): 58.6MM **Privately Held**
WEB: www.bchfs.org
SIC: 8322 Social service center
PA: Ohioguidestone
  434 Eastland Rd
  Berea OH 44017
  440 234-2006

(G-6198)
OLD DOMINION FREIGHT LINE INC
8055 Old Granger Rd (44125-4852)
PHONE.................................216 641-5566
Fax: 216 641-5606
Gary Huff, *Opers Mgr*
Jack Amato, *Manager*
Scott Carnahan, *Manager*
EMP: 34
SALES (corp-wide): 3.3B **Publicly Held**
WEB: www.odfl.com
SIC: 4213 Contract haulers
PA: Old Dominion Freight Line Inc
  500 Old Dominion Way
  Thomasville NC 27360
  336 889-5000

(G-6199)
OLD TIME POTTERY INC
7011 W 130th St Ste 1 (44130-7889)
PHONE.................................440 842-1244
Fax: 440 842-2187
Jack H Peterson, *Branch Mgr*
Dale Churnega, *Manager*
EMP: 82
SALES (corp-wide): 799.3MM **Privately Held**
WEB: www.oldtimepottery.com
SIC: 5999 5023 Art, picture frames & decorations; home furnishings
PA: Old Time Pottery, Llc
  480 River Rock Blvd
  Murfreesboro TN 37128
  615 890-6060

(G-6200)
OLYMPIC STEEL INC (PA)
22901 Millcreek Blvd # 650 (44122-5732)
PHONE.................................216 292-3800
Fax: 216 292-3513
Michael D Siegal, *Ch of Bd*
David A Wolfort, *President*
James D Post, *General Mgr*
Andrew S Greiff, *COO*
John W Brieck, *Vice Pres*
▲ EMP: 58
SQ FT: 127,000
SALES: 1.3B **Publicly Held**
WEB: www.olysteel.com
SIC: 5051 Steel; pipe & tubing, steel; iron or steel flat products

(G-6201)
OLYMPIC STEEL INC
5092 Richmond Rd (44146-1329)
PHONE.................................216 292-3800
Ray Walker, *Vice Pres*
EMP: 100
SALES (corp-wide): 1.3B **Publicly Held**
WEB: www.olysteel.com
SIC: 5051 Steel
PA: Olympic Steel, Inc.
  22901 Millcreek Blvd # 650
  Cleveland OH 44122
  216 292-3800

(G-6202)
OMNI INTERGLOBAL INC
600 Superior Ave E # 1300 (44114-2614)
P.O. Box 22896, Beachwood (44122-0896)
PHONE.................................216 239-3833
James B Abrams, *Principal*
EMP: 50 EST: 2015
SQ FT: 2,500
SALES (est): 2.2MM **Privately Held**
SIC: 4731 Freight transportation arrangement; domestic freight forwarding; foreign freight forwarding; customs clearance of freight

(G-6203)
ONCODIAGNOSTIC LABORATORY INC
812 Huron Rd E Ste 520 (44115-1126)
P.O. Box 117, Bolton MA (01740-0117)
PHONE.................................216 861-5846
Fax: 216 861-1720
Joseph Galang, *CEO*
Cirilo F Galang MD, *President*
Jennifer J Perry, *Business Mgr*
Heather Watt, *Vice Pres*
Ken Nodes, *Director*
EMP: 40
SQ FT: 3,000
SALES (est): 1.9MM **Privately Held**
WEB: www.oncodiagnostic.com
SIC: 8071 Pathological laboratory
PA: Predictive Biosciences, Inc.
  128 Spring St 400 Level B
  Lexington MA 02421

(G-6204)
ONE SKY FLIGHT LLC
26180 Curtiss Wright Pkwy (44143-1453)
PHONE.................................877 703-2348
Michael Silvestro, *CEO*
Kenneth Ricci, *Chairman*
Michael Rossi, *CFO*
Matthew Doyle, *VP Sales*
EMP: 860
SALES (est): 2.1MM
SALES (corp-wide): 91.1MM **Privately Held**
SIC: 4522 Flying charter service; non-scheduled charter services
PA: Flight Options, Inc.
  26180 Curtiss Wright Pkwy
  Richmond Heights OH 44143
  216 261-3880

(G-6205)
ONE SOURCE TECHNOLOGY LLC
Also Called: Asurint
1111 Superior Ave E # 2000 (44114-2522)
PHONE.................................216 420-1700
Fax: 216 621-4115
Gregg Gay, *CEO*
Connie Clore, *COO*
Steve Palek, *Exec VP*
Joe Dose, *Project Mgr*
Tracy Puzder, *QA Dir*
EMP: 50
SQ FT: 7,000
SALES (est): 10.5MM **Privately Held**
SIC: 7375 Data base information retrieval

(G-6206)
ONE WAY EXPRESS INCORPORATED
380 Solon Rd Ste 5 (44146-3809)
PHONE.................................440 439-9182
Fax: 440 439-9189
Cynthia Jackson, *President*
Richard Jackson, *Vice Pres*
Sue Oswick, *Manager*
Cindy Pavkov, *Office Admin*
EMP: 40
SQ FT: 2,500
SALES (est): 5.1MM **Privately Held**
WEB: www.onewayexpress.com
SIC: 4212 4213 Local trucking, without storage; trucking, except local

(G-6207)
ONX USA LLC (DH)
5910 Landerbrook Dr # 250 (44124-6508)
PHONE.................................440 569-2300
Mike Cox, *CEO*
Bart Foster, *Ch of Bd*
Paul Khawaja, *President*
Wayne Kiphart, *President*
Rosalind Lehman, *CFO*
EMP: 75
SQ FT: 20,000
SALES (est): 78.4MM
SALES (corp-wide): 1.2B **Publicly Held**
SIC: 7379 7372 Computer related consulting services; business oriented computer software
HQ: Onx Holdings Llc
  221 E 4th St
  Cincinnati OH 45202
  866 587-2287

(G-6208)
OPTIMA 777 LLC
Also Called: Westin Cleveland
777 Saint Clair Ave Ne (44114-1711)
PHONE.................................216 771-7700
Karolina Przybylska, *Supervisor*
Alan Feuerman,
Mark Anderson,
EMP: 49
SALES (est): 7.2MM **Privately Held**
SIC: 1522 Renovation, hotel/motel

(G-6209)
OPTIONS FLIGHT SUPPORT INC
26180 Curtiss Wright Pkwy (44143-1453)
PHONE.................................216 261-3500
Michael Scheerringa, *CEO*
Mark Brody, *CFO*
EMP: 160 EST: 1993
SALES (est): 14.2MM
SALES (corp-wide): 91.1MM **Privately Held**
SIC: 5599 4522 Aircraft dealers; air transportation, nonscheduled
PA: Flight Options, Inc.
  26180 Curtiss Wright Pkwy
  Richmond Heights OH 44143
  216 261-3880

(G-6210)
OR COLAN ASSOCIATES LLC
22710 Fairview Center Dr (44126-3607)
PHONE.................................440 827-6116
Tracy Jones, *Project Mgr*
EMP: 49
SALES (corp-wide): 16MM **Privately Held**
SIC: 8742 Management consulting services
PA: O.R. Colan Associates, Llc
  7005 Shannon Willow Rd # 100
  Charlotte NC 28226
  704 529-3115

(G-6211)
ORBIT INDUSTRIES INC (PA)
6840 Lake Abrams Dr (44130-3455)
PHONE.................................440 243-3311
Fax: 440 243-3379
Robert Aleksandrovic, *President*
EMP: 54 EST: 1965
SQ FT: 70,000
SALES (est): 8MM **Privately Held**
WEB: www.orbitndt.com
SIC: 7389 Industrial & commercial equipment inspection service

(G-6212)
ORCA HOUSE
1905 E 89th St (44106-2007)
PHONE.................................216 231-3772
Gregg Uhland, *Exec Dir*
Rochena Crosby, *Director*
Myrtle Latif, *Director*
EMP: 40
SQ FT: 24,030
SALES: 1.5MM **Privately Held**
WEB: www.orcahouse.org
SIC: 8093 Alcohol clinic, outpatient; rehabilitation center, outpatient treatment

(G-6213)
ORIANA HOUSE INC
1829 E 55th St (44103-3601)
PHONE.................................216 881-5440

Fax: 216 881-7896
Phil Nunes, *Manager*
EMP: 43
SALES (est): 674.2K
SALES (corp-wide): 48.4MM **Privately Held**
SIC: 8322 Substance abuse counseling
PA: Oriana House, Inc.
885 E Buchtel Ave
Akron OH 44305
330 535-8116

(G-6214)
ORIANA HOUSE INC
3540 Croton Ave (44115-3212)
PHONE..................216 361-9655
EMP: 215
SALES (corp-wide): 48.4MM **Privately Held**
SIC: 8069 Alcoholism rehabilitation hospital
PA: Oriana House, Inc.
885 E Buchtel Ave
Akron OH 44305
330 535-8116

(G-6215)
ORION CARE SERVICES LLC
18810 Harvard Ave (44122-6848)
PHONE..................216 752-3600
Sally Schwartz, *President*
Abram Schwartz, *Vice Pres*
Keith Yoder, *CFO*
Chris Ayewoh, *Administration*
EMP: 250
SALES (est): 3.7MM **Privately Held**
SIC: 8051 8052 Skilled nursing care facilities; intermediate care facilities

(G-6216)
OSBORN ENGINEERING COMPANY (PA)
1100 Superior Ave E # 300 (44114-2530)
PHONE..................216 861-2020
Fax: 216 861-3329
E P Baxendale, *President*
L V Hooper, *Vice Pres*
Douglas Lancashire, *Vice Pres*
Wayne A Twardokus, *Vice Pres*
Ramon E Campbell, *Opers Staff*
EMP: 90
SALES (est): 17.8MM **Privately Held**
WEB: www.osborn-eng.com
SIC: 8711 8712 Consulting engineer; architectural engineering

(G-6217)
OSTENDORF-MORRIS PROPERTIES
1100 Superior Ave E # 800 (44114-2518)
PHONE..................216 861-7200
Bill West, *President*
Mike Clegg, *Partner*
Michael Simonson, *Assistant VP*
Paul Misterka, *Vice Pres*
Frank Black, *Sales Associate*
EMP: 80
SALES (est): 7.4MM **Privately Held**
SIC: 6552 Land subdividers & developers, commercial

(G-6218)
OTIS ELEVATOR COMPANY
9800 Rockside Rd Ste 1200 (44125-6270)
PHONE..................216 573-2333
Fax: 216 573-2344
Matt Marketti, *Vice Pres*
Gordy Scll, *Manager*
Vince Ferro, *Manager*
EMP: 73
SALES (corp-wide): 59.8B **Publicly Held**
WEB: www.otis.com
SIC: 7699 1796 3534 Elevators: inspection, service & repair; elevator installation & conversion; elevators & equipment
HQ: Otis Elevator Company
1 Carrier Pl
Farmington CT 06032
860 674-3000

(G-6219)
OUTREACH PROFESSIONAL SVCS INC
Also Called: St. Vincent Medical Group
2351 E 22nd St (44115-3111)
PHONE..................216 472-4094
David F Perse, *President*
Beverly Lozar, *COO*
Theresa Wrabel, *Finance*
Vincent Farinacci, *Director*
Sharon Thomas, *Ch Nursing Ofcr*
EMP: 90
SQ FT: 3,700
SALES (est): 10.8MM
SALES (corp-wide): 142.3MM **Privately Held**
WEB: www.cpnmd.com
SIC: 8741 Office management
PA: St. Vincent Charity Medical Center
2351 E 22nd St
Cleveland OH 44115
216 861-6200

(G-6220)
OVATIONS
2000 Prospect Ave E (44115-2318)
PHONE..................216 687-9292
Wes Westley, *President*
EMP: 40
SALES (est): 2.1MM **Privately Held**
SIC: 7922 Concert management service

(G-6221)
OVERLOOK HOUSE
2187 Overlook Rd (44106-2323)
P.O. Box 161070, Rocky River (44116-7070)
PHONE..................216 795-3550
Linda Campana, *Trustee*
Julianne Wright, *Treasurer*
Kimberly Thorndike, *Director*
Diana Henn, *Administration*
EMP: 28
SQ FT: 20,000
SALES (est): 786.8K **Privately Held**
WEB: www.overlookhouse.org
SIC: 8059 8661 Nursing home, except skilled & intermediate care facility; religious organizations

(G-6222)
OWNERS MANAGEMENT
Also Called: Trans Con Buildings
25250 Rockside Rd Ste 1 (44146-1839)
PHONE..................440 439-3800
Fred Rzepka, *President*
Linda Tanella, *Opers Dir*
Paul Wilms, *Director*
EMP: 40
SALES (est): 1MM **Privately Held**
WEB: www.ownerslive.com
SIC: 8641 Condominium association

(G-6223)
OXCYON INC
17520 Engle Lake Dr Ste 1 (44130-8360)
PHONE..................440 239-3345
Fax: 440 239-8621
Samuel Keller, *CEO*
Joe Frey, *Prdtn Mgr*
James Kekic, *Sales Associate*
EMP: 42
SQ FT: 15,000
SALES (est): 5.4MM **Privately Held**
WEB: www.oxcyon.com
SIC: 4813

(G-6224)
OZANNE CONSTRUCTION CO INC
1635 E 25th St (44114-4214)
PHONE..................216 696-2876
Fax: 216 696-8613
Leroy Ozanne, *Ch of Bd*
Dominic L Ozanne, *President*
Robert E Fitzgerald, *Vice Pres*
Fred Rodgers, *Vice Pres*
Shermaine Hull, *Project Engr*
EMP: 40
SQ FT: 4,000
SALES (est): 17.3MM **Privately Held**
WEB: www.ozanne.com
SIC: 1542 Nonresidential construction

(G-6225)
P C VPA
16600 W Sprague Rd Ste 80 (44130-6318)
PHONE..................440 826-0500
EMP: 43 **Privately Held**
SIC: 8099 Medical services organization
PA: P C Vpa
500 Kirts Blvd Ste 200
Troy MI 48084

(G-6226)
P JS HAIR STYLING SHOPPE
20400 Lorain Rd (44126-3422)
PHONE..................440 333-1244
Fax: 440 333-7480
Peter J Holick, *Owner*
EMP: 25
SALES (est): 146K **Privately Held**
SIC: 7231 Hairdressers

(G-6227)
P-AMERICAS LLC
4561 Industrial Pkwy (44135-4541)
PHONE..................216 252-7377
Fax: 216 252-7392
Andy Connelly, *Principal*
Dennis Stanley, *Manager*
Fran Strazer, *Manager*
EMP: 60
SQ FT: 17,043
SALES (corp-wide): 63.5B **Publicly Held**
SIC: 5149 5499 Soft drinks; beverage stores
HQ: P-Americas Llc
1 Pepsi Way
Somers NY 10589
336 896-5740

(G-6228)
PAINTERS DISTRICT COUNCIL 6
8257 Dow Cir (44136-1761)
PHONE..................440 239-4575
Fax: 440 771-1970
Jim Nagy, *Accountant*
James Peppers, *Business Anlyst*
Terry Conroy, *Manager*
Joe Cryteser, *Manager*
George Boots, *Training Dir*
EMP: 29
SALES: 4.7MM **Privately Held**
SIC: 8631 Trade union

(G-6229)
PALADIN PROTECTIVE SYSTEMS INC
Also Called: Paladin Professional Sound
7680 Hub Pkwy (44125-5707)
PHONE..................216 441-6500
Fax: 216 441-5150
Calvin Corsi, *President*
Jeffrey L Kocian, *Principal*
Kevin Corsi, *Vice Pres*
Stefan Ebert, *Project Mgr*
Seth Green, *Project Mgr*
EMP: 50
SQ FT: 11,800
SALES (est): 20.6MM **Privately Held**
WEB: www.paladinps.com
SIC: 1731 Fire detection & burglar alarm systems specialization; closed circuit television installation; access control systems specialization; sound equipment specialization

(G-6230)
PALLADIUM HEALTHCARE LLC
16910 Harvard Ave (44128 2210)
PHONE..................216 644-4383
Lawanna Porter, *CEO*
Rose Radovanic, *CFO*
Kenneth Porter, *Director*
EMP: 200
SALES (est): 2.6MM **Privately Held**
SIC: 8082 Home health care services

(G-6231)
PARAGON CONSULTING INC
5900 Landerbrook Dr # 205 (44124-4085)
PHONE..................440 684-3101
Fax: 440 684-3102
Carmen Tulino, *President*
Larry Koester, *Principal*
Mark Atwood, *Vice Pres*
Susan Bene, *Human Resources*
Ray Modic, *Shareholder*
EMP: 30

SQ FT: 3,800
SALES (est): 5MM **Privately Held**
WEB: www.paragon-inc.com
SIC: 8742 General management consultant

(G-6232)
PARAGON TEC INC
3740 Carnegie Ave Ste 302 (44115-2756)
PHONE..................216 361-5555
Gail Dolman-Smith, *President*
Dorothy Watkins, *Business Mgr*
Dan Lawson, *VP Opers*
Bernice Alston, *Sr Project Mgr*
Gail Dolmansmith, *Manager*
EMP: 76
SALES (est): 4.4MM **Privately Held**
WEB: www.paragon-tec.com
SIC: 8742 General management consultant

(G-6233)
PARAN MANAGEMENT COMPANY LTD
2720 Van Aken Blvd # 200 (44120-2271)
PHONE..................216 921-5663
Fax: 216 921-0342
Stephen Niksa, *Senior VP*
Joseph Shafran,
Mark Zielinski,
EMP: 47
SQ FT: 3,500
SALES (est): 5.7MM **Privately Held**
WEB: www.paranmgt.com
SIC: 6531 Real estate managers

(G-6234)
PARK CORPORATION (PA)
6200 Riverside Dr (44135-3132)
P.O. Box 8678, South Charleston WV (25303-0678)
PHONE..................216 267-4870
Raymond P Park, *Ch of Bd*
Daniel K Park, *President*
Ricky L Bertrem, *Vice Pres*
Shelva J Davis, *Vice Pres*
Kelly C Park, *Vice Pres*
◆ **EMP:** 300
SQ FT: 2,500,000
SALES (est): 516.4MM **Privately Held**
WEB: www.parkcorp.com
SIC: 3547 1711 3443 5084 Rolling mill machinery; boiler maintenance contractor; mechanical contractor; boilers: industrial, power, or marine; industrial machinery & equipment; commercial & industrial building operation; exposition operation

(G-6235)
PARK CREEK RTIREMENT CMNTY INC
10064 N Church Dr (44130-4066)
PHONE..................440 842-5100
Fax: 440 842-5147
John D Spielbuger, *President*
Jessica Rowland, *Admin Sec*
Linda Fgoice, *Administration*
EMP: 30
SQ FT: 40,000
SALES (est): 1.1MM **Privately Held**
SIC: 8052 Intermediate care facilities

(G-6236)
PARK HOTELS & RESORTS INC
Also Called: Hilton
6200 Quarry Ln (44131-2218)
PHONE..................216 447-0020
Jock Litras, *General Mgr*
Don Rieger, *General Mgr*
Christopher Ellis, *Human Res Dir*
Lori Berhent, *Sales Dir*
EMP: 120
SALES (corp-wide): 2.7B **Publicly Held**
WEB: www.esirvine.com
SIC: 7011 Hotels & motels
PA: Park Hotels & Resorts Inc.
1600 Tysons Blvd Fl 10
Mc Lean VA 22102
703 584-7979

(G-6237)
PARK HOTELS & RESORTS INC
Also Called: Hilton
3663 Park East Dr (44122-4315)
PHONE..................216 464-5950
Fax: 216 464-6539

Cleveland - Cuyahoga County (G-6238)

Robert W Boykin, *General Mgr*
Emily Rhom, *Human Res Dir*
Jim Merrill, *Manager*
Guy Faraci, *Information Mgr*
Jessica Buttari, *Director*
EMP: 300
SALES (corp-wide): 2.7B Publicly Held
WEB: www.esirvine.com
SIC: 7011 5813 5812 Hotels; drinking places; eating places
PA: Park Hotels & Resorts Inc.
1600 Tysons Blvd Fl 10
Mc Lean VA 22102
703 584-7979

(G-6238)
PARK N FLY INC
19000 Snow Rd (44142-1412)
PHONE...................404 264-1000
Judy Behrend, *Branch Mgr*
Susan Brenders, *Manager*
Steven Dossa, *Manager*
Allen Ng, *Asst Mgr*
EMP: 30
SALES (corp-wide): 68.4MM Privately Held
WEB: www.parkholding.com
SIC: 7521 Parking lots
HQ: Park 'n Fly, Inc.
2060 Mount Paran Rd Nw # 207
Atlanta GA 30327
404 264-1000

(G-6239)
PARK PLACE MANAGEMENT INC
Also Called: Park Place Airport Parking
18975 Snow Rd (44142-1411)
P.O. Box 81376 (44181-0376)
PHONE...................216 362-1080
William Maloof, *President*
Walter J Himmelman, *CFO*
Shannon Saiko, *Manager*
EMP: 45
SQ FT: 2,000
SALES (est): 1.7MM Privately Held
SIC: 7521 Parking lots

(G-6240)
PARKER-HANNIFIN CORPORATION
Parker Service Center
6035 Parkland Blvd (44124-4186)
PHONE...................216 896-3000
Sherroll Manning, *Senior Buyer*
Tom Boyer, *Manager*
Edwin Thomas, *Manager*
EMP: 30
SALES (corp-wide): 12B Publicly Held
WEB: www.parker.com
SIC: 5084 Industrial machinery & equipment
PA: Parker-Hannifin Corporation
6035 Parkland Blvd
Cleveland OH 44124
216 896-3000

(G-6241)
PARKER-HANNIFIN CORPORATION
Motion & Control Training Div
6035 Parkland Blvd (44124-4186)
PHONE...................216 531-3000
Joe Bocian, *Branch Mgr*
EMP: 600
SALES (corp-wide): 12B Publicly Held
WEB: www.parker.com
SIC: 4225 3823 3714 General warehousing & storage; industrial instrmnts msrmnt display/control process variable; motor vehicle parts & accessories
PA: Parker-Hannifin Corporation
6035 Parkland Blvd
Cleveland OH 44124
216 896-3000

(G-6242)
PARKER-HANNIFIN INTL CORP (HQ)
6035 Parkland Blvd (44124-4186)
PHONE...................216 896-3000
Donald Washkewic, *President*
Thomas A Piraino Jr, *Vice Pres*
Cathy Suever, *Vice Pres*
Bill Erkkinen, *Purch Agent*
Evan Marks, *Design Engr*
EMP: 450
SALES (est): 33.4MM
SALES (corp-wide): 12B Publicly Held
SIC: 8741 Administrative management
PA: Parker-Hannifin Corporation
6035 Parkland Blvd
Cleveland OH 44124
216 896-3000

(G-6243)
PARKING COMPANY AMERICA INC
Also Called: Airport Pass Park
18899 Snow Rd (44142-1409)
PHONE...................216 265-0500
Fax: 216 265-0501
Lew Bodee, *Branch Mgr*
Marie Cunningham, *Manager*
Missy Kim, *Manager*
EMP: 30
SALES (corp-wide): 94.4MM Privately Held
WEB: www.airportfastparkandshuttle.com
SIC: 7521 Parking garage
PA: Parking Company Of America, Inc.
250 W Court St Ste 200e
Cincinnati OH 45202
513 241-0415

(G-6244)
PARKWOOD CORPORATION (PA)
1000 Lakeside Ave E (44114-1117)
PHONE...................216 875-6500
Fax: 216 875-6590
Morton L Mandel, *Ch of Bd*
Jack N Mandel, *Ch of Bd*
Thomas Mandel, *Vice Ch Bd*
Joseph C Mandel, *Chairman*
James R Fox, *Vice Pres*
EMP: 42
SQ FT: 13,680
SALES (est): 10.3MM Privately Held
WEB: www.parkwd.com
SIC: 6282 Investment advisory service

(G-6245)
PARMA CARE CENTER INC
Also Called: Parma Care Nursing & Rehab
5553 Broadview Rd (44134-1604)
PHONE...................216 661-6800
Fax: 216 661-6763
Mike Flank, *President*
Eitan Flank, *Owner*
David Farkas, *Vice Pres*
Brian Choleran, *Controller*
Grady Cowling, *CTO*
EMP: 125
SQ FT: 55,000
SALES (est): 10.2MM Privately Held
WEB: www.parmacarecenter.com
SIC: 8052 8051 Intermediate care facilities; skilled nursing care facilities

(G-6246)
PARMA CLINIC CANCER CENTER
Also Called: Parma Communirty Hospital
6525 Parma Blvd Fl 2 (44129)
PHONE...................440 743-4747
Laura Hinton, *Financial Exec*
Kim Monaco, *Manager*
Lisa Birklund, *Administration*
Oseitutu Owusu, *Oncology*
EMP: 25
SALES (est): 1MM Privately Held
SIC: 8069 Cancer hospital

(G-6247)
PARTNERS OF CITY VIEW LLC
Also Called: City View Nrsing Rhabilitation
6606 Carnegie Ave (44103-4622)
PHONE...................216 361-1414
Wendy Burrier, *Vice Pres*
Kevin Kilbane, *Director*
EMP: 150
SQ FT: 24,676
SALES (est): 5.7MM Privately Held
SIC: 8059 Nursing home, except skilled & intermediate care facility

(G-6248)
PARTNERSHIP LLC
29077 Clemens Rd (44145-1135)
PHONE...................440 471-8310
John J Finucane Jr, *President*
Chad Reusch, *Area Mgr*
Brad Alflen, *Vice Pres*
Laura Schramm, *Opers Mgr*
Jeff Smith, *Engineer*
EMP: 45
SALES (est): 8.6MM
SALES (corp-wide): 33.6MM Privately Held
SIC: 4213 Less-than-truckload (LTL) transport
PA: National Association Of College Stores, Inc.
500 E Lorain St
Oberlin OH 44074
207 287-3531

(G-6249)
PASSION TO HEAL HEALTHCARE
4228 W 58th St (44144-1713)
PHONE...................216 849-0180
Jacques Pollard, *Owner*
EMP: 25
SALES (est): 118.5K Privately Held
SIC: 8082 Home health care services

(G-6250)
PAT YOUNG SERVICE CO INC (PA)
6100 Hillcrest Dr (44125-4622)
PHONE...................216 447-8550
Derek W Young, *President*
Eugene Resovsky, *Vice Pres*
Kirk Young, *Vice Pres*
Fran Young, *Treasurer*
Rick Schmidt, *Manager*
▲ **EMP:** 49
SQ FT: 35,000
SALES (est): 55.8MM Privately Held
WEB: www.pysfederated.com
SIC: 5531 5013 Automotive parts; automotive supplies & parts

(G-6251)
PATHWAY HOUSE LLC
15539 Saranac Rd (44110-2458)
PHONE...................872 223-9797
James T Hemphil,
EMP: 26
SALES (corp-wide): 240K Privately Held
SIC: 7389 Telephone services
PA: Pathway House Llc
3126 W 101st St
Cleveland OH 44111
872 223-9797

(G-6252)
PAUL A ERTEL
Also Called: Nautica Queen
1153 Main Ave (44113-2324)
PHONE...................216 696-8888
Fax: 216 696-8890
Paul A Ertel, *Owner*
Colleen Grey, *Sales Mgr*
EMP: 65
SQ FT: 1,000
SALES (est): 1.5MM Privately Held
WEB: www.nauticaqueen.com
SIC: 5812 5813 7999 American restaurant; cocktail lounge; beach & water sports equipment rental & services

(G-6253)
PAYCOR INC
4500 Rockside Rd Ste 320 (44131-2170)
PHONE...................216 447-7913
Michael Yaquinto, *Branch Mgr*
EMP: 27
SALES (corp-wide): 105.2MM Privately Held
SIC: 8721 Payroll accounting service
PA: Paycor, Inc.
4811 Montgomery Rd
Cincinnati OH 45212
513 381-0505

(G-6254)
PAZCO INC
4500 Rockside Rd Ste 420 (44131-2180)
P.O. Box 830, Aurora (44202-0830)
PHONE...................216 447-9581
Scott Pavrish, *President*
Jeff Pavrish, *President*
EMP: 40 **EST:** 2001
SALES (est): 3.5MM Privately Held
WEB: www.pazco.com
SIC: 2899 8741 Plating compounds; management services

(G-6255)
PCM SALES INC
8200 Sweet Valley Dr # 108 (44125-4267)
PHONE...................501 342-1000
Fax: 216 642-9855
John Strauss, *Senior VP*
Fred Morey, *Sales Executive*
John Carsuo, *Manager*
EMP: 35
SALES (corp-wide): 2.1B Publicly Held
WEB: www.sarcom.com
SIC: 5045 Computers
HQ: Pcm Sales, Inc.
1940 E Mariposa Ave
El Segundo CA 90245
310 354-5600

(G-6256)
PCS COST
1360 E 9th St Ste 910 (44114-1719)
PHONE...................216 771-1090
Robert Strickland, *Principal*
EMP: 43
SALES: 950K Privately Held
SIC: 8742 Management consulting services

(G-6257)
PEARNE & GORDON LLP
Also Called: Pearne Gordon McCoy & Granger
1801 E 9th St Ste 1200 (44114-3108)
PHONE...................216 579-1700
Fax: 216 579-6073
David B Deioma, *Partner*
Richard Dickinson, *Partner*
James M Moore, *Partner*
John P Murtaugh, *Partner*
Carl Rankin, *Partner*
EMP: 50
SQ FT: 6,000
SALES (est): 7.8MM Privately Held
WEB: www.pearnegordon.com
SIC: 8111 General practice law office; patent solicitor

(G-6258)
PEASE & ASSOCIATES LLC (PA)
1422 Euclid Ave Ste 801 (44115-1902)
PHONE...................216 348-9600
Fax: 216 348-9610
Joseph Pease, *President*
Zachary Byham, *CFO*
Tina Moore, *CFO*
Beth Reimer, *Auditing Mgr*
Lindsay Arcuri, *Accountant*
EMP: 49
SALES (est): 6.4MM Privately Held
WEB: www.peasecpa.com
SIC: 8721 Accounting services, except auditing

(G-6259)
PEDIATRIC SERVICES INC (PA)
6707 Powers Blvd Ste 203 (44129-5494)
PHONE...................440 845-1500
Fax: 440 845-9227
Daniel Hostetler MD, *President*
Victoria Kaczynski, *Financial Exec*
Victoria Kazdynski, *Office Mgr*
Joanne M Hempel, *Med Doctor*
Jane A Flannigan, *Manager*
EMP: 38 **EST:** 1969
SQ FT: 4,000
SALES (est): 4.6MM Privately Held
WEB: www.pediatricservices.com
SIC: 8011 Pediatrician

GEOGRAPHIC SECTION

Cleveland - Cuyahoga County (G-6283)

(G-6260)
PEITRO PROPERTIES LTD PARTNR
Also Called: Comfort Inn
6191 Quarry Ln (44131-2203)
PHONE....................216 328-7777
Fax: 216 328-7777
Teresa Shaley, *Managing Prtnr*
Peter Maisano, *Partner*
EMP: 30
SQ FT: 1,000
SALES (est): 1.5MM Privately Held
SIC: 7011 Hotels & motels

(G-6261)
PEL LLC
4666 Manufacturing Ave (44135-2638)
PHONE....................216 267-5775
Fax: 216 267-6176
Michael Sotak, *President*
Jeff Simon, *Finance Dir*
Ronelle Peterson, *Mktg Dir*
Beverly Barnhardt, *Manager*
Janice Mullins, *Manager*
EMP: 38
SQ FT: 45,000
SALES (est): 12.1MM Privately Held
WEB: www.pelsupply.com
SIC: 5047 Artificial limbs

(G-6262)
PENSKE LOGISTICS LLC
7600 First Pl (44146-6700)
PHONE....................440 232-5811
Fax: 440 232-4623
Mark Oliver, *Manager*
Dan Florig,
EMP: 70
SALES (corp-wide): 2.9B Privately Held
WEB: www.penskelogistics.com
SIC: 7513 Truck leasing, without drivers
HQ: Penske Logistics Llc
Green Hls Rr 10
Reading PA 19603
800 529-6531

(G-6263)
PEPPER PIKE CLUB COMPANY INC
Also Called: PEPPER PIKE GOLF CLUB
2800 Som Center Rd (44124-4924)
PHONE....................216 831-9400
Fax: 216 831-3205
Dwayne Collins, *President*
Linda Wasco, *Controller*
EMP: 75
SQ FT: 10,000
SALES (est): 4MM Privately Held
SIC: 7997 8699 Golf club, membership; charitable organization

(G-6264)
PERCEPTIS LLC
1250 Old River Rd Ste 300 (44113-1244)
PHONE....................216 458-4122
Brittany McLaughlin, *Manager*
William Bradfield,
EMP: 150
SQ FT: 3,500
SALES (est): 9.8MM Privately Held
WEB: www.perceptis.net
SIC: 7379

(G-6265)
PERK COMPANY INC (PA)
8100 Grand Ave Ste 300 (44104-3164)
PHONE....................216 391-1444
Fax: 216 391-2233
Charles Perkins, *President*
Anthony Cifani, *Corp Secy*
Joseph Cifani, *Vice Pres*
Pam Fowler, *Manager*
Sastina Melcheski, *Manager*
EMP: 45
SQ FT: 15,000
SALES (est): 13.2MM Privately Held
WEB: www.perkcompany.com
SIC: 1611 General contractor, highway & street construction; concrete construction: roads, highways, sidewalks, etc.

(G-6266)
PERMANENT GEN ASRN CORP OHIO
9700 Rockside Rd (44125-6268)
PHONE....................216 986-3000
Steven Mason, *Ch of Bd*
Randy P Parker, *President*
David Hettinger, *Senior VP*
Brian Donovan, *Vice Pres*
EMP: 45
SQ FT: 15,000
SALES (est): 11.6MM
SALES (corp-wide): 9.3B Privately Held
WEB: www.pgac.com
SIC: 6331 Fire, marine & casualty insurance & carriers
HQ: Permanent General Companies, Inc.
2636 Elm Hill Pike # 510
Nashville TN 37214
615 242-1961

(G-6267)
PERSONAL TOUCH HM CARE IPA INC
4500 Rockside Rd Ste 460 (44131-6822)
PHONE....................216 986-0885
Sharon Tinsley, *Personnel Exec*
Noreen Scheck, *Manager*
Charlene Scunyog, *Administration*
EMP: 20
SALES (corp-wide): 363MM Privately Held
WEB: www.pthomecare.com
SIC: 8082 Home health care services
PA: Personal Touch Home Care Ipa, Inc.
1985 Marcus Ave Ste 202
New Hyde Park NY 11042
718 468-4747

(G-6268)
PERSONALIZED DATA CORPORATION
Also Called: Personalized Data Entry & Word
26155 Euclid Ave Uppr (44132-3366)
PHONE....................216 289-2200
Anthony Ruque, *President*
James Horne, *Vice Pres*
EMP: 40 EST: 1967
SQ FT: 2,100
SALES (est): 2.3MM Privately Held
WEB: www.personalizeddata.com
SIC: 7374 5734 Tabulating service; data punch service; data processing service; computer peripheral equipment

(G-6269)
PERSPECTUS ARCHITECTURE LLC (PA)
13212 Shaker Sq Ste 204 (44120-2398)
PHONE....................216 752-1800
Fax: 216 752-3833
Mike Lipowski, *Principal*
John Walkosak, *Project Dir*
Mary Seifert, *Accounts Mgr*
Marlene Fscher, *Manager*
Natalie Ata, *Director*
EMP: 40
SALES (est): 9MM Privately Held
SIC: 8712 Architectural engineering

(G-6270)
PETE BAUR BUICK GMC INC (PA)
14000 Pearl Rd (44136-8706)
PHONE....................440 238-5600
Fax: 440 238-6409
Daniel E Baur, *President*
Henry J Baur, *Vice Pres*
Pat Sims, *Sales Staff*
Michael Podany, *Sales Associate*
Mary Madal, *Manager*
EMP: 36
SQ FT: 26,000
SALES (est): 23.7MM Privately Held
WEB: www.petebaurpontiac.com
SIC: 5511 5531 7549 Automobiles, new & used; automobile & truck equipment & parts; automotive maintenance services

(G-6271)
PETERJ BRODHEAD
1001 Lakeside Ave E (44114-1158)
PHONE....................216 696-3232
Peter Brodhead, *Partner*
EMP: 30

SALES (est): 1.1MM Privately Held
SIC: 8111 General practice attorney, lawyer

(G-6272)
PETROS HOMES INC
10474 Broadview Rd (44147-3225)
PHONE....................440 546-9000
Fax: 440 546-9001
Sam Petros, *CEO*
Gary Naim, *President*
Dan Moorman, *Superintendent*
Chad Enders, *Opers Mgr*
Dan Smoulder, *Sales Staff*
EMP: 50
SQ FT: 9,216
SALES (est): 9.3MM Privately Held
WEB: www.petroshomes.com
SIC: 1521 6531 New construction, single-family houses; real estate agents & managers

(G-6273)
PHILIPS MEDICAL SYSTEMS CLEVEL (HQ)
Also Called: Medical Imaging Equipment
595 Miner Rd (44143-2131)
PHONE....................440 247-2652
David A Dripchak, *CEO*
Arlene Burnside, *General Mgr*
Jerry C Cirino, *Exec VP*
William J Cull Sr, *Vice Pres*
Hillary Sullivan, *Vice Pres*
◆ EMP: 500
SQ FT: 495,000
SALES (est): 621.4MM
SALES (corp-wide): 25.9B Privately Held
SIC: 3844 5047 5137 3842 X-ray apparatus & tubes; X-ray film & supplies; instruments, surgical & medical; hospital gowns, women's & children's; surgical appliances & supplies; laboratory apparatus & furniture; electrical equipment & supplies
PA: Koninklijke Philips N.V.
High Tech Campus 5
Eindhoven 5656
402 791-111

(G-6274)
PHILLIS WHEAT ASSOCIATION INC
Also Called: Kohler Day Care
4450 Cedar Ave Ste 1 (44103-4453)
PHONE....................216 391-4443
Thomas Harrington, *Chairman*
Paulette Shelton, *Manager*
Jacquelyn Bradshaw, *Exec Dir*
EMP: 25
SALES (est): 377.1K Privately Held
SIC: 8322 8299 Neighborhood center; adult day care center; music school

(G-6275)
PHOENIX RESIDENTIAL CENTERS
6465 Pearl Rd Ste 1 (44130-2979)
PHONE....................440 887-6097
Fax: 440 887-6403
Gary Toth, *Branch Mgr*
Ruth Cambell, *Administration*
EMP: 87
SQ FT: 5,845
SALES (est): 2.1MM
SALES (corp-wide): 3.6MM Privately Held
WEB: www.phoenixresidential.com
SIC: 6513 Apartment building operators
PA: Phoenix Residential Centers Inc
1954 Hubbard Rd Ste 1
Madison OH 44057
440 428-9082

(G-6276)
PHOENIX STEEL SERVICE INC
4679 Johnston Pkwy (44128-3221)
PHONE....................216 332-0600
Stuart Eisner, *President*
John Licastro, *Vice Pres*
EMP: 26
SQ FT: 102,000
SALES (est): 27.7MM Privately Held
WEB: www.phoenixsteelservice.com
SIC: 5051 Steel

(G-6277)
PHYCAL INC
51 Alpha Park (44143-2202)
PHONE....................440 460-2477
J Kevin Berner, *President*
Robert B Polak, *Chairman*
Deborah Klucho, *Accountant*
Richard Sayre, *CTO*
Lisa Richardson, *Administration*
EMP: 25
SALES (est): 1.7MM Privately Held
WEB: www.directcarbonenergy.com
SIC: 8731 Energy research
PA: Logos Energy, Inc.
51 Alpha Park
Cleveland OH

(G-6278)
PHYLLIS WHEATLEY ASSN DEV
Also Called: Phillis Wheatley Association
4450 Cedar Ave Ste 1 (44103-4453)
PHONE....................216 391-4443
Fax: 216 391-4543
EMP: 25
SQ FT: 1,504
SALES (est): 301.9K Privately Held
SIC: 8051 8399 Skilled Nursing Care Facility Social Services

(G-6279)
PHYSICIANS AMBULANCE SVC INC (PA)
Also Called: Physicians Medical Trnspt Team
4495 Cranwood Pkwy (44128-4003)
PHONE....................216 332-1667
Fax: 216 332-1669
Ron Hess, *President*
Terry Finnerty, *Vice Pres*
Jason Hess, *Vice Pres*
Jane Norvaisa, *Accounting Mgr*
Scott Wildenhim, *CIO*
EMP: 42
SALES (est): 8.5MM Privately Held
WEB: www.physiciansambulance.com
SIC: 4119 Ambulance service

(G-6280)
PINATA FOODS INC
Also Called: Festa Food Company
3590 W 58th St (44102-5663)
PHONE....................216 281-8811
Timothy Fagan, *President*
EMP: 30
SQ FT: 32,000
SALES (est): 16.5MM Privately Held
WEB: www.festafood.com
SIC: 5142 Packaged frozen goods

(G-6281)
PINS & NEEDLES INC (PA)
7300 Pearl Rd (44130-4807)
PHONE....................440 243-6400
Fax: 440 243-6696
Jim Brostek, *President*
Janice M Brostek, *Corp Secy*
EMP: 30
SALES (est): 5.9MM Privately Held
WEB: www.pinsandneedles.com
SIC: 5722 7219 5949 Sewing machines; garment making, alteration & repair; knitting goods & supplies

(G-6282)
PIONEER CLDDING GLZING SYSTEMS
5615 Cloverleaf Pkwy (44125-4816)
PHONE....................216 816-4242
Michael Robinson, *Branch Mgr*
EMP: 35
SALES (corp-wide): 56.9MM Privately Held
SIC: 1793 1741 3448 Glass & glazing work; masonry & other stonework; prefabricated metal components
PA: Pioneer Cladding And Glazing Systems
4074 Bethany Rd
Mason OH 45040
513 583-5925

(G-6283)
PIRHL CONTRACTORS LLC
800 W Saint Clair Ave 4 (44113-1266)
PHONE....................216 378-9690
David Burg, *Principal*
John Tarnowski, *CFO*

Cleveland - Cuyahoga County (G-6284)

Michelle Bockwich, *Controller*
David Uram,
EMP: 28
SALES (est): 4.1MM
SALES (corp-wide): 33.2MM **Privately Held**
SIC: 1521 Single-family housing construction
PA: Pirhl, Llc
  800 W Saint Clair Ave 4
  Cleveland OH 44113
  216 378-9690

(G-6284)
PITT-OHIO EXPRESS LLC
15225 Industrial Pkwy (44135-3307)
PHONE...............216 433-9000
Fax: 216 433-1197
Mike Todd, *Opers-Prdtn-Mfg*
Cheryl Groff, *Executive*
EMP: 300
SALES (corp-wide): 507.8MM **Privately Held**
SIC: 4231 4213 4212 Trucking terminal facilities; trucking, except local; local trucking, without storage
PA: Pitt-Ohio Express, Llc
  15 27th St
  Pittsburgh PA 15222
  412 232-3015

(G-6285)
PLANTSCAPING INC
Also Called: Blooms By Plantscaping
1865 E 40th St (44103-3552)
PHONE...............216 367-1200
Fax: 216 367-1211
Nancy Silverman, *President*
Todd Silverman, *Vice Pres*
Steven Bluestone, *Accounting Mgr*
Rachel Rosen, *Accounts Mgr*
Tim Reardon, *Manager*
EMP: 60
SQ FT: 31,800
SALES (est): 4.2MM **Privately Held**
WEB: www.plantscaping.com
SIC: 5193 Plants, potted

(G-6286)
PLAYHOUSE SQUARE FOUNDATION
1501 Euclid Ave Ste 200 (44115-2108)
PHONE...............216 771-4444
Fax: 216 771-3974
Art J Falco, *President*
Tom Einhouse, *Vice Pres*
Patricia Gaul, *Vice Pres*
Daniel Hahn, *Vice Pres*
Autumn Kiser, *Vice Pres*
EMP: 372
SALES: 77.7MM **Privately Held**
SIC: 7922 Entertainment promotion; amateur theatrical company

(G-6287)
PLAYHOUSE SQUARE HOLDG CO LLC (PA)
Also Called: PROP SHOP
1501 Euclid Ave Ste 200 (44115-2108)
PHONE...............216 771-4444
Fax: 216 771-0217
Patti Gaul, *CEO*
Art J Falco, *President*
Tom Einhouse, *Vice Pres*
Autumn Kiser, *Vice Pres*
Jody Dagg, *Prdtn Mgr*
EMP: 150
SQ FT: 10,000
SALES: 225.8K **Privately Held**
SIC: 8399 7922 Fund raising organization, non-fee basis; performing arts center production

(G-6288)
PLEASANT LAKE APARTMENTS LTD
10129 S Lake Blvd (44130-7552)
PHONE...............440 845-2694
Fax: 440 845-2163
Edward Marotta, *Branch Mgr*
EMP: 25
SALES (est): 1MM **Privately Held**
SIC: 6513 Apartment building operators

(G-6289)
PLEASANT LAKE NURSING HOME
Also Called: Pleasant Lake Villa
7260 Ridge Rd (44129-6636)
PHONE...............440 842-2273
Fax: 440 842-5809
Alex Daskal, *President*
Bruce Daskal, *Corp Secy*
David Farkas, *Vice Pres*
Harold Schachter, *Vice Pres*
Kelly Wright, *Administration*
EMP: 350
SQ FT: 65,000
SALES (est): 15MM **Privately Held**
SIC: 8051 8052 Skilled nursing care facilities; intermediate care facilities

(G-6290)
PORTER WRGHT MORRIS ARTHUR LLP
950 Main Ave Ste 500 (44113-7206)
PHONE...............216 443-2506
Fax: 216 443-9011
Hugh McKay, *Partner*
James Conroy,
Ezio A Listati,
Shawna Rosner,
David Lewis, *Sr Associate*
EMP: 75
SALES (corp-wide): 90.5MM **Privately Held**
SIC: 8111 General practice law office
PA: Porter, Wright, Morris & Arthur Llp
  41 S High St Ste 2900
  Columbus OH 43215
  614 227-2000

(G-6291)
POSITIVE EDUCATION PROGRAM
Also Called: Hopewell Day Treatment Center
11500 Franklin Blvd (44102-2335)
PHONE...............216 227-2730
Fax: 216 227-2740
Stephen Sheppard, *Director*
EMP: 40
SQ FT: 6,764
SALES (corp-wide): 43.3MM **Privately Held**
WEB: www.pepcleve.org
SIC: 8211 8322 Specialty education; self-help organization
PA: Positive Education Program Inc
  3100 Euclid Ave
  Cleveland OH 44115
  216 361-4400

(G-6292)
POSITIVE EDUCATION PROGRAM
Also Called: West Shore Day Treatment Ctr
4320 W 220th St (44126-1818)
PHONE...............440 471-8200
Fax: 440 331-3172
Ken Seiman,
EMP: 40
SALES (corp-wide): 43.3MM **Privately Held**
WEB: www.pepcleve.org
SIC: 8211 8093 Specialty education; specialty outpatient clinics
PA: Positive Education Program Inc
  3100 Euclid Ave
  Cleveland OH 44115
  216 361-4400

(G-6293)
POTTERY BARN INC
26300 Cedar Rd Ste 1010 (44122-8119)
PHONE...............216 378-1211
Fax: 216 378-1029
Lauren Grossi, *Manager*
EMP: 30
SALES (corp-wide): 5.2B **Publicly Held**
WEB: www.potterybarn.com
SIC: 5021 Furniture
HQ: Pottery Barn, Inc.
  3250 Van Ness Ave
  San Francisco CA 94109
  415 421-7900

(G-6294)
PRECIOUS ANGELS LRNG CTR INC
Also Called: Precious Angels Child Care I
5574 Pearl Rd (44129-2541)
PHONE...............440 886-1919
Fax: 440 884-6627
Kristen Little, *Principal*
EMP: 40
SALES (est): 501.6K **Privately Held**
SIC: 8351 Child day care services

(G-6295)
PRECISION WELDING CORPORATION
7900 Exchange St (44125-3334)
P.O. Box 25548 (44125-0548)
PHONE...............216 524-6110
Fax: 216 524-0456
Dennis Nader, *President*
Randy Nader, *Vice Pres*
Shonda Compton, *Manager*
Nick Julian, *Manager*
EMP: 32
SQ FT: 26,000
SALES (est): 4.5MM **Privately Held**
SIC: 7692 3444 3441 Welding repair; sheet metalwork; fabricated structural metal

(G-6296)
PREDICTIVE SERVICE LLC (PA)
25200 Chagrin Blvd # 300 (44122-5684)
PHONE...............866 772-6770
Ralph Delisio, *Exec VP*
Heidi Smith, *Mktg Dir*
Karina Diedrich, *Manager*
Derek Harrod, *Manager*
Joseph A Pitman, *Manager*
EMP: 51
SQ FT: 16,000
SALES (est): 20.9MM **Privately Held**
WEB: www.pscorp.com
SIC: 7389 Industrial & commercial equipment inspection service

(G-6297)
PREEMPTIVE SOLUTIONS LLC
767 Beta Dr (44143-2379)
PHONE...............440 443-7200
Fax: 216 460-0680
Gabriel Torok, *CEO*
Paul Ruflin, *President*
Andy Forsyth, *Vice Pres*
Keith Peer, *Vice Pres*
Jo Ramkumar, *QA Dir*
EMP: 30
SQ FT: 4,000
SALES (est): 3.8MM **Privately Held**
WEB: www.preemptive.com
SIC: 7372 Application computer software

(G-6298)
PREFERRED ACQUISITION CO LLC (PA)
4871 Neo Pkwy (44128-3101)
PHONE...............216 587-0957
Fax: 216 587-1169
Craig S Hartman, *CEO*
Mark Cline, *Vice Pres*
Brian Miller, *Vice Pres*
Susan Tubbs, *CFO*
Deborah Abbott, *Controller*
EMP: 59
SQ FT: 14,000
SALES (est): 16.9MM **Privately Held**
SIC: 1752 1721 Floor laying & floor work; commercial painting

(G-6299)
PREFERRED CAPITAL LENDING INC
200 Public Sq Ste 160 (44114-2398)
PHONE...............216 472-1391
Brian T Garelli, *Branch Mgr*
EMP: 26
SALES (corp-wide): 8MM **Privately Held**
SIC: 6153 Working capital financing
PA: Preferred Capital Lending, Inc.
  368 W Huron St Ste 200n
  Chicago IL 60654
  312 212-5000

(G-6300)
PREFERRED ROOFING OHIO INC
4871 Neo Pkwy (44128-3101)
PHONE...............216 587-0957
Fax: 216 663-6865
Thomas M Miller, *President*
Craig Sibbio, *Vice Pres*
Daniel Engle, *VP Opers*
Greg Derossett, *Project Mgr*
Heidi Berg, *Office Mgr*
EMP: 35
SALES (est): 3.2MM **Privately Held**
WEB: www.roofinghelp.com
SIC: 1761 Roofing & gutter work

(G-6301)
PREFERRED ROOFING SERVICES LLC
4871 Neo Pkwy (44128-3101)
PHONE...............216 587-0957
Craig Hartman, *Mng Member*
Brian Miller,
EMP: 35
SQ FT: 10,000
SALES (est): 1.9MM **Privately Held**
WEB: www.preferredcleveland.com
SIC: 1761 Roofing contractor

(G-6302)
PREMIER TRUCK PARTS INC
5800 W Canal Rd (44125-3341)
PHONE...............216 642-5000
Claude Humberson, *President*
Joey Lojek, *Corp Secy*
Brent Humberson, *Vice Pres*
Maggie Mogg, *Controller*
Larry Humberson, *Sales Staff*
EMP: 40
SQ FT: 17,000
SALES (est): 7.6MM **Privately Held**
SIC: 5531 5013 7513 Truck equipment & parts; truck parts & accessories; truck rental, without drivers

(G-6303)
PREMIER TRUCK SLS & RENTL INC
5800 W Canal Rd (44125-3327)
PHONE...............216 642-5000
Fax: 216 642-3038
Joey Lojek, *President*
Claude Humberson, *Corp Secy*
Brent Humberson, *Vice Pres*
Vicki Lojek, *Manager*
▼**EMP:** 35
SQ FT: 17,000
SALES (est): 6.4MM **Privately Held**
WEB: www.premiertrucksales.com
SIC: 5521 7513 Trucks, tractors & trailers: used; truck rental & leasing, no drivers

(G-6304)
PRESTIGE DELIVERY SYSTEMS LLC (HQ)
9535 Midwest Ave Ste 104 (44125-2457)
PHONE...............216 332-8000
Fax: 216 332-8030
Ronald Bernon, *Ch of Bd*
Joseph Bernon, *President*
Chip Newell, *Vice Pres*
Jim Shook, *Regl Sales Mgr*
Tim Roberts, *Sales Staff*
EMP: 60
SQ FT: 30,000
SALES: 52.1MM
SALES (corp-wide): 145.1MM **Privately Held**
SIC: 4513 4215 Package delivery, private air; package delivery, vehicular
PA: Lasership, Inc.
  1912 Woodford Rd Ste Ll
  Vienna VA 22182
  703 761-9030

(G-6305)
PRICEWATERHOUSECOOPERS LLP
200 Public Sq Fl 18 (44114-2310)
PHONE...............216 875-3000
John Duchnowski, *Purch Agent*
Richard P Stovsky, *Manager*
Brittany Bica, *Manager*
Anthony Dinardo, *Manager*
Jennifer Fleming, *Manager*

EMP: 300
SALES (corp-wide): 5.6B Privately Held
WEB: www.pwcglobal.com
SIC: 8721 Certified public accountant
PA: Pricewaterhousecoopers Llp
   300 Madison Ave Fl 24
   New York NY 10017
   646 471-4000

(G-6306)
PRIME TIME ENTERPRISES INC
Also Called: Prime Time Delivery & Whse
6410 Eastland Rd Ste A (44142-1306)
P.O. Box 811144 (44181-1144)
PHONE...................................440 891-8855
Dave Reichbaum, *President*
Lisa Levis, *President*
EMP: 35
SQ FT: 20,000
SALES (est): 5.1MM Privately Held
SIC: 4215 4225 4513 Courier services, except by air; general warehousing & storage; air courier services

(G-6307)
PRIVATE PRACTICE NURSES INC
403 Cary Jay Blvd (44143-1727)
PHONE...................................216 481-1305
Fax: 216 481-1305
Lisa Ashcroft, *President*
Susan Ashcroft, *Corp Secy*
Brent Crane, *Psychiatry*
EMP: 35
SALES (est): 1.5MM Privately Held
WEB: www.privatepracticenurses.com
SIC: 7361 Nurses' registry

(G-6308)
PRO ED COMMUNICATIONS INC
25101 Chagrin Blvd # 230 (44122-5688)
PHONE...................................216 595-7919
Fax: 216 595-7919
Marta Brookes, *President*
Mary Rofael, *Exec VP*
Greg Connel, *Senior VP*
Allison Huegel, *Vice Pres*
Laura McCormick, *Vice Pres*
EMP: 35
SQ FT: 4,000
SALES (est): 4.1MM Privately Held
WEB: www.proedcom.com
SIC: 8748 Communications consulting

(G-6309)
PROFESSIONAL SERVICE INDS INC
Also Called: PSI Testing and Engineering
5555 Canal Rd (44125-4874)
PHONE...................................216 447-1335
Fax: 216 642-7008
Chris Lopez, *Branch Mgr*
Wessam Mekhael, *Department Mgr*
Paul Bowyer, *Manager*
Jeanette Dezelan, *Receptionist*
EMP: 70
SALES (corp-wide): 731.5MM Privately Held
SIC: 8711 Consulting engineer
HQ: Professional Service Industries, Inc.
   545 E Algonquin Rd
   Arlington Heights IL 60005
   630 691-1490

(G-6310)
PROFIT RECOVERY OF OHIO
Also Called: Basista & Associates
16510 Webster Rd (44130-5464)
PHONE...................................440 243-1743
Amil E Basista, *Owner*
EMP: 115
SALES: 1.9MM Privately Held
SIC: 4813

(G-6311)
PROGRESSIVE AGENCY INC
Also Called: Progressive Insurance
6300 Wilson Mills Rd (44143-2109)
PHONE...................................440 461-5000
Fax: 440 395-2310
Peter B Lewis, *Chairman*
Jennifer West, *Corp Counsel*
Jason Dittmer, *Manager*
John Retton, *Manager*
Debbie Kraska, *Info Tech Dir*
EMP: 250

SALES (est): 92MM
SALES (corp-wide): 26.8B Publicly Held
SIC: 6331 Fire, marine & casualty insurance
PA: The Progressive Corporation
   6300 Wilson Mills Rd
   Mayfield Village OH 44143
   440 461-5000

(G-6312)
PROGRESSIVE BAYSIDE INSUR CO
Also Called: PROGRESSIVE INSURANCE
6300 Wilson Mills Rd (44143-2109)
P.O. Box W33, Mayfield Village (44143)
PHONE...................................440 395-4460
EMP: 261
SALES: 127.2MM
SALES (corp-wide): 26.8B Publicly Held
SIC: 6311 Life insurance
PA: The Progressive Corporation
   6300 Wilson Mills Rd
   Mayfield Village OH 44143
   440 461-5000

(G-6313)
PROGRESSIVE CASUALTY INSUR CO
Also Called: Progressive Insurance
651 Beta Dr 150 (44143-2318)
PHONE...................................440 683-8164
Jim Kaiser, *Manager*
Richard Burke, *Manager*
Ferhat Hoke, *Info Tech Mgr*
EMP: 30
SQ FT: 77,059
SALES (corp-wide): 26.8B Publicly Held
WEB: www.progressinsurance.com
SIC: 6331 6411 Fire, marine & casualty insurance; insurance agents & brokers
HQ: Progressive Casualty Insurance Company
   6300 Wilson Mills Rd
   Mayfield Village OH 44143
   440 461-5000

(G-6314)
PROGRESSIVE CASUALTY INSUR CO
Progressive Insurance
747 Alpha Dr Ste A21 (44143-2124)
PHONE...................................440 603-4033
William Kampf, *General Mgr*
Bradley A Granger, *Project Mgr*
Bradley Granger, *Project Mgr*
Neil Miklovic, *Auditing Mgr*
Elizabeth A Johnson, *Accounts Mgr*
EMP: 100
SALES (corp-wide): 26.8B Publicly Held
WEB: www.progressinsurance.com
SIC: 6331 6321 Automobile insurance; accident insurance carriers
HQ: Progressive Casualty Insurance Company
   6300 Wilson Mills Rd
   Mayfield Village OH 44143
   440 461-5000

(G-6315)
PROGRESSIVE CHOICE INSUR CO
6300 Wilson Mills Rd (44143-2109)
PHONE...................................440 461-5000
Steven A Broz, *President*
Denise Spies, *Technology*
EMP: 993
SALES (est): 151.8MM
SALES (corp-wide): 26.8B Publicly Held
SIC: 6331 Fire, marine & casualty insurance
HQ: Progressive Direct Holdings, Inc.
   6300 Wilson Mills Rd
   Cleveland OH

(G-6316)
PROGRESSIVE CORPORATION
Also Called: Progressive Insurance
600 Mills Rd (44101)
P.O. Box 6807 (44101-1807)
PHONE...................................800 925-2886
John Raguz, *Payroll Mgr*
EMP: 782
SALES (corp-wide): 26.8B Publicly Held
SIC: 6411 Insurance agents & brokers

PA: The Progressive Corporation
   6300 Wilson Mills Rd
   Mayfield Village OH 44143
   440 461-5000

(G-6317)
PROGRESSIVE CORPORATION
Also Called: Progressive Insurance
300 N Commons Blvd (44143-1589)
PHONE...................................440 461-5000
Fax: 440 446-7504
Leila Widgren, *QA Dir*
Carolyn Bowman, *Engineer*
Christopher Smith, *Engineer*
Stephen Adams, *Human Res Dir*
Pat Bemer, *Human Res Dir*
EMP: 391
SALES (corp-wide): 26.8B Publicly Held
SIC: 6331 6351 Fire, marine & casualty insurance; property damage insurance; credit & other financial responsibility insurance
PA: The Progressive Corporation
   6300 Wilson Mills Rd
   Mayfield Village OH 44143
   440 461-5000

(G-6318)
PROGRESSIVE HAWAII INSURANCE C
Also Called: PROGRESSIVE INSURANCE
6300 Wilson Mills Rd (44143-2109)
P.O. Box W33, Mayfield Village (44143)
PHONE...................................440 461-5000
Glenn M Renwick, *President*
EMP: 196
SALES: 197.9MM
SALES (corp-wide): 26.8B Publicly Held
SIC: 6411 Insurance agents, brokers & service
PA: The Progressive Corporation
   6300 Wilson Mills Rd
   Mayfield Village OH 44143
   440 461-5000

(G-6319)
PROGRESSIVE NORTHWESTERN INSUR
Also Called: PROGRESSIVE INSURANCE
6300 Wilson Mills Rd (44143-2109)
P.O. Box W33, Mayfield Village (44143)
PHONE...................................440 461-5000
Glenn Renwick, *CEO*
Robert Williams, *President*
Stephen Peterson, *Treasurer*
Dane Shrallow, *Admin Sec*
EMP: 25
SQ FT: 3,500
SALES: 1.5B
SALES (corp-wide): 26.8B Publicly Held
SIC: 6331 Fire, marine & casualty insurance
PA: The Progressive Corporation
   6300 Wilson Mills Rd
   Mayfield Village OH 44143
   440 461-5000

(G-6320)
PROGRESSIVE PARK LLC
Also Called: University Park Nursing Home
5553 Broadview Rd (44134-1604)
PHONE...................................330 434-4514
Pam Tunstall, *Corp Comm Staff*
Elisa Barton, *Marketing Staff*
Lina Bossmen, *Office Mgr*
Nancy Richiutti, *Office Mgr*
Jennifor Conloy,
EMP: 110
SALES (est): 4.7MM Privately Held
WEB: www.universityparknursing.com
SIC: 8051 Skilled nursing care facilities

(G-6321)
PROGRESSIVE PREMIER INSURANCE
Also Called: PROGRESSIVE INSURANCE
6300 Wilson Mills Rd W33 (44143-2109)
P.O. Box W33, Mayfield Village (44143)
PHONE...................................440 461-5000
Toby K Alfred, *CEO*
EMP: 196
SALES: 182MM
SALES (corp-wide): 26.8B Publicly Held
SIC: 6411 Insurance agents, brokers & service

PA: The Progressive Corporation
   6300 Wilson Mills Rd
   Mayfield Village OH 44143
   440 461-5000

(G-6322)
PROGRESSIVE SELECT INSUR CO
6300 Wilson Mills Rd (44143-2109)
PHONE...................................440 461-5000
James R Haas, *Principal*
EMP: 695
SALES: 173.5MM
SALES (corp-wide): 26.8B Publicly Held
SIC: 6331 Automobile insurance
HQ: Progressive Direct Holdings, Inc.
   6300 Wilson Mills Rd
   Cleveland OH

(G-6323)
PROJECT PACKAGING INC
Also Called: P P I
17877 Saint Clair Ave # 6 (44110-2632)
PHONE...................................216 451-7878
Fax: 216 451-4952
Ken Franklin, *President*
Roger Fischer, *Engineer*
Jim Reese, *VP Finance*
Stacy Passalaqua, *Manager*
Jeff Endemann, *CTO*
EMP: 50
SQ FT: 132,000
SALES (est): 3MM Privately Held
SIC: 7389 Packaging & labeling services

(G-6324)
PROTEM HOMECARE LLC
3535 Lee Rd (44120-5122)
PHONE...................................216 663-8188
Fax: 216 663-8884
Ada Nworie,
EMP: 30
SALES (est): 2.8MM Privately Held
SIC: 8052 Home for the mentally retarded, with health care

(G-6325)
PROTIVITI INC
1001 Lakeside Ave E (44114-1158)
PHONE...................................216 696-6010
Fax: 216 621-8643
Scott Laliberte, *Managing Dir*
Kathy Keller, *Pub Rel Dir*
Shannon Scopano, *Branch Mgr*
Mischa Goldhagen, *Manager*
EMP: 48
SALES (corp-wide): 5.2B Publicly Held
SIC: 8721 8742 Auditing services; industry specialist consultants
HQ: Protiviti Inc.
   2884 Sand Hill Rd Ste 200
   Menlo Park CA 94025
   650 234-6000

(G-6326)
PROVIDENCE HOUSE INC
Also Called: CRISIS NURSERY
2050 W 32nd St (44113-4018)
PHONE...................................216 651-5982
Fax: 216 651-0112
Natalie Leek-Nelson, *President*
Kathleen Miller, *Vice Pres*
James Rossman, *Treasurer*
James Kopniske, *Manager*
Carol Lowe, *Manager*
EMP: 37
SQ FT: 5,000
SALES: 2.4MM Privately Held
SIC: 8322 8361 Child related social services; residential care

(G-6327)
PRUDENTIAL INSUR CO OF AMER
5875 Landerbrook Dr # 110 (44124-4069)
PHONE...................................440 684-4409
Fax: 440 684-0492
Beth Smith, *Opers Mgr*
Mark Pietsch, *Manager*
David Lockman, *Advisor*
EMP: 40
SALES (corp-wide): 59.6B Publicly Held
SIC: 6411 Insurance agents, brokers & service

Cleveland - Cuyahoga County (G-6328)

HQ: The Prudential Insurance Company Of America
751 Broad St
Newark NJ 07102
973 802-6000

(G-6328)
PS LIFESTYLE LLC
Also Called: Salon PS
55 Public Sq Ste 1180 (44113-1901)
PHONE.................................440 600-1595
John J Polatz, *CEO*
Susan McDonough, *District Mgr*
Brett McMillan, *Exec VP*
Brian Goetz, *Vice Pres*
Shelley Edwards, *VP Opers*
EMP: 800
SQ FT: 4,000
SALES: 12MM **Privately Held**
SIC: 7231 Unisex hair salons; hairdressers

(G-6329)
PSC METALS INC
4250 E 68th Berdelle (44105)
PHONE.................................216 341-3400
Dusty Busser, *General Mgr*
Dustin Busser, *Branch Mgr*
EMP: 42
SQ FT: 3,384
SALES (corp-wide): 21.7B **Publicly Held**
WEB: www.pscmetals.com
SIC: 5093 Metal scrap & waste materials
HQ: Psc Metals, Inc.
5875 Landerbrook Dr # 200
Mayfield Heights OH 44124
440 753-5400

(G-6330)
PSE CREDIT UNION INC (PA)
5255 Regency Dr (44129-5453)
P.O. Box 29450 (44129-0450)
PHONE.................................440 843-8300
Fax: 440 843-7741
Janice L Thomas, *President*
Patricia Agardi, *Manager*
EMP: 50 EST: 1955
SQ FT: 9,206
SALES: 3.6MM **Privately Held**
WEB: www.psecuorg.net
SIC: 6062 State credit unions, not federally chartered

(G-6331)
PTC HOLDINGS INC
1422 Euclid Ave Ste 1130 (44115-2065)
PHONE.................................216 771-6960
Rocco Guarnaccia, *CEO*
Joe Maceda, *President*
EMP: 287
SALES (est): 234.6K **Publicly Held**
SIC: 6099 Clearinghouse associations, bank or check
PA: Lpl Financial Holdings Inc.
75 State St Ste 2401
Boston MA 02109

(G-6332)
PUBCO CORPORATION (PA)
3830 Kelley Ave (44114-4534)
PHONE.................................216 881-5300
William Dillingham, *President*
Stephen R Kalette, *Vice Pres*
Robert Turnbull, *Vice Pres*
Michael Knack, *Purchasing*
Maria Szubski, *CFO*
◆ EMP: 85
SQ FT: 312,000
SALES (est): 95MM **Privately Held**
SIC: 3531 6512 3955 Construction machinery; nonresidential building operators; carbon paper & inked ribbons

(G-6333)
QUALITY CEMENT INC
10840 Brookpark Rd (44130-1119)
PHONE.................................216 676-8838
Michael Chizmar, *President*
Eric Brenner, *Controller*
EMP: 35
SQ FT: 600
SALES: 8MM **Privately Held**
SIC: 1771 Concrete work

(G-6334)
QUALITY CONTROL INSPECTION (PA)
40 Tarbell Ave (44146-3615)
PHONE.................................440 359-1900
Fax: 440 359-1935
Rick Capone, *President*
Harold Miller, *Data Proc Staff*
Kris Kesich, *Admin Sec*
EMP: 60
SALES (est): 11MM **Privately Held**
WEB: www.qcigroup.com
SIC: 7389 8741 Building inspection service; construction management

(G-6335)
QUALITY SOLUTIONS INC
P.O. Box 40147 (44140-0147)
PHONE.................................440 933-9946
Francis P Toolan Jr, *Branch Mgr*
John Dickey, *Executive*
EMP: 27
SALES (corp-wide): 5.8MM **Privately Held**
SIC: 2741 8742 8732 Business service newsletters; publishing & printing; management consulting services; market analysis or research
PA: Quality Solutions Inc
44 Merrimac St Ste 22
Newburyport MA 01950
978 465-7755

(G-6336)
QUICKEN LOANS INC
100 Public Sq Ste 400 (44113-2207)
PHONE.................................216 586-8900
Christopher Mahnen, *President*
EMP: 33
SALES (corp-wide): 1.4B **Privately Held**
SIC: 6162 Mortgage bankers
HQ: Quicken Loans Inc.
1050 Woodward Ave
Detroit MI 48226
800 251-9080

(G-6337)
R AND G ENTERPRISES OF OHIO
9213 Harrow Dr (44129-1734)
PHONE.................................440 845-6870
Rita Assour, *President*
EMP: 30
SALES (est): 1.6MM **Privately Held**
SIC: 5092 Toys & games

(G-6338)
R B C APOLLO EQUITY PARTNERS (DH)
600 Superior Ave E # 2300 (44114-2612)
PHONE.................................216 875-2626
Brian Berry, *General Mgr*
Joseph Caruso, *Senior VP*
Kathy Beuck, *Asst Controller*
Joe Vanderdonck, *Manager*
Thomas Rini,
EMP: 36
SQ FT: 5,000
SALES (est): 6.5MM
SALES (corp-wide): 19.1B **Privately Held**
WEB: www.apollohousing.com
SIC: 6211 Investment bankers
HQ: Rbc Capital Markets Corporation
60 S 6th St Ste 700
Minneapolis MN 55402
612 371-2711

(G-6339)
R D D INC (PA)
Also Called: Power Direct
4719 Blythin Rd (44125-1209)
PHONE.................................216 781-5858
Daniel Delfino, *President*
Mindy Delfino, *Vice Pres*
Susan Ushek, *Exec Dir*
EMP: 120
SQ FT: 15,000
SALES (est): 17.3MM **Privately Held**
WEB: www.power-direct.com
SIC: 7389 8742 Telemarketing services; marketing consulting services

(G-6340)
R SQUARE INC
6100 Oak Tree Blvd # 200 (44131-2544)
PHONE.................................216 328-2077
Ravi Velu, *President*
EMP: 25
SQ FT: 1,500
SALES (est): 757.1K **Privately Held**
SIC: 7389 Business services

(G-6341)
R-CAP SECURITY LLC
7800 Superior Ave (44103-2858)
P.O. Box 10167 (44110-0167)
PHONE.................................216 761-6355
Fax: 216 881-7764
Velma Perkins, *Manager*
Charlotte Perkins,
Malinda Sutter, *Admin Sec*
EMP: 120
SALES (est): 3.8MM **Privately Held**
SIC: 7381 Security guard service

(G-6342)
RA STAFF COMPANY INC
Also Called: Staffco-Campisano
16500 W Sprague Rd (44130-6315)
PHONE.................................440 891-9900
Larry McHale, *President*
Heather Kantor, *Office Mgr*
Frank Campisano, *Manager*
Brian Conner, *Representative*
EMP: 25
SQ FT: 10,000
SALES (est): 3MM **Privately Held**
WEB: www.rastaffco.com
SIC: 8743 Sales promotion

(G-6343)
RADIO SEAWAY INC
Also Called: Radio Station Wclv
1375 Euclid Ave Ste 450 (44115-1839)
PHONE.................................216 916-6100
Fax: 216 464-2206
Robert D Conrad, *President*
Rich Marschner, *General Mgr*
Annie Bartlett, *Vice Pres*
Wiley Cornell, *Vice Pres*
Bill Oconnell, *Vice Pres*
EMP: 36 EST: 1962
SALES: 3MM **Privately Held**
WEB: www.wclv.com
SIC: 4832 7929 Radio broadcasting stations; entertainers & entertainment groups

(G-6344)
RADISSON HOTEL CLEVELAND GTWY
Also Called: Radisson Inn
651 Huron Rd E (44115-1116)
PHONE.................................216 377-9000
Fax: 216 377-9001
Megan Davis, *Sales Executive*
Liz Harman, *Office Mgr*
Donna White, *Director*
Megan Joyce, *Executive*
EMP: 70 EST: 1998
SALES (est): 1.9MM **Privately Held**
WEB: www.uctonline.org
SIC: 7011 Hotels & motels

(G-6345)
RADIX WIRE CO (PA)
Also Called: Radix Wire Company, The
26000 Lakeland Blvd (44132-2638)
PHONE.................................216 731-9191
Fax: 216 731-7082
Keith D Nootbaar, *President*
Jim Schaefer, *President*
Marylou Vermerris, *Chairman*
Brain Bukovec, *Vice Pres*
Steve Demko, *Vice Pres*
EMP: 60
SQ FT: 14,000
SALES (est): 21.5MM **Privately Held**
WEB: www.radix-wire.com
SIC: 3357 5051 Nonferrous wiredrawing & insulating; cable, wire

(G-6346)
RAE-ANN ENTERPRISES INC
Also Called: Rae-Ann Suburban
27310 W Oviatt Rd (44140-2139)
P.O. Box 40175 (44140-0175)
PHONE.................................440 249-5092
Ray Griffiths, *Vice Pres*

EMP: 55
SALES (est): 3.3MM **Privately Held**
SIC: 8059 Convalescent home

(G-6347)
RAE-ANN HOLDINGS INC
Also Called: Rae-Suburban
29505 Detroit Rd (44145-1932)
PHONE.................................440 871-5181
John Brutvan, *Purch Dir*
John Griffith, *Manager*
David Tolentino, *Director*
Debbie Wilson, *Director*
EMP: 99
SALES (corp-wide): 36.6MM **Privately Held**
SIC: 8059 8051 Nursing home, except skilled & intermediate care facility; skilled nursing care facilities
PA: Rae-Ann Holdings, Inc.
27310 W Oviatt Rd
Bay Village OH 44140
440 835-3004

(G-6348)
RAEANN INC (PA)
Also Called: Rae-Ann Center
P.O. Box 40175, Bay Village (44140-0175)
PHONE.................................440 871-5181
John Griffiths, *President*
Ray Griffiths, *President*
Mary Ann Griffiths, *Vice Pres*
Susan Griffiths, *Vice Pres*
Lee Mokry, *Controller*
EMP: 25
SQ FT: 2,000
SALES (est): 7.7MM **Privately Held**
SIC: 8051 Skilled nursing care facilities

(G-6349)
RAHIM INC
Also Called: R N R Consulting
1111 Superior Ave E # 1330 (44114-2541)
PHONE.................................216 621-8977
Fax: 216 621-8972
Abhijit Verekar, *CEO*
Jennifer Carrico, *Manager*
Aleksandra Gancheva, *Senior Mgr*
EMP: 29
SALES (est): 2.7MM **Privately Held**
WEB: www.rnrconsulting.com
SIC: 8742 Management consulting services

(G-6350)
RAKESH RANJAN MD & ASSOC INC (PA)
Also Called: Charak Ctr For Hlth & Wellness
12395 Mccracken Rd Ste A (44125-2946)
PHONE.................................216 375-9897
Fax: 330 764-9712
Ranjan Rakesh, *President*
Anish Ranjan, *Director*
EMP: 25
SQ FT: 20,000
SALES (est): 14.8MM **Privately Held**
SIC: 8011 Psychiatrist

(G-6351)
RAMOS TRUCKING CORPORATION
2890 W 3rd St (44113-2516)
PHONE.................................216 781-0770
Don Bugen, *President*
EMP: 25
SQ FT: 1,500
SALES (est): 1MM **Privately Held**
SIC: 4212 Local trucking, without storage

(G-6352)
RAN TEMPS INC
12800 Shaker Blvd (44120-2000)
PHONE.................................216 991-5500
Norman A Thomas, *President*
EMP: 38 EST: 1987
SALES (est): 1.9MM **Privately Held**
WEB: www.ran-associates.com
SIC: 7363 Temporary help service

(G-6353)
RATHBONE GROUP LLC
1100 Superior Ave E # 1850 (44114-2544)
PHONE.................................800 870-5521
Joel Rathbone, *CEO*
Jason Sullivan,
Adam Wilk,

GEOGRAPHIC SECTION   Cleveland - Cuyahoga County (G-6377)

John Lamerson, *Associate*
Matthew Zemanek, *Associate*
EMP: 63
SALES (est): 4.6MM **Privately Held**
SIC: 8111 General practice law office

(G-6354)
RAY FOGG BUILDING METHODS INC
981 Keynote Cir Ste 15 (44131-1842)
PHONE.................................216 351-7976
Fax: 216 351-5686
Raymon B Fogg Jr, *President*
Michael Merle, *President*
Richard Neiden, *Vice Pres*
Nicholas Poelking, *Project Mgr*
Virginia Fogg, *Admin Sec*
EMP: 25 **EST:** 1959
SQ FT: 5,700
SALES (est): 11.5MM **Privately Held**
SIC: 1541 1542 Industrial buildings, new construction; commercial & office building, new construction

(G-6355)
RAYCOM MEDIA INC
Also Called: W O I O
1717 E 12th St (44114-3246)
PHONE.................................216 367-7300
Fax: 216 436-5460
Bill Applegate, *Vice Pres*
Brian Sinclair, *Producer*
Lisa McManus, *Program Dir*
Judi Smith, *Executive Asst*
EMP: 225 **Privately Held**
WEB: www.kwwl.com
SIC: 4833 Television broadcasting stations
PA: Raycom Media, Inc.
   201 Monroe St Fl 20
   Montgomery AL 36104

(G-6356)
RDL ARCHITECTS INC
16102 Chagrin Blvd # 200 (44120-3708)
PHONE.................................216 752-4300
Fax: 216 663-9997
Ronald Lloyd, *President*
James Viviani, *Project Mgr*
Bob Reighard, *Design Engr*
Katherine Cunningham, *Office Mgr*
Jonathan Cana, *Sr Project Mgr*
EMP: 38
SALES (est): 2.6MM **Privately Held**
SIC: 8712 7389 Architectural services; interior design services

(G-6357)
REAL AMERICA INC
24555 Lake Shore Blvd (44123)
PHONE.................................216 261-1177
Edward Gudenas, *President*
EMP: 301
SALES (est): 17.8MM **Privately Held**
SIC: 5039 7033 Prefabricated buildings; campgrounds

(G-6358)
REAL ESTATE CAPITAL FUND LLC
Also Called: Taragon Advisors
20820 Chagrin Blvd # 300 (44122-5323)
PHONE.................................216 491-3990
William Soteroff, *Exec VP*
Adam Contos, *Vice Pres*
Tom Kramig, *Vice Pres*
Pat Lawrence, *Vice Pres*
Terence Sullivan,
EMP: 25 **EST:** 2001
SALES (est): 1.4MM **Privately Held**
SIC: 6531 8742 Real estate brokers & agents; financial consultant

(G-6359)
REALTY ONE INC
12333 Pearl Rd (44136-3412)
PHONE.................................440 238-1400
Fax: 440 238-2359
Martha Keene, *Manager*
Carol Barna, *Executive*
EMP: 100
SALES (corp-wide): 67.8MM **Privately Held**
WEB: www.realty-1st.com
SIC: 6531 Real estate agents & managers
HQ: Realty One, Inc.
   800 W Saint Clair Ave
   Cleveland OH 44113
   216 328-2500

(G-6360)
REBIZ LLC
1925 Saint Clair Ave Ne (44114-2028)
PHONE.................................844 467-3249
Junaid Hasan, *Mng Member*
Jessica Cornwell, *Manager*
EMP: 50 **EST:** 2014
SALES (est): 50.3K **Privately Held**
SIC: 8732 Business research service

(G-6361)
RECOVERY RESOURCES (PA)
3950 Chester Ave (44114-4625)
PHONE.................................216 431-4131
Debora Rodriguez, *President*
Charlotte Rerko, *COO*
William Morgan, *CFO*
Jason Joyce, *Director*
Donald Porach, *Director*
EMP: 48 **EST:** 1975
SQ FT: 6,800
SALES (est): 12.5MM **Privately Held**
SIC: 8093 Substance abuse clinics (outpatient)

(G-6362)
RECOVERY RESOURCES
4269 Pearl Rd Ste 300 (44109-4232)
PHONE.................................216 431-4131
Gordon Hewitt, *Branch Mgr*
Aileen Hernandez, *Med Doctor*
Richard R Hill, *Med Doctor*
Christina De Los Reyes, *Med Doctor*
Maureen Masterson, *Manager*
EMP: 65
SALES (corp-wide): 12.5MM **Privately Held**
SIC: 8093 Substance abuse clinics (outpatient)
PA: Recovery Resources
   3950 Chester Ave
   Cleveland OH 44114
   216 431-4131

(G-6363)
RED ROOF INNS INC
29595 Clemens Rd (44145-1056)
PHONE.................................440 892-7920
Fax: 440 892-7925
EMP: 28 **Privately Held**
WEB: www.redroof.com
SIC: 7011 Hotels & motels
HQ: Red Roof Inns, Inc.
   605 S Front St Ste 150
   Columbus OH 43215
   614 744-2600

(G-6364)
RED ROOF INNS INC
17555 Bagley Rd (44130-2551)
PHONE.................................440 243-5166
Fax: 440 243-2474
EMP: 26 **Privately Held**
WEB: www.redroof.com
SIC: 7011 Hotels & motels
HQ: Red Roof Inns, Inc.
   605 S Front St Ste 150
   Columbus OH 43215
   614 744-2600

(G-6365)
REED WESTLAKE LESKOSKY LTD (PA)
1422 Euclid Ave Ste 300 (44115-1912)
PHONE.................................216 522-0449
Paul Westlake Jr, *Managing Prtnr*
Phil Libassi, *Partner*
Ronald A Reed, *Partner*
Matthew Janiak, *Project Dir*
Glen Zeisset, *Project Dir*
EMP: 90
SQ FT: 20,000
SALES (est): 37.1MM **Privately Held**
WEB: www.vwrl.com
SIC: 8711 8712 Engineering services; architectural services

(G-6366)
REGAL CARPET CENTER INC
Also Called: Regal Carpet Co
5411 Northfield Rd (44146-1187)
PHONE.................................216 475-1844
Fax: 216 663-7738
Marvin Kinstlinger, *President*
Les Kinsley, *Treasurer*
Howard Kinstlinger, *Admin Sec*
EMP: 29
SQ FT: 15,000
SALES (est): 6.3MM **Privately Held**
SIC: 5713 5023 1752 Carpets; carpets; floor laying & floor work

(G-6367)
REGAL CINEMAS INC
18348 Bagley Rd (44130-3411)
PHONE.................................440 891-9845
Brian Kuhn, *Branch Mgr*
John Deluca, *Manager*
Justine Neligan, *Manager*
EMP: 35
SALES (corp-wide): 982.1MM **Privately Held**
WEB: www.regalcinemas.com
SIC: 7832 Motion picture theaters, except drive-in
HQ: Regal Cinemas, Inc.
   101 E Blount Ave Ste 100
   Knoxville TN 37920
   865 922-1123

(G-6368)
REID ASSET MANAGEMENT COMPANY
Also Called: Predict Technologies Div
9555 Rockside Rd Ste 350 (44125-6283)
PHONE.................................216 642-3223
Donald F Kautzman, *Principal*
Robert Shinn, *Project Mgr*
EMP: 40
SALES (est): 1.6MM
SALES (corp-wide): 9.9MM **Privately Held**
WEB: www.magnusequipment.com
SIC: 7389 8734 3826 5084 Industrial & commercial equipment inspection service; testing laboratories; analytical instruments; industrial machinery & equipment
PA: Reid Asset Management Company
   9555 Rockside Rd Ste 350
   Cleveland OH 44125
   216 642-3223

(G-6369)
REILLY SWEEPING INC
20350 Hannan Pkwy (44146-5353)
PHONE.................................440 786-8400
Fax: 440 786-8405
Patrick Reilly, *President*
Michael Reilly, *Vice Pres*
Sean Reilly, *Admin Sec*
EMP: 30
SALES (est): 5.4MM **Privately Held**
SIC: 4959 Sweeping service: road, airport, parking lot, etc.

(G-6370)
RELENTLESS RECOVERY INC
1898 Scranton Rd Uppr (44113-2434)
PHONE.................................216 621-8333
David Ziebro, *President*
Amy Osterling, *Vice Pres*
John Ziebro, *Manager*
EMP: 60
SALES (est): 20.2MM **Privately Held**
SIC: 6153 Credit card services, central agency collection

(G-6371)
RELIABILITY FIRST CORPORATION
3 Summit Park Dr Ste 600 (44131-6900)
PHONE.................................216 503-0600
Fax: 216 524-0603
Timothy R Gallagher, *President*
Raymond J Palmieri, *Vice Pres*
Scott Power, *Vice Pres*
Derek Kassimer, *Engineer*
Jill Lewton, *CFO*
EMP: 30
SALES (est): 19.2MM **Privately Held**
WEB: www.rfirst.org
SIC: 7539 Electrical services

(G-6372)
RELMEC MECHANICAL LLC
4975 Hamilton Ave (44114-3906)
PHONE.................................216 391-1030
Sharon Lunato, *CEO*
Layne Kendig, *President*
Jerry Mikus, *Vice Pres*
J Patrick O'Brien, *Vice Pres*
Pat Obrien, *Vice Pres*
EMP: 180
SALES (est): 27.7MM **Privately Held**
SIC: 1711 Mechanical contractor

(G-6373)
REMINGER CO LPA (PA)
101 W Prospect Ave # 1400 (44115-1074)
PHONE.................................216 687-1311
Stephen Walters, *President*
Leigh Anenson, *Editor*
William P Farrall, *Counsel*
William Meadows, *Vice Pres*
Donald Moracz, *Vice Pres*
EMP: 175 **EST:** 1958
SQ FT: 64,000
SALES (est): 59.8MM **Privately Held**
WEB: www.reminger.com
SIC: 8111 General practice law office

(G-6374)
RENAISSANCE HOTEL OPERATING CO
24 Public Sq Fl 1 (44113-2222)
PHONE.................................216 696-5600
Joseph Kendall, *Engineer*
Elizabeth Blackford, *Human Res Dir*
Pat Barrett, *Human Resources*
Frank McGee, *Sales Mgr*
Kristen Garcia, *Marketing Staff*
EMP: 650
SALES (corp-wide): 22.8B **Publicly Held**
WEB: www.renaissancehotel.com
SIC: 7011 7389 Hotels; office facilities & secretarial service rental
HQ: Renaissance Hotel Operating Company, Inc
   10400 Fernwood Rd
   Bethesda MD 20817
   301 380-3000

(G-6375)
RENNER OTTO BOISELLE & SKLAR
1621 Euclid Ave Ste 1900 (44115-2191)
PHONE.................................216 621-1113
Fax: 216 621-6165
Armand Boiselle, *Senior Partner*
John Renner, *Senior Partner*
Warren Sklar, *Senior Partner*
Donald Otto, *Partner*
Paul Steffes, *Engineer*
EMP: 35
SALES (est): 3.8MM **Privately Held**
WEB: www.rennerotto.com
SIC: 8111 General practice law office

(G-6376)
RENOVO NEURAL INC
10000 Cedar Ave (44106-2119)
PHONE.................................216 445-4252
Satish Medicetty, *President*
Bruce Trapp, *Chairman*
Caroline Lego, *Research*
Chris Ryan, *Exec Dir*
EMP: 29
SQ FT: 4,000
SALES: 3MM **Privately Held**
SIC: 8731 Commercial physical research
PA: Renovo Biosciences Inc
   10000 Cedar Ave
   Cleveland OH 44106
   216 445-4252

(G-6377)
RENTAL CONCEPTS INC (PA)
Also Called: Fleet Response
6450 Rockside Woods Blvd (44131-2237)
PHONE.................................216 525-3870
Fax: 216 887-2014
Ronald E Mawaka, *CEO*
Myron S Zadony, *President*
R Michael O'Neal, *Principal*
Scott Mawaka, *Chairman*
Kim Cassidy, *Controller*
EMP: 50
SQ FT: 11,000

Cleveland - Cuyahoga County (G-6378)

(G-6378)
REPRO ACQUISITION COMPANY LLC
Also Called: Reprocenter, The
25001 Rockwell Dr (44117-1239)
PHONE 216 738-3800
Fax: 216 738-3801
Ronald Smith,
▲ EMP: 40 EST: 1999
SQ FT: 32,000
SALES (est): 4.7MM Privately Held
WEB: www.reprocntr.com
SIC: 2752 7375 2789 Commercial printing, offset; information retrieval services; bookbinding & related work

(G-6379)
REPUBLIC SERVICES INC
8123 Jones Rd (44105-2046)
PHONE 216 741-4013
EMP: 34
SALES (corp-wide): 8.7B Publicly Held
SIC: 4953 Refuse System
PA: Republic Services, Inc.
18500 N Allied Way # 100
Phoenix AZ 85054
480 627-2700

(G-6380)
REPUBLIC SERVICES INC
8123 Jones Rd (44105-2046)
PHONE 216 741-4013
Doug Hay, Sales Staff
Matthew Mucha, Sales Staff
Allen Marino, Manager
Ken Ingle, Manager
Jack Simpson, Manager
EMP: 100
SALES (corp-wide): 10B Publicly Held
WEB: www.republicservices.com
SIC: 4953 Refuse collection & disposal services
PA: Republic Services, Inc.
18500 N Allied Way # 100
Phoenix AZ 85054
480 627-2700

(G-6381)
RESEARCH ASSOCIATES INC (PA)
Also Called: R A I
27999 Clemens Rd Frnt (44145-1182)
PHONE 440 892-1000
Fax: 440 892-9439
Kevin P Prendergast, President
Arthur L Sommer, Vice Pres
Shirley Kopp, Purch Agent
Donna Ogle, CFO
Brian Morog, Manager
EMP: 70
SQ FT: 10,800
SALES (est): 2.8MM Privately Held
WEB: www.raiglobal.com
SIC: 7299 Information services, consumer

(G-6382)
RESERS FINE FOODS INC
Also Called: Sidaris Italian Foods
1921 E 119th St (44106-1903)
PHONE 216 231-7112
Fax: 216 231-2647
Mardy Gilnut, Manager
EMP: 30
SQ FT: 22,726
SALES (corp-wide): 940.6MM Privately Held
SIC: 1541 Food products manufacturing or packing plant construction
PA: Reser's Fine Foods, Inc.
15570 Sw Jenkins Rd
Beaverton OR 97006
503 643-6431

(G-6383)
RESERVES NETWORK INC (PA)
22021 Brookpark Rd # 220 (44126-3100)
PHONE 440 779-1400
Fax: 440 779-1493
Neil Stallard, CEO
Donald L Stallard, Ch of Bd
Gordon Friedrich, Vice Pres
Nicholas Stallard, CFO
EMP: 30
SQ FT: 32,000
SALES (est): 31.1MM Privately Held
WEB: www.trnstaffing.com
SIC: 7363 7361 Temporary help service; placement agencies

(G-6384)
RESILIENCE CAPITL PARTNERS LLC (PA)
Also Called: Resilience Management
25101 Chagrin Blvd # 350 (44122-5643)
PHONE 216 292-0200
Fax: 216 292-4750
Robert Northrop, Senior VP
Doug Campbell, Vice Pres
Megan McPherson, Vice Pres
Robert Schwartz, Vice Pres
Robert Kay, Info Tech Mgr
EMP: 1898
SQ FT: 3,832
SALES (est): 98.4MM Privately Held
SIC: 7389 Financial services

(G-6385)
RESOURCE TITLE AGENCY INC (PA)
7100 E Pleasant Vly # 100 (44131-5545)
PHONE 216 520-0050
Leslie Rennell, President
Richard Rennell, Chairman
Raymond Bailey, CFO
Tim McFarland, Human Res Mgr
Megan Jenkins, Accounts Mgr
EMP: 87
SQ FT: 24,933
SALES (est): 21.2MM Privately Held
WEB: www.resourcetitle.com
SIC: 6361 6531 Real estate title insurance; escrow agent, real estate

(G-6386)
RESTAURANT DEPOT LLC
6150 Halle Dr (44125-4614)
PHONE 216 525-0101
Fax: 216 525-0202
Oaura, Branch Mgr
EMP: 25 Privately Held
SIC: 5141 4225 Groceries, general line; general warehousing & storage
HQ: Restaurant Depot, Llc
1524 132nd St
College Point NY 11356

(G-6387)
REVENUE ASSISTANCE CORPORATION
Also Called: Revenue Group
4780 Hinckley Indstrl 2 (44109-6003)
P.O. Box 93983 (44101-5983)
PHONE 216 763-2100
Trey Sheehan, President
Michael Sheehan, Vice Pres
John Tolaro, Vice Pres
Reza Gheitantschi, Director
Tammy Long, Analyst
EMP: 200
SALES (est): 24.4MM Privately Held
WEB: www.revenuegroup.com
SIC: 7322 Collection agency, except real estate

(G-6388)
REXEL USA INC
Also Called: Gexpro
5605 Granger Rd (44131-1213)
PHONE 216 778-6400
Jared Myers, Program Mgr
Scott Geraghty, Manager
EMP: 30
SALES (corp-wide): 3MM Privately Held
SIC: 5063 Electrical apparatus & equipment
HQ: Rexel Usa, Inc.
14951 Dallas Pkwy
Dallas TX 75254

(G-6389)
RICCO ENTERPRISES INCORPORATED
6010 Fleet Ave Frnt Ste (44105-3498)
PHONE 216 883-7775
EMP: 28 EST: 1969

(G-6390)
SALES (est): 1.4MM Privately Held
SIC: 6512 8741 Nonresidential Building Operator Management Services

RICHARD E JACOBS GROUP LLC
25425 Center Ridge Rd (44145-4122)
PHONE 440 871-4800
Judson E Smith, CEO
Richard Jacobs, Partner
Thomas Schmitz, COO
James F Eppele, Exec VP
William R Hansen, Exec VP
EMP: 50
SQ FT: 120,000
SALES (est): 5.7MM Privately Held
WEB: www.richardejacobsgroup.com
SIC: 6512 Nonresidential building operators

(G-6391)
RICHARD L BOWEN & ASSOC INC (PA)
13000 Shaker Blvd Ste 1 (44120-2098)
PHONE 216 491-9300
Fax: 216 491-8053
Richard L Bowen, President
Melanie Lewis, Senior Partner
Carol Padvorac, Vice Pres
Alex Dasco, Project Mgr
Angie Latessa, Project Mgr
EMP: 73 EST: 1943
SQ FT: 18,000
SALES (est): 14.7MM Privately Held
SIC: 8712 8741 8711 Architectural engineering; construction management; civil engineering

(G-6392)
RICHARD R JENCEN & ASSOCIATES
2850 Euclid Ave (44115-2414)
PHONE 216 781-0131
Fax: 216 781-0134
Jerry Rothenberg, Partner
E R Kanuer, Partner
E R Knauer, Partner
Nick Zalany, Partner
Amber Price, Project Mgr
EMP: 25
SALES (est): 3.4MM Privately Held
WEB: www.jencen.com
SIC: 8712 Architectural services

(G-6393)
RICHARD TOMM MD
Also Called: Tomm, Richard MD
1611 S Green Rd Ste 213 (44121-4138)
PHONE 216 297-3060
Fax: 216 691-3523
Michael Sheahan, President
Charlene Sapola, Manager
EMP: 65
SQ FT: 8,200
SALES (est): 4.1MM Privately Held
SIC: 8011 Internal medicine, physician/surgeon

(G-6394)
RICOH USA INC
Also Called: Nightrider Overnite Copy Svc
1360 E 9th St Bsmt 1 (44114-1779)
PHONE 216 574-9111
Fax: 216 574-2511
Michael Perkins, Manager
EMP: 80
SALES (corp-wide): 17.8B Privately Held
WEB: www.ikon.com
SIC: 7334 Photocopying & duplicating services
HQ: Ricoh Usa, Inc.
70 Valley Stream Pkwy
Malvern PA 19355
610 296-8000

(G-6395)
RIDGE PLEASANT VALLEY INC (PA)
Also Called: Pleasantview Nursing Home
7377 Ridge Rd (44129-6602)
PHONE 440 845-0200
Fax: 440 845-8037
Ester Daskal, Vice Pres
Becky Taylor, VP Human Res
Zorica Lukic, Human Res Dir
Janice Carlson, Director
Thomas Mandat, Director
EMP: 190
SQ FT: 60,000
SALES (est): 10.6MM Privately Held
SIC: 8051 8052 Extended care facility; intermediate care facilities

(G-6396)
RIDGEPARK MEDICAL ASSOCIATES
7575 Northcliff Ave # 307 (44144-3266)
PHONE 216 749-8256
Fax: 216 398-5292
Bruce Resnik, President
Laura Kenny, Office Mgr
Terence Witham, Psychiatry
EMP: 30
SALES (est): 2.9MM Privately Held
SIC: 8071 Blood analysis laboratory

(G-6397)
RIPCHO STUDIO
7630 Lorain Ave (44102-4297)
PHONE 216 631-0664
Fax: 216 281-2534
Bill Ripcho, Owner
Aireonna McCall, Senior Mgr
Josh Jasko, Graphic Designe
EMP: 45 EST: 1941
SQ FT: 20,000
SALES (est): 2.3MM Privately Held
WEB: www.ripchostudio.com
SIC: 7221 Photographer, still or video

(G-6398)
RIVER RECYCLING ENTPS LTD (PA)
4195 Bradley Rd (44109-3779)
PHONE 216 459-2100
Fax: 440 749-8107
William A Grodin, President
Kenneth Behrens, Corp Secy
James A Grodin, Vice Pres
Tom Villwock, Controller
▼ EMP: 26 EST: 1920
SQ FT: 76,000
SALES: 45MM Privately Held
WEB: www.rivershell.com
SIC: 5093 Ferrous metal scrap & waste

(G-6399)
RIVERSIDE DRIVES INC
Also Called: Riverside Drives Disc
4509 W 160th St (44135-2627)
P.O. Box 35166 (44135-0166)
PHONE 216 362-1211
Fax: 216 362-6836
Bernard Dillemuth, President
Robert Goodwin, General Mgr
Kathleen Dillemuth, Corp Secy
David Dillemuth, Vice Pres
Kathy Straka, Purchasing
▲ EMP: 28
SQ FT: 7,500
SALES (est): 22MM Privately Held
WEB: www.riversidedrives.com
SIC: 5063 3699 Power transmission equipment, electric; electrical equipment & supplies

(G-6400)
RIVERSIDE PARTNERS LLC
Also Called: Riverside Company, The
50 Public Sq Ste 2900 (44113-2284)
PHONE 216 344-1040
Fax: 216 344-1330
Stewart Kohl, CEO
Charlie Rial, Principal
Garrett Monda, Assistant VP
Timothy Tengea, Engineer
Rahul Mohan, Finance Mgr
EMP: 45
SALES (corp-wide): 3.7B Privately Held
WEB: www.riversidecompany.com
SIC: 6211 Investment bankers
PA: Riverside Partners L.L.C.
45 Rockefeller Plz # 400
New York NY 10111
212 265-6575

(G-6401)
RMS AQUACULTURE INC (PA)
6629 Engle Rd Ste 108 (44130-7943)
PHONE 216 433-1340

GEOGRAPHIC SECTION

Cleveland - Cuyahoga County (G-6424)

Fax: 216 433-1342
Steven Zarzeczny, *President*
Mike Daversa, *Vice Pres*
Robert Knyszek, *Treasurer*
Kimberly Kaszar, *Controller*
Sung Ho Shin, *Admin Sec*
EMP: 35
SALES (est): 3.6MM **Privately Held**
WEB: www.rmsaquaculture.com
SIC: 5999 0742 Tropical fish; veterinary services, specialties

(G-6402)
ROBERT HALF INTERNATIONAL INC
Rhi Consulting
1001 Lakeside Ave E 1320a (44114-1142)
PHONE 216 621-4253
Fax: 216 621-0418
Nancy Ramirez, *Manager*
EMP: 40
SALES (corp-wide): 5.2B **Publicly Held**
WEB: www.rhii.com
SIC: 7363 Temporary help service
PA: Robert Half International Inc.
2884 Sand Hill Rd Ste 200
Menlo Park CA 94025
650 234-6000

(G-6403)
ROBERT L STARK ENTERPRISES INC
1350 W 3rd St (44113-1806)
PHONE 216 292-0242
Robert L Stark, *President*
Steven Rubin, *COO*
Ted Kramer, *Vice Pres*
Raymond Weiss Jr, *CFO*
Marty Whims, *Controller*
EMP: 50
SQ FT: 11,000
SALES (est): 13.8MM **Privately Held**
SIC: 6552 Land subdividers & developers, commercial

(G-6404)
ROBERT W BAIRD & CO INC
200 Public Sq Ste 1650 (44114-2301)
PHONE 216 737-7330
Fax: 216 737-7370
Brian Kurtz, *Branch Mgr*
Joseph Kraft, *Manager*
Steve Milvet, *Manager*
Kevin Alberty, *Advisor*
EMP: 25
SALES (corp-wide): 715.8MM **Privately Held**
WEB: www.rwbaird.com
SIC: 6211 Brokers, security
HQ: Robert W. Baird & Co. Incorporated
777 E Wisconsin Ave Fl 29
Milwaukee WI 53202
414 765-3500

(G-6405)
ROBERT WILEY MD INC
Also Called: Cleveland Eye Clinic
2740 Carnegie Ave (44115-2627)
PHONE 216 621-3211
Robert G Wiley MD, *President*
Thomas Chester Od, *Principal*
Linda Georgia, *Manager*
Shamik Bafna, *Director*
EMP: 25
SQ FT: 1,000
SALES (est): 2MM **Privately Held**
WEB: www.clevelandeyeclinic.com
SIC: 8011 Ophthalmologist

(G-6406)
ROCK AND ROLL OF FAME AND MUSE
1100 Rock And Roll Blvd (44114-1023)
PHONE 216 781-7625
Fax: 216 515-1971
Greg Harris, *CEO*
Frank Suloivan, *Chairman*
Jann Wenner, *Chairman*
Peggy Vanrumppe, *Counsel*
Caprice Bragg, *Vice Pres*
EMP: 100
SQ FT: 150,000
SALES: 36.4MM **Privately Held**
WEB: www.rockhall.com
SIC: 8412 7922 Museum; theatrical producers & services

(G-6407)
ROCKPORT UNITED METHODIST CH
Also Called: Rockport Early Childhood Ctr
3301 Wooster Rd (44116-4195)
PHONE 440 331-9434
Fax: 440 331-0304
Valerie Norris, *Principal*
Keith Greiveldinger, *Regl Sales Mgr*
Sarah Sanderson, *Sales Staff*
Virginia Going, *Exec Dir*
Karen Hay, *Admin Asst*
EMP: 28
SALES (est): 1MM **Privately Held**
SIC: 8351 Preschool center

(G-6408)
ROCKSIDE CENTER LTD
6055 Rockside Woods Blvd (44131-2301)
PHONE 216 447-0070
Neil Viny,
Wynn Gerber,
EMP: 40
SQ FT: 7,500
SALES: 1,000K **Privately Held**
SIC: 6512 Commercial & industrial building operation

(G-6409)
ROCKWOOD EQUITY PARTNERS LLC (PA)
3201 Entp Pkwy Ste 370 (44122)
PHONE 216 378-9326
Fax: 216 378-9322
Owen M Colligan,
Brett Keith,
EMP: 50
SALES (est): 13.3MM **Privately Held**
SIC: 6726 Investment offices

(G-6410)
ROETZEL AND ANDRESS A LEGAL P
1375 E 9th St Fl 10 (44114-1788)
PHONE 216 623-0150
John J Schriner Jr, *Principal*
Paul Heuerman, *Corp Counsel*
Jenn Kline, *Technology*
Kim Brabham, *Legal Staff*
Lynn Browning, *Legal Staff*
EMP: 50
SALES (corp-wide): 53.4MM **Privately Held**
WEB: www.ralaw.com
SIC: 8111 General practice law office
PA: Roetzel And Andress, A Legal Professional Association
222 S Main St Ste 400
Akron OH 44308
330 376-2700

(G-6411)
ROSBY BROTHERS INC
Also Called: Rosby Brothers Grnhse & Grnhse
42 E Schaaf Rd (44131-1202)
PHONE 216 351-0850
Fax: 216 351-0847
Michael P Rosby, *President*
EMP: 30
SQ FT: 60,000
SALES (est): 1.1MM **Privately Held**
SIC: 5992 0181 Flowers, fresh; plants, potted; ornamental nursery products

(G-6412)
ROSE MARY JOHANNA GRASSELL (PA)
Also Called: Cedar House
2346 W 14th St (44113-3613)
PHONE 216 481-4823
A M Pilla Dd, *Principal*
EMP: 113
SALES (est): 2.9MM **Privately Held**
SIC: 8361 8052 Rehabilitation center, residential; health care incidental; intermediate care facilities

(G-6413)
ROSE PROPERTIES INC
Also Called: Rose Metal Industries
1536 E 43rd St (44103-2310)
PHONE 216 881-6000
Fax: 216 881-3689
Robert Rose, *President*

Kara Aberts, *General Mgr*
Joe Schirra, *Materials Mgr*
Tom Meakin, *Warehouse Mgr*
Bryan Bridgett, *Controller*
EMP: 50
SQ FT: 10,000
SALES (est): 1.9MM **Privately Held**
SIC: 6512 Commercial & industrial building operation

(G-6414)
ROULSTON RESEARCH CORP
1350 Euclid Ave Ste 400 (44115-1847)
PHONE 216 431-3000
Scott D Roulston, *President*
EMP: 30
SQ FT: 35,000
SALES (est): 1.7MM
SALES (corp-wide): 6.1MM **Privately Held**
WEB: www.roulston.com
SIC: 6799 Commodity contract pool operators
PA: Roulston & Company Inc
1350 Euclid Ave Ste 400
Cleveland OH

(G-6415)
ROYAL APPLIANCE MFG CO (HQ)
Also Called: TTI Floor Care North America
7005 Cochran Rd (44139-4303)
PHONE 440 996-2000
Fax: 440 996-2003
Chris Gurreri, *President*
Gary Dieterich, *Senior VP*
Dave Brickner, *Vice Pres*
Richard C Farone, *Vice Pres*
Keith T Moone, *Vice Pres*
◆ **EMP:** 250 **EST:** 1905
SQ FT: 458,000
SALES (est): 359.5MM
SALES (corp-wide): 6B **Privately Held**
WEB: www.dirtdevil.com
SIC: 5064 Vacuum cleaners, household
PA: Techtronic Industries Company Limited
29/F Kowloon Commerce Ctr Twr 2
Kwai Chung NT
240 268-88

(G-6416)
ROYAL MANOR HEALTH CARE INC (PA)
18810 Harvard Ave (44122-6848)
PHONE 216 752-3600
Abraham Schwartz, *President*
Dan Zawadzki, *COO*
Sally Schwartz, *Treasurer*
Dolores Wallace, *VP Mktg*
Josephine Deluca, *Director*
EMP: 50
SALES (est): 6.3MM **Privately Held**
SIC: 8051 8052 Skilled nursing care facilities; intermediate care facilities

(G-6417)
ROYAL OAK NRSING RHBLTTION CTR
Also Called: Royal Manor Homes
6973 Pearl Rd (44130-7831)
PHONE 440 884-9191
Andrea Pankhurst, *Personnel Exec*
Margaret Halas, *Director*
Gregory Davis, *Director*
EMP: 100
SALES (est): 4.7MM **Privately Held**
SIC: 8051 Convalescent home with continuous nursing care

(G-6418)
ROYAL REDEEMER LUTHERAN CHURCH
Also Called: Royal Redeemer Lutheran School
11680 Royalton Rd (44133-4461)
PHONE 440 237-7958
Fax: 440 237-6992
James Martin, *Pastor*
EMP: 40
SQ FT: 69,342
SALES (est): 810K **Privately Held**
SIC: 8661 8351 8211 Lutheran Church; preschool center; kindergarten

(G-6419)
ROYALTON FINANCIAL GROUP
Also Called: Gaydosh Associates
13374 Ridge Rd Ste 1 (44133-3803)
PHONE 440 582-3020
Fax: 440 582-3422
Edward Gaydosh, *President*
James E Gaydosh, *Vice Pres*
EMP: 30
SQ FT: 11,000
SALES (est): 2.3MM **Privately Held**
SIC: 8742 6411 Financial consultant; insurance agents, brokers & service

(G-6420)
RPC ELECTRONICS INC
Silicon Turnkey Express
749 Miner Rd Ste 4 (44143-2137)
PHONE 877 522-7927
Art Czarnitzki, *Sales Staff*
Ira Dryer, *Branch Mgr*
EMP: 31
SALES (corp-wide): 23.2MM **Privately Held**
WEB: www.rpcelectronics.com
SIC: 5064 Electrical appliances, television & radio
PA: Rpc Electronics, Inc.
749 Miner Rd
Highland Heights OH 44143
440 461-4700

(G-6421)
RSM US LLP
1001 Lakeside Ave E # 200 (44114-1158)
PHONE 216 523-1900
Penelope A Vitantonio, *Sales Executive*
John Balick, *Branch Mgr*
Kristina Fronczek, *Supervisor*
Loraine A Kalic, *Director*
Christine S Klaiber, *Director*
EMP: 125
SALES (corp-wide): 1.8B **Privately Held**
SIC: 8721 Accounting, auditing & bookkeeping; certified public accountant
PA: Rsm Us Llp
1 S Wacker Dr Ste 800
Chicago IL 60606
312 384-6000

(G-6422)
RUSSELL WEISMAN JR MD
11100 Euclid Ave (44106-1716)
PHONE 216 844-3127
Russell Jr Weisman, *Owner*
Patricia Hines, *Business Mgr*
John Thomas, *Director*
Ann Dragon, *Nurse*
EMP: 130
SALES (est): 17.8MM **Privately Held**
SIC: 8011 Physicians' office, including specialists

(G-6423)
RWK SERVICES INC (PA)
Also Called: Ductbreeze
4700 Rockside Rd Ste 330 (44131-2151)
PHONE 440 526-2144
William Wachs, *President*
Kerri Wachs, *Shareholder*
EMP: 29
SQ FT: 2,000
SALES (est): 2.8MM **Privately Held**
WEB: www.rwkservices.com
SIC: 7349 Janitorial service, contract basis; cleaning service, industrial or commercial

(G-6424)
RYDER TRUCK RENTAL INC
11250 Brookpark Rd (44130-1178)
PHONE 216 433-4700
Irisha Newton, *Human Resources*
James Yarwood, *Manager*
Paul Popely, *Manager*
Stuart Suls, *Manager*
Dewayne Watkins, *Manager*
EMP: 150
SQ FT: 15,240
SALES (corp-wide): 7.3B **Publicly Held**
SIC: 7513 Truck rental, without drivers
HQ: Ryder Truck Rental, Inc.
11690 Nw 105th St
Medley FL 33178
305 500-3726

(PA)=Parent Co (HQ)=Headquarters (DH)=Div Headquarters
◆ = New Business established in last 2 years

Cleveland - Cuyahoga County (G-6425)

(G-6425)
S & S INC
21300 Saint Clair Ave (44117-1024)
PHONE..................216 383-1880
Fax: 216 383-9597
Paul Nared, *President*
Nancy Kunes, *Vice Pres*
Patrick Hahn, *Portfolio Mgr*
Erin Dodson, *Sales Staff*
Don Dameiko, *Manager*
EMP: 25 **EST:** 1953
SQ FT: 17,000
SALES: 10.8MM **Privately Held**
WEB: www.sspackaging.com
SIC: 5199 5084 7699 Packaging materials; packaging machinery & equipment; industrial machinery & equipment repair

(G-6426)
S B MORABITO TRUCKING INC
3560 E 55th St (44105-1126)
PHONE..................216 441-3070
Fax: 216 441-6355
Sebastian Morabito Jr, *President*
Tony Morabito, *Vice Pres*
EMP: 100 **EST:** 1956
SQ FT: 20,000
SALES (est): 12MM **Privately Held**
WEB: www.sbmtruck.com
SIC: 4212 Local trucking, without storage

(G-6427)
S R RESTAURANT CORP
Also Called: Rascal House Pizza
1836 Euclid Ave Ste 800 (44115-2234)
PHONE..................216 781-6784
Mike Frangos, *President*
Fouly Frangos, *Vice Pres*
EMP: 50
SQ FT: 25,000
SALES (est): 2.4MM **Privately Held**
WEB: www.srrestaurant.com
SIC: 8641 Bars & restaurants, members only

(G-6428)
S S KEMP & COMPANY (DH)
Also Called: Trimark Ss Kemp
4567 Willow Pkwy (44125-1052)
PHONE..................216 271-7062
Fax: 216 271-5200
Mark Fishman, *President*
Howard Fishman, *Chairman*
Steven Fishman, *Vice Pres*
Brendan Ward, *Opers Mgr*
Kelsey Rankin, *Buyer*
EMP: 132
SQ FT: 70,000
SALES (est): 97.2MM
SALES (corp-wide): 6.7B **Privately Held**
WEB: www.sskemp.com
SIC: 5046 Commercial cooking & food service equipment
HQ: Trimark Usa, Llc
505 Collins St
Attleboro MA 02703
508 399-2400

(G-6429)
S&P DATA OHIO LLC
1500 W 3rd St Ste 130 (44113-1447)
PHONE..................216 965-0018
Dan Plashkes, *CEO*
Daniel Bemis, *President*
Kevin Lacomb, *Senior VP*
Mark Kulow, *Opers Mgr*
Brinda Joiner, *Human Res Mgr*
EMP: 400
SALES (est): 39.4MM **Privately Held**
SIC: 7389 Telemarketing services

(G-6430)
SABER HEALTHCARE GROUP LLC
Also Called: Crawford Manor Healthcare Ctr
1802 Crawford Rd (44106-2030)
PHONE..................216 795-5710
Cory Parish, *Administration*
EMP: 36
SALES (corp-wide): 68.5MM **Privately Held**
SIC: 8051 Skilled nursing care facilities
PA: Saber Healthcare Group, L.L.C.
26691 Richmond Rd Frnt
Bedford OH 44146
216 292-5706

(G-6431)
SABRY HOSPITAL
Also Called: Fairview Hospital
18101 Lorain Ave (44111-5612)
PHONE..................216 476-7052
Fax: 216 476-6967
Sabry Ayad, *Chairman*
EMP: 25 **EST:** 1970
SALES (est): 713.4K **Privately Held**
SIC: 8011 Anesthesiologist

(G-6432)
SAFEGARD BCKGRUND SCRENING LLC
3711 Chester Ave (44114-4623)
PHONE..................216 370-7345
Lana Iklodi, *Opers Mgr*
Norman James, *Accounts Exec*
Neil J Adelman,
EMP: 200
SALES (est): 5.1MM **Privately Held**
SIC: 7361 Employment agencies

(G-6433)
SAFEGUARD PROPERTIES LLC (HQ)
7887 Safeguard Cir (44125-5742)
PHONE..................216 739-2900
Alan Jaffa, *CEO*
Robert Klein, *Ch of Bd*
Michael Greenbaum, *VP Opers*
George Pilla, *VP Opers*
William Spellman, *Project Mgr*
EMP: 800
SQ FT: 33,600
SALES (est): 188.6MM
SALES (corp-wide): 242.1MM **Privately Held**
SIC: 8741 7382 7381 Management services; security systems services; detective & armored car services
PA: Safeguard Properties Management, Llc
7887 Hub Pkwy
Cleveland OH 44125
216 739-2900

(G-6434)
SAFEGUARD PROPERTIES MGT LLC (PA)
7887 Hub Pkwy (44125)
PHONE..................216 739-2900
Alan Jaffa, *CEO*
Dennis Howe, *Controller*
Oscar Nicholson, *Auditing Mgr*
Scott Heller, *Manager*
John Patriarche, *Manager*
EMP: 700
SALES (est): 242.1MM **Privately Held**
SIC: 1522 Residential construction; remodeling, multi-family dwellings

(G-6435)
SAFELITE FULFILLMENT INC
Also Called: Safelite Autoglass
6050 Towpath Dr Ste A (44125-4276)
PHONE..................216 475-7781
Fax: 216 643-1981
Randy George, *Manager*
EMP: 35
SALES (corp-wide): 3.1B **Privately Held**
WEB: www.belronus.com
SIC: 7536 4225 Automotive glass replacement shops; general warehousing & storage
HQ: Safelite Fulfillment, Inc.
7400 Safelite Way
Columbus OH 43235
614 210-9747

(G-6436)
SAINT FRANCIS DE SALES CHURCH
3434 George Ave (44134-2904)
PHONE..................440 884-2319
Rev Robert L Hoban, *Pastor*
EMP: 32
SALES (est): 754.9K **Privately Held**
SIC: 8661 6061 Catholic Church; federal credit unions

(G-6437)
SALEM MEDIA GROUP INC
Also Called: W F H M - F M 95.5
4 Summit Park Dr Ste 150 (44131-6921)
PHONE..................216 901-0921
Tim Vaughan, *Sales Mgr*
Mark Jaycox, *Manager*
EMP: 100
SALES (corp-wide): 263.7MM **Publicly Held**
WEB: www.srnradio.com
SIC: 4832 Radio broadcasting stations
PA: Salem Media Group, Inc.
4880 Santa Rosa Rd
Camarillo CA 93012
805 987-0400

(G-6438)
SALS HEATING AND COOLING INC
11701 Royalton Rd (44133-4210)
PHONE..................216 676-4949
Fax: 440 582-4995
Salvatore C Sidoti, *President*
Elaine Sidoti, *Vice Pres*
EMP: 25
SQ FT: 6,435
SALES (est): 5.4MM **Privately Held**
SIC: 1711 Warm air heating & air conditioning contractor

(G-6439)
SALVAGEDATA RECOVERY LLC (PA)
43 Alpha Park (44143-2202)
PHONE..................914 600-2434
Ralph Pierre, *President*
Avion McErgor, *Opers Mgr*
Caren McLeod, *Office Mgr*
Laura Taileur, *Manager*
EMP: 30
SQ FT: 6,000
SALES (est): 2.9MM **Privately Held**
WEB: www.salvagedata.com
SIC: 7375 Information retrieval services

(G-6440)
SALVATION ARMY
2507 E 22nd St (44115-3202)
P.O. Box 5847 (44101-0847)
PHONE..................216 861-8185
Fax: 216 861-2383
Ricardo Fernandez, *Manager*
EMP: 85
SQ FT: 28,928
SALES (corp-wide): 4.3B **Privately Held**
WEB: www.salvationarmy-usaeast.org
SIC: 8661 8641 8322 Religious organizations; civic social & fraternal associations; individual & family services
HQ: The Salvation Army
440 W Nyack Rd Ofc
West Nyack NY 10994
845 620-7200

(G-6441)
SAM-TOM INC
Also Called: Royce Security Services
3740 Euclid Ave Ste 102 (44115-2228)
PHONE..................216 426-7752
Fax: 216 426-7757
Joseph W Conley, *President*
EMP: 200
SQ FT: 2,000
SALES (est): 3.3MM **Privately Held**
SIC: 7381 Security guard service

(G-6442)
SAMSEL ROPE & MARINE SUPPLY CO (PA)
Also Called: Samsel Supply Company
1285 Old River Rd Uppr (44113-1279)
PHONE..................216 241-0333
Fax: 216 241-3426
Kathleen A Petrick, *President*
Larry E Nauth, *Principal*
Grace F Wilcox, *Principal*
Rosemary Woidke, *Principal*
F Michael Samsel, *Exec VP*
▲ **EMP:** 33
SQ FT: 100,000
SALES (est): 4.4MM **Privately Held**
WEB: www.samselsupply.com
SIC: 2394 5051 4959 5085 Canvas & related products; rope, wire (not insulated); miscellaneous nonferrous products; environmental cleanup services; industrial supplies; industrial tools; manufactured hardware (general); narrow fabric mills

(G-6443)
SANICO INC
7601 First Pl Ste 12 (44146-6702)
PHONE..................440 439-5686
Fax: 440 439-4332
Michael T Pallaise, *President*
M Terry Pallaise, *President*
EMP: 70
SQ FT: 2,000
SALES (est): 3.5MM **Privately Held**
WEB: www.saniko.com.pl
SIC: 6512 Nonresidential building operators

(G-6444)
SAW SERVICE AND SUPPLY COMPANY
11925 Zelis Rd (44135-4692)
PHONE..................216 252-5600
Fax: 216 252-7476
Robert Belock, *President*
Linda Belock, *Asst Sec*
▲ **EMP:** 50 **EST:** 1953
SQ FT: 30,000
SALES (est): 21.6MM **Privately Held**
WEB: www.sawservicesupply.com
SIC: 5072 7699 Power tools & accessories; power tool repair

(G-6445)
SAXON HOUSE CONDO
3167 Linden Rd (44116-4170)
PHONE..................440 333-8675
Dorothy O'Nill, *President*
EMP: 65
SALES (est): 529.8K **Privately Held**
SIC: 8641 Condominium association

(G-6446)
SCHINDLER ELEVATOR CORPORATION
Also Called: Millar Elevator Service
1100 E 55th St (44103-1027)
PHONE..................216 391-8600
Fax: 216 391-5006
Gerald Plezner, *Manager*
EMP: 60
SALES (corp-wide): 9.5B **Privately Held**
WEB: www.us.schindler.com
SIC: 7699 Elevators: inspection, service & repair
HQ: Schindler Elevator Corporation
20 Whippany Rd
Morristown NJ 07960
973 397-6500

(G-6447)
SCHINDLER ELEVATOR CORPORATION
18013 Clvlnd Pkw Dr 140 (44135)
PHONE..................216 370-9524
Scott Spieker, *Opers Mgr*
Miggy Torres, *Marketing Staff*
Jeff Davis, *Manager*
Nancy Bursa, *Manager*
EMP: 100
SALES (corp-wide): 9.5B **Privately Held**
WEB: www.us.schindler.com
SIC: 1796 Elevator installation & conversion
HQ: Schindler Elevator Corporation
20 Whippany Rd
Morristown NJ 07960
973 397-6500

(G-6448)
SCHNEIDER ELC SYSTEMS USA INC
6745 Engle Rd Ste 205 (44130-7993)
PHONE..................440 234-3900
John Soulliere, *General Mgr*
John Krause, *Manager*
EMP: 30
SALES (corp-wide): 241K **Privately Held**
WEB: www.foxboro.com
SIC: 8711 Industrial engineers
HQ: Schneider Electric Systems Usa, Inc.
38 Neponset Ave
Foxboro MA 02035
508 543-8750

GEOGRAPHIC SECTION
Cleveland - Cuyahoga County (G-6471)

(G-6449)
SCHOMER GLAUS PYLE
Also Called: Gpd Group
5595 Transportation Blvd (44125-5379)
PHONE.................216 518-5544
Stephen Schreiber, *Project Mgr*
Joseph Ciuni, *Branch Mgr*
Ed Franks, *Manager*
EMP: 50
SALES (corp-wide): 93.9MM Privately Held
SIC: 8711 8712 Civil engineering; architectural services
PA: Glaus, Pyle, Schomer, Burns & Dehaven, Inc.
520 S Main St Ste 2531
Akron OH 44311
330 572-2100

(G-6450)
SCHUSTERS GREENHOUSE LTD
9165 Columbia Rd (44138-2426)
PHONE.................440 235-2440
Fax: 440 235-2229
David Schuster, *Partner*
EMP: 25
SALES (est): 2.2MM Privately Held
WEB: www.schustersgreenhouse.com
SIC: 0181 Bedding plants, growing of; flowers: grown under cover (e.g. greenhouse production); foliage, growing of

(G-6451)
SCHWEIZER DIPPLE INC
7227 Division St (44146-5405)
PHONE.................440 786-8090
Fax: 440 786-8099
Michael J Kelley, *President*
Clark Dennis, *Exec VP*
Dennis J Clark, *Vice Pres*
James G Dwyer, *Vice Pres*
Peter A McGrogan, *Vice Pres*
EMP: 55
SQ FT: 27,000
SALES (est): 12.3MM
SALES (corp-wide): 42.6MM Privately Held
WEB: www.schweizer-dipple.com
SIC: 1711 3496 3444 3443 Mechanical contractor; miscellaneous fabricated wire products; sheet metalwork; fabricated plate work (boiler shop)
PA: Kelley Steel Erectors, Inc.
7220 Division St
Cleveland OH 44146
440 232-1573

(G-6452)
SCOTT FETZER COMPANY
Adalet
4801 W 150th St (44135-3301)
PHONE.................216 267-9000
Fax: 216 267-1681
Rob Klein, *Area Mgr*
Gene Shuster, *VP Opers*
Cherie Kmetz, *Purch Dir*
Janet Kelly, *Senior Buyer*
Keith Binnie, *Buyer*
EMP: 150
SALES (corp-wide): 242.1B Publicly Held
WEB: www.adalet.com
SIC: 5063 3469 3357 3613 Wire & cable; metal stampings; nonferrous wiredrawing & insulating; control panels, electric; metal housings, enclosures, casings & other containers
HQ: The Scott Fetzer Company
28800 Clemens Rd
Westlake OH 44145
440 892-3000

(G-6453)
SCOTT FETZER FINANCIAL GROUP
Also Called: Scott Fetzer Co
28800 Clemens Rd (44145-1197)
PHONE.................440 892-3000
Ken Semelberger, *CEO*
John Gretta, *Asst Treas*
EMP: 40
SALES (est): 3.9MM
SALES (corp-wide): 242.1B Publicly Held
WEB: www.scottfetzer.com
SIC: 6153 Short-term business credit

HQ: The Scott Fetzer Company
28800 Clemens Rd
Westlake OH 44145
440 892-3000

(G-6454)
SCRAP YARD LLC
Also Called: Cleveland Scrap
15000 Miles Ave (44128-2370)
PHONE.................216 271-5825
Fax: 216 271-5859
Allen Youngman, *President*
Jacobe Youngman, *Vice Pres*
Patrice Glause, *Controller*
Rob Petrilla, *Manager*
EMP: 25
SALES (est): 2.7MM Privately Held
SIC: 5093 Metal scrap & waste materials

(G-6455)
SCRIBES & SCRBBLR CHLD DEV CTR
14101 Uhlin Dr (44130-5604)
PHONE.................440 884-5437
Fax: 440 884-3009
Dennis Cox, *President*
Carol Cox, *Vice Pres*
EMP: 34
SQ FT: 31,000
SALES (est): 1MM Privately Held
SIC: 8351 7032 Nursery school; summer camp, except day & sports instructional

(G-6456)
SDC UNVRSITY CIR DEVELOPER LLC
Also Called: Courtyard By Marriott
2021 Cornell Rd (44106-3808)
PHONE.................216 791-5333
Dena Heinlein,
EMP: 99 EST: 2010
SALES (est): 2.7MM Privately Held
SIC: 7011 Hotels & motels

(G-6457)
SEAGATE HOSPITALITY GROUP LLC
Also Called: Holiday Inn
4181 W 150th St (44135-1303)
PHONE.................216 252-7700
Todd Middleton, *Branch Mgr*
Mackenzie Grill, *Manager*
EMP: 25
SALES (corp-wide): 14.4MM Privately Held
SIC: 7011 5812 Hotels; eating places
PA: Seagate Hospitality Group, Llc
400 Linden Oaks Ste 120
Rochester NY 14625
585 419-4000

(G-6458)
SEAMANS SERVICES
Also Called: Cleaveland Seaman's Service
1050 W 3rd St (44114-1002)
PHONE.................216 621-4107
Al Oberst, *President*
Homer Cook, *Vice Pres*
Donald Bisesi, *Treasurer*
EMP: 30
SALES (est): 577.4K Privately Held
SIC: 8322 Individual & family services

(G-6459)
SEARS ROEBUCK AND CO
Also Called: Sears Auto Center
17271 Southpark Ctr (44136-9311)
PHONE.................440 846-3595
Fax: 440 846-3539
Rick Goolie, *Manager*
Rebecca Thomas, *Manager*
EMP: 150
SALES (corp-wide): 16.7B Publicly Held
SIC: 7549 Automotive maintenance services
HQ: Sears, Roebuck And Co.
3333 Beverly Rd
Hoffman Estates IL 60179
847 286-2500

(G-6460)
SECURESTATE LLC
23340 Miles Rd (44128-5491)
PHONE.................216 927-0115
Fax: 216 927-0119

Ken Stasiak, *CEO*
Stephen Marchewitz, *President*
Sue Satink, *CFO*
Tom Eston, *Manager*
Eric Mone, *Sr Consultant*
EMP: 28 EST: 2001
SQ FT: 5,500
SALES (est): 5.1MM Privately Held
WEB: www.securestate.net
SIC: 7382 Security systems services

(G-6461)
SECURITAS SEC SVCS USA INC
3747 Euclid Ave (44115-2501)
PHONE.................216 431-3139
Fax: 216 431-3025
Cynthia Pacyga, *Branch Mgr*
EMP: 182
SALES (corp-wide): 9.5B Privately Held
SIC: 7381 Security guard service
HQ: Securitas Security Services Usa, Inc.
9 Campus Dr
Parsippany NJ 07054
973 267-5300

(G-6462)
SECURITAS SEC SVCS USA INC
Also Called: East Coast Region
12000 Snow Rd Ste 5 (44130-9314)
PHONE.................440 887-6800
AMI Hickman, *Vice Pres*
Scott Fry, *Branch Mgr*
Marion Olminsky, *Branch Mgr*
Paul Thomas, *Branch Mgr*
Maureen Budnie, *Manager*
EMP: 630
SALES (corp-wide): 9.5B Privately Held
WEB: www.securitasinc.com
SIC: 7381 Security guard service
HQ: Securitas Security Services Usa, Inc.
9 Campus Dr
Parsippany NJ 07054
973 267-5300

(G-6463)
SECURITAS SEC SVCS USA INC
Also Called: Shared Services
9885 Rockside Rd Ste 155 (44125-6272)
PHONE.................216 503-2021
Nick Riggs, *President*
Laura Svasta, *Branch Mgr*
Keith Lucas, *Branch Mgr*
Harold Wright, *Branch Mgr*
EMP: 116
SALES (corp-wide): 9.5B Privately Held
WEB: www.securitasinc.com
SIC: 7381 Security guard service
HQ: Securitas Security Services Usa, Inc.
9 Campus Dr
Parsippany NJ 07054
973 267-5300

(G-6464)
SEDLAK MANAGEMENT CONS INC
22901 Millcreek Blvd # 600 (44122-5728)
PHONE.................216 206-4700
Jeffrey B Graves, *President*
Joseph A Sedlak, *Chairman*
Ned N Sedlak, *Exec VP*
Jeff Mueller, *Vice Pres*
Patrick S Sedlak, *Vice Pres*
EMP: 32 EST: 1958
SQ FT: 18,500
SALES: 6.1MM Privately Held
WEB: www.jasedlak.com
SIC: 8742 7374 Planning consultant; industrial consultant; automation & robotics consultant; management information systems consultant; data processing & preparation

(G-6465)
SEELEY SVDGE EBERT GOURASH LPA
26600 Detroit Rd Fl 3 (44145-2395)
PHONE.................216 566-8200
Gregory Seeley, *Partner*
Gary Ebert, *Partner*
Daniel Gourash, *Partner*
Patrick J McIntyre, *Partner*
Keith Savidge, *Partner*
EMP: 30
SQ FT: 15,200

SALES (est): 4.7MM Privately Held
WEB: www.sse-law.com
SIC: 8111 General practice attorney, lawyer

(G-6466)
SELECT HOTELS GROUP LLC
Also Called: Hyatt Pl Clveland/Independence
6025 Jefferson Dr (44131-2145)
PHONE.................216 328-1060
Kevin Hastings, *Branch Mgr*
Barbara Yeater, *Manager*
EMP: 50
SALES (corp-wide): 4.6B Publicly Held
WEB: www.amerisuites.com
SIC: 7011 Hotels
HQ: Select Hotels Group, L.L.C.
71 S Wacker Dr
Chicago IL 60606
312 750-1234

(G-6467)
SELECT MEDICAL CORPORATION
Also Called: Kindred Hospital - Cleveland
11900 Fairhill Rd Ste 100 (44120-1063)
PHONE.................216 983-8030
Janet Mays, *Human Res Dir*
Despina Papouras, *Manager*
EMP: 218
SALES (corp-wide): 3.7B Publicly Held
SIC: 8062 General medical & surgical hospitals
HQ: Select Medical Corporation
4714 Gettysburg Rd
Mechanicsburg PA 17055
717 972-1100

(G-6468)
SELF-FUNDED PLANS INC (PA)
1432 Hamilton Ave (44114-1146)
PHONE.................216 566-1455
Fax: 216 566-1505
Donna B Luby, *President*
John Haines, *Vice Pres*
Marsha A Phillips, *Vice Pres*
Bredan Nugent, *Sales Mgr*
William Gorton, *Marketing Staff*
EMP: 45 EST: 1980
SQ FT: 25,000
SALES (est): 12.6MM Privately Held
WEB: www.sfpi.com
SIC: 6411 Insurance agents

(G-6469)
SELMAN & COMPANY (PA)
6110 Parkland Blvd (44124-4187)
PHONE.................440 646-9336
Fax: 440 646-9339
David Selman, *President*
John L Selman, *Chairman*
Cheryl M Ahmad, *Vice Pres*
Cheryl Ahmad, *Vice Pres*
Elizabeth M Boettcher, *Vice Pres*
EMP: 75
SQ FT: 26,000
SALES (est): 30.1MM Privately Held
WEB: www.sel-co.com
SIC: 6411 Insurance agents

(G-6470)
SENIOR OUTREACH SERVICES
Also Called: S.O.S.
2390 E 79th St (44104-2161)
P.O. Box 606177 (44106-0677)
PHONE.................216 421-6900
Ken Strother, *President*
Delores Lynch, *Director*
EMP: 50
SQ FT: 3,000
SALES: 1.2MM Privately Held
SIC: 8322 4119 Old age assistance; meal delivery program; local passenger transportation

(G-6471)
SERVICE CORPS RETIRED EXECS
Also Called: S C O R E
1350 Euclid Ave Ste 216 (44115-1815)
PHONE.................216 522-4194
Fax: 216 522-4844
Ron Grossman, *Treasurer*
Anita Khayat, *Branch Mgr*
EMP: 50

Cleveland - Cuyahoga County (G-6472)

SALES (corp-wide): 13.1MM **Privately Held**
WEB: www.score199.mv.com
SIC: 8611 Business associations
PA: Service Corps Of Retired Executives Association
1175 Herndon Pkwy Ste 900
Herndon VA 20170
703 487-3612

(G-6472)
SERVISAIR LLC (DH)
Also Called: Global Ground
5851 Cargo Rd (44135-3111)
P.O. Box 811150 (44181-1150)
PHONE.................................216 267-9910
Fax: 216 265-8140
Michael J Hancock, *President*
Maurice Nelson, *General Mgr*
Douglas Mc Connell, *Exec VP*
Timothy R Archer, *Senior VP*
Wes A Bement, *Senior VP*
EMP: 200
SQ FT: 10,000
SALES (est): 27.8MM **Privately Held**
SIC: 4581 Airport terminal services
HQ: Servisair Usa & Carribean
6065 Nw 18th St Bldg 716d
Miami FL 33126
305 262-4059

(G-6473)
SGT INC
21000 Brookpark Rd (44135-3127)
PHONE.................................216 433-3982
Bruce Macgregor, *Manager*
Dale Smejkal, *Technical Staff*
EMP: 348 **Privately Held**
WEB: www.sgt-inc.com
SIC: 8711 Engineering services
PA: Sgt, Inc.
7701 Greenbelt Rd Ste 400
Greenbelt MD 20770

(G-6474)
SHAIAS PARKING INC
812 Huron Rd E Ste 701 (44115-1165)
PHONE.................................216 621-0328
Fax: 216 621-2612
Victor Shaia, *President*
Tony Shala, *Manager*
EMP: 25
SQ FT: 1,000
SALES (est): 842.9K **Privately Held**
SIC: 7521 Parking lots

(G-6475)
SHAKER HOUSE
3700 Northfield Rd Ste 3 (44122-5240)
PHONE.................................216 991-6000
Robert Nash, *Mayor*
Craig Koslan, *Vice Pres*
EMP: 70
SQ FT: 7,897
SALES (est): 800K **Privately Held**
SIC: 7011 6513 Hotels; apartment building operators

(G-6476)
SHAKER VALLEY FOODS INC
3304 W 67th Pl (44102-5243)
PHONE.................................216 961-8600
Fax: 216 961-8077
Dean Comber, *President*
Jeff Koutris, *Purch Mgr*
EMP: 40
SQ FT: 30,000
SALES (est): 21.6MM **Privately Held**
WEB: www.shakervalleyfoods.com
SIC: 5141 2011 Food brokers; meat packing plants

(G-6477)
SHAPIRO SHAPIRO & SHAPIRO
Also Called: Kahan & Kahan
4469 Renaissance Pkwy (44128-5754)
PHONE.................................216 927-2030
Fax: 216 763-2620
Alan Shapiro, *President*
Mark Frank, *Personal Injury*
Wandra Evans, *Legal Staff*
EMP: 25
SALES (est): 2MM **Privately Held**
SIC: 8011 Occupational & industrial specialist, physician/surgeon

(G-6478)
SHIPPERS CONSOLIDATED DIST
Also Called: Shippers Cartage & Dist
1840 Carter Rd (44113-2402)
PHONE.................................216 579-9303
Fax: 216 566-0075
Robert Mangini, *President*
Charles H Glazer, *Corp Secy*
Mike Plnton, *Officer*
EMP: 41
SQ FT: 25,000
SALES (est): 4.6MM **Privately Held**
SIC: 4214 4213 Local trucking with storage; trucking, except local

(G-6479)
SHOREBY CLUB INC
40 Shoreby Dr (44108-1191)
PHONE.................................216 851-2587
Chris Mancusho, *General Mgr*
Erin Petre, *Manager*
Kimberly Coleman, *Admin Asst*
EMP: 60
SALES (est): 2.8MM **Privately Held**
SIC: 8699 5812 Personal interest organization; restaurant, family: independent

(G-6480)
SIEMENS INDUSTRY INC
Also Called: Siemens Fire Safety
5350 Trnsp Blvd Ste 9 (44125)
PHONE.................................216 365-7030
Fax: 216 332-7361
Richard Thomas, *Div Sub Head*
Mike McMichael, *Manager*
EMP: 60
SALES (corp-wide): 97.7B **Privately Held**
WEB: www.sibt.com
SIC: 5075 Warm air heating & air conditioning
HQ: Siemens Industry, Inc.
100 Technology Dr
Alpharetta GA 30005
770 740-3000

(G-6481)
SIEVERS SECURITY SYSTEMS INC (PA)
18210 Saint Clair Ave (44110-2626)
PHONE.................................216 383-1234
Michael Sievers, *President*
James Sievers, *Vice Pres*
Amy Sievers, *Treasurer*
Rob Sievers, *Admin Sec*
EMP: 30
SQ FT: 4,000
SALES (est): 14.4MM **Privately Held**
WEB: www.sieverssecurity.com
SIC: 5063 Burglar alarm systems

(G-6482)
SIGNAL PRODUCTIONS INC
1267 W 9th St (44113-1064)
PHONE.................................323 382-0000
Tyler Davidson, *Principal*
EMP: 50
SALES (est): 1MM **Privately Held**
SIC: 7819 Services allied to motion pictures

(G-6483)
SINGLETON HEALTH CARE CENTER
1867 E 82nd St (44103-4263)
PHONE.................................216 231-0076
Fax: 216 231-1761
Garth Ireland, *President*
Joseph Ireland, *Owner*
Channa Ireland, *Vice Pres*
Mary Ireland, *Vice Pres*
EMP: 50 EST: 1960
SQ FT: 15,000
SALES (est): 3.8MM **Privately Held**
SIC: 8052 8051 Personal care facility; skilled nursing care facilities

(G-6484)
SKODA MINOTTI HOLDINGS LLC (PA)
Also Called: Mayfield Village
6685 Beta Dr (44143-2320)
PHONE.................................440 449-6800
Gregory J Skoda, *Ch of Bd*
Michael Minotti, *President*
Arthur G Merriman, *Managing Prtnr*
Patrick Carney, *Vice Pres*
Robert E Coode, *Vice Pres*
EMP: 27
SQ FT: 25,939
SALES (est): 21.5MM **Privately Held**
WEB: www.skodaminotti.com
SIC: 7291 Tax return preparation services

(G-6485)
SKYE DEVELOPMENT COMPANY LLC
25001 Emery Rd Ste 420 (44128-5626)
PHONE.................................216 223-0160
Bradley N Sanders, *President*
Ken Adams, *Vice Pres*
Valerie Cotner, *Vice Pres*
Ben Lehrer, *Vice Pres*
Chris Wichmann, *Vice Pres*
EMP: 30
SALES (est): 1.9MM **Privately Held**
SIC: 6531 Real estate agents & managers

(G-6486)
SKYLIGHT FINANCIAL GROUP LLC
2012 W 25th St Ste 900 (44113-4124)
PHONE.................................216 621-5680
Pam Smith, *Vice Pres*
Mark Owens, *Mktg Dir*
Erin Stidham, *Manager*
Cathy Prather, *Agent*
Joseph Paulsey, *Info Tech Dir*
EMP: 31
SALES (est): 2.9MM **Privately Held**
SIC: 7389 Financial services

(G-6487)
SKYLINE CLVLAND RNAISSANCE LLC
Also Called: Renaissance Cleveland Hotel
24 Public Sq (44113-2213)
PHONE.................................216 696-5600
Fax: 216 696-7146
Michael Snegd, *President*
Steve Groppe, *General Mgr*
Joseph Kendall, *Engineer*
Patricia Barrett, *Human Res Dir*
Paul Kobayashi, *Sales Mgr*
EMP: 99 EST: 2015
SQ FT: 873,000
SALES (est): 485.2K **Privately Held**
SIC: 7011 Hotels

(G-6488)
SLAVIC VILLAGE DEVELOPMENT
5620 Broadway Ave Uppr Ste 200 (44127-1762)
PHONE.................................216 429-1182
Christopher Alvarado, *Principal*
Michael Geregach, *Principal*
Jim Oryl, *Safety Dir*
Andrew Kinney, *Marketing Mgr*
Ben Campbell, *Property Mgr*
EMP: 28
SALES (est): 1.8MM **Privately Held**
SIC: 6552 Land subdividers & developers, commercial

(G-6489)
SLAWSON EQUIPMENT CO INC
7851 Freeway Cir (44130-6308)
PHONE.................................216 391-7263
Thomas H Mc Clave, *President*
Gary L Mc Clave, *Corp Secy*
EMP: 38
SQ FT: 10,500
SALES (est): 7MM **Privately Held**
SIC: 5075 Warm air heating equipment & supplies; ventilating equipment & supplies; air conditioning equipment, except room units

(G-6490)
SLOVENE HOME FOR THE AGED
18621 Neff Rd (44119-3018)
PHONE.................................216 486-0268
Fax: 216 481-3771
Jeffrey Saf, *Administration*
EMP: 190
SQ FT: 77,000
SALES: 11.6MM **Privately Held**
SIC: 8051 Skilled nursing care facilities

(G-6491)
SM DOUBLE TREE HOTEL LAKE
Also Called: Doubletree Hotel
1111 Lakeside Ave E (44114-1130)
PHONE.................................216 241-5100
Carrie Borisa, *General Mgr*
Denise Beck, *Sales Mgr*
Leonard Clifton, *Manager*
EMP: 33
SALES (est): 1.9MM **Privately Held**
SIC: 7011 Hotels & motels

(G-6492)
SOCIETY ST VINCENT DE PAUL CLE (PA)
Also Called: St Vincent De Paul Society
6610 Biddulph Rd (44144-3303)
PHONE.................................216 696-6525
Lawrence G Lauter, *Exec Dir*
EMP: 70 EST: 1930
SQ FT: 500
SALES (est): 3.2MM **Privately Held**
SIC: 5932 8322 Clothing, secondhand; furniture, secondhand; individual & family services

(G-6493)
SOGETI USA LLC
6055 Rockside Woods # 170 (44131-2301)
PHONE.................................216 654-2230
Fax: 216 654-2250
Melinda White, *Principal*
EMP: 30
SALES (corp-wide): 353.3MM **Privately Held**
WEB: www.sogeti-usa.com
SIC: 7379
HQ: Sogeti Usa Llc
10100 Innovation Dr # 200
Miamisburg OH 45342
937 291-8100

(G-6494)
SOLIDARITY HEALTH NETWORK INC
4853 Galaxy Pkwy Ste K (44128-5939)
PHONE.................................216 831-1220
Fax: 216 834-4843
Anne Glorioso, *Principal*
Alexandra Granakis, *Manager*
EMP: 29
SQ FT: 4,500
SALES (est): 1.9MM **Privately Held**
SIC: 8399 Health systems agency

(G-6495)
SORBIR INC (PA)
Also Called: Marshall Ford
6200 Mayfield Rd (44124-3203)
PHONE.................................440 449-1000
Fax: 440 449-1000
Larry Elk, *President*
George Ducas, *Treasurer*
Dan Artino, *Sales Staff*
Jerry Sorkin, *Admin Sec*
EMP: 62
SQ FT: 40,000
SALES (est): 5.9MM **Privately Held**
SIC: 7515 5511 Passenger car leasing; automobiles, new & used

(G-6496)
SOUTH E HARLEY DAVIDSON SLS CO (PA)
Also Called: Southeast Golf Cars
23105 Aurora Rd (44146-1703)
PHONE.................................440 439-5300
Fax: 440 439-2919
Paul Meyers Sr, *CEO*
Paul Meyers Jr, *President*
Dave Baumgardner, *General Mgr*
Linda Russell, *Controller*
Diana Allie, *Manager*
EMP: 48
SQ FT: 20,000
SALES (est): 33MM **Privately Held**
WEB: www.southeastpolaris.com
SIC: 5571 7999 Motorcycle dealers; golf cart, power, rental

GEOGRAPHIC SECTION

Cleveland - Cuyahoga County (G-6520)

(G-6497)
SOUTH E HARLEY DAVIDSON SLS CO
Also Called: Southeast Golf Cars
23165 Aurora Rd (44146-1703)
PHONE..................440 439-3013
Paul Meyres, *Manager*
Todd Meyers, *Manager*
Paul Myers, *Manager*
EMP: 45
SALES (corp-wide): 33MM **Privately Held**
WEB: www.southeastpolaris.com
SIC: 4225 General warehousing
PA: South East Harley Davidson Sales Co.
23105 Aurora Rd
Cleveland OH 44146
440 439-5300

(G-6498)
SOUTH SHORE CABLE CNSTR INC
6400 Kolthoff Dr (44142-1310)
PHONE..................440 816-0033
Fax: 440 234-9850
Daniel Geib, *President*
James Stack, *Vice Pres*
Bill Sunderman, *Project Mgr*
Chris Yeager, *Project Mgr*
Bob Grubbs, *Opers Staff*
EMP: 70
SALES (est): 13.4MM **Privately Held**
SIC: 1623 Cable laying construction

(G-6499)
SOUTHWEST ASSOCIATES
Also Called: Century Oak Care Center
7250 Old Oak Blvd (44130-3341)
PHONE..................440 243-7888
Fax: 440 243-3944
David Crisafi, *Owner*
Stewart Bossel, *Partner*
Frank Crisafi, *Partner*
Danial Rocker, *Partner*
Senior H Ohio, *General Ptnr*
EMP: 120
SQ FT: 48,000
SALES (est): 9.7MM **Privately Held**
SIC: 6512 Commercial & industrial building operation

(G-6500)
SOUTHWEST CMNTY HLTH SYSTEMS
Also Called: Southwest General Hospital
18697 Bagley Rd (44130-3417)
PHONE..................440 816-8000
Thomas A Selden, *President*
Vasu Pandrangi, *Chairman*
James Bastian, *Treasurer*
Mark Pangersis, *Technology*
Stanley Trupo, *Admin Sec*
EMP: 1982
SQ FT: 567,121
SALES: 14.7K **Privately Held**
SIC: 8062 General medical & surgical hospitals

(G-6501)
SOUTHWEST FAMILY PHYSICIANS
7225 Old Oak Blvd A210 (44130-3339)
PHONE..................440 816-2750
Fax: 440 816-8025
David Lash, *President*
Steven Tymcio, *Vice Pres*
EMP: 48
SQ FT: 10,000
SALES (est): 5MM **Privately Held**
WEB: www.southwestfamilyphysicians.com
SIC: 8011 Physicians' office, including specialists

(G-6502)
SOUTHWEST GENERAL HEALTH CTR
Also Called: Lifeworks At Southwest General
7390 Old Oak Blvd (44130-3328)
PHONE..................440 816-4202
Fax: 440 816-4201
Shelly Murphy, *Office Mgr*
Dimitri Kontoveros, *Pharmacist*
Karen Siegel, *Manager*
Cara Padine, *Manager*
Sue McLaughlin, *Analyst*
EMP: 65
SALES (corp-wide): 315.6MM **Privately Held**
SIC: 8062 7991 General medical & surgical hospitals; health club
PA: Southwest General Health Center
18697 Bagley Rd
Cleveland OH 44130
440 816-8000

(G-6503)
SOUTHWEST GENERAL HEALTH CTR
Also Called: Southwest General Health Ctr
18697 Oak Vw (44130)
PHONE..................440 816-8200
Mary Freas, *CFO*
Christian Quinlan, *CFO*
James Bastian, *Asst Treas*
Jan Lasker, *Finance*
Cory Shaw, *Pharmacist*
EMP: 70
SQ FT: 83,892
SALES (corp-wide): 315.6MM **Privately Held**
SIC: 8062 8069 General medical & surgical hospitals; drug addiction rehabilitation hospital
PA: Southwest General Health Center
18697 Bagley Rd
Cleveland OH 44130
440 816-8000

(G-6504)
SOUTHWEST GENERAL HEALTH CTR (PA)
18697 Bagley Rd (44130-3417)
PHONE..................440 816-8000
Fax: 440 816-6263
L Jon Schurmeier, *President*
Donald Williams, *Trustee*
Albert Matyas, *Vice Pres*
Dave Ferris, *Project Mgr*
Linda Dudik, *Opers Mgr*
EMP: 2400
SQ FT: 150,000
SALES: 315.6MM **Privately Held**
SIC: 8062 General medical & surgical hospitals

(G-6505)
SOUTHWEST GENERAL HEALTH CTR
Also Called: Home Hlth Svcs Southwest Hosp
17951 Jefferson Park Rd (44130-8439)
PHONE..................440 816-8005
Fax: 440 816-6856
Lisa Goodlow, *Exec Dir*
Debbie Borowski, *Director*
Jackie Ball, *Director*
EMP: 40
SALES (corp-wide): 315.6MM **Privately Held**
SIC: 8062 General medical & surgical hospitals
PA: Southwest General Health Center
18697 Bagley Rd
Cleveland OH 44130
440 816-8000

(G-6506)
SOUTHWEST INTERNAL MEDICINE
7255 Old Oak Blvd C209 (44130-3329)
PHONE..................440 816-2777
James D Wismar, *Principal*
Kamesh Gundataneni MD, *Internal Med*
EMP: 25
SALES (est): 2.2MM **Privately Held**
WEB: www.southwestinternalmedicine.com
SIC: 8011 Internal medicine, physician/surgeon

(G-6507)
SOUTHWEST UROLOGY LLC (PA)
Also Called: Southwest Gastroenterology
6900 Pearl Rd Ste 200 (44130-3640)
PHONE..................440 845-0900
Fax: 440 845-7355
Michael Barkoukis MD, *President*
Arturo Bossa MD, *Principal*
Laurence Dervasi MD, *Principal*
Tim Sildor MD, *Principal*
Donna Reznik, *Office Mgr*
EMP: 30
SQ FT: 6,000
SALES (est): 6.3MM **Privately Held**
SIC: 8011 Urologist

(G-6508)
SP PLUS CORPORATION
Also Called: Standard Parking
9500 Euclid Ave Wb1 (44195-0001)
PHONE..................216 444-2255
Harold McMann, *Branch Mgr*
EMP: 90
SALES (corp-wide): 1.5B **Publicly Held**
SIC: 7521 Parking garage
PA: Sp Plus Corporation
200 E Randolph St # 7700
Chicago IL 60601
312 274-2000

(G-6509)
SP PLUS CORPORATION
1301 E 9th St Ste 1050 (44114-1888)
PHONE..................216 687-0141
Bob Kohler, *Regional Mgr*
Tom Svoboda, *Accountant*
EMP: 50
SALES (corp-wide): 1.5B **Publicly Held**
SIC: 7521 Parking garage
PA: Sp Plus Corporation
200 E Randolph St # 7700
Chicago IL 60601
312 274-2000

(G-6510)
SP PLUS CORPORATION
5300 Riverside Dr (44135-3130)
PHONE..................216 267-7275
Dennis McAndrew, *General Mgr*
EMP: 60
SALES (corp-wide): 1.5B **Publicly Held**
SIC: 7521 Parking lots
PA: Sp Plus Corporation
200 E Randolph St # 7700
Chicago IL 60601
312 274-2000

(G-6511)
SP PLUS CORPORATION
5300 Riverside Dr (44135-3130)
PHONE..................216 267-5030
Dennis McAndrew, *General Mgr*
EMP: 70
SALES (corp-wide): 1.5B **Publicly Held**
SIC: 7521 Parking lots
PA: Sp Plus Corporation
200 E Randolph St # 7700
Chicago IL 60601
312 274-2000

(G-6512)
SPANGENBERG SHIBLEY LIBER LLP
Also Called: Spangenberg Law Firm
1001 Lakeside Ave E # 1700 (44114-1158)
PHONE..................216 215-7445
Dennis Lansdowne, *Partner*
William Hawal, *Partner*
Justin Madden, *Partner*
Peter H Weinberger, *Partner*
Alex McLaughlin, *Director*
EMP: 32 **EST:** 1959
SALES (est): 5.1MM **Privately Held**
WEB: www.spanglaw.com
SIC: 8111 General practice law office

(G-6513)
SPANISH AMERICAN COMMITTEE (PA)
4407 Lorain Ave Fl 1 (44113-3779)
PHONE..................216 961-2100
Fax: 216 961-3305
Efrain Colon, *President*
Ramonita Vargas, *Principal*
Janice Cedeno, *Director*
EMP: 26 **EST:** 1966
SQ FT: 12,500
SALES (est): 1.2MM **Privately Held**
WEB: www.spanishamerican.org
SIC: 8322 8331 8351 Social service center; job training services; head start center, except in conjunction with school

(G-6514)
SPARKBASE INC
3615 Superior Ave E 4403d (44114-4139)
PHONE..................216 867-0877
Douglas Hardman, *CEO*
Geoffry Hardman, *President*
Andrew Kraynak, *VP Mktg*
Doug Pierce, *CTO*
EMP: 50
SQ FT: 6,800
SALES (est): 4.7MM **Privately Held**
SIC: 7389 Financial services

(G-6515)
SPECIALTY HOSP CLEVELAND INC
Also Called: Kindred Hosp - Clveland - Gtwy
2351 E 22nd St Fl 7 (44115-3111)
PHONE..................216 592-2830
Fax: 216 592-2831
Rothgerber L Arthur, *Senior VP*
EMP: 361
SALES (est): 3.9MM
SALES (corp-wide): 6B **Publicly Held**
SIC: 8062 General medical & surgical hospitals
PA: Kindred Healthcare, Inc.
680 S 4th St
Louisville KY 40202
502 596-7300

(G-6516)
SPECIALTY STEEL CO INC
18250 Miles Rd (44128-3439)
P.O. Box 28152 (44128-0152)
PHONE..................800 321-8500
Fax: 216 475-6332
Theodore Cohen Jr, *President*
Ronald De Camp, *Manager*
EMP: 40
SQ FT: 48,000
SALES (est): 6.9MM **Privately Held**
WEB: www.specialtysteel.com
SIC: 5051 Steel

(G-6517)
SPECTRUM SUPPORTIVE SERVICES
Also Called: Spectrum Supportive Services
4269 Pearl Rd Ste 300 (44109-4232)
PHONE..................216 875-0460
Stephen S Morse, *Exec Dir*
David Reichert, *Director*
EMP: 50
SALES (est): 497.5K
SALES (corp-wide): 897K **Privately Held**
WEB: www.spectrumsupport.org
SIC: 8331 8322 Vocational rehabilitation agency; association for the handicapped
PA: Spectrum Of Supportive Services
2900 Detroit Ave Fl 3
Cleveland OH 44113
216 761-2388

(G-6518)
SPECTRUM SUPPORTIVE SERVICES (PA)
Also Called: Careers Unlimited
2900 Detroit Ave Fl 3 (44113-2710)
PHONE..................216 761-2388
Fax: 440 939-2077
David Reichert, *Vice Pres*
Wil Cheeks, *Manager*
Stephen S Morse, *Exec Dir*
EMP: 105
SALES: 897K **Privately Held**
WEB: www.spectrumsupport.org
SIC: 8331 5149 Vocational rehabilitation agency; coffee & tea

(G-6519)
SPEEDEON DATA LLC
5875 Landerbrook Dr # 130 (44124-4069)
PHONE..................440 264-2100
Joshua Shale, *COO*
Linda Montgomery, *CFO*
Marc Jerauld, *Officer*
Gerard Daher,
EMP: 26 **EST:** 2008
SQ FT: 2,148
SALES (est): 3.7MM **Privately Held**
SIC: 7374 7379 Data processing service; computer data escrow service

(G-6520)
ST AUGUSTINE TOWERS
7821 Lake Ave Apt 304 (44102-6400)
PHONE..................216 634-7444
Fax: 216 634-2717

Cleveland - Cuyahoga County (G-6521)

Anita Newsham, *Principal*
Nancy Minerd, *Manager*
Anita Gerriasch, *Director*
Ali Schiallace, *Director*
Shalia Palmiero, *Nursing Dir*
EMP: 30
SALES: 1.9MM **Privately Held**
SIC: 8082 Home health care services

(G-6521)
ST CLAIR AUTO BODY
Also Called: St Clair Auto Body Shop
13608 Saint Clair Ave (44110-3547)
PHONE..................................216 531-7300
Fax: 216 851-5191
Norman Kirchner, *President*
Joe Zver, *Manager*
EMP: 25
SQ FT: 15,000
SALES (est): 3.9MM **Privately Held**
SIC: 7532 Body shop, automotive; paint shop, automotive

(G-6522)
ST REGIS INVESTMENT LLC
8111 Rockside Rd (44125-6129)
PHONE..................................216 520-1250
Frank Sinito,
EMP: 99 EST: 2015
SALES (est): 1.9MM **Privately Held**
SIC: 6513 Apartment building operators

(G-6523)
ST VINCENT CHARITY MED CTR (PA)
2351 E 22nd St (44115-3111)
PHONE..................................216 861-6200
Melvin G Pye Jr, *Ch of Bd*
David F Perse MD, *President*
Ross Joan, *COO*
Joan Ross, *COO*
John Marshall, *Vice Pres*
EMP: 974
SQ FT: 200,000
SALES: 142.3MM **Privately Held**
WEB: www.cccmhb.org
SIC: 8062 General medical & surgical hospitals

(G-6524)
STANTEC ARCH & ENGRG PC
3700 Park East Dr Ste 200 (44122-4339)
PHONE..................................216 454-2150
Christina Han, *Marketing Staff*
Lori Van Dermark, *Marketing Staff*
Amy Strasheim, *Branch Mgr*
Reshma Panjanani, *Information Mgr*
EMP: 25
SALES (corp-wide): 3.1B **Privately Held**
SIC: 8711 8712 Engineering services; architectural services
HQ: Stantec Architecture And Engineering P.C.
   311 Summer St
   Boston MA 02210

(G-6525)
STANTEC ARCHITECTURE INC
3700 Park East Dr Ste 200 (44122-4339)
PHONE..................................216 454-2150
Christina Han, *Marketing Staff*
Lori Van Dermark, *Marketing Staff*
Michael Carter, *Branch Mgr*
Reshma Panjanani, *Information Mgr*
EMP: 25
SALES (corp-wide): 3.1B **Privately Held**
WEB: www.burthill.com
SIC: 8712 8711 Architectural services; engineering services
HQ: Stantec Architecture Inc.
   224 S Michigan Ave # 1400
   Chicago IL 60604
   336 714-7413

(G-6526)
STANTEC CONSULTING SVCS INC
3700 Park East Dr Ste 200 (44122-4339)
PHONE..................................216 454-2150
Mike Carter, *Sls & Mktg Exec*
Christina Han, *Marketing Staff*
Lori Van Dermark, *Marketing Staff*
Amy Strasheim, *Manager*
Reshma Panjanani, *Information Mgr*
EMP: 25

SALES (corp-wide): 3.1B **Privately Held**
SIC: 8712 8711 Architectural services; engineering services
HQ: Stantec Consulting Services Inc.
   475 5th Ave Fl 12
   New York NY 10017
   212 352-5160

(G-6527)
STANTEC CONSULTING SVCS INC
1300 E 9th St Ste 1100 (44114-1506)
PHONE..................................216 621-2407
Robert Schubach, *Engineer*
Sven Wiberg, *Branch Mgr*
Anthony Green, *Architect*
James Harris, *Admin Sec*
EMP: 44
SALES (corp-wide): 3.1B **Privately Held**
WEB: www.mw.com
SIC: 8711 Engineering services
HQ: Stantec Consulting Services Inc.
   475 5th Ave Fl 12
   New York NY 10017
   212 352-5160

(G-6528)
STATE FARM MUTL AUTO INSUR CO
Also Called: State Farm Insurance
2700 W 25th St (44113-4710)
PHONE..................................216 621-3723
Kim Smith, *Office Mgr*
Andriann Dumar,
Dick McClement, *Manager*
EMP: 72
SALES (corp-wide): 39.5MM **Privately Held**
WEB: www.statefarm.com
SIC: 6411 Insurance agents & brokers
PA: State Farm Mutual Automobile Insurance Company
   1 State Farm Plz
   Bloomington IL 61710
   309 766-2311

(G-6529)
STATE FARM MUTL AUTO INSUR CO
Also Called: State Farm Insurance
2245 Warrensville Ctr Rd (44118-3145)
PHONE..................................216 321-1422
Fax: 216 321-2136
Linda Myers, *Branch Mgr*
Linda Meyers, *Agent*
EMP: 72
SALES (corp-wide): 39.5MM **Privately Held**
WEB: www.statefarm.com
SIC: 6411 Insurance agents & brokers
PA: State Farm Mutual Automobile Insurance Company
   1 State Farm Plz
   Bloomington IL 61710
   309 766-2311

(G-6530)
STATE INDUSTRIAL PRODUCTS CORP (PA)
Also Called: State Chemical Manufacturing
5915 Landerbrook Dr # 300 (44124-4039)
PHONE..................................877 747-6986
Fax: 216 574-9433
Harold Uhrman, *President*
Robert M San Julian, *President*
Kristin Miller, *District Mgr*
William Barnett, *Corp Secy*
Brian Limbert, *COO*
▼ **EMP:** 300 EST: 1911
SQ FT: 240,000
SALES: 107.9MM **Privately Held**
WEB: www.stateindustrial.com
SIC: 2841 5072 2842 2992 Soap: granulated, liquid, cake, flaked or chip; bolts, nuts & screws; specialty cleaning, polishes & sanitation goods; degreasing solvent; disinfectants, household or industrial plant; lubricating oils & greases; asphalt felts & coatings; chemical preparations

(G-6531)
STATE INDUSTRIAL PRODUCTS CORP
Also Called: U Z Engineered Products Co
12420 Plaza Dr (44130-1057)
PHONE..................................216 861-6363
Carroll Hulla, *Area Mgr*
Alan Kitchen, *Vice Pres*
Dave Debord, *Branch Mgr*
EMP: 200
SALES (corp-wide): 107.9MM **Privately Held**
WEB: www.stateindustrial.com
SIC: 5085 Fasteners, industrial: nuts, bolts, screws, etc.
PA: State Industrial Products Corporation
   5915 Landerbrook Dr # 300
   Cleveland OH 44124
   877 747-6986

(G-6532)
STATE-WIDE EXPRESS INC
5231 Engle Rd (44142-1531)
PHONE..................................216 676-4600
Fax: 216 433-9944
Tom Armanini, *President*
Dean Armanini, *Vice Pres*
EMP: 63
SQ FT: 25,000
SALES (est): 6.9MM **Privately Held**
SIC: 4214 4213 4212 Local trucking with storage; trucking, except local; local trucking, without storage

(G-6533)
STC TRANSPORATION INC
8806 Crane Ave (44105-1622)
PHONE..................................216 441-6217
Ernest Beardsley, *President*
Randall R Reed, *VP Sales*
EMP: 35
SQ FT: 120,000
SALES (est): 4.3MM
SALES (corp-wide): 79.7MM **Privately Held**
WEB: www.ncc-corp.com
SIC: 4213 Trucking, except local
PA: North Coast Container Corp.
   8806 Crane Ave
   Cleveland OH 44105
   216 441-6214

(G-6534)
STEEL WAREHOUSE CLEVELAND LLC
Also Called: Chesterfield Steel
3193 Independence Rd (44105-1045)
PHONE..................................888 225-3760
Fax: 216 481-8473
Bob Snyder, *Engineer*
Marc Stephens, *Engineer*
Hugh Garvey, *Mng Member*
Allan Maggied, *Manager*
William Dull, *Supervisor*
EMP: 50
SALES (est): 7.9MM **Privately Held**
SIC: 1541 Industrial buildings & warehouses
HQ: Steel Warehouse Company Llc
   2722 Tucker Dr
   South Bend IN 46619
   574 236-5100

(G-6535)
STEIN INC
1034 Holmden Ave (44109-1836)
PHONE..................................216 883-4277
Dave Bilez, *General Mgr*
Mark Benedict, *General Mgr*
EMP: 75
SALES (corp-wide): 83.5MM **Privately Held**
SIC: 1791 Structural steel erection
PA: Stein, Inc.
   1929 E Royalton Rd Ste C
   Cleveland OH 44147
   440 526-9301

(G-6536)
STELLA MARIS INC
Also Called: Stella Mris Detoxification Ctr
1320 Washington Ave (44113-2333)
PHONE..................................216 781-0550
Fax: 216 781-7501
Eric Shope, *Senior VP*

Bob Smith, *Opers Staff*
Roselyn Price, *Finance*
Margaret Roche, *Director*
Robert Fuecker, *Security Dir*
EMP: 30
SQ FT: 15,000
SALES: 3.2MM **Privately Held**
SIC: 8069 Substance abuse hospitals

(G-6537)
STEPHEN A RUDOLPH INC
1611 S Green Rd Ste 260 (44121-4192)
PHONE..................................216 381-1367
Stephen A Rudolph MD, *President*
EMP: 35
SALES (est): 1MM **Privately Held**
SIC: 8011 Internal medicine, physician/surgeon

(G-6538)
STEPSTONE GROUP REAL ESTATE LP
127 Public Sq Ste 5050 (44114-1246)
PHONE..................................216 522-0330
EMP: 30
SALES (est): 511.1K
SALES (corp-wide): 689.4K **Privately Held**
SIC: 8742 6282 Real estate consultant; investment advice
PA: Stepstone Group Real Estate Lp
   885 3rd Ave Fl 14
   New York NY 10022
   212 351-6100

(G-6539)
STERLING LTD CO
3550 Lander Rd Ste 200 (44124-5755)
PHONE..................................216 464-8850
Fax: 216 464-6901
John Burns, *President*
Ronald E Bates, *President*
Lisa Lipczynski, *Treasurer*
Jeffrey Biggar, *Director*
EMP: 34
SQ FT: 11,000
SALES (est): 4.6MM **Privately Held**
SIC: 6282 Investment advice; investment counselors

(G-6540)
STERN ADVERTISING INC (PA)
950 Main Ave Ste 700 (44113-7208)
PHONE..................................216 464-4850
Fax: 216 464-4850
Freda Royed, *CEO*
William J Stern, *President*
Kathryn Hanley, *Principal*
Joseph H Persky, *Principal*
Doug Cohen, *Exec VP*
EMP: 50
SQ FT: 15,000
SALES (est): 11.3MM **Privately Held**
SIC: 7311 Advertising consultant

(G-6541)
STONE GARDENS
27090 Cedar Rd (44122-8108)
PHONE..................................216 292-0070
Fax: 216 292-0033
Ross Wilkoff, *Administration*
EMP: 75
SALES (est): 3.5MM **Privately Held**
SIC: 8361 Residential care

(G-6542)
STONEWOOD RESIDENTIAL INC (PA)
6320 Smith Rd (44142-3711)
P.O. Box 42155 (44142-0155)
PHONE..................................216 267-9777
Fax: 216 267-5020
Bill Stacho, *President*
Beverly Krug, *Manager*
Lynn Urbanski, *Director*
EMP: 25
SQ FT: 5,800
SALES (est): 2MM **Privately Held**
SIC: 8361 Residential care for the handicapped

GEOGRAPHIC SECTION
Cleveland - Cuyahoga County (G-6566)

(G-6543)
STORER MEAT CO INC
Also Called: Five Star Brand
3700 Clark Ave (44109-1142)
P.O. Box 6242 (44101-1242)
PHONE.................216 621-7538
Fax: 216 361-0622
Robert Gutwein, *President*
Brad Herdman, *Controller*
Teresa Gutwein, *Admin Asst*
EMP: 40 EST: 1961
SQ FT: 33,000
SALES (est): 7.3MM **Privately Held**
SIC: 5147 Meats & meat products; meats, cured or smoked

(G-6544)
STOUT RISIUS ROSS LLC
600 Superior Ave E # 1700 (44114-2622)
PHONE.................216 685-5000
Fax: 216 685-5001
Michael L Kern III, *COO*
Jason Maracco, *Branch Mgr*
EMP: 25 **Privately Held**
SIC: 8748 Business consulting
PA: Stout Risius Ross, Llc
  1 S Wacker Dr Lbby 38
  Chicago IL 60606

(G-6545)
STRANG CORPORATION (PA)
Also Called: Don's Lighthouse Inn
8905 Lake Ave Fl 1 (44102-6319)
PHONE.................216 961-6767
Donald W Strang Jr, *Ch of Bd*
Donald W Strang III, *President*
Monica Stagg, *District Mgr*
Ed Copeland, *Vice Pres*
David Strang, *Vice Pres*
EMP: 50
SQ FT: 20,000
SALES (est): 17.3MM **Privately Held**
SIC: 7011 Hotels & motels

(G-6546)
SUMMERS ACQUISITION CORP (DH)
Also Called: Summers Rubber Company
12555 Berea Rd (44111-1619)
PHONE.................216 941-7700
Fax: 216 941-4673
Mike Summers, *President*
William M Summers, *Chairman*
Pete Haberbosch, *Vice Pres*
Eugene Mayo, *Vice Pres*
Gene Mayo, *Vice Pres*
▲ EMP: 26
SQ FT: 63,000
SALES (est): 22.3MM
SALES (corp-wide): 2.4B **Privately Held**
WEB: www.summersrubber.com
SIC: 5085 3429 Rubber goods, mechanical; manufactured hardware (general)
HQ: Hampton Rubber Company
  1669 W Pembroke Ave
  Hampton VA 23661
  757 722-9818

(G-6547)
SUMMIT ASSOCIATES INC
Also Called: Holiday Inn
3750 Orange Pl (44122-4404)
PHONE.................216 831-3300
Fax: 216 831-3300
Ken Hiller, *Manager*
EMP: 100
SALES (corp-wide): 39.8K **Privately Held**
WEB: www.sairealestate.com
SIC: 7011 5813 5812 Hotels & motels; drinking places; eating places
PA: Summit Associates Inc
  Raritan Plz 1 Raritan Ctr St Raritan Pla
  Edison NJ 08837
  732 225-2900

(G-6548)
SUMMIT HOTEL TRS 144 LLC
Also Called: Residence Inn By Marriott
527 Prospect Ave E (44115-1113)
PHONE.................216 443-9043
Tracy Sauers, *Principal*
Christopher Eng, *Principal*
EMP: 48
SALES (est): 180.6K **Privately Held**
SIC: 7011 Hotels & motels

(G-6549)
SUNBELT RENTALS INC
13800 Brookpark Rd (44135-5149)
PHONE.................216 362-0300
Robert Rogers, *Branch Mgr*
EMP: 30
SALES (corp-wide): 3.9B **Privately Held**
WEB: www.sunbeltrentals.com
SIC: 7353 7359 Heavy construction equipment rental; equipment rental & leasing
HQ: Sunbelt Rentals, Inc.
  2341 Deerfield Dr
  Fort Mill SC 29715
  803 578-5811

(G-6550)
SUNRISE LAND CO (DH)
1250 Trml Twr 50 Pub Sq 1250 Terminal Tower (44113)
PHONE.................216 621-6060
Robert Monchein, *President*
Wayne Danko, *Controller*
Layton Mc Cown, *Controller*
Mark Turnis, *VP Finance*
Darch Owf, *Admin Asst*
EMP: 39
SALES (est): 2.9MM
SALES (corp-wide): 911.9MM **Privately Held**
SIC: 6552 Land subdividers & developers, commercial; land subdividers & developers, residential
HQ: Forest City Enterprises, L.P.
  50 Public Sq Ste 1100
  Cleveland OH 44113
  216 621-6060

(G-6551)
SUNRISE SENIOR LIVING INC
Also Called: Sunrise At Shaker Heights
16333 Chagrin Blvd (44120-3711)
PHONE.................216 751-0930
Fax: 216 751-0980
Michelle Biro, *Sales Mgr*
Vesta Jones, *Exec Dir*
Pam Zivot Rn, *Exec Dir*
Deb Christian, *Administration*
EMP: 100
SALES (corp-wide): 4.3B **Publicly Held**
WEB: www.sunrise.com
SIC: 8051 Skilled nursing care facilities
HQ: Sunrise Senior Living, Llc
  7902 Westpark Dr
  Mc Lean VA 22102

(G-6552)
SUNRISE SENIOR LIVING LLC
Also Called: Sunrise At Parma
7766 Broadview Rd (44134-6743)
PHONE.................216 447-8909
Fax: 216 328-9272
Rima Hanson, *Manager*
EMP: 50
SQ FT: 20,703
SALES (corp-wide): 4.3B **Publicly Held**
WEB: www.sunrise.com
SIC: 8051 8361 Skilled nursing care facilities; residential care
HQ: Sunrise Senior Living, Llc
  7902 Westpark Dr
  Mc Lean VA 22102

(G-6553)
SUPERIOR APARTMENTS
1850 Superior Ave E 102a (44114-2130)
PHONE.................216 861-6405
Joseph Weiss, *President*
EMP: 30
SALES (est): 641.4K **Privately Held**
WEB: www.superiorapartments.net
SIC: 6513 Apartment building operators

(G-6554)
SUPERIOR PRODUCTS LLC
Also Called: Sp Medical
3786 Ridge Rd (44144-1127)
PHONE.................216 651-9400
Tomas Sarrel, *President*
Donald L Mottinger, *President*
Tim Austin, *Managing Dir*
Gregory K Gens, *Vice Pres*
Louise Egofske, *CFO*
◆ EMP: 80 EST: 1961

SALES (est): 17.8MM **Privately Held**
WEB: www.superiorprod.com
SIC: 3451 3494 5085 3492 Screw machine products; valves & pipe fittings; industrial fittings; fluid power valves & hose fittings

(G-6555)
SUPERIOR PRODUCTS LLC
3786 Ridge Rd (44144-1127)
PHONE.................216 651-9400
Fax: 440 602-6989
Donald L Mottinger, *President*
Tim Austin, *Managing Dir*
Gregory K Gens, *CFO*
Carolyn Gens, *Controller*
Tim Giesse, *Admin Sec*
EMP: 65
SQ FT: 75,000
SALES (est): 8.5MM
SALES (corp-wide): 171.5MM **Privately Held**
SIC: 3494 5085 3492 Valves & pipe fittings; industrial fittings; fluid power valves & hose fittings
HQ: Superior Holding, Llc
  3786 Ridge Rd
  Cleveland OH 44144
  216 651-9400

(G-6556)
SUPPLY TECHNOLOGIES LLC (HQ)
Also Called: I L S
6065 Parkland Blvd Ste 1 (44124-6145)
P.O. Box 248199 (44124-8199)
PHONE.................440 947-2100
Fax: 440 947-2299
Michael L Justice, *President*
Brad Hudson, *Vice Pres*
James Smetham, *Vice Pres*
Seth Swanner, *Vice Pres*
Tom Blevins, *Opers Mgr*
▲ EMP: 150 EST: 1998
SQ FT: 7,000
SALES (est): 39.4MM
SALES (corp-wide): 1.4B **Publicly Held**
WEB: www.deloscrew.com
SIC: 5085 3452 3469 Fasteners, industrial: nuts, bolts, screws, etc.; bolts, nuts, rivets & washers; screws, metal; nuts, metal; stamping metal for the trade
PA: Park-Ohio Holdings Corp.
  6065 Parkland Blvd Ste 1
  Cleveland OH 44124
  440 947-2000

(G-6557)
SUPPORT TO AT RISK TEENS
Also Called: Start
4515 Superior Ave (44103-1215)
PHONE.................216 696-5507
Mark Brauer, *Exec Dir*
EMP: 40
SALES: 2.6MM **Privately Held**
WEB: www.lmmyouth.org
SIC: 8322 Social service center

(G-6558)
SUPREME COURT UNITED STATES
Also Called: US Probation Office
801 W Superior Ave 20-100 (44113-1833)
PHONE.................216 357-7300
Greg Johnson, *Branch Mgr*
EMP: 27 **Publicly Held**
SIC: 8322 9211 Probation office; courts
HQ: Supreme Court, United States
  1 1st St Ne
  Washington DC 20543
  202 479-3000

(G-6559)
SURGERY CTR AN OHIO LTD PARTNR
Also Called: Surgery Center, The
19250 Bagley Rd (44130-3347)
PHONE.................440 826-3240
Barbara Draves, *Partner*
EMP: 60
SALES (est): 7.9MM
SALES (corp-wide): 19.3B **Publicly Held**
SIC: 8011 Surgeon

HQ: United Surgical Partners International, Inc.
  15305 Dallas Pkwy # 1600
  Addison TX 75001
  972 713-3500

(G-6560)
SWA INC
Also Called: Century Oak Care Center
7250 Old Oak Blvd (44130-3341)
PHONE.................440 243-7888
Stewart Bossel, *President*
Justin Winters, *Associate*
EMP: 116
SQ FT: 48,000
SALES (est): 2.9MM **Privately Held**
WEB: www.centuryoakcarecenter.com
SIC: 8051 Skilled nursing care facilities

(G-6561)
SWEENEY ROBERT E CO LPA
55 Public Sq Ste 1500 (44113-1998)
PHONE.................216 696-0606
Fax: 216 696-0679
Robert E Sweeney, *President*
Kevin E McDermott,
William A Sweeney,
EMP: 48
SQ FT: 10,000
SALES (est): 3.6MM **Privately Held**
SIC: 8111 General practice law office

(G-6562)
SYSTEM SEALS INC (HQ)
9505 Midwest Ave (44125-2421)
PHONE.................440 735-0200
Fax: 440 735-0288
Arnold V Engelbrechten, *President*
Jim Bell, *Controller*
Julian Gigg, *Regl Sales Mgr*
Julia Rumley, *Sales Associate*
▲ EMP: 60
SQ FT: 10,000
SALES (est): 9.4MM **Privately Held**
WEB: www.systemseals.com
SIC: 3953 5084 Embossing seals & hand stamps; hydraulic systems equipment & supplies

(G-6563)
T & F SYSTEMS INC
1599 E 40th St (44103-2389)
PHONE.................216 881-3525
Fax: 216 881-6763
Brian Stenger, *President*
Tatian Ebert, *Controller*
EMP: 100
SQ FT: 14,000
SALES: 8MM **Privately Held**
SIC: 1761 Roofing contractor

(G-6564)
T J NEFF HOLDINGS INC
Also Called: Neff & Associates
6405 York Rd (44130-3033)
PHONE.................440 884-3100
Fax: 440 884-6443
Daniel Neff, *President*
Daniel J Neff, *President*
Eric Witzke, *Research*
Mike Denallo, *Engineer*
Stefan Kloss, *Engineer*
EMP: 40
SALES (est): 4.2MM **Privately Held**
SIC: 8711 8713 Civil engineering; consulting engineer; surveying services

(G-6565)
T L C LANDSCAPING INC
Also Called: Park Place Nursery
38000 Aurora Rd (44139-4619)
PHONE.................440 248-4852
Fax: 440 498-4980
Gary S Stanek, *President*
Kathy Stanek, *Admin Sec*
EMP: 39
SQ FT: 5,000
SALES (est): 1.2MM **Privately Held**
SIC: 0782 4959 Landscape contractors; snowplowing

(G-6566)
T W I INTERNATIONAL INC (DH)
24460 Aurora Rd (44146-1728)
PHONE.................440 439-1830
Armond Waxman, *Ch of Bd*

Cleveland - Cuyahoga County (G-6567)

GEOGRAPHIC SECTION

Melvin Waxman, *President*
Mark Wester, *Finance Dir*
EMP: 110
SQ FT: 21,000
SALES (est): 7.3MM
SALES (corp-wide): 100MM **Privately Held**
SIC: 7389 Packaging & labeling services

(G-6567)
TAFT STETTINIUS HOLLISTER LLP
200 Public Sq Ste 3500 (44114-2317)
PHONE..................216 241-3141
Fax: 216 241-2837
Stephen M O'Bryan, *Managing Prtnr*
Louis George, *Managing Dir*
Tracy Betz, *Editor*
James Dawson, *Editor*
Allison Bruns, *Counsel*
EMP: 74
SALES (corp-wide): 104.2MM **Privately Held**
SIC: 8111 General practice law office
PA: Taft Stettinius & Hollister Llp
  425 Walnut St Ste 1800
  Cincinnati OH 45202
  513 381-2838

(G-6568)
TALERIS CREDIT UNION INC
1250 E Granger Rd (44131-1234)
P.O. Box 318072 (44131-8072)
PHONE..................216 739-2300
Robin D Thomas, *President*
James McKenzie, *Vice Pres*
Harley Hill, *CFO*
Ben Boggs, *Controller*
Rick Zimmerman, *Sales Dir*
EMP: 45
SQ FT: 11,000
SALES (est): 2.6MM **Privately Held**
WEB: www.tcuohio.com
SIC: 6062 State credit unions, not federally chartered

(G-6569)
TANOS SALON
24225 Chagrin Blvd (44122-5516)
PHONE..................216 831-7880
Fax: 216 464-2740
Leonard Cosentino, *Owner*
Elaine Kausman, *Admin Sec*
EMP: 35
SALES (est): 316.5K **Privately Held**
SIC: 7231 Beauty shops

(G-6570)
TARGET AUTO BODY INC
5005 Carnegie Ave (44103-4353)
PHONE..................216 391-1942
Misun Pak, *President*
EMP: 25
SALES (est): 917K **Privately Held**
SIC: 7532 Body shop, automotive

(G-6571)
TAYLOR MADE GRAPHICS
7921 Hollenbeck Cir (44129-6214)
PHONE..................440 882-6318
James Keserich, *Owner*
Danette Keserich, *Co-Owner*
EMP: 27
SALES (est): 1.1MM **Privately Held**
SIC: 7336 Graphic arts & related design

(G-6572)
TAYLOR MURTIS HUMAN SVCS SYS
12395 Mccracken Rd (44125-2967)
PHONE..................216 283-4400
Ella Thomas, *Director*
EMP: 175
SALES (corp-wide): 25.3MM **Privately Held**
SIC: 8099 Blood related health services
PA: Murtis Taylor Human Services System
  13422 Kinsman Rd
  Cleveland OH 44120
  216 283-4400

(G-6573)
TAYLOR MURTIS HUMAN SVCS SYS (PA)
13422 Kinsman Rd (44120-4410)
PHONE..................216 283-4400
Fax: 216 283-2099
Lovell J Custard, *CEO*
Muqit Sabur, *Chairman*
John Chan, *Senior VP*
Roberta Taliaferro, *Vice Pres*
John Chen, *CFO*
EMP: 70
SQ FT: 35,000
SALES: 25.3MM **Privately Held**
SIC: 8093 8322 Mental health clinic, outpatient; community center; social service center; child related social services; emergency social services

(G-6574)
TAYLOR MURTIS HUMAN SVCS SYS
3167 Fulton Rd (44109-1465)
PHONE..................216 281-7192
Murtis Taylor, *Owner*
EMP: 88
SALES (corp-wide): 25.3MM **Privately Held**
SIC: 8322 8093 Community center; mental health clinic, outpatient
PA: Murtis Taylor Human Services System
  13422 Kinsman Rd
  Cleveland OH 44120
  216 283-4400

(G-6575)
TEAM INDUSTRIAL SERVICES INC
5901 Harper Rd (44139-1834)
PHONE..................440 498-9494
Chuck Avis, *Branch Mgr*
EMP: 32
SALES (corp-wide): 1.2B **Publicly Held**
SIC: 7699 Industrial equipment services
HQ: Team Industrial Services, Inc.
  13131 Dairy Ashford Rd # 600
  Sugar Land TX 77478
  281 388-5525

(G-6576)
TEAM NEO
1111 Superior Ave E # 1600 (44114-2552)
PHONE..................216 363-5400
Bill Koehler, *CEO*
Jenny W Febbo, *Vice Pres*
Daila Shimek, *Research*
Mary Kulak, *Office Mgr*
Camille Billups, *Manager*
EMP: 26
SALES (est): 4.7MM **Privately Held**
SIC: 8748 8699 Economic consultant; charitable organization

(G-6577)
TECH MAHINDRA (AMERICAS) INC
200 W Prospect Ave (44113-1432)
PHONE..................216 912-2002
Sudhakar Shetty, *Branch Mgr*
EMP: 80
SALES (corp-wide): 3.4B **Privately Held**
SIC: 7371 Custom computer programming services
HQ: Tech Mahindra (Americas) Inc.
  4965 Preston Park Blvd # 500
  Plano TX 75093

(G-6578)
TELEMAXX COMMUNICATIONS LLC (PA)
2150 Lee Rd (44118-2908)
PHONE..................216 371-8800
Sam Odetallah, *Mng Member*
EMP: 30 **EST:** 1997
SQ FT: 6,500
SALES (est): 1.9MM **Privately Held**
SIC: 4813 Telephone communication, except radio

(G-6579)
TELEMESSAGING SERVICES INC
Also Called: Tasco Inc Ohio
7441 W Ridgewood Dr # 130 (44135-5544)
PHONE..................440 845-5400
Fax: 440 845-1414
Jerri Habbyshaw, *Branch Mgr*
EMP: 25
SALES (est): 1.3MM
SALES (corp-wide): 8.3MM **Privately Held**
WEB: www.tascoteleserve.com
SIC: 7389 Telephone answering service
PA: Telemessaging Services Inc
  6600 York Rd Ste 203
  Baltimore MD 21212
  410 377-3000

(G-6580)
TEN THOUSAND VILLAGES CLEVELAND
12425 Cedar Rd (44106-3155)
P.O. Box 18193 (44118-0193)
PHONE..................216 575-1058
EMP: 25
SALES: 139.7K **Privately Held**
SIC: 5023 Whol Homefurnishings

(G-6581)
TENABLE PROTECTIVE SVCS INC (PA)
2423 Payne Ave (44114-4428)
PHONE..................216 361-0002
Peter Miragliotta, *CEO*
Francis Crish, *President*
Todd Andersen, *Counsel*
Mary C Hammond, *Vice Pres*
Jonathan Matej, *Opers Mgr*
EMP: 2835
SQ FT: 12,000
SALES (est): 85.3MM **Privately Held**
WEB: www.ac-products.com
SIC: 7381 Security guard service; private investigator

(G-6582)
TENDON MANUFACTURING INC
20805 Aurora Rd (44146-1005)
PHONE..................216 663-3200
Fax: 216 663-6464
Gregory F Tench, *President*
Michael J Gordon, *Corp Secy*
Eric Dedic, *Opers Staff*
Thomas Tench, *Sls & Mktg Exec*
Kathy Thomas, *Office Mgr*
EMP: 46
SQ FT: 36,000
SALES (est): 9.4MM **Privately Held**
WEB: www.tendon.com
SIC: 3599 3479 1761 7692 Machine shop, jobbing & repair; painting of metal products; sheet metalwork; welding repair; sheet metalwork; automotive & apparel trimmings

(G-6583)
TERENCE ISAKOV MD
Also Called: Family Physicans Associates
5187 Mayfield Rd Ste 102 (44124-2467)
PHONE..................440 449-1014
Fax: 440 946-8879
Terence Isakov MD, *Partner*
EMP: 55
SALES (est): 2.3MM **Privately Held**
SIC: 8011 General & family practice, physician/surgeon

(G-6584)
TERMINIX INTL CO LTD PARTNR
5350 Transportation Blvd (44125-5327)
PHONE..................216 518-1091
Fax: 216 518-1612
Ron Trebec, *Manager*
EMP: 29
SALES (corp-wide): 2.9B **Publicly Held**
SIC: 7342 Pest control services
HQ: The Terminix International Company Limited Partnership
  860 Ridge Lake Blvd A3-4008
  Memphis TN 38120
  901 766-1400

(G-6585)
TERRACE CONSTRUCTION CO INC
3965 Pearl Rd (44109-3103)
PHONE..................216 739-3170
Fax: 216 739-3169
Jeffrey Nock, *Owner*
Mark Edzma, *Vice Pres*
Douglas Miller, *Safety Dir*
Albert Galati, *Treasurer*
Shadi Sarrouh, *Accounting Mgr*
EMP: 55
SQ FT: 7,500
SALES (est): 14.8MM **Privately Held**
WEB: www.terraceconstruction.com
SIC: 1623 Underground utilities contractor; water main construction; sewer line construction

(G-6586)
TERRY J REPPA & ASSOCIATES
7029 Pearl Rd Ste 350 (44130-4979)
P.O. Box 30247 (44130-0247)
PHONE..................440 888-8533
Fax: 440 888-7807
Terry Reppa, *President*
EMP: 26
SALES (est): 1.6MM **Privately Held**
SIC: 8742 8721 Management consulting services; billing & bookkeeping service

(G-6587)
TESAR INDUSTRIAL CONTRS INC (PA)
3920 Jennings Rd (44109-2860)
PHONE..................216 741-8008
Fax: 216 741-8353
James Tesar Jr, *President*
Sharon Tesar, *Vice Pres*
EMP: 30 **EST:** 1920
SQ FT: 20,000
SALES (est): 8.6MM **Privately Held**
WEB: www.tesarindustrialcontractors.com
SIC: 1796 4212 4213 Machinery installation; machinery dismantling; heavy machinery transport, local; heavy machinery transport

(G-6588)
TH MARTIN INC
8500 Brookpark Rd (44129-6806)
PHONE..................216 741-2020
Fax: 216 741-1166
Thomas H Martin, *President*
Michael Martin, *Vice Pres*
Darrell Manno, *Project Mgr*
Don Sewell, *Project Mgr*
Bonnie M Felice, *Controller*
EMP: 100
SQ FT: 66,000
SALES (est): 24.8MM **Privately Held**
SIC: 1711 Ventilation & duct work contractor

(G-6589)
THE ANTER BROTHERS COMPANY (PA)
Also Called: Davis Tobacco Co
12501 Elmwood Ave (44111-5909)
PHONE..................216 252-4555
Fax: 216 252-4566
Richard G Anter, *President*
Victor M Anter Jr, *Vice Pres*
George M Anter, *Treasurer*
Lester T Tolt, *Asst Sec*
EMP: 48 **EST:** 1912
SQ FT: 100,000
SALES (est): 6.1MM **Privately Held**
SIC: 5194 5145 Tobacco & tobacco products; confectionery

(G-6590)
THE CLEVELAND-CLIFFS IRON CO
1100 Superior Ave E # 1500 (44114-2530)
PHONE..................216 694-5700
J A Carrabba, *CEO*
D S Gallagher, *President*
Richard Fink, *General Mgr*
David Katsilometes, *General Mgr*
Brien Schacherer, *General Mgr*
EMP: 176
SQ FT: 40,000

GEOGRAPHIC SECTION
Cleveland - Cuyahoga County (G-6613)

SALES (est): 12.8MM
SALES (corp-wide): 2.3B **Publicly Held**
SIC: 1011 Iron ore mining; iron ore beneficiating
PA: Cleveland-Cliffs Inc.
200 Public Sq Ste 3300
Cleveland OH 44114
216 694-5700

(G-6591)
THERMAL TREATMENT CENTER INC (HQ)
Also Called: Nettleton Steel Treating Div
1101 E 55th St (44103-1026)
PHONE..................216 881-8100
Carmen Paponitti, *President*
Jack Luck, *Vice Pres*
Louise Profughi, *Treasurer*
EMP: 35 EST: 1945
SQ FT: 85,000
SALES (est): 6.4MM
SALES (corp-wide): 22.9MM **Privately Held**
WEB: www.htg.cc
SIC: 3398 8711 Metal heat treating; engineering services
PA: Hi Tecmetal Group Inc
1101 E 55th St
Cleveland OH 44103
216 881-8100

(G-6592)
THIRD FEDERAL SAVINGS (HQ)
7007 Broadway Ave (44105-1490)
PHONE..................800 844-7333
Fax: 216 441-7050
Marc A Stefanski, *Ch of Bd*
Judie Johnson, *General Mgr*
Calvin Kennedy, *Regional Mgr*
Michelle Hay, *Business Mgr*
Paul Huml, *COO*
EMP: 300 EST: 1938
SALES: 405.3MM
SALES (corp-wide): 834.2MM **Publicly Held**
SIC: 6035 Federal savings & loan associations
PA: Third Federal Savings
103 Foulk Rd Ste 101
Wilmington DE 19803
302 661-2009

(G-6593)
THIRD FEDERAL SAVINGS
5950 Ridge Rd (44129-3998)
PHONE..................440 885-4900
Fax: 440 842-2806
Donna Walraph, *Manager*
EMP: 26
SALES (corp-wide): 834.2MM **Publicly Held**
SIC: 6035 Federal savings & loan associations
HQ: Third Federal Savings And Loan Association Of Cleveland
7007 Broadway Ave
Cleveland OH 44105
800 844-7333

(G-6594)
THIRD FEDERAL SAVINGS
Also Called: Third Federal Savings & Loan
6849 Pearl Rd (44130-3616)
PHONE..................440 843-6300
Fax: 440 843-9159
Sandy Long, *Manager*
EMP: 26
SALES (corp wide): 834.2MM **Publicly Held**
SIC: 6035 Federal savings & loan associations
HQ: Third Federal Savings And Loan Association Of Cleveland
7007 Broadway Ave
Cleveland OH 44105
800 844-7333

(G-6595)
THISTLEDOWN INC
Also Called: Thistledown Racetrack
21501 Emery Rd (44128-4556)
PHONE..................216 662-8600
Fax: 216 662-5339
EMP: 200
SQ FT: 340,000
SALES (est): 13.3MM **Privately Held**
SIC: 7948 Racing Or Track Operation

(G-6596)
THOMPSON HINE LLP (PA)
127 Public Sq (44114-1217)
PHONE..................216 566-5500
Fax: 216 566-5583
Kip T Bollin, *President*
David J Hooker, *Managing Prtnr*
Deborah Z Read, *Managing Prtnr*
Michael L Hardy, *Partner*
James B Aronoff, *Partner*
EMP: 370
SQ FT: 145,000
SALES (est): 98.4MM **Privately Held**
WEB: www.thompsonhine.com
SIC: 8111 General practice law office

(G-6597)
THREE VILLAGE CONDOMINIUM
5150 Three Village Dr (44124-3772)
PHONE..................440 461-1483
Fax: 440 473-6970
V S Sagal, *President*
Harrison Fuerst, *President*
EMP: 37
SQ FT: 261,000
SALES (est): 1MM **Privately Held**
SIC: 8641 Condominium association

(G-6598)
THRIFTY RENT-A-CAR SYSTEM INC
Also Called: Thrifty Car Rental
7701 Day Dr (44129-5604)
PHONE..................440 842-1660
Joseph E Cappy, *Ch of Bd*
EMP: 30
SALES (corp-wide): 8.8B **Publicly Held**
SIC: 7514 Rent-a-car service
HQ: Thrifty Rent-A-Car System, Inc.
8501 Williams Rd
Estero FL 33928
239 301-7000

(G-6599)
THYSSENKRUPP MATERIALS NA INC
Ken-Mac Metals
17901 Englewood Dr (44130-3454)
PHONE..................440 234-7500
Fax: 440 891-1298
Randy Pengov, *Sales Mgr*
Judy Snyder, *Sales Staff*
Sherry Diperna, *Sales Associate*
Timothy Yost, *Branch Mgr*
Gary Halterman, *Manager*
EMP: 202
SALES (corp-wide): 48.7B **Privately Held**
SIC: 5051 Nonferrous metal sheets, bars, rods, etc.; aluminum bars, rods, ingots, sheets, pipes, plates, etc.
HQ: Thyssenkrupp Materials Na, Inc.
22355 W 11 Mile Rd
Southfield MI 48033
248 233-5600

(G-6600)
TILDEN MINING COMPANY LC (HQ)
Also Called: Cliffs Michigan Mining Company
200 Public Sq Ste 3300 (44114-2315)
PHONE..................216 694-5700
Lourenco Goncalves, *President*
P Kelly Tompkins, *COO*
Terry Fodor, *Exec VP*
Maurice Harapiak, *Exec VP*
Terrence Mee, *Exec VP*
EMP: 580
SALES (est): 379.7MM
SALES (corp-wide): 2.3B **Publicly Held**
SIC: 1011 Iron ore mining; iron ore pelletizing; iron ore beneficiating
PA: Cleveland-Cliffs Inc.
200 Public Sq Ste 3300
Cleveland OH 44114
216 694-5700

(G-6601)
TOLEDO INNS INC
Also Called: Crowne Plaza Cleveland Airport
7230 Engle Rd (44130-3427)
PHONE..................440 243-4040
J B Patel, *Principal*
Diane Calire, *Manager*
EMP: 32
SQ FT: 61,845
SALES (est): 3.5MM **Privately Held**
SIC: 7011 Hotels

(G-6602)
TOM PAIGE CATERING COMPANY
2275 E 55th St (44103-4452)
PHONE..................216 431-4236
Fax: 216 431-6272
Thomas E Paige, *President*
Ryan Strickland, *Vice Pres*
Roy Manley, *Controller*
Charleen Mitchell, *Admin Asst*
EMP: 35
SQ FT: 92,000
SALES (est): 4.1MM **Privately Held**
SIC: 8322 Meal delivery program

(G-6603)
TOSHIBA AMER BUS SOLUTIONS INC
7850 Hub Pkwy (44125-5711)
PHONE..................216 642-7555
Ned Bergen, *VP Sales*
Nick Kumar, *Sales Associate*
Gary Miller, *Branch Mgr*
Julie Turi, *Executive Asst*
EMP: 37
SALES (corp-wide): 42.8B **Privately Held**
WEB: www.levenstein.com
SIC: 5999 7629 Business machines & equipment; facsimile equipment; photocopy machines; telephone equipment & systems; business machine repair, electric
HQ: Toshiba America Business Solutions, Inc.
25530 Commercentre Dr
Lake Forest CA 92630
949 462-6000

(G-6604)
TOTAL TRANSPORTATION TRCKG INC
Also Called: R J W
5755 Granger Rd Ste 400 (44131-1456)
PHONE..................216 398-6090
Jeffrey Wenham, *President*
Ed Tovey, *Vice Pres*
EMP: 25
SQ FT: 6,000
SALES (est): 1.7MM **Privately Held**
SIC: 4789 Cabs, horse drawn: for hire

(G-6605)
TOTAL WHOLESALE INC
Also Called: Seaway Cash N Carry
3900 Woodland Ave (44115-3411)
PHONE..................216 361-5757
Fax: 216 361-5760
Ali Faraj, *President*
Pepe Faraj, *Office Mgr*
EMP: 30
SQ FT: 1,000
SALES (est): 10.3MM **Privately Held**
WEB: www.seawaycashncarry.com
SIC: 5141 Food brokers

(G-6606)
TOURS OF BLACK HERITAGE INC
Also Called: Tobh
8800 Woodland Ave (44104-3221)
PHONE..................440 247-2737
Arline Burks, *CEO*
Dakota Gant, *President*
EMP: 63
SQ FT: 5,000
SALES (est): 2.5MM **Privately Held**
SIC: 4725 Tour operators

(G-6607)
TOWARDS EMPLOYMENT INC
1255 Euclid Ave Ste 300 (44115-1807)
PHONE..................216 696-5750
Josefa Martinez-Cedeo, *Finance*
Angelo Degenaro, *CTO*
Scott Criswell, *Info Tech Mgr*
Josefa Martinez, *Info Tech Mgr*
Cynthia Huff, *IT/INT Sup*
EMP: 40
SQ FT: 12,500
SALES: 3.1MM **Privately Held**
WEB: www.towardsemployment.org
SIC: 8641 Civic social & fraternal associations

(G-6608)
TRAFFTECH INC
7000 Hubbard Ave (44127-1419)
PHONE..................216 361-8808
Fax: 216 361-8811
William J Porter, *President*
Carol Porter, *Vice Pres*
Micheal Moran, *Controller*
Kim Mc Peak, *Admin Sec*
Deb Willfong, *Admin Asst*
EMP: 50
SQ FT: 55,000
SALES (est): 7.6MM **Privately Held**
SIC: 1611 General contractor, highway & street construction

(G-6609)
TRANSCON BUILDERS INC (PA)
25250 Rockside Rd Ste 2 (44146-1839)
PHONE..................440 439-3400
Peter Rzepka, *Ch of Bd*
Fred Rzepka, *President*
Lawrence Apple, *Vice Pres*
Stanley Freeman, *Vice Pres*
David Rzepka, *Chief Mktg Ofcr*
EMP: 30
SQ FT: 14,000
SALES (est): 38.4MM **Privately Held**
WEB: www.transconbuilders.com
SIC: 6513 1522 Apartment building operators; residential construction

(G-6610)
TRANSCORE ITS LLC
Also Called: Trans Core
6930 Engle Rd Ste Y (44130-8459)
PHONE..................440 243-2222
Fax: 440 243-4250
Edward L Brisann Sr, *Manager*
EMP: 25
SALES (corp-wide): 4.6B **Publicly Held**
SIC: 8711 Engineering services
HQ: Transcore Its, Llc
3721 Tecport Dr Ste 102
Harrisburg PA 17111
717 561-5869

(G-6611)
TRANSDIGM GROUP INCORPORATED (PA)
1301 E 9th St Ste 3000 (44114-1871)
PHONE..................216 706-2960
W Nicholas Howley, *Ch of Bd*
Kevin Stein, *President*
Bernt G Iversen II, *Exec VP*
Roger V Jones, *Exec VP*
Peter Palmer, *Exec VP*
EMP: 117
SQ FT: 20,100
SALES: 3.5B **Publicly Held**
WEB: www.transdigm.com
SIC: 3728 5088 Aircraft parts & equipment; aircraft equipment & supplies

(G-6612)
TRANSPORT SERVICES INC
10499 Royalton Rd (44133-4432)
PHONE..................440 582-4900
Fax: 440 582-3726
Adam Therrien, *President*
Albert Therrien, *Chairman*
Tom Soggs, *Vice Pres*
Patricia Therrien, *Vice Pres*
Mike Collins, *CFO*
EMP: 42
SQ FT: 20,000
SALES (est): 18.3MM **Privately Held**
WEB: www.transportservices.net
SIC: 5013 7519 7539 Trailer parts & accessories; trailer rental; trailer repair

(G-6613)
TRANSPORTATION UNLIMITED INC (PA)
3740 Carnegie Ave Ste 101 (44115-2756)
PHONE..................216 426-0088
Fax: 216 426-2248
Samuel Lucarelli, *President*
Jason Lucarelli, *Corp Secy*
Michael Panzarelli, *Vice Pres*
Mel Jackson, *Manager*

Cleveland - Cuyahoga County (G-6614)

GEOGRAPHIC SECTION

EMP: 1450 EST: 1974
SQ FT: 40,000
SALES (est): 52.8MM Privately Held
SIC: 7363 4213 4212 Truck driver services; trucking, except local; local trucking, without storage

(G-6614)
TRANSYSTEMS CORPORATION
55 Public Sq Ste 1900 (44113-1906)
PHONE 216 861-1780
Fax: 216 861-1028
Tim Rock, *Assistant VP*
Don Derewecki, *Vice Pres*
Rick Rockich, *Vice Pres*
James Stanek, *Vice Pres*
William Glassmyer, *Engineer*
EMP: 30
SALES (corp-wide): 144.2MM Privately Held
SIC: 8711 Consulting engineer
PA: Transystems Corporation
2400 Pershing Rd Ste 400
Kansas City MO 64108
816 329-8700

(G-6615)
TRAVELERS PROPERTY CSLTY CORP
Also Called: Travelers Insurance
6150 Oak Tree Blvd # 400 (44131-6917)
PHONE 216 643-2100
Fax: 216 524-0698
Brett Behar, *Vice Pres*
Barton S Brown, *Vice Pres*
Maureen Beveridge, *Accounts Exec*
Rebecca Griswold, *Accounts Exec*
Paul Nebraska, *Manager*
EMP: 110
SALES (corp-wide): 28.9B Publicly Held
WEB: www.travelerspc.com
SIC: 6411 Insurance agents
HQ: Travelers Property Casualty Corp.
1 Tower Sq 8ms
Hartford CT 06183

(G-6616)
TRI ZOB INC
Also Called: West Park Animal Hospital
4117 Rocky River Dr (44135-1107)
PHONE 216 252-4500
Fax: 216 252-1114
Borys Pakush, *President*
EMP: 30
SALES (est): 1.3MM Privately Held
WEB: www.westparkanimalhospital.com
SIC: 0742 Animal hospital services, pets & other animal specialties

(G-6617)
TRIAD ENGINEERING & CONTG CO (PA)
9715 Clinton Rd (44144-1031)
PHONE 440 786-1000
Fax: 440 786-1133
Clifford J Kassouf, *President*
Ernest P Mansour, *Principal*
Philip Kassouf, *Treasurer*
Donna Michalski, *Manager*
Paul Kassouf, *Admin Sec*
EMP: 30
SQ FT: 5,600
SALES (est): 14.1MM Privately Held
WEB: www.triad-engineering.com
SIC: 1794 Excavation & grading, building construction

(G-6618)
TRIMARK USA LLC
Trimark S S Kemp
4567 Willow Pkwy (44125-1041)
PHONE 216 271-7700
Bob Davison, *Sales Staff*
Tomwine Claw, *Manager*
EMP: 100
SALES (corp-wide): 6.7B Privately Held
SIC: 5046 Restaurant equipment & supplies
HQ: Trimark Usa, Llc
505 Collins St
Attleboro MA 02703
508 399-2400

(G-6619)
TROLLEY TOURS OF CLEVELAND
Also Called: Lolly The Trolley
1790 Columbus Rd (44113-2412)
P.O. Box 91658 (44101-3658)
PHONE 216 771-4484
Fax: 216 771-1273
Sherrill Paul, *President*
Peter Paul, *Treasurer*
EMP: 40
SQ FT: 12,000
SALES (est): 4.6MM Privately Held
WEB: www.lollytrolley.com
SIC: 4725 Tours, conducted

(G-6620)
TRX GREAT PLAINS INC
6600 Bessemer Ave (44127-1804)
PHONE 855 259-9259
EMP: 75 EST: 2010
SALES (est): 6.2MM Privately Held
SIC: 4731 Freight Transportation Arrangement

(G-6621)
TUCKER ELLIS LLP
950 Main Ave Ste 1100 (44113-7213)
PHONE 720 897-4400
Lawrence Callaghan, *Counsel*
Frederick Wich, *Branch Mgr*
Andrea M Przybysz, *Associate*
EMP: 95
SALES (est): 3.6MM
SALES (corp-wide): 49.1MM Privately Held
SIC: 8111 General practice attorney, lawyer
PA: Tucker Ellis Llp
950 Main Ave Ste 1100
Cleveland OH 44113
216 592-5000

(G-6622)
TUCKER ELLIS LLP (PA)
950 Main Ave Ste 1100 (44113-7213)
PHONE 216 592-5000
Robert Tucker, *Partner*
Stephen Ellis, *Partner*
Kim West, *Partner*
William Berglund, *Editor*
Sarah Bunce, *Counsel*
EMP: 201
SQ FT: 100,000
SALES (est): 49.1MM Privately Held
WEB: www.tuckerellis.com
SIC: 8111 General practice attorney, lawyer

(G-6623)
TURNER CONSTRUCTION COMPANY
1422 Euclid Ave Ste 1400 (44115-2015)
PHONE 216 522-1180
Jeffery V Abke, *Project Mgr*
Deborah King, *Purch Agent*
Mark Dent, *Branch Mgr*
EMP: 50
SALES (corp-wide): 1.5B Privately Held
WEB: www.tcco.com
SIC: 1542 Commercial & office building, new construction
HQ: Turner Construction Company Inc
375 Hudson St Fl 6
New York NY 10014
212 229-6000

(G-6624)
TYRONE TOWNHOUSES PA INV LLC
8111 Rockside Rd (44125-6129)
PHONE 216 520-1250
Frank Sinito,
EMP: 99
SALES (est): 1.5MM Privately Held
SIC: 6513 Apartment building operators

(G-6625)
U S ASSOCIATES REALTY INC
4700 Rockside Rd Ste 150 (44131-2171)
PHONE 216 663-3400
Fax: 216 663-3405
Al Dailide, *President*
Susan Dailide, *Admin Sec*
EMP: 25 EST: 1973

SALES (est): 440K Privately Held
WEB: www.usassoc.com
SIC: 6531 Real estate brokers & agents

(G-6626)
U S LABORATORIES INC
33095 Bainbridge Rd (44139-2834)
PHONE 440 248-1223
Ratanjit S Sondhe, *President*
EMP: 30
SQ FT: 60,000
SALES (est): 1.7MM
SALES (corp-wide): 62.4B Publicly Held
SIC: 8731 Chemical laboratory, except testing
HQ: The Dow Chemical Company
2030 Dow Ctr
Midland MI 48674
989 636-1000

(G-6627)
U S TITLE AGENCY INC
1213 Prospect Ave E # 400 (44115-1260)
PHONE 216 621-1424
Gerald Goldberg, *President*
William Boukalik, *COO*
Michael Gerome, *Senior VP*
Robert Levine, *Senior VP*
EMP: 33
SALES (est): 13.2MM Privately Held
SIC: 6361 6531 Real estate title insurance; real estate agents & managers

(G-6628)
UBS FINANCIAL SERVICES INC
2000 Auburn Dr Ste 100 (44122-4328)
PHONE 216 831-3400
James Chandler, *Div Sub Head*
Gene Pucci, *Opers Mgr*
John Minnillo, *Manager*
Kevin Forney, *Agent*
EMP: 50
SALES (corp-wide): 28B Privately Held
SIC: 6211 Stock brokers & dealers
HQ: Ubs Financial Services Inc.
1285 Ave Of The Americas
New York NY 10019
212 713-2000

(G-6629)
UHMG DEPARTMENT OF UROLOGIST (PA)
11100 Euclid Ave (44106-1716)
PHONE 216 844-3009
Fax: 216 382-7832
Firouz Daneshgari, *President*
Brad Calabrese, *General Mgr*
Donna Harris, *Human Res Mgr*
Adonis Hijaz, *Med Doctor*
Wendy Chenney, *Manager*
EMP: 42
SQ FT: 2,500
SALES (est): 4.3MM Privately Held
SIC: 8011 Urologist

(G-6630)
ULMER & BERNE LLP (PA)
Also Called: Ulmer & Berne Illinois
1660 W 2nd St Ste 1100 (44113-1406)
PHONE 216 583-7000
Fax: 216 931-6001
Jeffrey S Dunlap, *Ch of Bd*
John J Haggerty, *Ch of Bd*
Richard T Hamilton, *Ch of Bd*
Richard G Hardy, *Ch of Bd*
Peter A Rome, *Ch of Bd*
EMP: 284
SQ FT: 65,000
SALES (est): 85.9MM Privately Held
SIC: 8111 General practice law office

(G-6631)
UNION CLUB COMPANY
1211 Euclid Ave (44115-1865)
PHONE 216 621-4230
Fax: 216 621-7440
John Wheeler, *President*
Lawrence McFadden, *General Mgr*
John Sherwood, *Vice Pres*
Scott Kissinger, *CFO*
Mary Laughlin, *Treasurer*
EMP: 75
SQ FT: 75,000

SALES (est): 3.7MM Privately Held
WEB: www.unionclub.com
SIC: 8641 5813 5812 Social club, membership; drinking places; eating places

(G-6632)
UNITED AGENCIES INC
1422 Euclid Ave Ste 510 (44115-1901)
PHONE 216 696-8044
John Boyle III, *President*
Ralph Malafronte, *Senior VP*
Marianne Gladhill, *Vice Pres*
Jeff Bader, *Broker*
Dawn Helwig, *Accounts Mgr*
EMP: 30
SALES (est): 7.2MM Privately Held
SIC: 6411 Insurance agents

(G-6633)
UNITED AIRLINES INC
Also Called: Continental Airlines
5970 Cargo Rd (44135-3110)
PHONE 216 501-4700
Connie Mutch, *Human Res Mgr*
Tom Braun, *Manager*
George Hujo, *Manager*
Adrienne Babis, *Supervisor*
Tolman Rick, *Technician*
EMP: 167
SALES (corp-wide): 37.7B Publicly Held
WEB: www.continental.com
SIC: 4512 Air passenger carrier, scheduled
HQ: United Airlines, Inc.
233 S Wacker Dr Ste 710
Chicago IL 60606
872 825-4000

(G-6634)
UNITED ATMTC HTNG SPPLY OF CLV (PA)
Also Called: United Electric Motor Repair
2125 Superior Ave E (44114-2101)
PHONE 216 621-5571
Fax: 216 621-2789
Michael Morris, *President*
Lionel Meister, *Vice Pres*
Elizabeth Morris, *Treasurer*
Joan Meister, *Admin Sec*
EMP: 40
SQ FT: 50,000
SALES (est): 5.5MM Privately Held
SIC: 5074 5075 Heating equipment (hydronic); air conditioning equipment, except room units

(G-6635)
UNITED CEREBRAL PALSY (PA)
10011 Euclid Ave (44106-4701)
PHONE 216 791-8363
Patricia S Otter, *President*
Laverne Law, *CFO*
Tammi Billingsley, *Manager*
Elizabeth Mellino, *Manager*
Norma Seevers, *Executive Asst*
EMP: 235 EST: 1950
SQ FT: 40,000
SALES (est): 8.9MM Privately Held
SIC: 8361 8331 Rehabilitation center, residential: health care incidental; vocational rehabilitation agency

(G-6636)
UNITED CEREBRAL PALSY
Also Called: Edendale House
1374 Edendale St (44121-1627)
PHONE 216 381-9993
Fax: 216 381-9994
Diane Mc Kenna, *Branch Mgr*
EMP: 60
SALES (corp-wide): 8.9MM Privately Held
SIC: 8361 8052 8059 Rehabilitation center, residential: health care incidental; intermediate care facilities; home for the mentally retarded, exc. skilled or intermediate
PA: United Cerebral Palsy Association Of Greater Cleveland, Inc.
10011 Euclid Ave
Cleveland OH 44106
216 791-8363

(G-6637)
UNITED CONSUMER FINCL SVCS CO
865 Bassett Rd (44145-1142)
PHONE 440 835-3230
Fax: 440 835-6657
Cliff Hooley, *CEO*
Bill Francis, *President*
Scott Wolf, *President*
William Ciszczon, *Vice Pres*
Michele Liebenauer, *Controller*
EMP: 200
SQ FT: 27,000
SALES (est): 44.9MM
SALES (corp-wide): 242.1B **Publicly Held**
SIC: 6141 Consumer finance companies
HQ: The Scott Fetzer Company
28800 Clemens Rd
Westlake OH 44145
440 892-3000

(G-6638)
UNITED FD COML WKRS LOCAL 880 (PA)
2828 Euclid Ave (44115-2455)
PHONE 216 241-5930
Fax: 216 241-2168
Thomas H Robertson, *President*
Valancia Livingston, *Manager*
Robert W Grauvogl, *Admin Sec*
EMP: 43
SQ FT: 30,000
SALES (est): 4.2MM **Privately Held**
SIC: 8631 6512 Labor union; commercial & industrial building operation

(G-6639)
UNITED GARAGE & SERVICE CORP (PA)
2069 W 3rd St (44113-2502)
PHONE 216 623-1550
Arthur B Mc Bride Jr, *President*
Brian Mc Bride, *Vice Pres*
William Klug, *Treasurer*
Edward J Mc Bride, *Admin Sec*
EMP: 60
SQ FT: 10,000
SALES (est): 14.1MM **Privately Held**
SIC: 4121 7539 Taxicabs; automotive repair shops

(G-6640)
UNITED HEALTHCARE OHIO INC
1001 Lkeside Ave Ste 1000 (44114)
PHONE 216 694-4080
Fax: 216 771-1737
Lisa Chapman-Smith, *CEO*
Brian Elter, *Vice Pres*
Marvin Gossett, *Technical Mgr*
Andrew Bren, *Investment Ofcr*
Chelsey Berstler, *Auditing Mgr*
EMP: 80
SALES (corp-wide): 201.1B **Publicly Held**
WEB: www.uhc.com
SIC: 6324 Group hospitalization plans
HQ: United Healthcare Of Ohio, Inc.
9200 Worthington Rd
Columbus OH 43085
614 410-7000

(G-6641)
UNITED LABOR AGENCY INC
1020 Bolivar Rd Fl 3 (44115-1204)
PHONE 216 664-3446
Fax: 216 391-6959
Gary Gargiulo, *Finance*
D Megenhardt, *Exec Dir*
David Megenhardt, *Exec Dir*
Thelma Campbell, *Bd of Directors*
EMP: 115
SQ FT: 20,000
SALES: 9.2MM **Privately Held**
WEB: www.ula-ohio.org
SIC: 8399 Community development groups

(G-6642)
UNITED OMAHA LIFE INSURANCE CO
6060 Rockside Woods # 330 (44131-7343)
PHONE 216 573-6900
Fax: 216 573-6910
Neil Chonofski, *Manager*
Richard Doyle, *Manager*
EMP: 25
SALES (corp-wide): 8.7B **Privately Held**
SIC: 6311 Life insurance carriers
HQ: United Of Omaha Life Insurance Company
Mutual Of Omaha Plaza
Omaha NE 68175
402 342-7600

(G-6643)
UNITED PARCEL SERVICE INC
Also Called: UPS
17940 Englewood Dr (44130-3463)
PHONE 440 826-2591
Oscar Vasquez, *Manager*
Don Herwerden, *Manager*
Tania Renko, *Manager*
EMP: 400
SALES (corp-wide): 65.8B **Publicly Held**
WEB: www.ups.com
SIC: 4215 Parcel delivery, vehicular
PA: United Parcel Service, Inc.
55 Glenlake Pkwy
Atlanta GA 30328
404 828-6000

(G-6644)
UNITED PARCEL SERVICE INC OH
Also Called: UPS
4300 E 68th St (44105-5797)
PHONE 800 742-5877
Jim Grant, *Human Res Mgr*
Tony Patton, *Persnl Mgr*
Al Ratt, *Human Resources*
Robert Martin, *Sales Mgr*
EMP: 158
SALES (corp-wide): 65.8B **Publicly Held**
SIC: 4215 Parcel delivery, vehicular; package delivery, vehicular
HQ: United Parcel Service, Inc. (Oh)
55 Glenlake Pkwy
Atlanta GA 30328
404 828-6000

(G-6645)
UNITED PARCEL SERVICE INC OH
Also Called: UPS
18685 Sheldon Rd (44130-2471)
PHONE 216 676-4560
EMP: 316
SALES (corp-wide): 65.8B **Publicly Held**
SIC: 7389 Mailing & messenger services
HQ: United Parcel Service, Inc. (Oh)
55 Glenlake Pkwy
Atlanta GA 30328
404 828-6000

(G-6646)
UNITED STATES CARGO & COURIER
Also Called: U S Cargo
4735 W 150th St Ste D (44135-3300)
PHONE 216 325-0483
Fax: 216 662-4805
Tim Pullman, *Branch Mgr*
Randy Cargo, *Manager*
EMP: 30
SALES (est): 1.7MM
SALES (corp-wide): 9.9MM **Privately Held**
WEB: www.usccs.com
SIC: 4215 4513 Courier services, except by air; air courier services
HQ: United States Cargo & Courier Service Incorporated
900 Williams Ave
Columbus OH
614 552-2746

(G-6647)
UNITED WAY GREATER CLEVELAND (PA)
1331 Euclid Ave (44115-1819)
PHONE 216 436-2100
Fax: 216 436-2255
William Kitson, *CEO*
John Saada, *Trustee*
Jason Daniels, *Exec VP*
Simon Bisson, *Vice Pres*
Judith G Simpson, *Vice Pres*
EMP: 121
SQ FT: 90,000
SALES: 43.2MM **Privately Held**
WEB: www.uws.org
SIC: 8399 United Fund councils

(G-6648)
UNIVERSAL GRINDING CORPORATION
1234 W 78th St (44102-1914)
PHONE 216 631-9410
Fax: 216 631-5264
Donald R Toth, *President*
Kevin Decaire, *Corp Secy*
Nancy Toth, *Vice Pres*
EMP: 49
SQ FT: 86,000
SALES: 7MM **Privately Held**
WEB: www.universalgrinding.com
SIC: 7389 Grinding, precision: commercial or industrial

(G-6649)
UNIVERSAL OIL INC
265 Jefferson Ave (44113-2594)
PHONE 216 771-4300
Fax: 216 771-1845
John J Purcell, *President*
Scott Fox, *COO*
Don Krance, *Sales Staff*
EMP: 30
SQ FT: 25,000
SALES (est): 30.9MM **Privately Held**
WEB: www.universaloil.com
SIC: 5171 2992 Petroleum bulk stations; lubricating oils

(G-6650)
UNIVERSAL STEEL COMPANY
6600 Grant Ave (44105-5692)
PHONE 216 883-4972
Fax: 216 341-0421
Richard W Williams, *President*
Dean Dolata, *General Mgr*
David P Miller, *Chairman*
Kevin Smith, *General Ptnr*
Jerry Kinder, *Purch Mgr*
▲ **EMP:** 100
SQ FT: 200,000
SALES (est): 23.2MM
SALES (corp-wide): 107.5MM **Privately Held**
WEB: www.univsteel.com
SIC: 3444 5051 Sheet metalwork; steel
PA: Columbia National Group, Inc.
6600 Grant Ave
Cleveland OH 44105
216 883-4972

(G-6651)
UNIVERSITIES SPACE RES ASSN
Also Called: National Center For Space Expl
10900 Euclid Ave (44106-1712)
PHONE 216 368-0750
Kenneth Basch, *Opers Staff*
Iwan Alexander, *Director*
EMP: 40
SALES (corp-wide): 115.8MM **Privately Held**
SIC: 8733 Scientific research agency
PA: Universities Space Research Association
7178 Columbia Gateway Dr
Columbia MD 21046
410 730-2656

(G-6652)
UNIVERSITY ANESTHESIOLOGISTS
11100 Euclid Ave Ste 2517 (44106-1716)
PHONE 216 844-3777
Fax: 216 844-3780
Helmut Cascorbi, *Med Doctor*
Matthew Norcia, *Med Doctor*
David Rapkin, *Med Doctor*
David Wallace, *Med Doctor*
Cindy Patrzyk, *Administration*
EMP: 50
SALES (est): 4.5MM **Privately Held**
SIC: 8011 Anesthesiologist

(G-6653)
UNIVERSITY CIRCLE INCORPORATED (PA)
Also Called: UCI
10831 Magnolia Dr (44106-1887)
PHONE 216 791-3900
Fax: 216 791-3935
Christopher Ronayne, *President*
Janet Ashe, *Trustee*
Daniel J Stahura, *CFO*
Lisa Sands, *Mktg Dir*
David Razum, *Comms Mgr*
EMP: 30
SQ FT: 10,000
SALES: 11.3MM **Privately Held**
SIC: 6531 Real estate agents & managers

(G-6654)
UNIVERSITY HOSPITALS
Also Called: U H Ahuja Medical Center
3999 Richmond Rd (44122-6046)
PHONE 216 593-5500
Susan Juris, *Branch Mgr*
EMP: 500
SALES (corp-wide): 2.3B **Privately Held**
SIC: 8062 General medical & surgical hospitals
PA: University Hospitals Health System, Inc.
3605 Warrensville Ctr Rd
Shaker Heights OH 44122
216 767-8900

(G-6655)
UNIVERSITY HOSPITALS
2915 Ludlow Rd (44120-2308)
P.O. Box 202625, Shaker Heights (44120-8127)
PHONE 216 536-3020
Charles Sullivan, *Principal*
EMP: 35 **EST:** 2015
SALES (est): 3.7MM **Privately Held**
SIC: 8062 General medical & surgical hospitals

(G-6656)
UNIVERSITY HOSPITALS
12200 Fairhill Rd Frnt (44120-1058)
PHONE 216 844-6400
Bill Ditirro, *Manager*
Harry Menegay, *Administration*
EMP: 40
SALES (corp-wide): 2.3B **Privately Held**
SIC: 8062 General medical & surgical hospitals
PA: University Hospitals Health System, Inc.
3605 Warrensville Ctr Rd
Shaker Heights OH 44122
216 767-8900

(G-6657)
UNIVERSITY HOSPITALS
Also Called: Ireland Cancer Center
11100 Euclid Ave Wrn5065 (44106-1716)
PHONE 216 844-8797
Fax: 216 844-7832
Ron Burlinghaus, *Accounting Mgr*
Barbara Guy, *Financial Exec*
Dr Danton Gerson, *Branch Mgr*
Clark W Distelhorst, *Manager*
John H Wilber, *Surgeon*
EMP: 85
SALES (corp-wide): 2.3B **Privately Held**
SIC: 8733 8011 8741 Medical research; offices & clinics of medical doctors; management services
PA: University Hospitals Health System, Inc.
3605 Warrensville Ctr Rd
Shaker Heights OH 44122
216 767-8900

(G-6658)
UNIVERSITY HOSPITALS
Healthmatch
11001 Euclid Ave (44106-1713)
PHONE 216 767-8500
Bruce Wilkinfield, *Partner*
Baruch Kleinman, *Engineer*
Grant Snider, *Engineer*
Barry Effron, *Med Doctor*
Josh Plessinger, *Network Analyst*
EMP: 25

Cleveland - Cuyahoga County (G-6659)

SALES (corp-wide): 2.3B **Privately Held**
SIC: 8011 Offices & clinics of medical doctors
PA: University Hospitals Health System, Inc.
3605 Warrensville Ctr Rd
Shaker Heights OH 44122
216 767-8900

(G-6659)
UNIVERSITY HOSPITALS CLEVELAND
11100 Euclid Ave (44106-1716)
PHONE.................................216 844-1000
Tom Zenty, *President*
Kim Bixenstine, *Vice Pres*
Brent Carson, *Vice Pres*
Maria Kamenos, *Vice Pres*
Julia Simms, *Project Mgr*
EMP: 656
SALES (corp-wide): 2.3B **Privately Held**
SIC: 8062 General medical & surgical hospitals
HQ: University Hospitals Of Cleveland
11100 Euclid Ave
Cleveland OH 44106
216 844-1000

(G-6660)
UNIVERSITY HOSPITALS CLEVELAND (HQ)
11100 Euclid Ave (44106-1716)
PHONE.................................216 844-1000
Fax: 216 844-8397
Thomas Zenty, *President*
Robert Cunningham, *Vice Chairman*
Mary A Annecharico, *Senior VP*
Kim Bixenstine, *Vice Pres*
Jason Elliott, *Vice Pres*
▲ EMP: 7000
SALES (est): 2B
SALES (corp-wide): 2.3B **Privately Held**
SIC: 8062 8069 General medical & surgical hospitals; specialty hospitals, except psychiatric
PA: University Hospitals Health System, Inc.
3605 Warrensville Ctr Rd
Shaker Heights OH 44122
216 767-8900

(G-6661)
UNIVERSITY HOSPITALS CLEVELAND
4510 Richmond Rd (44128-5757)
PHONE.................................216 844-4663
Mary Havannah, *Manager*
EMP: 70
SALES (corp-wide): 2.3B **Privately Held**
SIC: 8062 8082 General medical & surgical hospitals; home health care services
HQ: University Hospitals Of Cleveland
11100 Euclid Ave
Cleveland OH 44106
216 844-1000

(G-6662)
UNIVERSITY HOSPITALS CLEVELAND
Rainbow Babies and Chld Hosp
11100 Euclid Ave (44106-1716)
PHONE.................................216 844-3528
Gary Weimer, *Senior VP*
Roseann Longnecker, *Office Mgr*
Depas Quale, *Office Mgr*
Janet Rhyner, *Office Mgr*
Alan J Cohen, *Plastic Surgeon*
EMP: 25
SALES (corp-wide): 2.3B **Privately Held**
SIC: 8062 8741 General medical & surgical hospitals; management services
HQ: University Hospitals Of Cleveland
11100 Euclid Ave
Cleveland OH 44106
216 844-1000

(G-6663)
UNIVERSITY HOSPITALS HE
4510 Richmond Rd (44128-5757)
PHONE.................................216 844-4663
Fax: 216 595-7295
Mary Havannah, *Principal*
Cheryl Ressetar, *Purch Agent*
Becky Ivcic, *CFO*

Mary Havanas, *Office Mgr*
Ralph Portzer, *Manager*
EMP: 350
SALES (est): 23.3MM
SALES (corp-wide): 2.3B **Privately Held**
SIC: 8082 Home health care services
PA: University Hospitals Health System, Inc.
3605 Warrensville Ctr Rd
Shaker Heights OH 44122
216 767-8900

(G-6664)
UNIVERSITY HOSPITALS HEALTH SY
11100 Euclid Ave (44106-1716)
PHONE.................................216 844-4663
Thomas F Zenty III, *CEO*
Richard E Grant, *Med Doctor*
EMP: 25
SALES: 269.9MM **Privately Held**
SIC: 8062 General medical & surgical hospitals

(G-6665)
UNIVERSITY MANOR HLTH CARE CTR
2186 Ambleside Dr (44106-4620)
PHONE.................................216 721-1400
Fax: 216 421-1468
Suzanne Fromson, *President*
Patricia Weisberg, *Corp Secy*
Linda Nawalaniec, *Controller*
Milton Fromson, *Shareholder*
Dan McDonald, *Administration*
EMP: 240
SALES (est): 7.4MM **Privately Held**
SIC: 8051 8052 Skilled nursing care facilities; intermediate care facilities

(G-6666)
UNIVERSITY OPHTHALMOLOGY ASSOC
1611 S Green Rd Ste 306c (44121-4192)
PHONE.................................216 382-8022
Fax: 216 382-7667
William Annable, *President*
Ronald Price MD, *Office Mgr*
EMP: 25
SALES (est): 2.3MM **Privately Held**
SIC: 8011 Ophthalmologist

(G-6667)
UNIVERSITY ORTHPEDIC ASSOC INC (PA)
Also Called: University Hospital
11100 Euclid Ave Ste 3001 (44106-1716)
PHONE.................................216 844-1000
Fax: 216 844-1325
Fred C Rothstein, *President*
George Bakale, *General Mgr*
Nancy M Tinsley, *Vice Pres*
Abigail Williams, *Project Mgr*
Valerie Hayden, *Opers Staff*
EMP: 25 EST: 1969
SQ FT: 2,300
SALES (est): 34.4MM **Privately Held**
SIC: 8011 Orthopedic physician

(G-6668)
UNIVERSITY RDLGSTS OF CLVELAND
Also Called: Cleveland University
2485 Euclid Ave (44115)
PHONE.................................216 844-1700
Fax: 216 844-5479
John Haaga, *Principal*
Hui Zhu, *Med Doctor*
Carol Rosen, *Director*
Kady Lesnak, *Admin Asst*
Pratima Sood, *Endocrinology*
EMP: 25
SALES (est): 3.1MM **Privately Held**
SIC: 8011 Radiologist

(G-6669)
UNIVERSITY SETTLEMENT INC (PA)
4800 Broadway Ave (44127-1071)
PHONE.................................216 641-8948
Fax: 216 641-7971
Jofefa Martinez, *Finance*
Claire Blajsczak, *Manager*
Tracey Mason, *Director*
Bob Tobing, *Asst Director*

EMP: 40
SQ FT: 8,525
SALES (est): 2.4MM **Privately Held**
WEB: www.universitysettlement.net
SIC: 8399 Community development groups

(G-6670)
UNIVERSITY SUBURBAN HEALTH CTR (PA)
1611 S Green Rd Ste A61 (44121-4100)
PHONE.................................216 382-8920
Fax: 216 382-8380
John L Naylor Jr, *Principal*
Robert Thompson, *Treasurer*
Chuck Abbey, *Exec Dir*
EMP: 200
SQ FT: 27,500
SALES: 9.2MM **Privately Held**
SIC: 8011 Medical centers; ambulatory surgical center

(G-6671)
UNIVERSITY SURGEONS INC
11100 Euclid Ave 7002 (44106-1716)
PHONE.................................216 844-3021
Fax: 216 844-1385
Thomas Stellato, *President*
Cathy Korponic, *Office Mgr*
EMP: 25
SALES (est): 1.4MM **Privately Held**
SIC: 8011 Surgeon

(G-6672)
URBAN LEAGU OF GREATER CLEVLND
2930 Prospect Ave E (44115-2608)
PHONE.................................216 622-0999
Fax: 216 622-0997
Myron F Robinson, *President*
Gregory Johnson, *COO*
Frank Usowell, *Vice Pres*
Tim Haas, *CFO*
Deborah Gray, *Asst Controller*
EMP: 28
SQ FT: 1,800
SALES: 1.3MM **Privately Held**
WEB: www.ulcleveland.org
SIC: 8641 Civic associations

(G-6673)
URBAN ONE INC
Also Called: Wzak
6555 Carnegie Ave (44103-4619)
PHONE.................................216 579-1111
Eddiie Harreol, *Owner*
EMP: 52
SALES (corp-wide): 440MM **Publicly Held**
WEB: www.radio-one.com
SIC: 4832 Radio broadcasting stations
PA: Urban One, Inc.
1010 Wayne Ave Fl 14
Silver Spring MD 20910
301 429-3200

(G-6674)
URBAN ONE INC
Also Called: Were-AM
1041 Huron Rd E (44115-1706)
PHONE.................................216 861-0100
Fax: 216 348-3650
Tom Hershel, *General Mgr*
EMP: 70
SQ FT: 10,000
SALES (corp-wide): 440MM **Publicly Held**
WEB: www.radio-one.com
SIC: 4832 Radio broadcasting stations
PA: Urban One, Inc.
1010 Wayne Ave Fl 14
Silver Spring MD 20910
301 429-3200

(G-6675)
URS GROUP INC
1300 E 9th St Ste 500 (44114-1503)
PHONE.................................216 622-2300
Fax: 216 622-2428
Keith Mast, *Opers Mgr*
Joe Borzyn, *Electrical Engi*
Andrew Lariccia, *Electrical Engi*
Jeff Toney, *Electrical Engi*
William Laubscher, *Branch Mgr*
EMP: 100
SALES (corp-wide): 18.2B **Publicly Held**
SIC: 8711 Engineering services

HQ: Urs Group, Inc.
300 S Grand Ave Ste 1100
Los Angeles CA 90071
213 593-8000

(G-6676)
US COMMUNICATIONS AND ELC INC
4933 Neo Pkwy (44128-3103)
PHONE.................................440 519-0880
Patricia Connole, *CEO*
James Connole, *President*
Robert Williams, *Vice Pres*
Pam Ingles, *Project Mgr*
Tom Kaufhold, *Project Mgr*
EMP: 85
SQ FT: 50,000
SALES: 15MM **Privately Held**
WEB: www.uscande.com
SIC: 1731 Communications specialization

(G-6677)
USA PARKING SYSTEMS INC
1325 Carnegie Ave Frnt (44115-2836)
PHONE.................................216 621-9255
Lou Frangos, *President*
EMP: 80
SQ FT: 2,500
SALES (est): 4MM **Privately Held**
WEB: www.usaparking.com
SIC: 7521 Parking garage

(G-6678)
USF HOLLAND LLC
Also Called: USFreightways
10720 Memphis Ave (44144-2057)
PHONE.................................216 941-4340
Fax: 216 941-1966
Keith Berlan, *Accounts Exec*
Joe Goodall, *Manager*
EMP: 150
SQ FT: 51,207
SALES (corp-wide): 4.8B **Publicly Held**
WEB: www.usfc.com
SIC: 4731 4213 4212 Freight forwarding; trucking, except local; local trucking, without storage
HQ: Usf Holland Llc
700 S Waverly Rd
Holland MI 49423
616 395-5000

(G-6679)
USHC PHYSICIANS INC
1611 S Green Rd Ste 260 (44121-4192)
PHONE.................................216 382-2036
Fax: 216 297-2118
Dr Steven Rudolph, *President*
J Dennis Morton, *President*
Ginger Radcliffe, *Manager*
EMP: 25
SALES (est): 1.5MM **Privately Held**
SIC: 8011 Internal medicine, physician/surgeon

(G-6680)
UTILICON CORPORATION
888 E 70th St (44103-1764)
PHONE.................................216 391-8500
Fax: 216 391-6722
Kenneth Lavan, *President*
Barbara Brennan, *Accounts Mgr*
Karen Adams, *Payroll Mgr*
EMP: 50
SQ FT: 75,000
SALES (est): 11MM **Privately Held**
WEB: www.utiliconcorp.com
SIC: 1623 Underground utilities contractor

(G-6681)
VAHALLA COMPANY INC
Also Called: Environmental Engineering Cons
3257 E 139th St (44120-3971)
P.O. Box 201607 (44120-8110)
PHONE.................................216 326-2245
Joseph H Daniels Jr, *President*
Jasper Day, *Director*
Kennar Hairston, *Director*
EMP: 35 EST: 1993
SQ FT: 2,500
SALES: 100K **Privately Held**
WEB: www.vahalla.com
SIC: 8748 Environmental consultant

GEOGRAPHIC SECTION
Cleveland - Cuyahoga County (G-6706)

(G-6682)
VALLEJO COMPANY
4429 State Rd Ste 1 (44109-6401)
PHONE...................216 741-3933
Fax: 216 741-3997
Katharine Yaroshak, *President*
EMP: 26
SALES: 6.2MM **Privately Held**
SIC: 4212 1623 Local trucking, without storage; oil & gas pipeline construction; sewer line construction

(G-6683)
VALLEY FORD TRUCK INC (PA)
Also Called: Valley Sterling of Cleveland
5715 Canal Rd (44125-3494)
PHONE...................216 524-2400
Brian O'Donnell, *President*
Michelle Steibner, *Corp Secy*
Michele Stebner, *Finance*
Audrey Coffin, *Human Res Mgr*
Ross Chapman, *Accounts Mgr*
◆ **EMP:** 73 **EST:** 1964
SQ FT: 15,000
SALES: 125MM **Privately Held**
WEB: www.valley2.com
SIC: 5013 5511 5521 5531 Truck parts & accessories; automobiles, new & used; trucks, tractors & trailers: used; truck equipment & parts; automobiles & other motor vehicles

(G-6684)
VALLEY RIDING
Also Called: ROCKY RIVER RIDING
19901 Puritas Ave (44135-1095)
PHONE...................216 267-2525
Fax: 216 267-9743
Margaret Macelhany, *President*
Martha Costello, *Vice Pres*
Jeanette Swisher, *Treasurer*
Margaret McElhany, *Manager*
EMP: 25
SALES: 619.5K **Privately Held**
WEB: www.valleyriding.com
SIC: 7999 Riding stable

(G-6685)
VALLEY VIEW FIRE DEPT
6899 Hathaway Rd (44125-4705)
PHONE...................216 524-7200
Fax: 216 524-9364
Michael Tyna, *Finance Mgr*
Thomas Koscielski, *Manager*
EMP: 27
SALES (est): 2.5MM **Privately Held**
WEB: www.valleyview.net
SIC: 1542 Fire station construction

(G-6686)
VAND CORP
1301 E 9th St Ste 1900 (44114-1862)
PHONE...................216 481-3788
Fax: 216 481-3066
EMP: 26
SALES (est): 2.1MM **Privately Held**
SIC: 8742 Management Consulting Services

(G-6687)
VANDRA BROS CONSTRUCTION INC
24629 Broadway Ave (44146-6340)
PHONE...................440 232-3030
Fax: 440 232-7194
Anthony Melarango, *President*
Peter Melarango, *Vice Pres*
Victor Melaragno, *Treasurer*
Victor Melarango, *Treasurer*
Bruno Melarango, *Admin Sec*
EMP: 25
SQ FT: 10,000
SALES (est): 4.3MM **Privately Held**
SIC: 1771 Concrete work

(G-6688)
VEDISCOVERY LLC
Also Called: Visual Evidence/E-Discovery
1382 W 9th St Ste 400 (44113-1231)
PHONE...................216 241-3443
Ronald Copfer, *CEO*
Daniel Copfer, *President*
Hal Brooks, *Exec VP*
Manfred Troibner,
EMP: 26
SQ FT: 6,000
SALES (est): 2.1MM **Privately Held**
SIC: 7371 7374 8742 Custom computer programming services; data processing & preparation; management consulting services

(G-6689)
VERITIV OPERATING COMPANY
Also Called: Xpedx
9797 Sweet Valley Dr (44125-4241)
PHONE...................216 901-5700
Fax: 216 901-2600
Scott Dunlap, *Engineer*
Michael Doerrr, *Branch Mgr*
Jim Purcell, *Manager*
Mary J Tiderman, *Manager*
EMP: 100
SALES (corp-wide): 8.3B **Publicly Held**
WEB: www.internationalpaper.com
SIC: 5084 Processing & packaging equipment; printing trades machinery, equipment & supplies
HQ: Veritiv Operating Company
1000 Abernathy Rd
Atlanta GA 30328
770 391-8200

(G-6690)
VETERANS FGN WARS POST 2850
3296 W 61st St (44102-5614)
PHONE...................216 631-2585
George Dennison, *Principal*
EMP: 100
SQ FT: 6,215
SALES: 57.4K **Privately Held**
SIC: 8641 Veterans' organization

(G-6691)
VETERANS HEALTH ADMINISTRATION
Also Called: Louis Stokes Cleveland Vamc
10701 East Blvd (44106-1702)
PHONE...................216 791-3800
Fax: 440 546-2713
Joseph Potkay, *Research*
Mark Wallace, *Med Doctor*
Kristen Guadalupe, *Admin Mgr*
William Montague, *Director*
Dan Wolpaw, *Director*
EMP: 3200 **Publicly Held**
WEB: www.veterans-ru.org
SIC: 8011 9451 Medical centers;
HQ: Veterans Health Administration
810 Vermont Ave Nw
Washington DC 20420

(G-6692)
VETERANS HEALTH ADMINISTRATION
Also Called: McCafferty Community Based
4242 Lorain Ave (44113-3715)
PHONE...................216 939-0699
Dean Dilzell, *Nutritionist*
Jodell Howard, *Admin Asst*
Ingrid-Jane V Barcelona, *Nurse Practr*
Bruce Kafer, *Nurse*
Marevelyn McKee,
EMP: 264 **Publicly Held**
WEB: www.veterans-ru.org
SIC: 8011 9451 Clinic, operated by physicians; psychiatric clinic;
HQ: Veterans Health Administration
810 Vermont Ave Nw
Washington DC 20420

(G-6693)
VGS INC
2239 E 55th St (44103-4451)
PHONE...................216 431-7800
Robert Comben Jr, *President*
James Huduk, *Vice Pres*
Mick Latkovich, *Vice Pres*
Donald E Carlton, *CFO*
Betty Goodman, *CFO*
EMP: 200
SQ FT: 36,000
SALES: 4MM **Privately Held**
SIC: 8331 2326 2311 Job training & vocational rehabilitation services; work uniforms; military uniforms, men's & youths': purchased materials

(G-6694)
VICTORY WHITE METAL COMPANY (PA)
6100 Roland Ave (44127-1399)
PHONE...................216 271-1400
Fax: 216 271-6430
Alex J Stanwick, *President*
Bill Clarke, *General Mgr*
Jennifer Sturman, *Admin Sec*
▲ **EMP:** 60 **EST:** 1920
SQ FT: 60,000
SALES (est): 38MM **Privately Held**
WEB: www.vwmc.com
SIC: 5085 3356 Valves & fittings; solder: wire, bar, acid core, & rosin core; lead & zinc; tin

(G-6695)
VICTORY WHITE METAL COMPANY
3027 E 55th St (44127-1275)
PHONE...................216 271-7200
Fax: 216 883-0008
Tim Hess, *Manager*
EMP: 25
SQ FT: 50,000
SALES (corp-wide): 38MM **Privately Held**
WEB: www.vwmc.com
SIC: 3341 4941 4225 Lead smelting & refining (secondary); water supply; general warehousing & storage
PA: The Victory White Metal Company
6100 Roland Ave
Cleveland OH 44127
216 271-1400

(G-6696)
VIKING EXPLOSIVES LLC
25800 Science Park Dr (44122-7339)
PHONE...................218 263-8845
Mike Lownds, *Vice Pres*
Bob Prittinen, *Manager*
Elaine Prittinen, *Manager*
Joel Staeth, *Info Tech Mgr*
EMP: 28
SALES (corp-wide): 22.6MM **Privately Held**
SIC: 5169 2892 Explosives; explosives
HQ: Viking Explosives Llc
25800 Science Park Dr # 300
Cleveland OH
216 464-2400

(G-6697)
VILLAGE OF CUYAHOGA HEIGHTS (PA)
4863 E 71st St Frnt (44125-1080)
PHONE...................216 641-7020
Barbara Biro, *Principal*
Jack Bacci, *Mayor*
David Sammons, *Director*
EMP: 117 **Privately Held**
WEB: www.cuyahogaheights.com
SIC: 9111 8641 City & town managers' offices; ; civic social & fraternal associations

(G-6698)
VILLAGE OF VALLEY VIEW
6848 Hathaway Rd (44125-4767)
PHONE...................216 524-6511
Randall Westfall, *Mayor*
EMP: 150 **Privately Held**
SIC: 8741 Administrative management
PA: Village Of Valley View
6848 Hathaway Rd
Cleveland OH 44125
216 524-6511

(G-6699)
VIP RESTORATION INC
1375 E 55th St (44103-1301)
PHONE...................216 426-9500
Vincent Piscitello, *Branch Mgr*
EMP: 60
SALES (est): 4.2MM
SALES (corp-wide): 24.5MM **Privately Held**
SIC: 1542 Commercial & office buildings, renovation & repair
PA: V.I.P. Restoration, Inc.
650 Graham Rd Ste 106
Cuyahoga Falls OH 44221
216 426-9500

(G-6700)
VISCONSI COMPANIES LTD
30050 Chagrin Blvd # 360 (44124-5716)
PHONE...................216 464-5550
Fax: 216 464-5550
Dominic Visconsi Jr, *CEO*
Anthoni Visconsi II, *CEO*
Barry Fader, *Senior VP*
Michael Olsen, *Vice Pres*
Alan Prince, *CFO*
EMP: 30
SQ FT: 8,000
SALES (est): 5.4MM **Privately Held**
SIC: 6552 6531 Subdividers & developers; real estate agents & managers

(G-6701)
VISCONSI MANAGEMENT INC
Also Called: Visconsi Company
30050 Chagrin Blvd # 360 (44124-5716)
PHONE...................216 464-5550
Dominic A Visconsi, *CEO*
Anthoni Visconsi II, *Co-CEO*
EMP: 30
SALES (est): 35.2K **Privately Held**
WEB: www.visconsi.com
SIC: 6512 Commercial & industrial building operation

(G-6702)
VISITING NRSE ASSN OF CLVELAND (PA)
Also Called: V N A
2500 E 22nd St (44115-3204)
PHONE...................216 931-1400
Fax: 216 694-4182
Mary Lou Stricklin, *President*
Claire M Zangerle, *President*
John Lauer, *Chairman*
John Graham, *Chairman*
Sharon Jones, *COO*
EMP: 500
SALES: 18.6MM **Privately Held**
WEB: www.vnacareplus.com
SIC: 8082 Visiting nurse service

(G-6703)
VISITING NRSE ASSN OF MID-OHIO
Also Called: Vna
2500 E 22nd St (44115-3204)
PHONE...................216 931-1300
Claire Zangerle, *CEO*
James E Makee Jr, *Vice Pres*
Russell Dugger, *Project Mgr*
Michelle Cielma, *Purch Agent*
Trivison Michele, *Purch Agent*
EMP: 32
SALES: 13.3MM **Privately Held**
SIC: 8082 Visiting nurse service

(G-6704)
VISITING NURSE ASSOCIATION
2500 E 22nd St (44115-3205)
PHONE...................216 931-1300
Joann Z Glick, *Chairman*
EMP: 32
SALES: 7.1MM **Privately Held**
SIC: 8621 Professional membership organizations

(G-6705)
VITALYST
3615 Superior Ave E 4406a (44114-4139)
PHONE...................216 201-9070
Kevin P Walters, *Branch Mgr*
EMP: 75 **Privately Held**
SIC: 7379 Computer related consulting services
PA: Vitalyst, Llc
1 Bala Plz Ste 434
Bala Cynwyd PA 19004

(G-6706)
VITAS HEALTHCARE CORPORATION
600 E Granger Rd Ste 100 (44131-6706)
PHONE...................216 706-2100
Raul Gonzalez, *Director*
EMP: 29
SALES (corp-wide): 1.6B **Publicly Held**
WEB: www.vitasinnovativehospicecare.com
SIC: 8082 Home health care services

Cleveland - Cuyahoga County (G-6707) — GEOGRAPHIC SECTION

HQ: Vitas Healthcare Corporation
100 S Biscayne Blvd # 1600
Miami FL 33131
305 374-4143

(G-6707)
VITRAN EXPRESS INC
5300 Crayton Ave (44104-2832)
PHONE.................216 426-8584
Rich Huffman, *Manager*
EMP: 100
SQ FT: 25,271
SALES (corp-wide): 109.4MM **Privately Held**
SIC: 4213 Contract haulers
PA: Vitran Express, Inc.
12225 Stephens Rd
Warren MI 48089
317 803-4000

(G-6708)
VOCATIONAL GUIDANCE SERVICES (PA)
2239 E 55th St (44103-4451)
PHONE.................216 431-7800
Fax: 216 476-3435
Robert E Comben Jr, *President*
Et Al, *Principal*
Nadine Coffinberry, *Principal*
Cornelia Ginn, *Principal*
Miriam Norton, *Principal*
EMP: 608
SQ FT: 130,931
SALES: 10.7MM **Privately Held**
SIC: 8331 Community service employment training program

(G-6709)
VOCATIONAL SERVICES INC
2239 E 55th St (44103-4451)
PHONE.................216 431-8085
Robert Comben, *President*
Donald E Carlson, *CFO*
EMP: 150
SQ FT: 17,541
SALES: 1MM **Privately Held**
SIC: 2391 2511 8331 Curtains & draperies; wood household furniture; job training & vocational rehabilitation services

(G-6710)
VOCON DESIGN INC (PA)
3142 Prospect Ave E (44115-2612)
PHONE.................216 588-0800
Fax: 216 623-0410
Debbie Donley, *President*
David M Douglass, *Principal*
Debbie McCann, *Vice Pres*
Paul G Voinovich, *Vice Pres*
Lisa Dye, *Project Dir*
EMP: 65
SQ FT: 17,000
SALES (est): 18.4MM **Privately Held**
WEB: www.vocon.com
SIC: 7389 Interior design services

(G-6711)
VOLUNTERS OF AMER GREATER OHIO
775 E 152nd St (44110-2304)
PHONE.................216 541-9000
Fax: 216 541-5143
EMP: 75
SALES (corp-wide): 8MM **Privately Held**
SIC: 8322 Social service center
PA: Volunteers Of America Of Greater Ohio
1776 E Broad St
Columbus OH 43203
614 253-6100

(G-6712)
VORYS SATER SEYMOUR PEASE LLP
200 Public Sq Ste 1400 (44114-2327)
PHONE.................216 479-6100
Fax: 216 479-6060
F Daniel Balmert, *Partner*
Wendy Isaacs, *Executive*
Daniel Balmert,
Chas J French III,
John W Read,
EMP: 50

SALES (corp-wide): 133.4MM **Privately Held**
SIC: 8111 General practice law office
PA: Vorys, Sater, Seymour And Pease Llp
52 E Gay St
Columbus OH 43215
614 464-6400

(G-6713)
W B MASON CO INC
12985 Snow Rd (44130-1006)
PHONE.................216 267-5000
Richard C Voigt, *Branch Mgr*
EMP: 53
SALES (corp-wide): 702.7MM **Privately Held**
SIC: 5112 5044 5021 Stationery & office supplies; office equipment; office furniture
PA: W. B. Mason Co., Inc.
59 Center St
Brockton MA 02301
781 794-8800

(G-6714)
W R G INC
Also Called: Buckeye Metals
3961 Pearl Rd (44109-3103)
PHONE.................216 351-8494
Fax: 216 351-1984
Mike Rauch, *President*
Mildred Neumann, *Principal*
Nathan R Simon, *Principal*
Sandra L Sotos, *Principal*
Robert Rauch, *Vice Pres*
EMP: 25
SQ FT: 121,500
SALES (est): 12.3MM **Privately Held**
SIC: 5093 3341 Nonferrous metals scrap; secondary nonferrous metals

(G-6715)
WABUSH MINES CLIFFS MINING CO
200 Public Sq Ste 3300 (44114-2315)
PHONE.................216 694-5700
Terrance Taridei, *CFO*
John Tuomi, *Mng Member*
Sue McGovern, *Admin Asst*
EMP: 800
SALES (est): 15.8MM
SALES (corp-wide): 2.3B **Publicly Held**
SIC: 1011 Iron ore mining; iron ore pelletizing; iron ore beneficiating
PA: Cleveland-Cliffs Inc.
200 Public Sq Ste 3300
Cleveland OH 44114
216 694-5700

(G-6716)
WADE TRIM
1100 Superior Ave E # 1710 (44114-2518)
PHONE.................216 363-0300
Fax: 216 363-0303
J Howard Flower, *President*
Kenneth A Tyrpak, *Corp Secy*
David D Peitro, *Senior VP*
Richard J Allar, *Vice Pres*
Wendy Sherrill, *Mktg Dir*
EMP: 35
SQ FT: 17,000
SALES (est): 3.8MM **Privately Held**
SIC: 8711 8713 Civil engineering; surveying services

(G-6717)
WAELZHOLZ NORTH AMERICA LLC
5221 W 164th St (44142-1507)
PHONE.................216 267-5500
David Zenker, *Vice Pres*
Frank Kluwe, *Mng Member*
▲ **EMP:** 25 **EST:** 1953
SQ FT: 45,000
SALES (est): 13.4MM
SALES (corp-wide): 664.9MM **Privately Held**
SIC: 5051 Steel
PA: C.D. Walzholz Gmbh & Co. Kg
Feldmuhlenstr. 55
Hagen 58093
233 196-40

(G-6718)
WALGREEN CO
Also Called: Walgreens
25221 Miles Rd Unit H (44128-5474)
PHONE.................216 595-1407
Fax: 216 595-1508
Tony Nikolich, *District Mgr*
Tim Titus, *Branch Mgr*
EMP: 40
SALES (corp-wide): 118.2B **Publicly Held**
WEB: www.walgreens.com
SIC: 8742 Restaurant & food services consultants
HQ: Walgreen Co.
200 Wilmot Rd
Deerfield IL 60015
847 315-2500

(G-6719)
WALTER HAVERFIELD LLP (PA)
1301 E 9th St Ste 3500 (44114-1821)
PHONE.................216 781-1212
Karen Waldron, *President*
Ralph Cascarilla, *Managing Prtnr*
Douglas N Barr, *Partner*
Darrell A Clay, *Partner*
Michael A Cyphert, *Partner*
EMP: 66 **EST:** 1932
SQ FT: 24,500
SALES (est): 16.3MM **Privately Held**
WEB: www.walterhav.com
SIC: 8111 General practice law office

(G-6720)
WALTHALL LLP (PA)
6300 Rockside Rd Ste 100 (44131-2221)
PHONE.................216 573-2330
Richard T Lash CPA, *Partner*
Charles P Battiato Jr CPA, *Partner*
Richard H Cause CPA, *Partner*
Daniel B Holben CPA, *Partner*
Judith A Mondry CPA, *Partner*
EMP: 45
SQ FT: 10,000
SALES (est): 4.8MM **Privately Held**
WEB: www.walthall.com
SIC: 8721 Certified public accountant

(G-6721)
WALTON MANOR HEALTH CARE CTR
19859 Alexander Rd (44146-5345)
PHONE.................440 439-4433
Fax: 440 439-0691
Morton J Weisberg, *President*
Tiffany Hexter, *Purchasing*
Susan Waters, *Human Res Mgr*
Hathaim Azem, *Director*
Andy Liuzzo, *Director*
EMP: 125
SQ FT: 55,299
SALES (est): 6MM **Privately Held**
SIC: 8051 Convalescent home with continuous nursing care

(G-6722)
WARNER DENNEHEY MARSHALL
127 Public Sq Ste 3510 (44114-1250)
PHONE.................216 912-3787
EMP: 54
SALES (corp-wide): 170.5MM **Privately Held**
SIC: 8111 General practice law office
PA: Marshall Dennehey Warner Coleman & Goggin P.C.
2000 Market St Ste 2300
Philadelphia PA 19103
215 575-2600

(G-6723)
WARRENTON COPPER LLC
1240 Marquette St (44114-3920)
PHONE.................636 456-3488
Herbert Black,
◆ **EMP:** 50
SQ FT: 100,000
SALES (est): 3.5MM
SALES (corp-wide): 762.1MM **Privately Held**
WEB: www.warrentoncopper.com
SIC: 1021 Copper ore mining & preparation

PA: Compagnie Americaine De Fer & Metaux Inc, La
9100 Boul Henri-Bourassa E
Montreal-Est QC H1E 2
514 494-2000

(G-6724)
WATERWORKS AMERICA INC
Also Called: Waterworks Crystals
5005 Rcksde Rd Crwn Cn 6f Crown Centre (44131)
PHONE.................440 526-4815
Bruce S Wirtanen, *President*
Susan Peters, *VP Admin*
Gary Palinkas, *Vice Pres*
Barry Stevens, *VP Sales*
Byron Krantz, *Admin Sec*
EMP: 247
SQ FT: 160,000
SALES (est): 27.8MM **Privately Held**
WEB: www.1water.com
SIC: 5191 Chemicals, agricultural

(G-6725)
WAXMAN CONSUMER PDTS GROUP INC (HQ)
24455 Aurora Rd (44146-1727)
PHONE.................440 439-1830
Fax: 440 439-8678
Lawrence Waxman, *President*
Armond Waxman, *Chairman*
Melvin Waxman, *Chairman*
John Holzheimer, *Vice Pres*
Mark Wester, *Vice Pres*
▲ **EMP:** 75
SQ FT: 9,000
SALES: 38.3MM
SALES (corp-wide): 100MM **Privately Held**
WEB: www.waxmancpgvendor.com
SIC: 5072 5074 Casters & glides; furniture hardware; plumbing & hydronic heating supplies
PA: Waxman Industries, Inc.
24460 Aurora Rd
Cleveland OH 44146
440 439-1830

(G-6726)
WAXMAN INDUSTRIES INC (PA)
24460 Aurora Rd (44146-1794)
PHONE.................440 439-1830
Fax: 440 439-1262
Armond Waxman, *Ch of Bd*
Melvin Waxman, *Ch of Bd*
Larry Waxman, *President*
Laurence Waxman, *President*
Robert Feldman, *Senior VP*
▲ **EMP:** 110 **EST:** 1962
SQ FT: 21,000
SALES: 100MM **Privately Held**
WEB: www.waxmanind.com
SIC: 5072 5074 3494 3491 Hardware; plumbing & hydronic heating supplies; valves & pipe fittings; industrial valves; plumbing fixture fittings & trim

(G-6727)
WEGMAN HESSLER VANDERBURG
6055 Rockside Woods Blvd # 200 (44131-2302)
PHONE.................216 642-3342
Fax: 216 642-8826
David J Hessler, *President*
Robert McIntyre, *Counsel*
Mark Thornton, *VP Admin*
Peter A Hessler, *Treasurer*
Mark Thorton, *Office Mgr*
EMP: 60
SALES (est): 6.8MM **Privately Held**
WEB: www.wegmanlaw.com
SIC: 8111 General practice attorney, lawyer

(G-6728)
WEINBERG CAPITAL GROUP INC (PA)
5005 Rockside Rd Ste 1140 (44131-6815)
PHONE.................216 503-8307
Ronald E Weinberg Jr, *CEO*
EMP: 96 **EST:** 2012
SALES (est): 5.9MM **Privately Held**
SIC: 6799 Investors

GEOGRAPHIC SECTION — Cleveland - Cuyahoga County (G-6751)

(G-6729)
WEINER KEITH D CO L P A INC
Also Called: Keith D Weiner & Assoc Lpa
75 Public Sq Ste 600 (44113-2079)
PHONE..................216 771-6500
Keith D Weiner, *President*
Evelyn Schonberg, *Corp Secy*
Kathleen M Van Horn, *Controller*
Teresa Geyer, *Office Mgr*
Vicki Depould, *Legal Staff*
EMP: 45
SALES: 1MM **Privately Held**
WEB: www.weinerlaw.com
SIC: 8111 General practice attorney, lawyer

(G-6730)
WELLS FARGO CLEARING SVCS LLC
Also Called: Wells Fargo Advisors
30100 Chagrin Blvd # 200 (44124-5722)
PHONE..................216 378-2722
Marc Silbiger,
EMP: 40
SALES (corp-wide): 97.7B **Publicly Held**
WEB: www.wachoviasec.com
SIC: 6211 Security brokers & dealers
HQ: Wells Fargo Clearing Services, Llc
  1 N Jefferson Ave
  Saint Louis MO 63103
  314 955-3000

(G-6731)
WELLS FARGO CLEARING SVCS LLC
Also Called: Wells Fargo Advisors
950 Main Ave Ste 300 (44113-7204)
PHONE..................216 574-7300
Tom Freeman, *Vice Pres*
Jordan Lefko, *Vice Pres*
Marc Silbiger, *Manager*
Eric Nilson, *Director*
Abby Stancik, *Advisor*
EMP: 62
SALES (corp-wide): 97.7B **Publicly Held**
WEB: www.wachoviasec.com
SIC: 6211 6221 Stock brokers & dealers; commodity contracts brokers, dealers
HQ: Wells Fargo Clearing Services, Llc
  1 N Jefferson Ave
  Saint Louis MO 63103
  314 955-3000

(G-6732)
WELTMAN WEINBERG & REIS CO LPA (PA)
Also Called: WW&r
323 W Lkeside Ave Ste 200 (44113)
PHONE..................216 685-1000
Fax: 216 363-4121
Robert B Weltman, *President*
Holly Anderson, *President*
Michelle Raphael, *President*
Alan Weinberg, *Managing Prtnr*
Theresa Fortunato, *Partner*
EMP: 1250 **EST:** 1951
SQ FT: 36,412
SALES (est): 98.4MM **Privately Held**
SIC: 8111 General practice law office

(G-6733)
WELTMAN WEINBERG & REIS CO LPA
981 Keynote Cir (44131-1871)
PHONE..................216 459-8633
EMP: 110
SALES (corp-wide): 98.4MM **Privately Held**
SIC: 8111 General practice law office
PA: Weltman, Weinberg & Reis Co., L.P.A.
  323 W Lkeside Ave Ste 200
  Cleveland OH 44113
  216 685-1000

(G-6734)
WESCO DISTRIBUTION INC
4741 Hinckley Indus Pkwy (44109-6004)
PHONE..................216 741-0441
Fax: 216 741-0505
Justin Brewster, *Opers Mgr*
Vincent Lutman, *Opers Mgr*
Rob Eicher, *Sales Staff*
Sharon Batsch, *Sales Associate*
Terry Mason, *Sales Associate*
EMP: 27 **Publicly Held**
SIC: 5063 5085 Electrical supplies; industrial supplies
HQ: Wesco Distribution, Inc.
  225 W Station Square Dr # 700
  Pittsburgh PA 15219

(G-6735)
WEST DENISON BASEBALL LEAGUE
3556 W 105th St (44111-3838)
P.O. Box 44483 (44144-0483)
PHONE..................216 251-5790
Ralph J Lukich, *Principal*
Mike Balina, *Vice Pres*
John Deighton, *Treasurer*
EMP: 40
SQ FT: 2,692
SALES: 20.2K **Privately Held**
SIC: 7997 Outdoor field clubs

(G-6736)
WEST SHORE CHILD CARE CENTER
20401 Hilliard Blvd (44116-3506)
PHONE..................440 333-3490
Fax: 440 333-3490
Steve Meka, *Vice Pres*
Karen O'Hagan, *Director*
EMP: 30
SALES (est): 844K **Privately Held**
WEB: www.wschildcare.org
SIC: 8351 Child day care services

(G-6737)
WEST SIDE CARDIOLOGY ASSOC
Also Called: Cumberford & Watts
20455 Lorain Rd Fl 2 (44126-3530)
PHONE..................440 333-8600
Marcello Mellino, *President*
Thomas Comerford, *Vice Pres*
Jana Stump, *Admin Asst*
EMP: 30
SALES (est): 1.3MM **Privately Held**
WEB: www.wscardiology.com
SIC: 8011 Cardiologist & cardio-vascular specialist

(G-6738)
WEST SIDE CARDIOLOGY ASSOC
20455 Lorain Rd Fl 2 (44126-3530)
PHONE..................440 333-8600
Marcel Malino MD, *Chairman*
E Nukta, *Cardiology*
EMP: 40
SQ FT: 6,400
SALES (est): 2.6MM **Privately Held**
SIC: 8011 Cardiologist & cardio-vascular specialist

(G-6739)
WEST SIDE COMMUNITY HOUSE
9300 Lorain Ave (44102-4725)
PHONE..................216 771-7297
Fax: 216 771-0620
Ren Aten, *Consultant*
Dawn Kolograf, *Director*
Gretchen Myers, *Director*
Terry Weber, *Director*
EMP: 35
SQ FT: 4,620
SALES (est): 1.7MM **Privately Held**
WEB: www.wschouse.org
SIC: 8322 Social service center

(G-6740)
WEST SIDE ECUMENICAL MINISTRY (PA)
Also Called: W S E M
5209 Detroit Ave (44102-2224)
PHONE..................216 325-9369
Fax: 216 651-4145
Laura Chalker, *General Mgr*
Phil Buck, *Exec Dir*
Lou Keim, *Director*
EMP: 130
SQ FT: 29,075
SALES (est): 8.2MM **Privately Held**
SIC: 8322 8661 Individual & family services; religious organizations

(G-6741)
WESTERN MANAGEMENT INC (PA)
14577 Lorain Ave (44111-3156)
PHONE..................216 941-3333
John Turk, *President*
Thomas M Cawley, *Principal*
Eric George Turk, *Principal*
EMP: 45
SQ FT: 10,000
SALES (est): 9.1MM **Privately Held**
SIC: 8741 Management services

(G-6742)
WESTERN RESERVE AREA AGENCY (PA)
Also Called: Wraaa
925 Euclid Ave Ste 600 (44115-1405)
PHONE..................216 621-0303
E Douglas Beach, *CEO*
Eamon Carey, *Accountant*
Deatress Peto, *Accountant*
Christopher Hall, *Finance*
Colene Kerrick, *Human Resources*
EMP: 189
SQ FT: 44,000
SALES: 68.8MM **Privately Held**
SIC: 8322 8082 Senior citizens' center or association; home health care services

(G-6743)
WESTERN RESERVE AREA AGENCY
Also Called: Passport
925 Euclid Ave Ste 600 (44115-1405)
PHONE..................216 621-0303
Fax: 216 621-7174
Ron Hill, *Director*
EMP: 30 **Privately Held**
SIC: 8322 Senior citizens' center or association
PA: Western Reserve Area Agency On Aging
  925 Euclid Ave Ste 600
  Cleveland OH 44115

(G-6744)
WESTERN RESERVE HISTORICAL SOC (PA)
Also Called: HALE FARM & VILLAGE
10825 East Blvd (44106-1777)
PHONE..................216 721-5722
Fax: 216 721-0645
Gainor B Davis, *CEO*
Angela Broholm, *Business Mgr*
Richard Arlesic, *Vice Pres*
Kelly Falcone, *Vice Pres*
Timothy Mann, *Vice Pres*
EMP: 60
SALES: 6.6MM **Privately Held**
SIC: 8412 8231 Historical society; specialized libraries

(G-6745)
WESTERN RESERVE INTERIORS INC
7777 Exchange St Ste 7 (44125-3337)
PHONE..................216 447-1081
Fax: 216 447-5017
Leslie S Cooke, *President*
Tom Cooke, *Vice Pres*
Jo Ann Castelli, *Treasurer*
Kevin Allar, *Manager*
Bruce Cooke, *Executive*
EMP: 30
SQ FT: 25,000
SALES (est): 4.3MM **Privately Held**
WEB: www.wri-net.com
SIC: 1742 Plastering, plain or ornamental; drywall; acoustical & ceiling work

(G-6746)
WESTLAKE CAB SERVICE
2069 W 3rd St (44113-2502)
PHONE..................440 331-5000
Fax: 216 623-3183
Arthur McBride, *President*
Edward Mc Bride, *Principal*
EMP: 80
SQ FT: 14,984
SALES (est): 3.2MM
SALES (corp-wide): 14.1MM **Privately Held**
SIC: 4121 Taxicabs

PA: United Garage & Service Corporation
  2069 W 3rd St
  Cleveland OH 44113
  216 623-1550

(G-6747)
WESTLAKE VILLAGE INC
28550 Westlake Village Dr (44145-7608)
PHONE..................440 892-4200
Fax: 440 892-4756
Jeanne Barnard, *President*
EMP: 130
SQ FT: 125,000
SALES: 6.9MM
SALES (corp-wide): 4.7B **Publicly Held**
WEB: www.westlakevillage.com
SIC: 6513 Retirement hotel operation
HQ: American Retirement Corporation
  111 Westwood Pl Ste 200
  Brentwood TN 37027
  615 221-2250

(G-6748)
WESTON INC (PA)
Also Called: Property 3
4760 Richmond Rd Ste 200 (44128-5979)
PHONE..................440 349-9000
Ann S Asher, *President*
Joseph Panetta, *Vice Pres*
T J Asher, *Marketing Mgr*
Brian Caves, *Property Mgr*
Jeannine Soster, *Property Mgr*
EMP: 29
SALES (est): 21.6MM **Privately Held**
WEB: www.weston.com
SIC: 6512 6541 Commercial & industrial building operation; title search companies

(G-6749)
WFTS
W E W S - TV
3001 Euclid Ave (44115-2516)
PHONE..................216 431-5555
Fax: 216 431-3666
Steve Weinstein, *General Mgr*
Warren Happel, *VP Engrg*
John Lansing, *VP Engrg*
Franz Margitza, *Engineer*
Peter Gunn, *Sales Dir*
EMP: 200
SQ FT: 10,000
SALES (corp-wide): 3.1B **Publicly Held**
WEB: www.diytv.com
SIC: 4833 Television broadcasting stations
HQ: Wfts
  4045 N Himes Ave
  Tampa FL 33607
  813 354-2800

(G-6750)
WHITING-TURNER CONTRACTING CO
5875 Landerbrook Dr # 100 (44124-6513)
PHONE..................440 449-9200
Ronald Knight, *Superintendent*
Jeff Maeder, *Vice Pres*
Jason Gebhardt, *Project Mgr*
Matt Wilson, *Project Mgr*
Doug Zwilling, *Project Mgr*
EMP: 70
SALES (corp-wide): 5.5B **Privately Held**
WEB: www.whiting-turner.com
SIC: 1541 1542 1629 Industrial buildings & warehouses; nonresidential construction; industrial plant construction
PA: The Whiting-Turner Contracting Company
  300 E Joppa Rd Ste 800
  Baltimore MD 21286
  410 821-1100

(G-6751)
WHOLE HEALTH MANAGEMENT INC (DH)
1375 E 9th St Ste 2500 (44114-1743)
PHONE..................216 921-8601
Fax: 216 622-0888
James J Hummer, *President*
David Beech, *Vice Pres*
Martin Butler, *Vice Pres*
Lucy Crane, *Vice Pres*
Robert Farrar, *Vice Pres*
EMP: 40
SQ FT: 5,000

Cleveland - Cuyahoga County (G-6752)   GEOGRAPHIC SECTION

SALES (est): 18.4MM
SALES (corp-wide): 118.2B Publicly Held
WEB: www.wholehealthnet.com
SIC: 8011 Occupational & industrial specialist, physician/surgeon
HQ: Walgreen Co.
   200 Wilmot Rd
   Deerfield IL 60015
   847 315-2500

(G-6752)
WILDWOOD YACHT CLUB INC
P.O. Box 19001 (44119-0001)
PHONE.................................216 531-9052
Stan Powski, President
EMP: 83
SALES: 38.8K Privately Held
SIC: 7997 Yacht club, membership

(G-6753)
WINDY HILL LTD INC (PA)
Also Called: Transworld News
3700 Kelley Ave (44114-4533)
PHONE.................................216 391-4800
Fax: 216 391-9911
Joel Kaminsky, President
Jeffrey Gross, Admin Sec
EMP: 80
SQ FT: 55,000
SALES (est): 15.8MM Privately Held
SIC: 5192 5099 Magazines; video cassettes, accessories & supplies

(G-6754)
WINSTON PRODUCTS LLC
30339 Diamond Pkwy # 105 (44139-5473)
PHONE.................................440 478-1418
Winston Breeden, CEO
Scott Jared, President
Tiffani Henderson, Opers Mgr
Kevin Brooks, Opers Staff
Melissa Mirt, Purch Mgr
▲ EMP: 100
SQ FT: 115,000
SALES (est): 50.1MM Privately Held
SIC: 3556 5013 Food products machinery; automotive supplies

(G-6755)
WIRELESS CENTER INC (PA)
1925 Saint Clair Ave Ne (44114-2028)
PHONE.................................216 503-3777
Azam Kazmi, Principal
Chris Anders, District Mgr
Dave Phillips, District Mgr
Ali Zaidi, District Mgr
Tariq Khan, Vice Pres
EMP: 300
SQ FT: 10,000
SALES (est): 28MM Privately Held
SIC: 4812 Cellular telephone services

(G-6756)
WKYC-TV INC
Also Called: W K Y C Channel 3
1333 Lakeside Ave E (44114-1159)
PHONE.................................216 344-3300
Fax: 216 344-3477
Brooke Spectorsky, President
Dick Russ, Editor
Larry Giele, Business Mgr
David Goler, Accounts Exec
Diane Pollock, Manager
EMP: 220
SALES (est): 25.1MM
SALES (corp-wide): 1.9B Publicly Held
WEB: www.wkyc.com
SIC: 4833 Television broadcasting stations
PA: Tegna Inc.
   7950 Jones Branch Dr
   Mc Lean VA 22102
   703 873-6600

(G-6757)
WONG MARGARET W ASSOC CO LPA (PA)
3150 Chester Ave (44114-4617)
PHONE.................................313 527-9989
Fax: 216 566-1125
Margaret W Wong, President
Kathleen Hill, General Mgr
Kathy Hill, General Mgr
Brian Marek, Info Tech Dir
Sara Elaqad, Legal Staff
EMP: 36

SALES (est): 4.8MM Privately Held
WEB: www.imwong.com
SIC: 8111 General practice law office

(G-6758)
WORLD AUTO PARTS INC
1240 Carnegie Ave (44115-2808)
PHONE.................................216 781-8418
Fax: 216 781-8887
Michael Maloof, President
Michael D Maloof, President
Daniel Maloof, Vice Pres
EMP: 28 EST: 1979
SQ FT: 100,000
SALES (est): 3.8MM Privately Held
SIC: 5013 Automotive supplies & parts

(G-6759)
WORLD SHIPPING INC (PA)
1340 Depot St Ste 200 (44116-1741)
PHONE.................................440 356-7676
Fax: 216 356-4727
Frederick M Hunger, President
Daniel Ambroziak, Vice Pres
Denise Corbett, Vice Pres
Dennis Mahoney, Vice Pres
John E Hunger, CFO
EMP: 30
SQ FT: 15,000
SALES (est): 241.2MM Privately Held
WEB: www.worldshipping.com
SIC: 4213 4731 Trucking, except local; agents, shipping

(G-6760)
WRIGHT CENTER
Also Called: Wright Surgery Center
1611 S Green Rd Ste 124 (44121-4121)
PHONE.................................216 382-1868
Fax: 216 382-0584
Cassy Schilero, Director
Irving A Hirsch, Director
EMP: 45
SALES (est): 3.9MM Privately Held
WEB: www.wrightcenter.com
SIC: 8062 General medical & surgical hospitals

(G-6761)
WTB INC
Also Called: M&J Fox Investments
815 Superior Ave E (44114-2706)
Rural Route 2991 73rd (44104)
PHONE.................................216 298-1895
Matthew Fox, President
Jennifer Fox, Vice Pres
Ceda Sherman, CFO
EMP: 26
SQ FT: 1,200
SALES (est): 3.4MM Privately Held
SIC: 8748 7389 Business consulting;

(G-6762)
WTW DELAWARE HOLDINGS LLC
Also Called: Willis Towers Watson
1001 Lakeside Ave E (44114-1158)
PHONE.................................216 937-4000
Fax: 216 937-4101
James E Pearce, Marketing Mgr
Jason Masony, Consultant
Philip Katzan, Data Proc Staff
Mike Turk, Director
Larry Seman, Account Dir
EMP: 145 Privately Held
WEB: www.watsonwyatt.com
SIC: 8742 8999 7371 7361 Compensation & benefits planning consultant; human resource consulting services; actuarial consultant; computer software systems analysis & design, custom; computer software development; employment agencies
HQ: Wtw Delaware Holdings Llc
   800 N Glebe Rd
   Arlington VA 22203

(G-6763)
WUNDERLICH SECURITIES INC
5885 Landerbrook Dr # 304 (44124-4045)
PHONE.................................440 646-1400
EMP: 30 Publicly Held
SIC: 6211 Security brokers & dealers

HQ: Wunderlich Securities, Inc.
   6000 Poplar Ave Ste 150
   Memphis TN 38119
   901 251-1330

(G-6764)
WYNDHAM INTERNATIONAL INC
Also Called: Wyndham Hotels & Resorts
1260 Euclid Ave (44115-1837)
PHONE.................................216 615-7500
Fax: 216 621-8659
Brian Malone, General Mgr
Amanda Strieter, General Mgr
Victoria Bachtel, Manager
Beth Blankenship, Director
Jane Dominowski, Director
EMP: 175
SALES (corp-wide): 75.7MM Privately Held
WEB: www.wyndham.com
SIC: 7011 5812 Hotels; eating places
HQ: Wyndham International, Inc
   22 Sylvan Way
   Parsippany NJ 07054
   973 753-6000

(G-6765)
WYSE ADVERTISING INC (PA)
668 Euclid Ave Ste 100 (44114-3024)
PHONE.................................216 696-2424
Fax: 216 689-2900
Michael Marino, CEO
Sharyn F Hinman, Senior VP
David N Jankowski, Senior VP
Ryan Hagler, Production
Margaret Weitzel, CFO
EMP: 98
SQ FT: 56,000
SALES (est): 12.6MM Privately Held
WEB: www.wyseadvertising.com
SIC: 7311 Advertising consultant

(G-6766)
X-RAY INDUSTRIES INC
Also Called: Xri Testing
5403 E Schaaf Rd (44131-1337)
PHONE.................................216 642-0100
Fax: 216 642-0100
Bob Hensher, Manager
Bob Henchar, Manager
EMP: 25
SALES (corp-wide): 34.8MM Privately Held
SIC: 8071 8734 X-ray laboratory, including dental; testing laboratories
PA: X-Ray Industries, Inc.
   1961 Thunderbird
   Troy MI 48084
   248 362-2242

(G-6767)
XEROX CORPORATION
6000 Fredom Sq Dr Ste 100 (44131)
PHONE.................................216 642-7806
Fax: 216 642-7806
Jeff Collier, Manager
EMP: 100
SALES (corp-wide): 10.2B Publicly Held
WEB: www.xerox.com
SIC: 5044 7699 7378 5045 Photocopy machines; photocopy machine repair; computer maintenance & repair; computers, peripherals & software
PA: Xerox Corporation
   201 Merritt 7
   Norwalk CT 06851
   203 968-3000

(G-6768)
XO COMMUNICATIONS LLC
3 Summit Park Dr Ste 250 (44131-2598)
PHONE.................................216 619-3200
Chris Ryan, Branch Mgr
EMP: 40
SALES (corp-wide): 126B Publicly Held
SIC: 4813 Telephone communication, except radio
HQ: Xo Communications, Llc
   13865 Sunrise Valley Dr
   Herndon VA 20171
   703 547-2000

(G-6769)
YELLOW CAB CO OF CLEVELAND
2069 W 3rd St (44113-2593)
PHONE.................................216 623-1500
Arthur Mc Bride, President
Brian Mc Bride, Vice Pres
William Klug, Treasurer
Edward Mc Bride, Admin Sec
EMP: 65 EST: 1928
SQ FT: 10,000
SALES (est): 3.2MM
SALES (corp-wide): 14.1MM Privately Held
WEB: www.clevelandyellowcab.com
SIC: 4121 Taxicabs
PA: United Garage & Service Corporation
   2069 W 3rd St
   Cleveland OH 44113
   216 623-1550

(G-6770)
YORK BUILDING MAINTENANCE INC
4748 Broadview Rd (44109-4668)
PHONE.................................216 398-8100
Fax: 216 398-8102
Albert Tharp, President
Jim Kluter, Vice Pres
Kathy Brenkus, Manager
EMP: 120 EST: 1981
SQ FT: 3,200
SALES (est): 2.5MM Privately Held
SIC: 7349 Janitorial service, contract basis; window cleaning; office cleaning or charring; cleaning service, industrial or commercial

(G-6771)
YORK RISK SERVICES GROUP INC
16560 Commerce Ct Ste 100 (44130-6305)
PHONE.................................440 863-2500
Tom McArthur, Owner
EMP: 27
SALES (corp-wide): 3B Privately Held
SIC: 6411 Insurance claim adjusters, not employed by insurance company
HQ: York Risk Services Group, Inc.
   1 Upper Pond
   Parsippany NJ 07054
   973 404-1200

(G-6772)
YORK RITE
13512 Kinsman Rd (44120-4412)
PHONE.................................216 751-1417
Clerence Foxhall, President
EMP: 26
SQ FT: 8,646
SALES (est): 1.3MM Privately Held
WEB: www.yorkrite.com
SIC: 8641 Civic social & fraternal associations

(G-6773)
YOUNG MNS CHRSTN ASSN CLVELAND
Also Called: YMCA West Park
15501 Lorain Ave (44111-5539)
PHONE.................................216 941-4654
Fax: 216 941-1351
Joseph Cerny, Manager
Christopher Mehling, Exec Dir
Christine Vidal, Director
Meghan Scott, Director
John Graves, Program Dir
EMP: 25
SALES (corp-wide): 29.2MM Privately Held
SIC: 8641 8322 7997 Youth organizations; individual & family services; membership sports & recreation clubs
PA: Young Men's Christian Association Of Cleveland
   1801 Superior Ave E # 130
   Cleveland OH 44114
   216 781-1337

(G-6774)
YOUNG MNS CHRSTN ASSN CLVELAND
631 Babbitt Rd (44123-2025)
PHONE.................................216 731-7454

GEOGRAPHIC SECTION

Cleves - Hamilton County (G-6797)

Fax: 216 731-8331
John Reid, Director
EMP: 40
SQ FT: 17,240
SALES (corp-wide): 29.2MM **Privately Held**
SIC: 8641 7991 8351 7032 Youth organizations; physical fitness facilities; child day care services; youth camps; individual & family services
PA: Young Men's Christian Association Of Cleveland
 1801 Superior Ave E # 130
 Cleveland OH 44114
 216 781-1337

(G-6775)
YOUNG MNS CHRSTN ASSN CLVELAND
Also Called: Hillcrest Ymca-Adrian
5000 Mayfield Rd (44124-2605)
PHONE...................216 382-4300
Fax: 216 382-4383
Alan Armstrong, Mktg Dir
Jane Martin, Director
Carla Turner, Director
EMP: 60
SQ FT: 17,286
SALES (corp-wide): 29.2MM **Privately Held**
SIC: 8641 7997 7991 Youth organizations; membership sports & recreation clubs; physical fitness facilities
PA: Young Men's Christian Association Of Cleveland
 1801 Superior Ave E # 130
 Cleveland OH 44114
 216 781-1337

(G-6776)
YOUNG WOMENS CHRISTIAN ASSOCI (PA)
Also Called: YWCA of Cleveland
4019 Prospect Ave (44103-4317)
PHONE...................216 881-6878
Fax: 216 881-9922
Margaret Mitchell, President
Irene Collins, CFO
Shalah Turner, Manager
Jerome Baker, Supervisor
Barbara Danforth, Exec Dir
EMP: 42
SQ FT: 24,000
SALES: 3.1MM **Privately Held**
SIC: 8641 7991 8351 7032 Youth organizations; physical fitness facilities; child day care services; youth camps; individual & family services

(G-6777)
YOUTH OPPORTUNITIES UNLIMITED
1361 Euclid Ave (44115-1819)
PHONE...................216 566-5445
Carol Rizchun, President
Craig Dorn, Vice Pres
Maggie Simak, Controller
Jay Paciorek, VP Finance
Carol Rivchun, VP Mktg
EMP: 40
SQ FT: 4,000
SALES: 8.8MM **Privately Held**
WEB: www.youthopportunities.org
SIC: 7361 Placement agencies

(G-6778)
Z A F INC
Also Called: Markfrank Hair Salons
2165 S Green Rd (44121-3313)
P.O. Box 605, Gates Mills (44040-0605)
PHONE...................216 291-1234
Fax: 216 691-9184
Frank Alvarez, President
EMP: 30
SQ FT: 2,000
SALES (est): 560.1K **Privately Held**
WEB: www.markfrank.com
SIC: 7231 Unisex hair salons; manicurist, pedicurist

(G-6779)
ZAREMBA GROUP INCORPORATED
14600 Detroit Ave # 1500 (44107-4299)
PHONE...................216 221-6600
Walter Zaremba Jr, President
Robert Steadley, Vice Pres
EMP: 48
SALES (est): 2.9MM **Privately Held**
SIC: 6552 8111 6531 Land subdividers & developers, commercial; legal services; real estate managers; real estate agent, commercial

(G-6780)
ZAREMBA LLC
14600 Detroit Ave # 1500 (44107-4299)
PHONE...................216 221-6600
Realty I Limite, Partner
Realty I Limited, Partner
Eastlake Retail Investment Lim, Ltd Ptnr
Joseph Urbancic, Mng Member
Paula Cuesman, Manager
EMP: 100
SQ FT: 20,000
SALES (est): 6.3MM **Privately Held**
SIC: 6512 6531 Shopping center, property operation only; real estate brokers & agents

(G-6781)
ZASHIN & RICH CO LPA (PA)
950 Main Ave Fl 4 (44113-7215)
PHONE...................216 696-4441
Fax: 216 248-8861
Andrew Zashin, President
Gwen Johnston, Office Admin
Amy Keating,
Michele L Jakubs, Associate
EMP: 35
SALES (est): 3.9MM **Privately Held**
WEB: www.zrlaw.com
SIC: 8111 Labor & employment law

(G-6782)
ZAVARELLA BROTHERS CNSTR CO
5381 Erie St Ste B (44146-1739)
PHONE...................440 232-2243
Fax: 440 232-6465
Nicholas Zavarella, President
Daniel Zavarella, Vice Pres
Dennis Fiorilli, Project Mgr
Chuck Zavarella, Admin Sec
EMP: 50
SQ FT: 1,000
SALES (est): 4.4MM **Privately Held**
SIC: 1741 Masonry & other stonework; bricklaying; concrete block masonry laying; foundation building

(G-6783)
ZENITH SYSTEMS LLC (PA)
5055 Corbin Dr (44128-5462)
PHONE...................216 587-9510
Paul Francisco, President
David Weiland, President
Robert Heiser, General Mgr
Geoff Jecmen, Superintendent
Greg Ropple, Superintendent
EMP: 133
SALES (est): 103.2MM **Privately Held**
SIC: 1731 Electrical work; communications specialization

(G-6784)
ZEP INC
Zep Manufacturing
6777 Engle Rd Ste A (44130-7953)
PHONE...................440 239-1580
Fax: 216 267-4763
Scott Ward, Manager
EMP: 37
SALES (corp-wide): 922.8MM **Privately Held**
SIC: 5169 Chemicals & allied products
HQ: Zep Inc.
 3330 Cumberland Blvd Se # 700
 Atlanta GA 30339
 877 428-9937

(G-6785)
ZUCKER BUILDING COMPANY
Also Called: State Chemical
5915 Landerbrook Dr # 300 (44124-4039)
PHONE...................216 861-7114
Harold Uhrman, President
Malcolm Zucker, Principal
Andy Shipp, District Mgr
Morgan Hallman, Sales Mgr
William Nix, Sales Mgr
EMP: 58
SQ FT: 240,000
SALES (est): 5.4MM **Privately Held**
WEB: www.statechemical.com
SIC: 6512 Commercial & industrial building operation

Cleveland Heights
Cuyahoga County

(G-6786)
CENTER FOR FAMILIES & CHILDREN
Rapp Art Center
1941 S Taylor Rd Ste 225 (44118-2103)
PHONE...................216 932-9497
Pamela Bradford, Manager
EMP: 25
SALES (corp-wide): 26MM **Privately Held**
SIC: 8322 Individual & family services
PA: Center For Families & Children, Inc
 4500 Euclid Ave
 Cleveland OH 44103
 216 432-7200

(G-6787)
CITY OF CLEVELAND HEIGHTS
Community Relations Service
40 Severance Cir (44118-1501)
PHONE...................216 291-2323
Susanna O'Neal, Director
EMP: 30 **Privately Held**
WEB: www.clevelandheights.com
SIC: 8743 Public relations services
PA: City Of Cleveland Heights
 40 Severance Cir
 Cleveland Heights OH 44118
 216 291-4444

(G-6788)
CITY OF CLEVELAND HEIGHTS
Water Dept
40 Severance Cir (44118-1501)
PHONE...................216 291-5995
Fax: 216 291-5977
Dennis Zentarski, Principal
EMP: 35 **Privately Held**
WEB: www.clevelandheights.com
SIC: 4941 Water supply
PA: City Of Cleveland Heights
 40 Severance Cir
 Cleveland Heights OH 44118
 216 291-4444

(G-6789)
HEIGHTS LAUNDRY & DRY CLEANING (PA)
1863 Coventry Rd (44118-1610)
PHONE...................216 932-9666
Manning Dishler, President
Arlene Dishler, Vice Pres
EMP: 32
SQ FT: 3,000
SALES (est): 990.8K **Privately Held**
SIC: 7211 7216 Power laundries, family & commercial; drycleaning plants, except rugs

(G-6790)
HOME DEPOT USA INC
Also Called: Home Depot, The
3460 Mayfield Rd (44118-1405)
PHONE...................216 297-1303
Fax: 216 691-4096
Timothy E McCarthy, Manager
Maurice Kirkland, Manager
EMP: 150
SALES (corp-wide): 100.9B **Publicly Held**
WEB: www.homerentalsdepot.com
SIC: 5211 7359 Home centers; tool rental
HQ: Home Depot U.S.A., Inc.
 2455 Paces Ferry Rd Se
 Atlanta GA 30339

(G-6791)
JEWISH EDCATN CTR OF CLEVELAND
2030 S Taylor Rd (44118-2605)
PHONE...................216 371-0446
Yossi Israeli, Info Tech Dir
Ilya Kligman, Technology
Seymour Kopelowitz, Exec Dir
Jeffrey Schein, Director
Judith Schiller, Director
EMP: 75
SQ FT: 20,000
SALES: 5.8MM **Privately Held**
SIC: 8399 Council for social agency

(G-6792)
KAISER FOUNDATION HOSPITALS
Also Called: Cleveland Heights Medical Ctr
10 Severance Cir (44118-1533)
PHONE...................800 524-7377
EMP: 593
SALES (corp-wide): 82.6B **Privately Held**
SIC: 8011 Medical centers
HQ: Kaiser Foundation Hospitals Inc
 1 Kaiser Plz
 Oakland CA 94612
 510 271-6611

(G-6793)
MISSION PRIDE INC
3011 Berkshire Rd (44118-2421)
PHONE...................216 759-7404
Damon Cross, President
Reya lees, Vice Pres
EMP: 43
SALES (est): 1.3MM **Privately Held**
SIC: 8742 Marketing consulting services

(G-6794)
NOOR HOME HEALTH CARE
2490 Lee Blvd Ste 110 (44118-1255)
PHONE...................216 320-0803
Barkhad Abdullahi, Principal
EMP: 51 **Privately Held**
SIC: 9431 6321 5047 Administration of public health programs; accident & health insurance carriers; medical & hospital equipment

(G-6795)
REALTY CORPORATION OF AMERICA
3048 Meadowbrook Blvd (44118-2842)
PHONE...................216 522-0020
Fax: 216 522-0033
Anthony Viola, President
Sera Brewer, Director
EMP: 46
SQ FT: 50,000
SALES: 5MM **Privately Held**
WEB: www.realtycorpofamerica.com
SIC: 6162 Bond & mortgage companies

(G-6796)
REILLY PAINTING CO
1899 S Taylor Rd (44118-2160)
PHONE...................216 371-8160
Fax: 216 371-1302
Michael Reilly, President
Fiona Reilly, Vice Pres
Kiki Stout, Manager
Eve Prikryl, Administration
EMP: 30
SQ FT: 8,063
SALES (est): 2.5MM **Privately Held**
SIC: 1721 1761 Exterior residential painting contractor; interior residential painting contractor; exterior commercial painting contractor; interior commercial painting contractor; roofing, siding & sheet metal work

Cleves
Hamilton County

(G-6797)
BANTA ELECTRICAL CONTRS INC
5701 Hamilton Cleves Rd (45002-9504)
P.O. Box 377, Miamitown (45041-0377)
PHONE...................513 353-4446
Fax: 513 353-3708
Gale F Banta, President
Ed Ginter, Vice Pres
Mr Stephen Banta, Project Mgr
Dave Findley, Purchasing
Carolyn Banta, Info Tech Mgr
EMP: 100
SQ FT: 12,000

Cleves - Hamilton County (G-6798)

SALES (est): 15MM **Privately Held**
WEB: www.bantaelectric.com
SIC: **1731** General electrical contractor

(G-6798)
DAY PRECISION WALL INC
5715 Hamilton Cleves Rd (45002-9504)
PHONE....................513 353-2999
Fax: 513 353-3919
Jim Day, *President*
Joseph H Day, *Vice Pres*
Larry Day, *Vice Pres*
Sam Hirst, *Treasurer*
EMP: 30
SALES (est): 2.6MM **Privately Held**
SIC: **1771** Foundation & footing contractor

(G-6799)
EQUIPMENT MAINTENANCE INC (PA)
Also Called: Equipment Maintenance & Repair
5885 Hamilton Cleves Rd (45002-9529)
PHONE....................513 353-3518
Fax: 513 353-3582
Don Holden, *President*
Dave Holden, *Manager*
EMP: 34
SQ FT: 22,000
SALES (est): 2.5MM **Privately Held**
SIC: **7699** 5261 5082 Aircraft & heavy equipment repair services; general household repair services; lawn & garden equipment; construction & mining machinery

(G-6800)
KATHMAN ELECTRIC CO INC
8969 Harrison Pike (45002-9757)
PHONE....................513 353-3365
Fax: 513 353-3365
Raymond E Kathman, *President*
Thomas Kathman, *Vice Pres*
Gary Kathman, *Admin Sec*
EMP: 45
SQ FT: 3,000
SALES (est): 4.8MM **Privately Held**
SIC: **1731** General electrical contractor

(G-6801)
KEN NEYER PLUMBING INC
4895 Hamilton Cleves Rd (45002-9752)
PHONE....................513 353-3311
Fax: 513 353-3329
James Neyer, *President*
Ken Neyer Jr, *Vice Pres*
Janet Neyer, *Treasurer*
Cheryl Tucker, *Finance Mgr*
Rodney Deffinger, *Manager*
EMP: 150
SQ FT: 2,500
SALES (est): 32.8MM **Privately Held**
WEB: www.neyerplumbing.com
SIC: **1711** Plumbing contractors

(G-6802)
KINDERTOWN EDUCATIONAL CENTERS (PA)
Also Called: Biederman Educational Centers
8720 Bridgetown Rd (45002-1328)
PHONE....................859 344-8802
Fax: 859 344-0249
Stewart J Biederman, *President*
Amy Early, *Director*
Cheryl Lawrence, *Director*
Amy Morgan, *Director*
EMP: 48
SALES (est): 1.4MM **Privately Held**
WEB: www.biedermaneducationalcenters.com
SIC: **8351** Group day care center

(G-6803)
LARRY SMITH CONTRACTORS INC
Also Called: Larry Smith Plumbing
5737 Dry Fork Rd (45002-9730)
PHONE....................513 367-0218
Fax: 513 367-3585
Larry Smith, *President*
Marvin Smith, *Vice Pres*
Matthew Young, *Vice Pres*
EMP: 50
SQ FT: 4,000

SALES (est): 8.8MM **Privately Held**
SIC: **1623** Sewer line construction; water main construction

(G-6804)
MATTLIN CONSTRUCTION INC
5835 Hamilton Cleves Rd (45002-9529)
PHONE....................513 598-5402
Fax: 513 598-8014
C David Mattlin, *President*
David M Mattlin, *Vice Pres*
Tim Mattlin, *Admin Sec*
EMP: 30
SALES (est): 6.9MM **Privately Held**
WEB: www.mattlinconstruction.net
SIC: **1542** 1771 Commercial & office buildings, renovation & repair; concrete work

(G-6805)
REIS TRUCKING INC
10080 Valley Junction Rd (45002-9406)
PHONE....................513 353-1960
Fax: 513 353-4297
Paul A Reis, *President*
EMP: 28
SQ FT: 7,000
SALES: 6.8MM **Privately Held**
WEB: www.reistrucking.com
SIC: **4212** Local trucking, without storage

(G-6806)
WM KRAMER AND SONS INC
Also Called: W K S
9171 Harrison Pike # 12 (45002-9076)
PHONE....................513 353-1142
Steven M Kramer, *President*
Bruce Kramer, *Vice Pres*
Doug Kramer, *Vice Pres*
Kevin Kramer, *Vice Pres*
Tom Lehrter, *Project Mgr*
EMP: 75
SQ FT: 22,357
SALES (est): 11.8MM **Privately Held**
WEB: www.kramerroofing.com
SIC: **1761** Roofing contractor

Clinton
Summit County

(G-6807)
RESIDNTIAL COML RNOVATIONS INC
7686 S Clvland Msslion Rd (44216-8912)
PHONE....................330 815-1476
EMP: 50
SALES (est): 3.8MM **Privately Held**
SIC: **1521** 1522 1542 1761 Single-Family House Cnst Residential Construction Nonresidential Cnstn Roofing/Siding Contr

Clyde
Sandusky County

(G-6808)
ARBORS AT CLIDE ASSSTED LIVING
Also Called: Abror Health Care
700 Coulson St (43410-2065)
PHONE....................419 547-7746
Fax: 419 547-1605
Kelli Livas, *Exec Dir*
Ramonda Stahl, *Director*
EMP: 25
SALES (est): 956.2K **Privately Held**
SIC: **8361** Residential care

(G-6809)
ASTORIA PLACE OF CLYDE LLC
Also Called: Heritage Village of Clyde
700 Helen St (43410-2051)
PHONE....................419 547-9595
Jason Dipasqua, *COO*
Eric Hutchins, *Administration*
EMP: 70 EST: 2014
SALES (est): 1MM **Privately Held**
SIC: **8051** Skilled nursing care facilities

(G-6810)
BAKER BNNGSON RLTY AUCTIONEERS
1570 W Mcpherson Hwy (43410-1012)
PHONE....................419 547-7777
Fax: 419 547-7744
Bill Baker, *Partner*
Ken Bonnigson, *Partner*
Teri Meyer, *Office Mgr*
Dean Smith, *Real Est Agnt*
EMP: 25
SALES (est): 1.4MM **Privately Held**
WEB: www.bakerbonnigson.com
SIC: **6519** 6531 7359 7389 Real property lessors; appraiser, real estate; tent & tarpaulin rental; auctioneers, fee basis

(G-6811)
CHANEY ROOFING MAINTENANCE
Also Called: C R M
7040 State Route 101 N (43410-9636)
PHONE....................419 639-2761
Fax: 419 639-2799
Shawn Chaney, *President*
Gary S Chaney, *Chairman*
David Huffman, *Project Mgr*
Deb Snyder, *Office Mgr*
EMP: 30
SQ FT: 50,000
SALES: 3.9MM **Privately Held**
WEB: www.chaney-roofing.com
SIC: **1761** 1542 Roofing contractor; commercial & office building, new construction

(G-6812)
CLYDE-FINDLAY AREA CR UN INC (PA)
1455 W Mcpherson Hwy (43410-1009)
PHONE....................419 547-7781
Fax: 419 547-6669
Paul Howard, *President*
Scott Hicks, *President*
Smith Sonya, *Opers Mgr*
Kenneth Cobb, *Treasurer*
Holly Brawley, *Marketing Staff*
EMP: 28
SQ FT: 12,416
SALES: 4.1MM **Privately Held**
WEB: www.cfacu.com
SIC: **6061** 6163 Federal credit unions; loan brokers

(G-6813)
FULTZ & SON INC
Also Called: FSI Disposal
100 S Main St (43410-1633)
PHONE....................419 547-9365
Fax: 419 547-9594
Larry F Fultz, *President*
Audra Albright, *Admin Sec*
EMP: 28 EST: 1952
SQ FT: 22,000
SALES (est): 3.8MM **Privately Held**
WEB: www.fsidisposal.com
SIC: **4212** 4953 Garbage collection & transport, no disposal; recycling, waste materials

(G-6814)
HMSHOST CORPORATION
Also Called: Marriott
888 N County Road 260 (43410-8514)
PHONE....................419 547-8667
Tom Travis, *General Mgr*
John Mongiello, *Opers Mgr*
Carroll Timmons, *Site Mgr*
Frank Hercik, *Opers Staff*
Paula Miller, *Opers Staff*
EMP: 125
SALES (corp-wide): 9.1MM **Privately Held**
SIC: **7011** 8741 6531 Hotels & motels; management services; real estate agents & managers
HQ: Hmshost Corporation
6905 Rockledge Dr 1f
Bethesda MD 20817

(G-6815)
HOSPICE OF MEMORIAL HOSPITA L
430 S Main St (43410-2142)
PHONE....................419 334-6626
Fax: 419 547-9459

Anne Shelley, *Director*
EMP: 30
SALES (est): 252.2K **Privately Held**
SIC: **8082** Home health care services

(G-6816)
J B HUNT TRANSPORT INC
600 N Woodland Ave (43410-1054)
PHONE....................419 547-2777
Tracey Walker, *Branch Mgr*
EMP: 166
SALES (corp-wide): 7.1B **Publicly Held**
SIC: **4213** Trucking, except local
HQ: J. B. Hunt Transport, Inc.
615 J B Hunt Corporate Dr
Lowell AR 72745
479 820-0000

(G-6817)
KF CONSTRUCTION AND EXCVTG LLC
220 Norwest St (43410-2162)
PHONE....................419 547-7555
Michelle Bishop, *President*
EMP: 25
SALES: 950K **Privately Held**
SIC: **1521** New construction, single-family houses

(G-6818)
MEMORIAL HOSPITAL
Memorial Home Health & Hospice
430 S Main St (43410-2142)
PHONE....................419 547-6419
Anne Shelley, *Director*
Marianna Snavely, *Administration*
EMP: 40
SALES (corp-wide): 63MM **Privately Held**
SIC: **8062** 8082 General medical & surgical hospitals; home health care services
PA: Memorial Hospital
715 S Taft Ave
Fremont OH 43420
419 334-6657

(G-6819)
PENSKE LOGISTICS LLC
600 N Woodland Ave (43410-1054)
PHONE....................419 547-2615
Matt Barrown, *Manager*
EMP: 42
SALES (corp-wide): 2.9B **Privately Held**
WEB: www.penskelogistics.com
SIC: **7389** Field warehousing
HQ: Penske Logistics Llc
Green Hls Rr 10
Reading PA 19603
800 529-6531

(G-6820)
POLYCHEM CORPORATION
Also Called: Evergreen Plastics
202 Watertower Dr (43410-2154)
PHONE....................419 547-1400
Fax: 419 547-4551
Mark Jeckering, *General Mgr*
Howard Lamont, *Controller*
Brandon Golden, *Regl Sales Mgr*
Heidi Fratianne, *Sales Staff*
Tim Cross, *Manager*
EMP: 75
SALES (corp-wide): 153.7MM **Privately Held**
SIC: **3052** 4953 Plastic belting; recycling, waste materials
PA: Polychem Corporation
6277 Heisley Rd
Mentor OH 44060
440 357-1500

(G-6821)
ROCKWELL SPRINGS TROUT CLUB (PA)
1581 County Road 310 (43410-9733)
PHONE....................419 684-7971
Fax: 419 684-7928
Toni Borchardt, *Principal*
Kevin Ramsey, *Admin Sec*
Jeff Smith, *Asst Sec*
EMP: 41
SQ FT: 4,000
SALES: 1.2MM **Privately Held**
SIC: **7032** 7041 5812 Fishing camp; lodging house, organization; eating places

GEOGRAPHIC SECTION

Columbia Station - Lorain County (G-6844)

(G-6822)
SANDCO INDUSTRIES
567 Premier Dr (43410-2157)
PHONE..................................419 334-9090
Fax: 419 332-9571
Donald Nalley, *Director*
EMP: 130
SALES: 1.4MM **Privately Held**
WEB: www.sanmrdd.org
SIC: 8331 Sheltered workshop

(G-6823)
SPADER FREIGHT CARRIERS INC
1134 E Mcpherson Hwy (43410-9802)
P.O. Box 246 (43410-0246)
PHONE..................................419 547-1117
David Spader, *President*
David L Spader, *President*
Steve Spader, *Vice Pres*
Tom Spader, *Admin Sec*
EMP: 62
SQ FT: 58,000
SALES (est): 8.9MM **Privately Held**
SIC: 4213 Trucking, except local

(G-6824)
SPADER FREIGHT SERVICES INC (PA)
Also Called: S F S
1134 E Mcpherson Hwy (43410-9802)
P.O. Box 246 (43410-0246)
PHONE..................................419 547-1117
David Spader, *President*
Steve Spader, *Vice Pres*
Jeff Leopold, *Sales Staff*
Marsha Harmon, *Manager*
Adam Powell, *Manager*
EMP: 60
SQ FT: 60,000
SALES (est): 6.8MM **Privately Held**
WEB: www.spaderfreight.com
SIC: 4213 Contract haulers

(G-6825)
WHIRLPOOL CORPORATION
1081 W Mcpherson Hwy (43410-1001)
PHONE..................................419 547-2610
Joe Lafave, *Senior Engr*
Tom Borro, *Manager*
EMP: 125
SALES (corp-wide): 21.2B **Publicly Held**
WEB: www.whirlpoolcorp.com
SIC: 4225 General warehousing
PA: Whirlpool Corporation
    2000 N M 63
    Benton Harbor MI 49022
    269 923-5000

Coal Grove
Lawrence County

(G-6826)
TRI-STATE INDUSTRIES INC
606 Carlton Davidson Ln (45638-2926)
PHONE..................................740 532-0406
Fax: 740 532-0407
Paul Mollett, *Director*
EMP: 175
SQ FT: 30,000
SALES: 592.5K **Privately Held**
SIC: 8331 Sheltered workshop

Coldwater
Mercer County

(G-6827)
AYERS SERVICE GROUP LLC
Also Called: Cw Service
5215b State Route 118 (45828-9702)
PHONE..................................419 678-4811
Fax: 419 678-8417
Stan Ayers,
EMP: 25
SALES (est): 1.1MM **Privately Held**
SIC: 1521 Single-family housing construction

(G-6828)
COUNTY OF MERCER
Also Called: Coldwater Ems
510 W Main St (45828-1607)
PHONE..................................419 678-8071
Kevin Sanning, *Chief*
EMP: 25
WEB: www.mercercountyohio.org
SIC: 8322 Emergency social services
PA: County Of Mercer
    220 W Livingston St A201
    Celina OH 45822
    419 586-3178

(G-6829)
HCF OF BRIARWOOD INC
Also Called: Briarwood Mano
100 Don Desch Dr D (45828-1583)
PHONE..................................419 678-2311
Fax: 419 678-3491
Deb Post, *Financial Exec*
Janel Schulte, *Marketing Staff*
Shanna Holland, *Exec Dir*
Kristen Wynk, *Director*
EMP: 256
SALES (est): 5.2MM
SALES (corp-wide): 154.8MM **Privately Held**
WEB: www.hcfinc.com
SIC: 8051 Extended care facility
PA: Hcf Management, Inc.
    1100 Shawnee Rd
    Lima OH 45805
    419 999-2010

(G-6830)
HOSPICE OF DARKE COUNTY INC
Also Called: State of Heart HM Hlth Hospice
230 W Main St (45828-1703)
PHONE..................................419 678-4808
Diane Stevenson, *Exec Dir*
Tammy Fox, *Director*
EMP: 25 **Privately Held**
WEB: www.stateoftheheartcare.org
SIC: 8093 7361 Specialty outpatient clinics; employment agencies
PA: Hospice Of Darke County, Inc.
    1350 N Broadway St
    Greenville OH 45331

(G-6831)
LEFELD IMPLEMENT INC (PA)
Also Called: John Deere Authorized Dealer
5228 State Route 118 (45828-9702)
PHONE..................................419 678-2375
Fax: 419 678-8705
Steve Layfield, *President*
Judy Marbaugh, *Corp Secy*
Dan Lefeld, *Vice Pres*
Michael Lefeld, *Vice Pres*
Paul J Lefeld Jr, *Vice Pres*
▲ EMP: 28
SQ FT: 40,000
SALES (est): 5.2MM **Privately Held**
SIC: 5999 5082 Farm machinery; farm equipment & supplies; construction & mining machinery

(G-6832)
LEFELD WELDING & STL SUPS INC (PA)
Also Called: Lefeld Supplies Rental
600 N 2nd St (45828-9777)
PHONE..................................419 678-2397
Fax: 419 678-8279
Stanley C Lefeld, *CEO*
Gary Lefeld, *President*
Marge Lefeld, *Controller*
Cindy Myer, *Controller*
Chuck Meyer, *Accounts Mgr*
▲ EMP: 43 EST: 1953
SQ FT: 10,400
SALES (est): 25.1MM **Privately Held**
WEB: www.lefeld.com
SIC: 5084 7353 1799 3441 Welding machinery & equipment; heavy construction equipment rental; welding on site; fabricated structural metal

(G-6833)
MERCER CNTY JOINT TOWNSHP HOSP
Also Called: Mercer County Community Hosp
800 W Main St (45828-1613)
PHONE..................................419 678-2341
Fax: 419 678-3271
Cindy Berning, *CFO*
Donn Fishbein, *Pathologist*
Joseph Mesarvey, *Director*
Shelly Ro, *Director*
Terese Burnette, *Executive*
EMP: 88
SALES (est): 9.6MM
SALES (corp-wide): 50.6MM **Privately Held**
SIC: 8062 General medical & surgical hospitals
PA: Mercer County Joint Township Community Hospital
    800 W Main St
    Coldwater OH 45828
    419 678-2341

(G-6834)
PAX STEEL PRODUCTS INC
104 E Vine St (45828-1246)
PHONE..................................419 678-1481
Bill Kramer, *President*
Jerry Meyer, *Manager*
EMP: 50
SALES (est): 3MM **Privately Held**
SIC: 5083 Farm & garden machinery

(G-6835)
THE PEOPLES BANK CO INC (PA)
112 W Main St 114 (45828-1701)
P.O. Box 110 (45828-0110)
PHONE..................................419 678-2385
Jack A Hartings, *President*
Bob Thompson, *Treasurer*
Bruce Slavik, *Controller*
Connie Boeke, *Marketing Staff*
Sue Baldwin, *Director*
EMP: 29 EST: 1905
SQ FT: 8,000
SALES: 17.7MM **Privately Held**
SIC: 6022 8721 State trust companies accepting deposits, commercial; accounting, auditing & bookkeeping

(G-6836)
THE PEOPLES BANK CO INC
112 W Main St (45828-1701)
P.O. Box 110 (45828-0110)
PHONE..................................419 678-2385
Jack Hartings, *Manager*
EMP: 30
SALES (corp-wide): 17.7MM **Privately Held**
SIC: 6022 State commercial banks
PA: The Peoples Bank Co Inc
    112 W Main St 114
    Coldwater OH 45828
    419 678-2385

(G-6837)
VILLAGE OF COLDWATER
Also Called: Tax Department
610 W Sycamore St (45828-1662)
PHONE..................................419 678-2685
Eric Thomas, *Manager*
EMP: 80 **Privately Held**
WEB: www.villageofcoldwater.com
SIC: 7291 9111 Tax return preparation services; city & town managers' offices
PA: Village Of Coldwater
    610 W Sycamore St
    Coldwater OH 45828
    419 678-4881

College Corner
Butler County

(G-6838)
OHIO STATE PARKS INC
Also Called: Hueston Woods Lodge,
5201 Lodge Rd (45003-9038)
PHONE..................................513 664-3504
Susan Chapin, *Sales Staff*
Pamela Hodapp, *Sales Staff*
Tom Arvan, *Manager*
Katie Brown, *Manager*
Jim Henahan, *Manager*
EMP: 60
SALES (est): 3MM **Privately Held**
WEB: www.hwpaintball.com
SIC: 7011 7992 5813 5812 Vacation lodges; public golf courses; drinking places; eating places

Collins
Huron County

(G-6839)
CINC
14006 Bellamy Rd (44826-9627)
PHONE..................................419 663-6644
Dan Costner, *President*
EMP: 27
SALES (est): 2.3MM **Privately Held**
SIC: 5084 Industrial machinery & equipment

Columbia Station
Lorain County

(G-6840)
AMERI-LINE INC
27060 Royalton Rd (44028-9048)
P.O. Box 965 (44028-0965)
PHONE..................................440 316-4500
Fax: 440 236-3243
Joseph Michetti, *President*
Gregory Romanovich, *Corp Secy*
Jerome Santivasci, *Vice Pres*
Robert Komer, *Regl Sales Mgr*
Lucy Starnoni,
EMP: 30
SQ FT: 12,000
SALES: 2.7MM **Privately Held**
WEB: www.ameri-line.com
SIC: 4213 4731 Contract haulers; truck transportation brokers

(G-6841)
CAMILLUS VILLA INC
10515 East River Rd (44028-9541)
P.O. Box 880 (44028-0880)
PHONE..................................440 236-5091
Bruce A Schirhart, *President*
Suzanne Placko, *Manager*
Diana P Garven, *Director*
Natwarlal Jethva, *Director*
Barb West, *Director*
EMP: 90
SQ FT: 18,000
SALES (est): 3.8MM **Privately Held**
SIC: 8051 Skilled nursing care facilities

(G-6842)
CENTRAL COMMAND INC
33891 Henwell Rd (44028-9150)
PHONE..................................330 723-2062
Fax: 330 722-6517
Keith Peer, *President*
EMP: 25
SQ FT: 4,000
SALES (est): 2.1MM **Privately Held**
WEB: www.centralcommand.com
SIC: 7374 Data processing & preparation

(G-6843)
CLEVELAND PICK-A-PART INC
12420 Station Rd (44028-9501)
PHONE..................................440 236-5031
Fax: 440 236-6150
Richard Fragnoli, *President*
Rebecca Fragnoli, *Principal*
Brian Fragnoli, *Vice Pres*
EMP: 32
SQ FT: 10,000
SALES: 950K **Privately Held**
WEB: www.clevelandpickapart.com
SIC: 7549 Automotive maintenance services

(G-6844)
COLUMBIA HILLS COUNTRY CLB INC
16200 East River Rd (44028-9485)
PHONE..................................440 236-5051
Fax: 440 236-5054

Columbia Station - Lorain County (G-6845)

Michael Weinhardt, *President*
Karsen Eckweiler, *Manager*
Charles Sandio, *Manager*
Fred Ode, *Executive*
Jon Standen, *Executive*
EMP: 25
SQ FT: 43,000
SALES (est): 1.4MM **Privately Held**
WEB: www.columbiahills.org
SIC: 7997 Country club, membership

(G-6845)
DORLON GOLF CLUB
18000 Station Rd (44028-8726)
PHONE..................................440 236-8234
Fax: 440 236-5078
Debra Lontor, *Owner*
EMP: 25
SQ FT: 2,500
SALES (est): 768.4K **Privately Held**
WEB: www.dorlon.com
SIC: 7992 Public golf courses

(G-6846)
EMERALD WOODS GOLF COURSE
11464 Clarke Rd (44028-9231)
PHONE..................................440 236-8940
Fax: 440 236-5450
Richard McCoain, *President*
EMP: 25
SQ FT: 1,500
SALES (est): 1MM **Privately Held**
WEB: www.emeraldwoodsgc.com
SIC: 7992 5941 Public golf courses; sporting goods & bicycle shops

(G-6847)
J D S LEASING INC
27230 Royalton Rd (44028-9159)
PHONE..................................440 236-6575
Scott Mihu, *President*
Jeffrey Mihu, *Manager*
EMP: 33
SALES (est): 1.5MM **Privately Held**
WEB: www.jdstrucking.com
SIC: 7538 Truck engine repair, except industrial

(G-6848)
M & B TRUCKING EXPRESS CORP
27457 Royalton Rd (44028-9159)
P.O. Box 395 (44028-0395)
PHONE..................................440 236-8820
Fax: 440 236-8833
Michael A Bagi, *President*
Deborah Hawley, *Treasurer*
EMP: 26
SQ FT: 1,500
SALES: 1MM **Privately Held**
SIC: 4213 Trucking, except local

(G-6849)
MASLYK LANDSCAPING INC
12289 Eaton Commerce Pkwy (44028-9208)
PHONE..................................440 748-3635
Alan Maslyk, *President*
EMP: 30
SALES (est): 1.9MM **Privately Held**
SIC: 0781 Landscape services

(G-6850)
MORTONS LAWN SERVICE INC
Also Called: Morton Landscape Dev Co
11564 Station Rd (44028-9501)
P.O. Box 967 (44028-0967)
PHONE..................................440 236-3550
Fax: 440 236-3550
Barry J Morton, *President*
Melinda Heidecker, *Human Res Dir*
EMP: 50 EST: 1981
SQ FT: 3,000
SALES (est): 3.3MM **Privately Held**
WEB: www.mortonslandscaping.com
SIC: 0781 0782 Landscape services; fertilizing services, lawn

(G-6851)
PETITTI ENTERPRISES INC
Also Called: Casa Verde Growers
10310 East River Rd (44028-9531)
PHONE..................................440 236-5055
Fax: 440 236-5059
Gwain Coleson, *Manager*

Meg Vanderbilt, *Manager*
Ann Ward, *Manager*
EMP: 50
SALES (corp-wide): 20.1MM **Privately Held**
WEB: www.petittigardencenter.com
SIC: 5193 Flowers & nursery stock
PA: Petitti Enterprises, Inc.
25018 Broadway Ave
Oakwood Village OH 44146
440 439-8636

(G-6852)
TOTAL RHABILITATION SPECIALIST
23050 Louise Ln (44028-9474)
PHONE..................................440 236-8527
Ray Bilecky, *Principal*
David Chhoransky, *Principal*
Mizzy Chhoransky, *Principal*
EMP: 50
SALES (est): 479.9K **Privately Held**
SIC: 8049 Physical therapist

Columbiana
Columbiana County

(G-6853)
BUCKEYE COMPONENTS LLC (PA)
1340 State Route 14 (44408-9648)
PHONE..................................330 482-5163
Robert Holmes,
EMP: 29
SQ FT: 8,000
SALES (est): 2.9MM **Privately Held**
SIC: 5031 2439 Lumber, plywood & millwork; trusses, wooden roof

(G-6854)
C TUCKER COPE & ASSOC INC
170 Duquesne St (44408-1637)
PHONE..................................330 482-4472
Charles T Cope, *President*
Jim Bacon, *COO*
Linda Cope, *Vice Pres*
Jeanne Wright, *Controller*
Quinn Frease, *Administration*
EMP: 42
SALES (est): 11.9MM **Privately Held**
WEB: www.ctcope.com
SIC: 1611 1542 1541 Concrete construction: roads, highways, sidewalks, etc.; commercial & office building, new construction; industrial buildings, new construction

(G-6855)
COLUMBIANA BOILER COMPANY LLC
200 W Railroad St (44408-1281)
PHONE..................................330 482-3373
Fax: 330 482-3390
Michael J Sherwin, *President*
Wayne Good, *Vice Pres*
Chuck Gorby, *Vice Pres*
Gerianne Klepfer, *CFO*
John Bossone, *Director*
◆ EMP: 45 EST: 1894
SQ FT: 50,000
SALES: 9.5MM
SALES (corp-wide): 4.3MM **Privately Held**
SIC: 1791 3443 Storage tanks, metal: erection; process vessels, industrial: metal plate
PA: Columbiana Holding Co Inc
200 W Railroad St
Columbiana OH 44408
330 482-3373

(G-6856)
COLUMBIANA SERVICE COMPANY LLC
Also Called: Reichard Industries, LLC
338 S Main St (44408-1509)
PHONE..................................330 482-5511
James Hawkins,
EMP: 65
SALES: 2MM **Privately Held**
SIC: 7363 Employee leasing service

(G-6857)
D & V TRUCKING INC
12803 Clmbana Canfield Rd (44408-9769)
PHONE..................................330 482-9440
Fax: 330 482-4850
Danny W Fowler Jr, *President*
EMP: 50
SQ FT: 20,000
SALES (est): 6.3MM **Privately Held**
SIC: 4212 Dump truck haulage

(G-6858)
DAS DUTCH VILLAGE INN
150 E State Route 14 (44408-8425)
PHONE..................................330 482-5050
Fax: 330 482-4141
Ralph Witmer, *Partner*
Raymond Horst, *Partner*
David Stryffeler, *General Mgr*
Jacqueline Smith, *Chief Mktg Ofcr*
Rose Conrad, *Marketing Mgr*
EMP: 63
SQ FT: 3,400
SALES (est): 3.1MM **Privately Held**
WEB: www.dasdutchvillage.com
SIC: 7011 Vacation lodges

(G-6859)
FOUR WHEEL DRIVE HARDWARE LLC
Also Called: 4wd
44488 State Route 14 (44408-9540)
PHONE..................................330 482-4733
Fax: 330 482-5035
George Adler, *CEO*
Eb Peters, *President*
Pattie Keslar, *Controller*
Sean Campbell, *Sales Mgr*
Devin Black, *Sales Staff*
◆ EMP: 155 EST: 1976
SQ FT: 53,000
SALES (est): 31.3MM
SALES (corp-wide): 99.6B **Publicly Held**
WEB: www.performanceproduct.net
SIC: 5013 5531 Automotive supplies & parts; automotive parts; automotive accessories
HQ: Transamerican Dissolution Company, Llc
400 W Artesia Blvd
Compton CA 90220
310 900-5500

(G-6860)
MACO CONSTRUCTION SERVICES
170 Duquesne St (44408-1637)
PHONE..................................330 482-4472
Fax: 330 482-5037
Linda Cope, *President*
C Tucker Cope, *Corp Secy*
EMP: 35
SQ FT: 1,500
SALES (est): 4.3MM **Privately Held**
SIC: 1541 1611 Steel building construction; concrete construction: roads, highways, sidewalks, etc.

(G-6861)
MCMASTER FARMS
345 Old Fourteen Rd (44408-9493)
PHONE..................................330 482-2913
Fax: 330 482-0284
David McMaster, *Owner*
Jon Jesse McMaster, *Partner*
EMP: 69
SALES (est): 4.6MM **Privately Held**
SIC: 0161 0134 0119 Corn farm, sweet; pumpkin farm; Irish potatoes; feeder grains

(G-6862)
R & L TRANSFER INC
1320 Springfield Rd (44408)
PHONE..................................330 482-5800
Fax: 330 482-5814
Jeff Pickett, *General Mgr*
Timothy Oswald, *Manager*
EMP: 200 **Privately Held**
WEB: www.robertsarena.com
SIC: 4213 4212 Trucking, except local; local trucking, without storage

HQ: R & L Transfer, Inc.
600 Gilliam Rd
Wilmington OH 45177
937 382-1494

(G-6863)
STG COMMUNICATION SERVICES INC
1401 Wardinglsey Ave (44408-9756)
PHONE..................................330 482-0500
Fax: 330 482-4451
Mark Muzzane, *President*
Brien Meals, *Project Mgr*
Dylan Hipple, *Safety Mgr*
Teri Kechler, *Finance*
Sharon McDevitt, *Office Mgr*
EMP: 35
SALES (est): 4.3MM **Privately Held**
SIC: 8999 Communication services

(G-6864)
STG COMMUNICATION SERVICES INC
1401 Wardinglsey Ave (44408-9756)
PHONE..................................330 482-0500
Mark Muccana, *President*
M Scott Strong, *Vice Pres*
Ken Hall, *Manager*
EMP: 25
SQ FT: 10,000
SALES (est): 4.2MM **Privately Held**
WEB: www.stgcom.com
SIC: 1623 Transmitting tower (telecommunication) construction

(G-6865)
U S A CONCRETE SPECIALISTS
145 Nulf Dr (44408-9730)
PHONE..................................330 482-9150
Joseph L Rich, *President*
EMP: 30
SALES (est): 1.8MM **Privately Held**
SIC: 1771 Concrete work

(G-6866)
WINDSOR HOUSE INC
Also Called: Parkside Health Care Center
930 E Park Ave (44408-1452)
PHONE..................................330 482-1375
Fax: 330 482-0003
Wendy Dickson, *Human Res Dir*
Jennifer Connely, *Manager*
Laurice Haines Rn, *Nursing Dir*
Laurice Haynes, *Nursing Dir*
Diane Defrank, *Hlthcr Dir*
EMP: 100
SALES (corp-wide): 25.7MM **Privately Held**
SIC: 8051 Skilled nursing care facilities
PA: Windsor House, Inc.
101 W Liberty St
Girard OH
330 545-1550

(G-6867)
WINDSOR HOUSE INC
Also Called: Northeastern Ohio Alzheimer Ctr
1899 W Garfield Rd (44408-9785)
PHONE..................................330 549-9259
Fax: 330 549-0765
Kim Guarnieri, *Principal*
Robin Prince, *Nursing Dir*
Amy Foust, *Hlthcr Dir*
Roe Kelly, *Admin Sec*
Renee Manning, *Receptionist*
EMP: 125
SALES (corp-wide): 25.7MM **Privately Held**
SIC: 8051 8052 Skilled nursing care facilities; intermediate care facilities
PA: Windsor House, Inc.
101 W Liberty St
Girard OH
330 545-1550

Columbus
Delaware County

(G-6868)
ADENA COMMERCIAL LLC
Also Called: Colliers International
8800 Lyra Dr Ste 650 (43240-2107)
PHONE..................................614 436-9800

Richard B Schuen, CEO
Michael R Linder, Senior VP
EMP: 40
SQ FT: 7,500
SALES (est): 7MM
SALES (corp-wide): 1.9B Privately Held
WEB: www.adenarealty.com
SIC: 6531 Real estate agent, commercial
HQ: Colliers International Property Consultants Inc.
601 Union St Ste 3320
Seattle WA 98101
206 695-4200

(G-6869)
BANC ONE SERVICES CORPORATION (HQ)
1111 Polaris Pkwy Ste B3 (43240-2031)
P.O. Box 710638 (43271-0001)
PHONE..................614 248-5800
Fax: 614 213-4104
Neil Williams, Senior VP
Kristin Gibson, Financial Analy
Bill Hunt, Manager
Rob Holt, Network Mgr
EMP: 2855
SALES (est): 156.1MM
SALES (corp-wide): 99.6B Publicly Held
WEB: www.bancone.com
SIC: 7389 Financial services
PA: Jpmorgan Chase & Co.
270 Park Ave Fl 38
New York NY 10017
212 270-6000

(G-6870)
BANKERS LIFE & CASUALTY CO
8740 Orion Pl Ste 204 (43240-4063)
PHONE..................614 987-0590
Fax: 614 888-5240
Sandy Harned, Sales Staff
John M Kwasnik, Manager
Bryan Marshall, Agent
William McKinney, Agent
EMP: 37
SALES (corp-wide): 4.3B Publicly Held
WEB: www.bankerslife.com
SIC: 6311 Life insurance
HQ: Bankers Life & Casualty Co
111 E Wacker Dr Ste 2100
Chicago IL 60601
312 396-6000

(G-6871)
CAPITAL LIGHTING INC
901 Polaris Pkwy (43240-2035)
PHONE..................614 841-1200
Fax: 614 841-0826
Larry W King, President
David L Winks, Vice Pres
Ann Landis, Warehouse Mgr
Keith Shuck, Sales Staff
Alisha Meyer, Sales Executive
▲ EMP: 60
SQ FT: 32,000
SALES (est): 39.3MM Privately Held
WEB: www.capitallightinginc.com
SIC: 5063 5719 Lighting fixtures; lighting, lamps & accessories

(G-6872)
CENTER FOR DAGNSTC IMAGING INC
2141 Polaris Pkwy (43240-2022)
PHONE..................614 841-0800
EMP: 145 Privately Held
SIC: 8011 Offices & clinics of medical doctors
PA: Center For Diagnostic Imaging, Inc.
5775 Wayzata Blvd Ste 400
Minneapolis MN 55416

(G-6873)
CENTURY 21-JOE WALKER & ASSOC
Also Called: Century 21 - North Office
8800 Lyra Dr Ste 600 (43240-2120)
PHONE..................614 899-1400
Fax: 614 899-1400
Joseph Walker, President
Charity Walker, Vice Pres
Laura Oliva, Manager
Tom Newberry, Technology
Craig Balster, Real Est Agnt
EMP: 40

SALES: 3.5MM Privately Held
WEB: www.maxcopeland.com
SIC: 6531 Real estate agent, residential

(G-6874)
CGI TECHNOLOGIES SOLUTIONS INC
2000 Polaris Pkwy (43240-2108)
PHONE..................614 880-2200
Joyce Clause, Branch Mgr
EMP: 56
SALES (corp-wide): 8.6B Privately Held
SIC: 7379
HQ: Cgi Technologies And Solutions Inc.
11325 Random Hills Rd
Fairfax VA 22030
703 267-8000

(G-6875)
CHANGES HAIR DESIGNERS INC
Also Called: Changes Salon & Day Spa
2054 Polaris Pkwy (43240-2007)
PHONE..................614 846-6666
Fax: 614 846-3996
William Reichert, President
Sonya Pellegrini, Manager
EMP: 25
SQ FT: 3,200
SALES (est): 713.5K Privately Held
WEB: www.changessalon.com
SIC: 7991 7231 Spas; beauty shops

(G-6876)
CHASE EQUIPMENT FINANCE INC (HQ)
1111 Polaris Pkwy Ste A3 (43240-2031)
PHONE..................800 678-2601
Clif H Gottwals, CEO
Gary S Gage, Vice Pres
Verla Campbell, Manager
EMP: 230
SQ FT: 43,000
SALES (est): 64.4MM
SALES (corp-wide): 99.6B Publicly Held
SIC: 6021 National commercial banks
PA: Jpmorgan Chase & Co.
270 Park Ave Fl 38
New York NY 10017
212 270-6000

(G-6877)
COLUMBUS FINANCIAL GR
8425 Pulsar Pl Ste 450 (43240-2008)
PHONE..................614 785-5100
Fax: 614 785-4255
Jonathan Codispoti, Managing Dir
Paul J Vineis, Principal
Barbara De Francisco, Administration
William Ho, Advisor
EMP: 25
SALES (est): 5.1MM Privately Held
SIC: 6311 Life insurance

(G-6878)
CORPORATE ONE FEDERAL CR UN (PA)
8700 Orion Pl (43240-2078)
P.O. Box 2770 (43216-2770)
PHONE..................614 825-9314
Lee C Butke, CEO
Melissa Ashley, Exec VP
Tammy Cantrell, Exec VP
Joseph Ghammashi, Exec VP
Jim Horlacher, Exec VP
EMP: 98
SQ FT: 35,000
SALES (est): 27MM Privately Held
SIC: 6061 Federal credit unions

(G-6879)
CRANEL INCORPORATED (PA)
Also Called: Cranel Imaging
8999 Gemini Pkwy Ste A (43240-2250)
PHONE..................614 431-8000
Fax: 614 431-8388
Craig Wallace, President
James Wallace, Chairman
Dennis Fields, District Mgr
David Nguyen, Business Mgr
Leslie Duff, Vice Pres
EMP: 100
SQ FT: 65,000

SALES (est): 52.5MM Privately Held
WEB: www.adexisstorage.com
SIC: 5045 Computer peripheral equipment

(G-6880)
DUGAN & MEYERS CONSTRUCTION CO
8740 Orion Pl Ste 220 (43240-4063)
PHONE..................614 257-7430
Fax: 614 257-7432
Jeffery Kelly, President
Lincoln Ketterer, Vice Pres
Jeffrey Kelly, Treasurer
Jerome E Meyers, Admin Sec
EMP: 40
SQ FT: 2,500
SALES (est): 4.4MM
SALES (corp-wide): 103.1MM Privately Held
WEB: www.dugan-meyers.com
SIC: 1541 1542 Industrial buildings, new construction; commercial & office building, new construction
HQ: Dugan & Meyers Construction Co
11110 Kenwood Rd
Blue Ash OH 45242
513 891-4300

(G-6881)
EMERSON PROCESS MGT LLLP
8460 Orion Pl Ste 110 (43240)
PHONE..................877 468-6384
Chris Village, Manager
EMP: 50
SALES (corp-wide): 15.2B Publicly Held
SIC: 8711 Engineering services
HQ: Emerson Process Management Lllp
1100 W Louis Henna Blvd
Round Rock TX 78681

(G-6882)
HEALTH CARE PLUS (HQ)
1120 Polaris Pkwy Ste 204 (43240-4042)
PHONE..................614 340-7587
Fax: 614 340-7588
Randall A Mason, President
Yow Hong, Project Mgr
Robin Levalley, Manager
EMP: 27
SQ FT: 750
SALES (est): 4.1MM
SALES (corp-wide): 7.7MM Privately Held
WEB: www.mardencompanies.com
SIC: 8082 7361 8351 Home health care services; nurses' registry; child day care services
PA: Marden Rehabilitation Assoc
200 Putnam St Ste 800
Marietta OH 45750
740 373-9446

(G-6883)
HILTON GRDN INN CLMBUS POLARIS
8535 Lyra Dr (43240-2026)
PHONE..................614 846-8884
Dan Fox, Principal
Teresa S Tompkins, Sales Dir
Daphne Spencer, Manager
EMP: 25
SALES (est): 1.4MM Privately Held
SIC: 7011 Hotels

(G-6884)
HILTON POLARIS
Also Called: Hilton Columbus Polaris
8700 Lyra Dr (43240-2103)
PHONE..................614 885-1600
Jamie Johnson, Principal
EMP: 52 EST: 2008
SALES (est): 3.6MM Privately Held
SIC: 7011 Hotels & motels

(G-6885)
HTP INC
8720 Orion Pl Ste 300 (43240-2111)
PHONE..................614 885-1272
Ray Shealy, CEO
Dennis Swartzlander, Ch of Bd
Blair Baker, Vice Pres
Leigh Orlov, Vice Pres
Fred Richards, Vice Pres
EMP: 42
SQ FT: 13,968

SALES: 5.5MM Privately Held
WEB: www.htp-inc.com
SIC: 8999 Communication services

(G-6886)
INFOR (US) INC
Also Called: Tdci
8760 Orion Pl Ste 300 (43240-2109)
PHONE..................614 781-2325
Gloria Davis, Branch Mgr
EMP: 75
SALES (corp-wide): 2.8B Privately Held
WEB: www.tdci.com
SIC: 8742 7373 Management consulting services; systems software development services
HQ: Infor (Us), Inc.
13560 Morris Rd Ste 4100
Alpharetta GA 30004
678 319-8000

(G-6887)
JOSEPH WALKER INC
Also Called: Century 21
8800 Lyra Dr Ste 600 (43240-2120)
PHONE..................614 895-3840
Fax: 614 895-3839
Joseph Walker, President
EMP: 50
SQ FT: 3,050
SALES (est): 1.9MM Privately Held
WEB: www.plcox.com
SIC: 6531 Real estate agent, residential

(G-6888)
JPMORGAN CHASE BANK NAT ASSN (HQ)
1111 Polaris Pkwy (43240-2050)
PHONE..................614 436-3055
James Dimon, Ch of Bd
Sean Friedman, President
Ellyn Brognara, Managing Dir
Ajith Sundaresh, Managing Dir
David Lawton, Principal
◆ EMP: 1800
SALES: 81.8MM
SALES (corp-wide): 99.6B Publicly Held
WEB: www.chase.com
SIC: 6022 6099 6799 6211 State commercial banks; travelers' checks issuance; safe deposit companies; real estate investors, except property operators; investment bankers; mortgage bankers; credit card service
PA: Jpmorgan Chase & Co.
270 Park Ave Fl 38
New York NY 10017
212 270-6000

(G-6889)
JPMORGAN HIGH YIELD FUND
1111 Polaris Pkwy (43240-2031)
PHONE..................614 248-7017
Toni Demsky, Manager
EMP: 36
SALES (est): 255K
SALES (corp-wide): 99.6B Publicly Held
SIC: 6722 Money market mutual funds
HQ: Jpmorgan Investment Advisors Inc.
1111 Polaris Pkwy
Columbus OH 43240

(G-6890)
JPMORGAN INV ADVISORS INC (HQ)
1111 Polaris Pkwy (43240-2031)
P.O. Box 711235 (43271-0001)
PHONE..................614 248-5800
Fax: 614 213-9404
David J Kundert, President
Diana Westhoff, Manager
EMP: 550
SQ FT: 50,000
SALES (est): 95MM
SALES (corp-wide): 99.6B Publicly Held
SIC: 6282 Investment advisory service
PA: Jpmorgan Chase & Co.
270 Park Ave Fl 38
New York NY 10017
212 270-6000

(G-6891)
KARPINSKI ENGINEERING INC
8800 Lyra Dr Ste 530 (43240-2100)
PHONE..................614 430-9820
Ken Borah, Vice Pres

Columbus - Delaware County (G-6892)

Matt Garee, *Project Engr*
EMP: 30
SALES (corp-wide): 10.4MM **Privately Held**
SIC: 8711 Mechanical engineering
PA: Karpinski Engineering, Inc.
3135 Euclid Ave Ste 200
Cleveland OH 44115
216 391-3700

(G-6892)
LOWES HOME CENTERS LLC
1465 Polaris Pkwy (43240-6002)
PHONE..................................614 433-9957
Fax: 614 436-3672
Ryan Lane, *Office Mgr*
Chad Pratt, *Branch Mgr*
EMP: 150
SALES (corp-wide): 68.6B **Publicly Held**
SIC: 5211 5031 5722 5064 Home centers; building materials, exterior; building materials, interior; household appliance stores; electrical appliances, television & radio
HQ: Lowe's Home Centers, Llc
1605 Curtis Bridge Rd
Wilkesboro NC 28697
336 658-4000

(G-6893)
MANTA MEDIA INC
8760 Orion Pl Ste 200 (43240-2109)
PHONE..................................888 875-5833
John Swanciger, *CEO*
Peter Morse, *Vice Pres*
George Troutman, *CFO*
Ricannia Frates, *Natl Sales Mgr*
Joey Glowacki, *VP Sales*
EMP: 48
SQ FT: 5,000
SALES (est): 7.5MM **Privately Held**
WEB: www.ecnext.com
SIC: 7313 Printed media advertising representatives

(G-6894)
MEDICAL SPECIALTIES DISTRS LLC
400 Lazelle Rd Ste 13 (43240-4051)
PHONE..................................614 888-7939
EMP: 27
SALES (corp-wide): 474.2MM **Privately Held**
SIC: 8099 Childbirth preparation clinic
PA: Medical Specialties Distributors, Llc
800 Technology Center Dr # 3
Stoughton MA 02072
781 344-6000

(G-6895)
MERRILL LYNCH PIERCE FENNER
8425 Pulsar Pl Ste 200 (43240-4048)
PHONE..................................614 825-0350
Fax: 614 825-0389
Barry Casoli, *Vice Pres*
Leonard Barbe, *Investment Ofcr*
Jeff Daniels, *Investment Ofcr*
Patti Schultz, *Investment Ofcr*
Larry Tyree, *Manager*
EMP: 40
SALES (corp-wide): 100.2B **Publicly Held**
WEB: www.merlyn.com
SIC: 6211 Security brokers & dealers
HQ: Merrill Lynch, Pierce, Fenner & Smith Incorporated
111 8th Ave
New York NY 10011
800 637-7455

(G-6896)
MICROSOFT CORPORATION
8800 Lyra Dr Ste 400 (43240-2100)
PHONE..................................614 719-5900
Fax: 614 985-1832
Marrida Davis, *General Mgr*
Susan Leasure, *Accounts Mgr*
Doug Brennan, *Sales Staff*
Eric Savoldi, *Technical Staff*
EMP: 45
SALES (corp-wide): 89.9B **Publicly Held**
WEB: www.microsoft.com
SIC: 7372 Application computer software
PA: Microsoft Corporation
1 Microsoft Way
Redmond WA 98052
425 882-8080

(G-6897)
NEWCOME CORP
Also Called: Newcome Electronic Systems
9005 Antares Ave (43240-2012)
P.O. Box 12247 (43212-0247)
PHONE..................................614 848-5688
Fax: 614 848-9921
Timothy W Newcome, *President*
Grosh Tracy, *Marketing Staff*
David Oconnor, *Manager*
Fred Hamilton, *Technology*
EMP: 40
SQ FT: 8,500
SALES (est): 4.7MM **Privately Held**
WEB: www.newcome.com
SIC: 1731 Fiber optic cable installation; voice, data & video wiring contractor; computer installation

(G-6898)
OHIO FARMERS INSURANCE COMPANY
Also Called: Westfield Group
2000 Polaris Pkwy Ste 202 (43240-2006)
PHONE..................................614 848-6174
Fax: 614 848-6184
Keith Gilliam, *Manager*
Jennifer Stjohn, *Manager*
EMP: 75
SALES (corp-wide): 1.6B **Privately Held**
WEB: www.westfieldgrp.com
SIC: 6411 Property & casualty insurance agent
PA: Ohio Farmers Insurance Company
1 Park Cir
Westfield Center OH 44251
800 243-0210

(G-6899)
PACIFIC HERITG INN POLARIS LLC
9090 Lyra Dr (43240-2116)
PHONE..................................614 880-9080
Rachel Marchant, *Mng Member*
Juliann Beatty,
EMP: 50
SQ FT: 100,000
SALES (est): 757.5K **Privately Held**
SIC: 7011 Inns

(G-6900)
PETSMART INC
1184 Polaris Pkwy (43240-2024)
PHONE..................................614 433-9361
Barbara Fritzgerald, *Principal*
EMP: 32
SALES (corp-wide): 12.7B **Privately Held**
WEB: www.petsmart.com
SIC: 0752 Grooming services, pet & animal specialties
HQ: Petsmart, Inc.
19601 N 27th Ave
Phoenix AZ 85027
623 580-6100

(G-6901)
POLARIS TOWNE CENTER LLC
1500 Polaris Pkwy # 3000 (43240-2126)
PHONE..................................614 456-0123
Richard Hunt,
Richard Hunt,
EMP: 30
SALES (est): 967K
SALES (corp-wide): 843.4MM **Publicly Held**
WEB: www.glimcher.com
SIC: 6512 Nonresidential building operators
PA: Washington Prime Group Inc.
180 E Broad St Fl 21
Columbus OH 43215
614 621-9000

(G-6902)
PRIME AE GROUP INC
8415 Pulsar Pl Ste 300 (43240-4032)
PHONE..................................614 839-0250
Kumar Buvanendaran, *President*
Kerry Hogan, *Senior VP*
Jodie Bare, *Vice Pres*
Michael Rice, *Vice Pres*
Amit Joshi, *Project Engr*
EMP: 82 **Privately Held**
SIC: 8711 8712 Civil engineering; architectural engineering
PA: Prime Ae Group, Inc.
5521 Res Pk Dr Ste 300
Baltimore MD 21228

(G-6903)
RANDSTAD TECHNOLOGIES LLC
8425 Pulsar Pl Ste 110 (43240-4032)
PHONE..................................614 436-0961
Reanna Lancaster, *Branch Mgr*
EMP: 72
SALES (corp-wide): 27.4B **Privately Held**
SIC: 7361 Employment agencies
HQ: Randstad Technologies, Llc
150 Presidential Way # 300
Woburn MA 01801
781 938-1910

(G-6904)
RIGHT AT HOME LLC
8828 Commerce Loop Dr (43240-2121)
PHONE..................................614 734-1110
Kathy Noble,
EMP: 30
SALES (est): 562.1K **Privately Held**
SIC: 8082 Home health care services

(G-6905)
ROCKFORD HOMES INC (PA)
999 Polaris Pkwy Ste 200 (43240-2051)
PHONE..................................614 785-0015
Fax: 614 785-9181
Robert E Yoakam Sr, *CEO*
Robert Yoakam Jr, *President*
Don Wick, *Vice Pres*
Rita Yoakam, *Treasurer*
EMP: 62
SALES (est): 15.8MM **Privately Held**
WEB: www.rockfordhomes.net
SIC: 1521 1522 6552 New construction, single-family houses; residential construction; subdividers & developers

(G-6906)
SEARS ROEBUCK AND CO
1280 Polaris Pkwy (43240-2036)
PHONE..................................614 797-2095
Fax: 614 797-2295
Michael Ladd, *Manager*
EMP: 116
SALES (corp-wide): 16.7B **Publicly Held**
SIC: 7549 Automotive maintenance services
HQ: Sears, Roebuck And Co.
3333 Beverly Rd
Hoffman Estates IL 60179
847 286-2500

(G-6907)
SEQUENT INC (PA)
Also Called: SEQUENT INFORMATION SOLUTIONS
8425 Pulsar Pl Ste 200 (43240-4032)
PHONE..................................614 436-5880
Bill Hutter, *CEO*
Joseph W Cole, *President*
Timothy Reed, *VP Opers*
Paula Reed, *Accountant*
Audrey McClinton, *Human Res Dir*
EMP: 85
SQ FT: 12,000
SALES: 10.9MM **Privately Held**
WEB: www.sequent.com
SIC: 7363 8748 Employee leasing service; employee programs administration

(G-6908)
SWH MIMIS CAFE LLC
Also Called: Mimis Cafe 112
1428 Polaris Pkwy (43240-2040)
PHONE..................................614 433-0441
EMP: 69 **Privately Held**
WEB: www.mimiscafe.com
SIC: 5149 Groceries & related products
HQ: Swh Mimi's Cafe, Llc
12201 Merit Dr Ste 900
Dallas TX 75251
866 926-6636

(G-6909)
VENTECH SOLUTIONS INC (PA)
8425 Pulsar Pl Ste 300 (43240-2079)
PHONE..................................614 757-1167
Herb Jones, *CEO*
John Carrier, *President*
Robert Williams, *General Mgr*
Smokey Williams, *General Mgr*
Ravi Kunduru, *Chairman*
EMP: 85
SQ FT: 6,000
SALES: 118MM **Privately Held**
WEB: www.ventechsolutions.com
SIC: 7371 7373 7379 Custom computer programming services; systems engineering, computer related; systems integration services; computer related maintenance services

(G-6910)
WESTERN & SOUTHERN LF INSUR CO
8425 Pulsar Pl Ste 310 (43240-4041)
PHONE..................................614 898-1066
Fax: 614 898-0325
Terry Garner, *Manager*
EMP: 27 **Privately Held**
SIC: 6411 Life insurance agents
HQ: The Western & Southern Life Insurance Company
400 Broadway St
Cincinnati OH 45202
513 629-1800

(G-6911)
WESTFIELD SERVICES INC (PA)
2000 Polaris Pkwy Ste 202 (43240-2006)
P.O. Box 1690 (43216-1690)
PHONE..................................614 796-7700
Fax: 614 796-7779
Jon Park, *CEO*
Brian Bowerman, *Vice Pres*
EMP: 28 **EST:** 1998
SALES (est): 6.2MM **Privately Held**
WEB: www.westfieldservices.com
SIC: 6411 Property & casualty insurance agent

Columbus
Franklin County

(G-6912)
1522 HESS STREET LLC
1522 Hess St (43212-2642)
PHONE..................................614 291-6876
Jeffery Brown, *President*
EMP: 35
SALES (est): 2.6MM **Privately Held**
SIC: 1521 General remodeling, single-family houses

(G-6913)
5 STAR HOTEL MANAGEMENT IV LP
Also Called: Residence Inn By Marriott
6191 Quarter Horse Dr (43229-2568)
PHONE..................................614 431-1819
Fax: 614 431-2477
Stephanie Martin, *Principal*
EMP: 80
SALES (est): 1.8MM **Privately Held**
SIC: 7011 Hotels & motels

(G-6914)
50 S FRONT LLC
Also Called: Doubletree Suites by Hilton
50 S Front St (43215-4129)
PHONE..................................614 224-4600
Micheal Bulgarelli, *Principal*
David Buddemeyer, *Principal*
EMP: 66
SALES (est): 3.3MM **Privately Held**
SIC: 7011 Hotels

(G-6915)
6TH CIRCUIT COURT
Also Called: US Probation Office
85 Marconi Blvd Rm 546 (43215-2835)
PHONE..................................614 719-3100
Linda Wilmouth, *Manager*
Patrick Crowley, *Manager*
EMP: 34 **Publicly Held**
WEB: www.mied.uscourts.gov

GEOGRAPHIC SECTION

Columbus - Franklin County (G-6941)

SIC: **8322** Probation office
HQ: 6th Circuit Court
   601 W Broadway Bsmt
   Louisville KY 40202
   502 625-3800

(G-6916)
75 EAST STATE LLC
Also Called: Sheraton Clumbus At Capitol Sq
75 E State St (43215-4203)
PHONE.................................614 365-4500
Fax: 614 365-4696
David Buddemeyer, *President*
Mandy Berryman, *Manager*
Lynda Ciminello, *Manager*
Nicole Wellington, *Manager*
Cara Morrow, *Director*
EMP: 44
SALES (est): 3.7MM **Privately Held**
SIC: **7011** Hotels

(G-6917)
845 YARD STREET LLC (PA)
375 N Front St Ste 200 (43215-2258)
PHONE.................................614 857-2330
Brian Ellis,
Shelley Stevens, *Administration*
EMP: 60
SALES (est): 3.2MM **Privately Held**
SIC: **6798** Realty investment trusts

(G-6918)
A B INDUSTRIAL COATINGS
212 N Grant Ave (43215-2642)
PHONE.................................614 228-0383
James Volpe, *Owner*
David Halves, *Manager*
EMP: 35
SALES (est): 1MM **Privately Held**
SIC: **1721** Industrial painting

(G-6919)
A BETTER CHOICE CHILD CARE LLC
2572 Cleveland Ave (43211-1679)
PHONE.................................614 268-8503
Jama Farrah, *Branch Mgr*
EMP: 25
SALES (est): 434.3K **Privately Held**
SIC: **8322** Child related social services

(G-6920)
A T V INC
2047 Leonard Ave (43219-2277)
PHONE.................................614 252-5060
Paul Vellani, *President*
Davie Beickman, *Controller*
EMP: 115
SQ FT: 7,325
SALES: 3.9MM **Privately Held**
SIC: **4141** Local bus charter service

(G-6921)
A&R LOGISTICS INC
1230 Harmon Ave (43223-3307)
PHONE.................................614 444-4111
Fax: 614 444-1475
James Bedeker, *Manager*
EMP: 70
SALES (corp-wide): 293.1MM **Privately Held**
WEB: www.arpdsi.com
SIC: **4213** Contract haulers
PA: A&R Logistics, Inc.
   600 N Hurstbourne Pkwy # 110
   Louisville KY 40222
   815 941-5200

(G-6922)
A-1 NURSING CARE INC
2500 Corp Exchange Dr # 220 (43231-7601)
PHONE.................................614 268-3800
Naresh Patel, *President*
EMP: 200
SQ FT: 22,000
SALES (est): 11.4MM **Privately Held**
SIC: **7361** 8082 Nurses' registry; home health care services

(G-6923)
A-SONS CONSTRUCTION INC
6427 Busch Blvd (43229-1862)
PHONE.................................614 846-2438
Jeffrey Beeson, *Branch Mgr*
EMP: 61

SALES (corp-wide): 66.3MM **Privately Held**
SIC: **8741** 1521 Construction management; single-family housing construction
PA: A-Son's Construction, Inc.
   3100 S Tillotson Ave
   Muncie IN 47302
   888 463-2790

(G-6924)
ABBOTT LABORATORIES
Also Called: Abbott Nutrition
585 Cleveland Ave (43215-1755)
P.O. Box 16546 (43216-6546)
PHONE.................................614 624-3191
Fax: 614 624-3816
Chuck Mundy, *Principal*
Steve Nichols, *Plant Mgr*
Joe Ceddia, *Project Mgr*
Cindy Lyons, *Project Mgr*
Carol Marvin, *Project Mgr*
EMP: 550
SQ FT: 378,500
SALES (corp-wide): 27.3B **Publicly Held**
WEB: www.abbott.com
SIC: **8099** 2834 2087 2086 Nutrition services; pharmaceutical preparations; flavoring extracts & syrups; bottled & canned soft drinks; canned specialties
PA: Abbott Laboratories
   100 Abbott Park Rd
   Abbott Park IL 60064
   224 667-6100

(G-6925)
ABF FREIGHT SYSTEM INC
1720 Joyce Ave (43219-1026)
P.O. Box 24666 (43224-0666)
PHONE.................................614 294-3537
Fax: 614 294-6082
Rich Desantis, *General Mgr*
Patrick Petit, *Sales Mgr*
EMP: 45
SALES (corp-wide): 2.8B **Publicly Held**
WEB: www.abfs.com
SIC: **4213** Contract haulers
HQ: Abf Freight System, Inc.
   3801 Old Greenwood Rd
   Fort Smith AR 72903
   479 785-8700

(G-6926)
ABLE COMPANY LTD PARTNERSHIP (PA)
Also Called: Able Roofing
4777 Westerville Rd (43231-6042)
PHONE.................................614 478-4176
Fax: 614 478-4176
Paul Demboski, *President*
Jeff Kriegel, *Vice Pres*
Rich Smith, *Project Mgr*
Scott Henderson, *Prdtn Mgr*
Tiffany Riemenschneider, *Production*
EMP: 57
SQ FT: 23,000
SALES (est): 21.6MM **Privately Held**
SIC: **1761** 1741 Roofing contractor; chimney construction & maintenance

(G-6927)
ABLE ROOFING LLC
4777 Westerville Rd (43231-6042)
PHONE.................................614 444-7663
Paul Demboski, *Branch Mgr*
EMP: 50
SALES (corp-wide): 21.6MM **Privately Held**
SIC: **1761** Roofing contractor
PA: Able Company Limited Partnership
   4777 Westerville Rd
   Columbus OH 43231
   614 444-7663

(G-6928)
ABOVE & BEYOND CAREGIVERS LLC
2862 Johnstown Rd (43219-1793)
PHONE.................................614 478-1700
Crystal L Sillah,
Elisee Ndenga,
EMP: 28
SALES (est): 772.1K **Privately Held**
SIC: **8082** 4119 Home health care services; local passenger transportation

(G-6929)
ABSOLUTE CARE MANAGEMENT LLC (PA)
4618 Sawmill Rd (43220-2247)
PHONE.................................614 846-8053
Mark King, *CEO*
Amanda Hines, *Admin Asst*
EMP: 35
SALES (est): 1.5MM **Privately Held**
WEB: www.absolutecarecompany.com
SIC: **8322** Individual & family services

(G-6930)
ACADEMIC SUPPORT SERVICES LLC
Also Called: Janitorial Support Services
2958 Blossom Ave (43231-2925)
PHONE.................................740 274-6138
Audra Johnson, *Mng Member*
EMP: 31
SALES: 350K **Privately Held**
SIC: **8299** 7349 Tutoring school; janitorial service, contract basis

(G-6931)
ACADEMY KIDS LEARNING CTR INC
289 Woodland Ave (43203-1747)
PHONE.................................614 258-5437
Fax: 614 253-7115
David R Weaver, *President*
Carol Burns, *Director*
Annett Howell, *Administration*
EMP: 30
SALES (est): 884K **Privately Held**
SIC: **8351** Preschool center

(G-6932)
ACCELERATED MOVING & STOR INC
4001 Refugee Rd Ste 2 (43232-5187)
PHONE.................................614 836-1007
Todd G Wilson, *President*
Sherman Willis, *Assistant VP*
James Willis, *Vice Pres*
EMP: 25
SQ FT: 11,000
SALES (est): 2.3MM **Privately Held**
SIC: **4214** 4213 4212 Furniture moving & storage, local; household goods transport; moving services

(G-6933)
ACCENT DRAPERY CO INC
Also Called: Accent Drapery Supply Co
1180 Goodale Blvd (43212-3793)
PHONE.................................614 488-0741
Fax: 614 488-7809
Patrick Casbarro, *President*
Brian Whiteside, *Vice Pres*
Allyson Woods, *Mktg Coord*
Marie Buehler, *Manager*
EMP: 27
SQ FT: 19,500
SALES (est): 4.1MM **Privately Held**
SIC: **5714** 5023 2391 Draperies; draperies; curtains & draperies

(G-6934)
ACCENTURE LLP
400 W Nationwide Blvd # 100 (43215-2377)
PHONE.................................614 629-2000
Fax: 614 228-0692
James Struntz, *Managing Prtnr*
Gregg Bourdo, *Corp Comm Staff*
John Hrusovsky, *Branch Mgr*
Karen McDonnell, *Manager*
Todd Cameron, *Senior Mgr*
EMP: 215 **Privately Held**
WEB: www.wavesecurities.com
SIC: **8742** 8748 Business consultant; business consulting
HQ: Accenture Llp
   161 N Clark St Ste 1100
   Chicago IL 60601
   312 693-0161

(G-6935)
ACCOMODAIRE TOTAL CLEANING LLC
541 Kasons Way (43230-6278)
PHONE.................................614 367-1347
Sharon F Turner, *Partner*

EMP: 35
SALES (est): 998.5K **Privately Held**
SIC: **7349** Janitorial service, contract basis

(G-6936)
ACCURATE INVENTORY AND C
Also Called: Quantum Services
4284 N High St Fl 1 (43214-2695)
PHONE.................................800 777-9414
Fax: 614 261-8166
Ray Crook Jr, *President*
Randy Burke, *Vice Pres*
Pamela Hoyt, *Controller*
Patrick Mignogno, *Branch Mgr*
Mark Flynn, *CTO*
EMP: 355
SQ FT: 11,600
SALES (est): 26.4MM **Privately Held**
WEB: www.quantum-services.com
SIC: **7389** 8742 Inventory computing service; business consultant

(G-6937)
ACE BUILDING MAINTENANCE LLC
2565 Mccutcheon Rd (43219-3337)
P.O. Box 24190 (43224-0190)
PHONE.................................614 471-2223
Paul Greenland, *Vice Pres*
Raymond Doughty, *Supervisor*
Ruby J Doughty,
EMP: 37
SALES: 217K **Privately Held**
WEB: www.acebuildmaint.com
SIC: **7349** Building cleaning service; building maintenance, except repairs

(G-6938)
ACLOCHE LLC (PA)
Also Called: Academy Medical Staffing Svcs
1800 Watermark Dr Ste 430 (43215-1397)
PHONE.................................888 608-0889
Fax: 614 416-5774
Kim Shoemaker, *CEO*
Georgia Ruch, *Founder*
Betty Lou Ruch, *Founder*
Toni Good, *Purch Agent*
Gail Byrd, *Human Resources*
EMP: 33
SQ FT: 12,000
SALES (est): 13.4MM **Privately Held**
WEB: www.acloche.com
SIC: **7363** 8742 Temporary help service; human resource consulting services

(G-6939)
ACOCK ASSOC ARCHITECTS LLC
383 N Front St Ste 1 (43215-2251)
PHONE.................................614 228-1586
Fax: 614 228-2780
Jack Maki, *Principal*
Leonard Whitley, *Project Mgr*
Mike Perone, *Controller*
George Acock, *Mng Member*
Pavan Peter, *CTO*
EMP: 25
SQ FT: 30,000
SALES: 4.8MM **Privately Held**
SIC: **8712** Architectural engineering

(G-6940)
ACORN DISTRIBUTORS INC
5310 Crosswind Dr (43228-3600)
PHONE.................................614 294-6444
Fax: 614 737-3703
Jennifer Rosenberg, *President*
Jim Long, *Purchasing*
Stephanie Garrett, *HR Admin*
Craig Cottingham, *Sales Mgr*
Dennis Collins, *Sales Staff*
EMP: 40 EST: 2010
SQ FT: 100,000
SALES (est): 11.8MM **Privately Held**
SIC: **5113** 5087 5046 Disposable plates, cups, napkins & eating utensils; towels, paper; napkins, paper; janitors' supplies; commercial equipment

(G-6941)
ACTION FOR CHILDREN INC (PA)
78 Jefferson Ave (43215-3860)
PHONE.................................614 224-0222
Fax: 614 224-5437

Columbus - Franklin County (G-6942)

Rhonda Fraas, *President*
Phillip Deberry, *Finance*
Jessica Woodruff, *Program Mgr*
Diane Bennett, *Exec Dir*
Lou Briggs, *Bd of Directors*
EMP: 38
SALES: 3.5MM **Privately Held**
WEB: www.actionforchildren.com
SIC: 7299 8351 8322 Information services, consumer; child day care services; individual & family services

(G-6942)
AD FARROW LLC (PA)
491 W Broad St (43215-2755)
PHONE..................................614 228-6353
Fax: 614 228-8848
Cathy Ozborne, *General Mgr*
Andy Zakrajsek, *Senior VP*
Barb Baxter, *Controller*
Lisa Wallace, *Controller*
Kelli Flanagan, *Accountant*
EMP: 50 **EST:** 1912
SQ FT: 82,500
SALES (est): 11.3MM **Privately Held**
WEB: www.adfarrow.com
SIC: 5571 7699 Motorcycles; motorcycle repair service

(G-6943)
AD INVESTMENTS LLC
375 N Front St Ste 200 (43215-2258)
PHONE..................................614 857-2340
Brian Ellis, *CEO*
EMP: 50
SALES: 2.6MM
SALES (corp-wide): 26.6B **Privately Held**
SIC: 6512 Commercial & industrial building operation
HQ: Nationwide Realty Investors, Ltd.
 375 N Front St Ste 200
 Columbus OH 43215
 614 857-2330

(G-6944)
ADMINISTRATIVE SVCS OHIO DEPT
Also Called: Office of Procurement Services
4200 Surface Rd (43228-1313)
PHONE..................................614 466-5090
Fax: 614 485-1056
Wayne McCulty, *Principal*
EMP: 70 **Privately Held**
SIC: 7299 Consumer purchasing services
HQ: Ohio Department Of Administrative Services
 30 E Broad St
 Columbus OH 43215

(G-6945)
ADVANCE HOME CARE LLC (PA)
1191 S James Rd Ste D (43227-1800)
PHONE..................................614 436-3611
Saed Mohamed, *CEO*
Abdillahi Yusuf, *President*
Idil Abdukadir, *Principal*
EMP: 80
SQ FT: 2,000
SALES (est): 1.6MM **Privately Held**
SIC: 8082 Home health care services

(G-6946)
ADVANCED FACILITIES MAINT CORP (PA)
6171 Huntley Rd Ste G (43229-1079)
P.O. Box 91171 (43209-7171)
PHONE..................................614 389-3495
Ross Pappas, *President*
EMP: 34
SQ FT: 10,000
SALES (est): 6.9MM **Privately Held**
SIC: 7349 Building maintenance services

(G-6947)
ADVANTAGE AEROTECH INC
Also Called: Alliance Advantage
1400 Hollybrier Dr # 121 (43230-8472)
PHONE..................................614 759-8329
Pamela D Price, *President*
EMP: 40
SALES (est): 3.1MM **Privately Held**
SIC: 8733 8711 Noncommercial research organizations; engineering services

(G-6948)
ADVOCATE SOLUTIONS LLC
762 S Pearl St (43206-2032)
PHONE..................................614 444-5144
Dwaine Gould, *Partner*
Frank Carchedi, *Partner*
Alan Dillman, *Partner*
Rex Plouck, *Vice Pres*
Jack Joseph, *Project Mgr*
EMP: 50
SALES (est): 2.9MM **Privately Held**
WEB: www.gcrltd.com
SIC: 8742 Business consultant

(G-6949)
AEP ENERGY PARTNERS INC
1 Riverside Plz (43215-2355)
PHONE..................................614 716-1000
Nicholas K Akins, *CEO*
Ronnie Young, *Managing Dir*
Robert P Powers, *Exec VP*
Lonni Dieck, *Senior VP*
Joseph Hamrock, *Senior VP*
EMP: 45
SALES (est): 19.9MM **Privately Held**
SIC: 4911 Electric services

(G-6950)
AEP ENERGY SERVICES INC
155 W Nationwide Blvd (43215-2570)
PHONE..................................614 583-2900
Richard Freeman, *General Mgr*
Jay Godfrey, *Managing Dir*
Stephan T Haynes, *Vice Pres*
Rob Gladman, *Buyer*
Duane T Phlegar, *Plant Engr Mgr*
EMP: 260
SALES (est): 25.1MM
SALES (corp-wide): 15.4B **Publicly Held**
WEB: www.aep.com
SIC: 4924 Natural gas distribution
PA: American Electric Power Company, Inc.
 1 Riverside Plz Fl 1 # 1
 Columbus OH 43215
 614 716-1000

(G-6951)
AEP GENERATING COMPANY (HQ)
1 Riverside Plz Ste 1600 (43215-2355)
PHONE..................................614 223-1000
Nick Akins, *CEO*
E L Draper Jr, *President*
Gina Bivens, *Counsel*
Paul Burdeaux, *Counsel*
Heather Geiger, *Counsel*
EMP: 1800
SALES: 564MM
SALES (corp-wide): 15.4B **Publicly Held**
WEB: www.aepmedia1.com
SIC: 4911 Generation, electric power
PA: American Electric Power Company, Inc.
 1 Riverside Plz Fl 1 # 1
 Columbus OH 43215
 614 716-1000

(G-6952)
AEP POWER MARKETING INC (HQ)
Also Called: America Electric Power Texas
1 Riverside Plz Fl 1 (43215-2355)
PHONE..................................614 716-1000
Michael Morris, *President*
Gene Jensen, *Vice Pres*
William Singmon, *Vice Pres*
Mark Menezes, *Manager*
Sean Parcel, *Info Tech Dir*
EMP: 2000
SALES (est): 590.6MM
SALES (corp-wide): 15.4B **Publicly Held**
SIC: 4911 Electric services
PA: American Electric Power Company, Inc.
 1 Riverside Plz Fl 1 # 1
 Columbus OH 43215
 614 716-1000

(G-6953)
AETNA BUILDING MAINTENANCE INC (DH)
Also Called: Aetna Integrated Services
646 Parsons Ave (43206-1435)
PHONE..................................614 476-1818
Paul Greenland, *President*
Darick Brown, *President*
Sean Letwat, *Opers Staff*
Robert Perlman, *Opers Staff*
Rachel Lanham, *Human Resources*
EMP: 354 **EST:** 1959
SQ FT: 12,000
SALES (est): 67.6MM
SALES (corp-wide): 17.6MM **Privately Held**
WEB: www.aetnabuilding.com
SIC: 7349 1711 1731 Janitorial service, contract basis; window cleaning; plumbing, heating, air-conditioning contractors; electrical work
HQ: Atalian Global Services, Inc.
 417 5th Ave
 New York NY 10016
 212 251-7846

(G-6954)
AFLAC INCORPORATED
30 Northwoods Blvd # 100 (43235-4716)
PHONE..................................614 410-1696
Robert Hare, *Branch Mgr*
EMP: 107
SALES (corp-wide): 21.6B **Publicly Held**
SIC: 6411 Insurance agents, brokers & service
PA: Aflac Incorporated
 1932 Wynnton Rd
 Columbus GA 31999
 706 323-3431

(G-6955)
AGEE CLYMER MITCHELL & LARET (PA)
226 N 5th St Ste 501 (43215-2718)
PHONE..................................614 221-3318
James G Clymer, *Partner*
Russell Canestraro, *Partner*
Joffre Laret, *Partner*
Greg Mitchell, *Partner*
Susan Pride, *Bookkeeper*
EMP: 30
SALES (est): 5.3MM **Privately Held**
WEB: www.ageeclymer.com
SIC: 8111 General practice law office

(G-6956)
AGGRESSIVE MECHANICAL INC
638 Greenlawn Ave (43223-2635)
PHONE..................................614 443-3280
Fax: 614 443-5470
Kevin Hall, *President*
Dan Bosworth, *Vice Pres*
John Mills, *Treasurer*
Angie Kincaid, *Manager*
Russell Cochenour, *Admin Sec*
EMP: 25
SQ FT: 8,600
SALES (est): 5.2MM **Privately Held**
SIC: 1711 Heating & air conditioning contractors

(G-6957)
AGRI COMMUNICATORS INC
Also Called: Ohio's Country Journal
1625 Bethel Rd Ste 203 (43220-2071)
PHONE..................................614 273-0465
Fax: 614 273-0463
Bart Johnson, *President*
Kim Lemmon, *Editor*
Marilyn Johnson, *Corp Secy*
David Conley, *Controller*
Lori Lawrence, *Marketing Staff*
EMP: 25
SQ FT: 4,000
SALES (est): 2.2MM **Privately Held**
WEB: www.ocj.com
SIC: 7313 2721 Radio, television, publisher representatives; periodicals: publishing only

(G-6958)
AIRNET SYSTEMS INC (PA)
7250 Star Check Dr (43217-1025)
PHONE..................................614 409-4900
Joan C Makley, *Owner*
Jeffery B Harris, *COO*
Larry M Glasscock Jr, *Senior VP*
Wynn D Peterson, *Senior VP*
Tom Brennan, *Vice Pres*
EMP: 193
SALES (est): 146.9MM **Privately Held**
WEB: www.airnet.com
SIC: 4522 4731 Air transportation, non-scheduled; air cargo carriers, nonscheduled; freight transportation arrangement

(G-6959)
AIRPORT CORE HOTEL LLC (PA)
Also Called: Embassy Suites Columbus Arprt
2886 Airport Dr (43219-2240)
PHONE..................................614 536-0500
Michael Cooney, *General Mgr*
Tim Buchholz, *Bookkeeper*
Nicole Leonetti, *Meeting Planner*
EMP: 150 **EST:** 2009
SALES (est): 7.8MM **Privately Held**
SIC: 7011 Hotels

(G-6960)
AIRTRON LP
3021 International St (43228-4635)
PHONE..................................614 274-2345
Fax: 614 276-5767
Bill Fortner, *Vice Pres*
Bill Duecker, *Manager*
Doug Kilbourne, *Manager*
EMP: 80 **Privately Held**
SIC: 1711 5075 Warm air heating & air conditioning contractor; warm air heating & air conditioning
HQ: Airtron, Inc.
 9260 Marketpl Dr
 Miamisburg OH 45342
 937 898-0826

(G-6961)
AKSM/GENESIS MEDICAL SVCS INC
100 W 3rd Ave Ste 350 (43201-7205)
PHONE..................................614 447-0281
Ann Stevens, *President*
EMP: 25
SALES: 950K **Privately Held**
SIC: 8099 Medical services organization

(G-6962)
AKZO NOBEL COATINGS INC
1313 Windsor Ave (43211-2851)
P.O. Box 489 (43216-0489)
PHONE..................................614 294-3361
David Curl, *Opers Mgr*
Sherman Hanna, *Purchasing*
John Benson, *Sales Staff*
John Wolff, *Manager*
Tom Starcher, *Manager*
EMP: 200
SALES (corp-wide): 15B **Privately Held**
WEB: www.nam.sikkens.com
SIC: 2851 8734 Paints & allied products; testing laboratories
HQ: Akzo Nobel Coatings Inc.
 8220 Mohawk Dr
 Strongsville OH 44136
 440 297-5100

(G-6963)
ALDO PERAZA
5585 Ranchwood Dr (43228-6226)
PHONE..................................614 804-0403
Aldo Peraza, *President*
EMP: 60 **EST:** 2013
SALES (est): 88.3K **Privately Held**
SIC: 7363 Truck driver services

(G-6964)
ALL CRANE RENTAL CORP (PA)
683 Oakland Park Ave (43224-3936)
PHONE..................................614 261-1800
Fax: 614 261-4430
Michael C Liptak Jr, *President*
Mike Flanders, *General Mgr*
Stephanie Reynolds, *General Mgr*
Larry Liptak, *Vice Pres*
Todd Weakley, *Parts Mgr*
EMP: 60
SQ FT: 46,000
SALES (est): 9.6MM **Privately Held**
SIC: 7353 Heavy construction equipment rental

(G-6965)
ALL SECURED SECURITY SVCS LLC (PA)
343 E Barthman Ave (43207-1919)
PHONE..................................614 861-0482
Fax: 614 322-7233

▲ = Import ▼ = Export
◆ = Import/Export

GEOGRAPHIC SECTION
Columbus - Franklin County (G-6989)

Kris Zulandt, *Founder*
Kelly James, *VP Sales*
EMP: 26
SALES (est): 1.2MM **Privately Held**
SIC: 7381 Security guard service

(G-6966)
ALLEN GARDINER DEROBERTS
777 Goodale Blvd Ste 200 (43212-3862)
PHONE..................614 221-1500
Fax: 614 221-1580
Dan Berndt, *Agent*
Al Harris, *Agent*
Jeff Levy, *Agent*
Andrew Gardiner,
Stu Allen,
EMP: 37
SQ FT: 14,000
SALES (est): 6.8MM **Privately Held**
WEB: www.allengardiner.co.za
SIC: 6411 Insurance agents

(G-6967)
ALLEN KHNLE STOVALL NEUMAN LLP
Also Called: Aksn
17 S High St Ste 1220 (43215-3441)
PHONE..................614 221-8500
Thomas R Allen, *Partner*
EMP: 30
SALES: 1MM **Privately Held**
SIC: 8111 General practice attorney, lawyer

(G-6968)
ALLIANCE DATA SYSTEMS CORP
3075 Loyalty Cir (43219-3673)
P.O. Box 31262 (43219)
PHONE..................614 729-4000
Fax: 614 729-4509
Sheryl McKenzie, *Vice Pres*
Karen Morauski, *Vice Pres*
Eileen Ouellette, *Vice Pres*
Brian Showalter, *Opers Mgr*
Pete Poling, *Accounts Mgr*
EMP: 263 **Publicly Held**
WEB: www.alliancedatasystems.com
SIC: 7374 Data processing service
PA: Alliance Data Systems Corporation
7500 Dallas Pkwy Ste 700
Plano TX 75024

(G-6969)
ALLIED BUILDING PRODUCTS CORP
1055 Kinnear Rd (43212-1150)
PHONE..................614 488-0717
Fax: 614 488-0650
Gregg Elkins, *Opers Mgr*
Bill Howard, *VP Sales*
Rick Miller, *Manager*
EMP: 30
SALES (corp-wide): 4.3B **Publicly Held**
WEB: www.alliedbuilding.com
SIC: 5033 Roofing & siding materials
HQ: Allied Building Products Corp.
15 E Union Ave
East Rutherford NJ 07073
201 507-8400

(G-6970)
ALLIED FABRICATING & WLDG CO
5699 Chantry Dr (43232-4799)
PHONE..................614 751-6664
Fax: 614 868 0020
Thomas Caminiti, *CEO*
Jack Burgoon, *President*
Joseph Caminiti, *President*
Raymond Cunningham, *Vice Pres*
Gray Arthurs, *Engineer*
EMP: 34 **EST:** 1971
SQ FT: 30,000
SALES (est): 7.4MM **Privately Held**
WEB: www.afaw.net
SIC: 3444 7692 3535 3441 Sheet metal specialties, not stamped; welding repair; conveyors & conveying equipment; fabricated structural metal; rubber & plastics hose & beltings

(G-6971)
ALLIED INTERSTATE LLC
P.O. Box 561534
PHONE..................715 386-1810
EMP: 65
SALES (corp-wide): 1B **Privately Held**
SIC: 7322 Adjustment/Collection Services
HQ: Allied Interstate, Llc
12755 Hwy 55 Ste 300
Plymouth MN 55441
973 630-5720

(G-6972)
ALLPRO PARKING OHIO LLC
431 E Broad St (43215-4004)
PHONE..................614 221-9696
Richard A Serra, *CEO*
Thomas Eckl, *Vice Pres*
EMP: 30
SALES (est): 365.9K
SALES (corp-wide): 25.1MM **Privately Held**
SIC: 7521 Automobile parking
PA: Allpro Parking, Llc
465 Washington St Ste 100
Buffalo NY 14203
716 849-7275

(G-6973)
ALMOST FAMILY INC
Also Called: Home Care By Blackstone
445 Hutchinson Ave (43235-5677)
PHONE..................614 457-1900
Jennifer Lockard, *Branch Mgr*
EMP: 26
SALES (corp-wide): 796.9MM **Publicly Held**
SIC: 8082 Home health care services
PA: Almost Family, Inc.
9510 Ormsby Station Rd
Louisville KY 40223
502 891-1000

(G-6974)
ALPHA CHI OMEGA
103 E 15th Ave (43201-1601)
PHONE..................614 291-3871
Lesley King, *President*
EMP: 38
SQ FT: 10,268
SALES (est): 1MM **Privately Held**
SIC: 7041 Fraternities & sororities

(G-6975)
ALPHA EPSILON PHI
200 E 17th Ave (43201-1535)
PHONE..................614 294-5243
Rachel Campbell, *President*
Ashley Peterson, *Vice Pres*
Jessica Zuckerman, *Treasurer*
Daniele Lewis, *Admin Sec*
EMP: 46
SALES: 88.8K **Privately Held**
SIC: 7041 Sorority residential house

(G-6976)
ALPHA GROUP OF DELAWARE INC
85 Marconi Blvd (43215-2823)
PHONE..................614 222-1855
Laura Schick, *Branch Mgr*
EMP: 51
SALES (corp-wide): 3.6MM **Privately Held**
SIC: 8331 9111 Sheltered workshop; county supervisors' & executives' offices
PA: The Alpha Group Of Delaware Inc
1000 Alpha Dr
Delaware OH 43015
740 368-5810

(G-6977)
ALPINE INSULATION I LLC
495 S High St Ste (43215-5689)
PHONE..................614 221-3399
Jeffrey W Edwards, *President*
Jay P Elliott, *COO*
Michael T Miller, *CFO*
Todd R Fry,
EMP: 3675
SALES (est): 36.3MM
SALES (corp-wide): 1.1B **Publicly Held**
SIC: 5033 5211 Insulation materials; insulation material, building
PA: Installed Building Products, Inc.
495 S High St Ste 50
Columbus OH 43215
614 221-3399

(G-6978)
ALTIMATE CARE LLC (PA)
5869 Cleveland Ave (43231-2859)
PHONE..................614 794-9600
Ninell Drankwalter, *Owner*
Cathy Mitchell, *Office Mgr*
Irene Mendyuk, *Administration*
EMP: 31
SALES (est): 2.3MM **Privately Held**
SIC: 8082 Home health care services

(G-6979)
ALVIS INC
Also Called: Alvis House
844 Bryden Rd (43205-1728)
PHONE..................614 252-1788
Fax: 614 252-2025
Wendy Saez, *Manager*
Jeneen Peloquin, *Data Proc Dir*
EMP: 108
SALES (corp-wide): 22.3MM **Privately Held**
WEB: www.alvishouse.org
SIC: 8361 Halfway group home, persons with social or personal problems
PA: Alvis, Inc.
2100 Stella Ct
Columbus OH 43215
614 252-8402

(G-6980)
AMANDACARE INC
Also Called: Amandacare Home Health
2101 S Hamilton Rd # 212 (43232-4144)
PHONE..................614 884-8880
Paulene Crocco, *CEO*
Beverly Schaffer, *Vice Pres*
EMP: 120 **EST:** 1996
SALES (est): 3MM **Privately Held**
WEB: www.amandacare.com
SIC: 8082 Home health care services

(G-6981)
AMBER HOME CARE LLC
2800 Corp Exchange Dr # 100 (43231-7661)
PHONE..................614 523-0668
Douglas S Speelman,
Jason Huxley,
EMP: 30
SALES (est): 1MM **Privately Held**
SIC: 8082 Visiting nurse service

(G-6982)
AMC ENTERTAINMENT INC
6360 Busch Blvd (43229-1805)
PHONE..................614 846-6575
Michael Reid, *Branch Mgr*
EMP: 45 **Publicly Held**
WEB: www.amctheatres.com
SIC: 7832 Motion picture theaters, except drive-in
HQ: Amc Entertainment Inc.
11500 Ash St
Leawood KS 66211
913 213-2000

(G-6983)
AMC ENTERTAINMENT INC
275 Easton Town Ctr (43219-6077)
PHONE..................614 428-5716
Stephanie McClullan, *Manager*
EMP: 30 **Publicly Held**
WEB: www.amctheatres.com
SIC: 7832 Motion picture theaters, except drive-in
HQ: Amc Entertainment Inc.
11500 Ash St
Leawood KS 66211
913 213-2000

(G-6984)
AMC ENTERTAINMENT INC
777 Kinnear Rd (43212-1441)
PHONE..................614 429-0100
John Swaney, *Manager*
EMP: 27 **Publicly Held**
WEB: www.amctheatres.com
SIC: 7832 Exhibitors, itinerant: motion picture

HQ: Amc Entertainment Inc.
11500 Ash St
Leawood KS 66211
913 213-2000

(G-6985)
AMERICAN BOTTLING COMPANY
Also Called: 7 Up / R C/Canada Dry Btlg Co
950 Stelzer Rd (43219-3740)
PHONE..................614 237-4201
Fax: 614 231-6524
Mike Stall, *Branch Mgr*
EMP: 100 **Publicly Held**
WEB: www.cs-americas.com
SIC: 2086 5149 Soft drinks: packaged in cans, bottles, etc.; groceries & related products
HQ: The American Bottling Company
5301 Legacy Dr
Plano TX 75024

(G-6986)
AMERICAN COMMERCE INSURANCE CO (DH)
3590 Twin Creeks Dr (43204-1628)
PHONE..................614 272-6951
Greg Clark, *Vice Pres*
Perumal Ganesh, *Applctn Conslt*
Ganesh Perumal, *Applctn Conslt*
John Gardner, *Telecom Exec*
Lisa Celona, *Sr Associate*
EMP: 191
SQ FT: 39,000
SALES: 193.7MM
SALES (corp-wide): 72.6K **Privately Held**
WEB: www.acilink.com
SIC: 6331 6351 Automobile insurance; property damage insurance; liability insurance
HQ: The Commerce Insurance Company
211 Main St
Webster MA 01570
508 943-9000

(G-6987)
AMERICAN ELECTRIC POWER CO INC
5900 Refugee Rd (43232-4727)
PHONE..................614 856-2750
Daniel Cox, *Principal*
Tim Galecki, *Manager*
Mike Flowers, *Supervisor*
EMP: 30
SALES (corp-wide): 15.4B **Publicly Held**
SIC: 1731 Electrical work
PA: American Electric Power Company, Inc.
1 Riverside Plz Fl 1 # 1
Columbus OH 43215
614 716-1000

(G-6988)
AMERICAN ELECTRIC POWER CO INC
Also Called: Columbus Southern Power Co
1759 W Mound St (43223-1813)
PHONE..................614 351-3715
Doug Ickes, *General Mgr*
Scott Krueger, *Area Spvr*
EMP: 75
SALES (corp-wide): 15.4B **Publicly Held**
SIC: 4911 Distribution, electric power
PA: American Electric Power Company, Inc.
1 Riverside Plz Fl 1 # 1
Columbus OH 43215
614 716-1000

(G-6989)
AMERICAN ELECTRIC POWER CO INC
Also Called: AEP Pro Serv Rso
1 Riverside Plz Ste 1600 (43215-2355)
PHONE..................614 716-1000
David Bnks, *President*
John Powers, *President*
Mark W Marano, *Senior VP*
John Harper, *Vice Pres*
Mark James, *Vice Pres*
EMP: 30
SALES (corp-wide): 15.4B **Publicly Held**
SIC: 1731 General electrical contractor
PA: American Electric Power Company, Inc.
1 Riverside Plz Fl 1 # 1
Columbus OH 43215
614 716-1000

Columbus - Franklin County (G-6990)

(G-6990)
AMERICAN ELECTRIC PWR SVC CORP (HQ)
Also Called: AEP
1 Riverside Plz Fl 1 (43215-2373)
P.O. Box 16631 (43216-6631)
PHONE....................614 716-1000
Fax: 614 223-1823
Nicholas K Akins, *Ch of Bd*
Terri Berliner, *President*
Johnathan Powers, *President*
Paul Johnson, *Managing Dir*
Darren Kelsey, *Business Mgr*
▲ **EMP:** 500 **EST:** 1937
SQ FT: 800,000
SALES: 1.3B
SALES (corp-wide): 15.4B **Publicly Held**
WEB: www.myenviroassistant.com
SIC: 4911 8711 8713 8721 Distribution, electric power; engineering services; surveying services; accounting services, except auditing; auditing services; billing & bookkeeping service
PA: American Electric Power Company, Inc.
1 Riverside Plz Fl 1 # 1
Columbus OH 43215
614 716-1000

(G-6991)
AMERICAN ELECTRIC PWR SVC CORP
Also Called: AEP Service
825 Tech Center Dr (43230-6653)
PHONE....................614 582-1742
Ben Mehraban, *Project Mgr*
Steve Boyd, *Engineer*
Matthew Gauss, *Engineer*
Dustin Reynolds, *Engineer*
Brian Schell, *Engineer*
EMP: 29
SALES (corp-wide): 15.4B **Publicly Held**
SIC: 4911 Electric services
HQ: American Electric Power Service Corporation
1 Riverside Plz Fl 1 # 1
Columbus OH 43215
614 716-1000

(G-6992)
AMERICAN FIDELITY ASSURANCE CO
90 Northwoods Blvd Ste B (43235-4719)
PHONE....................800 437-1011
James Gray, *President*
Marc Marion, *Vice Pres*
EMP: 1000 **Privately Held**
WEB: www.afadvantage.com
SIC: 6411 Insurance agents
HQ: American Fidelity Assurance Company
9000 Cameron Pkwy
Oklahoma City OK 73114
405 523-2000

(G-6993)
AMERICAN HEALTH NETWORK INC
2500 Corp Exchange Dr # 100 (43231-7601)
PHONE....................614 794-4500
Fax: 614 794-4976
Jeff R Fisher, *Office Mgr*
Meckler Gary, *Med Doctor*
Kim Rittenhouse, *Manager*
Judy Labanz, *Manager*
Leslie Bright, *Info Tech Mgr*
EMP: 27
SALES (corp-wide): 201.1B **Publicly Held**
SIC: 8011 Offices & clinics of medical doctors
HQ: American Health Network, Inc.
10689 N Pennsylvna St # 200
Indianapolis IN 46280

(G-6994)
AMERICAN HEART ASSOCIATION INC
5455 N High St (43214-1127)
P.O. Box 163549 (43216-3549)
PHONE....................614 848-6676
Fax: 614 848-4227
Charles Romane, *Branch Mgr*
Alieen Meyer, *Exec Dir*
Charles C Tweel, *Director*
Bryce Morrice, *Admin Sec*
EMP: 50
SALES (corp-wide): 780.2MM **Privately Held**
WEB: www.americanheart.org
SIC: 8621 Professional membership organizations
PA: American Heart Association, Inc.
7272 Greenville Ave
Dallas TX 75231
214 373-6300

(G-6995)
AMERICAN HLTH NETWRK OHIO LLC (HQ)
2500 Corporate Exchange D (43231-7601)
PHONE....................614 794-4500
Ben Park, *CEO*
EMP: 80
SALES (est): 229.2MM
SALES (corp-wide): 201.1B **Publicly Held**
SIC: 8011 Offices & clinics of medical doctors
PA: Unitedhealth Group Incorporated
9900 Bren Rd E Ste 300w
Minnetonka MN 55343
952 936-1300

(G-6996)
AMERICAN HOME HEALTH CARE INC
Also Called: American Medical Equipment
861 Taylor Rd Unit I (43230-6275)
PHONE....................614 237-1133
Fax: 614 237-1177
Brad Yakam, *President*
Tushar Shah, *Vice Pres*
Adil Navid, *CFO*
Stewart Brownstein, *Accounts Mgr*
EMP: 30
SQ FT: 6,500
SALES (est): 9.4MM **Privately Held**
WEB: www.ame-medical.com
SIC: 7352 5999 5047 Medical equipment rental; medical apparatus & supplies; hospital equipment & furniture

(G-6997)
AMERICAN INSTITUTE RESEARCH
41 S High St Ste 2425 (43215-6148)
PHONE....................614 221-8717
Terry Salinger, *Branch Mgr*
EMP: 329
SALES (corp-wide): 474MM **Privately Held**
SIC: 8733 Noncommercial social research organization
PA: American Institutes For Research In The Behavioral Sciences
1000 Thmas Jfferson St Nw
Washington DC 20007
202 403-5000

(G-6998)
AMERICAN INSTITUTE RESEARCH
820 Freeway Dr N (43229-5440)
PHONE....................614 310-8982
EMP: 329
SALES (corp-wide): 474MM **Privately Held**
SIC: 8733 Research institute
PA: American Institutes For Research In The Behavioral Sciences
1000 Thmas Jfferson St Nw
Washington DC 20007
202 403-5000

(G-6999)
AMERICAN KIDNEY STONE MGT LTD (PA)
Also Called: Aksm
100 W 3rd Ave Ste 350 (43201-7205)
PHONE....................800 637-5188
Fax: 614 447-9374
Henry Wise II, *Chairman*
Bruce Campbell, *Regional Mgr*
Mike Waldschmidt, *Regional Mgr*
Alan Buergenthal, *Vice Pres*
Theresa Perry, *Vice Pres*
EMP: 30
SQ FT: 11,000
SALES (est): 15.1MM **Privately Held**
WEB: www.aksm.com
SIC: 8093 Specialty outpatient clinics

(G-7000)
AMERICAN LINEHAUL CORPORATION
1860 Williams Rd (43207-5113)
PHONE....................614 409-8568
Scott Scheurell, *President*
EMP: 27
SALES (corp-wide): 27.2MM **Privately Held**
SIC: 4789 Cargo loading & unloading services
PA: American Linehaul Corporation
9 Mount Bethel Rd Ste 206
Warren NJ 07059
973 589-0101

(G-7001)
AMERICAN MECHANICAL GROUP INC
Also Called: Honeywell Authorized Dealer
5729 Westbourne Ave (43213-1449)
PHONE....................614 575-3720
Brian Yockey, *President*
Michelle Hope, *Manager*
Kyle Murray, *Technician*
EMP: 32
SALES (est): 5.4MM **Privately Held**
WEB: www.american-mech.com
SIC: 8741 Business management

(G-7002)
AMERICAN MUNICIPAL POWER INC
Also Called: AMP-Ohio
1111 Schrock Rd Ste 100 (43229-1155)
PHONE....................614 540-1111
Fax: 614 540-1113
Jon Bisher, *Ch of Bd*
Marc Gerken, *President*
Dan Moats, *General Mgr*
John Bentine, *Senior VP*
Bobby Little, *Senior VP*
◆ **EMP:** 229
SQ FT: 100,000
SALES: 1.1B **Privately Held**
WEB: www.amppartners.org
SIC: 4911 Generation, electric power

(G-7003)
AMERICAN PRECAST REFRACTORIES
2700 Scioto Pkwy (43221-4657)
PHONE....................614 876-8416
Fax: 614 876-3133
John Turner, *President*
Suzanne T Deffet, *Vice Pres*
EMP: 275
SALES (est): 13MM
SALES (corp-wide): 123.3MM **Privately Held**
WEB: www.amprecast.com
SIC: 1611 Concrete construction: roads, highways, sidewalks, etc.; surfacing & paving
PA: Allied Mineral Products, Inc.
2700 Scioto Pkwy
Columbus OH 43221
614 876-0244

(G-7004)
AMERICAN RED CROSS OF GRTR COL (PA)
995 E Broad St (43205-1339)
PHONE....................614 253-7981
Fax: 614 253-1544
Michael Carroll, *CEO*
Mark Whitman, *Sls & Mktg Exec*
Jocelyn Bolin, *Accounts Mgr*
Mary E Wissel, *Med Doctor*
William Taylor, *Manager*
EMP: 40
SQ FT: 80,000
SALES (est): 5.3MM **Privately Held**
WEB: www.redcrosscolumbus.org
SIC: 8399 Community action agency

(G-7005)
AMERICAN REPROGRAPHICS CO LLC
Also Called: ARC
1159 Dublin Rd (43215-1874)
PHONE....................614 224-5149
Dave Gilbert, *Vice Pres*
Gerald Schueller, *Branch Mgr*
Debbie Engle, *Manager*
Rick Neuenschwander, *Manager*
Jerry Schueller, *Manager*
EMP: 25
SALES (corp-wide): 394.5MM **Publicly Held**
WEB: www.e-arc.com
SIC: 7334 Blueprinting service
HQ: American Reprographics Company, L.L.C.
1981 N Broadway Ste 385
Walnut Creek CA 94596
925 949-5100

(G-7006)
AMERICAN RESIDENTIAL SVCS LLC
Also Called: Rescue Rooter of Columbus
3050 Switzer Ave (43219-2316)
PHONE....................888 762-7752
Fax: 614 476-3393
Jason Norris, *General Mgr*
Ralph Fumo, *Sales Executive*
David Marcum, *Manager*
EMP: 50
SQ FT: 18,000
SALES (corp-wide): 2.6B **Privately Held**
WEB: www.ars.com
SIC: 7699 Sewer cleaning & rodding
PA: American Residential Services Llc
965 Ridge Lake Blvd # 201
Memphis TN 38120
901 271-9700

(G-7007)
AMERICAN SIGNATURE INC (HQ)
Also Called: Value City
4300 E 5th Ave (43219-1816)
PHONE....................614 449-6107
Tod H Friedman, *President*
Justin Rieger, *General Mgr*
Elizabeth Spuck, *General Mgr*
Lorraine Henicheck, *Regional Mgr*
Bryan Beam, *Exec VP*
EMP: 150
SALES (est): 535.7MM
SALES (corp-wide): 2.7B **Privately Held**
WEB: www.ashome.com
SIC: 7389 Furniture finishing
PA: Schottenstein Stores Corporation
4300 E 5th Ave
Columbus OH 43219
614 221-9200

(G-7008)
AMERICAN SOCIETY FOR NONDSTCTV
1711 Arlingate Ln (43228-4116)
P.O. Box 28518 (43228-0518)
PHONE....................614 274-6003
Fax: 614 274-6899
Haley Cowans, *Editor*
Lisa Brasche, *Research*
Mary M Potter, *CFO*
Matt Monta, *Manager*
Craig Phillips, *CIO*
EMP: 47
SQ FT: 18,000
SALES: 8.6MM **Privately Held**
WEB: www.asnt.net
SIC: 8621 Medical field-related associations

(G-7009)
AMERICAN SVCS & PROTECTION LLC
2572 Oakstone Dr 8 (43231-7614)
PHONE....................614 884-0177
Aaron Harper, *President*
Lovell Harper, *Vice Pres*
Philana Harper, *Finance*
Shawn Harper,
EMP: 80
SALES (est): 898.1K **Privately Held**
SIC: 7382 7381 Security systems services; guard services

GEOGRAPHIC SECTION
Columbus - Franklin County (G-7034)

(G-7010)
AMERICAS DREAM HOMES LLC
1336 E Main St Ste G (43205-2081)
PHONE.................................614 252-7834
Almondia White,
EMP: 32
SQ FT: 1,400
SALES (est): 142.7K Privately Held
SIC: 8059 Home for the mentally retarded, exc. skilled or intermediate

(G-7011)
AMERICAS FLOOR SOURCE LLC (PA)
3442 Millennium Ct (43219-5551)
PHONE.................................614 808-3915
Fax: 614 237-3405
Ron Rieger, Regional Mgr
Gina Hoffer, Exec VP
Dick Fadley, Vice Pres
Brandy Goldberg, Vice Pres
Cary Jerris, Vice Pres
▲ EMP: 58
SQ FT: 50,000
SALES: 65MM Privately Held
WEB: www.americasfloorsource.com
SIC: 5713 5023 Carpets; floor coverings

(G-7012)
AMERISOURCE HEALTH SVCS LLC
Also Called: American Health Packaging
2550 John Glenn Ave Ste A (43217-1188)
PHONE.................................614 492-8177
Fax: 614 492-1903
Rick Knight, President
Jeff Spencer, Vice Pres
John Swartz, Vice Pres
John Jasinski, Opers Mgr
Lewis Huber, Materials Mgr
▲ EMP: 89
SQ FT: 153,000
SALES (est): 22.5MM
SALES (corp-wide): 153.1B Publicly Held
WEB: www.healthpack.com
SIC: 2064 4783 Cough drops, except pharmaceutical preparations; packing goods for shipping
HQ: Amerisourcebergen Drug Corporation
  1300 Morris Dr Ste 100
  Chesterbrook PA 19087
  610 727-7000

(G-7013)
AMERISOURCEBERGEN CORPORATION
1200 E 5th Ave (43219-2410)
P.O. Box 870, Worthington (43085-0870)
PHONE.................................610 727-7000
Fax: 614 253-0181
Roger Cox, Division Mgr
Jon Briney, Vice Pres
Dennis Hone, Vice Pres
Gary Van Dyke, Sales Mgr
Elaine Yokosuk, Cust Mgr
EMP: 200
SALES (corp-wide): 153.1B Publicly Held
WEB: www.amerisourcebergen.net
SIC: 5122 Pharmaceuticals
PA: Amerisourcebergen Corporation
  1300 Morris Dr Ste 100
  Chesterbrook PA 19087
  610 727-7000

(G-7014)
AMETHYST INC
455 E Mound St (43215-5595)
PHONE.................................614 242-1284
Fax: 614 242-1285
Lois Hochstetler, Exec Dir
EMP: 55
SALES: 4.1MM Privately Held
WEB: www.amethyst-inc.org
SIC: 8322 8093 Alcoholism counseling, nontreatment; drug clinic, outpatient

(G-7015)
AMF BOWLING CENTERS INC
4825 Sawmill Rd (43235-7266)
PHONE.................................614 889-0880
Fax: 614 889-1226
Melvin Harrington, Manager
EMP: 50
SALES (corp-wide): 81.2MM Privately Held
WEB: www.kidsports.org
SIC: 7933 Ten pin center
HQ: Amf Bowling Centers, Inc.
  7313 Bell Creek Rd
  Mechanicsville VA 23111

(G-7016)
AMUSEMENTS OF AMERICA INC
717 E 17th Ave (43211-2494)
PHONE.................................614 297-8863
Karen Salas, Branch Mgr
EMP: 130
SALES (corp-wide): 7MM Privately Held
SIC: 7999 Carnival operation
PA: Amusements Of America Inc
  24 Federal Rd
  Monroe Township NJ 08831
  305 258-2020

(G-7017)
ANDERSON ALUMINUM CORPORATION
Also Called: Anderson Properties
2816 Morse Rd (43231-6034)
PHONE.................................614 476-4877
Helena Anderson, President
Bradley Anderson, Vice Pres
Nestor Perez, Project Mgr
Mike Daniel, Opers Mgr
George Deniro, Opers Mgr
EMP: 70 EST: 1980
SQ FT: 70,000
SALES (est): 17.8MM Privately Held
SIC: 1793 Glass & glazing work

(G-7018)
ANDERSON GLASS CO INC
2816 Morse Rd (43231-6094)
PHONE.................................614 476-4877
Fax: 614 471-4330
Bradley Anderson, President
Helena Anderson, Vice Pres
George Deniro, Opers Staff
Judy Mullen, Office Mgr
EMP: 30 EST: 1949
SQ FT: 32,000
SALES: 4MM Privately Held
WEB: www.andersonglassco.com
SIC: 5039 3231 3229 Exterior flat glass: plate or window; interior flat glass: plate or window; products of purchased glass; pressed & blown glass

(G-7019)
ANESTHESIOLOGY CONSULTANT INC
111 S Grant Ave (43215-4701)
PHONE.................................614 566-9983
Michael Romanelli Do, President
Joyce Brown, Office Mgr
Vernon Barney, Med Doctor
Shalini Reddy, Med Doctor
Sabmit K Barua, Anesthesiology
EMP: 30
SALES (est): 5MM Privately Held
SIC: 8011 Anesthesiologist

(G-7020)
ANGELOS CAULKING & SEALANTS CO
727 N James Rd (43219-1839)
PHONE.................................614 236-1350
Fax: 614 236-5001
Angelo Gesouras, President
Sandra Gesouras, Vice Pres
EMP: 26
SQ FT: 2,400
SALES (est): 2.1MM Privately Held
SIC: 1799 Caulking (construction)

(G-7021)
ANIMAL CARE UNLIMITED INC
2665 Billingsley Rd (43235-1904)
PHONE.................................614 766-2317
Fax: 614 766-4508
Donald Burton Dvm, President
EMP: 29
SALES (est): 2MM Privately Held
WEB: www.animalcareunlimited.com
SIC: 0742 0752 Veterinarian, animal specialties; animal hospital services, pets & other animal specialties; boarding services, kennels

(G-7022)
ANSPACH MEEKS ELLENBERGER LLP
175 S 3rd St Ste 285 (43215-5188)
PHONE.................................614 745-8350
Bob Anspach, Branch Mgr
EMP: 28
SALES (corp-wide): 10.1MM Privately Held
SIC: 8111 General practice attorney, lawyer
PA: Anspach Meeks Ellenberger Llp
  300 Madison Ave Ste 1600
  Toledo OH 43604
  419 447-6181

(G-7023)
AON CONSULTING INC
445 Hutchinson Ave # 900 (43235-8619)
PHONE.................................614 436-8100
C Bertram, Senior VP
Jasen Dashner, Consultant
Gary Hutchison, Info Tech Mgr
EMP: 27
SQ FT: 1,500
SALES (corp-wide): 11.6B Privately Held
WEB: www.radford.com
SIC: 6411 Insurance brokers
HQ: Aon Consulting, Inc.
  200 E Randolph St Ll3
  Chicago IL 60601
  312 381-1000

(G-7024)
AON CONSULTING INC
355 E Campus View Blvd (43235-5616)
PHONE.................................614 847-4670
EMP: 61
SALES (corp-wide): 11.6B Privately Held
SIC: 6411 Insurance brokers
HQ: Aon Consulting, Inc.
  200 E Randolph St Ll3
  Chicago IL 60601
  312 381-1000

(G-7025)
AP23 SPORTS COMPLEX LLC
775 Georgesville Rd (43228-2826)
PHONE.................................614 452-0760
Derrick Pryor,
EMP: 27
SQ FT: 204,000
SALES (est): 260.8K Privately Held
SIC: 7941 Sports clubs, managers & promoters

(G-7026)
APCO ALUMINUM AWNING CO
815 Michigan Ave (43215-1161)
PHONE.................................614 334-2726
Mark Mason, Owner
EMP: 38
SALES: 9MM Privately Held
SIC: 1799 Awning installation

(G-7027)
APCO INDUSTRIES INC
Also Called: Apco Window & Door Company
777 Michigan Ave (43215-1177)
PHONE.................................614 224-2345
Fax: 614 224-8165
Bill Clarken Jr, President
William M Clarkin, President
Warren C Gifford, President
Mark M Mason, President
Joe Lieonart, Vice Pres
EMP: 100 EST: 1902
SQ FT: 52,000
SALES (est): 21.3MM Privately Held
WEB: www.apco.com
SIC: 1761 5033 5039 5031 Gutter & downspout contractor; siding contractor; siding, except wood; eaves troughing, parts & supplies; doors; general remodeling, single-family houses; home centers

(G-7028)
APELLES LLC
3700 Corp Dr 2f Ste 240 (43231)
PHONE.................................614 899-7322
Michael Fitzmartin,
EMP: 30
SALES (est): 4.4MM Privately Held
WEB: www.apelles.com
SIC: 7322 Collection agency, except real estate

(G-7029)
APPALACHIAN POWER COMPANY (HQ)
Also Called: AEP
1 Riverside Plz (43215-2355)
PHONE.................................614 716-1000
Nicholas K Akins, Ch of Bd
Mark Dempsey, Vice Pres
Jeffery Lafleur, Vice Pres
Armando A Pe, Vice Pres
Barbara Radous, Vice Pres
▲ EMP: 170 EST: 1926
SALES: 2.9B
SALES (corp-wide): 15.4B Publicly Held
SIC: 4911 Electric services; distribution, electric power; generation, electric power; transmission, electric power
PA: American Electric Power Company, Inc.
  1 Riverside Plz Fl 1 # 1
  Columbus OH 43215
  614 716-1000

(G-7030)
APRIA HEALTHCARE LLC
4060 Business Park Dr A (43204-5047)
PHONE.................................614 351-5920
Fax: 614 351-5942
Christopher Bell, Branch Mgr
Patricia Mahon, Manager
EMP: 36 Privately Held
WEB: www.apria.com
SIC: 7352 Medical equipment rental
HQ: Apria Healthcare Llc
  26220 Enterprise Ct
  Lake Forest CA 92630
  949 616-2606

(G-7031)
AQUARIUS MARINE LLC
250 N Hartford Ave (43222-1100)
Po Box 1267
PHONE.................................614 875-8200
Steve McKinley, Facilities Mgr
Michael Coccia, Treasurer
Colin A McBride,
EMP: 25
SALES (est): 3MM Privately Held
SIC: 1629 Marine construction

(G-7032)
ARAMARK UNF & CAREER AP LLC
1900 Progress Ave (43207-1727)
PHONE.................................614 445-8341
Fax: 614 445-7366
Brad Gillespie, General Mgr
Ben Hartfile, Plant Engr
Bert Murray, Project Engr
Joe Carrothers, Manager
EMP: 250 Publicly Held
WEB: www.aramark-uniform.com
SIC: 7218 7213 Industrial launderers; uniform supply
HQ: Aramark Uniform & Career Apparel, Llc
  115 N First St Ste 203
  Burbank CA 91502
  818 973-3700

(G-7033)
ARBORS EAST LLC
5500 E Broad St (43213-1497)
PHONE.................................614 575-9003
Fax: 614 575-9101
John Dipietra, Director
Tina Keller, Director
Cindy Jeffers, Officer
Stacy Duncan, Administration
Lisa Chalk, Administration
EMP: 100
SALES (est): 5.2MM Privately Held
WEB: www.extendicarehealth.com
SIC: 8052 8051 Intermediate care facilities; skilled nursing care facilities

(G-7034)
ARC INDUSTRIES INCORPORATED O (PA)
2780 Airport Dr (43219-2289)
PHONE.................................614 479-2500
Geraldine C Nasse, Principal
EMP: 143
SQ FT: 8,976
SALES (est): 11.7MM Privately Held
WEB: www.arcind.com
SIC: 8331 Sheltered workshop

Columbus - Franklin County (G-7035)

(G-7035)
ARC INDUSTRIES INCORPORATED O
Also Called: ARC Industries North
6633 Doubletree Ave (43229-1156)
PHONE................................614 436-4800
Fax: 614 342-5350
Nan Burns, *Director*
EMP: 300
SALES (corp-wide): 11.7MM Privately Held
WEB: www.arcind.com
SIC: 8331 Sheltered workshop
PA: Arc Industries, Incorporated, Of Franklin County, Ohio
2780 Airport Dr
Columbus OH 43219
614 479-2500

(G-7036)
ARC INDUSTRIES INCORPORATED O
Also Called: ARC Industreis East
909 Taylor Station Rd (43230-6655)
PHONE................................614 864-2406
Fax: 614 342-5315
John Dixon, *Opers Staff*
Clarice Pavlick, *Manager*
EMP: 300
SALES (corp-wide): 11.7MM Privately Held
WEB: www.arcind.com
SIC: 8331 Sheltered workshop
PA: Arc Industries, Incorporated, Of Franklin County, Ohio
2780 Airport Dr
Columbus OH 43219
614 479-2500

(G-7037)
ARC INDUSTRIES INCORPORATED O
Also Called: ARC Industries West
250 W Dodridge St (43202-1599)
PHONE................................614 267-1207
Fax: 614 267-3762
Janet Montgomery, *Director*
EMP: 65
SALES (corp-wide): 11.7MM Privately Held
WEB: www.arcind.com
SIC: 8331 Sheltered workshop
PA: Arc Industries, Incorporated, Of Franklin County, Ohio
2780 Airport Dr
Columbus OH 43219
614 479-2500

(G-7038)
ARCHITCTURAL CON SOLUTIONS INC
1997 Harmon Ave (43223-3828)
P.O. Box 1056, Grove City (43123-6056)
PHONE................................614 940-5399
Brian Snyder, *President*
Andre Bondurant, *Principal*
Patrick Donahue, *Vice Pres*
EMP: 25
SALES (est): 1.9MM Privately Held
SIC: 1771 Patio construction, concrete

(G-7039)
ARDENT MILLS LLC
4200 Sullivant Ave (43228-4325)
PHONE................................614 274-2545
Fax: 614 274-0068
Richard Hooper, *Plant Mgr*
Richard Baillie, *Branch Mgr*
Dan Srouse, *Manager*
EMP: 32
SALES (corp-wide): 631.7MM Privately Held
WEB: www.conagra.com
SIC: 2041 5153 Flour; grain elevators
PA: Ardent Mills, Llc
1875 Lawrence St Ste 1400
Denver CO 80202
800 851-9618

(G-7040)
AREA WIDE PROTECTIVE INC
2439 Scioto Harper Dr (43204-3420)
PHONE................................614 272-7840
Del Sexton, *Principal*
EMP: 37 EST: 2013
SALES (est): 1.3MM Privately Held
SIC: 5999 5084 Safety supplies & equipment; safety equipment

(G-7041)
ARLEDGE CONSTRUCTION INC (PA)
2460 Performance Way (43207-2857)
PHONE................................614 732-4258
Fax: 614 875-9191
Craig Arledge, *President*
Craig Stover, *Manager*
EMP: 41
SALES: 5MM Privately Held
SIC: 1771 Foundation & footing contractor

(G-7042)
ARLINGTON CONTACT LENS SVC INC
Also Called: Discountcontactlenses.com
4265 Diplomacy Dr (43228-3834)
PHONE................................614 921-9894
Peter Clarkson, *President*
Phillip Dietrich, *Vice Pres*
Christine Vakaleris, *Vice Pres*
Melissa Smith, *Manager*
▲ EMP: 47
SQ FT: 21,000
SALES (est): 4.7MM
SALES (corp-wide): 1.2B Publicly Held
WEB: www.aclens.com
SIC: 5995 8011 Contact lenses, prescription; offices & clinics of medical doctors
HQ: National Vision, Inc.
2435 Commerce Ave # 2200
Duluth GA 30096
770 822-3600

(G-7043)
ARLINGTON TOWING INC
Also Called: Camcar Towing
2354 Wood Ave (43221-3520)
PHONE................................614 488-2006
Fax: 614 486-4113
Mike Davis, *President*
Rob Morris, *Manager*
EMP: 30
SALES (est): 1.3MM Privately Held
SIC: 7549 Towing service, automotive

(G-7044)
ARTHUR G JAMES CANCER
300 W 10th Ave Ste 519 (43210-1280)
PHONE................................614 293-4878
David E Schuller, *Director*
EMP: 700
SALES: 2.2MM Privately Held
WEB: www.jamesline.com
SIC: 8733 8731 8069 Medical research; commercial physical research; specialty hospitals, except psychiatric

(G-7045)
ARTHUR G JAMES CANCER HOSPITAL
300 W 10th Ave (43210-1280)
PHONE................................614 293-3300
Fax: 614 293-3080
Jan A Rupert, *Principal*
Keith Keplinger, *Ch Radiology*
Jill Hannah, *Human Res Dir*
Belinda R Avalos, *Manager*
Paul Monk, *Manager*
EMP: 25
SALES (est): 1.8MM Privately Held
SIC: 8069 Cancer hospital

(G-7046)
ARTISTIC DANCE ENTERPRISES
Also Called: Dublin Dance Center
2665 Farmers Dr (43235-2767)
PHONE................................614 761-2882
Fax: 614 761-7583
Teresa Crye, *President*
EMP: 25
SQ FT: 7,000
SALES (est): 984.5K Privately Held
WEB: www.dublindance.com
SIC: 7911 5621 5632 Children's dancing school; boutiques; dancewear

(G-7047)
ARVIND SAGAR INC
Also Called: Homewood Suites
2880 Airport Dr (43219-2240)
PHONE................................614 428-8800
Fax: 614 428-1044
Arvind Sagar, *Owner*
EMP: 25
SALES (est): 1.6MM Privately Held
WEB: www.arvindsagar.com
SIC: 7011 Hotels & motels

(G-7048)
ASC GROUP INC (PA)
800 Freeway Dr N Ste 101 (43229-5447)
PHONE................................614 268-2514
Shaune M Skinner, *President*
Debbie King, *Business Mgr*
Elsie Immel Blei, *Vice Pres*
Elsie Immel-Blei, *Vice Pres*
Annette Ericksen, *Manager*
EMP: 32
SQ FT: 10,000
SALES: 4MM Privately Held
WEB: www.ascgroup.net
SIC: 8713 8712 8731 8733 Surveying services; architectural services; environmental research; archeological expeditions; earth science services

(G-7049)
ASHLAND LLC
Also Called: Ashland Performance Materials
802 Harmon Ave (43223-2410)
PHONE................................614 232-8510
Fax: 614 232-8520
Paul W Chellgren, *Ch of Bd*
Harold Jenkins, *Controller*
Suzette Work, *Programmer Anys*
Sandra Derthick, *Relations*
EMP: 75
SQ FT: 19,378
SALES (corp-wide): 3.2B Publicly Held
WEB: www.ashland.com
SIC: 5169 Alkalines & chlorine
HQ: Ashland Llc
50 E Rivercenter Blvd # 1600
Covington KY 41011
859 815-3333

(G-7050)
ASHLAND LLC
Ashland Distribution
3849 Fisher Rd (43228-1015)
PHONE................................614 276-6144
Fax: 614 276-0884
Larry B Clark, *Branch Mgr*
EMP: 30
SQ FT: 4,656
SALES (corp-wide): 3.2B Publicly Held
WEB: www.ashland.com
SIC: 5169 Alkalines & chlorine
HQ: Ashland Llc
50 E Rivercenter Blvd # 1600
Covington KY 41011
859 815-3333

(G-7051)
ASPEN COMMUNITY LIVING
2021 E Dublin Granville R (43229-3552)
PHONE................................614 880-6000
Martha Clifford, *Manager*
EMP: 104
SALES (corp-wide): 137.4MM Privately Held
SIC: 7363 7361 Help supply services; employment agencies
HQ: Aspen Nursing Services, Inc.
2360 Edgerton St
Little Canada MN 55117
651 415-1444

(G-7052)
ASPLUNDH CONSTRUCTION CORP
481 Schrock Rd (43229-1027)
PHONE................................614 532-5224
Jarrod Wachter, *Branch Mgr*
EMP: 180
SALES (corp-wide): 4.3B Privately Held
SIC: 1521 Single-family housing construction
HQ: Asplundh Construction, Corp.
93 Sills Rd
Yaphank NY 11980
631 205-9340

(G-7053)
ASSISTNCE IN MKTG COLUMBUS INC
1 Easton Oval Ste 100 (43219-6062)
PHONE................................614 583-2100
Carl Iseman, *President*
EMP: 28
SALES: 1.2MM Privately Held
SIC: 8732 Market analysis or research

(G-7054)
ASSOC DVLPMTLY DISABLED
Also Called: Dahlberg Learning Center
1915 E Cooke Rd (43224-2266)
PHONE................................614 447-0606
Fax: 614 447-0609
Bernice Hagler-Cody, *Director*
EMP: 30
SQ FT: 22,213
SALES (corp-wide): 18.7MM Privately Held
WEB: www.add1.com
SIC: 8361 8351 Home for the mentally handicapped; preschool center
PA: Association For The Developmentally Disabled
769 Brooksedge Blvd
Westerville OH 43081
614 486-4361

(G-7055)
ASSOCIATED MATERIALS LLC
Also Called: Alside Supply Center
640 Dearborn Park Ln (43085-5701)
PHONE................................614 985-4611
Dan Dreyman, *Branch Mgr*
Michael Gerken, *Manager*
EMP: 25 Privately Held
WEB: www.associatedmaterials.com
SIC: 5033 Roofing & siding materials
HQ: Associated Materials, Llc
3773 State Rd
Cuyahoga Falls OH 44223
330 929-1811

(G-7056)
ASSOCIATED PRESS
1103 Schrock Rd Ste 300 (43229-1179)
PHONE................................614 885-3444
Fax: 614 885-3248
Eva Parziale, *Manager*
EMP: 25
SALES (corp-wide): 556.2MM Privately Held
WEB: www.apme.com
SIC: 7383 News reporting services for newspapers & periodicals
PA: The Associated Press
1 World Financial Ctr # 19
New York NY 10281
212 621-1500

(G-7057)
ASTORIA PLACE COLUMBUS LLC
Also Called: Columbus Rhbilitation Subacute
44 S Souder Ave (43222-1539)
PHONE................................614 228-5900
Matthew Macklin, *Mng Member*
Joseph Brandman, *Manager*
Yehudit Goldberg, *Manager*
Michael Nudell, *Manager*
Brittaney Crock, *Administration*
EMP: 99 EST: 2014
SQ FT: 52,000
SALES: 8.6MM Privately Held
SIC: 8051 Mental retardation hospital

(G-7058)
ASTUTE INC (PA)
Also Called: Astute Solutions
2400 Corp Exchange Dr # 150 (43231-7606)
PHONE................................614 508-6100
Fax: 614 508-6100
Joseph Sanda, *CEO*
Gregory Miller, *COO*
Liz Bailey, *Vice Pres*
Rob Barnhart, *Vice Pres*
Kathi Gabet, *Vice Pres*
EMP: 49
SQ FT: 12,230

GEOGRAPHIC SECTION

Columbus - Franklin County (G-7082)

SALES (est): 18.1MM **Privately Held**
WEB: www.astutesolutions.com
SIC: 7371 Computer software development

(G-7059)
ASYMMETRIC TECHNOLOGIES LLC
1395 Grandview Ave Ste 3 (43212-2859)
PHONE...................614 725-5310
Brian J Borkowski, *Managing Dir*
Cress Clanton, *Director*
EMP: 35
SQ FT: 2,000
SALES: 3.9MM **Privately Held**
SIC: 8731 Biological research

(G-7060)
AT T BROADBAND & INTERN
P.O. Box 182552 (43218-2552)
PHONE...................614 839-4271
EMP: 25
SALES (est): 2.4MM **Privately Held**
SIC: 4813

(G-7061)
AT&T CORP
3419 Indianola Ave (43214-4129)
PHONE...................614 223-6513
Ed Humeidan, *Branch Mgr*
EMP: 69
SALES (corp-wide): 160.5B **Publicly Held**
SIC: 4813 Telephone communication, except radio
HQ: At&T Corp.
1 At&T Way
Bedminster NJ 07921
800 403-3302

(G-7062)
AT&T CORP
150 E Gay St Ste 4a (43215-3130)
PHONE...................614 223-8236
Connie Browning, *President*
Cari Walters, *Assistant VP*
Michael Kehoe, *Vice Pres*
James Duncan, *Engineer*
Steven Kleinknecht, *Sls & Mktg Exec*
EMP: 1000
SALES (corp-wide): 160.5B **Publicly Held**
WEB: www.att.com
SIC: 7629 4813 2741 Telecommunication equipment repair (except telephones); telephone communication, except radio; miscellaneous publishing
HQ: At&T Corp.
1 At&T Way
Bedminster NJ 07921
800 403-3302

(G-7063)
AT&T CORP
2583 S Hamilton Rd (43232-4964)
PHONE...................614 575-3044
Dorothy Tanner, *Branch Mgr*
EMP: 97
SALES (corp-wide): 160.5B **Publicly Held**
SIC: 4812 Cellular telephone services
HQ: At&T Corp.
1 At&T Way
Bedminster NJ 07921
800 403-3302

(G-7064)
AT&T CORP
1649 Georgesville Sq Dr (43228-3689)
PHONE...................614 851-2400
Demond Chambliss, *Branch Mgr*
EMP: 97
SALES (corp-wide): 160.5B **Publicly Held**
SIC: 4812 Cellular telephone services
HQ: At&T Corp.
1 At&T Way
Bedminster NJ 07921
800 403-3302

(G-7065)
AT&T CORP
4300 Appian Way (43230-1446)
PHONE...................614 337-3902
John Jude, *Area Mgr*
EMP: 69

SALES (corp-wide): 160.5B **Publicly Held**
WEB: www.att.com
SIC: 4813 Telephone communication, except radio
HQ: At&T Corp.
1 At&T Way
Bedminster NJ 07921
800 403-3302

(G-7066)
AT&T MOBILITY LLC
1555 Olentangy River Rd (43212-1495)
PHONE...................614 291-2500
Mark Fragale, *Sales Mgr*
Ben Patrick, *Accounts Exec*
Ralkina Samuels, *Sales Staff*
EMP: 26
SALES (corp-wide): 160.5B **Publicly Held**
WEB: www.cingular.com
SIC: 4812 4813 Cellular telephone services; telephone communication, except radio
HQ: At&T Mobility Llc
1025 Lenox Park Blvd Ne
Brookhaven GA 30319
800 331-0500

(G-7067)
ATLAPAC CORP
2901 E 4th Ave Ste 5 (43219-2896)
PHONE...................614 252-2121
Fax: 614 252-7289
James R Staeck, *President*
Mike Mc Coy, *CFO*
Mike McCoy, *CFO*
▲ EMP: 70 **EST:** 1964
SQ FT: 50,000
SALES (est): 12.1MM **Privately Held**
WEB: www.atlapaccorp.com
SIC: 2673 5113 Plastic bags: made from purchased materials; cellophane bags, unprinted: made from purchased materials; bags, paper & disposable plastic

(G-7068)
ATLAS ADVISORS LLC
1795 S High St (43207-1865)
PHONE...................888 282-0873
Rick Abner, *COO*
Ken Szymborski, *CFO*
Anthony Abner, *Mng Member*
EMP: 35
SALES (est): 3.3MM **Privately Held**
SIC: 8742 Management consulting services

(G-7069)
ATLAS CAPITAL SERVICES INC (PA)
Also Called: Atlas Butler Heating & Cooling
4849 Evanswood Dr (43229-6206)
PHONE...................614 294-7373
Fax: 614 298-6977
Mark Swepston, *President*
George Hoskins, *Vice Pres*
James Smith, *Project Mgr*
Larry J Winner, *CFO*
Michael Bogartis, *Manager*
EMP: 80
SQ FT: 16,000
SALES (est): 22.2MM **Privately Held**
WEB: www.atlasbutler.com
SIC: 1711 Warm air heating & air conditioning contractor

(G-7070)
ATLAS CONSTRUCTION COMPANY
4672 Friendship Dr (43230-4302)
PHONE...................614 475-4705
Fax: 614 475-0570
Steven Testa, *President*
Richard Testa, *Vice Pres*
EMP: 60
SQ FT: 4,000
SALES (est): 7.6MM **Privately Held**
SIC: 1771 Concrete work

(G-7071)
ATLAS HOME MOVING & STORAGE
1570 Integrity Dr E (43209-2704)
PHONE...................614 445-8831

Jack Herring, *Owner*
Dave Woodhouse, *General Mgr*
EMP: 50
SALES (est): 2MM **Privately Held**
SIC: 4214 Local trucking with storage

(G-7072)
ATLAS INDUSTRIAL CONTRS LLC (HQ)
5275 Sinclair Rd (43229-5042)
PHONE...................614 841-4500
Fax: 614 841-4510
George Ghanem, *President*
Jeff Forgey, *Division Mgr*
Rich Wine, *Division Mgr*
Mike Gaydos, *Superintendent*
Rod Walton, *Superintendent*
EMP: 450
SQ FT: 20,000
SALES: 140.1MM **Privately Held**
WEB: www.atlascos.com
SIC: 1731 3498 1796 Electrical work; fabricated pipe & fittings; machine moving & rigging

(G-7073)
AUBURN DAIRY PRODUCTS INC
2200 Cardigan Ave (43215-1092)
PHONE...................614 488-2536
Douglas A Smith, *President*
Martin Lavine, *Vice Pres*
Thomas G Michaelides, *Treasurer*
G Frederick Smith, *Admin Sec*
EMP: 31
SQ FT: 10,300
SALES (est): 4.2MM
SALES (corp-wide): 44.3MM **Privately Held**
SIC: 2026 5143 Whipped topping, except frozen or dry mix; dairy products, except dried or canned
PA: Instantwhip Foods, Inc.
2200 Cardigan Ave
Columbus OH 43215
614 488-2536

(G-7074)
AUSSIEFIT I LLC
5929 E Main St (43213-3353)
PHONE...................614 755-4400
Geoff Dyer, *CEO*
Warren Montanyc, *Accountant*
EMP: 30
SQ FT: 28,700
SALES (est): 839.2K
SALES (corp-wide): 1MM **Privately Held**
SIC: 7991 Physical fitness clubs with training equipment
PA: I Aussiefit
497 1st St W
Saint Petersburg FL 33715
727 393-9484

(G-7075)
AUSTIN FOAM PLASTICS INC
Also Called: A F P Ohio
2200 International St (43228-4630)
PHONE...................614 921-0824
Fax: 614 527-7881
Dan Berona, *Manager*
EMP: 25
SALES (corp-wide): 51.6MM **Privately Held**
WEB: www.austinfoam.com
SIC: 3086 7336 Insulation or cushioning material, foamed plastic; package design
PA: Austin Foam Plastics, Inc.
2933 A W Grimes Blvd
Pflugerville TX 78660
512 251-6300

(G-7076)
AUTO BODY NORTH INC (PA)
Also Called: Auto Body Mill Run
8675 N High St (43235-1003)
P.O. Box 720, Worthington (43085-0720)
PHONE...................614 436-3700
Fax: 614 888-4622
Thomas Carpenter, *President*
Darryl Patterson, *President*
William L Denney, *Exec VP*
Robert Vance, *Vice Pres*
Ron Betz, *Manager*
EMP: 30
SQ FT: 1,800

SALES (est): 4.7MM **Privately Held**
WEB: www.autobodyofcolumbus.com
SIC: 7532 Collision shops, automotive

(G-7077)
AUTOMOTIVE DISTRIBUTORS CO INC (PA)
Also Called: Automotive Distributors Whse
2981 Morse Rd (43231-6098)
PHONE...................614 476-1315
Fax: 614 476-9469
Robert I Yeoman, *President*
Frank Schmidt, *Vice Pres*
Jim Ballweg, *Opers Mgr*
Joseph Clay, *Treasurer*
Paul Negulescu, *Regl Sales Mgr*
EMP: 65
SQ FT: 70,000
SALES: 132.8MM **Privately Held**
WEB: www.adw1.com
SIC: 5013 Automotive supplies & parts

(G-7078)
AVNET INC
Also Called: Avnet Computers
2800 Corp Exchange Dr # 160 (43231-7661)
PHONE...................614 865-1400
Gary Brady, *Branch Mgr*
Dan Maston, *Manager*
EMP: 26
SALES (corp-wide): 17.4B **Publicly Held**
WEB: www.avnet.com
SIC: 5065 Semiconductor devices
PA: Avnet, Inc.
2211 S 47th St
Phoenix AZ 85034
480 643-2000

(G-7079)
AXA ADVISORS LLC
7965 N High St Ste 140 (43235-8404)
PHONE...................614 985-3015
Fax: 614 985-3040
Christopher Polle, *Principal*
Joseph Messinger, *Vice Pres*
Katherine Fyffe, *Finance Mgr*
Michael Scherer, *Finance Mgr*
Tracy Drew, *Advisor*
EMP: 120
SALES (corp-wide): 3.8B **Publicly Held**
WEB: www.axacs.com
SIC: 6211 Mutual funds, selling by independent salesperson
HQ: Axa Advisors, Llc
1290 Ave Of Amrcs Fl Cnc1
New York NY 10104
212 554-1234

(G-7080)
AXIA CONSULTING INC
1391 W 5th Ave Ste 320 (43212-2902)
PHONE...................614 675-4050
Brian Pellot, *Human Resources*
Teresa Conroy-Roth, *Sales Dir*
Paul Grove, *Mng Member*
Paul D Grove, *Manager*
Kurt Domini, *Consultant*
EMP: 65
SALES: 24.9MM **Privately Held**
WEB: www.axiaconsulting.net
SIC: 7373 Systems integration services

(G-7081)
B & B PLASTICS RECYCLERS INC
3300 Lockbourne Rd (43207-3917)
PHONE...................614 409-2880
Maria Carreon, *Branch Mgr*
EMP: 110
SALES (corp-wide): 117.2MM **Privately Held**
SIC: 4953 Recycling, waste materials
PA: B & B Plastics Recyclers, Inc.
3040 N Locust Ave
Rialto CA 92377
909 829-3606

(G-7082)
BABBAGE-SIMMEL & ASSOC INC
Also Called: Babbage Simmel
2780 Airport Dr Ste 160 (43219-2291)
PHONE...................614 481-6555
Houshang Maani, *Ch of Bd*

Columbus - Franklin County (G-7083)

Louis Maani, *President*
Mal Owen, *Product Mgr*
EMP: 39
SALES (est): 3.3MM **Privately Held**
WEB: www.babsim.com
SIC: 8243 8743 Operator training, computer; public relations services

(G-7083)
BAILEY & LONG INC
Also Called: Goddard School
101 E Town St Ste 115 (43215-5247)
PHONE..............................614 937-9435
Malvin Long, *President*
Meredith C Bailey, *CFO*
EMP: 25 EST: 2010
SALES (est): 549.6K **Privately Held**
SIC: 8351 Preschool center

(G-7084)
BAILEY ASSOCIATES
6836 Caine Rd (43235-4290)
PHONE..............................614 760-7752
Rudy Bailey, *Owner*
EMP: 110
SALES: 3.2MM **Privately Held**
SIC: 8741 Financial management for business

(G-7085)
BAILEY CAVALIERI LLC (PA)
10 W Broad St Ste 2100 (43215-3455)
PHONE..............................614 221-3258
Michael Mahoney, *Managing Dir*
Joan Parrish, *Manager*
Brenda Barnett, *Office Admin*
Mike Toth, *Info Tech Mgr*
Michael P Mahoney, *Director*
EMP: 86
SQ FT: 45,000
SALES (est): 13.1MM **Privately Held**
SIC: 8111 General practice attorney, lawyer

(G-7086)
BAKER & HOSTETLER LLP
65 E State St Ste 2100 (43215-4213)
PHONE..............................614 228-1541
Fax: 614 462-2616
EMP: 123
SALES (corp-wide): 316.3MM **Privately Held**
SIC: 8111 Legal Services Office
PA: Baker & Hostetler Llp
     127 Public Sq Ste 2000
     Cleveland OH 44114
     216 621-0200

(G-7087)
BALL BOUNCE AND SPORT INC
3275 Alum Creek Dr (43207-3460)
PHONE..............................614 662-5381
Shaun Davis, *Branch Mgr*
EMP: 30
SALES (est): 1.4MM
SALES (corp-wide): 158.8MM **Privately Held**
SIC: 5092 Toys & hobby goods & supplies
PA: Ball, Bounce And Sport, Inc.
     1 Hedstrom Dr
     Ashland OH 44805
     419 289-9310

(G-7088)
BALLET METROPOLITAN INC
Also Called: Balletmet Columbus
322 Mount Vernon Ave (43215-2131)
PHONE..............................614 229-4860
Fax: 614 229-4858
Thomas Brinker, *Treasurer*
Elaine Kolb, *Accounting Mgr*
Terence Womble, *Mktg Dir*
Sue Porter, *Exec Dir*
Pam Bishop, *Director*
EMP: 140
SQ FT: 35,000
SALES: 7.3MM **Privately Held**
WEB: www.balletmet.org
SIC: 7922 7911 Ballet production; professional dancing school

(G-7089)
BARCUS COMPANY INC
1601 Bethel Rd Ste 100 (43220-2006)
PHONE..............................614 451-9000
Philip Barcus, *President*
EMP: 50
SQ FT: 10,000
SALES (est): 4.3MM **Privately Held**
WEB: www.barcuscompany.com
SIC: 6513 6512 Apartment building operators; commercial & industrial building operation

(G-7090)
BARKAN & NEFF CO LPA (PA)
250 E Broad St Fl 10 (43215-3708)
PHONE..............................614 221-4221
Fax: 614 221-5423
Frank J Neff, *President*
Bob Derose, *Senior Partner*
Eileen Goodin, *Principal*
Sanford Meizlish, *Principal*
Kathy Edmondson, *Accounting Mgr*
EMP: 40
SQ FT: 15,000
SALES (est): 13.9MM **Privately Held**
WEB: www.bnhmlaw.com
SIC: 8111 General practice law office

(G-7091)
BARR ENGINEERING INCORPORATED (PA)
Also Called: National Engrg Archtctral Svcs
2800 Corp Exchange Dr # 240 (43231-7628)
PHONE..............................614 714-0299
Jawdat Siddiqi, *President*
Enoch Chipukaizer, *Principal*
Robin Lamb, *Principal*
Jessica Cave, *Accountant*
Andrew Barr, *Financial Exec*
EMP: 35
SQ FT: 1,500
SALES (est): 9.4MM **Privately Held**
SIC: 8711 8713 8734 1799 Civil engineering; surveying services; testing laboratories; core drilling & cutting; nonmetallic minerals development & test boring

(G-7092)
BATTELLE MEMORIAL INSTITUTE (PA)
505 King Ave (43201-2681)
PHONE..............................614 424-6424
Fax: 614 424-3321
Lewis Von Thaer, *CEO*
John Welch, *Ch of Bd*
Russell Austin, *Senior VP*
Dave Evans, *CFO*
▲ EMP: 4712 EST: 1925
SQ FT: 3,810
SALES (est): 4.8B **Privately Held**
WEB: www.battelle.org
SIC: 8731 Commercial physical research; medical research, commercial; environmental research; electronic research

(G-7093)
BATTELLEED
505 King Ave (43201-2693)
PHONE..............................614 859-6433
Elizabeth Combs, *Administration*
EMP: 99
SALES (est): 2.9MM **Privately Held**
SIC: 8731 Biotechnical research, commercial

(G-7094)
BAY STATE GAS COMPANY
200 Civic Center Dr (43215-7510)
PHONE..............................614 460-4292
Steven Jablonski, *Branch Mgr*
EMP: 273
SALES (corp-wide): 4.8B **Publicly Held**
WEB: www.baystategas.com
SIC: 4924 Natural gas distribution
HQ: Bay State Gas Company
     4 Technology Dr
     Westborough MA 01581
     508 836-7000

(G-7095)
BBS PROFESSIONAL CORPORATION (DH)
1103 Schrock Rd Ste 400 (43229-1179)
PHONE..............................614 888-3100
Edward O Vance, *Ch of Bd*
Paul R Schlegel, *President*
Donald F Cuthbert, *Vice Pres*
EMP: 49
SQ FT: 19,000
SALES (est): 4.2MM
SALES (corp-wide): 10B **Publicly Held**
SIC: 8711 Consulting engineer
HQ: Ch2m Hill, Inc.
     9191 S Jamaica St
     Englewood CO 80112
     303 771-0900

(G-7096)
BDO USA LLP
300 Spruce St Ste 100 (43215-1173)
PHONE..............................614 488-3126
Mike Voinovich, *Managing Prtnr*
EMP: 45
SALES (corp-wide): 1.2B **Privately Held**
SIC: 8721 Accounting, auditing & bookkeeping
PA: Bdo Usa, Llp
     330 N Wabash Ave Ste 3200
     Chicago IL 60611
     312 240-1236

(G-7097)
BEECHWOLD VETERINARY HOSPITAL (PA)
4590 Indianola Ave (43214-2248)
PHONE..............................614 268-8666
Stephen D Wenger, *President*
Marilyn A Schwab, *Principal*
Bruce Wenger, *Principal*
Ed Winderl, *Corp Secy*
Robert Hanson, *Vice Pres*
EMP: 40
SQ FT: 6,000
SALES (est): 3.5MM **Privately Held**
WEB: www.beechwoldvet.vetsuite.com
SIC: 0742 Animal hospital services, pets & other animal specialties

(G-7098)
BELAYUSA CORPORATION
5197 Trabue Rd (43228-9498)
PHONE..............................614 878-8200
Carl Long, *President*
EMP: 31
SQ FT: 2,000
SALES (est): 396.4K **Privately Held**
SIC: 7381 Private investigator

(G-7099)
BELCAN CORPORATION
Also Called: Belcan Staffing Solutions
519 S High St (43215-5602)
PHONE..............................614 224-6080
EMP: 749
SALES (corp-wide): 666.9MM **Privately Held**
SIC: 7363 Engineering help service
PA: Belcan, Llc
     10200 Anderson Way
     Blue Ash OH 45242
     513 891-0972

(G-7100)
BENESCH FRIEDLANDER COPLAN &
41 S High St Ste 2600 (43215-6164)
PHONE..............................614 223-9300
David Paragas, *Partner*
N Victor Goodman, *Partner*
Kelly E Mulrane, *Associate*
EMP: 50
SALES (corp-wide): 57.2MM **Privately Held**
SIC: 8111 Legal services
PA: Benesch, Friedlander, Coplan & Aronoff Llp
     200 Public Sq Ste 2300
     Cleveland OH 44114
     216 363-4500

(G-7101)
BERARDI + PARTNERS
1398 Goodale Blvd (43212-3720)
PHONE..............................614 221-1110
Fax: 614 221-0831
George Berardi, *Partner*
Christopher Bruzzese, *Partner*
Jonathan Leonard, *Project Leader*
John Matthews, *Project Leader*
Dan Mayer, *Director*
EMP: 25
SQ FT: 9,000
SALES (est): 4.2MM **Privately Held**
WEB: www.bpiarch.com
SIC: 8712 Architectural engineering

(G-7102)
BERTEC CORPORATION
6171 Huntley Rd Ste J (43229-1047)
PHONE..............................614 543-0962
Fax: 614 430-5425
Necip Berme, *President*
Scott Barnes, *General Mgr*
Jeff S Sobotka, *Purch Mgr*
Martha Fitzgerald, *Engineer*
Kuba Ober, *Engineer*
EMP: 27
SQ FT: 12,000
SALES (est): 5.2MM **Privately Held**
WEB: www.bertec.com
SIC: 8711 Consulting engineer; mechanical engineering

(G-7103)
BEST WESTERN COLUMBUS N HOTEL
Also Called: Best Western Columbus North
888 E Dublin Granville Rd (43229-2416)
PHONE..............................614 888-8230
Fax: 614 888-8223
Shawn Chang, *General Mgr*
EMP: 40
SALES (est): 1.4MM **Privately Held**
SIC: 6512 7991 7011 5813 Nonresidential building operators; physical fitness facilities; hotels & motels; drinking places; eating places

(G-7104)
BETH-EL AGAPE CHRISTIAN CENTER
840 Mansfield Ave (43219-2453)
PHONE..............................614 445-0674
Benita Farve, *President*
Quanta Brown, *Corp Secy*
Rowena Bryant, *Admin Sec*
EMP: 25
SALES (est): 161.7K **Privately Held**
SIC: 8322 Outreach program

(G-7105)
BEYOND THE HORIZONS HOME HEALT
2645 Fairwood Ave (43207-2729)
PHONE..............................608 630-0617
William Reynolds, *Principal*
Julius Myricks, *Principal*
EMP: 25
SALES (est): 194.8K **Privately Held**
SIC: 8082 Home health care services

(G-7106)
BIG BROTH AND BIG SISTE OF CEN (PA)
Also Called: Mentoring Ctr For Centl Ohio
1855 E Dbln Grnvl Rd Fl 1 (43229)
PHONE..............................614 839-2447
Fax: 614 839-5437
Heather Campbell, *CEO*
Douglas Peterman Jr, *Chairman*
Dave Schirner, *Vice Pres*
Craig Marshall, *Treasurer*
Denise McConnell, *Treasurer*
EMP: 50
SQ FT: 11,000
SALES: 5.9MM **Privately Held**
WEB: www.bbbscolumbus.org
SIC: 8322 7033 Helping hand service (Big Brother, etc.); campgrounds

(G-7107)
BIG LOTS STORES INC (HQ)
300 Phillipi Rd (43228-5311)
PHONE..............................614 278-6800
David J Campisi, *CEO*
Richard Chene, *Exec VP*
Tim Johnson, *CFO*
▲ EMP: 500
SALES: 4.2B
SALES (corp-wide): 5.2B **Publicly Held**
WEB: www.biglots.com
SIC: 5331 5021 5044 5961 Variety stores; furniture; office equipment; catalog & mail-order houses

GEOGRAPHIC SECTION
Columbus - Franklin County (G-7131)

PA: Big Lots, Inc.
300 Phillipi Rd
Columbus OH 43228
614 278-6800

(G-7108)
BIG RED ROOSTER (HQ)
121 Thurman Ave (43206-2656)
PHONE................614 255-0200
Fax: 614 255-0205
Martin J Beck, *CEO*
Josh Broehl, *President*
Vicki Eickelberger, *President*
Don Hasulak, *President*
Stephen Jay, *President*
EMP: 54
SALES (est): 15.1MM
SALES (corp-wide): 7.9B **Publicly Held**
SIC: 8712 8748 7371 Architectural services; industrial development planning; computer software systems analysis & design, custom
PA: Jones Lang Lasalle Incorporated
200 E Randolph St # 4300
Chicago IL 60601
312 782-5800

(G-7109)
BIG WESTERN OPERATING CO INC
Also Called: Big Western Lanes
500 Georgesville Rd (43228-2421)
PHONE................614 274-1169
Fax: 614 274-5245
Paul Cusmano, *President*
EMP: 25
SQ FT: 45,000
SALES (est): 500.6K **Privately Held**
SIC: 7933 Ten pin center

(G-7110)
BIMBO BAKERIES USA INC
1020 Claycraft Rd Ste D (43230-6684)
PHONE................614 868-7565
Dave Melaragno, *Manager*
EMP: 30 **Privately Held**
WEB: www.gwbakeries.com
SIC: 5149 Bakery products
HQ: Bimbo Bakeries Usa, Inc
255 Business Center Dr # 200
Horsham PA 19044
215 347-5500

(G-7111)
BIO-BLOOD COMPONENTS INC
1393 N High St (43201-2459)
PHONE................614 294-3183
Fax: 614 294-2214
Jane Hancock, *Manager*
Shelly Heckert, *Manager*
EMP: 30
SALES (corp-wide): 18.6MM **Privately Held**
SIC: 8099 2836 Blood bank; biological products, except diagnostic
PA: Bio-Blood Components, Inc.
5700 Pleasant View Rd
Memphis TN 38134
901 384-6250

(G-7112)
BIO-MDCAL APPLCATIONS OHIO INC
Also Called: Fresenius Med Care Cntl Ohio E
4039 E Broad St (43213-1136)
PHONE................614 338-8202
Jim Barsanti, *Manager*
William H Bay, *Nephrology*
EMP: 25
SALES (corp-wide): 20.9B **Privately Held**
WEB: www.fresenius.org
SIC: 8092 Kidney dialysis centers
HQ: Bio-Medical Applications Of Ohio, Inc.
920 Winter St
Waltham MA 02451

(G-7113)
BKG HOLDINGS LLC
Also Called: Bartha Audio Visual
600 N Cassady Ave Ofc (43219-2790)
PHONE................614 252-7455
Fax: 614 252-7641
Cheryl Bright, *General Mgr*
Douglas Moore, *General Mgr*
Jason Brentlinger, *Prdtn Mgr*
Larry Spiess, *Controller*
Alan Shultz, *Accounts Mgr*
EMP: 45
SQ FT: 48,115
SALES (est): 7.3MM **Privately Held**
WEB: www.bartha.com
SIC: 7812 7359 Audio-visual program production; audio-visual equipment & supply rental

(G-7114)
BKG SERVICES INC
3948 Townsfair Way # 230 (43219-6096)
P.O. Box 307352 (43230-7352)
PHONE................614 476-1800
Fax: 614 476-3017
Benjamin Harper, *President*
EMP: 30
SQ FT: 500
SALES (est): 882.2K **Privately Held**
WEB: www.bkgservices.com
SIC: 7349 Janitorial service, contract basis

(G-7115)
BLACK & VEATCH CORPORATION
4449 Easton Way Ste 150 (43219-7002)
PHONE................614 473-0921
Pat Roman, *Manager*
Paul Smith, *Manager*
EMP: 30
SALES (corp-wide): 3.2B **Privately Held**
WEB: www.bv.com
SIC: 8711 Consulting engineer
HQ: Black & Veatch Corporation
11401 Lamar Ave
Overland Park KS 66211
913 458-2000

(G-7116)
BLACK SAPPHIRE C COLUMBUS UNIV
Also Called: Springhill Suites
1421 Olentangy River Rd (43212-1449)
PHONE................614 297-9912
Alan Schreiber, *General Mgr*
Dena St Clair, *Asst Director*
EMP: 100
SALES (est): 2.2MM **Privately Held**
SIC: 7011 Hotels & motels

(G-7117)
BLACKBURNS FABRICATION INC
2467 Jackson Pike (43223-3846)
PHONE................614 875-0784
Fax: 614 875-0337
Mark A Blackburn, *President*
Edsel L Blackburn Sr, *Vice Pres*
Bill Dawson, *Purchasing*
Steve Bosak, *Sales Associate*
Carolyn Blackburn, *Admin Sec*
EMP: 30
SQ FT: 50,000
SALES (est): 9.2MM **Privately Held**
WEB: www.blackburnsfab.com
SIC: 3441 5051 Fabricated structural metal; structural shapes, iron or steel

(G-7118)
BLASTMASTER HOLDINGS USA LLC
Also Called: Blast-One International
4510 Bridgeway Ave (43219)
PHONE................877 725-2781
Raj Govindaraj, *CFO*
Bryce Kenimer, *Controller*
Timothy D Gooden,
Andrew Gooden,
James Gooden,
◆ **EMP:** 100
SQ FT: 56,000
SALES (est): 55MM **Privately Held**
SIC: 5084 Industrial machinery & equipment

(G-7119)
BLOOD SERVICES CENTL OHIO REG (PA)
995 E Broad St (43205-1322)
PHONE................614 253-7981
Ambrose Ng, *CEO*
Kurt Anders, *Finance*
Rita Barns, *MIS Mgr*
David Gabriel, *Administration*
EMP: 200
SQ FT: 80,000
SALES (est): 2.8MM **Privately Held**
SIC: 8099 Blood related health services

(G-7120)
BMI FEDERAL CREDIT UNION (PA)
760 Kinnear Rd Frnt (43212-1487)
P.O. Box 3670, Dublin (43016-0340)
PHONE................614 298-8527
Fax: 614 291-1773
Sharon Custer, *President*
Stacy Toki, *Human Res Dir*
Connie Vradenburg, *Manager*
Greg Hopp, *Info Tech Dir*
EMP: 70
SQ FT: 18,000
SALES: 13.5MM **Privately Held**
WEB: www.bmifcu.com
SIC: 6061 Federal credit unions

(G-7121)
BNAI BRITH HILLEL FDN AT OSU
46 E 16th Ave (43201-1615)
PHONE................614 294-4797
Fax: 614 294-4796
Aaron Shocket, *President*
EMP: 36
SALES: 1.1MM **Privately Held**
SIC: 8661 8611 Religious organizations; community affairs & services

(G-7122)
BOB SUMEREL TIRE CO INC
2807 International St (43228-4616)
PHONE................614 527-9700
Fax: 614 527-1075
Lisa Smith, *General Mgr*
Timothy Hooker, *Manager*
Thomas Crnko, *Manager*
EMP: 32
SALES (corp-wide): 87.3MM **Privately Held**
WEB: www.bobsumereltire.com
SIC: 5014 5015 7534 Tires & tubes; batteries, used: automotive; tire retreading & repair shops
PA: Bob Sumerel Tire Co., Inc.
1257 Cox Ave
Erlanger KY 41018
859 283-2700

(G-7123)
BOBB AUTOMOTIVE INC
Also Called: Bobb Suzuki
4639 W Broad St (43228-1610)
P.O. Box 28148 (43228-0148)
PHONE................614 853-3000
Jeff May, *President*
Thomas O'Ryan, *Vice Pres*
Cindy Blagg, *Human Res Mgr*
Sam Ferroni, *Sales Associate*
Bob Frederick, *Sales Associate*
EMP: 50
SQ FT: 15,000
SALES (est): 69.2MM **Privately Held**
WEB: www.fetrucks.com
SIC: 5511 7515 5012 Automobiles, new & used; passenger car leasing; automobiles & other motor vehicles

(G-7124)
BONDED CHEMICALS INC (HQ)
Also Called: Chemgroup
2645 Charter St (43228-4605)
PHONE................614 777-9240
Fax: 614 777-9244
Marty Wehr, *President*
Sue Wiford, *Corp Secy*
Mason Chandler, *Manager*
Carol Cordell, *Manager*
Chris Davis, *Manager*
▲ **EMP:** 30 **EST:** 1945
SALES (est): 35.9MM
SALES (corp-wide): 125.6MM **Privately Held**
WEB: www.chemgroup.com
SIC: 5169 Sanitation preparations; industrial chemicals
PA: Chemgroup, Inc
2600 Thunderhawk Ct
Dayton OH 45414
937 898-5566

(G-7125)
BOWEN ENGINEERING CORPORATION
22 E Gay St Ste 700 (43215-3173)
PHONE................614 536-0273
EMP: 148
SALES (corp-wide): 396.2MM **Privately Held**
SIC: 8711 Engineering services
PA: Bowen Engineering Corporation
8802 N Meridian St Ste X
Indianapolis IN 46260
219 661-9770

(G-7126)
BOYD PROPERTY GROUP LLC
71 Winner Ave (43203-1956)
PHONE................614 725-5228
Kristin Dillard,
EMP: 25
SALES (est): 1.3MM **Privately Held**
SIC: 6531 7389 Real estate managers;

(G-7127)
BOYS & GIRLS CLUB OF COLUMBUS
1108 City Park Ave # 301 (43206-3686)
PHONE................614 221-8830
Fax: 614 221-1225
Drew Dimaccio, *President*
Rebecca Asmo, *Exec Dir*
Traci Callender, *Director*
Courtney Cooke, *Director*
Arielle Scott, *Director*
EMP: 46
SQ FT: 22,000
SALES (est): 2.1MM **Privately Held**
SIC: 8641 Youth organizations

(G-7128)
BP-LS-PT CO
5275 Sinclair Rd (43229-5042)
PHONE................614 841-4500
Peter C Taub, *President*
Randy Goddard, *Vice Pres*
Jim Harrison, *Manager*
EMP: 95
SALES (est): 4.4MM **Privately Held**
SIC: 1731 General electrical contractor

(G-7129)
BPM REALTY INC
195 N Grant Ave Fl 2a (43215-2855)
PHONE................614 221-6811
Frederick W Ziegler, *Ch of Bd*
John M Ziegler, *President*
Gloria McCoy, *Accountant*
EMP: 27
SQ FT: 43,000
SALES (est): 3MM **Privately Held**
WEB: www.buckeyepm.com
SIC: 7331 2752 Mailing service; commercial printing, offset

(G-7130)
BRADY WARE & SCHOENFELD INC
4249 Easton Way Ste 100 (43219-6170)
PHONE................614 885-7407
EMP: 65
SALES (corp-wide): 14.6MM **Privately Held**
SIC: 8721 Accounting/Auditing /Bookkeeping
PA: Brady, Ware & Schoenfeld, Inc.
3001 Rigby Rd Ste 400
Miamisburg OH 45342
937 223-5247

(G-7131)
BRADY WARE & SCHOENFELD INC
Also Called: Brady Ware
4249 Easton Way Ste 100 (43219-6170)
PHONE................614 825-6277
Bob Reynolds, *Branch Mgr*
EMP: 65
SALES (est): 3.5MM
SALES (corp-wide): 16.9MM **Privately Held**
SIC: 8721 Certified public accountant
PA: Brady, Ware & Schoenfeld, Inc.
3601 Rigby Rd Ste 400
Miamisburg OH 45342
937 223-5247

Columbus - Franklin County (G-7132)

(G-7132)
BREATHING ASSOCIATION
1520 Old Henderson Rd # 201 (43220-3639)
PHONE.................614 457-4570
Jeffery Schulze, *Accountant*
Marie E Collart, *Exec Dir*
Renee Kirwan, *Nurse Practr*
Jennifer Hutchinson, *Associate*
EMP: 27 **EST:** 1906
SQ FT: 1,800
SALES: 2MM **Privately Held**
SIC: 8621 Medical field-related associations

(G-7133)
BRIAR-GATE REALTY INC
1675 W Mound St (43223-1809)
P.O. Box 1150, Grove City (43123-6150)
PHONE.................614 299-2121
EMP: 27
SALES (corp-wide): 22MM **Privately Held**
SIC: 4225 General warehousing & storage
PA: Briar-Gate Realty, Inc.
3827 Brookham Dr
Grove City OH 43123
614 299-2121

(G-7134)
BRICKER & ECKLER LLP (PA)
100 S 3rd St Ste B (43215-4291)
PHONE.................614 227-2300
Fax: 614 227-2399
Richard C Simpson, *Partner*
Kimball H Carey, *Counsel*
Thomas J O'Brien, *Counsel*
Melinda Whitney, *QC Mgr*
Steve Odum, *Office Mgr*
EMP: 311 **EST:** 1997
SQ FT: 100,000
SALES (est): 46.5MM **Privately Held**
WEB: www.counselfor.net
SIC: 8111 General practice law office

(G-7135)
BRIGHT HORIZONS CHLD CTRS LLC
Also Called: Bright Horizons Battelle
835 Thomas Ln (43214-3905)
PHONE.................614 754-7023
Rebecca Komarov, *Director*
EMP: 40
SALES (corp-wide): 1.7B **Publicly Held**
SIC: 8351 Group day care center
HQ: Bright Horizons Children's Centers Llc
200 Talcott Ave
Watertown MA 02472
617 673-8000

(G-7136)
BRIGHT HORIZONS CHLD CTRS LLC
111 S Grant Ave (43215-4701)
PHONE.................614 566-9322
Fax: 614 566-8067
Karen Hughes, *Manager*
EMP: 27
SALES (corp-wide): 1.7B **Publicly Held**
WEB: www.atlantaga.ncr.com
SIC: 8351 Group day care center
HQ: Bright Horizons Children's Centers Llc
200 Talcott Ave
Watertown MA 02472
617 673-8000

(G-7137)
BRIGHT HORIZONS CHLD CTRS LLC
277 E Town St (43215-4627)
PHONE.................614 227-0550
Catherine Edgar, *Director*
EMP: 28
SALES (corp-wide): 1.7B **Publicly Held**
WEB: www.atlantaga.ncr.com
SIC: 8748 Business consulting
HQ: Bright Horizons Children's Centers Llc
200 Talcott Ave
Watertown MA 02472
617 673-8000

(G-7138)
BRIGHT HORIZONS CHLD CTRS LLC
835 Thomas Ln (43214-3905)
PHONE.................614 566-4847
Lori Ritter, *Manager*
EMP: 27
SALES (corp-wide): 1.7B **Publicly Held**
WEB: www.atlantaga.ncr.com
SIC: 8351 Child day care services
HQ: Bright Horizons Children's Centers Llc
200 Talcott Ave
Watertown MA 02472
617 673-8000

(G-7139)
BRIGHTVIEW LANDSCAPE SVCS INC
3001 Innis Rd (43224-3741)
PHONE.................614 801-1712
EMP: 38
SALES (corp-wide): 914MM **Privately Held**
SIC: 0781 Landscape services
HQ: Brightview Landscape Services, Inc.
24151 Ventura Blvd
Calabasas CA 91302
818 223-8500

(G-7140)
BRIGHTVIEW LANDSCAPE SVCS INC
3001 Innis Rd (43224-3741)
PHONE.................614 478-2085
Cory Foltz, *Sales Staff*
Larry Reasinger, *Sales Executive*
Maria Sanbuco, *Sales Executive*
Lara Moon, *Marketing Staff*
Joel Korte, *Manager*
EMP: 56
SQ FT: 845
SALES (corp-wide): 914MM **Privately Held**
SIC: 0781 Landscape services
HQ: Brightview Landscape Services, Inc.
24151 Ventura Blvd
Calabasas CA 91302
818 223-8500

(G-7141)
BRIGHTVIEW LANDSCAPE SVCS INC
3001 Innis Rd (43224-3741)
PHONE.................740 369-4800
EMP: 56
SALES (corp-wide): 914MM **Privately Held**
SIC: 0781 Landscape services
HQ: Brightview Landscape Services, Inc.
24151 Ventura Blvd
Calabasas CA 91302
818 223-8500

(G-7142)
BRIGHTVIEW LANDSCAPES LLC
2323 Performance Way (43207-2858)
PHONE.................301 987-9200
Fax: 614 445-7346
Joe Pistininzi, *Principal*
EMP: 36
SALES (corp-wide): 914MM **Privately Held**
SIC: 0781 Landscape services
HQ: Brightview Landscapes, Llc
401 Plymouth Rd Ste 500
Plymouth Meeting PA 19462
484 567-7204

(G-7143)
BRIGHTVIEW LANDSCAPES LLC
2240 Harper Rd (43204-3410)
PHONE.................614 276-5500
Fax: 614 276-5506
Jeff Rupp, *Principal*
Mark Kubasak, *Accounts Mgr*
EMP: 56
SALES (corp-wide): 914MM **Privately Held**
SIC: 0781 Landscape services
HQ: Brightview Landscapes, Llc
401 Plymouth Rd Ste 500
Plymouth Meeting PA 19462
484 567-7204

(G-7144)
BRINKS INCORPORATED
1362 Essex Ave (43211-2632)
PHONE.................614 291-1268
Fax: 614 291-1282
David Bramkamp, *Manager*
Debbie Stanton, *Executive*
EMP: 42
SALES (corp-wide): 3.3B **Publicly Held**
WEB: www.brinksinc.com
SIC: 7381 Armored car services
HQ: Brink's, Incorporated
1801 Bayberry Ct Ste 400
Richmond VA 23226
804 289-9600

(G-7145)
BRINKS INCORPORATED
506 E Starr Ave (43201-3618)
PHONE.................614 291-0624
Charles Redmond, *Principal*
EMP: 42
SALES (corp-wide): 3.3B **Publicly Held**
SIC: 7381 Armored car services
HQ: Brink's, Incorporated
1801 Bayberry Ct Ste 400
Richmond VA 23226
804 289-9600

(G-7146)
BROAD & JAMES INC
Also Called: Broad & James Towing
3502 E 7th Ave (43219-1735)
PHONE.................614 231-8697
Fax: 614 237-2310
Tim Shriner, *President*
Jim Shriner, *Vice Pres*
EMP: 30 **EST:** 1973
SQ FT: 2,500
SALES (est): 3.9MM **Privately Held**
SIC: 7549 7539 Towing service, automotive; automotive repair shops

(G-7147)
BROAD STREET HOTEL ASSOC LP
Also Called: Ramada Inn East - Airport
4801 E Broad St (43213-1356)
PHONE.................614 861-0321
Kevork Toroyian, *Partner*
Patrick Barrett, *Partner*
Barkev Kayajian, *Partner*
Bill Nikolis, *Partner*
EMP: 60
SQ FT: 15,000
SALES (est): 1.7MM **Privately Held**
WEB: www.endlessresin.com
SIC: 7011 7991 5813 5812 Hotels; physical fitness facilities; drinking places; eating places

(G-7148)
BROADSPIRE SERVICES INC
445 Hutchinson Ave # 550 (43235-5677)
PHONE.................614 436-8990
Michael Carney, *General Mgr*
EMP: 25
SALES (corp-wide): 1.1B **Privately Held**
WEB: www.choosebroadspire.com
SIC: 6331 8099 Workers' compensation insurance; medical services organization
HQ: Broadspire Services Inc
1391 Nw 136th Ave
Sunrise FL 33323
954 452-4000

(G-7149)
BROADVIEW NH LLC
5151 N Hamilton Rd (43230-1313)
PHONE.................614 337-1066
Mordecai Rosenberg, *President*
Lisa Schwartz, *Principal*
Ronald Swartz, *Principal*
Dawn Wozniak, *Opers Staff*
EMP: 99
SALES (est): 574.4K **Privately Held**
SIC: 8051 Skilled nursing care facilities

(G-7150)
BRON-SHOE COMPANY
Also Called: American Bronzing Company
1313 Alum Creek Dr (43209-2760)
P.O. Box 91135 (43209-7135)
PHONE.................614 252-0967
Fax: 614 252-4602
Robert J Kaynes Jr, *President*
Susan Lantz, *Treasurer*
▲ **EMP:** 25 **EST:** 1949
SQ FT: 40,000
SALES (est): 3.1MM **Privately Held**
WEB: www.abcbronze.com
SIC: 7389 3471 Bronzing, baby shoes; plating of metals or formed products

(G-7151)
BROOK WILLOW CHRSTN CMMUNITIES
Also Called: Willow Brook Christian Home
55 Lazelle Rd (43235-1402)
PHONE.................614 885-3300
Paula Jenner, *Director*
Terry Slayman, *Director*
Mary Calpin, *Food Svc Dir*
Tamara Eichenlaub, *Hlthcr Dir*
David Chappell, *Administration*
EMP: 65
SALES (corp-wide): 3.4MM **Privately Held**
WEB: www.willow-brook.org
SIC: 8052 8051 Intermediate care facilities; skilled nursing care facilities
PA: Willow Brook Christian Communities, Inc
100 Delaware Xing W
Delaware OH 43015
740 369-0048

(G-7152)
BROOKDALE LVING CMMUNITIES INC
Also Called: Brookdale Living Cmnty Ohio
3500 Trillium Xing (43235-7991)
PHONE.................614 734-1000
Debbie Castle, *Manager*
Kathy Loney, *Director*
EMP: 100
SALES (corp-wide): 4.7B **Publicly Held**
WEB: www.parkplace-spokane.com
SIC: 8059 Personal care home, with health care
HQ: Brookdale Living Communities, Inc.
515 N State St Ste 1750
Chicago IL 60654

(G-7153)
BROOKSIDE GOLF & CNTRY CLB CO
2770 W Dblin Granville Rd (43235-2785)
PHONE.................614 889-2581
Fax: 614 889-2749
James Rowlette, *President*
Kurt Burmeister, *General Mgr*
Kasey Counseller, *General Mgr*
Joe Furko, *General Mgr*
Joseph T Furko III, *General Mgr*
EMP: 150 **EST:** 1927
SQ FT: 75,000
SALES: 6.1MM **Privately Held**
WEB: www.brooksidegcc.com
SIC: 7997 Country club, membership; golf club, membership

(G-7154)
BRUSH CONTRACTORS INC
5000 Transamerica Dr (43228-9335)
P.O. Box 3213, Dublin (43016-0098)
PHONE.................614 850-8500
Fax: 614 850-8550
Stephen Brush, *President*
EMP: 65
SQ FT: 10,500
SALES (est): 8.2MM **Privately Held**
WEB: www.brushcontractors.com
SIC: 1731 Lighting contractor

(G-7155)
BUCKEYE ASSN SCHL ADMNSTRATORS
8050 N High St Ste 150 (43235-6486)
PHONE.................614 846-4080
Fax: 614 846-4081
Kathy Lowery, *Principal*
Dr Jerry Klenke, *Director*

EMP: 25
SALES: 2.8MM **Privately Held**
SIC: 8621 Education & teacher association

(G-7156)
BUCKEYE BOXES INC
601 N Hague Ave (43204-1498)
PHONE..................614 274-8484
Fax: 419 626-9635
EMP: 30
SALES (est): 1.8MM
SALES (corp-wide): 24.9MM **Privately Held**
SIC: 5113 2653 Industrial & personal service paper; corrugated & solid fiber boxes
PA: Buckeye Boxes, Inc.
    601 N Hague Ave
    Columbus OH 43204
    614 274-8484

(G-7157)
BUCKEYE CMNTY EIGHTY ONE LP
Also Called: Williams Street Apartments
3021 E Dblin Granville Rd (43231-4031)
PHONE..................614 942-2020
Brenda Jacques, *General Ptnr*
Steven Boone, *Ltd Ptnr*
EMP: 37
SALES (est): 559.1K **Privately Held**
SIC: 6513 Apartment building operators

(G-7158)
BUCKEYE CMNTY HOPE FOUNDATION (PA)
3021 E Dblin Grndville Rd (43231)
PHONE..................614 942-2014
Steve J Boone, *President*
Ian Maute, *Vice Pres*
Carlisa Stewart, *Vice Pres*
Dave Graber, *Project Mgr*
Anthony English, *Controller*
EMP: 102
SQ FT: 5,000
SALES: 19.6MM **Privately Held**
SIC: 1521 Single-family housing construction

(G-7159)
BUCKEYE CMNTY TWENTY SIX LP
Also Called: Montpelier Gardens
3021 E Dblin Granville Rd (43231-4031)
PHONE..................614 942-2020
Steven Boone, *President*
EMP: 30
SALES (est): 925.2K **Privately Held**
SIC: 6531 Real estate agents & managers

(G-7160)
BUCKEYE POWER INC (PA)
Also Called: Ohio Rural Electric Coops
6677 Busch Blvd (43229-1101)
PHONE..................614 781-0573
Steven Nelson, *Ch of Bd*
Anthony J Ahern, *President*
Bobby Daniel, *Vice Pres*
Jeff Brehm, *Comms Dir*
Patrick Higgins, *Comms Dir*
EMP: 28
SQ FT: 36,000
SALES (est): 575.9MM **Privately Held**
WEB: www.buckeyepower.com
SIC: 8611 4911 Trade associations; generation, electric power

(G-7161)
BUCKEYE RANCH INC
Also Called: Permanent Family Solutions
697 E Broad St (43215-3948)
PHONE..................614 384-7700
Steve Richard, *Branch Mgr*
Christie Laffin, *Nutritionist*
EMP: 55
SALES (corp-wide): 42.8MM **Privately Held**
SIC: 8361 Home for the emotionally disturbed; halfway group home, persons with social or personal problems; halfway home for delinquents & offenders; juvenile correctional home
PA: The Buckeye Ranch Inc
    5665 Hoover Rd
    Grove City OH 43123
    614 875-2371

(G-7162)
BUCKEYE TRUCK EQUIPMENT INC
Also Called: Buckeye Body and Equipment
939 E Starr Ave (43201-3042)
P.O. Box 1150 (43216-1150)
PHONE..................614 299-1136
Fax: 614 299-2314
Fred Bongiovanni, *President*
Jeffrey Massey, *Vice Pres*
Sherry Collopy, *Production*
Andy Easterday, *Inv Control Mgr*
Angelene McMickle, *Inv Control Mgr*
EMP: 34
SQ FT: 55,000
SALES: 9MM **Privately Held**
SIC: 5012 Truck bodies

(G-7163)
BUCKNER AND SONS MASONRY INC
3800 Sullivant Ave Ste A (43228-7608)
PHONE..................614 279-9777
Fax: 614 279-7855
Otis Buckner, *President*
Bailene Buckner, *Corp Secy*
EMP: 37
SQ FT: 3,200
SALES (est): 3MM **Privately Held**
SIC: 1741 Masonry & other stonework

(G-7164)
BUDENHEIM USA INC
2219 Westbrooke Dr (43228-9605)
PHONE..................614 345-2400
Douglas Lim, *Ch of Bd*
Harold Schaub, *President*
Jerry Cohen, *President*
Becca Beck, *General Mgr*
Michael Schmitt, *General Mgr*
◆ EMP: 25
SALES (est): 18MM
SALES (corp-wide): 222.7MM **Privately Held**
WEB: www.gallard.com
SIC: 5169 Industrial chemicals; food additives & preservatives
PA: Chemische Fabrik Budenheim Kg
    Rheinstr. 27
    Budenheim 55257
    613 989-0

(G-7165)
BUDROS RUHLIN & ROE INC
1801 Watermark Dr Ste 300 (43215-7088)
PHONE..................614 481-6900
Fax: 614 481-6919
James L Budros, *President*
Daniel Roe, *Principal*
Peggy Ruhlin, *Principal*
John Schuman, *Principal*
Joe Patracuollo, *Vice Pres*
EMP: 39
SALES: 3.3MM **Privately Held**
WEB: www.b-r-r.com
SIC: 8742 Financial consultant

(G-7166)
BUILDER SERVICES GROUP INC
Also Called: Gale Insulation
2365 Scioto Harper Dr (43204-3495)
PHONE..................614 263-9378
Fax: 614 263-1019
EMP: 70
SALES (corp-wide): 1.9B **Publicly Held**
WEB: www.galeind.com
SIC: 1742 Insulation, buildings
HQ: Builder Services Group, Inc.
    475 N Williamson Blvd
    Daytona Beach FL 32114
    386 304-2222

(G-7167)
BUILDERS TRASH SERVICE
1575 Harmon Ave (43223-3316)
PHONE..................614 444-7060
Fax: 614 444-5455
Mike Neri, *Owner*
EMP: 25
SALES (est): 2.5MM **Privately Held**
WEB: www.builderstrash.com
SIC: 4953 Refuse collection & disposal services

(G-7168)
BULKMATIC TRANSPORT COMPANY
2271 Williams Rd (43207-5121)
PHONE..................614 497-2372
Mickey Hancock, *Branch Mgr*
EMP: 30
SALES (corp-wide): 410.6MM **Privately Held**
SIC: 4213 Contract haulers
PA: Bulkmatic Transport Company Inc
    2001 N Cline Ave
    Griffith IN 46319
    800 535-8505

(G-7169)
BURGESS & NIPLE INC (PA)
5085 Reed Rd (43220-2513)
PHONE..................502 254-2344
Fax: 614 451-1385
Ronald R Schultz, *CEO*
Kenneth R Davis Jr, *President*
Charles Wilmut, *Opers Staff*
Dippel James, *Project Engr*
Vance Martin, *Electrical Engi*
EMP: 275
SQ FT: 60,000
SALES (est): 122.1MM **Privately Held**
WEB: www.burgessniple.com
SIC: 8711 8712 Consulting engineer; architectural engineering

(G-7170)
BURGESS & NIPLE / HEAPY ENGINE
5085 Reed Rd (43220-2513)
PHONE..................614 459-2050
Robert Draper,
Karen Anderson,
EMP: 99
SALES (est): 1.3MM **Privately Held**
SIC: 8711 8712 7389 Engineering services; architectural services;

(G-7171)
BUTLER ANIMAL HEALTH SUP LLC
Also Called: Henry Schein Animal Health
3820 Twin Creeks Dr (43204-5000)
PHONE..................614 718-2000
Kevin Eilerman, *Manager*
Mark Axelrod, *Manager*
Joshua Coates, *Manager*
Heidi Rudolph, *Asst Mgr*
Sharon Wray, *Programmer Anys*
EMP: 37
SALES (corp-wide): 12.4B **Publicly Held**
SIC: 5122 Drugs, proprietaries & sundries; biologicals & allied products; pharmaceuticals
HQ: Butler Animal Health Supply Llc
    400 Metro Pl N Ste 100
    Dublin OH 43017
    614 761-9095

(G-7172)
BUTLER CINCIONE AND DICUCCIO
556 E Town St 100 (43215-3337)
PHONE..................614 221-3151
Fax: 614 221-8196
Gerald N Dicaccio, *Partner*
Alphonse P Cincione, *Partner*
N Gerald Dicuccio, *Partner*
David Barnhardt, *Principal*
Renee Kimhle, *Manager*
EMP: 30
SQ FT: 10,000
SALES (est): 2.9MM **Privately Held**
WEB: www.bcdlaws.com
SIC: 8111 General practice attorney, lawyer

(G-7173)
C A E C INC
Also Called: Columbus Car Audio & ACC
2975 Morse Rd Ste A (43231-6051)
PHONE..................614 337-1091
Fax: 614 337-1093
Todd Hays, *President*
Jennifer Keeney, *Manager*
Danielle Hays, *Admin Sec*
EMP: 38
SQ FT: 14,000
SALES (est): 5.4MM **Privately Held**
SIC: 5731 5065 Sound equipment, automotive; sound equipment, electronic

(G-7174)
C M LIMITED
5255 Sinclair Rd (43229-5042)
PHONE..................614 888-4567
Max Brown, *President*
Herbert Cook Jr, *Principal*
EMP: 50
SQ FT: 60,000
SALES (est): 1.7MM **Privately Held**
SIC: 6512 Commercial & industrial building operation

(G-7175)
C T CORPORATION SYSTEM
Also Called: C T Columbus
4400 Easton Cmns Ste 300 (43219-6226)
PHONE..................614 473-9749
Ann Roberson, *Manager*
Ruth Lawrence, *Manager*
EMP: 50
SALES (corp-wide): 5.2B **Privately Held**
WEB: www.ctadvantage.com
SIC: 8111 Corporate, partnership & business law
HQ: C T Corporation System
    111 8th Ave Fl 13
    New York NY 10011
    212 894-8940

(G-7176)
C V PERRY & CO (PA)
370 S 5th St (43215-5408)
P.O. Box 20405 (43220-0405)
PHONE..................614 221-4131
Fax: 614 221-3293
Brian Vain, *President*
James Fry, *CFO*
Carlyle Perry, *Manager*
EMP: 47
SQ FT: 3,500
SALES (est): 4.7MM **Privately Held**
WEB: www.cvperry.com
SIC: 1521 6552 6531 New construction, single-family houses; land subdividers & developers, commercial; real estate brokers & agents

(G-7177)
CALFEE HALTER & GRISWOLD LLP
41 S High St Ste 1200 (43215-3465)
PHONE..................614 621-1500
Karen Scurlock, *Branch Mgr*
Michael Mitchell, *Corp Counsel*
Peter Rosato, *Corp Counsel*
Anne Will, *Corp Counsel*
EMP: 25
SALES (corp-wide): 49.3MM **Privately Held**
SIC: 8111 General practice attorney, lawyer
PA: Calfee, Halter & Griswold Llp
    1405 E 6th St Ste 1
    Cleveland OH 44114
    216 831-2732

(G-7178)
CALFEE HALGERR GRISWOLD LLC
41 S High St Ste 1200 (43215-3465)
PHONE..................614 621-7003
Fax: 614 621-0010
Brent Ballard,
EMP: 25 EST: 2010
SALES (est): 772.3K **Privately Held**
SIC: 8111 General practice attorney, lawyer

(G-7179)
CALYPSO LOGISTICS LLC
Also Called: Calypso Distribution Services
2035 Innis Rd (43224-3646)
PHONE..................614 262-8911
Fax: 614 262-9816
Thomas L Kelly, *Vice Pres*
Jerry M Socol, *Vice Pres*
Son Pham, *Info Tech Mgr*
Michael J Chambers, *Director*
Jason Sipos,
EMP: 120
SQ FT: 365,000

Columbus - Franklin County (G-7180)

SALES (est): 10.3MM **Privately Held**
WEB: www.calypsologistics.com
SIC: 4225 4783 General warehousing; packing & crating

(G-7180)
CAMERON MITCHELL REST LLC (PA)
Also Called: Ocean Prime
390 W Nationwide Blvd # 300 (43215-2337)
PHONE..................614 621-3663
Fax: 614 621-1020
David Miller, *President*
Stacey Connaughton, *Vice Pres*
Charles Kline, *Vice Pres*
Kimberly Ho, *Accounting Mgr*
Katie Laudick, *Human Res Dir*
EMP: 46 EST: 1998
SQ FT: 7,800
SALES (est): 130.9MM **Privately Held**
WEB: www.cameronmitchell.com
SIC: 8741 5812 Restaurant management; eating places

(G-7181)
CAMP PINECLIFF INC
277 S Cassingham Rd (43209-1804)
PHONE..................614 236-5698
EMP: 100
SALES (est): 1.6MM **Privately Held**
SIC: 7032 8661 Sporting And Recreational Camps, Nsk

(G-7182)
CANYON MEDICAL CENTER INC
5969 E Broad St Ste 200 (43213-1546)
PHONE..................614 864-6010
Fax: 614 864-0306
Stephen D Shell MD, *President*
Stephen Canowitz, *Med Doctor*
John Dipietra, *Med Doctor*
Paul E Shoaps, *Med Doctor*
Boris Valdman, *Med Doctor*
EMP: 40 EST: 1976
SQ FT: 18,000
SALES (est): 5.9MM **Privately Held**
WEB: www.canyonmc.com
SIC: 8011 Internal medicine, physician/surgeon

(G-7183)
CAPITAL FIRE PROTECTION CO (PA)
3360 Valleyview Dr (43204-1296)
PHONE..................614 279-9448
Fax: 614 279-6092
William P Jolley, *President*
Christian Bradford, *President*
Steve Stump, *Principal*
John C Falk Sr, *Co-President*
Mark E Hunnell, *Vice Pres*
EMP: 42 EST: 1963
SQ FT: 20,000
SALES (est): 9.9MM **Privately Held**
WEB: www.capfire.com
SIC: 1799 Coating, caulking & weather, water & fireproofing

(G-7184)
CAPITAL TRANSPORTATION INC
1170 N Cassady Ave (43219-2232)
PHONE..................614 258-0400
Richard M Crockett, *President*
David Evans, *Project Mgr*
EMP: 104
SQ FT: 70,000
SALES (est): 4MM **Privately Held**
SIC: 4119 Limousine rental, with driver

(G-7185)
CAPITAL WHOLESALE DRUG COMPANY
Also Called: Capital Drug
873 Williams Ave (43212-3850)
PHONE..................614 297-8225
Fax: 614 297-8224
George D Richards, *Ch of Bd*
George K Richards, *President*
Peter Behrent, *General Mgr*
Daniel G Macleod, *Principal*
Edgar P Stocker, *Principal*
EMP: 55
SQ FT: 45,000
SALES (est): 44.1MM **Privately Held**
SIC: 5122 Pharmaceuticals; druggists' sundries

(G-7186)
CAPITOL CITY CARDIOLOGY INC (PA)
5825 Westbourne Ave (43213-1459)
PHONE..................614 464-0884
Fax: 614 297-0340
Charles Noble MD, *President*
Loretta Harrison, *Manager*
Raj Patel MD, *Shareholder*
Ruben Sheares MD, *Shareholder*
EMP: 40
SQ FT: 3,000
SALES (est): 6.1MM **Privately Held**
WEB: www.capitolcitycardiology.com
SIC: 8011 Cardiologist & cardio-vascular specialist

(G-7187)
CAPITOL EXPRESS ENTPS INC (PA)
Also Called: Cisco Capitol Express
3815 Twin Creeks Dr (43204-5005)
P.O. Box 462, Hilliard (43026-0462)
PHONE..................614 279-2819
Fax: 614 279-5616
Kennon Wissinger, *President*
Linda Cose, *Vice Pres*
EMP: 60
SQ FT: 6,000
SALES (est): 5.5MM **Privately Held**
SIC: 4212 Delivery service, vehicular

(G-7188)
CAPITOL TUNNELING INC
2216 Refugee Rd (43207-2800)
PHONE..................614 444-0255
Fax: 614 444-4094
Kyle Lucas, *President*
Matt Jutte, *Project Mgr*
Christine Harris, *Accounting Mgr*
Ledia Hoagland, *Manager*
E Lucus, *Manager*
EMP: 30
SQ FT: 1,200
SALES (est): 7.5MM **Privately Held**
SIC: 1622 Tunnel construction

(G-7189)
CARCORP INC
Also Called: Dennis Mitsubishi
2900 Morse Rd (43231-6036)
P.O. Box 29365 (43229-0365)
PHONE..................877 857-2801
Fax: 614 478-4237
Keith Dennis, *President*
Aaron Masterson, *Vice Pres*
Kurt Dennis, *Systems Mgr*
Aaron Casto, *Director*
Jim Tigyer, *Director*
▼ EMP: 146
SQ FT: 12,000
SALES (est): 68.8MM **Privately Held**
SIC: 5511 5521 7515 5571 Automobiles, new & used; used car dealers; passenger car leasing; motorcycle dealers

(G-7190)
CARDINAL BUILDERS INC
4409 E Main St (43213-3061)
PHONE..................614 237-1000
Fax: 614 237-0569
Tim Coady, *President*
Tim Kane, *Shareholder*
EMP: 25 EST: 1965
SQ FT: 22,000
SALES (est): 6.5MM **Privately Held**
WEB: www.cardinalbuilders.com
SIC: 3541 1521 1522 1799 Machine tool replacement & repair parts, metal cutting types; general remodeling, single-family houses; patio & deck construction & repair; hotel/motel & multi-family home renovation & remodeling; kitchen & bathroom remodeling; siding contractor; roofing contractor

(G-7191)
CARDINAL CONTAINER CORPORATION
3700 Lockbourne Rd (43207-5133)
PHONE..................614 497-3033
Fax: 614 497-3335
Charles Marcum, *President*
Mike Marcum, *Vice Pres*
Brad Beck, *Sales Staff*
EMP: 50
SQ FT: 29,000
SALES (est): 31.1MM **Privately Held**
SIC: 5113 Boxes & containers

(G-7192)
CARDINAL HEALTH INC
2215 Citygate Dr Ste D (43219-3589)
PHONE..................614 473-0786
Ian McCreary, *Engng Exec*
Kristin Hogan, *HR Admin*
Lindsay Konopka, *Marketing Mgr*
Matt Hathaway, *Manager*
Tim Reed, *Manager*
EMP: 200
SALES (corp-wide): 129.9B **Publicly Held**
SIC: 8099 Blood related health services
PA: Cardinal Health, Inc.
    7000 Cardinal Pl
    Dublin OH 43017
    614 757-5000

(G-7193)
CARDINAL HEALTH INC
2088 West Case Rd Ste 110 (43235-2540)
PHONE..................614 757-7690
Sarah Creech, *Manager*
EMP: 74
SALES (corp-wide): 129.9B **Publicly Held**
SIC: 5122 Pharmaceuticals
PA: Cardinal Health, Inc.
    7000 Cardinal Pl
    Dublin OH 43017
    614 757-5000

(G-7194)
CARDINAL HEALTH 200 LLC
1548 Mcgaw Rd (43207)
PHONE..................614 491-0050
Mario Lombardi, *Manager*
EMP: 150
SQ FT: 18,750
SALES (corp-wide): 129.9B **Publicly Held**
WEB: www.allegiancehealth.com
SIC: 5047 Medical equipment & supplies
HQ: Cardinal Health 200, Llc
    3651 Birchwood Dr
    Waukegan IL 60085

(G-7195)
CARDINAL HEALTHCARE
P.O. Box 183005 (43218-3005)
PHONE..................954 202-1883
EMP: 30
SALES (est): 860K **Privately Held**
SIC: 8099 Health & allied services

(G-7196)
CARDINAL ORTHOPAEDIC GROUP INC
170 Taylor Station Rd (43213-4491)
PHONE..................614 759-1186
Fax: 614 864-7117
Dale Ingram, *President*
Brian L Davison, *Orthopedist*
EMP: 33
SQ FT: 16,000
SALES (est): 3.2MM **Privately Held**
SIC: 8011 Physicians' office, including specialists

(G-7197)
CARDIO THORACIC SURGERY
410 W 10th Ave (43210-1240)
PHONE..................614 293-4509
Fax: 614 293-4726
Benjamin Sun, *Director*
EMP: 40
SALES (est): 1.1MM **Privately Held**
SIC: 8011 Offices & clinics of medical doctors

(G-7198)
CAREER PARTNERS INTL LLC (PA)
20 S 3rd St Ste 210 (43215-4206)
PHONE..................919 401-4260
Terry Gillis, *Vice Ch Bd*
Doug Matthews, *President*
Michael Hazell, *Managing Prtnr*
Karen Romeo, *Senior VP*
Sue Rowley, *Senior VP*
EMP: 1600 EST: 1987
SALES (est): 80.2MM **Privately Held**
WEB: www.cpiworld.com
SIC: 8742 General management consultant

(G-7199)
CARFAGNAS INCORPORATED
Also Called: Carfagna's Cleve Meats
1405 E Dblin Granville Rd (43229-3357)
PHONE..................614 846-6340
Fax: 614 846-0937
Edward Carfagna, *CEO*
Dino Carfagna, *President*
Cecilia Carfagna, *Vice Pres*
Sam Carfagna, *Treasurer*
Julie Riley, *Financial Exec*
EMP: 50
SQ FT: 9,000
SALES (est): 6.4MM **Privately Held**
WEB: www.carfagnas.com
SIC: 5411 5147 Grocery stores, independent; meats & meat products

(G-7200)
CARLILE PATCHEN & MURPHY LLP (PA)
366 E Broad St (43215-3819)
PHONE..................614 228-6135
Fax: 614 221-0216
Ricky Hollenbaugh, *Partner*
Michael Igo, *Partner*
James R Moats, *Partner*
Kathy Benjamin, *Counsel*
Andrew J Federico, *Counsel*
EMP: 70
SQ FT: 24,000
SALES (est): 16.9MM **Privately Held**
WEB: www.cpmlaw.com
SIC: 8111 General practice law office

(G-7201)
CARLISLE HOTELS INC
Also Called: Hampton Inn
5625 Trabue Rd (43228-9567)
PHONE..................614 851-5599
Fax: 614 851-5590
Bikha Patel, *Branch Mgr*
EMP: 47
SALES (corp-wide): 146.8MM **Privately Held**
WEB: www.cheapaccommodation.com
SIC: 7011 Hotels & motels
HQ: Carlisle Hotels, Inc.
    263 Wagner Pl
    Memphis TN 38103
    901 526-5000

(G-7202)
CARPENTER LIPPS & LELAND LLP (PA)
280 N High St Ste 1300 (43215-7515)
PHONE..................614 365-4100
Michael H Carpenter, *Managing Prtnr*
Michael N Beekhuizen, *Counsel*
Jason Bennett, *Info Tech Mgr*
Mariann Fetty, *Director*
Jeffrey A Lipps, *Director*
EMP: 50
SALES (est): 8.3MM **Privately Held**
WEB: www.carpenterlipps.com
SIC: 8111 General practice law office

(G-7203)
CARRIER INDUSTRIES INC
1700 Georgesville Rd (43228-3620)
PHONE..................614 851-6363
Myron P Shevell, *Branch Mgr*
EMP: 394
SALES (corp-wide): 30.8MM **Privately Held**
SIC: 4213 4212 Trucking, except local; local trucking, without storage
PA: Carrier Industries, Inc.
    1-71 North Ave E
    Elizabeth NJ 07201
    908 965-0100

(G-7204)
CASKEY CLEANING CO
Also Called: Caskey Cleaners
47 W Gates St (43206-3441)
PHONE..................614 443-7448

Fax: 614 449-4065
Lloyd Hill, *Principal*
EMP: 67
SQ FT: 50,000
SALES (est): 2.3MM **Privately Held**
SIC: 7216 Cleaning & dyeing, except rugs

(G-7205)
CASLEO CORPORATION
Also Called: Global Meals
2741 E 4th Ave (43219-2824)
PHONE.....................614 252-6508
Nataliya Krylova, *CEO*
Olga Silvnyak, *President*
EMP: 30
SALES (est): 600K **Privately Held**
SIC: 8322 Meal delivery program

(G-7206)
CASS INFORMATION SYSTEMS INC
2644 Kirkwood Hyw Newark (43218)
PHONE.....................614 839-4503
Kathy Callanan, *Branch Mgr*
EMP: 40
SALES (corp-wide): 137.4MM **Publicly Held**
SIC: 4813 Telephone communication, except radio
PA: Cass Information Systems, Inc.
12444 Powerscort Dr # 550
Saint Louis MO 63131
314 506-5500

(G-7207)
CASS INFORMATION SYSTEMS INC
Also Called: Cass Logistics
2675 Corporate Exchange (43231-1662)
P.O. Box 182447 (43218-2447)
PHONE.....................614 766-2277
Fax: 614 791-3300
Harold Ellis, *Opers Mgr*
Jeff Nini, *CPA*
Monique Winston, *Human Res Mgr*
Paula Igo, *Human Resources*
Lani Wollam, *Accounts Mgr*
EMP: 131
SALES (corp-wide): 137.4MM **Publicly Held**
WEB: www.cassinfo.com
SIC: 7389 Personal service agents, brokers & bureaus
PA: Cass Information Systems, Inc.
12444 Powerscort Dr # 550
Saint Louis MO 63131
314 506-5500

(G-7208)
CASSADY VLG APRTMENTS OHIO LLC
3089 Cassady Village Trl (43219-3501)
PHONE.....................216 520-1250
Frnak Sinito,
EMP: 99
SALES (est): 789.1K **Privately Held**
SIC: 6513 Apartment building operators

(G-7209)
CASTO COMMUNITIES CNSTR LTD
191 W Nationwide Blvd # 200 (43215-2568)
PHONE.....................614 228-8545
Don M Casto, *Branch Mgr*
EMP: 381
SALES (corp-wide): 18.8MM **Privately Held**
SIC: 6512 Commercial & industrial building operation
PA: Casto Communities Construction Limited
191 W Nationwide Blvd # 200
Columbus OH 43215
614 228-5331

(G-7210)
CATHOLIC DIOCESE OF COLUMBUS
Also Called: Bishop Ready High School
707 Salisbury Rd (43204-2449)
PHONE.....................614 276-5263
Fax: 614 276-5116
Celene Seamen, *Principal*
Zhiwei Bi, *Librarian*
Matt Brickner, *Director*
Mike Rossetti, *Athletic Dir*
Michelle Kelly, *Asst Director*
EMP: 55
SALES (corp-wide): 6.7MM **Privately Held**
WEB: www.colscss.org
SIC: 8211 7929 Catholic elementary & secondary schools; entertainers & entertainment groups
PA: Catholic Diocese Of Columbus
198 E Broad St
Columbus OH 43215
614 224-2251

(G-7211)
CATHOLIC DIOCESE OF COLUMBUS
197 E Gay St Ste 1 (43215-3229)
PHONE.....................614 221-5891
Don Wisler, *President*
Tom Berg, *Director*
Robert Sisson, *Associate Dir*
Kellie Shonk, *Admin Asst*
EMP: 35
SALES (corp-wide): 6.7MM **Privately Held**
WEB: www.colscss.org
SIC: 8322 Social service center
PA: Catholic Diocese Of Columbus
198 E Broad St
Columbus OH 43215
614 224-2251

(G-7212)
CATHOLIC SOCIAL SERVICES INC
197 E Gay St (43215-3229)
PHONE.....................614 221-5891
Fax: 614 228-1125
Rachel Lustig, *President*
Sabree Akinyele, *Vice Pres*
Laura Campise, *Director*
Barbara McKenzie, *Director*
Ramona Reyes, *Director*
EMP: 85
SALES: 5.6MM **Privately Held**
SIC: 8322 Social service center

(G-7213)
CBC COMPANIES INC
1691 Nw Professional Plz (43220-3866)
PHONE.....................614 222-4343
Glenn Fitzgerald, *General Mgr*
Eric Duhon, *Vice Pres*
Steven Stauch, *Vice Pres*
William Webb, *Vice Pres*
Karenann Barth, *Opers Spvr*
EMP: 30
SQ FT: 19,560
SALES (corp-wide): 279.4MM **Privately Held**
SIC: 7323 Credit reporting services
PA: Cbc Companies, Inc.
250 E Broad St Fl 21
Columbus OH 43215
614 222-4343

(G-7214)
CBC COMPANIES INC
1651 Nw Professional Plz (43220-3866)
PHONE.....................614 538-6100
Fax: 614 538-6102
Gary Hughes, *Engineer*
Scott Webb, *Engineer*
Douglas Manger, *Sales Staff*
Jonathan Price, *Manager*
Michael Frabott, *Manager*
EMP: 80
SALES (corp-wide): 279.4MM **Privately Held**
SIC: 7323 7374 Credit bureau & agency; data processing & preparation
PA: Cbc Companies, Inc.
250 E Broad St Fl 21
Columbus OH 43215
614 222-4343

(G-7215)
CBCINNOVIS INTERNATIONAL INC (HQ)
250 E Broad St Fl 21 (43215-3770)
PHONE.....................614 222-4343
Jonathan Price, *President*
Leland Haydon, *Sr Corp Ofcr*
Bryan Stitt, *Accounting Mgr*
Kelley Masters, *Human Resources*
Pam Lahr, *VP Sales*
EMP: 41
SALES (est): 10.7MM
SALES (corp-wide): 279.4MM **Privately Held**
SIC: 7323 Credit bureau & agency
PA: Cbc Companies, Inc.
250 E Broad St Fl 21
Columbus OH 43215
614 222-4343

(G-7216)
CBRE INC
200 Civic Center Dr Ste 8 (43215-4234)
PHONE.....................614 438-5488
Barbara Frost, *Architect*
Rob Click, *Manager*
EMP: 80
SALES (corp-wide): 14.2B **Publicly Held**
HQ: Cbre, Inc.
400 S Hope St Ste 25
Los Angeles CA 90071
310 477-5876

(G-7217)
CD1025
Also Called: WWCD
1036 S Front St (43206-3402)
PHONE.....................614 221-9923
Fax: 614 227-0021
Randy Malloy, *President*
Leslie Edwards, *Sales Staff*
EMP: 25
SALES: 106.5K **Privately Held**
SIC: 4832 Radio broadcasting stations

(G-7218)
CDC MANAGEMENT CO
4949 Freeway Dr E (43229-5401)
PHONE.....................614 781-0216
Paul Jenkins Jr, *President*
Cindy Axthelm, *VP Opers*
Jim Stahl, *Finance Mgr*
EMP: 250
SQ FT: 24,019
SALES (est): 12MM **Privately Held**
SIC: 8741 5181 Management services; beer & ale

(G-7219)
CDM SMITH INC
445 Hutchinson Ave # 820 (43235-8633)
PHONE.....................614 847-8340
Rusty Neff, *Vice Pres*
Trent Branson, *Project Mgr*
Erin Stachler, *Project Engr*
Tom Jedlinsky, *Sales Executive*
Derek Wride, *Sr Project Mgr*
EMP: 33
SALES (corp-wide): 1.1B **Privately Held**
WEB: www.cdm.com
SIC: 8748 Environmental consultant
PA: Cdm Smith Inc
75 State St Ste 701
Boston MA 02109
617 452-6000

(G-7220)
CELLCO PARTNERSHIP
Also Called: Verizon Wireless
3985 Morse Xing (43219-6040)
PHONE.....................614 476-9786
Fax: 614 476-9127
Julia M Campbell, *Accounts Mgr*
EMP: 71
SALES (corp-wide): 120B **Publicly Held**
SIC: 4812 Cellular telephone services
HQ: Cellco Partnership
1 Verizon Way
Basking Ridge NJ 07920

(G-7221)
CELLCO PARTNERSHIP
Also Called: Verizon
2180 Henderson Rd (43220-2320)
PHONE.....................614 459-7200
Mike Demko, *Branch Mgr*
EMP: 25
SALES (corp-wide): 126B **Publicly Held**
SIC: 4812 5999 Cellular telephone services; mobile telephones & equipment
HQ: Cellco Partnership
1 Verizon Way
Basking Ridge NJ 07920

(G-7222)
CENTENNIAL PRSRVTION GROUP LLC
600 N Cassady Ave Ste D (43219-2789)
PHONE.....................614 238-0730
Matt Wolf, *CEO*
Susan Martinez, *Administration*
EMP: 38
SALES: 4MM **Privately Held**
SIC: 1741 Masonry & other stonework

(G-7223)
CENTER FOR COGNITIVE AND BEH (PA)
Also Called: Kevin D Arnold
4624 Sawmill Rd (43220-2247)
PHONE.....................614 459-4490
Fax: 614 457-3656
Kevin D Arnold, *President*
Shauna Springer, *Author*
EMP: 30
SALES (est): 2.1MM **Privately Held**
WEB: www.ccbtcolumbus.com
SIC: 8049 Clinical psychologist

(G-7224)
CENTER FOR COGNITV BEHAV PSYCH
4624 Sawmill Rd (43220-2247)
PHONE.....................614 459-4490
Sarah Shearer, *Council Mbr*
EMP: 30
SALES (est): 52K **Privately Held**
SIC: 8322 Individual & family services

(G-7225)
CENTER FOR EATING DISORDERS
Also Called: Center For Balanced Living
8001 Ravines Edge Ct # 201 (43235-5423)
PHONE.....................614 896-8222
Fax: 614 293-9549
Laura Hill, *Principal*
Lori Johnson, *Executive*
Patricia Forman, *Psychiatry*
EMP: 42
SALES (est): 3MM **Privately Held**
SIC: 8052 8731 Home for the mentally retarded, with health care; medical research, commercial

(G-7226)
CENTER OF VOCTNL ALTRNTVS MNTL (PA)
Also Called: Cova
3770 N High St (43214-3525)
PHONE.....................614 294-7117
Fax: 614 294-7443
Judy Braun, *President*
Joe Hauser, *Controller*
Martita Dougherty, *Accountant*
Janee Jenkins, *Program Mgr*
Jill Jones, *Program Dir*
EMP: 63
SQ FT: 3,500
SALES: 3MM **Privately Held**
SIC: 8331 Vocational rehabilitation agency

(G-7227)
CENTRAL CMNTY HSE OF COLUMBUS (PA)
1150 E Main St (43205-1902)
P.O. Box 7047 (43205-0047)
PHONE.....................614 253-7267
Fax: 614 252-9164
Tammy Hall, *Financial Exec*
Pamela McCarthy, *Director*
Jackie Calderone, *Director*
Peggy Roberts, *Executive Asst*
EMP: 40
SQ FT: 1,500
SALES: 1.6MM **Privately Held**
SIC: 8322 Social service center

(G-7228)
CENTRAL OH AREA AGENCY ON AGNG
Also Called: Passport
3776 S High St (43207-4012)
PHONE.....................614 645-7250
Fax: 614 645-3884
Patty Callahan, *Manager*
Amy Slocum, *Manager*
Cindy Farson, *Director*

Columbus - Franklin County (G-7229)

EMP: 150
SALES (est): 7.4MM Privately Held
WEB: www.coaaa.org
SIC: 8322 Senior citizens' center or association

(G-7229)
CENTRAL OHIO BUILDING CO INC
Also Called: Thor Construction
3756 Agler Rd (43219-3699)
PHONE..................................614 475-6392
Fax: 614 475-9827
Otis Wilbur Ronk, *President*
Jay Watkins, *President*
Sol Morton Isaac, *Principal*
C F O'Brien, *Principal*
William N Postlewaite, *Principal*
EMP: 35
SQ FT: 2,000
SALES (est): 11.1MM Privately Held
SIC: 1542 1541 Institutional building construction; industrial buildings, new construction

(G-7230)
CENTRAL OHIO HOSPITALISTS
3525 Olentangy River Rd # 4330 (43214-3937)
PHONE..................................614 255-6900
Joseph A Mack, *President*
Nicholas Nelson, *Treasurer*
Pamela Boyers, *Exec Dir*
John N Kwak, *Director*
EMP: 39
SALES (est): 2.2MM Privately Held
SIC: 7363 Medical help service

(G-7231)
CENTRAL OHIO MEDICAL TEXTILES
Also Called: COMTEX
575 Harmon Ave (43223-2449)
PHONE..................................614 453-9274
Ken Boock, *Chairman*
Myles Noel, *COO*
Becky Davis, *CFO*
Alex Boeriu, *Manager*
Kevin Kozak, *Manager*
EMP: 150
SQ FT: 100,000
SALES: 23.4MM Privately Held
WEB: www.comtex.com
SIC: 7219 Laundry, except power & coin-operated

(G-7232)
CENTRAL OHIO NUTRITION CENTER (PA)
Also Called: Conci
648 Taylor Rd (43230-3202)
PHONE..................................614 864-7225
Fax: 614 864-2207
Edward Baltes MD, *President*
J T Broyles MD, *Vice Pres*
Richard A Lutes MD, *Vice Pres*
Robert K May MD, *Vice Pres*
Karla Reedy, *Office Mgr*
EMP: 35
SQ FT: 2,500
SALES (est): 3MM Privately Held
WEB: www.buddywhite.com
SIC: 8049 Nutritionist

(G-7233)
CENTRAL OHIO POISON CENTER
Also Called: Childrens Hospital
700 Childrens Dr (43205-2664)
PHONE..................................800 222-1222
Fax: 614 221-2672
EMP: 30 EST: 1958
SQ FT: 19,950
SALES (est): 1.6MM Privately Held
WEB: www.copeds.org
SIC: 8099 Health/Allied Services

(G-7234)
CENTRAL OHIO PRIMARY CARE
770 Jasonway Ave Ste G2 (43214-4333)
PHONE..................................614 459-3687
Laura Dureu, *Office Mgr*
Drexdal Pratt, *Branch Mgr*
David Neiger, *Med Doctor*
EMP: 37 Privately Held
SIC: 8011 General & family practice, physician/surgeon
PA: Central Ohio Primary Care Physicians, Inc.
570 Polaris Pkwy Ste 250
Westerville OH 43082

(G-7235)
CENTRAL OHIO PRIMARY CARE
4885 Olentangy River Rd # 2 (43214-1952)
PHONE..................................614 451-1551
EMP: 43 Privately Held
SIC: 8011 Physical medicine, physician/surgeon
PA: Central Ohio Primary Care Physicians, Inc.
570 Polaris Pkwy Ste 250
Westerville OH 43082

(G-7236)
CENTRAL OHIO PRIMARY CARE
4885 Olentangy River Rd (43214-1952)
PHONE..................................614 268-6555
John W Wulf MD, *CEO*
Thomas Blosser, *Family Practiti*
EMP: 50 Privately Held
SIC: 8049 Acupuncturist
PA: Central Ohio Primary Care Physicians, Inc.
570 Polaris Pkwy Ste 250
Westerville OH 43082

(G-7237)
CENTRAL OHIO PRIMARY CARE
Also Called: Capital City Medical Assoc
2489 Stelzer Rd 101 (43219-4007)
PHONE..................................614 473-1300
Prisca Maynard, *Med Doctor*
Sheryl Moyer, *Manager*
Letheria Ayers, *Manager*
Kinika Hartley, *Nurse Practr*
EMP: 30 Privately Held
WEB: www.copcp.com
SIC: 8011 Internal medicine, physician/surgeon
PA: Central Ohio Primary Care Physicians, Inc.
570 Polaris Pkwy Ste 250
Westerville OH 43082

(G-7238)
CENTRAL OHIO PRIMARY CARE
3535 Olentangy River Rd (43214-3908)
PHONE..................................614 268-8164
Jonathan Matthew Enlow, *Principal*
Jonathan Thorne, *Research*
Dave Condon, *Med Doctor*
Donald Deep, *Med Doctor*
Ronald C Miller MD, *Med Doctor*
EMP: 105 Privately Held
SIC: 8011 Internal medicine, physician/surgeon
PA: Central Ohio Primary Care Physicians, Inc.
570 Polaris Pkwy Ste 250
Westerville OH 43082

(G-7239)
CENTRAL OHIO PRIMARY CARE
4030 Henderson Rd (43220-2287)
PHONE..................................614 442-7550
Fax: 614 442-4100
John Leff, *Med Doctor*
EMP: 35 Privately Held
SIC: 8049 8011 Acupuncturist; offices & clinics of medical doctors
PA: Central Ohio Primary Care Physicians, Inc.
570 Polaris Pkwy Ste 250
Westerville OH 43082

(G-7240)
CENTRAL OHIO SURGICAL ASSOC (PA)
750 Mount Carmel Mall # 380 (43222-1589)
PHONE..................................614 222-8000
Fax: 614 228-7381
Jeff Turner, *President*
Pamela Chambers, *Division Mgr*
Pam Abraham, *Office Mgr*
Ramona Penland, *Office Mgr*
Dr Ghalib A Hannun, *Med Doctor*
EMP: 31
SQ FT: 4,000
SALES (est): 4.6MM Privately Held
WEB: www.midohiosurgical.com
SIC: 8011 Cardiologist & cardio-vascular specialist; surgeon

(G-7241)
CENTRAL OHIO TRANSIT AUTHORITY
1333 Fields Ave (43201-2908)
PHONE..................................614 275-5800
Doug Moore, *Branch Mgr*
EMP: 143
SALES (est): 3.2MM
SALES (corp-wide): 64.7MM Privately Held
SIC: 4111 Bus line operations
PA: Central Ohio Transit Authority
33 N High St
Columbus OH 43215
614 275-5800

(G-7242)
CENTRAL OHIO TRANSIT AUTHORITY (PA)
Also Called: Cota
33 N High St (43215-3076)
PHONE..................................614 275-5800
Fax: 614 228-4106
W Curtis Stitt, *President*
Carol Wise, *COO*
Megan Kleinman, *Counsel*
Clinton Forbes, *Vice Pres*
Laura Koprowski, *Vice Pres*
EMP: 750
SQ FT: 390,000
SALES (est): 64.7MM Privately Held
WEB: www.cota.com
SIC: 4111 Bus line operations

(G-7243)
CENTRAL OHIO YOUTH FOR CHRIST
5000 Arlington Centre Blv (43220-3082)
P.O. Box 14804 (43214-0804)
PHONE..................................614 732-5260
Fax: 614 268-4110
Corey Caputo, *Opers Mgr*
Scott Arnold, *Director*
Bryan Brookes, *Director*
Greg Rodgers, *Director*
Jack Strack, *Director*
EMP: 41
SQ FT: 1,000
SALES: 2.7MM Privately Held
SIC: 8641 8322 Youth organizations; youth center

(G-7244)
CERTIFIED OIL INC
949 King Ave (43212-2662)
P.O. Box 182439 (43218-2439)
PHONE..................................614 421-7500
Peter Lacaillade, *President*
Carol Dillard, *Shareholder*
EMP: 100
SQ FT: 24,500
SALES (est): 5.6MM
SALES (corp-wide): 50.2MM Privately Held
SIC: 4212 Petroleum haulage, local
PA: Certified Oil Corporation
949 King Ave
Columbus OH 43212
614 421-7500

(G-7245)
CEVA LOGISTICS US INC
Also Called: Eagle USA Airfreight
2727 London Groveport Rd (43207)
PHONE..................................614 482-5107
Fax: 614 491-7844
Larry Savage, *Manager*
EMP: 50 Publicly Held
WEB: www.tntlogistics.com
SIC: 4731 Freight forwarding
HQ: Ceva Logistics U.S., Inc.
15350 Vickery Dr
Houston TX 77032
281 618-3100

(G-7246)
CGI TECHNOLOGIES SOLUTIONS INC
88 E Broad St Ste 1425 (43215-3506)
PHONE..................................614 228-2245
Nola Haug, *Manager*
EMP: 56
SALES (corp-wide): 8.6B Privately Held
SIC: 7379 Computer related consulting services
HQ: Cgi Technologies And Solutions Inc.
11325 Random Hills Rd
Fairfax VA 22030
703 267-8000

(G-7247)
CH RELTY IV/CLMBUS PARTNERS LP
Also Called: Doubletree Columbus Hotel
175 Hutchinson Ave (43235-1413)
PHONE..................................614 885-3334
Jayson Martin, *Marketing Staff*
Dan Ouellette, *Manager*
EMP: 100
SQ FT: 44,962 Privately Held
SIC: 7011 6512 5813 5812 Hotels; non-residential building operators; drinking places; eating places
PA: Ch Realty Iv/Columbus Partners, L.P.
3819 Maple Ave
Dallas TX 75219

(G-7248)
CH ROBINSON COMPANY INC
Also Called: C.H. Robinson 123
800 Yard St Ste 200 (43212-3882)
PHONE..................................614 933-5100
Scott Norris, *General Mgr*
EMP: 35
SALES (corp-wide): 14.8B Publicly Held
SIC: 4731 Freight transportation arrangement
HQ: C.H. Robinson Company, Inc.
14701 Charlson Rd Ste 200
Eden Prairie MN 55347

(G-7249)
CH2M HILL INC
2 Easton Oval Ste 125 (43219-6042)
PHONE..................................614 888-3100
Fax: 216 623-1624
Ian Hammons, *Electrical Engi*
Hansen Tjioeng, *Electrical Engi*
B Casey, *Branch Mgr*
EMP: 41
SALES (corp-wide): 10B Publicly Held
SIC: 8711 Engineering services
HQ: Ch2m Hill, Inc.
9191 S Jamaica St
Englewood CO 80112
303 771-0900

(G-7250)
CHAD DOWNING
Also Called: Point Plus Personnel
679 Rose Way (43230-5806)
PHONE..................................614 532-5127
Chad Downing, *Owner*
EMP: 25
SALES (est): 1MM Privately Held
SIC: 7361 Executive placement

(G-7251)
CHAMPAIGN RESIDENTIAL SERVICES
1350 W 5th Ave Ste 230 (43212-2907)
PHONE..................................614 481-5550
Fax: 614 481-5557
Scott Delong, *CFO*
Dan Johnson, *Exec Dir*
EMP: 35 EST: 1976
SALES (est): 840.1K Privately Held
SIC: 8322 Social services for the handicapped

(G-7252)
CHANGE HEALTHCARE TECH ENABLED
Also Called: Midwest Physicians
3535 Olentangy River Rd (43214-3908)
PHONE..................................614 566-5861
Fax: 614 566-6792
Scott Henderson, *Med Doctor*
Bev Myers, *Manager*
Phillip Shaffer, *Manager*
Nancy Buel, *Director*
EMP: 64

SALES (corp-wide): 198.5B **Publicly Held**
SIC: **8641** 8062 Civic social & fraternal associations; general medical & surgical hospitals
HQ: Change Healthcare Technology Enabled Services, Llc
5995 Windward Pkwy
Alpharetta GA 30005
770 237-4300

(G-7253)
CHASE MANHATTAN MORTGAGE CORP
200 E Campus View Blvd # 3 (43235-4678)
PHONE................614 422-7982
Patricia Caidy, *Assoc VP*
Caidy Patricia, *Branch Mgr*
EMP: 108
SALES (corp-wide): 99.6B **Publicly Held**
SIC: **6162** Mortgage bankers
HQ: Chase Manhattan Mortgage Corp
343 Thornall St Ste 7
Edison NJ 08837
732 205-0600

(G-7254)
CHASE MANHATTAN MORTGAGE CORP
3415 Vision Dr (43219-6009)
PHONE................614 422-6900
Fax: 614 422-6770
Theresa Wise, *Assistant VP*
Beverly Berry, *Branch Mgr*
Gary Gough, *Manager*
Kendall Kowalski, *CTO*
EMP: 3000
SALES (corp-wide): 99.6B **Publicly Held**
SIC: **6162** Mortgage bankers & correspondents
HQ: Chase Manhattan Mortgage Corp
343 Thornall St Ste 7
Edison NJ 08837
732 205-0600

(G-7255)
CHESROWN OLDSMOBILE GMC INC
Also Called: Chessrown Kia Town
4675 Karl Rd (43229-6456)
P.O. Box 160, Delaware (43015-0160)
PHONE................614 846-3040
Jim Gill, *President*
Terry Lynn, *Office Mgr*
EMP: 45
SQ FT: 55,000
SALES (est): 10.8MM **Privately Held**
WEB: www.chesrown.com
SIC: **5511** 7532 7515 5531 Automobiles, new & used; pickups, new & used; top & body repair & paint shops; passenger car leasing; automotive & home supply stores; used car dealers

(G-7256)
CHESTNUT HILL MANAGEMENT CO
Also Called: Inn At Chestnut Hill, The
5055 Thompson Rd (43230-6336)
PHONE................614 855-3700
Fax: 614 855-1328
Don Alspach, *President*
David Alspach, *Vice Pres*
Sandra Burton, *Persnl Mgr*
Todd Gabel, *Exec Dir*
Kim Waits, *Exec Dir*
EMP: 90
SALES (est): 2.6MM **Privately Held**
SIC: **8082** Home health care services

(G-7257)
CHICN FIXINS INC
2041 Pine Needle Ct (43232-2664)
PHONE................614 929-8431
Deric Butler, *CEO*
EMP: 35
SQ FT: 1,500
SALES (est): 547.3K **Privately Held**
SIC: **0251** Broiler, fryer & roaster chickens

(G-7258)
CHILD DVLPMNT CNCL OF FRNKLN (PA)
300 E Spring St (43215-2630)
PHONE................614 221-1709

Mattie James, *President*
Debbie Eiland, *Area Mgr*
Dave Proctor, *Area Mgr*
Brenda Rivers, *Senior VP*
Marlita Bartlett, *Vice Pres*
EMP: 60
SQ FT: 2,300
SALES: 26.2MM **Privately Held**
SIC: **8351** Head start center, except in conjunction with school

(G-7259)
CHILD DVLPMNT CNCL OF FRNKLN
Also Called: Cdc Capital Park Head St Ctr
2150 Agler Rd (43224-4523)
PHONE................614 416-5178
Fax: 614 337-3831
Carlene Ibenegbu, *Branch Mgr*
EMP: 30
SALES (corp-wide): 26.2MM **Privately Held**
SIC: **8351** Head start center, except in conjunction with school
PA: The Child Development Council Of Franklin County
300 E Spring St
Columbus OH 43215
614 221-1709

(G-7260)
CHILDREN FIRST INC
Also Called: CHILDREN FIRST DAY CARE
77 S High St Fl 7 (43215-6108)
PHONE................614 466-0945
Fax: 614 728-8355
Deanna Kropf, *Director*
EMP: 30
SQ FT: 9,000
SALES: 1MM **Privately Held**
SIC: **8351** Child day care services

(G-7261)
CHILDRENS HOMECARE SERVICES
455 E Mound St (43215-5595)
PHONE................614 355-1100
Fax: 614 460-6640
Heidi Drake, *Director*
EMP: 150
SQ FT: 7,000
SALES (est): 2.5MM
SALES (corp-wide): 1.3B **Privately Held**
SIC: **8082** 8322 Home health care services; individual & family services
PA: Nationwide Children's Hospital
700 Childrens Dr
Columbus OH 43205
614 722-2000

(G-7262)
CHILDRENS HOSPITAL FOUNDATION
700 Childrens Dr (43205-2664)
P.O. Box 16810 (43216-6810)
PHONE................614 355-0888
Fax: 614 722-6130
James Digan, *President*
Kevin Welch, *Vice Pres*
Tim Robinson, *Controller*
Jose Balderrama, *VP Human Res*
Katalin Koranyi, *Med Doctor*
EMP: 31
SALES (est): 3.8MM **Privately Held**
SIC: **8399** Fund raising organization, non-fee basis

(G-7263)
CHILDRENS HUNGER ALLIANCE (PA)
1105 Schrock Rd Ste 505 (43229-1181)
PHONE................614 341-7700
Jeff Hastings, *Principal*
Carol Looman, *Regional Mgr*
Stella Marshall, *Regional Mgr*
Shelly Beiting, *Senior VP*
Erin Flynn, *Senior VP*
EMP: 85
SQ FT: 5,900
SALES: 13.5MM **Privately Held**
SIC: **8322** 8399 Social service center; advocacy group

(G-7264)
CHILDRENS SURGERY CENTER INC
700 Childrens Dr (43205-2666)
PHONE................614 722-2920
D Alan Tingley, *Administration*
EMP: 60
SQ FT: 25,000
SALES (est): 3.2MM **Privately Held**
SIC: **8011** Ambulatory surgical center

(G-7265)
CHILLER LLC
3600 Chiller Ln (43219-6026)
PHONE................614 475-7575
Fax: 614 418-1990
Andy Deyo, *President*
Keith Newland, *Manager*
EMP: 50
SALES (corp-wide): 11.7MM **Privately Held**
WEB: www.chiller.com
SIC: **7999** Ice skating rink operation
PA: Chiller Llc
7001 Dublin Park Dr
Dublin OH 43016
614 764-1000

(G-7266)
CHOICE RECOVERY INC
1550 Old Henderson Rd S100 (43220-3662)
PHONE................614 358-9900
Chad Silverstein, *President*
Traci Jones, *Human Res Dir*
Tracy Jones, *Human Resources*
Meagen Lane, *VP Sales*
Joshua Atkinson, *Consultant*
EMP: 65
SALES: 15MM **Privately Held**
SIC: **7322** Collection agency, except real estate

(G-7267)
CHOICES FOR VCTIMS DOM VOLENCE
770 E Main St (43205-1715)
PHONE................614 258-6080
Gail Heller, *Exec Dir*
EMP: 60
SQ FT: 2,200
SALES: 1.1MM **Privately Held**
SIC: **8361** 8322 Residential care; individual & family services

(G-7268)
CHRISTIAN MISSIONARY ALLIANCE
Also Called: Sunshine Nursery School
3750 Henderson Rd (43220-2236)
PHONE................614 457-4085
Fax: 614 442-8472
Jennifer Rupert, *Director*
Doug Peterson, *Director*
EMP: 27
SALES (corp-wide): 49.4MM **Privately Held**
WEB: www.fac-columbus.org
SIC: **8351** Child day care services
PA: The Christian Missionary Alliance
8595 Explorer Dr
Colorado Springs CO 80920
719 599-5999

(G-7269)
CHRISTIAN WORTHINGTON VLG INC
165 Highbluffs Blvd (43235-1484)
PHONE................614 846-6076
Fax: 614 842-9541
Joan Yasses, *Manager*
Randall Richardson, *Exec Dir*
Richardson Randy, *Director*
Brian Cooper, *Administration*
EMP: 33
SALES: 3.8MM **Privately Held**
SIC: **8051** Skilled nursing care facilities

(G-7270)
CHRISTOPHER C KAEDING
2050 Kenny Rd Ste 3100 (43221-3502)
PHONE................614 293-3600
Christopher Kaeding, *Partner*
Dr Grant Jones, *Partner*
EMP: 50

SALES (est): 1.2MM **Privately Held**
SIC: **8011** Physicians' office, including specialists

(G-7271)
CHUTE GERDEMAN INC
455 S Ludlow St (43215-5647)
PHONE................614 469-1001
Fax: 614 469-1002
Brian Shafley, *CEO*
Jay Highland, *COO*
Wendy Johnson, *COO*
George Nauman, *Exec VP*
Elle C Gerdeman, *Vice Pres*
EMP: 64
SQ FT: 19,000
SALES (est): 9.1MM
SALES (corp-wide): 9.5MM **Privately Held**
WEB: www.chutegerdeman.com
SIC: **7389** 8712 Interior designer; architectural services
PA: Foote, Cone & Belding, Inc.
875 N Michigan Ave # 1850
Chicago IL 60611
312 425-5626

(G-7272)
CINEMARK USA INC
Also Called: Cinemark Carriage Pl Movies 12
2570 Bethel Rd (43220-2225)
PHONE................614 538-0403
Christa Sexton, *Manager*
EMP: 30 **Publicly Held**
SIC: **7832** Motion picture theaters, except drive-in
HQ: Cinemark Usa, Inc.
3900 Dallas Pkwy Ste 500
Plano TX 75093
972 665-1000

(G-7273)
CINEMARK USA INC
Also Called: Cinemark Movies 10
5275 Westpointe Plaza Dr (43228-9131)
PHONE................614 529-8547
Kevin Smith, *Manager*
EMP: 25 **Publicly Held**
SIC: **7832** Motion picture theaters, except drive-in
HQ: Cinemark Usa, Inc.
3900 Dallas Pkwy Ste 500
Plano TX 75093
972 665-1000

(G-7274)
CINTAS CORPORATION NO 2
1300 Boltonfield St (43228-3696)
P.O. Box 28246 (43228-0246)
PHONE................614 878-7313
Fax: 614 878-8965
John Borak, *Branch Mgr*
EMP: 98
SALES (corp-wide): 5.3B **Publicly Held**
WEB: www.cintas-corp.com
SIC: **7213** 7218 Uniform supply; industrial launderers
HQ: Cintas Corporation No. 2
6800 Cintas Blvd
Mason OH 45040

(G-7275)
CIRCLE BUILDING SERVICES INC
742 Harmon Ave (43223-2450)
P.O. Box 1473 (43216-1473)
PHONE................014 228-6090
Fax: 614 228-7411
Daniel M Litzinger, *President*
EMP: 90
SALES (est): 3.2MM **Privately Held**
WEB: www.circlebuildingservices.com
SIC: **7349** Building cleaning service

(G-7276)
CIRCLE S TRANSPORT INC
1008 Arcaro Dr (43230-3855)
PHONE................614 207-2184
Edward Saraniero, *President*
Lorana Basham, *Manager*
EMP: 45
SALES (est): 5.7MM **Privately Held**
SIC: **4213** 4212 Trucking, except local; local trucking, without storage

Columbus - Franklin County (G-7277)

(G-7277)
CITICORP CREDIT SERVICES INC
1500 Boltonfield St (43228-3669)
PHONE.................................212 559-1000
Ken Vanderoef, *Manager*
EMP: 303
SALES (corp-wide): 71.4B **Publicly Held**
SIC: 7389 Credit card service
HQ: Citicorp Credit Services, Inc.
One Court Square 25th Flr
Long Island City NY 11120
718 248-3192

(G-7278)
CITY OF COLUMBUS
Also Called: Public Utlties-Electricity Div
3500 Indianola Ave (43214-3702)
PHONE.................................614 645-7627
Kris Lower, *Manager*
Jeffery Hubbard, *Administration*
EMP: 120
SQ FT: 6,176 **Privately Held**
WEB: www.cityofcolumbus.org
SIC: 9631 4931 Regulation, administration of utilities; ; electric & other services combined
PA: City Of Columbus
90 W Broad St Rm B33
Columbus OH 43215
614 645-7671

(G-7279)
CITY OF COLUMBUS
Also Called: Dept of Public Utilities
910 Dublin Rd Ste 4050 (43215-1169)
PHONE.................................614 645-7490
Fax: 614 645-5814
Pamela Davis, *Purchasing*
Rita Stone, *Office Mgr*
Danella Pettenski, *Branch Mgr*
Thomas Finnegan, *Manager*
Jill Tapitch, *Manager*
EMP: 35 **Privately Held**
SIC: 4941 Water supply
PA: City Of Columbus
90 W Broad St Rm B33
Columbus OH 43215
614 645-7671

(G-7280)
CITY OF COLUMBUS
Also Called: Health Dept
3433 Agler Rd Ste 2800 (43219-3389)
PHONE.................................614 645-1600
Kate Ondra, *Administration*
EMP: 25 **Privately Held**
WEB: www.cityofcolumbus.org
SIC: 8011 9431 General & family practice, physician/surgeon; administration of public health programs;
PA: City Of Columbus
90 W Broad St Rm B33
Columbus OH 43215
614 645-7671

(G-7281)
CITY OF COLUMBUS
Also Called: Health Dept
1875 Morse Rd 235 (43229-6603)
PHONE.................................614 645-3072
EMP: 55 **Privately Held**
WEB: www.cityofcolumbus.org
SIC: 8399 9431 Fund raising organization, non-fee basis; administration of public health programs;
PA: City Of Columbus
90 W Broad St Rm B33
Columbus OH 43215
614 645-7671

(G-7282)
CITY OF COLUMBUS
Also Called: Health, Dept Of- Admin
240 Parsons Ave (43215-5331)
PHONE.................................614 645-7417
Dr Teresa Long, *Director*
Larry Thomas, *Admin Sec*
EMP: 100 **Privately Held**
WEB: www.cityofcolumbus.org
SIC: 8399 9431 Health & welfare council;
PA: City Of Columbus
90 W Broad St Rm B33
Columbus OH 43215
614 645-7671

(G-7283)
CITY OF COLUMBUS
910 Dublin Rd (43215-1169)
PHONE.................................614 645-8270
Chuck Turner, *Manager*
EMP: 69 **Privately Held**
WEB: www.cityofcolumbus.org
SIC: 9532 4941 ; water supply
PA: City Of Columbus
90 W Broad St Rm B33
Columbus OH 43215
614 645-7671

(G-7284)
CITY OF COLUMBUS
Also Called: City Attorney
375 S High St Fl 7 (43215-4520)
PHONE.................................614 645-6624
Lara Baker, *Branch Mgr*
EMP: 40 **Privately Held**
WEB: www.cityofcolumbus.org
SIC: 8111 9222 Legal services;
PA: City Of Columbus
90 W Broad St Rm B33
Columbus OH 43215
614 645-7671

(G-7285)
CITY OF COLUMBUS
Also Called: Public Utilities- Water Div
940 Dublin Rd (43215-1169)
PHONE.................................614 645-8297
Fax: 614 645-7119
Tom Camden, *Branch Mgr*
EMP: 35 **Privately Held**
WEB: www.cityofcolumbus.org
SIC: 4941 9511 Water supply; air, water & solid waste management;
PA: City Of Columbus
90 W Broad St Rm B33
Columbus OH 43215
614 645-7671

(G-7286)
CITY OF WHITEHALL
Also Called: Whitehall Division of Fire
390 S Yearling Rd (43213-1876)
PHONE.................................614 237-5478
Fax: 614 237-0236
Tim Tilton, *Chief*
EMP: 44 **Privately Held**
WEB: www.cityofwhitehall.com
SIC: 9224 8011 ; offices & clinics of medical doctors
PA: City Of Whitehall
360 S Yearling Rd
Columbus OH 43213
614 237-8613

(G-7287)
CITYNET OHIO LLC
343 N Front St Ste 400 (43215-2266)
PHONE.................................614 364-7881
James Martin, *Mng Member*
EMP: 30
SALES (est): 1.4MM **Privately Held**
SIC: 7372 Prepackaged software

(G-7288)
CJ MAHAN CONSTRUCTION CO LLC (PA)
250 N Hartford Ave (43222-1100)
PHONE.................................614 277-4545
Fax: 614 875-1175
Doug McCrae, *Managing Prtnr*
Mickey Humphrey, *Superintendent*
Ronnie Latham, *Superintendent*
Jared Althouse, *Project Mgr*
Mark Hutchins, *Project Mgr*
EMP: 99
SALES (est): 65.8MM **Privately Held**
SIC: 1622 Bridge, tunnel & elevated highway

(G-7289)
CLAIRE DE LEIGH CORP
Also Called: Figlio Wood Fired Pizza
3712 Riverside Dr (43221-1134)
PHONE.................................614 459-6575
Peter Ganis, *President*
John Franky, *Sales/Mktg Mgr*
EMP: 50
SALES (est): 1.4MM **Privately Held**
SIC: 5812 5813 7011 Pizza restaurants; drinking places; hotels & motels

(G-7290)
CLAPROOD ROMAN J CO
242 N Grant Ave (43215-2642)
PHONE.................................614 221-5515
Fax: 614 365-9321
Floyd R Claprood Sr, *President*
Raymond Claprood Jr, *Vice Pres*
F Raymond Claprood Jr, *Treasurer*
EMP: 30 **EST:** 1939
SQ FT: 25,000
SALES (est): 3.8MM **Privately Held**
SIC: 5193 Flowers, fresh; florists' supplies

(G-7291)
CLAREMONT RETIREMENT VILLAGE
7041 Bent Tree Blvd (43235-3916)
PHONE.................................614 761-2011
Fax: 614 761-1892
Clare Kilar, *Partner*
Kim Roberts, *Pub Rel Dir*
Christian Cottrell, *Administration*
EMP: 70
SALES (est): 4.4MM **Privately Held**
SIC: 6513 Retirement hotel operation

(G-7292)
CLARK SCHAEFER HACKETT & CO
4449 Easton Way Ste 400 (43219-7002)
PHONE.................................614 885-2208
Fax: 614 885-8159
Edward Walsh, *Managing Prtnr*
Edwad V Walsh, *Partner*
Daniel P Lacey, *CPA*
Paula Bedford, *Manager*
Ryan Kilpatrick, *Manager*
EMP: 87
SALES (corp-wide): 40.4MM **Privately Held**
WEB: www.cshco.com
SIC: 8721 Certified public accountant
PA: Clark, Schaefer, Hackett & Co.
1 E 4th St Ste 1200
Cincinnati OH 45202
513 241-3111

(G-7293)
CLASSIC DENTAL LABS INC
1252 S High St (43206-3446)
P.O. Box 6276 (43206-0276)
PHONE.................................614 443-0328
Fax: 614 443-7311
EMP: 34 **EST:** 1980
SALES (est): 2.2MM **Privately Held**
SIC: 8072 Dental Laboratory

(G-7294)
CLASSIC PAPERING & PAINTING
1061 Goodale Blvd (43212-3830)
PHONE.................................614 221-0505
Fax: 614 221-0513
Jeff Clifton, *President*
Melanie Crane, *Sls & Mktg Exec*
Stacia Clifton, *Human Resources*
Cheryl McFarland, *Administration*
EMP: 28
SALES (est): 1.9MM **Privately Held**
WEB: www.classicpaperingandpainting.com
SIC: 1721 Residential painting

(G-7295)
CLEAN INNOVATIONS (PA)
Also Called: Columbus Jan Healthnet Svcs
575 E 11th Ave (43215-2605)
P.O. Box 11399 (43211-0399)
PHONE.................................614 299-1187
Fax: 614 299-2011
Howard Cohen, *President*
Annette Cohen, *Corp Secy*
Susan Cohen Ungar, *Vice Pres*
Lois Clarke, *Opers Mgr*
Bill Daniels, *Accounts Exec*
EMP: 27
SQ FT: 26,000
SALES (est): 11.3MM **Privately Held**
WEB: www.cjs.net
SIC: 5087 Janitors' supplies; cleaning & maintenance equipment & supplies

(G-7296)
CLEAR CHANNEL OUTDOOR INC
770 Harrison Dr (43204-3513)
PHONE.................................614 276-9781
Robert Rankin III, *General Mgr*
Joyce Cook, *Manager*
Rick David, *Manager*
EMP: 34 **Publicly Held**
WEB: www.clearchanneloutdoor.com
SIC: 7312 Billboard advertising
HQ: Clear Channel Outdoor, Inc.
2325 E Camelback Rd # 400
Phoenix AZ 85016

(G-7297)
CLEVELAND CLINIC FOUNDATION
Also Called: Cleveland Clinic Star Imaging
921 Jasonway Ave (43214-2352)
PHONE.................................614 451-0489
EMP: 85
SALES (corp-wide): 8B **Privately Held**
SIC: 6733 Trusts
PA: The Cleveland Clinic Foundation
9500 Euclid Ave
Cleveland OH 44195
216 636-8335

(G-7298)
CLEVELAND CONSTRUCTION INC
6399 Broughton Ave (43213-1690)
PHONE.................................740 927-9000
Richard G Small, *Principal*
Elliot Christiansen, *Manager*
EMP: 30
SALES (corp-wide): 411.5MM **Privately Held**
SIC: 1542 1742 1752 Commercial & office building contractors; commercial & office building, new construction; commercial & office buildings, renovation & repair; specialized public building contractors; plastering, plain or ornamental; drywall; insulation, buildings; acoustical & ceiling work; floor laying & floor work
PA: Cleveland Construction, Inc.
8620 Tyler Blvd
Mentor OH 44060
440 255-8000

(G-7299)
CLEVELAND GLASS BLOCK INC
Also Called: Columbus Glass Block
3091 E 14th Ave (43219-2356)
PHONE.................................614 252-5888
Fax: 614 252-5661
John Krulcik, *Manager*
Greg Sutter, *Manager*
EMP: 25
SALES (corp-wide): 11.7MM **Privately Held**
WEB: www.clevelandglassblock.com
SIC: 5231 5039 Glass; glass construction materials
PA: Cleveland Glass Block, Inc.
4566 E 71st St
Cleveland OH 44105
216 531-6363

(G-7300)
CLIME LEASING CO LLC
Also Called: Columbus Healthcare Center
4301 Clime Rd N (43228-3403)
PHONE.................................614 276-4400
Fax: 614 278-7645
Cody Brown, *Mng Member*
Stephen Rosedale,
EMP: 99
SALES (est): 3.9MM
SALES (corp-wide): 103.9MM **Privately Held**
SIC: 8051 Skilled nursing care facilities
HQ: Health Care Facility Management, Llc
4700 Ashwood Dr Ste 200
Blue Ash OH 45241

(G-7301)
CLINIC5
1466 Northwest Blvd (43212-3063)
PHONE.................................614 598-9960
Xavier Salvatorino, *Mng Member*
Winston Vandesol,

GEOGRAPHIC SECTION

Columbus - Franklin County (G-7326)

EMP: 25 EST: 2010
SALES (est): 166.9K **Privately Held**
SIC: 8099 Health & allied services

(G-7302)
CLINICAL SPECIALTIES INC
Also Called: C S I
7654 Crosswoods Dr (43235-4621)
PHONE.................614 659-6580
Kevin Cunningham, *Branch Mgr*
EMP: 116
SALES (corp-wide): 20.1MM **Privately Held**
SIC: 5047 Medical & hospital equipment
PA: Clinical Specialties, Inc
    6955 Treeline Dr Ste A
    Brecksville OH 44141
    888 873-7888

(G-7303)
CLINTON-CARVELL INC
Also Called: Crystal Crystal Carpet Care
1131 Harrisburg Pike (43223-2835)
PHONE.................614 351-8858
Darryl C Reed, *President*
EMP: 30
SQ FT: 2,000
SALES (est): 2.2MM **Privately Held**
WEB: www.clintoncarvell.com
SIC: 8734 7349 8748 Testing laboratories; office cleaning or charring; environmental consultant

(G-7304)
CLINTONVILLE COMMUNITY MKT
Also Called: Clintonville Community Market
85 E Gay St Ste 1000 (43215-3118)
PHONE.................614 261-3663
Karen Hansen, *General Mgr*
Edward Bain, *Manager*
EMP: 30
SALES (est): 1.8MM **Privately Held**
WEB: www.communitymarket.org
SIC: 5149 5812 Natural & organic foods; eating places

(G-7305)
CLK MULTI-FAMILY MGT LLC
Also Called: Spring Creek Apts
5811 Spring Run Dr (43229-2890)
PHONE.................614 891-0011
EMP: 104
SALES (corp-wide): 26.4MM **Privately Held**
SIC: 8741 Management services
PA: Clk Multi-Family Management, Llc
    5545 Murray Ave Fl 3
    Memphis TN 38119
    901 435-9300

(G-7306)
CLM PALLET RECYCLING INC
4311 Janitrol Rd Ste 150 (43228-1389)
PHONE.................614 272-5761
Steve Foor, *Branch Mgr*
EMP: 93
SALES (corp-wide): 39MM **Privately Held**
SIC: 4953 Recycling, waste materials
PA: Clm Pallet Recycling, Inc.
    3103 W 1000 N
    Fortville IN 46040
    317 485-4080

(G-7307)
CLOSEOUT DISTRIBUTION INC (HQ)
300 Phillipi Rd (43228-1310)
PHONE.................614 278-6800
Michael J Potter, *CEO*
Jared A Poff, *Treasurer*
▲ EMP: 600
SALES (est): 221.5MM
SALES (corp-wide): 5.2B **Publicly Held**
SIC: 5092 Toys & games
PA: Big Lots, Inc.
    300 Phillipi Rd
    Columbus OH 43228
    614 278-6800

(G-7308)
CLOVVR LLC
1275 Kinnear Rd Ste 234 (43212-1180)
PHONE.................740 653-2224
Hanad Duale,

EMP: 32
SALES (est): 635.8K **Privately Held**
SIC: 7389

(G-7309)
CMP I COLUMBUS II OWNER LLC
Also Called: Courtyard Columbus Worthington
7411 Vantage Dr (43235-1415)
PHONE.................614 436-7070
Judy Lynam, *Manager*
EMP: 32
SALES (est): 552.8K
SALES (corp-wide): 50.6MM **Privately Held**
SIC: 7011 Hotels
PA: Cmp I Owner-T, Llc
    399 Park Ave Fl 18
    New York NY 10022
    212 547-2609

(G-7310)
CMP I OWNER-T LLC
7411 Vantage Dr (43235-1415)
PHONE.................614 436-7070
Judy Lynam, *Branch Mgr*
EMP: 32
SALES (corp-wide): 50.6MM **Privately Held**
SIC: 8741 Hotel or motel management
PA: Cmp I Owner-T, Llc
    399 Park Ave Fl 18
    New York NY 10022
    212 547-2609

(G-7311)
COAXIAL COMMUNICATIONS OF SOUT (PA)
700 Ackerman Rd Ste 280 (43202-1559)
PHONE.................513 797-4400
Dennis J Mc Gillicuddy, *Ch of Bd*
W Edward Wood, *President*
D Steven Mc Voy, *Exec VP*
Art Loescher, *Vice Pres*
Tom Wilson, *CFO*
EMP: 55 EST: 1985
SALES: 15.4MM **Privately Held**
SIC: 4841 Cable television services

(G-7312)
COBA/SELECT SIRES INC (PA)
1224 Alton Darby Creek Rd (43228-9792)
PHONE.................614 878-5333
Fax: 614 870-2622
Duane Logan, *President*
Kim M House, *CFO*
Chris Lahmers, *Marketing Staff*
Jim Ray, *Manager*
EMP: 100
SQ FT: 15,000
SALES: 22.1MM **Privately Held**
WEB: www.cobaselect.com
SIC: 0752 Artificial insemination services, animal specialties

(G-7313)
CODE ONE COMMUNICATIONS INC
2785 Castlewood Rd (43209-3140)
PHONE.................614 338-0321
F Leon Wilson, *CEO*
EMP: 26
SALES: 38MM **Privately Held**
WEB: www.blackagenda.com
SIC: 8743 Public relations services

(G-7314)
COFFMAN FAMILY PARTNERSHIP
5435 Nelsonia Pl (43213-3532)
PHONE.................614 864-5400
Tean Coffman, *Owner*
EMP: 50
SALES: 4MM **Privately Held**
SIC: 6531 Real estate leasing & rentals

(G-7315)
COILPLUS INC
Coilplus Berwick
5677 Alshire Rd (43232-4703)
PHONE.................614 866-1338
R Terry Harrold, *Division Pres*
Larry Apple, *QC Mgr*
EMP: 51

SALES (corp-wide): 56.5B **Privately Held**
SIC: 5051 Steel
HQ: Coilplus, Inc.
    6250 N River Rd Ste 6050
    Rosemont IL 60018
    847 384-3000

(G-7316)
COLDLINER EXPRESS INC
4921 Vulcan Ave (43228-9573)
P.O. Box 28767 (43228-0767)
PHONE.................614 570-0836
Marci S Hinton, *President*
Douglas Abel, *Principal*
EMP: 40
SQ FT: 5,000
SALES: 12MM **Privately Held**
SIC: 4789 Cargo loading & unloading services

(G-7317)
COLEETA DAYCARE LLC (PA)
4480 Refugee Rd Ste 201 (43232-4459)
PHONE.................614 310-6465
Coleeta Music, *President*
Brenda Scurlock, *Exec Dir*
EMP: 25
SALES (est): 519.9K **Privately Held**
SIC: 8351 Group day care center

(G-7318)
COLHOC LIMITED PARTNERSHIP
Also Called: Columbus Blue Jackets
200 W Nationwide Blvd (43215-2561)
PHONE.................614 246-4625
Fax: 614 246-4007
Craig L Leipold, *Owner*
Barry Brennan, *General Mgr*
Larry Hoepfner, *Exec VP*
Kathryn Dobbs, *Vice Pres*
Melissa Boyd, *Maint Spvr*
▲ EMP: 150 EST: 1998
SALES (est): 18.7MM **Privately Held**
WEB: www.bluejackets.com
SIC: 7941 Ice hockey club

(G-7319)
COLLECTIONS ACQUISITION CO LLC
2 Easton Oval Ste 350 (43219-6193)
PHONE.................614 944-5788
Brad West, *Senior VP*
Steven Balachovic, *Mng Member*
Lex Crosett, *CTO*
EMP: 125
SALES (est): 8.8MM **Privately Held**
SIC: 7389 Financial services

(G-7320)
COLLECTOR WELLS INTL INC
6360 Huntley Rd (43229-1008)
PHONE.................614 888-6263
Fax: 614 888-9208
Sam Stowe, *President*
Andrew Smith, *Corp Secy*
James French, *Vice Pres*
Henry Hunt, *Vice Pres*
Mark Nilges, *Vice Pres*
EMP: 30
SALES (est): 3.4MM
SALES (corp-wide): 475.5MM **Publicly Held**
WEB: www.collectorwellsint.com
SIC: 1781 Water well drilling
PA: Layne Christensen Company
    1800 Hughco Landing Blvd
    The Woodlands TX 77380
    281 475-2600

(G-7321)
COLUMBIA GAS OF OHIO INC (HQ)
290 W Nationwide Blvd # 114 (43215-4157)
P.O. Box 117 (43216-0117)
PHONE.................614 460-6000
Fax: 614 460-4947
Jack Partridge, *President*
Dick James, *President*
George Usner, *Vice Pres*
Devit Vajda, *Treasurer*
Ms Jaime Hartenback, *Accountant*
EMP: 30 EST: 1951
SQ FT: 50,000

SALES: 854MM
SALES (corp-wide): 4.8B **Publicly Held**
WEB: www.meterrepairshop.com
SIC: 4924 Natural gas distribution
PA: Nisource Inc.
    801 E 86th Ave
    Merrillville IN 46410
    877 647-5990

(G-7322)
COLUMBIA GAS OF OHIO INC
290 W Nationwide Blvd (43215-4157)
P.O. Box 2318 (43216-2318)
PHONE.................614 481-1000
Gary Schuler, *Principal*
EMP: 250
SALES (corp-wide): 4.8B **Publicly Held**
WEB: www.meterrepairshop.com
SIC: 4924 Natural gas distribution
HQ: Columbia Gas Of Ohio, Inc.
    290 W Nationwide Blvd # 114
    Columbus OH 43215
    614 460-6000

(G-7323)
COLUMBIA GAS TRANSMISSION LLC (DH)
Also Called: CPG
200 Cizzic Ctr Dr (43216)
PHONE.................614 460-6000
Glen L Kettering, *President*
Jeffrey W Grossman, *Vice Pres*
David J Vajda, *Treasurer*
Karen Townsend, *Controller*
Kathie Macgillivray, *HR Admin*
EMP: 50 EST: 1969
SALES: 1.1B
SALES (corp-wide): 9.2B **Privately Held**
SIC: 4922 Pipelines, natural gas; storage, natural gas
HQ: Columbia Pipeline Group, Inc.
    5151 San Felipe St
    Houston TX 77056
    713 386-3701

(G-7324)
COLUMBIA GAS TRANSMISSION LLC
Also Called: Columbia Energy
290 W Nationwide Blvd # 114 (43215-4157)
PHONE.................614 460-4704
Beverly J Hall, *Admin Asst*
EMP: 40
SALES (corp-wide): 9.2B **Privately Held**
SIC: 4922 Natural gas transmission
HQ: Columbia Gas Transmission, Llc
    200 Cizzic Ctr Dr
    Columbus OH 43216
    614 460-6000

(G-7325)
COLUMBS/WORTHINGTON HTG AC INC
Also Called: Columbus/Worthington Htg & AC
6363 Fiesta Dr (43235-5202)
PHONE.................614 771-5381
Fax: 614 771-7088
Jeff Ford, *President*
George Petty, *CFO*
Dorbee Codwel, *Controller*
Brian Rensi, *Sales Staff*
Kurt Holland, *Marketing Staff*
EMP: 45
SQ FT: 22,400
SALES (est): 7.3MM
SALES (corp-wide): 2.6B **Privately Held**
WEB: www.columbusmechanical.com
SIC: 1711 7623 7699 Warm air heating & air conditioning contractor; air conditioning repair; boiler & heating repair services
PA: American Residential Services Llc
    965 Ridge Lake Blvd # 201
    Memphis TN 38120
    901 271-9700

(G-7326)
COLUMBUS AIRPORT LTD PARTNR
Also Called: Columbus Airport Marriott
1375 N Cassady Ave (43219-1524)
PHONE.................614 475-7551
Janet Rhodes, *Principal*
Tyrone Crockwell, *Engineer*
Kathy Davis, *Bookkeeper*

Columbus - Franklin County (G-7327)

Erin Daniels, *Accounts Mgr*
Katherine Weislogel, *Director*
EMP: 160
SQ FT: 220,000
SALES (est): 7.6MM **Privately Held**
SIC: 7011 5813 5812 Hotels; drinking places; eating places

(G-7327)
COLUMBUS ALZHEIMERS CARE CTR
700 Jasonway Ave (43214-2458)
PHONE 614 459-7050
Tonia Hoak, *Exec Dir*
Mark Buddie, *Director*
Monica Wiess, *Administration*
Debbie Moran, *Administration*
Donna Lane,
EMP: 125
SQ FT: 41,654
SALES: 7.8MM **Privately Held**
SIC: 8059 8051 Nursing home, except skilled & intermediate care facility; skilled nursing care facilities

(G-7328)
COLUMBUS AREA
899 E Broad St Ste 100 (43205-1156)
PHONE 614 251-6561
Fax: 614 251-6580
Bailey Janie, *CEO*
Kristi Boger, *General Mgr*
Cassandra Ellis, *Financial Exec*
Betty Sellars, *Manager*
Sue Garas, *Psychiatry*
EMP: 65
SALES (corp-wide): 14.5MM **Privately Held**
SIC: 8093 8051 Mental health clinic, outpatient; mental retardation hospital
PA: Columbus Area Integrated Health Services, Inc.
1515 E Broad St
Columbus OH 43205
614 252-0711

(G-7329)
COLUMBUS AREA INC
Also Called: Pathways Center
1515 E Broad St (43205-1550)
PHONE 614 252-0711
Janie Bailey, *President*
EMP: 50
SALES (corp-wide): 14.5MM **Privately Held**
WEB: www.columbus-area.com
SIC: 8093 Mental health clinic, outpatient
PA: Columbus Area Integrated Health Services, Inc.
1515 E Broad St
Columbus OH 43205
614 252-0711

(G-7330)
COLUMBUS AREA INTEGRATED HEALT (PA)
Also Called: Columbus Area Community
1515 E Broad St (43205-1550)
PHONE 614 252-0711
Fax: 614 252-9250
Anthony L Penn, *President*
Marguerite Smith, *Pub Rel Mgr*
Cassandra A Ellis, *CFO*
Robin Peterfy, *Finance Mgr*
Beverly Perry, *Case Mgr*
EMP: 80
SQ FT: 80,000
SALES: 14.5MM **Privately Held**
WEB: www.columbus-area.com
SIC: 8093 8052 Mental health clinic, outpatient; drug clinic, outpatient; intermediate care facilities; home for the mentally retarded, with health care

(G-7331)
COLUMBUS ASSOCIATION FOR THE P (PA)
Also Called: Capa
55 E State St (43215-4203)
PHONE 614 469-1045
Fax: 614 469-0429
William B Conner Jr, *President*
Michael Petrecca, *Vice Chairman*
Greg Bryan, *Top Exec*
Chris Tewell, *Vice Pres*
Joy Demarchis, *Opers Staff*

EMP: 705
SALES: 5.9MM **Privately Held**
SIC: 6512 Theater building, ownership & operation

(G-7332)
COLUMBUS ASSOCIATION FOR THE P
39 E State St (43215-4203)
PHONE 614 469-0939
William Conner, *Director*
EMP: 90
SALES (corp-wide): 5.9MM **Privately Held**
SIC: 7922 7929 Legitimate live theater producers; entertainers & entertainment groups
PA: The Columbus Association For The Performing Arts
55 E State St
Columbus OH 43215
614 469-1045

(G-7333)
COLUMBUS BAR ASSOCIATION
175 S 3rd St Ste 1100 (43215-5197)
PHONE 614 221-4112
Kathy Wiesman, *Exec Dir*
Alex Lagusch, *Director*
Annette Hudson, *Director*
Stephen R Buchenroth, *Bd of Directors*
Thomas W Hill, *Bd of Directors*
EMP: 32
SALES: 2.9MM **Privately Held**
SIC: 8621 Bar association

(G-7334)
COLUMBUS BRIDE
34 S 3rd St (43215-4201)
PHONE 614 888-4567
Fax: 614 561-8746
Ray Tatrocki, *General Mgr*
Sherry Paprocki, *Editor*
Randy Beyer, *Controller*
Leanne Brandell, *Executive*
EMP: 60
SQ FT: 1,000
SALES (est): 4.9MM **Privately Held**
WEB: www.columbusalive.com
SIC: 2721 7389 Periodicals: publishing only; convention & show services

(G-7335)
COLUMBUS CARDIOLOGY CONS INC
85 Mcnaughten Rd Ste 300 (43213-5112)
PHONE 614 224-2281
Karen Kane, *Manager*
Jill Heller, *Cardiology*
EMP: 150 **Privately Held**
SIC: 8011 Cardiologist & cardio-vascular specialist
PA: Columbus Cardiology Consultants, Inc.
745 W State St Ste 750
Columbus OH 43222

(G-7336)
COLUMBUS CARDIOLOGY CONS INC (PA)
745 W State St Ste 750 (43222-1515)
PHONE 614 224-2281
Fax: 614 221-8869
F Kevin Hackett, *President*
EMP: 220
SQ FT: 20,000
SALES (est): 14.2MM **Privately Held**
SIC: 8011 Cardiologist & cardio-vascular specialist

(G-7337)
COLUMBUS CHRISTIAN CENTER INC (PA)
Also Called: Faith Christian Accademy
2300 N Cassady Ave (43219-1508)
P.O. Box 24009 (43224-0009)
PHONE 614 416-9673
David C Forbes, *Pastor*
EMP: 40
SALES (est): 2.2MM **Privately Held**
SIC: 8661 8351 Non-denominational church; child day care services

(G-7338)
COLUMBUS CITY TRNSP DIV
1800 E 17th Ave (43219-1007)
PHONE 614 645-3182
William Burns, *Opers Mgr*
Henry Gusman, *Director*
EMP: 150
SALES (est): 9.7MM **Privately Held**
SIC: 1542 Nonresidential construction

(G-7339)
COLUMBUS CLUB CO
181 E Broad St (43215-3788)
PHONE 614 224-4131
Fax: 614 224-4752
Steve Landerman, *President*
Nora Jurczak, *Office Mgr*
Carla Sokol, *Manager*
EMP: 30
SQ FT: 5,000
SALES (est): 1.6MM **Privately Held**
WEB: www.columbusclub.com
SIC: 8641 Business persons club

(G-7340)
COLUMBUS COAL & LIME CO (PA)
Also Called: Granville Builders Supply
1150 Sullivant Ave (43223-1427)
P.O. Box 23156 (43223-0156)
PHONE 614 224-9241
Fax: 614 224-1721
Katherine N Gatterdam, *CEO*
John Niermeyer, *Ch of Bd*
Rich Gatterdam, *President*
E L Humphreys, *Principal*
Carl H Niermeyer, *Principal*
EMP: 30
SQ FT: 20,000
SALES (est): 11.9MM **Privately Held**
WEB: www.columbuscoal.com
SIC: 5032 5211 Sand, construction; brick

(G-7341)
COLUMBUS COL-WELD CORPORATION
1515 Harrisburg Pike (43223-3609)
P.O. Box 23097 (43223-0097)
PHONE 614 276-5303
Fax: 614 276-1998
Charles Stump, *President*
Maynard Stump, *Vice Pres*
John W Stump, *Treasurer*
Roger Stump, *Admin Sec*
EMP: 40 **EST:** 1944
SQ FT: 40,000
SALES (est): 2MM **Privately Held**
SIC: 7538 Engine repair, except diesel: automotive

(G-7342)
COLUMBUS CONCORD LTD PARTNR
Also Called: Courtyard By Marriott
35 W Spring St (43215-2215)
PHONE 614 228-3200
Bob Micklash, *CEO*
Anne Turpin, *General Mgr*
Dan Peterson, *Manager*
Jacob Williams, *IT/INT Sup*
EMP: 70
SALES (est): 2.7MM **Privately Held**
SIC: 7011 Hotels & motels

(G-7343)
COLUMBUS COUNTRY CLUB
4831 E Broad St (43213-1390)
PHONE 614 861-1332
Fax: 614 861-0354
Eugnne Lweis, *President*
Dwight Penn, *President*
Jay Frank, *General Mgr*
Amanda Greenwood, *Sales Dir*
John Blute, *Manager*
EMP: 70
SQ FT: 14,000
SALES: 3.7MM **Privately Held**
WEB: www.columbuscc.com
SIC: 7997 7991 5941 5813 Country club, membership; physical fitness facilities; sporting goods & bicycle shops; drinking places; eating places

(G-7344)
COLUMBUS CTR FOR HUMN SVCS INC (PA)
Also Called: Cchs Johnstown Home
540 Industrial Mile Rd (43228-2413)
PHONE 614 641-2904
Fax: 614 278-9006
Rebecca Sharp, *CEO*
David McCarty, *President*
Brent Garland, *Vice Pres*
Kim Kehl, *Treasurer*
Thomas Caldwell, *Finance*
EMP: 145
SQ FT: 32,000
SALES: 7.7MM **Privately Held**
SIC: 8059 Home for the mentally retarded, exc. skilled or intermediate

(G-7345)
COLUMBUS DAY CARE CENTER
3389 Westerville Rd (43224-3052)
PHONE 614 269-8980
Iman Ali, *Director*
EMP: 27 **EST:** 2010
SALES (est): 407.4K **Privately Held**
SIC: 8351 Child day care services

(G-7346)
COLUMBUS DISTRIBUTING COMPANY (PA)
Also Called: Delmar Distributing
4949 Freeway Dr E (43229-5479)
PHONE 614 846-1000
Fax: 614 846-5293
Paul A Jenkins Jr, *Ch of Bd*
Barbara Jenkins, *Vice Ch Bd*
Paul Jenkins Jr, *President*
Debbie Smith, *Vice Pres*
Dave Lofhbough, *Accountant*
▲ **EMP:** 275
SQ FT: 130,000
SALES (est): 96.7MM **Privately Held**
WEB: www.delmardistributing.com
SIC: 5181 Beer & other fermented malt liquors

(G-7347)
COLUMBUS DRYWALL & INSULATION
876 N 19th St (43219-2417)
PHONE 614 257-0257
Fax: 614 257-0261
Steve Ostrander, *President*
EMP: 65 **EST:** 1969
SQ FT: 28,000
SALES (est): 3MM **Privately Held**
WEB: www.columbusinsulation.com
SIC: 1742 1521 Drywall; insulation, buildings; acoustical & ceiling work; single-family housing construction

(G-7348)
COLUMBUS DRYWALL INC
Also Called: Columbus Drywall Installation
876 N 19th St (43219-2417)
PHONE 614 257-0257
Steve Ostrander, *President*
Darvis Ostrander, *Vice Pres*
EMP: 50
SQ FT: 20,000
SALES (est): 3.3MM **Privately Held**
WEB: www.columbusdrywall.com
SIC: 1742 1521 Drywall; single-family housing construction

(G-7349)
COLUMBUS EASTON HOTEL LLC
Also Called: Marriott
3999 Easton Loop W (43219-6152)
PHONE 614 414-1000
Brad Gester, *General Mgr*
Kelly Vame, *Sales Mgr*
Brad Jester, *Manager*
EMP: 35
SALES (est): 1.1MM **Privately Held**
SIC: 7011 Hotels & motels

(G-7350)
COLUMBUS EASTON HOTEL LLC (PA)
Also Called: Hilton Columbus At Easton
3900 Chagrin Dr Fl 7 (43219-7100)
PHONE 614 414-5000

Fax: 614 416-8444
Carrie Richards, *General Mgr*
Janetta Tischer, *Principal*
Khau Tong, *Controller*
Tim Woodhall, *Sales Dir*
Pam Geis, *Sales Mgr*
EMP: 89
SALES (est): 11.8MM **Privately Held**
SIC: 7011 Hotels

(G-7351)
COLUMBUS EASTON HOTEL LLC
3900 Morse Xing (43219-6081)
PHONE..................614 383-2005
Mary Faust, *Human Res Dir*
Mort Olshan, *Branch Mgr*
EMP: 40
SALES (corp-wide): 11.8MM **Privately Held**
SIC: 7011 Hotels
PA: Columbus Easton Hotel Llc
3900 Chagrin Dr Fl 7
Columbus OH 43219
614 414-5000

(G-7352)
COLUMBUS EQUIPMENT COMPANY (PA)
Also Called: Kubota Authorized Dealer
2323 Performance Way (43207-2473)
PHONE..................614 437-0352
Fax: 614 443-8257
Josh Stivison, *President*
Ray Frase, *General Mgr*
Tim Albright, *Vice Pres*
Ernie Potter, *Vice Pres*
Jon St Julian, *Materials Mgr*
▼ **EMP:** 43 **EST:** 1951
SQ FT: 12,000
SALES (est): 84.2MM **Privately Held**
WEB: www.colsequipment.com
SIC: 5082 7353 General construction machinery & equipment; heavy construction equipment rental

(G-7353)
COLUMBUS EQUIPMENT COMPANY
2323 Performance Way (43207-2473)
PHONE..................614 443-6541
Luke Matheson, *Sales Staff*
Tom Fpvison, *Marketing Staff*
Albert Allen, *Branch Mgr*
Matt Norton, *Branch Mgr*
Josh Stidison, *Branch Mgr*
EMP: 45
SALES (corp-wide): 84.2MM **Privately Held**
WEB: www.colsequipment.com
SIC: 5082 7353 General construction machinery & equipment; heavy construction equipment rental
PA: The Columbus Equipment Company
2323 Performance Way
Columbus OH 43207
614 437-0352

(G-7354)
COLUMBUS FOUNDATION
1234 E Broad St (43205-1453)
PHONE..................614 251-4000
Fax: 614 251-4009
Douglas Kridler, *President*
Kelley Griesmer, *Senior VP*
Tamera Durrence, *Vice Pres*
Carol Harmon, *Vice Pres*
John McCoy, *Vice Pres*
EMP: 45
SQ FT: 20,000
SALES (est): 3.6MM **Privately Held**
SIC: 8322 Individual & family services

(G-7355)
COLUMBUS GREEN CABS INC (PA)
Also Called: Yellow Cabs
1989 Camaro Ave (43207-1716)
PHONE..................614 444-4444
Jeff Kates, *President*
Jeff R Glassman, *Vice Pres*
EMP: 40 **EST:** 1928
SQ FT: 26,000
SALES (est): 4.8MM **Privately Held**
SIC: 4121 Taxicabs

(G-7356)
COLUMBUS GSTRNTRLOGY GROUP INC
3820 Olentangy River Rd (43214-5403)
PHONE..................614 457-1213
Richard A Edgin, *President*
Richard Sheets, *Manager*
Gregory D Gibbons, *Gastroenterlgy*
EMP: 60
SQ FT: 3,545
SALES (est): 3MM **Privately Held**
SIC: 8011 Gastronomist

(G-7357)
COLUMBUS HEATING & VENT CO
182 N Yale Ave (43222-1127)
PHONE..................614 274-1177
Fax: 614 274-7873
Charles R Gulley, *President*
Greogy Yoak, *President*
Michael Blythe, *Corp Secy*
Anthony Staten, *Director*
Mikel Plythe, *Admin Sec*
EMP: 135 **EST:** 1874
SALES (est): 23.6MM **Privately Held**
WEB: www.columbusheat.com
SIC: 1711 3585 Warm air heating & air conditioning contractor; ventilation & duct work contractor; furnaces, warm air: electric

(G-7358)
COLUMBUS HOSPITALITY
775 Yard St Ste 180 (43212-3857)
PHONE..................614 461-2648
Charles Lagarce, *Owner*
Thomas Gurtler, *Managing Prtnr*
Dirk Bengel, *General Mgr*
Jessica Lagarce, *Counsel*
Gregg Gibson, *Facilities Dir*
EMP: 30
SALES (est): 3.9MM **Privately Held**
WEB: www.columbushospitality.com
SIC: 7011 Hotels & motels

(G-7359)
COLUMBUS HOTEL PARTNERSHIP LLC
Also Called: Embassy Suites Columbus
2700 Corporate Exch Dr (43231-1690)
PHONE..................614 890-8600
Lacey McLachlan, *Sales Mgr*
Alpesh Patel,
EMP: 85
SALES (est): 333.9K **Privately Held**
SIC: 7011 Resort hotel, franchised

(G-7360)
COLUMBUS HOUSING PARTNR INC
Also Called: C.H.P.
3443 Agler Rd Ste 200 (43219-3385)
PHONE..................614 221-8889
Fax: 614 221-8904
Bruce Luecke, *President*
Carrie A Hiatt, *COO*
Tania Young, *Opers Staff*
Dan Duffy, *CFO*
Valorie Schwarzmann, *CFO*
EMP: 58
SQ FT: 10,000
SALES (est): 6.9MM **Privately Held**
SIC: 6552 Land subdividers & developers, residential

(G-7361)
COLUMBUS JEWISH FEDERATION
1175 College Ave (43209-2827)
PHONE..................614 237-7686
Fax: 614 237-2221
Marsha Hurowitz, *President*
Hal Lewis, *President*
Bobby Covitz, *Vice Pres*
Mitchell J Orlik, *Vice Pres*
Donald Kelly, *CFO*
EMP: 30
SQ FT: 15,000
SALES (est): 4.5MM **Privately Held**
SIC: 8399 Fund raising organization, non-fee basis

(G-7362)
COLUMBUS LANDMARKS FOUNDATION
57 Jefferson Ave Fl 1 (43215-3866)
PHONE..................614 221-0227
Fax: 614 224-9619
Richard Stevens, *Vice Pres*
Bob Larkin, *Opers Staff*
Kathy M Kane, *Exec Dir*
Kathy Kane, *Exec Dir*
Becky West, *Exec Dir*
EMP: 26
SALES: 165.9K **Privately Held**
WEB: www.columbuslandmarks.org
SIC: 8699 8399 Automobile owners' association; historical club; advocacy group

(G-7363)
COLUMBUS LEASING LLC
Also Called: Crowne Plaza Columbus North
6500 Doubletree Ave (43229-1111)
PHONE..................614 885-1885
Daniel Ouellette,
EMP: 99
SALES (est): 6.4MM **Privately Held**
SIC: 7011 Hotels

(G-7364)
COLUMBUS MAENNERCHOR
Also Called: GERMAN SINGING SOCIETY
976 S High St (43206-2524)
PHONE..................614 444-3531
Fax: 614 444-3583
Rene V Blaha, *President*
Hannelore Holman, *Manager*
EMP: 35
SQ FT: 4,000
SALES: 225.8K **Privately Held**
WEB: www.maennerchor.com
SIC: 8641 Community membership club

(G-7365)
COLUMBUS MED ASSN FOUNDATION
1390 Dublin Rd (43215-1009)
PHONE..................614 240-7420
Julie Eikenberry, *CFO*
Cathy Thompson, *Program Mgr*
Phil Cass, *Director*
EMP: 30
SALES: 2.2MM **Privately Held**
SIC: 8621 Medical field-related associations

(G-7366)
COLUMBUS MEDICAL ASSOCIATION
1390 Dublin Rd (43215-1009)
PHONE..................614 240-7410
Phillip Cass, *CEO*
Gerald Penn, *President*
Olivia Thomas, *Trustee*
Warren Tyler, *Trustee*
Laurie Hawkins, *CFO*
EMP: 30
SQ FT: 12,432
SALES: 414.2K **Privately Held**
SIC: 8621 Health association

(G-7367)
COLUMBUS MEDICAL RHEUMATOLOGY
Also Called: Columbus Arthritis Center
1211 Dublin Rd Fl 1 (43215-1026)
P.O. Box 2097, Westerville (43086-2097)
PHONE..................614 486-5200
Fax: 614 486-9665
Sterling W Hedrick MD, *President*
Sarah Williams, *Human Res Mgr*
Melissa Wymer, *Office Mgr*
Jennifer Richardson, *Med Doctor*
Kevin Schlessel, *Med Doctor*
EMP: 25
SALES (est): 5.9MM **Privately Held**
WEB: www.columbusarthritis.com
SIC: 8011 Rheumatology specialist, physician/surgeon

(G-7368)
COLUMBUS METRO FEDERAL CR UN
4000 E Broad St (43213-1140)
P.O. Box 13240 (43213-0240)
PHONE..................614 239-0210

Tim Ritchey, *Principal*
EMP: 28
SALES (est): 7MM **Privately Held**
SIC: 6111 6211 Federal & federally sponsored credit agencies; security brokers & dealers
PA: Columbus Metro Federal Credit Union (Inc)
4000 E Broad St
Columbus OH 43213
614 239-0210

(G-7369)
COLUMBUS METRO FEDERAL CR UN (PA)
4000 E Broad St (43213-1140)
P.O. Box 13240 (43213-0240)
PHONE..................614 239-0210
Fax: 614 239-0988
Tim Richey, *President*
Jennifer Banker, *Vice Pres*
Jim Downey, *Manager*
Tim Ford, *Manager*
Tony Southall, *Director*
EMP: 33
SQ FT: 20,503
SALES: 7MM **Privately Held**
SIC: 6111 6163 Federal & federally sponsored credit agencies; loan brokers

(G-7370)
COLUMBUS MONTESSORI EDUCATION
979 S James Rd (43227-1071)
PHONE..................614 231-3790
Fax: 614 231-3780
Jill Aubert, *Finance Mgr*
Diane Bender, *Librarian*
Peggy Fein, *Director*
Susan Caskey, *Teacher*
Rachel Kaufman-Martin, *Teacher*
EMP: 40
SQ FT: 26,369
SALES: 2.8MM **Privately Held**
WEB: www.columbusmontessori.org
SIC: 8351 8299 Child day care services; Montessori child development center; educational service, nondegree granting: continuing educ.

(G-7371)
COLUMBUS MUNICIPAL EMPLOYEES (PA)
365 S 4th St (43215-5422)
PHONE..................614 224-8890
Fax: 614 322-0022
Jim Riederer, *President*
Tracy Cera, *CFO*
Jean Dunaway, *Accountant*
Amie Day, *Human Resources*
Brent Fisher, *Mktg Coord*
EMP: 31
SQ FT: 5,000
SALES: 9.6MM **Privately Held**
SIC: 6061 Federal credit unions

(G-7372)
COLUMBUS MUSEUM OF ART
480 E Broad St (43215-3886)
PHONE..................614 221-6801
Fax: 614 221-0226
Nannette Maciejunes, *General Mgr*
F C Sessions Et Al, *Principal*
W G Deshler, *Principal*
P W Huntington, *Principal*
David Leach, *Facilities Dir*
▲ **EMP:** 100
SQ FT: 89,000
SALES: 19.6MM **Privately Held**
WEB: www.cmaohio.org
SIC: 8412 5812 Art gallery; eating places

(G-7373)
COLUMBUS NEIGHBORHOOD HEALTH C
1905 Parsons Ave (43207-1933)
PHONE..................614 445-0685
EMP: 118
SALES (corp-wide): 31.7MM **Privately Held**
SIC: 8011 Clinic, operated by physicians

Columbus - Franklin County (G-7374)

PA: Columbus Neighborhood Health Center, Inc.
2780 Airport Dr Ste 100
Columbus OH 43219
614 645-5500

(G-7374)
COLUMBUS OBSTTRCANS GYNCLGISTS (PA)
Also Called: Columbus Obgyn
750 Mount Carmel Mall # 100 (43222-1553)
PHONE..................614 434-2400
Fax: 614 341-6713
Ralph R Ballenger MD, *President*
Mark Vanmeter, *COO*
R D Blose MD, *Vice Pres*
Charles A Caranna MD, *Vice Pres*
Larry A Simon MD, *Treasurer*
EMP: 26
SQ FT: 2,850
SALES (est): 7.2MM **Privately Held**
SIC: 8011 Obstetrician; gynecologist

(G-7375)
COLUMBUS ONCOLOGY ASSOCIATES
810 Jasonway Ave Ste A (43214-4359)
PHONE..................614 442-3130
Peter Kourlas, *President*
Christopher George, *Vice Pres*
John Kuebler, *Vice Pres*
Thomas Sweeney, *Treasurer*
Scott Blair, *Admin Sec*
▲ **EMP:** 51
SQ FT: 23,000
SALES (est): 6.9MM **Privately Held**
WEB: www.coainc.net
SIC: 8011 Hematologist; oncologist

(G-7376)
COLUMBUS PUBLIC SCHOOL DST
Also Called: Columbus Pub Schl Vhcl Maint
889 E 17th Ave (43211-2492)
PHONE..................614 365-5263
Nick Brown, *Maint Spvr*
Phil Downs, *Manager*
EMP: 200
SALES (corp-wide): 1B **Privately Held**
WEB: www.siebertschool.com
SIC: 5013 Automotive servicing equipment
PA: Columbus Public School District
270 E State St Fl 3
Columbus OH 43215
614 365-5000

(G-7377)
COLUMBUS PUBLIC SCHOOL DST
Also Called: Cassady Alternative Elementary
2500 N Cassady Ave (43219-1514)
PHONE..................614 365-5456
Fax: 614 365-8700
Natasha Shaefer, *Principal*
Carol Fluharty, *Advisor*
EMP: 40
SALES (corp-wide): 1B **Privately Held**
WEB: www.siebertschool.com
SIC: 8211 8351 Public elementary school; preschool center
PA: Columbus Public School District
270 E State St Fl 3
Columbus OH 43215
614 365-5000

(G-7378)
COLUMBUS PUBLIC SCHOOL DST
Also Called: Cols Boe Custodial Services
889 E 17th Ave (43211-2492)
PHONE..................614 365-5043
Fax: 614 365-5073
Chuck Holler, *Manager*
EMP: 500
SALES (corp-wide): 1B **Privately Held**
WEB: www.siebertschool.com
SIC: 7349 Building maintenance services
PA: Columbus Public School District
270 E State St Fl 3
Columbus OH 43215
614 365-5000

(G-7379)
COLUMBUS PUBLIC SCHOOL DST
Also Called: Food Service
450 E Fulton St (43215-5527)
PHONE..................614 365-5000
Dudley Hawkey, *Director*
Joe Brown, *Director*
EMP: 40
SALES (corp-wide): 1B **Privately Held**
WEB: www.siebertschool.com
SIC: 8742 Restaurant & food services consultants
PA: Columbus Public School District
270 E State St Fl 3
Columbus OH 43215
614 365-5000

(G-7380)
COLUMBUS PUBLIC SCHOOL DST
Also Called: Columbus Schl Dst Bus Compound
4001 Appian Way (43230-1469)
PHONE..................614 365-6542
Greg McCandless, *Manager*
EMP: 158
SALES (corp-wide): 1B **Privately Held**
WEB: www.siebertschool.com
SIC: 4111 Bus transportation
PA: Columbus Public School District
270 E State St Fl 3
Columbus OH 43215
614 365-5000

(G-7381)
COLUMBUS REGIONAL AIRPORT AUTH
4760 E 5th Ave Ste G (43219-1877)
PHONE..................614 239-4000
EMP: 31 **Privately Held**
SIC: 4581 Airport
PA: Columbus Regional Airport Authority
4600 Intl Gtwy Ste 2
Columbus OH 43219

(G-7382)
COLUMBUS REGIONAL AIRPORT AUTH (PA)
Also Called: John Glenn Columbus Intl Arprt
4600 Intl Gtwy Ste 2 (43219)
PHONE..................614 239-4015
Fax: 614 239-4066
Elaine Roberts, *President*
Michael Brady, *Business Mgr*
Joshua Burger, *Senior VP*
Torrance Richardson, *Vice Pres*
Brian Sarkis, *Vice Pres*
EMP: 320
SQ FT: 821,795
SALES: 88.1MM **Privately Held**
WEB: www.columbusairports.com
SIC: 4581 Airport

(G-7383)
COLUMBUS SAI MOTORS LLC
Also Called: Sonic Automotive 1400
1400 Auto Mall Dr (43228-3657)
PHONE..................614 851-3273
Keith Daniels, *President*
Bud C Hatfield, *Principal*
Scott Smith, *COO*
Gerald Curtis, *Sales Mgr*
Jeff Warrington, *Sales Mgr*
EMP: 50
SQ FT: 24,000
SALES (est): 5.9MM
SALES (corp-wide): 9.8B **Publicly Held**
SIC: 7538 5511 7515 5521 General automotive repair shops; automobiles, new & used; passenger car leasing; used car dealers
PA: Sonic Automotive, Inc.
4401 Colwick Rd
Charlotte NC 28211
704 566-2400

(G-7384)
COLUMBUS SERUM COMPANY (DH)
2025 S High St (43207-2426)
PHONE..................614 444-5211
Fax: 614 444-4974
Robert Peterson, *President*
Bruce A Peterson, *Vice Pres*
EMP: 138 **EST:** 1922
SQ FT: 30,000
SALES (est): 47.7MM
SALES (corp-wide): 5.5B **Publicly Held**
WEB: www.milburnequine.com
SIC: 5122 5199 Biologicals & allied products; pet supplies
HQ: Patterson Veterinary Supply, Inc.
137 Barnum Rd
Devens MA 01434
978 353-6000

(G-7385)
COLUMBUS SOUTHERN POWER CO (HQ)
1 Riverside Plz (43215-2355)
PHONE..................614 716-1000
Fax: 614 716-1823
Michael G Morris, *Ch of Bd*
Joseph Hamrock, *President*
Holly K Koeppel, *Exec VP*
Brian X Tierney, *CFO*
Timothy Bowman, *Finance Mgr*
EMP: 43
SALES (est): 44.5MM
SALES (corp-wide): 15.4B **Publicly Held**
SIC: 4911 Electric services; distribution, electric power; generation, electric power; transmission, electric power
PA: American Electric Power Company, Inc.
1 Riverside Plz Fl 1 # 1
Columbus OH 43215
614 716-1000

(G-7386)
COLUMBUS SPECH HEARING CTR CPD
510 E North Broadway St (43214-4114)
PHONE..................614 263-5151
Fax: 614 263-5365
Dawn Gleason, *President*
EMP: 79
SQ FT: 40,000
SALES: 4.5MM **Privately Held**
SIC: 8322 Social services for the handicapped

(G-7387)
COLUMBUS SQUARE BOWLING PALACE
5707 Forest Hills Blvd (43231-2990)
PHONE..................614 895-1122
Fax: 614 895-0106
William H Hadler, *President*
William N Hadler, *Vice Pres*
EMP: 48
SALES (est): 1.9MM **Privately Held**
WEB: www.palacelanes.com
SIC: 7933 5813 Ten pin center; cocktail lounge

(G-7388)
COLUMBUS STEEL ERECTORS INC
1700 Walcutt Rd (43228-9612)
PHONE..................614 876-5050
Lisa Runyon, *CEO*
Shawn Runyon, *President*
EMP: 25
SALES (est): 3.9MM **Privately Held**
WEB: www.columbussteelerectors.com
SIC: 1791 Iron work, structural

(G-7389)
COLUMBUS SYMPHONY ORCHESTRA
55 E State St Fl 5 (43215-4203)
PHONE..................614 228-9600
Fax: 614 224-7273
Pavana Stetzik, *General Mgr*
Chad Wintton, *CFO*
Merissa Mahoy, *Accountant*
Scott Davis, *Personnel Exec*
Norma Snyder, *Accounts Mgr*
EMP: 85
SALES: 7.8MM **Privately Held**
WEB: www.columbussymphony.com
SIC: 7929 Orchestras or bands

(G-7390)
COLUMBUS TEAM SOCCER LLC (PA)
Also Called: Columbus Crew, The
1 Black And Gold Blvd (43211-2091)
PHONE..................614 447-1301
Fax: 614 447-4114
Lisa Fricker, *General Mgr*
Liz Russell, *General Mgr*
Faith Shachter, *Human Res Mgr*
Jon Bromberg, *Accounts Exec*
Nathan Newcombe, *Accounts Exec*
▲ **EMP:** 40
SALES (est): 4.9MM **Privately Held**
SIC: 7941 Soccer club

(G-7391)
COLUMBUS URBAN LEAGUE INC
788 Mount Vernon Ave (43203-1408)
PHONE..................614 257-6300
Fax: 614 257-6327
Stephanie Hightower, *President*
Gready Pettigrew, *Principal*
Glenn Harris, *Director*
Lorretta King, *Director*
Linda Stallworth, *Director*
EMP: 50
SQ FT: 25,000
SALES: 5.3MM **Privately Held**
WEB: www.cul.org
SIC: 8399 Community development groups

(G-7392)
COLUMBUS W HLTH CARE CO PARTNR
2731 Clime Rd (43223-3625)
PHONE..................614 274-4005
Judith Camp, *Branch Mgr*
EMP: 47
SALES (corp-wide): 6.5MM **Privately Held**
SIC: 8082 Home health care services
PA: Columbus West Health Care Co. Ltd Partnership
1700 Heinzerling Dr
Columbus OH 43223
614 274-4222

(G-7393)
COLUMBUS W HLTH CARE CO PARTNR (PA)
Also Called: Columbus West Pk Nursing & Reh
1700 Heinzerling Dr (43223-3671)
PHONE..................614 274-4222
Fax: 614 275-3722
Thomas J Stewart, *Partner*
Gail Devaux, *Director*
Suzanne Smith, *Hlthcr Dir*
EMP: 107
SALES (est): 6.5MM **Privately Held**
WEB: www.columbuswestpark.com
SIC: 8051 Convalescent home with continuous nursing care

(G-7394)
COLUMBUS WORTHINGTON HOSPITALI
Also Called: Double Tree
175 Hutchinson Ave (43235-1413)
PHONE..................614 885-3334
Daniel Ouellette, *Manager*
Sattish Duggal,
EMP: 85 **EST:** 2013
SALES (est): 5.8MM **Privately Held**
SIC: 7011 Hotel, franchised

(G-7395)
COLUMBUS-RNA-DAVITA LLC
Also Called: Columbus Dialysis
226 Graceland Blvd (43214-1532)
PHONE..................614 985-1732
Fax: 614 538-6850
Zach King, *Director*
EMP: 25 **Publicly Held**
WEB: www.us.gambro.com
SIC: 8092 Kidney dialysis centers
HQ: Columbus-Rna-Davita, Llc
601 Hawaii St
El Segundo CA 90245

(G-7396)
COMBINED INSURANCE CO AMER
150 E Campus View Blvd # 230 (43235-6610)
PHONE..................614 210-6209
Domic Pallante, *Manager*
EMP: 85
SQ FT: 2,000

GEOGRAPHIC SECTION
Columbus - Franklin County (G-7420)

SALES (corp-wide): 28.7B **Privately Held**
SIC: 6411 Insurance agents; education services, insurance
HQ: Combined Insurance Company Of America
200 E Randolph St Lbby 10
Chicago IL 60601
800 225-4500

(G-7397) COMENITY SERVICING LLC
3095 Loyalty Cir (43219-3673)
PHONE 614 729-4000
Tim King, *Officer*
EMP: 142
SALES (est): 466.7K **Publicly Held**
SIC: 7389 Advertising, promotional & trade show services
HQ: Ads Alliance Data Systems, Inc.
7500 Dallas Pkwy Ste 700
Plano TX 75024
214 494-3000

(G-7398) COMFORT INNS
1213 E Dblin Granville Rd (43229-3301)
PHONE 614 885-4084
Dehesh Patle, *General Mgr*
Gagan Dada, *Manager*
Dehesh Patel, *Manager*
EMP: 25
SALES (est): 854.2K **Privately Held**
SIC: 7011 Hotels & motels

(G-7399) COMMERCIAL DEBT CUNSELING CORP
445 Hutchinson Ave # 500 (43235-5677)
PHONE 614 848-9800
Kenneth Monnett, *President*
Joe Caparros, *Regional Mgr*
Clark D Schaefer, *Regional Mgr*
Laura Columbro, *Personnel Exec*
Traci Parrill, *Marketing Mgr*
EMP: 75
SQ FT: 40,000
SALES (est): 7.6MM **Privately Held**
WEB: www.amerassist.com
SIC: 8742 Financial consultant

(G-7400) COMMERCIAL PARTS & SER
5033 Transamerica Dr (43228-9381)
PHONE 614 221-0057
Steve Weigel, *Branch Mgr*
EMP: 55
SALES (corp-wide): 17.9MM **Privately Held**
WEB: www.cpsohio.com
SIC: 5087 Restaurant supplies
PA: Commercial Parts & Service Of Cincinnati, Ohio, Inc.
10671 Techwood Cir Ste 1
Blue Ash OH 45242
513 984-1900

(G-7401) COMMUNITIES IN SCHOOLS
510 E North Broadway St (43214-4114)
PHONE 614 268-2472
Fax: 614 268-4260
Karen Lurvey, *Vice Pres*
Beth Urban, *Opers Staff*
Sarah Neikirk, *Exec Dir*
Derrick Fulton, *Exec Dir*
EMP: 54
SALES (est): 1MM **Privately Held**
WEB: www.cickido.org
SIC: 8641 Youth organizations

(G-7402) COMMUNITY CRIME PATROL
248 E 11th Ave (43201-2255)
PHONE 614 247-1765
Ellen Moore, *Asst Director*
Kevin Widmer, *Asst Director*
EMP: 40
SALES: 575.3K **Privately Held**
SIC: 7381 Protective services, guard

(G-7403) COMMUNITY DEV FOR ALL PEOPLE
946 Parsons Ave (43206-2346)
P.O. Box 6063 (43206-0063)
PHONE 614 445-7342

David Cofer, *Managing Dir*
John Edgar, *Exec Dir*
Katelin Hansen, *Director*
EMP: 28
SALES (est): 2.1MM **Privately Held**
SIC: 8699 Charitable organization

(G-7404) COMMUNITY EMRGCY MED SVCS OHIO
Also Called: Medcare Ambulance
3699 Paragon Dr (43228-9751)
PHONE 614 751-6651
Phil Koster, *Director*
EMP: 120
SALES (est): 20.3MM **Privately Held**
SIC: 5012 Ambulances

(G-7405) COMMUNITY HSING NETWRK DEV CO
1680 Watermark Dr (43215-1034)
PHONE 614 487-6700
Susan Weaver, *CEO*
Anthony Penn, *COO*
Don Hollenack, *CFO*
Chris Mitchell, *Manager*
Samantha Shuler, *Director*
EMP: 125
SALES (est): 15.1MM **Privately Held**
WEB: www.chninc.org
SIC: 8361 Home for the mentally handicapped

(G-7406) COMMUNITY LIVING EXPERIENCES
2939 Donnylane Blvd (43235-3228)
PHONE 614 588-0320
William H Campbell, *President*
Becky Campbell, *CFO*
Nancy Cooper, *Controller*
Renee Chandler, *Human Resources*
Jeanette McDonald, *Human Resources*
EMP: 30
SALES (est): 2.6MM **Privately Held**
SIC: 8361 Home for the mentally handicapped

(G-7407) COMMUNITY PRPTS OHIO III LLC
Also Called: Cpo3
42 N 17th St (43203)
PHONE 614 253-0984
Michelle Hert, *Principal*
Barry Stayer, *CFO*
Davita Tucker, *Marketing Staff*
Talisha Sealey, *Property Mgr*
Harry Post, *Director*
EMP: 55
SALES (est): 515K **Privately Held**
SIC: 6513 Apartment building operators

(G-7408) COMMUNITY PRPTS OHIO MGT SVCS
Also Called: Cpo Managmnt Services
910 E Broad St (43205-1150)
PHONE 614 253-0984
Isabel Toth, *President*
Chad Ketler, *Vice Pres*
Sharon Griffith, *CFO*
Michelle Hert, *Officer*
EMP: 55
SALES (est): 6.4MM **Privately Held**
SIC: 6513 Apartment building operators
PA: City Of Columbus
90 W Broad St Rm B33
Columbus OH 43215
614 645-7671

(G-7409) COMMUNITY REFUGEE & IMMIGATION
1925 E Dublin Granville R (43229-3517)
PHONE 614 235-5747
Fax: 614 235-6127
Ruby Wolfe, *General Mgr*
Karen Clarkcarpe, *Human Resources*
Dahir Adan, *Case Mgr*
Karin Blythe, *Program Mgr*
Abbu Babdugama, *Manager*
EMP: 75 **EST:** 1995

SALES: 3.8MM **Privately Held**
WEB: www.cris-ohio.com
SIC: 8322 Refugee service

(G-7410) COMMUNITY SHELTER BOARD
111 Liberty St Ste 150 (43215-5849)
PHONE 614 221-9195
Fax: 614 221-9199
Jeremiah Bakerstull, *Manager*
Michelle Hertigae, *Exec Dir*
Lianna Barbu, *Director*
Janet Bridges, *Director*
Pam Garrett, *Executive*
EMP: 25
SALES: 31.6MM **Privately Held**
WEB: www.csb.org
SIC: 8621 Professional membership organizations

(G-7411) COMMUNITY SRGL SPLY TOMS RVR
3823 Twin Creeks Dr (43204-5005)
PHONE 614 307-2975
Andy Tyler, *Branch Mgr*
EMP: 126
SALES (corp-wide): 176.7MM **Privately Held**
SIC: 5047 Medical equipment & supplies
PA: Community Surgical Supply Of Toms River Inc
1390 Rte 37 W
Toms River NJ 08755
732 349-2990

(G-7412) COMPDRUG (PA)
Also Called: YOUTH TO YOUTH
547 E 11th Ave (43211-2603)
PHONE 614 224-4506
Fax: 614 224-8451
Robert E Sweet, *President*
Dustin Mets, *Exec VP*
Ronald L Pogue, *Senior VP*
Mark Sellers, *Vice Pres*
Cheryl Sells, *Program Dir*
EMP: 60
SQ FT: 15,000
SALES: 13.5MM **Privately Held**
WEB: www.compdrug.org
SIC: 8322 8361 General counseling services; rehabilitation center, residential; health care incidental

(G-7413) COMPETITOR SWIM PRODUCTS INC
Also Called: Great American Woodies
5310 Career Ct (43213)
P.O. Box 12160 (43212-0160)
PHONE 800 888-7946
Brad Underwood, *President*
Alan Sprague, *CFO*
Richard Thomas, *VP Sales*
Richey Smith, *Director*
EMP: 85
SQ FT: 60,000
SALES (est): 20.2MM **Privately Held**
WEB: www.richeyind.com
SIC: 5091 Swimming pools, equipment & supplies

(G-7414) COMPLETE GENERAL CNSTR CO (PA)
1221 E 5th Ave (43219-2493)
PHONE 614 258-9515
Fax: 614 258-5398
Lee Guzzo, *Ch of Bd*
Gildo Guzzo Jr, *President*
Jim George, *Vice Pres*
John M Kinley, *Vice Pres*
Fred Lawson, *Vice Pres*
EMP: 150
SQ FT: 6,000
SALES (est): 67.4MM **Privately Held**
WEB: www.completegeneral.com
SIC: 1622 Bridge construction; highway construction, elevated

(G-7415) COMPREHENSIVE SERVICES INC
1555 Bethel Rd (43220-2003)
PHONE 614 442-0664
Fax: 614 442-0620
Richard C Davis, *President*
Susan Blacock, *Partner*
Jan Brewer, *Partner*
Louisa Celebrese, *Partner*
Edward Dagenfield, *Partner*
EMP: 30
SQ FT: 8,800
SALES (est): 1.9MM **Privately Held**
WEB: www.comprehensive-services.us
SIC: 8049 Clinical psychologist

(G-7416) COMPRODUCTS INC (PA)
Also Called: B & C COMMUNICATIONS
1740 Harmon Ave Ste F (43223-3355)
PHONE 614 276-5552
Fax: 614 276-0580
Thomas Harb, *CEO*
Leland Haydon, *President*
Steven Stauch, *Vice Pres*
Stac Sorrell, *Human Resources*
Gene Weimer, *Marketing Staff*
EMP: 27
SQ FT: 12,000
SALES (est): 12.6MM **Privately Held**
SIC: 5065 7622 Radio parts & accessories; radio receiving & transmitting tubes; radio repair & installation

(G-7417) COMPUTER HELPER PUBLISHING
450 Beecher Rd (43230-1797)
P.O. Box 30191, Gahanna (43230-0191)
PHONE 614 939-9094
Fax: 614 939-9004
Mel Wygant, *President*
EMP: 25
SQ FT: 3,300
SALES (est): 4.1MM **Privately Held**
SIC: 5045 7371 5734 Computer software; custom computer programming services; computer & software stores

(G-7418) COMRESOURCE INC
1159 Dublin Rd Ste 200 (43215-1874)
PHONE 614 221-6348
Fax: 614 221-6349
Gary L Potts, *President*
Richard C Hannon Jr, *Principal*
Dave Gilbert, *Vice Pres*
Matthew Dorsey, *Project Mgr*
Danny Puckett, *Engineer*
EMP: 45
SQ FT: 3,500
SALES (est): 10.7MM **Privately Held**
WEB: www.comresource.com
SIC: 7379

(G-7419) COMTECH GLOBAL INC
355 E Campus View Blvd # 195 (43235-8624)
PHONE 614 796-1148
Sridhar Nannapaneni, *President*
EMP: 72
SQ FT: 3,000
SALES (est): 8.2MM **Privately Held**
WEB: www.comtech-global.com
SIC: 7371 Computer software development

(G-7420) CONGRESSIONAL BANK
Also Called: American Federal Bank
4343 Easton Cmns Ste 150 (43219-6237)
PHONE 614 441-9230
Kris McCurry, *Broker*
Dan Snyder, *Manager*
EMP: 50 **Privately Held**
SIC: 6035 Federal savings banks
HQ: Congressional Bank
6701 Democracy Blvd # 400
Bethesda MD 20817
301 299-8810

Columbus - Franklin County (G-7421)

(G-7421)
CONNAISSANCE CONSULTING LLC
4071 Easton Way (43219-6087)
PHONE..................614 289-5200
Jeffrey Lussenhop, *CEO*
Harold Williams, *President*
Steven A Minick, *COO*
Tim Bosco, *CFO*
EMP: 113
SQ FT: 4,000
SALES (est): 3.5MM Privately Held
SIC: 8748 Business consulting

(G-7422)
CONNOR EVANS HAFENSTEIN LLP
2000 Henderson Rd Ste 460 (43220-2466)
PHONE..................614 464-2025
Fax: 614 224-8708
Daniel D Connor, *Managing Prtnr*
Robert Behal, *Partner*
EMP: 25 EST: 1970
SQ FT: 8,500
SALES (est): 2.6MM Privately Held
WEB: www.connorbehal.com
SIC: 8111 General practice attorney, lawyer

(G-7423)
CONSOLIDATED ELEC DISTRS INC
C E D
2101 S High St (43207-2428)
PHONE..................614 445-8871
Fax: 614 445-7165
Jim Bemiller, *Warehouse Mgr*
Ray Gillenwater, *Sales Staff*
Shawn Miller, *Sales Staff*
Sean O'Neil, *Sales Staff*
Tim Sedlock, *Sales Staff*
EMP: 50
SALES (corp-wide): 5.1B Privately Held
SIC: 5063 Electrical supplies
PA: Consolidated Electrical Distributors, Inc.
 1920 Westridge Dr
 Irving TX 75038
 972 582-5300

(G-7424)
CONSTRUCTION ONE INC
Also Called: Construction First
101 E Town St Ste 401 (43215-5247)
PHONE..................614 961-1140
Fax: 614 237-6769
William A Moberger, *President*
Paul Heatherly, *Superintendent*
Calvin Kelley, *Superintendent*
Sam Paratore, *Superintendent*
Vincent Wardle, *Superintendent*
EMP: 30
SQ FT: 7,500
SALES (est): 28.9MM Privately Held
SIC: 1542 Commercial & office building, new construction

(G-7425)
CONSTRUCTION SYSTEMS INC (PA)
2865 E 14th Ave (43219-2301)
PHONE..................614 252-0708
Fax: 614 251-8043
JD Flaherty Jr, *President*
Andrew Poczik, *Exec VP*
Tim Faherty, *Vice Pres*
Ted Roshon, *Vice Pres*
Randy Swoyer, *Vice Pres*
EMP: 68
SQ FT: 4,500
SALES (est): 19.4MM Privately Held
WEB: www.consysohio.com
SIC: 1742 Drywall; acoustical & ceiling work; plastering, plain or ornamental

(G-7426)
CONTAINERPORT GROUP INC
Also Called: Cpg
2400 Creekway Dr (43207-3431)
PHONE..................440 333-1330
Fax: 614 252-5144
Glenn Fehribach, *Senior VP*
Donna Izzo, *Transptn Dir*
Brad Ralston, *Project Mgr*
Ioana Sgondea, *Accountant*
Seth Skaggs, *Accounts Mgr*
EMP: 40
SALES (corp-wide): 241.2MM Privately Held
WEB: www.containerport.com
SIC: 4783 4212 4213 Containerization of goods for shipping; light haulage & cartage, local; trucking, except local
HQ: Containerport Group, Inc.
 1340 Depot St Fl 2
 Cleveland OH 44116
 440 333-1330

(G-7427)
CONTINENTAL BUSINESS SERVICES
Also Called: Continental Mewthod Solutions
41 S Grant Ave Fl 2 (43215-3979)
PHONE..................614 224-4534
Fax: 614 464-4730
Beau Hamer, *President*
Wendell R Kessler, *Corp Secy*
EMP: 30 EST: 1967
SQ FT: 5,000
SALES (est): 1.2MM Privately Held
SIC: 7389 Telephone answering service

(G-7428)
CONTINENTAL OFFICE FURN CORP (PA)
Also Called: Continntal Office Environments
5061 Freeway Dr E (43229-5401)
PHONE..................614 262-5010
Fax: 614 261-1261
Ira Sharfin, *CEO*
Franklin Kass, *Ch of Bd*
John Lucks Jr, *Ch of Bd*
Kyle Johnson, *President*
Nick Magoto, *Exec VP*
◆ EMP: 150 EST: 1941
SQ FT: 70,000
SALES: 110MM Privately Held
WEB: www.continentaloffice.com
SIC: 5021 1752 Office furniture; wood floor installation & refinishing

(G-7429)
CONTINENTAL OFFICE FURN CORP
Continental Office Moves
5063 Freeway Dr E (43229-5401)
PHONE..................614 781-0080
Fax: 614 786-1930
Jeff Leary, *Vice Pres*
Larry Snider, *Vice Pres*
Tim Conrad, *Manager*
EMP: 50
SALES (corp-wide): 110MM Privately Held
WEB: www.continentaloffice.com
SIC: 4212 Moving services
PA: Continental Office Furniture Corporation
 5061 Freeway Dr E
 Columbus OH 43229
 614 262-5010

(G-7430)
CONTINENTAL PROPERTIES
150 E Broad St Ste 700 (43215-3610)
P.O. Box 712 (43216-0712)
PHONE..................614 221-1800
Franklin Kass, *Managing Prtnr*
John Lucks Jr, *Partner*
John Shacklett, *Finance*
Angel Robbins, *Director*
Margaret McCandless, *Admin Sec*
EMP: 300
SALES (est): 21.8MM Privately Held
WEB: www.continental-communities.com
SIC: 6512 Commercial & industrial building operation

(G-7431)
CONTINENTAL RE COMPANIES (PA)
150 E Broad St Ste 200 (43215-3644)
PHONE..................614 221-1800
Franklin Kass, *Ch of Bd*
John Lucks Jr, *Vice Pres*
Brett Robinson, *Vice Pres*
Robert Lynch, *Project Mgr*
James Conway, *CFO*
EMP: 140
SALES (est): 105.6MM Privately Held
WEB: www.continental-realestate.com
SIC: 1542 1541 Commercial & office building, new construction; industrial buildings & warehouses

(G-7432)
CONTINENTAL REALTY LTD
180 E Broad St Ste 1708 (43215-3727)
PHONE..................614 221-6260
Angel Robbins, *Manager*
EMP: 29 Privately Held
SIC: 6531 Real estate brokers & agents
PA: Continental Realty Ltd
 150 E Gay St
 Columbus OH 43215

(G-7433)
CONTINENTAL/OLENTANGY HT LLC
1421 Olentangy River Rd (43212-1449)
PHONE..................614 297-9912
Dena Heinlein, *Marketing Staff*
EMP: 99
SALES (est): 894.5K Privately Held
SIC: 7011 Hotels & motels

(G-7434)
CONTINNTAL MSSAGE SOLUTION INC
Also Called: CMS Customer Solutions
41 S Grant Ave Fl 2 (43215-3979)
PHONE..................614 224-4534
Beau A Hamer, *President*
Andy Granger, *Controller*
Carol Lnd, *Manager*
EMP: 65
SALES (est): 7.4MM Privately Held
SIC: 8741 7299 Circuit management for motion picture theaters; personal document & information services

(G-7435)
CONTRACT SWEEPERS & EQP CO (PA)
2137 Parkwood Ave (43219-1145)
PHONE..................614 221-7441
Fax: 614 221-4241
Charles F Glander, *CEO*
Gerald Kesselring, *President*
Robert E Fultz, *Principal*
John C Hartranft, *Principal*
Mark Borden, *Area Mgr*
EMP: 50 EST: 1960
SQ FT: 10,000
SALES (est): 58.8MM Privately Held
WEB: www.sweepers.com
SIC: 4959 5084 Sweeping service: road, airport, parking lot, etc.; snowplowing; cleaning equipment, high pressure, sand or steam

(G-7436)
COOPER WODA COMPANIES INC (PA)
500 S Front St Fl 10 (43215-7619)
PHONE..................614 396-3200
Jeffrey J Woda, *Principal*
David Cooper, *Principal*
Sue Milner, *Controller*
Jennifer Ricci, *Agent*
EMP: 100 EST: 2007
SALES (est): 7.2MM Privately Held
SIC: 1522 1521 Apartment building construction; new construction, single-family houses

(G-7437)
COPART INC
1680 Williams Rd (43207-5111)
PHONE..................614 497-1590
Richard Hulker, *Manager*
EMP: 30
SALES (corp-wide): 1.4B Publicly Held
WEB: www.copart.com
SIC: 5012 Automobile auction
PA: Copart, Inc.
 14185 Dallas Pkwy Ste 300
 Dallas TX 75254
 972 391-5000

(G-7438)
COPC HOSPITALS
3555 Olentangy River Rd (43214-3912)
PHONE..................614 268-8164
Timothy Fallon, *President*
EMP: 27 EST: 2011
SALES (est): 1.9MM Privately Held
SIC: 8062 General medical & surgical hospitals

(G-7439)
CORI CARE INC
1060 Kingsmill Pkwy (43229-1143)
PHONE..................614 848-4357
Candace Allegra, *President*
Carrie Swank, *Office Mgr*
Jacki Frost, *Admin Asst*
EMP: 55
SALES (est): 2MM Privately Held
SIC: 8082 Home health care services

(G-7440)
CORK INC
2006 Kenton St (43205-1655)
PHONE..................614 253-8400
Charles Blauman, *President*
EMP: 50
SALES (est): 2.7MM Privately Held
SIC: 1521 Single-family housing construction

(G-7441)
CORPORATE CLEANING INC
781 Northwest Blvd # 103 (43212-3858)
PHONE..................614 203-6051
Crystal Hughey, *CEO*
Eugene Hughey, *COO*
EMP: 33 EST: 2010
SALES (est): 1.3MM Privately Held
SIC: 7699 7349 7342 1542 Cleaning services; building & office cleaning services; building cleaning service; rest room cleaning service; commercial & office building, new construction

(G-7442)
CORPORATE ENVIRONMENTS OF OHIO
Also Called: C E O
2899 Morse Rd (43231-6033)
PHONE..................614 358-3375
Fax: 614 358-8732
Mark Bailey, *President*
Linda Robbins, *Vice Pres*
Pat Bailey, *Finance*
EMP: 43
SQ FT: 33,000
SALES (est): 3.9MM Privately Held
SIC: 5712 1799 Office furniture; office furniture installation

(G-7443)
CORPORATE EXCHANGE HOTEL ASSOC
Also Called: Embassy Suites
2700 Corporate Exch Dr (43231-1690)
PHONE..................614 890-8600
Fax: 614 823-5438
Kendal Clay, *General Ptnr*
Andy Barrick, *Information Mgr*
EMP: 150
SALES (est): 6.5MM Privately Held
SIC: 7011 5812 5813 Hotels; eating places; cocktail lounge

(G-7444)
CORPORATE FIN ASSOC OF CLUMBUS
671 Camden Yard Ct (43235-3492)
PHONE..................614 457-9219
Charles E Washbush, *President*
EMP: 100
SQ FT: 750
SALES: 100MM Privately Held
SIC: 8742 7389 6211 Business consultant; brokers, business: buying & selling business enterprises; security brokers & dealers

(G-7445)
CORROSION FLUID PRODUCTS CORP (DH)
3000 E 14th Ave (43219-2355)
PHONE..................248 478-0100
Joseph V Andronaco, *CEO*
Joseph P Andronaco, *President*
Rich Catalano, *General Mgr*
Randy Dingman, *General Mgr*
Terry Massey, *Vice Pres*

▲ EMP: 30
SQ FT: 28,500
SALES (est): 57.5MM
SALES (corp-wide): 2.5B **Publicly Held**
WEB: www.corrosionfluid.com
SIC: 5084 5074 Pumps & pumping equipment; pipes & fittings, plastic; plumbing & heating valves
HQ: Fcx Performance, Inc
3000 E 14th Ave
Columbus OH 43219
614 324-6050

(G-7446)
COS EXPRESS INC
3616 Fisher Rd (43228-1012)
PHONE......................614 276-9000
Charles J Casey Jr, *President*
Ed Weisenberger, *Vice Pres*
EMP: 99
SQ FT: 5,460
SALES (est): 8.3MM **Privately Held**
SIC: 4731 Freight transportation arrangement

(G-7447)
COSMIC CONCEPTS LTD
399 E Main St Ste 140 (43215-5384)
PHONE......................614 228-1104
John Riddle, *Branch Mgr*
EMP: 142
SALES (corp-wide): 46MM **Privately Held**
SIC: 4822 Telegraph & other communications
PA: Cosmic Concepts, Ltd.
318 Clubhouse Rd
Hunt Valley MD 21031
410 825-8500

(G-7448)
COSTUME SPECIALISTS INC (PA)
211 N 5th St Ste 100 (43215-2722)
PHONE......................614 464-2115
Fax: 614 464-2114
Wendy C Goldstein, *President*
Steven Hudson, *Purch Agent*
Greg Manger, *Sales Staff*
Tracy Liberatore, *Admin Asst*
EMP: 36
SQ FT: 34,500
SALES (est): 3.1MM **Privately Held**
WEB: www.cospec.com
SIC: 2389 7299 Theatrical costumes; costume rental

(G-7449)
COTT SYSTEMS INC
2800 Corp Exchange Dr # 300 (43231-1678)
PHONE......................614 847-4405
Fax: 614 847-3737
Deborah A Ball, *CEO*
Karen L Bailey, *Exec VP*
Jodie Bare, *Vice Pres*
Bob Mains, *Vice Pres*
Richard J Miller, *Vice Pres*
EMP: 77
SQ FT: 20,000
SALES (est): 16.4MM **Privately Held**
WEB: www.cottsystems.com
SIC: 7373 7371 2789 Computer integrated systems design; computer software development & applications; beveling of cards

(G-7450)
COUNTRYSIDE ELECTRIC INC
2920 Switzer Ave (43219-2372)
PHONE......................614 478-7960
Fax: 614 478-8419
Glen Lehman, *President*
Vicki Lehman, *Corp Secy*
Eric Scott, *Manager*
EMP: 25
SALES (est): 4MM **Privately Held**
WEB: www.countrysideelectricinc.com
SIC: 1731 General electrical contractor

(G-7451)
COURTYARD MANAGEMENT CORP
Also Called: Courtyard By Marriott
2901 Airport Dr (43219-2299)
PHONE......................614 475-8530
Fax: 614 475-8599
Mark Laport, *Manager*
EMP: 50
SALES (corp-wide): 22.8B **Publicly Held**
SIC: 7011 Hotels & motels
HQ: Courtyard Management Corporation
10400 Fernwood Rd
Bethesda MD 20817

(G-7452)
COVENANT HOME HEALTH CARE LLC
5212 W Broad St Ste J (43228-1670)
PHONE......................614 465-2017
Zeinab A Ali, *Mng Member*
Zeinab Ali, *Mng Member*
Daniel Evans, *Executive*
EMP: 30
SALES (est): 595.3K **Privately Held**
SIC: 8099 Blood related health services

(G-7453)
COVENANT TRANSPORT INC
3825 Aries Brook Dr (43207-4696)
PHONE......................423 821-1212
EMP: 71 **Publicly Held**
WEB: www.covenanttransport.com
SIC: 4731 Brokers, shipping
HQ: Covenant Transport, Inc.
400 Birmingham Hwy
Chattanooga TN 37419
423 821-1212

(G-7454)
CRABBE BROWN & JAMES LLP (PA)
500 S Front St Ste 1200 (43215-7631)
PHONE......................614 229-4587
Fax: 614 229-4559
Larry James, *CEO*
Doreen Mazzanti, *Plant Mgr*
Vincent J Lodico, *Controller*
Robert Lewis, *Corp Counsel*
Carol Reinhart, *Manager*
EMP: 50
SALES (est): 7.9MM **Privately Held**
SIC: 8111 General practice law office

(G-7455)
CRAWFORD MECHANICAL SVCS INC
3445 Morse Rd (43231-6183)
PHONE......................614 478-9424
Fax: 614 478-9447
William T Crawford, *President*
Suzette Crawford, *Vice Pres*
Bill Blake, *Project Mgr*
Justin Doll, *Project Mgr*
Tony Young, *CFO*
EMP: 70
SALES (est): 15.6MM **Privately Held**
WEB: www.crawfordmech.com
SIC: 1711 Plumbing contractors

(G-7456)
CREATIVE LIVING INC
150 W 10th Ave (43201-2093)
PHONE......................614 421-1131
Fax: 614 421-9949
Todd D Ackerman, *President*
John Lepley, *Trustee*
Ron Mains, *Treasurer*
Marilyn Frank, *Exec Dir*
Jody Orsine Geiger, *Admin Sec*
EMP: 29 **EST:** 1969
SQ FT: 10,000
SALES: 300.2K **Privately Held**
WEB: www.creative-living.com
SIC: 6513 Retirement hotel operation

(G-7457)
CREATIVE LIVING HOUSING CORP
150 W 10th Ave Ofc (43201-7015)
PHONE......................614 421-1226
Anne Nagey, *President*
Marilyn Frank, *Director*
EMP: 25
SQ FT: 10,000
SALES: 396.4K **Privately Held**
SIC: 6513 Apartment building operators

(G-7458)
CREDIT BUR COLLECTN SVCS INC (HQ)
Also Called: Cbcs
236 E Town St (43215-4631)
PHONE......................614 223-0688
Larry Ebert, *President*
Jennifer Allen, *General Mgr*
Dirk Cantrell, *Corp Secy*
Brian Stryker, *Vice Pres*
Ki Sang, *Opers Staff*
EMP: 50
SQ FT: 60,000
SALES (est): 20MM
SALES (corp-wide): 279.4MM **Privately Held**
SIC: 7322 Collection agency, except real estate
PA: Cbc Companies, Inc.
250 E Broad St Fl 21
Columbus OH 43215
614 222-4343

(G-7459)
CREEKSIDE II LLC
Also Called: Pizzuti
2 Miranova Pl Ste 100 (43215-7003)
PHONE......................614 280-4000
Ronald Pizzuti, *CEO*
EMP: 45 **EST:** 1973
SALES (est): 2.4MM **Privately Held**
WEB: www.pizzuti.com
SIC: 6552 Land subdividers & developers, commercial

(G-7460)
CRESTLINE HOTELS & RESORTS LLC
7490 Vantage Dr (43235-1416)
PHONE......................614 846-4355
Liz Buxton, *Manager*
EMP: 34 **Publicly Held**
SIC: 8741 Hotel or motel management
HQ: Crestline Hotels & Resorts, Llc
3950 University Dr # 301
Fairfax VA 22030
571 529-6100

(G-7461)
CRETE CARRIER CORPORATION
5400 Crosswind Dr (43228-3778)
PHONE......................614 853-4500
Scott Clay, *Manager*
Randy James, *Manager*
EMP: 150
SALES (corp-wide): 984MM **Privately Held**
SIC: 4213 Refrigerated products transport
PA: Crete Carrier Corporation
400 Nw 56th St
Lincoln NE 68528
402 475-9521

(G-7462)
CREW SOCCER STADIUM LLC
1 Black And Gold Blvd (43211-2091)
PHONE......................614 447-2739
Andy Louthnane, *President*
Mark McCullers, *President*
EMP: 50
SALES (est): 3.6MM **Privately Held**
SIC: 7941 Sports field or stadium operator, promoting sports events

(G-7463)
CRITICAL CARE TRANSPORT INC
2936 E 14th Ave (43219-2304)
P.O. Box 360912 (43236-0912)
PHONE......................614 775-0564
William Staton, *President*
Christian Staton, *Principal*
Benjamin Leonard, *Opers Staff*
James Samuell, *Director*
EMP: 60
SALES (est): 2.5MM **Privately Held**
WEB: www.criticalcaretransport.net
SIC: 4119 Ambulance service

(G-7464)
CRITTENTON FAMILY SERVICES
1414 E Broad St (43205-1505)
PHONE......................614 251-0103
Fax: 614 251-1177
Steve Votow, *Director*
EMP: 35
SQ FT: 3,500
SALES: 7.1MM **Privately Held**
SIC: 8322 Youth center

(G-7465)
CROSSCHX INC
99 E Main St (43215-5115)
PHONE......................800 501-3161
Sean Lane, *CEO*
Brad Mascho, *President*
Carlton Fox, *COO*
Joel Crockett, *Vice Pres*
Bubba Fox, *Vice Pres*
EMP: 73
SQ FT: 5,500
SALES (est): 4MM **Privately Held**
SIC: 7371 Computer software development & applications

(G-7466)
CROWE HORWATH LLP
155 W Nationwide Blvd # 500 (43215-2570)
PHONE......................614 469-0001
Joseph Santucci, *Principal*
Dennis Obyc, *Accounting Mgr*
John Chen, *Auditing Mgr*
Jeff Nywening, *Auditing Mgr*
Dawena Lusk, *Tax Mgr*
EMP: 126
SQ FT: 6,600
SALES (corp-wide): 809.4MM **Privately Held**
SIC: 8721 Certified public accountant
PA: Crowe Horwath Llp
225 W Wacker Dr Ste 2600
Chicago IL 60606
312 899-7000

(G-7467)
CROWN DIELECTRIC INDS INC
Also Called: Crown Auto Top Mfg Co
830 W Broad St (43222-1421)
PHONE......................614 224-5161
Fax: 614 221-1384
Anthony Gurvis, *President*
Andrew M Kauffman, *Principal*
Ron Gurvis, *Vice Pres*
Andy Kauffman, *Controller*
EMP: 105 **EST:** 1931
SQ FT: 2,000
SALES (est): 6.9MM **Privately Held**
SIC: 2394 2399 2273 5013 Convertible tops, canvas or boat: from purchased materials; seat covers, automobile; automobile floor coverings, except rubber or plastic; automotive supplies & parts; automotive parts

(G-7468)
CROWN WESTFALEN LLC
1251 Dublin Rd (43215-7000)
PHONE......................614 488-1169
EMP: 197
SALES (est): 149.9K
SALES (corp-wide): 8MM **Privately Held**
SIC: 8742 Management consulting services
PA: Crown Northcorp, Inc.
1251 Dublin Rd Ste 100
Columbus OH 43215
614 488-1169

(G-7469)
CRP CONTRACTING
4477 E 5th Ave (43219-1817)
PHONE......................614 338-8501
James Head, *Partner*
Paul Ondera, *Partner*
EMP: 60
SALES (est): 1.5MM **Privately Held**
SIC: 1611 Airport runway construction

(G-7470)
CS HOTELS LIMITED PARTNERSHIP
Also Called: Courtyard Columbus West
2350 Westbelt Dr (43228-3822)
PHONE......................614 771-8999
EMP: 75 **Privately Held**
SIC: 7011 Hotels And Motels, Nsk
PA: Cs Hotels Limited Partnership
740 Centre View Blvd
Crestview Hills KY 41017

Columbus - Franklin County (G-7471) — GEOGRAPHIC SECTION

(G-7471)
CSL PLASMA INC
2650 N High St (43202-2520)
PHONE..................614 267-4982
Bruce Gasparollo, *General Mgr*
Carmen Fannin, *Branch Mgr*
Mark Leach, *Assistant*
EMP: 100
SQ FT: 3,000
SALES (corp-wide): 6.9B **Privately Held**
WEB: www.zlbplasma.com
SIC: 8099 Plasmapherous center
HQ: Csl Plasma Inc.
    900 Broken Sound Pkwy # 4
    Boca Raton FL 33487
    561 981-3700

(G-7472)
CSX CORPORATION
88 E Broad St Ste 1540 (43215-3550)
PHONE..................614 242-3932
EMP: 1000
SALES (corp-wide): 11.4B **Publicly Held**
SIC: 4789 Pipeline terminal facilities, independently operated
PA: Csx Corporation
    500 Water St Fl 15
    Jacksonville FL 32202
    904 359-3200

(G-7473)
CTD INVESTMENTS LLC (PA)
630 E Broad St (43215-3999)
PHONE..................614 570-9949
Richard L Gerhardt II,
Stephanie Jandik,
William Lewis,
EMP: 50
SQ FT: 6,000
SALES: 20MM **Privately Held**
SIC: 6799 5999 Investors; electronic parts & equipment

(G-7474)
CTL ENGINEERING INC (PA)
2860 Fisher Rd (43204-3538)
P.O. Box 44548 (43204-0548)
PHONE..................614 276-8123
Fax: 614 276-6377
C K Satyapriya, *CEO*
David Breitfeller, *Vice Pres*
Ali Jamshidi, *CFO*
Paul Douglas, *VP Mktg*
Donald C Dewey, *Branch Mgr*
EMP: 120
SQ FT: 35,000
SALES: 36.1MM **Privately Held**
WEB: www.ctleng.com
SIC: 8711 8731 8734 8713 Consulting engineer; commercial physical research; metallurgical testing laboratory; product testing laboratory, safety or performance; forensic laboratory; surveying services

(G-7475)
CV PERRY BUILDERS
370 S 5th St Ste 2 (43215-5433)
P.O. Box 20405 (43220-0405)
PHONE..................614 221-4131
Carlyle Perry Jr, *President*
James Fry, *CFO*
EMP: 35
SALES (est): 2MM
SALES (corp-wide): 4.7MM **Privately Held**
WEB: www.cvperry.com
SIC: 1531 6719 Operative builders; investment holding companies, except banks
PA: C. V. Perry & Co.
    370 S 5th St
    Columbus OH 43215
    614 221-4131

(G-7476)
D & D INVESTMENT CO
Also Called: Columbus Cold Storage
3080 Valleyview Dr (43204-2011)
PHONE..................614 272-6567
Donald Dick, *Partner*
Daniel Dick, *Partner*
Jason Dick, *Vice Pres*
EMP: 50
SALES (est): 8MM **Privately Held**
SIC: 5078 4222 5169 5999 Cold storage machinery; warehousing, cold storage or refrigerated; dry ice; ice

(G-7477)
D & J MASTER CLEAN INC
Also Called: Master Clean Carpet & Uphlstry
680 Dearborn Park Ln (43085-5701)
PHONE..................614 847-1181
Fax: 614 338-1122
Don Kessler, *CEO*
Theresa Kessler, *General Mgr*
Stephanie Kessler, *Corp Secy*
Van Wilcox, *Vice Pres*
Joe Wooster, *Vice Pres*
EMP: 100
SQ FT: 15,000
SALES (est): 7.6MM **Privately Held**
SIC: 7217 7349 Carpet & upholstery cleaning on customer premises; janitorial service, contract basis

(G-7478)
D & S PROPERTIES
Also Called: S & W Properties
854 E Broad St (43205-1110)
PHONE..................614 224-6663
David L Fisher, *Partner*
Suzanne P Fisher, *Partner*
EMP: 28
SQ FT: 900
SALES: 3.7MM **Privately Held**
SIC: 6513 Apartment hotel operation

(G-7479)
D H I COOPERATIVE INC
1224 Alton Darby Creek Rd A (43228-9813)
P.O. Box 28168 (43228-0168)
PHONE..................614 545-0460
Fax: 614 545-0468
Tony Broering, *President*
Brian Winters, *General Mgr*
Cathy Strong, *Accounting Mgr*
Julee Oreilly, *Manager*
Julee O'Reilly, *Lab Dir*
EMP: 65 **EST:** 1969
SQ FT: 7,200
SALES (est): 5.9MM **Privately Held**
WEB: www.dhiohio.com
SIC: 0751 Milk testing services

(G-7480)
D L A TRAINING CENTER
3990 E Brd St Bldg 11 5 (43213)
P.O. Box 3990 (43218-3990)
PHONE..................614 692-5986
Lori Beatty, *Med Doctor*
Kathleen Tuskas, *Director*
EMP: 100 **EST:** 1999
SALES (est): 5.2MM **Privately Held**
SIC: 8742 Training & development consultant

(G-7481)
D M I DISTRIBUTION INC
6150 Huntley Rd Ste A (43229-1000)
PHONE..................765 584-3234
Ray Waudby, *Warehouse Mgr*
Roger Stewart, *Manager*
EMP: 35 **Privately Held**
WEB: www.dmidistribution.com
SIC: 4225 5084 General warehousing & storage; brewery products manufacturing machinery, commercial
PA: D M I Distribution, Inc.
    990 Industrial Park Dr
    Winchester IN 47394

(G-7482)
D&T INSTALLED SIDING LLC
1325 Marion Rd (43207-2142)
PHONE..................614 444-8445
Tim Wiseman,
EMP: 30
SALES (est): 2.2MM **Privately Held**
SIC: 1761 Siding contractor

(G-7483)
DAILY SERVICES LLC (PA)
1110 Morse Rd Ste B1 (43229-6325)
PHONE..................614 431-5100
Ryan Cote, *President*
Lisa McEldowney, *District Mgr*
Rick Fazzina, *CFO*
Scott Holland, *Controller*
Ryan Mason, *Mng Member*
EMP: 250
SQ FT: 2,000

SALES (est): 22.3MM **Privately Held**
SIC: 7361 Executive placement

(G-7484)
DAN TOBIN PONTIAC BUICK GMC
Also Called: Tobin, Dan Pontiac
2539 Billingsley Rd (43235-5975)
PHONE..................614 889-6300
Fax: 614 793-4493
Daniel L Tobin, *CEO*
Nita Smith, *Controller*
Keith Chambers, *Sales Mgr*
Kyln Mitchell, *Sales Mgr*
Tate Cline, *Sales Staff*
EMP: 85
SQ FT: 40,000
SALES (est): 34.4MM **Privately Held**
WEB: www.dantobin.com
SIC: 5511 7538 7532 5521 Automobiles, new & used; general automotive repair shops; top & body repair & paint shops; used car dealers

(G-7485)
DANA & PARISER ATTYS
495 E Mound St (43215-5596)
PHONE..................614 253-1010
David Pariser, *Owner*
EMP: 40
SALES (est): 4.1MM **Privately Held**
WEB: www.dplawyers.com
SIC: 8111 General practice attorney, lawyer

(G-7486)
DANCOR INC
2155 Dublin Rd (43228-9668)
PHONE..................614 340-2155
Fax: 614 340-2156
Dan Fronk, *CEO*
Michael Michalski, *COO*
Dave Werner, *COO*
Nick Malagreca, *Sales Mgr*
Jae Ober, *Sales Mgr*
EMP: 35
SQ FT: 20,000
SALES (est): 4.9MM **Privately Held**
WEB: www.dancorinc.com
SIC: 8748 Business consulting

(G-7487)
DANIEL LOGISTICS INC
426 Mccormick Blvd (43213-1525)
PHONE..................614 367-9442
Ellen Cathers, *President*
Mick Bolon, *General Mgr*
Gay Cathers, *Corp Secy*
Seth Lingo, *Facilities Mgr*
Kevin Trent, *Treasurer*
EMP: 75
SQ FT: 14,000
SALES (est): 5.2MM **Privately Held**
WEB: www.daniellogistics.com
SIC: 4225 General warehousing & storage

(G-7488)
DANITE HOLDINGS LTD
Also Called: Danite Sign Co
1640 Harmon Ave (43223-3321)
PHONE..................614 444-3333
Fax: 614 444-3026
Tim McCord, *President*
C William Klausman, *Partner*
Tom Seymore, *COO*
James Detty, *Project Mgr*
Jeremy McCord, *Purchasing*
EMP: 50
SQ FT: 33,500
SALES (est): 8.1MM **Privately Held**
WEB: www.danitesign.com
SIC: 3993 1799 Electric signs; neon signs; sign installation & maintenance

(G-7489)
DAR PLUMBING
Also Called: D A R Plumbing
2230 Refugee Rd (43207-2843)
P.O. Box 7791 (43207-0791)
PHONE..................614 445-8243
Fax: 614 445-8207
Don Hughes, *Owner*
EMP: 27
SQ FT: 1,500
SALES (est): 2.3MM **Privately Held**
SIC: 1711 Plumbing contractors

(G-7490)
DAVEY TREE EXPERT COMPANY
Also Called: Davey Tree and Lawn Care
3603 Westerville Rd (43224-2538)
PHONE..................614 471-4144
Fax: 614 471-9126
Tom Bowman, *Manager*
EMP: 55
SQ FT: 1,445
SALES (corp-wide): 915.9MM **Privately Held**
SIC: 0782 0783 Landscape contractors; ornamental shrub & tree services
PA: The Davey Tree Expert Company
    1500 N Mantua St
    Kent OH 44240
    330 673-9511

(G-7491)
DAWSON RESOURCES (PA)
Also Called: Dawson Personnel Systems
1114 Dublin Rd (43215-1039)
PHONE..................614 255-1400
Fax: 614 255-1401
Michael Linton, *President*
Ian Dawson, *Managing Dir*
Christopher Decapua, *Principal*
David Decapua, *Principal*
Jonathan Clark, *Business Mgr*
EMP: 45
SQ FT: 5,000
SALES (est): 38.4MM **Privately Held**
WEB: www.dawsonworks.com
SIC: 7361 7363 Placement agencies; temporary help service; employee leasing service; office help supply service

(G-7492)
DAWSON RESOURCES
Also Called: Dawson Personnel
4184 W Broad St (43228-1671)
PHONE..................614 274-8900
Maurine Kenneley, *Branch Mgr*
EMP: 386
SALES (corp-wide): 38.4MM **Privately Held**
WEB: www.dawsonworks.com
SIC: 7361 Employment agencies
PA: Dawson Resources
    1114 Dublin Rd
    Columbus OH 43215
    614 255-1400

(G-7493)
DAYTON FREIGHT LINES INC
1406 Blatt Blvd (43230-6627)
PHONE..................614 860-1080
Fax: 614 860-1851
Grey Armstrong, *Manager*
EMP: 30
SALES (corp-wide): 1B **Privately Held**
SIC: 4213 Trucking, except local
PA: Dayton Freight Lines, Inc.
    6450 Poe Ave Ste 311
    Dayton OH 45414
    937 264-4060

(G-7494)
DAYTON HEIDELBERG DISTRG CO
3801 Parkwest Dr (43228-1457)
PHONE..................614 308-0400
Greg Maurer, *Branch Mgr*
EMP: 200
SALES (corp-wide): 369.4MM **Privately Held**
SIC: 5182 5181 Wine; beer & ale
PA: Dayton Heidelberg Distributing Co.
    3601 Dryden Rd
    Moraine OH 45439
    937 222-8692

(G-7495)
DB&P LOGISTICS INC
3544 Watkins Rd (43232-5544)
P.O. Box 32335 (43232-0335)
PHONE..................614 491-4035
Danie Barke, *Principal*
EMP: 30
SALES (est): 1.5MM **Privately Held**
WEB: www.pemberton-inc.com
SIC: 7011 Hotels

GEOGRAPHIC SECTION
Columbus - Franklin County (G-7519)

(G-7496)
DD&B INC
4449 Easton Way (43219-6093)
PHONE..................614 577-0550
Deric Butler, *CEO*
EMP: 50 **EST:** 2015
SQ FT: 3,500
SALES (est): 1MM **Privately Held**
SIC: 4212 Delivery service, vehicular

(G-7497)
DDR CORP
445 Hutchinson Ave # 800 (43235-5677)
PHONE..................614 785-6445
Steve Eroskey, *Principal*
EMP: 50
SALES (corp-wide): 921.5MM **Privately Held**
WEB: www.ddrc.com
SIC: 6798 Real estate investment trusts
PA: Ddr Corp.
   3300 Enterprise Pkwy
   Beachwood OH 44122
   216 755-5500

(G-7498)
DEARTH MANAGEMENT COMPANY (PA)
Also Called: Morning View Care Center
134 Northwoods Blvd Ste C (43235-4727)
P.O. Box 10, Marengo (43334-0010)
PHONE..................614 847-1070
Fax: 614 847-1393
Tammy Shepherd, *Vice Pres*
Glen H Dearth, *Administration*
EMP: 217
SQ FT: 10,000
SALES (est): 11.7MM **Privately Held**
WEB: www.schoenbrunnhealthcare.com
SIC: 8052 8741 Personal care facility; management services

(G-7499)
DEDICATED TECHNOLOGIES INC
580 N 4th St Ste 280 (43215-2154)
PHONE..................614 460-3200
Fax: 614 460-3201
Jeffrey P Dalton, *President*
Phillip Deskins, *Business Mgr*
Kate Thomas, *Business Mgr*
Patricia Lickliter, *Vice Pres*
Shadyne Nunley, *Project Mgr*
EMP: 82
SQ FT: 7,000
SALES (est): 10.7MM **Privately Held**
WEB: www.dedicatedtech.com
SIC: 8742 7361 8748 Industry specialist consultants; placement agencies; business consulting

(G-7500)
DEFENSE FIN & ACCOUNTING SVC
3990 E Broad St (43213-1152)
PHONE..................410 436-9740
Paul Fincato, *Principal*
Norman Noe, *Finance*
David Kane, *Manager*
Eric Swanson, *Prgrmr*
EMP: 50
SALES (est): 10.4MM **Privately Held**
SIC: 8721 Accounting, auditing & bookkeeping

(G-7501)
DEFENSE FIN & ACCOUNTING SVC
Also Called: West Entitlement Operations
3990 E Broad St (43213-1152)
PHONE..................614 693-6700
Jeff Boyd, *Supervisor*
Johnathan Witter, *Director*
EMP: 2900 **Publicly Held**
WEB: www.osd.pentagon.mil
SIC: 8721 9711 Accounting services, except auditing; national security;
HQ: Defense Finance & Accounting Service
   8899 E 56th St
   Indianapolis IN 46249

(G-7502)
DEFENSE INFO SYSTEMS AGCY
Also Called: D I S A D E C C Columbus
3990 E Broad St Bldg 20c (43213-1152)
P.O. Box 3990 (43218-3990)
PHONE..................614 692-4433
Brian States, *Network Enginr*
Michael Robertson, *Director*
EMP: 153 **Publicly Held**
WEB: www.scott.disa.mil
SIC: 6411 Insurance agents, brokers & service
HQ: Defense Information Systems Agency
   6910 Cooper Rd
   Fort Meade MD 20755

(G-7503)
DEL MONTE FRESH PRODUCE NA INC
2200 Westbelt Dr (43228-3820)
PHONE..................614 527-7398
Fax: 614 527-8575
Andrew Pschesang, *Manager*
EMP: 30 **Privately Held**
SIC: 5148 Fruits, fresh
HQ: Del Monte Fresh Produce N.A., Inc.
   241 Sevilla Ave Ste 200
   Coral Gables FL 33134
   305 520-8400

(G-7504)
DELILLE OXYGEN COMPANY (PA)
772 Marion Rd (43207-2595)
P.O. Box 7809 (43207-0809)
PHONE..................614 444-1177
Fax: 614 444-0733
Joseph R Smith, *Ch of Bd*
Tom Smith, *President*
Richard F Carlile, *Principal*
Jim Smith, *Vice Pres*
Josh Weinmann, *Vice Pres*
EMP: 30
SQ FT: 20,000
SALES (est): 19.8MM **Privately Held**
WEB: www.delille.com
SIC: 2813 5085 Acetylene; welding supplies

(G-7505)
DELOITTE & TOUCHE LLP
180 E Broad St Ste 1400 (43215-3611)
PHONE..................614 221-1000
Fax: 614 229-4647
Chad Fast, *Auditing Mgr*
Kevin Davis, *Auditor*
Breanne Walker, *Auditor*
Brian Maxwell, *Human Res Dir*
John McEwan, *Branch Mgr*
EMP: 250
SALES (corp-wide): 5.9B **Privately Held**
WEB: www.deloitte.com
SIC: 8721 Accounting services, except auditing; certified public accountant
HQ: Deloitte & Touche Llp
   30 Rockefeller Plz # 4350
   New York NY 10112
   212 492-4000

(G-7506)
DELTA AIR LINES INC
Also Called: Delta Airlines
4600 Intl Gtwy Ste 6 (43219)
PHONE..................614 239-4440
Felix Sciuloi, *General Mgr*
Joseph Farmer, *Senior Mgr*
EMP: 53
SALES (corp-wide): 41.2B **Publicly Held**
WEB: www.delta.com
SIC: 4512 Air passenger carrier, scheduled
PA: Delta Air Lines, Inc.
   1030 Delta Blvd
   Atlanta GA 30354
   404 715-2600

(G-7507)
DENT MAGIC
4629 Poth Rd (43213-1329)
PHONE..................614 864-3368
Fax: 614 759-8422
David Bradley Miller, *Owner*
EMP: 26
SALES (est): 729.8K **Privately Held**
SIC: 7532 Body shop, automotive

(G-7508)
DENTAL FACILITY
Also Called: DENTAL FACULTY PRACTICE
305 W 12th Ave Rm 1159 (43210-1267)
PHONE..................614 292-1472
Paul Casamassimo, *President*
EMP: 50
SALES: 8.7MM **Privately Held**
WEB: www.dentalfacility.com
SIC: 8021 Dentists' office

(G-7509)
DEPUY PAVING INC
1850 Mckinley Ave (43222-1004)
PHONE..................614 272-0256
Fax: 614 272-7144
Clyde Depuy, *President*
Laura Depuy, *Vice Pres*
EMP: 25
SQ FT: 6,400
SALES (est): 2.7MM **Privately Held**
SIC: 1771 Blacktop (asphalt) work

(G-7510)
DESIGN CENTRAL INC
6464 Presidential Gtwy (43231-7673)
PHONE..................614 890-0202
Fax: 614 890-5880
Rainer Teufel, *Chairman*
Deb Liviach, *Treasurer*
Pete Koloski, *Executive*
EMP: 35
SQ FT: 13,000
SALES (est): 3.9MM **Privately Held**
WEB: www.design-central.com
SIC: 7389 Design, commercial & industrial

(G-7511)
DEVCARE SOLUTIONS LTD
131 N High St Ste 640 (43215-3079)
PHONE..................614 221-2277
Janaki Thiru, *President*
Ramkumar Regupathy, *Bus Dvlpt Dir*
Iyyappan Amirthalingam, *Financial Analy*
Kiran Elan, *Manager*
Venkat SRI, *Manager*
EMP: 47
SQ FT: 600
SALES: 7.3MM **Privately Held**
SIC: 8748 7371 7373 Systems engineering consultant, ex. computer or professional; custom computer programming services; systems engineering, computer related; office computer automation systems integration

(G-7512)
DEVELPMNTAL DSBLTIES OHIO DEPT
Also Called: Youngstown Developmental Ctr
30 E Broad St Fl 8 (43215-3414)
PHONE..................330 544-2231
Cynthia Renner, *Superintendent*
Pat Negro, *Director*
EMP: 245 **Privately Held**
SIC: 9431 8361 Administration of public health programs; ; home for the mentally retarded
HQ: Ohio Department Of Developmental Disabilities
   30 E Broad St Fl 13
   Columbus OH 43215

(G-7513)
DEVELPMNTAL DSBLTIES OHIO DEPT
Also Called: Columbus Developmental Center
1601 W Broad St (43222-1054)
PHONE..................614 272-0509
Fax: 614 272-1054
Charles Flowers, *Manager*
Nicki Cross, *Nursing Dir*
Nickie Cross, *Nursing Dir*
Andy Chappella, *Executive*
EMP: 350 **Privately Held**
SIC: 9431 8063 8052 Administration of public health programs; ; psychiatric hospitals; intermediate care facilities
HQ: Ohio Department Of Developmental Disabilities
   30 E Broad St Fl 13
   Columbus OH 43215

(G-7514)
DEVELPMNTAL DSBLTIES OHIO DEPT
Also Called: Montgomery Developmental Ctr
30 E Broad St Fl 8 (43215-3414)
PHONE..................937 233-8108
Fax: 937 233-9020
Greg Darling, *Superintendent*
EMP: 200 **Privately Held**
SIC: 9431 8322 Administration of public health programs; ; individual & family services
HQ: Ohio Department Of Developmental Disabilities
   30 E Broad St Fl 13
   Columbus OH 43215

(G-7515)
DEVRY UNIVERSITY INC
1350 Alum Creek Dr (43209-2705)
PHONE..................614 251-6969
Scarlett Howery, *President*
Larry Stewart, *Facilities Mgr*
Galen Graham, *Pub Rel Mgr*
Sharon Steel, *Marketing Mgr*
EMP: 225
SQ FT: 92,000
SALES (corp-wide): 1.8B **Publicly Held**
WEB: www.devryuniversity.com
SIC: 8742 8221 Human resource consulting services; university
HQ: Devry University, Inc.
   3005 Highland Pkwy # 700
   Downers Grove IL 60515
   630 515-7700

(G-7516)
DIAMOND HILL CAPITAL MGT INC
325 John H Mcconnell Blvd (43215-2672)
PHONE..................614 255-3333
Ric Dillon, *President*
Lisa M Wesolek, *Managing Dir*
Richard Snowdon, *Vice Pres*
Brian Baker, *Research*
Daniel Kohnen, *Research*
EMP: 45
SALES (est): 9.5MM **Publicly Held**
SIC: 6211 Security brokers & dealers
PA: Diamond Hill Investment Group, Inc.
   325 John H Mcconnell Blvd # 200
   Columbus OH 43215

(G-7517)
DIAMOND HILL FUNDS
325 John H Mcconnell Blvd # 200 (43215-2677)
PHONE..................614 255-3333
Roderick Dillon, *Partner*
George S McElroy, *Managing Dir*
EMP: 30
SQ FT: 8,000
SALES (est): 4.1MM **Privately Held**
SIC: 6282 Investment advisory service

(G-7518)
DICKS SPORTING GOODS INC
Also Called: Dick's Sporting Goods 1166
4304 Easton Gateway Dr (43219-1544)
PHONE..................614 472-4250
Robert Nelson, *Branch Mgr*
EMP: 35
SALES (corp-wide): 8.5B **Publicly Held**
SIC: 7999 5699 Sporting goods rental; sports apparel
PA: Dick's Sporting Goods, Inc.
   345 Court St
   Coraopolis PA 15108
   724 273-3400

(G-7519)
DIGICO IMAGING INC
Also Called: DCI
3487 E Fulton St (43227-1126)
PHONE..................614 239-5200
Ira Nutis, *President*
Steve Spain, *Vice Pres*
Michael Eyer, *Prdtn Mgr*
Tred Rowland, *CIO*
Gary Hedrick, *Director*
EMP: 75 **EST:** 1997
SQ FT: 14,454

Columbus - Franklin County (G-7520) — GEOGRAPHIC SECTION

SALES (est): 13.8MM
SALES (corp-wide): 89.2MM Privately Held
WEB: www.digicoimaging.com
SIC: 7384 Photofinishing laboratory
PA: Nutis Press, Inc.
3540 E Fulton St
Columbus OH 43227
614 237-8626

(G-7520)
DIRECTIONS FOR YOUTH FAMILIES
657 S Ohio Ave (43205-2743)
PHONE..................614 258-8043
John Cervi, Manager
EMP: 34
SALES (corp-wide): 7.7MM Privately Held
SIC: 8322 Youth center
PA: Directions For Youth & Families Inc
1515 Indianola Ave
Columbus OH 43201
614 294-2661

(G-7521)
DIRECTIONS FOR YOUTH FAMILIES
3840 Kimberly Pkwy N (43232-4232)
PHONE..................614 694-0203
EMP: 27
SALES (corp-wide): 7.7MM Privately Held
SIC: 8322 Youth center
PA: Directions For Youth & Families Inc
1515 Indianola Ave
Columbus OH 43201
614 294-2661

(G-7522)
DIRECTIONS FOR YOUTH FAMILIES (PA)
1515 Indianola Ave (43201-2118)
PHONE..................614 294-2661
Fax: 614 294-3247
Duane Casares, CEO
Barbara Martin, Finance
Jamie McKenna, Finance
Patricia Lassiter, Corp Comm Staff
Peter Levites, Psychologist
EMP: 50
SQ FT: 1,000
SALES: 7.7MM Privately Held
WEB: www.directionsforyouth.org
SIC: 8322 General counseling services

(G-7523)
DISPATCH CONSUMER SERVICES (HQ)
Also Called: Dispatch Color Press
5300 Crosswind Dr (43228-3600)
PHONE..................740 548-5555
Fax: 740 548-4940
John Curtain, President
Steven G Cover, General Mgr
Pam Benoit, Vice Pres
J Russello, Vice Pres
Richard Hay, Opers Staff
EMP: 30
SQ FT: 63,000
SALES (est): 5.4MM
SALES (corp-wide): 600.6MM Privately Held
SIC: 7319 Distribution of advertising material or sample services
PA: The Dispatch Printing Company
62 E Broad St
Columbus OH 43215
614 461-5000

(G-7524)
DISPATCH PRINTING COMPANY (PA)
Also Called: Columbus Dispatch The
62 E Broad St (43215-3500)
PHONE..................614 461-5000
Fax: 614 461-7554
Michael J Fiorile, CEO
John F Wolfe, Ch of Bd
Joseph Y Gallo, President
J H Peterson Et Al, Principal
Joseph J Gill, Principal
EMP: 600
SQ FT: 200,000
SALES (est): 600.6MM Privately Held
WEB: www.columbusdispatch.com
SIC: 4833 Television broadcasting stations

(G-7525)
DISPATCH PRODUCTIONS INC
770 Twin Rivers Dr (43215-1127)
PHONE..................614 460-3700
Michael Fiorile, President
Tom Greece Dorn, General Mgr
John Butte, Vice Pres
Cynda Simmons, Technology
EMP: 80
SALES (est): 3.1MM
SALES (corp-wide): 600.6MM Privately Held
WEB: www.dispatchbroadcast.com
SIC: 8999 Radio & television announcing
PA: The Dispatch Printing Company
62 E Broad St
Columbus OH 43215
614 461-5000

(G-7526)
DIST-TRANS INC
1580 Williams Rd (43207-5183)
PHONE..................614 497-1660
Fax: 614 492-2191
John E Ness, President
Robert E Ness, Chairman
Theodore Waltz, Corp Secy
Dan Raver, Manager
EMP: 110 EST: 1978
SQ FT: 50,000
SALES (est): 244.1K
SALES (corp-wide): 266.3K Privately Held
SIC: 4213 Trucking, except local
PA: Jebren, Inc
1580 Williams Rd
Columbus OH 43207
614 497-1660

(G-7527)
DIVERSIFIED HEALTH MANAGEMENT
3569 Refugee Rd Ste C (43232-9306)
PHONE..................614 338-8888
Alex Thommasathit, CEO
Bounthanh Phommasathit, CFO
EMP: 26 EST: 2013
SALES (est): 1.2MM Privately Held
SIC: 8082 Home health care services

(G-7528)
DIVERSITY SEARCH GROUP LLC
2600 Corp Exchange Dr # 110 (43231-1670)
PHONE..................614 352-2988
Teresa Sherald, CEO
EMP: 273
SALES (est): 13.6MM Privately Held
WEB: www.diversitysearchgroup.com
SIC: 7361 Executive placement

(G-7529)
DIVINE HEALTHCARE SERVICES LLC
2374 E Dublin Granvl Rd (43229-3507)
PHONE..................614 899-6767
Sheillah Sowah, Owner
EMP: 50
SALES (est): 302.7K Privately Held
SIC: 8099 Health & allied services

(G-7530)
DIVISION DRNKING GROUND WATERS
Also Called: Ddhew
50 W Town St Ste 700 (43215-4173)
PHONE..................614 644-2752
Fax: 614 644-2909
Mike Baker, Chief
Michael Mead, Chief
Vandhana Veerni, CIO
Bill Ritter, IT/INT Sup
Chris Korleski, Director
EMP: 65
SALES (est): 418.3K Privately Held
SIC: 8641 1711 Environmental protection organization; plumbing, heating, air-conditioning contractors

(G-7531)
DIVISION OF GEOLOGICAL SURVEY
2045 Morse Rd Bldg C (43229-6693)
PHONE..................614 265-6576
Fax: 614 447-1918
Michael Angle, Principal
Thomas Serenko, Chief
EMP: 30 EST: 2010
SALES (est): 99K Privately Held
SIC: 8732 Research services, except laboratory

(G-7532)
DLZ AMERICAN DRILLING INC
6121 Huntley Rd (43229-1003)
PHONE..................614 888-0040
James May, Treasurer
Vicki Briggs, Controller
EMP: 26
SALES (est): 1.3MM
SALES (corp-wide): 93MM Privately Held
SIC: 8711 Engineering services
PA: Dlz Corporation
6121 Huntley Rd
Columbus OH 43229
614 888-0040

(G-7533)
DLZ CONSTRUCTION SERVICES INC
6121 Huntley Rd (43229-1003)
PHONE..................614 888-0040
Vikram Rajadhyaksha, CEO
Brian Funkhouser, Controller
Josh Varelmann, Services
EMP: 48
SQ FT: 80,000
SALES: 10MM
SALES (corp-wide): 93MM Privately Held
SIC: 8711 Engineering services
HQ: Dlz National, Inc.
6121 Huntley Rd
Columbus OH 43229

(G-7534)
DLZ NATIONAL INC (HQ)
6121 Huntley Rd (43229-1003)
PHONE..................614 888-0040
Vikram Rajadhyaksha, CEO
Brian Funkhouser, Controller
EMP: 25
SQ FT: 80,000
SALES (est): 13.5MM
SALES (corp-wide): 93MM Privately Held
WEB: www.dlznational.com
SIC: 8711 Consulting engineer
PA: Dlz Corporation
6121 Huntley Rd
Columbus OH 43229
614 888-0040

(G-7535)
DLZ OHIO INC (HQ)
6121 Huntley Rd (43229-1003)
PHONE..................614 888-0040
A James Siebert, President
Vikram Rajadhyaksha, Chairman
P V Rajadhyaksha, COO
David Cutlip, Vice Pres
Tom Hessler, Project Mgr
EMP: 200
SQ FT: 45,000
SALES (est): 24.6MM
SALES (corp-wide): 93MM Privately Held
SIC: 8711 1382 8712 8713 Consulting engineer; civil engineering; geophysical exploration, oil & gas field; architectural services; surveying services
PA: Dlz Corporation
6121 Huntley Rd
Columbus OH 43229
614 888-0040

(G-7536)
DNO INC
3650 E 5th Ave (43219-1805)
PHONE..................614 231-3601
Fax: 614 231-5032
Anthony Dinovo, President
Carol Dinovo, Vice Pres
James Griffin, Manager
Alex Dinovo, Director
EMP: 80
SQ FT: 10,000
SALES (est): 24MM Privately Held
WEB: www.dnoinc.com
SIC: 5148 2099 Fresh fruits & vegetables; fruits, fresh; salads, fresh or refrigerated

(G-7537)
DOCTORS OHIOHEALTH CORPORATION (HQ)
Also Called: Doctors Hospital North
5100 W Broad St (43228-1607)
PHONE..................614 544-5424
Fax: 614 294-5322
David Blom, CEO
Michael Bernstein, Senior VP
Steve Garlock, Senior VP
Cheryl Herbert, Senior VP
Barbara Otey, Senior VP
EMP: 1200
SQ FT: 270,000
SALES (est): 389.5MM
SALES (corp-wide): 3.7B Privately Held
SIC: 8062 8011 Hospital, medical school affiliated with residency; medical insurance plan
PA: Ohiohealth Corporation
180 E Broad St
Columbus OH 43215
614 788-8860

(G-7538)
DOCUMENT IMGING SPCIALISTS LLC
Also Called: Information Management Svcs
5047 Transamerica Dr (43228-9381)
P.O. Box 29230 (43229-0230)
PHONE..................614 868-9008
Olivia Leonard, Mktg Coord
Michael Iadarola, Mng Member
Timothy Stephens,
EMP: 29
SQ FT: 3,700
SALES (est): 6.8MM Privately Held
SIC: 5044 7699 Office equipment; office equipment & accessory customizing

(G-7539)
DOCUMENT SOLUTIONS OHIO LLC
Also Called: Document Solutions Group
100 E Campus View Blvd # 105 (43235-4647)
PHONE..................614 846-2400
Michael Barry, Technical Mgr
Laurel Lautensack, Accounts Exec
Jeff Lacy,
Mitch Brown,
Michael Tutko Jr,
EMP: 45
SQ FT: 3,500
SALES (est): 3.8MM Privately Held
SIC: 5044 Copying equipment

(G-7540)
DONALD BOWEN AND ASSOC DDS
2575 W Broad St Unit 3 (43204-3333)
PHONE..................614 274-0454
Donald Bowen, Owner
EMP: 45
SALES (est): 828.5K Privately Held
SIC: 8021 Dentists' office

(G-7541)
DOOLEY HEATING AND AC LLC
2010 Zettler Rd (43232-3834)
PHONE..................614 278-9944
Fax: 614 278-9955
Brian Dooley, Mng Member
Tonya Stewart, Director
EMP: 31
SALES (est): 3MM Privately Held
WEB: www.dooleyheating.com
SIC: 1711 Warm air heating & air conditioning contractor

(G-7542)
DOUBLE Z CONSTRUCTION COMPANY
2550 Harrison Rd (43204-3510)
PHONE..................614 274-9334
Fax: 614 274-2702

GEOGRAPHIC SECTION — Columbus - Franklin County (G-7567)

David Guzzo, *President*
Larry Lyons, *Vice Pres*
John T Stinson, *Vice Pres*
Vincent M Guzzo, *Chief Engr*
EMP: 60
SQ FT: 6,500
SALES (est): 14.2MM **Privately Held**
SIC: 1611 Highway & street construction

(G-7543)
DOVE BUILDING SERVICES INC
1691 Cleveland Ave (43211-2558)
PHONE 614 299-4700
Fax: 614 299-5599
Vernon L Gibson, *President*
EMP: 70 **EST:** 1977
SQ FT: 2,500
SALES (est): 2.9MM **Privately Held**
SIC: 7349 Janitorial service, contract basis

(G-7544)
DRS PAUL BOYLES & KENNEDY
Also Called: Paul, Elaine MD
3545 Olentangy River Rd (43214-3907)
PHONE 614 734-3347
Elaine Paul, *President*
EMP: 35
SALES (est): 794.3K **Privately Held**
SIC: 8011 Specialized medical practitioners, except internal

(G-7545)
DRURY HOTELS COMPANY LLC
Also Called: Drury Inn & Suites Clmbus Conv
88 E Nationwide Blvd (43215-2576)
PHONE 614 221-7008
Fax: 614 221-7008
Scott Bosak, *Manager*
EMP: 31
SALES (corp-wide): 397.4MM **Privately Held**
WEB: www.druryhotels.com
SIC: 7011 Hotels
PA: Drury Hotels Company, Llc
721 Emerson Rd Ste 400
Saint Louis MO 63141
314 429-2255

(G-7546)
DRY IT RITE LLC
Also Called: Rite Way Restoration
4330 Groves Rd (43232-4103)
PHONE 614 295-8135
Matt Schillig, *Manager*
John Phillippi,
EMP: 29
SALES: 2.5MM **Privately Held**
SIC: 1521 General remodeling, single-family houses

(G-7547)
DUANE MORRIS LLP
200 N High St (43215-2416)
PHONE 937 424-7086
Kathleen Deland, *Branch Mgr*
EMP: 36
SALES (corp-wide): 300MM **Privately Held**
SIC: 8111 General practice attorney, lawyer
PA: Duane Morris Llp
30 S 17th St Fl 5
Philadelphia PA 19103
215 979-1000

(G-7548)
DUBLIN CLEANERS INC (PA)
6845 Caine Rd (43235-4234)
PHONE 614 764-9934
Fax: 614 764-8806
Gregory J Butler, *President*
Ryan Brown, *Manager*
EMP: 55
SQ FT: 12,000
SALES (est): 2.6MM **Privately Held**
WEB: www.dublincleaners.com
SIC: 7216 Cleaning & dyeing, except rugs

(G-7549)
DUFFY HOMES INC
495 S High St Ste 270 (43215-7665)
PHONE 614 410-4100
Fax: 614 410-4101
Vince Kollar, *President*
Mark Grubb, *Senior VP*
Aaron Spencer, *Project Mgr*
Bill Bixler, *Prdtn Mgr*
Matt Horlacher, *Facilities Mgr*
EMP: 30
SQ FT: 4,700
SALES (est): 3.4MM **Privately Held**
WEB: www.duffyhomes.com
SIC: 1531 1521 Speculative builder, single-family houses; new construction, single-family houses

(G-7550)
DUMMEN NA INC (PA)
Also Called: Ecke Ranch
250 S High St Ste 650 (43215-4630)
PHONE 614 850-9551
Paul Ecke, *Ch of Bd*
Pete Chamberlain, *CFO*
Thom David, *Marketing Mgr*
Dan Windus, *MIS Mgr*
Ron Cramer, *Intl Dir*
▲ **EMP:** 57
SQ FT: 1,500,000
SALES (est): 39MM **Privately Held**
SIC: 0181 Flowers grown in field nurseries

(G-7551)
DUNBAR ARMORED INC
2300 Citygate Dr Unit B (43219-3665)
PHONE 614 475-1969
Fax: 614 475-2304
Matthew Lytle, *Manager*
Brian Baker, *Manager*
Trevor Rohe, *Manager*
EMP: 35
SALES (corp-wide): 700.1MM **Privately Held**
WEB: www.dunbararmored.com
SIC: 7381 Armored car services
PA: Dunbar Armored, Inc.
50 Schilling Rd
Hunt Valley MD 21031
410 584-9800

(G-7552)
DURABLE SLATE CO (PA)
Also Called: Durable Slate Company, The
3933 Groves Rd (43232-4138)
PHONE 614 299-7100
Fax: 614 299-7100
Michael Chan, *CEO*
Gary Wyan, *Sr Corp Ofcr*
John Chan, *Vice Pres*
Cherie Downey, *Pub Rel Dir*
Mark Sherby, *Executive*
▲ **EMP:** 70
SQ FT: 14,000
SALES (est): 21.5MM **Privately Held**
WEB: www.durableslate.com
SIC: 1761 Roofing contractor; roof repair; sheet metalwork

(G-7553)
DUTYS TOWING
Also Called: Duty's Towing & Auto Service
3288 E Broad St (43213-1006)
PHONE 614 252-3336
EMP: 30
SALES (est): 1.1MM **Privately Held**
SIC: 7549 Automotive Towing Service

(G-7554)
DWIGHT SPENCER & ASSOCIATES (PA)
Also Called: Spencer Research
1290 Grandview Ave (43212-3482)
PHONE 614 488-3123
Fax: 614 421-1154
George Maynard, *President*
Betty Spencer, *Vice Pres*
EMP: 34
SQ FT: 6,000
SALES (est): 4.8MM **Privately Held**
WEB: www.spencer-research.com
SIC: 8742 8732 Marketing consulting services; research services, except laboratory

(G-7555)
DYNALECTRIC COMPANY
1762 Dividend Dr (43228-3845)
PHONE 614 529-7500
Brad Baker, *Manager*
EMP: 35
SALES (corp-wide): 7.6B **Publicly Held**
WEB: www.dyna-fl.com
SIC: 1731 General electrical contractor
HQ: Dynalectric Company
22930 Shaw Rd Ste 100
Dulles VA 20166
703 288-2866

(G-7556)
DYNAMITE TECHNOLOGIES LLC (PA)
274 Marconi Blvd Ste 300 (43215-2363)
PHONE 614 538-0095
Jeff Nieman, *Business Mgr*
Kurt Stephens, *QC Mgr*
Jenna Stranges, *QC Mgr*
Gordon McKinney, *Engineer*
Mike Waclo, *Design Engr*
EMP: 80
SALES (est): 9.9MM **Privately Held**
SIC: 7371 Custom computer programming services

(G-7557)
DYNAMIX ENGINEERING LTD
855 Grandview Ave Ste 300 (43215-1193)
PHONE 614 443-1178
Fax: 614 443-1594
Eugene Griffin, *Partner*
Todd Mace, *Partner*
Lee A Dye, *Project Mgr*
Stuart Hill, *Project Mgr*
Kelechi Abakporo, *Engineer*
EMP: 55
SQ FT: 10,000
SALES (est): 8.9MM **Privately Held**
WEB: www.dynamix-ltd.com
SIC: 8711 Civil engineering

(G-7558)
DYNOTEC INC
2931 E Dublin Granv Rd (43231)
PHONE 614 880-7320
Fax: 614 880-7324
Tobias A Iloka, *President*
Omar Kanoun, *Vice Pres*
Jerry Mills, *Transptn Dir*
Don Cruden, *Project Mgr*
Alphonso Kolliesuah, *Engineer*
EMP: 40
SQ FT: 1,000
SALES (est): 5MM **Privately Held**
SIC: 8711 Civil engineering; consulting engineer

(G-7559)
E M COLUMBUS LLC
Also Called: Eastland Mall
2740 Eastland Mall Ste B (43232-4959)
PHONE 614 861-3232
Holly Dozer, *General Mgr*
Shirley Fix, *Office Mgr*
Herb Glimcher, *Mng Member*
EMP: 33
SALES (est): 1.8MM
SALES (corp-wide): 4.2MM **Privately Held**
WEB: www.shopeastland-oh.com
SIC: 6531 Real estate managers
PA: Glimcher Realty Trust
2740 Eastland Mall Ste B
Columbus OH 43232
614 861-3232

(G-7560)
E P FERRIS & ASSOCIATES INC
880 King Ave (43212-2654)
PHONE 614 299-2999
Edward P Ferris, *President*
Ridgeway Joseph, *Exec VP*
Matt Ferris, *Vice Pres*
Sean G Gillilan, *Manager*
Kay Ferris, *Admin Sec*
EMP: 25
SALES (est): 2.6MM **Privately Held**
WEB: www.epferris.com
SIC: 8711 8713 Civil engineering; surveying services

(G-7561)
E RETAILING ASSOCIATES LLC
Also Called: Customized Girl
2282 Westbrooke Dr (43228-9416)
PHONE 614 300-5785
Claire Stinedurf, *Production*
Cindy Terapak, *Cust Mgr*
Taj Schaffnit, *Mng Member*
Stephanie Schaffnit, *Manager*
Marty Laroche, *CTO*
EMP: 64
SALES (est): 8.6MM **Privately Held**
WEB: www.customisegirl.com
SIC: 8748 5961 2253 Business consulting; ; T-shirts & tops, knit

(G-7562)
E WYNN INC
Also Called: Columbus Window Cleaning Co
1851 S High St (43207-2372)
P.O. Box 2201 (43216-2201)
PHONE 614 444-5288
Fax: 614 445-3375
Lynn Elliott, *President*
Neil Schultz, *President*
James Waddy, *Sales Executive*
Rezella Fraley, *Office Mgr*
Terry Atkinson, *Exec Dir*
EMP: 30
SQ FT: 7,000
SALES (est): 1.2MM **Privately Held**
WEB: www.columbuswindowcleaning.com
SIC: 7349 Window cleaning; building cleaning service

(G-7563)
EARLY CHILDHOOD LEARNING COMMU
4141 Rudy Rd (43214-2943)
PHONE 614 451-6418
Fax: 614 451-3179
Becky Love, *Director*
Sally Harrington, *Deputy Dir*
EMP: 65
SALES (est): 701K **Privately Held**
SIC: 8351 Child day care services

(G-7564)
EASTERN HORIZON INC
Also Called: Urban Express Transportation
1640 E 5th Ave (43219-2554)
PHONE 614 253-7000
Qeis M Atieh, *President*
Pam Atieh, *Manager*
EMP: 45
SQ FT: 3,000
SALES (est): 1.6MM **Privately Held**
WEB: www.urbanexpress.biz
SIC: 4119 Limousine rental, with driver

(G-7565)
EASTLAND CRANE SERVICE INC
Also Called: Eastland Crane & Towing
2190 S Hamilton Rd (43232-4487)
PHONE 614 868-9750
Fax: 614 866-9758
Robert M Marshall, *President*
Brenda Marshall, *Corp Secy*
Rick Smith, *Manager*
EMP: 25
SQ FT: 1,500
SALES (est): 4.5MM **Privately Held**
SIC: 7353 7549 Cranes & aerial lift equipment, rental or leasing; towing service, automotive

(G-7566)
EASTLAND LANES INC
2666 Old Courtright Rd (43232-2603)
P.O. Box 735, Morgantown WV (26507-0735)
PHONE 614 868-9866
Fax: 614 868-9871
Steve Lorenze Jr, *President*
Jack Keener, *Corp Secy*
Ginger Lorenze, *Vice Pres*
Carol Clemens, *Manager*
EMP: 50
SQ FT: 62,000
SALES (est): 1.5MM **Privately Held**
WEB: www.eastlandlanes.com
SIC: 7933 Ten pin center

(G-7567)
EASTON TOWN CENTER II LLC
Also Called: Steiner Associates
160 Easton Town Ctr (43219-6074)
PHONE 614 416-7000
Fax: 614 416-7002
Roxanne Nally, *Manager*
Kristin Scott, *Director*
EMP: 60
SALES (est): 2.7MM **Privately Held**
SIC: 6512 Shopping center, property operation only

Columbus - Franklin County (G-7568) — GEOGRAPHIC SECTION

(G-7568)
EASTON TOWN CENTER LLC
Also Called: Easton Town Center Guest Svcs
4016 Townsfair Way # 201 (43219-6083)
PHONE.................................614 337-2560
Yaromir Steiner, *Mng Member*
Eddie Bauer,
EMP: 175
SQ FT: 10,000
SALES (est): 14.5MM **Privately Held**
WEB: www.eastontowncenter.com
SIC: 6512 Shopping center, regional (300,000 - 1,000,000 sq ft)

(G-7569)
EASTWAY SUPPLIES INC
1561 Alum Creek Dr (43209-2780)
PHONE.................................614 252-3650
Fax: 614 252-0021
Gary M Glanzman, *President*
John Edwards, *COO*
Jason Burton, *CFO*
Richard Lannon, *Credit Mgr*
Ken Kean, *Sales Staff*
EMP: 40 EST: 1971
SQ FT: 10,000
SALES (est): 33.7MM **Privately Held**
WEB: www.eastwaysupplies.com
SIC: 5074 Plumbing fittings & supplies

(G-7570)
ECHO RESIDENTIAL SUPPORT
6500 Busch Blvd Ste 215 (43229-6708)
PHONE.................................614 210-0944
Brad Kurash, *CEO*
Thomas Scarce, *President*
EMP: 35
SALES (est): 1.3MM **Privately Held**
WEB: www.ehos.org
SIC: 8361 Home for the mentally handicapped

(G-7571)
ECHO-TAPE LLC
651 Dearborn Park Ln (43085-5702)
PHONE.................................614 892-3246
Scott Taylor,
EMP: 25
SALES (est): 2.1MM **Privately Held**
SIC: 7379 Computer related maintenance services

(G-7572)
ECLIPSECORP LLC
825 Taylor Rd (43230-6235)
PHONE.................................614 626-8536
Stephanie Ryland, *Prdtn Mgr*
Ryan Srbljan, *Sales Staff*
Brooke Miller, *Marketing Staff*
Spenser Dickerson, *Manager*
Jamie Linscott, *Creative Dir*
EMP: 35
SALES (est): 2MM **Privately Held**
WEB: www.eclipse-studio.com
SIC: 7335 Photographic studio, commercial

(G-7573)
ECOMMERCE INC (PA)
Also Called: Hostexcellence.com
1774 Dividend Dr (43228-3845)
PHONE.................................800 861-9394
Fathi Said, *CEO*
Richard Simpson, *Superintendent*
Diane D Reynolds, *Vice Pres*
Christopher Testerman, *Sales Dir*
Kelsey Begin, *Marketing Staff*
EMP: 60
SALES (est): 42.6MM **Privately Held**
WEB: www.hostexcellence.com
SIC: 4813

(G-7574)
ECOMMERCE LLC
1774 Dividend Dr (43228-3845)
PHONE.................................800 861-9394
Fathi Said, *CEO*
EMP: 99 EST: 2010
SALES (est): 4.6MM **Privately Held**
SIC: 7375 Data base information retrieval

(G-7575)
ECONOMIC & CMNTY DEV INST INC
Also Called: ECDI
1655 Old Leonard Ave (43219-2541)
PHONE.................................614 559-0104
Inna Kinney, *President*
Eric Diamond, *Vice Pres*
Greg Zucca, *Vice Pres*
Sharelle Buyer, *Controller*
Tim Kehoe, *Portfolio Mgr*
EMP: 41
SALES (est): 6.8MM **Privately Held**
SIC: 8322 Community center

(G-7576)
EDDIE BAUER LLC
4599 Fisher Rd (43228-8921)
PHONE.................................614 278-9281
Fax: 614 278-7818
Rob McDougal, *Manager*
Jim Deem, *Executive*
EMP: 50
SALES (corp-wide): 7B **Privately Held**
SIC: 4226 Special warehousing & storage
HQ: Eddie Bauer Llc
   10401 Ne 8th St Ste 500
   Bellevue WA 98004

(G-7577)
EDISON EQUIPMENT (PA)
Also Called: EE
2225 Mckinley Ave (43204-3484)
PHONE.................................614 883-5710
Fax: 614 883-5711
Paul Collini, *President*
Todd Steltenkamp, *CFO*
Deboah Townsend, *Accountant*
Brad Burbacher, *Sales Associate*
Keith Hollingsworth, *Marketing Staff*
EMP: 36
SQ FT: 20,000
SALES (est): 14.1MM **Privately Held**
WEB: www.edisonequipment.com
SIC: 5063 Electrical supplies

(G-7578)
EDISON WELDING INSTITUTE INC (PA)
Also Called: E W I
1250 Arthur E Adams Dr (43221-3585)
PHONE.................................614 688-5000
Fax: 614 688-5001
Henry Cialone, *CEO*
Edward W Ungar, *Principal*
Mark Yadach, *Business Mgr*
Phil Weisenbach, *COO*
Jesse Bonfeld, *Vice Pres*
EMP: 145
SQ FT: 135,000
SALES: 33.7MM **Privately Held**
WEB: www.ewi.org
SIC: 8731 Commercial physical research

(G-7579)
EDMOND HOTEL INVESTORS LLC
24 E Lincoln St (43215-1586)
PHONE.................................614 891-2900
Scott Somerville, *President*
Robyn Asher, *CFO*
EMP: 65
SALES (est): 260.2K **Privately Held**
SIC: 7011 Hotels & motels

(G-7580)
EDUCATION FIRST CREDIT UN INC (PA)
399 E Livingston Ave (43215-5531)
PHONE.................................614 221-9376
Michael J Wettrich, *President*
June Tallman, *Principal*
Jared Elsass, *CFO*
Mallory Pierce, *Loan Officer*
Vicki Williams, *Accountant*
EMP: 25 EST: 1936
SQ FT: 4,000
SALES: 4.3MM **Privately Held**
WEB: www.educu.org
SIC: 6061 6062 Federal credit unions; state credit unions

(G-7581)
EDUCATIONAL SOLUTIONS CO
1155 Highland St (43201-3277)
PHONE.................................614 989-4588
Robert Stephens, *Exec Dir*
Estella Stephens, *Director*
EMP: 75
SALES (est): 2.6MM **Privately Held**
SIC: 8748 Business consulting

(G-7582)
EDWARDS MOONEY & MOSES
Also Called: Edwards Mooney & Moses of Ohio
1320 Mckinley Ave Ste B (43222-1155)
PHONE.................................614 351-1439
Randall Hall, *Officer*
EMP: 80
SALES (est): 4.5MM
SALES (corp-wide): 1.1B **Publicly Held**
WEB: www.ibpteam.com
SIC: 1742 Insulation, buildings
HQ: Installed Building Products Llc
   495 S High St Ste 50
   Columbus OH 43215
   614 221-3399

(G-7583)
EDWARDS CREATIVE LEARNING CTR
3858 Alum Creek Dr Ste A (43207-5135)
PHONE.................................614 492-8977
Shirley Atkins, *Owner*
EMP: 30
SALES (est): 628.3K **Privately Held**
SIC: 8351 Group day care center

(G-7584)
EDWARDS ELECTRICAL & MECH
685 Grandview Ave (43215-1119)
PHONE.................................614 485-2003
Fax: 614 485-2518
Matt Snyder, *Branch Mgr*
EMP: 40 **Privately Held**
WEB: www.edwards-elec.com
SIC: 2752 1711 Commercial printing, lithographic; mechanical contractor
HQ: Edwards Electrical & Mechanical Inc
   2350 N Shadeland Ave
   Indianapolis IN 46219
   317 543-3460

(G-7585)
EDWARDS LAND COMPANY
495 S High St Ste 150 (43215-5695)
PHONE.................................614 241-2070
Charlie Driscoll, *Chairman*
Charles Driscoll, *Chairman*
EMP: 27
SALES (est): 3MM
SALES (corp-wide): 14.9MM **Privately Held**
SIC: 6552 Subdividers & developers
PA: The Edwards Industries Inc
   495 S High St Ste 150
   Columbus OH 43215
   614 241-2070

(G-7586)
EFCO CORP
Also Called: Economy Forms
3900 Zane Trace Dr (43228-3833)
PHONE.................................614 876-1226
Fax: 614 876-1228
James Grubb, *Plant Mgr*
Robert Thrash, *Plant Mgr*
Jim Davis, *Manager*
Jim Grubb, *Manager*
EMP: 26
SALES (corp-wide): 258.7MM **Privately Held**
SIC: 5051 7353 4225 3444 Steel; heavy construction equipment rental; general warehousing; concrete forms, sheet metal; miscellaneous fabricated wire products; fabricated plate work (boiler shop)
HQ: Efco Corp
   1800 Ne Broadway Ave
   Des Moines IA 50313
   515 266-1141

(G-7587)
EFFICIENT ELECTRIC CORP
4800 Groves Rd (43232-4165)
PHONE.................................614 552-0200
Fax: 614 552-0201
Ken Havice, *President*
Jim Ruisinger, *Corp Secy*
Peggy Gabbert, *Manager*
Tom Leigel, *Bd of Directors*
EMP: 33
SQ FT: 15,000
SALES (est): 6MM **Privately Held**
WEB: www.efficient-electric.com
SIC: 1731 General electrical contractor

(G-7588)
ELFORD INC
Also Called: Elford Construction Services
1220 Dublin Rd (43215-1008)
PHONE.................................614 488-4000
Fax: 614 487-6600
Jeffrey L Copeland, *Ch of Bd*
James W Smith, *President*
Timothy Davis, *Exec VP*
James R Johnson, *Exec VP*
Robert Butler, *Vice Pres*
EMP: 200
SQ FT: 54,000
SALES (est): 150.7MM **Privately Held**
WEB: www.elford.com
SIC: 1542 1541 8741 Commercial & office building, new construction; institutional building construction; industrial buildings, new construction; construction management

(G-7589)
ELITE HOME REMODELING INC
6295a Busch Blvd Ste A (43229-1801)
PHONE.................................614 785-6700
Fax: 614 785-6701
Robert S Harmon, *President*
Susan B Harmon, *Admin Sec*
EMP: 35
SQ FT: 2,500
SALES (est): 3.5MM **Privately Held**
SIC: 1521 Single-family housing construction

(G-7590)
EMBRACING AUTISM INC
2491 W Dblin Granville Rd (43235-2708)
P.O. Box 29190 (43229-0190)
PHONE.................................614 559-0077
David Rastoka, *President*
Lora Montgomery, *Opers Staff*
Karrie Rios, *Case Mgr*
Laura Sanders, *Training Spec*
EMP: 30 EST: 2012
SALES (est): 691.4K
SALES (corp-wide): 137.4MM **Privately Held**
SIC: 8361 Residential care
HQ: Dungarvin Ohio, Llc
   6555 Busch Blvd Ste 110
   Columbus OH 43229

(G-7591)
EMCOR FCLITIES SVCS N AMER INC
280 N High St Ste 1700 (43215-7511)
PHONE.................................614 430-5078
Matthew Seguin, *Manager*
EMP: 90
SALES (corp-wide): 7.6B **Publicly Held**
SIC: 1711 Heating systems repair & maintenance
HQ: Emcor Facilities Services Of North America, Inc.
   306 Northern Ave Ste 5
   Boston MA 02210
   617 482-0100

(G-7592)
EMERGENCY SERVICES INC
2323 W 5th Ave Ste 220 (43204-4899)
PHONE.................................614 224-6420
Alen Gora, *President*
Barbara S Fisher, *Business Mgr*
EMP: 45
SALES (est): 53.3K **Privately Held**
SIC: 8011 Offices & clinics of medical doctors

GEOGRAPHIC SECTION
Columbus - Franklin County (G-7616)

(G-7593)
ENERVISE INCORPORATED
6663 Huntley Rd Ste K (43229-1038)
PHONE..................................614 885-9800
Fax: 614 885-6662
Brenda Burnette, *Manager*
EMP: 50
SALES (est): 4.7MM
SALES (corp-wide): 40.9MM **Privately Held**
WEB: www.engineeringexcellence.com
SIC: 1711 Mechanical contractor
PA: Enervise Incorporated
4360 Glendale Milford Rd
Blue Ash OH 45242
513 761-6000

(G-7594)
ENGAGED HEALTH CARE BUS SVCS
Also Called: Ppmc
4619 Kenny Rd Ste 100 (43220-2779)
PHONE..................................614 457-8180
Samuel J Kiehl III, *President*
Gary W Beauchamp, *President*
Craig A Adkins, *Vice Pres*
Jay W Eckersley, *Vice Pres*
Todd Rodriguez, *Cust Mgr*
EMP: 50
SQ FT: 10,000
SALES (est): 2.5MM **Privately Held**
WEB: www.ppmc.net
SIC: 8099 8742 Blood related health services; business consultant

(G-7595)
ENHANCED HOME HEALTH CARE LLC
700 Morse Rd Ste 206 (43214-1879)
PHONE..................................614 433-7266
Fax: 614 885-6665
Sadia Y Abdi, *Principal*
EMP: 80
SALES (est): 966.7K **Privately Held**
SIC: 8082 Visiting nurse service

(G-7596)
ENHANCED SOFTWARE INC
Also Called: Vsync
625 E North Broadway St (43214-4133)
PHONE..................................877 805-8388
James C McAllister, *CEO*
Bill Knapp, *President*
EMP: 25
SQ FT: 7,000
SALES (est): 2.8MM **Privately Held**
WEB: www.vsync.com
SIC: 5045 Computer software

(G-7597)
ENTRUST SOLUTIONS LLC
Also Called: Entrust Healthcare
20 S 3rd St Ste 210 (43215-4206)
PHONE..................................614 504-4900
Christopher Assif, *Mng Member*
Roger Allison, *Manager*
James Martini, *Manager*
EMP: 30
SALES: 3MM **Privately Held**
SIC: 7379 Computer related consulting services

(G-7598)
ENVIRO IT LLC
Also Called: Accurate It Services
3854 Fisher Rd (43228-1016)
PHONE..................................614 453-0709
Scott Weigand, *COO*
Sergey Zeleny, *Purch Mgr*
Michael Yankelevich, *Mng Member*
Shaun Taylor, *Manager*
Peter Digravio, *Admin Asst*
EMP: 30
SALES (est): 3.8MM **Privately Held**
WEB: www.accurateit.com
SIC: 7379 5065 ; modems, computer

(G-7599)
ENVIRONMENT CONTROL OF GREATER
2218 Dividend Dr (43228-3808)
PHONE..................................614 868-9788
Fax: 614 868-9219
Jonathan Hanks, *President*
Wendy Hanks, *Corp Secy*

Sean Frazier, *Opers Staff*
Steve Hawley, *Sales Staff*
Sharon Letner, *Sales Associate*
EMP: 80
SQ FT: 6,849
SALES (est): 4.8MM **Privately Held**
SIC: 4959 7349 Environmental cleanup services; building maintenance services

(G-7600)
ENVIRONMENTAL SYSTEMS RESEARCH
Also Called: Esri
1085 Beecher Xing N Ste A (43230-4563)
PHONE..................................614 933-8698
Steven Kenzie, *Manager*
EMP: 76
SALES (corp-wide): 1B **Privately Held**
WEB: www.esri.com
SIC: 5045 Computer software
PA: Environmental Systems Research Institute, Inc.
380 New York St
Redlands CA 92373
909 793-2853

(G-7601)
ENVOY AIR INC
Also Called: AMR Eagle
4100 E 5th Ave (43219-1802)
PHONE..................................614 231-4391
EMP: 54
SALES (corp-wide): 42.2B **Publicly Held**
SIC: 4512 Air passenger carrier, scheduled
HQ: Envoy Air Inc.
4301 Regent Blvd
Irving TX 75063
972 374-5200

(G-7602)
EQUITABLE MORTGAGE CORPORATION (PA)
3530 Snouffer Rd Ste 100 (43235-2702)
PHONE..................................614 764-1232
Fax: 614 764-1281
Bruce Calabrese, *President*
Steve Stasuilewicz, *Exec VP*
Richard Cercone, *Vice Pres*
John Stamolis, *Vice Pres*
Don Welling, *Vice Pres*
EMP: 28
SQ FT: 21,500
SALES (est): 5.5MM **Privately Held**
WEB: www.eqfin.com
SIC: 6163 Mortgage brokers arranging for loans, using money of others

(G-7603)
EQUITAS HEALTH INC
4400 N High St Ste 300 (43214-2635)
PHONE..................................614 299-2437
William Hardy, *CEO*
Peggy Anderson, *COO*
Carole Anderson, *Sr Corp Ofcr*
Aaron Clark, *Manager*
EMP: 235
SQ FT: 10,000
SALES: 29MM **Privately Held**
WEB: www.catf.net
SIC: 8322 8093 8011 8049 Individual & family services; mental health clinic, outpatient; primary care medical clinic; specialized medical practitioners, except internal; nurses & other medical assistants; specialized dental practitioners

(G-7604)
ERIE INSURANCE EXCHANGE
445 Hutchinson Ave (43235-5677)
PHONE..................................614 430-8530
EMP: 65
SALES (corp-wide): 374.1MM **Privately Held**
SIC: 6411 Insurance agents, brokers & service
PA: Erie Insurance Exchange
100 Erie Insurance Pl
Erie PA 16530
800 458-0811

(G-7605)
ERIE INSURANCE EXCHANGE
445 Hutchinson Ave # 350 (43235-5677)
P.O. Box 23, Worthington (43085-0023)
PHONE..................................614 436-0224
Fax: 614 436-0296

Paul Miller, *Manager*
EMP: 110
SQ FT: 5,000
SALES (corp-wide): 374.1MM **Privately Held**
WEB: www.erie-insurance.com
SIC: 6331 Reciprocal interinsurance exchanges: fire, marine, casualty
PA: Erie Insurance Exchange
100 Erie Insurance Pl
Erie PA 16530
800 458-0811

(G-7606)
ERNEST FRITSCH
6245 Sunderland Dr (43229-1977)
PHONE..................................614 436-5995
EMP: 50
SALES (est): 4.7MM **Privately Held**
SIC: 1542 Nonresidential Construction

(G-7607)
ERNST & YOUNG LLP
Also Called: Ey
800 Yard St Ste 200 (43212-3882)
PHONE..................................614 224-5678
Fax: 614 232-7939
Craig Marshall, *Managing Prtnr*
Daniel Eck, *Broker*
James Bachmann, *Manager*
Lori Maite, *Manager*
Jayson McCurdy, *IT/INT Sup*
EMP: 170
SALES (corp-wide): 5.3B **Privately Held**
WEB: www.ey.com
SIC: 8721 8742 Certified public accountant; auditing services; business consultant; management information systems consultant
PA: Ernst & Young Llp
5 Times Sq Fl Conlv1
New York NY 10036
212 773-3000

(G-7608)
ESC AND COMPANY INC
2000 Toronado Blvd A (43207-1755)
PHONE..................................614 794-0568
Fax: 614 794-0998
Emil S Colucci, *President*
Matt Colucci, *Vice Pres*
Melissa Colucci, *Vice Pres*
Melissa Hayes, *Vice Pres*
▲ EMP: 30
SALES (est): 7.2MM **Privately Held**
WEB: www.esctradingcompany.com
SIC: 5199 Gifts & novelties

(G-7609)
ESCAPE ENTERPRISES INC
Also Called: Steak Escape
222 Neilston St (43215-2609)
PHONE..................................614 224-0300
Fax: 614 224-6460
Mark Turner, *Principal*
Kennard Smith, *Chairman*
EMP: 35
SQ FT: 10,000
SALES (est): 1.9MM **Privately Held**
WEB: www.steakescape.com
SIC: 5812 6794 Fast food restaurants & stands; franchises, selling or licensing

(G-7610)
ESSENDANT CO
1634 Westbelt Dr (43228-3810)
PHONE..................................614 876-7774
Fax: 614 876-4922
Mike Huettel, *President*
Steve Isaacs, *Vice Pres*
Josh Howey, *Manager*
Michael Martin, *Manager*
Joe Rogers, *Senior Mgr*
EMP: 100
SQ FT: 126,000
SALES (corp-wide): 5B **Publicly Held**
WEB: www.ussco.com
SIC: 5112 5044 Office supplies; office equipment
HQ: Essendant Co.
1 Parkway North Blvd # 100
Deerfield IL 60015
847 627-7000

(G-7611)
ESSENTIALPROFILE1CORP
735 N Wilson Rd (43204-1463)
PHONE..................................614 805-4794
John Harris, *Principal*
EMP: 80
SALES: 350K **Privately Held**
SIC: 7349 Cleaning service, industrial or commercial

(G-7612)
ESSEX HEALTHCARE CORPORATION (PA)
2780 Airport Dr Ste 400 (43219-2289)
PHONE..................................614 416-0600
Don Finney, *President*
Francis J Crosby, *President*
Sue Malone, *Vice Pres*
Blaine W Sheffield, *Vice Pres*
Keith Yoder, *CFO*
EMP: 30
SQ FT: 15,000
SALES (est): 41.3MM **Privately Held**
WEB: www.atriumlivingcenters.com
SIC: 6531 Real estate agents & managers

(G-7613)
ESSILOR LABORATORIES AMER INC
Also Called: Top Network
3671 Interchange Rd (43204-1499)
PHONE..................................614 274-0840
Fax: 614 274-5414
Kathryn Rismiller, *Treasurer*
Don Lepore, *Manager*
Judy Ellis, *Manager*
Steve Hile, *Manager*
Wayne Phelps, *Manager*
EMP: 50 **Privately Held**
WEB: www.crizal.com
SIC: 3851 5049 Eyeglasses, lenses & frames; optical goods
HQ: Essilor Laboratories Of America, Inc.
13515 N Stemmons Fwy
Dallas TX 75234
972 241-4141

(G-7614)
ESTES EXPRESS LINES INC
1009 Frank Rd (43223-3858)
PHONE..................................614 275-6000
Fax: 614 275-4383
Linda Smith, *Sales Executive*
Tom Siefert, *Manager*
Scott Jeppesen, *Manager*
Annette Weiner, *Executive*
EMP: 105
SQ FT: 4,331
SALES (corp-wide): 2.4B **Privately Held**
WEB: www.estes-express.com
SIC: 4213 Less-than-truckload (LTL) transport
PA: Estes Express Lines, Inc.
3901 W Broad St
Richmond VA 23230
804 353-1900

(G-7615)
ETC GAMECO LLC
Also Called: Kdb
157 Easton Town Ctr (43219-6075)
PHONE..................................614 428-7529
Adam Kleinhenz, *General Mgr*
Sean Rogers, *Opers Mgr*
Lori Peare, *Accounts Mgr*
Ashlee Dickson, *Social Dir*
EMP: 80 EST: 2010
SALES (est): 1.5MM **Privately Held**
SIC: 7929 Entertainment service

(G-7616)
EXCEL DECORATORS INC
3910 Groves Rd Ste A (43232-4162)
PHONE..................................614 522-0056
Sonja Winscott, *Branch Mgr*
EMP: 128
SALES (corp-wide): 7.4MM **Privately Held**
SIC: 7299 Party planning service
PA: Excel Decorators Inc
3748 Kentucky Ave
Indianapolis IN 46221
317 856-1300

Columbus - Franklin County (G-7617) — GEOGRAPHIC SECTION

(G-7617)
EXCEL TRUCKING LLC
1000 Frank Rd (43223-3859)
PHONE..................................614 826-1988
Abdulla Abdi, *CEO*
EMP: 25 **EST:** 2011
SQ FT: 900
SALES: 13MM Privately Held
SIC: 4213 Trucking, except local

(G-7618)
EXECUTIVES AGENCIES
30 E Broad St Fl 26 (43215-3414)
PHONE..................................614 466-2980
Mathew Lamtke, *Exec Dir*
Peter Thomas, *Deputy Dir*
EMP: 35
SALES (est): 1.4MM Privately Held
SIC: 8111 Legal services

(G-7619)
EXEL FREIGHT CONNECT INC
226 N 5th St Ste 218 (43215-2780)
P.O. Box 15850 (43215-0850)
PHONE..................................855 393-5378
Brian Malinowski, *Director*
EMP: 68 **EST:** 2014
SALES (est): 16.4MM
SALES (corp-wide): 71.2B Privately Held
SIC: 4731 Freight forwarding
HQ: Exel Inc.
  570 Polaris Pkwy
  Westerville OH 43082
  614 865-8500

(G-7620)
EXEL GLOBAL LOGISTICS INC
2144a John Glenn Ave (43217-1154)
PHONE..................................614 409-4500
Roger Richard, *Branch Mgr*
EMP: 25
SALES (corp-wide): 71.2B Privately Held
WEB: www.exelgloballogistics.com
SIC: 4731 Domestic freight forwarding
HQ: Exel Global Logistics Inc.
  22879 Glenn Dr Ste 100
  Sterling VA 20164
  703 350-1298

(G-7621)
EXPERIS FINANCE US LLC
175 S 3rd St Ste 375 (43215-6196)
PHONE..................................614 223-2300
Rich Grunenwald, *Branch Mgr*
EMP: 63 Publicly Held
SIC: 8721 Accounting, auditing & bookkeeping
HQ: Experis Finance Us, Llc
  100 W Manpower Pl
  Milwaukee WI 53212

(G-7622)
EXPERIS US INC
175 S 3rd St Ste 375 (43215-6196)
PHONE..................................614 223-2300
Fax: 614 223-2301
Sisi Nguyen, *Branch Mgr*
EMP: 36 Publicly Held
SIC: 7361 Executive placement
HQ: Experis Us, Inc.
  100 W Manpower Pl
  Milwaukee WI 53212

(G-7623)
EXPONENTIA US INC
424 Beecher Rd Ste A (43230-3510)
PHONE..................................614 944-5103
Gira Suvramani, *President*
Veera Murugappan, *Controller*
EMP: 30
SQ FT: 5,200
SALES: 4.8MM Privately Held
SIC: 7372 Publishers' computer software

(G-7624)
EXXCEL PROJECT MANAGEMENT LLC
328 Civic Center Dr (43215-5087)
PHONE..................................614 621-4500
Fax: 614 621-4515
F Douglas Reardon, *President*
Mike Skunda, *Senior VP*
Douglas Kaiser, *Vice Pres*
William Daniel, *Project Mgr*
Bill Nahs, *Project Mgr*
EMP: 28
SQ FT: 10,000
SALES (est): 13.9MM Privately Held
WEB: www.exxcel.com
SIC: 1542 1541 Commercial & office building, new construction; industrial buildings, new construction

(G-7625)
EYE CENTER (PA)
Also Called: Ohio Eye Associates
262 Neil Ave (43215-7309)
PHONE..................................614 228-3937
Peter Utrata, *Principal*
Grace Kim, *Ophthalmology*
Mary Delong, *Administration*
EMP: 25
SQ FT: 2,200
SALES (est): 3.9MM Privately Held
WEB: www.eyesurgerycenterofohio.com
SIC: 3841 8011 Eye examining instruments & apparatus; offices & clinics of medical doctors

(G-7626)
F S T EXPRESS INC
1727 Georgesville Rd (43228-3619)
PHONE..................................614 529-7900
Arthur J Decrane, *President*
David S Kent, *CFO*
Anita Norris, *Controller*
EMP: 80
SQ FT: 12,000
SALES (est): 10.7MM
SALES (corp-wide): 80.3MM Privately Held
WEB: www.fstfst.com
SIC: 4213 Contract haulers
PA: Fst Logistics, Inc.
  2040 Atlas St
  Columbus OH 43228
  614 529-7900

(G-7627)
FACILITYSOURCE LLC
200 E Campus View Blvd (43235-4678)
PHONE..................................614 318-1700
Fax: 614 318-1701
Amy Fonzi, *President*
Peter Mohrhauser, *COO*
Tom Holden, *Vice Pres*
Mark Strayer, *Vice Pres*
Jon Nairn, *Project Mgr*
EMP: 374
SALES (corp-wide): 32.3MM Privately Held
SIC: 8744 Facilities support services
PA: Facilitysource Llc
  2020 N Central Ave # 1200
  Phoenix AZ 85004
  614 318-1700

(G-7628)
FAHLGREN INC (PA)
4030 Easton Sta Ste 300 (43219-7012)
PHONE..................................614 383-1500
Fax: 614 222-2200
H Smoot Fahlgren, *Ch of Bd*
Neil Mortine, *President*
Steve Drongowski, *President*
Alan Hoover, *General Mgr*
Sean Cowan, *Exec VP*
EMP: 40
SALES: 23MM Privately Held
WEB: www.fahlgren.com
SIC: 7311 Advertising consultant

(G-7629)
FAHLGREN INC
4030 Easton Sta Ste 300 (43219-7012)
PHONE..................................614 383-1500
Steve Drongowski, *CEO*
Wendy Cramer, *Vice Pres*
Ray Hancart, *Director*
Jay Karr, *Director*
Katie McGrath, *Director*
EMP: 60
SALES (corp-wide): 23MM Privately Held
WEB: www.fahlgren.com
SIC: 7311 8742 8743 Advertising consultant; marketing consulting services; public relations & publicity
PA: Fahlgren, Inc.
  4030 Easton Sta Ste 300
  Columbus OH 43219
  614 383-1500

(G-7630)
FAIRFELD INN STES CLMBUS ARPRT
4300 International Gtwy (43219-1749)
PHONE..................................614 237-2100
Stephen Schwartz, *CEO*
EMP: 30
SALES (est): 1MM Privately Held
SIC: 7011 Hotels & motels

(G-7631)
FAIRFIELD INN
3031 Olentangy River Rd (43202-1572)
PHONE..................................614 267-1111
Frank Stnichols, *Principal*
Tamika Glenn, *Supervisor*
Scott Lomax, *CIO*
EMP: 80
SALES (est): 2.3MM Privately Held
SIC: 7011 Hotels & motels

(G-7632)
FAIRWAY INDEPENDENT MRTG CORP
4215 Worth Ave Ste 220 (43219-1546)
PHONE..................................614 930-6552
EMP: 43 Privately Held
SIC: 6162 Mortgage bankers & correspondents
PA: Fairway Independent Mortgage Corporation
  4750 S Biltmore Ln
  Madison WI 53718

(G-7633)
FAITH MISSION INC (HQ)
245 N Grant Ave (43215-2641)
PHONE..................................614 224-6617
Fax: 614 221-0936
Nina Lewis, *Opers Staff*
Misty Decker, *Manager*
Mark McPherson, *Manager*
Josiah Sapp, *Manager*
John Dickey, *Exec Dir*
EMP: 50
SQ FT: 20,000
SALES: 8.1MM
SALES (corp-wide): 49.2MM Privately Held
SIC: 8322 Emergency shelters
PA: Lutheran Social Services Of Central Ohio
  500 W Wilson Bridge Rd
  Worthington OH 43085
  419 289-3523

(G-7634)
FAITH MISSION INC
245 N Grant Ave (43215-2641)
PHONE..................................614 224-6617
Ereuss Preuss, *Director*
EMP: 45
SQ FT: 15,708
SALES (corp-wide): 49.2MM Privately Held
SIC: 8322 Social service center
HQ: Faith Mission, Inc
  245 N Grant Ave
  Columbus OH 43215
  614 224-6617

(G-7635)
FAMILY HEALTH CARE CENTER INC
Also Called: Linden Medical Center
2800 W Broad St Ste B (43204-2600)
PHONE..................................614 274-4171
Fax: 614 274-4197
Michelle Washington, *President*
EMP: 43
SQ FT: 1,200
SALES (est): 2.3MM Privately Held
SIC: 8011 General & family practice, physician/surgeon

(G-7636)
FAMILY PHYSICIANS OF GAHANNA
535 Officenter Pl Ste A (43230-5341)
PHONE..................................614 471-9654
Fax: 614 471-9634
Michael Baehr, *Partner*
Joseph Lutz, *Partner*
Maria Sammarco, *Partner*
Evan Stathulis, *Partner*
John Tyznik, *Partner*
EMP: 30
SALES (est): 2.5MM Privately Held
WEB: www.fpoginc.com
SIC: 8011 General & family practice, physician/surgeon

(G-7637)
FARBER CORPORATION
Also Called: Honeywell Authorized Dealer
800 E 12th Ave (43211-2670)
PHONE..................................614 294-1626
Fax: 614 294-4825
Edward A Farber, *President*
Sandra B Farber, *Corp Secy*
Tim Farber, *Vice Pres*
Michael Klingler, *Vice Pres*
Rick Buck, *Project Mgr*
▲ **EMP:** 30
SQ FT: 12,000
SALES (est): 7.5MM Privately Held
WEB: www.farbercorp.com
SIC: 1711 Mechanical contractor

(G-7638)
FARMERS GROUP INC
Also Called: Farmers Insurance
2500 Farmers Dr (43235-5706)
PHONE..................................614 406-2424
Russell Powers, *Vice Pres*
Randall Dennison, *Technology*
David F Blunt, *Director*
EMP: 200
SALES (corp-wide): 68.4B Privately Held
WEB: www.farmers.com
SIC: 6311 6331 Life insurance; fire, marine & casualty insurance
HQ: Farmers Group, Inc.
  6301 Owensmouth Ave
  Woodland Hills CA 91367
  323 932-3200

(G-7639)
FARMERS GROUP INC
Also Called: Farmers Insurance
7400 Safelite Way (43235-5086)
PHONE..................................614 766-6005
Robert Fuller, *Branch Mgr*
EMP: 30
SALES (corp-wide): 68.4B Privately Held
WEB: www.farmers.com
SIC: 6411 Insurance agents, brokers & service
HQ: Farmers Group, Inc.
  6301 Owensmouth Ave
  Woodland Hills CA 91367
  323 932-3200

(G-7640)
FARMERS GROUP INC
Also Called: Farmers Insurance
2545 Farmers Dr Ste 440 (43235-2705)
P.O. Box 268994, Oklahoma City OK (73126-8994)
PHONE..................................614 799-3200
Craig Miller, *Manager*
EMP: 40
SALES (corp-wide): 68.4B Privately Held
WEB: www.farmers.com
SIC: 6411 Insurance agents, brokers & service
HQ: Farmers Group, Inc.
  6301 Owensmouth Ave
  Woodland Hills CA 91367
  323 932-3200

(G-7641)
FARMERS INSURANCE OF COLUMBUS (DH)
7400 Skyline Dr E (43235-2706)
P.O. Box 2910, Shawnee Mission KS (66201-1310)
PHONE..................................614 799-3200
Fax: 614 882-3537
Annette K Schons-Thompson, *President*
Martin D Feinstein, *Vice Pres*
John H Lynch, *Vice Pres*
Russell L Powers, *Vice Pres*
Warren B Tucker, *Vice Pres*
EMP: 400
SQ FT: 350,000

GEOGRAPHIC SECTION
Columbus - Franklin County (G-7663)

SALES (est): 212.5K
SALES (corp-wide): 68.4B **Privately Held**
SIC: 6411 Insurance agents, brokers & service
HQ: Farmers Insurance Exchange
6301 Owensmouth Ave # 300
Woodland Hills CA 91367
323 932-3200

(G-7642)
FARMERS NEW WORLD LF INSUR CO
Also Called: Farmers Insurance
2500 Farmers Dr (43235-5706)
P.O. Box 182325 (43218-2325)
PHONE.................................614 764-9975
Fax: 614 766-7519
Shawn Huffman, *Underwriter*
Lucile Vickia, *Manager*
Claudia Lozier, *Executive*
EMP: 130
SALES (corp-wide): 68.4B **Privately Held**
SIC: 6411 6321 Insurance agents, brokers & service; health insurance carriers
HQ: Farmers New World Life Insurance Co Inc
3003 77th Ave Se
Mercer Island WA 98040
206 232-1093

(G-7643)
FATHOM SEO LLC
1465 Northwest Blvd (43212-3062)
PHONE.................................614 291-8456
Phil Kopp, *Sales Staff*
Christopher Lowry, *Branch Mgr*
EMP: 72
SALES (corp-wide): 24.5MM **Privately Held**
SIC: 8742 Marketing consulting services
PA: Fathom Seo, Llc
8200 Sweet Valley Dr
Cleveland OH 44125
216 525-0510

(G-7644)
FAVRET COMPANY
Also Called: Favret Heating & Cooling
1296 Dublin Rd (43215-1008)
PHONE.................................614 488-5211
Fax: 614 487-4538
William Favret, *CEO*
Mark Favret, *President*
Philip Favret, *Vice Pres*
Jim Chesbrough, *Sales Staff*
Richard Sprowles, *Sales Staff*
EMP: 63
SQ FT: 20,000
SALES (est): 10.9MM **Privately Held**
WEB: www.favret.com
SIC: 1711 Warm air heating & air conditioning contractor; plumbing contractors

(G-7645)
FCX PERFORMANCE INC (HQ)
Also Called: Jh Instruments
3000 E 14th Ave (43219-2355)
PHONE.................................614 324-6050
Thomas Cox, *CEO*
Jeff Caswell, *President*
Amory Roach, *Area Mgr*
Russell S Frazee, *COO*
Chris Hill, *Exec VP*
▲ EMP: 40
SQ FT: 44,000
SALES (est): 307.3MM
SALES (corp-wide): 2.5B **Publicly Held**
WEB: www.fcxperformance.com
SIC: 5084 5085 3494 Instruments & control equipment; industrial supplies; valves & fittings; valves & pipe fittings
PA: Applied Industrial Technologies, Inc.
1 Applied Plz
Cleveland OH 44115
216 426-4000

(G-7646)
FEDERAL EXPRESS CORPORATION
Also Called: Fedex
7066 Cargo Rd (43217-1346)
PHONE.................................614 492-6106
EMP: 300
SALES (corp-wide): 47.4B **Publicly Held**
SIC: 4513 4512 4522 4215 Air And Ground Cargo Carrier/Warehouse

HQ: Federal Express Corporation
3610 Hacks Cross Rd
Memphis TN 38125
901 369-3600

(G-7647)
FEDERAL EXPRESS CORPORATION
Also Called: Fedex
2424 Citygate Dr (43219-3590)
PHONE.................................800 463-3339
Curt Zimbric, *Manager*
EMP: 109
SALES (corp-wide): 60.3B **Publicly Held**
WEB: www.federalexpress.com
SIC: 4513 Package delivery, private air
HQ: Federal Express Corporation
3610 Hacks Cross Rd
Memphis TN 38125
901 369-3600

(G-7648)
FEDERAL EXPRESS CORPORATION
Also Called: Fedex
2850 International St (43228-4612)
PHONE.................................800 463-3339
EMP: 109
SALES (corp-wide): 60.3B **Publicly Held**
WEB: www.federalexpress.com
SIC: 4513 Package delivery, private air
HQ: Federal Express Corporation
3610 Hacks Cross Rd
Memphis TN 38125
901 369-3600

(G-7649)
FEDEX GROUND PACKAGE SYS INC
4600 Poth Rd (43213-1328)
PHONE.................................614 863-8000
Fax: 614 863-8060
Jeff Neilan, *Engineer*
Dom Sakowski, *Accounts Exec*
Chris V Esche, *Manager*
Adam Stiffler, *Manager*
Kathy Ross, *Administration*
EMP: 146
SALES (corp-wide): 60.3B **Publicly Held**
SIC: 4213 Contract haulers
HQ: Fedex Ground Package System, Inc.
1000 Fed Ex Dr
Coraopolis PA 15108
412 269-1000

(G-7650)
FEDEX OFFICE & PRINT SVCS INC
180 N High St (43215-2403)
PHONE.................................614 621-1100
Leslie Benners, *CFO*
Joe Hunt, *Accounts Exec*
Trocon Brown, *Branch Mgr*
EMP: 32
SALES (corp-wide): 60.3B **Publicly Held**
WEB: www.kinkos.com
SIC: 7334 2791 Photocopying & duplicating services; typesetting
HQ: Fedex Office And Print Services, Inc.
7900 Legacy Dr
Plano TX 75024
214 550-7000

(G-7651)
FEDEX OFFICE & PRINT SVCS INC
4516 Kenny Rd (43220-3711)
PHONE.................................614 538-1429
Darrah Wright, *Principal*
Bobby Robison, *Manager*
EMP: 43
SALES (corp-wide): 60.3B **Publicly Held**
WEB: www.kinkos.com
SIC: 7334 Photocopying & duplicating services
HQ: Fedex Office And Print Services, Inc.
7900 Legacy Dr
Plano TX 75024
214 550-7000

(G-7652)
FEINKNOPF MACIOCE SCHAPPA ARC
995 W 3rd Ave (43212-3109)
PHONE.................................614 297-1020

Joseph F Schappa, *President*
David A Youse, *Vice Pres*
George Pack, *Project Mgr*
Vaughn Benson, *Manager*
EMP: 25 EST: 1928
SQ FT: 7,000
SALES (est): 3.7MM **Privately Held**
WEB: www.fmsarchitects.com
SIC: 8712 Architectural engineering

(G-7653)
FHC ENTERPRISES LLC
Also Called: Government Resource Partners
5489 Blue Ash Rd (43229-3630)
PHONE.................................614 271-3513
Jim Cieply,
EMP: 34
SQ FT: 1,400
SALES (est): 375K **Privately Held**
SIC: 7379 Computer related maintenance services

(G-7654)
FIFTH AVENUE LUMBER CO (HQ)
Also Called: Lumber Craft
479 E 5th Ave (43201-2876)
P.O. Box 8098 (43201-0098)
PHONE.................................614 294-0068
Fax: 614 294-4732
Wilbur C Strait Jr, *CEO*
William A Cady, *President*
Craig Mitchell, *Marketing Staff*
Todd Buxton, *Manager*
Chuck Stewart, *Manager*
EMP: 90
SQ FT: 8,000
SALES (est): 13MM
SALES (corp-wide): 39.1MM **Privately Held**
WEB: www.straitandlamp.com
SIC: 5211 5031 Lumber products; lumber, plywood & millwork
PA: The Strait & Lamp Lumber Company Incorporated
269 National Rd Se
Hebron OH 43025
740 928-4501

(G-7655)
FIFTH THIRD BNK OF COLUMBUS OH
21 E State St Fl 4 (43215-4208)
PHONE.................................614 744-7553
Fax: 614 341-2607
Jordan Miller, *President*
Jed Horowitz, *Editor*
Barb Pyke, *Manager*
Mollie Schooley, *Manager*
EMP: 900
SALES (est): 379.6MM
SALES (corp-wide): 7.7B **Publicly Held**
WEB: www.53.com
SIC: 6022 State trust companies accepting deposits, commercial
PA: Fifth Third Bancorp
38 Fountain Square Plz
Cincinnati OH 45202
800 972-3030

(G-7656)
FINE LINE GRAPHICS CORP (PA)
1481 Goodale Blvd (43212-3402)
P.O. Box 163370 (43216-3370)
PHONE.................................614 486-0276
Fax: 614 486-5012
James Basch, *President*
Mark Carro, *Principal*
Gregory Davis, *Vice Pres*
Allie Davis, *VP Human Res*
Tracy Phares, *Human Res Mgr*
▲ EMP: 151
SQ FT: 42,000
SALES (est): 39MM **Privately Held**
SIC: 2752 7331 Commercial printing, offset; business forms, lithographed; mailing service

(G-7657)
FINISHMASTER INC
Also Called: Autobody Supply Company
212 N Grant Ave (43215-2642)
PHONE.................................614 228-4328
James Volpe, *Branch Mgr*
EMP: 68

SALES (corp-wide): 1.4B **Privately Held**
SIC: 3563 5013 5198 Air & gas compressors including vacuum pumps; automotive supplies; paints, varnishes & supplies; paints; lacquers; enamels
HQ: Finishmaster, Inc.
115 W Washington St Fl 7
Indianapolis IN 46204
317 237-3678

(G-7658)
FIRM HAHN LAW
Also Called: Hahn Loeser & Parks
65 E State St Ste 1400 (43215-4209)
PHONE.................................614 221-0240
Arland Stein, *Partner*
Dale Hunt, *Manager*
Phillip G Eckenrode, *Associate*
Emily Ladky, *Associate*
Christopher Mykytiak, *Associate*
EMP: 25 EST: 2008
SALES (est): 1.7MM **Privately Held**
SIC: 8111 General practice law office

(G-7659)
FIRST ACCEPTANCE CORPORATION
895 S Hamilton Rd (43213-3069)
PHONE.................................614 237-9700
Fax: 614 237-9796
Joanne Wein, *Principal*
EMP: 31
SALES (corp-wide): 347.5MM **Publicly Held**
SIC: 6411 Insurance agents
PA: First Acceptance Corporation
3813 Green Hills Vlg Dr
Nashville TN 37215
615 844-2800

(G-7660)
FIRST ACCEPTANCE CORPORATION
3497 Parsons Ave (43207-3883)
PHONE.................................614 492-1446
Donna Jones, *Manager*
EMP: 31
SALES (corp-wide): 347.5MM **Publicly Held**
SIC: 6411 Insurance agents, brokers & service
PA: First Acceptance Corporation
3813 Green Hills Vlg Dr
Nashville TN 37215
615 844-2800

(G-7661)
FIRST ACCEPTANCE CORPORATION
4898 W Broad St (43228-1602)
PHONE.................................614 853-3344
Fax: 614 851-9970
Ken Hollister, *Principal*
EMP: 41
SALES (corp-wide): 347.5MM **Publicly Held**
SIC: 6411 Insurance agents, brokers & service
PA: First Acceptance Corporation
3813 Green Hills Vlg Dr
Nashville TN 37215
615 844-2800

(G-7662)
FIRST COMMUNITY CHURCH (PA)
1320 Cambridge Blvd (43212-3200)
PHONE.................................614 488-2763
Fax: 614 488-2763
Ruth Decker, *Ch of Bd*
David Hett, *Minister*
Richard Wing, *Minister*
Cynthia Harsany, *Finance*
Michael Barber, *Mktg Dir*
EMP: 48
SQ FT: 56,796
SALES (est): 4.7MM **Privately Held**
SIC: 8661 8351 Community church; child day care services

(G-7663)
FIRST COMMUNITY CHURCH
Also Called: Mary Evans Childcare Center
3777 Dublin Rd (43221-4915)
PHONE.................................614 488-0681

Columbus - Franklin County (G-7664)

Fax: 614 777-4098
Jamy Zambito, *Director*
EMP: 26
SQ FT: 17,424
SALES (corp-wide): 4.7MM **Privately Held**
SIC: 8661 8351 Community church; child day care services
PA: The First Community Church
1320 Cambridge Blvd
Columbus OH 43212
614 488-0681

(G-7664)
FIRST COMMUNITY VILLAGE
Also Called: NATIONAL CHURCH RESIDENCES FIRST COMMUNITY VILLAGE
1800 Riverside Dr Ofc (43212-1819)
PHONE..............................614 324-4455
Fax: 614 486-5628
Tanya Kim Hahn, *President*
Harold G Edwards, *Principal*
Jane Nash, *Principal*
Edward D Schorr Jr, *Principal*
Diane Tomlinson, *Senior VP*
EMP: 300 **EST:** 1963
SQ FT: 1,269
SALES: 26.9MM
SALES (corp-wide): 44.4MM **Privately Held**
WEB: www.firstcommunityvillage.org
SIC: 8082 8051 8059 8322 Home health care services; skilled nursing care facilities; nursing home, except skilled & intermediate care facility; outreach program; geriatric residential care
PA: National Church Residences
2335 N Bank Dr
Columbus OH 43220
614 451-2151

(G-7665)
FIRST HOTEL ASSOCIATES LP
Also Called: Westin Hotel
310 S High St (43215-4508)
PHONE..............................614 228-3800
Deborah Brown, *General Mgr*
Steve Dietrich, *Controller*
Carl Palmer, *Human Res Dir*
Carla A Farmer, *Sales Dir*
Molly Gribbin, *Director*
EMP: 100
SALES (est): 2.7MM **Privately Held**
SIC: 7011 5813 5812 Hotels; drinking places; eating places

(G-7666)
FIRST MERCHANTS BANK
2130 Tremont Ctr (43221-3110)
PHONE..............................614 486-9000
EMP: 30
SALES (corp-wide): 385.9MM **Publicly Held**
SIC: 6029 6163 Commercial banks; loan brokers
HQ: First Merchants Bank
189 W Market St
Wabash IN 46992
260 563-4116

(G-7667)
FISHEL COMPANY (PA)
Also Called: FISHEL TECHNOLOGIES
1366 Dublin Rd (43215-1093)
PHONE..............................614 274-8100
John E Phillips, *President*
Bob Dinuoscio, *Division Mgr*
Ruben Garcia, *Division Mgr*
Tracy Pate, *Division Mgr*
Mark Vucko, *Division Mgr*
EMP: 60
SQ FT: 22,000
SALES: 341.9MM **Privately Held**
WEB: www.fishelco.com
SIC: 1623 1731 8711 Telephone & communication line construction; electric power line construction; cable television line construction; gas main construction; general electrical contractor; engineering services

(G-7668)
FISHEL COMPANY
1600 Walcutt Rd (43228-9394)
PHONE..............................614 850-9012
Craig Mathes, *Human Res Dir*
Richard Keeler, *Marketing Staff*
Scott Homberger, *Manager*
Stewart Beckett, *Manager*
James Geddes, *Manager*
EMP: 130
SALES (corp-wide): 341.9MM **Privately Held**
WEB: www.fishelco.com
SIC: 1623 Underground utilities contractor
PA: The Fishel Company
1366 Dublin Rd
Columbus OH 43215
614 274-8100

(G-7669)
FISHEL COMPANY
Johnson Brothers Construction
1600 Walcutt Rd (43228-9394)
PHONE..............................614 850-4400
Fax: 614 850-4419
Ed Evans, *Manager*
Angi Storino, *IT/INT Sup*
EMP: 65
SALES (corp-wide): 341.9MM **Privately Held**
WEB: www.fishelco.com
SIC: 1623 8711 1731 3612 Telephone & communication line construction; electric power line construction; cable television line construction; gas main construction; engineering services; electrical work; transformers, except electric
PA: The Fishel Company
1366 Dublin Rd
Columbus OH 43215
614 274-8100

(G-7670)
FITCH INC (DH)
585 Suth Front St Ste 300 (43215)
PHONE..............................614 885-3453
Simon Bolton, *CEO*
Dan Stanek, *Partner*
Rick Redpath, *Managing Dir*
Gregory Vick, *Exec VP*
Nick Griggs, *Project Mgr*
EMP: 60 **EST:** 1960
SQ FT: 40,000
SALES (est): 14.3MM
SALES (corp-wide): 17.7B **Privately Held**
SIC: 7336 Graphic arts & related design
HQ: Wpp Clapton Square, Llc
100 Park Ave Fl 4
New York NY 10017
212 632-2200

(G-7671)
FIVE STAR SENIOR LIVING INC
Also Called: Forum At Knightsbridge
4590 Knightsbridge Blvd (43214-4327)
PHONE..............................614 451-6793
Fax: 614 273-2450
Jennifer Saunders, *Personnel Exec*
Catherine Miller, *Marketing Staff*
Rebecca Converse, *Exec Dir*
EMP: 63 **Publicly Held**
WEB: www.fivestarqualitycare.com
SIC: 8051 Skilled nursing care facilities
PA: Five Star Senior Living Inc.
400 Centre St
Newton MA 02458

(G-7672)
FIXARI FAMILY DENTAL INC (PA)
4241 Kimberly Pkwy (43232-7225)
PHONE..............................614 866-7445
Fax: 614 866-8750
Mark Fixari, *President*
Shane Fixari, *Vice Pres*
EMP: 30
SQ FT: 2,700
SALES (est): 4.1MM **Privately Held**
SIC: 8021 Dentists' office

(G-7673)
FLAIRSOFT LTD (PA)
7720 Rivers Edge Dr Ste 2 (43235-1361)
PHONE..............................614 888-0700
Fax: 614 573-7255
Dheeraj Kulshrestha, *Partner*
Bryan Corson, *Vice Pres*
Nick Kulshrestha, *Vice Pres*
Geoff Wilhelm, *Vice Pres*
Nandini Kondagari, *Accounting Mgr*
EMP: 50
SALES: 9.5MM **Privately Held**
SIC: 7371 Computer software development

(G-7674)
FLEETWOOD MANAGEMENT INC
1675 Old Henderson Rd (43220-3644)
PHONE..............................614 538-1277
Robert J Beggs, *President*
Joseph E Scruggs, *Vice Pres*
Juli A Difolco, *CFO*
EMP: 40 **EST:** 1996
SQ FT: 2,850
SALES (est): 2.2MM **Privately Held**
SIC: 6531 Real estate managers

(G-7675)
FLIGHT EXPRESS INC (HQ)
7250 Star Check Dr (43217-1025)
PHONE..............................305 379-8686
Pat Hawk, *President*
Stephanie Banning, *Opers Staff*
Stephen Howery, *Treasurer*
Bradley Marcantelli, *Controller*
EMP: 80
SALES (est): 13.9MM
SALES (corp-wide): 483MM **Privately Held**
SIC: 4512 Air cargo carrier, scheduled
PA: Bayside Capital, Inc.
1450 Brickell Ave Fl 31
Miami FL 33131
305 379-8686

(G-7676)
FLODRAULIC GROUP INCORPORATED
765 N Hague Ave (43204-1424)
PHONE..............................614 276-8141
Henrietta Blair, *Branch Mgr*
EMP: 25
SALES (corp-wide): 2.5B **Privately Held**
WEB: www.flodraulicgroup.com
SIC: 5085 Industrial supplies
PA: Flodraulic Group Incorporated
3539 N 700 W
Greenfield IN 46140
317 890-3700

(G-7677)
FLOWER FACTORY INC
4395 Clime Rd (43228-3406)
PHONE..............................614 275-6220
Bruce Mann, *Manager*
EMP: 60
SALES (corp-wide): 140.6MM **Privately Held**
SIC: 5199 5193 5092 Gifts & novelties; general merchandise, non-durable; artificial flowers; arts & crafts equipment & supplies
PA: Flower Factory, Inc.
5655 Whipple Ave Nw
North Canton OH 44720
330 494-7978

(G-7678)
FMW RRI OPCO LLC (PA)
Also Called: Red Roof Inn
605 S Front St Ste 150 (43215-5809)
PHONE..............................614 744-2659
James G Glasgow Jr, *President*
EMP: 36
SALES (est): 8.9MM **Privately Held**
SIC: 7011 Inns

(G-7679)
FOOD FOR GOOD THOUGHT INC
4185 N High St (43214-3011)
PHONE..............................614 447-0424
Audrey Todd, *President*
EMP: 30
SALES: 22.4K **Privately Held**
SIC: 8331 Vocational rehabilitation agency

(G-7680)
FOOD SAFETY NET SERVICES LTD
4130 Fisher Rd (43228-1022)
PHONE..............................614 274-2070
Steve Palmer, *Branch Mgr*
EMP: 35
SALES (corp-wide): 32.3MM **Privately Held**
SIC: 8734 Food testing service
PA: Food Safety Net Services, Ltd.
199 W Rhapsody Dr
San Antonio TX 78216
888 525-9788

(G-7681)
FORTUNE BRANDS WINDOWS INC (DH)
Also Called: Simonton Windows
3948 Townsfair Way # 200 (43219-6095)
PHONE..............................614 532-3500
Mark Savan, *President*
Michael S Petersen, *Vice Pres*
Greg Schorr, *Vice Pres*
Matthew C Lenz, *Treasurer*
Steve Hiley, *Manager*
▲ **EMP:** 400
SALES (est): 90.9MM
SALES (corp-wide): 2B **Publicly Held**
WEB: www.simontonwindows.com
SIC: 1751 5211 Window & door installation & erection; window & door (prefabricated) installation; door & window products
HQ: Ply Gem Industries, Inc.
5020 Weston Pkwy Ste 400
Cary NC 27513
919 677-3900

(G-7682)
FRANKLIN CNTY BD COMMISSIONERS
Also Called: County Engineers Office
970 Dublin Rd (43215-1169)
PHONE..............................614 462-3030
Fax: 614 462-3359
Dean Ringle, *Principal*
Nick Menedis, *Human Res Mgr*
Amy Lowe, *Comms Dir*
Michael Phelps, *Manager*
Marty Hughes, *Clerk*
EMP: 180
SQ FT: 8,040
SALES (corp-wide): 1.2B **Privately Held**
SIC: 1611 9111 Highway & street construction; county supervisors' & executives' offices
PA: Franklin County Board Of Commissioners
373 S High St Fl 26
Columbus OH 43215
614 525-3322

(G-7683)
FRANKLIN CNTY BD COMMISSIONERS
Franklin County Chld Svcs Bd
855 W Mound St (43223-2208)
PHONE..............................614 275-2571
James Stephenson, *Purch Mgr*
Penny Miller, *Supervisor*
Rob Nieman, *Supervisor*
Michele Bullock, *Technology*
Chip Spinning, *Director*
EMP: 200
SALES (corp-wide): 1.2B **Privately Held**
SIC: 8322 Children's aid society; adoption services
PA: Franklin County Board Of Commissioners
373 S High St Fl 26
Columbus OH 43215
614 525-3322

(G-7684)
FRANKLIN CNTY BD COMMISSIONERS
Franklin County Facility MGT
373 S High St Fl 2 (43215-4591)
PHONE..............................614 462-3800
Fax: 614 525-3180
Maryann Barnhart, *Director*
EMP: 250
SALES (corp-wide): 1.2B **Privately Held**
SIC: 8744 Facilities support services
PA: Franklin County Board Of Commissioners
373 S High St Fl 26
Columbus OH 43215
614 525-3322

GEOGRAPHIC SECTION
Columbus - Franklin County (G-7708)

(G-7685)
FRANKLIN CNTY BD COMMISSIONERS
Also Called: Child Support Enforcement Agcy
80 E Fulton St (43215-5128)
PHONE..................614 462-3275
Chad Davidson, *Network Tech*
Joe Pilat, *Director*
EMP: 300
SALES (corp-wide): 1.2B **Privately Held**
SIC: 8322 Child related social services
PA: Franklin County Board Of Commissioners
373 S High St Fl 26
Columbus OH 43215
614 525-3322

(G-7686)
FRANKLIN CNTY BD COMMISSIONERS
Also Called: Juvenile Detention Center
399 S Front St (43215-5389)
PHONE..................614 462-3429
Kathryn Lias, *Principal*
EMP: 30
SALES (corp-wide): 1.2B **Privately Held**
SIC: 8361 Juvenile correctional facilities
PA: Franklin County Board Of Commissioners
373 S High St Fl 26
Columbus OH 43215
614 525-3322

(G-7687)
FRANKLIN CNTY BD COMMISSIONERS
Also Called: Franklin County Childrens Svcs
4071 E Main St (43213-2952)
PHONE..................614 229-7100
Fax: 614 575-3600
Chip Spinning, *Director*
EMP: 500
SALES (corp-wide): 1.2B **Privately Held**
SIC: 8322 Child related social services
PA: Franklin County Board Of Commissioners
373 S High St Fl 26
Columbus OH 43215
614 525-3322

(G-7688)
FRANKLIN CNTY BD COMMISSIONERS
Also Called: Franklin County Pub Defender
373 S High St Fl 12 (43215-4591)
PHONE..................614 462-3194
Fax: 614 462-6470
Judith M Stevenson, *Manager*
EMP: 145
SALES (corp-wide): 1.2B **Privately Held**
SIC: 8111 Legal services
PA: Franklin County Board Of Commissioners
373 S High St Fl 26
Columbus OH 43215
614 525-3322

(G-7689)
FRANKLIN CNTY BD COMMISSIONERS
1731 Alum Creek Dr (43207-1708)
PHONE..................614 462-4360
Patricia Sphar, *President*
EMP: 33
SALES (corp-wide): 1.2B **Privately Held**
SIC: 8699 Animal humane society
PA: Franklin County Board Of Commissioners
373 S High St Fl 26
Columbus OH 43215
614 525-3322

(G-7690)
FRANKLIN CNTY CRT COMMON PLEAS
Division of Domestic Relations
373 S High St Fl 6 (43215-4591)
PHONE..................614 525-5775
Dana Preisse,
EMP: 30 **Privately Held**
SIC: 7363 Domestic help service

PA: Franklin County Court Of Common Pleas
373 S High St Fl 6
Columbus OH 43215
614 525-5775

(G-7691)
FRANKLIN COMMUNICATIONS INC
Also Called: W S N Y F M Sunny 95
4401 Carriage Hill Ln (43220-3837)
PHONE..................614 451-2191
Alan Goodman, *President*
Jody Wigton, *Manager*
EMP: 100
SALES (est): 6.2MM **Privately Held**
WEB: www.columbusradiogroup.com
SIC: 4832 Radio broadcasting stations

(G-7692)
FRANKLIN COMMUNICATIONS INC
Also Called: Wsny FM
4401 Carriage Hill Ln (43220-3837)
PHONE..................614 459-9769
Fax: 614 821-9595
Edward K Christian, *CEO*
Alan Goodman, *President*
John Marocchi, *Chief Engr*
EMP: 65
SQ FT: 10,000
SALES (est): 2.1MM **Publicly Held**
WEB: www.sagacommunications.com
SIC: 4832 2711 Radio broadcasting stations; newspapers
HQ: Saga Communications Of New England, Inc.
73 Kercheval Ave Ste 201
Grosse Pointe Farms MI 48236
313 886-7070

(G-7693)
FRANKLIN COMMUNITY BASE CORREC
1745 Alum Creek Dr (43207-1708)
PHONE..................614 525-4600
Fax: 614 462-4606
Gayle Dittmer, *Principal*
Jacki Dickinson,
Ricky Hodge, *Clerk*
EMP: 75
SALES (est): 2.1MM **Privately Held**
WEB: www.fccourts.org
SIC: 8744 Correctional facility

(G-7694)
FRANKLIN COUNTY ADAMH BOARD
447 E Broad St (43215-3822)
PHONE..................614 224-1057
Fax: 614 224-0991
David Royer, *CEO*
Mitzi Moody, *Project Mgr*
Vincent Sabino, *Project Mgr*
Justin Curtis, *Research*
John Logan, *Financial Analy*
EMP: 50
SALES (est): 932.8K **Privately Held**
SIC: 8099 Health & allied services

(G-7695)
FRANKLIN COUNTY HISTORICAL SOC
Also Called: Cosi
333 W Broad St (43215-2738)
PHONE..................614 228-2674
Fax: 614 228-6363
David Chesebrough, *CEO*
Bernie Ostrowski, *Partner*
Kimberly Pratt, *Principal*
James Brewster, *District Mgr*
Joseph Dunsmore, *District Mgr*
◆ **EMP:** 124
SQ FT: 200,000
SALES: 16.9MM **Privately Held**
WEB: www.mail.cosi.org
SIC: 8412 Museum

(G-7696)
FRANKLIN COUNTY RESIDENTIAL S
1021 Checkrein Ave (43229-1106)
PHONE..................614 844-5847
Patty Howe, *Business Mgr*
Gaines Strouse, *Manager*

Debi Atkinson, *Asst Mgr*
Margaret Padgett, *Asst Mgr*
Ed Harper, *Director*
EMP: 285
SALES: 21.7MM **Privately Held**
WEB: www.fcres.com
SIC: 8361 Home for the mentally handicapped

(G-7697)
FRANKLIN IMAGING LLC (PA)
500 Schrock Rd (43229-1028)
PHONE..................614 885-6894
Fax: 614 885-2823
Emily Williamson,
Joe Williamson,
EMP: 30
SQ FT: 14,400
SALES (est): 6.2MM **Privately Held**
WEB: www.franklinimaging.com
SIC: 7334 5044 5049 Blueprinting service; blueprinting equipment; engineers' equipment & supplies

(G-7698)
FRANKLIN SHCP INC
Also Called: Crown Pointe Care Center
1850 Crown Park Ct (43235-2400)
PHONE..................440 614-0160
Fax: 614 459-1721
Brian Colleran, *President*
Winnie Moazampour, *Director*
Tabitha Meyer, *Social Dir*
Janet Hornet, *Executive*
EMP: 99
SALES: 6.6MM **Privately Held**
SIC: 8051 Convalescent home with continuous nursing care

(G-7699)
FRANKLIN SPECIALTY TRNSPT INC (HQ)
2040 Atlas St (43228-9645)
PHONE..................614 529-7900
Arthur J Decrane, *President*
David S Kent, *CFO*
EMP: 100
SQ FT: 42,000
SALES: 21MM
SALES (corp-wide): 80.3MM **Privately Held**
WEB: www.fstfst.com
SIC: 4213 Less-than-truckload (LTL) transport; refrigerated products transport
PA: Fst Logistics, Inc.
2040 Atlas St
Columbus OH 43228
614 529-7900

(G-7700)
FRATERNAL ORDER OF POLICE OF O (PA)
222 E Town St Fl 1e (43215-4611)
PHONE..................614 224-5700
Fax: 614 224-5775
Jay McDonald, *President*
Mark Drum, *Treasurer*
Gwen Callender,
Kay Cremeans,
Mike Piotrowski,
EMP: 74
SQ FT: 6,500
SALES: 1.1MM **Privately Held**
SIC: 8641 Fraternal associations

(G-7701)
FREEDOM SPECIALTY INSURANCE CO (DH)
Also Called: Travelers Insurance
1 W Nationwide Blvd (43215-2752)
P.O. Box 4120, Scottsdale AZ (85261-4120)
PHONE..................614 249-1545
Chris Watson, *President*
▲ **EMP:** 202 **EST:** 1976
SQ FT: 96,000
SALES (est): 37.8MM
SALES (corp-wide): 26.6B **Privately Held**
WEB: www.atlanticinsurancecompany.com
SIC: 6411 Insurance agents
HQ: Scottsdale Insurance Company
8877 N Gainey Center Dr
Scottsdale AZ 85258
480 365-4000

(G-7702)
FREELAND CONTRACTING CO
2100 Integrity Dr S (43209-2752)
PHONE..................614 443-2718
Fax: 614 443-2738
James R Fry, *President*
Brenda Fry, *Vice Pres*
EMP: 32
SQ FT: 19,200
SALES (est): 8.9MM **Privately Held**
SIC: 1711 Plumbing contractors

(G-7703)
FRESENIUS MED CARE HLDINGS INC
Also Called: Liberty Dlysis Md-Mrica Dlysis
2355 S Hamilton Rd (43232-4305)
PHONE..................800 881-5101
EMP: 30
SALES (corp-wide): 20.9B **Privately Held**
SIC: 8092 Kidney dialysis centers
HQ: Fresenius Medical Care Holdings, Inc.
920 Winter St
Waltham MA 02451

(G-7704)
FRESHEALTH LLC
3650 E 5th Ave (43219-1805)
PHONE..................614 231-3601
James Griffin, *CFO*
Alex Dinovo, *Mng Member*
EMP: 80
SALES (est): 1.1MM **Privately Held**
SIC: 0723 Fruit crops market preparation services

(G-7705)
FRIEDMAN MANAGEMENT COMPANY
50 W Broad St Ste 200 (43215-5942)
PHONE..................614 224-2424
Andrew Rausthe, *Branch Mgr*
EMP: 57 **Privately Held**
SIC: 6512 Property operation, retail establishment
PA: Friedman Management Company
34975 W 12 Mile Rd # 100
Farmington Hills MI 48331

(G-7706)
FRIENDS OF ART FOR CULTURAL
Also Called: F A C E
191 Melyers Ct (43235-6418)
PHONE..................614 888-9929
Caffan T Willis, *Vice Pres*
EMP: 25
SALES: 84K **Privately Held**
SIC: 8641 Youth organizations

(G-7707)
FRIENDSHIP VLG OF CLUMBUS OHIO
5757 Ponderosa Dr (43231-3102)
PHONE..................614 890-8287
Fax: 614 890-2661
Amanda Trzcinski, *Principal*
Jennifer Sanchez, *Executive*
Kristen Parker, *Advisor*
EMP: 92
SALES (corp-wide): 16.8MM **Privately Held**
SIC: 8051 Convalescent home with continuous nursing care
PA: Friendship Village Of Columbus Ohio, Inc
5800 Frest Hills Blvd Ofc
Columbus OH 43231
614 890-8282

(G-7708)
FRIENDSHIP VLG OF CLUMBUS OHIO (PA)
5800 Frest Hills Blvd Ofc (43231)
PHONE..................614 890-8282
Chris Harbert, *Opers Staff*
Nancy Nelson, *Sls & Mktg Exec*
Neil Edelson, *Mktg Dir*
Joy Hall, *Office Mgr*
Thomas Miller, *Exec Dir*
EMP: 205
SQ FT: 265,000

Columbus - Franklin County (G-7709)

SALES: 16.8MM **Privately Held**
WEB: www.friendshipvillageoh.com
SIC: 8361 8051 Home for the aged; skilled nursing care facilities

(G-7709)
FRITO-LAY NORTH AMERICA INC
6611 Broughton Ave (43213-1523)
PHONE 614 508-3004
Don Jacklich, *Sales/Mktg Mgr*
EMP: 165
SALES (corp-wide): 63.5B **Publicly Held**
WEB: www.fritolay.com
SIC: 5145 Snack foods
HQ: Frito-Lay North America, Inc.
7701 Legacy Dr
Plano TX 75024

(G-7710)
FRITZ-RUMER-COOKE CO INC
635 E Woodrow Ave (43207-2030)
PHONE 614 444-8844
Clement C Cooke, *President*
Gordon Webster, *General Mgr*
Ben Swope, *COO*
Karen Cooke, *Vice Pres*
Tom Willhelm, *Project Engr*
EMP: 35
SQ FT: 1,500
SALES (est): 10.3MM **Privately Held**
SIC: 1629 Railroad & railway roadbed construction

(G-7711)
FROST BROWN TODD LLC
1 Columbus Ste 2300 10 W (43215)
PHONE 614 464-1211
Fax: 614 464-1737
Thomas V Willams, *Branch Mgr*
Jeffrey Lindemann, *Corp Counsel*
Jeffery Rupert, *Corp Counsel*
Carol Dunn, *Executive*
William Harter, *Sr Associate*
EMP: 38
SALES (corp-wide): 153.4MM **Privately Held**
WEB: www.fbtextra.com
SIC: 8111 General practice attorney, lawyer
PA: Frost Brown Todd Llc
3300 Grt Amrcn Towe 301e
Cincinnati OH 45202
513 651-6800

(G-7712)
FTM ASSOCIATES LLC
150 E Campus View Blvd (43235-4648)
PHONE 614 846-1834
David B Friedman,
EMP: 80
SQ FT: 134,000
SALES (est): 2.4MM **Privately Held**
SIC: 6513 Apartment building operators

(G-7713)
FUJIYAMA INTERNATIONAL INC
5755 Cleveland Ave (43231-2831)
PHONE 614 891-2224
Bill Marcum, *President*
Myung Kim, *Vice Pres*
EMP: 30
SALES: 1.5MM **Privately Held**
SIC: 6531 Real estate agents & managers

(G-7714)
FUNNY BONE COMEDY CLUB & CAFE
145 Easton Town Ctr (43219-6075)
PHONE 614 471-5653
Fax: 614 471-0557
Dave Stroupe, *Owner*
EMP: 35
SALES (est): 794.8K **Privately Held**
WEB: www.gofunnybone.com
SIC: 7922 Theatrical producers & services

(G-7715)
FURNITURE BANK CENTRAL OHIO
Also Called: Furniture With A Heart
118 S Yale Ave (43222-1369)
PHONE 614 272-9544
James C Stein, *President*
Steve Votaw, *President*
Racheal Dellon, *Manager*
John Vidosh, *Director*
James C Henderson, *Bd of Directors*
EMP: 25
SQ FT: 1,820
SALES (est): 5MM **Privately Held**
WEB: www.mapfurniturebank.org
SIC: 8322 Social service center

(G-7716)
FUTURE POLY TECH INC (PA)
2215 Citygate Dr Ste D (43219-3589)
PHONE 614 942-1209
Ron Anderko, *President*
EMP: 30
SALES (est): 3.5MM **Privately Held**
SIC: 7389 Packaging & labeling services

(G-7717)
G AND H MANAGEMENT
Also Called: Capital Care Women's Center
1243 E Broad St (43205-1404)
PHONE 614 268-2273
Fax: 614 430-3744
Kathleen Glover, *President*
EMP: 25
SQ FT: 5,000
SALES: 1.6MM **Privately Held**
WEB: www.capitalcarewomenscenter.com
SIC: 8099 Medical services organization

(G-7718)
G III REITTER WALLS LLC
1759 Old Leonard Ave (43219-2561)
PHONE 614 545-4444
Dave Reitter,
EMP: 27 **EST:** 2013
SALES: 2MM **Privately Held**
SIC: 1522 1542 Residential construction; nonresidential construction

(G-7719)
G MECHANICAL INC
6635 Singletree Dr (43229-1120)
PHONE 614 844-6750
Fax: 614 844-6754
Christopher Giannetto, *President*
Dianne Coberson, *Controller*
EMP: 42
SALES: 7.5MM **Privately Held**
SIC: 1711 Heating & air conditioning contractors

(G-7720)
G STEPHENS INC
1175 Dublin Rd Ste 2 (43215-1252)
PHONE 614 227-0304
Glenn Stephens, *Branch Mgr*
EMP: 65
SALES (est): 2.5MM **Privately Held**
SIC: 8741 Construction management
PA: G. Stephens, Inc.
133 N Summit St
Akron OH 44304

(G-7721)
G-COR AUTOMOTIVE CORP (PA)
2100 Refugee Rd (43207-2841)
PHONE 614 443-6735
Fax: 614 443-6718
Stanley Greenblott, *President*
Donald L Feinstein, *Principal*
Kenny Greenblott, *Vice Pres*
Stacy Swaney, *Manager*
▼ **EMP:** 45
SQ FT: 250,000
SALES (est): 27.6MM **Privately Held**
SIC: 5013 5015 5093 Automotive supplies & parts; automotive parts & supplies, used; metal scrap & waste materials

(G-7722)
G4S SECURE SOLUTIONS (USA)
Also Called: Wackenhut
2211 Lake Club Dr Ste 105 (43232-3204)
PHONE 614 322-5100
Fax: 614 322-5110
Graham Gibson, *Branch Mgr*
EMP: 150
SALES (corp-wide): 9.3B **Privately Held**
SIC: 7382 Security systems services
HQ: G4s Secure Solutions (Usa) Inc.
1395 University Blvd
Jupiter FL 33458
561 622-5656

(G-7723)
GAHANNA HEALTH CARE CENTER
Also Called: Rocky Creek Hlth Rhabilitation
121 James Rd (43230-2825)
PHONE 614 475-7222
Brian Colleran, *President*
Galvin Baumgardner, *Director*
Helen Nojay, *Executive*
EMP: 50
SALES (est): 1.1MM **Privately Held**
SIC: 8051 Skilled nursing care facilities

(G-7724)
GAHANNA-JEFFERSON PUB SCHL DST
Also Called: Bus Transportation Department
782 Science Blvd (43230-6641)
PHONE 614 751-7581
Robert McCafferty, *Principal*
EMP: 60
SALES (corp-wide): 95.7MM **Privately Held**
SIC: 4151 School buses
PA: Gahanna-Jefferson Public School District
160 S Hamilton Rd
Gahanna OH 43230
614 471-7065

(G-7725)
GALLAGHER GAMS PRYOR TALLAN
471 E Broad St Fl 19 (43215-3864)
PHONE 614 228-5151
Laurie Duckworth, *President*
James R Gallagher, *Partner*
Brian Gallagher, *Partner*
Mark H Gams, *Partner*
Barry Littrell, *Partner*
EMP: 26
SALES (est): 3.5MM **Privately Held**
WEB: www.ggptl.com
SIC: 8111 General practice law office

(G-7726)
GARDA CL GREAT LAKES INC
Also Called: At Systems
201 Schofield Dr (43213-3831)
PHONE 614 863-4044
Ron Drener, *Manager*
EMP: 30
SALES (corp-wide): 69.3K **Privately Held**
WEB: www.gocashlink.com
SIC: 7381 Armored car services
HQ: Garda Cl Great Lakes, Inc.
201 Schofield Dr
Columbus OH 43213
561 939-7000

(G-7727)
GARDA CL GREAT LAKES INC (DH)
Also Called: United Armored Services
201 Schofield Dr (43213-3831)
PHONE 561 939-7000
Fax: 614 575-2386
Stephan Cretier, *President*
Tim Henry, *President*
Chris W Jamroz, *President*
Don Debord, *Business Mgr*
Patrice Boily, *Vice Pres*
EMP: 400 **EST:** 1971
SQ FT: 60,000
SALES (est): 20.4MM
SALES (corp-wide): 69.3K **Privately Held**
SIC: 7381 7389 7359 Armored car services; packaging & labeling services; equipment rental & leasing

(G-7728)
GARDNER INC (PA)
3641 Interchange Rd (43204-1499)
PHONE 614 456-4000
Fax: 614 456-4001
John F Finn, *CEO*
James P Finn, *Vice Pres*
Michael L Finn, *Vice Pres*
John T Finn, *CFO*
Mark Greiner, *Credit Mgr*
EMP: 222
SQ FT: 204,000
SALES (est): 56.2MM **Privately Held**
SIC: 6512 5084 Nonresidential building operators; engines, gasoline

(G-7729)
GARDNER-CONNELL LLC
3641 Interchange Rd (43204-1499)
PHONE 614 456-4000
Gary Muehlbauer, *Area Mgr*
Mark Greiner, *Credit Mgr*
Bill Shamon, *Branch Mgr*
EMP: 37 **Privately Held**
SIC: 5191 5083 Farm supplies; farm & garden machinery
PA: Gardner-Connell, Llc
125 Constitution Blvd
Franklin MA 02038

(G-7730)
GARLAND GROUP INC
Also Called: Buckeye Real Estate
48 E 15th Ave Frnt (43201-1679)
P.O. Box 8310 (43201-0310)
PHONE 614 294-4411
Fax: 614 299-3754
Wayne Garland, *President*
Lorie Garland, *Vice Pres*
Robert Hendershot, *Treasurer*
EMP: 50 **EST:** 1975
SQ FT: 7,300
SALES (est): 5.6MM **Privately Held**
WEB: www.buckeyere.com
SIC: 6513 1522 6531 Apartment building operators; remodeling, multi-family dwellings; real estate brokers & agents

(G-7731)
GBQ CONSULTING LLC
230 West St Ste 700 (43215-2663)
PHONE 614 221-1120
Darci Congrove, *CEO*
Cara Hounshell,
EMP: 61 **EST:** 2005
SALES (est): 440.7K
SALES (corp-wide): 20.2MM **Privately Held**
SIC: 8742 Management consulting services
PA: Gbq Holdings, Llc
230 West St Ste 700
Columbus OH 43215
614 221-1120

(G-7732)
GBQ HOLDINGS LLC (PA)
230 West St Ste 700 (43215-2663)
PHONE 614 221-1120
Darci Congrove, *Principal*
Andrew Arend, *COO*
Shaun Powell, *Controller*
Debra Reese, *Accountant*
Cheryl Hooker, *Human Res Mgr*
EMP: 57
SQ FT: 39,178
SALES (est): 20.2MM **Privately Held**
SIC: 8721 Accounting, auditing & bookkeeping

(G-7733)
GEM CITY HOME CARE LLC
4020 Venture Ct (43228-9600)
PHONE 614 588-0228
Juli Walder, *Branch Mgr*
EMP: 28
SALES (corp-wide): 4.5MM **Privately Held**
SIC: 8059 Personal care home, with health care
PA: Gem City Home Care Llc
1700 Lyons Rd Unit A
Dayton OH 45458
937 438-9100

(G-7734)
GENERAL PARTS INC
Also Called: Carquest Auto Parts
2825 Silver Dr (43211-1052)
PHONE 614 267-5197
Kendra Reiss, *Branch Mgr*
Dave Hirst, *Manager*
EMP: 25
SALES (corp-wide): 9.3B **Publicly Held**
WEB: www.carquest.com
SIC: 5013 5531 Automotive supplies; automotive parts
HQ: General Parts, Inc.
2635 E Millbrook Rd Ste C
Raleigh NC 27604
919 573-3000

GEOGRAPHIC SECTION

Columbus - Franklin County (G-7757)

(G-7735)
GENERAL SERVICES CLEANING CO
8111 Blind Brook Ct (43235-1203)
P.O. Box 1052, Powell (43065-1052)
PHONE..............................614 840-0562
Fax: 614 840-0576
Brad Kilgore, *President*
Becky Kilgore, *Vice Pres*
EMP: 30
SQ FT: 3,000
SALES (est): 1MM **Privately Held**
SIC: 7349 Janitorial service, contract basis

(G-7736)
GENERAL THEMING CONTRS LLC
Also Called: GTC Artist With Machines
3750 Courtright Ct (43227-2253)
PHONE..............................614 252-6342
Fax: 614 252-6297
Richard D Rogovin, *Principal*
Joe Barton, *Controller*
April Andrck, *Accounts Mgr*
Erin Fisher, *Manager*
Phil Reynolds, *Executive*
EMP: 105
SQ FT: 60,000
SALES (est): 17.9MM **Privately Held**
WEB: www.theming.net
SIC: 7389 7336 2759 2396 Sign painting & lettering shop; commercial art & graphic design; commercial printing; automotive & apparel trimmings

(G-7737)
GENERATION HEALTH CORP
Also Called: Broadview Health Center
5151 N Hamilton Rd (43230-1313)
PHONE..............................614 337-1066
Fax: 614 337-1013
George R Powell, *President*
Renee M Hott, *Vice Pres*
Kelly C McGee, *Treasurer*
Ted R Williams, *Accountant*
Edward Powell Jr, *Admin Sec*
EMP: 130
SQ FT: 57,946
SALES (est): 7.9MM **Privately Held**
WEB: www.broadviewhealth.com
SIC: 8051 Skilled nursing care facilities

(G-7738)
GENESIS CORP
Also Called: Genesis 10
4449 Easton Way (43219-6093)
PHONE..............................614 934-1211
Kim Murgas, *Branch Mgr*
Sachin Khanijow, *Tech Recruiter*
EMP: 35
SALES (corp-wide): 179.7MM **Privately Held**
SIC: 7379 8742 Computer related consulting services; management consulting services
PA: Genesis Corp.
950 3rd Ave Ste 900
New York NY 10022
212 688-5522

(G-7739)
GENPAK LLC
845 Kaderly Dr (43228-1033)
PHONE..............................614 276-5156
Fax: 614 276-7670
Scott Wilson, *Manager*
Lori Kear, *Manager*
Clarence Barnard, *Maintence Staff*
EMP: 50
SALES (corp-wide): 12B **Privately Held**
WEB: www.genpak.com
SIC: 4783 Packing & crating
HQ: Genpak Llc
10601 Westlake Dr
Charlotte NC 28273
980 256-7729

(G-7740)
GENUINE PARTS COMPANY
Also Called: NAPA Distribution Center
2665 W Dblin Granville Rd (43235-2710)
PHONE..............................614 766-6865
Ron Koenigshofer, *General Mgr*
Grant Morris, *Vice Pres*
Tracey Kyler, *Human Res Mgr*
John Cavender, *Branch Mgr*
Spencer Abbott, *Manager*
EMP: 300
SALES (corp-wide): 16.3B **Publicly Held**
WEB: www.genpt.com
SIC: 5531 5013 Automotive parts; automotive supplies & parts
PA: Genuine Parts Company
2999 Wildwood Pkwy
Atlanta GA 30339
770 953-1700

(G-7741)
GEO BYERS SONS HOLDING INC
Also Called: Hertz
4185 E 5th Ave (43219-1813)
PHONE..............................614 239-1084
Fax: 614 236-4410
Wares Valerie, *Personnel Exec*
Blaine Byers, *Manager*
EMP: 30
SALES (corp-wide): 191.9MM **Privately Held**
SIC: 7514 7513 Rent-a-car service; truck rental, without drivers
PA: Geo. Byers Sons Holding, Inc.
427 S Hamilton Rd
Columbus OH 43213
614 228-5111

(G-7742)
GEORGE J IGEL & CO INC
2040 Alum Creek Dr (43207-1714)
PHONE..............................614 445-8421
Fax: 614 445-8205
Tim Cunningham, *Superintendent*
Rod Henwood, *Superintendent*
Harry Howard, *Superintendent*
Bob Kees, *Superintendent*
Brad Swallie, *Superintendent*
EMP: 892 EST: 1911
SQ FT: 50,000
SALES (est): 158.5MM **Privately Held**
WEB: www.igelco.com
SIC: 1794 1623 6552 Excavation & grading, building construction; sewer line construction; water main construction; subdividers & developers

(G-7743)
GEORGE KUHN ENTERPRISES INC
Also Called: A J Asphalt Maintenance & Pav
2200 Mckinley Ave (43204-3417)
PHONE..............................614 481-8838
Fax: 614 481-8839
Margaret Kuhn, *CEO*
James Kuhn, *President*
Kevin George, *Vice Pres*
EMP: 50
SQ FT: 8,000
SALES (est): 5MM **Privately Held**
SIC: 1771 1611 Blacktop (asphalt) work; highway & street maintenance

(G-7744)
GEORGE W MC CLOY
921 Chatham Ln Ste 302 (43221-2482)
PHONE..............................614 457-6233
George W Mc Cloy, *Owner*
EMP: 70
SQ FT: 53,000
SALES (est): 7.3MM **Privately Held**
SIC: 6411 6163 Insurance agents & brokers; loan brokers

(G-7745)
GEOTEX CONSTRUCTION SVCS INC
1025 Stimmel Rd (43223-2911)
P.O. Box 16331 (43216-6331)
PHONE..............................614 444-5690
Fax: 614 444-5691
Richard Clark, *President*
James W Jordan, *Principal*
Pete Kelley, *Vice Pres*
EMP: 50
SQ FT: 6,000
SALES (est): 8.4MM **Privately Held**
SIC: 1794 1623 Excavation work; excavation & grading, building construction; underground utilities contractor

(G-7746)
GERLACH JOHN J CENTER FOR SEN
Also Called: Ohio Health
180 E Broad St Fl 34 (43215-3707)
PHONE..............................614 566-5858
Fax: 614 566-1916
Robert Shuemak, *Vice Chairman*
Jennifer Day, *COO*
Terry Oliver, *Prdtn Mgr*
J Steele, *Manager*
Michelle Stokes, *Director*
EMP: 30
SALES (est): 751.6K **Privately Held**
SIC: 8322 Senior citizens' center or association

(G-7747)
GERMAIN FORD LLC
7250 Sawmill Rd (43235-1942)
PHONE..............................614 889-7777
Shane Kitts, *Finance Mgr*
Melissa McDowell, *Accountant*
Lee Green, *Sales Staff*
Scott Cropper, *Sales Associate*
Mitchell Gadd, *Manager*
EMP: 135
SQ FT: 41,000
SALES (est): 46.6MM **Privately Held**
SIC: 5511 7539 Automobiles, new & used; automotive repair shops

(G-7748)
GERMAIN ON SCARBOROUGH LLC
Also Called: Germain Toyota
5711 Scarborough Blvd (43232-4748)
PHONE..............................614 868-0300
Fax: 614 868-0701
Brian Kramer, *General Mgr*
Craig Ferguson, *Plant Mgr*
Tessa L Pekarcik, *Human Res Dir*
Blaine Burgess, *Sales Staff*
Angelina Fiera, *Sales Staff*
EMP: 150
SALES (corp-wide): 133MM **Privately Held**
WEB: www.germainbmw.com
SIC: 5511 7538 5531 7515 Automobiles, new & used; general automotive repair shops; automotive & home supply stores; passenger car leasing
PA: Germain On Scarborough, Llc
4250 Morse Xing
Columbus OH 43219
239 592-5550

(G-7749)
GETHSEMANE LUTHERAN CHURCH
35 E Stanton Ave (43214-1198)
PHONE..............................614 885-4319
Karen Asmus-Alsnauer, *Pastor*
Diane Gutgesell, *Admin Sec*
EMP: 25
SQ FT: 10,000
SALES (est): 795.6K **Privately Held**
SIC: 8661 8351 Lutheran Church; child day care services

(G-7750)
GILBANE BUILDING COMPANY
145 E Rich St Fl 4 (43215-5253)
PHONE..............................614 948-4000
Walt McKelvey, *Branch Mgr*
EMP: 30
SALES (corp-wide): 4.8B **Privately Held**
WEB: www.gilbaneco.com
SIC: 8741 1542 Construction management; nonresidential construction
HQ: Gilbane Building Company
7 Jackson Walkway Ste 2
Providence RI 02903
401 456-5800

(G-7751)
GIRL SCOUTS OF THE US AMER
Girl Scouts Ohio's Heartland
1700 Watermark Dr (43215-1097)
PHONE..............................614 487-8101
Tammy Wharton, *CEO*
Keri Campbell, *Development*
Mark Clatney, *Manager*
Elizabeth Frey, *Manager*
Pierre Laurin, *Director*
EMP: 102
SALES (corp-wide): 92.4MM **Privately Held**
SIC: 8641 Girl Scout organization
PA: Girl Scouts Of The United States Of America
420 5th Ave Fl 13
New York NY 10018
212 852-8000

(G-7752)
GIRL SCUTS OHIOS HEARTLAND INC (PA)
1700 Watermark Dr (43215-1097)
PHONE..............................614 340-8820
Fax: 614 487-8189
Tammy Wharton, *CEO*
Tony Doye, *COO*
EMP: 93
SALES: 7.8MM **Privately Held**
SIC: 8641 Girl Scout organization

(G-7753)
GLADDEN COMMUNITY HOUSE
183 Hawkes Ave (43223-1533)
P.O. Box 23030 (43223-0030)
PHONE..............................614 221-7801
Fax: 614 227-1648
Joy Chivers, *President*
Kevin Ballard, *Vice Pres*
Mardi Ciriaco, *Vice Pres*
EMP: 30
SQ FT: 40,000
SALES: 1.7MM **Privately Held**
SIC: 8322 Neighborhood center

(G-7754)
GLAVAN & ACCOCIATES ARCHITECTS
107 S High St Ste 200 (43215-3492)
PHONE..............................614 205-4060
Fax: 614 228-3337
Jeffrey L Glavan, *President*
Jay Edward Feher, *Vice Pres*
EMP: 30
SQ FT: 10,000
SALES: 2.7MM **Privately Held**
WEB: www.glavan.com
SIC: 8712 Architectural services

(G-7755)
GLEN WESLEY INC
Also Called: WESLEY RIDGE
5155 N High St (43214-1694)
PHONE..............................614 888-7492
Fax: 614 436-6012
Margeret Carmany, *CEO*
Africa Thomas, *Principal*
Tina Cassady, *Principal*
Lauren Croman, *Principal*
Patricia Banzhof, *Vice Pres*
EMP: 100 EST: 1967
SQ FT: 279,000
SALES: 19.8MM **Privately Held**
WEB: www.glenwesley.com
SIC: 8051 6513 8361 Skilled nursing care facilities; apartment building operators; retirement hotel operation; geriatric residential care; home for the aged; rehabilitation center, residential: health care incidental

(G-7756)
GODMAN GUILD (PA)
303 E 6th Ave (43201-2888)
PHONE..............................614 294-5476
Fax: 614 299-4080
Erin Fay, *General Mgr*
Greta Rzymek, *Senior VP*
Linda Silva, *Senior VP*
Janis Dean, *Opers Staff*
Jessica Burchard, *Manager*
EMP: 30
SALES: 4.2MM **Privately Held**
WEB: www.godmanguild.com
SIC: 8322 Social service center; community center

(G-7757)
GOLD STAR INSULATION L P
495 S High St (43215-5689)
PHONE..............................614 221-3241
Pam Henson, *General Mgr*
Pam Hanson, *Admin Sec*
EMP: 40

SALES: 5MM **Privately Held**
SIC: 1542 1521 Commercial & office building, new construction; new construction; single-family houses

(G-7758)
GOLDEN ENDINGS GOLDEN RET RESC
1043 Elmwood Ave (43212-3255)
PHONE.............................614 486-0773
Kay Hirsch, *President*
EMP: 50
SALES: 79.5K **Privately Held**
SIC: 6732 Trusts: educational, religious, etc.

(G-7759)
GOLDEN LIVING LLC
Also Called: Beverly
1425 Yorkland Rd (43232-1686)
PHONE.............................614 861-6666
Brenda Clagg, *Human Res Mgr*
Robert Brooks, *Exec Dir*
EMP: 110
SALES (corp-wide): 7.4MM **Privately Held**
SIC: 8059 8052 8051 Convalescent home; intermediate care facilities; skilled nursing care facilities
PA: Golden Living Llc
5220 Tennyson Pkwy # 400
Plano TX 75024
972 372-6300

(G-7760)
GOODWILL INDS CENTL OHIO INC (PA)
Also Called: Goodwill Columbus
1331 Edgehill Rd (43212-3123)
PHONE.............................614 294-5181
Fax: 614 294-6895
Marjory Pizzuti, *President*
Holly Gross, *President*
David Armstrong, *COO*
Anthony Hartley, *COO*
Hartley Anthony, *Vice Pres*
EMP: 275
SQ FT: 185,000
SALES: 45.1MM **Privately Held**
SIC: 8331 5399 Job training services; vocational rehabilitation agency; surplus & salvage goods

(G-7761)
GOODWILL INDS CENTL OHIO INC
Also Called: Working Community Services
890 N Hague Ave (43204-2174)
PHONE.............................614 274-5296
Timmy Hughes, *Manager*
Melinda Collins, *Director*
EMP: 50
SALES (corp-wide): 45.1MM **Privately Held**
SIC: 8331 Job training services
PA: Goodwill Industries Of Central Ohio, Inc.
1331 Edgehill Rd
Columbus OH 43212
614 294-5181

(G-7762)
GOSH ENTERPRISES INC (PA)
Also Called: Charley's Steakery
2500 Farmers Dr 140 (43235-5706)
PHONE.............................614 923-4700
Charley Shin, *President*
Bob Wright, *President*
Joe Hoock, *Managing Prtnr*
Cody Garner, *General Mgr*
Rick Long, *General Mgr*
EMP: 42
SQ FT: 4,000
SALES (est): 14.6MM **Privately Held**
SIC: 5812 6794 Grills (eating places); franchises, selling or licensing

(G-7763)
GOVERNAN LLC
Also Called: Glomark-Governan
4862 Pleasant Valley Dr (43220-5409)
PHONE.............................614 761-2400
Ana L Bermudez, *Vice Pres*
Gary Casale, *Vice Pres*
Rueben Melendez,

EMP: 42
SALES (est): 2.9MM **Privately Held**
SIC: 8748 Business consulting

(G-7764)
GOWDY PARTNERS LLC
1533 Lake Shore Dr Ste 50 (43204-3897)
PHONE.............................614 488-4424
Conrad Wisinger, *Principal*
EMP: 32
SALES (est): 2.7MM **Privately Held**
SIC: 1542 Commercial & office building, new construction

(G-7765)
GRAF AND SONS INC
Also Called: Overhead Door Company
2300 International St (43228-4621)
PHONE.............................614 481-2020
Fax: 614 486-6888
Dean Monnin, *President*
Jeff Giles, *Site Mgr*
Brian Ruhi, *Manager*
EMP: 30
SQ FT: 30,000
SALES (est): 3.9MM **Privately Held**
WEB: www.grafsons.com
SIC: 1751 5031 Garage door, installation or erection; doors, garage; doors

(G-7766)
GRANDVIEW FAMILY PRACTICE
1550 W 5th Ave Lowr (43212-2474)
PHONE.............................740 258-9267
Fax: 614 488-0226
Dr Charles May, *President*
Bonnie C May, *Office Mgr*
EMP: 25
SQ FT: 4,000
SALES (est): 2.6MM **Privately Held**
SIC: 8031 8011 Offices & clinics of osteopathic physicians; general & family practice, physician/surgeon

(G-7767)
GRANGE INDEMNITY INSURANCE CO
Also Called: Grange Mutual Casualty Company
671 S High St (43206-1066)
P.O. Box 1218 (43216-1218)
PHONE.............................614 445-2900
Fax: 614 445-2619
Tom Welch, *President*
Martin J Dinehart, *Vice Pres*
David T Roark, *Vice Pres*
Randall J Montelone, *Treasurer*
Brian Smith, *Regl Sales Mgr*
EMP: 52
SQ FT: 9,500
SALES (est): 15.3MM
SALES (corp-wide): 1.2B **Privately Held**
SIC: 6311 Life insurance
PA: Grange Mutual Casualty Company
671 S High St
Columbus OH 43206
614 445-2900

(G-7768)
GRANGE LIFE INSURANCE COMPANY
671 S High St (43206-1066)
PHONE.............................800 445-3030
Thomas Welch, *CEO*
Mark Phillips, *Sales Staff*
EMP: 39 **EST:** 2014
SALES (est): 21MM **Privately Held**
SIC: 6311 Life insurance

(G-7769)
GRANGE MUTUAL CASUALTY COMPANY (PA)
Also Called: Grange Insurance Companies
671 S High St (43206-1049)
P.O. Box 1218 (43216-1218)
PHONE.............................614 445-2900
Fax: 614 444-7777
Tom Welch, *CEO*
David Berentz, *President*
John R Delucia, *President*
Scott Drab, *President*
Brent Lombardi, *President*
EMP: 850
SQ FT: 212,000

SALES (est): 1.2B **Privately Held**
SIC: 6331 Automobile insurance; fire, marine & casualty insurance: mutual

(G-7770)
GRAYBAR ELECTRIC COMPANY INC
1200 Kinnear Rd (43212-1154)
PHONE.............................614 486-4391
Fax: 614 486-0117
Lance Gross, *Marketing Staff*
Rick Dannhausen, *Branch Mgr*
Harodl Yarborough, *Supervisor*
EMP: 44
SALES (corp-wide): 6.6B **Privately Held**
WEB: www.graybar.com
SIC: 5063 Electrical supplies
PA: Graybar Electric Company, Inc.
34 N Meramec Ave
Saint Louis MO 63105
314 573-9200

(G-7771)
GREAT NTHRN CNSULTING SVCS INC (PA)
200 E Campus View Blvd # 200 (43235-4678)
PHONE.............................614 890-9999
Fax: 614 899-1807
James C Deboard, *Principal*
Jeffrey Jones, *CFO*
Travis Gamble, *Sales Associate*
Vernon Brown, *Manager*
Anna Mary Abel, *Administration*
EMP: 50
SQ FT: 4,000
SALES (est): 8.3MM **Privately Held**
WEB: www.gnorth.com
SIC: 7379

(G-7772)
GREAT VALUE STORAGE
5301 Tamarack Cir E (43229-4501)
PHONE.............................614 848-8420
EMP: 33
SALES (corp-wide): 33.8MM **Privately Held**
SIC: 4226 4225 Household goods & furniture storage; general warehousing & storage
PA: Great Value Storage
401 Congress Ave Fl 33
Austin TX 78701
512 327-3300

(G-7773)
GREATER CLUMBUS CONVENTION CTR
400 N High St Fl 4 (43215-2078)
PHONE.............................614 827-2500
Craig Liston, *General Mgr*
Lauren Carter, *Sales Mgr*
Scott Keeton, *Manager*
Art McAndew, *Manager*
Kristin Moore, *Social Dir*
EMP: 189 **EST:** 1974
SALES (est): 20.2MM **Privately Held**
SIC: 6512 Commercial & industrial building operation

(G-7774)
GREATER COLUMBUS CHMBR COMMRCE
150 S Front St Ste 200 (43215-7107)
PHONE.............................614 221-1321
Fax: 614 221-1669
Ty Marsh, *President*
Sally A Jackson, *President*
Michael Hartley, *Vice Pres*
Michelle Bretscher, *Mktg Dir*
Troy Jackson, *Marketing Staff*
EMP: 40
SQ FT: 23,000
SALES: 3.2MM **Privately Held**
WEB: www.columbus.org
SIC: 8611 Chamber of Commerce

(G-7775)
GREATER COLUMBUS REGIONAL
285 E State St Ste 170 (43215-4322)
PHONE.............................614 228-9114
Fax: 614 228-9120
Tracy Khalchik, *Manager*
Kris Stelzer, *Director*

DH Ventures,
EMP: 70
SALES (est): 1.6MM **Privately Held**
SIC: 8092 Kidney dialysis centers

(G-7776)
GREATR COLUMBUS CONVENTN & VIS (PA)
Also Called: GCCVB
277 W Nationwide Blvd (43215-2853)
PHONE.............................614 221-6623
Paul Astleford, *President*
Paul Nakamoto, *Exec VP*
Jodi Beekman, *Vice Pres*
Arica CTA, *Natl Sales Mgr*
Brian Ross, *VP Sales*
EMP: 38
SQ FT: 17,000
SALES: 15.1MM **Privately Held**
WEB: www.experiencecolumbus.com
SIC: 8699 Personal interest organization

(G-7777)
GREEN LAWN CEMETERY ASSN
1000 Greenlawn Ave (43223-2618)
PHONE.............................614 444-1123
Fax: 614 444-9815
Linda Burkey, *General Mgr*
Joesph Glandon, *Manager*
EMP: 25
SALES: 535.5K **Privately Held**
WEB: www.greenlawncolumbus.org
SIC: 6553 Cemetery association

(G-7778)
GREENSCAPES LANDSCAPE COMPANY
Also Called: Greenscapes Landscape Arch
4220 Winchester Pike (43232-5612)
PHONE.............................614 837-1869
Fax: 614 837-2393
William A Gerhardt, *President*
Tom Kuhn, *Sales Executive*
EMP: 70
SQ FT: 3,000
SALES (est): 9.2MM **Privately Held**
SIC: 0782 0781 4959 Landscape contractors; landscape architects; snowplowing

(G-7779)
GREYHOUND LINES INC
111 E Town St Ste 100 (43215-5153)
PHONE.............................614 221-0577
Fax: 614 221-7468
Dole Butterball, *Branch Mgr*
EMP: 40
SALES (corp-wide): 7B **Privately Held**
SIC: 4142 4131 Bus charter service, except local; intercity & rural bus transportation
HQ: Greyhound Lines, Inc.
350 N Saint Paul St # 300
Dallas TX 75201
214 849-8000

(G-7780)
GTE INTERNET
6816 Lauffer Rd (43231-1623)
PHONE.............................614 508-6000
Scott Klabunde, *Owner*
EMP: 70
SALES (est): 1.2MM **Privately Held**
SIC: 8011 Offices & clinics of medical doctors

(G-7781)
GUARDIAN BUSINESS SERVICES
3948 Townsfair Way # 220 (43219-6095)
PHONE.............................614 416-6090
Rick Wayman, *CEO*
Dale Bring, *President*
EMP: 25
SALES (est): 1MM **Privately Held**
SIC: 6411 Insurance agents, brokers & service

(G-7782)
GUARDIAN CARE SERVICES
665 E Dublin Granville Rd # 330 (43229-3334)
PHONE.............................614 436-8500
Sean Smar, *Owner*
Tamika Smar, *Co-Owner*
EMP: 30

GEOGRAPHIC SECTION   Columbus - Franklin County (G-7806)

SALES: 400K **Privately Held**
SIC: 7349 Building cleaning service

(G-7783)
GUARDIAN ELDER CARE COLUMBUS
2425 Kimberly Pkwy E (43232-4271)
PHONE..................614 868-9306
Brian Rendos, *CFO*
Brian Bosak, *Accounting Mgr*
EMP: 73 EST: 2016
SALES (est): 336.1K **Privately Held**
SIC: 8059 Nursing & personal care

(G-7784)
GUARDIAN ENTERPRISE GROUP INC
3948 Townsfair Way # 220 (43219-6095)
P.O. Box 1497, Westerville (43086-1497)
PHONE..................614 416-6080
Richard Schilg, *President*
EMP: 42
SALES (est): 5.7MM
SALES (corp-wide): 2.4MM **Privately Held**
WEB: www.guardianstudios.com
SIC: 7311 Advertising consultant
PA: Guardian Vision International, Inc.
   3948 Townsfair Way # 220
   Columbus OH 43219
   614 416-6080

(G-7785)
GUARDIAN WATER & POWER INC (PA)
1160 Goodale Blvd (43212-3728)
PHONE..................614 291-3141
Harry Apostolos, *President*
Patricia Apostolos, *Treasurer*
Sean Dicks, *Natl Sales Mgr*
Marc Norland, *Accounts Exec*
Branham Stovall, *Accounts Exec*
EMP: 60
SQ FT: 8,000
SALES (est): 7.1MM **Privately Held**
WEB: www.guardianwp.com
SIC: 7389 7322 Meter readers, remote; adjustment & collection services

(G-7786)
GUDENKAUF CORPORATION (PA)
2679 Mckinley Ave (43204-3898)
PHONE..................614 488-1776
Fax: 614 488-2723
Jeffrey Gudenkauf, *President*
Sandy Potterton, *President*
Bill Adkins, *Regional Mgr*
Vince Paxton, *Assistant VP*
Susan Gudenkauf, *Vice Pres*
EMP: 130 EST: 1977
SQ FT: 10,000
SALES (est): 45.3MM **Privately Held**
WEB: www.gudenkauf.com
SIC: 1623 Telephone & communication line construction; underground utilities contractor; gas main construction

(G-7787)
GUTKNECHT CONSTRUCTION COMPANY
2280 Citygate Dr (43219-3588)
PHONE..................614 532-5410
Jeff Feinman, *President*
Ben Lindsay, *Vice Pres*
Jamie Weisent, *Vice Pres*
Tom Deddow, *Project Mgr*
Anthony Howes, *Project Mgr*
EMP: 44
SQ FT: 7,500
SALES (est): 21.1MM **Privately Held**
WEB: www.gutknecht.com
SIC: 1542 Commercial & office building, new construction; commercial & office buildings, renovation & repair

(G-7788)
H & M PATCH COMPANY
Also Called: Gooseberry Patch
2500 Farmers Dr 110 (43235-5706)
PHONE..................614 339-8950
Fax: 740 363-7225
Shelby V Hutchins, *CEO*
Vickie Hutchins, *Principal*
Joann Martin, *Principal*

Cindy Watson, *Accounts Mgr*
Jen Licon-Conner, *Manager*
▲ EMP: 70
SQ FT: 52,000
SALES (est): 9.2MM **Privately Held**
WEB: www.gooseberrypatch.com
SIC: 5961 5192 5947 Gift items, mail order; books; gift shop

(G-7789)
H & M PLUMBING CO
4015 Alum Creek Dr (43207-5161)
PHONE..................614 491-4880
Fax: 614 491-5209
Doug Houchard, *President*
William Severns, *Vice Pres*
EMP: 40
SQ FT: 6,000
SALES (est): 4.5MM **Privately Held**
SIC: 1711 Plumbing contractors

(G-7790)
HABITAT FOR HUMANITY MID OHIO (PA)
3140 Westerville Rd (43224-3749)
PHONE..................614 422-4828
E J Thomas, *CEO*
Brian Canavan, *Vice Pres*
Mike Cosgrove, *CFO*
Phil Washburn, *Program Mgr*
Kate Ames, *Manager*
EMP: 50
SQ FT: 45,000
SALES: 7.3MM **Privately Held**
SIC: 1522 Residential construction

(G-7791)
HADLER REALTY COMPANY
Also Called: Hadler Company
2000 Henderson Rd Ste 500 (43220-2496)
PHONE..................614 457-6650
Fax: 614 457-0095
William N Hadler, *Owner*
Mindy Leroy, *Admin Asst*
EMP: 42 EST: 1945
SQ FT: 5,500
SALES (est): 6.2MM **Privately Held**
SIC: 6531 Real estate agent, commercial; real estate managers

(G-7792)
HADLER-ZIMMERMAN INC
2000 Henderson Rd Ste 500 (43220-2497)
PHONE..................614 457-6650
William H Hadler, *CEO*
George Hadler, *President*
David McKean, *Advt Staff*
EMP: 25
SQ FT: 7,500
SALES (est): 1.6MM **Privately Held**
SIC: 6512 Commercial & industrial building operation

(G-7793)
HAGGLUNDS DRIVES INC (DH)
2275 International St (43228-4632)
PHONE..................614 527-7400
Fax: 614 527-7401
Ted Bojanowski, *President*
Dave Bradford, *Managing Dir*
Arvind Singhal, *Managing Dir*
Takaaki Takanose, *Managing Dir*
Randy Hipp, *Business Mgr*
▲ EMP: 31
SQ FT: 20,000
SALES (est): 17.2MM
SALES (corp-wide): 261.7MM **Privately Held**
WEB: www.hagglunds.com
SIC: 5084 Hydraulic systems equipment & supplies
HQ: Bosch Rexroth Corporation
   14001 S Lakes Dr
   Charlotte NC 28273
   847 645-3600

(G-7794)
HAIKU
800 N High St (43215-1430)
P.O. Box 532, New Albany (43054-0532)
PHONE..................614 294-8168
Fax: 614 294-3868
Paul Liu, *Owner*
Jason Zishka, *General Mgr*
EMP: 30

SALES (est): 1.4MM **Privately Held**
SIC: 8741 5813 5812 Restaurant management; drinking places; eating places

(G-7795)
HALLMARK HOME MORTGAGE LLC
7965 N High St Ste 100 (43235-8402)
PHONE..................614 568-1960
Jack Ammons, *Branch Mgr*
EMP: 30 **Privately Held**
SIC: 6162 Mortgage bankers
PA: Hallmark Home Mortgage, Llc
   7421 Coldwater Rd
   Fort Wayne IN 46825

(G-7796)
HAMILTON HOMECARE INC
Also Called: Hamilton Healthcare
309 S 4th St (43215-5428)
PHONE..................614 221-0022
Fax: 614 221-0085
Lisa Hamilton, *President*
EMP: 35
SALES (est): 1.6MM **Privately Held**
SIC: 8082 Home health care services

(G-7797)
HAMILTON-PARKER COMPANY (PA)
1865 Leonard Ave (43219-4500)
PHONE..................614 358-7800
Fax: 614 358-2315
Adam Lewin, *President*
Kevin Bussert, *Opers Staff*
Michelle Brokaw, *Purchasing*
Swieterman Doug, *Purchasing*
Justin Perry, *CFO*
▲ EMP: 95
SQ FT: 50,000
SALES (est): 25.6MM **Privately Held**
WEB: www.hamiltonparker.com
SIC: 5211 5075 5032 5031 Lumber & other building materials; brick; tile, ceramic; warm air heating & air conditioning; brick, stone & related material; lumber, plywood & millwork

(G-7798)
HANDSON CENTRAL OHIO INC
195 N Grant Ave (43215-2855)
PHONE..................614 221-2255
Marilee Chinnici-Zuercher, *President*
Marilee Zuercher, *President*
Joseph J Patrick Jr, *Vice Pres*
Bridget Wolf, *CFO*
Carl Konopka, *Info Tech Mgr*
EMP: 50
SQ FT: 8,400
SALES: 2.8MM **Privately Held**
WEB: www.firstlink.org
SIC: 8322 8331 Social service center; job training & vocational rehabilitation services

(G-7799)
HANLIN-RAINALDI CONSTRUCTION
6610 Singletree Dr (43229-1121)
PHONE..................614 436-4204
Grant L Douglass, *Ch of Bd*
Marty Romine, *Superintendent*
Ed Rainaldi, *Vice Pres*
Michael O Hanlin, *Treasurer*
Michael Rainaldi, *Treasurer*
EMP: 34
SQ FT: 8,000
SALES (est): 9.3MM **Privately Held**
WEB: www.hanlinrainaldi.com
SIC: 1542 Commercial & office building, new construction

(G-7800)
HANSON CONCRETE PRODUCTS OHIO
Also Called: Hanson Pipe & Products
1500 Haul Rd (43207-1888)
PHONE..................614 443-4846
Terry Feather, *Manager*
EMP: 35 **Privately Held**
SIC: 1771 3441 3272 Concrete work; fabricated structural metal; concrete products
PA: Hanson Concrete Products Ohio, Inc
   6055 150th St W
   Saint Paul MN 55124

(G-7801)
HARDLINES DESIGN COMPANY (PA)
4608 Indianola Ave Ste D (43214-2287)
PHONE..................614 784-8733
Fax: 614 784-9336
Charissa W Durst, *President*
Mej Stokes, *Office Mgr*
EMP: 25
SQ FT: 7,000
SALES (est): 3.2MM **Privately Held**
WEB: www.hardlinesdesign.com
SIC: 8712 Architectural engineering

(G-7802)
HAROLD K PHLLIPS RSTRATION INC
972 Harmon Ave (43223-2414)
PHONE..................614 443-5699
Fax: 614 443-9040
Spike Phillips, *President*
Geneva Phillips, *Admin Sec*
EMP: 30
SQ FT: 7,000
SALES (est): 3.5MM **Privately Held**
WEB: www.phillipsrestoration.com
SIC: 1741 Tuckpointing or restoration

(G-7803)
HAWA INCORPORATED (PA)
980 Old Henderson Rd C (43220-3723)
PHONE..................614 451-1711
Douglas S Coffey, *President*
Jane Newkirk, *Business Mgr*
Chris A Pore, *Exec VP*
Neb Heminger, *Vice Pres*
James R Lockad, *Vice Pres*
EMP: 30 EST: 1954
SQ FT: 10,000
SALES: 7.5MM **Privately Held**
SIC: 8711 Consulting engineer; mechanical engineering; industrial engineers; electrical or electronic engineering

(G-7804)
HAYDOCY AUTOMOTIVE INC
Also Called: Haydocy Automotors
3895 W Broad St (43228-1444)
P.O. Box 28125 (43228-0125)
PHONE..................614 279-8880
Fax: 614 255-5890
Chris Haydocy, *President*
Bob Park, *General Mgr*
Rita Fitch, *Corp Secy*
Ed Gabel, *Sales Mgr*
Dan Lynch, *Sales Mgr*
EMP: 60
SALES (est): 7.8MM **Privately Held**
WEB: www.haydocy.com
SIC: 7538 5511 7532 5531 General automotive repair shops; automobiles, new & used; pickups, new & used; vans, new & used; top & body repair & paint shops; automotive & home supply stores; automobiles & other motor vehicles

(G-7805)
HAYWARD DISTRIBUTING CO (PA)
4061 Perimeter Dr (43228-1048)
PHONE..................614 272-5953
Fax: 614 272-5959
John M Budde, *Ch of Bd*
Ronald L Monroe, *President*
Mark Roberts, *Opers Mgr*
Mark Adameck, *Buyer*
Eric Vanorder, *Purchasing*
▲ EMP: 35 EST: 1947
SQ FT: 36,000
SALES: 35.2MM **Privately Held**
WEB: www.haydist.com
SIC: 5083 5023 Lawn machinery & equipment; garden machinery & equipment; grills, barbecue

(G-7806)
HBI PAYMENTS LTD
Also Called: Purepay
3 Easton Oval Ste 210 (43219-6011)
PHONE..................614 944-5788
John Cullen, *Partner*
Brad West, *Partner*
EMP: 75

Columbus - Franklin County (G-7807)

SALES (est): 5.1MM **Privately Held**
SIC: 6211 Investment firm, general brokerage

(G-7807)
HDR ENGINEERING INC
2800 Corp Exchange Dr # 100 (43231-7661)
PHONE..................614 839-5770
Matt Selhorst, *Manager*
EMP: 41
SALES (corp-wide): 2.3B **Privately Held**
SIC: 8742 8711 Management consulting services; engineering services
HQ: Hdr Engineering, Inc.
8404 Indian Hills Dr
Omaha NE 68114
402 399-1000

(G-7808)
HEAD INC
4477 E 5th Ave (43219-1817)
PHONE..................614 338-8501
Fax: 614 338-8514
Middleton E Head Jr, *Ch of Bd*
James M Head, *President*
Jim Head, *President*
Paul Ondera, *Vice Pres*
Matt Reardon, *Project Mgr*
EMP: 50
SQ FT: 6,000
SALES (est): 24.7MM **Privately Held**
WEB: www.headinc.com
SIC: 1541 1542 Industrial buildings, new construction; institutional building construction

(G-7809)
HEALTH CARE DATAWORKS INC
4215 Worth Ave Ste 320 (43219-1546)
PHONE..................614 255-5400
Charles Birminghan, *CEO*
Charles Birminghan, *CEO*
Jason Buskirk, *COO*
Jessica V Gerken, *Vice Pres*
Michael Ostrander, *Vice Pres*
EMP: 62
SQ FT: 13,000
SALES (est): 7.8MM
SALES (corp-wide): 63.4MM **Privately Held**
SIC: 7371 Computer software development
PA: Health Catalyst, Inc.
3165 E Millrock Dr # 400
Salt Lake City UT 84121
801 708-6800

(G-7810)
HEALTH CARE DEPO OF OHIO LLC
1570 E Dblin Grndville Rd (43229)
PHONE..................614 776-3333
Fatai Adesiji,
EMP: 65
SALES (est): 1.3MM **Privately Held**
SIC: 8082 Home health care services

(G-7811)
HEALTH CARE RTREMENT CORP AMER
Also Called: Heartland - Victorian Village
920 Thurber Dr W (43215-1247)
PHONE..................614 464-2273
Fax: 614 464-3037
Gretchen Mangone, *Branch Mgr*
Janice Berridge, *Manager*
EMP: 100
SQ FT: 31,974
SALES (corp-wide): 3.6B **Publicly Held**
WEB: www.hrc-manorcare.com
SIC: 8051 Convalescent home with continuous nursing care
HQ: Health Care And Retirement Corporation Of America
333 N Summit St Ste 103
Toledo OH 43604
419 252-5500

(G-7812)
HEALTHCARE AND SOCIAL
Also Called: Ohio Health Care Employees
1395 Dublin Rd (43215-1086)
PHONE..................614 461-1199

Tom Woodruff, *Principal*
Delores Brantley, *Vice Pres*
Larry Daniels, *Vice Pres*
Renee Hamrick, *Vice Pres*
Cheryl Hill, *Vice Pres*
EMP: 33
SALES (est): 1.1MM **Privately Held**
SIC: 8631 Labor union

(G-7813)
HEALTHY LIFE HM HEALTHCARE LLC
5454 Cleveland Ave # 201 (43231-4021)
PHONE..................614 865-3368
Peter Arhin, *Mng Member*
EMP: 30
SALES (est): 127K **Privately Held**
SIC: 8361 Training school for delinquents

(G-7814)
HEART OHIO FAMILY HEALTH CTRS
882 S Hamilton Rd (43213-3003)
PHONE..................614 235-5555
Jenn Schehl, *General Mgr*
Maggie Bornhorst, *Project Mgr*
Kylie Noble, *Project Mgr*
Christopher Penrod, *CFO*
Alison Purdon, *Sr Project Mgr*
EMP: 31
SQ FT: 2,925
SALES (est): 4.7MM **Privately Held**
SIC: 8011 Clinic, operated by physicians

(G-7815)
HEART SPECIALISTS OF OHIO
3650 Olentangy River Rd # 300 (43214-3464)
P.O. Box 59, Plain City (43064-0059)
PHONE..................614 538-0527
Fax: 614 538-0530
Timothy Obarski, *President*
Dr Michael R Jennings, *President*
Dr Lawrence Murcko, *Corp Secy*
Dr Debbra Debates, *Vice Pres*
Dr Tim Obarski, *Vice Pres*
EMP: 25
SALES (est): 3.5MM **Privately Held**
WEB: www.heartspecialistsofohio.com
SIC: 8011 Cardiologist & cardio-vascular specialist

(G-7816)
HEARTBEAT INTERNATIONAL INC
5000 Arlington Centre Blv (43220-3083)
PHONE..................614 885-7577
Fax: 614 885-8746
Margaret H Hartshorn, *President*
Jor-El Godsey, *President*
Lisa Dudley, *Opers Staff*
Gary Thome, *Treasurer*
Tony Gruber, *Controller*
EMP: 45
SALES (est): 3MM **Privately Held**
WEB: www.heartbeatinternational.org
SIC: 8661 8322 Religious organizations; adoption services

(G-7817)
HEARTLAND EXPRESS INC
1800 Lone Eagle St (43228-3646)
PHONE..................614 870-8628
Thomas Kasenberg, *Manager*
EMP: 101
SALES (corp-wide): 607.3MM **Publicly Held**
SIC: 4212 Local trucking, without storage
PA: Heartland Express, Inc.
901 N Kansas Ave
North Liberty IA 52317
319 626-3600

(G-7818)
HEARTLAND HOME CARE LLC
Also Called: Heartland Home Health Care
6500 Busch Blvd Ste 210 (43229-1738)
PHONE..................614 433-0423
Fax: 614 433-0640
Susan Abbott, *Branch Mgr*
EMP: 50
SALES (corp-wide): 3.6B **Publicly Held**
SIC: 8082 Home health care services

HQ: Heartland Home Care, Llc
333 N Summit St
Toledo OH 43604

(G-7819)
HEARTLAND HOSPICE SERVICES LLC
Also Called: Heartland HM Hlth Care Hospice
6500 Busch Blvd Ste 210 (43229-1738)
PHONE..................614 433-0423
Fax: 614 433-0641
Chrissy Goelz, *Branch Mgr*
EMP: 98
SALES (corp-wide): 3.6B **Publicly Held**
SIC: 8082 Home health care services
HQ: Heartland Hospice Services, Llc
333 N Summit St
Toledo OH 43604

(G-7820)
HEARTLAND PETROLEUM LLC (PA)
4001 E 5th Ave (43219-1812)
PHONE..................614 441-4001
William C Snedegar, *CEO*
Donna Weeda, *General Mgr*
Rex Snedegar, *VP Sales*
Cheri Puckett, *Office Mgr*
Gary Snider, *Manager*
EMP: 47
SQ FT: 9,400
SALES (est): 15.7MM **Privately Held**
WEB: www.heartland-petroleum.com
SIC: 5172 Petroleum brokers

(G-7821)
HEINZERLING FOUNDATION (PA)
Also Called: Heinzerling Mem Foundation
1800 Heinzerling Dr (43223-3642)
PHONE..................614 272-8888
Fax: 614 272-6863
N Christan Raseld, *Manager*
Dennis Sites, *Manager*
Robert Heninzerli, *Exec Dir*
Brian Asbury, *Director*
EMP: 250
SQ FT: 67,000
SALES: 25.1MM **Privately Held**
SIC: 8059 8052 Home for the mentally retarded, exc. skilled or intermediate; intermediate care facilities

(G-7822)
HEINZERLING FOUNDATION
Also Called: Heinzerling Developmental Ctr
1755 Heinzerling Dr (43223-3672)
PHONE..................614 272-2000
Fax: 614 272-2050
Ken Hibbert, *Facilities Dir*
Bob Heinzerling, *Director*
Patrick Doyle, *Director*
Jane Martin, *Director*
Linda Taylor, *Food Svc Dir*
EMP: 550
SQ FT: 40,300
SALES (corp-wide): 25.1MM **Privately Held**
SIC: 8059 8361 Home for the mentally retarded, exc. skilled or intermediate; residential care
PA: Heinzerling Foundation
1800 Heinzerling Dr
Columbus OH 43223
614 272-8888

(G-7823)
HEISER STAFFING SERVICES LLC
330 W Spring St Ste 205 (43215-7300)
PHONE..................614 800-4188
Karla Heiser, *Mng Member*
EMP: 33 EST: 2014
SALES: 354K **Privately Held**
SIC: 7363 Temporary help service

(G-7824)
HELMSMAN MANAGEMENT SVCS LLC
700 Taylor Rd Ste 220 (43230-3318)
P.O. Box 307230, Gahanna (43230-7230)
PHONE..................614 478-8282
Fax: 614 478-8283
Michael Topin, *Branch Mgr*
EMP: 85

SALES (corp-wide): 38.3B **Privately Held**
SIC: 8741 Management services
HQ: Helmsman Management Services Llc
175 Berkeley St
Boston MA 02116
857 224-1970

(G-7825)
HENDERSON ROAD REST SYSTEMS (PA)
Also Called: Hyde Park Grille
1615 Old Henderson Rd (43220-3617)
PHONE..................614 442-3310
Fax: 614 442-3318
Joseph Soccone, *President*
Richard Hauck, *Vice Pres*
EMP: 40
SQ FT: 6,516
SALES (est): 1MM **Privately Held**
SIC: 5812 4119 7542 American restaurant; limousine rental, with driver; car-washes

(G-7826)
HER INC
Also Called: Her Real Living
583 1/2 S 3rd St (43215-5755)
PHONE..................614 240-7400
Fax: 614 221-9017
Ronnie Woodrow, *Broker*
Louise Potter, *Manager*
EMP: 25
SQ FT: 993
SALES (corp-wide): 14.3MM **Privately Held**
WEB: www.eassent.com
SIC: 6531 Real estate agent, residential
PA: Her, Inc
4261 Morse Rd
Columbus OH 43230
614 221-7400

(G-7827)
HER INC (PA)
4261 Morse Rd (43230-1522)
PHONE..................614 221-7400
Fax: 614 442-2907
George W Smith, *CEO*
Harley E Rouda Sr, *Ch of Bd*
Harley E Rouda Jr, *President*
Geri Van Lent, *Senior VP*
Robert E Zellar, *Senior VP*
EMP: 27
SQ FT: 9,800
SALES (est): 14.3MM **Privately Held**
WEB: www.eassent.com
SIC: 6531 Real estate agent, residential

(G-7828)
HER INC
Also Called: H E R Realtors
2815 E Main St (43209-2520)
PHONE..................614 239-7400
Fax: 614 239-7233
Kathy Landry, *Manager*
EMP: 40
SALES (corp-wide): 14.3MM **Privately Held**
WEB: www.eassent.com
SIC: 6531 Real estate brokers & agents
PA: Her, Inc
4261 Morse Rd
Columbus OH 43230
614 221-7400

(G-7829)
HER INC
Also Called: H E R Realtors
4680 W Broad St (43228-1611)
PHONE..................614 878-4734
Fax: 614 878-8795
Art Travis, *Manager*
EMP: 25
SALES (corp-wide): 14.3MM **Privately Held**
WEB: www.eassent.com
SIC: 6531 Real estate agents & managers
PA: Her, Inc
4261 Morse Rd
Columbus OH 43230
614 221-7400

(G-7830)
HERITAGE DAY HEALTH CENTERS (HQ)
Also Called: NATIONAL CHURCH RESIDENCES CENTER FOR SENIOR HEALTH
2335 N Bank Dr (43220-5423)
PHONE.................................614 451-2151
Fax: 614 338-2350
Tanya Kim Hahn, *President*
Rebecca Baker, *Vice Pres*
David Driver, *Vice Pres*
Pamela Monroe, *Vice Pres*
Amy Rosenthal, *Senior Mgr*
EMP: 32
SQ FT: 4,200
SALES (corp-wide): 44.4MM **Privately Held**
SIC: 8082 Home health care services
PA: National Church Residences
2335 N Bank Dr
Columbus OH 43220
614 451-2151

(G-7831)
HERITAGE MARBLE OF OHIO INC
Also Called: Heritage Marbles
7086 Huntley Rd (43229-1022)
PHONE.................................614 436-1464
Fax: 614 436-9874
Gene Daniels, *President*
Jim Franklin, *Controller*
EMP: 25
SQ FT: 22,000
SALES (est): 1.9MM **Privately Held**
WEB: www.heritagemarble.com
SIC: 3281 1411 Marble, building: cut & shaped; dimension stone

(G-7832)
HIDDEN LAKE CONDOMINIUMS
Also Called: Real Property Management
1363 Lake Shore Dr (43204-3640)
PHONE.................................614 488-1131
Dwight Penn, *CEO*
Brent Vanoss, *Administration*
EMP: 85
SALES (est): 2.1MM **Privately Held**
SIC: 6531 Condominium manager

(G-7833)
HIGHBANKS CARE CENTER LLC
111 Lazelle Rd (43235-1419)
PHONE.................................614 888-2021
Aimee Palmer, *Office Mgr*
Brian Colleran, *Mng Member*
Richard A Schloss,
EMP: 62
SALES: 4.2MM **Privately Held**
WEB: www.highbanks-care.net
SIC: 8051 Convalescent home with continuous nursing care

(G-7834)
HIGHLAND RELIEF ORGANIZATION
2761 Regaldo Dr (43219-8131)
PHONE.................................614 843-5152
Farah Elmi, *President*
EMP: 40
SALES (est): 126.4K **Privately Held**
SIC: 8641 Civic social & fraternal associations

(G-7835)
HILL BARTH & KING LLC
Also Called: Hbk CPA & Consultants
226 N 5th St Ste 500 (43215-2784)
PHONE.................................614 228-4000
Paul Ritchui, *Manager*
Amy Moore, *Admin Asst*
EMP: 71
SALES (corp-wide): 49.7MM **Privately Held**
SIC: 8721 Certified public accountant
PA: Hill, Barth & King Llc
6603 Summit Dr
Canfield OH 44406
330 758-6213

(G-7836)
HILL MANOR 1 INC
3244 Southfield Dr E (43207-3341)
Drawer 2409 St Rd, Delaware (43015)
PHONE.................................740 972-3227
Fannie Mills, *President*
EMP: 36
SQ FT: 2,994
SALES (est): 463.1K **Privately Held**
SIC: 8361 8093 Residential care; rehabilitation center, outpatient treatment

(G-7837)
HILTON GARDEN INN
3232 Olentangy River Rd (43202-1519)
PHONE.................................614 263-7200
John Businger, *Manager*
EMP: 80
SALES (est): 2.2MM **Privately Held**
SIC: 7011 Hotels

(G-7838)
HILTON GRDN INN COLUMBUS ARPRT
4265 Sawyer Rd (43219-3812)
PHONE.................................614 231-2869
Fax: 614 235-1590
Paul Malcolm, *General Mgr*
Jenkins Bernadette, *Manager*
EMP: 80
SALES (est): 2.5MM **Privately Held**
SIC: 7011 Hotels

(G-7839)
HIT PORTFOLIO I MISC TRS LLC
Also Called: Hyatt Pl Columbus Worthington
7490 Vantage Dr (43235-1416)
PHONE.................................614 846-4355
Liz Buxton, *General Mgr*
Sarah Hughes, *Sales Dir*
Bo Hagood, *Branch Mgr*
EMP: 25
SALES (corp-wide): 4.6B **Publicly Held**
SIC: 7011 Hotels
HQ: Hit Portfolio I Misc Trs, Llc
150 N Riverside Plz
Chicago IL 60606
312 750-1234

(G-7840)
HIT PORTFOLIO I MISC TRS LLC
Also Called: Hyatt On Capitol Square
75 E State St (43215-4203)
PHONE.................................614 228-1234
Fax: 614 365-4508
Bruce Flyer, *General Mgr*
Jeff Donahoe, *Sales Dir*
Bryan King, *Sales Dir*
Karen Theis, *Branch Mgr*
Abbie Dalton, *Manager*
EMP: 200
SALES (corp-wide): 4.6B **Publicly Held**
WEB: www.hyatt.com
SIC: 6512 7011 5812 5813 Nonresidential building operators; hotels; eating places; drinking places
HQ: Hit Portfolio I Misc Trs, Llc
150 N Riverside Plz
Chicago IL 60606
312 750-1234

(G-7841)
HIT SWN TRS LLC
Also Called: Courtyard Columbus Downtown
35 W Spring St (43215-2215)
PHONE.................................614 228-3200
Jennifer Moss, *Sales Dir*
Anne Turpin, *Manager*
EMP: 30
SALES (corp-wide): 621MM **Privately Held**
SIC: 7011 Hotels
HQ: Hit Swn Trs, Llc
450 Park Ave Ste 14
New York NY 10022
212 415-6500

(G-7842)
HITE PARTS EXCHANGE INC
2235 Mckinley Ave (43204-3400)
PHONE.................................614 272-5115
Fax: 614 272-9808
Thomas A Blake, *President*
Chris Allred, *Sales Staff*
Dona Blake, *Admin Sec*
EMP: 30
SQ FT: 14,000
SALES (est): 4.4MM **Privately Held**
WEB: www.hiteparts.com
SIC: 5013 3714 3625 3594 Automotive supplies & parts; pumps, oil & gas; clutches; motor vehicle engines & parts; clutches, motor vehicle; relays & industrial controls; fluid power pumps & motors; carburetors, pistons, rings, valves; power transmission equipment

(G-7843)
HOCKADEN & ASSOCIATES INC
883 N Cassady Ave (43219-2203)
PHONE.................................614 252-0993
Fax: 614 252-0444
Gurgun Muharrem, *President*
Mark Schroeder, *Vice Pres*
Kurt Ziessler, *Project Engr*
EMP: 40
SALES (est): 3.4MM **Privately Held**
WEB: www.hockaden.com
SIC: 8711 Civil engineering

(G-7844)
HOGAN SERVICES INC
1500 Obetz Rd (43207-4477)
PHONE.................................614 491-8402
Max Baker, *Branch Mgr*
EMP: 30
SALES (est): 732.5K **Privately Held**
SALES (corp-wide): 13.3MM **Privately Held**
SIC: 4789 Pipeline terminal facilities, independently operated
PA: Hogan Services, Inc
2150 Schuetz Rd Ste 210
Saint Louis MO 63146
314 421-6000

(G-7845)
HOLIDAY INN EXPRESS
3045 Olentangy River Rd (43202-1516)
PHONE.................................614 447-1212
Amber Franklin, *General Mgr*
Jagdeep Singh,
EMP: 25
SALES (est): 1.1MM **Privately Held**
SIC: 7011 Hotels & motels

(G-7846)
HOLIDAY LANES INC
4589 E Broad St (43213-3852)
PHONE.................................614 861-1600
Fax: 614 861-2478
Rick Kennedy, *President*
Joseph E Ducey, *Principal*
Helen P Price, *Principal*
William E Shirk, *Principal*
EMP: 42 EST: 1956
SQ FT: 50,000
SALES (est): 1.6MM **Privately Held**
SIC: 7933 5813 5812 Ten pin center; cocktail lounge; snack bar

(G-7847)
HOLLAND ROOFING INC
Also Called: Holland Roofing of Columbus
3494 E 7th Ave (43219-1735)
PHONE.................................614 430-3724
Fax: 614 430-3725
Clayton Marshall, *Principal*
Peter Romans, *Sales Mgr*
Mark W Tingler, *Manager*
EMP: 40
SALES (corp-wide): 46.6MM **Privately Held**
WEB: www.pondliners.com
SIC: 1761 Roofing contractor
PA: Holland Roofing, Inc.
7450 Industrial Rd
Florence KY 41042
859 525-0887

(G-7848)
HOME DEPOT USA INC
Also Called: Home Depot, The
6333 Cleveland Ave (43231-1617)
PHONE.................................614 523-0600
Fax: 614 901-0416
Jason Gage, *Manager*
Jack McEwoen, *Manager*
Mark Smith, *Manager*
Jason Werny, *Manager*
Melissa Ruh, *Executive*
EMP: 150
SALES (corp-wide): 100.9B **Publicly Held**
WEB: www.homerentalsdepot.com
SIC: 5211 7359 Home centers; tool rental
HQ: Home Depot U.S.A., Inc.
2455 Paces Ferry Rd Se
Atlanta GA 30339

(G-7849)
HOME DEPOT USA INC
Also Called: Home Depot, The
100 S Grener Ave (43228-1922)
PHONE.................................614 878-9150
Fax: 614 853-4416
Dan Hernan, *Manager*
EMP: 150
SALES (corp-wide): 100.9B **Publicly Held**
WEB: www.homerentalsdepot.com
SIC: 5211 7359 Home centers; tool rental
HQ: Home Depot U.S.A., Inc.
2455 Paces Ferry Rd Se
Atlanta GA 30339

(G-7850)
HOME DEPOT USA INC
Also Called: Home Depot, The
5200 N Hamilton Rd (43230-1316)
PHONE.................................614 939-5036
Fax: 614 855-6436
Chuck Fry, *Manager*
EMP: 120
SALES (corp-wide): 100.9B **Publicly Held**
WEB: www.homerentalsdepot.com
SIC: 5211 7359 Home centers; tool rental
HQ: Home Depot U.S.A., Inc.
2455 Paces Ferry Rd Se
Atlanta GA 30339

(G-7851)
HOME MOVING & STORAGE CO INC
1570 Integrity Dr E (43209-2704)
PHONE.................................614 445-6377
Fax: 614 445-6972
Jay K Fuson, *President*
Jack L Herring, *President*
Tami Marlow, *General Mgr*
EMP: 25
SQ FT: 20,500
SALES (est): 3.5MM **Privately Held**
WEB: www.homerelocation.com
SIC: 4213 Trucking, except local

(G-7852)
HOMELESS FAMILIES FOUNDATION
33 N Grubb St (43215-2748)
PHONE.................................614 461-9427
Fax: 614 461-9234
Jim Hopkins, *Chairman*
Beth Fetzer-Rice, *Manager*
Adrian Corbet, *Exec Dir*
Louise Seipel, *Director*
EMP: 25
SALES: 2.2MM **Privately Held**
SIC: 8322 Social service center

(G-7853)
HOMETOWN IMPROVEMENT CO
1430 Halfhill Way (43207-4494)
PHONE.................................614 846-1060
Fax: 614 501-9405
Richard Hatfield, *Owner*
EMP: 25
SALES: 35MM **Privately Held**
SIC: 1521 General remodeling, single-family houses

(G-7854)
HOMETOWN URGENT CARE
4400 N High St Ste 101 (43214-2635)
PHONE.................................614 263-4400
Fax: 614 263-4401
Wendy Melick, *Branch Mgr*
EMP: 150
SALES (corp-wide): 73.2MM **Privately Held**
SIC: 8011 Medical centers
PA: Hometown Urgent Care
2400 Corp Exchange Dr # 102
Columbus OH 43231
614 505-7633

Columbus - Franklin County (G-7855)

(G-7855)
HOMETOWN URGENT CARE
2880 Stelzer Rd (43219-3133)
PHONE..................614 472-2880
George Thomas, *Branch Mgr*
EMP: 126
SALES (corp-wide): 73.2MM **Privately Held**
SIC: 8011 Primary care medical clinic
PA: Hometown Urgent Care
2400 Corp Exchange Dr # 102
Columbus OH 43231
614 505-7633

(G-7856)
HOMETOWN URGENT CARE
4300 Clime Rd Ste 110 (43228-6491)
PHONE..................614 272-1100
Janet Pettiford, *Office Mgr*
Bill Stricker, *Branch Mgr*
EMP: 125
SALES (corp-wide): 73.2MM **Privately Held**
SIC: 8011 Medical centers
PA: Hometown Urgent Care
2400 Corp Exchange Dr # 102
Columbus OH 43231
614 505-7633

(G-7857)
HOMEWOOD CORPORATION (PA)
2700 E Dublin Granville R (43231-4089)
PHONE..................614 898-7200
Fax: 614 451-1197
John H Bain, *CEO*
George Anthony Skestos, *President*
Robert Story, *Info Tech Dir*
Bob Story, *Technology*
EMP: 120
SQ FT: 20,000
SALES (est): 49.3MM **Privately Held**
WEB: www.homewood-homes.com
SIC: 1522 Apartment building construction

(G-7858)
HONEYWELL INTERNATIONAL INC
2080 Arlingate Ln (43228-4112)
PHONE..................614 717-2270
Fax: 614 717-2269
Ronald Vogt,
EMP: 50
SALES (corp-wide): 40.5B **Publicly Held**
WEB: www.honeywell.com
SIC: 5075 5065 7382 Warm air heating & air conditioning; security control equipment & systems; security systems services
PA: Honeywell International Inc.
115 Tabor Rd
Morris Plains NJ 07950
973 455-2000

(G-7859)
HORIZON HM HLTH CARE AGCY LLC
3035 W Broad St Ste 102 (43204-2653)
PHONE..................614 279-2933
Ibrahim Osman, *Mng Member*
EMP: 40
SALES (est): 256.1K **Privately Held**
SIC: 8082 Home health care services

(G-7860)
HOTEL 50 S FRONT OPCO LP
50 S Front St (43215-4129)
PHONE..................614 228-4600
Jan Hando, *Controller*
Raymond Schulte, *Manager*
EMP: 85
SALES (est): 250.9K **Privately Held**
SIC: 7011 Resort hotel

(G-7861)
HUCKLEBERRY HOUSE
1421 Hamlet St (43201-2599)
PHONE..................614 294-5553
Fax: 614 294-6109
Tom Meers, *Partner*
Rebecca Westerfelt, *Director*
EMP: 60 EST: 1970
SQ FT: 9,000
SALES: 3MM **Privately Held**
WEB: www.huckhouse.org
SIC: 8322 Crisis center

(G-7862)
HUGHES & KNOLLMAN CONSTRUCTION
4601 E 5th Ave (43219-1819)
P.O. Box 360415 (43236-0415)
PHONE..................614 237-6167
Terry Hughes, *President*
EMP: 55
SALES (est): 5MM **Privately Held**
SIC: 1542 1742 Commercial & office building, new construction; drywall

(G-7863)
HUNTINGTON AUTO TRUST 2015-1
Huntington Ctr 41 S High (43287-0001)
PHONE..................302 636-5401
Fax: 614 480-5467
EMP: 188
SALES (est): 125.2K
SALES (corp-wide): 4.7B **Publicly Held**
SIC: 6733 Trusts
PA: Huntington Bancshares Incorporated
41 S High St
Columbus OH 43215
614 480-8300

(G-7864)
HUNTINGTON AUTO TRUST 2016-1
41 S High St (43215-6170)
PHONE..................302 636-5401
EMP: 125
SALES (est): 76.6K
SALES (corp-wide): 4.7B **Publicly Held**
SIC: 6733 Trusts
PA: Huntington Bancshares Incorporated
41 S High St
Columbus OH 43215
614 480-8300

(G-7865)
HUNTINGTON BANCSHARES INC (PA)
41 S High St (43215-6170)
PHONE..................614 480-8300
Stephen D Steinour, *Ch of Bd*
Julie C Tutkovics, *Exec VP*
Howell D McCullough III, *CFO*
Richard Remiker, *Director*
Jana J Litsey, *Executive*
EMP: 116
SALES: 4.7B **Publicly Held**
WEB: www.huntington.com
SIC: 6021 National commercial banks

(G-7866)
HUNTINGTON INSURANCE INC
7 Easton Oval (43219-6010)
PHONE..................614 480-3800
Fax: 614 331-5862
Candi Moore, *Principal*
Sharon Lint, *Payroll Mgr*
Dawn Cutcher, *Manager*
Dee Gargac, *Manager*
Chris McCoy, *Software Engr*
EMP: 37
SALES (corp-wide): 4.7B **Publicly Held**
SIC: 6411 6211 Insurance agents; security brokers & dealers
HQ: Huntington Insurance, Inc.
519 Madison Ave
Toledo OH 43604
419 720-7900

(G-7867)
HUNTINGTON INSURANCE INC
37 W Broad St Ste 1100 (43215-4159)
PHONE..................614 899-8500
Steven W Weiler, *Senior VP*
Gail Boucher, *Accounts Mgr*
Tom Weissling, *Manager*
Donna Wares, *Manager*
EMP: 100
SALES (corp-wide): 4.7B **Publicly Held**
WEB: www.skyinsure.com
SIC: 6411 Insurance agents, brokers & service

HQ: Huntington Insurance, Inc.
519 Madison Ave
Toledo OH 43604
419 720-7900

(G-7868)
HUNTINGTON NATIONAL BANK
4078 Powell Ave (43213-2321)
PHONE..................614 480-0067
Jenne Roboerts, *Principal*
EMP: 100
SALES (corp-wide): 4.7B **Publicly Held**
SIC: 6099 Check clearing services
HQ: The Huntington National Bank
17 S High St Fl 1
Columbus OH 43215
614 480-4293

(G-7869)
HUNTINGTON NATIONAL BANK (PA)
17 S High St Fl 1 (43215-3413)
PHONE..................614 480-4293
EMP: 27
SALES (est): 1.5MM **Privately Held**
SIC: 6029 Commercial Banks, Not Chartered

(G-7870)
HUNTINGTON NATIONAL BANK (HQ)
17 S High St Fl 1 (43215-3413)
PHONE..................614 480-4293
Fax: 614 480-4548
Stephen D Steinour, *President*
Renee Csuhran, *President*
William C Shivers, *President*
Paul Heller, *COO*
Richard A Cheap, *Exec VP*
EMP: 300
SQ FT: 190,000
SALES: 3.6B
SALES (corp-wide): 4.7B **Publicly Held**
WEB: www.huntingtonnationalbank.com
SIC: 6029 Commercial banks
PA: Huntington Bancshares Incorporated
41 S High St
Columbus OH 43215
614 480-8300

(G-7871)
HUNTINGTON NATIONAL BANK
2361 Morse Rd (43229-5856)
PHONE..................614 480-8300
Beth Schenz, *Counsel*
Susan Brueckman, *Senior VP*
Bayard King, *Senior VP*
Jeffrey Lafferty, *Senior VP*
Brian Marshall, *Senior VP*
EMP: 54
SALES (corp-wide): 4.7B **Publicly Held**
WEB: www.huntingtonnationalbank.com
SIC: 6021 National commercial banks
HQ: The Huntington National Bank
17 S High St Fl 1
Columbus OH 43215
614 480-4293

(G-7872)
HUNTINGTON TECHNOLOGY FINANCE
37 W Broad St (43215-4132)
PHONE..................614 480-5169
Aaron Johann, *Vice Pres*
EMP: 251
SALES (est): 226.6K
SALES (corp-wide): 4.7B **Publicly Held**
SIC: 6021 National commercial banks
PA: Huntington Bancshares Incorporated
41 S High St
Columbus OH 43215
614 480-8300

(G-7873)
HY-TEK MATERIAL HANDLING INC (PA)
2222 Rickenbacker Pkwy W (43217-5002)
PHONE..................614 497-2500
Fax: 614 497-0311
Samuel Grooms, *President*
Chris Connor, *General Mgr*
Mark Bruner, *Vice Pres*
Donnie Johnson, *Vice Pres*
Tony Murray, *Vice Pres*
▲ EMP: 76

SQ FT: 55,000
SALES (est): 81.4MM **Privately Held**
WEB: www.hy-tek.net
SIC: 5084 5013 7538 7513 Materials handling machinery; conveyor systems; lift trucks & parts; truck parts & accessories; truck engine repair, except industrial; truck rental, without drivers; machinery installation

(G-7874)
HYATT CORPORATION
Also Called: Hyatt Hotel
350 N High St (43215-2006)
PHONE..................614 463-1234
Fax: 614 280-3034
Stephen Stewart, *General Mgr*
Charles Lutrick, *Controller*
Pierre Le, *Sales Mgr*
Jennifer Pringle, *Sales Mgr*
Kevin McCarty, *Supervisor*
EMP: 300
SALES (corp-wide): 4.6B **Publicly Held**
WEB: www.hyatt.com
SIC: 7011 5813 5812 Hotel, franchised; bar (drinking places); diner
HQ: Hit Portfolio I Misc Trs, Llc
150 N Riverside Plz
Chicago IL 60606
312 750-1234

(G-7875)
HYATT REGENCY COLUMBUS
350 N High St (43215-2006)
PHONE..................614 463-1234
Fax: 614 469-9664
Hyatt Columbus Corp, *General Ptnr*
Mike Oconner, *Purch Dir*
Charles Lutrick, *Controller*
Donald Frey, *Human Res Dir*
Jeff Rutter, *Manager*
EMP: 325
SALES (est): 13.4MM **Privately Held**
SIC: 7011 Hotels

(G-7876)
HYPERLOGISTICS GROUP INC (PA)
9301 Intermodal Ct N (43217-6101)
PHONE..................614 497-0800
Seatta K Layland, *President*
James Brooks, *Warehouse Mgr*
Marina Apple, *Accountant*
Sandi Conti, *Accountant*
Dreama Lolan, *Manager*
EMP: 45 EST: 1973
SALES (est): 6MM **Privately Held**
SIC: 4225 General warehousing

(G-7877)
I H SCHLEZINGER INC
Also Called: Schlezinger Metals
1041 Joyce Ave (43219-2448)
P.O. Box 83624 (43203-0624)
PHONE..................614 252-1188
Fax: 614 252-1180
Kenneth Cohen, *President*
Jack Joseph, *Vice Pres*
John Miller, *Vice Pres*
Donald Zulanch, *Vice Pres*
Robert Joseph, *Treasurer*
EMP: 42
SQ FT: 9,000
SALES (est): 13.6MM **Privately Held**
WEB: www.ihschlezinger.com
SIC: 3341 5093 Secondary nonferrous metals; ferrous metal scrap & waste

(G-7878)
I VRABLE INC
Also Called: Heritage Manor Skilled Nursing
3248 Henderson Rd (43220-7337)
PHONE..................614 545-5500
Allan Vrable, *President*
James Merrill, *CFO*
William Linden, *Auditing Mgr*
EMP: 133
SALES: 7MM **Privately Held**
SIC: 8051 Skilled nursing care facilities
PA: Vrable Healthcare, Inc.
3248 Henderson Rd
Columbus OH 43220

GEOGRAPHIC SECTION
Columbus - Franklin County (G-7903)

(G-7879)
I-FORCE LLC
Also Called: Iforce
1110 Morse Rd Ste 200 (43229-6325)
PHONE..................614 431-5100
Ryan Cote, *President*
David Stearns, *Controller*
Jill Weitzel, *Branch Mgr*
Kornelia Hryniewiecka, *Manager*
Adam Kendall, *Manager*
EMP: 150
SALES (est): 165.8K Privately Held
SIC: 7361 Employment agencies

(G-7880)
IACOVETTA BUILDERS INC
2525 Fisher Rd (43204-3533)
PHONE..................614 272-6464
Eugene Iacovetta, *President*
Perry Dematteo, *QC Mgr*
R A Pritchard, *Treasurer*
EMP: 50
SQ FT: 1,200
SALES (est): 3.3MM Privately Held
SIC: 1522 6513 Multi-family dwelling construction; apartment building operators

(G-7881)
ICE MILLER LLP
250 West St Ste 700 (43215-7509)
PHONE..................614 462-2700
Joanne Pastwa, *President*
Tonya Toops, *President*
Angela Parkhill, *Managing Prtnr*
James Burns, *Counsel*
Jodi Johnson, *Counsel*
EMP: 100
SALES (corp-wide): 98.4MM Privately Held
SIC: 8111 General practice law office
PA: Ice Miller Llp
1 American Sq Ste 2900
Indianapolis IN 46282
317 236-2100

(G-7882)
IHEARTCOMMUNICATIONS INC
92.3 Wcol FM
2323 W 5th Ave Ste 200 (43204-4988)
PHONE..................614 486-6101
Fax: 614 487-3553
Tom Thon, *General Mgr*
Brian Dytko, *General Mgr*
Lisa Dollinger, *Vice Pres*
Bruce Kamp, *Director*
David Newman, *Associate*
EMP: 100 Publicly Held
SIC: 4832 Radio broadcasting stations
HQ: Iheartcommunications, Inc.
20880 Stone Oak Pkwy
San Antonio TX 78258
210 822-2828

(G-7883)
IHG MANAGEMENT (MARYLAND) LLC
Also Called: Crowne Plaza Columbus Downtown
33 E Nationwide Blvd (43215-2512)
PHONE..................614 461-4100
Juan Laginia, *Branch Mgr*
EMP: 145
SALES (corp-wide): 1.7B Privately Held
SIC: 7011 Hotels
HQ: Maryland Llc Ihg Management
8844 Columbia 100 Pkwy
Columbia MD 21045

(G-7804)
ILLINOIS & MIDLAND RR INC (HQ)
4349 Easton Way Ste 110 (43219-6114)
PHONE..................217 670-1242
Fax: 217 788-8660
Spencer D White, *President*
Jenice Davis, *Accountant*
Teri Waganer, *Human Res Mgr*
EMP: 67
SALES (est): 8.7MM
SALES (corp-wide): 2.2B Publicly Held
SIC: 4011 Railroads, line-haul operating
PA: Genesee & Wyoming Inc.
20 West Ave
Darien CT 06820
203 202-8900

(G-7885)
IMPACT COMMUNITY ACTION
700 Bryden Rd Fl 2 (43215-4839)
PHONE..................614 252-2799
Robert E Chilton, *CEO*
Anita Maldonado, *Vice Pres*
McLain Davis, *Project Mgr*
Charline Jordan, *QC Mgr*
Sue Petersen, *CFO*
EMP: 75
SALES: 6.9MM Privately Held
SIC: 8322 Community center

(G-7886)
IMPROVE IT HOME REMODELING INC (PA)
40 W 1st Ave (43201-3402)
PHONE..................614 297-5121
Seth Cammeyer, *President*
Brian Leader, *Vice Pres*
Barry Dix, *Director*
Phil Wiley, *Director*
EMP: 39
SQ FT: 14,000
SALES: 12MM Privately Held
SIC: 1521 General remodeling, single-family houses

(G-7887)
IN HIS PRSENCE MINISTRIES INTL
Also Called: Inprem Hlstic Cmnty Rsurce Ctr
5757 Karl Rd (43229-3603)
PHONE..................614 516-1812
Alex-Eric Clottey, *Pastor*
Alex-Eric Abrokwa-Clottey, *Pastor*
Angela Gibbs, *Admin Asst*
Pranklina Sowah, *Assistant*
EMP: 25
SALES (est): 2.5MM Privately Held
SIC: 8661 8611 Non-denominational church; community affairs & services

(G-7888)
INC/BALLEW A HEAD JOINT VENTR
4477 E 5th Ave (43219-1817)
PHONE..................614 338-5801
James Head, *Partner*
Paul Ondera, *Vice Pres*
EMP: 55
SALES (est): 1.7MM Privately Held
SIC: 6531 Real estate leasing & rentals

(G-7889)
INDIANA MICHIGAN POWER COMPANY (HQ)
Also Called: AEP
1 Riverside Plz (43215-2355)
PHONE..................614 716-1000
Nicholas K Akins, *Ch of Bd*
Paul Chodak III, *President*
Archie Pugh, *Managing Dir*
Ed Ehler, *Vice Pres*
Thomas A Kratt, *Vice Pres*
EMP: 123 EST: 1907
SALES: 2.1B
SALES (corp-wide): 15.4B Publicly Held
SIC: 4911 Electric services; distribution, electric power; generation, electric power; transmission, electric power
PA: American Electric Power Company, Inc.
1 Riverside Plz Fl 1 # 1
Columbus OH 43215
614 716-1000

(G-7890)
INDUS AIRPORT HOTEL II LLC
Also Called: Hampton Inn
4280 International Gtwy (43219-1747)
PHONE..................614 235-0717
Janet Boissy, *Principal*
Matthew Shier, *Principal*
EMP: 55
SALES (est): 195.3K Privately Held
SIC: 7011 Hotels & motels

(G-7891)
INDUS AIRPORT HOTELS I LLC
Also Called: Hilton Grdn Inn Columbus Arprt
4265 Sawyer Rd (43219-3812)
PHONE..................614 231-2869
Janet Boissy, *Principal*
Matthew Shier, *Principal*
EMP: 55 EST: 2016
SALES (est): 430.9K Privately Held
SIC: 7011 Inns

(G-7892)
INDUS TRADE & TECHNOLOGY LLC
Also Called: Stone Mart
2249 Westbrooke Dr Bldg H (43228-9643)
PHONE..................614 527-0257
Yash Lunkad, *General Mgr*
Surendra Kankriya, *Mng Member*
Surendra Kentkerya, *Mng Member*
▲ **EMP:** 26
SQ FT: 5,000
SALES: 17.5MM Privately Held
SIC: 5032 Granite building stone

(G-7893)
INDUSTRIAL AIR CENTERS INC
Also Called: Columbus Air Center
2840 Fisher Rd Ste E (43204-3559)
PHONE..................614 274-9171
George Burch, *President*
Dave Parke, *Manager*
EMP: 50 Privately Held
WEB: www.iacserv.com
SIC: 5084 Compressors, except air conditioning
PA: Industrial Air Centers Inc.
731 E Market St
Jeffersonville IN 47130

(G-7894)
INDUSTRY INSIGHTS INC
6235 Emerald Pkwy (43235)
P.O. Box 4330, Dublin (43016-0708)
PHONE..................614 389-2100
Fax: 614 802-2309
Thomas J Noon, *Ch of Bd*
Stephen Kretzer, *Vice Pres*
Shawn Six, *Vice Pres*
Michael Woods, *Manager*
Ben Fair, *Web Dvlpr*
EMP: 25
SQ FT: 3,500
SALES (est): 2.2MM Privately Held
WEB: www.industryinsights.com
SIC: 8742 Business consultant

(G-7895)
INFOQUEST INFORMATION SERVICES
2000 Henderson Rd Ste 300 (43220-2453)
PHONE..................614 761-3003
John Hughes, *President*
EMP: 25
SALES (est): 5.6MM Privately Held
SIC: 6411 Insurance claim processing, except medical

(G-7896)
INFOR (US) INC
2800 Corp Exchange Dr # 350 (43231-7661)
PHONE..................678 319-8000
David Coffey, *Vice Pres*
EMP: 350
SALES (corp-wide): 2.8B Privately Held
SIC: 7373 7371 Systems software development services; computer system selling services; custom computer programming services
HQ: Infor (Us), Inc.
13560 Morris Rd Ste 4100
Alpharetta GA 30004
678 319-8000

(G-7891)
INFORMATION CONTROL CORP
Also Called: Clutch Interactive
2500 Corporate Exch Dr (43231-7665)
PHONE..................614 523-3070
Fax: 614 523-1314
Steven Glaser, *CEO*
Blane Walter, *Ch of Bd*
John Kratz, *President*
Janet Arnette, *President*
Terry Slabaugh, *Principal*
EMP: 500 EST: 1978
SQ FT: 35,000
SALES (est): 73.3MM Privately Held
WEB: www.iccohio.com
SIC: 7379

(G-7898)
INGLESIDE INVESTMENTS INC
Also Called: Ww CD Radio
1036 S Front St (43206-3402)
PHONE..................614 221-1025
Fax: 614 224-4334
Roger Vaughan, *President*
EMP: 35
SALES (est): 1.6MM Privately Held
WEB: www.cd101.com
SIC: 4832 8742 Radio broadcasting stations; new business start-up consultant

(G-7899)
INLAND PRODUCTS INC (PA)
599 Frank Rd (43223-3813)
PHONE..................614 443-3425
Gary H Baas, *President*
Tom Pegan, *Controller*
David Bass, *Finance Dir*
EMP: 26
SQ FT: 40,000
SALES (est): 5.4MM Privately Held
SIC: 2077 5159 Grease rendering, inedible; tallow rendering, inedible; bone meal, except as animal feed; meat meal & tankage, except as animal feed; hides

(G-7900)
INNOVATIVE ARCHITECTURAL
Also Called: Iap Government Services Group
2740 Airport Dr Ste 300 (43219-2295)
PHONE..................614 416-0614
Thomas G Banks, *CEO*
Jennifer Schneider, *Senior VP*
EMP: 25
SQ FT: 5,000
SALES: 19.9MM Privately Held
WEB: www.iaparchitectural.com
SIC: 8741 Construction management

(G-7901)
INNOVEL SOLUTIONS INC
Also Called: Sears
5330 Crosswind Dr (43228-3600)
PHONE..................614 878-2092
Tom Dardis, *Manager*
EMP: 99
SALES (corp-wide): 16.7B Publicly Held
WEB: www.slslogistics.com+%22sears+logistics+servi
SIC: 4731 Agents, shipping
HQ: Innovel Solutions, Inc.
3333 Beverly Rd
Hoffman Estates IL 60179
847 286-2500

(G-7902)
INNOVEL SOLUTIONS INC
Also Called: Sears
4100 Lockbourne Industria (43207-4377)
PHONE..................614 492-5304
Fax: 614 492-5305
John Mannella, *Manager*
Bill Enderle, *IT/INT Sup*
EMP: 600
SALES (corp-wide): 16.7B Publicly Held
WEB: www.slslogistics.com+%22sears+logistics+servi
SIC: 4731 Agents, shipping
HQ: Innovel Solutions, Inc.
3333 Beverly Rd
Hoffman Estates IL 60179
847 286-2500

(G-7903)
INNOVIS DATA SOLUTIONS INC
250 E Broad St (43215-3708)
PHONE..................614 222-4343
Jonathan H Price, *President*
Dirk Cantrell, *Vice Pres*
Keith Kotrowicsz, *Treasurer*
Bob Ezely, *Sales Mgr*
Terry Bangasser, *Accounts Exec*
EMP: 35 EST: 1999
SALES: 4.4MM
SALES (corp-wide): 279.4MM Privately Held
WEB: www.innovis.com
SIC: 7323 Credit bureau & agency
PA: Cbc Companies, Inc.
250 E Broad St Fl 21
Columbus OH 43215
614 222-4343

Columbus - Franklin County (G-7904)

(G-7904)
INQUIRY SYSTEMS INC
1195 Goodale Blvd (43212-3730)
PHONE..................................614 464-3800
Carey Hindall, *President*
Kathy Hindall, *Vice Pres*
EMP: 30
SQ FT: 14,000
SALES: 529.2K **Privately Held**
WEB: www.inquirysys.com
SIC: 8742 4783 7311 7389 Marketing consulting services; packing goods for shipping; advertising agencies; subscription fulfillment services: magazine, newspaper, etc.

(G-7905)
INSIGHT COMMUNICATIONS OF CO
Also Called: Insight Ohio
3770 E Livingston Ave (43227-2280)
PHONE..................................614 236-1200
Stephen Crane, *Vice Pres*
Bob Lau, *Vice Pres*
Jim Mundy, *Manager*
Dan Mannino,
Pat Elztroth,
EMP: 200 EST: 1998
SALES (est): 5.6MM **Privately Held**
SIC: 4841 1731 Cable television services; electrical work

(G-7906)
INSIGHT DIRECT USA INC
375 N Front St (43215-2232)
PHONE..................................614 456-0423
Fax: 614 228-7505
Tom Montes, *Branch Mgr*
EMP: 60 **Publicly Held**
SIC: 5045 Computer software
HQ: Insight Direct Usa, Inc.
   6820 S Harl Ave
   Tempe AZ 85283
   480 333-3000

(G-7907)
INSTALLED BUILDING PDTS II LLC
Also Called: Insulation Northwest
495 S High St Ste 50 (43215-5689)
PHONE..................................626 812-6070
Pamela Henson, *Partner*
Todd Fry, *Chief Acct*
EMP: 97
SALES (est): 8.4MM
SALES (corp-wide): 1.1B **Publicly Held**
SIC: 1742 Insulation, buildings
PA: Installed Building Products, Inc.
   495 S High St Ste 50
   Columbus OH 43215
   614 221-3399

(G-7908)
INSTALLED BUILDING PDTS INC (PA)
495 S High St Ste 50 (43215-5689)
PHONE..................................614 221-3399
Jeffrey W Edwards, *Ch of Bd*
Jay P Elliott, *COO*
Jason R Niswonger, *Senior VP*
Michael T Miller, *CFO*
Todd R Fry, *Treasurer*
EMP: 151
SALES: 1.1B **Publicly Held**
SIC: 1522 5033 5211 Residential construction; insulation materials; insulation material, building

(G-7909)
INSTALLED BUILDING PDTS LLC
Also Called: IBP Columbus
1320 Mckinley Ave Ste A (43222-1155)
PHONE..................................614 308-9900
Duane Clark, *Prdtn Mgr*
Kelly Clifford, *Marketing Mgr*
Mark Lomax, *Branch Mgr*
EMP: 27
SALES (corp-wide): 1.1B **Publicly Held**
SIC: 1742 Insulation, buildings
HQ: Installed Building Products Llc
   495 S High St Ste 50
   Columbus OH 43215
   614 221-3399

(G-7910)
INSTITUTE FOR HUMAN SERVICES (PA)
1706 E Broad St (43203-2039)
PHONE..................................614 251-6000
Fax: 614 251-6005
Keith Hughes, *Psychologist*
Patti Beekman, *Manager*
Sandra Parker, *Manager*
Lois Tyler, *Manager*
Mason Landrum, *Technology*
EMP: 28
SALES: 7.4MM **Privately Held**
SIC: 8742 Human resource consulting services

(G-7911)
INSURANCE INTERMEDIARIES INC
280 N High St Ste 300 (43215-2535)
PHONE..................................614 846-1111
Fax: 614 846-2111
David S Schmidt, *President*
Duane Knauer, *President*
Larry Bobb, *Vice Pres*
EMP: 65
SQ FT: 14,000
SALES (est): 12.5MM
SALES (corp-wide): 26.6B **Privately Held**
WEB: www.nirassn.com
SIC: 6411 Insurance brokers
PA: Nationwide Mutual Insurance Company
   1 Nationwide Plz
   Columbus OH 43215
   614 249-7111

(G-7912)
INTER HEALT CARE OF CAMBR ZANE (PA)
Also Called: Interim Services
960 Checkrein Ave Ste A (43229-1107)
PHONE..................................614 436-9404
Michael W Hartshorn, *President*
Harold A Salo, *President*
Tom Kirker, *Principal*
Linda Martin, *Principal*
Thomas Di Marco, *Corp Secy*
EMP: 36
SQ FT: 7,500
SALES: 11.7MM **Privately Held**
SIC: 8082 Home health care services

(G-7913)
INTERBAKE FOODS LLC
1740 Joyce Ave (43219-1026)
PHONE..................................614 294-4931
Raymond Baxter, *President*
Harry Seniea, *Vice Pres*
Steve Randall, *Purch Agent*
Art Barr, *Manager*
Andrew Callahan, *Manager*
EMP: 128
SALES (corp-wide): 35.5B **Privately Held**
WEB: www.interbake.com
SIC: 5149 Bakery products
HQ: Interbake Foods Llc
   3951 Westerre Pkwy # 200
   Henrico VA 23233
   804 755-7107

(G-7914)
INTERBAKE FOODS LLC
Norse Dairy Systems
1700 E 17th Ave (43219-1005)
P.O. Box 1869 (43216-1869)
PHONE..................................614 294-4931
Scott Fullbright, *Vice Pres*
Andrew Callahan, *MIS Staff*
EMP: 600
SALES (corp-wide): 35.5B **Privately Held**
WEB: www.interbake.com
SIC: 5149 Bakery products
HQ: Interbake Foods Llc
   3951 Westerre Pkwy # 200
   Henrico VA 23233
   804 755-7107

(G-7915)
INTERIOR SUPPLY CINCINNATI LLC
481 E 11th Ave (43211-2601)
PHONE..................................614 424-6611
Robert Pickard, *President*
Brian McAndrew, *Sales Mgr*
Kelly Garland, *Office Mgr*
Jessica Strandwitz, *Manager*
Timothy Flynn,
EMP: 30
SALES (est): 3.6MM **Privately Held**
SIC: 7389 Interior design services

(G-7916)
INTERNAL MDCINE CONS OF CLMBUS
104 N Murray Hill Rd (43228-1524)
PHONE..................................614 878-6413
Fax: 614 878-1159
Robert A Palma, *President*
Peter Pema, *Vice Pres*
Jeffrey Kaufman, *Treasurer*
Thomas E Wanko, *Admin Sec*
EMP: 30
SQ FT: 5,000
SALES (est): 2.1MM **Privately Held**
SIC: 8031 8011 Offices & clinics of osteopathic physicians; internal medicine, physician/surgeon

(G-7917)
INTERNATIONAL MASONRY INC
135 Spruce St (43215-1623)
P.O. Box 1598 (43216-1598)
PHONE..................................614 469-8338
Fax: 614 469-0139
John C Casey, *Chairman*
Mitchell Casey, *Corp Secy*
Brian Casey, *Vice Pres*
Douglas Casey, *Vice Pres*
Eric J Casey, *Vice Pres*
EMP: 90
SQ FT: 7,500
SALES (est): 7.7MM **Privately Held**
WEB: www.imi-smc.com
SIC: 1741 Bricklaying

(G-7918)
INTERNATIONAL UN ELEV CONSTRS
Also Called: International Union Elvtor Cns
23 W 2nd Ave Ste C (43201-3406)
PHONE..................................614 291-5859
John Neil Rouse III, *Manager*
EMP: 122
SALES (corp-wide): 11.9MM **Privately Held**
SIC: 8641 Civic associations
PA: International Union Of Elevator Constructors
   7154 Columbia Gateway Dr
   Columbia MD 21046
   410 953-6150

(G-7919)
INTERSTATE TRUCKWAY INC
5440 Renner Rd (43228-8941)
PHONE..................................614 771-1220
Willy Walraven, *Branch Mgr*
EMP: 32 **Privately Held**
WEB: www.itdsdedicated.com
SIC: 3799 5012 Trailers & trailer equipment; automobiles & other motor vehicles
PA: Interstate Truckway Inc
   1755 Dreman Ave
   Cincinnati OH 45223

(G-7920)
INTERTEK TESTING SVCS NA INC
Also Called: Etl
1717 Arlingate Ln (43228-4116)
PHONE..................................614 279-8090
Jennifer Chandler, *Vice Pres*
Vo That, *Project Engr*
Darren Varga, *Project Engr*
Kenneth Klinner, *Accounts Mgr*
Sam Peck, *Accounts Mgr*
EMP: 40
SALES (corp-wide): 3.1B **Privately Held**
WEB: www.intertektestingservices.com
SIC: 8734 Testing laboratories
HQ: Intertek Testing Services Na, Inc.
   3933 Us Route 11
   Cortland NY 13045
   607 753-6711

(G-7921)
IQ INNOVATIONS LLC
580 N 4th St Ste 560 (43215-2158)
PHONE..................................614 222-0882
Zita Hunt, *CEO*

Greg Dye, *Vice Pres*
William Lager,
EMP: 33
SALES (est): 6MM **Privately Held**
SIC: 7371 8299 Computer software development; educational services

(G-7922)
IRON MOUNTAIN INFO MGT LLC
4848 Evanswood Dr (43229-6207)
PHONE..................................614 840-9321
John Furgus, *Manager*
EMP: 38
SALES (corp-wide): 3.8B **Publicly Held**
SIC: 4226 Special warehousing & storage
HQ: Iron Mountain Information Management, Llc
   1 Federal St
   Boston MA 02110
   800 899-4766

(G-7923)
IRTH SOLUTIONS INC (PA)
5009 Horizons Dr Ste 100 (43220-5284)
PHONE..................................614 459-2328
Jason Adams, *CEO*
G Brent Bishop, *President*
Jessica Thomas, *Manager*
Matthew Abbitt, *Director*
EMP: 29
SQ FT: 12,100
SALES (est): 8.6MM **Privately Held**
WEB: www.irth.com
SIC: 7371 Computer software development

(G-7924)
ISAAC BRANT LEDMAN TEETOR LLP
2 Miranova Pl Ste 700 (43215-3742)
PHONE..................................614 221-2121
Fax: 614 365-9516
Angela Reed, *President*
Dennis Newman, *Partner*
Donald Anspaugh, *Partner*
Charles Brant, *Partner*
Frederick Isaac, *Partner*
EMP: 70
SALES (est): 7.4MM **Privately Held**
WEB: www.isaacbrant.com
SIC: 8111 General practice law office

(G-7925)
ISAAC WILES BURKHOLDER & TEETO
2 Miranova Pl Ste 700 (43215-5098)
PHONE..................................614 221-5216
Isaac Wiles, *Principal*
Cindy Roberts, *Counsel*
Denise Herald, *Human Res Mgr*
EMP: 51
SALES (est): 8MM **Privately Held**
SIC: 8111 General practice law office

(G-7926)
ISABELLE RIDGWAY CARE CTR INC
1520 Hawthorne Ave (43203-1762)
PHONE..................................614 252-4931
Fax: 614 252-5911
Patricia Mullins, *CEO*
John Atala, *CFO*
Darrell E Elliott, *Treasurer*
Teresa Travis, *Hlthcr Dir*
Alanna M Morgan, *Administration*
EMP: 140 EST: 1912
SQ FT: 70,400
SALES (est): 6.9MM **Privately Held**
WEB: www.isabelleridgway.com
SIC: 8051 8052 Convalescent home with continuous nursing care; intermediate care facilities

(G-7927)
ISLAND HOSPITALITY MGT LLC
Also Called: Columbus-Gatehouse Inn
2084 S Hamilton Rd (43232-4302)
PHONE..................................614 864-8844
Bryan Zeitlin, *Branch Mgr*
Jason Everson, *Manager*
EMP: 25

GEOGRAPHIC SECTION

Columbus - Franklin County (G-7952)

SALES (corp-wide): 832.9MM **Privately Held**
WEB: www.napleshamptoninn.com
SIC: 8742 7991 7011 Management consulting services; physical fitness facilities; hotels
PA: Island Hospitality Management, Llc
222 Lakeview Ave Ste 200
West Palm Beach FL 33401
561 832-6132

(G-7928)
ITICKETSCOM
700 Taylor Rd Ste 210 (43230-3318)
PHONE..............................614 410-4140
Cindy Novak, *Vice Pres*
EMP: 25 **EST:** 2013
SALES (est): 313.4K **Privately Held**
SIC: 7999 Ticket sales office for sporting events, contract

(G-7929)
J & J CARRIERS LLC
2572 Cleveland Ave Ste 5 (43211-1679)
PHONE..............................614 447-2615
Fax: 614 261-0520
Charmaine Kimble, *Partner*
April L Boykins, *Partner*
Jerry B Boykins, *Partner*
Jason D Kimble, *Partner*
EMP: 50
SQ FT: 1,000
SALES (est): 2.6MM **Privately Held**
SIC: 4213 Contract haulers

(G-7930)
J & T WASHES INC
1319 W 5th Ave (43212-2902)
PHONE..............................614 486-9093
Jeff Randolph, *President*
EMP: 25
SALES (est): 322.6K **Privately Held**
SIC: 7542 Carwashes; washing & polishing, automotive

(G-7931)
J K ENTERPRISES INC
Also Called: A & J Asphalt
2200 Mckinley Ave (43204-3417)
PHONE..............................614 481-8838
James Kuhn, *President*
EMP: 55
SALES (est): 5.4MM **Privately Held**
SIC: 1771 1611 Blacktop (asphalt) work; highway & street maintenance

(G-7932)
J S P A INC
2717 Burnaby Dr (43209-3200)
PHONE..............................407 957-6664
Fax: 614 236-5772
Joel Slaven, *President*
EMP: 40 **EST:** 1997
SALES (est): 418.7K **Privately Held**
WEB: www.jspa.com
SIC: 7929 Entertainers & entertainment groups

(G-7933)
JACK CONIE & SONS CORP
Also Called: Conie Construction Company
1340 Windsor Ave (43211-2852)
PHONE..............................614 291-5931
Fax: 614 291-9054
Richard P Conie, *Ch of Bd*
Michael C Conie, *President*
Carol Conie, *Treasurer*
Tim Berg, *Controller*
Darroll Kunze, *Manager*
EMP: 75 **EST:** 1971
SQ FT: 10,000
SALES (est): 15.8MM **Privately Held**
SIC: 1623 1629 Sewer line construction; earthmoving contractor

(G-7934)
JAMES POWERS
340 E Town St Ste 8700 (43215-4660)
PHONE..............................614 566-9397
James Powers, *Med Doctor*
EMP: 25
SALES (est): 61K **Privately Held**
SIC: 8322 Rehabilitation services

(G-7935)
JARED GALLERIA OF JEWELERY
4159 Morse Xing (43219-6015)
PHONE..............................614 476-6532
Jared Gambino, *Principal*
EMP: 99
SALES: 950K **Privately Held**
SIC: 7322 Adjustment & collection services

(G-7936)
JAVITCH BLOCK LLC
140 E Town St Ste 1250 (43215-4268)
PHONE..............................216 623-0000
Bruce A Block, *Branch Mgr*
EMP: 87
SALES (corp-wide): 58.1MM **Privately Held**
SIC: 8111 General practice attorney, lawyer
PA: Javitch Block Llc
1100 Superior Ave E Fl 19
Cleveland OH 44114
216 623-0000

(G-7937)
JB HUNT TRANSPORT SVCS INC
5435 Crosswind Dr (43228-3654)
PHONE..............................614 335-6681
Fax: 614 870-6640
John Schaar, *Accounts Mgr*
Matthew Burns, *Manager*
Mark Brewer, *Director*
EMP: 1448
SALES (corp-wide): 7.1B **Publicly Held**
SIC: 4213 4731 Trucking, except local; freight transportation arrangement
PA: J. B. Hunt Transport Services, Inc.
615 Jb Hunt Corp Dr
Lowell AR 72745
479 820-0000

(G-7938)
JDEL INC
200 W Nationwide Blvd # 1 (43215-2561)
PHONE..............................614 436-2418
EMP: 25
SQ FT: 4,500
SALES (est): 2MM
SALES (corp-wide): 96MM **Privately Held**
SIC: 6211 Security Broker/Dealer
PA: Jmac Inc.
200 W Nationwide Blvd # 1
Columbus OH 43215
614 436-2418

(G-7939)
JETSELECT LLC (PA)
4130 E 5th Ave (43219-1802)
PHONE..............................614 338-4380
Robert Austin, *CEO*
Gregory Marcussen, *Opers Staff*
Steve Lister, *VP Sales*
Shawn Wilkinson, *Sales Staff*
Nathan Batty, *Director*
EMP: 54
SALES (est): 15.1MM **Privately Held**
WEB: www.jetselect.net
SIC: 4522 Flying charter service

(G-7940)
JEWISH FAMILY SERVICES
1070 College Ave Ste A (43209-2489)
PHONE..............................614 231-1890
Fax: 614 231-4978
Andrea Applegate, *COO*
Oleg Vaisberg, *Vice Pres*
Ruth Bigus, *Pub Rel Dir*
Jim Hatch, *Consultant*
Ahmadou Kane, *Consultant*
EMP: 60
SALES: 3.1MM **Privately Held**
WEB: www.jfscolumbus.org
SIC: 8322 8331 Social service center; family (marriage) counseling; settlement house; vocational rehabilitation agency

(G-7941)
JIM KEIM FORD
Also Called: Keim, Jim Ford Sales
5575 Keim Cir (43228-7328)
PHONE..............................614 888-3333
Fax: 614 841-0314
James Keim, *President*
L D Pellissier III, *Corp Secy*

Nancy Joseph, *Controller*
Scott Simpson, *Finance Mgr*
Jack Dematteo, *Sales Mgr*
EMP: 100 **EST:** 1922
SQ FT: 40,000
SALES (est): 42.4MM **Privately Held**
SIC: 5511 7538 5521 Automobiles, new & used; pickups, new & used; general automotive repair shops; used car dealers

(G-7942)
JOHN A BECKER CO
Also Called: Becker Electric Supply
3825 Business Park Dr (43204-5007)
PHONE..............................614 272-8800
Fax: 614 272-5999
James Becker, *General Mgr*
Dennis Shireman, *Technical Staff*
EMP: 38
SALES (corp-wide): 239.6MM **Privately Held**
WEB: www.beckerelectric.com
SIC: 5063 1731 Electrical supplies; electrical work
PA: The John A Becker Co
1341 E 4th St
Dayton OH 45402
937 226-1341

(G-7943)
JOHNSON & FISCHER INC
Also Called: J F Painting Co
5303 Trabue Rd (43228-9783)
PHONE..............................614 276-8868
Fax: 614 276-8889
Robert J Johnson, *President*
Terry Pierce, *Office Mgr*
EMP: 45
SQ FT: 3,000
SALES (est): 4.3MM **Privately Held**
WEB: www.jfpaintingcompany.com
SIC: 1721 Commercial painting; industrial painting

(G-7944)
JOHNSON MIRMIRAN THOMPSON INC
Also Called: Barr & Prevost, A Jmt Division
2800 Corp Exchange Dr # 250 (43231-7661)
PHONE..............................614 714-0270
Fax: 614 714-0322
Jack Moeller, *President*
Andrew Barr, *Manager*
Fred Mirmiran, *Director*
EMP: 86
SALES (corp-wide): 224.9MM **Privately Held**
SIC: 8711 8712 8742 4785 Construction & civil engineering; civil engineering; architectural engineering; management engineering; highway bridge operation
PA: Johnson, Mirmiran & Thompson, Inc.
40 Wight Ave
Hunt Valley MD 21030
410 329-3100

(G-7945)
JOHNSON MIRMIRAN THOMPSON INC
Also Called: Jmt
2800 Corp Exchange Dr (43231-7661)
PHONE..............................614 714-0270
EMP: 30
SALES (corp-wide): 124.8MM **Privately Held**
SIC: 8711 Engineering Services
PA: Johnson, Mirmiran & Thompson, Inc.
72 Loveton Cir
Sparks MD 21030
410 329-3100

(G-7946)
JOLLY TOTS TOO INC
5511 N Hamilton Rd (43230-1321)
PHONE..............................614 471-0688
Fax: 614 471-0693
Brenda Warnock, *President*
EMP: 33
SALES (est): 1MM **Privately Held**
SIC: 8351 Group day care center

(G-7947)
JONES DAY LIMITED PARTNERSHIP
325 John H Mcconnell Blvd # 600 (43215-2672)
P.O. Box 165017 (43216-5017)
PHONE..............................614 469-3939
Fax: 614 461-4198
Fordham Huffman, *Manager*
Nancy Clark, *Manager*
Cynthia Gifford, *Manager*
Jason Grove, *Manager*
Brian Hannan, *Manager*
EMP: 200
SALES (corp-wide): 926MM **Privately Held**
SIC: 8111 General practice attorney, lawyer
PA: Jones Day Limited Partnership
901 Lakeside Ave E Ste 2
Cleveland OH 44114
216 586-3939

(G-7948)
JONES LAW GROUP LLC
513 E Rich St Ste 100 (43215-5376)
PHONE..............................614 545-9998
Eric Jones, *Principal*
EMP: 25
SALES (est): 372K **Privately Held**
SIC: 8111 General practice law office

(G-7949)
JONES TRUCK & SPRING REPR INC
350 Frank Rd (43207-2423)
PHONE..............................614 443-4619
John Richard Jones, *President*
Jack E Fink, *Vice Pres*
EMP: 70
SQ FT: 12,000
SALES (est): 6.6MM **Privately Held**
WEB: www.jonesspring.com
SIC: 7539 Trailer repair

(G-7950)
JOSEPH T RYERSON & SON INC
555 N Yearling Rd (43213-1395)
P.O. Box 145484, Cincinnati (45250-5484)
PHONE..............................513 542-5800
Fax: 513 542-4413
Edward J Lehner, *President*
Mark Oswald, *General Mgr*
Phil Kennedy, *Sales Staff*
Kurt Balder, *Clerk*
EMP: 80
SQ FT: 480,000 **Publicly Held**
SIC: 5051 3444 Iron & steel (ferrous) products; aluminum bars, rods, ingots, sheets, pipes, plates, etc.; sheet metalwork
HQ: Joseph T. Ryerson & Son, Inc.
227 W Monroe St Fl 27
Chicago IL 60606
312 292-5000

(G-7951)
JOSHUA INVESTMENT COMPANY INC
Also Called: Joshua Homes
3065 Mcctcheon Crssing Dr (43219-5054)
PHONE..............................614 428-5555
Eric Schottenstein, *President*
▲ **EMP:** 45
SALES (est): 4.1MM **Privately Held**
WEB: www.joshuahomes.com
SIC: 1521 New construction, single-family houses

(G-7952)
JPMORGAN CHASE BANK NAT ASSN
4000 Morse Xing (43219-6037)
PHONE..............................614 476-1910
EMP: 26
SALES (corp-wide): 99.6B **Publicly Held**
SIC: 6021 National commercial banks
HQ: Jpmorgan Chase Bank, National Association
1111 Polaris Pkwy
Columbus OH 43240
614 436-3055

Columbus - Franklin County (G-7953)

(G-7953)
JPMORGAN CHASE BANK NAT ASSN
3415 Vision Dr (43219-6009)
PHONE.....................216 781-2127
John Barth, *Senior VP*
Clinton Sampson, *Manager*
EMP: 26
SALES (corp-wide): 99.6B **Publicly Held**
WEB: www.chase.com
SIC: 6021 National commercial banks
HQ: Jpmorgan Chase Bank, National Association
1111 Polaris Pkwy
Columbus OH 43240
614 436-3055

(G-7954)
JPMORGAN CHASE BANK NAT ASSN
100 E Broad St Ste 2460 (43215-3618)
PHONE.....................614 248-5391
Bob Skea, *COO*
Cris Gossard, *Vice Pres*
EMP: 26
SALES (corp-wide): 99.6B **Publicly Held**
SIC: 6021 National commercial banks
HQ: Jpmorgan Chase Bank, National Association
1111 Polaris Pkwy
Columbus OH 43240
614 436-3055

(G-7955)
JPMORGAN CHASE BANK NAT ASSN
Also Called: Chase HM Mrtgages Florence Off
3415 Vision Dr (43219-6009)
PHONE.....................843 679-3653
Sharon Hardee, *Principal*
Michael Lichwa, *Assistant VP*
Robert Blankenship, *Vice Pres*
Christina Copeland, *Vice Pres*
Lauren Hammons, *Vice Pres*
EMP: 400
SALES (corp-wide): 99.6B **Publicly Held**
SIC: 6411 Insurance agents
HQ: Jpmorgan Chase Bank, National Association
1111 Polaris Pkwy
Columbus OH 43240
614 436-3055

(G-7956)
JPMORGAN CHASE BANK NAT ASSN
1199 Corrugated Way (43201-2901)
PHONE.....................614 248-2083
Lori Walkowiak, *Branch Mgr*
EMP: 26
SQ FT: 13,170
SALES (corp-wide): 99.6B **Publicly Held**
WEB: www.chase.com
SIC: 6021 National commercial banks
HQ: Jpmorgan Chase Bank, National Association
1111 Polaris Pkwy
Columbus OH 43240
614 436-3055

(G-7957)
JUICE TECHNOLOGIES INC
Also Called: Plug Smart
350 E 1st Ave Ste 210 (43201-3792)
PHONE.....................800 518-5576
Richard Housh, *CEO*
Dave Zehala, *President*
Tom Martin, *COO*
Duane Dickey, *Vice Pres*
Justin Eschman, *Project Mgr*
EMP: 27 EST: 2008
SALES: 6.3MM **Privately Held**
SIC: 8711 8748 7389 8734 Engineering services; mechanical engineering; energy conservation engineering; consulting engineer; business consulting; ; product certification, safety or performance; management services

(G-7958)
JULIAN SPEER CO
Also Called: Speer Mechanical
5255 Sinclair Rd (43229-5042)
PHONE.....................614 261-6331
Fax: 614 261-6330
Dennis Shuman, *President*
John Harper, *Vice Pres*
Michael A Shuman, *Vice Pres*
Dale Witte, *Vice Pres*
Tom Hangen, *Purch Mgr*
EMP: 55 EST: 1957
SALES (est): 6.4MM
SALES (corp-wide): 41.2MM **Privately Held**
WEB: www.speermechanical.com
SIC: 1711 Mechanical contractor
PA: Speer Industries Incorporated
5255 Sinclair Rd
Columbus OH 43229
614 261-6331

(G-7959)
JUMPLINECOM INC
5000 Arlngton Centre Blvd (43220-3075)
PHONE.....................614 859-1170
Rick Barber, *President*
Derek Hopper, *CFO*
Marc Hardgrove, *Treasurer*
Jason Beyke, *Director*
Robert Kaufman, *Admin Sec*
EMP: 26
SQ FT: 4,500
SALES (est): 3MM **Privately Held**
WEB: www.jumpline.com
SIC: 4813

(G-7960)
JURUS STANLEY R ATTY AT LAW
Also Called: Jurus Law Office
1375 Dublin Rd (43215-1074)
PHONE.....................614 486-0297
Fax: 614 486-8580
Stanley R Jurus, *Owner*
John R Workman,
EMP: 29
SALES (est): 2.7MM **Privately Held**
SIC: 8111 Labor & employment law

(G-7961)
JUST IN TIME CARE INC
Also Called: Just In Time Care Services
5320 E Main St Ste 200 (43213-2567)
PHONE.....................614 985-3555
Dr David Orgen, *President*
Dr David Rex Orgen, *President*
Sarah Orgen, *Vice Pres*
EMP: 30 EST: 2007
SALES: 1MM **Privately Held**
SIC: 8059 8049 Personal care home, with health care; speech therapist

(G-7962)
KAPPA KAPPA GAMMA FOUNDATION (PA)
Also Called: Kappa Kappa Gamma Fraternity
530 E Town St (43215-4820)
P.O. Box 38 (43216-0038)
PHONE.....................614 228-6515
Fax: 614 228-7809
Kari Kittrell, *Director*
Mary Cunnyngham, *Administration*
Marsha Jones, *Administration*
EMP: 30
SQ FT: 15,000
SALES: 3.5MM **Privately Held**
WEB: www.kappa.org
SIC: 8641 University club

(G-7963)
KARE A LOT
1030 King Ave (43212-2609)
PHONE.....................614 298-8933
Fax: 614 298-8934
Milagros Neuman, *President*
EMP: 30 EST: 1984
SALES (est): 966.4K **Privately Held**
SIC: 8351 Group day care center

(G-7964)
KARE A LOT INFNT TDDLR DEV CTR
Also Called: Kare A Lot Child Care Center
3164 Riverside Dr (43221-2540)
PHONE.....................614 481-7532
Fax: 614 481-9532
Milagros Neuman, *President*
EMP: 28
SQ FT: 2,700
SALES (est): 1.1MM **Privately Held**
SIC: 8351 Group day care center

(G-7965)
KARL HC LLC
Also Called: Villa Angela Care Center
5700 Karl Rd (43229-3602)
PHONE.....................614 846-5420
James Griffiths, *Mng Member*
Dianna Bozek, *Mng Member*
Brian Colleran, *Mng Member*
EMP: 350
SQ FT: 102,000
SALES: 16.1MM **Privately Held**
WEB: www.villa-angela.net
SIC: 8051 Skilled nursing care facilities

(G-7966)
KARLSBERGER COMPANIES (PA)
99 E Main St (43215-5115)
P.O. Box 340130 (43234-0130)
PHONE.....................614 461-9500
Fax: 614 461-6324
Michael Tyne, *Ch of Bd*
Richard Barger, *COO*
William O Anderson, *CFO*
Val Carvalho, *Financial Exec*
EMP: 105 EST: 1927
SQ FT: 32,000
SALES (est): 12.1MM **Privately Held**
SIC: 8712 8742 7389 Architectural services; planning consultant; hospital & health services consultant; interior decorating

(G-7967)
KARRINGTON OPERATING CO INC (DH)
919 Old Henderson Rd (43220-3722)
PHONE.....................614 324-5951
Richard R Slager, *Ch of Bd*
Pete Klisares, *President*
Richard J Clark, *COO*
Robin Holderman, *Exec VP*
Stephen Lewis, *Senior VP*
EMP: 55
SQ FT: 14,000
SALES (est): 10.7MM
SALES (corp-wide): 4.3B **Publicly Held**
WEB: www.karrington.com
SIC: 8059 Personal care home, with health care

(G-7968)
KASTLE TECHNOLOGIES CO LLC
185-H Huntley Rd (43229)
PHONE.....................614 433-9860
Dennis Quebe, *CEO*
William Page, *CFO*
EMP: 25
SALES (corp-wide): 83.3MM **Privately Held**
SIC: 1731 Electrical work
HQ: Kastle Technologies Co., Llc
100 Cart Path Dr
Monroe OH 45050
513 360-2901

(G-7969)
KE GUTRIDGE LLC
1111 Rarig Ave (43219-2357)
PHONE.....................614 252-0420
Fax: 614 252-0653
Gil Gutridge, *Owner*
Richard Stover, *General Mgr*
EMP: 138
SALES (corp-wide): 4.4MM **Privately Held**
SIC: 1711 Plumbing contractors
PA: Ke Gutridge, Llc
88 S 2nd St
Newark OH 43055
740 349-9411

(G-7970)
KEGLER BROWN HL RITTER CO LPA (PA)
65 E State St Ste 1800 (43215-4294)
PHONE.....................614 462-5400
Elise Elman, *President*
Wendy Schmidt, *President*
Michael E Zatezalo, *Managing Prtnr*
Luis M Alcalde, *Counsel*
Luis Alcalde, *Counsel*
EMP: 142
SQ FT: 51,000
SALES (est): 30.5MM **Privately Held**
WEB: www.keglerbrown.com
SIC: 8111 General practice attorney, lawyer

(G-7971)
KELLER GROUP LIMITED
Also Called: Keller Farms Landscape & Nurs
3909 Groves Rd (43232-4138)
PHONE.....................614 866-9551
Fax: 614 866-9602
Mike Terry, *Opers Mgr*
Kimberly Donnelli, *Purchasing*
Michael Hartmann, *Controller*
Bernard W Fleming,
EMP: 36
SQ FT: 11,400
SALES (est): 4.1MM **Privately Held**
WEB: www.kellerfarmslandscaping.com
SIC: 0782 Landscape contractors; lawn care services

(G-7972)
KELLER WILLIAMS CLASSIC PRO
1510 W Lane Ave (43221-3960)
PHONE.....................614 451-8500
Fax: 614 451-1213
Samuel Mathoslah, *Manager*
Susan Parrish,
Bobbi Evans, *Real Est Agnt*
Stacy H McVey, *Real Est Agnt*
Chip Parrish, *Real Est Agnt*
EMP: 75
SALES (est): 3MM **Privately Held**
WEB: www.kellerwilliamsclassicproperties.yourk-woff
SIC: 6531 Real estate agent, residential

(G-7973)
KEMBA FINANCIAL CREDIT UN INC
4311 N High St (43214-2609)
PHONE.....................614 235-2395
Fax: 614 235-2395
Gerald Guy, *CEO*
Steve Liard, *Manager*
EMP: 78
SALES (corp-wide): 40.5MM **Privately Held**
SIC: 6282 Investment advice
PA: Kemba Financial Credit Union, Inc,
555 Officenter Pl Ste 100
Gahanna OH 43230
614 235-2395

(G-7974)
KEMBA FINANCIAL CREDIT UN INC
55 Office Centre Pl (43228)
PHONE.....................614 853-9774
Gerald D Guy, *President*
EMP: 125 EST: 1935
SQ FT: 38,292
SALES: 30.7MM **Privately Held**
SIC: 6062 State credit unions, not federally chartered

(G-7975)
KEMBA FINANCIAL CREDIT UNION
4220 E Broad St (43213-1216)
P.O. Box 307370 (43230-7370)
PHONE.....................614 235-2395
Fax: 614 324-8365
Jerry Guy, *CEO*
EMP: 69
SQ FT: 1,200
SALES (est): 8.9MM **Privately Held**
SIC: 6062 State credit unions, not federally chartered

(G-7976)
KENDALL HOLDINGS LTD (PA)
Also Called: Phpk Technologies
2111 Builders Pl (43204-4886)
PHONE.....................614 486-4750
Richard Coleman, *Partner*
Mike Agosta, *Project Engr*
Steve Willming, *Design Engr*
Julie Battles, *Controller*

GEOGRAPHIC SECTION
Columbus - Franklin County (G-8000)

Tim Savely, *Marketing Mgr*
▲ **EMP:** 45
SQ FT: 60,000
SALES (est): 10.8MM **Privately Held**
SIC: 3443 8711 Fabricated plate work (boiler shop); engineering services

(G-7977)
KENDRICK-MOLLENAUER PNTG CO
1099 Stimmel Rd (43223-2911)
PHONE..............................614 443-7037
Fax: 614 443-8128
Howard Kendrick, *President*
Rose M Kendrick, *Corp Secy*
James W Kendrick Jr, *Vice Pres*
Jerry Sahr, *Vice Pres*
EMP: 35
SALES (est): 3.4MM **Privately Held**
SIC: 1721 Residential painting; commercial painting

(G-7978)
KENNETHS HAIR SALONS & DAY SP (PA)
Also Called: Kenneth's Design Group
5151 Reed Rd Ste 250b (43220-2594)
PHONE..............................614 457-7712
Fax: 614 457-7794
Kenneth Anders, *President*
Kathy Masters, *Marketing Staff*
John Fitzgerald, *Manager*
Emily Harrison, *Manager*
Steve McElheny, *Manager*
EMP: 310
SQ FT: 46,000
SALES (est): 11.5MM **Privately Held**
WEB: www.kenneths.com
SIC: 7231 5999 Beauty shops; hair dressing school; facial salons; beauty culture school; toiletries, cosmetics & perfumes

(G-7979)
KENOSHA BEEF INTERNATIONAL LTD
Birchwood Meats & Provisions
1821 Dividend Dr (43228-3848)
PHONE..............................614 771-1330
Fax: 614 771-9590
Ken Fudy, *Principal*
Ken Fude, *COO*
Mike Marquardt, *Vice Pres*
Troy Maynard, *Opers Staff*
Ray Green, *Manager*
EMP: 107
SQ FT: 10,000
SALES (est): 16.1MM
SALES (corp-wide): 187.4MM **Privately Held**
WEB: www.bwfoods.com
SIC: 5147 2013 Meats, fresh; sausages & other prepared meats
PA: Kenosha Beef International, Ltd.
3111 152nd Ave
Kenosha WI 53144
800 541-1684

(G-7980)
KENSINGTON PLACE INC
1001 Parkview Blvd (43219-2270)
PHONE..............................614 252-5276
Fax: 614 251-7690
Larry Crowell, *President*
Phil Helser, *CFO*
Penny Smith, *Director*
EMP: 26
SALES: 803.7K **Privately Held**
SIC: 6513 Retirement hotel operation

(G-7981)
KENT PLACE HOUSING
Also Called: Buckeye Community Forty Four
1414 Gault St (43205-2933)
PHONE..............................614 942-2020
Steve Boone, *Partner*
Trenda Cooper, *Clerk*
EMP: 99
SQ FT: 1,445
SALES (est): 2MM **Privately Held**
SIC: 6514 Dwelling operators, except apartments

(G-7982)
KEVIN KENNEDY ASSOCIATES INC
275 Outerbelt St (43213-1529)
PHONE..............................317 536-7000
Sharon Kennedy, *CEO*
Randy Clarksean, *President*
Tom Weisgerber, *President*
Jacque Bader, *Treasurer*
Bob Russell, *Consultant*
EMP: 37
SALES (est): 3.8MM **Privately Held**
WEB: www.kkai.com
SIC: 8711 Consulting engineer

(G-7983)
KEY BLUE PRINTS INC (PA)
Also Called: Key Color
195 E Livingston Ave (43215-5793)
PHONE..............................614 228-3285
David M Key III, *President*
Mark R Lasek, *Managing Dir*
Rod Macdonald, *Managing Dir*
Daniel Brown, *Vice Pres*
Robert Levy, *Vice Pres*
▲ **EMP:** 54
SQ FT: 18,000
SALES (est): 30.9MM **Privately Held**
WEB: www.key-evidence.com
SIC: 5049 7334 Drafting supplies; blue-printing service

(G-7984)
KEYSTONE FREIGHT CORP
2545 Parsons Ave (43207-2974)
PHONE..............................614 542-0320
John Dietz, *Branch Mgr*
EMP: 30
SQ FT: 8,772
SALES (corp-wide): 258.1MM **Privately Held**
SIC: 4213 Trucking, except local
HQ: Keystone Freight Corp.
611 Us Highway 46 W # 301
Hasbrouck Heights NJ 07604
201 330-1900

(G-7985)
KFORCE INC
200 E Campus View Blvd # 225 (43235-6619)
PHONE..............................614 436-4027
EMP: 30
SALES (corp-wide): 1.3B **Publicly Held**
SIC: 7361 Staffing Services
PA: Kforce Inc.
1001 E Palm Ave
Tampa FL 33605
813 552-5000

(G-7986)
KIDDIE WEST PEDIATRIC CENTER
4766 W Broad St (43228-1613)
PHONE..............................614 276-7733
Fax: 614 276-0702
Carl R Backes Do, *President*
Dawn Dilling, *Med Doctor*
Alicia M Kuper, *Pediatrics*
Benjamin Liston, *Nurse Practr*
EMP: 30
SALES (est): 3.6MM **Privately Held**
SIC: 8011 Pediatrician

(G-7987)
KIDNEY CENTER OF BEXLEY LLC
1151 College Ave (43209-2827)
PHONE..............................614 231-2200
EMP: 116
SALES (est): 280.6K **Publicly Held**
SIC: 8092 Kidney dialysis centers
PA: American Renal Associates Holdings, Inc.
500 Cummings Ctr Ste 6550
Beverly MA 01915

(G-7988)
KIDS WORLD
2812 Morse Rd (43231-6034)
PHONE..............................614 473-9229
Yna Ness, *President*
EMP: 25
SALES (est): 593.5K **Privately Held**
SIC: 8351 Child day care services

(G-7989)
KINDERCARE LEARNING CTRS LLC
Also Called: Mount Carmel Kindercare
5959 E Broad St (43213-1501)
PHONE..............................614 759-6622
Fax: 614 759-6105
Misty Perry, *Manager*
Shawna Tahl, *Manager*
Laquanta Austin, *Director*
EMP: 30
SALES (corp-wide): 1.2B **Privately Held**
WEB: www.kindercare.com
SIC: 8351 Child day care services
HQ: Kindercare Learning Centers, Llc
650 Ne Holladay St # 1400
Portland OR 97232
503 872-1300

(G-7990)
KINDRED HEALTHCARE OPER INC
Also Called: Minerva Park
5460 Cleveland Ave (43231-4005)
PHONE..............................614 882-2490
Fax: 614 818-0638
William Altman, *Vice Pres*
Joseph Landenwich, *Vice Pres*
Teresa Garvey, *Office Mgr*
Valarie Youell, *Administration*
EMP: 80
SALES (corp-wide): 6B **Publicly Held**
WEB: www.salemhaven.com
SIC: 8051 Skilled nursing care facilities
HQ: Kindred Healthcare Operating, Inc.
680 S 4th St
Louisville KY 40202
502 596-7300

(G-7991)
KINDRED NURSING CENTERS E LLC
Also Called: Kindred Transitional Care
2770 Clime Rd (43223-3626)
PHONE..............................614 276-8222
Carissa Moses, *Sls & Mktg Exec*
Dawn Lewis, *Manager*
Janice Kelly, *Director*
Dane Plumly, *Director*
Raymond Pongonis, *Director*
EMP: 100
SALES (corp-wide): 6B **Publicly Held**
WEB: www.salemhaven.com
SIC: 8051 Convalescent home with continuous nursing care
HQ: Kindred Nursing Centers East, L.L.C.
680 S 4th St
Louisville KY 40202
502 596-7300

(G-7992)
KING BUSINESS INTERIORS INC
1400 Goodale Blvd Ste 102 (43212-3777)
PHONE..............................614 430-0020
Fax: 614 430-0022
Darla J King, *President*
David R King, *Vice Pres*
Jerry Hagan, *Project Mgr*
Tony Casey, *Accounts Mgr*
Ashley Barcus, *Sales Staff*
EMP: 36
SQ FT: 10,000
SALES (est): 32.2MM **Privately Held**
WEB: www.kbiinc.com
SIC: 5021 Office furniture

(G-7993)
KING MEMORY LLC
380 Morrison Rd Ste A (43213-1430)
PHONE..............................614 418-6044
Darryl Tanner, *CEO*
▲ **EMP:** 25
SALES (est): 5.7MM **Privately Held**
SIC: 5045 Computers, peripherals & software

(G-7994)
KING TUT LOGISTICS LLC
Also Called: Cleopatra Trucking
3600 Enterprise Ave (43228-1047)
PHONE..............................614 538-0509
Mike Roahrig, *Safety Dir*
Jesse Brown, *Mng Member*
Mark Gabriel,
Maged Tadros,
Michael G Wessa,
EMP: 50
SALES (est): 6.1MM **Privately Held**
SIC: 4214 4225 7389 Local trucking with storage; general warehousing & storage; packaging & labeling services

(G-7995)
KLARNA INC
629 N High St Ste 300 (43215-2025)
PHONE..............................614 615-4705
Brian Billingsley, *CEO*
Brian Brady, *Finance*
EMP: 37
SQ FT: 3,300
SALES (est): 9.9MM
SALES (corp-wide): 383MM **Privately Held**
SIC: 6099 Electronic funds transfer network, including switching
HQ: Klarna Bank Ab
Sveavagen 46
Stockholm 111 3
812 012-000

(G-7996)
KLEAN A KAR INC (PA)
8251 Windsong Ct (43235-1491)
PHONE..............................614 221-3145
Fax: 614 221-3183
Dennis Ramsey, *President*
Doug Ramsey, *Vice Pres*
Dan Ramsey, *Treasurer*
EMP: 40
SALES (est): 4.4MM **Privately Held**
WEB: www.kleanakar.com
SIC: 7542 Washing & polishing, automotive

(G-7997)
KLINGBEIL MANAGEMENT GROUP CO (PA)
21 W Broad St Fl 10 (43215-4172)
PHONE..............................614 220-8900
James D Klingbeil, *President*
Richard J Dishnica, *Agent*
EMP: 30
SALES (est): 2.8MM **Privately Held**
SIC: 6531 1522 8742 8721 Real estate managers; remodeling, multi-family dwellings; administrative services consultant; accounting services, except auditing

(G-7998)
KLINGBEIL MULTIFAMILTY FUND IV
21 W Broad St Fl 11 (43215-4100)
PHONE..............................415 398-0106
Paul Rose, *Branch Mgr*
EMP: 100
SALES (corp-wide): 33.2MM **Privately Held**
WEB: www.kcmapts.com
SIC: 6513 Apartment building operators
PA: Klingbeil Multifamily Fund Iv
200 California St Ste 300
San Francisco CA 94111
415 398-3590

(G-7999)
KM2 SOLUTIONS LLC
Also Called: Technology Hub
2400 Corp Exchange Dr # 210 (43231-7605)
PHONE..............................610 213-1408
EMP: 460
SALES (corp-wide): 41.3MM **Privately Held**
SIC: 8742 Financial consultant
PA: Km2 Solutions, Llc
100 Park Ave Rm 1600
New York NY 10017
404 848-8886

(G-8000)
KMI INC
5025 Arlington Centre Blv (43220-2959)
PHONE..............................614 326-6304
Mark Colasante, *Principal*
Joel Copeland, *COO*
Greg Wasylik, *Accounts Mgr*
EMP: 38
SQ FT: 10,000

Columbus - Franklin County (G-8001) — GEOGRAPHIC SECTION

SALES (est): 1.4MM **Privately Held**
SIC: **7371** Computer software development & applications

(G-8001)
KNAPP VETERINARY HOSPITAL INC
596 Oakland Park Ave (43214-4199)
PHONE..................614 267-3124
Fax: 614 267-0049
Paul H Knapp Dvm, *President*
Robert Knapp, *Vice Pres*
John C Munsell, *Vice Pres*
EMP: 29 EST: 1945
SQ FT: 5,000
SALES (est): 2.1MM **Privately Held**
SIC: **0742** Animal hospital services, pets & other animal specialties

(G-8002)
KNIGHT TRANSPORTATION INC
4275 Westward Ave (43228-1045)
PHONE..................614 308-4900
Dan Kutter, *Branch Mgr*
EMP: 78
SALES (corp-wide): 2.4B **Publicly Held**
SIC: **4213** 4212 Heavy hauling; local trucking, without storage
HQ: Knight Transportation, Inc.
20002 N 19th Ave
Phoenix AZ 85027
602 269-2000

(G-8003)
KNIGHT-SWIFT TRNSP HLDGS INC
4141 Parkwest Dr (43228-1400)
PHONE..................614 274-5204
Fax: 614 308-2380
Dale Cooley, *General Mgr*
Patricia Rooney, *Human Res Dir*
Michael Click, *Manager*
EMP: 75
SQ FT: 1,364
SALES (corp-wide): 2.4B **Publicly Held**
SIC: **4213** Contract haulers
PA: Knight-Swift Transportation Holdings Inc.
2200 S 75th Ave
Phoenix AZ 85043
602 269-9700

(G-8004)
KNOLLMAN CONSTRUCTION LLC
4601 E 5th Ave (43219-1819)
P.O. Box 360415 (43236-0415)
PHONE..................614 841-0130
Tom Ray, *VP Opers*
Eric Bobbitt, *Controller*
Trey Knollman,
EMP: 200
SALES (est): 11.6MM **Privately Held**
WEB: www.knollmanconstruction.com
SIC: **1742** Drywall

(G-8005)
KNOWLEDGE MGT INTERACTIVE INC
Also Called: K M I
330 W Spring St Ste 320 (43215-7305)
PHONE..................614 224-0664
Fax: 614 224-0665
Mark Colasante, *CEO*
Kristin Davis, *Prdtn Mgr*
Tanya Zarnitsa, *QC Mgr*
Eric Blevins, *Engineer*
Denise Bishop, *Manager*
EMP: 35
SQ FT: 6,800
SALES (est): 5.1MM **Privately Held**
WEB: www.kmionline.com
SIC: **7371** Computer software development

(G-8006)
KOHR ROYER GRIFFITH DEV CO LLC
1480 Dublin Rd (43215-1068)
PHONE..................614 228-2471
Fax: 614 228-8550
Richard L Royer, *CEO*
EMP: 47
SQ FT: 4,500

SALES (est): 1.9MM **Privately Held**
SIC: **6512** Commercial & industrial building operation

(G-8007)
KOKOSING CONSTRUCTION CO INC (HQ)
886 Mckinley Ave (43222-1187)
P.O. Box 226, Fredericktown (43019-0226)
PHONE..................614 228-1029
Fax: 614 212-5711
W Barth Burgett, *CEO*
Joe A Celuch, *General Mgr*
Bart Moody, *Area Mgr*
Marsha Rinehart, *Exec VP*
Daniel J Compston, *Senior VP*
▲ EMP: 200
SALES (est): 513.2MM
SALES (corp-wide): 674.3MM **Privately Held**
WEB: www.kokosing-inc.com
SIC: **1611** 1622 1629 1542 General contractor; highway & street construction; highway & street paving contractor; bridge construction; waste water & sewage treatment plant construction; commercial & office building, new construction; industrial buildings, new construction; renovation, remodeling & repairs: industrial buildings; sewer line construction; water main construction
PA: Kokosing Inc.
6235 Wstrville Rd Ste 200
Westerville OH 43081
614 212-5700

(G-8008)
KOKOSING CONSTRUCTION CO INC
886 Mckinley Ave (43222-1187)
PHONE..................614 228-1029
Mike Helbing, *Manager*
EMP: 25
SQ FT: 2,527
SALES (corp-wide): 674.3MM **Privately Held**
WEB: www.kokosing-inc.com
SIC: **1611** 1622 General contractor, highway & street construction; bridge, tunnel & elevated highway
HQ: Kokosing Construction Company, Inc.
886 Mckinley Ave
Columbus OH 43222
614 228-1029

(G-8009)
KOORSEN FIRE & SECURITY INC
727 Manor Park Dr (43228-9522)
PHONE..................614 878-2228
Dale Underwood, *Branch Mgr*
George Hinkle, *Manager*
EMP: 45
SALES (corp-wide): 264.3MM **Privately Held**
WEB: www.koorsen.com
SIC: **5099** Fire extinguishers
PA: Koorsen Fire & Security, Inc.
2719 N Arlington Ave
Indianapolis IN 46218
317 542-1800

(G-8010)
KOORSEN FIRE & SECURITY INC
727 Manor Park Dr (43228-9522)
PHONE..................614 878-2228
Fred Hillma, *Branch Mgr*
EMP: 25
SALES (corp-wide): 264.3MM **Privately Held**
SIC: **5099** Fire extinguishers; lifesaving & survival equipment (non-medical)
PA: Koorsen Fire & Security, Inc.
2719 N Arlington Ave
Indianapolis IN 46218
317 542-1800

(G-8011)
KORMAN CONSTRUCTION CORP
3695 Interchange Rd (43204-1499)
PHONE..................614 274-2170
Fax: 614 274-3427
Young Bok Lee, *President*

EMP: 30
SQ FT: 10,560
SALES (est): 4.1MM **Privately Held**
SIC: **1761** 1799 Roofing contractor; kitchen & bathroom remodeling

(G-8012)
KPMG LLP
191 W Nationwide Blvd # 500 (43215-2575)
PHONE..................614 249-2300
Fax: 614 249-2348
Harold I Zeidman, *Partner*
Todd Babione, *Managing Dir*
Brett Hoke, *Auditing Mgr*
Masako Narita, *Financial Exec*
Cynthia Thompson, *Human Res Mgr*
EMP: 160
SALES (corp-wide): 5.3B **Privately Held**
SIC: **8721** Accounting services, except auditing; certified public accountant
PA: Kpmg Llp
345 Park Ave Lowr Ll4
New York NY 10154
212 758-9700

(G-8013)
KREBER GRAPHICS INC (PA)
2580 Westbelt Dr (43228-3827)
PHONE..................614 529-5701
Jim Kreber, *CEO*
Jynne Harris, *President*
Todd Alexander, *Exec VP*
Jeremy Gustafson, *Senior VP*
Jeremy Gufstason, *Vice Pres*
EMP: 90 EST: 1947
SQ FT: 86,000
SALES (est): 19MM **Privately Held**
WEB: www.kreber.com
SIC: **7311** Advertising consultant

(G-8014)
KRIEGER FORD INC (PA)
1800 Morse Rd (43229-6691)
PHONE..................614 888-3320
Fax: 614 847-8033
G Douglas Krieger, *President*
Harold Samour, *Business Mgr*
Brent Ferguson, *Corp Secy*
John Jeffrey Krieger, *Vice Pres*
William Coultas, *Store Mgr*
▲ EMP: 160 EST: 1965
SQ FT: 50,000
SALES (est): 69.2MM **Privately Held**
SIC: **5511** 7515 7538 7513 Automobiles, new & used; passenger car leasing; general automotive repair shops; truck rental & leasing, no drivers

(G-8015)
KROGER CO
850 S Hamilton Rd (43213-3000)
PHONE..................614 759-2745
Fax: 614 759-2756
Lou Gilliam, *Manager*
EMP: 173
SALES (corp-wide): 122.6B **Publicly Held**
WEB: www.kroger.com
SIC: **5411** 5141 5912 Supermarkets, chain; supermarkets, 66,000-99,000 square feet; convenience stores, chain; groceries, general line; drug stores & proprietary stores
PA: The Kroger Co
1014 Vine St Ste 1000
Cincinnati OH 45202
513 762-4000

(G-8016)
KROGER REFILL CENTER
2270 Rickenbacker Pkwy W (43217-5002)
PHONE..................614 333-5017
Marette Parry, *CEO*
Chong Lin, *Pharmacist*
EMP: 50
SALES (est): 3.6MM **Privately Held**
SIC: **8742** Human resource consulting services

(G-8017)
KST SECURITY INC
727 Manor Park Dr (43228-9522)
PHONE..................614 878-2228
Constance A Morgan, *Administration*
EMP: 38 **Privately Held**

SIC: **7382** Security systems services
PA: Kst Security, Inc.
6121 E 30th St
Indianapolis IN 46219

(G-8018)
KUSAN INC
Also Called: Quality Air Heating and AC
4060 Indianola Ave (43214-3160)
PHONE..................614 262-1818
Thomas Kusan, *President*
Nick Kusan, *Vice Pres*
Robert Willis, *Sales Mgr*
EMP: 27
SQ FT: 5,000
SALES (est): 4.5MM **Privately Held**
WEB: www.qualityairandheat.com
SIC: **1711** Warm air heating & air conditioning contractor

(G-8019)
L & W SUPPLY CORPORATION
1150 Mckinley Ave (43222-1113)
PHONE..................614 276-6391
Bernie Van, *General Mgr*
Jon Tribbie, *Manager*
EMP: 25
SALES (corp-wide): 4.3B **Privately Held**
WEB: www.lwsupply.com
SIC: **5032** Drywall materials
HQ: L & W Supply Corporation
300 S Riverside Plz # 200
Chicago IL 60606
312 606-4000

(G-8020)
L BRANDS SERVICE COMPANY LLC
Also Called: Limited Services Corporation
3 Limited Pkwy (43230-1467)
PHONE..................614 415-7000
Leslie H Wexner, *Ch of Bd*
Sarah Bonnaud, *Assoc VP*
Nathaniel Beegle, *Director*
Tiffany Luckhaupt, *Recruiter*
EMP: 94
SALES (est): 4.7MM
SALES (corp-wide): 12.6B **Publicly Held**
WEB: www.limited.com
SIC: **6512** 8743 Nonresidential building operators; public relations services
PA: L Brands, Inc.
3 Limited Pkwy
Columbus OH 43230
614 415-7000

(G-8021)
L BRANDS STORE DSIGN CNSTR INC
Also Called: Limited
3 Ltd Pkwy (43230)
PHONE..................614 415-7000
Fax: 614 479-7440
Gene Torcha, *President*
Peter M Horvath, *Exec VP*
Martyn Redgrave, *Exec VP*
Scott Taylor, *Exec VP*
Margaret M Wright, *Exec VP*
▲ EMP: 230
SALES (est): 120.2MM
SALES (corp-wide): 12.6B **Publicly Held**
WEB: www.limited.com
SIC: **1542** Commercial & office building, new construction
PA: L Brands, Inc.
3 Limited Pkwy
Columbus OH 43230
614 415-7000

(G-8022)
L J NAVY TRUCKING COMPANY
2365 Performance Way (43207-2858)
PHONE..................614 754-8929
Fax: 740 894-5203
Thad Blatt, *President*
Carolyn Blatt, *Corp Secy*
EMP: 25
SALES (est): 4.5MM **Privately Held**
SIC: **4213** Trucking, except local

(G-8023)
L JACK RUSCILLI
Also Called: Ruscilli Investment Co
2041 Arlingate Ln (43228-4113)
PHONE..................614 876-9484
L Jack Ruscilli, *Owner*

Chuck Wiseman, *Opers Mgr*
Doug Garey, *Manager*
EMP: 50
SALES (est): 3MM **Privately Held**
SIC: 1542 Nonresidential construction

(G-8024)
L V TRUCKING INC
Also Called: L V Trckng
2440 Harrison Rd (43204-3508)
PHONE..................614 275-4994
Fax: 614 275-3019
Brad Moore, *President*
L Vince Moore, *Vice Pres*
Neil Hever, *Opers Mgr*
Shawn Kelly, *Opers Mgr*
Cheryl Criss, *Mktg Dir*
EMP: 41
SQ FT: 3,000
SALES (est): 6.2MM **Privately Held**
WEB: www.lvtrucking.com
SIC: 4213 4212 Contract haulers; local trucking, without storage

(G-8025)
L3 AVIATION PRODUCTS INC
Also Called: Goodrich Avionics
1105 Schrock Rd Ste 800 (43229-1154)
PHONE..................614 825-2001
James Gregg, *Engineer*
Billie Stevens, *Manager*
EMP: 60
SALES (corp-wide): 9.5B **Publicly Held**
SIC: 3812 8711 Aircraft flight instruments; gyroscopes; automatic pilots, aircraft; radar systems & equipment; engineering services
HQ: L3 Aviation Products, Inc.
5353 52nd St Se
Grand Rapids MI 49512
616 977-6837

(G-8026)
LA-Z-BOY INCORPORATED
4228 Easton Gateway Dr (43219-1543)
PHONE..................614 478-0898
EMP: 203
SALES (corp-wide): 1.5B **Publicly Held**
SIC: 5021 Furniture
PA: La-Z-Boy Incorporated
1 La Z Boy Dr
Monroe MI 48162
734 242-1444

(G-8027)
LABORATORY CORPORATION AMERICA
941 E Johnstown Rd (43230-1851)
PHONE..................614 475-7852
Fax: 614 475-7863
James Duff, *Principal*
EMP: 25 **Publicly Held**
SIC: 8071 Blood analysis laboratory
HQ: Laboratory Corporation Of America
358 S Main St Ste 458
Burlington NC 27215
336 229-1127

(G-8028)
LABORATORY CORPORATION AMERICA
5888 Cleveland Ave (43231-2860)
PHONE..................614 882-6278
Angela Myers, *Branch Mgr*
Michael Longstreth, *Technician*
EMP: 25 **Publicly Held**
SIC: 8071 Testing laboratories
HQ: Laboratory Corporation Of America
358 S Main St Ste 458
Burlington NC 27215
336 229-1127

(G-8029)
LADAN LEARNING CENTER
6028 Cleveland Ave (43231-2230)
PHONE..................614 426-4306
Hibo Omar, *Owner*
EMP: 35
SALES (est): 124.7K **Privately Held**
SIC: 8351 Child day care services

(G-8030)
LADERA HEALTHCARE COMPANY
1661 Old Henderson Rd (43220-3644)
PHONE..................614 459-1313
Ralph Hazelbaker, *Partner*
Diane Haemmerly, *Partner*
John Haemmerly, *Partner*
Billie Hazelbaker, *Partner*
EMP: 30
SALES (est): 1.6MM **Privately Held**
SIC: 6512 Nonresidential building operators

(G-8031)
LAKEFRONT LINES INC
Also Called: Lakefront Trailways
3152 E 17th Ave (43219-2353)
P.O. Box 360556 (43236-0556)
PHONE..................614 476-1113
Fax: 614 476-1482
Christopher McCrady, *Branch Mgr*
EMP: 25
SALES (corp-wide): 4.9B **Privately Held**
WEB: www.lakefrontlines.com
SIC: 4119 4142 Local passenger transportation; bus charter service, except local
HQ: Lakefront Lines, Inc.
13315 Brookpark Rd
Brookpark OH 44142
216 267-8810

(G-8032)
LANCASTER COMMERCIAL PDTS LLC
2353 Westbrooke Dr (43228-9557)
P.O. Box 870, Worthington (43085-0870)
PHONE..................740 286-5081
Kenneth Evans, *President*
Anish Mistry, *Managing Prtnr*
Robert Mills, *Executive*
◆ **EMP:** 34
SALES (est): 15.7MM **Privately Held**
SIC: 5085 3089 Industrial supplies; injection molding of plastics

(G-8033)
LANCASTER POLLARD & CO LLC (HQ)
65 E State St Ste 1600 (43215-4237)
PHONE..................614 224-8800
Thomas Green, *CEO*
T Brian Pollard, *President*
Grant T Goodman, *Vice Pres*
Tanya Hahn, *Vice Pres*
Ross Holland, *Vice Pres*
EMP: 25
SALES (est): 10.8MM **Privately Held**
WEB: www.lancasterpollard.com
SIC: 6211 Investment bankers

(G-8034)
LANCASTER POLLARD MRTG CO LLC (PA)
65 E State St Ste 1600 (43215-4237)
PHONE..................614 224-8800
Thomas R Green, *CEO*
Timothy J Dobyns, *Exec VP*
Shelly Harvey, *Vice Pres*
Kevin J Beerman, *CFO*
EMP: 70
SALES (est): 43.6MM **Privately Held**
SIC: 6159 6162 6282 Intermediate investment banks; mortgage bankers; investment advisory service

(G-8035)
LANCE A1 CLEANING SERVICES LLC
342 Hanton Way (43213-4430)
PHONE..................614 370-0550
Lance Owens,
EMP: 100
SALES (est): 44K **Privately Held**
SIC: 7699 Cleaning services

(G-8036)
LANE ALTON & HORST LLC
2 Miranova Pl Ste 220 (43215-7050)
PHONE..................614 228-6885
Fax: 614 228-0146
Kortnee Hardin, *President*
Catherine Park, *President*
Joseph Gerling, *Managing Prtnr*
James W Lewis, *Counsel*
Joseph Winner, *Human Res Dir*
EMP: 45
SQ FT: 24,000
SALES (est): 304.2K **Privately Held**
WEB: www.lah4law.com
SIC: 8111 General practice law office

(G-8037)
LANE AVIATION CORPORATION
4389 International Gtwy # 228 (43219-3819)
P.O. Box 360420 (43236-0420)
PHONE..................614 237-3747
Fax: 614 231-4741
Donna L Earl, *CEO*
Brad Primm, *President*
Bob Wing, *Business Mgr*
Timothy Bertrand, *Parts Mgr*
Glenn Blashford, *Sales Staff*
EMP: 130 **EST:** 1935
SQ FT: 172,000
SALES (est): 48.1MM **Privately Held**
WEB: www.laneaviation.com
SIC: 5599 4581 4522 4512 Aircraft, self-propelled; aircraft servicing & repairing; air passenger carriers, nonscheduled; air transportation, scheduled

(G-8038)
LANG STONE COMPANY INC (PA)
4099 E 5th Ave (43219-1812)
P.O. Box 360747 (43236-0747)
PHONE..................614 235-4099
Fax: 614 224-5264
E Dean Coffman, *President*
Bryan Bragg, *COO*
Joan First, *VP Admin*
Joann Coffman, *Vice Pres*
Tom Coffman, *Vice Pres*
▲ **EMP:** 55 **EST:** 1856
SQ FT: 10,000
SALES (est): 20.3MM **Privately Held**
WEB: www.langstone.com
SIC: 5032 5211 3281 3272 Building stone; marble building stone; granite building stone; lumber & other building materials; masonry materials & supplies; cut stone & stone products; concrete products; crushed & broken limestone

(G-8039)
LAPHAM-HICKEY STEEL CORP
753 Marion Rd (43207-2554)
PHONE..................614 443-4881
James Derry, *COO*
Gary West, *Plant Mgr*
George Keel, *Safety Mgr*
Casey Stedman, *Accounts Mgr*
Joni Fritz, *Sales Associate*
EMP: 25
SQ FT: 110,000
SALES (corp-wide): 305.3MM **Privately Held**
WEB: www.lapham-hickey.com
SIC: 5051 3443 3441 3398 Steel; fabricated plate work (boiler shop); fabricated structural metal; metal heat treating; blast furnaces & steel mills
PA: Lapham-Hickey Steel Corp.
5500 W 73rd St
Chicago IL 60638
708 496-6111

(G-8040)
LARRIMER & LARRIMER LLC
165 N High St (43215-2486)
PHONE..................419 222-6266
Darla Kaikis, *Branch Mgr*
EMP: 28
SALES (corp-wide): 5.8MM **Privately Held**
SIC: 8111 Labor & employment law
PA: Larrimer & Larrimer, Llc
165 N High St Fl 3
Columbus OH 43215
614 221-7548

(G-8041)
LARRIMER & LARRIMER LLC (PA)
165 N High St Fl 3 (43215-2486)
PHONE..................614 221-7548
Fax: 614 221-8659
Gavin R Larrimer, *Partner*
Terrence W Larrimer, *Partner*
David France, *Librarian*
Megan Hovanes, *Legal Staff*
EMP: 50 **EST:** 1960
SQ FT: 7,500
SALES (est): 5.8MM **Privately Held**
WEB: www.larrimer.com
SIC: 8111 General practice law office

(G-8042)
LASTING IMPRESSIONS EVENT
Also Called: Lasting Imprssions Event Rentl
5080 Sinclair Rd Ste 200 (43229-5412)
PHONE..................614 252-5400
Fax: 614 252-8755
James P Fritz, *President*
J P Fritz, *President*
Melissa Elison, *Accountant*
Jim Gernstetter, *Sales Mgr*
Carrie Meyer, *Sales Staff*
EMP: 78
SQ FT: 105,000
SALES (est): 3.5MM **Privately Held**
WEB: www.lirents.net
SIC: 7359 Dishes, silverware, tables & banquet accessories rental

(G-8043)
LAW OFFCES RBERT A SCHRGER LPA
81 S 5th St Ste 400 (43215-4323)
PHONE..................614 824-5731
Robert A Schuerger, *President*
Bruce Gurwin, *Opers Staff*
Kelly Hart, *Administration*
Lance Thompson, *Administration*
EMP: 30
SQ FT: 13,500
SALES (est): 3.6MM **Privately Held**
SIC: 8111 General practice law office

(G-8044)
LAWHON AND ASSOCIATES INC (PA)
1441 King Ave (43212-2108)
PHONE..................614 481-8600
Susan Daniels, *President*
Karrie Bontrager, *Exec VP*
Tim Price, *Project Mgr*
Richard Isaly, *CFO*
Michele Glinsky, *Human Res Mgr*
EMP: 38
SQ FT: 16,300
SALES (est): 5.4MM **Privately Held**
WEB: www.lawhon-assoc.com
SIC: 8748 Environmental consultant

(G-8045)
LAWRENCE M SHELL DDS
Also Called: Dental Associates
2862 E Main St Ste A (43209-3709)
PHONE..................614 235-3444
Fax: 614 235-3495
Lawrence M Shell DDS, *Owner*
Cheryl Devore, *Admin Sec*
Lewis Claman, *Fmly & Gen Dent*
Steven Young, *Fmly & Gen Dent*
EMP: 27
SQ FT: 5,000
SALES (est): 1.3MM **Privately Held**
WEB: www.dentalassociatesbexley.com
SIC: 8021 Dentists' office

(G-8046)
LBI STARBUCKS DC 3
3 Limited Pkwy (43230-1467)
PHONE..................614 415-6363
Edward Razek, *Principal*
Boris Sherman, *Senior VP*
Thomas Javitch, *Vice Pres*
Brad Kramer, *Vice Pres*
Paula Leachman, *Vice Pres*
EMP: 230 **EST:** 2013
SALES (est): 13MM **Privately Held**
SIC: 8041 Offices & clinics of chiropractors

(G-8047)
LEADER PROMOTIONS INC (PA)
Also Called: Leaderpromos.com
790 E Johnstown Rd (43230-2116)
PHONE..................614 416-6565
Stephanie Leader, *CEO*
Kathy Weible, *CFO*
Amber Brown, *Controller*
Sune Akarri, *Accountant*

Columbus - Franklin County (G-8048)

David Broxterman, *Accountant*
▲ **EMP:** 75
SQ FT: 14,000
SALES (est) 40.8MM **Privately Held**
WEB: www.leaderpromos.com
SIC: 5199 Advertising specialties

(G-8048)
LEGACY COMMERCIAL FLOORING LTD (PA)
Also Called: Legacy Commercial Finishes
800 Morrison Rd (43230-6643)
PHONE 614 476-1043
Tony Nixon, *President*
Cara Hinkle, *Business Mgr*
George Holinga, *Vice Pres*
Robert McKelvey, *Vice Pres*
Tom Crowley, *Accounts Mgr*
EMP: 251
SQ FT: 6,500
SALES (est) 22.4MM **Privately Held**
WEB: www.legacycommercialflooring.com
SIC: 1752 Carpet laying

(G-8049)
LEGACY FREEDOM TREATMENT CTR
751 Northwest Blvd # 200 (43212-1977)
PHONE 614 741-2100
Alli Becker, *CEO*
Alli Beckerm, *CEO*
EMP: 50 **EST:** 2015
SALES (est) 344.8K **Privately Held**
SIC: 8093 Substance abuse clinics (outpatient)

(G-8050)
LEGAL AID SOCIETY OF COLUMBUS (PA)
1108 City Park Ave # 100 (43206-3583)
PHONE 614 737-0139
Thomas Weeks, *Director*
Eric J Hoffman, *Bd of Directors*
Matthew Krejci, *Bd of Directors*
Joseph L Piccin, *Bd of Directors*
Nicole E Rager, *Bd of Directors*
EMP: 68 **EST:** 1954
SALES: 4.3MM **Privately Held**
SIC: 8111 Legal aid service

(G-8051)
LEIDOS INC
4449 Easton Way Ste 150 (43219-7002)
PHONE 858 826-6000
Fax: 614 473-8859
John Jumper, *CEO*
Christopher Brewster, *Manager*
EMP: 350
SALES (corp-wide): 10.1B **Publicly Held**
WEB: www.saic.com
SIC: 7373 Systems engineering, computer related
HQ: Leidos, Inc.
 11951 Freedom Dr Ste 500
 Reston VA 20190
 571 526-6000

(G-8052)
LEO YANNENOFF JEWISH COMMUNITY (PA)
1125 College Ave (43209-7802)
PHONE 614 231-2731
Fax: 614 231-8222
Tina Rice, *Facilities Mgr*
Ellen Kozberg, *Site Mgr*
Louise Young, *CFO*
Sharon Sadlowski, *Accounting Mgr*
Pamela Andrews, *Human Res Dir*
EMP: 137
SQ FT: 106,000
SALES: 10.2MM **Privately Held**
WEB: www.columbusjcc.org
SIC: 8641 8699 Social club, membership; recreation association; charitable organization

(G-8053)
LEVY & ASSOCIATES LLC
4645 Executive Dr (43220-3601)
PHONE 614 898-5200
Kenneth Santuzzi, *Opers Staff*
Denise Brooks, *Director*
Yale Levy, *Director*
EMP: 47
SQ FT: 12,000
SALES (est) 5.9MM **Privately Held**
SIC: 8111 General practice attorney, lawyer

(G-8054)
LEWIS & MICHAEL MVG & STOR CO
845 Harrisburg Pike (43223-2526)
PHONE 614 275-2997
Charles M Lewis, *President*
David M Lewis, *Vice Pres*
William E Lewis, *Vice Pres*
EMP: 45
SQ FT: 50,000
SALES (est) 3.6MM
SALES (corp-wide): 8MM **Privately Held**
WEB: www.atlaslm.com
SIC: 4212 Moving services
PA: Lewis & Michael, Inc.
 1827 Woodman Dr
 Dayton OH 45420
 937 252-6683

(G-8055)
LEXTANT CORPORATION
250 S High St Ste 600 (43215-4622)
PHONE 614 228-9711
Fax: 614 228-9715
Chris Rockwell, *President*
Spencer Murrell, *Vice Pres*
Paul Rockwell, *CFO*
Holley Smith, *Finance Mgr*
Sherri Dorsch, *Finance*
EMP: 48 **EST:** 2000
SALES (est) 2MM **Privately Held**
WEB: www.lextant.com
SIC: 8748 Business consulting

(G-8056)
LIBERTY COMM SFTWR SLTIONS INC
Also Called: Newfound Technologies
1050 Kingsmill Pkwy (43229-1143)
PHONE 614 318-5000
Padmanbhan Sathyanarayana, *CEO*
Gary Olander, *Principal*
Rodger Marting, *CFO*
Cindy Smith, *Finance Mgr*
Shalini Sathyanarayana, *Director*
EMP: 25
SQ FT: 8,300
SALES (est) 2.3MM **Privately Held**
WEB: www.nfti.com
SIC: 7371 Computer software development

(G-8057)
LIBERTY MORTGAGE COMPANY INC
473 E Rich St (43215-5300)
PHONE 614 224-4000
Fax: 614 227-6776
Karen Richmond, *President*
Dean Richards, *General Mgr*
John Vlahos, *Director*
Mary Fallieros, *Admin Sec*
Jason Lehman, *Administration*
EMP: 49
SQ FT: 4,500
SALES (est) 7.8MM **Privately Held**
SIC: 6162 Mortgage bankers & correspondents

(G-8058)
LICKING-KNOX GOODWILL INDS INC
3990 E Broad St (43213-1152)
PHONE 614 235-7675
Fax: 614 231-8955
Benny White, *Principal*
EMP: 60
SALES (corp-wide): 8.8MM **Privately Held**
SIC: 7349 Building maintenance services
PA: Licking-Knox Goodwill Industries, Inc.
 65 S 5th St
 Newark OH 43055
 740 345-9861

(G-8059)
LIEBERT CORPORATION (DH)
Also Called: Vertiv
1050 Dearborn Dr (43085-4709)
P.O. Box 29186 (43229-0186)
PHONE 614 888-0246
Fax: 614 841-6973
Rob Johnson, *CEO*
◆ **EMP:** 1300
SQ FT: 330,000
SALES (est) 2B **Privately Held**
WEB: www.liebert.com
SIC: 3585 3613 7629 Air conditioning equipment, complete; regulators, power; electronic equipment repair
HQ: Vertiv Group Corporation
 1050 Dearborn Dr
 Columbus OH 43085
 614 888-0246

(G-8060)
LIEBERT CORPORATION
Also Called: Liebert Learning Center
6700 Huntley Rd Ste A (43229-1186)
P.O. Box 29186 (43229-0186)
PHONE 614 841-6104
Fax: 614 841-6107
Cathy Edly, *Manager*
EMP: 60 **Privately Held**
WEB: www.liebert.com
SIC: 7629 Electronic equipment repair
HQ: Liebert Corporation
 1050 Dearborn Dr
 Columbus OH 43085
 614 888-0246

(G-8061)
LIFE CARE CENTERS AMERICA INC
Also Called: Mayfare Village
3000 Bethel Rd (43220-2262)
PHONE 614 889-6320
Amanda Grether, *Office Mgr*
Julie Klein, *Manager*
Charles Tweel, *Director*
Julie Kline, *Administration*
EMP: 100
SALES (corp-wide): 101MM **Privately Held**
SIC: 8051 Convalescent home with continuous nursing care
PA: Life Care Centers Of America, Inc.
 3570 Keith St Nw
 Cleveland TN 37312
 423 472-9585

(G-8062)
LIFE TIME FITNESS INC
Also Called: Lifetime Fitness
3900 Easton Sta (43219-6064)
PHONE 614 428-6000
Wright Josh, *Financial Exec*
Rob Zwelling, *Manager*
Dean Hilton, *Manager*
EMP: 250
SALES (corp-wide): 773.5MM **Privately Held**
WEB: www.ltfcorporatewellness.com
SIC: 7991 7299 Health club; personal appearance services
HQ: Life Time Fitness, Inc.
 2902 Corporate Pl
 Chanhassen MN 55317

(G-8063)
LIFECARE ALLIANCE
Also Called: MEALS ON WHEELS
1699 W Mound St (43223-1855)
PHONE 614 278-3130
Fax: 614 278-3143
Charles W Gehring, *CEO*
Robert Click, *President*
Joseph W Cole II, *Chairman*
John Gregory, *Senior VP*
Andrea Albanese, *Vice Pres*
EMP: 210
SQ FT: 33,000
SALES: 12.6MM **Privately Held**
WEB: www.lifecarealliance.org
SIC: 8082 Home health care services

(G-8064)
LIFECARE MEDICAL SERVICES
3065 E 14th Ave (43219-2356)
PHONE 614 258-2545
EMP: 30
SALES (est) 910K **Privately Held**
SIC: 4119 Local Passenger Transportation

(G-8065)
LIFESTYLE COMMUNITIES LTD (PA)
230 West St Ste 200 (43215-2655)
PHONE 614 918-2000
Michael J Deasecentis Jr, *Partner*
Michael J Deasecentis Sr, *Partner*
Julie Mickley, *Regional Mgr*
Brent Miller, *COO*
Maria Gargrave, *Counsel*
EMP: 53
SQ FT: 40,000
SALES (est) 21.8MM **Privately Held**
SIC: 1522 Multi-family dwellings, new construction

(G-8066)
LIMBACH COMPANY LLC
851 Williams Ave (43212-3849)
PHONE 614 299-2175
Fax: 614 299-4825
Richard Schneider, *Opers Mgr*
William Meadows, *Branch Mgr*
EMP: 28 **Privately Held**
SIC: 1711 Warm air heating & air conditioning contractor; plumbing contractors
HQ: Limbach Company Llc
 31 35th St
 Pittsburgh PA 15201
 412 359-2173

(G-8067)
LIMBACH COMPANY LLC
822 Cleveland Ave (43201-3612)
PHONE 614 299-2175
Terry Griffith, *Controller*
Brian Gifford, *Accounts Mgr*
Jay Sharp, *Branch Mgr*
Heath Wolfe, *Technology*
EMP: 110 **Privately Held**
SIC: 1711 Mechanical contractor
HQ: Limbach Company Llc
 31 35th St
 Pittsburgh PA 15201
 412 359-2173

(G-8068)
LIMITLESS SOLUTIONS INC
600 Claycraft Rd (43230-5328)
PHONE 614 577-1550
Fax: 614 577-1575
Tom Kuhnash, *President*
EMP: 25
SALES (est) 2MM **Privately Held**
WEB: www.limitless-solutions.net
SIC: 7389 Personal service agents, brokers & bureaus

(G-8069)
LINCOLN FINCL ADVISORS CORP
7650 Rivers Edge Dr # 200 (43235-1342)
PHONE 614 888-6516
Terry Sanders, *Financial Exec*
Allmon Jamie, *Personnel Exec*
Jamie Allmon, *Manager*
Edwin Shaffer, *Manager*
Amy Giller, *Admin Mgr*
EMP: 100
SALES (corp-wide): 14.2B **Publicly Held**
SIC: 6411 Insurance agents, brokers & service
HQ: Lincoln Financial Advisors Corporation
 1300 S Clinton St
 Fort Wayne IN 46802
 800 237-3813

(G-8070)
LINDSEY ACCURA INC
Also Called: Hbl Automotive
5880 Scarborough Blvd (43232-4746)
PHONE 800 980-8199
Burt Lindsey, *President*
Kim Blackman, *Executive*
EMP: 45
SALES (est) 7MM **Privately Held**
SIC: 5511 7538 5599 Automobiles, new & used; general automotive repair shops; automotive dealers

(G-8071)
LIQUI-BOX INTERNATIONAL INC
480 Schrock Rd Ste G (43229-1092)
PHONE 614 888-9280
Stewart Grave, *President*

EMP: 100
SQ FT: 63,000
SALES (corp-wide): 228.8MM **Privately Held**
WEB: www.liquibox.com
SIC: **6719** Investment holding companies, except banks
PA: Liqui-Box Corporation
901 E Byrd St Ste 1105
Richmond VA 23219
804 325-1400

(G-8072)
LITHKO RESTORATION TECH LLC
1059 Cable Ave (43222-1201)
PHONE..................................614 221-0711
Fax: 614 221-0769
Scott Rees, *Branch Mgr*
EMP: 40
SALES (est): 2.2MM
SALES (corp-wide): 23.1MM **Privately Held**
SIC: **1771** Concrete repair
PA: Lithko Restoration Technologies, Llc
990 N Main St
Monroe OH 45050
513 863-5500

(G-8073)
LITTLE DREAMERS BIG BELIEVERS
1077 N High St (43201-2439)
PHONE..................................614 294-2922
Sarah Delay, *Director*
EMP: 31
SALES (est): 194.8K **Privately Held**
SIC: **8351** Child day care services

(G-8074)
LIVE TECHNOLOGIES HOLDINGS INC
3445 Millennium Ct (43219-5550)
PHONE..................................614 278-7777
Michael L Ranney Jr, *President*
Thomas Marks, *CFO*
EMP: 100 EST: 2016
SALES (est): 2.6MM **Privately Held**
SIC: **1731** 7359 5099 7819 Sound equipment specialization; lighting contractor; audio-visual equipment & supply rental; video & audio equipment; sound (effects & music production), motion picture; investment holding companies, except banks

(G-8075)
LOEB ELECTRIC COMPANY (PA)
Also Called: Unistrut-Columbus
1800 E 5th Ave Ste A (43219-2592)
PHONE..................................614 294-6351
Fax: 614 291-4129
Charles A Loeb, *President*
Debbie Coffmon, *General Mgr*
M J Walsh, *Principal*
William Adams, *Editor*
Lon Smith, *Vice Pres*
▲ EMP: 95 EST: 1911
SQ FT: 220,000
SALES (est): 180.8MM **Privately Held**
WEB: www.loebelectric.com
SIC: **5063** Electrical supplies; lighting fixtures; circuit breakers; wire & cable

(G-8076)
LONGTERM LODGING INC
Also Called: Abaco Rhbltion Nursing Fcilty
721 S Souder Ave (43223)
PHONE..................................614 224-0614
Mary Rhinehart, *President*
Nellie Burdick, *General Mgr*
EMP: 106
SQ FT: 30,000
SALES (est): 6.4MM **Privately Held**
WEB: www.wecarehealthfacility.com
SIC: **8051** Skilled nursing care facilities

(G-8077)
LOTH INC
Also Called: T W Ruff
855 Grandview Ave Ste 2 (43215-1102)
PHONE..................................614 487-4000
Jason Walaler, *General Mgr*
EMP: 55

SALES (corp-wide): 62.3MM **Privately Held**
WEB: www.lothmbi.com
SIC: **5021** 5712 Office furniture; office furniture
PA: Loth, Inc.
3574 E Kemper Rd
Cincinnati OH 45241
513 554-4900

(G-8078)
LOTH INC
855 Grandview Ave Ste 2 (43215-1102)
PHONE..................................614 225-1933
Fax: 614 460-7747
John Johnson V, *Branch Mgr*
EMP: 55
SALES (corp-wide): 62.3MM **Privately Held**
SIC: **5021** Office furniture
PA: Loth, Inc.
3574 E Kemper Rd
Cincinnati OH 45241
513 554-4900

(G-8079)
LOWES HOME CENTERS LLC
1675 Georgesville Sq Dr (43228-3689)
PHONE..................................614 853-6200
Fax: 614 853-6218
Billy Houghton, *Manager*
EMP: 175
SALES (corp-wide): 68.6B **Publicly Held**
SIC: **5211** 5031 5722 5064 Home centers; building materials, exterior; building materials, interior; household appliance stores; electrical appliances, television & radio
HQ: Lowe's Home Centers, Llc
1605 Curtis Bridge Rd
Wilkesboro NC 28697
336 658-4000

(G-8080)
LOWES HOME CENTERS LLC
3616 E Broad St (43213-1154)
PHONE..................................614 238-2601
Fax: 614 238-2621
Jason Cressy, *Manager*
Shane Thompson, *Manager*
EMP: 150
SALES (corp-wide): 68.6B **Publicly Held**
SIC: **5211** 5031 5722 5064 Home centers; building materials, exterior; building materials, interior; household appliance stores; electrical appliances, television & radio
HQ: Lowe's Home Centers, Llc
1605 Curtis Bridge Rd
Wilkesboro NC 28697
336 658-4000

(G-8081)
LOWES HOME CENTERS LLC
3899 S High St (43207-4013)
PHONE..................................614 497-6170
Fax: 614 497-6173
Dan Gather, *Office Mgr*
Jason Altemose, *Branch Mgr*
EMP: 150
SALES (corp-wide): 68.6B **Publicly Held**
SIC: **5211** 5031 5722 5064 Home centers; building materials, exterior; building materials, interior; household appliance stores; electrical appliances, television & radio
HQ: Lowe's Home Centers, Llc
1605 Curtis Bridge Rd
Wilkesboro NC 28697
336 658-4000

(G-8082)
LOWES HOME CENTERS LLC
2345 Silver Dr (43211-1050)
PHONE..................................614 447-2851
Fax: 614 447-2865
Ed Wuthrich, *Manager*
EMP: 150
SALES (corp-wide): 68.6B **Publicly Held**
SIC: **5211** 5031 5722 5064 Home centers; building materials, exterior; building materials, interior; household appliance stores; electrical appliances, television & radio

HQ: Lowe's Home Centers, Llc
1605 Curtis Bridge Rd
Wilkesboro NC 28697
336 658-4000

(G-8083)
LOWES HOME CENTERS LLC
4141 Morse Xing (43219-6015)
PHONE..................................614 476-7100
Fax: 614 476-7130
Edward Kotalo, *Human Res Mgr*
Mike Cuellar, *Branch Mgr*
EMP: 150
SALES (corp-wide): 68.6B **Publicly Held**
SIC: **5211** 5031 5722 5064 Home centers; building materials, exterior; building materials, interior; household appliance stores; electrical appliances, television & radio
HQ: Lowe's Home Centers, Llc
1605 Curtis Bridge Rd
Wilkesboro NC 28697
336 658-4000

(G-8084)
LSI ADL TECHONOLOGY LLC
2727 Scioto Pkwy (43221-4658)
PHONE..................................614 345-9040
Fax: 614 345-9041
Kevin Kelly, *President*
Dave Feeney, *COO*
Craig Miller, *Vice Pres*
Nick Klein, *Engineer*
Jeff Stonebraker, *Engineer*
EMP: 45
SQ FT: 56,000
SALES (est): 10.7MM **Privately Held**
WEB: www.adltech.com
SIC: **8711** Designing: ship, boat, machine & product

(G-8085)
LTI INC
3445 Millennium Ct (43219-5550)
PHONE..................................614 278-7777
Michael L Ranney Jr, *President*
Andrew Linck, *Vice Pres*
David Zuppo, *Vice Pres*
Ted Karl, *Project Mgr*
Chad Higgins, *Opers Mgr*
EMP: 70
SQ FT: 35,000
SALES (est): 3.2MM **Privately Held**
WEB: www.livetechnologiesinc.com
SIC: **6799** Commodity investors

(G-8086)
LUMENANCE LLC (PA)
4449 Easton Way Fl 2 (43219-7005)
PHONE..................................319 541-6811
Theordore J Messerly,
Mark Luo,
Sharon Pope, *Author*
EMP: 30
SALES (est): 2.5MM **Privately Held**
SIC: **8748** Systems analysis & engineering consulting services

(G-8087)
LUPER NEIDENTAL & LOGAN A LEG
1160 Dublin Rd Ste 400 (43215-1052)
PHONE..................................614 221-7663
Fax: 614 464-2425
Frederick M Luper, *President*
Roger T Whitaker, *Corp Secy*
William B Logan Jr, *Vice Pres*
K Wallace Neidenthal, *Vice Pres*
Jack L Stewart, *Vice Pres*
EMP: 45
SQ FT: 20,000
SALES (est): 5.9MM **Privately Held**
WEB: www.lnlattorneys.com
SIC: **8111** General practice law office

(G-8088)
LUSK & HARKIN LTD
Also Called: Lusk Hrkin Architects Planners
35 N 4th St Fl 5 (43215-3625)
PHONE..................................614 221-3707
Fax: 614 827-6001
Michael Lusk, *Partner*
James L Harkin, *Partner*
Steve McCoppin, *Partner*
James Harkin, *Principal*
EMP: 26

SQ FT: 5,000
SALES (est): 2.2MM **Privately Held**
WEB: www.luskharkin.com
SIC: **8712** Architectural engineering

(G-8089)
LUTHERAN SENIOR CITY INC (HQ)
Also Called: Lutheran Village Courtyard
935 N Cassady Ave (43219-2283)
PHONE..................................614 228-5200
Larry Crowell, *President*
Rev Thomas Hudson, *Chairman*
Phil Helser, *CFO*
Terry Beichtel, *Data Proc Exec*
EMP: 299
SQ FT: 121,000
SALES: 13.2MM
SALES (corp-wide): 49.2MM **Privately Held**
SIC: **8051** Convalescent home with continuous nursing care
PA: Lutheran Social Services Of Central Ohio
500 W Wilson Bridge Rd
Worthington OH 43085
419 289-3523

(G-8090)
LYONS DOUGHTY & VELDHUIS PC
471 E Broad St Fl 12 (43215-3806)
PHONE..................................614 229-3888
EMP: 35 **Privately Held**
SIC: **8111** General practice law office; debt collection law
PA: Lyons, Doughty & Veldhuis Pc
136 Gaither Dr Ste 100
Mount Laurel NJ 08054

(G-8091)
M & A DISTRIBUTING CO INC
871 Michigan Ave (43215-1108)
PHONE..................................614 294-3555
John M Antonucci, *Branch Mgr*
EMP: 98
SALES (corp-wide): 53.7MM **Privately Held**
SIC: **5182** Wine & distilled beverages
PA: M. & A. Distributing Co., Inc.
31031 Diamond Pkwy
Solon OH 44139
440 703-4580

(G-8092)
M J S HOLDING
Also Called: Instanceworkplace
226 N 5th St (43215-2656)
PHONE..................................614 410-2512
EMP: 25 **Privately Held**
SIC: **6719** Holding Company

(G-8093)
M P DORY CO
2001 Integrity Dr S (43209-2729)
PHONE..................................614 444-2138
Fax: 614 444-2130
Thomas Kuhn, *President*
Jeff Kuhn, *Corp Secy*
Chris Cebull, *Vice Pres*
Dean Eschliman, *Project Mgr*
Kevin Kuhn, *Manager*
EMP: 80
SQ FT: 11,000
SALES (est): 14.7MM **Privately Held**
SIC: **1611** Guardrail construction, highways

(G-8094)
M/I FINANCIAL LLC (HQ)
3 Easton Oval Ste 340 (43219-6011)
PHONE..................................614 418-8650
Fax: 614 418-8776
Paul Rosen, *President*
Derek Klutch, *COO*
Kate Elmquist, *Vice Pres*
Philip G Creek, *CFO*
Susan Depuy, *Manager*
EMP: 53
SALES (est): 23.9MM
SALES (corp-wide): 1.9B **Publicly Held**
SIC: **6162** Mortgage bankers & correspondents; mortgage brokers, using own money

Columbus - Franklin County (G-8095) — GEOGRAPHIC SECTION

PA: M/I Homes, Inc.
3 Easton Oval Ste 500
Columbus OH 43219
614 418-8000

(G-8095)
M/I HOMES INC (PA)
3 Easton Oval Ste 500 (43219-6011)
PHONE...........................614 418-8000
Fax: 614 418-8080
Robert H Schottenstein, *Ch of Bd*
Paul S Rosen, *Senior VP*
Marilou Gonzalez, *Vice Pres*
Greg Jones, *Vice Pres*
Bryan Poche, *Vice Pres*
EMP: 290 EST: 1973
SQ FT: 85,000
SALES: 1.9B Publicly Held
WEB: www.mihomes.com
SIC: 1531 6162 Speculative builder, single-family houses; townhouse developers; mortgage bankers & correspondents

(G-8096)
M/I HOMES OF AUSTIN LLC
3 Easton Oval Ste 500 (43219-6011)
PHONE...........................614 418-8000
Irving Schottenstein, *Principal*
EMP: 25
SALES (est): 3.1MM
SALES (corp-wide): 1.9B Publicly Held
SIC: 1531 Operative builders
PA: M/I Homes, Inc.
3 Easton Oval Ste 500
Columbus OH 43219
614 418-8000

(G-8097)
MAGIC INDUSTRIES INC
Also Called: Dent Magic
4651 Poth Rd (43213-1396)
PHONE...........................614 759-8422
David B Miller, *President*
Derrick C Osborne, *Vice Pres*
Roy Gelin, *Manager*
EMP: 50
SQ FT: 6,000
SALES (est): 7.2MM Privately Held
SIC: 7532 5999 Body shop, automotive; mobile telephones & equipment

(G-8098)
MAGNETIC SPRINGS WATER COMPANY (PA)
1917 Joyce Ave (43219-1029)
P.O. Box 182076 (43218-2076)
PHONE...........................614 421-1780
Fax: 614 421-1681
Jeffrey Allison, *President*
Kim Vansickle, *General Mgr*
James E Allison, *Chairman*
Beverly Allison, *Corp Secy*
Sherry Allison, *Vice Pres*
EMP: 70
SQ FT: 100,000
SALES (est): 62.2MM Privately Held
WEB: www.magneticsprings.com
SIC: 5149 5499 Mineral or spring water bottling; water: distilled mineral or spring

(G-8099)
MAGUIRE & SCHNEIDER LLP
1650 Lake Shore Dr # 150 (43204-4942)
PHONE...........................614 224-1222
Fax: 614 224-1236
Patrick Maguire, *Partner*
Paul Schneider, *Partner*
Andrew Maletz, *Vice Pres*
Donald Andrews, *Marketing Staff*
Gayna Strachota, *Receptionist*
EMP: 30
SALES (est): 4.1MM Privately Held
WEB: www.maguire-schneider.com
SIC: 8111 General practice attorney, lawyer

(G-8100)
MAIN STREET FMLY MEDICINE LLC
881 E Main St (43205-1713)
PHONE...........................614 253-8537
Fax: 614 253-8539
Chandre C Gowda, *Principal*
EMP: 26
SALES (est): 1.2MM Privately Held
SIC: 8082 Home health care services

(G-8101)
MAJIDZADEH ENTERPRISES INC (PA)
Also Called: Resource International
6350 Presidential Gtwy (43231-7653)
PHONE...........................614 823-4949
Farah Majidzadeh, *Ch of Bd*
Kamran Majidzadeh, *President*
Steve Johnson, *Vice Pres*
Steven Johnson, *Vice Pres*
Dominic Maxwell, *CFO*
EMP: 50
SALES (est): 29.3MM Privately Held
WEB: www.smpscolumbus.org
SIC: 8711 Consulting engineer

(G-8102)
MANAGEMENT RECRUITERS INTL INC
Also Called: Management Recruiters Intl
800 E Broad St (43205-1015)
PHONE...........................614 252-6200
Fax: 614 252-4744
John Zambito, *Sales/Mktg Mgr*
EMP: 40
SALES (corp-wide): 864.3MM Privately Held
WEB: www.mrwg.com
SIC: 7361 Executive placement
HQ: Management Recruiters International, Inc.
1735 Market St Ste 200
Philadelphia PA 19103
800 875-4000

(G-8103)
MANLEY DEAS & KOCHALSKI LLC (PA)
1555 Lake Shore Dr (43204-3825)
P.O. Box 165028 (43216-5028)
PHONE...........................614 220-5611
Brian T Deas, *Managing Prtnr*
Kate Vanderzee, *Info Tech Mgr*
Edward M Kochalski,
EMP: 58
SALES (est): 35.1MM Privately Held
SIC: 8111 General practice law office

(G-8104)
MAPSYS INC (PA)
Also Called: MAP SYSTEMS AND SOLUTIONS
920 Michigan Ave (43215-1165)
PHONE...........................614 255-7258
Steve Bernard, *President*
Paul Neal, *Corp Secy*
Jim Heiberger, *Vice Pres*
Terry Payne, *Vice Pres*
Scott Abrams, *Engineer*
EMP: 40
SQ FT: 6,000
SALES: 19.3MM Privately Held
WEB: www.mapsysinc.com
SIC: 7372 7371 5045 Business oriented computer software; custom computer programming services; computers, peripherals & software

(G-8105)
MARATHON PETROLEUM COMPANY LP
Lincoln Village Sta (43228)
PHONE...........................614 274-1125
J F Grant, *District Mgr*
EMP: 25 Publicly Held
WEB: www.mapllc.com
SIC: 5172 Gasoline
HQ: Marathon Petroleum Company Lp
539 S Main St
Findlay OH 45840

(G-8106)
MARCUS HOTELS INC
Also Called: Westin Columbus
310 S High St (43215-4508)
PHONE...........................614 228-3800
Tom Baker, *Manager*
Carol Keene, *Admin Asst*
EMP: 43
SALES (corp-wide): 622.7MM Publicly Held
SIC: 7011 Hotels & motels
HQ: Marcus Hotels Inc
100 E Wisconsin Ave
Milwaukee WI 53202

(G-8107)
MARCUS MLLCHAP RE INV SVCS INC
230 West St Ste 100 (43215-2391)
PHONE...........................614 360-9800
Nandy Hart, *Branch Mgr*
EMP: 30
SALES (corp-wide): 719.7MM Publicly Held
SIC: 6531 Real estate agent, commercial
HQ: Marcus & Millichap Real Estate Investment Services, Inc.
23975 Park Sorrento # 400
Calabasas CA 91302

(G-8108)
MARCUS THEATRES CORPORATION
Also Called: Crosswoods Ultrascreen Cinema
200 Hutchinson Ave (43235-4687)
PHONE...........................614 436-9818
Tim Burn, *Branch Mgr*
EMP: 100
SALES (corp-wide): 622.7MM Publicly Held
SIC: 7832 5813 5812 Motion picture theaters, except drive-in; tavern (drinking places); fast food restaurants & stands
HQ: Marcus Theatres Corporation
100 E Wisconsin Ave
Milwaukee WI 53202
414 905-1500

(G-8109)
MARFO COMPANY (PA)
Also Called: Trading Corp of America
799 N Hague Ave (43204-1424)
PHONE...........................614 276-3352
Fax: 614 276-2279
Bill Giovanello, *CEO*
Cheryl Beery, *President*
Carol Gatzke, *Vice Pres*
Carla Jay, *Buyer*
Mary Montgomery, *Buyer*
EMP: 100
SQ FT: 41,000
SALES (est): 21.9MM Privately Held
WEB: www.marsala.com
SIC: 5094 3911 Jewelry; jewelry apparel

(G-8110)
MARION ROAD ENTERPRISES
Also Called: Wasserstom Disrtributing Ofc
477 S Front St (43215-5625)
PHONE...........................614 228-6525
Reid Wasserstrom, *Partner*
EMP: 200
SQ FT: 250,000
SALES (est): 5.6MM Privately Held
SIC: 6512 Nonresidential building operators

(G-8111)
MARKETING RESULTS LTD
3985 Groves Rd (43232-4138)
PHONE...........................614 575-9300
Fax: 614 575-9390
Brady Churches, *Principal*
Karen Waldmann, *Vice Pres*
Jerry Sommers,
◆ EMP: 25
SQ FT: 130,000
SALES (est): 21.1MM Privately Held
SIC: 5023 Home furnishings

(G-8112)
MARRIOTT INTERNATIONAL INC
695 Taylor Rd (43230-6203)
PHONE...........................614 861-1400
EMP: 173
SALES (corp-wide): 22.8B Publicly Held
SIC: 7011 Hotels & motels
PA: Marriott International, Inc.
10400 Fernwood Rd
Bethesda MD 20817
301 380-3000

(G-8113)
MARRIOTT INTERNATIONAL INC
50 N 3rd St (43215-3510)
PHONE...........................614 228-5050
Fax: 614 233-7555
Carol Packett, *Finance Mgr*

Courtney Baker, *Financial Exec*
Jamie Everhardt, *Financial Exec*
Laura Whitehead, *Sales Dir*
Gerie Lonbarob, *Manager*
EMP: 275
SALES (corp-wide): 22.8B Publicly Held
SIC: 7011 Hotels & motels
PA: Marriott International, Inc.
10400 Fernwood Rd
Bethesda MD 20817
301 380-3000

(G-8114)
MARRIOTT INTERNATIONAL INC
7411 Vantage Dr (43235-1415)
PHONE...........................614 436-7070
Fax: 614 436-4970
Shane Ewald, *General Mgr*
Shanna Draper, *Executive*
EMP: 30
SALES (corp-wide): 22.8B Publicly Held
SIC: 7011 Hotels & motels
PA: Marriott International, Inc.
10400 Fernwood Rd
Bethesda MD 20817
301 380-3000

(G-8115)
MARRIOTT INTERNATIONAL INC
2901 Airport Dr (43219-2299)
PHONE...........................614 475-8530
Becky Krieger, *Manager*
EMP: 167
SALES (corp-wide): 22.8B Publicly Held
SIC: 7011 Hotels & motels
PA: Marriott International, Inc.
10400 Fernwood Rd
Bethesda MD 20817
301 380-3000

(G-8116)
MARRIOTT INTERNATIONAL INC
Also Called: Residence Inn By Marriott
2084 S Hamilton Rd (43232-4302)
PHONE...........................614 864-8844
Fax: 614 864-4572
Patty Bollinger, *Sales Dir*
Rob Kennedy, *Branch Mgr*
EMP: 167
SALES (corp-wide): 22.8B Publicly Held
SIC: 7011 Hotels & motels
PA: Marriott International, Inc.
10400 Fernwood Rd
Bethesda MD 20817
301 380-3000

(G-8117)
MARRIOTT INTERNATIONAL INC
Also Called: Residence Inn By Marriott
36 E Gay St (43215-3108)
PHONE...........................614 222-2610
Joey Guiyab, *Branch Mgr*
EMP: 167
SALES (corp-wide): 22.8B Publicly Held
SIC: 7011 Hotels & motels
PA: Marriott International, Inc.
10400 Fernwood Rd
Bethesda MD 20817
301 380-3000

(G-8118)
MARRIOTT INTERNATIONAL INC
Also Called: Residence Inn By Marriott
7300 Huntington Park Dr (43235-5718)
PHONE...........................614 885-0799
Tim Whitehead, *General Mgr*
Christine Clement, *Manager*
EMP: 40
SALES (corp-wide): 22.8B Publicly Held
SIC: 7011 Hotels & motels
PA: Marriott International, Inc.
10400 Fernwood Rd
Bethesda MD 20817
301 380-3000

(G-8119)
MARSH USA INC
325 John H Mcconnell Blvd # 350 (43215-7644)
PHONE...........................614 227-6200

GEOGRAPHIC SECTION

Columbus - Franklin County (G-8140)

Fax: 614 227-6201
Kyle Ewart, *Facilities Mgr*
Tom Hayden, *Branch Mgr*
EMP: 64
SALES (corp-wide): 14B **Publicly Held**
WEB: www.marsh.com
SIC: 6411 Insurance brokers
HQ: Marsh Usa Inc.
1166 Ave Of The Americas
New York NY 10036
212 345-6000

(G-8120)
MARSHALL INFORMATION SVCS LLC
Also Called: Primary Solutions
6665 Busch Blvd (43229-1767)
PHONE 614 430-0355
Molly Oddi, *Human Res Dir*
Brian Marshall, *Mng Member*
Derek Hammonds, *Software Engr*
Kurt Bresko, *Database Admin*
Joanne Marshall,
EMP: 31
SALES (est): 3.6MM **Privately Held**
WEB: www.primarysolutions.net
SIC: 7371 Computer software development

(G-8121)
MARTIN CARPET CLEANING COMPANY
795 S Wall St (43206-1995)
PHONE 614 443-4655
Fax: 614 443-2722
John Martin, *Ch of Bd*
Brent Martin, *Vice Pres*
Chad Martin, *Vice Pres*
Sheila Szabo, *Info Tech Mgr*
EMP: 28
SQ FT: 8,030
SALES (est): 1.3MM **Privately Held**
SIC: 7217 Carpet & rug cleaning plant; upholstery cleaning on customer premises

(G-8122)
MARY KELLEYS INC
Also Called: Mary Kelley's Restaurant
1013 Highland St (43201-3421)
PHONE 614 760-7041
Fax: 614 760-9211
Richard Hammond, *President*
Mary Kelley, *Manager*
EMP: 70
SQ FT: 7,000
SALES (est): 4.4MM **Privately Held**
SIC: 8748 5812 Business consulting; eating places

(G-8123)
MARYHAVEN INC (PA)
1791 Alum Creek Dr (43207-1757)
PHONE 614 449-1530
Fax: 614 444-3541
Paul Coleman, *CEO*
Ron Kerr, *Vice Pres*
Tom Lianez, *Vice Pres*
Michael Cheatham, *Facilities Mgr*
Vivian Russell, *Controller*
EMP: 116 **EST:** 1959
SQ FT: 100,000
SALES: 21.9MM **Privately Held**
WEB: www.maryhaven.com
SIC: 8069 Alcoholism rehabilitation hospital; drug addiction rehabilitation hospital

(G-8124)
MAST INDUSTRIES INC (DH)
Also Called: L Brands
2 Limited Pkwy (43230-1445)
PHONE 614 415-7000
Fax: 614 337-5080
Leslie H Wexner, *CEO*
James M Schwartz, *President*
Ed Schaffer, *Business Mgr*
Mike Koempel, *Exec VP*
Stuart Burgdoerfer, *Vice Pres*
▲ **EMP:** 125
SALES (est): 396.9MM
SALES (corp-wide): 12.6B **Publicly Held**
WEB: www.mast.com
SIC: 5137 5136 Women's & children's clothing; men's & boys' clothing

(G-8125)
MAST LOGISTICS SERVICES INC
2 Limited Pkwy (43230-1445)
PHONE 614 415-7500
Fax: 614 415-7525
Bruce Mosier, *President*
Greg Cunningham, *Assistant VP*
Bernie Brown, *Vice Pres*
Tom Ramsey, *VP Mktg*
Lindsay Chastain, *Marketing Staff*
▲ **EMP:** 150
SALES (est): 176MM
SALES (corp-wide): 12.6B **Publicly Held**
WEB: www.ldsltd.com
SIC: 5113 Shipping supplies
PA: L Brands, Inc.
3 Limited Pkwy
Columbus OH 43230
614 415-7000

(G-8126)
MAST TECHNOLOGY SERVICES INC
Also Called: Limited Technology Svcs Inc
3 Limited Pkwy (43230-1467)
PHONE 614 415-7000
Fax: 614 415-7238
Jon Ricker, *President*
Barbara Golder, *Manager*
EMP: 800
SALES (est): 80.2MM
SALES (corp-wide): 12.6B **Publicly Held**
WEB: www.limited.com
SIC: 7374 Data processing & preparation
PA: L Brands, Inc.
3 Limited Pkwy
Columbus OH 43230
614 415-7000

(G-8127)
MATERN OHIO MANAGEMENT INC
Also Called: Maternohio Management Services
1241 Dublin Rd Ste 200 (43215-7062)
PHONE 614 457-7660
Fax: 614 457-7640
Christophe M Copeland MD, *President*
EMP: 65
SALES (est): 5.3MM **Privately Held**
WEB: www.maternohio.com
SIC: 8011 Clinic, operated by physicians

(G-8128)
MATERNOHIO CLINICAL ASSOICATES
1241 Dublin Rd Ste 102 (43215-7048)
PHONE 614 457-7660
Dan Shemenski, *Principal*
EMP: 25
SALES (est): 2.3MM **Privately Held**
SIC: 8071 Medical laboratories

(G-8129)
MATRIX MEDIA SERVICES INC
463 E Town St Ste 200 (43215-4706)
PHONE 614 228-2200
Fax: 614 228-8404
Charles Mc Crimmon, *President*
Brian Tankersley, *Vice Pres*
Marty Blanton, *Production*
Ashley Griffith, *Buyer*
Catherine Hill, *CFO*
EMP: 30
SQ FT: 15,000
SALES (est): 7.9MM **Privately Held**
WEB: www.matrixmediaservices.com
SIC: 7311 7312 Advertising consultant; outdoor advertising services; billboard advertising

(G-8130)
MATVEST INC
Also Called: Bermex
1380 Dublin Rd Ste 200 (43215-1025)
PHONE 614 487-8720
Fax: 614 487-8783
Mark Everly, *General Mgr*
David Mack, *Opers Mgr*
Chris Covey, *Branch Mgr*
Raymond Tackett, *Manager*
EMP: 30

SALES (corp-wide): 12MM **Privately Held**
WEB: www.bermexinc.com
SIC: 3545 7389 Machine tool accessories; meter readers, remote
PA: Matvest, Inc.
37244 S Groesbeck Hwy A
Clinton Township MI 48036
586 461-2051

(G-8131)
MAXIMATION LLC
2257 A Wstbroke Dr Bldg H (43228)
PHONE 614 526-2260
Fax: 614 777-7967
Ronald Brown, *Owner*
Rick Brown, *Vice Pres*
Kathy Horst, *CFO*
Chad White, *VP Mktg*
Pamela Kolb, *Director*
EMP: 70
SQ FT: 10,000
SALES (est): 4.8MM **Privately Held**
WEB: www.maximation.com
SIC: 7371 Computer software development & applications

(G-8132)
MAYFAIR NURSING CARE CENTERS
Also Called: Mayfair Village
3000 Bethel Rd (43220-2262)
PHONE 614 889-6320
Fax: 614 889-7532
J Edwin Farmer, *President*
EMP: 100
SQ FT: 10,000
SALES: 8.3MM **Privately Held**
SIC: 8051 Convalescent home with continuous nursing care

(G-8133)
MC CLOY FINANCIAL SERVICES
Also Called: New Enland Life Ins Co
921 Chatham Ln Ste 300 (43221-2418)
PHONE 614 457-6233
Fax: 614 442-4594
George W McCloy, *President*
Jeffrey Logan, *General Ptnr*
Teresa Rusell, *Marketing Staff*
Jeff Logan, *Council Mbr*
EMP: 65
SQ FT: 21,000
SALES: 2.5MM **Privately Held**
WEB: www.columbusoh.nef.com
SIC: 6211 6411 8742 Security brokers & dealers; insurance agents; financial consultant

(G-8134)
MCDANIELS CNSTR CORP INC
1069 Woodland Ave (43219-2177)
PHONE 614 252-5852
Fax: 614 258-3097
Dan Moncrief III, *CEO*
Eric Girard, *President*
Ryan Embrey, *General Mgr*
Ken Jones, *General Mgr*
Keith Mathias, *General Mgr*
EMP: 60
SQ FT: 12,000
SALES (est): 15.8MM **Privately Held**
WEB: www.mcdanielsconstruction.com
SIC: 1611 8741 General contractor; highway & street construction; construction management

(G-8135)
MCDONALDS CORPORATION
2600 Corporate Exch Dr (43231-7683)
PHONE 614 682-1128
EMP: 38
SALES (corp-wide): 25.4B **Publicly Held**
SIC: 5812 6794 Operates & Franchises Restaurants
PA: Mcdonald's Corporation
1 Mcdonalds Dr
Oak Brook IL 60523
630 623-3000

(G-8136)
MCGILL AIRCLEAN LLC
1777 Refugee Rd (43207-2119)
PHONE 614 829-1200
Fax: 614 542-2616
James D McGill, *President*

Tom Maurer, *Engineer*
T J Shay, *Sales Mgr*
Tj Shay, *Sales Mgr*
Paul R Hess, *Mng Member*
◆ **EMP:** 70
SQ FT: 15,000
SALES (est): 18.2MM
SALES (corp-wide): 61.5MM **Privately Held**
WEB: www.mcgillairclean.com
SIC: 3564 1796 Precipitators, electrostatic; pollution control equipment installation
HQ: United Mcgill Corporation
1 Mission Park
Groveport OH 43125
614 829-1200

(G-8137)
MCNAUGHTON-MCKAY ELC OHIO INC (HQ)
Also Called: McNaughton-Mckay Electric Ohio
2255 Citygate Dr (43219-3567)
P.O. Box 849 (43216-0849)
PHONE 614 476-2800
Fax: 614 476-2882
Donald D Slominski Jr, *CEO*
William Parsons, *General Mgr*
Michael G Mimnaugh, *Corp Secy*
Richard M Dahlstrom, *Exec VP*
John R McNaughton III, *Exec VP*
▲ **EMP:** 70 **EST:** 1996
SQ FT: 65,000
SALES (est): 101.2MM
SALES (corp-wide): 724.3MM **Privately Held**
WEB: www.mc.mc.com
SIC: 5063 Electrical supplies
PA: Mcnaughton-Mckay Electric Co.
1357 E Lincoln Ave
Madison Heights MI 48071
248 399-7500

(G-8138)
MCR SERVICES INC
638 E 5th Ave (43201-2965)
PHONE 614 421-0860
Fax: 614 421-0865
Wade F Hungerford, *President*
Del Smith, *General Mgr*
Scott Gallagher, *Vice Pres*
Buddy Radebaugh, *Sales Staff*
EMP: 32
SQ FT: 14,000
SALES (est): 13.8MM **Privately Held**
WEB: www.mcrservices.com
SIC: 1542 Commercial & office building, new construction; commercial & office buildings, renovation & repair

(G-8139)
MEACHAM & APEL ARCHITECTS INC
Also Called: MA Architects
775 Yard St Ste 325 (43212-3890)
PHONE 614 764-0407
Fax: 614 764-0237
Mark Daniels, *President*
Jim Mitchell, *Exec VP*
Seth Oakley, *Project Mgr*
Carrie Boyd, *Director*
John Eymann, *Admin Sec*
EMP: 65
SQ FT: 18,000
SALES: 4.5MM **Privately Held**
WEB: www.meachamapel.com
SIC: 8712 Architectural engineering

(G-8140)
MEADOWBROOK MEAT COMPANY INC
M B M
4300 Diplomacy Dr (43228-3804)
PHONE 614 771-9660
Al Monzo, *General Mgr*
Al Monsaw, *Manager*
EMP: 220
SQ FT: 80,000
SALES (corp-wide): 242.1B **Publicly Held**
WEB: www.mbmlc.com
SIC: 5147 5141 Meats & meat products; groceries, general line

Columbus - Franklin County (G-8141)

HQ: Meadowbrook Meat Company, Inc.
2641 Meadowbrook Rd
Rocky Mount NC 27801
252 985-7200

(G-8141)
MED CLEAN
5725 Westbourne Ave (43213-1449)
PHONE...................................614 207-3317
Anthony Christopher, Owner
EMP: 107
SQ FT: 14,000
SALES: 7.2MM Privately Held
SIC: 7699 Cleaning services

(G-8142)
MED RIDE EMS
2741 E 4th Ave (43219-2824)
P.O. Box 30754, Gahanna (43230-0754)
PHONE...................................614 747-9744
Fax: 614 352-2887
Ibrahim Y Halloway, CEO
Abe Halloway, CEO
Robert Oros, Director
EMP: 55 EST: 2007
SQ FT: 12,000
SALES: 2MM Privately Held
SIC: 4119 Ambulance service

(G-8143)
MEDICAL MUTUAL OF OHIO
10 W Broad St Ste 1400 (43215-3469)
PHONE...................................614 621-4585
Fax: 614 932-7255
Mickie Byas, Vice Pres
Sharon Gillespie, Client Mgr
John Stofa, Manager
Pj Apostle, Network Enginr
EMP: 35
SALES (corp-wide): 1.4B Privately Held
SIC: 8011 Medical insurance plan
PA: Medical Mutual Of Ohio
2060 E 9th St Frnt Ste
Cleveland OH 44115
216 687-7000

(G-8144)
MEDIGISTICS INC (PA)
1111 Schrock Rd Ste 200 (43229-1155)
PHONE...................................614 430-5700
Susan Long, President
Roger Broome, Vice Pres
Don Kyle, Vice Pres
Michael Poling, Vice Pres
Judy Cznadel, Purchasing
EMP: 65
SQ FT: 30,000
SALES (est): 9MM Privately Held
SIC: 7389 8721 Charge account service; accounting, auditing & bookkeeping

(G-8145)
MEDONE HOSPITAL PHYSICIANS
3525 Olentangy River Rd (43214-3937)
PHONE...................................314 255-6900
Christine C Quilling, Principal
EMP: 34
SALES (est): 2.5MM Privately Held
SIC: 8062 General medical & surgical hospitals

(G-8146)
MENARD INC
6800 E Broad St (43213-1515)
PHONE...................................614 501-1654
Scott Sirsich, President
EMP: 256
SALES (corp-wide): 13.8B Privately Held
SIC: 7299 Home improvement & renovation contractor agency
PA: Menard, Inc.
5101 Menard Dr
Eau Claire WI 54703
715 876-5911

(G-8147)
MENTAL HEALTH AND ADDI SERV
Also Called: Twin Vly Behavioral Healthcare
2200 W Broad St (43223-1297)
PHONE...................................614 752-0333
Terry Jacobs, Vice Pres
Steven Swartzmiller, Safety Dir
Richard Freeland, Branch Mgr
Dusan Makel, Case Mgr
Missy McGarvey, MIS Dir
EMP: 51 Privately Held
SIC: 8063 9431 Psychiatric hospitals; mental health agency administration, government;
HQ: Ohio Department Of Mental Health And Addiction Services
30 E Broad St Fl 8
Columbus OH 43215

(G-8148)
MENTAL HEALTH AND ADDI SERV
Also Called: Twin Vly Behavioral Hlth Care
2200 W Broad St (43223-1297)
PHONE...................................614 752-0333
Fax: 614 752-0386
Gil Murphy, Personnel Exec
Bob Short, Branch Mgr
Pam Morse, Clerk
EMP: 190 Privately Held
SIC: 8062 9431 8093 General medical & surgical hospitals; administration of public health programs; ; mental health clinic, outpatient
HQ: Ohio Department Of Mental Health And Addiction Services
30 E Broad St Fl 8
Columbus OH 43215

(G-8149)
MERRILL LYNCH PIERCE FENNER
65 E State St Ste 2600 (43215-4254)
PHONE...................................614 225-3152
Jeffrey Wolfe, Vice Pres
Mike Elsner, CFO
Christopher Boyd, Investment Ofcr
Michael Elsner, Investment Ofcr
Kelly Kashmiry, Investment Ofcr
EMP: 60
SALES (corp-wide): 100.2B Publicly Held
WEB: www.ml.com
SIC: 6282 Investment advice
HQ: Merrill Lynch, Pierce, Fenner & Smith Incorporated
111 8th Ave
New York NY 10011
800 637-7455

(G-8150)
MERRILL LYNCH PIERCE FENNER
2 Easton Oval Ste 100 (43219-6036)
PHONE...................................614 475-2798
Fax: 614 475-6469
Alan Beymer, Investment Ofcr
Scott Mann, Investment Ofcr
Thomas Puleri, Investment Ofcr
Beverly Ressler, Investment Ofcr
Valerie Smith, Investment Ofcr
EMP: 48
SALES (corp-wide): 100.2B Publicly Held
WEB: www.merlyn.com
SIC: 6211 Security brokers & dealers
HQ: Merrill Lynch, Pierce, Fenner & Smith Incorporated
111 8th Ave
New York NY 10011
800 637-7455

(G-8151)
MERRILL LYNCH PIERCE FENNER
4661 Sawmill Rd Ste 200 (43220-6123)
PHONE...................................614 225-3000
Fax: 614 225-3166
Chris Brooks, Assistant VP
Clayton Jones, Vice Pres
Jim White III, Vice Pres
Jim Schaine, Exec Dir
EMP: 90
SALES (corp-wide): 100.2B Publicly Held
WEB: www.merlyn.com
SIC: 6211 8742 6282 Security brokers & dealers; financial consultant; investment advice
HQ: Merrill Lynch, Pierce, Fenner & Smith Incorporated
111 8th Ave
New York NY 10011
800 637-7455

(G-8152)
MESSER CONSTRUCTION CO
3705 Business Park Dr (43204-5007)
PHONE...................................614 275-0141
Fax: 614 275-0145
Jason Brett, Regional Mgr
James R Hess, Vice Pres
Kevin Donahue, Project Mgr
Mike Hann, Project Mgr
Sarah Warner, Project Engr
EMP: 100
SALES (corp-wide): 1B Privately Held
WEB: www.messer.com
SIC: 1542 Commercial & office building, new construction
PA: Messer Construction Co.
643 W Court St
Cincinnati OH 45203
513 242-1541

(G-8153)
METAMATERIA PARTNERS LLC
1275 Kinnear Rd (43212-1180)
PHONE...................................614 340-1690
J Richard Schorr, Partner
Diane Gay, Manager
EMP: 27
SQ FT: 3,000
SALES (est): 1.6MM Privately Held
WEB: www.metamateria.com
SIC: 8711 Consulting engineer

(G-8154)
METRO SAFETY AND SECURITY LLC
5785 Emporium Sq (43231-2802)
PHONE...................................614 792-2770
Jeff Clark, Mng Member
EMP: 65
SQ FT: 3,000
SALES: 1.4MM Privately Held
SIC: 7382 7381 Security systems services; fire alarm maintenance & monitoring; protective services, guard; security guard service

(G-8155)
MEYERS + ASSOCIATES ARCH LLC
232 N 3rd St Ste 300 (43215-2786)
PHONE...................................614 221-9433
Dottie Cocola, Accountant
Christopher P Meyers,
EMP: 28
SALES (est): 59.6K Privately Held
SIC: 8712 Architectural services

(G-8156)
MGF SOURCING US LLC (HQ)
4200 Regent St Ste 205 (43219-6229)
PHONE...................................614 904-3300
James Schwartz, President
Dan Bloch, President
Jennie Wilson, CFO
Anna Autullo, Accounts Mgr
▲ EMP: 775
SQ FT: 16,000
SALES: 1.2B Privately Held
SIC: 5137 5136 Women's & children's clothing; men's & boys' clothing

(G-8157)
MICHAEL A GARCIA SALON
2440 E Main St (43209-2441)
PHONE...................................614 235-1605
Fax: 614 235-1065
Michael Garcia, Owner
Leslie Garcia, Co-Owner
EMP: 30
SALES (est): 635.8K Privately Held
SIC: 7231 Hairdressers

(G-8158)
MICHAEL BAKER INTL INC
250 West St Ste 420 (43215-7527)
PHONE...................................614 418-1773
Bill Arrighi, Branch Mgr
EMP: 239
SALES (corp-wide): 592.9MM Privately Held
WEB: www.michaelbaker.com
SIC: 8711 Consulting engineer
HQ: Baker Michael International Inc
500 Grant St Ste 5400
Pittsburgh PA 15219
412 269-6300

(G-8159)
MICRO CENTER ONLINE INC
747 Bethel Rd (43214-1901)
P.O. Box 1143, Hilliard (43026-6143)
PHONE...................................614 326-8500
R Dale Brown, CEO
John F Baker, Ch of Bd
T James Koehler, CFO
Charlene Walker, CFO
Chuck Gammello, Business Dir
EMP: 150
SALES (est): 11.6MM
SALES (corp-wide): 3.3B Privately Held
SIC: 5045 5734 Computer peripheral equipment; personal computers
PA: Micro Electronics, Inc.
4119 Leap Rd
Hilliard OH 43026
614 850-3000

(G-8160)
MICRO ELECTRONICS INC
Also Called: Microcenter DC
2701 Charter St Ste B (43228-4639)
PHONE...................................614 334-1430
Steve Lancaster, Manager
EMP: 80
SALES (corp-wide): 3.3B Privately Held
WEB: www.microcenter.com
SIC: 5045 5734 4225 Computer peripheral equipment; computer & software stores; general warehousing & storage
PA: Micro Electronics, Inc.
4119 Leap Rd
Hilliard OH 43026
614 850-3000

(G-8161)
MICROWAVE LEASING SERVICES LLC
Also Called: M L S
2860 Fisher Rd (43204-3538)
PHONE...................................614 308-5433
C K Satyapriyam,
John Werner,
EMP: 30
SQ FT: 37,000
SALES (est): 7.2MM
SALES (corp-wide): 36.1MM Privately Held
WEB: www.ctleng.com
SIC: 1623 Communication line & transmission tower construction
PA: Ctl Engineering, Inc.
2860 Fisher Rd
Columbus OH 43204
614 276-8123

(G-8162)
MID OHIO EMERGENCY SVCS LLC
3525 Olentangy Blvd # 4330 (43214-4022)
PHONE...................................614 566-5070
Fax: 614 265-2639
Jennifer Bailey, Principal
Tom Nolan, COO
EMP: 25
SALES (est): 1.1MM Privately Held
SIC: 8999 Services

(G-8163)
MID-AMERICAN CLG CONTRS INC
1046 King Ave (43212-2609)
PHONE...................................614 291-7170
Fax: 614 291-4962
Tony Cordoso, Manager
Susan Smetanko, Manager
EMP: 200 Privately Held
WEB: www.corporatesupportinc.com
SIC: 7349 Janitorial service, contract basis
PA: Mid-American Cleaning Contractors, Inc.
447 N Elizabeth St
Lima OH 45801

GEOGRAPHIC SECTION
Columbus - Franklin County (G-8187)

(G-8164)
MID-OHIO AIR CONDITIONING
456 E 5th Ave (43201-2971)
P.O. Box 8397 (43201-0397)
PHONE.................614 291-4664
Fax: 614 291-2365
Rod Burkett, *President*
Jim Jude, *Sales Engr*
Karen York, *Office Mgr*
Matthew Trubee, *Admin Sec*
EMP: 34
SQ FT: 16,000
SALES (est): 7MM **Privately Held**
WEB: www.midohioac.com
SIC: 7623 Air conditioning repair

(G-8165)
MID-OHIO ELECTRIC CO
1170 Mckinley Ave (43222-1113)
PHONE.................614 274-8000
Fax: 614 274-1671
Cynthia Langhirt, *President*
Bruce A Langhirt, *Vice Pres*
Vince Langhirt, *Vice Pres*
Bret Law, *Accountant*
Bob Calkins, *Sales Staff*
EMP: 26
SQ FT: 13,800
SALES (est): 5.8MM **Privately Held**
WEB: www.mid-ohioelectric.com
SIC: 7694 5063 7629 8711 Electric motor repair; motors, electric; circuit board repair; generator repair; electrical or electronic engineering

(G-8166)
MID-STATE BOLT AND NUT CO INC (PA)
1575 Alum Creek Dr (43209-2712)
PHONE.................614 253-8631
Fax: 614 253-1585
David R Broehm, *President*
Stephen English, *Vice Pres*
Curt McCullough, *Vice Pres*
William C McCullough, *Vice Pres*
David A Breault, *Treasurer*
▲ **EMP:** 43 **EST:** 1946
SQ FT: 85,000
SALES (est): 30.3MM **Privately Held**
WEB: www.msbolt.com
SIC: 5085 5072 Fasteners, industrial: nuts, bolts, screws, etc.; bolts

(G-8167)
MIDOHIO CRDIOLGY VASCULAR CONS (PA)
3705 Olentangy River Rd # 100 (43214-3467)
PHONE.................614 262-6772
Anthony T Chapekis, *President*
Becky Olson, *Project Mgr*
Linda Pinkerman, *Office Mgr*
Joseph Mayo, *Med Doctor*
Emile G Daoud, *Director*
EMP: 125
SQ FT: 42,000
SALES (est): 8.6MM **Privately Held**
WEB: www.mocvc.com
SIC: 8011 Cardiologist & cardio-vascular specialist

(G-8168)
MIDWEST ALLERGY ASSOCIATES (PA)
Also Called: Bullock, Jos D MD
8080 Ravines Edge Ct # 100 (43235-5424)
PHONE.................614 846-5944
Joseph D Bullock MD, *Vice Pres*
Lori Knisley, *Office Mgr*
EMP: 25
SQ FT: 9,600
SALES (est): 6.6MM **Privately Held**
SIC: 8011 Physicians' office, including specialists

(G-8169)
MIDWEST FRESH FOODS INC
38 N Glenwood Ave (43222-1206)
PHONE.................614 469-1492
Fax: 614 469-1701
Charles Giller, *President*
Taylor Hunt, *General Mgr*
Cliff Richey, *General Mgr*
Stan Hunt, *Vice Pres*
Ken Roth, *Vice Pres*
EMP: 35
SQ FT: 7,000
SALES (est): 24.6MM **Privately Held**
WEB: www.midwestfresh.com
SIC: 5148 Fruits, fresh; vegetables, fresh

(G-8170)
MIDWEST MOTOR SUPPLY CO (PA)
Also Called: Kimball Midwest
4800 Roberts Rd (43228-9791)
P.O. Box 2470 (43216-2470)
PHONE.................800 233-1294
Fax: 614 219-6101
Patrick J McCurdy Jr, *President*
A Glenn McClelland, *Principal*
Steve Crispin, *District Mgr*
Charles McCurdy, *Vice Pres*
Chas McCurdy, *Vice Pres*
▲ **EMP:** 200
SQ FT: 85,000
SALES (est): 147.9MM **Privately Held**
WEB: www.kimballmidwest.com
SIC: 3965 3399 8742 Fasteners; metal fasteners; materials mgmt. (purchasing, handling, inventory) consultant

(G-8171)
MIDWEST PHYSCANS ANSTHSIA SVCS
5151 Reed Rd Ste 225c (43220-2553)
PHONE.................614 884-0641
Daniel Hiestand, *President*
Jean Davis, *Manager*
Shannon Kuhn, *Manager*
Dustin Arnold, *Anesthesiology*
Edward Chen, *Anesthesiology*
EMP: 98
SALES (est): 13.6MM **Privately Held**
SIC: 8011 Anesthesiologist

(G-8172)
MIDWEST ROOFING & FURNACE CO
Also Called: Midwest Heating & Cooling
646 S Nelson Rd (43205-2599)
PHONE.................614 252-5241
Fax: 614 252-5260
H Terry Hoover, *President*
Ben Davidson, *General Mgr*
Donna Hoover, *Principal*
Leon C Hoover, *Corp Secy*
EMP: 25
SQ FT: 9,000
SALES (est): 3.2MM **Privately Held**
SIC: 1711 1761 1521 1542 Warm air heating & air conditioning contractor; roofing contractor; sheet metalwork; general remodeling, single-family houses; commercial & office building, new construction

(G-8173)
MILES-MCCLELLAN CNSTR CO INC (PA)
2100 Builders Pl (43204-4885)
PHONE.................614 487-7744
Fax: 614 487-7747
Lonnie Miles, *CEO*
Matthew Q McClellan, *President*
Dave McIntosh, *Vice Pres*
Mike Rodriguez, *Vice Pres*
Ted Tinkler, *Vice Pres*
EMP: 28 **EST:** 1978
SQ FT: 19,000
SALES (est): 31.6MM **Privately Held**
WEB: www.miles-mcclellan.com
SIC: 1542 1541 Commercial & office building, new construction; commercial & office buildings, renovation & repair; industrial buildings, new construction; renovation, remodeling & repairs: industrial buildings

(G-8174)
MILLCRAFT PAPER COMPANY
4311 Janitrol Rd Ste 600 (43228-1389)
PHONE.................740 924-9470
Jeff Hannah, *Branch Mgr*
EMP: 28 **Privately Held**
SIC: 5111 Printing paper
HQ: The Millcraft Paper Company
6800 Grant Ave
Cleveland OH 44105
216 441-5505

(G-8175)
MILLCRAFT PAPER COMPANY
Also Called: Columbus Division
4311 Janitorl Rd Ste 600 (43228-1389)
PHONE.................614 675-4800
James G Lovensheimer, *VP Opers*
Bob Moran, *Accounts Mgr*
Eric Michel, *Branch Mgr*
EMP: 28 **Privately Held**
WEB: www.millcraft.com
SIC: 5111 5113 Printing paper; industrial & personal service paper
HQ: The Millcraft Paper Company
6800 Grant Ave
Cleveland OH 44105
216 441-5505

(G-8176)
MIMRX CO INC
Also Called: Scrip Pharmacy
2787 Charter St (43228-4607)
PHONE.................614 850-6672
Rich Friedman, *President*
Al Corfera, *Vice Pres*
Ambu Patel, *Cert Phar Tech*
Anita Roberts, *Cert Phar Tech*
Shauna Setty, *Cert Phar Tech*
EMP: 500
SALES (est): 37MM **Privately Held**
SIC: 5122 Druggists' sundries

(G-8177)
MINAMYER RESIDENTIAL MR/DD SVC
967 Worthington Woods Loo (43085-4816)
PHONE.................614 802-0190
Fax: 614 802-0198
Darla Minamyer, *President*
Dean Minamyer, *Vice Pres*
EMP: 33
SALES (est): 1.4MM **Privately Held**
SIC: 8059 Home for the mentally retarded, exc. skilled or intermediate

(G-8178)
MIRCALE HEALTH CARE
3245 E Livingston Ave # 108 (43227-1947)
PHONE.................614 237-7702
Fax: 614 235-5383
Tedila Zacchaues, *Partner*
Cathy Comer, *Director*
Janie Hampton, *Executive*
EMP: 200
SALES (est): 3MM **Privately Held**
WEB: www.miraclehealthcarecolumbus.com
SIC: 8082 Home health care services

(G-8179)
MISPACE INC
5954 Rockland Ct (43221)
PHONE.................614 626-2602
Aleta Baird, *CEO*
Emily Van, *Admin Asst*
EMP: 30 **EST:** 2009
SQ FT: 800
SALES (est): 556K **Privately Held**
SIC: 7699 Cleaning services

(G-8180)
MJ BAUMANN CO INC
Also Called: M J Baumann
6400 Broughton Ave (43213-1524)
PHONE.................614 759-7100
Lawrence Irwin, *President*
Jean Reed, *Controller*
Bob A Irwin, *Executive*
EMP: 67
SQ FT: 7,200
SALES (est): 8.7MM **Privately Held**
SIC: 1711 Plumbing contractors

(G-8181)
MODLICH STONEWORKS INC
Also Called: Modlich Stone Works
2255 Harper Rd (43204-3411)
PHONE.................614 276-2848
Fax: 614 276-3115
Linus Modlich, *President*
Mark Modlich, *Corp Secy*
Chris Modlich, *Vice Pres*
Chris Di Renzo, *Project Mgr*
Chris D Rienzo, *Project Mgr*
▲ **EMP:** 25
SQ FT: 15,000
SALES (est): 4.6MM **Privately Held**
SIC: 5211 1799 Counter tops; counter top installation

(G-8182)
MOHUN HEALTH CARE CENTER
Also Called: MOHUN HEALTH CARE CENTER GIFT
2320 Airport Dr (43219-2059)
PHONE.................614 416-6132
Fax: 614 251-0338
Maureen Trimble, *Human Res Dir*
Christine Warren, *Human Res Mgr*
Angie Schwart, *Director*
Miranda Fraunfelter, *Hlthcr Dir*
Sister Jacqueline Baum, *Administration*
EMP: 39
SALES (est): 6.6MM **Privately Held**
SIC: 8059 5947 Nursing home, except skilled & intermediate care facility; greeting cards; novelties

(G-8183)
MOLINA HEALTHCARE INC
Also Called: Molina Healthcare of Ohio
3000 Corp Exchange Dr # 100 (43231-7689)
PHONE.................800 642-4168
Scott Merriman, *Project Mgr*
Kathy Mancini, *Branch Mgr*
Sarah McGreevy, *Pharmacist*
Virginia P Fuentes, *Director*
Augustus Parker, *Director*
EMP: 695
SALES (corp-wide): 19.8B **Publicly Held**
SIC: 6324 Hospital & medical service plans
PA: Molina Healthcare, Inc.
200 Oceangate Ste 100
Long Beach CA 90802
562 435-3666

(G-8184)
MONESI TRUCKING & EQP REPR INC
1715 Atlas St (43228-9648)
PHONE.................614 921-9183
Fax: 614 921-9498
Donald Monesi, *President*
Marlene Monesi, *Vice Pres*
Tim Zugaro, *Safety Dir*
Matt Malone, *Traffic Dir*
EMP: 40
SQ FT: 5,000
SALES (est): 5.2MM **Privately Held**
SIC: 4212 Dump truck haulage

(G-8185)
MONRO INC
Also Called: Monro Muffler Brake
4570 W Broad St (43228-1644)
PHONE.................614 360-3883
EMP: 98
SALES (corp-wide): 1B **Publicly Held**
SIC: 7539 Brake services
PA: Monro, Inc.
200 Holleder Pkwy
Rochester NY 14615
585 647-6400

(G-8186)
MOODY NAT CY DT CLUMBUS MT LLC
Also Called: Courtyard By Mrt Clmbs Dwntwn
35 W Spring St (43215-2215)
PHONE.................614 228-3200
Ann Turpin, *General Mgr*
Rabina Colson, *Sales Dir*
EMP: 65
SALES (est): 2.1MM **Privately Held**
SIC: 7011 Hotels

(G-8187)
MOODY-NOLAN INC (PA)
300 Spruce St Ste 300 (43215-1175)
PHONE.................614 461-4664
Fax: 614 280-8881
Curtis J Moody, *CEO*
John William Miller, *Principal*
Paul F Pryor, *Principal*
Wardell Ross, *Project Mgr*
Roger Watson, *Project Mgr*
EMP: 115
SQ FT: 77,000

Columbus - Franklin County (G-8188)

SALES (est): 33.3MM **Privately Held**
WEB: www.moodynolan.com
SIC: **8712** 8711 Architectural engineering; engineering services

(G-8188)
MORGAN STANLEY
4449 Easton Way Ste 300 (43219-7001)
PHONE 614 473-2086
Beth Caravati, *Office Mgr*
EMP: 72
SALES (est): 2.4MM **Privately Held**
SIC: **6282** 6211 Investment advice; stock brokers & dealers

(G-8189)
MORGAN STANLEY & CO LLC
41 S High St Ste 2700 (43215-6104)
PHONE 614 228-0600
Fax: 614 227-2000
Andy Crunpins, *Branch Mgr*
EMP: 50
SALES (corp-wide): 43.6B **Publicly Held**
WEB: www.msvp.com
SIC: **6211** Investment firm, general brokerage
HQ: Morgan Stanley & Co. Llc
  1585 Broadway
  New York NY 10036
  212 761-4000

(G-8190)
MOTEL 6 OPERATING LP
7474 N High St (43235-1446)
PHONE 614 431-2525
Jim Hanson, *Branch Mgr*
EMP: 50
SQ FT: 8,160
SALES (corp-wide): 646MM **Privately Held**
WEB: www.motel6.com
SIC: **7011** Motels
HQ: Motel 6 Operating L.P.
  4001 Intl Pkwy Ste 500
  Carrollton TX 75007
  972 360-9000

(G-8191)
MOTORISTS COML MUTL INSUR CO (PA)
Also Called: MOTORISTS INSURANCE GROUP
471 E Broad St Bsmt (43215-3852)
PHONE 614 225-8211
John J Bishop, *Ch of Bd*
David L Kaufman, *President*
Susan E Haack, *CFO*
Cynthia Feldner, *Manager*
EMP: 32
SQ FT: 300,000
SALES: 133.6MM **Privately Held**
SIC: **6331** Fire, marine & casualty insurance: mutual

(G-8192)
MOTORISTS LIFE INSURANCE CO
Also Called: MOTORISTS INSURANCE GROUP
471 E Broad St Ste 200 (43215-3842)
PHONE 614 225-8211
David Kaufman, *CEO*
John Bishop, *Ch of Bd*
Michael Agan, *President*
Susan Haack, *CFO*
Jim Vermillion, *Accountant*
EMP: 48
SQ FT: 5,000
SALES: 66.4MM
SALES (corp-wide): 494.7MM **Privately Held**
SIC: **6311** Life insurance
PA: Motorists Mutual Insurance Company
  471 E Broad St Ste 200
  Columbus OH 43215
  614 225-8211

(G-8193)
MOTORISTS MUTUAL INSURANCE CO (PA)
Also Called: MOTORISTS INSURANCE GROUP
471 E Broad St Ste 200 (43215-3805)
PHONE 614 225-8211
Fax: 800 876-8407
David Kaufman, *CEO*
Gregory Burton, *Ch of Bd*
Michael J Agan, *President*
Larry Conner, *President*
Thomas Obrokta Jr, *President*
EMP: 550
SQ FT: 300,000
SALES: 494.7MM **Privately Held**
SIC: **6331** Fire, marine & casualty insurance: mutual; automobile insurance; property damage insurance; burglary & theft insurance

(G-8194)
MOUNT CARMEL E DIALYSIS CLNC
Also Called: Fersenius Medical Center
85 Mcnaughten Rd (43213-2174)
PHONE 614 322-0433
Fax: 614 322-0434
Natasha Shaas, *Office Mgr*
Dottie Camiscione, *Director*
EMP: 30
SALES (est): 764.9K **Privately Held**
SIC: **8092** Kidney dialysis centers

(G-8195)
MOUNT CARMEL EAST HOSPITAL
6001 E Broad St (43213-1570)
PHONE 614 234-6000
Fax: 614 234-6611
Joseph Calvaruso, *CEO*
Katie Barga, *QA Dir*
Laura Mangia, *Human Resources*
Jenni Wai, *Pharmacist*
Thomas Brady, *Med Doctor*
EMP: 1100
SALES (est): 144.8MM
SALES (corp-wide): 16.3B **Privately Held**
WEB: www.mountcarmelhealth.com
SIC: **8062** General medical & surgical hospitals
HQ: Niagara Health Corporation
  6150 E Broad St
  Columbus OH 43213
  614 898-4000

(G-8196)
MOUNT CARMEL HEALTH (DH)
793 W State St (43222-1551)
PHONE 614 234-5000
Fax: 614 225-1257
Marcia Ladue, *Principal*
Sloan A Fache, *COO*
Lisa Wallschlaeger, *Project Mgr*
Glenn Shaw, *Engineer*
Jackie Prineau, *CFO*
EMP: 1600
SQ FT: 17,236
SALES (est): 312MM
SALES (corp-wide): 16.3B **Privately Held**
SIC: **8062** General medical & surgical hospitals; hospital, professional nursing school
HQ: Niagara Health Corporation
  6150 E Broad St
  Columbus OH 43213
  614 898-4000

(G-8197)
MOUNT CARMEL HEALTH
730 W Rich St (43222-1620)
PHONE 614 234-8170
Fax: 614 234-6623
Lisa Wallschlaeger, *Project Mgr*
Dave Yoder, *Branch Mgr*
EMP: 110
SQ FT: 3,036
SALES (corp-wide): 16.3B **Privately Held**
SIC: **8322** Senior citizens' center or association
HQ: Mount Carmel Health
  793 W State St
  Columbus OH 43222
  614 234-5000

(G-8198)
MOUNT CARMEL HEALTH SYSTEM (HQ)
6150 E Broad St (43213-1574)
PHONE 614 234-6000
Fax: 614 234-7908
Claus Von Zychlin, *CEO*
Douglas H Stine, *President*
Hugh Jones, *Senior VP*
Kahy Blair, *Vice Pres*
David Cozier, *Vice Pres*
EMP: 800
SALES: 1.2B
SALES (corp-wide): 16.3B **Privately Held**
SIC: **8062** General medical & surgical hospitals
PA: Trinity Health Corporation
  20555 Victor Pkwy
  Livonia MI 48152
  734 343-1000

(G-8199)
MOUNT CARMEL IMAGING & THERAPY
Also Called: Horizons Imaging & Therapy Ctr
5969 E Broad St Ste 100 (43213-1546)
PHONE 614 234-8080
Fax: 614 234-8098
Barbara Emmets, *Manager*
Roger Stile, *Exec Dir*
Brian P Biernat, *Dermatology*
Paul T Heban, *Internal Med*
EMP: 35
SQ FT: 15,000
SALES (est): 2.6MM **Privately Held**
SIC: **8071** X-ray laboratory, including dental

(G-8200)
MOUNT CRMEL HOSPICE EVRGRN CTR
1144 Dublin Rd (43215-1039)
PHONE 614 234-0200
Fax: 614 234-0201
Lorie Yosick, *Director*
EMP: 67
SALES: 6MM **Privately Held**
SIC: **8099** 8082 Medical services organization; home health care services

(G-8201)
MOWERYS COLLISION INC
155 Phillipi Rd (43228-1383)
PHONE 614 274-6072
Fax: 614 274-6601
Richard Mowery, *President*
Jerome Mitchell, *Vice Pres*
Paula Mowery, *Admin Sec*
EMP: 27
SQ FT: 20,000
SALES: 2MM **Privately Held**
SIC: **7532** Body shop, automotive

(G-8202)
MRAP LLC
Also Called: Market Ready Services
1721 Westbelt Dr (43228-3811)
PHONE 614 545-3190
Jeffrey Wilkins, *CEO*
Leah Balcer, *Accountant*
Matt Fulton, *Manager*
John Marihugh, *Info Tech Mgr*
Felicia Harr, *Admin Asst*
EMP: 50
SALES (est): 4.9MM **Privately Held**
SIC: **1799** 1721 7349 6531 Exterior cleaning, including sandblasting; exterior residential painting contractor; interior residential painting contractor; building maintenance services; building cleaning service; buying agent, real estate; real estate agent, residential; selling agent, real estate

(G-8203)
MS CONSULTANTS INC
2221 Schrock Rd (43229-1547)
PHONE 614 898-7100
Fax: 614 898-7570
Thomas E Mozier, *President*
Jason Longbrake, *Business Mgr*
Ed Randall, *Vice Pres*
Bill Steinmetz, *Vice Pres*
Donald Killmeyer, *Transptn Dir*
EMP: 105
SALES (est): 11.8MM
SALES (corp-wide): 39.8MM **Privately Held**
WEB: www.moshsolutions.com
SIC: **8711** Consulting engineer
PA: Ms Consultants, Inc
  333 E Federal St
  Youngstown OH 44503
  330 744-5321

(G-8204)
MSA GROUP INC
Also Called: Crown Logistics
2839 Charter St (43248-4607)
P.O. Box 20405 (43220-0405)
PHONE 614 334-0400
Jeff Hoover, *CEO*
James Carmody Jr, *COO*
EMP: 300
SQ FT: 40,000
SALES: 6MM **Privately Held**
SIC: **5087** 5122 Beauty parlor equipment & supplies; drugs & drug proprietaries

(G-8205)
MUETZEL PLUMBING & HEATING CO
1661 Kenny Rd (43212-2264)
P.O. Box 12489 (43212-0489)
PHONE 614 299-7700
Fax: 614 299-9389
John R Muetzel, *President*
Robert Muetzel, *Corp Secy*
Thomas C Muetzel, *Vice Pres*
Susie Lewis, *Purch Agent*
Dan Muetzel, *Manager*
EMP: 52 EST: 1967
SQ FT: 16,000
SALES (est): 11.2MM **Privately Held**
WEB: www.muetzel.com
SIC: **1711** Plumbing contractors; hydronics heating contractor; warm air heating & air conditioning contractor; process piping contractor

(G-8206)
MULTICON BUILDERS INC (PA)
495 S High St Ste 150 (43215-5695)
PHONE 614 241-2070
Charles P Driscoll, *President*
Peter H Edwards, *Chairman*
Douglas A Hill, *CFO*
Tom Markworth, *Admin Sec*
EMP: 30
SQ FT: 3,000
SALES (est): 3.1MM **Privately Held**
SIC: **6552** 1542 Land subdividers & developers, commercial; commercial & office building contractors

(G-8207)
MULTICON BUILDERS INC
Also Called: Multicon Construction
503 S High St (43215-5660)
PHONE 614 463-1142
Fax: 614 463-9523
Peter H Edward, *Ch of Bd*
EMP: 27
SALES (corp-wide): 3.1MM **Privately Held**
SIC: **6552** 1542 Land subdividers & developers, commercial; commercial & office building contractors
PA: Multicon Builders Inc
  495 S High St Ste 150
  Columbus OH 43215
  614 241-2070

(G-8208)
MULTICON CONSTRUCTION CO
Also Called: Eclipse Real Estate Group
1320 Mckinley Ave Ste C (43222-1155)
PHONE 614 351-2683
Fax: 614 351-2960
Randy Bosscawen, *President*
EMP: 25
SALES (est): 3.6MM **Privately Held**
WEB: www.multiconstruction.com
SIC: **1531** Operative builders

(G-8209)
MUNICH REINSURANCE AMERICA INC
471 E Broad St Fl 17 (43215-3842)
PHONE 614 221-7123
Fax: 614 228-2342
Gordon Avron, *Senior VP*
Robert Beck, *Senior VP*
Michael Kisly, *Vice Pres*
Richard Schultz, *Manager*
Jeffrey Pritektt, *Manager*
EMP: 26 **Privately Held**
SIC: **6331** Fire, marine & casualty insurance & carriers

HQ: Munich Reinsurance America, Inc.
555 College Rd E
Princeton NJ 08540
609 243-4200

(G-8210)
MXD GROUP INC
1650 Watermark Dr Ste 100 (43215-1043)
PHONE..................................614 801-0621
Frank Gaura, *Vice Pres*
Ken Mangen, *VP Opers*
Wendy Brimmer, *Opers Mgr*
Randy James, *Opers Mgr*
Tim Steele, *Opers Mgr*
EMP: 27 **Privately Held**
SIC: 4225 8742 General warehousing; transportation consultant
PA: Mxd Group, Inc.
7795 Walton Pkwy Ste 400
New Albany OH 43054
866 711-3129

(G-8211)
MYERS/SCHMALENBERGER INC (PA)
Also Called: M S I Design
462 S Ludlow St (43215-5647)
PHONE..................................614 621-2796
Tim Schmalenberger, *President*
Keith Myers, *Principal*
Chris Hostettler, *CFO*
Rachael Harkleroad, *Consultant*
Kristy Quinn, *Director*
EMP: 38
SALES (est): 3.2MM **Privately Held**
WEB: www.msidesign.com
SIC: 0781 Landscape counseling & planning

(G-8212)
N WASSERSTROM & SONS INC (HQ)
Also Called: Wasserstrom Marketing Division
2300 Lockbourne Rd (43207-6111)
PHONE..................................614 228-5550
Fax: 614 443-6499
William Wasserstrom, *President*
John H Mc Cormick, *Senior VP*
John H McCormick, *Senior VP*
Craig Dietz, *Vice Pres*
Jim Scott, *Purch Dir*
◆ **EMP:** 250
SQ FT: 175,000
SALES (est): 137.4MM
SALES (corp-wide): 792.7MM **Privately Held**
SIC: 3556 5046 3444 Food products machinery; restaurant equipment & supplies; sheet metalwork
PA: The Wasserstrom Company
4500 E Broad St
Columbus OH 43213
614 228-6525

(G-8213)
NAS VENTURES
4477 E 5th Ave (43219-1817)
PHONE..................................614 338-8501
James Head, *Partner*
Paul Ondera, *Partner*
EMP: 60
SALES (est): 1.5MM **Privately Held**
SIC: 1611 Airport runway construction

(G-8214)
NATIONAL BOARD OF BOILER (PA)
1055 Crupper Ave (43229-1108)
PHONE..................................614 888-8320
Fax: 614 888-0750
Marsha Harvey, *General Mgr*
Michael A Mess, *Principal*
Judy Longhenry, *Facilities Mgr*
Robert Ferrell, *Senior Engr*
Tim Gardner, *Senior Engr*
EMP: 61
SQ FT: 5,000
SALES: 18.6MM **Privately Held**
SIC: 7389 Inspection & testing services

(G-8215)
NATIONAL CHURCH RESIDENCES (PA)
2335 N Bank Dr (43220-5423)
PHONE..................................614 451-2151
Fax: 614 451-0351
Mark Ricketts, *President*
Tim Slemmer, *President*
Jerry B Kuyoth, *COO*
Jacci Nickell, *Senior VP*
Jeff Wolf, *Senior VP*
EMP: 193
SQ FT: 20,000
SALES: 44.4MM **Privately Held**
SIC: 6513 8051 8059 6531 Apartment building operators; apartment hotel operation; retirement hotel operation; skilled nursing care facilities; convalescent home with continuous nursing care; convalescent home; nursing home, except skilled & intermediate care facility; real estate agents & managers

(G-8216)
NATIONAL CHURCH RESIDENCES
2335 N Bank Dr (43220-5423)
PHONE..................................614 451-2151
Steve Bodkin, *President*
Colleen Luft, *Vice Pres*
Jodi Naderhoff, *Treasurer*
EMP: 27
SALES: 332.2K
SALES (corp-wide): 44.4MM **Privately Held**
SIC: 8082 Home health care services
PA: National Church Residences
2335 N Bank Dr
Columbus OH 43220
614 451-2151

(G-8217)
NATIONAL ELECTRIC COIL INC (PA)
Also Called: N E C Columbus
800 King Ave (43212-2644)
P.O. Box 370 (43216-0370)
PHONE..................................614 488-1151
Fax: 614 488-2063
Robert Barton, *CEO*
William Wentz, *General Mgr*
Athena Amaxas, *Principal*
Robert Hodge, *Senior VP*
Danial Bucklew, *Vice Pres*
◆ **EMP:** 300
SQ FT: 500,000
SALES (est): 69.9MM **Privately Held**
WEB: www.national-electric-coil.com
SIC: 7694 Electric motor repair

(G-8218)
NATIONAL GUARD OHIO
Also Called: Air National Guard Med Clinic
7370 Minuteman Way (43217-1161)
PHONE..................................614 492-3166
Bob Schraft, *Manager*
EMP: 86 **Privately Held**
WEB: www.ohionationalguard.com
SIC: 9711 8011 National Guard; ; offices & clinics of medical doctors
HQ: Ohio National Guard
2825 W Dblin Granville Rd
Columbus OH 43235

(G-8219)
NATIONAL HIGHWAY EQUIPMENT CO
971 Old Henderson Rd (43220-3722)
P.O. Box 20262 (43220-0262)
PHONE..................................614 459-4900
Fax: 614 459-4945
William S Dutcher, *President*
Greg Buckey, *Vice Pres*
Terry Miller, *Controller*
EMP: 61
SALES (est): 9.9MM **Privately Held**
WEB: www.nationalhighwayexpress.com
SIC: 4212 4213 Local trucking, without storage; trucking, except local

(G-8220)
NATIONAL HOUSING CORPORATION (PA)
45 N 4th St Ste 200 (43215-3602)
PHONE..................................614 481-8106
H Burkley Showe, *President*
Showe Builders, *Principal*
Betty Hays, *Principal*
Andrew Showe, *Vice Pres*
Hugh B Showe II, *Vice Pres*
EMP: 40 **EST:** 1963
SQ FT: 5,000
SALES (est): 96MM **Privately Held**
WEB: www.nationalhousingcorp.com
SIC: 1522 1542 6513 Apartment building construction; commercial & office building, new construction; apartment building operators

(G-8221)
NATIONAL HOUSING TR LTD PARTNR
Also Called: Nht
2335 N Bank Dr (43220-5423)
PHONE..................................614 451-9929
James Bowman, *President*
Lori Little, *Director*
EMP: 45
SQ FT: 800
SALES: 6.1MM **Privately Held**
SIC: 6726 Management investment funds, closed-end

(G-8222)
NATIONAL REALTY SERVICES INC (HQ)
2261 Sandover Rd (43220-2919)
PHONE..................................614 798-0971
Ronald E Scherer, *Ch of Bd*
Ronald A Huff, *President*
Arnie Berman, *Purchasing*
David B Thompson, *Treasurer*
Thomas Logsdon, *Senior Mgr*
EMP: 25
SQ FT: 8,000
SALES (est): 2MM
SALES (corp-wide): 4.3MM **Privately Held**
WEB: www.nationalrsi.com
SIC: 6531 Real estate brokers & agents; real estate managers; real estate leasing & rentals
PA: National/Rs Inc
5131 Post Rd
Dublin OH
614 798-0971

(G-8223)
NATIONAL RENTAL (US) INC
Also Called: National Rent A Car
4600 International Gtwy (43219-1779)
PHONE..................................614 239-3270
Fax: 614 237-4907
Natilie Martin, *Manager*
Mike Samson, *Manager*
EMP: 30
SALES (corp-wide): 6.1B **Privately Held**
WEB: www.specialtyrentals.com
SIC: 7514 Rent-a-car service
HQ: National Rental (Us) Inc.
6929 N Lakewood Ave # 100
Tulsa OK 74117

(G-8224)
NATIONAL RGSTRY EMRGNCY MDCL
Also Called: National Registry-Emergency
6610 Busch Blvd (43229-1740)
P.O. Box 29233 (43229-0233)
PHONE..................................614 888-4484
Fax: 614 888-8920
Douglas Ehlert, *Business Mgr*
Mark Terry, *Treasurer*
Sara Hammond, *Info Tech Mgr*
Terry Markwood, *Info Tech Mgr*
Severo Rodriguez, *Exec Dir*
EMP: 35
SALES: 14.4MM **Privately Held**
SIC: 8732 8011 Market analysis, business & economic research; offices & clinics of medical doctors

(G-8225)
NATIONAL YOUTH ADVOCATE PROGRA (PA)
1801 Watermark Dr Ste 200 (43215-7088)
PHONE..................................614 487-8758
Kate Riznyk, *Opers Spvr*
Linda Hawk, *QA Dir*
Robert Clay, *CFO*
Jean Sandler, *Controller*
Joyette Smith-Ross, *Human Res Dir*
EMP: 42
SALES: 53.3MM **Privately Held**
WEB: www.iyaf.org
SIC: 8322 Child related social services

(G-8226)
NATIONAL YOUTH ADVOCATE PROGRA
1303 E Main St (43205-2047)
PHONE..................................614 252-6927
Jen Tala, *Director*
EMP: 85
SALES (corp-wide): 53.3MM **Privately Held**
WEB: www.iyaf.org
SIC: 8322 Social service center
PA: National Youth Advocate Program, Inc.
1801 Watermark Dr Ste 200
Columbus OH 43215
614 487-8758

(G-8227)
NATIONS TITLE AGENCY OF OHIO (HQ)
3700 Corporate Dr Ste 200 (43231-4996)
PHONE..................................614 839-3848
Fax: 614 839-3850
Robert Berryman, *President*
EMP: 25
SALES (est): 2.5MM
SALES (corp-wide): 50MM **Privately Held**
SIC: 6411
PA: Nations Holding Company
5370 W 95th St
Prairie Village KS 66207
913 383-8185

(G-8228)
NATIONSTAR MORTGAGE LLC
150 E Campus View Blvd (43235-4648)
PHONE..................................614 985-9500
EMP: 87
SALES (corp-wide): 1.6B **Publicly Held**
SIC: 6162 6163 Mortgage bankers; loan brokers
HQ: Nationstar Mortgage Llc
8950 Cypress Waters Blvd
Coppell TX 75019
469 549-2000

(G-8229)
NATIONWIDE CHILDRENS HOSPITAL
Also Called: Short and Sweet
700 Childrens Dr (43205-2639)
PHONE..................................614 722-2700
Roy Lucas, *Finance*
EMP: 200
SALES (corp-wide): 1.3B **Privately Held**
SIC: 8069 8731 8071 8399 Children's hospital; commercial physical research; medical laboratories; fund raising organization, non-fee basis
PA: Nationwide Children's Hospital
700 Childrens Dr
Columbus OH 43205
614 722-2000

(G-8230)
NATIONWIDE CHILDRENS HOSPITAL
Also Called: Caniano Bsner Pdiatrics Clinic
555 S 18th St Ste 6g (43205-2654)
PHONE..................................614 722-5750
Fax: 614 722-3903
Thomas Hansen, *CEO*
Karen E Hisr, *Vice Pres*
Jon Anderegg, *Research*
Karen Ratliff-Schaub, *Med Doctor*
Jim Jones, *Manager*
EMP: 473
SALES (corp-wide): 1.3B **Privately Held**
SIC: 8069 Children's hospital
PA: Nationwide Children's Hospital
700 Childrens Dr
Columbus OH 43205
614 722-2000

(G-8231)
NATIONWIDE CHILDRENS HOSPITAL (PA)
700 Childrens Dr (43205-2639)
PHONE..................................614 722-2000
Steve Allen, *CEO*
Donna A Caniano, *Chief*

Columbus - Franklin County (G-8232)

Rick Miller, *COO*
Brian Huck, *Bishop*
Theodore L Adams, *Trustee*
◆ **EMP:** 12000
SQ FT: 1,324,000
SALES: 1.3B **Privately Held**
SIC: 8069 Children's hospital

(G-8232)
NATIONWIDE CHILDRENS HOSPITAL
Also Called: Wexner Research Institute
700 Childrens Dr (43205-2639)
PHONE..................614 722-2000
Fax: 614 722-2774
Patty McClimon, *Senior VP*
John Clark, *Vice Pres*
Eric Vaughn, *Vice Pres*
Robert Frietag, *Project Mgr*
Lola Popcevski, *Project Mgr*
EMP: 3000
SALES (corp-wide): 1.3B **Privately Held**
SIC: 8069 8733 Children's hospital; research institute
PA: Nationwide Children's Hospital
    700 Childrens Dr
    Columbus OH 43205
    614 722-2000

(G-8233)
NATIONWIDE CHILDRENS HOSPITAL
Also Called: Columbus Childrens Hospital
655 E Livingston Ave (43205-2618)
PHONE..................614 722-8200
John T Clark Jr, *Senior VP*
Karen Days, *Branch Mgr*
Debbie Quinn, *Anesthesiology*
Ebony Cherry, *Director*
Dana S Hardin, *Endocrinology*
EMP: 473
SALES (corp-wide): 1.3B **Privately Held**
SIC: 8069 8399 Children's hospital; advocacy group
PA: Nationwide Children's Hospital
    700 Childrens Dr
    Columbus OH 43205
    614 722-2000

(G-8234)
NATIONWIDE CHILDRENS HOSPITAL
3433 Agler Rd Ste 1400 (43219-3388)
PHONE..................614 355-0802
Steve Allen, *Branch Mgr*
EMP: 830
SALES (corp-wide): 1.3B **Privately Held**
SIC: 8069 Children's hospital
PA: Nationwide Children's Hospital
    700 Childrens Dr
    Columbus OH 43205
    614 722-2000

(G-8235)
NATIONWIDE CHILDRENS HOSPITAL
Also Called: Close To Home Health Care Ctr
6435 E Broad St (43213-1507)
PHONE..................614 355-8100
Steve Allen, *Branch Mgr*
Jodie Bookman, *Manager*
James Ranjitsingh, *Manager*
Michael Keeley, *Analyst*
EMP: 473
SALES (corp-wide): 1.3B **Privately Held**
SIC: 8069 Children's hospital
PA: Nationwide Children's Hospital
    700 Childrens Dr
    Columbus OH 43205
    614 722-2000

(G-8236)
NATIONWIDE CHILDRENS HOSPITAL
1125 E Main St (43205-1931)
PHONE..................614 355-9200
Steve Allen, *Branch Mgr*
EMP: 473
SALES (corp-wide): 1.3B **Privately Held**
SIC: 8069 Children's hospital
PA: Nationwide Children's Hospital
    700 Childrens Dr
    Columbus OH 43205
    614 722-2000

(G-8237)
NATIONWIDE CHILDRENS HOSPITAL
Also Called: Childrens Hosp Guidance Ctrs
495 E Main St (43215-5349)
PHONE..................614 355-8000
Fax: 614 221-9523
Regina Dewitt, *Vice Pres*
Jamie C Phillips, *Vice Pres*
Marybeth Camboni, *Research*
Melissa Ginn, *Research*
Jessica Prescod, *Research*
EMP: 473
SALES (corp-wide): 1.3B **Privately Held**
SIC: 8069 8093 Children's hospital; mental health clinic, outpatient
PA: Nationwide Children's Hospital
    700 Childrens Dr
    Columbus OH 43205
    614 722-2000

(G-8238)
NATIONWIDE CORPORATION (HQ)
1 Nationwide Plz (43215-2226)
PHONE..................614 249-7111
Fax: 614 249-2134
Steve Rasmussen, *CEO*
Cathy Ellwood, *President*
Damon R McFerson, *President*
Brian O'Dell, *President*
Duncan Griffin, *Division Mgr*
EMP: 27 **EST:** 1947
SQ FT: 9,500
SALES: 25.9B
SALES (corp-wide): 26.6B **Privately Held**
WEB: www.nationwide.com
SIC: 6411 6321 Insurance agents, brokers & service; accident insurance carriers; health insurance carriers
PA: Nationwide Mutual Insurance Company
    1 Nationwide Plz
    Columbus OH 43215
    614 249-7111

(G-8239)
NATIONWIDE CORPORATION
1 Nationwide Plz (43215-2226)
P.O. Box 182794 (43218-2794)
PHONE..................614 249-4302
Paula Edwards, *Manager*
Patricia Szlosek, *Director*
Janice Toomey, *Executive Asst*
EMP: 80
SALES (corp-wide): 26.6B **Privately Held**
WEB: www.nationwide.com
SIC: 6411 Insurance agents, brokers & service
HQ: Nationwide Corporation
    1 Nationwide Plz
    Columbus OH 43215
    614 249-7111

(G-8240)
NATIONWIDE ENERGY PARTNERS LLC
230 West St Ste 150 (43215-2785)
PHONE..................614 918-2031
Dan Lhota, *President*
Jay Tribbie, *Project Mgr*
Robert Davis, *CFO*
Rick Eurich, *Controller*
David Johnson, *Controller*
EMP: 36
SALES (est): 4.5MM **Privately Held**
WEB: www.nationwideenergypartners.com
SIC: 1731 8748 Electrical work; energy conservation consultant

(G-8241)
NATIONWIDE FIN INST DIS AGENCY
1 Nationwide Plz 2-0501 (43215-2226)
PHONE..................614 249-6825
Mark R Thresher, *CEO*
David L Giertz, *President*
Richard Karas, *President*
Barb Boyd, *Assistant VP*
Conrad Bubis, *Manager*
EMP: 60
SQ FT: 10,000
SALES (est): 6.9MM
SALES (corp-wide): 26.6B **Privately Held**
SIC: 6411 Mutual funds, selling by independent salesperson

HQ: Nationwide Corporation
    1 Nationwide Plz
    Columbus OH 43215
    614 249-7111

(G-8242)
NATIONWIDE FINANCIAL SVCS INC (DH)
1 Nationwide Plz (43215-2226)
P.O. Box 182049 (43218-2049)
PHONE..................614 249-7111
Fax: 614 249-4553
Mark R Thresher, *President*
Vince Antonucci, *President*
Keith D Bernard, *President*
Cortez Crosby, *President*
Eric Freud, *President*
EMP: 117
SQ FT: 898,000
SALES (est): 15.9B
SALES (corp-wide): 26.6B **Privately Held**
WEB: www.nationwidefinancial.com
SIC: 6311 6411 8742 Life insurance; pension & retirement plan consultants; life insurance agents; advisory services, insurance; banking & finance consultant
HQ: Nationwide Corporation
    1 Nationwide Plz
    Columbus OH 43215
    614 249-7111

(G-8243)
NATIONWIDE GENERAL INSUR CO
1 W Nationwide Blvd # 100 (43215-2752)
P.O. Box 182171 (43218-2171)
PHONE..................614 249-7111
Harold Weihl, *Ch of Bd*
Dimon Richard Mc Frson, *President*
Richard D Crabtree, *President*
Dimon Richard Mc Ferson, *President*
Brenda L Ross-Mathes, *President*
EMP: 75
SQ FT: 10,000
SALES (est): 52.7MM
SALES (corp-wide): 26.6B **Privately Held**
WEB: www.nirassn.com
SIC: 6311 6331 7389 8741 Life insurance; fire, marine & casualty insurance; financial services; administrative management
PA: Nationwide Mutual Insurance Company
    1 Nationwide Plz
    Columbus OH 43215
    614 249-7111

(G-8244)
NATIONWIDE INV SVCS CORP
2 Nationwide Plz (43215-2534)
PHONE..................614 249-7111
Duane Meek, *President*
EMP: 75
SALES (est): 12.2MM
SALES (corp-wide): 26.6B **Privately Held**
WEB: www.nationwideinsurance.com
SIC: 6211 Security brokers & dealers
HQ: Nationwide Life Insurance Company
    1 Nationwide Plz
    Columbus OH 43215
    877 669-6877

(G-8245)
NATIONWIDE LIFE INSUR CO AMER
P.O. Box 182928 (43218-2928)
PHONE..................800 688-5177
Fax: 610 407-1322
Gary D McMahan, *President*
James G Potter Jr, *Exec VP*
Joan Tucker, *Exec VP*
Sarah Coxe Lange, *Senior VP*
Jim Benson, *Vice Pres*
◆ **EMP:** 1500 **EST:** 1865
SQ FT: 110,000
SALES (est): 211.1MM
SALES (corp-wide): 26.6B **Privately Held**
SIC: 6411 6211 6719 Insurance agents; brokers, security; investment holding companies, except banks
HQ: Nationwide Financial Services, Inc.
    1 Nationwide Plz
    Columbus OH 43215

(G-8246)
NATIONWIDE MUTL FIRE INSUR CO (HQ)
1 W Nationwide Blvd # 100 (43215-2752)
P.O. Box 182171 (43218-2171)
PHONE..................614 249-7111
Dimon R Mc Ferson, *Ch of Bd*
Richard D Crabtree, *President*
Gordon E Mc Cutchan, *Exec VP*
Robert J Woodward Jr, *Exec VP*
Duane M Campbell, *Vice Pres*
EMP: 33
SALES: 4.3B
SALES (corp-wide): 26.6B **Privately Held**
SIC: 6411 Insurance agents
PA: Nationwide Mutual Insurance Company
    1 Nationwide Plz
    Columbus OH 43215
    614 249-7111

(G-8247)
NATIONWIDE MUTUAL INSURANCE CO (PA)
1 Nationwide Plz (43215-2226)
P.O. Box 182171 (43218-2171)
PHONE..................614 249-7111
Fax: 614 791-0203
Steve Rasmussen, *CEO*
Anne Arvia, *President*
Erik Bennett, *President*
Larry Hilsheimer, *President*
Angie Klett, *President*
EMP: 6953
SQ FT: 1,328,797
SALES: 26.6B **Privately Held**
WEB: www.nirassn.com
SIC: 6331 6311 6321 6531 Fire, marine & casualty insurance: mutual; property damage insurance; automobile insurance; life insurance carriers; accident insurance carriers; health insurance carriers; real estate agents & managers

(G-8248)
NATIONWIDE RLTY INVESTORS LTD (HQ)
Also Called: N R I
375 N Front St Ste 200 (43215-2258)
PHONE..................614 857-2330
Fax: 614 857-2346
Brian Ellis, *Managing Prtnr*
Tina Guegold, *Treasurer*
Stephen Simms, *Manager*
Erin Uritus, *Manager*
Shelley Stevens, *Administration*
EMP: 29
SALES (est): 2.6MM
SALES (corp-wide): 26.6B **Privately Held**
SIC: 6552 Subdividers & developers
PA: Nationwide Mutual Insurance Company
    1 Nationwide Plz
    Columbus OH 43215
    614 249-7111

(G-8249)
NATURAL RESOURCES OHIO DEPT
Also Called: Division of Engineering
2045 Morse Rd Bldg C (43229-6693)
PHONE..................614 265-6948
Steve Manila, *Chief*
EMP: 40 **Privately Held**
WEB: www.ohiostateparks.com
SIC: 8711 9512 9199 Engineering services; civil engineering; land, mineral & wildlife conservation;
HQ: Ohio Department Of Natural Resources
    2045 Morse Rd Bldg D-3
    Columbus OH 43229

(G-8250)
NATURAL RESOURCES OHIO DEPT
Also Called: Odnr Computer Communication
1894 Fountain Square Ct (43224-1360)
PHONE..................614 265-6852
Greg Mountz, *Manager*
Mark Ogden, *Administration*
EMP: 39 **Privately Held**
WEB: www.ohiostateparks.com

GEOGRAPHIC SECTION
Columbus - Franklin County (G-8274)

SIC: 7379 9512 8731 7373 Computer related consulting services; land, mineral & wildlife conservation; ; commercial physical research; computer integrated systems design
HQ: Ohio Department Of Natural Resources
2045 Morse Rd Bldg D-3
Columbus OH 43229

(G-8251)
NAVIGTOR MGT PRTNERS LTD LBLTY
1400 Goodale Blvd Ste 100 (43212-3777)
PHONE..................614 796-0090
David K Schoettmer, *Senior Partner*
Arturo Sanabria, *General Mgr*
Heather Bodak, *Finance*
Kristen Kipnes, *Human Resources*
Kristen Phelps, *Human Resources*
EMP: 43
SQ FT: 3,500
SALES: 39.4MM **Privately Held**
WEB: www.navmp.com
SIC: 7379 8742 Computer related consulting services; management consulting services

(G-8252)
NBBJ LLC (PA)
Also Called: NBBJ Construction Services
250 S High St Ste 300 (43215-4629)
PHONE..................206 223-5026
Fax: 614 224-9907
Brenda Clark, *Controller*
Debra Castle, *Manager*
Meredith Doppelt, *Manager*
David Lenox, *Manager*
Jejett Miller, *Manager*
EMP: 150
SALES: 26.5MM **Privately Held**
WEB: www.nbbj.com
SIC: 8712 Architectural engineering

(G-8253)
NCR AT HOME HEALTH & WELLNESS
2335 N Bank Dr (43220-5423)
PHONE..................614 451-2151
Teresa Alltton, *President*
Tanya K Hahn, *Senior VP*
Jacci Nickell, *Senior VP*
Tara Wenger, *QA Dir*
Megan Searles, *Human Resources*
EMP: 75
SALES: 323.9K
SALES (corp-wide): 44.4MM **Privately Held**
SIC: 8082 Home health care services
PA: National Church Residences
2335 N Bank Dr
Columbus OH 43220
614 451-2151

(G-8254)
NCS HEALTHCARE OF OHIO LLC
Also Called: Omnicare of Central Ohio
2305 Westbrooke Dr Bldg C (43228-9624)
P.O. Box 520, Hilliard (43026-0520)
PHONE..................614 534-0400
Stefan Stewart, *Branch Mgr*
EMP: 49
SALES (corp-wide): 184.7B **Publicly Held**
SIC: 5122 Drugs, proprietaries & sundries
HQ: Ncs Healthcare Of Ohio, Llc
201 E 4th St Ste 900
Cincinnati OH 45202

(G-8255)
NEACE ASSOC INSUR AGCY OF OHIO
285 Cozzins St (43215-2334)
PHONE..................614 224-0772
Jeff Kurz, *Manager*
EMP: 48 **Privately Held**
WEB: www.neacelukens.com
SIC: 6411 Insurance agents, brokers & service
PA: Neace & Associates Insurance Agency Of Ohio, Inc
5905 E Galbraith Rd
Cincinnati OH 45236

(G-8256)
NEIGHBORHOOD HOUSE (PA)
1000 Atcheson St (43203-1353)
P.O. Box 555, Blacklick (43004-0555)
PHONE..................614 252-4941
Fax: 614 252-7919
Charles Wheeler, *President*
Tony Ransom, *Director*
EMP: 51
SQ FT: 30,000
SALES (est): 1.8MM **Privately Held**
SIC: 8351 8093 8322 Child day care services; specialty outpatient clinics; individual & family services; senior citizens' center or association; settlement house

(G-8257)
NEST TENDERS LIMITED
Also Called: Two Men & A Truck
5083 Westerville Rd (43231-4909)
PHONE..................614 901-1570
Fax: 614 901-1577
Gail Kelley, *President*
Steve Barton, *General Mgr*
Rob Wallace, *General Mgr*
John Kelley, *Vice Pres*
Stephanie Clarey, *Sales Staff*
EMP: 100
SQ FT: 22,000
SALES (est): 10.1MM **Privately Held**
SIC: 4212 Moving services

(G-8258)
NETCARE CORPORATION (PA)
Also Called: Netcare Access
199 S Cent Ave (43223)
PHONE..................614 274-9500
A King Stumpp, *President*
P G Baynes, *Principal*
J A Bonham, *Principal*
W Brannon, *Principal*
W Colwell, *Principal*
EMP: 100
SQ FT: 30,000
SALES: 14.1MM **Privately Held**
SIC: 8049 Psychologist, psychotherapist & hypnotist

(G-8259)
NETCARE CORPORATION
741 E Broad St (43205-1001)
PHONE..................614 274-9500
Diane Durkim, *Branch Mgr*
EMP: 40
SALES (corp-wide): 14.1MM **Privately Held**
SIC: 8049 Psychologist, psychotherapist & hypnotist
PA: Netcare Corporation
199 S Cent Ave
Columbus OH 43223
614 274-9500

(G-8260)
NETJETS ASSN SHRED ARCFT PLOTS
Also Called: Njasap
2740 Airport Dr (43219-2286)
PHONE..................614 863-2008
John Malmborg, *President*
Paul Konrath, *Vice Pres*
Jason Layman, *Vice Pres*
Chip Johnson, *Accountant*
Brooke Scherer, *Accountant*
EMP: 75
SALES: 5.1MM **Privately Held**
SIC: 7363 Pilot service, aviation

(G-8261)
NETJETS INC (HQ)
4111 Bridgeway Ave (43219-1882)
PHONE..................614 239-5500
Adam Johnson, *CEO*
Bill Noe, *President*
Eric Blind, *Editor*
Robert Molsbergen, *COO*
Nathan Speiser, *Counsel*
EMP: 25
SALES: 3.8B
SALES (corp-wide): 242.1B **Publicly Held**
WEB: www.netjets.com
SIC: 4522 5088 7359 Flying charter service; aircraft & parts; aircraft rental

PA: Berkshire Hathaway Inc.
3555 Farnam St Ste 1140
Omaha NE 68131
402 346-1400

(G-8262)
NETJETS INTERNATIONAL INC (DH)
4111 Bridgeway Ave (43219-1882)
PHONE..................614 239-5500
Lesha Thorpe, *Treasurer*
EMP: 665 EST: 1995
SQ FT: 22,500
SALES (est): 33.1MM
SALES (corp-wide): 242.1B **Publicly Held**
SIC: 4522 Flying charter service
HQ: Netjets Inc.
4111 Bridgeway Ave
Columbus OH 43219
614 239-5500

(G-8263)
NETJETS LARGE AIRCRAFT INC
4111 Bridgeway Ave (43219-1882)
PHONE..................614 239-4853
Michael Wargotz, *Principal*
Peter S Richards, *Senior VP*
Richard G Smith, *Manager*
Steve Ohl, *Administration*
David Beach, *Assistant*
EMP: 71
SALES (est): 5.2MM **Privately Held**
SIC: 4581 Aircraft maintenance & repair services

(G-8264)
NETJETS SALES INC
4111 Bridgeway Ave (43219-1882)
P.O. Box 369099 (43236-9099)
PHONE..................614 239-5500
Bill Noe, *President*
Ed Bensen, *Senior VP*
Rick Montgomery, *QA Dir*
Lesha Thorpe, *Treasurer*
Greg Rapp, *Manager*
EMP: 200
SALES (est): 118.3MM
SALES (corp-wide): 242.1B **Publicly Held**
SIC: 5088 4522 Aircraft & parts; air transportation, nonscheduled
HQ: Netjets Inc.
4111 Bridgeway Ave
Columbus OH 43219
614 239-5500

(G-8265)
NETWORK HOUSING 2005 INC
1680 Watermark Dr (43215-1034)
PHONE..................614 487-6700
Susan E Weaver, *Exec Dir*
EMP: 99
SQ FT: 1,024
SALES: 117.1K **Privately Held**
SIC: 8361 Home for the mentally handicapped

(G-8266)
NETWORK RESTORATIONS II
Also Called: Nr2
129 E 7th Ave (43201-2589)
PHONE..................614 253-0984
Michelle Hert, *Principal*
EMP: 55
SALES: 060K **Privately Held**
SIC: 6513 Apartment building operators

(G-8267)
NETWORK RESTORATIONS III LLC
Also Called: Nr3
910 E Broad St (43205-1150)
PHONE..................614 253-0984
Michelle Hert,
EMP: 55
SALES: 950K **Privately Held**
SIC: 6513 Apartment building operators

(G-8268)
NEUROLOGICAL ASSOCIATES INC
931 Chatham Ln Ste 200 (43221-2486)
PHONE..................614 544-4455

Fax: 614 326-0018
Jeff Ubank, *President*
J Alan Logeay, *COO*
Edward J Kosnik, *Treasurer*
Laura A Popelr, *Manager*
Michele J Meagher, *Admin Sec*
EMP: 60
SALES (est): 5MM **Privately Held**
WEB: www.neuroassociates.com
SIC: 8011 Neurologist; surgeon

(G-8269)
NEUROSCIENCE CENTER INC
Also Called: Department of Neurology
1654 Upham Dr Fl 4 (43210-1250)
PHONE..................614 293-8930
Fax: 614 293-6111
Jerry Mendell, *President*
Andrew P Slivka Jr, *Med Doctor*
EMP: 85
SALES (est): 2.5MM **Privately Held**
SIC: 8062 General medical & surgical hospitals

(G-8270)
NEW ALBANY CARE CENTER LLC
5691 Thompson Rd (43230-1345)
PHONE..................614 855-8866
Fax: 614 855-8880
Melanie O'Neil, *Principal*
Chelsea Jackson, *Financial Exec*
Ashely Mans, *Manager*
EMP: 125
SALES (est): 4.7MM **Privately Held**
SIC: 8051 Convalescent home with continuous nursing care

(G-8271)
NEW BGNNNGS ASSEMBLY OF GOD CH
492 Williams Rd (43207-5156)
PHONE..................614 497-2658
Fax: 614 497-2171
Samuel J Kirk Jr, *President*
Margaret Kirk, *VP Mktg*
Charlotte Roff, *VP Mktg*
EMP: 25
SQ FT: 3,640
SALES: 180K **Privately Held**
SIC: 8661 8351 Assembly of God Church; child day care services

(G-8272)
NEW ENGLAND LIFE INSURANCE CO
Also Called: New England Securities
921 Chatham Ln Ste 300 (43221-2418)
PHONE..................614 457-6233
Fax: 614 457-8525
Yolande Circosta, *Manager*
EMP: 50
SALES (corp-wide): 63.4B **Publicly Held**
WEB: www.thehoovercompanies.com
SIC: 6411 Insurance agents
HQ: The New England Life Insurance Company
501 Boylston St Ste 500
Boston MA 02116
617 578-2000

(G-8273)
NEW JERSEY AQUARIUM LLC
4016 Townsfair Way # 201 (43219-6083)
PHONE..................614 414-7300
Yaromir Steiner, *Mng Member*
Sheri Kamer, *Manager*
EMP: 100
SALES (est): 2.2MM **Privately Held**
WEB: www.adventureaquarium.com
SIC: 7299 Banquet hall facilities

(G-8274)
NEWARK PARCEL SERVICE COMPANY
640 N Cassady Ave (43219-2721)
PHONE..................614 253-3777
Fax: 614 253-1330
Patrick Sullivan, *President*
EMP: 33
SQ FT: 60,000
SALES (est): 7.3MM **Privately Held**
WEB: www.npsfrt.com
SIC: 4731 Freight transportation arrangement

Columbus - Franklin County (G-8275)

(G-8275)
NEXSTAR BROADCASTING INC
Also Called: Wcmh
3165 Olentangy River Rd (43202-1518)
PHONE 614 263-4444
Fax: 614 447-9107
Steve King, Engineer
Jody Van Fossen, Manager
Dan Rositano, Manager
Anthony Weems, CIO
EMP: 151
SALES (corp-wide): 2.4B Publicly Held
WEB: www.media-general.com
SIC: 4833 Television broadcasting stations
HQ: Nexstar Broadcasting, Inc.
545 E John Carpenter Fwy # 700
Irving TX 75062
972 373-8800

(G-8276)
NEXUS COMMUNICATIONS INC
Also Called: Reachout Wireless
2631 Morse Rd (43231-5931)
PHONE 740 549-1092
Steve Fenker, President
Steve Crea, CFO
EMP: 50
SALES (est): 5.5MM Privately Held
SIC: 8748 Business consulting

(G-8277)
NIAGARA HEALTH CORPORATION (HQ)
6150 E Broad St (43213-1574)
PHONE 614 898-4000
Randall E Moore, Principal
Jessica Amendolare, Marketing Mgr
Brandi Pennington, Marketing Mgr
Jillian Buschman, Manager
Lora Miller, Manager
EMP: 200
SALES (est): 459MM
SALES (corp-wide): 16.3B Privately Held
WEB: www.mchs.com
SIC: 8741 8062 Hospital management; general medical & surgical hospitals
PA: Trinity Health Corporation
20555 Victor Pkwy
Livonia MI 48152
734 343-1000

(G-8278)
NICHOLSON BUILDERS INC
6525 Busch Blvd Ste 101 (43229-1789)
PHONE 614 846-8621
Fax: 614 846-7390
William Nicholson, Owner
Mike Fought, General Mgr
Mike Cairns, Executive
EMP: 47
SALES (est): 6.2MM Privately Held
SIC: 1521 New construction, single-family houses

(G-8279)
NIGHTINGALE HOME CARE
3380 Tremont Rd Ste 270 (43221-2140)
PHONE 614 457-6006
Fax: 614 442-2020
Judy Dorsi, President
Sandy Dillion, Executive
EMP: 35
SALES: 2.2MM Privately Held
SIC: 8082 Home health care services

(G-8280)
NISOURCE INC
290 W Nationwide Blvd (43215-2561)
PHONE 614 460-4878
Todd M Rodgers, Counsel
Charles Shafer, Vice Pres
Joseph M Siget Jr, Auditing Mgr
Julie Benner, Human Resources
Sarah M Perry, Corp Comm Staff
EMP: 34
SALES (corp-wide): 4.8B Publicly Held
SIC: 4911 Electric services
PA: Nisource Inc.
801 E 86th Ave
Merrillville IN 46410
877 647-5990

(G-8281)
NITSCHKE SAMPSON DIETZ INC
990 W 3rd Ave (43212-3127)
PHONE 614 464-1933
Fax: 614 298-2149
Thomas Sampson, CEO
John Behal, Principal
Keith De Voe III, Principal
James F Dietz, Treasurer
Brad Wilson, Controller
EMP: 25
SQ FT: 9,500
SALES (est): 4.6MM Privately Held
WEB: www.bsdarchitects.com
SIC: 1521 8712 1542 1522 General remodeling, single-family houses; architectural services; nonresidential construction; residential construction

(G-8282)
NJ EXECUTIVE SERVICES INC
4111 Bridgeway Ave (43219-1882)
PHONE 614 239-2996
Steve Ohl, Administration
EMP: 42
SALES (est): 4.6MM Privately Held
SIC: 5088 Aircraft equipment & supplies

(G-8283)
NL OF KY INC
Also Called: Neace Lukens
285 Cozzins St (43215-2334)
PHONE 614 224-0772
Linda Dvorak, Accounts Mgr
Aimee Geraci, Accounts Exec
Clete Richardson, Accounts Exec
Jeff Kurz, Manager
EMP: 49 Privately Held
SIC: 6411 Insurance agents
HQ: Nl Of Ky, Inc.
2305 River Rd
Louisville KY 40206

(G-8284)
NORFOLK SOUTHERN CORPORATION
Also Called: Tarsec
3329 Thoroughbred Dr (43217-1200)
PHONE 614 251-2684
Fax: 614 251-2688
Steve Gray, Principal
EMP: 100
SALES (corp-wide): 10.5B Publicly Held
WEB: www.nscorp.com
SIC: 4011 Railroads, line-haul operating
PA: Norfolk Southern Corporation
3 Commercial Pl Ste 1a
Norfolk VA 23510
757 629-2680

(G-8285)
NORMAN JONES ENLOW & CO (PA)
226 N 5th St Ste 500 (43215-2784)
PHONE 614 228-4000
Fax: 614 228-4040
EMP: 40 EST: 1954
SALES (est): 6.8MM Privately Held
SIC: 8721 Accounting/Auditing/Bookkeeping

(G-8286)
NORTH AMERICAN BROADCASTING
Also Called: Wrkz
1458 Dublin Rd (43215-1010)
PHONE 614 481-7800
Fax: 614 481-8070
Matthew Minich, President
Nick Reed, Treasurer
Tom Miller, Natl Sales Mgr
Nanette Wickline, Accounts Mgr
Lori Whisman, Accounts Exec
EMP: 60 EST: 1956
SQ FT: 11,000
SALES (est): 6.4MM Privately Held
WEB: www.nabco-inc.com
SIC: 4832 Radio broadcasting stations

(G-8287)
NORTH BROADWAY CHILDRENS CTR
48 E North Broadway St (43214-4112)
PHONE 614 262-6222
Rebecca McCoy, Owner
Ed Delehanty, Finance Mgr
EMP: 40
SALES (est): 1.2MM Privately Held
SIC: 8351 Preschool center

(G-8288)
NORTH CNTL MNTAL HLTH SVCS INC (PA)
Also Called: NCC ASSOCIATES
1301 N High St (43201-2460)
PHONE 614 227-6865
Fax: 614 299-9007
Don Wood, CEO
John Hunter, Vice Pres
Joseph Niedzwidski, CFO
Joseph Niedzwiedski, CFO
Cheryl Roush, Controller
EMP: 80
SQ FT: 21,500
SALES: 16.9MM Privately Held
SIC: 8093 8361 Mental health clinic, outpatient; residential care

(G-8289)
NORTH COMMUNITY COUNSELING CTR (PA)
4897 Karl Rd (43229-5147)
PHONE 614 846-2588
Fax: 614 846-9759
David Kittridge, President
Davis Kittridge, President
Courtney Cornell, Pub Rel Mgr
Audrey Knaff, Program Dir
Sandy Wood, Admin Asst
EMP: 55
SQ FT: 3,500
SALES (est): 2.5MM Privately Held
SIC: 8093 Mental health clinic, outpatient

(G-8290)
NORTHERN AUTOMOTIVE INC (PA)
Also Called: Saturn-West
8600 N High St (43235-1004)
PHONE 614 436-2001
Fax: 614 842-4116
Thomas Carpenter, President
William L Denney, Exec VP
Robert Vance, Exec VP
Robert Stoll, Controller
Al Clapsaddle, Sales Associate
EMP: 50
SQ FT: 29,000
SALES (est): 32.5MM Privately Held
SIC: 5511 7538 5521 Automobiles, new & used; general automotive repair shops; used car dealers

(G-8291)
NORTHLAND BRDG FRANKLIN CNTY
Also Called: Bridge Counseling Center
4897 Karl Rd (43229-5147)
PHONE 614 846-2588
David Kittredge, President
EMP: 30
SQ FT: 4,158
SALES (est): 421.5K Privately Held
WEB: www.bridgecounselingcenter.com
SIC: 8322 General counseling services

(G-8292)
NORTHLAND HOTEL INC
Also Called: Super 8 Motel Columbus North
1078 E Dblin Granville Rd (43229-2503)
PHONE 614 885-1601
Fax: 614 885-1601
Ray Lin, President
Eddie Stanley, General Mgr
Xuan Liu, Manager
EMP: 30
SALES (est): 1.6MM Privately Held
SIC: 7011 Hotels & motels

(G-8293)
NORTHPOINTE PLAZA
Also Called: Departmental Store
191 W Nationwide Blvd # 200 (43215-2568)
PHONE 614 744-2229
Nancy Novatney, Manager
EMP: 70
SALES (est): 2.1MM Privately Held
WEB: www.departmentalstore.com
SIC: 6531 Real estate agent, commercial

(G-8294)
NORTHPOINTE PROPERTY MGT LLC
3250 Henderson Rd Ste 103 (43220-2398)
PHONE 614 579-9712
Aniko Marcy, Principal
EMP: 197
SALES (est): 113.1K Privately Held
SIC: 7349 1799 Building maintenance services; exterior cleaning, including sandblasting; cleaning new buildings after construction; construction site cleanup

(G-8295)
NORTHWEST EYE SURGEONS INC (PA)
2250 N Bank Dr (43220-5420)
PHONE 614 451-7550
Fax: 614 451-8642
Robert Lembach, President
Jaimye Weaver, Financial Exec
Todd Whitaker, Med Doctor
Sue Hersey, Admin Asst
EMP: 32
SALES (est): 6.6MM Privately Held
WEB: www.northwesteyesurgeons.com
SIC: 8011 Ophthalmologist

(G-8296)
NORTHWEST HTS TITLE AGCY LLC
4200 Regent St Ste 210 (43219-6229)
PHONE 614 451-6313
Beverly Harris, Principal
Elizabeth Davis, Principal
EMP: 25
SALES (est): 3.3MM Privately Held
SIC: 6361 Title insurance

(G-8297)
NORTHWEST MENTAL HEALTH SVCS
Also Called: Northwest Counseling Services
1560 Fishinger Rd Ste 100 (43221-2108)
PHONE 614 457-7876
Fax: 614 457-7896
Susan Hunt, Human Res Dir
Kay Sims, MIS Dir
A King Stumpp, Exec Dir
Hollie Goldberg, Exec Dir
Mary Brett, Director
EMP: 50
SALES: 772.5K Privately Held
WEB: www.northwestcounselingservices.org
SIC: 8093 8322 Mental health clinic, outpatient; individual & family services

(G-8298)
NORTHWEST SWIM CLUB INC
1064 Bethel Rd (43220-2610)
P.O. Box 20015 (43220-0015)
PHONE 614 442-8716
Barb Fleeter, Vice Pres
Mike O'Leary, Vice Pres
Doug Cowgill, Treasurer
Deb Juracich, Treasurer
Mary Carlton, Manager
EMP: 40
SALES: 451.9K Privately Held
WEB: www.northwestswimclub.com
SIC: 7997 Swimming club, membership

(G-8299)
NORTHWESTERN MUTL LF INSUR CO
Also Called: Central Ohio Financial Group
800 Yard St Ste 300 (43212-3882)
PHONE 614 221-5287
Fax: 614 221-0235
Steve Childers, COO
Steve Shoulders, Manager
Kevin Drewyor, Officer
Patrick Lucas, Officer
Jason Swanson, Officer
EMP: 48
SALES (corp-wide): 28.1B Privately Held
WEB: www.nmfn.com
SIC: 6311 Life insurance
PA: The Northwestern Mutual Life Insurance Company
720 E Wisconsin Ave
Milwaukee WI 53202
414 271-1444

GEOGRAPHIC SECTION

Columbus - Franklin County (G-8323)

(G-8300)
NOVOTEC RECYCLING LLC
3960 Groves Rd (43232-4137)
PHONE..............................614 231-8326
Tom Bolon, *CEO*
David Robbins, *Controller*
Mayling Inthisarn, *Admin Dir*
EMP: 27
SALES (est): 6.4MM Privately Held
SIC: 4953 Recycling, waste materials

(G-8301)
NRT COMMERCIAL UTAH LLC
Also Called: Bexley
2288 E Main St (43209-2335)
PHONE..............................614 239-0808
Mark Kraus, *Manager*
EMP: 55 Publicly Held
WEB: www.nrtinc.com
SIC: 6531 Real estate agent, residential
HQ: Nrt Commercial Utah Llc
175 Park Ave
Madison NJ 07940

(G-8302)
NTK HOTEL GROUP II LLC
Also Called: Hampton Inn
501 N High St (43215-2008)
PHONE..............................614 559-2000
Fax: 614 559-2001
Andrew Hann, *General Mgr*
Maria Schroeder, *Manager*
Matthew Kolbrich, *Executive*
David Patel,
EMP: 60
SALES (est): 4.1MM Privately Held
SIC: 7011 Hotels

(G-8303)
NUCON INTERNATIONAL INC
6800 Huntley Rd (43229-1018)
PHONE..............................614 846-5710
Louis Kovach, *Branch Mgr*
EMP: 26
SALES (est): 1.5MM
SALES (corp-wide): 9.1MM Privately Held
WEB: www.nucon-int.com
SIC: 8734 Testing laboratories
PA: Nucon International, Inc.
7000 Huntley Rd
Columbus OH 43229
614 846-5710

(G-8304)
NUETERRA HOLDINGS LLC
Also Called: Ohio Surgery Center
930 Bethel Rd (43214-1906)
PHONE..............................614 451-0500
Kim Esteph, *Manager*
EMP: 40
SALES (corp-wide): 58MM Privately Held
WEB: www.findlaysurgerycenter.com
SIC: 8011 Surgeon
PA: Nueterra Holdings, Llc
11221 Roe Ave Ste 1a
Leawood KS 66211
913 387-0500

(G-8305)
NUGROWTH SOLUTIONS LLC (PA)
Also Called: Strategic Insurance Software
4181 Arlingate Plz (43228-4115)
PHONE..............................800 747-9273
Adam Rapp, *Accounts Mgr*
Eric Weisgarber, *Sales Staff*
Kate Gluck, *Mktg Dir*
Jessica Deal, *Marketing Staff*
Daniel Kear, *Marketing Staff*
EMP: 28
SALES (est): 5.3MM Privately Held
SIC: 8743 8748 Sales promotion; business consulting

(G-8306)
NURSES HEART MED STAFFING LLC
1100 Morse Rd Ste 104 (43229-1170)
PHONE..............................614 648-5111
James Teague, *Principal*
Rosaland Berenguer, *Principal*
Vanessa Garnes, *Principal*
EMP: 40 **EST:** 2016

SALES (est): 1MM Privately Held
SIC: 7361 Employment agencies

(G-8307)
NUTIS PRESS INC (PA)
Also Called: Printed Resources
3540 E Fulton St (43227-1100)
P.O. Box 27248 (43227-0248)
PHONE..............................614 237-8626
Fax: 614 239-0564
Ira Nutis, *President*
Gary Abrams, *President*
Jay Rosner, *Managing Dir*
Mark Chernis, *COO*
Timothy Conroy, *Exec VP*
▼ **EMP:** 193 **EST:** 1961
SQ FT: 95,000
SALES (est): 89.2MM Privately Held
WEB: www.nutispress.com
SIC: 5199 Advertising specialties

(G-8308)
NWD ARENA DISTRICT II LLC
375 N Front St Ste 200 (43215-2258)
PHONE..............................614 857-2330
Brian Ellis,
EMP: 50
SQ FT: 7,250
SALES: 1,000K Privately Held
SIC: 6531 Real estate leasing & rentals

(G-8309)
O S U FACULTY CLUB
Also Called: OHIO STATE UNIVERSITY FACULTY
181 S Oval Mall (43210-1325)
PHONE..............................614 292-2262
Fax: 614 292-1144
Goeffrey White, *Manager*
Bill Hiser, *Manager*
Yeerong Sweetland, *Director*
Andrea Bakker, *Asst Director*
Kelly Neriani, *Research Analys*
EMP: 50
SQ FT: 7,500
SALES (est): 2.2MM Privately Held
WEB: www.ohio-statefacultyclub.com
SIC: 8641 Community membership club; social club, membership

(G-8310)
OAKLAND NURSERY INC (PA)
1156 Oakland Park Ave (43224-3317)
PHONE..............................614 268-3834
Fax: 614 268-3003
Paul S Reiner, *President*
John G Reiner, *Co-President*
Genevieve Mills, *COO*
Mark Reiner, *VP Opers*
Matt Moser, *Store Mgr*
▲ **EMP:** 50
SQ FT: 5,000
SALES (est): 12.2MM Privately Held
WEB: www.oaklandnursery.com
SIC: 5261 0781 Nursery stock, seeds & bulbs; lawnmowers & tractors; garden supplies & tools; landscape services

(G-8311)
OAKLEAF VILLAGE LTD
5500 Karl Rd Apt 113 (43229-3664)
PHONE..............................614 431-1739
Fax: 614 431-0247
Michelle Spiert, *Office Mgr*
Dawn Nero, *Manager*
EMP: 60
SQ FT: 110,000
SALES (est): 5.1MM Privately Held
WEB: www.oakleafvillage.com
SIC: 8361 Geriatric residential care

(G-8312)
OCCUPATIONAL HEALTH LINK (PA)
445 Hutchinson Ave # 205 (43235-5677)
PHONE..............................614 885-0039
Fax: 614 825-1459
Karen Conger, *Partner*
Sandy Devery, *CFO*
Occupational Health Research I,
William L Newkirk,
EMP: 28
SQ FT: 8,500

SALES (est): 11.9MM Privately Held
WEB: www.oehpmco.com
SIC: 6331 8399 Workers' compensation insurance; health systems agency

(G-8313)
ODW LOGISTICS INC (PA)
Also Called: O D W
400 W Nationwide Blvd # 200 (43215-2394)
PHONE..............................614 549-5000
Jason Poot, *President*
Chris Copsey, *General Mgr*
Eric Isakson, *General Mgr*
Scott Leonard, *General Mgr*
Patrick Porter, *General Mgr*
EMP: 300
SQ FT: 1,000,000
SALES (est): 197.4MM Privately Held
SIC: 4225 4226 General warehousing; special warehousing & storage

(G-8314)
ODYSSEY CONSULTING SERVICES
2531 Oakstone Dr (43231-7612)
PHONE..............................614 523-4248
Fax: 614 523-4249
Mike McGovern, *President*
Kevin Martinez, *Assistant VP*
Diana McGovern, *Vice Pres*
Bonnie Harmor, *Director*
EMP: 110
SQ FT: 4,000
SALES (est): 5.5MM Privately Held
SIC: 7371 Computer software systems analysis & design, custom

(G-8315)
OHIC INSURANCE COMPANY (HQ)
155 E Broad St Fl 10 (43215-3614)
PHONE..............................614 221-7777
Fax: 614 461-1120
Jerry Cassidy, *Ch of Bd*
Mark Anderson, *Vice Pres*
Jim Daldyga, *Vice Pres*
Nancy Libke, *Vice Pres*
Darrell Rainum, *Vice Pres*
EMP: 80
SQ FT: 19,000
SALES (est): 8.9MM
SALES (corp-wide): 393.6MM Privately Held
WEB: www.ohic.com
SIC: 6331 6411 8742 Fire, marine & casualty insurance & carriers; insurance claim adjusters, not employed by insurance company; hospital & health services consultant
PA: The Doctors' Company An Interinsurance Exchange
185 Greenwood Rd
Napa CA 94558
707 226-0100

(G-8316)
OHIO ACADEMY OF SCIENCE
1500 W 3rd Ave Ste 228 (43212-2817)
P.O. Box 12519 (43212-0519)
PHONE..............................614 488-2228
Fax: 614 488-2228
Stephen McConoughey, *CEO*
Dr Richard Janson, *President*
Jeff Jahn, *Manager*
Kirk Schwall, *Manager*
Cindy Stoker, *Manager*
EMP: 25 **EST:** 1891
SQ FT: 1,200
SALES (est): 1.7MM Privately Held
WEB: www.heartlandscience.org
SIC: 8211 8699 Academy; charitable organization

(G-8317)
OHIO ASSN PUB SCHL EMPLOYEES (PA)
Also Called: Oapse-Local 4
6805 Oak Creek Dr Ste 1 (43229-1501)
PHONE..............................614 890-4770
Sue Soabaugh, *Accounts Mgr*
Courtney Belcher, *Corp Counsel*
Robert Fantauzzo, *Consultant*
Joe Rugola, *Exec Dir*
Kathy Malone, *Director*
EMP: 32

SQ FT: 18,000
SALES (est): 9.2MM Privately Held
SIC: 8631 Labor union

(G-8318)
OHIO ASSOCIATION OF FOODBANKS
101 E Town St Ste 540 (43215-5119)
PHONE..............................614 221-4336
Fax: 614 221-4338
Joree Jacobs, *Comms Dir*
Joree Novotny, *Comms Dir*
Charles Barber, *Manager*
Kathryn Meyers, *Manager*
Erin Wright, *Manager*
EMP: 32
SQ FT: 8,700
SALES: 29.9MM Privately Held
SIC: 8621 Professional membership organizations

(G-8319)
OHIO ASSOCIATION REALTORS INC
200 E Town St (43215-4608)
PHONE..............................614 228-6675
Fax: 614 228-2601
Robert E Fletcher, *CEO*
Robin Jennings, *VP Opers*
Denis Nowacki, *Treasurer*
Lisa Picklesimer, *Marketing Staff*
Chrissy Rose, *Marketing Staff*
EMP: 25 **EST:** 1911
SQ FT: 15,168
SALES: 4.4MM Privately Held
WEB: www.ohiorealtor.com
SIC: 8611 2721 Trade associations; trade journals; publishing & printing

(G-8320)
OHIO AUTOMOBILE CLUB
Also Called: AAA Car Care Plus
2400 Sobeck Rd (43232-3801)
PHONE..............................614 559-0000
Fax: 614 559-0006
Mark Boyer, *Manager*
EMP: 30
SQ FT: 18,200
SALES (corp-wide): 55.9MM Privately Held
SIC: 7538 General automotive repair shops
PA: The Ohio Automobile Club
90 E Wilson Bridge Rd # 1
Worthington OH 43085
614 431-7901

(G-8321)
OHIO CHAMBER OF COMMERCE INC
230 E Town St Ste 300 (43215-4657)
P.O. Box 15159 (43215-0159)
PHONE..............................614 228-4201
Andrew E Doehrel, *President*
Linda Woggon, *Vice Pres*
Michelle Anderson, *Technology*
Anthonio Fiore, *Director*
Allan Brown, *General Counsel*
EMP: 25
SALES: 3.3MM Privately Held
WEB: www.ohiochamber.com
SIC: 8611 Chamber of Commerce

(G-8322)
OHIO CON SAWING & DRLG INC
2935 E 14th Ave Ste 200 (43219 2364)
PHONE..............................614 252-1122
Tom Lenix, *Manager*
EMP: 25
SALES (corp-wide): 14.5MM Privately Held
WEB: www.gp-radar.com
SIC: 1771 Concrete repair
PA: Ohio Concrete Sawing And Drilling, Inc.
8534 Central Ave
Sylvania OH 43560
419 841-1330

(G-8323)
OHIO CUSTODIAL MAINTENANCE
Also Called: Ohio Custodial Management
1291 S High St (43206-3472)
PHONE..............................614 443-1232
John Tucker, *CEO*

Columbus - Franklin County (G-8324)

Scott Tucker, *President*
Bill Weaver, *Project Mgr*
EMP: 120
SQ FT: 7,000
SALES (est): 2.9MM
SALES (corp-wide): 5.7MM **Privately Held**
WEB: www.ohiocustodial.com
SIC: 7349 8742 Janitorial service, contract basis; management consulting services
PA: Ohio Support Services Corp.
   1291 S High St
   Columbus OH 43206
   614 443-0291

(G-8324)
OHIO DEPARTMENT OF AGING
246 N High St Fl 1 (43215-3363)
PHONE 614 466-5500
Fax: 614 466-5741
Cathy McNamara, *Accounting Mgr*
Kevin Flanagan, *Manager*
Barbara Riley, *Director*
EMP: 100
SQ FT: 35,000
SALES (est): 4.9MM **Privately Held**
SIC: 8361 9441 Home for the aged; old soldiers' home; administration of social & manpower programs;
HQ: Executive Office State Of Ohio
   30 E Broad St
   Columbus OH 43215

(G-8325)
OHIO DEPARTMENT OF COMMERCE
Division of Securities
77 S High St Fl 22 (43215-6108)
PHONE 614 644-7381
Fax: 614 466-3316
Joe Bishop, *Commissioner*
EMP: 39 **Privately Held**
SIC: 9311 6211 Finance, taxation & monetary policy; ; security brokers & dealers
HQ: Department Of Commerce Ohio
   6606 Tussing Rd
   Reynoldsburg OH 43068

(G-8326)
OHIO DEPARTMENT OF COMMERCE
Division Fincl Institutions
77 S High St Fl 21 (43215-6108)
PHONE 614 728-8400
Fax: 614 644-1631
Charles Dolezal, *Superintendent*
EMP: 115 **Privately Held**
SIC: 9611 8611 Administration of general economic programs; ; business associations
HQ: Department Of Commerce Ohio
   6606 Tussing Rd
   Reynoldsburg OH 43068

(G-8327)
OHIO DEPARTMENT OF HEALTH
Also Called: Wic
3850 Sullivant Ave # 102 (43228-4327)
PHONE 614 645-3621
Fax: 614 645-2476
EMP: 269 **Privately Held**
SIC: 8322 Individual & family services
HQ: Department Of Health Ohio
   246 N High St
   Columbus OH 43215

(G-8328)
OHIO DEPARTMENT OF HEALTH
Also Called: Bureau Information & Support
246 N High St (43215-2406)
P.O. Box 118 (43216-0118)
PHONE 614 466-1521
Nick Baird, *Director*
EMP: 200 **Privately Held**
WEB: www.jchealth.com
SIC: 8621 9431 Health association; administration of public health programs;
HQ: Department Of Health Ohio
   246 N High St
   Columbus OH 43215

(G-8329)
OHIO DEPARTMENT OF HEALTH
Also Called: Rehabilitation Services
400 E Campus View Blvd (43235-4685)
PHONE 614 438-1255

Bill Mc Mc Farland, *Accounts Mgr*
John Connelly, *Director*
EMP: 800 **Privately Held**
WEB: www.jchealth.com
SIC: 8322 9431 Rehabilitation services; administration of public health programs;
HQ: Department Of Health Ohio
   246 N High St
   Columbus OH 43215

(G-8330)
OHIO DEPARTMENT TRANSPORTATION
Also Called: Material Management
1600 W Broad St (43223-1202)
PHONE 614 275-1324
James Beasley, *Director*
EMP: 65 **Privately Held**
SIC: 9621 8734 Regulation, administration of transportation; ; automobile proving & testing ground
HQ: Ohio Department Of Transportation
   1980 W Broad St
   Columbus OH 43223

(G-8331)
OHIO DEPARTMENT VETERANS SVCS
77 S High St Fl 7 (43215-6108)
PHONE 614 644-0898
Michael Liptay, *Controller*
Tom Mefarland, *Office Mgr*
Thomas Moe, *Director*
Sandra Hamilton, *Nurse*
EMP: 800
SALES: 199.2K **Privately Held**
WEB: www.governor.ohio.gov
SIC: 8051 Skilled nursing care facilities
HQ: Executive Office State Of Ohio
   30 E Broad St
   Columbus OH 43215

(G-8332)
OHIO DEPARTMENT YOUTH SERVICES
Also Called: Freedom Center
51 N High St Fl 5 (43215-3012)
PHONE 740 881-3337
Joyce Bednerek, *Superintendent*
EMP: 30 **Privately Held**
SIC: 9431 8069 Public health agency administration, government; ; substance abuse hospitals
HQ: Department Of Youth Service, Ohio
   30 W Spring St Fl 5
   Columbus OH 43215

(G-8333)
OHIO DEPT AMVET SVC FOUNDATION (PA)
1395 E Dublin Granville R (43229-3314)
PHONE 614 431-6990
Donald Limer, *President*
David Salisbury, *Opers Mgr*
Jane Brown, *Admin Sec*
EMP: 75
SQ FT: 3,024
SALES (est): 3.2MM **Privately Held**
WEB: www.ohamvets.org
SIC: 8641 Veterans' organization

(G-8334)
OHIO DEPT OF JOB & FMLY SVCS
Also Called: Bureau Labor Market Info
4300 Kimberly Pkwy N (43232-8296)
PHONE 614 752-9494
Keith Ewald, *Director*
EMP: 50 **Privately Held**
WEB: www.job.com
SIC: 8331 9441 Community service employment training program;
HQ: The Ohio Department Of Job And Family Services
   30 E Broad St Fl 32
   Columbus OH 43215

(G-8335)
OHIO DEPT OF JOB & FMLY SVCS
Also Called: Office For Children Fmly Svcs
255 E Main St Fl 3 (43215-5222)
PHONE 614 466-1213
Rick Smith, *Manager*
EMP: 120 **Privately Held**

WEB: www.job.com
SIC: 8351 9441 8322 Child day care services; administration of social & manpower programs; ; individual & family services
HQ: The Ohio Department Of Job And Family Services
   30 E Broad St Fl 32
   Columbus OH 43215

(G-8336)
OHIO DEPT RHBILITATION CORECTN
Also Called: Parole & Community Services
770 W Broad St (43222-1419)
PHONE 614 274-9000
Jannet Morman, *Chief*
EMP: 300 **Privately Held**
SIC: 8322 9223 Parole office; correctional institutions;
HQ: Ohio Department Of Rehabilitation And Correction
   770 W Broad St
   Columbus OH 43222

(G-8337)
OHIO DISABILITY RIGHTS LAW POL
Also Called: Disabillity Rights Ohio
200 Civic Center Dr (43215-7510)
PHONE 614 466-7264
Michael Kirkman, *Exec Dir*
EMP: 45 **EST:** 2012
SALES: 4.6MM **Privately Held**
SIC: 8111 Legal services

(G-8338)
OHIO EDUCATION ASSOCIATION
Also Called: E-Tech Ohio Commision
2470 North Star Rd (43221-3405)
PHONE 614 485-6000
Larry Koslap, *Project Mgr*
Kate BR, *Manager*
EMP: 60
SALES (corp-wide): 59.2MM **Privately Held**
SIC: 8631 Labor union
PA: Ohio Education Association Inc
   225 E Broad St Fl 2
   Columbus OH 43215
   614 228-4526

(G-8339)
OHIO EDUCATION ASSOCIATION (PA)
225 E Broad St Fl 2 (43215-3709)
P.O. Box 2550 (43216-2550)
PHONE 614 228-4526
Patricia F Brooks, *President*
Pete Scully, *Vice Pres*
Maureen Patrick, *Production*
Russ Harris, *Research*
Jim Timlin, *Treasurer*
EMP: 60
SQ FT: 5,734
SALES: 59.2MM **Privately Held**
SIC: 8631 Labor union

(G-8340)
OHIO EQUITIES LLC
6210 Busch Blvd (43229-1804)
PHONE 614 207-1805
EMP: 45
SALES (corp-wide): 14.6MM **Privately Held**
SIC: 8742 Real estate consultant
PA: Ohio Equities, Llc
   605 S Front St Ste 200
   Columbus OH 43215
   614 224-2400

(G-8341)
OHIO EQUITIES LLC
Also Called: Nai Ohio Equities, Realtors
17 S High St Ste 799 (43215-3450)
PHONE 614 469-0058
Amy Karnes, *Mktg Dir*
Amber Frilling, *Property Mgr*
Marla McGraw, *Property Mgr*
David Wakeman, *Property Mgr*
Lynne Raduege, *Manager*
EMP: 61

SALES (corp-wide): 14.6MM **Privately Held**
WEB: www.ohioequities.com
SIC: 6531 Real estate brokers & agents
PA: Ohio Equities, Llc
   605 S Front St Ste 200
   Columbus OH 43215
   614 224-2400

(G-8342)
OHIO EXPOSITION CENTER
717 E 17th Ave (43211-2494)
PHONE 614 644-4000
Fax: 614 644-4031
Virgil Strickler, *CEO*
Birgil Strickler, *General Mgr*
EMP: 75
SALES (est): 3.1MM **Privately Held**
SIC: 7999 Exposition operation

(G-8343)
OHIO EXTERMINATING CO INC
1347 N High St (43201-2497)
PHONE 614 294-6311
Fax: 614 291-5444
Thomas Christman, *President*
Jim Witt, *Accounts Mgr*
Brooke Christman, *Manager*
EMP: 30
SQ FT: 10,000
SALES (est): 2.1MM **Privately Held**
WEB: www.ohioexterminating.com
SIC: 7342 Termite control; pest control in structures

(G-8344)
OHIO FAIR PLAN UNDWRT ASSN
2500 Corp Exchange Dr # 250 (43231-8616)
PHONE 614 839-6446
Fax: 614 839-2882
Norman E Beal, *Partner*
David Culler, *Partner*
David Engleson, *Partner*
Ellen Leslie, *Partner*
Chris Beha, *Auditing Mgr*
EMP: 38 **EST:** 1968
SALES (est): 15.9MM **Privately Held**
WEB: www.ohiofairplan.com
SIC: 6331 Property damage insurance

(G-8345)
OHIO FARM BUR FEDERATION INC (PA)
Also Called: Our Ohio Communications
280 N High St Fl 6 (43215-2594)
P.O. Box 182383 (43218-2383)
PHONE 614 249-2400
Frank Burkett, *President*
Steve Hirsch, *President*
Lynn Snyder, *Editor*
Roger Baker, *Trustee*
Adam Sharp, *Exec VP*
EMP: 55
SQ FT: 12,700
SALES (est): 12MM **Privately Held**
WEB: www.ohioapples.com
SIC: 8611 Trade associations

(G-8346)
OHIO GSTROENTEROLOGY GROUP INC
815 W Broad St Ste 220 (43222-1478)
PHONE 614 221-8355
Edward Brand, *Branch Mgr*
EMP: 28 **Privately Held**
SIC: 8011 Cardiologist & cardio-vascular specialist; gastronomist
PA: Ohio Gastroenterology Group, Inc.
   3400 Olentangy River Rd
   Columbus OH 43202

(G-8347)
OHIO GSTROENTEROLOGY GROUP INC
85 Mcnaughten Rd Ste 320 (43213-5111)
PHONE 614 754-5500
Fax: 614 868-0436
Edward Brand, *Principal*
Seth Hoffman, *Med Doctor*
Michael Taxier, *Med Doctor*
Scott Young, *Med Doctor*
May Meeks, *Office Spvr*
EMP: 33 **Privately Held**
SIC: 8011 Gastronomist

GEOGRAPHIC SECTION

Columbus - Franklin County (G-8371)

PA: Ohio Gastroenterology Group, Inc.
3400 Olentangy River Rd
Columbus OH 43202

(G-8348)
OHIO GSTROENTEROLOGY GROUP INC (PA)
3400 Olentangy River Rd (43202-1523)
PHONE................................614 754-5500
Fax: 614 457-8438
Thomas Ransbottom, *President*
Frank J Chapman, *COO*
Megan Dana, *Human Res Mgr*
Heather Foisset, *Human Res Mgr*
May Meeks, *Office Mgr*
EMP: 69
SALES (est): 16.5MM **Privately Held**
WEB: www.ohiogastro.com
SIC: 8011 Gastronomist

(G-8349)
OHIO HEALTH COUNCIL
155 E Broad St Ste 301 (43215-3640)
PHONE................................614 221-7614
John Callender, *Ch of Bd*
Rosalie Weakland, *Director*
EMP: 70
SALES: 11.2K **Privately Held**
SIC: 8621 Health association

(G-8350)
OHIO HEALTH GROUP LLC
155 E Broad St Ste 1700 (43215-3673)
PHONE................................614 566-0010
Fax: 614 566-0403
Tom Thompson,
EMP: 40
SQ FT: 36,000
SALES (est): 5.8MM **Privately Held**
WEB: www.ohiohealthgroup.com
SIC: 8011 Medical insurance associations

(G-8351)
OHIO HEATING AND REFRIGERATION
1465 Clara St (43211-2623)
P.O. Box 91203 (43209-7203)
PHONE................................614 863-6666
Sam Goldstein Norman, *President*
Ken Scott, *Project Mgr*
Tom Sefchick, *Project Mgr*
Demetria Summers, *Office Mgr*
Dan Clifford, *Manager*
EMP: 26
SALES (est): 11.6MM **Privately Held**
SIC: 1711 Warm air heating & air conditioning contractor; plumbing contractors

(G-8352)
OHIO HISTORICAL SOCIETY (PA)
Also Called: OHIO HISTORY CONNECTION
800 E 17th Ave (43211-2497)
PHONE................................614 297-2300
Fax: 614 297-2367
Glenda S Greenwood, *President*
David Simmons, *Editor*
Ronald J Ungvarsky, *Vice Pres*
Andy Hite, *Site Mgr*
Thomas W Johnson, *Treasurer*
EMP: 200 **EST:** 1885
SQ FT: 50,000
SALES: 21MM **Privately Held**
WEB: www.ohiotimelessadventures.com
SIC: 8412 Museum

(G-8353)
OHIO HOSPITAL ASSOCIATION
155 E Broad St Ste 301 (43215-3640)
PHONE................................614 221-7614
Fax: 614 221-4771
James R Castle, *President*
Mike Abrams, *President*
Ryan Biles, *Exec VP*
Ronald D Wade Sr, *Exec VP*
Sarah Cansler, *Manager*
EMP: 62 **EST:** 1935
SQ FT: 9,000
SALES: 17MM **Privately Held**
SIC: 8621 Health association

(G-8354)
OHIO HOSPITAL FOR PSYCHIATRY
880 Greenlawn Ave (43223-2616)
PHONE................................877 762-9026
Marcia Berch, *CEO*
Gerry Breen, *Executive*
EMP: 50
SALES (est): 7MM **Publicly Held**
SIC: 8063 Psychiatric hospitals
HQ: Behavioral Centers Of America, Llc
830 Crescent Centre Dr # 610
Franklin TN 37067
615 292-9514

(G-8355)
OHIO INDEMNITY COMPANY
250 E Broad St Fl 7 (43215-3708)
PHONE................................614 228-1601
John Sokol, *Ch of Bd*
Sally Cress, *Corp Secy*
David Juredine, *Div Sub Head*
Daniel J Stephan, *Senior VP*
Stephen J Toth, *Vice Pres*
EMP: 25
SQ FT: 12,000
SALES (est): 13.1MM
SALES (corp-wide): 46.1MM **Privately Held**
WEB: www.ohioindemnity.com
SIC: 6331 6411 Automobile insurance; property damage insurance; insurance agents, brokers & service
PA: Bancinsurance Corporation
250 E Broad St Fl 7
Columbus OH 43215
614 220-5200

(G-8356)
OHIO LEGAL RIGHTS SERVICE
50 W Broad St Ste 1400 (43215-2999)
PHONE................................614 466-7264
Paula Jones, *CFO*
Michael Kirkman, *Exec Dir*
Jeffrey Folkerth, *Administration*
EMP: 47
SQ FT: 17,694
SALES (est): 1.6MM **Privately Held**
WEB: www.governor.ohio.gov
SIC: 8399 Advocacy group
HQ: Executive State Of Ohio
30 E Broad St
Columbus OH 43215

(G-8357)
OHIO LIVING
Also Called: Westminster Thurber
645 Neil Ave Ofc (43215-1624)
PHONE................................614 224-1651
Fax: 614 228-8898
Kay Howard, *Pub Rel Dir*
Lovely Belfance, *Director*
EMP: 300
SQ FT: 8,728 **Privately Held**
WEB: www.nwo.oprs.org
SIC: 6513 8051 8052 Retirement hotel operation; skilled nursing care facilities; intermediate care facilities
PA: Ohio Living
1001 Kingsmill Pkwy
Columbus OH 43229

(G-8358)
OHIO LIVING (PA)
1001 Kingsmill Pkwy (43229-1129)
PHONE................................614 888-7800
Fax: 614 888-6864
Laurence Gumina, *CEO*
Dana Ullom-Vucelich, *Opers Staff*
Robert Stillman, *CFO*
Tom Kelly, *Controller*
Cathy Koerner, *Marketing Staff*
EMP: 50
SQ FT: 12,000
SALES: 226.4MM **Privately Held**
WEB: www.nwo.oprs.org
SIC: 8361 Rest home, with health care incidental

(G-8359)
OHIO MACHINERY CO
Ohio Cat
5252 Walcutt Ct (43228-9641)
PHONE................................614 878-2287
Fax: 614 851-3736
Kelly Love, *Vice Pres*
Tom Abel, *Sales Mgr*
Craig Curtis, *Sales Mgr*
Ed Buerger, *Sales Staff*
Jeff Frank, *Sales Staff*
EMP: 300
SALES (corp-wide): 222.7MM **Privately Held**
WEB: www.enginesnow.com
SIC: 5082 General construction machinery & equipment
PA: Ohio Machinery Co.
3993 E Royalton Rd
Broadview Heights OH 44147
440 526-6200

(G-8360)
OHIO MEDICAL TRNSP INC (PA)
Also Called: MEDFLIGHT OF OHIO
2827 W Dblin Granville Rd (43235-2712)
PHONE................................614 791-4400
Fax: 614 734-8080
Rod Crane, *President*
Frank Brisker, *Business Mgr*
Lindsey Castle, *Vice Pres*
Sam Kennedy, *Safety Mgr*
Rick Leaver, *Maint Spvr*
EMP: 200
SALES: 44.4MM **Privately Held**
WEB: www.medflight.com
SIC: 4522 4119 Ambulance services, air; ambulance service

(G-8361)
OHIO MULCH SUPPLY INC (PA)
1600 Universal Rd (43207-1733)
PHONE................................614 445-4455
Fax: 614 445-4464
James A Weber II, *President*
Anthony S Elia, *Principal*
Ralph T Spencer, *Principal*
David McClure, *Opers Mgr*
Samuel J Agresti, *CFO*
EMP: 70
SQ FT: 2,000
SALES (est): 52MM **Privately Held**
SIC: 0782 Garden planting services

(G-8362)
OHIO NEWS NETWORK
Also Called: Ohio News Network, The
770 Twin Rivers Dr (43215-1127)
PHONE................................614 460-3700
Fax: 614 280-6305
Tom Greidorn, *General Mgr*
Vince Jones, *Vice Pres*
Thomas Banks, *Engineer*
Scott Brandenburg, *Accounts Exec*
Molly Pensyl, *Accounts Exec*
EMP: 80
SALES (est): 3.7MM **Privately Held**
WEB: www.onnnews.com
SIC: 7383 2711 4841 News syndicates; newspapers; cable & other pay television services

(G-8363)
OHIO OPERATING ENGINEERS APPRN
1184 Dublin Rd (43215-7004)
PHONE................................614 487-6531
Don Black, *Principal*
EMP: 30
SALES (est): 3.4MM **Privately Held**
SIC: 8631 Labor union

(G-8364)
OHIO ORTHPD SURGERY INST LLC
4605 Sawmill Rd (43220-2246)
PHONE................................614 827-8777
Fax: 614 488-7864
A S C Group Lc, *Mng Membor*
Dianna Iannarino, *Manager*
Geoff Omiatek, *Director*
William Fitz MD,
EMP: 30
SALES: 400K **Privately Held**
WEB: www.ohio-ortho-surg.com
SIC: 8011 Orthopedic physician

(G-8365)
OHIO OSTEOPATHIC HOSPITAL ASSN
52 W 3rd Ave (43201)
P.O. Box 8130 (43201-0130)
PHONE................................614 299-2107
Jon F Wills, *Principal*
EMP: 26

SALES: 79.3K **Privately Held**
SIC: 8062 General medical & surgical hospitals

(G-8366)
OHIO POWER COMPANY (HQ)
Also Called: AEP
1 Riverside Plz (43215-2355)
PHONE................................614 716-1000
Nicholas K Akins, *Ch of Bd*
Brian X Tierney, *CFO*
Joseph M Buonaiuto,
EMP: 170
SALES: 2.8B
SALES (corp-wide): 15.4B **Publicly Held**
SIC: 4911 Electric services; distribution, electric power; generation, electric power; transmission, electric power
PA: American Electric Power Company, Inc.
1 Riverside Plz Fl 1 # 1
Columbus OH 43215
614 716-1000

(G-8367)
OHIO POWER COMPANY
215 N Front St (43215-2255)
PHONE................................614 836-2570
Fax: 614 464-7144
Lionel Highley, *Branch Mgr*
EMP: 41
SALES (corp-wide): 15.4B **Publicly Held**
SIC: 4911 Generation, electric power; transmission, electric power; distribution, electric power
HQ: Ohio Power Company
1 Riverside Plz
Columbus OH 43215
614 716-1000

(G-8368)
OHIO PRESBT RETIREMENT SVCS
Also Called: Westminster Thurber Community
717 Neil Ave (43215-1609)
PHONE................................614 228-8888
Leslie Belfance, *Exec Dir*
EMP: 174 **Privately Held**
SIC: 8049 Acupuncturist
PA: Ohio Living
1001 Kingsmill Pkwy
Columbus OH 43229

(G-8369)
OHIO PRESBYTERIAN RTR SVCS
Also Called: OPRS FOUNDATION
1001 Kingsmill Pkwy (43229-1129)
PHONE................................614 888-7800
Thomas G Hofmann, *President*
Dan O'Connor, *Vice Pres*
Sandy Simpson, *Vice Pres*
Sue Welty, *Vice Pres*
Ann Otto, *Human Resources*
EMP: 38
SALES: 11.6MM **Privately Held**
SIC: 7389 Fund raising organizations

(G-8370)
OHIO PUB EMPLYEES RTREMENT SYS
277 E Town St (43215-4627)
PHONE................................614 228-8471
Fax: 614 857-1172
Sharon Downs, *Principal*
Cinthia Sledz, *Chairman*
Blake W Sherry, *COO*
Jenny Starr, *CFO*
Brad Sturm, *Portfolio Mgr*
EMP: 468
SQ FT: 145,404
SALES (est): 326.2MM **Privately Held**
WEB: www.opers.org
SIC: 6371 9441 Pension funds; administration of social & manpower programs;
HQ: Executive Office State Of Ohio
30 E Broad St
Columbus OH 43215

(G-8371)
OHIO RURAL ELECTRIC COOPS INC
Also Called: Country Living
6677 Busch Blvd (43229-1101)
P.O. Box 26036 (43226)
PHONE................................614 846-5757

Columbus - Franklin County (G-8372)

Anthony J Ahern, *President*
EMP: 25 **EST:** 1941
SALES: 6MM **Privately Held**
SIC: 8611 5063 Trade associations; electrical apparatus & equipment; electrical supplies

(G-8372)
OHIO SCHOOL BOARDS ASSOCIATION
8050 N High St Ste 100 (43235-6481)
PHONE 614 540-4000
Cheryl Ryan, *Consultant*
Rick Lewis, *Exec Dir*
EMP: 48 **EST:** 1955
SALES: 7.9MM **Privately Held**
SIC: 8699 Animal humane society

(G-8373)
OHIO SCHOOL BOARDS ASSOCIATION
8050 N High St Ste 100 (43235-6481)
PHONE 614 540-4000
Rick Lewis, *Exec Dir*
EMP: 44
SALES: 215K **Privately Held**
SIC: 8699 Charitable organization

(G-8374)
OHIO SCHOOL PSYCHOLOGISTS ASSN
4449 Easton Way Fl 2offi (43219)
PHONE 614 414-5980
Cheryl Vandenburg, *Principal*
EMP: 44
SALES: 312.2K **Privately Held**
WEB: www.ospaonline.org
SIC: 8211 8621 Elementary & secondary schools; professional membership organizations

(G-8375)
OHIO SENIOR HOME HLTH CARE LLC
6004 Cleveland Ave (43231-2230)
PHONE 614 470-6070
Saeed Ali, *CEO*
EMP: 80 **EST:** 2015
SALES (est): 326.8K **Privately Held**
SIC: 8082 Home health care services

(G-8376)
OHIO SOC OF CRTIF PUB ACCNTNTS
Also Called: Ohio Soceity of Cpas
4249 Easton Way Ste 150 (43219-6163)
P.O. Box 1810, Dublin (43017-7810)
PHONE 614 764-2727
Fax: 614 764-5880
Scott Wiley, *President*
Laura Hay, *COO*
Boyd Search, *Vice Pres*
Judy Schiewer, *Financial Exec*
Clarke J Price, *Exec Dir*
EMP: 53
SQ FT: 13,500
SALES: 9.5MM **Privately Held**
SIC: 8621 Accounting association

(G-8377)
OHIO STATE BAR ASSOCIATION
Also Called: Ohio Cle Institute
1700 Lake Shore Dr (43204-4895)
PHONE 614 487-2050
Fax: 614 487-8808
Victoria Robertson, *COO*
Shane Zatezalo, *Engng Exec*
Mike Oldfield, *Sls & Mktg Exec*
Alicia Blair, *Accounting Mgr*
Judy Hall, *Accounting Mgr*
EMP: 37
SQ FT: 13,338
SALES (est): 6.7MM **Privately Held**
SIC: 8111 Legal services

(G-8378)
OHIO STATE BAR ASSOCIATION
1700 Lake Shore Dr (43204-4895)
P.O. Box 16562 (43216-6562)
PHONE 614 487-2050
Keith Ashman, *President*
Desiree Blankenship, *Counsel*
Reginal Jackson, *Vice Pres*
Mandy Fowler-Aquilina, *Accounts Exec*
Heather Sowald, *Corp Counsel*
EMP: 55
SALES: 10.3MM **Privately Held**
WEB: www.ohiostatebarassociation.com
SIC: 8621 Bar association

(G-8379)
OHIO STATE UNIV ALUMNI ASSN
Also Called: ALUMNI ASSOCIATION, THE
2200 Olentangy River Rd (43210-1035)
PHONE 614 292-2200
Archie Griffin, *President*
Andy Gurd, *COO*
Julia Wolf, *Accounts Exec*
Jennifer Russell, *Sales Staff*
Steve Proctor, *VP Corp Comm*
EMP: 60 **EST:** 1910
SQ FT: 9,600
SALES: 11.4MM **Privately Held**
WEB: www.ohiostatealumni.org
SIC: 8641 8661 Alumni association; religious organizations

(G-8380)
OHIO STATE UNIV MANAGED HEALTH
1900 Kenny Rd (43210-1016)
PHONE 614 292-8405
Jeff Walters, *President*
EMP: 40 **EST:** 1991
SALES (est): 1.8MM **Privately Held**
WEB: www.osumhcs.com
SIC: 8011 Medical insurance plan

(G-8381)
OHIO STATE UNIV RES FOUNDATION
1960 Kenny Rd (43210-1016)
PHONE 614 292-3815
Caroline Whitacre, *Principal*
Pranab Bhattacharya, *Treasurer*
Susan Imel, *Info Tech Mgr*
Christine Hamble, *Director*
Richard Bradbury, *Admin Sec*
EMP: 105
SQ FT: 40,000
SALES: 13.2MM **Privately Held**
SIC: 8741 Administrative management

(G-8382)
OHIO STATE UNIV WEXNER MED CTR
369 Grenadine Way (43235-5742)
PHONE 614 293-2663
Fax: 614 293-6250
Anne Sullivan, *Surgeon*
Maria A Barnett, *Family Practiti*
EMP: 135
SALES (corp-wide): 2.6B **Privately Held**
SIC: 8011 Medical centers
PA: The Ohio State University Wexner
Medical Center
410 W 10th Ave
Columbus OH 43210
614 293-8000

(G-8383)
OHIO STATE UNIV WEXNER MED CTR
915 Olentangy River Rd # 5000 (43212-3153)
PHONE 614 227-0562
Michaelle Palmer, *Principal*
Stephen Smith, *Med Doctor*
EMP: 5009
SALES (corp-wide): 2.6B **Privately Held**
SIC: 8011 Medical centers
PA: The Ohio State University Wexner
Medical Center
410 W 10th Ave
Columbus OH 43210
614 293-8000

(G-8384)
OHIO STATE UNIV WEXNER MED CTR (PA)
410 W 10th Ave (43210-1240)
PHONE 614 293-8000
Fax: 614 257-3750
Michael V Drake, *President*
Sunny Lambson, *Facilities Mgr*
Lydia Hill, *Buyer*
Denny Sweet, *Human Res Dir*
Lisa Green, *Marketing Mgr*
EMP: 1000 **EST:** 1910

SALES: 2.6B **Privately Held**
SIC: 8062 General medical & surgical hospitals

(G-8385)
OHIO STATE UNIV WEXNER MED CTR
320 W 10th Ave (43210-1280)
PHONE 614 293-7521
Leona Ayers, *Branch Mgr*
EMP: 5018
SALES (corp-wide): 2.6B **Privately Held**
SIC: 8221 8011 Colleges universities & professional schools; offices & clinics of medical doctors
PA: The Ohio State University Wexner
Medical Center
410 W 10th Ave
Columbus OH 43210
614 293-8000

(G-8386)
OHIO STATE UNIV WEXNER MED CTR
Also Called: Otolaryngology Department
1492 E Broad St (43205-1546)
PHONE 614 366-3687
Michelle Schnurr, *Branch Mgr*
EMP: 188
SALES (corp-wide): 2.6B **Privately Held**
SIC: 8062 General medical & surgical hospitals
PA: The Ohio State University Wexner
Medical Center
410 W 10th Ave
Columbus OH 43210
614 293-8000

(G-8387)
OHIO STATE UNIV WEXNER MED CTR
Also Called: Division of Gastroenterology
410 W 10th Ave (43210-1240)
PHONE 614 293-6255
Darwin L Conwell, *Director*
EMP: 574
SALES (corp-wide): 2.6B **Privately Held**
WEB: www.ohio-state.edu
SIC: 8011 8221 Offices & clinics of medical doctors; university
PA: The Ohio State University Wexner
Medical Center
410 W 10th Ave
Columbus OH 43210
614 293-8000

(G-8388)
OHIO STATE UNIVERSITY
Also Called: Dodd Hall Inptent Rhbilitation
480 Medical Center Dr (43210-1229)
PHONE 614 366-3692
Fax: 614 293-4409
Dwight Owen, *Development*
Martin Joyce, *CFO*
Mark Larmore, *CFO*
Janelle Janowiecki, *Nursing Mgr*
Jessica Macdonald, *Psychologist*
EMP: 547
SALES (corp-wide): 5.5B **Privately Held**
SIC: 8011 8049 8322 Medical centers; physical therapist; rehabilitation services
PA: The Ohio State University
Student Acade Servi Bldg
Columbus OH 43210
614 292-6446

(G-8389)
OHIO STATE UNIVERSITY
Also Called: Schottenstein Center, The
555 Borror Dr (43210-1187)
PHONE 614 688-3939
Joe Odoguardi, *Finance Dir*
Mike Gatto, *Exec Dir*
EMP: 730
SALES (corp-wide): 5.5B **Privately Held**
WEB: www.ohio-state.edu
SIC: 6512 8221 Property operation, auditoriums & theaters; university
PA: The Ohio State University
Student Acade Servi Bldg
Columbus OH 43210
614 292-6446

(G-8390)
OHIO STATE UNIVERSITY
Also Called: Internal Medicine
410 W 10th Ave Rm 205 (43210-1240)
PHONE 614 293-8045
Fax: 614 293-8153
Georgia Bishop, *Vice Chairman*
Robert McKenney, *Assistant VP*
Patricia M Hill-Callahan, *Vice Pres*
Joddi Giacobbi, *Project Mgr*
Daisy Sinha, *Project Mgr*
EMP: 574
SALES (corp-wide): 5.5B **Privately Held**
SIC: 8011 Internal medicine, physician/surgeon
PA: The Ohio State University
Student Acade Servi Bldg
Columbus OH 43210
614 292-6446

(G-8391)
OHIO STATE UNIVERSITY
Also Called: Osu Cnter For Wllness Prvntion
2050 Kenny Rd Ste 1010 (43221-3502)
PHONE 614 293-2800
Fax: 614 293-2801
Grant L Jones MD, *Med Doctor*
Patricia Neel, *Manager*
Trish Neal, *Director*
EMP: 40
SALES (corp-wide): 5.5B **Privately Held**
WEB: www.ohio-state.edu
SIC: 7991 8221 Physical fitness facilities; university
PA: The Ohio State University
Student Acade Servi Bldg
Columbus OH 43210
614 292-6446

(G-8392)
OHIO STATE UNIVERSITY
Also Called: College of Dentistry
305 W 12th Ave (43210-1267)
PHONE 614 292-5578
Gordon Gee, *President*
Priyangi Pereya, *Manager*
Isabelle Denry, *Professor*
Angelo Mariotti, *Assoc Prof*
Henry W Fields Jr, *Fmly & Gen Dent*
EMP: 60
SALES (corp-wide): 5.5B **Privately Held**
WEB: www.ohio-state.edu
SIC: 8021 8221 Prosthodontist; university
PA: The Ohio State University
Student Acade Servi Bldg
Columbus OH 43210
614 292-6446

(G-8393)
OHIO STATE UNIVERSITY
University Hospitals East
300 W 10th Ave (43210-1280)
PHONE 614 257-3000
Karen Miawsky, *CFO*
Robert Salmen, *Financial Exec*
Thoma Spackman, *Branch Mgr*
Ben Leonard, *Food Svc Dir*
EMP: 800
SALES (corp-wide): 5.5B **Privately Held**
WEB: www.ohio-state.edu
SIC: 8062 8093 8049 8011 General medical & surgical hospitals; rehabilitation center, outpatient treatment; physical therapist; oncologist
PA: The Ohio State University
Student Acade Servi Bldg
Columbus OH 43210
614 292-6446

(G-8394)
OHIO STATE UNIVERSITY
Also Called: Medohio Family Care Center
1615 Fishinger Rd (43221-2103)
PHONE 614 293-7417
Fax: 614 457-2012
William Padamadan, *Principal*
Kendra McCamey MD, *Med Doctor*
EMP: 574
SQ FT: 1,677
SALES (corp-wide): 5.5B **Privately Held**
WEB: www.ohio-state.edu
SIC: 8011 8221 Offices & clinics of medical doctors; university

PA: The Ohio State University
Student Acade Servi Bldg
Columbus OH 43210
614 292-6446

(G-8395)
OHIO STATE UNIVERSITY
Also Called: Medical Center
480 W 9th Ave (43210-1245)
PHONE..................614 293-8750
Fax: 614 293-5220
Robert Vanecko, *Branch Mgr*
EMP: 188
SALES (corp-wide): 5.5B **Privately Held**
WEB: www.ohio-state.edu
SIC: 8062 8221 General medical & surgical hospitals; university
PA: The Ohio State University
Student Acade Servi Bldg
Columbus OH 43210
614 292-6446

(G-8396)
OHIO STATE UNIVERSITY
Also Called: Glaucoma Consultants
915 Olentangy River Rd (43212-3153)
PHONE..................614 293-8116
Paul Weber,
EMP: 523
SALES (corp-wide): 5.5B **Privately Held**
SIC: 8011 Ophthalmologist
PA: The Ohio State University
Student Acade Servi Bldg
Columbus OH 43210
614 292-6446

(G-8397)
OHIO STATE UNIVERSITY
Also Called: Department of Human Nutrition
350 Campbell Hl (43210)
PHONE..................614 292-5504
James Kinder, *Chairman*
Angela Wendel, *Manager*
Helen Everts, *Professor*
John N Rayer, *Professor*
EMP: 50
SALES (corp-wide): 5.5B **Privately Held**
WEB: www.ohio-state.edu
SIC: 8099 8221 Nutrition services; university
PA: The Ohio State University
Student Acade Servi Bldg
Columbus OH 43210
614 292-6446

(G-8398)
OHIO STATE UNIVERSITY
Also Called: College Engineering/Aerospace
2300 West Case Rd (43235-7531)
PHONE..................614 292-5491
MO Samimy, *Director*
EMP: 75
SALES (corp-wide): 5.5B **Privately Held**
WEB: www.ohio-state.edu
SIC: 8221 8732 Colleges universities & professional schools; educational research
PA: The Ohio State University
Student Acade Servi Bldg
Columbus OH 43210
614 292-6446

(G-8399)
OHIO STATE UNIVERSITY
Also Called: Osu Industrial Welding Sy
1248 Arthur E Adams Dr (43221-3560)
PHONE..................614 292-4139
Richard A Miller, *Chairman*
EMP: 32
SALES (corp-wide): 5.5B **Privately Held**
WEB: www.ohio-state.edu
SIC: 7692 8221 Welding repair; university
PA: The Ohio State University
Student Acade Servi Bldg
Columbus OH 43210
614 292-6446

(G-8400)
OHIO STATE UNIVERSITY
Also Called: Osu Value City Arena
555 Borror Dr Ste 1030 (43210-1187)
PHONE..................614 292-2624
Lin Yuan, *Software Engr*
Michael Gatto, *Director*
Justin Doyle, *Business Dir*
EMP: 37

SALES (corp-wide): 5.5B **Privately Held**
WEB: www.ohio-state.edu
SIC: 7941 8221 Sports field or stadium operator, promoting sports events; university
PA: The Ohio State University
Student Acade Servi Bldg
Columbus OH 43210
614 292-6446

(G-8401)
OHIO STATE UNIVERSITY
Also Called: Nisonger Center
1581 Dodd Dr Ste 321 (43210-1257)
PHONE..................614 685-3192
Halley Dawson, *Director*
Kyle Jamison, *Administration*
Lacramioara Spetie, *Psychiatry*
EMP: 60
SALES (corp-wide): 5.5B **Privately Held**
WEB: www.ohio-state.edu
SIC: 8331 8221 Job training & vocational rehabilitation services; university
PA: The Ohio State University
Student Acade Servi Bldg
Columbus OH 43210
614 292-6446

(G-8402)
OHIO STATE UNIVERSITY
Also Called: Mershon Center For Education
1501 Neil Ave (43201-2602)
PHONE..................614 292-1681
Richard Harman, *Director*
EMP: 70
SALES (corp-wide): 5.5B **Privately Held**
WEB: www.ohio-state.edu
SIC: 8733 8221 Noncommercial research organizations; university
PA: The Ohio State University
Student Acade Servi Bldg
Columbus OH 43210
614 292-6446

(G-8403)
OHIO STATE UNIVERSITY
Also Called: Medical Center
1375 Perry St (43201-3177)
P.O. Box 183111 (43218-3111)
PHONE..................614 293-3860
Paula Sulcebarger, *Project Mgr*
Burdge McLean, *Manager*
Todd Neffenger, *Manager*
David Niemeyer, *Manager*
Wesley Stahler, *Manager*
EMP: 5249
SALES (corp-wide): 5.5B **Privately Held**
WEB: www.ohio-state.edu
SIC: 8011 8221 Medical centers; university
PA: The Ohio State University
Student Acade Servi Bldg
Columbus OH 43210
614 292-6446

(G-8404)
OHIO STATE UNIVERSITY
Also Called: Blackwell Inn, The
2110 Tuttle Park Pl (43210-1137)
PHONE..................614 247-4000
Fax: 614 247-4040
Eric Adelman, *General Mgr*
Trevor Sudano, *Marketing Staff*
Joel Broughton, *Web Dvlpr*
Neil Hoyng, *Technical Staff*
Nathan Smith, *Software Dev*
EMP: 26
SALES (corp-wide): 5.5B **Privately Held**
WEB: www.ohio-state.edu
SIC: 7011 8221 Hotels; university
PA: The Ohio State University
Student Acade Servi Bldg
Columbus OH 43210
614 292-6446

(G-8405)
OHIO STATE UNIVERSITY
Also Called: Ohio State Univ Child Care
725 Ackerman Rd (43202-1502)
PHONE..................614 292-4453
Andrew McFaddin, *Manager*
John Turvy, *Manager*
Maggie Sommers, *Director*
Gus CHI, *Admin Asst*
Rebecca Levitt, *Assistant*
EMP: 75

SALES (corp-wide): 5.5B **Privately Held**
WEB: www.ohio-state.edu
SIC: 8351 8221 Child day care services; colleges universities & professional schools
PA: The Ohio State University
Student Acade Servi Bldg
Columbus OH 43210
614 292-6446

(G-8406)
OHIO STATE UNIVERSITY
Also Called: Wosu Am-FM TV
2400 Olentangy River Rd (43210-1027)
PHONE..................614 292-4510
Fax: 614 292-7625
Tom Rieland, *General Mgr*
Dale Ouzts, *General Mgr*
Tom Borgerding, *Editor*
Mary Alice Akins, *Finance*
Theresa Ravencraft, *Program Mgr*
EMP: 120
SALES (corp-wide): 5.5B **Privately Held**
WEB: www.ohio-state.edu
SIC: 4832 4833 Radio broadcasting stations; television translator station
PA: The Ohio State University
Student Acade Servi Bldg
Columbus OH 43210
614 292-6446

(G-8407)
OHIO STATE UNIVERSITY
Also Called: University Tech Service
1121 Kinnear Rd Bldg E (43212-1153)
PHONE..................614 292-4843
Eileen Strider, *Principal*
Scott Johnson, *Manager*
Mark A Carey, *CTO*
Peter B McMeen, *Admin Asst*
EMP: 250
SALES (corp-wide): 5.5B **Privately Held**
WEB: www.ohio-state.edu
SIC: 8221 7379 University; computer related consulting services
PA: The Ohio State University
Student Acade Servi Bldg
Columbus OH 43210
614 292-6446

(G-8408)
OHIO STATE UNIVERSITY
Also Called: Accounts Payable Department
901 Woody Hayes Dr (43210-4013)
PHONE..................614 292-6831
Ronald Holland, *Manager*
EMP: 35
SALES (corp-wide): 5.5B **Privately Held**
WEB: www.ohio-state.edu
SIC: 8721 Accounting services, except auditing
PA: The Ohio State University
Student Acade Servi Bldg
Columbus OH 43210
614 292-6446

(G-8409)
OHIO STATE UNIVERSITY
Also Called: Veterans ADM Out Ptient Clinic
420 N James Rd (43219-1834)
PHONE..................614 257-5200
Bernard F Williams, *Manager*
EMP: 52
SALES (corp-wide): 5.5B **Privately Held**
WEB: www.ohio-state.edu
SIC: 8099 8221 Blood related health services; university
PA: The Ohio State University
Student Acade Servi Bldg
Columbus OH 43210
614 292-6446

(G-8410)
OHIO STATE UNIVERSITY
Also Called: Center Ed/Train Employmnt
1900 Kenny Rd (43210-1016)
PHONE..................614 292-4353
Fax: 614 292-1260
Ray D Ryan, *Exec Dir*
EMP: 75
SALES (corp-wide): 5.5B **Privately Held**
WEB: www.ohio-state.edu
SIC: 8732 8331 Educational research; job training services

PA: The Ohio State University
Student Acade Servi Bldg
Columbus OH 43210
614 292-6446

(G-8411)
OHIO STATE UNIVERSITY
Also Called: Osu Obgyn
395 W 12th Ave (43210-1267)
PHONE..................614 293-4997
Fax: 614 293-3073
Larry Copeland, *Chairman*
Subha Raman, *Cardiology*
Sheri Hart, *Neurology*
James Moore, *Neurology*
John G Oas, *Neurology*
EMP: 50
SALES (corp-wide): 5.5B **Privately Held**
WEB: www.ohio-state.edu
SIC: 8011 8221 Obstetrician; university
PA: The Ohio State University
Student Acade Servi Bldg
Columbus OH 43210
614 292-6446

(G-8412)
OHIO STATE UNIVERSITY
Also Called: Osu Personnel
2130 Neil Ave (43210-1296)
PHONE..................614 293-2494
William E Kerwan, *President*
EMP: 600
SALES (corp-wide): 5.5B **Privately Held**
WEB: www.ohio-state.edu
SIC: 7361 8221 Employment agencies; colleges universities & professional schools
PA: The Ohio State University
Student Acade Servi Bldg
Columbus OH 43210
614 292-6446

(G-8413)
OHIO STATE UNIVERSITY
Also Called: O S U Telephone Service
320 W 8th Ave (43201-2331)
PHONE..................614 292-7788
BJ Reeb, *Engineer*
Elizabeth Boster, *Manager*
Jamie Lambert, *Manager*
John Marlow, *Manager*
Bob Corben, *Director*
EMP: 75
SALES (corp-wide): 5.5B **Privately Held**
WEB: www.ohio-state.edu
SIC: 8331 8221 Manpower training; university
PA: The Ohio State University
Student Acade Servi Bldg
Columbus OH 43210
614 292-6446

(G-8414)
OHIO STATE UNIVERSITY
Also Called: Center For Human Resource RES
921 Chatham Ln Ste 100 (43221-2418)
PHONE..................614 442-7300
Brent Bogrees, *Engineer*
Randell Olson, *Director*
EMP: 60
SALES (corp-wide): 5.5B **Privately Held**
WEB: www.ohio-state.edu
SIC: 8732 8221 Economic research; university
PA: The Ohio State University
Student Acade Servi Bldg
Columbus OH 43210
614 292-6446

(G-8415)
OHIO STATE UNIVERSITY
Also Called: Infectious Diseases Department
N.1135 Doan Hl (43210)
PHONE..................614 293-8732
Robert J Fass, *Director*
EMP: 40
SALES (corp-wide): 5.5B **Privately Held**
WEB: www.ohio-state.edu
SIC: 8011 8221 Infectious disease specialist, physician/surgeon; university
PA: The Ohio State University
Student Acade Servi Bldg
Columbus OH 43210
614 292-6446

Columbus - Franklin County (G-8416)

(G-8416)
OHIO STATE UNIVERSITY
Also Called: Communiction/Journalism
3007 Derby Rd (43221-2607)
PHONE.................................614 292-6291
Don Dell, *Principal*
EMP: 36
SALES (corp-wide): 5.5B Privately Held
WEB: www.ohio-state.edu
SIC: 4813 8221 Telephone communication, except radio; university
PA: The Ohio State University
Student Acade Servi Bldg
Columbus OH 43210
614 292-6446

(G-8417)
OHIO STATE UNIVERSITY
Also Called: Osu Medical Staff ADM
410 W 10th Ave Rm 130 (43210-1240)
PHONE.................................614 293-8158
Janet Combs, *Office Mgr*
Antonio E Chiocca, *Med Doctor*
Tim Rumfield, *Manager*
Iouri Ivanov, *Pathologist*
Andrew Thomas, *Director*
EMP: 35
SALES (corp-wide): 5.5B Privately Held
WEB: www.ohio-state.edu
SIC: 8062 8221 Hospital, medical school affiliation; university
PA: The Ohio State University
Student Acade Servi Bldg
Columbus OH 43210
614 292-6446

(G-8418)
OHIO STATE UNIVERSITY
Also Called: Student Wilce Health Center
1875 Millikin Rd Fl 3 (43210-2200)
PHONE.................................614 292-0110
Melissa Ames, *Manager*
Margot Sandler, *Manager*
Ted W Grace, *Director*
Rose Dodson, *Admin Sec*
EMP: 100
SALES (corp-wide): 5.5B Privately Held
WEB: www.ohio-state.edu
SIC: 8099 8221 Health screening service; university
PA: The Ohio State University
Student Acade Servi Bldg
Columbus OH 43210
614 292-6446

(G-8419)
OHIO STATE UNIVERSITY
Also Called: Osu Dept Psychology
Ps Pschology Rm 225 (43210)
PHONE.................................614 292-6741
Dr Gifford Weary, *Chairman*
Chad Carpenter, *Manager*
Richard E Petty, *Administration*
Barbara Andersen, *Professor*
EMP: 60
SALES (corp-wide): 5.5B Privately Held
WEB: www.ohio-state.edu
SIC: 8049 8221 Clinical psychologist; university
PA: The Ohio State University
Student Acade Servi Bldg
Columbus OH 43210
614 292-6446

(G-8420)
OHIO STATE UNIVERSITY
Oral and Maxillofacial Surgery
305 W 12th Ave Ste 2131 (43210-1267)
P.O. Box 907, Hilliard (43026-0907)
PHONE.................................614 292-5144
Dr Gregory Ness, *Director*
EMP: 27
SALES (corp-wide): 5.5B Privately Held
WEB: www.ohio-state.edu
SIC: 8021 8221 Dental surgeon; maxillofacial specialist; university
PA: The Ohio State University
Student Acade Servi Bldg
Columbus OH 43210
614 292-6446

(G-8421)
OHIO STATE UNIVERSITY
Also Called: Osu-Infectious Diseases
456 W 10th Ave Rm 4725 (43210-1240)
PHONE.................................614 293-8732
Fax: 614 293-8102
Kottil Rammohan, *Med Doctor*
James L Moore, *Neurology*
EMP: 37
SALES (corp-wide): 5.5B Privately Held
WEB: www.ohio-state.edu
SIC: 4959 8221 Disease control; university
PA: The Ohio State University
Student Acade Servi Bldg
Columbus OH 43210
614 292-6446

(G-8422)
OHIO STATE UNIVERSITY
Also Called: Medical Center
410 W 10th Ave (43210-1240)
PHONE.................................614 293-8588
Carl Story, *Manager*
EMP: 40
SALES (corp-wide): 5.5B Privately Held
WEB: www.ohio-state.edu
SIC: 5047 8221 Medical & hospital equipment; university
PA: The Ohio State University
Student Acade Servi Bldg
Columbus OH 43210
614 292-6446

(G-8423)
OHIO STATE UNIVERSITY
Also Called: School Edctl Policy Leadership
29 W Woodruff Ave Ofc 121 (43210-1116)
PHONE.................................614 688-5721
Robert Lawson, *Director*
EMP: 50
SALES (corp-wide): 5.5B Privately Held
WEB: www.ohio-state.edu
SIC: 8221 8641 University; educator's association
PA: The Ohio State University
Student Acade Servi Bldg
Columbus OH 43210
614 292-6446

(G-8424)
OHIO STATE UNIVERSITY
University Hospital
650 Ackerman Rd Ste 135 (43202-4500)
PHONE.................................614 293-3737
Beth Necamp, *Principal*
Lori E Smith, *Corp Comm Staff*
Darrell Ward, *Director*
Sherri Kirk, *Associate Dir*
Ron Kibbe, *Asst Director*
EMP: 40
SALES (corp-wide): 5.5B Privately Held
WEB: www.ohio-state.edu
SIC: 8743 8221 Public relations services; university
PA: The Ohio State University
Student Acade Servi Bldg
Columbus OH 43210
614 292-6446

(G-8425)
OHIO STATE UNIVERSITY
Also Called: Nuclear Reactor Laboratory
1298 Kinnear Rd (43212-1154)
PHONE.................................614 688-8220
Thomas E Blue, *Director*
EMP: 101
SALES (corp-wide): 5.5B Privately Held
SIC: 8731 Chemical laboratory, except testing
PA: The Ohio State University
Student Acade Servi Bldg
Columbus OH 43210
614 292-6446

(G-8426)
OHIO STATE UNIVERSITY
Also Called: Transportation Department
2578 Kenny Rd (43210-1038)
PHONE.................................614 292-6122
Steve Basinger, *Director*
EMP: 35
SALES (corp-wide): 5.5B Privately Held
WEB: www.ohio-state.edu
SIC: 4789 8221 Cargo loading & unloading services; university
PA: The Ohio State University
Student Acade Servi Bldg
Columbus OH 43210
614 292-6446

(G-8427)
OHIO STATE UNIVERSITY
Also Called: Fawcett Center For Tomorrow
2400 Olentangy River Rd (43210-1027)
PHONE.................................614 292-3238
Fax: 614 292-3389
Diane Whitbeck, *Principal*
Amy Palermo, *Exec Dir*
EMP: 300
SALES (corp-wide): 5.5B Privately Held
WEB: www.ohio-state.edu
SIC: 8221 7991 7011 5813 Colleges universities & professional schools; physical fitness facilities; hotels & motels; drinking places; eating places
PA: The Ohio State University
Student Acade Servi Bldg
Columbus OH 43210
614 292-6446

(G-8428)
OHIO STATE UNIVERSITY
Also Called: Ohio State Univ Vtrnarian Hosp
601 Vernon Tharp St (43210-4007)
PHONE.................................614 292-6661
Fax: 614 292-9982
Cheryl Holloway, *Manager*
Dr Richard M Bednarski, *Director*
Alicia Bertone, *Professor*
Mary A McLoughlin,
Pam Walker,
EMP: 150
SALES (corp-wide): 5.5B Privately Held
WEB: www.ohio-state.edu
SIC: 0742 8221 Animal hospital services, pets & other animal specialties; university
PA: The Ohio State University
Student Acade Servi Bldg
Columbus OH 43210
614 292-6446

(G-8429)
OHIO STATE UNIVERSITY
Osu Center Automotive Research
930 Kinnear Rd (43212-1443)
PHONE.................................614 292-5990
David Cooke, *Manager*
Giorgio Rizzoni, *Director*
EMP: 149
SALES (corp-wide): 5.5B Privately Held
SIC: 8733 8221 Research institute; university
PA: The Ohio State University
Student Acade Servi Bldg
Columbus OH 43210
614 292-6446

(G-8430)
OHIO STATE UNIVERSITY
Also Called: Delta Theta Sigma Fraternity
80 E 13th Ave (43201-1808)
PHONE.................................614 294-2635
Fax: 614 297-5429
Austin Kirk, *President*
Kathryn Jones, *Meeting Planner*
EMP: 25
SALES (corp-wide): 5.5B Privately Held
WEB: www.ohio-state.edu
SIC: 7041 8221 Fraternities & sororities; university
PA: The Ohio State University
Student Acade Servi Bldg
Columbus OH 43210
614 292-6446

(G-8431)
OHIO STATE UNIVERSITY
Also Called: Speech Language Hearing Clinic
1070 Carmack Rd (43210-1002)
PHONE.................................614 292-6251
Jennifer Forsythe, *Manager*
Gail Whitelaw, *Director*
EMP: 188
SALES (corp-wide): 5.5B Privately Held
WEB: www.ohio-state.edu
SIC: 8062 8221 Hospital, medical school affiliation; colleges universities & professional schools
PA: The Ohio State University
Student Acade Servi Bldg
Columbus OH 43210
614 292-6446

(G-8432)
OHIO STATE UNIVERSITY
Also Called: Oarnet
1224 Kinnear Rd (43212-1154)
PHONE.................................614 728-8100
Fax: 614 728-8174
Kevin Earp, *Manager*
Douglas Gale, *Director*
EMP: 45
SALES (corp-wide): 5.5B Privately Held
WEB: www.ohio-state.edu
SIC: 7373 8742 Computer integrated systems design; management consulting services
PA: The Ohio State University
Student Acade Servi Bldg
Columbus OH 43210
614 292-6446

(G-8433)
OHIO STATE UNIVERSITY
Also Called: Ohio State Univ Spt Mdcine Ctr
2050 Kenny Rd Fl 3 (43221-3502)
PHONE.................................614 293-2222
Fax: 614 293-4399
Terry Hazucha, *Principal*
Steve Hewitt, *Project Mgr*
EMP: 60
SALES (corp-wide): 5.5B Privately Held
WEB: www.ohio-state.edu
SIC: 8011 8221 Sports medicine specialist, physician; university
PA: The Ohio State University
Student Acade Servi Bldg
Columbus OH 43210
614 292-6446

(G-8434)
OHIO STATE UNIVERSITY
Also Called: Dept of Surgery
410 W 10th Ave Fl 7 (43210-1240)
PHONE.................................614 293-8133
Christopher Ellison, *Chairman*
Mark W Arnold, *Professor*
EMP: 350
SALES (corp-wide): 5.5B Privately Held
WEB: www.ohio-state.edu
SIC: 8011 8221 Physicians' office, including specialists; university
PA: The Ohio State University
Student Acade Servi Bldg
Columbus OH 43210
614 292-6446

(G-8435)
OHIO STATE UNIVERSITY
Also Called: Nat'l Rglartory RES Institutue
1080 Carmack Rd (43210-1002)
PHONE.................................614 292-9404
EMP: 30
SALES (corp-wide): 5.1B Privately Held
SIC: 8732 8221 Commercial Nonphysical Research College/University
PA: The Ohio State University
Student Acade Servi Bldg
Columbus OH 43210
614 292-6446

(G-8436)
OHIO STATE UNIVERSITY
Also Called: James Cancer Center
300 W 10th Ave 924 (43210-1280)
PHONE.................................614 293-5066
John Biancamano, *Vice Pres*
Steven Gabbe, *Vice Pres*
Zachary Rossfeld, *Vice Pres*
Marie Kaufman, *Purch Agent*
Charles Borden, *QA Dir*
EMP: 574
SALES (corp-wide): 5.5B Privately Held
SIC: 8011 8221 Oncologist; university
PA: The Ohio State University
Student Acade Servi Bldg
Columbus OH 43210
614 292-6446

(G-8437)
OHIO STATE UNIVERSITY
Also Called: Medical Records Department
410 W 10th Ave Rm 140 (43210-1240)
PHONE.................................614 293-8419
Tony Fragle, *Manager*
Liz Curtis, *Director*
Hagop S Mekhjian, *Director*
EMP: 35

GEOGRAPHIC SECTION
Columbus - Franklin County (G-8459)

SALES (corp-wide): 5.5B **Privately Held**
WEB: www.ohio-state.edu
SIC: **8062** 8221 General medical & surgical hospitals; university
PA: The Ohio State University
Student Acade Servi Bldg
Columbus OH 43210
614 292-6446

(G-8438)
OHIO STATE UNIVERSITY
Also Called: Osu Physics Dept, The
191 W Woodruff Ave (43210-1117)
PHONE..................614 292-0476
William Saam, *Principal*
Justin North, *Manager*
Richard D Kass, *Professor*
Steven A Ringel, *Professor*
EMP: 66
SALES (corp-wide): 5.5B **Privately Held**
SIC: **8732** Commercial nonphysical research
PA: The Ohio State University
Student Acade Servi Bldg
Columbus OH 43210
614 292-6446

(G-8439)
OHIO STATE UNIVERSITY
Also Called: Osu Faculty Practice
305 W 12th Ave (43210-1267)
PHONE..................614 292-1472
Jennifer Small, *Manager*
Kelly Shader DDS, *Director*
EMP: 62
SALES (corp-wide): 5.5B **Privately Held**
WEB: www.ohio-state.edu
SIC: **8021** 8221 Prosthodontist; university
PA: The Ohio State University
Student Acade Servi Bldg
Columbus OH 43210
614 292-6446

(G-8440)
OHIO STATE UNIVERSITY
Also Called: Surgical Oncology Division
N924 Doan Hall 410 W 10 (43210)
PHONE..................614 293-8196
William Farrar, *Director*
Henry Zheng, *Director*
EMP: 35
SALES (corp-wide): 5.5B **Privately Held**
WEB: www.ohio-state.edu
SIC: **8062** 8221 General medical & surgical hospitals; university
PA: The Ohio State University
Student Acade Servi Bldg
Columbus OH 43210
614 292-6446

(G-8441)
OHIO STATE UNIVERSITY
Also Called: Medical Center Security
450 W 10th Ave (43210-1240)
PHONE..................614 293-8333
Peter Baker, *Med Doctor*
Spero Vasila, *Director*
EMP: 47
SALES (corp-wide): 5.5B **Privately Held**
WEB: www.ohio-state.edu
SIC: **8062** 8221 General medical & surgical hospitals; colleges universities & professional schools
PA: The Ohio State University
Student Acade Servi Bldg
Columbus OH 43210
614 292-6446

(G-8442)
OHIO STATE UNIVERSITY
Also Called: Osu Hospitals
450 W 10th Ave (43210-1240)
PHONE..................614 293-8000
Peter Geier, *CEO*
Dan Tippett, *Human Res Dir*
David Crawford, *Marketing Staff*
Stephen Schaal, *Med Doctor*
Tammy Moore, *Director*
EMP: 1000
SALES (corp-wide): 5.5B **Privately Held**
WEB: www.ohio-state.edu
SIC: **8062** 8221 General medical & surgical hospitals; university

PA: The Ohio State University
Student Acade Servi Bldg
Columbus OH 43210
614 292-6446

(G-8443)
OHIO STATE UNIVERSITY
305 W 12th Ave (43210-1267)
PHONE..................614 292-2751
Dean Henry Fields, *Manager*
EMP: 100
SALES (corp-wide): 5.5B **Privately Held**
WEB: www.ohio-state.edu
SIC: **8021** 8221 Offices & clinics of dentists; university
PA: The Ohio State University
Student Acade Servi Bldg
Columbus OH 43210
614 292-6446

(G-8444)
OHIO STATE UNIVERSITY
Also Called: Department of Internal Med Div
473 W 12th Ave (43210-1252)
PHONE..................614 293-4967
Fax: 614 292-4818
Patricia Caldwell, *Med Doctor*
Emile Daoud II, *Med Doctor*
John Larry, *Med Doctor*
Angie Crespin, *Manager*
EMP: 574
SALES (corp-wide): 5.5B **Privately Held**
SIC: **8011** Cardiologist & cardio-vascular specialist
PA: The Ohio State University
Student Acade Servi Bldg
Columbus OH 43210
614 292-6446

(G-8445)
OHIO STATE UNIVERSITY
Also Called: Facilities Operation and Dev
2003 Millikin Rd Rm 150 (43210-1243)
PHONE..................614 292-6158
Mellisa Belleney, *Vice Pres*
EMP: 2000
SALES (corp-wide): 5.5B **Privately Held**
WEB: www.ohio-state.edu
SIC: **7629** 7349 Electronic equipment repair; cleaning service, industrial or commercial
PA: The Ohio State University
Student Acade Servi Bldg
Columbus OH 43210
614 292-6446

(G-8446)
OHIO STATE UNIVERSITY
Also Called: Osu Division of Pulmonary
2050 Kenny Rd Ste 2200 (43221-3502)
PHONE..................614 293-4925
Carl V Leier, *Med Doctor*
Tim Mazik, *Administration*
EMP: 50
SALES (corp-wide): 5.5B **Privately Held**
WEB: www.ohio-state.edu
SIC: **8069** 8221 Specialty hospitals, except psychiatric; university
PA: The Ohio State University
Student Acade Servi Bldg
Columbus OH 43210
614 292-6446

(G-8447)
OHIO STATE UNIVERSITY
915 Olentangy River Rd (43212-3153)
PHONE..................614 293-8074
Mark Inman, *Branch Mgr*
EMP: 52
SALES (corp-wide): 5.5B **Privately Held**
SIC: **8099** Medical services organization
PA: The Ohio State University
Student Acade Servi Bldg
Columbus OH 43210
614 292-6446

(G-8448)
OHIO SUPPORT SERVICES CORP (PA)
1291 S High St (43206-3445)
PHONE..................614 443-0291
Fax: 614 443-0293
John W Tucker, *CEO*
Scott Tucker, *President*
EMP: 235
SQ FT: 7,000

SALES (est): 5.7MM **Privately Held**
WEB: www.ohiosupport.com
SIC: **7381** Security guard service

(G-8449)
OHIO SURGERY CENTER LTD
930 Bethel Rd (43214-1906)
PHONE..................614 451-0500
Jeffrey Hiltbrand, *Partner*
Diana Doane, *Controller*
EMP: 60
SQ FT: 17,000
SALES (est): 7.9MM **Privately Held**
SIC: **8011** Ambulatory surgical center

(G-8450)
OHIO TECHNICAL SERVICES INC
1949 Camaro Ave (43207-1716)
PHONE..................614 372-0829
Fax: 614 372-0933
Brian Hatfield, *President*
William Lawhon, *President*
Kim Metheny, *Manager*
EMP: 39
SQ FT: 11,000
SALES (est): 11.1MM **Privately Held**
WEB: www.ohiotechserv.com
SIC: **1542** Commercial & office building contractors

(G-8451)
OHIO TRANSMISSION CORPORATION (HQ)
Also Called: Otp Industrial Solutions
1900 Jetway Blvd (43219-1681)
PHONE..................614 342-6247
Fax: 614 342-6351
Philip Derrow, *CEO*
David D Derrow, *Chairman*
Dan Benjamin, *Area Mgr*
Darin Bushong, *Area Mgr*
Kurt Lang, *Exec VP*
◆ EMP: 110 EST: 1963
SQ FT: 40,000
SALES (est): 365.5MM **Privately Held**
WEB: www.otpnet.com
SIC: **5084** 5085 Industrial machinery & equipment; materials handling machinery; compressors, except air conditioning; pumps & pumping equipment; power transmission equipment & apparatus; bearings

(G-8452)
OHIO TRANSMISSION CORPORATION
Also Called: Air Technologies
1900 Jetway Blvd (43219-1681)
PHONE..................614 342-6247
Kurt Lang, *Branch Mgr*
EMP: 33 **Privately Held**
WEB: www.otpnet.com
SIC: **7537** Automotive transmission repair shops
HQ: Ohio Transmission Corporation
1900 Jetway Blvd
Columbus OH 43219
614 342-6247

(G-8453)
OHIO YOUTH ADVOCATE PROGRAM INC
1303 E Main St (43205-2047)
PHONE..................614 252-6927
Fax: 614 252-4367
Scott Timmerman, *Director*
EMP: 64
SALES (corp-wide): 2.6MM **Privately Held**
SIC: **8322** Child related social services
PA: Ohio Youth Advocate Program, Inc.
1801 Watermark Dr Ste 200
Columbus OH 43215
614 487-8758

(G-8454)
OHIOHEALTH CORPORATION
Also Called: Community Medicine
3595 Olentangy River Rd (43214-3440)
PHONE..................614 566-5456
Kim Jordan, *Med Doctor*
John Boswell, *Manager*
Bev Meyer, *Manager*
EMP: 108

SALES (corp-wide): 3.7B **Privately Held**
WEB: www.ohiohealth.com
SIC: **8062** General medical & surgical hospitals
PA: Ohiohealth Corporation
180 E Broad St
Columbus OH 43215
614 788-8860

(G-8455)
OHIOHEALTH CORPORATION
180 E Broad St (43215-3707)
P.O. Box 8 (43216-0008)
PHONE..................614 566-2124
Bosse Shawna, *President*
Charles Wagner, *Vice Pres*
Pennylane Lowe, *Opers Mgr*
Missy Gleason, *Pub Rel Mgr*
Betsy Joseph, *Human Resources*
EMP: 107
SALES (corp-wide): 3.7B **Privately Held**
SIC: **8062** General medical & surgical hospitals
PA: Ohiohealth Corporation
180 E Broad St
Columbus OH 43215
614 788-8860

(G-8456)
OHIOHEALTH CORPORATION
3333 Chippewa St (43204-1654)
PHONE..................614 566-3500
Mary Jo McElroy, *Branch Mgr*
EMP: 65
SALES (corp-wide): 3.7B **Privately Held**
WEB: www.ohiohealth.com
SIC: **8742** Hospital & health services consultant
PA: Ohiohealth Corporation
180 E Broad St
Columbus OH 43215
614 788-8860

(G-8457)
OHIOHEALTH CORPORATION (PA)
180 E Broad St (43215-3707)
PHONE..................614 788-8860
David Blom, *President*
Kay Holland, *Regional Mgr*
Bruce Hagen, *COO*
Michael W Louge, *COO*
Robert P Millen, *COO*
EMP: 1500
SALES: 3.7B **Privately Held**
WEB: www.ohiohealth.com
SIC: **8049** 8062 8082 8051 Occupational therapist; general medical & surgical hospitals; home health care services; convalescent home with continuous nursing care

(G-8458)
OHIOHEALTH CORPORATION
Also Called: Distrubution Center
2601 Silver Dr (43211-1056)
PHONE..................614 566-5977
Stevo Stefanovski, *Purch Dir*
Thomas Sherrin, *Director*
Kenneth Boock, *Director*
Deborah Hetrick, *Director*
Jamie Yolles, *Director*
EMP: 60
SALES (corp-wide): 3.7B **Privately Held**
WEB: www.ohiohealth.com
SIC: **8062** General medical & surgical hospitals
PA: Ohiohealth Corporation
180 E Broad St
Columbus OH 43215
614 788-8860

(G-8459)
OHIOHEALTH CORPORATION
755 Thomas Ln (43214-3903)
PHONE..................614 566-4800
Sally Robinson, *General Mgr*
Mary McElroy, *Senior VP*
Larry Brown, *Project Mgr*
Valerie Fridley, *Project Mgr*
Chuck Baker, *Manager*
EMP: 200
SALES (corp-wide): 3.7B **Privately Held**
WEB: www.ohiohealth.com
SIC: **8062** General medical & surgical hospitals

Columbus - Franklin County (G-8460)

PA: Ohiohealth Corporation
180 E Broad St
Columbus OH 43215
614 788-8860

(G-8460)
OHIOHEALTH CORPORATION
697 Thomas Ln (43214-3931)
PHONE.................................614 566-5414
Edward T Bope, *Director*
EMP: 30
SALES (corp-wide): 3.7B Privately Held
WEB: www.ohiohealth.com
SIC: 8062 Hospital, medical school affiliated with residency
PA: Ohiohealth Corporation
180 E Broad St
Columbus OH 43215
614 788-8860

(G-8461)
OHIOHEALTH RESEARCH INSTITUTE
3545 Olentangy River Rd # 328 (43214-3907)
PHONE.................................614 566-4297
Jennifer Griggs, *Manager*
John Niles, *Director*
Christine Hotz, *Administration*
EMP: 40
SALES (est): 1,000K Privately Held
SIC: 8733 Noncommercial research organizations

(G-8462)
OHIOHLTH RVERSIDE METHDST HOSP
3535 Olentangy River Rd (43214-3908)
PHONE.................................614 566-5000
Fax: 614 566-6747
Brian D Jepson, *President*
Steve Markovitch, *Senior VP*
Lee Davis, *Vice Pres*
Marci Dop, *Vice Pres*
Carolyn Ettinger, *Vice Pres*
EMP: 944 **EST:** 1884
SQ FT: 327,886
SALES (est): 1.2B Privately Held
SIC: 8062 General medical & surgical hospitals

(G-8463)
OLD DOMINION FREIGHT LINE INC
2885 Alum Creek Dr (43207-2818)
PHONE.................................614 491-3903
Fax: 614 491-5633
Bill Appoloni, *Chief Mktg Ofcr*
Bill Pressler, *Manager*
EMP: 260
SALES (corp-wide): 3.3B Publicly Held
WEB: www.odfl.com
SIC: 4213 Less-than-truckload (LTL) transport
PA: Old Dominion Freight Line Inc
500 Old Dominion Way
Thomasville NC 27360
336 889-5000

(G-8464)
OLD TIME POTTERY INC
2200 Morse Rd (43229-5821)
PHONE.................................614 337-1258
Fax: 614 337-1268
John Thaden, *Div Sub Head*
David Sidall, *Manager*
EMP: 80
SALES (corp-wide): 799.3MM Privately Held
WEB: www.oldtimepottery.com
SIC: 5999 5023 Art, picture frames & decorations; home furnishings
PA: Old Time Pottery, Llc
480 River Rock Blvd
Murfreesboro TN 37128
615 890-6060

(G-8465)
OLENTANGY VILLAGE ASSOCIATES
Also Called: Olentangy Village Apartments
2907 N High St (43202-1101)
PHONE.................................614 515-4680
Fax: 614 261-7742
John W Kessler, *Partner*
Kerry Wintrich, *General Mgr*
Jeremy Smith, *Controller*
Michelle Fairchild, *Marketing Mgr*
EMP: 40
SQ FT: 2,100
SALES (est): 3.3MM Privately Held
WEB: www.olentangyvillage.com
SIC: 6513 6512 Apartment hotel operation; commercial & industrial building operation

(G-8466)
OLOGIE LLC
447 E Main St Ste 122 (43215-5661)
PHONE.................................614 221-1107
Fax: 614 221-1108
Bill Faust, *Managing Prtnr*
Bev Ryan, *Senior Partner*
Cathy Predmore, *Managing Dir*
Emily Holt, *Editor*
Timothy Straker, *COO*
EMP: 51
SALES: 12.1MM Privately Held
WEB: www.ologie.com
SIC: 8742 Marketing consulting services

(G-8467)
OLSHAN HOTEL MANAGEMENT INC
Also Called: Residence Inn By Marriott
3999 Easton Loop W (43219-6152)
PHONE.................................614 414-1000
Fax: 614 414-1040
Michael Gouzie, *Branch Mgr*
EMP: 40
SALES (corp-wide): 13.9MM Privately Held
WEB: www.hiltoncolumbus.com
SIC: 7011 Hotels & motels
HQ: Olshan Hotel Management, Inc.
560 S Collier Blvd
Marco Island FL 34145

(G-8468)
OLSHAN HOTEL MANAGEMENT INC
Also Called: Courtyard Easton
3900 Morse Xing (43219-6081)
PHONE.................................614 416-8000
Brad Jester, *Manager*
EMP: 25
SALES (corp-wide): 13.9MM Privately Held
WEB: www.hiltoncolumbus.com
SIC: 7011 Resort hotel
HQ: Olshan Hotel Management, Inc.
560 S Collier Blvd
Marco Island FL 34145

(G-8469)
OPEN ARMS HEALTH SYSTEMS LLC
868 Freeway Dr N (43229-5420)
PHONE.................................614 385-8354
Natalie Bartholomew, *Director*
EMP: 31
SALES (est): 1.8MM Privately Held
SIC: 8082 Home health care services

(G-8470)
OPEN ONLINE LLC (PA)
Also Called: Openonline
1650 Lake Shore Dr # 350 (43204-4978)
PHONE.................................614 481-6999
Fax: 614 481-6980
Nick Vanoff, *CEO*
Richard Henderson, *COO*
James Thompson, *Controller*
EMP: 31
SQ FT: 4,100
SALES (est): 4.6MM Privately Held
SIC: 7323 Credit reporting services

(G-8471)
OPERS LEGAL DEPT
277 E Town St (43215-4642)
PHONE.................................614 227-0550
Fax: 614 227-0089
Cinthia Sledz, *Principal*
Sphr Wilson, *Human Res Dir*
Katherine Edgar, *Manager*
Gretchen Feldmann, *Manager*
Ted Meisky, *Asst Director*
EMP: 29
SALES (est): 4.4MM Privately Held
SIC: 8111 Legal services

(G-8472)
OPHTHLMIC SRGEONS CONS OF OHIO
262 Neil Ave Ste 430 (43215-7312)
PHONE.................................614 221-7464
John Burns, *President*
Alice Epitropoulos, *Principal*
Jill Foster MD, *Principal*
David M Lehmann, *Principal*
Jackie Lee, *Business Mgr*
EMP: 38
SQ FT: 14,000
SALES (est): 5.3MM Privately Held
WEB: www.ohioeyesurgeons.com
SIC: 8011 Ophthalmologist

(G-8473)
OPPORTUNITIES FOR OHIOANS (DH)
400 E Campus View Blvd (43235-4685)
PHONE.................................614 438-1200
Christina Wendell, *Counsel*
Therese Dyer, *CFO*
Janine Salloum Ashanin, *Human Resources*
Brad Reynolds, *Commissioner*
Tim Nguyen, *CIO*
EMP: 31
SALES (est): 8.8MM Privately Held
WEB: www.rsc.ohio.gov
SIC: 8322 Social services for the handicapped; rehabilitation services

(G-8474)
OPTIMUM TECHNOLOGY INC (PA)
Also Called: O T I
100 E Campus View Blvd # 380 (43235-4702)
PHONE.................................614 785-1110
Fax: 614 547-0063
Jagdish M Davda, *President*
Nick Kitchen, *QA Dir*
Renae Gross, *Business Anlyst*
Shobhana Davda, *Psychologist*
Karen Vincent, *Manager*
EMP: 30
SQ FT: 6,581
SALES: 9.4MM Privately Held
SIC: 7379

(G-8475)
OPTION CARE INFUSION SVCS INC
7654 Crosswoods Dr (43235-4621)
PHONE.................................614 431-6453
Fax: 614 236-6210
Brian J Tybor, *Pharmacist*
Nancy Creadon, *Manager*
Treasa Badger, *Executive*
EMP: 30
SALES (corp-wide): 1.7B Privately Held
SIC: 8082 Home health care services
HQ: Option Care Infusion Services, Inc.
3000 Lakeside Dr Ste 300n
Bannockburn IL 60015
312 940-2500

(G-8476)
OPTION LINE
665 E Dublin Granville Rd # 290 (43229-3245)
PHONE.................................614 586-1380
EMP: 30
SALES (est): 412.3K Privately Held
SIC: 8322 Individual/Family Services

(G-8477)
ORANGE BARREL MEDIA LLC
250 N Hartford Ave (43222-1100)
PHONE.................................614 294-4898
Peter Scantland, *Principal*
Robert Ackerman, *Opers Mgr*
James Wooster, *Opers Staff*
Adam Borchers, *CFO*
Chad Truitt, *Asst Controller*
EMP: 25
SALES (est): 2.5MM Privately Held
WEB: www.orangebarrelmedia.com
SIC: 3993 7312 Signs & advertising specialties; outdoor advertising services

(G-8478)
ORCHARD HILTZ & MCCLIMENT INC
580 N 4th St Ste 610 (43215-2157)
PHONE.................................614 418-0600
Gerry Bird, *Chairman*
EMP: 65
SALES (corp-wide): 47.4MM Privately Held
SIC: 8712 Architectural services; architectural engineering
PA: Orchard, Hiltz & Mccliment, Inc.
34000 Plymouth Rd
Livonia MI 48150
734 522-6711

(G-8479)
ORDER OF UNITE COMMERCIAL TRA (PA)
Also Called: FRATERNAL INSURANCE
1801 Watermark Dr Ste 100 (43215-7088)
P.O. Box 159019 (43215-8619)
PHONE.................................614 487-9680
Ron Hunt, *CEO*
Kevin Hecker, *Vice Pres*
Ron Ives, *Vice Pres*
Martha Tate Horn, *Treasurer*
Mindy Van Order, *Accountant*
EMP: 58 **EST:** 1888
SQ FT: 33,000
SALES: 20.4MM Privately Held
SIC: 8641 Fraternal associations

(G-8480)
OREILLY AUTOMOTIVE INC
1455 Parsons Ave (43207-1247)
PHONE.................................614 444-5352
Danny Lemley, *Branch Mgr*
EMP: 46 Publicly Held
SIC: 7538 General automotive repair shops
PA: O'reilly Automotive, Inc.
233 S Patterson Ave
Springfield MO 65802

(G-8481)
ORKIN LLC
Also Called: Orkin Pest Control 561
6230 Huntley Rd (43229-1006)
PHONE.................................614 888-5811
Fax: 614 888-0293
Bob Toledo, *Branch Mgr*
EMP: 30
SALES (corp-wide): 1.6B Publicly Held
WEB: www.orkin.com
SIC: 7342 Exterminating & fumigating
HQ: Orkin, Llc
2170 Piedmont Rd Ne
Atlanta GA 30324
404 888-2000

(G-8482)
ORTHONEURO
4420 Refugee Rd (43232-4416)
PHONE.................................614 890-6555
EMP: 65
SALES (corp-wide): 25.1MM Privately Held
SIC: 8011 8049 Offices And Clinics Of Medical Doctors, N
PA: Orthoneuro
70 S Cleveland Ave
Westerville OH 43081
614 839-3203

(G-8483)
ORTHONEURO
Also Called: Christopher D Cannell
1313 Olentangy River Rd (43212-3120)
PHONE.................................614 890-6555
Charles Cure, *President*
Heather Benjamin, *COO*
Michael B Cannone, *Med Doctor*
Paula Murphy, *Manager*
Michael Hurlburt, *Obstetrician*
EMP: 100
SALES (corp-wide): 19.3MM Privately Held
SIC: 8011 Neurologist
PA: Orthoneuro
70 S Cleveland Ave
Westerville OH 43081
614 890-6555

GEOGRAPHIC SECTION
Columbus - Franklin County (G-8510)

(G-8484)
ORTHOPEDIC ONE INC
4605 Sawmill Rd (43220-2246)
PHONE.................614 827-8700
Tom Ellis, *President*
EMP: 90 **Privately Held**
SIC: 8011 Orthopedic physician; surgeon
PA: Orthopedic One, Inc.
170 Taylor Station Rd
Columbus OH 43213

(G-8485)
ORTHOPEDIC ONE INC (PA)
Also Called: CARDINAL ORTHOPAEDIC INSTITUTE, THE
170 Taylor Station Rd (43213-4491)
PHONE.................614 545-7900
Dale Ingram, *CEO*
EMP: 48
SALES (est): 1.9MM **Privately Held**
SIC: 8069 Orthopedic hospital

(G-8486)
OSU EMERGENCY MEDICINE LLC
700 Ackerman Rd Ste 270 (43202-1553)
PHONE.................614 947-3700
Tammie Adkins, *Principal*
Douglas Rund,
EMP: 99
SALES (est): 4.2MM
SALES (corp-wide): 5.5B **Privately Held**
SIC: 8011 Medical centers
HQ: Ohio State University Physicians, Inc.
700 Ackerman Rd Ste 600
Columbus OH 43202

(G-8487)
OSU NEPHROLOGY MEDICAL CTR
410 W 10th Ave (43210-1240)
PHONE.................614 293-8300
Fax: 614 293-0990
Brad Rovin, *Director*
EMP: 25 **EST:** 1939
SALES (est): 2.3MM **Privately Held**
SIC: 8062 8299 General medical & surgical hospitals; educational services

(G-8488)
OSU ORTHODONTIC CLINIC
2010 901 Woody Hayes Dr (43210)
PHONE.................614 292-1058
Henry Fields, *Ch of Bd*
EMP: 32
SALES (est): 498.2K **Privately Held**
SIC: 8021 Orthodontist

(G-8489)
OSU PATHOLOGY SERVICES LLC
410 W 10th Ave (43210-1240)
PHONE.................614 293-5905
Harry Pukay-Martin,
EMP: 99
SALES (est): 2.1MM
SALES (corp-wide): 5.5B **Privately Held**
SIC: 8071 Pathological laboratory
HQ: Ohio State University Physicians, Inc.
700 Ackerman Rd Ste 600
Columbus OH 43202

(G-8490)
OSU PATHOLOGY SERVICES LLC
1645 Neil Ave Rm 129 (43210-1218)
PHONE.................614 247-6461
Fax: 614 293-3227
Bs Duff, *Hum Res Coord*
Daniel Sedmak, *Mng Member*
Sanford Barsky, *Mng Member*
Amy Giwirtz,
EMP: 300
SALES (est): 4.5MM **Privately Held**
SIC: 8071 Pathological laboratory

(G-8491)
OSU PHYSICAL MEDICINE LLC
480 Medical Center Dr # 1036 (43210-1229)
PHONE.................614 366-6398
William S Pease MD, *President*
Joyce Martin, *CFO*
EMP: 25

SALES: 950K
SALES (corp-wide): 5.5B **Privately Held**
SIC: 8011 Medical centers
HQ: Ohio State University Physicians, Inc.
700 Ackerman Rd Ste 600
Columbus OH 43202

(G-8492)
OSU PSYCHIATRY LLC
700 Ackerman Rd Ste 600 (43202-1559)
PHONE.................614 794-1818
Vanessa Armentrout, *Controller*
Radu Saveanu, *Exec Dir*
EMP: 31
SALES: 950K
SALES (corp-wide): 5.5B **Privately Held**
SIC: 8011 Psychiatric clinic
HQ: Ohio State University Physicians, Inc.
700 Ackerman Rd Ste 600
Columbus OH 43202

(G-8493)
OSU RADIOLOGY LLC
395 W 12th Ave (43210-1267)
PHONE.................614 293-8315
Fax: 614 293-6935
Kevin Crofoot, *Business Mgr*
Ruth Hackman, *Business Mgr*
Glen E Cooke, *Cardiovascular*
EMP: 32
SALES (est): 1.1MM
SALES (corp-wide): 5.5B **Privately Held**
SIC: 8011 Radiologist
HQ: Ohio State University Physicians, Inc.
700 Ackerman Rd Ste 600
Columbus OH 43202

(G-8494)
OSU SPT MDCINE PHYSCIANS INC
2835 Fred Taylor Dr (43202-1552)
PHONE.................614 293-3600
Chris Kaeding, *Principal*
Garth Dahdah, *Program Dir*
Jennifer Carter, *Sports Medicine*
EMP: 33
SALES (est): 2.8MM **Privately Held**
SIC: 8011 Sports medicine specialist, physician

(G-8495)
OSU SURGERY LLC
Genrl Srgry Dept OH State Univ
915 Olentangy River Rd # 2100 (43212-3154)
PHONE.................614 293-8116
Sheldon Simon, *Managing Dir*
Chris Kaiser, *CFO*
Amy Gellegani, *VP Mktg*
Scott Melvin, *Branch Mgr*
Kristy Fox, *Administration*
EMP: 50
SQ FT: 3,000
SALES (corp-wide): 25MM **Privately Held**
SIC: 8011 Surgeon
PA: Osu Surgery, Llc
700 Ackerman Rd Ste 350
Columbus OH 43202
614 261-1141

(G-8496)
OSU SURGERY LLC (PA)
700 Ackerman Rd Ste 350 (43202-1583)
PHONE.................614 261-1141
Fax: 614 261-8159
Chris Kaiser, *CFO*
E C Ellison MD,
Robert L Rubert MD,
EMP: 150
SQ FT: 6,700
SALES: 25MM **Privately Held**
SIC: 8011 Surgeon

(G-8497)
OSUP COMMUNITY OUTREACH LLC
700 Ackerman Rd Ste 600 (43202-1559)
PHONE.................614 685-1542
Alisa A Schueneman,
EMP: 30 **EST:** 2015
SALES (est): 1.3MM **Privately Held**
SIC: 8011 Physicians' office, including specialists

(G-8498)
OTIS ELEVATOR COMPANY
777 Dearborn Park Ln L (43085-5716)
PHONE.................614 777-6500
Fax: 614 777-6509
Tim Collins, *Manager*
EMP: 50
SALES (corp-wide): 59.8B **Publicly Held**
WEB: www.otis.com
SIC: 5084 7699 Elevators; elevators: inspection, service & repair
HQ: Otis Elevator Company
1 Carrier Pl
Farmington CT 06032
860 674-3000

(G-8499)
OUR LADY OF BETHLEHEM SCHOOLS
4567 Olentangy River Rd (43214-2499)
PHONE.................614 459-8285
Fax: 614 451-3706
Marilyn Dono, *Principal*
Lauren Don, *Marketing Staff*
Gina Wachinger, *Tech/Comp Coord*
EMP: 30
SALES (est): 1.3MM **Privately Held**
WEB: www.cdeducation.org
SIC: 8211 8661 8351 Catholic elementary & secondary schools; Catholic Church; child day care services

(G-8500)
P & D TRANSPORTATION INC
Also Called: Putnam Logistics
4274 Groves Rd (43232-4103)
PHONE.................614 577-1130
Earl Taylor, *Manager*
EMP: 30
SALES (corp-wide): 21.3MM **Privately Held**
SIC: 4213 4212 Trucking, except local; local trucking, without storage
PA: P & D Transportation, Inc.
1705 Moxahala Ave
Zanesville OH 43701
740 454-1221

(G-8501)
P C C REFRIGERATED EX INC
Also Called: PCC Transportation
2365 Performance Way (43207-2858)
PHONE.................614 754-8929
Robert Perry Jr, *President*
Eric Lubold, *Manager*
EMP: 30
SQ FT: 5,000
SALES (est): 8.2MM **Privately Held**
SIC: 4213 Refrigerated products transport

(G-8502)
P E MILLER & ASSOC
1341 S Hamilton Rd (43227-1304)
P.O. Box 1898, Buckeye Lake (43008-1898)
PHONE.................614 231-4743
Fax: 614 231-9529
Petty Miller, *President*
EMP: 80
SALES (est): 1.7MM **Privately Held**
SIC: 8082 7361 Home health care services; nurses' registry

(G-8503)
P E MILLER & ASSOCIATES INC
1341 S Hamilton Rd (43227-1304)
P.O. Box 1808, Buckeye Lake (43008-1898)
PHONE.................614 231-4743
Peggy E Miller, *President*
Charles Miller, *Vice Pres*
Jonathan Miller, *Treasurer*
Harriette Blaskis, *Admin Sec*
Harriet Hill, *Admin Sec*
EMP: 100
SALES (est): 3.1MM **Privately Held**
SIC: 7363 8082 Help supply services; home health care services

(G-8504)
PACHE MANAGEMENT COMPANY INC
5026 Dierker Rd Ofc (43220-5278)
PHONE.................614 451-9236
Paul C Herreid, *CEO*

Dorrit Herreid, *Vice Pres*
EMP: 50
SQ FT: 1,000
SALES (est): 3.3MM **Privately Held**
WEB: www.pachemgmt.com
SIC: 6531 Real estate managers

(G-8505)
PACTIV LLC
2120 Westbelt Dr (43228-3820)
P.O. Box 28147 (43228-0147)
PHONE.................614 771-5400
Joe Deal, *Opers Mgr*
Ed Steeberger, *Opers Mgr*
Lynn Morgan, *Purch Agent*
Gary White, *Buyer*
Toni Caniglia, *Human Res Dir*
EMP: 240 **Privately Held**
WEB: www.pactiv.com
SIC: 2631 7389 Paperboard mills; packaging & labeling services
HQ: Pactiv Llc
1900 W Field Ct
Lake Forest IL 60045
847 482-2000

(G-8506)
PACTIV LLC
1999 Dividend Dr (43228-3849)
PHONE.................614 777-4019
See Berger, *Manager*
EMP: 200 **Privately Held**
WEB: www.pactiv.com
SIC: 7389 Packaging & labeling services
HQ: Pactiv Llc
1900 W Field Ct
Lake Forest IL 60045
847 482-2000

(G-8507)
PAGETECH LTD
951 Robinwood Ave Ste F (43213-6707)
P.O. Box 9870 (43209-0870)
PHONE.................614 238-0518
Maureen Menzel, *Manager*
John W Page,
EMP: 60
SQ FT: 10,000
SALES (est): 3.2MM **Privately Held**
SIC: 7812 Audio-visual program production

(G-8508)
PAIN CONTROL CONSULTANTS INC
1680 Watermark Dr 100 (43215-1034)
PHONE.................614 430-5727
Fax: 614 358-7260
W David Leak, *President*
Vijay Upadhyaya, *Controller*
Bob Volk, *Manager*
EMP: 30
SQ FT: 12,000
SALES (est): 1.6MM **Privately Held**
SIC: 8011 Offices & clinics of medical doctors

(G-8509)
PAIN NET INC
99 N Brice Rd Ste 270 (43213-6525)
PHONE.................614 481-5960
Fax: 614 481-5964
W David Leak, *President*
Elizabeth Ansel, *Exec VP*
EMP: 54
SQ FT: 25,000
SALES (est): 4.6MM **Privately Held**
SIC: 8011 8621 Offices & clinics of medical doctors; professional membership organizations

(G-8510)
PALMER VOLKEMA THOMAS INC
140 E Town St Ste 1100 (43215-5183)
PHONE.................614 221-4400
Elizabeth Burkett, *President*
Robert Gray Palmer, *Partner*
Craig Scott, *Partner*
Warner R Thomas, *Partner*
Daniel P Volkema, *Partner*
EMP: 25
SALES (est): 2.4MM **Privately Held**
WEB: www.vt-law.com
SIC: 8111 General practice law office

Columbus - Franklin County (G-8511) — GEOGRAPHIC SECTION

(G-8511)
PALMER-DONAVIN MFG CO (PA)
3210 Centerpoint Dr (43212)
P.O. Box 2109 (43216-2109)
PHONE..........................614 486-0975
Fax: 614 486-5073
Robert J Woodward Jr, *Ch of Bd*
Ronald Calhoun, *President*
Eric Belke, *Vice Pres*
Bob Icenhour, *Vice Pres*
Robert J McCollow, *Vice Pres*
▲ **EMP:** 143
SQ FT: 73,000
SALES (est): 220MM **Privately Held**
WEB: www.palmerdonavin.com
SIC: 5033 Roofing & siding materials

(G-8512)
PALMETTO CONSTRUCTION SVCS LLC
892 Scott St (43222-1233)
PHONE..........................614 503-7150
Anthony Howes, *Project Mgr*
Jerry Diodore, *Mng Member*
Casey Cusack,
EMP: 36
SQ FT: 15,000
SALES: 22MM **Privately Held**
SIC: 1541 1542 Industrial buildings, new construction; commercial & office building contractors

(G-8513)
PANACEA PRODUCTS CORPORATION (PA)
Also Called: J-Mak Industries
2711 International St (43228-4604)
PHONE..........................614 850-7000
Fax: 614 850-7111
Frank A Paniccia, *President*
Louis Calderone, *Principal*
Fred Pagura, *Principal*
Jim Fancelli, *Vice Pres*
Gregg Paniccia, *Vice Pres*
◆ **EMP:** 40
SALES (est): 29.4MM **Privately Held**
WEB: www.panac.com
SIC: 3496 2542 5051 Miscellaneous fabricated wire products; shelving, made from purchased wire; shelving, office & store: except wood; metals service centers & offices

(G-8514)
PAPPAS LEAH
41 S High St Fl 12 (43215-3406)
PHONE..........................614 621-7007
Leah Pappas, *Owner*
EMP: 25
SALES (est): 646.2K **Privately Held**
SIC: 8111 Legal services

(G-8515)
PARK NATIONAL BANK
140 E Town St Ste 1400 (43215-5114)
PHONE..........................614 228-0063
Fax: 614 228-0205
Ralph Root, *Branch Mgr*
Megan Gadke, *Trust Officer*
EMP: 25
SALES (corp-wide): 367MM **Publicly Held**
WEB: www.parknationalbank.com
SIC: 6021 National commercial banks
HQ: The Park National Bank
50 N 3rd St
Newark OH 43055
740 349-8451

(G-8516)
PARKER-HANNIFIN CORPORATION
Also Called: Tube Fittings Division
3885 Gateway Blvd (43228-9723)
PHONE..........................614 279-7070
Fax: 614 279-7685
Wendy Moore, *Safety Mgr*
Ted Amling, *Engineer*
Dan Domanowski, *Engineer*
Nathan Green, *Engineer*
Eric Grimes, *Engineer*
EMP: 120
SALES (corp-wide): 12B **Publicly Held**
WEB: www.parker.com
SIC: 3494 5074 Pipe fittings; plumbing fittings & supplies
PA: Parker-Hannifin Corporation
6035 Parkland Blvd
Cleveland OH 44124
216 896-3000

(G-8517)
PARKING SOLUTIONS INC (HQ)
Also Called: Parking Sltions For Healthcare
353 W Nationwide Blvd (43215-2311)
P.O. Box 906, New Albany (43054-0906)
PHONE..........................614 469-7000
Fax: 614 469-7694
Aaron D Shocket, *President*
Gwynn Haven, *General Mgr*
Rudy Touvell, *General Mgr*
Kristen Bitonte, *Accounting Mgr*
EMP: 600
SALES (est): 23.6MM
SALES (corp-wide): 481.2MM **Privately Held**
WEB: www.parkingsolutionsinc.com
SIC: 7299 Valet parking
PA: Towne Park, Llc
1 Park Pl Ste 200
Annapolis MD 21401
410 267-6111

(G-8518)
PARKOPS COLUMBUS LLC
56 E Long St (43215-2911)
PHONE..........................877 499-9155
Joe Furnl, *Mng Member*
EMP: 500
SALES: 7.5MM **Privately Held**
SIC: 8741 Management services

(G-8519)
PARMAN GROUP INC (PA)
4501 Hilton Corporate Dr (43232-4154)
P.O. Box 360687 (43236-0687)
PHONE..........................513 673-0077
Jamie L Parman, *President*
Jeremy Duffield, *Opers Mgr*
Antonio Collura, *Data Proc Exec*
EMP: 50
SQ FT: 22,000
SALES (est): 2.6MM **Privately Held**
SIC: 8742 Compensation & benefits planning consultant

(G-8520)
PATIENT ACCOUNT MGT SVCS LLC
950 Taylor Station Rd I (43230-6670)
PHONE..........................614 575-0044
Jess Ellerdrock, *Manager*
EMP: 25
SALES (est): 1.1MM
SALES (corp-wide): 198.5B **Publicly Held**
WEB: www.per-se.com
SIC: 8742 Hospital & health services consultant
HQ: Change Healthcare Technologies, Llc
5995 Windward Pkwy
Alpharetta GA 30005

(G-8521)
PATRICK MAHONEY
Also Called: Physical Thrapy Consulting Svc
1223 Neil Ave (43201-3119)
PHONE..........................614 292-5766
Patrick Mahoney, *Owner*
EMP: 40
SALES (est): 2MM **Privately Held**
WEB: www.patrickmahoney.com
SIC: 8742 Personnel management consultant

(G-8522)
PAUL PETERSON COMPANY (PA)
950 Dublin Rd (43215-1169)
P.O. Box 1510 (43216-1510)
PHONE..........................614 486-4375
Fax: 614 486-5517
Paul Peterson Jr, *CEO*
Parr Peterson, *President*
Andrew J White Jr, *Principal*
Richard L Miller, *Principal*
Grant S Richards, *Principal*
EMP: 47
SALES (est): 15.2MM **Privately Held**
WEB: www.ppco.net
SIC: 1611 1799 3669 5084 Guardrail construction, highways; highway & street sign installation; waterproofing; traffic signals, electric; safety equipment; work zone traffic equipment (flags, cones, barrels, etc.)

(G-8523)
PAUL PETERSON SAFETY DIV INC
950 Dublin Rd (43215-1169)
P.O. Box 1510 (43216-1510)
PHONE..........................614 486-4375
Paul Peterson Jr, *President*
Colette Peterson, *Corp Secy*
Gary Boylan, *Vice Pres*
Parr Peterson, *Vice Pres*
EMP: 30
SQ FT: 3,800
SALES (est): 180.7K
SALES (corp-wide): 15.2MM **Privately Held**
WEB: www.ppco.net
SIC: 3993 5999 7359 Signs, not made in custom sign painting shops; safety supplies & equipment; work zone traffic equipment (flags, cones, barrels, etc.)
PA: The Paul Peterson Company
950 Dublin Rd
Columbus OH 43215
614 486-4375

(G-8524)
PAUL WERTH ASSOCIATES INC (PA)
10 N High St Ste 300 (43215-3497)
PHONE..........................614 224-8114
Fax: 614 224-8509
Sandra W Harbrecht, *President*
Karl Gebhardt, *Vice Pres*
Carl West, *CFO*
Margaret Werth, *Treasurer*
Melina Metzger, *Accounting Mgr*
EMP: 28
SALES (est): 5.8MM **Privately Held**
WEB: www.paulwerth.com
SIC: 8743 7319 Public relations & publicity; transit advertising services

(G-8525)
PCA-CORRECTIONS LLC
Also Called: Choice Pharmacy Services
4014 Venture Ct (43228-9600)
PHONE..........................614 297-8244
Fax: 614 297-8239
Connie O'Connell, *Branch Mgr*
Jordan Prozialeck, *Exec Dir*
Sandy Smith, *Admin Asst*
EMP: 50 **Privately Held**
SIC: 5122 Pharmaceuticals
PA: Pca-Corrections, Llc
2701 Chestnut Station Ct
Louisville KY 40299

(G-8526)
PEABODY LANDSCAPE CNSTR INC
Also Called: Peabody Landscape Group
2253 Dublin Rd (43228-9629)
PHONE..........................614 488-2877
Fax: 614 488-3543
David G Peabody, *President*
Cheryl Brammer, *Vice Pres*
Cindy Clay, *Controller*
David Veppert, *Controller*
Dave Smith, *Sales Staff*
EMP: 64
SQ FT: 2,000
SALES (est): 10.4MM **Privately Held**
WEB: www.peabodylandscape.com
SIC: 0782 Landscape contractors

(G-8527)
PEARL INTERACTIVE NETWORK INC
1103 Schrock Rd Ste 109 (43229-1177)
PHONE..........................614 258-2943
Merry Korn, *CEO*
Brian Nimmo, *Vice Pres*
Diane Schrimpf, *Vice Pres*
David Logan, *CFO*
Gina Beyer, *Sales Executive*
EMP: 350
SALES (est): 33.5MM **Privately Held**
WEB: www.pearlinter.org
SIC: 4813 7361 Telephone communication, except radio; voice telephone communications; employment agencies

(G-8528)
PECO II INC
7060 Huntley Rd (43229-1082)
PHONE..........................614 431-0694
Rich Powell, *Opers Mgr*
EMP: 55
SALES (corp-wide): 122B **Publicly Held**
WEB: www.peco2.com
SIC: 3661 8711 7372 3822 Telephone & telegraph apparatus; engineering services; prepackaged software; auto controls regulating residntl & coml environmt & applncs; relays & industrial controls
HQ: Peco Ii, Inc.
601 Shiloh Rd
Plano TX 75074
972 284-8449

(G-8529)
PEDERSEN INSULATION COMPANY
2901 Johnstown Rd (43219-1719)
P.O. Box 30744 (43230-0744)
PHONE..........................614 471-3788
Fax: 614 471-0114
Gregory Pedersen, *President*
Jared Goodsite, *Vice Pres*
Valerie Pedersen, *Admin Sec*
EMP: 40 **EST:** 1963
SQ FT: 7,200
SALES (est): 4.8MM **Privately Held**
SIC: 1742 1799 Insulation, buildings; asbestos removal & encapsulation

(G-8530)
PEDIATRIC ASSOCIATES INC (PA)
1021 Country Club Rd A (43213-2484)
PHONE..........................614 501-7337
Malcolm Robbins MD, *President*
William Fernald MD, *Corp Secy*
Sandra Boyle MD, *Vice Pres*
Anne Croft MD, *Vice Pres*
Althea Clarke, *Controller*
EMP: 44
SQ FT: 3,000
SALES (est): 9.5MM **Privately Held**
SIC: 8011 Pediatrician

(G-8531)
PENSKE TRUCK LEASING CO LP
2470 Westbelt Dr (43228-3825)
PHONE..........................614 658-0000
Tim Burke, *District Mgr*
Dennis Day, *Manager*
Maria Chandler, *Manager*
Phil Freeman, *Manager*
Randy Ljubi, *Executive*
EMP: 50
SQ FT: 22,480
SALES (corp-wide): 2.9B **Privately Held**
WEB: www.pensketruckleasing.com
SIC: 7513 Truck leasing, without drivers
PA: Penske Truck Leasing Co., L.P.
2675 Morgantown Rd
Reading PA 19607
610 775-6000

(G-8532)
PEOPLE TO MY SITE LLC
Also Called: People To Site
580 N 4th St Ste 500 (43215-2158)
PHONE..........................614 452-8179
Toodd Swicker, *Mng Member*
Karin Oliver-Kreft, *Supervisor*
Ben Clarke, *CIO*
Terrence Tuy, *Web Dvlpr*
Peter Boyuk, *Director*
EMP: 49
SALES (est): 5.9MM **Privately Held**
WEB: www.i16y.net
SIC: 7311 Advertising agencies

GEOGRAPHIC SECTION
Columbus - Franklin County (G-8558)

(G-8533)
PEOPLETOMYSITECOM LLC (PA)
Also Called: Shipyard, The
580 N 4th St Ste 500 (43215-2158)
PHONE................................800 295-4519
Jason Walker, *Managing Prtnr*
Stephen Howell, *Project Mgr*
Tiffanie Hiibner, *Ch Credit Ofcr*
Jen Lyttle, *Consultant*
Zachary Yurch, *Consultant*
EMP: 48 EST: 2005
SALES (est): 7.9MM Privately Held
SIC: 8742 Marketing consulting services

(G-8534)
PEP BOYS - MANNY MOE & JACK
2830 S Hamilton Rd (43232-4906)
PHONE................................614 864-2092
Fax: 614 864-8372
Greg Miller, *Manager*
EMP: 30
SQ FT: 22,400
SALES (corp-wide): 21.7B Publicly Held
SIC: 5531 7538 Automotive parts; general automotive repair shops
HQ: Pep Boys - Manny, Moe & Jack Of Delaware, Inc
3111 W Allegheny Ave
Philadelphia PA 19132

(G-8535)
PERCEPTIONIST INC
1010 Taylor Station Rd A (43230-6676)
PHONE................................614 384-7500
Tiger Downey, *President*
Lisa Dulay, *Treasurer*
Scott Mackenzie, *Shareholder*
EMP: 26
SQ FT: 3,000
SALES: 1.4MM Privately Held
SIC: 7389 Telephone answering service

(G-8536)
PERKFECT DESIGN SOLUTIONS
308 E 9th Ave (43201-2207)
PHONE................................614 778-3560
Bert Perkins III, *Principal*
EMP: 25
SALES (est): 1.2MM Privately Held
SIC: 8712 Architectural services

(G-8537)
PERRY CONTRACT SERVICES INC
2319 Scioto Harper Dr (43204-3495)
PHONE................................614 274-4350
Anthony Perry, *President*
Liz Perry, *General Mgr*
EMP: 60
SALES (est): 1.5MM Privately Held
SIC: 7349 Janitorial service, contract basis; window cleaning

(G-8538)
PERSONAL SERVICE INSURANCE CO
2760 Airport Dr Ste 130 (43219-2294)
P.O. Box 105021, Atlanta GA (30348-5021)
PHONE................................800 282-9416
William Lockhorn, *President*
EMP: 380
SQ FT: 10,000
SALES (est): 89MM Privately Held
WEB: www.personalserviceinsurance.com
SIC: 6331 Property damage insurance; fire, marine & casualty insurance & carriers; automobile insurance

(G-8539)
PERSONAL TOUCH HM CARE IPA INC
454 E Main St Ste 227 (43215-5372)
PHONE................................614 227-6952
Patti Malm, *Manager*
EMP: 51
SALES (corp-wide): 363MM Privately Held
WEB: www.pthomecare.com
SIC: 8082 Home health care services

PA: Personal Touch Home Care Ipa, Inc.
1985 Marcus Ave Ste 202
New Hyde Park NY 11042
718 468-4747

(G-8540)
PETSMART INC
3713 Easton Market (43219-6023)
PHONE................................614 418-9389
Fax: 614 418-0153
Craig Samet, *Manager*
Lisa Mack, *Manager*
EMP: 55
SALES (corp-wide): 12.7B Privately Held
WEB: www.petsmart.com
SIC: 5999 0752 0742 Pet food; pet supplies; grooming services, pet & animal specialties; veterinary services, specialties
HQ: Petsmart, Inc.
19601 N 27th Ave
Phoenix AZ 85027
623 580-6100

(G-8541)
PHANTOM TECHNICAL SERVICES INC
111 Outerbelt St (43213-1548)
PHONE................................614 868-9920
William G Yates Jr, *President*
Tracy Sheward, *Manager*
EMP: 30
SQ FT: 7,500
SALES (est): 2MM Privately Held
WEB: www.phantomtechnical.com
SIC: 8711 Electrical or electronic engineering; mechanical engineering

(G-8542)
PHINNEY INDUSTRIAL ROOFING
700 Hadley Dr (43228-1030)
PHONE................................614 308-9000
Fax: 614 308-9595
Mike Phinney, *President*
Mike Decrane, *Vice Pres*
Kathey Phinney, *Vice Pres*
Mark Allen, *Project Mgr*
Shaun Andrews, *Project Mgr*
▼ **EMP:** 65
SQ FT: 20,000
SALES (est): 16.1MM Privately Held
WEB: www.phinneyindustrial.com
SIC: 1761 Roofing contractor; sheet metalwork

(G-8543)
PIERCE CLEANERS INC
5205 N High St (43214-1201)
P.O. Box 14371 (43214-0371)
PHONE................................614 888-4225
Fax: 614 888-4029
Robert Pierce, *President*
Craig R Yoder, *Senior VP*
Diane Landauer, *Treasurer*
EMP: 29
SALES (est): 1.1MM Privately Held
SIC: 7216 Drycleaning plants, except rugs; drycleaning collecting & distributing agency

(G-8544)
PILLAR TECHNOLOGY GROUP LLC
580 N 4th St (43215-2106)
PHONE................................614 535-7868
Bob Myers, *CEO*
FMP: 62 Privately Held
SIC: 7371 Custom computer programming services
PA: Pillar Technology Group Llc
580 N 4th St Ste 190
Columbus OH 43215

(G-8545)
PILOT DOGS INCORPORATED
625 W Town St (43215-4496)
PHONE................................614 221-6367
Fax: 614 221-1577
James G Langford, *Vice Pres*
Stan Topy, *Treasurer*
Ben Zox, *Treasurer*
Dawn Dent, *Manager*
J Jay Gray, *Exec Dir*
EMP: 26
SQ FT: 7,000

SALES: 3.8MM Privately Held
WEB: www.pilotdogs.org
SIC: 8399 Health systems agency

(G-8546)
PIZZUTI BUILDERS LLC
2 Miranova Pl Ste 800 (43215-3719)
PHONE................................614 280-4000
James Cramer, *Treasurer*
Ronald Pizzuti,
Richard Daley,
EMP: 40
SQ FT: 16,000
SALES (est): 2.5MM Privately Held
SIC: 6552 Subdividers & developers

(G-8547)
PIZZUTI INC (PA)
629 N High St 500 (43215-2025)
PHONE................................614 280-4000
Fax: 614 280-5000
Ronald A Pizzuti, *CEO*
Joel S Pizzuti, *President*
James S Russell, *COO*
Michael A Chivini, *Exec VP*
Scott B West, *Exec VP*
EMP: 50
SQ FT: 12,000
SALES (est): 49.1MM Privately Held
WEB: www.twomiranovaplace.com
SIC: 6552 6531 Subdividers & developers; real estate managers

(G-8548)
PLANES MVG & STOR CO COLUMBUS
2000 Dividend Dr (43228-3847)
PHONE................................614 777-9090
Fax: 614 777-0444
John J Planes, *CEO*
John Sabatalo, *President*
Jim Reed, *Warehouse Mgr*
Raymond Gundrum, *Treasurer*
Mark Geis, *Controller*
EMP: 51
SQ FT: 75,000
SALES: 10.1MM Privately Held
SIC: 4213 4214 Household goods transport; local trucking with storage

(G-8549)
PLANNED PRENTHOOD GREATER OHIO (PA)
206 E State St (43215-4311)
PHONE................................614 224-2235
Stephanie Kight, *CEO*
Lillian Williams, *Principal*
Erica Wilson-Domer, *Vice Pres*
Barbara L Singhaus, *CFO*
Susan Hirt, *Director*
EMP: 30
SALES (est): 20.7MM Privately Held
SIC: 8093 Family planning clinic

(G-8550)
PLATINUM PRESTIGE PROPERTY
4120 Beechbank Rd (43213-2378)
PHONE................................614 705-2251
Delmar Williams, *Principal*
K E Williams, *Principal*
Kchina Williams, *Principal*
Kvontae Williams, *Principal*
EMP: 26
SALES (est): 421.5K Privately Held
SIC: 7389

(G-8551)
PLAYTIME PRESCHOOL LLC
1030 Alum Creek Dr (43209-2701)
PHONE................................614 975-1005
Elisabeth Lawson, *Mng Member*
Kelly Lawson,
EMP: 25
SQ FT: 10,000
SALES (est): 1.2MM Privately Held
SIC: 8351 Preschool center

(G-8552)
PLAZA PROPERTIES INC (PA)
Also Called: Bexley Plaza Apartments
3016 Maryland Ave (43209-1591)
P.O. Box 9601 (43209-0601)
PHONE................................614 237-3726
Larry Ruben, *Ch of Bd*

Bernard R Ruben, *Ch of Bd*
Lawrence G Ruben, *President*
Florine C Ruben, *Vice Pres*
Erica Brown, *Human Resources*
EMP: 50
SQ FT: 5,000
SALES (est): 10.3MM Privately Held
WEB: www.plazaproperties.com
SIC: 6513 6531 Apartment building operators; real estate managers

(G-8553)
POTTERY BARN INC
3945 Easton Square Pl W H-1 (43219-6072)
PHONE................................614 478-3154
Jean Gilbert, *General Mgr*
Tammy Mullins, *Sales Staff*
EMP: 25
SALES (corp-wide): 5.2B Publicly Held
WEB: www.potterybarn.com
SIC: 5719 5023 Kitchenware; kitchenware
HQ: Pottery Barn, Inc.
3250 Van Ness Ave
San Francisco CA 94109
415 421-7900

(G-8554)
POWER DISTRIBUTORS LLC (PA)
Also Called: Central Power Systems
3700 Paragon Dr (43228-9750)
PHONE................................614 876-3533
Matthew Finn, *President*
Mark Greiner, *Credit Staff*
Tim Snell, *Natl Sales Mgr*
Kristen Powell, *Sales Staff*
James Tokarski, *Sales Staff*
▲ **EMP:** 84
SALES (est): 120.6MM Privately Held
SIC: 5084 3524 Engines & parts, air-cooled; lawn & garden equipment; lawn & garden tractors & equipment

(G-8555)
PREMIER BROADCASTING CO INC
Also Called: Massey's Pizza
5310 E Main St Ste 101 (43213-2598)
PHONE................................614 866-0700
David Pallone, *President*
James Pallone, *Corp Secy*
Kristen Carter, *Accounts Mgr*
EMP: 35
SQ FT: 1,200
SALES: 4MM Privately Held
SIC: 5812 6794 Pizza restaurants; franchises, selling or licensing

(G-8556)
PREMIER PRPTS CENTL OHIO INC
5674 Westbourne Ave (43213-1448)
PHONE................................614 755-4275
Kathryn S Harr, *President*
Christopher D Harr, *Vice Pres*
EMP: 25
SALES (est): 1.7MM Privately Held
SIC: 6531 Real estate agents & managers

(G-8557)
PREMIERFIRST HOME HEALTH CARE
1430 S High St (43207-1045)
PHONE................................614 443-3110
Gary F Woods, *Controller*
Tammy Seymour, *Manager*
Tim Smith, *Administration*
EMP: 35
SQ FT: 1,200
SALES (est): 1.4MM Privately Held
SIC: 8082 Home health care services

(G-8558)
PREVENT BLINDNESS - OHIO
1500 W 3rd Ave Ste 200 (43212-2817)
PHONE................................614 464-2020
Fax: 614 481-9670
Sherill K Williams, *President*
EMP: 26
SQ FT: 4,016
SALES: 1.6MM Privately Held
SIC: 8399 Health systems agency

Columbus - Franklin County (G-8559) — GEOGRAPHIC SECTION

(G-8559)
PRICEWATERHOUSECOOPERS LLP
41 S High St Ste 25 (43215-6113)
PHONE................................614 225-8700
Carrie L Clay, *Partner*
Michael Gebbie, *Managing Dir*
John Moore, *Mktg Dir*
Jim Robbins, *Branch Mgr*
Ben Addison, *Manager*
EMP: 200
SALES (corp-wide): 5.6B **Privately Held**
WEB: www.pwcglobal.com
SIC: 8721 Certified public accountant
PA: Pricewaterhousecoopers Llp
    300 Madison Ave Fl 24
    New York NY 10017
    646 471-4000

(G-8560)
PRIMATECH INC (PA)
50 Northwoods Blvd Ste A (43235-4717)
PHONE................................614 841-9800
Fax: 614 841-9805
Paul Baybutt, *President*
Daniel Ini, *Vice Pres*
Daniel J Pissini, *Vice Pres*
Steven Baybutt, *Opers Mgr*
Kimberly Mullins, *Engng Exec*
EMP: 30
SQ FT: 3,500
SALES: 3.8MM **Privately Held**
WEB: www.primatech.com
SIC: 8748 8711 Systems engineering consultant, ex. computer or professional; computer software systems analysis & design, custom; professional engineer

(G-8561)
PRIORITY DESIGNS INC
100 S Hamilton Rd (43213-2013)
PHONE................................614 337-9979
Fax: 614 337-9499
Paul Kolada, *President*
Lois Kolada, *Corp Secy*
Laura Alexander, *Engineer*
Chris Cicenas, *Engineer*
Ryan Crisp, *Engineer*
EMP: 55
SQ FT: 55,000
SALES (est): 6.9MM **Privately Held**
WEB: www.prioritydesigns.com
SIC: 7389 Design, commercial & industrial

(G-8562)
PRN NURSE INC
Also Called: Health Care Personnel
6161 Radekin Rd (43232-2921)
PHONE................................614 864-9292
Sandra K Shane, *President*
Wilson Jeff, *Project Mgr*
Connie Barnes, *Office Mgr*
George E Erdy, *Contractor*
EMP: 300
SALES: 3.1MM **Privately Held**
SIC: 7363 7361 Medical help service; employment agencies

(G-8563)
PRO-TOUCH INC
721 N Rose Ave (43219-2522)
PHONE................................614 586-0303
Fax: 614 586-0314
Nancy Brugler, *CEO*
Douglas Brugler, *President*
Donna Blake, *Manager*
EMP: 150
SQ FT: 6,500
SALES: 2.2MM **Privately Held**
WEB: www.pro-touchinc.com
SIC: 7349 5087 Janitorial service, contract basis; janitors' supplies

(G-8564)
PRO-TOW INC
1669 Harmon Ave (43223-3320)
PHONE................................614 444-8697
James Whittredge, *President*
EMP: 25
SQ FT: 5,000
SALES (est): 2.2MM **Privately Held**
SIC: 7549 Towing services

(G-8565)
PRODUCERS CREDIT CORPORATION
Also Called: PCC
8351 N High St Ste 250 (43235-1440)
PHONE................................614 433-2150
Dennis Bolling, *President*
Ron Williams, *Pastor*
Irvin Porteus, *Director*
EMP: 32
SALES: 1.4MM
SALES (corp-wide): 123.4MM **Privately Held**
SIC: 7389 6159 Financial services; livestock loan companies
PA: United Producers, Inc.
    8351 N High St Ste 250
    Columbus OH 43235
    614 433-2150

(G-8566)
PROFESSIONAL DRIVERS GA INC
Also Called: Prodrivers
4251 Diplomacy Dr (43228-3803)
PHONE................................614 529-8282
Kelly Garbrandt, *Sales Mgr*
EMP: 31
SALES (corp-wide): 547.8MM **Privately Held**
SIC: 7363 Truck driver services
HQ: Professional Drivers Of Georgia, Inc.
    1040 Crown Pointe Pkwy
    Atlanta GA 30338

(G-8567)
PROFESSIONAL MAINT OF COLUMBUS
541 Stimmel Rd (43223-2901)
PHONE................................614 443-6528
Fax: 614 443-0069
Eldon L Hall, *Ch of Bd*
Dale Barnette, *President*
Eldon Hall Jr, *Vice Pres*
Robert L White, *Vice Pres*
Susie McVay, *Office Mgr*
EMP: 190
SQ FT: 9,500
SALES (est): 5.1MM **Privately Held**
SIC: 7349 Janitorial service, contract basis

(G-8568)
PROFESSIONAL SERVICE INDS INC
Also Called: Professional Service Inds
4960 Vulcan Ave Ste C (43228-9614)
PHONE................................614 876-8000
Fax: 614 876-0548
Cathy Brandi, *Principal*
Charles Helm, *Principal*
Paul Hundley, *Business Mgr*
John Xu, *Department Mgr*
Michael Mazzoli, *Manager*
EMP: 25
SALES (corp-wide): 731.5MM **Privately Held**
SIC: 8711 8734 Consulting engineer; testing laboratories
HQ: Professional Service Industries, Inc.
    545 E Algonquin Rd
    Arlington Heights IL 60005
    630 691-1490

(G-8569)
PROFESSIONALS FOR WOMENS HLTH (PA)
921 Jasonway Ave Ste B (43214-2456)
PHONE................................614 268-8800
Fax: 614 268-8249
Kevin Hacket MD, *Owner*
Kevin Hackett MD, *Owner*
Ann Wurst MD, *Co-Owner*
Ranie Cropper, *Manager*
Susan Harding, *Manager*
EMP: 35
SQ FT: 10,000
SALES (est): 6.5MM **Privately Held**
WEB: www.pwhealth.com
SIC: 8011 Gynecologist

(G-8570)
PROLOGUE RESEARCH INTL INC
580 N 4th St Ste 270 (43215-2158)
PHONE................................614 324-1500
Fax: 614 324-0686
Tom Ludlam Jr, *President*
Krystyna Kowalczyk, *Exec VP*
Kathleen Zajd, *Senior VP*
Jane Bentley, *Vice Pres*
EMP: 60
SQ FT: 12,443
SALES (est): 4MM **Publicly Held**
WEB: www.procro.com
SIC: 8733 Medical research
HQ: Novella Clinical Inc.
    1700 Perimeter Park Dr
    Morrisville NC 27560
    919 484-1921

(G-8571)
PROMOHOUSE INC
Also Called: Axis Advertising
515 Park St (43215-2039)
PHONE................................614 324-9200
Fax: 614 324-9211
Matthew Grossman, *President*
Ron Bott, *Exec VP*
Michelle Guetle, *Exec VP*
Michael Levin, *Vice Pres*
Michael Levins, *CFO*
EMP: 45
SQ FT: 17,000
SALES (est): 1.5MM **Privately Held**
SIC: 7389 Personal service agents, brokers & bureaus

(G-8572)
PROSPERITY CARE SERVICE
2021 Dublin Rd (43228-8900)
PHONE................................614 430-8626
Sallamadou Bangoura, *President*
EMP: 40
SALES (est): 1.1MM **Privately Held**
SIC: 8099 Medical services organization

(G-8573)
PROVIDENCE REES INC
2111 Builders Pl (43204-4886)
P.O. Box 12535 (43212-0535)
PHONE................................614 833-6231
Fax: 614 487-6184
Billy Parsley, *Corp Secy*
Herbert Brown, *Vice Pres*
John Oneal, *Opers Mgr*
Lee Nichols, *Production*
Catherine Vance, *Purch Agent*
EMP: 35
SQ FT: 36,000
SALES: 4.7MM **Privately Held**
SIC: 3496 8711 Wire winding; engineering services

(G-8574)
PROVIDER PHYSICIANS INC
Also Called: Physician Providers North
6096 E Main St Ste 112 (43213-4302)
PHONE................................614 755-3000
Dr Charles Block, *President*
Sue Ferrell, *Manager*
James R Dorado, *Pediatrics*
EMP: 63
SALES (est): 3.7MM **Privately Held**
SIC: 8011 Surgeon

(G-8575)
PROVIDER SERVICES INC
Also Called: High Banks Care Centre
111 Lazelle Rd (43235-1419)
PHONE................................614 888-2021
Aimee Palmer, *Manager*
Winnie Mozampour, *Director*
Paula Bourne, *Administration*
EMP: 75
SALES (est): 1.7MM **Privately Held**
SIC: 8399 8059 Social change association; convalescent home

(G-8576)
PSC METALS INC
1283 Joyce Ave (43219-2134)
PHONE................................614 299-4175
Kevin Ringle, *Manager*
EMP: 38
SALES (corp-wide): 21.7B **Publicly Held**
SIC: 5093 Metal scrap & waste materials
HQ: Psc Metals, Inc.
    5875 Landerbrook Dr # 200
    Mayfield Heights OH 44124
    440 753-5400

(G-8577)
PUBLIC SAFETY OHIO DEPARTMENT
Also Called: Licensing Section
1970 W Broad St (43223-1102)
P.O. Box 16520 (43216-6520)
PHONE................................614 752-7600
James Chisman, *Branch Mgr*
EMP: 1100 **Privately Held**
SIC: 7299 9621 Personal document & information services; motor vehicle licensing & inspection office, government;
HQ: Ohio Department Of Public Safety
    1970 W Broad St Fl 5
    Columbus OH 43223

(G-8578)
PUBLIC SERVICE COMPANY OKLA (HQ)
Also Called: AEP
1 Riverside Plz (43215-2355)
PHONE................................614 716-1000
Nicholas K Akins, *CEO*
Bill McKamey, *Vice Pres*
Tommy Slater, *Vice Pres*
Jason Pound, *Buyer*
Brian X Tierney, *CFO*
EMP: 170
SALES: 1.4B
SALES (corp-wide): 15.4B **Publicly Held**
WEB: www.psoklahoma.com
SIC: 4911 Electric services; distribution, electric power; generation, electric power; transmission, electric power
PA: American Electric Power Company, Inc.
    1 Riverside Plz Fl 1 # 1
    Columbus OH 43215
    614 716-1000

(G-8579)
QUAD/GRAPHICS INC
4051 Fondorf Dr (43228-1025)
PHONE................................614 276-4800
Pat Seymour, *Human Res Dir*
Norm Phristoffersem, *Manager*
EMP: 250
SALES (corp-wide): 4.1B **Publicly Held**
WEB: www.vertisinc.com
SIC: 7311 2791 2752 Advertising agencies; typesetting; commercial printing, lithographic
PA: Quad/Graphics Inc.
    N61w23044 Harrys Way
    Sussex WI 53089
    414 566-6000

(G-8580)
QUALITY ASSURED CLEANING INC
6407 Nicholas Dr (43235-5204)
P.O. Box 1250, Powell (43065-1250)
PHONE................................614 798-1505
Fax: 614 798-1509
Eric Hassen, *Vice Pres*
EMP: 99
SALES (est): 4.1MM **Privately Held**
SIC: 7349 Janitorial service, contract basis

(G-8581)
QUANTUM HEALTH INC
7450 Huntington Park Dr (43235-5617)
PHONE................................614 846-4318
Kara J Trott, *CEO*
Randy Gebhardt, *President*
Shannon Skaggs, *President*
Ryan Whiteleather, *President*
Amy Crowell, *Exec VP*
EMP: 99
SQ FT: 25,000
SALES (est): 13.8MM **Privately Held**
WEB: www.qh-quantum.com
SIC: 8082 Home health care services

(G-8582)
QUINCY MALL INC (PA)
191 W Nationwide Blvd # 200 (43215-2568)
PHONE................................614 228-5331
Don M Casto III, *President*
Frank S Benson III, *Vice Pres*

EMP: 25
SQ FT: 1,500
SALES (est): 1.2MM **Privately Held**
WEB: www.cullprop.com
SIC: 6512 Shopping center, property operation only

(G-8583)
RACKSQUARED LLC
325 E Spring St (43215-2629)
PHONE..............................614 737-8812
Brad Wasserstrom, *President*
Brad Wasferstrom, *President*
Phil Smith, *COO*
Gary Mangelson, *CFO*
Gary Ferguson, *Technology*
EMP: 28
SQ FT: 10,000
SALES: 3MM **Privately Held**
SIC: 7374 8742 Data processing & preparation; business consultant

(G-8584)
RADIOHIO INCORPORATED
Also Called: Wbns-AM Sports Radio 1460 Fan
605 S Front St Fl 3 (43215-5198)
PHONE..............................614 460-3850
Fax: 614 460-3757
John F Wolfe, *Ch of Bd*
Jeanine Porter, *Traffic Mgr*
Todd Markiewicz, *Sales Mgr*
Randy Parker, *Sales Mgr*
Don Snyder, *Sales Mgr*
EMP: 75
SQ FT: 24,000
SALES (est): 6.5MM **Privately Held**
WEB: www.radiohio.com
SIC: 4832 Radio broadcasting stations

(G-8585)
RAINBOW FLEA MARKET INC (PA)
Also Called: Livinginston Court Flea Market
865 King Ave (43212-2653)
PHONE..............................614 291-3133
Solly L Yassenoff, *President*
Karen Yassenoff, *Admin Sec*
EMP: 30
SQ FT: 5,000
SALES (est): 1.4MM **Privately Held**
SIC: 7389 Flea market

(G-8586)
RAINBOW LANES INC
Also Called: Rainbow Bowling Lanes
3224 S High St (43207-3695)
PHONE..............................614 491-7155
Fax: 614 491-6901
Bob McCracken, *President*
EMP: 30 EST: 1959
SQ FT: 45,000
SALES (est): 667.1K **Privately Held**
WEB: www.rainbowbowling.com
SIC: 7933 5813 Ten pin center; cocktail lounge

(G-8587)
RAMA INC
Also Called: Staybrdge Sites Columbus Arprt
2890 Airport Dr (43219-2240)
PHONE..............................614 473-9888
Fax: 614 471-9617
Bill Patel, *President*
Tim Breen, *General Mgr*
Kalpen Patel, *Sales Mgr*
EMP: 25
SALES (est): 1.3MM **Privately Held**
WEB: www.wm.staybridge.com
SIC: 7011 Hotels

(G-8588)
RANDOLPH AND ASSOCIATES RE
Also Called: Randolph & Assoc Real Estate
239 Buttonwood Ct (43230-6229)
PHONE..............................614 269-8418
Kevin Randolph, *President*
EMP: 30
SQ FT: 1,100
SALES (est): 1.6MM **Privately Held**
SIC: 6531 Real estate brokers & agents

(G-8589)
RAYMOND RECEPTON HOUSE
3860 Trabue Rd (43228-9559)
PHONE..............................614 276-6127
Stefanie Green, *Principal*
EMP: 30 EST: 2010
SALES (est): 297.2K **Privately Held**
SIC: 7299 Banquet hall facilities

(G-8590)
RBP ATLANTA LLC
4100 Regent St Ste G (43219-6160)
PHONE..............................614 246-2522
James Merkel,
EMP: 87 EST: 2011
SALES (est): 8.8MM
SALES (corp-wide): 48.8MM **Privately Held**
SIC: 8741 Hotel or motel management
PA: Rockbridge Capital, Llc
4100 Regent St Ste G
Columbus OH 43219
614 246-2400

(G-8591)
RCS ENTERPRISES INC
Also Called: Next Generation
139 W Johnstown Rd (43230-2700)
P.O. Box 30979 (43230-0979)
PHONE..............................614 337-8520
Fax: 614 337-8691
Larry Dempsey, *President*
Ryan Schmidt, *Vice Pres*
EMP: 70
SALES (est): 2MM **Privately Held**
WEB: www.rpigraphic.com
SIC: 7349 Office cleaning or charring

(G-8592)
RCWC COL INC
Also Called: Bar 145
955 W 5th Ave Ste 7 (43212-2635)
PHONE..............................614 564-9344
Jeremy Fitzgerald, *President*
Johnny Runckel, *General Mgr*
EMP: 60
SALES (est): 653K **Privately Held**
SIC: 5812 7929 Eating places; entertainment service

(G-8593)
RDP FOODSERVICE LTD
620 Oakland Park Ave (43214-4128)
P.O. Box 14866 (43214-0866)
PHONE..............................614 261-5661
Fax: 614 261-5672
Mark Mizer, *President*
Christopher Dipaolo, *Exec VP*
Paul Di Paolo, *Mng Member*
Jim Randall,
Jim Solitro,
EMP: 72
SQ FT: 30,000
SALES (est): 28MM **Privately Held**
SIC: 5149 5087 Pizza supplies; restaurant supplies

(G-8594)
REAL ESTATE INVESTORS MGT INC (PA)
Also Called: Chimney Hill Apartments
4041 Roberts Rd (43228-9536)
PHONE..............................614 777-2444
Herm Gelliand, *President*
EMP: 25
SALES (est): 1.1MM **Privately Held**
SIC: 6513 Apartment building operators

(G-8595)
REAL LIVING TITLE AGENCY LTD (PA)
77 E Nationwide Blvd (43215-2512)
PHONE..............................614 459-7400
Fax: 216 621-2551
Dan Riley, *President*
Chris Riordan, *Executive Asst*
EMP: 60
SALES (est): 24.2MM **Privately Held**
SIC: 6541 6531 Title search companies; escrow agent, real estate

(G-8596)
RECOVERY ONE LLC
3240 Henderson Rd Ste A (43220-2300)
PHONE..............................614 336-4207

Fax: 614 336-1150
Steve Jones, *Manager*
Shelly Kallon, *Manager*
Albert F Cameron III,
EMP: 67
SALES (est): 5.5MM **Privately Held**
SIC: 7322 8111 Collection agency, except real estate; legal services

(G-8597)
RED CAPITAL MARKETS LLC
10 W Broad St Ste 1800 (43215-3420)
PHONE..............................614 857-1400
James Croft, *CEO*
James Murphy, *President*
Andrew Steiner, *Vice Pres*
Brian Kelleher, *CFO*
Lisa Boecher, *Manager*
EMP: 234
SALES (est): 25.5MM
SALES (corp-wide): 18B **Publicly Held**
WEB: www.allegiantbank.com
SIC: 6211 Investment firm, general brokerage
HQ: Pnc Bank, National Association
222 Delaware Ave
Wilmington DE 19801
877 762-2000

(G-8598)
RED CAPITAL PARTNERS LLC (DH)
Also Called: Red Capital Advisors
10 W Broad St Fl 8 (43215-3418)
PHONE..............................614 857-1400
Ted Meylor, *CEO*
Thomas Line, *CFO*
Richard Coomber, *Office Mgr*
Lisa Borchers, *Executive Asst*
Ciera Adams, *Admin Asst*
EMP: 75
SALES (est): 38.5MM
SALES (corp-wide): 23.5B **Privately Held**
WEB: www.redcapitalgroup.com
SIC: 6282 Investment advisory service
HQ: Red Capital Group Llc
10 W Broad St Fl 8
Columbus OH 43215
614 857-1400

(G-8599)
RED MORTGAGE CAPITAL LLC (DH)
10 W Broad St Ste 1800 (43215-3420)
PHONE..............................614 857-1400
Fax: 614 857-1660
Edward Meylor, *CEO*
Trent Brooks, *President*
Jordan Rowsey, *Assistant VP*
Barry A Fuller, *Director*
Kathryn Burton Gray, *Director*
EMP: 50
SALES (est): 36.4MM
SALES (corp-wide): 23.5B **Privately Held**
WEB: www.allegiantbank.com
SIC: 6162 Mortgage brokers, using own money
HQ: Red Capital Group Llc
10 W Broad St Fl 8
Columbus OH 43215
614 857-1400

(G-8600)
RED ROOF INNS INC (HQ)
605 S Front St Ste 150 (43215-5809)
PHONE..............................614 744-2600
Fax: 614 224-9724
Andrew Alexander, *CEO*
John Campbell, *General Mgr*
Erwan Garnier, *General Mgr*
Robert Hoffman, *General Mgr*
Jeff Horne, *General Mgr*
EMP: 525
SALES (est): 484.9MM **Privately Held**
WEB: www.redroof.com
SIC: 7011 Hotels & motels

(G-8601)
RED ROOF INNS INC
111 Nationwide Plz (43215)
PHONE..............................614 224-6539
Fax: 614 224-6573
Jeffrey Schwartz, *Manager*
Marcelo Cacciola, *Director*
EMP: 33 **Privately Held**
WEB: www.redroof.com

SIC: 7011 Hotels & motels
HQ: Red Roof Inns, Inc.
605 S Front St Ste 150
Columbus OH 43215
614 744-2600

(G-8602)
REFECTORY RESTAURANT INC
1092 Bethel Rd (43220-2610)
PHONE..............................614 451-9774
Fax: 614 451-4434
Kamal Boulos, *President*
EMP: 50
SQ FT: 10,000
SALES (est): 2MM **Privately Held**
WEB: www.therefectoryrestaurant.com
SIC: 5812 7299 French restaurant; banquet hall facilities

(G-8603)
REFRIGERATION SYSTEMS COMPANY (HQ)
1770 Genessee Ave (43211-1650)
PHONE..............................614 263-0913
Fax: 614 263-6660
Thomas A Leighty, *CEO*
Robert A Appleton, *President*
Ronald B Odom, *Vice Pres*
Yukari Niki, *Human Res Mgr*
EMP: 63 EST: 1961
SQ FT: 20,000
SALES (est): 32.4MM
SALES (corp-wide): 51.2MM **Privately Held**
WEB: www.rsc-gc.com
SIC: 1541 7623 Industrial buildings & warehouses; food products manufacturing or packing plant construction; industrial buildings, new construction; warehouse construction; refrigeration repair service
PA: Manweb Services, Inc.
11800 Exit 5 Pkwy Ste 106
Fishers IN 46037
317 863-0007

(G-8604)
REGAL CINEMAS INC
Also Called: Regal Entertainment Group
1800 Georgesville Sq (43228-3695)
PHONE..............................614 853-0850
Josh Dinan, *Manager*
EMP: 36
SALES (corp-wide): 982.1MM **Privately Held**
WEB: www.regalcinemas.com
SIC: 7832 Motion picture theaters, except drive-in
HQ: Regal Cinemas, Inc.
101 E Blount Ave Ste 100
Knoxville TN 37920
865 922-1123

(G-8605)
REGAL HOSPITALITY LLC
Also Called: Sheraton Suites Columbus
201 Hutchinson Ave (43235-4689)
PHONE..............................614 436-0004
Elizabeth Procaccianti, *Manager*
EMP: 28
SALES (corp-wide): 2.1MM **Privately Held**
SIC: 8741 Hotel or motel management
PA: Regal Hospitality, Llc
6840 Caine Rd
Columbus OH 43235
614 389-1916

(G-8606)
REGENCY LEASING CO LLC
Also Called: Regency Manor Rehab
2000 Regency Manor Cir (43207-1777)
PHONE..............................614 542-3100
Fax: 614 445-8050
Jay Hicks, *President*
Doug Rowe, *President*
Samantha Banks, *Human Res Dir*
Pamela Sams, *Marketing Mgr*
Sam Powers, *Executive*
EMP: 300
SALES (est): 10.8MM
SALES (corp-wide): 103.9MM **Privately Held**
WEB: www.communicarehealth.com
SIC: 8051 Skilled nursing care facilities

Columbus - Franklin County (G-8607)   GEOGRAPHIC SECTION

PA: Communicare Health Services, Inc.
4700 Ashwood Dr Ste 200
Blue Ash OH 45241
513 530-1654

(G-8607)
REGENSIS STNA TRAINING PROGRAM
415 E Mound St (43215-5532)
PHONE.............................614 849-0115
Mark Glover, *Owner*
EMP: 50 **EST:** 2008
SALES (est): 347.6K **Privately Held**
SIC: 8099 Health & allied services

(G-8608)
REHABLTATION CORECTN OHIO DEPT
Also Called: Columbus Regional Office
1030 Alum Creek Dr (43209-2701)
PHONE.............................614 752-0800
Fax: 614 752-0900
Lee Sampson, *Manager*
Kim Oats, *Administration*
EMP: 100 **Privately Held**
SIC: 8322 9223 Parole office; offender self-help agency;
HQ: Ohio Department Of Rehabilitation And Correction
770 W Broad St
Columbus OH 43222

(G-8609)
REITTER STUCCO INC
1100 King Ave (43212-2262)
PHONE.............................614 291-2212
Fax: 614 291-2602
Frederick J Reitter, *President*
John Spangler, *Superintendent*
Lynn Alexander, *Purchasing*
John E Reitter, *Treasurer*
Johnny Buzzelli, *Cust Mgr*
EMP: 40
SQ FT: 30,000
SALES (est): 6.3MM **Privately Held**
WEB: www.reitterstucco.com
SIC: 1771 5072 Exterior concrete stucco contractor; hardware

(G-8610)
REITTER WALL SYSTEMS INC
1178 Joyce Ave (43219-2135)
PHONE.............................614 545-4444
R Gabe Reitter II, *President*
Brett Hoerig, *Vice Pres*
EMP: 54
SQ FT: 16,000
SALES (est): 5.1MM **Privately Held**
WEB: www.reitterwall.com
SIC: 1771 Exterior concrete stucco contractor

(G-8611)
RELAY GEAR LTD
3738 Paragon Dr (43228-9750)
PHONE.............................888 735-2943
Mark Betts, *Partner*
Duane Hickerson, *Partner*
Bob Southard, *Partner*
Derek Betts, *General Ptnr*
▲ **EMP:** 32
SQ FT: 25,000
SALES (est): 2.4MM **Privately Held**
WEB: www.relaygear.com
SIC: 5199 7389 Advertising specialties; advertising, promotional & trade show services

(G-8612)
RELIABLE APPL INSTALLATION INC
3736 Paragon Dr (43228-9750)
PHONE.............................614 246-6840
Fax: 614 246-6487
Randy James, *Branch Mgr*
EMP: 36
SALES (corp-wide): 10.7MM **Privately Held**
SIC: 4212 Local trucking, without storage
PA: Reliable Appliance Installation, Inc.
604 Office Pkwy
Westerville OH 43082
614 794-3307

(G-8613)
RENIER CONSTRUCTION CORP
2164 Citygate Dr (43219-3556)
PHONE.............................614 866-4580
Fax: 614 866-0115
William R Heifner, *President*
Joe Ross, *General Mgr*
Lee Braswell, *Superintendent*
Timothy D Dever, *Vice Pres*
Thomas Rice, *Vice Pres*
EMP: 25
SQ FT: 8,500
SALES (est): 14.1MM **Privately Held**
WEB: www.renier.com
SIC: 1542 8741 Commercial & office building, new construction; construction management

(G-8614)
REPUBLIC SERVICES INC
933 Frank Rd (43223-3856)
PHONE.............................614 308-3000
Fax: 614 272-1058
Joe Ditommaso, *General Mgr*
Beth Martin, *General Mgr*
Michael Davis, *Principal*
Chris Coyle, *Regional Mgr*
Joe Cobryn, *Opers Spvr*
EMP: 50
SALES (corp-wide): 10B **Publicly Held**
SIC: 4953 Rubbish collection & disposal
PA: Republic Services, Inc.
18500 N Allied Way # 100
Phoenix AZ 85054
480 627-2700

(G-8615)
REPUBLIC SERVICES INC
933 Frank Rd (43223-3856)
PHONE.............................740 969-4487
Earl Kennedy, *Facilities Mgr*
Mike Varney, *Branch Mgr*
EMP: 60
SALES (corp-wide): 10B **Publicly Held**
WEB: www.republicservices.com
SIC: 4953 Refuse collection & disposal services
PA: Republic Services, Inc.
18500 N Allied Way # 100
Phoenix AZ 85054
480 627-2700

(G-8616)
REPUBLICAN STATE CENTRAL EXECU
Also Called: Ohio Republican Party
211 S 5th St (43215-5203)
PHONE.............................614 228-2481
Robert Bennet, *Chairman*
Kaye Ayres, *Vice Chairman*
Max Docksey, *Director*
Ruth Wray, *Admin Asst*
EMP: 30 **EST:** 1858
SALES: 50.2K **Privately Held**
WEB: www.ohiogop.org
SIC: 8651 Political campaign organization

(G-8617)
RESEARCH INSTITUTE AT NATION
700 Childrens Dr (43205-2664)
PHONE.............................614 722-2700
John Barnard, *President*
Sherwood L Fawcett, *Principal*
Robert Lazarus Jr, *Principal*
Janet E Porter, *Principal*
William Wise, *Principal*
EMP: 140
SQ FT: 106,000
SALES (est): 22.7MM
SALES (corp-wide): 1.3B **Privately Held**
SIC: 8062 8733 General medical & surgical hospitals; medical research
PA: Nationwide Children's Hospital
700 Childrens Dr
Columbus OH 43205
614 722-2000

(G-8618)
RESIDENCE INN
Also Called: Residence Inn By Marriott
36 E Gay St (43215-3108)
PHONE.............................614 222-2610
Fax: 614 222-2611
Troy Chontas, *General Mgr*

Joey Guiyab, *Principal*
EMP: 40
SALES: 950K **Privately Held**
SIC: 7011 Hotels & motels

(G-8619)
RESIDENTIAL FINANCE CORP (PA)
1 Easton Oval Ste 400 (43219-6092)
PHONE.............................614 324-4700
Fax: 614 324-4718
David Stein, *President*
Michael Isaacs, *President*
Douglas Harris, *COO*
Obiora Egbuna, *Vice Pres*
Barry Habib, *Vice Pres*
EMP: 300
SQ FT: 36,000
SALES (est): 62.2MM **Privately Held**
WEB: www.myrfc.com
SIC: 6162 Bond & mortgage companies

(G-8620)
RESIDENTIAL ONE REALTY INC (PA)
Also Called: Prudential
8351 N High St Ste 150 (43235-1409)
PHONE.............................614 436-9830
Joanne Figge, *President*
Michael Mahon, *Broker*
Betsy McCloskey, *Manager*
EMP: 40
SQ FT: 4,500
SALES (est): 1.5MM **Privately Held**
SIC: 6531 Real estate brokers & agents

(G-8621)
RESOURCE INTERACTIVE
250 S High St Ste 400 (43215-4622)
PHONE.............................614 621-2888
Nancy J Kramer, *CEO*
Kelly Moony, *President*
Jan Berardi, *Facilities Dir*
Rob Pettit, *Manager*
Lisa Richardson, *Manager*
EMP: 41
SALES (est): 5.3MM **Privately Held**
SIC: 7389 7331 Advertising, promotional & trade show services; direct mail advertising services

(G-8622)
RESOURCE INTERNATIONAL INC (HQ)
Also Called: Rii
6350 Presidential Gtwy (43231-7653)
PHONE.............................614 823-4949
Fax: 614 823-4990
Kamran Majidzadeh, *CEO*
Farah B Majidzadeh, *CEO*
Sam Khorshidi, *President*
Todd Majidzadeh, *Exec VP*
Robert Hart, *Vice Pres*
EMP: 120
SQ FT: 20,000
SALES (est): 29.3MM **Privately Held**
WEB: www.resourceinternational.com
SIC: 7371 8734 8713 1799 Custom computer programming services; testing laboratories; surveying services; spraying contractor, non-agricultural; consulting engineer; management services
PA: Majidzadeh Enterprises, Inc.
6350 Presidential Gtwy
Columbus OH 43231
614 823-4949

(G-8623)
RESOURCE VENTURES LTD (HQ)
Also Called: Resource Interactive
250 S High St Ste 400 (43215-4622)
PHONE.............................614 621-2888
Kelly Mooney, *CEO*
Rob Heckman, *Vice Pres*
Shannon Clear, *Project Mgr*
Ramesh Rajan, *CFO*
Anu Hariharan, *Controller*
EMP: 81
SQ FT: 27,880
SALES (est): 45.4MM
SALES (corp-wide): 79.1B **Publicly Held**
WEB: www.resourceinteractive.com
SIC: 8742 Marketing consulting services

PA: International Business Machines Corporation
1 New Orchard Rd Ste 1 # 1
Armonk NY 10504
914 499-1900

(G-8624)
RESTAURANT EQUIPPERS INC
Also Called: Warehouse
635 W Broad St (43215-2711)
PHONE.............................614 358-6622
Charlie Shaikov, *Manager*
EMP: 40
SALES (corp-wide): 45MM **Privately Held**
WEB: www.equippers.com
SIC: 4225 5046 General warehousing; commercial equipment
PA: Restaurant Equippers, Inc.
635 W Broad St
Columbus OH 43215
800 235-3325

(G-8625)
RETAIL FORWARD INC
Also Called: Tns Retail Forward
2 Easton Oval Ste 500 (43219-6036)
PHONE.............................614 355-4000
Daniel Boehm, *President*
Al Meyers, *Vice Pres*
Paul Casper, *CFO*
EMP: 37
SQ FT: 10,500
SALES: 7.7MM
SALES (corp-wide): 17.7B **Privately Held**
WEB: www.retailforward.com
SIC: 8742 Planning consultant
HQ: Tns North America, Inc.
11 Madison Ave Fl 12
New York NY 10010
212 991-6100

(G-8626)
RETINA GROUP INC (PA)
262 Neil Ave Ste 220 (43215-7310)
PHONE.............................614 464-3937
Fax: 614 464-0088
Jester Ribenour Do, *President*
E Mitchell Opremcakm, *Vice Pres*
Chet D Riedenour, *Treasurer*
Wayn Howlet, *Manager*
Tracy Schiefferle, *Exec Dir*
EMP: 25
SQ FT: 20,000
SALES (est): 3.5MM **Privately Held**
WEB: www.theretinagroup.com
SIC: 8011 Offices & clinics of medical doctors

(G-8627)
REV1 VENTURES
Also Called: Platform Lab
1275 Kinnear Rd (43212-1180)
PHONE.............................614 487-3700
Ted Ford, *President*
Parker Macdonell, *Managing Dir*
Wayne Embree, *Exec VP*
Mike Blackwell, *Senior VP*
Ryan Helon, *Senior VP*
EMP: 25
SQ FT: 62,000
SALES (est): 7.7MM **Privately Held**
WEB: www.techcolumbus.org
SIC: 6799 8299 8741 8734 Venture capital companies; educational services; business management; testing laboratories

(G-8628)
RIDGEWOOD AT FRIENDSHIP VLG
5675 Ponderosa Dr Ofc (43231-6765)
PHONE.............................614 890-8285
Mick Feauto, *Principal*
Carol Gilbert, *Director*
EMP: 35 **EST:** 2001
SALES (est): 883.9K **Privately Held**
WEB: www.fvcolumbus.com
SIC: 8052 Intermediate care facilities

(G-8629)
RIGHTER CO INC
2424 Harrison Rd (43204-3508)
PHONE.............................614 272-9700
Fax: 614 274-3325
Bradley R Nadolson, *President*
Jerry Yantes, *Vice Pres*

Tracy Ferguson, *Treasurer*
Bill Wyner, *Manager*
Melinda Righter, *Asst Sec*
EMP: 45
SQ FT: 6,400
SALES: 17.3MM **Privately Held**
WEB: www.rightercompany.com
SIC: 1622 1542 Bridge construction; highway construction, elevated; tunnel construction; nonresidential construction

(G-8630)
RIGHTER CONSTRUCTION SVCS INC
Also Called: Piling & Shoring Services
2424 Harrison Rd (43204-3557)
PHONE 614 272-9700
Brad Nadolson, *CEO*
Bradley Nadolson, *President*
EMP: 50
SALES (est): 3.4MM **Privately Held**
SIC: 1622 1541 1542 1629 Bridge construction; highway construction, elevated; tunnel construction; industrial buildings & warehouses; nonresidential construction; pile driving contractor; dock construction; industrial plant construction

(G-8631)
RINKOV EYECARE CENTER (PA)
Also Called: Rinkov, Mark H Od
81 E Gay St (43215-3103)
PHONE 614 224-2414
Fax: 614 224-5916
Mark H Rinkov, *President*
Claudia Rinkov, *Vice Pres*
Tricia Burroughs, *Med Doctor*
EMP: 25
SQ FT: 1,500
SALES (est): 2.4MM **Privately Held**
WEB: www.rinkoveyecare.com
SIC: 8042 Specialized optometrists

(G-8632)
RITE RUG CO
5465 N Hamilton Rd (43230-1319)
PHONE 614 478-3365
Joel Wood, *Manager*
EMP: 35
SALES (corp-wide): 82.2MM **Privately Held**
SIC: 7389 5713 Interior design services; floor covering stores
PA: Rite Rug Co.
4450 Poth Rd Ste A
Columbus OH 43213
614 261-6060

(G-8633)
RIVER CONSULTING LLC (DH)
445 Hutchinson Ave # 740 (43235-5677)
PHONE 614 797-2480
Fax: 614 890-1883
Gregory Dirfank, *President*
John Strayer, *Senior Partner*
Nancy Moorman, *Business Mgr*
Walter Martin, *Vice Pres*
Mike Patena, *Vice Pres*
EMP: 85 **EST:** 1981
SQ FT: 16,000
SALES (est): 33MM **Publicly Held**
WEB: www.rci-columbus.com
SIC: 8711 Consulting engineer
HQ: Kinder Morgan Energy Partners, L.P.
1001 La St Ste 1000
Houston TX 77002
713 369-9000

(G-8634)
RIVER ROAD HOTEL CORP
Also Called: University Plz Ht Cnfrence Ctr
3110 Olentangy River Rd (43202-1517)
PHONE 614 267-7461
Fax: 614 263-5299
James L Nichols, *President*
Timothy Michael, *Corp Secy*
EMP: 50
SQ FT: 35,000
SALES (est): 1.7MM
SALES (corp-wide): 5.5B **Privately Held**
WEB: www.universityplazaosu.com
SIC: 5812 7011 5813 American restaurant; hotels; drinking places

PA: The Ohio State University
Student Acade Servi Bldg
Columbus OH 43210
614 292-6446

(G-8635)
RIVERSIDE NEPHROLOGY ASSOC INC
929 Jasonway Ave (43214-2464)
PHONE 614 538-2250
Fax: 614 538-2256
Kevin Schroeder, *President*
Ronald Deandre Jr, *Vice Pres*
Julie Barnes, *Manager*
EMP: 25
SQ FT: 4,000
SALES (est): 4MM **Privately Held**
WEB: www.riversidenephrology.com
SIC: 8011 Nephrologist; physicians' office, including specialists

(G-8636)
RIVERSIDE RADIOLOGY AND (PA)
100 E Campus View Blvd # 100 (43235-4647)
PHONE 614 340-7747
Fax: 614 566-6647
Marsha Flarghty, *President*
Matthew Studer, *Engineer*
Kelli Lieb, *Controller*
Julie Landholt, *Human Resources*
Mike Suddendorf, *Mktg Dir*
EMP: 145
SALES (est): 39.9MM **Privately Held**
WEB: www.riversiderad.com
SIC: 8011 Radiologist

(G-8637)
RIVERVIEW HOTEL LLC
Also Called: Hampton Inn
3160 Olentangy River Rd (43202-1517)
PHONE 614 268-8700
Janet Boissy, *Owner*
Andrew Hann, *General Mgr*
EMP: 46
SQ FT: 106,000
SALES (est): 1.5MM **Privately Held**
SIC: 7011 Hotels & motels

(G-8638)
RLJ III - EM CLMBUS LESSEE LLC
Also Called: Embassy Suites Columbus
2700 Corporate Exch Dr (43231-1690)
PHONE 614 890-8600
Don Gantt, *General Mgr*
Lacey McLachlan, *Sales Mgr*
Moly Curnutte, *Sales Staff*
EMP: 99
SALES (est): 4.4MM **Privately Held**
SIC: 7011 Hotels & motels

(G-8639)
RLJ MANAGEMENT CO INC (PA)
3021 E Dblin Granville Rd (43231-4031)
PHONE 614 942-2020
Fax: 614 942-2000
Steve Boone, *President*
Bill Harvey, *Vice Pres*
Daniel Slane, *Treasurer*
Bobbi England, *Director*
EMP: 207
SQ FT: 5,200
SALES (est): 16.3MM **Privately Held**
WEB: www.rljmgmt.com
SIC: 6531 8721 Real estate managers; accounting services, except auditing

(G-8640)
ROBERT HALF INTERNATIONAL INC
277 W Nationwide Blvd (43215-2853)
PHONE 614 221-8326
Chris Ferguson, *Director*
Kim Swartzmiller, *Executive*
EMP: 93
SALES (corp-wide): 5.2B **Publicly Held**
SIC: 7361 Placement agencies
PA: Robert Half International Inc.
2884 Sand Hill Rd Ste 200
Menlo Park CA 94025
650 234-6000

(G-8641)
ROBERT HALF INTERNATIONAL INC
277 W Nationwide Blvd # 200 (43215-2853)
PHONE 614 221-1544
Lami Beck, *Manager*
EMP: 91
SALES (corp-wide): 5.2B **Publicly Held**
WEB: www.rhii.com
SIC: 7361 Executive placement
PA: Robert Half International Inc.
2884 Sand Hill Rd Ste 200
Menlo Park CA 94025
650 234-6000

(G-8642)
ROBERT M NEFF INC
711 Stimmel Rd (43223-2905)
PHONE 614 444-1562
Fax: 614 444-1596
Phillip Dante Berkhmeir, *Principal*
EMP: 64
SQ FT: 2,400
SALES (corp-wide): 9MM **Privately Held**
SIC: 4213 4215 4212 Contract haulers; courier services, except by air; mail carriers, contract
PA: Robert M Neff Inc
1955 James Pkwy
Heath OH 43056
740 928-4393

(G-8643)
ROCKBRIDGE CAPITAL LLC (PA)
4100 Regent St Ste G (43219-6160)
PHONE 614 246-2400
James T Merkel, *CEO*
Ronald L Callentine, *Chairman*
Stephen C Denz, *Exec VP*
Kenneth J Krebs, *Exec VP*
Christopher Dusseau, *Senior VP*
EMP: 42
SQ FT: 7,000
SALES (est): 48.8MM **Privately Held**
WEB: www.rockbridgecapital.com
SIC: 6726 Investment offices

(G-8644)
ROEHRENBECK ELECTRIC INC
2525 English Rd (43207-2899)
PHONE 614 443-9709
Fax: 614 443-9723
Richard Roehrenbeck, *President*
Nick Garner, *Engineer*
Lana Harison, *Controller*
Kirk Lier, *Controller*
Carolyn Rogers, *Accounting Mgr*
EMP: 44 **EST:** 1964
SQ FT: 10,000
SALES (est): 7.7MM **Privately Held**
SIC: 1731 General electrical contractor

(G-8645)
ROETZEL AND ANDRESS A LEGAL P
41 S High St Fl 21 (43215-3406)
PHONE 614 463-9489
Fax: 614 463-9792
Gilda Palange, *Credit Staff*
Beth Breier, *Office Mgr*
Angela Ratajczak, *Office Mgr*
Thomas Dillon, *Branch Mgr*
Dena Thompson, *Corp Counsel*
EMP: 40
SALES (corp-wide): 53.4MM **Privately Held**
WEB: www.ralaw.com
SIC: 8111 Corporate, partnership & business law
PA: Roetzel And Andress, A Legal Professional Association
222 S Main St Ste 400
Akron OH 44308
330 376-2700

(G-8646)
RON FOTH RETAIL INC
Also Called: Ron Foth Advertising
8100 N High St (43235-6475)
PHONE 614 888-7771
Fax: 614 888-5933
Kay Foth, *President*
Larry Row, *Senior VP*

Mike Foth Jr, *Vice Pres*
Ron Foth Jr, *Vice Pres*
Kim Moore, *Vice Pres*
EMP: 55
SQ FT: 23,500
SALES (est): 12.3MM **Privately Held**
WEB: www.ronfoth.com
SIC: 7311 7812 Advertising consultant; audio-visual program production

(G-8647)
ROOFING SUPPLY GROUP LLC
1288 Essex Ave (43201-2928)
PHONE 614 239-1111
Thomas Lecorchick, *Owner*
Jose Trevino, *Warehouse Mgr*
Brian Takaki, *Credit Mgr*
Paula Choate, *Sales Staff*
Gary Gilmore, *Sales Staff*
EMP: 32
SALES (est): 6.7MM **Privately Held**
SIC: 5099 Durable goods

(G-8648)
ROSE GRACIAS
Also Called: Hilton Homewood Suites
115 Hutchinson Ave 101-136 (43235-1413)
PHONE 614 785-0001
Rose Gracias, *General Mgr*
Anna Toth, *Principal*
Greg Huss, *Manager*
Gacias Rose, *Manager*
EMP: 45
SALES (est): 1.2MM **Privately Held**
SIC: 7011 Hotels

(G-8649)
ROSE PRODUCTS AND SERVICES INC
545 Stimmel Rd (43223-2901)
PHONE 614 443-7647
Fax: 614 443-2771
Robert Roth, *President*
Sue Brennan, *Manager*
EMP: 50 **EST:** 1926
SQ FT: 50,000
SALES (est): 7.9MM **Privately Held**
SIC: 5087 2842 Janitors' supplies; specialty cleaning preparations

(G-8650)
ROSEVILLE MOTOR EXPRESS INC
2720 Westbelt Dr (43228-3871)
PHONE 614 921-2121
Bill Moore, *President*
Terry Vanholmes, *Manager*
EMP: 50
SALES (est): 4MM **Privately Held**
SIC: 4213 Trucking, except local

(G-8651)
ROSSFORD GRTRIC CARE LTD PRTNR
Also Called: Heatherdowns Nursing Center
1661 Old Henderson Rd (43220-3644)
PHONE 614 459-0445
Ralph E Hazelbaker, *Partner*
Heatherdown Health Care Corp, *General Ptnr*
Carol Campbell, *Ltd Ptnr*
EMP: 110
SALES (est): 5.6MM **Privately Held**
SIC: 8051 Skilled nursing care facilities

(G-8652)
ROTO-ROOTER SERVICES COMPANY
4480 Bridgeway Ave Ste B (43219-1886)
PHONE 614 238-8006
Fax: 614 351-6315
Dennis Giffin, *Manager*
EMP: 40
SALES (corp-wide): 1.6B **Publicly Held**
SIC: 7699 Sewer cleaning & rodding
HQ: Roto-Rooter Services Company
255 E 5th St Ste 2500
Cincinnati OH 45202
513 762-6690

(G-8653)
ROYAL ELECTRIC CNSTR CORP
1250 Memory Ln N (43209-2749)
PHONE 614 253-6600
Fax: 614 253-8680

Columbus - Franklin County (G-8654)

Susan Ernst, *President*
Gregory Ernst, *Vice Pres*
Douglas Hoferkamp, *Manager*
EMP: 30
SQ FT: 33,000
SALES (est): 6.1MM **Privately Held**
WEB: www.royalcorp.com
SIC: 1731 General electrical contractor

(G-8654)
ROYAL HEALTH SERVICES LLC
3556 Sullivant Ave # 203 (43204-1153)
PHONE..................614 826-1316
Mohamed Hared, *Administration*
EMP: 33 **Privately Held**
SIC: 9431 6321 Administration of public health programs; accident & health insurance carriers

(G-8655)
ROYAL PAPER STOCK COMPANY INC (PA)
1300 Norton Rd (43228-3640)
PHONE..................614 851-4714
Fax: 614 851-4715
Michael Radtke, *President*
Richard Dahn, *Vice Pres*
John Daly, *CFO*
Martha Radke, *Treasurer*
Mickey Bowman, *Sales Associate*
EMP: 70
SQ FT: 80,000
SALES (est): 52.9MM **Privately Held**
WEB: www.royalpaperstock.com
SIC: 5093 Waste paper

(G-8656)
RSM US LLP
250 West St Ste 200 (43215-7538)
PHONE..................614 224-7722
William Petrus, *Manager*
Leonard Kummerer, *Supervisor*
Jacqueline Hudak, *Admin Asst*
EMP: 40
SALES (corp-wide): 1.8B **Privately Held**
SIC: 8721 Certified public accountant
PA: Rsm Us Llp
  1 S Wacker Dr Ste 800
  Chicago IL 60606
  312 384-6000

(G-8657)
RTW INC
544 W Walnut St (43215-4480)
PHONE..................614 594-9217
Rod Warrix, *Principal*
EMP: 28
SALES (corp-wide): 570MM **Publicly Held**
SIC: 6331 Assessment associations: fire, marine & casualty insurance
HQ: Rtw, Inc
  8500 Normandale Lake Blvd # 1400
  Minneapolis MN 55437
  952 893-0403

(G-8658)
RUSCILLI CONSTRUCTION CO INC (PA)
5000 Arlngtn Ctr Blvd # 300 (43220-3075)
PHONE..................614 876-9484
Fax: 614 876-0253
Louis V Ruscilli, *CEO*
L Jack Ruscilli, *Ch of Bd*
Robert A Ruscilli Jr, *President*
Jeremy Crawford, *Superintendent*
Phillip Miller, *Superintendent*
EMP: 80
SQ FT: 35,000
SALES (est): 52.3MM **Privately Held**
WEB: www.ruscilli.com
SIC: 1541 8741 1542 Industrial buildings, new construction; warehouse construction; construction management; commercial & office building, new construction; school building construction; institutional building construction

(G-8659)
RUSH MOTOR SALES INC
Also Called: Rush Lincoln Mercury
2350 Morse Rd (43229-5801)
P.O. Box 29286 (43229-0286)
PHONE..................614 471-9980
Carol Overfield, *Corp Secy*
Mark Rush, *Manager*

EMP: 40
SQ FT: 35,000
SALES (est): 8.9MM **Privately Held**
WEB: www.ronrushlm.com
SIC: 5511 7538 Automobiles, new & used; general automotive repair shops

(G-8660)
RUSH TRUCK LEASING INC (HQ)
Also Called: Columbus Idealease West
4200 Currency Dr (43228-3802)
PHONE..................614 876-3500
EMP: 27
SALES (est): 13.8MM
SALES (corp-wide): 4.7B **Publicly Held**
SIC: 5012 7538 5531 5014 Automobiles & other motor vehicles; general automotive repair shops; automotive & home supply stores; tires & tubes; truck rental & leasing, no drivers
PA: Rush Enterprises, Inc.
  555 S Ih 35 Ste 500
  New Braunfels TX 78130
  830 302-5200

(G-8661)
RUSTYS TOWING SERVICE INC
4845 Obetz Reese Rd (43207-4831)
PHONE..................614 491-6288
Fax: 614 491-3511
Russ Mc Quirt, *President*
EMP: 54
SQ FT: 1,200
SALES (est): 5MM **Privately Held**
SIC: 7549 Towing service, automotive

(G-8662)
RUTHERFORD FUNERAL HOME INC (PA)
2383 N High St (43202-2921)
PHONE..................614 451-0593
Fax: 614 299-1114
William P Rutherford, *President*
Helen M Rutherford, *Admin Sec*
EMP: 29
SQ FT: 2,500
SALES (est): 2.7MM **Privately Held**
SIC: 7261 Funeral home; crematory

(G-8663)
RXP OHIO LLC
Also Called: Rxp Wireless
630 E Broad St (43215-3999)
PHONE..................614 937-2844
Stephanie Jandik, *Mng Member*
EMP: 80
SQ FT: 15,000
SALES (est): 665.5K **Privately Held**
SIC: 4813 Telephone communications broker

(G-8664)
RYBAC INC
407 E Livingston Ave (43215-5531)
PHONE..................614 228-3578
Lawrence D Schaffer, *President*
EMP: 35
SALES (est): 1.6MM **Privately Held**
SIC: 6531 Real estate brokers & agents

(G-8665)
RYDER TRUCK RENTAL INC
775 Schrock Rd (43229-1124)
P.O. Box 29623 (43229-0623)
PHONE..................614 846-6780
Fax: 614 431-8772
Rick Lenkey, *Branch Mgr*
Jonathan Reed, *Business Dir*
EMP: 45
SALES (corp-wide): 7.3B **Publicly Held**
SIC: 7513 7519 Truck rental, without drivers; utility trailer rental
HQ: Ryder Truck Rental, Inc.
  11690 Nw 105th St
  Medley FL 33178
  305 500-3726

(G-8666)
RYDER TRUCK RENTAL INC
2600 Westbelt Dr (43228-3829)
PHONE..................614 876-0405
Fax: 614 876-7696
Amber Cerana, *Accounts Mgr*
Michael Thompson, *Manager*
EMP: 30

SALES (corp-wide): 7.3B **Publicly Held**
SIC: 7513 Truck rental, without drivers
HQ: Ryder Truck Rental, Inc.
  11690 Nw 105th St
  Medley FL 33178
  305 500-3726

(G-8667)
S & T TRUCK AND AUTO SVC INC
Also Called: Silvan Trucking Company Ohio
3150 Valleyview Dr Rm 8 (43204-2002)
PHONE..................614 272-8163
Fax: 614 272-8319
Brent Greek, *President*
Glenda Purdy, *Vice Pres*
Jeremy Garrett, *Opers Mgr*
Gail Grabovich, *Manager*
Debbie Groves, *Administration*
EMP: 39
SQ FT: 8,000
SALES (est): 10.2MM **Privately Held**
SIC: 4213 Contract haulers

(G-8668)
SAFE AUTO INSURANCE COMPANY (HQ)
Also Called: S A
4 Easton Oval (43219-6010)
P.O. Box 182109 (43218-2109)
PHONE..................614 231-0200
Ronald H Davies, *CEO*
Shawn M Flahive, *Principal*
Anne C Griffin, *Principal*
James A Yano, *Principal*
Tara Baxley, *Senior VP*
EMP: 258
SQ FT: 50,000
SALES (est): 678.8MM **Privately Held**
SIC: 6411 Insurance agents, brokers & service
PA: Safe Auto Insurance Group, Inc.
  4 Easton Oval
  Columbus OH 43219
  614 231-0200

(G-8669)
SAFE AUTO INSURANCE GROUP INC (PA)
4 Easton Oval (43219-6010)
PHONE..................614 231-0200
Fax: 614 231-4650
Ronald H Davies, *CEO*
ARI Deshe, *Ch of Bd*
Jon P Diamond, *Ch of Bd*
Jonathan P Diamond, *Vice Chairman*
Jack H Coolidge, *Senior VP*
EMP: 59
SQ FT: 45,000
SALES (est): 678.8MM **Privately Held**
SIC: 6331 6411 Automobile insurance; insurance agents, brokers & service

(G-8670)
SAFELITE FULFILLMENT INC
Also Called: Safelite Autoglass
760 Dearborn Park Ln (43085-5703)
PHONE..................614 781-5449
Fax: 614 228-5815
Brenton Carr, *Branch Mgr*
Joel Marsh, *Manager*
EMP: 25
SALES (corp-wide): 3.1B **Privately Held**
WEB: www.belronus.com
SIC: 7536 4225 Automotive glass replacement shops; general warehousing & storage
HQ: Safelite Fulfillment, Inc.
  7400 Safelite Way
  Columbus OH 43235
  614 210-9747

(G-8671)
SAFELITE FULFILLMENT INC
Accounts Payable Department
7400 Safelite Way (43235-5086)
P.O. Box 182827 (43218-2827)
PHONE..................614 210-9050
Kaleisha Johnson, *Principal*
EMP: 25
SALES (corp-wide): 3.1B **Privately Held**
SIC: 8721 Accounting, auditing & bookkeeping

HQ: Safelite Fulfillment, Inc.
  7400 Safelite Way
  Columbus OH 43235
  614 210-9747

(G-8672)
SAFELITE GROUP INC (DH)
Also Called: Safelite Autoglass
7400 Safelite Way (43235-5086)
P.O. Box 182827 (43218-2827)
PHONE..................614 210-9000
Fax: 614 761-4992
Thomas Feeney, *CEO*
Michelle Beiter, *President*
Ron Duncan, *President*
Paul Groves, *President*
Kerry Hurff, *President*
▲ **EMP:** 1000
SALES (est): 2.2B
SALES (corp-wide): 3.1B **Privately Held**
WEB: www.safelitegroup.com
SIC: 7536 3231 6411 Automotive glass replacement shops; windshields, glass: made from purchased glass; insurance claim processing, except medical
HQ: Belron Sa
  Boulevard Du Prince Henri 9b
  Luxembourg
  274 788-60

(G-8673)
SAFELITE SOLUTIONS LLC
7400 Safelite Way (43235-5086)
PHONE..................614 210-9000
Dan Wislon, *President*
Douglas A Jenny Cain, *CFO*
Douglas A Herron, *CFO*
EMP: 3500
SALES (est): 98.4MM
SALES (corp-wide): 3.1B **Privately Held**
WEB: www.safelitegroup.com
SIC: 8742 Management consulting services
HQ: Safelite Group, Inc.
  7400 Safelite Way
  Columbus OH 43235
  614 210-9000

(G-8674)
SAFEWAY ELECTRIC COMPANY INC
1973 Lockbourne Rd (43207-1488)
PHONE..................614 443-7672
Fax: 614 443-2442
Andy Untch, *President*
David Muncy, *Admin Sec*
EMP: 36
SQ FT: 22,000
SALES (est): 6MM **Privately Held**
SIC: 1731 General electrical contractor

(G-8675)
SAGA COMMUNICATIONS NENG INC
Also Called: Wsny Radio Station
4401 Carriage Hill Ln (43220-3837)
PHONE..................614 451-2191
Alan Goodman, *Manager*
EMP: 80 **Publicly Held**
WEB: www.sagacommunications.com
SIC: 4832 Radio broadcasting stations
HQ: Saga Communications Of New England, Inc.
  73 Kercheval Ave Ste 201
  Grosse Pointe Farms MI 48236
  313 886-7070

(G-8676)
SAIA MOTOR FREIGHT LINE LLC
1717 Krieger St (43228-3623)
PHONE..................614 870-8778
Fax: 614 870-0267
Myles Hook, *Manager*
EMP: 80
SALES (corp-wide): 1.3B **Publicly Held**
WEB: www.saia.com
SIC: 4213 Contract haulers
HQ: Saia Motor Freight Line, Llc
  11465 Johns Creek Pkwy # 400
  Duluth GA 30097
  770 232-5067

GEOGRAPHIC SECTION
Columbus - Franklin County (G-8701)

(G-8677)
SAINT CECILIA CHURCH
Also Called: St Cecilia School
440 Norton Rd (43228-7602)
PHONE.................................614 878-5353
Fax: 614 878-0459
Leo Connolly, *Pastor*
Carolyn Hughes, *Librarian*
Trisha Jakubick, *Director*
Jim Martin, *Director*
Katie Wohrle, *Director*
EMP: 42
SALES: 1MM **Privately Held**
SIC: 8211 8661 8351 Catholic elementary & secondary schools; religious organizations; preschool center

(G-8678)
SALLY BEAUTY SUPPLY LLC
Also Called: Sally Beauty Supply 9927
4309 Janitrol Rd (43228-1301)
PHONE.................................614 278-1691
Fax: 614 351-0514
Tom Brown, *Director*
EMP: 250 **Publicly Held**
WEB: www.sallybeauty.com
SIC: 4225 5087 General warehousing & storage; service establishment equipment
HQ: Sally Beauty Supply Llc
3001 Colorado Blvd
Denton TX 76210
940 898-7500

(G-8679)
SALO INC (PA)
Also Called: INTERIM HEALTHCARE
960 Checkrein Ave Ste A (43229-1107)
PHONE.................................614 436-9404
Fax: 614 888-3686
Kathleen Gilmartin, *CEO*
Michael Hartshorn, *Ch of Bd*
Max Hahnen, *Vice Pres*
Sonya Hinds, *Vice Pres*
Christine Oswald, *Vice Pres*
EMP: 93
SQ FT: 7,500
SALES: 24.4MM **Privately Held**
WEB: www.salo.com
SIC: 8082 Home health care services

(G-8680)
SALON COMMUNICATION SERVICES
Also Called: Jacob Neal Salon
650 N High St (43215-1547)
PHONE.................................614 233-8500
Fax: 614 233-8501
Jacob Neal, *President*
Jody Dierksheide, *Manager*
EMP: 26
SQ FT: 1,300
SALES (est): 809.6K **Privately Held**
WEB: www.jacobneal.com
SIC: 7231 Unisex hair salons

(G-8681)
SALVATION ARMY
966 E Main St (43205-2339)
PHONE.................................614 252-7171
Fax: 614 221-1896
Frank Kirk, *Principal*
EMP: 60
SALES (corp-wide): 4.3B **Privately Held**
WEB: www.salvationarmy-usaeast.org
SIC: 8322 8399 Multi-service center; advocacy group
HQ: The Salvation Army
440 W Nyack Rd Ofc
West Nyack NY 10994
845 620-7200

(G-8682)
SALVATION ARMY
1675 S High St (43207-1863)
P.O. Box 7827 (43207-0827)
PHONE.................................800 728-7825
Maj Dennis Gensler, *Manager*
EMP: 67
SALES (corp-wide): 4.3B **Privately Held**
WEB: www.salvationarmy-usaeast.org
SIC: 8322 8399 Multi-service center; community development groups
HQ: The Salvation Army
440 W Nyack Rd Ofc
West Nyack NY 10994
845 620-7200

(G-8683)
SAMKEL INC
Also Called: Children's Academy
100 Obetz Rd (43207-4031)
PHONE.................................614 491-3270
Fax: 614 492-0035
Ronald Sams, *President*
Barbara A Sams, *Corp Secy*
EMP: 50
SQ FT: 10,000
SALES (est): 2.1MM **Privately Held**
SIC: 8351 8211 Preschool center; group day care center; private elementary school

(G-8684)
SANDS DECKER CPS LLC (PA)
1495 Old Henderson Rd (43220-3613)
PHONE.................................614 459-6992
Glenn E Decker, *Principal*
Rick Cox, *Project Mgr*
Brenton McCuskey, *Engineer*
Sarah Stephens, *Mktg Coord*
Kathy Zalmon, *Office Mgr*
EMP: 28
SQ FT: 1,000
SALES (est): 4.7MM **Privately Held**
WEB: www.sandsdecker.com
SIC: 8711 8713 Civil engineering; surveying services

(G-8685)
SAUER GROUP INC
1801 Lone Eagle St (43228-3647)
PHONE.................................614 853-2500
Charles D Steitz, *President*
Dennis Hartz, *VP Opers*
Terry Kilinay, *CFO*
EMP: 200 **EST:** 2007
SQ FT: 23,000
SALES (est): 48.2MM
SALES (corp-wide): 120.8MM **Privately Held**
SIC: 1711 Mechanical contractor
PA: Sauer Holdings, Inc.
30 51st St
Pittsburgh PA 15201
412 687-4100

(G-8686)
SAUER INCORPORATED
1801 Lone Eagle St (43228-3647)
PHONE.................................614 853-2500
Charles Steitz, *Branch Mgr*
EMP: 75
SALES (corp-wide): 120.8MM **Privately Held**
WEB: www.sauerinc.com
SIC: 1711 Mechanical contractor
HQ: Sauer Incorporated
30 51st St
Pittsburgh PA 15201
412 687-4100

(G-8687)
SAVARE CORPORATION (DH)
230 West St Ste 700 (43215-2663)
PHONE.................................770 517-3749
Rick Schwieterman, *CEO*
Laura Savare, *CFO*
Domenico Boffelli, *Admin Sec*
EMP: 87
SQ FT: 52,650
SALES (corp-wide): 342.8K **Privately Held**
SIC: 6719 Investment holding companies, except banks
HQ: Savare' I.C. Srl
Via Polidoro Da Caravaggio 3
Milano MI 20156
023 086-993

(G-8688)
SAX 5TH AVE CAR WASH INC (PA)
Also Called: Sax Car Wash
1319 W 5th Ave (43212-2902)
PHONE.................................614 486-9093
Fax: 614 488-8857
Jeff Randolph, *President*
Bob Morgan, *President*
EMP: 25
SQ FT: 3,500
SALES (est): 1.9MM **Privately Held**
WEB: www.saxcarwash.com
SIC: 7542 Carwashes

(G-8689)
SAYLES COMPANY LLC
Also Called: Miracle Method of Columbus
1575 Integrity Dr E (43209-2707)
PHONE.................................614 801-0432
Mary Sayles, *General Mgr*
Leo Sayles, *Mng Member*
Emily Sayles,
EMP: 25
SQ FT: 2,500
SALES: 3MM **Privately Held**
SIC: 1799 Bathtub refinishing

(G-8690)
SB CAPITAL ACQUISITIONS LLC
Also Called: Jc's 5 Star Outlet
4010 E 5th Ave (43219-1811)
PHONE.................................614 443-4080
Jay L Schottenstein, *Principal*
Amanda Harvey, *Accountant*
EMP: 1500 **EST:** 2011
SQ FT: 15,125
SALES: 353.4K **Privately Held**
SIC: 8742 Retail trade consultant
PA: Sb Capital Group Llc
4300 E 5th Ave
Columbus OH 43219

(G-8691)
SB CAPITAL GROUP LLC (PA)
Also Called: Retail 4 Less
4300 E 5th Ave (43219-1816)
PHONE.................................516 829-2400
Fax: 614 449-4869
Jay L Schottenstein, *Ch of Bd*
David Bernstein, *President*
Steve Haransky, *Managing Dir*
Dirk E Greene, *Vice Pres*
Stephen Jenkins, *Vice Pres*
EMP: 25
SQ FT: 325,000
SALES (est): 83.3MM **Privately Held**
WEB: www.sbcapitalgroup.com
SIC: 7389 Merchandise liquidators

(G-8692)
SBC ADVERTISING LTD
333 W Nationwide Blvd (43215-2311)
PHONE.................................614 891-7070
Fax: 614 891-3664
David Dennis, *President*
Neil Widerschen, *Principal*
Matt Wilson, *Principal*
Jill Jameson, *Med Doctor*
Jeremy Rosario, *Director*
EMP: 110
SQ FT: 20,000
SALES (est): 32.4MM **Privately Held**
WEB: www.sbcadv.com
SIC: 7311 8742 8743 Advertising consultant; marketing consulting services; public relations & publicity

(G-8693)
SCARBROUGH E TENNIS FITNES CTR
Also Called: Scarbrough E Tennis Fitnes CLB
5641 Alshire Rd (43232-4703)
PHONE.................................614 751-2597
Fax: 614 868-5957
Robert Weiler, *Partner*
Bob Kelly, *Partner*
Rita Brown, *Vice Pres*
Robert Hilborn, *Manager*
EMP: 50
SALES (est): 1.6MM **Privately Held**
SIC: 7997 Tennis club, membership

(G-8694)
SCHINDLER ELEVATOR CORPORATION
3607 Interchange Rd (43204-1499)
PHONE.................................614 573-2777
Sean Walsh, *Manager*
EMP: 45
SALES (corp-wide): 9.5B **Privately Held**
WEB: www.us.schindler.com
SIC: 7699 5084 1796 Elevators: inspection, service & repair; elevators; installing building equipment
HQ: Schindler Elevator Corporation
20 Whippany Rd
Morristown NJ 07960
973 397-6500

(G-8695)
SCHLEE MALT HOUSE CONDO ASSN
Also Called: Equip Estate Group
495 S High St Ste 10 (43215-5689)
PHONE.................................614 463-1999
Kim Ulle, *President*
EMP: 26 **EST:** 1989
SALES (est): 361.2K **Privately Held**
SIC: 8641 Fraternal associations

(G-8696)
SCHMID MECHANICAL CO
5255 Sinclair Rd (43229-5042)
PHONE.................................614 261-6331
Dennis Shuman, *President*
Dustin Fishburn, *Vice Pres*
Timothy Schmid, *Vice Pres*
Daniel Shuman, *Vice Pres*
EMP: 50
SALES (est): 683.6K
SALES (corp-wide): 41.2MM **Privately Held**
SIC: 1711 Mechanical contractor
PA: Speer Industries Incorporated
5255 Sinclair Rd
Columbus OH 43229
614 261-6331

(G-8697)
SCHNEIDER DOWNS & CO INC
65 E State St Ste 2000 (43215-4271)
PHONE.................................614 621-4060
Fax: 614 621-4062
Joe Patrick, *Manager*
EMP: 75
SALES (corp-wide): 45.6MM **Privately Held**
SIC: 8721 Certified public accountant
PA: Schneider Downs & Co., Inc.
1 Ppg Pl Ste 1700
Pittsburgh PA 15222
412 261-3644

(G-8698)
SCHODORF TRUCK BODY & EQP CO
885 Harmon Ave (43223-2411)
P.O. Box 23322 (43223-0322)
PHONE.................................614 228-6793
Fax: 614 228-6775
Joe Schodorf, *President*
Paul F Schodorf, *Vice Pres*
Mattday Schodorfwinches, *Parts Mgr*
EMP: 40
SQ FT: 52,000
SALES (est): 10.3MM **Privately Held**
WEB: www.schodorftruck.com
SIC: 5012 3713 3211 Truck bodies; truck bodies (motor vehicles); flat glass

(G-8699)
SCHOMER GLAUS PYLE
Also Called: Gpd Group
1801 Watermark Dr Ste 210 (43215-1096)
PHONE.................................614 210-0751
Darrin Kotecki, *President*
Kayla Stucke, *Marketing Staff*
EMP: 85
SALES (corp-wide): 93.9MM **Privately Held**
SIC: 8711 8712 Consulting engineer; architectural services
PA: Glaus, Pyle, Schomer, Burns & Dehaven, Inc.
520 S Main St Ste 2531
Akron OH 44311
330 572-2100

(G-8700)
SCHOOL CHOICE OHIO INC
88 E Broad St Ste 640 (43215-3506)
PHONE.................................614 223-1555
Lois Graham, *Office Mgr*
Matt Cox, *Exec Dir*
Kaleigh Lemaster, *Exec Dir*
EMP: 50
SALES: 603.6K **Privately Held**
SIC: 8699 Charitable organization

(G-8701)
SCHOOL EMPLOYEES RETIREMENT
300 E Broad St Ste 100 (43215-3747)
PHONE.................................614 222-5853

Columbus - Franklin County (G-8702)

Alan Tharp, *Vice Pres*
Tim Fox, *Engineer*
Virginia Briszendine, *CFO*
Tracy Valentino, *CFO*
Judi Masri, *Investment Ofcr*
EMP: 166
SQ FT: 197,980
SALES (est): 1.4B **Privately Held**
WEB: www.governor.ohio.gov
SIC: 6371 9441 Pension, health & welfare funds; administration of social & manpower programs;
HQ: Executive Office State Of Ohio
30 E Broad St
Columbus OH 43215

(G-8702)
SCHOOLEY CALDWELL ASSOCIATES
300 Marconi Blvd Ste 100 (43215-2329)
PHONE..............................614 628-0300
Fax: 614 628-0311
Robert D Loversidge, *President*
Jayne M Vandenburgh, *COO*
Vincent A Bednar, *Vice Pres*
Robert K Smith, *Vice Pres*
Terence J Sullivan, *Vice Pres*
EMP: 55
SQ FT: 17,255
SALES (est): 6MM **Privately Held**
WEB: www.sca-ae.com
SIC: 8748 8711 8712 City planning; consulting engineer; architectural engineering

(G-8703)
SCHOTTENSTEIN RE GROUP LLC
2 Easton Oval Ste 510 (43219-6013)
PHONE..............................614 418-8900
Fax: 614 418-8920
Brett Kaufman, *President*
Wes Smith, *President*
George Harmanis, *Senior VP*
Brian Schottenstein, *Vice Pres*
Deborah Wilson, *Vice Pres*
EMP: 38
SQ FT: 15,000
SALES (est): 5.9MM **Privately Held**
WEB: www.srealestateg.com
SIC: 6531 Real estate managers; real estate brokers & agents

(G-8704)
SCHOTTENSTEIN REALTY LLC
Also Called: Schottenstein Property Group
4300 E 5th Ave (43219-1816)
PHONE..............................614 445-8461
Dirk Greene, *Senior VP*
Bill Kugel, *Vice Pres*
Amy Romanowski, *Vice Pres*
Chuck Seall, *Vice Pres*
Mike Cahill, *Opers Mgr*
EMP: 50
SALES (est): 4.6MM **Privately Held**
SIC: 6519 6512 Sub-lessors of real estate; shopping center, property operation only; shopping center, regional (300,000 - 1,000,000 sq ft); shopping center, neighborhood (30,000 - 100,000 sq ft)

(G-8705)
SCIENTIFIC FORMING TECH CORP (PA)
Also Called: Deform
2545 Farmers Dr Ste 200 (43235-3713)
PHONE..............................614 451-8330
Andy Tang, *President*
Misty Engelbrecht, *Controller*
EMP: 29
SALES (est): 4.9MM **Privately Held**
WEB: www.deform.com
SIC: 7371 Custom computer programming services; computer software development

(G-8706)
SCIOTO DOWNS INC
6000 S High St (43207)
P.O. Box 7823 (43207-0823)
PHONE..............................614 295-4700
Fax: 614 491-4626
Edward T Ryan, *President*
Troy J Buswell, *Vice Pres*
Richard Fiore, *Controller*
Donna Hundley, *Sales Executive*
Steven Carpenito, *Director*
EMP: 1000

SALES (est): 2.4MM
SALES (corp-wide): 1.4B **Publicly Held**
WEB: www.sciotodowns.com
SIC: 7948 Horse race track operation; harness horse racing
HQ: Mtr Gaming Group, Inc.
Hc 2 Box S
Chester WV 26034
304 387-8000

(G-8707)
SCIOTO PACKAGING INC
6969 Alum Creek Dr (43217-1244)
PHONE..............................614 491-1500
Dennis Hickox, *President*
Isaac Macie, *Manager*
Steve Burelison, *Admin Sec*
EMP: 50
SALES (est): 2.1MM **Privately Held**
WEB: www.sciotopackaging.com
SIC: 8748 Business consulting

(G-8708)
SCOTT SCRIVEN & WAHOFF LLP
250 E Broad St Ste 900 (43215-3725)
PHONE..............................614 222-8686
Fax: 614 222-8688
Greg Scott, *Partner*
Day Jones, *Vice Pres*
Brent Leiter, *Vice Pres*
Paul Elder, *Manager*
Rick Hill, *Manager*
EMP: 28
SALES (est): 3.4MM **Privately Held**
WEB: www.sswlaw.com
SIC: 8111 Labor & employment law

(G-8709)
SEA LTD (PA)
7001 Buffalo Pkwy (43229-1157)
PHONE..............................614 888-4160
Fax: 614 885-8014
Glenn Baker, *CEO*
Jason Baker, *CEO*
Robert K Rupp, *Principal*
Kirk Wolf, *Research*
Elaine Castro, *Engineer*
EMP: 100
SQ FT: 56,526
SALES (est): 72.5MM **Privately Held**
SIC: 8711 Consulting engineer

(G-8710)
SECURITY CHECK LLC (PA)
2 Easton Oval Ste 350 (43219-6193)
P.O. Box 1211, Oxford MS (38655-1211)
PHONE..............................614 944-5788
Joan Rasbery, *COO*
Dewitt Lovelace, *CFO*
John Lewis, *Mng Member*
Thomas Weldon, *Director*
William Alias Jr,
EMP: 150
SQ FT: 6,000
SALES (est): 10.2MM **Privately Held**
WEB: www.security-check.net
SIC: 7389 7322 Check validation service; collection agency, except real estate

(G-8711)
SEG OF OHIO INC (PA)
4016 Townsfair Way # 201 (43219-6083)
PHONE..............................614 414-7300
Fax: 614 414-7311
Yaromir Steiner, *CEO*
Barry Rosenberg, *President*
Beau Arnason, *Exec VP*
Anne Mastin, *Exec VP*
Patricia Curry, *Senior VP*
EMP: 35
SQ FT: 8,035
SALES (est): 73.6MM **Privately Held**
WEB: www.steiner.com
SIC: 6552 Subdividers & developers

(G-8712)
SELECT SPECIALTY HOSP COLUMBUS
1087 Dennison Ave (43201-3201)
PHONE..............................614 291-8467
Fax: 614 291-9626
William Eckle, *Purch Dir*
Deb Raykovich, *VP Finance*
Mary Burkett, *Branch Mgr*
Lin Record, *Quality Imp Dir*

Lin P Sawley, *Quality Imp Dir*
EMP: 88
SALES (corp-wide): 3.7B **Publicly Held**
WEB: www.selectmedicalcorp.com
SIC: 8062 General medical & surgical hospitals
HQ: Select Specialty Hospital - Columbus, Inc.
4716 Old Gettysburg Rd
Mechanicsburg PA 17055
336 718-6300

(G-8713)
SEQUOIA PRO BOWL
5501 Sandalwood Blvd (43229-4476)
PHONE..............................614 885-7043
Fax: 614 885-3745
Tim Boss, *Owner*
EMP: 25
SQ FT: 32,000
SALES (est): 500K **Privately Held**
WEB: www.sequoiaprobowl.com
SIC: 7933 Ten pin center

(G-8714)
SERENITY CENTER INC
Also Called: Forest Hills Center
2841 E Dblin Granville Rd (43231-4037)
PHONE..............................614 891-1111
Cynthia Lawes, *President*
Deb Gibson, *Personnel Exec*
EMP: 110
SALES (est): 3.5MM **Privately Held**
SIC: 8059 Nursing home, except skilled & intermediate care facility

(G-8715)
SERVICE EXPERTS HTG & AC LLC
Also Called: Service Experts of Columbus
1751 Dividend Dr (43228-3899)
PHONE..............................614 859-6993
Rick Rogers, *Branch Mgr*
EMP: 30
SALES (corp-wide): 736.6MM **Privately Held**
SIC: 1711 Heating & air conditioning contractors
HQ: Service Experts Heating & Air Conditioning Llc
3820 American Dr Ste 200
Plano TX 75075
972 535-3800

(G-8716)
SERVICE PRONET INC
1535 Georgesville Rd (43228-3615)
P.O. Box 28339 (43228)
PHONE..............................614 874-4300
Richard Deering, *President*
Tim Custer, *Vice Pres*
Andrew Deering, *Vice Pres*
Randy Hames, *Sales Mgr*
Rafael Zumbado, *Technology*
EMP: 35
SALES: 5MM **Privately Held**
WEB: www.theservicepro.net
SIC: 7374 7371 7389 Computer graphics service; computer software development & applications;

(G-8717)
SETIAWAN ASSOCIATES LLC
50 W Broad St Ste 1800 (43215-5910)
PHONE..............................614 285-5815
EMP: 25
SQ FT: 1,000
SALES (est): 738.4K **Privately Held**
SIC: 7359 Equipment Rental/Leasing

(G-8718)
SETTLE MUTER ELECTRIC LTD (PA)
Also Called: S M E
711 Claycraft Rd (43230-6631)
PHONE..............................614 866-7554
Fax: 614 866-7541
Mark Muter, *President*
Bill Muter, *Vice Pres*
William Muter, *Vice Pres*
Charles Settle, *Vice Pres*
Bryan Eckert, *Project Mgr*
EMP: 113
SQ FT: 15,000

SALES (est): 28.4MM **Privately Held**
WEB: www.settlemuter.com
SIC: 1731 General electrical contractor

(G-8719)
SHADE TREE COOL LIVING LLC
6317 Busch Blvd (43229-1802)
PHONE..............................614 844-5990
Colin Leveque, *Mng Member*
▲ **EMP:** 25
SALES (est): 2MM **Privately Held**
SIC: 1521 Patio & deck construction & repair

(G-8720)
SHADOART PRODUCTIONS INC
503 S Front St Ste 260 (43215-5662)
PHONE..............................614 227-6125
Steven F Guyer, *President*
Stacie V Boord, *Corp Secy*
Julie A Klein, *Vice Pres*
Billy Depetro, *Mktg Coord*
EMP: 68
SALES (est): 3.4MM **Privately Held**
SIC: 7812 Motion picture & video production

(G-8721)
SHAFFER DISTRIBUTING COMPANY (PA)
1100 W 3rd Ave (43212-3113)
P.O. Box 12427 (43212-0427)
PHONE..............................614 421-6800
Fax: 614 294-1040
Steven W Shaffer, *CEO*
William H Kraft, *President*
Paul T Westbrock, *Exec VP*
Charles Ropke, *Vice Pres*
Chuck Ropke, *Vice Pres*
▲ **EMP:** 58 **EST:** 1929
SQ FT: 63,000
SALES (est): 41.8MM **Privately Held**
WEB: www.shafferindy.com
SIC: 5087 Vending machines & supplies

(G-8722)
SHALOM HOUSE INC (HQ)
Also Called: HERITAGE HOUSE NURSING HOME
1135 College Ave (43209-7802)
PHONE..............................614 239-1999
Fax: 614 239-1367
David Rosen, *President*
Pamela Lamb, *Controller*
Ruth Dodge, *Administration*
EMP: 35
SALES: 2.7MM
SALES (corp-wide): 15.9MM **Privately Held**
SIC: 8361 Residential care
PA: Wexner Heritage Village
1151 College Ave
Columbus OH 43209
614 231-4900

(G-8723)
SHAMROCK TAXI LTD
P.O. Box 360363 (43236-0363)
PHONE..............................614 263-8294
T Nagasi, *CEO*
EMP: 38
SALES (est): 698.8K **Privately Held**
SIC: 4121 Taxicabs

(G-8724)
SHEEDY PAVING INC
730 N Rose Ave (43219-2523)
PHONE..............................614 252-2111
Fax: 614 252-0363
James P Sheedy, *President*
Mark J Sheedy, *Vice Pres*
Michael Sheedy, *Vice Pres*
Tom Coalter, *Project Mgr*
Alex Sheedy, *Mktg Dir*
EMP: 36 **EST:** 1941
SQ FT: 3,400
SALES (est): 5.4MM **Privately Held**
SIC: 1771 Blacktop (asphalt) work

(G-8725)
SHELLY AND SANDS INC
1515 Harmon Ave (43223-3309)
P.O. Box 2469 (43216-2469)
PHONE..............................614 444-5100
Doug Howell, *Branch Mgr*

GEOGRAPHIC SECTION
Columbus - Franklin County (G-8748)

EMP: 50
SALES (corp-wide): 260.8MM **Privately Held**
WEB: www.shellyandsands.com
SIC: 1611 1771 1542 Highway & street paving contractor; concrete work; nonresidential construction
PA: Shelly And Sands, Inc.
3570 S River Rd
Zanesville OH 43701
740 453-0721

(G-8726)
SHG WHITEHALL HOLDINGS LLC
Also Called: Manor At Whitehall, The
4805 Langley Ave (43213-6125)
PHONE.................................216 292-5706
Fax: 614 861-3033
George Repchick, *President*
EMP: 120
SQ FT: 55,000
SALES: 11.5MM
SALES (corp-wide): 10.8MM **Privately Held**
SIC: 8051 Skilled nursing care facilities
PA: Saber Healthcare Holdings, Llc
26691 Richmond Rd Frnt
Bedford Heights OH 44146
216 292-5706

(G-8727)
SHINING COMPANY
3739 Wynds Dr (43232-4244)
PHONE.................................614 588-4115
Wendell Hill, *President*
Tracie Moore, *Co-Owner*
EMP: 214
SQ FT: 1,200,000
SALES: 4MM **Privately Held**
SIC: 7349 Building maintenance services

(G-8728)
SHOEMAKER ELECTRIC COMPANY
Also Called: Shoemaker Industrial Solutions
831 Bonham Ave (43211-2999)
PHONE.................................614 294-5626
Fax: 614 294-6330
Fred N Kletrovets, *President*
Teri Richardson, *Treasurer*
Betty Kletrovets, *Admin Sec*
▲ **EMP:** 29 **EST:** 1935
SQ FT: 16,000
SALES (est): 7.4MM **Privately Held**
WEB: www.shoemakerindustrial.com
SIC: 7694 5063 Electric motor repair; motors, electric

(G-8729)
SHOWE BUILDERS INC (HQ)
45 N 4th St (43215-3602)
PHONE.................................614 481-8106
Fax: 614 481-3416
Hugh B Showe, *President*
Scott Hunley, *Vice Pres*
David M Showe, *Vice Pres*
Hugh B Showe II, *Treasurer*
Chris Gahn, *Accountant*
EMP: 26
SQ FT: 5,000
SALES (est): 7.2MM
SALES (corp-wide): 96MM **Privately Held**
SIC: 1522 Apartment building construction
PA: National Housing Corporation
45 N 4th St Ste 200
Columbus OH 43215
614 481-8106

(G-8730)
SIGMA CHI FRAT
260 E 15th Ave (43201-1902)
PHONE.................................614 297-8783
Jeoff Korff, *President*
Todd Yarros, *President*
EMP: 50
SALES: 338.3K **Privately Held**
SIC: 8641 7041 University club; fraternities & sororities

(G-8731)
SIGNATURE CONTROL SYSTEMS LLC
Also Called: Signature Controls
2228 Citygate Dr (43219-3565)
PHONE.................................614 864-2222
Toll Free:.................................877 -
Tom Foster, *General Mgr*
Bryan Roche, *VP Opers*
Chris Popovich, *Project Mgr*
Cory Lacrosse, *CFO*
Bob Schmidt, *CFO*
EMP: 50
SQ FT: 20,000
SALES (est): 16MM **Privately Held**
WEB: www.signaturecontrols.com
SIC: 5063 1799 Control & signal wire & cable, including coaxial; parking facility equipment installation

(G-8732)
SILLIKER LABORATORIES OHIO INC
2057 Builders Pl (43204-4886)
PHONE.................................614 486-0150
Fax: 614 486-0151
Stephanie Campbell, *Manager*
Lori Benz, *Supervisor*
Michele Smoot, *Director*
Amitha Miele, *Lab Dir*
EMP: 30
SQ FT: 4,700
SALES (est): 3.6MM **Privately Held**
WEB: www.silliker.com
SIC: 8734 Testing laboratories; food testing service
HQ: Silliker, Inc.
111 E Wacker Dr Ste 2300
Chicago IL 60601
312 938-5151

(G-8733)
SIMCO SUPPLY CO
Also Called: Simco Controls
3000 E 14th Ave (43219-2355)
PHONE.................................614 253-1999
Fax: 614 253-2033
Charles M Simon, *President*
Don P Simon, *Vice Pres*
Julie Fields, *Controller*
EMP: 50
SQ FT: 50,000
SALES (est): 8.6MM **Privately Held**
WEB: www.simcosupply.com
SIC: 5084 Instruments & control equipment

(G-8734)
SIMON KNTON CNCIL BYSCUTS AMER (PA)
Also Called: BOY SCOUTS OF AMERICA
807 Kinnear Rd (43212-1490)
PHONE.................................614 436-7200
Fax: 614 436-7917
E Linn Draper, *President*
Randy Bly, *Vice Pres*
Andy Paterson, *Purch Agent*
Jeff Pearson, *Controller*
Randy Larson, *Director*
EMP: 54
SQ FT: 20,000
SALES: 4.5MM **Privately Held**
WEB: www.skcbsa.org
SIC: 8641 Boy Scout organization

(G-8735)
SIMONE HEALTH MANAGEMENT INC
750 E Broad St Ste 300 (43205-1126)
PHONE.................................614 224-1347
Viengkeo Vilay, *CEO*
EMP: 35
SALES (est): 790.9K **Privately Held**
SIC: 8082 Home health care services

(G-8736)
SIMPLIFI ESO LLC
2 Miranova Pl Ste 500 (43215-7052)
PHONE.................................614 635-8679
William Rowland, *CFO*
Kim Dibella, *Mng Member*
Donna Roby, *Executive Asst*
EMP: 120
SQ FT: 3,700
SALES (est): 9.3MM **Privately Held**
SIC: 8748 Employee programs administration

(G-8737)
SIMPSON STRONG-TIE COMPANY INC
2600 International St (43228-4617)
PHONE.................................614 876-8060
Fax: 614 876-0636
Shane Vilasineekul, *Engineer*
Sharon Bott, *Human Res Dir*
Rick Reid, *Sales Staff*
Dave Williams, *Branch Mgr*
Jerry Gridley, *Manager*
EMP: 120
SALES (corp-wide): 977MM **Publicly Held**
SIC: 5082 3643 3452 Construction & mining machinery; current-carrying wiring devices; bolts, nuts, rivets & washers
HQ: Simpson Strong-Tie Company Inc.
5956 W Las Positas Blvd
Pleasanton CA 94588
925 560-9000

(G-8738)
SINCLAIR MEDIA II INC
Also Called: Wwho TV
1261 Dublin Rd (43215-7000)
PHONE.................................614 481-6666
Fax: 740 485-5339
Bill Davis, *Engineer*
Elen Daly, *Branch Mgr*
Danielle Turner, *Supervisor*
EMP: 110
SALES (corp-wide): 2.7B **Publicly Held**
SIC: 4833 Television broadcasting stations
HQ: Sinclair Media Ii, Inc
4990 Mobile Hwy
Pensacola FL 32506
850 456-3333

(G-8739)
SINCLAIR MEDIA II INC
Also Called: Wsyx and ABC 6
1261 Dublin Rd (43215-7000)
PHONE.................................614 481-6666
Wendy Vaughan, *Accounts Exec*
Dan Mellon, *Manager*
Rick Smith, *Director*
EMP: 176
SQ FT: 31,942
SALES (corp-wide): 2.7B **Publicly Held**
WEB: www.kvbw.com
SIC: 4833 Television broadcasting stations
HQ: Sinclair Media Ii, Inc.
10706 Beaver Dam Rd
Hunt Valley MD 21030
513 641-4400

(G-8740)
SINCLAIR MEDIA II INC
1261 Dublin Rd (43215-7000)
PHONE.................................614 481-6666
Dan Mellon, *Manager*
EMP: 55
SALES (corp-wide): 2.7B **Publicly Held**
WEB: www.weartv.com
SIC: 4833 Television broadcasting stations
HQ: Sinclair Media Ii, Inc
4990 Mobile Hwy
Pensacola FL 32506
850 456-3333

(G-8741)
SKINNER DIESEL SERVICES INC (PA)
Also Called: Commercial Radiator
2440 Lockbourne Rd (43207-2168)
PHONE.................................614 491-8785
Fax: 614 491-9931
Mike L Skinner, *President*
EMP: 50
SQ FT: 12,000
SALES (est): 7.4MM **Privately Held**
WEB: www.quickwinch.com
SIC: 7538 7532 Diesel engine repair: automotive; truck engine repair, except industrial; body shop, trucks

(G-8742)
SKY FINANCIAL CAPITAL TR III
41 S High St (43215-6170)
PHONE.................................614 480-3278
EMP: 125

SALES (est): 91.2K
SALES (corp-wide): 4.7B **Publicly Held**
SIC: 6733 Trusts
PA: Huntington Bancshares Incorporated
41 S High St
Columbus OH 43215
614 480-8300

(G-8743)
SLEEP CARE INC
985 Schrock Rd (43229-1180)
PHONE.................................614 901-8989
Craig Pickerill, *President*
EMP: 42
SALES (est): 332.5K **Privately Held**
SIC: 8093 Biofeedback center

(G-8744)
SMG HOLDINGS INC
Also Called: Greater Clumbus Convention Ctr
400 N High St Fl 2 (43215-2096)
PHONE.................................614 827-2500
John Page, *General Mgr*
Bill Clark, *Finance*
EMP: 130
SALES (corp-wide): 24.5B **Privately Held**
WEB: www.smgworld.com
SIC: 8741 6512 Management services; nonresidential building operators
HQ: Smg Holdings, Llc
300 Cnshohckn State Rd # 450
Conshohocken PA 19428

(G-8745)
SMITH & ASSOCIATES EXCAVATING
2765 Drake Rd (43219-1603)
PHONE.................................740 362-3355
Fax: 740 362-3022
Ken Belczak, *President*
EMP: 40 **EST:** 1976
SQ FT: 9,600
SALES (est): 6.2MM **Privately Held**
WEB: www.smithexc.com
SIC: 1794 Excavation & grading, building construction

(G-8746)
SMITH TANDY COMPANY
555 City Park Ave (43215-5737)
PHONE.................................614 224-9255
Fax: 614 224-9258
Michael J Weisz, *Partner*
Steven Stieglitz, *Financial Analy*
Edward Friedman, *Associate*
EMP: 25
SALES (est): 1.9MM **Privately Held**
WEB: www.smithtandy.com
SIC: 6513 Apartment building operators

(G-8747)
SMOOT CONSTRUCTION CO OHIO (PA)
1907 Leonard Ave Ste 200 (43219-4506)
PHONE.................................614 257-0032
Mark Cain, *President*
Lewis R Smoot Sr, *Partner*
Thomas J Fitzpatrick, *Partner*
Lewis R Smoot Jr, *Senior VP*
EMP: 50
SALES (est): 27.3MM **Privately Held**
SIC: 8742 Construction project management consultant

(G-8748)
SONIC AUTOMOTIVE
Also Called: Toyota West
1500 Auto Mall Dr (43228-3660)
PHONE.................................614 870-8200
Fax: 614 870-9595
Scott Smith, *Vice Pres*
Donnie Hoover, *Parts Mgr*
Terrence Olaoye, *Parts Mgr*
Dave Rona, *Parts Mgr*
Gabor Rona, *Parts Mgr*
EMP: 94
SALES (est): 31.8MM
SALES (corp-wide): 9.8B **Publicly Held**
SIC: 5511 7538 7515 5531 Automobiles, new & used; general automotive repair shops; passenger car leasing; automotive & home supply stores; used car dealers
PA: Sonic Automotive, Inc.
4401 Colwick Rd
Charlotte NC 28211
704 566-2400

Columbus - Franklin County (G-8749)

(G-8749)
SONIC AUTOMOTIVE-1495 AUTOMALL
Also Called: Hatfield Lincoln Mercury
1495 Auto Mall Dr (43228-3658)
PHONE..................614 317-4326
Fax: 614 870-5488
Scott Penn, *Manager*
Jay J Fraley, *Manager*
EMP: 30
SALES (est): 4MM
SALES (corp-wide): 9.8B **Publicly Held**
SIC: 5511 5561 5571 7532 Automobiles, new & used; travel trailers: automobile, new & used; motorcycle dealers; top & body repair & paint shops; passenger car leasing; used car dealers
PA: Sonic Automotive, Inc.
4401 Colwick Rd
Charlotte NC 28211
704 566-2400

(G-8750)
SOPHISTICATED SYSTEMS INC (PA)
2191 Citygate Dr (43219-3564)
PHONE..................614 418-4600
Fax: 614 418-4610
Dwight Smith, *President*
Dwight E Smith, *President*
Jane L Borgelt, *CFO*
Connie Taylor, *Branch Mgr*
EMP: 76
SQ FT: 10,000
SALES (est): 18.1MM **Privately Held**
WEB: www.ssicom.com
SIC: 7379 5045 Computer related consulting services; computers, peripherals & software

(G-8751)
SOUTHAST CMNTY MENTAL HLTH CTR (PA)
16 W Long St (43215-2815)
PHONE..................614 225-0980
Steven Atwood, *CFO*
Charlie Hickman, *Finance*
Miranda Cox, *Manager*
Sandra Stephenson, *Exec Dir*
Melissa Shelek, *Director*
EMP: 250
SQ FT: 67,988
SALES (est): 12.5MM **Privately Held**
WEB: www.southeastinc.com
SIC: 8093 8361 8011 Mental health clinic, outpatient; substance abuse clinics (outpatient); residential care; offices & clinics of medical doctors

(G-8752)
SOUTHAST CMNTY MENTAL HLTH CTR
1455 S 4th St (43207-1011)
PHONE..................614 444-0800
Fax: 614 444-1036
Diane Sadler, *Branch Mgr*
EMP: 40
SQ FT: 10,191
SALES (corp-wide): 12.5MM **Privately Held**
WEB: www.southeastinc.com
SIC: 8063 8322 8093 8069 Psychiatric hospitals; family counseling services; mental health clinic, outpatient; alcoholism rehabilitation hospital
PA: Southeast Community Mental Health Center Inc
16 W Long St
Columbus OH 43215
614 225-0980

(G-8753)
SOUTHAST CMNTY MENTAL HLTH CTR
Community Treatment
1705 S High St (43207-1864)
PHONE..................614 445-6832
Don Strasser, *Associate Dir*
EMP: 40
SALES (corp-wide): 12.5MM **Privately Held**
WEB: www.southeastinc.com
SIC: 8093 8322 Mental health clinic, outpatient; telephone counseling service

PA: Southeast Community Mental Health Center Inc
16 W Long St
Columbus OH 43215
614 225-0980

(G-8754)
SOUTHERN GLZERS DSTRS OHIO LLC (HQ)
Also Called: Glazer's of Ohio
4800 Poth Rd (43213-1332)
PHONE..................614 552-7900
Bennett Glazer, *President*
Mike Maxwell, *COO*
Stanton Robins, *Vice Pres*
Scott Westerman, *Vice Pres*
Rachelle Roberts, *Portfolio Mgr*
▲ EMP: 77
SQ FT: 100,000
SALES (est): 80.6MM
SALES (corp-wide): 5.8B **Privately Held**
SIC: 5181 5182 Beer & ale; wine
PA: Southern Glazer's Wine And Spirits, Llc
1600 Nw 163rd St
Miami FL 33169
305 625-4171

(G-8755)
SOUTHSIDE LEARNING & DEV CTR
280 Reeb Ave (43207-1936)
PHONE..................614 444-1529
Fax: 614 444-5436
Roberta Bishop, *Director*
Amy Valentine, *Admin Asst*
EMP: 27
SALES: 1.2MM **Privately Held**
SIC: 8351 Preschool center

(G-8756)
SOUTHWESTERN ELECTRIC POWER CO (HQ)
Also Called: AEP
1 Riverside Plz (43215-2355)
PHONE..................614 716-1000
Nicholas K Akins, *Ch of Bd*
Dan Lee, *Engineer*
Brian X Tierney, *CFO*
Richard Turner, *Manager*
Johnny McGatlin, *Supervisor*
EMP: 135
SALES: 1.7B
SALES (corp-wide): 15.4B **Publicly Held**
WEB: www.swepco.com
SIC: 4911 Generation, electric power; distribution, electric power; transmission, electric power
PA: American Electric Power Company, Inc.
1 Riverside Plz Fl 1 # 1
Columbus OH 43215
614 716-1000

(G-8757)
SOUTHWESTERN TILE AND MBL CO
1030 Cable Ave (43222-1202)
PHONE..................614 464-1257
Fax: 614 464-4037
Vaughn Fowler Jr, *President*
Robert Fowler, *Vice Pres*
Bill Rogers, *Manager*
Judith Vest, *Admin Sec*
EMP: 30
SQ FT: 10,000
SALES: 2.6MM **Privately Held**
SIC: 1743 Tile installation, ceramic; marble installation, interior

(G-8758)
SPARTAN WHSE & DIST CO INC (PA)
Also Called: Spartan Logistics
4140 Lockbourne Rd (43207-4221)
PHONE..................614 497-1777
Fax: 614 497-1808
Ed Harmon, *Ch of Bd*
Steve Harmon, *President*
Chris Toler, *General Mgr*
Josh Ledford, *Vice Pres*
Mark Philyaw, *Warehouse Mgr*
EMP: 85
SQ FT: 1,000,000
SALES (est): 53.6MM **Privately Held**
SIC: 4214 Local trucking with storage

(G-8759)
SPECTRUM MGT HOLDG CO LLC
Also Called: Time Warner
3760 Interchange Rd (43204-4131)
PHONE..................614 481-5408
Cindy Powell, *Opers Staff*
Gerald Capehart, *Manager*
Derrick Bohlin, *Manager*
EMP: 83
SALES (corp-wide): 41.5B **Publicly Held**
SIC: 4841 Cable television services
HQ: Spectrum Management Holding Company, Llc
400 Atlantic St
Stamford CT 06901
203 905-7801

(G-8760)
SPECTRUM MGT HOLDG CO LLC
Also Called: Time Warner
1015 Olentangy River Rd (43212-3148)
PHONE..................614 344-4159
Rhonda Frost, *President*
Randy Hall, *Vice Pres*
Jitesh Bhayani, *Human Res Mgr*
Michael McBrayer, *Senior Mgr*
Robert Finney, *Director*
EMP: 50
SALES (corp-wide): 41.5B **Publicly Held**
SIC: 4841 Cable television services
HQ: Spectrum Management Holding Company, Llc
400 Atlantic St
Stamford CT 06901
203 905-7801

(G-8761)
SPEER INDUSTRIES INCORPORATED (PA)
Also Called: Speer Mechanical
5255 Sinclair Rd (43229-5042)
PHONE..................614 261-6331
Samuel A Shuman, *Ch of Bd*
Tom Hangan, *President*
Dennis Shuman, *President*
Phil McEvoy, *COO*
John Harper, *Vice Pres*
EMP: 150
SQ FT: 60,000
SALES (est): 41.2MM **Privately Held**
SIC: 1711 Mechanical contractor

(G-8762)
SPILLMAN COMPANY
1701 Moler Rd (43207-1684)
P.O. Box 7847 (43207-0847)
PHONE..................614 444-2184
Fax: 614 444-1231
Ted Coons, *CEO*
Don McNutt, *President*
Theodore W Coons, *Principal*
Lynn Coons, *Treasurer*
Abby Aitchison, *Sales Mgr*
◆ EMP: 34 EST: 1948
SQ FT: 37,000
SALES: 7.9MM **Privately Held**
WEB: www.spillmanform.com
SIC: 1771 5084 3446 Concrete work; cement making machinery; architectural metalwork

(G-8763)
SPORTS MEDICINE GRANT INC (PA)
Also Called: Smgoa
323 E Town St Ste 100 (43215-4753)
PHONE..................614 461-8174
Raymond J Tesner, *President*
Sid Canter,
EMP: 60
SQ FT: 8,600
SALES (est): 6.5MM **Privately Held**
WEB: www.smgoa.com
SIC: 8031 Offices & clinics of osteopathic physicians

(G-8764)
SPRAY A TREE INC
Also Called: S A T Landscaping
1585 Pemberton Dr (43221-1443)
PHONE..................614 457-8257
Fortunato Merullo, *President*
Renee Merullo, *Vice Pres*
EMP: 25
SQ FT: 8,000
SALES (est): 1.9MM **Privately Held**
SIC: 0782 Landscape contractors

(G-8765)
SPRINT SPECTRUM LP
2367 S Hamilton Rd (43232-4305)
PHONE..................614 575-5500
Fax: 614 861-5516
Mike Schull, *Branch Mgr*
EMP: 30
SALES (corp-wide): 78.3B **Publicly Held**
WEB: www.sprintpcs.com
SIC: 4813 4812 Local & long distance telephone communications; cellular telephone services
HQ: Sprint Spectrum L.P.
6800 Sprint Pkwy
Overland Park KS 66251

(G-8766)
SPRINT SPECTRUM LP
6614 Sawmill Rd (43235-4943)
PHONE..................614 793-2500
Fax: 614 799-1309
David Starcher, *Manager*
EMP: 30
SALES (corp-wide): 78.3B **Publicly Held**
WEB: www.sprintpcs.com
SIC: 4813 Local & long distance telephone communications
HQ: Sprint Spectrum L.P.
6800 Sprint Pkwy
Overland Park KS 66251

(G-8767)
SPRINT SPECTRUM LP
3918 Townsfair Way (43219-6067)
PHONE..................614 428-2300
Fax: 614 428-2301
Jeff Stalcup, *Manager*
EMP: 30
SALES (corp-wide): 78.3B **Publicly Held**
WEB: www.sprintpcs.com
SIC: 4813 4812 Local & long distance telephone communications; cellular telephone services
HQ: Sprint Spectrum L.P.
6800 Sprint Pkwy
Overland Park KS 66251

(G-8768)
SPRUCE BOUGH HOMES LLC
Also Called: Sbh I & II
18 E 3rd Ave (43201-3532)
PHONE..................614 253-0984
Sarah French, *Principal*
EMP: 55
SALES: 944K **Privately Held**
SIC: 6513 Apartment building operators

(G-8769)
SSTH LLC
Also Called: Central Ohio Home Help Agency
739 S James Rd Ste 100 (43227-1098)
PHONE..................614 884-0793
Tim Hanners,
EMP: 64
SQ FT: 1,800
SALES: 900K **Privately Held**
WEB: www.cohha.org
SIC: 8082 Visiting nurse service

(G-8770)
ST STEPHENS COMMUNITY HOUSE
Also Called: ST STEPHENS COMMUNITY SERVICE
1500 E 17th Ave (43219-1002)
PHONE..................614 294-6347
Fax: 614 294-0258
Tim Kelly, *President*
Michelle Mills, *General Mgr*
Akeem Jones, *Trustee*
Marilyn Mehaffie, *Vice Pres*
Ray Thomas, *Vice Pres*
EMP: 80
SQ FT: 41,000
SALES: 4.9MM **Privately Held**
WEB: www.saintstephensch.org
SIC: 8322 8351 Community center; child day care services

GEOGRAPHIC SECTION
Columbus - Franklin County (G-8792)

(G-8771)
ST VINCENT FAMILY CENTERS (PA)
1490 E Main St (43205-2140)
PHONE..................614 252-0731
Fax: 614 252-8468
Anne Ransone, *President*
Debbie Elkins, *President*
Pat Dutson, *Trustee*
Michael Edwards, *Trustee*
Matt Kyle, *Trustee*
EMP: 180
SALES: 12MM **Privately Held**
SIC: 8322 8361 8093 Social service center; residential care for the handicapped; specialty outpatient clinics

(G-8772)
STAID LOGIC LLC (PA)
595 E Broad St Ste 206 (43215-4043)
PHONE..................309 807-0575
Kiran Basireddy, *CEO*
Meghana Penubolu, *President*
Linda Ryan, *Financial Exec*
EMP: 35
SALES (est): 2.1MM **Privately Held**
SIC: 7379 7371 Computer related maintenance services; computer related consulting services; custom computer programming services

(G-8773)
STANTEC ARCH & ENGRG PC
1500 Lake Shore Dr # 100 (43204-3800)
PHONE..................614 486-4383
Christina Han, *Marketing Staff*
Lori Van Dermark, *Marketing Staff*
Amy Strasheim, *Manager*
Reshma Panjanani, *Information Mgr*
EMP: 25
SALES (corp-wide): 3.1B **Privately Held**
SIC: 8711 8712 Engineering services; architectural services
HQ: Stantec Architecture And Engineering P.C.
311 Summer St
Boston MA 02210

(G-8774)
STANTEC CONSULTING SVCS INC
1500 Lake Shore Dr # 100 (43204-3800)
PHONE..................614 486-4383
Christina Han, *Marketing Staff*
Lori Van Dermark, *Marketing Staff*
Matt Tin, *Manager*
Reshma Panjanani, *Information Mgr*
EMP: 123
SALES (corp-wide): 3.1B **Privately Held**
WEB: www.fmsm.com
SIC: 8712 8711 Architectural services; engineering services
HQ: Stantec Consulting Services Inc.
475 5th Ave Fl 12
New York NY 10017
212 352-5160

(G-8775)
STAPLES INC
700 Taylor Rd Ste 100 (43230-3318)
PHONE..................614 472-2014
Susie Petrak, *Branch Mgr*
EMP: 35
SALES (corp-wide): 18.2B **Privately Held**
WEB: www.corporate-express.com
SIC: 5943 5021 Stationery stores; furniture
HQ: Staples, Inc.
500 Staples Dr
Framingham MA 01702
508 253-5000

(G-8776)
STAR LEASING CO (PA)
4080 Business Park Dr (43204-5023)
PHONE..................614 278-9999
Fax: 614 278-9998
Steve Jackson, *President*
Thomas C Copeland III, *Principal*
Jeffrey H Rosen, *Senior VP*
Jeffrey D Egle, *Vice Pres*
Michael Hensley, *Vice Pres*
EMP: 75

SALES (est): 52.7MM **Privately Held**
WEB: www.starleasing.com
SIC: 7513 7539 7549 Truck leasing, without drivers; automotive turbocharger & blower repair; towing services

(G-8777)
STAR PACKAGING INC
1796 Frebis Ave (43206-3729)
PHONE..................614 564-9936
Fax: 614 876-0271
James R Tata, *President*
Chad Bartling, *Vice Pres*
EMP: 32
SQ FT: 53,000
SALES (est): 13.8MM **Privately Held**
SIC: 5199 4783 Packaging materials; packing goods for shipping

(G-8778)
STARWOOD HOTELS & RESORTS
3030 Plaza Prpts Blvd (43219)
PHONE..................614 345-9291
Laurie Hess, *Principal*
EMP: 195
SALES (corp-wide): 22.8B **Publicly Held**
SIC: 7011 Hotels & motels
HQ: Starwood Hotels & Resorts Worldwide, Llc
1 Star Pt
Stamford CT 06902
203 964-6000

(G-8779)
STARWOOD HOTELS & RESORTS
888 E Dublin Granville Rd (43229-2416)
PHONE..................614 888-8230
Steve Marangoni, *Manager*
EMP: 120
SALES (corp-wide): 22.8B **Publicly Held**
SIC: 7011 Hotels & motels
HQ: Starwood Hotels & Resorts Worldwide, Llc
1 Star Pt
Stamford CT 06902
203 964-6000

(G-8780)
STATE AUTO FINANCIAL CORP (HQ)
Also Called: STATE AUTO INSURANCE COMPANIES
518 E Broad St (43215-3901)
P.O. Box 182822 (43218-2822)
PHONE..................614 464-5000
Fax: 614 464-5325
Michael E Larocco, *Ch of Bd*
Alita Burke, *President*
Jason E Berkey, *Senior VP*
Melissa A Centers, *Senior VP*
Kim B Garland, *Senior VP*
EMP: 47
SQ FT: 280,000
SALES: 1.4B
SALES (corp-wide): 570MM **Publicly Held**
SIC: 6331 Fire, marine & casualty insurance
PA: State Automobile Mutual Insurance Co Inc
518 E Broad St
Columbus OH 43215
833 724-3577

(G-8781)
STATE AUTOMOBILE MUTL INSUR CO (PA)
Also Called: State Auto Insurance Companies
518 E Broad St (43215-3901)
P.O. Box 182822 (43218-2822)
PHONE..................833 724-3577
Mike Larocco, *Ch of Bd*
Bob Bachtell, *President*
Jessica E Buss, *Senior VP*
Lyle D Rhodebeck, *Senior VP*
James A Yano, *Senior VP*
EMP: 1500
SQ FT: 270,000

SALES: 570MM **Publicly Held**
WEB: www.stfc.com
SIC: 6331 6411 6351 Fire, marine & casualty insurance & carriers; automobile insurance; insurance agents, brokers & service; surety insurance

(G-8782)
STATE OF OHIO
4200 Surface Rd (43228-1313)
PHONE..................614 466-3455
Charles Wheeler, *Principal*
Kevin Kelly, *Purchasing*
Doug Smith, *Recruiter*
EMP: 199 **Privately Held**
SIC: 8742 Human resource consulting services
PA: State Of Ohio
30 E Broad St Fl 40
Columbus OH 43215
614 466-3455

(G-8783)
STATE TCHERS RTREMENT SYS OHIO (HQ)
Also Called: Strs Ohio
275 E Broad St (43215-3703)
PHONE..................614 227-4090
Fax: 614 227-2952
Robert Stein, *Chairman*
Corey Geog, *Top Exec*
Christine Leslie, *Vice Pres*
Edward Zimmer, *Vice Pres*
Julie H Frazier, *Project Mgr*
EMP: 146
SQ FT: 176,000
SALES (est): 8.2B **Privately Held**
SIC: 6371 Pension funds
PA: State Of Ohio
30 E Broad St Fl 40
Columbus OH 43215
614 466-3455

(G-8784)
STATECO FINANCIAL SERVICES
518 E Broad St (43215-3901)
P.O. Box 182822 (43218-2822)
PHONE..................614 464-5000
Robert Moone, *President*
Urlin G Harris Jr, *CFO*
Terry Bowshier, *Treasurer*
Robert L Bailey Jr, *Director*
John R Lowther, *Admin Sec*
EMP: 200
SALES (est): 15.3MM
SALES (corp-wide): 570MM **Publicly Held**
SIC: 6211 Investment firm, general brokerage
HQ: State Auto Financial Corporation
518 E Broad St
Columbus OH 43215

(G-8785)
STAUFS COFFEE ROASTERS II INC (PA)
705 Hadley Dr (43228-1029)
PHONE..................614 487-6050
Andy Tang, *CEO*
Mark J Swanson, *President*
William Strugis, *CFO*
Robert Metzager, *Sales Executive*
Shawn Schultze, *Manager*
EMP: 40
SQ FT: 4,400
SALES (est): 3.1MM **Privately Held**
WEB: www.staufs.com
SIC: 5499 5722 5149 5084 Gourmet food stores; coffee; tea; household appliance stores; coffee & tea; brewery products manufacturing machinery, commercial

(G-8786)
STERLING PAPER CO (HQ)
1845 Progress Ave (43207-1726)
PHONE..................614 443-0303
Fax: 614 443-7125
Robert Rosenfeld, *President*
Ron Duncan, *Marketing Staff*
Joey Sucgang, *Technology*
▲ **EMP:** 45
SALES (est): 116MM **Privately Held**
SIC: 5111 5199 Printing paper; packaging materials

PA: Rosemark Paper, Inc.
1845 Progress Ave
Columbus OH 43207
614 443-0303

(G-8787)
STEVE SHAFFER
Also Called: Orkin
3905 Sullivant Ave (43228-4326)
PHONE..................614 276-6355
Steve Shaffer, *Principal*
EMP: 30
SALES (est): 1.1MM **Privately Held**
SIC: 7342 Exterminating & fumigating

(G-8788)
STEVEN H BYERLY INC
Also Called: Steve Byerly Masonry
4890 Cleveland Ave (43231-4757)
P.O. Box 29133 (43229-0133)
PHONE..................614 882-0092
Fax: 614 885-9876
Steve Byerly, *Owner*
EMP: 25
SALES (est): 1.4MM **Privately Held**
SIC: 1741 7699 Masonry & other stonework; cleaning services

(G-8789)
STILSON & ASSOCIATES INC
6121 Huntley Rd (43229-1003)
PHONE..................614 847-0300
Fax: 614 436-9876
Vikram V Rajadhysha, *President*
Kevin M Bainter, *Vice Pres*
John Salman, *Vice Pres*
Manoj Sethi, *Vice Pres*
A J Siebert III, *Vice Pres*
EMP: 40
SQ FT: 40,000
SALES (est): 3MM
SALES (corp-wide): 93MM **Privately Held**
SIC: 8712 8711 Architectural services; consulting engineer
PA: Dlz Corporation
6121 Huntley Rd
Columbus OH 43229
614 888-0040

(G-8790)
STONEHENGE CAPITAL COMPANY LLC
191 W Nationwide Blvd (43215-2568)
PHONE..................614 246-2456
Lucinda Jackson, *Vice Pres*
Thomas Adamak, *Branch Mgr*
Gordon S Leblanc Jr, *Manager*
William Owens, *Director*
EMP: 32
SALES (corp-wide): 1.8MM **Privately Held**
SIC: 6282 Investment advice
PA: Stonehenge Capital Company Llc
236 3rd St
Baton Rouge LA 70801
225 408-3000

(G-8791)
STONEHENGE FINCL HOLDINGS INC (PA)
191 W Nationwide Blvd # 600 (43215-2568)
PHONE..................614 246-2500
Fax: 614 246-2441
David R Meuse, *President*
Ronald D Brooks, *Vice Pres*
Michael J Endres, *Vice Pres*
James Henson, *Vice Pres*
Brad L Pospichel, *Vice Pres*
EMP: 50
SQ FT: 17,000
SALES (est): 11.2MM **Privately Held**
WEB: www.Stonehengepartners.com
SIC: 6211 Security brokers & dealers

(G-8792)
STRADERS GARDEN CENTERS INC (PA)
Also Called: Strader's Green House
5350 Riverside Dr (43220-1700)
PHONE..................614 889-1314
Fax: 614 889-2546
Jack D Strader, *President*
Ruth E Strader, *Corp Secy*

Columbus - Franklin County (G-8793) — GEOGRAPHIC SECTION

Mary Brennen, *Vice Pres*
Bethany Broderick, *Human Resources*
▲ **EMP:** 125
SQ FT: 30,625
SALES: 10MM **Privately Held**
SIC: 5261 5193 Nurseries; plants, potted

(G-8793)
STRADERS NRTHWST SCHWINN
5350 Riverside Dr (43220-1700)
PHONE...................................614 889-2453
Jack Strader, *Owner*
EMP: 25
SALES: 300K **Privately Held**
SIC: 7699 5941 Bicycle repair shop; bicycle & bicycle parts

(G-8794)
STRATEGIC INSURANCE SFTWR INC
Also Called: SIS
4181 Arlingate Plz (43228-4115)
PHONE...................................614 915-9769
Robert Moone, *President*
Doug Allen, *COO*
Craig Segbers, *Vice Pres*
Terrance Bowshier, *Controller*
John Lowther, *Council Mbr*
EMP: 30
SQ FT: 11,000
SALES (est): 1.3MM
SALES (corp-wide): 5.3MM **Privately Held**
WEB: www.sisware.com
SIC: 7371 Computer software development
PA: Nugrowth Solutions, Llc
  4181 Arlingate Plz
  Columbus OH 43228
  800 747-9273

(G-8795)
STRATEGIC RESEARCH GROUP INC
995 Goodale Blvd Ste 1 (43212-3865)
PHONE...................................614 220-8860
Fax: 614 220-8845
Kathleen Carr, *President*
Michaela Herrick, *Research*
EMP: 30 **EST:** 1999
SQ FT: 4,200
SALES (est): 5.2MM **Privately Held**
WEB: www.strategicresearchgroup.com
SIC: 6411 Research services, insurance

(G-8796)
STRAWSER CONSTRUCTION INC (HQ)
1392 Dublin Rd (43215-1009)
PHONE...................................614 276-5501
Pierre Peltier, *President*
Chris Anspaugh, *General Mgr*
Dave Kiser, *Vice Pres*
Tim Herbst, *Sales Mgr*
EMP: 32
SALES (est): 47.6MM **Privately Held**
SIC: 1522 Residential construction
PA: Barrett Industries Corp
  1392 Dublin Rd
  Columbus OH 43215
  614 485-9168

(G-8797)
STRAWSER EQUIPMENT & LSG INC
1235 Stimmel Rd (43223-2915)
PHONE...................................614 444-2521
Fax: 614 444-2523
David Strawser, *President*
Kiendra Strawser, *Admin Sec*
EMP: 60
SQ FT: 50,000
SALES: 7MM **Privately Held**
SIC: 4212 Dump truck haulage

(G-8798)
STYLE-LINE INCORPORATED (PA)
Also Called: Chelsea House Fabrics
901 W 3rd Ave Ste A (43212-3131)
P.O. Box 2706 (43216-2706)
PHONE...................................614 291-0600
Fax: 614 291-0700
Laura R Prophater, *President*
William H Prophater, *Vice Pres*
EMP: 45
SQ FT: 54,000
SALES (est): 6.1MM **Privately Held**
SIC: 5023 5131 2391 1799 Venetian blinds; vertical blinds; window shades; window covering parts & accessories; drapery material, woven; curtains, window: made from purchased materials; drapery track installation

(G-8799)
SUCCESS KIDZ 24-HR ENRCHMT CTR
1800 Parsons Ave (43207-1929)
PHONE...................................614 419-2276
Wynter Kirkbride, *Director*
EMP: 30
SALES (est): 1.7MM **Privately Held**
SIC: 8351 Child day care services

(G-8800)
SUMMERFIELD HOMES LLC
27 Linwood Ave (43205-1512)
PHONE...................................614 253-0984
Michelle Hert, *Principal*
EMP: 55
SALES: 906K **Privately Held**
SIC: 6513 Apartment building operators

(G-8801)
SUMMIT FINANCIAL STRATEGIES
7965 N High St Ste 350 (43235-8446)
PHONE...................................614 885-1115
Samantha Maccia, *President*
Samantha M Macchia, *COO*
Liam J Hurley, *Vice Pres*
Brian Sutliff, *Vice Pres*
Chris Cea, *Office Mgr*
EMP: 30 **EST:** 1994
SALES (est): 2.6MM **Privately Held**
WEB: www.summitfin.com
SIC: 6282 Investment advisory service

(G-8802)
SUMTOTAL SYSTEMS LLC
100 E Campus View Blvd # 250 (43235-4682)
PHONE...................................352 264-2800
Bruce Duff, *Senior VP*
Emily McCarty, *Sales Staff*
Joshua Roberts, *Sr Project Mgr*
Justin Dopiriak, *Manager*
Connie Mazza, *Manager*
EMP: 218 **Privately Held**
SIC: 7371 Computer software development
HQ: Sumtotal Systems Llc
  2850 Nw 43rd St Ste 150
  Gainesville FL 32606
  352 264-2800

(G-8803)
SUNRISE CONNECTICUT AVENUE ASS
Also Called: Forum At Knightsbridge
4590 Knightsbridge Blvd (43214-4327)
PHONE...................................614 451-6766
Fax: 614 442-2280
Cathy Miller, *Marketing Staff*
Donna Lane, *Exec Dir*
Beckey Converse, *Director*
Mark Evans, *Director*
EMP: 30
SQ FT: 4,000
SALES (corp-wide): 4.3B **Publicly Held**
SIC: 8051 Skilled nursing care facilities
HQ: Sunrise Connecticut Avenue Assisted Living, L.L.C.
  5111 Connecticut Ave Nw
  Washington DC 20008
  202 966-8020

(G-8804)
SUPER LAUNDRY INC
Also Called: Ohio Laundry
2268 Westbrooke Dr (43228-9416)
PHONE...................................614 258-5147
Fax: 614 258-5476
Mithch Blatt, *President*
Thomas Duckworth, *Regional Mgr*
EMP: 25
SQ FT: 22,000
SALES (est): 10.2MM
SALES (corp-wide): 387.4MM **Privately Held**
SIC: 5064 Clothes dryers, electric & gas
HQ: Coinmach Laundry Corporation
  1017 E Morehead St # 100
  Charlotte NC 28204

(G-8805)
SUPERIOR GROUP
740 Waterman Ave (43215-1155)
PHONE...................................614 488-8035
Greg Stewart, *CEO*
Bryan Stewart, *President*
Suzanne Stewart, *Exec VP*
Ted Bader, *Vice Pres*
Rich Hartman, *Vice Pres*
EMP: 180
SALES (est): 46.2MM **Privately Held**
WEB: www.electricalspecialists.com
SIC: 1731 Electrical work

(G-8806)
SUPPLY NETWORK INC
Viking Supply Net
2353 International St (43228-4622)
PHONE...................................614 527-5800
Fax: 614 527-5818
Paul Slivka, *Opers Mgr*
Tommy Haberman, *Sales Staff*
Jamey Wright, *Sales Staff*
Gary Stumph, *Branch Mgr*
Sandy Bryer, *Manager*
EMP: 30
SQ FT: 15,800 **Privately Held**
WEB: www.vikingsupplynet.com
SIC: 1711 Sprinkler contractors
HQ: Supply Network, Inc.
  210 Industrial Park Dr
  Hastings MI 49058
  269 945-9501

(G-8807)
SUPPLY TECH OF COLUMBUS LLC
5197 Trabue Rd (43228-9498)
PHONE...................................614 299-0184
Jeffrey Saley, *Principal*
EMP: 50 **EST:** 2012
SALES (est): 1.6MM **Privately Held**
SIC: 1731 Voice, data & video wiring contractor

(G-8808)
SUPREME COURT UNITED STATES
Also Called: Federal Probation
85 Marconi Blvd Rm 546 (43215-2835)
PHONE...................................614 719-3107
Pat Crowley, *Manager*
EMP: 69 **Publicly Held**
WEB: www.supremecourtus.gov
SIC: 8322 Probation office
HQ: Supreme Court, United States
  1 1st St Ne
  Washington DC 20543
  202 479-3000

(G-8809)
SUPREME COURT OF OHIO
Also Called: Court of Claims of Ohio
65 S Front St Fl 1 (43215-3431)
PHONE...................................614 387-9800
Fax: 614 644-8553
Miles Durfey, *Clerk*
EMP: 40 **Privately Held**
WEB: www.judicialstudies.com
SIC: 9199 6411 General government administration; ; insurance claim adjusters, not employed by insurance company
HQ: The Supreme Court Of Ohio
  65 S Front St Fl 1
  Columbus OH 43215
  614 387-9000

(G-8810)
SUPREME TOUCH HOME HEALTH SVCS
2547 W Broad St (43204-3324)
PHONE...................................614 783-1115
Gbolaga Akinboyede, *President*
Sefinat Akinboyede, *Vice Pres*
Jason Felix, *Administration*
EMP: 98
SALES (est): 3.5MM **Privately Held**
SIC: 8082 Home health care services

(G-8811)
SURE HOME IMPROVMENTS LLC
6031 E Main St Ste 222 (43213-3356)
PHONE...................................614 586-0610
Joseph Schuer, *Branch Mgr*
EMP: 26 **Privately Held**
SIC: 1521 General remodeling, single-family houses
PA: Sure Home Improvments, Llc
  6031 E Main St
  Columbus OH 43213

(G-8812)
SURGERY AND GYNECOLOGY INC (PA)
114r W 3rd Ave (43201-3211)
PHONE...................................614 294-1603
Fax: 614 294-4468
Judy Hutton, *General Mgr*
Scott D Barkin, *Urology*
EMP: 25
SQ FT: 5,000
SALES (est): 1MM **Privately Held**
SIC: 8062 General medical & surgical hospitals

(G-8813)
SVH HOLDINGS LLC
Also Called: Miracle Health Care
4322 N Hamilton Rd (43230-1710)
PHONE...................................844 560-7775
Suzanne Horn, *COO*
Verlin Horn, *Administration*
EMP: 99 **EST:** 2014
SQ FT: 1,900
SALES (est): 369.4K **Privately Held**
SIC: 8082 Home health care services

(G-8814)
SYGMA NETWORK INC
2400 Harrison Rd (43204-3508)
PHONE...................................614 771-3801
Colleen McGinnis, *Opers Spvr*
Kerry Dunn, *Opers Staff*
Bob Johnson, *Branch Mgr*
Toni Saitta, *Manager*
EMP: 117
SQ FT: 10,000
SALES (corp-wide): 55.3B **Publicly Held**
WEB: www.sygmanetwork.com
SIC: 5141 Food brokers
HQ: The Sygma Network Inc
  5550 Blazer Pkwy Ste 300
  Dublin OH 43017

(G-8815)
SYNORAN
2389 Bryden Rd (43209-2131)
PHONE...................................614 236-4014
Jeff Wagner, *CFO*
William M Randle,
Mark Quinlan,
EMP: 30 **EST:** 2000
SQ FT: 10,000
SALES: 4.1MM **Privately Held**
WEB: www.synoran.com
SIC: 7371 Software programming applications

(G-8816)
SYSCO CENTRAL OHIO INC
2400 Harrison Rd (43204-3508)
P.O. Box 94570, Cleveland (44101-4570)
PHONE...................................614 272-0658
Debra Hamernick, *President*
Lynn Zullo, *Sr Corp Ofcr*
Michael Haunert, *Senior VP*
Charlie Anderson, *Vice Pres*
Mark Eggett, *Vice Pres*
EMP: 300
SQ FT: 308,000
SALES (est): 100.1MM
SALES (corp-wide): 55.3B **Publicly Held**
WEB: www.abbott.sysco.com
SIC: 5141 5142 Groceries, general line; packaged frozen goods
PA: Sysco Corporation
  1390 Enclave Pkwy
  Houston TX 77077
  281 584-1390

GEOGRAPHIC SECTION
Columbus - Franklin County (G-8840)

(G-8817)
T K EDWARDS LLC
782 N High St (43215-1430)
PHONE.....................614 406-8064
Don Roberts, *General Ptnr*
EMP: 38
SALES (est): 2.1MM **Privately Held**
SIC: 8741 Restaurant management

(G-8818)
T&L GLOBAL MANAGEMENT LLC
Also Called: Pro-Touch
1572 Lafayette Dr (43220-3867)
PHONE.....................614 586-0303
Liton K Bhowmick,
Liton Bhowmick,
Doug Brugler,
EMP: 86
SALES (est): 1.4MM **Privately Held**
SIC: 7349 5169 Janitorial service, contract basis; chemicals & allied products

(G-8819)
TAFT STETTINIUS HOLLISTER LLP
65 E State St Ste 1000 (43215-4221)
PHONE.....................614 221-4000
Leon D Bass, *Counsel*
Chou-IL Lee, *Counsel*
Roderick H Willcox, *Counsel*
David Johnson, *Branch Mgr*
Alycen Cummings, *Legal Staff*
EMP: 75
SALES (corp-wide): 104.2MM **Privately Held**
SIC: 8111 General practice law office
PA: Taft Stettinius & Hollister Llp
425 Walnut St Ste 1800
Cincinnati OH 45202
513 381-2838

(G-8820)
TAILORED MANAGEMENT SERVICES (PA)
1165 Dublin Rd (43215-1005)
PHONE.....................614 859-1500
Brad Beach, *President*
Adam Fleming, *Accounts Mgr*
Marcie Sakash, *Accounts Mgr*
Christine McCoy, *Office Mgr*
Kelly Spencer, *Manager*
EMP: 85
SALES (est): 8.9MM **Privately Held**
SIC: 7361 Employment agencies

(G-8821)
TANGOE INC
200 E Campus View Blvd # 150 (43235-4700)
PHONE.....................614 842-9918
Shawn Page, *Technology*
EMP: 75
SALES (corp-wide): 311MM **Privately Held**
WEB: www.profitline.com
SIC: 8748 Telecommunications consultant
HQ: Tangoe Us, Inc.
169 Lackawanna Ave Ste 2b
Parsippany NJ 07054
973 257-0300

(G-8822)
TARGET STORES INC
3720 Soldano Blvd (43228-1422)
PHONE.....................614 279-4224
Fax: 614 279-4224
EMP: 220
SALES (corp-wide): 69.5B **Publicly Held**
SIC: 5311 7384 5912 Department Store Photofinishing Laboratory Ret Drugs/Sundries
HQ: Target Stores, Inc.
1000 Nicollet Mall
Minneapolis MN 55403

(G-8823)
TARRIER FOODS CORP
2700 International St # 100 (43228-2640)
PHONE.....................614 876-8594
Fax: 614 876-3038
Timothy A Tarrier, *President*
Chuck Zigler, *General Mgr*
Julia A Grooms, *Principal*
Ann Tarrier, *Principal*
Jordan T Tarrier, *Project Dir*
EMP: 42
SQ FT: 54,000
SALES (est): 23.2MM **Privately Held**
WEB: www.tarrierfoods.com
SIC: 5149 5145 2099 Dried or canned foods; nuts, salted or roasted; food preparations

(G-8824)
TAYLOR STN SURGICAL CTR LTD
275 Taylor Station Rd Ab (43213-2927)
PHONE.....................614 751-4466
Barbara Irish, *Project Mgr*
Jane Ann Mead, *Opers Mgr*
Linda Meikle, *Director*
Mount Carmel Health System,
EMP: 60
SQ FT: 1,728
SALES (est): 9.9MM **Privately Held**
SIC: 8011 Surgeon

(G-8825)
TAYLOR STRATEGY PARTNERS LLC (PA)
8000 Ravines Edge Ct # 200 (43235-5422)
PHONE.....................614 436-6650
Mike Gamble, *President*
Jon Dewitt, *Managing Prtnr*
William Taylor, *Managing Prtnr*
Katherine McAllister, *Managing Dir*
Kathleen McCutcheon, *Vice Pres*
EMP: 33
SALES (est): 1.7MM **Privately Held**
WEB: www.taylorsearchpartners.com
SIC: 7361 8742 Placement agencies; executive placement; management consulting services; human resource consulting services; personnel management consultant; training & development consultant

(G-8826)
TDS DOCUMENT MANAGEMENT LTD
Also Called: Shred It
161 Jackson St (43206-1124)
PHONE.....................614 367-9633
Fax: 614 751-9713
Shelley Barney, *Principal*
Jennifer McKeithen, *Sales Staff*
Thomas S Elsass, *Manager*
Bob Jeene, *Manager*
Thomas Elsass,
EMP: 28 EST: 1997
SALES (est): 4.2MM **Privately Held**
SIC: 7389 Document & office record destruction

(G-8827)
TEAM MANAGEMENT INC
Also Called: T M I
2018 N 4th St (43201-1730)
PHONE.....................614 486-0864
Charles Belding, *President*
Tim Spang, *COO*
EMP: 150
SQ FT: 5,000
SALES (est): 7.3MM **Privately Held**
SIC: 7319 Display advertising service

(G-8828)
TEK-COLLECT INCORPORATED
871 Park St (43215-1441)
PHONE.....................614 299-2766
Nicole Buhr, *President*
David McDonald, *General Mgr*
Carl Peterson, *Regional Mgr*
Michelle Mooney, *District Mgr*
Jon Ressler, *District Mgr*
EMP: 35
SQ FT: 5,500
SALES (est): 5.5MM **Privately Held**
WEB: www.tekcollect.com
SIC: 7322 Collection agency, except real estate

(G-8829)
TELHIO CREDIT UNION INC (PA)
96 N 4th St (43215-3163)
P.O. Box 1449 (43216-1449)
PHONE.....................614 221-3233
Fax: 614 222-6898
Leslie Bumgarner, *President*
Kristen Scott, *President*
Troy Hall, *Senior VP*
Ed Smallwood, *Senior VP*
Karen Daniels, *Assistant VP*
EMP: 50
SQ FT: 24,000
SALES (est): 23.2MM **Privately Held**
WEB: www.telhio.org
SIC: 6062 State credit unions, not federally chartered

(G-8830)
TELHIO CREDIT UNION INC
201 Outerbelt St (43213-1560)
PHONE.....................614 221-3233
Fax: 614 575-5454
Daniel Jurcich, *Banking Exec*
Susan Tinnerello, *Manager*
Carolyn Younkin, *Supervisor*
EMP: 25
SALES (est): 2.5MM
SALES (corp-wide): 23.2MM **Privately Held**
WEB: www.telhio.org
SIC: 6062 State credit unions, not federally chartered
PA: Telhio Credit Union, Inc.
96 N 4th St
Columbus OH 43215
614 221-3233

(G-8831)
TELLIGEN TECH INC
2740 Airport Dr Ste 190 (43219-2286)
PHONE.....................614 934-1554
Krishna Pandeswara, *President*
Ashwin Telligentechinc, *Info Tech Dir*
Rahul Telligentech, *Tech Recruiter*
EMP: 47 EST: 2012
SALES (est): 3.4MM **Privately Held**
SIC: 7373 7379 Systems engineering, computer related; office computer automation systems integration; computer related consulting services;

(G-8832)
TERRAFIRM CONSTRUCTION LLC
250 N Hartford Ave (43222-1100)
PHONE.....................913 433-2998
Jim Morgan, *Project Mgr*
George Schuler, *Project Engr*
Michael Coccia, *Treasurer*
Clay Rathbun, *Sales Dir*
Shannon Smith, *Manager*
EMP: 30 EST: 2014
SQ FT: 5,000
SALES (est): 3.5MM
SALES (corp-wide): 65.8MM **Privately Held**
SIC: 1799 Caulking (construction)
PA: C.J. Mahan Construction Company, Llc
250 N Hartford Ave
Columbus OH 43222
614 277-4545

(G-8833)
TFH-EB INC
Also Called: Waterworks, The
550 Schrock Rd (43229-1062)
PHONE.....................614 253-7246
Thomas F Havens, *Ch of Bd*
David R Specht, *President*
Ellen Hardymon, *Corp Secy*
EMP: 80 EST: 1935
SQ FT: 25,000
SALES: 9.7MM **Privately Held**
WEB: www.thewaterworks.com
SIC: 7099 4212 1711 Sewer cleaning & rodding; hazardous waste transport; plumbing, heating, air-conditioning contractors

(G-8834)
THE COTTINGHAM PAPER CO
Also Called: Cottingham Party Savers
324 E 2nd Ave (43201-3624)
PHONE.....................614 294-6444
Fax: 614 294-7042
Richard S Cottingham, *President*
Craig Cottingham, *Vice Pres*
Mary Beth Willis, *CFO*
EMP: 45
SQ FT: 48,000
SALES (est): 6.2MM **Privately Held**
WEB: www.cottinghampaper.com
SIC: 5046 5113 5087 Restaurant equipment & supplies; industrial & personal service paper; janitors' supplies

(G-8835)
THE DAIMLER GROUP INC
1533 Lake Shore Dr (43204-3897)
PHONE.....................614 488-4424
Fax: 614 488-0603
Robert C White, *Ch of Bd*
Conrad W Wisinger, *President*
Herman Ziegler, *COO*
Todd Sloan, *Exec VP*
Larry Wendling, *CFO*
EMP: 31
SQ FT: 7,000
SALES (est): 10.4MM **Privately Held**
WEB: www.daimlergroup.com
SIC: 6552 Land subdividers & developers, commercial; land subdividers & developers, residential

(G-8836)
THE HUNTINGTON INVESTMENT CO (HQ)
41 S High St Fl 7 (43215-6116)
PHONE.....................614 480-3600
Fax: 614 480-4187
Michael Miroballi, *President*
Raymond Closz, *COO*
Jeri Ball, *Vice Pres*
Karl Hamilton, *Vice Pres*
Jay O'Malley, *Vice Pres*
EMP: 50
SQ FT: 110,000
SALES (est): 56.4MM
SALES (corp-wide): 4.7B **Publicly Held**
SIC: 6211 Brokers, security
PA: Huntington Bancshares Incorporated
41 S High St
Columbus OH 43215
614 480-8300

(G-8837)
THOMAS DOOR CONTROLS INC
4196 Indianola Ave (43214-2858)
PHONE.....................614 263-1756
Fax: 614 267-6345
Scott Thomas, *President*
Todd Sackett, *Vice Pres*
David Gregg, *Project Mgr*
Brian Bolyard, *Parts Mgr*
Karen Davis, *Accountant*
▲ EMP: 36
SQ FT: 10,000
SALES: 19.8MM **Privately Held**
SIC: 5063 7699 Electrical apparatus & equipment; door & window repair

(G-8838)
THOMAS W RUFF AND COMPANY
Also Called: Office Furniture USA
855 Grandview Ave Ste 2 (43215-1102)
PHONE.....................800 828-0234
John V Johnson II, *President*
EMP: 260 EST: 2007
SALES (est): 21.8MM **Privately Held**
SIC: 5021 5712 Office & public building furniture; office furniture

(G-8839)
THOMPSON CAPRI LANES INC
5860 Roche Dr (43229-3208)
PHONE.....................614 888-3159
Fax: 614 888-5820
Daniel Thompson, *President*
Rob Foote, *Manager*
EMP: 25
SQ FT: 12,500
SALES (est): 921.5K **Privately Held**
SIC: 7933 Ten pin center

(G-8840)
THOMPSON HINE LLP
10 W Broad St Ste 700 (43215-3476)
PHONE.....................614 469-3200
Fax: 614 469-3361
Samuel Michel, *Editor*
Bradley Vogel, *Editor*
Elizabeth Blattner, *Counsel*
Cassandra Borchers, *Counsel*
Nathan Hunt, *Counsel*
EMP: 125

Columbus - Franklin County (G-8841) GEOGRAPHIC SECTION

SALES (corp-wide): 98.4MM Privately Held
SIC: 8111 General practice attorney, lawyer
PA: Thompson Hine Llp
127 Public Sq
Cleveland OH 44114
216 566-5500

(G-8841)
THOMPSON HINE LLP
41 S High St Ste 1700 (43215-6157)
PHONE 614 469-3200
Anthony White, *Branch Mgr*
Mary Baranyai, *Admin Sec*
Stephanie Cox, *Administration*
Nick Seabold, *Administration*
EMP: 123
SALES (corp-wide): 98.4MM Privately Held
SIC: 8111 General practice attorney, lawyer
PA: Thompson Hine Llp
127 Public Sq
Cleveland OH 44114
216 566-5500

(G-8842)
THREE C BODY SHOP INC (PA)
2300 Briggs Rd (43223-3218)
PHONE 614 274-9700
Fax: 614 274-0611
Robert Juniper Jr, *President*
EMP: 65
SQ FT: 40,000
SALES (est): 7.8MM Privately Held
SIC: 7532 7539 Body shop, automotive; frame repair shops, automotive

(G-8843)
THREE C BODY SHOP INC
8321 N High St (43235-6459)
PHONE 614 885-0900
Juniper Bob, *General Mgr*
EMP: 35
SALES (corp-wide): 7.8MM Privately Held
SIC: 7532 Paint shop, automotive
PA: Three C Body Shop Inc
2300 Briggs Rd
Columbus OH 43223
614 274-9700

(G-8844)
THURNS BAKERY & DELI
541 S 3rd St (43215-5721)
PHONE 614 221-9246
Fax: 614 221-3510
Marilyn Plank, *President*
Bill Plank, *Vice Pres*
Chris Plank, *Vice Pres*
Dan Plank, *Vice Pres*
EMP: 25 **EST:** 1972
SQ FT: 2,100
SALES (est): 1.1MM Privately Held
SIC: 5461 5149 2051 Bakeries; bakery products; bread, cake & related products

(G-8845)
TIME WARNER CABLE ENTPS LLC
1600 Dublin Rd (43215-1076)
PHONE 614 255-6289
Rhonda Frost, *President*
EMP: 3000
SALES (corp-wide): 41.5B Publicly Held
SIC: 4841 Cable television services
HQ: Time Warner Cable Enterprises Llc
400 Atlantic St Ste 6
Stamford CT 06901

(G-8846)
TIME WARNER CABLE ENTPS LLC
1125 Chambers Rd (43212-1701)
PHONE 614 481-5072
John Uversagtz, *Manager*
John Unverzagt, *Executive*
EMP: 50
SQ FT: 11,813
SALES (corp-wide): 41.5B Publicly Held
SIC: 4841 Cable television services
HQ: Time Warner Cable Enterprises Llc
400 Atlantic St Ste 6
Stamford CT 06901

(G-8847)
TIME WARNER CABLE INC
Also Called: Insight Communications
3770 E Livingston Ave (43227-2246)
PHONE 614 236-1200
Jeff Talente, *Purchasing*
Stephanie Stokes, *VP Finance*
Cathy Dysart, *Sales Mgr*
Joe Zink, *Program Mgr*
Jim Hires, *Manager*
EMP: 25
SALES (corp-wide): 41.5B Publicly Held
SIC: 4841 Cable television services
HQ: Spectrum Management Holding Company, Llc
400 Atlantic St
Stamford CT 06901
203 905-7801

(G-8848)
TIME WARNER CABLE INC
1980 Alum Creek Dr (43207-1792)
PHONE 614 481-5050
Fax: 614 481-5283
Pete Spicer, *Systems Mgr*
EMP: 60
SALES (corp-wide): 41.5B Publicly Held
WEB: www.rrbiznet.com
SIC: 4841 Cable television services
HQ: Spectrum Management Holding Company, Llc
400 Atlantic St
Stamford CT 06901
203 905-7801

(G-8849)
TIME WARNER CABLE INC
1266 Dublin Rd (43215-1008)
P.O. Box 2553 (43216-2553)
PHONE 614 481-5000
Fax: 614 481-5644
Rhonda Frost, *President*
David Eastburn, *Vice Pres*
Steve Bertsch, *Manager*
Dan Sheehan, *Director*
EMP: 600
SALES (corp-wide): 41.5B Publicly Held
SIC: 4841 Cable television services
HQ: Spectrum Management Holding Company, Llc
400 Atlantic St
Stamford CT 06901
203 905-7801

(G-8850)
TITLE FIRST AGENCY INC (PA)
3650 Olentangy River Rd # 400 (43214-3654)
PHONE 614 224-9207
Fax: 614 224-1423
Sean Stoner, *President*
James Hewit, *President*
Paul Thompson, *President*
Tony Nauta, *Senior VP*
Tammy Leach, *Opers Staff*
EMP: 30 **EST:** 1956
SQ FT: 7,500
SALES (est): 37.5MM Privately Held
WEB: www.titlefirst.com
SIC: 6361 7375 Real estate title insurance; data base information retrieval

(G-8851)
TJM CLMBUS LLC TJM CLUMBUS LLC
6500 Doubletree Ave (43229-1111)
PHONE 614 885-1885
Steve Petrucelli, *General Mgr*
EMP: 99
SQ FT: 594,507
SALES (est): 1.3MM Privately Held
SIC: 8741 Hotel or motel management

(G-8852)
TNT EQUIPMENT COMPANY (PA)
6677 Broughton Ave (43213-1523)
PHONE 614 882-1549
Anthony J Valentine, *President*
Michael Solomon, *Sales Mgr*
Joel Baileys, *Marketing Staff*
Joe Valentine, *Marketing Staff*
Lisa Brooks, *Office Mgr*
EMP: 25
SQ FT: 7,000
SALES (est): 14.8MM Privately Held
WEB: www.tntequip.com
SIC: 5082 7353 7699 General construction machinery & equipment; heavy construction equipment rental; construction equipment repair

(G-8853)
TOM PROPERTIES LLC
777 Dearborn Park Ln A (43085-5716)
PHONE 614 781-0055
Kim Brown, *District Mgr*
Sue Pickering, *VP Human Res*
James Redd, *Manager*
Pat Smith, *Manager*
John Sutherland, *Manager*
EMP: 100
SQ FT: 5,000
SALES (est): 5.2MM Privately Held
WEB: www.tomproperties.com
SIC: 6531 Rental agent, real estate

(G-8854)
TOMMY BAHAMA GROUP INC
4185 The Strand (43219-6120)
PHONE 614 750-9668
EMP: 112
SALES (corp-wide): 1B Publicly Held
SIC: 7389 Apparel designers, commercial
HQ: Tommy Bahama Group, Inc.
400 Fairview Ave N # 488
Seattle WA 98109

(G-8855)
TOTH RENOVATION LLC
444 Siebert St (43206-2721)
PHONE 614 542-9683
EMP: 25
SALES (est): 3.1MM Privately Held
SIC: 1521 General remodeling, single-family houses

(G-8856)
TOWLIFT INC
1200 Milepost Dr (43228-9862)
PHONE 614 851-1001
Fax: 614 851-4160
Dave Shearer, *Materials Mgr*
Craig Reich, *Manager*
EMP: 70
SALES (corp-wide): 106.6MM Privately Held
SIC: 5084 7699 Lift trucks & parts; industrial equipment services
PA: Towlift, Inc.
1395 Valley Belt Rd
Brooklyn Heights OH 44131
216 749-6800

(G-8857)
TOWN INN CO LLC
Also Called: Holiday Inn
175 E Town St (43215-4609)
PHONE 614 221-3281
Gene Calloway, *Branch Mgr*
Louis Potvin, *Executive*
EMP: 79
SQ FT: 124,294
SALES (est): 1.5MM Privately Held
SIC: 7011 Hotels & motels
HQ: Town Inn Co Llc
3850 Bird Rd Ste 302
Miami FL 33146
614 221-3281

(G-8858)
TOWNHOMES MANAGEMENT INC
407 E Livingston Ave (43215-5587)
PHONE 614 228-3578
Fax: 614 228-1393
Lawrence D Schaffer, *President*
Darrell Spegal, *Vice Pres*
EMP: 29
SQ FT: 1,500
SALES (est): 2.2MM Privately Held
WEB: www.ktohio.com
SIC: 6513 6531 Apartment building operators; real estate brokers & agents

(G-8859)
TP MECHANICAL CONTRACTORS INC
Also Called: T P McHncal Cntrs Svc Fbrction
2130 Franklin Rd (43209-2724)
PHONE 614 253-8556
Aaron Thomas, *Superintendent*
Steve Blust, *Vice Pres*
Tom Martin, *Vice Pres*
Rick Absher, *Safety Dir*
Mark Moler, *Controller*
EMP: 250 Privately Held
SIC: 6552 Subdividers & developers
PA: Tp Mechanical Contractors, Inc.
1500 Kemper Meadow Dr
Cincinnati OH 45240

(G-8860)
TPUSA INC
Also Called: Teleperformance USA
4335 Equity Dr (43228-3842)
PHONE 614 621-5512
Trevor Ferger, *Exec VP*
Richard Matlock, *CIO*
EMP: 800
SALES (corp-wide): 74.7MM Privately Held
WEB: www.teleperformanceusa.com
SIC: 4813 Telephone/video communications
HQ: Tpusa, Inc.
5295 S Commerce Dr # 600
Murray UT 84107
801 257-5800

(G-8861)
TRADER BUDS WESTSIDE DODGE
4000 W Broad St (43228-1449)
PHONE 614 272-0000
Fax: 614 272-5430
B S Smith, *President*
Nelson Bowers, *Vice Pres*
EMP: 85
SQ FT: 22,000
SALES: 77.6MM
SALES (corp-wide): 9.8B Publicly Held
WEB: www.traderbuds.com
SIC: 5511 7538 Automobiles, new & used; general automotive repair shops
PA: Sonic Automotive, Inc.
4401 Colwick Rd
Charlotte NC 28211
704 566-2400

(G-8862)
TRADESOURCE INC
1550 Old Henderson Rd (43220-3626)
PHONE 614 824-3883
EMP: 140 Privately Held
SIC: 7361 Labor contractors (employment agency)
PA: Tradesource, Inc.
205 Hallene Rd Unit 211
Warwick RI 02886

(G-8863)
TRADITIONS AT STYGLER ROAD
Also Called: National Ch Rsdnces Stygler Rd
167 N Stygler Rd (43230-2434)
PHONE 614 475-8778
Fax: 614 337-1199
Steve Bodkin, *President*
Gale Cochran, *Manager*
Terri Martin, *Nursing Dir*
Kelly Welsh, *Administration*
EMP: 32 **EST:** 1994
SALES (est): 5.1MM
SALES (corp-wide): 44.4MM Privately Held
SIC: 8082 Home health care services
PA: National Church Residences
2335 N Bank Dr
Columbus OH 43220
614 451-2151

(G-8864)
TRANSAMERICA PREMIER LF INSUR
1335 Dublin Rd Ste 200c (43215-7008)
PHONE 614 488-5983
Fax: 614 488-7912
Raymond De Piro, *Branch Mgr*
EMP: 34
SALES (corp-wide): 593.2MM Privately Held
WEB: www.monlife.com
SIC: 6311 6321 Life insurance carriers; accident & health insurance

HQ: Transamerica Premier Life Insurance Company
4333 Edgewood Rd Ne
Cedar Rapids IA 52499
319 355-8511

(G-8865)
TRANSPORTATION OHIO DEPARTMENT
1600 W Broad St (43223-1202)
PHONE..................614 275-1300
Fax: 614 275-1354
Jerry Wray, *Director*
EMP: 40 Privately Held
SIC: 9199 8734 ; automobile proving & testing ground
HQ: Ohio Department Of Transportation
1980 W Broad St
Columbus OH 43223

(G-8866)
TRANSYSTEMS CORPORATION
400 W Nationwide Blvd # 225 (43215-4373)
PHONE..................614 433-7800
Aaron Grilliot, *Manager*
David Shipps, *Administration*
Andrew Schneider, *Associate*
EMP: 25
SALES (corp-wide): 144.2MM Privately Held
SIC: 8711 Consulting engineer
PA: Transystems Corporation
2400 Pershing Rd Ste 400
Kansas City MO 64108
816 329-8700

(G-8867)
TRI MODAL SERVICE INC
2015 Walcutt Rd (43228-9575)
P.O. Box 109, Worthington (43085-0109)
PHONE..................614 876-6325
Fax: 614 876-2128
Mark Stewart, *President*
John S Stewart, *Vice Pres*
Wilma S Stewart, *Treasurer*
Bernie Mauck, *Manager*
Richard Elliott, *Admin Sec*
EMP: 29
SQ FT: 2,500
SALES: 1.6MM
SALES (corp-wide): 35.1MM Privately Held
WEB: www.trnj.com
SIC: 4214 Local trucking with storage
PA: Transinternational System, Inc.
130 E Wilson Bridge Rd # 150
Worthington OH 43085
614 891-4942

(G-8868)
TRIAD TRANSPORT INC
1484 Williams Rd (43207-5178)
P.O. Box 818, McAlester OK (74502-0818)
PHONE..................614 491-9497
Jim Painter, *Branch Mgr*
EMP: 42
SALES (est): 1.8MM
SALES (corp-wide): 28MM Privately Held
WEB: www.triadtransport.com
SIC: 4213 4953 Trucking, except local; hazardous waste collection & disposal
PA: Triad Transport, Inc.
1630 Diesel Ave
Mcalester OK 74501
918 421-2429

(G-8869)
TRICONT TRUCKING COMPANY
2200 Westbelt Dr (43228-3820)
PHONE..................614 527-7398
Jerry Baker, *General Mgr*
EMP: 181
SALES (corp-wide): 17.6MM Privately Held
SIC: 4212 Local trucking, without storage
PA: Tricont Trucking Company
241 Sevilla Ave
Coral Gables FL 33134
305 520-8400

(G-8870)
TRIDENT USA HEALTH SVCS LLC
Also Called: Mobilex USA
6185 Huntley Rd Ste Q (43229-1094)
PHONE..................614 888-2226
Fax: 614 888-0027
Rick Lang, *Manager*
EMP: 50 Privately Held
SIC: 8071 X-ray laboratory, including dental
PA: Trident Usa Health Services, Llc
930 Ridgebrook Rd Fl 3
Sparks MD 21152

(G-8871)
TRINITY CONTRACTING INC
4878 Mgnolia Blossom Blvd (43230-1025)
PHONE..................614 905-4410
David Albrecht, *Principal*
EMP: 99
SALES (est): 3MM Privately Held
SIC: 1799 Special trade contractors

(G-8872)
TRINITY HEALTH CORPORATION
5700 Karl Rd (43229-3602)
PHONE..................614 846-5420
James Griffith, *Director*
EMP: 350
SALES (corp-wide): 16.3B Privately Held
WEB: www.trinity-health.com
SIC: 8051 8092 8069 Skilled nursing care facilities; kidney dialysis centers; specialty hospitals, except psychiatric
PA: Trinity Health Corporation
20555 Victor Pkwy
Livonia MI 48152
734 343-1000

(G-8873)
TRINITY HEALTH GROUP LTD
827 Yard St (43212-3886)
PHONE..................614 899-4830
Fax: 614 899-4831
John Chory,
Junita Chory, *Administration*
Robert Gesing,
EMP: 42
SQ FT: 70,000
SALES: 6.7MM Privately Held
WEB: www.trinityhealthgroup.com
SIC: 8712 Architectural services

(G-8874)
TRINITY HOME BUILDERS INC
2700 E Dublin Granville (43231-4094)
PHONE..................614 889-7830
Jim Phieffer, *President*
Keith Pecinovski, *Principal*
William Moorhead, *Treasurer*
Mark Vouis, *VP Sales*
Scott Esker, *Sales Associate*
EMP: 25
SALES (est): 3MM Privately Held
SIC: 1521 New construction, single-family houses

(G-8875)
TRUBUILT CONSTRUCTION SVCS LLC
Also Called: Rezod
777 Harrison Dr (43204-3507)
PHONE..................614 279-4800
Charles Dozer, *Mng Member*
EMP: 35
SALES (est): 2.8MM Privately Held
SIC: 1542 Commercial & office building, new construction

(G-8876)
TRUE NORTH ENERGY LLC
631 S High St (43215-5620)
PHONE..................614 222-0198
Muasta Dabos, *Principal*
EMP: 39
SALES (corp-wide): 274.9MM Privately Held
SIC: 4925 Gas production and/or distribution
PA: True North Energy, Llc
10346 Brecksville Rd
Brecksville OH 44141
877 245-9336

(G-8877)
TUCKER ELLIS LLP
175 S 3rd St Ste 520 (43215-7101)
PHONE..................614 358-9717
Eric Weldele, *Manager*
EMP: 95
SALES (corp-wide): 49.1MM Privately Held
SIC: 8111 General practice attorney, lawyer
PA: Tucker Ellis Llp
950 Main Ave Ste 1100
Cleveland OH 44113
216 592-5000

(G-8878)
TURN-KEY INDUSTRIAL SVCS LLC
820 Distribution Dr (43228-1004)
PHONE..................614 274-1128
Gregory Less, *Mng Member*
EMP: 52
SQ FT: 10,000
SALES: 7.6MM Privately Held
SIC: 7692 3441 Automotive welding; building components, structural steel

(G-8879)
TURNER CONSTRUCTION COMPANY
262 Hanover St (43215-2332)
PHONE..................614 984-3000
Fax: 614 781-8553
Joe Dziengelewski, *Superintendent*
Litany Zenz, *Superintendent*
Rik Labardi, *Vice Pres*
Rita Reed, *Financial Analy*
Kurt Smith, *Manager*
EMP: 75
SALES (corp-wide): 1.5B Privately Held
WEB: www.tcco.com
SIC: 1542 Commercial & office building, new construction
HQ: Turner Construction Company Inc
375 Hudson St Fl 6
New York NY 10014
212 229-6000

(G-8880)
TURNKEY NETWORK SOLUTIONS LLC
3450 Millikin Ct Ste A (43228-9378)
PHONE..................614 876-9944
Michael Trudeau, *Branch Mgr*
EMP: 25
SALES (corp-wide): 1.2MM Privately Held
WEB: www.tkns.net
SIC: 8711 8748 Engineering services; telecommunications consultant
PA: Turnkey Network Solutions, Llc
7020 Southbelt Dr Se
Caledonia MI 49316
616 455-9840

(G-8881)
TWO MEN & A VACUUM LLC
81 S 4th St Ste 100 (43215-4355)
PHONE..................614 300-7970
Cody Warren,
EMP: 52
SALES: 700K Privately Held
SIC: 7349 7359 Cleaning service, industrial or commercial; home cleaning & maintenance equipment rental services

(G-8882)
U S A PLUMBING COMPANY
1425 Community Park Dr (43229-2258)
PHONE..................614 882-6402
Fax: 614 882-5936
Larry Miller, *CEO*
Matt McGee, *President*
EMP: 27
SQ FT: 1,400
SALES (est): 1.7MM Privately Held
SIC: 1711 Plumbing contractors

(G-8883)
UBS FINANCIAL SERVICES INC
41 S High St Ste 3300 (43215-6104)
PHONE..................614 460-6559
EMP: 50
SALES (corp-wide): 28B Privately Held
SIC: 6211 Security Broker/Dealer

HQ: Ubs Financial Services Inc.
1285 Ave Of The Americas
New York NY 10019
212 713-2000

(G-8884)
UBS FINANCIAL SERVICES INC
5025 Arlngtn Ctr Blvd # 120 (43220-2959)
PHONE..................614 442-6240
Ken Dorsch, *Manager*
Susan Surtman, *Advisor*
EMP: 30
SALES (corp-wide): 28B Privately Held
SIC: 6211 Security brokers & dealers
HQ: Ubs Financial Services, Inc.
1285 Ave Of The Americas
New York NY 10019
212 713-2000

(G-8885)
UCT PROPERTY INC
1801 Watermark Dr Ste 100 (43215-7088)
PHONE..................614 228-3276
Ron Hunt, *Vice Pres*
EMP: 40
SALES: 136.7K
SALES (corp-wide): 20.4MM Privately Held
SIC: 6411 Insurance agents & brokers
PA: The Order Of Unite Commercial Tra
1801 Watermark Dr Ste 100
Columbus OH 43215
614 487-9680

(G-8886)
ULMER & BERNE LLP
65 E State St Ste 1100 (43215-4213)
PHONE..................614 229-0000
Fax: 614 228-8561
Alexander Andrews, *Principal*
Rebecca B Swanson,
Jeri Murray, *Legal Staff*
Teresa Scharf, *Legal Staff*
Brian E Linhart, *Associate*
EMP: 27
SALES (corp-wide): 85.9MM Privately Held
SIC: 8111 General practice attorney, lawyer
PA: Ulmer & Berne Llp
1660 W 2nd St Ste 1100
Cleveland OH 44113
216 583-7000

(G-8887)
UNICO ALLOYS & METALS INC
Also Called: United Alloys and Metals
1177 Joyce Ave Ste B (43219-1900)
PHONE..................614 299-0545
Fax: 614 299-2524
Dane Germuska, *President*
Frank Santorio, *Vice Pres*
Phil Boston, *Opers Mgr*
Mike Fagan, *Finance*
John Churley, *Admin Sec*
◆ EMP: 76
SQ FT: 450,000
SALES (est): 44.1MM
SALES (corp-wide): 1.7B Privately Held
SIC: 5093 Ferrous metal scrap & waste
HQ: Cronimet Ferroleg. Gmbh
Sudbeckenstr. 22
Karlsruhe 76189
721 952-250

(G-8888)
UNICON INTERNATIONAL INC (PA)
241 Outerbelt St (43213-1529)
PHONE..................614 861-7070
Fax: 614 861-7096
Peichen Jane Lee, *President*
Sherman Lau, *Senior VP*
Li-Hung David Lee, *Vice Pres*
Michael McAlear, *Vice Pres*
Rachel Fuhrman, *HR Admin*
EMP: 126
SQ FT: 10,000
SALES (est): 17.8MM Privately Held
WEB: www.unicon-intl.com
SIC: 7371 7379 Computer software systems analysis & design, custom; computer related consulting services

Columbus - Franklin County (G-8889)

(G-8889)
UNION MORTGAGE SERVICES INC (PA)
Also Called: First Community Mortgage Svcs
1080 Fishinger Rd (43221-2302)
PHONE 614 457-4815
James P Simpson, *President*
W Matthew Baker, *Vice Pres*
Denis Faherty, *Manager*
EMP: 40
SQ FT: 1,200
SALES: 5MM **Privately Held**
SIC: 6163 Mortgage brokers arranging for loans, using money of others

(G-8890)
UNITED FOOD COMML WRKRS UN
Also Called: UFCW LOCAL 1059
4150 E Main St Fl 2 (43213-2953)
PHONE 614 235-3635
Rebecca A Berroyer, *President*
Jason Kaseman, *Director*
Tina Morgan, *Director*
Gregory J Behnke, *Admin Sec*
EMP: 27 **EST:** 1941
SQ FT: 3,700
SALES: 10.7MM **Privately Held**
WEB: www.ufcw1059.com
SIC: 8631 Labor union

(G-8891)
UNITED HEALTHCARE OHIO INC (DH)
9200 Worthington Rd (43085)
PHONE 614 410-7000
Tom Brady, *CEO*
G David Shafer, *President*
Thomas Sullivan, *COO*
Mark Woessner, *Vice Pres*
Chris Timpson, *Accounts Exec*
EMP: 350
SQ FT: 72,000
SALES (est): 955.1MM
SALES (corp-wide): 201.1B **Publicly Held**
WEB: www.uhc.com
SIC: 6324 Group hospitalization plans; health maintenance organization (HMO), insurance only
HQ: United Healthcare Services Inc.
9900 Bren Rd E Ste 300w
Minnetonka MN 55343
952 936-1300

(G-8892)
UNITED HOME HEALTH SERVICES
297 Woodland Ave (43203-1747)
PHONE 614 880-8686
Fax: 614 372-0665
David R Weaver, *President*
Sopheap Som, *Administration*
EMP: 85
SALES: 500K **Privately Held**
SIC: 8082 Home health care services

(G-8893)
UNITED INSULATION CO INC
Also Called: Mascals Contracting Services
1985 Oakland Park Ave (43224-3636)
PHONE 614 263-9378
Scott Hershiser, *CEO*
Chuck Moreland, *Principal*
Chuck Woland, *Principal*
EMP: 40
SQ FT: 34,000
SALES: 11MM
SALES (corp-wide): 1.9B **Publicly Held**
WEB: www.galeind.com
SIC: 1742 Insulation, buildings
HQ: Topbuild Services Group Corp.
475 N Williamson Blvd
Daytona Beach FL 32114
386 304-2200

(G-8894)
UNITED MANAGEMENT INC (PA)
Also Called: Casto
250 Civic Center Dr (43215-5086)
PHONE 614 228-5371
Fax: 614 229-4368
Don M Casto III, *President*
Shannon Dixon, *President*
Brett Hutchens, *Partner*

Paul Lukeman, *Partner*
Neisha Vitello, *General Mgr*
EMP: 75 **EST:** 1955
SALES (est): 70.2MM **Privately Held**
WEB: www.castosoutheast.com
SIC: 6512 Shopping center, property operation only

(G-8895)
UNITED PARCEL SERVICE INC
Also Called: UPS
1711 Georgesville Rd (43228-3619)
PHONE 614 385-9100
Corey Thompson, *General Mgr*
John Cummins, *Branch Mgr*
EMP: 60
SALES (corp-wide): 65.8B **Publicly Held**
WEB: www.ups.com
SIC: 4513 Letter delivery, private air; package delivery, private air; parcel delivery, private air
PA: United Parcel Service, Inc.
55 Glenlake Pkwy
Atlanta GA 30328
404 828-6000

(G-8896)
UNITED PARCEL SERVICE INC
Also Called: UPS
118 Graceland Blvd (43214-1530)
PHONE 614 431-0600
Fax: 614 431-0602
Vinu Patel, *Branch Mgr*
EMP: 38
SALES (corp-wide): 65.8B **Publicly Held**
WEB: www.ups.com
SIC: 4215 Package delivery, vehicular
PA: United Parcel Service, Inc.
55 Glenlake Pkwy
Atlanta GA 30328
404 828-6000

(G-8897)
UNITED PARCEL SERVICE INC OH
Also Called: UPS
100 E Campus View Blvd # 300 (43235-8602)
PHONE 614 841-7159
James Stickradt, *Manager*
Ray Turner, *Info Tech Mgr*
EMP: 158
SALES (corp-wide): 65.8B **Publicly Held**
WEB: www.upsscs.com
SIC: 4215 Package delivery, vehicular; parcel delivery, vehicular
HQ: United Parcel Service, Inc. (Oh)
55 Glenlake Pkwy
Atlanta GA 30328
404 828-6000

(G-8898)
UNITED PARCEL SERVICE INC OH
Also Called: UPS
5101 Trabue Rd (43228-9481)
PHONE 614 870-4111
Ray Turner, *Supervisor*
EMP: 316
SALES (corp-wide): 65.8B **Publicly Held**
WEB: www.upsscs.com
SIC: 7389 Mailing & messenger services
HQ: United Parcel Service, Inc. (Oh)
55 Glenlake Pkwy
Atlanta GA 30328
404 828-6000

(G-8899)
UNITED PRODUCERS INC (PA)
8351 N High St Ste 250 (43235-1440)
PHONE 614 433-2150
Mike Bumgarner, *President*
Dennis Bolling, *President*
Bob Siegel, *Vice Pres*
Doyle Devers, *Facilities Mgr*
Joe Werstak, *CFO*
EMP: 131
SALES (est): 123.4MM **Privately Held**
WEB: www.uproducers.com
SIC: 5154 Hogs

(G-8900)
UNITED STATES CARGO & COURIER
2036 Williams Rd (43207-5117)
PHONE 614 449-2854
Alice Wassel, *Manager*
EMP: 45
SALES (corp-wide): 9.9MM **Privately Held**
WEB: www.usccs.com
SIC: 4215 Courier services, except by air
HQ: United States Cargo & Courier Service Incorporated
900 Williams Ave
Columbus OH
614 552-2746

(G-8901)
UNITED STATES TROTTING ASSN
800 Michigan Ave (43215-1595)
PHONE 614 224-2291
Fred Noe, *Exec VP*
Tc Lane, *Director*
EMP: 78
SALES (corp-wide): 7.9MM **Privately Held**
WEB: www.ustrotting.com
SIC: 8743 Public relations & publicity
PA: United States Trotting Association (Inc)
6130 S Sunbury Rd
Westerville OH 43081
614 224-2291

(G-8902)
UNITED STEELWORKERS
Also Called: Uswa
4467 Village Park Dr (43228-6430)
PHONE 614 272-8609
S Kidwell, *Branch Mgr*
EMP: 50
SALES (corp-wide): 61.5K **Privately Held**
WEB: www.uswa.org
SIC: 8631 Labor union
PA: United Steelworkers
60 Bolevard Of The Allies
Pittsburgh PA 15222
412 562-2400

(G-8903)
UNITED STTES BOWL CONGRESS INC
643 S Hamilton Rd (43213-3176)
PHONE 614 237-3716
J E Dimond, *Branch Mgr*
EMP: 51
SALES (corp-wide): 32.9MM **Privately Held**
SIC: 8699 Athletic organizations
PA: United States Bowling Congress, Inc.
621 Six Flags Dr
Arlington TX 76011
817 385-8200

(G-8904)
UNITED WAY CENTRAL OHIO INC
360 S 3rd St (43215-5412)
PHONE 614 227-2700
Fax: 614 224-5835
Janet E Jackson, *President*
Helen Ninos, *COO*
Susan Tomasky, *Exec VP*
Michael Robinson, *Assistant VP*
Angel Towns, *Assistant VP*
EMP: 78
SQ FT: 10,000
SALES (est): 28.6MM **Privately Held**
WEB: www.uwcentralohio.org
SIC: 8399 United Fund councils

(G-8905)
UNIVERSAL FABG CNSTR SVCS INC
Also Called: UNI-Facs
1241 Mckinley Ave (43222-1114)
PHONE 614 274-1128
Steve Finkel, *President*
Robert Watts, *Treasurer*
Jodi Sinclair, *Director*
▲ **EMP:** 86
SQ FT: 120,000

SALES (est): 25.1MM **Privately Held**
WEB: www.unifacs.com
SIC: 1541 3441 3599 1799 Renovation, remodeling & repairs: industrial buildings; building components, structural steel; expansion joints (structural shapes), iron or steel; catapults; sandblasting of building exteriors

(G-8906)
UNIVERSAL HEALTH CARE SVCS INC
2873 Suwanee Rd (43224-4469)
PHONE 614 547-0282
Suliman Ahmed, *President*
Aden J Abu, *CFO*
EMP: 120
SQ FT: 3,600
SALES (est): 3.7MM **Privately Held**
SIC: 8082 Home health care services

(G-8907)
UNIVERSAL RECOVERY SYSTEMS
Also Called: Stat Communications
5197 Trabue Rd (43228-9498)
PHONE 614 299-0184
Fax: 614 299-0380
Jeff Saley, *President*
Dave Ackerman, *Project Mgr*
Natalie Price, *Finance*
Carly Kepick, *Manager*
Bill Clevenger, *Maintence Staff*
EMP: 54
SALES (est): 11MM **Privately Held**
SIC: 1623 1731 Cable laying construction; fiber optic cable installation

(G-8908)
UNIVERSITY EYE SURGEONS
Also Called: Eye Physicians & Surgeons
456 W 10th Ave Ste 5241 (43210-1240)
PHONE 614 293-5635
Fax: 614 293-4579
Thomas Mauger, *Principal*
EMP: 150
SALES (est): 3.5MM **Privately Held**
SIC: 8011 Physicians' office, including specialists

(G-8909)
UNIVERSITY GYN&OB CNSLTNTS INC (PA)
1654 Upham Dr Rm N500 (43210-1250)
PHONE 614 293-8697
Fax: 614 293-8993
L Copeland, *President*
M Landon, *Corp Secy*
William G Dodds, *Obstetrician*
Dan Pierce, *Administration*
EMP: 50
SALES (est): 1.5MM **Privately Held**
SIC: 8011 Gynecologist; obstetrician

(G-8910)
UNIVERSITY OTOLARYNGOLOGISTS (PA)
Also Called: E N T
810 Mackenzie Dr (43220)
PHONE 614 273-2241
Fax: 614 293-3193
David E Schuller MD, *President*
David R Kelly MD, *Vice Pres*
Amy Barrett, *Marketing Staff*
Keith Nistor, *Director*
Linda Hawkey,
EMP: 40
SALES (est): 6MM **Privately Held**
WEB: www.excel-ent.com
SIC: 8011 5999 Ears, nose & throat specialist: physician/surgeon; hearing aids

(G-8911)
UNUM LIFE INSURANCE CO AMER
445 Hutchinson Ave # 300 (43235-5677)
PHONE 614 807-2500
Fax: 614 807-2599
R G Peterson, *Manager*
Janice McCarthy, *Manager*
EMP: 39 **Publicly Held**
WEB: www.benuckrainey.com
SIC: 6411 Insurance agents

HQ: Unum Life Insurance Company Of
America
2211 Congress St
Portland ME 04122
207 575-2211

(G-8912)
UPGRADE HOMES
586 Blenheim Rd (43214-3264)
PHONE..................614 975-8532
Jeff Trickett, *President*
EMP: 50
SALES (est): 1.6MM Privately Held
SIC: 1522 Residential construction

(G-8913)
UPH HOLDINGS LLC
Also Called: Marriott Columbus Univ Area
3100 Olentangy River Rd (43202-1517)
PHONE..................614 447-9777
Dena St Clair, *Director*
EMP: 99
SALES (est): 533.8K Privately Held
SIC: 7011 Hotels & motels

(G-8914)
UPPER ARLINGTON CITY SCHL DST
Also Called: School Age Child Care
4770 Burbank Dr (43220-2800)
PHONE..................614 487-5133
Fax: 614 487-5192
Kathy Ficell, *Director*
EMP: 30
SALES (corp-wide): 59MM Privately Held
SIC: 8211 8351 Public elementary school; child day care services
PA: Upper Arlington City School District
1950 N Mallway Dr
Columbus OH 43221
614 487-5000

(G-8915)
UPPER ARLINGTON LUTHERAN CH (PA)
2300 Lytham Rd (43220-4699)
PHONE..................614 451-3736
Fax: 614 451-0993
Paul Uring, *Pastor*
Brittany Timm, *Director*
EMP: 35
SALES (est): 1.9MM Privately Held
WEB: www.ualc.org
SIC: 8661 8351 Lutheran Church; preschool center

(G-8916)
UPPER ARLINGTON SURGERY CENTER
2240 N Bank Dr (43220-5420)
PHONE..................614 442-6515
Mary Ann Cooney, *President*
EMP: 48
SQ FT: 24,000
SALES (est): 3.6MM
SALES (corp-wide): 3.7B Privately Held
WEB: www.ohiohealth.com
SIC: 8093 Specialty outpatient clinics
PA: Ohiohealth Corporation
180 E Broad St
Columbus OH 43215
614 788-8860

(G-8917)
UPREACH LLC
4488 Mobile Dr (43220-3713)
PHONE..................614 442-7702
Melissa Gourley, *Mng Member*
Beth Hunter, *Mng Member*
Tamara Bokor, *Manager*
EMP: 300
SQ FT: 5,937
SALES (est): 5.8MM Privately Held
SIC: 8322 Social services for the handicapped

(G-8918)
URBAN ONE INC
Also Called: Wckx-FM
350 E 1st Ave Ste 100 (43201-3792)
PHONE..................614 487-1444
Fax: 614 487-5863
Skip Bednarczyk, *Advt Staff*
Tara Berman, *Manager*
EMP: 40
SALES (corp-wide): 440MM Publicly Held
WEB: www.radio-one.com
SIC: 4832 Radio broadcasting stations
PA: Urban One, Inc.
1010 Wayne Ave Fl 14
Silver Spring MD 20910
301 429-3200

(G-8919)
URBANCREST AFFRDBL HSING LLC
3443 Agler Rd Ste 200 (43219-3385)
PHONE..................614 228-3578
Amy Klaben, *President*
Carrie Hiatt, *Director*
Stacy York, *Administration*
EMP: 55
SALES (est): 1.8MM Privately Held
SIC: 6513 Apartment building operators

(G-8920)
UROLOGICAL ASSOCIATES INC
750 Mount Carmel Mall # 350 (43222-1553)
PHONE..................614 221-5189
Fax: 614 221-0463
Stephen P Smith, *President*
R Daniel Bohl, *Treasurer*
Kenneth J Wright, *Vascular Srgry*
EMP: 35 EST: 1948
SALES (est): 2.6MM Privately Held
SIC: 8011 Urologist

(G-8921)
URS GROUP INC
277 N Nationwide Blvd (43215-2853)
PHONE..................614 464-4500
Jeff Williamson, *Vice Pres*
Jeff Kerr, *Project Mgr*
Albert King, *Project Mgr*
Somasundaram Natarajan, *Engineer*
James R Linthicum, *Branch Mgr*
EMP: 150
SALES (corp-wide): 18.2B Publicly Held
SIC: 8711 8712 Engineering services; architectural services
HQ: Urs Group, Inc.
300 S Grand Ave Ste 1100
Los Angeles CA 90071
213 593-8000

(G-8922)
URS-SMITH GROUP VA IDIQ JOINT
277 W Nationwide Blvd (43215-2853)
PHONE..................614 464-4500
Nicholas Nash, *CEO*
EMP: 50
SALES (est): 3.3MM Privately Held
SIC: 8711 Engineering services

(G-8923)
US DENTAL CARE/M D GELENDER
Also Called: U S Dental Care
949 E Livingston Ave (43205-2795)
PHONE..................614 252-3181
Fax: 614 252-1549
Martin D Gelender DDS, *Owner*
EMP: 25 EST: 1962
SQ FT: 21,700
SALES (est): 1.6MM Privately Held
WEB: www.usdentalcare.com
SIC: 8021 Dentists' office

(G-8924)
US HOME CENTER LLC (PA)
Also Called: Owens Corning Basement Finishi
2050 Integrity Dr S (43209-2728)
PHONE..................614 737-9000
Fax: 614 737-9001
Stephen Brookes, *President*
EMP: 27
SQ FT: 7,000
SALES (est): 2.4MM Privately Held
SIC: 8748 1521 Business consulting; single-family home remodeling, additions & repairs

(G-8925)
US SECURITY HOLDINGS INC
1350 W 5th Ave Ste 300 (43212-2907)
PHONE..................614 488-6110
EMP: 100
SALES (corp-wide): 307MM Privately Held
SIC: 7381 Security guard service
HQ: U.S. Security Holdings, Inc.
200 Mansell Ct E Ste 500
Roswell GA 30076
770 625-1400

(G-8926)
USF HOLLAND LLC
Also Called: USFreightways
4800 Journal St (43228-4611)
PHONE..................614 529-9300
Fax: 614 529-6191
J D Barnes, *Manager*
EMP: 250
SALES (corp-wide): 4.8B Publicly Held
WEB: www.usfc.com
SIC: 4213 4212 Less-than-truckload (LTL) transport; local trucking, without storage
HQ: Usf Holland Llc
700 S Waverly Rd
Holland MI 49423
616 395-5000

(G-8927)
USI INSURANCE SERVICES NAT
580 N 4th St Ste 400 (43215-2153)
PHONE..................614 228-5565
Patty Woo, *Branch Mgr*
Barbara Rhymer, *Agent*
EMP: 43 Privately Held
SIC: 6411 Insurance agents, brokers & service
HQ: Usi Insurance Services National, Inc
150 N Michigan Ave # 3900
Chicago IL 60601
866 294-2571

(G-8928)
UTICA NATIONAL INSURANCE GROUP
2600 Corp Exchange Dr # 200 (43231-1672)
PHONE..................614 823-5300
Ralph Laspina, *Senior VP*
Doug Randolph, *Branch Mgr*
EMP: 48
SALES (corp-wide): 932.2MM Privately Held
SIC: 6331 Assessment associations: fire, marine & casualty insurance
HQ: Utica National Insurance Group
180 Genesee St
New Hartford NY 13413
315 734-2000

(G-8929)
V VRABLE INC
Also Called: Beeghly Oaks Skilled
3248 Henderson Rd Ste 104 (43220-7337)
PHONE..................614 545-5500
Allan Vrable, *President*
James Merrill, *CFO*
EMP: 109
SQ FT: 56,000
SALES (est): 7.2MM Privately Held
SIC: 8051 Skilled nursing care facilities
PA: Vrable Healthcare, Inc.
3248 Henderson Rd
Columbus OH 43220

(G-8930)
VALLEY INTERIOR SYSTEMS INC
Also Called: Price Thrice Supply
3840 Fisher Rd (43228-1016)
PHONE..................614 351-8440
Fax: 614 351-1769
Brian Robberts, *Superintendent*
John Strawser Jr, *COO*
Teresa Tannon, *Purchasing*
Jim Melaragno, *Manager*
EMP: 150
SALES (corp-wide): 70.7MM Privately Held
SIC: 1742 Drywall; acoustical & ceiling work; plastering, plain or ornamental
PA: Valley Interior Systems, Inc.
2203 Fowler St
Cincinnati OH 45206
513 961-0400

(G-8931)
VALUE RECOVERY GROUP INC (PA)
919 Old Henderson Rd (43220-3722)
PHONE..................614 324-5959
Barry Fromm, *Ch of Bd*
James Sisto, *COO*
Sharon Gorby, *Senior VP*
Halle B Hahn, *Vice Pres*
Bob Herington, *CFO*
EMP: 30
SALES (est): 7.7MM Privately Held
WEB: www.valuerecovery.com
SIC: 8111 Debt collection law

(G-8932)
VAN DYNE-CROTTY CO (PA)
Also Called: Spirit Services Company
2150 Fairwood Ave (43207-1736)
PHONE..................614 684-0048
Fax: 614 431-8107
Timothy F Crotty, *CEO*
Mike Crotty, *President*
Eugene A Mayl, *Principal*
R Frank Crotty, *Chairman*
Brandy Grace, *Controller*
EMP: 25
SQ FT: 107,000
SALES (est): 39MM Privately Held
WEB: www.getspirit.com
SIC: 7218 7213 7219 Industrial uniform supply; wiping towel supply; treated equipment supply: mats, rugs, mops, cloths, etc.; industrial clothing launderers; uniform supply; accessory & non-garment cleaning & repair; glove mending for individuals

(G-8933)
VAN DYNE-CROTTY CO
Also Called: Spirit Services Company
2150 Fairwood Ave (43207-1736)
P.O. Box 28506 (43228-0506)
PHONE..................614 491-3903
Toll Free:..................877 -
John R Crotty, *CFO*
Bob Jackson, *Credit Mgr*
Dennis Fremrood, *Branch Mgr*
EMP: 150
SALES (est): 1.2MM
SALES (corp-wide): 39MM Privately Held
WEB: www.getspirit.com
SIC: 7218 7213 Industrial uniform supply; uniform supply
PA: Van Dyne-Crotty Co.
2150 Fairwood Ave
Columbus OH 43207
614 684-0048

(G-8934)
VANGUARD WINES LLC (PA)
1020 W 5th Ave (43212-2630)
PHONE..................614 291-3493
Fax: 614 291-3634
Drew Neiman, *CEO*
Scott Eaton, *Opers Mgr*
Eric Stewart, *Human Resources*
Joan Braun, *Sales Staff*
Mike Harvey, *Sales Staff*
▲ EMP: 80
SALES (est): 30.8MM Privately Held
WEB: www.vanguardwines.com
SIC: 5182 Wine

(G-8935)
VERITIV OPERATING COMPANY
525 N Nelson Rd (43219-2949)
PHONE..................614 251-7100
Rhonda Yates, *Director*
EMP: 39
SALES (corp-wide): 8.3B Publicly Held
SIC: 5113 Industrial & personal service paper
HQ: Veritiv Operating Company
1000 Abernathy Rd
Atlanta GA 30328
770 391-8200

Columbus - Franklin County (G-8936)

(G-8936)
VERTI INSURANCE COMPANY
3590 Twin Creeks Dr (43204-1628)
PHONE..................844 448-3784
Marcos March, *Branch Mgr*
EMP: 60
SALES (corp-wide): 15.8MM **Privately Held**
SIC: 6331 Automobile insurance
PA: Verti Insurance Company
211 Main St
Webster MA 01570
844 448-3784

(G-8937)
VETERANS HEALTH ADMINISTRATION
Also Called: Chalmers P Wylie VA
420 N James Rd (43219-1834)
PHONE..................614 257-5524
Teri Mzozoyana, *Manager*
EMP: 250 **Publicly Held**
WEB: www.veterans-ru.org
SIC: 8011 9451 Clinic, operated by physicians; psychiatric clinic;
HQ: Veterans Health Administration
810 Vermont Ave Nw
Washington DC 20420

(G-8938)
VIBO CONSTRUCTION INC
266 N 4th St Ste 100 (43215-2565)
PHONE..................614 210-6780
Tania Prespia, *President*
Greg Pezzo, *Manager*
EMP: 35 **EST:** 2011
SQ FT: 800
SALES: 4MM **Privately Held**
SIC: 1521 Single-family housing construction

(G-8939)
VICTORY FTNES CTRS OF COLUMBUS (PA)
3427 South Blvd (43204-1213)
PHONE..................614 351-1688
Bob Brown, *President*
Dawn Wilson, *General Mgr*
▼ **EMP:** 25
SALES (est): 380.6K **Privately Held**
WEB: www.victoryfitnesscenter.net
SIC: 7991 Physical fitness clubs with training equipment; weight reducing clubs

(G-8940)
VIDEO DUPLICATION SERVICES INC (PA)
Also Called: Vds
3777 Busineoh Pk Dr Ste A (43204)
PHONE..................614 871-3827
Peter A Stock, *President*
Christian Stock, *Vice Pres*
Maria Vera, *Manager*
▲ **EMP:** 37
SQ FT: 47,000
SALES (est): 1.3MM **Privately Held**
SIC: 7812 Video tape production

(G-8941)
VILLA MILANO INC
Also Called: Villa Mlano Bnquet Cnfrnce Ctr
1630 Schrock Rd (43229-8220)
PHONE..................614 882-2058
Fax: 614 882-2491
Joseph Milano Jr, *President*
Dina Milano, *Treasurer*
Tina Milano, *Manager*
EMP: 30 **EST:** 1982
SQ FT: 20,000
SALES (est): 1.5MM **Privately Held**
WEB: www.villamilano.com
SIC: 7299 Banquet hall facilities

(G-8942)
VINTAGE WINE DISTRIBUTOR INC
2277 Westbrooke Dr (43228-9368)
PHONE..................614 876-2580
Fax: 614 876-1038
Bill Forbes, *Sales/Mktg Mgr*
Jay Valerio, *Manager*
EMP: 40

SALES (corp-wide): 25MM **Privately Held**
WEB: www.vintwine.com
SIC: 5182 Wine
PA: Vintage Wine Distributor, Inc.
6555 Davis Indus Pkwy
Solon OH 44139
440 248-1750

(G-8943)
VISION & VOCATIONAL SERVICES (PA)
1393 N High St (43201-2459)
P.O. Box 7, Ostrander (43061-0007)
PHONE..................614 294-5571
Andrew Grywalsky, *Finance*
Martin Gaudiose, *Director*
Mike Hanes, *Director*
Becky Noack, *Director*
Bob Turner, *Director*
EMP: 40
SQ FT: 30,000
SALES: 989.7K **Privately Held**
WEB: www.visioncenter.org
SIC: 8331 Job training & vocational rehabilitation services

(G-8944)
VISION SERVICE PLAN
3400 Morris Xing (43219)
PHONE..................614 471-7511
Fax: 614 225-6278
Roger Valine, *Branch Mgr*
EMP: 180
SALES (corp-wide): 3.2B **Privately Held**
WEB: www.vsp.com
SIC: 6411 Insurance agents
PA: Vision Service Plan
3333 Quality Dr
Rancho Cordova CA 95670
916 851-5000

(G-8945)
VISTA INDUSTRIAL PACKAGING LLC
Also Called: Vista Packaging & Logistics
4700 Fisher Rd (43228-9752)
PHONE..................800 454-6117
Tina Defluiter, *Opers Mgr*
Sarah Eckhoff, *Accounting Mgr*
Martha J Cahall,
J Matthew Cahall,
Kyle A Cahall,
EMP: 65
SQ FT: 350,000
SALES (est): 25.5MM **Privately Held**
SIC: 4783 7389 4226 2679 Packing & crating; inspection & testing services; special warehousing & storage; pressed fiber & molded pulp products except food products

(G-8946)
VISTACARE USA INC
540 Officenter Pl Ste 100 (43230-5332)
PHONE..................614 975-3230
Gay Rogers, *Branch Mgr*
EMP: 35
SALES (corp-wide): 6B **Publicly Held**
SIC: 8082 Home health care services
HQ: Vistacare Usa Inc
4800 N Scottsdale Rd # 5000
Scottsdale AZ 85251
480 648-4545

(G-8947)
VITRAN EXPRESS INC
5075 Krieger Ct (43228-3652)
PHONE..................614 870-2255
Bill Veris, *Sales Executive*
John Swanson, *Branch Mgr*
EMP: 200
SALES (corp-wide): 109.4MM **Privately Held**
SIC: 4212 Local trucking, without storage
PA: Vitran Express, Inc.
12225 Stephens Rd
Warren MI 48089
317 803-4000

(G-8948)
VJP HOSPITALITY LTD
Also Called: Four Points By Sheritan
3030 Plaza Prpts Blvd (43219)
PHONE..................614 475-8383
Paul Patel, *General Ptnr*

Laurie Hess, *Director*
EMP: 25
SALES: 300K **Privately Held**
SIC: 7011 Hotels & motels

(G-8949)
VOLUNTERS OF AMER GREATER OHIO
4280 Macsway Ave (43232-4257)
PHONE..................614 861-8551
Fax: 614 861-8651
Chris Westernburger, *Manager*
EMP: 36
SQ FT: 17,776
SALES (corp-wide): 8MM **Privately Held**
WEB: www.voa.org
SIC: 8322 Individual & family services
PA: Volunteers Of America Of Greater Ohio
1776 E Broad St
Columbus OH 43203
614 253-6100

(G-8950)
VOLUNTERS OF AMER GREATER OHIO
2335 N Bank Dr (43220-5423)
PHONE..................614 372-3120
Dennis Kresak, *Manager*
EMP: 200
SALES (corp-wide): 8MM **Privately Held**
WEB: www.voa.org
SIC: 8322 Individual & family services
PA: Volunteers Of America Of Greater Ohio
1776 E Broad St
Columbus OH 43203
614 253-6100

(G-8951)
VOLUNTERS OF AMER GREATER OHIO (PA)
1776 E Broad St (43203-1787)
PHONE..................614 253-6100
Sherry Keyes-Hebron, *President*
Christopher England, *CFO*
Caroline Mazur, *Assistant*
EMP: 120 **EST:** 1904
SQ FT: 8,000
SALES (est): 8MM **Privately Held**
SIC: 8322 8361 5932 5521 Social service center; alcoholism counseling, nontreatment; home for destitute men & women; clothing, secondhand; furniture, secondhand; automobiles, used cars only

(G-8952)
VOLUNTERS OF AMER GREATER OHIO
3620 Indianola Ave (43214-3758)
PHONE..................614 263-9134
Fax: 614 263-9138
Ray Ramons, *Director*
EMP: 30
SALES (corp-wide): 8MM **Privately Held**
SIC: 8322 Social service center
PA: Volunteers Of America Of Greater Ohio
1776 E Broad St
Columbus OH 43203
614 253-6100

(G-8953)
VOYA FINANCIAL INC
7965 N High St (43235-8402)
PHONE..................614 431-5000
Nicholas Disalle, *Manager*
EMP: 25
SALES (corp-wide): 8.6B **Publicly Held**
SIC: 6311 6411 Life insurance; insurance agents, brokers & service
PA: Voya Financial, Inc.
230 Park Ave Fl 14
New York NY 10169
212 309-8200

(G-8954)
VRABLE HEALTHCARE INC (PA)
3248 Henderson Rd (43220-7337)
PHONE..................614 545-5500
Fax: 614 538-2399
Allan K Vrable, *President*
Linda S Vrable, *Vice Pres*
James P Merrill, *CFO*
Todd Frasure, *Manager*
Kathleen Gregory, *Manager*
EMP: 30

SALES: 39.5MM **Privately Held**
WEB: www.vrablehealthcare.com
SIC: 8051 Convalescent home with continuous nursing care

(G-8955)
VRABLE II INC
Also Called: Southern Hills Skilled
3248 Henderson Rd (43220-7337)
PHONE..................614 545-5502
Allan K Vrable, *President*
Jim Merrill, *CFO*
EMP: 93
SQ FT: 40,000
SALES: 7.6MM **Privately Held**
SIC: 8051 Skilled nursing care facilities
PA: Vrable Healthcare, Inc.
3248 Henderson Rd
Columbus OH 43220

(G-8956)
VRABLE IV INC (HQ)
Also Called: Pembrooke Place Skilled
3248 Henderson Rd (43220-7337)
PHONE..................614 545-5502
Allan Vrable, *President*
James Merrill, *CFO*
EMP: 89
SQ FT: 52,000
SALES: 7.2MM **Privately Held**
SIC: 8051 Skilled nursing care facilities

(G-8957)
W D TIRE WAREHOUSE INC (PA)
Also Called: Convenient Tire Service
3805 E Livingston Ave (43227-2359)
PHONE..................614 461-8944
Fax: 614 461-0136
Doug Reed, *Principal*
Thomas J Brown Jr, *Principal*
Amy Reed, *Corp Secy*
▲ **EMP:** 32
SQ FT: 80,000
SALES (est): 51.3MM **Privately Held**
WEB: www.wdtire.net
SIC: 5014 Tires & tubes

(G-8958)
W F BOLIN COMPANY INC
4100 Fisher Rd (43228-1039)
PHONE..................614 276-6397
Wilbur F Bolin Jr, *President*
Bill Bolin, *Vice Pres*
William F Bolin, *Vice Pres*
EMP: 25
SQ FT: 4,500
SALES: 3MM **Privately Held**
SIC: 1721 Commercial painting; industrial painting

(G-8959)
W W WILLIAMS COMPANY LLC (DH)
835 Goodale Blvd (43212-3870)
PHONE..................614 228-5000
Fax: 614 228-4490
John Simmons, *CEO*
Tom Stocker, *Opers Staff*
Andy Gasser, *CFO*
Greg Wainer, *Sales Mgr*
Tom Ikegami, *Sales Staff*
EMP: 60 **EST:** 2016
SQ FT: 75,000
SALES (est): 218.9MM
SALES (corp-wide): 2.1B **Privately Held**
SIC: 7538 7537 Diesel engine repair: automotive; automotive transmission repair shops
HQ: Power Acquisition Llc
835 Goodale Blvd
Columbus OH 43212
614 228-5000

(G-8960)
W W WILLIAMS COMPANY LLC
Also Called: W. W. Wllams LLC - Lgstics Div
835 Goodale Blvd (43212-3870)
PHONE..................614 228-5000
Alan Gatlin, *CEO*
David Jackson, *Manager*
Dorian Norstrom, *Administration*
EMP: 25
SALES (corp-wide): 2.1B **Privately Held**
SIC: 4225 General warehousing & storage

GEOGRAPHIC SECTION — Columbus - Franklin County (G-8983)

HQ: The W W Williams Company Llc
  835 Goodale Blvd
  Columbus OH 43212
  614 228-5000

(G-8961)
WALGREEN CO
Also Called: Walgreens
3015 E Livingston Ave (43209-3047)
PHONE..................614 236-8622
Fax: 614 236-9355
Ryan Serfin, Branch Mgr
EMP: 30
SALES (corp-wide): 118.2B Publicly Held
WEB: www.walgreens.com
SIC: 5912 7384 Drug stores; photofinishing laboratory
HQ: Walgreen Co.
  200 Wilmot Rd
  Deerfield IL 60015
  847 315-2500

(G-8962)
WALKER NATIONAL INC
2195 Wright Brothers Ave (43217-1157)
PHONE..................614 492-1614
Richard Longo, President
Deborah Krikorian, CFO
Laurie Efteves, Accountant
Joy Keller, Credit Staff
Doug Bailey, Executive
◆ EMP: 30
SALES: 8MM
SALES (corp-wide): 45MM Privately Held
WEB: www.walkernational.com
SIC: 3499 7699 Magnets, permanent: metallic; industrial equipment services
HQ: Walker Magnetics Group, Inc.
  60 Solferino St Ste C
  Worcester MA 01604
  508 853-3232

(G-8963)
WALLACE F ACKLEY CO (PA)
695 Kenwick Rd (43209-2592)
PHONE..................614 231-3661
Fax: 614 231-7424
Gill Kirk, Partner
Stanford Ackley, Principal
Sandra Kirk, Principal
Brent Howard, Accounting Mgr
EMP: 51
SQ FT: 1,500
SALES (est): 4.4MM Privately Held
WEB: www.wallacefackleyco.com
SIC: 6513 Apartment building operators

(G-8964)
WALNUT HILLS PHYSICAL THERAPY
Also Called: Mount Carmel/Walnut Hills
5965 E Broad St Ste 390 (43213-1565)
PHONE..................614 234-8000
Fax: 614 234-8020
Anna May Balmaseda, President
Laura Miller, Principal
Jean Waddell, Vice Pres
EMP: 28
SALES (est): 830.7K Privately Held
SIC: 8049 Physical therapist

(G-8965)
WALTEK INC
399 W State St (43215-4008)
PHONE..................614 469-0156
Mike Graham, Branch Mgr
EMP: 42
SALES (corp-wide): 10.7MM Privately Held
SIC: 1611 General contractor, highway & street construction
PA: Waltek Inc.
  14310 Sunfish Lake Blvd
  Ramsey MN 55303
  763 427-3181

(G-8966)
WARD TRUCKING LLC
1601 Mckinley Ave (43222-1045)
PHONE..................614 275-3800
Fax: 614 275-3855
Mike Stone, Manager
EMP: 45
SALES (corp-wide): 153.4MM Privately Held
SIC: 4213 Contract haulers
PA: Ward Trucking, Llc
  1436 Ward Trucking Dr
  Altoona PA 16602
  814 944-0803

(G-8967)
WASHINGTON PRI (HQ)
Also Called: Glimcher Properties Ltd Partnr
180 E Broad St Fl 22 (43215-3714)
PHONE..................614 621-9000
Fax: 614 621-9321
Herbert Glimcher, Partner
Jeff Palley, Controller
EMP: 102
SQ FT: 35,248
SALES (est): 26.8MM
SALES (corp-wide): 843.4MM Publicly Held
WEB: www.almedamall.com
SIC: 6512 Commercial & industrial building operation
PA: Washington Prime Group Inc.
  180 E Broad St Fl 21
  Columbus OH 43215
  614 621-9000

(G-8968)
WASHINGTON PRIME GROUP LP (HQ)
180 E Broad St (43215-3707)
PHONE..................614 621-9000
Louis G Conforti, CEO
Robert J Laikin, Ch of Bd
Robert P Demchak, Exec VP
Melissa A Indest, Senior VP
Mark E Yale, CFO
EMP: 940
SALES: 758.1MM
SALES (corp-wide): 843.4MM Publicly Held
WEB: www.washingtonprime.com
SIC: 6798 Real estate investment trusts; realty investment trusts
PA: Washington Prime Group Inc.
  180 E Broad St Fl 21
  Columbus OH 43215
  614 621-9000

(G-8969)
WASHINGTON PRIME GROUP INC (PA)
180 E Broad St Fl 21 (43215-3714)
PHONE..................614 621-9000
Louis G Conforti, CEO
Robert J Laikin, Ch of Bd
Keric M Knerr, COO
Paul Ajdaharian, Exec VP
Robert P Demchak, Exec VP
EMP: 70
SALES: 843.4MM Publicly Held
SIC: 6512 6798 Property operation, retail establishment; realty investment trusts

(G-8970)
WASSERSTROM COMPANY (PA)
Also Called: National Smallwares
4500 E Broad St (43213-1360)
PHONE..................614 228-6525
Fax: 614 228-2165
Rodney Wasserstrom, President
Dave Lewellen, General Mgr
Mark Medonich, General Mgr
David A Tumen, Principal
Shelly Meyers, Exec VP
◆ EMP: 395 EST: 1902
SQ FT: 250,000
SALES (est): 792.7MM Privately Held
WEB: www.wasserstrom.com
SIC: 5087 3566 5021 5046 Restaurant supplies; speed changers, drives & gears; office furniture; commercial cooking & food service equipment; office supplies; kitchenware

(G-8971)
WASSERSTROM COMPANY
Also Called: Wassarstrom Rest Sup Super Str
2777 Silver Dr (43211-1054)
PHONE..................614 228-6525
Susan Coffman, Manager
EMP: 25

SALES (corp-wide): 792.7MM Privately Held
WEB: www.wasserstrom.com
SIC: 5149 Pizza supplies
PA: The Wasserstrom Company
  4500 E Broad St
  Columbus OH 43213
  614 228-6525

(G-8972)
WASSERSTROM HOLDINGS INC
477 S Front St (43215-5625)
P.O. Box 182056 (43218-2056)
PHONE..................614 228-6525
Rodney Wasserstrom, Co-COB
Alan Wasserstrom, Co-COB
EMP: 180 Privately Held
SIC: 6719 Investment holding companies, except banks

(G-8973)
WBNS TV INC
Also Called: Channel 10
770 Twin Rivers Dr (43215-1159)
P.O. Box 1010 (43216-1010)
PHONE..................614 460-3700
Fax: 614 460-2809
John F Wolfe, Ch of Bd
Micheal J Fiorile, President
Michael J Fiorile, President
Dustin Strah, Editor
Chris Walsh, Editor
EMP: 220 EST: 1965
SQ FT: 40,000
SALES (est): 31.6MM
SALES (corp-wide): 600.6MM Privately Held
WEB: www.wbns10tv.com
SIC: 4833 Television broadcasting stations
PA: The Dispatch Printing Company
  62 E Broad St
  Columbus OH 43215
  614 461-5000

(G-8974)
WEBER PARTNERS LTD (PA)
Also Called: Weber Associates
775 Yard St Ste 350 (43212-3892)
PHONE..................614 222-6806
Fax: 614 222-6808
Luke Smith, President
Tom Parry, Partner
Koichi Kiyohara, Partner
Andrew Leatherman, Partner
Brad Dresbach, Vice Pres
EMP: 30
SALES (est): 2.9MM Privately Held
SIC: 8742 Marketing consulting services

(G-8975)
WEILANDS FINE MEATS INC
Also Called: Weiland's Gourmet Market
3600 Indianola Ave (43214-3758)
PHONE..................614 267-9910
John Williams, President
Tim Teegardin, Vice Pres
EMP: 47
SQ FT: 15,000
SALES (est): 4.2MM Privately Held
WEB: www.weilandsgourmetmarket.com
SIC: 5421 5411 5147 Meat & fish markets; delicatessens; meats & meat products

(G-8976)
WELLS FARGO CLEARING SVCS LLC
Also Called: Wells Fargo Advisors
41 S High St Ste 1550 (43215-3406)
PHONE..................614 221-8371
Fax: 614 221-5809
Garrett Venetta, Branch Mgr
EMP: 25
SALES (corp-wide): 97.7B Publicly Held
SIC: 6211 Stock brokers & dealers; bond dealers & brokers
HQ: Wells Fargo Clearing Services, Llc
  1 N Jefferson Ave
  Saint Louis MO 63103
  314 955-3000

(G-8977)
WENDT-BRISTOL HEALTH SERVICES (PA)
921 Jasonway Ave Ste B (43214-2456)
PHONE..................614 403-9966

Marvin D Kantor, Ch of Bd
Sheldon A Gold, President
EMP: 25 EST: 1966
SALES (est): 3.6MM Privately Held
SIC: 8093 Specialty outpatient clinics

(G-8978)
WENGER TEMPERATURE CONTROL
Also Called: Honeywell Authorized Dealer
2005 Progress Ave (43207-1759)
PHONE..................614 586-4016
Fax: 614 443-2230
Joseph E Wenger III, President
George Wenger, Vice Pres
Bill Browning, Project Mgr
EMP: 25 EST: 1977
SQ FT: 13,000
SALES (est): 3MM Privately Held
WEB: www.wengertempcontrol.com
SIC: 1711 1542 Heating & air conditioning contractors; refrigeration contractor; design & erection, combined: non-residential

(G-8979)
WESBANCO INC
2000 Henderson Rd Ste 100 (43220-2453)
PHONE..................614 208-7298
Fax: 614 755-4094
Jerry Cox, Vice Pres
EMP: 38
SALES (corp-wide): 421.2MM Publicly Held
SIC: 6029 Commercial banks
PA: Wesbanco, Inc.
  1 Bank Plz
  Wheeling WV 26003
  304 234-9000

(G-8980)
WESTMINSTER MANAGEMENT COMPANY
2731 Clime Rd (43223-3625)
PHONE..................614 274-5154
Thomas J Stewart, President
Dawn Miller, Vice Pres
EMP: 108
SQ FT: 1,200
SALES (est): 4.8MM Privately Held
SIC: 8741 Nursing & personal care facility management

(G-8981)
WESTPATRICK CORP
250 N Hartford Ave 300 (43222-1100)
PHONE..................614 875-8200
Charles Jeffrey Mahan, President
Douglas R McCrae, Partner
Gary D Yancer, Partner
Bradley Prewitt, General Mgr
Michael Coccia, Corp Secy
EMP: 40
SQ FT: 7,000
SALES (est): 10.2MM Privately Held
SIC: 1622 1611 Bridge construction; general contractor, highway & street construction

(G-8982)
WESTPOST COLUMBUS LLC
6500 Doubletree Ave (43229-1111)
PHONE..................614 885-1885
Daniel Ouellette, Principal
Firoz Howlader, Controller
EMP: 99
SALES: 950K Privately Held
SIC: 7011 Hotels & motels

(G-8983)
WESTSIDE FAMILY PRACTICE INC
5206 Chaps Ct (43221-5706)
PHONE..................614 878-4541
Fax: 614 878-6228
Wesley Hard MD, President
EMP: 29
SALES (est): 2.3MM Privately Held
SIC: 8011 General & family practice, physician/surgeon

Columbus - Franklin County (G-8984)

(G-8984)
WEXNER HERITAGE VILLAGE (PA)
Also Called: HERITAGE HOUSE NURSING HOME
1151 College Ave (43209-2827)
PHONE..........................614 231-4900
Fax: 614 338-2399
Chris Christian, *Senior VP*
Erin Keller, *Senior VP*
Cheryl Howard, *Vice Pres*
Cheri Shrider, *Opers Staff*
David Driver, *CFO*
EMP: 500
SQ FT: 224,000
SALES: 15.9MM **Privately Held**
SIC: 8052 8051 Intermediate care facilities; skilled nursing care facilities

(G-8985)
WHETSTONE CARE CENTER LLC
Also Called: Whetstone Center
3710 Olentangy River Rd (43214-3426)
PHONE..........................614 457-1100
Fax: 614 457-0173
Michele Engelbach, *Principal*
Erin Hennesy, *Exec Dir*
Christina Thrope, *Social Dir*
EMP: 210
SQ FT: 62,000
SALES (corp-wide): 22.4MM **Privately Held**
WEB: www.macintoshcompany.com
SIC: 8051 8059 Convalescent home with continuous nursing care; convalescent home
PA: Whetstone Care Center Llc
3863 Trueman Ct
Hilliard OH 43026
614 345-9500

(G-8986)
WHITE CASTLE SYSTEM INC (PA)
555 W Goodale St (43215-1104)
P.O. Box 1498 (43216-1498)
PHONE..........................614 228-5781
Fax: 614 464-0596
Edgar W Ingram III, *Ch of Bd*
Bette Everson, *President*
Elizabeth Ingram, *President*
Shelly Frazier, *General Mgr*
Gail Gurney, *General Mgr*
▲ **EMP:** 275
SQ FT: 143,000
SALES (est): 636.6MM **Privately Held**
WEB: www.whitecastle.com
SIC: 5812 5142 2051 2013 Fast-food restaurant, chain; meat, frozen: packaged; bread, cake & related products; sausages & other prepared meats

(G-8987)
WHITE OAK INVESTMENTS INC
3730 Lockbourne Rd (43207-5133)
P.O. Box 182022 (43218-2022)
PHONE..........................614 491-1000
Fax: 614 492-2462
Joseph C Bowman, *President*
Maureen Travis, *Human Res Dir*
Nikki Vanderbeek, *Sales Mgr*
Kathy Angers, *Regl Sales Mgr*
Christina Carr, *Regl Sales Mgr*
EMP: 65
SQ FT: 65,000
SALES (est): 10.4MM **Privately Held**
WEB: www.cenres.com
SIC: 7389 Fund raising organizations

(G-8988)
WHITEHALL CITY SCHOOLS
Also Called: C Ray Wllams Erly Chldhood Ctr
4738 Kae Ave (43213-6100)
PHONE..........................614 417-5680
Fax: 614 559-0085
Shirley Drakes, *Principal*
Steve McAfee, *CFO*
EMP: 40
SALES (corp-wide): 46.4MM **Privately Held**
WEB: www.whitehall.k12.oh.us
SIC: 8351 8211 Preschool center; kindergarten

PA: Whitehall City Schools
625 S Yearling Rd
Columbus OH 43213
614 417-5000

(G-8989)
WHITEHALL FRMENS BNVLENCE FUND
390 S Yearling Rd (43213-1876)
PHONE..........................614 237-5478
Tim Tilton, *Chief*
EMP: 43
SALES (est): 321.3K **Privately Held**
SIC: 8641 Civic social & fraternal associations

(G-8990)
WHITESTONE GROUP INC
4100 Regent St Ste C (43219-6156)
PHONE..........................614 501-7007
John Clark, *President*
Pam Gentile, *President*
R Gene Hart, *Vice Pres*
Bill Smith, *CFO*
EMP: 300
SQ FT: 2,500
SALES (est): 33MM **Privately Held**
SIC: 7382 Security systems services

(G-8991)
WICKERTREE TNNIS FTNES CLB LLC
5760 Maple Canyon Ave (43229-2894)
PHONE..........................614 882-5724
Fax: 614 891-8442
Marvin Williams, *President*
Janet Craycraft, *Vice Pres*
Ravi Thenappan, *Mng Member*
Dough Birosario, *Manager*
Arnie Jones, *Manager*
EMP: 28
SQ FT: 60,000
SALES (est): 1.2MM **Privately Held**
WEB: www.wickertree.com
SIC: 7997 Tennis club, membership

(G-8992)
WIDEPINT INTGRTED SLTIONS CORP
8351 N High St Ste 200 (43235-1501)
PHONE..........................614 410-1587
Todd McMillen, *Manager*
EMP: 45 **Publicly Held**
WEB: www.isysllc.com
SIC: 7371 Computer software development
HQ: Widepoint Integrated Solutions Corp.
7926 Jones Branch Dr # 520
Mc Lean VA 22102
703 349-5644

(G-8993)
WILES BOYLE BURKHOLDER &
Also Called: Wiles Doucher
2 Miranova Pl Ste 700 (43215-5098)
PHONE..........................614 221-5216
Fax: 614 221-5692
James M Wiles, *Co-President*
Daniel Wiles, *Co-President*
Thomas E Boyle, *Corp Secy*
Peg Lowry, *Accounting Mgr*
EMP: 67
SQ FT: 25,000
SALES (est): 8.9MM **Privately Held**
SIC: 8111 General practice attorney, lawyer

(G-8994)
WILLGLO SERVICES INC
Also Called: BURGE SERVICE
995 Thurman Ave (43206-3133)
P.O. Box 77469 (43207-7469)
PHONE..........................614 443-3020
William Burge, *President*
Gloria Burge, *Administration*
EMP: 50
SALES (est): 1.6MM **Privately Held**
SIC: 8052 Home for the mentally retarded, with health care

(G-8995)
WILLIAM I NOTZ
Also Called: Department of Statistics
1958 Neil Ave Rm 319 (43210-1247)
PHONE..........................614 292-3154

William I Notz, *Principal*
Paul Brower, *Chairman*
EMP: 40
SALES (est): 2.4MM **Privately Held**
SIC: 8621 Professional standards review board

(G-8996)
WILLIAM SYDNEY DRUEN
85 E Deshler Ave (43206-2655)
PHONE..........................614 444-7655
William Sydney Druen, *Owner*
EMP: 25
SALES (est): 1.1MM **Privately Held**
SIC: 8748 Business consulting

(G-8997)
WILLIS OF OHIO INC (DH)
775 Yard St Ste 200 (43212-3891)
PHONE..........................614 457-7000
John Chaney, *CEO*
Michael Connelly, *Managing Prtnr*
Charles Black, *Exec VP*
Ken Sweeney, *Exec VP*
Paul Case, *Senior VP*
EMP: 25 **EST:** 1922
SALES (est): 9.5MM **Privately Held**
SIC: 6411 Insurance agents, brokers & service
HQ: Willis North America Inc.
200 Liberty St Fl 7
New York NY 10281
212 915-8888

(G-8998)
WILLO SECURITY INC
1989 W 5th Ave Ste 3 (43212-1912)
PHONE..........................614 481-9456
Steven Alan, *Manager*
EMP: 143
SALES (corp-wide): 7.4MM **Privately Held**
WEB: www.willosecurity.com
SIC: 7381 Security guard service
PA: Willo Security, Inc.
38230 Glenn Ave
Willoughby OH 44094
440 953-9191

(G-8999)
WILSON ENTERPRISES INC
Also Called: Wilson's Turf
1600 Universal Rd (43207-1733)
PHONE..........................614 444-8873
Richard B Wilson, *President*
Richard Wilson, *President*
Daniel Wilson, *Vice Pres*
Phil Paolini, *Treasurer*
EMP: 40
SQ FT: 4,000
SALES (est): 4.9MM **Privately Held**
WEB: www.wilsonsturf.com
SIC: 0782 Sodding contractor

(G-9000)
WINGLER CONSTRUCTION CORP
Also Called: One Stop Remodeling
771 S Hamilton Rd (43213-3001)
PHONE..........................614 626-8546
Fax: 614 947-7007
Ronald E Wingler, *President*
EMP: 25
SQ FT: 13,000
SALES (est): 4MM **Privately Held**
SIC: 1521 1542 General remodeling, single-family houses; commercial & office buildings, renovation & repair

(G-9001)
WM COLUMBUS HOTEL LLC
Also Called: Westin Columbus
310 S High St (43215-4508)
PHONE..........................614 228-3800
Janet Rhodes, *General Mgr*
Mark Zettl, *COO*
Doug Denyer, *CFO*
Marci Bussart, *Accountant*
Carl Palmer, *Human Res Dir*
EMP: 250
SQ FT: 200,000
SALES: 13.3MM
SALES (corp-wide): 622.7MM **Publicly Held**
SIC: 7011 Hotels

PA: The Marcus Corporation
100 E Wisconsin Ave # 1
Milwaukee WI 53202
414 905-1000

(G-9002)
WODA CONSTRUCTION INC
500 S Front St Fl 10 (43215-7619)
PHONE..........................614 396-3200
Jeffrey Woda, *President*
David Cooper Jr, *Exec VP*
Bruce Moffat, *Vice Pres*
Susan Milner, *Controller*
Tammy Greene, *Manager*
EMP: 47
SQ FT: 3,000
SALES: 42.4MM
SALES (corp-wide): 7.2MM **Privately Held**
WEB: www.wodagroup.com
SIC: 1522 1521 Apartment building construction; new construction, single-family houses
PA: Cooper Woda Companies Inc
500 S Front St Fl 10
Columbus OH 43215
614 396-3200

(G-9003)
WOMEN PHYSICANS OF OB/GYN INC (PA)
3525 Olentangy River Rd # 6350 (43214-3937)
PHONE..........................614 734-3340
Elaine Paul, *President*
Rebecca Gallagher, *Manager*
Alicia M Shanks, *Nurse Practr*
EMP: 33
SALES (est): 5.5MM **Privately Held**
SIC: 8011 Offices & clinics of medical doctors

(G-9004)
WOODLAND ASSISTED LIVING RESI
Also Called: Woodlands of Columbus
5380 E Broad St Ofc (43213-3848)
PHONE..........................614 755-7591
Fax: 614 755-7595
Thomas J Smith,
Richard Osbourne,
EMP: 50
SALES (est): 2.5MM **Privately Held**
SIC: 8051 Skilled nursing care facilities

(G-9005)
WOOLPERT INC
1 Easton Oval Ste 310 (43219-6062)
PHONE..........................614 476-6000
Fax: 614 476-6225
Bridget Prosch, *Branch Mgr*
EMP: 50
SALES (corp-wide): 99MM **Privately Held**
WEB: www.woolpert.com
SIC: 8711 Civil engineering
PA: Woolpert, Inc.
4454 Idea Center Blvd
Beavercreek OH 45430
937 461-5660

(G-9006)
WORKERS COMPENSATION OHIO BUR
30 W Spring St (43215-2216)
PHONE..........................800 644-6292
Stephen Buehrer, *Administration*
EMP: 2300 **Privately Held**
SIC: 6411 Insurance agents, brokers & service
HQ: Ohio Bureau Of Workers' Compensation
30 W Spring St Fl 2-29
Columbus OH 43215
614 644-6292

(G-9007)
WORKERS COMPENSATION OHIO BUR (DH)
30 W Spring St Fl 2-29 (43215-2216)
PHONE..........................614 644-6292
Mike Brown, *Project Mgr*
Tracy Rhodes, *Purch Agent*
Babara Young, *Persnl Dir*
Toni Brokaw, *Human Res Mgr*

Sharon Csonka, *Manager*
EMP: 1500
SALES (est): 2.2B **Privately Held**
SIC: 6331 9199 Workers' compensation insurance; general government administration

(G-9008)
WORLY PLUMBING SUPPLY INC (PA)
400 Greenlawn Ave (43223-2611)
PHONE..................................614 445-1000
Fax: 614 445-4900
Jay Worly, *President*
Jeff Worly, *COO*
Bradley Simms, *Plant Mgr*
Lena Brown, *Purchasing*
Judith Tompkins, *Controller*
EMP: 54 EST: 1952
SQ FT: 96,000
SALES (est): 54.6MM **Privately Held**
WEB: www.worly.com
SIC: 5074 Plumbing fittings & supplies; heating equipment (hydronic)

(G-9009)
WORTHNGTON STELPAC SYSTEMS LLC (HQ)
1205 Dearborn Dr (43085-4769)
PHONE..................................614 438-3205
Mark Russell, *CEO*
EMP: 250
SALES (est): 47.5MM
SALES (corp-wide): 3B **Publicly Held**
SIC: 3325 5051 Steel foundries; metals service centers & offices
PA: Worthington Industries, Inc.
  200 W Old Wlson Bridge Rd
  Worthington OH 43085
  614 438-3210

(G-9010)
WW GRAINGER INC
Also Called: Grainger 176
3640 Interchange Rd (43204-1434)
PHONE..................................614 276-5231
Fax: 614 274-7335
Rich Herron, *Manager*
EMP: 35
SALES (corp-wide): 10.4B **Publicly Held**
WEB: www.grainger.com
SIC: 5063 5084 5075 5078 Motors, electric; motor controls, starters & relays: electric; power transmission equipment, electric; generators; fans, industrial; pumps & pumping equipment; compressors, except air conditioning; pneumatic tools & equipment; warm air heating equipment & supplies; air conditioning equipment, except room units; refrigeration equipment & supplies; electric tools; power tools & accessories; hand tools
PA: W.W. Grainger, Inc.
  100 Grainger Pkwy
  Lake Forest IL 60045
  847 535-1000

(G-9011)
WYANDOTTE ATHLETIC CLUB
5198 Riding Club Ln (43213-3202)
PHONE..................................614 861-6303
Fax: 614 861-0669
Todd Decker, *President*
Rafael Lisboa, *Sales Dir*
EMP: 50
SALES (est): 2.2MM **Privately Held**
WEB: www.wyandotteathleticclub.com
SIC: 7991 Health club

(G-9012)
X F CONSTRUCTION SVCS INC
Also Called: X F Petroleum Equipment
1120 Claycraft Rd (43230-6640)
PHONE..................................614 575-2700
Fax: 614 575-0603
William R Patrick, *President*
James Fairchild, *Vice Pres*
Lucille Stallard, *Vice Pres*
Robert Patrick, *Treasurer*
Brinda Nussdaun, *Manager*
EMP: 35
SQ FT: 20,000
SALES (est): 6MM **Privately Held**
SIC: 1731 1799 5172 General electrical contractor; service station equipment installation, maintenance & repair; service station supplies, petroleum

(G-9013)
XENTRY SYSTEMS INTEGRATION LLC (HQ)
771 Dearborn Park Ln N (43085-5720)
PHONE..................................614 452-7300
John Nemerofsky, *President*
Johnathan Smith, *Project Mgr*
Victor Borsukevich, *Manager*
EMP: 26
SALES (est): 8.3MM
SALES (corp-wide): 33.9MM **Privately Held**
SIC: 7382 Security systems services
PA: Sgi Matrix, Llc
  1041 Byers Rd
  Miamisburg OH 45342
  937 438-9033

(G-9014)
XPO LOGISTICS FREIGHT INC
2625 Westbelt Dr (43228-3828)
PHONE..................................614 876-7100
Fax: 614 771-0211
Freda Hayner, *Manager*
EMP: 172
SQ FT: 6,460
SALES (corp-wide): 15.3B **Publicly Held**
WEB: www.con-way.com
SIC: 4231 4213 4212 Trucking terminal facilities; trucking, except local; local trucking, without storage
HQ: Xpo Logistics Freight, Inc.
  2211 Old Earhart Rd # 100
  Ann Arbor MI 48105
  734 998-4200

(G-9015)
YORK TEMPLE COUNTRY CLUB INC
Also Called: YORK GOLF CLUB
7459 N High St (43235-1412)
PHONE..................................614 885-5459
Fax: 614 885-5942
Chuck Dahn, *General Mgr*
Glenn Johnson, *VP Finance*
EMP: 40
SQ FT: 18,000
SALES: 1.9MM **Privately Held**
WEB: www.yorkgolfclub.com
SIC: 7997 5812 Country club, membership; golf club, membership; eating places

(G-9016)
YORKLAND HEALTH CARE INC
Also Called: Yorkland Park Care Center
1425 Yorkland Rd (43232-1686)
PHONE..................................614 751-2525
Brian Colleran, *President*
Charles Baughman, *Director*
EMP: 99
SQ FT: 2,561
SALES: 12.3MM **Privately Held**
WEB: www.yorkland-park.net
SIC: 8059 Nursing home, except skilled & intermediate care facility

(G-9017)
YOUNG MENS CHRISTIAN ASSOC
Also Called: YMCA
1640 Sandalwood Pl (43229-3640)
PHONE..................................614 885-4252
Fax: 614 885-6244
Chloe Viers, *Director*
EMP: 170
SQ FT: 7,700
SALES (corp-wide): 44.9MM **Privately Held**
WEB: www.ymca-columbus.com
SIC: 8641 8322 7032 7999 Youth organizations; individual & family services; sporting & recreational camps; recreation center
PA: Young Men's Christian Association Of Central Ohio
  40 W Long St
  Columbus OH 43215
  614 389-4409

(G-9018)
YOUNG MENS CHRISTIAN ASSOC
Also Called: Hilltop
2879 Valleyview Dr (43204-2010)
PHONE..................................614 276-8224
Fax: 614 276-5579
Glenn Davis, *Maintenance Dir*
Cheryl Nielson, *Branch Mgr*
Katrina Hacker, *Director*
Carol Parlette, *Director*
EMP: 100
SALES (corp-wide): 44.9MM **Privately Held**
WEB: www.ymca-columbus.com
SIC: 8641 7999 8322 Youth organizations; recreation center; individual & family services
PA: Young Men's Christian Association Of Central Ohio
  40 W Long St
  Columbus OH 43215
  614 389-4409

(G-9019)
YOUNG MENS CHRISTIAN ASSOC
Also Called: YMCA
130 Woodland Ave (43203-1774)
PHONE..................................614 252-3166
Fax: 614 252-3169
Kim Jordan, *Branch Mgr*
Winifred Simpson, *Director*
EMP: 65
SALES (corp-wide): 44.9MM **Privately Held**
WEB: www.ymca-columbus.com
SIC: 8641 7991 8351 7032 Youth organizations; physical fitness facilities; child day care services; youth camps; individual & family services
PA: Young Men's Christian Association Of Central Ohio
  40 W Long St
  Columbus OH 43215
  614 389-4409

(G-9020)
YOUNG MENS CHRISTIAN ASSOC
Also Called: YMCA
600 Fox Ridge St (43228-2213)
PHONE..................................614 878-7269
Fax: 614 878-0086
Elana Lehihan, *Director*
EMP: 25
SALES (corp-wide): 44.9MM **Privately Held**
WEB: www.ymca-columbus.com
SIC: 8641 7997 Civic social & fraternal associations; swimming club, membership
PA: Young Men's Christian Association Of Central Ohio
  40 W Long St
  Columbus OH 43215
  614 389-4409

(G-9021)
YOUNG WOMENS CHRISTIAN ASSN (PA)
Also Called: YWCA
65 S 4th St (43215-4356)
PHONE..................................614 224-9121
Fax: 614 224-2522
Elfi Di Bella, *President*
Terri W Ifeduba, *Vice Pres*
Joyce Swayne, *Opers Staff*
Valerie Henthorn, *Accounting Mgr*
Michelle Chieffo, *Property Mgr*
EMP: 60
SQ FT: 100,880
SALES: 14.1MM **Privately Held**
SIC: 8641 7991 8351 7032 Youth organizations; physical fitness facilities; child day care services; youth camps; individual & family services

(G-9022)
YOUTH ADVOCATE SERVICES
825 Grandview Ave (43215-1123)
PHONE..................................614 258-9927
Fax: 614 258-5719
Sarah Cochey, *CEO*
Glenn Richard, *CFO*
Ann Hemphill, *Manager*
Korlyn Davis, *Director*
EMP: 28
SQ FT: 10,500
SALES: 3.9MM **Privately Held**
WEB: www.youthad.org
SIC: 8322 Child related social services

(G-9023)
YRC INC
Also Called: Yellow Transportation
5400 Fisher Rd (43228-9771)
P.O. Box 28188 (43228-0188)
PHONE..................................614 878-9281
Fax: 614 851-6150
Chuck Zinsmayer, *Manager*
James McDonald, *Systems Staff*
EMP: 56
SQ FT: 6,800
SALES (corp-wide): 4.8B **Publicly Held**
WEB: www.roadway.com
SIC: 4231 4213 Trucking terminal facilities; trucking, except local
HQ: Yrc Inc.
  10990 Roe Ave
  Overland Park KS 66211
  913 696-6100

(G-9024)
Z PRODUCE CO INC
720 Harmon Ave (43223-2450)
PHONE..................................614 224-4373
Fax: 614 224-4301
Dean Zaglanis, *President*
Helen C Zaglanis, *Admin Sec*
EMP: 35
SQ FT: 28,000
SALES (est): 7.5MM **Privately Held**
WEB: www.zproduce.com
SIC: 5148 5149 5142 Banana ripening; fruits, fresh; potatoes, fresh; vegetables, fresh; canned goods: fruit, vegetables, seafood, meats, etc.; packaged frozen goods

(G-9025)
ZANER-BLOSER INC (HQ)
1400 Goodale Blvd Ste 200 (43212-3777)
P.O. Box 16764 (43216-6764)
PHONE..................................614 486-0221
Fax: 614 487-2699
Robert Page, *President*
Thomas Mason, *Treasurer*
Jennifer Ayers, *Accountant*
Rita Cook, *Sales Staff*
Lee Shaler, *Sales Associate*
▲ **EMP:** 61
SQ FT: 15,000
SALES (est): 88.3MM
SALES (corp-wide): 235.3MM **Privately Held**
WEB: www.zaner-bloser.com
SIC: 5192 5049 8249 2731 Books; school supplies; correspondence school; book publishing
PA: Highlights For Children, Inc.
  1800 Watermark Dr
  Columbus OH 43215
  614 486-0631

(G-9026)
ZEIGER TIGGES & LITTLE LLP
41 S High St Ste 3500 (43215-6110)
PHONE..................................614 365-9900
Bradley T Ferrell, *Partner*
Marion H Little Jr, *Partner*
Stuart G Parsell, *Partner*
Steven W Tigges, *Partner*
John Zeiger, *General Ptnr*
EMP: 27
SQ FT: 16,000
SALES: 8MM **Privately Held**
WEB: www.litohio.com
SIC: 8111 General practice attorney, lawyer

(G-9027)
ZIPLINE LOGISTICS LLC
2300 W 5th Ave (43215-1003)
PHONE..................................888 469-4754
Walter Lynch, *CEO*
Andrew Lynch, *President*
John Rodeheffer,
EMP: 54
SQ FT: 3,600

Columbus - Franklin County (G-9028)

SALES (est): 11.1MM **Privately Held**
WEB: www.ziplinelogistics.com
SIC: 4213 Trucking, except local

(G-9028)
ZUSMAN COMMUNITY HOSPICE
1151 College Ave (43209-2827)
PHONE..................614 559-0350
Fax: 614 338-2379
Amy Kramer, *Info Tech Mgr*
April Mock, *Director*
EMP: 30 EST: 2007
SALES (est): 542.9K **Privately Held**
SIC: 8052 Personal care facility

Columbus Grove
Putnam County

(G-9029)
CARPE DIEM INDUSTRIES LLC (PA)
Also Called: Colonial Surface Solutions
4599 Campbell Rd (45830-9403)
PHONE..................419 659-5639
Patricia Langhals, *President*
Gene Heitmeyer, *General Mgr*
Darren Langhals, *Corp Secy*
Brian Langhals, *Facilities Mgr*
Tammy Whitlow, *Human Res Mgr*
EMP: 55
SQ FT: 750
SALES (est): 18.1MM **Privately Held**
WEB: www.colonialsurfacesolutions.com
SIC: 3479 3471 3398 1799 Painting of metal products; cleaning & descaling metal products; sand blasting of metal parts; tumbling (cleaning & polishing) of machine parts; metal heat treating; tempering of metal; coating of metal structures at construction site

(G-9030)
HALKER DRYWALL INC
Also Called: Halker Drywall & Plastering
21457 Road 15u (45830-9244)
PHONE..................419 646-3679
Fax: 419 646-3679
Vickie Halker, *President*
Job Halker, *Corp Secy*
David Halker, *Vice Pres*
Sara Scheroder, *Manager*
EMP: 45
SALES (est): 3.9MM **Privately Held**
WEB: www.halkerdrywall.com
SIC: 1742 Drywall; exterior insulation & finish (EIFS) applicator

(G-9031)
TOM LANGHALS
Also Called: Colonial Farms
4599 Campbell Rd (45830-9403)
PHONE..................419 659-5629
Tom Langhals, *Owner*
Janice Langhals, *Co-Owner*
EMP: 30
SALES (est): 3.9MM **Privately Held**
SIC: 5084 0115 Cleaning equipment, high pressure, sand or steam; corn

Concord Township
Lake County

(G-9032)
KAISER FOUNDATION HOSPITALS
Also Called: Healthspan-Concord Med Offs
7536 Fredle Dr (44077-9406)
PHONE..................440 350-3614
Amanda Currence, *Director*
EMP: 593
SALES (corp-wide): 82.6B **Privately Held**
SIC: 8011 Offices & clinics of medical doctors
HQ: Kaiser Foundation Hospitals Inc
1 Kaiser Plz
Oakland CA 94612
510 271-6611

Concord Twp
Lake County

(G-9033)
GARDENLIFE INC
Also Called: Grimes Seeds
11335 Concord Hambden Rd (44077-9704)
PHONE..................440 352-6195
Fax: 440 352-1800
Gary S Grimes, *Ch of Bd*
Rodney Ledrew, *Vice Pres*
EMP: 35
SQ FT: 9,000
SALES (est): 19.5MM **Privately Held**
WEB: www.grimeseeds.com
SIC: 5191 Seeds: field, garden & flower; garden supplies

(G-9034)
QH MANAGEMENT COMPANY LLC
Also Called: Quail Hollow Resort
11080 Concord Hambden Rd (44077-9704)
PHONE..................440 497-1100
Fax: 440 350-3558
Mukiv Rahmen, *General Mgr*
Paul Brushwood, *Vice Pres*
Tom Korth, *Controller*
Mike Kelly,
EMP: 99
SALES (est): 1,000K **Privately Held**
SIC: 7011 Resort hotel

Conesville
Coshocton County

(G-9035)
AMERICAN ELECTRIC POWER CO INC
47201 County Road 273 (43811-9701)
PHONE..................740 829-4129
Ronald Borton, *Production*
Bill Miller, *Electrical Engi*
Dan Lambert, *Manager*
Daniel Moyer, *Manager*
Clarence Sidwell, *Manager*
EMP: 30
SALES (corp-wide): 15.4B **Publicly Held**
WEB: www.aep.com
SIC: 1731 Electrical work
PA: American Electric Power Company, Inc.
1 Riverside Plz Fl 1 # 1
Columbus OH 43215
614 716-1000

(G-9036)
COLUMBUS SOUTHERN POWER CO
47201 County Road 273 (43811-9701)
PHONE..................740 829-2378
Fax: 740 829-4000
Michael Zwick, *Plant Mgr*
G H Tharp, *Finance Other*
Royal Wilson, *Human Res Mgr*
Dan Lambert, *Manager*
EMP: 100
SALES (corp-wide): 15.4B **Publicly Held**
SIC: 4911 Electric services
HQ: Columbus Southern Power Company
1 Riverside Plz
Columbus OH 43215
614 716-1000

Conneaut
Ashtabula County

(G-9037)
ASHTABULA COUNTY COMMNTY ACTN
Also Called: Conneaut Senior Services
327 Mill St (44030-2439)
PHONE..................440 593-6441
Persela Airhart, *Manager*
EMP: 100
SALES (corp-wide): 92.1K **Privately Held**
SIC: 8399 8322 Antipoverty board; senior citizens' center or association
PA: Ashtabula County Community Action Agency Properties Corporation
6920 Austinburg Rd
Ashtabula OH 44004
440 997-1721

(G-9038)
ASHTABULA COUNTY RESIDENTIAL I (PA)
29 Parrish Rd (44030-1146)
PHONE..................440 593-6404
Fax: 440 593-6007
Charlotte Lovas, *President*
EMP: 35
SQ FT: 1,000
SALES (est): 2.1MM **Privately Held**
SIC: 8361 Home for the mentally handicapped

(G-9039)
BESSEMER AND LAKE ERIE RR CO
Also Called: Pittsburgh & Conneaut Dock
950 Ford Ave (44030-1867)
P.O. Box 90 (44030-0090)
PHONE..................440 593-1102
Fax: 216 593-1102
Robert S Rosati, *Branch Mgr*
EMP: 150
SALES (corp-wide): 10.2B **Privately Held**
SIC: 6519 Real property lessors
HQ: Bessemer And Lake Erie Railroad Company
17641 Ashland Ave
Homewood IL 60430
708 206-6708

(G-9040)
BROWN MEMORIAL HOSPITAL
Also Called: University Hosp Hlth Sys Inc
158 W Main Rd (44030-2039)
PHONE..................440 593-1131
Fax: 440 593-6710
Robert David, *President*
Mike McGrath, *CFO*
Barbara Gurto, *Human Res Dir*
Tammi Lewis, *Marketing Staff*
Bradley Best, *Manager*
EMP: 300
SQ FT: 97,000
SALES (est): 20MM
SALES (corp-wide): 2.3B **Privately Held**
SIC: 8062 General medical & surgical hospitals
PA: University Hospitals Health System, Inc.
3605 Warrensville Ctr Rd
Shaker Heights OH 44122
216 767-8900

(G-9041)
CONNEAUT TELEPHONE COMPANY
Also Called: Suite224 and Cablesuite541
224 State St (44030-2637)
P.O. Box 579 (44030-0579)
PHONE..................440 593-7140
Fax: 440 593-5544
Ray Rapose, *Ch of Bd*
P Tom Picard, *General Mgr*
James Haney, *Vice Pres*
Karen Picard, *CFO*
Karen Arcaro, *Accountant*
EMP: 50
SQ FT: 8,000
SALES (est): 12.6MM **Privately Held**
WEB: www.conneauttelephone.com
SIC: 4841 4813 Cable & other pay television services; local telephone communications

(G-9042)
ES3 MANAGEMENT INC
Also Called: Lake Pnte Rhbltion Nrsing Ctr
22 Parrish Rd (44030-1178)
PHONE..................440 593-6266
Joyce M Humphrey, *President*
Robin L Hillier, *Shareholder*
EMP: 90
SALES (est): 2.5MM **Privately Held**
SIC: 8051 Skilled nursing care facilities

(G-9043)
MANAGEMENT & TRAINING CORP
Also Called: Lake Erie Correctional Fcilty
501 Thompson Rd (44030-8668)
P.O. Box 8000 (44030-8000)
PHONE..................801 693-2600
Fax: 440 599-2704
Teresa Aramaki, *Vice Pres*
Rich Gansheihmer, *Branch Mgr*
R Gansheimer, *Manager*
Paul Sackett, *Manager*
Bill Thompson, *Manager*
EMP: 207
SALES (corp-wide): 667.6MM **Privately Held**
WEB: www.mtctrains.com
SIC: 8744 Correctional facility
PA: Management & Training Corporation
500 N Market Place Dr # 100
Centerville UT 84014
801 693-2600

(G-9044)
MERLENE ENTERPRISES INC
Also Called: Stanley Steemer
734 Harbor St (44030-1839)
PHONE..................440 593-6771
Fax: 440 599-2879
Jeffrey Merlene, *Owner*
Rachael Merlene, *Treasurer*
EMP: 42
SALES: 173K **Privately Held**
SIC: 7217 Carpet & furniture cleaning on location

(G-9045)
ODD FELLOWS HALL
Also Called: Independent Order-Odd Fellows
253 Liberty St (44030-2705)
PHONE..................440 599-7973
Harry Church, *Principal*
EMP: 45
SALES (est): 575.1K **Privately Held**
SIC: 8611 Business associations

(G-9046)
SHELDON HARRY E CALVARY CAMP
4411 Lake Rd (44030-1013)
PHONE..................440 593-4381
Dave Dix, *President*
Tim Green, *Exec Dir*
EMP: 60
SALES: 400K **Privately Held**
WEB: www.calvarycamp.com
SIC: 7032 8661 Bible camp; religious organizations

(G-9047)
SUITE 224 INTERNET
224 State St (44030-2637)
PHONE..................440 593-7113
Tom Ticard, *General Mgr*
Ken Johnson, *General Mgr*
Anne M Zeitler, *Superintendent*
Lou-Ann Wilkinson, *Research*
Daniel Patchin, *Engineer*
EMP: 30
SALES (est): 2.8MM **Privately Held**
WEB: www.suite224.com
SIC: 7373 4813 Computer integrated systems design;

(G-9048)
THE VILLA AT LAKE MGT CO
48 Parrish Rd Ofc (44030-1197)
PHONE..................440 599-1999
Fax: 440 593-1259
Willa Hummer, *Director*
EMP: 65
SALES (est): 793.8K **Privately Held**
SIC: 8059 8052 Nursing home, except skilled & intermediate care facility; intermediate care facilities

GEOGRAPHIC SECTION

Continental
Putnam County

(G-9049)
HOMIER & SONS INC (PA)
Also Called: Homier Implement Company
21133 State Route 613 (45831-8968)
P.O. Box 340 (45831-0340)
PHONE....................................419 596-3965
Fax: 419 596-3964
Raymond Homier, *President*
John Bibler, *Corp Secy*
Dan Homier, *Vice Pres*
Wilfred Homier, *Vice Pres*
EMP: 28
SQ FT: 18,000
SALES: 7MM **Privately Held**
SIC: 5083 Farm implements

Convoy
Van Wert County

(G-9050)
VANCREST LTD
Also Called: Vancrest of Convoy
510 E Tully St (45832-8876)
PHONE....................................419 749-2194
Fax: 419 749-2424
Denise Wehri, *Principal*
Jessica England, *Administration*
EMP: 123
SALES (corp-wide): 16.3MM **Privately Held**
SIC: 8051 Convalescent home with continuous nursing care
PA: Vancrest, Inc.
120 W Main St Ste 200
Van Wert OH 45891
419 238-0715

Copley
Summit County

(G-9051)
ANTECH DIAGNOSTICS INC
1321 Centerview Cir (44321-1627)
PHONE....................................330 665-4996
Robert Antin, *CEO*
Neil Tauber, *Vice Pres*
Tomas Fuller, *CFO*
Kim Calogar, *Manager*
EMP: 26
SALES (corp-wide): 1.1MM **Privately Held**
SIC: 8734 Assaying service
HQ: Antech Diagnostics, Inc.
17620 Mount Herrmann St
Fountain Valley CA 92708
800 745-4725

(G-9052)
APOSTOLOS GROUP INC
Also Called: Thomarios
1122 Jacoby Rd (44321-1758)
PHONE....................................330 670-9900
Fax: 330 253-6424
Paul Thomarios, *President*
EMP: 90 **Privately Held**
SIC: 1721 Bridge painting
PA: The Apostolos Group Inc
1 Canal Square Plz
Akron OH 44308

(G-9053)
BENEFIT SERVICES INC (PA)
3636 Copley Rd Ste 201 (44321-1602)
PHONE....................................330 666-0337
Connie Frazier, *President*
Jerry Newbauer, *COO*
Jeanne Dambrogi, *Director*
EMP: 100
SQ FT: 18,000
SALES (est): 29.4MM **Privately Held**
WEB: www.benefit-services.com
SIC: 6324 Health maintenance organization (HMO), insurance only

(G-9054)
CENTURION OF AKRON INC
1062 Jacoby Rd (44321-1711)
PHONE....................................330 645-6699
Fax: 330 645-0370
James Gebbie, *CEO*
Rich Gebbie, *President*
EMP: 85
SQ FT: 38,000
SALES (est): 3.6MM **Privately Held**
SIC: 7331 Mailing service

(G-9055)
COPLEY HEALTH CENTER INC
155 Heritage Woods Dr (44321-2791)
PHONE....................................330 666-0980
Terri Gironda, *Marketing Staff*
Edward Parisi, *Director*
Alicia Holland, *Administration*
EMP: 170
SALES (corp-wide): 36.7MM **Privately Held**
WEB: www.copleyhealthcenter.com
SIC: 8051 Skilled nursing care facilities
PA: Copley Health Center Inc
155 Heritage Woods Dr
Copley OH 44321
330 666-0980

(G-9056)
DOMOKUR ARCHITECTS INC
4651 Medina Rd (44321-3130)
PHONE....................................330 666-7878
Fax: 330 666-6061
Michael Domokur, *President*
Dennis W Edwards, *Principal*
Jessica Riley, *Bd of Directors*
EMP: 25
SQ FT: 12,000
SALES (est): 5.1MM **Privately Held**
WEB: www.domokur.com
SIC: 8712 Architectural engineering

(G-9057)
KELLEY COMPANIES
Also Called: Northwestern Mutual Life
190 Montrose West Ave # 200 (44321-1372)
PHONE....................................330 668-6100
Donald E Kelley, *Owner*
EMP: 70
SALES (est): 3.4MM **Privately Held**
SIC: 8742 6311 6324 Financial consultant; life insurance; group hospitalization plans

(G-9058)
LEWIS LANDSCAPING INC
3606 Minor Rd (44321-2414)
PHONE....................................330 666-2655
Fax: 330 666-7601
Wilson Lewis, *Owner*
EMP: 40
SALES: 1.5MM **Privately Held**
SIC: 0782 Landscape contractors

(G-9059)
LORANTFFY CARE CENTER INC
2631 Copley Rd (44321-2198)
P.O. Box 4017 (44321-0017)
PHONE....................................330 666-2631
Elizabeth Domotor, *President*
Elizabeth Schmidt, *Administration*
EMP: 90
SQ FT: 19,000
SALES: 4MM **Privately Held**
SIC: 8051 Convalescent home with continuous nursing care

(G-9060)
MARRIOTT INTERNATIONAL INC
Also Called: Residence Inn By Marriott
120 Montrose West Ave (44321-1372)
PHONE....................................330 666-4811
Fax: 330 666-8029
Ray Merle, *Principal*
John Sukola, *Manager*
EMP: 50
SALES (corp-wide): 22.8B **Publicly Held**
SIC: 7011 Hotels & motels
PA: Marriott International, Inc.
10400 Fernwood Rd
Bethesda MD 20817
301 380-3000

(G-9061)
METROPLTAN VTERINARY MED GROUP
Also Called: Metropolitan Veterinary Hosp
1053 S Clvland Mssllon Rd (44321-1659)
PHONE....................................330 253-2544
Fax: 330 666-0519
Sheldon Padgett, *Med Doctor*
James M Sumner, *Director*
EMP: 25
SQ FT: 10,000
SALES (est): 770K **Privately Held**
WEB: www.metropolitanvet.com
SIC: 0742 Veterinarian, animal specialties

(G-9062)
SALON WARE INC
1298 Centerview Cir (44321-1632)
PHONE....................................330 665-2244
Rod Hatch, *President*
Karen Hatch, *Corp Secy*
EMP: 38
SQ FT: 20,000
SALES (est): 6.1MM **Privately Held**
WEB: www.salonware.com
SIC: 5087 7231 Beauty parlor equipment & supplies; beauty shops

(G-9063)
SHELLS INC (PA)
1245 S Cleveland Massillo (44321-1680)
PHONE....................................330 808-5558
Fax: 330 335-1566
Henry C Bray Jr, *President*
Henry Bray Jr, *President*
John Edminister, *Vice Pres*
Toby Neher, *Plant Mgr*
Jama Neher, *Human Res Mgr*
EMP: 75 **EST:** 1972
SQ FT: 85,000
SALES (est): 28.7MM **Privately Held**
WEB: www.shells.com
SIC: 5051 3543 Foundry products; industrial patterns

(G-9064)
SHETLERS SALES & SERVICE INC
Also Called: John Deere Authorized Dealer
3500 Copley Rd (44321-1609)
PHONE....................................330 760-3358
Fax: 330 668-9073
Leonard Shetler, *President*
EMP: 27
SQ FT: 9,760
SALES (est): 2.1MM **Privately Held**
SIC: 5261 5082 Lawnmowers & tractors; construction & mining machinery

(G-9065)
SUMNER HOME FOR THE AGED INC (PA)
Also Called: Sumner On Merriman
4327 Cobblestone Dr (44321-2930)
PHONE....................................330 666-2952
Ted Pappas, *CEO*
Robert D Wetter Jr, *Finance*
EMP: 199 **EST:** 1911
SQ FT: 25,000
SALES (est): 3.4MM **Privately Held**
WEB: www.sumnerhome.com
SIC: 8051 Skilled nursing care facilities

(G-9066)
SUMNER ON RIDGEWOOD
970 Sumner Pkwy (44321-1693)
PHONE....................................330 664-1360
Fax: 330 664-1197
Shane Gabis, *Principal*
EMP: 29 **EST:** 2009
SALES: 31.8MM **Privately Held**
SIC: 8059 Nursing & personal care

(G-9067)
TOWNSHIP OF COPLEY
Road Maintenance
1540 S Clvlnd Mssllon Rd (44321-1908)
PHONE....................................330 666-1853
Al James, *Manager*
EMP: 80 **Privately Held**
SIC: 1611 9111 Highway & street construction; mayors' offices

PA: Township Of Copley
1540 S Clvland Mssllon Rd
Copley OH 44321
330 666-1853

(G-9068)
VETERINARY RFRRL&EMER CTR OF
1321 Centerview Cir (44321-1627)
PHONE....................................330 665-4996
Rod Ferguson, *President*
James Voge, *Principal*
Shaun McWilliams, *Exec Dir*
Bill Weber, *Principal*
EMP: 30
SALES (est): 2.2MM **Privately Held**
WEB: www.akronvet.com
SIC: 0742 8011 Animal hospital services, pets & other animal specialties; internal medicine, physician/surgeon

(G-9069)
WYNDHAM INTERNATIONAL INC
200 Montrose West Ave (44321-2788)
PHONE....................................330 666-9300
Chris Bitikofer, *General Mgr*
EMP: 46
SALES (corp-wide): 75.7MM **Privately Held**
WEB: www.wyndham.com
SIC: 7011 5813 5812 Hotels & motels; drinking places; eating places
HQ: Wyndham International, Inc
22 Sylvan Way
Parsippany NJ 07054
973 753-6000

(G-9070)
YRC INC
1275 Oh Ave (44321-1531)
PHONE....................................330 665-0274
Bill Gordon, *Branch Mgr*
EMP: 250
SALES (corp-wide): 4.8B **Publicly Held**
SIC: 4213 Contract haulers
HQ: Yrc Inc.
10990 Roe Ave
Overland Park KS 66211
913 696-6100

(G-9071)
YRC INC
Also Called: Yrc Ubc Cargo Claim Dept
1275 Oh Ave (44321-1531)
P.O. Box 7903, Overland Park KS (66207-0903)
PHONE....................................913 344-5174
EMP: 35
SALES (corp-wide): 4.8B **Publicly Held**
SIC: 4731 Freight transportation arrangement
HQ: Yrc Inc.
10990 Roe Ave
Overland Park KS 66211
913 696-6100

Cortland
Trumbull County

(G-9072)
ARROWHEAD TRANSPORT CO
2555 Greenville Rd (44410-9648)
PHONE....................................330 638-2900
Fax: 330 638-2806
Robert H Burn, *President*
EMP: 40
SQ FT: 3,000
SALES: 3MM **Privately Held**
SIC: 4212 5032 Light haulage & cartage, local; aggregate; gravel; sand, construction

(G-9073)
BOWERS INSURANCE AGENCY INC
339 N High St (44410-1022)
P.O. Box 280 (44410-0280)
PHONE....................................330 638-6146
Fax: 330 638-8198
Ben Bowers, *President*
Matt Parise, *Partner*
Gene Francisco, *Exec VP*
Dina Hodnicky, *Controller*

Cortland - Trumbull County (G-9074) — GEOGRAPHIC SECTION

Rob Hoy, *Accounts Mgr*
EMP: 30
SQ FT: 4,100
SALES (est): 5.3MM
SALES (corp-wide): 104.5MM **Publicly Held**
WEB: www.thebowersagency.com
SIC: 6411 6211 Insurance agents; security brokers & dealers
HQ: The Farmers National Bank Of Canfield
20 S Broad St
Canfield OH 44406
330 533-3341

(G-9074)
BURNETT POOLS INC (PA)
Also Called: Burnett Pools and Spas
2498 State Route 5 (44410-9339)
PHONE 330 372-1725
Fax: 330 372-1723
Alan Burnett, *President*
Myra May, *Corp Secy*
Gary P Burnett, *Vice Pres*
Holly Hess, *Treasurer*
Holly Burnett, *Personnel Exec*
EMP: 40 **EST:** 1948
SQ FT: 8,400
SALES: 6MM **Privately Held**
WEB: www.burnettpoolsandspas.com
SIC: 5999 1799 5941 Swimming pool chemicals, equipment & supplies; swimming pool construction; pool & billiard tables

(G-9075)
CONTINENT HLTH CO CORTLAND LLC
Also Called: Concord Care Center Cortland
4250 Sodom Hutchings Rd (44410-9790)
PHONE 330 637-7906
Marla Fife, *Business Mgr*
Jessica Hunter, *Mktg Dir*
John Aldrich, *Manager*
Alexander Sherman,
EMP: 50
SALES (est): 1.8MM **Privately Held**
SIC: 8051 Skilled nursing care facilities

(G-9076)
J GILMORE DESIGN LIMITED
Also Called: Green Gate
3172 Niles Cortland Rd Ne (44410-1738)
P.O. Box 400 (44410-0400)
PHONE 330 638-8224
Fax: 330 638-3580
James Gilmore, *Principal*
Michelle Lewis, *Manager*
Sandra Gilmore,
EMP: 25
SQ FT: 8,600
SALES (est): 1.8MM **Privately Held**
SIC: 0782 Landscape contractors

(G-9077)
MARK THOMAS FORD INC
3098 State Route 5 (44410-9207)
PHONE 330 638-1010
Tom Levak, *President*
Mark Makatura, *Finance Mgr*
James Goddard, *Sales Staff*
Robert V Mines, *Sales Staff*
Linda Helmuth, *Office Mgr*
EMP: 45
SQ FT: 27,700
SALES (est): 22.4MM **Privately Held**
SIC: 5511 7538 7532 5521 Automobiles, new & used; general automotive repair shops; top & body repair & paint shops; used car dealers

(G-9078)
MARYANN MCEOWEN
272 Wae Trl (44410-1642)
PHONE 330 638-6385
Maryann McEowen, *Owner*
EMP: 80
SALES (est): 1.5MM **Privately Held**
SIC: 6531 Real estate agent, residential

(G-9079)
MILLER YOUNT PAVING INC
2295 Hagland Blackstub Rd (44410-9318)
PHONE 330 372-4408
Fax: 330 372-3525
Herbert Cottrell, *President*

David A Grayson, *Vice Pres*
EMP: 35
SALES (est): 6.2MM **Privately Held**
SIC: 1794 1771 Excavation work; blacktop (asphalt) work

(G-9080)
OHIO DEPARTMENT TRANSPORTATION
310 2nd St (44410-1539)
PHONE 330 637-5951
Greg Solarz, *General Mgr*
EMP: 45 **Privately Held**
SIC: 9621 7521 Regulation, administration of transportation; ; parking garage
HQ: Ohio Department Of Transportation
1980 W Broad St
Columbus OH 43223

(G-9081)
OHIO LIVING
303 N Mecca St (44410-1074)
PHONE 330 638-2420
Mary Cochran, *Exec Dir*
Troy Snyder, *Exec Dir*
EMP: 653 **Privately Held**
SIC: 6519 Real property lessors
PA: Ohio Living
1001 Kingsmill Pkwy
Columbus OH 43229

(G-9082)
SABER HEALTHCARE GROUP LLC
Also Called: Cortland Healthcare Center
369 N High St (44410-1022)
PHONE 330 638-4015
Fax: 330 638-4628
Dale Sanders, *Administration*
EMP: 36
SALES (corp-wide): 68.5MM **Privately Held**
SIC: 8051 Skilled nursing care facilities
PA: Saber Healthcare Group, L.L.C.
26691 Richmond Rd Frnt
Bedford OH 44146
216 292-5706

(G-9083)
THE CORTLAND SAV & BNKG CO (HQ)
Also Called: CORTLAND BANKS
194 W Main St (44410-1445)
P.O. Box 98 (44410-0098)
PHONE 330 637-8040
Fax: 330 638-3018
James M Gasior, *CEO*
Lawrence A Fantauzzi, *President*
Kennith Stady, *Dean*
Timothy Carney, *COO*
Tim Carney, *Exec VP*
EMP: 100
SQ FT: 22,000
SALES: 28.5MM
SALES (corp-wide): 28.6MM **Publicly Held**
WEB: www.cortland-banks.com
SIC: 6022 State trust companies accepting deposits, commercial
PA: Cortland Bancorp
194 W Main St
Cortland OH 44410
330 637-8040

(G-9084)
TRUMBULL-MAHONING MED GROUP
Also Called: Trumbll-Mhoning Med Group Phrm
2600 State Route 5 (44410-9393)
PHONE 330 372-8800
Mary Younger, *CFO*
Selena Serotko, *Human Resources*
Leonard Kanterman, *Director*
Andrew Marakas, *Director*
Ruth Quarles, *Family Practiti*
EMP: 84
SALES (est): 10.3MM **Privately Held**
SIC: 8011 5912 Medical centers; drug stores

(G-9085)
WIN TAMER CORPORATION
Also Called: Tamer Win Golf & Country Club
2940 Niles Cortland Rd Ne (44410-1734)
PHONE 330 637-2881
Deborah A Rura, *President*
Charles D Winch, *Vice Pres*
EMP: 30
SQ FT: 4,400
SALES (est): 1.2MM **Privately Held**
SIC: 7992 Public golf courses

Coshocton
Coshocton County

(G-9086)
ALPHA NURSING HOMES INC
Also Called: Autumn Health Care
1991 Otsego Ave (43812-9370)
PHONE 740 622-2074
Fax: 740 622-5501
Judy Moore, *Branch Mgr*
Virginia King, *Nursing Dir*
Karri Wisecarver, *Social Dir*
Rebecca Moore, *Administration*
EMP: 100
SALES (est): 1.5MM
SALES (corp-wide): 3.1MM **Privately Held**
WEB: www.alphanursingservice.com
SIC: 8052 8059 Intermediate care facilities; nursing home, except skilled & intermediate care facility
PA: Alpha Nursing Homes, Inc
419 E Main St
Lancaster OH

(G-9087)
AMERICAN ELECTRIC POWER CO INC
405 Brewer Ln (43812-8965)
PHONE 740 295-3070
Bret Berry, *Supervisor*
EMP: 33
SALES (corp-wide): 15.4B **Publicly Held**
SIC: 1731 Electrical work
PA: American Electric Power Company, Inc.
1 Riverside Plz Fl 1 # 1
Columbus OH 43215
614 716-1000

(G-9088)
BORAL RESOURCES LLC
48699 County Rd 275 (43812)
PHONE 740 622-8042
Doug Rixters, *Branch Mgr*
Donna Wright, *Manager*
EMP: 51
SALES (corp-wide): 3.1B **Privately Held**
SIC: 5032 4953 8711 Cement; masons' materials; refuse systems; engineering services
HQ: Boral Resources, Llc
10701 S River Front Pkwy
South Jordan UT 84095
801 984-9400

(G-9089)
BPO ELKS OF USA
Also Called: Brotherhd Frtrnl Ordr
434 Chestnut St (43812-1134)
PHONE 740 622-0794
Beverly Blair, *Manager*
EMP: 25
SQ FT: 4,500
SALES (est): 350.2K **Privately Held**
SIC: 8641 5812 5813 Fraternal associations; restaurant, lunch counter; bar (drinking places)

(G-9090)
CITY OF COSHOCTON
Also Called: Auditor's Ofiice
760 Chestnut St Lbby (43812-1269)
PHONE 740 622-1763
Timothy Turner, *Mayor*
EMP: 100 **Privately Held**
WEB: www.coshoctoncityhall.com
SIC: 8748 City planning
PA: City Of Coshocton
760 Chestnut St Lbby
Coshocton OH 43812
740 622-1763

(G-9091)
COLLEGE PARK INC
Also Called: College Park HM Hlth Care Plus
380 Browns Ln Ste 7 (43812-2075)
PHONE 740 623-4607
Fax: 740 623-4618
Tim Postlewaite, *President*
EMP: 48
SALES (corp-wide): 3.9MM **Privately Held**
SIC: 8361 Geriatric residential care
PA: College Park, Inc
21990 Orchard St
West Lafayette OH
740 623-4612

(G-9092)
COLUMBUS & OHIO RIVER RR CO
47849 Papermill Rd (43812-9724)
PHONE 740 622-8092
Jerry J Jacobson, *CEO*
Mike Connor, *Vice Pres*
Jerry Sattora, *CFO*
Denise Seal, *Bookkeeper*
EMP: 90
SALES (est): 6MM
SALES (corp-wide): 9.9MM **Privately Held**
SIC: 4011 Railroads, line-haul operating
PA: Summit View, Inc.
47849 Papermill Rd
Coshocton OH
740 622-8092

(G-9093)
COSHOCTON BOWLING CENTER
775 S 2nd St (43812-1979)
PHONE 740 622-6332
Fax: 740 622-9336
EMP: 25
SALES (est): 874K **Privately Held**
SIC: 7933 5812 Bowling Center Eating Place

(G-9094)
COSHOCTON CNTY EMRGNCY MED SVC (HQ)
Also Called: Ccems
513 Chestnut St (43812-1210)
PHONE 740 622-4294
Fax: 740 622-4917
Rick Cosmar, *QA Dir*
Todd Shrower, *Director*
Cathy Cosmar, *Admin Asst*
EMP: 50
SQ FT: 2,500
SALES (est): 3.1MM **Privately Held**
WEB: www.cc-ems.com
SIC: 4119 Ambulance service
PA: County Of Coshocton
401 1/2 Main St
Coshocton OH 43812
740 622-1753

(G-9095)
COSHOCTON COUNTY HEAD START
3201 County Road 16 (43812-9123)
PHONE 740 622-3667
Fax: 740 622-0402
Sheryl Hardesty, *CFO*
Suzy Lapp, *CFO*
Patricia Bachert, *Director*
EMP: 38
SALES: 2.5MM **Privately Held**
SIC: 8351 Head start center, except in conjunction with school

(G-9096)
COSHOCTON OPCO LLC
Also Called: Coshocton Healthcare and
100 S Whitewoman St (43812-1068)
PHONE 740 622-1220
Fax: 740 622-6384
Scott Burleyson,
EMP: 99
SALES (est): 2.2MM **Privately Held**
SIC: 8051 Skilled nursing care facilities

GEOGRAPHIC SECTION

Coshocton - Coshocton County (G-9121)

(G-9097)
COSHOCTON TRUCKING SOUTH INC
2702 S 6th St (43812-9776)
P.O. Box 1210 (43812-6210)
PHONE..................740 622-1311
Fax: 740 622-6066
C James Woodie, *President*
Deanna Woodie, *Vice Pres*
Tracy Hunt, *Manager*
EMP: 102
SALES (est): 11.2MM **Privately Held**
SIC: 4212 Dump truck haulage

(G-9098)
COSHOCTON VILLAGE INN SUITES
Also Called: Coshocton Village Inn & Suites
115 N Water St (43812-1004)
PHONE..................740 622-9455
Fax: 740 623-0873
Jennifer Sigman, *General Mgr*
Megan Bradison, *Manager*
EMP: 25
SALES (est): 1MM **Privately Held**
SIC: 7011 7299 7991 Resort hotel; banquet hall facilities; physical fitness facilities

(G-9099)
COUNTY OF COSHOCTON
Also Called: County Engineer's Office
23194 County Road 621 (43812-8903)
PHONE..................740 622-2135
Fred Wahtel, *Principal*
EMP: 30 **Privately Held**
SIC: 8711 Engineering services
PA: County Of Coshocton
  401 1/2 Main St
  Coshocton OH 43812
  740 622-1753

(G-9100)
COUNTY OF COSHOCTON
Also Called: Child Support Agency
725 Pine St (43812-2318)
PHONE..................740 622-1020
Melinda Fehrman, *Director*
EMP: 80 **Privately Held**
WEB: www.coshoctonlakepark.com
SIC: 8322 9111 Child related social services; county supervisors' & executives' offices
PA: County Of Coshocton
  401 1/2 Main St
  Coshocton OH 43812
  740 622-1753

(G-9101)
COVINGTON SQUARE SENIOR APT
380 Browns Ln (43812-2073)
PHONE..................740 623-4603
Tim Omlewey, *Owner*
EMP: 25
SALES (est): 203.4K **Privately Held**
SIC: 8082 Home health care services

(G-9102)
FAMILY PHYSICIANS OF COSHOCTON
440 Browns Ln (43812-2071)
PHONE..................740 622-0332
Fax: 740 622-0335
Jerold A Meyer, *President*
Gloria Jewett, *Manager*
David J Luzowski, *Gnrl Med Prac*
EMP: 28
SQ FT: 2,400
SALES (est): 1.8MM **Privately Held**
SIC: 8011 General & family practice, physician/surgeon

(G-9103)
FRONTIER POWER COMPANY
770 S 2nd St (43812-1978)
P.O. Box 280 (43812-0280)
PHONE..................740 622-6755
Fax: 740 622-0711
Robert E Wise, *President*
Steve Nelson, *General Mgr*
Blair Porteus, *Corp Secy*
Martin Daugherty, *Vice Pres*
John Powell, *Vice Pres*
EMP: 34

SQ FT: 8,000
SALES: 15.4MM **Privately Held**
WEB: www.frontier-power.com
SIC: 4911 Distribution, electric power

(G-9104)
HEALTH SERVICES COSHOCTON CNTY
230 S 4th St (43812-2019)
PHONE..................740 622-7311
Barbara B Emmons, *Director*
EMP: 38
SALES: 2.6MM **Privately Held**
SIC: 8082 Visiting nurse service

(G-9105)
HILSCHER-CLARKE ELECTRIC CO
572 S 3rd St (43812-2057)
PHONE..................740 622-5557
Kellee Slack, *Project Mgr*
Rod Bruning, *Foreman/Supr*
Ted Foster, *Manager*
Brad A Reynolds, *Technical Staff*
EMP: 53
SALES (corp-wide): 48.2MM **Privately Held**
WEB: www.hilscher-clarke.com
SIC: 1731 General electrical contractor
PA: Hilscher-Clarke Electric Company
  519 4th St Nw
  Canton OH 44703
  330 452-9806

(G-9106)
HOME LOAN FINANCIAL CORP (PA)
Also Called: Home Loan Savings Bank
413 Main St Ste 1 (43812-1556)
PHONE..................740 622-0444
Robert C Hamilton, *Ch of Bd*
Kyle R Hamilton, *Vice Pres*
Preston W Bair, *CFO*
EMP: 45 EST: 1997
SALES: 9.6MM **Publicly Held**
WEB: www.homeloansavingsbank.com
SIC: 6162 6311 Mortgage bankers; life insurance

(G-9107)
HOPEWELL INDUSTRIES INC (PA)
637 Chestnut St (43812-1212)
PHONE..................740 622-3563
Fax: 740 622-3531
Diane Williams, *Safety Mgr*
EMP: 150 EST: 1971
SQ FT: 14,000
SALES: 1.1MM **Privately Held**
WEB: www.hopewellind.org
SIC: 8331 7349 2789 0782 Sheltered workshop; building maintenance services; bookbinding & related work; lawn & garden services

(G-9108)
ITM MARKETING INC
Also Called: Intellitarget Marketing Svcs
470 Downtowner Plz (43812-1929)
PHONE..................740 295-3575
Fax: 740 295-3581
Lawrence W Farrell, *President*
Bruce Collen, *CFO*
Suzanne Afterkirk, *Human Res Mgr*
EMP: 124
SQ FT: 10,200
SALES (est): 16.8MM **Privately Held**
WEB: www.itmmarketing.com
SIC: 8742 Marketing consulting services

(G-9109)
JACOBS DWELLING NURSING HOME
25680 Bethlehem Township (43812)
PHONE..................740 824-3635
Huldah Chestnut, *Administration*
Cynthia Trail, *Admin Sec*
Huldah Chesnut, *Administration*
EMP: 30
SALES (est): 294.5K **Privately Held**
WEB: www.supremecouncilhouseofjacob.com
SIC: 8059 8051 Nursing home, except skilled & intermediate care facility; skilled nursing care facilities

(G-9110)
KNO-HO-CO- ASHLAND COMMUNITY A (PA)
120 N 4th St (43812-1504)
PHONE..................740 622-9801
Michael Stephens, *CEO*
Donna Denning, *Director*
John Flexter, *Administration*
EMP: 180
SQ FT: 2,000
SALES: 9.9MM **Privately Held**
SIC: 8322 Social service center

(G-9111)
MCWANE INC
Clow Water Systems Company
2266 S 6th St (43812-8906)
P.O. Box 6001 (43812-6001)
PHONE..................740 622-6651
Fax: 740 622-8551
Frank Eschleman, *President*
Neil Sampsel, *Dept Chairman*
Jeff Otterstedt, *Vice Pres*
Mike Parker, *Safety Dir*
Andy Boise, *Foreman/Supr*
EMP: 400
SALES (corp-wide): 1.2B **Privately Held**
WEB: www.mcwane.com
SIC: 3321 5085 5051 3444 Cast iron pipe & fittings; industrial supplies; pipe & tubing, steel; sheet metalwork; fabricated structural metal; blast furnaces & steel mills
PA: Mcwane, Inc.
  2900 Highway 280 S # 300
  Birmingham AL 35223
  205 414-3100

(G-9112)
MUSKINGUM COACH COMPANY (PA)
Also Called: Eagle Rock Tours
1662 S 2nd St (43812-1950)
PHONE..................740 622-2545
Fax: 740 622-4349
Deborah Brown, *President*
Donna Harber, *Sales Mgr*
EMP: 26
SQ FT: 2,500
SALES (est): 4.6MM **Privately Held**
WEB: www.muskingumcoach.com
SIC: 4131 4724 Interstate bus line; travel agencies

(G-9113)
NOVELTY ADVERTISING CO INC
Also Called: Kenyon Co
1148 Walnut St (43812-1769)
P.O. Box 250 (43812-0250)
PHONE..................740 622-3113
Fax: 740 622-5286
Gregory Coffman, *President*
Mark Clark, *Vice Pres*
James McConnel, *Vice Pres*
Dick Emerson, *Marketing Staff*
Emily Heithaus, *Director*
◆ EMP: 50
SQ FT: 100,000
SALES (est): 10.6MM **Privately Held**
WEB: www.noveltyadv.com
SIC: 2752 5199 Calendars, lithographed; advertising specialties

(G-9114)
OXFORD MIN CMPANY-KENTUCKY LLC
544 Chestnut St (43812-1209)
PHONE..................740 622-6302
EMP: 183
SALES (est): 87.7MM
SALES (corp-wide): 1.3B **Publicly Held**
SIC: 1221 Strip mining, bituminous
HQ: Westmoreland Resource Partners, Lp
  9540 Maroon Cir Unit 200
  Englewood CO 80112

(G-9115)
RESIDENTIAL HOME FOR THE DEVLP (PA)
925 Chestnut St (43812-1302)
P.O. Box 997 (43812-0997)
PHONE..................740 622-9778
Fax: 740 622-4642
Rita Shaw, *President*
Marylin Shroyer, *President*

Kelly Workman, *Manager*
Darla Foster, *Prgrmr*
Michael Dennis, *Exec Dir*
EMP: 172
SQ FT: 1,200
SALES: 8.4MM **Privately Held**
WEB: www.reliabledist.com
SIC: 8361 Home for the mentally handicapped

(G-9116)
ROSCOE VILLAGE FOUNDATION
Also Called: Village Inn Restaurant
200 N Whitewoman St (43812-1059)
PHONE..................740 622-2222
Fax: 740 623-6568
Joel Hampton, *CEO*
EMP: 60
SALES (corp-wide): 968.5K **Privately Held**
WEB: www.roscoevillage.com
SIC: 5812 7299 5813 Restaurant, family; chain; banquet hall facilities; tavern (drinking places)
PA: Roscoe Village Foundation, Inc
  600 N Whitewoman St
  Coshocton OH 43812
  740 622-7644

(G-9117)
SALO INC
232 Chestnut St (43812-1164)
PHONE..................740 623-2331
EMP: 1299
SALES (corp-wide): 24.4MM **Privately Held**
SIC: 7363 Medical help service
PA: Salo, Inc.
  960 Checkrein Ave Ste A
  Columbus OH 43229
  614 436-9404

(G-9118)
THOMPKINS CHILD ADLESCENT SVCS
1199 S 2nd St (43812-1920)
PHONE..................740 622-4470
Fax: 740 622-5580
EMP: 68
SALES (corp-wide): 4.9MM **Privately Held**
SIC: 8093 Mental health clinic, outpatient
PA: Thompkins Child And Adolescent Services
  2845 Bell St
  Zanesville OH 43701
  740 454-0738

(G-9119)
THREE RIVERS ENERGY LLC
18137 County Road 271 (43812-9465)
PHONE..................740 623-3035
Eamonn Byrne, *CEO*
Keith Reuter, *Administration*
EMP: 38
SALES (est): 5.7MM **Privately Held**
SIC: 4613 Refined petroleum pipelines

(G-9120)
UNITED STEELWORKERS
Also Called: Uswa
1048 S 6th St (43812-2804)
PHONE..................740 622-8860
Don Freed, *Branch Mgr*
EMP: 44
SALES (corp-wide): 61.5K **Privately Held**
WEB: www.uswa.org
SIC: 8631 Labor union
PA: United Steelworkers
  60 Bolevard Of The Allies
  Pittsburgh PA 15222
  412 562-2400

(G-9121)
WINDSORWOOD PLACE INC
255 Browns Ln (43812-2063)
PHONE..................740 623-4600
Fax: 740 623-4610
John Humersley, *President*
Robert Guilliams, *Manager*
Stacy Guilliams, *Administration*
Stacy A Guilliams, *Administration*
EMP: 25
SALES (est): 905.4K **Privately Held**
SIC: 6513 8059 Retirement hotel operation; nursing & personal care

Coventry Township
Summit County

(G-9122)
AKRON AUTO AUCTION INC
2471 Ley Dr (44319-1100)
PHONE....................330 724-7708
Fax: 330 773-1641
Jeff Bailey, *President*
Howard Campbell, *Vice Pres*
Gary Listed, *Treasurer*
Mike Waseity, *Manager*
EMP: 116
SQ FT: 2,000
SALES (est): 22.9MM Privately Held
WEB: www.akronautoauction.com
SIC: **5521** 5012 Used car dealers; automobiles & other motor vehicles

(G-9123)
BUCKEYE WASTE INDUSTRIES INC
2430 S Main St (44319-1154)
P.O. Box 1262, Cuyahoga Falls, (44223-0262)
PHONE....................330 645-9900
Fax: 330 645-9474
Gerry Konn, *President*
Diane Miller, *Corp Secy*
EMP: 25
SQ FT: 5,000
SALES (est): 4.8MM Privately Held
SIC: **4213** Contract haulers

(G-9124)
FRED W ALBRECHT GROCERY CO
Also Called: Acme
3235 Manchester Rd Unit A (44319-1459)
PHONE....................330 645-6222
Fax: 330 644-4304
Bernie King, *Branch Mgr*
Joe Lamb, *Manager*
Gail Meadows, *Executive*
EMP: 150
SALES (corp-wide): 339.6MM Privately Held
WEB: www.acmefreshmarket.com
SIC: **5912** 5411 7384 5992 Drug stores & proprietary stores; grocery stores; photofinish laboratories; florists; eating places
PA: The Fred W Albrecht Grocery Company
2700 Gilchrist Rd Ste A
Akron OH 44305
330 733-2861

(G-9125)
HI-WAY DISTRIBUTING CORP AMER
3716 E State St (44203-4548)
PHONE....................330 645-6633
Fax: 330 645-6795
Jeff Hornak, *President*
J L Miller, *Principal*
Joseph P Mueller, *Principal*
Dominic A Musitano Jr, *Principal*
Eric Emerson, *Regl Sales Mgr*
▲ EMP: 60
SQ FT: 48,000
SALES (est): 33.5MM Privately Held
WEB: www.hiwaydist.com
SIC: **5199** 5731 General merchandise, non-durable; sound equipment, automotive

(G-9126)
INTERVAL BROTHERHOOD HOMES
Also Called: IBH
3445 S Main St (44319-3028)
PHONE....................330 644-4095
Fax: 330 644-2031
Deborah Foster-Koch, *Exec Dir*
Father Samuel Ciccolini, *Director*
EMP: 72
SQ FT: 1,626

SALES: 5.7MM Privately Held
WEB: www.ibh.org
SIC: **8361** 8211 Rehabilitation center, residential: health care incidental; elementary & secondary schools

(G-9127)
K COMPANY INCORPORATED
Also Called: Honeywell Authorized Dealer
2234 S Arlington Rd (44319-1929)
PHONE....................330 773-5125
Fax: 330 773-2962
Thomas Bauer, *CEO*
Christopher Martin, *President*
Thomas G Bauer, *Principal*
Jerry L Kriebel, *Principal*
Daniel Bauer, *Vice Pres*
EMP: 110
SQ FT: 43,000
SALES: 35MM Privately Held
SIC: **1711** Warm air heating & air conditioning contractor

(G-9128)
LAKES HEATING AND AC
Also Called: Honeywell Authorized Dealer
2476 N Turkeyfoot Rd (44319-1139)
PHONE....................330 644-7811
Fax: 330 644-8823
Brian F Cuthbert, *President*
EMP: 25 EST: 1974
SQ FT: 2,500
SALES (est): 4.6MM Privately Held
WEB: www.lakeshtg.com
SIC: **1711** Warm air heating & air conditioning contractor

(G-9129)
NEW DIAMOND LINE CONT CORP
760 Killian Rd Ste B (44319-2560)
PHONE....................330 644-9993
Fax: 330 644-2305
Barb Bishop, *President*
Shayne Bishop, *Manager*
Glenn Witchey, *Manager*
Ron Bender, *Director*
◆ EMP: 30
SQ FT: 160,000
SALES (est): 5.2MM Privately Held
WEB: www.diamondline.com
SIC: **5193** Florists' supplies

(G-9130)
OHIO HICKORY HARVEST BRAND PRO
Also Called: Hickory Harvest Foods
90 Logan Pkwy (44319-1177)
PHONE....................330 644-6266
Fax: 330 644-2501
Darlene Swiatkowski, *CEO*
Joseph Swiatkowski, *President*
Michael Swiatkowski, *Vice Pres*
Shellie Beck, *Office Mgr*
EMP: 32 EST: 1972
SQ FT: 32,000
SALES: 17.7MM Privately Held
WEB: www.hickoryharvest.com
SIC: **5145** 5149 2099 Nuts, salted or roasted; candy; fruits, dried; food preparations

(G-9131)
REM-OHIO INC
470 Portage Lakes Dr # 207 (44319-2290)
PHONE....................330 644-9730
Fax: 330 644-6695
Neil Brendmoen, *Director*
EMP: 100
SALES (corp-wide): 2.8MM Privately Held
WEB: www.remohio.com
SIC: **8361** 8721 Home for the mentally retarded; accounting, auditing & bookkeeping
PA: Rem-Ohio, Inc
6921 York Ave S
Minneapolis MN 55435
952 925-5067

(G-9132)
SCHOMER GLAUS PYLE
Also Called: Gpd Group
470 Portage Lakes Dr (44319-2290)
PHONE....................330 645-2131
David B Granger, *President*

EMP: 63
SALES (corp-wide): 93.9MM Privately Held
SIC: **8711** Consulting engineer
PA: Glaus, Pyle, Schomer, Burns & Dehaven, Inc.
520 S Main St Ste 2531
Akron OH 44311
330 572-2100

(G-9133)
STANLEY STEMER OF AKRON CANTON
Also Called: C K M
76 Hanna Pkwy (44319-1165)
PHONE....................330 785-5005
Fax: 330 785-5009
Craig Pucci, *President*
Kevin M Pucci, *Vice Pres*
Melvin Paul Pucci, *Treasurer*
EMP: 30
SQ FT: 3,000
SALES (est): 1.6MM Privately Held
SIC: **7217** 7349 1799 Carpet & furniture cleaning on location; upholstery cleaning on customer premises; floor waxing; post-disaster renovations

(G-9134)
TERIK ROOFING INC
72 Hanna Pkwy (44319-1165)
PHONE....................330 785-0060
Fax: 330 785-0070
Terry Clark, *President*
Eric Gelal, *Vice Pres*
Lisa Raresheid, *Office Admin*
EMP: 30
SQ FT: 4,000
SALES (est): 4.2MM Privately Held
WEB: www.terikroofing.com
SIC: **1761** Roofing contractor

Covington
Miami County

(G-9135)
APPLE FARM SERVICE INC (PA)
Also Called: Apple Farm Service Infc
10120 W Versailles Rd (45318-9618)
PHONE....................937 526-4851
Fax: 937 526-5241
William Apple, *President*
Gary Schumacher, *General Mgr*
Linda Apple, *Corp Secy*
INA Pearl Apple, *Vice Pres*
EMP: 40
SQ FT: 16,875
SALES (est): 22.1MM Privately Held
WEB: www.applefarmservice.com
SIC: **5083** 7699 Agricultural machinery; tractors, agricultural; farm implements; farm machinery repair; tractor repair

(G-9136)
BUFFALO JACKS
137 S High St (45318-1311)
PHONE....................937 473-2524
Fax: 937 473-2425
Jack Maier, *Owner*
EMP: 25
SQ FT: 2,400
SALES (est): 701.6K Privately Held
SIC: **5812** 7299 Family restaurants; American restaurant; banquet hall facilities

(G-9137)
LAVY CONCRETE CONSTRUCTION
7277 W Piqua Clayton Rd (45318-9698)
P.O. Box 9023, Dayton (45409-9023)
PHONE....................937 606-4754
Terry Lavy, *President*
Jane Lavy, *Corp Secy*
EMP: 40
SQ FT: 14,000
SALES (est): 3.3MM Privately Held
WEB: www.lavyconcrete.com
SIC: **1771** Concrete work

(G-9138)
R W EARHART COMPANY
700 Mote Dr (45318-1231)
PHONE....................937 753-1191

EMP: 38 EST: 2016
SALES (est): 1.6MM Privately Held
SIC: **8711** Petroleum, mining & chemical engineers
PA: Mansfield Energy Corp.
1025 Airport Pkwy
Gainesville GA 30501

(G-9139)
STAR-EX INC
1600 Mote Dr (45318-1213)
PHONE....................937 473-2397
Fax: 937 473-3638
Lester Stacy, *President*
Kyla Manson, *Corp Secy*
Gary Manson, *Vice Pres*
EMP: 25
SQ FT: 2,000
SALES: 8MM Privately Held
SIC: **1794** Excavation work

(G-9140)
UVMC NURSING CARE INC
Also Called: Covington Care Center
75 Mote Dr (45318-1245)
PHONE....................937 473-2075
Fax: 937 473-2963
Lisa Cecil, *Chf Purch Ofc*
Julie Young, *Financial Exec*
Brenda Lewis, *Branch Mgr*
Lisa Beanblossom, *Director*
Timothy Schultz, *Administration*
EMP: 103
SQ FT: 30,672
SALES (est): 3.2MM
SALES (corp-wide): 20.3MM Privately Held
SIC: **8059** 8069 8051 Nursing home, except skilled & intermediate care facility; specialty hospitals, except psychiatric; skilled nursing care facilities
PA: Uvmc Nursing Care, Inc.
3130 N County Road 25a
Troy OH 45373
937 440-4000

Creola
Vinton County

(G-9141)
AHOY TRANSPORT LLC
301 E Main St (45622)
PHONE....................740 596-0536
Arretha Hoy, *Mng Member*
EMP: 28
SALES (est): 402.4K Privately Held
SIC: **4789** Cargo loading & unloading services

Crestline
Crawford County

(G-9142)
CONSULATE MANAGEMENT CO LLC
327 W Main St (44827-1434)
PHONE....................419 683-3436
Susan Bacin, *CFO*
EMP: 606
SALES (corp-wide): 581.9MM Privately Held
SIC: **8741** Management services
PA: Consulate Management Company, Llc
800 Concourse Pkwy S
Maitland FL 32751
407 571-1550

(G-9143)
CONSULATE MANAGEMENT CO LLC
Also Called: Crestline Nursing Center
327 W Main St (44827-1434)
PHONE....................419 683-3255
Fax: 419 683-4118
Joseph Conte, *Principal*
Phil Critcher, *Administration*
EMP: 106
SALES (corp-wide): 581.9MM Privately Held
SIC: **8051** Skilled nursing care facilities

GEOGRAPHIC SECTION

Cuyahoga Falls - Summit County (G-9164)

PA: Consulate Management Company, Llc
800 Concourse Pkwy S
Maitland FL 32751
407 571-1550

(G-9144)
CRESTLINE NURSING HOME INC
327 W Main St (44827-1488)
PHONE.................................419 683-3255
Fax: 419 683-3114
Brent Riefe, *Principal*
Suzie Bacin, *Office Mgr*
Virginia Webber, *Director*
Heidi Heiby, *Hlthcr Dir*
Lisa Davis, *Records Dir*
EMP: 50
SQ FT: 20,000
SALES (est): 1.8MM
SALES (corp-wide): 581.9MM **Privately Held**
WEB: www.tandemhealthcare.com
SIC: 8051 Skilled nursing care facilities
PA: Consulate Management Company, Llc
800 Concourse Pkwy S
Maitland FL 32751
407 571-1550

(G-9145)
GOLDEN HAWK INC
4594 Lincoln Hwy 30 (44827-9685)
PHONE.................................419 683-3304
Raymond Miller, *President*
Rhonda Furr, *Accountant*
EMP: 75 EST: 1976
SALES (est): 3.5MM **Privately Held**
SIC: 4212 Local trucking, without storage
PA: Golden Hawk Transportation Co.
4594 Lincoln Hwy
Crestline OH 44827

(G-9146)
GOLDEN HAWK TRANSPORTATION CO (PA)
4594 Lincoln Hwy (44827-9685)
PHONE.................................419 683-3304
Fax: 419 683-3835
Raymond Miller, *President*
Richard Rowen, *General Mgr*
Rhonda Furr, *Accountant*
EMP: 70
SQ FT: 10,000
SALES (est): 10.3MM **Privately Held**
SIC: 4213 Heavy hauling; contract haulers

(G-9147)
MEDCENTRAL HEALTH SYSTEM
Also Called: Crestline Hospital
291 Heiser Ct (44827-1453)
PHONE.................................419 683-1040
Fax: 419 683-7077
Susan Brown, *CEO*
Marte Alsleben, *Finance Mgr*
Carla Pindel, *Manager*
Sally Ingalls, *Data Proc Staff*
Cindy Jakubick, *Director*
EMP: 120
SALES (corp-wide): 3.7B **Privately Held**
SIC: 8062 8093 8049 General medical & surgical hospitals; rehabilitation center, outpatient treatment; physical therapist
HQ: Medcentral Health System
335 Glessner Ave
Mansfield OH 44903
419 526-8000

(G-9148)
MOSIER INDUSTRIAL SERVICES
900 S Wiley St (44827-1766)
PHONE.................................419 683-4000
Rod Mosier, *Owner*
Dennis Hickman, *Project Mgr*
Bill Graaf, *Office Mgr*
Terri Mosier, *Office Mgr*
EMP: 26
SALES: 3.5MM **Privately Held**
SIC: 1795 Wrecking & demolition work

(G-9149)
P-N-D COMMUNICATIONS INC
7900 Middletown Rd (44827-9795)
P.O. Box 956, Galion (44833-0956)
PHONE.................................419 683-1922
Fax: 419 683-0232
Cathy Pollock, *President*
Rick Pollock, *Vice Pres*
Kevin Pollock, *Treasurer*

Ray Canter, *Sales Staff*
EMP: 25
SQ FT: 850
SALES: 1.3MM **Privately Held**
SIC: 5044 1799 Office equipment; office furniture installation

Creston
Wayne County

(G-9150)
HAWKINS MARKETS INC
Also Called: Hawks Nest Golf Club
2800 E Pleasant Home Rd (44217-9434)
PHONE.................................330 435-4611
Fax: 330 435-4511
Chris McCormick, *Manager*
EMP: 30
SALES (corp-wide): 1MM **Privately Held**
WEB: www.hawksnestgc.com
SIC: 7992 Public golf courses
PA: Hawkins Markets, Inc.
2033 Portage Rd
Wooster OH
330 262-4023

Cridersville
Auglaize County

(G-9151)
CRIDERSVILLE HEALTH CARE CTR
Also Called: Cridersville Nursing Home
603 E Main St Frnt (45806-2411)
PHONE.................................419 645-4468
Fax: 419 645-4648
Greg Costello, *Director*
Suman Mishar, *Director*
EMP: 42
SALES (est): 2.1MM **Privately Held**
SIC: 8052 8051 Intermediate care facilities; skilled nursing care facilities

(G-9152)
OTTERBEIN SNIOR LFSTYLE CHICES
Also Called: Otterbein Cridersville
100 Red Oak Dr (45806-9618)
PHONE.................................419 645-5114
Fax: 419 645-5115
Leeann Collins, *Marketing Staff*
Kristen Haer, *Program Mgr*
Adam Neubauer, *Manager*
Tabby Samuel, *Senior Mgr*
Debbie King, *Info Tech Mgr*
EMP: 130
SQ FT: 50,000
SALES (corp-wide): 43.8MM **Privately Held**
SIC: 8361 8051 Home for the aged; skilled nursing care facilities
PA: Senior Otterbein Lifestyle Choices
585 N State Route 741
Lebanon OH 45036
513 933-5400

Crooksville
Perry County

(G-9153)
VALUE AUTO AUCTION LLC
3776 Hc 93 (43731)
PHONE.................................740 982-3030
Fax: 740 982-3055
Adam Metzder, *CFO*
Scott Hamilton, *Manager*
Chris Fahey,
Robert J Fahey Jr,
EMP: 100
SALES (est): 4.2MM **Privately Held**
SIC: 5012 Automobile auction

Croton
Licking County

(G-9154)
OHIO FRESH EGGS LLC (PA)
11212 Croton Rd (43013-9725)
PHONE.................................740 893-7200
Donald Hersey, *General Mgr*
Gary Bethel, *Mng Member*
▲ EMP: 250
SQ FT: 5,000
SALES (est): 24.3MM **Privately Held**
SIC: 5144 2015 Eggs; egg processing

Crown City
Gallia County

(G-9155)
GIORGI OF CHESAPEAKE INC
21019 State Route 7 S (45623-9085)
PHONE.................................740 256-1724
Robert Thoman, *President*
Arno Lucas, *Vice Pres*
EMP: 40
SQ FT: 500
SALES (est): 750K **Privately Held**
SIC: 1742 1761 Drywall; acoustical & ceiling work; architectural sheet metal work

Cutler
Washington County

(G-9156)
ALAN STONE CO INC
1324 Ellis Run Rd (45724-5041)
PHONE.................................740 448-1100
Claudia Staley, *President*
EMP: 40 EST: 1960
SALES: 9.4MM **Privately Held**
SIC: 1771 Concrete work

(G-9157)
ALAN STONE COMPANY
1324 Ellis Run Rd (45724-5041)
PHONE.................................740 448-1100
Claudio Staley, *President*
EMP: 60
SALES (est): 4.4MM **Privately Held**
SIC: 1611 General contractor, highway & street construction

Cuyahoga Falls
Summit County

(G-9158)
AJAX COMMERCIAL CLEANING INC
3566 State Rd Ste 5 (44223-2600)
P.O. Box 4031 (44223-4031)
PHONE.................................330 928-4543
Fax: 330 923-6671
William J Berger, *President*
Thomas Potts, *Sales Mgr*
EMP: 99
SALES: 950K **Privately Held**
WEB: www.ajaxcommercialcleaning.com
SIC: 7349 Cleaning service, industrial or commercial

(G-9159)
AKRON GEN EDWIN SHAW RHBLTTION
330 Broadway St E (44221-3312)
PHONE.................................330 375-1300
William G Frantz, *Ch of Bd*
EMP: 104
SALES (est): 4.5MM
SALES (corp-wide): 8B **Privately Held**
SIC: 8069 Drug addiction rehabilitation hospital
HQ: Akron General Medical Center Inc
1 Akron General Ave
Akron OH 44307
330 344-6000

(G-9160)
ALRO STEEL CORPORATION
4787 State Rd (44223)
P.O. Box 3555 (44223-7555)
PHONE.................................330 929-4660
Fax: 330 929-3936
Todd Rumler, *Manager*
Thomas Saunders, *Executive*
EMP: 40
SQ FT: 77,094
SALES (corp-wide): 1.6B **Privately Held**
WEB: www.alro.com
SIC: 5051 Steel
PA: Alro Steel Corporation
3100 E High St
Jackson MI 49203
517 787-5500

(G-9161)
ASSOCIATED MATERIALS LLC (DH)
3773 State Rd (44223-2603)
P.O. Box 2010, Akron (44309-2010)
PHONE.................................330 929-1811
Erik D Ragatz, *Ch of Bd*
Brian C Strauss, *President*
William L Topper, *Exec VP*
Philippe Bourbonniere, *Senior VP*
Adam D Casebere, *Senior VP*
▲ EMP: 277
SQ FT: 63,000
SALES: 1.1B **Privately Held**
WEB: www.associatedmaterials.com
SIC: 3089 5033 5031 3442 Plastic hardware & building products; siding, plastic; windows, plastic; fences, gates & accessories: plastic; roofing & siding materials; siding, except wood; roofing, asphalt & sheet metal; insulation materials; windows; kitchen cabinets; metal doors, sash & trim

(G-9162)
ASSOCIATED MATERIALS GROUP INC (PA)
3773 State Rd (44223-2603)
PHONE.................................330 929-1811
Brian C Strauss, *President*
EMP: 37
SALES (est): 1.5B **Privately Held**
SIC: 3089 5033 5031 3442 Plastic hardware & building products; siding, plastic; windows, plastic; fences, gates & accessories: plastic; roofing & siding materials; siding, except wood; roofing, asphalt & sheet metal; insulation materials; windows; kitchen cabinets; metal doors, sash & trim

(G-9163)
ASSOCIATED MTLS HOLDINGS LLC
3773 State Rd (44223-2603)
P.O. Box 2010, Akron (44309-2010)
PHONE.................................330 929-1811
Ira D Kleinman, *Ch of Bd*
James Bussman, *Exec VP*
Warren Arthur, *Senior VP*
Paul Pratt, *Vice Pres*
Scott Harcek, *VP Opers*
EMP: 2000
SALES (est): 132.3MM **Privately Held**
SIC: 3089 5033 5031 5063 Plastic hardware & building products; siding, plastic; windows, plastic; fences, gates & accessories: plastic; roofing & siding materials; siding, except wood; roofing, asphalt & sheet metal; insulation materials; windows; kitchen cabinets; wire & cable; metal doors, sash & trim
PA: Associated Materials Group, Inc.
3773 State Rd
Cuyahoga Falls OH 44223

(G-9164)
BARRETT & ASSOCIATES INC (PA)
Also Called: B & A
1060 Graham Rd Ste C (44224-2960)
PHONE.................................330 928-2323
Gerald Barrett, *President*
Gary Roos, *Human Resources*
EMP: 42
SQ FT: 5,220

Cuyahoga Falls - Summit County (G-9165)

SALES (est): 4.3MM **Privately Held**
WEB: www.barrett-associates.com
SIC: 8742 Human resource consulting services

(G-9165)
BECKER PUMPS CORPORATION
100 E Ascot Ln (44223-3768)
PHONE....................................330 928-9966
Fax: 330 928-7065
Dr Dorothee Becker, *President*
Jason Rathbun, *Managing Dir*
Roy Cedarstrom, *Area Mgr*
Steve Gilliam, *Area Mgr*
Josh Lancaster, *Area Mgr*
▲ **EMP:** 46
SQ FT: 33,400
SALES (est): 26.2MM **Privately Held**
WEB: www.beckerpumps.com
SIC: 5084 Compressors, except air conditioning; pumps & pumping equipment

(G-9166)
BIO-MDCAL APPLCATIONS OHIO INC
Also Called: Fresenius Kidney Care
320 Broadway St E (44221)
PHONE....................................330 928-4511
EMP: 25
SALES (corp-wide): 17.5B **Privately Held**
SIC: 8092 Kidney Dialysis Centers
HQ: Bio-Medical Applications Of Ohio, Inc.
  920 Winter St
  Waltham MA 02451

(G-9167)
BRIDGESTONE RET OPERATIONS LLC
Also Called: Firestone
2761 State Rd (44223)
PHONE....................................330 929-3391
EMP: 30
SALES (corp-wide): 35.8B **Privately Held**
SIC: 5531 7539 Ret Auto/Home Supplies Automotive Repair
HQ: Bridgestone Retail Operations, Llc
  333 E Lake St Ste 300
  Bloomingdale IL 60108
  630 259-9000

(G-9168)
CARDINAL RETIREMENT VILLAGE
171 Graham Rd (44223-1773)
PHONE....................................330 928-7888
Fax: 330 928-0334
Scott Phillips, *Partner*
Kim Richards, *Principal*
EMP: 30
SALES (est): 1.6MM **Privately Held**
SIC: 6513 8052 8361 Retirement hotel operation; intermediate care facilities; residential care

(G-9169)
CASCADE GROUP INC
Also Called: Cascade Audi
4149 State Rd (44223-2611)
PHONE....................................330 929-1861
Michelle Primm, *President*
Michael Primm, *Corp Secy*
Donald T Primm, *Vice Pres*
Patrick Primm, *Vice Pres*
Chris Hawkins, *Sales Staff*
EMP: 50
SQ FT: 15,000
SALES (est): 14.7MM **Privately Held**
WEB: www.cascadeautogroup.com
SIC: 5511 7538 5531 5521 Automobiles, new & used; general automotive repair shops; automotive & home supply stores; used car dealers

(G-9170)
CELLCO PARTNERSHIP
Also Called: Verizon Wireless
371 Howe Ave (44221-4900)
PHONE....................................330 928-4382
Fax: 330 928-4850
EMP: 71
SALES (corp-wide): 126B **Publicly Held**
SIC: 4812 Cellular telephone services
HQ: Cellco Partnership
  1 Verizon Way
  Basking Ridge NJ 07920

(G-9171)
CHAPEL HL CHRSTN SCHL ENDWMENT
1090 Howe Ave (44221-5130)
PHONE....................................330 929-1901
Donald Lichi, *President*
Shelby Morgan, *President*
Sharon Ausdury, *Principal*
Everett Prentice, *Treasurer*
Brian Wilson, *Manager*
EMP: 60
SQ FT: 20,000
SALES (est): 2.1MM **Privately Held**
SIC: 7389 Fund raising organizations

(G-9172)
CIRCLE PRIME MANUFACTURING
2114 Front St (44221-3220)
P.O. Box 112 (44222-0112)
PHONE....................................330 923-0019
Fax: 330 923-8249
James Mothersbaugh, *President*
Jeanette Federico, *General Mgr*
Dale Mitchell, *Vice Pres*
Robert Mothersbaugh, *Vice Pres*
Chris Zentz, *Materials Mgr*
EMP: 27
SQ FT: 50,000
SALES (est): 5.1MM **Privately Held**
WEB: www.circleprime.com
SIC: 8731 3672 3812 3663 Commercial physical research; printed circuit boards; antennas, radar or communications; radio broadcasting & communications equipment; electrical equipment & supplies; engineering services

(G-9173)
CITY OF CUYAHOGA FALLS
Also Called: Electric Services
2550 Bailey Rd (44221-2950)
PHONE....................................330 971-8000
Fax: 330 971-8040
Robert L Bye, *Superintendent*
EMP: 50 **Privately Held**
WEB: www.cfmunicourt.com
SIC: 4911 Distribution, electric power
PA: City Of Cuyahoga Falls
  2310 2nd St
  Cuyahoga Falls OH 44221
  330 971-8230

(G-9174)
CITY OF CUYAHOGA FALLS
Also Called: Brookledge Golf Club
1621 Bailey Rd (44221-5209)
PHONE....................................330 971-8416
Fax: 330 971-8430
Steve Black, *President*
Vince Randazzo, *Manager*
EMP: 40 **Privately Held**
WEB: www.cfmunicourt.com
SIC: 7992 9111 Public golf courses; mayors' offices
PA: City Of Cuyahoga Falls
  2310 2nd St
  Cuyahoga Falls OH 44221
  330 971-8230

(G-9175)
CITY OF CUYAHOGA FALLS
Also Called: Water Department
2310 Second St (44221-2583)
PHONE....................................330 971-8130
Fax: 330 971-8129
John Christopher, *Manager*
EMP: 30 **Privately Held**
WEB: www.cfmunicourt.com
SIC: 4941 Water supply
PA: City Of Cuyahoga Falls
  2310 2nd St
  Cuyahoga Falls OH 44221
  330 971-8230

(G-9176)
CITY OF CUYAHOGA FALLS
Also Called: Street Department
2560 Bailey Rd (44221-2950)
PHONE....................................330 971-8030
Fax: 330 971-8028
Charles J Mobak, *Manager*
EMP: 35 **Privately Held**
WEB: www.cfmunicourt.com
SIC: 1611 Highway & street construction

PA: City Of Cuyahoga Falls
  2310 2nd St
  Cuyahoga Falls OH 44221
  330 971-8230

(G-9177)
COMMUNITY HOME CARE
1900 23rd St (44221-1404)
PHONE....................................330 971-7011
Fax: 330 971-7620
EMP: 30
SALES (est): 1.1MM **Privately Held**
SIC: 8082 7361 Home Health Care Services Employment Agency

(G-9178)
DAVIS EYE CENTER
789 Graham Rd (44221-1045)
PHONE....................................330 923-5676
Charles H Davis, *Owner*
EMP: 50
SALES (est): 2.9MM **Privately Held**
SIC: 8031 8011 Offices & clinics of osteopathic physicians; offices & clinics of medical doctors

(G-9179)
DENTRONIX INC
235 Ascot Pkwy (44223-3701)
PHONE....................................330 916-7300
Fax: 330 916-7333
Jerry Sullivan, *President*
Joseph Fasano, *Treasurer*
EMP: 50
SQ FT: 16,000
SALES: 5.5MM
SALES (corp-wide): 169.9MM **Privately Held**
WEB: www.dentronix.com
SIC: 3843 5047 3842 3841 Orthodontic appliances; dental equipment & supplies; surgical appliances & supplies; surgical & medical instruments; analytical instruments; laboratory apparatus & furniture
HQ: Coltene/Whaledent Inc.
  235 Ascot Pkwy
  Cuyahoga Falls OH 44223
  330 916-8800

(G-9180)
DIANE VISHNIA RN AND ASSOC
Also Called: Professional Nursing Service
2497 State Rd (44223-1503)
PHONE....................................330 929-1113
Diane Vishnia Rn, *President*
Patty Genitan, *IT/INT Sup*
EMP: 100
SQ FT: 3,100
SALES (est): 1.7MM **Privately Held**
SIC: 8082 Visiting nurse service

(G-9181)
DOCUMENT TECH SYSTEMS LTD
Also Called: Dts
525 Portage Trail Ext W (44223-2541)
PHONE....................................330 928-5311
Fax: 330 928-5318
Pat Kelly, *Principal*
Mark Milosovic, *Sales Dir*
Jodi Wiff, *Manager*
Nina Aust, *Technology*
Michael Hornsby, *Technology*
EMP: 42
SQ FT: 2,700
SALES (est): 5.7MM **Privately Held**
WEB: www.dts-doc.com
SIC: 7373 Computer integrated systems design

(G-9182)
FALLS FAMILY PRACTICE INC (PA)
Also Called: Falls Dermatology
857 Graham Rd (44221-1170)
PHONE....................................330 923-9585
Fax: 330 923-2290
A Hugh McLaughlin, *President*
EMP: 40
SALES (est): 4.4MM **Privately Held**
WEB: www.fallsfamilypractice.com
SIC: 8011 General & family practice, physician/surgeon

(G-9183)
FALLS HEATING & COOLING INC
Also Called: Honeywell Authorized Dealer
461 Munroe Falls Ave (44221-3407)
PHONE....................................330 929-8777
Fax: 330 929-2171
Larry Burris, *President*
Marge Laria, *Treasurer*
Alex Clause, *Sales Staff*
Paul Burris, *Admin Sec*
EMP: 35
SQ FT: 4,069
SALES (est): 5.5MM **Privately Held**
SIC: 1711 Mechanical contractor

(G-9184)
FALLS MOTOR CITY INC
Also Called: Falls Chrysler Jeep Dodge
4100 State Rd (44223-2612)
PHONE....................................330 929-3066
Fax: 330 923-3294
Paul Hrnchar, *President*
Ron Davis, *General Mgr*
EMP: 50
SALES (est): 20.8MM **Privately Held**
SIC: 5511 7514 Automobiles, new & used; rent-a-car service

(G-9185)
FALLS STAMPING & WELDING CO (PA)
2900 Vincent St (44221-1954)
P.O. Box 153 (44222-0153)
PHONE....................................330 928-1191
Fax: 330 928-1196
David Cesar, *CEO*
Rick Boettner, *Chairman*
Kenneth J Laino, *Counsel*
Charlie Williams, *Plant Mgr*
Kellie Smith, *Materials Mgr*
EMP: 125 EST: 1919
SQ FT: 95,000
SALES (est): 39.7MM **Privately Held**
WEB: www.falls-stamping.com
SIC: 3465 3469 3544 3711 Automotive stampings; stamping metal for the trade; special dies, tools, jigs & fixtures; chassis, motor vehicle; motor vehicle parts & accessories; welding repair

(G-9186)
FALLS SUPERSONIC CAR WASH INC
2720 2nd St (44221-2202)
PHONE....................................330 928-1657
Richard Sengpiel, *President*
Tim Sengpiel, *Vice Pres*
EMP: 25
SQ FT: 4,160
SALES (est): 1MM **Privately Held**
SIC: 7542 Carwash, automatic

(G-9187)
FALLS VILLAGE RETIREMENT CMNTY
330 Broadway St E (44221-3312)
PHONE....................................330 945-9797
Fax: 330 920-6483
Miceahel Francis, *Managing Dir*
EMP: 100
SQ FT: 77,000
SALES (est): 6.2MM **Privately Held**
SIC: 8051 8052 Convalescent home with continuous nursing care; intermediate care facilities

(G-9188)
FIFTH THIRD BANK
4070 Fishcreek Rd (44224-5402)
PHONE....................................330 686-0511
Fax: 330 686-4679
Andrew Karis, *Manager*
EMP: 64
SALES (corp-wide): 7.7B **Publicly Held**
WEB: www.53rd.com
SIC: 6022 State trust companies accepting deposits, commercial
HQ: The Fifth Third Bank
  38 Fountain Square Plz
  Cincinnati OH 45202
  513 579-5203

GEOGRAPHIC SECTION
Cuyahoga Falls - Summit County (G-9213)

(G-9189)
FLYTZ GYMNASTICS INC
Also Called: Flytz UAS Training Center
2900 State Rd Unit A (44223-1299)
PHONE..........................330 926-2900
John King, *President*
EMP: 25
SALES (est): 773.2K **Privately Held**
SIC: 7999 Gymnastic instruction, non-membership

(G-9190)
FRIENDS OF THE LIB CYAHOGA FLS
2015 3rd St (44221-3205)
PHONE..........................330 928-2117
Mary Ann Kenny, *President*
Robert Swedenborg, *Vice Pres*
Deborah Ziccardi, *Treasurer*
Wes Johnston, *Admin Sec*
EMP: 200
SALES: 5K **Privately Held**
SIC: 5942 5192 Book stores; books, periodicals & newspapers

(G-9191)
GARDENS WESTERN RESERVE INC
45 Chart Rd (44223-2821)
PHONE..........................330 928-4500
Fax: 330 928-4900
Steve Tartaglione, *Maintenance Dir*
Toni Cerrito, *Purch Agent*
Rich Piekarski, *Branch Mgr*
Melissa Cook, *Nursing Dir*
Hanna Schindley, *Administration*
EMP: 75
SALES (est): 1.7MM
SALES (corp-wide): 4.4MM **Privately Held**
SIC: 8082 Home health care services
PA: Gardens Of Western Reserve, Inc.
 9975 Greentree Pkwy
 Streetsboro OH 44241
 330 342-9100

(G-9192)
GENERAL ELECTRIC COMPANY
2914 Cedar Hill Rd (44223-1300)
PHONE..........................330 256-5331
EMP: 51
SALES (corp-wide): 122B **Publicly Held**
SIC: 1731 Electrical work
PA: General Electric Company
 41 Farnsworth St
 Boston MA 02210
 617 443-3000

(G-9193)
HANDELS HOMEMADE ICE CREAM
2922 State Rd (44223-1244)
PHONE..........................330 922-4589
Fax: 330 922-4589
Amy Rosen, *Owner*
EMP: 25
SALES (est): 1.4MM **Privately Held**
SIC: 5143 Ice cream & ices

(G-9194)
HOME DEPOT USA INC
Also Called: Home Depot, The
325 Howe Ave (44223-4959)
PHONE..........................330 922-3448
Fax: 330 916-9416
Daniel Berend, *Manager*
EMP: 200
SALES (corp-wide): 100.0B **Publicly Held**
WEB: www.homerentaldepot.com
SIC: 5211 7359 Home centers; tool rental
HQ: Home Depot U.S.A., Inc.
 2455 Paces Ferry Rd Se
 Atlanta GA 30339

(G-9195)
ILLUMETEK CORP
121 E Ascot Ln (44223-3769)
P.O. Box 1147 (44223-0147)
PHONE..........................330 342-7582
Fax: 330 926-8944
James M Pulk, *President*
Roger Griffin, *Corp Secy*
J Anthe, *Vice Pres*
EMP: 26
SQ FT: 20,000
SALES (est): 6.5MM **Privately Held**
WEB: www.illumetek.com
SIC: 8741 Management services

(G-9196)
INTERNATIONAL FRAT OF DEL
2735 Elmwood St (44221-2307)
PHONE..........................330 922-5959
Carla Edwards, *Admin Sec*
EMP: 25
SALES (est): 166.5K **Privately Held**
SIC: 8641 University club

(G-9197)
J&J PRECISION MACHINE LTD
1474 Main St (44221-4927)
PHONE..........................330 923-5783
Fax: 330 923-5905
Hans R Leitner, *CEO*
Hans Leitner, *CEO*
EMP: 38
SALES (est): 7.1MM **Privately Held**
SIC: 3441 7699 Building components, structural steel; industrial machinery & equipment repair

(G-9198)
JPMORGAN CHASE BANK NAT ASSN
2647 Bailey Rd (44221-2272)
PHONE..........................330 972-1905
Fax: 330 972-1842
Tim Bruzeski, *Principal*
EMP: 26
SALES (corp-wide): 99.6B **Publicly Held**
SIC: 6021 National commercial banks
HQ: Jpmorgan Chase Bank, National Association
 1111 Polaris Pkwy
 Columbus OH 43240
 614 436-3055

(G-9199)
JULIUS ZORN INC
Also Called: Juzo
3690 Zorn Dr (44223-3580)
P.O. Box 1088 (44223-1088)
PHONE..........................330 923-4999
Fax: 330 916-9165
Anne Rose Zorn, *President*
Petra Zorn, *Vice Pres*
Nancy Schnarr, *Purch Mgr*
Raymond Gornik, *CFO*
Uwe Schettler, *Treasurer*
▲ **EMP:** 75
SQ FT: 30,000
SALES (est): 31.2MM
SALES (corp-wide): 86.6MM **Privately Held**
WEB: www.juzousa.com
SIC: 5047 3842 Medical equipment & supplies; hosiery, support; supports: abdominal, ankle, arch, kneecap, etc.; socks, stump
PA: Julius Zorn Gmbh
 Juliusplatz 1
 Aichach 86551
 825 190-10

(G-9200)
K H F INC
Also Called: Klassic Hardwood Flooring
3884 State Rd (44223-2606)
PHONE..........................330 928-0694
Fax: 330 928-8499
Thomas Kaser, *President*
Sue Kaser, *Sales Executive*
EMP: 27
SALES (est): 2.7MM **Privately Held**
SIC: 1752 Wood floor installation & refinishing

(G-9201)
KARAM & SIMON REALTY INC
207 Portage Trail Ext W # 101 (44223-1297)
PHONE..........................330 929-0707
Fax: 330 929-0980
John G Simon, *Vice Pres*
Paul Simon, *Director*
EMP: 30
SALES (est): 2.4MM **Privately Held**
WEB: www.karamcompanies.com
SIC: 6531 Real estate agent, residential

(G-9202)
KEUCHEL & ASSOCIATES INC
Also Called: Spunfab
175 Muffin Ln (44223-3359)
PHONE..........................330 945-9455
Fax: 330 945-7588
Ken Keuchel, *President*
Herbert W Keuchel, *Principal*
Richard W Staehle, *Principal*
Herb Keuchel, *Shareholder*
◆ **EMP:** 50
SQ FT: 40,000
SALES (est): 7.8MM **Privately Held**
WEB: www.spunfab.com
SIC: 2241 8711 Narrow fabric mills; consulting engineer

(G-9203)
KYOCERA SGS PRECISION TOOLS
22 Marc Dr (44223-2628)
PHONE..........................330 686-4151
John A Haag, *Ch of Bd*
Richard Tichon, *Manager*
Richard Hunter, *Director*
Stephanie Stuhldreher, *Administration*
EMP: 99
SALES (corp-wide): 78.5MM **Privately Held**
WEB: www.sgstool.com
SIC: 5084 Machine tools & accessories
PA: Kyocera Sgs Precision Tools
 55 S Main St
 Munroe Falls OH 44262
 330 688-6667

(G-9204)
KYOCERA SGS PRECISION TOOLS
238 Marc Dr (44223-2651)
PHONE..........................330 922-1953
David Bradley, *Sales Engr*
Richard G Tichon, *Branch Mgr*
EMP: 50
SALES (corp-wide): 78.5MM **Privately Held**
WEB: www.sgstool.com
SIC: 4225 General warehousing & storage
PA: Kyocera Sgs Precision Tools
 55 S Main St
 Munroe Falls OH 44262
 330 688-6667

(G-9205)
LINDEN INDUSTRIES INC
137 Ascot Pkwy (44223-3355)
PHONE..........................330 928-4064
Peter Tilgner, *President*
Ken Erwin, *Vice Pres*
Bob Hughey, *CFO*
Robert Hughey, *Controller*
Scott Erwin, *Sales Executive*
EMP: 42
SQ FT: 26,000
SALES (est): 9.9MM **Privately Held**
WEB: www.lindenindustries.com
SIC: 3559 5084 Plastics working machinery; robots, molding & forming plastics; industrial machinery & equipment

(G-9206)
M C HAIR CONSULTANTS INC
833 Portage Trl (44221-3004)
PHONE..........................234 678-3987
Fax: 330 945-7170
Marcy Cona, *President*
Carol A Cogdeill, *Corp Secy*
Kathy Casper, *Vice Pres*
Sharon Roberson, *Admin Sec*
EMP: 40
SQ FT: 4,000
SALES (est): 1.7MM **Privately Held**
WEB: www.mchair.com
SIC: 7231 Cosmetology & personal hygiene salons

(G-9207)
MAPLEWOOD AT BATH CREEK LLC
Also Called: Maplewood At Cuyahoga Falls
190 W Bath Rd (44223-2516)
PHONE..........................234 208-9872
Donna Palmieri, *Human Resources*
Gregory Smith,
EMP: 99
SALES (est): 362K **Privately Held**
SIC: 8059 Nursing home, except skilled & intermediate care facility

(G-9208)
MENORAH PARK CENTER FOR SENIO
Also Called: Summit Home Health Care Svcs
960 Graham Rd 3 (44221-1149)
PHONE..........................330 867-2143
Fax: 330 867-2350
Teresa Williams, *Manager*
EMP: 54
SALES (corp-wide): 71.1MM **Privately Held**
WEB: www.menorahpark.org
SIC: 8082 Home health care services
PA: Menorah Park Center For Senior Living Bet Moshav Zekenim Hadati
 27100 Cedar Rd
 Cleveland OH 44122
 216 831-6500

(G-9209)
MICNAN INC (PA)
Also Called: Ace Mitchell Bowlers Mart
3365 Cavalier Trl (44224-4905)
P.O. Box 3168 (44223-0468)
PHONE..........................330 920-6200
David Grau, *President*
Mary E Limbach, *Principal*
Karen Grau, *Vice Pres*
Tanja McCoy, *Office Mgr*
▲ **EMP:** 50
SQ FT: 26,000
SALES (est): 41MM **Privately Held**
WEB: www.acemitchell.com
SIC: 5091 Bowling equipment

(G-9210)
MIDWAY BOWLING LANES INC
Also Called: Acne Bowling Supply
1925 20th St (44223-1966)
PHONE..........................330 762-7477
Richard Ray Stalnaker, *President*
Morris Laatsch, *Vice Pres*
EMP: 25
SALES: 1.3MM **Privately Held**
SIC: 7933 Bowling centers

(G-9211)
MILL POND FAMILY PHYSICIANS
265 Portage Trail Ext W (44223-3613)
PHONE..........................330 928-3111
Donald A Dahlen, *President*
Dawn Hubbard, *Assistant VP*
Mary Rabolinsky, *Vice Pres*
Ross Black, *Admin Sec*
Ross R Black II, *Admin Sec*
EMP: 30
SALES (est): 2.1MM **Privately Held**
SIC: 8011 General & family practice, physician/surgeon

(G-9212)
PETSMART INC
355 Howe Ave (44221-4900)
PHONE..........................330 922-4114
Fax: 330 630-0874
Richard Jacobs, *Manager*
EMP: 30
SALES (corp-wide): 12.7B **Privately Held**
WEB: www.petsmart.com
SIC: 5999 0752 Pet food; animal specialty services
HQ: Petsmart, Inc.
 19601 N 27th Ave
 Phoenix AZ 85027
 623 580-6100

(G-9213)
PRC MEDICAL LLC (PA)
111 Stow Ave Ste 200 (44221-2560)
PHONE..........................330 493-9004
Harry Curley, *President*
EMP: 75
SQ FT: 10,000
SALES (est): 4.7MM **Privately Held**
WEB: www.prcontrol.com
SIC: 7322 Collection agency, except real estate

Cuyahoga Falls - Summit County (G-9214)

(G-9214)
PROSPECT MOLD & DIE COMPANY
1100 Main St (44221-4922)
PHONE..................330 929-3311
Bruce W Wright, *CEO*
Brandon Wenzlik, *President*
Jeff Glick, *Vice Pres*
Jim Vanmeter, *Engineer*
Thomas M Orr, *CFO*
▲ **EMP:** 100 **EST:** 1945
SQ FT: 100,000
SALES (est): 94.7MM **Privately Held**
WEB: www.prospectmold.com
SIC: 5084 3544 Industrial machinery & equipment; forms (molds), for foundry & plastics working machinery

(G-9215)
RIVERSIDE CMNTY URBAN REDEV
Also Called: Sheraton Suites Akron
1989 Front St (44221-3811)
PHONE..................330 929-3000
Fax: 330 920-7524
Thomas J Dillon, *Ch of Bd*
Abe Moses, *President*
Bill Reider, *Regional Mgr*
Brijette Gojkov, *Human Res Mgr*
Michele Ingersol, *Human Res Mgr*
EMP: 180
SQ FT: 255,000
SALES: 11.2MM **Privately Held**
WEB: www.sheratonakron.com
SIC: 5813 7011 5812 7299 Cocktail lounge; hotel, franchised; restaurant, family: independent; banquet hall facilities

(G-9216)
RON MARHOFER AUTOMALL INC
1260 Main St (44221-4923)
PHONE..................330 835-6707
Fax: 330 923-1301
Mike Bell, *Sales Associate*
Ronald L Marhofer, *Branch Mgr*
Chuck Tepus, *Manager*
EMP: 253
SALES (corp-wide): 77.4MM **Privately Held**
SIC: 7532 5511 Body shop, automotive; automobiles, new & used
PA: Ron Marhofer Automall, Inc
    1350 Main St
    Cuyahoga Falls OH 44221
    330 923-5059

(G-9217)
RON MARHOFER AUTOMALL INC (PA)
Also Called: Ron Marhofer Lincoln Mercury
1350 Main St (44221-4925)
PHONE..................330 923-5059
Fax: 330 923-3597
Ron Marhofer, *President*
EMP: 50
SQ FT: 20,000
SALES (est): 77.4MM **Privately Held**
SIC: 5511 7538 7532 7515 Automobiles, new & used; general automotive repair shops; top & body repair & paint shops; passenger car leasing

(G-9218)
RV PROPERTIES LLC
Also Called: Carginal Retirement Village
171 Graham Rd (44223-1773)
PHONE..................330 928-7888
W Scot Phillips, *President*
EMP: 40
SALES (est): 345.6K **Privately Held**
SIC: 6514 Residential building, four or fewer units: operation

(G-9219)
SOUNDTRACK PRINTING
1400 Sackett Ave (44221-2355)
PHONE..................330 606-7117
Andrew Moore, *Owner*
EMP: 125
SALES (est): 3.8MM **Privately Held**
SIC: 5699 7389 T-shirts, custom printed;

(G-9220)
STATE VALLEY DENTAL CENTER
63 Graham Rd Ste 3 (44223-1294)
PHONE..................330 920-8060
Fax: 330 928-5379
Christopher Nassif, *President*
EMP: 35
SQ FT: 3,800
SALES (est): 1.4MM **Privately Held**
SIC: 8021 8072 Dental clinic; dental laboratories

(G-9221)
SUMMA HEALTH
2345 4th St (44221-2573)
PHONE..................330 926-0384
Fax: 330 926-1032
Joseph P Myers, *Vice Pres*
Judy Bishop, *Human Res Mgr*
Lesley Peacock, *Marketing Staff*
John A Fink, *Med Doctor*
Susan M Clark, *Manager*
EMP: 491
SALES (corp-wide): 1B **Privately Held**
SIC: 8049 Occupational therapist
PA: Summa Health System
    525 E Market St
    Akron OH 44304
    330 375-3000

(G-9222)
SUMMIT ENVIRONMENTAL TECH INC (PA)
3310 Win St (44223-3790)
PHONE..................330 253-8211
Mohamed Osman, *President*
Holly Florea, *Project Mgr*
Ron Gibas, *QC Mgr*
Elvin Chavez, *Manager*
Jeff Nottingham, *Manager*
EMP: 50
SQ FT: 20,000
SALES (est): 10.3MM **Privately Held**
SIC: 8734 Testing laboratories

(G-9223)
SUNRISE SENIOR LIVING LLC
Also Called: Sunrise of Cuyahoga Falls
1500 State Rd (44223-1302)
PHONE..................330 929-8500
Fax: 330 929-2090
Bethany Hall, *Manager*
EMP: 60
SALES (corp-wide): 4.3B **Publicly Held**
WEB: www.sunrise.com
SIC: 8051 Skilled nursing care facilities
HQ: Sunrise Senior Living, Llc
    7902 Westpark Dr
    Mc Lean VA 22102

(G-9224)
TECHNICAL CONSTRUCTION SPC
Also Called: Ohio Pressure Grouting
3341 Cavalier Trl (44224-4905)
PHONE..................330 929-1088
Fax: 330 929-1053
Edward R Sheeler, *President*
Jacky Gibsom, *Manager*
EMP: 25
SQ FT: 10,000
SALES (est): 2.6MM **Privately Held**
WEB: www.tcsdivisions.com
SIC: 1741 1771 8711 Tuckpointing or restoration; flooring contractor; foundation & footing contractor; structural engineering

(G-9225)
TESTA ENTERPRISES INC
2335 2nd St Ste A (44221-2529)
PHONE..................330 926-9060
Fax: 330 926-9453
Paul Testa, *President*
Ryan Landi, *Vice Pres*
EMP: 35
SALES (est): 4.4MM **Privately Held**
SIC: 1541 Industrial buildings, new construction

(G-9226)
TRADITIONS AT BATH RD INC
Also Called: National Church
300 E Bath Rd (44223-2510)
PHONE..................330 929-6272
Fax: 330 945-3404
Tom Slemmer, *President*
Joni Dyer, *Personnel Exec*
Betty Bramlett, *Corp Comm Staff*
Carol Campbell, *Director*
Daniel Cannone, *Director*
EMP: 140
SALES (est): 6.1MM **Privately Held**
SIC: 8051 8361 Skilled nursing care facilities; residential care

(G-9227)
TRILLIUM FAMILY SOLUTIONS INC
Also Called: FAMILY COUNSELING SERVICES OF
111 Stow Ave Ste 100 (44221-2560)
PHONE..................330 454-7066
Cathy Trubisay, *CEO*
Scott Erickson, *Vice Pres*
Lisa Garnes, *Vice Pres*
Pam Hendershot, *Accounting Mgr*
Stephen Board, *Exec Dir*
EMP: 100
SALES (est): 2.4MM **Privately Held**
WEB: www.familyservicesinc.org
SIC: 8322 Family (marriage) counseling

(G-9228)
ULTRA TECH MACHINERY INC
297 Ascot Pkwy (44223-3701)
PHONE..................330 929-5544
Fax: 330 923-7527
Don Hagarty, *President*
Jim Hagarty, *Vice Pres*
Robert Hagarty, *Vice Pres*
Dave Monter, *Engineer*
John Monahan, *Design Engr*
▲ **EMP:** 30
SQ FT: 11,000
SALES (est): 7.8MM **Privately Held**
WEB: www.utmachinery.com
SIC: 3599 7389 Machine shop, jobbing & repair; design, commercial & industrial

(G-9229)
UNITY HEALTH NETWORK LLC (PA)
3033 State Rd (44223-3614)
PHONE..................330 923-5899
Robert A Kent, *Principal*
Lori McGarvey, *Office Mgr*
Janelle Van Meter, *Assistant*
EMP: 51
SALES (est): 14.5MM **Privately Held**
SIC: 8099 Blood related health services

(G-9230)
VALLEY VIEW GOLF CLUB INC
3600 Haas Rd (44223-2903)
PHONE..................330 928-9034
Fax: 330 928-0108
Joanne Springer, *President*
Gary Springer, *Treasurer*
EMP: 36
SQ FT: 2,000
SALES (est): 1.5MM **Privately Held**
SIC: 7992 Public golf courses

(G-9231)
VALUE CITY FURNITURE INC
790 Howe Ave (44221-5124)
PHONE..................330 929-2111
Fax: 330 929-0152
Amy Rogers, *Manager*
EMP: 35
SALES (corp-wide): 2.7B **Privately Held**
WEB: www.vcf.com
SIC: 5021 Furniture
HQ: Value City Furniture, Inc..
    4300 E 5th Ave
    Columbus OH 43219

(G-9232)
VIP RESTORATION INC (PA)
Also Called: VIP Building Exteriors Contrs
650 Graham Rd Ste 106 (44221-1051)
PHONE..................216 426-9500
Fax: 216 426-9502
Rick Semersky, *President*

Bethany Friedlander, *COO*
Bethany Criscione, *Treasurer*
EMP: 85
SQ FT: 8,000
SALES (est): 24.5MM **Privately Held**
WEB: www.viprestoration.com
SIC: 1542 1741 Nonresidential construction; commercial & office buildings, renovation & repair; masonry & other stonework

(G-9233)
VISHNIA & ASSOCIATES INC
Also Called: Professional Nursing Service
2497 State Rd (44223-1503)
PHONE..................330 929-5512
Fax: 330 929-7732
Diane Vishnia, *President*
Sandy Moran, *Office Mgr*
EMP: 75
SQ FT: 1,500
SALES (est): 1.7MM **Privately Held**
SIC: 8082 7361 Visiting nurse service; nurses' registry

(G-9234)
W B N X T V 55
2690 State Rd (44223-1644)
PHONE..................330 922-5500
Eddie Brown, *Sales Mgr*
Patty Armstrong, *Director*
Julie Wertheimer, *Admin Asst*
EMP: 50
SALES (est): 4.6MM **Privately Held**
SIC: 4833 Television broadcasting stations

(G-9235)
WALGREEN CO
Also Called: Walgreens
2645 State Rd (44223-1642)
PHONE..................330 928-5444
Fax: 330 928-5300
Monica Allebach, *Manager*
Tara Hubert, *Manager*
EMP: 25
SALES (corp-wide): 118.2B **Publicly Held**
WEB: www.walgreens.com
SIC: 5912 7384 Drug stores; photofinishing laboratory
HQ: Walgreen Co.
    200 Wilmot Rd
    Deerfield IL 60015
    847 315-2500

(G-9236)
WINSTON BRDCSTG NETWRK INC (PA)
Also Called: Wbnx TV 55
2690 State Rd (44223-1644)
PHONE..................330 928-5711
Fax: 330 920-1057
Eddie Brown, *President*
Dave Armstrong, *Prdtn Mgr*
Patty Armstron, *Engineer*
Cori McGowan, *Accounts Exec*
Tony Nichols, *Accounts Exec*
EMP: 50
SQ FT: 10,000
SALES (est): 41.7MM **Privately Held**
WEB: www.wbnx.com
SIC: 4833 Television broadcasting stations

(G-9237)
YOUNG MENS CHRISTIAN ASSOC
Also Called: YMCA Cuyahoga Falls Branch
544 Broad Blvd (44221-3836)
PHONE..................330 923-5223
Adam Clutts, *Exec Dir*
Jill Kolesar, *Exec Dir*
EMP: 60
SQ FT: 36,237
SALES (corp-wide): 16.8MM **Privately Held**
WEB: www.campynoah.com
SIC: 8641 7991 8351 7032 Youth organizations; physical fitness facilities; child day care services; youth camps; individual & family services
PA: The Young Men's Christian Association Of Akron Ohio
    50 S Mn St Ste LI100
    Akron OH 44308
    330 376-1335

GEOGRAPHIC SECTION
Dayton - Greene County (G-9261)

Cygnet
Wood County

(G-9238)
ALABAMA FARMERS COOP INC
Also Called: Bonnie Plant Farm
12419 Jerry City Rd (43413-9749)
PHONE..........................419 655-2289
Fax: 419 655-2696
Tommy Paulk, *President*
EMP: 30
SALES (corp-wide): 12.7MM **Privately Held**
WEB: www.alafarm.com
SIC: 5191 Farm supplies
PA: Alabama Farmers Cooperative, Inc.
121 Somerville Rd Ne
Decatur AL 35601
256 353-6843

Dalton
Wayne County

(G-9239)
A PROVIDE CARE INC
Also Called: Shady Lawn Nursing Home
15028 Old Lincoln Way (44618-9731)
PHONE..........................330 828-2278
Fax: 330 828-2041
David J Lipins, *President*
Reuven Dessler, *Corp Secy*
Nathan Levitansky, *VP Admin*
Steven Murray, *Director*
EMP: 150
SQ FT: 50,000
SALES (est): 12.1MM **Privately Held**
SIC: 8052 8051 Intermediate care facilities; skilled nursing care facilities

(G-9240)
DAS DUTCH KITCHEN INC
14278 Lincoln Way E (44618-9717)
PHONE..........................330 683-0530
Fax: 330 683-3114
Larry Kannal, *President*
Donna Kannal, *Vice Pres*
Dennis Horst, *Controller*
EMP: 70
SQ FT: 9,000
SALES (est): 5.5MM **Privately Held**
WEB: www.dasdutch.com
SIC: 8741 Restaurant management

(G-9241)
GERBER FEED SERVICE INC
3094 Moser Rd (44618-9074)
P.O. Box 509 (44618-0509)
PHONE..........................330 857-4421
Brad Gerber, *President*
Fae Gerber, *Vice Pres*
John Nussbaum, *Vice Pres*
Harley Gerber, *Treasurer*
Michelle Nussbaum, *Admin Sec*
EMP: 45
SQ FT: 250,000
SALES (est): 18.6MM **Privately Held**
SIC: 5191 Feed

(G-9242)
PETER GRAHAM DUNN INC
1417 Zuercher Rd (44618-9776)
PHONE..........................330 816-0035
Fax: 330 857-5455
Peter G Dunn, *President*
Leanna Dunn, *Corp Secy*
Elisa Stoyle, *Office Mgr*
▲ EMP: 50
SQ FT: 36,000
SALES: 9.3MM **Privately Held**
WEB: www.pgrahamdunn.com
SIC: 3499 5199 Novelties & giftware, including trophies; advertising specialties

(G-9243)
WENGER ASPHALT INC
Also Called: North Star Asphalt
26 N Cochran St (44618-9808)
PHONE..........................330 837-4767
Howard J Wenger, *President*
EMP: 35
SQ FT: 6,000
SALES (est): 1.7MM **Privately Held**
SIC: 1771 Blacktop (asphalt) work

(G-9244)
WENGER EXCAVATING INC
26 N Cochran St (44618-9808)
P.O. Box 499 (44618-0499)
PHONE..........................330 837-4767
Howard J Wenger, *President*
Clair Good, *Vice Pres*
Sandra Wenger, *Treasurer*
EMP: 45
SQ FT: 6,000
SALES (est): 6.1MM **Privately Held**
SIC: 1794 1623 Excavation & grading, building construction; sewer line construction; water main construction

---

Danville
Knox County

(G-9245)
CRST INTERNATIONAL INC
16559 Skyline Dr (43014-8620)
PHONE..........................740 599-0008
Glenn Nyhart, *Branch Mgr*
EMP: 54
SALES (corp-wide): 2.1B **Privately Held**
SIC: 4213 Automobiles, transport & delivery
PA: Crst International, Inc.
201 1st St Se
Cedar Rapids IA 52401
319 396-4400

(G-9246)
CUDDY FARMS INC
15835 Danville Jelloway R (43014-9611)
PHONE..........................740 599-7979
Fax: 740 599-6200
Sigrid Boersma, *Manager*
EMP: 36
SALES (corp-wide): 63.1MM **Privately Held**
WEB: www.cuddyfarms.com
SIC: 0254 Poultry hatcheries
HQ: Cuddy Farms, Inc.
2205 Blair Rd
Marshville NC
704 694-6501

(G-9247)
SELECT GENETICS LLC
15835 Dnville Jelloway Rd (43014)
PHONE..........................740 599-7979
Judy Goare, *Administration*
EMP: 42
SALES (corp-wide): 2.2B **Privately Held**
SIC: 0254 Chicken hatchery
HQ: Select Genetics, Llc
1800 Tech Dr Fl 2 Flr 2
Willmar MN 56201
320 235-8850

Dayton
Darke County

(G-9248)
POULTRY SERVICE ASSOCIATES
9317 Young Rd (45390-8620)
PHONE..........................937 968-3339
Fax: 937 968-3331
Don Belt, *President*
EMP: 40
SALES (est): 1.9MM **Privately Held**
SIC: 0751 Poultry services

Dayton
Greene County

(G-9249)
AFIT LS USAF
2950 Hobson Way (45433-7765)
PHONE..........................937 255-3636
Billy Burt, *Principal*
Wanda Markowski, *Analyst*
Marc Shaver, *Instructor*
EMP: 30 EST: 2011
SALES (est): 4MM **Privately Held**
SIC: 5192 Books

(G-9250)
AH STURGILL ROOFING INC
4358 Springfield St B (45431-1089)
PHONE..........................937 254-2955
Fax: 937 254-2956
Allen H Sturgill, *President*
Jeremy Sturgill, *Principal*
EMP: 25
SALES (est): 3.5MM **Privately Held**
WEB: www.sturgillroofing.com
SIC: 1761 Roofing contractor

(G-9251)
AIR FORCE US DEPT OF
4225 Logistics Ave (45433-5769)
PHONE..........................937 656-2354
EMP: 254 **Publicly Held**
SIC: 9711 7372 Air Force; business oriented computer software
HQ: United States Department Of The Air Force
1000 Air Force Pentagon
Washington DC 20330

(G-9252)
AIR FORCE US DEPT OF
Also Called: Naf Wright Patterson Afb
5215 Thurlow St 2 (45433-5547)
PHONE..........................937 257-6068
Ron Canady, *Branch Mgr*
EMP: 99 **Publicly Held**
WEB: www.af.mil
SIC: 7041 9711 Lodging house, organization; Air Force
HQ: United States Department Of The Air Force
1000 Air Force Pentagon
Washington DC 20330

(G-9253)
AIR FRCE MUSEUM FOUNDATION INC
1100 Spaatz St Bldg 489 (45433-7102)
PHONE..........................937 258-1218
Fax: 937 258-3816
Tracy Clifton, *Purch Agent*
Katherine Kirsch, *Purch Agent*
Sarah Shatzkin, *Human Res Mgr*
Kim Pierre, *Sales Mgr*
Bill Horner, *Manager*
EMP: 40
SQ FT: 5,500
SALES: 6MM **Privately Held**
SIC: 8399 Fund raising organization, non-fee basis

(G-9254)
AMERICAN SALES INC
Also Called: A S I
1755 Spaulding Rd (45432-3727)
P.O. Box 1105 (45401-1105)
PHONE..........................937 253-9520
David Goldenberg, *President*
Judith Goldenberg, *Chairman*
Tim Philley, *Vice Pres*
Robert Goldenberg, *Treasurer*
David F Drake, *VP Sales*
EMP: 35 EST: 1908
SQ FT: 18,000
SALES (est): 1.4MM **Privately Held**
SIC: 7215 5087 Laundry, coin-operated; laundry equipment & supplies

(G-9255)
ARMY & AIR FORCE EXCHANGE SVC
Also Called: Wright Patterson Afb Lodging
2439 Schlatter Dr (45433-5519)
PHONE..........................937 257-2928
Mary Drury, *Branch Mgr*
EMP: 150 **Publicly Held**
WEB: www.aafes.com
SIC: 7011 9711 Hotels & motels; Air Force;
HQ: Army & Air Force Exchange Service
3911 S Walton Walker Blvd
Dallas TX 75236
214 312-2011

(G-9256)
ARMY & AIR FORCE EXCHANGE SVC
Also Called: Air Force Morale Welfare Rec
5215 Thurlow St Ste 2 (45433-5547)
PHONE..........................937 257-7736
Ronald Tarmelle, *Branch Mgr*
EMP: 900 **Publicly Held**
WEB: www.aafes.com
SIC: 7999 9711 Recreation services; Air Force
HQ: Army & Air Force Exchange Service
3911 S Walton Walker Blvd
Dallas TX 75236
214 312-2011

(G-9257)
BATTELLE MEMORIAL INSTITUTE
Also Called: Battelle Dayton Operations
5100 Sprngfeld St Ste 110 (45431)
PHONE..........................937 254-0880
Fax: 937 254-8583
Donald Culp, *Senior Engr*
Pam Peets, *Branch Mgr*
EMP: 28
SALES (corp-wide): 4.8B **Privately Held**
WEB: www.battelle.org
SIC: 8731 Commercial physical research; medical research, commercial; environmental research; electronic research
PA: Battelle Memorial Institute Inc
505 King Ave
Columbus OH 43201
614 424-6424

(G-9258)
BRINKS INCORPORATED
4395 Springfield St (45431-1077)
PHONE..........................937 253-9777
Fax: 937 253-2670
Glen Reno, *Manager*
Donna Justice, *Admin Sec*
EMP: 50
SALES (corp-wide): 3.3B **Publicly Held**
WEB: www.brinksinc.com
SIC: 7381 Armored car services
HQ: Brink's, Incorporated
1801 Bayberry Ct Ste 400
Richmond VA 23226
804 289-9600

(G-9259)
BUTT CONSTRUCTION COMPANY INC
3858 Germany Ln (45431-1607)
P.O. Box 31306 (45437-0306)
PHONE..........................937 426-1313
Fax: 937 426-5323
Bill Butt, *President*
David S Butt, *Exec VP*
Chuck Cheadle, *Planning*
EMP: 35 EST: 1927
SQ FT: 4,400
SALES (est): 12.6MM **Privately Held**
WEB: www.buttconstruction.com
SIC: 1542 1541 Institutional building construction; industrial buildings, new construction

(G-9260)
CDO TECHNOLOGIES INC (PA)
Also Called: C D O
5200 Sprngfeld St Ste 320 (45431)
PHONE..........................937 258-0022
Fax: 937 258-1614
Alphonso Wofford, *President*
Don Ertel, *Senior VP*
Greg Greening, *Vice Pres*
Mary L Tingle, *Controller*
Gary B Volz, *VP Finance*
EMP: 75
SQ FT: 6,000
SALES (est): 60.8MM **Privately Held**
WEB: www.cdotech.com
SIC: 7371 7373 Computer software systems analysis & design, custom; computer integrated systems design

(G-9261)
CHILDERS PHOTOGRAPHY
5616 Burkhardt Rd (45431-2202)
PHONE..........................937 256-0501
Fax: 937 252-5111
Charles Childers, *Owner*

Dayton - Greene County (G-9262)   GEOGRAPHIC SECTION

EMP: 30
SQ FT: 1,800
SALES (est): 1.1MM **Privately Held**
WEB: www.childersphoto.com
SIC: 7221 7335 Photographer, still or video; photographic studio, commercial

(G-9262)
COMPUTER SCIENCES CORPORATION
2435 5th St Bldg 676 (45433-7802)
PHONE..................937 904-5113
Donna Klecka, *Principal*
EMP: 50
SALES (corp-wide): 23.5B **Publicly Held**
WEB: www.csc.com
SIC: 7376 Computer facilities management
HQ: Computer Sciences Corporation
   1775 Tysons Blvd Ste 219
   Tysons VA 22102
   703 245-9675

(G-9263)
DAYTON INDUSTRIAL DRUM INC
1880 Radio Rd (45431-1099)
PHONE..................937 253-8933
Fax: 937 253-8656
David Hussong, *President*
Phillip Sievering, *General Mgr*
Ruth M Hussong, *Corp Secy*
Kylene Hussong, *Vice Pres*
David Kotchka, *Sales Associate*
EMP: 25
SQ FT: 25,000
SALES (est): 4.6MM **Privately Held**
WEB: www.daytonindustrialdrum.com
SIC: 7699 5085 5113 2673 Industrial equipment services; drums, new or reconditioned; industrial & personal service paper; bags: plastic, laminated & coated; fiber cans, drums & similar products

(G-9264)
DAYTON POWER AND LIGHT COMPANY (DH)
1065 Woodman Dr (45432-1423)
PHONE..................937 224-6000
Fax: 937 339-8351
Andrew M Vesey, *Ch of Bd*
Tom Raga, *President*
Bryce Nickel, *Assistant VP*
Dave Crusey, *Vice Pres*
Teresa Marrinan, *Vice Pres*
EMP: 200 **EST:** 1911
SALES: 720MM
SALES (corp-wide): 10.5B **Publicly Held**
WEB: www.waytogo.com
SIC: 4911 4931 Generation, electric power; transmission, electric power; distribution, electric power; ; electric & other services combined
HQ: Dpl Inc.
   1065 Woodman Dr
   Dayton OH 45432
   937 331-4063

(G-9265)
DEFENSE RESEARCH ASSOC INC
3915 Germany Ln Ste 102 (45431-1688)
PHONE..................937 431-1644
Fax: 937 427-4526
Leroy E Anderson, *CEO*
Ray Trimmer, *Vice Pres*
Jeanette Anderson, *Treasurer*
Jeannette Watkins, *Human Res Mgr*
Rebecca Trimmer, *Admin Sec*
EMP: 38
SQ FT: 15,000
SALES (est): 5.6MM **Privately Held**
WEB: www.dra-inc.net
SIC: 8731 Commercial physical research

(G-9266)
DPL INC (DH)
1065 Woodman Dr (45432-1438)
PHONE..................937 331-4063
Fax: 937 224-6500
Phil Herrington, *President*
Derek Porter, *President*
Bryce Nickel, *Assistant VP*
Gregory S Campbell, *Vice Pres*
Shirish Desai, *Vice Pres*
EMP: 31

SALES: 1.2B
SALES (corp-wide): 10.5B **Publicly Held**
WEB: www.dpl.com
SIC: 4911 Generation, electric power; transmission, electric power; distribution, electric power
HQ: Aes Dpl Holdings, Llc
   4300 Wilson Blvd
   Arlington VA 22203
   703 522-1315

(G-9267)
DUNCAN OIL CO (PA)
849 Factory Rd (45434-6134)
PHONE..................937 426-5945
Roger McDaniel, *President*
Ryan McDaniel, *COO*
Dan Gose, *Vice Pres*
Jeremy Willman, *Opers Mgr*
Steven Heck, *CFO*
EMP: 28
SQ FT: 5,000
SALES (est): 104MM **Privately Held**
WEB: www.duncan-oil.com
SIC: 5172 5411 5983 1542 Gasoline; fuel oil; convenience stores; fuel oil dealers; service station construction

(G-9268)
EAST DAYTON CHRISTIAN SCHOOL
999 Spinning Rd (45431-2847)
PHONE..................937 252-5400
Stacey Auvil, *Principal*
Stan Ellingson, *Principal*
Rachelle Svoboda, *Business Mgr*
Diane Turner, *Librarian*
Cory Ferguson, *Director*
EMP: 40
SALES (est): 1.9MM **Privately Held**
WEB: www.eastdaytonchristian.org
SIC: 8211 8351 Private combined elementary & secondary school; preschool center

(G-9269)
EVANHOE & ASSOCIATES INC
Also Called: Aidc Solutions
5089 Norman Blvd (45431-1224)
PHONE..................937 235-2995
Charles E Evanhoe, *President*
Anita S Evanhoe, *Vice Pres*
Bob Fudge, *Vice Pres*
Robert Fudge, *Vice Pres*
Dale Kirby, *Vice Pres*
EMP: 25
SQ FT: 6,000
SALES (est): 6.4MM **Privately Held**
WEB: www.evanhoe.com
SIC: 7373 7371 7376 7379 Value-added resellers, computer systems; custom computer programming services; computer facilities management; ; computer maintenance & repair; computers, peripherals & software

(G-9270)
GROVE WALNUT COUNTRY CLUB INC
5050 Linden Ave (45432-1898)
PHONE..................937 253-3109
Fax: 937 253-1260
Robert Reahling, *President*
EMP: 50 **EST:** 1935
SQ FT: 26,000
SALES (est): 1.7MM **Privately Held**
SIC: 7997 Country club, membership

(G-9271)
HEALTH CARE RTREMENT CORP AMER
Also Called: Heartland - Beavercreek
1974 N Fairfield Rd (45432)
PHONE..................937 429-1106
Marilyn Akers, *Facilities Dir*
Sherriann Wood, *Branch Mgr*
Karen Davis, *Director*
Gary Palmer, *Director*
Janice Sherman, *Social Dir*
EMP: 145
SALES (corp-wide): 3.6B **Publicly Held**
WEB: www.hrc-manorcare.com
SIC: 8051 Convalescent home with continuous nursing care

HQ: Health Care And Retirement Corporation Of America
   333 N Summit St Ste 103
   Toledo OH 43604
   419 252-5500

(G-9272)
HIDY MOTORS INC (PA)
Also Called: Hidy Honda
2300 Hller Drv Bevr Crk Beaver Creek (45434)
PHONE..................937 426-9564
Fax: 937 427-5958
David Hidy, *President*
Rita Mayes, *CFO*
Rita Mays, *Office Mgr*
Chris Noland, *Manager*
EMP: 88
SQ FT: 33,000
SALES (est): 31.6MM **Privately Held**
WEB: www.hidyhonda.com
SIC: 5511 5012 7515 Automobiles, new & used; pickups, new & used; vans, new & used; automobiles & other motor vehicles; passenger car leasing

(G-9273)
HILTON GARDEN INN BEAVERCREEK
3498 Pentagon Park Blvd (45431)
PHONE..................937 458-2650
Rob Hale, *Principal*
EMP: 80
SALES (est): 2.3MM **Privately Held**
SIC: 7011 Hotels

(G-9274)
INFOCISION MANAGEMENT CORP
101 Woodman Dr (45431-1422)
PHONE..................937 259-2400
Robert King, *Branch Mgr*
EMP: 182
SALES (corp-wide): 242.3MM **Privately Held**
SIC: 8741 Management services
PA: Infocision Management Corporation
   325 Springside Dr
   Akron OH 44333
   330 668-1411

(G-9275)
INNOVATIVE TECHNOLOGIES CORP (PA)
Also Called: Itc
1020 Woodman Dr Ste 100 (45432-1410)
PHONE..................937 252-2145
Fax: 937 254-6853
Ramesh K Mehan, *President*
Ramesh Mehan, *President*
Jerry Hamilton, *COO*
Renee Mehan, *Vice Pres*
Anita Barrett, *Purch Agent*
EMP: 70
SQ FT: 16,000
SALES (est): 11.1MM **Privately Held**
WEB: www.itc-1.com
SIC: 8742 7375 Management consulting services; information retrieval services

(G-9276)
LANDING GEAR TEST FACILITY
Also Called: Safety and Sustainment Branch
1981 5th St (45433-7202)
PHONE..................937 255-5740
J Greer McClain, *Chief*
Martin Vogel, *Opers Staff*
EMP: 30
SQ FT: 60,000
SALES (est): 1.6MM **Privately Held**
SIC: 8734 Testing laboratories

(G-9277)
MECHANICAL SYSTEMS DAYTON INC
Also Called: Msd
4401 Springfield St (45431-1040)
PHONE..................937 254-3235
Fax: 937 254-4295
Beverly Stewart, *CEO*
John Stewart, *Vice Pres*
Ray Layne, *Project Mgr*
Phil Smith, *Safety Mgr*
Sara Sowers, *Engineer*
EMP: 100 **EST:** 1984

SQ FT: 40,000
SALES (est): 30.7MM **Privately Held**
WEB: www.msdinc.net
SIC: 1711 Mechanical contractor

(G-9278)
NELSON FINANCIAL GROUP
Also Called: Successful Eductl Seminars
3195 Dayton Xenia Rd # 900 (45434-6390)
PHONE..................513 686-7800
William Nelson, *CEO*
Phyllis Nelson, *President*
Ed Severt, *COO*
EMP: 25
SALES (est): 353.1K **Privately Held**
SIC: 7299 Personal financial services

(G-9279)
OHIO ASSN PUB SCHL EMPLOYEES
Also Called: Oapse
1675 Woodman Dr (45432-3336)
PHONE..................937 253-5100
Karen Bosk, *Principal*
Gary Martin, *Associate Dir*
Nina Calabria, *Admin Asst*
EMP: 55
SALES (corp-wide): 9.2MM **Privately Held**
SIC: 8631 Labor union
PA: Ohio Association Of Public School Employees
   6805 Oak Creek Dr Ste 1
   Columbus OH 43229
   614 890-4770

(G-9280)
P E SYSTEMS INC
5100 Sprngfield St Ste 510 (45431)
PHONE..................937 258-0141
Fax: 937 254-0302
Kathy Anderson, *General Mgr*
William Goetz, *Vice Pres*
Kelly Rutledge, *Human Resources*
Larry Bogemann, *Branch Mgr*
Leonard Gulley, *Database Admin*
EMP: 100 **Privately Held**
WEB: www.pesystems-ne.com
SIC: 8711 Consulting engineer
PA: P E Systems, Inc.
   10201 Fairfax Blvd # 400
   Fairfax VA 22030

(G-9281)
PAIN MANAGEMENT ASSOCIATES INC
Also Called: Dayton Outpatien Practice
1010 Woodman Dr Ste 100 (45432-1429)
PHONE..................937 252-2000
Suresh Gupta, *President*
EMP: 30
SQ FT: 36,000
SALES (est): 953.7K
SALES (corp-wide): 287.4MM **Privately Held**
SIC: 8093 Specialty outpatient clinics
HQ: Team Health Holdings, Inc.
   265 Brookview Centre Way
   Knoxville TN 37919
   865 693-1000

(G-9282)
RXOC INFORMATION OPERATIONS
2977 Hobson Way (45433-7733)
PHONE..................937 255-1151
Brian A Stucke, *Manager*
EMP: 32 **EST:** 2011
SALES (est): 508.4K **Privately Held**
SIC: 8999 Information bureau

(G-9283)
S & S REAL ESTATE MANAGERS LLC
4996 Woodman Park Dr # 13 (45432-1244)
PHONE..................937 256-7000
Stephany Warren, *Accountant*
Traci Monhollen,
EMP: 62
SALES (est): 2.8MM **Privately Held**
SIC: 6531 Real estate managers

GEOGRAPHIC SECTION
Dayton - Montgomery County (G-9308)

(G-9284)
SUPERIOR MECHANICAL SVCS INC
Also Called: Honeywell Authorized Dealer
3100 Plainfield Rd Ste C (45432-3725)
PHONE 937 259-0082
Fax: 937 259-0700
Steve Heidenreich, *President*
Mark Rath, *Vice Pres*
David Heidenreich, *Admin Sec*
Theresa Rosenthal, *Admin Asst*
EMP: 26
SQ FT: 6,000
SALES (est): 4.4MM **Privately Held**
SIC: **1711** 8711 Warm air heating & air conditioning contractor; ventilation & duct work contractor; mechanical contractor; engineering services

(G-9285)
UNISON INDUSTRIES LLC
Elano Div
2455 Dayton Xenia Rd (45434-7148)
PHONE 937 426-0621
Fax: 937 427-0288
Tim Hudson, *General Mgr*
Linda Revis, *Materials Mgr*
Corrie Burgess, *Senior Buyer*
Jessica Haines, *Buyer*
Alex Byrd, *Engineer*
EMP: 400
SALES (corp-wide): 122B **Publicly Held**
WEB: www.unisonindustries.com
SIC: **3728** 4581 3714 3498 Aircraft parts & equipment; aircraft servicing & repairing; motor vehicle parts & accessories; fabricated pipe & fittings; steel pipe & tubes
HQ: Unison Industries, Llc
 7575 Baymeadows Way
 Jacksonville FL 32256
 904 739-4000

(G-9286)
UNITED STATES DEPT OF NAVY
Also Called: Namru-Dayton
2624 Q St Bldg 851 Area B (45433)
PHONE 937 938-3926
Rees Lee, *President*
Keith Wallace, *Purch Mgr*
Nicholas Roberts, *Persnl Mgr*
EMP: 40 **Publicly Held**
SIC: **9711** 8733 Navy; ; medical research
HQ: United States Department Of The Navy
 1200 Navy Pentagon
 Washington DC 20350

(G-9287)
US DEPT OF THE AIR FORCE
Also Called: Usaf-Medical Center
4881 Sug Mple Dr Bldg 830 (45433)
PHONE 937 257-0837
Fax: 937 656-1102
Gary Walker, *Branch Mgr*
Peter H Mason, *Podiatrist*
James T Dunlap, *Surgeon*
Eric W Fester, *Surgeon*
Paul D Gleason, *Surgeon*
EMP: 90 **Publicly Held**
WEB: www.af.mil
SIC: **8011** 9711 Offices & clinics of medical doctors; Air Force;
HQ: United States Department Of The Air Force
 1000 Air Force Pentagon
 Washington DC 20330

(G-9288)
US DEPT OF THE AIR FORCE
2856 G St (45433-7400)
PHONE 937 255-5150
Richarard Stotts, *Director*
EMP: 391 **Publicly Held**
WEB: www.af.mil
SIC: **8733** 9711 Medical research; Air Force
HQ: United States Department Of The Air Force
 1000 Air Force Pentagon
 Washington DC 20330

(G-9289)
USAF SCTT
4180 Watson Way (45433-5648)
PHONE 937 257-0228
Beverly Brown, *Principal*

Steven Rice, *Engineer*
EMP: 31
SALES (est): 2.3MM **Privately Held**
SIC: **8711** Engineering services

(G-9290)
WRIGHT STATE UNIVERSITY
Also Called: Mini University
3640 Colonel Glenn Hwy (45435-0002)
PHONE 937 775-4070
Fax: 937 775-2832
Kevin Lorson, *Vice Chairman*
James Tomlin, *Opers Staff*
Ran Raider, *Manager*
Camy Scheffield, *Director*
James Brown, *Director*
EMP: 30
SQ FT: 8,982
SALES (corp-wide): 238.1MM **Privately Held**
SIC: **8351** Child day care services
PA: Wright State University
 3640 Colonel Glenn Hwy
 Dayton OH 45435
 937 775-3333

Dayton
Montgomery County

(G-9291)
10 WILMINGTON PLACE
10 Wilmington Ave (45420-1877)
PHONE 937 253-1010
Fax: 937 253-3982
Barry Humphries, *Owner*
Barry Humprys, *Manager*
EMP: 90
SQ FT: 300,000
SALES (est): 5.5MM **Privately Held**
WEB: www.10wilmingtonplace.com
SIC: **8051** 8052 Skilled nursing care facilities; intermediate care facilities

(G-9292)
1ST ADVNCE SEC INVSTGTIONS INC
111 W 1st St Ste 101 (45402-1137)
P.O. Box 61128 (45406-9128)
PHONE 937 317-4433
Darryl Johnson, *President*
EMP: 49 EST: 2013
SALES (est): 281.9K **Privately Held**
SIC: **7381** 8742 Guard services; training & development consultant

(G-9293)
5440 CHARLESGATE RD OPER LLC
Also Called: Rehab & Nursing Ctr Sprng Crk
5440 Charlesgate Rd (45424-1049)
PHONE 937 236-6707
Elizabeth Toohill, *Director*
EMP: 80
SALES (est): 2.2MM **Privately Held**
SIC: **8051** Skilled nursing care facilities

(G-9294)
6TH CIRCUIT COURT
Also Called: US Federal District Court
200 W 2nd St Ste 702 (45402-1472)
PHONE 614 719-3100
Larry England, *Manager*
Tracey Whibb, *Officer*
EMP: 25 **Publicly Held**
WEB: www.mied.uscourts.gov
SIC: **9211** 8322 Federal courts; ; probation office
HQ: 6th Circuit Court
 601 W Broadway Bsmt
 Louisville KY 40202
 502 625-3800

(G-9295)
7NT ENTERPRISES LLC (PA)
531 E 3rd St (45402-2280)
PHONE 937 435-3200
Pratap Rajadhyaksha, *CEO*
Travis Burr, *COO*
Rose O'Grady, *Office Mgr*
EMP: 45
SALES (est): 2MM **Privately Held**
SIC: **8711** 8713 Engineering services; surveying services

(G-9296)
A & D DAYCARE AND LEARNING CTR
1049 Infirmary Rd (45417-5450)
PHONE 937 263-4447
Andrew Peterson, *President*
Dorothy Peterson, *Vice Pres*
EMP: 30
SALES (est): 1.1MM **Privately Held**
SIC: **8351** Preschool center

(G-9297)
A B S TEMPS INC
2770 Wilmington Pike (45419-2141)
PHONE 937 252-9888
Fax: 937 252-9869
Mike Nicks, *President*
EMP: 25
SALES (est): 1MM **Privately Held**
SIC: **7363** Temporary help service

(G-9298)
A PLUS EXPEDITING & LOGISTICS
2947 Boulder Ave (45414-4846)
P.O. Box 570 (45404-0570)
PHONE 937 424-0220
Billy E Back, *President*
Betty Jones, *Manager*
EMP: 32
SALES (est): 3.5MM **Privately Held**
SIC: **4214** Local trucking with storage

(G-9299)
A TO Z GOLF MANAGMENT CO
Also Called: Rollandia Golf & Magic Castle
4990 Wilmington Pike (45440-2100)
PHONE 937 434-4911
Zachary Fink, *Owner*
Cindy Cook, *Office Mgr*
EMP: 30
SALES (est): 1.3MM **Privately Held**
WEB: www.gorollandia.com
SIC: **7929** 7992 Entertainment service; public golf courses

(G-9300)
AAA MIAMI VALLEY (PA)
Also Called: AAA Travel Agency
825 S Ludlow St (45402-2612)
P.O. Box 1801 (45401-1801)
PHONE 937 224-2896
Fax: 937 224-2890
Gus Geil, *Ch of Bd*
John E Horn, *Vice Ch Bd*
Raymond Keyton, *President*
James Moses, *CFO*
Witt Darner, *Treasurer*
EMP: 80 EST: 1920
SQ FT: 15,000
SALES (est): 28.9MM **Privately Held**
WEB: www.aaamiamivalley.com
SIC: **4724** 8699 Travel agencies; automobile owners' association

(G-9301)
ABF FREIGHT SYSTEM INC
8051 Center Point 70 Blvd (45424-6374)
PHONE 937 236-2210
Fax: 937 237-0932
Nick Dinapoli, *President*
Tim Magoto, *Sales/Mktg Mgr*
Dayna Slutterbeck, *Accounts Mgr*
EMP: 28
SALES (corp-wide): 2.8B **Publicly Held**
WEB: www.abfs.com
SIC: **4213** Contract haulers
HQ: Abf Freight System, Inc.
 3801 Old Greenwood Rd
 Fort Smith AR 72903
 479 785-8700

(G-9302)
ABM PARKING SERVICES INC
40 N Main St Ste 1540 (45423-1043)
PHONE 937 461-2113
Fax: 937 461-2958
Alan Barnett, *Manager*
EMP: 30
SALES (corp-wide): 5.4B **Publicly Held**
WEB: www.meyers.net
SIC: **7521** Parking lots

HQ: Abm Parking Services, Inc.
 1150 S Olive St Fl 19
 Los Angeles CA 90015
 213 284-7600

(G-9303)
ACCESS CLEANING SERVICE INC
5045 N Main St Ste 100 (45415-3637)
P.O. Box 5782 (45405-0782)
PHONE 937 276-2605
Fax: 937 276-5199
Spencer L Johnson, *President*
Cynthia Johnson, *Admin Sec*
EMP: 46
SQ FT: 1,600
SALES (est): 1.1MM **Privately Held**
SIC: **7349** Janitorial service, contract basis

(G-9304)
ACCESS HOME CARE LLC
2555 S Dixie Dr Ste 100 (45409-1532)
PHONE 937 224-9991
Michael Biggs, *Mng Member*
EMP: 40
SALES (est): 1.2MM **Privately Held**
SIC: **8059** 4789 Personal care home, with health care; transportation services

(G-9305)
ACCURATE LUBR & MET WKG FLUIDS (PA)
Also Called: Acculube
403 Homestead Ave (45417-3921)
P.O. Box 3807 (45401-3807)
PHONE 937 461-9906
Fax: 937 461-9917
Marilyn Kinne, *President*
Chris Fisk, *Vice Pres*
Kyle Morison, *Vice Pres*
Jay E Webb, *Vice Pres*
Ryan Welborn, *Sales Mgr*
EMP: 39
SQ FT: 80,000
SALES (est): 17.3MM **Privately Held**
WEB: www.acculube.com
SIC: **5169** 5172 Industrial chemicals; lubricating oils & greases

(G-9306)
ACUREN INSPECTION INC
705 Albany St (45417-3460)
PHONE 937 228-9729
Jim Bailey, *President*
Ricki Miller, *Controller*
EMP: 52
SALES (corp-wide): 1.6B **Privately Held**
SIC: **1389** Testing, measuring, surveying & analysis services
HQ: Acuren Inspection, Inc.
 30 Main St Ste 402
 Danbury CT 06810
 203 702-8740

(G-9307)
ACUREN INSPECTION INC
Also Called: Eastern Region Department
7333 Paragon Rd Ste 240 (45459-4157)
PHONE 937 228-9729
Ricki Miller, *Branch Mgr*
EMP: 50
SALES (corp-wide): 1.6B **Privately Held**
SIC: **7389** Inspection & testing services
HQ: Acuren Inspection, Inc.
 30 Main St Ste 402
 Danbury CT 06810
 203 702-8740

(G-9308)
ADAMS-ROBINSON ENTERPRISES INC (PA)
Also Called: Adams Robinson Construction
2735 Needmore Rd (45414-4207)
PHONE 937 274-5318
Fax: 937 274-0836
Michael Adams, *CEO*
Mark Harris, *Superintendent*
M Bradley Adams, *Vice Pres*
Patrick Ludwig, *Project Mgr*
Chris Rahtes, *Project Mgr*
EMP: 150
SQ FT: 10,324
SALES (est): 93.9MM **Privately Held**
SIC: **1623** Water, sewer & utility lines

Dayton - Montgomery County (G-9309)

(G-9309)
ADVANCE HOME CARE LLC
1250 W Dorothy Ln (45409-1317)
PHONE 937 723-6335
Karima Moudjud, *Branch Mgr*
EMP: 60
SALES (corp-wide): 1.6MM **Privately Held**
SIC: 8082 Home health care services
PA: Advance Home Care Llc
 1191 S James Rd Ste D
 Columbus OH 43227
 614 436-3611

(G-9310)
ADVANCED TOOL & SUPPLY INC
4530 Wadsworth Rd (45414-4226)
PHONE 937 278-7337
Charles Allen, *President*
Robert Wall, *Treasurer*
EMP: 48
SQ FT: 120,000
SALES: 7.6MM **Privately Held**
SIC: 5085 5084 1796 Industrial supplies; machine tools & accessories; machine moving & rigging

(G-9311)
AECOM GLOBAL II LLC
7333 Paragon Rd Ste 175 (45459-4173)
PHONE 937 233-1230
Fax: 937 436-7403
Tim Koch, *Principal*
EMP: 35
SALES (corp-wide): 18.2B **Publicly Held**
WEB: www.wcc.com
SIC: 8711 Consulting engineer
HQ: Aecom Global Ii, Llc
 1999 Avenue Of The Stars
 Los Angeles CA 90067
 213 593-8100

(G-9312)
AETNA BUILDING MAINTENANCE INC
2044 Wayne Ave (45410-2140)
PHONE 866 238-6201
Hugh Bledle, *Manager*
EMP: 130
SALES (corp-wide): 17.6MM **Privately Held**
WEB: www.aetnabuilding.com
SIC: 7349 Janitorial service, contract basis
HQ: Aetna Building Maintenance, Inc.
 646 Parsons Ave
 Columbus OH 43206
 614 476-1818

(G-9313)
AHF OHIO INC
264 Wilmington Ave (45420-1989)
PHONE 937 256-4663
Rick Cordonnier, *Administration*
EMP: 89
SALES (corp-wide): 21MM **Privately Held**
SIC: 8051 8361 Skilled nursing care facilities; residential care
PA: Ahf Ohio, Inc.
 5920 Venture Dr Ste 100
 Dublin OH 43017
 614 760-7352

(G-9314)
ALCOHOL DRUG ADDCTION & MENTAL
Also Called: Adamhs Bd For Montgomery Cnty
409 E Monument Ave # 102 (45402-1482)
PHONE 937 443-0416
Fax: 937 461-2204
Helen Jones-Kelley, *CEO*
Jonathan Parks, *CFO*
Joseph Szoke, *Exec Dir*
Larry Akers, *Director*
Andrea Doolittle, *Director*
EMP: 30
SALES: 40MM **Privately Held**
WEB: www.adamhs.co.montgomery.oh.us
SIC: 8069 8093 Drug addiction rehabilitation hospital; mental health clinic, outpatient

(G-9315)
ALL ABOUT HOME CARE SVCS LLC
1307 E 3rd St (45403-1816)
PHONE 937 222-2980
Patty L Shepherd,
EMP: 37
SALES (est): 256.3K **Privately Held**
SIC: 8082 Home health care services

(G-9316)
ALLIED BUILDERS INC (PA)
Also Called: Allied Fence Builders
1644 Kuntz Rd (45404-1234)
P.O. Box 94 (45404-0094)
PHONE 937 226-0311
Fax: 937 236-8747
Linda S Helton, *President*
Bill Helton Jr, *Vice Pres*
EMP: 47
SQ FT: 25,500
SALES: 4.5MM **Privately Held**
WEB: www.allied-fence.com
SIC: 1799 Fence construction

(G-9317)
ALLIED SUPPLY COMPANY INC (PA)
Also Called: Johnson Contrls Authorized Dlr
1100 E Monument Ave (45402-1343)
PHONE 937 224-9833
Fax: 937 224-5648
William V Homan, *Ch of Bd*
Thomas E Homan, *President*
Craig Anderson, *General Mgr*
J W Van De Grift, *Principal*
Ryan Courtney, *Warehouse Mgr*
EMP: 40 EST: 1948
SQ FT: 65,000
SALES (est): 33.1MM **Privately Held**
WEB: www.alliedsupply.com
SIC: 5078 5075 5085 Refrigeration equipment & supplies; warm air heating equipment & supplies; air conditioning & ventilation equipment & supplies; mill supplies

(G-9318)
ALLIED WASTE SYSTEMS INC
Dempsey Waste Systems
1577 W River Rd (45417-6740)
PHONE 937 268-8110
Fax: 937 268-6407
Mark E Crowe, *Sales/Mktg Mgr*
EMP: 35
SQ FT: 25,000
SALES (corp-wide): 10B **Publicly Held**
SIC: 4953 Refuse collection & disposal services
HQ: Allied Waste Systems, Inc.
 18500 N Allied Way # 100
 Phoenix AZ 85054
 480 627-2700

(G-9319)
ALLOYD INSULATION CO INC
5734 Webster St (45414-3521)
P.O. Box 13299 (45413-0299)
PHONE 937 890-7900
Fax: 937 890-6223
Thomas Wolfe, *President*
Martha Wolfe, *Vice Pres*
Dave Schenck, *Project Mgr*
Tom Wills, *Project Mgr*
Kirk Crafton, *Opers Mgr*
EMP: 25
SQ FT: 30,000
SALES (est): 3.2MM **Privately Held**
WEB: www.alloydco.com
SIC: 1799 Insulation of pipes & boilers

(G-9320)
ALPHA & OMEGA BLDG SVCS INC
1529 Brown St Rm 223 (45469-3401)
PHONE 937 229-3536
Mike Crotty, *Vice Pres*
EMP: 74
SALES (corp-wide): 9.5MM **Privately Held**
WEB: www.aobuildingservices.com
SIC: 7349 Building maintenance, except repairs
PA: Alpha & Omega Building Services, Inc.
 2843 Culver Ave Ste B
 Dayton OH 45429
 937 298-2125

(G-9321)
ALPHA & OMEGA BLDG SVCS INC (PA)
2843 Culver Ave Ste B (45429-3720)
PHONE 937 298-2125
James Baker, *President*
Cindy Landerer, *Treasurer*
EMP: 300
SQ FT: 7,000
SALES (est): 9.5MM **Privately Held**
WEB: www.aobuildingservices.com
SIC: 7349 Janitorial service, contract basis

(G-9322)
ALPHA MEDIA LLC
Also Called: Wing-FM
717 E David Rd (45429-5218)
PHONE 937 294-5858
Fax: 937 297-5233
John King, *General Mgr*
Ryan Osborne, *General Mgr*
Jim Richards, *Sales Mgr*
Jamey Zell, *CTO*
Mark Neal, *Director*
EMP: 40 **Privately Held**
SIC: 4832 Radio broadcasting stations
PA: Alpha Media Llc
 1211 Sw 5th Ave Ste 600
 Portland OR 97204

(G-9323)
ALRO STEEL CORPORATION
Also Called: Arlo Aluminum & Steel
821 Springfield St (45403-1252)
PHONE 937 253-6121
Fax: 937 253-6126
Tim Elliott, *Manager*
David Zontek, *Manager*
EMP: 40
SQ FT: 120,000
SALES (corp-wide): 1.6B **Privately Held**
WEB: www.alro.com
SIC: 5051 3441 3317 3316 Steel; fabricated structural metal; steel pipe & tubes; cold finishing of steel shapes; blast furnaces & steel mills
PA: Alro Steel Corporation
 3100 E High St
 Jackson MI 49203
 517 787-5500

(G-9324)
ALTERNATE SLTIONS PRIVATE DUTY (PA)
1251 E Dorothy Ln (45419-2106)
PHONE 937 298-1111
David Ganzsarto, *CEO*
Chad Creech, *Opers Staff*
Steve Helton, *Controller*
EMP: 70
SALES (est): 1.8MM **Privately Held**
WEB: www.ashomecare.com
SIC: 8082 Home health care services

(G-9325)
ALTERNATE SOLUTIONS FIRST LLC
1251 E Dorothy Ln (45419-2106)
PHONE 937 298-1111
Fax: 937 298-7210
David Ganzsarto,
EMP: 200
SQ FT: 2,000
SALES: 1MM **Privately Held**
SIC: 8082 7361 Home health care services; nurses' registry

(G-9326)
ALTERNATE SOLUTIONS HEALTHCARE
1050 Forrer Blvd (45420-1472)
PHONE 937 299-1111
David Ganzsarto, *CEO*
Scott Becker, *COO*
Eric Masters, *Vice Pres*
Al Lefeld, *CFO*
BSN L Erickson Rn MN, *Manager*
EMP: 65
SALES (est): 3.8MM **Privately Held**
SIC: 7363 Temporary help service

(G-9327)
ALTICK & CORWIN CO LPA
1 S Main St Ste 1590 (45402-2035)
PHONE 937 223-1201
Fax: 937 223-5100
Marshal Ruchmann, *Principal*
Marshall D Ruchman, *Shareholder*
Dennis J Adkins, *Shareholder*
Deborah J Adler, *Shareholder*
Philip B Herron, *Shareholder*
EMP: 25 EST: 1930
SQ FT: 15,750
SALES: 2.9MM **Privately Held**
WEB: www.altickcorwin.com
SIC: 8111 General practice attorney, lawyer

(G-9328)
AMERICAN CITY BUS JOURNALS INC
Also Called: Dayton Business Journal
40 N Main St Ste 800 (45423-1053)
PHONE 937 528-4400
Fax: 937 222-8595
Dave Smith, *Publisher*
Caleb Stephens, *Editor*
Neil Arthur, *Manager*
Arthur Porter, *Supervisor*
EMP: 26
SALES (corp-wide): 1.4B **Privately Held**
SIC: 2711 7313 Newspapers: publishing only, not printed on site; newspaper advertising representative
HQ: American City Business Journals, Inc.
 120 W Morehead St Ste 400
 Charlotte NC 28202
 704 973-1000

(G-9329)
AMERICAN FEDERATION OF STATE
15 Gates St (45402-2917)
PHONE 937 461-9983
Marcia Knox, *Director*
EMP: 37
SALES: 100.9K **Privately Held**
SIC: 8631 Employees' association

(G-9330)
AMERICAN NURSING CARE INC
5335 Far Hills Ave # 103 (45429-2317)
PHONE 937 438-3844
Fax: 937 438-3764
Kitty Makley, *Branch Mgr*
Kevin Adams, *Admin Asst*
EMP: 37 **Privately Held**
WEB: www.americannursingcare.com
SIC: 8051 8082 Skilled nursing care facilities; home health care services
HQ: American Nursing Care, Inc.
 1700 Edison Dr Ste 300
 Milford OH 45150
 513 576-0262

(G-9331)
AMERICAN POWER LLC
1819 Troy St (45404-2400)
PHONE 937 235-0418
Adil Baguirov,
Islom Shakhbandarov,
EMP: 25 EST: 2013
SALES (est): 813.9K **Privately Held**
SIC: 4213 Trailer or container on flat car (TOFC/COFC); heavy machinery transport; refrigerated products transport; less-than-truckload (LTL) transport

(G-9332)
AMERICAN RED CROSS (HQ)
370 W 1st St (45402-3006)
P.O. Box 517 (45401-0517)
PHONE 937 222-0124
Fax: 937 445-0577
Tom Foder, *CEO*
Ronald Horvat, *Vice Pres*
Lillia Griffin, *CFO*
Kathy Umstead, *Controller*
EMP: 50
SQ FT: 2,500
SALES (est): 3.6MM
SALES (corp-wide): 2.5B **Privately Held**
SIC: 8322 Individual & family services

GEOGRAPHIC SECTION
Dayton - Montgomery County (G-9358)

PA: The American National Red Cross
430 17th St Nw
Washington DC 20006
202 737-8300

(G-9333)
AMERIPRO LOGISTICS LLC
6754 Stovall Dr (45424-7216)
PHONE..................................410 375-3469
Sevil Shakhmamov, *Principal*
Aziz Magjaigov, *Controller*
EMP: 25 **EST:** 2010
SALES (est): 1.4MM **Privately Held**
SIC: 4789 Car loading

(G-9334)
AMF FACILITY SERVICES INC
844 Oakleaf Dr (45417-3544)
PHONE..................................800 991-2273
A Mark Fowler, *President*
David Crouch, *Project Mgr*
EMP: 44
SALES: 3MM **Privately Held**
SIC: 7349 Building maintenance, except repairs

(G-9335)
AMG INC (PA)
Also Called: AMG-Eng
1497 Shoup Mill Rd (45414-3903)
PHONE..................................937 260-4646
Fax: 937 274-3870
Alberto G Mendez, *President*
Julieta Davis, *Vice Pres*
Scott Feller, *Vice Pres*
John Haas, *Vice Pres*
Maria C Mendez, *Treasurer*
EMP: 45
SQ FT: 26,796
SALES (est): 20MM **Privately Held**
SIC: 8711 Consulting engineer

(G-9336)
ANDERSEN DISTRIBUTION INC
8569 N Dixie Dr (45414-2463)
PHONE..................................937 898-7844
Joe Klosterman, *Manager*
EMP: 200
SALES (corp-wide): 2.9B **Privately Held**
SIC: 5031 8741 4225 Doors & windows; management services; general warehousing & storage
HQ: Andersen Distribution Inc.
100 4th Ave N
Bayport MN 55003
651 264-5150

(G-9337)
ANESTHESIOLOGY SERVICES NETWRK
1 Wyoming St (45409-2722)
P.O. Box 632317, Cincinnati (45263-2317)
PHONE..................................937 208-6173
Fax: 937 208-2450
Charles Cardone, *President*
EMP: 50
SALES (est): 4.6MM **Privately Held**
WEB: www.asndayton.com
SIC: 8011 Anesthesiologist

(G-9338)
APPLIED RESEARCH ASSOC INC
Also Called: Berriehill
7735 Paragon Rd (45459-4051)
PHONE..................................937 435-1016
EMP: 30
SALES (corp wide): 229.9MM **Privately Held**
SIC: 8731 Commercial physical research
PA: Applied Research Associates, Inc.
4300 San Mateo Blvd Ne A220
Albuquerque NM 87110
505 883-3636

(G-9339)
APPLIED RESEARCH ASSOC INC
7735 Paragon Rd (45459-4051)
PHONE..................................937 873-8166
Wally Zukauskas, *Manager*
EMP: 36

SALES (corp-wide): 229.9MM **Privately Held**
WEB: www.ara.com
SIC: 8731 8732 Engineering laboratory, except testing; commercial nonphysical research
PA: Applied Research Associates, Inc.
4300 San Mateo Blvd Ne A220
Albuquerque NM 87110
505 883-3636

(G-9340)
ARAMARK UNF & CAREER AP LLC
1200 Webster St (45404-1500)
P.O. Box 139 (45404-0139)
PHONE..................................937 223-6667
Jarrod Burch, *General Mgr*
Michelle Stout, *Site Mgr*
Lisa Qvick, *Sales Staff*
Sonya Crum, *Telecom Exec*
EMP: 100 **Publicly Held**
WEB: www.aramark-uniform.com
SIC: 7218 7213 7216 Industrial uniform supply; uniform supply; drycleaning plants, except rugs
HQ: Aramark Uniform & Career Apparel, Llc
115 N First St Ste 203
Burbank CA 91502
818 973-3700

(G-9341)
ARC DOCUMENT SOLUTIONS INC
222 N Saint Clair St (45402-1230)
PHONE..................................937 277-7930
EMP: 27
SALES (corp-wide): 406.1MM **Publicly Held**
SIC: 7334 Photocopying Services
PA: Arc Document Solutions, Inc.
1981 N Broadway Ste 385
Walnut Creek CA 94596
925 949-5100

(G-9342)
ARDENT TECHNOLOGIES INC
6234 Far Hills Ave (45459-1927)
PHONE..................................937 312-1345
Srinivas Appalaneni, *President*
Ronald Hartke, *Business Mgr*
S R Ancha, *Human Res Mgr*
EMP: 125
SALES (est): 12MM **Privately Held**
WEB: www.ardentinc.com
SIC: 8748 Business consulting

(G-9343)
AREA AGENCY ON AGING PLANNI
Also Called: Area Agency On Aging P S A 2
40 W 2nd St Ste 400 (45402-1873)
PHONE..................................800 258-7277
Cathie Hoffman, *Supervisor*
Doug McGarry, *Exec Dir*
Harriet Napier, *Officer*
EMP: 126
SALES: 44.7MM **Privately Held**
WEB: www.info4seniors.org
SIC: 8322 8082 Senior citizens' center or association; home health care services

(G-9344)
ARK FOUNDATION OF DAYTON
Also Called: ARKY BOOK STORE
2002 S Smithville Rd (45420-2804)
P.O. Box 20069 (45420-0069)
PHONE..................................937 256-2759
Ronnie E Cooper, *President*
Brenda Cooper, *Manager*
EMP: 25
SALES: 30.9K **Privately Held**
WEB: www.arky.org
SIC: 8412 8661 Museum; religious organizations

(G-9345)
ASSOCIATED SPECIALISTS
7707 Paragon Rd Ste 101 (45459-4070)
PHONE..................................937 208-7272
Roger H Griffin MD, *President*
EMP: 25
SALES (est): 2.4MM **Privately Held**
SIC: 8011 Internal medicine, physician/surgeon

(G-9346)
ASSURED HEALTH CARE INC
Also Called: Assured Hlth Care HM Care Svcs
1250 W Dorothy Ln Ste 200 (45409-1317)
P.O. Box 143, Tipp City (45371-0143)
PHONE..................................937 294-2803
Fax: 937 294-4946
Mary J Fair, *President*
EMP: 32
SALES (est): 1MM **Privately Held**
WEB: www.assuredhealth.net
SIC: 8082 7361 Home health care services; nurses' registry

(G-9347)
AUMAN MAHAN & FURRY A LEGAL
110 N Main St Ste 1000 (45402-3703)
PHONE..................................937 223-6003
Fax: 937 223-8550
Robert Dunlevey, *President*
Gary Auaman, *Vice Pres*
Gary Auman, *Vice Pres*
Stephen Watring, *Vice Pres*
Steve Watring, *Vice Pres*
EMP: 28
SALES (est): 3.7MM **Privately Held**
WEB: www.dmfdayton.com
SIC: 8111 General practice attorney, lawyer

(G-9348)
B AND D INVESTMENT PARTNERSHIP
Also Called: Danbarry Dollar Svr Cinema
7650 Waynetowne Blvd (45424-2000)
PHONE..................................937 233-6698
Tom Sanders, *General Mgr*
EMP: 25
SALES (corp-wide): 1.4MM **Privately Held**
WEB: www.danberrycinemas.com
SIC: 7832 Exhibitors, itinerant: motion picture
PA: B And D Investment Partnership
8050 Hosbrook Rd Ste 203
Cincinnati OH 45236
513 784-1521

(G-9349)
BATHROOM ALTERNATIVES INC
Also Called: Bath Fitter
85 Westpark Rd (45459-4812)
PHONE..................................937 434-1984
Jason Haught, *President*
Mark Clausing, *Prdtn Mgr*
EMP: 30
SALES (est): 6.9MM **Privately Held**
SIC: 5211 1799 Bathroom fixtures, equipment & supplies; kitchen & bathroom remodeling

(G-9350)
BDTK PRIVATE SECURITY
4950 Sweetbirch Dr (45424-4827)
PHONE..................................937 520-1784
Bradley White, *Principal*
EMP: 30
SALES (est): 331.6K **Privately Held**
SIC: 7381 Guard services

(G-9351)
BEAVERCREEK YMCA
111 W 1st St Ste 207 (45402-1154)
PHONE..................................937 426-9622
Fax: 937 426-4103
Karen Early, *Manager*
Greg Ulliman, *Business Dir*
EMP: 90
SALES (est): 3MM **Privately Held**
SIC: 8351 8322 Child day care services; individual & family services

(G-9352)
BECKER CONSTRUCTION INC
525 Gargrave Rd (45449-5401)
PHONE..................................937 859-8308
Timothy J Becker, *President*
EMP: 30
SALES (est): 6.1MM **Privately Held**
SIC: 1542 Commercial & office building, new construction; commercial & office buildings, renovation & repair; institutional building construction

(G-9353)
BELCAN SVCS GROUP LTD PARTNR
Also Called: Belcan Staffing Services
832 S Ludlow St Ste 1 (45202-2651)
PHONE..................................937 586-5053
Erica King, *Branch Mgr*
EMP: 150
SALES (corp-wide): 666.9MM **Privately Held**
SIC: 7363 Temporary help service
HQ: Belcan Services Group Limited Partnership
10200 Anderson Way
Blue Ash OH 45242
513 891-0972

(G-9354)
BELLAZIO SALON & DAY SPA
101 E Alex Bell Rd # 127 (45459-2779)
PHONE..................................937 432-6722
Fax: 937 432-6722
Eleanor Timmerman, *Owner*
Amy Powell, *Manager*
EMP: 44 **EST:** 2000
SALES (est): 695.6K **Privately Held**
WEB: www.bellaziosalondayspa.com
SIC: 7231 Manicurist, pedicurist

(G-9355)
BIESER GREER & LANDIS LLP
6 N Main St Ste 400 (45402-1914)
PHONE..................................937 223-3277
Fax: 937 223-6339
Charles Shook, *Partner*
Irvin Bieser, *Partner*
David Greer, *Partner*
James Greer, *Partner*
John Haviland, *Partner*
EMP: 46
SALES (est): 5.9MM **Privately Held**
WEB: www.biesergreer.com
SIC: 8111 General practice law office

(G-9356)
BIG HILL REALTY CORP (PA)
Also Called: Federer Homes and Gardens RE
5580 Far Hills Ave (45429-2285)
PHONE..................................937 435-1177
Fax: 937 435-2790
William Ryan, *CEO*
Jeffrey Owens, *President*
Kathy Rice, *COO*
George Long, *Vice Pres*
Jeff Owens, *Vice Pres*
EMP: 170
SQ FT: 3,500
SALES (est): 9.3MM **Privately Held**
WEB: www.bighillmac.com
SIC: 6531 Real estate agent, residential

(G-9357)
BIGGER ROAD VETERINARY CLINIC (PA)
5655 Bigger Rd (45440-2714)
PHONE..................................937 435-3262
Fax: 937 435-1319
E Eugene Snyder Dvm, *President*
Christine Snyder, *Corp Secy*
Kelly Searles, *Practice Mgr*
Jesse Dorland, *Administration*
Nichole Olp, *Associate*
EMP: 35
SQ FT: 2,200
SALES (est): 2.1MM **Privately Held**
SIC: 0742 Animal hospital services, pets & other animal specialties; veterinarian, animal specialties

(G-9358)
BILLBACK SYSTEMS LLC
8000 Millers Farm Ln (45458-7310)
PHONE..................................937 433-1844
Fax: 937 433-1855
Julie Goetz, *Controller*
Terry O Brien, *Manager*
Andrew Moon,
David Alspach,
Larry Paule,
EMP: 25
SQ FT: 400
SALES (est): 1.9MM **Privately Held**
WEB: www.billback.com
SIC: 7371 Computer software development

Dayton - Montgomery County (G-9359)

GEOGRAPHIC SECTION

HQ: Espreon Pty Limited
L 37 680 George St
Sydney NSW 2000
282 066-060

(G-9359)
BILTMORE APARTMENTS LTD
Also Called: Biltmore Towers
210 N Main St (45402-1234)
PHONE..................937 461-9695
Fax: 937 461-1811
Jennifer Hardee, *Principal*
Leeann Morein, *Vice Pres*
Cheryl L Johnson, *Manager*
EMP: 99
SALES (est): 3.4MM **Publicly Held**
SIC: 6513 Apartment building operators
HQ: Aimco Properties, L.P.
4582 S Ulster St Ste 1100
Denver CO 80237

(G-9360)
BLADECUTTERS LAWN SERVICE INC
Also Called: Bladecutters Lawn and Ldscpg
5440 N Dixie Dr (45414-3947)
P.O. Box 403 (45405-0403)
PHONE..................937 274-3861
Fax: 937 274-9306
John Scott, *President*
EMP: 25
SQ FT: 608
SALES: 626K **Privately Held**
WEB: www.bladecutters.com
SIC: 0782 5099 0781 4959 Lawn services; firewood; landscape counseling & planning; snowplowing; top soil; wrecking & demolition work

(G-9361)
BOB SUMEREL TIRE CO INC
7711 Center Point 70 Blvd (45424-6368)
PHONE..................937 235-0062
Fax: 937 235-0064
Dennis Lavoie, *Manager*
EMP: 25
SALES (corp-wide): 87.3MM **Privately Held**
WEB: www.bobsumereltire.com
SIC: 5531 7534 Automotive tires; tire retreading & repair shops
PA: Bob Sumerel Tire Co., Inc.
1257 Cox Ave
Erlanger KY 41018
859 283-2700

(G-9362)
BOMBECK FAMILY LEARNING CENTER
941 Alberta St (45409-2806)
PHONE..................937 229-2158
Ashley Smith, *Director*
Diana Smith, *Director*
Melissa Flanagan, *Asst Director*
EMP: 27
SALES (est): 351.8K **Privately Held**
SIC: 8351 Preschool center

(G-9363)
BONBRIGHT DISTRIBUTORS INC
1 Arena Park Dr (45417-4678)
PHONE..................937 222-1001
Fax: 937 222-0138
H Brock Anderson, *President*
Richard B Pohl Jr, *Corp Secy*
John Dimario, *Vice Pres*
Jim Brown, *CFO*
Mark Brown, *Sales Mgr*
▲ **EMP:** 125
SQ FT: 70,000
SALES (est): 61.3MM **Privately Held**
WEB: www.bonbright.com
SIC: 5181 Beer & other fermented malt liquors

(G-9364)
BOOST TECHNOLOGIES LLC
Also Called: Shumsky Promotional
811 E 4th St (45402-2227)
PHONE..................800 223-2203
Anita Emoff, *CEO*
Shannon Kesson, *Project Mgr*
Melissa Morgan, *Office Admin*
Anthony Poly, *CTO*

Brandon Wyen, *IT/INT Sup*
EMP: 74
SALES (est): 17.5MM **Privately Held**
SIC: 5199 Advertising specialties

(G-9365)
BOX 21 RESCUE SQUAD INC
100 E Helena St 120 (45404-1002)
PHONE..................937 223-2821
Karen Beavers, *President*
Ralph Wilhelm, *COO*
Lisa Sorrell, *Opers Staff*
Barb Fletcher, *Treasurer*
Bill Wentling, *Treasurer*
EMP: 50
SALES (est): 240K **Privately Held**
WEB: www.box21rescue.org
SIC: 8322 Individual & family services

(G-9366)
BRIGHTVIEW LANDSCAPES LLC
38 Brandt St (45404-2047)
PHONE..................937 235-9595
Rich Martell, *Manager*
EMP: 36
SALES (corp-wide): 914MM **Privately Held**
SIC: 0781 Landscape services
HQ: Brightview Landscapes, Llc
401 Plymouth Rd Ste 500
Plymouth Meeting PA 19462
484 567-7204

(G-9367)
BRIXX ICE COMPANY
500 E 1st St (45402-1221)
PHONE..................937 222-2257
Chris Bahi, *Owner*
EMP: 50
SALES (est): 794.1K **Privately Held**
WEB: www.brixxicecompany.com
SIC: 7941 Sports field or stadium operator; promoting sports events

(G-9368)
BUCKEYE CHARTER SERVICE INC
Also Called: Buckeye Charters
8240 Expansion Way (45424-6382)
PHONE..................937 879-3000
Fax: 937 233-4316
Jerry Biedenharn, *Principal*
Dale Stern, *Opers Mgr*
Lisa Tilley, *Sales Executive*
Lisa Pierce, *Office Mgr*
EMP: 30 **Privately Held**
WEB: www.buckeyecharterservice.com
SIC: 4142 Bus charter service, except local
PA: Buckeye Charter Service, Inc
1235 E Hanthorn Rd
Lima OH 45804

(G-9369)
BUCKEYE HOME HEALTH CARE (PA)
7700 Paragon Rd Ste A (45459-4081)
PHONE..................937 291-3780
Fax: 937 291-3789
Tina Hardwick, *Principal*
Stacey Bennett, *Sales Associate*
Crystal Burst, *Manager*
Lauren Adams, *Occ Therapy Dir*
Trish Bennett, *Administration*
EMP: 32
SALES: 9.7MM **Privately Held**
SIC: 8059 Nursing home, except skilled & intermediate care facility

(G-9370)
BUCKEYE POOL INC
486 Windsor Park Dr (45459-4111)
P.O. Box 750548 (45475-0548)
PHONE..................937 434-7916
Fax: 937 434-0232
Gary Aiken, *President*
Terry Blair, *General Mgr*
Chris Durbin, *Sales Mgr*
EMP: 25 **EST:** 1959
SQ FT: 3,200
SALES (est): 2.3MM **Privately Held**
SIC: 7389 1799 Swimming pool & hot tub service & maintenance; swimming pool construction

(G-9371)
BUCKEYE TRILS GIRL SCOUT CNCIL (PA)
450 Shoup Mill Rd (45415-3518)
PHONE..................937 275-7601
Fax: 937 275-1147
Barbara Bonisas, *CEO*
Kelly Bowlds, *Manager*
Marcia Dowds, *Manager*
Romona Roberts, *Director*
EMP: 41
SQ FT: 40,000
SALES (est): 1.6MM **Privately Held**
WEB: www.btgirlscouts.org
SIC: 8641 Girl Scout organization

(G-9372)
BUDDE SHEET METAL WORKS INC (PA)
305 Leo St (45404-1083)
PHONE..................937 224-0868
Fax: 937 224-1356
Thomas Budde, *President*
William R Budde Jr, *Corp Secy*
Stephen L Budde, *Vice Pres*
Angie Budde- Obrien, *Manager*
Bill Budde Jr, *Admin Sec*
EMP: 39
SQ FT: 20,000
SALES: 6MM **Privately Held**
WEB: www.buddesheetmetal.com
SIC: 1761 3444 1711 Sheet metalwork; sheet metalwork; plumbing, heating, air-conditioning contractors

(G-9373)
BURD BROTHERS INC
1789 Stanley Ave (45404-1116)
PHONE..................513 708-7787
Tyler Burdick, *Branch Mgr*
EMP: 33 **Privately Held**
SIC: 4731 Truck transportation brokers
PA: Burd Brothers, Inc.
4005 Borman Dr
Batavia OH 45103

(G-9374)
BURKHARDT SPRINGFIELD NEIGHBOR
735 Huffman Ave (45403-2651)
PHONE..................937 252-7076
Lodia Furnas, *President*
Terry Middleton, *Vice Pres*
EMP: 40
SALES (est): 523.8K **Privately Held**
SIC: 8641 Civic social & fraternal associations

(G-9375)
BUSINESS FURNITURE LLC
8 N Main St (45402-1904)
PHONE..................937 293-1010
Debra M Oakes, *Branch Mgr*
EMP: 50
SALES (corp-wide): 65.4MM **Privately Held**
SIC: 5021 7641 5023 Office furniture; furniture repair & maintenance; carpets
PA: Business Furniture, Llc
8421 Bearing Dr Ste 200
Indianapolis IN 46268
317 216-4844

(G-9376)
CALIBER HOME LOANS INC
8534 Yankee St (45458-1888)
PHONE..................937 435-5363
EMP: 42
SALES (corp-wide): 2.4B **Privately Held**
SIC: 6163 6141 Loan brokers; personal credit institutions
PA: Caliber Home Loans, Inc.
1525 S Belt Line Rd
Coppell TX 75019
800 401-6587

(G-9377)
CALVIN LANIER
5363 Birdland Ave (45417-8848)
PHONE..................937 952-4221
Calvin Lanier, *Principal*
EMP: 25
SALES (est): 946.9K **Privately Held**
SIC: 3423 7389 Plumbers' hand tools;

(G-9378)
CAPITAL HEALTH SERVICES INC (PA)
5040 Philadelphia Dr (45415-3604)
PHONE..................937 278-0404
Ken Bernsen, *CEO*
Joshua Huff, *Vice Pres*
Kara Bernsen, *Treasurer*
Vicki Hawkins, *Controller*
Pamela Cooke, *Director*
EMP: 34
SALES (est): 6.3MM **Privately Held**
SIC: 8051 8059 Skilled nursing care facilities; personal care home, with health care

(G-9379)
CAPRI BOWLING LANES INC
2727 S Dixie Dr (45409-1506)
PHONE..................937 832-4000
Fax: 937 298-7486
Ernie Talos, *President*
Thomas Mantia, *Corp Secy*
EMP: 30 **EST:** 1959
SQ FT: 30,000
SALES (est): 871.5K **Privately Held**
SIC: 7933 5813 5812 Ten pin center; cocktail lounge; eating places

(G-9380)
CARE ONE LLC
Also Called: Spring Creek Nursing Center
5440 Charlesgate Rd (45424-1049)
PHONE..................937 236-6707
Fax: 937 236-4802
Karma Winburn, *Principal*
Robert Hunter, *Director*
EMP: 160
SALES (corp-wide): 422.3MM **Privately Held**
SIC: 8051 Convalescent home with continuous nursing care
PA: Care One, Llc
173 Bridge Plz N
Fort Lee NJ 07024
201 242-4000

(G-9381)
CARESOURCE MANAGEMENT GROUP CO (PA)
230 N Main St (45402-1263)
P.O. Box 8738 (45401-8738)
PHONE..................937 224-3300
Pamela B Morris, *CEO*
Bobby Jones, *COO*
Bobby L Jones, *COO*
Leslie W Naamon, *COO*
David Finkel, *Exec VP*
EMP: 800
SALES: 1.1B **Privately Held**
WEB: www.caresource.com
SIC: 6321 Health insurance carriers

(G-9382)
CARESOURCE MANAGEMENT GROUP CO
230 N Main St (45402-1263)
PHONE..................937 224-3300
Michael E Ervin, *Ch of Bd*
EMP: 40 **Privately Held**
SIC: 6321 Health insurance carriers
PA: Caresource Management Group Co.
230 N Main St
Dayton OH 45402

(G-9383)
CARLS BODY SHOP INC
Also Called: Carl's Body Shop & Towing
1120 Wayne Ave (45410-1406)
PHONE..................937 253-5166
Fax: 937 253-9371
Matt Miller, *President*
Jill Oberschlake, *Manager*
Lee Miller, *Admin Sec*
EMP: 32
SQ FT: 10,000
SALES (est): 4.4MM **Privately Held**
WEB: www.carlsbodyshop.com
SIC: 7532 Body shop, automotive

(G-9384)
CARRIAGE INN OF TROTWOOD INC
Also Called: Shiloh Springs Care Center
5020 Philadelphia Dr (45415-3653)
PHONE..................937 277-0505

GEOGRAPHIC SECTION

Dayton - Montgomery County (G-9409)

Ken Bernsen, *President*
EMP: 100
SALES: 6MM **Privately Held**
SIC: 8051 Convalescent home with continuous nursing care

(G-9385)
CARRIAGE INN RETIREMENT CMNTY
5040 Philadelphia Dr (45415-3604)
PHONE.................................937 278-0404
Fax: 937 278-0092
Joshua Huff, *Vice Pres*
James Nagle, *Director*
Wayne Davis, *Administration*
EMP: 130
SALES (est): 5.8MM **Privately Held**
WEB: www.capitalhs.com
SIC: 8051 Convalescent home with continuous nursing care

(G-9386)
CARRY TRANSPORT INC
5536 Brentlinger Dr (45414-3510)
PHONE.................................937 236-0026
Fax: 937 236-9472
Don Linder, *Branch Mgr*
EMP: 25 **Privately Held**
SIC: 4213 Contract haulers
PA: Carry Transport Inc
2630 Kindustry Park Rd
Keokuk IA 52632

(G-9387)
CASHLAND FINANCIAL SVCS INC (DH)
100 E 3rd St Ste 200 (45402-2128)
PHONE.................................937 253-7842
Fax: 937 853-2173
Steve McAllister, *President*
Carolyn Gibbs, *Site Mgr*
EMP: 40
SALES (est): 65.7MM
SALES (corp-wide): 1.7B **Publicly Held**
SIC: 6099 Check cashing agencies
HQ: Frontier Merger Sub Llc
1600 W 7th St
Fort Worth TX 76102
800 223-8738

(G-9388)
CASSANOS INC (PA)
Also Called: Cassano's Pizza & Subs
1700 E Stroop Rd (45429-5095)
PHONE.................................937 294-8400
Fax: 937 294-8107
Vic Cassano Jr, *Ch of Bd*
Chris Cassano, *Vice Pres*
Pat Dillon, *Maint Spvr*
Kent Warner, *Purchasing*
Timothy Sayer, *Controller*
EMP: 45 **EST:** 1949
SQ FT: 37,500
SALES (est): 13.3MM **Privately Held**
SIC: 5812 5149 6794 Pizzeria, chain; sandwiches & submarines shop; baking supplies; pizza supplies; franchises, selling or licensing

(G-9389)
CATALYST PAPER (USA) INC
7777 Wash Vlg Dr Ste 210 (45459-3995)
PHONE.................................937 528-3800
Linda McClinchy, *Vice Pres*
EMP: 50
SALES (corp-wide): 886.4MM **Privately Held**
SIC: 5111 Finc paper
HQ: Catalyst Paper (Usa) Inc.
2200 6th Ave Ste 800
Seattle WA 98121
206 838-2070

(G-9390)
CATHOLIC SOCIAL SVC MIAMI VLY (PA)
Also Called: Miami Valley Family Care Ctr
922 W Riverview Ave (45402-6424)
PHONE.................................937 223-7217
Cathy Guerrant, *Human Res Mgr*
Andrea Skrlac, *Corp Comm Staff*
Marilyn Horton, *Case Mgr*
Nympha Clark, *Manager*
Carolyn Craig, *Manager*
EMP: 30

SALES: 18.2MM **Privately Held**
SIC: 8322 8351 Family service agency; child guidance agency; adoption services; child day care services

(G-9391)
CBC ENGINEERS & ASSOCIATES LTD (PA)
125 Westpark Rd (45459-4814)
PHONE.................................937 428-6150
Fax: 937 428-6154
Alvin C Banner, *President*
Mitch Hardert, *Chief Engr*
Bill Robertson, *Director*
EMP: 30
SALES (est): 4.3MM **Privately Held**
SIC: 8711 Consulting engineer

(G-9392)
CDC TECHNOLOGIES INC
7100 Corporate Way Ste C (45459-4284)
PHONE.................................937 886-9713
Jerry Czmiel, *President*
Angie Czmie, *Treasurer*
EMP: 60
SALES (est): 3.2MM **Privately Held**
WEB: www.cdctechinc.com
SIC: 7389 Design services

(G-9393)
CENTERVILLE CHILD DEVELOPMENT
8095 Garnet Dr (45458-2140)
PHONE.................................937 434-5949
Fax: 937 434-5556
Joseph Valentour, *Partner*
Catherine Valentour, *Partner*
EMP: 30
SQ FT: 4,700
SALES: 1MM **Privately Held**
SIC: 8351 Group day care center

(G-9394)
CENTRIC CONSULTING LLC (PA)
Also Called: Practical Solution
1215 Lyons Rd F (45458-1858)
PHONE.................................888 781-7567
Mike Brannan, *President*
Art Chwalek, *Vice Pres*
Michael Murphy, *Vice Pres*
Chris Szaz, *Vice Pres*
Bonnie Bruce, *Project Mgr*
EMP: 86
SQ FT: 1,000
SALES (est): 37.5MM **Privately Held**
WEB: www.centricconsulting.com
SIC: 8748 Systems engineering consultant, ex. computer or professional

(G-9395)
CH2M HILL CONSTRUCTORS INC
1 S Main St Ste 1100 (45402-2074)
PHONE.................................937 228-4285
S Wanders, *Branch Mgr*
EMP: 30
SALES (corp-wide): 10B **Publicly Held**
SIC: 1623 8711 Water, sewer & utility lines; engineering services
HQ: Ch2m Hill Constructors, Inc.
9189 S Jamaica St
Englewood CO 80112

(G-9396)
CHAMPIONS GYM
6559 Brantford Rd (45414-2301)
PHONE.................................937 294-8202
Fax: 937 294-8155
Larry Pacifico, *President*
EMP: 45
SQ FT: 10,000
SALES: 1.3MM **Privately Held**
WEB: www.championsgym.com
SIC: 7991 Health club

(G-9397)
CHAPEL ELECTRIC CO LLC
1985 Founders Dr (45420-4012)
PHONE.................................937 222-2290
Fax: 937 222-1759
Gregory P Ross, *President*
Dennis F Quebe, *Chairman*
Van Der, *Vice Pres*
Roger Van Der Horst, *Vice Pres*

Richard E Penewit, *Vice Pres*
EMP: 115
SQ FT: 40,000
SALES (est): 44.7MM
SALES (corp-wide): 83.3MM **Privately Held**
WEB: www.chapel.com
SIC: 1731 General electrical contractor
PA: Quebe Holdings, Inc.
1985 Founders Dr
Dayton OH 45420
937 222-2290

(G-9398)
CHAPEL-ROMANOFF TECH LLC
1985 Founders Dr (45420-4012)
PHONE.................................937 222-9840
Jeffrey Carr, *Superintendent*
CJ Withrow, *Manager*
Sam Warwar,
Gregory P Ross,
Dennis Severance,
EMP: 25
SQ FT: 40,000
SALES (est): 4.7MM
SALES (corp-wide): 83.3MM **Privately Held**
WEB: www.quebe.com
SIC: 1731 Telephone & telephone equipment installation
PA: Quebe Holdings, Inc.
1985 Founders Dr
Dayton OH 45420
937 222-2290

(G-9399)
CHARLES F JERGENS CNSTR INC
1280 Brandt Pike (45404-2468)
PHONE.................................937 233-1830
Fax: 937 233-2075
Phillip Jergens, *President*
Charles F Jergens, *Vice Pres*
Dennis McCreight, *Controller*
Connie Bales, *Manager*
Kerry Jergens, *Administration*
EMP: 30
SQ FT: 1,500
SALES: 6.8MM **Privately Held**
SIC: 1794 1795 Excavation work; wrecking & demolition work

(G-9400)
CHARLES JERGENS CONTRACTOR
1280 Brandt Pike (45404-2468)
PHONE.................................937 233-1830
Charles F Jergens, *President*
Patricia Jergens, *Vice Pres*
EMP: 40 **EST:** 1939
SQ FT: 1,500
SALES (est): 4.8MM **Privately Held**
SIC: 7353 1794 Heavy construction equipment rental; excavation work

(G-9401)
CHEMICAL SERVICES INC
2600 Thunderhawk Ct (45414-3459)
PHONE.................................937 898-5566
Fax: 937 898-7602
Martin J Wehr, *President*
Matt Schneider, *Purch Mgr*
Sue Wiford, *Controller*
George Lueking, *Sales Executive*
EMP: 26
SQ FT: 40,000
SALES (est): 23.6MM
SALES (corp-wide): 125.6MM **Privately Held**
WEB: www.chemicalservices.com
SIC: 5169 Industrial chemicals
PA: Chemgroup, Inc
2600 Thunderhawk Ct
Dayton OH 45414
937 898-5566

(G-9402)
CHILDRENS HOME CARE DAYTON
18 Childrens Plz (45404-1867)
PHONE.................................937 641-4663
Fax: 937 463-5339
Susan Chandler, *Pharmacist*
Susan Powell, *CTO*
Peggy Dolye, *Exec Dir*
Vicki Peoples, *Exec Dir*

Vickie Peoples, *Exec Dir*
EMP: 65
SALES: 8.2MM **Privately Held**
SIC: 7361 8082 Nurses' registry; home health care services

(G-9403)
CHILDRENS MEDICAL CTR TOLEDO
Also Called: Dayton Children
1 Childrens Plz (45404-1873)
PHONE.................................937 641-3000
David Kensaul, *CEO*
Bonnie Summerville, *Vice Pres*
CJ Guarasci, *Manager*
Jemma Reiedinger, *Admin Asst*
EMP: 1500
SALES (est): 30.7MM **Privately Held**
SIC: 8069 Children's hospital

(G-9404)
CHIMNEYS INN
767 Mmsburg Cnterville Rd (45459)
PHONE.................................937 567-7850
Philip Hayden, *President*
Matt Hayden, *General Mgr*
EMP: 25
SALES: 250K **Privately Held**
WEB: www.chimneysinn.com
SIC: 7011 Inns

(G-9405)
CHOICES IN COMMUNITY LIVING (PA)
1651 Needmore Rd Ste B (45414-3801)
PHONE.................................937 898-3655
Fax: 937 898-3553
W Thomas Weaver, *President*
Shannon Link, *Finance*
Kelly Lance, *Volunteer Dir*
EMP: 200
SQ FT: 2,000
SALES: 11.4MM **Privately Held**
WEB: www.choicesincl.com
SIC: 8361 8052 Home for the mentally retarded; home for the mentally handicapped; intermediate care facilities

(G-9406)
CHRISTIAN TWIGS GYMNASTICS CLB
Also Called: Twigs Kids
1900 S Alex Rd (45449-5371)
P.O. Box 348, Miamisburg (45343-0348)
PHONE.................................937 866-8356
Fax: 937 866-3079
Bob Putman, *President*
EMP: 28
SQ FT: 9,400
SALES: 250K **Privately Held**
WEB: www.twigskids.com
SIC: 7999 Gymnastic instruction, non-membership

(G-9407)
CHS OF BOWERSTON OPER CO INC
Also Called: Sunny Slope Nursing Home
5020 Philadelphia Dr (45415-3653)
PHONE.................................937 277-0505
Kenneth Bernsen, *President*
Kara Bernsen, *Shareholder*
Josh Huff, *Shareholder*
Sarah Manning, *Shareholder*
EMP: 60
SALES (est): 513.5K **Privately Held**
SIC: 8051 Skilled nursing care facilities

(G-9408)
CITY CASTERS
Also Called: Clear Channel
101 Pine St Ste 300 (45402-2948)
PHONE.................................937 224-1137
EMP: 50 **EST:** 2009
SALES (est): 2.6MM **Privately Held**
SIC: 4832 Radio Broadcast Station

(G-9409)
CITY OF CENTERVILLE
Also Called: Golf Course At Yankee Trace
10000 Yankee St (45458-3520)
PHONE.................................937 438-3585
Steve Shull, *Director*
Matthew Scharrer, *Assistant*
EMP: 75 **Privately Held**

Dayton - Montgomery County (G-9410)

GEOGRAPHIC SECTION

WEB: www.ci.centerville.oh.us
SIC: 5812 7299 Eating places; banquet hall facilities
PA: City Of Centerville
100 W Spring Valley Pike
Dayton OH 45458
937 433-7151

(G-9410)
CITY OF DAYTON
Also Called: Water Department
320 W Monument Ave (45402-3017)
PHONE..........................937 333-3725
Fax: 937 228-2833
Scott Holmes, *Chief Engr*
William Zilli, *Branch Mgr*
Tammi Clements, *Director*
EMP: 40
SQ FT: 14,000 **Privately Held**
WEB: www.daytonconventioncenter.com
SIC: 1623 4941 Water, sewer & utility lines; water supply
PA: City Of Dayton
101 W 3rd St
Dayton OH 45402
937 333-3333

(G-9411)
CITY OF DAYTON
Also Called: Dayton Wastewater Trtmnt Plant
2800 Guthrie Rd Ste A (45417-6700)
PHONE..........................937 333-1837
Fax: 937 333-1826
Chris Clark, *Branch Mgr*
Mark Varvel, *Manager*
Jerry Overton, *Supervisor*
EMP: 72 **Privately Held**
WEB: www.daytonconventioncenter.com
SIC: 4952 Sewerage systems
PA: City Of Dayton
101 W 3rd St
Dayton OH 45402
937 333-3333

(G-9412)
CITY OF DAYTON
Also Called: Dayton City Water Department
3210 Chuck Wagner Ln (45414-4401)
PHONE..........................937 333-6070
George Crosby, *Manager*
Shannon Zell, *Manager*
EMP: 125 **Privately Held**
WEB: www.daytonconventioncenter.com
SIC: 4941 Water supply
PA: City Of Dayton
101 W 3rd St
Dayton OH 45402
937 333-3333

(G-9413)
CITY OF DAYTON
Also Called: City Dayton Water Distribution
945 Ottawa St (45402-1365)
PHONE..........................937 333-7138
Wayne Simpson, *Manager*
EMP: 95 **Privately Held**
WEB: www.daytonconventioncenter.com
SIC: 4971 Water distribution or supply systems for irrigation
PA: City Of Dayton
101 W 3rd St
Dayton OH 45402
937 333-3333

(G-9414)
COCA-COLA BOTTLING CO CNSLD
1000 Coca Cola Blvd (45424-6375)
PHONE..........................937 878-5000
Fax: 937 879-1005
Bob Tiootson, *Manager*
Diana Huffman, *Manager*
EMP: 95
SALES (corp-wide): 4.3B **Publicly Held**
WEB: www.colasic.net
SIC: 5149 2086 Soft drinks; carbonated beverages, nonalcoholic: bottled & canned
PA: Coca-Cola Bottling Co. Consolidated
4100 Coca Cola Plz # 100
Charlotte NC 28211
704 557-4400

(G-9415)
COLDWELL BNKR HRITG RLTORS LLC
8534 Yankee St Ste 1b (45458-1889)
PHONE..........................937 304-8500
Fax: 937 439-6355
Stephen Ericson, *Buyer*
Tom Bechtel, *Sales/Mktg Mgr*
Jeff Spring, *Manager*
Eric Cole, *Real Est Agnt*
Dana Wice, *Real Est Agnt*
EMP: 40
SALES (est): 1.4MM
SALES (corp-wide): 7.5MM **Privately Held**
WEB: www.coldwellbankerdayton.com
SIC: 6531 Real estate agent, residential
PA: Coldwell Banker Heritage Realtors Llc
2000 Hewitt Ave
Dayton OH 45440
937 434-7600

(G-9416)
COLDWELL BNKR HRITG RLTORS LLC (PA)
2000 Hewitt Ave (45440-2917)
PHONE..........................937 434-7600
Fax: 937 434-0300
Jean Walsh, *Sales Associate*
Beth Edgar, *Branch Mgr*
Vicki James, *Manager*
Georgiana Nye, *Manager*
Evelyn Davidson, *Consultant*
EMP: 40 **EST:** 1967
SQ FT: 10,000
SALES (est): 7.5MM **Privately Held**
WEB: www.coldwellbankerdayton.com
SIC: 6531 6512 Real estate agent, residential; commercial & industrial building operation

(G-9417)
COLDWELL BNKR HRITG RLTORS LLC
8534 Yankee St Ste 1b (45458-1889)
PHONE..........................937 439-4500
Fax: 937 439-6369
Sip Miller, *Office Mgr*
Jennifer Danishek, *Asst Broker*
Jamie Wilson, *Asst Broker*
Morgan Walz, *Real Est Agnt*
EMP: 25
SALES (est): 1.1MM
SALES (corp-wide): 7.5MM **Privately Held**
WEB: www.coldwellbankerdayton.com
SIC: 6531 Real estate agent, residential
PA: Coldwell Banker Heritage Realtors Llc
2000 Hewitt Ave
Dayton OH 45440
937 434-7600

(G-9418)
COMMUNITY MERCY FOUNDATION
Also Called: Mercy Siena Woods
235 W Orchard Springs Dr (45415)
PHONE..........................937 278-8211
Fax: 937 278-8046
Pamela Brown, *Director*
Susan Hayes, *Administration*
EMP: 120
SQ FT: 56,000
SALES (corp-wide): 4.2B **Privately Held**
SIC: 8051 Skilled nursing care facilities
HQ: The Community Mercy Foundation
1 S Limestone St Ste 700
Springfield OH 45502

(G-9419)
COMMUNITY MERCY FOUNDATION
Also Called: Mercy Sienna Spring II
6125 N Main St (45415-3110)
PHONE..........................937 274-1569
James Gravell, *Manager*
EMP: 100
SALES (corp-wide): 4.2B **Privately Held**
SIC: 8741 Hospital management; nursing & personal care facility management
HQ: The Community Mercy Foundation
1 S Limestone St Ste 700
Springfield OH 45502

(G-9420)
COMPTECH COMPUTER TECH INC
7777 Washington Village D (45459-3975)
PHONE..........................937 228-2667
Allan Stephen, *CEO*
EMP: 25
SQ FT: 1,200
SALES: 5.3MM **Privately Held**
SIC: 7379 Computer related consulting services

(G-9421)
COMPUNET CLINICAL LABS LLC
2508 Sandride Dr (45439)
PHONE..........................937 208-3555
Vicki Studebaker, *Vice Pres*
Ed Doucette, *Branch Mgr*
EMP: 400
SALES (corp-wide): 354MM **Privately Held**
SIC: 8071 Medical laboratories
HQ: Compunet Clinical Laboratories, Llc
2308 Sandridge Dr
Moraine OH 45439
937 296-0844

(G-9422)
CONCORD DAYTON HOTEL II LLC
Also Called: Dayton Marriott
1414 S Patterson Blvd (45409-2105)
PHONE..........................937 223-1000
Fax: 937 223-7853
Patrick McGaha, *General Mgr*
Dena St Clair, *Principal*
EMP: 99 **EST:** 2014
SALES (est): 4MM **Privately Held**
SIC: 5812 7011 American restaurant; hotels & motels

(G-9423)
CONNOR CONCEPTS INC
Also Called: Chop House Restaurant
7727 Washington Vlg Dr (45459-3954)
PHONE..........................937 291-1661
Fax: 937 291-0660
Jeff Roberts, *Manager*
Jeff Wagoner, *Manager*
EMP: 65 **Privately Held**
SIC: 5812 7299 American restaurant; banquet hall facilities
PA: Connor Concepts, Inc.
10911 Turkey Dr
Knoxville TN 37934

(G-9424)
CONSUMER ADVOCACY MODEL
Also Called: CAM Program. The
601 S Edwin C Moses Blvd (45417-3424)
PHONE..........................937 222-2400
Fax: 937 222-7522
Melissa Jones, *Director*
Kristen Dunn, *Administration*
EMP: 25
SALES (est): 440.6K **Privately Held**
SIC: 8093 Specialty outpatient clinics

(G-9425)
COOLIDGE LAW
33 W 1st St Ste 600 (45402-1235)
PHONE..........................937 223-8177
Richard Schwartz, *Partner*
EMP: 68
SALES (est): 2.1MM **Privately Held**
SIC: 8111 General practice law office

(G-9426)
COOLIDGE WALL CO LPA (PA)
33 W 1st St Ste 600 (45402-1289)
PHONE..........................937 223-8177
Fax: 937 223-6705
J Stephen Herbert, *President*
James W Walworth, *COO*
Robert Bartlett, *Manager*
Marilyn Bourdow, *Manager*
Christopher Conard, *Manager*
EMP: 30 **EST:** 1853
SQ FT: 30,000
SALES (est): 8.5MM **Privately Held**
SIC: 8111 General practice law office

(G-9427)
COPP SYSTEMS INC
Also Called: Copp Systems Integrator
123 S Keowee St (45402-2240)
PHONE..........................937 228-4188
Fax: 937 228-2901
Bill Defries, *Principal*
Daniel J Hilbert, *Vice Pres*
Rocale Bumpus, *Opers Staff*
Tom Gilfoyle, *Purchasing*
John Harrell, *Engineer*
EMP: 32
SQ FT: 12,000
SALES (est): 20.3MM **Privately Held**
SIC: 5065 1731 Intercommunication equipment, electronic; paging & signaling equipment; closed circuit television; sound equipment, electronic; electrical work

(G-9428)
CORBUS LLC (HQ)
1129 Miamisbrg Cntrvle Rd Ste (45449)
PHONE..........................937 226-7724
Fax: 937 586-3059
Rajesh K Soin, *Ch of Bd*
Steve Catanzarita, *Principal*
Joseph A Basalla, *COO*
Kevin Robie, *Vice Pres*
EMP: 85
SQ FT: 12,500
SALES (est): 73MM
SALES (corp-wide): 118.3MM **Privately Held**
WEB: www.corbus.com
SIC: 8742 Management consulting services
PA: Soin International, Llc
1129 Miamsbg Ctrvl Rd 1 Ste
Dayton OH 45449
937 427-7646

(G-9429)
COTTAGES OF CLAYTON
8212 N Main St (45415-1641)
PHONE..........................937 280-0300
Fax: 937 280-0301
Amber Stevens, *Financial Exec*
Nick Anderson, *Exec Dir*
Sarah Zerale, *Administration*
EMP: 45
SALES (est): 2MM **Privately Held**
SIC: 8082 Home health care services

(G-9430)
COUNTERTOP ALTERNATIVES INC
Also Called: Granite Transformations
2325 Woodman Dr (45420-1479)
PHONE..........................937 254-3334
Jayson Grothjan, *President*
Grothjan Jason, *Manager*
EMP: 30
SALES (est): 2.8MM **Privately Held**
WEB: www.countertopalternatives.com
SIC: 1799 1751 Counter top installation; cabinet & finish carpentry

(G-9431)
COUNTY OF MONTGOMERY
Also Called: Sheriff's Office
345 W 2nd St (45422-6401)
PHONE..........................937 225-4192
Phil Plummer, *Sheriff*
EMP: 75 **Privately Held**
SIC: 9221 8399 Sheriffs' offices; community action agency
PA: County Of Montgomery
451 W 3rd St Fl 4
Dayton OH 45422
937 225-4000

(G-9432)
COUNTY OF MONTGOMERY
Also Called: Montgomery Cnty Children Svcs
3304 N Main St (45405-2709)
PHONE..........................937 224-5437
Fax: 937 277-1127
Mary Ann Nelson, *Principal*
Helen Kelly-Jones, *Human Res Mgr*
EMP: 450 **Privately Held**
WEB: www.mcmrdd.org
SIC: 8322 Individual & family services

GEOGRAPHIC SECTION
Dayton - Montgomery County (G-9457)

PA: County Of Montgomery
451 W 3rd St Fl 4
Dayton OH 45422
937 225-4000

(G-9433)
COUNTY OF MONTGOMERY
Also Called: Engineering Department
5625 Little Richmond Rd (45426-3219)
PHONE.................937 854-4576
Fax: 937 854-3413
Jerry Crane, *Foreman/Supr*
Mark Hartung, *Manager*
Anthony Pagan, *Technology*
EMP: 70
SQ FT: 5,000 **Privately Held**
WEB: www.mcmrdd.org
SIC: 8711 Engineering services
PA: County Of Montgomery
451 W 3rd St Fl 4
Dayton OH 45422
937 225-4000

(G-9434)
COUNTY OF MONTGOMERY
Also Called: Stillwater Center
8100 N Main St (45415-1702)
PHONE.................937 264-0460
Fax: 937 890-9579
Catina Lofton, *Supervisor*
Michelle Pierce Mobley, *Director*
Robin Miller, *Food Svc Dir*
EMP: 251
SQ FT: 108,000 **Privately Held**
WEB: www.mcmrdd.org
SIC: 8051 8052 Mental retardation hospital; home for the mentally retarded, with health care
PA: County Of Montgomery
451 W 3rd St Fl 4
Dayton OH 45422
937 225-4000

(G-9435)
COUNTY OF MONTGOMERY
Also Called: Treasurers Office
451 W 3rd St Fl 2 (45422-0001)
P.O. Box 972 (45422)
PHONE.................937 225-4010
Fax: 937 496-7122
Marsha Shaffer, *Senior Buyer*
Hugh Quill, *Treasurer*
EMP: 32 **Privately Held**
WEB: www.mcmrdd.org
SIC: 9111 8611 County supervisors' & executives' offices; business associations
PA: County Of Montgomery
451 W 3rd St Fl 4
Dayton OH 45422
937 225-4000

(G-9436)
COUNTY OF MONTGOMERY
Also Called: Montgomery County Dept of Job
1111 Edwin C Moses Blvd (45422-3600)
PHONE.................937 225-4804
Fax: 937 225-5087
Kim Bridges, *Principal*
David Hess, *Director*
EMP: 300 **Privately Held**
WEB: www.mcmrdd.org
SIC: 8331 8322 Job training & vocational rehabilitation services; individual & family services
PA: County Of Montgomery
451 W 3rd St Fl 4
Dayton OH 45422
937 225-4000

(G-9437)
COUNTY OF MONTGOMERY
Also Called: Montgomery Cnty Prosecutors Off
301 W 3rd St Fl 5 (45402-1446)
P.O. Box 972 (45402)
PHONE.................937 225-5623
Fax: 937 496-6555
George B Patricoff, *Director*
EMP: 200 **Privately Held**
WEB: www.mcmrdd.org
SIC: 8111 General practice attorney, lawyer
PA: County Of Montgomery
451 W 3rd St Fl 4
Dayton OH 45422
937 225-4000

(G-9438)
COUNTY OF MONTGOMERY
Also Called: Children Services
3501 Merrimac Ave (45405-2646)
PHONE.................937 224-5437
Shannon Jones, *Principal*
EMP: 75 **Privately Held**
WEB: www.is-partner.com
SIC: 8322 Child related social services
PA: County Of Montgomery
451 W 3rd St Fl 4
Dayton OH 45422
937 225-4000

(G-9439)
COUNTY OF MONTGOMERY
Also Called: Management Information Svcs
41 N Perry St Rm 1 (45422-2000)
PHONE.................937 496-3103
Joseph Pecquet, *Manager*
EMP: 300 **Privately Held**
WEB: www.mcmrdd.org
SIC: 7378 7371 Computer maintenance & repair; custom computer programming services
PA: County Of Montgomery
451 W 3rd St Fl 4
Dayton OH 45422
937 225-4000

(G-9440)
COUNTY OF MONTGOMERY
Also Called: Coroner
361 W 3rd St (45402-1418)
PHONE.................937 225-4156
James Davis, *Principal*
Bryan Casto, *Med Doctor*
Kent Harshbarger, *Med Doctor*
Russell Uptegrove, *Med Doctor*
Alee Steuer, *Admin Asst*
EMP: 34 **Privately Held**
WEB: www.mcmrdd.org
SIC: 8011 Pathologist
PA: County Of Montgomery
451 W 3rd St Fl 4
Dayton OH 45422
937 225-4000

(G-9441)
COURTYARD BY MARRIOTT DAYTON
2006 S Edwin C Moses Blvd (45417-4675)
PHONE.................937 220-9060
Fax: 937 220-9233
Karen Younce, *Principal*
EMP: 25
SALES (est): 1.2MM **Privately Held**
SIC: 7011 Hotels

(G-9442)
COX COMMUNICATIONS INC
1611 S Main St (45409-2547)
PHONE.................937 222-5700
David Dashewich, *Vice Pres*
Doug Franklin, *Branch Mgr*
EMP: 76
SALES (corp-wide): 33B **Privately Held**
SIC: 4841 Cable television services
HQ: Cox Communications, Inc.
6205 B Pchtree Dunwody Ne
Atlanta GA 30328

(G-9443)
CREATIVE IMAGES COLLEGE OF B (PA)
Also Called: Creative Imges Inst Csmetology
7535 Poe Ave (45414-2557)
PHONE.................937 478-7922
Fax: 937 415-3658
Nicholas Schindler, *President*
Angie Copeland, *Director*
Angie Wright, *Director*
EMP: 30
SALES (est): 1.1MM **Privately Held**
SIC: 7231 Cosmetology school

(G-9444)
CREDIT BUR COLLECTN SVCS INC
Also Called: Cbcs
11 W Monument Ave Ste 200 (45402-1233)
PHONE.................937 496-2577
Fax: 937 496-2582
Kevin Kastl, *Principal*
Kevin Castle, *Manager*
Earl Thomas, *Manager*
EMP: 35
SALES (corp-wide): 279.4MM **Privately Held**
SIC: 7322 Collection agency, except real estate
HQ: Credit Bureau Collection Services, Inc.
236 E Town St
Columbus OH 43215
614 223-0688

(G-9445)
CREDIT INFONET INC
4540 Honeywell Ct (45424-5760)
PHONE.................937 235-2546
Thomas L Midkiff, *President*
Jean Midkiff, *Corp Secy*
Ahvai Taylor, *Sales Associate*
Dave Danielson, *Chief Mktg Ofcr*
Jason Coen, *Data Proc Exec*
EMP: 25
SALES (est): 4.2MM **Privately Held**
SIC: 7323 Credit reporting services

(G-9446)
CROSWELL OF WILLIAMSBURG LLC
4828 Wolf Creek Pike (45417-9438)
PHONE.................800 782-8747
John W Croswell, *Branch Mgr*
EMP: 65
SALES (corp-wide): 7MM **Privately Held**
SIC: 4724 Travel agencies
PA: Croswell Of Williamsburg Llc
975 W Main St
Williamsburg OH 45176
513 724-2206

(G-9447)
CSA ANIMAL NUTRITION LLC
6640 Poe Ave Ste 225 (45414-2678)
PHONE.................866 615-8084
Brett Hartman, *Finance*
Charles Schininger, *Mng Member*
EMP: 30
SQ FT: 11,000
SALES: 3MM **Privately Held**
SIC: 0752 Animal specialty services

(G-9448)
CSL PLASMA INC
850 N Main St (45405-4629)
PHONE.................937 331-9186
Sashia Linder, *Branch Mgr*
Brad Patton, *Manager*
EMP: 79
SALES (corp-wide): 6.9B **Privately Held**
WEB: www.zlbplasma.com
SIC: 8099 Blood bank
HQ: Csl Plasma Inc.
900 Broken Sound Pkwy # 4
Boca Raton FL 33487
561 981-3700

(G-9449)
DAHM BROTHERS COMPANY INC
743 Valley St (45404-1957)
PHONE.................937 461-5627
Fax: 937 461-5628
Steve Dahm, *President*
Christopher Dahm, *President*
EMP: 25 EST: 1929
SQ FT: 4,500
SALES (est): 2.7MM **Privately Held**
SIC: 1761 Roofing contractor

(G-9450)
DAIKIN APPLIED AMERICAS INC
Also Called: Daikin Applied Parts Warehouse
2915 Needmore Rd (45414-4303)
PHONE.................763 553-5009
Fax: 937 233-7969
Walt Moulton, *Branch Mgr*
EMP: 25
SALES (corp-wide): 17.9B **Privately Held**
SIC: 5075 4225 Warm air heating & air conditioning; general warehousing & storage
HQ: Daikin Applied Americas Inc.
13600 Industrial Pk Blvd
Minneapolis MN 55441
763 553-5330

(G-9451)
DAVID CAMPBELL
Also Called: Cold Well Banker Realty
2000 Hewitt Ave (45440-2917)
PHONE.................937 266-7064
Ron Sweenny, *Managing Prtnr*
Steve Arman, *Partner*
Thomas R Weaver, *Real Est Agnt*
EMP: 25
SALES (est): 593.6K **Privately Held**
SIC: 6531 Real estate agent, residential

(G-9452)
DAVITA INC
Also Called: Davita Dialysis
5721 Bigger Rd (45440-2752)
PHONE.................937 435-4030
Fax: 937 435-4140
David Howdyshell, *Administration*
EMP: 27 **Publicly Held**
SIC: 8092 Kidney dialysis centers
PA: Davita Inc.
2000 16th St
Denver CO 80202

(G-9453)
DAVUE OB-GYN ASSOCIATES INC (PA)
2200 Philadelphia Dr # 101 (45406-1840)
PHONE.................937 277-8988
James Huey Jr, *President*
Druce J Bernie, *Vice Pres*
Stewart Weprin MD, *Treasurer*
EMP: 58
SQ FT: 5,220
SALES (est): 1.6MM **Privately Held**
SIC: 8011 Obstetrician; gynecologist

(G-9454)
DAY AIR CREDIT UNION INC (PA)
3501 Wilmington Pike (45429-4840)
P.O. Box 292980 (45429-8980)
PHONE.................937 643-2160
Fax: 937 297-3436
William J Burke, *President*
Don McCauley, *Chairman*
Paul Hauck, *Senior VP*
Richard Spyker, *Treasurer*
Charlette Leasure, *Administration*
EMP: 43 EST: 1945
SQ FT: 16,000
SALES: 13.4MM **Privately Held**
WEB: www.dayair.com
SIC: 6062 State credit unions, not federally chartered

(G-9455)
DAYBREAK INC (PA)
605 S Patterson Blvd (45402-2649)
PHONE.................937 395-4600
Fax: 937 461-6582
Linda Kramer, *CEO*
Joanne Taylor, *Facilities Mgr*
Ginny Glass, *Supervisor*
Matt West, *Supervisor*
Liz Wilson, *Director*
EMP: 48 EST: 1975
SQ FT: 53,681
SALES: 8.3MM **Privately Held**
WEB: www.daybreakdayton.org
SIC: 8399 Fund raising organization, non-fee basis

(G-9456)
DAYTON ANIMAL HOSPITAL ASSOC
Also Called: North Main Animal Clinic
8015 N Main St (45415-2250)
PHONE.................937 890-4744
Fax: 937 890-3911
Beth S Weiseerger, *President*
EMP: 27
SQ FT: 4,920
SALES (est): 1.8MM **Privately Held**
SIC: 0742 0752 Animal hospital services, pets & other animal specialties; grooming services, pet & animal specialties

(G-9457)
DAYTON ANTHEM
Also Called: Well Point Anthem
1222 S Patterson Blvd # 4 (45402-2684)
PHONE.................937 428-8000
Fax: 937 428-8128

Dayton - Montgomery County (G-9458)

GEOGRAPHIC SECTION

Rich Gunza, *Director*
EMP: 60
SALES (est): 3.7MM **Privately Held**
SIC: 8621 Health association

(G-9458)
DAYTON APPLIANCE PARTS CO (PA)
122 Sears St (45402-1765)
PHONE 937 224-0487
Fax: 937 224-3437
Timothy Houtz, *President*
James C Houtz, *Vice Pres*
David Heizman, *Accounts Mgr*
Hank Wolf, *Manager*
Joe Lapensee, *Exec Dir*
EMP: 35 **EST:** 1938
SQ FT: 15,000
SALES (est): 17.2MM **Privately Held**
WEB: www.partwizard.com
SIC: 5064 5722 Appliance parts, household; appliance parts

(G-9459)
DAYTON AREA CHAMBER COMMERCE
22 E 5th St Ste 200 (45402-2413)
PHONE 937 226-1444
Fax: 937 226-8254
Phil Parker, *President*
Natalie King-Albert, *Vice Pres*
Marcia Bostick, *Admin Mgr*
Holly Allen, *Director*
EMP: 28
SQ FT: 7,000
SALES: 2.4MM **Privately Held**
SIC: 8611 Chamber of Commerce

(G-9460)
DAYTON ART INSTITUTE
456 Belmonte Park N (45405-4700)
PHONE 937 223-5277
Fax: 937 223-3140
David Stacy, *CFO*
Alexander L Nyerges, *Director*
Janice Driesbach, *Director*
▲ **EMP:** 100
SQ FT: 105,000
SALES: 4.1MM **Privately Held**
WEB: www.daytonartinstitute.org
SIC: 8412 Museum

(G-9461)
DAYTON BAG & BURLAP CO (PA)
322 Davis Ave (45403-2900)
P.O. Box 8 (45401-0008)
PHONE 937 258-8000
Fax: 937 258-0029
Sam Lumby, *President*
Scott Owen, *COO*
Jeffery S Rutter, *COO*
Charlie Cretcher, *CFO*
Kevin Rutter, *Accountant*
▲ **EMP:** 105 **EST:** 1910
SQ FT: 140,000
SALES: 41.2MM **Privately Held**
SIC: 5199 Burlap; dressed furs; baskets

(G-9462)
DAYTON CARDIOLOGY CONSULTANTS (PA)
Also Called: Dayton Crdiolgy Vascular Cons
1126 S Main St (45409-2616)
PHONE 937 223-3053
Raymond Pratt MD, *President*
Holy Cross, *Administration*
Sukirtharan Sinnthamby, *Cardiovascular*
EMP: 47
SQ FT: 10,000
SALES: 8MM **Privately Held**
WEB: www.daytoncardiology.com
SIC: 8011 Cardiologist & cardio-vascular specialist

(G-9463)
DAYTON CHILDRENS HOSPITAL
1 Childrens Plz (45404-1873)
PHONE 937 641-3376
Gary A Mueller, *Principal*
EMP: 30
SALES (est): 118.9K **Privately Held**
SIC: 8011 Internal medicine, physician/surgeon

(G-9464)
DAYTON CHILDRENS HOSPITAL (PA)
Also Called: CHILDREN'S MEDICAL CENTER
1 Childrens Plz (45404-1873)
PHONE 937 641-3000
Fax: 937 463-5400
Deborah A Feldman, *CEO*
David Kinsaul, *President*
Karen Braun, *Business Mgr*
Matt Graybill, *COO*
Lynn Peters, *Senior VP*
▲ **EMP:** 1000
SQ FT: 345,000
SALES: 253.7MM **Privately Held**
SIC: 8069 Children's hospital

(G-9465)
DAYTON CHOA
Also Called: Hotel Dayton
2301 Wagner Ford Rd (45414-5006)
PHONE 937 278-4871
Helen Cho, *Owner*
EMP: 30
SALES (est): 1.3MM **Privately Held**
SIC: 7011 Hotels & motels

(G-9466)
DAYTON CITY PARKS GOLF MAINT
Also Called: Kittyhawk Golf Course
3383 Chuck Wagner Ln (45414-4402)
PHONE 937 333-3378
Fax: 937 237-5224
Tom Getts, *Superintendent*
Phillip Cline, *Superintendent*
Maria Oria, *Superintendent*
William Stutz, *Superintendent*
Kevin Moore, *Manager*
EMP: 30
SALES (est): 753.4K **Privately Held**
SIC: 0781 Landscape services

(G-9467)
DAYTON COUNTRY CLUB COMPANY
555 Kramer Rd (45419-3399)
PHONE 937 294-3352
Fax: 937 294-4151
Steven Gongola, *General Mgr*
Jeffrey Grant, *General Mgr*
Cindy Gardner, *Mktg Dir*
EMP: 90
SALES: 3.8MM **Privately Held**
WEB: www.daytoncountryclub.com
SIC: 7997 Country club, membership

(G-9468)
DAYTON CVB
Also Called: Dayton Convention Visitors Bur
1 Chamber Plz Ste A (45402-2426)
PHONE 937 226-8211
Fax: 937 226-8294
Jacquelyn Powell, *President*
EMP: 40
SALES (est): 1.4MM **Privately Held**
SIC: 7389 Tourist information bureau

(G-9469)
DAYTON DIGITAL MEDIA INC
Also Called: Dayton Digital.com
2212 Patterson Rd (45420-3061)
PHONE 937 223-8335
Joseph Lutz, *Principal*
EMP: 50
SALES (est): 1.9MM **Privately Held**
WEB: www.buyfireproducts.com
SIC: 7389 8742 Advertising, promotional & trade show services; training & development consultant

(G-9470)
DAYTON DMH INC
Also Called: Wood Glenn Nursing Center
3800 Summit Glen Rd (45449-3647)
PHONE 937 436-2273
Fax: 937 436-4771
Carmen Winburn, *Administration*
EMP: 170
SALES (corp-wide): 1.3MM **Privately Held**
SIC: 8051 Skilled nursing care facilities

PA: Dayton Dmh Inc
12348 High Bluff Dr # 100
San Diego CA 92130
858 350-4400

(G-9471)
DAYTON DOOR SALES INC (PA)
Also Called: Overhead Door Co of Dayton
1112 Springfield Rd (45403-1405)
P.O. Box 134 (45404-0134)
PHONE 937 253-9181
Fax: 937 253-9222
Kenneth F Monnin, *CEO*
Dean Monnin, *President*
Lawrence J Becker, *Vice Pres*
Shawna Fuquea, *Credit Mgr*
Lawrence Becker, *MIS Dir*
EMP: 40
SQ FT: 8,800
SALES (est): 16.2MM **Privately Held**
WEB: www.daytondoorsales.com
SIC: 5211 7699 5031 1751 Garage doors, sale & installation; doors, wood or metal, except storm; doors, storm: wood or metal; windows, storm: wood or metal; garage door repair; door & window repair; doors, garage; doors; windows; window & door (prefabricated) installation

(G-9472)
DAYTON DOOR SALES INC
Also Called: Overhead Door Co Springfield
1112 Springfield Rd (45403-1405)
P.O. Box 134 (45404-0134)
PHONE 937 253-9181
Dean Monnin, *Manager*
EMP: 50
SALES (corp-wide): 16.2MM **Privately Held**
WEB: www.daytondoorsales.com
SIC: 5211 5031 7699 Garage doors, sale & installation; doors, garage; garage door repair

PA: Dayton Door Sales, Inc.
1112 Springfield St
Dayton OH 45403
937 253-9181

(G-9473)
DAYTON EAR NOSE THROAT SRGEONS
7076 Corporate Way Ste 1 (45459-4246)
P.O. Box 522 (45409-0522)
PHONE 937 434-0555
Dr John H Boyles Jr, *President*
Charles Zeller IV, *Executive*
EMP: 39
SQ FT: 17,000
SALES (est): 3.4MM **Privately Held**
WEB: www.daytonent.com
SIC: 8011 Ears, nose & throat specialist: physician/surgeon

(G-9474)
DAYTON FOUNDATION INC
Also Called: DISABILITY FOUNDATION THE
40 N Main St Ste 500 (45423-1038)
PHONE 937 222-0410
Fax: 937 222-0636
Michael Parks, *Chairman*
Steve Darnell, *VP Finance*
Latonya McCane, *HR Admin*
Carol Hicks, *VP Mktg*
Melissa Gray, *Technical Staff*
EMP: 30
SQ FT: 5,000
SALES: 4.3MM **Privately Held**
SIC: 8741 8733 8742 Management services; noncommercial research organizations; management consulting services

(G-9475)
DAYTON FREIGHT LINES INC
6265 Executive Blvd Ste A (45424-1400)
PHONE 937 236-4880
Fax: 937 236-7768
Art Hollrah, *Financial Exec*
Jill Heggem, *Office Mgr*
Brian Gratch, *Manager*
Jack Barry, *Manager*
James Ross, *Manager*
EMP: 70
SALES (corp-wide): 1B **Privately Held**
SIC: 4213 4731 4231 Less-than-truckload (LTL) transport; freight consolidation; trucking terminal facilities

PA: Dayton Freight Lines, Inc.
6450 Poe Ave Ste 311
Dayton OH 45414
937 264-4060

(G-9476)
DAYTON HARA ARENA CONF EXHIBTN
1001 Shiloh Springs Rd (45415-2727)
P.O. Box 188, Brookville (45309-0188)
PHONE 937 278-4776
Fax: 937 278-4633
Tom Carroll, *General Mgr*
Ralph Wampler Sr, *Vice Pres*
Karen Wampler, *Human Res Mgr*
Brooke Folkerth, *Marketing Mgr*
Bob Flanagan, *Manager*
EMP: 40
SQ FT: 165,000
SALES (est): 3MM **Privately Held**
WEB: www.haracomplex.com
SIC: 6512 Auditorium & hall operation

(G-9477)
DAYTON HEART CENTER INC (PA)
1530 Needmore Rd Ste 300 (45414-3980)
PHONE 937 277-4274
Davic Joffe, *President*
C David Joffe, *President*
Henry H Chong, *Partner*
Gary J Fishbein, *Partner*
Amit Goyal, *Partner*
EMP: 60
SQ FT: 38,000
SALES (est): 9.8MM **Privately Held**
SIC: 8011 Cardiologist & cardio-vascular specialist

(G-9478)
DAYTON HISTORY
Also Called: Carillon Historical Park
1000 Carillon Blvd (45409-2023)
PHONE 937 293-2841
Fax: 937 293-5798
Brady Kress, *CEO*
Eric Cluxton, *Chairman*
Chris Taylor, *Facilities Dir*
Steve Lucht, *Site Mgr*
Alexandra Ollinger, *Treasurer*
EMP: 125
SALES: 6.6MM **Privately Held**
SIC: 8412 7999 Museum; tourist attractions, amusement park concessions & rides

(G-9479)
DAYTON HOSPICE INCORPORATED (PA)
Also Called: Hospice Butler and Warren Cnty
324 Wilmington Ave (45420-1890)
PHONE 937 256-4490
Fax: 937 256-9802
Deborah Dailey, *President*
William H Macbeth, *Principal*
Steve Wetterhan, *Pastor*
Vicky Forrest, *Vice Pres*
Ken Forrer, *Purch Agent*
EMP: 275
SQ FT: 85,000
SALES: 53.2MM **Privately Held**
WEB: www.hospicedayton.com
SIC: 8082 Home health care services

(G-9480)
DAYTON MAILING SERVICES INC
100 S Keowee St (45402-2241)
P.O. Box 2436 (45401-2436)
PHONE 937 222-5056
Fax: 937 222-2696
Christine Soward, *President*
Jim Hoffman, *Vice Pres*
Tom Cooper, *Manager*
Lori Heineman, *Officer*
EMP: 30
SQ FT: 100,000
SALES (est): 9MM **Privately Held**
WEB: www.daytonmailing.com
SIC: 7331 2759 Mailing service; commercial printing

GEOGRAPHIC SECTION
Dayton - Montgomery County (G-9503)

(G-9481)
DAYTON MEDICAL IMAGING
Also Called: U S Diagnostics
7901 Schatz Pointe Dr (45459-3826)
PHONE...................937 439-0390
Fax: 937 439-4082
Jeffrey Sergent, *Manager*
Mindy Nemon, *Director*
EMP: 96
SQ FT: 3,372
SALES: 2MM Privately Held
SIC: 8011 8071 Radiologist; X-ray laboratory, including dental

(G-9482)
DAYTON METRO CHAPTER
Also Called: Society For Prsrvtion Encurage
3816 Robertann Dr (45420-1053)
PHONE...................937 294-0192
William Carver, *President*
Willam Rohr, *Director*
EMP: 25
SALES (est): 650K Privately Held
SIC: 7929 Entertainers

(G-9483)
DAYTON NWBORN CARE SPCLSTS INC
1 Childrens Plz Rm 4085 (45404-1873)
PHONE...................937 641-3329
Deborah Feldman, *President*
EMP: 501
SALES (est): 1.7MM Publicly Held
SIC: 8051 Skilled nursing care facilities
PA: Mednax, Inc.
1301 Concord Ter
Sunrise FL 33323

(G-9484)
DAYTON OSTEOPATHIC HOSPITAL (HQ)
Also Called: Grandview Hospital & Med Ctr
405 W Grand Ave (45405-7538)
PHONE...................937 762-1629
Fax: 937 461-0020
Fred Manchur, *CEO*
Jim Porter, *President*
Russell J Wetherell, *President*
Jon Larrabee, *Vice Pres*
Todd Anderson, *CFO*
EMP: 1134
SQ FT: 700,000
SALES (est): 118.5MM
SALES (corp-wide): 1.7B Privately Held
WEB: www.gvh-svh.org
SIC: 8062 General medical & surgical hospitals
PA: Kettering Adventist Healthcare
3535 Southern Blvd
Dayton OH 45429
937 298-4331

(G-9485)
DAYTON PERFORMING ARTS ALIANCE
126 N Main St Ste 210 (45402-1766)
PHONE...................937 224-3521
Fax: 937 223-9189
Wendy Campbell, *Chairman*
Raymond Lane, *Vice Pres*
Peter Klosterman, *CFO*
Teri Warwick, *CFO*
Daniel Deitz, *Treasurer*
EMP: 100
SQ FT: 2,022
SALES: 4.7MM Privately Held
WEB: www.daytonphilharmonic.com
SIC: 7929 Symphony orchestras

(G-9486)
DAYTON PHYSICIANS LLC (PA)
6680 Poe Ave Ste 200 (45414-2855)
PHONE...................937 280-8400
Pam Cornelius, *Opers Mgr*
Dawn Koesters, *Opers Mgr*
James Moore, *Opers Mgr*
Jeffery Sergent, *Opers Mgr*
Holly Card, *Site Mgr*
EMP: 58
SQ FT: 5,000
SALES (est): 25.8MM Privately Held
SIC: 8011 Oncologist

(G-9487)
DAYTON PRIMARY & URGENT CARE
301 W 1st St Ste 100 (45402-3046)
PHONE...................937 461-0800
Fax: 937 461-4669
Morris Brown, *President*
EMP: 28
SALES (est): 1.8MM Privately Held
SIC: 8011 Gastronomist

(G-9488)
DAYTON PROF BASBAL CLB LLC
Also Called: Dayton Dragons Baseball
220 N Patterson Blvd (45402-1279)
P.O. Box 2107 (45401-2107)
PHONE...................937 228-2287
Fax: 937 228-2284
Robert Murphy, *President*
Eric Deutsch, *Exec VP*
Jeff Webb, *Vice Pres*
Dave Mayse, *VP Opers*
Joe Eaglowski, *Opers Mgr*
EMP: 28
SALES (est): 2.7MM Privately Held
WEB: www.daytondragons.com
SIC: 7941 Baseball club, professional & semi-professional

(G-9489)
DAYTON PUBLIC SCHOOL DISTRICT
Also Called: Service Building
115 S Ludlow St (45402-1812)
PHONE...................937 542-3000
Cheryl Wilson, *Plant Mgr*
Lori Ward, *Manager*
Teresa Leo, *Webmaster*
EMP: 80
SALES (corp-wide): 319MM Privately Held
WEB: www.dps.k12.oh.us
SIC: 4832 Educational
PA: Dayton Public School District
115 S Ludlow St
Dayton OH 45402
937 542-3000

(G-9490)
DAYTON REGIONAL DIALYSIS INC (PA)
8701 Old Troy Pike Ste 10 (45424-1053)
PHONE...................937 898-5526
Lawrence W Klein, *President*
EMP: 33
SQ FT: 7,600
SALES (est): 1.1MM Privately Held
WEB: www.naod-drd.org
SIC: 8092 8011 Kidney dialysis centers; nephrologist

(G-9491)
DAYTON SOCIETY NATURAL HISTORY (PA)
Also Called: BOONSHOFT MUSEUM OF DISCOVERY
2600 Deweese Pkwy (45414-5400)
PHONE...................937 275-7431
Fax: 937 275-5811
Mark J Meister, *President*
Frieda Brigner, *General Mgr*
Lynn Hanson, *Vice Pres*
Lynn Simonelli, *Vice Pres*
Dona Vella, *Vice Pres*
▲ EMP: 80
SQ FT: 75
SALES: 5MM Privately Held
WEB: www.sunwatch.org
SIC: 8412 Museum

(G-9492)
DAYTON TORO MOTORCYCLE CLUB
1536 W 3rd St (45402-6717)
PHONE...................937 723-9133
John Clork, *CEO*
Shawn Jones, *President*
Fox Rose, *President*
EMP: 25
SQ FT: 2,425
SALES (est): 1.9MM Privately Held
SIC: 7997 Membership sports & recreation clubs

(G-9493)
DAYTON URBAN LEAGUE (PA)
907 W 5th St (45402-8306)
PHONE...................937 226-1513
Fax: 937 220-6666
Sheldon Mitchell, *President*
Clarence Ray III, *Vice Pres*
Willie F Walker, *Vice Pres*
Yvette R Fields, *Treasurer*
Yvette Kelly-Fields, *Director*
EMP: 25
SQ FT: 25,000
SALES: 3.8MM Privately Held
WEB: www.duleague.org
SIC: 8322 8331 Public welfare center; job training & vocational rehabilitation services

(G-9494)
DAYTON WALLS & CEILINGS INC
4328 Webster St (45414-4936)
P.O. Box 13561 (45413-0561)
PHONE...................937 277-0531
Fax: 937 278-5326
Eric Peterson, *President*
Robert Coyle, *Exec VP*
John Peterson, *Vice Pres*
Huffman Ken, *Administration*
EMP: 82
SQ FT: 14,000
SALES: 11.4MM Privately Held
WEB: www.dwceiling.com
SIC: 1742 Drywall; acoustical & ceiling work

(G-9495)
DAYTON WINDUSTRIAL CO
137 E Helena St (45404-1052)
P.O. Box 1127 (45401-1127)
PHONE...................937 461-2603
Fax: 937 461-2994
Greg Jackson, *President*
Dennis Cole, *Sales Staff*
Jeremy Jackson, *Sales Staff*
Brad Williams, *Sales Associate*
Theresa Sherritt, *Manager*
EMP: 30
SALES (est): 3.3MM
SALES (corp-wide): 2.7B Privately Held
WEB: www.daytonwindustrial.com
SIC: 5085 Valves & fittings
PA: Winsupply Inc.
3110 Kettering Blvd
Moraine OH 45439
937 294-5331

(G-9496)
DELOITTE & TOUCHE LLP
220 E Monu Ave Ste 500 (45402)
PHONE...................937 223-8821
Fax: 937 223-8583
Sara Hunt, *Accountant*
Rodney Berning, *Auditor*
Edward T Bentley, *Manager*
Edward Bentley, *IT/INT Sup*
Scott A Snodgress, *IT/INT Sup*
EMP: 100
SALES (corp-wide): 5.9B Privately Held
WEB: www.deloitte.com
SIC: 8721 8742 Certified public accountant; management consulting services
HQ: Deloitte & Touche Llp
30 Rockefeller Plz # 4350
New York NY 10112
212 492-4000

(G-9497)
DELOITTE CONSULTING LLP
711 E Monu Ave Ste 201 (45402)
PHONE...................937 223-8821
Mark A Danis, *Principal*
Susan Kline, *Opers Mgr*
EMP: 150
SALES (corp-wide): 5.9B Privately Held
WEB: www.dctoolset.com
SIC: 8742 8748 Management consulting services; business consulting
HQ: Deloitte Consulting Llp
30 Rockefeller Plz
New York NY 10112
212 492-4000

(G-9498)
DERMATLGISTS OF SOUTHWEST OHIO (PA)
5300 Far Hills Ave # 100 (45429-2381)
PHONE...................937 435-2094
Fax: 937 433-9612
Stephen B Levitt MD, *President*
Thomas G Olsen, *Vice Pres*
John Lepage, *Med Doctor*
John Mackie, *Executive*
Paula Taylor, *Administration*
EMP: 45 EST: 1978
SQ FT: 3,000
SALES (est): 8.2MM Privately Held
WEB: www.dermswohio.com
SIC: 8011 Dermatologist

(G-9499)
DESIGN HOMES & DEVELOPMENT CO
Also Called: Dhdc
8534 Yankee St Ste A (45458-1889)
PHONE...................937 438-3667
Fax: 937 435-1606
Shery Oakes, *President*
Angela Clark, *VP Sls/Mktg*
Scott Denlinger, *Manager*
Laura Sweney, *Manager*
Chelsey Giotta, *Executive Asst*
EMP: 35
SALES (est): 6.6MM Privately Held
WEB: www.designhomesco.com
SIC: 8711 1542 1521 6531 Civil engineering; commercial & office building contractors; single-family housing construction; real estate agents & managers

(G-9500)
DIALYSIS CENTER OF DAYTON EAST
1431 Business Center Ct (45410-3300)
PHONE...................937 252-1867
Fax: 937 254-9312
EMP: 30
SALES (est): 1.2MM Privately Held
SIC: 8092 Dialysis Center

(G-9501)
DIGESTIVE SPECIALISTS INC
Also Called: Digestive Endoscopy Center
999 Brubaker Dr Ste 1 (45429-3505)
PHONE...................937 534-7330
Fax: 937 293-8772
Ramesh Gandhi, *President*
Harold Fishman, *Vice Pres*
Linda Fowler, *CFO*
Cindy Klink, *Finance Mgr*
Cindy Millikin, *Marketing Staff*
▲ EMP: 30
SALES (est): 8.7MM Privately Held
SIC: 8011 Physicians' office, including specialists

(G-9502)
DIVERSCARE HEALTHCARE SVCS INC
6125 N Main St (45415-3110)
PHONE...................937 278-8211
Loren Martin, *Branch Mgr*
EMP: 36
SALES (corp-wide): 574.7MM Publicly Held
SIC: 8051 8322 Skilled nursing care facilities; extended care facility; rehabilitation services
PA: Diversicare Healthcare Services, Inc.
1621 Galleria Blvd
Brentwood TN 37027
615 771-7575

(G-9503)
DOLING & ASSOCIATES DENTAL LAB
3318 Successful Way (45414-4318)
PHONE...................937 254-0075
Fax: 937 254-3256
Ted Doling, *President*
Joe Wiener, *Vice Pres*
Joyce Doling, *Finance Mgr*
EMP: 25
SQ FT: 3,000

Dayton - Montgomery County (G-9504)

SALES (est): 1.5MM Privately Held
SIC: 8072 3842 Dental laboratories; crown & bridge production; surgical appliances & supplies

(G-9504)
DOMESTIC RELATIONS
301 W 3rd St Ste 500 (45402-1446)
PHONE....................937 225-4063
Mike Howley, *Director*
EMP: 50
SALES (est): 2.5MM Privately Held
SIC: 8743 Public relations & publicity

(G-9505)
DRT HOLDINGS INC (PA)
618 Greenmount Blvd (45419-3271)
PHONE....................937 298-7391
Gary Van Gundy, *President*
Greg Martin, *Senior VP*
Sean McBermott, *Engineer*
John Penrod, *Engineer*
Joseph Zehenny, *CFO*
EMP: 60
SALES (est): 189.9MM Privately Held
SIC: 6719 Investment holding companies, except banks

(G-9506)
DRURY HOTELS COMPANY LLC
Also Called: Drury Inn & Suites Dayton N
6616 Miller Ln (45414-2663)
PHONE....................937 454-5200
Fax: 937 454-5200
Steven Patton, *Manager*
EMP: 39
SALES (corp-wide): 397.4MM Privately Held
WEB: www.druryhotels.com
SIC: 7011 Hotels
PA: Drury Hotels Company, Llc
  721 Emerson Rd Ste 400
  Saint Louis MO 63141
  314 429-2255

(G-9507)
DUCRU SPE LLC
1 S Main St (45402-2024)
PHONE....................937 228-2224
Arleen Brothers, *Manager*
Harold Gootrad,
EMP: 25
SALES (est): 2.2MM Privately Held
SIC: 6531 Real estate leasing & rentals

(G-9508)
DUNSIANE SWIM CLUB
600 W Spring Valley Pike (45458-3617)
P.O. Box 41003 (45441-0003)
PHONE....................937 433-7946
Rockne Morrissey, *Treasurer*
EMP: 31
SALES: 233.5K Privately Held
SIC: 7997 Swimming club, membership; tennis club, membership

(G-9509)
DUPONT INC
1515 Nicholas Rd (45417-6712)
PHONE....................937 268-3411
Jeremy Crouch, *Sales Staff*
Richard Russell, *Manager*
William Kohl, *Admin Asst*
EMP: 55
SALES (est): 5.3MM Privately Held
SIC: 5169 Chemicals & allied products

(G-9510)
E-MEK TECHNOLOGIES LLC
7410 Webster St (45414-5816)
PHONE....................937 424-3163
Fax: 937 424-3167
Larry Crossley, *President*
EMP: 60
SALES (est): 12.1MM Privately Held
SIC: 7379

(G-9511)
EARLY EXPRESS SERVICES INC
Also Called: Early Express Mail Services
1333 E 2nd St (45403-1020)
P.O. Box 2422 (45401-2422)
PHONE....................937 223-5801
Fax: 937 223-5549
Karen Sensel, *CEO*
Cindy Woodward, *President*
Beth Wright, *Accountant*
Casey Cook, *Sr Project Mgr*
Matt Thompson, *Art Dir*
EMP: 39
SQ FT: 17,000
SALES (est): 5.7MM Privately Held
WEB: www.earlyexpress.com
SIC: 7331 4212 7374 Mailing service; mailing list compilers; delivery service, vehicular; data processing service

(G-9512)
EARLY LEARNING TREE CHLD CTR (PA)
2332 N Main St (45405-3439)
PHONE....................937 276-3221
Fax: 937 293-1488
Jan Kalbfleisch, *Executive*
Dorothy Pultz,
EMP: 55 EST: 1971
SQ FT: 7,200
SALES (est): 2.5MM Privately Held
SIC: 8351 Group day care center

(G-9513)
EARLY LEARNING TREE CHLD CTR
2332 N Main St (45405-3439)
PHONE....................937 293-7907
Dorothy Pultz, *Owner*
EMP: 56
SALES (est): 3.3MM
SALES (corp-wide): 2.5MM Privately Held
SIC: 8741 8351 Business management; preschool center
PA: Early Learning Tree Children's Center
  2332 N Main St
  Dayton OH 45405
  937 276-3221

(G-9514)
EAST END COMMUNITY SVCS CORP
624 Xenia Ave (45410-1826)
PHONE....................937 259-1898
Fax: 937 222-7316
Cheryl Brookes, *Business Mgr*
Michelle Johnson, *Program Mgr*
Jan Lepore-Jentleson, *Exec Dir*
Stephanie Smith, *Exec Dir*
Jean Berry, *Director*
EMP: 48
SQ FT: 3,706
SALES: 2MM Privately Held
WEB: www.east-end.org
SIC: 8322 8399 Social service center; community development groups

(G-9515)
EAST WAY BEHAVIORAL HLTH CARE
600 Wayne Ave (45410-1122)
PHONE....................937 222-4900
Jonh Strahm, *President*
Bob Groskops, *Treasurer*
Helen Bailey, *Manager*
EMP: 200
SQ FT: 25,000
SALES: 63.9K
SALES (corp-wide): 20.3MM Privately Held
SIC: 8093 8742 8249 Mental health clinic, outpatient; hospital & health services consultant; medical training services
PA: Eastway Corporation
  600 Wayne Ave
  Dayton OH 45410
  937 496-2000

(G-9516)
EASTWAY CORPORATION (PA)
Also Called: Eastway Behavorial Healthcare
600 Wayne Ave (45410-1199)
P.O. Box 983 (45401-0983)
PHONE....................937 496-2000
Fax: 937 496-2028
John F Strahm, *CEO*
Elnar Salamzade, *General Mgr*
Robert E Jaeger, *Principal*
R J Stubbs, *Principal*
Mary Louise Van Doren, *Principal*
EMP: 115 EST: 1957
SALES: 20.3MM Privately Held
SIC: 8063 8322 Hospital for the mentally ill; individual & family services

(G-9517)
EASTWAY CORPORATION
Also Called: Eastco
600 Wayne Ave (45410-1199)
PHONE....................937 531-7000
Fax: 937 496-2035
Joe Pesch, *Info Tech Mgr*
James Sherman, *Director*
EMP: 224
SQ FT: 9,100
SALES (corp-wide): 20.3MM Privately Held
SIC: 8063 8093 Hospital for the mentally ill; specialty outpatient clinics
PA: Eastway Corporation
  600 Wayne Ave
  Dayton OH 45410
  937 496-2000

(G-9518)
ECHOING HILLS VILLAGE INC
Also Called: Echoing Wood Residential Cntr
5455 Salem Bend Dr (45426-1609)
PHONE....................937 854-5151
Fax: 937 854-5153
Robert Gardner, *Med Doctor*
Rose Barber, *Manager*
Julie Grace, *Program Dir*
Timothy Dotson, *Administration*
Alice Byrd, *Clerk*
EMP: 60
SALES (corp-wide): 25.3MM Privately Held
WEB: www.echoinghillsvillage.org
SIC: 7032 8051 Sporting & recreational camps; skilled nursing care facilities
PA: Echoing Hills Village, Inc.
  36272 County Road 79
  Warsaw OH 43844
  740 327-2311

(G-9519)
ECHOING HILLS VILLAGE INC
Also Called: Echoing Valley
7040 Union Schoolhouse Rd (45424-5207)
PHONE....................937 237-7881
Fax: 937 237-0803
Jeanine Purdum, *Project Mgr*
Timothy Dotson, *Human Res Mgr*
Rose Barber, *Manager*
EMP: 50
SALES (corp-wide): 25.3MM Privately Held
WEB: www.echoinghillsvillage.org
SIC: 7032 8059 Sporting & recreational camps; home for the mentally retarded, exc. skilled or intermediate
PA: Echoing Hills Village, Inc.
  36272 County Road 79
  Warsaw OH 43844
  740 327-2311

(G-9520)
EDAPTIVE COMPUTING INC
1245 Lyons Rd Ste G (45458-1818)
PHONE....................937 433-0477
Fax: 937 433-7366
Anju Chawla, *CEO*
Praveen Chawla, *President*
Steve Hoblit, *Accountant*
Jeff Akers, *Director*
Michael Hucul, *Director*
EMP: 70
SQ FT: 10,000
SALES: 15MM Privately Held
WEB: www.edaptive.com
SIC: 7371 Computer software systems analysis & design, custom

(G-9521)
ELITE ISG
Also Called: Elite Investigations SEC Group
7825 N Dixie Dr Ste C (45414-2778)
PHONE....................937 668-6858
Aw Powers, *Partner*
EMP: 35
SALES: 700K Privately Held
SIC: 7381 Security guard service

(G-9522)
ELIZABETH PLACE HOLDINGS LLC
1 Elizabeth Pl (45417-3445)
PHONE....................323 300-3700
Sheral Bateman, *Accountant*
Troy Campbell,
Odet Mkrtchyan,
EMP: 30 EST: 2013
SALES (est): 3.4MM Privately Held
SIC: 8011 Physicians' office, including specialists

(G-9523)
ELIZABETHS NEW LIFE CENTER INC
Also Called: ELIZABETH'S NEW LIFE WOMEN'S C
2201 N Main St (45405-3528)
PHONE....................937 226-7414
Fax: 937 226-1682
Rosemary Prier, *Opers Staff*
Kimberly Horner, *Human Res Dir*
Dominique Koukol, *Human Res Dir*
Julie Myers, *Manager*
Vivian Koob, *Exec Dir*
EMP: 54
SALES: 2.2MM Privately Held
SIC: 8699 Charitable organization

(G-9524)
ELLIOTT TOOL TECHNOLOGIES LTD (PA)
1760 Tuttle Ave (45403-3428)
PHONE....................937 253-6133
Fax: 937 253-9189
Joseph W Smith, *President*
Roger Lall, *General Mgr*
Rob Glenn, *Area Mgr*
John Stoll, *Area Mgr*
Jason Triche, *Area Mgr*
EMP: 68
SQ FT: 37,000
SALES (est): 16MM Privately Held
WEB: www.elliott-tool.com
SIC: 7359 3542 5072 3541 Equipment rental & leasing; machine tools, metal forming type; hand tools; machine tools, metal cutting type; fabricated pipe & fittings

(G-9525)
ELLIPSE SOLUTIONS LLC
7917 Washington Woods Dr (45459-4026)
PHONE....................937 312-1547
Kevin Davies, *Director*
EMP: 50
SALES (est): 2.5MM Privately Held
SIC: 8748 Systems engineering consultant, ex. computer or professional

(G-9526)
EMERGENCY MEDICINE SPECIALISTS
8280 Yankee St (45458-1806)
PHONE....................937 438-8910
Richard Garrson, *President*
Debra Edwards, *Emerg Med Spec*
EMP: 56
SALES (est): 2MM Privately Held
SIC: 8011 Freestanding emergency medical center

(G-9527)
ENVIRNMENTAL ENGRG SYSTEMS INC
Also Called: Honeywell Authorized Dealer
17 Creston Ave (45404-1701)
PHONE....................937 228-6492
Fax: 937 228-8994
Eric Miske, *President*
Jeredythe Miske, *Vice Pres*
Thomas J Miske, *Vice Pres*
Martin Stewart, *Vice Pres*
Deborah Fin, *Finance Mgr*
EMP: 30
SQ FT: 10,000
SALES (est): 5.2MM Privately Held
WEB: www.envengsys.com
SIC: 1711 Mechanical contractor

GEOGRAPHIC SECTION
Dayton - Montgomery County (G-9553)

(G-9528)
ENVISION HEALTHCARE CORP
1530 Needmore Rd Ste 101 (45414-3900)
PHONE.....................937 534-7330
Fax: 937 279-9936
Julie Sprenkel, *Manager*
Julie Sprenkle, *Manager*
EMP: 1027
SALES (corp-wide): 7.8B **Publicly Held**
SIC: 8011 Offices & clinics of medical doctors
PA: Envision Healthcare Corporation
1a Burton Hills Blvd
Nashville TN 37215
615 665-1283

(G-9529)
EQUITAS HEALTH INC
Also Called: Equitas Health Pharmacy
15 W 4th St Ste 200 (45402-2051)
PHONE.....................937 461-2437
Fax: 937 424-8952
William J Hardy, *Exec Dir*
Julie Embree, *Director*
EMP: 200
SALES (est): 8.4MM **Privately Held**
SIC: 8322 Individual & family services

(G-9530)
ERIE CONSTRUCTION MID-WEST INC
Also Called: Erie Construction Co
3520 Sudachi Dr (45414-2435)
PHONE.....................937 898-4688
Jeff Block, *Manager*
EMP: 35
SALES (corp-wide): 40.4MM **Privately Held**
SIC: 1521 5211 1799 1761 General remodeling, single-family houses; door & window products; kitchen & bathroom remodeling; siding contractor
PA: Erie Construction Mid-West, Inc.
4271 Monroe St
Toledo OH 43606
419 472-4200

(G-9531)
ESSEX AND ASSOCIATES INC
7501 Paragon Rd Ste 100 (45459-5319)
PHONE.....................937 432-1040
Wayne Essex, *President*
Ryan Phillips, *Business Mgr*
Nancy Bonfield, *Executive Asst*
Karen Bonfield, *Admin Sec*
EMP: 30
SALES (est): 3MM **Privately Held**
SIC: 8721 Certified public accountant

(G-9532)
EVANGELICAL RETIREMENT
Also Called: Friendship Village of Dayton
5790 Denlinger Rd (45426-1838)
PHONE.....................937 837-5581
Fax: 937 854-4203
Rev Henry Gathagan, *President*
Ron Shroder, *Vice Pres*
Robert Hunter, *Director*
Barb Morris, *Director*
EMP: 230 **EST:** 1972
SQ FT: 439,000
SALES (est): 13.2MM **Privately Held**
SIC: 8361 Home for the aged

(G-9533)
EXCELLENCE IN MOTIVATION INC
6 N Main St Ste 370 (45402-1908)
PHONE.....................763 445-3000
Fax: 937 222-9259
Robert Miller, *President*
John Kernan, *CFO*
Ron Moore, *Accounts Mgr*
Molly Sandquist, *Accounts Exec*
Kim Riley, *Manager*
EMP: 144
SALES (est): 17.5MM
SALES (corp-wide): 100MM **Privately Held**
WEB: www.eim-inc.com
SIC: 8748 8741 Business consulting; management services
PA: One10 Llc
100 N 6th St Ste 700b
Minneapolis MN 55403
763 445-3000

(G-9534)
EXCLUSIVE HOMECARE SERVICES
4699 Salem Ave Ste 1 (45416-1724)
PHONE.....................937 236-6750
Fax: 937 222-8190
Sylvia Grubbs, *CEO*
EMP: 70
SALES (est): 962.9K **Privately Held**
SIC: 8082 Home health care services

(G-9535)
EXEL N AMERCN LOGISTICS INC
5522 Little Richmond Rd (45426-3218)
PHONE.....................937 854-7900
Scott Marcus, *Manager*
Jennifer Schaffranker, *Executive*
EMP: 150
SALES (corp-wide): 71.2B **Privately Held**
SIC: 4222 Storage, frozen or refrigerated goods
HQ: Exel North American Logistics, Inc.
570 Players Pkwy
Westerville OH 43081
800 272-1052

(G-9536)
EXPEDATA LLC
8073 Washington Vlg Dr (45458-1847)
PHONE.....................937 439-6767
Andrea Litle, *Accounting Mgr*
Doug Patterson, *Mng Member*
Ira Goldstein, *CTO*
Denis Manceau, *Director*
Amy Schear, *Administration*
EMP: 30
SALES (est): 3.1MM **Privately Held**
SIC: 7374 Data processing & preparation

(G-9537)
FACILITIES KAHN MANAGEMENT
121 Springboro Pike (45449-3639)
P.O. Box 253 (45401-0253)
PHONE.....................313 202-7607
EMP: 27
SALES (est): 1.4MM **Privately Held**
SIC: 8741 Management Services

(G-9538)
FAIRBORN SFTBALL OFFCIALS ASSN
8740 Cannondale Ln (45424-6460)
PHONE.....................937 902-9920
Sterling Kaimimoku, *President*
EMP: 40
SALES (est): 727.2K **Privately Held**
SIC: 4832 Sports

(G-9539)
FAR OAKS ORTHOPEDISTS INC
3737 Sthern Blvd Ste 2100 (45429)
PHONE.....................937 433-5309
Daniel J Dunaway MD, *Principal*
EMP: 29
SALES (est): 1.9MM
SALES (corp-wide): 6.5MM **Privately Held**
SIC: 8011 Sports medicine specialist, physician
PA: Far Oaks Orthopedists, Inc.
6490 Centervl Bus Pkwy
Dayton OH 45459
937 433-5309

(G-9540)
FAR OAKS ORTHOPEDISTS INC (PA)
6490 Centervl Bus Pkwy (45459-2633)
PHONE.....................937 433-5309
Daniel Dunaway MD, *President*
Donald Ames MD, *Vice Pres*
Steven Klenhenz MD, *Vice Pres*
John Lochner MD, *Vice Pres*
Timothy Quinn MD, *Vice Pres*
EMP: 35
SQ FT: 10,600
SALES (est): 6.5MM **Privately Held**
SIC: 8011 Orthopedic physician

(G-9541)
FARUKI IRELAND & COX PLLC (PA)
500 Courthouse Plz 10 (45402-1122)
PHONE.....................937 227-3700
Teri Seabold, *President*
Charles J Faruki, *Partner*
John Kendall, *Director*
Wanda Works, *Administration*
Erik Gainer, *Legal Staff*
EMP: 50
SALES (est): 6.1MM **Privately Held**
WEB: www.fgilaw.com
SIC: 8111 Corporate, partnership & business law

(G-9542)
FED/MATRIX A JOINT VENTURE LLC
249 Wayne Ave (45402-2939)
PHONE.....................863 665-6363
James Faulkner, *Managing Prtnr*
Karen Rooney, *Accounting Mgr*
Kimberly Goodman, *Office Mgr*
Monika Slowinski, *Office Mgr*
EMP: 25
SALES (corp-wide): 1MM **Privately Held**
SIC: 8712 8711 Architectural engineering; engineering services
PA: Fed/Matrix, A Joint Venture, Llc
255 County Road 555 S
Bartow FL 33830
863 667-1491

(G-9543)
FEDEX FREIGHT INC
8101 Terminal Ln (45424-1457)
PHONE.....................937 233-4826
Fax: 937 233-4858
EMP: 120
SALES (corp-wide): 47.4B **Publicly Held**
SIC: 4213 Nonlocal Trucking Operator
HQ: Fedex Freight, Inc.
2200 Forward Dr
Harrison AR 72601
870 741-9000

(G-9544)
FEDEX OFFICE & PRINT SVCS INC
1189 Mmsburg Cntrville Rd (45459)
PHONE.....................937 436-0677
EMP: 30
SALES (corp-wide): 47.4B **Publicly Held**
SIC: 7334 2791 2789 Photocopying Services Typesetting Services Bookbinding/Related Work
HQ: Fedex Office And Print Services, Inc.
7900 Legacy Dr
Dallas TX 75024
214 550-7000

(G-9545)
FERGUSON CONSTRUCTION COMPANY
2201 Embury Park Rd (45414-5544)
PHONE.....................937 274-1173
Fax: 937 277-1379
Kevin McCormick, *Project Mgr*
Brett Sutherly, *Project Mgr*
Jay T Gearon, *Sales & Mktg St*
Tom Pleiman, *CFO*
Jay Grieshop, *Controller*
EMP: 70
SQ FT: 4,424
SALES (est): 3.7MM
SALES (corp-wide): 128.4MM **Privately Held**
WEB: www.ferguson-construction.com
SIC: 1541 1542 Industrial buildings, new construction; nonresidential construction
PA: Ferguson Construction Company Inc
400 Canal St
Sidney OH 45365
937 498-2381

(G-9546)
FERGUSON HILLS INC
Also Called: Caesar Creek Flea Market
7812 Mcewen Rd Ste 200 (45459-4069)
PHONE.....................513 539-4497
Louis Levin, *CEO*
Allen Levin, *Vice Pres*
EMP: 77
SQ FT: 3,000
SALES (est): 5.3MM **Privately Held**
WEB: www.levininc.com
SIC: 7389 Flea market

(G-9547)
FIRST COMMUNITY HLTH SVCS LLC
Also Called: Fchs
3634 Watertower Ln Ste 1 (45449-4000)
PHONE.....................937 247-0400
Selina Asamoah,
Yao Ayitey,
EMP: 50
SQ FT: 3,000
SALES: 1.5MM **Privately Held**
SIC: 8082 Home health care services

(G-9548)
FIRST DAY FINCL FEDERAL CR UN (PA)
1030 N Main St (45405-4212)
P.O. Box 407 (45405-0407)
PHONE.....................937 222-4546
Ben Roth, *President*
EMP: 30
SQ FT: 6,000
SALES (est): 4.3MM **Privately Held**
SIC: 6061 6162 Federal credit unions; mortgage bankers & correspondents

(G-9549)
FIRST MENTAL RETARDATION CORP
3827 W 3rd St (45417-1842)
PHONE.....................937 262-3077
Fax: 937 262-3081
Janice Smith, *CEO*
EMP: 28
SALES: 17.9K **Privately Held**
SIC: 8361 Residential care

(G-9550)
FIRST SCHOOL CORP
7659 Mcewen Rd (45459-3907)
PHONE.....................937 433-3455
Fax: 937 439-5845
Mark Stone, *President*
EMP: 26 **EST:** 1971
SQ FT: 6,000
SALES (est): 794K **Privately Held**
SIC: 8351 8211 Preschool center; elementary & secondary schools

(G-9551)
FISHEL COMPANY
7651 Center Point 70 Blvd (45424-5193)
PHONE.....................937 233-2268
Fax: 937 233-2183
Darrell Rice, *Division Mgr*
Rick Druin, *Regional Mgr*
Chris Sands, *Manager*
EMP: 110
SALES (corp-wide): 341.9MM **Privately Held**
WEB: www.fishelco.com
SIC: 1623 1794 Gas main construction; excavation work
PA: The Fishel Company
1366 Dublin Rd
Columbus OH 43215
614 274-8100

(G-9552)
FIVE RIVERS HEALTH CENTERS (PA)
2261 Philadelphia Dr # 200 (45406-1814)
PHONE.....................937 734-6841
Gina McFarlane-El, *CEO*
Thomas Duncan, *President*
Ann Schuerman, *Principal*
David Bridge, *CFO*
Jane A Clifton, *Manager*
EMP: 29
SALES: 15.9MM **Privately Held**
SIC: 8011 Clinic, operated by physicians

(G-9553)
FIVE SEASONS SPT CNTRY CLB INC
4242 Clyo Rd (45440-6101)
PHONE.....................937 848-9200
Fax: 937 848-9201
Bruce Stapleton, *Manager*
EMP: 100 **Privately Held**
WEB: www.fiveseasonsday.com

Dayton - Montgomery County (G-9554)

SIC: 7997 7941 Country club, membership; sports clubs, managers & promoters
HQ: Five Seasons Sports Country Club, Inc.
100 E Rivercenter Blvd # 1100
Covington KY 41011

(G-9554)
FLANAGAN LBERMAN HOFFMAN SWAIM
15 W 4th St Ste 100 (45402-2019)
PHONE................................937 223-5200
Fax: 937 223-3335
Patrick A Flanagan, *Partner*
Thomas Angelo, *Partner*
Charles Geidner, *Partner*
Robert Goelz, *Partner*
David Grieshop, *Partner*
EMP: 45
SQ FT: 11,000
SALES (est): 5.2MM **Privately Held**
WEB: www.flhslaw.com
SIC: 8111 General practice law office

(G-9555)
FOODLINER INC
5560 Brentlinger Dr (45414-3510)
PHONE................................563 451-1047
Dwain Minor, *General Mgr*
Lowell Stepp, *Manager*
Todd Hiel, *Manager*
EMP: 25
SALES (corp-wide): 99.1MM **Privately Held**
SIC: 4213 Contract haulers
PA: Foodliner, Inc.
2099 Southpark Ct Ste 1
Dubuque IA 52003
563 584-2670

(G-9556)
FORMSOFT GROUP LTD
10863 Yankee St (45458-3574)
PHONE................................937 885-5015
Fax: 937 885-5320
Janet Popson, *General Mgr*
Randy Popson, *Principal*
EMP: 25
SALES (est): 1.9MM **Privately Held**
WEB: www.formsoftgroup.com
SIC: 7371 Computer software development; software programming applications

(G-9557)
FORRER DEVELOPMENT LTD
7625 Paragon Rd Ste E (45459-4063)
PHONE................................937 431-6489
David Nianouris, *President*
EMP: 30
SQ FT: 100,000
SALES: 250K **Privately Held**
SIC: 6552 Land subdividers & developers, residential

(G-9558)
FOUNDATION FOR COMMUNIT (PA)
349 S Main St (45402-2715)
PHONE................................937 461-3450
Fax: 937 461-9217
David M Smith, *CEO*
Jodi L Minneman, *COO*
Diane L Wilson, *COO*
Clow Andrew, *Facilities Dir*
Norman Green, *Senior Buyer*
EMP: 250
SQ FT: 110,000
SALES: 0 **Privately Held**
SIC: 8099 Blood bank; organ bank

(G-9559)
FOX CLEANERS INC (PA)
4333 N Main St (45405-5035)
PHONE................................937 276-4171
Fax: 937 276-2267
John Roberts, *President*
Donna Manns, *Office Mgr*
EMP: 72
SQ FT: 30,000
SALES (est): 1.9MM **Privately Held**
SIC: 7216 7215 Drycleaning plants, except rugs; laundry, coin-operated

(G-9560)
FRANCISCAN AT ST LEONARD
8100 Clyo Rd (45458-2720)
PHONE................................937 433-0480
Fax: 937 439-7165
Patricia Ioas, *Treasurer*
Marie Clinger, *Human Res Dir*
Mary Houston, *Manager*
Timothy Dressman, *Exec Dir*
Jack Harless, *Director*
EMP: 360
SALES (est): 8.7MM **Privately Held**
WEB: www.stleonard.net
SIC: 8059 8052 Personal care home, with health care; intermediate care facilities

(G-9561)
FRANKLIN IRON & METAL CORP
1939 E 1st St (45403-1131)
PHONE................................937 253-8184
Fax: 937 253-2030
Jack Edelman, *President*
Greg Clouse, *General Mgr*
Debra Edelman, *Treasurer*
Justin Smith, *Manager*
▲ **EMP:** 105
SQ FT: 60,000
SALES (est): 46.1MM **Privately Held**
SIC: 5093 3341 3312 Ferrous metal scrap & waste; secondary nonferrous metals; blast furnaces & steel mills

(G-9562)
FREEZE/ARNOLD A FREUND LEGAL (PA)
1 S Main St Ste 1800 (45402-2043)
PHONE................................937 222-2424
Fax: 937 222-5369
Neil F Freund, *CEO*
Stephen V Freeze, *President*
Cheryl Leavell, *President*
Christopher Carigg, *COO*
Thomas B Bruns, *Vice Pres*
EMP: 90
SQ FT: 40,000
SALES (est): 19MM **Privately Held**
WEB: www.ffalaw.com
SIC: 8111 General practice attorney, lawyer

(G-9563)
FRITO-LAY NORTH AMERICA INC
49 Kelly Ave (45404-1256)
PHONE................................937 224-8716
Fax: 937 224-3742
Al Schretter, *Project Mgr*
John Dean, *Manager*
Mike Powers, *Manager*
EMP: 42
SALES (corp-wide): 63.5B **Publicly Held**
WEB: www.fritolay.com
SIC: 5145 Snack foods
HQ: Frito-Lay North America, Inc.
7701 Legacy Dr
Plano TX 75024

(G-9564)
FRYMAN-KUCK GENERAL CONTRS INC
5150 Webster St (45414-4228)
P.O. Box 13655 (45413-0655)
PHONE................................937 274-2892
Fax: 937 274-9485
Paul Kuck, *President*
Amy Gostolsky, *Vice Pres*
Kent Kuck, *Vice Pres*
Kurt Kuck, *Vice Pres*
Randy Kuck, *Vice Pres*
EMP: 50 **EST:** 1945
SALES: 5MM **Privately Held**
WEB: www.fryman-kuck.com
SIC: 1542 1541 1629 1622 Commercial & office buildings, renovation & repair; commercial & office building, new construction; religious building construction; school building construction; renovation, remodeling & repairs; industrial buildings; industrial buildings, new construction; waste water & sewage treatment plant construction; highway construction, elevated; general contractor, highway & street construction

(G-9565)
FUTURA DESIGN SERVICE INC
6001 N Dixie Dr (45414-4017)
PHONE................................937 890-5252
Fax: 937 890-5255
Dennis Tresslar, *President*
EMP: 25
SQ FT: 6,500
SALES (est): 2.7MM **Privately Held**
SIC: 8711 Engineering services

(G-9566)
FUYAO GLASS AMERICA INC (HQ)
2801 W Stroop Rd (45439)
PHONE................................937 496-5777
Frank Welling, *President*
EMP: 207 **EST:** 2014
SALES (est): 184.1MM
SALES (corp-wide): 2.8B **Privately Held**
SIC: 3231 5013 Products of purchased glass; automobile glass
PA: Fuyao Glass Industry Group Co., Ltd.
Area 1 Fuyao Industrial Village
Ronggiao Economic & Techological
Fuqing 35030
591 853-8377

(G-9567)
G & C FINISHES FROM THE FUTURE (PA)
Also Called: Car Paint
6897 N Dixie Dr (45414-3263)
PHONE................................937 890-3002
Fax: 937 890-2768
James M Volpe, *CEO*
Greg Mc Gathen, *President*
Chris Gardner, *Vice Pres*
EMP: 26 **EST:** 1981
SQ FT: 4,000
SALES (est): 2.4MM **Privately Held**
WEB: www.carpaintstore.net
SIC: 5013 5531 Body repair or paint shop supplies, automotive; automotive & home supply stores

(G-9568)
GE AVIATION SYSTEMS LLC
111 River Park Dr (45409-2109)
PHONE................................937 474-9397
Renee Waag,
Derek Busboom,
EMP: 99
SALES (est): 8MM **Privately Held**
SIC: 8711 Engineering services

(G-9569)
GEM CITY WATERPROOFING
1424 Stanley Ave (45404-1111)
PHONE................................937 220-6800
Mike Ferraro, *Owner*
EMP: 30
SALES (est): 837K **Privately Held**
SIC: 1799 Waterproofing

(G-9570)
GENERAL ELECTRIC COMPANY
950 Forrer Blvd (45420-1469)
P.O. Box 8726 (45401-8726)
PHONE................................937 534-6920
Glen Marino, *Division Pres*
Jeff Loar, *Manager*
EMP: 1200
SALES (corp-wide): 122B **Publicly Held**
WEB: www.gecommercialfinance.com
SIC: 7389 6153 Packaging & labeling services; short-term business credit
PA: General Electric Company
41 Farnsworth St
Boston MA 02210
617 443-3000

(G-9571)
GENERAL ELECTRIC COMPANY
950 Forrer Blvd (45420-1469)
PHONE................................937 534-2000
Michael Sanders, *President*
Bill Ellingwood, *Manager*
EMP: 48
SALES (corp-wide): 122B **Publicly Held**
WEB: www.gecapital.com
SIC: 6153 Short-term business credit

PA: General Electric Company
41 Farnsworth St
Boston MA 02210
617 443-3000

(G-9572)
GERMAIN & CO INC
Also Called: Germane Solutions
10552 Success Ln Ste A (45458-3664)
PHONE................................937 885-5827
Art Boll, *CEO*
James Brown, *President*
Thomas Gentile, *Principal*
Bruce Deighton, *Vice Pres*
Tracy Kulik, *Vice Pres*
EMP: 25
SALES (est): 2MM **Privately Held**
SIC: 8742 Hospital & health services consultant

(G-9573)
GLOBAL GRAPHENE GROUP INC
1240 Mccook Ave (45404-1059)
PHONE................................937 331-9884
Bor Jang, *CEO*
Jennifer Smallwood, *Controller*
Aruna Zhamu, *CTO*
EMP: 40 **EST:** 2016 **Privately Held**
SIC: 6719 Investment holding companies, except banks

(G-9574)
GLOBAL GVRNMENT EDCATN SLTIONS
6450 Poe Ave Ste 200 (45414-2655)
PHONE................................937 368-2308
Richard Leeds, *President*
Shelly Rohr, *Business Mgr*
Steve Goldschein, *Vice Pres*
Curt Rush, *Treasurer*
Brenda Brandyberry, *Accounts Mgr*
EMP: 70
SQ FT: 275,000
SALES: 36MM **Publicly Held**
WEB: www.globalgoved.com
SIC: 5045 Computers, peripherals & software; computer peripheral equipment; printers, computer; computers & accessories, personal & home entertainment
PA: Systemax Inc.
11 Harbor Park Dr
Port Washington NY 11050

(G-9575)
GMS INC
Also Called: United Building Materials
1509 Stanley Ave (45404-1112)
PHONE................................937 222-4444
Fax: 937 222-2221
Barbara Omer, *Controller*
Chris Peters, *Sales Staff*
David Elliott, *Marketing Staff*
David Stawser, *Branch Mgr*
Jon Crawford, *Manager*
EMP: 30
SALES (corp-wide): 2.3B **Publicly Held**
SIC: 5211 5032 Lumber products; drywall materials
PA: Gms Inc.
100 Crescent Center Pkwy
Tucker GA 30084
800 392-4619

(G-9576)
GOOD SAMARITAN HOSPITAL
Also Called: Samaritan Crisiscare
1 Elizabeth Pl (45417-3445)
PHONE................................937 224-4646
Fax: 937 224-1625
Dr Bryan Dyer, *Branch Mgr*
Sidney F Miller, *Surgeon*
EMP: 32 **Privately Held**
SIC: 8062 General medical & surgical hospitals
HQ: Good Samaritan Hospital
2222 Philadelphia Dr
Dayton OH 45406
937 278-2612

(G-9577)
GOOD SAMARITAN HOSPITAL (DH)
2222 Philadelphia Dr (45406-1891)
PHONE................................937 278-2612

GEOGRAPHIC SECTION
Dayton - Montgomery County (G-9600)

Fax: 937 276-8337
Mark S Shaker, *President*
Mary Lousandra, *Facilities Mgr*
Kim Strahl, *Purch Dir*
Betsy Street, *Buyer*
Joel Tooley, *Buyer*
EMP: 900
SQ FT: 1,000,000
SALES: 321.5MM **Privately Held**
SIC: 8062 Hospital, affiliated with AMA residency
HQ: Samaritan Health Partners
2222 Philadelphia Dr
Dayton OH 45406
937 208-8400

(G-9578)
GOOD SAMARITAN HOSPITAL
40 W 4th St Ste 1202 (45402-1857)
PHONE 937 734-2612
Larry Henry, *Human Res Mgr*
Kerney Mosbey, *Branch Mgr*
Michael Meed, *Comp Lab Dir*
EMP: 32 **Privately Held**
SIC: 8062 General medical & surgical hospitals
HQ: Good Samaritan Hospital
2222 Philadelphia Dr
Dayton OH 45406
937 278-2612

(G-9579)
GOODWILL ESTER SEALS MIAMI VLY (PA)
Also Called: Easter Seal
660 S Main St (45402-2708)
PHONE 937 461-4800
Lance W Detrick, *President*
Denise Watts, *General Mgr*
Leo Dugdale, *Sr Corp Ofcr*
Kathy Rearick, *Vice Pres*
Steve Budde, *Facilities Dir*
EMP: 210
SQ FT: 105,000
SALES: 44.5MM **Privately Held**
WEB: www.ohiogoodwills.org
SIC: 8331 Vocational rehabilitation agency

(G-9580)
GOODWILL ESTER SEALS MIAMI VLY
Goodwill Inds of Miami Vly
660 S Main St (45402-2708)
PHONE 937 461-4800
Fax: 937 461-1414
Kennedy Legler Jr, *Senior Partner*
Leo E Dugdale III, *CFO*
Leo Dugdale, *CFO*
Bill Hines, *Human Res Mgr*
Amy Luttrell, *Branch Mgr*
EMP: 300
SALES (corp-wide): 44.5MM **Privately Held**
WEB: www.ohiogoodwills.org
SIC: 4225 General warehousing & storage
PA: Easter Goodwill Seals Miami Valley
660 S Main St
Dayton OH 45402
937 461-4800

(G-9581)
GOSIGER INC (PA)
108 Mcdonough St (45402-2267)
P.O. Box 533 (45401-0533)
PHONE 937 228-5174
Fax: 937 228-5189
Peter G Haley, *President*
John Haley, *Managing Prtnr*
Peter Haley, *Managing Prtnr*
Jane Haley, *Chairman*
Josh Collins, *Regional Mgr*
◆ EMP: 130
SQ FT: 60,000
SALES (est): 144.1MM **Privately Held**
WEB: www.gosiger.com
SIC: 5084 Machine tools & accessories

(G-9582)
GOSIGER INC
108 Mcdonough St (45402-2267)
P.O. Box 533 (45401-0533)
PHONE 937 228-5174
Jerry Pressel, *Branch Mgr*
EMP: 100

SALES (corp-wide): 144.1MM **Privately Held**
WEB: www.gosiger.com
SIC: 5084 Machine tools & accessories
PA: Gosiger, Inc.
108 Mcdonough St
Dayton OH 45402
937 228-5174

(G-9583)
GRACEWORKS LUTHERAN SERVICES
Also Called: Bethany Village Linden
6443 Bethany Village Dr (45459-3571)
PHONE 937 436-6850
John Brinkman, *Administration*
EMP: 500
SALES (corp-wide): 45.6MM **Privately Held**
SIC: 8082 Home health care services
PA: Graceworks Lutheran Services
6430 Inner Mission Way
Dayton OH 45459
937 433-2140

(G-9584)
GRACEWORKS LUTHERAN SERVICES (PA)
6430 Inner Mission Way (45459-7400)
PHONE 937 433-2140
Willis O Serr II, *President*
Michael W Allen, *Vice Pres*
Jim Bosse, *Vice Pres*
Cheryl Robinson, *Project Mgr*
David Wood, *Project Mgr*
EMP: 550
SQ FT: 250,000
SALES: 45.6MM **Privately Held**
SIC: 8051 Skilled nursing care facilities

(G-9585)
GRACEWORKS LUTHERAN SERVICES
6430 Inner Mission Way (45459-7400)
PHONE 937 433-2110
Michael Allen, *Branch Mgr*
EMP: 118
SALES (corp-wide): 45.6MM **Privately Held**
SIC: 8322 Individual & family services
PA: Graceworks Lutheran Services
6430 Inner Mission Way
Dayton OH 45459
937 433-2140

(G-9586)
GREATER DAYTON MVG & STOR CO
3516 Wright Way Rd Ste 2 (45424-5164)
PHONE 937 235-0011
Ira Morgan, *President*
Orville Morgan Sr, *Chairman*
Barb Sigmon, *Bookkeeper*
EMP: 50
SQ FT: 6,000
SALES (est): 5MM **Privately Held**
SIC: 4214 4213 Household goods moving & storage, local; household goods transport; moving services

(G-9587)
GREATER DAYTON PUBLIC TV (PA)
Also Called: THINK TV
110 S Jefferson St (45402-2402)
PHONE 937 220-1600
Fax: 937 220-1642
David M Fogarty, *President*
Sue Brinson, *Editor*
Kolanko Taylor, *Editor*
Kitty Lensman, *COO*
Fred H Stone, *Chief Engr*
EMP: 90
SQ FT: 24,500
SALES (est): 4.6MM **Privately Held**
SIC: 4833 Television broadcasting stations

(G-9588)
GREATER DAYTON RTA
4 S Main St (45402-2055)
PHONE 937 425-8400
Fax: 937 425-8413
Allison Ledford, *Opers Staff*
Pete Trick, *Project Engr*
Mary Stanforth, *CFO*

Carla Lakatos, *Financial Exec*
Anthony Whitmore, *Mktg Dir*
EMP: 680
SALES (est): 34.4MM **Privately Held**
SIC: 4131 Intercity & rural bus transportation

(G-9589)
GREATER DAYTON SURGERY CTR LLC
1625 Delco Park Dr (45420-1391)
PHONE 937 535-2200
Teresa Day, *Materials Mgr*
Tonya Reynolds, *Manager*
Todd Evans, *Exec Dir*
Norbert Mertzman, *Director*
Lawrence Fischer, *Administration*
EMP: 35
SQ FT: 15,000
SALES (est): 7MM **Privately Held**
WEB: www.daytonsurgerycenter.com
SIC: 8062 General medical & surgical hospitals

(G-9590)
GREATER DYTON RGNAL TRNST AUTH (PA)
Also Called: R T A
4 S Main St Ste C (45402-2052)
PHONE 937 425-8310
Mark Donaghy, *CEO*
Robert Ruzinsky, *General Mgr*
Joann Oliver, *Purch Agent*
Joe Swisshelm, *Purch Agent*
Tamea Wiesman, *Purch Agent*
EMP: 100
SALES (est): 8.5MM **Privately Held**
WEB: www.mvrta.org
SIC: 4111 Bus line operations

(G-9591)
GREENTREE GROUP INC (PA)
1360 Tech Ct Ste 100 (45430)
PHONE 937 490-5500
Fax: 937 490-5510
Travis Greenwood, *CEO*
Samuel Greenwood, *Ch of Bd*
Rick Daprato, *Principal*
Tammy Whitaker, *Business Mgr*
Paul Matthews, *Project Mgr*
EMP: 65
SQ FT: 25,000
SALES (est): 19.3MM **Privately Held**
SIC: 7379 8742 Computer related maintenance services; management consulting services

(G-9592)
GS1 US INC
7887 Wash Vlg Dr Ste 300 (45459-3988)
PHONE 609 620-0200
Laura Disciullo, *Vice Pres*
Luiz Martins, *VP Opers*
Hermetz Henry, *Finance Mgr*
Laura Incorvia, *Human Resources*
Mia Franklin, *Accounts Mgr*
EMP: 60
SALES (corp-wide): 54.8MM **Privately Held**
WEB: www.uniformcodecouncil.com
SIC: 8611 Trade associations
PA: Gs1 Us, Inc.
1009 Lenox Dr Ste 202
Lawrenceville NJ 08648
937 435-3870

(G-9593)
GYPC INC
Also Called: Marquette Group
475 Stonehaven Rd (45429-1645)
PHONE 309 677-0405
Christopher F Cummings, *CEO*
Chris Cummings, *CEO*
Eric Webb, *President*
Chris Harkins, *Business Mgr*
Stephanie Rosebrough, *Opers Mgr*
EMP: 225
SALES (est): 60.4MM **Privately Held**
WEB: www.mqgroup.com
SIC: 7311 Advertising consultant

(G-9594)
H & R CONCRETE INC
9120 State Route 48 (45458-5127)
PHONE 937 885-2910
Fax: 937 885-5106

Hershell Williams, *President*
Carol Ferrell, *Admin Sec*
EMP: 35
SQ FT: 480
SALES (est): 4.9MM **Privately Held**
SIC: 1771 1794 Concrete work; excavation work

(G-9595)
HADASSAH DAYTON CHAPTER
880 Fernshire Dr (45459-2310)
PHONE 937 275-0227
Dena Briskin, *Principal*
EMP: 30 EST: 2003
SALES (est): 990K **Privately Held**
SIC: 8699 Charitable organization

(G-9596)
HAFENBRACK MKTG CMMNCTIONS INC
Also Called: Genessa Health Marketing
116 E 3rd St (45402-2130)
PHONE 937 424-8950
Fax: 937 859-3021
Dave Hafenbrack, *President*
John Fimiani, *Senior Partner*
Hans Wagner, *Principal*
Elise Hafenbrack, *Vice Pres*
Erin Rogers, *Project Mgr*
EMP: 26
SQ FT: 3,000
SALES (est): 2.3MM **Privately Held**
SIC: 8742 Marketing consulting services

(G-9597)
HAHN AUTOMOTIVE WAREHOUSE INC
Also Called: Genuine Auto Parts 864
32 Franklin St (45422-2633)
P.O. Box 2909 (45401-2909)
PHONE 937 223-1068
Rick Bowman, *Sales Mgr*
Max Williams, *Sales Mgr*
Rob Zimmer, *Manager*
EMP: 30
SALES (corp-wide): 323.3MM **Privately Held**
WEB: www.iautoparts.com
SIC: 5013 5531 Automotive supplies & parts; automotive parts
PA: Hahn Automotive Warehouse, Inc.
415 W Main St
Rochester NY 14608
585 235-1595

(G-9598)
HAND CTR AT ORTHOPAEDIC INST
3205 Woodman Dr (45420-1143)
PHONE 937 298-4417
Gary Giffen, *Personnel Exec*
Todd Evans, *Administration*
EMP: 60
SALES (est): 871.7K **Privately Held**
SIC: 8011 Orthopedic physician

(G-9599)
HANS ZWART MD & ASSOCIATES (PA)
1520 S Main St Ste 3 (45409-2643)
PHONE 937 433-4183
Jeffrey K Hoffman, *President*
Jeffrey Hoffman MD, *President*
EMP: 40
SALES (est): 2MM **Privately Held**
WEB: www.mail2.erint.com
SIC: 8011 Cardiologist & cardio-vascular specialist; thoracic physician

(G-9600)
HARBORSIDE HEALTHCARE CORP
Also Called: Laurelwood, The
3797 Summit Glen Rd Frnt (45449-3663)
PHONE 937 436-6155
Fax: 937 436-0480
Deborah Schott, *Branch Mgr*
EMP: 70 **Publicly Held**
WEB: www.harborsideuniversity.com
SIC: 8741 Hospital management; nursing & personal care facility management
HQ: Harborside Healthcare Corporation
5100 Sun Ave Ne
Albuquerque NM

Dayton - Montgomery County (G-9601)

(G-9601)
HAVEN BHAVIORAL HEALTHCARE INC
1 Elizabeth Pl Ste A (45417-3445)
PHONE..................937 234-0100
EMP: 446 Privately Held
SIC: 8322 Senior citizens' center or association
PA: Haven Behavioral Healthcare, Inc.
3102 West End Ave # 1000
Nashville TN 37203

(G-9602)
HDI LTD
Also Called: Crowne Plaza Dayton
33 E 5th St (45402-2403)
PHONE..................937 224-0800
Don Bramer, Partner
Kris Davis, Sales Dir
Nicole Presley, Accounts Mgr
Jeff Baumgartner, Manager
EMP: 135
SALES (est): 5.9MM Privately Held
WEB: www.cpdayton.com
SIC: 7011 Hotels

(G-9603)
HEALING TOUCH HEALTHCARE
627 S Edwin C Moses Blvd 3l (45417-3461)
PHONE..................937 610-5555
Fax: 937 610-5554
Faisal M Ali, Principal
Danish Ali, Director
EMP: 35
SALES (est): 1.7MM Privately Held
SIC: 8099 Health screening service

(G-9604)
HEALTH CARE RTREMENT CORP AMER
Also Called: Heartland of Kettering
3313 Wilmington Pike (45429-4023)
PHONE..................937 298-8084
Nancy Mendehall, Purchasing
Alexis Welsh, Human Res Dir
Jennifer Woodward, Administration
EMP: 107
SQ FT: 26,152
SALES (corp-wide): 3.6B Publicly Held
WEB: www.hrc-manorcare.com
SIC: 8051 Skilled nursing care facilities
HQ: Health Care And Retirement Corporation Of America
333 N Summit St Ste 103
Toledo OH 43604
419 252-5500

(G-9605)
HEALTHSOUTH
1 Elizabeth Pl (45417-3445)
PHONE..................937 424-8200
Fax: 937 424-8250
John Pierson, CEO
Kim Stucker, Human Res Dir
Gayle Marlin, Admin Asst
EMP: 102
SALES (est): 7.8MM Privately Held
WEB: www.daytonrehab.com
SIC: 8069 Specialty hospitals, except psychiatric

(G-9606)
HEART HOSPITAL OF DTO LLC
Also Called: Dayton Heart & Vascular Hosp
2222 Philadelphia Dr (45406-1813)
PHONE..................937 734-8000
Chad Carpenter, Mng Member
Chad Patrick, Mng Member
Margaret Ballanger, Director
EMP: 300 EST: 1999
SQ FT: 128,000
SALES (est): 7.6MM Privately Held
WEB: www.daytonhearthospital.com
SIC: 8062 8069 General medical & surgical hospitals; specialty hospitals, except psychiatry
HQ: Good Samaritan Hospital
2222 Philadelphia Dr
Dayton OH 45406
937 278-2612

(G-9607)
HEARTLAND HOSPICE SERVICES LLC
Also Called: Heartland HM Hlth Care Hospice
580 Lincoln Park Blvd # 320 (45429-3493)
PHONE..................937 299-6980
Fax: 937 395-0254
Stephanie Rich, Administration
Jana Miller, Administration
EMP: 25
SALES (corp-wide): 3.6B Publicly Held
SIC: 8082 Home health care services
HQ: Heartland Hospice Services, Llc
333 N Summit St
Toledo OH 43604

(G-9608)
HEARTSPRING HOME HLTH CARE LLC
1251 E Dorothy Ln (45419-2106)
PHONE..................937 531-6920
EMP: 90
SALES (est): 2.4MM Privately Held
SIC: 8099 Health/Allied Services

(G-9609)
HEIDER CLEANERS INC
3720 Wilmington Pike (45429-4856)
PHONE..................937 298-6631
Fax: 937 298-2742
F Joseph Heider, President
Francis J Heider, Exec VP
Rita Heider, Vice Pres
Joan Rauch, Admin Sec
EMP: 26
SQ FT: 7,000
SALES (est): 868K Privately Held
WEB: www.heidercleaners.com
SIC: 7216 Drycleaning plants, except rugs; curtain cleaning & repair

(G-9610)
HEYMAN RALPH E ATTORNEY AT LAW
10 N Ludlow St (45402-1854)
PHONE..................937 449-2820
Ralph E Heyman, Partner
Richard Chernasky, Partner
EMP: 60
SALES (est): 2.8MM Privately Held
SIC: 8111 General practice attorney, lawyer

(G-9611)
HIGH VOLTAGE MAINTENANCE CORP (DH)
Also Called: Vertiv
5100 Energy Dr (45414-3525)
P.O. Box 13059 (45413-0059)
PHONE..................937 278-0811
Fax: 937 278-7791
Charles S Helldoerfer, President
Jim Buczek, COO
Thomas E Nation, Vice Pres
Doug Combs, Foreman/Supr
Becky Bistreck, Human Res Mgr
EMP: 35 EST: 1966
SQ FT: 10,000
SALES (est): 28.6MM Privately Held
WEB: www.hvmcorp.com
SIC: 8734 8711 Testing laboratories; electrical or electronic engineering
HQ: Vertiv Group Corporation
1050 Dearborn Dr
Columbus OH 43085
614 888-0246

(G-9612)
HOLIDAY INN EXPRESS
5655 Wilmington Pike (45459-7102)
PHONE..................937 424-5757
Fax: 937 424-5758
Angela Shockley, Director
EMP: 28
SALES (est): 1.3MM Privately Held
SIC: 7011 Hotels & motels

(G-9613)
HOME CARE NETWORK INC (PA)
190 E Spring Valley Pike A (45458-3803)
PHONE..................937 435-1142
Fax: 937 258-8711
Betty Martin, President
Betty Adams, Vice Pres
Dawn Dilorenzo, Payroll Mgr
Carter Ledbetter, Info Tech Dir
Lisa D Priest, Admin Asst
EMP: 79
SALES (est): 21MM Privately Held
SIC: 8082 7361 Visiting nurse service; nurses' registry

(G-9614)
HOME DEPOT USA INC
Also Called: Home Depot, The
345 N Springboro Pike (45449-3644)
PHONE..................937 312-9053
Fax: 937 312-2726
Darryl Sanders, Manager
EMP: 123
SALES (corp-wide): 100.9B Publicly Held
WEB: www.homerentalsdepot.com
SIC: 5211 7359 Home centers; tool rental
HQ: Home Depot U.S.A., Inc.
2455 Paces Ferry Rd Se
Atlanta GA 30339

(G-9615)
HOME DEPOT USA INC
Also Called: Home Depot, The
5860 Wilmington Pike (45459-7004)
PHONE..................937 312-9076
Fax: 937 312-2746
Kelly Cassidy, Manager
EMP: 130
SALES (corp-wide): 100.9B Publicly Held
WEB: www.homerentalsdepot.com
SIC: 5211 7359 Home centers; tool rental
HQ: Home Depot U.S.A., Inc.
2455 Paces Ferry Rd Se
Atlanta GA 30339

(G-9616)
HOME DEPOT USA INC
Also Called: Home Depot, The
5200 Salem Ave Unit A (45426-1700)
PHONE..................937 837-1551
Fax: 937 837-9082
Rick Goodrich, President
Brian Boots, General Mgr
Thomas Gargano, General Mgr
Paula Capozza, Business Mgr
Kirk Kaiser, Vice Pres
EMP: 100
SALES (corp-wide): 100.9B Publicly Held
WEB: www.homerentalsdepot.com
SIC: 5211 7359 Home centers; tool rental
HQ: Home Depot U.S.A., Inc.
2455 Paces Ferry Rd Se
Atlanta GA 30339

(G-9617)
HOME TOWN REALTORS LLC
9201 N Dixie Dr (45414-1862)
PHONE..................937 890-9111
Keller Williams,
EMP: 75
SALES (est): 2.4MM Privately Held
SIC: 6531 Real estate agents & managers

(G-9618)
HOMEFULL
33 W 1st St Ste 100 (45402-1243)
PHONE..................937 293-1945
Steve Cartright, Principal
Russell W Morgan, Principal
Karen M Shepler, Principal
Candace High, CFO
Terry Smith, Treasurer
EMP: 70
SALES (est): 2.9MM Privately Held
WEB: www.theotherplace.org
SIC: 8322 Emergency shelters

(G-9619)
HOMETOWN URGENT CARE
6210 Brandt Pike (45424-4019)
PHONE..................937 236-8630
Fax: 937 236-8635
Lisa Kay, Branch Mgr
EMP: 175
SALES (corp-wide): 73.2MM Privately Held
SIC: 8011 Freestanding emergency medical center
PA: Hometown Urgent Care
2400 Corp Exchange Dr # 102
Columbus OH 43231
614 505-7633

(G-9620)
HORENSTEIN NICHO & BLUME A L
124 E 3rd St Fl 5 (45402-2186)
PHONE..................937 224-7200
Steven V Hornstein, Partner
Gary Blumenthal, Partner
Bruce Nicholson, Partner
Wilbur S Lang, Principal
Jessica Shaffer, Corp Counsel
EMP: 38
SALES (est): 4MM Privately Held
WEB: www.hnb-law.com
SIC: 8111 General practice law office

(G-9621)
HORIZON PAYROLL SERVICES INC
2700 Miamisburg Centervil (45459-3705)
P.O. Box 751053 (45475-1053)
PHONE..................937 434-8244
Fax: 937 434-8145
Marilynne Saliwanchik, President
Alan Saliwanchik, Vice Pres
Stephanie Webster, Opers Mgr
Becky Sortman, Tax Mgr
Ann Fleischer, HR Admin
EMP: 300
SQ FT: 3,000
SALES (est): 40MM Privately Held
WEB: www.gohorizon.com
SIC: 7371 5045 Custom computer programming services; computers, peripherals & software

(G-9622)
HOSS VALUE CARS & TRUCKS INC (PA)
Also Called: Voss Hyundai
766 Mmsburg Cnterville Rd (45459)
PHONE..................937 428-2400
John E Voss, President
David Flanders, Business Mgr
Kevin Murvay, Info Tech Dir
EMP: 49
SALES (est): 10.1MM Privately Held
WEB: www.vosshyundai.com
SIC: 5511 7538 Automobiles, new & used; general automotive repair shops

(G-9623)
HUBER HEIGHTS YMCA
7251 Shull Rd (45424-1234)
PHONE..................937 236-9622
Fax: 937 236-9627
Josh Sullenberger, Principal
Cindy Edwards, Exec Dir
EMP: 64
SALES (est): 709.9K Privately Held
SIC: 8641 7991 8351 7032 Youth organizations; physical fitness facilities; child day care services; youth camps; individual & family services

(G-9624)
HUBER INVESTMENT CORPORATION (PA)
5550 Huber Rd (45424-2099)
PHONE..................937 233-1122
Fax: 937 235-8002
Charles H Huber, President
Terry Huber, Vice Pres
Cindy Roads, Manager
Rich Williams, Admin Sec
EMP: 50
SQ FT: 1,552
SALES (est): 4.3MM Privately Held
SIC: 6514 6513 Residential building, four or fewer units: operation; apartment building operators

(G-9625)
HUFFMAN HEALTH CARE INC
Also Called: Livingston Care Center
20 Livingston Ave (45403-2938)
PHONE..................937 476-1000
Fax: 937 476-1006
Harold Sosna, President
Kris Rolfsen, Director
EMP: 105

SALES: 5.7MM **Privately Held**
SIC: 8051 Skilled nursing care facilities

(G-9626)
IHEARTCOMMUNICATIONS INC
Also Called: Wize-AM
101 Pine St (45402-2948)
PHONE.................................937 224-1137
Lisa Rice, *President*
Rita Sinsouno, *Executive*
EMP: 50 **Publicly Held**
SIC: 4832 Radio broadcasting stations
HQ: Iheartcommunications, Inc.
    20880 Stone Oak Pkwy
    San Antonio TX 78258
    210 822-2828

(G-9627)
IHEARTCOMMUNICATIONS INC
Also Called: Wxeg-FM
101 Pine St Ste 300 (45402-2948)
PHONE.................................937 224-1137
Fax: 937 222-5483
Nick Gnau, *Sales Mgr*
Aaron Klauber, *Marketing Staff*
Robert Zuroweste, *Manager*
Paul Brigitzer, *Info Tech Mgr*
John Beaulieu, *Exec Dir*
EMP: 150 **Publicly Held**
SIC: 4832 7313 Radio broadcasting stations; radio advertising representative
HQ: Iheartcommunications, Inc.
    20880 Stone Oak Pkwy
    San Antonio TX 78258
    210 822-2828

(G-9628)
IMPACT SALES INC
2501 Neff Rd (45414-5001)
PHONE.................................937 274-1905
Carl Pennington, *Manager*
EMP: 95
SALES (corp-wide): 51MM **Privately Held**
SIC: 5141 Food brokers
PA: Impact Sales, Inc
    915 W Jefferson St Ste A
    Boise ID 83702
    208 343-5800

(G-9629)
INDUS VALLEY CONSULTANTS INC (PA)
1430 Yankee Park Pl Ste A (45458-1829)
PHONE.................................937 660-4748
Srikanth Paladugu, *President*
Madhavi Latha, *Human Res Mgr*
Anupama Reddy, *Human Res Mgr*
Raghavaram Arepalli, *Accounts Mgr*
Sujatha Katuri, *Accounts Mgr*
EMP: 104
SALES (est): 8.4MM **Privately Held**
WEB: www.indusvalley.com
SIC: 7379

(G-9630)
INDUSTRIAL FIBERGLASS SPC INC
Also Called: Fiber Systems
521 Kiser St (45404-1641)
PHONE.................................937 222-9000
Theodore Morton, *Ch of Bd*
Diana Hall, *President*
Janice Morton, *Corp Secy*
Diana Partin, *Purchasing*
Rose Marie Wiliams, *Accounting Mgr*
EMP: 35 **EST:** 1978
SQ FT: 122,000
SALES (est): 6.5MM **Privately Held**
WEB: www.ifs-frp.com
SIC: 3229 1799 Glass fiber products; service station equipment installation, maintenance & repair

(G-9631)
INTEGRATED DATA SERVICES INC
111 Harries St Apt 202 (45402-1889)
PHONE.................................937 656-5496
Jerry W Murray, *Principal*
EMP: 57
SALES (corp-wide): 15.1MM **Privately Held**
SIC: 7374 Data processing service

PA: Integrated Data Services, Inc.
    2141 Rosecrans Ave # 2050
    El Segundo CA 90245
    310 647-3439

(G-9632)
INTEGRATED SOLUTIONS AND
1430 Yankee Park Pl (45458-1829)
PHONE.................................513 826-1932
Clarence McGill, *President*
Vernice Taylor, *Vice Pres*
EMP: 27
SALES (est): 3.2MM **Privately Held**
WEB: www.iss-unlimited.com
SIC: 7379 8748 Computer related consulting services; business consulting

(G-9633)
INTEGRITY HOTEL GROUP
Also Called: Crowne Plaza Dayton Hotel
33 E 5th St (45402-2403)
PHONE.................................937 224-0800
Michael Larsen, *General Mgr*
Abdul Aziz Rupani, *Principal*
EMP: 112
SALES: 950K **Privately Held**
SIC: 7011 Hotels

(G-9634)
INTERIM HEALTHCARE OF DAYTON
Also Called: Medical Prsnnel Pool of Dayton
30 W Rahn Rd Ste 2 (45429-2238)
PHONE.................................937 291-5330
Fax: 937 291-5336
Thomas J Dimarco, *President*
Craig Smith,
EMP: 299
SQ FT: 2,500
SALES: 2.3MM
SALES (corp-wide): 24.4MM **Privately Held**
WEB: www.salo.com
SIC: 7363 Temporary help service
PA: Salo, Inc.
    960 Checkrein Ave Ste A
    Columbus OH 43229
    614 436-9404

(G-9635)
INTERNTIONAL MOLASSES CORP LTD
4744 Wolf Creek Pike (45417-9436)
PHONE.................................937 276-7980
Fax: 937 276-7986
Doug Harrison, *President*
Penny Childers, *Office Mgr*
▲ **EMP:** 30 **EST:** 2000
SALES (est): 9MM **Privately Held**
WEB: www.internationalmolasses.com
SIC: 5149 Molasses, industrial

(G-9636)
INTOWN SUITES MANAGEMENT INC
8981 Kingsridge Dr (45458-1624)
PHONE.................................937 433-9038
Tracey Rahe, *Manager*
EMP: 28 **Privately Held**
SIC: 6513 Apartment hotel operation
HQ: Intown Suites Management, Inc.
    980 Hammond Dr Ste 1400
    Atlanta GA 30328
    800 769-1670

(G-9637)
IRONGATE INC
Also Called: Irongate Inc Realtors
4461 Far Hills Ave (45429-2405)
PHONE.................................937 298-6000
Fax: 937 298-5341
Tim Hagedorn, *Sales Associate*
Pat Colman, *Manager*
Bob Wilson, *Manager*
Chad Christian, *Asst Director*
Steven A Bitonti, *Real Est Agnt*
EMP: 50
SALES (corp-wide): 12.9MM **Privately Held**
WEB: www.irongate-realtors.com
SIC: 6531 Real estate agents & managers
PA: Irongate, Inc
    122 N Main St
    Centerville OH 45459
    937 433-3300

(G-9638)
IRONGATE INC
1353 Lyons Rd (45458-1822)
PHONE.................................937 432-3432
Fax: 937 436-3908
Steven Brown, *President*
Dale Berry, *COO*
Sally Garofoli, *Sales Associate*
Leslie Walker, *Sales Associate*
April Hauser, *Administration*
EMP: 95
SALES (corp-wide): 12.9MM **Privately Held**
WEB: www.irongate-realtors.com
SIC: 6531 Real estate agents & managers
PA: Irongate, Inc
    122 N Main St
    Centerville OH 45459
    937 433-3300

(G-9639)
JAMES L JACOBSON
40 N Main St Ste 2700 (45423-1005)
PHONE.................................937 223-1130
Andy Storar, *Principal*
EMP: 50
SALES (est): 1.2MM **Privately Held**
SIC: 8111 General practice attorney, lawyer

(G-9640)
JET EXPRESS INC (PA)
4518 Webster St (45414-4940)
PHONE.................................937 274-7033
Fax: 937 274-1658
Kevin Burch, *President*
Greg Atkinson, *Vice Pres*
Roger Atkinson Jr, *Vice Pres*
Brad Bradley, *Safety Dir*
John Garrett, *Terminal Mgr*
EMP: 60
SQ FT: 36,000
SALES (est): 22.3MM **Privately Held**
WEB: www.jetexpressinc.com
SIC: 4212 4213 Local trucking, without storage; trucking, except local

(G-9641)
JEWISH FDRTION OF GRTER DAYTON
Also Called: Covenant House
4911 Covenant House Dr (45426-2007)
PHONE.................................937 837-2651
Fax: 937 837-5831
Arthur Cohn, *Manager*
Art Cohen, *Exec Dir*
Peter Wells, *Exec Dir*
Morris Brown, *Director*
Kim Brown, *Social Dir*
EMP: 95
SALES (corp-wide): 4.9MM **Privately Held**
SIC: 8322 8051 Community center; skilled nursing care facilities
PA: Jewish Federation Of Greater Dayton, Inc
    525 Versailles Dr
    Dayton OH 45459
    937 610-1555

(G-9642)
JOE AND JILL LEWIS INC
Also Called: J & J
716 N Broadway St (45402-6245)
P.O. Box 60183 (45406-0183)
PHONE.................................937 718-8829
Joseph W Lewis, *President*
EMP: 99
SALES: 100K **Privately Held**
SIC: 8331 Job training & vocational rehabilitation services

(G-9643)
JOHN A BECKER CO (PA)
Also Called: Becker Electric Supply
1341 E 4th St (45402-2235)
P.O. Box 247 (45401-0247)
PHONE.................................937 226-1341
Fax: 937 226-1790
Thomas J Becker, *CEO*
David Adkinson, *President*
James Becker, *Vice Pres*
Mark Covey, *Vice Pres*
James Dichito, *Vice Pres*
EMP: 62 **EST:** 1920
SQ FT: 65,000

SALES (est): 239.6MM **Privately Held**
WEB: www.beckerelectric.com
SIC: 5063 Electrical construction materials

(G-9644)
JOHN O BOSTOCK JR
Also Called: Total Carpet & Cleaning Svc
5107 Midway Ave (45417-9068)
PHONE.................................937 263-8540
John O Bostock Jr, *Owner*
EMP: 28
SALES: 300K **Privately Held**
SIC: 7349 Building maintenance services

(G-9645)
JOSLIN DIABETES CENTER INC
1989 Miambrg Ctrvl Rd 2 Ste (45459)
PHONE.................................937 401-7575
Fax: 937 401-7579
Jannene Reibert, *Branch Mgr*
EMP: 25
SALES (corp-wide): 83.7MM **Privately Held**
SIC: 8011 Endocrinologist; diabetes specialist, physician/surgeon
PA: Joslin Diabetes Center, Inc.
    1 Joslin Pl
    Boston MA 02215
    617 732-2400

(G-9646)
JPMORGAN CHASE BANK NAT ASSN
950 Forrer Blvd (45420-1469)
P.O. Box 8726 (45401-8726)
PHONE.................................937 534-8218
Jack Peltier, *Manager*
EMP: 1300
SALES (corp-wide): 99.6B **Publicly Held**
WEB: www.chase.com
SIC: 6021 National commercial banks
HQ: Jpmorgan Chase Bank, National Association
    1111 Polaris Pkwy
    Columbus OH 43240
    614 436-3055

(G-9647)
JYG INNOVATIONS LLC
6450 Poe Ave Ste 103 (45414-2667)
PHONE.................................937 630-3858
Jacqueline Gamblin, *CEO*
Merrill Osterman, *Vice Pres*
EMP: 28
SQ FT: 3,000
SALES: 2.4MM **Privately Held**
SIC: 8742 8748 7371 7379 Management consulting services; systems engineering consultant, ex. computer or professional; custom computer programming services; computer related maintenance services; computer facilities management; clinic, operated by physicians

(G-9648)
KEANEY INVESTMENT GROUP LLC
Also Called: Dayton Precision Services
1440 Nicholas Rd (45417-6711)
PHONE.................................937 263-6429
Fax: 937 263-6525
Linda Keaney, *CEO*
James Keaney, *President*
Brett Mitchell, *Accounts Mgr*
Karen Parons, *Manager*
Karen Parsons, *Manager*
EMP: 26
SQ FT: 20,000
SALES (est): 6.4MM **Privately Held**
SIC: 7699 Valve repair, industrial

(G-9649)
KETTERING ADVENTIST HEALTHCARE
3965 Southern Blvd (45429-1229)
PHONE.................................937 298-4331
EMP: 50
SALES (corp-wide): 1.7B **Privately Held**
SIC: 8741 Hospital management
PA: Kettering Adventist Healthcare
    3535 Southern Blvd
    Dayton OH 45429
    937 298-4331

Dayton - Montgomery County (G-9650)

(G-9650)
KETTERING ANESTHESIA ASSOC INC
3533 Sthern Blvd Ste 5200 (45429)
PHONE.................937 298-4331
Laurence J Holland, *President*
EMP: 94
SALES (est): 6.3MM **Privately Held**
SIC: **8011** Anesthesiologist

(G-9651)
KETTERING ANIMAL HOSPITAL INC
1600 Delco Park Dr (45420-1198)
PHONE.................937 294-5211
Fax: 937 294-5201
Dennis A Kulasa, *President*
Dawn M Stiens, *Principal*
Alan Schulze, *Vice Pres*
EMP: 25
SALES (est): 1.9MM **Privately Held**
SIC: **0742** 0752 Veterinarian, animal specialties; boarding services, kennels

(G-9652)
KETTERING CITY SCHOOL DISTRICT
Also Called: Kettering School Maintainence
2636 Wilmington Pike (45419-2455)
PHONE.................937 297-1990
Tom Lee, *Manager*
EMP: 75
SALES (corp-wide): 112.3MM **Privately Held**
WEB: www.kettering.k12.oh.us
SIC: **8211** 7349 Public elementary school; building maintenance services
PA: Kettering City School District
3750 Far Hills Ave
Dayton OH 45429
937 499-1400

(G-9653)
KETTERING CITY SCHOOL DISTRICT
Also Called: Transportation Dept
2640 Wilmington Pike (45419-2455)
PHONE.................937 499-1770
Fax: 513 297-1994
Dan Girbin, *General Mgr*
EMP: 81
SALES (corp-wide): 112.3MM **Privately Held**
WEB: www.kettering.k12.oh.us
SIC: **8211** 4789 Public elementary & secondary schools; cargo loading & unloading services
PA: Kettering City School District
3750 Far Hills Ave
Dayton OH 45429
937 499-1400

(G-9654)
KETTERING MEDICAL CENTER
Also Called: Kettering College Medical Art
3535 Southern Blvd (45429-1298)
PHONE.................937 298-4331
Fax: 937 296-4273
Frank Perez, *CEO*
Steve Huckabaa, *Vice Pres*
Brad Mader, *Mktg Dir*
Frank Engler, *Marketing Staff*
Melissa Walters, *Manager*
EMP: 50
SALES (corp-wide): 1.7B **Privately Held**
WEB: www.kmcfoundation.org
SIC: **8099** Medical services organization
HQ: Kettering Medical Center
3535 Southern Blvd
Kettering OH 45429
937 298-4331

(G-9655)
KETTERING MEDICAL CENTER
Also Called: Kbec Sugarcreek Health Center
580 Lincoln Park Blvd # 200 (45429-3474)
PHONE.................937 299-0099
Julie Hilman, *Branch Mgr*
EMP: 50
SALES (corp-wide): 1.7B **Privately Held**
WEB: www.kmcfoundation.org
SIC: **8099** Physical examination & testing services
HQ: Kettering Medical Center
3535 Southern Blvd
Kettering OH 45429
937 298-4331

(G-9656)
KETTERING MEDICAL CENTER
Also Called: Kettering Health Network
1251 E Dorothy Ln (45419-2106)
PHONE.................937 384-8750
Fax: 937 384-8780
Jarrod McNaughton, *Vice Pres*
Tere Kendel, *Human Resources*
Eileen Corwin, *Med Doctor*
Heather Craft, *Practice Mgr*
Rita E Kaveney, *Manager*
EMP: 30
SALES (corp-wide): 1.7B **Privately Held**
WEB: www.kmcfoundation.org
SIC: **8062** Hospital, professional nursing school
HQ: Kettering Medical Center
3535 Southern Blvd
Kettering OH 45429
937 298-4331

(G-9657)
KETTERING RECREATION CENTER
2900 Glengarry Dr (45420-1225)
PHONE.................937 296-2587
Fax: 937 296-3297
Jim Garges, *President*
Sonja Rom, *Principal*
Jena Bosworth, *Manager*
Jim Englehardt, *Manager*
Mary Beth Thaman, *Director*
EMP: 50
SALES (est): 1.4MM **Privately Held**
SIC: **8322** 7999 7991 Senior citizens' center or association; amusement & recreation; physical fitness facilities

(G-9658)
KETTERING TENNIS CENTER
Also Called: Ktc Quell
4565 Gateway Cir (45440-1790)
PHONE.................937 434-6602
Linda Heinz, *Owner*
EMP: 27
SALES (est): 622.9K **Privately Held**
WEB: www.ktcquail.com
SIC: **7997** Tennis club, membership

(G-9659)
KINDERCARE LEARNING CTRS INC
Also Called: Kindercare Center 1480
951 E Rahn Rd (45429-5927)
PHONE.................937 435-2353
Fax: 937 435-2354
Sherlynn Mullen, *Director*
EMP: 25
SALES (corp-wide): 1.2B **Privately Held**
WEB: www.kindercare.com
SIC: **8351** Group day care center
HQ: Kindercare Learning Centers, Llc
650 Ne Holladay St # 1400
Portland OR 97232
503 872-1300

(G-9660)
KINDRED HEALTHCARE INC
Also Called: Kindred Hospital
707 S Edwin C Moses Blvd (45417-3462)
PHONE.................937 222-5963
Fax: 937 222-5968
Susan Davis, *Manager*
Bruce Moman, *Manager*
Timothy Phoenix, *Director*
Richard Brown, *Radiology Dir*
EMP: 81
SALES (corp-wide): 6B **Publicly Held**
SIC: **8062** 8051 8011 General medical & surgical hospitals; skilled nursing care facilities; dispensary, operated by physicians
PA: Kindred Healthcare, Inc.
680 S 4th St
Louisville KY 40202
502 596-7300

(G-9661)
KINDRED HEALTHCARE INC
Also Called: Kindred At Home
7887 Washington Vlg Dr (45459-3900)
PHONE.................937 433-2400
EMP: 592
SALES (corp-wide): 6B **Publicly Held**
SIC: **9431** 8099 8082 Cancer detection program administration, government; childbirth preparation clinic; oxygen tent service
PA: Kindred Healthcare, Inc.
680 S 4th St
Louisville KY 40202
502 596-7300

(G-9662)
KINDRED HEALTHCARE INC
Also Called: Kindred Hospital-Dayton
601 S Edwin C Moses Blvd (45417-3424)
PHONE.................937 222-5963
Christina Stover, *CEO*
EMP: 81
SALES (corp-wide): 6B **Publicly Held**
WEB: www.kindredhealthcare.com
SIC: **8062** General medical & surgical hospitals
PA: Kindred Healthcare, Inc.
680 S 4th St
Louisville KY 40202
502 596-7300

(G-9663)
KING TREE LEASING CO LLC
Also Called: Riverside Nrsing Rhabilitation
1390 King Tree Dr (45405-1401)
PHONE.................937 278-0723
Fax: 937 276-8675
Stephen Rosedale,
EMP: 99
SQ FT: 71,560
SALES (est): 10.1MM **Privately Held**
SIC: **8051** Convalescent home with continuous nursing care

(G-9664)
KNIGHTS OF COLUMBUS
6050 Dog Leg Rd (45415-2513)
PHONE.................937 890-2971
John Grady, *Principal*
EMP: 50
SALES (corp-wide): 2.2B **Privately Held**
WEB: www.kofc.org
SIC: **8641** Fraternal associations
PA: Knights Of Columbus
1 Columbus Plz Ste 1700
New Haven CT 06510
203 752-4000

(G-9665)
KOHLER FOODS INC (PA)
Also Called: Kohler Catering
4572 Presidential Way (45429-5751)
PHONE.................937 291-3600
Erwin Kohler Jr, *President*
Betty Kohler, *Corp Secy*
Craig Kohler, *Vice Pres*
Kellie Daab, *Sales Mgr*
Sue Delaney, *Sales Mgr*
EMP: 50
SQ FT: 9,000
SALES (est): 3.6MM **Privately Held**
WEB: www.kohlercatering.net
SIC: **7299** 5812 Banquet hall facilities; caterers

(G-9666)
KROGER CO
2917 W Alex Bell Rd (45459-1127)
PHONE.................937 294-7210
Fax: 937 294-1703
Doug Palman, *Manager*
EMP: 187
SALES (corp-wide): 122.6B **Publicly Held**
WEB: www.kroger.com
SIC: **5411** 7384 5912 Supermarkets, chain; photofinishing laboratory; drug stores
PA: The Kroger Co
1014 Vine St Ste 1000
Cincinnati OH 45202
513 762-4000

(G-9667)
KROGER CO
6480 Wilmington Pike (45459-7010)
PHONE.................937 848-5990
Fax: 937 848-6769
Martin Crump, *Principal*
Ziu Lin, *Pharmacist*
Ryan Burkhart, *Manager*
EMP: 100
SALES (corp-wide): 122.6B **Publicly Held**
WEB: www.kroger.com
SIC: **5411** 5141 Supermarkets, chain; supermarkets, 66,000-99,000 square feet; convenience stores, chain; groceries, general line
PA: The Kroger Co
1014 Vine St Ste 1000
Cincinnati OH 45202
513 762-4000

(G-9668)
L R G INC
3795 Wyse Rd (45414-2540)
PHONE.................937 890-0510
Fax: 937 890-3094
Gale Shoup, *President*
Bruce Black, *Superintendent*
David Christian, *Superintendent*
Heath Peters, *Vice Pres*
Roland Peters, *Vice Pres*
EMP: 27
SQ FT: 2,500
SALES (est): 7.1MM **Privately Held**
WEB: www.glrinc.net
SIC: **8711** Construction & civil engineering

(G-9669)
LABORATORY OF DERMATOPATHOLOGY
7835 Paragon Rd (45459-4021)
PHONE.................937 434-2351
Thomas G Olsen, *Principal*
Shawn Nicholson, *Sales Mgr*
Christine Anthony, *Mktg Dir*
Michael Conroy, *Med Doctor*
Theresa A Feeser, *Manager*
EMP: 40
SQ FT: 3,000
SALES (est): 5.2MM **Privately Held**
SIC: **8071** Testing laboratories

(G-9670)
LAKESHORE DIALYSIS LLC
Also Called: Five Rivers Dialysis
4750 N Main St (45405-5021)
PHONE.................937 278-0516
James K Hilger,
EMP: 33
SALES (est): 642.5K **Publicly Held**
SIC: **8092** Kidney dialysis centers
PA: Davita Inc.
2000 16th St
Denver CO 80202

(G-9671)
LAKEWOODS II LTD
980 Wilmington Ave (45420-1686)
PHONE.................937 254-6141
Frank Sinito, *General Ptnr*
EMP: 99
SALES (est): 3MM **Privately Held**
SIC: **6513** Apartment building operators

(G-9672)
LANCO GLOBAL SYSTEMS INC
1430c Yankee Park Pl (45458-1829)
PHONE.................937 660-8090
Venkat Kadiyala, *Branch Mgr*
EMP: 87
SALES (corp-wide): 10.1MM **Privately Held**
SIC: **7379**
PA: Lanco Global Systems, Inc.
21515 Ridgetop Cir # 150
Sterling VA 20166
703 953-2157

(G-9673)
LAP TECHNOLOGY LLC
6101 Webster St (45414-3435)
PHONE.................937 415-5794
Dilip Patel, *Mng Member*
Mike Patel,
Frank Penn,
EMP: 30

GEOGRAPHIC SECTION

Dayton - Montgomery County (G-9697)

SALES (est): 2.5MM **Privately Held**
SIC: 7371 Computer software systems analysis & design, custom

(G-9674)
LASER HAIR REMOVAL CENTER
Also Called: Hair Removal Center of So
5300 Far Hills Ave # 250 (45429-2347)
PHONE.................................937 433-7536
Carla Miracle, *Manager*
EMP: 85 **EST:** 1999
SALES (est): 760K **Privately Held**
SIC: 8011 7231 Dermatologist; beauty shops

(G-9675)
LAURITO & LAURITO LLC
7550 Paragon Rd (45459-5317)
PHONE.................................937 743-4878
Jeffrey Laurito, *Mng Member*
September Paul, *Manager*
Erin Laurito,
EMP: 35
SQ FT: 6,000
SALES (est): 3.7MM **Privately Held**
WEB: www.lauritolaw.com
SIC: 8111 General practice law office

(G-9676)
LEGRAND NORTH AMERICA LLC
1501 Webster St (45404-1559)
PHONE.................................937 224-0639
Fax: 937 223-6385
Geoffrey Hyman, *Principal*
EMP: 159
SALES (corp-wide): 16.3MM **Privately Held**
WEB: www.lastar.com
SIC: 1731 Communications specialization
HQ: Legrand North America, Llc
60 Woodlawn St
West Hartford CT 06110
860 233-6251

(G-9677)
LENZ INC
Also Called: Lenz Company
3301 Klepinger Rd (45406-1823)
P.O. Box 1044 (45401-1044)
PHONE.................................937 277-9364
Fax: 937 277-6516
Robert Wagner, *President*
Grace Campbell, *Human Resources*
Rick Brown, *Sales Staff*
EMP: 50
SQ FT: 15,000
SALES (est): 6.5MM **Privately Held**
WEB: www.thelenz.com
SIC: 6531 3089 Real estate brokers & agents; fittings for pipe, plastic

(G-9678)
LEWARO-D&J-A JOINT VENTURE CO
Also Called: Lewaro Contsruction
1436 Yankee Park Pl Ste A (45458-1893)
PHONE.................................937 443-0000
Phillip Moore, *President*
EMP: 50
SQ FT: 1,200
SALES (est): 1.3MM **Privately Held**
SIC: 8741 8742 8711 1542 Construction management; construction project management consultant; construction & civil engineering; commercial & office building, new construction; highway & street construction

(G-9679)
LEWIS & MICHAEL INC (PA)
1827 Woodman Dr (45420-2937)
P.O. Box 97 (45401-0097)
PHONE.................................937 252-6683
Fax: 937 252-7678
Charles M Lewis, *Ch of Bd*
David Lewis, *President*
Jamie Terebinski, *Vice Pres*
Jackie Ridenour, *Finance*
Pam Heuing, *Admin Asst*
EMP: 30 **EST:** 1941
SQ FT: 40,000
SALES: 8MM **Privately Held**
SIC: 4213 4214 4225 Household goods transport; household goods moving & storage, local; general warehousing

(G-9680)
LIFE CONNECTION OF OHIO INC
40 Wyoming St (45409-2721)
PHONE.................................937 223-8223
Fax: 937 223-8955
Michael Phillips, *CEO*
EMP: 36
SALES (est): 1MM **Privately Held**
SIC: 8099 Organ bank

(G-9681)
LIFESTGES SMRTAN CTR FOR WOMEN
Also Called: Lifestgs-Smrtan Ctrs For Women
2200 Philadelphia Dr # 101 (45406-1840)
PHONE.................................937 277-8988
Bruce Bernie, *Principal*
Maria Kong MD, *Med Doctor*
William Rettig MD, *Med Doctor*
EMP: 50
SQ FT: 5,220
SALES (est): 2.4MM **Privately Held**
SIC: 8099 8011 Medical services organization; offices & clinics of medical doctors

(G-9682)
LIFETOUCH INC
3701 Wilmington Pike (45429-4844)
PHONE.................................937 298-6275
Kenneth Molz, *Manager*
EMP: 33
SALES (corp-wide): 856.2MM **Privately Held**
SIC: 7221 Photographer, still or video
PA: Lifetouch Inc.
11000 Viking Dr
Eden Prairie MN 55344
952 826-4000

(G-9683)
LINCOLN PARK ASSOCIATES II LP
Also Called: Lincoln Park Manor
694 Isaac Prugh Way (45429-3481)
PHONE.................................937 297-4300
Fax: 513 297-4397
Charles Osborn Jr, *Partner*
Miami Valley Hospital Extended, *General Ptnr*
Miami Valley Hospital, *Ltd Ptnr*
Anita Theis, *Manager*
EMP: 130
SQ FT: 40,000
SALES (est): 7.4MM **Privately Held**
SIC: 8051 8059 8052 Convalescent home with continuous nursing care; nursing home, except skilled & intermediate care facility; intermediate care facilities

(G-9684)
LINK IQ LLC (PA)
125 Westpark Rd (45459-4814)
PHONE.................................859 983-6080
Andy Myers,
EMP: 25 **EST:** 2011
SQ FT: 8,000
SALES (est): 3MM **Privately Held**
SIC: 4813 7379 ; computer related maintenance services

(G-9685)
LION GROUP INC (DH)
7200 Poe Ave Ste 400 (45414-2798)
PHONE.................................937 898-1949
Richard Harris, *Research*
Cassandra Whitley, *Research*
James Disanto, *Treasurer*
Richard Musick, *Treasurer*
Leslie Gass, *Accountant*
EMP: 90
SQ FT: 3,700
SALES (est): 106.2MM **Privately Held**
SIC: 6719 Investment holding companies, except banks
HQ: Haagen Rookgeneratoren B.V.
Industrieweg 5
Baarle Nassau 5111
135 076-800

(G-9686)
LION-VALLEN LTD PARTNERSHIP (PA)
Also Called: L V I
7200 Poe Ave Ste 400 (45414-2798)
PHONE.................................937 898-1949
Stephen Schwartz, *Partner*
Terry Smith, *Senior VP*
Mark Boyed, *Vice Pres*
Dennis Dudek, *Vice Pres*
Alan Nash, *Vice Pres*
▼ **EMP:** 300
SALES (est): 40.4MM **Privately Held**
WEB: www.lionapparel.com
SIC: 5136 5137 Uniforms, men's & boys'; uniforms, women's & children's

(G-9687)
LORENZ CORPORATION (PA)
Also Called: Show What You Know
501 E 3rd St (45402-2280)
P.O. Box 802 (45401-0802)
PHONE.................................937 228-6118
Fax: 937 223-2042
Geoffrey R Lorenz, *Ch of Bd*
Reiff Lorenz, *President*
Jean A Shafferman, *Editor*
Tom Borchers, *Corp Secy*
Barbara Meaks, *Vice Pres*
▲ **EMP:** 68 **EST:** 1890
SQ FT: 55,000
SALES (est): 9.1MM **Privately Held**
WEB: www.lorenz.com
SIC: 2741 5049 2721 Music, sheet: publishing only, not printed on site; school supplies; periodicals: publishing only

(G-9688)
LOWES HOME CENTERS LLC
8421 Old Troy Pike (45424-1029)
PHONE.................................937 235-2920
Fax: 937 235-1803
Benjamin Bolin, *Store Mgr*
Rob Kalp, *Manager*
Patricia Burrows, *Executive*
EMP: 150
SALES (corp-wide): 68.6B **Publicly Held**
SIC: 5211 5031 5722 5064 Home centers; building materials, exterior; building materials, interior; household appliance stores; electrical appliances, television & radio
HQ: Lowe's Home Centers, Llc
1605 Curtis Bridge Rd
Wilkesboro NC 28697
336 658-4000

(G-9689)
LOWES HOME CENTERS LLC
2900 Martins Dr (45449-3602)
PHONE.................................937 438-4900
Fax: 937 438-4915
Steve Dolan, *Manager*
EMP: 150
SALES (corp-wide): 68.6B **Publicly Held**
SIC: 5211 5031 5722 5064 Home centers; building materials, exterior; building materials, interior; household appliance stores; electrical appliances, television & radio
HQ: Lowe's Home Centers, Llc
1605 Curtis Bridge Rd
Wilkesboro NC 28697
336 658-4000

(G-9690)
LOWES HOME CENTERS LLC
6300 Wilmington Pike (45459-7009)
PHONE.................................937 848-5600
Fax: 937 848-5615
Jim Dougherty, *Branch Mgr*
EMP: 165
SALES (corp-wide): 68.6B **Publicly Held**
SIC: 5211 5031 5722 5064 Home centers; building materials, exterior; building materials, interior; household appliance stores; electrical appliances, television & radio
HQ: Lowe's Home Centers, Llc
1605 Curtis Bridge Rd
Wilkesboro NC 28697
336 658-4000

(G-9691)
LOWES HOME CENTERS LLC
5252 Salem Ave (45426-1702)
PHONE.................................937 854-8200
Fax: 937 854-8011
Michael Sturtz, *Office Mgr*
EMP: 150

SALES (corp-wide): 68.6B **Publicly Held**
SIC: 5211 5031 5722 5064 Lumber & other building materials; building materials, exterior; building materials, interior; household appliance stores; electrical appliances, television & radio
HQ: Lowe's Home Centers, Llc
1605 Curtis Bridge Rd
Wilkesboro NC 28697
336 658-4000

(G-9692)
M & R ELECTRIC MOTOR SVC INC
1516 E 5th St (45403-2397)
PHONE.................................937 222-6282
Fax: 937 222-1901
Charles Mader, *Corp Secy*
Ronald Mader, *Vice Pres*
Anthony Mader, *Vice Pres*
Craig Mader, *Treasurer*
EMP: 28 **EST:** 1949
SQ FT: 8,000
SALES: 4MM **Privately Held**
SIC: 5063 7694 Motors, electric; electric motor repair

(G-9693)
M K MOORE & SONS INC
5150 Wagner Ford Rd (45414-3662)
P.O. Box 13149 (45413-0149)
PHONE.................................937 236-1812
Fax: 937 236-0490
Michael K Moore, *President*
Christoher Moore, *Vice Pres*
EMP: 30
SQ FT: 10,000
SALES (est): 2.2MM **Privately Held**
SIC: 1799 1742 1711 Insulation of pipes & boilers; insulation, buildings; plumbing, heating, air-conditioning contractors

(G-9694)
MAGIC CASTLE INC
4990 Wilmington Pike (45440-2100)
PHONE.................................937 434-4911
Fax: 937 428-5959
Scott Callabouno, *President*
EMP: 30
SALES (est): 551.2K **Privately Held**
SIC: 7999 7993 Golf services & professionals; coin-operated amusement devices

(G-9695)
MAIN LINE SUPPLY CO INC (PA)
300 N Findlay St (45403-1256)
PHONE.................................937 254-6910
Fax: 937 254-3224
Mike O'Brien, *CEO*
Tim Kroger, *President*
Steve Ireland, *Vice Pres*
Jeff Poast, *Controller*
Kelly Solomon, *Finance Mgr*
◆ **EMP:** 40 **EST:** 1955
SQ FT: 70,000
SALES (est): 32.1MM **Privately Held**
WEB: www.mainlinesupply.com
SIC: 5085 Valves & fittings

(G-9696)
MALL REALTY INC
Also Called: Barnes Cope
862 Watertower Ln (45449-2413)
PHONE.................................937 866-3700
Fax: 937 859-1249
Barry Barnes, *President*
Lois Barnes, *Treasurer*
Anna Hartsouk, *Info Tech Mgr*
Tom Freeman, *Admin Sec*
EMP: 45
SQ FT: 6,000
SALES (est): 2.6MM **Privately Held**
SIC: 6531 Real estate agent, residential

(G-9697)
MANUFACTURING SERVICES INTL
15 W Dorothy Ln (45429-1446)
PHONE.................................937 299-9922
Fax: 937 226-7642
William Hart, *Principal*
EMP: 25
SALES (est): 2.3MM **Privately Held**
SIC: 8711 Engineering services

Dayton - Montgomery County (G-9698)

(G-9698)
MARCA TERRACE WIDOWS
50 S Findlay St (45403-2023)
PHONE..................937 252-1661
Mike Freeman, *Principal*
EMP: 80
SALES (est): 451K **Privately Held**
SIC: 8093 Rehabilitation center, outpatient treatment

(G-9699)
MARSH & MCLENNAN AGENCY LLC
409 E Monu Ave Ste 400 (45402)
PHONE..................937 228-4135
Nick Dattilo, *Senior VP*
David Griffin, *Senior VP*
Julie Rose, *Accounts Mgr*
Karen Harker, *Branch Mgr*
Rhonda Hess, *Director*
EMP: 125
SALES (corp-wide): 14B **Publicly Held**
SIC: 6411 Insurance brokers; property & casualty insurance agent; life insurance agents
HQ: Marsh & Mclennan Agency Llc
360 Hamilton Ave Ste 930
White Plains NY 10601

(G-9700)
MARSH BUILDING PRODUCTS INC (PA)
2030 Winners Cir (45404-1130)
PHONE..................937 222-3321
Fax: 937 222-3797
Ken Middleton, *President*
Mary C Gronefeld, *Principal*
Mike Middleton, *Vice Pres*
Matt Keiber, *Controller*
Tim Mac Veigh, *Financial Exec*
EMP: 25
SQ FT: 15,000
SALES (est): 23.2MM **Privately Held**
WEB: www.marshbuild.com
SIC: 5031 7699 5211 Building materials, exterior; building materials, interior; door & window repair; siding

(G-9701)
MARY C ENTERPRISES INC (PA)
Also Called: Dots Market
2274 Patterson Rd (45420-3061)
PHONE..................937 253-6169
Fax: 937 253-1057
Rob Bernhard, *President*
Frankie Davis, *Vice Pres*
Brad Medlin, *Manager*
EMP: 80
SQ FT: 18,000
SALES (est): 12.5MM **Privately Held**
WEB: www.dotsmarket.com
SIC: 5411 6099 5421 Supermarkets, independent; electronic funds transfer network, including switching; meat markets, including freezer provisioners

(G-9702)
MARY SCOTT NURSING HOME INC
3109 Campus Dr (45406-4100)
PHONE..................937 278-0761
Peggy Rainey, *Manager*
Kenneth Crawford, *Exec Dir*
Timothy Miller, *Exec Dir*
EMP: 98
SALES (est): 5.2MM
SALES (corp-wide): 7.5MM **Privately Held**
WEB: www.msnc.org
SIC: 8052 Personal care facility
PA: Mary Scott Centers Inc
3109 Campus Dr
Dayton OH 45406
937 278-0761

(G-9703)
MAXWELL LIGHTNING PROTECTION
621 Pond St (45402-1348)
PHONE..................937 228-7350
Fax: 937 228-1508
Wayne S Maxwell, *President*
Lynn Busse, *Corp Secy*
Lee Maxwell, *Supervisor*
Caralee Fox, *Admin Sec*
Brad Ratliff, *Administration*
EMP: 40
SQ FT: 7,200
SALES (est): 6.1MM **Privately Held**
WEB: www.maxwell-lp.com
SIC: 1799 Lightning conductor erection

(G-9704)
MBC CARDIOLOGIST INC
122 Wyoming St (45409-2731)
PHONE..................937 223-4461
Fax: 937 449-7603
James M Pacenta MD, *Principal*
EMP: 55 EST: 2001
SALES (est): 1.3MM **Privately Held**
SIC: 8011 Offices & clinics of medical doctors

(G-9705)
MBI SOLUTIONS INC
332 Congress Park Dr (45459-4133)
PHONE..................937 619-4000
Fax: 937 619-4020
Paul Kolodzik MD, *CEO*
Steve Broughton, *President*
Tom Grile, *President*
Terry Heineman, *COO*
Robert Voss, *CFO*
EMP: 112
SQ FT: 22,000
SALES (est): 8.7MM
SALES (corp-wide): 15.1MM **Privately Held**
WEB: www.premierhcs.net
SIC: 8721 Billing & bookkeeping service
PA: Premier Health Care System, Inc.
332 Congress Park Dr
Dayton OH
937 312-3627

(G-9706)
MCAFEE HEATING & AC CO INC
Also Called: McAfee Air Duct Cleaning
4750 Hempstead Station Dr (45429-5164)
PHONE..................937 438-1976
Gregory K McAfee, *President*
Angela Downey, *President*
Naomi McAfee, *Vice Pres*
Patti McDaniel, *Manager*
EMP: 45
SQ FT: 3,500
SALES (est): 8.4MM **Privately Held**
WEB: www.mcair.com
SIC: 1711 Warm air heating & air conditioning contractor

(G-9707)
MCH SERVICES INC
190 E Spring Valley Pike (45458-3803)
PHONE..................260 432-9699
Melisa Roysdon, *Manager*
EMP: 118
SALES (corp-wide): 4.3MM **Privately Held**
SIC: 8082 Home health care services
HQ: Mch Services Inc
108 Lundy Ln
Hattiesburg MS

(G-9708)
MCM ELECTRONICS INC
Also Called: M C M & One Com
650 Congress Park Dr (45459-4072)
PHONE..................937 434-0031
Fax: 937 743-3826
Amy Cale, *Project Mgr*
Jeff Schillo, *Controller*
Renee Jolley, *Marketing Staff*
George Boyle, *Manager*
Norm Stepp, *Executive*
EMP: 60
SQ FT: 130,980 **Privately Held**
WEB: www.mcmelectronics.com
SIC: 5065 4225 Electronic parts; general warehousing
HQ: Mcm Electronics, Inc.
650 Congress Park Dr
Centerville OH 45459

(G-9709)
MECHANICAL CNSTR MANAGERS LLC (PA)
Also Called: Rieck Services
5245 Wadsworth Rd (45414-3507)
P.O. Box 13565 (45413-0565)
PHONE..................937 274-1987
Fax: 937 274-7392
Steven B Mayers, *Vice Pres*
Jim Mobley, *Vice Pres*
Douglas Wallker, *Vice Pres*
Nate Lewis, *Project Mgr*
Steve Willis, *Project Mgr*
EMP: 200 EST: 1949
SQ FT: 50,000
SALES: 38.9MM **Privately Held**
SIC: 1711 1761 Mechanical contractor; sheet metalwork; roofing contractor

(G-9710)
MED AMERICA HLTH SYSTEMS CORP (PA)
1 Wyoming St (45409-2722)
PHONE..................937 223-6192
Fax: 937 220-2454
T G Breitenbach, *President*
Sarah Maurer, *Editor*
Timothy Jackson, *CFO*
Anita Hamlin, *Accountant*
Kimberly Hottell, *Manager*
EMP: 4700
SQ FT: 1,000,000
SALES: 968.3MM **Privately Held**
SIC: 8062 8741 8082 General medical & surgical hospitals; management services; home health care services

(G-9711)
MED-PASS INCORPORATED
1 Reynolds Way (45430-1586)
PHONE..................937 438-8884
Lisa Hanauer, *President*
Susan Spiegel, *Corp Secy*
Kim Buckingham, *Vice Pres*
Doug Harlow, *Vice Pres*
Valerie Hill, *Finance Mgr*
EMP: 40
SQ FT: 40,000
SALES (est): 9.3MM **Privately Held**
WEB: www.med-pass.com
SIC: 5112 8742 Computer & photocopying supplies; management consulting services

(G-9712)
MEDCATH INTERMEDIATE HOLDINGS
Also Called: Dayton Heart Hospital
707 S Edwin Moses Blvd (45408)
PHONE..................937 221-8016
EMP: 370
SALES (corp-wide): 331MM **Privately Held**
SIC: 8062 8069 General Hospital Specialty Hospital
HQ: Medcath Intermediate Holdings Inc
10720 Sikes Pl Ste 300
Charlotte NC

(G-9713)
MEDICAL CENTER AT ELIZABETH PL
Also Called: McEp
1 Elizabeth Pl (45417-3445)
PHONE..................937 223-6237
Fax: 937 660-3111
John Fleishman MD, *President*
Jessica Bent, *HR Admin*
Greg Barnett, *Nursing Mgr*
Alex Rintoul, *Mng Member*
Denisa Fox, *Manager*
EMP: 120
SALES: 18.7MM **Privately Held**
SIC: 8062 General medical & surgical hospitals

(G-9714)
MEDICAL ONCLGY-HEMATOLOGY ASSN
3737 Sthern Blvd Ste 4200 (45429)
PHONE..................937 223-2183
Basel Yanes, *President*
Laura Francis, *Office Mgr*
Alejandro R Calvo, *Oncology*
Ali H Kanbar, *Oncology*
Stuart A Merl, *Oncology*
EMP: 25
SQ FT: 2,000
SALES (est): 2.4MM **Privately Held**
SIC: 8011 Hematologist

(G-9715)
MEDICINE MIDWEST LLC
Also Called: Primed At Congress Park
979 Congress Park Dr (45459-4009)
PHONE..................937 435-8786
Sherrie McKinney, *Human Resources*
Leslie Schrager, *Manager*
EMP: 25
SALES (est): 811.6K
SALES (corp-wide): 3.6MM **Privately Held**
SIC: 8011 General & family practice, physician/surgeon
PA: Medicine Midwest Llc
4700 Smith Rd Ste A
Cincinnati OH 45212
513 533-1199

(G-9716)
MEDWORK LLC
Also Called: Medwork Occupational Hlth Care
1435 Cincinnati St # 100 (45417-4614)
PHONE..................937 449-0800
Dean Imbrogno, *President*
EMP: 58
SALES (est): 2.6MM **Privately Held**
SIC: 8049 Occupational therapist

(G-9717)
MEGACITY FIRE PROTECTION INC (PA)
8210 Expansion Way (45424-6382)
PHONE..................937 335-0775
Fax: 937 879-5050
Larry Gagnon, *President*
Kathleen Gagnon, *Vice Pres*
Emily Goubeaux, *Project Mgr*
Dale Shuster, *Opers Staff*
Cathy Petitto, *Human Resources*
EMP: 40 EST: 1970
SQ FT: 15,000
SALES (est): 5.8MM **Privately Held**
WEB: www.megacityfire.com
SIC: 7389 5085 1731 Fire extinguisher servicing; industrial supplies; fire detection & burglar alarm systems specialization

(G-9718)
MENDELSON ELECTRONICS CO INC
Also Called: Mendelson Liquidation Outlet
340 E 1st St (45402-1250)
PHONE..................937 461-3525
Fax: 937 461-3391
Sanford Mendelson, *President*
Terry Pinsky, *Vice Pres*
Harlan Mendelson, *Sales Executive*
Doris Theodald, *Manager*
EMP: 39
SQ FT: 517,000
SALES: 2.9MM **Privately Held**
WEB: www.meci.com
SIC: 5999 5065 Electronic parts & equipment; electronic parts

(G-9719)
MENDELSON REALTY LTD
340 E 1st St (45402-1250)
PHONE..................937 461-3525
Sanford Mendelson, *Partner*
EMP: 50 EST: 1975
SALES (est): 3.2MM **Privately Held**
WEB: www.mendelsons.com
SIC: 6512 6531 Commercial & industrial building operation; real estate brokers & agents

(G-9720)
MERCHANTS SCRTY SRVC OF DAYTON
2015 Wayne Ave (45410-2134)
P.O. Box 432 (45409-0432)
PHONE..................937 256-9373
Fax: 937 256-8385
James Houpt, *President*
Shanon Be, *Human Res Mgr*
Sandra K Houpt, *Admin Sec*
EMP: 300
SQ FT: 1,500
SALES (est): 8.9MM **Privately Held**
WEB: www.merchantssecurity.com
SIC: 7381 Security guard service

GEOGRAPHIC SECTION
Dayton - Montgomery County (G-9743)

(G-9721)
MESSER CONSTRUCTION CO
4801 Hempstead Station Dr A (45429-5171)
PHONE..................................937 291-1300
Fax: 937 291-4900
Matthew Verst, *Vice Pres*
Eric Wainscott, *Vice Pres*
Matthew Schnelle, *Project Mgr*
Michael King, *Engineer*
David Kylander, *Sls & Mktg Exec*
EMP: 100
SALES (corp-wide): 1B **Privately Held**
WEB: www.messer.com
SIC: 1542 Commercial & office building, new construction
PA: Messer Construction Co.
  643 W Court St
  Cincinnati OH 45203
  513 242-1541

(G-9722)
METLIFE AUTO HM INSUR AGCY INC (HQ)
9797 Springboro Pike (45448-0001)
PHONE..................................815 266-5301
Stephen Klingel, *Ch of Bd*
Darla Fitchum, *COO*
Howard Dalton, *Senior VP*
Andrew Douglass, *Senior VP*
Ruby Schroeder, *Vice Pres*
EMP: 700 EST: 1915
SQ FT: 180,000
SALES (est): 264.5MM
SALES (corp-wide): 63.4B **Publicly Held**
WEB: www.metlifeautoandhome.com
SIC: 6411 Insurance agents & brokers
PA: Metlife, Inc.
  200 Park Ave
  New York NY 10166
  212 578-9500

(G-9723)
MFH INC (PA)
Also Called: Media Group At Michael's, The
241 E Alex Bell Rd (45459-2706)
PHONE..................................937 435-4701
Fax: 937 435-4272
Michael Schuh Jr, *President*
Kathleen Lee, *General Mgr*
Kim Yedlosky, *Opers Dir*
Rosalind Ross, *Accountant*
Sarah Delaney, *Marketing Mgr*
EMP: 33
SQ FT: 3,000
SALES: 3.5MM **Privately Held**
WEB: www.michaelssalons.com
SIC: 7231 7241 Beauty shops; barber shops

(G-9724)
MFH INC
Also Called: Michaels For Hair
241 E Alex Bell Rd (45459-2706)
PHONE..................................937 435-4701
Fax: 937 435-6688
Kathleen Lee, *Manager*
EMP: 100
SALES (corp-wide): 3.5MM **Privately Held**
WEB: www.michaelssalons.com
SIC: 7231 Beauty shops
PA: Mfh, Inc.
  241 E Alex Bell Rd
  Dayton OH 45459
  937 435-4701

(G-9725)
MH EQUIPMENT COMPANY
Also Called: M H Equipment - Ohio
3000 Production Ct (45414-3514)
P.O. Box 13030 (45413-0030)
PHONE..................................937 890-6800
Doug Davis, *Parts Mgr*
Ken Mauch, *Branch Mgr*
EMP: 50
SALES (corp-wide): 237.2MM **Privately Held**
HQ: Mh Equipment Company
  8901 N Industrial Rd
  Peoria IL 61615
  309 579-8020

(G-9726)
MIAMI VALLEY BEKINS INC
Also Called: Miami Valley Moving & Storage
5941 Milo Rd (45414-3415)
P.O. Box 13191 (45413-0191)
PHONE..................................937 278-4296
Sheila Westray, *President*
Michelle Scott, *Treasurer*
EMP: 25
SQ FT: 43,000
SALES (est): 2.3MM **Privately Held**
SIC: 4214 4213 Local trucking with storage; contract haulers

(G-9727)
MIAMI VALLEY BROADCASTING CORP (HQ)
Also Called: Oldies 95
1611 S Main St (45409-2547)
PHONE..................................937 259-2111
Fax: 937 259-2024
Edrew Fichser, *President*
Karen Klimowicz, *Controller*
Eric Zwarg, *Controller*
Ron Taylor, *Manager*
James Hatcher, *Admin Sec*
EMP: 160
SQ FT: 54,000
SALES (est): 25.3MM
SALES (corp-wide): 33B **Privately Held**
SIC: 4833 Television broadcasting stations
PA: Cox Enterprises, Inc.
  6205 Pachtree Dunwoody Rd
  Atlanta GA 30328
  678 645-0000

(G-9728)
MIAMI VALLEY COMMUNITY ACTION (PA)
Also Called: Miami Valley Cap
719 S Main St (45402-2709)
PHONE..................................937 222-1009
Cherish Cronmiller, *CEO*
Joyce E Price, *COO*
Augusta Dent, *Vice Pres*
Stephen V Pipenger, *CFO*
Stephen Pipenger, *Finance*
EMP: 60 EST: 1964
SQ FT: 21,000
SALES: 13MM **Privately Held**
SIC: 8399 8322 6732 Community action agency; antipoverty board; individual & family services; trusts: educational, religious, etc.

(G-9729)
MIAMI VALLEY FAMILY CARE CTR
4100 W 3rd St (45428-9000)
PHONE..................................937 268-0336
Diana Hankie, *Principal*
Susan Johnson, *Principal*
Deb Ruscitelli, *Principal*
Mary Burns, *Director*
Linda Simms, *Director*
EMP: 32
SALES (est): 570.3K **Privately Held**
SIC: 8351 Preschool center

(G-9730)
MIAMI VALLEY GOLF CLUB (PA)
3311 Salem Ave (45406-2699)
PHONE..................................937 278-7381
Fax: 937 274-9121
Mel Cloud, *Manager*
Hale Chris, *Manager*
Nick Fonner, *Manager*
Pat Mahon, *Executive*
EMP: 75
SQ FT: 35,000
SALES: 1.8MM **Privately Held**
WEB: www.miamivalleygolfclub.com
SIC: 7997 Country club, membership

(G-9731)
MIAMI VALLEY HOSPITAL
Also Called: Miami Valley South Campus
2400 Miami Valley Dr (45459-4774)
PHONE..................................937 436-5200
Fax: 937 438-2829
Joanne Ringer, *Vice Pres*
EMP: 250
SALES (corp-wide): 968.3MM **Privately Held**
SIC: 8062 General medical & surgical hospitals
HQ: Miami Valley Hospital
  1 Wyoming St
  Dayton OH 45409
  937 208-8000

(G-9732)
MIAMI VALLEY HOSPITAL (HQ)
1 Wyoming St (45409-2711)
PHONE..................................937 208-8000
Fax: 937 208-6300
Bobbie Gerhart, *President*
Mark Shaker, *President*
Barbara Johnson, *COO*
Makkie Clancy, *Vice Pres*
Diane Pleiman, *Vice Pres*
EMP: 5000
SQ FT: 1,000,000
SALES: 809.9MM
SALES (corp-wide): 968.3MM **Privately Held**
WEB: www.mvafp.com
SIC: 8062 General medical & surgical hospitals
PA: Med America Health Systems Corporation
  1 Wyoming St
  Dayton OH 45409
  937 223-6192

(G-9733)
MIAMI VALLEY HOSPITAL
Also Called: Child Care Center
28 Hill St (45409-2922)
PHONE..................................937 224-3916
Fax: 937 224-0230
Angela Collins, *Director*
EMP: 30
SQ FT: 1,068
SALES (corp-wide): 968.3MM **Privately Held**
WEB: www.mvafp.com
SIC: 8351 Child day care services
HQ: Miami Valley Hospital
  1 Wyoming St
  Dayton OH 45409
  937 208-8000

(G-9734)
MIAMI VALLEY HOSPITALIST GROUP
30 E Apple St Ste 3300 (45409-2939)
PHONE..................................937 208-8394
Angela Black, *Principal*
EMP: 100
SALES (est): 616.5K **Privately Held**
SIC: 6324 Hospital & medical service plans

(G-9735)
MIAMI VALLEY HSING ASSN I INC
907 W 5th St (45402-8306)
PHONE..................................937 263-4449
Connie Isaac, *CEO*
Connie Isaacs, *CFO*
Dan Swan, *Director*
EMP: 44
SQ FT: 1,000
SALES (est): 47.9K **Privately Held**
SIC: 8052 Home for the mentally retarded, with health care

(G-9736)
MIAMI VALLEY MEMORY GRDNS ASSN (DH)
1639 E Lytle 5 Points Rd (45458-5203)
PHONE..................................937 885-7779
Lona Jones, *General Mgr*
David Carroll, *General Mgr*
EMP: 30
SALES (est): 5.2MM
SALES (corp-wide): 3.1B **Publicly Held**
SIC: 6553 0782 Cemetery association; lawn & garden services

(G-9737)
MIAMI VALLEY REGIONAL PLG COMM
10 N Ludlow St Ste 700 (45402-1855)
PHONE..................................937 223-6323
Mark Barry, *General Mgr*
Carol Aquilino, *Controller*
Laura Henry, *Marketing Staff*
Paul Arnold, *Manager*
Brian Martin, *Exec Dir*
EMP: 25
SQ FT: 11,000
SALES (est): 2.6MM **Privately Held**
WEB: www.mvrpc.org
SIC: 8748 Economic consultant

(G-9738)
MIAMI VALLEY SCHOOL
5151 Denise Dr (45429-1999)
PHONE..................................937 434-4444
Fax: 937 434-1033
Jay Scheurle, *Principal*
Peter B Benedict II, *Principal*
Debbie Spiegel, *Dean*
Jennifer Papadakis, *Comms Dir*
Caitlin Wissler, *Librarian*
EMP: 26
SALES (est): 7.1MM **Privately Held**
SIC: 8351 8211 Preschool center; elementary & secondary schools

(G-9739)
MIAMI VALLEY URGENT CARE
6229 Troy Pike (45424-3646)
PHONE..................................937 252-2000
Suresh Gupta, *President*
EMP: 30
SALES (est): 427.1K **Privately Held**
SIC: 8059 Rest home, with health care

(G-9740)
MIAMI VLY CHILD DEV CTRS INC (PA)
Also Called: MVCDC
215 Horace St (45402-8318)
PHONE..................................937 226-5664
Marry Burn, *President*
Dayvenia Chesney, *COO*
William Hewitt, *COO*
Lakendra Moore, *Opers Mgr*
Scott Siegfried, *QC Dir*
EMP: 85 EST: 1964
SQ FT: 22,000
SALES: 32MM **Privately Held**
WEB: www.mvcdc.org
SIC: 8351 Head start center, except in conjunction with school

(G-9741)
MIAMI VLY CHILD DEV CTRS INC
Also Called: Miami View Head Start
215 Horace St (45402-8318)
PHONE..................................937 228-1644
Fax: 937 226-5665
Wilma Cade, *Manager*
Kim Johnson, *Manager*
EMP: 33
SALES (corp-wide): 32MM **Privately Held**
WEB: www.mvcdc.org
SIC: 8351 Head start center, except in conjunction with school
PA: Miami Valley Child Development Centers, Inc.
  215 Horace St
  Dayton OH 45402
  937 226-5664

(G-9742)
MIAMI VLY HSING OPRTUNTIES INC (PA)
Also Called: MVHO
907 W 5th St (45402-8306)
PHONE..................................937 263-4449
Fax: 937 263-9873
Debbie Watts Robinson, *CEO*
Donna Everson, *COO*
EMP: 34
SQ FT: 1,000
SALES: 7.1MM **Privately Held**
SIC: 8361 Home for the mentally handicapped

(G-9743)
MID-AMERICAN CLG CONTRS INC
360 Gargrave Rd Ste E (45449-5405)
PHONE..................................937 859-6222
Nuesmeyer Kermit, *Branch Mgr*
EMP: 105 **Privately Held**
SIC: 7699 Cleaning services

Dayton - Montgomery County (G-9744)

PA: Mid-American Cleaning Contractors, Inc.
447 N Elizabeth St
Lima OH 45801

(G-9744)
MIDWEST BEHAVIORAL CARE LTD
3821 Little York Rd (45414-2409)
PHONE 937 454-0092
Fax: 937 434-6840
Steve Pearce, *Partner*
Phyllis Kuehnl-Walters, *Partner*
Debra Sowald, *Partner*
EMP: 25
SALES (est): 1.2MM **Privately Held**
SIC: 8093 8322 8049 Mental health clinic, outpatient; general counseling services; clinical psychologist

(G-9745)
MIDWEST IRON AND METAL CO
461 Homestead Ave (45417-3921)
P.O. Box 546 (45401-0546)
PHONE 937 222-5992
Fax: 937 222-5233
Joel Frydman, *CEO*
Farley Frydman, *President*
Bert Appel, *Principal*
Judy Griffith, *Principal*
Miriam Jacobs, *Principal*
EMP: 65
SQ FT: 150,000
SALES (est): 18.5MM **Privately Held**
SIC: 3341 5093 Secondary nonferrous metals; scrap & waste materials

(G-9746)
MIKE RENNIE
Also Called: Imagistics International
300 E Bus Way Ste 270 (45401)
PHONE 513 830-0020
Dan Baker, *Principal*
John Curtis, *Principal*
James Tucker, *Vice Pres*
James Stocker, *Sales Mgr*
Mike Rennie, *Manager*
EMP: 35
SALES (est): 1.5MM **Privately Held**
SIC: 7334 Photocopying & duplicating services

(G-9747)
MIKE-SELLS POTATO CHIP CO (HQ)
333 Leo St (45404-1080)
P.O. Box 115 (45404-0115)
PHONE 937 228-9400
Fax: 937 461-5707
Dennis Franklin, *General Mgr*
D W Mikesell, *Principal*
Martha J Mikesell, *Principal*
Philip Kazer, *Exec VP*
Joe Gauthier, *Vice Pres*
EMP: 30
SQ FT: 95,000
SALES (est): 65.7MM **Privately Held**
SIC: 2096 5145 Potato chips & other potato-based snacks; snack foods; pretzels; corn chips
PA: Mike-Sell's West Virginia, Inc.
333 Leo St
Dayton OH 45404
937 228-9400

(G-9748)
MILLCRAFT PAPER COMPANY
1200 Leo St (45404-1650)
PHONE 937 222-7829
Fax: 937 461-0900
Evan Baker, *Accounts Mgr*
Michael A McCaughey, *Branch Mgr*
EMP: 27
SQ FT: 6,600 **Privately Held**
SIC: 5111 5113 Fine paper; paper & products, wrapping or coarse; pressure sensitive tape
HQ: The Millcraft Paper Company
6800 Grant Ave
Cleveland OH 44105
216 441-5505

(G-9749)
MILLER-VALENTINE CONSTRUCTION
137 N Main St Ste 900 (45402-1846)
PHONE 937 293-0900
Bill Krul, *CEO*
Chris Knueven, *President*
David Settles, *Sr Project Mgr*
Sharon Rislund, *Manager*
Dave Selby, *Manager*
EMP: 100
SQ FT: 25,000
SALES (est): 15.4MM **Privately Held**
SIC: 1541 1542 8011 Industrial buildings, new construction; nonresidential construction; commercial & office building, new construction; commercial & office buildings, renovation & repair; shopping center construction; medical centers

(G-9750)
MILLER-VLENTINE OPERATIONS INC (PA)
Also Called: Miller Valentine Group
137 N Main St Ste 900 (45402-1846)
PHONE 937 293-0900
Fax: 937 299-1564
Bill Krul, *CEO*
William Krul, *CEO*
Dina Rancourt, *President*
William Schneider, *Senior Partner*
Larry Hedger, *Superintendent*
EMP: 35
SALES: 153MM **Privately Held**
SIC: 6552 6531 Subdividers & developers; real estate managers

(G-9751)
MILLER-VLENTINE OPERATIONS INC
Also Called: Miller Valentine Group
9435 Waterstone Blvd (45409)
PHONE 513 771-0900
Bill Krul, *Branch Mgr*
EMP: 510
SALES (corp-wide): 153MM **Privately Held**
SIC: 6552 6531 Subdividers & developers; real estate managers
PA: Miller-Valentine Operations, Inc.
137 N Main St Ste 900
Dayton OH 45402
937 293-0900

(G-9752)
MITOSIS LLC
14 W 1st St Ste 302 (45402-1259)
PHONE 937 557-3440
Tyler Back, *Mng Member*
EMP: 25
SALES (est): 50.4K **Privately Held**
SIC: 7336 7812 7371 Graphic arts & related design; video production; computer software development & applications

(G-9753)
MODERN BUILDERS SUPPLY INC
2627 Stanley Ave (45404-2732)
P.O. Box 155 (45404-0155)
PHONE 937 222-2627
Fax: 937 222-8441
Mike Schweigert, *Regional Mgr*
Kerry Linsenbigler, *Site Mgr*
Richard Baindge, *Manager*
EMP: 31
SALES (corp-wide): 437.3MM **Privately Held**
WEB: www.polaristechnologies.com
SIC: 5033 Roofing & siding materials
PA: Modern Builders Supply, Inc.
302 Mcclurg Rd
Youngstown OH 44512
330 729-2690

(G-9754)
MONCO ENTERPRISES INC (PA)
700 Liberty Ln (45449-2135)
PHONE 937 461-0034
Fax: 937 461-6554
Phil Hartje, *General Mgr*
Joe Akakpo, *Facilities Mgr*
Tom Digiovanna, *Info Tech Mgr*
Elvia Thomas, *Director*
EMP: 850

SQ FT: 50,000
SALES: 38.6K **Privately Held**
SIC: 8331 2789 Sheltered workshop; community service employment training program; bookbinding & related work

(G-9755)
MONTGOMERY IRON & PAPER CO INC
Also Called: Montgomery Paper Co Div
400 E 4th St (45402-2110)
PHONE 937 222-4059
Steven Jacobs, *President*
Mitchell Jacobs, *General Mgr*
Victor Jacobs, *Vice Pres*
Charles Jacobs, *Director*
Claire Jacobs, *Director*
EMP: 64
SQ FT: 17,000
SALES (est): 12.6MM **Privately Held**
SIC: 5093 Scrap & waste materials

(G-9756)
MORAINE COUNTRY CLUB
4075 Southern Blvd Unit 1 (45429-1199)
PHONE 937 294-6200
Fax: 937 297-6350
Jack E King, *President*
Jack Proud, *President*
Phil Zwierzchowski, *General Mgr*
Marianne Speranza, *Business Mgr*
John Giering, *Treasurer*
EMP: 35
SQ FT: 20,000
SALES: 5MM **Privately Held**
WEB: www.morainecountryclub.com
SIC: 7997 Country club, membership

(G-9757)
MORGAN SERVICES INC
817 Webster St (45404-1529)
PHONE 937 223-5241
Alan Hartzell, *Branch Mgr*
EMP: 90
SALES (corp-wide): 38.6MM **Privately Held**
SIC: 7213 Linen supply
PA: Morgan Services, Inc.
323 N Michigan Ave
Chicago IL 60601
312 346-3181

(G-9758)
MOTO FRANCHISE CORPORATION (PA)
Also Called: Motophoto
7086 Corporate Way Ste 2 (45459-4298)
PHONE 937 291-1900
Harry D Loyle, *President*
Ron Mohney, *Vice Pres*
Joseph M O'Hara, *Vice Pres*
EMP: 32
SQ FT: 3,500
SALES (est): 10.1MM **Privately Held**
SIC: 6794 Franchises, selling or licensing

(G-9759)
MOTORISTS MUTUAL INSURANCE CO
Also Called: Motorists Life Ins Co
8255 Yankee St (45458-1807)
P.O. Box 750306 (45475-0306)
PHONE 937 435-5540
Fax: 937 435-6073
Brent Morrison, *Branch Mgr*
EMP: 30
SALES (corp-wide): 494.7MM **Privately Held**
SIC: 6331 6411 Fire, marine & casualty insurance: mutual; insurance agents, brokers & service
PA: Motorists Mutual Insurance Company
471 E Broad St Ste 200
Columbus OH 43215
614 225-8211

(G-9760)
MUHA CONSTRUCTION INC
Also Called: Midwest Painting
855 Congress Park Dr # 101 (45459-4096)
PHONE 937 435-0678
David J Muha, *President*
Rhonda K Cox, *Exec VP*
Chuck Albert, *Vice Pres*
Greg Beem, *Project Mgr*

Jeff Paden, *Project Mgr*
EMP: 46
SQ FT: 40,000
SALES: 10MM **Privately Held**
WEB: www.muhaconstruction.com
SIC: 1721 1542 Commercial painting; commercial & office building contractors

(G-9761)
MULLINS INTERNATIONAL SLS CORP
2949 Valley Pike (45404-2609)
P.O. Box 24113 (45424-0113)
PHONE 937 233-4213
William R Mullins, *President*
Dennis D Mullins, *Vice Pres*
Richard F Mullins, *Vice Pres*
▲ **EMP:** 60 **EST:** 1972
SQ FT: 75,000
SALES: 1MM **Privately Held**
SIC: 5085 Rubber goods, mechanical

(G-9762)
MUTUAL ELECTRIC COMPANY
3660 Dayton Park Dr (45414-4406)
P.O. Box 131222 (45413-1222)
PHONE 937 254-6211
Ted Michel, *President*
Belinda Michel, *Vice Pres*
Robert Kreitzer, *Admin Sec*
EMP: 32 **EST:** 1944
SQ FT: 7,000
SALES: 2.2MM **Privately Held**
WEB: www.mutual-electric.com
SIC: 1731 General electrical contractor

(G-9763)
MV COMMERCIAL CONSTRUCTION LLC
Also Called: Miller Valentin Construction
137 N Main St Ste 900 (45402-1846)
PHONE 937 293-0900
Christopher Knueven, *President*
Tony Beach, *Superintendent*
Nick Beach, *Vice Pres*
Jerry Kronenberger, *Controller*
Jane Marx, *Controller*
EMP: 125
SALES: 125MM **Privately Held**
SIC: 1541 Industrial buildings & warehouses

(G-9764)
MV LAND DEVELOPMENT COMPANY
Also Called: Valentine Group
137 N Main St Ste 900 (45402-1846)
PHONE 937 293-0900
Bill Krul, *CEO*
Joanne Evans-Nesby, *Personnel Assit*
EMP: 450
SALES (est): 8.4MM **Privately Held**
SIC: 6531 Real estate agent, commercial

(G-9765)
MVHE INC (HQ)
110 N Main St Ste 370 (45402-3729)
PHONE 937 499-8211
Ken Prunier, *President*
David Sturgeon, *CFO*
Joseph Mendhall, *Director*
EMP: 40
SQ FT: 2,100
SALES (est): 24.8MM
SALES (corp-wide): 968.3MM **Privately Held**
SIC: 8099 8011 Medical services organization; offices & clinics of medical doctors
PA: Med America Health Systems Corporation
1 Wyoming St
Dayton OH 45409
937 223-6192

(G-9766)
N C R EMPLOYEE BENEFIT ASSN
Also Called: NCR Country Club
4435 Dogwood Trl (45429-1239)
PHONE 937 299-3571
Fax: 937 643-6900
Steve Scarpino, *President*
Michelle Fornes, *Accountant*
Glenn Thompson, *Manager*
Ron Wilson, *Manager*

GEOGRAPHIC SECTION

Dayton - Montgomery County (G-9794)

Lisa Snapp, *Director*
EMP: 150
SQ FT: 44,000
SALES (est): 10.4MM **Privately Held**
WEB: www.ncrcountryclub.com
SIC: 7997 7991 5812 Country club, membership; physical fitness facilities; eating places

(G-9767)
NASA-TRMI GROUP INC
7918 N Main St (45415-2328)
PHONE.................................937 387-6517
Deborah Young, *Principal*
EMP: 99
SQ FT: 1,000
SALES (est): 606K **Privately Held**
SIC: 7381 Guard services

(G-9768)
NATIONAL ALLIANCE SEC AGCY INC
7918 N Main St (45415-2328)
PHONE.................................937 387-6517
Frederick Conner, *Principal*
EMP: 135 **Privately Held**
SIC: 7381 Protective services, guard
PA: National Alliance Security Agency, Inc.
7918 N Main St
Dayton OH 45415

(G-9769)
NATIONAL HERITG ACADEMIES INC
Also Called: Emerson Academy
501 Hickory St (45410-1232)
PHONE.................................937 223-2889
Alison Foreman, *Branch Mgr*
EMP: 54 **Privately Held**
SIC: 8741 Management services
PA: National Heritage Academies, Inc.
3850 Broadmoor Ave Se # 201
Grand Rapids MI 49512

(G-9770)
NATIONAL HERITG ACADEMIES INC
Also Called: Pathway School of Discovery
173 Avondale Dr (45404-2123)
PHONE.................................937 235-5498
Keith Colbert, *Branch Mgr*
EMP: 54 **Privately Held**
SIC: 8741 Management services
PA: National Heritage Academies, Inc.
3850 Broadmoor Ave Se # 201
Grand Rapids MI 49512

(G-9771)
NATIONAL HERITG ACADEMIES INC
Also Called: North Dayton School Discovery
3901 Turner Rd (45415-3654)
PHONE.................................937 278-6671
Ron Albino, *Branch Mgr*
EMP: 54 **Privately Held**
SIC: 8741 Management services
PA: National Heritage Academies, Inc.
3850 Broadmoor Ave Se # 201
Grand Rapids MI 49512

(G-9772)
NELSON TREE SERVICE INC (DH)
3300 Office Park Dr # 205 (45439-2394)
PHONE.................................937 294-1313
Fax: 937 294-8673
Lou Nekola, *President*
Jeff Jones, *Exec VP*
Mike Laughman, *Sls & Mktg Exec*
Bev Nelson, *Manager*
EMP: 35
SQ FT: 4,000
SALES (est): 19.9MM
SALES (corp-wide): 4.3B **Privately Held**
WEB: www.nelsontree.com
SIC: 0783 Tree trimming services for public utility lines

(G-9773)
NICHOLAS E DAVIS
Also Called: Taft Law
40 N Main St Ste 1700 (45423-1029)
PHONE.................................937 228-2838
Nicholas Davis, *Partner*
EMP: 48

SALES (est): 90.9K **Privately Held**
SIC: 8111 General practice law office

(G-9774)
NICKOLAS RSIDENTIAL TRTMNT CTR
5581 Dayton Liberty Rd (45417-5403)
PHONE.................................937 496-7100
Fax: 937 496-7315
Dedrick Howard, *Superintendent*
EMP: 33
SALES (est): 1.1MM **Privately Held**
SIC: 8361 Residential care for children

(G-9775)
NORMAN-SPENCER AGENCY INC (PA)
Also Called: Miami Valley Insurance Assoc
8075 Washington Vlg Dr (45458-1847)
PHONE.................................937 432-1600
Paul J Norman, *Ch of Bd*
Brian Norman, *President*
Phil Keeter, *Vice Pres*
Sandy Welker, *Vice Pres*
Pat Malone, *CFO*
EMP: 25
SQ FT: 9,000
SALES (est): 21.2MM **Privately Held**
SIC: 5088 Marine supplies

(G-9776)
NORTHWEST CHILD DEVELOPMENT AN ✪
2823 Campus Dr (45406-4103)
PHONE.................................937 559-9565
Matthew C Boykin,
EMP: 40 EST: 2017
SALES (est): 141K **Privately Held**
SIC: 8351 Child day care services

(G-9777)
NVR INC
2094 Northwest Pkwy (45426-3200)
PHONE.................................937 529-7000
Kenneth Thomas, *Branch Mgr*
EMP: 122 **Publicly Held**
SIC: 1531 Operative builders
PA: Nvr, Inc.
11700 Plaza America Dr # 500
Reston VA 20190

(G-9778)
OAK CREEK TERRACE INC
2316 Springmill Rd (45440-2504)
PHONE.................................937 439-1454
Fax: 937 439-5920
Barry A Kohn, *President*
Samuel Boymel, *Chairman*
Harold J Sosna, *Vice Pres*
James Nagle, *Director*
EMP: 101
SALES (est): 2.9MM **Privately Held**
WEB: www.oakcreekterrace.com
SIC: 8051 Convalescent home with continuous nursing care

(G-9779)
OAK CREEK UNITED CHURCH
5280 Bigger Rd (45440-2658)
PHONE.................................937 434-3941
Kim Leetch, *Director*
Kenny Roaden, *Director*
Cinda Tyler, *Director*
EMP: 30
SQ FT: 42,000
SALES (est): 587.9K **Privately Held**
SIC: 8061 8351 Church of Christ; child day care services

(G-9780)
OAKS OF WEST KETTERING INC
1150 W Dorothy Ln (45409-1305)
PHONE.................................937 293-1152
Kenneth J Bernsen, *Principal*
Melissa Whitaker, *Manager*
EMP: 118
SQ FT: 47,752
SALES (est): 5.3MM **Privately Held**
SIC: 8322 Rehabilitation services

(G-9781)
OBERERS FLOWERS INC (PA)
1448 Troy St (45404-2725)
PHONE.................................937 223-1253

Fax: 937 449-8207
Richard A Oberer, *President*
Ann R Oberer, *Corp Secy*
Rhonda Oberer Dunn, *Vice Pres*
Randall Oberer, *Vice Pres*
Keith Fields, *Store Mgr*
▲ **EMP:** 32
SALES (est): 10.3MM **Privately Held**
WEB: www.oberers.com
SIC: 5992 5193 Flowers, fresh; flowers, fresh; florists' supplies

(G-9782)
OBSTETRICS & GYNECOLOGY S INC (PA)
3533 Sthern Blvd Ste 4600 (45429)
PHONE.................................937 296-0167
Art Altman, *President*
Mary Adams, *Office Mgr*
Becky Ivey, *Manager*
EMP: 26
SALES (est): 2.7MM **Privately Held**
SIC: 8011 Obstetrician; gynecologist

(G-9783)
ODYSSEY HEALTHCARE INC
3085 Woodman Dr Ste 200 (45420-1193)
PHONE.................................937 298-2800
Fax: 937 298-2801
Donna Martz, *Branch Mgr*
EMP: 30
SALES (corp-wide): 6B **Publicly Held**
SIC: 8093 Specialty outpatient clinics
HQ: Odyssey Healthcare, Inc.
7801 Mesquite Bend Dr # 105
Irving TX 75063

(G-9784)
OHIO DEPARTMENT OF HEALTH
1323 W 3rd St (45402-6714)
PHONE.................................937 285-6250
Fax: 937 285-6303
Barbara Nixon, *Branch Mgr*
EMP: 68 **Privately Held**
WEB: www.jchealth.com
SIC: 9431 8322 Administration of public health programs; ; individual & family services
HQ: Department Of Health Ohio
246 N High St
Columbus OH 43215

(G-9785)
OHIO HOME HEALTH CARE INC
5050 Nebraska Ave Ste 5 (45424-6197)
PHONE.................................937 853-0271
Fax: 937 853-0274
Vickey Siegel, *President*
EMP: 40
SALES (est): 1.4MM **Privately Held**
SIC: 8082 Visiting nurse service

(G-9786)
OHIO IRRIGATION LAWN SPRINKLER (PA)
Also Called: O-Heil Irrigation
2109 E Social Row Rd (45458-4803)
PHONE.................................937 432-9911
Jeffrey W Heil, *President*
Justin Heil, *Vice Pres*
Jane Pummill, *Manager*
Jen Lamb, *Admin Asst*
EMP: 25
SQ FT: 5,800
SALES (est): 5.1MM **Privately Held**
SIC: 1711 5083 4959 1629 Irrigation sprinkler system installation; lawn & garden machinery & equipment; snowplowing; drainage system construction

(G-9787)
OHIO PEDIATRICS INC
7200 Poe Ave Ste 201 (45414-2799)
PHONE.................................937 299-2339
Dee Speaks, *Manager*
EMP: 30
SALES (corp-wide): 7.5MM **Privately Held**
SIC: 8011 Pediatrician
PA: Ohio Pediatrics Inc
1775 Delco Park Dr
Dayton OH 45420
937 299-2743

(G-9788)
OHIO PEDIATRICS INC (PA)
1775 Delco Park Dr (45420-1398)
PHONE.................................937 299-2743
James Bryant, *President*
Lida King, *Nurse Practr*
EMP: 45
SALES (est): 7.5MM **Privately Held**
SIC: 8011 Pediatrician

(G-9789)
OHIO PRESBT RETIREMENT SVCS
6520 Poe Ave (45414-2792)
PHONE.................................937 415-5666
EMP: 218 **Privately Held**
SIC: 8059 Convalescent home
PA: Ohio Living
1001 Kingsmill Pkwy
Columbus OH 43229

(G-9790)
OLD DOMINION FREIGHT LINE INC
3100 Transportation Rd (45404-2359)
PHONE.................................937 235-1596
Fax: 937 235-9316
Jason Back, *Manager*
EMP: 48
SALES (corp-wide): 3.3B **Publicly Held**
WEB: www.odfl.com
SIC: 4213 Contract haulers
PA: Old Dominion Freight Line Inc
500 Old Dominion Way
Thomasville NC 27360
336 889-5000

(G-9791)
ONE LINCOLN PARK
590 Isaac Prugh Way (45429-3482)
PHONE.................................937 298-0594
Fax: 937 297-4135
Miller Valentine, *Partner*
Charles A Osborn Jr, *Partner*
Miami Valley Hospital Extended, *Ltd Ptnr*
Chris Loch, *Director*
EMP: 100
SALES (est): 7MM **Privately Held**
WEB: www.lincolnparkseniors.com
SIC: 6513 6531 Retirement hotel operation; real estate agents & managers

(G-9792)
ONE10 LLC
130 W 2nd St Ste 500 (45402-1547)
PHONE.................................763 445-3000
EMP: 80
SALES (corp-wide): 1.8B **Privately Held**
SIC: 8742 Management And Marketing Consulting Services
HQ: One10 Llc
100 N 6th St Ste 700b
Minneapolis MN 55403
763 445-3000

(G-9793)
ORBIT MOVERS & ERECTORS INC
1101 Negley Pl (45402-6258)
PHONE.................................937 277-8080
Fax: 937 277-2686
James Arnett Jr, *CEO*
Jay Hahn, *President*
David Grayson, *CFO*
Donald Roberts, *Admin Sec*
EMP: 50
SQ FT: 125,000
SALES (est): 5.9MM
SALES (corp-wide): 15.5MM **Privately Held**
SIC: 1796 1791 Millwright; machine moving & rigging; iron work, structural
PA: Unitize Company, Inc.
1101 Negley Pl
Dayton OH 45402
937 277-2686

(G-9794)
ORTHOPEDIC ASSOCIATES DAYTON
7980 N Main St (45415-2328)
PHONE.................................937 280-4988
Thomas Cook, *Owner*
EMP: 25 EST: 2010

SALES (est): 3.5MM **Privately Held**
SIC: **8011** Orthopedic physician

(G-9795)
OSTERFELD CHAMPION SERVICE
121 Commerce Park Dr (45404-1213)
PHONE.................................937 254-8437
Fax: 937 254-8439
Barbara Smith, *CEO*
Warren Smith, *President*
Mack Spears, *Project Mgr*
Fawnie Brown, *Controller*
Rick Borgman, *Sales Executive*
EMP: 25
SALES (est): 5MM **Privately Held**
WEB: www.osterfeld.us
SIC: **1711 7699 7623** Mechanical contractor; boiler repair shop; air conditioning repair

(G-9796)
P & R COMMUNICATIONS SVC INC (PA)
Also Called: First Page
700 E 1st St (45402-1383)
PHONE.................................937 222-0861
Fax: 937 512-8101
Steve Reeves, *President*
David Reeves, *Vice Pres*
Katie Ward, *VP Sales*
Chris Hanes, *Sales Mgr*
Carla Reedy, *Account Dir*
EMP: 45 EST: 1964
SQ FT: 30,000
SALES (est): 5.3MM **Privately Held**
WEB: www.prcdayton.com
SIC: **7622 5065** Radio repair shop; radio parts & accessories

(G-9797)
PACCAR LEASING CORPORATION
Also Called: PacLease
7740 Center Point 70 Blvd (45424-6367)
PHONE.................................937 235-2589
Bill Evans, *Branch Mgr*
EMP: 25
SALES (corp-wide): 19.4B **Publicly Held**
WEB: www.glsayre.com
SIC: **7513** Truck leasing, without drivers
HQ: Paccar Leasing Corporation
    777 106th Ave Ne
    Bellevue WA 98004
    425 468-7400

(G-9798)
PAE & ASSOCIATES INC
7925 Paragon Rd (45459-4019)
PHONE.................................937 833-0013
Fax: 937 833-6334
John P Elder, *President*
Patrick A Elder, *Chairman*
Doug Mitchell, *Vice Pres*
Jay Willen, *Vice Pres*
Mary Thomas, *Officer*
EMP: 30
SQ FT: 5,700
SALES (est): 9.4MM **Privately Held**
WEB: www.paeassociates.com
SIC: **1629** Industrial plant construction

(G-9799)
PALMER TRUCKS INC
Also Called: Kenthworth of Dayton
7740 Center Point 70 Blvd (45424-6367)
PHONE.................................937 235-3318
John Sidebottom, *Branch Mgr*
Scott Nichols, *Manager*
EMP: 30
SALES (corp-wide): 228.9MM **Privately Held**
WEB: www.palmertrucks.com
SIC: **7538 7532 5531 5511** General automotive repair shops; truck painting & lettering; truck equipment & parts; pickups, new & used
PA: Palmer Trucks, Inc.
    2929 S Holt Rd
    Indianapolis IN 46241
    317 243-1668

(G-9800)
PANINI NORTH AMERICA INC
577 Congress Park Dr (45459-4036)
PHONE.................................937 291-2195
Fax: 937 291-2197
Michael Pratt, *CEO*
Ugo Panini, *President*
Douglas L Roberts, *President*
Caleb Miller, *Opers Staff*
Giuseppe Frenza, *Engineer*
▲ EMP: 37
SQ FT: 10,000
SALES (est): 19.5MM **Privately Held**
WEB: www.paninina.com
SIC: **5049** Bank equipment & supplies
PA: D21 Holding Spa
    Via Po 39
    Torino TO
    011 817-6011

(G-9801)
PARADIGM INDUSTRIAL LLC
1345 Stanley Ave (45404-1015)
PHONE.................................937 224-4415
Fax: 937 224-4423
Flem Messer, *General Mgr*
Ashley Webb, *Principal*
Daniel Ervin, *Vice Pres*
Greg Day, *Opers Mgr*
Shanna Bennett, *Info Tech Mgr*
EMP: 40
SQ FT: 14,000
SALES (est): 5.8MM **Privately Held**
WEB: www.paradigm-industrial.com
SIC: **7699 7363** Industrial machinery & equipment repair; employee leasing service

(G-9802)
PARK RACEWAY INC
777 Hollywood Blvd (45414-3698)
PHONE.................................419 476-7751
Arnold Stansley, *President*
Cheri Lenavitt, *Vice Pres*
Jack M Lenavitt, *Treasurer*
EMP: 110
SQ FT: 50,000
SALES (est): 2.4MM
SALES (corp-wide): 3.1B **Publicly Held**
WEB: www.racewayparktoledo.com
SIC: **7948 5812 5813** Horse race track operation; eating places; drinking places
PA: Penn National Gaming, Inc.
    825 Berkshire Blvd # 200
    Wyomissing PA 19610
    610 373-2400

(G-9803)
PARKS RECREATION DIVISION
455 Infirmary Rd (45417-8748)
PHONE.................................937 496-7135
Kim Farrell, *Principal*
Allen Leab, *Administration*
EMP: 30
SALES: 100K **Privately Held**
SIC: **8641** Recreation association

(G-9804)
PATRICIA A DICKERSON MD
1299 E Alex Bell Rd (45459-2658)
PHONE.................................937 436-1117
Fax: 937 436-9576
Patricia A Dickerson, *Owner*
EMP: 28
SALES (est): 1.1MM **Privately Held**
SIC: **8011** Dermatologist

(G-9805)
PAWS INN INC
8926 Kingsridge Dr (45458-1619)
PHONE.................................937 435-1500
Fax: 937 435-2366
Raymond Fournier, *President*
Ronda Sprague, *Manager*
EMP: 25
SALES (est): 769.3K **Privately Held**
WEB: www.pawsinnah.com
SIC: **0752 0742** Boarding services, kennels; grooming services, pet & animal specialties; veterinarian, animal specialties

(G-9806)
PEPSI-COLA METRO BTLG CO INC
526 Milburn Ave (45404-1678)
PHONE.................................937 461-4664
Tim Trant, *General Mgr*
Cheryl Fuson, *Human Res Mgr*
Richard Hargenrader, *Sales Executive*
Phillip Beach, *Manager*
Michael Sidenstick, *Manager*
EMP: 300
SQ FT: 115,000
SALES (corp-wide): 63.5B **Publicly Held**
WEB: www.joy-of-cola.com
SIC: **2086 5149** Soft drinks: packaged in cans, bottles, etc.; groceries & related products
HQ: Pepsi-Cola Metropolitan Bottling Company, Inc.
    1111 Westchester Ave
    White Plains NY 10604
    914 767-6000

(G-9807)
PERMA-FIX OF DAYTON INC
300 Cherokee Dr (45417-8113)
PHONE.................................937 268-6501
Fax: 937 268-5734
Brad Malatesta, *President*
Richard Kelecy, *Vice Pres*
Andy Owens, *QC Mgr*
Alison Arrowsmith, *Manager*
Kim Black, *Manager*
EMP: 42 EST: 1941
SQ FT: 25,000
SALES (est): 6.5MM **Privately Held**
SIC: **4953 2992** Recycling, waste materials; lubricating oils & greases
PA: Ogm, Ltd.
    2480 Jackson Pike
    Columbus OH 43223
    614 539-8238

(G-9808)
PICKREL BROTHERS INC
901 S Perry St (45402-2589)
PHONE.................................937 461-5960
Fax: 937 461-1280
Thomas Pickrel, *President*
James L Pickrel, *Vice Pres*
Mike Hochwalt, *Opers Mgr*
Greg Pickrel, *Purch Agent*
Phil Hoke, *Sales Associate*
EMP: 50
SQ FT: 25,000
SALES (est): 33.4MM **Privately Held**
WEB: www.pickrelbros.com
SIC: **5074** Plumbing fittings & supplies

(G-9809)
PICKREL SCHAEFFER EBELING LPA
40 N Main St Ste 2700 (45423-2700)
PHONE.................................937 223-1130
Fax: 937 223-0339
Paul Zimmer, *President*
Paul Winterhalter, *Project Mgr*
Andrew C Storar, *Manager*
Michele King, *Shareholder*
Jon Rosmeyer, *Admin Sec*
EMP: 52
SQ FT: 16,000
SALES (est): 6.7MM **Privately Held**
WEB: www.pselaw.com
SIC: **8111** General practice law office

(G-9810)
PLACES INC
11 W Monument Ave Ste 700 (45402-1245)
PHONE.................................937 461-4300
Fax: 937 461-0443
Dave Nuscher, *Accounting Mgr*
Penney Kramer, *Manager*
Barb Stokoe, *Info Tech Mgr*
Roy Craig, *Exec Dir*
EMP: 62
SALES: 3.4MM **Privately Held**
SIC: **8052** Home for the mentally retarded, with health care

(G-9811)
PLANNED PARENTHOOD ASSOCIATION (PA)
Also Called: Planned Prnthood of Grter Mami
224 N Wilkinson St (45402-3096)
PHONE.................................937 226-0780
Fax: 937 226-0328
Noreen Willhelm, *Acting CEO*
Ron Hursh, *Facilities Mgr*
EMP: 33
SQ FT: 14,000
SALES: 568K **Privately Held**
SIC: **8093 8322** Family planning clinic; individual & family services

(G-9812)
PLATINUM EXPRESS INC
2549 Stanley Ave (45404-2730)
PHONE.................................937 235-9540
Mina Burba, *President*
EMP: 60 EST: 1999
SALES (est): 9MM **Privately Held**
SIC: **4213** Trucking, except local

(G-9813)
POELKING BOWLING CENTERS
8871 Kingsridge Dr (45458-1617)
PHONE.................................937 435-3855
Fax: 937 435-1830
Joe Poelking, *Owner*
Tracy Wolfe, *Manager*
EMP: 25 EST: 1976
SALES (est): 880.6K **Privately Held**
SIC: **7933** Ten pin center

(G-9814)
POELKING LANES INC (PA)
1403 Wilmington Ave (45420-1542)
PHONE.................................937 299-5573
Fax: 937 299-2330
Jon P Poelking, *President*
Jayson Poelking, *General Mgr*
Michael Poelking, *Treasurer*
Doug Cooper, *Manager*
Joe Taylor, *Manager*
EMP: 64 EST: 1951
SQ FT: 38,000
SALES (est): 4MM **Privately Held**
SIC: **7933 5813** Ten pin center; cocktail lounge

(G-9815)
PORTER WRGHT MORRIS ARTHUR LLP
Also Called: Attorneys-At-Law
1 S Main St Ste 1600 (45402-2088)
P.O. Box 1805 (45401-1805)
PHONE.................................937 449-6810
Fax: 937 449-6820
R Bruce Snyder, *Managing Prtnr*
Molly Deverse, *Pastor*
David G Zimmerman, *Personnel*
Joanna Arnason, *Marketing Mgr*
Christina M Miller, *Manager*
EMP: 35
SQ FT: 25,500
SALES (corp-wide): 90.5MM **Privately Held**
SIC: **8111** General practice law office
PA: Porter, Wright, Morris & Arthur Llp
    41 S High St Ste 2900
    Columbus OH 43215
    614 227-2000

(G-9816)
POSITIVE ELECTRIC INC
4738 Gateway Cir Ste C (45440-1724)
PHONE.................................937 428-0606
Fax: 937 428-0617
Guy Monnin, *President*
EMP: 25
SQ FT: 2,000
SALES: 1.6MM **Privately Held**
SIC: **1731** General electrical contractor

(G-9817)
POWER MANAGEMENT INC (PA)
420 Davis Ave (45403-2912)
PHONE.................................937 222-2909
Fax: 937 258-5495
Reece Powers, *President*
EMP: 28
SQ FT: 24,000

GEOGRAPHIC SECTION
Dayton - Montgomery County (G-9842)

SALES (est): 3.1MM **Privately Held**
SIC: 6512 6513 2752 7331 Nonresidential building operators; apartment building operators; offset & photolithographic printing; mailing service; management consulting services; commercial nonphysical research

(G-9818)
PRECISION MTAL FABRICATION INC (PA)
191 Heid Ave (45404-1217)
PHONE................937 235-9261
Fax: 937 233-0906
Jim Hackenberger, *President*
John Limberg, *Corp Secy*
Drew Hackenberger, *QC Mgr*
Mike Desch, *Sales Staff*
Rick Miller, *Manager*
EMP: 53
SQ FT: 30,000
SALES (est): 6.8MM **Privately Held**
WEB: www.premetfab.com
SIC: 7692 3444 Welding repair; sheet metalwork

(G-9819)
PREMIER HEALTH GROUP LLC
110 N Main St Ste 350 (45402-3735)
PHONE................937 535-4100
James R Pancoast, *Principal*
Thomas M Duncan, *Senior VP*
Mary H Boosalis, *Vice Pres*
EMP: 38 **EST:** 2014
SALES (est): 13.1MM **Privately Held**
SIC: 8011 Offices & clinics of medical doctors

(G-9820)
PREMIER HEALTH PARTNERS (PA)
Also Called: Miami Valley
110 N Main St Ste 450 (45402-3712)
PHONE................937 499-9596
Fax: 937 223-9750
James R Pancoast, *President*
Sharon Rector, *Principal*
Mikki Clancy, *COO*
Mark Shaker, *Senior VP*
Mary H Boosalis, *Vice Pres*
EMP: 636
SALES (est): 354MM **Privately Held**
SIC: 8082 Home health care services

(G-9821)
PREMIER HEALTH SPECIALISTS INC (HQ)
110 N Main St Ste 350 (45402-3735)
PHONE................937 223-4518
Thomas Thorton, *President*
Keith Wisenberg, *Med Doctor*
EMP: 50
SALES (est): 10.5MM
SALES (corp-wide): 968.3MM **Privately Held**
WEB: www.mvcdayton.com
SIC: 8011 Surgeon
PA: Med America Health Systems Corporation
1 Wyoming St
Dayton OH 45409
937 223-6192

(G-9822)
PREMIER HEART ASSOCIATES INC
6251 Cood Samaritan Way # 220 (45424-5464)
PHONE................937 832-2425
Steve Stratton, *Manager*
EMP: 30 **EST:** 2000
SALES (est): 3.6MM **Privately Held**
WEB: www.premierheartassociates.com
SIC: 8011 Cardiologist & cardio-vascular specialist

(G-9823)
PRIMARY CR NTWRK PRMR HLTH PRT
Also Called: Needmore Road Primary Care
1530 Needmore Rd Ste 200 (45414-3957)
PHONE................937 278-5854
Kenneth Prunier, *CEO*
EMP: 48

SALES (corp-wide): 33.7MM **Privately Held**
SIC: 8011 General & family practice, physician/surgeon
PA: Primary Care Network Of Premier Health Partners
110 N Main St Ste 350
Dayton OH 45402
937 226-7085

(G-9824)
PRIMARY CR NTWRK PRMR HLTH PRT
1222 S Patterson Blvd # 120 (45402-2684)
PHONE................937 208-9090
EMP: 56
SALES (corp-wide): 33.7MM **Privately Held**
SIC: 8011 General & family practice, physician/surgeon
PA: Primary Care Network Of Premier Health Partners
110 N Main St Ste 350
Dayton OH 45402
937 226-7085

(G-9825)
PRIMARY CR NTWRK PRMR HLTH PRT (PA)
Also Called: Samanritan Family Care
110 N Main St Ste 350 (45402-3735)
PHONE................937 226-7085
Ken Prunier, *President*
Dave Sturgeon, *CFO*
EMP: 30
SALES (est): 33.7MM **Privately Held**
SIC: 8011 General & family practice, physician/surgeon

(G-9826)
PRIMARY CR NTWRK PRMR HLTH PRT
Also Called: Perinatal Partners
2350 Miami Valley Dr # 410 (45459-4778)
PHONE................937 424-9800
Terri L Stuerman, *Vice Pres*
EMP: 56
SALES (corp-wide): 33.7MM **Privately Held**
SIC: 8011 Gynecologist
PA: Primary Care Network Of Premier Health Partners
110 N Main St Ste 350
Dayton OH 45402
937 226-7085

(G-9827)
PRIMARY DAYTON INNKEEPERS LLC
7701 Washington Vlg Dr (45459-3954)
PHONE................937 938-9550
Rob Hale, *Principal*
EMP: 27
SALES (est): 1.6MM **Privately Held**
SIC: 7011 Hotels

(G-9828)
PRIMED
979 Congress Park Dr (45459-4009)
PHONE................937 435-9013
Fax: 937 435-1458
Carrol H Estep, *Principal*
EMP: 25 **EST:** 2001
SALES (est): 739.7K **Privately Held**
SIC: 8011 General & family practice, physician/surgeon

(G-9829)
PRIMED PHYSICIANS
540 Lincoln Park Blvd # 390 (45429-6408)
PHONE................937 298-8058
John E Mauer MD, *Partner*
Malak Adib, *Partner*
Tamara Togliatti, *Partner*
EMP: 40
SALES (est): 4.6MM **Privately Held**
SIC: 8011 General & family practice, physician/surgeon

(G-9830)
PRIMED PREMIER INTEGRATED MED (PA)
Also Called: Primed Physicians
6520 Acro Ct (45459-2679)
PHONE................937 291-6893

Karen Davis, *Director*
EMP: 250
SALES (est): 13.9MM **Privately Held**
SIC: 8011 Cardiologist & cardio-vascular specialist

(G-9831)
PRODUCE ONE INC
904 Woodley Rd (45403-1444)
PHONE................931 253-4749
Gary Pavlofsky, *President*
Rob Stichweh, *Senior VP*
Jeanie Hargrove, *Vice Pres*
Ervin Pavlofsky, *Vice Pres*
Jay Crabtree, *VP Opers*
EMP: 75
SQ FT: 14,000
SALES (est): 29.3MM **Privately Held**
WEB: www.produceone.com
SIC: 5148 5142 5147 5149 Fruits, fresh; fish, frozen: packaged; meats, fresh; canned goods: fruit, vegetables, seafood, meats, etc.
PA: Premier Produce Properties Ltd
4500 Willow Pkwy
Cleveland OH 44125
800 229-5517

(G-9832)
PRODUCTION DESIGN SERVICES INC (PA)
Also Called: Pdsi Technical Services
313 Mound St (45402-8370)
PHONE................937 866-3377
Fax: 937 866-3437
John H Schultz, *President*
Jeffrey R Schultz, *Vice Pres*
Pat Moore, *Plant Mgr*
Jim Hite, *Engineer*
Kevin Sizemore, *Engineer*
EMP: 80
SQ FT: 48,000
SALES (est): 24.9MM **Privately Held**
WEB: www.p-d-s-i.com
SIC: 3569 8711 7363 3823 Robots, assembly line: industrial & commercial; industrial engineers; mechanical engineering; temporary help service; industrial instrmnts msrmnt display/control process variable; machine tool accessories; special dies, tools, jigs & fixtures

(G-9833)
PRODUCTIVITY QULTY SYSTEMS INC (PA)
Also Called: PQ Systems
210b E Spring Valley Pike (45458-2653)
P.O. Box 750010 (45475-0010)
PHONE................937 885-2255
Michael J Cleary, *President*
Barbara Cleary, *Vice Pres*
EMP: 25
SQ FT: 20,000
SALES (est): 4.8MM **Privately Held**
WEB: www.pqsystems.com
SIC: 7371 5046 8742 Computer software development; teaching machines, electronic; productivity improvement consultant

(G-9834)
PROFESSIONAL MAINT DAYTON
223 E Helena St (45404-1003)
PHONE................937 461-5259
Fax: 937 461-5260
John E Thompson, *President*
EMP: 85
SQ FT: 3,000
SALES (est): 800K **Privately Held**
WEB: www.pmdayton.com
SIC: 7349 Janitorial service, contract basis

(G-9835)
PROFILE DIGITAL PRINTING LLC
5449 Marina Dr (45449-1833)
PHONE................937 866-4241
Terry Harmeyer, *General Mgr*
Tom Helmers, *Principal*
Carol Fiorentino, *Prdtn Mgr*
June Helmers,
EMP: 25
SALES (est): 4.1MM **Privately Held**
WEB: www.profiledpi.com
SIC: 7334 2759 2752 Blueprinting service; commercial printing; commercial printing, lithographic

(G-9836)
PROJECT C U R E INC
200 Daruma Pkwy (45439-7909)
PHONE................937 262-3500
Fax: 937 262-3523
Herman Erving, *Opers Spvr*
Hasani Hayden, *Human Res Dir*
Jean Rhodes, *Manager*
Michael Williams, *Manager*
Linda Bostick, *Supervisor*
EMP: 50 **EST:** 1970
SQ FT: 14,280
SALES: 4MM **Privately Held**
WEB: www.projectcure.com
SIC: 8093 Substance abuse clinics (outpatient); alcohol clinic, outpatient; drug clinic, outpatient; rehabilitation center, outpatient treatment

(G-9837)
QUANEXUS INC
571 Congress Park Dr (45459-4036)
PHONE................937 885-7272
Jack Gerbs, *Principal*
Chris Elrod, *Marketing Staff*
Eli Branum, *Network Enginr*
EMP: 37
SALES (est): 7.4MM **Privately Held**
SIC: 4813 7379 Data telephone communications; voice telephone communications; computer related consulting services

(G-9838)
QUEBE HOLDINGS INC (PA)
Also Called: Chapel Electric Co.
1985 Founders Dr (45420-4012)
PHONE................937 222-2290
Dennis F Quebe, *Ch of Bd*
Gregory P Ross, *President*
Richard E Penewit, *Vice Pres*
Roger Vanderhorst, *Vice Pres*
Kenny Lowery, *Project Mgr*
EMP: 100
SQ FT: 40,000
SALES (est): 83.3MM **Privately Held**
WEB: www.quebe.com
SIC: 1731 Lighting contractor

(G-9839)
R L O INC (PA)
Also Called: Great Clips
466 Windsor Park Dr (45459-4111)
PHONE................937 620-9998
Clara Osterhage, *President*
Raymond Osterhage, *Vice Pres*
EMP: 35
SALES (est): 749.6K **Privately Held**
SIC: 7231 Unisex hair salons

(G-9840)
RAHN DENTAL GROUP INC
5660 Far Hills Ave (45429-2206)
PHONE................937 435-0324
Douglas Patton, *President*
Dr Paul Unverferth, *Vice Pres*
Adrienne Wright, *Practice Mgr*
Dr Richard C Quinttus, *Admin Sec*
EMP: 32
SALES (est): 1.8MM **Privately Held**
SIC: 8021 Dentists' office

(G-9841)
RAM RESTORATION LLC
Also Called: Ram Resources
11125 Yankee St Ste A (45458-3698)
PHONE................937 347-7418
Trish Jackson, *COO*
Dave Weir, *Sales Mgr*
Randy Mount,
Regis Robbins,
Tom Weir,
EMP: 36
SQ FT: 2,500
SALES (est): 2.7MM **Privately Held**
SIC: 1799 1521 1522 Home/office interiors finishing, furnishing & remodeling; kitchen & bathroom remodeling; single-family home remodeling, additions & repairs; hotel/motel & multi-family home renovation & remodeling

(G-9842)
RAPID MORTGAGE COMPANY
Also Called: Rapid Aerial Imaging
9537 Gem Stone Dr (45458-4942)
PHONE................937 748-8888

Dayton - Montgomery County (G-9843)

Dennis M Fisher, *President*
Nancy Mackenzie, *Business Mgr*
Chris Howard, *Vice Pres*
David Rawson, *Vice Pres*
Linda Wacker, *Broker*
EMP: 50
SALES (est): 7.2MM **Privately Held**
WEB: www.rapidmortgagecompany.com
SIC: 6162 7335 7389 7221 Bond & mortgage companies; commercial photography; mapmaking or drafting, including aerial; photographer, still or video

(G-9843)
RDE SYSTEM CORPORATION
Also Called: Sonshine Commercial Cleaning
986 Windsor Ave (45402-5750)
PHONE 513 933-8000
Bob Espepp, *President*
Ryan Zeman, *Manager*
EMP: 100
SALES (est): 1.5MM **Privately Held**
SIC: 7349 Cleaning service, industrial or commercial

(G-9844)
REAL ART DESIGN GROUP INC (PA)
520 E 1st St (45402-1221)
PHONE 937 223-9955
Fax: 937 223-3013
Christopher Wire, *President*
Matt Zolman, *Project Mgr*
Betsy McFaddin, *Prdtn Mgr*
Betsy McSaddin, *Prdtn Mgr*
Casie Lord, *Human Res Dir*
EMP: 33
SQ FT: 25,000
SALES: 1.5MM **Privately Held**
WEB: www.realartusa.com
SIC: 7336 7311 Graphic arts & related design; advertising consultant

(G-9845)
REGENT SYSTEMS INC
Also Called: RSI
7590 Paragon Rd (45459-4065)
PHONE 937 640-8010
Fax: 937 640-8011
Michael A Bernal, *CEO*
Richard Nagel, *President*
Wilma M Bernal, *Corp Secy*
Dawn A Bernal, *Vice Pres*
Tony Dicioccio, *Vice Pres*
EMP: 65
SQ FT: 8,000
SALES: 9.6MM **Privately Held**
WEB: www.regentsystems.com
SIC: 7379 8742 ; hospital & health services consultant

(G-9846)
RELIABLE CONTRACTORS INC
Also Called: Rave - Rlable Audio Video Elec
94 Compark Rd Ste 200 (45459-4853)
PHONE 937 433-0262
Joe Ryan, *President*
Matt Minor, *Project Mgr*
Dave White, *Department Mgr*
EMP: 60
SQ FT: 12,500
SALES (est): 12.4MM **Privately Held**
WEB: www.reliable-contractors.com
SIC: 1731 General electrical contractor

(G-9847)
RENTHOTEL DAYTON LLC
Also Called: Doubletree Hotel
11 S Ludlow St (45402-1810)
PHONE 937 461-4700
Fax: 937 461-6981
Robert Holsten, *Principal*
Dwight Crawford, *Marketing Mgr*
Jennifer Brown, *Director*
C H Corp,
EMP: 95
SQ FT: 184,000
SALES (est): 2.3MM **Privately Held**
SIC: 7011 Hotels & motels

(G-9848)
RENTZ CORP (PA)
Also Called: Metropolitan Cleaners
759 Grants Trl (45459-3123)
PHONE 937 434-2774
Fax: 937 434-7780

Richard J Rentz, *President*
Barbara Rentz, *Corp Secy*
EMP: 50
SALES (est): 1.7MM **Privately Held**
SIC: 7216 Drycleaning plants, except rugs

(G-9849)
REPUBLIC SERVICES INC
Also Called: Allied Waste Division
1577 W River Rd (45417-6740)
PHONE 937 268-8110
Don Baer, *Branch Mgr*
EMP: 34
SALES (corp-wide): 10B **Publicly Held**
SIC: 4953 Refuse collection & disposal services
PA: Republic Services, Inc.
    18500 N Allied Way # 100
    Phoenix AZ 85054
    480 627-2700

(G-9850)
RESIDENT HOME ASSOCIATION
3661 Salem Ave (45406-1661)
PHONE 937 278-0791
Fax: 937 278-2240
Rhonda Rich, *Accountant*
Brenda Whitney, *Director*
EMP: 65
SQ FT: 4,582
SALES: 5.1MM **Privately Held**
SIC: 8621 Professional membership organizations

(G-9851)
RICHARD A BROOCK
10 N Ludlow St (45402-1854)
PHONE 937 449-2840
Richard A Broock, *Principal*
EMP: 50
SALES (est): 1.9MM **Privately Held**
SIC: 8111 Corporate, partnership & business law

(G-9852)
RIVERVIEW HEALTH INSTITUTE
1 Elizabeth Pl (45417-3445)
PHONE 937 222-5390
Fax: 937 222-5332
Ethan Fallang, *CEO*
EMP: 48
SALES (est): 10.6MM **Privately Held**
WEB: www.riverviewhealthinstitute.com
SIC: 8011 Medical centers

(G-9853)
RMS OF OHIO INC
5335 Far Hills Ave # 306 (45429-2317)
PHONE 937 291-3622
Fax: 937 291-3537
Joseph Cozzolino, *President*
Bobbi Malloy, *CFO*
Briget Forsythe, *Director*
EMP: 55
SALES (est): 1.8MM **Privately Held**
SIC: 8082 Home health care services

(G-9854)
ROBERT HALF INTERNATIONAL INC
1 S Main St Ste 300 (45402-2065)
PHONE 937 224-7376
Jill Crowe, *Manager*
EMP: 92
SALES (corp-wide): 5.2B **Publicly Held**
SIC: 7361 Executive placement
PA: Robert Half International, Inc.
    2884 Sand Hill Rd Ste 200
    Menlo Park CA 94025
    650 234-6000

(G-9855)
ROMITECH INC (PA)
2000 Composite Dr (45420-1493)
PHONE 937 297-9529
Fax: 937 435-2430
EMP: 32
SQ FT: 45,000
SALES (est): 4.8MM **Privately Held**
SIC: 5999 8748 Ret Misc Merchandise Business Consulting Services

(G-9856)
RUMPKE TRANSPORTATION CO LLC
Also Called: Rumpke Container Service
1932 E Monument Ave (45402-1359)
PHONE 937 461-0004
Fax: 937 461-3716
Carolyn Lane, *Controller*
Yvette Bennett, *Human Res Dir*
Kyle Aughe, *Manager*
EMP: 38 **Privately Held**
SIC: 4953 7359 Refuse collection & disposal services; portable toilet rental
HQ: Rumpke Transportation Company, Llc
    10795 Hughes Rd
    Cincinnati OH 45251
    513 851-0122

(G-9857)
RUSH EXPEDITING INC
2619 Needmore Rd (45414-4205)
PHONE 937 885-0894
Jan E Parker, *President*
EMP: 30
SALES (est): 4MM **Privately Held**
SIC: 4212 Carpool/vanpool arrangement

(G-9858)
RUSH PACKAGE DELIVERY INC (PA)
Also Called: Rush Trnsp & Logistics
2619 Needmore Rd (45414-4205)
P.O. Box 2810 (45401-2810)
PHONE 937 224-7874
Fax: 937 293-7466
Steve Parker, *CEO*
Ashley Parker, *President*
Jan Parker, *Principal*
Jennifer Keish, *Accounts Mgr*
EMP: 150
SQ FT: 5,500
SALES (est): 14.6MM **Privately Held**
WEB: www.rush-delivery.com
SIC: 4215 Courier services, except by air

(G-9859)
RUSH PACKAGE DELIVERY INC
Also Called: Rush Trnsp & Logistics
2619 Needmore Rd (45414-4205)
PHONE 937 297-6182
Ron Hanyke, *General Mgr*
EMP: 80
SALES (est): 3.9MM
SALES (corp-wide): 14.6MM **Privately Held**
WEB: www.rush-delivery.com
SIC: 4212 7389 Delivery service, vehicular; courier or messenger service
PA: Rush Package Delivery, Inc.
    2619 Needmore Rd
    Dayton OH 45414
    937 224-7874

(G-9860)
RYDER TRUCK RENTAL INC
3580 Needmore Rd (45414-4316)
PHONE 937 236-1650
Fax: 937 236-1418
Greg Stone, *General Mgr*
Ray Viers, *CFO*
EMP: 30
SALES (corp-wide): 7.3B **Publicly Held**
SIC: 7513 Truck rental, without drivers
HQ: Ryder Truck Rental, Inc.
    11690 Nw 105th St
    Medley FL 33178
    305 500-3726

(G-9861)
S & S MANAGEMENT INC
Also Called: Holiday Inn
5612 Merily Way (45424-2065)
PHONE 937 235-2000
Fax: 937 235-2600
Brian McKenzie, *Manager*
EMP: 30
SALES: 1.3MM
SALES (corp-wide): 8.6MM **Privately Held**
SIC: 7011 Hotels
PA: S & S Management Inc
    550 Folkerth Ave 100
    Sidney OH 45365
    937 498-9645

(G-9862)
S&D/OSTERFELD MECH CONTRS INC
1101 Negley Pl (45402-6258)
PHONE 937 277-1700
Fax: 937 254-8506
Jeff Arthur, *CEO*
James Arnett Jr, *CEO*
Lisa Schneider, *President*
Carl Crawford, *Vice Pres*
David Grayson, *CFO*
EMP: 50
SQ FT: 125,000
SALES (est): 5.4MM
SALES (corp-wide): 15.5MM **Privately Held**
WEB: www.unitize.com
SIC: 1711 Plumbing contractors; heating & air conditioning contractors
PA: Unitize Company, Inc.
    1101 Negley Pl
    Dayton OH 45402
    937 277-2686

(G-9863)
SALVATION ARMY
1000 N Keowee St (45404-1520)
P.O. Box 10007 (45402-7007)
PHONE 937 528-5100
Thomas Depreis, *Branch Mgr*
Desiree Hogsett, *Admin Asst*
EMP: 30
SALES (corp-wide): 4.3B **Privately Held**
WEB: www.salvationarmy-usaeast.org
SIC: 8322 8661 Family service agency; miscellaneous denomination church
HQ: The Salvation Army
    440 W Nyack Rd Ofc
    West Nyack NY 10994
    845 620-7200

(G-9864)
SAMARITAN BEHAVIORAL HEALTH (DH)
601 Enid Ave (45429-5413)
PHONE 937 276-8333
Sue McGatha, *CEO*
Marilyn Houser, *Vice Pres*
Janet Rogers, *Treasurer*
EMP: 26
SALES (est): 11.2MM **Privately Held**
SIC: 8093 Mental health clinic, outpatient
HQ: Samaritan Health Partners
    2222 Philadelphia Dr
    Dayton OH 45406
    937 208-8400

(G-9865)
SAMARITAN HEALTH PARTNERS (HQ)
2222 Philadelphia Dr (45406-1813)
PHONE 937 208-8400
Fax: 937 293-0960
K Douglas Deck, *President*
Tom Curtin, *CFO*
Thomas M Duncan, *CFO*
Janet Rogers, *Treasurer*
Lisa Smith, *Info Tech Mgr*
EMP: 2165
SQ FT: 1,000,000
SALES (est): 353.2MM **Privately Held**
SIC: 8062 General medical & surgical hospitals

(G-9866)
SAMPLE MACHINING INC
Also Called: Bitec
220 N Jersey St (45403-1220)
PHONE 937 258-3338
Fax: 937 258-3840
Beverly Bleicher, *President*
Kevin Bleicher, *Vice Pres*
David Calmes, *Mfg Mgr*
Chris Bell, *QC Mgr*
Jeremy Royse, *QC Mgr*
EMP: 45
SQ FT: 19,000
SALES: 7MM **Privately Held**
WEB: www.bitecsmi.com
SIC: 3599 8734 Custom machinery; testing laboratories

GEOGRAPHIC SECTION
Dayton - Montgomery County (G-9892)

(G-9867)
SANCTUARY AT WILMINGTON PLACE
264 Wilmington Ave (45420-1989)
PHONE.....................937 256-4663
Robert Banasik, *President*
Ronda Lee, *Human Res Mgr*
Julie Justice, *Corp Comm Staff*
Kevin Kauffman, *Administration*
EMP: 60
SALES (est): 3.1MM Privately Held
SIC: 8051 Skilled nursing care facilities

(G-9868)
SATURN ELECTRIC INC
2628 Nordic Rd (45414-3424)
P.O. Box 13830 (45413-0830)
PHONE.....................937 278-2580
Fax: 937 278-0220
Doug Kash, *President*
Chris Galloway, *Manager*
EMP: 50
SQ FT: 10,000
SALES (est): 9.8MM Privately Held
SIC: 1731 Electrical work

(G-9869)
SCOTT INDUSTRIAL SYSTEMS INC (PA)
4433 Interpoint Blvd (45424-5708)
P.O. Box 1387 (45401-1387)
PHONE.....................937 233-8146
Fax: 937 233-1020
Randall Scott, *Ch of Bd*
Dave Baumann, *President*
Mark Bryan, *President*
Chuck Volpe, *President*
Tim Hermann, *District Mgr*
EMP: 75
SQ FT: 63,000
SALES (est): 65.4MM Privately Held
WEB: www.scottindustrialsystems.com
SIC: 5084 Hydraulic systems equipment & supplies; pneumatic tools & equipment

(G-9870)
SCREEN WORKS INC (PA)
3970 Image Dr (45414-2524)
PHONE.....................937 264-9111
Fax: 937 264-9100
Jeff Cottrell, *Principal*
Beth Nealeigh, *Sales Mgr*
Debbie Smith, *Marketing Staff*
Jeff Kotak, *Director*
EMP: 50
SQ FT: 42,000
SALES (est): 4.7MM Privately Held
WEB: www.screenworksinc.com
SIC: 7336 5199 7389 3993 Silk screen design; advertising specialties; embroidering of advertising on shirts, etc.; signs & advertising specialties; automotive & apparel trimmings

(G-9871)
SEBALY SHILLITO & DYER LPA (PA)
1900 Kettering Tower 40n (45423-1013)
PHONE.....................937 222-2500
Jon M Sebaly, *President*
Mike Maloney, *Managing Prtnr*
Peter Donahue, *Counsel*
Melissa Mills, *CFO*
Heather Welbaum, *Manager*
EMP: 48
SALES (est): 7.7MM Privately Held
SIC: 8111 General practice attorney, lawyer

(G-9872)
SECOND MENTAL RETARDATION
Also Called: First Mental Retardation
3827 W 3rd St (45417-1842)
PHONE.....................937 262-3077
Janice Smith, *Exec Dir*
EMP: 30
SALES (est): 47.5K Privately Held
SIC: 8361 Residential care

(G-9873)
SECURITAS SEC SVCS USA INC
Automotive Services Division
118 W 1st St (45402-1150)
PHONE.....................937 224-7432
William Mangus, *Business Mgr*
Tammy Glover, *Human Res Mgr*
Kathy Hudwig, *Human Res Mgr*
Gary Burkeholder, *Persnl Mgr*
Bill Mangus, *Sales Mgr*
EMP: 110
SALES (corp-wide): 9.5B Privately Held
SIC: 7382 Protective devices, security
HQ: Securitas Security Services Usa, Inc.
9 Campus Dr
Parsippany NJ 07054
973 267-5300

(G-9874)
SELECT INDUSTRIES CORP
60 Heid Ave (45404-1216)
PHONE.....................937 233-9191
Mike Ryan, *Principal*
EMP: 27
SALES (est): 16.5MM Privately Held
SIC: 5084 Industrial machinery & equipment

(G-9875)
SENIOR RESOURCE CONNECTION (PA)
Also Called: Meals On Wheels
222 Salem Ave (45406-5805)
PHONE.....................937 223-8246
Roger Davis, *Business Mgr*
Chuck Comp, *Vice Pres*
Susan Dickey, *Human Res Dir*
Lisa Garvic, *Human Res Dir*
Cristal Fillers, *Office Mgr*
EMP: 195
SQ FT: 25,000
SALES: 8.3MM Privately Held
SIC: 8322 Senior citizens' center or association

(G-9876)
SERENITY HM HALTHCARE SVCS LLC
33 White Allen Ave (45405-4930)
PHONE.....................937 222-0002
EMP: 80
SALES (est): 633.1K Privately Held
SIC: 8099 Blood related health services

(G-9877)
SERVICE CENTER TITLE AGENCY
Also Called: Vantage Land Title
6718 Loop Rd (45459-2161)
PHONE.....................937 312-3080
Andy Morgan, *President*
EMP: 27
SALES (est): 2.5MM Privately Held
SIC: 6361 Title insurance

(G-9878)
SFA ARCHITECTS INC
120 W 2nd St Ste 1800 (45402-1603)
PHONE.....................937 281-0600
E Thomas Fernandez, *CEO*
Dave F Freeman, *General Mgr*
Dave B Breda, *COO*
EMP: 36
SALES (est): 1.5MM Privately Held
SIC: 8712 Architectural engineering

(G-9879)
SHR MANAGEMENT RESOURCES CORP
2222 Philadelphia Dr (45406-1813)
PHONE.....................937 274-1546
Doug Deck, *CEO*
John P Mason, *President*
Carolyn Harpel, *Treasurer*
EMP: 30
SALES (est): 711.3K Privately Held
SIC: 8093 5912 Specialty outpatient clinics; drug stores
HQ: Samaritan Health Partners
2222 Philadelphia Dr
Dayton OH 45406
937 208-8400

(G-9880)
SHUMSKY ENTERPRISES INC (PA)
Also Called: Boost Technologies
811 E 4th St (45402-2227)
P.O. Box 36 (45401-0036)
PHONE.....................937 223-2203
Fax: 937 223-2252
Anita Emoff, *CEO*
Michael J Emoff, *Ch of Bd*
William Diederich, *President*
Tricia Hillard, *General Mgr*
Matty Toomb, *Vice Pres*
▲ EMP: 66
SQ FT: 19,500
SALES (est): 32.9MM Privately Held
WEB: www.pointsdemo.com
SIC: 5199 Advertising specialties

(G-9881)
SIBCY CLINE INC
8353 Yankee St (45458-1809)
PHONE.....................937 610-3404
Fax: 937 432-3706
Irma Wise, *Branch Mgr*
Kenneth E Brown, *Manager*
Pamela H Phillips, *Administration*
EMP: 42
SALES (corp-wide): 2.1B Privately Held
SIC: 6531 Real estate brokers & agents
PA: Sibcy Cline, Inc.
8044 Montgomery Rd # 300
Cincinnati OH 45236
513 984-4100

(G-9882)
SIEBENTHALER COMPANY (PA)
Also Called: Siebenthaler's Garden Center
3001 Catalpa Dr (45405-1745)
PHONE.....................937 427-4110
Fax: 937 274-9448
Jeff Siebenthaler, *President*
R Jeffrey Siebenthaler, *President*
Michael Fanning, *Vice Pres*
David C Ruppert, *Vice Pres*
John Lee, *Treasurer*
EMP: 53 EST: 1870
SQ FT: 3,000
SALES (est): 8.6MM Privately Held
WEB: www.siebenthaler.com
SIC: 0782 5193 5261 Landscape contractors; nursery stock; nurseries & garden centers

(G-9883)
SIENA SPRINGS II
6217 N Main St (45415-3157)
PHONE.....................513 639-2800
Laura Brown Wells, *Manager*
EMP: 28
SALES (est): 248.3K Privately Held
SIC: 6531 Real estate agents & managers

(G-9884)
SIGNATURE CONCRETE INC
517 Windsor Park Dr (45459-4112)
PHONE.....................937 723-8435
Fax: 937 415-1325
Michael Leach, *President*
Jeffrey Mullins, *Vice Pres*
EMP: 26
SQ FT: 2,400
SALES (est): 4.4MM Privately Held
SIC: 1771 Concrete pumping

(G-9885)
SKATEWORLD INC (PA)
Also Called: Skateworld of Kettering
1601 E David Rd (45429-5709)
PHONE.....................937 294-4032
Rick Corson, *President*
Jessica Fuller, *Manager*
Corey Trhlik, *Manager*
EMP: 25
SQ FT: 26,000
SALES (est): 1.7MM Privately Held
SIC: 7999 5812 Roller skating rink operation; skating instruction, ice or roller; fast-food restaurant, independent

(G-9886)
SMS TRANSPORT LLC
8235 Old Troy Pike 272 (45424-1025)
PHONE.....................937 813-8897
Sevil Shakhmanov,
Karla Howell, *Assistant*
EMP: 25
SALES (est): 1.8MM Privately Held
SIC: 4213 4215 4731 Contract haulers; courier services, except by air; freight forwarding

(G-9887)
SOGETI USA LLC
6494 Centervl Bus Pkwy (45459-2633)
PHONE.....................937 433-3334
Fax: 937 433-4048
William Blaxton, *Senior VP*
John Dial, *Vice Pres*
Rajesh Eshwar, *Vice Pres*
Brian Hammond, *Vice Pres*
Benassis Jacques, *Project Dir*
EMP: 56
SALES (corp-wide): 353.3MM Privately Held
SIC: 7379
HQ: Sogeti Usa Llc
10100 Innovation Dr # 200
Miamisburg OH 45342
937 291-8100

(G-9888)
SONOCO PRTECTIVE SOLUTIONS INC
R P A Packaging Division
6061 Milo Rd (45414-3417)
PHONE.....................937 890-7628
EMP: 35
SALES (corp-wide): 4.9B Publicly Held
SIC: 7389 Packing And Crating Service
HQ: Sonoco Protective Solutions, Inc.
1 N 2nd St
Hartsville SC 29550
843 383-7000

(G-9889)
SOUTH COMMUNITY INC
Also Called: Youth Partial Hospitalization
2745 S Smthvle Rd Ste 14 (45420)
PHONE.....................937 252-0100
Fax: 937 256-2867
Melissa Buck, *Principal*
Lisa Carter, *Director*
Lee Dunham, *Director*
EMP: 45
SALES (corp-wide): 19MM Privately Held
SIC: 8093 Mental health clinic, outpatient
PA: South Community, Inc.
3095 Kettering Blvd Ste 1
Moraine OH 45439
937 293-8300

(G-9890)
SOUTH DAYTON ACUTE CARE CONS
33 W Rahn Rd (45429-2219)
PHONE.....................937 433-8990
Fax: 937 433-8691
Robert L Barker, *President*
Dr Jeffrey Weinstein, *Corp Secy*
Dr George Crespo, *Vice Pres*
Dr Shachi Rattan, *Vice Pres*
Luann Miller, *Project Mgr*
EMP: 36
SQ FT: 10,000
SALES (est): 10MM Privately Held
WEB: www.sdacc.com
SIC: 8011 Physicians' office, including specialists

(G-9891)
SOUTH DYTON URLGCAL ASSCATIONS (PA)
10 Southmoor Cir Nw Ste 1 (45429-2444)
PHONE.....................937 294-1489
Fax: 937 294-7999
Juan M Palomar MD, *President*
Sammy Hemway MD, *Vice Pres*
Ralph M Cruz MD, *Treasurer*
Sharat C Kalvakota MD, *Admin Sec*
Raymond S Russell, *Urology*
EMP: 30
SQ FT: 5,000
SALES (est): 2.5MM Privately Held
SIC: 8011 Urologist

(G-9892)
SOUTHWEST OHIO ENT SPCLSTS INC (PA)
1222 S Patterson Blvd # 400 (45402-2642)
PHONE.....................937 496-2600
Hugh E Wall Jr, *Principal*
Robert B Matusoff, *Principal*
Nathan Soifer, *Principal*
Dan Young, *Office Mgr*
Robert A Goldenberg, *Otolaryngology*

Dayton - Montgomery County (G-9893)

EMP: 40
SALES (est): 10.5MM **Privately Held**
SIC: 8011 Offices & clinics of medical doctors

(G-9893)
SOWDER CONCRETE CORPORATION
Also Called: Sowder Concrete Contractors
8510 N Dixie Dr (45414-2451)
PHONE..................937 890-1633
Fax: 937 890-1648
EMP: 30
SQ FT: 5,000
SALES: 6.5MM **Privately Held**
SIC: 1771 Concrete Contractor

(G-9894)
SPACE MANAGEMENT INC
Also Called: Professional Building Maint
2109 S Smithville Rd (45420-2805)
PHONE..................937 254-6622
Fax: 937 252-6622
Kevin Ray Findlay, *President*
EMP: 50
SQ FT: 5,000
SALES (est): 4.1MM **Privately Held**
SIC: 8744 Facilities support services

(G-9895)
SPEARS TRANSF & EXPEDITING INC
2637 Nordic Rd (45414-3423)
PHONE..................937 275-2443
Mike Spears, *Branch Mgr*
EMP: 25
SALES (corp-wide): 8MM **Privately Held**
WEB: www.spearsexpedite.com
SIC: 4212 4214 Local trucking, without storage; local trucking with storage
PA: Spears Transfer & Expediting, Inc.
303 Corporate Dr Ste 101b
Vandalia OH 45377
937 898-9700

(G-9896)
SPECTRUM MGT HOLDG CO LLC
Time Warner
275 Leo St (45404-1005)
PHONE..................937 684-8891
Tim Cuss, *Branch Mgr*
EMP: 80
SALES (corp-wide): 41.5B **Publicly Held**
SIC: 4841 Cable television services
HQ: Spectrum Management Holding Company, Llc
400 Atlantic St
Stamford CT 06901
203 905-7801

(G-9897)
SPECTRUM MGT HOLDG CO LLC
Also Called: Time Warner
3691 Turner Rd (45415-3690)
PHONE..................937 294-6800
Richard S Hutchinson, *Principal*
Timothy Cuss, *Manager*
EMP: 83
SALES (corp-wide): 41.5B **Publicly Held**
SIC: 4841 Cable television services
HQ: Spectrum Management Holding Company, Llc
400 Atlantic St
Stamford CT 06901
203 905-7801

(G-9898)
SPRINGFIELD CARTAGE LLC
1546 Stanley Ave (45414-1113)
P.O. Box 1263 (45401-1263)
PHONE..................937 222-2120
Nello Adduccio, *Mng Member*
Tracy Nungester, *Advisor*
EMP: 86
SALES: 13MM **Privately Held**
SIC: 7359 Industrial truck rental

(G-9899)
SPRINGHILLS LLC
Also Called: Spring Hills At Singing Woods
140 E Woodbury Dr (45415-2841)
PHONE..................937 274-1400
Fax: 937 274-8759

John Steiner, *Principal*
Cindi McBarron, *Corp Comm Staff*
EMP: 171
SALES (est): 3.9MM **Privately Held**
SIC: 8051 Convalescent home with continuous nursing care
PA: Springhills Llc
515 Plainfield Ave
Edison NJ 08817

(G-9900)
SPURLOCK TRUCK SERVICE
Also Called: Summit Towing
129 Lincoln Park Blvd (45429-2717)
PHONE..................937 268-6100
Fax: 937 228-6212
Robert Spurlock, *President*
Dr Karen Garner, *Admin Sec*
EMP: 34 EST: 1927
SQ FT: 7,000
SALES: 1MM **Privately Held**
SIC: 7538 7549 General automotive repair shops; towing service, automotive

(G-9901)
SSS CONSULTING INC
Also Called: H R Chally Group
3123 Res Blvd Ste 250 (45420)
PHONE..................937 259-1200
Fax: 937 259-5757
Howard P Stevens, *Ch of Bd*
Gerald M Lerer, *President*
Bruce Sevy, *Managing Dir*
Brenda Routt, *Exec VP*
Christopher Holmes, *Vice Pres*
EMP: 35 EST: 1973
SQ FT: 15,000
SALES (est): 4.8MM **Privately Held**
WEB: www.chally.com
SIC: 8748 8732 8742 Testing services; market analysis or research; management consulting services

(G-9902)
ST VINCENT DE PAUL SCL SVS
1133 S Edwin C Moses Blvd (45417-4094)
PHONE..................937 222-7349
Christine Hampton, *Controller*
Hannah Krafka, *Marketing Staff*
Leigh Sempeles, *Exec Dir*
EMP: 78
SALES (est): 4.3MM **Privately Held**
SIC: 8322 Individual & family services

(G-9903)
STANDARD REGISTER INC
Also Called: Taylor Communications
600 Albany St (45417-3442)
PHONE..................937 221-1000
Fax: 937 443-1973
Debra L Taylor, *CEO*
Gregory W Jackson, *Exec VP*
Gregory J Greve, *Vice Pres*
Suzanne M Spellacy, *Vice Pres*
Larry D Taylor, *Vice Pres*
EMP: 2860
SALES (est): 448.3K
SALES (corp-wide): 4.3B **Privately Held**
SIC: 8742 Management consulting services
PA: Taylor Corporation
1725 Roe Crest Dr
North Mankato MN 56003
507 625-2828

(G-9904)
STARWIN INDUSTRIES INC
3387 Woodman Dr (45429-4100)
PHONE..................937 293-8568
Fax: 937 299-0698
Norman Staub, *CEO*
Rick Little, *President*
John Whitaker, *General Mgr*
Mark Belt, *Vice Pres*
Bill Anderson, *Project Mgr*
EMP: 40
SQ FT: 30,000
SALES (est): 7.5MM **Privately Held**
WEB: www.starwin-ind.com
SIC: 3599 7372 Machine shop, jobbing & repair; prepackaged software

(G-9905)
STATE FARM LIFE INSURANCE CO
Also Called: State Farm Insurance
1436 Needmore Rd (45414-3965)
PHONE..................937 276-1900
Fax: 937 276-1901
Jim McGhee, *Manager*
EMP: 60
SALES (corp-wide): 39.5MM **Privately Held**
WEB: www.davidvetch.com
SIC: 6411 Insurance agents & brokers
HQ: State Farm Life Insurance Company Inc
1 State Farm Plz
Bloomington IL 61701
309 766-2311

(G-9906)
STERLING LAND TITLE AGENCY
7016 Corporate Way Ste B (45459-4351)
PHONE..................937 438-2000
Alex P Katona, *President*
Phil Long, *Marketing Staff*
Pam Folino, *Manager*
EMP: 30
SQ FT: 12,500
SALES (est): 11MM **Privately Held**
SIC: 6361 Real estate title insurance

(G-9907)
STEVE BROWN
1353 Lyons Rd (45458-1822)
PHONE..................937 436-2700
Steve Brown, *Partner*
EMP: 60
SALES (est): 164.4K **Privately Held**
SIC: 6531 Real estate brokers & agents

(G-9908)
STONEMOR PARTNERS LP
Also Called: West Memory Gardens
6722 Hemple Rd (45439-6648)
PHONE..................937 866-4135
Fax: 937 866-2176
Glenna Wall, *Principal*
EMP: 50
SALES (corp-wide): 326.2MM **Publicly Held**
WEB: www.stonemor.com
SIC: 6553 Cemetery subdividers & developers
PA: Stonemor Partners L.P.
3600 Horizon Blvd Ste 100
Trevose PA 19053
215 826-2800

(G-9909)
STOOPS FRGHTLNR-QLITY TRLR INC
Also Called: Stoops Freightliner of Dayton
7800 Center Point 70 Blvd (45424-6369)
PHONE..................937 236-4092
Jeff Gast, *Manager*
EMP: 50
SALES (corp-wide): 531.9MM **Privately Held**
WEB: www.stoops.com
SIC: 5511 5531 7538 7539 Trucks, tractors & trailers: new & used; automotive parts; general truck repair; trailer repair; automobiles & other motor vehicles
HQ: Truck Country Of Indiana, Inc.
1851 W Thompson Rd
Indianapolis IN 46217
317 788-1533

(G-9910)
STRATACACHE INC (PA)
Also Called: Stratacache Products
2 Emmet St Ste 200 (45405-4958)
PHONE..................937 224-0485
Chris Riegel, *CEO*
Ken Boyle, *Senior VP*
Russell Young, *Senior VP*
Ken Cates, *Vice Pres*
John Rau, *Vice Pres*
▲ EMP: 110
SQ FT: 65,000
SALES (est): 81.2MM **Privately Held**
WEB: www.stratacache.com
SIC: 5734 4822 Software, business & non-game; nonvocal message communications

(G-9911)
STUDEBAKER ELECTRIC COMPANY
8459 N Main St Ste 114 (45415-1382)
PHONE..................937 890-9510
Fax: 937 890-9644
David L Studebaker, *CEO*
Shannon Saksaka, *Business Mgr*
Phillip Lahrmer, *CFO*
Scott Searcy, *Controller*
EMP: 100
SQ FT: 1,600
SALES (est): 4.8MM **Privately Held**
WEB: www.studebakerelectric.com
SIC: 1731 General electrical contractor

(G-9912)
SUBURBAN VETERINARIAN CLINIC
102 E Spring Valley Pike (45458-3803)
PHONE..................937 433-2160
Dan Lokai, *Owner*
Christine Livingston, *Manager*
EMP: 30
SQ FT: 6,200
SALES (est): 1.3MM **Privately Held**
SIC: 0742 Animal hospital services, pets & other animal specialties; veterinarian, animal specialties

(G-9913)
SUMMIT SOLUTIONS INC
Also Called: Summit Quest
446 Windsor Park Dr (45459-4111)
PHONE..................937 291-4333
Fax: 937 291-1666
Jeff S Lafave, *CEO*
Aaron Lafave, *Consultant*
EMP: 40 EST: 1998
SALES (est): 4MM **Privately Held**
WEB: www.summitqwest.com
SIC: 8748 Business consulting

(G-9914)
SUMMITT OHIO LEASING CO LLC
Also Called: Wood Glen Alzheimers Community
3800 Summit Glen Rd (45449-3647)
PHONE..................937 436-2273
Steve Rosedale, *CEO*
Meenakshi Patel, *Director*
Stephen Rosedale,
EMP: 220
SALES (est): 7.1MM **Privately Held**
SIC: 8051 Convalescent home with continuous nursing care

(G-9915)
SUNRISE SENIOR LIVING INC
Also Called: Brighton Gardens Wash Township
6800 Paragon Rd Ofc (45459-3164)
PHONE..................937 438-0054
Fax: 937 438-5203
Sharon Hammond, *Sales Staff*
Rose Marie Caldwell, *Manager*
Jenni Clark, *Manager*
Shelly Henderson, *Exec Dir*
EMP: 86
SALES (corp-wide): 4.3B **Publicly Held**
WEB: www.sunrise.com
SIC: 8051 Skilled nursing care facilities
HQ: Sunrise Senior Living, Llc
7902 Westpark Dr
Mc Lean VA 22102

(G-9916)
SUPERIOR DENTAL CARE INC
6683 Centervl Bus Pkwy (45459-2634)
PHONE..................937 438-0283
Fax: 937 438-0288
Traci Harrell, *CEO*
Richard W Portune DDS, *President*
Bettina Imes, *Publisher*
Douglas R Hoefling DDS, *Treasurer*
Anne Wassum, *Controller*
EMP: 31
SQ FT: 7,878
SALES (est): 18.3MM **Privately Held**
WEB: www.superiordental.com
SIC: 6321 Health insurance carriers

GEOGRAPHIC SECTION
Dayton - Montgomery County (G-9941)

(G-9917)
SWN COMMUNICATIONS INC
Also Called: One Call Now
6450 Poe Ave Ste 500 (45414-2648)
PHONE..................877 698-3262
Shannon Bailey, *Senior VP*
Ruth Cox, *Manager*
EMP: 30
SALES (corp-wide): 580.9MM **Privately Held**
SIC: 4813 Data telephone communications
HQ: Swn Communications Inc.
500 Plaza Dr Ste 205
Secaucus NJ 07094
212 379-4900

(G-9918)
SYNERGY HOMECARE SOUTH DAYTON
501 Windsor Park Dr (45459-4112)
PHONE..................937 610-0555
Fax: 937 610-0541
Tim Homer, *President*
EMP: 35
SQ FT: 1,000
SALES: 100K **Privately Held**
SIC: 8082 Home health care services

(G-9919)
SYSTEMAX MANUFACTURING INC
6450 Poe Ave Ste 200 (45414-2655)
PHONE..................937 368-2300
Tammy Moore, *Warehouse Mgr*
Linda Owens, *Accounting Mgr*
Jennifer Harlow, *Accountant*
Pam Shablin, *Sales Mgr*
Skip Murray, *Mktg Dir*
▲ **EMP:** 200
SQ FT: 185,000
SALES (est): 26.6MM **Publicly Held**
WEB: www.systemax.com
SIC: 5045 5961 7373 3577 Computers, peripherals & software; computer peripheral equipment; printers, computer; computers & accessories, personal & home entertainment; computers & peripheral equipment, mail order; systems integration services; computer peripheral equipment; electronic computers
PA: Systemax Inc.
11 Harbor Park Dr
Port Washington NY 11050

(G-9920)
TALMAGE N PORTER MD
979 Congress Park Dr (45459-4009)
PHONE..................937 435-9013
Talmage Porter, *Principal*
EMP: 25 **EST:** 2001
SALES (est): 550K **Privately Held**
SIC: 8011 General & family practice, physician/surgeon

(G-9921)
TEAM RAHAL OF DAYTON INC (PA)
Also Called: Lexus of Dayton
8111 Yankee St (45458-1962)
PHONE..................937 438-3800
Fax: 937 438-3027
John Higgins, *President*
Janet Struve, *Sales Associate*
Scott D Gomez, *Sales Executive*
Tom Meininger Jr, *Manager*
Emilio Perez, *Consultant*
EMP: 30
SQ FT: 12,000
SALES (est): 12.3MM **Privately Held**
SIC: 5511 7515 Automobiles, new & used; passenger car leasing

(G-9922)
TEKNOL INC (PA)
Also Called: Rubber Seal Products
5751 Webster St (45414-3520)
P.O. Box 13387 (45413-0387)
PHONE..................937 264-0190
Fax: 937 890-6320
Kent Von Behren, *President*
Dan Popper, *Nat'l Sales Mgr*
David Rants, *Sales Mgr*
Jim Testa, *Marketing Staff*
R Von Behren, *Shareholder*
▲ **EMP:** 57 **EST:** 1976
SQ FT: 60,000
SALES: 31MM **Privately Held**
WEB: www.rubber-seal.com
SIC: 2899 2891 5198 2851 Chemical preparations; sealants; paints, varnishes & supplies; paints & allied products

(G-9923)
TELAMON CORPORATION
600 N Irwin St (45403-1337)
PHONE..................937 254-2004
Sean Quinn, *Owner*
EMP: 25
SALES (corp-wide): 497.5MM **Privately Held**
SIC: 7361 Employment agencies
PA: Telamon Corporation
1000 E 116th St
Carmel IN 46032
317 818-6888

(G-9924)
THE FOODBANK INC
56 Armor Pl (45417-1187)
PHONE..................937 461-0265
Burma Thomas, *CEO*
Michelle Riley, *CEO*
Carlos Rodriguez, *Exec Dir*
Aaron Hill, *Volunteer Dir*
EMP: 29
SALES: 11.5MM **Privately Held**
SIC: 8322 Social service center

(G-9925)
THE FOR NATIONAL ASSOCIATION
4215 Breezewood Ave (45406-1313)
PHONE..................937 470-1059
Jean Foward, *Branch Mgr*
EMP: 25
SALES (corp-wide): 22.8MM **Privately Held**
SIC: 8641 Social associations
PA: National Association For The Advancement Of Colored People
4805 Mount Hope Dr
Baltimore MD 21215
410 580-5777

(G-9926)
THE MARIA-JOSEPH CENTER
Also Called: CHI
4830 Salem Ave (45416-1716)
P.O. Box 636000, Littleton CO (80163-6000)
PHONE..................937 278-2692
Fax: 937 277-1259
Sharon Thornton, *President*
Betsey Peterson, *Manager*
EMP: 400
SQ FT: 500,000
SALES: 20.3MM **Privately Held**
WEB: www.mariajoseph.org
SIC: 8052 8051 Intermediate care facilities; skilled nursing care facilities
PA: Catholic Health Initiatives
198 Inverness Dr W
Englewood CO 80112

(G-9927)
THINKTV NETWORK
110 S Jefferson St (45402-2402)
PHONE..................937 220-1600
David Fogarty, *President*
Lorrence Kellar, *Vice Pres*
Travis Greenwood, *Treasurer*
Sue Brinson, *Comms Mgr*
EMP: 50
SALES (est): 1.7MM **Privately Held**
SIC: 4833 7313 Television broadcasting stations; television & radio time sales

(G-9928)
THOMPSON STEEL COMPANY INC
Also Called: Dayton Steel Service
3911 Dayton Park Dr (45414-4411)
PHONE..................937 236-6940
Fax: 937 236-0724
Dave Berie, *General Mgr*
Earl Hicks, *Principal*
EMP: 30
SALES (corp-wide): 78.6MM **Privately Held**
SIC: 5051 Steel
PA: Thompson Steel Company, Inc.
120 Royall St Ste 2
Canton MA 02021
781 828-8800

(G-9929)
TIPHARAH GROUP CORP (PA)
Also Called: Tipharah Designs
252 Burgess Ave (45415-2630)
PHONE..................937 430-6266
Deirdre Brown Postell, *President*
EMP: 168
SQ FT: 2,200
SALES (est): 3.8MM **Privately Held**
SIC: 8748 Business consulting

(G-9930)
TIPHARAH GROUP CORP
Also Called: Tipharah Hospitality
252 Burgess Ave (45415-2630)
PHONE..................937 430-6266
Deirdre Postell, *President*
EMP: 152
SALES (corp-wide): 3.8MM **Privately Held**
SIC: 8748 Business consulting
PA: The Tipharah Group Corp
252 Burgess Ave
Dayton OH 45415
937 430-6266

(G-9931)
TIPP MACHINE & TOOL INC
4201 Little York Rd (45414-2507)
PHONE..................937 890-8428
Richard L Snell, *Ch of Bd*
Gary Van Gundy, *President*
Charles E Snell, *Principal*
Robert J Moorman, *Principal*
Viola M Snell, *Principal*
EMP: 124
SQ FT: 52,000
SALES (est): 11.1MM **Privately Held**
WEB: www.tippmachine.com
SIC: 3544 3599 7389 Special dies & tools; industrial molds; jigs & fixtures; machine shop, jobbing & repair; grinding, precision: commercial or industrial
PA: Drt Holdings, Inc.
618 Greenmount Blvd
Dayton OH 45419

(G-9932)
TOP TIER SOCCER LLC
1268 Walnut Valley Ln (45458-9683)
PHONE..................937 903-6114
Colin Jones, *Mng Member*
EMP: 29
SALES: 498K **Privately Held**
SIC: 5947 7389 Novelties;

(G-9933)
TOTAL RENAL CARE INC
Also Called: Linden Home Dialysis
1431 Business Center Ct (45410-3300)
PHONE..................937 252-1867
Jim Hilger, *Branch Mgr*
EMP: 30 **Publicly Held**
SIC: 8092 Kidney dialysis centers
HQ: Total Renal Care, Inc.
2000 16th St
Denver CO 80202
303 405-2100

(G-9934)
TOULA INDUSTRIES LTD LLC
1019 Valley Vista Way (45429 6130)
PHONE..................937 689-1818
Martin Mershad, *President*
EMP: 150
SALES (est): 7.4MM **Privately Held**
SIC: 4412 Deep sea foreign transportation of freight

(G-9935)
TOYOTA INDUSTRIES N AMER INC
Also Called: Prolift Industrial Equipment
6254 Executive Blvd (45424-1423)
PHONE..................937 237-0976
Fax: 937 237-0978
Stephen Ford, *Manager*
EMP: 27
SALES (corp-wide): 19.8B **Privately Held**
SIC: 5084 7699 Lift trucks & parts; industrial truck repair
HQ: Toyota Industries North America, Inc.
3030 Barker Dr
Columbus IN 47201
812 341-3810

(G-9936)
TRAME MECHANICAL INC
Also Called: Honeywell Authorized Dealer
2721 Timber Ln (45414-4735)
P.O. Box 13596 (45413-0596)
PHONE..................937 258-1000
Fax: 937 258-2898
Steve Walton, *CEO*
EMP: 25 **EST:** 1979
SQ FT: 9,000
SALES: 3.9MM **Privately Held**
WEB: www.trame.com
SIC: 1711 Mechanical contractor

(G-9937)
TRIANGLE PRECISION INDUSTRIES
1650 Delco Park Dr (45420-1392)
PHONE..................937 299-6776
Fax: 937 299-7340
Gerald D Schriml, *President*
Paul S Holzinger, *Vice Pres*
EMP: 57
SQ FT: 23,400
SALES (est): 10.2MM **Privately Held**
WEB: www.triangleprecision.com
SIC: 3599 7692 3446 3444 Machine shop, jobbing & repair; welding repair; architectural metalwork; sheet metalwork; fabricated plate work (boiler shop); fabricated structural metal

(G-9938)
TRIMBLE ENGINEERING & CNSTR
5475 Kellenburger Rd (45424-1013)
PHONE..................937 233-8921
Fax: 937 233-9441
Madolyn Trimble, *Principal*
Kimberly Rife, *Manager*
Ron Reames, *Analyst*
▲ **EMP:** 31
SALES (est): 6.9MM **Privately Held**
SIC: 5712 7353 Office furniture; heavy construction equipment rental

(G-9939)
TRUGREEN LIMITED PARTNERSHIP
Also Called: Tru Green-Chemlawn
767 Liberty Ln (45449-2134)
PHONE..................937 866-8399
Dan Brodbeck, *Manager*
Susan Allen, *Manager*
EMP: 40
SALES (corp-wide): 4B **Privately Held**
SIC: 0782 Lawn care services
HQ: Trugreen Limited Partnership
1790 Kirby Pkwy
Memphis TN 38138
901 251-4128

(G-9940)
TRUSTED HOMECARE SOLUTIONS
2324 Stanley Ave Ste 115 (45404-1202)
PHONE..................937 506-7063
Viktoria E Peck, *Principal*
EMP: 25
SALES (est): 165.9K **Privately Held**
SIC: 8082 Home health care services

(G-9941)
TV MINORITY COMPANY INC
1700 E Monument Ave (45402-1364)
PHONE..................937 226-1559
Dan Schreier, *General Mgr*
EMP: 50
SALES (corp-wide): 46.6MM **Privately Held**
WEB: www.ilgi.com
SIC: 4212 Local trucking, without storage
PA: T.V. Minority Company, Inc.
9400 Pelham Rd
Taylor MI 48180
313 386-1048

Dayton - Montgomery County (G-9942)

(G-9942)
UBS FINANCIAL SERVICES INC
7887 Wash Vlg Dr Ste 100 (45459-3998)
PHONE...................................937 428-1300
Timothy Van Simaeys, *Principal*
EMP: 25
SALES (corp-wide): 28B **Privately Held**
SIC: 6211 Security brokers & dealers
HQ: Ubs Financial Services Inc.
1285 Ave Of The Americas
New York NY 10019
212 713-2000

(G-9943)
UFCW 75 REAL ESTATE CORP
7250 Poe Ave Ste 400 (45414-2698)
PHONE...................................937 677-0075
EMP: 60
SALES: 305.1K **Privately Held**
SIC: 6531 Real estate agents & managers

(G-9944)
UNION SAVINGS BANK
5651 Far Hills Ave (45429-2205)
PHONE...................................937 434-1254
Fax: 937 434-7103
Debbie Tchorz, *Facilities Mgr*
Kevin Grooms, *Loan Officer*
Melodie Sexten, *Loan Officer*
Ione Potter, *Broker*
Chris Gibbs, *VP Sales*
EMP: 60
SQ FT: 2,620
SALES (corp-wide): 147.9MM **Privately Held**
SIC: 6036 6035 Savings & loan associations, not federally chartered; federal savings banks
PA: Union Savings Bank
8534 E Kemper Rd Fl 1
Cincinnati OH 45249
513 489-1955

(G-9945)
UNITED ART AND EDUCATION INC
799 Lyons Rd (45459-3980)
PHONE...................................800 322-3247
Fax: 937 432-6473
Justin Hunt, *Manager*
David Kirkwood, *Manager*
Kelly Warnen, *Director*
EMP: 41
SALES (corp-wide): 24.1MM **Privately Held**
SIC: 5999 7389 5943 Artists' supplies & materials; laminating service; school supplies
PA: United Art And Education, Inc.
4413 Airport Expy
Fort Wayne IN 46809
260 478-1121

(G-9946)
UNITED FOOD AND COML WKRS
Also Called: Ufcw Local No. 75
7250 Poe Ave Ste 400 (45414-2698)
PHONE...................................937 665-0075
Fax: 513 539-9964
Lennie Wyatt, *President*
Joy Church, *Office Mgr*
Linda Welborne, *Agent*
EMP: 65
SQ FT: 1,500
SALES: 13.5MM **Privately Held**
SIC: 8631 Trade union

(G-9947)
UNITED REHABILITATION SERVICES
4710 Troy Pike (45424-5740)
PHONE...................................937 233-1230
Fax: 937 236-8930
Ashley Crawford, *Corp Comm Staff*
Kelly Lockwood, *Manager*
Jeremy Nelson, *Manager*
Tracy Pohlabel, *Manager*
Tara Speidel, *Manager*
EMP: 74
SQ FT: 37,000
SALES: 7.6MM **Privately Held**
SIC: 8399 8351 8322 8093 United Fund councils; child day care services; individual & family services; rehabilitation center, outpatient treatment; speech pathologist; hearing aids

(G-9948)
UNITED TELEMANAGEMENT CORP
6450 Poe Ave Ste 401 (45414-2665)
PHONE...................................937 454-1888
Fax: 937 890-7742
Terry L Henley, *CEO*
Don Campbell, *President*
Patricia D Milthaler, *General Mgr*
Jerry Tishkoff, *Exec VP*
James Hague, *CFO*
EMP: 25
SQ FT: 5,000
SALES (est): 3.2MM **Privately Held**
WEB: www.telelink-usa.com
SIC: 8741 Management services

(G-9949)
UNITED WAY OF THE GREATER DAYT (PA)
33 W 1st St Ste 500 (45402-1235)
P.O. Box 634625, Cincinnati (45263-4625)
PHONE...................................937 225-3060
Fax: 937 456-5622
Tom Maultsby, *President*
Bruce Brown, *Vice Pres*
Terri Leputa, *Assoc VP*
Jeffery Sellers, *Assoc VP*
Brent Byerly, *VP Finance*
EMP: 35
SALES: 9MM **Privately Held**
SIC: 8399 8322 United Fund councils; individual & family services

(G-9950)
UNIVERSAL 1 CREDIT UNION INC (PA)
1 River Park Dr (45409-2104)
P.O. Box 467 (45409-0467)
PHONE...................................800 762-9555
Fax: 937 225-9266
Loren A Rush, *President*
Glenn Kershner, *Exec VP*
Steve Shore, *Exec VP*
Ann Parrish, *Treasurer*
Alicia Hershberger, *Branch Mgr*
EMP: 73
SALES: 15.2MM **Privately Held**
WEB: www.universal1cu.biz
SIC: 6062 State credit unions, not federally chartered

(G-9951)
UNIVERSITY OF DAYTON
300 College Park Ave (45469-0002)
PHONE...................................937 255-3141
Bernard Ploeger, *Branch Mgr*
EMP: 150
SALES (corp-wide): 521.5MM **Privately Held**
WEB: www.udayton.edu
SIC: 8742 8221 Management consulting services; university
PA: The University Of Dayton
300 College Park Ave
Dayton OH 45469
937 229-2919

(G-9952)
UNIVERSITY OF DAYTON (PA)
300 College Park Ave (45469-0002)
PHONE...................................937 229-2919
Fax: 937 229-4461
Dr Daniel J Curran, *President*
Phillip Chick, *President*
Rob Durkle, *President*
Todd Imwalle, *President*
Jane Perrich, *President*
EMP: 2000
SQ FT: 25,000
SALES: 521.5MM **Privately Held**
WEB: www.udayton.edu
SIC: 8221 8733 University; noncommercial research organizations

(G-9953)
UNIVERSITY OF DAYTON
Also Called: University of Dyton Schl Engrg
300 College St (45402-8002)
PHONE...................................937 229-2113
Fax: 937 229-3433
Alison Borgerding, *Opers Staff*
Christopher Bruening, *Engineer*
Jeff Dennis, *Engineer*
James Sebastian, *Engineer*
Scott D Stouffer, *Engineer*
EMP: 250
SALES (corp-wide): 521.5MM **Privately Held**
WEB: www.udayton.edu
SIC: 8733 8221 Research institute; university
PA: The University Of Dayton
300 College Park Ave
Dayton OH 45469
937 229-2919

(G-9954)
UNIVERSITY OF DAYTON
Also Called: University Dayton RES Inst
711 E Monu Ave Ste 101 (45469-0001)
PHONE...................................937 229-3822
Daniel Kramer, *Div Sub Head*
John Ruschau, *Div Sub Head*
Andrew Abbott, *Engineer*
Chris Buck, *Engineer*
Jeremy Cain, *Engineer*
EMP: 400
SALES (corp-wide): 521.5MM **Privately Held**
SIC: 8733 8221 Research institute; university
PA: The University Of Dayton
300 College Park Ave
Dayton OH 45469
937 229-2919

(G-9955)
UNIVERSITY OF DAYTON
Also Called: Research Institute
1529 Brown St (45469-3401)
PHONE...................................937 229-3913
Rachel Bryant, *Facilities Mgr*
Ken Soucy, *Manager*
Carlos Stewart, *Asst Director*
Gwyn E Fox Stump, *Asst Director*
EMP: 150
SALES (corp-wide): 521.5MM **Privately Held**
WEB: www.udayton.edu
SIC: 8742 8221 Management consulting services; university
PA: The University Of Dayton
300 College Park Ave
Dayton OH 45469
937 229-2919

(G-9956)
UNIVERSITY WOMENS HEALTHCARE
627 S Edwin C Moses Blvd (45417-3461)
PHONE...................................937 208-2948
Gail Smith, *Office Mgr*
Janice Duke, *Med Doctor*
Jack Gruber, *Med Doctor*
Bruce Johnson, *Manager*
Sheila Barhan, *Obstetrician*
EMP: 42
SALES (est): 827.5K **Privately Held**
SIC: 8099 Medical services organization

(G-9957)
UPS GROUND FREIGHT INC
3730 Valley St (45424-5144)
PHONE...................................937 236-4700
Todd Fleharty, *Sales Staff*
Scott Gettys, *Manager*
EMP: 50
SALES (corp-wide): 65.8B **Publicly Held**
WEB: www.overnite.com
SIC: 4213 4212 Contract haulers; local trucking, without storage
HQ: Ups Ground Freight, Inc.
1000 Semmes Ave
Richmond VA 23224
866 372-5619

(G-9958)
US INSPECTION SERVICES INC (DH)
Also Called: Acuren Inspection
7333 Paragon Rd Ste 240 (45459-4157)
PHONE...................................937 660-9879
Jim Bailey, *President*
Peter Scannell, *President*
Ricki Miller, *Controller*
Larry Jeffries, *Manager*
Michelle Pritchard, *Administration*
EMP: 50
SQ FT: 18,000
SALES (est): 20.4MM
SALES (corp-wide): 1.6B **Privately Held**
SIC: 8734 Testing laboratories
HQ: Acuren Inspection, Inc.
30 Main St Ste 402
Danbury CT 06810
203 702-8740

(G-9959)
USF HOLLAND LLC
Also Called: USFreightways
2700 Valley Pike (45404-2695)
PHONE...................................937 233-7600
Bob Bayless, *Sales Executive*
Frank Blizzard, *Manager*
EMP: 150
SALES (corp-wide): 4.8B **Publicly Held**
WEB: www.usfc.com
SIC: 4212 4213 Local trucking, without storage; trucking, except local
HQ: Usf Holland Llc
700 S Waverly Rd
Holland MI 49423
616 395-5000

(G-9960)
VALENTOUR EDUCATION INC
Also Called: Ccdc
8095 Garnet Dr (45458-2140)
PHONE...................................937 434-5949
Kathy Valentour, *Exec Dir*
EMP: 35
SALES (est): 843.6K **Privately Held**
SIC: 8351 Preschool center

(G-9961)
VALLEY INTERIOR SYSTEMS INC
2760 Thunderhawk Ct (45414-3464)
PHONE...................................937 890-7319
Fax: 937 890-7367
Terry Gyetvai, *Branch Mgr*
EMP: 50
SALES (corp-wide): 70.7MM **Privately Held**
SIC: 1742 Drywall; acoustical & ceiling work; plastering, plain or ornamental
PA: Valley Interior Systems, Inc.
2203 Fowler St
Cincinnati OH 45206
513 961-0400

(G-9962)
VAN CON INC
8535 N Dixie Dr Ste B (45414-2474)
PHONE...................................937 890-8400
Fax: 937 890-4916
Samuel L Moorman, *Ch of Bd*
Jean L Maychack, *President*
Jack Moorman, *Vice Pres*
Sean Olson, *Vice Pres*
Norma Moorman, *Treasurer*
EMP: 29 **EST:** 1978
SQ FT: 13,000
SALES (est): 9.2MM **Privately Held**
WEB: www.van-con.com
SIC: 1542 1521 Commercial & office building, new construction; new construction, single-family houses

(G-9963)
VAN HOWARDS LINES INC
Also Called: Morgan & Sons Moving & Storage
3516 Wright Way Rd Ste 2 (45424-5164)
PHONE...................................937 235-0007
Fax: 937 235-0426
Orville Morgan Sr, *President*
Orville Morgan Jr, *Corp Secy*
Ira Morgan, *Vice Pres*
Crystal Farmer, *Bookkeeper*
EMP: 47

GEOGRAPHIC SECTION
Dayton - Montgomery County (G-9986)

SQ FT: 26,000
SALES: 1.7MM **Privately Held**
SIC: **4213** 4214 4212 Household goods transport; local trucking with storage; local trucking; without storage; furniture moving, local; without storage

(G-9964)
VANCE ROAD ENTERPRISES INC
1431 N Gettysburg Ave (45417-9517)
PHONE..............................937 268-6953
Troy Peavy, *President*
EMP: 28
SALES (est): 5MM **Privately Held**
SIC: **4213** Trucking, except local

(G-9965)
VANDALIA BLACKTOP SEAL COATING
6740 Webster St (45414-2613)
PHONE..............................937 454-0571
Fax: 937 454-1250
H David Brusman Jr, *President*
Tony Koehl, *Vice Pres*
Ron Cantrell, *Foreman/Supr*
Leon Davis, *Sales Staff*
EMP: 50
SQ FT: 2,000
SALES (est): 9.6MM **Privately Held**
WEB: www.vandaliablacktop.com
SIC: **1611** 1794 Highway & street paving contractor; excavation work

(G-9966)
VANGUARD IMAGING PARTNERS
6251 Good Samaritan Way # 140 (45424-5254)
PHONE..............................937 236-4780
Scott Buchanen, *President*
EMP: 60
SALES (est): 2.9MM **Privately Held**
SIC: **8011** Radiologist

(G-9967)
VARTEK SERVICES INC
4770 Hempstead Station Dr (45429-5164)
PHONE..............................937 438-3550
Fax: 937 438-3972
Michael Hosford, *CEO*
Darlene Waite, *President*
Don Purvis, *Opers Mgr*
Dan Molloy, *Technical Mgr*
Sarah Hallum, *Accountant*
EMP: 35
SQ FT: 15,000
SALES (est): 6.9MM **Privately Held**
WEB: www.vartek.com
SIC: **8742** Management information systems consultant

(G-9968)
VEOLIA ES INDUSTRIAL SVCS INC
6151 Executive Blvd (45424-1440)
PHONE..............................937 425-0512
Jeff Geibel, *Safety Mgr*
Chris McCollum, *Site Mgr*
George Levi Jr, *Purch Dir*
Mike Webb, *Branch Mgr*
Dave Weaver, *Manager*
EMP: 120
SALES (corp-wide): 572.2MM **Privately Held**
WEB: www.onyxindustrial.com
SIC: **7349** Cleaning service, industrial or commercial
HQ: Veolia Es Industrial Services, Inc.
4760 World Houston Pkwy # 100
Houston TX 77032
713 672-8004

(G-9969)
VERIZON WIRELESS INC
2799 Mmsburg Cntrville Rd (45459)
PHONE..............................937 434-2355
Fax: 937 291-7759
EMP: 55
SALES (corp-wide): 125.9B **Publicly Held**
SIC: **4812** Radiotelephone Communication
HQ: Verizon Wireless, Inc.
1 Verizon Way
Basking Ridge NJ 07920

(G-9970)
VERNON F GLASER & ASSOCIATES
3085 Woodman Dr Ste 250 (45420-1181)
PHONE..............................937 298-5536
Fax: 937 298-5596
Vernon F Glaser, *President*
Eileen Mroz, *Financial Exec*
Traci Fischer, *Accounts Mgr*
Thomas Finkenstatt, *Info Tech Mgr*
EMP: 30
SQ FT: 8,500
SALES (est): 4.2MM **Privately Held**
SIC: **8742** 8721 Hospital & health services consultant; accounting, auditing & bookkeeping

(G-9971)
VETERAN SECURITY PATROL CO
601 S E C Moses Blvd # 170 (45417-3424)
PHONE..............................937 222-7333
Fax: 937 424-5406
Roy Belcher, *Branch Mgr*
EMP: 40 **Privately Held**
WEB: www.veteransecurity.com
SIC: **7381** Detective & armored car services
PA: Veteran Security Patrol Co.
215 Taylor Ave
Bellevue KY 41073

(G-9972)
VETERANS AFFAIRS US DEPT
Also Called: Dayton V A Medical Center
4100 W 3rd St (45428-9000)
PHONE..............................937 268-6511
Fax: 937 267-5372
Nick McCray, *General Mgr*
Lawrence Tucker, *Marketing Mgr*
Francis Beavers, *Office Mgr*
Jodi Cokl, *Branch Mgr*
Terri Dalton, *Nursing Mgr*
EMP: 2000 **Publicly Held**
WEB: www.veterans-ru.org
SIC: **8011** 9451 Medical centers; administration of veterans' affairs;
HQ: United States Dept Of Veterans Affairs
810 Vermont Ave Nw
Washington DC 20420
202 273-5400

(G-9973)
VIVIAL MEDIA LLC
3100 Res Blvd Ste 250 (45420)
PHONE..............................937 610-4100
EMP: 61
SALES (corp-wide): 31.3MM **Privately Held**
SIC: **7311** Advertising agencies
PA: Vivial Media Llc
160 Inverness Dr W # 250
Englewood CO 80112
303 867-1600

(G-9974)
VOCALINK INC
405 W 1st St Ste A (45402-3007)
PHONE..............................937 223-1415
Amelia Rodriguez, *President*
Ray Reyes, *Vice Pres*
Bruce Smith, *Research*
Steve Jeanmougin, *Controller*
Christina Brownlee, *Mktg Dir*
EMP: 405
SALES (est): 3.5MM **Privately Held**
SIC: **7389** Translation services

(G-9975)
VOLVO BMW DYTON EVANS VOLKSWAG
Also Called: Evans Motor Works
7124 Poe Ave (45414-2546)
PHONE..............................937 890-6200
Jim Evans, *President*
Jims Evans, *President*
Nathan Willis, *General Mgr*
Jim Corwin, *Parts Mgr*
Brian Hogarth, *Sales Mgr*
EMP: 50 EST: 2009
SALES (est): 2.1MM **Privately Held**
SIC: **5511** 7538 Automobiles, new & used; general automotive repair shops

(G-9976)
VOSS AUTO NETWORK INC (PA)
Also Called: Hoss
766 Mmsburg Cnterville Rd (45459)
PHONE..............................937 428-2447
Fax: 937 434-7472
Chuck Belk, *President*
John Voss, *President*
Dick Lange, *General Mgr*
Teresa Haynes, *Principal*
Michelle Mills, *Financial Exec*
EMP: 50
SQ FT: 45,288
SALES (est): 155.1MM **Privately Held**
WEB: www.vossauto.net
SIC: **5511** 7538 7513 5521 Automobiles, new & used; general automotive repair shops; truck rental & leasing, no drivers; used car dealers; automobiles & other motor vehicles

(G-9977)
VOSS AUTO NETWORK INC
100 Loop Rd (45459-2142)
PHONE..............................937 433-1444
Craig Voss, *General Mgr*
Greg Stout, *VP Finance*
Teresa Haines, *Human Resources*
Chad Minkner, *Sales Mgr*
Jennifer Miller, *Sales Executive*
EMP: 450
SALES (corp-wide): 155.1MM **Privately Held**
WEB: www.vossauto.net
SIC: **7532** 5521 Body shop, automotive; automobiles, used cars only
PA: Voss Auto Network, Inc.
766 Mmsburg Cnterville Rd
Dayton OH 45459
937 428-2447

(G-9978)
VOSS CHEVROLET INC
100 Loop Rd (45459-2197)
PHONE..............................937 428-2500
Fax: 937 433-9872
John E Voss, *President*
Greg Stout, *Finance*
Teresa Haines, *Human Res Mgr*
Susan Haught, *Human Res Mgr*
Jenny Miller, *Sales Executive*
EMP: 190
SQ FT: 55,000
SALES (est): 54.8MM **Privately Held**
SIC: **5511** 5521 5012 Automobiles, new & used; used car dealers; automobiles & other motor vehicles

(G-9979)
VOSS DODGE (PA)
90 Loop Rd (45459-2140)
PHONE..............................937 435-7800
Fax: 937 428-6302
John E Voss, *President*
Brooke Baker, *Accounting Mgr*
EMP: 50
SQ FT: 26,000
SALES (est): 7.8MM **Privately Held**
WEB: www.vossdodge.com
SIC: **5511** 5521 5012 Automobiles, new & used; used car dealers; automobiles & other motor vehicles

(G-9980)
W2005/FARGO HOTELS (POOL C)
Also Called: Courtyard Dayton
7087 Miller Ln (45414-2653)
PHONE..............................937 890-6112
Fax: 937 890-6112
David Smith, *Manager*
EMP: 40
SALES (corp-wide): 16.5MM **Privately Held**
WEB: www.daytonraiders.com
SIC: **7011** Hotels & motels
HQ: W2005/Fargo Hotels (Pool C) Realty, L.P.
5851 Legacy Cir Ste 400
Plano TX 75024

(G-9981)
WALGREEN CO
Also Called: Walgreens
6485 Wilmington Pike (45459-7110)
PHONE..............................937 433-5314
Fax: 937 433-4058
Michelle Motil, *Pharmacist*
Cecil Perry, *Manager*
Rebecca Hasbrook, *Manager*
EMP: 40
SALES (corp-wide): 118.2B **Publicly Held**
WEB: www.walgreens.com
SIC: **5912** 7384 Drug stores; photofinishing laboratory
HQ: Walgreen Co.
200 Wilmot Rd
Deerfield IL 60015
847 315-2500

(G-9982)
WALGREEN CO
Also Called: Walgreens
2600 S Smithville Rd (45420-2642)
PHONE..............................937 781-9561
Fax: 937 781-9387
Amy Hall, *Pharmacist*
Cristy Loebrich, *Manager*
EMP: 30
SALES (corp-wide): 118.2B **Publicly Held**
WEB: www.walgreens.com
SIC: **5912** 7384 Drug stores; photofinishing laboratory
HQ: Walgreen Co.
200 Wilmot Rd
Deerfield IL 60015
847 315-2500

(G-9983)
WALGREEN CO
Also Called: Walgreens
2710 Salem Ave (45406-2730)
PHONE..............................937 277-6022
Fax: 937 277-0288
Bryan Astor, *Manager*
Bryan Regin, *Manager*
EMP: 25
SALES (corp-wide): 118.2B **Publicly Held**
WEB: www.walgreens.com
SIC: **5912** 7384 Drug stores; photofinishing laboratory
HQ: Walgreen Co.
200 Wilmot Rd
Deerfield IL 60015
847 315-2500

(G-9984)
WASHINGTON MANOR INC (PA)
Also Called: Washington Manor Nursing Ctr
7300 Mcewen Rd (45459-3903)
PHONE..............................937 433-3441
Fax: 937 433-6027
Linda Kurke, *Owner*
EMP: 25
SQ FT: 52,000
SALES (est): 3.3MM **Privately Held**
WEB: www.libertynursingcenters.com
SIC: **8361** 8052 8051 Geriatric residential care; intermediate care facilities; skilled nursing care facilities

(G-9985)
WASHINGTON TOWNSHIP PARK DST (PA)
Also Called: Centerville Washington Pk Dst
221 S Main St (45402-2407)
PHONE..............................937 433-5155
Fax: 937 433-6564
Michael J Rice, *Vice Pres*
Loann Castillo, *Program Mgr*
Arnie Biono, *Director*
Carol Kennard, *Director*
EMP: 30
SQ FT: 3,500
SALES (est): 1.6MM **Privately Held**
WEB: www.cwpd.org
SIC: **7999** Recreation services

(G-9986)
WASHINGTON TWNSHIP MNTGOMERY
Also Called: Washington Twnship Rcrtion Ctr
895 Mmsburg Cnterville Rd (45459)
PHONE..............................937 433-0130
Fax: 937 438-2755
Joyce Fronzaglia, *Office Mgr*
Tom Cote, *Manager*
Mark Metzger, *Manager*
Rich Palmer, *Webmaster*

Dayton - Montgomery County (G-9987)

David Paice, *Director*
EMP: 125
SQ FT: 20,000 **Privately Held**
WEB: www.washingtontwp.org
SIC: 7999 7991 Recreation center; physical fitness facilities
PA: Washington Township, Montgomery County
8200 Mcewen Rd
Dayton OH 45458
937 435-2376

(G-9987)
WEB YOGA INC
938 Senate Dr (45459-4017)
PHONE 937 428-0000
Fax: 937 428-0171
Vijay Vallabhaneni, *President*
Robin Davenport, *Manager*
Tamiko Lawton, *Manager*
EMP: 30
SQ FT: 2,400
SALES (est): 3.4MM **Privately Held**
WEB: www.webyoga.com
SIC: 7379 Computer related consulting services

(G-9988)
WEE CARE LEARNING CENTER
9675 N Dixie Dr (45414-1818)
PHONE 937 454-9363
Helene Gross, *Director*
EMP: 30
SALES (est): 192.5K **Privately Held**
SIC: 8351 Preschool center

(G-9989)
WELCH PACKAGING LLC
321 Hopeland St (45417-4027)
PHONE 937 223-3958
Scott Welch, *President*
EMP: 48
SALES (corp-wide): 225MM **Privately Held**
SIC: 5113 Corrugated & solid fiber boxes
HQ: Welch Packaging, Llc
1020 Herman St
Elkhart IN 46516
574 295-2460

(G-9990)
WENZLER DAYCARE LEARNING CTR
Also Called: Wenzler Daycare & Learning Ctr
4535 Presidential Way (45429-5752)
PHONE 937 435-8200
Fax: 937 435-1415
Brenda Wenzler, *President*
Benita Wenzler, *Vice Pres*
EMP: 30
SALES (est): 1.1MM **Privately Held**
SIC: 8351 Child day care services

(G-9991)
WESCO DISTRIBUTION INC
2080 Winners Cir (45404-1130)
P.O. Box 119 (45404-0119)
PHONE 937 228-9668
Fax: 419 222-5787
Robin Miller, *Sales Executive*
Mark Boytim, *Branch Mgr*
EMP: 25 **Publicly Held**
SIC: 5063 5085 Electrical apparatus & equipment; industrial supplies
HQ: Wesco Distribution, Inc.
225 W Station Square Dr # 700
Pittsburgh PA 15219

(G-9992)
WESLEY COMMUNITY CENTER INC
3730 Delphos Ave (45417-1647)
PHONE 937 263-3556
Fax: 937 263-9582
Harris Tay, *Exec Dir*
Harris K Tay, *Exec Dir*
EMP: 29
SALES: 978.6K **Privately Held**
SIC: 8641 Civic associations

(G-9993)
WESTERN & SOUTHERN LF INSUR CO
1964 E Whipp Rd (45440-2921)
PHONE 937 435-1964
Fax: 937 435-2399
Mark J Cook, *Manager*
EMP: 30 **Privately Held**
SIC: 6411 Life insurance agents
HQ: The Western & Southern Life Insurance Company
400 Broadway St
Cincinnati OH 45202
513 629-1800

(G-9994)
WESTMINSTER FINANCIAL COMPANY
125 N Wilkinson St (45402-1423)
PHONE 937 898-5010
Lawrence Miles, *CEO*
Larry Landford, *Agent*
EMP: 50
SALES (est): 8.6MM **Privately Held**
SIC: 6282 Investment advice; investment advisory service

(G-9995)
WESTMNSTER FNCL SECURITIES INC
Also Called: Westminster Fincl Companies
40 N Main St Ste 2400 (45423-1004)
PHONE 937 898-5010
Miles Brazie, *CEO*
Lawrence Miles Brazie, *President*
Elizabeth Amundson, *Senior VP*
Kirk Stager, *Vice Pres*
Jessica Trunck, *Opers Mgr*
EMP: 50
SQ FT: 10,000
SALES (est): 9MM **Privately Held**
WEB: www.westminsterfinancial.com
SIC: 6211 Brokers, security

(G-9996)
WHITE FAMILY COMPANIES INC
Also Called: White Allen Chevrolet
442 N Main St (45405-4923)
PHONE 937 222-3701
Fax: 937 220-6318
Howard Monk, *General Mgr*
Nick Monk, *General Mgr*
Tim White, *Manager*
EMP: 160
SALES (corp-wide): 83.4MM **Privately Held**
WEB: www.whitecars.com
SIC: 5511 7513 5012 Automobiles, new & used; truck rental & leasing, no drivers; automobiles & other motor vehicles
PA: The White Family Companies Inc
2 River Pl Ste 444
Dayton OH 45405
937 220-6394

(G-9997)
WIDOWS HOME OF DAYTON OHIO
50 S Findlay St (45403-2091)
PHONE 937 252-1661
Fax: 937 252-0448
Antonette Flohre, *President*
Everett Telljohann, *President*
Paul Heinrich, *Vice Pres*
Dale Heinz, *Treasurer*
Lisa Heitzman, *Office Mgr*
EMP: 70
SQ FT: 50,000
SALES: 6.1MM **Privately Held**
SIC: 8361 8051 Residential care; home for the aged; skilled nursing care facilities

(G-9998)
WIGGINS CLG & CRPT SVC INC (PA)
4699 Salem Ave Ste 2 (45416-1724)
PHONE 937 279-9080
Jewel Wiggins, *President*
Brenda Wiggins, *Corp Secy*
EMP: 62
SQ FT: 2,400
SALES (est): 1.6MM **Privately Held**
WEB: www.wigginscleaning.com
SIC: 7349 7217 Cleaning service, industrial or commercial; building cleaning service; carpet & furniture cleaning on location

(G-9999)
WILLIAMS BROS ROOFG SIDING CO
3600 Valley St (45424-5142)
P.O. Box 24589 (45424-0589)
PHONE 937 434-3838
Fax: 937 236-4744
Martin E Williams, *President*
Theresa S Williams, *Corp Secy*
Greg Oldiges, *Vice Pres*
Steve Krammer, *Manager*
EMP: 25 EST: 1937
SQ FT: 5,500
SALES (est): 2.1MM **Privately Held**
WEB: www.williamsbrosroofing.com
SIC: 1751 1761 Window & door (prefabricated) installation; roofing contractor; siding contractor; gutter & downspout contractor

(G-10000)
WILMER CUTLER PICK HALE DORR
Also Called: Wilmerhale
3139 Research Blvd (45420-4006)
PHONE 937 395-2100
Matthew Coatney, *Vice Pres*
Donna Smith, *Branch Mgr*
Chris Southern, *Manager*
Charles S Beene, *Sr Associate*
Amanda L Major, *Sr Associate*
EMP: 270
SALES (corp-wide): 98.4MM **Privately Held**
SIC: 8111 Specialized law offices, attorneys
PA: Wilmer Cutler Pickering Hale And Dorr Llp
1875 Pennsylvania Ave Nw
Washington DC 20006
202 663-6000

(G-10001)
WISE SERVICES INC
1705 Guenther Rd (45417-9344)
P.O. Box 17159 (45417-0159)
PHONE 937 854-0281
David F Abney II, *President*
EMP: 45
SALES (est): 8.6MM **Privately Held**
SIC: 1542 Commercial & office building contractors

(G-10002)
WOMENS CENTERS-DAYTON
359 Forest Ave Ste 106 (45405-4559)
PHONE 937 228-2222
Vivian Koob, *Principal*
EMP: 50 EST: 2010
SALES (est): 676.2K **Privately Held**
SIC: 8071 Ultrasound laboratory

(G-10003)
WOODY TREE MEDICS
Also Called: Tru-Gro Landscaping
4350 Delco Dell Rd (45429-1211)
PHONE 937 298-5316
Fax: 937 298-3860
William F Wesig, *President*
EMP: 25
SQ FT: 34,680
SALES (est): 795.1K **Privately Held**
SIC: 0782 0783 Lawn & garden services; ornamental shrub & tree services

(G-10004)
WRIGHT BROTHERS AERO INC
Also Called: Logistics Department
3700 Mccall St (45417-1942)
PHONE 937 454-8475
Fax: 937 454-8401
Kevin Keeley Jr, *Principal*
EMP: 25
SALES (corp-wide): 8.1MM **Privately Held**
SIC: 4212 Delivery service, vehicular
PA: Wright Brothers Aero, Inc.
3700 Mccauley Dr Ste C
Vandalia OH 45377
937 890-8900

(G-10005)
XPO LOGISTICS FREIGHT INC
3410 Stop 8 Rd (45414-3428)
PHONE 937 898-9808
Fax: 937 898-4522
John Crowley, *Sls & Mktg Exec*
John Crawley, *Manager*
EMP: 35
SQ FT: 18,920
SALES (corp-wide): 15.3B **Publicly Held**
WEB: www.con-way.com
SIC: 4212 Local trucking, without storage
HQ: Xpo Logistics Freight, Inc.
2211 Old Earhart Rd # 100
Ann Arbor MI 48105
734 998-4200

(G-10006)
YEARWOOD CORPORATION (PA)
Also Called: Carousel Beauty College
125 E 2nd St (45402-1701)
P.O. Box 750144 (45475-0144)
PHONE 937 223-3572
Fax: 937 223-8951
Donald Yearwood, *President*
EMP: 33
SQ FT: 5,000
SALES (est): 2.2MM **Privately Held**
WEB: www.carouselbeauty.com
SIC: 7231 Beauty culture school

(G-10007)
YODER INDUSTRIES INC (PA)
2520 Needmore Rd (45414-4204)
PHONE 937 278-5769
Fax: 937 278-6321
Ron Zeverka, *President*
Janet E Roush, *Principal*
Ron Veverka, *Principal*
J B Yoder, *Principal*
Charles W Slicer, *Chairman*
EMP: 110 EST: 1956
SQ FT: 32,000
SALES (est): 13MM **Privately Held**
WEB: www.yoderindustries.com
SIC: 3369 3363 3365 3471 Nonferrous foundries; aluminum die-castings; aluminum foundries; plating & polishing; testing laboratories; nonferrous die-castings except aluminum

(G-10008)
YOUNG & ALEXANDER CO LPA (PA)
130 W 2nd St Ste 1500 (45402-1502)
PHONE 937 224-9291
Fax: 937 224-9679
Mark R Chilson, *President*
Steven Dean, *Vice Pres*
Christie McIntosh, *Legal Staff*
EMP: 53
SALES (est): 4.6MM **Privately Held**
SIC: 8111 General practice attorney, lawyer

(G-10009)
YOUNG MENS CHRISTIAN ASSOC (PA)
Also Called: YMCA of Greater Dayton
118 W St Ste 300 (45402)
PHONE 937 223-5201
Fax: 937 463-4880
Dale Brunner, *CEO*
Neal Pemberton, *Vice Pres*
Leann Krintzline, *Manager*
Leon Doiley, *Director*
Dusty Geer, *Admin Asst*
EMP: 1250 EST: 1882
SQ FT: 9,000
SALES: 26.1MM **Privately Held**
WEB: www.daytonymca.org
SIC: 8641 7991 8351 7032 Youth organizations; physical fitness facilities; child day care services; youth camps; individual & family services

(G-10010)
YOUNG MENS CHRISTIAN ASSOC
Also Called: South Cmty Family YMCA Cdc
4545 Marshall Rd (45429-5716)
PHONE 937 312-1810
Fax: 937 434-1975
Kelley Ingram, *Engrg Dir*
EMP: 25

GEOGRAPHIC SECTION

Defiance - Defiance County (G-10032)

SALES (corp-wide): 26.1MM **Privately Held**
WEB: www.daytonymca.org
SIC: **8641** 7991 8351 7032 Youth organizations; physical fitness facilities; child day care services; youth camps; individual & family services
PA: Young Men's Christian Association Of Greater Dayton
118 W St Ste 300
Dayton OH 45402
937 223-5201

(G-10011)
YOUNG MENS CHRISTIAN ASSOC
Also Called: Beavercreek YMCA Sch's Out I
111 W 1st St Ste 207 (45402-1154)
PHONE..................................937 426-9622
Tom Feller, *Exec Dir*
Stacy Wentzell, *Director*
EMP: 80
SALES (corp-wide): 26.1MM **Privately Held**
WEB: www.daytonymca.org
SIC: **8641** 7997 Youth organizations; membership sports & recreation clubs
PA: Young Men's Christian Association Of Greater Dayton
118 W St Ste 300
Dayton OH 45402
937 223-5201

(G-10012)
YOUNG MENS CHRISTIAN ASSOC
Also Called: YMCA Crayon Club Chld Care
316 N Wilkinson St (45402-3060)
PHONE..................................937 228-9622
Nancy Hudecek, *Director*
EMP: 40
SALES (corp-wide): 26.1MM **Privately Held**
WEB: www.daytonymca.org
SIC: **8641** 8351 7997 7991 Youth organizations; child day care services; membership sports & recreation clubs; physical fitness facilities; recreation center
PA: Young Men's Christian Association Of Greater Dayton
118 W St Ste 300
Dayton OH 45402
937 223-5201

(G-10013)
YOUNG WOMENS CHRISTIAN
Also Called: YWCA of Dayton
141 W 3rd St (45402-1814)
PHONE..................................937 461-5550
Donna Audette, *CEO*
Michelle Riley, *COO*
Marissa Buckles, *Manager*
Stacy Shern, *Manager*
Deven Warvel, *Info Tech Mgr*
EMP: 79 EST: 1871
SQ FT: 100,000
SALES: 3.1MM **Privately Held**
SIC: **8641** 7991 8351 7032 Youth organizations; physical fitness facilities; child day care services; youth camps; individual & family services

(G-10014)
YWCA SHELTER & HOUSING NETWORK
141 W 3rd St (45402-1814)
PHONE..................................937 222-6333
Fax: 937 222-0610
Donna Audette, *CEO*
EMP: 30
SALES (est): 234.2K **Privately Held**
SIC: **8641** 7991 8351 7032 Youth organizations; physical fitness facilities; child day care services; youth camps; individual & family services

(G-10015)
ZIKS FAMILY PHARMACY 100
1130 W 3rd St (45402-6812)
PHONE..................................937 225-9350
Nnodum Iheme, *CEO*
Nnenna Iheme, *Vice Pres*
EMP: 30
SQ FT: 5,500

SALES (est): 5MM **Privately Held**
SIC: **5912** 5047 8082 Drug stores; medical & hospital equipment; home health care services

De Graff
Logan County

(G-10016)
SCHINDEWOLF EXPRESS INC
200 S Boggs St (43318-7905)
PHONE..................................937 585-5919
Suzie Schindewolf, *CEO*
Dan Schindewolf, *President*
Casey Schindewolf, *Corp Secy*
David Breneck, *Vice Pres*
Chad Shindewolf, *Vice Pres*
EMP: 52
SALES (est): 2.2MM **Privately Held**
SIC: **4213** 4212 Contract haulers; local trucking, without storage

Deerfield
Portage County

(G-10017)
CHEVRON AE RESOURCES LLC
1823 State Route 14 (44411)
P.O. Box 160 (44411-0160)
PHONE..................................330 654-4343
EMP: 30
SALES (corp-wide): 129.9B **Publicly Held**
SIC: **1311** 1382 Crude Petroleum/Natural Gas Production Oil/Gas Exploration Services
HQ: Chevron Ae Resources Llc
1000 Commerce Dr Fl 4
Pittsburgh PA 15275
800 251-0171

(G-10018)
DEERFIELD FARMS
9041 State Route 224 (44411-8715)
P.O. Box 155 (44411-0155)
PHONE..................................330 584-4715
B William Wallbrown, *President*
John Wallbrown, *Vice Pres*
EMP: 32
SQ FT: 5,000
SALES (est): 2.4MM **Privately Held**
SIC: **0191** 1799 1521 General farms, primarily crop; fence construction; patio & deck construction & repair

(G-10019)
DEERFIELD FARMS SERVICE INC (PA)
9041 State Route 224 (44411-8715)
P.O. Box 155 (44411-0155)
PHONE..................................330 584-4715
Fax: 330 584-6420
B William Wallbrown, *President*
Joan Wallbrown, *Corp Secy*
John Wallbrown, *Vice Pres*
Travis Wright, *Project Mgr*
Ben Gage, *Opers Mgr*
EMP: 63
SQ FT: 25,000
SALES: 52MM **Privately Held**
WEB: www.deerfieldfarms.com
SIC: **5153** 5191 4221 5083 Grain elevators; fertilizer & fertilizer materials; grain elevator, storage only; agricultural machinery & equipment

Defiance
Defiance County

(G-10020)
BROOKVIEW HEALTHCARE CTR
Also Called: Brookview Healthcare Center
214 Harding St (43512-1381)
PHONE..................................419 784-1014
Paul Dauerman, *President*
Samer Obri, *Director*
EMP: 90

SALES (est): 5MM **Privately Held**
WEB: www.brookview.com
SIC: **8059** 8051 Convalescent home; skilled nursing care facilities

(G-10021)
CELLCO PARTNERSHIP
Also Called: Verizon Wireless
1007 N Clinton St Ste 1 (43512-4608)
PHONE..................................419 784-3800
Fax: 419 784-3900
Judy Aden, *Branch Mgr*
EMP: 71
SALES (corp-wide): 126B **Publicly Held**
SIC: **4812** Cellular telephone services
HQ: Cellco Partnership
1 Verizon Way
Basking Ridge NJ 07920

(G-10022)
CITY BEVERAGE COMPANY
8283 N State Route 66 (43512-6612)
P.O. Box 432 (43512-0432)
PHONE..................................419 782-7065
Fax: 419 782-9426
Thomas Sauer, *President*
Mike Klepper, *COO*
Larry Venter, *Opers Mgr*
Rachel Sternberg, *Inv Control Mgr*
Scott Harlow, *CFO*
▲ EMP: 25 EST: 1960
SQ FT: 33,000
SALES (est): 5.8MM **Privately Held**
WEB: www.citybev.com
SIC: **5181** Beer & other fermented malt liquors

(G-10023)
CONSOLIDATED GRAIN & BARGE CO
Also Called: CGB -Defiance
11859 Krouse Rd (43512-8618)
PHONE..................................419 785-1941
Kevin D Adams, *CEO*
EMP: 51 **Privately Held**
SIC: **5153** 4221 Grains; grain elevator, storage only
HQ: Consolidated Grain & Barge Company
1127 Hwy 190 E Service Rd
Covington LA 70433
985 867-3500

(G-10024)
CREDIT ADJUSTMENTS INC (PA)
330 Florence St (43512-2512)
PHONE..................................419 782-3709
Fax: 419 784-9784
Dexter Smith, *President*
Jason Osborne, *Vice Pres*
Gayle Carter, *Vice Pres*
Shelah Cheek, *Credit Mgr*
Amy Bains, *Human Res Mgr*
EMP: 53
SQ FT: 10,000
SALES: 11.1MM **Privately Held**
WEB: www.credit-adjustments.com
SIC: **7322** Collection agency, except real estate

(G-10025)
DEFIANCE CNTY BD COMMISSIONERS
Also Called: Defiance County Senior Center
140 E Broadway St (43512-1639)
PHONE..................................419 782-3233
Fax: 419 782-7610
Tina Hilcr, *Director*
EMP: 26 **Privately Held**
SIC: **8322** Individual & family services
PA: Defiance County Board Of Commissioners
500 Court St Ste A
Defiance OH 43512
419 782-4761

(G-10026)
DEFIANCE FAMILY PHYSICIANS
1250 Ralston Ave Ste 104 (43512-5308)
PHONE..................................419 785-3281
Fax: 419 784-1606
Robert Barnett MD, *Partner*
Hacker Lisa, *Manager*
Sharon Jewel, *Receptionist*
Nancy Hard, *Receptionist Se*
EMP: 26 EST: 1982

SALES (est): 1.9MM **Privately Held**
SIC: **8011** General & family practice, physician/surgeon

(G-10027)
DEFIANCE HOSPITAL INC
Also Called: DEFIANCE REGIONAL MEDICAL CENTER
1200 Ralston Ave (43512-1396)
PHONE..................................419 782-6955
Tim Jakacki, *President*
Carl A Sixeas, *Principal*
Nighat Hashmi, *Ch Pathology*
Ed Ferguson, *Ch Radiology*
Sandy Warren, *Purch Mgr*
EMP: 359
SQ FT: 150,000
SALES: 56.3MM
SALES (corp-wide): 1.5B **Privately Held**
SIC: **8062** General medical & surgical hospitals
PA: Promedica Health Systems, Inc.
100 Madison Ave
Toledo OH 43604
567 585-7454

(G-10028)
DILLY DOOR CO
1640 Baltimore St (43512-1963)
PHONE..................................419 782-1181
Fax: 419 782-1495
Gary Konst, *President*
Robert Eugene Andrews, *Vice Pres*
Diane Pittman, *Manager*
Mae Luderman, *Shareholder*
Tommy A Clark, *Admin Sec*
EMP: 40
SQ FT: 35,000
SALES (est): 6.6MM **Privately Held**
SIC: **5211** 1751 Lumber & other building materials; door & window products; window & door (prefabricated) installation

(G-10029)
ELLERBROCK HEATING & AC
13055 Dohoney Rd (43512-8716)
PHONE..................................419 782-1834
Fax: 419 782-7919
Scott Wagner, *President*
EMP: 25
SALES (est): 1.2MM **Privately Held**
SIC: **1711** Heating & air conditioning contractors

(G-10030)
FAUSTER-CAMERON INC (PA)
Also Called: Defiance Clinic
1400 E 2nd St (43512-2440)
PHONE..................................419 784-1414
Fax: 419 783-3380
Chad L Peter, *CEO*
Allen Gaspar, *Ch of Bd*
Nathan Fogt, *Corp Secy*
John Racciato, *Vice Pres*
Virinder K Bhardwaj MD, *Med Doctor*
EMP: 310
SQ FT: 101,908
SALES (est): 29.1MM **Privately Held**
WEB: www.defianceclinic.com
SIC: **8011** Medical centers

(G-10031)
FIRST FEDERAL BANK OF MIDWEST (HQ)
Also Called: FIRST DEFIANCE
601 Clinton St Ste 1 (43512-2661)
P.O. Box 240 (43512-0248)
PHONE..................................419 782-5015
William J Small, *Ch of Bd*
James L Rohrs, *President*
Gregory R Allen, *Exec VP*
Dennis Rose, *Exec VP*
Kevin Thompson, *Exec VP*
EMP: 50
SQ FT: 10,000
SALES: 110.3MM **Publicly Held**
SIC: **6035** Federal savings & loan associations

(G-10032)
FITZENRIDER INC
827 Perry St (43512-2738)
PHONE..................................419 784-0828
Fax: 419 782-7385
John Jacob, *President*
Philip Fitzenrider, *Vice Pres*

Defiance - Defiance County (G-10033)

Ron Huner, *Manager*
Kevin Meyer, *IT/INT Sup*
EMP: 30 **EST:** 1955
SQ FT: 15,000
SALES (est): 6.2MM **Privately Held**
SIC: 1711 Warm air heating & air conditioning contractor; ventilation & duct work contractor; mechanical contractor

(G-10033)
FOUNTAIN CITY LEASING INC
2060 E 2nd St Ste 101 (43512-9208)
PHONE..................419 785-3100
Fax: 419 267-5535
Sam Hornish, *President*
Richard Miller, *Controller*
Janet Liffick, *Accountant*
Bill Turner, *Manager*
Jo Ellen Hornish, *Admin Sec*
EMP: 82
SQ FT: 14,000
SALES (est): 7.7MM **Privately Held**
SIC: 7513 Truck leasing, without drivers

(G-10034)
HUBBARD COMPANY
612 Clinton St (43512-2637)
P.O. Box 100 (43512-0100)
PHONE..................419 784-4455
Fax: 419 782-1662
E Keith Hubbard, *Ch of Bd*
Thomas K Hubbard, *President*
Jean A Hubbard, *Treasurer*
Dick Anderson, *Sales Staff*
Blayne Robbins, *Sales Staff*
EMP: 44
SQ FT: 20,000
SALES (est): 7.2MM **Privately Held**
WEB: www.hubbardcompany.com
SIC: 5943 5192 2752 2732 Office forms & supplies; books; commercial printing, offset; book printing; book publishing

(G-10035)
HUNTINGTON NATIONAL BANK
405 W 3rd St (43512-2136)
PHONE..................419 782-5050
Robert Degler, *Manager*
EMP: 35
SALES (corp-wide): 4.7B **Publicly Held**
WEB: www.huntingtonnationalbank.com
SIC: 6029 6022 Commercial banks; state commercial banks
HQ: The Huntington National Bank
17 S High St Fl 1
Columbus OH 43215
614 480-4293

(G-10036)
IDEAL SETECH LLC
24862 Elliott Rd (43512-9217)
PHONE..................419 782-5522
John McCarthey, *Branch Mgr*
EMP: 25 **Privately Held**
SIC: 8741 Management services
PA: Ideal Setech, L.L.C.
2525 Clark St
Detroit MI 48209

(G-10037)
IHEARTCOMMUNICATIONS INC
2110 Radio Dr (43512-1977)
PHONE..................419 782-9336
Bob Climanas, *Manager*
EMP: 61 **Publicly Held**
SIC: 4832 Radio broadcasting stations
HQ: Iheartcommunications, Inc.
20880 Stone Oak Pkwy
San Antonio TX 78258
210 822-2828

(G-10038)
JOHNS MANVILLE CORPORATION
600 Jackson Ave (43512-2769)
PHONE..................419 784-7000
Jerry Henry, *Branch Mgr*
EMP: 54
SALES (corp-wide): 242.1B **Publicly Held**
SIC: 5033 5211 Roofing, siding & insulation; roofing material; insulation material, building

HQ: Johns Manville Corporation
717 17th St Ste 800
Denver CO 80202
303 978-2000

(G-10039)
KELLER LOGISTICS GROUP INC
24862 Elliott Rd Ste 101 (43512-9237)
PHONE..................419 784-4805
Fax: 419 782-3277
Scott J Galbraith, *Branch Mgr*
EMP: 67 **Privately Held**
SIC: 4215 Courier services, except by air
PA: Keller Logistics Group, Inc.
24862 Elliott Rd Ste 101
Defiance OH 43512

(G-10040)
KELLER LOGISTICS GROUP INC (PA)
24862 Elliott Rd Ste 101 (43512-9237)
PHONE..................866 276-9486
Bryan Keller, *Principal*
Dawn Nye, *Principal*
Nate Schaublin, *Principal*
Beth Woodbury, *Principal*
Aaron Keller, *Vice Pres*
EMP: 46
SALES (est): 44.4MM **Privately Held**
SIC: 4731 7389 Freight transportation arrangement; packaging & labeling services

(G-10041)
KELLER WAREHOUSING & DIST LLC
1160 Carpenter Rd (43512-1727)
PHONE..................419 784-4805
EMP: 125
SQ FT: 7,000
SALES (est): 4.3MM **Privately Held**
SIC: 4225 General Warehouse/Storage

(G-10042)
KETTENRING COUNTRY CLUB INC
1124 Powell View Dr (43512-3084)
PHONE..................419 782-2101
Fax: 419 784-5613
Tom Callan, *President*
EMP: 35
SQ FT: 14,000
SALES (est): 1MM **Privately Held**
SIC: 7997 Country club, membership

(G-10043)
KIRK & BLUM MANUFACTURING CO
Also Called: Kirk and Blum
24226 Bowman Rd (43512-6819)
PHONE..................419 782-9885
Fax: 419 782-9888
George Nelson, *Manager*
EMP: 38
SALES (corp-wide): 345MM **Publicly Held**
SIC: 1761 3444 3443 Sheet metalwork; sheet metal specialties, not stamped; fabricated plate work (boiler shop)
HQ: The Kirk & Blum Manufacturing Company
4625 Red Bank Rd Ste 200
Cincinnati OH 45227
513 458-2600

(G-10044)
LAUREL HEALTHCARE
Also Called: Laurels of Defiance
1701 Jefferson Ave (43512-3493)
PHONE..................419 782-7879
Fax: 419 782-6520
Dennis G Sherman, *President*
Lori Murphy, *Financial Exec*
Heather Maag, *Director*
EMP: 120
SALES: 10MM **Privately Held**
SIC: 8051 Convalescent home with continuous nursing care

(G-10045)
LOWES HOME CENTERS LLC
1831 N Clinton St (43512-8555)
PHONE..................419 782-9000
Fax: 419 782-1838

Gail Post, *Branch Mgr*
EMP: 150
SALES (corp-wide): 68.6B **Publicly Held**
SIC: 5211 5031 5722 5064 Home centers; building materials, exterior; building materials, interior; household appliance stores; electrical appliances, television & radio
HQ: Lowe's Home Centers, Llc
1605 Curtis Bridge Rd
Wilkesboro NC 28697
336 658-4000

(G-10046)
MAUMEE VALLEY GUIDANCE CENTER (PA)
211 Biede Ave (43512-2497)
PHONE..................419 782-8856
Fax: 419 784-4506
Rachelle McDonald, *Manager*
William Bierie, *Exec Dir*
Sheryl Nusbaum, *Admin Sec*
EMP: 40
SQ FT: 6,000
SALES: 3.6MM **Privately Held**
SIC: 8093 Mental health clinic, outpatient

(G-10047)
MCDONALDS DESIGN & BUILD INC
101 Clinton St Ste 2200 (43512-2173)
PHONE..................419 782-4191
Fax: 419 782-7435
Kevin R McDonald, *President*
Scott McDonald II, *Vice Pres*
Ann Westrick, *Treasurer*
Brenda Mathewson, *Admin Sec*
EMP: 30
SQ FT: 3,500
SALES (est): 5MM **Privately Held**
SIC: 1542 1541 Commercial & office building, new construction; industrial buildings, new construction

(G-10048)
MERCY HOSPITAL OF DEFIANCE
1400 E 2nd St (43512-2440)
PHONE..................419 782-8444
Fax: 419 783-3003
Chad L Peter, *CEO*
EMP: 156
SALES: 23.7MM **Privately Held**
SIC: 8062 General medical & surgical hospitals

(G-10049)
METAL MANAGEMENT OHIO INC
Also Called: Simms Metal Management Ohio
27063 State Route 281 (43512-8963)
PHONE..................419 782-7791
Tim Weisman, *Plant Mgr*
Tim Wiseman, *Manager*
EMP: 50
SALES (corp-wide): 3.8B **Privately Held**
SIC: 5093 Ferrous metal scrap & waste
HQ: Metal Management Ohio, Inc.
3100 Lonyo St
Detroit MI 48209
313 841-1800

(G-10050)
MIDWEST CMNTY FEDERAL CR UN
1481 Deerwood Dr (43512-6738)
P.O. Box 608 (43512-0608)
PHONE..................419 782-9856
Gina Medley, *President*
EMP: 30
SQ FT: 5,300
SALES (est): 3.5MM **Privately Held**
SIC: 6061 Federal credit unions

(G-10051)
NORTHWESTRN OH COMMUNTY ACTION (PA)
1933 E 2nd St (43512-2503)
PHONE..................419 784-2150
Dean Genter, *President*
Deborah Gerken, *Exec Dir*
EMP: 150
SQ FT: 8,000

SALES: 7.3MM **Privately Held**
WEB: www.nocac.org
SIC: 8399 8322 Community action agency; individual & family services

(G-10052)
POSTEMA INSURANCE & INVESTMENT
2014 Baltimore St (43512-1918)
PHONE..................419 782-2500
Fax: 419 782-0645
Dennis Postema, *Owner*
EMP: 30
SALES (est): 3.7MM **Privately Held**
SIC: 6411 Insurance agents

(G-10053)
RELIANCE FINANCIAL SERVICES NA
401 Clinton St (43512-2632)
P.O. Box 467 (43512-0467)
PHONE..................419 783-8007
Jeffrey D Sewell, *CEO*
Gregory Marquiss, *President*
David S Bell, *Exec VP*
Chris Hubbard, *Bd of Directors*
EMP: 30
SALES (est): 1.1MM
SALES (corp-wide): 49.7MM **Publicly Held**
SIC: 7389 Financial services
HQ: The State Bank And Trust Company
401 Clinton St
Defiance OH 43512
419 783-8950

(G-10054)
RICHLAND CO & ASSOCIATES INC (PA)
101 Clinton St Ste 2200 (43512-2173)
PHONE..................419 782-0141
Douglas A Mc Donald, *President*
Douglas McDonald, *Vice Pres*
Kevin R McDonald, *Vice Pres*
Ann Westrick, *Treasurer*
Brenda Mathewson, *Admin Sec*
EMP: 44
SQ FT: 3,500
SALES: 3MM **Privately Held**
SIC: 1761 Roofing contractor; sheet metalwork

(G-10055)
RURBANC DATA SERVICES INC
Also Called: Rdsi Banking Systems
7622 N State Route 66 (43512-6715)
PHONE..................419 782-2530
Fax: 419 782-1442
Kurt Kratzer, *President*
Gwen Anderson, *Vice Pres*
Karen Oskey, *Vice Pres*
Gary Saxman, *CFO*
Joe Buerkle, *Info Tech Mgr*
EMP: 60
SALES: 21.6MM
SALES (corp-wide): 49.7MM **Publicly Held**
WEB: www.rdsiweb.com
SIC: 7374 Data processing service
PA: Sb Financial Group, Inc.
401 Clinton St
Defiance OH 43512
419 783-8950

(G-10056)
SB FINANCIAL GROUP INC (PA)
401 Clinton St (43512-2632)
P.O. Box 467 (43512-0467)
PHONE..................419 783-8950
Fax: 419 784-4085
Mark A Klein, *Ch of Bd*
Jonathan R Gathman, *Exec VP*
Anthony V Cosentino, *CFO*
Cyndi Ensign, *Sales Mgr*
Tim Moser, *CIO*
EMP: 192
SALES: 49.7MM **Publicly Held**
WEB: www.rurban.net
SIC: 6022 State trust companies accepting deposits, commercial

GEOGRAPHIC SECTION

Delaware - Delaware County (G-10078)

(G-10057)
SERVICEMASTER OF DEFIANCE INC
1255 Carpenter Rd (43512-8505)
PHONE..............................419 784-5570
Fax: 419 784-0307
Richard F McCann, *President*
Richard F Mc Cann, *President*
Michael Mc Cann, *Corp Secy*
Pat McFarland, *Mktg Dir*
Roseann Barth, *Office Mgr*
EMP: 100
SQ FT: 1,400
SALES (est): 3MM **Privately Held**
WEB: www.fortsm.com
SIC: 7349 6794 5087 Janitorial service, contract basis; franchises, selling or licensing; janitors' supplies

(G-10058)
STATE BANK AND TRUST COMPANY (HQ)
401 Clinton St (43512-2662)
P.O. Box 467 (43512-0467)
PHONE..............................419 783-8950
Fax: 419 784-4034
Mark A Klein, *CEO*
Steven D Vandemark, *Ch of Bd*
David Anderson, *President*
David Homoelle, *President*
Mark A Soukup, *President*
◆ EMP: 35
SQ FT: 10,000
SALES: 49MM
SALES (corp-wide): 49.7MM **Publicly Held**
SIC: 6022 6163 State trust companies accepting deposits, commercial; loan brokers
PA: Sb Financial Group, Inc.
  401 Clinton St
  Defiance OH 43512
  419 783-8950

(G-10059)
STYKEMAIN PNTIAC-BUICK-GMC LTD (PA)
25124 Elliott Rd (43512-9003)
PHONE..............................419 784-5252
Dustin Cantrell, *Parts Mgr*
Todd Bartley, *Sales Mgr*
Ethan Stykemain, *Cust Mgr*
Tom Davis, *Manager*
James Stykemain,
EMP: 100
SQ FT: 30,000
SALES (est): 28.7MM **Privately Held**
WEB: www.stykemain.com
SIC: 5511 5012 Automobiles, new & used; automobiles

(G-10060)
SUN HEALTHCARE GROUP INC
Also Called: Twin Rvers Care Rhbltation Ctr
395 Harding St (43512-1315)
PHONE..............................419 784-1450
Michael Adams, *Manager*
Sarah Stauffer, *Manager*
Mike Adams, *Administration*
EMP: 130 **Publicly Held**
WEB: www.harborsidehealthcare.com
SIC: 8051 Skilled nursing care facilities
HQ: Sun Healthcare Group, Inc.
  27442 Portola Pkwy # 200
  Foothill Ranch CA 92610

(G-10061)
THOMAS E KELLER TRUCKING INC
24862 Elliott Rd (43512-9217)
PHONE..............................419 784-4805
Fax: 419 782-3834
Bryan Keller, *President*
Scott Galbraith, *Controller*
Lori Adams, *Hum Res Coord*
Meredith Mickey, *Marketing Staff*
Chris Hattemer, *Supervisor*
EMP: 110
SALES (est): 20.5MM **Privately Held**
SIC: 4213 Contract haulers

(G-10062)
UNITED PARCEL SERVICE INC OH
Also Called: UPS
820 Carpenter Rd (43512-1726)
PHONE..............................419 782-3552
Mike Kenneth, *Manager*
Raymond Blakely, *Manager*
Jack Long, *Supervisor*
EMP: 70
SALES (corp-wide): 65.8B **Publicly Held**
WEB: www.martrac.com
SIC: 4215 4513 Package delivery, vehicular; air courier services
HQ: United Parcel Service, Inc. (Oh)
  55 Glenlake Pkwy
  Atlanta GA 30328
  404 828-6000

(G-10063)
WERLOR INC
Also Called: Werlor Waste Control
1420 Ralston Ave (43512-1380)
PHONE..............................419 784-4285
Fax: 419 782-9188
Gerald Wertz, *President*
Judy Wertz, *Corp Secy*
Mark Hageman, *Vice Pres*
Tom Taylor, *Vice Pres*
Casey Wertz, *Vice Pres*
EMP: 40
SQ FT: 8,000
SALES (est): 5.5MM **Privately Held**
WEB: www.werlor.com
SIC: 4212 2875 Garbage collection & transport, no disposal; compost

Delaware
Delaware County

(G-10064)
A L K INC
Also Called: Wintersong Village of Delaware
462 W Central Ave (43015-1405)
PHONE..............................740 369-8741
Fax: 740 363-8359
Charles Summers, *President*
Diane Summers, *Corp Secy*
Gerald Kremer, *Director*
EMP: 60
SQ FT: 14,000
SALES (est): 3.5MM **Privately Held**
SIC: 8051 Skilled nursing care facilities

(G-10065)
ACI INDUSTRIES LTD (PA)
970 Pittsburgh Dr (43015-3872)
PHONE..............................740 368-4160
Fax: 740 764-7803
Ralph Paglieri, *Partner*
Scott H Fischer, *Partner*
Helen Harper, *Partner*
Shreelal Bhatter, *Vice Pres*
Michael Blanton, *Plant Mgr*
◆ EMP: 50
SQ FT: 225,000
SALES (est): 3.8MM **Privately Held**
WEB: www.aci-industries.com
SIC: 3341 5093 3339 Secondary nonferrous metals; scrap & waste materials; primary nonferrous metals

(G-10066)
ACI INDUSTRIES CONVERTING LTD (HQ)
Also Called: J and J Sales
970 Pittsburgh Dr (43015-3872)
PHONE..............................740 368-4160
Fax: 740 368-4181
Mike Paglieri, *General Ptnr*
Mark Arcaro, *Vice Pres*
Todd Zimdars, *VP Opers*
John T Griffo, *Controller*
Cathy Arcaro, *Manager*
◆ EMP: 33
SQ FT: 232,000
SALES (est): 2.7MM
SALES (corp-wide): 3.8MM **Privately Held**
SIC: 2676 5113 Towels, napkins & tissue paper products; towels, paper
PA: Aci Industries, Ltd.
  970 Pittsburgh Dr
  Delaware OH 43015
  740 368-4160

(G-10067)
ADVANCE STORES COMPANY INC
Advance Auto Parts
1675 Us Highway 42 S (43015-8285)
PHONE..............................740 369-4491
Fax: 740 362-9722
Chris Hagestad, *President*
Bob Scott, *Manager*
Jeff Monahan, *Data Proc Exec*
Betsy Linkous, *Administration*
EMP: 125
SALES (corp-wide): 9.3B **Publicly Held**
SIC: 5013 Automotive supplies
HQ: Advance Stores Company Incorporated
  5008 Airport Rd Nw
  Roanoke VA 24012
  540 362-4911

(G-10068)
AFTERMARKET PARTS COMPANY LLC (HQ)
Also Called: New Flyer
3229 Sawmill Pkwy (43015-7541)
PHONE..............................888 333-6224
Jim Marcotuli, *President*
▲ EMP: 83
SALES (est): 220.2MM
SALES (corp-wide): 2.2B **Privately Held**
SIC: 5013 Motor vehicle supplies & new parts; automotive brakes
PA: New Flyer Industries Inc
  711 Kernaghan Ave
  Winnipeg MB R2C 3
  204 224-1251

(G-10069)
ALPHA GROUP OF DELAWARE INC (PA)
1000 Alpha Dr (43015-8642)
PHONE..............................740 368-5810
Fax: 740 368-5819
Dave Nuscher, *CEO*
Joseph Leonard, *CEO*
James Cornett, *Opers Mgr*
Lois Oswald, *Bookkeeper*
Curt Gwinn, *Finance*
EMP: 55
SALES (est): 3.6MM **Privately Held**
WEB: www.alphagroup.net
SIC: 8331 9111 Sheltered workshop; county supervisors' & executives' offices

(G-10070)
ALPHA GROUP OF DELAWARE INC
Also Called: Ergon
1000 Alpha Dr (43015-8642)
PHONE..............................740 368-5820
Fax: 740 368-5829
Laura Schick, *Manager*
EMP: 47
SALES (corp-wide): 3.6MM **Privately Held**
WEB: www.alphagroup.net
SIC: 8331 9111 Job training & vocational rehabilitation services; county supervisors' & executives' offices
PA: The Alpha Group Of Delaware Inc
  1000 Alpha Dr
  Delaware OH 43015
  740 368-5810

(G-10071)
AMERICAN HEALTH NETWORK INC
104 N Union St (43015-1706)
PHONE..............................740 363-5437
Fax: 740 369-5123
Nancy Schuler, *Branch Mgr*
Eileen Bolton, *Med Doctor*
EMP: 27
SALES (corp-wide): 201.1B **Publicly Held**
SIC: 8011 Offices & clinics of medical doctors
HQ: American Health Network, Inc.
  10689 N Pennsylvna St # 200
  Indianapolis IN 46280

(G-10072)
ATLANTIC COASTAL TRUCKING
Also Called: Atlantic Triangle Trucking
222 E William St (43015-3282)
PHONE..............................201 438-6500
Peter Dykstra, *President*
Josephine Dykstra, *Corp Secy*
Mark Dykstra, *Vice Pres*
Steven McGorty, *Manager*
Cheryl Kerin, *Executive*
EMP: 110
SALES (est): 5.4MM **Privately Held**
WEB: www.act-tri.com
SIC: 4212 Local trucking, without storage

(G-10073)
AUTHENTIC FOOD LLC
Also Called: Corner Cafe
535 Sunbury Rd (43015-8656)
PHONE..............................740 369-0377
Dimitri Velalis, *Mng Member*
Maria Velalis, *Mng Member*
Tom Velalis,
EMP: 25
SQ FT: 2,560
SALES (est): 1.6MM **Privately Held**
SIC: 8741 Restaurant management

(G-10074)
BRIDGES TO INDEPENDENCE INC (PA)
61 W William St (43015-2338)
PHONE..............................740 362-1996
Fax: 740 362-1997
Chris Ritchie, *President*
Michelle Ferguson, *Office Admin*
Bunny Ambro, *Exec Dir*
Lisa Morgan, *Director*
Traci Pigg, *Director*
EMP: 120
SALES (est): 4.7MM **Privately Held**
WEB: www.bridgestoindependence.com
SIC: 8322 Social services for the handicapped

(G-10075)
BUNS OF DELAWARE INC
Also Called: Buns Restaurant & Bakery
14 W Winter St (43015-1919)
PHONE..............................740 363-2867
Fax: 740 363-1756
Vasili Konstantinidis, *President*
EMP: 40
SQ FT: 11,184
SALES (est): 1.1MM **Privately Held**
SIC: 5812 5461 7299 2051 Eating places; bakeries; banquet hall facilities; bread, cake & related products

(G-10076)
CARRIAGE TOWN CHRYSLER PLYMOUTH
2815 Stratford Rd (43015-2951)
P.O. Box 420 (43015-0420)
PHONE..............................740 369-9611
James R Pancake Jr, *President*
Kim Bloom, *Vice Pres*
EMP: 70
SALES (est): 8.1MM **Privately Held**
SIC: 6411 Life insurance agents

(G-10077)
CELLCO PARTNERSHIP
Also Called: Verizon Wireless
1100 Sunbury Rd Ret702 (43015-6040)
PHONE..............................740 362-2400
Fax: 740 369-0318
EMP: 76
SALES (corp-wide): 126B **Publicly Held**
SIC: 4812 Cellular telephone services
HQ: Cellco Partnership
  1 Verizon Way
  Basking Ridge NJ 07920

(G-10078)
CENTRAL OHIO CONTRACTORS INC
888 Us Highway 42 N (43015-9014)
PHONE..............................740 369-7700
Joe Corwin, *Principal*
Karen Smith, *Sales Associate*
EMP: 70

Delaware - Delaware County (G-10079)

SALES (corp-wide): 1.9MM **Privately Held**
SIC: 1522 4953 Residential construction; refuse collection & disposal services
PA: Central Ohio Contractors, Inc.
2879 Jackson Pike
Grove City OH 43123
614 539-2579

(G-10079)
CENTRAL OHIO MENTAL HEALTH CTR (PA)
250 S Henry St (43015-2978)
PHONE..................740 368-7831
Fax: 740 369-4908
Neil Tolbert, *CFO*
Ron Lane, *Controller*
Wendy Williams, *VP Human Res*
Karen Cowie, *Manager*
Tom Sefcik, *Director*
EMP: 105
SQ FT: 6,000
SALES: 5.6MM **Privately Held**
SIC: 8093 Mental health clinic, outpatient

(G-10080)
CITIGROUP INC
310 Greif Pkwy (43015-8260)
PHONE..................740 548-0594
Diane Matton, *Branch Mgr*
EMP: 380
SALES (corp-wide): 71.4B **Publicly Held**
WEB: www.citigroup.com
SIC: 7389 Telephone services
PA: Citigroup Inc.
388 Greenwich St
New York NY 10013
212 559-1000

(G-10081)
CONSOLIDATED ELECTRIC COOP
680 Sunbury Rd (43015-9555)
P.O. Box 630 (43015-0630)
PHONE..................740 363-2641
Fax: 740 947-3082
Brian Newton, *President*
EMP: 43 EST: 1936
SQ FT: 19,000
SALES (est): 5.3MM **Privately Held**
SIC: 4911 Distribution, electric power

(G-10082)
COUNTY OF DELAWARE
50 Channing St (43015-2050)
P.O. Box 614, Lewis Center (43035-0614)
PHONE..................740 833-2240
Fax: 740 368-5851
Chad Antel, *Manager*
EMP: 110 **Privately Held**
SIC: 1623 Water, sewer & utility lines
PA: County Of Delaware
101 N Sandusky St
Delaware OH 43015
740 368-1800

(G-10083)
COUNTY OF DELAWARE
Also Called: Delaware County Engineers
50 Channing St (43015-2050)
PHONE..................740 833-2400
Fax: 740 833-2399
Chris Bauserman, *Manager*
EMP: 70 **Privately Held**
WEB: www.delawarecountysheriff.com
SIC: 8711 1611 Engineering services; highway & street construction
PA: County Of Delaware
101 N Sandusky St
Delaware OH 43015
740 368-1800

(G-10084)
COUNTY OF DELAWARE
Also Called: Delaware General Health Dst
1 W Winter St Fl 2 (43015-1918)
P.O. Box 570 (43015-0570)
PHONE..................740 203-2040
Fax: 740 203-2003
Frances M Veverka, *President*
Burgess Castle, *Cnty Cmsnr*
Kerr Murray, *Cnty Cmsnr*
EMP: 70
SQ FT: 15,000
SALES: 6.4MM **Privately Held**
SIC: 8011 Clinic, operated by physicians

(G-10085)
CREATIVE FOUNDATIONS INC (PA)
57 N Sandusky St (43015-1925)
PHONE..................740 362-5102
Diane Kopf, *QA Dir*
David Robbins, *Exec Dir*
EMP: 100 EST: 2001
SQ FT: 6,000
SALES (est): 9.9MM **Privately Held**
SIC: 8322 Social service center

(G-10086)
DEL-CO WATER COMPANY INC (PA)
6658 Olentangy River Rd (43015-9211)
PHONE..................740 548-7746
Fax: 740 548-6203
Timothy D McNamara, *President*
Kenneth Zarbaugh, *President*
Glenn Marzluf, *General Mgr*
P K Tudor, *General Mgr*
Robert Jenkins, *Corp Secy*
EMP: 103
SQ FT: 8,000
SALES: 27.5MM **Privately Held**
WEB: www.delcowater.com
SIC: 4941 Water supply

(G-10087)
DELAWARE CITY SCHOOL DISTRICT
Also Called: Delaware City School Garage
2462 Liberty Rd (43015-8810)
PHONE..................740 363-5901
Fax: 740 362-2452
Christy Cobb, *Manager*
Larry Davis, *Director*
EMP: 30
SALES (corp-wide): 66.6MM **Privately Held**
WEB: www.dcs.k12.oh.us
SIC: 8211 7538 Public elementary school; general automotive repair shops
PA: Delaware City School District
74 W William St
Delaware OH 43015
740 833-1100

(G-10088)
DELAWARE COUNTY HISTORICAL SOC
2690 Stratford Rd (43015-2948)
PHONE..................740 369-3831
Kris Thomas, *President*
EMP: 60
SQ FT: 2,244
SALES: 77.5K **Privately Held**
SIC: 8412 Historical society

(G-10089)
DELAWARE GOLF CLUB INC
Also Called: Tnr Properties
3326 Columbus Pike (43015)
PHONE..................740 362-2582
Robert Mirferendeski, *Manager*
John Miller, *Director*
EMP: 40
SALES (est): 3MM **Privately Held**
SIC: 5941 7999 7299 Golf goods & equipment; golf services & professionals; golf driving range; wedding chapel, privately operated

(G-10090)
DELAWARE OPCO LLC
Also Called: ARBORS AT DELAWARE
2270 Warrensburg Rd (43015-1336)
PHONE..................502 429-8062
Fax: 740 363-5881
Robert Norcross, *CEO*
Benjamin Sparks, *Clerk*
EMP: 99 EST: 2014
SQ FT: 60,000
SALES: 6.4MM **Privately Held**
SIC: 8051 Skilled nursing care facilities

(G-10091)
DORNOCH GOLF CLUB INC
3329 Columbus Pike (43015-8963)
PHONE..................740 369-0863
Fax: 614 457-3874
Gary Bachinski, *President*
Bill Bonds, *CPA*
EMP: 25

SALES (est): 1.2MM **Privately Held**
SIC: 7997 Golf club, membership

(G-10092)
EDS TREE & TURF
Also Called: Maple Crest Builders
5801 S Section Line Rd (43015-9489)
PHONE..................740 881-5800
Mark E Ross, *Owner*
Ed Ross, *Exec Dir*
EMP: 40
SQ FT: 5,500
SALES: 1MM **Privately Held**
SIC: 0782 Sodding contractor; seeding services, lawn

(G-10093)
EXCEL HEALTH SERVICES LLC
163 N Sandusky St Ste 201 (43015-1771)
PHONE..................614 794-0006
Fax: 614 794-2735
Emiliah Oduah,
Lkenna Nzeogu,
EMP: 99
SALES (est): 3.6MM **Privately Held**
SIC: 8082 Visiting nurse service

(G-10094)
FIRST COMMONWEALTH BANK
100 Delaware Xing W (43015-7853)
PHONE..................740 548-3340
Alfred Wise, *Branch Mgr*
EMP: 27
SALES (corp-wide): 330.8MM **Publicly Held**
SIC: 6022 State commercial banks
HQ: First Commonwealth Bank
601 Philadelphia St
Indiana PA 15701
724 349-7220

(G-10095)
FIRST COMMONWEALTH BANK
100 Willow Brook Way S (43015-3249)
PHONE..................740 369-0048
David Eedwards, *Branch Mgr*
EMP: 27
SALES (corp-wide): 330.8MM **Publicly Held**
SIC: 6022 State trust companies accepting deposits, commercial
HQ: First Commonwealth Bank
601 Philadelphia St
Indiana PA 15701
724 349-7220

(G-10096)
FIRSTENTERPRISES INC
2000 Nutter Farms Ln (43015-9195)
PHONE..................740 369-5100
Mike Doyle, *Principal*
EMP: 389
SALES (corp-wide): 421.8MM **Privately Held**
SIC: 4213 Trucking, except local
PA: Firstenterprises, Inc.
202 Heritage Park Dr
Murfreesboro TN 37129
615 890-9229

(G-10097)
FLOYD BROWNE GROUP INC
Also Called: Floyd Brown Group
585 Sunbury Rd (43015-9795)
PHONE..................740 363-6792
Fax: 740 363-6536
Daniel Whited, *Branch Mgr*
EMP: 50
SALES (corp-wide): 43.6MM **Privately Held**
SIC: 8748 Environmental consultant
HQ: Floyd Browne Group, Inc.
7965 N High St Ste 340
Columbus OH 43235
740 363-6792

(G-10098)
FOOR CONCRETE CO INC (PA)
5361 State Route 37 E (43015-9684)
PHONE..................740 513-4346
Fax: 740 513-4353
Archie E Foor Jr, *President*
Cass Budde, *Controller*
EMP: 55

SALES: 7.4MM **Privately Held**
WEB: www.foorconcrete.com
SIC: 1771 Concrete pumping

(G-10099)
FREDERICK C SMITH CLINIC INC
6 Lexington Blvd (43015-1047)
PHONE..................740 363-9021
Linda Lowry, *Manager*
Elena Sutherland, *Psychiatry*
EMP: 50
SALES (corp-wide): 32.7MM **Privately Held**
WEB: www.marionareahealth.com
SIC: 8011 General & family practice, physician/surgeon
PA: Frederick C Smith Clinic Inc
1040 Delaware Ave
Marion OH 43302
740 383-7000

(G-10100)
GANZFAIR INVESTMENT INC
Also Called: Shamrock Golf Club
231 Clubhouse Dr (43015-8490)
PHONE..................614 792-6630
Fax: 614 792-6250
Gary Bachinski, *President*
EMP: 25
SQ FT: 5,000
SALES: 1.4MM **Privately Held**
WEB: www.shamrockgc.com
SIC: 7992 7997 Public golf courses; membership sports & recreation clubs

(G-10101)
GLOBAL MALL UNLIMITED
1423 Missouri Ave (43015-2990)
PHONE..................740 533-7203
EMP: 35
SALES: 950K **Privately Held**
SIC: 5045 Whol Computers/Peripherals

(G-10102)
GRADY MEMORIAL HOSPITAL (PA)
561 W Central Ave (43015-1489)
PHONE..................740 615-1000
David Blom, *CEO*
Johnni Beckel, *Senior VP*
Mike Bateman, *Manager*
Anita Grillot, *Manager*
David W Nardin, *Director*
EMP: 37
SQ FT: 124,740
SALES: 92MM **Privately Held**
SIC: 8062 General medical & surgical hospitals

(G-10103)
HEALTH WORKS MSO INC (PA)
561 W Central Ave (43015-1410)
PHONE..................740 368-5366
Fax: 740 368-5442
Steven Garlock, *President*
EMP: 47
SALES (est): 1.5MM **Privately Held**
SIC: 8011 Physicians' office, including specialists

(G-10104)
HELP LINE OF DLWARE MRROW CNTY
Also Called: HELPLINE
11 N Franklin St (43015-1913)
PHONE..................740 369-3316
Fax: 740 363-1835
Leslie Baldwin, *Financial Exec*
Lauren Macdade, *Program Mgr*
Michelle Price, *Manager*
Susan Hanson, *Exec Dir*
Julianna Nemeth, *Director*
EMP: 25
SQ FT: 3,187
SALES: 2.1MM **Privately Held**
SIC: 8322 Crisis intervention center; referral service for personal & social problems

(G-10105)
HENDERSON TRUCKING INC
124 Henderson Ct (43015-8479)
PHONE..................740 369-6100
Fax: 740 363-8625
Jack Henderson, *President*
Joyce Henderson, *Admin Sec*
EMP: 40

GEOGRAPHIC SECTION

Delaware - Delaware County (G-10129)

SQ FT: 8,400
SALES (est): 4.9MM **Privately Held**
SIC: 4214 4212 Local trucking with storage; local trucking, without storage; dump truck haulage

(G-10106)
HOMELIFE COMPANIES INC (PA)
13 E Winter St (43015-1978)
PHONE..................740 369-1297
Fax: 614 363-1577
Donald E Rankey Jr, *President*
Pamela Hertwig-Rankey, *Shareholder*
EMP: 26
SQ FT: 12,000
SALES (est): 3.5MM **Privately Held**
SIC: 8742 6531 Real estate consultant; real estate agents & managers

(G-10107)
HOMETOWN URGENT CARE
1100 Sunbury Rd Ste 706 (43015-6040)
PHONE..................740 363-3133
EMP: 100
SALES (corp-wide): 73.2MM **Privately Held**
SIC: 8049 8011 7291 Occupational therapist; medical centers; tax return preparation services
PA: Hometown Urgent Care
2400 Corp Exchange Dr # 102
Columbus OH 43231
614 505-7633

(G-10108)
INCUBIT LLC
40 N Sandusky St Ste 200 (43015-1973)
PHONE..................740 362-1401
Dorian Wolter, *CEO*
EMP: 100
SQ FT: 2,000
SALES: 15MM **Privately Held**
SIC: 8742 7371 Business consultant; computer software development

(G-10109)
INNO-PAK LLC (PA)
1932 Pittsburgh Dr (43015-3868)
PHONE..................740 363-0090
Denny Tao, *General Mgr*
Todd Miles, *Managing Dir*
Adam Bechtold, *Vice Pres*
Nick Healey, *Vice Pres*
Nathan Sill, *Vice Pres*
▲ **EMP:** 43
SALES (est): 80MM **Privately Held**
SIC: 5162 Plastics materials

(G-10110)
JEGS AUTOMOTIVE INC (PA)
Also Called: Jeg's High-Performance Center
101 Jegs Pl (43015-9279)
PHONE..................614 294-5050
Fax: 740 362-7017
Edward James Coughlin, *President*
Todd Iden, *General Mgr*
Jeg Coughlin, *Vice Pres*
John Coughlin, *Vice Pres*
Michael Coughlin, *Vice Pres*
▲ **EMP:** 150
SQ FT: 200,000
SALES (est): 206.6MM **Privately Held**
SIC: 5013 5961 5531 Automotive supplies & parts; automotive supplies & equipment, mail order; automotive parts

(G-10111)
JENNINGS & ASSOCIATES
26 Northwood Dr (43015-1502)
PHONE..................740 369-4426
Michael Jennings, *Partner*
EMP: 35
SALES (est): 2.3MM **Privately Held**
SIC: 8721 8748 7291 Accounting, auditing & bookkeeping; business consulting; tax return preparation services

(G-10112)
JPMORGAN CHASE BANK NAT ASSN
61 N Sandusky St (43015-1925)
P.O. Box 710573, Columbus (43271-0001)
PHONE..................740 363-8032
Rhonda Uttam, *Vice Pres*
Mindy Hoffman, *Manager*
EMP: 800
SALES (corp-wide): 99.6B **Publicly Held**
WEB: www.firstusa.com
SIC: 6021 National commercial banks
HQ: Jpmorgan Chase Bank, National Association
1111 Polaris Pkwy
Columbus OH 43240
614 436-3055

(G-10113)
KHEMPCO BLDG SUP CO LTD PARTNR (PA)
Also Called: Arlington-Blaine Lumber Co
130 Johnson Dr (43015-8699)
PHONE..................740 549-0465
Fax: 614 294-3163
Donny Bowman, *Partner*
Richard Robinson, *Partner*
James D Klingbeil Jr, *General Ptnr*
Michael Michalski, *Controller*
EMP: 40
SALES (est): 22.7MM **Privately Held**
SIC: 5031 5211 2439 2431 Lumber: rough, dressed & finished; building materials, exterior; building materials, interior; lumber & other building materials; trusses, except roof: laminated lumber; trusses, wooden roof; doors, wood; hardware

(G-10114)
KROGER CO
1840 Columbus Pike (43015-2728)
PHONE..................740 363-4398
Fax: 614 363-4279
Emily Rice, *Pharmacist*
Brenda Young, *Manager*
EMP: 100
SALES (corp-wide): 122.6B **Publicly Held**
WEB: www.kroger.com
SIC: 5411 5141 Supermarkets, chain; supermarkets, 66,000-99,000 square feet; convenience stores, chain; groceries, general line
PA: The Kroger Co
1014 Vine St Ste 1000
Cincinnati OH 45202
513 762-4000

(G-10115)
LEVERING MANAGEMENT INC
Also Called: Delaware Court Health Care Ctr
4 New Market Dr (43015-2258)
PHONE..................740 369-6400
Fax: 614 369-6401
William Levering, *President*
Frederic Zuspan, *Senior VP*
Leah Cottrill, *Manager*
Jack Fling, *Manager*
Thomas Hubbell, *Director*
EMP: 85
SALES (est): 2.7MM
SALES (est): 32.8MM **Privately Held**
SIC: 8059 8052 8051 Nursing home, except skilled & intermediate care facility; intermediate care facilities; skilled nursing care facilities
PA: Levering Management, Inc.
201 N Main St
Mount Vernon OH 43050
740 397-3897

(G-10116)
LIBERTY CASTING COMPANY LLC
407 Curtis St (43015-2439)
P.O. Box 1368 (43015-8368)
PHONE..................740 363-1941
Lonnie Buckner, *Manager*
EMP: 31
SALES (corp-wide): 25.6MM **Privately Held**
SIC: 7699 7692 5085 Cleaning services; welding repair; industrial supplies
PA: Liberty Casting Company Llc
550 Liberty Rd
Delaware OH 43015
740 363-1941

(G-10117)
NATIONAL LIME AND STONE CO
Also Called: National Lime Stone Clmbus Reg
2406 S Section Line Rd (43015-9518)
P.O. Box 537 (43015-0537)
PHONE..................740 548-4206
Fax: 614 363-0325
Michael Geckle, *Site Mgr*
Chris Barks, *Opers Staff*
Carolyn Coder, *Office Mgr*
Chad Doll, *Manager*
EMP: 40
SALES (corp-wide): 3.2B **Privately Held**
WEB: www.natlime.com
SIC: 1422 Crushed & broken limestone
PA: The National Lime And Stone Company
551 Lake Cascade Pkwy
Findlay OH 45840
419 422-4341

(G-10118)
NORTHPOINT SENIOR SERVICES LLC
Also Called: Arbors of Delaware
2270 Warrensburg Rd (43015-1336)
PHONE..................740 369-9614
Bob Jablonfis, *Manager*
Frances Voegele, *Director*
EMP: 100
SALES (corp-wide): 37.8MM **Privately Held**
WEB: www.extendicarehealth.com
SIC: 8051 8093 Skilled nursing care facilities; specialty outpatient clinics
PA: Senior Northpoint Services Llc
7400 New Lagrange 100
Louisville KY 40222
502 429-8062

(G-10119)
OHIO DEPARTMENT TRANSPORTATION
Also Called: District 6
400 E William St (43015-2199)
PHONE..................740 363-1251
Michael C Flynn, *Manager*
EMP: 150
SQ FT: 71,438 **Privately Held**
SIC: 9621 1611 Regulation, administration of transportation; ; highway & street maintenance
HQ: Ohio Department Of Transportation
1980 W Broad St
Columbus OH 43223

(G-10120)
PIONEER HI-BRED INTL INC
59 Greif Pkwy Ste 200 (43015-7205)
P.O. Box 1000, Johnston IA (50131-9411)
PHONE..................740 657-6120
Donna Dugas, *Branch Mgr*
EMP: 30
SALES (corp-wide): 62.4B **Publicly Held**
SIC: 5191 Seeds: field, garden & flower
HQ: Pioneer Hi-Bred International, Inc.
7100 Nw 62nd Ave
Johnston IA 50131
515 535-3200

(G-10121)
RADIOLOGY PHYSICIANS INC
3769 Columbus Pike # 220 (43015-7213)
PHONE..................614 717-9840
Michael Gregg, *Med Doctor*
EMP: 29
SALES (est): 1.6MM **Privately Held**
SIC: 8011 Radiologist

(G-10122)
RECOVERY PRV RES OF DEL & MOR
118 Stover Dr (43015-8601)
PHONE..................740 369-6811
Tony Williams, *CEO*
Kristyn Dahler, *Info Tech Mgr*
Jeni Biancki, *Administration*
EMP: 29
SQ FT: 20,000
SALES: 1.4MM **Privately Held**
SIC: 8093 Alcohol clinic, outpatient; drug clinic, outpatient

(G-10123)
REFLEKTIONS LTD
560 Sunbury Rd Ste 1 (43015-8692)
PHONE..................614 560-6994
Justin B Livingston, *Owner*
Janette Faut, *Partner*
EMP: 30
SALES: 500K **Privately Held**
SIC: 8082 Home health care services

(G-10124)
RJW TRUCKING COMPANY LTD
Also Called: Henderson Trucking
124 Henderson Ct (43015-8479)
PHONE..................740 363-5343
Jack Henderson, *Mng Member*
Shaun Henderson,
EMP: 25
SALES (est): 2.1MM **Privately Held**
SIC: 1442 4212 Construction sand & gravel; local trucking, without storage; dump truck haulage

(G-10125)
SARAH MOORE HLTH CARE CTR INC
Also Called: SARAH MOORE COMMUNITY
26 N Union St (43015-1922)
PHONE..................740 362-9641
Fax: 614 369-2834
Ronald White, *President*
Thomas W Hess, *Principal*
EMP: 100
SQ FT: 30,000
SALES: 2.7MM **Privately Held**
SIC: 8059 8052 Nursing home, except skilled & intermediate care facility; intermediate care facilities

(G-10126)
SCHNEIDER NAT CARRIERS INC
600 London Rd (43015-3839)
PHONE..................740 362-6910
Jerry Jackson, *Manager*
EMP: 30
SALES (corp-wide): 4.3B **Publicly Held**
SIC: 4731 4213 Truck transportation brokers; trucking, except local
HQ: Schneider National Carriers, Inc.
3101 Packerland Dr
Green Bay WI 54313
920 592-2000

(G-10127)
SKY CLIMBER TWR SOLUTIONS LLC
1800 Pittsburgh Dr (43015-3870)
PHONE..................740 203-3900
Thomas Warchol, *General Mgr*
EMP: 30
SQ FT: 10,000
SALES (est): 1.4MM **Privately Held**
SIC: 1623 Transmitting tower (telecommunication) construction

(G-10128)
SOURCEPOINT
800 Cheshire Rd (43015-6038)
PHONE..................740 363-6677
Fax: 740 363-7588
Robert Horrocks, *Exec Dir*
Kimberly Clewell, *Director*
Fara Waugh, *Director*
Jill Smith, *Recruiter*
EMP: 90
SQ FT: 58,000
SALES: 9.6MM **Privately Held**
WEB: www.growingolder.org
SIC: 8322 Senior citizens' center or association

(G-10129)
THORSENS GREENHOUSE LLC
2069 Hyatts Rd (43015-9215)
PHONE..................740 363-5069
Doug Thorsen, *Partner*
Allison Thorsen, *Sales Mgr*
▲ **EMP:** 35
SQ FT: 140,000
SALES: 3MM **Privately Held**
WEB: www.thorsensgreenhouse.com
SIC: 0181 5193 Flowers: grown under cover (e.g. greenhouse production); nursery stock

Delaware - Delaware County (G-10130)

(G-10130)
TRUCCO CONSTRUCTION CO INC
3531 Airport Rd (43015-9467)
PHONE.................................740 417-9010
Fax: 740 417-9040
Mark Trucco, *CEO*
Mitchell Trucco, *President*
John Bland, *Safety Dir*
Nate Gold, *Project Mgr*
Randy Rice, *Project Mgr*
EMP: 130
SQ FT: 24,470
SALES: 72.3MM **Privately Held**
WEB: www.truccoconstruction.com
SIC: 1623 1711 1794 1611 Underground utilities contractor; concrete work; excavation & grading, building construction; highway & street construction

(G-10131)
TWOK GENERAL CO
Also Called: Two K General Company
19 Gruber St Bldg B (43015-2424)
PHONE.................................740 417-9195
Fax: 740 657-1223
William Morgan Jr, *President*
Gary Daubenspeck, *Owner*
Don Kitchen, *Project Mgr*
Matt Moran, *Project Mgr*
EMP: 25
SQ FT: 2,500
SALES (est): 7.3MM **Privately Held**
WEB: www.2kgeneral.com
SIC: 1542 Commercial & office building, new construction; commercial & office buildings, renovation & repair

(G-10132)
U S XPRESS INC
2000 Nutter Farms Ln (43015-9195)
PHONE.................................740 363-0700
Scott Cluff, *Branch Mgr*
EMP: 50 **Privately Held**
SIC: 4213 Contract haulers
HQ: U. S. Xpress, Inc.
4080 Jenkins Rd
Chattanooga TN 37421
866 266-7270

(G-10133)
UNITED PARCEL SERVICE INC OH
Also Called: UPS
1675 Us Highway 42 S (43015-8285)
PHONE.................................740 363-0636
Richard Gammons, *Branch Mgr*
EMP: 316
SALES (corp-wide): 65.8B **Publicly Held**
SIC: 7389 4731 4512 4215 Mailbox rental & related service; transportation agents & brokers; air cargo carrier, scheduled; courier services, except by air
HQ: United Parcel Service, Inc. (Oh)
55 Glenlake Pkwy
Atlanta GA 30328
404 828-6000

(G-10134)
WALGREEN CO
Also Called: Walgreens
19 London Rd (43015-2613)
PHONE.................................740 368-9380
Fax: 740 363-9780
Sandera Jenamore, *Manager*
EMP: 30
SALES (corp-wide): 118.2B **Publicly Held**
WEB: www.walgreens.com
SIC: 5912 7384 Drug stores; photofinishing laboratory
HQ: Walgreen Co.
200 Wilmot Rd
Deerfield IL 60015
847 315-2500

(G-10135)
WILLOW BROOK CHRSTN CMMUNITIES (PA)
Also Called: Willow Brook Christian Village
100 Delaware Xing W (43015-7853)
PHONE.................................740 369-0048
Fax: 740 369-7037
Larry Harris, *CEO*
Lauri Mosher, *Purch Agent*
Joyce Stambaugh, *Director*
EMP: 60
SQ FT: 21,780
SALES: 3.4MM **Privately Held**
WEB: www.willow-brook.org
SIC: 8052 8051 Intermediate care facilities; skilled nursing care facilities

(G-10136)
WOMEN HEALTH PARTNERS
Also Called: Smith Clinic
6 Lexington Blvd (43015-1047)
PHONE.................................740 363-9021
Fax: 740 363-7962
David S Smith, *Partner*
Bruce Barker MD, *Med Doctor*
Robert R Crowell, *Surgeon*
Gerald L Kremer, *Director*
Elaine Thompson, *Nursing Dir*
EMP: 50
SALES (est): 3.6MM **Privately Held**
SIC: 8011 Obstetrician; gynecologist

Delphos
Allen County

(G-10137)
ALL TEMP REFRIGERATION INC
Also Called: Tdk Refrigeration Leasing
18996 State Route 66 (45833-9326)
PHONE.................................419 692-5016
Fax: 419 692-5537
Keith Pohlman, *President*
Mary Pohlman, *Vice Pres*
Steve Conley, *CFO*
Dan Krietemeyer, *Manager*
Kim Larue, *Manager*
EMP: 50
SQ FT: 11,900
SALES (est): 12.5MM **Privately Held**
WEB: www.alltemprefrigeration.org
SIC: 1711 7359 Refrigeration contractor; equipment rental & leasing

(G-10138)
CITY OF DELPHOS
Also Called: Engineer Department
608 N Canal St (45833-2401)
PHONE.................................419 695-4010
Gerald Neumeier, *Principal*
EMP: 50 **Privately Held**
SIC: 8711 Engineering services
PA: City Of Delphos
608 N Canal St
Delphos OH 45833
419 695-4010

(G-10139)
COMMUNITY HLTH PRFSSIONALS INC
602 E 5th St (45833-1510)
PHONE.................................419 695-8101
Amy Zalar, *Manager*
EMP: 32
SALES (corp-wide): 14MM **Privately Held**
SIC: 8082 Visiting nurse service
PA: Community Health Professionals, Inc.
1159 Westwood Dr
Van Wert OH 45891
419 238-9223

(G-10140)
D&D TRUCKING AND SERVICES INC
5191 Kill Rd (45833-9460)
PHONE.................................419 692-3205
John Miller, *CEO*
Jackie Mason, *Opers Mgr*
Joyce Schimmoller, *Admin Sec*
EMP: 26 **EST:** 1996
SQ FT: 10,000
SALES: 2MM **Privately Held**
SIC: 4212 Local trucking, without storage

(G-10141)
DELPHOS AMBULATORY CARE CENTER
1800 E 5th St Ste 1 (45833-9180)
PHONE.................................419 692-2662
Fax: 419 996-5458
Jim Reber, *President*
Lisa Metre, *Vice Pres*
Sonya Selhorst, *Manager*
EMP: 35
SALES (est): 1.6MM **Privately Held**
SIC: 8062 General medical & surgical hospitals

(G-10142)
DOUBLE A TRAILER SALES INC (PA)
1750 E 5th St (45833-9138)
P.O. Box 129 (45833-0129)
PHONE.................................419 692-7626
Fax: 419 695-4520
Mark A Wannemacher, *President*
Dan Brickner, *Vice Pres*
Charles Wannemacher, *Vice Pres*
Leann Wannemacher, *Vice Pres*
Nathan Wannemacher, *Purch Dir*
▲ **EMP:** 29
SQ FT: 14,000
SALES (est): 10.4MM **Privately Held**
WEB: www.doubleatrailer.com
SIC: 5084 7539 Industrial machine parts; trailer repair

(G-10143)
FIRST FEDERAL BANK OF MIDWEST
230 E 2nd St (45833-1701)
PHONE.................................419 695-1055
Cindy Metzger, *Sales Executive*
Becky Minnig, *Manager*
EMP: 40 **Publicly Held**
SIC: 6035 6162 6022 Federal savings & loan associations; mortgage bankers & correspondents; state commercial banks
HQ: First Federal Bank Of The Midwest
601 Clinton St Ste 1
Defiance OH 43512
419 782-5015

(G-10144)
FOR SPECIALIZED ALTERNATIVES (PA)
Also Called: S A F Y
10100 Elida Rd (45833-9056)
PHONE.................................419 695-8010
Scott Spangler, *President*
Jim Sherman, *Senior VP*
Marc Bloomingdale, *Vice Pres*
Tonya Brooks-Thomas, *Vice Pres*
Jane Wintz, *Vice Pres*
EMP: 50
SQ FT: 4,800
SALES: 7.4MM **Privately Held**
WEB: www.safy.org
SIC: 8322 Child related social services

(G-10145)
K & M TIRE INC (PA)
965 Spencerville Rd (45833-2351)
P.O. Box 279 (45833-0279)
PHONE.................................419 695-1061
Ken Langhals, *President*
Cheryl Gossard, *Vice Pres*
Paul Zurcher, *Vice Pres*
Dan Lucke, *Controller*
Mel Donnelly, *Sales Mgr*
▲ **EMP:** 130 **EST:** 1977
SQ FT: 150,000
SALES: 451.1MM **Privately Held**
SIC: 5014 7538 5531 Automobile tires & tubes; general automotive repair shops; automotive tires

(G-10146)
K & M TIRE INC
502 N Main St (45833-1594)
PHONE.................................419 695-1060
Fax: 419 695-9519
Ken Langhols, *Owner*
Jeff Musselman, *General Mgr*
EMP: 29
SALES (corp-wide): 451.1MM **Privately Held**
SIC: 5014 Automobile tires & tubes
PA: K & M Tire, Inc.
965 Spencerville Rd
Delphos OH 45833
419 695-1061

(G-10147)
MENKE BROS CONSTRUCTION CO
24266 Road T (45833-9330)
P.O. Box 158, Fort Jennings (45844-0158)
PHONE.................................419 286-2086
Fax: 419 286-2087
Craig Menke, *President*
Eugene P Menke, *President*
Matt Menke, *Vice Pres*
Thomas J Menke, *Vice Pres*
Connie Knott, *Project Mgr*
EMP: 40 **EST:** 1949
SQ FT: 4,500
SALES: 1MM **Privately Held**
SIC: 1771 1794 Foundation & footing contractor; excavation work

(G-10148)
PALMER-DONAVIN MFG CO
Lima Div
911 Spencerville Rd (45833-2351)
PHONE.................................419 692-5000
Jerry Miner, *Manager*
EMP: 35
SALES (corp-wide): 220MM **Privately Held**
WEB: www.palmerdonavin.com
SIC: 5039 5074 Prefabricated structures; heating equipment (hydronic)
PA: The Palmer-Donavin Manufacturing Company
3210 Centerpoint Dr
Columbus OH 43212
614 486-0975

(G-10149)
PHOENIX HOMES INC (PA)
238 N Main St (45833-1767)
PHONE.................................419 692-2421
Fax: 419 695-1895
Bruce Maag, *CEO*
Veronica Conley, *Controller*
Karrie Gruvenhoff, *Manager*
EMP: 40
SALES (est): 991.1K **Privately Held**
WEB: www.phnxgroup.com
SIC: 8082 Home health care services

(G-10150)
SARAH JANE LIVING CENTER LTD
328 W 2nd St (45833-1671)
PHONE.................................419 692-6618
Fax: 419 692-2654
Kimberly Ousley, *Director*
Mick Murphy, *Administration*
Ginnie Hellman, *Administration*
EMP: 45
SALES (est): 1.7MM **Privately Held**
SIC: 8051 Convalescent home with continuous nursing care

(G-10151)
SPECIALIZED ALTERNATIVES FOR F (PA)
Also Called: Safy
10100 Elida Rd (45833-9056)
PHONE.................................419 695-8010
Fax: 419 695-8010
Scott Spangler, *COO*
Karen Niese, *Controller*
John Hollenkamp, *Financial Exec*
Dana Watson, *Psychologist*
Ryann Verneston, *Manager*
EMP: 525
SALES: 18.8MM **Privately Held**
SIC: 8322 Child related social services

(G-10152)
TOLEDO MOLDING & DIE INC
Also Called: Delphos Plant 2
24086 State Route 697 (45833-9203)
P.O. Box 393 (45833-0393)
PHONE.................................419 692-6022
Fax: 419 692-8058
Craig Norbeck, *Plant Mgr*
Troy Burns, *Engineer*
Steve Cleaves, *Engineer*
Brian Hohenbrink, *Engineer*
Robert Whitney, *Engineer*
EMP: 85

GEOGRAPHIC SECTION

Dillonvale - Jefferson County (G-10174)

SALES (corp-wide): 377.7MM **Privately Held**
WEB: www.tmdinc.com
SIC: 5031 3714 Molding, all materials; motor vehicle parts & accessories
PA: Toledo Molding & Die, Inc.
1429 Coining Dr
Toledo OH 43612
419 470-3950

(G-10153)
VANCREST LTD
Also Called: Vancrest Healthcare Cntr
1425 E 5th St (45833-9142)
PHONE..................................419 695-2871
Cindy Langenkamp, *Manager*
Eric Burk, *Director*
Perry Hux, *Medical Dir*
Greg Seller, *Medical Dir*
EMP: 185
SQ FT: 1,306
SALES (corp-wide): 16.3MM **Privately Held**
WEB: www.vancrest.com
SIC: 8051 Convalescent home with continuous nursing care
PA: Vancrest, Ltd.
120 W Main St Ste 200
Van Wert OH 45891
419 238-0715

(G-10154)
VANCREST APTS
310 Elida Rd (45833-9134)
PHONE..................................419 695-7335
Rene Mueller, *Director*
EMP: 35
SALES (est): 1MM **Privately Held**
SIC: 6513 Apartment building operators

Delta
Fulton County

(G-10155)
AECOM GLOBAL II LLC
605 Taylor St (43515-1045)
PHONE..................................419 774-9862
James Page, *Manager*
EMP: 93
SALES (corp-wide): 18.2B **Publicly Held**
SIC: 8748 Systems engineering consultant, ex. computer or professional
HQ: Aecom Global Ii, Llc
1999 Avenue Of The Stars
Los Angeles CA 90067
213 593-8100

(G-10156)
BEROSKE FARMS & GREENHOUSE INC
12647 County Road 5 (43515-9202)
PHONE..................................419 826-4547
Theodore Beroske, *President*
Denise Snclair, *Office Mgr*
EMP: 50
SALES (est): 4.6MM **Privately Held**
WEB: www.beroskesgreenhouse.com
SIC: 0181 5193 Bedding plants, growing of; nursery stock

(G-10157)
EDW C LEVY CO
Also Called: Fullton Mill Services
6565 County Road 9 (43515-9449)
P.O. Box 86 (43515-0086)
PHONE..................................419 822-8286
Paul Ruffner, *Manager*
EMP: 30
SALES (corp-wide): 368.7MM **Privately Held**
WEB: www.edwclevy.com
SIC: 4212 3295 Dump truck haulage; minerals, ground or treated
PA: Edw. C. Levy Co.
9300 Dix
Dearborn MI 48120
313 429-2200

(G-10158)
FIRST FDRAL SVING LN ASSN DLTA (PA)
Also Called: FIRST FEDERAL SAVINGS AND LOAN
404 Main St (43515-1350)
PHONE..................................419 822-3131
Fax: 419 822-5611
James E Coe, *President*
John Brady, *Chairman*
Karen West, *Assistant VP*
Kerry Vandock, *CFO*
Louise Gilson, *Controller*
EMP: 48 EST: 1934
SQ FT: 10,000
SALES: 5.2MM **Privately Held**
WEB: www.firstfeddelta.com
SIC: 6035 Federal savings & loan associations

(G-10159)
INDUSTRIAL REPAIR & MFG INC (PA)
1140 E Main St Ste A (43515-8401)
PHONE..................................419 822-4232
Toll Free:..................................877 -
William H Toedter, *President*
Peggy J Toedter, *Vice Pres*
▲ EMP: 42
SQ FT: 48,000
SALES (est): 6MM **Privately Held**
SIC: 7699 7363 3443 Industrial equipment services; truck driver services; containers, shipping (bombs, etc.): metal plate

(G-10160)
K & L TRUCKING INC
490 W Main St (43515-9490)
PHONE..................................419 822-3836
Fax: 419 822-3184
Greg A Stickley, *President*
Dustin Stacekly, *Manager*
Debra Stickley, *Admin Sec*
EMP: 25
SQ FT: 300
SALES (est): 4.8MM **Privately Held**
SIC: 4213 Contract haulers

(G-10161)
NATURE FRESH FARMS USA INC
9250 Us Highway 20a (43515-9441)
PHONE..................................419 330-5080
Peter Quiring, *President*
Mj Kim, *Human Res Mgr*
EMP: 36
SALES (est): 984.6K
SALES (corp-wide): 32.4MM **Privately Held**
SIC: 0182 Vegetable crops grown under cover
PA: Nature Fresh Farms Inc
634 Mersea Road 7
Leamington ON N8H 3
519 326-8603

(G-10162)
NRI GLOBAL INC
3401 Rodgers Rd (43515)
PHONE..................................905 790-2828
Sarah Couto-Viera, *Principal*
EMP: 50 EST: 2010 **Privately Held**
SIC: 6719 Investment holding companies, except banks

Dennison
Tuscarawas County

(G-10163)
FIRST NATIONAL BNK OF DENNISON (HQ)
105 Grant St (44621-1247)
P.O. Box 31 (44621-0031)
PHONE..................................740 922-2532
Blair Hillyer, *President*
Larry J Mosher, *Exec VP*
Debbie Lukens, *Assistant VP*
Linda Clouse, *Vice Pres*
R E Wise, *Vice Pres*
EMP: 40 EST: 1933
SQ FT: 6,200
SALES: 9.5MM
SALES (corp-wide): 8.7MM **Privately Held**
SIC: 6021 National commercial banks
PA: Fnb, Inc.
105 Grant St
Dennison OH 44621
740 922-2532

(G-10164)
FNB INC (PA)
105 Grant St (44621-1247)
P.O. Box 31 (44621-0031)
PHONE..................................740 922-2532
Fax: 740 922-6376
Blair Hillyer, *President*
Robert Michels, *Assistant VP*
Linda Clouse, *Vice Pres*
Teresa Moore, *Bookkeeper*
Scott Bradley, *Branch Mgr*
EMP: 30
SALES: 8.7MM **Privately Held**
SIC: 7389 Financial services

(G-10165)
IONNO PROPERTIES S CORP
Also Called: Tank Services Company
4412 Pleasant Vly Rd Se (44621-9038)
P.O. Box 71 (44621-0071)
PHONE..................................330 479-9267
Fax: 330 479-9271
John Ionno, *President*
Mike La Croix, *Vice Pres*
Dan Fletchenger, *Manager*
EMP: 45
SQ FT: 37,000
SALES (est): 5MM **Privately Held**
SIC: 1799 1721 Sandblasting of building exteriors; commercial painting

(G-10166)
TRINITY HOSPITAL TWIN CITY
819 N 1st St (44621-1003)
PHONE..................................740 922-2800
Michael Zilm, *CEO*
Joseph J Mitchell, *President*
Lorna Morrow, *CFO*
Robert Tracz, *CFO*
Halli Sell, *Controller*
EMP: 263
SQ FT: 52,127
SALES: 110.9K **Privately Held**
SIC: 8011 8062 Medical centers; hospital, AMA approved residency
HQ: Sylvania Franciscan Health
1715 Indian Wood Cir # 200
Maumee OH 43537
419 882-8373

(G-10167)
TUSCO GROCERS INC
30 S 4th St (44621-1412)
PHONE..................................740 922-8721
Fax: 740 922-4443
Gregory W Kimble, *CEO*
Jayn Devney, *President*
Mike Oberholzer, *Treasurer*
Jennifer Raber, *Finance Dir*
Fred Bollon, *Director*
▼ EMP: 65
SQ FT: 259,000
SALES (est): 10.4MM
SALES (corp-wide): 413.2MM **Privately Held**
WEB: www.tuscogrocers.com
SIC: 5141 Groceries, general line
PA: Laurel Grocery Company Llc
120 Barbourville Rd
London KY 40744
606 878-6601

(G-10168)
UTICA EAST OHIO MIDSTREAM LLC
8349 Azalea Rd Sw (44621-9100)
PHONE..................................740 431-4168
EMP: 505
SALES (est): 4.2MM
SALES (corp-wide): 8B **Publicly Held**
SIC: 4922 Pipelines, natural gas
HQ: Utica Gas Services, L.L.C.
525 Central Park Dr # 1005
Oklahoma City OK 73105
877 413-1023

Deshler
Henry County

(G-10169)
EAST WATER LEASING CO LLC
Also Called: Communicare Health Services
620 E Water St (43516-1327)
PHONE..................................419 278-6921
Stephen L Rosedale, *CEO*
EMP: 99
SALES (est): 1.9MM **Privately Held**
SIC: 8051 Convalescent home with continuous nursing care

Dexter City
Noble County

(G-10170)
B&N COAL INC
38455 Marietta Rte (45727)
P.O. Box 100 (45727-0100)
PHONE..................................740 783-3575
Fax: 740 783-5455
Carl Baker, *President*
Bob Cunningham, *Corp Secy*
Roger Osborne, *Vice Pres*
Robert Cunningham, *Admin Sec*
EMP: 64 EST: 1962
SQ FT: 21,000
SALES: 18MM **Privately Held**
SIC: 1221 8711 Strip mining, bituminous; engineering services

(G-10171)
WARREN DRILLING CO INC
Also Called: Warren Trucking
305 Smithson St (45727-9749)
P.O. Box 103 (45727-0103)
PHONE..................................740 783-2775
Fax: 740 783-0016
Dan R Warren, *President*
Lewis D Warren, *Principal*
Paul H Warren, *Principal*
W T Warren, *Principal*
Randy C Warren, *Vice Pres*
EMP: 110 EST: 1939
SALES (est): 27.5MM **Privately Held**
WEB: www.warrendrilling.biz
SIC: 1381 Directional drilling oil & gas wells

Diamond
Portage County

(G-10172)
SDS EARTH MOVING INC
3966 Wayland Rd (44412-8737)
PHONE..................................330 358-2132
James W Sanders, *President*
EMP: 35
SALES: 8MM **Privately Held**
SIC: 4212 Local trucking, without storage

Dillonvale
Jefferson County

(G-10173)
COLAIANNI CONSTRUCTION INC
2141 State Route 150 (43917-7889)
PHONE..................................740 769-2362
Fax: 740 769-2069
Vincent Colaianni, *President*
Mary Ann Colaianni, *Corp Secy*
Dino Colaianni, *Vice Pres*
EMP: 40
SALES (est): 8.6MM **Privately Held**
WEB: www.colaianniconst.com
SIC: 1542 Nonresidential construction

(G-10174)
COLERAIN VOLUNTEER FIRE CO
72555 Colerain Rd (43917-9547)
PHONE..................................740 738-0735

Dover - Tuscarawas County (G-10175)

Fax: 740 635-4857
Ty Wilson, *President*
Robert Finney, *Treasurer*
EMP: 32
SALES: 259K **Privately Held**
SIC: 7389 8049 Fire protection service other than forestry or public; paramedic

Dover
Tuscarawas County

(G-10175)
ADVENTURE HARLEY DAVIDSON
Also Called: H & M Harley Davidson
1465 State Route 39 Nw (44622-7336)
PHONE.................................330 343-2295
Fax: 330 343-5839
Sarah Andreas, *Site Mgr*
Larry Browning, *CFO*
Karen Oberhaus, *Bookkeeper*
Olga Bell, *Human Res Dir*
Mike Davis, *Sales Mgr*
EMP: 26
SQ FT: 14,000
SALES (est): 7.2MM **Privately Held**
WEB: www.hmhd.com
SIC: 5571 7699 Motorcycles; motorcycle repair service

(G-10176)
BARKETT FRUIT CO INC (PA)
Also Called: Farmer Smiths Market
1213 E 3rd St (44622-1227)
PHONE.................................330 364-6645
Fax: 330 364-7683
William Barkett, *CEO*
James Barkett, *President*
Thomas Barkett, *Vice Pres*
Ronald Barkett, *Treasurer*
Ashley Winter, *Manager*
EMP: 36
SQ FT: 20,000
SALES (est): 12.3MM **Privately Held**
WEB: www.barkettfruit.com
SIC: 5148 5143 5144 2099 Vegetables; fruits; dairy products, except dried or canned; eggs; salads, fresh or refrigerated

(G-10177)
BELDEN & BLAKE CORPORATION
1748 Saltwell Rd Nw (44622-7471)
PHONE.................................330 602-5551
Fax: 330 602-5554
Tim McConah, *Branch Mgr*
EMP: 30
SQ FT: 4,500 **Privately Held**
WEB: www.beldenblake.com
SIC: 1311 1389 4922 5082 Crude petroleum production; natural gas production; oil field services; natural gas transmission; oil field equipment; oil & gas exploration services
HQ: Belden & Blake Corporation
1001 Fannin St Ste 800
Houston TX 77002
713 659-3500

(G-10178)
BERNER TRUCKING INC
5885 Crown Rd Nw (44622-9610)
P.O. Box 660 (44622-0660)
PHONE.................................330 343-5812
James E Knisely, *President*
John M Berner, *Vice Pres*
Kimberly Hobart, *Controller*
Tim Goehring, *Finance Mgr*
Jim Kenisley, *Financial Exec*
EMP: 150
SQ FT: 22,500
SALES: 22MM **Privately Held**
WEB: www.bernertrucking.com
SIC: 4212 Dump truck haulage

(G-10179)
BUEHLER FOOD MARKETS INC
Also Called: Buehler 10
3000 N Wooster Ave (44622-9469)
PHONE.................................330 364-3079
Fax: 330 364-1731
Doug Wills, *Manager*
EMP: 220
SALES (corp-wide): 455.8MM **Privately Held**
SIC: 5411 7384 5992 5912 Grocery stores, independent; photofinish laboratories; florists; drug stores & proprietary stores; eating places; gasoline service stations
HQ: Buehler Food Markets Incorporated
1401 Old Mansfield Rd
Wooster OH 44691
330 264-4355

(G-10180)
CHUCK NICHOLSON PNTC-GMC TRCKS
135 W Broadway St (44622-1916)
PHONE.................................330 343-7781
Fax: 330 364-4879
Charles Nicholson, *President*
Ron Garbrandt, *President*
Dan Kiethley, *President*
Bryan Kohler, *VP Sls/Mktg*
Ashley Manor, *VP Sls/Mktg*
EMP: 40 **EST:** 1945
SQ FT: 25,000
SALES (est): 12.5MM **Privately Held**
SIC: 5511 5521 5012 Automobiles, new & used; used car dealers; automobiles & other motor vehicles

(G-10181)
COMMUNITY MENTAL HEALTHCARE (PA)
201 Hospital Dr (44622-2058)
PHONE.................................330 343-1811
Fax: 330 343-8188
Gregg Martini, *General Mgr*
Cindy Hisrich, *Human Res Mgr*
Thomas L Reynolds, *Child Psycholgy*
J Boroski, *Exec Dir*
Joseph Gavin PHD, *Director*
EMP: 40 **EST:** 1969
SQ FT: 10,841
SALES: 5MM **Privately Held**
SIC: 8063 Hospital for the mentally ill

(G-10182)
COUNTRY CLUB CENTER HOMES INC
Also Called: COUNTRY CLUB RETIREMENT CENTER
860 E Iron Ave (44622-2082)
PHONE.................................330 343-6351
Fax: 330 343-0514
Jeffrey Holland, *President*
John E Holland, *Treasurer*
Paul McFadden, *Director*
Steve Harlan, *Food Svc Dir*
Michael Hohman, *Administration*
EMP: 100
SALES: 6.3MM **Privately Held**
SIC: 8051 8059 8052 Convalescent home with continuous nursing care; convalescent home; intermediate care facilities

(G-10183)
DISCOUNT DRUG MART INC
3015 N Wooster Ave (44622-9491)
PHONE.................................330 343-7700
Fax: 330 343-9908
Mike Lantree, *Manager*
EMP: 30
SALES (corp-wide): 747.4MM **Privately Held**
WEB: www.discount-drugmart.com
SIC: 5912 7384 Drug stores; photofinishing laboratory
PA: Discount Drug Mart, Inc.
211 Commerce Dr
Medina OH 44256
330 725-2340

(G-10184)
DOVER CITY SCHOOLS
Also Called: New Dawn Child Care Center
865 1/2 E Iron Ave (44622-2099)
PHONE.................................330 343-8880
Fax: 330 343-5599
Sue Mathews, *Director*
EMP: 67
SALES (corp-wide): 29.3MM **Privately Held**
SIC: 8211 8351 Public elementary & secondary schools; child day care services
PA: Dover City Schools
219 W 6th St
Dover OH 44622
330 364-1906

(G-10185)
DOVER HYDRAULICS INC (PA)
Also Called: Dover Hydraulics South
2996 Progress St (44622-9639)
P.O. Box 2239 (44622-1000)
PHONE.................................330 364-1617
Fax: 330 343-4994
Robert D Sensel, *President*
Rich Engstrom, *General Mgr*
Shane Hammonds, *General Mgr*
Eric Kinsey, *Corp Secy*
Dayne Thomas, *Vice Pres*
▲ **EMP:** 79
SQ FT: 25,000
SALES (est): 12.3MM **Privately Held**
WEB: www.doverhydraulics.com
SIC: 7699 Hydraulic equipment repair

(G-10186)
DOVER NURSING CENTER
Also Called: Park Village Health Care Ctr
1525 N Crater Ave (44622-9558)
PHONE.................................330 364-4436
EMP: 81
SQ FT: 32,000
SALES (est): 4.8MM **Privately Held**
SIC: 8052 8051 Intermediate Care Facility Skilled Nursing Care Facility

(G-10187)
DOVER PHILA FEDERAL CREDIT UN (PA)
119 Filmore Ave (44622-2061)
PHONE.................................330 364-8874
Fax: 330 343-7270
Jack Dooling, *President*
Jason Garner, *CFO*
Megan Bender, *Accountant*
Kelsey McConaha, *Marketing Staff*
Wendy Slates, *Marketing Staff*
EMP: 80
SQ FT: 9,000
SALES: 11.2MM **Privately Held**
SIC: 6061 Federal credit unions

(G-10188)
FIRST FEDERAL CMNTY BNK ASSN (HQ)
321 N Wooster Ave (44622-2949)
P.O. Box 38 (44622-0038)
PHONE.................................330 364-7777
Fax: 330 364-7779
Trent B Troyer, *CEO*
Edwin Rivera, *Area Mgr*
Matthew Miller, *Assistant VP*
Michele Larkin, *Vice Pres*
Sally O'Donnell, *Vice Pres*
EMP: 58
SALES: 14.8MM
SALES (corp-wide): 11.7MM **Publicly Held**
WEB: www.ffsbd.com
SIC: 6035 Federal savings & loan associations
PA: Ffd Financial Corporation
321 N Wooster Ave
Dover OH 44622
330 364-7777

(G-10189)
FLICKINGER PIPING COMPANY INC
439 S Tuscarawas Ave (44622-2360)
PHONE.................................330 364-4224
Fax: 330 364-4122
Joel D Flickinger, *President*
EMP: 25
SALES (est): 4.7MM **Privately Held**
SIC: 1711 Plumbing contractors

(G-10190)
GIANT EAGLE INC
515 Union Ave Ste 243 (44622-3000)
PHONE.................................330 364-5301
Fax: 330 602-8523
Cindy Stoll, *Human Res Dir*
Jason Lanzer, *Manager*
EMP: 100
SALES (corp-wide): 7.6B **Privately Held**
SIC: 5411 5912 5193 Supermarkets; drug stores; flowers & florists' supplies
PA: Giant Eagle, Inc.
101 Kappa Dr
Pittsburgh PA 15238
800 362-8899

(G-10191)
HENNIS NURSING HOME
Also Called: Hennis Care Centre At Dover
1720 N Cross St (44622-1044)
PHONE.................................330 364-8849
Fax: 330 364-2128
Harry Hennis IL, *President*
Harry Hennis II, *President*
Debbie Edwards, *Facilities Dir*
Harold Baker, *Manager*
Stephanie Fortner, *Manager*
EMP: 180
SALES: 11.4MM **Privately Held**
SIC: 8051 8052 Convalescent home with continuous nursing care; intermediate care facilities

(G-10192)
HORN ELECTRIC COMPANY
Also Called: Horn Engineering
608 S Tuscarawas Ave (44622-2346)
P.O. Box 493 (44622-0493)
PHONE.................................330 364-7784
Robert A Horn, *President*
EMP: 32 **EST:** 1953
SQ FT: 2,100
SALES (est): 3MM **Privately Held**
WEB: www.hornengineering.com
SIC: 8711 Engineering services

(G-10193)
HUNTINGTON NATIONAL BANK
232 W 3rd St Ste 207 (44622-2969)
P.O. Box 100 (44622-0100)
PHONE.................................330 343-6611
Fax: 330 343-8379
Katherine Fausnight, *Principal*
Lawrence Markworth, *Counsel*
Carla Schlegel, *Branch Mgr*
Kay Whitlach, *Manager*
Lori James, *Admin Asst*
EMP: 35
SALES (corp-wide): 4.7B **Publicly Held**
WEB: www.huntingtonnationalbank.com
SIC: 6029 6021 Commercial banks; national commercial banks
HQ: The Huntington National Bank
17 S High St Fl 1
Columbus OH 43215
614 480-4293

(G-10194)
KIMBLE COMPANIES INC (PA)
Also Called: Ace Disposal
3596 State Route 39 Nw (44622-7232)
P.O. Box 448 (44622-0448)
PHONE.................................330 343-5665
Fax: 330 343-0411
Keith Kimble, *President*
Scott Walter, *General Mgr*
Tom Wiseman, *General Mgr*
Don Zaucha, *General Mgr*
Davin Kimble, *Editor*
EMP: 191
SQ FT: 2,300
SALES (est): 55.3MM **Privately Held**
SIC: 4953 Garbage: collecting, destroying & processing

(G-10195)
KNISELY INC
Also Called: Berner Trucking
5885 Crown Rd Nw (44622-9610)
P.O. Box 660 (44622-0660)
PHONE.................................330 343-5812
James E Knisely, *President*
EMP: 100
SQ FT: 22,500
SALES (est): 9MM **Privately Held**
WEB: www.knisely.com
SIC: 7389 5172 7513 Brokers' services; diesel fuel; truck leasing, without drivers

(G-10196)
L AND C SOFT SERVE INC
Also Called: Dover Softies
717 N Wooster Ave (44622-2866)
PHONE.................................330 364-3823

Cathy M Lawless, *President*
Luke Lawless, *Owner*
EMP: 25
SALES (est): 1.1MM **Privately Held**
SIC: 8742 Restaurant & food services consultants

(G-10197)
MARMON HIGHWAY TECH LLC
6332 Columbia Rd Nw (44622-7676)
P.O. Box 525 (44622-0525)
PHONE..................330 878-5595
EMP: 40
SQ FT: 2,725
SALES (corp-wide): 210.8B **Publicly Held**
SIC: 7539 3714 Automotive Repair Mfg Motor Vehicle Parts/Accessories
HQ: Marmon Highway Technologies Llc
5915 Chalkville Rd 300
Birmingham AL 35235
205 508-2000

(G-10198)
METAL MASTERS INC
125 Williams Dr Nw (44622-7662)
PHONE..................330 343-3515
Fax: 330 343-4965
Matthew Fox, *President*
Mary Lou Miller, *Treasurer*
Bret Kettlewell, *Controller*
EMP: 45
SALES (est): 7.7MM **Privately Held**
WEB: www.metal-masters.net
SIC: 1711 Warm air heating & air conditioning contractor

(G-10199)
MID-OHIO CONTRACTING INC
1817 Horns Ln Nw (44622-7314)
PHONE..................330 343-2925
Fax: 330 364-4784
EMP: 150 **EST:** 1981
SQ FT: 3,200
SALES (est): 34.4MM **Privately Held**
SIC: 1623 Oil & gas pipeline construction

(G-10200)
MINNESOTA LIMITED LLC
2198 Donald Dr (44622-7493)
PHONE..................330 343-4612
Gary Hawk, *Branch Mgr*
EMP: 107
SALES (corp-wide): 183.1MM **Privately Held**
SIC: 1623 Oil & gas pipeline construction
PA: Minnesota Limited, Llc
18640 200th St Nw
Big Lake MN 55309
763 262-7000

(G-10201)
NCS HEALTHCARE OF OHIO LLC
Also Called: Omnicare of Dover
219 W 12th St (44622-2606)
PHONE..................330 364-5011
Jerry Marlowe, *Director*
EMP: 44
SALES (corp-wide): 184.7B **Publicly Held**
SIC: 5122 Pharmaceuticals
HQ: Ncs Healthcare Of Ohio, Llc
201 E 4th St Ste 900
Cincinnati OH 45202

(G-10202)
NEW DAWN HEALTH CARE INC
Also Called: New Dawn Retirement Community
865 E Iron Ave (44622-2099)
PHONE..................330 343-5521
Fax: 330 343-5526
Daniel Hershberger, *President*
Harry Hershberger, *Vice Pres*
Perry Hershberger, *Vice Pres*
Sandra Hershberger, *Treasurer*
Susan Matthews, *Exec Dir*
EMP: 187 **EST:** 1976
SQ FT: 73,000
SALES (est): 12MM **Privately Held**
WEB: www.new-dawn.net
SIC: 8051 8361 8351 8052 Skilled nursing care facilities; home for the aged; children's home; child day care services; intermediate care facilities

(G-10203)
NICK STRIMBU INC
303 Oxford St (44622-1976)
PHONE..................330 448-4046
EMP: 79
SALES (corp-wide): 23.9MM **Privately Held**
SIC: 4213 Trucking, except local
PA: Nick Strimbu, Inc.
3500 Parkway Dr
Brookfield OH 44403
330 448-4046

(G-10204)
OHIO CARRIERS CORP
6531 Mckracken Dr Nw (44622-7682)
PHONE..................330 878-5311
William Von Kaenel, *President*
Ronald V Kaenel, *Vice Pres*
Ronald Von Kaenel, *Vice Pres*
EMP: 75
SQ FT: 4,000
SALES (est): 2.6MM
SALES (corp-wide): 3.5MM **Privately Held**
WEB: www.ohiocarrier.com
SIC: 4213 Trucking, except local
PA: Beller-Von Kaenel Trucking Inc
6531 Mckracken Dr Nw
Dover OH 44622
330 878-5311

(G-10205)
PACE SANKAR LANDSCAPING INC
Also Called: Pace-Sankar Landscaping
4005 Johnstown Rd Ne (44622-7562)
PHONE..................330 343-0858
Fax: 330 343-7567
Michael Pace, *President*
Rick Charnock, *Financial Exec*
Beth Stoll, *Office Mgr*
Jason Hull, *Manager*
Michelle Leone, *Manager*
EMP: 35
SALES (est): 2.4MM **Privately Held**
SIC: 0782 Landscape contractors

(G-10206)
PETERMAN PLUMBING AND HTG INC
525 W 15th St (44622-9711)
P.O. Box 278 (44622-0278)
PHONE..................330 364-4497
Fax: 330 364-3922
Douglas L Peterman, *President*
Thomas Hisrich, *Vice Pres*
Natalie Peterman, *Mktg Dir*
Mark Sutterluety, *Manager*
EMP: 25
SQ FT: 14,000
SALES (est): 4.5MM **Privately Held**
SIC: 1711 Plumbing contractors; warm air heating & air conditioning contractor

(G-10207)
RANGE RSURCES - APPALACHIA LLC
1748 Saltwell Rd Nw (44622-7471)
PHONE..................330 866-3301
Woody McDaniels, *Manager*
EMP: 41
SALES (corp-wide): 2.6B **Publicly Held**
WEB: www.gl-energy.com
SIC: 1382 Oil & gas exploration services
HQ: Range Resources - Appalachia, Llc.
3000 Town Center Blvd
Canonsburg PA 15317
724 743-6700

(G-10208)
RE/MAX EXPERTS REALTY
720 N Wooster Ave (44622-2871)
PHONE..................330 364-7355
Fax: 330 364-3192
Kathy Pietro, *President*
Jennifer Hitchcock, *Partner*
EMP: 35
SQ FT: 2,000
SALES (est): 1.6MM **Privately Held**
SIC: 6531 Real estate agent, residential

(G-10209)
REPUBLICAN HEADQUARTERS
203 S Wooster Ave (44622-1942)
P.O. Box 542 (44622-0542)
PHONE..................330 343-6131
Doug Wills, *President*
EMP: 40
SALES (est): 587.2K **Privately Held**
SIC: 8651 Political action committee

(G-10210)
RUSSELL HAWK ENTERPRISES INC
2198 Donald Dr (44622-7493)
PHONE..................330 343-4612
Russell Hawk, *President*
Gary Hawk, *Vice Pres*
Wilma Hawk, *Vice Pres*
EMP: 35 **EST:** 1960
SQ FT: 4,000
SALES (est): 3.5MM **Privately Held**
SIC: 1623 Oil & gas pipeline construction

(G-10211)
SCHOENBRUNN LANDSCAPING INC
Also Called: Schoenbrunn Ldscp & Lawn Svc
1505 State Route 39 Nw (44622-7337)
PHONE..................330 364-3688
Fax: 330 343-0647
Marty Kamban, *President*
Randy Kamban, *Vice Pres*
Lisa Clum, *Manager*
Judy Felton, *Manager*
EMP: 30
SQ FT: 1,500
SALES (est): 2.7MM **Privately Held**
WEB: www.schoenbrunnlandscaping.com
SIC: 0781 0782 Landscape services; lawn services

(G-10212)
SMITH AMBULANCE SERVICE INC
214 W 3rd St (44622-2965)
PHONE..................330 825-0205
Robert L Smith, *Branch Mgr*
EMP: 28 **Privately Held**
SIC: 4119 Ambulance service
PA: Smith Ambulance Service, Inc
214 W 3rd St
Dover OH 44622

(G-10213)
SMITH AMBULANCE SERVICE INC (PA)
214 W 3rd St (44622-2965)
PHONE..................330 602-0050
Robert L Smith, *President*
Rick Annen, *Vice Pres*
Bob Stanley, *Human Res Dir*
Cristinia Westlake, *Training Spec*
EMP: 30
SALES (est): 6.1MM **Privately Held**
WEB: www.smithambulanceservice.com
SIC: 4119 Ambulance service

(G-10214)
SMITH CONCRETE CO (PA)
Also Called: Division of Selling Materials
2301 Progress St (44622-9641)
P.O. Box 356, Marietta (45750-0356)
PHONE..................740 373-7441
Fax: 740 373-7446
Mike Murphy, *General Mgr*
Amelia Fouss, *Managor*
EMP: 50 **EST:** 1922
SQ FT: 2,000
SALES (est): 5.6MM **Privately Held**
WEB: www.smithconcreteco.com
SIC: 3272 3273 1442 Dry mixture concrete; ready-mixed concrete; construction sand & gravel

(G-10215)
SPEEDIE AUTO SALVAGE LTD
6995 Eberhart Rd Nw (44622-7000)
PHONE..................330 878-9961
Fax: 330 878-5532
Gregory Bender, *President*
Greg Bender, *President*
Matt Bender, *President*
EMP: 25
SQ FT: 2,178,000
SALES: 5MM **Privately Held**
WEB: www.speedieauto.com
SIC: 5015 Automotive supplies, used

(G-10216)
TEATER ORTHOPEDIC SURGEONS
Also Called: Dover Orthopedic Center
515 Union Ave Ste 167 (44622-3005)
PHONE..................330 343-3335
Fax: 330 364-5720
Scott F Holder, *President*
James McQuillan, *Med Doctor*
Marilyn Orr, *Orthopedist*
EMP: 25
SQ FT: 4,879
SALES (est): 1.6MM **Privately Held**
SIC: 8011 Orthopedic physician

(G-10217)
TUSCARAWAS COUNTY COMMITEE
Also Called: TUSCARAWAS COUNTY SENIOR CENTE
425 Prospect St (44622-2224)
PHONE..................330 364-6611
Pam Ferrell, *Exec Dir*
Pam Serrelle, *Exec Dir*
EMP: 80
SALES (est): 2MM **Privately Held**
SIC: 8322 Senior citizens' center or association

(G-10218)
UNION COUNTRY CLUB
1000 N Bellevue Ave (44622-9457)
PHONE..................330 343-5544
Fax: 330 343-4660
Jim Miller, *President*
Dave Garnett, *Accountant*
Kate Morgan, *Finance*
Paul Block, *Director*
EMP: 40
SQ FT: 1,092
SALES (est): 1.5MM **Privately Held**
SIC: 7997 Country club, membership

(G-10219)
UNION HOSPITAL ASSOCIATION (PA)
659 Boulevard St (44622-2077)
PHONE..................330 343-3311
Fax: 330 364-0863
William W Harding, *CEO*
Cathy Corbett, *President*
Bruece James, *President*
David Brown, *Ch Pathology*
Stephen Sabo, *Ch Radiology*
EMP: 83
SQ FT: 280,000
SALES: 109.9MM **Privately Held**
WEB: www.uhcareers.com
SIC: 8062 8011 General medical & surgical hospitals; offices & clinics of medical doctors

(G-10220)
UNION HOSPITAL ASSOCIATION
500 Medical Park Dr (44622-3204)
PHONE..................330 602-0719
Fax: 330 602-0721
Steven Chismar, *Med Doctor*
Marcel Nwizu, *Med Doctor*
Rick Cole, *Director*
EMP: 909
SALES (corp-wide): 109.9MM **Privately Held**
SIC: 8621 Professional membership organizations
PA: Union Hospital Association
659 Boulevard St
Dover OH 44622
330 343-3311

(G-10221)
UNION HOSPITAL HOME HLTH CARE
659 Boulevard St (44622-2077)
PHONE..................330 343-6909
Fax: 330 343-4883
Anne Phillips, *Human Resources*
Rick Cole, *Manager*
Debra Albaugh, *Exec Dir*
EMP: 28

Dover - Tuscarawas County (G-10222)   **GEOGRAPHIC SECTION**

SALES (est): 474.9K Privately Held
SIC: 8082 Home health care services

(G-10222)
VERIZON NEW YORK INC
715 Commercial Pkwy (44622-3151)
PHONE...................330 364-0508
Daryl Croley, Manager
EMP: 45
SALES (corp-wide): 126B Publicly Held
SIC: 4812 Radio telephone communication
HQ: Verizon New York Inc.
140 West St
New York NY 10007
212 395-1000

Doylestown
Wayne County

(G-10223)
BEHEYDTS AUTO WRECKING
15475 Serfass Rd (44230-9345)
PHONE...................330 658-6109
Maxwell Beheydt, Owner
EMP: 50
SALES (est): 389.9K Privately Held
SIC: 7542 7389 5015 Carwashes; business services; motor vehicle parts, used

(G-10224)
CHIPPEWA GOLF CORP
Also Called: Chippewa Golf Club
12147 Shank Rd (44230-9707)
PHONE...................330 658-2566
Fax: 330 658-3127
Kevin Larizza, President
EMP: 30
SQ FT: 4,800
SALES (est): 1.7MM Privately Held
WEB: www.chippewagolfclub.com
SIC: 7992 Public golf courses

(G-10225)
CHIPPEWA SCHOOL DISTRICT
Also Called: SC Chippewa Preschool
165 Brooklyn Ave (44230-1204)
PHONE...................330 658-4868
Ronna Haer, Principal
EMP: 36
SALES (est): 647.4K
SALES (corp-wide): 20.3MM Privately Held
SIC: 8351 Preschool center
PA: Chippewa School District
56 N Portage St
Doylestown OH 44230
330 658-6700

(G-10226)
DOYLESTOWN COMMUNICATIONS
Also Called: Doylestown Cable TV
81 N Portage St (44230-1349)
PHONE...................330 658-7000
Thomas Brockman, President
Sandra S Brockman, Vice Pres
EMP: 40
SQ FT: 4,400
SALES: 400K
SALES (corp-wide): 11.1MM Privately Held
WEB: www.doylestowncommunications.com
SIC: 4841 7375 Cable television services; on-line data base information retrieval
PA: Doylestown Telephone Company Inc
81 N Portage St
Doylestown OH 44230
330 658-2121

(G-10227)
DOYLESTOWN HEALTH CARE CENTER
95 Black Dr (44230-1300)
PHONE...................330 658-1533
Fax: 330 658-3332
John J Masternick, President
Angie Watkins, Personnel
Don Brobes, CTO
Leo Grimes, Exec Dir
Freeland Oliverio, Director
EMP: 105

SALES (est): 3MM Privately Held
SIC: 8051 8052 Convalescent home with continuous nursing care; intermediate care facilities

(G-10228)
DOYLESTOWN TELEPHONE COMPANY (PA)
Also Called: Doylestown Communications
81 N Portage St (44230-1349)
PHONE...................330 658-2121
Fax: 330 658-3344
Tom Brockman, President
Joaquin Savage, Senior VP
Sandra Brockman, Vice Pres
EMP: 38
SQ FT: 4,400
SALES (est): 11.1MM Privately Held
WEB: www.neobright.net
SIC: 4813 Local telephone communications

(G-10229)
DOYLESTOWN TELEPHONE COMPANY
Also Called: Doylestown Cable
28 E Marion St (44230-1348)
PHONE...................330 658-6666
Dennis Hartman, General Mgr
EMP: 40
SALES (corp-wide): 11.1MM Privately Held
WEB: www.neobright.net
SIC: 4813 4225 Local telephone communications; general warehousing
PA: Doylestown Telephone Company Inc
81 N Portage St
Doylestown OH 44230
330 658-2121

Dresden
Muskingum County

(G-10230)
AEP DRESDEN PLANT
9595 Mcglade School Rd (43821-9457)
PHONE...................740 450-1964
Melissa Helmick, General Mgr
Ron Borton, Opers Staff
Robert Dillon, Maintence Staff
EMP: 32 EST: 2007
SALES (est): 1.4MM Privately Held
SIC: 4931

Dublin
Franklin County

(G-10231)
3SG CORPORATION (PA)
344 Cramer Creek Ct (43017-2585)
PHONE...................614 761-8394
Fax: 614 761-2716
Rangan Manoranjan, CEO
Nanda Nair, President
Cleo Fernando, CFO
Anton Rasiah, CFO
EMP: 38 EST: 1999
SALES (est): 19.9MM Privately Held
WEB: www.3sg.com
SIC: 7379 Computer related consulting services

(G-10232)
3SG CORPORATION
344 Cramer Creek Ct (43017-2585)
PHONE...................614 309-3600
Adam Uhrig, Manager
EMP: 132
SALES (corp-wide): 19.9MM Privately Held
SIC: 5045 Computers, peripherals & software
PA: 3sg Corporation
344 Cramer Creek Ct
Dublin OH 43017
614 761-8394

(G-10233)
ACADIA SOLUTIONS INC
6751 Burnside Ln (43016-8015)
PHONE...................614 505-6135
Frank Wang, President
Bence Toth, Vice Pres
EMP: 25
SALES (est): 2MM Privately Held
SIC: 7373 7371 8748 5065 Local area network (LAN) systems integrator; computer software development & applications; telecommunications consultant; telephone & telegraphic equipment

(G-10234)
ADVANCED PRGRM RESOURCES INC (PA)
Also Called: Touchmark
2715 Tuller Pkwy (43017-2310)
PHONE...................614 761-9994
Fax: 614 761-3397
Danial Chacho, CEO
Larry Dado, President
Douglas Heagren, Treasurer
Jennifer Heagren, Director
Karen Smith, Administration
EMP: 47
SQ FT: 5,100
SALES (est): 4.3MM Privately Held
SIC: 7379 7373 8742 7372 Computer related consulting services; systems integration services; management consulting services; application computer software; custom computer programming services

(G-10235)
AECOM GLOBAL II LLC
5550 Blazer Pkwy Ste 175 (43017-3495)
PHONE...................614 726-3500
Frank Ambrosio, Branch Mgr
EMP: 268
SALES (corp-wide): 18.2B Publicly Held
SIC: 8712 Architectural engineering
HQ: Aecom Global Ii, Llc
1999 Avenue Of The Stars
Los Angeles CA 90067
213 593-8100

(G-10236)
AFFILIATED RESOURCE GROUP INC
5700 Perimeter Dr Ste H (43017-3247)
P.O. Box 491 (43017-0491)
PHONE...................614 889-6555
Fax: 614 448-9949
Mike Moran, President
Chris Drew, Director
John Proffitt, Director
EMP: 51
SQ FT: 7,500
SALES: 4.2MM Privately Held
WEB: www.aresgrp.com
SIC: 8742 Management information systems consultant

(G-10237)
AHF OHIO INC
4880 Tuttle Rd (43017-7566)
PHONE...................614 760-8870
Justin Moore, Administration
EMP: 97
SALES (corp-wide): 21MM Privately Held
SIC: 8051 8361 Skilled nursing care facilities; residential care
PA: Ahf Ohio, Inc.
5920 Venture Dr Ste 100
Dublin OH 43017
614 760-7352

(G-10238)
AHF/CENTRAL STATES INC
Also Called: Belcourt Terracenursing Home
5920 Venture Dr Ste 100 (43017-2236)
PHONE...................615 383-3570
Brian Vermillion, Director
Tom Cox, Director
Robert Quinn, Director
EMP: 62
SQ FT: 23,780
SALES (corp-wide): 11.6MM Privately Held
SIC: 8051 Skilled nursing care facilities

PA: Ahf/Central States, Inc.
249 W Mcmurray Rd
Canonsburg PA 15317
724 941-7150

(G-10239)
ALCATEL-LUCENT USA INC
5475 Rings Rd Ste 101 (43017-7564)
PHONE...................614 860-2000
Fax: 614 868-3956
James Hines, Dept Chairman
Susan Vance-Johnson, Vice Pres
Mike Tom, Opers Spvr
Dave Markley, QC Mgr
Sugato Ganguly, Technical Mgr
EMP: 450
SALES (corp-wide): 24.9B Privately Held
WEB: www.lucent.com
SIC: 8731 Commercial physical research
HQ: Nokia Of America Corporation
600 Mountain Ave Ste 700
New Providence NJ 07974

(G-10240)
ALEXSON SERVICES INC
Also Called: Via Quest
525 Metro Pl N Ste 300 (43017-5320)
PHONE...................614 889-5837
Richard Johnson, President
EMP: 37
SALES (est): 1.6MM Privately Held
SIC: 8322 Social services for the handicapped

(G-10241)
ALKON CORPORATION
6750 Crosby Ct (43016-7644)
PHONE...................614 799-6650
Fax: 614 793-0608
Mark Marino, Branch Mgr
EMP: 35
SALES (corp-wide): 24.2MM Privately Held
WEB: www.alkoncorp.com
SIC: 3491 3082 5084 5085 Industrial valves; unsupported plastics profile shapes; industrial machinery & equipment; industrial supplies
PA: Alkon Corporation
728 Graham Dr
Fremont OH 43420
419 335-9111

(G-10242)
ALLIANCE MEDICAL INC (DH)
Also Called: Allmed
5000 Tuttle Crossing Blvd (43016-1534)
PHONE...................800 890-3092
Larry Dahl, President
Cindy Dahl, Vice Pres
Adrea Lind, Payroll Mgr
Michelle Collins, Manager
Marsha Everts, Manager
EMP: 35
SQ FT: 10,000
SALES (est): 7.3MM Privately Held
WEB: www.alliancemed.com
SIC: 5192 5047 Books; medical equipment & supplies
HQ: Bound Tree Medical, Llc
5000 Tuttle Crossing Blvd
Dublin OH 43016
614 760-5000

(G-10243)
ALTERNATIVE CARE MGT SYSTEMS
Also Called: Alternative Care MGT Systs
4789 Rings Rd (43017-1513)
PHONE...................614 761-0035
Fax: 614 761-0452
EMP: 25
SQ FT: 8,000
SALES (est): 21.4K
SALES (corp-wide): 42.8K Privately Held
SIC: 8742 6411 Management Consulting Services-Health Care
PA: Employee Benefit Management Corp
4789 Rings Rd
Dublin OH 43017
614 766-5800

(G-10244)
AMAXX INC
5975 Wilcox Pl Ste B (43016-8728)
PHONE...................614 486-3481

GEOGRAPHIC SECTION

Dublin - Franklin County (G-10267)

Nicole Hall, *Principal*
Eric Hall, *Vice Pres*
Pat Mullen, *Sales Staff*
EMP: 35
SALES (est): 5.7MM Privately Held
SIC: 7375 On-line data base information retrieval

(G-10245)
AMERICAN CANCER SOCIETY EAST
5555 Frantz Rd Frnt Frnt (43017-4184)
PHONE..................888 227-6446
Fax: 614 889-6578
Gary Pincock, *CEO*
Daniel Wiant, *CPA*
Diane Burack, *MIS Dir*
Robert Gerbasi, *Technology*
John Alduino, *Director*
EMP: 262
SALES (corp-wide): 91.7MM Privately Held
SIC: 8733 Noncommercial research organizations
PA: American Cancer Society, East Central Division, Inc.
Sipe Ave Rr 422
Hershey PA 17033
717 533-6144

(G-10246)
AMERICAN CLLEGE CRDLGY FNDTION
Also Called: Accf Accreditation
6161 Riverside Dr (43017-5102)
PHONE..................614 442-5950
Abe Joseph, *Branch Mgr*
EMP: 40
SALES (corp-wide): 88.5MM Privately Held
SIC: 8621 Medical field-related associations
PA: American College Of Cardiology Foundation
2400 N St Nw
Washington DC 20037
202 375-6000

(G-10247)
AMERICAN EQUITY MORTGAGE INC
6465 Reflections Dr # 240 (43017-2375)
PHONE..................800 236-2600
Dave Azzano, *General Mgr*
Clay Baker, *Managing Dir*
EMP: 89 Privately Held
SIC: 6162 Mortgage bankers
PA: American Equity Mortgage, Inc.
11933 Westline Indus Dr
Saint Louis MO 63146

(G-10248)
AMERICAN INSUR ADMINISTRATORS
5455 Rings Rd Ste 200 (43017-7529)
PHONE..................614 486-5388
Jon Boes, *COO*
Kathy Russell, *Assistant VP*
Yvonne Weatherford, *Accounts Mgr*
Paul Maddy, *Info Tech Dir*
EMP: 30 **EST:** 2012
SALES (est): 4.5MM Privately Held
SIC: 6411 Insurance agents
PA: Usi, Inc.
200 Summit Lake Dr # 350
Valhalla NY 10595

(G-10249)
AMERICAN ITALIAN GOLF
Also Called: Riviera Country Club
545 Metro Pl S Ste 100 (43017-5353)
PHONE..................614 889-2551
Fax: 614 889-5820
Steve N Verberis, *General Mgr*
Amy Brown, *Manager*
EMP: 60 **EST:** 1949
SQ FT: 2,793
SALES (est): 2.4MM Privately Held
SIC: 7997 Golf club, membership

(G-10250)
AMERICAN MULTI-CINEMA INC
Also Called: AMC
6700 Village Pkwy (43017-2073)
PHONE..................614 889-0580
Stephanie McClullan, *General Mgr*
EMP: 50 Publicly Held
WEB: www.arrowheadtownecenter.com
SIC: 7832 Exhibitors, itinerant: motion picture
HQ: American Multi-Cinema, Inc.
1 Amc Way
Leawood KS 66211
913 213-2000

(G-10251)
AMERICAN MUTL SHARE INSUR CORP (PA)
Also Called: AMERICAN SHARE INSURANCE
5656 Frantz Rd (43017-2552)
PHONE..................614 764-1900
Fax: 614 764-1493
Dennis R Adams, *President*
G Duane Welsh, *Vice Pres*
Curtis L Robson, *Treasurer*
Eva Chung, *Asst Controller*
John Dorsey, *Sales Mgr*
EMP: 32
SQ FT: 10,000
SALES: 3.1MM Privately Held
WEB: www.americanshare.com
SIC: 6399 Deposit insurance

(G-10252)
AMERICAN SYSTEMS CNSULTING INC
Also Called: Asci
5777 Frantz Rd Ste 150 (43017-1885)
PHONE..................614 282-7180
Cliff A Gallatin, *President*
Daryl L Mayfield, *Senior VP*
Patrick Gemperline, *Vice Pres*
Tim Calvin, *Info Tech Mgr*
Evelyn Singer, *Admin Asst*
EMP: 62
SQ FT: 29,000
SALES (est): 3.9MM Privately Held
WEB: www.asci.net
SIC: 7371 7379 Custom computer programming services; data processing consultant

(G-10253)
AMERIPRISE FINANCIAL SVCS INC
655 Metro Pl S Ste 450 (43017-3388)
PHONE..................614 934-4057
Sandy Yinger, *Manager*
Jason Gilbert, *Advisor*
EMP: 45
SALES (corp-wide): 12B Publicly Held
WEB: www.amps.com
SIC: 8742 6282 Financial consultant; investment advice
HQ: Ameriprise Financial Services Inc.
500 2nd St S Ste 101
La Crosse WI 54601
608 783-2639

(G-10254)
AP/AIM DUBLIN SUITES TRS LLC
Also Called: Embassy Suites Columbus Dublin
5100 Upper Metro Pl (43017-3384)
PHONE..................614 790-9000
Cheree Goodall, *Principal*
Kristy Adams-Clay, *Sales Dir*
Jamie Grittman, *Director*
EMP: 99
SALES (est): 4MM Privately Held
SIC: 7011 Hotels

(G-10255)
ARLINGWORTH HOME HEALTH INC
6479 Reflections Dr # 100 (43017-2354)
PHONE..................614 659-0961
Fax: 614 923-7001
Michael Legg, *Administration*
EMP: 40
SQ FT: 2,700
SALES (est): 1.8MM Privately Held
SIC: 8082 Home health care services

(G-10256)
ASHLAND LLC
Also Called: Ashland Distribution
5200 Blazer Pkwy (43017-3309)
P.O. Box 2219, Columbus (43216-2219)
PHONE..................614 790-3333
Fax: 614 790-3173
Sherri Nelson, *President*
Leonard R Gelosa, *Senior VP*
Ted Harris, *Vice Pres*
Fred Good, *Vice Pres*
Micheal Brown, *Engineer*
EMP: 150
SALES (corp-wide): 3.2B Publicly Held
WEB: www.ashland.com
SIC: 2899 5169 Chemical preparations; chemicals & allied products
HQ: Ashland Llc
50 E Rivercenter Blvd # 1600
Covington KY 41011
859 815-3333

(G-10257)
AT&T CORP
7497 Sawmill Rd (43016-9616)
PHONE..................614 798-3898
Tisha Miller, *Manager*
EMP: 97
SALES (corp-wide): 160.5B Publicly Held
SIC: 4812 Cellular telephone services
HQ: At&T Corp.
1 At&T Way
Bedminster NJ 07921
800 403-3302

(G-10258)
AURORA IMAGING COMPANY
344 Cramer Creek Ct (43017-2585)
PHONE..................614 761-1390
Nanda Nair, *President*
Ranjan Manorjan, *Chairman*
EMP: 35
SQ FT: 1,800
SALES (est): 1.1MM Privately Held
SIC: 7374 Optical scanning data service; computer graphics service

(G-10259)
BBC&M ENGINEERING INC (PA)
6190 Enterprise Ct (43016-7297)
PHONE..................614 793-2226
Fax: 614 793-2410
Stephen C Pasternack, *President*
Timothy A Van Echo, *Exec VP*
Ronald T Erb, *Vice Pres*
Daniel A Furgason, *Vice Pres*
Stephen L Loskota, *Vice Pres*
EMP: 65 **EST:** 1957
SQ FT: 25,000
SALES: 7.7MM Privately Held
WEB: www.bbcm.com
SIC: 8711 Consulting engineer

(G-10260)
BEECHWOLD VETERINARY HOSPITAL
Also Called: Riverside Veterinary Hospital
6924 Riverside Dr (43017-9519)
PHONE..................614 766-1222
Dave McGuffin, *Manager*
EMP: 42
SQ FT: 1,509
SALES (corp-wide): 3.5MM Privately Held
WEB: www.beechwoldvet.vetsuite.com
SIC: 0742 Animal hospital services, pets & other animal specialties
PA: Beechwold Veterinary Hospital Inc
4590 Indianola Ave
Columbus OH 43214
614 268-8666

(G-10261)
BENCO DENTAL SUPPLY CO
4333 Tuller Rd Ste E (43017-5064)
PHONE..................614 761-1053
Fax: 614 761-1401
Vickie Pfahler, *Manager*
EMP: 98
SALES (corp-wide): 512.1MM Privately Held
SIC: 5047 Dental equipment & supplies
PA: Benco Dental Supply Co.
295 Centerpoint Blvd
Pittston PA 18640
570 602-7781

(G-10262)
BENEFIT ADM AGCY LLC
5880 Venture Dr (43017-6140)
PHONE..................614 791-1143
Courtlann Atkinson, *President*
Bob Santilli, *Director*
EMP: 25
SALES (est): 1.7MM Privately Held
SIC: 6411 Insurance brokers

(G-10263)
BIOSORTIA PHARMACEUTICALS INC
4266 Tuller Rd (43017-5007)
PHONE..................614 636-4850
Ross O Youngs, *President*
Haiyin He, *Vice Pres*
Derek Ailts, *Opers Dir*
Rob Brammer, *Purch Mgr*
Guy T Carter, *CFO*
EMP: 25
SALES (est): 2.6MM Privately Held
SIC: 8731 Biological research

(G-10264)
BMI FEDERAL CREDIT UNION
6165 Emerald Pkwy (43016-3248)
P.O. Box 3670 (43016-0340)
PHONE..................614 707-4000
Fax: 614 707-4195
William Allender, *President*
Sharon Custer, *President*
Dawn Shafer, *Accountant*
Joseph Corna, *Asst Mgr*
Amy Hatfield, *Assistant*
EMP: 100 **EST:** 1934
SQ FT: 44,000
SALES: 15.1MM Privately Held
SIC: 6061 Federal credit unions

(G-10265)
BMW FINANCIAL SERVICES NA LLC
5515 Parkcenter Cir (43017-3533)
PHONE..................614 718-6900
Chris Bennett, *Vice Pres*
James Edgerton, *Vice Pres*
Brian Smith, *Project Mgr*
Robert Kodger, *Facilities Mgr*
Bernard De Souza, *Sls & Mktg Exec*
EMP: 150
SALES (corp-wide): 116.3B Privately Held
SIC: 6159 Automobile finance leasing
HQ: Bmw Financial Services Na, Llc
5550 Britton Pkwy
Hilliard OH 43026

(G-10266)
BOUND TREE MEDICAL LLC (HQ)
5000 Tuttle Crossing Blvd (43016-1534)
P.O. Box 8023 (43016-2023)
PHONE..................614 760-5000
Keith Cony, *Regional Mgr*
Jeff Plumb, *Regional Mgr*
Cecilia Ochoa, *Opers Mgr*
Rosa Castro, *Purch Mgr*
Jimmy Greene, *Buyer*
▲ **EMP:** 80
SQ FT: 30,000
SALES (est): 97.4MM Privately Held
WEB: www.boundtree.com
SIC: 5047 Medical equipment & supplies

(G-10267)
BRENTLINGER ENTERPRISES
Also Called: Midwestern Auto Group
6335 Perimeter Loop Rd (43017-3207)
PHONE..................614 889-2571
Fax: 614 761-2381
Mark Brentlinger, *Partner*
Alain Bennett, *Sales Staff*
Megan Bruzzese, *Sales Staff*
David Perry, *Sales Staff*
Mike Schroeder, *Sales Staff*
▲ **EMP:** 160
SQ FT: 100,000

Dublin - Franklin County (G-10268)

SALES (est): 59.8MM **Privately Held**
WEB: www.magcars.com
SIC: 5511 7538 Automobiles, new & used; general automotive repair shops

(G-10268)
BRINKS INCORPORATED
7293 Sawmill Rd (43016-9684)
PHONE..................614 761-1205
Marshall Goatley, *Opers Staff*
Kevin Neu, *Branch Mgr*
Bill Vechiarella, *Manager*
EMP: 42
SALES (corp-wide): 3.3B **Publicly Held**
WEB: www.brinksinc.com
SIC: 7381 Armored car services
HQ: Brink's, Incorporated
 1801 Bayberry Ct Ste 400
 Richmond VA 23226
 804 289-9600

(G-10269)
BROOKDALE SENIOR LIVING INC
7220 Muirfield Dr (43017-2862)
PHONE..................614 336-3677
Heidi Strawn, *Office Mgr*
EMP: 36
SALES (corp-wide): 4.7B **Publicly Held**
SIC: 8082 Home health care services
PA: Brookdale Senior Living
 111 Westwood Pl Ste 400
 Brentwood TN 37027
 615 221-2250

(G-10270)
BROWN AND CALDWELL
4700 Lakehurst Ct Ste 100 (43016-2249)
PHONE..................614 410-6144
Tim Block, *Manager*
Michael O'Shaughnessy, *Administration*
EMP: 32
SALES (corp-wide): 540.3MM **Privately Held**
SIC: 8711 Professional engineer
PA: Brown And Caldwell
 201 N Civic Dr Ste 115
 Walnut Creek CA 94596
 925 937-9010

(G-10271)
BUCKEYE CHECK CASHING INC (HQ)
Also Called: First Virginia
6785 Bobcat Way Ste 200 (43016-1443)
PHONE..................614 798-5900
Ted Saunders, *CEO*
Eric Austin, *President*
Kyle Hanson, *President*
Robert Grieser, *Senior VP*
Rob Grieser, *Vice Pres*
EMP: 200
SALES (est): 102.2MM **Privately Held**
WEB: www.buckeyecheckcashing.com
SIC: 6099 Check cashing agencies

(G-10272)
BUCKEYE DRMTLOGY DRMTHPHTHLOGY (PA)
5720 Blazer Pkwy (43017-3566)
PHONE..................614 389-6331
Julio Cruz, *Principal*
Adam Hessel MD, *Principal*
Sandra Jones-Wu MD, *Principal*
Mohammad S Diab, *Dermatology*
Yang Shen, *Dermatology*
EMP: 30
SALES (est): 3.6MM **Privately Held**
SIC: 8011 Dermatologist

(G-10273)
BUTLER ANIMAL HEALTH SUP LLC (DH)
Also Called: Henry Schein Animal Health
400 Metro Pl N Ste 100 (43017-3340)
PHONE..................614 761-9095
Francis Dirksmeier, *President*
Matt Bridges, *Regional Mgr*
Anthony Johnson, *Exec VP*
Fred Bravo, *Vice Pres*
Sean Henderson, *CFO*
◆ EMP: 170

SALES (est): 1.3B
SALES (corp-wide): 12.4B **Publicly Held**
SIC: 5122 5047 Drugs, proprietaries & sundries; biologicals & allied products; pharmaceuticals; veterinarians' equipment & supplies
HQ: Butler Animal Health Holding Company Llc
 400 Metro Pl N Ste 150
 Dublin OH 43017
 614 761-9095

(G-10274)
BUTLER ANIMAL HLTH HOLDG LLC (HQ)
Also Called: Butler Animal Supply
400 Metro Pl N Ste 150 (43017-3392)
PHONE..................614 761-9095
Dale Dye, *Regional Mgr*
Hornsby Williams, *Purch Mgr*
Leo McNeil, *CFO*
Liz Bell, *Sales Mgr*
Derek Card, *Sales Mgr*
▼ EMP: 40
SALES (est): 1.3B
SALES (corp-wide): 12.4B **Publicly Held**
SIC: 5122 5149 5047 Drugs, proprietaries & sundries; pharmaceuticals; biologicals & allied products; pet foods; veterinarians' equipment & supplies
PA: Henry Schein, Inc.
 135 Duryea Rd
 Melville NY 11747
 631 843-5500

(G-10275)
CARDINAL HEALTH INC (PA)
7000 Cardinal Pl (43017-1091)
PHONE..................614 757-6000
Fax: 614 757-6000
Jon L Giacomin, *CEO*
George S Barrett, *Ch of Bd*
Donald M Casey Jr, *President*
Michele A M Holcomb, *Exec VP*
Michele Holcomb, *Exec VP*
◆ EMP: 2800
SALES: 129.9B **Publicly Held**
WEB: www.cardinal.com
SIC: 5122 5047 8741 3842 Drugs, proprietaries & sundries; pharmaceuticals; druggists' sundries; blood plasma; surgical equipment & supplies; hospital equipment & supplies; management services; surgical appliances & supplies

(G-10276)
CARDINAL HEALTH 100 INC (HQ)
Also Called: Bindley Western Drug
7000 Cardinal Pl (43017-1091)
PHONE..................614 757-5000
William E Bindley, *Ch of Bd*
Keith W Burks, *Exec VP*
Gregory S Beyerl, *Vice Pres*
Kathy Byrne, *Vice Pres*
Michael L Shinn, *Treasurer*
EMP: 280
SQ FT: 70,000
SALES (est): 194.3MM
SALES (corp-wide): 129.9B **Publicly Held**
WEB: www.bindley.com
SIC: 5122 5047 Drugs, proprietaries & sundries; pharmaceuticals; cosmetics, perfumes & hair products; druggists' sundries; medical & hospital equipment
PA: Cardinal Health, Inc.
 7000 Cardinal Pl
 Dublin OH 43017
 614 757-5000

(G-10277)
CARDINAL HEALTH 301 LLC (HQ)
Also Called: Pyxis Data Systems
7000 Cardinal Pl (43017-1091)
PHONE..................614 757-5000
R Kerry Clark, *CEO*
Robert D Walter, *Ch of Bd*
Stephen S Thomas, *President*
Steve Bain, *Cardinal*
Kaushik Ghosh, *Cardinal*
▲ EMP: 600

SALES (est): 200.4MM
SALES (corp-wide): 129.9B **Publicly Held**
SIC: 5047 Medical & hospital equipment; dental equipment & supplies
PA: Cardinal Health, Inc.
 7000 Cardinal Pl
 Dublin OH 43017
 614 757-5000

(G-10278)
CARDIO PARTNERS INC
5000 Tuttle Crossing Blvd (43016-1534)
P.O. Box 8023 (43016-2023)
PHONE..................614 760-5038
Dan Connor, *CEO*
Jeff Prestel, *President*
EMP: 100
SALES (est): 21.5MM **Privately Held**
SIC: 5047 7389 Medical equipment & supplies;

(G-10279)
CARE INFORMATION SYSTEMS LLC
5723 Dalymount Dr (43016-3234)
PHONE..................614 496-4338
Krishna Char, *CEO*
EMP: 65
SALES: 750K **Privately Held**
SIC: 7371 Custom computer programming services

(G-10280)
CAREWORKS OF OHIO INC (PA)
Also Called: Vocworks
5555 Glendon Ct Ste 300 (43016-3302)
P.O. Box 182726, Columbus (43218-2726)
PHONE..................614 792-1085
William W Pfeiffer, *President*
Danielle Dresden, *Regional Mgr*
Sharon Kitsonas, *Regional Mgr*
Richard J Poach, *COO*
Tim James, *Senior VP*
EMP: 450
SQ FT: 85,000
SALES (est): 44.6MM **Privately Held**
WEB: www.careworks.com
SIC: 8059 7361 8741 6411 Personal care home, with health care; employment agencies; management services; insurance agents, brokers & service

(G-10281)
CELLCO PARTNERSHIP
Also Called: Verizon
5165 Emerald Pkwy (43017-1063)
PHONE..................614 560-2000
Fax: 614 560-2222
Dennis F Strigl, *President*
Catherine Passmore, *Marketing Staff*
Steven Watson, *Marketing Staff*
Doreen Lucas, *Associate Dir*
Amy Vollkommer, *Associate Dir*
EMP: 500
SALES (corp-wide): 126B **Publicly Held**
SIC: 4812 Cellular telephone services
HQ: Cellco Partnership
 1 Verizon Way
 Basking Ridge NJ 07920

(G-10282)
CELLCO PARTNERSHIP
Also Called: Verizon Wireless
5520 Blazer Pkwy (43016-1525)
PHONE..................614 793-8989
Marcy Geiger, *Branch Mgr*
EMP: 57
SALES (corp-wide): 126B **Publicly Held**
SIC: 4899 Data communication services
HQ: Cellco Partnership
 1 Verizon Way
 Basking Ridge NJ 07920

(G-10283)
CELLCO PARTNERSHIP
Also Called: Verizon
5035 Post Rd (43017-1115)
PHONE..................614 793-8989
Walter Abood, *Branch Mgr*
EMP: 30
SALES (corp-wide): 126B **Publicly Held**
SIC: 4812 5999 5731 Cellular telephone services; telephone equipment & systems; radio, television & electronic stores

HQ: Cellco Partnership
 1 Verizon Way
 Basking Ridge NJ 07920

(G-10284)
CENTRAL OHIO ICE RINKS INC
7001 Dublin Park Dr (43016-8340)
PHONE..................614 475-7575
Fax: 614 791-9302
Windy Herb, *President*
Greg Kirstein, *President*
EMP: 30
SQ FT: 70,000
SALES (est): 199.2K **Privately Held**
SIC: 7999 Ice skating rink operation

(G-10285)
CENTRAL OHIO POURED WALLS INC
7627 Fishel Dr N (43016-8747)
PHONE..................614 889-0505
Fax: 614 761-0669
Mark Del Col, *President*
Lena D Col, *Project Mgr*
EMP: 30
SQ FT: 6,000
SALES (est): 3MM **Privately Held**
SIC: 1771 Foundation & footing contractor

(G-10286)
CENTURYLINK INC
4650 Lakehurst Ct (43016-3252)
PHONE..................614 215-4223
William G Bogantz, *Project Mgr*
Tracy Auborn, *Human Resources*
Carlos Stuart, *Branch Mgr*
Mark Maglott, *Sr Project Mgr*
Robert Mulvaney, *Program Mgr*
EMP: 3000
SALES (corp-wide): 17.6B **Publicly Held**
SIC: 7629 Telecommunication equipment repair (except telephones)
PA: Centurylink, Inc.
 100 Centurylink Dr
 Monroe LA 71203
 318 388-9000

(G-10287)
CHAMPAIGN NATIONAL BANK URBANA
6400 Perimeter Loop Rd (43017-3205)
PHONE..................614 798-1321
Brian Dupont, *Branch Mgr*
Jacquey Yoder, *Manager*
EMP: 30 **Privately Held**
WEB: www.champaignbank.com
SIC: 6021 National commercial banks
HQ: Champaign National Bank Of Urbana
 601 Scioto St
 Urbana OH 43078
 937 653-1100

(G-10288)
CHECKFREE SERVICES CORPORATION
Also Called: Fiserv
6000 Perimeter Dr (43017-3233)
PHONE..................614 564-3000
Fax: 614 564-3427
Bridie Fanning, *Exec VP*
Jason Tolan, *Facilities Mgr*
Delinda Bing, *Business Anlyst*
Brian Forrest, *Business Anlyst*
Michael Kingery, *Business Anlyst*
EMP: 1000
SALES (corp-wide): 5.7B **Publicly Held**
SIC: 7371 Computer software systems analysis & design, custom
HQ: Checkfree Services Corporation
 2900 Westside Pkwy
 Alpharetta GA 30004
 678 375-3000

(G-10289)
CHECKSMART FINANCIAL COMPANY (DH)
6785 Bobcat Way Ste 200 (43016-1443)
PHONE..................614 798-5900
Rob Grieser, *Principal*
Bridgette Roman, *Executive*
EMP: 25
SALES (est): 78.3MM **Privately Held**
SIC: 6099 Check cashing agencies

HQ: Checksmart Financial Holdings Corp.
6785 Bobcat Way Ste 200
Dublin OH 43016
614 798-5900

(G-10290)
CHEMCOTE INC
Also Called: Cicar
7599 Fishel Dr N (43016-8818)
PHONE..................614 792-2683
Frank Bucci, *President*
Joseph Bucci, *Vice Pres*
Drew Dimaccio, *Vice Pres*
Joe Sanderlin, *Vice Pres*
Doug Hobson, *Opers Mgr*
EMP: 120
SQ FT: 6,000
SALES (est): 27.1MM **Privately Held**
SIC: 1611 Highway & street paving contractor

(G-10291)
CHEMCOTE ROOFING COMPANY
7599 Fishel Dr N (43016-8818)
PHONE..................614 792-2683
Fax: 614 792-0688
Frank Bucci, *President*
Drew Dimaccio, *Treasurer*
EMP: 70
SQ FT: 2,000
SALES (est): 5.9MM **Privately Held**
WEB: www.chemcote.com
SIC: 1761 Roofing contractor

(G-10292)
CHILLER LLC (PA)
7001 Dublin Park Dr (43016-8340)
PHONE..................614 764-1000
Wendy Herb, *President*
David A Paitson, *Principal*
Mazin Habash, *Manager*
Kurt Kramer, *Manager*
Michael Sims, *Director*
EMP: 75 EST: 1997
SQ FT: 76,000
SALES (est): 11.7MM **Privately Held**
WEB: www.chiller.com
SIC: 7999 Ice skating rink operation

(G-10293)
CISCO SYSTEMS INC
5400 Frantz Rd Ste 200 (43016-4147)
PHONE..................614 764-4987
Bill Taylor, *Principal*
Dana Daum, *Engineer*
Vince Hartsook, *Engineer*
Tom Herrli, *Engineer*
Jason Houx, *Engineer*
EMP: 98
SALES (corp-wide): 48B **Publicly Held**
WEB: www.cisco.com
SIC: 5045 Computer peripheral equipment
PA: Cisco Systems, Inc.
170 W Tasman Dr
San Jose CA 95134
408 526-4000

(G-10294)
CITY OF DUBLIN
Also Called: Division Streets & Utilities
6555 Shier Rings Rd (43016-8716)
PHONE..................614 410-4750
Fax: 614 761-6512
Ron Burns, *Director*
Megan O'Callaghan, *Deputy Dir*
EMP: 50
SQ FT: 3,052 **Privately Held**
SIC: 4911 Electric services
PA: City Of Dublin
5200 Emerald Pkwy
Dublin OH 43017
614 410-4400

(G-10295)
CLEMANS NELSON & ASSOC INC (PA)
485 Metro Pl S Ste 200 (43017-5333)
PHONE..................614 923-7700
Fax: 614 847-7411
Mark J Lucas, *President*
Brett Geary, *Regional Mgr*
Howard D Heffelfinger, *Exec VP*
David S Beauguard, *Vice Pres*
John J Krock, *Vice Pres*
EMP: 39 EST: 1976
SQ FT: 6,928
SALES (est): 3.4MM **Privately Held**
SIC: 8742 Human resource consulting services

(G-10296)
CLOSE TO HOME HEALTH CARE CTR
Also Called: Children's Hospital Northwest
5675 Venture Dr (43017-2159)
PHONE..................614 932-9013
Fax: 614 760-1601
Larry Long, *Director*
Dennis Bartholomew, *Director*
Daniel Boue, *Director*
EMP: 50
SALES (est): 13MM **Privately Held**
SIC: 6324 Hospital & medical service plans

(G-10297)
CMP I COLUMBUS I OWNER LLC
Also Called: Courtyard Columbus Dublin
5175 Post Rd (43017-2125)
PHONE..................614 764-9393
Nichole Brinker, *Manager*
Allen Turpin, *Director*
EMP: 37
SALES (est): 1.2MM
SALES (corp-wide): 50.6MM **Privately Held**
SIC: 7011 Hotels
PA: Cmp I Owner-T, Llc
399 Park Ave Fl 18
New York NY 10022
212 547-2609

(G-10298)
CMP I OWNER-T LLC
5175 Post Rd (43017-2125)
PHONE..................614 764-9393
Nichole Brinker, *Manager*
EMP: 37
SALES (corp-wide): 50.6MM **Privately Held**
SIC: 8741 Hotel or motel management
PA: Cmp I Owner-T, Llc
399 Park Ave Fl 18
New York NY 10022
212 547-2609

(G-10299)
COLONIAL LF ACCIDENT INSUR CO
485 Metro Pl S Ste 150 (43017-5300)
PHONE..................614 793-8622
Christopher McKee, *General Mgr*
EMP: 400 **Publicly Held**
SIC: 6411 Insurance agents
HQ: Colonial Life & Accident Insurance Company Inc
1200 Colonial Life Blvd W
Columbia SC 29210
803 798-7000

(G-10300)
COLUMBUS AAA CORP
Also Called: AAA Rental & Sales
2502 Starford Dr (43016-9247)
PHONE..................614 889-2840
Helen Mc Carthy, *CEO*
Michael Mc Carthy, *President*
Michael M Carthy, *President*
Timothy Mc Carthy, *President*
Joseph Mc Carthy, *Vice Pres*
EMP: 25
SQ FT: 21,000
SALES (est): 2.6MM **Privately Held**
SIC: 7359 5712 Party supplies rental services; furniture stores

(G-10301)
COLUMBUS SURGICAL CENTER LLP
5005 Parkcenter Ave (43017-3582)
PHONE..................614 932-9503
Kim Heimlich, *Principal*
EMP: 50
SALES (est): 1.6MM **Privately Held**
SIC: 8011 8399 Ambulatory surgical center; social services

(G-10302)
COMMAND ALKON INCORPORATED
6750 Crosby Ct (43016-7644)
PHONE..................614 799-0600
Randy Willaman, *Branch Mgr*
EMP: 60
SALES (corp-wide): 111.4MM **Privately Held**
WEB: www.commandalkon.com
SIC: 3823 7371 3625 Industrial process measurement equipment; custom computer programming services; relays & industrial controls
PA: Command Alkon Incorporated
1800 Intl Pk Dr Ste 400
Birmingham AL 35243
205 879-3282

(G-10303)
COMMONWEALTH HOTELS LLC
Also Called: Embassy Suites
5100 Upper Metro Pl (43017-3384)
PHONE..................614 790-9000
Fax: 614 790-9001
Lee Palaschak, *Branch Mgr*
EMP: 125
SALES (corp-wide): 91.6MM **Privately Held**
WEB: www.commonwealth-hotels.com
SIC: 7011 5813 5812 Hotels; drinking places; eating places
PA: Commonwealth Hotels, Llc
100 E Rivercenter Blvd # 1050
Covington KY 41011
859 392-2264

(G-10304)
COMMUNITY CHOICE FINANCIAL INC (PA)
Also Called: EASY MONEY
6785 Bobcat Way Ste 200 (43016-1443)
PHONE..................614 798-5900
William E Saunders Jr, *CEO*
Kyle Hanson, *President*
Ted Saunders, *Principal*
Marshall Davis, *Vice Pres*
Robert Grieser, *Vice Pres*
EMP: 78
SALES: 364MM **Privately Held**
SIC: 6799 Investors

(G-10305)
COMPASS CONSTRUCTION INC
7670 Fishel Dr S (43016-8820)
PHONE..................614 761-7800
Fax: 614 761-2063
Larry Mirgon, *President*
Guy Detrick, *Asst Supt*
Frank Reynolds, *Vice Pres*
Scott Fandrich, *Manager*
Kerry Dobbins, *Executive*
EMP: 80
SQ FT: 14,400
SALES (est): 7.4MM **Privately Held**
WEB: www.compassconstruction.com
SIC: 1742 Drywall; acoustical & ceiling work

(G-10306)
COMPMANAGEMENT INC (HQ)
6377 Emerald Pkwy (43016-3272)
P.O. Box 884 (43017-6884)
PHONE..................614 376-5300
Fax: 614 766-6888
Stephen Brown, *CEO*
Cheryl Powers, *President*
Jonathan Wagner, *President*
Richard Kurth, *Exec VP*
Daniel Sullivan, *Senior VP*
EMP: 40
SALES (est): 211.9MM
SALES (corp-wide): 3.4B **Privately Held**
WEB: www.compmgt.com
SIC: 6411 Insurance agents, brokers & service
PA: Sedgwick Cms Holdings, Inc.
1100 Ridgeway Loop Rd # 200
Memphis TN 38120
901 415-7400

(G-10307)
COMPMANAGEMENT HEALTH SYSTEMS
6377 Emerald Pkwy (43016-3272)
P.O. Box 1040 (43017-6040)
PHONE..................614 766-5223
Robert J Bossart, *CEO*
Lance Watkins, *Assistant VP*
Jolin Wall, *Controller*
Rob Rissmeyer, *VP Human Res*
Brent Isler, *Accounts Exec*
EMP: 100
SALES (est): 4.4MM
SALES (corp-wide): 3.4B **Privately Held**
WEB: www.chsmco.com
SIC: 8748 Employee programs administration
HQ: Compmanagement, Inc.
6377 Emerald Pkwy
Dublin OH 43016
614 376-5300

(G-10308)
CONSOLIDATED LEARNING CTRS INC
Also Called: Jelly Bean Junction Lrng Ctr
7100 Muirfield Dr Ste 200 (43017-3807)
PHONE..................614 791-0050
Jeffry Roby, *CEO*
Bonnie Roby, *President*
Jessica Hoffman, *Principal*
EMP: 115
SQ FT: 4,000
SALES (est): 2.5MM **Privately Held**
SIC: 8351 Child day care services

(G-10309)
CONSTRUCTION LABOR CONTRS LLC
Also Called: CLC
5930 Wilcox Pl Ste F (43016-6804)
PHONE..................614 932-9937
Fax: 614 932-9938
Steve Dorsey, *General Mgr*
M Columbus, *Executive*
Darrel Madsen, *Executive*
EMP: 100 **Privately Held**
WEB: www.constructionlaborcontractors.com
SIC: 7361 Employment agencies
HQ: Construction Labor Contractors, Llc
3380 Brecksville Rd # 200
Richfield OH 44286
330 247-1080

(G-10310)
COUNTRY CLUB AT MUIRFIELD VLG
Also Called: Country Club, The
8715 Muirfield Dr (43017-9600)
PHONE..................614 764-1714
Fax: 614 764-4717
Jim Hughes, *CEO*
John Blute, *General Mgr*
Alissa Klein, *Comms Dir*
Mike Greeny, *Manager*
D Mancini, *Manager*
EMP: 30
SQ FT: 35,000
SALES (est): 2.3MM **Privately Held**
WEB: www.tccmv.com
SIC: 7997 Country club, membership

(G-10311)
COVELLI ENTERPRISES INC
6693 Sawmill Rd (43017-9009)
PHONE..................614 889-7802
EMP: 79
SALES (corp-wide): 414.5MM **Privately Held**
SIC: 7389 Personal service agents, brokers & bureaus
PA: Covelli Enterprises, Inc.
3900 E Market St Ste 1
Warren OH 44484
330 856-3176

(G-10312)
CRAWFORD HOYING LTD
6640 Riverside Dr Ste 500 (43017-9534)
PHONE..................614 335-2020
Chris Lanning, *President*
Brent D Crawford, *Chairman*
Robert C Hoying, *Chairman*
Mark Mayers, *COO*

Dublin - Franklin County (G-10313) GEOGRAPHIC SECTION

Don Brokaw, *Vice Pres*
EMP: 215
SALES (est): 23.8MM **Privately Held**
SIC: 6531 Real estate agents & managers

(G-10313)
CRESTTEK LLC (PA)
565 Metro Pl S Ste 420 (43017-7321)
PHONE..................................248 602-2083
Madhu Naidu, *Mng Member*
Girish Gowda,
Walter Muccino,
EMP: 40
SQ FT: 2,800
SALES: 4MM **Privately Held**
SIC: 7549 Automotive customizing services, non-factory basis

(G-10314)
CUTLER REAL ESTATE INC
6375 Riverside Dr Ste 210 (43017-5241)
PHONE..................................614 339-4664
Doug Green, *General Mgr*
EMP: 45
SALES (est): 218.9K **Privately Held**
SIC: 6531 6519 Real estate brokers & agents; real property lessors

(G-10315)
CWB PROPERTY MANAGMENT INC (PA)
5775 Perimeter Dr Ste 290 (43017-3224)
PHONE..................................614 793-2244
Fax: 614 793-2328
William W Wolfe, *President*
Kenneth J Castrop, *Corp Secy*
Connie Burkett, *COO*
Christopher D Conrath, *Vice Pres*
Marina Rabkin, *Accounting Mgr*
EMP: 30
SQ FT: 2,400
SALES (est): 2.6MM **Privately Held**
WEB: www.cwbpm.com
SIC: 6513 6514 7011 6531 Apartment building operators; dwelling operators, except apartments; hotels & motels; real estate agents & managers

(G-10316)
DATALYSYS LLC
6063 Frantz Rd Ste 206 (43017-3370)
PHONE..................................614 495-0260
Rajneesh Katarapu, *Manager*
Mayuri Sriram,
Raj Katarapu,
EMP: 40
SALES: 4MM **Privately Held**
SIC: 7379

(G-10317)
DEDICATED TECH SERVICES INC
545 Metro Pl S Ste 100 (43017-5353)
PHONE..................................614 309-0059
Patricia E Lickliter, *President*
Jeffrey Dalton, *Treasurer*
EMP: 55
SALES: 100K **Privately Held**
SIC: 7371 7373 7376 7379 Computer software development; local area network (LAN) systems integrator; computer facilities management; computer related maintenance services; usher service; management consulting services

(G-10318)
DELTA ENERGY LLC
5555 Perimeter Dr (43017-3219)
PHONE..................................614 761-3603
Fax: 614 339-2700
Justin McMaster, *President*
Sheri Tackett,
EMP: 45
SQ FT: 8,000
SALES (est): 9.7MM **Privately Held**
WEB: www.deltaenergyllc.com
SIC: 4924 8742 Natural gas distribution; management consulting services

(G-10319)
DEMARIUS CORPORATION
Also Called: Progressive Medical Intl
5000 Tuttle Crossing Blvd (43016-1534)
PHONE..................................760 957-5500
Marc Lawrence, *President*
Barbara Nelson, *Accounts Mgr*

Heather Miller, *Manager*
▲ **EMP:** 40
SQ FT: 35,000
SALES (est): 6.5MM **Privately Held**
WEB: www.progressivemed.com
SIC: 5047 Medical equipment & supplies

(G-10320)
DEPENDBLE BLDRS RENOVATORS LLC
4555 Summit View Rd (43016-9525)
PHONE..................................614 761-8250
Pete Hamer,
EMP: 26
SQ FT: 360
SALES: 540K **Privately Held**
SIC: 1522 Hotel/motel & multi-family home renovation & remodeling

(G-10321)
DIMENSION SERVICE CORPORATION
Also Called: D S C
5500 Frantz Rd Ste 100 (43017-3545)
P.O. Box 2082 (43017-7082)
PHONE..................................614 226-7455
Fax: 614 792-8027
Bradley Hunter, *President*
Al Stein, *COO*
Kenny Halfpap, *Vice Pres*
Alan Weiner, *Treasurer*
Mike Murphy, *Chief Acct*
EMP: 125
SQ FT: 25,000
SALES (est): 65.5MM **Privately Held**
WEB: www.dimensionservice.com
SIC: 6399 Warranty insurance, automobile

(G-10322)
DOCTORS CONSULTING SERVICE
200 Bradenton Ave (43017-3513)
PHONE..................................614 793-1980
Fax: 614 793-1985
Jerry Snively, *President*
Terrence Fickel, *Vice Pres*
EMP: 25
SQ FT: 4,120
SALES (est): 1.8MM **Privately Held**
SIC: 8721 Billing & bookkeeping service

(G-10323)
DOMINION HOMES INC (HQ)
4900 Tuttle Crossing Blvd (43016-1532)
PHONE..................................614 356-5000
Fax: 614 356-6010
Donn Borror, *Ch of Bd*
Jeffrey Croft, *President*
Mike Schultz, *Business Mgr*
Holly Fasone, *COO*
David S Borror, *Exec VP*
EMP: 100
SALES (est): 82.6MM **Privately Held**
SIC: 1521 Single-family housing construction

(G-10324)
DRURY HOTELS COMPANY LLC
Also Called: Drury Inn & Suites Columbus NW
6170 Parkcenter Cir (43017-3583)
PHONE..................................614 798-8802
Jessica Baker, *Manager*
EMP: 28
SALES (corp-wide): 397.4MM **Privately Held**
WEB: www.druryhotels.com
SIC: 7011 Inns
PA: Drury Hotels Company, Llc
721 Emerson Rd Ste 400
Saint Louis MO 63141
314 429-2255

(G-10325)
DUBLIN BUILDING SYSTEMS CO
6233 Avery Rd (43016-8788)
P.O. Box 370 (43017-0370)
PHONE..................................614 760-5831
Fax: 614 889-5437
Thomas W Irelan, *President*
Jim Simpson, *Superintendent*
C Stanley Taylor, *Principal*
Victor D Irelan, *Chairman*
Robert J Howe, *Vice Pres*
EMP: 44

SQ FT: 5,000
SALES (est): 14.7MM **Privately Held**
WEB: www.dublinbuilding.com
SIC: 1791 1521 Structural steel erection; single-family housing construction

(G-10326)
DUBLIN CITY SCHOOLS
6371 Shier Rings Rd (43016-9498)
PHONE..................................614 764-5926
Victor Dodds, *Director*
Andrea McCullough, *Teacher*
Mary A Petty, *Assistant*
EMP: 150
SALES (corp-wide): 234.1MM **Privately Held**
SIC: 4151 School buses
PA: Dublin City Schools
7030 Coffman Rd
Dublin OH 43017
614 764-5913

(G-10327)
DUBLIN FAMILY CARE INC
250 W Bridge St Ste 101 (43017-1172)
PHONE..................................614 761-2244
James J Barr MD, *President*
Dr Joseph Carducci, *Vice Pres*
EMP: 25
SALES (est): 3.4MM **Privately Held**
SIC: 8011 General & family practice, physician/surgeon

(G-10328)
DUBLIN GERIATRIC CARE CO LP
Also Called: Convalarium At Indian Run
6430 Post Rd (43016-1226)
PHONE..................................614 761-1188
Fax: 614 761-0410
Ralph E Hazelbaker, *Partner*
Dennison Health Ventures, *Partner*
Dublin Health Care Corp, *General Ptnr*
EMP: 50
SALES (est): 2.1MM **Privately Held**
SIC: 8059 8051 Convalescent home; skilled nursing care facilities

(G-10329)
DUBLIN LATCHKEY INC
5970 Venture Dr Ste A (43017-2263)
PHONE..................................614 793-0871
Moreen Bruce, *Director*
Shirley Place, *Director*
Cris Williams, *Director*
EMP: 60
SALES: 2MM **Privately Held**
WEB: www.dublinlatchkey.com
SIC: 8351 Preschool center

(G-10330)
DUBLIN LEARNING ACADEMY
5900 Cromdale Dr (43017-8751)
PHONE..................................614 761-1800
Cathy Holbert, *President*
EMP: 25
SALES (est): 550.1K **Privately Held**
SIC: 8351 Preschool center

(G-10331)
DUBLIN MILLWORK CO INC
7575 Fishel Dr S (43016-8821)
PHONE..................................614 889-7776
Fax: 614 889-8206
Wilbur C Strait, *Ch of Bd*
Scott Evisol, *General Mgr*
Scott Ebersole, *Manager*
Chuck Dearth, *Info Tech Mgr*
Andy Castle, *Executive*
EMP: 30 **EST:** 1981
SQ FT: 100,000
SALES (est): 4.5MM
SALES (corp-wide): 39.1MM **Privately Held**
WEB: www.dublinmillwork.com
SIC: 5031 2431 Trim, sheet metal; doors & windows; millwork
PA: The Strait & Lamp Lumber Company Incorporated
269 National Rd Se
Hebron OH 43025
740 928-4501

(G-10332)
DUBLIN SURGICAL CENTER LLC
5005 Parkcenter Ave (43017-3582)
PHONE..................................614 932-9548
Fax: 614 932-9549
William Emlich, *Mng Member*
Stephen Fisher, *Mng Member*
Steven Miller, *Mng Member*
Marsha Browning, *Manager*
EMP: 28
SALES (est): 5.3MM **Privately Held**
SIC: 8011 Ambulatory surgical center

(G-10333)
DUKE REALTY CORPORATION
Also Called: Duke-Weeks Realty
6640 Riverside Dr Ste 320 (43017-0406)
PHONE..................................614 932-6000
Don Hunter, *President*
EMP: 75
SALES (corp-wide): 780.9MM **Privately Held**
WEB: www.dukereit.com
SIC: 6512 Commercial & industrial building operation
PA: Duke Realty Corporation
600 E 96th St Ste 100
Indianapolis IN 46240
317 808-6000

(G-10334)
EDUCATION INNOVATIONS INTL LLC
655 Metro Pl S Ste 750 (43017-5306)
P.O. Box 266, Amlin (43002-0266)
PHONE..................................614 339-3676
James E McCord, *CEO*
Judy McCord, *CFO*
EMP: 120
SQ FT: 75,000
SALES: 10MM **Privately Held**
SIC: 8741 Management services

(G-10335)
EMERALD PEDIATRICS
5695 Innovation Dr (43016-3312)
PHONE..................................614 932-5050
Fye Dennis, *Financial Exec*
Donna Hickel, *Manager*
Kristen E Thompson, *Pediatrics*
EMP: 35
SALES (est): 2.8MM **Privately Held**
WEB: www.emeraldpediatrics.com
SIC: 8011 Pediatrician

(G-10336)
EMPLOYEE BENEFIT MANAGEMENT (PA)
Also Called: Ebmc
4789 Rings Rd (43017-1513)
PHONE..................................614 766-5800
Fax: 614 766-0901
Tom Jack, *President*
Bob Ochall, *President*
Kenneth Patrick, *President*
James Armstrong, *CFO*
Roger Munday, *Manager*
EMP: 34
SQ FT: 33,000
SALES: 42.8K **Privately Held**
SIC: 8748 6411 Employee programs administration; insurance agents, brokers & service

(G-10337)
EPCON CMMNTIES FRANCHISING INC
500 Stonehenge Pkwy (43017-7572)
PHONE..................................614 761-1010
Philip Fankhauser, *CEO*
Ed Bacome, *President*
Linda Peck, *Sls & Mktg Exec*
David Blackmore, *CFO*
Julie Jensen, *Sales Mgr*
EMP: 87
SQ FT: 10,000
SALES (est): 9.3MM **Privately Held**
WEB: www.epcongroup.com
SIC: 1531 6794 Condominium developers; franchises, selling or licensing

GEOGRAPHIC SECTION
Dublin - Franklin County (G-10359)

(G-10338)
EPCON COMMUNITIES INC
500 Stonehenge Pkwy (43017-7572)
PHONE..................614 761-1010
Phil Fankhauser, *President*
Ed Bacome, *Vice Pres*
David P Blackmore, *CFO*
Angela Brown, *Sales Associate*
Cindy Harsany, *Manager*
EMP: 70
SQ FT: 10,500
SALES (est): 26.9MM **Privately Held**
WEB: www.epconcommunities.com
SIC: 1531 Condominium developers

(G-10339)
ERP ANALYSTS INC
425 Metro Pl N Ste 510 (43017-7328)
PHONE..................614 718-9222
Srikanth Gaddam, *President*
Ranjith K Reddy, *Business Mgr*
Dick Kelley, *Vice Pres*
Manohar Vedula, *Assoc VP*
Harsha Roddam, *Opers Mgr*
EMP: 499
SALES: 76MM **Privately Held**
WEB: www.erpanalysts.com
SIC: 7371 Custom computer programming services

(G-10340)
EVERRIS NA INC (DH)
4950 Blazer Pkwy (43017-3305)
PHONE..................614 726-7100
Ariana Cohen, *President*
Hadia Lefavre, *Exec VP*
Dana Pearson, *Marketing Mgr*
◆ EMP: 25
SQ FT: 73,000
SALES (est): 34.1MM
SALES (corp-wide): 5.4B **Privately Held**
WEB: www.everris.com
SIC: 1479 Fertilizer mineral mining; fertilizer mineral mining

(G-10341)
EXACT SOFTWARE NORTH AMER LLC (DH)
5455 Rings Rd Ste 100 (43017-7519)
PHONE..................978 539-6186
Lisa Wise, *General Mgr*
Mariette Hoogenboom, *Finance Mgr*
Mitchell Alcon,
Alex Braverman,
James A Workman,
EMP: 170
SQ FT: 30,000
SALES (est): 78.7MM
SALES (corp-wide): 216.4MM **Privately Held**
WEB: www.exactamerica.com
SIC: 7371 7372 5045 2759 Computer software development; prepackaged software; computer software; letterpress printing
HQ: Exact Holding B.V.
Molengraaffsingel 33
Delft 2629
152 613-714

(G-10342)
EXACT SOFTWARE NORTH AMER LLC
5455 Rings Rd Ste 100 (43017-7519)
PHONE..................614 410-2600
Peter Dudek, *Senior Partner*
Lisa M Wise, *Senior Partner*
Tammy Guarino, *Project Mgr*
Angie Phillians, *Opers Staff*
Zach Bergman, *QC Mgr*
EMP: 150
SQ FT: 30,000
SALES (corp-wide): 216.4MM **Privately Held**
WEB: www.exactamerica.com
SIC: 7373 Computer integrated systems design
HQ: Exact Software North America, Llc
5455 Rings Rd Ste 100
Dublin OH 43017
978 539-6186

(G-10343)
EXCESS SHARE INSURANCE CORP
Also Called: AMERICAN SHARE INSURANCE
5656 Frantz Rd (43017-2552)
PHONE..................614 764-1900
Dennis Adams, *President*
Gerald D Welsh, *Corp Secy*
Curt Robson, *Treasurer*
EMP: 35
SQ FT: 10,000
SALES: 2.5MM
SALES (corp-wide): 3.1MM **Privately Held**
WEB: www.excessshare.com
SIC: 6399 Deposit insurance
PA: American Mutual Share Insurance Corporation
5656 Frantz Rd
Dublin OH 43017
614 764-1900

(G-10344)
F DOHMEN CO
F D C O Data Processing
7000 Cardinal Pl (43017-1091)
PHONE..................614 757-5000
John Dohmen, *Principal*
EMP: 200
SALES (corp-wide): 162.5MM **Privately Held**
WEB: www.dohmen.com
SIC: 5122 Drugs & drug proprietaries
PA: The F Dohmen Co
190 N Milwaukee St
Milwaukee WI 53202
866 336-1336

(G-10345)
FANNING/HOWEY ASSOCIATES INC
4930 Bradenton Ave (43017-7599)
PHONE..................614 764-4661
Fax: 614 764-7894
Jim Moll, *Financial Exec*
Alan Esparza, *Manager*
Dean Yuricich, *Manager*
David Sundersingh, *Information Mgr*
EMP: 60
SALES (corp-wide): 37.5MM **Privately Held**
WEB: www.fhai.com
SIC: 8712 Architectural engineering
PA: Fanning/Howey Associates, Inc.
1200 Irmscher Blvd
Celina OH 45822
419 586-2292

(G-10346)
FANNING/HOWEY ASSOCIATES INC
4930 Bradenton Ave (43017-7599)
PHONE..................919 831-1831
Roger Brown, *Accounts Exec*
Wayne R Roberts, *Branch Mgr*
EMP: 60
SALES (corp-wide): 37.5MM **Privately Held**
SIC: 8712 Architectural services
PA: Fanning/Howey Associates, Inc.
1200 Irmscher Blvd
Celina OH 45822
419 586-2292

(G-10347)
FAST SWITCH LTD
4900 Blazer Pkwy (43017-3305)
P.O. Box 99 (43017-0099)
PHONE..................614 336-1122
Fax: 614 336-3695
Mark Pukita, *CEO*
Benjamin Lagemann, *Vice Pres*
Kristin Buck, *Controller*
Ryan Freas, *Accounts Mgr*
Ken Hamilton, *Accounts Mgr*
EMP: 300
SQ FT: 1,200
SALES: 51.1MM **Privately Held**
WEB: www.fastswitch.com
SIC: 7361 Executive placement

(G-10348)
FLEX FUND INC
6125 Memorial Dr (43017-9000)
PHONE..................614 766-7000
Robert S Meeder Jr, *President*
EMP: 45
SQ FT: 10,000
SALES (est): 2.9MM **Privately Held**
WEB: www.flexfunds.com
SIC: 6289 8721 Security transfer agents; accounting services, except auditing

(G-10349)
FORESIGHT CORPORATION
655 Metro Pl S Ste 900 (43017-3398)
PHONE..................614 791-1600
Fax: 614 791-1609
Robert Fisher, *President*
Douglas Spence, *Exec VP*
Ken Kaiser, *Vice Pres*
Elaine White, *Vice Pres*
Kristin Maxwell, *CFO*
EMP: 43
SALES (est): 2.3MM
SALES (corp-wide): 3B **Privately Held**
WEB: www.foresightcorp.com
SIC: 7371 Computer software development & applications
HQ: Tibco Software Inc.
3307 Hillview Ave
Palo Alto CA 94304

(G-10350)
FRANK GATES SERVICE COMPANY (DH)
Also Called: Avizent
5000 Bradenton Ave # 100 (43017-3534)
P.O. Box 182364, Columbus (43218-2364)
PHONE..................614 793-8000
Fax: 614 791-7650
Daniel R Sullivan, *President*
Madeleine Melancon, *Principal*
Harrison W Smith, *Principal*
Robert Zamary, *COO*
EMP: 300
SQ FT: 66,000
SALES (est): 87.6MM
SALES (corp-wide): 3B **Privately Held**
WEB: www.fgsc.com
SIC: 8742 Management consulting services
HQ: York Risk Services Group, Inc.
1 Upper Pond
Parsippany NJ 07054
973 404-1200

(G-10351)
FRIENDSHIP VLG OF DUBLIN OHIO
6000 Riverside Dr Ofc Ofc (43017-5073)
PHONE..................614 764-1600
Fax: 614 764-1600
Sheri Meier, *COO*
Charles Ansley, *Treasurer*
Lisa Everson, *Human Res Dir*
Dan Nase, *Mktg Dir*
Steve Love, *Marketing Mgr*
EMP: 250
SALES: 20.5MM **Privately Held**
WEB: www.fvdublin.org
SIC: 8059 8051 Rest home, with health care; skilled nursing care facilities

(G-10352)
GALLAGHER BASSETT SERVICES
545 Metro Pl S Ste 250 (43017-5310)
PHONE..................614 764-7616
Richard Komparens, *Manager*
Leslie Corwin, *Executive*
EMP: 35
SALES (corp-wide): 6.1B **Publicly Held**
WEB: www.atlantisad.com
SIC: 6411 Insurance agents & brokers
HQ: Gallagher Bassett Services, Inc.
2850 Golf Rd Ste 1000
Rolling Meadows IL 60008
630 773-3800

(G-10353)
GEMINI PROPERTIES
Also Called: G P M C
6470 Post Rd Ofc (43016-7206)
PHONE..................614 764-2800
Fax: 614 761-7504
Ron Keller, *Director*
Beth Baker, *Director*
EMP: 50
SALES (corp-wide): 6.2MM **Privately Held**
WEB: www.geminiproperties.com
SIC: 6513 Retirement hotel operation
PA: Gemini Properties
1516 S Boston Ave Ste 301
Tulsa OK 74119
918 592-4400

(G-10354)
GOLF CLUB OF DUBLIN LLC
5805 Eiterman Rd (43016-8004)
PHONE..................614 889-5469
Fax: 614 874-3825
Wes Widdows, *Manager*
Shannon Gerasimchik, *Director*
Jared Wong, *Director*
Tom Anderson,
EMP: 50
SALES (est): 2.3MM **Privately Held**
WEB: www.golfclubofdublin.net
SIC: 7992 Public golf courses

(G-10355)
GUILD ASSOCIATES INC (PA)
Also Called: Guild Biosciences
5750 Shier Rings Rd (43016-1234)
PHONE..................614 798-8215
Fax: 614 798-1972
Dominic Dinovo, *President*
Dolores Dinovo, *Treasurer*
Kyle Evans, *Asst Controller*
Robert L Freeburn II, *Manager*
◆ EMP: 80
SQ FT: 53,000
SALES: 33MM **Privately Held**
SIC: 3559 8731 Chemical machinery & equipment; chemical laboratory, except testing; biotechnical research, commercial

(G-10356)
HANOVER INSURANCE COMPANY
545 Metro Pl S Ste 380 (43017-5316)
PHONE..................614 408-9000
Paula Leger, *Branch Mgr*
EMP: 75 **Publicly Held**
SIC: 6411 Insurance agents
HQ: The Hanover Insurance Company
440 Lincoln St
Worcester MA 01653
508 853-7200

(G-10357)
HARDAGE HOTELS I LLC
Also Called: Chase Suite Hotel
4130 Tuller Rd (43017-9502)
PHONE..................614 766-7762
William Quigley, *Manager*
EMP: 30 **Privately Held**
WEB: www.woodfinsuitehotels.com
SIC: 7011 Hotel, franchised
PA: Hardage Hotels I, Llc
12555 High Bluff Dr # 330
San Diego CA 92130

(G-10358)
HASLETT HEATING & COOLING INC
Also Called: Honeywell Authorized Dealer
7686 Fishel Dr N A (43016-8746)
PHONE..................614 299-2133
Fax: 614 299-4490
Jeff Florer, *President*
Bruce Ames, *Vice Pres*
Marcie Arnold, *Manager*
EMP: 38
SALES (est): 8.8MM **Privately Held**
WEB: www.haslettmechanical.com
SIC: 1711 Warm air heating & air conditioning contractor

(G-10359)
HER INC
Also Called: H E R Realtors
5725 Perimeter Dr (43017-3216)
PHONE..................614 889-7400
Matthew Long, *Exec VP*
Mike Peebles, *Vice Pres*
Elia Hughes, *Senior Buyer*
Susan Crank, *Broker*
Randal Miller, *Sales Mgr*

(PA)=Parent Co (HQ)=Headquarters (DH)=Div Headquarters
✪ = New Business established in last 2 years

Dublin - Franklin County (G-10360)

EMP: 120
SALES (corp-wide): 14.3MM Privately Held
WEB: www.eassent.com
SIC: 6531 Real estate brokers & agents
PA: Her, Inc
4261 Morse Rd
Columbus OH 43230
614 221-7400

(G-10360)
HERITAGE WRRANTY INSUR RRG INC
Also Called: Heritage Administration Svcs
400 Metro Pl N Ste 300 (43017-3377)
PHONE 800 753-5236
Haytham H Elzayn, *CEO*
Larry S Roseberry, *President*
Stephen E Goodrich, *Vice Pres*
Ronald L Uhing, *CFO*
Gary H Osborne, *Asst Treas*
EMP: 73 EST: 1998
SQ FT: 15,000
SALES (est): 19.7MM Privately Held
WEB: www.heritagewarranty.com
SIC: 6399 Warranty insurance, automobile

(G-10361)
HILL DISTRIBUTING COMPANY
5080 Tuttle Crossing Blvd # 100 (43016-3541)
PHONE 614 276-6533
Fax: 614 276-8888
Charles D Hill Jr, *Ch of Bd*
Cynthia Hill Conie, *President*
Christine Hill Wilson, *Vice Pres*
Cammi Rose, *Manager*
▲ **EMP:** 90
SQ FT: 50,400
SALES (est): 14.5MM Privately Held
WEB: www.hilldist
SIC: 5181 5149 Beer & other fermented malt liquors; mineral or spring water bottling

(G-10362)
HIT PORTFOLIO I HIL TRS LLC
Also Called: Hampton Inn Columbus Airport
3920 Tuller Rd (43017-5020)
PHONE 614 235-0717
Fax: 614 792-6652
Sandy Jervis, *Sales Executive*
Ken Morgan, *Manager*
EMP: 31
SALES (corp-wide): 621MM Privately Held
SIC: 7011 Hotels
HQ: Hit Portfolio I Hil Trs, Llc
3950 University Dr # 301
Fairfax VA 22030
212 415-6500

(G-10363)
HLG ENGINEERING & SURVEY INC
5980 Wilcox Pl Ste G (43016-6809)
PHONE 614 760-8320
Charlie Rollings, *President*
EMP: 40
SALES (est): 3.3MM Privately Held
SIC: 8711 Engineering services

(G-10364)
HOLO PUNDITS INC
425 Metro Pl N Ste 440 (43017-5325)
PHONE 614 707-5225
Vinod Dega, *CEO*
EMP: 50 EST: 2013
SALES: 20K Privately Held
SIC: 7371 Computer software writing services

(G-10365)
HOTEL 2345 LLC
Also Called: Cloverleaf Suites
4130 Tuller Rd (43017-9502)
PHONE 614 766-7762
Ritesh Jariwala,
EMP: 30
SALES (est): 623.7K Privately Held
SIC: 7011 Inns

(G-10366)
HR BUTLER LLC
63 Corbins Mill Dr Ste A (43017-8314)
PHONE 614 923-2900
Thomas Hedge, *President*
EMP: 25 EST: 2000
SALES (est): 1.5MM Privately Held
SIC: 8721 8742 Payroll accounting service; human resource consulting services

(G-10367)
HULL & ASSOCIATES INC (PA)
6397 Emerald Pkwy Ste 200 (43016-2231)
PHONE 614 793-8777
Fax: 614 793-9070
John H Hull, *Ch of Bd*
Craig A Kasper, *President*
Michael C Cermak, *Vice Pres*
David L Richards, *Vice Pres*
Jenny Lupescu, *Manager*
EMP: 50
SQ FT: 9,180
SALES (est): 39.8MM Privately Held
WEB: www.hullinc.com
SIC: 8711 8748 Consulting engineer; environmental consultant

(G-10368)
HUMANA INC
485 Metro Pl S Ste 410 (43017-5366)
PHONE 614 210-1038
Jane Hirsch, *Manager*
EMP: 41
SALES (corp-wide): 53.7B Publicly Held
SIC: 6324 Health maintenance organization (HMO), insurance only
PA: Humana Inc.
500 W Main St Ste 300
Louisville KY 40202
502 580-1000

(G-10369)
HUNTINGTON NATIONAL BANK
4300 Tuller Rd (43017-5008)
PHONE 614 336-4620
EMP: 100
SALES (corp-wide): 3.7B Publicly Held
SIC: 6099 Depository Banking Services
HQ: The Huntington National Bank
17 S High St Fl 1
Columbus OH 43215
614 480-4293

(G-10370)
HUSKY MARKETING AND SUPPLY CO
Also Called: Husky Energy
5550 Blazer Pkwy Ste 200 (43017-3478)
PHONE 614 210-2300
Scott Howard, *General Mgr*
Rod Cundiff, *Business Mgr*
Stephan Kessen, *Maint Spvr*
Jon Frueh, *Engineer*
Brook Urban, *Engineer*
EMP: 40
SALES (est): 191.6K
SALES (corp-wide): 9.5B Privately Held
SIC: 1321 1382 Natural gasoline production; oil & gas exploration services
PA: Husky Energy Inc
707 8 Ave Sw
Calgary AB T2P 1
403 298-6111

(G-10371)
HYLANT GROUP INC
Also Called: Hylant Group of Columbus
565 Metro Pl S Ste 450 (43017-5386)
PHONE 614 932-1200
Craig Markos, *Manager*
EMP: 30
SALES (corp-wide): 122MM Privately Held
WEB: www.hylant.com
SIC: 6411 Insurance agents
PA: Hylant Group, Inc.
811 Madison Ave Fl 11
Toledo OH 43604
419 255-1020

(G-10372)
HYLANT-MACLEAN INC
Also Called: Hylant Group
565 Metro Pl S Ste 450 (43017-5386)
PHONE 614 932-1200
Fax: 614 932-1299
Craig Markos, *President*
Steve Federer, *Vice Pres*
Rebecca Salvato, *Client Mgr*
Cathy Alexa, *Manager*
Heather Oder, *Executive*
EMP: 43
SALES (est): 1.4MM Privately Held
SIC: 6411 Insurance agents

(G-10373)
IGS SOLAR LLC
6100 Emerald Pkwy (43016-3248)
PHONE 844 447-7652
Scott H White, *President*
EMP: 31 EST: 2014
SALES (est): 11.4MM Privately Held
SIC: 4911 Electric services

(G-10374)
INDECON SOLUTIONS LLC
655 Metro Pl S Ste 740 (43017-3356)
PHONE 614 799-1850
Fax: 614 799-3505
Lily Comisso, *Accounts Exec*
Edward Haas, *Manager*
Haley Moore, *Info Tech Dir*
Phil Dauphin, *Executive*
Kayla Gully, *Tech Recruiter*
EMP: 50
SALES (corp-wide): 46.7MM Privately Held
WEB: www.indeconinc.com
SIC: 7371 7379 8748 Custom computer programming services; data processing consultant; systems engineering consultant, ex. computer or professional
HQ: Indecon Solutions, Llc
115 W Washington St # 1310
Indianapolis IN 46204
317 634-9482

(G-10375)
INFOVERITY LLC
5131 Post Rd Ste 220 (43017-2194)
PHONE 614 327-5173
Matthew Wienke, *Partner*
Paras Baral, *Consultant*
Turner Engle, *Consultant*
Enrique Guzman, *Consultant*
David Nacy, *Consultant*
EMP: 40
SQ FT: 2,500
SALES: 1MM Privately Held
SIC: 8748 7389 Business consulting;

(G-10376)
INFOVISION 21 INC
6077 Frantz Rd Ste 105 (43017-3373)
PHONE 614 761-8844
Bapaiah Koneru, *President*
Naveen Paruchuri, *Programmer Anys*
Marc Bandman, *Director*
EMP: 44 EST: 1996
SQ FT: 2,500
SALES: 5MM Privately Held
WEB: www.infovision21.com
SIC: 7374 7371 7379 Data processing & preparation; computer software development; computer related consulting services

(G-10377)
INTEGRA CNCINNATI/COLUMBUS INC
Also Called: Dublin
6241 Riverside Dr (43017-5068)
PHONE 614 764-8040
Bruce Daubner, *President*
Mariann Bellman, *Office Mgr*
Gary Wright, *Director*
EMP: 30
SALES (est): 1.6MM Privately Held
SIC: 6531 Real estate agents & managers

(G-10378)
INTERSTATE GAS SUPPLY INC (PA)
6100 Emerald Pkwy (43016-3248)
P.O. Box 9060 (43017-0960)
PHONE 614 659-5000
Fax: 614 659-5993
Scott White, *President*
Jim Baich, *COO*
Doug Austin, *Exec VP*
Jason Moore, *Vice Pres*
Patrick Smith, *Vice Pres*
EMP: 190
SQ FT: 100,000
SALES: 1.4B Privately Held
WEB: www.igsenergy.com
SIC: 1311 Natural gas production

(G-10379)
JACKSON I-94 LTD PARTNERSHIP
Also Called: Rodeway Inn
6059 Frantz Rd Ste 205 (43017-3368)
PHONE 614 793-2244
Earl Blinn, *Owner*
Castrop Wolfe, *General Ptnr*
EMP: 28
SQ FT: 2,400
SALES (est): 323K Privately Held
SIC: 7011 5812 Hotels & motels; eating places

(G-10380)
JOHNSON CNTRLS SEC SLTIONS LLC
6175 Shamrock Ct Ste S (43016-1224)
PHONE 561 988-3600
Fax: 614 771-8598
Edwina Simpson, *Human Res Mgr*
Mark Williamson, *Branch Mgr*
Taylor Youtzy, *Manager*
EMP: 134 Privately Held
WEB: www.adt.com
SIC: 7382 Burglar alarm maintenance & monitoring; fire alarm maintenance & monitoring
HQ: Johnson Controls Security Solutions Llc
4700 Exchange Ct Ste 300
Boca Raton FL 33431
561 264-2071

(G-10381)
JOHNSON CONTROLS
6175 Shamrock Ct Ste S (43016-1224)
PHONE 614 602-2000
Fax: 614 481-8945
Tom Rosenberger, *Project Mgr*
Eric Cowan, *Sales Staff*
Christopher Landes, *Sales Staff*
Tom Clapp, *Manager*
Stephen Hicks, *Manager*
EMP: 55 Privately Held
WEB: www.simplexgrinnell.com
SIC: 1711 5999 Fire sprinkler system installation; fire extinguishers
HQ: Johnson Controls Fire Protection Lp
4700 Exchange Ct Ste 300
Boca Raton FL 33431
561 988-7200

(G-10382)
JOHNSON CONTROLS
6175 Shamrock Ct (43016-1200)
PHONE 614 717-9079
Herbert Reinhold, *Vice Pres*
Tom Rosenberger, *Project Mgr*
Mike Skunza, *Sales & Mktg St*
Eric Cowan, *Sales Staff*
Charlotte Knakiewicz, *Sales Staff*
EMP: 99 Privately Held
WEB: www.simplexgrinnell.com
SIC: 1711 Fire sprinkler system installation
HQ: Johnson Controls Fire Protection Lp
4700 Exchange Ct Ste 300
Boca Raton FL 33431
561 988-7200

(G-10383)
JUNIPER NETWORKS INC
545 Metro Pl S Ste 164 (43017-5316)
PHONE 614 932-1432
Mike Isler, *Manager*
EMP: 72 Publicly Held
WEB: www.juniper.net
SIC: 7373 7372 Local area network (LAN) systems integrator; prepackaged software
PA: Juniper Networks, Inc.
1133 Innovation Way
Sunnyvale CA 94089

(G-10384)
L&T TECHNOLOGY SERVICES LTD
5550 Blazer Pkwy Ste 125 (43017-3482)
PHONE 732 688-4402
Feroz Reza, *Manager*
EMP: 50

GEOGRAPHIC SECTION
Dublin - Franklin County (G-10407)

SALES (corp-wide): 465.1MM **Privately Held**
SIC: 8711 Acoustical engineering
PA: L&T Technology Services Limited
  5th, Floor, West Block-Ii, L&T Knowledge City (It/Ites) Sez
  Vadodara GJ 39001
  265 670-5000

(G-10385)
LABORATORY CORPORATION AMERICA
5920 Wilcox Pl Ste F (43016-6802)
PHONE..................614 336-3993
Fax: 614 761-1855
Dwobeng Owusu-Nyamekye, *Opers Mgr*
Jimmy Seipel, *Human Res Mgr*
Pam Oliver, *Branch Mgr*
Steve Jones, *Manager*
Michelle Troyer, *Info Tech Mgr*
EMP: 608
SQ FT: 82,000 **Publicly Held**
WEB: www.labcorp.com
SIC: 8071 8731 Testing laboratories; commercial physical research
HQ: Laboratory Corporation Of America
  358 S Main St Ste 458
  Burlington NC 27215
  336 229-1127

(G-10386)
LEE & ASSOCIATES INC
Also Called: Lee & Associates - Columbus
5100 Prkcnter Ave Ste 100 (43017)
PHONE..................614 923-3300
Tim Kelton, *Principal*
EMP: 32 **Privately Held**
SIC: 6531 Real estate brokers & agents
PA: Lee & Associates Inc.
  3200 E Camelback Rd # 100
  Phoenix AZ 85018

(G-10387)
LIBERTY VLG SENIOR COMMUNITIES
Also Called: Liberty Village Manor
4248 Tuller Rd Ste 201 (43017-5025)
PHONE..................614 889-5002
John M Haemmerle, *President*
EMP: 40
SALES (est): 558.8K **Privately Held**
SIC: 8059 Personal care home, with health care

(G-10388)
LIFE TIME FITNESS INC
3825 Hard Rd (43016-8335)
PHONE..................952 229-7158
Rob Zwelling, *Principal*
EMP: 132
SALES (corp-wide): 773.5MM **Privately Held**
SIC: 7991 Health club
HQ: Life Time Fitness, Inc.
  2902 Corporate Pl
  Chanhassen MN 55317

(G-10389)
LIGHTWELL INC (PA)
565 Metro Pl S Ste 220 (43017-5380)
PHONE..................614 310-2700
Michelle Abreu, *Ch of Bd*
Michelle Kerr, *Chairman*
Bryan Scott, *Accounts Exec*
Susan Sever, *Accounts Exec*
Mike Warvel, *Accounts Exec*
EMP: 46
SQ FT: 7,500
SALES (est): 16.8MM **Privately Held**
WEB: www.oxford-consulting.com
SIC: 7379

(G-10390)
LODGING FIRST LLC
94 N High St Ste 250 (43017-1110)
PHONE..................614 792-2770
Brian Moloney, *Vice Pres*
Patrick Quinn, *Vice Pres*
Jessica Distel, *Asst Controller*
Terri Beckett, *Sales Mgr*
Sindy Radcliff, *Sales Staff*
EMP: 50
SALES (est): 1MM **Privately Held**
WEB: www.fighospitality.com
SIC: 7021 Rooming & boarding houses

(G-10391)
LOGIC SOFT INC
Also Called: Www.logicsoftusa.com
5900 Sawmill Rd Ste 200 (43017-2588)
PHONE..................614 884-5544
Ketan Shah, *CEO*
Satish Barapatre, *President*
Harish Kukreja, *Exec VP*
EMP: 55
SQ FT: 3,000
SALES (est): 9.3MM **Privately Held**
SIC: 7371 Computer software systems analysis & design, custom

(G-10392)
LOWES HOME CENTERS LLC
6555 Dublin Center Dr (43017-5016)
PHONE..................614 659-0530
Fax: 614 659-0547
Shane Thompson, *Manager*
EMP: 150
SALES (corp-wide): 68.6B **Publicly Held**
SIC: 5211 5031 5722 5064 Home centers; building materials, exterior; building materials, interior; household appliance stores; electrical appliances, television & radio
HQ: Lowe's Home Centers, Llc
  1605 Curtis Bridge Rd
  Wilkesboro NC 28697
  336 658-4000

(G-10393)
MEDCO HEALTH SOLUTIONS INC
Also Called: Express Script
5151 Blazer Pkwy Ste B (43017-9307)
PHONE..................614 822-2000
William Kelly, *Manager*
Mark Klopfer, *Manager*
Amy Aldighere, *Director*
Christopher Mulier, *Director*
EMP: 800
SALES (corp-wide): 100B **Publicly Held**
WEB: www.merck-medco.com
SIC: 5961 8742 Pharmaceuticals, mail order; management consulting services
HQ: Medco Health Solutions, Inc.
  100 Parsons Pond Dr
  Franklin Lakes NJ 07417
  201 269-3400

(G-10394)
MEEDER ASSET MANAGEMENT INC
6125 Memor Dr (43017)
P.O. Box 7177 (43017-0777)
PHONE..................614 760-2112
Robert S Meeder Jr, *President*
Donald F Meeder, *Vice Pres*
EMP: 58
SQ FT: 10,000
SALES (est): 6.1MM **Privately Held**
WEB: www.meederadvisoryservices.com
SIC: 6282 Investment counselors

(G-10395)
MERRILL LYNCH PIERCE FENNER
555 Metro Pl N Ste 550 (43017-5303)
PHONE..................614 798-4354
Fax: 614 798-4398
Ted L Altenburg, *Vice Pres*
Robert Bishop, *Vice Pres*
David Morosky, *Manager*
EMP: 25
SALES (corp-wide): 100.2B **Publicly Held**
WEB: www.merlyn.com
SIC: 6211 Brokers, security
HQ: Merrill Lynch, Pierce, Fenner & Smith Incorporated
  111 8th Ave
  New York NY 10011
  800 637-7455

(G-10396)
METROPOLITAN LIFE INSUR CO
Also Called: MetLife
5600 Blazer Pkwy Ste 100 (43017-7525)
PHONE..................614 792-1463
Michael A Schlegel, *General Mgr*
Liz Tambellini, *Accounts Mgr*
Cheryl Eveas, *Manager*
Richard Lee, *Prgrmr*
EMP: 100
SALES (corp-wide): 63.4B **Publicly Held**
SIC: 6411 Insurance agents & brokers
HQ: Metropolitan Life Insurance Company (Inc)
  501 Us Highway 22
  Bridgewater NJ 08807
  212 578-2211

(G-10397)
MICROMAN INC (PA)
Also Called: Telephony & Data Solutions
4393 Tuller Rd Ste A (43017-5106)
PHONE..................614 923-8000
Fax: 614 792-6868
Bradford Mandell, *COO*
Carles Dalmau, *Vice Pres*
Ian Lloyd, *Project Mgr*
Frank Roberto, *Project Mgr*
Amber Brown, *Purchasing*
EMP: 42
SQ FT: 23,873
SALES: 14.9MM **Privately Held**
WEB: www.tel-dat.com
SIC: 5734 7373 Computer & software stores; computer peripheral equipment; software, business & non-game; computer integrated systems design

(G-10398)
MIDWEST GYMNSTICS CHEERLEADING
Also Called: Mgc
9361 Pratolino Villa Dr (43016-7376)
PHONE..................614 764-0775
Fax: 614 764-7344
Louis Robinson, *President*
Carol Robinson, *Exec VP*
EMP: 28
SQ FT: 18,500
SALES (est): 906.4K **Privately Held**
WEB: www.midwestgymandcheer.com
SIC: 7032 7999 7997 Sporting & recreational camps; gymnastic instruction, non-membership; membership sports & recreation clubs

(G-10399)
MITSUBSHI INTL FD INGRDNTS INC (DH)
5080 Tuttle Crossing Blvd (43016-3540)
PHONE..................614 652-1111
Gerry McKiernan, *CEO*
Montgomery Emmanuel, *CFO*
Bridget Shrigley, *Accounts Mgr*
Hai Vo, *Accounts Mgr*
Saurav Goyal, *Sales Staff*
▲ **EMP:** 35
SQ FT: 10,800
SALES (est): 150MM
SALES (corp-wide): 56.5B **Privately Held**
SIC: 5169 Food additives & preservatives
HQ: Mitsubishi Corporation (Americas)
  655 3rd Ave
  New York NY 10017
  212 605-2000

(G-10400)
MORGAN STANLEY & CO LLC
545 Metro Pl S Ste 300 (43017-3385)
PHONE..................614 798-3100
Michael Zid, *Branch Mgr*
EMP: 35
SALES (corp-wide): 43.6B **Publicly Held**
WEB: www.msvp.com
SIC: 6211 Security brokers & dealers
HQ: Morgan Stanley & Co. Llc
  1585 Broadway
  New York NY 10036
  212 761-4000

(G-10401)
MUIRFIELD ASSOCIATION INC
8372 Muirfield Dr (43017-8590)
PHONE..................614 889-0922
Fax: 614 889-1142
Warren Fishman, *President*
Walter Zeier, *Manager*
EMP: 30
SQ FT: 2,500
SALES (est): 1.1MM **Privately Held**
WEB: www.muirfieldassociation.com
SIC: 8641 Homeowners' association

(G-10402)
MUIRFIELD VILLAGE GOLF CLUB
Also Called: Memorial Tournament, The
5750 Memorial Dr (43017-9742)
PHONE..................614 889-6700
Fax: 614 889-0084
Jack Nicklaus, *President*
Nicholas La Rocca, *General Mgr*
Nicholas Larocca, *General Mgr*
Kevin Kennebeck, *COO*
John G Hines, *Vice Pres*
EMP: 50 **EST:** 1972
SQ FT: 40,000
SALES (est): 10.2MM **Privately Held**
WEB: www.muirfieldvillagegolfclub.com
SIC: 7997 Golf club, membership

(G-10403)
NATIONAL ADMINISTATIVE SVC LLC
400 Metro Pl N Ste 360 (43017-3318)
PHONE..................614 358-3607
Michelle Defouw, *Manager*
Haytham Elzayn,
EMP: 25
SQ FT: 10,000
SALES (est): 1.3MM **Privately Held**
SIC: 8742 Administrative services consultant

(G-10404)
NATIONAL CITY MORTGAGE
545 Metro Pl S Ste 100 (43017-5353)
PHONE..................614 401-5030
George Maloof, *Vice Pres*
EMP: 32
SALES (est): 2.2MM **Privately Held**
SIC: 6021 National commercial banks

(G-10405)
NATIONWIDE RTIREMENT SOLUTIONS (DH)
5900 Parkwood Pl (43016-1216)
P.O. Box 182171, Columbus (43218-2171)
PHONE..................614 854-8300
Duane Meek, *President*
Chris Cole, *Manager*
EMP: 125
SQ FT: 7,000
SALES (est): 32.6MM
SALES (corp-wide): 26.6B **Privately Held**
WEB: www.pebscomo.com
SIC: 6371 8748 8742 6411 Pension funds; employee programs administration; management consulting services; insurance agents, brokers & service
HQ: Nationwide Corporation
  1 Nationwide Plz
  Columbus OH 43215
  614 249-7111

(G-10406)
NESTLE USA INC
Also Called: Nestle Quality Assurance Ctr
6625 Eiterman Rd (43016-8727)
PHONE..................614 526-5300
Les Smoot, *Manager*
Timothy Jackson, *Manager*
Todd Tritcak, *Manager*
EMP: 85
SALES (corp-wide): 88.4B **Privately Held**
WEB: www.nestleusa.com
SIC: 8734 Food testing service
HQ: Nestle Usa, Inc.
  1812 N Moore St
  Rosslyn VA 22209
  818 549-6000

(G-10407)
NETSMART TECHNOLOGIES INC
5455 Rings Rd (43017-3573)
PHONE..................614 764-0143
Rick Bennett, *Engineer*
Thomas Bown, *Engineer*
Joshua Bradley, *Engineer*
Shawn Martin, *Engineer*
Dj Nauta, *Engineer*
EMP: 60 **Privately Held**
SIC: 7371 8742 5045 7373 Custom computer programming services; management consulting services; computers, peripherals & software; value-added resellers, computer systems

Dublin - Franklin County (G-10408)   GEOGRAPHIC SECTION

PA: Netsmart Technologies, Inc.
4950 College Blvd
Overland Park KS 66211

(G-10408)
NETWAVE CORPORATION
6457 Reflections Dr # 130 (43017-2352)
PHONE..............................614 850-6300
Fax: 614 771-9056
Steve Hoffman, *President*
Mark Goodson, *Vice Pres*
Joe Dipiero, *Accounts Mgr*
EMP: 26
SQ FT: 13,000
SALES (est): 5.1MM **Privately Held**
WEB: www.netwavecorp.com
SIC: 7379 5045 Computer related consulting services; computers, peripherals & software

(G-10409)
NIGHTINGALE HOME HEALTHCARE
Also Called: Aspire Home Healthcare of Ohio
5945 Wilcox Pl Ste C (43016-8713)
PHONE..............................614 408-0104
Dev A Brar MD, *Owner*
EMP: 36 **Privately Held**
SIC: 8082 Home health care services
PA: Nightingale Home Healthcare Inc
1036 S Rangeline Rd
Carmel IN 46032

(G-10410)
NORTHWODS CNSLTING PRTNERS INC
Also Called: Cabin In The Wood
5815 Wall St (43017-3264)
PHONE..............................614 781-7800
Fax: 614 781-7801
Gary Heinze, *President*
David Michael George, *President*
Chris McConnell, *Business Mgr*
Chris Carlson, *COO*
Jon Petersen, *Vice Pres*
EMP: 118
SQ FT: 4,000
SALES (est): 20.3MM **Privately Held**
WEB: www.teamnorthwoods.com
SIC: 7371 Computer software development

(G-10411)
NRT COMMERCIAL UTAH LLC
Also Called: Coldwell Banker
4535 W Dblin Granville Rd (43017-2081)
PHONE..............................614 889-0808
Sheri Cook, *President*
Jerry White, *Exec VP*
Lanae Aulino, *Sales Staff*
Michael Busch, *Sales Staff*
Herman England, *Sales Staff*
EMP: 28 **Publicly Held**
WEB: www.nrtinc.com
SIC: 6531 Real estate agent, residential
HQ: Nrt Commercial Utah Llc
175 Park Ave
Madison NJ 07940

(G-10412)
OCLC INC (PA)
6565 Kilgour Pl (43017-3395)
PHONE..............................614 764-6000
Fax: 614 764-6096
David A Prichard, *President*
Susan Walker, *President*
Norbert Weinberger, *Managing Dir*
Pat Ring, *Principal*
Antonio Jose A Santana, *Regional Mgr*
EMP: 860
SQ FT: 350,000
SALES: 208.3MM **Privately Held**
WEB: www.purl.org
SIC: 7375 On-line data base information retrieval

(G-10413)
OHIO HEALTHCARE FEDERAL CR UN (PA)
3955 W Dblin Granville Rd (43017-1435)
PHONE..............................614 737-6034
William Butler, *President*
Christy Oconnell, *CFO*
Samantha Smith,
EMP: 31

SALES: 3.6MM **Privately Held**
SIC: 6061 Federal credit unions

(G-10414)
OHIO SEED IMPROVEMENT ASSN
6150 Avery Rd (43016-8760)
P.O. Box 477 (43017-0477)
PHONE..............................614 889-1136
Fax: 614 889-8979
Howard Tallman, *President*
Ned Thurn, *President*
John Armstrong, *Admin Sec*
EMP: 59
SALES: 709.8K **Privately Held**
SIC: 8733 Research institute

(G-10415)
OHIO STATE MEDICAL ASSOCIATION (PA)
Also Called: OSMA
5115 Prkcnter Ave Ste 200 (43017)
PHONE..............................614 527-6762
Fax: 614 527-6763
Richard R Ellison, *President*
Kelsey Hardin, *Research*
Lisa Miller, *Accountant*
Peggy Sears, *Sales Staff*
Reginald Fields, *Comms Dir*
EMP: 53 EST: 1904
SQ FT: 35,000
SALES: 6MM **Privately Held**
WEB: www.osma.org
SIC: 8621 Medical field-related associations

(G-10416)
OHIOHEALTH CORPORATION
Also Called: Dublin Methodist Hospital
7500 Hospital Dr (43016-8518)
PHONE..............................614 544-8000
Cheryl Herbert, *President*
Harry Trombitas, *Vice Pres*
Renee Pharris, *Opers Mgr*
Jason McGuire, *Materials Mgr*
Diane Shaub, *Human Res Dir*
EMP: 500
SALES (corp-wide): 3.7B **Privately Held**
WEB: www.ohiohealth.com
SIC: 8062 General medical & surgical hospitals
PA: Ohiohealth Corporation
180 E Broad St
Columbus OH 43215
614 788-8860

(G-10417)
ORTHOPAEDIC & SPINE CENTER AT
6810 Perimeter Dr 200a (43016-8013)
PHONE..............................614 468-0300
Heather Gore,
EMP: 28
SALES (est): 3.5MM **Privately Held**
WEB: www.orthopaedicandspinecenter.com
SIC: 8011 Orthopedic physician

(G-10418)
OSU INTERNAL MEDICINE LLC (PA)
3900 Stoneridge Ln Ste B (43017-2289)
PHONE..............................614 293-0080
Fax: 614 366-9339
Earnest Mazzaferri MD, *President*
Earl Metz MD, *Vice Pres*
Joyce Martin, *CFO*
John Fromkes MD, *Treasurer*
Melissa Hall, *Mktg Dir*
EMP: 55
SQ FT: 17,500
SALES (est): 11.2MM **Privately Held**
SIC: 8741 Business management

(G-10419)
OXFORD BLAZER COMPANY INC
5700 Blazer Pkwy Ste B (43017-3665)
PHONE..............................614 792-2220
Rochelle Kiner, *Principal*
Christopher Black, *Principal*
EMP: 26
SQ FT: 85,263

SALES (est): 1.3MM **Privately Held**
SIC: 8351 6324 Preschool center; health maintenance organization (HMO), insurance only

(G-10420)
PACE ANALYTICAL SERVICES INC
4860 Blazer Pkwy (43017-3302)
PHONE..............................614 486-5421
Fax: 614 487-1480
Harry M Borg, *General Mgr*
Alicia Barnes, *Project Mgr*
Eric Nielsen, *Marketing Staff*
EMP: 35
SALES (corp-wide): 65.2MM **Privately Held**
SIC: 8734 Testing laboratories
HQ: Pace Analytical Services, Llc
1800 Elm St Se
Minneapolis MN 55414

(G-10421)
PARALLEL TECHNOLOGIES INC
4868 Blazer Pkwy (43017-3302)
PHONE..............................614 798-9700
Fax: 614 798-1701
Joseph Redman, *President*
Martin B Jacobs, *Senior VP*
Sarah Redman, *Personnel Exec*
Tori Lewis, *Sales Staff*
Todd Poling, *Manager*
EMP: 80
SQ FT: 8,500
SALES (est): 15.2MM **Privately Held**
WEB: www.paralleltech.com
SIC: 1623 7372 Telephone & communication line construction; business oriented computer software
PA: R C I Communications Inc
4868 Blazer Pkwy
Dublin OH 43017
614 798-9700

(G-10422)
PARKS DRILLING COMPANY (PA)
5745 Avery Rd (43016-8756)
PHONE..............................614 761-7707
Fax: 614 761-9379
Jim Parks, *CEO*
Danel Duff, *President*
David Bhornbeck, *Principal*
Trent Southworth, *Vice Pres*
Jim Hathaway, *Project Mgr*
EMP: 25 EST: 1971
SQ FT: 8,000
SALES (est): 7.5MM **Privately Held**
SIC: 1629 Caisson drilling

(G-10423)
PAYCHEX INC
5080 Tuttle Crossing Blvd # 450 (43016-3500)
PHONE..............................614 210-0400
Fax: 614 734-9862
Jim McElwain, *CPA*
Michael Boczek, *Sales Mgr*
Rose Roesch, *Sales Associate*
Dana Abramski, *Sales Executive*
Scott Muenzer, *Manager*
EMP: 83
SALES (corp-wide): 3.1B **Publicly Held**
WEB: www.paychex.com
SIC: 8721 Payroll accounting service
PA: Paychex, Inc.
911 Panorama Trl S
Rochester NY 14625
585 385-6666

(G-10424)
PCCW TELESERVICES (US) INC (PA)
Also Called: Influent
5200 Rings Rd (43017-3557)
PHONE..............................614 652-6300
Fax: 614 280-1610
Andrew C Jacobs, *Ch of Bd*
Mark K Attinger, *President*
Scott P Lee, *Corp Secy*
Ken Cross, *Vice Pres*
Jim Garwood, *Vice Pres*
EMP: 1300
SQ FT: 10,000

SALES (est): 66.7MM **Privately Held**
WEB: www.influentinc.com
SIC: 7299 7389 Personal financial services; telemarketing services

(G-10425)
PEPPER CNSTR CO OHIO LLC
495 Metro Pl S Ste 350 (43017-5399)
PHONE..............................614 793-4477
Paul Francois, *President*
Christopher Averill, *Exec VP*
Debbie Connolly, *Admin Asst*
Kate Holstein, *Administration*
EMP: 40
SALES: 84.6MM
SALES (corp-wide): 1.1B **Privately Held**
SIC: 1542 1541 Commercial & office building, new construction; industrial buildings & warehouses
HQ: Pepper Construction Group, Llc
643 N Orleans St
Chicago IL 60654
312 266-4700

(G-10426)
PERIO INC (PA)
Also Called: Franklin Dental Manufacturing
6156 Wilcox Rd (43016-1265)
PHONE..............................614 791-1207
Fax: 614 792-0484
Tom Murray, *CEO*
John Price, *Principal*
Melanie Murray, *Corp Secy*
Don Buckingham, *Vice Pres*
Chad Beining, *Accountant*
◆ EMP: 37
SQ FT: 14,000
SALES (est): 21.8MM **Privately Held**
WEB: www.barbasol.com
SIC: 5047 5087 8052 Dentists' professional supplies; beauty parlor equipment & supplies; personal care facility

(G-10427)
PMI SUPPLY INC
Also Called: Progressive Medical Intl
5000 Tuttle Crossing Blvd (43016-1534)
PHONE..............................760 598-1128
Mark Cervenka, *Vice Pres*
Steve Carbone, *Controller*
Barbara Nelson, *Manager*
Kim Gardner, *Technician*
▲ EMP: 60
SALES (est): 10.2MM **Privately Held**
SIC: 5047 Medical equipment & supplies
PA: Sarnova Inc.
5000 Tuttle Crossing Blvd
Dublin OH 43016

(G-10428)
POPPER & ASSOCIATES MSRP LLC
7153 Timberview Dr (43017-1017)
PHONE..............................614 798-8991
John Popper, *CEO*
EMP: 50
SALES (est): 1.6MM **Privately Held**
SIC: 7331 7389 Direct mail advertising services;

(G-10429)
PRESIDIO INFRASTRUCTURE
5025 Bradenton Ave Ste B (43017-3506)
PHONE..............................614 381-1400
Fax: 614 336-7807
Melissa Curtis, *Project Mgr*
Chris Couch, *Engineer*
Michael Duffer, *Engineer*
Kristen Kropat, *Engineer*
Adam Perkins, *Engineer*
EMP: 36
SALES (corp-wide): 1.1B **Publicly Held**
SIC: 7373 Computer integrated systems design
HQ: Presidio Infrastructure Solutions Llc
6355 E Paris Ave Se
Caledonia MI 49316
616 871-1500

(G-10430)
PRIMARY CARE NURSING SERVICES
3140 Lilly Mar Ct (43017-5075)
PHONE..............................614 764-0960
Fax: 614 761-0696
Susan M Sharpe, *President*

▲ = Import ▼ = Export
◆ = Import/Export

GEOGRAPHIC SECTION
Dublin - Franklin County (G-10454)

Susan Sharp, *Admin Asst*
EMP: 52
SALES (est): 1.6MM **Privately Held**
WEB: www.pcnsohio.com
SIC: 8082 8011 Visiting nurse service; offices & clinics of medical doctors

(G-10431)
PRIMERO HOME LOANS LLC
4725 Lakehurst Ct Ste 400 (43016-2251)
PHONE.................877 959-2921
Robert Griffith, *CEO*
Brian Folwarezy, *Exec VP*
Tom Guy, *Project Mgr*
Debbie Foley, *Manager*
Brian Folwarczny, *Officer*
EMP: 80
SQ FT: 240,000
SALES (est): 20MM **Privately Held**
WEB: www.fearonfinancial.com
SIC: 6162 Mortgage bankers

(G-10432)
PSI SUPPLY CHAIN SOLUTIONS LLC
5050 Bradenton Ave (43017-3520)
P.O. Box 130 (43017-0130)
PHONE.................614 389-4717
Stuart A Bishop, *Ch of Bd*
Michael P McCarrell, *President*
EMP: 25
SALES (est): 291.7K
SALES (corp-wide): 76.9MM **Privately Held**
SIC: 8742 Hospital & health services consultant
HQ: Pharmacy Systems, Inc.
5050 Bradenton Ave
Dublin OH
614 766-0101

(G-10433)
QUALITY SUPPLY CHAIN CO-OP INC
1 Dave Thomas Blvd (43017-5452)
PHONE.................614 764-3124
John Inwright, *President*
Ed Medlock, *Senior VP*
Amy Bertke, *Vice Pres*
Lorraine Green, *Vice Pres*
David Kourie, *Vice Pres*
EMP: 40
SALES (est): 5.1MM **Privately Held**
SIC: 8741 Business management

(G-10434)
QUEST SOFTWARE INC
Also Called: Aeilita Div
6500 Emerald Pkwy Ste 400 (43016-6234)
PHONE.................614 336-9223
Yinghua Qin, *Research*
Alan Burden, *Accounts Mgr*
Kevin Moore, *Accounts Mgr*
Eric Rowe, *Accounts Mgr*
Gib Patt, *Sales Staff*
EMP: 70
SALES (corp-wide): 1.6B **Privately Held**
WEB: www.quest.com
SIC: 7371 Computer software development
HQ: Quest Software, Inc.
4 Polaris Way
Aliso Viejo CA 92656
949 754-8000

(G-10435)
QWEST CORPORATION
4650 Lakehurst Ct Ste 100 (43016-3254)
PHONE.................614 793-9258
Marshall Hanno, *Vice Pres*
James D Heflinger, *Vice Pres*
Tom Wynne, *Branch Mgr*
James T Bartlett, *Director*
Stephen W Fillo, *Director*
EMP: 59
SALES (corp-wide): 17.6B **Publicly Held**
SIC: 4813 Telephone communication, except radio
HQ: Qwest Corporation
100 Centurylink Dr
Monroe LA 71203
318 388-9000

(G-10436)
RACAZA INTERNATIONAL LLC
555 N Metro Pls Ste 245 (43017)
PHONE.................614 973-9266
Dyna Bala, *Principal*
Ila Mistry, *Principal*
Siva Bala, *Director*
EMP: 45 **EST:** 2010
SALES (est): 1.8MM **Privately Held**
SIC: 8711 Engineering services

(G-10437)
RANDALL MORTGAGE SERVICES (PA)
655 Metro Pl S Ste 600 (43017-3394)
PHONE.................614 336-7948
Fax: 614 923-4701
Robert R Shepherd, *President*
Eric D Anderson, *Assistant VP*
Thomas A Clarkson, *Vice Pres*
Barb Shepard, *Human Res Dir*
Matthew Schwadd, *Info Tech Mgr*
EMP: 123
SALES (est): 19.3MM **Privately Held**
SIC: 6163 Mortgage brokers arranging for loans, using money of others

(G-10438)
REA & ASSOCIATES INC
Also Called: Beall Rose Crtif Pub Accntants
5775 Perimeter Dr Ste 200 (43017-3224)
PHONE.................614 889-8725
Fax: 614 889-0159
Mark Beebe, *Accountant*
Leman G Beall, *Branch Mgr*
Tim McDaniel, *Director*
EMP: 33
SALES (corp-wide): 32.3MM **Privately Held**
WEB: www.reacpa.com
SIC: 8721 Certified public accountant
PA: Rea & Associates, Inc.
419 W High Ave
New Philadelphia OH 44663
330 339-6651

(G-10439)
REAL PROPERTY MANAGEMENT INC (PA)
5550 Blazer Pkwy Ste 175 (43017-3495)
PHONE.................614 766-6500
Matt Steele, *President*
Chad Reed, *Property Mgr*
Michelle Lowe, *Manager*
Brett Vanoss, *Administration*
EMP: 38
SQ FT: 10,000
SALES (est): 7.8MM **Privately Held**
WEB: www.rpmanagement.com
SIC: 6531 8721 Real estate managers; billing & bookkeeping service

(G-10440)
RICH CRITES & DITTMER LLC
6400 Rverside Dr Ste D100 (43017)
PHONE.................614 228-5822
Jeff Rich, *Manager*
Jeffrey A Rich,
Karol L Fox,
Mark H Gillis,
D Michael Crites,
EMP: 25
SQ FT: 7,700
SALES (est): 1.5MM **Privately Held**
WEB: www.richcrites.com
SIC: 8111 General practice attorney, lawyer

(G-10441)
RIVERSIDE DRV ANIMAL CARE CTR
6924 Riverside Dr (43017-9519)
PHONE.................614 414-2668
Fax: 614 766-7904
Becky Marsh, *Practice Mgr*
Jane Bock, *Administration*
David Abvp,
Robert A Hnson,
EMP: 50
SALES (est): 1.9MM **Privately Held**
SIC: 0742 Veterinarian, animal specialties

(G-10442)
ROBERT HALF INTERNATIONAL INC
5550 Blazer Pkwy Ste 250 (43017-3481)
PHONE.................614 602-0505
Krista Groves, *Branch Mgr*
EMP: 92
SALES (corp-wide): 5.2B **Publicly Held**
SIC: 7361 Labor contractors (employment agency)
PA: Robert Half International Inc.
2884 Sand Hill Rd Ste 200
Menlo Park CA 94025
650 234-6000

(G-10443)
ROLLING HOCEVAR & ASSOCIA
5980 Wilcox Pl Ste G (43016-6809)
PHONE.................614 760-8320
June Leader, *Principal*
Chris Rolling, *Principal*
EMP: 37
SALES (est): 2MM **Privately Held**
SIC: 7389 Business services

(G-10444)
ROTO GROUP LLC
7001 Discovery Blvd Fl 2 (43017-3261)
PHONE.................614 760-8690
Fax: 614 760-8691
Joseph Wisne, *President*
Steve Langsdorf, *Vice Pres*
Julia McAllister, *Project Mgr*
Janet Hurt, *CFO*
Jennifer Ives, *Controller*
EMP: 80
SQ FT: 60,000
SALES (est): 7MM **Privately Held**
WEB: www.rotostudio.com
SIC: 7999 Exhibition operation

(G-10445)
S&ME INC
6190 Enterprise Ct (43016-3293)
PHONE.................614 793-2226
Stephen C Pasternack, *Branch Mgr*
EMP: 76 **Privately Held**
SIC: 8711 Consulting engineer
PA: S&Me, Inc.
3201 Spring Forest Rd
Raleigh NC 27616

(G-10446)
SAFETY SOLUTIONS INC (HQ)
6161 Shamrock Ct (43016-1293)
P.O. Box 8100 (43016-2100)
PHONE.................614 799-9900
Fax: 614 799-9901
David L Forsthoffer, *President*
Mike Boone, *Vice Pres*
John Perrin, *Vice Pres*
Ann Bauman, *Sls & Mktg Exec*
Sid Alexander, *Manager*
EMP: 72
SQ FT: 65,000
SALES (est): 80.6MM
SALES (corp-wide): 10.4B **Publicly Held**
WEB: www.safetysolutions.com
SIC: 5084 5136 5139 Safety equipment; gloves, men's & boys'; shoes; boots
PA: W.W. Grainger, Inc.
100 Grainger Pkwy
Lake Forest IL 60045
847 535-1000

(G-10447)
SANCTUARY AT TUTTLE CROSSING
4880 Tuttle Rd (43017-7566)
PHONE.................614 408-0182
Fax: 614 336-4187
Robert Banasik, *President*
Amy Kerske, *Financial Exec*
EMP: 68
SALES (est): 3.3MM **Privately Held**
SIC: 8051 Skilled nursing care facilities

(G-10448)
SARNOVA INC (PA)
5000 Tuttle Crossing Blvd (43016-1534)
P.O. Box 8023 (43016-2023)
PHONE.................614 760-5000
Dan Connors, *CEO*
Brian Laduke, *President*
Tom Metcalf, *President*

Rick Barber, *General Mgr*
Kim Rosser, *Business Mgr*
EMP: 80
SALES (est): 153.7MM **Privately Held**
SIC: 5999 5047 Medical apparatus & supplies; medical equipment & supplies

(G-10449)
SB HOTEL LLC (PA)
Also Called: Ramada Inn
5775 Perimeter Dr Ste 290 (43017-3224)
PHONE.................614 793-2244
Tari McNamara, *Managing Dir*
Kenneth J Castrop, *Mng Member*
Jim Bednar, *Manager*
Michael Miller, *Manager*
Douglas Pollock, *Manager*
EMP: 50
SQ FT: 100,000
SALES (est): 2.1MM **Privately Held**
WEB: www.hamptoninnsouthbend.com
SIC: 7011 5812 5813 Hotels & motels; family restaurants; cocktail lounge

(G-10450)
SEARS ROEBUCK AND CO
4975 Tuttle Crossing Blvd (43016-1531)
PHONE.................614 760-7195
Fax: 614 760-7156
John Osborn, *Manager*
EMP: 93
SALES (corp-wide): 16.7B **Publicly Held**
SIC: 7549 Automotive maintenance services
HQ: Sears, Roebuck And Co.
3333 Beverly Rd
Hoffman Estates IL 60179
847 286-2500

(G-10451)
SELECT HOTELS GROUP LLC
Also Called: Hyatt Place Columbus/Dublin
6161 Parkcenter Cir (43017-4701)
PHONE.................614 799-1913
Ryan Fisher, *Branch Mgr*
EMP: 25
SALES (corp-wide): 4.6B **Publicly Held**
WEB: www.amerisuites.com
SIC: 7011 7991 Hotels; physical fitness facilities
HQ: Select Hotels Group, L.L.C.
71 S Wacker Dr
Chicago IL 60606
312 750-1234

(G-10452)
SHEPHERD EXCAVATING INC
6295 Cosgray Rd (43016-8737)
PHONE.................614 889-1115
Jerry Semon, *President*
Robert Toombs, *Vice Pres*
Rebecca Miller, *Sls & Mktg Exec*
Lisa Davidson, *Executive*
Melissa Chapman, *Receptionist*
EMP: 90
SQ FT: 4,000
SALES (est): 9.4MM **Privately Held**
SIC: 1771 Concrete work; foundation & footing contractor

(G-10453)
SIGNATURE INC
5115 Prkcnter Ave Ste 200 (43017)
PHONE.................614 734-0010
Fax: 614 766-9419
Don Farrell, *President*
Steve Wolever, *COO*
Dave Hamilton, *Senior VP*
Scott Schilling, *Vice Pres*
Jeff Scholes, *CFO*
EMP: 250
SALES (est): 27.6MM **Privately Held**
WEB: www.signature-training.com
SIC: 8741 Management services

(G-10454)
SIMON PROPERTY GROUP
Also Called: Tuttle Crossing Associates
5043 Tuttle Crossing Blvd (43016-1511)
PHONE.................614 717-9300
Peter Cooper, *General Mgr*
Steven Hinkle, *Director*
EMP: 39 **EST:** 1995
SALES (est): 4MM **Privately Held**
SIC: 6512 Shopping center, property operation only

Dublin - Franklin County (G-10455)

(G-10455)
SOCIUS1 LLC (PA)
5747 Perimeter Dr Ste 200 (43017-3258)
PHONE 614 280-9880
Jeff Geisler, *CEO*
Tricia Jarvis, *CFO*
Gloria Sniter, *Accountant*
Jeff Smith, *Sales Executive*
McKes Son, *Marketing Mgr*
EMP: 58
SALES (est): 14.4MM **Privately Held**
WEB: www.socius1.com
SIC: 8742 Business consultant

(G-10456)
SOLENIS LLC
5200 Blazer Pkwy (43017-3309)
PHONE 614 336-1101
EMP: 40 EST: 2014
SALES (est): 12MM **Privately Held**
SIC: 8742 Business consultant

(G-10457)
SONESTA INTL HOTELS CORP
435 Metro Pl S (43017-5315)
PHONE 614 791-8554
EMP: 121
SALES (corp-wide): 226.6MM **Privately Held**
SIC: 7011 Hotels
PA: Sonesta International Hotels Corporation
  255 Washington St Ste 270
  Newton MA 02458
  770 923-1775

(G-10458)
SOUTHEASTERN EQUIPMENT CO INC
6390 Shier Rings Rd (43016-5204)
P.O. Box 368 (43017-0368)
PHONE 614 889-1073
Fax: 614 761-1156
Thomas Truck, *Opers-Prdtn-Mfg*
EMP: 156
SQ FT: 12,000 **Privately Held**
WEB: www.southeasternequip.com
SIC: 5082 General construction machinery & equipment
PA: Southeastern Equipment Company, Inc.
  10874 E Pike Rd
  Cambridge OH 43725

(G-10459)
SRINSOFT INC
7243 Sawmill Rd Ste 205 (43016-5016)
PHONE 614 893-6535
Padma Hari, *President*
Prasanna Ramamurthy, *Business Mgr*
EMP: 29
SALES (est): 3.2MM **Privately Held**
SIC: 7371 Computer software development

(G-10460)
STANDLEY LAW GROUP LLP
6300 Riverside Dr (43017-5043)
PHONE 614 792-5555
Fax: 614 792-5536
Jeff Norris, *Partner*
Trisha Beachy-Bryant, *General Mgr*
Deanna Barnett, *Manager*
Steve Grant, *Professor*
Heidi Beachy, *Legal Staff*
EMP: 26
SQ FT: 7,000
SALES: 7MM **Privately Held**
WEB: www.standleyllp.com
SIC: 8111 Patent, trademark & copyright law

(G-10461)
STANLEY STEEMER INTL INC (PA)
Also Called: Stanley Steemer Carpet Cleaner
5800 Innovation Dr (43016-3271)
P.O. Box 8004 (43016-2004)
PHONE 614 764-2007
Fax: 614 764-1506
Wesley C Bates, *CEO*
Jack A Bates, *President*
Justin Bates, *President*
Ron Cochran, *General Mgr*
Mike Fazzari, *General Mgr*
EMP: 250
SQ FT: 55,000
SALES: 241.9MM **Privately Held**
WEB: www.stanley-steemer.com
SIC: 7217 3635 6794 5713 Carpet & furniture cleaning on location; upholstery cleaning on customer premises; household vacuum cleaners; franchises, selling or licensing; carpets

(G-10462)
STANLEY STEEMER INTL INC
Also Called: Stanley Steemer Carpet Clr 05
5500 Stanley Steemer Pkwy (43016-1210)
PHONE 614 652-2241
Fax: 614 761-3176
Billy Dean, *General Mgr*
Fred McCoy, *General Mgr*
Danny Sylwestrak, *General Mgr*
Eric Ford, *District Mgr*
Arnold Nunez, *Business Mgr*
EMP: 50
SALES (corp-wide): 241.9MM **Privately Held**
WEB: www.stanley-steemer.com
SIC: 7217 Carpet & furniture cleaning on location
PA: Stanley Steemer International, Inc.
  5800 Innovation Dr
  Dublin OH 43016
  614 764-2007

(G-10463)
STANTEC CONSULTING SVCS INC
6465 Reflections Dr # 150 (43017-2355)
PHONE 614 210-2000
Christina Han, *Marketing Staff*
Lori Van Dermark, *Marketing Staff*
EMP: 39
SALES (corp-wide): 3.1B **Privately Held**
SIC: 8711 Engineering services
HQ: Stantec Consulting Services Inc.
  475 5th Ave Fl 12
  New York NY 10017
  212 352-5160

(G-10464)
STRATEGIC SYSTEMS INC
485 Metro Pl S Ste 270 (43017-7325)
PHONE 614 717-4774
Jyothsna Vadada, *CEO*
Brent Dyke, *Vice Pres*
Sankar Mangapuram, *CFO*
Ram Kola, *Tech Recruiter*
Joseph Oelke, *Tech Recruiter*
EMP: 116
SQ FT: 1,200
SALES (est): 17.4MM **Privately Held**
WEB: www.strategicsystems.com
SIC: 7379

(G-10465)
SUNNY DAY ACADEMY LLC (PA)
Also Called: SDA
255 Bradenton Ave (43017-2673)
PHONE 614 718-1717
Debbie Ziegler, *Treasurer*
Sara Miller, *Mng Member*
Karen Bass, *Admin Sec*
Lou Hight, *Admin Sec*
Karen Oldenborg, *Admin Sec*
EMP: 25 EST: 2010
SALES (est): 707.4K **Privately Held**
SIC: 8351 Group day care center

(G-10466)
SUNRISE SENIOR LIVING LLC
Also Called: Sunrise of Dublin
4175 Stoneridge Ln (43017-2080)
PHONE 614 718-2062
EMP: 49
SALES (corp-wide): 4.3B **Publicly Held**
WEB: www.sunrise.com
SIC: 8361 Home for the aged
HQ: Sunrise Senior Living, Llc
  7902 Westpark Dr
  Mc Lean VA 22102

(G-10467)
SUPPORTCARE INC (PA)
Also Called: Supportcare Ohio
525 Metro Pl N Ste 350 (43017-5451)
PHONE 614 889-5837
Richard Johnson, *President*
Alberta Austin, *Accounts Mgr*
EMP: 35
SALES (est): 8.6MM **Privately Held**
SIC: 8082 Home health care services

(G-10468)
SUTPHEN CORPORATION (PA)
6450 Eiterman Rd (43016-8711)
P.O. Box 158, Amlin (43002-0158)
PHONE 800 726-7030
Fax: 614 889-0874
Drew Sutphen, *President*
Thomas C Sutphen, *Chairman*
Julie S Phelps, *Vice Pres*
Greg Mallon, *CFO*
Jill Dorne, *Controller*
◆ EMP: 180
SQ FT: 90,000
SALES (est): 49.5MM **Privately Held**
WEB: www.sutpheneast.com
SIC: 3711 5087 Fire department vehicles (motor vehicles), assembly of; firefighting equipment

(G-10469)
SYGMA NETWORK INC
5550 Blazer Pkwy Ste 300 (43017-3478)
PHONE 614 734-2500
Fax: 614 529-1566
Rick Tarantelli, *Human Res Mgr*
Chet Minor, *Branch Mgr*
EMP: 320
SALES (corp-wide): 55.3B **Publicly Held**
WEB: www.sygmanetwork.com
SIC: 4225 General warehousing
HQ: The Sygma Network Inc
  5550 Blazer Pkwy Ste 300
  Dublin OH 43017

(G-10470)
SYGMA NETWORK INC (HQ)
5550 Blazer Pkwy Ste 300 (43017-3478)
P.O. Box 7327 (43017-0709)
PHONE 614 734-2500
Fax: 614 734-2550
Thomas Russell, *CEO*
Steven Deasey, *President*
Mike Wren, *General Mgr*
Joseph A Sugar, *Chairman*
Robert Johnson, *Business Mgr*
▲ EMP: 150
SQ FT: 30,000
SALES (est): 3.1B
SALES (corp-wide): 55.3B **Publicly Held**
WEB: www.sygmanetwork.com
SIC: 5149 Groceries & related products
PA: Sysco Corporation
  1390 Enclave Pkwy
  Houston TX 77077
  281 584-1390

(G-10471)
SYNTERO INC (PA)
Also Called: DUBLIN COUNSELING CENTER
299 Cramer Creek Ct (43017-2586)
PHONE 614 889-5722
Julie E Rinaldi, *General Mgr*
Alissa Reynolds, *Program Mgr*
Kim Vance, *Manager*
Wendy Vernon, *Info Tech Mgr*
Katherine Mihelich-Helms, *Director*
EMP: 45
SALES: 5.6MM **Privately Held**
WEB: www.dublincounselingcenter.org
SIC: 8093 8322 8069 Mental health clinic, outpatient; general counseling services; drug addiction rehabilitation hospital

(G-10472)
T & R PROPERTIES (PA)
Also Called: T & R Property Management
3895 Stoneridge Ln (43017-2152)
PHONE 614 923-4000
P Ronald Sabatino, *President*
Lisa Stickley, *General Mgr*
Tamara Potts, *CFO*
Tamra L Potts, *CFO*
Kayla Chapman, *Human Res Mgr*
EMP: 30
SQ FT: 1,200
SALES (est): 16.4MM **Privately Held**
WEB: www.trprop.com
SIC: 6531 Real estate managers

(G-10473)
TARTAN FIELDS GOLF CLUB LTD
8070 Tartan Fields Dr (43017-8780)
PHONE 614 792-0900
Fax: 614 792-0752
Joe Flynn, *General Mgr*
Stacy Grogan, *General Mgr*
Mark Kelley, *General Mgr*
Bill Stevenson, *General Mgr*
Nicola Harmon, *Controller*
EMP: 100
SALES (est): 7.1MM **Privately Held**
WEB: www.tartanfields.com
SIC: 7997 5941 5813 5812 Golf club, membership; sporting goods & bicycle shops; drinking places; eating places

(G-10474)
TEK SYSTEMS
5115 Prkcnter Ave Ste 170 (43017)
PHONE 614 789-6200
Darren Yeager, *Principal*
EMP: 75
SALES (est): 228.4K **Privately Held**
SIC: 8742 Management information systems consultant

(G-10475)
TELECMMNCTONS STFFING SLUTIONS
Also Called: TSS Resources
8191 Glencree Pl (43016-9523)
PHONE 614 799-9300
Fax: 614 799-1012
Ginny Berke, *President*
EMP: 25
SALES (est): 1.3MM **Privately Held**
SIC: 7361 Executive placement

(G-10476)
THE NATURE CONSERVANCY
Also Called: Ohio Field Office
6375 Riverside Dr Ste 100 (43017-5045)
PHONE 614 717-2770
Fax: 614 717-2777
Marianne Gabel, *Ch of Bd*
Mark Schmaltz, *Opers Staff*
Justin Cox, *Manager*
Ross Lebold, *Comp Spec*
Gerry Bird, *Director*
EMP: 30
SALES (corp-wide): 1.1B **Privately Held**
WEB: www.nature.org
SIC: 8641 Environmental protection organization
PA: The Nature Conservancy
  4245 Fairfax Dr Ste 100
  Arlington VA 22203
  703 841-5300

(G-10477)
TRI-ANIM HEALTH SERVICES INC (HQ)
5000 Tuttle Crossing Blvd (43016-1534)
P.O. Box 8023 (43016-2023)
PHONE 614 760-5000
Jeff Prestel, *President*
Rick Barber, *General Mgr*
Rob Boudeau, *General Mgr*
Dale Clendon, *Principal*
Dan L Pister, *COO*
▲ EMP: 50
SQ FT: 38,600
SALES (est): 39.8MM **Privately Held**
WEB: www.trianim.com
SIC: 5047 Medical equipment & supplies

(G-10478)
UNIVENTURE INC (PA)
Also Called: Univenture CD Packg & Systems
4266 Tuller Rd Ste 101 (43017-5007)
PHONE 937 645-4600
Fax: 614 529-2110
Ross O Youngs, *CEO*
Michele Cole, *President*
Larry George, *Vice Pres*
Timothy Williams, *Project Mgr*
Laura Nault, *Materials Mgr*
EMP: 95
SQ FT: 100,000
SALES (est): 45.9MM **Privately Held**
WEB: www.univenture.com
SIC: 7389 7336 Packaging & labeling services; package design

GEOGRAPHIC SECTION

Dunkirk - Hardin County (G-10501)

(G-10479)
UNIVENTURE INC
4266 Tuller Rd Ste 101 (43017-5007)
PHONE..................................937 645-4600
Rick Nichols, *Manager*
EMP: 35
SALES (corp-wide): 45.9MM **Privately Held**
WEB: www.univenture.com
SIC: 7389 Packaging & labeling services
PA: Univenture, Inc.
  4266 Tuller Rd Ste 101
  Dublin OH 43017
  937 645-4600

(G-10480)
URBAN OASSIS INC
Also Called: Spa At River Ridge Salon, The
5555 Wall St (43017-3244)
PHONE..................................614 766-9946
Fax: 614 760-1898
Peggi Fisher-Hanson, *President*
Abbey Martini, *Mktg Dir*
Emily Armstrong, *Manager*
Jackie Clark, *Art Dir*
Melanie Lloyd, *Master*
EMP: 30
SALES (est): 701.7K **Privately Held**
SIC: 7231 Hairdressers

(G-10481)
VIAQUEST INC (PA)
525 Metro Pl N Ste 300 (43017-5320)
PHONE..................................614 889-5837
Richard Johnson, *President*
Melissa Pittman, *Program Dir*
Janet Pell, *Admin Sec*
EMP: 38
SALES: 4.1MM **Privately Held**
WEB: www.viaquestinc.com
SIC: 8741 Business management

(G-10482)
VIAQUEST BEHAVIORAL HEALTH LLC (PA)
Also Called: Summit Quest Academy
525 Metro Pl N Ste 450 (43017-5321)
PHONE..................................614 339-0868
Richard Johnson, *President*
EMP: 33
SQ FT: 1,500
SALES (est): 27.7MM **Privately Held**
WEB: www.magcorp.com
SIC: 8741 8742 Hospital management; nursing & personal care facility management; management consulting services

(G-10483)
VIAQUEST HOME HEALTH LLC (HQ)
525 Metro Pl N (43017-5342)
PHONE..................................800 645-3267
Richard D Johnson, *President*
EMP: 25 **EST:** 2005
SALES (est): 4.1MM **Privately Held**
SIC: 8059 Personal care home, with health care

(G-10484)
VOC WORKS LTD
5555 Glendon Ct Ste 300 (43016-3302)
P.O. Box 182848, Columbus (43218-2848)
PHONE..................................614 760-3515
William Pfeiffer, *President*
L T Nichols, *Vice Pres*
Thomas R Brownlee,
EMP: 90
SALES (est): 1.6MM **Privately Held**
SIC: 8331 8741 Vocational rehabilitation agency; management services

(G-10485)
W T SPORTS INC
5288 Aryshire Dr (43017-9424)
PHONE..................................740 654-0035
Ed Thompson, *President*
EMP: 40
SQ FT: 17,000
SALES: 500K **Privately Held**
SIC: 7991 Physical fitness clubs with training equipment

(G-10486)
W2005/FARGO HOTELS (POOL C)
Also Called: Homewood Suites Dublin
5300 Parkcenter Ave (43017-7555)
PHONE..................................614 791-8675
Janna Mertenf, *Manager*
EMP: 80
SALES (corp-wide): 16.5MM **Privately Held**
WEB: www.daytonraiders.com
SIC: 7011 Inns
HQ: W2005/Fargo Hotels (Pool C) Realty, L.P.
  5851 Legacy Cir Ste 400
  Plano TX 75024

(G-10487)
WALGREEN CO
Also Called: Walgreens
6805 Hospital Dr (43016-8556)
PHONE..................................614 336-0431
Fax: 614 336-0442
Mike Strawser, *Manager*
EMP: 25
SALES (corp-wide): 118.2B **Publicly Held**
WEB: www.walgreens.com
SIC: 5912 7384 Drug stores; photofinishing laboratory
HQ: Walgreen Co.
  200 Wilmot Rd
  Deerfield IL 60015
  847 315-2500

(G-10488)
WD PARTNERS INC
7007 Discovery Blvd (43017-3218)
PHONE..................................614 634-7000
Scott Hathaway, *Manager*
EMP: 35
SALES (corp-wide): 67.1MM **Privately Held**
SIC: 8712 Architectural services
PA: Wd Partners, Inc.
  7007 Discovery Blvd
  Dublin OH 43017
  614 634-7000

(G-10489)
WELLS FARGO CLEARING SVCS LLC
Also Called: Wells Fargo Advisors
485 Metro Pl S Ste 300 (43017-1882)
PHONE..................................614 764-2040
Montford S Will,
EMP: 80
SALES (corp-wide): 97.7B **Publicly Held**
WEB: www.wachoviasec.com
SIC: 6211 Stock brokers & dealers
HQ: Wells Fargo Clearing Services, Llc
  1 N Jefferson Ave
  Saint Louis MO 63103
  314 955-3000

(G-10490)
WELLS FARGO HOME MORTGAGE INC
485 Metro Pl S Ste 300 (43017-1882)
PHONE..................................614 781-8847
Toll Free:..................................877 -
Fax: 614 436-2744
EMP: 30
SALES (corp-wide): 90B **Publicly Held**
SIC: 6162 Mortgage Banker/Correspondent
HQ: Wells Fargo Home Mortgage Inc
  1 Home Campus
  Des Moines IA 50328
  515 324-3707

(G-10491)
WENDYS COMPANY (PA)
1 Dave Thomas Blvd (43017-5452)
PHONE..................................614 764-3100
Nelson Peltz, *Ch of Bd*
Todd A Penegor, *President*
Robert D Wright, *COO*
Scott A Kriss, *Senior VP*
Dana Klein, *Vice Pres*
◆ **EMP:** 475 **EST:** 1929
SQ FT: 324,025

SALES: 1.2B **Publicly Held**
WEB: www.wendysarbys.com
SIC: 5812 6794 Fast-food restaurant, chain; franchises, selling or licensing

(G-10492)
WENDYS RESTAURANTS LLC (HQ)
1 Dave Thomas Blvd (43017-5452)
PHONE..................................614 764-3100
Emil J Brolick, *President*
Emil Brolick, *President*
Chris Houston, *General Mgr*
Donald F Calhoun, *Exec VP*
Ed Choe, *Exec VP*
EMP: 120 **EST:** 2008
SQ FT: 249,025
SALES (est): 2.3B
SALES (corp-wide): 1.2B **Publicly Held**
WEB: www.wendysarbys.com
SIC: 5812 6794 Fast-food restaurant, chain; franchises, selling or licensing
PA: The Wendy's Company
  1 Dave Thomas Blvd
  Dublin OH 43017
  614 764-3100

(G-10493)
WINEGARDNER & HAMMONS INC
Also Called: Marriott
5605 Paul G Blzr Mmrl Pkw (43017)
PHONE..................................614 791-1000
Rich Byrd, *Manager*
Tana Gilmore, *Executive*
EMP: 150
SALES (corp-wide): 84.3MM **Privately Held**
WEB: www.whihotels.com
SIC: 7011 Hotels & motels
PA: Req/Jqh Holdings, Inc.
  4243 Hunt Rd Ste 2
  Blue Ash OH 45242
  513 891-1066

(G-10494)
XPO INTERMODAL INC (HQ)
5165 Emerald Pkwy 300 (43017-1063)
PHONE..................................614 717-4131
Fax: 614 923-1400
Daniel L Gardner, *CEO*
John T Hickerson, *Ch of Bd*
M Sean Fernandez, *President*
Larry Savage, *President*
Jeffrey Brashares, *COO*
EMP: 80
SALES (est): 385MM
SALES (corp-wide): 15.3B **Publicly Held**
WEB: www.pacer-international.com
SIC: 4731 Freight transportation arrangement
PA: Xpo Logistics, Inc.
  5 American Ln
  Greenwich CT 06831
  844 742-5976

(G-10495)
XPO INTERMODAL SOLUTIONS INC (DH)
Also Called: Pacer
5165 Emerald Pkwy (43017-1063)
PHONE..................................614 923-1400
Daniel W Avramovich, *President*
Charles Hoffman, *President*
Jeffrey Smith, *General Mgr*
Michael F Killea, *Exec VP*
James E Ward, *Exec VP*
EMP: 550
SQ FT: 107,000
SALES (est): 89.2MM
SALES (corp-wide): 15.3B **Publicly Held**
SIC: 4731 Agents, shipping
HQ: Xpo Intermodal, Inc.
  5165 Emerald Pkwy 300
  Dublin OH 43017
  614 923-1400

(G-10496)
XPO STACKTRAIN LLC
Also Called: Pacer Stacktrain
5165 Emerald Pkwy (43017-1063)
PHONE..................................614 923-1400
Patricia Hutchinson, *Accounts Exec*
Barny Carter, *Systems Staff*
EMP: 32

SALES (corp-wide): 15.3B **Publicly Held**
WEB: www.pacerstack.com
SIC: 4731 Freight transportation arrangement
HQ: Xpo Stacktrain, Llc
  5165 Emerald Pkwy
  Dublin OH 43017
  925 887-1400

(G-10497)
YORK RISK SERVICES GROUP INC
5555 Glendon Ct (43016-3304)
PHONE..................................866 391-9675
Layton McCallum, *Principal*
EMP: 250
SALES (corp-wide): 3B **Privately Held**
SIC: 6411 Insurance agents, brokers & service
HQ: York Risk Services Group, Inc.
  1 Upper Pond
  Parsippany NJ 07054
  973 404-1200

Duncan Falls
Muskingum County

(G-10498)
DUNCAN FALLS ASSOC
Water St (43734)
PHONE..................................740 674-7105
Vernan Trout, *President*
EMP: 82
SALES (est): 2.7MM **Privately Held**
SIC: 8742 Management consulting services

Dundee
Tuscarawas County

(G-10499)
ALPINE STRUCTURES LLC
2675 Us Route 62 (44624-9235)
PHONE..................................330 359-5708
Fax: 330 893-2655
Jaban Miller, *General Mgr*
Sam Yoder, *General Mgr*
Moses Miller, *Mng Member*
Javan Miller, *Mng Member*
Ranita Yoder, *Admin Sec*
EMP: 25
SQ FT: 37,396
SALES (est): 5.8MM **Privately Held**
WEB: www.alpinestructures.com
SIC: 1542 Garage construction

(G-10500)
HRH DOOR CORP
Also Called: Wayne - Dalton
2589 County Road 168 (44624-9217)
PHONE..................................330 893-3233
Fax: 330 893-3371
Donald Diglew, *Manager*
Donald Diglaw, *Manager*
EMP: 39
SALES (corp-wide): 618.8MM **Privately Held**
WEB: www.waynedalton.com
SIC: 5031 Doors
PA: Hrh Door Corp.
  1 Door Dr
  Mount Hope OH 44660
  850 208-3400

Dunkirk
Hardin County

(G-10501)
BALL BOUNCE AND SPORT INC
Also Called: Diamond Plastics
211 W Geneva St (45836-1008)
PHONE..................................419 759-3838
EMP: 50
SALES (corp-wide): 148.6MM **Privately Held**
SIC: 5092 Whol Toys/Hobby Goods

East Canton - Stark County (G-10502)

PA: Ball, Bounce And Sport, Inc.
1 Hedstrom Dr
Ashland OH 44805
419 759-3838

East Canton
Stark County

(G-10502)
AMERICAN LEGION
Also Called: American Legion Post 667
204 Wood St S (44730-1326)
PHONE 330 488-0119
Clifford F Tolston, *President*
EMP: 70
SALES (est): 373.5K **Privately Held**
SIC: 8641 Veterans' organization

(G-10503)
FTS INTERNATIONAL INC
1520 Wood Ave Se (44730-9591)
PHONE 330 754-2375
Richard Jelley, *Branch Mgr*
EMP: 629 **Publicly Held**
SIC: 1389 Measurement of well flow rates, oil & gas
PA: Fts International, Inc.
777 Main St Ste 2900
Fort Worth TX 76102

(G-10504)
KOCH KNIGHT LLC (DH)
5385 Orchardview Dr Se (44730-9568)
P.O. Box 30070 (44730-0070)
PHONE 330 488-1651
Fax: 330 488-1656
Mike Graeff, *President*
Mathew Phayer, *Vice Pres*
Jeremy Heestand, *Project Mgr*
Roy Williams, *Project Mgr*
Greg Carle, *Opers Mgr*
◆ **EMP:** 80
SALES (est): 30.3MM
SALES (corp-wide): 45.4B **Privately Held**
WEB: www.kochknight.com
SIC: 2911 5172 5169 4922 Petroleum refining; petroleum products; chemicals & allied products; natural gas transmission; crude petroleum production; natural gas production; refinery, chemical processing & similar machinery
HQ: Koch-Glitsch, Lp
4111 E 37th St N
Wichita KS 67220
316 828-5110

East Fultonham
Muskingum County

(G-10505)
CHESTERHILL STONE CO
Also Called: Shelly Materials
6305 Saltillo Rd (43735)
P.O. Box 28 (43735-0028)
PHONE 740 849-2338
Fax: 740 849-2599
George Hill, *Superintendent*
EMP: 29
SALES (corp-wide): 9MM **Privately Held**
SIC: 1422 Crushed & broken limestone
PA: Chesterhill Stone Co
773 E State Route 60 Ne
Mcconnelsville OH

(G-10506)
COLUMBIA RECREATION ASSN
Also Called: Lake Isabella Recreation Assn
5960 Fourth St (43735)
P.O. Box 56 (43735-0056)
PHONE 740 849-2466
Alan Reed, *President*
Carl Border, *Principal*
Lou Willard, *Treasurer*
Lester Adolth, *Manager*
EMP: 35
SALES: 219.7K **Privately Held**
SIC: 7997 Hunting club, membership

East Liberty
Logan County

(G-10507)
CEVA LOGISTICS US INC
26230 Stokes Rd (43319-9501)
PHONE 937 578-1160
Sonny Goings, *Personnel Exec*
Chris McKenrick, *Manager*
EMP: 40 **Publicly Held**
WEB: www.tntlogistics.com
SIC: 4213 Trucking, except local
HQ: Ceva Logistics U.S., Inc.
15350 Vickery Dr
Houston TX 77032
281 618-3100

(G-10508)
CLARK TRUCKING INC (DH)
11590 Township Road 157 (43319-8500)
PHONE 937 642-0335
Fax: 937 642-3028
Kaneo Meguro, *President*
John Jenkins, *Vice Pres*
Albert Wittkopp, *Vice Pres*
Edward Allison, *Treasurer*
Steve Fuchik, *Manager*
EMP: 145 **EST:** 1954
SQ FT: 4,000
SALES (est): 14.9MM
SALES (corp-wide): 123.1B **Privately Held**
WEB: www.clarktrucking.com
SIC: 4214 4213 Local trucking with storage; contract haulers
HQ: Midwest Express Inc.
11590 Township Road 298
East Liberty OH 43319
937 642-0335

(G-10509)
HONDA LOGISTICS NORTH AMER INC (DH)
11590 Township Road 298 (43319-9487)
PHONE 937 642-0335
Tamaki Hashimoto, *President*
Pam Pickens, *Purchasing*
Steve Fuchik, *Finance Mgr*
Kristi Warren, *Human Resources*
Tom Collins, *Manager*
EMP: 1338
SALES (est): 227.5MM
SALES (corp-wide): 123.1B **Privately Held**
SIC: 4226 Special warehousing & storage
HQ: Honda Logistics Inc.
6, Ichibancho
Chiyoda-Ku TKY 102-0
353 571-041

(G-10510)
MIDWEST EXPRESS INC (DH)
11590 Township Road 298 (43319-9450)
PHONE 937 642-0335
Fax: 937 645-7145
Tamaki Hashimoto, *President*
Tadao Endo, *Principal*
Ed Allison, *Vice Pres*
Brian Blair, *Vice Pres*
Robert Overbaugh, *Vice Pres*
EMP: 950
SQ FT: 1,833,902
SALES (est): 218.8MM
SALES (corp-wide): 123.1B **Privately Held**
SIC: 4226 Special warehousing & storage
HQ: Honda Logistics North America, Inc.
11590 Township Road 298
East Liberty OH 43319
937 642-0335

(G-10511)
MPW INDUSTRIAL SERVICES INC
Also Called: Facility MGT & Support Svcs
11000 State Route 347 (43319-9470)
PHONE 937 644-0200
Fax: 937 645-8101
Dan Smith, *Plant Mgr*
Duane Jolliff, *Manager*
Bryan Nichols, *IT/INT Sup*
Keith Smith, *IT/INT Sup*
Lee Howdyshell, *Data Proc Staff*
EMP: 100
SALES (corp-wide): 257.9MM **Privately Held**
SIC: 7349 7363 Cleaning service, industrial or commercial; help supply services
HQ: Mpw Industrial Services, Inc.
9711 Lancaster Rd
Hebron OH 43025
800 827-8790

(G-10512)
NEX TRANSPORT INC
13900 State Route 287 (43319-9466)
PHONE 937 645-3761
Fax: 937 642-8837
Tosaki Watanabe, *President*
Fumio Moriyama, *President*
Toshiaki Watanabe, *President*
Tomie Mori, *Exec VP*
Teizo Kanda, *Vice Pres*
EMP: 220
SQ FT: 400,000
SALES: 39.3MM
SALES (corp-wide): 16.4B **Privately Held**
WEB: www.nextransport.com
SIC: 4226 Special warehousing & storage
HQ: Nippon Express U.S.A., Inc.
2401 44th Rd Fl 14
Long Island City NY 11101
212 758-6100

East Liverpool
Columbiana County

(G-10513)
AARONS INC
16240 Dresden Ave Ste A (43920-8603)
PHONE 330 385-7201
Steven Harrington, *Branch Mgr*
EMP: 25
SALES (corp-wide): 3.3B **Publicly Held**
WEB: www.aaronrents.com
SIC: 7359 Furniture rental
PA: Aaron's, Inc.
400 Galleria Pkwy Se # 300
Atlanta GA 30339
678 402-3000

(G-10514)
ALSAN CORPORATION
Also Called: East Liverpool Motor Lodge
900 W 8th St (43920-2303)
PHONE 330 385-3636
Alfred C Gloeckner, *President*
EMP: 100 **EST:** 1980
SQ FT: 87,000
SALES (est): 2.7MM **Privately Held**
WEB: www.elmotorlodge.com
SIC: 5812 7011 7991 7231 Restaurant, family: independent; motels; spas; hairdressers

(G-10515)
ANKLE AND FOOT CARE CENTER (PA)
Also Called: Foot & Ankle Clinic
16844 Saint Clair Ave # 2 (43920-4278)
PHONE 330 385-2413
Fax: 330 385-6870
Lawrence Didomenico, *Partner*
Kenneth Emch, *Partner*
Christian Carbonell, *Med Doctor*
Betty Emch, *Manager*
Lawrence D Didomenico, *Podiatrist*
EMP: 25
SALES (est): 2.2MM **Privately Held**
SIC: 8043 Offices & clinics of podiatrists

(G-10516)
BLOSSOM HILL ELDERLY HOUSING L
100 Wilbert Ave (43920-4091)
PHONE 330 385-4310
Steve Boone, *Exec Dir*
EMP: 90
SALES (est): 2.4MM **Privately Held**
SIC: 6531 Real estate leasing & rentals

(G-10517)
CITY HOSPITAL ASSOCIATION
Also Called: EAST LIVERPOOL CITY HOSPITAL
425 W 5th St (43920-2405)
PHONE 330 385-7200
Fax: 330 386-2048
Kenneth J Cochran, *CEO*
Patrick Beaver, *Vice Pres*
Kyle Johnson, *Vice Pres*
Pamela Smith, *Vice Pres*
Anthony Puorro, *Controller*
EMP: 600
SQ FT: 226,660
SALES: 75.2MM **Privately Held**
SIC: 8062 General medical & surgical hospitals

(G-10518)
COMMUNITY ACTION COLUMBIANA CT
Also Called: Y M C A-Head Start
134 E 4th St (43920-3044)
PHONE 330 385-7251
Fax: 330 385-4408
Joyce Lapura, *Director*
EMP: 28
SALES (corp-wide): 15.2MM **Privately Held**
SIC: 7999 8641 Recreation center; youth organizations
PA: Community Action Agency Of Columbiana County, Inc.
7880 Lincole Pl
Lisbon OH 44432
330 424-7221

(G-10519)
DUQUESNE LIGHT COMPANY
626 Saint Clair Ave (43920-3077)
PHONE 330 385-6103
EMP: 147 **Privately Held**
SIC: 4911 Electric services
HQ: Duquesne Light Company
411 7th Ave 6-1
Pittsburgh PA 15219
412 393-6000

(G-10520)
EAST LIVERPOOL WATER DEPT
2220 Michigan Ave (43920-3638)
PHONE 330 385-8812
Keith Clark, *Superintendent*
Scott McNicol, *Superintendent*
EMP: 26 **EST:** 1915
SALES (est): 3.4MM **Privately Held**
SIC: 4941 Water supply

(G-10521)
FARMERS NATIONAL BANK
16924 Saint Clair Ave (43920-4255)
P.O. Box 555, Canfield (44406-0555)
PHONE 330 385-9200
Fax: 330 386-7459
Kevin Helmick, *President*
EMP: 70
SALES (corp-wide): 104.5MM **Publicly Held**
SIC: 6021 National trust companies with deposits, commercial
HQ: The Farmers National Bank Of Canfield
20 S Broad St
Canfield OH 44406
330 533-3341

(G-10522)
HILL INTL TRCKS NA LLC (PA)
47866 Y And O Rd (43920-8724)
P.O. Box 2170 (43920-0170)
PHONE 330 386-6440
Fax: 330 386-3336
Michael Barber, *VP Opers*
Tony Sorge, *Finance*
Mike Chronister, *Human Res Mgr*
Jeff Mundy, *VP Sales*
Fred Biscella, *Sales Executive*
▼ **EMP:** 100 **EST:** 1890
SQ FT: 30,000
SALES (est): 92.7MM **Privately Held**
WEB: www.hillinternationaltrucks.com
SIC: 5511 5531 7538 Trucks, tractors & trailers: new & used; truck equipment & parts; general automotive repair shops

GEOGRAPHIC SECTION

Eastlake - Lake County (G-10545)

(G-10523)
LIFETEAM EMS INC
Also Called: Lifeteam Ambulance Service
740 Dresden Ave Ste A (43920-4309)
P.O. Box 362 (43920-5362)
PHONE..................................330 386-9284
Fax: 330 386-7425
Raymond Strohacker, CEO
Kelly Betteridge, President
Bob Swickard, Opers Staff
EMP: 42
SQ FT: 15,000
SALES: 1.7MM Privately Held
WEB: www.lifeteamems.com
SIC: 4119 8049 Ambulance service; paramedic

(G-10524)
MARTIN ALTMEYER FUNERAL HOME
15872 Saint Clair Ave (43920-8984)
PHONE..................................330 385-3650
Fax: 330 385-3619
James Altmeyer Jr, President
EMP: 30 EST: 1936
SQ FT: 4,358
SALES (est): 1.4MM Privately Held
SIC: 7261 Funeral home

(G-10525)
MIKE PUSATERI EXCAVATING INC
16363 Saint Clair Ave (43920-9124)
P.O. Box 2136 (43920-0136)
PHONE..................................330 385-5221
Fax: 330 385-6903
Michael J Pusateri, President
James V Pusateri, Vice Pres
Michael Pusateri, Treasurer
Debra Smith, Admin Sec
EMP: 35
SQ FT: 4,800
SALES (est): 8.4MM Privately Held
SIC: 1794 Excavation work

(G-10526)
MURRAY LEASING INC
14778 E Liverpool Rd (43920-9712)
P.O. Box 2138 (43920-0138)
PHONE..................................330 386-4757
H B Murray, President
Betty Murray, Vice Pres
EMP: 125
SQ FT: 10,000
SALES (est): 7.4MM Privately Held
SIC: 7513 4213 4212 Truck leasing, without drivers; trucking, except local; local trucking, without storage

(G-10527)
NENTWICK CONVALESCENT HOME
500 Selfridge St (43920-1997)
PHONE..................................330 385-5001
Fax: 330 385-2441
Rev John Nentwick, President
Mary Nentwick Tambellini, Corp Secy
Alfred Tambellini, Vice Pres
Carla Disch, Director
EMP: 105
SQ FT: 28,000
SALES (est): 4.4MM Privately Held
SIC: 8059 8051 Convalescent home; skilled nursing care facilities

(G-10528)
NORTH STAR CRITICAL CARE LLC
16356 State Route 267 (43920-3932)
P.O. Box 2011 (43920-0011)
PHONE..................................330 386-9110
Elio P Lerussi, Mng Member
Lee Lerussi, Manager
Christine Lerussi,
EMP: 28
SALES (est): 810K Privately Held
SIC: 4119 Ambulance service

(G-10529)
OHIO VALLEY HOME CARE LLC
425 W 5th St (43920-2405)
P.O. Box 80 (43920-5080)
PHONE..................................330 385-2333
Keith Richardson, CEO
Richard Adkins, Admin Asst
Amy Palmer, Administration
EMP: 34
SQ FT: 800
SALES (est): 285.8K Privately Held
SIC: 8082 Home health care services

(G-10530)
OHIO VALLEY HOME HLTH SVCS INC (PA)
425 W 5th St (43920-2405)
PHONE..................................330 385-2333
Fax: 330 385-9034
Keith Richardson, CEO
Barbara Reed, Treasurer
Susan Drysdale, VP Mktg
Jannet McCoy, Manager
Richard Adkins, Supervisor
EMP: 28
SQ FT: 1,500
SALES (est): 2.1MM Privately Held
WEB: www.ovhhs.com
SIC: 8082 Visiting nurse service

(G-10531)
OS HILL LEASING INC
47866 Y And O Rd (43920-8724)
P.O. Box 2170 (43920-0170)
PHONE..................................330 386-6440
Jack I Hill, President
Mike Fisher, Corp Secy
Gary Malonne, Vice Pres
EMP: 40
SQ FT: 30,000
SALES (est): 2.4MM
SALES (corp-wide): 92.7MM Privately Held
WEB: www.hillintltrucks.com
SIC: 7513 Truck leasing, without drivers
PA: Hill International Trucks N.A., Llc
47866 Y And O Rd
East Liverpool OH 43920
330 386-6440

(G-10532)
P N P INC
Also Called: Chcc Home Health Care
48444 Bell School Rd (43920-9646)
PHONE..................................330 386-1231
Joseph Cilone, President
EMP: 100 EST: 2011
SQ FT: 144
SALES (est): 2.9MM
SALES (corp-wide): 3.6MM Privately Held
SIC: 8099 Health screening service
PA: Jcth Holdings, Inc.
48444 Bell School Rd
East Liverpool OH 43920
330 386-1231

(G-10533)
PRECESION FINNING BENDING INC
1250 Saint George St # 6 (43920-3400)
PHONE..................................330 382-9351
Fax: 330 382-9354
Mark Anderson, President
Jason Anderson, Vice Pres
Kelly Smith, Manager
EMP: 25
SQ FT: 70,000
SALES (est): 2MM Privately Held
SIC: 5051 Steel

(G-10534)
SH BELL COMPANY
2217 Michigan Ave (43920-3637)
PHONE..................................412 963-9910
Fax: 330 385-8120
Adam Bell, Sales Mgr
Vince Monte, Sales Staff
Rusty Davis, Manager
Jill Tillman, Manager
Doris Thayer, Director
EMP: 37
SALES (corp-wide): 22.8MM Privately Held
SIC: 3479 4226 4225 Aluminum coating of metal products; special warehousing & storage; general warehousing & storage
PA: S.H. Bell Company
644 Alpha Dr
Pittsburgh PA 15238
412 963-9910

(G-10535)
SOARING EAGLE INC
Also Called: Newbold Technologies
114 W 5th St (43920-2920)
PHONE..................................330 385-5579
Fax: 330 385-3672
Craig Newbold, President
Susan Cogswell, Manager
Lisa McKee, Sr Consultant
EMP: 30
SQ FT: 20,360
SALES (est): 6MM Privately Held
SIC: 7373 Systems software development services

(G-10536)
YMCA INC
Also Called: YMCA of East Liverpool Ohio
15655 State Route 170 A2 (43920-9672)
PHONE..................................330 385-6400
Fax: 330 385-4534
Robert O'Hara, Principal
EMP: 64
SALES (est): 1.3MM Privately Held
SIC: 8641 7991 8351 7032 Youth organizations; physical fitness facilities; child day care services; youth camps; individual & family services

East Palestine
Columbiana County

(G-10537)
COVINGTON SNF INC
Also Called: Covington Skilled Nursing
100 Covington Dr (44413-1007)
PHONE..................................330 426-2920
Timothy A Chesney, Vice Pres
Nicole Jablonski, Admin Asst
EMP: 27
SALES: 5.5MM Privately Held
SIC: 8051 Convalescent home with continuous nursing care

(G-10538)
JASAR RECYCLING INC
183 Edgeworth Ave (44413-1554)
PHONE..................................864 233-5421
Fax: 330 426-9461
Ed McNee, President
Chris Toy, Human Res Mgr
Kelley Lester, Nat'l Sales Mgr
John Cote, Sales Mgr
Jeri Crum, Sales Mgr
▼ EMP: 70
SQ FT: 240,000
SALES (est): 44.3MM Privately Held
WEB: www.jasarrecycling.com
SIC: 5093 Metal scrap & waste materials

(G-10539)
SMS TECHNICAL SERVICES LLC
49560 State Route 14 (44413-9725)
PHONE..................................330 426-4126
Ron Sattler, Buyer
Ken Heestend, Branch Mgr
Ken Heestand, Director
Connie Berresford, Executive
EMP: 35
SQ FT: 16,000 Privately Held
SIC: 7699 Industrial machinery & equipment repair
HQ: Sms Technical Services Llc
100 Sandusky St
Pittsburgh PA 15212
724 553-3420

East Sparta
Stark County

(G-10540)
MALAVITE EXCAVATING INC
5508 Ridge Ave Se (44626-9702)
PHONE..................................330 484-1274
Fax: 330 484-3089
Gust Malavite, President
Gust Malavite Jr, Vice Pres
Kevin Malavite, Treasurer
EMP: 25 EST: 1978
SQ FT: 10,000
SALES: 1MM Privately Held
SIC: 7353 Earth moving equipment, rental or leasing

(G-10541)
STANLEY MILLER CONSTRUCTION CO
2250 Howenstine Dr Se (44626-9538)
PHONE..................................330 484-2229
David S Miller, President
Steven Miller, Vice Pres
Brian Sudduth, Vice Pres
Terri Krupar, Project Mgr
Craig McGuire, Project Mgr
EMP: 25
SQ FT: 10,000
SALES (est): 8.9MM Privately Held
WEB: www.smillerconst.com
SIC: 1542 1541 Commercial & office building, new construction; commercial & office buildings, renovation & repair; industrial buildings, new construction; renovation, remodeling & repairs: industrial buildings

(G-10542)
WILLIAMS SUPER SERVICE INC
Also Called: Williams Toyota Lift
9462 Main Ave Se (44626-9583)
P.O. Box 359 (44626-0359)
PHONE..................................330 733-7750
Paul Williams, President
Rod Lancaster, Sales Mgr
John Visner, Sales Executive
Jason Pratt, Marketing Staff
Jason Froman, Manager
EMP: 27
SQ FT: 6,000
SALES (est): 5.4MM Privately Held
WEB: www.williamstoyotalift.com
SIC: 7699 5084 Industrial machinery & equipment repair; lift trucks & parts

East Springfield
Jefferson County

(G-10543)
SPRING HILLS GOLF CLUB
99 Corder Dr (43925)
PHONE..................................740 543-3270
Charlie Corder Sr, Principal
EMP: 25
SALES (est): 452K Privately Held
SIC: 7999 Golf services & professionals

Eastlake
Lake County

(G-10544)
AVNET INC
Also Called: Avnet Computers
34201 Melinz Pkwy Unit D (44095-4018)
PHONE..................................440 479-3607
EMP: 27
SALES (corp-wide): 17.4B Publicly Held
SIC: 5065 Electronic parts
PA: Avnet, Inc.
2211 S 47th St
Phoenix AZ 85034
480 643-2000

(G-10545)
DISASTER RECONSTRUCTION INC
Also Called: Servicmaster By Disaster Recon
33851 Curtis Blvd Ste 202 (44095-4003)
PHONE..................................440 918-1523
Greg Dennison, President
EMP: 31
SQ FT: 3,000
SALES (est): 2.9MM Privately Held
SIC: 1521 1542 1799 General remodeling, single-family houses; commercial & office buildings, renovation & repair; post-disaster renovations

Eastlake - Lake County (G-10546)

(G-10546)
EASTLAKE LODGING LLC
Also Called: Radisson Eastlake
35000 Curtis Blvd (44095-4019)
PHONE...................440 953-8000
Mike Madonna, *General Mgr*
EMP: 50
SALES (est): 2.7MM **Privately Held**
SIC: 7011 Bed & breakfast inn
PA: Concord Hospitality Enterprises Company
11410 Common Oaks Dr
Raleigh NC 27614

(G-10547)
JOHN F GALLAGHER PLUMBING CO
36360 Lakeland Blvd (44095-5314)
PHONE...................440 946-4256
Fax: 440 946-0918
Michael J Gallagher, *President*
Meg Radtke, *Accounts Mgr*
John Gallagher II, *Shareholder*
Patrick F Gallagher, *Shareholder*
Thomas E Gallagher, *Shareholder*
EMP: 45
SQ FT: 10,000
SALES: 8.4MM **Privately Held**
WEB: www.jfgallagherco.com
SIC: 1711 1794 Mechanical contractor; plumbing contractors; warm air heating & air conditioning contractor; fire sprinkler system installation; excavation work

(G-10548)
MAJOR ELECTRONIX CORP
33801 Curtis Blvd Ste 110 (44095-4045)
PHONE...................440 942-0054
William Rowell, *President*
J R Rowell, *Vice Pres*
Michael Rowell, *Sales Mgr*
Kristen Burkley, *Sales Staff*
Chris Cleary, *Sales Staff*
▲ **EMP:** 25
SQ FT: 12,500
SALES (est): 7.1MM **Privately Held**
WEB: www.majorelectronix.com
SIC: 5065 5063 Electronic parts; electrical apparatus & equipment

(G-10549)
MILLENIUM CONTROL SYSTEMS LLC
34525 Melinz Pkwy Ste 205 (44095-4037)
PHONE...................440 510-0055
Fax: 440 510-0055
Mike Upholz, *Project Dir*
Scot Poore, *Electrical Engi*
Carol Caimi, *Office Mgr*
Toni Chuhran, *Software Dev*
Patrick Gallagher,
EMP: 37
SQ FT: 12,000
SALES (est): 12.1MM **Privately Held**
WEB: www.millenniumcontrols.com
SIC: 7373 Systems integration services

(G-10550)
NORTHERN OHIO PLUMBING CO
35601 Curtis Blvd Unit 1 (44095-4128)
PHONE...................440 951-3370
Fax: 440 951-6952
James J Roddy, *President*
John Roddy Jr, *Corp Secy*
Roddy Frank, *Vice Pres*
Frank Roddy, *Vice Pres*
Mark Wilson, *Vice Pres*
EMP: 50
SQ FT: 12,000
SALES (est): 7.8MM **Privately Held**
SIC: 1711 Plumbing contractors

(G-10551)
UNIVAR INC
Also Called: Southern Mill Creek Pdts Ohio
33851 Curtis Blvd Ste 208 (44095-4003)
PHONE...................440 510-1259
Kris Joos, *Finance Mgr*
Sam Hartwell, *Branch Mgr*
EMP: 40
SALES (corp-wide): 8.2B **Publicly Held**
SIC: 5191 Pesticides

PA: Univar Inc.
3075 Highland Pkwy # 200
Downers Grove IL 60515
331 777-6000

Eaton
Preble County

(G-10552)
ANCILLARY MEDICAL INVESTMENTS
Also Called: Gary's Prescription Pharmacy
125 Amelia Dr (45320-9508)
PHONE...................937 456-5520
Fax: 937 456-4984
S Gary Pieratt, *President*
Bret Frence, *Principal*
EMP: 31
SQ FT: 6,000
SALES (est): 4.9MM **Privately Held**
SIC: 5912 7352 Drug stores; medical equipment rental

(G-10553)
AT&T SERVICES INC
1338 N Barron St (45320-1016)
PHONE...................937 456-2330
Karen Williams, *Manager*
EMP: 187
SALES (corp-wide): 160.5B **Publicly Held**
SIC: 4813 4812 Local & long distance telephone communications; cellular telephone services
HQ: At&T Services, Inc.
208 S Akard St Ste 110
Dallas TX 75202
210 821-4105

(G-10554)
COLONIAL BANC CORP (PA)
110 W Main St (45320-1746)
P.O. Box 309 (45320-0309)
PHONE...................937 456-5544
Joan Kreitzer, *President*
Amy Aldridge, *Exec VP*
Dan Daugherty, *Assistant VP*
Amy Fouche, *Manager*
Susan Landgrave, *Admin Asst*
EMP: 36
SALES (est): 7.3MM **Privately Held**
WEB: www.enbbank.com
SIC: 6021 7291 National commercial banks; tax return preparation services

(G-10555)
DAVITA INC
105 E Wash Jackson Rd (45320-9789)
PHONE...................937 456-1174
Susan Dynes, *President*
EMP: 27 **Publicly Held**
SIC: 8092 Kidney dialysis centers
PA: Davita Inc.
2000 16th St
Denver CO 80202

(G-10556)
DAYTEP INC
1816 Alexander Rd (45320-9222)
PHONE...................937 456-5860
Jayme M Day, *President*
James G Day, *Treasurer*
EMP: 35 **EST:** 1997
SQ FT: 22,500
SALES: 6.4MM **Privately Held**
WEB: www.daytep.com
SIC: 1542 Commercial & office building, new construction

(G-10557)
DRAKE STATE AIR
3711 Ozias Rd (45320-9750)
PHONE...................937 472-3740
Steve Christer, *CEO*
EMP: 50
SALES (est): 1.6MM **Privately Held**
SIC: 1711 Heating & air conditioning contractors

(G-10558)
DRAKE STATE AIR SYSTEMS INC
1417 E Main St (45320-2231)
PHONE...................937 472-0640
Steve Chrismer, *President*
Sherry Loveless, *Opers Staff*
Lisa Soullivan, *Controller*
Chelsea Chrismer, *Manager*
EMP: 26
SALES (est): 2.4MM **Privately Held**
WEB: www.drakecomfort.com
SIC: 1711 Warm air heating & air conditioning contractor

(G-10559)
EATON GARDENS REHABILITATION A
Also Called: Maple Gardens Rehab
515 S Maple St (45320-9413)
PHONE...................937 456-5537
Ephram Lahasky,
EMP: 85
SALES (est): 777.1K **Privately Held**
SIC: 8051 Skilled nursing care facilities

(G-10560)
EATON RESCUE SQUAD
Also Called: Eaton Fire Division
391 W Lexington Rd (45320-9275)
P.O. Box 27 (45320-0027)
PHONE...................937 456-5361
Brian Smith, *Branch Mgr*
EMP: 32 **Privately Held**
WEB: www.eatonmunicipalcourt.com
SIC: 9224 4119 Fire department, not including volunteer; ambulance service
PA: Eaton Rescue Squad
328 N Maple St
Eaton OH 45320
937 456-5310

(G-10561)
GARYS PHARMACY INC
125 Amelia Dr (45320-9508)
PHONE...................937 456-5777
Gary Pieratt, *President*
EMP: 31
SALES: 7MM **Privately Held**
SIC: 5912 5999 5947 5499 Drug stores; hospital equipment & supplies; greeting cards; health & dietetic food stores; hospital equipment & furniture; agents, shipping

(G-10562)
HEALTH CARE RTREMENT CORP AMER
Also Called: Heartland of Eaton
515 S Maple St (45320-9413)
PHONE...................937 456-5537
Tom Nielander, *Manager*
EMP: 100
SALES (corp-wide): 3.6B **Publicly Held**
WEB: www.hrc-manorcare.com
SIC: 8051 Skilled nursing care facilities
HQ: Health Care And Retirement Corporation Of America
333 N Summit St Ste 103
Toledo OH 43604
419 252-5500

(G-10563)
KRAMER & KRAMER INC
Also Called: Kramer & Kramer Realtors
420 N Barron St (45320-1708)
P.O. Box 85 (45320-0085)
PHONE...................937 456-1101
Fax: 937 456-1201
Horace J Kramer Sr, *President*
H John Kramer, *Vice Pres*
Debbie Kramer, *Treasurer*
Janet EBY, *Manager*
EMP: 30
SQ FT: 3,000
SALES (est): 2.1MM **Privately Held**
WEB: www.kramerauctions.com
SIC: 7389 6531 Auctioneers, fee basis; real estate brokers & agents

(G-10564)
L & M PRODUCTS INC
1407 N Barron St (45320-1017)
PHONE...................937 456-7141
Fax: 937 456-7143

Ben Hollinger, *President*
EMP: 150
SQ FT: 14,000
SALES: 1.6MM **Privately Held**
SIC: 8331 Vocational rehabilitation agency

(G-10565)
LCNB NATIONAL BANK
110 W Main St (45320-1746)
PHONE...................937 456-5544
Michele Kreitzer, *Officer*
EMP: 59
SALES (corp-wide): 54.9MM **Publicly Held**
SIC: 6021 National commercial banks
HQ: Lcnb National Bank
2 N Broadway St Lowr
Lebanon OH 45036
513 932-1414

(G-10566)
MARONDA HOMES INC FLORIDA
Also Called: Imperial Lumber
1050 S Barron St (45320-9387)
PHONE...................937 472-3907
Larry Taylor, *Manager*
EMP: 100
SALES (corp-wide): 166.1MM **Privately Held**
WEB: www.maronda.com
SIC: 1521 New construction, single-family houses
HQ: Maronda Homes Inc Of Florida
11 Timberglen Dr
Imperial PA 15126
724 695-1200

(G-10567)
MEDPRO LLC
251 W Lexington Rd (45320-9282)
PHONE...................937 336-5586
Gina Hatmaker, *CEO*
Patrick Caylor, *COO*
Erica Fisher, *Human Resources*
Ernest Hatmaker, *Officer*
EMP: 75
SALES (est): 890.9K **Privately Held**
SIC: 4119 Local passenger transportation; ambulance service

(G-10568)
MENTAL RTRDTION PREBLE CNTY BD (PA)
201 E Lexington Rd Ste A (45320-1578)
PHONE...................937 456-5891
Diane Knupp, *Superintendent*
Shirley Turner, *Superintendent*
EMP: 60
SALES (est): 1.1MM **Privately Held**
SIC: 8051 8211 Mental retardation hospital; school for the retarded; public special education school

(G-10569)
MIAMI VALLEY COMMUNITY ACTION
308 Eaton Lewisburg Rd (45320-1105)
PHONE...................937 456-2800
Fax: 937 456-3164
Rita Daily, *Director*
EMP: 45
SALES (corp-wide): 13MM **Privately Held**
SIC: 8322 Social service center
PA: Miami Valley Community Action Partnership
719 S Main St
Dayton OH 45402
937 222-1009

(G-10570)
NAMI OF PREBLE COUNTY OHIO
800 E Saint Clair St (45320-2433)
PHONE...................937 456-4947
Shelly Ratliff, *Director*
EMP: 50 **EST:** 2013
SALES (est): 273.9K **Privately Held**
SIC: 8322 8699 Old age assistance; senior citizens' center or association; charitable organization

▲ = Import ▼ = Export
◆ = Import/Export

GEOGRAPHIC SECTION
Elyria - Lorain County (G-10593)

(G-10571)
OCTOBER ENTERPRISES INC
Also Called: Greenbriar Nursing Center, The
501 W Lexington Rd (45320-9274)
PHONE................937 456-9535
Fax: 937 456-9530
Paul De Palma, *President*
Jennifer Besecker, *Admin Asst*
EMP: 125
SQ FT: 27,660
SALES (est): 5.8MM Privately Held
WEB: www.greenbriarcampus.com
SIC: 8051 8052 Convalescent home with continuous nursing care; intermediate care facilities

(G-10572)
PARKER-HANNIFIN CORPORATION
Tube Fittings Division
725 N Beech St (45320-1499)
PHONE................937 456-5571
Fax: 937 456-5696
Dave Stover, *Prdtn Mgr*
Jay Studer, *Mfg Mgr*
Debrah Burleson, *Purchasing*
Paul Farno, *Purchasing*
Tom Fox, *QC Dir*
EMP: 400
SALES (corp-wide): 12B Publicly Held
WEB: www.parker.com
SIC: 3494 5074 3498 3492 Pipe fittings; couplings, except pressure & soil pipe; plumbing & heating valves; plumbing fittings & supplies; tube fabricating (contract bending & shaping); fluid power valves & hose fittings
PA: Parker-Hannifin Corporation
6035 Parkland Blvd
Cleveland OH 44124
216 896-3000

(G-10573)
PERSONAL TOUCH HM CARE IPA INC
Also Called: Health Force
302 Eaton Lewisburg Rd (45320-1105)
PHONE................937 456-4447
Ann Koller, *Personnel Exec*
Patty Guthrie, *Manager*
Annette Owens, *Manager*
Susan Moore, *Director*
EMP: 40
SALES (corp-wide): 363MM Privately Held
WEB: www.pthomecare.com
SIC: 8082 7361 Visiting nurse service; nurses' registry
PA: Personal Touch Home Care Ipa, Inc.
1985 Marcus Ave Ste 202
New Hyde Park NY 11042
718 468-4747

(G-10574)
PREBLE COUNTY COUNCIL ON AGING
800 E Saint Clair St (45320-2433)
PHONE................937 456-4947
Fax: 937 456-6565
Shelley Ratliff, *Exec Dir*
Alice Mc Mann, *Director*
EMP: 25
SALES: 1.2MM Privately Held
SIC: 8322 Social worker

(G-10575)
PREBLE COUNTY GENERAL HLTH DST
Also Called: Erik Balster Hlth Commissioner
615 Hillcrest Dr (45320-8559)
PHONE................937 472-0087
Fax: 937 456-6350
Erik Balster, *Principal*
Lorraine Cheek, *Facilities Mgr*
Sarah Hays, *Finance Dir*
Pamela Heiser, *Accountant*
Marilyn Wilson, *Consultant*
EMP: 28
SALES (est): 1.3MM Privately Held
SIC: 8011 Obstetrician

(G-10576)
REID PHYSICIAN ASSOCIATES INC
Also Called: Reid Physicians Associates
109b Wash Jackson Rd (45320-9793)
PHONE................937 456-4400
Joellen Tapalman, *Manager*
EMP: 414
SALES (corp-wide): 40MM Privately Held
SIC: 8011 General & family practice, physician/surgeon
PA: Reid Physician Associates, Inc.
1100 Reid Pkwy
Richmond IN 47374
765 983-3000

(G-10577)
TIME WARNER CABLE INC
419 S Barron St (45320-2401)
P.O. Box 348 (45320-0348)
PHONE................937 471-1572
Fax: 937 456-9439
Kathi Hollenbauga, *Manager*
EMP: 33
SQ FT: 2,500
SALES (corp-wide): 41.5B Publicly Held
SIC: 4841 Cable television services
HQ: Spectrum Management Holding Company, Llc
400 Atlantic St
Stamford CT 06901
203 905-7801

(G-10578)
TRINITY ACTION PARTNERSHIP
308 Eaton Lewisburg Rd (45320-1105)
PHONE................937 456-2800
John Dollenn, *CEO*
Joyce Price, *COO*
Steve Dipender, *CFO*
Rita Daily, *Director*
EMP: 50
SALES (est): 1.7MM Privately Held
WEB: www.cap-dayton.org
SIC: 8322 Meal delivery program

(G-10579)
UNITED PRODUCERS INC
617 S Franklin St (45320-9419)
PHONE................937 456-4161
John Raile, *Accounting Mgr*
Harry O'Call, *Manager*
EMP: 25
SALES (corp-wide): 123.4MM Privately Held
WEB: www.uproducers.com
SIC: 5154 Auctioning livestock
PA: United Producers, Inc.
8351 N High St Ste 250
Columbus OH 43235
614 433-2150

(G-10580)
VANCREST LTD
Also Called: Vancrest Healthcare Cntr Eaton
1600 Park Ave (45320-9674)
PHONE................937 456-3010
Brenda Newman, *Mktg Dir*
Lori Nelson, *Records Dir*
Rosemarie Dennis, *Administration*
EMP: 60
SALES (corp-wide): 16.3MM Privately Held
WEB: www.vancrest.com
SIC: 8051 Convalescent home with continuous nursing care
PA: Vancrest, Ltd.
120 W Main St Ste 200
Van Wert OH 45891
419 238-0715

Edgerton
Williams County

(G-10581)
ALL HEART HOME CARE LLC
143 N Michigan Ave (43517-9322)
P.O. Box 896 (43517-0896)
PHONE................419 298-0034
Kelly Wilhelm, *Mng Member*
EMP: 44
SALES (est): 158.2K Privately Held
SIC: 8082 Home health care services

(G-10582)
ANGELS VISITING
143 N Michigan Ave (43517-9322)
P.O. Box 896 (43517-0896)
PHONE................419 298-0034
Kelly Wilhelm, *Owner*
EMP: 60
SALES (est): 129.9K Privately Held
SIC: 8082 Home health care services

(G-10583)
MATERIAL SUPPLIERS INC
2444 State Route 49 (43517-9551)
P.O. Box 340 (43517-0340)
PHONE................419 298-2440
Gerry Weber, *President*
Dean Weber, *Vice Pres*
EMP: 30 EST: 1997
SALES (est): 2.5MM Privately Held
SIC: 4213 Trucking, except local

(G-10584)
PEREGRINE HEALTH SERVICES INC
Also Called: Park View Nursing Center
328 W Vine St (43517-9600)
PHONE................419 298-2321
Fax: 419 298-2512
Ed Fodrea, *Manager*
EMP: 100
SALES (corp-wide): 7MM Privately Held
WEB: www.nursinghomeinfo.org
SIC: 8099 Health screening service
PA: Peregrine Health Services, Inc.
1661 Old Henderson Rd
Columbus OH 43220
614 459-2656

Edon
Williams County

(G-10585)
AGRIDRY LLC
3460 Us Highway 20 (43518-9733)
P.O. Box 336 (43518-0336)
PHONE................419 459-4399
Bruce Silcott, *Office Mgr*
Eli P Troyer, *Mng Member*
EMP: 45
SALES (est): 10.7MM Privately Held
SIC: 3567 1541 Driers & redriers, industrial process; grain elevator construction

Elida
Allen County

(G-10586)
BOARD AMERCN TOWNSHIP TRUSTEES
102 Pioneer Rd (45807-1106)
PHONE................419 331-8651
Fax: 419 331-7047
G B Bowers, *President*
Paul Basinger, *Principal*
Darell Long, *Principal*
Larry Van Demark, *Principal*
Laurie Swick, *Treasurer*
EMP: 50
SALES (est): 4.4MM Privately Held
SIC: 4959 Road, airport & parking lot maintenance services

Elmore
Ottawa County

(G-10587)
CHIPMATIC TOOL & MACHINE INC
212 Ottawa St (43416-7710)
P.O. Box 87 (43416-0087)
PHONE................419 862-2737
Fax: 419 862-2769
Mike Detzel, *President*
Bob Babjack, *General Mgr*
John Hansen, *Purch Mgr*
Duane Glase, *Purch Agent*
Chris Lajoie, *QC Mgr*
EMP: 67
SQ FT: 30,000
SALES (est): 10.4MM Privately Held
WEB: www.chipmatic.com
SIC: 3599 8711 7692 3544 Machine shop, jobbing & repair; mechanical engineering; welding repair; special dies, tools, jigs & fixtures

(G-10588)
INTERNATIONAL ORDR OF RNBOW FO
Also Called: Genoa Assembly 107
18706 W State Route 105 (43416-9525)
PHONE................419 862-3009
Brenda Roadarmel, *Director*
EMP: 30 EST: 1926
SALES (est): 306K Privately Held
SIC: 8641 Civic social & fraternal associations

(G-10589)
ROTHERT FARM INC
1084 S Opfer Lentz Rd (43416-9789)
PHONE................419 467-0095
Trent Rothert, *President*
Susan Rohtert, *Treasurer*
EMP: 87
SALES (est): 7MM Privately Held
SIC: 0161 Cabbage farm

Elyria
Lorain County

(G-10590)
AA FIRE PROTECTION LLC
620 Sugar Ln (44035-6310)
PHONE................440 327-0060
Scott McMillen, *CEO*
EMP: 25
SALES (est): 2.2MM Privately Held
SIC: 7389 Fire protection service other than forestry or public

(G-10591)
ABBEWOOD LIMITED PARTNERSHIP
Also Called: The Abbewood
1210 Abbe Rd S Ofc (44035-7276)
PHONE................440 366-8980
Fax: 440 365-5165
Logan Sexton, *General Ptnr*
EMP: 27
SALES (est): 2.1MM Privately Held
SIC: 8361 Home for the aged

(G-10592)
ABRAHAM FORD LLC
Also Called: Elyria Ford
1115 E Broad St (44035-6305)
PHONE................440 233-7402
Nick Abraham, *President*
Kris Allegretto, *Manager*
Kyle Klekota, *Manager*
Chad Whitacre, *Manager*
EMP: 30
SQ FT: 16,000
SALES (est): 2.5MM Privately Held
SIC: 7389 7538 5531 5521 Personal service agents, brokers & bureaus; general automotive repair shops, automotive & home supply stores; used car dealers

(G-10593)
AMERICAN HOOD SYSTEMS INC
177 Reaser Ct (44035-6285)
P.O. Box 1377 (44036-1377)
PHONE................440 365-4567
Michael Maynard, *President*
Daniel Reaser, *Principal*
Angela Mullen, *Buyer*
Samantha Hamilton, *Manager*
EMP: 40
SQ FT: 40,000
SALES: 1MM Privately Held
WEB: www.americanhood.com
SIC: 5075 Ventilating equipment & supplies

Elyria - Lorain County (G-10594) GEOGRAPHIC SECTION

(G-10594)
ARCH ABRAHAM SUSUKI LTD
Also Called: Arch Abraham Nissan & Susuki
1111 E Broad St (44035-6305)
PHONE.....................440 934-6001
Archie Abraham, *Owner*
Nancy McGreevy, *Accountant*
EMP: 32
SQ FT: 9,600
SALES (est): 6.1MM **Privately Held**
SIC: 5511 7532 5521 Automobiles, new & used; top & body repair & paint shops; used car dealers

(G-10595)
ATLAS ELECTRICAL CONSTRUCTION
7974 Murray Ridge Rd (44035-2065)
P.O. Box 695 (44036-0695)
PHONE.....................440 323-5418
Fax: 440 323-4944
Pearl Myers, *President*
Rowena Myers, *Corp Secy*
Charles R Myers Jr, *Vice Pres*
EMP: 25
SQ FT: 5,700
SALES (est): 2.9MM **Privately Held**
SIC: 1731 General electrical contractor

(G-10596)
BELLMAN PLUMBING INC
7520 W Ridge Rd (44035-1960)
PHONE.....................440 324-4477
Robert Bellman, *President*
EMP: 28
SQ FT: 13,400
SALES (est): 3.9MM **Privately Held**
WEB: www.bellmanplumbing.com
SIC: 1711 Plumbing contractors

(G-10597)
BENDIX COML VHCL SYSTEMS LLC (DH)
901 Cleveland St (44035-4153)
P.O. Box 4016 (44036-2016)
PHONE.....................440 329-9000
Fax: 440 329-9203
Christian Fischer, *President*
Lance Hansen, *Managing Dir*
Paul Johnson, *Managing Dir*
Carlos Hungria, *COO*
Claus Beyer, *Vice Pres*
◆ **EMP:** 350 **EST:** 1930
SALES (est): 1.1B **Privately Held**
SIC: 5013 8711 Automotive supplies & parts; engineering services
HQ: Knorr Brake Truck Systems Company
748 Starbuck Ave
Watertown NY 13601
315 786-5200

(G-10598)
BINDU ASSOCIATES LLC
Also Called: Country Suites By Carlson
645 Griswold Rd (44035-2394)
PHONE.....................440 324-0099
Fax: 440 324-1199
Kiran Patel, *President*
Sam Patel,
EMP: 25
SALES: 1MM **Privately Held**
SIC: 7011 Hotels & motels

(G-10599)
BRADY PLUMBING & HEATING INC
43191 N Ridge Rd (44035-1058)
PHONE.....................440 324-4261
Fax: 440 324-9987
Ken Brady, *President*
Loretta Brady, *Vice Pres*
EMP: 30
SALES (est): 2MM **Privately Held**
SIC: 1711 Plumbing contractors

(G-10600)
C&K TRUCKING LLC
41387 Schadden Rd (44035-2222)
PHONE.....................440 657-5249
EMP: 31 **Privately Held**
SIC: 4213 Contract haulers
PA: C&K Trucking, Llc
6205 W 101st St
Chicago Ridge IL 60415

(G-10601)
CELLCO PARTNERSHIP
Also Called: Verizon
1621 W River Rd N (44035-2715)
PHONE.....................440 324-9479
Fax: 440 324-1294
Joy Heldt, *Manager*
EMP: 30
SALES (corp-wide): 126B **Publicly Held**
SIC: 4812 Cellular telephone services
HQ: Cellco Partnership
1 Verizon Way
Basking Ridge NJ 07920

(G-10602)
CENTRO PROPERTIES GROUP LLC
3343 Midway Mall (44035-9003)
P.O. Box 7674, Merrifield VA (22116-7674)
PHONE.....................440 324-6610
Mark Bressler, *Manager*
EMP: 50
SALES (corp-wide): 2.2MM **Privately Held**
SIC: 5311 6512 Department stores; non-residential building operators
PA: Centro Properties Group Llc
1 Fayette St Ste 300
Conshohocken PA 19428
610 941-9304

(G-10603)
CHEMICAL BANK
111 Antioch Dr (44035-9104)
PHONE.....................440 323-7451
Matt Clark, *Manager*
EMP: 36
SALES (corp-wide): 776.1MM **Publicly Held**
SIC: 6035 Federal savings & loan associations
HQ: Chemical Bank
333 E Main St
Midland MI 48640
989 631-9200

(G-10604)
CITY OF ELYRIA
Also Called: Elyria Waste Water Plant
1194 Gulf Rd (44035-1752)
PHONE.....................440 366-2211
Fax: 440 366-0787
Gregory Worcester, *Manager*
EMP: 52 **Privately Held**
WEB: www.elyriahealth.com
SIC: 4953 Refuse systems
PA: City Of Elyria
131 Court St
Elyria OH 44035
440 326-1402

(G-10605)
CLEVELAND CLINIC FOUNDATION
303 Chestnut Commons Dr (44035-9607)
PHONE.....................440 366-9444
John Secrist, *Branch Mgr*
EMP: 85
SALES (corp-wide): 8B **Privately Held**
SIC: 6733 Trusts
PA: The Cleveland Clinic Foundation
9500 Euclid Ave
Cleveland OH 44195
216 636-8335

(G-10606)
COBOS INSURANCE CENTRE LLC
41436 Griswold Rd (44035-2324)
PHONE.....................440 324-3732
Fax: 440 324-2584
Deborah Fischer, *Accountant*
Caitlyn Baird, *Agent*
Macario Cobos, *Agent*
Matthew Grattan, *Agent*
Roberto Cobos,
EMP: 25
SQ FT: 2,000
SALES (est): 3.6MM **Privately Held**
SIC: 6411 Insurance agents

(G-10607)
COMPREHENSIVE HEALTH CARE (HQ)
Also Called: Emh Regional Healthcare System
630 E River St (44035-5902)
PHONE.....................440 329-7500
Fax: 440 329-7372
Donald Sheldon, *President*
Jill Cooksey, *Vice Pres*
Daniel N Miller, *Vice Pres*
Don Miller, *VP Opers*
Jeff Hahn, *Facilities Dir*
EMP: 1200
SQ FT: 450,000
SALES: 18.2MM
SALES (corp-wide): 2.3B **Privately Held**
WEB: www.emh-healthcare.org
SIC: 8741 Hospital management
PA: University Hospitals Health System, Inc.
3605 Warrensville Ctr Rd
Shaker Heights OH 44122
216 767-8900

(G-10608)
CONSUMER FOODS
123 Gateway Blvd N (44035-4923)
PHONE.....................440 284-5972
Dennis Walter, *President*
EMP: 40
SALES (est): 254.7K **Privately Held**
SIC: 7542 Carwashes

(G-10609)
COUNTY OF LORAIN
Also Called: Lorain County Sani Engineers
247 Hadaway St (44035-7760)
PHONE.....................440 329-5584
Fax: 440 329-5587
Kenneth P Carney Sr, *Principal*
EMP: 85 **Privately Held**
WEB: www.lcmhb.org
SIC: 4952 Sewerage systems
PA: County Of Lorain
226 Middle Ave
Elyria OH 44035
440 329-5201

(G-10610)
COUNTY OF LORAIN
Also Called: Lorain Cnty Brd Mntl Rtrdtn
1091 Infirmary Rd (44035-4804)
PHONE.....................440 329-3734
Fax: 440 322-2683
Amber Fisher PHD, *Superintendent*
Thaddeus G Chmura, *Asst Supt*
John Boncok, *Director*
EMP: 50 **Privately Held**
WEB: www.lcmhb.org
SIC: 8322 8361 Social service center; general counseling services; home for the mentally handicapped; home for the physically handicapped
PA: County Of Lorain
226 Middle Ave
Elyria OH 44035
440 329-5201

(G-10611)
COUNTY OF LORAIN
Also Called: Adult Probation Department
308 2nd St (44035-5506)
PHONE.....................440 326-4700
Bart Hobart, *Director*
EMP: 30 **Privately Held**
WEB: www.lcmhb.org
SIC: 8322 Probation office
PA: County Of Lorain
226 Middle Ave
Elyria OH 44035
440 329-5201

(G-10612)
COUNTY OF LORAIN
Also Called: Lorain County Engineers
247 Hadaway St (44035-7760)
PHONE.....................440 326-5884
Fax: 440 323-3357
Ken Carney, *Manager*
EMP: 29 **Privately Held**
WEB: www.lcmhb.org
SIC: 8711 Engineering services

PA: County Of Lorain
226 Middle Ave
Elyria OH 44035
440 329-5201

(G-10613)
COUNTY OF LORAIN
Also Called: Lorain Country Job & Fmly Svcs
42495 N Ridge Rd Ste A (44035-1045)
PHONE.....................440 284-1830
Jeff King, *Branch Mgr*
Michael Longo, *Director*
EMP: 100 **Privately Held**
SIC: 8322 Social service center
PA: County Of Lorain
226 Middle Ave
Elyria OH 44035
440 329-5201

(G-10614)
COUNTY OF LORAIN
Also Called: Drug and Alcohol
120 East Ave (44035-5652)
PHONE.....................440 989-4900
Vesta Warner, *Director*
EMP: 50 **Privately Held**
WEB: www.lcmhb.org
SIC: 8093 Alcohol clinic, outpatient
PA: County Of Lorain
226 Middle Ave
Elyria OH 44035
440 329-5201

(G-10615)
COUNTY OF LORAIN
Also Called: Lorain County Garage
42100 Russia Rd (44035-6813)
PHONE.....................440 326-5880
Fax: 440 284-1062
Mike Rodak, *Superintendent*
EMP: 55 **Privately Held**
WEB: www.lcmhb.org
SIC: 7538 General automotive repair shops
PA: County Of Lorain
226 Middle Ave
Elyria OH 44035
440 329-5201

(G-10616)
COUNTY OF LORAIN
Also Called: Lorain County Childrens Svcs
226 Middle Ave Fl 4 (44035-5629)
PHONE.....................440 329-5340
Fax: 440 329-5378
Donald Starett, *Human Res Mgr*
Robert Milovich, *Data Proc Staff*
Dr Gary Crow, *Director*
EMP: 140 **Privately Held**
WEB: www.lcmhb.org
SIC: 8322 8361 Adoption services; group foster home
PA: County Of Lorain
226 Middle Ave
Elyria OH 44035
440 329-5201

(G-10617)
DOT DIAMOND CORE DRILLING INC (PA)
780 Sugar Ln (44035-6312)
P.O. Box 683 (44036-0683)
PHONE.....................440 322-6466
Jeannie Nolan, *President*
Krista Phillips, *General Mgr*
Pat Nolan, *Principal*
Matt Nolan, *Vice Pres*
Ryan Nolan, *Vice Pres*
EMP: 28 **EST:** 1974
SQ FT: 7,200
SALES (est): 7.6MM **Privately Held**
WEB: www.dotdrilling.com
SIC: 1771 Concrete work

(G-10618)
DYNATECH SYSTEMS INC
161 Reaser Ct (44035-6285)
P.O. Box 1589 (44036-1589)
PHONE.....................440 365-1774
Fax: 440 365-1717
Sue A Everett, *President*
EMP: 25
SQ FT: 5,000

GEOGRAPHIC SECTION

Elyria - Lorain County (G-10643)

SALES (est): 3.3MM **Privately Held**
WEB: www.diamonddrillbit.com
SIC: 3425 5085 Saw blades & handsaws; industrial supplies

(G-10619)
EDUCATONAL SVC CTR LORAIN CNTY (PA)
1885 Lake Ave (44035-2551)
PHONE..................440 244-1659
Fax: 440 324-7355
Thomas Rockwell, *Superintendent*
Moira Erwine, *Director*
Diane Koski, *Admin Asst*
Debra Greszler, *Education*
Mary Kaminski, *Education*
EMP: 25
SALES (est): 10.4MM **Privately Held**
SIC: 8741 8211 Administrative management; elementary & secondary schools

(G-10620)
EJQ HOME HEALTH CARE INC
800 Middle Ave (44035-5855)
PHONE..................440 323-7004
Eva Boone, *President*
EMP: 75
SALES (est): 1.7MM **Privately Held**
WEB: www.ejqhomehealthcare.com
SIC: 8082 Visiting nurse service

(G-10621)
ELYRIA COUNTRY CLUB COMPANY
41625 Oberlin Elyria Rd (44035-7599)
PHONE..................440 322-6391
Fax: 440 322-2083
Eric Toth, *Controller*
Kimberly Violo, *Manager*
Kimberly Viola, *Manager*
EMP: 125
SQ FT: 19,892
SALES: 2.8MM **Privately Held**
SIC: 7997 Country club, membership

(G-10622)
ELYRIA FOUNDRY HOLDINGS LLC
120 Filbert St (44035-5357)
PHONE..................440 322-4657
L Bevington, *Vice Pres*
Doug Varney, *VP Opers*
Debbie Murawski, *Purchasing*
Bruce Smith,
EMP: 300 **Privately Held**
SIC: 6719 Investment holding companies, except banks

(G-10623)
ELYRIA-LORAIN BROADCASTING CO (HQ)
Also Called: Elts Broadcasting
538 Broad St 400 (44035-5508)
PHONE..................440 322-3761
George Hudnutt, *President*
Philip Kelly, *Treasurer*
Starr Davril, *Info Tech Mgr*
EMP: 50 EST: 1945
SQ FT: 3,000
SALES (est): 11.4MM
SALES (corp-wide): 12.7MM **Privately Held**
WEB: www.wnwv.com
SIC: 4832 Radio broadcasting stations
PA: Lorain County Printing & Publishing Co Inc
225 East Ave
Elyria OH
440 329-7000

(G-10624)
ELYRIA-LORAIN BROADCASTING CO
Also Called: Weol/Wnwv Radio
538 Broad St 400 (44035-5508)
PHONE..................440 322-3761
Fax: 440 284-3189
Gary L Kneisley, *President*
Renee McKinley, *Sales Staff*
EMP: 25
SALES (corp-wide): 12.7MM **Privately Held**
WEB: www.wnwv.com
SIC: 7319 Media buying service

HQ: Elyria-Lorain Broadcasting Company
538 Broad St 400
Elyria OH 44035
440 322-3761

(G-10625)
EMH REGIONAL HOMECARE AGENCY
90 E Broad St (44035-5521)
PHONE..................440 329-7519
Fax: 440 284-5769
Don Sheldon, *President*
Rae Vandemotter, *Manager*
EMP: 30
SALES (est): 845K **Privately Held**
SIC: 8082 Home health care services

(G-10626)
EMPLOYMENT NETWORK
42495 N Ridge Rd (44035-1045)
PHONE..................440 324-5244
Fax: 440 324-5266
Linda Brown, *Vice Pres*
Diana Mishlannau, *Manager*
Jan Rybarczyk, *Director*
EMP: 35
SALES (est): 1.2MM **Privately Held**
SIC: 7361 Placement agencies

(G-10627)
ENVELOPE MART OF NORTH E OHIO
Also Called: Em Print Group
1540 Lowell St (44035-4869)
PHONE..................440 322-8862
Robert Thompson, *CEO*
Bradley Thompson, *President*
Andrew Thompson, *Vice Pres*
Brian Thompson, *VP Opers*
Chris Arnold, *Sales Mgr*
EMP: 40
SQ FT: 80,000
SALES (est): 11.2MM **Privately Held**
WEB: www.envmart.com
SIC: 5112 Envelopes

(G-10628)
ENVELOPE MART OF OHIO INC
1540 Lowell St (44035-4869)
P.O. Box 808 (44036-0808)
PHONE..................440 365-8177
Fax: 800 214-1733
Robert T Thompson, *President*
Chris Arnold, *President*
EMP: 50
SALES (est): 9MM **Privately Held**
SIC: 5112 2677 Envelopes; envelopes

(G-10629)
ENVIROTEST SYSTEMS CORP
128 Reaser Ct (44035-6285)
PHONE..................330 963-4464
EMP: 34 **Privately Held**
WEB: www.il.etest.com
SIC: 7549 Emissions testing without repairs, automotive
HQ: Envirotest Systems Corp.
7 Kripes Rd
East Granby CT 06026

(G-10630)
GLOBAL TCHNICAL RECRUITERS INC
366 Chestnut Commons Dr (44035-9604)
PHONE..................440 365-1670
Robert Murphy, *Manager*
EMP: 36
SALES (corp-wide): 7.8MM **Privately Held**
SIC: 7361 Executive placement
PA: Global Technical Recruiters Inc.
27887 Clemens Rd Ste 1
Westlake OH 44145
216 251-9560

(G-10631)
GOODWILL INDS LORAIN CNTY INC (PA)
145 Keep Ct (44035-2214)
PHONE..................440 242-2124
Fax: 440 245-2670
Nancy Everman, *Finance*
Sherwin Case, *Manager*
Gina Ciuca, *Manager*
Mona Finlayson, *Manager*

Jennifer Kozak, *Manager*
EMP: 32 EST: 1928
SQ FT: 27,000
SALES: 4MM **Privately Held**
WEB: www.goodwillofloraincounty.com
SIC: 8331 Job training services

(G-10632)
GROSS PLUMBING INCORPORATED
Also Called: Gross Supply
6843 Lake Ave (44035-2149)
PHONE..................440 324-9999
Fax: 440 324-3366
Daniel Gross, *President*
Edward J Gross, *Vice Pres*
Guy Gross, *Vice Pres*
Martha Taylor, *Treasurer*
Pam Pierce, *Admin Sec*
EMP: 50 EST: 1956
SQ FT: 25,000
SALES (est): 9.9MM **Privately Held**
SIC: 1711 5999 Plumbing contractors; mechanical contractor; plumbing & heating supplies

(G-10633)
HOME DEPOT USA INC
Also Called: Home Depot, The
150 Market Dr (44035-2885)
PHONE..................440 324-7222
Fax: 440 326-0416
James Meiden, *Manager*
Tom Davis, *Manager*
EMP: 135
SALES (corp-wide): 100.9B **Publicly Held**
WEB: www.homerentalsdepot.com
SIC: 5211 7359 Home centers; tool rental
HQ: Home Depot U.S.A., Inc.
2455 Paces Ferry Rd Se
Atlanta GA 30339

(G-10634)
HORIZON EDUCATION CENTERS
Also Called: Allen Horizon Center
10347 Dewhurst Rd (44035-8403)
PHONE..................440 458-5115
Fax: 440 458-5130
Donna Trent, *Branch Mgr*
EMP: 27
SALES (est): 408.4K
SALES (corp-wide): 6.1MM **Privately Held**
SIC: 8322 Adult day care center
PA: Horizon Education Centers
29510 Lorain Rd
North Olmsted OH 44070
440 779-1930

(G-10635)
IMMACULATE INTERIORS
123 Brace Ave (44035-2659)
PHONE..................440 324-9300
Russ Baldwin, *Owner*
EMP: 50
SALES (est): 1.8MM **Privately Held**
SIC: 1742 Acoustical & insulation work

(G-10636)
IMPACT MEDICAL MGT GROUP
1120 E Broad St (44035-6306)
P.O. Box 30 (44036-0030)
PHONE..................440 365-7014
Fax: 440 365-7178
Kathy George, *President*
EMP: 35
SQ FT: 1,200
SALES (est): 2.8MM **Privately Held**
SIC: 8748 Business consulting

(G-10637)
JERSEY CENTRAL PWR & LIGHT CO
Also Called: Firstenergy
6326 Lake Ave (44035-1116)
PHONE..................440 326-3222
Tony Alexander, *President*
EMP: 65 **Publicly Held**
WEB: www.jersey-central-power-light.monmouth.n
SIC: 4911 Electric services

HQ: Jersey Central Power & Light Company
76 S Main St
Akron OH 44308
800 736-3402

(G-10638)
KOKOSING CONSTRUCTION CO INC
1539 Lowell St (44035-4868)
PHONE..................440 323-9346
Fax: 440 322-2710
Brian Burgett, *President*
EMP: 50
SQ FT: 12,440
SALES (est): 2.6MM **Privately Held**
SIC: 1629 1521 Heavy construction; single-family housing construction

(G-10639)
KS ASSOCIATES INC
260 Burns Rd Ste 100 (44035-1513)
PHONE..................440 365-4730
Fax: 440 365-4790
Lynn Miggins, *President*
Rich Librach, *Vice Pres*
Tod Odonoghue, *Vice Pres*
Mark Skellenger, *Vice Pres*
Doug Dunn, *Engineer*
EMP: 55
SALES (est): 8MM **Privately Held**
SIC: 8711 8713 Civil engineering; surveying services

(G-10640)
LIFE CARE CENTERS AMERICA INC
1212 Abbe Rd S (44035-7269)
PHONE..................440 365-5200
Fax: 440 365-5266
Judy Harvey, *Purch Agent*
Marcy Szuch, *Financial Exec*
Vanessa Martin, *Persnl Dir*
Douglas McDermott, *Branch Mgr*
Robert Taylor, *CIO*
EMP: 119
SALES (corp-wide): 101MM **Privately Held**
SIC: 8051 Convalescent home with continuous nursing care
PA: Life Care Centers Of America, Inc.
3570 Keith St Nw
Cleveland TN 37312
423 472-9585

(G-10641)
LIFECARE AMBULANCE INC
598 Cleveland St (44035-4144)
PHONE..................440 323-2527
Fax: 440 365-2266
Peter De La Porte, *Branch Mgr*
EMP: 53
SALES (corp-wide): 13MM **Privately Held**
SIC: 4119 Ambulance service
PA: Lifecare Ambulance Inc.
640 Cleveland St
Elyria OH 44035
440 323-6111

(G-10642)
LIFECARE AMBULANCE INC (PA)
Also Called: Lorain Lifecare Ambulance
640 Cleveland St (44035-4104)
P.O. Box 993 (44036-0993)
PHONE..................440 323-6111
Peter De La Porte, *President*
Herbert De La Porte, *Vice Pres*
David Richards, *CFO*
EMP: 25
SQ FT: 15,000
SALES (est): 13MM **Privately Held**
WEB: www.lifecareambulance.com
SIC: 4119 4111 Ambulance service; local & suburban transit

(G-10643)
LIFESHARE CMNTY BLOOD SVCS INC (PA)
105 Cleveland St Ste 101 (44035-6166)
PHONE..................440 322-6159
Richard Cluck, *President*
Michael Dash, *Vice Pres*
Donyah Perine, *Finance*

Elyria - Lorain County (G-10644)

Ruby Nelson, *Executive Asst*
EMP: 35
SQ FT: 10,000
SALES: 15.9MM **Privately Held**
SIC: 8099 Blood bank

(G-10644)
LIFESHARE COMMUNITY BLOOD SVCS
105 Cliffland St (44035)
PHONE 440 322-6573
Richard Cluck, *Manager*
EMP: 45
SALES (corp-wide): 15.9MM **Privately Held**
SIC: 8099 Blood bank
PA: Lifeshare Community Blood Services, Inc.
105 Cleveland St Ste 101
Elyria OH 44035
440 322-6159

(G-10645)
LODGING INDUSTRY INC
Also Called: Econo Lodge
523 Griswold Rd (44035-2306)
PHONE 440 324-3911
Fax: 440 324-3911
Melyndy Brown, *General Mgr*
Scott Poldena, *Manager*
EMP: 25
SALES (corp-wide): 1.5MM **Privately Held**
SIC: 7011 Hotels & motels
PA: Lodging Industry Inc
910 Lorain Blvd Ste N
Elyria OH
440 323-9820

(G-10646)
LORAIN COUNTY BOARD
1091 Infirmary Rd (44035-4804)
PHONE 440 329-3734
Fax: 440 322-7659
Amber Fisher, *Superintendent*
Jodi Denes, *Manager*
Heather Gurchik, *Director*
Ashley Bunch, *Asst Director*
EMP: 34
SALES (est): 700.6K **Privately Held**
SIC: 8093 8331 Mental health clinic, outpatient; sheltered workshop

(G-10647)
LOWES HOME CENTERS LLC
646 Midway Blvd (44035-2442)
PHONE 440 324-5004
Fax: 440 324-4361
Paul Fran, *Branch Mgr*
Thomas Kilroy, *Department Mgr*
EMP: 200
SALES (corp-wide): 68.6B **Publicly Held**
SIC: 5211 5031 5722 Home centers; building materials, exterior; building materials, interior; household appliance stores
HQ: Lowe's Home Centers, Llc
1605 Curtis Bridge Rd
Wilkesboro NC 28697
336 658-4000

(G-10648)
MAINTENANCE SYSTERMS OF N OHIO
42208 Albrecht Rd Ste 1 (44035-8925)
P.O. Box 1203 (44036-1203)
PHONE 440 323-1291
Fax: 440 323-5293
Frank Rybarcyk Jr, *President*
EMP: 25
SQ FT: 5,200
SALES (est): 4.1MM **Privately Held**
WEB: www.maintenancesystemsco.com
SIC: 1611 1771 Surfacing & paving; highway & street maintenance; blacktop (asphalt) work

(G-10649)
MATCO PROPERTIES INC
823 Leona St (44035-2300)
PHONE 440 366-5501
Jack Matia, *President*
Debby Kurauz, *Human Res Dir*
EMP: 65
SQ FT: 50,000
SALES (est): 3.2MM **Privately Held**
SIC: 6512 Nonresidential building operators

(G-10650)
MATIA MOTORS INC
Also Called: Jack Matia Honda
823 Leona St (44035-2300)
PHONE 440 365-7311
Jack Matia, *President*
Barbara Matia, *Vice Pres*
Jim Vankeuren, *Parts Mgr*
Bonny Bowlling, *Finance*
Jon Bakeman, *Sales Mgr*
EMP: 38
SQ FT: 10,000
SALES (est): 17MM **Privately Held**
WEB: www.jackmatia.com
SIC: 5511 7538 7532 5531 Automobiles, new & used; general automotive repair shops; top & body repair & paint shops; automotive & home supply stores

(G-10651)
MERCY HEALTH
1120 E Broad St Fl 2 (44035-6306)
PHONE 440 336-2239
Edwin M Oley, *CEO*
EMP: 35
SALES (corp-wide): 4.2B **Privately Held**
SIC: 8011 Offices & clinics of medical doctors
PA: Mercy Health
1701 Mercy Health Pl
Cincinnati OH 45237
513 639-2800

(G-10652)
MERCY HEALTH
41201 Schadden Rd (44035-2249)
PHONE 440 324-0400
Joan Cikra, *Admin Dir*
EMP: 48
SALES (corp-wide): 4.2B **Privately Held**
SIC: 8099 8322 Medical services organization; general counseling services
PA: Mercy Health
1701 Mercy Health Pl
Cincinnati OH 45237
513 639-2800

(G-10653)
MIDWAY MALL MERCHANTS ASSOC
3343 Midway Mall (44035-9003)
PHONE 440 244-1245
Mark Bressler, *Manager*
Suzy Davis, *Admin Sec*
Cindy Simms, *Admin Sec*
EMP: 50
SALES (est): 3.9MM **Privately Held**
SIC: 8743 Promotion service

(G-10654)
MIDWAY REALTY COMPANY
Also Called: Sommers Mobil Leasing
1800 Lorain Blvd (44035-2407)
P.O. Box 84 (44036-0084)
PHONE 440 324-2404
Kenneth Sommer, *President*
Kent Sommer, *Vice Pres*
Ron Sommer, *Vice Pres*
Todd Sommer, *Vice Pres*
EMP: 45
SQ FT: 1,000
SALES (est): 2.2MM **Privately Held**
SIC: 6519 Real property lessors

(G-10655)
MOLLY MAID OF LORAIN COUNTY
753 Leona St (44035-2350)
PHONE 440 327-0000
Craig P Zoladz, *President*
Molly Zoladz, *Vice Pres*
EMP: 30
SQ FT: 1,700
SALES (est): 720K **Privately Held**
SIC: 7349 Maid services, contract or fee basis

(G-10656)
MULTILINK INC
Also Called: Multifab
580 Ternes Ln (44035-6252)
PHONE 440 366-6966
Fax: 440 366-6802
Steven Kaplan, *President*
Bernadette Golas, *COO*
Mike French, *Senior VP*
Kathy Kaplan, *Vice Pres*
Will Lundstrom, *Vice Pres*
▲ **EMP:** 140
SQ FT: 110,000
SALES (est): 147.4MM **Privately Held**
WEB: www.multilinkbroadband.com
SIC: 5063 3829 Wire & cable; cable testing machines

(G-10657)
MURRAY RIDGE PRODUCTION CENTER
1091 Infirmary Rd (44035-4804)
PHONE 440 329-3734
Amber Fischer, *Superintendent*
Gerry Findlan, *Human Res Mgr*
David Blevins, *Marketing Staff*
John Bonko, *Pharmacy Dir*
EMP: 500
SQ FT: 100,000
SALES (est): 10MM **Privately Held**
WEB: www.mrpcinc.com
SIC: 8331 8322 Vocational rehabilitation agency; social services for the handicapped

(G-10658)
NC HHA INC
Also Called: Intrepid USA Healthcare Svcs
1170 E Broad St Ste 101 (44035-6351)
PHONE 216 593-7750
Adrienne Adkins, *Principal*
Cecellia Callis, *Vice Pres*
Kajsa Keane,
EMP: 80
SALES (est): 1MM
SALES (corp-wide): 4.2B **Privately Held**
SIC: 8082 Home health care services
HQ: Intrepid U.S.A., Inc.
4055 Valley View Ln # 500
Dallas TX 75244
214 445-3750

(G-10659)
NOR CORP
Also Called: Northern Ohio Realty
10247 Dewhurst Rd Ste 101 (44035-8950)
PHONE 440 366-0099
Fax: 440 366-6350
Lorene Albert, *President*
Ken Keffer, *Manager*
Sheri O'Conner, *Executive*
EMP: 28
SALES (est): 1.3MM **Privately Held**
WEB: www.northernohiorealty.com
SIC: 6531 Real estate brokers & agents

(G-10660)
NORTH OHIO HEART CENTER INC
10325 Dewhurst Rd (44035-8403)
PHONE 440 366-3600
Patricia Cathcart, *Branch Mgr*
EMP: 47
SALES (corp-wide): 13.5MM **Privately Held**
SIC: 8011 Cardiologist & cardio-vascular specialist
PA: North Ohio Heart Center, Inc
3600 Kolbe Rd Ste 127
Lorain OH 44053
440 204-4000

(G-10661)
NORTH OHIO HEART CENTER INC
125 E Broad St Ste 305 (44035-6447)
PHONE 440 326-4120
Fax: 440 322-3454
Kenneth J Bescak, *Med Doctor*
Gary Ghome, *Manager*
Brahim Hassan, *Cardiology*
Stephen Moore Do, *Osteopathy*
EMP: 50
SALES (corp-wide): 13.5MM **Privately Held**
WEB: www.nohc.com
SIC: 8011 Cardiologist & cardio-vascular specialist
PA: North Ohio Heart Center, Inc
3600 Kolbe Rd Ste 127
Lorain OH 44053
440 204-4000

(G-10662)
NORTH SHORE DOOR CO INC
Also Called: Nsd
162 Edgewood St (44035-4006)
PHONE 800 783-6112
Fax: 440 365-3514
EMP: 36
SQ FT: 9,000
SALES (est): 12.1MM **Privately Held**
SIC: 5031 Whol Lumber/Plywood/Millwork

(G-10663)
NORTHCUTT TRUCKING INC
40259 Butternut Ridge Rd (44035-7905)
P.O. Box 82 (44036-0082)
PHONE 440 458-5139
Charles Northcutt, *Principal*
Alisa Bailes, *Office Mgr*
EMP: 40
SALES: 1.1MM **Privately Held**
SIC: 4212 Local trucking, without storage

(G-10664)
NORTHERN OHIO ROOFG SHTMTL INC
Also Called: Norfab
880 Infirmary Rd (44035-4884)
PHONE 440 322-8262
Fax: 440 322-5212
David Phiel, *President*
Joseph A Blaszak, *Corp Secy*
Susan Haynel, *Manager*
EMP: 30
SQ FT: 12,000
SALES (est): 4MM **Privately Held**
WEB: www.northernohioroofing.com
SIC: 1761 Roofing contractor; sheet metalwork

(G-10665)
NORTHWEST LIMOUSINE INC
642 Sugar Ln Ste 207 (44035-6310)
P.O. Box 513 (44036-0513)
PHONE 440 322-5804
Johnathan Squires, *President*
Brian Humphrey, *Manager*
EMP: 33
SQ FT: 300,000
SALES (est): 840K **Privately Held**
SIC: 4119 Limousine rental, with driver

(G-10666)
OPEN DOOR CHRISTIAN SCHOOL
8287 W Ridge Rd (44035-4498)
PHONE 440 322-6386
Fax: 440 284-6033
Tarrell Dunckel, *Principal*
Angie Lowe, *Principal*
Walter Sheffield, *Human Res Mgr*
Stacey Zaborowski, *Librarian*
Wendi Phillips, *Manager*
EMP: 62
SQ FT: 42,000
SALES: 3.7MM **Privately Held**
WEB: www.odcs.org
SIC: 8211 8351 Private combined elementary & secondary school; private elementary school; private junior high school; private senior high school; preschool center

(G-10667)
PACIFIC MGT HOLDINGS LLC
Also Called: Pharmacy-Lite Packaging
250 Warden Ave (44035-2650)
P.O. Box 775 (44036-0775)
PHONE 440 324-3339
Fax: 440 324-6116
Angel Velez, *Manager*
Jack Brennan,
Ian Brennan,
▼ **EMP:** 30
SQ FT: 90,000
SALES (est): 12.7MM **Privately Held**
WEB: www.pharmacylite.com
SIC: 5199 Packaging materials

GEOGRAPHIC SECTION
Elyria - Lorain County (G-10692)

(G-10668)
PALM CREST EAST INC
Also Called: Palm Crest Nursing Homes
1251 East Ave (44035-7674)
PHONE..................440 322-0726
Fax: 440 322-2810
Sally Schwartz, *President*
Abraham Schwartz, *Corp Secy*
Edgar Torres, *Director*
Dan Zawaddski, *Administration*
EMP: 40
SALES (est): 1.4MM **Privately Held**
SIC: 8052 Intermediate care facilities; home for the mentally retarded, with health care
PA: Royal Manor Health Care Inc
18810 Harvard Ave
Cleveland OH 44122

(G-10669)
PEPSI-COLA METRO BTLG CO INC
925 Lorain Blvd (44035-2819)
PHONE..................440 323-5524
Fax: 440 323-2997
Mike Schonberg, *Branch Mgr*
Cooper Don, *Manager*
EMP: 50
SALES (corp-wide): 63.5B **Publicly Held**
WEB: www.joy-of-cola.com
SIC: 4225 5149 General warehousing & storage; soft drinks
HQ: Pepsi-Cola Metropolitan Bottling Company, Inc.
1111 Westchester Ave
White Plains NY 10604
914 767-6000

(G-10670)
PLATINUM RESTORATION CONTRS
104 Reaser Ct (44035-6285)
PHONE..................440 327-0699
Fax: 440 366-5496
Michelle Brooks, *President*
EMP: 33 EST: 2010
SALES (est): 13.4MM **Privately Held**
SIC: 6331 Property damage insurance

(G-10671)
PLATINUM RESTORATION INC
104 Reaser Ct (44035-6285)
PHONE..................440 327-0699
Wayne Hudspath, *President*
Matthew Benedict, *Business Mgr*
Michelle Brooks, *Vice Pres*
Randy Price, *Project Mgr*
Nathan Stipcic, *Project Mgr*
EMP: 30
SQ FT: 5,000
SALES (est): 4.3MM **Privately Held**
SIC: 1741 1629 Tuckpointing or restoration; waste water & sewage treatment plant construction

(G-10672)
PURPLE MARLIN INC
Also Called: Maintenance Systems Nthrn Ohio
42208 Albrecht Rd Ste 1 (44035-8925)
P.O. Box 1203 (44036-1203)
PHONE..................440 323-1291
Frank Rybarcyk, *President*
Rodney Nacanon, *Sales Staff*
EMP: 25
SALES (est): 2.4MM **Privately Held**
SIC: 1799 Parking facility equipment & maintenance

(G-10673)
RAY ESSER & SONS INC
830 Walnut St Ste 1 (44035-3353)
PHONE..................440 324-2018
Fax: 440 323-6894
Ray Esser, *President*
Richard Esser, *Treasurer*
Randy Esser, *Admin Sec*
EMP: 30
SALES (est): 4MM **Privately Held**
WEB: www.rayesserandsons.com
SIC: 1711 Hydronics heating contractor; fire sprinkler system installation

(G-10674)
REALTY ONE INC
1240 Abbe Rd N (44035-1649)
PHONE..................440 365-8392
Fax: 440 365-2769
Russ Throne, *Manager*
Megan O'Neill, *Office Admin*
EMP: 40
SALES (corp-wide): 67.8MM **Privately Held**
WEB: www.realty-1st.com
SIC: 6531 Real estate brokers & agents
HQ: Realty One, Inc.
800 W Saint Clair Ave
Cleveland OH 44113
216 328-2500

(G-10675)
REGAL CINEMAS INC
Also Called: Cobblestone Square 20
5500 Abbe Rd (44035)
PHONE..................440 934-3356
Steve Flauto, *Branch Mgr*
EMP: 35
SALES (corp-wide): 982.1MM **Privately Held**
WEB: www.regalcinemas.com
SIC: 7832 Motion picture theaters, except drive-in
HQ: Regal Cinemas, Inc.
101 E Blount Ave Ste 100
Knoxville TN 37920
865 922-1123

(G-10676)
REPUBLIC SERVICES INC
40195 Butternut Ridge Rd (44035-7903)
P.O. Box 4011 (44036-2011)
PHONE..................440 458-5191
Keith Cordesman, *Branch Mgr*
EMP: 34
SALES (corp-wide): 10B **Publicly Held**
SIC: 4953 Refuse collection & disposal services
PA: Republic Services, Inc.
18500 N Allied Way # 100
Phoenix AZ 85054
480 627-2700

(G-10677)
SANTANTONIO DIANA AND ASSOC
Also Called: Psychiatric Psychological Svcs
750 Abbe Rd S (44035-7246)
PHONE..................440 323-5121
Diana Santantonio, *Owner*
EMP: 25
SALES (est): 1.1MM **Privately Held**
WEB: www.psychandpsych.com
SIC: 8322 General counseling services

(G-10678)
SCHOOL EMPLOYEES LORAIN COUNTY
340 Griswold Rd (44035-2301)
PHONE..................440 324-3400
Fax: 440 324-3292
Edward Enyedi, *CEO*
Brent Binkley, *COO*
Karen Akers, *CFO*
Shannon Boesel, *Manager*
Mary Vaughan, *Director*
EMP: 40
SALES: 4.1MM **Privately Held**
WEB: www.selccu.org
SIC: 6061 Federal credit unions

(G-10679)
SENSI CARE 3
1243 East Ave (44035-7674)
PHONE..................440 323-6310
Dolores Wallace, *Manager*
Wendy Morris, *Director*
EMP: 40
SALES (est): 795.1K **Privately Held**
SIC: 8051 8052 Convalescent home with continuous nursing care; intermediate care facilities

(G-10680)
SMINK ELECTRIC INC
215 Winckles St (44035-6129)
P.O. Box 1103 (44036-1103)
PHONE..................440 322-5518
Fax: 440 322-6492
John Smink, *President*
Greg Smink, *Vice Pres*
Donna Smink, *Accountant*
EMP: 25
SQ FT: 2,200
SALES (est): 3.6MM **Privately Held**
WEB: www.sminkelectric.com
SIC: 1731 General electrical contractor

(G-10681)
SOUTH SHORE ELECTRIC INC
589 Ternes Ln (44035-6251)
P.O. Box 321 (44036-0321)
PHONE..................440 366-6289
Fax: 440 366-6940
Paul Zielazienski, *President*
Kathryn Zielazienski, *Corp Secy*
Keith Buckley, *Project Mgr*
Mike German, *Project Mgr*
Freda Verburg, *Controller*
EMP: 40
SQ FT: 11,000
SALES (est): 7.2MM **Privately Held**
WEB: www.southshoreelectric.com
SIC: 1731 General electrical contractor

(G-10682)
SPORTS FACILITY ACOUSTICS INC
801 Bond St (44035-3318)
PHONE..................440 323-1400
Chris Kysela, *President*
EMP: 35
SALES (est): 1.2MM **Privately Held**
SIC: 1742 Acoustical & ceiling work

(G-10683)
ST JUDE SOCIAL CONCERN HOT
636 Sycamore St (44035-4050)
PHONE..................440 365-7971
Jean Koch, *Principal*
EMP: 80
SALES: 3K **Privately Held**
SIC: 8399 Social services

(G-10684)
TIME WARNER CABLE INC
578 Ternes Ln (44035-6252)
PHONE..................440 366-0416
Chris Potts, *Branch Mgr*
EMP: 83
SALES (corp-wide): 41.5B **Publicly Held**
SIC: 4841 Cable television services
HQ: Spectrum Management Holding Company, Llc
400 Atlantic St
Stamford CT 06901
203 905-7801

(G-10685)
TRUGREEN LIMITED PARTNERSHIP
Also Called: Tru Green-Chemlawn
151 Keep Ct (44035-2214)
PHONE..................440 540-4209
Fax: 440 324-6203
Matthew Rehlander, *Branch Mgr*
EMP: 70
SQ FT: 12,000
SALES (corp-wide): 4B **Privately Held**
SIC: 0782 Lawn care services
HQ: Trugreen Limited Partnership
1790 Kirby Pkwy
Memphis TN 38138
901 251-4128

(G-10686)
VANTAGE AGING
42495 N Ridge Rd (44035-1045)
PHONE..................440 324-3588
Mary Ensman, *Principal*
EMP: 620
SALES (corp-wide): 13.1MM **Privately Held**
SIC: 8322 Public welfare center
PA: Vantage Aging
2279 Romig Rd
Akron OH 44320
330 253-4597

(G-10687)
VOCATIONAL GUIDANCE SERVICES
Also Called: Vocational Services
359 Lowell St (44035-4935)
PHONE..................440 322-1123
Fax: 440 322-3417
Lynn Merholz, *Manager*
EMP: 30
SALES (corp-wide): 10.7MM **Privately Held**
SIC: 8331 Vocational training agency; community service employment training program; sheltered workshop; vocational rehabilitation agency
PA: Vocational Guidance Services Inc
2239 E 55th St
Cleveland OH 44103
216 431-7800

(G-10688)
WEOL
Also Called: Lorraine Elyria Broadcasting
538 Broad St (44035-5508)
PHONE..................440 236-9283
Gary Knisley, *President*
Bill Forthofer, *Sales Mgr*
EMP: 50
SALES (est): 2.5MM **Privately Held**
WEB: www.weol.com
SIC: 4832 Radio broadcasting stations

(G-10689)
WESLEYAN SENIOR LIVING (PA)
Also Called: WESLEYAN VILLAGE
807 West Ave (44035-5893)
PHONE..................440 284-9000
Michael Rogan, *President*
Tina Gendics, *General Mgr*
Dianne Koletti, *VP Finance*
Meg Nieberding, *Mktg Dir*
Threse Meyer, *Manager*
EMP: 100
SALES: 19.1MM **Privately Held**
SIC: 8361 Residential care

(G-10690)
WESLEYAN VILLAGE
807 West Ave (44035-5898)
PHONE..................440 284-9000
Michael Rogan, *CEO*
Leonard Budd, *Chairman*
Peter Duffield, *CFO*
Cherlie Bauer, *Accounts Mgr*
EMP: 400 EST: 1923
SQ FT: 226,000
SALES: 273.9K
SALES (corp-wide): 19.1MM **Privately Held**
WEB: www.villageliving.com
SIC: 8361 Home for the aged
PA: Senior Wesleyan Living
807 West Ave
Elyria OH 44035
440 284-9000

(G-10691)
WESTERN & SOUTHERN LF INSUR CO
347 Midway Blvd Ste 101 (44035-2496)
PHONE..................440 324-2626
Dennis Dickerson, *Sales Mgr*
Paul Herman, *Manager*
EMP: 25 **Privately Held**
SIC: 6411 Life insurance agents
HQ: The Western & Southern Life Insurance Company
400 Broadway St
Cincinnati OH 45202
513 629-1800

(G-10692)
WILLIAMS BROS BUILDERS INC
686 Sugar Ln (44035-6310)
PHONE..................440 365-3261
Fax: 440 365-5674
Bart Williams, *President*
Donald L Lemons, *Superintendent*
Jonathan R Traut, *Treasurer*
EMP: 30
SQ FT: 2,000

Elyria - Lorain County (G-10693)

GEOGRAPHIC SECTION

SALES (est): 6.1MM **Privately Held**
WEB: www.williamsbrothersbuilders.com
SIC: **1541** 1542 Industrial buildings, new construction; commercial & office building contractors

(G-10693)
WINDSTREAM OHIO LLC (HQ)
363 3rd St (44035-5632)
PHONE.................................440 329-4000
Dave Thomas, *President*
John Mueller, *Corp Secy*
Gordan Gatien, *Vice Pres*
George Lee, *Vice Pres*
EMP: 140
SQ FT: 15,000
SALES (est): 52.5MM
SALES (corp-wide): 5.8B **Publicly Held**
SIC: **4813** Local telephone communications
PA: Windstream Holdings, Inc.
  4001 N Rodney Parham Rd # 101
  Little Rock AR 72212
  501 748-7000

(G-10694)
WISE CHOICES IN LEARNING LTD
352 Griswold Rd (44035-2301)
PHONE.................................440 324-6056
Karen Wise,
EMP: 27
SALES (est): 544.2K **Privately Held**
SIC: **8351** Child day care services

(G-10695)
ZONE TRANSPORTATION CO
41670 Schadden Rd (44035-2229)
P.O. Box 1379 (44036-1379)
PHONE.................................440 324-3544
Robert J Lehman Sr, *President*
EMP: 100
SQ FT: 55,000
SALES (est): 8.2MM **Privately Held**
SIC: **4213** 4212 Trucking, except local; local trucking, without storage

---

Englewood
Montgomery County

(G-10696)
ANALYTICAL PACE SERVICES LLC
25 Holiday Dr (45322-2706)
PHONE.................................937 832-8242
Brooke Chandler, *Manager*
EMP: 30
SALES (corp-wide): 65.2MM **Privately Held**
SIC: **8734** Soil analysis; water testing laboratory
HQ: Pace Analytical Services, Llc
  1800 Elm St Se
  Minneapolis MN 55414

(G-10697)
AVI-SPL EMPLOYEE
35 Rockridge Rd Ste B (45322-2738)
PHONE.................................937 836-4787
EMP: 45
SALES (corp-wide): 596.9MM **Privately Held**
SIC: **4813** Telephone Communications
HQ: Avi-Spl Employee Emergency Relief Fund, Inc.
  6301 Benjamin Rd Ste 101
  Tampa FL 33634
  813 884-7168

(G-10698)
BROOKDALE SNIOR LVING CMMNTIES
350 Union Blvd (45322-2196)
PHONE.................................937 832-8500
Fax: 937 832-0056
Britney Jaco, *Corp Comm Staff*
Wendy Haines, *Director*
EMP: 30
SALES (corp-wide): 4.7B **Publicly Held**
WEB: www.assisted.com
SIC: **8059** Rest home, with health care
HQ: Brookdale Senior Living Communities, Inc.
  6737 W Wa St Ste 2300
  Milwaukee WI 53214
  414 918-5000

(G-10699)
CASTILIAN & CO
Also Called: Castilian Hair & Skin Center
848 Union Blvd (45322-2101)
PHONE.................................937 836-9671
Barbara E Crabtree, *Owner*
EMP: 25 EST: 1970
SALES (est): 621.9K **Privately Held**
SIC: **7231** Hairdressers

(G-10700)
CITY OF ENGLEWOOD
Also Called: Englewood, City of
333 W National Rd Ofc (45322-1495)
PHONE.................................937 836-2434
Vernon Brown, *Superintendent*
Corey Stone, *Info Tech Mgr*
EMP: 50 **Privately Held**
SIC: **1623** Water, sewer & utility lines
PA: City Of Englewood
  333 W National Rd Ofc
  Englewood OH 45322
  937 836-1732

(G-10701)
CREATIVE MICROSYSTEMS INC
Also Called: Civica CMI
52 Hillside Ct (45322-2745)
PHONE.................................937 836-4499
Fax: 937 836-1036
James T Hodges, *CEO*
Susan M Neuman, *Corp Secy*
Joe Patterson, *Project Mgr*
Missy Matherne, *Purchasing*
David Swigart, *Finance*
EMP: 80 EST: 1979
SQ FT: 14,400
SALES (est): 12MM **Privately Held**
WEB: www.creativemicrosystems.com
SIC: **7373** 7372 Systems integration services; prepackaged software

(G-10702)
DAYTON HOTELS LLC
Also Called: Best Western
20 Rockridge Rd (45322-2710)
PHONE.................................937 832-2222
Abhijit Vasani, *CEO*
EMP: 25
SALES (est): 1.5MM
SALES (corp-wide): 1.3MM **Privately Held**
WEB: www.hamptoninndaytonnorth.com
SIC: **7011** Hotels & motels
PA: Indiana Motel Developers
  2595 Eastwood Dr
  Columbus IN 47203
  812 372-1541

(G-10703)
ENGLEWOOD SQUARE LTD
Also Called: Englewood Square Apartments
150 Chris Dr Apt 119 (45322-1117)
PHONE.................................937 836-4117
Leonard Gorsuch, *President*
Elizabeth Clark, *Manager*
EMP: 100
SALES (est): 3.3MM **Privately Held**
SIC: **6513** Apartment building operators

(G-10704)
GARBER ELECTRICAL CONTRS INC
Also Called: Garber Connect
100 Rockridge Rd (45322-2737)
PHONE.................................937 771-5202
Fax: 937 771-5205
Gary A Garber, *President*
Dean Balsbaugh, *Project Mgr*
Justin Flory, *Project Mgr*
Ryan Gotthardt, *Project Mgr*
Terry Cool, *Sales Mgr*
EMP: 60
SALES (est): 15.6MM **Privately Held**
SIC: **1731** General electrical contractor; electric power systems contractors

(G-10705)
GEM CITY UROLOGIST INC (PA)
9000 N Main St Ste 333 (45415-1185)
PHONE.................................937 832-8400
Fax: 937 832-8711
Ahmad Abouhossein MD, *Principal*
Jan Bernie MD, *Exec VP*
Howard B Abromowitz, *Treasurer*
EMP: 27
SALES (est): 2.3MM **Privately Held**
WEB: www.gemcityurology.com
SIC: **8011** Urologist

(G-10706)
GOOD SAMARITAN HOSPITAL
Also Called: Good Samaritan Health Center
9000 N Main St Ofc (45415-1168)
PHONE.................................937 276-6784
Fax: 937 279-5704
Anita Adams, *Vice Pres*
EMP: 250 **Privately Held**
SIC: **8062** 8011 Hospital, affiliated with AMA residency; offices & clinics of medical doctors
HQ: Good Samaritan Hospital
  2222 Philadelphia Dr
  Dayton OH 45406
  937 278-2612

(G-10707)
GRACE BRETHREN VILLAGE INC
1010 Taywood Rd Ofc (45322-2415)
PHONE.................................937 836-4011
Fax: 937 836-7230
Gurjeet Kahlon, *Director*
Mike Montgomery, *Administration*
EMP: 48
SALES (est): 2.8MM **Privately Held**
WEB: www.gbvillage.com
SIC: **8051** Convalescent home with continuous nursing care

(G-10708)
HOLIDAY INN OF ENGLEWOOD
10 Rockridge Rd (45322-2797)
PHONE.................................937 832-1234
Fax: 937 832-3548
Roy Smith, *Owner*
Angela Williams, *Manager*
EMP: 75
SALES (est): 1.3MM **Privately Held**
SIC: **7011** Hotels & motels

(G-10709)
IDEAL IMAGE INC
115 Haas Dr (45322-2845)
PHONE.................................937 832-1660
Fax: 937 832-5270
Dale Paugh, *President*
Belinda Paugh, *Vice Pres*
J Belinda Paugh, *Treasurer*
Tom Walker, *Sales Executive*
Jenny Sutter, *Mktg Dir*
EMP: 77
SQ FT: 40,000
SALES (est): 12.3MM **Privately Held**
WEB: www.idealimageinc.com
SIC: **7335** Photographic studio, commercial

(G-10710)
INNOVATIVE LOGISTICS GROUP INC
30 Lau Pkwy (45315-8777)
PHONE.................................937 832-9350
Brad Eib, *Branch Mgr*
EMP: 40
SALES (corp-wide): 10.5MM **Privately Held**
SIC: **4731** Domestic freight forwarding
HQ: Innovative Logistics Group, Inc.
  9850 Pelham Rd
  Taylor MI 48180

(G-10711)
KING KOLD INC
331 N Main St (45322-1333)
PHONE.................................937 836-2731
Fax: 937 836-5919
Douglas Smith, *President*
Robert L Smith, *Corp Secy*
Nancy Beckman, *Office Mgr*
EMP: 25
SQ FT: 5,210
SALES (est): 2.4MM **Privately Held**
SIC: **2038** 2013 2011 5142 Frozen specialties; cooked meats from purchased meat; meat packing plants; fish, frozen: packaged

(G-10712)
LIBERTY NURSING CENTER
Also Called: Englewood Manor
425 Lauricella Ct (45322)
P.O. Box 340 (45322-0340)
PHONE.................................937 836-5143
Fax: 937 836-1799
Linda Black-Kurek, *President*
Linda Black Kurek, *President*
Kirk Smith, *Director*
EMP: 34 EST: 1962
SALES (est): 3.1MM **Privately Held**
WEB: www.englewoodmanor.com
SIC: **8051** 8052 Convalescent home with continuous nursing care; intermediate care facilities

(G-10713)
NORTHMONT SERVICE CENTER
7277 Hoke Rd (45315-8845)
PHONE.................................937 832-5050
Jason Watson, *Director*
John Blessing, *Director*
EMP: 100
SALES (est): 4.3MM **Privately Held**
SIC: **4151** School buses

(G-10714)
PARKVIEW MANOR INC (PA)
425 Lauricella Ct (45322)
PHONE.................................937 296-1550
James A Lauricella Sr, *President*
Lena M Lauricella, *Vice Pres*
EMP: 90 EST: 1997
SALES (est): 3.1MM **Privately Held**
SIC: **8052** 8051 Intermediate care facilities; skilled nursing care facilities

(G-10715)
PEDIATRIC ASSOCIATES OF DAYTON (PA)
9000 N Main St Ste 332 (45415-1185)
PHONE.................................937 832-7337
Gary Youra, *President*
Richard Smith, *Vice Pres*
David Roer, *Treasurer*
Jackie Myers, *Nursing Dir*
EMP: 25
SQ FT: 2,600
SALES (est): 3.7MM **Privately Held**
SIC: **8011** Pediatrician

(G-10716)
POLYCOM INC
35 Rockridge Rd Ste A (45322-2767)
PHONE.................................937 245-1853
David Allen, *Branch Mgr*
James Downs, *Director*
EMP: 35
SALES (corp-wide): 284.3MM **Privately Held**
WEB: www.polycom.com
SIC: **5065** Telephone equipment
HQ: Polycom, Inc.
  6001 America Center Dr
  San Jose CA 95002
  408 586-6000

(G-10717)
PREMIER HEART INC
9000 N Main St Ste 101 (45415-1184)
PHONE.................................937 832-2425
Fax: 937 832-9804
Ahmad Karim, *President*
EMP: 35
SALES (est): 2MM **Privately Held**
SIC: **8011** Cardiologist & cardio-vascular specialist

(G-10718)
PRISTINE SNIOR LVING ENGLEWOOD
425 Lauricella Ct (45322)
PHONE.................................937 836-5143
Jensen Glaze,
EMP: 200 EST: 2016
SALES: 9.7MM **Privately Held**
SIC: **8361** Home for the aged

GEOGRAPHIC SECTION

(G-10719)
SAMARITAN N SURGERY CTR LTD
9000 N Main St (45415-1180)
PHONE..........................937 567-6100
Fax: 937 279-5798
David P Kelly, *Principal*
Carita Lawrence, *Office Mgr*
EMP: 31
SALES (est): 3.5MM **Privately Held**
SIC: 8062 General medical & surgical hospitals

(G-10720)
SUNRISE SENIOR LIVING LLC
95 W Wenger Rd (45322-2723)
PHONE..........................937 836-9617
Jennifer Tibbettgrady, *Branch Mgr*
EMP: 50
SALES (corp-wide): 4.3B **Publicly Held**
SIC: 8361 Home for the aged
HQ: Sunrise Senior Living, Llc
    7902 Westpark Dr
    Mc Lean VA 22102

(G-10721)
SUNSET CARPET CLEANING
Also Called: E Z Cleaners
9 Beckenham Rd (45322-1262)
PHONE..........................937 836-5531
Fax: 937 339-6777
Bill Minnich, *President*
Fred Minnich, *Vice Pres*
EMP: 36
SQ FT: 5,100
SALES (est): 1.5MM **Privately Held**
WEB: www.sunsetcarpetcleaning.com
SIC: 7216 7217 Drycleaning plants, except rugs; carpet & upholstery cleaning

(G-10722)
TV MINORITY COMPANY INC
Dayton Origin Distribution Ctr
30 Lau Pkwy (45315-8777)
PHONE..........................937 832-9350
Fax: 937 832-8445
Brad Eib, *Branch Mgr*
EMP: 50
SALES (corp-wide): 46.6MM **Privately Held**
WEB: www.ilgi.com
SIC: 4731 8742 Freight forwarding; transportation consultant
PA: T.V. Minority Company, Inc.
    9400 Pelham Rd
    Taylor MI 48180
    313 386-1048

(G-10723)
UPTOWN HAIR STUDIO INC
Also Called: Uptown Hair & Day Spa
390 W National Rd (45322-1401)
PHONE..........................937 832-2111
Fax: 937 836-7951
Linda S Harlamert, *President*
Theresa Bowers, *Vice Pres*
EMP: 35
SQ FT: 1,800
SALES (est): 795.5K **Privately Held**
SIC: 7231 7991 Beauty shops; manicurist, pedicurist; spas

(G-10724)
WEIFFENBACH MARBLE & TILE CO
150 Lau Pkwy (45315-8787)
PHONE..........................937 832-7055
Fax: 937 832-7005
Craig Lindsey, *President*
Jill Lindsey, *General Mgr*
Anne Lindsey, *Executive*
EMP: 40
SALES (est): 6.2MM **Privately Held**
SIC: 1752 Floor laying & floor work

(G-10725)
YOUNG MENS CHRISTIAN ASSOC
Also Called: Metropolitan YMCA
1200 W National Rd (45315-9504)
P.O. Box 38 (45322-0038)
PHONE..........................937 836-9622
Fax: 937 836-3035
April Turner, *Director*
EMP: 65
SALES (corp-wide): 26.1MM **Privately Held**
WEB: www.daytonymca.org
SIC: 8641 8661 7997 Community membership club; religious organizations; membership sports & recreation clubs
PA: Young Men's Christian Association Of Greater Dayton
    118 W St Ste 300
    Dayton OH 45402
    937 223-5201

Enon
Clark County

(G-10726)
CONCRETE CORING COMPANY INC
400 E Main St (45323-1042)
P.O. Box 308 (45323-0308)
PHONE..........................937 864-7325
Fax: 937 864-2007
Terry D Holmes, *President*
Sharon Murphy, *Accountant*
EMP: 30
SQ FT: 1,996
SALES (est): 4.1MM **Privately Held**
SIC: 1771 Concrete work

(G-10727)
ENON FIREMANS ASSOCIATION
260 E Main St (45323-1054)
PHONE..........................937 864-7429
Fax: 937 864-2143
Maxine McKee, *President*
Don Ingram, *Treasurer*
EMP: 40 EST: 2001
SALES (est): 338.1K **Privately Held**
SIC: 8641 8611 Fraternal associations; business associations

Etna
Franklin County

(G-10728)
FIVE SEASONS LANDSCAPE MGT INC
9886 Mink St Sw Rear (43068-3812)
PHONE..........................740 964-2915
Fax: 740 964-2918
Bill Leidecker, *President*
Steve Woods, *Vice Pres*
Andrea L Snider, *Sls & Mktg Exec*
John Josephson, *Controller*
Josh Gilbert, *Accounts Mgr*
EMP: 100
SQ FT: 5,000
SALES (est): 7.5MM **Privately Held**
WEB: www.fiveseasonslandscape.com
SIC: 0781 Landscape services

(G-10729)
HARRIS & HEAVENER EXCAVATING
149 Humphries Dr (43068-6801)
PHONE..........................740 927-1423
Fax: 740 927-1427
Steven Heavener, *President*
Tom Evans, *Assistant VP*
Dallas Goins, *Administration*
EMP: 28
SQ FT: 3,000
SALES (est): 5.1MM **Privately Held**
SIC: 1794 Excavation & grading, building construction

(G-10730)
MOO MOO NORTH HAMILTON LLC (PA)
Also Called: Moo Moo Carwash
13375 National Rd Sw D (43068-3388)
PHONE..........................614 751-9274
John Rousch, *Mng Member*
EMP: 46
SALES (est): 3.9MM **Privately Held**
SIC: 7542 Washing & polishing, automotive

Etna
Licking County

(G-10731)
B & D CONCRETE FOOTERS INC
12897 National Rd Sw (43062-9281)
P.O. Box 400, Kirkersville (43033-0400)
PHONE..........................740 964-2294
Fax: 740 964-2229
Jason Deskins, *President*
EMP: 45
SALES (est): 4.8MM **Privately Held**
SIC: 1771 Concrete work

(G-10732)
BEST LIGHTING PRODUCTS INC (DH)
1213 Etna Pkwy (43062-8041)
PHONE..........................740 964-0063
Fax: 740 964-1132
Jeffrey S Katz, *CEO*
George Jue, *President*
Lynne Bauman, *CFO*
Howard Hopkins, *Accounts Mgr*
Eddie Trachtenberg, *Accounts Mgr*
◆ EMP: 61 EST: 1997
SQ FT: 60,000
SALES (est): 15.5MM **Privately Held**
WEB: www.bestlighting.net
SIC: 3646 5063 Commercial indusl & institutional electric lighting fixtures; electrical apparatus & equipment
HQ: Wafra Investment Advisory Group Inc.
    345 Park Ave Fl 4100
    New York NY 10154
    212 515-7600

(G-10733)
CUMBERLAND TRAIL GOLF CLB CRSE
8244 Columbia Rd Sw (43062-9290)
PHONE..........................740 964-9336
Fax: 740 964-5970
Mike Tickett, *Principal*
EMP: 50
SALES (est): 1.8MM **Privately Held**
SIC: 7997 Golf club, membership

(G-10734)
EXEL INC
127 Heritage Dr (43062-9805)
PHONE..........................740 927-1762
EMP: 64
SALES (corp-wide): 71.2B **Privately Held**
SIC: 4225 General warehousing
HQ: Exel Inc.
    570 Polaris Pkwy
    Westerville OH 43082
    614 865-8500

(G-10735)
K & W ROOFING INC
Also Called: K and W Roofing
8356 National Rd Sw (43062-9034)
PHONE..........................740 927-3122
Fax: 740 964-6368
Bill Kilcoyne, *President*
Tricia Kilcoyne, *Corp Secy*
EMP: 25
SQ FT: 3,000
SALES (est): 4MM **Privately Held**
SIC: 1761 Roofing contractor

(G-10736)
MENLO LOGISTICS INC
107 Heritage Dr (43062-9805)
PHONE..........................740 963-1154
Robert Bianco, *President*
Timothy Wilson, *Office Mgr*
EMP: 99 EST: 2015
SQ FT: 350,000
SALES (est): 5.2MM **Privately Held**
SIC: 4225 General warehousing & storage

(G-10737)
OHIO HIGH SCHOOL FOOTBALL COAC
138 Purple Finch Loop (43062-8974)
PHONE..........................419 673-1286
Paul Farrah, *President*
Michael Mauk, *Treasurer*
Gerald Cooke, *Bd of Directors*
EMP: 25
SALES: 125.7K **Privately Held**
SIC: 7941 Football club

(G-10738)
PROGRESSIVE FLOORING SVCS INC
100 Heritage Dr (43062-8042)
PHONE..........................614 868-9005
Richard A South, *CEO*
Richard J South, *President*
Nino A Cervi, *Vice Pres*
Matthew Teets, *Project Mgr*
Bill Twinam, *Project Mgr*
EMP: 28
SQ FT: 45,300
SALES (est): 7MM **Privately Held**
WEB: www.progressiveflooringservices.com
SIC: 1752 Carpet laying

(G-10739)
TEREX UTILITIES INC
Also Called: Columbus Division
110 Venture Dr (43062-9239)
PHONE..........................614 444-7373
Fax: 614 444-4565
Brian Blind, *Sales Staff*
George Barr, *Branch Mgr*
EMP: 30
SALES (corp-wide): 4.3B **Publicly Held**
WEB: www.craneamerica.com
SIC: 7699 Industrial truck repair
HQ: Terex Utilities, Inc.
    12805 Sw 77th Pl
    Tigard OR 97223
    503 620-0611

(G-10740)
WILLIAM D TAYLOR SR INC (PA)
Also Called: Jericho Investments Company
263 Trail E (43062-9680)
PHONE..........................614 653-6683
William D Taylor, *Principal*
EMP: 51
SQ FT: 1,800
SALES (est): 2.6MM **Privately Held**
WEB: www.realmoments.net
SIC: 6163 6411 6282 Mortgage brokers arranging for loans, using money of others; insurance agents; investment advice

Euclid
Cuyahoga County

(G-10741)
A W S INC
Also Called: Euclid Adult Training Center
1490 E 191st St (44117-1321)
PHONE..........................216 486-0600
Fax: 216 486-2331
Daisy Maleckar, *General Mgr*
EMP: 50
SALES (corp-wide): 7.8MM **Privately Held**
SIC: 8331 8322 Vocational rehabilitation agency; rehabilitation services
PA: A W S Inc
    1275 Lakeside Ave E
    Cleveland OH 44114
    216 861-0250

(G-10742)
ALL STATE HOME MORTGAGE INC
26250 Euclid Ave Ste 901 (44132-3696)
PHONE..........................216 261-7700
Michael McCandless, *President*
George Marlowe, *Corp Secy*
Sandy Marlowe, *Human Res Dir*
EMP: 100
SQ FT: 17,000
SALES (est): 7.1MM **Privately Held**
WEB: www.ashm.us
SIC: 6163 Mortgage brokers arranging for loans, using money of others

(G-10743)
ASV SERVICES LLC
27801 Euclid Ave Ste 420 (44132-3547)
PHONE..........................216 797-1701
EMP: 35

Euclid - Cuyahoga County (G-10744) **GEOGRAPHIC SECTION**

SALES (est): 458.5K **Privately Held**
SIC: **7521** 4119 Automobile parking; local passenger transportation

(G-10744)
B H C SERVICES INC
Also Called: Brason's Willcare
26250 Euclid Ave Ste 901 (44132-3696)
PHONE..................................216 289-5300
David Brason, *President*
Todd Brason, *Principal*
EMP: 2000
SALES: 11MM **Privately Held**
WEB: www.bhcservices.com
SIC: **8082** Visiting nurse service

(G-10745)
BP
Also Called: Aquasonic Car Wash
24310 Lakeland Blvd (44132-2658)
PHONE..................................216 731-3826
Fax: 216 731-4367
John Attwood Jr, *President*
EMP: 40
SQ FT: 80,000
SALES (est): 427.9K **Privately Held**
SIC: **7542** 5541 Carwashes; gasoline service stations

(G-10746)
BRACOR INC
Also Called: Willcare
26250 Euclid Ave Ste 901 (44132-3696)
PHONE..................................216 289-5300
Edward Casey, *Manager*
EMP: 31
SALES (corp-wide): 796.9MM **Publicly Held**
SIC: **8082** Visiting nurse service
HQ: Bracor, Inc.
346 Delaware Ave
Buffalo NY 14202
716 856-7500

(G-10747)
CONTAINERPORT GROUP INC
24881 Rockwell Dr (44117-1243)
PHONE..................................216 692-3124
Stan Jurcevic, *Branch Mgr*
EMP: 55
SALES (corp-wide): 241.2MM **Privately Held**
SIC: **4212** 4731 Draying, local; without storage; freight transportation arrangement
HQ: Containerport Group, Inc.
1340 Depot St Fl 2
Cleveland OH 44116
440 333-1330

(G-10748)
DAUGHERTY CONSTRUCTION INC
Also Called: Daugherty Roofing
22460 Lakeland Blvd (44132-2655)
PHONE..................................216 731-9444
Fax: 216 731-9644
Harold Daugherty, *President*
EMP: 35
SQ FT: 6,600
SALES (est): 5.2MM **Privately Held**
SIC: **1761** 1521 1542 5211 Roofing contractor; siding contractor; new construction, single-family houses; general remodeling, single-family houses; commercial & office buildings, renovation & repair; door & window products; siding

(G-10749)
DEACON 10
1353 E 260th St Ste 1 (44132-2818)
PHONE..................................216 731-4000
Neal Alexander, *CEO*
Debra Fikaris, *Manager*
EMP: 99 EST: 2011
SALES (est): 2.5MM **Privately Held**
SIC: **7381** Security guard service

(G-10750)
DEE JAY CLEANERS INC
878 E 222nd St (44123-3316)
PHONE..................................216 731-7060
Fax: 216 731-4736
David Sabel, *President*
EMP: 25

SALES (est): 1.1MM **Privately Held**
WEB: www.jaydeecleaners.com
SIC: **7216** 7211 Cleaning & dyeing, except rugs; power laundries, family & commercial

(G-10751)
EUCLID CITY SCHOOLS
Also Called: Service Center Warehouse
463 Babbitt Rd (44123-1640)
PHONE..................................216 261-2900
Pat Blach, *Manager*
EMP: 70 **Privately Held**
WEB: www.euclid.k12.oh.us
SIC: **5049** School supplies
PA: Euclid City Schools
651 E 222nd St
Euclid OH 44123

(G-10752)
EUCLID HEAT TREATING CO
Also Called: E H T Company
1408 E 222nd St (44117-1108)
PHONE..................................216 481-8444
Fax: 216 481-3473
John H Vanas, *President*
Dan Lipnicki, *Vice Pres*
Roger Robbins, *Manager*
EMP: 55 EST: 1946
SQ FT: 45,000
SALES (est): 14MM **Privately Held**
WEB: www.euclidheattreating.com
SIC: **3398** 1711 Metal heat treating; plumbing, heating, air-conditioning contractors

(G-10753)
EUCLID HOSPITAL (HQ)
Also Called: CLEVELAND CLINIC HEALTH SYSTEM
18901 Lake Shore Blvd (44119-1078)
PHONE..................................216 531-9000
Fax: 216 692-7425
Tom Selden, *CEO*
Mark Froimson, *President*
Warren Rock, *Managing Dir*
Lauren Rock, *COO*
Smion Jin, *Engineer*
EMP: 69
SQ FT: 14,144
SALES: 110.4MM
SALES (corp-wide): 8B **Privately Held**
WEB: www.cchseast.org
SIC: **8062** General medical & surgical hospitals
PA: The Cleveland Clinic Foundation
9500 Euclid Ave
Cleveland OH 44195
216 636-8335

(G-10754)
EUCLID HOSPITAL
Also Called: Euclid Finance Division
18901 Lake Shore Blvd # 4 (44119-1078)
PHONE..................................216 445-6440
Fax: 216 692-7524
Charles Miner, *Branch Mgr*
EMP: 140
SALES (corp-wide): 8B **Privately Held**
SIC: **8721** Accounting, auditing & bookkeeping
HQ: Euclid Hospital
18901 Lake Shore Blvd
Euclid OH 44119
216 531-9000

(G-10755)
FIRST FRUITS CHILD DEV CTR I
21877 Euclid Ave (44117-1515)
P.O. Box 17438 (44117-0438)
PHONE..................................216 862-4715
Chelsea Pernell, *President*
Felicia Murrell, *Director*
Chelsea T Pernell,
EMP: 30
SALES: 2MM **Privately Held**
SIC: **8351** Child day care services

(G-10756)
GATEWAY FAMILY HOUSE
1 Gateway (44119-2447)
PHONE..................................216 531-5400
Fax: 216 486-1922
Paul Voniinovich, *Partner*
EMP: 40

SALES (est): 1.6MM **Privately Held**
SIC: **8051** Skilled nursing care facilities

(G-10757)
HELP FOUNDATION INC
27348 Oak Ct (44132-2114)
PHONE..................................216 289-7710
Doug Knoop, *Director*
EMP: 46
SALES (corp-wide): 8.3MM **Privately Held**
SIC: **8641** Civic social & fraternal associations
PA: Help Foundation, Inc
26900 Euclid Ave
Euclid OH 44132
216 432-4810

(G-10758)
HELP FOUNDATION INC (PA)
26900 Euclid Ave (44132-3404)
PHONE..................................216 432-4810
Fax: 216 361-2608
Daniel J Rice, *CEO*
Michael Brink, *Counsel*
Tara Nieberding, *Vice Pres*
Joann Hirsh, *Treasurer*
Liz Linder, *Finance*
EMP: 200
SALES: 8.3MM **Privately Held**
SIC: **8741** Administrative management

(G-10759)
HGR INDUSTRIAL SURPLUS INC (PA)
Also Called: H G R
20001 Euclid Ave (44117-1480)
PHONE..................................216 486-4567
Fax: 216 486-4779
Brian Krueger, *CEO*
Paul Betori, *President*
Jeff McLain, *Principal*
Jessica Greggs, *Inv Control Mgr*
Jason Arnett, *Buyer*
▼EMP: 47
SQ FT: 250,000
SALES (est): 31.6MM **Privately Held**
WEB: www.hgrindustrialsurplus.com
SIC: **5084** Materials handling machinery

(G-10760)
HILLCREST AMBULANCE SVC INC
26420 Lakeland Blvd (44132-2642)
PHONE..................................216 797-4000
Edward Patriarca Sr, *President*
Marie Niebes, *Accountant*
Tony Mannarino, *MIS Dir*
EMP: 180
SQ FT: 3,500
SALES (est): 5.4MM **Privately Held**
SIC: **4119** Ambulance service

(G-10761)
HOME CARE RELIEF INC
753 E 200th St (44119-2504)
PHONE..................................216 692-2270
Fax: 216 692-2273
Darlene Kennedy, *CEO*
EMP: 100
SALES (est): 1.8MM **Privately Held**
SIC: **8082** Home health care services

(G-10762)
HOME DEPOT USA INC
Also Called: Home Depot, The
877 E 200th St (44119-2515)
PHONE..................................216 692-2780
Fax: 216 404-2017
Ron Lockhart, *Manager*
EMP: 200
SALES (corp-wide): 100.9B **Publicly Held**
WEB: www.homerentalsdepot.com
SIC: **5211** 7359 Home centers; tool rental
HQ: Home Depot U.S.A., Inc.
2455 Paces Ferry Rd Se
Atlanta GA 30339

(G-10763)
INDIAN HILLS SENIOR COMMUNITY
1541 E 191st St (44117-1330)
PHONE..................................216 486-7700
Juan Villaneuva, *President*

EMP: 36
SQ FT: 7,000
SALES (est): 2MM **Privately Held**
SIC: **6513** Apartment building operators

(G-10764)
INTEGRITY ENTERPRIZES (PA)
27801 Euclid Ave Ste 440 (44132-3547)
PHONE..................................216 289-8801
London Margerum, *Mng Member*
EMP: 50
SALES (est): 275K **Privately Held**
SIC: **7361** Employment agencies

(G-10765)
J RAYL TRANSPORT INC
Jrayl Drayage
24881 Rockwell Dr (44117-1243)
PHONE..................................330 940-1668
Stan Jurcevic, *Manager*
EMP: 25
SALES (corp-wide): 40.6MM **Privately Held**
SIC: **4731** Truck transportation brokers
PA: J. Rayl Transport, Inc.
1016 Triplett Blvd 1
Akron OH 44306
330 784-1134

(G-10766)
KITCHEN KATERING INC
Also Called: Manor, The
24111 Rockwell Dr (44117-1200)
PHONE..................................216 481-8080
Fax: 216 481-4549
Richard G Eberhard, *President*
EMP: 50 EST: 1961
SQ FT: 22,000
SALES (est): 2.3MM **Privately Held**
SIC: **7299** 5812 Banquet hall facilities; caterers

(G-10767)
LIONS GATE SEC SOLUTIONS INC
Also Called: Lion's Gate Trning SEC Sltions
295 E 208th St (44123-1852)
PHONE..................................440 539-8382
Charisse Montgomery, *President*
Richard Montgomery, *Vice Pres*
Joeseph Hodges, *Director*
EMP: 50
SALES (est): 641.1K **Privately Held**
SIC: **7389**

(G-10768)
MULTICARE HOME HEALTH SERVICES
27691 Euclid Ave Ste B-1 (44132-3546)
PHONE..................................216 731-8900
Fax: 216 731-8972
Lorenza Henderson, *President*
EMP: 70
SALES (est): 2.7MM **Privately Held**
SIC: **8082** Home health care services

(G-10769)
NATIONAL HERITG ACADEMIES INC
Also Called: Pinnacle Academy
860 E 222nd St (44123-3317)
PHONE..................................216 731-0127
Jennifer Littlefield, *Branch Mgr*
EMP: 54 **Privately Held**
SIC: **8741** Management services
PA: National Heritage Academies, Inc.
3850 Broadmoor Ave Se # 201
Grand Rapids MI 49512

(G-10770)
OMNI PARK HEALTH CARE LLC
Also Called: Get Help Home
27801 Euclid Ave Ste 600 (44132-3548)
PHONE..................................216 289-8963
Rosezetta Scott, *Vice Pres*
Lisa Burton, *Accountant*
Terry Maynard, *Mng Member*
EMP: 115
SQ FT: 4,200
SALES (est): 4.8MM **Privately Held**
SIC: **8082** Home health care services

▲ = Import ▼=Export
◆ =Import/Export

GEOGRAPHIC SECTION

Fairborn - Greene County (G-10793)

(G-10771)
PIONEER SOLUTIONS LLC
24800 Rockwell Dr (44117-1203)
PHONE..................216 383-3400
Fax: 216 383-3413
Earl Lancaster, *Chief Engr*
Dean House, *Engineer*
Andrew Papcun, *Engineer*
Joe Kaltenbach, *Engng Exec*
Chris Althausen, *Sales Executive*
EMP: 30
SQ FT: 10,000
SALES (est): 5.1MM **Privately Held**
SIC: 8711 Consulting engineer

(G-10772)
POLLAK DISTRIBUTING CO INC
Also Called: Pollak Foods
1200 Babbitt Rd (44132-2704)
P.O. Box 17485 (44117-0485)
PHONE..................216 851-9911
Fax: 216 851-9939
Arthur Pollak, *President*
Basya Gifter, *Purchasing*
Marel Hirsch, *Manager*
EMP: 25
SQ FT: 45,000
SALES (est): 18.2MM **Privately Held**
WEB: www.pollakdist.com
SIC: 5141 5113 Groceries, general line; industrial & personal service paper

(G-10773)
R & A SPORTS INC
Also Called: Adler Team Sports
23780 Lakeland Blvd (44132-2615)
PHONE..................216 289-2254
Fax: 216 289-6392
John Domo, *President*
Richard Domo, *Vice Pres*
Ruth Ann Domo, *Admin Sec*
EMP: 25
SQ FT: 16,000
SALES: 3.9MM **Privately Held**
SIC: 5091 5136 5137 2396 Sporting & recreation goods; sportswear, men's & boys'; sportswear, women's & children's; screen printing on fabric articles

(G-10774)
ROSEMARY CENTER
19350 Euclid Ave (44117-1425)
PHONE..................216 481-4823
Fax: 216 481-4154
Patricia Colombo, *Principal*
John P Fleischer, *Treasurer*
Christine Picard, *Finance*
William Liptak, *VP Human Res*
Bill Liptak, *HR Admin*
EMP: 29
SALES (est): 3.9MM **Privately Held**
SIC: 8399 Community development groups

(G-10775)
SABER HEALTHCARE GROUP LLC
Also Called: Willows Health and Rehab Ctr
1500 E 191st St (44117-1398)
PHONE..................216 486-5736
Nick Gulich, *Administration*
EMP: 36
SALES (corp-wide): 68.5MM **Privately Held**
SIC: 8051 Skilled nursing care facilities
PA: Saber Healthcare Group, L.L.C.
26691 Richmond Rd Frnt
Bedford OH 44146
216 292-5706

(G-10776)
SISTERS OD SAINT JOSEPH OF SAI
Also Called: MOUNT ST JOSEPH NURSING HOME
21800 Chardon Rd (44117-2125)
PHONE..................216 531-7426
Fax: 216 531-4033
SIS Paschal Yap, *Treasurer*
Angelo Costa, *Controller*
Juanita Castaneda, *Director*
Katie Heglaw, *Records Dir*
Mother M Raphael, *Administration*
EMP: 255
SQ FT: 90,000
SALES: 8.3MM **Privately Held**
SIC: 8051 Convalescent home with continuous nursing care

(G-10777)
STACK CONTAINER SERVICE INC
24881 Rockwell Dr (44117-1243)
P.O. Box 202, Chesterland (44026-0202)
PHONE..................216 531-7555
Stan Jurcevic, *President*
Michael Fugate, *General Mgr*
John Jurcevic, *Exec VP*
Marko Bartulovic, *Vice Pres*
John Pavlik, *Vice Pres*
EMP: 55
SQ FT: 4,600
SALES (est): 6.2MM **Privately Held**
SIC: 4731 4212 Freight transportation arrangement; draying, local: without storage

(G-10778)
SUBURBAN MEDICAL LABORATORY
26300 Euclid Ave Ste 810 (44132-3708)
PHONE..................330 929-7992
Fax: 330 929-0826
Sandra Fishel, *President*
Patina Olinger, *Human Res Mgr*
Dr Mark Greenberg, *Director*
John Nehrer, *Admin Sec*
EMP: 120
SQ FT: 15,000
SALES (est): 2.5MM **Privately Held**
WEB: www.smlab.com
SIC: 8071 Testing laboratories

(G-10779)
THERMO-TEC INSULATION INC
1415 E 222nd St (44117-1107)
PHONE..................216 663-3842
Fax: 216 663-3843
Margaret Scarl, *President*
Charles Scarl, *Vice Pres*
EMP: 25
SALES (est): 3.1MM **Privately Held**
SIC: 1742 Insulation, buildings

(G-10780)
UNIVERSITY MEDNET (PA)
18599 Lake Shore Blvd (44119-1093)
PHONE..................216 383-0100
Fax: 216 383-6092
Seth Eisengart MD, *Ch of Bd*
Richard Hammond, *President*
Kenneth Spano MD, *Treasurer*
Diane Burgin, *Manager*
Arnold Rozensweig MD, *Admin Sec*
EMP: 300
SQ FT: 124,000
SALES (est): 11.6MM **Privately Held**
SIC: 8069 8082 5999 Specialty hospitals, except psychiatric; home health care services; medical apparatus & supplies

(G-10781)
ZAK ENTERPRISES LTD (PA)
Also Called: Clinical Health Laboratories
26250 Euclid Ave Ste 810 (44132-3718)
PHONE..................216 261-9700
Fax: 216 261-3955
Alan Firestone, *Ch of Bd*
Carol A Zarlenga, *President*
Igor Porthoy, *Opers Mgr*
EMP: 75
SQ FT: 15,000
SALES (est): 3.4MM **Privately Held**
WEB: www.cakenterprises.com
SIC: 8071 Testing laboratories

Fairborn
Greene County

(G-10782)
ADVANCE MECHANICAL PLBG & HTG
235 Glaser St Ste B (45324-5170)
PHONE..................937 879-9405
Robert Burrowes, *Owner*
EMP: 32
SQ FT: 6,000
SALES (est): 1.7MM **Privately Held**
SIC: 1711 Plumbing contractors; boiler & furnace contractors

(G-10783)
ADVANCED MECHANICAL SVCS INC
Also Called: Honeywell Authorized Dealer
575 Sports St (45324-5138)
P.O. Box 68 (45324-0068)
PHONE..................937 879-7426
Fax: 937 879-7428
William Burrowes, *President*
William D Parsons, *Principal*
▲ EMP: 32
SALES (est): 6.7MM **Privately Held**
SIC: 1711 Mechanical contractor

(G-10784)
AFFINITY SPECIALTY APPAREL INC (PA)
Also Called: Affinity Apparel
1202 E Dayton Yllow Spgs (45324-6326)
PHONE..................866 548-8434
Robert McIntire, *President*
Marcia Hischke, *Vice Pres*
Will Vereen, *Vice Pres*
Bill Tucker, *CFO*
Brittanie Stacy, *Human Res Mgr*
◆ EMP: 61
SALES (est): 18.9MM **Privately Held**
SIC: 5699 7389 Uniforms; textile & apparel services

(G-10785)
BRILLIGENT SOLUTIONS INC (PA)
1130 Channingway Dr (45324-9240)
PHONE..................937 879-4148
David Geloneck, *President*
Doug Henry, *Vice Pres*
James Blair, *Engineer*
Aaron Burke, *Engineer*
Timothy Meade, *Engineer*
EMP: 27
SQ FT: 7,400
SALES (est): 4MM **Privately Held**
SIC: 8711 8731 Consulting engineer; commercial physical research

(G-10786)
BROOKDALE SENIOR LIVING INC
Also Called: Brookdale Fox Run
7800 Dyton Springfield Rd (45324-1997)
PHONE..................937 864-1500
EMP: 27
SALES (corp-wide): 4.7B **Publicly Held**
SIC: 8322 Old age assistance
PA: Brookdale Senior Living
111 Westwood Pl Ste 400
Brentwood TN 37027
615 221-2250

(G-10787)
COMBS INTERIOR SPECIALTIES INC
475 W Funderburg Rd (45324-2359)
PHONE..................937 879-2047
Fax: 937 879-0003
Marcus Combs, *President*
Jaden Callahan, *Purchasing*
Tiffany Ross, *Controller*
Chris McFadden, *Executive*
Byron Hubbard,
EMP: 75
SALES (est): 14.4MM **Privately Held**
SIC: 1542 1751 1521 Nonresidential construction; carpentry work; single-family housing construction

(G-10788)
COVENANT CARE OHIO INC
Wright Nursing Center
829 Yllow Sprng Frfeld Rd (45324)
PHONE..................937 878-7046
Fax: 937 878-4860
Bryan Ernst, *Facilities Dir*
Dan Bautista, *Director*
Jenny Hoffman, *Director*
Nedra Polk, *Social Dir*
Greg Nijack, *Administration*
EMP: 90 **Privately Held**
WEB: www.villagegeorgetown.com
SIC: 8052 8069 8051 Intermediate care facilities; specialty hospitals, except psychiatric; skilled nursing care facilities
HQ: Covenant Care Ohio, Inc.
27071 Aliso Creek Rd # 100
Aliso Viejo CA 92656
949 349-1200

(G-10789)
CURTISS-WRIGHT CONTROLS
2600 Paramount Pl Ste 200 (45324-6816)
PHONE..................937 252-5601
Ron Taulton, *Branch Mgr*
Gorky Chin, *Manager*
Paul Davis, *Manager*
Julie Trotter, *Manager*
Eric Freeman, *Info Tech Dir*
EMP: 50
SALES (corp-wide): 2.2B **Publicly Held**
SIC: 8711 8731 3769 3625 Consulting engineer; commercial physical research; guided missile & space vehicle parts & auxiliary equipment; relays & industrial controls
HQ: Curtiss-Wright Controls Electronic Systems, Inc.
28965 Avenue Penn
Santa Clarita CA 91355
661 702-1494

(G-10790)
DAVE MARSHALL INC (PA)
Also Called: Ziebart
1448 Kauffman Ave (45324-3108)
PHONE..................937 878-9135
Fax: 614 878-1526
David Marshall, *President*
Susan Marshall, *Admin Sec*
EMP: 90
SALES (est): 5.5MM **Privately Held**
WEB: www.davemarshall.com
SIC: 7549 Undercoating/rustproofing cars

(G-10791)
DAVITA INC
1266 N Broad St (45324-5549)
PHONE..................937 879-0433
Fax: 937 879-0589
Jeffrey Spears, *Administration*
EMP: 27 **Publicly Held**
SIC: 8092 Kidney dialysis centers
PA: Davita Inc.
2000 16th St
Denver CO 80202

(G-10792)
DAYSPRING HEALTH CARE CENTER
8001 Dyton Springfield Rd (45324-1907)
PHONE..................937 864-5800
Fax: 937 864-2495
Matt Walters, *President*
Barry Bortz, *Vice Pres*
John Hoenemeyer, *Administration*
George Miu, *Administration*
EMP: 135
SALES (est): 6.3MM
SALES (corp-wide): 74MM **Privately Held**
SIC: 8051 8052 Skilled nursing care facilities; intermediate care facilities
PA: Carespring Health Care Management, Llc
390 Wards Corner Rd
Loveland OH 45140
513 943-4000

(G-10793)
DETMER & SONS INC (PA)
Also Called: Detmer & Sons Heating & AC
1170 Channingway Dr (45324-9240)
PHONE..................937 879-2373
Frank Detmer Jr, *President*
Eric Detmer, *President*
Jim Streck, *Vice Pres*
Matt Detmer, *Manager*
Nate Raberding, *Consultant*
EMP: 26
SQ FT: 3,000
SALES (est): 6.2MM **Privately Held**
WEB: www.detmersons.com
SIC: 1711 1761 Warm air heating & air conditioning contractor; sheet metalwork

Fairborn - Greene County (G-10794)

GEOGRAPHIC SECTION

(G-10794)
FAIRBORN FISH
Also Called: Fairborn Fish Organization
101 Mann Ave (45324-5020)
P.O. Box 1484 (45324-1484)
PHONE.................................937 879-1313
Beth Player, *Principal*
EMP: 50
SALES (est): 182.7K **Privately Held**
SIC: 8322 Social service center

(G-10795)
FAIRBORN ST LUKE UNTD MTHDST
Also Called: Fairborn Pre School & Day Care
100 N Broad St (45324-4804)
PHONE.................................937 878-5042
Fax: 937 878-3029
Mary Gale, *Director*
EMP: 25
SALES: 374.2K **Privately Held**
SIC: 8351 Preschool center

(G-10796)
FAIRBORN YMCA
Also Called: Young Mens Christn Assosiation
300 S Central Ave (45324-4721)
PHONE.................................937 754-9622
Fax: 937 878-6480
Larry Dryden, *Director*
Lori Setherolf, *Director*
EMP: 30 **EST:** 1949
SALES (est): 482.6K **Privately Held**
WEB: www.ymcaofgreenecounty.org
SIC: 8641 8322 Youth organizations; youth center

(G-10797)
G&K SERVICES INC
Also Called: Lion Uniform Group
1202 Dyton Yllow Sprng Rd (45324-6326)
PHONE.................................937 873-4500
EMP: 52
SALES (corp-wide): 5.3B **Publicly Held**
SIC: 7218 Industrial uniform supply
HQ: G&K Services, Llc
    5995 Opus Pkwy Ste 500
    Minnetonka MN 55343
    952 912-5500

(G-10798)
I SUPPLY CO
1255 Spangler Rd (45324-9768)
P.O. Box 1739 (45324-7739)
PHONE.................................937 878-5240
Fax: 937 878-9236
Jerry Parisi, *CEO*
Gerald Parisi, *President*
Joe Parisi, *President*
Mario Parisi, *President*
Tim Detrick, *Vice Pres*
EMP: 175 **EST:** 1974
SQ FT: 109,000
SALES (est): 186.4M **Privately Held**
WEB: www.isupplyco.com
SIC: 5087 5113 Janitors' supplies; containers, paper & disposable plastic

(G-10799)
K & R DISTRIBUTORS INC
Also Called: Aqua Falls Bottled Watrer
7606 Dayton Rd (45324-5944)
PHONE.................................937 864-5495
Bob Kennedy, *President*
Katie Jones, *Manager*
Dylan Thomas, *Manager*
EMP: 45
SALES (est): 3.1MM **Privately Held**
SIC: 5963 5961 7389 Bottled water delivery; cheese, mail order; coffee service

(G-10800)
KETTERING ADVENTIST HEALTHCARE
1045 Channingway Dr (45324-9252)
PHONE.................................937 878-8644
EMP: 70
SALES (corp-wide): 1.7B **Privately Held**
SIC: 8062 General medical & surgical hospitals
PA: Kettering Adventist Healthcare
    3535 Southern Blvd
    Dayton OH 45429
    937 298-4331

(G-10801)
KLEIN ASSOCIATES INC
1750 Commerce Center Blvd (45324-6362)
PHONE.................................937 873-8166
Fax: 937 873-8258
Floyd D Reed, *President*
Dr Gary A Klein, *Chairman*
Dr Helen Klein, *Vice Pres*
Cheryl Cain, *Accounting Mgr*
EMP: 36 **EST:** 1978
SQ FT: 9,800
SALES (est): 3.1MM **Privately Held**
SIC: 8732 Sociological research

(G-10802)
MANZANO DIALYSIS LLC
Also Called: Midwest Fairborn Dialysis
1266 N Broad St (45324-5549)
PHONE.................................937 879-0433
George Carghese, *Principal*
EMP: 45
SALES (est): 767.9K **Publicly Held**
SIC: 8092 Kidney dialysis centers
PA: Davita Inc.
    2000 16th St
    Denver CO 80202

(G-10803)
RITE RUG CO
2015 Commerce Center Blvd (45324-6335)
PHONE.................................937 318-9197
EMP: 35
SALES (corp-wide): 82.2MM **Privately Held**
SIC: 5713 1752 Carpets; floor laying & floor work
PA: Rite Rug Co.
    4450 Poth Rd Ste A
    Columbus OH 43213
    614 261-6060

(G-10804)
STICKELMAN SCHNEIDER ASSOC LLC (HQ)
1130 Channingway Dr (45324-9240)
PHONE.................................513 475-6000
Fax: 937 873-9901
Doreen Worch, *Bd of Directors*
Ronald Stickelman Jr,
Dirk Schneider,
Sarah Stickelman,
EMP: 35
SQ FT: 3,200
SALES (est): 2.1MM
SALES (corp-wide): 6MM **Privately Held**
WEB: www.stickelman.com
SIC: 6531 Appraiser, real estate
PA: Stickelman, Schneider & Association Inc.
    1130 Channingway Dr
    Fairborn OH 45324
    937 873-9900

(G-10805)
SUMMIT AT PARK HILLS LLC
2270 Park Hills Dr Ofc (45324-5900)
PHONE.................................317 462-8048
Fax: 937 754-9830
Todd Spittal,
EMP: 45
SALES (est): 1.6MM **Privately Held**
SIC: 8059 Nursing home, except skilled & intermediate care facility

(G-10806)
UNITED CHURCH HOMES INC
Also Called: Patriot Ridge Community
789 Stoneybrook Trl (45324-6021)
PHONE.................................937 878-0262
Brian Allen, *Manager*
John Sefton, *Director*
Laura Ferrell, *Administration*
EMP: 110
SALES (corp-wide): 78.1MM **Privately Held**
WEB: www.altenheimcommunity.org
SIC: 8052 8051 Intermediate care facilities; skilled nursing care facilities
PA: United Church Homes Inc
    170 E Center St
    Marion OH 43302
    740 382-4885

(G-10807)
US BANK NATIONAL ASSOCIATION
Also Called: US Bank
1 W Main St (45324-4741)
PHONE.................................937 873-7845
Robert Carico, *Manager*
EMP: 100
SALES (corp-wide): 22.7B **Publicly Held**
WEB: www.firstar.com
SIC: 6021 National commercial banks
HQ: U.S. Bank National Association
    425 Walnut St Fl 1
    Cincinnati OH 45202
    513 632-4234

(G-10808)
VALENTINE BUICK GMC INC
1105 N Central Ave (45324-5668)
P.O. Box 432 (45324-0432)
PHONE.................................937 878-7371
Fax: 937 878-0804
Dennis Valentine, *President*
Deborah Burton, *Business Mgr*
Bette Green, *Corp Secy*
Anthony Homan, *Sales Dir*
Shannon Ciarletta, *Clerk*
EMP: 60
SALES (est): 17.8MM **Privately Held**
SIC: 5511 7538 Automobiles, new & used; general automotive repair shops

(G-10809)
VISICON INC
Also Called: Hope Hotel & Conference Center
Area A Bldg 823 (45324)
PHONE.................................937 879-2696
David Meyers, *President*
Micki Witter, *General Mgr*
EMP: 100
SQ FT: 132,000
SALES (est): 849.6K **Privately Held**
SIC: 7011 Hotels

(G-10810)
W2005/FARGO HOTELS (POOL C)
Also Called: Hampton Inn Fairborn
2550 Paramount Pl (45324-6789)
PHONE.................................937 429-5505
Lisa Deen, *Manager*
Victoria Kinney, *Manager*
EMP: 25
SALES (corp-wide): 16.5MM **Privately Held**
WEB: www.daytonraiders.com
SIC: 7011 Hotels
HQ: W2005/Fargo Hotels (Pool C) Realty, L.P.
    5851 Legacy Cir Ste 400
    Plano TX 75024

(G-10811)
WASTE MANAGEMENT OHIO INC
1700 N Broad St (45324-9747)
P.O. Box 1799 (45324-7799)
PHONE.................................800 343-6047
Fax: 937 878-3172
Ginger Kaladas, *Credit Staff*
Thomas Koogler, *Manager*
EMP: 100
SALES (corp-wide): 14.4B **Publicly Held**
SIC: 7359 4212 Portable toilet rental; local trucking, without storage
HQ: Waste Management Of Ohio, Inc.
    1700 N Broad St
    Fairborn OH 45324

(G-10812)
WASTE MANAGEMENT OHIO INC (HQ)
1700 N Broad St (45324-9747)
P.O. Box 4648, Carol Stream IL (60197-4648)
PHONE.................................800 343-6047
Paul Pistono, *President*
Robert Adams, *Plant Mgr*
Ginger Kaladas, *Credit Staff*
Thomas Koogler, *Manager*
Keith Gregory, *Maintence Staff*
EMP: 120

SALES (est): 39.4MM
SALES (corp-wide): 14.4B **Publicly Held**
WEB: www.wm.com
SIC: 4953 4212 Refuse collection & disposal services; local trucking, without storage
PA: Waste Management, Inc.
    1001 Fannin St Ste 4000
    Houston TX 77002
    713 512-6200

(G-10813)
WELLS & SONS JANITORIAL SVC
1877 S Maple Ave Ste 250 (45324-3487)
PHONE.................................937 878-4375
Fax: 937 878-4336
Kenneth Wells, *President*
Janet H Wells, *Corp Secy*
Edwin Wells, *Vice Pres*
James L Wells, *Vice Pres*
Rich Lutz, *Executive*
EMP: 42
SQ FT: 3,600
SALES: 869.4K **Privately Held**
SIC: 7349 Janitorial service, contract basis

Fairfield
Butler County

(G-10814)
AB MARKETING LLC
Also Called: Sphere, The
1211 Symmes Rd Apt B (45014-9501)
PHONE.................................513 385-6158
Theresa Hughes, *General Mgr*
Darroll Alexander, *Mng Member*
EMP: 50
SALES: 500K **Privately Held**
SIC: 5091 Sporting & recreation goods

(G-10815)
ACPX2
1750 Garrett House Ln (45014-8654)
PHONE.................................513 829-2100
Mike Pennington, *CEO*
Lisa Pennington, *Admin Sec*
EMP: 30
SALES (est): 1.6MM **Privately Held**
SIC: 7699 Cleaning services

(G-10816)
AFC INDUSTRIES INC (PA)
Also Called: Advanced Fastener
3795 Port Union Rd (45014-2207)
PHONE.................................513 874-7456
Fax: 513 874-9009
Robert T Tomlinson, *President*
Steve Sullivan, *Exec VP*
Tom Riley, *VP Opers*
Renee Elam, *Buyer*
Curt Robertson, *VP Finance*
▲ **EMP:** 28
SQ FT: 27,000
SALES (est): 22.2MM **Privately Held**
WEB: www.pintech.com
SIC: 5085 Fasteners, industrial: nuts, bolts, screws, etc.

(G-10817)
AFFILIATES IN ORAL & MAXLOFCL (PA)
Also Called: Doctors Weaver Wallace Conley
5188 Winton Rd (45014-2900)
PHONE.................................513 829-8080
Fax: 513 829-8080
Dr David A Weaver, *Partner*
David Weaver, *Principal*
Timothy Conley, *Principal*
Douglas Wallace, *Principal*
Sherry Weaver, *Manager*
EMP: 30
SQ FT: 7,000
SALES (est): 3.5MM **Privately Held**
SIC: 8069 8062 Specialty hospitals, except psychiatric; general medical & surgical hospitals

(G-10818)
ALBA MANUFACTURING INC
8950 Seward Rd (45011-9109)
PHONE.................................513 874-0551
Tom Moon, *President*

GEOGRAPHIC SECTION

Fairfield - Butler County (G-10840)

Thomas N Inderhees, *President*
Mike Kroger, *Vice Pres*
Jerry Heneerlight, *Safety Mgr*
Mike Kees, *Purchasing*
EMP: 52
SQ FT: 67,000
SALES (est): 30.3MM **Privately Held**
WEB: www.albamfg.com
SIC: 3535 5084 3312 Conveyors & conveying equipment; conveyor systems; blast furnaces & steel mills

(G-10819)
ALEXSON SERVICES INC
Also Called: Fairfield Center
350 Kolb Dr (45014-5357)
PHONE.................513 874-0423
Andrea Levenson, *CEO*
Carl Hampton, *Manager*
EMP: 263
SALES (est): 6.2MM
SALES (corp-wide): 4MM **Privately Held**
WEB: www.fairfieldcenter.com
SIC: 8361 8052 8051 Home for the mentally retarded; intermediate care facilities; skilled nursing care facilities
PA: Manor Home Ownership Of Facilities Inc
246 N Broadway
Geneva OH

(G-10820)
AREA WIDE PROTECTIVE INC
9500 Le Saint Dr (45014-2253)
PHONE.................513 321-9889
Fax: 513 321-9891
EMP: 48
SALES (corp-wide): 111.4MM **Privately Held**
SIC: 3669 7381 7382 Mfg Communications Equip Detective/Armor Car Svcs Security System Svcs
HQ: Area Wide Protective, Inc.
826 Overholt Rd
Kent OH 44240
330 644-0655

(G-10821)
AURGROUP FINANCIAL CREDIT UN
8811 Holden Blvd (45014-2109)
PHONE.................513 942-4422
Gareda Guecking, *President*
Kelly Culp, *Mktg Dir*
EMP: 63
SALES (est): 9.6MM **Privately Held**
SIC: 6061 Federal credit unions

(G-10822)
BANSAL CONSTRUCTION INC
3263 Homeward Way Ste A (45014-4237)
P.O. Box 132, West Chester (45071-0132)
PHONE.................513 874-5410
Anurag Bansal, *President*
Ambrish K Bansal, *Vice Pres*
Tracey Powell, *Admin Sec*
EMP: 35
SQ FT: 5,000
SALES (est): 12.7MM **Privately Held**
SIC: 1731 1794 General electrical contractor; excavation work

(G-10823)
BELL MOVING AND STORAGE INC (PA)
4075 Port Union Rd (45014-2205)
PHONE.................513 942-7500
Fax: 513 942-7600
Tamara Kissel, *President*
William Kissel, *Vice Pres*
Frieda Abell, *Manager*
Angie Padgett, *Manager*
EMP: 25
SQ FT: 25,000
SALES (est): 4.2MM **Privately Held**
WEB: www.bellmoving.com
SIC: 4214 4213 4212 Household goods moving & storage, local; trucking, except local; local trucking, without storage

(G-10824)
BROCK & SONS INC
8731 N Gilmore Rd (45014-2105)
PHONE.................513 874-4555
Fax: 513 874-6824
Linda Brock, *President*
Jeff Brock, *Vice Pres*
Geoffrey Brock, *Treasurer*
EMP: 40 **EST:** 1937
SQ FT: 1,500
SALES (est): 6.9MM **Privately Held**
WEB: www.brockandsons.com
SIC: 1623 1611 Water main construction; sewer line construction; oil & gas pipeline construction; underground utilities contractor; general contractor, highway & street construction

(G-10825)
BUSAM FAIRFIELD LLC
Also Called: Busam Subaru/Suzuki
6195 Dixie Hwy (45014-4249)
PHONE.................513 771-8100
Cathy L Tamm, *Controller*
Cathy Tamm, *Controller*
David Little, *Manager*
Ted Seibert, *Manager*
Greg Frye, *Consultant*
EMP: 27
SALES (est): 6.7MM **Privately Held**
SIC: 5511 7532 Automobiles, new & used; body shop, automotive

(G-10826)
BUTLER COUNTY BOARD OF DEVELOP
Also Called: Community Supports Services
441 Patterson Blvd (45014-2511)
PHONE.................513 867-5913
Fax: 513 867-5669
Christina Hurr, *Superintendent*
Ted McGuire, *Exec Dir*
EMP: 47
SALES (corp-wide): 5.9MM **Privately Held**
SIC: 8361 9111 8052 Home for the mentally retarded; county supervisors' & executives' offices; intermediate care facilities
PA: Butler County Board Of Developmental Disabilities
282 N Fair Ave Ste 1
Hamilton OH 45011
513 785-2815

(G-10827)
C & K INDUSTRIAL SERVICES INC
4980 Factory Dr (45014-1945)
PHONE.................513 829-5353
Fax: 513 829-0604
Kirby Bolton, *Branch Mgr*
EMP: 40
SALES (corp-wide): 119.5MM **Privately Held**
SIC: 4959 Sweeping service: road, airport, parking lot, etc.
PA: C & K Industrial Services, Inc.
5617 E Schaaf Rd
Independence OH 44131
216 642-0055

(G-10828)
CALVARY INDUSTRIES INC (PA)
9233 Seward Rd (45014-5407)
PHONE.................513 874-1113
Fax: 513 860-6184
John P Morelock Jr, *CEO*
Ivan Byers, *President*
Kimberly Fraley, *General Mgr*
Eric Meade, *Business Mgr*
Dan Mitten, *Business Mgr*
▲ **EMP:** 60
SQ FT: 100,000
SALES (est): 34.6MM **Privately Held**
WEB: www.calvaryindustries.com
SIC: 2819 5169 Industrial inorganic chemicals; chemicals & allied products

(G-10829)
CAPITAL SENIOR LIVING CORP
1400 Corydale Dr (45014-3361)
PHONE.................513 829-6200
Fax: 513 829-6203
Connie Reed, *Marketing Staff*
Sheryl Withrow, *Director*
Danielle Pietak, *Director*
Brett Miles, *Food Svc Dir*
EMP: 315
SALES (corp-wide): 467MM **Publicly Held**
SIC: 8052 Intermediate care facilities

PA: Capital Senior Living Corp
14160 Dallas Pkwy Ste 300
Dallas TX 75254
972 770-5600

(G-10830)
CHILDRENS HOSPITAL MEDICAL CTR
Also Called: Cincinatti Chld Hosp Med Ctr
3050 Mack Rd Ste 105 (45014-5375)
PHONE.................513 636-6400
Fax: 513 636-6436
John Linser, *Branch Mgr*
Kimberly Denning, *Manager*
Robert J Hill, *Surgeon*
Avril Mortellite, *Nurse*
EMP: 30
SALES (corp-wide): 1.6B **Privately Held**
WEB: www.cincinnatichildrens.org
SIC: 8733 8071 Medical research; medical laboratories
PA: Children's Hospital Medical Center
3333 Burnet Ave
Cincinnati OH 45229
513 636-4200

(G-10831)
CIMA INC
4416 Dixie Hwy (45014-1114)
PHONE.................513 682-5900
Tom Uhl, *President*
▲ **EMP:** 30
SALES (est): 4.9MM **Privately Held**
WEB: www.cima-kdt.com
SIC: 3561 7363 Industrial pumps & parts; temporary help service

(G-10832)
CINCINNATI CASUALTY COMPANY
6200 S Gilmore Rd (45014-5141)
P.O. Box 145496, Cincinnati (45250-5496)
PHONE.................513 870-2000
James E Benoski, *Vice Ch Bd*
Larry Plum, *President*
Thomas A Joseph, *President*
Teresa L Cracas, *Counsel*
Robert B Morgan, *Senior VP*
EMP: 80
SQ FT: 370,000
SALES (est): 38.2MM
SALES (corp-wide): 5.7B **Publicly Held**
WEB: www.cib-online.com
SIC: 6331 Fire, marine & casualty insurance & carriers
HQ: Cincinnati Insurance Company
6200 S Gilmore Rd
Fairfield OH 45014
513 870-2000

(G-10833)
CINCINNATI FINANCIAL CORP (PA)
6200 S Gilmore Rd (45014-5141)
P.O. Box 145496, Cincinnati (45250-5496)
PHONE.................513 870-2000
Fax: 513 870-2900
Kenneth W Stecher, *Ch of Bd*
Steven J Johnston, *President*
Scott Gilliam, *President*
John Ohara, *Superintendent*
Blake Slater, *Exec VP*
EMP: 3201
SQ FT: 1,508,200
SALES: 5.7B **Publicly Held**
WEB: www.cinfin.com
SIC: 0331 6311 6411 6211 Fire, marine & casualty insurance; fire, marine & casualty insurance & carriers; property damage insurance; life insurance carriers; property & casualty insurance agent; investment firm, general brokerage; financial services

(G-10834)
CINCINNATI GYMNASTICS ACADEMY
3635 Woodridge Blvd (45014-8521)
PHONE.................513 860-3082
Fax: 513 870-3831
Mary Lee Tracy, *President*
Mandi Hinson, *Director*
EMP: 50
SQ FT: 20,000

SALES: 194.3K **Privately Held**
WEB: www.cincinnatigymnastics.com
SIC: 7999 8661 Gymnastic instruction, non-membership; religious organizations

(G-10835)
CINCINNATI INDEMINTY CO
6200 S Gilmore Rd (45014-5141)
P.O. Box 145496, Cincinnati (45250-5496)
PHONE.................513 870-2000
James E Benoski, *Vice Ch Bd*
John Schiff, *President*
Brad E Behringer, *Senior VP*
T F Elchynski, *Senior VP*
Martin Mullen, *Senior VP*
EMP: 600
SALES (est): 143.5MM
SALES (corp-wide): 5.7B **Publicly Held**
WEB: www.cib-online.com
SIC: 6331 Fire, marine & casualty insurance & carriers
HQ: Cincinnati Insurance Company
6200 S Gilmore Rd
Fairfield OH 45014
513 870-2000

(G-10836)
CINCINNATI LIFE INSURANCE CO
6200 S Gilmore Rd (45014-5141)
P.O. Box 145496, Cincinnati (45250-5496)
PHONE.................513 870-2000
David M Popplewell, *President*
Teresa L Cracas, *Counsel*
Stephen C Roach, *Counsel*
Eric N Mathews, *Senior VP*
Brad E Behringer, *Vice Pres*
EMP: 950
SQ FT: 383,000
SALES (est): 329.7MM
SALES (corp-wide): 5.7B **Publicly Held**
WEB: www.cib-online.com
SIC: 6311 Life insurance
HQ: Cincinnati Insurance Company
6200 S Gilmore Rd
Fairfield OH 45014
513 870-2000

(G-10837)
CLAYTON WEAVER TRUCKING INC
3043 Lelia Ln (45014-1204)
PHONE.................513 896-6932
Fax: 513 896-4207
Clayton Weaver, *President*
Brenda Weaver, *Corp Secy*
Steve Bowden, *Manager*
EMP: 40
SQ FT: 864
SALES (est): 5.5MM **Privately Held**
SIC: 4213 4212 Trucking, except local; local trucking, without storage

(G-10838)
CPC LOGISTICS INC
Also Called: Pds
8695 Seward Rd (45011-9716)
PHONE.................513 874-5787
Fax: 513 682-7555
EMP: 51 **EST:** 1972
SALES (est): 1.9MM **Privately Held**
SIC: 8742 7363 3674 Management Consulting Services Help Supply Services Mfg Semiconductors/Related Devices

(G-10839)
DAVITA INC
1210 Hicks Blvd (45014-1921)
PHONE.................513 939-1110
Tracie Metz, *Manager*
Sarah Waits, *Administration*
EMP: 27 **Publicly Held**
SIC: 8092 Kidney dialysis centers
PA: Davita Inc.
2000 16th St
Denver CO 80202

(G-10840)
DEUFOL WORLDWIDE PACKAGING LLC ✪
4380 Dixie Hwy (45014-1119)
PHONE.................414 967-8000
EMP: 54 **EST:** 2017
SALES (est): 1MM **Privately Held**
SIC: 4783 5113 Packing And Crating, Nsk

Fairfield - Butler County (G-10841) — GEOGRAPHIC SECTION

(G-10841)
DIALYSIS SPECIALISTS FAIRFIELD
4750 Dixie Hwy (45014-1848)
PHONE 513 863-6331
Fax: 513 863-6898
Laura Nortman, *Manager*
EMP: 25
SALES (est): 890K **Privately Held**
SIC: 8092 Kidney dialysis centers

(G-10842)
DNA DIAGNOSTICS CENTER INC (HQ)
Also Called: Dna Technology Park
1 Ddc Way (45014-2281)
PHONE 513 881-7800
Lori Tauber Marcus, *Ch of Bd*
Peter Vitulli, *President*
Dustyn Bunsold, *Business Mgr*
Jerry Watkins, *COO*
Daniel Leigh, *Vice Pres*
EMP: 185
SQ FT: 66,000
SALES (est): 42.6MM
SALES (corp-wide): 13.3MM **Privately Held**
WEB: www.paternite.com
SIC: 8734 Testing laboratories

(G-10843)
DYNAMIC MECHANICAL SYSTEMS
5623 Sigmon Way (45014-3946)
PHONE 513 858-6722
Fax: 513 874-6390
Gregory P Dinkel, *President*
EMP: 30
SQ FT: 6,000
SALES (est): 2.1MM **Privately Held**
WEB: www.dynamicmechanical.com
SIC: 1731 1711 General electrical contractor; plumbing contractors; heating & air conditioning contractors

(G-10844)
EAGLE INDUSTRIES OHIO INC
Also Called: Allgood Home Improvements
275 Commercial Dr (45014-5565)
PHONE 513 247-2900
Edward Grant, *President*
John Hoerst, *Accounts Mgr*
EMP: 35 **EST:** 1995
SQ FT: 5,114
SALES: 5.5MM **Privately Held**
SIC: 7299 Home improvement & renovation contractor agency

(G-10845)
ELEMENT CINCINNATI
3701 Port Union Rd (45014-2200)
PHONE 513 984-4112
EMP: 39
SALES (est): 7.7MM **Privately Held**
SIC: 8734 Testing laboratories

(G-10846)
ELEMENT MTLS TECH CNCNNATI INC (PA)
3701 Port Union Rd (45014-2200)
PHONE 513 771-2536
Fax: 513 771-2564
Charles Noall, *CEO*
Steven Etter, *CEO*
Michael Janssen, *General Mgr*
Phil Steele, *General Mgr*
Thomas Walsh, *General Mgr*
EMP: 45
SQ FT: 11,000
SALES (est): 16.6MM **Privately Held**
WEB: www.mar-test.com
SIC: 8734 Testing laboratories

(G-10847)
EMBASSY HEALTHCARE INC
Also Called: Parkside Nrsing Rehabilitation
908 Symmes Rd (45014-1842)
PHONE 513 868-6500
Aaron Handler, *President*
Janet Bresnahan, *Administration*
EMP: 64
SALES (est): 3.4MM **Privately Held**
SIC: 8051 Convalescent home with continuous nursing care

(G-10848)
ERIC BOEPPLER FMLY LTD PARTNR
Also Called: A Savannah Nite Limousine Svcs
9331 Seward Rd Ste A (45014-2272)
PHONE 513 336-8108
Lynn Boeppler, *Partner*
Eric Boeppler, *General Ptnr*
EMP: 60
SALES (est): 571.9K **Privately Held**
SIC: 4119 Limousine rental, with driver

(G-10849)
ESJ CARRIER CORPORATION
3240 Production Dr (45014-4230)
P.O. Box 181060 (45018-1060)
PHONE 513 728-7388
Eva Ambrose, *CEO*
Sandra Ambrose, *President*
Don McKinney, *VP Opers*
Robert Roth, *Manager*
Greg Maschinot, *Senior Mgr*
EMP: 40 **EST:** 1998
SALES (est): 12.5MM **Privately Held**
SIC: 4731 Truck transportation brokers

(G-10850)
FAIRFIELD TEMPO CLUB
8800 Holden Blvd (45014-2100)
PHONE 513 863-2081
Carl Lampl, *Principal*
EMP: 28
SALES: 750.6K **Privately Held**
SIC: 7997 Membership sports & recreation clubs

(G-10851)
FEHR SERVICES LLC
6200 Pleasant Ave Ste 3 (45014-4671)
PHONE 513 829-9333
Paul Fehring,
EMP: 38 **EST:** 1995
SQ FT: 1,100
SALES (est): 2.2MM **Privately Held**
WEB: www.drsbillinginc.com
SIC: 8721 Accounting services, except auditing

(G-10852)
GOZA DIALYSIS LLC
Also Called: Ross Dialysis
3825 Kraus Ln Ste S (45014-5867)
PHONE 513 738-0276
James K Hilger,
EMP: 29
SALES (est): 302.8K **Publicly Held**
SIC: 8092 Kidney dialysis centers
PA: Davita Inc.
2000 16th St
Denver CO 80202

(G-10853)
GREAT AMERICAN INSURANCE CO
9450 Seward Rd (45014-5412)
P.O. Box 188060 (45018-8060)
PHONE 513 603-2570
Rick Weber, *Manager*
EMP: 75 **Publicly Held**
SIC: 6331 Fire, marine & casualty insurance
HQ: Great American Insurance Company
301 E 4th St Fl 8
Cincinnati OH 45202
513 369-5000

(G-10854)
GREAT MIAMI VALLEY YMCA
Also Called: Fairfield YMCA Pre-School
5220 Bibury Rd (45014-3665)
PHONE 513 829-3091
Fax: 513 829-3519
Julia Brant, *Director*
EMP: 100
SALES (corp-wide): 13.3MM **Privately Held**
SIC: 8641 7991 8351 7032 Youth organizations; physical fitness facilities; child day care services; youth camps; individual & family services
PA: Great Miami Valley Ymca
105 N 2nd St
Hamilton OH 45011
513 887-0001

(G-10855)
H & O DISTRIBUTION INC
325 Osborne Dr (45014-2250)
PHONE 513 874-2090
Fax: 513 874-5170
Brad Osborne, *CEO*
Keith Emmons, *Vice Pres*
John Holmes, *Vice Pres*
Bill Lansaw, *Sls & Mktg Exec*
John Banfield, *Controller*
EMP: 25
SQ FT: 510,000
SALES (est): 4.3MM
SALES (corp-wide): 10.6MM **Privately Held**
SIC: 4225 General warehousing
PA: Osborne Trucking Company
325 Osborne Dr
Fairfield OH 45014
513 874-2090

(G-10856)
HALCOMB CONCRETE CONSTRUCTION
1409 Veterans Dr (45014-1905)
PHONE 513 829-3576
Richard Halcomb, *President*
EMP: 25
SQ FT: 2,500
SALES (est): 1.5MM **Privately Held**
SIC: 1771 Foundation & footing contractor

(G-10857)
HANOVER INSURANCE COMPANY
6061 Winton Rd (45014-4946)
PHONE 513 829-4555
EMP: 75 **Publicly Held**
SIC: 6411 Insurance agents
HQ: The Hanover Insurance Company
440 Lincoln St
Worcester MA 01653
508 853-7200

(G-10858)
HERZIG-KRALL MEDICAL GROUP
5150 Sandy Ln (45014-2738)
PHONE 513 896-9595
Fax: 513 896-4171
Edward Herzig, *President*
William Krall, *Vice Pres*
Ray Inders, *Manager*
Anthony Behler, *Admin Sec*
Vickie Kling, *Administration*
EMP: 40
SQ FT: 10,000
SALES (est): 2.9MM **Privately Held**
SIC: 8011 Offices & clinics of medical doctors

(G-10859)
HOGAN TRUCK LEASING INC
2001 Ddc Way (45014-2285)
PHONE 513 454-3500
Jeff Buhraw, *Manager*
EMP: 33
SALES (corp-wide): 88.1MM **Privately Held**
SIC: 7513 7363 Truck rental & leasing, no drivers; truck driver services
PA: Hogan Truck Leasing, Inc.
2150 Schuetz Rd Ste 210
Saint Louis MO 63146
314 421-6000

(G-10860)
HOWDEN AMERICAN FAN COMPANY
Woods Fan Division
3235 Homeward Way (45014-4237)
PHONE 513 874-2400
Fax: 513 870-6249
Kirk Shaper, *Manager*
EMP: 31
SALES (corp-wide): 75.8MM **Privately Held**
WEB: www.amfan-woods.com
SIC: 5084 Fans, industrial
HQ: Howden American Fan Company
2933 Symmes Rd
Fairfield OH 45014
513 874-2400

(G-10861)
HOWDEN NORTH AMERICA INC
2933 Symmes Rd (45014-2001)
PHONE 513 874-2400
Karl Kimmerling, *President*
Lori Beans, *General Mgr*
Kirk Schaeper, *Safety Mgr*
Guiseppe Blanchard, *Purch Mgr*
Brett Fargo, *Buyer*
▲ **EMP:** 170
SALES (est): 32.4MM
SALES (corp-wide): 3.3B **Publicly Held**
WEB: www.howdenbuffalo.com
SIC: 5084 Industrial machinery & equipment
HQ: Howden North America Inc.
2475 George Urban Blvd # 120
Depew NY 14043
803 741-2700

(G-10862)
INTERCOASTAL TRNSP SYSTEMS
Also Called: Universal Transportation
5284 Winton Rd (45014-3912)
PHONE 513 829-1287
Tom Burer, *President*
EMP: 60
SQ FT: 6,000
SALES (est): 2.8MM **Privately Held**
SIC: 4111 4119 Local & suburban transit; local passenger transportation

(G-10863)
INTERSTATE WAREHOUSING VA LLC
110 Distribution Dr (45014-4257)
PHONE 513 874-6500
Fax: 513 874-6775
Paul Hanna, *General Mgr*
Matt Suttman, *Safety Mgr*
Kevin Bowden, *Manager*
EMP: 80
SALES (corp-wide): 122.1MM **Privately Held**
WEB: www.tippmanngroup.com
SIC: 4222 4226 Warehousing, cold storage or refrigerated; special warehousing & storage
HQ: Interstate Warehousing Of Virginia, L.L.C.
9009 Coldwater Rd Ste 300
Fort Wayne IN 46825
260 490-3000

(G-10864)
J FELDKAMP DESIGN BUILD LTD
3239 Profit Dr (45014-4239)
PHONE 513 870-0601
Jody Feldkamp, *President*
Robert Boggs, *Principal*
Jonathan Feldkamp, *Vice Pres*
Elisa Feldkamp, *CFO*
Steve Habard, *Manager*
EMP: 42
SQ FT: 18,000
SALES: 3.7MM **Privately Held**
SIC: 1711 3499 Heating & air conditioning contractors; plumbing contractors; aerosol valves, metal

(G-10865)
JACO WATERPROOFING LLC
4350 Wade Mill Rd (45014-5853)
P.O. Box 865, Ross (45061-0865)
PHONE 513 738-0084
Fax: 513 738-0087
Bill Sackenheim, *President*
David Yeager, *Opers Mgr*
Ron Smith, *Accounts Mgr*
Andrea Hartmann, *Admin Asst*
EMP: 27
SALES (est): 3.8MM **Privately Held**
WEB: www.appliedtechnologies.com
SIC: 1799 Waterproofing

(G-10866)
JTF CONSTRUCTION INC
4235 Muhlhauser Rd (45014-5450)
PHONE 513 860-9835
Gregory W Fisher, *President*
Patrick Mullen, *Vice Pres*
Michelle Franchini, *Manager*
EMP: 70

GEOGRAPHIC SECTION
Fairfield - Butler County (G-10890)

SQ FT: 6,900
SALES (est): 15.4MM **Privately Held**
SIC: **1542** Commercial & office buildings, renovation & repair

(G-10867)
JWF TECHNOLOGIES LLC (PA)
6820 Fairfield Bus Ctr (45014)
PHONE..................513 769-9611
Dominic Dipilla, *President*
Scott Johnson, *QC Mgr*
Christopher Pollitt, *Engineer*
Lisa Kreutz, *Controller*
John Lampe, *Sales Dir*
▲ EMP: 26 EST: 1998
SQ FT: 30,000
SALES (est): 20.1MM **Privately Held**
WEB: www.jwftechnologies.com
SIC: **5084** Hydraulic systems equipment & supplies

(G-10868)
KELLEY BROTHERS ROOFING INC
4905 Factory Dr (45014-1916)
PHONE..................513 829-7717
Fax: 513 829-7737
Robert Kelley, *President*
George Horton, *General Mgr*
Michael Kelley, *COO*
Steven Gebing, *Vice Pres*
John Newlon, *CFO*
EMP: 100 EST: 1978
SQ FT: 25,000
SALES (est): 22.8MM **Privately Held**
WEB: www.kbroof.com
SIC: **1761** Roofing contractor

(G-10869)
KENS BEVERAGE INC
3219 Homeward Way (45014-4237)
PHONE..................513 874-8200
Fax: 513 874-8201
Ken Reimer, *Managing Dir*
Phil Morris, *Branch Mgr*
Angel Tudor, *Manager*
EMP: 40
SALES (corp-wide): 51.3MM **Privately Held**
WEB: www.kensbeverage.com
SIC: **1799** 7699 Food service equipment installation; restaurant equipment repair
PA: Ken's Beverage, Inc.
10015 S Mandel St
Plainfield IL 60585
630 904-1555

(G-10870)
KINGS COVE AUTOMOTIVE LLC
Also Called: Performance Lexus
5726 Dixie Hwy (45014-4204)
PHONE..................513 677-0177
Phyllis Hackman, *Consultant*
Michael Dever,
EMP: 60
SALES (est): 16.9MM **Privately Held**
SIC: **5511** 6159 7539 Automobiles, new & used; automobile finance leasing; automotive repair shops

(G-10871)
KOCH MEAT CO INC
Also Called: Cooked Foods
4100 Port Union Rd (45014-2293)
PHONE..................513 874-3500
Monty Lobb, *Human Res Mgr*
Brian Reisen, *Manager*
EMP: 400
SALES (corp-wide): 2.2B **Privately Held**
SIC: **5142** 5144 2015 Packaged frozen goods; poultry & poultry products; poultry slaughtering & processing
HQ: Koch Meat Co., Inc.
1300 Higgins Rd Ste 100
Park Ridge IL 60068
847 384-8018

(G-10872)
LAKEFRONT LINES INC
Also Called: Lakefront Trailways
4991 Factory Dr (45014-1946)
P.O. Box 18613 (45018-0613)
PHONE..................513 829-8290
Fax: 513 829-7049
Jerry Stedy, *Branch Mgr*
EMP: 80
SALES (corp-wide): 4.9B **Privately Held**
WEB: www.lakefrontlines.com
SIC: **4119** 4141 Local passenger transportation; local bus charter service
HQ: Lakefront Lines, Inc.
13315 Brookpark Rd
Brookpark OH 44142
216 267-8810

(G-10873)
LOVELAND EXCAVATING INC
Also Called: Loveland Excavating and Paving
260 Osborne Dr (45014-2246)
PHONE..................513 965-6600
Matthew J Brennan, *CEO*
Bryan Shepherd, *Vice Pres*
Mike Moeller, *Project Mgr*
Jeremy Redmon, *Project Mgr*
Sharon Rasnic, *Controller*
EMP: 45
SQ FT: 3,000
SALES (est): 7.4MM **Privately Held**
SIC: **1794** Excavation & grading, building construction
PA: Ohio Heavy Equipment Leasing, Llc
9520 Le Saint Dr
Fairfield OH 45014
513 965-6600

(G-10874)
MARTIN LS DDS MS (PA)
Also Called: Martin Periodontics
1211 Nilles Rd (45014-2911)
PHONE..................513 829-8999
L S Martin DDS Ms, *Owner*
EMP: 26
SALES (est): 1.2MM **Privately Held**
SIC: **8021** Offices & clinics of dentists; periodontist

(G-10875)
MARTIN MARIETTA MATERIALS INC
Also Called: Fairfield Gravel
107 River Cir Bldg 1 (45014-2333)
PHONE..................513 829-6446
Robert Lance, *Branch Mgr*
Jody Barker, *Manager*
EMP: 50
SQ FT: 1,344 **Publicly Held**
WEB: www.martinmarietta.com
SIC: **5032** Aggregate
PA: Martin Marietta Materials Inc
2710 Wycliff Rd
Raleigh NC 27607

(G-10876)
MASTER-HALCO INC
620 Commerce Center Dr (45011-8664)
PHONE..................513 869-7600
Mark Stockton, *Superintendent*
Paul Smith, *Manager*
EMP: 35
SALES (corp-wide): 42.5B **Privately Held**
WEB: www.fenceonline.com
SIC: **3315** 5051 Steel wire & related products; fence gates posts & fittings: steel; steel
HQ: Master-Halco, Inc.
3010 Lbj Fwy Ste 800
Dallas TX 75234
972 714-7300

(G-10877)
MCCLOY ENGINEERING LLC
Also Called: Accutek Testing Laboratory
3701 Port Union Rd (45014-2200)
PHONE..................513 984-4112
John McCloy, *President*
Andrew Kiddon, *Project Engr*
John M Mitchell, *Sales Dir*
Ben Kaiser, *Sales Staff*
Eric Dahman, *Sales Executive*
EMP: 45
SALES (est): 6.9MM **Privately Held**
WEB: www.accutektesting.com
SIC: **8734** Product testing laboratories
HQ: Element Materials Technology Huntington Beach Inc.
15062 Bolsa Chica St
Huntington Beach CA 92649
714 892-1961

(G-10878)
MERCY HAMILTON HOSPITAL
3000 Mack Rd (45014-5335)
PHONE..................513 603-8600
Dave Ferrell, *President*
Matt Eversole, *Vice Pres*
Mike Hibbard, *Vice Pres*
Joseph H Brandabur, *Pathologist*
Pamela Justice, *Infect Cntl Dir*
EMP: 50
SALES (est): 231.3MM **Privately Held**
SIC: **8062** General medical & surgical hospitals

(G-10879)
MERCY HEALTH
2960 Mack Rd Ste 201 (45014-5300)
PHONE..................513 829-1700
Vijay Rajan, *President*
EMP: 48
SALES (corp-wide): 4.2B **Privately Held**
SIC: **8011** Offices & clinics of medical doctors
PA: Mercy Health
1701 Mercy Health Pl
Cincinnati OH 45237
513 639-2800

(G-10880)
MERCY HEALTH
3000 Mack Rd (45014-5335)
PHONE..................513 870-7008
Dianne Raanz, *President*
Bob Feldbauer, *COO*
Patricia Davis-Hagens, *Vice Pres*
Sheila McAdams, *Manager*
Robert Hill, *Surgeon*
EMP: 30
SQ FT: 13,800
SALES (corp-wide): 4.2B **Privately Held**
SIC: **8641** Social associations
PA: Mercy Health
1701 Mercy Health Pl
Cincinnati OH 45237
513 639-2800

(G-10881)
MERCY HEALTHPLEXM LLC
3050 Mack Rd Ste 210 (45014-5375)
PHONE..................513 870-7101
Schmidt Craig, *Manager*
Sean Slovenski, *Director*
Mike Combes, *Director*
EMP: 50
SALES (est): 1.2MM **Privately Held**
WEB: www.emercy.com
SIC: **8093** Specialty outpatient clinics

(G-10882)
MIDDLETOWN INNKEEPERS INC
Also Called: Hampton Inn Cinc Nw/Fairfield
430 Kolb Dr (45014-5361)
PHONE..................513 942-3440
Fax: 513 942-3441
Har S Bharnagar, *President*
EMP: 40
SALES (est): 2.5MM **Privately Held**
SIC: **7011** Hotels & motels

(G-10883)
MULTICARE MANAGEMENT GROUP
Also Called: Parkside Nrsing Rhbltation Ctr
908 Symmes Rd (45014-1842)
PHONE..................513 868-6500
Aaron B Handler, *President*
Cathy Lnd, *Office Mgr*
EMP: 105
SQ FT: 27,000
SALES: 950K **Privately Held**
WEB: www.communitymulticarecenter.com
SIC: **8051** Convalescent home with continuous nursing care

(G-10884)
NORTH STAR REALTY INCORPORATED
3501 Tylersville Rd Ste G (45011-8005)
PHONE..................513 737-1700
Fax: 513 737-9527
Lonnie Lewis, *President*
EMP: 28
SALES: 585K **Privately Held**
SIC: **6531** Real estate agents & managers

(G-10885)
NURSES CARE INC
1083 Hicks Blvd Ste 140 (45014-2884)
PHONE..................513 424-1141
Fax: 513 829-2241
Sheila Rush, *Branch Mgr*
EMP: 30
SALES (corp-wide): 3.9MM **Privately Held**
WEB: www.nursescareinc.com
SIC: **8082** Home health care services
PA: Nurses Care, Inc
9009 Springboro Pike
Miamisburg OH 45342
513 424-1141

(G-10886)
OBSTETRICS & GYNECOLOGY ASSOC (PA)
3050 Mack Rd Ste 375 (45014-5378)
PHONE..................513 221-3800
Fax: 513 682-4520
Lawrence Freeman, *Vice Pres*
Jerry A Goodman, *Vice Pres*
Mike Gruga, *Project Mgr*
Stephen A Straubing, *Treasurer*
Judy Teeple, *Manager*
EMP: 60
SALES (est): 10.2MM **Privately Held**
SIC: **8011** Physicians' office, including specialists; obstetrician; gynecologist

(G-10887)
OHIO CASUALTY INSURANCE CO (DH)
Also Called: Liberty Mutual
9450 Seward Rd (45014-5412)
PHONE..................800 843-6446
Fax: 513 603-7900
Dan R Carmichael, *CEO*
Debra K Crane, *Senior VP*
Ralph G Goode, *Senior VP*
John S Kellington, *Senior VP*
Thomas E Schadler, *Senior VP*
EMP: 1200
SQ FT: 3,379
SALES (est): 337.5MM
SALES (corp-wide): 38.3B **Privately Held**
WEB: www.oci.com
SIC: **6331** 6311 Fire, marine & casualty insurance; workers' compensation insurance; fire, marine & casualty insurance: stock; life insurance carriers
HQ: Liberty Mutual Insurance Company
175 Berkeley St
Boston MA 02116
617 357-9500

(G-10888)
OHIO HEAVY EQUIPMENT LSG LLC (PA)
9520 Le Saint Dr (45014-2253)
PHONE..................513 965-6600
Matthew Brennan, *Owner*
EMP: 30 EST: 2006
SALES (est): 7.4MM **Privately Held**
SIC: **1794** Excavation work

(G-10889)
ONE WAY FARM OF FAIRFIELD INC
Also Called: ONE WAY FARM CHILDREN'S HOME
6131 E River Rd (45014-3241)
P.O. Box 18637 (45018-0637)
PHONE..................513 829-3276
Fax: 513 829-2150
Jane Holmes, *President*
Ronda Croucher, *Marketing Staff*
Barbara Condo, *Exec Dir*
EMP: 35
SALES: 1.3MM **Privately Held**
WEB: www.onewayfarm.org
SIC: **8361** Children's boarding home

(G-10890)
OSBORNE TRUCKING COMPANY (PA)
325 Osborne Dr (45014-2250)
PHONE..................513 874-2090
Fax: 513 881-7391
Brad Osborne, *President*
John Holmes, *Vice Pres*
Michael Heller, *VP Opers*
Gary Banfield, *Safety Dir*

Fairfield - Butler County (G-10891)

Brad Osbourne, *Sls & Mktg Exec*
EMP: 69
SQ FT: 510,000
SALES (est): 10.6MM **Privately Held**
WEB: www.osborneho.com
SIC: 4213 4225 Trucking, except local; general warehousing

(G-10891)
OSF INTERNATIONAL INC
6320 S Gilmore Rd (45014-5125)
PHONE 513 942-6620
Fax: 513 942-3982
Chris Dussin, *Branch Mgr*
EMP: 40
SALES (corp-wide): 156.3MM **Privately Held**
SIC: 5149 Spaghetti
PA: Osf International, Inc.
  0715 Sw Bancroft St
  Portland OR 97239
  503 222-5375

(G-10892)
PAKMARK LLC
Also Called: Innomark Communications
420 Distribution Cir (45014-5473)
PHONE 513 285-1040
Troy Born, *Production*
Bill Witters, *Controller*
John Henderson, *Manager*
Gary Boens,
Bill Fair,
▼ **EMP:** 35
SQ FT: 20,000
SALES (est): 9.8MM **Privately Held**
SIC: 5199 Packaging materials

(G-10893)
PEDIATRIC ASSOC OF FAIRFIELD
5502 Dixie Hwy Ste A (45014-4297)
PHONE 513 874-9460
Jean Janelle, *President*
Dr Robert Lerer, *Treasurer*
Thomas J Catalanottomd, *Director*
Jennifer S Hakell, *Director*
Dr Warren Webb, *Admin Sec*
EMP: 40
SQ FT: 8,200
SALES (est): 7MM **Privately Held**
WEB: www.pedsfairfield.com
SIC: 8011 Pediatrician

(G-10894)
PENNINGTON SEED INC
9530 Le Saint Dr (45014-2253)
PHONE 513 642-8980
Grayson Godley, *General Mgr*
EMP: 93
SALES (corp-wide): 2B **Publicly Held**
SIC: 0181 Bulbs & seeds
HQ: Pennington Seed, Inc.
  1280 Atlanta Hwy
  Madison GA 30650
  706 342-1234

(G-10895)
PERFORMANCE AUTOPLEX LLC
Also Called: Performance Automotive Network
5726 Dixie Hwy (45014-4204)
PHONE 513 870-5033
Joyce Heineman, *Business Mgr*
Cathy Munoz, *Finance*
Patrick Disney, *Technology*
Verna Jaqui, *Executive*
Michael Dever,
EMP: 90
SALES (est): 26.4MM **Privately Held**
SIC: 5012 Automobiles

(G-10896)
PREMIER CONSTRUCTION COMPANY
9361 Seward Rd (45014-5409)
PHONE 513 874-2611
Fax: 513 874-4893
Jan Gilkey, *President*
Dennis Long, *Manager*
EMP: 35 **EST:** 1959
SQ FT: 10,000
SALES (est): 8.2MM **Privately Held**
SIC: 5031 1751 2452 Lumber: rough, dressed & finished; plywood; carpentry work; panels & sections, prefabricated, wood

(G-10897)
R B DEVELOPMENT COMPANY INC
5200 Camelot Dr (45014-4009)
P.O. Box 18040 (45018-0040)
PHONE 513 829-8100
Didon Eldad, *President*
EMP: 300
SQ FT: 120,000
SALES (est): 16.6MM **Privately Held**
SIC: 1542 Shopping center construction

(G-10898)
RAY ST CLAIR ROOFING INC
3810 Port Union Rd (45014-2202)
PHONE 513 874-1234
Fax: 513 682-4695
Raymond J St Clair, *President*
Mike Wehring, *Senior VP*
Kevin S Clair, *Vice Pres*
Kevin St Clair, *Vice Pres*
EMP: 35 **EST:** 1956
SQ FT: 7,000
SALES (est): 4.9MM **Privately Held**
WEB: www.raystclairroofing.com
SIC: 1761 1751 1741 Roofing contractor; siding contractor; window & door (prefabricated) installation; chimney construction & maintenance

(G-10899)
RIEMAN ARSZMAN CSTM DISTRS INC
9190 Seward Rd (45014-5406)
PHONE 513 874-5444
Ken Rieman, *President*
Richard Arszman, *Vice Pres*
Rebecca Rolfert, *Opers Mgr*
Tom Knodel, *Accounts Mgr*
Rob Saunders, *Accounts Mgr*
EMP: 34
SQ FT: 15,000
SALES (est): 30.3MM **Privately Held**
SIC: 5064 Electrical appliances, major; dishwashers; refrigerators & freezers; washing machines

(G-10900)
RIVER CITY PHARMA
8695 Seward Rd (45011-9716)
PHONE 513 870-1680
Danny Smith, *President*
Jason Smith, *Vice Pres*
EMP: 75
SALES (est): 5.7MM **Privately Held**
SIC: 2834 5122 Pharmaceutical preparations; pharmaceuticals

(G-10901)
ROBERT F ARROM MD INC
1020 Symmes Rd (45014-1844)
PHONE 513 893-4107
Fax: 513 863-3053
Robert F Arrom MD, *Owner*
EMP: 30
SQ FT: 1,492
SALES (est): 2.2MM **Privately Held**
SIC: 8011 Offices & clinics of medical doctors

(G-10902)
SAFETY-KLEEN SYSTEMS INC
4120 Thunderbird Ln (45014-2235)
PHONE 513 563-0931
Fax: 513 563-4763
Rich Goodwin, *Manager*
Gena Maras, *Admin Sec*
EMP: 30
SALES (corp-wide): 2.9B **Publicly Held**
SIC: 8748 Environmental consultant
HQ: Safety-Kleen Systems, Inc.
  2600 N Central Expy # 400
  Richardson TX 75080
  972 265-2000

(G-10903)
SCHIFF JOHN J & THOMAS R & CO
Also Called: Schiff Agency
6200 S Gilmore Rd (45014-5141)
P.O. Box 145496, Cincinnati (45250-5496)
PHONE 513 870-2580
Fax: 513 870-2063
John J Schiff Jr, *Ch of Bd*
Raymond E Broerman, *President*
Jeff Lutter, *General Mgr*
Mike Tiemeier, *Vice Pres*
Michael Lint, *Sales Staff*
EMP: 28
SALES (est): 4.8MM **Privately Held**
SIC: 6411 Property & casualty insurance agent; life insurance agents

(G-10904)
SHARPS VALET PARKING
Also Called: Sharp's Valet Parkg
843 Southwind Dr (45014-2755)
PHONE 513 863-1777
Jeff Anders, *Owner*
EMP: 30 **EST:** 1978
SALES (est): 615.9K **Privately Held**
WEB: www.sharpsvalet.com
SIC: 7521 Automobile parking

(G-10905)
SHIP-PAQ INC
3845 Port Union Rd (45014-2208)
PHONE 513 860-0700
Fax: 513 682-2208
James R Jarboe, *President*
Nancy L Jarboe, *VP Admin*
Manford Yoho, *Vice Pres*
Kyle Jarboe, *Info Tech Mgr*
▲ **EMP:** 28
SQ FT: 46,500
SALES (est): 9.9MM **Privately Held**
WEB: www.shippaq.com
SIC: 5199 Packaging materials

(G-10906)
SHRED-IT USA LLC
6838 Firfield Bus Ctr Dr (45014)
PHONE 847 288-0377
Sean Wynn, *Branch Mgr*
EMP: 53
SALES (corp-wide): 3.5B **Publicly Held**
SIC: 8741 Management services
HQ: Shred-It Usa Llc
  6838 Firfield Bus Ctr Dr
  Fairfield OH 45014
  800 697-4733

(G-10907)
SHRED-IT USA LLC (HQ)
6838 Firfield Bus Ctr Dr (45014)
PHONE 800 697-4733
Charles A Alutto, *President*
Brent Arnold, *COO*
Brenda Frank, *Vice Pres*
Christopher Stevens, *Project Mgr*
Dan Ginnetti, *CFO*
EMP: 36
SALES (est): 1B
SALES (corp-wide): 3.5B **Publicly Held**
SIC: 7389 Document & office record destruction
PA: Stericycle, Inc.
  28161 N Keith Dr
  Lake Forest IL 60045
  847 367-5910

(G-10908)
SIBCY CLINE INC
600 Wessel Dr (45014-3600)
PHONE 513 385-3330
Fax: 513 385-9673
Rob Stix, *Manager*
EMP: 45
SALES (corp-wide): 2.1B **Privately Held**
WEB: www.sibcycline.com
SIC: 6531 Real estate agent, residential
PA: Sibcy Cline, Inc.
  8044 Montgomery Rd # 300
  Cincinnati OH 45236
  513 984-4100

(G-10909)
SIBCY CLINE INC
600 Wessel Dr (45014-3600)
PHONE 513 829-0044
Fax: 513 829-4360

Thomas Hasselbeck, *Manager*
EMP: 55
SALES (corp-wide): 2.1B **Privately Held**
WEB: www.sibcycline.com
SIC: 6531 Real estate brokers & agents
PA: Sibcy Cline, Inc.
  8044 Montgomery Rd # 300
  Cincinnati OH 45236
  513 984-4100

(G-10910)
SKYLINE CHILI INC (PA)
4180 Thunderbird Ln (45014-2235)
PHONE 513 874-1188
Fax: 513 874-3591
Kevin R Mc Donnell, *President*
Philip M Lewis, *Senior VP*
Kenneth E Davis, *Vice Pres*
Charles L Harnist, *Vice Pres*
Jim Konves, *Vice Pres*
▲ **EMP:** 120 **EST:** 1949
SQ FT: 42,000
SALES (est): 60.9MM **Privately Held**
WEB: www.skylinechili.com
SIC: 5812 2038 6794 5149 Restaurant, family: chain; frozen specialties; franchises, selling or licensing; groceries & related products; dried or canned foods; canned goods: fruit, vegetables, seafood, meats, etc.; canned specialties

(G-10911)
STEVEN L SAWDAI
6120 Pleasant Ave (45014-4623)
PHONE 513 829-3830
Steven L Sawdai, *Partner*
EMP: 26
SALES (est): 388.5K **Privately Held**
SIC: 0742 Veterinarian, animal specialties

(G-10912)
SUNESIS ENVIRONMENTAL LLC
325 Commercial Dr (45014-5567)
PHONE 513 326-6000
Richard E Jones Jr, *President*
Andrea Strunk, *Administration*
EMP: 92 **EST:** 2015
SALES (est): 2.6MM **Privately Held**
SIC: 1623 1629 1795 Water, sewer & utility lines; sewer line construction; dams, waterways, docks & other marine construction; earthmoving contractor; wrecking & demolition work

(G-10913)
TERMINIX INTL CO LTD PARTNR
4305 Muhlhauser Rd Ste 2 (45014-2265)
PHONE 513 942-6670
Fax: 513 942-6712
Kelvin Colter, *Manager*
EMP: 35
SALES (corp-wide): 2.9B **Publicly Held**
SIC: 7342 Pest control services
HQ: The Terminix International Company Limited Partnership
  860 Ridge Lake Blvd A3-4008
  Memphis TN 38120
  901 766-1400

(G-10914)
THERMAL SOLUTIONS INC
9491 Seward Rd (45014-5411)
PHONE 513 742-2836
Fax: 513 742-2465
Tom Wiest, *President*
Mary C Guy, *Treasurer*
Russell Wiest, *Financial Exec*
James Diersing, *Executive*
Lisa Diersing, *Admin Sec*
EMP: 55
SQ FT: 2,100
SALES (est): 4.8MM **Privately Held**
SIC: 1742 Insulation, buildings

(G-10915)
TORIS STATION
Also Called: Fairfield Bnquet Convention Ctr
74 Donald Dr (45014-3003)
PHONE 513 829-7815
Fax: 513 829-1958
Sam Minnielli, *Owner*
Christa Carnahan, *Director*
David Richards, *Director*
Barb Wyrick, *Director*
EMP: 30

Fairlawn - Summit County (G-10938)

SALES (est): 962.2K **Privately Held**
SIC: 7299 Banquet hall facilities

(G-10916)
TRI COUNTY ASSEMBLY OF GOD
7350 Dixie Hwy (45014-5597)
PHONE.................513 874-8575
Fax: 513 874-4521
Rev Brad H Rosenberg, *Pastor*
Rev Hugh H Rosenberg, *Pastor*
Marcella Boston, *Admin Asst*
EMP: 35 EST: 1961
SQ FT: 200,000
SALES (est): 2.1MM **Privately Held**
WEB: www.tcalife.com
SIC: 8661 8351 Assembly of God Church; preschool center

(G-10917)
TRI COUNTY EXTENDED CARE CTR
5200 Camelot Dr (45014-4009)
P.O. Box 18040 (45018-0040)
PHONE.................513 829-3555
Fax: 513 829-5852
Gidon Eltad, *CEO*
Samuel Boymel, *President*
Peggy Morris, *Vice Pres*
Tonya Bower, *Purch Agent*
Rachel Boymel, *Treasurer*
EMP: 250
SQ FT: 120,000
SALES: 17.3MM **Privately Held**
WEB: www.tcecc.com
SIC: 8051 Extended care facility

(G-10918)
TRUGREEN LIMITED PARTNERSHIP
Also Called: Tru Green-Chemlawn
4041 Thunderbird Ln (45014-2232)
PHONE.................513 223-3707
Fax: 513 942-0278
Jeff Kozakiewicz, *General Mgr*
Melinda Parks, *Info Tech Mgr*
EMP: 40
SQ FT: 2,000
SALES (corp-wide): 4B **Privately Held**
SIC: 0782 Lawn care services
HQ: Trugreen Limited Partnership
    1790 Kirby Pkwy
    Memphis TN 38138
    901 251-4128

(G-10919)
UNICUSTOM INC
3263 Homeward Way (45014-4237)
P.O. Box 74, West Chester (45071-0074)
PHONE.................513 874-9806
Fax: 513 870-5932
Avnish K Bansal, *President*
Veena Bansal, *Vice Pres*
Ambrish Bansal, *CFO*
EMP: 30
SQ FT: 7,000
SALES (est): 2.5MM **Privately Held**
SIC: 1731 1611 General electrical contractor; highway & street construction

(G-10920)
UNIVERSAL TRANSPORTATION SYSTE (PA)
Also Called: Uts
5284 Winton Rd (45014-3912)
PHONE.................513 829-1287
Fax: 513 829-4763
Melissa Ziepfel, *Human Res Mgr*
Sean Davidson, *Manager*
Carolyn Burer,
Diana Navey, *Executive Asst*
EMP: 200
SQ FT: 1,200
SALES (est): 18.3MM **Privately Held**
WEB: www.utswct.com
SIC: 4111 8742 Local & suburban transit; transportation consultant

(G-10921)
US BRONCO SERVICES INC
280 Donald Dr (45014-3007)
P.O. Box 181418 (45018-1418)
PHONE.................513 829-9880
Joseph Kulifay, *President*
Kelly Grant, *Administration*

EMP: 50
SALES (est): 2.3MM **Privately Held**
SIC: 7389 Meter readers, remote

(G-10922)
VERITIV OPERATING COMPANY
Also Called: International Paper
6120 S Gilmore Rd (45014-5162)
PHONE.................513 285-0999
Chuck Helmes, *Vice Pres*
John Nelson, *Human Res Mgr*
Elizabeth Rhoden, *Program Mgr*
Jim Baumer, *Manager*
Gene Bartholomen, *Manager*
EMP: 133
SALES (corp-wide): 8.3B **Publicly Held**
WEB: www.internationalpaper.com
SIC: 5113 Industrial & personal service paper
HQ: Veritiv Operating Company
    1000 Abernathy Rd
    Atlanta GA 30328
    770 391-8200

(G-10923)
ZEBEC OF NORTH AMERICA INC
210 Donald Dr (45014-3007)
P.O. Box 181570 (45018-1570)
PHONE.................513 829-5533
Ed Synder, *President*
Chris Snyder, *Vice Pres*
Scott Snyder, *Vice Pres*
Danielle Koroschetz, *Office Mgr*
▲ EMP: 35
SQ FT: 7,000
SALES (est): 3.6MM **Privately Held**
WEB: www.zebec.com
SIC: 3949 5091 Sporting & athletic goods; sporting & recreation goods

Fairfield Township
Butler County

(G-10924)
BETHESDA HOSPITAL INC
Also Called: Bethesda Butler Hospital
3125 Hamilton Mason Rd (45011-5307)
PHONE.................513 894-8888
Greg Owens, *Medical Dir*
EMP: 28 **Privately Held**
SIC: 8062 General medical & surgical hospitals
HQ: Bethesda Hospital, Inc.
    619 Oak St
    Cincinnati OH 45206
    513 569-6100

(G-10925)
BURCHWOOD CARE CENTER
Also Called: Hellandale Community
4070 Hamilton Mason Rd (45011-5414)
PHONE.................513 868-3300
Jane Gegner, *Pub Rel Dir*
Brent Dixon, *Director*
Gregg Dixon, *Director*
Valerie Glen, *Director*
EMP: 50
SALES (est): 2.1MM **Privately Held**
SIC: 8059 Rest home, with health care

(G-10926)
BUTLER COUNTY OF OHIO
Also Called: Butler County Care Facility
1800 Princeton Rd (45011-4742)
PHONE.................513 887-3728
Fax: 513 785-6626
Belle Qusenberry, *Human Resources*
Charles Demidovich, *Director*
EMP: 180
SQ FT: 33,000 **Privately Held**
WEB: www.butlercountyclerk.org
SIC: 8052 9111 8322 8051 Intermediate care facilities; county supervisors' & executives' offices; individual & family services; skilled nursing care facilities
PA: Butler, County Of Ohio
    315 High St Fl 6
    Hamilton OH 45011
    513 887-3278

(G-10927)
BUTLER COUNTY BD OF MENTAL RE
Liberty Center
5645 Liberty Fairfield Rd (45011-2251)
PHONE.................513 785-2870
Fax: 513 867-5989
Sherry Dillon, *Manager*
EMP: 105
SALES (corp-wide): 5.9MM **Privately Held**
SIC: 8361 9111 8331 Home for the mentally retarded; county supervisors' & executives' offices; job training services
PA: Butler County Board Of Developmental Disabilities
    282 N Fair Ave Ste 1
    Hamilton OH 45011
    513 785-2815

(G-10928)
CREEKSIDE GOLF LTD
Also Called: Walden Ponds Golf Club
6090 Golf Club Ln (45011-7816)
PHONE.................513 785-2999
Fax: 513 868-1037
Ken Johnston, *General Mgr*
Cheryl Ackerman, *General Mgr*
Allison Rhodis, *Sales Dir*
Andrew Crum, *Manager*
EMP: 50
SALES (est): 2.9MM **Privately Held**
SIC: 7992 Public golf courses

(G-10929)
GLENWARD INC
Also Called: Glen Meadows
3472 Hamilton Mason Rd (45011-5437)
PHONE.................513 863-3100
Fax: 513 867-7897
Glyndon Powell, *President*
Wanda Rice, *Controller*
Chuck Powell, *Administration*
EMP: 150
SQ FT: 4,000
SALES (est): 6.3MM **Privately Held**
WEB: www.glenmeadows.com
SIC: 8051 Skilled nursing care facilities

(G-10930)
GREAT MIAMI VALLEY YMCA
Also Called: East Butler County YMCA
6645 Morris Rd (45011-5417)
PHONE.................513 892-9622
Cindy Koenig, *Branch Mgr*
EMP: 136
SALES (corp-wide): 13.3MM **Privately Held**
SIC: 8641 7991 8351 7032 Youth organizations; physical fitness facilities; child day care services; youth camps; individual & family services
PA: Great Miami Valley Ymca
    105 N 2nd St
    Hamilton OH 45011
    513 887-0001

(G-10931)
HOME DEPOT USA INC
Also Called: Home Depot, The
6562 Winford Ave (45011-0547)
PHONE.................513 887-1450
Fax: 513 785-4702
Michael Yudt, *Manager*
EMP: 200
SALES (corp-wide): 100.9B **Publicly Held**
WEB: www.homerentalsdepot.com
SIC: 5211 7359 Home centers; tool rental
HQ: Home Depot U.S.A., Inc.
    2455 Paces Ferry Rd Se
    Atlanta GA 30339

(G-10932)
KERRINGTON HEALTH SYSTEMS INC
Also Called: Wellington Manor
2923 Hamilton Mason Rd (45011-5355)
PHONE.................513 863-0360
Fax: 513 867-7886
Yvette Ross, *Social Dir*
Darla Mull, *Food Svc Dir*
Charles Powell, *Administration*
John Hill, *Maintence Staff*
EMP: 150

SALES (est): 10MM **Privately Held**
SIC: 8741 Nursing & personal care facility management

(G-10933)
KINDERCARE EDUCATION LLC
Also Called: Kinder Care Learning Center
7939 Morris Rd (45011-7715)
PHONE.................513 896-4769
Wendy Welch, *Director*
EMP: 25
SALES (corp-wide): 1.2B **Privately Held**
WEB: www.knowledgelearning.com
SIC: 8351 Group day care center
PA: Kindercare Education Llc
    650 Ne Holladay St # 1400
    Portland OR 97232
    503 872-1300

(G-10934)
MENARD INC
2865 Princeton Rd (45011-5342)
PHONE.................513 737-2204
EMP: 120
SALES (corp-wide): 13.8B **Privately Held**
SIC: 5211 1521 Home centers; single-family home remodeling, additions & repairs
PA: Menard, Inc.
    5101 Menard Dr
    Eau Claire WI 54703
    715 876-5911

(G-10935)
ROBIDEN INC
Also Called: Red Squirrel
6059 Creekside Way (45011-7882)
PHONE.................513 421-0000
Fax: 513 671-3006
Dennis Kurlas, *President*
Peter Lamb, *General Mgr*
EMP: 27
SALES (est): 878.9K **Privately Held**
SIC: 0782 Lawn & garden services

(G-10936)
TRANSITIONAL LIVING INC (HQ)
2052 Princeton Rd (45011-4746)
PHONE.................513 863-6383
Fax: 513 863-9882
Mike Francis, *CFO*
David F Craft, *Exec Dir*
Angie Turner, *Nursing Dir*
Peter A Ramirez, *Psychiatry*
EMP: 65
SQ FT: 20,000
SALES: 3.3MM **Privately Held**
SIC: 8069 Alcoholism rehabilitation hospital
PA: Community Health Alliance
    1020 Symmes Rd
    Fairfield OH 45014
    513 896-3458

Fairlawn
Summit County

(G-10937)
ANGMAR MEDICAL HOLDINGS INC
3480 W Market St (44333-3316)
PHONE.................330 835-9663
EMP: 73
SALES (corp-wide): 52.4MM **Privately Held**
SIC: 9431 8082 Administration of public health programs; home health care services
PA: Angmar Medical Holdings Inc
    2301 Highway 1187 Ste 203
    Mansfield TX 76063
    817 539-2400

(G-10938)
BOBER MARKEY FEDOROVICH (PA)
Also Called: Bmf
3421 Ridgewood Rd Ste 300 (44333-3180)
PHONE.................330 762-9785
Fax: 330 762-3108
Stanley M Bober, *President*
Richard C Fedorovich, *Managing Prtnr*
Richard C Fedorovih, *Managing Prtnr*

Fairlawn - Summit County (G-10939)   GEOGRAPHIC SECTION

Danielle J Kimmell, *Partner*
Michael R Lee, *Partner*
EMP: 69
SQ FT: 11,000
SALES (est): 12MM **Privately Held**
WEB: www.bmfadvisors.com
SIC: 8721 Certified public accountant

(G-10939)
BRUNSWICK COMPANIES (PA)
2857 Riviera Dr Ste 100 (44333-3474)
PHONE................................330 864-8800
Todd Stein, *President*
Michelle Hirsch, *Senior VP*
Donna Schroeder, *Senior VP*
Julie Phillips, *Vice Pres*
Rachel Weinberg, *Vice Pres*
EMP: 29
SQ FT: 7,000
SALES (est): 31.1MM **Privately Held**
WEB: www.brunswickcompany.com
SIC: 6411 Insurance agents

(G-10940)
CADNA RUBBER COMPANY INC
Also Called: Cadna Automotive
703 S Clvland Mssillon Rd (44333-3023)
PHONE................................901 566-9090
Fax: 901 255-1162
Devin Hart, *CEO*
Tom Griffin, *CFO*
▲ **EMP:** 30
SQ FT: 50,000
SALES (est): 10.4MM
SALES (corp-wide): 51.9B **Privately Held**
WEB: www.cadna.com
SIC: 5013 Automotive engines & engine parts
HQ: Contitech Ag
 Vahrenwalder Str. 9
 Hannover 30165
 511 938-02

(G-10941)
CELLCO PARTNERSHIP
Also Called: Verizon
3750 W Market St Unit C (44333-4801)
PHONE................................330 665-5220
Fax: 330 665-4917
Greg Rugabber, *Branch Mgr*
EMP: 25
SALES (corp-wide): 126B **Publicly Held**
SIC: 4812 Cellular telephone services
HQ: Cellco Partnership
 1 Verizon Way
 Basking Ridge NJ 07920

(G-10942)
CHIMA TRAVEL BUREAU INC (PA)
55 Merz Blvd Unit B (44333-2895)
PHONE................................330 867-4770
Fax: 330 867-4281
Craig P Chima, *President*
Derek Chima, *Vice Pres*
Lance Chima, *Vice Pres*
Nancy Rettkowski, *Manager*
EMP: 29
SQ FT: 2,000
SALES (est): 5.8MM **Privately Held**
WEB: www.chimatravel.net
SIC: 4724 Tourist agency arranging transport, lodging & car rental

(G-10943)
CUTLER REAL ESTATE (PA)
2800 W Market St (44333-4007)
PHONE................................330 836-9141
Jay Cutler, *President*
William H Marting, *President*
Dana E Gechoff, *Treasurer*
Sandra Gri, *Manager*
Bud Marting, *Manager*
EMP: 177
SQ FT: 10,000
SALES (est): 6.9MM **Privately Held**
SIC: 6531 Real estate agent, residential

(G-10944)
DENTAL HEALTH SERVICES (PA)
110 N Miller Rd Ste 200 (44333-3787)
PHONE................................330 864-9090
Fax: 330 864-2626
Franchesk Dearlo, *Owner*
Marvin D Cohen DDS, *Owner*
▲ **EMP:** 30

SALES (est): 2MM **Privately Held**
WEB: www.dentalhealthservicesinc.com
SIC: 8021 Dentists' office

(G-10945)
DIALAMERICA MARKETING INC
3090 W Market St Ste 210 (44333-3616)
PHONE................................330 836-5293
Fax: 330 869-9416
Ted Herik, *Manager*
EMP: 180
SALES (corp-wide): 395.1MM **Privately Held**
WEB: www.dialupamerica.net
SIC: 7389 Telemarketing services; telephone services
PA: Dialamerica Marketing, Inc.
 960 Macarthur Blvd
 Mahwah NJ 07430
 201 327-0200

(G-10946)
E & L PREMIER CORPORATION
Also Called: Snelling
3250 W Market St Ste 102 (44333-3319)
PHONE................................330 863-9910
Fax: 330 863-9910
Esther Gotschall, *President*
Lindsay Beaver, *Admin Asst*
Christopher Bennis, *Recruiter*
Kyle David, *Recruiter*
Sherry Samms, *Recruiter*
EMP: 150
SQ FT: 7,703
SALES (est): 6.1MM **Privately Held**
SIC: 7363 7361 Temporary help service; employment agencies

(G-10947)
ELIOKEM INC (HQ)
175 Ghent Rd (44333-3330)
PHONE................................330 734-1100
Fax: 330 734-1101
John F Malloy, *President*
Veronique Le Du, *Vice Pres*
Robert Smith, *Vice Pres*
▲ **EMP:** 85
SQ FT: 100,000
SALES (est): 20.9MM
SALES (corp-wide): 783.1MM **Publicly Held**
WEB: www.eliokem.com
SIC: 5169 Industrial chemicals
PA: Omnova Solutions Inc.
 25435 Harvard Rd
 Beachwood OH 44122
 216 682-7000

(G-10948)
EMERALD HEALTH NETWORK INC (HQ)
3320 W Market St 100 (44333-3306)
PHONE................................216 479-2030
Fax: 216 479-2039
Peter Osner, *President*
Deanna Webber, *Senior VP*
John Gudel, *Info Tech Mgr*
Robert G Halcik, *Info Tech Mgr*
Stephen Halliburton, *Info Tech Mgr*
EMP: 65
SQ FT: 26,000
SALES (est): 4.9MM **Privately Held**
WEB: www.emeraldhealth.com
SIC: 8742 Hospital & health services consultant

(G-10949)
FAIRLAWN ASSOCIATES LTD
Also Called: Hilton Akron Fairlawn
3180 W Market St (44333-3314)
PHONE................................330 867-5000
Fred Todd, *Chief Engr*
Emily Roberts, *Sls & Mktg Exec*
Mary Seman, *Human Res Mgr*
Julie Costello, *Sales Mgr*
Cassandra White, *Sales Mgr*
EMP: 150
SQ FT: 250,000
SALES (est): 11.2MM **Privately Held**
SIC: 7011 5812 6519 6512 Inns; restaurant, family: chain; real property lessors; commercial & industrial building operation; drinking places

(G-10950)
FAIRLAWN OPCO LLC
Also Called: ARBORS AT FAIRLAWN
575 S Clvland Mssillon Rd (44333-3019)
PHONE................................502 429-8062
Fax: 330 666-3215
Robert Norcross, *CEO*
Rosanne Shovlin, *Director*
Benjamin Sparks, *Clerk*
EMP: 99
SQ FT: 60,000
SALES: 7.4MM **Privately Held**
SIC: 8051 Skilled nursing care facilities

(G-10951)
FAMILY DENTAL TEAM INC (PA)
620 Ridgewood Xing Ste K (44333-3531)
PHONE................................330 733-7911
Fax: 330 376-2298
Mark Grucella, *Principal*
Lanny Cortez, *Fmly & Gen Dent*
EMP: 30
SQ FT: 4,000
SALES (est): 4.4MM **Privately Held**
SIC: 8021 Dentists' office

(G-10952)
FIRST CHOICE MED STAFF OF OHIO
3200 W Market St Ste 1 (44333-3315)
PHONE................................330 867-1409
Cammy Davis, *Branch Mgr*
EMP: 25
SALES (corp-wide): 4.6MM **Privately Held**
SIC: 8099 Medical services organization
PA: First Choice Medical Staffing Of Ohio, Inc.
 1457 W 117th St
 Cleveland OH 44107
 216 521-2222

(G-10953)
FIRST COMMUNICATIONS LLC
3340 W Market St (44333-3381)
PHONE................................330 835-2323
Keith Harrison, *General Mgr*
Barbara Jamaleddin, *Senior VP*
Tom Jones, *Senior VP*
Thomas Simone, *Vice Pres*
Kelly Rosen, *Project Mgr*
EMP: 29
SALES (corp-wide): 70.1MM **Privately Held**
SIC: 4813 Long distance telephone communications
PA: First Communications, Llc
 3340 W Market St
 Fairlawn OH 44333
 330 835-2323

(G-10954)
FIRST COMMUNICATIONS LLC (PA)
3340 W Market St (44333-3381)
PHONE................................330 835-2323
Toll Free:................................888 -
Fax: 330 835-2330
Raymond Hexamer, *CEO*
Margi Shaw, *President*
Mark Sollenberger, *CFO*
Andrea Desando, *Sales Mgr*
Nick Marema, *Accounts Exec*
▲ **EMP:** 310
SALES (est): 70.1MM **Privately Held**
SIC: 4813 Long distance telephone communications

(G-10955)
HERNANDEZ CNSTR SVCS INC
33 Merz Blvd Ste 2 (44333-3641)
PHONE................................330 796-0500
Scott Hernandez, *President*
EMP: 50 **EST:** 2005
SQ FT: 9,600
SALES (est): 9MM **Privately Held**
SIC: 8741 Construction management

(G-10956)
HOSPICE CARE OHIO (PA)
Also Called: Hospice Visiting Nurse Service
3358 Ridgewood Rd (44333-3118)
PHONE................................330 665-1455
Fax: 330 668-4680
Karen Mullen, *President*

Tracey Nauer, *Director*
EMP: 26
SALES (est): 11.8MM **Privately Held**
SIC: 8082 Visiting nurse service

(G-10957)
INNOVAIRRE COMMUNICATIONS LLC
3200 W Market St Ste 302 (44333-3326)
PHONE................................330 869-8500
Paul Noonan, *Managing Dir*
EMP: 56
SALES (corp-wide): 79.1MM **Privately Held**
SIC: 7389 Fund raising organizations
PA: Innovairre Communications, Llc
 2 Executive Campus # 200
 Cherry Hill NJ 08002
 856 663-2500

(G-10958)
INTERIM HALTHCARE COLUMBUS INC
Also Called: Interim Services
3040 W Market St Ste 1 (44333-3642)
PHONE................................330 836-5571
Fax: 216 836-5721
Thomas J Dimarco, *President*
Jan Pike, *Manager*
Craig Smith,
EMP: 30
SALES (corp-wide): 24.4MM **Privately Held**
SIC: 8082 7361 7363 Home health care services; nurses' registry; medical help service
HQ: Interim Healthcare Of Columbus, Inc.
 784 Morrison Rd
 Gahanna OH 43230
 614 888-3130

(G-10959)
INTERNATIONAL DATA MGT INC (PA)
3200 W Market St Ste 302 (44333-3326)
PHONE................................330 869-8500
Paul Noonan, *President*
Derrick Bell, *Vice Pres*
Chris Moore, *Vice Pres*
Janis Watson, *Controller*
Andy Kepley, *Human Res Mgr*
EMP: 50
SQ FT: 24,000
SALES (est): 4.5MM **Privately Held**
WEB: www.idmi.com
SIC: 7374 Computer graphics service

(G-10960)
JERSEY CENTRAL PWR & LIGHT CO
Also Called: Firstenergy
395 Ghent Rd Rm 407 (44333-2678)
PHONE................................330 315-6713
Doug Elliott, *Manager*
EMP: 45 **Publicly Held**
WEB: www.jersey-central-power-light.monmouth.n
SIC: 4911 8742 4939 Electric services; management consulting services; combination utilities
HQ: Jersey Central Power & Light Company
 76 S Main St
 Akron OH 44308
 800 736-3402

(G-10961)
KAISER FOUNDATION HOSPITALS
Also Called: Fairlawn Medical Offices
4055 Embassy Pkwy Ste 110 (44333-1781)
PHONE................................800 524-7377
EMP: 593
SALES (corp-wide): 82.6B **Privately Held**
SIC: 8011 Offices & clinics of medical doctors
HQ: Kaiser Foundation Hospitals Inc
 1 Kaiser Plz
 Oakland CA 94612
 510 271-6611

GEOGRAPHIC SECTION

Findlay - Hancock County (G-10987)

(G-10962)
KENNETH ZERRUSEN
Also Called: K and R
3412 W Market St (44333-3308)
PHONE.................330 869-9007
Kenneth Zerrusen, *Principal*
Brandy Brewer, *Opers Staff*
Kevin Thompson, *Business Dir*
Amber Angelilli, *Admin Sec*
EMP: 70
SALES (est): 2MM **Privately Held**
SIC: 8111 General practice attorney, lawyer

(G-10963)
KLAIS AND COMPANY INC (PA)
3320 W Market St 100 (44333-3306)
PHONE.................330 867-8443
Fax: 330 867-0827
Nancy Archibald, *Principal*
Debbie Vespoint, *Manager*
Stan Lippian, *MIS Dir*
EMP: 37 **EST:** 1966
SALES (est): 5.3MM **Privately Held**
WEB: www.klais.com
SIC: 8748 Employee programs administration

(G-10964)
MET GROUP
2640 W Market St (44333-4202)
PHONE.................330 864-1916
Dean Erickson, *President*
EMP: 36
SALES (est): 853.4K **Privately Held**
WEB: www.metgroup.com
SIC: 8093 Specialty outpatient clinics

(G-10965)
MIDWEST EMERGENCY SERVICES LLC
3585 Ridge Park Dr (44333-8203)
PHONE.................586 294-2700
Larry Gazdick, *General Mgr*
Traci Vostenak, *Vice Pres*
Patricia J Weddel, *Human Res Mgr*
Mark Evans, *Mktg Dir*
James M Fox, *Mng Member*
EMP: 45
SQ FT: 8,000
SALES (est): 2.3MM **Privately Held**
SIC: 8721 7361 Billing & bookkeeping service; employment agencies

(G-10966)
MONTROSE FORD INC (PA)
Also Called: MTA Leasing
3960 Medina Rd (44333-2495)
P.O. Box 5260, Akron (44334-0260)
PHONE.................330 666-0711
Fax: 330 666-2793
Michael Thompson, *Ch of Bd*
Christopher Mills, *General Mgr*
Brent Normando, *Business Mgr*
Chris Mills, *Vice Pres*
Joseph Stefanini, *Vice Pres*
EMP: 86
SQ FT: 20,000
SALES (est): 94.7MM **Privately Held**
SIC: 5511 5521 7515 7513 Automobiles, new & used; used car dealers; passenger car leasing; truck rental & leasing, no drivers; general automotive repair shops; top & body repair & paint shops

(G-10967)
NATIONAL MENTOR HOLDINGS INC
3085 W Market St (44333-3652)
PHONE.................330 835-1468
Hamali Kachalia, *Branch Mgr*
EMP: 1278
SALES (corp-wide): 741.5MM **Privately Held**
SIC: 8082 Home health care services
PA: National Mentor Holdings, Inc.
313 Congress St Fl 5
Boston MA 02210
617 790-4800

(G-10968)
PREMIX HOLDING COMPANY
3637 Ridgewood Rd (44333-3123)
PHONE.................330 666-3751
EMP: 320 **EST:** 2016

SALES (corp-wide): 2.4B **Publicly Held**
SIC: 6719 Investment holding companies, except banks
HQ: Hpc Holdings, Llc
3637 Ridgewood Rd
Fairlawn OH 44333

(G-10969)
RISK INTERNATIONAL SVCS INC (HQ)
4055 Embassy Pkwy Ste 100 (44333-1781)
PHONE.................216 255-3400
David O'Brien, *Ch of Bd*
Michael D Davis, *President*
Eric Krieg, *Managing Dir*
Beau Rowell, *Managing Dir*
James Meehan, *Counsel*
EMP: 33
SALES (est): 6.8MM **Privately Held**
WEB: www.riskinternational.com
SIC: 8742 Management consulting services
PA: Risk International Holdings, Inc.
4055 Embassy Pkwy Ste 100
Fairlawn OH 44333
216 255-3400

(G-10970)
RWDOP LLC
Also Called: Orchards of Ridgewood Livin
3558 Ridgewood Rd (44333-3122)
PHONE.................330 666-3776
Adrin Chelzean, *Administration*
EMP: 160
SALES (est): 12.2MM **Privately Held**
SIC: 8051 Skilled nursing care facilities

(G-10971)
SAINT EDWARD HOUSING CORP
Also Called: Village At St Edward Ind Lving
3125 Smith Rd Ofc (44333-2671)
PHONE.................330 668-2828
John Hennelly, *President*
EMP: 38
SALES (est): 1.9MM **Privately Held**
SIC: 6513 Retirement hotel operation

(G-10972)
SANCTUARY SOFTWARE STUDIO INC
3560 W Market St Ste 100 (44333-2660)
PHONE.................330 666-9690
Michael J Terry, *President*
Stacey Simonton, *Manager*
Corey Smith, *Software Engr*
Stacy Simontom, *Director*
EMP: 28
SQ FT: 2,200
SALES (est): 2MM **Privately Held**
WEB: www.sancsoft.com
SIC: 7372 7371 Application computer software; computer software development

(G-10973)
SAND RUN SUPPORTS LLC
2695 Sand Run Pkwy (44333-3762)
PHONE.................330 256-2127
Rich Willse,
EMP: 50
SALES (est): 463.7K **Privately Held**
WEB: www.sandrunsupports.com
SIC: 8082 Home health care services

(G-10974)
SEIBERT-KECK INSURANCE AGENCY (PA)
2950 W Market St Ste A (44333-3600)
PHONE.................330 867-3140
Fax: 330 867-0291
Craig Hassinger, *President*
Johanne Williams, *COO*
David Critchfield, *Exec VP*
Shelley C White, *Assistant VP*
Cliff Baseler, *Vice Pres*
EMP: 38
SQ FT: 17,000
SALES (est): 17.7MM **Privately Held**
WEB: www.seibertkeck.com
SIC: 6411 Insurance agents; insurance brokers

(G-10975)
SENIOR INDEPENDENCE
Also Called: Rockynol
83 N Miller Rd Ste 101 (44333-3729)
PHONE.................330 873-3468
Sheila Flannery, *Exec Dir*
Audrey M Coy, *Admin Asst*
EMP: 60
SALES (est): 3.4MM **Privately Held**
SIC: 8399 8082 Community development groups; home health care services

(G-10976)
SENIOR SELECT HOME HEALTH CARE
3009 Smith Rd Ste 25 (44333-2694)
PHONE.................330 665-4663
Jim Licitri, *President*
Brian Conners, *Finance*
EMP: 30
SALES (est): 1.1MM **Privately Held**
WEB: www.seniorselecthomecare.com
SIC: 8082 Home health care services

(G-10977)
ST EDWARD HOME
Also Called: VILLAGE AT SAINT EDWARD
3131 Smith Rd (44333-2697)
PHONE.................330 668-2828
Fax: 330 666-2721
John J Hennelly, *President*
Danielle Maur, *VP Opers*
Elizabeth Weinhold, *CFO*
Melanie Gladden, *Accounting Mgr*
Ingrid McCaman, *Bookkeeper*
EMP: 200
SQ FT: 210,000
SALES (est): 13.3MM **Privately Held**
SIC: 8051 8361 Skilled nursing care facilities; residential care

(G-10978)
STOUFFER REALTY INC (PA)
130 N Miller Rd Ste A (44333-3728)
PHONE.................330 835-4900
Gary D Stouffer, *President*
Jim Fox, *Vice Pres*
Dana Gechoff, *Financial Exec*
Dan Salmons, *Regl Sales Mgr*
Sandy Locascio, *Sales Staff*
EMP: 47
SALES (est): 6.9MM **Privately Held**
WEB: www.stoufferrealty.com
SIC: 6531 Real estate brokers & agents

(G-10979)
SUMMIT ADVANTAGE LLC
3340 W Market St Ste 100 (44333-3381)
PHONE.................330 835-2453
Jessica Newman, *President*
EMP: 75 **EST:** 2012
SALES (est): 4.1MM **Privately Held**
SIC: 7389 8741 Telemarketing services; telephone services; telephone answering service; office management

(G-10980)
VEYANCE INDUSTRIAL SVCS INC (PA)
703 S Clvland Mssillon Rd (44333-3023)
PHONE.................307 682-7855
Alison Boesch, *Principal*
Charles Seymour, *Vice Pres*
Timothy Jarvis, *Mfg Dir*
John Bass, *Purch Mgr*
Mark Trowbridge, *Engineer*
EMP: 233 **EST:** 2007
SALES (est): 17.1MM **Privately Held**
SIC: 4212 Baggage transfer

(G-10981)
WELTY BUILDING COMPANY LTD (PA)
3421 Ridgewood Rd Ste 200 (44333-3165)
PHONE.................330 867-2400
Donzell S Taylor, *President*
Bradley Ewing, *President*
Ed Paparone, *President*
Mike Melnyk, *General Mgr*
Scott Brady, *Superintendent*
EMP: 75
SQ FT: 2,400

SALES (est): 35.6MM **Privately Held**
SIC: 1542 Commercial & office building, new construction; commercial & office buildings, renovation & repair

(G-10982)
WEST MONTROSE PROPERTIES (PA)
2841 Riviera Dr Ste 300 (44333-3413)
PHONE.................330 867-4013
Micheal Gallucci Jr, *Partner*
John Bresnahan, *Vice Pres*
EMP: 100
SQ FT: 5,000
SALES (est): 528.9K **Privately Held**
SIC: 7011 Hotel, franchised

Farmersville
Montgomery County

(G-10983)
FARMERSVILLE FIRE ASSN INC
Also Called: Farmersville Fire Department
207 N Elm St (45325-1120)
PHONE.................937 696-2863
Tom Wallace, *Chief*
Chisty Smith,
EMP: 27
SALES: 429.4K **Privately Held**
WEB: www.station67.com
SIC: 8641 Civic associations

Fayetteville
Brown County

(G-10984)
MEDIADVERTISER COMPANY
337 Lorelei Dr (45118-8498)
PHONE.................513 651-0265
Tom Nelson, *President*
EMP: 28
SQ FT: 400
SALES: 2.5MM **Privately Held**
SIC: 8748 Business consulting; communications consulting

Felicity
Clermont County

(G-10985)
FRANKLIN TOWNSHIP FIRE AND EMS
718 Market St (45120)
P.O. Box 58 (45120-0058)
PHONE.................513 876-2996
Fax: 513 876-2996
Diane Seibert, *Manager*
Bradley Moore, *Asst Chief*
EMP: 25
SALES (est): 887.4K **Privately Held**
SIC: 4119 Ambulance service

Findlay
Hancock County

(G-10986)
1 AMAZING PLACE CO
207 E Foulke Ave (45840-3754)
PHONE.................419 420-0424
Fax: 419 420-0780
Elizabeth A Manley, *President*
EMP: 34
SALES (est): 796.5K **Privately Held**
SIC: 8351 Preschool center

(G-10987)
631 SOUTH MAIN STREET DEV LLC
Also Called: Hancock Hotel
631 S Main St (45840-3127)
PHONE.................419 423-0631
Rodney Nichols, *Mng Member*
Donald Malarky,
Kelly Niese,
Shane Pfleiderer,

Findlay - Hancock County (G-10988)

Marland Turner,
EMP: 70
SALES (est): 557.4K **Publicly Held**
SIC: 7011 Hotels
PA: Marathon Petroleum Corporation
539 S Main St
Findlay OH 45840

(G-10988)
A B M INC
119 E Sandusky St (45840-4901)
PHONE.................................419 421-2292
Toni Cramer, *Accounts Mgr*
Wayne Mitrick, *Manager*
EMP: 40 **Privately Held**
WEB: www.lakes-mortgage.com
SIC: 7349 Cleaning service, industrial or commercial
PA: A B M, Inc.
180 N Lasalle St Ste 1700
Chicago IL 60601

(G-10989)
ACT I TEMPORARIES FINDLAY INC
2017 Tiffin Ave (45840-9502)
PHONE.................................419 423-0713
Fax: 419 423-4029
Angela Robinson, *President*
William Robinson, *Principal*
EMP: 425
SQ FT: 750
SALES (est): 8.8MM **Privately Held**
SIC: 7363 Temporary help service

(G-10990)
AMERICAN ELECTRIC POWER CO INC
430 Emma St (45840-1736)
PHONE.................................419 420-3011
Louann Hampshire, *Branch Mgr*
EMP: 37
SALES (corp-wide): 15.4B **Publicly Held**
WEB: www.aep.com
SIC: 4911 Electric services; distribution, electric power; generation, electric power; transmission, electric power
PA: American Electric Power Company, Inc.
1 Riverside Plz Fl 1 # 1
Columbus OH 43215
614 716-1000

(G-10991)
APPRAISAL RESEARCH CORPORATION (PA)
101 E Sandusky St Ste 408 (45840-3257)
P.O. Box 1002 (45839-1002)
PHONE.................................419 423-3582
Fax: 419 423-2637
Richard Hoffman, *President*
Janice A Hoffman, *Admin Sec*
EMP: 110 **EST:** 1978
SQ FT: 3,600
SALES (est): 6.9MM **Privately Held**
WEB: www.appraisalresearch.cc
SIC: 6531 Appraiser, real estate

(G-10992)
BACK IN BLACK CO
2100 Fostoria Ave (45840-8758)
P.O. Box 842 (45839-0842)
PHONE.................................419 425-5555
Rob Hayward, *President*
EMP: 40
SALES (est): 1.5MM **Privately Held**
SIC: 4212 Heavy machinery transport, local

(G-10993)
BASOL MAINTENANCE SERVICE INC
1333 Trenton Ave (45840-1923)
P.O. Box 613 (45839-0613)
PHONE.................................419 422-0946
Fax: 419 422-0167
Judith A McMahon, *President*
Patricia Tisci, *Vice Pres*
Colleen Peterman, *Treasurer*
EMP: 60 **EST:** 1963
SQ FT: 25,000
SALES: 1.4MM **Privately Held**
SIC: 7349 Janitorial service, contract basis

(G-10994)
BIOLIFE PLASMA SERVICES LP
1789 E Melrose Ave (45840-4415)
PHONE.................................419 425-8680
Matt Walter, *Branch Mgr*
Matt Walters, *Manager*
EMP: 51
SALES (corp-wide): 11.4B **Privately Held**
WEB: www.biolifeplasma.com
SIC: 5122 8099 Blood plasma; plasmapherous center
HQ: Biolife Plasma Services L.P.
1435 Lake Cook Rd
Philadelphia PA 19182
847 940-5559

(G-10995)
BIRCHAVEN VILLAGE
415 College St (45840-3619)
PHONE.................................419 424-3000
Robert Benson, *Principal*
EMP: 210
SALES (corp-wide): 9.1MM **Privately Held**
SIC: 8059 Convalescent home
PA: Birchaven Village
15100 Birchaven Ln Ofc C
Findlay OH 45840
419 424-3000

(G-10996)
BIRCHAVEN VILLAGE (PA)
15100 Birchaven Ln Ofc C (45840-9779)
P.O. Box 1425 (45839-1425)
PHONE.................................419 424-3000
Fax: 419 425-3070
Bridget Mundy, *Vice Pres*
Barbara Pasztor, *Ch Nursing Ofcr*
Tim Storer, *Administration*
EMP: 74
SQ FT: 75,000
SALES (est): 9.1MM **Privately Held**
SIC: 8051 6514 Skilled nursing care facilities; dwelling operators, except apartments

(G-10997)
BLANCHARD VALLEY HEALTH SYSTEM (PA)
1900 S Main St (45840-1214)
PHONE.................................419 423-4500
Scott Malaney, *President*
Duane Jebbett, *Chairman*
Micheline Kerr, *Business Mgr*
Mary Jo, *Dean*
Chris Keller, *Vice Pres*
EMP: 1700
SQ FT: 50,000
SALES: 32.5MM **Privately Held**
SIC: 8741 7349 Hospital management; building maintenance, except repairs

(G-10998)
BLANCHARD VALLEY HEALTH SYSTEM
Also Called: Bridge Home Health & Hostice
15100 Birchaven Ln (45840-9773)
P.O. Box 1425 (45839-1425)
PHONE.................................419 424-3000
Robert Westphal, *President*
EMP: 70
SALES (corp-wide): 32.5MM **Privately Held**
SIC: 8741 7361 8082 Hospital management; nurses' registry; home health care services
PA: Blanchard Valley Health System
1900 S Main St
Findlay OH 45840
419 423-4500

(G-10999)
BLANCHARD VALLEY HOSPITAL
Also Called: Nearly New Shop
306 Lima Ave (45840-3042)
PHONE.................................419 423-4335
Dorthy Staley, *President*
EMP: 25
SALES (est): 625K **Privately Held**
WEB: www.blanchardvalleyhospital.com
SIC: 5932 8011 Used merchandise stores; general & family practice, physician/surgeon

(G-11000)
BLANCHARD VALLEY INDUSTRIES
1700 N Sandusky St (45840-6463)
PHONE.................................419 422-6386
Mike Chiarelli, *CEO*
Dedra Estep, *Manager*
EMP: 80
SALES: 1.3MM **Privately Held**
SIC: 7361 Employment agencies

(G-11001)
BLANCHARD VALLEY MEDICAL ASSOC
200 W Pearl St (45840-1394)
PHONE.................................419 424-0380
Gary E Hirschfeld MD, *President*
Mary Ann Tucker, *Pharmacist*
Kathy Mills, *Diabetes*
Beth Wilhelm,
Stacey Leist, *Lic Prac Nurse*
EMP: 90 **EST:** 1971
SQ FT: 14,000
SALES (est): 10MM **Privately Held**
WEB: www.bvma.com
SIC: 8011 Internal medicine, physician/surgeon

(G-11002)
BLANCHARD VLY RESIDENTIAL CTR
Also Called: Blanchard Valley School
1705 E Main Cross St (45840-7064)
PHONE.................................419 422-6503
Fax: 419 425-7053
Jammy Bonifas, *Director*
EMP: 60
SALES (est): 2.7MM **Privately Held**
SIC: 8051 Mental retardation hospital

(G-11003)
BLANCHARD VLY RGIONAL HLTH CTR
1800 N Blanchard St # 121 (45840-4503)
PHONE.................................419 427-0809
Brenda Sciranka, *Branch Mgr*
EMP: 150
SALES (corp-wide): 32.5MM **Privately Held**
SIC: 8011 Medical centers
HQ: Blanchard Valley Regional Health Center
1900 S Main St
Findlay OH 45840
419 423-4500

(G-11004)
BLANCHARD VLY RGIONAL HLTH CTR (HQ)
Also Called: Blanchard Valley Hospital
1900 S Main St (45840-1214)
PHONE.................................419 423-4500
Fax: 419 423-5358
John Bookmyer, *COO*
Karen Gerardi, *Pharmacist*
Rhonda Siefker, *Pharmacist*
Marcia Bello, *Manager*
Sally Gockstetter, *Manager*
▲ **EMP:** 750
SQ FT: 50,000
SALES: 219.5MM
SALES (corp-wide): 32.5MM **Privately Held**
SIC: 8062 Hospital, affiliated with AMA residency
PA: Blanchard Valley Health System
1900 S Main St
Findlay OH 45840
419 423-4500

(G-11005)
BOB MILLER RIGGING INC
Also Called: Hrm Leasing
11758 Township Road 100 (45840-9730)
P.O. Box 1445 (45839-1445)
PHONE.................................419 422-7477
Fax: 419 422-9454
H Robert Miller, *President*
EMP: 27
SALES (est): 4.8MM **Privately Held**
SIC: 4212 Heavy machinery transport, local

(G-11006)
BOLOTIN LAW OFFICES
612 S Main St Ste 201 (45840-3153)
PHONE.................................419 424-9800
Toll Free:.................................888 -
EMP: 42
SALES (est): 1.3MM **Privately Held**
SIC: 8111 Legal Services Office

(G-11007)
BPREX PLASTIC PACKAGING INC
170 Stanford Pkwy (45840-1732)
PHONE.................................419 423-3271
John Lindy, *Manager*
EMP: 200 **Publicly Held**
SIC: 5162 Plastics products
HQ: Bprex Plastic Packaging Inc.
1 Seagate Ste 10
Toledo OH 43604

(G-11008)
BROOKDALE SENIOR LIVING INC
Also Called: Grand Court, The
600 Fox Run Rd Ofc (45840-7403)
PHONE.................................419 422-8657
Fax: 419 422-0606
John P Rijos, *President*
Kristin A Ferge, *Exec VP*
Bryan D Richardson, *Exec VP*
Lorrel Filliater, *Exec Dir*
Margaret Malloy, *Director*
EMP: 90
SALES (corp-wide): 4.7B **Publicly Held**
WEB: www.grandcourtlifestyles.com
SIC: 8361 Home for the aged
PA: Brookdale Senior Living
111 Westwood Pl Ste 400
Brentwood TN 37027
615 221-2250

(G-11009)
BROOKDALE SNIOR LVING CMMNTIES
Also Called: Sterling House of Findlay
725 Fox Run Rd (45840-8403)
PHONE.................................419 423-4440
Fax: 419 423-7471
Robin Dilley, *Manager*
EMP: 35
SALES (corp-wide): 4.7B **Publicly Held**
WEB: www.assisted.com
SIC: 8059 Rest home, with health care
HQ: Brookdale Senior Living Communities, Inc.
6737 W Wa St Ste 2300
Milwaukee WI 53214
414 918-5000

(G-11010)
BULLDAWG HOLDINGS LLC (PA)
Also Called: Flag City Mack
151 Stanford Pkwy (45840-1731)
PHONE.................................419 423-3131
Charles D Walter, *Ch of Bd*
James Hoffman, *President*
Greg Jack, *General Mgr*
Mark Stechschulte, *Sales Staff*
Aaron Koogler, *Marketing Staff*
EMP: 34
SQ FT: 36,900
SALES (est): 11.1MM **Privately Held**
WEB: www.flagcitymack.com
SIC: 5012 5531 Truck tractors; truck equipment & parts

(G-11011)
CELLCO PARTNERSHIP
Also Called: Verizon
15073 E Us Route 224 (45840-7764)
PHONE.................................419 424-2351
Fax: 419 424-9313
Barry Alspth, *Branch Mgr*
EMP: 25
SALES (corp-wide): 126B **Publicly Held**
SIC: 4812 5999 Cellular telephone services; telephone equipment & systems
HQ: Cellco Partnership
1 Verizon Way
Basking Ridge NJ 07920

GEOGRAPHIC SECTION
Findlay - Hancock County (G-11034)

(G-11012)
CENTURY HEALTH INC (PA)
1918 N Main St (45840-3818)
PHONE..............................419 425-5050
Fax: 419 423-4092
Colleen Schlea, *CEO*
Carletta Capes, *Corp Secy*
Nida Rider, *Vice Pres*
David Bruns, *Finance*
Basanti Basu, *Psychiatry*
EMP: 65
SQ FT: 11,700
SALES: 5.7MM Privately Held
SIC: 8093 Alcohol clinic, outpatient; drug clinic, outpatient

(G-11013)
CITY OF COMPASSION
1624 Tiffin Ave (45840-6852)
PHONE..............................419 422-7800
EMP: 51 Privately Held
SIC: 9111 8699 City & town managers' offices; charitable organization

(G-11014)
CITY OF FINDLAY
Also Called: Findlay Waste Water Treatment
1201 S River Rd (45840)
PHONE..............................419 424-7179
Fax: 419 424-7823
Randy Greeno, *Superintendent*
David Beach, *Supervisor*
EMP: 33 Privately Held
SIC: 4952 Sewerage systems
PA: City Of Findlay
318 Dorney Plz Ste 313
Findlay OH 45840
419 424-7114

(G-11015)
COLUMBIA GAS OF OHIO INC
1800 Broad Ave (45840-2722)
P.O. Box 2318, Columbus (43216-2318)
PHONE..............................419 435-7725
Fax: 419 427-3240
H R Rowe, *Branch Mgr*
H R Null Rowe, *Branch Mgr*
EMP: 50
SALES (corp-wide): 4.8B Publicly Held
WEB: www.meterrepairshop.com
SIC: 4924 Natural gas distribution
HQ: Columbia Gas Of Ohio, Inc.
290 W Nationwide Blvd # 114
Columbus OH 43215
614 460-6000

(G-11016)
COUNTY OF HANCOCK
Also Called: Blanchard Valley Industries
1700 E Sandusky St (45840-6463)
PHONE..............................419 422-6387
Dedra Estep, *General Mgr*
Wendy Rizor, *Human Res Mgr*
Sheryl Cotter, *Manager*
Rebecca McAdams, *Manager*
Kim Tabor, *Director*
EMP: 50 Privately Held
WEB: www.hancockparks.com
SIC: 8361 8331 Home for the physically handicapped; job training & vocational rehabilitation services
PA: County Of Hancock
300 S Main St
Findlay OH 45840
419 424-7015

(G-11017)
COUNTY OF HANCOCK
Also Called: Hancock County Home
7746 County Road 140 A (45840-1978)
PHONE..............................419 424-7050
Dan Cox, *Manager*
EMP: 58 Privately Held
WEB: www.hancockparks.com
SIC: 8361 Residential care
PA: County Of Hancock
300 S Main St
Findlay OH 45840
419 424-7015

(G-11018)
COUNTY OF HANCOCK
Also Called: Hancock County Engineer
1900 Lima Ave (45840-1439)
P.O. Box 828 (45839-0828)
PHONE..............................419 422-7433

Fax: 419 424-5057
Chris Long, *Director*
EMP: 34 Privately Held
WEB: www.hancockparks.com
SIC: 8711 4214 Structural engineering; local trucking with storage
PA: County Of Hancock
300 S Main St
Findlay OH 45840
419 424-7015

(G-11019)
COUNTY OF HANCOCK
Also Called: Hancock Park District
1424 E Main Cross St (45840-7006)
PHONE..............................419 425-7275
Fax: 419 423-5811
Tifani Boltz, *Manager*
Gary Pruitt, *Director*
EMP: 25 Privately Held
WEB: www.hancockparks.com
SIC: 7999 9512 Recreation services; recreational program administration, government
PA: County Of Hancock
300 S Main St
Findlay OH 45840
419 424-7015

(G-11020)
DANBY PRODUCTS INC (DH)
1800 Production Dr (45840-5445)
P.O. Box 669 (45839-0669)
PHONE..............................519 425-8627
Fax: 419 425-8629
James Estill, *President*
Shauna Gamble, *COO*
Andrew Raymond, *CFO*
Linh Phan, *Marketing Staff*
▲ EMP: 43
SQ FT: 155,948
SALES (est): 148MM
SALES (corp-wide): 255.3K Privately Held
WEB: www.danbyproducts.com
SIC: 5064 Electrical appliances, major
HQ: Danby Products Limited
5070 Whitelaw Rd
Guelph ON N1H 6
519 837-0920

(G-11021)
EBSO INC
Also Called: Administrative Service Cons
215 Stanford Pkwy (45840-1733)
PHONE..............................419 423-3823
Fax: 419 423-7097
Cori Guagenti, *Branch Mgr*
EMP: 39
SALES (corp-wide): 9.2MM Privately Held
SIC: 6324 6411 Hospital & medical service plans; insurance agents, brokers & service
PA: Ebso Inc.
7020 N Pt Wshngton Rd 2
Glendale WI 53217
414 410-1802

(G-11022)
FABCO INC
616 N Blanchard St (45840-5706)
PHONE..............................419 427-0872
Jon Ballinger, *President*
EMP: 60
SALES (corp-wide): 49.7MM Privately Held
SIC: 5082 Excavating machinery & equipment
HQ: Fabco, Inc.
616 N Blanchard St
Findlay OH 45840
419 421-4740

(G-11023)
FAMILY RSOURCE CTR NW OHIO INC
Also Called: Family Resource Centers
1941 Carlin St (45840-1460)
PHONE..............................419 422-8616
Fax: 419 423-9221
Tonnie Guagenta, *General Mgr*
Melissa Meyer, *Senior VP*
EMP: 30

SALES (corp-wide): 3.9MM Privately Held
WEB: www.frcohio.com
SIC: 8093 Mental health clinic, outpatient
PA: Family Resource Center Of Northwest Ohio, Inc.
530 S Main St
Lima OH 45804
419 222-1168

(G-11024)
FIELD & STREAM BOWHUNTERS
1023 Cypress Ave (45840-4726)
PHONE..............................419 423-9861
Harlod Spence, *President*
EMP: 80
SALES (est): 903.7K Privately Held
SIC: 7997 Gun & hunting clubs

(G-11025)
FINDLAY COUNTRY CLUB
1500 Country Club Dr (45840-6369)
PHONE..............................419 422-9263
Fax: 419 422-9291
James Price, *COO*
Geoffrey Wedwaldt, *Executive*
EMP: 40
SQ FT: 5,000
SALES: 2.1MM Privately Held
WEB: www.findlaycc.com
SIC: 7997 7991 5813 5812 Country club, membership; physical fitness facilities; drinking places; eating places

(G-11026)
FINDLAY IMPLEMENT CO (PA)
Also Called: John Deere Authorized Dealer
1640 Northridge Rd (45840-1902)
P.O. Box 824 (45839-0824)
PHONE..............................419 424-0471
Fax: 419 424-1044
Craig L Holmes, *CEO*
William Stall, *President*
Ralph Philips, *Manager*
EMP: 39
SQ FT: 30,000
SALES (est): 12.1MM Privately Held
WEB: www.findlay-imp.com
SIC: 5261 5082 Lawnmowers & tractors; construction & mining machinery

(G-11027)
FINDLAY INN & CONFERENCE CTR
200 E Main Cross St (45840-4819)
PHONE..............................419 422-5682
Fax: 419 422-5581
Ralph Russo, *Partner*
Todd McCracken, *General Mgr*
Lolie Anez, *Financial Exec*
John Wengrow, *Sales Executive*
Bruce Schroder, *Manager*
EMP: 60
SALES (est): 4.4MM Privately Held
WEB: www.findlayinn.com
SIC: 7011 7299 6512 5812 Resort hotel; banquet hall facilities; nonresidential building operators; eating places

(G-11028)
FINDLAY PUBLISHING COMPANY
Also Called: Wfin AM
551 Lake Cascade Pkwy (45840-1388)
P.O. Box 1507 (45839-1507)
PHONE..............................419 422-4545
Fax: 419 422-6736
Roger Kranz, *Prdtn Dir*
Mary Yarris, *Marketing Staff*
Sandra J Kozlevcar, *Manager*
EMP: 35
SALES (corp-wide): 14.3MM Privately Held
WEB: www.thecourier.com
SIC: 4832 Radio broadcasting stations
PA: Findlay Publishing Company, The (Inc)
701 W Sandusky St
Findlay OH
419 422-5151

(G-11029)
FINDLAY TRUCK LINE INC
106 W Front St (45840-3408)
P.O. Box 1362 (45839-1362)
PHONE..............................419 422-1945
Fax: 419 422-0380
Gregory J Cassidy, *President*
Brian Adams, *Vice Pres*
EMP: 86
SQ FT: 10,000
SALES (est): 7.2MM Privately Held
WEB: www.ftlco.com
SIC: 4212 Local trucking, without storage

(G-11030)
FINDLAY WOMENS CARE LLC (PA)
Also Called: Tiffin Womens Care
1917 S Main St (45840-1208)
PHONE..............................419 420-0904
Krista Montes, *Business Mgr*
Carmen Doty-Armstrong, *Mng Member*
EMP: 30
SALES (est): 3.2MM Privately Held
SIC: 8011 Gynecologist

(G-11031)
FINDLAY Y M C A CHILD DEV
231 E Lincoln St (45840-4940)
PHONE..............................419 422-3174
Vicki Montgomery, *Data Proc Exec*
Susan Stitnale, *Director*
EMP: 50
SALES (est): 741.6K Privately Held
SIC: 8641 7991 8351 7032 Youth organizations; physical fitness facilities; child day care services; youth camps; individual & family services

(G-11032)
FIVE & COMPANY REALTY INC
Also Called: Re/Max Realty/Findlay
1621 Tiffin Ave (45840-6848)
PHONE..............................419 423-8004
Fax: 419 423-9707
Iveadean Wolber, *President*
Kathy Williams, *Vice Pres*
Josie Lentz, *Broker*
Charity Ritzler, *Broker*
Greg Williams, *Real Est Agnt*
EMP: 28
SQ FT: 3,000
SALES (est): 2.2MM Privately Held
WEB: www.findlayrealtor.net
SIC: 6531 Real estate agent, residential

(G-11033)
FRIENDS SERVICE CO INC (PA)
Also Called: Friends Business Source
2300 Bright Rd (45840-5432)
PHONE..............................419 427-1704
Fax: 419 425-9432
Kenneth J Schroeder, *President*
Dale Alt, *President*
Betsy Hughes, *Vice Pres*
Peg Schroeder, *Human Res Dir*
Dennis Mitchell, *Human Resources*
EMP: 80
SQ FT: 65,000
SALES: 30MM Privately Held
WEB: www.friendsoffice.com
SIC: 5112 5021 5044 5087 Stationery & office supplies; furniture; office equipment; janitors' supplies; photolithographic printing

(G-11034)
G S WIRING SYSTEMS INC (HQ)
1801 Production Dr (45840-5446)
P.O. Box 1045 (45839-1045)
PHONE..............................419 423-7111
George Suzuki, *President*
Shinichi Inagaki, *President*
Yukinobu Ukai, *Treasurer*
Annette Edgington, *Accountant*
Masami Kunimi, *Sales Mgr*
▲ EMP: 412
SQ FT: 72,000
SALES (est): 46MM
SALES (corp-wide): 242.9MM Privately Held
WEB: www.gswiring.com
SIC: 3714 5013 Automotive wiring harness sets; motor vehicle supplies & new parts

Findlay - Hancock County (G-11035)

PA: G.S.Electech,Inc.
58-1, Hirako, Yoshiwaracho
Toyota AIC 473-0
565 782-800

(G-11035)
GARNER TRUCKING INC
Also Called: Garner Transportation Group
9291 County Road 313 (45840-9005)
P.O. Box 1506 (45839-1506)
PHONE..............................419 422-5742
Fax: 419 422-8085
Jean Garner, *CEO*
Sherri Brumbaugh, *President*
Stephanie Kramer, *Vice Pres*
Don Perkins, *Vice Pres*
Nicole Stewart, *Vice Pres*
EMP: 136
SQ FT: 19,000
SALES: 20MM **Privately Held**
WEB: www.garnertrucking.com
SIC: 4213 4731 4212 Contract haulers; truck transportation brokers; local trucking, without storage

(G-11036)
GENE STEVENS AUTO & TRUCK CTR
Also Called: Gene Stevens Honda
1033 Bright Rd (45840-6978)
PHONE..............................419 429-2000
Fax: 419 422-3375
Gene Stevens, *President*
Scott Stevens, *Vice Pres*
Elaine Stevens, *Treasurer*
Carol Taylor, *Admin Asst*
EMP: 50
SALES (est): 16.1MM **Privately Held**
WEB: www.genestevensauto.com
SIC: 5511 5521 5012 Automobiles, new & used; used car dealers; automobiles & other motor vehicles

(G-11037)
GRAHAM PACKG PLASTIC PDTS INC
170 Stanford Pkwy (45840-1732)
PHONE..............................419 423-3271
John Lindy, *Plant Mgr*
Cris Ricker, *Plant Mgr*
Allen Reinhart, *Engineer*
Nancy Cole, *Accountant*
Natoshia Kelly, *Human Resources*
EMP: 200
SALES (est): 30.7MM **Privately Held**
WEB: www.grahampackaging.com
SIC: 5199 Packaging materials
HQ: Graham Packaging Company, L.P.
700 Indian Springs Dr # 100
Lancaster PA 17601
717 849-8500

(G-11038)
GRANGER ELC HANCOCK CNTY LLC
3763 County Road 140 (45840)
PHONE..............................517 371-9765
Ray A Easton, *CFO*
EMP: 25
SALES (est): 1.3MM **Privately Held**
SIC: 4911 Electric services

(G-11039)
H T I EXPRESS
110 Bentley Ct (45840-1779)
PHONE..............................419 423-9555
Jeff Hall, *President*
EMP: 26
SALES (est): 1.3MM **Privately Held**
SIC: 4212 Local trucking, without storage

(G-11040)
HANCO AMBULANCE INC
417 6th St (45840-5198)
PHONE..............................419 423-2912
Fax: 419 423-7254
Duane Donaldson, *President*
Rob Martin, *President*
Shirley Moore, *President*
EMP: 48
SQ FT: 4,200
SALES (est): 1.8MM **Privately Held**
WEB: www.hancoems.com
SIC: 4119 Ambulance service

(G-11041)
HANCOCK FEDERAL CREDIT UNION
1701 E Melrose Ave (45840-4415)
P.O. Box 1623 (45839-1623)
PHONE..............................419 420-0338
Fax: 419 424-0124
Joyce Mohr, *CEO*
Donna Litchle, *Principal*
Suzzette Boyd, *Senior VP*
Greg Harris, *Vice Pres*
John Holzwart, *Vice Pres*
EMP: 25
SALES: 2.8MM **Privately Held**
WEB: www.hancockfcu.com
SIC: 6062 State credit unions, not federally chartered

(G-11042)
HANCOCK HARDIN WYANDOT PUTNAM (PA)
Also Called: Community Action Commission
122 Jefferson St (45840-4843)
P.O. Box 179 (45839-0179)
PHONE..............................419 423-4115
Fax: 419 423-4115
Dennis La Rocco, *Exec Dir*
Dave Salucci, *Deputy Dir*
EMP: 125
SQ FT: 6,300
SALES (est): 8.7MM **Privately Held**
SIC: 8399 Community action agency

(G-11043)
HANCOCK JOB & FAMILY SERVICES
7814 County Road 140 (45840-1819)
PHONE..............................419 424-7022
Judy Wauford, *Administration*
EMP: 88
SALES (est): 1.1MM **Privately Held**
SIC: 8322 Child related social services

(G-11044)
HCF OF FINDLAY INC
Also Called: Fox Run Manor
11745 Township Road 145 (45840-1093)
PHONE..............................419 999-2010
Barbara Masella, *Vice Pres*
Shane Stewart, *Administration*
EMP: 99
SALES (est): 1MM
SALES (corp-wide): 154.8MM **Privately Held**
SIC: 8059 Nursing home, except skilled & intermediate care facility
PA: Hcf Management, Inc.
1100 Shawnee Rd
Lima OH 45805
419 999-2010

(G-11045)
HCF OF FOX RUN INC
Also Called: Fox Run Manor
11745 Township Road 145 (45840-1093)
PHONE..............................419 424-0832
Fax: 419 424-3560
Lisa Line, *Sls & Mktg Exec*
Shane Stewart, *Administration*
EMP: 99
SALES (est): 4MM
SALES (corp-wide): 154.8MM **Privately Held**
SIC: 8051 8059 Convalescent home with continuous nursing care; nursing home, except skilled & intermediate care facility
PA: Hcf Management, Inc.
1100 Shawnee Rd
Lima OH 45805
419 999-2010

(G-11046)
HELTON ENTERPRISES INC (PA)
151 Stanford Pkwy (45840-1731)
PHONE..............................419 423-4180
Fax: 419 424-5134
Charles D Walter, *Ch of Bd*
James Hoffman, *President*
Dan Campling, *Corp Secy*
EMP: 38
SQ FT: 39,600
SALES (est): 2.9MM **Privately Held**
SIC: 7513 5012 5531 Truck leasing, without drivers; truck tractors; trailers for trucks, new & used; truck equipment & parts

(G-11047)
HTI - HALL TRUCKING INC
110 Bentley Ct (45840-1779)
PHONE..............................419 423-9555
Fax: 419 423-1587
Jeffrey A Hall, *President*
Cassandra Hall, *Admin Sec*
EMP: 40
SALES (est): 6.2MM **Privately Held**
SIC: 4213 Trucking, except local

(G-11048)
HUNTINGTON INSURANCE INC
Also Called: Huntington Bank
236 S Main St (45840-3352)
PHONE..............................419 429-4627
Donald Bledsoe, *Broker*
Marcia Walton, *Branch Mgr*
EMP: 46
SALES (corp-wide): 4.7B **Publicly Held**
WEB: www.skyinsure.com
SIC: 6029 Commercial banks
HQ: Huntington Insurance, Inc.
519 Madison Ave
Toledo OH 43604
419 720-7900

(G-11049)
HYWAY TRUCKING COMPANY
10060 W Us Route 224 (45840-1914)
P.O. Box 416 (45839-0416)
PHONE..............................419 423-7145
Fax: 419 423-6654
Matt Lenhart, *President*
EMP: 100
SALES (est): 13.8MM **Privately Held**
WEB: www.hywaytrucking.com
SIC: 4213 4212 Contract haulers; local trucking, without storage

(G-11050)
INTER HEALT CARE OF NORTH OH I
Also Called: Interim Services
2129 Stephen Ave Ste 3 Ste 2 (45840)
PHONE..............................419 422-5328
Fax: 419 422-4924
Krista Finsto, *Manager*
EMP: 50
SALES (corp-wide): 24.4MM **Privately Held**
SIC: 7363 Temporary help service
HQ: Interim Health Care Of Northwestern Ohio, Inc
3100 W Central Ave # 250
Toledo OH 43606

(G-11051)
JK-CO LLC
16960 E State Route 12 (45840-9744)
PHONE..............................419 422-5240
Fax: 419 422-5260
Joseph L Kurtz, *President*
C Leon Thornton, *Vice Pres*
Tony Butz, *Project Mgr*
Chuck Brothers, *Buyer*
Jody Karg, *Accountant*
▼ EMP: 45
SQ FT: 40,000
SALES (est): 11.7MM **Privately Held**
SIC: 3743 4789 Railroad car rebuilding; railroad car repair

(G-11052)
JPMORGAN CHASE BANK NAT ASSN
1971 Broad Ave (45840-2723)
PHONE..............................419 424-7570
Fax: 419 424-7555
Jeff Hire, *Branch Mgr*
EMP: 26
SALES (corp-wide): 99.6B **Publicly Held**
SIC: 6021 National commercial banks
HQ: Jpmorgan Chase Bank, National Association
1111 Polaris Pkwy
Columbus OH 43240
614 436-3055

(G-11053)
JPMORGAN CHASE BANK NAT ASSN
500 S Main St (45840-3230)
PHONE..............................419 424-7512
Anna Bretzing, *Manager*
EMP: 26
SALES (corp-wide): 99.6B **Publicly Held**
WEB: www.chase.com
SIC: 6021 National commercial banks
HQ: Jpmorgan Chase Bank, National Association
1111 Polaris Pkwy
Columbus OH 43240
614 436-3055

(G-11054)
JUDSON PALMER HOME CORP
2911 N Main St (45840-4099)
P.O. Box 119 (45839-0119)
PHONE..............................419 422-9656
Fax: 419 422-9656
Rebecca Rademacher, *Principal*
EMP: 25
SQ FT: 30,000
SALES: 1.4MM **Privately Held**
WEB: www.judsonpalmer.com
SIC: 8059 Rest home, with health care

(G-11055)
KRAMER ENTERPRISES INC (PA)
Also Called: City Laundry & Dry Cleaning Co
116 E Main Cross St (45840-4817)
PHONE..............................419 422-7924
Fax: 419 422-8332
Paul T Kramer, *President*
Carl P Kramer, *Principal*
Rich Kramer, *Vice Pres*
Brandon Salyer, *Supervisor*
Pamela E Kramer, *Admin Sec*
EMP: 70
SQ FT: 6,500
SALES (est): 10.8MM **Privately Held**
WEB: www.kramerenterprises.com
SIC: 7213 7216 Uniform supply; drycleaning plants, except rugs

(G-11056)
LARICHE SUBARU INC
Also Called: Lariche Chevrolet-Cadillac
215 E Main Cross St (45840-4818)
PHONE..............................419 422-1855
Fax: 419 422-6760
Lou Lariche, *President*
Bob Lariche, *General Mgr*
Scott Lariche, *Corp Secy*
John Lariche, *Vice Pres*
Clyde Geiser, *CPA*
EMP: 72
SQ FT: 25,000
SALES (est): 31.7MM **Privately Held**
WEB: www.larichechevrolet.com
SIC: 5511 5521 7515 7538 Automobiles, new & used; pickups, new & used; used car dealers; passenger car leasing; general automotive repair shops

(G-11057)
LOWES HOME CENTERS LLC
1077 Bright Rd (45840-6978)
PHONE..............................419 420-7531
Fax: 419 420-7548
Scott Adkins, *Store Mgr*
Mary Parkins, *Executive*
EMP: 150
SALES (corp-wide): 68.6B **Publicly Held**
SIC: 5211 5031 5722 5064 Home centers; building materials, exterior; building materials, interior; household appliance stores; electrical appliances, television & radio
HQ: Lowe's Home Centers, Llc
1605 Curtis Bridge Rd
Wilkesboro NC 28697
336 658-4000

(G-11058)
LOWES HOME CENTERS LLC
12700 County Road 212 (45840-9718)
PHONE..............................419 429-5700
Thys Visser, *Branch Mgr*
Mark Stewart, *Manager*
Jason Griffith, *Manager*
EMP: 236

SALES (corp-wide): 68.6B **Publicly Held**
SIC: 4225 General warehousing & storage
HQ: Lowe's Home Centers, Llc
  1605 Curtis Bridge Rd
  Wilkesboro NC 28697
  336 658-4000

(G-11059)
LUKE THEIS ENTERPRISES INC
Also Called: Luke Theis Contractors
14120 State Route 568 (45840-9428)
PHONE..................419 422-2040
Luke Theis, *President*
EMP: 57
SALES: 122MM **Privately Held**
SIC: 1542 1541 1521 Nonresidential construction; industrial buildings & warehouses; new construction, single-family houses

(G-11060)
MANLEYS MANOR NURSING HOME INC
Also Called: Heritage, The
2820 Greenacre Dr (45840-4157)
PHONE..................419 424-0402
L Don Manley, *President*
Karen Manley, *Corp Secy*
Dawn Harris, *Network Mgr*
Jolynda Timmerman, *Exec Dir*
Deb Creager, *Administration*
EMP: 150
SQ FT: 1,200,000
SALES (est): 6.6MM **Privately Held**
SIC: 8051 6512 Convalescent home with continuous nursing care; commercial & industrial building operation

(G-11061)
MARATHON PETROLEUM CORPORATION (PA)
539 S Main St (45840-3229)
PHONE..................419 422-2121
Fax: 330 273-0972
Gary R Heminger, *Ch of Bd*
Adam Rhoden, *Port Captain*
Rodney P Nichols, *Exec VP*
Randy Nickerson, *Exec VP*
Donald C Templin, *Exec VP*
▲ **EMP:** 277
SALES: 75.3B **Publicly Held**
SIC: 2911 5172 Petroleum refining; gasoline

(G-11062)
MARATHON PIPE LINE LLC (HQ)
539 S Main St Ste 7614 (45840-3229)
PHONE..................419 422-2121
Fax: 419 421-4018
Gary R Heminger, *CEO*
Pamela K Beall, *Vice Pres*
Clifford C Cook, *Vice Pres*
R K McCord, *Vice Pres*
Rodney P Nichols, *Vice Pres*
▲ **EMP:** 107
SQ FT: 25,000
SALES: 467.9MM **Publicly Held**
WEB: www.mapl.com
SIC: 4612 4613 Crude petroleum pipelines; refined petroleum pipelines

(G-11063)
MAY JIM AUTO SALES LLC
Also Called: Jim May Auto Sales & Svc Ctr
3690 Speedway Dr (45840-7246)
PHONE..................419 422-9797
Fax: 419 422-9798
Jim May, *Managing Prtnr*
EMP: 25
SQ FT: 6,000
SALES (est): 4.4MM **Privately Held**
SIC: 5521 7538 Automobiles, used cars only; general automotive repair shops

(G-11064)
MCNAUGHTON-MCKAY ELC OHIO INC
1950 Industrial Dr (45840-5441)
PHONE..................419 422-2984
Timothy J Krucki, *Principal*
EMP: 30
SQ FT: 35,000

SALES (corp-wide): 724.3MM **Privately Held**
WEB: www.mc.mc.com
SIC: 5063 Electrical supplies
HQ: Mcnaughton-Mckay Electric Company Of Ohio, Inc.
  2255 Citygate Dr
  Columbus OH 43219
  614 476-2800

(G-11065)
MEDCORP INC
330 N Cory St (45840-3566)
PHONE..................419 425-9700
Dick Bage, *Owner*
EMP: 198 **Privately Held**
SIC: 4119 8082 Ambulance service; home health care services
PA: Medcorp, Inc.
  745 Medcorp Dr
  Toledo OH 43608

(G-11066)
MIAMI INDUSTRIAL TRUCKS INC
130 Stanford Pkwy (45840-1732)
PHONE..................419 424-0042
Fax: 419 421-0174
Rob Gibson, *Opers Mgr*
Eric Risner, *Accounts Mgr*
Larry McLaughlin, *Regl Sales Mgr*
Michael Wechta, *Manager*
EMP: 40
SALES (corp-wide): 51.9MM **Privately Held**
WEB: www.mitlift.com
SIC: 7353 Heavy construction equipment rental; cranes & aerial lift equipment, rental or leasing
PA: Miami Industrial Trucks, Inc.
  2830 E River Rd
  Moraine OH 45439
  937 293-4194

(G-11067)
MID-AMERICAN CLG CONTRS INC
1648 Tiffin Ave (45840-6849)
PHONE..................419 429-6222
John Whitaker, *Branch Mgr*
EMP: 117 **Privately Held**
SIC: 7349 Janitorial service, contract basis
PA: Mid-American Cleaning Contractors, Inc.
  447 N Elizabeth St
  Lima OH 45801

(G-11068)
NAPOLEON WASH-N-FILL INC (PA)
Also Called: Flag City Auto Wash
339 E Main Cross St (45840-4820)
PHONE..................419 422-7216
Fax: 419 422-7699
Randy Miller, *President*
Leo Snyder, *President*
Michael Snyder, *Vice Pres*
Chauncey Morse, *Treasurer*
EMP: 125
SALES (est): 2.8MM **Privately Held**
WEB: www.flagcityautowash.com
SIC: 7542 Washing & polishing, automotive

(G-11069)
NATIONAL LIME AND STONE CO
9860 County Road 313 (45840-9003)
P.O. Box 120 (45839-0120)
PHONE..................419 423-3400
Fax: 419 423-1313
Gary Eisenhart, *Credit Mgr*
Tim Federici, *Sales Staff*
Denny Swick, *Branch Mgr*
Jeannine Clark, *Director*
EMP: 31
SALES (corp-wide): 3.2B **Privately Held**
WEB: www.natlime.com
SIC: 3273 1422 Ready-mixed concrete; crushed & broken limestone
PA: The National Lime And Stone Company
  551 Lake Cascade Pkwy
  Findlay OH 45840
  419 422-4341

(G-11070)
NOAKES ROONEY RLTY & ASSOC CO
Also Called: ERA
2113 Tiffin Ave Ste 103 (45840-8516)
PHONE..................419 423-4861
Fax: 419 423-7712
Greta Noakes, *President*
Gary Noakes, *Vice Pres*
David Hindall, *Manager*
Brad Lemos, *Real Est Agnt*
EMP: 25
SQ FT: 2,500
SALES (est): 1.1MM **Privately Held**
WEB: www.noakesrooney.com
SIC: 6531 Real estate agent, residential

(G-11071)
NORTHWEST OHIO ORTHOPEDIC & SP
7595 County Road 236 (45840-8738)
PHONE..................419 427-1984
Fax: 419 427-2864
James D Egleston, *President*
Amy Young, *Office Mgr*
Kim Smith, *Podiatrist*
Michelle Colvin,
EMP: 110
SALES (est): 13.7MM **Privately Held**
SIC: 8069 Orthopedic hospital

(G-11072)
OHIO AUTOMOTIVE SUPPLY CO
525 W Main Cross St (45840-3370)
P.O. Box 209 (45839-0209)
PHONE..................419 422-1655
Fax: 419 422-9670
Thomas E Winklejohn, *President*
J Theodore Winklejohn, *Vice Pres*
EMP: 29
SQ FT: 3,500
SALES (est): 6MM **Privately Held**
WEB: www.ohioautomotive.com
SIC: 5013 Truck parts & accessories; automotive supplies & parts; automotive supplies

(G-11073)
PETERBILT OF NORTHWEST OHIO
1330 Trenton Ave (45840-1924)
PHONE..................419 423-3441
Fax: 419 422-2904
Alvin Daugherty, *CEO*
Rick Daugherty, *President*
Daryl Daugherty, *Treasurer*
Nan Daugherty, *Controller*
EMP: 35
SQ FT: 30,000
SALES (est): 9.6MM **Privately Held**
WEB: www.peterbiltofnwohio.com
SIC: 5012 Truck tractors; trailers for trucks, new & used

(G-11074)
PETERMAN ASSOCIATES INC
3480 N Main St (45840-4207)
PHONE..................419 722-9566
Fax: 419 422-9466
Nick Nigh, *President*
Jud Taylor, *Manager*
EMP: 40
SQ FT: 2,400
SALES (est): 4.4MM **Privately Held**
WEB: www.petermanaes.com
SIC: 8711 8713 Consulting engineer; civil engineering; surveying services

(G-11075)
PETSMART INC
2330 Tiffin Ave (45840-9507)
PHONE..................419 423-6869
Rodman Saint, *Branch Mgr*
EMP: 32
SALES (corp-wide): 12.7B **Privately Held**
SIC: 0752 Grooming services, pet & animal specialties
HQ: Petsmart, Inc.
  19601 N 27th Ave
  Phoenix AZ 85027
  623 580-6100

(G-11076)
PLUMBLINE SOLUTIONS INC
Also Called: Solomon Cloud Solutions
1219 W Main Cross St # 101 (45840-0707)
PHONE..................419 581-2963
Vern Strong, *CEO*
Gary Harpst, *Chairman*
EMP: 50
SALES (est): 761.7K **Privately Held**
SIC: 7371 Computer software development

(G-11077)
PRIDE TRANSPORTATION INC
611 Howard St (45840-2529)
PHONE..................419 424-2145
Jonathan E Ruehle, *President*
Sara Jones, *Corp Secy*
Richard R Ruehle, *Vice Pres*
Tom Erdman, *Vice Pres*
EMP: 32
SQ FT: 9,600
SALES (est): 5.4MM **Privately Held**
WEB: www.pridetransportation.com
SIC: 4731 4212 4213 Truck transportation brokers; local trucking, without storage; trucking, except local

(G-11078)
QUALITY LINES INC
2440 Bright Rd (45840-5436)
P.O. Box 904 (45839-0904)
PHONE..................740 815-1165
Fax: 419 429-1336
Ronald Smith, *President*
EMP: 122
SQ FT: 6,000
SALES: 20MM **Privately Held**
WEB: www.qualitylines.net
SIC: 1623 7389 Pipeline construction;

(G-11079)
RIGHTTHING LLC (HQ)
Also Called: Rightthing, The
3401 Technology Dr (45840-9547)
PHONE..................419 420-1830
Fax: 419 420-3720
Terry Terhark, *CEO*
Cooper C Care, *General Mgr*
John Hess, *Senior VP*
Jeffrey A Martin, *VP Finance*
Elaine Kaiser, *Accounts Mgr*
EMP: 360
SQ FT: 43,000
SALES (est): 27.8MM
SALES (corp-wide): 12.3B **Publicly Held**
WEB: www.rightthinginc.com
SIC: 7361 Employment agencies
PA: Automatic Data Processing, Inc.
  1 Adp Blvd Ste 1 # 1
  Roseland NJ 07068
  973 974-5000

(G-11080)
SHELLY COMPANY
Also Called: Findlay Division
1700 Fostoria Ave Ste 200 (45840-6218)
PHONE..................419 422-8854
Don Webber, *Branch Mgr*
Dave Fogg, *Manager*
Tom Good, *Manager*
EMP: 70
SALES (corp-wide): 29.7B **Privately Held**
SIC: 1611 Surfacing & paving
HQ: Shelly Company
  80 Park Dr
  Thornville OH 43076
  740 246-6315

(G-11081)
SIX DISCIPLINES LLC (PA)
1219 W Main Cross St # 205 (45840-0702)
PHONE..................419 424-6647
Scott Boley, *Partner*
Dan Gonder, *COO*
Clark Brian, *Financial Exec*
Scott Gray, *Sales Dir*
Gary Harpst, *Mng Member*
EMP: 47
SALES (est): 3.7MM **Privately Held**
WEB: www.sixdisciplines.com
SIC: 8748 Business consulting

Findlay - Hancock County (G-11082)

(G-11082)
SOMETHING SPECIAL LRNG CTR INC
655 Fox Run Rd Ste J (45840-8401)
PHONE..................................419 422-1400
Fax: 419 420-0684
Kathleen Brandle, *Director*
EMP: 25
SALES (corp-wide): 2.9MM **Privately Held**
SIC: 8351 Child day care services
PA: Something Special Learning Center, Inc.
   8251 Wterville Swanton Rd
   Waterville OH 43566
   419 878-4190

(G-11083)
SPECTRUM EYE CARE INC
15840 Medical Dr S Ste A (45840-7833)
PHONE..................................419 423-8665
Paul Armstrong, *President*
Jack G Hendershot Jr, *President*
Candice Hendershot, *Corp Secy*
EMP: 50
SQ FT: 2,000
SALES: 5.8MM **Privately Held**
SIC: 8011 Ophthalmologist

(G-11084)
ST CATHERINES CARE CTR FINDLAY
8455 County Road 140 (45840-1828)
PHONE..................................419 422-3978
Fax: 419 422-9507
Albert E Jenkins III, *President*
EMP: 110
SQ FT: 8,500
SALES (est): 2MM **Privately Held**
SIC: 8051 Convalescent home with continuous nursing care

(G-11085)
STEARNS COMPANIES LLC
4404 Township Road 142 (45840-9607)
PHONE..................................419 422-0241
Erik Stearns,
EMP: 35
SALES (est): 1.1MM **Privately Held**
SIC: 7361 Labor contractors (employment agency)

(G-11086)
STONECO INC (DH)
1700 Fostoria Ave Ste 200 (45840-6218)
P.O. Box 865 (45839-0865)
PHONE..................................419 422-8854
Fax: 419 429-3444
John T Bearss, *President*
Don Weber, *Vice Pres*
Jack Zouhary, *Admin Sec*
EMP: 99
SQ FT: 34,000
SALES (est): 69.3MM
SALES (corp-wide): 29.7B **Privately Held**
WEB: www.stoneco.net
SIC: 2951 1411 Asphalt & asphaltic paving mixtures (not from refineries); limestone, dimension-quarrying
HQ: Shelly Company
   80 Park Dr
   Thornville OH 43076
   740 246-6315

(G-11087)
STREACKER TRACTOR SALES INC
Also Called: Kubota Authorized Dealer
1218 Trenton Ave (45840-1922)
PHONE..................................419 422-6973
Fax: 419 422-5084
Karl Streacker, *Sales Executive*
Joe Streacker, *Manager*
EMP: 25
SALES (corp-wide): 14.7MM **Privately Held**
WEB: www.streackertractor.com
SIC: 5999 5083 Farm equipment & supplies; farm & garden machinery
PA: Streacker Tractor Sales, Inc.
   1400 N 5th St
   Fremont OH 43420
   419 334-9775

(G-11088)
SUNRISE SENIOR LIVING LLC
Also Called: Sunrise of Findlay
401 Lake Cascade Pkwy (45840-1378)
PHONE..................................419 425-3440
Mari Comer, *Project Mgr*
Charles Latta, *Exec Dir*
Maryann Koppman, *Director*
Robyn Naraine, *Director*
Joanne Marcario, *Admin Asst*
EMP: 45
SALES (corp-wide): 4.3B **Publicly Held**
WEB: www.sunrise.com
SIC: 8051 8361 Skilled nursing care facilities; residential care
HQ: Sunrise Senior Living, Llc
   7902 Westpark Dr
   Mc Lean VA 22102

(G-11089)
SWS ENVIRONMENTAL SERVICES
3820 Ventura Dr (45840-7200)
PHONE..................................254 629-1718
Fax: 419 425-5851
John Seifert, *Manager*
EMP: 32 **Privately Held**
WEB: www.ecesi.com
SIC: 1794 1521 Excavation work; single-family housing construction
HQ: Sws Environmental Services
   9204 Us Highway 287
   Fort Worth TX 76131
   850 234-8428

(G-11090)
T J D INDUSTRIAL CLG & MAINT
12340 Township Road 109 (45840-7685)
PHONE..................................419 425-5025
Fax: 419 425-5024
Timothy Durbin, *President*
Jeannie Durbin, *Corp Secy*
EMP: 30
SALES (est): 3.2MM **Privately Held**
SIC: 4959 Sweeping service: road, airport, parking lot, etc.

(G-11091)
TAYLOR CORPORATION
Also Called: Taylor House
1920 Breckenridge Rd # 110 (45840-8111)
PHONE..................................419 420-0790
Fax: 419 420-9627
Jamie Rush, *Director*
EMP: 25
SALES (est): 1.1MM **Privately Held**
SIC: 8322 Old age assistance

(G-11092)
TOUR DE FORCE CRM INC
14601 County Road 212 # 1 (45840-7749)
P.O. Box 1262 (45839-1262)
PHONE..................................419 425-4800
Matt Hartman, *President*
Terry Kin, *VP Opers*
Jerrod Hartman, *Regl Sales Mgr*
Ashley Kurtzman, *Sales Staff*
Ashley Heath, *Marketing Staff*
EMP: 28
SALES (est): 6.5MM **Privately Held**
WEB: www.mrhtech.com
SIC: 7373 Systems software development services

(G-11093)
TOWNEPLACE SUITES BY MARRIOTT
2501 Tiffin Ave (45840-9512)
PHONE..................................419 425-9545
Fax: 419 425-9742
Traci Binkley, *Principal*
EMP: 26
SALES (est): 1.4MM **Privately Held**
SIC: 7011 Hotel, franchised

(G-11094)
TROY BUILT BUILDING LLC
1001 Fishlock Ave (45840-6427)
PHONE..................................419 425-1093
Troy Greer, *Mng Member*
EMP: 67
SALES (est): 4.2MM **Privately Held**
SIC: 1541 Industrial buildings, new construction

(G-11095)
UNITED PARCEL SERVICE INC OH
Also Called: UPS
1301 Commerce Pkwy (45840-1971)
PHONE..................................419 424-9494
EMP: 158
SALES (corp-wide): 65.8B **Publicly Held**
SIC: 4215 7521 Courier services, except by air; automobile storage garage
HQ: United Parcel Service, Inc. (Oh)
   55 Glenlake Pkwy
   Atlanta GA 30328
   404 828-6000

(G-11096)
UNIVERSITY OF FINDLAY
1015 N Main St (45840-3671)
PHONE..................................419 434-4516
Dr Katherine Fell, *Branch Mgr*
EMP: 200
SALES (corp-wide): 94.7MM **Privately Held**
SIC: 8641 Alumni association
PA: The University Of Findlay
   1000 N Main St
   Findlay OH 45840
   419 422-8313

(G-11097)
UNIVERSITY OF FINDLAY
Also Called: John & Hester Powell Grimm
1000 N Main St (45840-3653)
PHONE..................................419 434-4531
Jack Grimm, *Branch Mgr*
Randall Langston, *Director*
Philip Lucas, *Education*
EMP: 160
SALES (corp-wide): 94.7MM **Privately Held**
SIC: 7922 Performing arts center production
PA: The University Of Findlay
   1000 N Main St
   Findlay OH 45840
   419 422-8313

(G-11098)
VCA ANIMAL HOSPITALS INC
Also Called: VCA Findlay Animal Hospital
2141 Bright Rd (45840-5433)
PHONE..................................419 423-7232
Fax: 419 423-1215
Annette Augsberger, *Branch Mgr*
Alexandra Tyzzer,
David Calland,
Tony Fuller,
EMP: 30
SALES (corp-wide): 1.1MM **Privately Held**
SIC: 0742 Veterinary services, specialties
HQ: Vca Animal Hospitals, Inc.
   12401 W Olympic Blvd
   Los Angeles CA 90064

(G-11099)
WARNER BUICK-NISSAN INC
Also Called: Warner Nissan
1060 County Road 95 (45840)
PHONE..................................419 423-7161
Fax: 419 422-6149
Larry R Warner, *President*
Chris Phillips, *Corp Secy*
Brian Miller, *Store Mgr*
Jason Deitrick, *Manager*
Bruce Herrig, *Director*
EMP: 42
SQ FT: 17,000
SALES (est): 16.7MM **Privately Held**
WEB: www.warnerbuicknissan.com
SIC: 5511 7538 7532 5521 Automobiles, new & used; general automotive repair shops; top & body repair & paint shops; used car dealers; automobiles & other motor vehicles

(G-11100)
WHIRLPOOL CORPORATION
4325 County Road 86 (45840-9327)
PHONE..................................419 423-6097
Fax: 419 423-6095
James Dillon, *Engineer*
Rod Opelt, *Manager*
EMP: 60
SQ FT: 553,000
SALES (corp-wide): 21.2B **Publicly Held**
WEB: www.whirlpoolcorp.com
SIC: 5064 Washing machines
PA: Whirlpool Corporation
   2000 N M 63
   Benton Harbor MI 49022
   269 923-5000

(G-11101)
WOLFF BROS SUPPLY INC
6000 Fostoria Ave (45840-9776)
PHONE..................................419 425-8511
Fax: 419 425-8512
Pete Doyles, *Branch Mgr*
Carl Wohlford, *Manager*
Shawnee Richey, *Training Spec*
EMP: 40
SALES (corp-wide): 114.4MM **Privately Held**
SIC: 5074 5075 5063 Plumbing fittings & supplies; air conditioning & ventilation equipment & supplies; electrical apparatus & equipment
PA: Wolff Bros. Supply, Inc
   6078 Wolff Rd
   Medina OH 44256
   330 725-3451

(G-11102)
YOUNG MNS CHRISTN ASSN FINDLAY (PA)
Also Called: YMCA OF FINDLAY
300 E Lincoln St (45840-4943)
PHONE..................................419 422-4424
Jamie Stall, *Treasurer*
Jack Schuett, *Manager*
Bent Finlay, *Exec Dir*
Kallie Allen, *Director*
Jerry McNamee, *Director*
EMP: 100
SQ FT: 70,000
SALES: 4.3MM **Privately Held**
SIC: 8641 7997 7991 Youth organizations; membership sports & recreation clubs; physical fitness facilities

Flat Rock
Seneca County

(G-11103)
FLAT ROCK CARE CENTER
7353 County Rd 29 (44828)
PHONE..................................419 483-7330
Fax: 419 483-7244
Rev Nancy S Hull, *President*
Tami Kirkham, *Human Res Mgr*
Jason Grant, *Director*
Jeanise Hoeffel, *Director*
Suzy McKinney, *Associate*
EMP: 120
SALES: 4.2MM **Privately Held**
WEB: www.flatrockhomes.org
SIC: 8361 8741 Residential care for the handicapped; management services

Flushing
Belmont County

(G-11104)
HILLANDALE FARMS INC
72165 Mrrstown Flshing Rd (43977-9706)
PHONE..................................740 968-3597
Fax: 740 968-3082
Orland Bethel, *President*
Gary Bethel, *Corp Secy*
EMP: 50
SALES (est): 11.9MM **Privately Held**
SIC: 5144 Eggs

(G-11105)
JACK A HAMILTON & ASSOC INC
342 High St (43977-9750)
P.O. Box 471 (43977-0471)
PHONE..................................740 968-4947
Fax: 740 968-4225
Paul Hamilton, *CEO*
Charles Garvick, *President*
Rachel L Hamilton, *Corp Secy*
Ray L Luyster, *Vice Pres*
Ray Luyster, *Vice Pres*

EMP: 31
SQ FT: 3,100
SALES (est): 2.8MM Privately Held
WEB: www.hamiltonandassoc.com
SIC: 8711 8713 Civil engineering; consulting engineer; surveying services

(G-11106)
RES-CARE INC
41743 Mount Hope Rd (43977-9777)
PHONE...................740 968-0181
EMP: 47
SALES (corp-wide): 24.5B Privately Held
SIC: 8052 Home for the mentally retarded, with health care
HQ: Res-Care, Inc.
9901 Linn Station Rd
Louisville KY 40223
502 394-2100

Forest
Hardin County

(G-11107)
WAMPUM HARDWARE CO
Also Called: Northern Ohio Explosives
17507 Township Road 50 (45843-9602)
P.O. Box 155 (45843-0155)
PHONE...................419 273-2542
Fax: 419 273-3324
Gerald Davis, President
EMP: 39
SALES (corp-wide): 37.9MM Privately Held
WEB: www.wampumhardware.com
SIC: 5169 Explosives
PA: Wampum Hardware Co.
636 Paden Rd
New Galilee PA 16141
724 336-4501

Fort Jennings
Putnam County

(G-11108)
FORT JENNINGS STATE BANK (PA)
120 N Water St (45844-9657)
P.O. Box 186 (45844-0186)
PHONE...................419 286-2527
Fax: 419 286-2409
Lawrence Schimmoler, President
Joann Beam, Executive
EMP: 30 EST: 1918
SALES: 8MM Privately Held
WEB: www.fjsb.com
SIC: 6036 6022 State savings banks, not federally chartered; state commercial banks

(G-11109)
NORTHWEST BUILDING RESOURCES (HQ)
23734 State Route 189 (45844-9510)
PHONE...................419 286-5400
Mike Nichols, President
Steve Nichols, Corp Secy
Joe Nichols, Vice Pres
EMP: 30
SQ FT: 10,000
SALES (est): 12MM Privately Held
SIC: 5031 Building materials, exterior

Fort Loramie
Shelby County

(G-11110)
DISTRIBUTION AND TRNSP SVC INC (PA)
401 S Main St (45845-8716)
PHONE...................937 295-3343
Fax: 937 295-2213
Susan A Burke, President
James Burke, Vice Pres
EMP: 30
SQ FT: 60,000
SALES (est): 9.7MM Privately Held
SIC: 4214 4213 4512 4226 Local trucking with storage; trucking, except local; air transportation, scheduled; special warehousing & storage

(G-11111)
SELECT-ARC INC
600 Enterprise Dr (45845)
P.O. Box 259 (45845-0259)
PHONE...................937 295-5215
Fax: 937 295-5217
Dale Stager, President
Scott Sager, Vice Pres
Melvin Seitz, QC Mgr
Ottmar Marko, CFO
Stacy Tangeman, Credit Staff
◆ EMP: 125
SQ FT: 67,000
SALES (est): 32.9MM Privately Held
WEB: www.select-arc.com
SIC: 3548 6719 Welding apparatus; personal holding companies, except banks

(G-11112)
WAYNE TRAIL TECHNOLOGIES INC
203 E Park St (45845-9303)
P.O. Box 257 (45845-0257)
PHONE...................937 295-2120
Fax: 937 295-2642
David M Knapke, President
Craig Olberding, Safety Mgr
Brooke Broerman, Purchasing
Dave Ruhenkamp, Purchasing
Mike Bollheimer, Engineer
EMP: 100 EST: 1962
SQ FT: 82,000
SALES (est): 31.3MM
SALES (corp-wide): 2.6B Publicly Held
WEB: www.waynetrail.com
SIC: 3728 3599 7692 3544 Aircraft parts & equipment; tubing, flexible metallic; welding repair; special dies, tools, jigs & fixtures
PA: Lincoln Electric Holdings, Inc.
22801 Saint Clair Ave
Cleveland OH 44117
216 481-8100

Fort Recovery
Mercer County

(G-11113)
C W EGG PRODUCTS LLC
2360 Wabash Rd (45846-9586)
PHONE...................419 375-5800
Jim Cooper, Mng Member
EMP: 50
SALES (est): 1.2MM Privately Held
SIC: 5144 Eggs

(G-11114)
CHEESEMAN LLC (HQ)
2200 State Route 119 (45846-9713)
P.O. Box 656 (45846-0656)
PHONE...................419 375-4132
Ed Zumstein, President
Craig Watcke, COO
Doug Wall, CFO
Tyler Hazel, Accounts Mgr
Tom Vehorn, Sales Staff
EMP: 350
SALES (est): 40.7MM
SALES (corp-wide): 55.7MM Privately Held
SIC: 4212 Local trucking, without storage
PA: Zumstein, Inc.
2200 State Route 119
Fort Recovery OH 45846
419 375-4132

(G-11115)
COOPER FARMS INC (PA)
2321 State Route 49 (45846-9501)
P.O. Box 339 (45846-0339)
PHONE...................419 375-4116
James R Cooper, President
Brian Donley, General Ptnr
Gary A Cooper, Vice Pres
Vic Cooper, Project Mgr
Justin Kremer, Prdtn Mgr
EMP: 100 EST: 1940
SQ FT: 38,000
SALES (est): 32.6MM Privately Held
WEB: www.cooperfarms.com
SIC: 2048 5191 Poultry feeds; feed

(G-11116)
FORT RECOVERY EQUIPMENT INC
1201 Industrial Dr (45846-8046)
P.O. Box 646 (45846-0646)
PHONE...................419 375-1006
Fax: 419 375-4404
Cyril G Le Fevre, President
Helen Le Fevere, Vice Pres
Greg Le Fevre, Vice Pres
Chad Guggenbiller, CFO
◆ EMP: 50 EST: 1970
SQ FT: 30,000
SALES (est): 12.4MM Privately Held
WEB: www.fortrecoveryequipment.com
SIC: 5083 3523 Livestock equipment; barn, silo, poultry, dairy & livestock machinery

(G-11117)
FORT RECOVERY EQUITY INC (PA)
2351 Wabash Rd (45846-9586)
PHONE...................419 375-4119
Fax: 419 375-4838
William Glass, CEO
Arnie Sumner, President
EMP: 165
SQ FT: 15,000
SALES (est): 18.6MM Privately Held
SIC: 2015 5153 Egg processing; grain elevators

(G-11118)
HULL BROS INC
Also Called: Kubota Authorized Dealer
520 E Boundary St (45846-9795)
P.O. Box 634 (45846-0634)
PHONE...................419 375-2827
Fax: 419 375-4730
Richard D Hull, President
Norman F Hull Jr, Vice Pres
Paul Evans, Treasurer
EMP: 27
SQ FT: 30,000
SALES (est): 4MM Privately Held
SIC: 5999 5261 5722 5083 Farm equipment & supplies; lawn & garden equipment; household appliance stores; farm & garden machinery

(G-11119)
MIDWEST POULTRY SERVICES LP
Also Called: Sunny Side Farms
374 New Wston Ft Lrmie Rd (45846-9105)
PHONE...................419 375-4417
Fax: 419 375-4127
Leon Lamontagne, Manager
EMP: 25
SQ FT: 35,000
SALES (corp-wide): 174.9MM Privately Held
SIC: 0254 Poultry hatcheries
PA: Midwest Poultry Services, L.P.
9951 W State Road 25
Mentone IN 46539
574 353-7232

(G-11120)
V H COOPER & CO INC (HQ)
Also Called: Cooper Foods
2321 State Route 49 (45846-9501)
P.O. Box 339 (45846-0339)
PHONE...................419 375-4116
Fax: 419 375-4200
James R Cooper, President
Gary A Cooper, COO
Neil Diller, CFO
Anada E Cooper, Treasurer
Dale Siebeneck, Director
EMP: 150
SQ FT: 4,400

SALES (est): 124MM
SALES (corp-wide): 256.7MM Privately Held
WEB: www.cooperfoods.com
SIC: 0253 2015 2011 Turkeys & turkey eggs; chicken slaughtering & processing; pork products from pork slaughtered on site; hams & picnics from meat slaughtered on site
PA: Cooper Hatchery, Inc.
22348 Road 140
Oakwood OH 45873
419 594-3325

(G-11121)
WENDEL POULTRY SERVICE INC
1860 Union City Rd (45846)
P.O. Box 267 (45846-0267)
PHONE...................419 375-2439
Fax: 419 375-2439
Randall Wendel, President
Gary Wendel, Vice Pres
Pam Hicks, Admin Sec
EMP: 45
SALES (est): 3MM Privately Held
SIC: 4212 Live poultry haulage

Fostoria
Seneca County

(G-11122)
AVIATION MANUFACTURING CO INC
901 S Union St (44830-2561)
P.O. Box 1127 (44830-1127)
PHONE...................419 435-7448
Richard W Norton Jr, President
Lisa Adams, Plant Mgr
Leslie Lipski, CFO
EMP: 80 EST: 1996
SALES (est): 5.9MM Privately Held
SIC: 4581 Airports, flying fields & services

(G-11123)
BODIE ELECTRIC INC
1109 N Main St (44830-1979)
P.O. Box 1043 (44830-1043)
PHONE...................419 435-3672
Fax: 419 435-1521
Marianne Bodie, President
R Scott Bodie, President
Pete Finch, Vice Pres
Scott Bodie, Financial Exec
Kristy Deeter, Office Mgr
EMP: 40
SQ FT: 8,200
SALES (est): 6MM Privately Held
WEB: www.bodieelectric.com
SIC: 1731 General electrical contractor

(G-11124)
BOWLING TRANSPORTATION INC (PA)
1827 Sandusky St (44830-2754)
PHONE...................419 436-9590
Bill J Bowling, President
Don Bowling, Vice Pres
Jeff Beck, Manager
Jo Ann May, Admin Sec
EMP: 100
SQ FT: 4,250
SALES (est): 16.5MM Privately Held
WEB: www.bowtran.com
SIC: 4213 4212 Contract haulers; local trucking, without storage

(G-11125)
COUNTY OF SENECA
602 S Corporate Dr W (44830-9456)
PHONE...................419 435-0729
Kathy Nye, Manager
EMP: 75 Privately Held
WEB: www.senecapros.org
SIC: 8331 Sheltered workshop
PA: County Of Seneca
111 Madison St
Tiffin OH 44883
419 447-4550

Fostoria - Seneca County (G-11126)

(G-11126)
FOSTORIA HOSPITAL ASSOCIATION (HQ)
Also Called: Fostoria Community Hospital
501 Van Buren St (44830-1534)
P.O. Box 907 (44830-0907)
PHONE.....................419 435-7734
Fax: 419 436-6602
Dan Schwanke, *President*
Peg Frankart, *Vice Pres*
Linda Wagner, *Prdtn Mgr*
Lori Clouse, *Human Res Mgr*
David Borgman, *Office Mgr*
EMP: 253
SQ FT: 68,000
SALES: 34MM
SALES (corp-wide): 1.5B Privately Held
WEB: www.grosenfeld.com
SIC: 8062 Hospital, affiliated with AMA residency
PA: Promedica Health Systems, Inc.
100 Madison Ave
Toledo OH 43604
567 585-7454

(G-11127)
FRUTH & CO (PA)
601 Parkway Dr Ste A (44830-1592)
P.O. Box 854 (44830-0854)
PHONE.....................419 435-8541
Fax: 419 435-0747
Ronald Brown,
Chris Chalsim,
David Miller,
Donald Yarris,
EMP: 28
SQ FT: 4,000
SALES (est): 1.9MM Privately Held
WEB: www.fruthpll.com
SIC: 8721 Certified public accountant

(G-11128)
GEARY FAMILY YMCA FOSTRIA
154 W Center St (44830-2201)
PHONE.....................419 435-6608
Eric Stinehelfer, *Director*
EMP: 45
SALES: 1.1MM Privately Held
WEB: www.gearyfamilyymca.org
SIC: 8641 8351 Recreation association; child day care services

(G-11129)
GOOD SHEPHERD HOME
725 Columbus Ave (44830-3255)
PHONE.....................419 937-1801
Fax: 419 435-1594
Carol Jenot, *Accounting Dir*
Crystal Macias, *Human Res Dir*
Janet Rhodes, *Data Proc Staff*
Chris Widman, *Director*
Dick Cook, *Director*
EMP: 145
SQ FT: 75,000
SALES: 12.7MM Privately Held
WEB: www.goodshepherdhome.com
SIC: 8052 8051 Intermediate care facilities; skilled nursing care facilities

(G-11130)
HANSON DISTRIBUTING CO INC
Also Called: Beerco Distributing Co
22116 Township Road 218 (44830-9612)
P.O. Box 590 (44830-0590)
PHONE.....................419 435-3214
Fax: 419 435-0925
Kent Allen Brodbeck, *President*
Kris Klepper, *Vice Pres*
Mike Klepper, *Treasurer*
Robbie Maassel, *Office Mgr*
EMP: 75
SQ FT: 25,600
SALES (est): 22.5MM Privately Held
SIC: 5181 Ale; beer & other fermented malt liquors
PA: Superior Distributing Co Inc
22116 Township Road 218
Fostoria OH 44830
419 435-3214

(G-11131)
HCF MANAGEMENT INC
25 Christopher Dr (44830-3318)
PHONE.....................419 435-8112
Sandy Hatfield, *Human Res Dir*
Paula Kirkpatrick, *Branch Mgr*
EMP: 90
SALES (corp-wide): 154.8MM Privately Held
SIC: 8059 Convalescent home
PA: Hcf Management, Inc.
1100 Shawnee Rd
Lima OH 45805
419 999-2010

(G-11132)
HOOSIER EXPRESS INC (PA)
1827 Sandusky St (44830-2754)
PHONE.....................419 436-9590
Bill J Bowling, *President*
Joann May, *Corp Secy*
EMP: 29
SALES (est): 1.6MM Privately Held
SIC: 4213 Contract haulers

(G-11133)
INDEPENDENCE CARE COMMUNITY
Also Called: Independence House
1000 Independence Ave (44830-9614)
PHONE.....................419 435-8505
Fax: 419 435-0829
Cheryl Buckland, *President*
Darlene Delarosa, *Principal*
Tim Beidelschies, *Director*
Larry D Manley, *Admin Sec*
EMP: 61
SQ FT: 40,000
SALES (est): 3.4MM Privately Held
WEB: www.independence-house.com
SIC: 8051 Skilled nursing care facilities

(G-11134)
LIFETOUCH INC
922 Springville Ave Ste B (44830-3240)
PHONE.....................419 435-2646
Fax: 419 435-8870
Doug Smith, *Manager*
EMP: 50
SALES (corp-wide): 856.2MM Privately Held
WEB: www.lifetouch.com
SIC: 7221 Photographer, still or video
PA: Lifetouch Inc.
11000 Viking Dr
Eden Prairie MN 55344
952 826-4000

(G-11135)
NATIONAL MENTOR HOLDINGS INC
526 Plaza Dr (44830-1352)
PHONE.....................419 443-0867
EMP: 799
SALES (corp-wide): 741.5MM Privately Held
SIC: 8082 8361 Home health care services; home for the mentally handicapped
PA: National Mentor Holdings, Inc.
313 Congress St Fl 5
Boston MA 02210
617 790-4800

(G-11136)
NORFOLK SOUTHERN CORPORATION
Also Called: Fostoria Mixing Center
3101 N Township Road 47 (44830-9381)
PHONE.....................419 436-2408
Tim Dennis, *Project Engr*
Tom Siler, *Manager*
EMP: 100
SALES (corp-wide): 10.5B Publicly Held
WEB: www.nscorp.com
SIC: 4011 Railroads, line-haul operating
PA: Norfolk Southern Corporation
3 Commercial Pl Ste 1a
Norfolk VA 23510
757 629-2680

(G-11137)
OK INDUSTRIES INC
2307 W Corporate Dr W (44830-9449)
PHONE.....................419 435-2361
James Kenyon, *President*
Jim Kenyon, *President*
Nila Rehus, *Administration*
EMP: 45
SQ FT: 100,000
SALES (est): 10.6MM Privately Held
WEB: www.okindustries.com
SIC: 4953 Recycling, waste materials

(G-11138)
RES-CARE INC
Also Called: Dillon Group Homes
1016 Dillon Cir (44830-3395)
PHONE.....................419 435-6620
Fax: 419 435-6558
Denise Tucker, *Manager*
Wanda Bates, *Manager*
Wanda Tucker, *Supervisor*
EMP: 48
SALES (corp-wide): 24.5B Privately Held
SIC: 8052 Home for the mentally retarded, with health care
HQ: Res-Care, Inc.
9901 Linn Station Rd
Louisville KY 40223
502 394-2100

(G-11139)
ROPPE HOLDING COMPANY
Also Called: Roppe Distribution
1500 Sandusky St (44830-2753)
PHONE.....................419 435-9335
Fax: 419 435-9377
Vickie Kent, *Human Res Mgr*
Angie Welly, *Branch Mgr*
Larry Nester Sr, *Technology*
EMP: 30
SALES (est): 2.9MM
SALES (corp-wide): 132.9MM Privately Held
WEB: www.roppe.com
SIC: 4225 General warehousing & storage
PA: Roppe Holding Company
1602 N Union St
Fostoria OH 44830
419 435-8546

(G-11140)
SENECA RE ADS IND FOSTORIA DIV
602 S Corporate Dr W (44830-9456)
PHONE.....................419 435-0729
Laurie Fretz, *Division Mgr*
Rodney Biggert, *Director*
EMP: 110 **EST:** 2010
SALES (est): 533.1K Privately Held
SIC: 8699 Charitable organization

(G-11141)
ST CATHERINES CARE CENTERS O
Also Called: St Catherine's Manor
25 Christopher Dr (44830-3399)
PHONE.....................419 435-8112
Fax: 419 435-0334
Jim Unverferth, *President*
EMP: 110
SQ FT: 34,000
SALES (est): 3.8MM Privately Held
SIC: 8051 Convalescent home with continuous nursing care

(G-11142)
VOCA OF OHIO
Also Called: Dillon R D
1021 Dillon Rd (44830-4604)
PHONE.....................419 435-5836
Fax: 419 435-5762
Porcia Tucker, *Manager*
Robeta Walthour, *Director*
EMP: 45
SALES (est): 572K Privately Held
SIC: 8052 Home for the mentally retarded, with health care

(G-11143)
ZENDER ELECTRIC
966 Springville Ave (44830-3268)
P.O. Box 568 (44830-0568)
PHONE.....................419 436-1538
Buddy Zender, *Owner*
Tony Heidetriem, *Office Mgr*
EMP: 25
SQ FT: 3,000
SALES (est): 3.7MM Privately Held
SIC: 1731 7538 Electrical work; general automotive repair shops

Fowler
Trumbull County

(G-11144)
MEADOWBROOK MANOR OF HARTFORD
Also Called: Concord Health Center Hartford
3090 Five Pnts Hrtford Rd (44418-9726)
PHONE.....................330 772-5253
Fax: 330 772-7771
Debra Ifft, *President*
Amanda Smith, *Hlthcr Dir*
EMP: 66
SQ FT: 15,000
SALES (est): 3MM Privately Held
SIC: 8051 Skilled nursing care facilities

Frankfort
Ross County

(G-11145)
DAVID W MILLIKEN (PA)
Also Called: Milliken's Dairy Cone
2 S Main St (45628-8018)
P.O. Box 427 (45628-0427)
PHONE.....................740 998-5023
David W Milliken, *Owner*
EMP: 30
SALES (est): 1.2MM Privately Held
SIC: 5812 1521 Ice cream, soft drink & soda fountain stands; ice cream stands or dairy bars; new construction, single-family houses; general remodeling, single-family houses

(G-11146)
VALLEY VIEW ALZHIMERS CARE CTR
3363 Ragged Ridge Rd (45628-9551)
PHONE.....................740 998-2948
Fax: 740 998-2940
Judith Heimerl-Brown, *President*
Marge Poyner, *Vice Pres*
Jo Morris-Sandorn, *Human Res Mgr*
Dirk Juschka, *Director*
Tammy Robertson, *Admin Sec*
EMP: 60
SALES: 3.6MM Privately Held
WEB: www.valleyviewalz.com
SIC: 8059 8051 Rest home, with health care; skilled nursing care facilities

Franklin
Warren County

(G-11147)
3-D TECHNICAL SERVICES COMPANY
Also Called: 3-Dmed
255 Industrial Dr (45005-4429)
PHONE.....................937 746-2901
Fax: 513 746-5071
Robert Aumann, *President*
Bill Wurzelbacher, *Opers Mgr*
Ashley Albanese, *Sales Staff*
Becky Larson, *Sales Staff*
Jennifer Theriault, *Info Tech Mgr*
EMP: 25
SQ FT: 15,000
SALES (est): 3.1MM Privately Held
WEB: www.3-dtechnicalservices.com
SIC: 7389 2542 3999 Building scale models; design, commercial & industrial; partitions & fixtures, except wood; models, general, except toy

(G-11148)
ADESA CORPORATION LLC
4400 William C Good Blvd (45005-4438)
PHONE.....................937 746-5361
G Parker, *Branch Mgr*
Laura Schatz, *Manager*
EMP: 107 Publicly Held
SIC: 5012 Automobile auction
HQ: Adesa Corporation, Llc
13085 Hamilton Crossing B
Carmel IN 46032

Franklin Furnace - Scioto County (G-11171)

(G-11149)
ASBUILT CONSTRUCTION LTD
29 Eagle Ct (45005-6322)
PHONE..................................937 550-4900
Fax: 513 424-2444
Martha Baldwin, *Partner*
Sharlene Norman, *Manager*
EMP: 25
SQ FT: 3,500
SALES (est): 1.5MM **Privately Held**
SIC: 1522 Residential construction

(G-11150)
BOBS MORAINE TRUCKING INC
8251 Claude Thomas Rd (45005-1412)
PHONE..................................937 746-8420
Fax: 513 743-7740
Rita Maschmeier, *President*
Bob Maschmeier, *Vice Pres*
Robert Maschmeier, *Treasurer*
EMP: 30
SQ FT: 15,000
SALES (est): 3.9MM **Privately Held**
WEB: www.bmtinc.us
SIC: 4212 Liquid haulage, local

(G-11151)
CARINGTON HEALTH SYSTEMS
Also Called: Franklin Ridge Care Facility
421 Mission Ln (45005-2327)
PHONE..................................937 743-2754
Sylvia Sipe, *Branch Mgr*
Richard Chamberlain, *Director*
Kim Sells, *Hlthcr Dir*
EMP: 130
SALES (corp-wide): 85.7MM **Privately Held**
SIC: 8051 8052 Convalescent home with continuous nursing care; intermediate care facilities
PA: Carington Health Systems
8200 Beckett Park Dr
Hamilton OH 45011
513 682-2700

(G-11152)
CENTIMARK CORPORATION
Also Called: Centimark Roofing Systems
319 Industrial Dr (45005-4431)
PHONE..................................937 704-9909
Fax: 937 704-9919
Mark Moore, *Sales/Mktg Mgr*
EMP: 30
SQ FT: 5,000
SALES (corp-wide): 625.8MM **Privately Held**
WEB: www.centimark.com
SIC: 1761 Roofing contractor
PA: Centimark Corporation
12 Grandview Cir
Canonsburg PA 15317
724 514-8700

(G-11153)
DAYTON HOSPICE INCORPORATED
5940 Long Meadow Dr (45005-9689)
PHONE..................................513 422-0300
Amy Wagner, *Vice Pres*
Vicky Forrest, *Branch Mgr*
Kenneth Forrer, *Director*
EMP: 225
SALES (corp-wide): 53.2MM **Privately Held**
SIC: 8082 Home health care services
PA: Hospice Of Dayton, Incorporated
324 Wilmington Ave
Dayton OH 45420
937 256-4490

(G-11154)
EAGLE EQUIPMENT CORPORATION
Also Called: Fluid Power Components
245 Industrial Dr (45005-4429)
PHONE..................................937 746-0510
Fax: 937 746-1656
Jeff Fronk, *President*
Chuck Docken, *Sales Staff*
EMP: 30
SQ FT: 7,000
SALES (est): 2.7MM
SALES (corp-wide): 9.2MM **Privately Held**
WEB: www.eaglequip.com
SIC: 5085 Valves & fittings
PA: Eagle Equipment Corporation
666 Brooksedge Blvd
Westerville OH 43081
614 882-9200

(G-11155)
FRIENDLY NURSING HOME INC
4339 State Route 122 (45005-9762)
PHONE..................................937 855-2363
Fax: 937 855-4679
Barbara Lindsey, *President*
Kirk Smith, *Director*
Tina Parker, *Admin Sec*
EMP: 40
SALES (est): 2.2MM **Privately Held**
SIC: 8051 Skilled nursing care facilities

(G-11156)
GREENPRO SERVICES INC
2969 Beal Rd (45005-4603)
PHONE..................................937 748-1559
Tod R Hernerson, *President*
Jeremy Anspach, *Division Mgr*
Lori Bolin, *Finance*
Brad Meyer, *Sales Executive*
Miranda Dawn, *Manager*
EMP: 30
SQ FT: 1,000
SALES (est): 2.8MM **Privately Held**
SIC: 0781 Landscape services

(G-11157)
GREENSPACE ENTERPRISE TECH INC
8401 Claude Thomas Rd # 28 (45005-1497)
PHONE..................................888 309-8517
Jason Terry, *President*
EMP: 40 EST: 2014
SQ FT: 1,500
SALES (est): 914.1K **Privately Held**
SIC: 7389

(G-11158)
HENDERSON TURF FARM INC
2969 Beal Rd (45005-4603)
PHONE..................................937 748-1559
Fax: 513 748-1568
Marvin N Kolstein, *President*
Todd Henderson, *President*
Trent Gillam, *Division Mgr*
Reita C Henderson, *Principal*
Timothy Luers, *Sales Mgr*
EMP: 40
SQ FT: 1,600
SALES (est): 5.7MM **Privately Held**
SIC: 0191 0181 0782 0711 General farms, primarily crop; sod farms; lawn services; fertilizer application services; local trucking, without storage

(G-11159)
JOINT EMERGENCY MED SVC INC
201 E 6th St (45005-2580)
P.O. Box 525 (45005-0525)
PHONE..................................937 746-3471
Fax: 937 746-1501
Andrew J Riddiough, *Chief*
Brandon Saylor, *Manager*
Scott Fromeyer, *Officer*
Jesse Madde, *Asst Chief*
EMP: 47
SQ FT: 4,600
SALES: 572.8K **Privately Held**
SIC: 8099 Medical services organization; freestanding emergency medical center

(G-11160)
KOEHLKE COMPONENTS INC
1201 Commerce Center Dr (45005-7206)
PHONE..................................937 435-5435
Tom Koehlke, *President*
Glenn Davis, *Regional Mgr*
Shirley F Koehlke, *Corp Secy*
Lisa Palmer, *Buyer*
Doris Lin, *Accountant*
▲ EMP: 26
SQ FT: 10,000
SALES (est): 21.8MM **Privately Held**
WEB: www.koehlke.com
SIC: 5065 Electronic parts

(G-11161)
OHIO-KENTUCKY STEEL CORP
2001 Commerce Center Dr (45005-1478)
PHONE..................................937 743-4600
Fax: 937 743-4605
Christopher Fiora, *CEO*
Brian Baker, *Vice Pres*
EMP: 30 EST: 1974
SQ FT: 84,000
SALES: 3MM **Privately Held**
WEB: www.ohkysteel.com
SIC: 7389 Metal slitting & shearing

(G-11162)
PATRICK STAFFING INC (PA)
1200 E 2nd St Ste B (45005-1974)
PHONE..................................937 743-5585
Joy Patrick, *President*
EMP: 35
SQ FT: 3,672
SALES (est): 2.9MM **Privately Held**
SIC: 7363 Manpower pools

(G-11163)
PEOPLES BANK NATIONAL ASSN
1400 E 2nd St (45005-1811)
PHONE..................................937 746-5733
EMP: 41
SALES (corp-wide): 182.1MM **Publicly Held**
SIC: 6021 National commercial banks
HQ: Peoples Bank
138 Putnam St
Marietta OH 45750
740 373-3155

(G-11164)
PRIMARY CR NTWRK PRMR HLTH PRT
8401 Claude Thomas Rd (45005-1497)
PHONE..................................937 743-5965
Jerome Yount, *Branch Mgr*
EMP: 33
SALES (corp-wide): 33.7MM **Privately Held**
SIC: 8011 Offices & clinics of medical doctors
PA: Primary Care Network Of Premier Health Partners
110 N Main St Ste 350
Dayton OH 45402
937 226-7085

(G-11165)
SIDE EFFECTS INC
259 Industrial Dr (45005-4429)
PHONE..................................937 704-9696
Fax: 937 704-9146
Bob Westerfield, *President*
Kylene Pippin, *President*
Scott Griswold, *General Mgr*
Jennifer Kuhn, *Exec VP*
Kelli Adkins, *Project Mgr*
EMP: 25
SALES (est): 3.3MM **Privately Held**
WEB: www.sideeffectsinc.com
SIC: 7389 Athletic equipment inspection service

(G-11166)
UNIFIRST CORPORATION
265 Industrial Dr (45005 4429)
PHONE..................................937 746-0531
Fax: 513 746-7045
Chris Martin, *Sales Associate*
John Leugers, *Branch Mgr*
Frank Keslind, *Manager*
Rodney Stebelton, *Manager*
EMP: 75
SQ FT: 38,000
SALES (corp-wide): 1.5B **Publicly Held**
WEB: www.unifirst.com
SIC: 7218 7213 Industrial uniform supply; uniform supply
PA: Unifirst Corporation
68 Jonspin Rd
Wilmington MA 01887
978 658-8888

(G-11167)
WALTER F STEPHENS JR INC
415 South Ave (45005-3647)
PHONE..................................937 746-0521
Fax: 513 746-0947
Ruth Ann Stephens, *Ch of Bd*
Carla Baker, *President*
Walter F Stephens Jr, *President*
Diane Stephens Maloney, *Corp Secy*
Patty Gleason, *Vice Pres*
EMP: 50
SQ FT: 45,000
SALES (est): 6.8MM **Privately Held**
SIC: 5999 2389 5122 5023 Police supply stores; uniforms & vestments; toiletries; toothbrushes, except electric; kitchenware; uniforms, men's & boys'; mattresses & foundations

Franklin Furnace
Scioto County

(G-11168)
BIG SANDY DISTRIBUTION INC (PA)
Also Called: Big Sandy Superstores
8375 Gallia Pike (45629-8989)
PHONE..................................740 574-2113
Fax: 740 574-1078
Rober Vanhoose III, *President*
Robert Van Hoose Jr, *Chairman*
Daniel Evans, *District Mgr*
Derek Janey, *Opers Mgr*
Sandi Peyton, *Opers Mgr*
EMP: 200
SQ FT: 150,000
SALES (est): 151.4MM **Privately Held**
SIC: 4225 General warehousing & storage

(G-11169)
BIG SANDY FURNITURE INC (HQ)
Also Called: Big Sandy Service Company
8375 Gallia Pike (45629-8989)
PHONE..................................740 574-2113
Robert W Vanhoose Jr, *Ch of Bd*
John C Stewart Jr, *President*
Trey Vanhoose, *Buyer*
Jennifer Lambert, *Payroll Mgr*
Greg Flannery, *Manager*
EMP: 100
SQ FT: 250,000
SALES (est): 48.8MM **Privately Held**
WEB: www.bigsandyfurniture.com
SIC: 4225 5712 5995 5999 General warehousing & storage; furniture stores; optical goods stores; toiletries, cosmetics & perfumes; gas household appliances; electric household appliances, major

(G-11170)
FOUNTAINHEAD NURSING HOME INC
4734 Gallia Pike (45629-8600)
PHONE..................................740 354-9113
Fax: 740 354-9096
Jerry Ledingham, *President*
EMP: 34
SALES: 1MM **Privately Held**
SIC: 8051 Skilled nursing care facilities

(G-11171)
G & J PEPSI-COLA BOTTLERS INC
Also Called: Pepsico
4587 Gallia Pike (45629-8777)
P.O. Box 299 (45629-0299)
PHONE..................................740 354-9191
Fax: 740 354-9217
Don Chalfant, *VP Sales*
Robert Ross, *Branch Mgr*
EMP: 350
SALES (corp-wide): 475.8MM **Privately Held**
WEB: www.gjpepsi.com
SIC: 2086 5149 Carbonated soft drinks, bottled & canned; groceries & related products
PA: G & J Pepsi-Cola Bottlers Inc
9435 Waterstone Blvd # 390
Cincinnati OH 45249
513 785-6060

Franklin Furnace - Scioto County (G-11172)

(G-11172)
HAVERHILL COKE COMPANY LLC
Also Called: Sun Coke Energy
2446 Gallia Pike (45629-8837)
PHONE...................740 355-9819
James Skipworth, *General Mgr*
Steve Baker, *Vice Pres*
Chris Collier, *Opers Mgr*
Jason Crum, *Manager*
Dovie Majors,
▲ **EMP:** 65
SALES (est): 55.4MM
SALES (corp-wide): 1.3B Publicly Held
SIC: 5051 Steel
HQ: Suncoke Energy Partners, L.P.
  1011 Warrenville Rd # 600
  Lisle IL 60532
  630 824-1000

(G-11173)
R & M DELIVERY
8375 Gallia Pike (45629-8989)
PHONE...................740 574-2113
Robert W Meredith, *Partner*
Phillip Robinson, *Partner*
EMP: 25
SALES: 1.4MM Privately Held
SIC: 4212 Delivery service, vehicular

Frazeysburg
Muskingum County

(G-11174)
CALVARY CHRISTIAN CH OF OHIO
Also Called: Frazeysburg Restaurant & Bky
338 W 3rd St (43822-9785)
PHONE...................740 828-9000
Rev Scott Egbert, *President*
Robert McGraw, *Vice Pres*
Mari Anne Holbrook, *Treasurer*
Faith O'Leary, *Manager*
Faith Oleary, *Manager*
EMP: 40
SQ FT: 2,500
SALES: 55.4K Privately Held
SIC: 2051 8661 5541 0241 Bakery: wholesale or wholesale/retail combined; Christian & Reformed Church; filling stations, gasoline; milk production

(G-11175)
FRAZEYSBURG LIONS CLUB INC
12355 Scout Rd (43822-9713)
PHONE...................740 828-2313
Dan Osborn, *Corp Secy*
EMP: 34
SALES (est): 304.9K Privately Held
SIC: 8699 Personal interest organization

(G-11176)
REM CORP
26 E 3rd St (43822-9651)
P.O. Box 3 (43822-0003)
PHONE...................740 828-2601
Faith Oleary, *Manager*
EMP: 40
SALES (corp-wide): 3.1MM Privately Held
SIC: 8082 Home health care services
PA: Rem Corp.
  265 S Pioneer Blvd
  Springboro OH
  800 990-0302

Fredericksburg
Wayne County

(G-11177)
IVAN WEAVER CONSTRUCTION CO (PA)
124 N Mill St (44627-9593)
P.O. Box 258 (44627-0258)
PHONE...................330 695-3461
Fax: 330 695-7545
Ivan Weaver, *President*
Clara Weaver, *Corp Secy*
Mark Weaver, *Sales Executive*

EMP: 38 **EST:** 1964
SQ FT: 1,892
SALES (est): 10.2MM Privately Held
SIC: 1542 1521 Commercial & office building, new construction; new construction; single-family houses

Fredericktown
Knox County

(G-11178)
BURCH HYDRO INC
17860 Ankneytown Rd (43019-8065)
P.O. Box 230 (43019-0230)
PHONE...................740 694-9146
Fax: 740 694-4188
Michael R Burch, *President*
Patricia A Burch, *Corp Secy*
EMP: 30
SALES (est): 5.9MM Privately Held
WEB: www.burchhydro.com
SIC: 4212 7699 Light haulage & cartage, local; machinery cleaning

(G-11179)
BURCH HYDRO TRUCKING INC
17860 Ankneytown Rd (43019-8065)
P.O. Box 230 (43019-0230)
PHONE...................740 694-9146
Michael R Burch, *President*
Patricia A Burch, *Corp Secy*
Judy Williams, *Clerk*
EMP: 30
SQ FT: 3,200
SALES (est): 3.7MM Privately Held
SIC: 4212 Light haulage & cartage, local

(G-11180)
INTEGRITY KOKOSING PIPELINE SV
Also Called: Ikps
17531 Waterford Rd (43019-9561)
P.O. Box 226 (43019-0226)
PHONE...................740 694-6315
Marsha Rinehart, *CEO*
Timothy Seibert, *President*
Adams Potes, *Manager*
EMP: 175 **EST:** 2012
SQ FT: 16,000
SALES: 64MM Privately Held
SIC: 4613 Gasoline pipelines (common carriers)

Freeport
Harrison County

(G-11181)
ROSEBUD MINING COMPANY
28490 Birmingham Rd (43973-9754)
PHONE...................740 658-4217
EMP: 35
SALES (corp-wide): 672.6MM Privately Held
SIC: 1222 Bituminous coal-underground mining
PA: Rosebud Mining Company
  301 Market St
  Kittanning PA 16201
  724 545-6222

Fremont
Sandusky County

(G-11182)
ADVANTAGE FORD LINCOLN MERCURY
885 Hagerty Dr (43420-9162)
P.O. Box 1167 (43420-8167)
PHONE...................419 334-9751
Fax: 419 334-8809
Merlton Brandenburg, *President*
John McGlynn, *Vice Pres*
Herbert D Stump, *Vice Pres*
David Root, *Sales Staff*
Bob Ochs, *Manager*
EMP: 40
SQ FT: 23,000

SALES (est): 15.3MM Privately Held
WEB: www.advantagefordlm.com
SIC: 5511 7538 7532 Automobiles, new & used; general automotive repair shops; top & body repair & paint shops

(G-11183)
ALFRED NICKLES BAKERY INC
721 White Rd (43420-1544)
PHONE...................419 332-6418
David Owen, *Principal*
Dave Roth, *Manager*
EMP: 29
SALES (corp-wide): 205MM Privately Held
WEB: www.nicklesbakery.com
SIC: 5149 Bakery products
PA: Alfred Nickles Bakery, Inc.
  26 Main St N
  Navarre OH 44662
  330 879-5635

(G-11184)
ALKON CORPORATION (PA)
728 Graham Dr (43420-4073)
PHONE...................419 355-9111
Mark Winter, *President*
Wayne Morroney, *President*
Prakash Jog, *Vice Pres*
Mark Radloff, *Vice Pres*
Dave Kowalski, *Opers Mgr*
▲ **EMP:** 60 **EST:** 1968
SQ FT: 40,000
SALES (est): 24.2MM Privately Held
WEB: www.alkoncorp.com
SIC: 3491 3082 5084 5085 Valves, nuclear; tubes, unsupported plastic; industrial machinery & equipment; pistons & valves; valves & fittings; fluid power valves & hose fittings

(G-11185)
BAUMAN CHRYSLER JEEP DODGE
2577 W State St (43420-1444)
P.O. Box 1127 (43420-8127)
PHONE...................419 332-8291
Albert Bauman III, *President*
Diamond Jim, *Treasurer*
Buck Baumann, *Manager*
EMP: 34
SQ FT: 13,000
SALES (est): 9.9MM Privately Held
SIC: 5511 7532 Automobiles, new & used; body shop, automotive

(G-11186)
CARITAS INC
Also Called: PARKVIEW CARE CENTER
1406 Oak Harbor Rd (43420-1025)
PHONE...................419 332-2589
Fax: 419 332-0121
Patrick Kriner, *President*
Mary Arnold, *Exec Dir*
Diane Bath, *Director*
Jennifer Schwartz, *Director*
Charles Valone, *Director*
EMP: 46
SQ FT: 15,000
SALES: 2.5MM Privately Held
SIC: 8051 8361 Convalescent home with continuous nursing care; home for the aged

(G-11187)
CELLCO PARTNERSHIP
Also Called: Verizon
2140 Enterprise St Ste C (43420-8530)
PHONE...................419 333-1009
Chris Webb, *Principal*
Tim Wisler, *Sales Staff*
EMP: 71
SALES (corp-wide): 126B Publicly Held
SIC: 4812 5999 Cellular telephone services; telephone equipment & systems
HQ: Cellco Partnership
  1 Verizon Way
  Basking Ridge NJ 07920

(G-11188)
COMMUNITY & RURAL HEALTH SVCS (PA)
Also Called: Community Hlth Svcs Dntl Clinic
2221 Hayes Ave (43420-2632)
PHONE...................419 334-8943
Fax: 419 334-8619

J Liszak, *President*
Bonnie Bane, *CFO*
Tiffany Tipple, *Human Res Dir*
Emily Brickner, *Supervisor*
Annette Moore, *Supervisor*
EMP: 50
SALES: 8MM Privately Held
SIC: 8099 Medical services organization

(G-11189)
COUNTY ENGINEERING OFFICE
2500 W State St (43420-1445)
PHONE...................419 334-9731
Chad Fisher, *Superintendent*
Christopher Verdette, *Office Mgr*
James Moyer, *Director*
EMP: 34
SALES (est): 1.5MM Privately Held
SIC: 8711 7538 Civil engineering; general automotive repair shops

(G-11190)
COUNTY OF SANDUSKY
Also Called: School of Hope
1001 Castalia St (43420-4015)
PHONE...................419 637-2243
Jayne Repp, *Principal*
Cathy Glassford, *Info Tech Mgr*
Kim Jenkins, *Info Tech Mgr*
EMP: 100 Privately Held
WEB: www.sanduskycohd.org
SIC: 8331 Sheltered workshop
PA: County Of Sandusky
  622 Croghan St
  Fremont OH 43420
  419 334-6100

(G-11191)
COUNTY OF SANDUSKY
Also Called: Countyside Continuing Care
1865 Countryside Dr (43420-8748)
PHONE...................419 334-2602
Fax: 419 334-6287
Linda Black-Kurek, *President*
Lori Cress, *Director*
EMP: 99
SALES (est): 1,000K Privately Held
SIC: 8051 Convalescent home with continuous nursing care

(G-11192)
COUNTY OF SANDUSKY
Also Called: Countryside Cntinuing Care Ctr
1865 Countryside Dr (43420-8748)
PHONE...................419 334-2602
James Fischer, *Administration*
EMP: 125 Privately Held
WEB: www.sanduskycohd.org
SIC: 8051 9111 Skilled nursing care facilities; county supervisors' & executives' offices
PA: County Of Sandusky
  622 Croghan St
  Fremont OH 43420
  419 334-6100

(G-11193)
CROGHAN COLONIAL BANK (HQ)
323 Croghan St (43420-3088)
P.O. Box C (43420-0557)
PHONE...................419 332-7301
Fax: 419 355-2266
Steven C Futrell, *President*
John C Barrington, *Principal*
Ted L Hilty, *Principal*
J Phillip Keller, *Principal*
Don W Miller, *Principal*
EMP: 45
SQ FT: 39,500
SALES: 39.3MM Publicly Held
WEB: www.croghan.com
SIC: 6022 State trust companies accepting deposits, commercial

(G-11194)
DAMSCHRODER ROOFING INC
2228 Hayes Ave Ste D (43420-2699)
PHONE...................419 332-5000
Fax: 419 334-5000
Dana Howell, *President*
Jonathan Barnes, *Accountant*
Melissa Cruz, *Human Resources*
Ian Rammel, *Social Dir*
EMP: 28

GEOGRAPHIC SECTION

Fremont - Sandusky County (G-11217)

SALES: 4.7MM **Privately Held**
SIC: 1761 Roofing contractor

(G-11195)
DOEPKER GROUP INC
Also Called: Time Staffing
1303 W State St (43420-2016)
PHONE..............................419 355-1409
Jeffrey Doepker, *President*
Scott Root, *Manager*
Cierra Bishop, *Admin Asst*
Kristina Fuller, *Recruiter*
Betty Taschler, *Associate*
EMP: 27
SALES: 20MM **Privately Held**
SIC: 7363 Temporary help service

(G-11196)
EASTER SEALS METRO CHICAGO INC
Also Called: Easter Seal Northwestern Ohio
101 S Stone St (43420-2651)
PHONE..............................419 332-3016
Fax: 419 332-5921
Jennifer Lewis, *Manager*
EMP: 40
SALES (corp-wide): 40MM **Privately Held**
WEB: www.eastersealsnwohio.org
SIC: 8399 Fund raising organization, non-fee basis
PA: Easter Seals Metropolitan Chicago, Inc.
1939 W 13th St Ste 300
Chicago IL 60608
312 491-4110

(G-11197)
FIRELANDS REGIONAL HEALTH SYS
Also Called: Firelnds Cnsling Recovery Svcs
675 Bartson Rd (43420-9672)
PHONE..............................419 332-5524
Dawn Kroh, *Superintendent*
EMP: 30
SALES (corp-wide): 15.5K **Privately Held**
SIC: 8093 8069 8062 Mental health clinic, outpatient; drug addiction rehabilitation hospital; general medical & surgical hospitals
PA: Firelands Regional Health System
1111 Hayes Ave
Sandusky OH 44870
419 557-7400

(G-11198)
FIRST CHOICE PACKAGING INC (PA)
Also Called: First Choice Packg Solutions
1501 W State St (43420-1629)
PHONE..............................419 333-4100
Fax: 419 334-6564
Paul W Tomick, *President*
Frank Wolfinger, *Vice Pres*
Charlie Bently, *Purchasing*
Greg Walters, *Design Engr*
Joyce Menekey, *Admin Sec*
▲ EMP: 105
SALES (est): 33.2MM **Privately Held**
WEB: www.firstchoicepackaging.com
SIC: 3089 7389 Thermoformed finished plastic products; packaging & labeling services

(G-11199)
FLEX TEMP EMPLOYMENT SERVICES
Also Called: Pagan
524 W State St (43420-2532)
PHONE..............................419 355-9675
Fax: 419 355-1580
Larry Aaron, *Manager*
EMP: 143
SALES (corp-wide): 5.8MM **Privately Held**
WEB: www.flextemp.com
SIC: 7363 Temporary help service
PA: Flex Temp Employment Services Inc
1514 E Farwell St Frnt
Sandusky OH 44870
419 625-3470

(G-11200)
FRATERNAL ORDER EAGLES INC
Also Called: Foe 712
2570 W State St (43420-1445)
PHONE..............................419 332-3961
Fax: 419 332-6333
James Hoffman, *President*
EMP: 27
SALES (corp-wide): 11MM **Privately Held**
WEB: www.fraternalorderofeagles.tribe.net
SIC: 8641 Fraternal associations
HQ: Fraternal Order Of Eagles Inc.
1623 Gateway Cir
Grove City OH 43123
614 883-2200

(G-11201)
FREMONT FEDERAL CREDIT UNION (PA)
315 Croghan St (43420-3013)
P.O. Box 1208 (43420-8208)
PHONE..............................419 334-4434
Fax: 419 334-7883
Anthony Camilleri, *President*
Joseph Saalman, *Exec VP*
Kelly Calmes, *Office Mgr*
Maria Ranker, *Director*
EMP: 115
SALES: 7.8MM **Privately Held**
WEB: www.fremontfcu.com
SIC: 6061 6163 Federal credit unions; loan brokers

(G-11202)
FREMONT LOGISTICS LLC
1301 Heinz Rd (43420-8584)
PHONE..............................419 333-0669
Kristy McKenzie, *Supervisor*
Scott Ellithorpe,
EMP: 100
SALES (est): 5.6MM
SALES (corp-wide): 43.7MM **Privately Held**
WEB: www.es3.com
SIC: 4225 General warehousing & storage
PA: Es3, Llc
6 Optical Ave
Keene NH 03431
603 354-6100

(G-11203)
GOODNIGHT INN INC
Also Called: Days Inn
3701 N State Route 53 (43420-9318)
PHONE..............................419 334-9551
Fax: 419 334-9551
Kerri Henry, *Manager*
Katina Kayden, *Manager*
EMP: 40
SALES (corp-wide): 5.3MM **Privately Held**
SIC: 7011 Hotels & motels
PA: Goodnight Inn, Inc.
11313 Us Highway 250 N
Milan OH 44846
419 626-3610

(G-11204)
GOODWILL INDUSTRIES OF ERIE
1040 Oak Harbor Rd (43420-1017)
PHONE..............................419 355-1579
Nicole Rinebold, *Manager*
EMP: 63
SALES (corp-wide): 8.9MM **Privately Held**
SIC: 8322 Individual & family services
PA: Goodwill Industries Of Erie, Huron, Ottawa And Sandusky Counties, Inc.
419 W Market St
Sandusky OH 44870
419 625-4744

(G-11205)
GOODWILL INDUSTRIES OF ERIE
Also Called: Fremont Plant Operations
1597 Pontiac Ave (43420-9792)
PHONE..............................419 334-7566
Fax: 419 334-8671
T Burnsderter, *Branch Mgr*
EMP: 75
SALES (corp-wide): 8.9MM **Privately Held**
SIC: 8322 Individual & family services
PA: Goodwill Industries Of Erie, Huron, Ottawa And Sandusky Counties, Inc.
419 W Market St
Sandusky OH 44870
419 625-4744

(G-11206)
HOLIDAY INN EXPRESS
1501 Hospitality Ct (43420-8306)
PHONE..............................419 332-7700
Shanda McCluty, *General Mgr*
EMP: 50
SALES (est): 1MM **Privately Held**
SIC: 7011 Hotels & motels

(G-11207)
IN HOME HEALTH LLC
Also Called: Heartland HM Hlth Care Hospice
907 W State St Ste A (43420-2548)
PHONE..............................419 355-9209
Fax: 419 355-9425
Ann Wright, *Principal*
EMP: 38
SALES (corp-wide): 3.6B **Publicly Held**
SIC: 8082 Home health care services
HQ: In Home Health, Llc
333 N Summit St
Toledo OH 43604

(G-11208)
KELLER OCHS KOCH INC
Also Called: SCI
416 S Arch St (43420-2965)
PHONE..............................419 332-8288
Fax: 419 332-7308
John P Keller, *President*
Lawrence L Koch, *Vice Pres*
Lee Smith, *Manager*
EMP: 30
SQ FT: 20,000
SALES: 800K
SALES (corp-wide): 3.1B **Publicly Held**
WEB: www.keller-ochs-kochfuneralhome.com
SIC: 7261 Funeral home
PA: Service Corporation International
1929 Allen Pkwy
Houston TX 77019
713 522-5141

(G-11209)
KINSWA DIALYSIS LLC
Also Called: Fremont Regional Dialysis
100 Pinnacle Dr (43420-7400)
PHONE..............................419 332-0310
James K Hilger,
EMP: 33
SALES (est): 790.6K **Publicly Held**
SIC: 8092 Kidney dialysis centers
PA: Davita Inc.
2000 16th St
Denver CO 80202

(G-11210)
LOWES HOME CENTERS LLC
1952 N State Route 53 (43420-8637)
PHONE..............................419 355-0221
Fax: 419 355-0253
Lori Thomas, *Branch Mgr*
Corrina O'Connell, *Executive*
EMP: 150
SALES (corp-wide): 68.6B **Publicly Held**
SIC: 5211 5031 5722 5064 Home centers; building materials, exterior; building materials, interior; household appliance stores; electrical appliances, television & radio
HQ: Lowe's Home Centers, Llc
1605 Curtis Bridge Rd
Wilkesboro NC 28697
336 658-4000

(G-11211)
MADISON MOTOR SERVICE INC
2921 W State St (43420-6600)
PHONE..............................419 332-0727
Fax: 419 334-1309
Richard Seitz, *President*
EMP: 31
SQ FT: 4,800
SALES (est): 2.7MM **Privately Held**
SIC: 7549 7538 Towing service, automotive; general automotive repair shops

(G-11212)
MEMORIAL HOSPITAL (PA)
Also Called: MEMORIAL HOSPITAL HEALTHLINK
715 S Taft Ave (43420-3296)
PHONE..............................419 334-6657
Fax: 419 334-6693
Pamella Jensen, *CEO*
John Al Gorman, *Principal*
Andy Smith, *Mktg Dir*
Fateh Ahmed, *Med Doctor*
Kelly Randall, *Med Doctor*
EMP: 550 EST: 1915
SQ FT: 197,000
SALES: 63MM **Privately Held**
SIC: 8062 General medical & surgical hospitals

(G-11213)
MICHAEL BROTHERS INC
Also Called: Sycamore Hills Golf Club
3728 Hayes Ave (43420-9717)
PHONE..............................419 332-5716
Douglas A Michael, *President*
Douglas A Micahel Jr, *President*
Tonny Michael, *Vice Pres*
Douglas Michael Sr, *Treasurer*
Wayne Michael, *Admin Sec*
EMP: 35
SQ FT: 5,000
SALES (est): 2.1MM **Privately Held**
SIC: 7997 Golf club, membership

(G-11214)
MOTION CONTROLS ROBOTICS INC
1500 Walter Ave (43420-1449)
PHONE..............................419 334-5886
Fax: 419 334-5639
Scott D Lang, *President*
Tim Ellenberger, *Vice Pres*
Julie Beaschler, *Project Mgr*
Yvette Howey, *Accounting Mgr*
Walker Davenport, *Prgrmr*
EMP: 32
SQ FT: 57,000
SALES (est): 7.6MM **Privately Held**
WEB: www.motioncontrolsplus.com
SIC: 8742 Automation & robotics consultant

(G-11215)
OHIO DEPT OF JOB & FMLY SVCS
Also Called: Sandusky Cnty Job & Fmly Svcs
2511 Countryside Dr (43420-9016)
PHONE..............................419 334-3891
Peter Cantu, *Branch Mgr*
EMP: 28 **Privately Held**
WEB: www.job.com
SIC: 9441 7363 ; help supply services
HQ: The Ohio Department Of Job And Family Services
30 E Broad St Fl 32
Columbus OH 43215

(G-11216)
RK FAMILY INC
1800 E State St (43420-4000)
PHONE..............................419 355-8230
Tim Lodes, *Principal*
EMP: 219
SALES (corp-wide): 1.2B **Privately Held**
SIC: 5099 Firearms & ammunition, except sporting
PA: Rk Family, Inc.
4216 Dewitt Ave
Mattoon IL 61938
217 235-7102

(G-11217)
RTHRFORD B HAYES PRSDNTIAL CTR
Also Called: Hayes, Rutherford B Pres Lib Spiegel Grv (43420)
PHONE..............................419 332-2081
Fax: 419 332-4952
Christy Weininger, *Exec Dir*
Christie Weininger, *Exec Dir*
Christie M Weininger, *Exec Dir*
Kathy Boukissen, *Director*
EMP: 43
SALES: 2.1MM **Privately Held**
SIC: 8231 8412 Libraries; museum

Fremont - Sandusky County (G-11218)

(G-11218)
SABROSKE ELECTRIC INC
115 Lincoln St (43420-2852)
PHONE.............................419 332-6444
Fax: 419 332-6945
Thomas P Decker, *President*
Eric Smart, *Vice Pres*
Linda E Decker, *Admin Sec*
EMP: 25 **EST:** 1930
SQ FT: 6,000
SALES: 2.5MM **Privately Held**
SIC: 1731 5063 General electrical contractor; electrical supplies

(G-11219)
SANDUSKY COUNTY ENGR & HWY GAR
2500 W State St (43420-1445)
PHONE.............................419 334-9731
Fax: 419 334-9733
James Moyer, *Principal*
Rich Randolph, *Design Engr*
EMP: 25
SALES (est): 2.2MM **Privately Held**
SIC: 8711 Consulting engineer

(G-11220)
SIERRA LOBO INC (PA)
102 Pinnacle Dr (43420-7400)
PHONE.............................419 332-7101
Fax: 419 332-1619
George A Satornino, *President*
Rich Christiansen, *Vice Pres*
Nabil Kattouah, *Vice Pres*
Daniel R Lowe, *Vice Pres*
Nathan Campbell, *Engineer*
EMP: 32
SALES (est): 92.2MM **Privately Held**
SIC: 8711 Consulting engineer

(G-11221)
SISTERS OF MERCY
Also Called: Sisters of Mercy Fremont, Ohio
1220 Tiffin St (43420-3562)
PHONE.............................419 332-8208
Fax: 419 332-4423
Janette Tahy, *Manager*
EMP: 35
SALES (corp-wide): 17.4MM **Privately Held**
SIC: 8361 Home for the aged
HQ: Sisters Of Mercy Of The Americas
South Central Community, Inc
2335 Grandview Ave
Cincinnati OH
513 221-1800

(G-11222)
STYLE CREST INC
605 Hagerty Dr (43420-9100)
P.O. Box A (43420-0555)
PHONE.............................419 332-7369
Bryan Kern, *Vice Pres*
Ty Franz, *CFO*
Steve Grine, *Manager*
George Gray,
Robert Hoffman,
EMP: 150
SALES (corp-wide): 174.8MM **Privately Held**
SIC: 5075 Warm air heating & air conditioning
HQ: Style Crest, Inc.
2450 Enterprise St
Fremont OH 43420
419 332-7369

(G-11223)
STYLE CREST INC (HQ)
2450 Enterprise St (43420-8553)
P.O. Box A (43420-0555)
PHONE.............................419 332-7369
Thomas Kern, *CEO*
Henry Valle, *President*
Phillip Burton, *Corp Secy*
William Goad, *Exec VP*
Bryan T Kern, *Exec VP*
◆ **EMP:** 277
SALES (est): 165.5MM
SALES (corp-wide): 174.8MM **Privately Held**
SIC: 3089 5075 5031 8361 Siding, plastic; warm air heating & air conditioning; building materials, exterior; building materials, interior; residential care
PA: Style Crest Enterprises, Inc.
2450 Enterprise St
Fremont OH 43420
419 355-8586

(G-11224)
STYLE CREST ENTERPRISES INC (PA)
2450 Enterprise St (43420-8553)
P.O. Box A (43420-0555)
PHONE.............................419 355-8586
Thomas L Kern, *CEO*
Henry Valle, *President*
Phillip Burton, *Corp Secy*
Bryan T Kern, *Exec VP*
Stephen Crokie, *Mfg Spvr*
EMP: 70
SQ FT: 40,000
SALES (est): 174.8MM **Privately Held**
SIC: 3089 5075 Plastic hardware & building products; awnings, fiberglass & plastic combination; siding, plastic; warm air heating & air conditioning

(G-11225)
STYLE CREST TRANSPORT INC
2450 Enterprise St (43420-8553)
P.O. Box A (43420-0555)
PHONE.............................419 332-7369
Thomas L Kern, *CEO*
Henry Valle, *President*
Phillip Burton, *Corp Secy*
Bryan T Kern, *Exec VP*
Tyrone G Frantz, *CFO*
EMP: 51
SQ FT: 1,500
SALES (est): 4.7MM
SALES (corp-wide): 174.8MM **Privately Held**
SIC: 4213 4212 Trucking, except local; local trucking, without storage
PA: Style Crest Enterprises, Inc.
2450 Enterprise St
Fremont OH 43420
419 355-8586

(G-11226)
VOLUNTERS AMER CARE FACILITIES
Also Called: Bethesda Care Center
600 N Brush St (43420-1402)
PHONE.............................419 334-9521
Fax: 419 334-2045
Laura Moyer, *Human Resources*
Roger Wyman, *Exec Dir*
David Wassil, *Director*
EMP: 110
SALES (corp-wide): 66.7MM **Privately Held**
SIC: 8051 Convalescent home with continuous nursing care
PA: Volunteers Of America Care Facilities
7530 Market Place Dr
Eden Prairie MN 55344
952 941-0305

(G-11227)
W S O S COMMUNITY A (PA)
109 S Front St (43420-3021)
P.O. Box 590 (43420-0590)
PHONE.............................419 333-6068
Fax: 419 334-8919
Ruthann House, *CEO*
David R Kipplen, *Vice Pres*
Jaime Munoz, *Controller*
Andrea Carter, *Accountant*
Adrienne Fausey, *Human Res Dir*
EMP: 70
SQ FT: 17,000
SALES: 33.3MM **Privately Held**
WEB: www.wsos.org
SIC: 8351 8322 8331 Head start center, except in conjunction with school; individual & family services; job training services

(G-11228)
W S O S COMMUNITY A
Also Called: Fremont TMC Head Start
765 S Buchanan St (43420-4903)
PHONE.............................419 334-8511
Fax: 419 332-7966
Brenda Barton, *Director*
Kathy Morrison, *Director*
EMP: 60
SALES (corp-wide): 33.3MM **Privately Held**
SIC: 8351 8331 Head start center, except in conjunction with school; job training services
PA: W. S. O. S. Community Action Commission, Inc.
109 S Front St
Fremont OH 43420
419 333-6068

(G-11229)
WARNER MECHANICAL CORPORATION
1609 Dickinson St (43420-1119)
P.O. Box 747 (43420-0747)
PHONE.............................419 332-7116
Fax: 419 332-6370
Scott Warner, *CEO*
James Krock, *President*
Kevin Reed, *Project Mgr*
James H Warner, *Treasurer*
EMP: 30 **EST:** 1946
SQ FT: 10,000
SALES (est): 6.9MM **Privately Held**
WEB: www.warnermech.com
SIC: 1711 Mechanical contractor

(G-11230)
WSOS CHILD DEVELOPMENT PROGRAM
Also Called: Wcdp
765 S Buchanan St (43420-4903)
PHONE.............................419 334-8511
Penny Moore, *Director*
Kathy Morrison, *Director*
EMP: 45
SALES (est): 1.4MM **Privately Held**
SIC: 8351 8661 Child day care services; head start center, except in conjunction with school; Presbyterian Church

(G-11231)
YOUNG MENS CHRISTIAN ASSN
Also Called: YMCA
1000 North St (43420-1131)
PHONE.............................419 332-9622
Fax: 419 332-5973
Samantha Winke, *Bookkeeper*
Denise Reiter, *Exec Dir*
EMP: 50 **EST:** 1953
SALES (est): 1.1MM **Privately Held**
SIC: 8641 8322 7997 Youth organizations; individual & family services; membership sports & recreation clubs

---

Gahanna
Franklin County

(G-11232)
1ST ADVANCED EMS LLC
735 Taylor Rd Ste 210 (43230-6274)
PHONE.............................614 348-9991
Lucy Kimkhe, *Financial Exec*
Yuri Fish, *Mng Member*
Mike Moore, *Manager*
Joshua Schooley, *Exec Dir*
EMP: 78
SALES (est): 3.1MM **Privately Held**
SIC: 4119 Ambulance service

(G-11233)
ARROW GLOBL ASSET DSPSTION INC
Also Called: Retrobox.com
1120 Morrison Rd Ste A (43230-6646)
PHONE.............................614 328-4100
Fax: 614 866-1298
Dave Ryan, *Principal*
Casson Jen, *Human Res Dir*
Scott Sedon, *Data Proc Exec*
Spengler John, *Exec Dir*
EMP: 70
SALES (corp-wide): 26.8B **Publicly Held**
WEB: www.intechra.com
SIC: 5045 Computers
HQ: Arrow Global Asset Disposition, Inc.
9101 Burnet Rd Ste 203
Austin TX 78758
800 378-6897

(G-11234)
CINEMARK USA INC
Also Called: Cinemark Stnrdge Plz Movies 16
323 Stoneridge Ln (43230-6783)
PHONE.............................614 471-7620
Scott Smith, *Manager*
EMP: 25 **Publicly Held**
SIC: 7832 Motion picture theaters, except drive-in
HQ: Cinemark Usa, Inc.
3900 Dallas Pkwy Ste 500
Plano TX 75093
972 665-1000

(G-11235)
COLUMBUS ASPHALT PAVING INC
1196 Technology Dr (43230-6607)
PHONE.............................614 759-9800
Fax: 614 759-9611
David J Power, *President*
Kevin Power, *Sr Corp Ofcr*
Christopher Batdorff, *Vice Pres*
Gary Pisano, *Opers Mgr*
EMP: 40 **EST:** 1975
SQ FT: 5,200
SALES (est): 8.9MM **Privately Held**
WEB: www.capasphalt.com
SIC: 1611 Highway & street paving contractor

(G-11236)
COLUMBUS OH-16 AIRPORT GAHANNA
Also Called: Springhill Suites
665 Taylor Rd (43230-6203)
PHONE.............................614 501-4770
Fax: 614 501-4750
Brian Moore, *Principal*
Greg Moundas, *Vice Pres*
Cheree Goodall, *Office Mgr*
EMP: 29
SALES (est): 2.1MM **Privately Held**
SIC: 7011 Hotels & motels

(G-11237)
CONSUMER CREDIT COUN (PA)
Also Called: Apprisen
690 Taylor Rd Ste 110 (43230-3520)
PHONE.............................614 552-2222
Michael Kappas, *CEO*
Karl Hoffmann, *Division Mgr*
Lisa Piercefield, *Opers Mgr*
Victor Russell, *Opers Mgr*
Christopher Kallay, *CFO*
EMP: 43
SQ FT: 50,000
SALES: 8.8MM **Privately Held**
WEB: www.cccservices.com
SIC: 7299 Debt counseling or adjustment service, individuals

(G-11238)
CUSTOM AC & HTG CO
Also Called: Honeywell Authorized Dealer
935 Claycraft Rd (43230-6650)
PHONE.............................614 552-4822
Fax: 614 552-2837
Patrick Halaiko, *President*
Leon Blalock, *COO*
Jeff Reed, *Vice Pres*
John Meredith, *Engineer*
Bonnie Green, *Sales Staff*
EMP: 75
SQ FT: 7,500
SALES (est): 15.7MM **Privately Held**
WEB: www.customairco.com
SIC: 1711 Warm air heating & air conditioning contractor

(G-11239)
DEEMSYS INC
800 Cross Pointe Rd Ste A (43230-6688)
PHONE.............................614 322-9928
Vijiayarani Benjamin, *Ch of Bd*
Jacob Benjamin, *President*
Dexter Benjamin, *Vice Pres*
Rt Rajan, *Manager*
EMP: 82
SQ FT: 5,100

GEOGRAPHIC SECTION
Gahanna - Franklin County (G-11264)

SALES: 7.8MM **Privately Held**
WEB: www.deemsysinc.com
SIC: 8748 2741 7373 8299 Business consulting; ; systems software development services; educational service, non-degree granting: continuing educ.; computer software development & applications

(G-11240)
EQUITY CENTRAL LLC
81 Mill St Ste 206 (43230-1718)
PHONE..................614 861-7777
Mekel Henderson,
EMP: 25
SQ FT: 1,300
SALES (est): 1.4MM **Privately Held**
WEB: www.equitycentralrealty.com
SIC: 6531 1521 1522 Real estate brokers & agents; single-family housing construction; residential construction

(G-11241)
ESTATE INFORMATION SVCS LLC
Also Called: Eis
670 Morrison Rd Ste 300 (43230-5324)
PHONE..................614 729-1700
J C Gunnell, *CEO*
Victoria Edwards, *Exec VP*
Victoria M Edwards, *Exec VP*
Michael Lame, *CFO*
Kip Randal, *Financial Exec*
EMP: 70
SQ FT: 20,000
SALES (est): 9.5MM **Privately Held**
SIC: 7322 Collection agency, except real estate

(G-11242)
FUN DAY EVENTS LLC
947 E Johnstown Rd # 163 (43230-1851)
PHONE..................740 549-9000
Michael Ross, *Manager*
EMP: 30
SQ FT: 10,000
SALES (est): 1.1MM **Privately Held**
WEB: www.fundayevents.com
SIC: 7299 Facility rental & party planning services

(G-11243)
GAHANNA ANIMAL HOSPITAL INC
144 W Johnstown Rd (43230-2773)
PHONE..................614 471-2201
Fax: 614 471-1907
John Worman Dvm, *President*
Julie Radabaugh, *Treasurer*
EMP: 50
SQ FT: 1,704
SALES (est): 1.8MM **Privately Held**
WEB: www.gahannaanimalhospital.com
SIC: 0742 Animal hospital services, pets & other animal specialties

(G-11244)
GENERATIONS FAMILY MEDICINE
765 N Hamilton Rd Ste 255 (43230-8703)
PHONE..................614 337-1282
Jeffery Miller MD, *President*
Craig W O Sullivan MD, *Treasurer*
Robert Zaino MD, *Admin Sec*
John Zaino, *Family Practiti*
Leanne Benson, *Assistant*
EMP: 26
SQ FT: 4,100
SALES: 1.2MM **Privately Held**
SIC: 8011 General & family practice, physician/surgeon

(G-11245)
GULF SOUTH MEDICAL SUPPLY INC
915 Taylor Rd Unit A (43230-3292)
PHONE..................614 501-9080
Fax: 614 501-9088
Mickey Gilson, *Accounts Exec*
Michael Evans, *Manager*
EMP: 40
SALES (corp-wide): 198.5B **Publicly Held**
WEB: www.gsms.com
SIC: 5047 Medical equipment & supplies
HQ: Gulf South Medical Supply Inc
4345 Sthpint Blvd Ste 100
Jacksonville FL 32216
904 332-3000

(G-11246)
HEART CARE
765 N Hamilton Rd Ste 120 (43230-8707)
PHONE..................614 533-5000
Twilla Lee, *Manager*
Peter B Amsterdam MD, *Manager*
Lora Siner, *Manager*
David Nicholson, *Cardiovascular*
Kim Anderson, *Assistant*
EMP: 51
SALES (est): 3.9MM **Privately Held**
SIC: 8011 Cardiologist & cardio-vascular specialist

(G-11247)
HEARTLAND BANK (PA)
850 N Hamilton Rd (43230-1757)
PHONE..................614 337-4600
Fax: 614 337-4608
G Scott McComb, *Ch of Bd*
Jay Eggspuehler, *Vice Ch Bd*
Tiney M Mc Comb, *President*
Steve Hines, *COO*
Joe Gottron, *Exec VP*
EMP: 50 **EST:** 1988
SQ FT: 15,000
SALES: 40.6MM **Privately Held**
WEB: www.heartlandbank.com
SIC: 6022 State trust companies accepting deposits, commercial

(G-11248)
IJUS LLC (PA)
Also Called: Innovative Joint Utility Svcs
690 Taylor Rd Ste 100 (43230-3520)
PHONE..................614 470-9882
William Schulze, *President*
Eric Young, *Area Mgr*
Scott Schulze, *Safety Dir*
Mike Miller, *Project Mgr*
Kerry Jonker, *Opers Spvr*
EMP: 85
SQ FT: 15,000
SALES (est): 22.1MM **Privately Held**
WEB: www.ijus.net
SIC: 8711 Consulting engineer

(G-11249)
INTERIM HALTHCARE COLUMBUS INC (HQ)
784 Morrison Rd (43230-6642)
PHONE..................614 888-3130
Thomas J Dimarco, *President*
Michael W Hartshorn, *Principal*
Richard Nielsen, *Principal*
Tyler Rader, *Info Tech Mgr*
Craig Smith,
EMP: 30
SQ FT: 3,400
SALES: 19.7MM
SALES (corp-wide): 24.4MM **Privately Held**
SIC: 8082 Home health care services
PA: Salo, Inc.
960 Checkrein Ave Ste A
Columbus OH 43229
614 436-9404

(G-11250)
KINDERCARE EDUCATION LLC
Also Called: Childrens World Lrng Ctr 177
4885 Cherry Bottom Rd (43230-4535)
PHONE..................614 337-2035
EMP: 25
SALES (corp-wide): 1B **Privately Held**
SIC: 8351 Child Day Care Services
PA: Kindercare Education Llc
650 Ne Holladay St # 1400
Portland OR 97232
503 872-1300

(G-11251)
KONE INC
735 Cross Pointe Rd Ste G (43230-6786)
PHONE..................614 866-1751
Tony Crumley, *Manager*
EMP: 34
SALES (corp-wide): 650.6MM **Privately Held**
WEB: www.us.kone.com
SIC: 7699 Elevators: inspection, service & repair
HQ: Kone Inc.
4225 Naperville Rd # 400
Lisle IL 60532
630 577-1650

(G-11252)
LANDSEL TITLE AGENCY INC (PA)
961 N Hamilton Rd Ste 100 (43230-1758)
PHONE..................614 337-1928
Fax: 614 337-9206
Randall L Craycraft, *President*
Rick Brown, *Business Mgr*
Lisa Tomba, *Controller*
Paul Wittenberg, *Accounts Mgr*
Britney Choina, *Accounts Exec*
EMP: 45
SQ FT: 7,000
SALES: 3.5MM **Privately Held**
SIC: 6361 6541 Real estate title insurance; title & trust companies

(G-11253)
LIBERTY MUTUAL INSURANCE CO
630 Morrison Rd Ste 300 (43230-5318)
PHONE..................614 864-4100
Fax: 614 864-0376
Chingyee Lam, *Investment Ofcr*
Laura Glatts, *Human Resources*
Bryan Graham, *Manager*
EMP: 65
SALES (corp-wide): 38.3B **Privately Held**
WEB: www.libertymutual.com
SIC: 6331 Fire, marine & casualty insurance
HQ: Liberty Mutual Insurance Company
175 Berkeley St
Boston MA 02116
617 357-9500

(G-11254)
LITTLE LAMBS CHILDRENS CENTER
425 S Hamilton Rd (43230-3474)
PHONE..................614 471-9269
Stacy Barrett, *Principal*
EMP: 35
SALES: 995.4K **Privately Held**
SIC: 8351 Child day care services

(G-11255)
LIVING IN FAMILY ENVIRONMENT
142 N High St (43230-3032)
P.O. Box 307416 (43230-7416)
PHONE..................614 475-5305
Fax: 614 471-6912
Mary Bill, *Manager*
Mary Mooneybiel, *Manager*
EMP: 60 **EST:** 1997
SALES (est): 1.5MM **Privately Held**
SIC: 8322 Social service center

(G-11256)
MARK-L INC
Also Called: Mark-L Construction
1180 Claycraft Rd (43230-6640)
PHONE..................614 863-8832
Fax: 614 863-9008
Mark A Laivins Sr, *President*
Keith Judy, *Project Mgr*
EMP: 32
SQ FT: 8,000
SALES (est): 22.3MM **Privately Held**
WEB: www.mark-l.com
SIC: 1542 Commercial & office building, new construction

(G-11257)
MAXIM HEALTHCARE SERVICES INC
735 Taylor Rd (43230-6274)
PHONE..................614 986-3001
EMP: 94
SALES (corp-wide): 1.3B **Privately Held**
SIC: 8099 Blood related health services
PA: Maxim Healthcare Services, Inc.
7227 Lee Deforest Dr
Columbia MD 21046
410 910-1500

(G-11258)
MPOWER INC
4643 Winery Way (43230-4232)
PHONE..................614 783-0478
Dejuante McKee, *President*
EMP: 30
SALES: 1.4MM **Privately Held**
SIC: 1542 Nonresidential construction

(G-11259)
NETJETS AVIATION INC
760 Morrison Rd Ste 250 (43230-6652)
PHONE..................614 239-5501
Pete Richards, *Manager*
EMP: 40
SALES (corp-wide): 242.1B **Publicly Held**
SIC: 8741 Administrative management; office management
HQ: Netjets Aviation, Inc.
4111 Bridgeway Ave
Columbus OH 43219
614 239-5500

(G-11260)
ODYSSEY HEALTHCARE INC
Also Called: Odyssey Healthcare of Columbus
540 Officenter Pl Ste 295 (43230-5323)
PHONE..................614 414-0500
Holly Franko, *General Mgr*
Marcy Gillis, *Manager*
EMP: 120
SALES (corp-wide): 6B **Publicly Held**
SIC: 8082 Home health care services
HQ: Odyssey Healthcare, Inc.
7801 Mesquite Bend Dr # 105
Irving TX 75063

(G-11261)
OHIO PIA SERVICE CORPORATION
600 Cross Pointe Rd (43230-6696)
PHONE..................614 552-8000
George Haenzel, *President*
Becca Calkins, *Accountant*
EMP: 26
SALES: 3.3MM **Privately Held**
SIC: 6311 Life insurance

(G-11262)
OHIO POWER COMPANY
700 Morrison Rd (43230-6642)
PHONE..................614 836-2570
EMP: 41
SALES (corp-wide): 15.4B **Publicly Held**
SIC: 4911 Transmission, electric power
HQ: Ohio Power Company
1 Riverside Plz
Columbus OH 43215
614 716-1000

(G-11263)
PARKSIDE BEHAVIORAL HEALTHCARE
349 Olde Ridenour Rd (43230-2528)
PHONE..................614 471-2552
EMP: 50
SALES (est): 2.2MM **Privately Held**
SIC: 8069 Specialty Hospital

(G-11264)
RELIANT CAPITAL SOLUTIONS LLC
Also Called: Reliant Recovery Solutions
670 Cross Pointe Rd (43230-6862)
P.O. Box 30469, Columbus (43230-0469)
PHONE..................614 452-6100
David Shull, *CFO*
Aneta Turner, *Accountant*
Micah Bradford, *Accounts Mgr*
Tamra Chambers, *Manager*
Joe Hindes, *Manager*
EMP: 185
SQ FT: 20,000
SALES: 9.9MM **Privately Held**
WEB: www.reliantcapitalsolutions.com
SIC: 7322 Collection agency, except real estate

Gahanna - Franklin County (G-11265)

(G-11265)
ROCKWOOD DRY CLEANERS CORP
171 Granville St (43230-3005)
PHONE..........................614 471-3700
Robert Rings, *President*
Justin Rings, *Vice Pres*
EMP: 28
SALES (est): 1.6MM **Privately Held**
SIC: **7216** Cleaning & dyeing, except rugs

(G-11266)
ROMANOFF ELECTRIC INC (PA)
1288 Research Rd (43230-6625)
PHONE..........................614 755-4500
Fax: 614 755-4510
Matthew Romanoff, *President*
Jin OH, *Safety Dir*
Deb Anderson, *Controller*
Heather Baytos, *Personnel Exec*
Paul Ackerman, *Assistant*
EMP: 133
SQ FT: 14,000
SALES (est): 62.5MM **Privately Held**
SIC: **1731** General electrical contractor

(G-11267)
SANDEL CORP
152 N High St (43230-3032)
P.O. Box 307262 (43230-7262)
PHONE..........................614 475-5898
Fax: 614 475-6790
Walter P Sandel, *President*
Kathryn Sandel, *Treasurer*
EMP: 25
SQ FT: 2,000
SALES (est): 2.6MM **Privately Held**
SIC: **1742** Insulation, buildings

(G-11268)
SOLAR IMAGING LLC
825 Taylor Rd (43230-6235)
PHONE..........................614 626-8536
Paul Hartong, *Prdtn Mgr*
Jeffrey B Burt, *Mng Member*
Mike Barrett, *Manager*
Stephanie Ryland, *Manager*
Sandra G Burt, *Admin Sec*
EMP: 40
SALES (est): 3.4MM **Privately Held**
SIC: **7384** Photofinishing laboratory

(G-11269)
STAR GROUP LTD
Also Called: Holiday Inn
460 Waterbury Ct (43230-3450)
PHONE..........................614 428-8678
Fax: 614 428-9839
Richard Chen,
EMP: 25
SALES (est): 2.1MM **Privately Held**
SIC: **7011** Hotels & motels

(G-11270)
STONE COFFMAN COMPANY LLC
6015 Taylor Rd (43230-3211)
PHONE..........................614 861-4668
Fax: 614 861-4655
Christy Elswick, *Sales Staff*
Roger Lutz, *Sales Staff*
Tammy Lytle, *Sales Staff*
Charley McDill, *Sales Staff*
Thomas Coffman,
EMP: 25
SALES (est): 3.2MM **Privately Held**
WEB: www.coffmanstone.com
SIC: **5032** 5211 Brick, stone & related material; masonry materials & supplies; paving stones

(G-11271)
SUNRISE MORTGAGE SERVICES INC
3596 Ringling Ln (43230-4609)
PHONE..........................614 989-5412
Richard Greer, *President*
EMP: 70
SALES (est): 5.2MM **Privately Held**
SIC: **6162** Mortgage bankers & correspondents

(G-11272)
SUNRISE SENIOR LIVING INC
Also Called: Sunrise of Gahanna
775 E Johnstown Rd (43230-2115)
PHONE..........................614 418-9775
Fax: 614 418-9799
Todd Gable, *Manager*
EMP: 35
SALES (corp-wide): 4.3B **Publicly Held**
WEB: www.sunrise.com
SIC: **8051** 8361 Skilled nursing care facilities; residential care
HQ: Sunrise Senior Living, Llc
7902 Westpark Dr
Mc Lean VA 22102

(G-11273)
TERRACON CONSULTANTS INC
Also Called: Terracon Consultants N4
800 Morrison Rd (43230-6643)
PHONE..........................614 863-3113
Fax: 614 863-0475
Kevin Ernst, *Manager*
EMP: 35
SALES (corp-wide): 654.9MM **Privately Held**
SIC: **8711** 8731 Consulting engineer; environmental research
PA: Terracon Consultants, Inc.
18001 W 106th St Ste 300
Olathe KS 66061
913 599-6886

(G-11274)
VMA INC
Also Called: Animal Care At Cherry Way
1353 Cherry Way Dr (43230-6775)
PHONE..........................614 475-7300
Fax: 614 475-7337
Trina Ferrell, *Manager*
EMP: 25 EST: 1997
SALES (est): 1.1MM **Privately Held**
SIC: **0742** Veterinarian, animal specialties

(G-11275)
WINN-SCAPES INC
Also Called: Winnscapes Inc/Schmidt Nurs Co
6079 Taylor Rd (43230-3211)
PHONE..........................614 866-9466
Richard Winnestaffer, *CEO*
Carl Morris Jr, *President*
Thomas Becker, *Accounts Mgr*
Mike Clapper, *Sales Staff*
Robert Parsons, *Sales Staff*
EMP: 51
SQ FT: 6,000
SALES (est): 4.7MM **Privately Held**
WEB: www.winnscapes.com
SIC: **0782** Landscape contractors

(G-11276)
YOUNG MENS CHRISTIAN ASSOC
Also Called: YMCA
555 Ymca Pl (43230-6851)
PHONE..........................614 416-9622
Chris Angelletta, *Manager*
Brenda Conner, *Director*
EMP: 160
SALES (corp-wide): 44.9MM **Privately Held**
WEB: www.ymca-columbus.com
SIC: **8641** 7991 8351 7032 Youth organizations; physical fitness facilities; child day care services; youth camps; individual & family services
PA: Young Men's Christian Association Of Central Ohio
40 W Long St
Columbus OH 43215
614 389-4409

Galena
Delaware County

(G-11277)
ACORN FARMS INC
7679 Worthington Rd B (43021-9412)
PHONE..........................614 891-9348
Fax: 614 891-1002
Paul Reiner, *President*
Marge Bland, *Opers Mgr*
Barbara Bromley, *Engineer*
Lisa Maxwell, *Controller*
Charity A Raimond, *Financial Exec*
▲ EMP: 150
SQ FT: 3,200
SALES (est): 13MM **Privately Held**
WEB: www.acornfarms.com
SIC: **0181** Nursery stock, growing of

(G-11278)
AMERICAN GOLF CORPORATION
Also Called: Royal American Links Golf Club
3300 Miller Paul Rd (43021-9243)
PHONE..........................740 965-5122
Dave Philsburg, *Owner*
Josh Bryant, *Superintendent*
Jason Shelton, *Manager*
EMP: 46
SALES (corp-wide): 621.9MM **Privately Held**
WEB: www.americangolf.com
SIC: **7997** 7992 Golf club, membership; public golf courses
PA: American Golf Corporation
6080 Center Dr Ste 500
Los Angeles CA 90045
310 664-4000

(G-11279)
B2B POWER PARTNERS
5647 Summer Blvd (43021-9003)
PHONE..........................614 309-6964
Craig Owens, *President*
EMP: 30
SALES (est): 844.3K **Privately Held**
SIC: **8748** Business consulting

(G-11280)
BIG RED LP
Also Called: Double Eagle Club
6025 Cheshire Rd (43021-9408)
PHONE..........................740 548-7799
Fax: 740 548-7083
John H McConnell, *Partner*
Bruce Ruhl, *General Mgr*
Rick Mellen, *Executive*
EMP: 75
SQ FT: 5,731
SALES: 1.8MM **Privately Held**
SIC: **7997** Golf club, membership

(G-11281)
DIVISION 7 INC
Also Called: Division 7 Roofing
72 Holmes St (43021-9414)
P.O. Box 366 (43021-0366)
PHONE..........................740 965-1970
George W Reiss, *CEO*
John Kiesel, *President*
John C Seitzinger, *Vice Pres*
Sarah Loney, *Manager*
EMP: 40
SALES (est): 7.4MM **Privately Held**
SIC: **1761** 7389 Roofing contractor; sheet metalwork; crane & aerial lift service

(G-11282)
FOXRIDGE FARMS CORP
7273 Cheshire Rd (43021-9409)
PHONE..........................740 965-1369
Fax: 740 848-4099
Kathy Dixon, *President*
EMP: 30
SALES (est): 599.6K **Privately Held**
WEB: www.foxridgefarms.com
SIC: **7999** 0752 Riding stable; animal specialty services

(G-11283)
HEAT TTAL FCLTY SLUTIONS INC
5064 Red Bank Rd (43021-8603)
PHONE..........................740 965-3005
Ron Thomas, *President*
Ray Robinson, *Vice Pres*
Diana Spiers, *Manager*
Laurie Steller, *Consultant*
EMP: 30
SALES (est): 4.4MM **Privately Held**
SIC: **1711** 7359 Heating & air conditioning contractors; sound & lighting equipment rental

(G-11284)
J R MEAD INDUSTRIAL CONTRS
6606 Lake Of The Woods Pt (43021-9616)
PHONE..........................614 891-4466
Joanie R Mead, *President*
James E Mead, *Vice Pres*
EMP: 50
SQ FT: 12,000
SALES (est): 3.4MM **Privately Held**
SIC: **1799** 1796 Rigging & scaffolding; machinery dismantling

(G-11285)
LAKES COUNTRY CLUB INC
Also Called: Lakes Golf and Country Club
7129 Africa Rd (43021-9581)
PHONE..........................614 882-4167
Todd Ortlip, *President*
Chris Haunty, *Administration*
EMP: 150
SALES (est): 2.3MM **Privately Held**
WEB: www.lakescc.com
SIC: **7997** Golf club, membership

(G-11286)
LAZER KRAZE
6075 Braymoore Dr (43021-9093)
PHONE..........................513 339-1030
Robin Wilcox, *CEO*
Dave Wilcox, *Vice Pres*
EMP: 30
SALES: 110K **Privately Held**
SIC: **7299** Facility rental & party planning services

(G-11287)
SPELLACYS TURF-LAWN INC
6555 Plumb Rd (43021-9442)
PHONE..........................740 965-5508
Fax: 740 965-5507
Christopher Spellacy, *President*
John O'Neill, *Opers Mgr*
Brian Van Voorhis, *Sales Staff*
EMP: 40
SQ FT: 15,240
SALES (est): 1.9MM **Privately Held**
WEB: www.turflawn.com
SIC: **0781** 0782 4959 1711 Landscape architects; lawn care services; fertilizing services, lawn; mowing services, lawn; snowplowing; irrigation sprinkler system installation

Galion
Crawford County

(G-11288)
A & G MANUFACTURING CO INC (PA)
Also Called: A G Mercury
280 Gelsanliter Rd (44833-2234)
P.O. Box 935 (44833-0935)
PHONE..........................419 468-7433
Fax: 419 468-3990
Arvin Shifley, *President*
Glen Shifley Sr, *Principal*
Doug Shifley, *Treasurer*
Jim Streib, *Sales Mgr*
Karin Baldwin, *Accounts Mgr*
▲ EMP: 40
SQ FT: 100,000
SALES (est): 10.4MM **Privately Held**
WEB: www.agmercury.com
SIC: **3599** 7692 3446 3444 Machine shop, jobbing & repair; welding repair; architectural metalwork; sheet metalwork; fabricated plate work (boiler shop); fabricated structural metal

(G-11289)
A M COMMUNICATIONS LTD (PA)
5707 State Route 309 (44833-9541)
PHONE..........................419 528-3051
Alan Miller, *President*
Hilary Grooms, *Opers Mgr*
Nick Quintel, *Opers Mgr*
Nicia Cary, *Human Res Dir*
Dennis Broski, *Manager*
EMP: 59
SQ FT: 8,000

GEOGRAPHIC SECTION

SALES (est): 22.2MM **Privately Held**
WEB: www.amcable.com
SIC: 8748 Communications consulting

(G-11290)
AVITA HEALTH SYSTEM
Also Called: Robert L Dawson M.D., James
955 Hosford Rd (44833-9325)
PHONE.................................419 468-7059
James H Wurm, *Partner*
EMP: 184
SALES (corp-wide): 22.9MM **Privately Held**
SIC: 8322 Community center
PA: Avita Health System
 269 Portland Way S
 Galion OH 44833
 419 468-4841

(G-11291)
AVITA HEALTH SYSTEM (PA)
269 Portland Way S (44833-2312)
PHONE.................................419 468-4841
Jerry Morasko, *CEO*
Eric Draime, *CFO*
Alex Reed, *Director*
Rhonda Ridenour, *Director*
Besy Carpenter, *Executive Asst*
EMP: 106
SALES: 22.9MM **Privately Held**
SIC: 8011 Internal medicine, physician/surgeon

(G-11292)
BAILLIE LUMBER CO LP
3953 County Road 51 (44833-9630)
PHONE.................................419 462-2000
Russel Jones, *Branch Mgr*
EMP: 40
SALES (corp-wide): 304.5MM **Privately Held**
SIC: 5031 2426 2421 Lumber: rough, dressed & finished; hardwood dimension & flooring mills; sawmills & planing mills, general
PA: Baillie Lumber Co., L.P.
 4002 Legion Dr
 Hamburg NY 14075
 800 950-2850

(G-11293)
CRAWFORD CNTY SHARED HLTH SVCS
1220 N Market St (44833-1443)
P.O. Box 327 (44833-0327)
PHONE.................................419 468-7985
Bert Maglott, *Exec Dir*
EMP: 44
SALES: 4.2MM **Privately Held**
SIC: 8082 Home health care services

(G-11294)
FIRST FDRAL SAV LN ASSN GALION
140 N Columbus St (44833-1909)
PHONE.................................419 468-1518
Fax: 419 468-2973
Eric Geyer, *Principal*
EMP: 75
SALES (est): 5.8MM **Privately Held**
SIC: 6035 Federal savings & loan associations

(G-11295)
FIRST FEDERAL BANK OF OHIO (PA)
140 N Columbus St (44833-1909)
P.O. Box 957 (44833-0957)
PHONE.................................419 468-1518
David B Beach, *CEO*
Thomas Moore, *President*
Eric S Geyer, *Chairman*
David Schockman, *Vice Pres*
Rodney J Vose, *Vice Pres*
EMP: 60 EST: 1891
SQ FT: 12,000
SALES: 8.3MM **Privately Held**
WEB: www.firstfederalbankofohio.com
SIC: 6035 Federal savings & loan associations

(G-11296)
FLICK LUMBER CO INC
Also Called: Flick Packaging
340 S Columbus St (44833-2624)
P.O. Box 296 (44833-0296)
PHONE.................................419 468-6278
Fax: 419 468-4752
Gary G Flick, *President*
Erik Flick, *Vice Pres*
George Flick, *Vice Pres*
Brian Coon, *Sales Mgr*
Kristi Stief, *Office Mgr*
EMP: 30
SQ FT: 35,200
SALES (est): 6.3MM **Privately Held**
WEB: www.flickpackaging.com
SIC: 4783 Packing goods for shipping; crating goods for shipping

(G-11297)
GALION COMMUNITY CENTER YMCA
500 Gill Ave (44833-1213)
PHONE.................................419 468-7754
Fax: 419 468-4738
Terry Gribble, *CEO*
EMP: 25
SALES: 1.2MM **Privately Held**
SIC: 8641 7991 8351 7032 Youth organizations; physical fitness facilities; child day care services; youth camps; individual & family services

(G-11298)
GALION COMMUNITY HOSPITAL
269 Portland Way S (44833-2399)
PHONE.................................419 468-4841
Fax: 419 468-2381
Lamar Wyse, *President*
Eric Draime, *Vice Pres*
Robert Melaragno, *CFO*
Rhonda Ridenouer, *Office Mgr*
Joseph Guth, *Med Doctor*
EMP: 465
SQ FT: 165,219
SALES: 106.5MM **Privately Held**
WEB: www.galionhospital.org
SIC: 8062 8051 Hospital, affiliated with AMA residency; skilled nursing care facilities

(G-11299)
GALION EAST OHIO I LP
1300 Harding Way E (44833-3063)
PHONE.................................216 520-1250
Frank Sinito, *General Ptnr*
EMP: 99
SALES (est): 789.1K **Privately Held**
SIC: 6513 Apartment building operators

(G-11300)
GMC EXCAVATION & TRUCKING
1859 Biddle Rd (44833-8962)
P.O. Box 203, Iberia (43325-0203)
PHONE.................................419 468-0121
Fax: 419 462-2231
Steven J Beck, *Partner*
Mindy Beck, *Partner*
Lynn Dovenbarger, *Admin Sec*
EMP: 40
SALES (est): 3.2MM **Privately Held**
SIC: 4213 1794 4212 Trucking, except local; excavation work; local trucking, without storage

(G-11301)
GOUDY INTERNAL MEDICINE INC
Also Called: Goudy, James A II MD
270 Portland Way S Rear (44833-2395)
PHONE.................................419 468-8323
James A Goudy II, *President*
EMP: 100
SALES (est): 2.5MM **Privately Held**
SIC: 8011 Internal medicine, physician/surgeon

(G-11302)
MILL CREEK NURSING
900 Wedgewood Cir (44833-8815)
PHONE.................................419 468-4046
Brian Colleran, *President*
EMP: 50
SALES: 5.6MM **Privately Held**
SIC: 8051 Skilled nursing care facilities

(G-11303)
OHIO HRTLAND CMNTY ACTION COMM
Also Called: Salvation Army
124 Buehler St (44833-2248)
PHONE.................................419 468-5121
Karen Wise, *VP Finance*
Frances Horton, *Manager*
EMP: 25
SALES (corp-wide): 10MM **Privately Held**
SIC: 8399 8322 Community action agency; individual & family services
PA: Ohio Heartland Community Action Commission
 372 E Center St
 Marion OH 43302
 740 387-1039

(G-11304)
OHIO TRANSMISSION CORPORATION
Otp Industrial Solutions
1311 Freese Works Pl (44833-9368)
P.O. Box 73278, Cleveland (44193-0002)
PHONE.................................419 468-7866
David Falk, *Branch Mgr*
EMP: 25 **Privately Held**
SIC: 5084 5085 Pumps & pumping equipment; power transmission equipment & apparatus
HQ: Ohio Transmission Corporation
 1900 Jetway Blvd
 Columbus OH 43219
 614 342-6247

(G-11305)
STEELE DIALYSIS LLC
Also Called: Galion Dialysis
865 Harding Way W (44833-1637)
PHONE.................................419 462-1028
James K Hilger,
EMP: 33 EST: 2013
SALES (est): 485.5K **Publicly Held**
SIC: 8092 Kidney dialysis centers
PA: Davita Inc.
 2000 16th St
 Denver CO 80202

(G-11306)
SURFSIDE MOTORS INC (PA)
Also Called: Craig Smith Auto Group
7459 State Route 309 (44833-9735)
P.O. Box 850 (44833-0850)
PHONE.................................419 462-1746
Toll Free:...............................866 -
Fax: 419 462-1653
Craig A Smith, *President*
Matt Wilson, *Parts Mgr*
Bill Willis, *CFO*
Jeff Caldwell, *Sales Mgr*
Artty Mayse, *Sales Staff*
EMP: 50
SQ FT: 21,000
SALES (est): 15.3MM **Privately Held**
WEB: www.craigsmithrvcenter.com
SIC: 5511 5521 7538 7532 Automobiles, new & used; used car dealers; general automotive repair shops; top & body repair & paint shops; recreational vehicle dealers

(G-11307)
TSI INC
1263 State Route 598 (44833-9367)
P.O. Box 687 (44833-0687)
PHONE.................................419 468-1855
George Dallas, *President*
Rita Masucci, *Vice Pres*
Bob Lynch, *Sales Executive*
EMP: 30
SALES (est): 3MM **Privately Held**
SIC: 8711 7373 Engineering services; computer integrated systems design

Gallipolis
Gallia County

(G-11308)
AREA AGENCY ON AGING DST 7 INC
Also Called: Galia County Council On Aging
1167 State Route 160 (45631-8407)
PHONE.................................740 446-7000
Fax: 740 446-7008
Shirley Doff, *Branch Mgr*
EMP: 29
SALES: 833.3K
SALES (corp-wide): 61MM **Privately Held**
SIC: 8322 Senior citizens' center or association
PA: Area Agency On Aging District 7, Inc.
 160 Dorsey Dr
 Rio Grande OH 45674
 800 582-7277

(G-11309)
BIMBO BAKERIES USA INC
1708 Eastern Ave (45631-1739)
PHONE.................................740 446-4552
Tracy Montgomery, *Branch Mgr*
EMP: 30 **Privately Held**
SIC: 5149 Bakery products
HQ: Bimbo Bakeries Usa, Inc
 255 Business Center Dr # 200
 Horsham PA 19044
 215 347-5500

(G-11310)
CITY OF GALLIPOLIS
Also Called: Gallipolis Municipal Pool
2501 Ohio Ave (45631-1656)
PHONE.................................740 441-6003
Bradd Bostic, *Director*
EMP: 33 **Privately Held**
SIC: 7999 Swimming pool, non-membership
PA: City Of Gallipolis
 333 3rd Third Ave # 3
 Gallipolis OH 45631
 740 441-6003

(G-11311)
COUNTY OF GALLIA
Also Called: Gallia County Human Services
848 3rd Ave (45631-1625)
P.O. Box 339 (45631-0339)
PHONE.................................740 446-3222
Fax: 740 446-8942
Kathy McCalla, *Director*
EMP: 55 **Privately Held**
SIC: 6371 9111 Pension, health & welfare funds; county supervisors' & executives' offices
PA: County Of Gallia
 18 Locust St Ste 1292
 Gallipolis OH 45631
 740 446-4612

(G-11312)
COUNTY OF GALLIA
Also Called: State Highway Dept Gallia
1107 State Route 160 (45631-8407)
PHONE.................................740 446-2665
Bob Howard, *Superintendent*
EMP: 32 **Privately Held**
SIC: 0782 9111 Highway lawn & garden maintenance services; county supervisors' & executives' offices
PA: County Of Gallia
 18 Locust St Ste 1292
 Gallipolis OH 45631
 740 446-4612

(G-11313)
COUNTY OF GALLIA
Also Called: Gallia County Engineer
1167 State Route 160 (45631-8407)
PHONE.................................740 446-4009
Fax: 740 441-2032
Bret Boothe, *Engineer*
Glen Smith, *Engineer*
Lewis Shelton, *Manager*
EMP: 29 **Privately Held**
SIC: 8711 Engineering services

Gallipolis - Gallia County (G-11314)   GEOGRAPHIC SECTION

PA: County Of Gallia
18 Locust St Ste 1292
Gallipolis OH 45631
740 446-4612

(G-11314)
DEVELPMNTAL DSBLTIES OHIO DEPT
Also Called: Gallipolis Developmental Ctr
2500 Ohio Ave (45631-1656)
PHONE.................................740 446-1642
Fax: 740 446-1341
Sam Matthews, *Persnl Mgr*
Don Walker, *Branch Mgr*
Chip Kirby, *Director*
Mary Holly, *Admin Sec*
EMP: 510 **Privately Held**
SIC: 9431 8063 8052 Administration of public health programs; ; psychiatric hospitals; intermediate care facilities
HQ: Ohio Department Of Developmental Disabilities
30 E Broad St Fl 13
Columbus OH 43215

(G-11315)
FAMILY SENIOR CARE INC
859 3rd Ave (45631-1624)
PHONE.................................740 441-1428
Teri Pearson, *Administration*
EMP: 27
SALES (est): 784.6K **Privately Held**
WEB: www.familyseniorcare.com
SIC: 8322 8082 Senior citizens' center or association; home health care services

(G-11316)
GALLCO INC
Also Called: GALLCO INDUSTRIES
77 Mill Creek Rd (45631-8423)
PHONE.................................740 446-3775
Robert Burlile, *President*
Bernard Miehm, *Vice Pres*
Timothy Stout, *Director*
EMP: 55
SALES: 134.9K **Privately Held**
SIC: 8331 Sheltered workshop

(G-11317)
GALLIPOLIS AUTO AUCTION INC
286 Upper River Rd (45631-1839)
P.O. Box 421 (45631-0421)
PHONE.................................740 446-1576
Fax: 740 446-6318
Bonnie Shelton, *President*
Don Shelton, *Corp Secy*
Roger Stover, *Manager*
EMP: 28
SQ FT: 10,000
SALES: 2.9MM **Privately Held**
SIC: 5012 Automobile auction

(G-11318)
GALLIPOLIS CARE LLC
Also Called: PRESTIGE HEALTHCARE
170 Pinecrest Dr (45631-1347)
PHONE.................................740 446-7112
Fax: 740 446-9088
Melvin Rhinelander, *Ch of Bd*
Elyse Aasen, *Council Mbr*
Charlene Smith, *Hlthcr Dir*
Nathan Wedge, *Hlthcr Dir*
Amanda Wray, *Administration*
EMP: 110
SALES: 6.9MM
SALES (corp-wide): 37.8MM **Privately Held**
SIC: 8051 Convalescent home with continuous nursing care
PA: Senior Northpoint Services Llc
7400 New Lagrange 100
Louisville KY 40222
502 429-8062

(G-11319)
GALLIPOLIS HOSPITALITY INC
Also Called: Holiday Inn
577 State Route 7 N (45631-5921)
PHONE.................................740 446-0090
Fax: 740 446-0090
Anthony Etnyre, *President*
Gary Kilgore, *General Mgr*
EMP: 40
SQ FT: 50,000
SALES (est): 1.2MM **Privately Held**
SIC: 7011 5813 5812 Hotels; drinking places; eating places

(G-11320)
HOLZER CLINIC LLC
100 Jackson Pike (45631-1560)
PHONE.................................304 746-3701
Fax: 740 441-3433
Ralph Fisher, *Purch Dir*
Debbie Caldwell, *Controller*
Matt Johnson, *Branch Mgr*
Lori Cremeans, *Manager*
Bonnie McFarland, *Director*
EMP: 112
SALES (corp-wide): 323.8MM **Privately Held**
SIC: 8011 Clinic, operated by physicians
HQ: Holzer Clinic Llc
90 Jackson Pike
Gallipolis OH 45631
740 446-5411

(G-11321)
HOLZER CLINIC LLC (HQ)
Also Called: Holzer Health Center
90 Jackson Pike (45631-1562)
PHONE.................................740 446-5411
Fax: 740 446-5082
Christopher T Meyer, *CEO*
Craig Strafford, *President*
Jon Sullivan, *Treasurer*
William Miller, *Psychologist*
Naci I Bozkir, *Ophthalmology*
EMP: 566
SQ FT: 95,000
SALES (est): 78.6MM
SALES (corp-wide): 323.8MM **Privately Held**
WEB: www.holzerclinic.com
SIC: 8011 8741 Physicians' office, including specialists; management services
PA: Holzer Health System
100 Jackson Pike
Gallipolis OH 45631
740 446-5060

(G-11322)
HOLZER CLINIC LLC
100 Jackson Pike (45631-1560)
PHONE.................................304 744-2300
Marietta Babayev, *Branch Mgr*
Marianna Massey, *Manager*
EMP: 112
SALES (corp-wide): 323.8MM **Privately Held**
SIC: 8011 Physical medicine, physician/surgeon
HQ: Holzer Clinic Llc
90 Jackson Pike
Gallipolis OH 45631
740 446-5411

(G-11323)
HOLZER CLINIC LLC
Also Called: Holzer Hospital
90 Jackson Pike (45631-1562)
PHONE.................................740 446-5412
Lamar Wyfe, *CEO*
EMP: 43
SALES (corp-wide): 323.8MM **Privately Held**
WEB: www.holzerclinic.com
SIC: 8011 7991 Clinic, operated by physicians; health club
HQ: Holzer Clinic Llc
90 Jackson Pike
Gallipolis OH 45631
740 446-5411

(G-11324)
HOLZER HEALTH SYSTEM (PA)
Also Called: HOLZER CONSOLIDATED HEALTH SYS
100 Jackson Pike (45631-1560)
PHONE.................................740 446-5060
Fax: 740 446-5892
Brent Saundrs, *President*
Linda Stanley, *Financial Analy*
Lisa Halley, *VP Human Res*
Sheila Whiteley, *Med Doctor*
Kim Caldwell, *Payroll Mgr*
EMP: 32
SALES: 323.8MM **Privately Held**
SIC: 8062 General medical & surgical hospitals

(G-11325)
HOLZER HOSPITAL FOUNDATION (HQ)
Also Called: Holzer Medical Center
100 Jackson Pike (45631-1560)
PHONE.................................740 446-5000
Fax: 740 446-5522
Christopher T Meyer, *CEO*
Brent A Saunders, *Ch of Bd*
Ronald Saunders, *COO*
Tom Judy, *Sr Corp Ofcr*
John Cunningham, *Exec VP*
EMP: 898
SQ FT: 254,000
SALES: 154.4MM
SALES (corp-wide): 323.8MM **Privately Held**
WEB: www.holzer.org
SIC: 8062 General medical & surgical hospitals
PA: Holzer Health System
100 Jackson Pike
Gallipolis OH 45631
740 446-5060

(G-11326)
HOLZER HOSPITAL FOUNDATION
90 Jackson Pike (45631-1560)
PHONE.................................740 446-5000
Kenneth Coughenour, *Branch Mgr*
Sarah Deel, *Case Mgr*
Micheal Lovell, *Info Tech Mgr*
Brandon Coughenour, *Director*
Sarah Harrigan, *Director*
EMP: 457
SALES (corp-wide): 323.8MM **Privately Held**
SIC: 8062 General medical & surgical hospitals
HQ: Holzer Hospital Foundation Inc
100 Jackson Pike
Gallipolis OH 45631
740 446-5000

(G-11327)
LOCAL 911 UNITED MINE WORKERS
5102 State Route 218 (45631-8906)
PHONE.................................740 256-6083
Allen Wauth, *President*
Mike Dammeter, *Vice Pres*
Bryan Wood, *Treasurer*
EMP: 40
SALES (est): 1.9MM **Privately Held**
SIC: 8631 Labor unions & similar labor organizations

(G-11328)
MEDI HOME HEALTH AGENCY INC
Also Called: Medi Home Care
412 2nd Ave (45631-1130)
PHONE.................................740 441-1779
Fax: 740 441-1979
Diana Harless, *Manager*
EMP: 25
SALES (corp-wide): 193.8MM **Privately Held**
SIC: 8082 Home health care services
HQ: Medi Home Health Agency Inc
105 Main St
Steubenville OH 43953
740 266-3977

(G-11329)
MRM CONSTRUCTION INC
110 Bellomy Dr (45631-8998)
PHONE.................................740 388-0079
Patricia Luckeydoo, *CEO*
Will Luckeydoo, *General Mgr*
EMP: 25
SQ FT: 3,000
SALES (est): 2.9MM **Privately Held**
SIC: 1799 Construction site cleanup

(G-11330)
OHIO VALLEY BANK COMPANY
Also Called: Inside Foodland
236 2nd Ave (45631-1022)
PHONE.................................740 446-2168
Fax: 740 446-2185
Julia Slone, *Branch Mgr*
EMP: 60 **Publicly Held**
WEB: www.ovbc.com

SIC: 6022 State trust companies accepting deposits, commercial
HQ: The Ohio Valley Bank Company
420 3rd Ave
Gallipolis OH 45631
740 446-2631

(G-11331)
OHIO VALLEY BANK COMPANY (HQ)
420 3rd Ave (45631-1135)
P.O. Box 240 (45631-0240)
PHONE.................................740 446-2631
Fax: 740 446-6279
Thomas E Wiseman, *President*
Jeffrey E Smith, *Chairman*
Katrinka V Hart, *Exec VP*
E Richard Mahan, *Exec VP*
Larry E Miller II, *Exec VP*
EMP: 188
SALES: 43.5MM **Publicly Held**
WEB: www.ovbc.com
SIC: 6022 State commercial banks

(G-11332)
OHIO VALLEY BANK COMPANY
100 Jackson Pike (45631-1560)
PHONE.................................740 446-1646
Rebecca Nesbitt, *Director*
EMP: 27 **Publicly Held**
SIC: 6022 State trust companies accepting deposits, commercial
HQ: The Ohio Valley Bank Company
420 3rd Ave
Gallipolis OH 45631
740 446-2631

(G-11333)
OHIO VALLEY BANK COMPANY
143 3rd Ave (45631-1023)
PHONE.................................740 446-2631
Lawrencene Miller, *Senior VP*
EMP: 27 **Publicly Held**
SIC: 6022 State commercial banks
HQ: The Ohio Valley Bank Company
420 3rd Ave
Gallipolis OH 45631
740 446-2631

(G-11334)
OHIO VALLEY HOME HEALTH INC (PA)
Also Called: Family Home Health Plus
1480 Jackson Pike (45631-2602)
P.O. Box 274 (45631-0274)
PHONE.................................740 441-1393
Don Corbin, *CEO*
Michael Valley, *President*
EMP: 43
SALES (est): 5MM **Privately Held**
SIC: 8082 Home health care services

(G-11335)
PIERCETON TRUCKING CO INC
4311 State Route 160 (45631-9814)
PHONE.................................740 446-0114
Fax: 740 446-9511
Flem Meade, *Manager*
EMP: 35
SALES (corp-wide): 5.3MM **Privately Held**
SIC: 4212 Local trucking, without storage
PA: Pierceton Trucking Co Inc
10322 N Troyer Rd
Laketon IN 46943
260 982-2175

(G-11336)
REPUBLIC SERVICES INC
97 Hubbard Ave (45631-1920)
PHONE.................................800 331-0988
EMP: 34
SALES (corp-wide): 10B **Publicly Held**
SIC: 4953 Refuse collection & disposal services
PA: Republic Services, Inc.
18500 N Allied Way # 100
Phoenix AZ 85054
480 627-2700

(G-11337)
RES-CARE INC
8204 Carla Dr (45631-8769)
PHONE.................................740 446-7549
Colleen Houck, *Sales Executive*
Roberta Vangundy, *Manager*

GEOGRAPHIC SECTION

Geneva - Ashtabula County (G-11361)

EMP: 65
SALES (corp-wide): 24.5B **Privately Held**
WEB: www.rescare.com
SIC: 8052 Home for the mentally retarded, with health care
HQ: Res-Care, Inc.
9901 Linn Station Rd
Louisville KY 40223
502 394-2100

(G-11338)
RICK EPLION PAVING
7159 State Route 7 S (45631-8925)
P.O. Box 712, Proctorville (45669-0712)
PHONE..................................740 446-3000
Rick Eplion, *Owner*
EMP: 25
SALES: 3MM **Privately Held**
SIC: 1611 Surfacing & paving

(G-11339)
THOMAS DO-IT CENTER INC (PA)
Also Called: Thomas Rental
176 Mccormick Rd (45631-8745)
PHONE..................................740 446-2002
Fax: 740 446-6761
Jim Thomas, *President*
Lee Cyrus, *President*
Jay Hall, *Principal*
Marlene Hall, *Vice Pres*
▲ EMP: 45
SQ FT: 85,000
SALES (est): 15.4MM **Privately Held**
SIC: 5211 5251 7359 2439 Lumber & other building materials; lumber products; hardware; builders' hardware; equipment rental & leasing; lawn & garden equipment rental; trusses, wooden roof

(G-11340)
USF HOLLAND INC
Also Called: USFreightways
95 Holland Dr (45631-8241)
PHONE..................................740 441-1200
Fax: 740 441-1210
Paul Williamson, *Opers Mgr*
Andy Koziel, *Branch Mgr*
Mike Mathers, *Manager*
EMP: 75
SALES (corp-wide): 4.8B **Publicly Held**
WEB: www.usfc.com
SIC: 4213 4212 Less-than-truckload (LTL) transport; local trucking, without storage
HQ: Usf Holland Llc
700 S Waverly Rd
Holland MI 49423
616 395-5000

(G-11341)
WOODLAND CENTERS INC (PA)
3086 State Route 160 (45631-8409)
PHONE..................................740 446-5500
Fax: 740 441-4202
Louella M Stover, *CFO*
Kevin Mock, *Human Res Dir*
Amanda Brumfield, *Manager*
Legea McAvena, *Manager*
Regina Smith, *Manager*
EMP: 90
SQ FT: 18,000
SALES: 5.9MM **Privately Held**
SIC: 8093 Mental health clinic, outpatient

Galloway
Franklin County

(G-11342)
COLUMBUS FRKLN CNTY PK
1775 Darby Creek Dr (43119-9171)
PHONE..................................614 891-0700
Fax: 614 878-2866
EMP: 27
SALES (corp-wide): 18.3MM **Privately Held**
SIC: 7996 Amusement parks
PA: Columbus & Franklin County Metropolitan Park District
1069 W Main St Unit B
Westerville OH 43081
614 891-0700

(G-11343)
DEDICATED NURSING ASSOC INC
5672 W Broad St (43119-8127)
PHONE..................................877 411-8350
EMP: 41 **Privately Held**
SIC: 7361 7363 8051 Nurses' registry; medical help service; skilled nursing care facilities
PA: Dedicated Nursing Associates, Inc.
6536 State Route 22
Delmont PA 15626

(G-11344)
JPMORGAN CHASE BANK NAT ASSN
5684 W Broad St (43119-8127)
PHONE..................................614 853-2999
Alicia Jones, *Manager*
Julie Feeler, *Manager*
EMP: 26
SALES (corp-wide): 99.6B **Publicly Held**
WEB: www.chase.com
SIC: 6021 National commercial banks
HQ: Jpmorgan Chase Bank, National Association
1111 Polaris Pkwy
Columbus OH 43240
614 436-3055

(G-11345)
LIBERTY TAX INC
942 Galloway Rd (43119-8293)
PHONE..................................614 853-1090
Fax: 614 853-9910
Richard Looby, *Branch Mgr*
EMP: 49
SALES (corp-wide): 173.9MM **Publicly Held**
SIC: 7291 Tax return preparation services
PA: Liberty Tax, Inc.
1716 Corp Landing Pkwy
Virginia Beach VA 23454
757 493-8855

(G-11346)
MIKES TRUCKING LTD
570 Plain City Grgsvlle (43119)
PHONE..................................614 879-8808
Fax: 614 879-7667
Terri Roberts, *Office Mgr*
Mike Culbertson,
Mary Culbertson,
EMP: 35
SALES (est): 5.1MM **Privately Held**
WEB: www.mikestrucking.com
SIC: 4212 Dump truck haulage

Gambier
Knox County

(G-11347)
HOCHSTEDLER CONSTRUCTION LTD
24761 Dennis Church Rd (43022-8706)
PHONE..................................740 427-4880
Edward Hochstedler, *President*
Jeremy Hochstedler, *Vice Pres*
Matthew Hochstedler, *Vice Pres*
Paul Hochstedler, *Vice Pres*
EMP: 35
SALES (est): 2.9MM **Privately Held**
SIC: 1521 7389 Single-family housing construction;

(G-11348)
KENYON COLLEGE
Also Called: Kenyon Inn
100 W Wegan St (43022)
P.O. Box 273 (43022-0273)
PHONE..................................740 427-2202
Fax: 740 427-2392
Tristen Haas, *Manager*
Lisa Train, *Asst Director*
Babette Cichanowicz, *Admin Asst*
EMP: 30
SALES (corp-wide): 124.3MM **Privately Held**
WEB: www.kenyon.edu
SIC: 7011 8221 Hotels & motels; college, except junior

PA: Kenyon College
1 Kenyon College
Gambier OH 43022
740 427-5000

(G-11349)
SMALL SAND & GRAVEL INC
10229 Killduff Rd (43022-9657)
P.O. Box 617 (43022-0617)
PHONE..................................740 427-3130
Michael W Small, *President*
Wiiliam T Small, *Treasurer*
Sharon Mills, *Office Mgr*
Carol Small, *Admin Sec*
EMP: 35
SALES (est): 8.6MM **Privately Held**
SIC: 1442 Sand mining; gravel mining

(G-11350)
SMALLS ASPHALT PAVING INC
10229 Killduff Rd (43022-9657)
P.O. Box 552 (43022-0552)
PHONE..................................740 427-4096
Robert E Small, *President*
Michael Small, *Vice Pres*
William T Small, *Treasurer*
Carol Small, *Admin Sec*
EMP: 25
SALES (est): 2.5MM **Privately Held**
SIC: 1771 2951 1611 Blacktop (asphalt) work; asphalt paving mixtures & blocks; highway & street construction

Garfield Heights
Cuyahoga County

(G-11351)
CLOCKWORK LOGISTICS INC
4765 E 131st St (44105-7131)
PHONE..................................216 587-5371
Frank Ilkanich Jr, *President*
Steve Toth, *VP Admin*
EMP: 47
SQ FT: 3,500
SALES (est): 5.4MM **Privately Held**
WEB: www.cwlog.com
SIC: 4215 Package delivery, vehicular

Garrettsville
Portage County

(G-11352)
SKYLANE LLC
Also Called: Sky Lane Drive-Thru
8311 Windham St (44231-9406)
PHONE..................................330 527-9999
Fax: 330 527-0408
Aaron King,
Rob Murray,
Tracy Murray,
Brittain Paul,
Matthew Paul,
EMP: 26
SQ FT: 120,000
SALES (est): 875.2K **Privately Held**
SIC: 5812 7933 Restaurant, family: chain; bowling centers

(G-11353)
SUGARBUSH GOLF INC
Also Called: Sugarbush Golf Club
11186 State Route 88 (44231-9601)
PHONE..................................330 527-4202
Fax: 330 527-5919
Mike Koval, *President*
Lilian M Koval, *Corp Secy*
William Kothera, *Vice Pres*
EMP: 30
SALES (est): 1.4MM **Privately Held**
WEB: www.sugarbushgolfclub.com
SIC: 7992 Public golf courses

(G-11354)
TLC HEALTH WELLNESS & FITNESS
1 Memory Ln (44231-9443)
PHONE..................................330 527-4852
Annette Andrews, *Owner*
EMP: 25
SALES (est): 395.8K **Privately Held**
SIC: 7991 Health club

Gates Mills
Cuyahoga County

(G-11355)
ARBOR REHABILITATION & HEALTCR
45125 Fairmount Blvd (44040)
P.O. Box 99 (44040-0099)
PHONE..................................440 423-0206
Robert Vadas, *President*
Cathy Stitts, *Opers Staff*
Phil Stitts, *VP Finance*
Allison Collins, *Technology*
Mark Stapleton, *Director*
EMP: 275
SALES: 7MM **Privately Held**
WEB: www.arborrehab.com
SIC: 8322 Rehabilitation services

(G-11356)
CHAGRIN VALLEY HUNT CLUB
7620 Old Mill Rd (44040-9700)
P.O. Box 159 (44040-0159)
PHONE..................................440 423-4414
Fred Floyd, *President*
EMP: 40
SQ FT: 7,463
SALES: 2.1MM **Privately Held**
WEB: www.chagrinvalleyhunt.com
SIC: 7997 Country club, membership

Geneva
Ashtabula County

(G-11357)
599 W MAIN CORPORATION
Also Called: Homestead
599 W Main St (44041-1252)
PHONE..................................440 466-5901
Fax: 440 466-2081
Jamie Miller, *President*
Margie Miller, *Administration*
EMP: 50
SALES (est): 2.7MM **Privately Held**
SIC: 8052 Home for the mentally retarded, with health care

(G-11358)
A2 SERVICES LLC
Also Called: Geneva Pipeline
4749 N Ridge Rd E (44041-8293)
PHONE..................................440 466-6611
Fax: 440 466-5044
Llevelyn Rhone,
EMP: 60
SALES (est): 9.5MM **Privately Held**
WEB: www.genevapipeline.com
SIC: 1542 Nonresidential construction

(G-11359)
BUILDING TECHNICIANS CORP
4500 Clay St (44041-8107)
PHONE..................................440 466-1651
Fax: 440 466-8107
Ellen Cumpston, *President*
Larry Cumpston, *Corp Secy*
Janet Cumpston, *Vice Pres*
EMP: 25 EST: 1976
SQ FT: 6,000
SALES (est): 3.5MM **Privately Held**
SIC: 1761 Roofing contractor

(G-11360)
COMMUNITY IMPROVEMENT CORP
44 N Forest St (44041-1371)
PHONE..................................440 466-4675
Jim Pearson, *Manager*
EMP: 50
SALES: 50.1K **Privately Held**
SIC: 1521 General remodeling, single-family houses

(G-11361)
FERRANTE WINE FARM INC
558 Rte 307 (44041)
PHONE..................................440 466-8466
Fax: 440 466-7370
Nicholas Ferrante, *President*

Geneva - Ashtabula County (G-11362)

Nicholas Farrante, *President*
Mary Jo Ferrante, *Principal*
Peter Ferrante, *Principal*
Charles Rehor, *Principal*
EMP: 40
SQ FT: 3,023
SALES (est): 2.4MM **Privately Held**
WEB: www.ferrantewinery.com
SIC: 0172 2084 5812 Grapes; wines; eating places

(G-11362)
GENEVA AREA CITY SCHOOL DST
Also Called: Bus Garage
75 North Ave E (44041-1154)
PHONE................................440 466-2684
Charlotte Lenard, *Admin Sec*
EMP: 42
SALES (corp-wide): 26.8MM **Privately Held**
SIC: 4151 School buses
PA: Geneva Area City Schools
135 S Eagle St
Geneva OH 44041
440 466-4831

(G-11363)
GENEVA AREA RECREATIONAL
Also Called: Gareat Sports Complex
1822 S Broadway (44041-7129)
PHONE................................440 466-1002
Fax: 440 415-1087
Ronald W Clutter, *Ch of Bd*
Bruce Scott, *Controller*
EMP: 25
SQ FT: 750,000
SALES: 9.5MM **Privately Held**
SIC: 7997 Membership sports & recreation clubs

(G-11364)
HUNTER REALTY INC
Also Called: Coldwell Banker
385 S Broadway (44041-1808)
PHONE................................440 466-9177
Fax: 440 466-7478
William Drenik, *Manager*
Michelle Collins, *Real Est Agnt*
Vincent Fusco, *Real Est Agnt*
Jamie Kelley, *Real Est Agnt*
Andrew Polony, *Real Est Agnt*
EMP: 25
SALES (corp-wide): 2.6MM **Privately Held**
WEB: www.cbhunter.com
SIC: 6531 Real estate agent, residential
PA: Hunter Realty Inc
24600 Detroit Rd Ste 240
Westlake OH 44145
440 892-7040

(G-11365)
LOUIS ARTHUR STEEL COMPANY (PA)
185 Water St (44041-1199)
P.O. Box 229 (44041-0229)
PHONE................................440 997-5545
Fax: 440 992-9726
J Trombley Kanicki, *President*
Andy Housel, *General Mgr*
J Matthew Kanicki, *Vice Pres*
Matthew Kanicki, *Vice Pres*
Sandra Kanicki, *Vice Pres*
EMP: 54 **EST:** 1949
SQ FT: 80,000
SALES (est): 18.9MM **Privately Held**
SIC: 3441 5051 3444 3443 Building components, structural steel; steel; sheet metalwork; fabricated plate work (boiler shop)

(G-11366)
NEIGHBORHOOD LOGISTICS CO INC
Also Called: Truckmen
5449 Bishop Rd (44041-9600)
PHONE................................440 466-0020
Jeff Jenks, *CEO*
Bruce Fleischmann, *President*
Julie Lefelhoc, *Corp Secy*
Dave Jewell, *Engrg Mgr*
David Jewell, *Director*
EMP: 34
SQ FT: 110,000
SALES (est): 10.1MM **Privately Held**
WEB: www.truckmen.com
SIC: 4213 4214 4212 Contract haulers; local trucking with storage; local trucking, without storage

(G-11367)
NURSING HOME MANAGEMENT INC
Also Called: Esther Marie Nursing Home
60 West St (44041-9723)
PHONE................................440 466-1181
Susan Knowson, *Owner*
Betty Velardo, *Office Mgr*
Sandy Szoka, *Director*
Mary Tobias, *Nursing Dir*
Rebecca Kahnell, *Social Dir*
EMP: 100
SALES (corp-wide): 5.2MM **Privately Held**
WEB: www.nursinghomemanagement.com
SIC: 8051 Skilled nursing care facilities
PA: Nursing Home Management Inc
2012 W War Memorial Dr
Peoria IL

(G-11368)
RAEANN INC
Also Called: Rae-Ann Geneva Skld Nrsng/Rehb
839 W Main St (44041-1218)
PHONE................................440 466-5733
Fax: 440 466-7944
Kathy Potter, *Facilities Dir*
Beth Cheney, *Pub Rel Dir*
John Griffiths, *Manager*
Theresa Jones, *Director*
Yasser Mikhail, *Director*
EMP: 80
SQ FT: 12,000
SALES (corp-wide): 7.7MM **Privately Held**
SIC: 8052 8051 Intermediate care facilities; skilled nursing care facilities
PA: Raeann Inc
Cleveland OH 44135
440 871-5181

(G-11369)
TEGAM INC (PA)
10 Tegam Way (44041-1144)
PHONE................................440 466-6100
Fax: 440 466-6110
Andrew Brush, *CEO*
Adam Fleder, *President*
Jacque Kato'schaefer, *Accountant*
EMP: 43
SQ FT: 28,600
SALES (est): 9.1MM **Privately Held**
WEB: www.tegam.com
SIC: 3829 7629 Measuring & controlling devices; electrical measuring instrument repair & calibration

(G-11370)
THIRD DIMENSION INC (PA)
633 Pleasant Ave (44041-1176)
PHONE................................877 926-3223
Fax: 440 466-3032
Jeanette De Jesus, *President*
Louis De Jesus, *Corp Secy*
Kyle Dejesus, *Opers Mgr*
Richard Patterson, *Controller*
Lori Brown, *Human Res Mgr*
EMP: 50
SQ FT: 180,000
SALES (est): 26.7MM **Privately Held**
WEB: www.dimensionthird.com
SIC: 7389 5199 7336 Packaging & labeling services; packaging materials; graphic arts & related design

(G-11371)
UHHS-MEMORIAL HOSP OF GENEVA
870 W Main St (44041-1219)
PHONE................................440 466-1141
Lisa Exl, *Human Res Dir*
Stephanie Truckey, *Nursing Mgr*
Stephanie Cleversy, *Manager*
John Baron, *Director*
Lori Boyce, *Director*
EMP: 183
SQ FT: 56,391
SALES (est): 10.6MM **Privately Held**
SIC: 8062 General medical & surgical hospitals

(G-11372)
VECTOR SECURITY INC
50 E Main St (44041-1347)
PHONE................................440 466-7233
Christine Longley, *Branch Mgr*
EMP: 32
SALES (corp-wide): 438MM **Privately Held**
SIC: 7382 1731 Burglar alarm maintenance & monitoring; fire detection & burglar alarm systems specialization
HQ: Vector Security Inc.
2000 Ericsson Dr Ste 250
Warrendale PA 15086
724 741-2200

(G-11373)
WASTE MANAGEMENT OHIO INC
4339 Tuttle Rd (44041-9231)
PHONE................................440 285-6767
Jan McCombs, *Branch Mgr*
Lee Hicks, *Contract Law*
EMP: 49
SALES (corp-wide): 14.4B **Publicly Held**
SIC: 4953 Refuse systems
HQ: Waste Management Of Ohio, Inc.
1700 N Broad St
Fairborn OH 45324

Genoa
Ottawa County

(G-11374)
ACCELERANT TECHNOLOGIES LLC
Also Called: Accelerant Solutions
2257 N Manor Dr (43430-9755)
PHONE................................419 236-8768
Larry Sanders, *President*
Gary Wylie, *Vice Pres*
Tyler Ball, *CFO*
Lynn Wight, *Manager*
Rudy Arn, *Director*
EMP: 58
SQ FT: 2,000
SALES: 20MM **Privately Held**
WEB: www.accelleranttech.com
SIC: 8711 8999 8742 Engineering services; energy conservation engineering; nuclear consultant; management consulting services

(G-11375)
CIMARRON EXPRESS INC
21611 State Route 51 W (43430-1245)
P.O. Box 185 (43430-0185)
PHONE................................419 855-7713
Fax: 419 855-7510
Glenn Grady, *President*
James Shepperd, *Senior VP*
Gale Johnson, *Vice Pres*
Bob Werth, *Vice Pres*
Mike Nopper, *Transptn Dir*
EMP: 65
SQ FT: 800
SALES: 25MM **Privately Held**
WEB: www.cimarronexpress.com
SIC: 4213 Contract haulers; automobiles, transport & delivery

(G-11376)
FIRST FEDERAL BANK OF MIDWEST
22020 Main St (43430)
PHONE................................419 855-8326
Jennifer Creager, *Branch Mgr*
EMP: 61 **Publicly Held**
SIC: 6035 Federal savings & loan associations
HQ: First Federal Bank Of The Midwest
601 Clinton St Ste 1
Defiance OH 43512
419 782-5015

(G-11377)
GENBANC
801 Main St (43430-1637)
P.O. Box 98 (43430-0098)
PHONE................................419 855-8381
Fax: 419 855-9006
Martin P Sutter, *President*
Margaret Haar, *Assistant VP*
Jean Holcombe, *Assistant VP*
Patricia Kelley, *Assistant VP*
Rochelle Wheeler, *Assistant VP*
EMP: 50 **Privately Held**
SIC: 6712 Bank holding companies

(G-11378)
GENOA BANKING COMPANY (PA)
801 Main St (43430-1637)
P.O. Box 98 (43430-0098)
PHONE................................419 855-8381
Fax: 419 855-3789
Martin Sutter, *President*
Ron Gladieux, *Chairman*
Jaime Buhrow, *Assistant VP*
Barbara Fleitz, *Assistant VP*
Tom Milam, *Assistant VP*
EMP: 29
SQ FT: 10,000
SALES: 15.5MM **Privately Held**
WEB: www.genoabank.com
SIC: 6022 State trust companies accepting deposits, commercial

(G-11379)
GENOA LEGION POST 324
302 West St (43430)
PHONE................................419 855-7049
Virgil Roecker, *President*
EMP: 30
SALES (est): 290.4K **Privately Held**
WEB: www.genoavetshome.us
SIC: 8641 Veterans' organization

(G-11380)
JAMES RECKER
Also Called: Recker Brothers
1446 Ottawa Rd (43430-9502)
PHONE................................419 837-5378
James Recker, *Owner*
Jack Recker, *Partner*
EMP: 25
SALES (est): 654.9K **Privately Held**
SIC: 0171 Strawberry farm

(G-11381)
MCCLELLAN MANAGEMENT INC
Also Called: Genoa Care Center
300 Cherry St (43430-1823)
PHONE................................419 855-7755
Fax: 419 855-4047
William Mc Clellan, *President*
Rhonda Mull, *Human Res Dir*
Julie McKitrick, *Director*
Duane Sander, *Director*
Josh Mc Clellan, *Administration*
EMP: 124
SQ FT: 20,000
SALES (est): 2.5MM **Privately Held**
SIC: 8051 8052 Convalescent home with continuous nursing care; intermediate care facilities

(G-11382)
MIKE GEORGE EXCAVATING
24366 W Hellwig Rd (43430-9720)
PHONE................................419 855-4147
Mike George, *Owner*
EMP: 35
SALES (est): 1.2MM **Privately Held**
SIC: 1794 Excavation work

Georgetown
Brown County

(G-11383)
ADAMS & BROWN COUNTIES ECONOMI (PA)
406 W Plum St (45121-1056)
PHONE................................937 378-6041
Fax: 937 378-3039
Alvin M Norris, *Director*

Loriane Hafitald, *Admin Sec*
EMP: 230
SQ FT: 10,000
SALES: 10.4MM *Privately Held*
SIC: 8399 Community action agency

(G-11384)
BROWN CNTY BD MNTAL RTARDATION
325 W State St Ste A2 (45121-1262)
PHONE.................................937 378-4891
Theresa Armstrong, *Principal*
Lena Bradford, *Principal*
EMP: 35
SQ FT: 100,000
SALES: 131.9K *Privately Held*
SIC: 8331 3993 2396 Sheltered workshop; signs & advertising specialties; automotive & apparel trimmings

(G-11385)
BROWN CNTY SNIOR CTZEN COUNCIL
505 N Main St (45121-1029)
PHONE: 937 378-6603
Fax: 937 378-2560
Sue Brooks, *Director*
Conney Taylor, *Administration*
EMP: 50
SALES: 1.1MM *Privately Held*
SIC: 8322 Senior citizens' center or association

(G-11386)
BROWN CO ED SERVICE CENTER
9231b Hamer Rd (45121-1527)
PHONE.................................937 378-6118
James D Fraizer, *Superintendent*
James Frazier, *Superintendent*
Robert Henry, *Superintendent*
Robin Tore, *Principal*
Sally Frydryk, *Purch Dir*
EMP: 100
SALES: 4.7MM *Privately Held*
WEB: www.brown.k12.oh.us
SIC: 8211 8741 Specialty education; management services

(G-11387)
BROWN COUNTY ASPHALT INC
11254 Hamer Rd (45121-8840)
PHONE.................................937 446-2481
Fax: 937 446-2481
Thomas Sawyer, *President*
Andrew Sawyers, *Vice Pres*
Duane Sawyers, *Vice Pres*
Joseph Sawyers, *Vice Pres*
Connie Sawyer, *Treasurer*
EMP: 25 EST: 1976
SALES (est): 2.8MM *Privately Held*
SIC: 1771 Blacktop (asphalt) work

(G-11388)
CAHALL BROS INC (PA)
Also Called: John Deere Authorized Dealer
50 Cahall Brothers Ln (45121-9077)
PHONE.................................937 378-4439
Fax: 937 378-4283
Calvin H Cahall, *President*
Roland Cahall, *Corp Secy*
Kyle Cahall, *Vice Pres*
Beth Louden, *Manager*
EMP: 25
SQ FT: 43,000
SALES (est): 6.8MM *Privately Held*
WEB: www.cahallbrosinc.com
SIC: 5083 Farm implements

(G-11389)
CHARLES D MCINTOSH TRCKG INC
669 E State St (45121-9323)
P.O. Box 21399 (45121-0399)
PHONE.................................937 378-3803
Donald Layman, *President*
EMP: 40
SALES: 2MM *Privately Held*
SIC: 4212 Local trucking, without storage

(G-11390)
COUNTY OF BROWN
Also Called: Brown County Engineers Office
25 Veterans Blvd (45121-7417)
PHONE.................................937 378-6456
Fax: 937 378-4175
Todd Cluxton, *Chief Engr*
James Beasley, *Branch Mgr*
EMP: 35 *Privately Held*
WEB: www.browncohd.org
SIC: 8711 Engineering services
PA: Brown County
  800 Mount Orab Pike
  Georgetown OH 45121
  937 378-3956

(G-11391)
COUNTY OF BROWN
Also Called: Department of Human Services
775 Mount Orab Pike (45121-1123)
P.O. Box 21169 (45121-0169)
PHONE.................................937 378-6104
Fax: 937 378-4753
David M Sharp, *Branch Mgr*
EMP: 45 *Privately Held*
WEB: www.browncohd.org
SIC: 8322 9111 Public welfare center; county supervisors' & executives' offices
PA: Brown County
  800 Mount Orab Pike
  Georgetown OH 45121
  937 378-3956

(G-11392)
COVENANT CARE OHIO INC
Also Called: Villa Georgetown
8065 Dr Faul Rd (45121-8811)
PHONE.................................937 378-0188
Fax: 937 378-3107
Sandra Leedy, *Manager*
Jeffery Donahoo, *Director*
Tracy White Rn, *Nursing Dir*
EMP: 75 *Privately Held*
WEB: www.villageorgetown.com
SIC: 8051 Skilled nursing care facilities
HQ: Covenant Care Ohio, Inc.
  27071 Aliso Creek Rd # 100
  Aliso Viejo CA 92656
  949 349-1200

(G-11393)
DAVITA INC
458 Home St (45121-1408)
PHONE.................................615 341-6311
James Hilger, *Branch Mgr*
EMP: 25 *Publicly Held*
SIC: 8011 Offices & clinics of medical doctors
PA: Davita Inc.
  2000 16th St
  Denver CO 80202

(G-11394)
GEORGETOWN LIFE SQUAD
301 S Main St Unit 1 (45121-1500)
P.O. Box 21184 (45121-0184)
PHONE.................................937 378-3082
Fax: 937 378-4709
Brian Dutlinger, *Director*
Anita McKenzie, *Admin Sec*
EMP: 30
SALES (est): 272.5K *Privately Held*
SIC: 4119 Ambulance service

(G-11395)
HEALTHSOURCE OF OHIO INC
Also Called: Southern Ohio Health
631 E State St (45121-1437)
PHONE.................................937 392-4381
Fax: 937 392-4383
Tammy Thackston, *Office Mgr*
Broderick King, *Internal Med*
Samantha King, *Pediatrics*
Angie Berryman, *Nurse*
Angie King, *Assistant*
EMP: 36
SALES (corp-wide): 38.7MM *Privately Held*
SIC: 8011 Pediatrician; internal medicine, physician/surgeon
PA: Healthsource Of Ohio, Inc.
  5400 Dupont Cir Ste A
  Milford OH 45150
  513 576-7700

(G-11396)
RELIABLE TRNSP SOLUTIONS LLC
Also Called: RTS
642 E State St (45121-9317)
P.O. Box 507, Amelia (45102-0507)
PHONE.................................937 378-2700
Fax: 937 378-5376
Ben Bird, *COO*
Matt Moss, *Executive*
Lucas Brown,
Garry Fletcher,
EMP: 47
SQ FT: 5,000
SALES (est): 19.3MM *Privately Held*
SIC: 4731 Transportation agents & brokers

(G-11397)
RUMPKE WASTE INC
9427 Beyers Rd (45121-9301)
PHONE.................................937 378-4126
Fax: 937 378-4799
Ronda Yates, *Manager*
Jerry Metzger, *Manager*
EMP: 55 *Privately Held*
SIC: 4953 4212 Refuse collection & disposal services; local trucking, without storage
HQ: Rumpke Waste, Inc.
  10795 Hughes Rd
  Cincinnati OH 45251
  513 851-0122

(G-11398)
SOUTHWEST HEALTHCARE OF BROWN
Also Called: Southwest Regional Medical Ctr
425 Home St (45121-1407)
P.O. Box 62609, Cincinnati (45262-0609)
PHONE.................................937 378-7800
Fax: 937 378-1431
Neil Cutter, *Regional Mgr*
Charles Hatfield, *Controller*
Matt Hess, *Personnel Exec*
Leonard Horwitz, *Med Doctor*
James Leonard, *Med Doctor*
EMP: 82 EST: 1952
SQ FT: 120,000
SALES: 25.2MM *Privately Held*
SIC: 8062 General medical & surgical hospitals

Germantown
Montgomery County

(G-11399)
OREILLY AUTOMOTIVE INC
2381 Beechwood Dr (45327-9463)
PHONE.................................937 660-3040
Tobias Vaughn, *Owner*
EMP: 35 *Publicly Held*
SIC: 7538 General automotive repair shops
PA: O'reilly Automotive, Inc.
  233 S Patterson Ave
  Springfield MO 65802

(G-11400)
ORWELL COMMUNICATIONS INC
Also Called: Fairpoint Long Distance
48130102 (45327)
PHONE.................................937 855-6511
EMP: 49
SALES (est): 828.1K
SALES (corp-wide): 1B *Publicly Held*
SIC: 4813 Local telephone communications
HQ: Fairpoint Communications, Inc.
  121 S 17th St
  Mattoon IL 61938

(G-11401)
QUALITY ONE TECHNOLOGIES INC
Also Called: Fairpoint Long Distance
36 N Plum St (45327-1358)
PHONE.................................937 855-6511
EMP: 49
SALES (est): 1MM
SALES (corp-wide): 1B *Publicly Held*
SIC: 4813 Local telephone communications
HQ: Fairpoint Communications, Inc.
  121 S 17th St
  Mattoon IL 61938

Gibsonburg
Sandusky County

(G-11402)
GIBSONBURG HEALTH LLC
Also Called: Windsor Lane Health Care
355 Windsor Ln (43431-1446)
PHONE.................................419 637-2104
Jack Hereth, *Mng Member*
Angela Ickes, *Food Svc Dir*
Darla Boster, *Hlthcr Dir*
EMP: 110
SALES (est): 6MM *Privately Held*
SIC: 8051 Skilled nursing care facilities

(G-11403)
MIARER TRANSPORTATION INC
2930 County Road 69 (43431-9709)
PHONE.................................419 665-2334
Fax: 419 665-2456
Thomas H Miarer, *President*
Anida Miarer, *Vice Pres*
EMP: 30
SQ FT: 5,500
SALES: 2MM *Privately Held*
SIC: 4213 Trucking, except local

(G-11404)
STOUT LORI CLEANING & SUCH
503 N Main St (43431-1113)
PHONE.................................419 637-7644
Lori Stout, *Owner*
EMP: 40
SALES (est): 717K *Privately Held*
SIC: 7349 7359 Building cleaning service; home cleaning & maintenance equipment rental services

(G-11405)
WESTFIELD ELECTRIC INC
2995 State Route 51 (43431-9710)
P.O. Box 93 (43431-0093)
PHONE.................................419 862-0078
Fax: 419 862-0079
Sheri M Busdeker, *CEO*
Thomas R Busdeker, *President*
Brian Freeman, *Vice Pres*
Ty Hamman, *Project Mgr*
Mark Younker, *Project Mgr*
EMP: 35
SQ FT: 10,000
SALES: 5MM *Privately Held*
SIC: 1731 5063 General electrical contractor; electrical construction materials

Girard
Trumbull County

(G-11406)
AIM INTEGRATED LOGISTICS INC
Also Called: NationaLease
1500 Trumbull Ave (44420-3453)
PHONE.................................330 759-0438
Thomas J Fleming, *President*
EMP: 400
SALES (est): 46.8MM
SALES (corp-wide): 279.8MM *Privately Held*
WEB: www.aimnationalease.com
SIC: 4212 7513 8741 Truck rental with drivers; truck leasing, without drivers; management services
PA: Aim Leasing Company
  1500 Trumbull Ave
  Girard OH 44420
  330 759-0438

(G-11407)
AIM LEASING COMPANY (PA)
Also Called: NationaLease
1500 Trumbull Ave (44420-3453)
PHONE.................................330 759-0438

Girard - Trumbull County (G-11408)

Fax: 330 759-3721
Thomas Fleming, *President*
David Gurska, *President*
Rudy Corpus, *Business Mgr*
Terry Dimascio, *Vice Pres*
Bob Penton, *Vice Pres*
EMP: 60
SQ FT: 10,000
SALES (est): 279.8MM **Privately Held**
WEB: www.aimnationalease.com
SIC: 7513 7538 4212 5983 Truck leasing, without drivers; general truck repair; truck rental with drivers; fuel oil dealers

(G-11408)
BOARDMAN MEDICAL SUPPLY CO (HQ)
Also Called: Innovative Concept
300 N State St (44420-2595)
PHONE 330 545-6700
Fax: 330 545-8601
Felix S Savon, *President*
Robin S Ivany, *Vice Pres*
Christine E Savon, *Treasurer*
Tess Crofford, *Exec Sec*
▲ **EMP:** 130
SQ FT: 3,400
SALES (est): 39.1MM **Privately Held**
WEB: www.boardmanmedicalsupply.com
SIC: 5999 7352 Hospital equipment & supplies; medical equipment rental
PA: Sateri Home Inc
  7246 Ronjoy Pl
  Youngstown OH 44512
  330 758-8106

(G-11409)
CINTAS CORPORATION NO 2
1061 Trumbull Ave (44420-3484)
PHONE 440 746-7777
EMP: 88
SALES (corp-wide): 5.3B **Publicly Held**
SIC: 7218 Industrial uniform supply
HQ: Cintas Corporation No. 2
  6800 Cintas Blvd
  Mason OH 45040

(G-11410)
COMDOC INC
6790 Belmont Ave (44420-1306)
PHONE 330 539-4822
Fax: 330 539-4754
Syl Frazzini, *Manager*
Carol Jackson, *Admin Asst*
EMP: 50
SALES (corp-wide): 10.2B **Publicly Held**
SIC: 5044 Photocopy machines
HQ: Comdoc, Inc.
  3458 Massillon Rd
  Uniontown OH 44685
  330 896-2346

(G-11411)
COMMERCIAL TRUCK & TRAILER
Also Called: Commercial Truck & Trlr Parts
313 N State St (44420-2539)
P.O. Box 179 (44420-0179)
PHONE 330 545-9717
Fax: 330 545-2314
Orren W Zook Jr, *President*
Dan Gleydura, *General Mgr*
Bruce Zook, *Vice Pres*
Kevin Zook, *Manager*
EMP: 26
SQ FT: 19,600
SALES (est): 5.6MM **Privately Held**
WEB: www.goctt.com
SIC: 5013 7538 Truck parts & accessories; general truck repair

(G-11412)
CREEKSIDE GOLF DOME
1300 N State St (44420-3642)
PHONE 330 545-5000
Fax: 330 545-5052
Tonny Latell, *President*
Jim St George, *President*
Todd Latell, *Principal*
Paul Latell, *Corp Secy*
EMP: 25
SALES (est): 640.8K **Privately Held**
WEB: www.creeksidegolfdome.com
SIC: 7999 Golf services & professionals; golf driving range; miniature golf course operation

(G-11413)
FIRE FOE CORP
999 Trumbull Ave (44420-3400)
PHONE 330 759-9834
Earnest A Nicholas, *President*
Jim Caldwell, *Division Mgr*
Thomas Spain, *Safety Dir*
Jamie Wilcox, *Controller*
Mary Nicholas, *Admin Sec*
EMP: 35
SQ FT: 18,000
SALES (est): 4.5MM **Privately Held**
WEB: www.firefoe.com
SIC: 3569 7699 Sprinkler systems, fire: automatic; fire control (military) equipment repair

(G-11414)
INDUSTRIAL INSUL COATINGS LLC
142 E 2nd St (44420-2905)
P.O. Box 154 (44420-0154)
PHONE 800 506-1399
Richard Marchese,
Edward Zajac,
John Zajac,
EMP: 28
SALES: 5.5MM **Privately Held**
SIC: 1742 7389 Insulation, buildings;

(G-11415)
INTERSTATE SHREDDING LLC
27 Furnace Ln (44420-3214)
P.O. Box 29 (44420-0029)
PHONE 330 545-5477
Gary Chandler, *General Mgr*
Gary Clayman, *Mng Member*
Barbara Ruftner, *Manager*
Michael Clayman,
Ron Hulett, *Regional*
▲ **EMP:** 40
SQ FT: 14,374
SALES (est): 9.1MM **Privately Held**
SIC: 4953 Recycling, waste materials

(G-11416)
JPMORGAN CHASE BANK NAT ASSN
43 W Liberty St (44420-2842)
PHONE 330 545-2551
Gene Tropf, *Manager*
EMP: 26
SALES (corp-wide): 99.6B **Publicly Held**
WEB: www.chase.com
SIC: 6021 National commercial banks
HQ: Jpmorgan Chase Bank, National Association
  1111 Polaris Pkwy
  Columbus OH 43240
  614 436-3055

(G-11417)
JUNIOR ACHVMENT MHNING VLY INC
1601 Motor Inn Dr Ste 305 (44420-2483)
PHONE 330 539-5268
Michele Merkel, *President*
Brian Hoopes, *Chairman*
Kevin Murphy, *Admin Sec*
EMP: 30
SQ FT: 1,200
SALES: 323.5K **Privately Held**
SIC: 8641 Educator's association

(G-11418)
K & M CONTRACTING OHIO INC
5635 Sampson Dr (44420-3510)
P.O. Box 528, Vienna (44473-0528)
PHONE 330 759-1090
Fax: 330 759-1091
Kristenlynn Chizmar, *President*
Michael Chizmar, *Project Mgr*
Ken Slanco, *Project Mgr*
EMP: 35
SQ FT: 2,200
SALES (est): 14.9MM **Privately Held**
SIC: 5082 General construction machinery & equipment

(G-11419)
KEYSTONE AUTOMOTIVE INDS INC
1282 Trumbull Ave Ste C (44420-3475)
PHONE 330 759-8019
Fax: 330 759-8492
Marty Grzybowski, *Manager*
EMP: 27
SALES (corp-wide): 9.7B **Publicly Held**
WEB: www.kool-vue.com
SIC: 5013 Motor vehicle supplies & new parts
HQ: Keystone Automotive Industries, Inc.
  655 Grassmere Park
  Nashville TN 37211
  615 781-5200

(G-11420)
MAHONING COUNTRY CLUB INC
710 E Liberty St (44420-2310)
PHONE 330 545-2517
Fax: 330 545-2501
John Ezzo, *President*
Dave Ezzo, *Vice Pres*
Susan Sigulee, *Admin Sec*
EMP: 30
SQ FT: 50,000
SALES (est): 1.5MM **Privately Held**
WEB: www.mahoningcountryclub.com
SIC: 5812 7992 5941 Eating places; public golf courses; sporting goods & bicycle shops

(G-11421)
OHIO MACHINERY CO
Also Called: Caterpillar Authorized Dealer
1 Ohio Machinery Blvd (44420-3198)
PHONE 330 530-9010
Fax: 330 530-9102
Sandy Federico, *Credit Staff*
Joe Mashchak, *Sales Staff*
Bob Reninger, *Sales Staff*
Ralph Binder, *Marketing Staff*
Glen Smith, *Manager*
EMP: 50
SQ FT: 10,000
SALES (corp-wide): 222.7MM **Privately Held**
WEB: www.enginesnow.com
SIC: 7699 5082 7353 Construction equipment repair; general construction machinery & equipment; heavy construction equipment rental
PA: Ohio Machinery Co.
  3993 E Royalton Rd
  Broadview Heights OH 44147
  440 526-6200

(G-11422)
OLD DOMINION FREIGHT LINE INC
1730 N State St (44420-1026)
PHONE 330 545-8628
Fax: 330 545-8670
Dave Robert, *Manager*
EMP: 48
SQ FT: 960
SALES (corp-wide): 3.3B **Publicly Held**
WEB: www.odfl.com
SIC: 4213 Less-than-truckload (LTL) transport
PA: Old Dominion Freight Line Inc
  500 Old Dominion Way
  Thomasville NC 27360
  336 889-5000

(G-11423)
OMNI MANOR INC (PA)
101 W Liberty St (44420-2844)
PHONE 330 545-1550
John Masternick, *President*
Leo Grimes, *Vice Pres*
Dorothy Masternick, *Treasurer*
Kelly Russ, *Hum Res Coord*
EMP: 200
SALES: 57.8MM **Privately Held**
SIC: 8051 Convalescent home with continuous nursing care

(G-11424)
PREMIER INTEGRATION
50 Harry St (44420-1709)
PHONE 330 545-8690
Fax: 330 545-8691
Richard Deeds, *Principal*
Dave Stierheim, *Electrical Engi*
EMP: 26
SALES (est): 4.6MM **Privately Held**
SIC: 8711 Professional engineer

(G-11425)
RICKS HAIR CENTER
27 Churchill Rd (44420-1864)
PHONE 330 545-5120
Richard Calve, *Principal*
EMP: 25
SALES (est): 194.6K **Privately Held**
SIC: 7241 Barber shops

(G-11426)
SOFT TOUCH WOOD LLC
Also Called: Soft Tuch Furn Repr Rfinishing
1560 S State St (44420-3315)
PHONE 330 545-4204
Fax: 330 288-0083
Terry Chudakoff, *President*
Anne Kirkpatrick, *Sales Associate*
Bob Leer, *Manager*
EMP: 40
SQ FT: 5,000
SALES (est): 2MM **Privately Held**
WEB: www.softtouchwood.com
SIC: 7641 2531 Furniture refinishing; public building & related furniture

(G-11427)
UNITED PARCEL SERVICE INC OH
Also Called: UPS
800 Trumbull Ave (44420-3445)
PHONE 330 545-0177
Paul Hammond, *Manager*
EMP: 209
SALES (corp-wide): 65.8B **Publicly Held**
WEB: www.upsscs.com
SIC: 4215 Parcel delivery, vehicular
HQ: United Parcel Service, Inc. (Oh)
  55 Glenlake Pkwy
  Atlanta GA 30328
  404 828-6000

(G-11428)
UNIVERSAL DEVELOPMENT MGT INC (PA)
Also Called: Howard Johnson
1607 Motor Inn Dr Ste 1 (44420-2496)
PHONE 330 759-7017
Fax: 330 759-4254
Ronald R Anderson, *President*
Gayle Anderson, *Managing Prtnr*
Melissa Anderson, *Managing Prtnr*
Harold J Anderson, *Vice Pres*
Dave Tybursky, *Controller*
EMP: 30
SQ FT: 12,000
SALES (est): 8.9MM **Privately Held**
SIC: 6513 1542 Apartment building operators; nonresidential construction

(G-11429)
VALLEY ELECTRICAL CNSLD INC
977 Tibbetts Wick Rd (44420-1133)
PHONE 330 539-4044
Fax: 330 539-4030
Rex Ferry, *President*
Tom Markovich, *General Mgr*
Jack Morse, *Business Mgr*
Mary Ferry, *Corp Secy*
Jeff Barber, *Exec VP*
EMP: 135
SQ FT: 17,200
SALES: 18.9MM **Privately Held**
WEB: www.vecohio.com
SIC: 1731 General electrical contractor

(G-11430)
VEC INC
977 Tibbetts Wick Rd (44420-1133)
PHONE 330 539-4044
Rex A Ferry, *President*
Jeff Barber, *General Mgr*
Mark Davis, *Superintendent*
Keith Frederick, *Superintendent*
Jason McClellan, *Opers Mgr*
EMP: 50 **EST:** 1965
SQ FT: 8,000
SALES: 71MM **Privately Held**
WEB: www.evetselectric.com
SIC: 1731 General electrical contractor

GEOGRAPHIC SECTION

Grand Rapids - Wood County (G-11454)

(G-11431)
YOUNGSTOWN WINDOW CLEANING CO
1057 Trumbull Ave Ste G (44420-3489)
PHONE..................330 743-3880
Fax: 330 743-6296
Steven Altman, *President*
Sandra Altman, *President*
Carol Altamn, *Vice Pres*
Stacy Lynn, *Office Mgr*
Gary Barker, *Manager*
EMP: 150
SQ FT: 12,000
SALES (est): 2.8MM **Privately Held**
SIC: 7349 Janitorial service, contract basis; window cleaning

Glandorf
Putnam County

(G-11432)
ST RITAS MEDICAL CENTER
Also Called: Catholic Health Partners
601 Us 224 (45848)
P.O. Box 100 (45848-0100)
PHONE..................419 538-6288
Karen Zorst, *Manager*
EMP: 50
SALES (corp-wide): 4.2B **Privately Held**
SIC: 8062 General medical & surgical hospitals
HQ: St. Rita's Medical Center
730 W Market St
Lima OH 45801
419 227-3361

Glenford
Perry County

(G-11433)
PIONEER SANDS LLC
Also Called: Glassrock Plant
2446 State Route 204 (43739-9789)
PHONE..................740 659-2241
Fax: 740 659-2348
Paul Currant, *Maint Mgr*
Jennifer Mulherin, *Financial Exec*
Wayn Dailey, *Manager*
EMP: 40
SALES (corp-wide): 5.4B **Publicly Held**
SIC: 3295 1446 Minerals, ground or treated; industrial sand
HQ: Pioneer Sands Llc
5205 N O Connor Blvd # 200
Irving TX 75039
972 444-9001

Glouster
Athens County

(G-11434)
HOCKING COLLEGE ADDC
19234 Taylor Ridge Rd (45732-9258)
PHONE..................740 541-2221
Larry Sisson, *Owner*
EMP: 40
SALES (est): 245.6K **Privately Held**
SIC: 8322 Drug abuse counselor, nontreatment

(G-11435)
HOCKINGTHENSPERRY CMNTY ACTION (PA)
3 Cardaras Dr (45732-8011)
P.O. Box 220 (45732-0220)
PHONE..................740 767-4500
Joyce Rinehart, *Payroll Mgr*
Diana Campbell, *Manager*
Doug Stanley, *Exec Dir*
Douglas Stanley, *Exec Dir*
Chris Delamatre, *Director*
EMP: 40 **EST:** 1966
SQ FT: 7,400
SALES: 12MM **Privately Held**
SIC: 8399 8331 8322 Community action agency; job training & vocational rehabilitation services; individual & family services

(G-11436)
U S ARMY CORPS OF ENGINEERS
23560 Jenkins Dam Rd (45732-9727)
PHONE..................740 767-3527
EMP: 66 **Publicly Held**
SIC: 8711 Engineering Services
HQ: U S Army Corps Of Engineers
441 G Street Nw
Washington DC 20314
804 435-9362

Goshen
Clermont County

(G-11437)
NORTHERN PLUMBING SYSTEMS
1708 State Route 28 (45122-9754)
PHONE..................513 831-5111
Fax: 513 831-5101
Timothy Moss,
Steward Moss Jr,
EMP: 31
SALES (est): 3.6MM **Privately Held**
SIC: 1711 Plumbing contractors

(G-11438)
PETERMAN
Also Called: School Bus Garage
6757 Linton Rd (45122-9402)
PHONE..................513 722-2229
Janet Wilson, *Principal*
EMP: 40
SALES (est): 925.2K **Privately Held**
WEB: www.peterman.com
SIC: 4151 School buses

(G-11439)
SDR SERVICES LLC
2109 State Route 28 B (45122-9561)
PHONE..................513 625-0695
Amber Stephens, *CEO*
Greg Pilot, *CFO*
EMP: 34
SALES (est): 1.4MM **Privately Held**
SIC: 7631 Jewelry repair services

Grafton
Lorain County

(G-11440)
CHEMICAL BANK
351 Main St (44044-1203)
PHONE..................440 926-2191
Gretchan Francis, *Branch Mgr*
EMP: 39
SALES (corp-wide): 776.1MM **Publicly Held**
SIC: 6035 Federal savings & loan associations
HQ: Chemical Bank
333 E Main St
Midland MI 48640
989 631-9200

(G-11441)
JOSEPH RUSSO
Also Called: Eaton Tire & Auto Parts
12044 Island Rd (44044-9538)
PHONE..................440 748-2690
Fax: 440 748-2690
Joseph Russo, *Owner*
EMP: 26
SQ FT: 30,000
SALES (est): 1.7MM **Privately Held**
WEB: www.josephrusso.com
SIC: 5531 5013 5014 7538 Automotive parts; automotive tires; automotive supplies & parts; tires & tubes; general automotive repair shops

(G-11442)
M P & A FIBERS INC
1024 Commerce Dr (44044-1277)
PHONE..................440 926-1074
Bill Crosby, *President*
Kristen Hardman, *Manager*
EMP: 35
SALES (est): 1.1MM **Privately Held**
SIC: 7389 Packaging & labeling services

(G-11443)
PINE BROOK GOLF CLUB INC
11043 Durkee Rd (44044-9108)
PHONE..................440 748-2939
EMP: 30
SQ FT: 4,800
SALES (est): 646.7K **Privately Held**
SIC: 7992 5812 5941 Public Golf Course Catering Facilities Snack Bar And Pro Shop

(G-11444)
ROSS CONSOLIDATED CORP (PA)
36790 Giles Rd (44044-9125)
PHONE..................440 748-5800
Maureen Cromling, *President*
Andy Janish, *Engineer*
Irene Garsky, *Personnel*
Bob Browne, *Sr Project Mgr*
Tony Fought, *Supervisor*
EMP: 70
SQ FT: 3,008
SALES (est): 65.2MM **Privately Held**
SIC: 4953 4212 8741 Incinerator operation; local trucking, without storage; management services

(G-11445)
ROSS INCINERATION SERVICES INC
36790 Giles Rd (44044-9125)
PHONE..................440 366-2000
Arthur Hargate, *CEO*
Maureen M Cromling, *Ch of Bd*
James Larson, *President*
Cliff Goytowski, *Exec VP*
Pat Lawson, *VP Admin*
▼ **EMP:** 115 **EST:** 1981
SALES (est): 32.4MM
SALES (corp-wide): 65.2MM **Privately Held**
SIC: 4953 Incinerator operation
PA: Ross Consolidated Corp
36790 Giles Rd
Grafton OH 44044
440 748-5800

(G-11446)
ROSS TRANSPORTATION SVCS INC
36790 Giles Rd (44044-9125)
PHONE..................440 748-5900
Fax: 440 366-2322
William E Cromling II, *President*
Joe Calderoni, *Regl Sales Mgr*
Dawn Palmer, *Executive Asst*
EMP: 250 **EST:** 1981
SALES (est): 32.1MM
SALES (corp-wide): 65.2MM **Privately Held**
WEB: www.rosstransportation.com
SIC: 4213 Contract haulers
PA: Ross Consolidated Corp
36790 Giles Rd
Grafton OH 44044
440 748-5800

Grand Rapids
Wood County

(G-11447)
4 PAWS SAKE INC
13244 Neowash Rd (43522-9657)
PHONE..................419 304-7139
Cindy Smith, *President*
Linda Boyle, *Vice Pres*
EMP: 50
SALES: 13.2K **Privately Held**
SIC: 0752 Grooming services, pet & animal specialties

(G-11448)
AE ELECTRIC INC
T483 County Road 1 (43522-9507)
P.O. Box 2744, Whitehouse (43571-0744)
PHONE..................419 392-8468
Fax: 419 392-2260
Ken Bialecki, *President*
Lori Womack, *Bookkeeper*
EMP: 25
SALES: 1.5MM **Privately Held**
SIC: 1731 Electrical work

(G-11449)
HALL NAZARETH INC
21211 W State Route 65 (43522-9818)
PHONE..................419 832-2900
Fax: 419 832-3700
Robert Bettinger, *Admin Sec*
EMP: 100
SALES (est): 7.6MM **Privately Held**
WEB: www.nazarethhall.com
SIC: 6512 7299 Auditorium & hall operation; wedding chapel, privately operated

(G-11450)
HERTZFELD POULTRY FARMS INC
15799 Milton Rd (43522-9761)
PHONE..................419 832-2070
Dave Hertzfeld, *Owner*
Shawna Gebhart, *Controller*
Kathleen Hertzfeld, *Manager*
EMP: 80
SALES (corp-wide): 6MM **Privately Held**
WEB: www.hpfeggs.com
SIC: 0191 0751 0119 General farms, primarily crop; poultry services; popcorn farm
PA: Hertzfeld Poultry Farms, Inc.
8525 Schadel Rd
Waterville OH

(G-11451)
KERR HOUSE INC
17777 Beaver St (43522-9496)
P.O. Box 363 (43522-0363)
PHONE..................419 832-1733
Fax: 419 832-4303
EMP: 30
SQ FT: 10,000
SALES (est): 920K **Privately Held**
SIC: 7991 7231 Physical Fitness Facility Beauty Shop

(G-11452)
PIONEER HI-BRED INTL INC
15180 Henry Wood Rd (43522-9772)
PHONE..................419 748-8051
Scott Millikan, *Manager*
EMP: 35
SQ FT: 6,000
SALES (corp-wide): 62.4B **Publicly Held**
WEB: www.pioneer.com
SIC: 5191 5153 2075 2041 Seeds: field, garden & flower; corn; soybeans; soybean oil mills; flour & other grain mill products
HQ: Pioneer Hi-Bred International, Inc.
7100 Nw 62nd Ave
Johnston IA 50131
515 535-3200

(G-11453)
RAPIDS NURSING HOMES INC
Also Called: Grand Rapids Care Center
24201 W 3rd St (43522-8702)
PHONE..................216 292-5706
Fax: 419 832-4205
Robert Tebeau, *President*
Ernest Tebeau, *Corp Secy*
Ronald Tebeau, *Vice Pres*
Barb Brigode, *Manager*
EMP: 50
SALES (est): 2.1MM **Privately Held**
SIC: 0051 Skilled nursing care facilities

(G-11454)
SABER HEALTHCARE GROUP LLC
Also Called: Grand Rapids Care Center
24201 W 3rd St (43522-8702)
PHONE..................419 484-1111
Natasha Bailey, *Administration*
EMP: 50
SALES (corp-wide): 68.5MM **Privately Held**
SIC: 8051 Skilled nursing care facilities
PA: Saber Healthcare Group, L.L.C.
26691 Richmond Rd Frnt
Bedford OH 44146
216 292-5706

Grand River
Lake County

(G-11455)
101 RIVER INC
Also Called: Grand River Seafood Supply
101 River St (44045-8212)
P.O. Box 120 (44045-0120)
PHONE..................................440 352-6343
Fax: 440 352-0904
Gerald Powell, *President*
Thomas O'Neil, *Accountant*
Marilyn Merker, *Office Mgr*
Jerry Powell, *Executive*
EMP: 50
SQ FT: 7,000
SALES (est): 2MM Privately Held
WEB: www.101riverviews.com
SIC: 5812 5146 Steak & barbecue restaurants; fish & seafoods

(G-11456)
JED INDUSTRIES INC
320 River St (44045-8214)
P.O. Box 369 (44045-0369)
PHONE..................................440 639-9973
Fax: 440 639-9796
Donald Nye, *President*
Barb Nye, *Manager*
EMP: 25
SQ FT: 27,000
SALES (est): 4MM Privately Held
WEB: www.jedindustries.com
SIC: 3599 5084 Machine & other job shop work; industrial machinery & equipment

(G-11457)
OSBORNE MATERIALS COMPANY (PA)
1 Williams St (44045-8253)
P.O. Box 248 (44045-0248)
PHONE..................................440 357-7026
Harold T Larned, *President*
Gary D Bradler, *President*
David Baczek, *Accountant*
▼ EMP: 41
SQ FT: 2,500
SALES (est): 7.1MM Privately Held
SIC: 1442 Sand mining; gravel mining

Granville
Licking County

(G-11458)
BIG O REFUSE INC
1919 Lancaster Rd Ste B (43023-9417)
P.O. Box 625, New Lexington (43764-0625)
PHONE..................................740 344-7544
Sherman Adkins Sr, *President*
Ralph Adkins Sr, *Vice Pres*
EMP: 30
SALES (est): 5.6MM Privately Held
SIC: 4953 Rubbish collection & disposal

(G-11459)
BUXTON INN INC
313 Broadway E (43023-1307)
PHONE..................................740 587-0001
Fax: 740 587-1460
Audrey V Orr, *Vice Pres*
Orville O Orr, *Manager*
EMP: 40
SQ FT: 20,000
SALES (est): 1.6MM Privately Held
WEB: www.buxtoninn.com
SIC: 5812 7011 Eating places; hotels

(G-11460)
CENTRAL OHIO GERIATRICS LLC
590 Newark Granville Rd (43023-1436)
PHONE..................................614 530-4077
John Weigand, *CEO*
EMP: 36 EST: 2009
SALES (est): 432.6K Privately Held
SIC: 8011 Primary care medical clinic

(G-11461)
CHESROWN OLDSMOBILE CADILLAC
Also Called: Chesrown Cadillac
371 Bryn Du Dr (43023-1512)
PHONE..................................740 366-7373
Fax: 740 366-5685
David T Chesrown, *President*
Janet Chesrown, *Corp Secy*
EMP: 25
SQ FT: 25,000
SALES (est): 6.5MM Privately Held
WEB: www.chesrownnewark.com
SIC: 5511 7549 Automobiles, new & used; high performance auto repair & service

(G-11462)
CLGT SOLUTIONS LLC
1670 Columbus Rd Ste C (43023-1232)
PHONE..................................740 920-4795
Frank Marois, *President*
Francis Marois, *Mng Member*
Ronnie Chaney,
Ann Graff,
Martin Graff,
EMP: 39
SQ FT: 150
SALES (est): 6MM Privately Held
WEB: www.clgtsolutions.com
SIC: 7389 8748 8742 Translation services; testing service, educational or personnel; management consulting services

(G-11463)
COUNTRY GARDENS
Also Called: Facklers
2326 Newark Granville Rd (43023-9290)
PHONE..................................740 522-8810
George Fackler, *CEO*
Danny Ghiloni, *Vice Pres*
EMP: 40
SALES (est): 837.8K Privately Held
SIC: 0781 Landscape services

(G-11464)
CRISPIN IRON & METAL CO LLC
190 Victoria Dr (43023-9106)
PHONE..................................740 616-6213
Todd Londot,
EMP: 25
SALES (est): 1MM Privately Held
SIC: 5093 Scrap & waste materials

(G-11465)
FACKLER COUNTRY GARDENS INC (PA)
Also Called: Kubota Authorized Dealer
2326 Newark Granville Rd (43023-9290)
PHONE..................................740 522-3128
George H Fackler III, *President*
Beth Jenkins, *Corp Secy*
Denny Ghiloni, *Vice Pres*
EMP: 40
SQ FT: 4,000
SALES (est): 5.5MM Privately Held
SIC: 5261 0782 5083 Garden supplies & tools; lawn care services; landscape contractors; farm & garden machinery

(G-11466)
GRANVILLE HOSPITALITY LLC
314 Broadway E (43023-1308)
PHONE..................................740 587-3333
Fax: 740 587-3333
Sean Mulryan, *General Mgr*
Linda Turk, *Sales Dir*
Matthew McComb, *Director*
Tim Lepontois, *Food Svc Dir*
Chad Lavely, *Executive*
EMP: 80
SQ FT: 50,000
SALES (est): 3.6MM Privately Held
WEB: www.granvilleinn.com
SIC: 5812 7011 5813 Restaurant, family: independent; hotels; drinking places

(G-11467)
KENDAL AT GRANVILLE
2158 Columbus Rd (43023-1242)
PHONE..................................740 321-0400
Fax: 740 587-3602
Jennifer Boback, *Finance*
Douglas Helman, *Exec Dir*
EMP: 130 EST: 1999
SALES: 13.8MM Privately Held
WEB: www.kag.kendal.org
SIC: 8361 Rehabilitation center, residential: health care incidental

(G-11468)
KRAJEWSKI CORP
Also Called: Universal Veneer
2825 Hallie Ln (43023-9256)
PHONE..................................740 522-2000
Fax: 740 788-9442
Dieter Heren, *CEO*
Kevin Robberts, *Facilities Mgr*
Doug Beal, *Director*
EMP: 50
SALES (est): 3MM Privately Held
SIC: 8743 Sales promotion
PA: Krajewski Corp
1776 Tamarack Rd
Newark OH 43055

(G-11469)
LARRIMER & LARRIMER LLC
2000 Newark Granville Rd # 200 (43023-7009)
PHONE..................................740 366-0184
Terrence Larrimer, *Partner*
EMP: 25
SALES (corp-wide): 5.8MM Privately Held
SIC: 8111 Patent, trademark & copyright law
PA: Larrimer & Larrimer, Llc
165 N High St Fl 3
Columbus OH 43215
614 221-7548

(G-11470)
MID-OHIO MECHANICAL INC
1844 Lancaster Rd (43023-9411)
PHONE..................................740 587-3362
Fax: 740 587-9834
Neal Hartfield, *President*
Douglas Hartfield, *Manager*
EMP: 30
SALES (corp-wide): 7.2MM Privately Held
WEB: www.midohiomechanical.com
SIC: 1711 4225 Plumbing, heating, air-conditioning contractors; general warehousing & storage
PA: Mid-Ohio Mechanical Incorporated
1264 Weaver Dr
Granville OH 43023
740 587-3362

(G-11471)
OWENS CORNING SALES LLC
Owens Corning Science and Tech
2790 Columbus Rd (43023-1200)
PHONE..................................740 587-3562
Fax: 740 321-7677
Frank O'Brien Bernin, *Vice Pres*
David Roth, *Vice Pres*
Warren Wolf, *Vice Pres*
Beth Ansley, *Opers Dir*
Paul Borders, *Plant Mgr*
EMP: 400 Publicly Held
WEB: www.owenscorning.com
SIC: 8731 2221 Commercial physical research; broadwoven fabric mills, man-made
HQ: Owens Corning Sales, Llc
1 Owens Corning Pkwy
Toledo OH 43659
419 248-8000

(G-11472)
VARO ENGINEERS INC
2790 Columbus Rd (43023-1252)
PHONE..................................740 587-2228
Fax: 740 587-2358
Dane Cox, *Branch Mgr*
Dan Keller, *Manager*
David A Macynski, *Software Dev*
EMP: 35
SALES (est): 2MM
SALES (corp-wide): 27.4MM Privately Held
WEB: www.varoeng.com
SIC: 8711 Consulting engineer
PA: Varo Engineers, Inc.
2751 Tuller Pkwy
Dublin OH 43017
614 459-0424

Gratis
Preble County

(G-11473)
GRATIS EMS
405 Harrison St (45330)
PHONE..................................937 787-4285
Joan Vance, *Officer*
EMP: 30
SALES (est): 314.4K Privately Held
SIC: 8099 Medical rescue squad

Green Springs
Seneca County

(G-11474)
ELMWOOD CENTER INC (PA)
Also Called: Elm Springs
441 N Broadway St (44836-9689)
PHONE..................................419 639-2581
Judy Blaha, *CEO*
Judy Downey, *CEO*
Kathy Hunt, *CEO*
Kim Prueter, *Pub Rel Dir*
Robin Hade, *Manager*
EMP: 67
SQ FT: 4,000
SALES (est): 9.2MM Privately Held
WEB: www.elmwoodassistedliving.com
SIC: 8052 Personal care facility

(G-11475)
ELMWOOD CENTER INC
Also Called: Elmwood At The Springs
401 N Broadway St (44836-9653)
PHONE..................................419 639-2626
Kathy Hunt, *Branch Mgr*
EMP: 60
SALES (corp-wide): 9.2MM Privately Held
SIC: 8052 Intermediate care facilities; personal care facility
PA: Elmwood Center Inc
441 N Broadway St
Green Springs OH 44836
419 639-2581

(G-11476)
ELMWOOD OF GREEN SPRINGS LTD
401 N Broadway St (44836-9653)
PHONE..................................419 639-2626
Kathy Hunt,
EMP: 99
SALES (est): 5.1MM Privately Held
SIC: 8062 General medical & surgical hospitals

(G-11477)
GREEN SPRINGS RESIDENTIAL LTD
430 N Broadway St (44836-9734)
PHONE..................................419 639-2581
Kathy Hunt, *President*
Robin Hade, *Manager*
EMP: 250
SALES (est): 4.9MM Privately Held
SIC: 6531 Rental agent, real estate

(G-11478)
KENNETH G MYERS CNSTR CO INC
201 Smith St (44836-9669)
P.O. Box 37 (44836-0037)
PHONE..................................419 639-2051
Fax: 419 639-3802
Todd E Myers, *President*
Dan Willey, *Principal*
Ronald Rowe, *Vice Pres*
Brent Myers, *Shareholder*
EMP: 100
SQ FT: 3,200
SALES (est): 15MM Privately Held
SIC: 1623 Telephone & communication line construction

(G-11479)
MILLER CABLE COMPANY
210 S Broadway St (44836-9635)
P.O. Box 68 (44836-0068)
PHONE.....................419 639-2091
Don W Miller, *Ch of Bd*
Jim Chamberlin, *President*
Thomas Sprow, *Corp Secy*
James Chamberlin Jr, *Vice Pres*
John Hartley, *Vice Pres*
EMP: 62
SQ FT: 2,500
SALES: 17.5MM **Privately Held**
WEB: www.millercable.com
SIC: 1731 General electrical contractor

(G-11480)
W S O S COMMUNITY A
Also Called: Quilter Cvlian Cnsrvation Camp
1518 E County Road 113 (44836-9606)
P.O. Box 590, Fremont (43420-0590)
PHONE.....................419 639-2802
Fax: 419 639-2255
Tim Havice, *Branch Mgr*
EMP: 50
SALES (corp-wide): 33.3MM **Privately Held**
SIC: 8331 Job training services
PA: W. S. O. S. Community Action Commission, Inc.
   109 S Front St
   Fremont OH 43420
   419 333-6068

(G-11481)
WYNN-REETH INC
Also Called: Remote Support Services
137 S Broadway St (44836-9319)
P.O. Box 785 (44836-0785)
PHONE.....................419 639-2094
Bruce Hunt, *President*
Jodi Bryan, *Case Mgr*
Destiny Pierce, *Case Mgr*
Adrian Smith, *Program Mgr*
Joy Sharp, *Manager*
EMP: 50
SALES (est): 2.3MM **Privately Held**
WEB: www.wynn-reeth.com
SIC: 8361 Home for the mentally handicapped

Greenfield
Highland County

(G-11482)
ADENA HEALTH SYSTEM
Also Called: Adena Fmly Medicine-Greenfield
1075 N Washington St (45123-9780)
PHONE.....................937 981-9444
Keith Coleman, *Branch Mgr*
EMP: 213
SALES (corp-wide): 111.9MM **Privately Held**
SIC: 8062 Hospital, medical school affiliated with nursing & residency
PA: Adena Health System
   272 Hospital Rd
   Chillicothe OH 45601
   740 779-7360

(G-11483)
COMMERCIAL CLEANING SOLUTIONS
10965 State Route 138 Sw (45123-8103)
PHONE.....................937 981-4870
Daniel Kinzer, *President*
EMP: 33
SALES (est): 606.7K **Privately Held**
SIC: 7349 Janitorial service, contract basis

(G-11484)
DALE ROSS TRUCKING INC
11408 State Route 41 S (45123-9385)
PHONE.....................937 981-2168
Lee Ann Ross, *President*
Dale Ross, *Corp Secy*
EMP: 30
SQ FT: 7,200
SALES: 500K **Privately Held**
SIC: 4212 Local trucking, without storage

(G-11485)
GREENFIELD AREA MEDICAL CTR
550 Mirabeau St (45123-1617)
PHONE.....................937 981-9400
Fax: 937 981-9339
Mark Shuter, *CEO*
Sandra McNeil, *Trustee*
Carla Sauer, *Human Res Mgr*
Wilbur Bill Sever, *Surgeon*
Dave Olaker, *Asst Mgr*
EMP: 100
SQ FT: 32,000
SALES: 14.8MM
SALES (corp-wide): 111.9MM **Privately Held**
WEB: www.adena.org
SIC: 8062 General medical & surgical hospitals
PA: Adena Health System
   272 Hospital Rd
   Chillicothe OH 45601
   740 779-7360

(G-11486)
GREENFIELD PRODUCTS INC
1230 N Washington St (45123-9783)
P.O. Box 99 (45123-0099)
PHONE.....................937 981-2696
Fax: 937 981-3466
Ann Gessner Pence, *President*
Wesley Pence, *Vice Pres*
Steve McCoy, *Opers Staff*
Tammy Wilson, *QC Mgr*
Paul Scott, *Accountant*
▲ **EMP:** 51 **EST:** 1959
SQ FT: 12,000
SALES (est): 24.5MM **Privately Held**
WEB: www.greenfieldfinishing.com
SIC: 5088 Transportation equipment & supplies

(G-11487)
HEALTHSOURCE OF OHIO INC
Also Called: Greenfield Family Health Ctr
1075 N Washington St (45123-9780)
PHONE.....................937 981-7707
Fax: 937 981-7129
Mellisa Garland, *Manager*
EMP: 25
SALES (corp-wide): 38.7MM **Privately Held**
SIC: 8093 8011 8082 Specialty outpatient clinics; general & family practice, physician/surgeon; home health care services
PA: Healthsource Of Ohio, Inc.
   5400 Dupont Cir Ste A
   Milford OH 45150
   513 576-7700

(G-11488)
MCMULLEN TRANSPORTATION LLC
11350 State Route 41 (45123-8562)
Rural Route 11892 Plea, Chillicothe (45601)
PHONE.....................937 981-4455
Lindsay Russell, *Opers Mgr*
Jamey Popp,
EMP: 27
SQ FT: 7,680
SALES (est): 2.9MM **Privately Held**
SIC: 4213 Contract haulers

Greenville
Darke County

(G-11489)
BISTRO OFF BROADWAY
117 E 5th St (45331-1935)
PHONE.....................937 316-5000
CJ Jones, *Principal*
EMP: 35
SALES (est): 659.5K **Privately Held**
SIC: 5812 8741 Family restaurants; restaurant management

(G-11490)
BROOKDALE SENIOR LIVING COMMUN
Also Called: Sterling House of Greenville
1401 N Broadway St (45331-4300)
PHONE.....................937 548-6800
Fax: 937 548-6740
Amy M Schwieterman, *Marketing Staff*
Vicky Ahlering, *Office Mgr*
Ida Hecht, *Manager*
Cassie Besecker, *Director*
Sharmain Allen, *Nursing Dir*
EMP: 40
SALES (corp-wide): 4.7B **Publicly Held**
WEB: www.assisted.com
SIC: 8059 8082 Rest home, with health care; home health care services
HQ: Brookdale Senior Living Communities, Inc.
   6737 W Wa St Ste 2300
   Milwaukee WI 53214
   414 918-5000

(G-11491)
BROTHERS PUBLISHING CO LLC
Also Called: Early Bird, The
5312 Sebring Warner Rd (45331-8787)
PHONE.....................937 548-3330
Fax: 937 548-3376
Ryan Berry, *Editor*
Keith Foutz, *Mng Member*
Clinton Randall, *Webmaster*
EMP: 45 **EST:** 1898
SALES (est): 2.4MM **Privately Held**
SIC: 2711 2791 7331 Newspapers: publishing only, not printed on site; typesetting; mailing list compilers

(G-11492)
CHAMBERS LEASING SYSTEMS
5187 Chld Hm Bradford Rd (45331)
PHONE.....................937 547-9777
Curt Betts, *Manager*
Jason Nichoals, *Manager*
EMP: 45
SALES (est): 1.7MM **Privately Held**
SIC: 4213 Contract haulers

(G-11493)
CHN INC - ADULT DAY CARE
Also Called: Comprensive Health Network
5420 State Route 571 (45331-9606)
PHONE.....................937 548-0506
Fax: 937 548-3468
Nancy Zechar, *President*
Cynthia L Scott, *Vice Pres*
Coy Boroff, *CFO*
Pamela Place, *Mktg Dir*
EMP: 35
SQ FT: 5,000
SALES: 5MM **Privately Held**
SIC: 8322 Adult day care center

(G-11494)
DARKE CNTY MENTAL HLTH CLINIC (PA)
212 E Main St (45331-1913)
P.O. Box 895 (45331-0895)
PHONE.....................937 548-1635
Ron Monroe, *Manager*
Lyn McArdle, *Exec Dir*
James Moore, *Exec Dir*
EMP: 27
SALES: 6.9K **Privately Held**
WEB: www.dcmhc.org
SIC: 8093 Mental health clinic, outpatient

(G-11495)
DARKE COUNTY SHERIFFS PATROL
5185 County Home Rd (45331-9753)
PHONE.....................937 548-3399
Fax: 937 548-9307
Toby Spencer, *Sheriff*
EMP: 75
SALES: 243.6K **Privately Held**
SIC: 7381 Protective services, guard

(G-11496)
DAVE KNAPP FORD LINCOLN INC (PA)
500 Wagner Ave (45331-2539)
PHONE.....................937 547-3000
Fax: 937 547-2228
David O Knapp, *President*
Dale Mansfield, *Inv Control Mgr*
Rodney Fisher, *Finance Mgr*
Jake Cabay, *Sales Mgr*
Chris Heidenreich, *Sales Mgr*
EMP: 42
SALES (est): 17.5MM **Privately Held**
WEB: www.daveknappford.com
SIC: 5511 5531 5012 Automobiles, new & used; automotive & home supply stores; automobiles & other motor vehicles

(G-11497)
DAYTON PHYSICIANS LLC
1111 Sweitzer St Ste C (45331-1189)
PHONE.....................937 547-0563
Pilar Gonzalez-Monk, *Branch Mgr*
EMP: 182
SALES (corp-wide): 25.8MM **Privately Held**
SIC: 8011 Primary care medical clinic
PA: Dayton Physicians, Llc
   6680 Poe Ave Ste 200
   Dayton OH 45414
   937 280-8400

(G-11498)
DICKMAN SUPPLY INC
1425 Sater St (45331-1672)
PHONE.....................937 492-6166
Fax: 937 548-7030
Roger Clevenger, *Engineer*
Logan Fair, *Human Res Mgr*
Brad Holzapfel, *Sales Staff*
Phil Shiverdecker, *Sales Staff*
Mark Winner, *Manager*
EMP: 25
SALES (est): 5.1MM
SALES (corp-wide): 114MM **Privately Held**
WEB: www.electro-controls.com
SIC: 5063 5084 Electrical apparatus & equipment; drilling bits; paper, sawmill & woodworking machinery
PA: Dickman Supply, Inc.
   1991 St Marys Ave
   Sidney OH 45365
   937 492-6166

(G-11499)
DREW AG-TRANSPORT INC
5450 Sebring Warner Rd (45331-8800)
PHONE.....................937 548-3200
Fax: 937 547-0532
Rod Drew, *President*
Cortnie Drew, *CFO*
EMP: 53
SALES (est): 8.8MM **Privately Held**
SIC: 4213 Contract haulers

(G-11500)
FAMILY HLTH SVCS DRKE CNTY INC (PA)
5735 Meeker Rd (45331-1180)
PHONE.....................937 548-3806
Fax: 937 548-3552
Mitch Eiting, *President*
Michael Rieman, *Vice Pres*
Kent James, *Treasurer*
Jean Young, *Exec Dir*
Coy Broff, *Executive*
EMP: 180
SQ FT: 43,000
SALES: 21.4MM **Privately Held**
WEB: www.familyhealthwebsite.com
SIC: 8011 Clinic, operated by physicians; primary care medical clinic

(G-11501)
GARBER AG FREIGHT INC
4667 Us Route 127 (45331-8806)
PHONE.....................937 548-8400
Fax: 937 540-0514
Ben Garber, *President*
Charles Garber, *Exec VP*
Jason Garber, *Vice Pres*
Ivan Garber, *Admin Sec*
EMP: 40
SALES (est): 4.6MM **Privately Held**
SIC: 4212 4213 Local trucking, without storage; trucking, except local

(G-11502)
GEORGE KNICK
2637 Hllgrove Wdington Rd (45331-9417)
PHONE.....................937 548-2832
George Knick, *Owner*
EMP: 25
SALES (est): 1.4MM **Privately Held**
SIC: 0191 0161 General farms, primarily crop; tomato farm

Greenville - Darke County (G-11503) GEOGRAPHIC SECTION

(G-11503)
GRACE RESURRECTION ASSOCIATION
Also Called: Grace Resurrection Cmnty Ctr
Grace Rsrrction Cmnty Ctr (45331)
PHONE 937 548-2595
Peggy Follrod, *Exec Dir*
EMP: 26
SALES: 110.1K **Privately Held**
SIC: 8322 Social service center

(G-11504)
GREENVILLE FEDERAL
690 Wagner Ave (45331-2649)
PHONE 937 548-4158
Fax: 937 548-6981
Jeff Knisi, *CEO*
Betty Hartzell, *Vice Pres*
Susan Allread, *CFO*
Brian Beam, *Marketing Mgr*
Nicholas Good, *Manager*
EMP: 40 **EST:** 1883
SQ FT: 11,000
SALES: 7.3MM
SALES (corp-wide): 6.8MM **Privately Held**
SIC: 6035 Federal savings & loan associations
HQ: Greenville Federal Financial Corporation
690 Wagner Ave
Greenville OH 45331
937 548-4158

(G-11505)
GREENVILLE NATIONAL BANCORP (PA)
446 S Bwy St (45331)
PHONE 937 548-1114
Steve Burns, *President*
Kent A James, *Vice Pres*
Douglas M Custenborder, *Treasurer*
EMP: 48
SQ FT: 7,500
SALES: 18.2MM **Privately Held**
SIC: 6712 Bank holding companies

(G-11506)
GREENVILLE NATIONAL BANK
446 S Broadway St (45331-1960)
P.O. Box 190 (45331-0190)
PHONE 937 548-1114
Steve Burns, *Manager*
EMP: 50
SALES (corp-wide): 18.2MM **Privately Held**
WEB: www.greenvillenationalbank.com
SIC: 6021 National commercial banks
HQ: Greenville National Bank (Inc)
446 S Broadway St
Greenville OH

(G-11507)
GREENVILLE TOWNSHIP RESCUE
Also Called: Rescue Squad
1401 Sater St (45331-1672)
P.O. Box 188 (45331-0188)
PHONE 937 548-9339
Mark Dotson, *Principal*
Steve Wenning, *Chief*
Leroy Murphy, *Manager*
Gregg Livingston, *Exec Dir*
EMP: 30
SQ FT: 2,400
SALES (est): 810K **Privately Held**
SIC: 4119 Ambulance service

(G-11508)
H & M PRECISION CONCRETE LLC
7805 Arcanum Bearsmill Rd (45331-9256)
PHONE 937 547-0012
Fax: 937 548-8598
Jason Haworth,
Todd Miller,
EMP: 32
SQ FT: 3,000
SALES: 4MM **Privately Held**
WEB: www.slabdocs.com
SIC: 1771 Concrete pumping

(G-11509)
HEALTH CARE RTREMENT CORP AMER
Also Called: Heartland of Greenville
243 Marion Dr (45331-2613)
PHONE 937 548-3141
Kara Hoernemann, *General Mgr*
EMP: 115
SALES (corp-wide): 3.6B **Publicly Held**
WEB: www.hrc-manorcare.com
SIC: 8051 Skilled nursing care facilities
HQ: Health Care And Retirement Corporation Of America
333 N Summit St Ste 103
Toledo OH 43604
419 252-5500

(G-11510)
HOSPICE OF DARKE COUNTY INC (PA)
Also Called: STATE OF THE HEART HOSPICE
1350 N Broadway St (45331-2461)
PHONE 937 548-2999
Fax: 937 548-7114
Ted Bauer, *Exec Dir*
Edward Hosbach II, *Director*
EMP: 40
SQ FT: 5,000
SALES: 8.6MM **Privately Held**
WEB: www.stateoftheheartcare.org
SIC: 8059 Personal care home, with health care

(G-11511)
JRB INDUSTRIES LLC
3425 State Route 571 (45331-3247)
PHONE 567 825-7022
James Bates,
EMP: 25
SALES (est): 609.6K **Privately Held**
SIC: 7389

(G-11512)
KTM ENTERPRISES INC
Also Called: Janitorial Management Services
120 W 3rd St (45331-1409)
P.O. Box 896 (45331-0896)
PHONE 937 548-8357
Rick Lundy, *President*
Tj Richardson, *Treasurer*
EMP: 31
SALES (est): 591K **Privately Held**
SIC: 7349 Janitorial service, contract basis

(G-11513)
LOWES HOME CENTERS LLC
1550 Wagner Ave (45331-2892)
PHONE 937 547-2400
Fax: 937 547-2403
Gerald Carroll, *Branch Mgr*
EMP: 105
SALES (corp-wide): 68.6B **Publicly Held**
SIC: 5211 5031 5722 5064 Home centers; building materials, exterior; building materials, interior; household appliance stores; electrical appliances, television & radio
HQ: Lowe's Home Centers, Llc
1605 Curtis Bridge Rd
Wilkesboro NC 28697
336 658-4000

(G-11514)
MIAMI VALLEY COMMUNITY ACTION
Metropolitan Housing
1469 Sweitzer St (45331-1029)
PHONE 937 548-8143
Janey Christman, *Director*
EMP: 62
SALES (corp-wide): 13MM **Privately Held**
SIC: 8322 Senior citizens' center or association
PA: Miami Valley Community Action Partnership
719 S Main St
Dayton OH 45402
937 222-1009

(G-11515)
OHIO DEPARTMENT TRANSPORTATION
Also Called: Hwy. Department
1144 Martin St (45331-9686)
PHONE 937 548-3015
Fax: 937 497-6987
Jeff Wetstone, *Manager*
EMP: 30 **Privately Held**
SIC: 9621 1611 Regulation, administration of transportation; ; highway & street maintenance
HQ: Ohio Department Of Transportation
1980 W Broad St
Columbus OH 43223

(G-11516)
REST HAVEN NURSING HOME INC
1096 N Ohio St (45331-2999)
PHONE 937 548-1138
Fax: 937 547-1049
Tom Lisowski, *Human Resources*
Michelle Bruns, *Administration*
EMP: 125
SQ FT: 20,000
SALES (est): 4.6MM **Privately Held**
SIC: 8052 8059 8051 Intermediate care facilities; rest home, with health care; skilled nursing care facilities

(G-11517)
RUMPKE WASTE INC
5474 Jaysville St John Rd (45331-9704)
PHONE 937 548-1939
Fax: 937 548-8874
Bruce Truman, *Manager*
EMP: 120 **Privately Held**
SIC: 4953 7359 4212 Refuse systems; equipment rental & leasing; local trucking, without storage
HQ: Rumpke Waste, Inc.
10795 Hughes Rd
Cincinnati OH 45251
513 851-0122

(G-11518)
SALLY BEAUTY SUPPLY LLC
Also Called: Beauty Systems Group
5805 Jaysville St John Rd (45331-8342)
PHONE 937 548-7684
Fax: 937 548-8431
Tim Gibson, *Manager*
Holly Lawrence, *Admin Asst*
EMP: 220 **Publicly Held**
WEB: www.sallybeauty.com
SIC: 4225 5087 General warehousing & storage; service establishment equipment
HQ: Sally Beauty Supply Llc
3001 Colorado Blvd
Denton TX 76210
940 898-7500

(G-11519)
SECOND NATIONAL BANK (HQ)
499 S Broadway St (45331-1961)
P.O. Box 130 (45331-0130)
PHONE 937 548-6687
Fax: 937 548-6687
John E Swallow, *CEO*
Marvin J Stammen, *President*
Ray Lear, *Chairman*
Leila English, *Trustee*
James Willock, *Trustee*
EMP: 40
SQ FT: 7,500
SALES (est): 1.6MM
SALES (corp-wide): 367MM **Publicly Held**
WEB: www.secondnational.com
SIC: 6021 6163 National commercial banks; loan brokers
PA: Park National Corporation
50 N 3rd St
Newark OH 43055
740 349-8451

(G-11520)
SPIRIT MEDICAL TRANSPORT LLC
5484 S State Route 49 (45331-1032)
PHONE 937 548-2800
Fax: 937 548-2826
Justin Staten, *COO*
Sally Wilson, *Human Resources*
Dan Winner, *Info Tech Mgr*
Brian Hathaway,
Darleen Wilcox, *Executive Asst*
EMP: 72
SALES (est): 3.4MM **Privately Held**
SIC: 4119 Ambulance service

(G-11521)
TELECOM EXPERTISE INDS INC (PA)
Also Called: T X I
5879 Jysville St Johns Rd (45331-9398)
P.O. Box 67 (45331-0067)
PHONE 937 548-5254
Fax: 937 548-5666
Jack Born, *President*
Imelda Pope, *Corp Secy*
Dave Pope, *Vice Pres*
Christopher Pope, *Project Mgr*
Max Rowe, *Manager*
EMP: 100
SQ FT: 38,000
SALES (est): 12.6MM **Privately Held**
WEB: www.txiinc.com
SIC: 1731 8711 Communications specialization; engineering services

(G-11522)
VALVOLINE INSTANT OIL CHANGE
661 Wagner Ave (45331-2648)
PHONE 937 548-0123
EMP: 190
SALES (corp-wide): 12.8MM **Privately Held**
SIC: 7549 Automotive maintenance services
PA: Valvoline Instant Oil Change Inc
7391 Bltmore Annplis Blvd
Glen Burnie MD 21061
410 760-5344

(G-11523)
VILLAGE GREEN HEALTHCARE CTR
Also Called: Gade Nursing Home 2
405 Chestnut St (45331-1306)
PHONE 937 548-1993
Fax: 937 548-2569
Martha Gade, *President*
Cheryl Stump, *Vice Pres*
Shane Sampson, *Director*
EMP: 70
SALES (est): 2.3MM **Privately Held**
SIC: 8051 Convalescent home with continuous nursing care

(G-11524)
WAYNE HEALTHCARE (PA)
835 Sweitzer St (45331-1007)
PHONE 937 548-1141
Fax: 937 547-5712
Wayne Deschambeau, *President*
W H Matchett Et Al, *Principal*
S A Hawes, *Principal*
E G Husted, *Principal*
George Massar, *COO*
EMP: 396 **EST:** 1920
SALES: 55.4MM **Privately Held**
SIC: 8062 General medical & surgical hospitals

(G-11525)
WAYNE INDUSTRIES INC
5844 Jysville St Johns Rd (45331-9398)
PHONE 937 548-6025
Fax: 937 548-5458
Mary Brennan, *Director*
EMP: 45
SALES: 291K **Privately Held**
SIC: 7363 Temporary help service

Greenwich
Huron County

(G-11526)
JOHNSON BROS RUBBER CO INC
Also Called: Johnson Bros Greenwich
41 Center St (44837-1049)
PHONE 419 752-4814
Fax: 419 752-7705

Grove City - Franklin County (G-11550)

Ken Bostic, *Manager*
EMP: 30
SALES (corp-wide): 54.4MM **Privately Held**
SIC: 5199 3743 3634 3545 Foams & rubber; railroad equipment; electric housewares & fans; machine tool accessories; gaskets, packing & sealing devices
PA: Johnson Bros. Rubber Co., Inc.
  42 W Buckeye St
  West Salem OH 44287
  419 853-4122

Grove City
Franklin County

(G-11527)
ACE TRUCK BODY INC
1600 Thrailkill Rd (43123-9733)
P.O. Box 459 (43123-0459)
PHONE..................................614 871-3100
Fax: 614 871-3860
Gary L Leasure, *President*
Ruth Ross, *Principal*
Robert D Beitzel, *Chairman*
David R Peitzel, *Vice Pres*
Ken Maynard, *Parts Mgr*
EMP: 25
SQ FT: 18,000
SALES: 10.4MM **Privately Held**
WEB: www.acetruck.com
SIC: 5012 5013 Truck bodies; motor vehicle supplies & new parts

(G-11528)
AMERICAN AIR FURNACE COMPANY
Also Called: American Air Comfort Tech
3945 Brookham Dr (43123-9741)
PHONE..................................614 876-1702
Fax: 614 876-1702
Steve Sliemers, *President*
Michael Sliemers, *Vice Pres*
EMP: 63
SQ FT: 24,000
SALES (est): 10.7MM **Privately Held**
WEB: www.americanairheating.com
SIC: 1711 Heating systems repair & maintenance

(G-11529)
AMERICAN GOLF CORPORATION
Also Called: Oakhurst Country Club
3223 Norton Rd (43123-9695)
PHONE..................................310 664-4278
Phylis Cain, *Accountant*
Shawn Logan, *Manager*
EMP: 35
SALES (corp-wide): 621.9MM **Privately Held**
SIC: 7997 Country club, membership
PA: American Golf Corporation
  6080 Center Dr Ste 500
  Los Angeles CA 90045
  310 664-4000

(G-11530)
AMERICAN MULTI-CINEMA INC
4218 Buckeye Pkwy (43123-8377)
PHONE..................................614 801-9130
EMP: 61 **Publicly Held**
SIC: 7832 Exhibitors, itinerant: motion picture
HQ: American Multi-Cinema, Inc.
  1 Amc Way
  Leawood KS 66211
  913 213-2000

(G-11531)
APEX GEAR
2375 Harrisburg Pike (43123-1057)
PHONE..................................614 539-3002
Jeremy Hamilton, *Owner*
EMP: 30
SALES (est): 1.2MM **Privately Held**
SIC: 5085 Gears

(G-11532)
AT&T CORP
4108 Buckeye Pkwy (43123-8175)
P.O. Box 908 (43123-0908)
PHONE..................................614 539-0165
Wendy Stalcup, *Branch Mgr*
EMP: 97
SALES (corp-wide): 160.5B **Publicly Held**
WEB: www.cingular.com
SIC: 4812 Cellular telephone services
HQ: At&T Corp.
  1 At&T Way
  Bedminster NJ 07921
  800 403-3302

(G-11533)
BERLIN PACKAGING LLC
3423 Southpark Pl C (43123-4828)
PHONE..................................614 777-6282
Andrew T Berlin, *Branch Mgr*
EMP: 47
SALES (corp-wide): 1B **Privately Held**
SIC: 5199 Packaging materials
PA: Berlin Packaging L.L.C.
  525 W Monroe St Ste 1400
  Chicago IL 60661
  312 876-9292

(G-11534)
BIG RUN URGENT CARE CENTER
3000 Meadow Pond Ct # 200 (43123-9827)
PHONE..................................614 871-7130
M Smith MD, *Principal*
Janice Piscitelli, *Relations*
EMP: 30
SALES (est): 947.9K **Privately Held**
SIC: 8011 Medical centers

(G-11535)
BOSCH REXROTH CORPORATION
3940 Gantz Rd Ste F (43123-4845)
PHONE..................................614 527-7400
Ted Bojanowski, *President*
EMP: 50
SALES (corp-wide): 261.7MM **Privately Held**
SIC: 5084 Hydraulic systems equipment & supplies
HQ: Bosch Rexroth Corporation
  14001 S Lakes Dr
  Charlotte NC 28273
  847 645-3600

(G-11536)
BRIAR-GATE REALTY INC
Also Called: Fireproof Records Center
3655 Brookham Dr (43123-4852)
PHONE..................................614 299-2122
Michael James, *Manager*
EMP: 27
SALES (corp-wide): 22MM **Privately Held**
WEB: www.fireproof.com
SIC: 4226 Document & office records storage
PA: Briar-Gate Realty, Inc.
  3827 Brookham Dr
  Grove City OH 43123
  614 299-2121

(G-11537)
BRIAR-GATE REALTY INC (PA)
Also Called: Fireproof Record Center
3827 Brookham Dr (43123-4827)
P.O. Box 1150 (43123-6150)
PHONE..................................614 299-2121
Fax: 614 421-4526
Michael James, *CEO*
Edward F James, *President*
C M Gibson, *Principal*
Sally R Gibson, *Principal*
Helen M Watkins, *Principal*
EMP: 66
SQ FT: 80,000
SALES (est): 22MM **Privately Held**
WEB: www.fireproof.com
SIC: 4226 Document & office records storage

(G-11538)
BROCON CONSTRUCTION INC
2120 Hardy Parkway St (43123-1240)
PHONE..................................614 871-7300
George Brobst, *President*
George M Brobst Jr, *President*
EMP: 45
SALES (est): 14.6MM **Privately Held**
WEB: www.brocon.net
SIC: 1542 Commercial & office building, new construction

(G-11539)
BROOKDALE SENIOR LIVING INC
1305 Lamplighter Dr (43123-8199)
PHONE..................................614 277-1200
Fax: 614 277-1299
EMP: 85
SALES (corp-wide): 4.7B **Publicly Held**
SIC: 6531 Real estate agents & managers
PA: Brookdale Senior Living
  111 Westwood Pl Ste 400
  Brentwood TN 37027
  615 221-2250

(G-11540)
BUCK EQUIPMENT INC
1720 Feddern Ave (43123-1206)
PHONE..................................614 539-3039
Fax: 614 539-3040
Dennis Hamilton, *CEO*
Steve Sunderland, *Controller*
Lee Nanzo, *Accounts Mgr*
Jamie Odell, *Sales Executive*
Chris Nichols, *Manager*
▲ EMP: 35
SQ FT: 60,000
SALES (est): 9.4MM **Privately Held**
WEB: www.buckequipment.com
SIC: 3531 3743 3441 5088 Logging equipment; railroad equipment; fabricated structural metal; railroad equipment & supplies

(G-11541)
BUCKEYE DRMTLOGY DRMTHPHTHLOGY
1933 Ohio Dr (43123-4835)
PHONE..................................614 317-9630
Carlos Rodriguez, *Branch Mgr*
EMP: 25
SALES (est): 1.7MM
SALES (corp-wide): 3.6MM **Privately Held**
SIC: 8011 Dermatologist
PA: Buckeye Dermatology & Dermathophathology Inc
  5720 Blazer Pkwy
  Dublin OH 43017
  614 389-6331

(G-11542)
BUCKEYE RANCH INC (PA)
5665 Hoover Rd (43123-9280)
PHONE..................................614 875-2371
Fax: 614 875-2366
D Nicholas Rees, *CEO*
Stephen Richard, *President*
Richard Rieser, *President*
Roger Minner, *Vice Pres*
Nick Rees, *Vice Pres*
EMP: 435 EST: 1961
SQ FT: 182,023
SALES: 42.8MM **Privately Held**
SIC: 8361 Home for the emotionally disturbed; halfway group home, persons with social or personal problems; halfway home for delinquents & offenders; juvenile correctional home

(G-11543)
C H BRADSHAW CO
2004 Hendrix Dr (43123-1278)
PHONE..................................614 871-2087
Fax: 614 871-2628
Robert Slack, *President*
Ron Johnson, *General Mgr*
Jeanne Slack, *Vice Pres*
EMP: 27
SQ FT: 22,000
SALES (est): 9.2MM **Privately Held**
WEB: www.chbradshaw.com
SIC: 5084 7699 Petroleum industry machinery; tank repair

(G-11544)
CELLCO PARTNERSHIP
Also Called: Verizon Wireless
3043 Turnberry Ct (43123-1789)
PHONE..................................614 277-2900
EMP: 71
SALES (est): 14.6MM **Privately Held**
SALES (corp-wide): 126B **Publicly Held**
SIC: 4812 Cellular telephone services
HQ: Cellco Partnership
  1 Verizon Way
  Basking Ridge NJ 07920

(G-11545)
CENTRAL OHIO CONTRACTORS INC (PA)
2879 Jackson Pike (43123-9737)
PHONE..................................614 539-2579
Fax: 614 539-2590
Ralph D Loewendick, *President*
Luanne Sigman, *Corp Secy*
EMP: 70
SALES: 1.9MM **Privately Held**
WEB: www.coc-inc.com
SIC: 4953 Sanitary landfill operation

(G-11546)
CIRCLE S FARMS INC
9015 London Groveport Rd (43123-8818)
PHONE..................................614 878-9462
Ethel Sullivan, *Principal*
EMP: 28
SQ FT: 1,500
SALES (est): 1.1MM **Privately Held**
SIC: 7999 5431 5148 5992 Festival operation; fruit & vegetable markets; fresh fruits & vegetables; flowers, fresh; general farms, primarily crop; groceries, general line

(G-11547)
COLUMBUS MOTOR SPEEDWAY INC
1882 Timber Haven Ct (43123-7909)
PHONE..................................614 491-1047
Fax: 614 491-6010
Jerry Nuckles, *President*
Barbara Nuckles, *Sales Staff*
EMP: 65
SQ FT: 250
SALES: 2.5MM **Privately Held**
SIC: 7948 Automotive race track operation

(G-11548)
COMPUTER SCIENCES CORPORATION
3940 Gantz Rd Ste F (43123-4845)
PHONE..................................614 801-2343
Charlene Stanley, *Director*
EMP: 145
SALES (corp-wide): 23.5B **Publicly Held**
WEB: www.csc.com
SIC: 7376 Computer facilities management
HQ: Computer Sciences Corporation
  1775 Tysons Blvd Ste 219
  Tysons VA 22102
  703 245-9675

(G-11549)
CONVERSE ELECTRIC INC
3783 Gantz Rd Ste A (43123-1892)
PHONE..................................614 808-4377
Fax: 614 871-8726
Jerry Converse, *President*
Chris Converse, *Vice Pres*
Bill Mount, *Vice Pres*
Dave Novontny, *Vice Pres*
Dave Miller, *Purchasing*
EMP: 100
SALES (est): 18.3MM **Privately Held**
WEB: www.converseelectric.com
SIC: 1731 General electrical contractor

(G-11550)
COX AUTOMOTIVE INC
Also Called: Ohio Auto Auction
3905 Jackson Pike (43123-9731)
PHONE..................................614 871-2771
Fax: 614 871-6894
Debbie Mc Bride, *Sales Executive*
John Deck, *Manager*
EMP: 450
SALES (corp-wide): 33B **Privately Held**
WEB: www.manheim.com
SIC: 5012 5531 Automobile auction; automotive accessories
HQ: Cox Automotive, Inc.
  6205-A Pchtree Dnwoody Rd
  Atlanta GA 30328
  404 843-5000

Grove City - Franklin County (G-11551)

(G-11551)
DAKOTA GIRLS LLC
Also Called: Goddard School
2585 London Groveport Rd (43123-9035)
PHONE....................614 801-2558
Fax: 614 801-0065
Kelly Vansyckle, *Owner*
Samantha Elliot,
EMP: 25
SALES (est): 886.8K **Privately Held**
SIC: 8351 Preschool center

(G-11552)
DECISION ONE
3423 Southpark Pl (43123-4828)
PHONE....................614 883-0215
Nick Sharma, *President*
Dick Interim, *Owner*
Jackie Marchitell, *Personnel Exec*
Kevin Folk, *Director*
▲ **EMP:** 37 **EST:** 1998
SALES (est): 10.4MM **Privately Held**
SIC: 5045 Computers, peripherals & software

(G-11553)
DENIER ELECTRIC CO INC
4000 Gantz Rd Ste C (43123-4844)
PHONE....................614 338-4664
Chuck Bull, *Vice Pres*
Clay Carroll, *Opers Mgr*
Mike Kallmeyer, *Branch Mgr*
John Birkenhauer, *Manager*
EMP: 50
SALES (corp-wide): 58.1MM **Privately Held**
SIC: 1731 General electrical contractor
PA: Denier Electric Co., Inc.
10891 State Route 128
Harrison OH 45030
513 738-2641

(G-11554)
DISCOVER TRAINING INC
4882 Rheims Way (43123-7903)
PHONE....................614 871-0010
Kristine H Kursinskis, *President*
EMP: 70
SALES: 3.5MM **Privately Held**
SIC: 7361 Employment agencies

(G-11555)
DOCTORS HOSPITAL HEALTH CENTER
Also Called: Doctors Hospital Fmly Practice
2030 Stringtown Rd Fl 3 (43123-3993)
PHONE....................614 544-0101
William Burke, *Principal*
Amy Jackson DDS, *Fmly & Gen Dent*
EMP: 35
SALES (est): 1.2MM **Privately Held**
WEB: www.doctorsfp.com
SIC: 8031 Offices & clinics of osteopathic physicians

(G-11556)
DRURY HOTELS COMPANY LLC
Also Called: Drury Inn & Suites Columbus S
4109 Parkway Centre Dr (43123-8095)
PHONE....................614 798-8802
Sam Gregory, *Branch Mgr*
EMP: 30
SALES (corp-wide): 397.4MM **Privately Held**
WEB: www.druryhotels.com
SIC: 7011 Hotels
PA: Drury Hotels Company, Llc
721 Emerson Rd Ste 400
Saint Louis MO 63141
314 429-2255

(G-11557)
DSI SYSTEMS INC
3650 Brookham Dr Ste K (43123-4929)
PHONE....................614 871-1456
Fax: 614 871-4643
Traci Fusner, *Manager*
Donna Bocox, *Admin Sec*
▲ **EMP:** 30
SALES (est): 1.3MM **Privately Held**
SIC: 4841 Satellite master antenna systems services (SMATV)

(G-11558)
ESEC CORPORATION
Also Called: Columbus Peterbilt
6240 Enterprise Pkwy (43123-9272)
PHONE....................614 875-3732
Fax: 614 875-9920
Tim Darr, *Manager*
EMP: 29
SQ FT: 26,480
SALES (est): 2MM
SALES (corp-wide): 7.6MM **Privately Held**
SIC: 5084 5012 5531 Industrial machinery & equipment; trucks, commercial; truck equipment & parts
PA: Esec Corporation
44 Victoria Rd
Youngstown OH 44515
330 799-1536

(G-11559)
FEDEX CORPORATION
3423 Southpark Pl (43123-4828)
PHONE....................614 801-0953
EMP: 34
SALES (corp-wide): 47.4B **Publicly Held**
SIC: 4513 Courier Services
PA: Fedex Corporation
942 Shady Grove Rd S
Memphis TN 38120
901 818-7500

(G-11560)
FEDEX GROUND PACKAGE SYS INC
6120 S Meadows Dr (43123-9298)
PHONE....................800 463-3339
Fax: 614 875-6596
James Primm, *Manager*
Mark Forsythe, *Manager*
Don Linder, *Manager*
Betsy Murrow, *Admin Sec*
William Lafferty, *Maintence Staff*
EMP: 500
SALES (corp-wide): 60.3B **Publicly Held**
SIC: 4213 4212 Contract haulers; local trucking, without storage
HQ: Fedex Ground Package System, Inc.
1000 Fed Ex Dr
Coraopolis PA 15108
412 269-1000

(G-11561)
FEDEX SMARTPOST INC
2969 Lewis Centre Way (43123-1782)
PHONE....................800 463-3339
Angela Julian, *HR Admin*
Chris Heine, *Branch Mgr*
EMP: 82
SALES (corp-wide): 60.3B **Publicly Held**
SIC: 4215 Parcel delivery, vehicular
HQ: Fedex Smartpost, Inc.
16555 W Rogers Dr
New Berlin WI 53151
800 463-3339

(G-11562)
FLOWERS FAMILY PRACTICE INC
3667 Marlane Dr (43123-8895)
PHONE....................614 277-9631
Stephanie Flowers, *Owner*
Hooley Barbara, *Manager*
Kim Bosley, *Assistant*
EMP: 25
SALES (est): 1.3MM **Privately Held**
SIC: 8011 General & family practice, physician/surgeon

(G-11563)
FRATERNAL ORDER EAGLES INC (HQ)
Also Called: F O E
1623 Gateway Cir (43123-9309)
PHONE....................614 883-2200
Fax: 614 883-2201
Chris Lainas, *President*
Chuck Cunnigham, *Vice Pres*
Tim Lewis, *Treasurer*
Mike Shonk, *Info Tech Dir*
Bob Wahls, *Admin Sec*
EMP: 33
SQ FT: 21,000
SALES: 3.2MM
SALES (corp-wide): 11MM **Privately Held**
WEB: www.fraternalorderofeagles.tribe.net
SIC: 8641 Fraternal associations
PA: Grand Aerie Of The Fraternal Order Of Eagles
1623 Gateway Cir
Grove City OH 43123
614 883-2200

(G-11564)
FRESENIUS MEDICAL CARE VRO LLC
Also Called: Fresenius Med Care Grove Cy
3149 Farm Bank Way (43123-1258)
PHONE....................614 875-2349
Mary Garber, *Manager*
Ron Kuerbitz,
EMP: 25
SALES (est): 715.4K **Privately Held**
SIC: 8092 Kidney dialysis centers

(G-11565)
GOODYEAR TIRE & RUBBER COMPANY
1950 Hendrix Dr (43123-1215)
PHONE....................614 871-1881
Kevin Klein, *Branch Mgr*
EMP: 42
SALES (corp-wide): 15.3B **Publicly Held**
WEB: www.wingfootc.com
SIC: 7534 Tire retreading & repair shops
PA: The Goodyear Tire & Rubber Company
200 E Innovation Way
Akron OH 44316
330 796-2121

(G-11566)
GRAND AERIE OF THE FRATERNAL (PA)
1623 Gateway Cir (43123-9309)
PHONE....................614 883-2200
Edgar L Bollenbacher, *Ch of Bd*
David Tice, *President*
Chris Lainas Jr, *Chairman*
Bob Larsen, *Treasurer*
Donald R Jim West, *Treasurer*
EMP: 42
SALES: 11MM **Privately Held**
WEB: www.foe.com
SIC: 8641 University club

(G-11567)
GROVE CITY COMMUNITY CLUB
3397 Civic Pl (43123-3137)
P.O. Box 434 (43123-0434)
PHONE....................614 875-6074
EMP: 45
SALES: 53.5K **Privately Held**
SIC: 8641 7997 Civic/Social Association Membership Sport/Recreation Club

(G-11568)
GROVE CY CHRSTN CHILD CARE CTR
4770 Hoover Rd (43123-8504)
PHONE....................614 875-2551
Fax: 614 875-1988
Kellie Castle, *Principal*
Jessica Rose, *Principal*
Jan Bowman, *Manager*
Susan Feisert, *Director*
Susan Sienert, *Director*
EMP: 80
SALES (est): 1.5MM **Privately Held**
SIC: 8322 Child related social services

(G-11569)
H O C J INC
2135 Hardy Parkway St (43123-1213)
PHONE....................614 539-4601
EMP: 31 **Privately Held**
SIC: 4213 Trucking, except local
PA: H O C J Inc
323 Cash Memorial Blvd
Forest Park GA 30297

(G-11570)
HOKUTO USA INC
2200 Southwest Blvd Ste F (43123-2854)
PHONE....................614 782-6200
Robin Hughes, *CEO*
Yoshimasa Sekiguchi, *President*
EMP: 42
SALES: 14MM
SALES (corp-wide): 77.2MM **Privately Held**
SIC: 8711 Engineering services
PA: Hokuto Corporation
155, Gonishicho
Komaki AIC 485-0
568 785-555

(G-11571)
INSTANTWHIP-COLUMBUS INC (HQ)
3855 Marlane Dr (43123-9224)
P.O. Box 249 (43123-0249)
PHONE....................614 871-9447
Fax: 614 871-8759
Douglas A Smith, *President*
Rusty Tuggle, *General Mgr*
Tom G Michaelides, *Senior VP*
Vinson Lewis, *Vice Pres*
Ken Temple, *Controller*
EMP: 32
SQ FT: 10,300
SALES (est): 5.6MM
SALES (corp-wide): 44.3MM **Privately Held**
SIC: 2026 5143 2023 8741 Whipped topping, except frozen or dry mix; dairy products, except dried or canned; dietary supplements, dairy & non-dairy based; management services
PA: Instantwhip Foods, Inc.
2200 Cardigan Ave
Columbus OH 43215
614 488-2536

(G-11572)
INTERSTATE CONSTRUCTION INC
3511 Farm Bank Way (43123-1970)
PHONE....................614 539-1188
Fax: 614 539-0880
Dwight Kincaid, *President*
EMP: 25
SQ FT: 8,000
SALES (est): 5.6MM **Privately Held**
WEB: www.interstateconstruction.net
SIC: 1522 1542 Multi-family dwellings, new construction; remodeling, multi-family dwellings; commercial & office building, new construction; commercial & office buildings, renovation & repair

(G-11573)
KIRK WILLIAMS COMPANY INC
2734 Home Rd (43123-1701)
P.O. Box 189 (43123-0189)
PHONE....................614 875-9023
Fax: 614 871-9214
James K Williams Jr, *President*
James K Williams II, *Corp Secy*
Nic Williams, *Project Mgr*
Patrick Williams, *Project Mgr*
Stephen Miller, *Sales Associate*
EMP: 80
SQ FT: 40,000
SALES (est): 31.3MM **Privately Held**
WEB: www.kirkwilliamsco.com
SIC: 1711 3564 3444 Mechanical contractor; warm air heating & air conditioning contractor; ventilation & duct work contractor; blowers & fans; sheet metalwork

(G-11574)
LA FORCE INC
3940 Gantz Rs Unit E (43123)
PHONE....................614 875-2545
Tom Gaible, *Branch Mgr*
EMP: 100
SALES (corp-wide): 156.3MM **Privately Held**
SIC: 5072 Builders' hardware
PA: La Force, Inc.
1060 W Mason St
Green Bay WI 54303
920 497-7100

(G-11575)
LENNOX INDUSTRIES INC
3750 Brookham Dr Ste A (43123-4850)
PHONE....................614 871-3017
Fax: 614 871-0854
Mark Miltko, *Manager*
EMP: 35

GEOGRAPHIC SECTION
Grove City - Franklin County (G-11599)

SALES (corp-wide): 3.8B **Publicly Held**
WEB: www.davelennox.com
SIC: 5075 Warm air heating & air conditioning
HQ: Lennox Industries Inc.
2100 Lake Park Blvd
Richardson TX 75080
972 497-5000

(G-11576)
LIBERTY TIRE RECYCLING LLC
3041 Jackson Pike (43123-9737)
PHONE..........................614 871-8097
Thomas Elder, *Cust Mgr*
Ed Kincaid, *Branch Mgr*
Rick Douglas, *Manager*
Jeffrey Kendall, *Manager*
Donald E REA, *Manager*
EMP: 26 **Privately Held**
SIC: 4953 Recycling, waste materials
HQ: Liberty Tire Recycling, Llc
600 River Ave Ste 3
Pittsburgh PA 15212
412 562-1700

(G-11577)
LINEMASTER SERVICES LLC
5736 Buckeye Pkwy (43123-9177)
PHONE..........................614 507-9945
David T Ehrenberg II,
EMP: 28
SALES (est): 1.6MM **Privately Held**
SIC: 8999 Services

(G-11578)
LITTLE THEATER OFF BROADWAY
Also Called: L T O B
3981 Broadway (43123-2639)
P.O. Box 504 (43123-0504)
PHONE..........................614 875-3919
Cathy Hyghland, *President*
Jane Mixer, *Principal*
Ruby Callison, *Vice Pres*
James Schmitt, *Treasurer*
Rosemary Tulseln, *Admin Sec*
EMP: 30
SALES: 63.8K **Privately Held**
WEB: www.ltob.org
SIC: 7922 Legitimate live theater producers

(G-11579)
MARTIN MARIETTA MATERIALS INC
Also Called: Martin Marietta Aggregates
3300 Jackson Pike (43123-8875)
PHONE..........................614 871-6708
Mike Matoszkia, *Manager*
EMP: 40
SQ FT: 420 **Publicly Held**
WEB: www.martinmarietta.com
SIC: 5032 Aggregate
PA: Martin Marietta Materials Inc
2710 Wycliff Rd
Raleigh NC 27607

(G-11580)
MH EQUIPMENT COMPANY
2055 Hardy Parkway St (43123-1213)
PHONE..........................614 871-1571
Dennis Dmytryk, *Manager*
EMP: 35
SALES (corp-wide): 237.2MM **Privately Held**
SIC: 5084 Materials handling machinery
HQ: Mh Equipment Company
8901 N Industrial Rd
Peoria IL 61615
309 579-8020

(G-11581)
MID-OHIO FOODBANK
3960 Brookham Dr (43123-9741)
PHONE..........................614 317-9400
Fax: 614 274-8063
Mathew Habash, *President*
Kimberly Dorniden, *Principal*
Lyn Hang, *COO*
Bridget Decrane, *Vice Pres*
Marilyn Tomasi, *Vice Pres*
EMP: 118
SQ FT: 204,500
SALES: 91.2MM **Privately Held**
SIC: 8322 Meal delivery program

(G-11582)
MYERS MACHINERY MOVERS INC
2210 Hardy Parkway St (43123-1243)
PHONE..........................614 871-5052
Fax: 614 871-8104
Gary Myers, *President*
Butch Myers, *Vice Pres*
Stacie Cope, *Admin Sec*
EMP: 50
SQ FT: 10,000
SALES (est): 10MM **Privately Held**
WEB: www.myersmachinerymovers.com
SIC: 4213 1796 4212 Heavy machinery transport; machine moving & rigging; local trucking, without storage

(G-11583)
NATIONWIDE CORPORATION
3400 Southpark Pl Ste A (43123-4856)
PHONE..........................614 277-5103
Steve Schick, *Manager*
Rob Allen, *Administration*
EMP: 350
SALES (corp-wide): 26.6B **Privately Held**
SIC: 6411 Insurance agents, brokers & service
HQ: Nationwide Corporation
1 Nationwide Plz
Columbus OH 43215
614 249-7111

(G-11584)
NEXTEL COMMUNICATIONS INC
1727 Stringtown Rd (43123-9125)
PHONE..........................614 801-9267
Fax: 614 801-9283
Trent Burke, *Manager*
EMP: 60
SALES (corp-wide): 78.3B **Publicly Held**
WEB: www.nextel.com
SIC: 4812 Cellular telephone services
HQ: Nextel Communications, Inc.
12502 Sunrise Valley Dr
Reston VA 20191
703 433-4000

(G-11585)
NIPPON EXPRESS USA INC
3705 Urbancrest Indus Dr (43123-1772)
PHONE..........................614 801-5695
Fax: 614 801-5686
Hediki Takami, *Manager*
EMP: 60
SALES (corp-wide): 16.4B **Privately Held**
SIC: 4731 Freight forwarding
HQ: Nippon Express U.S.A., Inc.
2401 44th Rd Fl 14
Long Island City NY 11101
212 758-6100

(G-11586)
NURSE MEDICIAL HEALTHCARE SVCS
3421 Farm Bank Way (43123-1974)
P.O. Box 801 (43123-0801)
PHONE..........................614 801-1300
Johnnie Berry, *President*
EMP: 90 **EST:** 2009
SALES: 5MM **Privately Held**
SIC: 8082 Visiting nurse service

(G-11587)
OHIO AUTO DELIVERY INC
Also Called: Oad
1700 Feddern Ave (43123-1206)
P.O. Box 268 (43123-0268)
PHONE..........................614 277-1445
Fax: 614 277-1450
David Stynchula, *President*
Kevin M Loychik, *Vice Pres*
Valerie Stynchula, *Admin Sec*
EMP: 30
SQ FT: 6,000
SALES (est): 5MM **Privately Held**
WEB: www.ohioautodelivery.com
SIC: 4213 Automobiles, transport & delivery

(G-11588)
OHIO AUTOMOBILE CLUB
4750 Big Run South Rd B (43123-9692)
PHONE..........................614 277-1310
Natalie Nassie, *Branch Mgr*
EMP: 43

SALES (corp-wide): 55.9MM **Privately Held**
SIC: 7997 Membership sports & recreation clubs
PA: The Ohio Automobile Club
90 E Wilson Bridge Rd # 1
Worthington OH 43085
614 431-7901

(G-11589)
OHIO CITRUS JUICES INC
2201 Hardy Parkway St (43123-1219)
PHONE..........................614 539-0030
Fax: 614 539-0278
Les Clark, *President*
Steve Clark, *General Mgr*
Kevin Jones, *Business Mgr*
Thomas Mathes, *Vice Pres*
EMP: 30
SQ FT: 11,000
SALES (est): 5MM **Privately Held**
WEB: www.ohiocitrus.com
SIC: 5149 Juices

(G-11590)
PAVEMENT PROTECTORS INC
Also Called: M & D Blacktop Sealing
2020 Longwood Ave (43123-1218)
PHONE..........................614 875-9989
Fax: 614 875-8649
Steve Bernsdorf, *President*
Chad Bernsdorf, *Vice Pres*
Mark Nance, *Sales Mgr*
Cindy Wahite-Gregory, *Administration*
EMP: 27 **EST:** 1964
SQ FT: 10,000
SALES (est): 4.6MM **Privately Held**
WEB: www.mdblacktop.com
SIC: 1771 Blacktop (asphalt) work

(G-11591)
PHOENIX GOLF LINKS
4239 London Groveport Rd (43123-9522)
PHONE..........................614 539-3636
Fax: 614 539-3366
Eric Mather, *President*
Barry Fisher, *Principal*
Katie Siebenthaler, *Relations*
EMP: 40 **EST:** 2000
SALES (est): 1MM
SALES (corp-wide): 8MM **Privately Held**
WEB: www.phoenixgl.com
SIC: 7992 5941 Public golf courses; golf, tennis & ski shops
PA: Petro Environmental Technologies, Inc
8160 Corp Pk Dr Ste 300
Cincinnati OH 45242
513 489-6789

(G-11592)
PITT-OHIO EXPRESS LLC
2101 Hardy Parkway St (43123-1213)
PHONE..........................614 801-1064
Fax: 614 801-1073
Rich Hassit, *General Mgr*
Richard Hazelet, *Manager*
EMP: 140
SALES (corp-wide): 507.8MM **Privately Held**
SIC: 4213 Heavy hauling
PA: Pitt-Ohio Express, Llc
15 27th St
Pittsburgh PA 15222
412 232-3015

(G-11593)
RR DONNELLEY & SONS COMPANY
Also Called: Wallace
3801 Gantz Rd Ste A (43123-4915)
PHONE..........................614 539-5527
Fax: 614 539-5687
Jeremy Liening, *Manager*
Craig Thorpe, *Executive*
EMP: 25
SALES (corp-wide): 6.9B **Publicly Held**
WEB: www.rrdonnelley.com
SIC: 4225 General warehousing & storage
PA: R. R. Donnelley & Sons Company
35 W Wacker Dr Ste 3650
Chicago IL 60601
312 326-8000

(G-11594)
S G LOEWENDICK AND SONS INC
2877 Jackson Pike (43123-9737)
PHONE..........................614 539-2582
Fax: 614 539-2585
David Loewendick, *President*
Fred Loewendick, *Vice Pres*
Karl Loewendick, *Vice Pres*
Lynn Riley, *Office Mgr*
EMP: 30 **EST:** 1937
SQ FT: 25,000
SALES: 2.2MM **Privately Held**
SIC: 1795 Demolition, buildings & other structures

(G-11595)
SAFETY TODAY INC (HQ)
Also Called: Midwest Service Center
3287 Southwest Blvd (43123-2210)
PHONE..........................614 409-7200
Fax: 614 409-7201
Edward Gustafson, *Principal*
Anthony Spearing, *Vice Pres*
▲ **EMP:** 30 **EST:** 1946
SQ FT: 90,000
SALES (est): 20.9MM **Privately Held**
WEB: www.safetytoday.com
SIC: 5084 5047 5099 Safety equipment; instruments & control equipment; measuring & testing equipment, electrical; noise control equipment; industrial safety devices: first aid kits & masks; safety equipment & supplies; fire extinguishers; lifesaving & survival equipment (non-medical); reflective road markers

(G-11596)
SAXTON REAL ESTATE CO (PA)
3703 Broadway (43123-2201)
PHONE..........................614 875-2327
Fax: 614 875-9670
William E Saxton, *President*
Marilyn Phillips, *Sales Staff*
Sydnie Padamadan, *Agent*
Shawn Barton, *Real Est Agnt*
Linda Clagg, *Real Est Agnt*
EMP: 60
SQ FT: 1,500
SALES (est): 4.7MM **Privately Held**
WEB: www.saxtonrealestate.com
SIC: 6531 Real estate agent, residential

(G-11597)
SECURITAS SEC SVCS USA INC
Also Called: East Central Region
2180 Southwest Blvd (43123-1893)
PHONE..........................614 871-6051
Jeremy Simpson, *Branch Mgr*
Wayne Bailey, *Manager*
Michael Hartsock, *Supervisor*
EMP: 116
SALES (corp-wide): 9.5B **Privately Held**
WEB: www.securitasinc.com
SIC: 7381 Security guard service
HQ: Securitas Security Services Usa, Inc.
9 Campus Dr
Parsippany NJ 07054
973 267-5300

(G-11598)
SOLID WASTE AUTH CENTL OHIO
Also Called: Swaco
4239 London Groveport Rd (43123-9522)
PHONE..........................614 871-5100
David J Bush, *Chairman*
Paul Koehler, *CFO*
Elizabeth Holser, *Manager*
Jeffrey Cahill, *Consultant*
Ronald J Mills, *Exec Dir*
EMP: 120
SQ FT: 7,500
SALES (est): 31.4MM **Privately Held**
SIC: 4953 Sanitary landfill operation

(G-11599)
SOUTH- WESTERN CITY SCHOOL DST
Also Called: South Western Head Start
4308 Haughn Rd (43123-3239)
PHONE..........................614 801-8438
Margie Bramel, *Director*
EMP: 70

Grove City - Franklin County (G-11600)

SALES (corp-wide): 303.6MM **Privately Held**
WEB: www.swcs.k12.oh.us
SIC: 8351 Head start center, except in conjunction with school
PA: South- Western City School District
3805 Marlane Dr
Grove City OH 43123
614 801-3000

(G-11600)
SOUTHWESTERN OBSTETRICIANS & G
Also Called: Grogg, Terry W MD
4461 Broadway 200 (43123-3064)
PHONE................614 875-0444
Diane Fitter, *President*
EMP: 25
SALES (est): 1.4MM **Privately Held**
SIC: 8011 Gynecologist; obstetrician

(G-11601)
SPERIAN PROTECTION USA INC
3325 Lewis Centre Way (43123-1786)
PHONE................614 539-5056
Ted Wenger, *Branch Mgr*
Eric Stipp, *Manager*
EMP: 70
SALES (corp-wide): 40.5B **Publicly Held**
SIC: 8741 Management services
HQ: Sperian Protection Usa, Inc.
900 Douglas Pike
Smithfield RI 02917

(G-11602)
STATE OF OHIO
Also Called: Ohio Board of Cosmetology
1929 Gateway Cir (43123-9587)
PHONE................614 466-3834
C Logston, *Exec Dir*
EMP: 38 **Privately Held**
SIC: 8621 Professional membership organizations
PA: State Of Ohio
30 E Broad St Fl 40
Columbus OH 43215
614 466-3455

(G-11603)
SYNNEX CORPORATION
Also Called: Grove City-Doh
4001 Gantz Rd Ste A (43123-4833)
PHONE................614 539-6995
Fax: 614 539-8148
Ruby Ray Ezell, *Branch Mgr*
EMP: 25
SALES (corp-wide): 17B **Publicly Held**
WEB: www.newageinc.com
SIC: 4225 General warehousing
PA: Synnex Corporation
44201 Nobel Dr
Fremont CA 94538
510 656-3333

(G-11604)
T N C CONSTRUCTION INC
Also Called: T N C Recovery and Maintenance
6058 Winnebago St (43123-9076)
PHONE................614 554-5330
Fax: 614 539-1032
Terry Whitt, *President*
EMP: 28
SQ FT: 1,200
SALES: 750K **Privately Held**
SIC: 7349 Building maintenance services

(G-11605)
TMARZETTI COMPANY
Also Called: Marzetti Distribution Center
5800 N Meadows Dr (43123-8600)
PHONE................614 277-3577
Joyce Decker, *Purch Mgr*
Jake Dean, *Research*
Mark Norman, *Branch Mgr*
Jeff Burkhart, *Manager*
Stephanie Gleason, *Manager*
EMP: 122
SALES (corp-wide): 1.2B **Publicly Held**
SIC: 4225 2035 General warehousing & storage; pickles, sauces & salad dressings

HQ: T.Marzetti Company
380 Polaris Pkwy Ste 400
Westerville OH 43082
614 846-2232

(G-11606)
TOSOH AMERICA INC (HQ)
3600 Gantz Rd (43123-1895)
PHONE................614 539-8622
Fax: 614 539-8722
Jan Top, *President*
Ryan Hannigan, *Buyer*
Andrew Hill, *Buyer*
Dan Rowell, *Controller*
Jessica Newsome, *Accounting Mgr*
▲ EMP: 350
SQ FT: 250,000
SALES (est): 215.4MM
SALES (corp-wide): 6.5B **Privately Held**
SIC: 5169 3564 5047 5052 Industrial chemicals; blowers & fans; diagnostic equipment, medical; coal & other minerals & ores
PA: Tosoh Corporation
3-8-2, Shiba
Minato-Ku TKY 105-0
354 275-103

(G-11607)
USHER TRANSPORT INC
2040 Hendrix Dr (43123-1215)
PHONE................614 875-0528
EMP: 25
SALES (corp-wide): 45MM **Privately Held**
SIC: 4925 Gas production and/or distribution
PA: Usher Transport, Inc.
3801 Shanks Ln
Louisville KY 40216
502 449-4000

(G-11608)
VALMER LAND TITLE AGENCY
3383 Farm Bank Way (43123-1973)
PHONE................614 875-7001
Stephanie Pietrocini, *Branch Mgr*
EMP: 33
SALES (corp-wide): 20MM **Privately Held**
SIC: 6361 Real estate title insurance
PA: Valmer Land Title Agency
2227 State Route 256 B
Reynoldsburg OH 43068
614 860-0005

(G-11609)
VOLUNTERS OF AMERICA CNTL OHIO
4026 Mcdowell Rd (43123-3942)
PHONE................614 801-1655
EMP: 75
SALES (corp-wide): 8MM **Privately Held**
SIC: 8322 Individual & family services
PA: Volunteers Of America Of Greater Ohio
1776 E Broad St
Columbus OH 43203
614 253-6100

(G-11610)
WALLICK PROPERTIES MIDWEST LLC
Also Called: Parkmead Apartments
4243 Farr Ct (43123-3951)
PHONE................614 539-9041
Cindy Byers, *Branch Mgr*
EMP: 113
SALES (corp-wide): 46MM **Privately Held**
SIC: 6531 Real estate managers
PA: Wallick Properties Midwest Llc
160 W Main St Ste 200
New Albany OH 43054
614 863-4640

(G-11611)
WALMART INC
3880 Southwest Blvd (43123-9071)
PHONE................614 871-7094
Fax: 614 871-7065
Mitch Hall, *Manager*
Bridget Dill, *Manager*
EMP: 1200

SALES (corp-wide): 500.3B **Publicly Held**
WEB: www.walmartstores.com
SIC: 4225 General warehousing & storage
PA: Walmart Inc.
702 Sw 8th St
Bentonville AR 72716
479 273-4000

(G-11612)
WATERBEDS N STUFF INC (PA)
Also Called: Beds N Stuff
3933 Brookham Dr (43123-9295)
PHONE................614 871-1171
Fax: 614 871-2413
Gerald Spero, *President*
Barry Lange, *General Mgr*
Earl Lloyd, *Purchasing*
▲ EMP: 35
SQ FT: 25,500
SALES (est): 19.1MM **Privately Held**
SIC: 5947 5712 5199 Gift shop; novelties; waterbeds & accessories; gifts & novelties

(G-11613)
WELSPUN USA INC
3901 Gantz Rd Ste A (43123-4914)
PHONE................614 945-5100
Cheryl Edmonds, *Controller*
Devesh Shriv, *Branch Mgr*
EMP: 30
SALES (corp-wide): 786.1MM **Privately Held**
SIC: 5131 Textiles, woven
HQ: Welspun Usa, Inc.
295 Textile Bldg 5th Ave # 5
New York NY 10016
212 620-2000

(G-11614)
WELTMAN WEINBERG & REIS CO LPA
3705 Marlane Dr (43123-8895)
PHONE................614 801-2600
Allen Reis, *Branch Mgr*
EMP: 132
SALES (est): 10.4MM
SALES (corp-wide): 98.4MM **Privately Held**
SIC: 8111 General practice law office
PA: Weltman, Weinberg & Reis Co., L.P.A.
323 W Lkeside Ave Ste 200
Cleveland OH 44113
216 685-1000

(G-11615)
WESTERN & SOUTHERN LF INSUR CO
Also Called: Western-Southern Life Insur
1931 Ohio Dr (43123-4835)
PHONE................614 277-4800
Fax: 614 277-4820
Frank Runion, *District Mgr*
EMP: 40 **Privately Held**
SIC: 6311 Life insurance
HQ: The Western & Southern Life Insurance Company
400 Broadway St
Cincinnati OH 45202
513 629-1800

(G-11616)
WHETSTONE CARE CENTER LLC
Also Called: Monterey Care Center
3929 Hoover Rd (43123-2853)
PHONE................614 875-7700
Sonia Merryman, *Personnel*
Bob Brooks, *Manager*
Gregory Runser, *Director*
Tricia Zelenak, *Executive*
EMP: 210
SALES (corp-wide): 22.4MM **Privately Held**
WEB: www.macintoshcompany.com
SIC: 8051 8069 Convalescent home with continuous nursing care; specialty hospitals, except psychiatric
PA: Whetstone Care Center Llc
3863 Trueman Ct
Hilliard OH 43026
614 345-9500

(G-11617)
WHITE GLOVE EXECUTIVE SERVICES
2647 Bryan Cir (43123-3526)
PHONE................614 226-2553
Gary Holland, *President*
EMP: 25
SALES: 280K **Privately Held**
WEB: www.whiteglovemaintenance.com
SIC: 7349 Building maintenance services

(G-11618)
WOMENS CIVIC CLUB GROVE CITY
3881 Tamara Dr (43123-2864)
PHONE................614 871-0145
Carolyn Kromer, *President*
Rosemary Barkes, *President*
Carol Rorick, *Vice Pres*
Susan Norris, *Treasurer*
Ada Weygandt, *Admin Sec*
EMP: 40
SALES (est): 484.9K **Privately Held**
SIC: 8699 Charitable organization

(G-11619)
WOODLAND RUN EQUIN VET FACILTY
1474 Borror Rd (43123-8972)
PHONE................614 871-4919
Fax: 614 871-2672
Richard C Mather II, *President*
Robert Buell, *Vice Pres*
EMP: 25
SQ FT: 856
SALES (est): 1MM **Privately Held**
SIC: 0742 Veterinarian, animal specialties

(G-11620)
YOUNG MENS CHRISTIAN ASSOC
Also Called: Urban Craft
3600 Discovery Dr (43123-9482)
PHONE................614 871-9622
Erica Hickox, *Director*
EMP: 180
SALES (corp-wide): 44.9MM **Privately Held**
WEB: www.ymca-columbus.com
SIC: 8641 7991 8351 7032 Youth organizations; physical fitness facilities; child day care services; youth camps; individual & family services
PA: Young Men's Christian Association Of Central Ohio
40 W Long St
Columbus OH 43215
614 389-4409

Groveport
Franklin County

(G-11621)
AIRE-TECH INC
4681 Homer Ohio Ln (43125-9231)
PHONE................614 836-5670
Fax: 614 836-5671
Suzie Tamborelle, *President*
Helena Rivera, *Office Mgr*
EMP: 30
SQ FT: 6,000
SALES: 3MM **Privately Held**
SIC: 1711 Warm air heating & air conditioning contractor

(G-11622)
AMSTED INDUSTRIES INCORPORATED
Also Called: Griffin Wheel
3900 Bixby Rd (43125-9510)
PHONE................614 836-2323
Fax: 614 836-2377
Joe Cuske, *Plant Mgr*
Mark S Shirley, *Plant Mgr*
Chris Grys, *Production*
Jesse Lepart, *Research*
Carrie Goss, *Personnel*
EMP: 181

GEOGRAPHIC SECTION

Groveport - Franklin County (G-11646)

SALES (corp-wide): 2.2B **Privately Held**
SIC: **3321** 5088 3743 3714 Railroad car wheels & brake shoes, cast iron; railroad equipment & supplies; railroad equipment; motor vehicle parts & accessories
PA: Amsted Industries Incorporated
180 N Stetson Ave # 1800
Chicago IL 60601
312 645-1700

(G-11623)
ARC INDUSTRIES INCORPORATED O
Also Called: ARC Industries South
4395 Marketing Pl (43125-9556)
PHONE..................614 836-0700
Fax: 614 342-5607
Dan Darling, *Human Res Dir*
Al Brehl, *Info Tech Mgr*
Sharon Evrard, *Technology*
Kurt Smith, *Director*
EMP: 290
SALES (corp-wide): 11.7MM **Privately Held**
WEB: www.arcind.com
SIC: **8322** 8331 Social services for the handicapped; job training & vocational rehabilitation services
PA: Arc Industries, Incorporated, Of Franklin County, Ohio
2780 Airport Dr
Columbus OH 43219
614 479-2500

(G-11624)
ARC INDUSTRIES INCORPORATED O
Also Called: Bixby Living Skills Center
4200 Bixby Rd (43125-9509)
PHONE..................614 836-6050
Fax: 614 342-5020
David Pisdale, *Manager*
Linda Monroe, *Director*
EMP: 50
SALES (corp-wide): 11.7MM **Privately Held**
WEB: www.arcind.com
SIC: **8399** Council for social agency
PA: Arc Industries, Incorporated, Of Franklin County, Ohio
2780 Airport Dr
Columbus OH 43219
614 479-2500

(G-11625)
BOARS HEAD PROVISIONS CO INC
2225 Spiegel Dr (43125-9036)
PHONE..................614 662-5300
Tiffany Ackley, *Hum Res Coord*
EMP: 301
SALES (corp-wide): 221.8MM **Privately Held**
SIC: **5147** Lard
PA: Boar's Head Provisions Co., Inc.
1819 Main St Ste 800
Sarasota FL 34236
941 955-0994

(G-11626)
C & R INC (PA)
5600 Clyde Moore Dr (43125-1081)
PHONE..................614 497-1130
Ronald E Murphy, *President*
Christina M Murphy, *Corp Secy*
Phillip Lee Mc Kitrick, *Vice Pres*
Toni Simmions, *Manager*
EMP: 47
SALES (est): 9.7MM **Privately Held**
WEB: www.crproducts.com
SIC: **3444** 7692 3443 3312 Sheet metal specialties, not stamped; welding repair; fabricated plate work (boiler shop); blast furnaces & steel mills

(G-11627)
CEVA FREIGHT LLC
Also Called: Ceva Ocean Line
2727 London Groveport Rd (43125-9304)
PHONE..................614 482-5100
Greg Russo, *Manager*
EMP: 75 **Publicly Held**
WEB: www.tntlogistics.com
SIC: **4731** Domestic freight forwarding

HQ: Ceva Freight, Llc
15350 Vickery Dr
Houston TX 77032

(G-11628)
CEVA LOGISTICS LLC
2727 London Groveport Rd (43125-9304)
PHONE..................614 482-5000
Robert Harper, *Branch Mgr*
EMP: 300 **Publicly Held**
SIC: **4731** Freight forwarding
HQ: Ceva Logistics, Llc
15350 Vickery Dr
Houston TX 77032
281 618-3100

(G-11629)
COMMERCIAL WAREHOUSE & CARTAGE
6295 Commerce Center Dr (43125-1160)
PHONE..................614 409-3901
EMP: 69
SALES (corp-wide): 92.1MM **Privately Held**
SIC: **4789** Pipeline terminal facilities, independently operated
PA: Commercial Warehouse & Cartage Inc
3402 Meyer Rd
Fort Wayne IN 46803
260 426-7825

(G-11630)
CRAFT WHOLESALERS INC
Also Called: Craft Catalog
4600 S Hamilton Rd (43125-9636)
PHONE..................740 964-6210
Fax: 740 964-6212
Tara Parker, *President*
Ariane Hutchinson, *Exec VP*
Steven Reichardt, *Human Res Mgr*
Mariah Ragan, *Marketing Staff*
Dawn Long, *Director*
▼ EMP: 108 EST: 1981
SQ FT: 50,000
SALES (est): 21.9MM **Privately Held**
WEB: www.craftwholesalers.com
SIC: **5092** 5961 Arts & crafts equipment & supplies; arts & crafts equipment & supplies, mail order

(G-11631)
CUTHBERT GREENHOUSE INC (PA)
4900 Hendron Rd (43125-9506)
PHONE..................614 836-3866
Fax: 614 836-3767
Wayne Cuthbert, *President*
David Cuthbert, *President*
Brett Cuthbert, *Corp Secy*
Grogery Cuthbert, *Vice Pres*
Ron Storm, *Sales Staff*
▲ EMP: 39
SQ FT: 518,000
SALES (est): 5MM **Privately Held**
WEB: www.cuthbertgreenhouse.com
SIC: **0181** Flowers: grown under cover (e.g. greenhouse production)

(G-11632)
DECKERS NURSERY INC
6239 Rager Rd (43125-9266)
PHONE..................614 836-2130
Fax: 614 836-1558
Brian M Decker, *President*
Patricia D Decker, *Corp Secy*
Adam Brown, *Sales Staff*
EMP: 25
SQ FT: 10,000
SALES (est): 3.5MM **Privately Held**
WEB: www.deckersnursery.com
SIC: **0181** Nursery stock, growing of

(G-11633)
DHL SUPPLY CHAIN (USA)
6390 Commerce Ct (43125-1158)
PHONE..................614 836-1265
EMP: 60
SALES (corp-wide): 71.2B **Privately Held**
SIC: **4731** Freight forwarding
HQ: Exel Inc.
570 Polaris Pkwy
Westerville OH 43082
614 865-8500

(G-11634)
DHL SUPPLY CHAIN (USA)
Also Called: Exel Logistics
2829 Rohr Rd (43125-9305)
PHONE..................614 662-9247
Steven Duncan, *General Mgr*
Chris Young, *Opers Spvr*
Wellman Dale, *Manager*
Mark Spencer, *Director*
EMP: 300
SALES (corp-wide): 71.2B **Privately Held**
WEB: www.exel-logistics.com
SIC: **4225** General warehousing
HQ: Exel Inc.
570 Polaris Pkwy
Westerville OH 43082
614 865-8500

(G-11635)
DWYER CONCRETE LIFTING INC
5650 Groveport Rd (43125-1003)
PHONE..................614 501-0998
Fax: 614 491-8828
Bryan Dwyer, *President*
EMP: 45
SALES (est): 1.4MM **Privately Held**
SIC: **1771** Concrete work

(G-11636)
EMERITUS CORPORATION
Also Called: Emeritus At Lakeview
4000 Lakeview Xing (43125-9059)
PHONE..................614 836-5990
Jill Wallace, *Branch Mgr*
EMP: 43
SALES (corp-wide): 4.7B **Publicly Held**
SIC: **8052** Personal care facility
HQ: Emeritus Corporation
3131 Elliott Ave Ste 500
Milwaukee WI 53214

(G-11637)
ESSILOR OF AMERICA INC
2400 Spiegel Dr Ste A (43125-9132)
PHONE..................614 492-0888
Fax: 614 497-3453
Dave Mann, *Facilities Mgr*
Robyn Taylor, *Human Res Mgr*
Den Lucas, *Manager*
Cindy McNeal, *Manager*
Mark Nicolia, *Analyst*
EMP: 250 **Privately Held**
WEB: www.essilor.com
SIC: **7389** 4225 Personal service agents, brokers & bureaus; general warehousing & storage
HQ: Essilor Of America, Inc.
13555 N Stemmons Fwy
Dallas TX 75234
214 496-4000

(G-11638)
FAF INC
6800 Port Rd (43125-9109)
PHONE..................800 496-4696
Mona Pritchard, *Principal*
Mary Walker, *Manager*
EMP: 755
SALES (est): 177.2MM
SALES (corp-wide): 1.1B **Publicly Held**
SIC: **4731** Freight transportation arrangement
PA: Forward Air Corporation
1915 Snapps Ferry Rd N
Greeneville TN 37745
423 636-7000

(G-11639)
FARO SERVICES INC (PA)
7070 Pontius Rd (43125-7504)
PHONE..................614 497-1700
Rich Ashton, *President*
Matthew Shaw, *Sales Mgr*
Tim Thomas, *Branch Mgr*
Lori Jones, *Manager*
EMP: 350
SQ FT: 322,000
SALES (est): 78.9MM **Privately Held**
SIC: **4225** 4731 General warehousing; freight transportation arrangement

(G-11640)
FEDEX SUP CHAIN DIST SYS INC
5765 Green Pointe Dr N (43125-1097)
PHONE..................614 277-3970

Fax: 614 277-3990
Gary Forsythe, *Manager*
Roy Haynes, *Asst Mgr*
EMP: 150
SALES (corp-wide): 60.3B **Publicly Held**
WEB: www.genco.com
SIC: **4225** General warehousing
HQ: Fedex Supply Chain Distribution System, Inc.
700 Cranberry Woods Dr
Cranberry Township PA 16066

(G-11641)
FUNAI SERVICE CORPORATION
2425 Spiegel Dr (43125-9278)
PHONE..................614 409-2600
Takashi Miyamoto, *President*
Yoshihiro Sasaki, *CFO*
Ai Collin, *Accounts Mgr*
Steve Pickett, *Manager*
▲ EMP: 25
SALES (est): 10MM **Privately Held**
SIC: **5065** Electronic parts

(G-11642)
HAGUE WATER CONDITIONING INC (PA)
4581 Homer Ohio Ln (43125-9082)
PHONE..................614 482-8121
Fax: 614 836-8900
William Hague, *President*
Joyce Hague, *Corp Secy*
Jeff Hague, *Vice Pres*
Julie Daniel, *Office Mgr*
Lisa Yacomino, *Info Tech Mgr*
EMP: 26
SALES (est): 5.6MM **Privately Held**
SIC: **7389** 5074 Water softener service; water softeners

(G-11643)
HD SUPPLY INC
6200 Commerce Center Dr (43125-1093)
PHONE..................614 771-4849
Mike Phillips, *President*
EMP: 41 **Publicly Held**
SIC: **5031** 5033 Building materials, exterior; building materials, interior; doors & windows; roofing, siding & insulation
HQ: Hd Supply, Inc.
3100 Cumberland Blvd Se # 1700
Atlanta GA 30339
770 852-9000

(G-11644)
HOME CITY ICE COMPANY
4505 S Hamilton Rd (43125-9335)
PHONE..................614 836-2877
Fax: 614 836-7523
Tony Bakes, *Branch Mgr*
EMP: 50
SQ FT: 12,000
SALES (corp-wide): 314.5MM **Privately Held**
WEB: www.homecityice.com
SIC: **5199** 5999 2097 Ice, manufactured or natural; ice; manufactured ice
PA: The Home City Ice Company
6045 Bridgetown Rd Ste 1
Cincinnati OH 45248
513 574-1800

(G-11645)
HOMETOWN URGENT CARE
3813 S Hamilton Rd (43125-9330)
PHONE..................614 835-0400
EMP: 126
SALES (corp-wide): 73.2MM **Privately Held**
SIC: **8011** Primary care medical clinic
PA: Hometown Urgent Care
2400 Corp Exchange Dr # 102
Columbus OH 43231
614 505-7633

(G-11646)
INN AT LAKEVIEW
4000 Lakeview Xing Ofc (43125-9060)
PHONE..................614 836-2866
Kelly Wilson, *Vice Pres*
Jill Wallace, *Administration*
EMP: 60 EST: 1998
SQ FT: 56,000
SALES (est): 1.5MM **Privately Held**
SIC: **8052** Intermediate care facilities

Groveport - Franklin County (G-11647)

(G-11647)
INNOVTIVE CRTIVE SOLUTIONS LLC
Also Called: I C S
5835 Green Pointe Dr S B (43125-2000)
PHONE..................614 491-9638
Bob Pushay, *Mng Member*
EMP: 38
SALES (est): 1.2MM **Privately Held**
SIC: 2759 7336 Screen printing; commercial art & graphic design

(G-11648)
ISOMEDIX OPERATIONS INC
Also Called: Steris Isomedix
4405 Marketing Pl (43125-9556)
PHONE..................614 836-5757
Fax: 614 836-9829
John M Schweers, *Principal*
Bryan Courtright, *Production*
Bill Williams, *Manager*
EMP: 30
SQ FT: 2,197
SALES (corp-wide): 2.6B **Privately Held**
WEB: www.isomedix.com
SIC: 8734 Industrial sterilization service
HQ: Isomedix Operations Inc.
5960 Heisley Rd
Mentor OH 44060

(G-11649)
J C DIRECT MAIL INC
4241 Williams Rd (43125-9029)
PHONE..................614 836-4848
Fax: 614 836-4847
Wayne Caltrider, *President*
EMP: 200
SQ FT: 76,736
SALES (est): 17MM **Privately Held**
WEB: www.wcnjcd.com
SIC: 7331 Mailing service

(G-11650)
JACOBSON WAREHOUSE COMPANY INC
Also Called: Xpo Logistics
2450 Spiegel Dr Ste H (43125-9120)
PHONE..................614 409-0003
Judith Jacobsen, *Branch Mgr*
EMP: 26
SALES (corp-wide): 15.3B **Publicly Held**
SIC: 4225 General warehousing & storage
HQ: Jacobson Warehouse Company, Inc.
3811 Dixon St
Des Moines IA 50313
515 265-6171

(G-11651)
JACOBSON WAREHOUSE COMPANY INC
Also Called: Xpo Logistics
6600 Port Rd Ste 200 (43125-9129)
PHONE..................614 497-6300
John Kettman, *Branch Mgr*
EMP: 80
SALES (corp-wide): 15.3B **Publicly Held**
WEB: www.jacobsonco.com
SIC: 4225 General warehousing & storage
HQ: Jacobson Warehouse Company, Inc.
3811 Dixon St
Des Moines IA 50313
515 265-6171

(G-11652)
K & M KLEENING SERVICE INC
4429 Professional Pkwy (43125-9228)
PHONE..................614 737-3750
Morris Berkley, *President*
Carolyn Berkley, *Vice Pres*
Randall Parker, *Vice Pres*
Michelle White, *Admin Sec*
EMP: 62
SALES (est): 1.9MM **Privately Held**
SIC: 7349 Janitorial service, contract basis

(G-11653)
KENCO GROUP INC
5235 Westpoint Dr Bldg 1 (43125-1189)
PHONE..................614 409-8754
Bill Harper, *Branch Mgr*
EMP: 30
SALES (corp-wide): 1.6B **Privately Held**
SIC: 4225 4783 Warehousing, self-storage; crating goods for shipping
PA: Kenco Group, Inc.
2001 Rverside Dr Ste 3100
Chattanooga TN 37406
423 622-1113

(G-11654)
KMART CORPORATION
4400 S Hamilton Rd (43125-9559)
PHONE..................614 836-5000
Fax: 614 836-2070
Gene Chlanese, *Manager*
Gene Chianese, *Manager*
Chuck Derr, *Manager*
EMP: 381
SALES (corp-wide): 16.7B **Publicly Held**
WEB: www.kmart.com
SIC: 4225 General warehousing & storage
HQ: Kmart Corporation
3333 Beverly Rd
Hoffman Estates IL 60179
847 286-2500

(G-11655)
KRAFT ELECTRICAL CONTG INC
4407 Professional Pkwy (43125-9228)
PHONE..................614 836-9300
EMP: 36
SALES (corp-wide): 13.4MM **Privately Held**
SIC: 4813 3699 Telephone communication, except radio; electrical equipment & supplies
PA: Kraft Electrical Contracting, Inc.
5710 Hillside Ave
Cincinnati OH 45233
513 467-0500

(G-11656)
LKQ CORPORATION
5830 Green Pointe Dr S A (43125-1188)
PHONE..................614 575-8200
Gary Miller, *Manager*
EMP: 30
SALES (corp-wide): 9.7B **Publicly Held**
SIC: 5093 Scrap & waste materials
PA: Lkq Corporation
500 W Madison St Ste 2800
Chicago IL 60661
312 621-1950

(G-11657)
MID-OHIO DEVELOPMENT CORP (PA)
Also Called: Mid-Ohio Properties
4393 Arbor Lake Dr (43125-9224)
P.O. Box 32449, Columbus (43232-0449)
PHONE..................614 836-0606
Fax: 614 836-4400
Herbert J Murphy Jr, *Ch of Bd*
Roney Murphy, *President*
Tom Denison, *Senior VP*
Larry Parr, *Vice Pres*
Steve Woellert, *CFO*
EMP: 60
SQ FT: 4,800
SALES (est): 15MM **Privately Held**
WEB: www.midohiodevelopment.com
SIC: 6552 6512 4225 Land subdividers & developers, commercial; commercial & industrial building operation; general warehousing

(G-11658)
NEW WORLD VAN LINES OHIO INC
4633 Homer Ohio Ln (43125-9231)
PHONE..................614 836-5720
Fax: 614 836-0600
Michael M Marx, *President*
Richard Wilkus, *CFO*
EMP: 35
SALES (est): 2.9MM **Privately Held**
SIC: 4213 Household goods transport

(G-11659)
NIFCO AMERICA CORPORATION
Also Called: Groveport Warehouse
2435 Spiegel Dr (43125-9278)
PHONE..................614 836-8733
John Deiker, *CFO*
EMP: 200
SALES (corp-wide): 2.2B **Privately Held**
SIC: 4225 General warehousing
HQ: Nifco America Corporation
8015 Dove Pkwy
Canal Winchester OH 43110
614 920-6800

(G-11660)
OHIO POWER COMPANY
4500 S Hamilton Rd (43125-9563)
PHONE..................614 836-2570
Dwight Snowden, *Branch Mgr*
Mike Hire, *Planning*
EMP: 100
SALES (corp-wide): 15.4B **Publicly Held**
SIC: 4911 Generation, electric power; transmission, electric power; distribution, electric power
HQ: Ohio Power Company
1 Riverside Plz
Columbus OH 43215
614 716-1000

(G-11661)
PETSMART INC
6499 Adelaide Ct (43125-9635)
PHONE..................614 497-3001
Fax: 614 409-2855
San Juana Silos, *Branch Mgr*
Rusty Roof, *Manager*
EMP: 48
SALES (corp-wide): 12.7B **Privately Held**
WEB: www.petsmart.com
SIC: 5999 0752 Pet food; animal specialty services
HQ: Petsmart, Inc.
19601 N 27th Ave
Phoenix AZ 85027
623 580-6100

(G-11662)
PRESORT AMERICA LTD
4227 Williams Rd (43125-9029)
PHONE..................614 836-5120
Fax: 614 836-4832
Wayne Caltrider, *Partner*
B W Caltride,
EMP: 60
SALES (est): 4.7MM **Privately Held**
SIC: 7331 Mailing service

(G-11663)
PRESTIGE DELIVERY SYSTEMS LLC
4279 Directors Blvd (43125-9504)
PHONE..................614 836-8980
Jeff Spocker, *Manager*
EMP: 30
SQ FT: 70,400
SALES (corp-wide): 145.1MM **Privately Held**
SIC: 4212 Delivery service, vehicular
HQ: Prestige Delivery Systems, Llc
9535 Midwest Ave Ste 104
Cleveland OH 44125
216 332-8000

(G-11664)
PRO HEALTH CARE SERVICES LTD
270 Main St Ste A (43125-1180)
P.O. Box 472 (43125-0472)
PHONE..................614 856-9111
Fax: 614 482-8051
Marco A Quezada, *Partner*
Maria Delaluz-Munoz, *General Ptnr*
Edward Lott, *COO*
EMP: 50
SALES (est): 1.6MM **Privately Held**
SIC: 8082 Visiting nurse service

(G-11665)
RADIAL SOUTH LP
6360-6440 Port Rd (43125)
PHONE..................678 584-4047
Steve Bolin, *Manager*
EMP: 200
SALES (corp-wide): 305.3MM **Privately Held**
WEB: www.innotrac.com
SIC: 5045 4226 Computers, peripherals & software; special warehousing & storage
HQ: Radial South, L.P.
935 1st Ave
King Of Prussia PA 19406
610 491-7000

(G-11666)
RENTOKIL NORTH AMERICA INC
Also Called: Initial Tropical Plant Svcs
6300 Commerce Center Dr G (43125-1183)
PHONE..................614 837-0099
Monica Garrison, *Vice Pres*
Monica Desch, *Manager*
Sue Riegel, *Admin Asst*
EMP: 35
SALES (corp-wide): 2.6B **Privately Held**
WEB: www.primescapeproducts.com
SIC: 5193 0781 Flowers & nursery stock; landscape services
HQ: Rentokil North America, Inc.
1125 Berkshire Blvd # 150
Wyomissing PA 19610
610 372-9700

(G-11667)
RICART FORD INC
Also Called: Ricart Automotive
4255 S Hamilton Rd (43125-9332)
PHONE..................614 836-5321
Fax: 614 836-6480
Rhett C Ricart, *President*
Jeffrey Becker, *Business Mgr*
Paul F Ricart Jr, *Vice Pres*
Jon Funderburk, *Parts Mgr*
Larry Mills, *Parts Mgr*
▲ EMP: 460 EST: 1953
SQ FT: 13,000
SALES (est): 71.8MM **Privately Held**
SIC: 5511 7538 Automobiles, new & used; general automotive repair shops

(G-11668)
RYDER TRUCK RENTAL INC
6500 Port Rd (43125-9103)
PHONE..................614 409-6550
Fax: 614 409-9917
Gregory Swienton, *Branch Mgr*
EMP: 40
SALES (corp-wide): 7.3B **Publicly Held**
SIC: 7513 Truck rental, without drivers
HQ: Ryder Truck Rental, Inc.
11690 Nw 105th St
Medley FL 33178
305 500-3726

(G-11669)
S&P GLOBAL INC
6405 Commerce Ct (43125-1187)
PHONE..................614 835-2444
EMP: 149
SALES (corp-wide): 6B **Publicly Held**
SIC: 6282 Investment advisory service
PA: S&P Global Inc.
55 Water St Ste Conc2
New York NY 10041
212 438-1000

(G-11670)
SCHENKER INC
2842 Spiegel Dr (43125-9012)
PHONE..................614 662-7217
Byron Howard, *Opers Mgr*
Joyce Michles, *Manager*
EMP: 30 **Privately Held**
SIC: 4789 Pipeline terminal facilities, independently operated
HQ: Schenker, Inc.
150 Albany Ave
Freeport NY 11520
757 821-3400

(G-11671)
SHAKLEE CORPORATION
5650 Green Pointe Dr N A (43125-1063)
PHONE..................614 409-2953
Gregg Wilson, *Branch Mgr*
EMP: 200
SALES (corp-wide): 129.7MM **Privately Held**
WEB: www.shaklee.net
SIC: 5122 Vitamins & minerals
PA: Shaklee Corporation
4747 Willow Rd
Pleasanton CA 94588
925 924-2000

GEOGRAPHIC SECTION

Hamilton - Butler County (G-11696)

(G-11672)
SHERMCO INDUSTRIES INC
Also Called: 8094
4383 Professional Pkwy (43125-9035)
PHONE..................614 836-8556
Brent McManan, *Branch Mgr*
EMP: 60
SALES (corp-wide): 150MM **Privately Held**
SIC: 8742 Maintenance management consultant
PA: Shermco Industries, Inc.
2425 E Pioneer Dr
Irving TX 75061
972 793-5523

(G-11673)
SPRINGS WINDOW FASHIONS LLC
6295 Commerce Center Dr (43125-1160)
PHONE..................614 492-6770
Mike Mehring, *Manager*
EMP: 66 **Privately Held**
WEB: www.springs.com
SIC: 4225 General warehousing & storage
HQ: Springs Window Fashions, Llc
7549 Graber Rd
Middleton WI 53562
608 836-1011

(G-11674)
STEDMAN FLOOR CO INC
420 Lowery Ct (43125-9567)
P.O. Box 418 (43125-0418)
PHONE..................614 836-3190
Fax: 614 836-0113
Richard Stedman, *President*
Tammy Dorion, *Bookkeeper*
Wanda Stedman, *Admin Sec*
EMP: 30
SQ FT: 26,000
SALES: 3.9MM **Privately Held**
SIC: 1752 Floor laying & floor work

(G-11675)
STRAND ASSOCIATES INC
4433 Professional Pkwy (43125-9228)
PHONE..................614 835-0460
Richard Sanson, *Vice Pres*
EMP: 36
SALES (corp-wide): 55.2MM **Privately Held**
SIC: 8711 Consulting engineer
PA: Strand Associates, Inc.
910 W Wingra Dr
Madison WI 53715
608 251-4843

(G-11676)
TNT POWER WASH INC
Also Called: TNT Services
3220 Toy Rd (43125-9297)
PHONE..................614 662-3110
Seth Bromberg, *President*
EMP: 26
SALES: 9.8MM **Privately Held**
SIC: 7349 Cleaning service, industrial or commercial

(G-11677)
TNT POWER WASH INC (PA)
Also Called: TNT Services
3220 Toy Rd (43125-9297)
PHONE..................614 662-3110
Seth Bromberg, *President*
Angela Root, *Sales Mgr*
Alicia Alexander, *Accounts Mgr*
Ricky Martin, *Accounts Mgr*
Michael McLean, *Accounts Mgr*
EMP: 26
SALES: 9.8MM **Privately Held**
SIC: 7349 Cleaning service, industrial or commercial

(G-11678)
TRILOGY FULFILLMENT LLC
6600 Alum Creek Dr (43125-9420)
PHONE..................614 491-0553
Charles Flannigan Jr,
EMP: 28
SALES (est): 70.3MM
SALES (corp-wide): 1.5B **Privately Held**
SIC: 8742 Distribution channels consultant

PA: Golden Gate Private Equity Incorporated
1 Embarcadero Ctr # 3900
San Francisco CA 94111
415 983-2706

(G-11679)
TRUGREEN LIMITED PARTNERSHIP
Also Called: Tru Green-Chemlawn
4045 Lakeview Xing (43125-9039)
PHONE..................614 610-4142
Fax: 614 836-0821
Tom Kiener, *Branch Mgr*
EMP: 45
SALES (corp-wide): 4B **Privately Held**
SIC: 0782 Lawn care services
HQ: Trugreen Limited Partnership
1790 Kirby Pkwy
Memphis TN 38138
901 251-4128

(G-11680)
UNION SUPPLY GROUP INC
Also Called: Food Express US
3321 Toy Rd (43125-9363)
PHONE..................614 409-1444
Fax: 614 409-1445
Guy Steele, *COO*
EMP: 30 **Privately Held**
SIC: 5084 Industrial machinery & equipment
PA: Union Supply Group, Inc.
2301 E Pacifica Pl
Rancho Dominguez CA 90220

(G-11681)
UNITED MCGILL CORPORATION (HQ)
1 Mission Park (43125-1100)
PHONE..................614 445-6850
Fax: 614 836-0113
James D McGill, *President*
Kathleen Cauley, *Personnel*
Tim Baltzer, *Programmer Anys*
Norman L Boyer, *Director*
Patrick Brooks, *Director*
▲ **EMP:** 30 **EST:** 1951
SQ FT: 13,000
SALES (est): 61.5MM **Privately Held**
WEB: www.unitedmcgill.com
SIC: 3444 3564 5169 3567 Ducts, sheet metal; precipitators, electrostatic; air purification equipment; sealants; industrial furnaces & ovens; adhesives & sealants
PA: The Mcgill Corporation
1 Mission Park
Groveport OH 43125
614 829-1200

(G-11682)
USAVINYL LLC
Also Called: Weatherables
5795 Green Pointe Dr S (43125-1083)
PHONE..................614 771-4805
Karla Norris, *Controller*
Brad Halley,
◆ **EMP:** 26
SALES: 10MM **Privately Held**
SIC: 5211 5031 Fencing; building materials, exterior

(G-11683)
UTILITY TECHNOLOGIES INTL CORP
4700 Homer Ohio Ln (43125-9230)
PHONE..................614 870-7624
Richard D Dickerson, *CEO*
Richard Dickerson, *CEO*
Hobart Griset, *President*
Rodney V Bennett, *Vice Pres*
Jason Julian, *Vice Pres*
EMP: 50
SALES (est): 9MM **Privately Held**
WEB: www.uti-corp.com
SIC: 8711 Consulting engineer

(G-11684)
VILLAGE OF GROVEPORT
655 Blacklick St (43125-1200)
PHONE..................614 830-2060
Anthony Bales, *Branch Mgr*
EMP: 34 **Privately Held**
SIC: 8322 Senior citizens' center or association

PA: Village Of Groveport
655 Blacklick St
Groveport OH 43125
614 836-5301

(G-11685)
W C NATIONAL MAILING CORP
4241 Williams Rd (43125-9573)
PHONE..................614 836-5703
Fax: 614 836-2076
Wayne Caltrider, *President*
Coy Walker, *Manager*
EMP: 300
SQ FT: 30,000
SALES (est): 24.2MM **Privately Held**
SIC: 7331 Mailing service

(G-11686)
WAXMAN CONSUMER PDTS GROUP INC
5920 Green Pointe Dr S A (43125-1182)
PHONE..................614 491-0500
Fax: 614 491-3027
Jeff Willey, *Manager*
Cong Lu, *Manager*
EMP: 60
SALES (corp-wide): 100MM **Privately Held**
WEB: www.waxmancpgvendor.com
SIC: 5074 5072 Plumbing fittings & supplies; casters & glides; furniture hardware
HQ: Waxman Consumer Products Group Inc.
24455 Aurora Rd
Cleveland OH 44146

Hamden
Vinton County

(G-11687)
HUSTON NURSING HOME
38500 State Route 160 (45634-8805)
P.O. Box 327 (45634-0327)
PHONE..................740 384-3485
Fax: 740 384-3324
Marjorie Houston, *President*
EMP: 90
SALES (est): 3.8MM **Privately Held**
SIC: 8051 Convalescent home with continuous nursing care

(G-11688)
SANDS HILL COAL HAULING CO INC (PA)
38701 State Route 160 (45634-8700)
PHONE..................740 384-4211
Alan Arthur, *President*
Diane Derrow, *Accountant*
EMP: 142 **EST:** 1946
SQ FT: 3,500
SALES (est): 7.2MM **Privately Held**
SIC: 1221 Strip mining, bituminous

Hamilton
Butler County

(G-11689)
AIRGAS SAFETY INC
N Park Business (45011)
PHONE..................513 942-1465
Hap Pfiefer, *Branch Mgr*
EMP: 50
SALES (corp-wide): 163.9MM **Privately Held**
WEB: www.airgas.com
SIC: 5169 Industrial gases
HQ: Airgas Safety, Inc.
2501 Green Ln
Levittown PA 19057

(G-11690)
ALAN WOODS TRUCKING INC
3592 Herman Rd (45013-9534)
PHONE..................513 738-3314
Alan Woods, *President*
Mary Lou Woods, *Corp Secy*
Audra Woods, *Manager*
EMP: 28
SALES (est): 2.7MM **Privately Held**
SIC: 4212 Dump truck haulage

(G-11691)
ALLAN MILLER INSURANCE AGENCY
185 N Brookwood Ave (45013-1211)
PHONE..................513 863-2629
Fax: 513 863-3899
Gary Miller, *President*
Allan Miller, *President*
Rob Wile, *Vice Pres*
Margie Miller, *Admin Sec*
EMP: 30
SQ FT: 750
SALES: 550K **Privately Held**
SIC: 6411 Insurance agents

(G-11692)
APPLAUSE TALENT PRESENTATION
1525 Singer Ave (45011-4420)
PHONE..................513 844-6788
Fax: 513 844-6840
Mary Anne Weisbrod, *President*
EMP: 25 **EST:** 1988
SALES (est): 858.6K **Privately Held**
WEB: www.applausetalent.com
SIC: 7911 Dance hall services

(G-11693)
AS LOGISTICS INC (DH)
Also Called: Amstan Logistics
101 Knightsbridge Dr (45011-3166)
PHONE..................513 863-4627
Fax: 513 863-0866
Jim Manfra, *President*
Ryan Ward, *Business Mgr*
Douglas Brown, *Opers Mgr*
Steve Kaiser, *Controller*
Ken Hurley, *Accountant*
EMP: 70 **EST:** 1974
SQ FT: 28,000
SALES: 76.5MM
SALES (corp-wide): 15.7B **Privately Held**
WEB: www.amstan.com
SIC: 4213 Contract haulers

(G-11694)
AUR GROUP FINANCIAL CREDIT UN
1401 Nw Washington Blvd (45013-1748)
PHONE..................513 737-0508
Fax: 513 894-3916
Tim Boellner, *Branch Mgr*
EMP: 32
SALES (corp-wide): 39K **Privately Held**
SIC: 6061 6062 Federal credit unions; state credit unions
PA: Aurgroup Financial Credit Union, Inc.
8811 Holden Blvd
Fairfield OH 45014
513 942-4422

(G-11695)
BUILDER SERVICES GROUP INC
Also Called: Gale Insulation
28 Keisland Ct (45015)
PHONE..................513 942-2204
Fax: 513 942-7535
Patrick Flanagan, *Division Mgr*
Sandra Parkinson, *Production*
Russ Miller, *Branch Mgr*
Dave Slesher, *Manager*
EMP: 25
SALES (corp-wide): 1.9B **Publicly Held**
WEB: www.galeind.com
SIC: 1742 Insulation, buildings
HQ: Builder Services Group, Inc.
475 N Williamson Blvd
Daytona Beach FL 32114
386 304-2222

(G-11696)
BUTLER COUNTY OF OHIO
Also Called: Auditors Office
130 High St Fl 4 (45011-2728)
PHONE..................513 887-3154
Fax: 513 887-3149
Kay Roger, *Manager*
EMP: 90 **Privately Held**
WEB: www.butlercountyclerk.org
SIC: 6531 Auction, real estate
PA: Butler, County Of Ohio
315 High St Fl 6
Hamilton OH 45011
513 887-3278

Hamilton - Butler County (G-11697)

(G-11697)
BUTLER COUNTY OF OHIO
Also Called: Workforce One
4631 Dixie Hwy (45014-1845)
PHONE.................................513 785-6500
Donald Kell, *Supervisor*
EMP: 25 **Privately Held**
WEB: www.butlercountyclerk.org
SIC: 8331 Job training & vocational rehabilitation services; job counseling
PA: Butler, County Of Ohio
315 High St Fl 6
Hamilton OH 45011
513 887-3278

(G-11698)
BUTLER BHAVIORAL HLTH SVCS INC (PA)
Also Called: HAMILTON COUNSELING CENTER T/S
1490 University Blvd (45011-3305)
PHONE.................................513 896-7887
Fax: 513 896-5682
Kimball Stricklin, *CEO*
Francis Koboenzer, *Med Doctor*
Alysha Haury, *Program Mgr*
EMP: 28
SALES: 8.4MM **Privately Held**
SIC: 8093 Mental health clinic, outpatient

(G-11699)
BUTLER CNTY CMNTY HLTH CNSRTM
300 High St 4 (45011-6078)
PHONE.................................513 454-1460
Fax: 513 887-3748
Donald Reimer, *Director*
EMP: 65
SQ FT: 22,000
SALES: 9.7MM **Privately Held**
SIC: 8011 General & family practice, physician/surgeon

(G-11700)
BUTLER COUNTY BD OF MENTAL RE
Also Called: Janat Clemmons Center
282 N Fair Ave Ste 1 (45011-4252)
PHONE.................................513 785-2815
Fax: 513 887-1527
Lisa Guliano, *Superintendent*
Mary May, *Principal*
Hailey Quinn, *Accounting Mgr*
Colleen Mercuri, *Psychologist*
Gina Frankenfield, *Education*
EMP: 28
SALES (corp-wide): 5.9MM **Privately Held**
SIC: 8361 8351 Home for the mentally retarded; preschool center
PA: Butler County Board Of Developmental Disabilities
282 N Fair Ave Ste 1
Hamilton OH 45011
513 785-2815

(G-11701)
BUTLER COUNTY CLERK OF COURTS
315 High St Ste 550 (45011-6063)
PHONE.................................513 887-3282
Kornhaus Justin, *Project Mgr*
Mary Swain, *Clerk*
EMP: 80 **EST:** 1889 **Privately Held**
SIC: 9211 8111 9621 9199 Local courts; administrative & government law; motor vehicle licensing & inspection office, government; general government administration

(G-11702)
BUTLER COUNTY EDUCTL SVC CTR
Also Called: Butler County Eductl Svcs Ctr
23 S Front St Fl 3 (45011-2819)
PHONE.................................513 737-2817
Fax: 513 737-2490
Kelly Hubbard, *Branch Mgr*
EMP: 35
SALES (corp-wide): 13.6MM **Privately Held**
SIC: 8351 Head start center, except in conjunction with school

PA: Butler County Educational Service Center
400 N Erie Hwy Ste A
Hamilton OH 45011
513 887-3710

(G-11703)
BUTLER COUNTY OF OHIO
Also Called: Butler County Engineers Office
1921 Fairgrove Ave (45011-1965)
PHONE.................................513 867-5744
Fax: 513 867-5849
Greg Wilkens, *Manager*
Jerry Jackson, *Supervisor*
EMP: 75 **Privately Held**
WEB: www.butlercountyclerk.org
SIC: 8711 Engineering services
PA: Butler, County Of Ohio
315 High St Fl 6
Hamilton OH 45011
513 887-3278

(G-11704)
BUTLER COUNTY OF OHIO
Also Called: Butler County Courts
315 High St Fl 5 (45011-6063)
PHONE.................................513 887-3090
Fax: 513 887-3970
Cindi Carpenter, *Principal*
EMP: 40 **Privately Held**
WEB: www.butlercountyclerk.org
SIC: 9211 8111 ; legal services
PA: Butler, County Of Ohio
315 High St Fl 6
Hamilton OH 45011
513 887-3278

(G-11705)
BUTLER COUNTY OF OHIO
Also Called: Butler County Information Svcs
315 High St Fl 2 (45011-6097)
PHONE.................................513 887-3418
Greg Sullivan, *Director*
EMP: 30 **Privately Held**
WEB: www.butlercountyclerk.org
SIC: 7378 Computer maintenance & repair
PA: Butler, County Of Ohio
315 High St Fl 6
Hamilton OH 45011
513 887-3278

(G-11706)
CARINGTON HEALTH SYSTEMS (PA)
Also Called: Franklin Ridge Care Facility
8200 Beckett Park Dr (45011)
PHONE.................................513 682-2700
Fax: 513 682-2701
Glyndon Powell, *President*
Edward Byington, *Vice Pres*
Sharon Wilburn, *Human Res Dir*
Linda Thiel, *Director*
Tammy Smith, *Nursing Dir*
EMP: 35
SALES (est): 85.7MM **Privately Held**
SIC: 8741 8051 Hospital management; nursing & personal care facility management; skilled nursing care facilities

(G-11707)
CENTURY EQUIPMENT INC
8650 Bilstein Blvd (45015-2204)
P.O. Box 62148, Cincinnati (45262-0148)
PHONE.................................513 285-1800
Ed Etton, *Branch Mgr*
EMP: 35
SALES (corp-wide): 41.7MM **Privately Held**
WEB: www.centuryequip.com
SIC: 5083 5087 Mowers, power; service establishment equipment
PA: Century Equipment, Inc.
5959 Angola Rd
Toledo OH 43615
419 865-7400

(G-11708)
CHACO CREDIT UNION INC (PA)
100 S 3rd St (45011-2816)
PHONE.................................513 785-3500
Fax: 513 785-3590
Ronald Lang, *President*
Dan Daily, *Vice Pres*
Kurt Winkler, *Vice Pres*
Peggy Klinzing, *Opers Mgr*
George Gordon, *CFO*

EMP: 50
SALES: 6.1MM **Privately Held**
WEB: www.chacocu.org
SIC: 6062 State credit unions, not federally chartered

(G-11709)
CITY OF HAMILTON
Also Called: City Dept Streets and Sewers
2210 S Erie Hwy (45011-4128)
PHONE.................................513 785-7551
Fax: 513 868-5907
Bob Sutton, *Superintendent*
EMP: 31 **Privately Held**
WEB: www.ci.hamilton.oh.us
SIC: 4952 9621 Sewerage systems; transportation department: government, non-operating
PA: City Of Hamilton
345 High St Fl 3
Hamilton OH 45011
513 785-7000

(G-11710)
CITY OF HAMILTON
Also Called: City of Hamilton Waste Water
2451 River Rd (45015-1432)
PHONE.................................513 868-5971
Fax: 513 868-5965
Thomas Hildebrand, *Manager*
EMP: 31 **Privately Held**
WEB: www.ci.hamilton.oh.us
SIC: 4952 Sewerage systems
PA: City Of Hamilton
345 High St Fl 3
Hamilton OH 45011
513 785-7000

(G-11711)
CITY OF HAMILTON
Also Called: Municipal Power Plant
960 N 3rd St (45011-1515)
PHONE.................................513 785-7450
Fax: 513 867-7343
Daniel Moats, *Branch Mgr*
EMP: 63 **Privately Held**
WEB: www.ci.hamilton.oh.us
SIC: 4911 Generation, electric power
PA: City Of Hamilton
345 High St Fl 3
Hamilton OH 45011
513 785-7000

(G-11712)
CLOSSMAN CATERING INCORPORATED
3725 Symmes Rd (45015-3305)
PHONE.................................513 942-7744
Fax: 513 942-7788
David Closky, *President*
Elizabeth Forman, *Vice Pres*
Sean Snyder, *Vice Pres*
David Vogt, *Vice Pres*
EMP: 40
SALES (est): 1.5MM **Privately Held**
SIC: 8322 Meal delivery program

(G-11713)
COLONIAL SENIOR SERVICES INC
Also Called: Berkeley Square Retirement Ctr
100 Berkley Dr (45013-1787)
PHONE.................................513 856-8600
Fax: 513 856-8324
Jim Mayer, *Branch Mgr*
Daniel Niehaus, *Director*
James Mayer, *Administration*
EMP: 130 **Privately Held**
SIC: 8741 8211 8399 8351 Management services; kindergarten; fund raising organization, non-fee basis; preschool center
PA: Colonial Senior Services, Inc.
520 Eaton Ave
Hamilton OH 45013

(G-11714)
COLONIAL SENIOR SERVICES INC
Also Called: Westover Preparatory School
855 Stahlheber Rd (45013-1963)
PHONE.................................513 867-4006
Fax: 513 867-4006
Kathleen Jackman, *Director*
EMP: 130 **Privately Held**

SIC: 8741 8211 8351 Management services; kindergarten; preschool center
PA: Colonial Senior Services, Inc.
520 Eaton Ave
Hamilton OH 45013

(G-11715)
COLONIAL SENIOR SERVICES INC
Also Called: Westover Retirement Community
855 Stahlheber Rd (45013-1963)
PHONE.................................513 844-8004
Fax: 513 895-0102
David Mancuso, *Manager*
Sucharitha Nalagatla, *Director*
Jim Mayer, *Administration*
EMP: 130 **Privately Held**
SIC: 8741 Management services
PA: Colonial Senior Services, Inc.
520 Eaton Ave
Hamilton OH 45013

(G-11716)
COMMUNITY BEHAVIORAL HLTH INC
824 S Martin Luther King (45011-3216)
PHONE.................................513 887-8500
Mark Zoellner, *Branch Mgr*
Kenneth E Tepe, *Psychiatry*
EMP: 160
SALES (corp-wide): 11.9MM **Privately Held**
SIC: 8093 Substance abuse clinics (outpatient)
PA: Community Behavioral Health, Inc.
520 Eaton Ave
Hamilton OH 45011
513 785-4783

(G-11717)
CONCORD HAMILTONIAN RVRFRNT HO
Also Called: Courtyard By Marriott
1 Riverfront Plz (45011-2712)
PHONE.................................513 896-6200
Carmam Johnson, *Principal*
Jamie Campbell, *Executive*
Mark G Laport, *Executive*
EMP: 60
SALES (est): 1.9MM **Privately Held**
SIC: 7011 Hotels

(G-11718)
COOLANTS PLUS INC (PA)
Also Called: Starfire
2570 Van Hook Ave (45015-1582)
PHONE.................................513 892-4000
Kurt D Deimer, *President*
Darrin Ward, *General Mgr*
Shelly Conrad, *Accounting Mgr*
Leigh Smith, *VP Sales*
JP Henderson, *Associate*
▲ **EMP:** 38
SQ FT: 9,000
SALES (est): 59.1MM **Privately Held**
WEB: www.coolantsplus.com
SIC: 5172 Fuel oil

(G-11719)
CREATIVE CENTER FOR CHILDREN
23 Court St (45011-2801)
PHONE.................................513 867-1118
Fax: 513 867-5417
Jennifer Dunkin, *Principal*
EMP: 45
SALES (est): 1.4MM **Privately Held**
SIC: 8351 Child day care services

(G-11720)
DARANA HYBRID INC
345 High St Fl 5 (45011-6086)
PHONE.................................513 785-7540
Darryl Cuttell, *President*
Rodney Caudill, *Vice Pres*
Gene Mercer, *Vice Pres*
Bart Tolleson, *Vice Pres*
Wayne Nelums, *Project Mgr*
▲ **EMP:** 75
SQ FT: 20,000
SALES (est): 17.6MM **Privately Held**
SIC: 1731 General electrical contractor

GEOGRAPHIC SECTION
Hamilton - Butler County (G-11744)

(G-11721)
DENNY R KING
325 N 10th St (45011-3411)
PHONE..................513 917-7968
Denny R King, *Principal*
EMP: 42
SALES (est): 2.7MM **Privately Held**
SIC: 1521 Single-family housing construction

(G-11722)
DIEBOLD NIXDORF INCORPORATED
8509 Bilstein Blvd (45015-2213)
PHONE..................513 870-1400
Daniel Kelly, *Sales Executive*
Greg Welsh, *Branch Mgr*
Eric Benson, *Manager*
EMP: 75
SALES (corp-wide): 4.6B **Publicly Held**
WEB: www.diebold.com
SIC: 5049 1731 7378 Bank equipment & supplies; banking machine installation & service; computer maintenance & repair
PA: Diebold Nixdorf, Incorporated
 5995 Mayfair Rd
 North Canton OH 44720
 330 490-4000

(G-11723)
DIVERSCARE HEALTHCARE SVCS INC
1302 Millville Ave (45013-3961)
PHONE..................513 867-4100
EMP: 30
SALES (corp-wide): 574.7MM **Publicly Held**
SIC: 8099 Blood related health services
PA: Diversicare Healthcare Services, Inc.
 1621 Galleria Blvd
 Brentwood TN 37027
 615 771-7575

(G-11724)
DON S CISLE CONTRACTOR INC (PA)
1714 Fairgrove Ave (45011-1962)
PHONE..................513 867-1400
Don M Cisle, *President*
Elizabeth Messeloing, *Manager*
EMP: 65
SQ FT: 2,400
SALES (est): 4.5MM **Privately Held**
WEB: www.cisle.com
SIC: 1611 General contractor, highway & street construction

(G-11725)
ELLISON TECHNOLOGIES INC
5333 Muhlhauser Rd (45011-9349)
PHONE..................310 323-2121
Art Seyler, *Branch Mgr*
EMP: 25
SALES (corp-wide): 38.4B **Privately Held**
WEB: www.ellisonmw.com
SIC: 5085 Industrial supplies
HQ: Ellison Technologies, Inc.
 9912 Pioneer Blvd
 Santa Fe Springs CA 90670
 562 949-8311

(G-11726)
EMPLOYMENT RELATIONS BOARD
Southwest Regional Water Dst
3640 Old Oxford Rd (45013-9382)
PHONE..................513 863-0828
Tom Yeager, *General Mgr*
Sherry Fry, *Human Resources*
EMP: 40 **Privately Held**
WEB: www.swwater.org
SIC: 4941 9199 Water supply; general government administration;
HQ: Employment Relations Board, Ohio State
 65 E State St Ste 1200
 Columbus OH 43215

(G-11727)
FORT HAMILTON HOSP FOUNDATION
630 Eaton Ave (45013-2767)
PHONE..................513 867-5492
EMP: 392

SALES (est): 686.7K
SALES (corp-wide): 1.7B **Privately Held**
SIC: 8399 Fund raising organization, non-fee basis
HQ: The Fort Hamilton Hospital
 630 Eaton Ave
 Hamilton OH 45013
 513 867-2000

(G-11728)
FORT HAMILTON HOSPITAL (DH)
Also Called: CHARLES F KETTERING MEMORIAL H
630 Eaton Ave (45013-2767)
PHONE..................513 867-2000
Alex Rodriguez, *President*
Michael Mewhirter, *VP Opers*
Peter J King, *VP Finance*
Lesley Snyder, *Finance Dir*
Joseph Geigle, *Human Res Dir*
EMP: 65 EST: 1925
SQ FT: 350,000
SALES: 119.4MM
SALES (corp-wide): 1.7B **Privately Held**
WEB: www.forthamiltonhospital.com
SIC: 8062 General medical & surgical hospitals
HQ: Kettering Medical Center
 3535 Southern Blvd
 Kettering OH 45429
 937 298-4331

(G-11729)
FORT HMLTN-HGHES HLTHCARE CORP (PA)
630 Eaton Ave (45013-2767)
PHONE..................513 867-2000
Fax: 513 867-2172
James A Kingsbury, *President*
Carol Huges, *Accountant*
Ronald Sundernaus, *Marketing Staff*
Robert McCollum, *Manager*
EMP: 1100
SQ FT: 350,000
SALES: 3.3MM **Privately Held**
SIC: 8741 Management services

(G-11730)
FRESENIUS MED CARE BUTLER CTY
Also Called: Fresenius Kdney Care W Hmilton
890 Nw Washington Blvd (45013-1281)
PHONE..................513 737-1415
Michelle Smallwood, *Branch Mgr*
Mary Garber, *Manager*
EMP: 30
SALES (corp-wide): 944.2K **Privately Held**
SIC: 8092 Kidney dialysis centers
PA: Fresenius Medical Care Butler County, Llc
 920 Winter St
 Waltham MA 02451
 781 699-4000

(G-11731)
GE ENGINE SERVICES LLC
3024 Symmes Rd (45015-1331)
PHONE..................513 243-9404
John Ousley, *Branch Mgr*
EMP: 300
SALES (corp-wide): 122B **Publicly Held**
SIC: 5088 Aircraft equipment & supplies
HQ: Ge Engine Services, Llc
 1 Neumann Way
 Cincinnati OH 45215
 513 243-2000

(G-11732)
GOLDEN YEARS NURSING HOME INC
Also Called: Golden Years Health Care
2436 Old Oxford Rd (45013-9332)
PHONE..................513 893-0471
Fax: 513 737-7620
Kyra Hornsby, *Administration*
EMP: 40
SQ FT: 15,000
SALES (est): 2.2MM
SALES (corp-wide): 85.7MM **Privately Held**
SIC: 8051 Extended care facility

PA: Carington Health Systems
 8200 Beckett Park Dr
 Hamilton OH 45011
 513 682-2700

(G-11733)
GREAT MIAMI VALLEY YMCA (PA)
Also Called: Fairfield YMCA
105 N 2nd St (45011-2701)
PHONE..................513 887-0001
Fax: 513 887-0960
Daven W Fippon, *President*
Jenny McGinnis, *CFO*
Dawn Knochenmuss, *Finance*
EMP: 60
SQ FT: 60,000
SALES: 13.3MM **Privately Held**
SIC: 8641 7991 8351 7032 Youth organizations; physical fitness facilities; child day care services; youth camps; individual & family services

(G-11734)
GREAT MIAMI VALLEY YMCA
Also Called: YMCA Camp Campbell Gard
4803 Augspurger Rd (45011-9547)
PHONE..................513 867-0600
Rick Taylor, *Branch Mgr*
EMP: 30
SALES (corp-wide): 13.3MM **Privately Held**
SIC: 8641 7033 Youth organizations; campsite
PA: Great Miami Valley Ymca
 105 N 2nd St
 Hamilton OH 45011
 513 887-0001

(G-11735)
GREAT MIAMI VALLEY YMCA
Also Called: Central Hamilton YMCA
105 N 2nd St (45011-2701)
PHONE..................513 887-0014
Dawn Knochenmuss, *Finance Mgr*
Angela Howard, *Branch Mgr*
Marlene Gillespie, *Director*
EMP: 60
SALES (est): 199.8K
SALES (corp-wide): 13.3MM **Privately Held**
SIC: 8641 7991 8351 7032 Youth organizations; physical fitness facilities; child day care services; youth camps; individual & family services
PA: Great Miami Valley Ymca
 105 N 2nd St
 Hamilton OH 45011
 513 887-0001

(G-11736)
GREAT MIAMI VALLEY YMCA
Also Called: Fitton Family YMCA
1307 Nw Washington Blvd (45013-1207)
PHONE..................513 868-9622
Ron Thunderhouse, *Exec Dir*
EMP: 100
SALES (corp-wide): 13.3MM **Privately Held**
SIC: 8641 7991 8351 7032 Youth organizations; physical fitness facilities; child day care services; youth camps; individual & family services
PA: Great Miami Valley Ymca
 105 N 2nd St
 Hamilton OH 45011
 513 887-0001

(G-11737)
H & R BLOCK INC
2304a Dixie Hwy (45015-1613)
PHONE..................513 868-1818
Fax: 513 868-1617
Mike Wilson, *Branch Mgr*
EMP: 30
SALES (corp-wide): 3B **Publicly Held**
SIC: 7291 Tax return preparation services
PA: H&R Block, Inc.
 1 H&R Block Way
 Kansas City MO 64105
 816 854-3000

(G-11738)
HAMILTON AUTOMOTIVE WAREHOUSE
Also Called: Savage Auto Supply Div
630 Maple Ave Ste 36 (45011-6001)
PHONE..................513 896-4000
Kathie Wallen, *Financial Exec*
Mark Wesendorf, *Manager*
EMP: 70
SALES (corp-wide): 15.1MM **Privately Held**
SIC: 5013 Automotive supplies & parts
PA: Hamilton Automotive Warehouse Inc
 630 Maple Ave
 Hamilton OH 45011
 513 896-4100

(G-11739)
HAMILTON AUTOMOTIVE WAREHOUSE (PA)
Also Called: Savage Auto Supply Div
630 Maple Ave (45011-6001)
PHONE..................513 896-4100
Jared Licklitter, *General Mgr*
Mark Wessendorf, *Manager*
EMP: 75
SQ FT: 20,000
SALES (est): 15.1MM **Privately Held**
SIC: 5013 5531 Automotive supplies & parts; automotive parts

(G-11740)
HAMILTON PARKS CONSERVANCY
106 N 2nd St (45011-2702)
PHONE..................513 785-7055
William Timmer, *Director*
EMP: 28
SALES: 1.9MM **Privately Held**
SIC: 8742 Maintenance management consultant

(G-11741)
HAMILTON SCRAP PROCESSORS
134 Hensel Pl (45011-1508)
PHONE..................513 863-3474
Neil Cohen, *President*
Wilbur Cohen, *Corp Secy*
Kenneth Cohen, *Vice Pres*
Pauline Koehler, *Manager*
EMP: 30
SQ FT: 140,000
SALES (est): 4MM **Privately Held**
SIC: 5093 Waste paper; metal scrap & waste materials; plastics scrap

(G-11742)
HOSPICE OF HAMILTON
1010 Eaton Ave (45013-4640)
PHONE..................513 895-1270
Nancy Glorius, *Opers Staff*
Victoria Ott, *Exec Dir*
Donna Prickel, *Director*
EMP: 30
SALES (est): 1.3MM **Privately Held**
SIC: 8741 Management services

(G-11743)
IMFLUX INC
3550 Symmes Rd Ste 100 (45015-1498)
PHONE..................513 488-1017
Nathan Estruth, *CEO*
Dave Le Neveu, *CFO*
EMP: 32
SALES (est): 7.1MM
SALES (corp-wide): 65B **Publicly Held**
SIC: 7371 8741 Computer software development & applications; management services; business management
PA: The Procter & Gamble Company
 1 Procter And Gamble Plz
 Cincinnati OH 45202
 513 983-1100

(G-11744)
INLOES MECHANICAL INC
Also Called: Inloes Heating and Cooling
157 N B St (45013-3102)
PHONE..................513 896-9499
Fax: 513 896-4320
Ryan Inloes, *President*
Richard A Inloes, *Vice Pres*
EMP: 28 EST: 1979
SQ FT: 32,000

Hamilton - Butler County (G-11745)

SALES: 5MM **Privately Held**
WEB: www.inloesheating.com
SIC: **1711** Warm air heating & air conditioning contractor

(G-11745)
INNOVATIVE ENRGY SOLUTIONS LLC
3680 Symmes Rd (45015-1380)
PHONE.............................937 228-3044
Fax: 937 874-8911
Mark Putnam,
John Brofft,
EMP: 31
SALES (est): 11.6MM **Privately Held**
SIC: **5084** Controlling instruments & accessories

(G-11746)
INTEGRATED POWER SERVICES LLC
2175a Schlichter Dr (45015-1482)
PHONE.............................513 863-8816
Jason Reynolds, *Branch Mgr*
EMP: 28
SQ FT: 20,500
SALES (corp-wide): 1.3B **Privately Held**
WEB: www.integratedps.com
SIC: **7694** Rebuilding motors, except automotive
HQ: Integrated Power Services Llc
3 Independence Pt Ste 100
Greenville SC 29615

(G-11747)
IRON MOUNTAIN INFO MGT LLC
3790 Symmes Rd (45015-1372)
PHONE.............................513 942-7300
Sandy Freeman, *Manager*
EMP: 25
SALES (corp-wide): 3.8B **Publicly Held**
SIC: **4226** Document & office records storage
HQ: Iron Mountain Information Management, Llc
1 Federal St
Boston MA 02110
800 899-4766

(G-11748)
JOSEPH T RYERSON & SON INC
Also Called: Ryerson Coil Processing
1108 Central Ave (45011-3823)
PHONE.............................513 896-4600
Eli Taylor, *Purch Mgr*
Dave Winkler, *Branch Mgr*
EMP: 30 **Publicly Held**
SIC: **5051** Steel; iron & steel (ferrous) products; aluminum bars, rods, ingots, sheets, pipes, plates, etc.; nonferrous metal sheets, bars, rods, etc.
HQ: Joseph T. Ryerson & Son, Inc.
227 W Monroe St Fl 27
Chicago IL 60606
312 292-5000

(G-11749)
KAROPA INCORPORATE
Also Called: Comfort Keepers
3987 Hmiltn Mddltwn Rd (45011-2297)
P.O. Box 18156, Fairfield (45018-0156)
PHONE.............................513 860-1616
Ron Rosenberg, *CEO*
Karen Rosenburg, *Vice Pres*
EMP: 45
SALES (est): 1.3MM **Privately Held**
SIC: **8082** Visiting nurse service

(G-11750)
KINGDOM KIDS INC
6106 Havenwood Ct (45011-7835)
PHONE.............................513 851-6400
Fax: 513 851-3396
EMP: 32
SALES (est): 934.5K **Privately Held**
SIC: **8351** Daycare Center

(G-11751)
LAIRSON TRUCKING LLC
99 N Riverside Dr (45011-5741)
PHONE.............................513 894-0452
Fax: 513 894-0321
Robert Lairson, *Partner*
Brenda Lairson, *Partner*
EMP: 25
SALES (est): 2MM **Privately Held**
SIC: **4212** Local trucking, without storage

(G-11752)
LARRY L MINGES
Also Called: Minges Drywall
4396 Wade Mill Rd (45014-5854)
PHONE.............................513 738-4901
Larry L Minges, *Owner*
EMP: 25
SALES (est): 1MM **Privately Held**
SIC: **1742** Drywall

(G-11753)
LCD HOME HEALTH AGENCY LLC
Also Called: Lcd Nurse Aide Academy
6 S 2nd St Ste 409 (45011-2865)
PHONE.............................513 497-0441
Lamonda Dye, *Mng Member*
EMP: 26
SQ FT: 1,500
SALES: 125K **Privately Held**
SIC: **8059** 8249 Convalescent home; practical nursing school

(G-11754)
LIFESPAN INCORPORATED (PA)
1900 Fairgrove Ave (45011-1966)
PHONE.............................513 868-3210
Cynthia Stever, *CEO*
Mary Royer, *Project Mgr*
Joyce Kachelries, *Director*
William Staler, *Director*
EMP: 74 **EST**: 1945
SQ FT: 21,000
SALES: 3.9MM **Privately Held**
WEB: www.lifespanohio.org
SIC: **8322** Family service agency; general counseling services

(G-11755)
LOWES HOME CENTERS LLC
1495 Main St (45013-1075)
PHONE.............................513 737-3700
Fax: 513 737-9175
Jeff Orvechowski, *Manager*
EMP: 150
SALES (corp-wide): 68.6B **Publicly Held**
SIC: **5211** 5031 5722 5064 Home centers; building materials, exterior; building materials, interior; household appliance stores; electrical appliances, television & radio
HQ: Lowe's Home Centers, Llc
1605 Curtis Bridge Rd
Wilkesboro NC 28697
336 658-4000

(G-11756)
M A FOLKES COMPANY INC
3095 Mcbride Ct (45011-5375)
P.O. Box 425 (45012-0425)
PHONE.............................513 785-4200
Fax: 513 785-4205
Michael Folkes, *President*
Jami Ambrosini, *Sls & Mktg Exec*
Barb Morgan, *Controller*
Barbara Morgan, *Personnel Exec*
Monica Robinson, *Executive*
EMP: 45
SQ FT: 200,000
SALES (est): 4.6MM **Privately Held**
WEB: www.mafolkes.com
SIC: **7389** 4225 8741 Packaging & labeling services; general warehousing & storage; management services

(G-11757)
MATANDY STEEL & METAL PDTS LLC
Also Called: Matandy Steel Sales
1200 Central Ave (45013-3825)
P.O. Box 1186 (45012-1186)
PHONE.............................513 844-2277
Fax: 513 844-6120
Andrew Schuster, *President*
Aaron Higdon, *General Mgr*
Melissa Holder, *Controller*
Matthew Pfirman, *Finance*
Julie Andrews, *Manager*
EMP: 100
SQ FT: 125,000
SALES (est): 104.8MM **Privately Held**
WEB: www.matandy.com
SIC: **5051** 3312 3444 3399 Steel; sheet or strip, steel, cold-rolled: own hot-rolled; studs & joists, sheet metal; nails: aluminum, brass or other nonferrous metal or wire

(G-11758)
MCCULLOUGH-HYDE MEM HOSP INC
1390 Eaton Ave (45013-1407)
PHONE.............................513 863-2215
Fax: 513 863-3338
Peter Towne, *Owner*
EMP: 355
SALES (corp-wide): 23.2MM **Privately Held**
SIC: **8062** General medical & surgical hospitals
PA: The Mccullough-Hyde Memorial Hospital Incorporated
110 N Poplar St
Oxford OH 45056
513 523-2111

(G-11759)
MILLIKIN AND FITTON LAW FIRM (PA)
Also Called: Millikin & Fitton
232 High St (45011-2711)
P.O. Box 598 (45012-0598)
PHONE.............................513 829-6700
Fax: 513 863-0031
John J Reister, *Partner*
John H Clemmons, *Partner*
Michael A Fulton, *Partner*
J S Irwin, *Partner*
William Keck, *Partner*
EMP: 28
SALES (est): 4.6MM **Privately Held**
WEB: www.mfitton.com
SIC: **8111** General practice law office

(G-11760)
MILLIS TRANSFER INC
1982 Jackson Rd (45011-9058)
PHONE.............................513 863-0222
Fax: 513 863-1934
Randy Purkey, *Manager*
EMP: 25
SALES (corp-wide): 108.2MM **Privately Held**
WEB: www.millistransfer.com
SIC: **4213** Contract haulers
PA: Millis Transfer, Inc.
121 Gebhardt Rd
Black River Falls WI 54615
715 284-4384

(G-11761)
OHIO CASUALTY INSURANCE CO
136 N 3rd St (45011-2726)
PHONE.............................513 867-3000
Fax: 513 867-2979
Jim Mc Goldrick, *Vice Pres*
Rick Thomas, *Personnel Exec*
Hal Goode, *Manager*
EMP: 148
SALES (corp-wide): 38.3B **Privately Held**
WEB: www.oci.com
SIC: **6331** Automobile insurance
HQ: The Ohio Casualty Insurance Company
9450 Seward Rd
Fairfield OH 45014
800 843-6446

(G-11762)
PEAK 10 INC
5307 Muhlhauser Rd (45011-9349)
PHONE.............................513 645-2900
Ernest Leffler, *Branch Mgr*
Alvaro Gonzalez, *Business Dir*
EMP: 70
SALES (corp-wide): 88.7MM **Privately Held**
SIC: **8748** Systems engineering consultant, ex. computer or professional
HQ: Peak 10, Inc.
8910 Lenox Pointe Dr G
Charlotte NC 28273

(G-11763)
PERSONAL TOUCH HM CARE IPA INC
7924 Jessies Way C (45011-1336)
PHONE.............................513 868-2272
Rob Swartz, *Marketing Staff*
Jenny Justice, *Manager*
Elizabeth Peters,
EMP: 150
SALES (corp-wide): 363MM **Privately Held**
WEB: www.pthomecare.com
SIC: **8082** Home health care services
PA: Personal Touch Home Care Ipa, Inc.
1985 Marcus Ave Ste 202
New Hyde Park NY 11042
718 468-4747

(G-11764)
PRESSLEY RIDGE FOUNDATION
734 Dayton St (45011-3460)
PHONE.............................513 737-0400
Fax: 513 785-3892
Anna Robinson, *Manager*
EMP: 30 **Privately Held**
SIC: **8082** Home health care services
PA: Pressley Ridge Foundation
5500 Corporate Dr Ste 400
Pittsburgh PA 15237

(G-11765)
R E WATSON INC
2728 Hamilton Cleves Rd (45013-9452)
P.O. Box 277, Ross (45061-0277)
PHONE.............................513 863-0070
Fax: 513 887-2327
Ronald E Watson, *President*
Michael Watson, *Vice Pres*
Janet Meyers, *Admin Sec*
EMP: 25 **EST**: 1964
SQ FT: 2,000
SALES: 5MM **Privately Held**
SIC: **4212** 4213 Dump truck haulage; trucking, except local

(G-11766)
RACK & BALLAUER EXCVTG CO INC
11321 Paddys Run Rd (45013-9403)
PHONE.............................513 738-7000
Larry Ballauer, *President*
Randy Rack, *Vice Pres*
Scot Rack, *Vice Pres*
EMP: 50
SQ FT: 4,000
SALES: 18.2MM **Privately Held**
SIC: **1794** Excavation work

(G-11767)
RAPIER ELECTRIC INC
4845 Augspurger Rd (45011-9547)
PHONE.............................513 868-9087
Fax: 513 868-9295
N Lynn Rapier, *President*
Lynn Rapier, *President*
Daniel Rapier, *Vice Pres*
EMP: 61
SQ FT: 2,100
SALES (est): 7.4MM **Privately Held**
SIC: **1731** General electrical contractor

(G-11768)
RESCARE OHIO INC
5099 Camelot Dr (45014-7423)
PHONE.............................513 829-8992
Melissa Moore, *Manager*
Dwight Finch, *Manager*
Lynne Hibbard, *Director*
EMP: 70
SALES (corp-wide): 24.5B **Privately Held**
SIC: **8361** Self-help group home
HQ: Rescare Ohio Inc
348 W Main St
Williamsburg OH 45176

(G-11769)
RESIDENCE AT KENSINGTON PLACE
Also Called: Residence At Huntington Court
350 Hancock Ave (45011-4448)
PHONE.............................513 863-4218
Larry Schindler, *Manager*
Sandy Smiley, *Food Svc Dir*
EMP: 125

SALES (corp-wide): 5.8MM **Privately Held**
SIC: 8059 Nursing home, except skilled & intermediate care facility
PA: The Residence At Kensington Place
751 Kensington St
Middletown OH 45044
513 424-3511

(G-11770)
RK FAMILY INC
1416 Main St (45013-1004)
PHONE..................513 737-0436
David Pfeiffer, *Principal*
EMP: 219
SALES (corp-wide): 1.2B **Privately Held**
SIC: 5083 Farm equipment parts & supplies
PA: Rk Family, Inc.
4216 Dewitt Ave
Mattoon IL 61938
217 235-7102

(G-11771)
RUMPKE CNSLD COMPANIES INC (PA)
Also Called: Rumpke Waste and Recycl Svcs
3963 Kraus Ln (45014-5841)
PHONE..................513 738-0800
Fax: 513 742-2900
William Rumpke Jr, *President*
Jeff Rumpke, *Vice Pres*
Todd Rumpke, *Vice Pres*
Anne Gray, *Site Mgr*
Richard J Roberts, *Engineer*
EMP: 200
SQ FT: 25,000
SALES (est): 1.6B **Privately Held**
SIC: 4953 Recycling, waste materials

(G-11772)
SALVAGNINI AMERICA INC (DH)
27 Bicentennial Ct (45015-1382)
PHONE..................513 874-8284
Fax: 513 874-2229
Eugenio Bassan, *CEO*
Vicente Undurraga, *Ch of Bd*
Doug Johnson, *Vice Pres*
Acosta Carlos, *Engineer*
▲ EMP: 40
SQ FT: 60,000
SALES (est): 34.6MM **Privately Held**
WEB: www.salvagnini.com
SIC: 5084 Machine tools & accessories; metalworking machinery
HQ: Salvagnini Italia Spa
Via Ingegnere Guido Salvagnini 51
Sarego VI 36040
044 472-5111

(G-11773)
SOJOURNER RECOVERY SERVICES (PA)
Also Called: Sojourner Home
294 N Fair Ave (45011-4222)
PHONE..................513 868-7654
Fax: 513 868-8091
Scott Dehring, *CEO*
Jan Day, *Sales Executive*
Leslye Simak, *Manager*
EMP: 80
SALES: 5.8MM **Privately Held**
WEB: www.sojournerrecovery.org
SIC: 8322 Alcoholism counseling, nontreatment

(G-11774)
STAARMANN CONCRETE INC
4316 Stahlheber Rd (45013-8912)
PHONE..................513 756-9191
Joseph Staarmann, *President*
Lynn Staarmann, *Admin Sec*
EMP: 30
SALES (est): 1.6MM **Privately Held**
SIC: 1771 Concrete work

(G-11775)
STAHLHEBER & SONS INC
Also Called: Stahlheber Excavating
4205 Hamilton Eaton Rd (45011-9643)
PHONE..................513 726-4446
Fax: 513 726-4600
Douglas W Stahlheber, *President*
Dave Long, *Vice Pres*
Chris Stahlheber, *Vice Pres*
Debra Stahlheber, *Admin Sec*

EMP: 28
SQ FT: 4,080
SALES: 1.4MM **Privately Held**
SIC: 1794 Excavation work

(G-11776)
SUNRISE SENIOR LIVING LLC
Also Called: Sunrise of Hamilton
896 Nw Washington Blvd (45013-1281)
PHONE..................513 893-9000
Fax: 513 893-9001
Jamie Cianciolo, *Exec Dir*
Natalie May, *Director*
Liz Peters, *Administration*
EMP: 50
SALES (corp-wide): 4.3B **Publicly Held**
WEB: www.sunrise.com
SIC: 8051 Skilled nursing care facilities
HQ: Sunrise Senior Living, Llc
7902 Westpark Dr
Mc Lean VA 22102

(G-11777)
TERRY ASPHALT MATERIALS INC (DH)
8600 Bilstein Blvd (45015-2204)
PHONE..................513 874-6192
Dan Koeninger, *CEO*
Dave Shaw, *Asst Supt*
Mike Haag, *Terminal Mgr*
Jim Monroe, *Terminal Mgr*
Andrew Sigafoos, *Terminal Mgr*
EMP: 25
SALES (est): 38.3MM
SALES (corp-wide): 95.5MM **Privately Held**
SIC: 5082 2952 Road construction & maintenance machinery; asphalt felts & coatings
HQ: Barrett Industries Corporation
73 Headquarters Plz
Morristown NJ 07960
973 533-1001

(G-11778)
THYSSENKRUPP BILSTEIN AMER INC (HQ)
8685 Bilstein Blvd (45015-2205)
PHONE..................513 881-7600
Fabian Schmahl, *President*
Hendrik Walde, *Opers Mgr*
Markus Mencher, *Opers Staff*
Ben Fisher, *Purch Mgr*
James Sagedal, *Purch Agent*
◆ EMP: 212
SQ FT: 115,000
SALES (est): 87.7MM
SALES (corp-wide): 48.7B **Privately Held**
SIC: 3714 5013 Shock absorbers, motor vehicle; springs, shock absorbers & struts
PA: Thyssenkrupp Ag
Thyssenkrupp Allee 1
Essen 45143
201 844-0

(G-11779)
TRUTEAM LLC
Also Called: Gale Insulation
28 Kiesland Ct (45015-1374)
PHONE..................513 942-2204
EMP: 25
SALES (corp-wide): 2.3B **Publicly Held**
SIC: 1742 Drywall/Insulating Contractor
HQ: Truteam, Llc
260 Jimmy Ann Dr
Daytona Beach FL 32114

(G-11780)
TWINBROOK HILLS BAPTIST CHURCH
40 Wrenwood Dr (45013-2499)
PHONE..................513 863-3107
Fax: 513 863-3991
Richard Riddick, *Pastor*
EMP: 40 EST: 1935
SALES (est): 899.6K **Privately Held**
WEB: www.twinbrook.net
SIC: 8661 8351 8211 Baptist Church; preschool center; kindergarten; private combined elementary & secondary school; private junior high school; private senior high school

(G-11781)
UNITED PARCEL SERVICE INC OH
Also Called: UPS
1951 Logan Ave (45015-1020)
PHONE..................513 863-1681
Fax: 513 863-1987
Bryan Zelen, *Manager*
EMP: 72
SALES (corp-wide): 65.8B **Publicly Held**
WEB: www.upsscs.com
SIC: 4215 Parcel delivery, vehicular
HQ: United Parcel Service, Inc. (Oh)
55 Glenlake Pkwy
Atlanta GA 30328
404 828-6000

(G-11782)
UNITED PERFORMANCE METALS INC (HQ)
3475 Symmes Rd (45015-1363)
PHONE..................513 860-6500
Tom Kennard, *President*
Craft O'Neal, *Chairman*
Greg Chase, *Vice Pres*
Peter Hackman, *Vice Pres*
Ray Miranda, *Plant Mgr*
◆ EMP: 141
SQ FT: 110,000
SALES (est): 99.7MM
SALES (corp-wide): 2.1B **Privately Held**
WEB: www.upmet.com
SIC: 5051 Steel
PA: O'neal Industries, Inc
2311 Highland Ave S # 200
Birmingham AL 35205
205 721-2880

(G-11783)
UNIVAR USA INC
12 Standen Dr (45015-2208)
PHONE..................513 870-4050
Bill Spangler, *Plant Mgr*
John Baird, *Branch Mgr*
EMP: 40
SALES (corp-wide): 8.2B **Publicly Held**
SIC: 5169 Industrial chemicals
HQ: Univar Usa Inc.
17411 Ne Union Hill Rd
Redmond WA 98052
425 889-3400

(G-11784)
WATSON GRAVEL INC (PA)
2728 Hamilton Cleves Rd (45013-9452)
PHONE..................513 863-0070
Ronald E Watson, *President*
Janet L Meyers, *Corp Secy*
Michael T Watson, *Vice Pres*
Labreeska Stanifer, *Human Res Mgr*
Brian Bottoms, *Manager*
EMP: 55
SQ FT: 2,000
SALES (est): 10.6MM **Privately Held**
WEB: www.watsongravel.com
SIC: 1442 Gravel mining

(G-11785)
YWCA OF HAMILTON
Also Called: Y W C A
244 Dayton St (45011-1634)
PHONE..................513 856-9800
Fax: 513 856-9803
Jane Rose, *President*
EMP: 29
SQ FT: 10,000
SALES: 1.2MM **Privately Held**
SIC: 8641 7999 Youth organizations; recreation center

Hammondsville
Jefferson County

(G-11786)
SALINE TOWNSHIP
Also Called: Emergency Medical Services
164 Main St (43930)
P.O. Box 177 (43930-0177)
PHONE..................330 532-2195
Marsha Plunket, *Chief*
EMP: 28
SALES (est): 799.1K **Privately Held**
SIC: 8322 Emergency social services

Hanoverton
Columbiana County

(G-11787)
SPREAD EAGLE TAVERN INC
10150 Plymouth St (44423-9623)
PHONE..................330 223-1583
Fax: 330 223-1445
David Johnson, *President*
Rod Chapman, *General Mgr*
Mark Webb, *Admin Sec*
EMP: 40
SALES (est): 1.5MM
SALES (corp-wide): 33.8MM **Privately Held**
WEB: www.spreadeagletavern.com
SIC: 7011 5812 Bed & breakfast inn; eating places
PA: Summitville Tiles, Inc
15364 State Rte 644
Summitville OH 43962
330 223-1511

Harrison
Hamilton County

(G-11788)
3S INCORPORATED (HQ)
8686 Southwest Pkwy (45030-2109)
PHONE..................513 202-5070
Matthew M Euson, *President*
Thomas Euson, *Vice Pres*
Simon Brakhage, *Project Mgr*
Michael Davis, *Asst Controller*
Sean Copenhaver, *Accounts Mgr*
EMP: 26
SQ FT: 10,000
SALES: 23MM
SALES (corp-wide): 2.6B **Privately Held**
SIC: 5099 Fire extinguishers
PA: Api Group Inc.
1100 Old Highway 8 Nw
Saint Paul MN 55112
651 636-4320

(G-11789)
ALLIANCE KNIFE INC
124 May Dr (45030-2024)
P.O. Box 729 (45030-0729)
PHONE..................513 367-9000
Fax: 513 367-2233
William L Keith, *President*
Sharon Keith, *Corp Secy*
Sheryl Becker, *Sales Associate*
Jackie Elmore, *Sales Associate*
Joe Daughery, *Sales Executive*
◆ EMP: 50
SALES (est): 7.4MM **Privately Held**
WEB: www.allianceknife.com
SIC: 3545 5085 3541 3423 Machine knives, metalworking; knives, industrial; machine tools, metal cutting type; hand & edge tools; cutlery

(G-11790)
ALTAQUIP LLC (DH)
100 Production Dr (45030-1477)
PHONE..................513 674-6464
Fax: 513 674-6468
Jeff Wedele, *Controller*
Mike King, *Mng Member*
EMP: 50
SALES (est): 58.7MM
SALES (corp-wide): 242.1B **Publicly Held**
SIC: 7699 Lawn mower repair shop
HQ: The Scott Fetzer Company
28800 Clemens Rd
Westlake OH 44145
440 892-3000

(G-11791)
ARCHWAYS BROOKVILLE INC
375 Industrial Dr (45030-1483)
P.O. Box 218 (45030-0218)
PHONE..................513 367-2649
Robert Cummings, *President*
EMP: 60

Harrison - Hamilton County (G-11792)

SALES (est): 2.9MM **Privately Held**
SIC: 8721 Accounting, auditing & bookkeeping

(G-11792)
BRIDGESTONE RET OPERATIONS LLC
Also Called: Michel Tires Plus 227925
10606 New Haven Rd (45030-2777)
PHONE.................513 367-7888
Fax: 513 202-5473
Cody George, *Manager*
EMP: 30
SALES (corp-wide): 32.5B **Privately Held**
WEB: www.tiresplus.com
SIC: 7534 Tire retreading & repair shops
HQ: Bridgestone Retail Operations, Llc
333 E Lake St Ste 300
Bloomingdale IL 60108
630 259-9000

(G-11793)
CINCINNATI EARLY LEARNING CTR
498 S State St (45030-1446)
PHONE.................513 367-2129
Fax: 513 367-2214
April Stewart, *Director*
EMP: 30
SALES (corp-wide): 5.1MM **Privately Held**
SIC: 8351 Preschool center
PA: Early Cincinnati Learning Center Inc
1301 E Mcmillan St
Cincinnati OH 45206
513 961-2690

(G-11794)
CIRCLING HILLS GOLF COURSE
10240 Carolina Trace Rd (45030-1604)
PHONE.................513 367-5858
Fax: 513 367-0838
John E Minges, *President*
Ed Minges, *Principal*
Gloria Minges, *Principal*
EMP: 40
SALES (est): 1.3MM **Privately Held**
WEB: www.circlinghills.com
SIC: 7992 5812 Public golf courses; eating places

(G-11795)
CORNELIUS JOEL ROOFING INC
Also Called: Home Improvement Center
9107 Kilby Rd (45030-2018)
P.O. Box 211 (45030-0211)
PHONE.................513 367-4401
Fax: 513 367-4482
Joel Cornelius, *President*
Keith Cornelius, *Vice Pres*
Doug Nagle, *Vice Pres*
Mary Jo Cornelius, *Admin Sec*
EMP: 25
SQ FT: 4,000
SALES (est): 3MM **Privately Held**
WEB: www.joelcornelius.com
SIC: 1761 5211 5251 Roofing contractor; gutter & downspout contractor; roofing material; hardware

(G-11796)
DENIER ELECTRIC CO INC (PA)
Also Called: Denier Technologies Div
10891 State Route 128 (45030-9236)
PHONE.................513 738-2641
Dennis J Denier, *CEO*
George D Roberts, *President*
Dave Eastabrooks, *Pastor*
Steve Johantges, *Pastor*
Diane K Herbort, *Exec VP*
EMP: 215
SQ FT: 40,000
SALES: 58.1MM **Privately Held**
WEB: www.denier.com
SIC: 1731 General electrical contractor

(G-11797)
F & M MAFCO INC (PA)
9149 Dry Fork Rd (45030-1901)
P.O. Box 11013, Cincinnati (45211-0013)
PHONE.................513 367-2151
Fax: 513 367-0363
Daniel Mc Kenna, *President*
Scott Speigle, *General Mgr*
Brenda Mittelstadt, *Sr Corp Ofcr*
Pat Mc Kenna, *Exec VP*
Robert W Mc Kenna Jr, *Exec VP*
◆ EMP: 186
SQ FT: 85,000
SALES: 76.9MM **Privately Held**
WEB: www.fmmafco.com
SIC: 5085 5072 7353 5082 Welding supplies; hardware; heavy construction equipment rental; general construction machinery & equipment

(G-11798)
FAIRWAY INDEPENDENT MRTG CORP
1180 Stone Dr (45030-1658)
PHONE.................513 367-6344
EMP: 34 **Privately Held**
SIC: 6162 Mortgage bankers
PA: Fairway Independent Mortgage Corporation
4750 S Biltmore Ln
Madison WI 53718

(G-11799)
GREER & WHITEHEAD CNSTR INC
510 S State St Ste D (45030-1494)
PHONE.................513 202-1757
Fax: 513 202-1757
Steven Whitehead, *President*
EMP: 35
SALES (est): 5.7MM **Privately Held**
SIC: 1711 1389 Mechanical contractor; building oil & gas well foundations on site

(G-11800)
HARRISON AVE ASSEMBLY OF GOD
Also Called: Hilltop Nursery School
949 Harrison Ave (45030-1520)
PHONE.................513 367-6100
Fax: 513 367-7280
Shirley Greene, *Principal*
John R Hembree, *Principal*
Dr John Hembree, *Pastor*
EMP: 30
SQ FT: 10,000
SALES (est): 1.7MM **Privately Held**
SIC: 8661 8351 8211 Churches, temples & shrines; nursery school; elementary & secondary schools

(G-11801)
HARRISON BUILDING AND LN ASSN (PA)
10490 New Haven Rd (45030-1657)
PHONE.................513 367-2015
Fax: 513 367-6590
Randall Grubbs, *President*
Robert Means, *Vice Pres*
Ray Ferneding, *Controller*
Jerry Heartmann, *CIO*
EMP: 28 EST: 1916
SALES: 7.6MM **Privately Held**
SIC: 6036 6035 Savings & loan associations, not federally chartered; federal savings & loan associations

(G-11802)
HUBERT COMPANY LLC (HQ)
9555 Dry Fork Rd (45030-1994)
PHONE.................513 367-8600
Fax: 513 367-8619
Mark Rudy, *President*
Chris Lewis, *General Mgr*
Ken Shaner, *Business Mgr*
Charles Dennis, *Vice Pres*
Rodger Reed, *Warehouse Mgr*
◆ EMP: 306 EST: 1946
SQ FT: 453,000
SALES (est): 187.7MM **Privately Held**
SIC: 5046 Store fixtures; store equipment; display equipment, except refrigerated

(G-11803)
JAMES H ALVIS TRUCKING INC
Also Called: Alvis Lndcape Golf Curses Mtls
9570 State Route 128 (45030-9706)
P.O. Box 243, Miamitown (45041-0243)
PHONE.................513 623-7211
Fax: 513 738-6116
James H Alvis, *President*
EMP: 28
SQ FT: 84,000
SALES (est): 2.3MM **Privately Held**
SIC: 4212 Dump truck haulage

(G-11804)
K&K TECHNICAL GROUP INC
10053 Simonson Rd Ste 2 (45030-2194)
PHONE.................513 202-1300
James Kennedy, *President*
Lindsey Skeens, *Vice Pres*
Mindy Beeson, *Accounting Mgr*
EMP: 200
SQ FT: 200
SALES: 15MM **Privately Held**
WEB: www.kandktechnical.com
SIC: 8711 Engineering services

(G-11805)
M & S DRYWALL INC
10999 State Route 128 (45030-9237)
PHONE.................513 738-1510
Fax: 513 738-3740
Paul Spaulding, *President*
Terry Spaulding, *Vice Pres*
EMP: 26
SALES: 1.5MM **Privately Held**
SIC: 1742 Drywall

(G-11806)
MODERN DAY CONCRETE CNSTR
9773 Crosby Rd (45030-9707)
PHONE.................513 738-1026
Fax: 513 738-4643
Thomas Weisman, *President*
Frank Klosterman, *Chairman*
David Sellet, *Vice Pres*
Gail Evans, *Admin Sec*
EMP: 30 EST: 1964
SQ FT: 2,500
SALES (est): 3.8MM **Privately Held**
SIC: 1771 Concrete work

(G-11807)
NVR INC
9439 Tebbs Ct (45030-2822)
PHONE.................513 202-0323
EMP: 112
SALES (corp-wide): 5B **Publicly Held**
SIC: 1531 Operative Builders
PA: Nvr, Inc.
11700 Plaza America Dr # 500
Reston VA 20190
703 956-4000

(G-11808)
SCHERZINGER DRILLING INC
9629 State Route 128 (45030-9226)
P.O. Box 202, Miamitown (45041-0202)
PHONE.................513 738-2000
Fax: 513 738-3100
Kenneth E Scherzinger, *President*
Kathleen Scherzinger, *Vice Pres*
Greg Nagele, *Opers Mgr*
Josh Trauger, *Administration*
EMP: 25
SQ FT: 7,000
SALES: 6.5MM **Privately Held**
WEB: www.scherzingerdrilling.com
SIC: 1629 Caisson drilling; pier construction

(G-11809)
T J WILLIAMS ELECTRIC CO
7925 New Haven Rd (45030-9205)
P.O. Box 586, Miamitown (45041-0586)
PHONE.................513 738-5366
Fax: 513 738-5375
Joyce Meyer, *President*
Teresa Vogelsang, *Vice Pres*
Diane Vogelsang, *Manager*
EMP: 25
SQ FT: 6,000
SALES (est): 4.5MM **Privately Held**
SIC: 1731 General electrical contractor

(G-11810)
TAKKT AMERICA HOLDING INC (PA)
9555 Dry Fork Rd (45030-1906)
PHONE.................513 367-8600
C Bart Kohler, *Principal*
Jeff Shelton, *Treasurer*
Janet McGuffey, *Controller*
Connie Rawb, *Accountant*
Jennifer M Clements, *Admin Sec*
▲ EMP: 187
SQ FT: 576,715
SALES (est): 39MM **Privately Held**
SIC: 5046 Store fixtures; store equipment; display equipment, except refrigerated

(G-11811)
TRIUMPH ENERGY CORPORATION
9171 Dry Fork Rd (45030-1901)
PHONE.................513 367-9900
Fax: 513 367-1556
Gerry Francis, *President*
Ronald Wittekind, *Chairman*
EMP: 50
SQ FT: 14,500
SALES: 39.4MM
SALES (corp-wide): 82.1MM **Privately Held**
SIC: 5172 5541 Petroleum products; gasoline service stations
PA: Hawkstone Associates, Inc.
9171 Dry Fork Rd
Harrison OH
513 367-9900

(G-11812)
WAYNE/SCOTT FETZER COMPANY
Also Called: Wayne Water Systems
101 Production Dr (45030-1477)
PHONE.................800 237-0987
Fax: 513 367-3229
Duane Johnson, *President*
Melissa Pasmore, *Mfg Spvr*
Susan Wilcox, *VP Finance*
Jim Hudson, *Human Res Dir*
Deb Dils, *Sales Staff*
▲ EMP: 200
SQ FT: 160,000
SALES (est): 86MM
SALES (corp-wide): 242.1B **Publicly Held**
SIC: 3561 5074 Pumps, domestic: water or sump; water purification equipment
HQ: The Scott Fetzer Company
28800 Clemens Rd
Westlake OH 44145
440 892-3000

Harrod
Allen County

(G-11813)
R D JONES EXCAVATING INC
10225 Alger Rd (45850-9792)
P.O. Box 127 (45850-0127)
PHONE.................419 648-5870
Randy Jones, *President*
David Sehlhorst, *Project Mgr*
Dana Jones, *Admin Sec*
EMP: 50
SQ FT: 1,200
SALES (est): 13.4MM **Privately Held**
SIC: 1794 Excavation & grading, building construction

Hartville
Stark County

(G-11814)
AKA WIRELESS INC
Also Called: Z Wireless
882 W Maple St (44632-9088)
PHONE.................216 213-8040
EMP: 26 **Privately Held**
SIC: 5999 4812 Mobile telephones & equipment; cellular telephone services
HQ: Aka Wireless, Inc.
7505 S Louise Ave
Sioux Falls SD 57108
605 275-3733

(G-11815)
BRENCKLE FARMS INC
12434 Duquette Ave Ne (44632-9329)
PHONE.................330 877-4426
Thomas Brenckle, *President*
EMP: 30
SALES (est): 2.4MM **Privately Held**
SIC: 0161 Vegetables & melons

GEOGRAPHIC SECTION

Heath - Licking County (G-11838)

(G-11816)
CONGRESS LAKE CLUB COMPANY
1 East Dr (44632-8890)
P.O. Box 370 (44632-0370)
PHONE..................330 877-9318
Fax: 330 877-1867
Fred Zollinger III, *President*
Paul Showalter, *Manager*
EMP: 40 EST: 1896
SQ FT: 40,000
SALES: 3.3MM **Privately Held**
WEB: www.congresslakeclub.org
SIC: 7997 Golf club, membership

(G-11817)
GENTLEBROOK INC (PA)
880 Sunnyside St Sw (44632-9087)
PHONE..................330 877-3694
Fax: 330 244-0038
Norman Wengerd, *CEO*
Mike Sleutz, *COO*
Phil Stauffer, *Exec Dir*
EMP: 220
SALES: 11.8MM **Privately Held**
SIC: 8361 8741 Home for the mentally retarded; management services

(G-11818)
GFS LEASING INC
Also Called: Altercare Hartville
1420 Smith Kramer St Ne (44632-8730)
PHONE..................330 877-2666
Fax: 330 877-2838
Alisa Tramontana, *Office Mgr*
Mark Smith, *Director*
Chelle Sink, *Administration*
Paige Owen, *Administration*
Paige Powell, *Administration*
EMP: 100
SALES (est): 1.5MM
SALES (corp-wide): 2.8MM **Privately Held**
SIC: 8051 Convalescent home with continuous nursing care
PA: Gfs Leasing Inc
1463 Tallmadge Rd
Kent OH 44240
330 296-6415

(G-11819)
GOODWILL IDSTRS GRTR CLVLND L
864 W Maple St Ste A (44632-8508)
PHONE..................330 877-7921
Fax: 330 877-7983
Dennis Dell, *Branch Mgr*
Dennis Odell, *Manager*
EMP: 27
SALES (corp-wide): 27.6MM **Privately Held**
SIC: 8331 Vocational rehabilitation agency
PA: Goodwill Industries Of Greater Cleveland And East Central Ohio, Inc.
408 9th St Sw
Canton OH 44707
330 454-9461

(G-11820)
HARTVILLE HARDWARE INC
Also Called: John Deere Authorized Dealer
1315 Edison St Nw (44632-9046)
PHONE..................330 877-4690
Fax: 330 877-4692
Howard Miller Jr, *President*
Wayne Miller, *Vice Pres*
Melanie Wagner, *Buyer*
Chris Wilson, *Financial Exec*
Susan Shea, *Human Resources*
▲ EMP: 210
SALES (est): 62.5MM **Privately Held**
WEB: www.hartvillehardware.com
SIC: 5251 5082 Hardware; construction & mining machinery
PA: Hrm Enterprises, Inc.
1015 Edison St Nw
Hartville OH 44632
330 877-9353

(G-11821)
HEALTHSPAN INTEGRATED CARE
Also Called: Kaiser Foundation Health Plan
900 W Maple St (44632-9088)
PHONE..................330 877-4018
Jim Innes, *Branch Mgr*
EMP: 29
SALES (corp-wide): 4.2B **Privately Held**
SIC: 6324 Hospital & medical service plans
HQ: Healthspan Integrated Care
1001 Lakeside Ave E # 1200
Cleveland OH 44114
216 621-5600

(G-11822)
HERSH CONSTRUCTION INC
Also Called: Homes By John Hershberger
650 S Prospect Ave # 200 (44632-8904)
PHONE..................330 877-1515
John Hershberger, *President*
EMP: 25
SQ FT: 20,000
SALES (est): 2.1MM **Privately Held**
SIC: 1521 New construction, single-family houses

(G-11823)
HRM ENTERPRISES INC (PA)
Also Called: True Value
1015 Edison St Nw (44632-8509)
PHONE..................330 877-9353
William J Howard, *President*
Wayne Miller, *Vice Pres*
Gary Summers, *Controller*
Jean Taliaferro, *Controller*
Elise Harper, *Human Res Dir*
▲ EMP: 160
SQ FT: 85,000
SALES (est): 62.5MM **Privately Held**
WEB: www.hartvilletool.com
SIC: 5947 5812 7389 Gift shop; American restaurant; flea market

(G-11824)
HUMANA INC
1289 Edison St Nw (44632-8942)
PHONE..................330 877-5464
EMP: 43
SALES (corp-wide): 53.7B **Publicly Held**
SIC: 6324 Health maintenance organization (HMO), insurance only
PA: Humana Inc.
500 W Main St Ste 300
Louisville KY 40202
502 580-1000

(G-11825)
K W ZELLERS & SON INC
13494 Duquette Ave Ne (44632-8820)
PHONE..................330 877-9371
Fax: 330 877-0243
Jeffrey Zellers, *President*
Cecil Kene, *Vice Pres*
Kenneth Zellers Jr, *Treasurer*
Richard Zellers, *Shareholder*
EMP: 25
SQ FT: 20,000
SALES: 10MM **Privately Held**
SIC: 0181 Ornamental nursery products; seeds, vegetable: growing of

(G-11826)
LAKE LOCAL BOARD OF EDUCATION
13188 Kent Ave Ne (44632-9666)
PHONE..................330 877-9383
Stella Loebmunson, *Owner*
EMP: 445
SALES (corp-wide): 16.3MM **Privately Held**
SIC: 4789 Pipeline terminal facilities, independently operated
PA: Lake Local Board Of Education
436 King Church Ave Sw
Uniontown OH 44685
330 877-9383

(G-11827)
NILCO LLC (HQ)
Also Called: Erie Lumber Co Division
1221 W Maple St Ste 100 (44632-8550)
PHONE..................888 248-5151
Jim Smith, *CEO*
EMP: 35
SQ FT: 66,670
SALES (est): 77.3MM
SALES (corp-wide): 800MM **Privately Held**
SIC: 5031 5251 Lumber: rough, dressed & finished; building materials, exterior; hardware
PA: U.S. Lumber Group, Llc
2160 Satellite Blvd # 450
Duluth GA 30097
678 474-4577

(G-11828)
OREILLY AUTOMOTIVE INC
1196 W Maple St (44632-9080)
PHONE..................330 267-4383
Mike Hobbs, *President*
EMP: 46 **Publicly Held**
SIC: 7538 General automotive repair shops
PA: O'reilly Automotive, Inc.
233 S Patterson Ave
Springfield MO 65802

(G-11829)
SABLE CREEK GOLF COURSE INC
5942 Edison St Ne (44632-9175)
PHONE..................330 877-9606
Fax: 330 877-9606
Robert Frase, *President*
Jeff Fraze, *Vice Pres*
Theresa Headley, *Admin Sec*
EMP: 35
SQ FT: 4,844
SALES (est): 1.9MM **Privately Held**
WEB: www.sablecreekgolf.com
SIC: 7992 Public golf courses

(G-11830)
SCHONER CHEVROLET INC
720 W Maple St (44632-8504)
P.O. Box 9 (44632-0009)
PHONE..................330 877-6731
Fax: 330 877-9656
Mark E Hanlon, *President*
Dorothy Hanlon, *Corp Secy*
Joe Memmer, *Store Mgr*
Ruth Cole, *Manager*
EMP: 30 EST: 1936
SQ FT: 20,000
SALES (est): 11.8MM **Privately Held**
WEB: www.schonerchevrolet.com
SIC: 5511 7514 7538 7515 Automobiles, new & used; pickups, new & used; vans, new & used; rent-a-car service; general automotive repair shops; passenger car leasing; truck rental & leasing, no drivers; used car dealers

(G-11831)
SOMMERS MARKET LLC (PA)
Also Called: Grocery Outlet Supermarket
214 Market Ave Sw (44632-8545)
PHONE..................330 352-7470
Roland Sommers, *President*
David J Sommers, *Vice Pres*
Phil Weidler,
EMP: 56 EST: 2007
SQ FT: 6,000
SALES: 3.5MM **Privately Held**
SIC: 5411 5141 Grocery stores, independent; groceries, general line

(G-11832)
VIETNAM VETERANS AMERICA INC
874 Marigold St Nw (44632-9032)
P.O. Box 6018, Akron (44312-0018)
PHONE..................330 877-6017
Lee Fisher, *President*
EMP: 26
SALES (corp-wide): 8.7MM **Privately Hold**
SIC: 8641 Veterans' organization
PA: Vietnam Veterans Of America, Inc.
8719 Colesville Rd # 100
Silver Spring MD 20910
301 585-4000

(G-11833)
WHOLESALE DECOR LLC
650 S Prospect Ave # 200 (44632-8904)
PHONE..................330 587-7100
Philip Daetwyler, *CEO*
EMP: 26
SALES (corp-wide): 20MM **Privately Held**
SIC: 5023 Home furnishings
PA: Wholesale Decor Llc
286 W Greenwich Rd
Seville OH 44273
877 745-5050

Hayesville
Ashland County

(G-11834)
IMPRESSIVE PACKAGING INC
Also Called: Ipi
627 County Rd 30 A (44838)
P.O. Box 325 (44838-0325)
PHONE..................419 368-6808
Fax: 419 368-4728
Wayne Willis, *President*
EMP: 33
SALES (est): 4.1MM **Privately Held**
WEB: www.impressivepackaging.com
SIC: 5199 5113 Packaging materials; corrugated & solid fiber boxes

Heath
Licking County

(G-11835)
BIONETICS CORPORATION
813 Irving Wick Dr W (43056-1199)
PHONE..................757 873-0900
Fax: 757 873-0900
Frankie Savage, *Marketing Staff*
W J Silvey, *Branch Mgr*
EMP: 25
SALES (corp-wide): 43.1MM **Privately Held**
WEB: www.bionetics.com
SIC: 8732 8742 8734 Market analysis, business & economic research; management consulting services; product testing laboratory, safety or performance
PA: The Bionetics Corporation
101 Production Dr Ste 100
Yorktown VA 23693
757 873-0900

(G-11836)
DICKS SPORTING GOODS INC
Also Called: Dick's Sporting Goods 1021
771 S 30th St Ste 9007 (43056-1252)
PHONE..................740 522-5555
Dave Schwabe, *Branch Mgr*
EMP: 35
SALES (corp-wide): 8.5B **Publicly Held**
SIC: 7999 5699 Sporting goods rental; sports apparel
PA: Dick's Sporting Goods, Inc.
345 Court St
Coraopolis PA 15108
724 273-3400

(G-11837)
GLEMSURE REALTY TRUST
Also Called: Indian Mound Mall
771 S 30th St Ste 9001 (43056-1252)
PHONE..................740 522-6620
Fax: 740 522-5171
John Guminski, *President*
Joseph Williams, *General Mgr*
Billy Anderson, *Manager*
EMP: 50
SALES (est): 2.1MM **Privately Held**
WEB: www.indianmoundmall.com
SIC: 6512 Shopping center, property operation only

(G-11838)
GUMMER WHOLESALE INC (PA)
1945 James Pkwy (43056-4000)
P.O. Box 2288 (43056-0288)
PHONE..................740 928-0415
Fax: 740 928-6727
Chad Gummer, *President*
Lillian Gummer, *Corp Secy*
Michael Gummer, *Vice Pres*
Bill Yost, *Purchasing*
Lou Dellapina, *CFO*
EMP: 67
SQ FT: 50,000
SALES (est): 45.8MM **Privately Held**
WEB: www.gummerwholesale.com
SIC: 5194 5145 5199 5141 Cigarettes; candy; novelties, paper; groceries, general line

Heath - Licking County (G-11839)

(G-11839)
MISTRAS GROUP INC
1480 James Pkwy (43056-4018)
PHONE..................740 788-9188
Fax: 614 788-9188
Larry Galloway, *Opers Mgr*
Bret Kraner, *Engineer*
Audrey Frye, *Financial Exec*
Dennis Bertolotti, *Sales Staff*
Dave Rywalski, *Sales Staff*
EMP: 35
SQ FT: 13,000 **Publicly Held**
SIC: 8734 Testing laboratories
PA: Mistras Group, Inc.
    195 Clarksville Rd Ste 2
    Princeton Junction NJ 08550

(G-11840)
MPLX TERMINALS LLC
840 Heath Rd (43056-1175)
PHONE..................504 252-8064
EMP: 33
SALES (corp-wide): 3.8B **Publicly Held**
SIC: 5172 Gasoline
HQ: Mplx Terminals Llc
    200 E Hardin St
    Findlay OH

(G-11841)
NUWAY INCORPORATED
996 Thornwood Dr (43056-9333)
P.O. Box 498, Granville (43023-0498)
PHONE..................740 587-2452
Dannette McInturff, *President*
Kody McInturff, *Vice Pres*
Kristopher McInturff, *Vice Pres*
Ashley McInturff, *Admin Sec*
EMP: 25
SQ FT: 1,600
SALES: 3.4MM **Privately Held**
SIC: 1794 Excavation & grading, building construction

(G-11842)
ROBERTSON CNSTR SVCS INC
1801 Thornwood Dr (43056-9311)
PHONE..................740 929-1000
Christian H Robertson, *President*
Kenneth Williams, *Safety Dir*
Daniel Moore, *Project Mgr*
Dean Locher, *Opers Mgr*
Michele Robertson, *Treasurer*
EMP: 100
SQ FT: 6,000
SALES (est): 45.2MM **Privately Held**
SIC: 1541 Industrial buildings & warehouses

(G-11843)
SAMUEL STRAPPING SYSTEMS INC
1455 James Pkwy (43056-4007)
PHONE..................740 522-2500
Matthew Taylor, *Accounting Mgr*
Jay Jones, *Manager*
David Joos, *Manager*
EMP: 100
SALES (corp-wide): 975.8MM **Privately Held**
WEB: www.samuelstrapping.com
SIC: 3565 3089 5085 5084 Wrapping machines; plastic processing; industrial supplies; industrial machinery & equipment; packaging materials
HQ: Samuel, Son & Co. (Usa) Inc.
    1401 Davey Rd Ste 300
    Woodridge IL 60517
    630 783-8900

(G-11844)
SIGNATURE HEALTH SERVICES LLC
675 Hopewell Dr (43056-1579)
PHONE..................740 522-6017
Jack Goldsberry, *Branch Mgr*
EMP: 25
SALES (corp-wide): 6B **Publicly Held**
SIC: 8082 Home health care services
HQ: Signature Health Services Llc
    300 N Cleveland Massillon
    Akron OH

Hebron
Licking County

(G-11845)
BAYER HERITAGE FEDERAL CR UN
1111 O Neill Dr (43025-9409)
PHONE..................740 929-2015
Rod Herrick, *Manager*
EMP: 132
SALES (corp-wide): 14.1MM **Privately Held**
WEB: www.bayerefcu.com
SIC: 6061 Federal credit unions
PA: Bayer Heritage Federal Credit Union
    178 N State Route 2
    New Martinsville WV 26155
    304 455-4029

(G-11846)
CLEAN HARBORS ENVMTL SVCS INC
581 Milliken Dr (43025-9657)
PHONE..................740 929-3532
Monte Londot, *General Mgr*
EMP: 43
SALES (corp-wide): 2.9B **Publicly Held**
SIC: 4953 Hazardous waste collection & disposal
HQ: Clean Harbors Environmental Services, Inc.
    42 Longwater Dr
    Norwell MA 02061
    781 792-5000

(G-11847)
DDM-DIGITAL IMAGING DATA
Also Called: Ddm Direct of Ohio
190 Milliken Dr (43025-9657)
PHONE..................740 928-1110
Eill Hillard, *Branch Mgr*
EMP: 60
SALES (corp-wide): 10MM **Privately Held**
WEB: www.ddmdirect.com
SIC: 7331 Direct mail advertising services
PA: Ddm-Digital Imaging, Data Processing And Mailing Services, L C
    1223 William St
    Buffalo NY 14206
    716 893-8671

(G-11848)
DHL SUPPLY CHAIN (USA)
200 Arrowhead Blvd (43025-9466)
PHONE..................740 929-2113
John Wolfe, *General Mgr*
Jim Guidice, *Vice Pres*
Giancarlo Delon, *Opers Mgr*
Doug Linzinmeir, *Opers Mgr*
Jordan Bonifas, *Opers Spvr*
EMP: 70
SALES (corp-wide): 71.2B **Privately Held**
WEB: www.exel-logistics.com
SIC: 4225 General warehousing
HQ: Exel Inc.
    570 Polaris Pkwy
    Westerville OH 43082
    614 865-8500

(G-11849)
HENDRICKSON INTERNATIONAL CORP
Also Called: Hendrickson Auxiliary Axles
277 N High St (43025-8008)
PHONE..................740 929-5600
Fax: 740 929-5601
Mike Keeler, *General Mgr*
Bill Lewis, *Mfg Dir*
Sherrill Moore, *Opers Mgr*
Mark Dankow, *Engineer*
Gregory Reiss, *Engineer*
EMP: 78
SALES (corp-wide): 1B **Privately Held**
SIC: 3714 3493 3089 5084 Motor vehicle parts & accessories; steel springs, except wire; plastic containers, except foam; industrial machinery & equipment; truck & bus bodies
HQ: Hendrickson International Corporation
    500 Park Blvd Ste 450
    Itasca IL 60143
    630 874-9700

(G-11850)
HERITAGE SPORTSWEAR INC (PA)
Also Called: Virginia T'S
102 Reliance Dr (43025-9204)
P.O. Box 760 (43025-0760)
PHONE..................740 928-7771
Fax: 740 928-3223
Michael Jurden, *President*
ARA Graves, *Opers Mgr*
Sarah Shifflett, *Purch Mgr*
Jennifer Starr, *Purchasing*
Jeff Meena, *Controller*
EMP: 75
SQ FT: 75,000
SALES (est): 197.1MM **Privately Held**
WEB: www.heritagesportswear.com
SIC: 5136 5137 Sportswear, men's & boys'; sportswear, women's & children's

(G-11851)
LEGEND SMELTING AND RECYCL INC (PA)
Also Called: L S R
717 Oneill Dr (43025)
PHONE..................740 928-0139
Fax: 740 928-0473
Randy Hess, *President*
Mark Sasko, *Vice Pres*
Paul Leary, *CFO*
Sandy Dilts, *Accountant*
Stephanie Starkey, *Human Resources*
▲ EMP: 60
SQ FT: 90,000
SALES (est): 24.1MM **Privately Held**
WEB: www.tarulli-tire.com
SIC: 5093 Nonferrous metals scrap

(G-11852)
MAXIM HEALTHCARE SERVICES INC
96 Integrity Dr Ste A (43025-7013)
PHONE..................740 522-6094
EMP: 80
SALES (corp-wide): 1.3B **Privately Held**
SIC: 8099 Blood related health services
PA: Maxim Healthcare Services, Inc.
    7227 Lee Deforest Dr
    Columbia MD 21046
    410 910-1500

(G-11853)
MID STATE SYSTEMS INC
9455 Lancaster Rd (43025-9640)
P.O. Box 926 (43025-0926)
PHONE..................740 928-1115
Fax: 740 928-1112
Leon Zazworsky, *President*
Judy K Zazworsky, *Vice Pres*
Laurie Montgomery, *Accounts Mgr*
Danny Wright, *Manager*
Sandy Erlenvach, *Director*
EMP: 78
SQ FT: 11,500
SALES (est): 12.6MM **Privately Held**
WEB: www.midstatesystems.com
SIC: 4213 Contract haulers

(G-11854)
MPW INDUSTRIAL SERVICES INC (HQ)
9711 Lancaster Rd (43025-9764)
P.O. Box 10 (43025-0010)
PHONE..................800 827-8790
Monte Black, *CEO*
John Cihon, *Business Mgr*
Kristen Hargus, *Vice Pres*
Curt Ruff, *Maintenance Dir*
Tony Donnadio, *Engineer*
EMP: 600
SQ FT: 75,000
SALES (est): 254.8MM
SALES (corp-wide): 257.9MM **Privately Held**
SIC: 7349 Cleaning service, industrial or commercial
PA: Mpw Industrial Services Group, Inc.
    9711 Lancaster Rd
    Hebron OH 43025
    740 927-8790

(G-11855)
MPW INDUSTRIAL SVCS GROUP INC (PA)
9711 Lancaster Rd (43025-9764)
PHONE..................740 927-8790
Fax: 740 928-1077
Monte R Black, *CEO*
Jared Black, *President*
David Furcolow, *District Mgr*
Ron Wells, *District Mgr*
Gary Babaryk, *Area Mgr*
EMP: 89 EST: 1972
SQ FT: 24,000
SALES (est): 257.9MM **Privately Held**
WEB: www.mpwgroup.com
SIC: 7349 8744 3589 Cleaning service, industrial or commercial; facilities support services; commercial cleaning equipment

(G-11856)
MPW INDUSTRIAL WATER SVCS INC
9711 Lancaster Rd (43025-9764)
P.O. Box 10 (43025-0010)
PHONE..................800 827-8790
Monte R Black, *President*
Robert Morris, *Safety Mgr*
EMP: 176
SALES: 45MM
SALES (corp-wide): 257.9MM **Privately Held**
SIC: 4499 Water transportation cleaning services
HQ: Mpw Management Services Corp.
    9711 Lancaster Rd
    Hebron OH 43025

(G-11857)
NATIONAL GAS OIL CORP
120 O Neill Dr (43025-9680)
PHONE..................740 348-1243
Dave Detty, *Manager*
EMP: 50
SALES: 11.7MM **Privately Held**
SIC: 4924 Natural gas distribution

(G-11858)
NATIONAL HOT ROD ASSOCIATION
Also Called: National Trail Raceway
2650 National Rd Sw Ste B (43025-9639)
PHONE..................740 928-5706
Fax: 740 928-2922
Mike Fornataro, *General Mgr*
Jim Layton, *General Mgr*
EMP: 139
SALES (corp-wide): 99.2MM **Privately Held**
WEB: www.nhra.com
SIC: 7948 8611 Dragstrip operation; business associations
PA: National Hot Rod Association
    2035 E Financial Way
    Glendora CA 91741
    626 914-4761

(G-11859)
S R DOOR INC (PA)
Also Called: Seal-Rite Door
1120 O Neill Dr (43025-9409)
P.O. Box 460 (43025-0460)
PHONE..................740 927-3558
Fax: 740 927-3690
Scott A Miller, *President*
Glen Miller, *Vice Pres*
EMP: 80
SQ FT: 75,000
SALES (est): 12.6MM **Privately Held**
WEB: www.seal-ritedoor.com
SIC: 2431 3442 3211 5031 Doors, wood; metal doors; construction glass; lumber, plywood & millwork

(G-11860)
SAFETY-KLEEN SYSTEMS INC
581 Milliken Dr (43025-9687)
PHONE..................740 929-3532
Fax: 740 928-1347
Steve Moyer, *Branch Mgr*
EMP: 61
SALES (corp-wide): 2.9B **Publicly Held**
SIC: 7389 4953 Solvents recovery service; refuse systems

GEOGRAPHIC SECTION

Hilliard - Franklin County (G-11884)

HQ: Safety-Kleen Systems, Inc.
2600 N Central Expy # 400
Richardson TX 75080
972 265-2000

(G-11861)
TRUCKOMAT CORPORATION
Also Called: Iowa 80 Group
10707 Lancaster Rd Ste 37 (43025-9622)
P.O. Box 837 (43025-0837)
PHONE..................................740 467-2818
Fax: 740 467-3330
Jeff Corley, *General Mgr*
EMP: 30
SALES (corp-wide): 367.4MM **Privately Held**
WEB: www.truckomat.com
SIC: 7542 5013 Truck wash; motor vehicle supplies & new parts
HQ: Truckomat Corporation
515 Sterling Dr
Walcott IA 52773
563 284-6965

Hicksville
Defiance County

(G-11862)
COMMUNITY MEMORIAL HOSPITAL (PA)
208 Columbus St (43526-1299)
PHONE..................................419 542-6692
Fax: 419 542-5673
Mel Fahs, *CEO*
Chuck Bohlmann, *Senior VP*
Michelle Waggoner, *Vice Pres*
Susan Hobeck, *CFO*
Judith Bowers, *Persnl Dir*
EMP: 119
SQ FT: 100,000
SALES: 24.6MM **Privately Held**
WEB: www.cmhosp.com
SIC: 8062 Hospital, affiliated with AMA residency

(G-11863)
FETTERS CONSTRUCTION INC
945 E High St (43526-1270)
PHONE..................................419 542-0944
EMP: 120 **Privately Held**
SIC: 1521 Single-Family House Construction
PA: Fetters Construction, Inc.
5417 County Road 427
Auburn IN 46706

(G-11864)
HICKORY CREEK HEALTHCARE
Also Called: Creek At Hicksburg
401 Fountain St (43526-1337)
PHONE..................................419 542-7795
Fax: 419 542-9765
Bill Langschiet, *Manager*
Helen Wiles Rn, *Nursing Dir*
EMP: 60
SALES (corp-wide): 24MM **Privately Held**
SIC: 8051 Skilled nursing care facilities
PA: Hickory Creek Healthcare Foundation, Inc.
5555 Glenridge Connector # 650
Atlanta GA 30342
678 990-7262

(G-11865)
HICKSVILLE BANK INC (HQ)
144 E High St (43526-1163)
P.O. Box 283 (43526-0283)
PHONE..................................419 542-7726
Fax: 419 542-9546
Anthony Primack, *President*
Larry Coburn, *President*
Cheryl Davis, *Exec VP*
Lucy Hilbert, *Senior VP*
Mary K Shinko, *Senior VP*
EMP: 46
SQ FT: 5,000
SALES: 4.5MM **Privately Held**
WEB: www.thehicksvillebank.com
SIC: 6022 State trust companies accepting deposits, commercial

(G-11866)
NEMCO INC
Also Called: Nemco Food Equipment
301 Meuse Argonne St (43526-1169)
P.O. Box 305 (43526-0305)
PHONE..................................419 542-7751
Fax: 419 542-6690
Kenny Moffatt, *CEO*
Stan Guillam, *President*
Todd Davis, *Purch Agent*
Janis Edwards, *Human Res Mgr*
Angie Slattery, *Office Mgr*
EMP: 70
SALES (est): 13MM **Privately Held**
SIC: 5046 Commercial cooking & food service equipment

(G-11867)
WHOLESALE HOUSE INC (PA)
Also Called: Twh
503 W High St (43526-1063)
P.O. Box 268 (43526-0268)
PHONE..................................419 542-1315
Fax: 419 542-6632
Marcy Keesbury, *President*
Stephen D Height, *President*
Nick Vasu, *Purchasing*
Jason Wisecup, *Sales Staff*
Rick Klein, *Manager*
◆ EMP: 70
SQ FT: 74,000
SALES (est): 54.9MM **Privately Held**
WEB: www.twhouse.com
SIC: 5065 Electronic parts & equipment

Highland Heights
Cuyahoga County

(G-11868)
C & S ASSOCIATES INC
Also Called: National Lien Digest
729 Miner Rd (44143-2117)
P.O. Box 24101, Cleveland (44124-0101)
PHONE..................................440 461-9661
Fax: 440 461-0822
Mary B Cowan, *President*
Delores A Cowan, *President*
Cathleen M Cowan, *Principal*
Bernard J Cowan, *Exec VP*
Greg Powelson, *Vice Pres*
EMP: 50 EST: 1974
SQ FT: 9,000
SALES (est): 6.8MM **Privately Held**
SIC: 7322 2721 Collection agency, except real estate; periodicals: publishing only

(G-11869)
HOME DEPOT USA INC
Also Called: Home Depot, The
6199 Wilson Mills Rd (44143-2101)
PHONE..................................440 684-1343
Fax: 440 720-1416
Rick Evans, *Manager*
Phil Monroe, *Manager*
EMP: 140
SALES (corp-wide): 100.9B **Publicly Held**
WEB: www.homerentalsdepot.com
SIC: 5211 7359 Home centers; tool rental
HQ: Home Depot U.S.A., Inc.
2455 Paces Ferry Rd Se
Atlanta GA 30339

(G-11870)
PHILIPS HEALTHCARE CLEVELAND
595 Miner Rd (44143-2131)
PHONE..................................440 483-3235
George M Albertson, *Principal*
Stephen Curtis, *Engineer*
Ronald Julian, *Engineer*
Matthew Rous, *Controller*
◆ EMP: 77
SALES (est): 8.4MM **Privately Held**
SIC: 8099 Blood related health services

(G-11871)
PROVIDIAN MED FIELD SVC LLC
5335 Avion Park Dr Unit A (44143-1916)
PHONE..................................440 833-0460
Michael Skok, *President*
David Skok, *Vice Pres*
Amy Murray, *Controller*
EMP: 26
SALES (est): 670K **Privately Held**
SIC: 7699 Hospital equipment repair services

(G-11872)
THINGS REMEMBERED INC (PA)
5500 Avion Park Dr (44143-1992)
PHONE..................................440 473-2000
Fax: 216 621-9377
Nelson Tejada, *President*
Beth Feldman, *District Mgr*
David Myers, *District Mgr*
Lisa Williams, *District Mgr*
Dave J Helkey, *COO*
EMP: 170
SQ FT: 55,000
SALES (est): 1.1B **Privately Held**
WEB: www.thingsremembered.com
SIC: 7389 5947 Engraving service; gift shop

Hilliard
Franklin County

(G-11873)
24 - SEVEN HOME HLTH CARE LLC
5064 Edgeley Dr (43026-3410)
PHONE..................................614 794-0325
Ahmed M Guntane, *Mng Member*
EMP: 47 EST: 2010
SALES: 1.2MM **Privately Held**
SIC: 8099 Blood related health services

(G-11874)
A JACOBS INC
4410 Hansen Dr (43026-2461)
PHONE..................................614 774-6757
Andrew Jacobs, *President*
EMP: 26
SALES: 1.9MM **Privately Held**
SIC: 7363 Truck driver services

(G-11875)
ABILITY MATTERS LLC
6058 Heritage View Ct (43026-7614)
PHONE..................................614 214-9652
Kristyn Miller, *CEO*
EMP: 50
SALES (est): 202.9K **Privately Held**
SIC: 8059 8082 Personal care home, with health care; home health care services

(G-11876)
ACCELERATED HEALTH SYSTEMS LLC
3780 Ridge Mill Dr (43026-7458)
PHONE..................................614 334-5135
EMP: 79
SALES (corp-wide): 25.1MM **Privately Held**
SIC: 8093 Rehabilitation center, outpatient treatment
PA: Accelerated Health Systems, Llc
625 Enterprise Dr
Oak Brook IL 60523
630 575-6200

(G-11877)
ALL MY SONS MOVING & STORGE OF
4401 Lyman Dr Ste D (43026-2201)
PHONE..................................014 405-7202
EMP: 35
SALES (est): 4.2MM **Privately Held**
SIC: 4214 Local trucking with storage

(G-11878)
APPLIANCE RECYCL CTRS AMER INC
A R C A Ohio
3700 Parkway Ln Ste D&G (43026-1238)
PHONE..................................614 876-8771
Fax: 614 777-5669
Dan Chuhna, *Manager*
EMP: 100
SALES (corp-wide): 103.5MM **Publicly Held**
WEB: www.arcainc.com
SIC: 5722 4953 Household appliance stores; recycling, waste materials
PA: Appliance Recycling Centers Of America, Inc.
175 Jackson Ave N Ste 102
Hopkins MN 55343
952 930-9000

(G-11879)
ARCTIC EXPRESS INC
4277 Lyman Dr (43026-1227)
P.O. Box 129 (43026-0129)
PHONE..................................614 876-4008
Fax: 614 876-0985
Richard E Durst, *Ch of Bd*
Jay Durst, *Safety Dir*
Denver Fannin, *Maintenance Dir*
William Elephant, *Controller*
Charlene Bauer, *Manager*
EMP: 111
SQ FT: 12,100
SALES: 20.1MM **Privately Held**
WEB: www.arcticexpress.com
SIC: 4213 Contract haulers; refrigerated products transport

(G-11880)
BANC CERTIFIED MERCH SVCS LLC
5006 Cemetery Rd (43026-1640)
PHONE..................................614 850-2740
Fax: 614 850-0850
Ali Razi, *Mng Member*
EMP: 46 EST: 2000
SQ FT: 1,500
SALES (est): 3.3MM **Privately Held**
WEB: www.banccertified.net
SIC: 7389 Credit card service

(G-11881)
BEHAVIORAL TREATMENTS
5275 Norwich St (43026-1424)
P.O. Box 430 (43026-0430)
PHONE..................................614 558-1968
William Jamison, *President*
EMP: 50
SALES (est): 627.6K **Privately Held**
SIC: 8322 Individual & family services

(G-11882)
BMW FINANCIAL SERVICES NA LLC (DH)
Also Called: Alphera Financial Services
5550 Britton Pkwy (43026-7456)
PHONE..................................614 718-6900
Fax: 614 718-6100
Ed Robinson, *CEO*
Steven Swecker, *General Mgr*
Tyler Weight, *Bishop*
Chris Bennett, *Vice Pres*
Ian Smith, *Vice Pres*
EMP: 45
SQ FT: 118,000
SALES (est): 487.2MM
SALES (corp-wide): 116.3B **Privately Held**
SIC: 6159 Automobile finance leasing
HQ: Bmw Of North America, Llc
300 Chestnut Ridge Rd
Woodcliff Lake NJ 07677
201 307-4000

(G-11883)
BROOKSEDGE DAY CARE CENTER
2185 Hilliard Rome Rd (43026-9068)
PHONE..................................614 529-0077
Fax: 614 529-8477
Carol Rezentes, *President*
Samuel Rezentes, *Vice Pres*
EMP: 30
SQ FT: 10,000
SALES (est): 682K **Privately Held**
SIC: 8351 Group day care center

(G-11884)
BRUNER CORPORATION (PA)
Also Called: Honeywell Authorized Dealer
3637 Lacon Rd (43026-1202)
PHONE..................................614 334-9000
Randy Sleeper, *CEO*
Mark Wenger, *President*
Lowell McElroy, *Division Mgr*
Brooks Robinson, *General Mgr*
Alex Grant, *Business Mgr*
EMP: 198
SQ FT: 4,200

Hilliard - Franklin County (G-11885) GEOGRAPHIC SECTION

SALES: 63MM Privately Held
WEB: www.brunercorp.com
SIC: 1711 Plumbing contractors; warm air heating & air conditioning contractor

(G-11885)
BUCK AND SONS LANDSCAPE SVC
7147 Hayden Run Rd (43026-7792)
P.O. Box 1119 (43026-6119)
PHONE 614 876-5359
Fax: 614 876-4991
Charles William Buck, *CEO*
Steven A Buck, *President*
Mark Meyers, *Vice Pres*
Lisa Myers, *Office Mgr*
Joe Kaltenbach, *Manager*
EMP: 45
SQ FT: 20,000
SALES: 2.6MM Privately Held
WEB: www.buckandsons.com
SIC: 0782 1711 Landscape contractors; garden planting services; garden maintenance services; irrigation sprinkler system installation

(G-11886)
BUCKHOLZ WALL SYSTEMS LLC
Also Called: Buckholz Wall Systems
4160 Anson Dr (43026-2206)
P.O. Box 229, Galloway (43119-0229)
PHONE 614 870-1775
Fax: 614 870-1968
Robert Johnson, *Vice Pres*
John Buckholz,
EMP: 50
SALES (est): 4.9MM Privately Held
SIC: 1771 1742 Stucco, gunite & grouting contractors; insulation, buildings

(G-11887)
CACHE NEXT GENERATION LLC
Also Called: C N G
3974 Brown Park Dr Ste D (43026-1168)
PHONE 614 850-9444
Saranat Annamalai, *Mng Member*
Shan Saravnan,
EMP: 98
SQ FT: 2,800
SALES (est): 3.9MM Privately Held
WEB: www.cachegroups.com
SIC: 7374 7379 Data entry service; computer related consulting services

(G-11888)
CARESOURCE MANAGEMENT GROUP CO
3455 Mill Run Dr (43026-9078)
PHONE 614 221-3370
Carrol Beaufay, *Branch Mgr*
Eric Sandkuhl, *Manager*
EMP: 40 Privately Held
SIC: 6321 Health insurance carriers
PA: Caresource Management Group Co.
    230 N Main St
    Dayton OH 45402

(G-11889)
CBIZ MED MGT PROFESSIONALS INC
3455 Mill Run Dr Ste 450 (43026-9083)
PHONE 614 771-2222
Mark Hamon, *Manager*
EMP: 30
SALES (corp-wide): 137.5MM Privately Held
WEB: www.llms.net
SIC: 8721 Billing & bookkeeping service
HQ: Cbiz Medical Management Professionals, Inc.
    5959 Shallowford Rd # 575
    Chattanooga TN 37421

(G-11890)
CINEMARK USA INC
Also Called: Cinemark Movies 12 At Mill Run
3773 Ridge Mill Dr (43026-9554)
PHONE 614 527-3773
EMP: 30
SALES (corp-wide): 2.9B Publicly Held
SIC: 7832 Motion Picture Theatre

HQ: Cinemark Usa, Inc.
    3900 Dallas Pkwy Ste 500
    Plano TX 75093
    972 665-1000

(G-11891)
COBALT GROUP INC
Integralink
4635 Trueman Blvd Ste 100 (43026-2491)
PHONE 614 876-4013
EMP: 85
SALES (corp-wide): 11.6B Publicly Held
SIC: 7375 Information Retrieval Services
HQ: The Cobalt Group Inc
    605 5th Ave S Ste 800
    Seattle WA 98104

(G-11892)
CREDIT UNION OF OHIO INC (PA)
5500 Britton Pkwy (43026-7456)
P.O. Box 165006, Columbus (43216-5006)
PHONE 614 487-6650
Susan Birkhimer, *CEO*
Tami Peyton, *Vice Pres*
Lisa Reynolds, *Accounting Mgr*
Melinda Roark, *Accountant*
Jill Gerschutz, *Mktg Dir*
EMP: 45 EST: 1967
SQ FT: 10,000
SALES: 4.6MM Privately Held
WEB: www.cuofohio.org
SIC: 6062 State credit unions, not federally chartered

(G-11893)
CUMMINS BRIDGEWAY COLUMBUS LLC
4000 Lyman Dr (43026-1212)
PHONE 614 771-1000
Fax: 614 771-0769
Tammy Fawley, *General Mgr*
Brian Grodesky, *Director*
Bill Bergner,
EMP: 60
SALES (est): 7.4MM
SALES (corp-wide): 20.4B Publicly Held
WEB: www.bridgewaypower.com
SIC: 5084 3519 Engines & parts, diesel; internal combustion engines
PA: Cummins Inc.
    500 Jackson St
    Columbus IN 47201
    812 377-5000

(G-11894)
CUMMINS INC
4000 Lyman Dr (43026-1212)
PHONE 614 771-1000
Fax: 614 771-0716
Greg Bowl, *Branch Mgr*
EMP: 25
SALES (corp-wide): 20.4B Publicly Held
WEB: www.bridgewaypower.com
SIC: 5084 7538 3519 Engines & parts, diesel; diesel engine repair: automotive; internal combustion engines
PA: Cummins Inc.
    500 Jackson St
    Columbus IN 47201
    812 377-5000

(G-11895)
DFS CORPORATE SERVICES LLC
Also Called: Discover Card Services
3311 Mill Meadow Dr (43026-9083)
P.O. Box 3025, New Albany (43054-3025)
PHONE 614 777-7020
Mike Devario, *Manager*
Mike Daverio, *CTO*
EMP: 300
SALES (corp-wide): 11.5B Publicly Held
WEB: www.discovercard.com
SIC: 7389 7322 Credit card service; adjustment & collection services
HQ: Dfs Corporate Services Llc
    2500 Lake Cook Rd 2
    Riverwoods IL 60015
    224 405-0900

(G-11896)
DISH NETWORK CORPORATION
3315 Mill Meadow Dr (43026-9088)
PHONE 614 534-2001

Randy Cox, *Manager*
Deborah Hampton, *Manager*
EMP: 52 Publicly Held
WEB: www.dishnetwork.com
SIC: 4841 Direct broadcast satellite services (DBS)
PA: Dish Network Corporation
    9601 S Meridian Blvd
    Englewood CO 80112

(G-11897)
E-CYCLE LLC
4105 Leap Rd (43026-1117)
PHONE 614 832-7032
Christopher J Irion, *CEO*
Craig Wolpert, *President*
Jennifer Myers, *COO*
John Jakovlic, *Vice Pres*
Tony Jerig, *Vice Pres*
EMP: 55
SALES (est): 34MM Privately Held
WEB: www.e-cycle.com
SIC: 5065 Telephone & telegraphic equipment

(G-11898)
EASTER SEALS CENTER
3830 Trueman Ct (43026-2496)
PHONE 614 228-5523
Pandora Shaw-Dupras, *CEO*
EMP: 99
SALES: 4.9MM
SALES (corp-wide): 73MM Privately Held
SIC: 8322 Social service center
PA: Easter Seals, Inc.
    141 W Jackson Blvd 1400a
    Chicago IL 60604
    312 726-6200

(G-11899)
ECOPLUMBERS INC
4691 Northwest Pkwy (43026-1126)
PHONE 614 299-9903
Michael Burnhart, *CFO*
Michael Barnhart, *CFO*
Braun Bocook, *Manager*
Roslyn Levasseur, *Manager*
EMP: 34
SALES: 4MM Privately Held
SIC: 1711 Plumbing contractors

(G-11900)
EQUITY INC (PA)
Also Called: Equity Real Estate
4653 Trueman Blvd Ste 100 (43026-2490)
PHONE 614 802-2900
Fax: 614 802-2901
Steve Wathen, *CEO*
James W Haring Jr, *COO*
Andy Johanni, *Exec VP*
Melanie B Wollenberg, *Exec VP*
Ted Dowding, *Senior VP*
EMP: 48
SQ FT: 9,000
SALES (est): 37.4MM Privately Held
SIC: 1541 1542 6552 Industrial buildings, new construction; commercial & office building, new construction; subdividers & developers

(G-11901)
FERGUSON ENTERPRISES INC
Also Called: Ferguson 124
4363 Lyman Dr (43026-1266)
P.O. Box 211000, Columbus (43221-8000)
PHONE 614 876-8555
Fax: 614 876-0156
Ron Sima, *Branch Mgr*
Ryan Burke, *Manager*
EMP: 25
SALES (corp-wide): 19.2B Privately Held
WEB: www.ferguson.com
SIC: 5074 5999 Plumbing fittings & supplies; heating equipment (hydronic); plumbing & heating supplies
HQ: Ferguson Enterprises, Inc.
    12500 Jefferson Ave
    Newport News VA 23602
    757 874-7795

(G-11902)
GENERAL ELECTRIC COMPANY
3455 Mill Run Dr (43026-9078)
PHONE 614 527-1078
EMP: 25

SALES (corp-wide): 123.6B Publicly Held
SIC: 1731 Electrical Contractor
PA: General Electric Company
    41 Farnsworth St
    Boston MA 02210
    617 443-3000

(G-11903)
GLENMONT
4599 Avery Rd (43026-9786)
PHONE 614 876-0084
Fax: 614 876-7095
Sara Faye Thorndike, *Principal*
Norrene McLaughlin, *Office Mgr*
Katherine Lundberg, *Director*
EMP: 43
SQ FT: 1,008
SALES: 3.2MM Privately Held
SIC: 8062 General medical & surgical hospitals

(G-11904)
GREAT DANE COLUMBUS INC
4080 Lyman Dr (43026-1287)
P.O. Box 9 (43026-0009)
PHONE 614 876-0666
Henry T Skipper Jr, *President*
Donald L Ottney, *Vice Pres*
D J O'Connor, *Admin Sec*
William H Oliphant, *Asst Sec*
EMP: 45
SQ FT: 14,200
SALES (est): 18.9MM
SALES (corp-wide): 1.5B Privately Held
SIC: 5012 Trailers for trucks, new & used
HQ: Great Dane Llc
    222 N Lasalle St Ste 920
    Chicago IL 60601

(G-11905)
GREAT DANE LLC
Also Called: Great Dane Trailers
4080 Lyman Dr (43026-1287)
PHONE 614 876-0666
Fax: 614 876-7689
Gary Blackburn, *Manager*
EMP: 38
SQ FT: 21,088
SALES (corp-wide): 1.5B Privately Held
WEB: www.greatdanetrailers.com
SIC: 5012 Trailers for trucks, new & used
HQ: Great Dane Llc
    222 N Lasalle St Ste 920
    Chicago IL 60601

(G-11906)
HAMILTON SAFE PRODUCTS CO INC
4770 Northwest Pkwy (43026-1131)
PHONE 614 268-5530
Brad Hunter, *President*
Dale Peters, *Regional Mgr*
Eric Bellis, *Vice Pres*
Eric De Bellis, *Vice Pres*
Fran Wooddrif, *Admin Sec*
EMP: 25
SQ FT: 13,500
SALES (est): 10.3MM Privately Held
SIC: 5049 Bank equipment & supplies

(G-11907)
HER INC
Also Called: H E R Realtors
3499 Main St (43026-1319)
PHONE 614 771-7400
Fax: 614 771-2417
Sherol Saxton Mulligan, *Principal*
EMP: 40
SALES (corp-wide): 14.3MM Privately Held
WEB: www.eassent.com
SIC: 6531 Real estate agent, residential
PA: Her, Inc
    4261 Morse Rd
    Columbus OH 43230
    614 221-7400

(G-11908)
HERITAGE GOLF CLUB LTD PARTNR
3525 Heritage Club Dr (43026-1313)
PHONE 614 777-1690
Fax: 614 777-1689
Dan O'Brien, *Partner*
EMP: 100

GEOGRAPHIC SECTION

Hilliard - Franklin County (G-11932)

SALES (est): 5.6MM
SALES (corp-wide): 433.7MM **Privately Held**
WEB: www.heritagegolfclub.com
SIC: 7992 5812 7997 5941 Public golf courses; eating places; membership sports & recreation clubs; sporting goods & bicycle shops
HQ: Clubcorp Holdings, Inc.
3030 Lbj Fwy Ste 600
Dallas TX 75234
972 243-6191

(G-11909)
HEYBURN DIALYSIS LLC
Also Called: Hilliard Station Dialysis
2447 Hilliard Rome Rd (43026-8194)
PHONE...................614 876-3610
James K Hilger, *Vice Pres*
EMP: 33
SALES (est): 446.5K **Publicly Held**
SIC: 8092 Kidney dialysis centers
PA: Davita Inc.
2000 16th St
Denver CO 80202

(G-11910)
HI-WAY PAVING INC
4343 Weaver Ct N (43026-1193)
P.O. Box 550 (43026-0550)
PHONE...................614 876-1700
Fax: 614 876-1899
Charles L Keith, *CEO*
James Taylor, *President*
Gail E Griffith, *Principal*
Brad Allison, *Exec VP*
Mark Lamonte, *CFO*
EMP: 100
SQ FT: 9,500
SALES (est): 41MM **Privately Held**
WEB: www.hiwaypaving.com
SIC: 1611 Concrete construction: roads, highways, sidewalks, etc.

(G-11911)
HOME DEPOT USA INC
Also Called: Home Depot, The
4101 Trueman Blvd (43026-2479)
PHONE...................614 876-5558
Fax: 614 850-4315
Wendy Ramjas, *Manager*
EMP: 150
SALES (corp-wide): 100.9B **Publicly Held**
WEB: www.homerentalsdepot.com
SIC: 5211 7359 Home centers; tool rental
HQ: Home Depot U.S.A., Inc.
2455 Paces Ferry Rd Se
Atlanta GA 30339

(G-11912)
HYO OK INC
4315 Cosgray Rd (43026-7786)
PHONE...................614 876-7644
Yun Kin, *President*
EMP: 30
SALES (est): 263.9K **Privately Held**
SIC: 7219 Garment alteration & repair shop

(G-11913)
INDUS HILLIARD HOTEL LLC
Also Called: Hampton Inn Stes Clmbus Hllard
3950 Lyman Dr (43026-1210)
PHONE...................614 334-1800
Janet Boissy, *Principal*
David Patel, *Principal*
EMP: 50
SALES (est): 344.9K **Privately Held**
SIC: 7011 Inns

(G-11914)
INLINER AMERICAN INC
4143 Weaver Ct S (43026-1119)
PHONE...................614 529-6440
Kathy Jarrell, *Manager*
David B Berger, *Director*
Carmen Wallace, *Admin Sec*
EMP: 29
SALES (corp-wide): 475.5MM **Publicly Held**
SIC: 1623 Water main construction; pipeline construction

HQ: Inliner American, Inc.
2601 W Lake Mary Blvd # 129
Lake Mary FL 32746
407 472-0014

(G-11915)
J M TOWNING INC
3690 Lacon Rd (43026-1223)
PHONE...................614 876-7335
Mike Towning, *President*
Erika Towning, *Corp Secy*
Charles Reichman, *Vice Pres*
Karen Riechman, *Manager*
EMP: 25
SALES (est): 1.5MM **Privately Held**
SIC: 4212 Truck rental with drivers

(G-11916)
JOHN ERAMO & SONS INC
3670 Lacon Rd (43026-1223)
PHONE...................614 777-0020
Fax: 614 527-1084
Anthony J Eramo, *President*
Rocco A Eramo, *Chairman*
John T Eramo, *Exec VP*
Brian R Eramo, *Vice Pres*
Micheal G Eramo, *Vice Pres*
EMP: 70
SQ FT: 6,000
SALES (est): 14.1MM **Privately Held**
WEB: www.eramo.com
SIC: 1794 Excavation & grading, building construction

(G-11917)
JPMORGAN CHASE BANK NAT ASSN
6364 Scioto Darby Rd (43026-9726)
PHONE...................614 876-7650
Richard Cundiff, *Branch Mgr*
EMP: 26
SALES (corp-wide): 99.6B **Publicly Held**
SIC: 6021 National commercial banks
HQ: Jpmorgan Chase Bank, National Association
1111 Polaris Pkwy
Columbus OH 43240
614 436-3055

(G-11918)
K M T SERVICE
3786 Fishinger Blvd (43026-8549)
P.O. Box 606 (43026-0606)
PHONE...................614 777-7770
Karl Trajcevski, *Owner*
EMP: 29
SALES (est): 5.4MM **Privately Held**
SIC: 7622 Video repair

(G-11919)
L & J FASTENERS INC
3636 Lacon Rd (43026-1223)
PHONE...................614 876-7313
Katherine Jenkins, *Ch of Bd*
John Jenkins, *President*
Sharyn Beene, *General Mgr*
Karen York, *General Mgr*
EMP: 30
SQ FT: 37,000
SALES (est): 4.6MM **Privately Held**
WEB: www.ljfasteners.com
SIC: 5085 Fasteners, industrial: nuts, bolts, screws, etc.

(G-11920)
LASERFLEX CORPORATION (HQ)
3649 Parkway Ln (43026-1214)
PHONE...................614 850-9600
Fax: 614 850-9635
Ken Kinkopf, *President*
Gene White, *Vice Pres*
Anthony Pinti, *Plant Mgr*
Brad Chandler, *QC Mgr*
Jerome Durham, *QC Mgr*
EMP: 62
SQ FT: 75,000
SALES (est): 34.1MM **Publicly Held**
WEB: www.customlasercuttingservices.com
SIC: 7389 7699 7692 3599 Metal cutting services; finishing services; industrial machinery & equipment repair; welding repair; machine shop, jobbing & repair; fabricated structural metal; metallizing of fabrics

(G-11921)
LIGHTHOUSE MEDICAL STAFFING
Also Called: Ambassador Nursing
3970 Brown Park Dr Ste B (43026-1166)
PHONE...................614 937-6259
James Burk, *CEO*
Greg Burk, *President*
EMP: 60
SQ FT: 1,000
SALES (est): 634.9K **Privately Held**
SIC: 8082 Home health care services

(G-11922)
LIN R ROGERS ELEC CONTRS INC
5050 Nike Dr Ste C (43026-7447)
PHONE...................614 876-9336
Bobby Yeary, *Branch Mgr*
EMP: 333
SALES (est): 8.6MM
SALES (corp-wide): 131.4MM **Privately Held**
SIC: 1731 General electrical contractor
PA: Lin R. Rogers Electrical Contractors, Inc.
2050 Marconi Dr Ste 100
Alpharetta GA 30005
770 772-3400

(G-11923)
LOWES HOME CENTERS LLC
3600 Park Mill Run Dr (43026-8123)
PHONE...................614 529-5900
Fax: 614 529-5930
Tom Worth, *Manager*
EMP: 150
SALES (corp-wide): 68.6B **Publicly Held**
SIC: 5211 5031 5722 5064 Home centers; building materials, exterior; building materials, interior; household appliance stores; electrical appliances, television & radio
HQ: Lowe's Home Centers, Llc
1605 Curtis Bridge Rd
Wilkesboro NC 28697
336 658-4000

(G-11924)
MAKOY CENTER INC
5462 Center St (43026-1068)
PHONE...................614 777-1211
Fax: 614 777-1211
George Yoakam, *President*
Clay Daniel, *General Mgr*
Aaron Vance, *Manager*
EMP: 35
SQ FT: 29,000
SALES (est): 1.4MM **Privately Held**
WEB: www.makoy.com
SIC: 7999 7299 6512 Recreation center; banquet hall facilities; auditorium & hall operation

(G-11925)
MATHESON TRI-GAS INC
4579 Sutphen Ct (43026-1224)
PHONE...................614 771-1311
Fax: 614 771-1286
Melissa Diehl, *Manager*
EMP: 30
SALES (corp-wide): 29.7B **Privately Held**
WEB: www.vngas.com
SIC: 5169 5084 Gases, compressed & liquefied; welding machinery & equipment
HQ: Matheson Tri-Gas, Inc.
150 Allen Rd Ste 302
Basking Ridge NJ 07920
908 991-9200

(G-11926)
MAXIM TECHNOLOGIES INC
3960 Brown Park Dr Ste D (43026-1161)
PHONE...................614 457-6325
Vijayalakshmi Chillakuru, *President*
Rajagopal Chillakuru, *COO*
Raj Chilla, *Vice Pres*
EMP: 30
SALES: 3MM **Privately Held**
SIC: 7379 Computer related consulting services

(G-11927)
MECHANICAL SUPPORT SVCS INC
4641 Northwest Pkwy (43026-1126)
P.O. Box 1475 (43026-6475)
PHONE...................614 777-8808
Craig F Bateman, *President*
EMP: 25
SQ FT: 2,500
SALES: 1.8MM **Privately Held**
WEB: www.mechanicalsupportservices.com
SIC: 8711 Mechanical engineering

(G-11928)
MERRY MOPPETS EARLY LEARNING
5075 Britton Pkwy (43026-9447)
PHONE...................614 529-1730
Fax: 614 529-6795
Gary Estep, *President*
Mytle Estep, *Principal*
Sue Kreft, *Exec Dir*
EMP: 35
SQ FT: 1,792
SALES (est): 744.9K **Privately Held**
WEB: www.merrymoppet.com
SIC: 8351 Preschool center

(G-11929)
METRO HEATING AND AC CO
Also Called: Metro Air
4731 Northwest Pkwy (43026-3102)
PHONE...................614 777-1237
Fax: 614 777-9276
Frank J Tate Jr, *President*
Dan Meszaros, *Vice Pres*
Kathryn Black, *Controller*
John Doughty, *Sales Staff*
Trish Roberts, *Manager*
EMP: 35
SQ FT: 5,000
SALES (est): 7.3MM **Privately Held**
SIC: 1711 Warm air heating & air conditioning contractor

(G-11930)
METROPOLITAN ENVMTL SVCS INC
5055 Nike Dr (43026-9692)
PHONE...................614 771-1881
Rick Gaffey, *President*
James Aman, *Corp Secy*
Erick Zeigler, *Vice Pres*
EMP: 90
SQ FT: 10,000
SALES (est): 6.6MM
SALES (corp-wide): 137MM **Privately Held**
WEB: www.metenviro.com
SIC: 7349 1794 1629 Cleaning service, industrial or commercial; excavation work; dredging contractor
PA: Carylon Corporation
2500 W Arthington St
Chicago IL 60612
312 666-7700

(G-11931)
MICRO CENTER INC
4119 Leap Rd (43026-1117)
PHONE...................614 850-3000
Richard Mershad, *CEO*
Brett Patton, *Human Resources*
EMP: 300
SALES (oct): 10.3MM
SALES (corp-wide): 3.3B **Privately Held**
SIC: 5734 5045 Computer & software stores; computers, peripherals & software
PA: Micro Electronics, Inc.
4119 Leap Rd
Hilliard OH 43026
614 850-3000

(G-11932)
MICRO ELECTRONICS INC (PA)
Also Called: Micro Center
4119 Leap Rd (43026-1117)
P.O. Box 910 (43026-0910)
PHONE...................614 850-3000
Fax: 614 850-3002
Richard M Mershad, *President*
Red Calub, *General Mgr*
Mark Hawes, *General Mgr*
Peggy Wolfe, *COO*

Hilliard - Franklin County (G-11933)

Kevin Hollingshead, *Vice Pres*
▲ **EMP:** 400
SALES (est): 3.3B **Privately Held**
WEB: www.microcenter.com
SIC: 5045 5734 Computer peripheral equipment; personal computers

(G-11933)
MICRO ELECTRONICS INC
Also Called: Micro Thinner
4055 Leap Rd (43026-1115)
P.O. Box 848 (43026-0848)
PHONE...............614 850-3500
James Kayler, *CFO*
Dennis Jackson, *Merchandise Mgr*
Jim Koehler, *Manager*
Jay Price, *Planning*
EMP: 79
SALES (corp-wide): 3.3B **Privately Held**
SIC: 5734 5045 Personal computers; computer software & accessories; computer peripheral equipment; computers & accessories, personal & home entertainment
PA: Micro Electronics, Inc.
4119 Leap Rd
Hilliard OH 43026
614 850-3000

(G-11934)
MICROANALYSIS SOCIETY INC
3405 Scioto Run Blvd (43026-3005)
PHONE...............614 256-8063
Dan Kremser, *Treasurer*
EMP: 500
SALES (est): 3.3MM **Privately Held**
SIC: 8299 7389 Educational services;

(G-11935)
MILL RUN CARE CENTER LLC
Also Called: Mill Run Gardens & Care Center
3399 Mill Run Dr (43026-9078)
PHONE...............614 527-3000
Fax: 614 527-7199
Laura Sandy, *Mng Member*
Maryanne Struck, *Manager*
Christophe Hudson, *Data Proc Dir*
Nicole Speakman, *Director*
EMP: 100
SALES (est): 5MM **Privately Held**
SIC: 8059 8052 8051 Nursing home, except skilled & intermediate care facility; intermediate care facilities; skilled nursing care facilities

(G-11936)
MILLER PIPELINE LLC
5000 Scioto Darby Rd (43026-1513)
PHONE...............614 777-8377
Scott Miller, *Manager*
EMP: 300
SALES (corp-wide): 2.6B **Publicly Held**
WEB: www.millerpipeline.com
SIC: 1623 Pipeline construction
HQ: Miller Pipeline, Llc
8850 Crawfordsville Rd
Indianapolis IN 46234
317 293-0278

(G-11937)
MILLS/JAMES INC
Also Called: Mills James Productions
3545 Fishinger Blvd (43026-9550)
PHONE...............614 777-9933
Fax: 614 777-9943
Cameron James, *CEO*
Ken Mills, *President*
Brian Alexander, *Editor*
Thomas Baumann, *Editor*
Robert Dixon, *Editor*
EMP: 130
SQ FT: 47,000
SALES: 21.3MM **Privately Held**
WEB: www.mjp.com
SIC: 7819 7812 Services allied to motion pictures; motion picture production & distribution; video tape production

(G-11938)
NORWICH ELEMENTARY PTO
4454 Davidson Rd (43026-9647)
PHONE...............614 921-6000
Abbe Kehler, *Principal*
EMP: 25
SALES: 28.6K **Privately Held**
SIC: 8641 Parent-teachers' association

(G-11939)
OHIO LAMINATING & BINDING INC
4364 Reynolds Dr (43026-1260)
PHONE...............614 771-4868
Fax: 614 771-0271
Jim Ondecko, *President*
Jimmy R Ondecko, *Vice Pres*
Jan McKee, *Manager*
EMP: 40
SQ FT: 5,000
SALES (est): 3.3MM **Privately Held**
WEB: www.ohiolaminatingandbinding.com
SIC: 7389 2789 2672 Laminating service; bookbinding & related work; coated & laminated paper

(G-11940)
OHIO STATE HOME SERVICES INC
Everdry Waterproofing Columbus
4271 Weaver Ct N (43026-1132)
PHONE...............614 850-5600
Ken Barnett, *Sales/Mktg Mgr*
Ken Barnette, *Manager*
EMP: 80
SQ FT: 1,700
SALES (corp-wide): 32.5MM **Privately Held**
WEB: www.ohiostatewaterproofing.com
SIC: 1799 1794 1741 Waterproofing; excavation & grading, building construction; foundation building
PA: Ohio State Home Services, Inc.
365 Highland Rd E
Macedonia OH 44056
330 467-1055

(G-11941)
OPEN TEXT INC
3671 Ridge Mill Dr (43026-7752)
PHONE...............614 658-3588
Anik Ganguly, *Manager*
Mike Nappi, *Manager*
Justin Zerby, *Manager*
Terry W Weirick, *Director*
EMP: 50
SALES (corp-wide): 2.2B **Privately Held**
SIC: 7372 Prepackaged software
HQ: Open Text Inc.
2950 S Delaware St
San Mateo CA 94403
650 645-3000

(G-11942)
PARKINS INCORPORATED
Also Called: Hampton Inn
3950 Lyman Dr (43026-1210)
PHONE...............614 334-1800
Fax: 614 334-1801
Tarun Patel, *President*
Vijay Zaver, *Vice Pres*
Amanda Sparks, *Branch Mgr*
EMP: 27
SALES (est): 2.4MM **Privately Held**
SIC: 7011 Hotels & motels

(G-11943)
PMWI LLC
3177 Overbridge Dr (43026-8091)
PHONE...............614 975-5004
Pavan Mehra, *Principal*
EMP: 99
SALES (est): 3.9MM **Privately Held**
SIC: 8711 7389 Engineering services;

(G-11944)
PREMIUM BEVERAGE SUPPLY LTD
3701 Lacon Rd (43026-1202)
PHONE...............614 777-1007
Ron Wilson, *Owner*
Dan Turi, *Opers Mgr*
▲ **EMP:** 38
SALES (est): 13.9MM **Privately Held**
WEB: www.premiumbeveragesupply.com
SIC: 5099 Wood & wood by-products

(G-11945)
PRUDENTIAL CALHOON CO REALTORS
3535 Fishinger Blvd # 100 (43026-7504)
PHONE...............614 777-1000
Fax: 614 777-6590
Thomas F Calhoon II, *President*
Samuel Calhoon, *Vice Pres*
Crystal Buess, *Broker*
Kenneth Coleman, *Broker*
Kathryn Eshelman, *Broker*
EMP: 36
SALES (est): 2.8MM **Privately Held**
WEB: www.prucalhoonrealtors.com
SIC: 6531 Real estate agent, residential

(G-11946)
QUALITY LIFE PROVIDERS LLC
Also Called: Comfort Keepers
3974 Brown Park Dr Ste E (43026-1168)
PHONE...............614 527-9999
Tina Murkowski, *Mng Member*
Bill Murkowski,
EMP: 25
SALES (est): 837.3K **Privately Held**
SIC: 8082 Visiting nurse service

(G-11947)
R & S HALLEY & CO INC
Also Called: Darby Creek Nursery
6368 Scioto Darby Rd (43026-9726)
PHONE...............614 771-0388
Fax: 614 771-6165
Jeffrey Turnbull, *President*
Lucinda Turnbull, *Admin Sec*
EMP: 35
SALES (est): 2.2MM **Privately Held**
WEB: www.darbycreek.org
SIC: 0181 0782 Nursery stock, growing of; landscape contractors

(G-11948)
RANDSTAD TECHNOLOGIES LP
3750 Fishinger Blvd (43026-8549)
PHONE...............614 552-3280
EMP: 42
SALES (corp-wide): 27.4B **Privately Held**
SIC: 7361 Employment agencies
HQ: Randstad Technologies, Llc
150 Presidential Way # 300
Woburn MA 01801
781 938-1910

(G-11949)
REXEL USA INC
3670 Parkway Ln Ste A (43026-1237)
PHONE...............614 771-7373
Gary L Martin, *Sales/Mktg Mgr*
EMP: 50
SQ FT: 36,000
SALES (corp-wide): 3MM **Privately Held**
SIC: 5063 Electrical supplies
HQ: Rexel Usa, Inc.
14951 Dallas Pkwy
Dallas TX 75254

(G-11950)
RIEPENHOFF LANDSCAPE LTD
3872 Scoto Darby Creek Rd (43026-9702)
PHONE...............614 876-4683
Fax: 614 876-4862
Steve Purcell, *President*
Ellen Purcell, *Vice Pres*
EMP: 25
SQ FT: 2,500
SALES (est): 1.5MM **Privately Held**
WEB: www.riepenhofflandscape.com
SIC: 0782 1629 Landscape contractors; irrigation system construction

(G-11951)
SCIOTO-DARBY CONCRETE INC
4540 Edgewyn Ave (43026-1222)
PHONE...............614 876-3114
Fax: 614 876-3117
David M Hamilton, *President*
Ronald Rak, *Controller*
EMP: 30
SQ FT: 20,000
SALES (est): 4.2MM **Privately Held**
WEB: www.sciotodarby.com
SIC: 1771 Concrete pumping

(G-11952)
SPECTRUM MGT HOLDG CO LLC
3652 Main St (43026-1359)
PHONE...............614 503-4153
EMP: 82
SALES (corp-wide): 41.5B **Publicly Held**
SIC: 4841 Cable television services

HQ: Spectrum Management Holding Company, Llc
400 Atlantic St
Stamford CT 06901
203 905-7801

(G-11953)
SPIRES MOTORS INC
Also Called: Buckeye Honda
3820 Parkway Ln (43026-1217)
P.O. Box 189, Lancaster (43130-0189)
PHONE...............614 771-2345
Fax: 740 653-4880
Gerald J Spires, *President*
Steve Ilich, *General Mgr*
William B Schuck, *Principal*
Dennis E Spires, *Senior VP*
Tim Spires, *Vice Pres*
EMP: 40
SQ FT: 10,000
SALES (est): 18.5MM **Privately Held**
WEB: www.buckeyehonda.com
SIC: 5511 7538 Automobiles, new & used; general automotive repair shops

(G-11954)
STAR DYNAMICS CORPORATION (PA)
Also Called: Aeroflex Powell
4455 Reynolds Dr (43026-1261)
PHONE...............614 334-4510
Jerry Jost, *President*
Andy Bell, *General Mgr*
Chris Fox, *General Mgr*
Robert Reynolds, *Vice Pres*
Bob Fresco, *VP Opers*
▲ **EMP:** 74
SQ FT: 20,000
SALES (est): 28.7MM **Privately Held**
WEB: www.isarinc.com
SIC: 5088 Navigation equipment & supplies

(G-11955)
STOVER TRANSPORTATION INC
3710 Lacon Rd (43026-1207)
P.O. Box 1328 (43026-6328)
PHONE...............614 777-4184
Fax: 614 777-4363
Raymond Stover, *President*
Rynda Stover, *Corp Secy*
EMP: 25
SALES (est): 4.7MM **Privately Held**
WEB: www.stovertransportation.com
SIC: 4231 Trucking terminal facilities

(G-11956)
TALX CORPORATION
3455 Mill Run Dr (43026-9078)
PHONE...............614 527-9404
German Matamoros, *Human Res Dir*
Kathy Couglin, *Manager*
Philip Russo, *Manager*
EMP: 42
SALES (corp-wide): 3.3B **Publicly Held**
WEB: www.talx.com
SIC: 7373 Systems software development services
HQ: Talx Corporation
11432 Lackland Rd
Saint Louis MO 63146
314 214-7000

(G-11957)
TEAM RAHAL INC
Also Called: Rahal Land and Racing
4601 Lyman Dr (43026-1249)
PHONE...............614 529-7000
Robert W Rahal, *President*
Steve Dickson, *General Mgr*
Brian Marks, *Vice Pres*
Clay Filson, *Project Mgr*
Dave Cline, *Purchasing*
◆ **EMP:** 65
SQ FT: 30,000
SALES (est): 176.2K **Privately Held**
WEB: www.rahal.com
SIC: 7948 Motor vehicle racing & drivers; race car drivers

(G-11958)
THOMAS AND KING INC
5561 Wstchester Woods Blvd (43026-7970)
PHONE...............614 527-0571
Steve Totillo, *General Mgr*
Amy Lee, *Manager*

GEOGRAPHIC SECTION
Hillsboro - Highland County (G-11979)

EMP: 101
SALES (corp-wide): 154.6MM **Privately Held**
WEB: www.tandk.com
SIC: 8742 Restaurant & food services consultants
PA: Thomas And King, Inc.
249 E Main St Ste 101
Lexington KY 40507
859 254-2180

(G-11959)
TODD A RUCK INC
5100 Harvest Meadow Ct (43026-9076)
P.O. Box 1327 (43026-6327)
PHONE 614 527-9927
Todd A Ruck, *President*
EMP: 31
SALES: 1.6MM **Privately Held**
SIC: 4212 Local trucking, without storage

(G-11960)
TRADITIONS AT MILL RUN
Also Called: National Ch Rsidences Mill Run
3550 Fishinger Blvd (43026-2100)
PHONE 614 771-0100
Fax: 614 529-2584
Tanya Kim Hahn, *CEO*
EMP: 60
SQ FT: 19,432
SALES: 3.7MM
SALES (corp-wide): 44.4MM **Privately Held**
SIC: 8059 Nursing home, except skilled & intermediate care facility
PA: National Church Residences
2335 N Bank Dr
Columbus OH 43220
614 451-2151

(G-11961)
TRUGREEN LIMITED PARTNERSHIP
Also Called: Tru Green-Chemlawn
5150 Nike Dr (43026-7448)
P.O. Box 1120 (43026-6120)
PHONE 614 527-7070
Joe Muller, *Manager*
EMP: 80
SALES (corp-wide): 4B **Privately Held**
SIC: 0782 Lawn care services
HQ: Trugreen Limited Partnership
1790 Kirby Pkwy
Memphis TN 38138
901 251-4128

(G-11962)
VARGO INTEGRATED SYSTEMS INC
3709 Parkway Ln (43026-1216)
PHONE 614 876-1163
J Michael Vargo, *President*
Bart J Cera, *COO*
Carlos Ysasi, *Vice Pres*
Scott Shaw, *Project Dir*
Ron Maynard, *Controller*
EMP: 40
SQ FT: 16,000
SALES: 72.1MM **Privately Held**
SIC: 5084 Conveyor systems

(G-11963)
VERIZON BUSINESS GLOBAL LLC
5000 Britton Pkwy (43026-9445)
PHONE 614 219-2317
David Hoppe, *Engineer*
Cory McCoy, *Sales Engr*
Sander Veraar, *Manager*
Zena Waters, *Info Tech Dir*
John Pries, *Technology*
EMP: 49
SALES (corp-wide): 126B **Publicly Held**
WEB: www.mccmt.com
SIC: 4813 8721 4822 7375 Local & long distance telephone communications; accounting, auditing & bookkeeping; telegraph & other communications; information retrieval services
HQ: Verizon Business Global Llc
22001 Loudoun County Pkwy
Ashburn VA 20147
703 886-5600

(G-11964)
VERIZON NEW YORK INC
5000 Britton Pkwy (43026-9445)
PHONE 614 301-2498
Janet Brumfield, *President*
Joseph Barbarita, *Branch Mgr*
Keith Dinucci, *Technology*
John Pries, *Technology*
EMP: 139
SALES (corp-wide): 126B **Publicly Held**
SIC: 7389 Personal service agents, brokers & bureaus
HQ: Verizon New York Inc.
140 West St
New York NY 10007
212 395-1000

(G-11965)
W W WILLIAMS COMPANY LLC
Also Called: W W Wllams Company-Midwest Div
3535 Parkway Ln (43026-1214)
PHONE 614 527-9400
Alan Gatlin, *President*
Andrea Douglass, *Principal*
L Ed McIntyre, *Manager*
Perry Rice, *Manager*
Dorian Norstrom, *Administration*
EMP: 50
SALES (corp-wide): 2.1B **Privately Held**
WEB: www.williamsdistribution.com
SIC: 7538 General truck repair
HQ: The W W Williams Company Llc
835 Goodale Blvd
Columbus OH 43212
614 228-5000

(G-11966)
YASHCO SYSTEMS INC
3974 Brown Park Dr (43026-1168)
PHONE 614 467-4600
Simren Datta, *President*
Firoz Saifee, *Business Mgr*
Pankaj Nagrath, *Sales Mgr*
Rajendra Gupta, *Programmer Anys*
Amish Shukla, *Programmer Anys*
EMP: 25
SALES (est): 2.2MM **Privately Held**
WEB: www.yashco.com
SIC: 8748 7371 Business consulting; custom computer programming services

(G-11967)
YOUNG MENS CHRISTIAN ASSOC
Also Called: YMCA
4515 Cosgray Rd (43026-7787)
PHONE 614 334-9622
Fax: 614 334-0173
Jan Fetters Sr, *VP*
Steve Gunn, *Vice Pres*
Jean Tom Sr, *Vice Pres*
Larry Lake, *Facilities Dir*
William Oliver, *Branch Mgr*
EMP: 175
SALES (corp-wide): 44.9MM **Privately Held**
WEB: www.ymca-columbus.com
SIC: 8641 7991 8351 7032 Youth organizations; physical fitness facilities; child day care services; youth camps; individual & family services
PA: Young Men's Christian Association Of Central Ohio
40 W Long St
Columbus OH 43215
614 389-4409

Hillsboro
Highland County

(G-11968)
CLASSIC REAL ESTATE CO
123 W Main St (45133-1452)
PHONE 937 393-3416
Fax: 937 393-1333
Joyce Fender, *President*
Jenny Cameron, *Owner*
Jenny Hilterbran, *Broker*
Shannon Chain, *Sales Executive*
Kimberly Abbott, *Agent*
EMP: 25
SQ FT: 1,800
SALES (est): 1.8MM **Privately Held**
SIC: 6531 8742 Real estate brokers & agents; real estate agent, commercial; real estate agent, residential; real estate consultant

(G-11969)
CONGREGATE LIVING OF AMERICA
Also Called: Crestwood RDG Skilled Nursing
141 Willetsville Pike (45133-9476)
PHONE 937 393-6700
David Gunderman, *Director*
Kimberly Jackson, *Nursing Dir*
Ramona Stapleton, *Administration*
EMP: 50
SALES (corp-wide): 4.4MM **Privately Held**
SIC: 8052 8051 Intermediate care facilities; skilled nursing care facilities
PA: Congregate Living Of America, Inc
463 E Pike St
Morrow OH 45152
513 899-2801

(G-11970)
COUNTY OF HIGHLAND
Also Called: Child Sup Dept of Job & Family
1575 N High St Ste 100 (45133-8286)
P.O. Box 809 (45133-0809)
PHONE 937 393-4278
Nancy Wisecup, *Director*
EMP: 25 **Privately Held**
WEB: www.co.highland.oh.us
SIC: 8322 Individual & family services
PA: County Of Highland
1575 N High St Ste 200
Hillsboro OH 45133
937 393-1911

(G-11971)
CRESTVIEW RIDGE NURSING
141 Willetsville Pike (45133-9476)
PHONE 937 393-6700
Fax: 937 393-4325
Tracy Hughey, *Director*
Michael Harrison, *Administration*
Benjamin Parsons,
EMP: 50
SALES (est): 510.2K **Privately Held**
SIC: 8051 Convalescent home with continuous nursing care

(G-11972)
DENSO INTERNATIONAL AMER INC
Also Called: Weastec
1600 N High St (45133-8259)
PHONE 937 393-6800
Adam Koloff, *Design Engr*
Karl Steinhauser, *Design Engr*
Larry Akers, *Manager*
Yuri Nease, *Senior Mgr*
Justin Cooper, *Teacher*
EMP: 500
SALES (corp-wide): 39.8B **Privately Held**
WEB: www.densocorp-na.com
SIC: 5013 Automotive supplies & parts
HQ: Denso International America, Inc.
24777 Denso Dr
Southfield MI 48033
248 350-7500

(G-11973)
F R S CONNECTIONS
Also Called: Frs Counselling
149 Chillicothe Ave (45133-1530)
P.O. Box 823 (45133-0823)
PHONE 937 393-9662
Ellen Butcher, *Principal*
EMP: 40
SALES (est): 522.9K **Privately Held**
SIC: 8099 8093 8322 Medical services organization; mental health clinic, outpatient; general counseling services

(G-11974)
FIFTH THIRD BANK OF STHRN OH (HQ)
511 N High St (45133-1134)
PHONE 937 840-5353
Fax: 937 840-5201
Raymond Webb, *President*
Diane Bailey, *Finance Mgr*
EMP: 27
SQ FT: 18,000
SALES (est): 58.2MM
SALES (corp-wide): 7.7B **Publicly Held**
SIC: 6022 6162 State trust companies accepting deposits, commercial; mortgage bankers & correspondents
PA: Fifth Third Bancorp
38 Fountain Square Plz
Cincinnati OH 45202
800 972-3030

(G-11975)
FRS COUNSELING INC (PA)
104 Erin Ct (45133-8591)
P.O. Box 823 (45133-0823)
PHONE 937 393-0585
Joe Adray, *CEO*
Tom Tise, *CFO*
Kimberly Dye, *Human Res Mgr*
Charles Gorman, *Director*
EMP: 30
SQ FT: 3,800
SALES: 6.2MM **Privately Held**
WEB: www.frshighland.org
SIC: 8093 8322 8069 Mental health clinic, outpatient; alcohol clinic, outpatient; detoxification center, outpatient; family counseling services; alcoholism rehabilitation hospital

(G-11976)
HANSON AGGREGATES EAST LLC
Plum Run Stone Division
4281 Roush Rd (45133-9147)
PHONE 937 364-2311
Hanson Div, *COO*
Lee Robb, *Maint Spvr*
Dennis Mount, *Sales Mgr*
J Craig Morgan, *Manager*
Butch Farmer, *Manager*
EMP: 35
SALES (corp-wide): 16B **Privately Held**
SIC: 3281 3273 1422 Stone, quarrying & processing of own stone products; ready-mixed concrete; crushed & broken limestone
HQ: Hanson Aggregates East Llc
3131 Rdu Center Dr
Morrisville NC 27560
919 380-2500

(G-11977)
HEALTH CARE RTREMENT CORP AMER
Also Called: Heartland of Hillsboro
1141 Northview Dr (45133-8525)
PHONE 937 393-5766
Antonio Stewart, *Branch Mgr*
EMP: 95
SALES (corp-wide): 3.6B **Publicly Held**
WEB: www.hrc-manorcare.com
SIC: 8051 Convalescent home with continuous nursing care
HQ: Health Care And Retirement Corporation Of America
333 N Summit St Ste 103
Toledo OH 43604
419 252-5500

(G-11978)
HIGHLAND COUNTY FAMILY YMCA
201 Diamond Dr (45133-5398)
PHONE 937 840-9622
Fax: 937 840-9626
Terry Mull, *Director*
EMP: 30
SALES: 675.2K **Privately Held**
SIC: 8641 7991 8351 7032 Youth organizations; physical fitness facilities; child day care services; youth camps; individual & family services

(G-11979)
HIGHLAND COUNTY JOINT
Also Called: Highland District Hospital
1275 N High St (45133-8273)
PHONE 937 393-6100
Fax: 937 393-6278
Jim Baer, *CEO*
Thomas Degen, *Principal*
Paula Detterman, *Principal*
Neil Miller, *Plant Mgr*
Jesse Ruble, *Purchasing*
EMP: 400

Hillsboro - Highland County (G-11980)

GEOGRAPHIC SECTION

SALES: 42.8MM **Privately Held**
SIC: **8062** Hospital, affiliated with AMA residency

(G-11980)
HIGHLAND COUNTY WATER CO INC (PA)
6686 Us Highway 50 (45133-7938)
P.O. Box 940 (45133-0940)
PHONE.................................937 393-4281
Fax: 937 393-5121
Larry Cockrell, *General Mgr*
Hattie Lovedahl, *Supervisor*
EMP: 26
SQ FT: 28,000
SALES: 1.5MM **Privately Held**
SIC: **4941** Water supply

(G-11981)
HIGHLND CNTY COMMNTY ACTION OR (PA)
Also Called: Hccao
1487 N High St Ste 500 (45133-6812)
PHONE.................................937 393-3060
Fax: 937 393-7707
Fred Berry, *President*
Richard Graves, *Corp Secy*
Greg Barr, *Vice Pres*
Jennifer Baker, *Finance Dir*
Brenda Woods, *Human Res Mgr*
EMP: 35
SALES: 5.6MM **Privately Held**
WEB: www.hccao.com
SIC: **8322** Social service center

(G-11982)
HILLSBORO HEALTH CENTER INC
1108 Northview Dr Ste 1 (45133-1191)
PHONE.................................937 393-5781
Rene Hawthorne, *President*
EMP: 25
SALES (est): 1.8MM **Privately Held**
SIC: **8011** General & family practice, physician/surgeon

(G-11983)
HOME HELPERS
Also Called: Home Helpers and Direct Link
503 E Main St (45133-1585)
PHONE.................................937 393-8600
Janet Dean, *Owner*
EMP: 64
SALES (est): 423K **Privately Held**
SIC: **8082** Home health care services

(G-11984)
JERRY HAAG MOTORS INC
1475 N High St (45133-9473)
PHONE.................................937 402-2090
Fax: 937 393-1142
Steven R Haag, *President*
Mindy Sanders, *Technology*
EMP: 32
SQ FT: 17,700
SALES (est): 12.7MM **Privately Held**
WEB: www.jerryhaagmotors.com
SIC: **5511** 7538 5531 Automobiles, new & used; general automotive repair shops; automotive & home supply stores

(G-11985)
LAURELS OF HILLSBORO
Also Called: LOURIES OF HILLSBORO
175 Chillicothe Ave (45133-1533)
PHONE.................................937 393-1925
Kathy Moore, *VP Finance*
Christy Garrison, *Office Mgr*
Dave Gunderman, *Director*
Lori Byron, *Administration*
Aj Stout, *Administration*
EMP: 70
SQ FT: 18,000
SALES: 8.1MM **Privately Held**
SIC: **8052** 8051 Intermediate care facilities; skilled nursing care facilities
PA: Laurel Health Care Company Of North Worthtington
8181 Worthington Rd
Westerville OH 43082

(G-11986)
LUCAS & CLARK FAMILY DENTISTRY
624 S High St (45133-1433)
P.O. Box 310 (45133-0310)
PHONE.................................937 393-3494
Fax: 937 393-6864
Lynne Lucas, *Vice Pres*
Laura Turner, *Office Mgr*
M Glenn Lucas DDS, *Director*
▲ EMP: 25
SQ FT: 3,000
SALES (est): 1.4MM **Privately Held**
SIC: **8021** Dentists' office

(G-11987)
MERCHANTS NATIONAL BANK (HQ)
100 N High St (45133-1152)
P.O. Box 10 (45133-0010)
PHONE.................................937 393-1134
Fax: 937 393-9425
Don Fender, *Ch of Bd*
Paul Pence Jr, *President*
Brock Burcham, *Assistant VP*
John Storrs, *Vice Pres*
Scott J Hopf, *CFO*
EMP: 50
SALES: 30.2MM
SALES (corp-wide): 28.8MM **Privately Held**
SIC: **6021** National commercial banks
PA: Merchants Bancorp Inc
100 N High St
Hillsboro OH 45133
937 393-1993

(G-11988)
NATIONAL CONSUMER COOP BNK
139 S High St (45133-1442)
PHONE.................................937 393-4246
Dami Odetola, *Vice Pres*
Carrie Hesler, *CFO*
Ernie Blankenship, *HR Admin*
Michael J Merce, *Branch Mgr*
Cecil Greene, *Manager*
EMP: 27
SALES (corp-wide): 103.7MM **Privately Held**
SIC: **6099** Check clearing services
PA: National Consumer Cooperative Bank
1901 Penn Ave Nw Ste 300
Washington DC 20006
202 349-7444

(G-11989)
NATIONAL COOPERATIVE BANK NA (HQ)
Also Called: N C B-F S B
139 S High St Ste 1 (45133-1442)
PHONE.................................937 393-4246
Fax: 937 393-4064
Charles E Snyder, *President*
Steven Brookner, *President*
Chris Goettke, *Co-President*
Kathleen H Luzik, *COO*
Patrick N Connealy, *Exec VP*
EMP: 63 EST: 1890
SQ FT: 20,000
SALES (est): 81.1MM
SALES (corp-wide): 103.7MM **Privately Held**
SIC: **6111** National Consumer Cooperative Bank
PA: National Consumer Cooperative Bank
1901 Penn Ave Nw Ste 300
Washington DC 20006
202 349-7444

(G-11990)
NB AND T INSURANCE AGENCY INC
Also Called: Steele, George R Co
111 Governor Foraker Pl (45133-1054)
PHONE.................................937 393-1985
Fax: 937 393-1501
Mike Phillips, *President*
George Phillips, *President*
S Davis, *Vice Pres*
Kelly Ward, *Manager*
EMP: 28
SALES (est): 2.6MM **Privately Held**
SIC: **6411** Insurance agents

(G-11991)
PAS TECHNOLOGIES INC
214 Hobart Dr (45133-9487)
PHONE.................................937 840-1000
Deanne Miller, *Purch Mgr*
Joshua Ayers, *Engineer*
James Heiser, *Engineer*
Nathanael Young, *Engineer*
Mark Greene, *Manager*
EMP: 100 **Privately Held**
WEB: www.pas-technologies.com
SIC: **3724** 7699 Aircraft engines & engine parts; aircraft & heavy equipment repair services
HQ: Pas Technologies Inc.
1234 Atlantic Ave
North Kansas City MO 64116

(G-11992)
WESTERN & SOUTHERN LF INSUR CO
902 N High St Ste B (45133-8501)
PHONE.................................937 393-1969
Robert Miller, *Manager*
EMP: 25 **Privately Held**
SIC: **6411** Life insurance agents
HQ: The Western & Southern Life Insurance Company
400 Broadway St
Cincinnati OH 45202
513 629-1800

(G-11993)
XPO LOGISTICS FREIGHT INC
5215 Us Route 50 (45133-9166)
PHONE.................................937 364-2361
Fax: 937 364-6369
James New, *Manager*
EMP: 27
SALES (corp-wide): 15.3B **Publicly Held**
WEB: www.con-way.com
SIC: **4212** Local trucking, without storage
HQ: Xpo Logistics Freight, Inc.
2211 Old Earhart Rd # 100
Ann Arbor MI 48105
734 998-4200

Hinckley
Medina County

(G-11994)
ALDI INC
1319 W 130th St (44233-9500)
PHONE.................................330 273-7351
Thomas Behtz, *Vice Pres*
EMP: 80 **Privately Held**
WEB: www.aldi.com
SIC: **5411** 4225 Grocery stores, chain; general warehousing & storage
HQ: Aldi Inc.
1200 N Kirk Rd
Batavia IL 60510
630 879-8100

(G-11995)
BLACK HORSE CARRIERS INC
1319 W 130th St (44233-9500)
PHONE.................................330 225-2250
Roger Foulk, *Branch Mgr*
EMP: 125
SALES (corp-wide): 121.9MM **Privately Held**
SIC: **4213** Trucking, except local
PA: Black Horse Carriers Inc.
455 Kehoe Blvd Ste 105
Carol Stream IL 60188
630 690-8900

(G-11996)
CLINICAL RESEARCH MGT INC (HQ)
1265 Ridge Rd Ste 2 (44233-9806)
PHONE.................................330 278-2343
Victoria Tifft, *CEO*
Joseph Sgherza, *President*
Jeff Burdine, *Vice Pres*
Claudia Christian, *Vice Pres*
Kathy Freeman, *Vice Pres*
EMP: 356
SALES: 64.1MM **Privately Held**
WEB: www.clinicalrm.com
SIC: **8731** 8732 Medical research, commercial; commercial nonphysical research

(G-11997)
ENVIRONMENTAL MATERIALS LLC
Also Called: Environmental Stone Works
2699 Center Rd (44233-9562)
PHONE.................................330 558-9168
Jon Burns,
EMP: 25
SALES (corp-wide): 261.7MM **Privately Held**
SIC: **1521** Single-family housing construction
PA: Environmental Materials, Llc
7306 S Alton Way Ste B
Centennial CO 80112
303 309-6610

(G-11998)
HEALTHSOURCE INC
1313 Ridge Rd (44233-9701)
P.O. Box 308 (44233-0308)
PHONE.................................330 278-2781
Jesse Dickerson, *President*
EMP: 125
SQ FT: 1,800
SALES (est): 1.8MM **Privately Held**
WEB: www.healthsourceinc.org
SIC: **8049** Physical therapist

(G-11999)
PINE HILLS GOLF CLUB INC
433 W 130th St (44233-9566)
PHONE.................................330 225-4477
Fax: 330 225-3196
William Gertrack, *President*
Scott Forester, *Corp Secy*
EMP: 40 EST: 1955
SQ FT: 5,820
SALES (est): 2MM **Privately Held**
WEB: www.golfpinehills.net
SIC: **7992** Public golf courses

(G-12000)
VALLEAIRE GOLF CLUB INC
6969 Boston Rd (44233-9402)
PHONE.................................440 237-9191
Fax: 440 230-1280
Mike Burns, *General Mgr*
EMP: 50 EST: 1964
SALES (est): 2MM **Privately Held**
SIC: **7997** Golf club, membership

(G-12001)
VANS EXPRESS INC
222 Concord Ln (44233-9662)
P.O. Box 53 (44233-0053)
PHONE.................................216 224-5388
Gary Van Den Haute, *President*
Don Vandenhaute, *Vice Pres*
EMP: 26
SALES (est): 3.3MM **Privately Held**
SIC: **8748** Business consulting

Hiram
Portage County

(G-12002)
GREAT LAKES CHEESE CO INC (PA)
17825 Great Lakes Pkwy (44234-9677)
P.O. Box 1806 (44234-1806)
PHONE.................................440 834-2500
Gary Vanic, *President*
Marcel Dasen, *Principal*
Hans Epprecht, *Principal*
Albert Z Meyers, *Principal*
John Epprecht, *Corp Secy*
◆ EMP: 500
SQ FT: 218,000
SALES (est): 1.6B **Privately Held**
WEB: www.greatlakescheese.com
SIC: **5143** 2022 Cheese; natural cheese

Holgate
Henry County

(G-12003)
MERCY HEALTH
106 N Wilhelm St (43527-7734)
PHONE.................................419 264-5800

GEOGRAPHIC SECTION

Holland - Lucas County (G-12026)

EMP: 55
SALES (corp-wide): 4.2B **Privately Held**
SIC: 8031 8011 Offices & clinics of osteopathic physicians; offices & clinics of medical doctors
PA: Mercy Health
1701 Mercy Health Pl
Cincinnati OH 45237
513 639-2800

(G-12004)
VANCREST HEALTH CARE CENTER
600 Joe E Brown Ave (43527-9803)
PHONE.................................419 264-0700
Fax: 419 264-0800
Mark White, *Principal*
Wendy Rollins, *Nursing Dir*
Kim Ricker, *Hlthcr Dir*
Amber Merriman, *Administration*
EMP: 60
SALES (est): 1.4MM **Privately Held**
SIC: 8082 Home health care services

Holland
Lucas County

(G-12005)
3C TECHNOLOGIES INC
6834 Spring Valley Dr # 202 (43528-7864)
PHONE.................................419 868-8999
Dave Capur, *President*
Matt Bublick, *Exec VP*
EMP: 65
SQ FT: 9,000
SALES (est): 3MM **Privately Held**
WEB: www.3ctech.com
SIC: 8741 8299 Business management; educational services

(G-12006)
ALLIED PAVING INC
Also Called: Allied Paving Company
8406 Airport Hwy (43528-8638)
PHONE.................................419 666-3100
Fax: 419 866-5022
Thomas Buck, *President*
Louann Buck, *Vice Pres*
Heather Buck, *Manager*
Heather Sealing, *Manager*
EMP: 25
SQ FT: 3,000
SALES (est): 3.9MM **Privately Held**
WEB: www.alliedpavingcompany.com
SIC: 1611 1771 Highway & street paving contractor; driveway, parking lot & blacktop contractors

(G-12007)
ALTERNATIVE SERVICES INC
7710 Hill Ave (43528-7607)
PHONE.................................419 861-2121
Janice Porter, *President*
Sarah York, *IT/INT Sup*
EMP: 35
SQ FT: 60,000
SALES (est): 2.2MM **Privately Held**
SIC: 7389 Packaging & labeling services

(G-12008)
ANNE GRADY CORPORATION
1645 Trade Rd (43528-8204)
PHONE.................................419 867-7501
Steve King, *CFO*
David A Boston, *Exec Dir*
EMP: 50
SQ FT: 20,000
SALES (corp-wide): 17.3MM **Privately Held**
SIC: 8331 Job training & vocational rehabilitation services
PA: Anne Grady Corporation
1525 Eber Rd
Holland OH 43528
419 380-8985

(G-12009)
ANNE GRADY CORPORATION (PA)
1525 Eber Rd (43528-9616)
P.O. Box 1297 (43528-1297)
PHONE.................................419 380-8985
Fax: 419 866-4326

Steve King, *Finance Dir*
Larry White, *Finance*
Velma Brown, *Human Res Mgr*
Mary Debmroz, *Human Res Mgr*
Linda Torbet, *Human Res Mgr*
EMP: 250
SQ FT: 70,000
SALES: 17.3MM **Privately Held**
WEB: www.annegrady.org
SIC: 8361 8052 Home for the mentally retarded; intermediate care facilities

(G-12010)
BLACK SWAMP STEEL INC
1761 Commerce Rd (43528-9789)
P.O. Box 1180 (43528-1180)
PHONE.................................419 867-8050
Fax: 419 865-9509
Dave Coronado, *President*
Steve Sieracke, *President*
Brad Carpenter, *Principal*
Jon West, *Principal*
EMP: 25 **EST:** 1991
SALES (est): 4.5MM **Privately Held**
SIC: 1791 Structural steel erection

(G-12011)
BLANCHARD TREE AND LAWN INC
1530 Kieswetter Rd (43528-8677)
P.O. Box 1100 (43528-1100)
PHONE.................................419 865-7071
Fax: 419 865-2822
James D Blanchard, *President*
EMP: 60 **EST:** 1958
SQ FT: 12,000
SALES (est): 2.4MM **Privately Held**
WEB: www.blanchardtree.com
SIC: 0783 0782 0781 0711 Ornamental shrub & tree services; mowing services, lawn; landscape services; fertilizer application services

(G-12012)
BRENNAN INDUSTRIAL TRUCK CO
Also Called: Brennan Equipment Services
6940 Hall St (43528-9485)
PHONE.................................419 867-6000
Fax: 419 867-6667
James H Brennan Jr, *President*
Thomas J Backoff, *Vice Pres*
Mike Fisher, *Controller*
EMP: 30 **EST:** 1957
SQ FT: 35,000
SALES (est): 18MM **Privately Held**
WEB: www.brennanindtrk.com
SIC: 5084 7359 Materials handling machinery; lift trucks & parts; industrial truck rental

(G-12013)
BRENNAN-EBERLY TEAM SPORTS INC (PA)
6144 Merger Dr (43528-8438)
PHONE.................................419 865-8326
Fax: 419 865-3596
Bob Eberly, *President*
Jay Lehman, *General Mgr*
Carol L Eberly, *Vice Pres*
Gary Ludwig, *Treasurer*
Dave Glore, *Sales Staff*
EMP: 25
SQ FT: 8,500
SALES (est): 7.5MM **Privately Held**
SIC: 5091 5139 5136 5137 Sporting & recreation goods; footwear, athletic; men's & boys' sportswear & work clothing; women's & children's sportswear & swimsuits

(G-12014)
CARDINAL HEALTH 414 LLC
6156 Trust Dr Ste B (43528-7860)
PHONE.................................419 867-1077
Mike Smith, *Manager*
Michael Smith, *Pharmacy Dir*
EMP: 29
SALES (corp-wide): 129.9B **Publicly Held**
WEB: www.syncor.com
SIC: 5122 Pharmaceuticals
HQ: Cardinal Health 414, Llc
7000 Cardinal Pl
Dublin OH 43017
614 757-5000

(G-12015)
CHILDRENS DISCOVERY CENTER
Also Called: Discovery Express Child Care
1640 Timber Wolf Dr (43528-8303)
PHONE.................................419 861-1060
Fax: 419 861-1063
Mona Taylor, *Director*
Lisa Hornyak, *Administration*
Cindi Taylor, *Administration*
EMP: 30
SQ FT: 10,829
SALES (corp-wide): 8MM **Privately Held**
WEB: www.discovery-express.com
SIC: 8351 Preschool center
PA: Childrens Discovery Center
6450 Weatherfield Ct 1a
Maumee OH 43537
419 867-8570

(G-12016)
COUNTY OF LUCAS
Also Called: Lucas County Engineer
1049 S Mccord Rd Bldg A (43528-7020)
PHONE.................................419 213-2892
Fax: 419 213-4598
Thomas Jameson, *Project Mgr*
Chris Zimo, *Opers Mgr*
Mark Drennen, *Financial Exec*
Mike Bays, *Manager*
CJ Holly, *Technology*
EMP: 58 **Privately Held**
SIC: 8711 Engineering services
PA: County Of Lucas
1 Government Ctr Ste 600
Toledo OH 43604
419 213-4406

(G-12017)
CREATIVE PRODUCTS INC
Also Called: CPI
1430 Kieswetter Rd (43528-9785)
PHONE.................................419 866-5501
Marvin Smith, *President*
EMP: 33
SQ FT: 26,000
SALES (est): 2.2MM **Privately Held**
SIC: 5023 5211 2541 Kitchen tools & utensils; cabinets, kitchen; counter tops; wood partitions & fixtures

(G-12018)
DANA HEAVY VEHICLE SYSTEMS
Also Called: Dana Spicer Service Parts
6936 Airport Hwy (43528)
PHONE.................................419 866-3900
Fax: 419 866-3924
Brad Ncgibney, *Development*
Len Newblom, *Development*
Suan Herring, *Sales Staff*
Tory Newton, *Sales Staff*
Sharon Rohr, *Marketing Staff*
EMP: 52 **Publicly Held**
SIC: 5013 Automotive supplies & parts
HQ: Dana Heavy Vehicle Systems Group, Llc
3939 Technology Dr
Maumee OH 43537

(G-12019)
DEVIRSIFIED MATERIAL HANDLING
Also Called: Interstate Lift Truck
8310 Airport Hwy (43528-8637)
PHONE.................................419 865-8025
Fax: 419 865-3836
Phil Graffy, *President*
Ted Wente, *Vice Pres*
Julie Hood, *Controller*
▼**EMP:** 26
SALES (est): 5.3MM **Privately Held**
SIC: 5084 Materials handling machinery

(G-12020)
DIANE BABIUCH
Also Called: Camelot Hair Tanning & Nails
7409 International Dr (43528-8623)
PHONE.................................419 867-8837
Fax: 419 578-0517
Diane Babiuch, *Owner*
Ray Babiuch, *Co-Owner*
EMP: 35
SQ FT: 3,000

SALES (est): 930K **Privately Held**
SIC: 7231 7299 Hairdressers; manicurist, pedicurist; tanning salon

(G-12021)
DOUGLAS COMPANY (PA)
1716 Prrysburg Holland Rd (43528-9581)
PHONE.................................419 865-8600
Peter Douglas, *President*
Dennis Robinson, *Exec VP*
Brian McCarthy, *Vice Pres*
Ronald Siebenaler, *Vice Pres*
Dennis Voss, *Project Mgr*
EMP: 25 **EST:** 1976
SQ FT: 14,000
SALES (est): 25.2MM **Privately Held**
WEB: www.douglascompany.com
SIC: 1542 1522 Commercial & office building, new construction; hotel/motel & multi-family home construction

(G-12022)
DOUGLAS CONSTRUCTION COMPANY
Also Called: Design Services Cnstr Co
1716 Prrysburg Holland Rd (43528-9581)
PHONE.................................419 865-8600
Peter Douglas, *President*
David Bockbrader, *Treasurer*
EMP: 25
SQ FT: 7,000
SALES (est): 1.6MM **Privately Held**
SIC: 1522 1531 Multi-family dwellings, new construction; remodeling, multi-family dwellings; condominium developers

(G-12023)
DYNAMIC CURRENTS CORP
1761 Commerce Rd (43528-9789)
PHONE.................................419 861-2036
David P Coronado, *President*
Rachael M Mendoza, *Corp Secy*
Lorie Siler, *Office Mgr*
EMP: 50
SALES (est): 3MM **Privately Held**
WEB: www.dynamiccurrents.com
SIC: 1731 Electrical work

(G-12024)
GLEASON CONSTRUCTION CO INC
540 S Centennial Rd (43528-8400)
PHONE.................................419 865-7480
Fax: 419 865-5526
James F Gleason, *President*
Joe Monks, *Controller*
Carol S Gleason, *Admin Sec*
EMP: 60
SQ FT: 20,000
SALES (est): 8.6MM **Privately Held**
SIC: 1623 Underground utilities contractor

(G-12025)
HABITEC SECURITY INC (PA)
1545 Timber Wolf Dr (43528-9130)
P.O. Box 352497, Toledo (43635-2497)
PHONE.................................419 537-6768
Fax: 419 582-3677
Nancy Smythe, *CEO*
John Smythe, *President*
Donald Kraatz, *Opers Mgr*
James M Sythe, *Personnel Exec*
Dennis Velliquette, *Human Resources*
EMP: 85
SQ FT: 9,000
SALES (est): 12.1MM **Privately Held**
WEB: www.habitecsecurity.com
SIC: 7382 Burglar alarm maintenance & monitoring

(G-12026)
HAMILTON MANUFACTURING CORP
1026 Hamilton Dr (43528-8210)
PHONE.................................419 867-4858
Fax: 419 867-4850
Robin Ritz, *CEO*
Steve Alt, *President*
Bonnie Osborne, *Exec VP*
Jill Snyder, *Buyer*
Bill Irwin, *Engineer*
▲**EMP:** 45 **EST:** 1921
SQ FT: 32,000

Holland - Lucas County (G-12027)

SALES (est): 10.2MM **Privately Held**
WEB: www.hamiltonmfg.com
SIC: **3172** 8711 Coin purses; designing; ship, boat, machine & product

(G-12027)
HOBBY LOBBY STORES INC
6645 Airport Hwy (43528-8419)
PHONE..................................419 861-1862
EMP: 55
SALES (corp-wide): 4.5B **Privately Held**
SIC: **6794** 5945 Patent owners & lessors; children's toys & games, except dolls
PA: Hobby Lobby Stores, Inc.
   7707 Sw 44th St
   Oklahoma City OK 73179
   405 745-1100

(G-12028)
HRP CAPITAL INC
Also Called: PhyCor
6855 Spring Valley Dr # 120 (43528-8039)
PHONE..................................419 865-3111
Pat Montgomery, *Branch Mgr*
Robin Graham, *Manager*
EMP: 26
SALES (corp-wide): 12.4MM **Privately Held**
SIC: **8741** 8011 Nursing & personal care facility management; physicians' office, including specialists
PA: Hrp Capital, Inc.
   173 Bridge Plz N
   Fort Lee NJ 07024
   201 242-4938

(G-12029)
I L T DIVERSIFIED MTL HDLG
8310 Airport Hwy (43528-8637)
PHONE..................................419 865-8025
Phillip Graffy, *President*
EMP: 27 EST: 1972
SQ FT: 16,000
SALES (est): 2.8MM **Privately Held**
SIC: **5084** 7359 7699 Lift trucks & parts; industrial truck rental; industrial truck repair

(G-12030)
ITS TECHNOLOGIES INC (PA)
7060 Spring Meadows Dr W D (43528-8093)
PHONE..................................419 842-2100
Roger L Radeloff, *President*
Allison Schock, *Division Mgr*
Barrie Howell, *Treasurer*
Carol Kurtz, *Sales Staff*
Jeff Frantz, *Director*
EMP: 100
SALES (est): 17MM **Privately Held**
SIC: **7363** 7361 Temporary help service; employment agencies

(G-12031)
KEY REALTY LTD
130 Fountain Dr (43528-9061)
PHONE..................................419 270-7445
Anissa Yoder, *Manager*
Phil Henderson,
EMP: 150 EST: 2008
SALES (est): 4MM **Privately Held**
SIC: **6531** Real estate agent, residential

(G-12032)
LAKE ERIE MED SURGICAL SUP INC
6920 Hall St (43528-9485)
P.O. Box 1267 (43528-1267)
PHONE..................................734 847-3847
Jeannie Sieren, *Branch Mgr*
EMP: 40
SALES (corp-wide): 16.4MM **Privately Held**
SIC: **5047** Medical & hospital equipment
PA: Lake Erie Medical & Surgical Supply, Inc.
   7560 Lewis Ave
   Temperance MI 48182
   734 847-3847

(G-12033)
LUTHERAN VILLAGE AT WOLF CREEK
Also Called: CREEKSIDE CONDOMINIUMS
2001 Prrysbrg Hllnd Ofc (43528-8001)
PHONE..................................419 861-2233
Fax: 419 861-2234
Mark Gavorski, *Principal*
Amanda Karamol, *Chf Purch Ofc*
E Stott, *Human Res Mgr*
Bob Burns, *Director*
EMP: 160
SQ FT: 113,154
SALES (est): 10.5MM **Privately Held**
WEB: www.creeksidecondominiums.com
SIC: **8059** 8361 8052 8051 Rest home, with health care; residential care; intermediate care facilities; skilled nursing care facilities

(G-12034)
MAC QUEEN ORCHARDS INC
7605 Garden Rd (43528-8538)
PHONE..................................419 865-2916
Fax: 419 865-1832
Robert H Mac Queen, *President*
Bernice Mac Queen, *Vice Pres*
Robert Mac Queen II, *Treasurer*
Jeffery Mac Queen, *Officer*
Lynn Mac Queen, *Admin Sec*
EMP: 45
SALES: 1MM **Privately Held**
WEB: www.macqueenorchards.com
SIC: **0175** Apple orchard; peach orchard; pear orchard; plum orchard

(G-12035)
MARRIOTT INTERNATIONAL INC
Also Called: Courtyard By Marriott
1435 E Mall Dr (43528-9490)
PHONE..................................419 866-1001
Fax: 419 866-9869
Rebecca Call, *Accounts Exec*
Jamie Talberth, *Manager*
EMP: 167
SALES (corp-wide): 22.8B **Publicly Held**
SIC: **7011** Hotels & motels
PA: Marriott International, Inc.
   10400 Fernwood Rd
   Bethesda MD 20817
   301 380-3000

(G-12036)
MC CLURG & CREAMER INC
7450 Hill Ave (43528-8751)
PHONE..................................419 866-7080
Fax: 419 866-3686
Marshall Mc Clurg, *President*
Curt Creamer, *Vice Pres*
EMP: 26
SALES (est): 1.7MM **Privately Held**
WEB: www.mcclurg-creamer.com
SIC: **0781** 0782 1711 4959 Landscape architects; lawn care services; irrigation sprinkler system installation; snowplowing

(G-12037)
MIDWEST CONTRACTING INC
1428 Albon Rd (43528-8683)
PHONE..................................419 866-4560
Fax: 419 866-4570
Aaron Koder, *President*
Rob Lowenstein, *Project Mgr*
Marcus Price, *Project Mgr*
Jennifer Koder, *Office Mgr*
Tom Dubois, *Sr Project Mgr*
EMP: 28 EST: 1996
SALES (est): 5.3MM **Privately Held**
SIC: **1799** Antenna installation

(G-12038)
MIDWEST TAPE LLC
1417 Timber Wolf Dr (43528-8302)
P.O. Box 820 (43528-0820)
PHONE..................................419 868-9370
Sue Bascuk, *General Mgr*
Brad Rose, *Vice Pres*
Mike Matney, *Project Mgr*
Kelsey Whitmore, *Receiver*
Brian Maroszek, *Buyer*
▲ EMP: 330
SQ FT: 100,000
SALES (est): 95.1MM **Privately Held**
WEB: www.midwesttapes.com
SIC: **7822** 5099 8741 7389 Video tapes, recorded: wholesale; motion picture distribution; video cassettes, accessories & supplies; administrative management; packaging & labeling services; ; data processing service

(G-12039)
MILLER FIREWORKS COMPANY INC (PA)
Also Called: Miller Fireworks Novelty
501 Glengary Rd (43528-9416)
PHONE..................................419 865-7329
John F Miller III, *President*
Gregory Ball, *Manager*
Jason Copeland, *Manager*
▲ EMP: 35
SQ FT: 2,520
SALES (est): 5.1MM **Privately Held**
WEB: www.millerfireworks.com
SIC: **5092** 5999 Fireworks; fireworks

(G-12040)
NATIONAL COMPRESSOR SVCS LLC (PA)
10349 Industrial St (43528-9791)
P.O. Box 760 (43528-0760)
PHONE..................................419 868-4980
Brenda Sevenski, *Purch Mgr*
Jaymi Crossfield, *Accounts Mgr*
Tracy Denney, *Accounts Mgr*
Mark Doty, *Accounts Mgr*
Ann Jeffries, *Office Mgr*
EMP: 39
SQ FT: 60,000
SALES: 11MM **Privately Held**
SIC: **7699** Compressor repair

(G-12041)
NORTHWEST ELECTRICAL CONTG INC
1617 Shanrock Dr (43528-8368)
PHONE..................................419 865-4757
Fax: 419 865-4722
Jody Mc Collum, *President*
Nick Nemire, *Project Mgr*
Kathy McCollum, *Financial Exec*
Kathy Mc Collum, *Admin Sec*
▲ EMP: 30
SQ FT: 8,800
SALES (est): 5.5MM **Privately Held**
WEB: www.nwelect.com
SIC: **1731** Electrical work

(G-12042)
NORTHWSTERN OHIO ADMNISTRATORS
7142 Nightingale Dr 1 (43528-7822)
P.O. Box 1330 (43528-1330)
PHONE..................................419 248-2401
Fax: 419 255-7136
Nick Madden, *President*
EMP: 25
SQ FT: 46,000
SALES (est): 3.9MM **Privately Held**
SIC: **6411** Insurance agents, brokers & service

(G-12043)
OCP CONTRACTORS INC (PA)
Also Called: O C P
1740 Commerce Rd (43528-9789)
PHONE..................................419 865-7168
Fax: 419 865-1284
Matthew Townsend, *President*
Sandy Gilday, *Business Mgr*
Pam Hepburn, *Vice Pres*
Matthew Giambrone, *Project Mgr*
Ray McKenzie, *Project Mgr*
EMP: 25
SQ FT: 8,000
SALES: 58MM **Privately Held**
WEB: www.ocp-contractors.com
SIC: **1742** 1751 1752 1743 Drywall; lightweight steel framing (metal stud) installation; floor laying & floor work; tile installation, ceramic; coating, caulking & weather, water & fireproofing

(G-12044)
OFFICE PRODUCTS TOLEDO INC
Also Called: M T Business Technologies
1205 Corporate Dr (43528-9590)
PHONE..................................419 865-7001
Susan Carl, *President*
Patrick Okuley, *Business Mgr*
Michael Pfeifer, *Technical Mgr*
Bill Ewers, *Sales Mgr*
Jack Jolley, *Sales Mgr*
EMP: 50
SALES (est): 17MM **Privately Held**
SIC: **5044** 7359 Copying equipment; office machine rental, except computers

(G-12045)
PETSMART INC
1450 Spring Meadows Dr (43528-9478)
PHONE..................................419 865-3941
EMP: 32
SALES (corp-wide): 12.7B **Privately Held**
SIC: **0752** Grooming services, pet & animal specialties
HQ: Petsmart, Inc.
   19601 N 27th Ave
   Phoenix AZ 85027
   623 580-6100

(G-12046)
PLASTIC TECHNOLOGIES INC (PA)
Also Called: Pti
1440 Timber Wolf Dr (43528-8301)
P.O. Box 964 (43528-0964)
PHONE..................................419 867-5400
Fax: 419 867-7700
Craig S Barrow, *President*
Gary Weaver, *President*
Tom Brady, *Chairman*
Dan Witham, *Business Mgr*
Elizabeth Brady, *Vice Pres*
EMP: 95
SQ FT: 46,000
SALES (est): 22.6MM **Privately Held**
WEB: www.plastictechnologies.com
SIC: **8734** 8731 Product testing laboratory, safety or performance; commercial physical research

(G-12047)
R & F INC
Also Called: Allied Home Health Services
6228 Merger Dr (43528-9593)
PHONE..................................419 868-2909
Fax: 419 861-9137
Tom Leffler, *Manager*
Nicole Howard, *Director*
EMP: 25
SALES (corp-wide): 13MM **Privately Held**
WEB: www.aprn1.com
SIC: **8049** 8051 8082 Physical therapist; skilled nursing care facilities; home health care services
PA: R & F Inc
   1133 Corporate Dr Ste B
   Holland OH 43528
   419 882-9870

(G-12048)
R & R HVAC SYSTEMS
1650 Eber Rd Ste E (43528-9793)
PHONE..................................419 861-0266
Ron Reid, *President*
Pat Reid, *Admin Sec*
EMP: 25
SALES (est): 2.2MM **Privately Held**
SIC: **1711** Heating & air conditioning contractors

(G-12049)
R L KING INSURANCE AGENCY
7723 Airport Hwy Ste F (43528-7602)
P.O. Box 1265 (43528-1265)
PHONE..................................419 255-9947
Ronald L King, *President*
EMP: 25
SQ FT: 3,000
SALES (est): 5.4MM **Privately Held**
SIC: **6411** Insurance agents

(G-12050)
R P MARKETING PUBLIC RELATIONS
1500 Timber Wolf Dr (43528-9129)
PHONE..................................419 241-2221
Martha Vetter, *President*
Stan Massey, *Vice Pres*
Laila Waggoner, *Vice Pres*
Susan Gdowik, *Director*
David Proudfoot, *Creative Dir*
EMP: 30
SALES (est): 2.7MM **Privately Held**
SIC: **8742** 7389 Marketing consulting services; advertising, promotional & trade show services

(G-12051)
ROMAN/PESHOFF INC
1500 Timber Wolf Dr (43528-9129)
PHONE..............................419 241-2221
Martha Vetter, *President*
Timothy Langhorst, *Vice Pres*
Stan Massey, *Vice Pres*
Laila Waggoner, *Vice Pres*
Jean Rogers, *Office Mgr*
EMP: 32
SQ FT: 8,800
SALES: 8.6MM **Privately Held**
WEB: www.r-p.com
SIC: 8743 7311 Public relations & publicity; advertising agencies

(G-12052)
SAWYER STEEL ERECTORS INC
1761 Commerce Rd (43528-9789)
PHONE..............................419 867-8050
John Isola, *President*
EMP: 50
SALES (est): 3.1MM **Privately Held**
SIC: 1791 Structural steel erection

(G-12053)
SCHINDLER ELEVATOR CORPORATION
Millar Elevator Service
1530 Timber Wolf Dr (43528-9161)
P.O. Box 960 (43528-0960)
PHONE..............................419 867-5100
Fax: 419 867-5101
Louis Haefner, *General Mgr*
Vanessa Herrero, *Sales Staff*
D Kornowa, *Marketing Staff*
Tim Shaey, *Manager*
Ed Isaac, *Supervisor*
EMP: 110
SQ FT: 2,000
SALES (corp-wide): 9.5B **Privately Held**
WEB: www.us.schindler.com
SIC: 1796 Elevator installation & conversion
HQ: Schindler Elevator Corporation
20 Whippany Rd
Morristown NJ 07960
973 397-6500

(G-12054)
SCHINDLER ELEVATOR CORPORATION
1530 Timber Wolf Dr (43528-9161)
P.O. Box 960 (43528-0960)
PHONE..............................419 861-5900
Fax: 419 867-5901
Don Mette, *Facilities Mgr*
Dennis Meyer, *Warehouse Mgr*
Brian Robbins, *Human Resources*
Mark Kershner, *Manager*
Cathie Teachout, *Manager*
EMP: 26
SALES (corp-wide): 9.5B **Privately Held**
WEB: www.us.schindler.com
SIC: 3534 7699 Elevators & equipment; escalators, passenger & freight; elevators: inspection, service & repair
HQ: Schindler Elevator Corporation
20 Whippany Rd
Morristown NJ 07960
973 397-6500

(G-12055)
SEAGATE OFFICE PRODUCTS INC
1044 Hamilton Dr (43528-8166)
PHONE..............................419 861-6161
Connie Leonardi, *President*
Sally Wagner, *Accountant*
Jackie Leonardi, *Accounts Mgr*
EMP: 25
SQ FT: 10,000
SALES (est): 9MM **Privately Held**
WEB: www.seagateop.com
SIC: 5112 5021 Office supplies; office furniture

(G-12056)
SPONSELLER GROUP INC (PA)
1600 Timber Wolf Dr (43528-8303)
PHONE..............................419 861-3000
Fax: 419 861-3004
Keith Sponseller, *President*
Harold P Sponseller, *Chairman*
Kevin R Nevius, *Vice Pres*
David Nowak, *Vice Pres*
Joe Jackson, *Project Mgr*
EMP: 44
SQ FT: 8,900
SALES (est): 8.7MM **Privately Held**
SIC: 8711 3599 Consulting engineer; machine shop, jobbing & repair

(G-12057)
SPRING MEADOW EXTENDED CARE CE (PA)
1125 Clarion Ave (43528-8107)
PHONE..............................419 866-6124
Fax: 419 866-2070
John H Stone, *President*
Jay Daniels, *Maintenance Dir*
Roxanne Warr, *Human Resources*
Davida Tucker, *Director*
Melinda Turpening, *Director*
EMP: 63
SQ FT: 50,000
SALES: 1.4MM **Privately Held**
SIC: 8052 8051 Intermediate care facilities; skilled nursing care facilities

(G-12058)
STONE OAK COUNTRY CLUB
100 Stone Oak Blvd (43528-9131)
PHONE..............................419 867-0969
Fax: 419 867-1011
Keith Olander, *President*
Chuck Radabaugh, *Sales Staff*
Beth Bazeley, *Sales Executive*
Nora Kelly, *Manager*
Julie Smith, *Manager*
EMP: 100
SQ FT: 25,517
SALES: 4.1MM **Privately Held**
SIC: 7997 Golf club, membership

(G-12059)
TEAM SPORTS LLC
6232 Merger Dr (43528-9593)
PHONE..............................419 865-8326
Jay Lehman,
Et Al,
L J Archambeau,
Roger Reese,
EMP: 25
SALES (est): 984K
SALES (corp-wide): 7.5MM **Privately Held**
SIC: 7389 Lettering service
PA: Brennan-Eberly Team Sports, Inc.
6144 Merger Dr
Holland OH 43528
419 865-8326

(G-12060)
TEKNI-PLEX INC
Also Called: Global Technology Center
1445 Timber Wolf Dr (43528-8302)
PHONE..............................419 491-2407
Paul J Young, *CEO*
Phil Bourgeois, *Vice Pres*
EMP: 25 **EST:** 1967
SALES (est): 5.5MM
SALES (corp-wide): 1B **Privately Held**
SIC: 2679 7389 2672 Egg cartons, molded pulp: made from purchased material; packaging & labeling services; cloth lined paper: made from purchased paper
PA: Tekni-Plex, Inc.
460 E Swedesford Rd # 3000
Wayne PA 19087
484 690-1520

(G-12061)
TOLEDO CLINIC INC
6135 Trust Dr Ste 230 (43528-9360)
PHONE..............................419 865-3111
Fax: 419 861-7862
Robin Graham, *Branch Mgr*
Jodee Ahrens, *Med Doctor*
EMP: 231
SALES (corp-wide): 119.2MM **Privately Held**
SIC: 8099 Blood related health services
PA: Toledo Clinic, Inc.
4235 Secor Rd
Toledo OH 43623
419 473-3561

(G-12062)
TOLEDO EDISON COMPANY
Also Called: Holland Operations Center
6099 Angola Rd (43528-9595)
PHONE..............................419 249-5364
Richard Reineck, *Accounts Mgr*
Trent Smith, *Manager*
EMP: 75
SQ FT: 92,928 **Publicly Held**
SIC: 4911 Distribution, electric power
HQ: The Toledo Edison Company
76 S Main St Bsmt
Akron OH 44308
800 447-3333

(G-12063)
TOTAL FLEET SOLUTIONS LLC
7050 Spring Meadows Dr W A (43528-7203)
PHONE..............................419 868-8853
Fax: 419 868-8912
Doug Heerdegen, *Vice Pres*
Ed Kelly, *Vice Pres*
David Alexander, *Sales Dir*
Mark Augustyniak, *Cust Mgr*
Heather Johnson, *Cust Mgr*
▲ **EMP:** 50 **EST:** 1995
SQ FT: 5,000
SALES (est): 40.7MM **Privately Held**
WEB: www.tfsglobal.com
SIC: 5084 Materials handling machinery

(G-12064)
TOYOTA INDUSTRIAL EQP DLR
Also Called: Dmh Toyota Lift
8310 Airport Hwy (43528-8637)
PHONE..............................419 865-8025
Philip Graffy, *President*
Julie Hood, *Manager*
EMP: 25
SALES (est): 5.6MM **Privately Held**
SIC: 5084 Materials handling machinery

(G-12065)
UNION CNSTR WKRS HLTH PLAN
Also Called: NORTHWESTERN OHIO ADMINISTRATO
7142 Nightingale Dr Ste 1 (43528-7822)
P.O. Box 1330 (43528-1330)
PHONE..............................419 248-2401
Nick Madden, *Financial Exec*
Bill Topel, *Administration*
Richard Watkins, *Administration*
EMP: 25
SALES: 22.1MM **Privately Held**
WEB: www.nwoadm.com
SIC: 8631 Labor union

(G-12066)
VELOCITY GRTEST PHONE EVER INC
7130 Spring Meadows Dr W (43528-9296)
P.O. Box 1179 (43528-1179)
PHONE..............................419 868-9983
Fax: 419 868-9986
Gregory Kiley, *President*
Kelly Greco, *Vice Pres*
John Meyers, *VP Opers*
Judi Reed, *Accountant*
Grant Smith, *Accountant*
EMP: 243
SALES: 175MM **Privately Held**
WEB: www.velocity.org
SIC: 7373 4899 Computer system selling services; data communication services

(G-12067)
VINYL DESIGN CORPORATION
7856 Hill Ave (43528-9181)
PHONE..............................419 283-4009
Fax: 419 865-4453
Patrick J Trompeter, *President*
Joe Shoots, *General Mgr*
EMP: 29
SQ FT: 36,000
SALES (est): 5.4MM **Privately Held**
WEB: www.vinyldesigncorp.com
SIC: 3089 5033 2452 Windows, plastic; siding, except wood; prefabricated wood buildings

(G-12068)
WAREHOUSE SERVICES GROUP LLC
6145 Merger Dr (43528-8430)
P.O. Box 965 (43528-0965)
PHONE..............................419 868-6400
Dan Kurz,
Mary Lou Anderson,
Craig Kurz,
George Kurz,
Kim Kurz,
EMP: 45
SQ FT: 70,000
SALES (est): 3.1MM **Privately Held**
SIC: 4225 General warehousing & storage

(G-12069)
YODER MACHINERY SALES COMPANY
1500 Holloway Rd (43528-9542)
P.O. Box 100 (43528-0100)
PHONE..............................419 865-5555
Timothy A Yoder, *President*
Timothy Yoder, *President*
Kory Yoder, *Vice Pres*
Ryan Yoder, *Vice Pres*
Terry Yoder, *Vice Pres*
EMP: 25
SQ FT: 106,000
SALES (est): 16.5MM **Privately Held**
WEB: www.yodermachinery.com
SIC: 5084 Machine tools & accessories

Holmesville
Holmes County

(G-12070)
ACTION COUPLING & EQP INC
8248 County Road 245 (44633-9724)
P.O. Box 99 (44633-0099)
PHONE..............................330 279-4242
Fax: 330 279-4208
Scott Eliot, *President*
David Eliot, *General Mgr*
Mike Franks, *Purchasing*
Jean Elliot, *Accounts Mgr*
▲ **EMP:** 80
SQ FT: 75,000
SALES (est): 19.4MM **Privately Held**
WEB: www.actiongolfcarts.com
SIC: 3569 5087 3429 Firefighting apparatus & related equipment; firefighting equipment; manufactured hardware (general)

(G-12071)
COUNTY OF HOLMES
Also Called: Holmes County Home
7260 State Route 83 (44633-9749)
PHONE..............................330 279-2801
Fax: 330 279-2050
Leslee Mast, *Superintendent*
EMP: 32
SQ FT: 40,000 **Privately Held**
WEB: www.district1fire.com
SIC: 8361 9111 Home for the mentally handicapped; county supervisors' & executives' offices
PA: County Of Holmes
2 Court St Ste 14
Millersburg OH 44654
330 674-1896

(G-12072)
HOLMES COUNTY BOARD OF DD
8001 Township Road 574 (44633-9751)
PHONE..............................330 674-8045
Scott F Brace, *Superintendent*
Curtis Goehring, *Treasurer*
David Cleveland, *Human Res Mgr*
EMP: 99
SALES (est): 2.6MM **Privately Held**
SIC: 8331 Job training & vocational rehabilitation services

(G-12073)
LYNN HOPE INDUSTRIES INC
Also Called: HOLMES COUNTY TRAINING CENTER
8001 Township Rd Ste 574 (44633)
PHONE..............................330 674-8045
Fax: 330 674-5182

Holmesville - Holmes County (G-12074)

Sherry Martin, *Director*
EMP: 75
SALES: 362.6K **Privately Held**
SIC: 8331 Sheltered workshop

(G-12074)
MILLER LOGGING INC
8373 State Route 83 (44633-9726)
PHONE..................330 279-4721
Fax: 330 279-3865
Roy A Miller Jr, *President*
Levi Miller, *Corp Secy*
Barbara Miller, *Vice Pres*
EMP: 28
SALES: 1.7MM **Privately Held**
SIC: 2421 1629 2411 Wood chips, produced at mill; land clearing contractor; logging

Homer
Licking County

(G-12075)
COLUMBIA GAS TRANSMISSION LLC
Also Called: Columbia Energy
1608 Homer Rd Nw (43027)
PHONE..................740 892-2552
Fax: 740 892-3836
Rod Graham, *Manager*
EMP: 25
SALES (corp-wide): 9.2B **Privately Held**
SIC: 4922 Pipelines, natural gas
HQ: Columbia Gas Transmission, Llc
200 Cizzic Ctr Dr
Columbus OH 43216
614 460-6000

Hooven
Hamilton County

(G-12076)
BUSY BEE ELECTRIC INC
100 Washington St (45033-7600)
PHONE..................513 353-3553
Fax: 513 353-3872
James R Oehlschlaeger, *President*
David Talbot, *Project Mgr*
Kathy Wiethe, *Treasurer*
Gary Buckhave, *Executive*
EMP: 25
SALES (est): 4.8MM **Privately Held**
WEB: www.busybeeelectric.com
SIC: 1731 General electrical contractor

(G-12077)
SEHLHORST EQUIPMENT SVCS INC
4450 Monroe Ave (45033-7640)
PHONE..................513 353-9300
Douglas Sehlhorst, *President*
Mark Billman, *Vice Pres*
Daniel Sehlhorst Jr, *Vice Pres*
David Sehlhorst, *Vice Pres*
Anne Rosenfeldt, *Office Mgr*
EMP: 30
SQ FT: 5,000
SALES (est): 5.4MM **Privately Held**
SIC: 1794 Excavation & grading, building construction

Hopedale
Harrison County

(G-12078)
GABLES CARE CENTER INC
351 Lahm Dr (43976-9761)
PHONE..................740 937-2900
Fax: 740 937-2939
Robert Huff, *President*
Lynn Huff, *Vice Pres*
Leona Smith, *Manager*
Kim Turnbull, *Director*
EMP: 105
SQ FT: 26,000
SALES (est): 5.6MM **Privately Held**
SIC: 8051 Convalescent home with continuous nursing care

(G-12079)
HOPEDALE MINING LLC
86900 Sinfield Rd (43976)
P.O. Box 415 (43976-0415)
PHONE..................740 937-2225
David G Zatezalo,
EMP: 40
SALES (est): 5.9MM **Privately Held**
SIC: 1081 Metal mining services

(G-12080)
WATER TRANSPORT LLC
100 Sammi Dr (43976-7713)
PHONE..................740 937-2199
Fax: 740 937-2888
Michael Kuester, *Mng Member*
EMP: 50
SQ FT: 15,000
SALES: 5MM **Privately Held**
SIC: 4789 Cargo loading & unloading services

Howard
Knox County

(G-12081)
PIONEER SANDS LLC
Also Called: Millwood Plant
26900 Coshocton Rd (43028-9216)
PHONE..................740 599-7773
Fax: 740 599-5134
Steven Bell, *Manager*
EMP: 30
SALES (corp-wide): 5.4B **Publicly Held**
SIC: 3295 1446 1442 Minerals, ground or treated; industrial sand; construction sand & gravel
HQ: Pioneer Sands Llc
5205 N O Connor Blvd # 200
Irving TX 75039
972 444-9001

Hubbard
Trumbull County

(G-12082)
BLUE BEACON OF HUBBARD INC
7044 Truck World Blvd (44425-3253)
PHONE..................330 534-4419
Charles Walker, *President*
EMP: 30 **EST:** 1979
SQ FT: 4,000
SALES (est): 372K **Privately Held**
SIC: 7542 Truck wash

(G-12083)
BLUE BEACON USA LP II
Also Called: Blue Beacon Truck Wash
7044 Truck World Blvd (44425-3253)
PHONE..................330 534-4419
Fax: 330 534-5203
Bill Rigley, *Manager*
EMP: 37
SALES (corp-wide): 88.4MM **Privately Held**
WEB: www.bluebeacon.com
SIC: 7542 Truck wash
PA: Blue Beacon U.S.A., L.P. Ii
500 Graves Blvd
Salina KS 67401
785 825-2221

(G-12084)
CONNIE PARKS (PA)
Also Called: Biomedical Laboratory
4504 Logan Way Ste B (44425-3345)
PHONE..................330 759-8334
Fax: 330 759-0780
Connie Parks, *Owner*
Kristen Zocco, *Manager*
EMP: 40
SALES (est): 2.1MM **Privately Held**
WEB: www.metalworkinggroup.com
SIC: 8071 Testing laboratories

(G-12085)
DESALVO CONSTRUCTION COMPANY
1491 W Liberty St (44425-3310)
PHONE..................330 759-8145
Fax: 330 759-7275
Joseph A Desalvo, *President*
Joseph K Desalvo, *Vice Pres*
Mark Dodd, *Vice Pres*
Sandra S Algoe, *Treasurer*
Sandra Algoe, *Office Mgr*
EMP: 45
SQ FT: 12,320
SALES: 17.7MM **Privately Held**
SIC: 1541 1542 Industrial buildings, new construction; commercial & office building, new construction

(G-12086)
ERIE INSURANCE EXCHANGE
5676 Everett East Rd (44425-2826)
PHONE..................330 568-1802
EMP: 62
SALES (corp-wide): 374.1MM **Privately Held**
WEB: www.erie-insurance.com
SIC: 6331 Reciprocal interinsurance exchanges: fire, marine, casualty
PA: Erie Insurance Exchange
100 Erie Insurance Pl
Erie PA 16530
800 458-0811

(G-12087)
GREENWOODS HUBBARD CHEVY-OLDS
Also Called: Greenwood's Oldsmobile
2635 N Main St (44425-3247)
P.O. Box 290 (44425-0290)
PHONE..................330 568-4335
Greg Greenwood, *President*
EMP: 35
SQ FT: 10,000
SALES (est): 6.6MM **Privately Held**
SIC: 5511 7538 7515 Automobiles, new & used; general automotive repair shops; passenger car leasing

(G-12088)
INDUSTRIAL AIR CONTROL INC
1276 Brookfield Rd (44425-3068)
P.O. Box 56 (44425-0056)
PHONE..................330 772-6422
Elmer Takash, *President*
Mary Langley, *Corp Secy*
Jim Davidson, *Vice Pres*
EMP: 60
SQ FT: 6,000
SALES (est): 2.4MM **Privately Held**
SIC: 7349 7699 Cleaning service, industrial or commercial; industrial equipment cleaning

(G-12089)
LIBERTY STEEL PRODUCTS INC
7193 Masury Rd (44425-9756)
P.O. Box 175, North Jackson (44451-0175)
PHONE..................330 534-7998
Fax: 330 534-8957
Bill McCullough, *Manager*
EMP: 200
SALES (corp-wide): 74MM **Privately Held**
SIC: 5051 Steel
PA: Liberty Steel Products, Inc.
11650 Mahoning Ave
North Jackson OH 44451
330 538-2236

(G-12090)
OHIO STEEL SHEET & PLATE INC
7845 Chestnut Ridge Rd (44425-9702)
P.O. Box 1146, Warren (44482-1146)
PHONE..................800 827-2401
Fax: 330 534-3204
John Rebhan, *President*
Mike Link, *Vice Pres*
Eric Rebhan, *Vice Pres*
Paul Musante, *Engineer*
Marie Cline, *Sales Staff*
EMP: 45
SQ FT: 320,000

SALES (est): 12.9MM **Privately Held**
WEB: www.ohiosteelplate.com
SIC: 3312 5051 3444 Sheet or strip, steel, hot-rolled; plate, steel; metals service centers & offices; sheet metalwork

(G-12091)
S & B TRUCKING INC (PA)
3045 Gale Dr (44425-1012)
PHONE..................614 554-4090
Fax: 330 759-8590
Charles Bosco, *President*
Robert Julius, *Corp Secy*
EMP: 26
SQ FT: 5,000
SALES (est): 4.3MM **Privately Held**
SIC: 7363 Truck driver services

(G-12092)
W W WILLIAMS COMPANY LLC
7125 Masury Rd (44425-9756)
P.O. Box 71 (44425-0071)
PHONE..................330 534-1161
Alan Gatlin, *CEO*
L Ed McIntyre, *Branch Mgr*
Dorian Norstrom, *Administration*
Megan Wajda, *Administration*
EMP: 26
SALES (corp-wide): 2.1B **Privately Held**
WEB: www.williamsdistribution.com
SIC: 5084 Engines & parts, diesel
HQ: The W W Williams Company Llc
835 Goodale Blvd
Columbus OH 43212
614 228-5000

(G-12093)
YOUNGSTOWN-KENWORTH INC (PA)
Also Called: All-Line Truck Sales
7255 Hubbard Masury Rd (44425-9757)
PHONE..................330 534-9761
Fax: 330 534-2966
Tomiel Mikes, *President*
Geraldine Mikes, *Principal*
Randall R Fiest, *Vice Pres*
Jerry Bell, *Sales Staff*
Dave Claypool, *Sales Staff*
EMP: 35
SQ FT: 14,900
SALES (est): 8.4MM **Privately Held**
WEB: www.youngstownkenworth.com
SIC: 5013 5012 7538 3713 Truck parts & accessories; trucks, commercial; general automotive repair shops; truck & bus bodies; industrial trucks & tractors

Huber Heights
Montgomery County

(G-12094)
CLARKE POWER SERVICES INC
6061 Executive Blvd (45424-1441)
PHONE..................937 684-4402
Chris Hager, *Manager*
Peter Saage, *Manager*
EMP: 34
SALES (corp-wide): 252.9MM **Privately Held**
SIC: 5084 Industrial machinery & equipment; engines & parts, diesel
PA: Clarke Power Services, Inc.
3133 E Kemper Rd
Cincinnati OH 45241
513 771-2200

(G-12095)
ESTES EXPRESS LINES INC
6295 Executive Blvd (45424-1439)
PHONE..................937 237-7536
Joe Ketring, *Branch Mgr*
EMP: 59
SALES (corp-wide): 2.4B **Privately Held**
SIC: 4213 Contract haulers
PA: Estes Express Lines, Inc.
3901 W Broad St
Richmond VA 23230
804 353-1900

GEOGRAPHIC SECTION

Hudson - Summit County (G-12121)

(G-12096)
JAMES D EGBERT OPTOMETRIST (PA)
Also Called: Gemini Eye Care Center
6557 Brandt Pike (45424-3353)
PHONE.................................937 236-1770
James D Egbert, *President*
Anna R Egbert, *Corp Secy*
Dr Steven Connett, *Vice Pres*
William Hancock, *Administration*
EMP: 40
SALES (est): 3.7MM **Privately Held**
WEB: www.geminieyecarecenters.com
SIC: 5995 8042 Contact lenses, prescription; offices & clinics of optometrists

(G-12097)
PENDSTER DIALYSIS LLC
Also Called: Huber Heights Dialysis
7769 Old Country Ct (45424-2097)
PHONE.................................937 237-0769
James K Hilger,
EMP: 25
SALES (est): 192.9K **Publicly Held**
SIC: 8092 Kidney dialysis centers
PA: Davita Inc.
  2000 16th St
  Denver CO 80202

(G-12098)
PETSMART INC
8281 Old Troy Pike (45424-1025)
PHONE.................................937 236-1335
Fax: 937 236-9268
Kami Mezcar, *Manager*
EMP: 30
SALES (corp-wide): 12.7B **Privately Held**
WEB: www.petsmart.com
SIC: 5999 0752 Pet food; animal specialty services
HQ: Petsmart, Inc.
  19601 N 27th Ave
  Phoenix AZ 85027
  623 580-6100

(G-12099)
TRIDEC TECHNOLOGIES LLC
4764 Fishburg Rd Ste D (45424-5456)
PHONE.................................937 938-8160
Leslie Godzik, *Office Mgr*
Brad Pfefferle, *Director*
Robert A Fritschie,
EMP: 25
SALES (est): 3.2MM **Privately Held**
SIC: 7371 Computer software systems analysis & design, custom

Hudson
Summit County

(G-12100)
A P O HOLDINGS INC (PA)
Also Called: A P O Pumps and Compressors
6607 Chittenden Rd (44236-2025)
PHONE.................................330 650-1330
Ted Mailey, *President*
Dave Murari, *Vice Pres*
Rick Pyles, *Administration*
EMP: 51
SALES (est): 47.6MM **Privately Held**
WEB: www.airpowerofohio.com
SIC: 5084 7699 Compressors, except air conditioning; compressor repair

(G-12101)
ADAPTIVE CORPORATION (PA)
118 W Streetsboro St (44236-2752)
PHONE.................................440 257-7460
Eric Doubell, *CEO*
Frank Thomas, *President*
Margie Ator, *CFO*
Curt Gallo, *Software Dev*
EMP: 25
SALES (est): 10MM **Privately Held**
SIC: 8711 Engineering services

(G-12102)
ALLSTATE INSURANCE COMPANY
75 Milford Dr Ste 222 (44236-2778)
PHONE.................................330 650-2917
Tracy L Mc Kenica, *Principal*
Joseph Yesko, *Agent*
EMP: 30
SALES (est): 1.2MM **Privately Held**
SIC: 6411 6311 7389 Insurance agents; property & casualty insurance agent; life insurance; financial services

(G-12103)
ALLSTATE INSURANCE COMPANY
75 Executive Pkwy (44237-0002)
PHONE.................................330 656-6000
William McCary, *Opers Staff*
Andrea Archer, *VP Mktg*
Doug Carpenter, *Manager*
Gay Yager, *Manager*
John Cannon, *Consultant*
EMP: 55 **Publicly Held**
WEB: www.allstate.com
SIC: 6411 Insurance agents, brokers & service
HQ: Allstate Insurance Company
  2775 Sanders Rd
  Northbrook IL 60062
  847 402-5000

(G-12104)
ALPHA FREIGHT SYSTEMS INC
5876 Darrow Rd (44236-3864)
PHONE.................................800 394-9001
Paul Kithcart, *President*
Dawn Marino, *Sales Mgr*
EMP: 69
SQ FT: 10,000
SALES (est): 10.1MM **Privately Held**
WEB: www.alphafreight.com
SIC: 4731 4213 Brokers, shipping; contract haulers
PA: Group Transportation Services, Inc.
  5876 Darrow Rd
  Hudson OH 44236

(G-12105)
BROWN DERBY ROADHOUSE
72 N Main St Ste 208 (44236-2883)
PHONE.................................330 528-3227
Fax: 330 626-1916
Parris Girvas, *President*
Leo Carmelli, *Manager*
EMP: 46
SALES (est): 1.5MM **Privately Held**
SIC: 5812 7299 Steak restaurant; banquet hall facilities

(G-12106)
C M M INC
546 Meadowridge Way (44236-1182)
PHONE.................................330 656-3820
Fax: 216 429-7405
Ronald Mamula, *President*
Robert Tierney, *General Mgr*
Joe Prementine, *Project Mgr*
EMP: 27
SALES (est): 4MM **Privately Held**
SIC: 8741 Construction management

(G-12107)
CELCO LTD
1140 Terex Rd (44236-3771)
PHONE.................................330 655-7000
Peter Spitalieri, *President*
EMP: 25
SALES (est): 1.1MM **Privately Held**
SIC: 7322 Collection agency, except real estate

(G-12108)
CHANGE HEALTHCARE HOLDINGS INC
300 Executive Pkwy W (44236-1690)
PHONE.................................330 405-0001
Marsha Andzelik, *Office Mgr*
Allen Hughes, *Manager*
Thomas T Winter, *Manager*
Kenneth Lucas, *Director*
Lisa Roseman, *Director*
EMP: 37
SALES (corp-wide): 1.9B **Privately Held**
SIC: 7374 Data processing service
HQ: Change Healthcare Holdings, Inc.
  3055 Lebanon Pike # 1000
  Nashville TN 37214
  615 932-3000

(G-12109)
CHARLES L MACCALLUM MD INC
5778 Darrow Rd Ste D (44236-3808)
PHONE.................................330 655-2161
Charles L Maccallum MD, *President*
EMP: 25
SQ FT: 2,500
SALES (est): 878K **Privately Held**
SIC: 8011 Offices & clinics of medical doctors

(G-12110)
CHASE TRANSCRIPTIONS INC (PA)
1737 Georgetown Rd Ste G (44236-5013)
PHONE.................................330 650-0539
Michael C Geaney, *President*
Kim Waterhouse, *Office Mgr*
Cynthia Boyle, *Supervisor*
EMP: 34
SQ FT: 4,000
SALES: 4.5MM **Privately Held**
WEB: www.chasetranscriptions.com
SIC: 7338 Secretarial & typing service; stenographic services

(G-12111)
CHOICE HOTELS INTL INC
Also Called: Clarion Hotel
6625 Dean Memorial Pkwy (44236-1157)
PHONE.................................330 656-1252
Debby Sankoe, *Branch Mgr*
EMP: 68
SALES (corp-wide): 1B **Publicly Held**
SIC: 7011 Hotels & motels
PA: Choice Hotels International, Inc.
  1 Choice Hotels Cir
  Rockville MD 20850
  301 592-5000

(G-12112)
CITY OF HUDSON VILLAGE
Also Called: Service Department
95 Owen Brown St (44236-2855)
PHONE.................................330 650-1052
Fax: 330 342-1761
Dan Roth, *Asst Supt*
Jay Carter, *Director*
Ryan Doran, *Officer*
Heather Heller,
EMP: 55 **Privately Held**
WEB: www.ellsworthmeadows.com
SIC: 4911 Electric services
PA: City Of Hudson Village
  115 Executive Pkwy # 400
  Hudson OH 44236
  330 650-1799

(G-12113)
COUNTRY CLUB OF HUDSON
2155 Middleton Rd (44236-1434)
P.O. Box 533 (44236-0533)
PHONE.................................330 650-1188
Fax: 330 342-0418
Karen Twedell, *Manager*
EMP: 45
SQ FT: 2,000
SALES (est): 2.2MM **Privately Held**
WEB: www.cchudson.com
SIC: 7997 5812 Country club, membership; eating places

(G-12114)
DREW MEDICAL INC (PA)
75 Milford Dr Ste 201 (44236-2778)
PHONE.................................407 363-6700
Michael Dinkel, *President*
Doug Dinkel, *Manager*
EMP: 30
SALES (est): 3.2MM **Privately Held**
SIC: 8071 Medical laboratories

(G-12115)
EDWARDS GEM INC
Also Called: Gemco Medical
5640 Hudson Indus Pkwy (44236-5011)
P.O. Box 429 (44236-0429)
PHONE.................................330 342-8300
Fax: 330 342-9444
Toni Edwards, *President*
Dee Edwards, *General Mgr*
George Edwards, *Exec VP*
Bill Baker, *Vice Pres*
David Draluck, *Vice Pres*
▲ **EMP:** 100
SQ FT: 80,000
SALES (est): 54.9MM **Privately Held**
SIC: 5122 5961 5999 5047 Pharmaceuticals; patent medicines; proprietary (patent) medicines; medicinals & botanicals; pharmaceuticals, mail order; cosmetics & perfumes, mail order; incontinent care products; medical equipment & supplies

(G-12116)
ESSENDANT CO
100 E Highland Rd (44236)
PHONE.................................330 650-9361
Dave Martin, *Manager*
EMP: 96
SALES (corp-wide): 5B **Publicly Held**
WEB: www.ussco.com
SIC: 5112 Office supplies
HQ: Essendant Co.
  1 Parkway North Blvd # 100
  Deerfield IL 60015
  847 627-7000

(G-12117)
FORTEC MEDICAL INC (PA)
6245 Hudson Crossing Pkwy (44236-4348)
PHONE.................................330 463-1265
Fax: 330 655-8894
Drew Forhan, *President*
John Voyzey, *President*
Mike Stickler, *Managing Dir*
Jake Barth, *Regional Mgr*
Clark Dunn, *Regional Mgr*
EMP: 30
SQ FT: 69,000
SALES (est): 16.3MM **Privately Held**
SIC: 7352 Medical equipment rental

(G-12118)
GIAMBRONE MASONRY INC
10000 Aurora Hudson Rd (44236-2520)
P.O. Box 810, Aurora (44202-0810)
PHONE.................................216 475-1200
David Giambrone, *President*
Matthew Birch, *Vice Pres*
Howard Kopit, *CPA*
Junior Fuller, *Sales Executive*
EMP: 80
SQ FT: 2,500
SALES (est): 6.1MM **Privately Held**
WEB: www.giambrone.com
SIC: 1741 Bricklaying

(G-12119)
GROUP TRANSPORTATION SVCS INC (PA)
Also Called: GTS
5876 Darrow Rd (44236-3864)
PHONE.................................800 689-6255
Fax: 330 342-8701
Michael Valentine, *President*
Paul Kithcart, *Vice Pres*
Brian Pollock, *Opers Staff*
Craig Estep, *Marketing Staff*
Kay Friend, *Manager*
EMP: 40
SQ FT: 24,780
SALES (est): 21.4MM **Privately Held**
WEB: www.onestopshipping.com
SIC: 8742 Transportation consultant

(G-12120)
HEALTH DESIGN PLUS INC
1755 Georgetown Rd (44236-4057)
PHONE.................................330 656-1072
Fax: 330 656-9387
Ruth Coleman, *CEO*
William Coleman, *President*
Roberta Kordish, *Vice Pres*
Noreen Sussman, *Vice Pres*
Sandra Pogozelski, *Opers Staff*
EMP: 92
SQ FT: 18,500
SALES (est): 35.2MM **Privately Held**
WEB: www.hdplus.com
SIC: 6411 Medical insurance claim processing, contract or fee basis

(G-12121)
HUDSON CITY ENGINEERING DEPT
115 Executive Pkwy # 400 (44236-1693)
PHONE.................................330 342-1770
Cathy Clark, *Principal*

Hudson - Summit County (G-12122)   GEOGRAPHIC SECTION

EMP: 28
SALES (est): 2.2MM Privately Held
SIC: 8322 Community center

(G-12122)
HUDSON MONTESSORI ASSOCIATION
Also Called: HUDSON MONTESSORI SCHOOL
7545 Darrow Rd (44236-1305)
PHONE..................................330 650-0424
Fax: 330 656-1870
Mat Virgil, Principal
Julia Brown, Principal
Peter Larrow, Principal
Patricia Ludick, Manager
EMP: 38
SALES: 3MM Privately Held
WEB: www.hudsonmontessori.org
SIC: 8351 8211 Preschool center; private elementary school

(G-12123)
HYDROGEOLOGIC INC
581 Boston Mills Rd # 600 (44236-1196)
PHONE..................................330 463-3303
Peter S Huyakorn, President
EMP: 31
SALES (corp-wide): 67MM Privately Held
SIC: 8731 Environmental research
PA: Hydrogeologic, Inc.
    11107 Sunset Hills Rd # 400
    Reston VA 20190
    703 478-5186

(G-12124)
INTEGRATED TELEHEALTH INC
Also Called: Global Telehealth Services
75 Milford Dr Ste 201 (44236-2778)
PHONE..................................216 373-2221
Michael A Miller, CEO
Christopher T Beseda, COO
EMP: 25 EST: 2015
SQ FT: 2,800
SALES: 50K Privately Held
SIC: 7371 Computer software development

(G-12125)
J NAN ENTERPRISES LLC
Also Called: Goddard Schools
5601 Darrow Rd (44236-4087)
PHONE..................................330 653-3766
Fax: 330 653-5757
Jeffery A Lutz, Owner
Nancy E Lutz, Vice Pres
EMP: 26
SQ FT: 8,000
SALES (est): 1.1MM Privately Held
SIC: 8351 Preschool center

(G-12126)
JPMORGAN CHASE BANK NAT ASSN
136 W Streetsboro St (44236-2746)
PHONE..................................330 650-0476
Fax: 330 655-5783
Paula Gianinni, Branch Mgr
EMP: 26
SALES (corp-wide): 99.6B Publicly Held
SIC: 6021 National commercial banks
HQ: Jpmorgan Chase Bank, National Association
    1111 Polaris Pkwy
    Columbus OH 43240
    614 436-3055

(G-12127)
KGK GARDENING DESIGN CORP
1975 Norton Rd (44236-4100)
PHONE..................................330 656-1709
Kenneth Kuryla, President
Joyce Kuryla, Vice Pres
EMP: 40
SALES (est): 1.5MM Privately Held
SIC: 0782 Landscape contractors

(G-12128)
KINGS MEDICAL COMPANY
1920 Georgetown Rd A (44236-4060)
PHONE..................................330 653-3968
Fax: 330 656-0600
Joe Betro, Vice Pres
Clark Labaski, Controller
William E Beattie, Director
Dennis R Abbuhl, Incorporator
EMP: 130
SALES (est): 12.7MM
SALES (corp-wide): 55MM Privately Held
WEB: www.kingsmedical.com
SIC: 8742 Banking & finance consultant; marketing consulting services
PA: King's Medical Group, Inc.
    1920 Georgetown Rd A
    Hudson OH 44236
    330 528-1765

(G-12129)
KRISTIE WARNER
Also Called: Gavin Scott Salon & Spa
4960 Darrow Rd (44224-1406)
PHONE..................................330 650-4450
Kristie Warner, Owner
EMP: 25
SALES (est): 575.9K Privately Held
SIC: 7231 7991 Manicurist, pedicurist; spas

(G-12130)
LAUREL LK RETIREMENT CMNTY INC
Also Called: Crown Center
200 Laurel Lake Dr Rear (44236-2132)
PHONE..................................330 650-0681
Fax: 330 650-6725
Michael Lesleins, Controller
Sue Maskiell, Marketing Staff
Charlene Kulesza, Office Mgr
David A Oster, Exec Dir
Sre A Diederich, Director
EMP: 350
SQ FT: 440,000
SALES: 24.4MM Privately Held
SIC: 8361 8051 Rest home, with health care incidental; skilled nursing care facilities

(G-12131)
LEAFFILTER NORTH LLC (PA)
1595 Georgetown Rd Ste G (44236-4045)
PHONE..................................330 655-7950
David Miller, Regional Mgr
Peter Adam, Opers Mgr
Bob Hare, Opers Mgr
Jay McClung, Opers Mgr
Michael Wilkins, Opers Mgr
EMP: 89
SALES (est): 56.2MM Privately Held
SIC: 1761 Gutter & downspout contractor

(G-12132)
MERRILL LYNCH PIERCE FENNER
10 W Streetsboro St # 305 (44236-2850)
PHONE..................................330 655-2312
Fax: 330 655-2104
Anastasia Kozer, Manager
EMP: 25
SALES (corp-wide): 100.2B Publicly Held
WEB: www.merlyn.com
SIC: 6211 8742 Security brokers & dealers; financial consultant
HQ: Merrill Lynch, Pierce, Fenner & Smith Incorporated
    111 8th Ave
    New York NY 10011
    800 637-7455

(G-12133)
MEYER DECORATIVE SURFACES USA (HQ)
Also Called: Mayer Laminates MA
300 Executive Pkwy W # 100 (44236-1690)
PHONE..................................800 776-3900
David Sullivan, President
▲ EMP: 25
SQ FT: 25,000
SALES (est): 48.6MM
SALES (corp-wide): 185.8MM Privately Held
SIC: 5031 Building materials, interior
PA: Compagnie De Saint-Gobain
    Les Miroirs La Defense 3
    Courbevoie 92400
    147 623-000

(G-12134)
MH LOGISTICS CORP
Also Called: M H Equipment
1892 Georgetown Rd (44236-4058)
PHONE..................................330 425-2476
Mike Young, Sales Mgr
Harry Bruno, Branch Mgr
Denny Dnytryk, Manager
Chris Merrick, Manager
EMP: 30
SALES (corp-wide): 237.2MM Privately Held
WEB: www.mhlogistics.com
SIC: 5084 7359 Industrial machinery & equipment; materials handling machinery; processing & packaging equipment; waste compactors; equipment rental & leasing
PA: M.H. Logistics Corp.
    8901 N Industrial Rd
    Peoria IL 61615
    309 579-8030

(G-12135)
MILLENNIUM CPITL RECOVERY CORP
95 Executive Pkwy Ste 100 (44236-5400)
PHONE..................................330 528-1450
Robert Bronchetti, President
Jayne Bronchetti, Exec VP
Rick O'Connell, Sales Staff
Charvene Eberhardt, Case Mgr
Lisa Johnson, Case Mgr
EMP: 40
SALES (est): 4.2MM Privately Held
WEB: www.automgmt.net
SIC: 7389 Repossession service

(G-12136)
NORANDEX BLDG MTLS DIST INC
Also Called: Norandex Building Mtls Dist
300 Executive Park Ste 100 (44236)
P.O. Box 860, Valley Forge PA (19482-0860)
PHONE..................................330 656-8924
Glenn Knowlton, President
Russ Kershaw, Business Mgr
Rebecca Faulk, Vice Pres
Ron Pearl, Branch Mgr
Audie Stein, Branch Mgr
EMP: 1000
SQ FT: 35,000
SALES (est): 13.3MM
SALES (corp-wide): 185.8MM Privately Held
WEB: www.norandex.com
SIC: 5033 5031 Siding, except wood; doors & windows
HQ: Saint-Gobain Corporation
    20 Moores Rd
    Malvern PA 19355

(G-12137)
NORTHWEST BANK
Also Called: Morgan Bank National Assn
178 W Streetsboro St # 1 (44236-2754)
PHONE..................................330 342-4018
Kevin Nelson, Exec VP
EMP: 300
SQ FT: 1,200
SALES (est): 5.5MM Publicly Held
WEB: www.morganbank.net
SIC: 6021 National commercial banks
PA: Northwest Bancshares, Inc.
    100 Liberty St
    Warren PA 16365

(G-12138)
PASCO INC
Also Called: G M A C Insurance Center
1140 Terex Rd (44236-3798)
PHONE..................................330 650-0613
Peter Spitalieri, President
Howard Essner, Senior VP
Dennis Duffield, Vice Pres
Scott Keller, Manager
Jay Moore, Senior Mgr
EMP: 300
SQ FT: 30,000
SALES (est): 66.1MM Privately Held
SIC: 6411 7323 Insurance information & consulting services; credit reporting services

(G-12139)
PAYCHEX INC
100 E Hines Hill Rd (44236-1115)
PHONE..................................330 342-0530
Martin Mucci, Branch Mgr
David Dennison, Consultant
EMP: 123
SALES (corp-wide): 3.1B Publicly Held
SIC: 8721 Payroll accounting service
PA: Paychex, Inc.
    911 Panorama Trl S
    Rochester NY 14625
    585 385-6666

(G-12140)
PETERMANN LTD
91 Owen Brown St (44236-2809)
PHONE..................................330 653-3323
Kimberly Lane, Manager
EMP: 80
SALES (est): 1.4MM Privately Held
SIC: 4151 School buses
HQ: Petermann Ltd
    8041 Hosbrook Rd Ste 330
    Cincinnati OH 45236

(G-12141)
RESTORATION RESOURCES INC
Also Called: SERVPRO
1546 Georgetown Rd (44236-4067)
PHONE..................................330 650-4486
Fax: 330 650-2321
Bruce Johnson, President
Terri Johnson, Vice Pres
EMP: 35
SQ FT: 2,700
SALES (est): 1.4MM Privately Held
WEB: www.restorationresources.com
SIC: 7349 Building maintenance services

(G-12142)
SABER HEALTHCARE GROUP LLC
Also Called: Hudson Elms Skilled Nursing
563 W Streetsboro St (44236-2050)
PHONE..................................330 650-0436
Tara Price, Administration
EMP: 36
SALES (corp-wide): 68.5MM Privately Held
SIC: 8051 Skilled nursing care facilities
PA: Saber Healthcare Group, L.L.C.
    26691 Richmond Rd Frnt
    Bedford OH 44146
    216 292-5706

(G-12143)
SETON CATHOLIC SCHOOL HUDSON
6923 Stow Rd (44236-3240)
PHONE..................................330 342-4200
Fax: 330 342-4276
SIS M Damicone, Principal
Pat Fritz, Comms Dir
Evelyn Kremyar, Librarian
Celeste Cappotto, Director
Paula Worhatch, Admin Sec
EMP: 30
SQ FT: 20,624
SALES (est): 359.3K Privately Held
WEB: www.setoncatholicschool.org
SIC: 8211 8351 Private elementary & secondary schools; child day care services

(G-12144)
SHIELD SECURITY SERVICE
P.O. Box 1001 (44236-6201)
PHONE..................................330 650-2001
Fax: 330 650-2442
Ray Hutchinson, Owner
Holly Stepnicki, Co-Owner
Sandra Hutchinson, Vice Pres
EMP: 25
SALES: 200K Privately Held
SIC: 7381 Security guard service

(G-12145)
STRUCTURAL BUILDING SYSTEMS
5802 Akron Cleveland Rd (44236-2010)
P.O. Box 463 (44236-0463)
PHONE..................................330 656-9353
Paul Mills, President
EMP: 95

GEOGRAPHIC SECTION

Huron - Erie County (G-12167)

SALES (est): 7.1MM Privately Held
SIC: 1541 Industrial buildings & warehouses

(G-12146)
T L C CHILD DEVELOPMENT CENTER
Also Called: Academy For Young Chldrn
187 Ravenna St (44236-3466)
PHONE.................................330 655-2797
Fax: 330 655-2294
Alison Pfeister, *President*
EMP: 25
SQ FT: 7,262
SALES (est): 1.1MM Privately Held
WEB: www.onlinewithtlc.com
SIC: 8351 Preschool center; nursery school

(G-12147)
UBS FINANCIAL SERVICES INC
43 Village Way Ste 201 (44236-5383)
PHONE.................................330 655-8319
EMP: 43
SALES (corp-wide): 28B Privately Held
SIC: 7389 Business Services
HQ: Ubs Financial Services Inc.
1285 Ave Of The Americas
New York NY 10019
212 713-2000

(G-12148)
UNITY HEALTH NETWORK LLC
5655 Hudson Dr Ste 110 (44236-4454)
PHONE.................................330 655-3820
Laurie Swinehart, *Branch Mgr*
EMP: 34
SALES (corp-wide): 14.5MM Privately Held
SIC: 8099 Blood related health services
PA: Unity Health Network, Llc
3033 State Rd
Cuyahoga Falls OH 44223
330 923-5899

(G-12149)
VERITIV PUBG & PRINT MGT INC (DH)
Also Called: Graphic Cmmnctons Holdings Inc
5700 Darrow Rd Ste 110 (44236-5026)
PHONE.................................330 650-5522
Fax: 330 650-8998
Mary A Laschinger, *CEO*
Allan Dragone, *CEO*
Matt Dawley, *President*
Mike Nash, *President*
Ken Flajs, *COO*
◆ **EMP:** 40
SALES (est): 273.4MM
SALES (corp-wide): 8.3B Publicly Held
SIC: 5111 7389 Fine paper; printing broker
HQ: Veritiv Operating Company
1000 Abernathy Rd
Atlanta GA 30328
770 391-8200

(G-12150)
WBC GROUP LLC (PA)
Also Called: Meyerpt
6333 Hudson Crossing Pkwy (44236-4346)
PHONE.................................866 528-2144
Ron Harrington, *CEO*
Elizabeth Cross, *Treasurer*
Kelly Eterovich, *Natl Sales Mgr*
Aaron Carino, *Accounts Mgr*
Andrea Scala, *Director*
▲ **EMP:** 95
SQ FT: 50,000
SALES (est): 129.2MM Privately Held
WEB: www.indemed.com
SIC: 5122 5047 3843 Vitamins & minerals; pharmaceuticals; medical & hospital equipment; dental equipment & supplies

(G-12151)
WESTERN & SOUTHERN LF INSUR CO
85 Executive Pkwy Ste 200 (44236-1691)
PHONE.................................234 380-4525
Fax: 330 688-6938
Joseph Parker, *Manager*
Michelle A Herd, *Senior Mgr*
Deanna May, *Officer*
EMP: 25 Privately Held
SIC: 6411 6311 Insurance agents; life insurance
HQ: The Western & Southern Life Insurance Company
400 Broadway St
Cincinnati OH 45202
513 629-1800

(G-12152)
WINDSTREAM OHIO LLC
100 Owen Brown St (44236-2812)
PHONE.................................330 650-8436
Bryan Fonner, *Opers Staff*
Rusty Hopkins, *Manager*
Lynn Bittinger, *Manager*
Steve Spence, *Manager*
EMP: 100
SALES (corp-wide): 5.8B Publicly Held
SIC: 4813 Telephone communication, except radio
HQ: Windstream Ohio, Llc
363 3rd St
Elyria OH 44035
440 329-4000

(G-12153)
WINDSTREAM WESTERN RESERVE LLC
245 N Main St (44236-2807)
PHONE.................................330 650-8000
Fax: 330 656-8456
John P Fletcher, *President*
Dennis McGiles, *VP Finance*
John Kaidner, *Marketing Staff*
Kurt Schlumberger, *Consultant*
Kay Fallon, *Nurse*
EMP: 120
SQ FT: 10,000
SALES (est): 42.5MM
SALES (corp-wide): 5.8B Publicly Held
WEB: www.windstreamcomm.com
SIC: 4813 Local telephone communications; long distance telephone communications
PA: Windstream Holdings, Inc.
4001 N Rodney Parham Rd # 101
Little Rock AR 72212
501 748-7000

(G-12154)
WOLTERS KLUWER CLINICAL DRUG
1100 Terex Rd (44236-3771)
PHONE.................................330 650-6506
Fax: 330 656-4307
Denise Basow, *President*
David A Del Toro, *Vice Pres*
Chris Madjerich, *Regl Sales Mgr*
Jerry Reeves, *Regl Sales Mgr*
Gregg Thompson, *Network Mgr*
EMP: 65
SQ FT: 24,000
SALES (est): 11.2MM
SALES (corp-wide): 5.2B Privately Held
SIC: 2731 2791 7379 Books: publishing only; typesetting, computer controlled; computer related maintenance services
HQ: Wolters Kluwer Health, Inc.
2001 Market St Ste 5
Philadelphia PA 19103
215 521-8300

(G-12155)
WONDERWORKER INC
Also Called: Sky Zone Boston Heights
6217 Chittenden Rd (44236-2021)
PHONE.................................234 249-3030
Charlee Hollio, *President*
Ivana Matyas, *Corp Secy*
EMP: 80
SQ FT: 24,000
SALES (est): 1.9MM Privately Held
SIC: 7999 Trampoline operation

Huntsburg
Geauga County

(G-12156)
ARMS TRUCKING CO INC (PA)
14818 Mayfield Rd (44046-8770)
PHONE.................................800 362-1343
Fax: 440 635-0980
Howard W Bates, *President*
Rick Humphries, *Vice Pres*
David W Ronyak, *Vice Pres*
Brian Bates, *Treasurer*
Stephanie Ronyak, *Controller*
EMP: 40
SQ FT: 21,000
SALES (est): 9MM Privately Held
SIC: 4213 4214 Contract haulers; local trucking with storage

(G-12157)
BLOSSOM HILLS NURSING HOME
Also Called: Blossom Hill Care Center
12496 Princeton Rd (44046-9792)
P.O. Box 369 (44046-0369)
PHONE.................................440 635-5567
Fax: 440 636-5601
Donald Gray, *President*
George Ohman, *Corp Secy*
Charles Ohman, *Vice Pres*
Theresa Weber, *Supervisor*
Lori Hess, *Director*
EMP: 85
SQ FT: 18,500
SALES (est): 3.7MM Privately Held
SIC: 8051 8052 Convalescent home with continuous nursing care; intermediate care facilities

(G-12158)
MAN GOLF OHIO LLC
14107 Mayfield Rd (44046-8722)
PHONE.................................440 635-5178
Robert Nance,
EMP: 35
SALES (est): 273.9K Privately Held
SIC: 7999 Golf services & professionals

Huron
Erie County

(G-12159)
AERIE FRTNRL ORDER EGLES 2875
2902 Cleveland Rd W (44839-1011)
P.O. Box 454 (44839-0454)
PHONE.................................419 433-4611
Jeff Widman, *President*
EMP: 35
SQ FT: 5,000
SALES: 325.1K Privately Held
SIC: 8641 University club

(G-12160)
AMERICAN PUBLISHERS LLC
2401 Sawmill Pkwy Ste 10 (44839-2284)
PHONE.................................419 626-0623
Fax: 419 621-4300
Steven Ester, *President*
John P Loughlin, *Vice Pres*
John Rohan Jr, *Treasurer*
Janet Ruffing, *Asst Treas*
Catherine Bostron, *Admin Sec*
EMP: 100 **EST:** 1918
SQ FT: 25,000
SALES (est): 7MM
SALES (corp-wide): 6.7B Privately Held
WEB: www.ppsb.com
SIC: 7389 Telemarketing services
PA: The Hearst Corporation
300 W 57th St Fl 42
New York NY 10019
212 649-2000

(G-12161)
BARNES NURSERY INC (PA)
3511 Cleveland Rd W (44839-1025)
PHONE.................................800 421-8722
Fax: 419 433-3555
Robert Barnes, *President*
Jarret Barnes, *Vice Pres*
Tyler Brown, *Store Mgr*
Julie Barnes, *Treasurer*
Sean Henrichs, *Manager*
EMP: 45
SQ FT: 5,000
SALES (est): 6.9MM Privately Held
WEB: www.barnesnursery.com
SIC: 0782 0181 5261 Landscape contractors; nursery stock, growing of; garden supplies & tools

(G-12162)
CHEFS GARDEN INC
9009 Huron Avery Rd (44839-2448)
PHONE.................................419 433-4947
Fax: 419 433-2403
Barbara Jones, *President*
Rose Halsey, *General Mgr*
Bob L Jones, *Vice Pres*
Mike Ineson, *Opers Staff*
Lee Jones, *Treasurer*
EMP: 130
SQ FT: 1,684
SALES (est): 10MM Privately Held
WEB: www.chefsgardeninc.com
SIC: 5148 Fruits, fresh

(G-12163)
CITY OF HURON
Water Department
417 Main St (44839-1652)
PHONE.................................419 433-5000
Ron Marsinick, *Principal*
EMP: 100 Privately Held
WEB: www.cityofhuron.org
SIC: 4941 Water supply
PA: City Of Huron
417 Main St
Huron OH 44839
419 433-5000

(G-12164)
COUNTY OF ERIE
Also Called: Erie County Care Facility
3916 Perkins Ave (44839-1059)
PHONE.................................419 627-8733
Fax: 419 627-1614
Marian Hill, *Admin Director*
EMP: 155 Privately Held
WEB: www.gem.org
SIC: 8051 9111 Convalescent home with continuous nursing care; county supervisors' & executives' offices
PA: County Of Erie
2900 Columbus Ave
Sandusky OH 44870
419 627-7682

(G-12165)
HUMANTICS INNOVATIVE SOLUTIONS
900 Denton Dr (44839-8922)
PHONE.................................567 265-5200
EMP: 33 Privately Held
SIC: 8748 Business consulting
PA: Humanetics Innovative Solutions, Inc
23300 Haggerty Rd
Farmington Hills MI 48335

(G-12166)
HURON CEMENT PRODUCTS COMPANY (PA)
Also Called: H & C Building Supplies
617 Main St (44839-2593)
PHONE.................................419 433-4161
Fax: 419 433-4690
John Caporini, *President*
Peggy Day, *Vice Pres*
Lauren Jones, *Controller*
Vince Thompson, *Admin Asst*
EMP: 38 **EST:** 1914
SQ FT: 37,800
SALES (est): 9.4MM Privately Held
SIC: 5211 5032 3273 3546 Cement; sand & gravel; cement; gravel; ready-mixed concrete; power-driven handtools; concrete products; cement, hydraulic

(G-12167)
HURON HEALTH CARE CENTER INC
Also Called: Admirals Pnte Nrsing Rhbltton
1920 Cleveland Rd W (44839-1211)
PHONE.................................419 433-4990
Fax: 419 433-5400
Jody Corsillas, *Mktg Dir*
Kelly Cook, *Director*
Carl Oberer, *Director*
Roy Sosa, *Director*
Amy Donaldson, *Administration*
EMP: 125
SALES: 584.9MM Privately Held
SIC: 8051 Convalescent home with continuous nursing care

Huron - Erie County (G-12168)

GEOGRAPHIC SECTION

(G-12168)
NORTH POINT EDUCTL SVC CTR
Also Called: Erie Co Office of Ed
710 Cleveland Rd W (44839-1546)
PHONE.....................440 967-0904
Fax: 419 433-3215
Susan Peterson, *Principal*
EMP: 43
SALES (corp-wide): 11.9MM **Privately Held**
WEB: www.ehove.net
SIC: 8211 8052 9111 School for physically handicapped; home for the mentally retarded, with health care; county supervisors' & executives' offices
PA: North Point Educational Service Center
1210 E Bogart Rd
Sandusky OH 44870
419 627-3900

(G-12169)
SANDUSKY ROTARY CLUB CHARITABL
1722 Sandpiper Ct (44839-9134)
P.O. Box 717, Sandusky (44871-0717)
PHONE............................419 625-1707
Cynthia Ball, *Principal*
EMP: 41
SALES: 69.7K **Privately Held**
SIC: 7997 Membership sports & recreation clubs

(G-12170)
SAW MILL CREEK LTD
Also Called: Lodge At Saw Mill Creek, The
400 Sawmill Creek Dr W (44839-2261)
PHONE............................419 433-3800
Fax: 419 433-7610
Greg Hill, *Partner*
Tom Bleile, *Partner*
Tammy Drosfman, *Manager*
Rick Ehrbar, *Technology*
EMP: 150
SALES (est): 5.2MM **Privately Held**
WEB: www.sawmillcreek.com
SIC: 7011 6512 5813 5812 Hotels & motels; nonresidential building operators; drinking places; eating places; marinas

(G-12171)
SAWMILL CREEK GOLF RACQUET CLB
Also Called: Sawmill Creek Shops
2401 Cleveland Rd W (44839-1066)
PHONE............................419 433-4945
Greg Hill, *President*
EMP: 80
SALES (corp-wide): 1MM **Privately Held**
SIC: 7997 Golf club, membership; tennis club, membership
PA: Sawmill Creek Golf & Racquet Club Inc
600 Harbor Vlg
Huron OH 44839
419 433-4945

(G-12172)
SAWMILL CREEK RESORT LTD
400 Sawmill Creek Dr W (44839-2261)
PHONE............................419 433-3800
Fax: 419 433-2761
Greg Hill, *President*
Jeff Oococo, *COO*
Jim Hill, *CFO*
Sandy Billetter-Zuber, *Finance*
Bruce Lingsweiler, *Sales Dir*
EMP: 170
SALES (est): 6.5MM **Privately Held**
WEB: www.greatlakesresorts.com
SIC: 5812 7011 Eating places; resort hotel

(G-12173)
SAWMILL GREEK GOLF RACQUET CLB
Also Called: Sawmill Creek Golf Racquet CLB
300 Sawmill Creek Dr W (44839-2260)
PHONE............................419 433-3789
Ryan Spicer, *Treasurer*
Barbara Durnwald, *Sales Mgr*
Jim Harmon, *Marketing Staff*
Chris Bleile, *Director*
EMP: 90
SALES (est): 1.8MM **Privately Held**
SIC: 7997 Golf club, membership

(G-12174)
SOUTH SHORE MARINE SERVICES
1611 Sawmill Pkwy (44839-2247)
P.O. Box 25 (44839-0025)
PHONE............................419 433-5798
Fax: 419 433-8020
Thomas Mack, *President*
Norm Baur, *Opers Mgr*
Nikki Baney, *Parts Mgr*
Cory Frankboner, *Accountant*
Stephanie Payne, *Human Resources*
EMP: 35
SQ FT: 9,000
SALES (est): 6.1MM **Privately Held**
WEB: www.southshoremarine.com
SIC: 4499 5551 Boat cleaning; motor boat dealers

(G-12175)
VITAL RESOURCES INC
1119 Sheltered Brook Dr (44839-2824)
PHONE............................440 614-5150
Charlene R Connell, *CEO*
Bruce Mihalick, *Vice Pres*
Anita Woodworth, *Accountant*
Betty Zelinsky, *Systems Staff*
EMP: 25
SALES (est): 2.4MM **Privately Held**
SIC: 7379 Computer related consulting services

(G-12176)
WILKES & COMPANY INC
205 Sprowl Rd (44839-2635)
P.O. Box 98 (44839-0098)
PHONE............................419 433-2325
Glen Ginesi, *President*
David Rengel, *Vice Pres*
EMP: 25 **EST:** 1912
SQ FT: 18,600
SALES (est): 5.7MM **Privately Held**
WEB: www.wilkesandcompany.com
SIC: 1711 Plumbing contractors

Independence
Cuyahoga County

(G-12177)
ACCEL PERFORMANCE GROUP LLC (DH)
6100 Oak Tree Blvd # 200 (44131-6914)
PHONE............................216 658-6413
Robert Tobey, *CEO*
Robert Romanelli, *President*
Bob Bruegging, *Vice Pres*
Leanne Verdile, *Buyer*
Michael Gretchko, *Engineer*
▲ **EMP:** 180
SQ FT: 200,000
SALES (est): 50.5MM **Privately Held**
WEB: www.mrgasket.com
SIC: 3714 5013 3053 Motor vehicle parts & accessories; automotive supplies & parts; gaskets, packing & sealing devices
HQ: Msdp Group Llc
1350 Pullman Dr Dr14
El Paso TX 79936
915 857-5200

(G-12178)
ACCURATE GROUP HOLDINGS INC (PA)
6000 Freedom Square Dr # 300 (44131-2547)
PHONE............................216 520-1740
Paul Doman, *President*
Matthew Lichtner, *Senior VP*
Michael Lynch, *CFO*
EMP: 59
SALES (est): 28.7MM **Privately Held**
SIC: 6361 6411 Real estate title insurance;

(G-12179)
ACXIOM CORPORATION
5005 Rockside Rd Ste 600 (44131-6827)
PHONE............................216 520-3181
Christina Basmagy, *COO*
EMP: 240
SALES (corp-wide): 880.2MM **Publicly Held**
WEB: www.acxiom.com
SIC: 7375 On-line data base information retrieval
PA: Acxiom Corporation
301 E Dave Ward Dr
Conway AR 72032
501 342-1000

(G-12180)
ACXIOM INFO SEC SVCS INC
6111 Oak Tree Blvd (44131-2589)
PHONE............................216 685-7600
Fax: 216 615-7677
Rodger Kline, *President*
Michelle Beben, *Superintendent*
Michael Cool, *Senior VP*
Kevin Zuffaroni, *Vice Pres*
Bob Campbell, *Opers Mgr*
EMP: 350
SQ FT: 15,000
SALES (est): 21.8MM
SALES (corp-wide): 264.7MM **Privately Held**
WEB: www.acxiom.com
SIC: 7389 Tenant screening service
HQ: Sterling Infosystems, Inc.
1 State St Fl 24
New York NY 10004
800 899-2272

(G-12181)
AEROTEK INC
Also Called: Aerotek 58
5990 W Creek Rd Ste 150 (44131-2181)
PHONE............................216 573-5520
Ken Sesco, *Principal*
EMP: 30
SALES (corp-wide): 11.5B **Privately Held**
WEB: www.searchhomesmn.com
SIC: 7363 Temporary help service
HQ: Aerotek, Inc.
7301 Parkway Dr
Hanover MD 21076
410 694-5100

(G-12182)
AGILE GLOBAL SOLUTIONS INC
5755 Granger Rd Ste 610 (44131-1458)
PHONE............................916 655-7745
EMP: 29
SALES (corp-wide): 5.2MM **Privately Held**
SIC: 7372 Business oriented computer software
PA: Agile Global Solutions, Inc.
13405 Folsom Blvd Ste 515
Folsom CA 95630
916 353-1780

(G-12183)
AIRGAS USA LLC
6055 Rockside Woods (44131-2301)
PHONE............................216 642-6600
EMP: 287
SALES (corp-wide): 163.9MM **Privately Held**
SIC: 5169 5084 5087 Compressed gas; industrial gases; industrial chemicals; welding machinery & equipment; safety equipment; janitors' supplies
HQ: Airgas Usa, Llc
259 N Radnor Chester Rd # 100
Radnor PA 19087
610 687-5253

(G-12184)
ALLIANCE LEGAL SOLUTIONS LLC
Also Called: Major Legal Services
6161 Oak Tree Blvd # 300 (44131-2581)
PHONE............................216 525-0100
Matt Lyon, *CFO*
EMP: 57
SQ FT: 2,000
SALES (est): 1.7MM **Privately Held**
SIC: 7361 Labor contractors (employment agency)

(G-12185)
ALLIANCE SOLUTIONS GROUP LLC (PA)
6161 Oak Tree Blvd (44131-2516)
PHONE............................216 525-0100
Aaron Grossman, *President*
Matt Lyon, *CFO*
Carmen Martin, *Consultant*
Lisa Tosado, *Recruiter*
EMP: 39
SQ FT: 7,000
SALES (est): 4.8MM **Privately Held**
WEB: www.alliancestaffingsolutions.com
SIC: 7363 7361 Temporary help service; employment agencies

(G-12186)
AP/AIM INDPNDNCE SITES TRS LLC
Also Called: Embassy Suites
5800 Rckside Woods Blvd N (44131-2346)
PHONE............................216 986-9900
Richard Somsak, *General Mgr*
Randy Torres,
EMP: 99
SALES: 950K **Privately Held**
SIC: 7011 Hotels & motels

(G-12187)
AREA TEMPS INC (PA)
4511 Rockside Rd Ste 190 (44131-2157)
PHONE............................216 781-5350
Raymond Castelluccio, *CEO*
Kent Castelluccio, *President*
Tom Corrigan, *Vice Pres*
Gail Rodgers, *Vice Pres*
Connie Gramoy, *Controller*
EMP: 40
SALES (est): 87.8MM **Privately Held**
WEB: www.areatemps.com
SIC: 7363 Temporary help service; office help supply service

(G-12188)
ARYSEN INC
Also Called: Dynamic Solution Associates
5005 Rockside Rd Ste 600 (44131-6827)
PHONE............................440 230-4400
Richard Ken Hartman, *Managing Dir*
EMP: 57
SALES: 20MM **Privately Held**
WEB: www.dsasite.com
SIC: 8742 Business consultant

(G-12189)
BMCH INC
Also Called: Triad Staffing
6100 Rksde Woods Blv N405 Ste 405 (44131)
PHONE............................216 642-1300
Debbie Santora, *President*
EMP: 60 **EST:** 2011
SALES (est): 1.6MM **Privately Held**
SIC: 7361 Employment agencies

(G-12190)
BOBBY TRIPODI FOUNDATION INC (PA)
Also Called: CORNERSTONE OF HOPE BEREAVEMEN
5905 Brecksville Rd (44131-1517)
P.O. Box 31555 (44131-0555)
PHONE............................216 524-3787
Mark Tripodi, *Exec Dir*
EMP: 26
SALES: 1.6MM **Privately Held**
SIC: 8322 General counseling services

(G-12191)
BUTTERFLY INC
8200 E Pleasant Valley Rd (44131-5523)
PHONE............................440 892-7777
Jim Eble, *President*
EMP: 30 **EST:** 2009
SALES (est): 4.4MM **Privately Held**
SIC: 4911 Electric services

(G-12192)
C & K INDUSTRIAL SERVICES INC (PA)
5617 E Schaaf Rd (44131-1334)
PHONE............................216 642-0055
Fax: 216 642-0059
Arthur Karas, *President*
Beau Barker, *Exec VP*

GEOGRAPHIC SECTION

Independence - Cuyahoga County (G-12215)

George Karas, *Vice Pres*
Cody Malkemus, *Project Mgr*
Daniel Mitchem, *Safety Mgr*
EMP: 100
SQ FT: 8,000
SALES (est): 119.5MM **Privately Held**
WEB: www.ckindustrial.com
SIC: 4959 7349 Sweeping service: road, airport, parking lot, etc.; building maintenance services

(G-12193)
CANON SOLUTIONS AMERICA INC
6100 Oak Tree Blvd (44131-2544)
PHONE.....................216 446-3830
Craig Palmer, *Branch Mgr*
EMP: 75
SALES (corp-wide): 36.4B **Privately Held**
SIC: 7389 Personal service agents, brokers & bureaus
HQ: Canon Solutions America, Inc.
 1 Canon Park
 Melville NY 11747
 631 330-5000

(G-12194)
CANON SOLUTIONS AMERICA INC
Also Called: Dps
6161 Oak Tree Blvd # 301 (44131-2516)
PHONE.....................216 750-2980
EMP: 27
SALES (corp-wide): 36.4B **Privately Held**
WEB: www.imagistics.com
SIC: 5112 Computer & photocopying supplies; computer paper; photocopying supplies
HQ: Canon Solutions America, Inc.
 1 Canon Park
 Melville NY 11747
 631 330-5000

(G-12195)
CELLCO PARTNERSHIP
Also Called: Verizon Wireless
6712 Rockside Rd (44131-2323)
PHONE.....................216 573-5880
Fax: 216 447-6016
Robert Moretti, *Manager*
EMP: 30
SALES (corp-wide): 126B **Publicly Held**
SIC: 4812 5999 Cellular telephone services; telephone equipment & systems
HQ: Cellco Partnership
 1 Verizon Way
 Basking Ridge NJ 07920

(G-12196)
CERTIFIED SEC SOLUTIONS INC (PA)
6050 Oak Tree Blvd (44131-6927)
PHONE.....................216 785-2986
Kevin Von Keyserling, *President*
Keith Peer, *COO*
Judah Aspler, *Vice Pres*
Chris Hickman, *Vice Pres*
Thomas Amato, *VP Opers*
EMP: 50
SQ FT: 6,000
SALES (est): 11.5MM **Privately Held**
WEB: www.css-security.com
SIC: 7371 Computer software systems analysis & design, custom

(G-12197)
CIGNA CORPORATION
3 Summit Park Dr Ste 250 (44131-2598)
PHONE.....................216 642-1700
Fax: 216 642-1820
Douglas Daubenspeck, *Branch Mgr*
Dave Barchet, *Manager*
Terri Kozmon, *Manager*
Melissa Liampetch, *Manager*
Nancy Stinnett, *Consultant*
EMP: 226
SALES (corp-wide): 41.6B **Publicly Held**
SIC: 6324 Health maintenance organization (HMO), insurance only
PA: Cigna Corporation
 900 Cottage Grove Rd
 Bloomfield CT 06002
 860 226-6000

(G-12198)
CLEVELAND ANESTHESIA GROUP
6701 Rockside Rd Ste 200 (44131-2316)
P.O. Box 94908, Cleveland (44101-4908)
PHONE.....................216 901-5706
Fax: 216 928-0141
John Bastulli, *President*
Keith Levendorf, *Treasurer*
Joyce Hardaway, *Med Doctor*
Robert Rogoff, *Med Doctor*
EMP: 42
SALES (est): 3.2MM **Privately Held**
SIC: 8011 Anesthesiologist

(G-12199)
CLEVELAND CLINIC COMMUNITY ONC
6100 W Creek Rd Ste 15 (44131-2133)
PHONE.....................216 447-9747
Sue Peterson, *Office Mgr*
Kenneth Weiss, *Podiatrist*
Nanette Rock, *Director*
EMP: 35
SALES (est): 2.4MM **Privately Held**
SIC: 8011 Offices & clinics of medical doctors

(G-12200)
CLEVELAND CLINIC FOUNDATION
Also Called: Cleveland Clinic Health System
6801 Brecksville Rd # 10 (44131-5058)
PHONE.....................216 986-4000
Tony Hrudka, *Finance*
Bertram Sue, *Branch Mgr*
Mary Hodgson, *Info Tech Dir*
Sue Bertram, *Director*
EMP: 85
SALES (corp-wide): 8B **Privately Held**
SIC: 6733 Trusts
PA: The Cleveland Clinic Foundation
 9500 Euclid Ave
 Cleveland OH 44195
 216 636-8335

(G-12201)
COOK PAVING AND CNSTR CO
4545 Spring Rd (44131-1023)
PHONE.....................216 267-7705
Fax: 216 267-7595
Linda Fletcher, *President*
Jim Matheos, *COO*
Michael Alex, *Vice Pres*
Keith L Rogers, *Admin Sec*
EMP: 50 **EST:** 1941
SQ FT: 12,000
SALES (est): 8.4MM **Privately Held**
SIC: 1771 1623 8741 1795 Concrete work; blacktop (asphalt) work; sewer line construction; underground utilities contractor; construction management; wrecking & demolition work; highway & street construction

(G-12202)
DAVITA INC
4801 Acorn Dr Ste 1 (44131-2576)
PHONE.....................216 525-0990
Ted Vancs, *Mktg Dir*
Bob Badal, *Branch Mgr*
EMP: 27 **Publicly Held**
SIC: 8092 Kidney dialysis centers
PA: Davita Inc.
 2000 16th St
 Denver CO 80202

(G-12203)
DENTAL ONE INC
6200 Oak Tree Blvd # 220 (44131-6937)
PHONE.....................216 584-1000
Andrew Pishkula, *Purchasing*
Kathleen Stautihar, *QA Dir*
Donna Sears, *Office Mgr*
Deborah Costanzo, *Manager*
Tom Nemcek, *Manager*
EMP: 50
SALES (corp-wide): 64.7MM **Privately Held**
SIC: 8742 8021 Business consultant; offices & clinics of dentists; dentists' office
PA: Dental One, Inc.
 17300 Dallas Pkwy # 1070
 Dallas TX 75248
 972 755-0800

(G-12204)
DIGERONIMO AGGREGATES LLC
8900 Hemlock Rd (44131-5012)
PHONE.....................216 524-2950
Vic Digeronimo, *President*
Keith McCabe, *Sales Mgr*
EMP: 28
SALES (est): 8MM **Privately Held**
SIC: 5032 Aggregate

(G-12205)
DOUGLAS R DENNY
6480 Rckside Woods Blvd S (44131-2233)
PHONE.....................216 236-2400
Douglas Denny, *Principal*
EMP: 42
SALES (est): 831.6K **Privately Held**
SIC: 7389 Personal service agents, brokers & bureaus

(G-12206)
EMC CORPORATION
6480 Rcksde Wds Blvd S # 330 (44131-2222)
PHONE.....................216 606-2000
Fax: 216 573-0872
Peter Bell, *District Mgr*
Tom Weldon, *Manager*
David Boje, *Manager*
Mitchell Breen, *Manager*
Karl Federmann, *Manager*
EMP: 39
SALES (corp-wide): 78.6B **Publicly Held**
WEB: www.emc.com
SIC: 3572 7372 Computer storage devices; prepackaged software
HQ: Emc Corporation
 176 South St
 Hopkinton MA 01748
 508 435-1000

(G-12207)
EMPLOYEESCREENIQ INC
Also Called: Background Information Svcs
6111 Oak Tree Blvd # 400 (44131-2585)
PHONE.....................216 514-2800
Les Fishman, *CEO*
Jason B Morris, *President*
Kevin W Bachman, *Opers Staff*
Nick Fishman, *Chief Mktg Ofcr*
Norene Katz, *Manager*
EMP: 80
SQ FT: 16,000
SALES (est): 9MM
SALES (corp-wide): 264.7MM **Privately Held**
WEB: www.employeescreen.com
SIC: 7389 Personal investigation service
HQ: Sterling Infosystems, Inc.
 1 State St Fl 24
 New York NY 10004
 800 899-2272

(G-12208)
EMPLOYERS SELECT PLAN AGCY INC
6480 Rcksde Wds Blvd S # 210 (44131-2233)
PHONE.....................216 642-4200
Charles Farro, *CEO*
Joseph R Crea, *President*
Mark Hinkel, *COO*
Jocelyn A Bradford, *Treasurer*
Keith W Reeves, *Director*
EMP: 33
SQ FT: 5,000
SALES (est): 4.2MM
SALES (corp-wide): 1.4B **Privately Held**
SIC: 6411 Insurance brokers
PA: Medical Mutual Of Ohio
 2060 E 9th St Frnt Ste
 Cleveland OH 44115
 216 687-7000

(G-12209)
ENTITLE DIRECT GROUP INC (HQ)
3 Summit Park Dr Ste 525 (44131-6900)
PHONE.....................216 236-7800
Timothy Dwyer, *CEO*
Lee Baskey, *COO*
Karen Leonard, *Manager*
EMP: 158
SALES (est): 2.1MM **Publicly Held**
SIC: 6361 Guarantee of titles

(G-12210)
ESC OF CUYAHOGA COUNTY
6393 Oak Tree Blvd # 300 (44131-6957)
PHONE.....................216 524-3000
Dr B Menderink, *Superintendent*
Dr Bob Menderink, *Superintendent*
EMP: 90
SALES (est): 707K **Privately Held**
SIC: 8331 Manpower training

(G-12211)
FARMERS GROUP INC
Also Called: Farmers Insurance
5990 W Creek Rd Ste 160 (44131-2181)
PHONE.....................216 750-4010
Larry Gallagher, *Manager*
EMP: 30
SALES (corp-wide): 68.4B **Privately Held**
WEB: www.farmers.com
SIC: 6411 Insurance agents, brokers & service
HQ: Farmers Group, Inc.
 6301 Owensmouth Ave
 Woodland Hills CA 91367
 323 932-3200

(G-12212)
FOREMOST INSURANCE COMPANY
Also Called: Bristol West Casualty Insur Co
5990 W Creek Rd Ste 160 (44131-2181)
PHONE.....................216 674-7000
Frank Formichelli, *Branch Mgr*
Tina Austin, *Technology*
EMP: 90
SALES (corp-wide): 68.4B **Privately Held**
SIC: 6331 Fire, marine & casualty insurance
HQ: Foremost Insurance Company
 5600 Beechtree Ln Se
 Caledonia MI 49316
 616 942-3000

(G-12213)
GALLERY HOLDINGS LLC
Also Called: Hr Plus
6111 Oak Tree Blvd (44131-2589)
PHONE.....................773 693-6220
William J Tate, *President*
James P Bar, *Vice Pres*
Kevin Haney, *Controller*
John Lange, *Mktg Dir*
Janet Hahn, *Admin Sec*
EMP: 55
SQ FT: 10,500
SALES (est): 1.2MM
SALES (corp-wide): 264.7MM **Privately Held**
WEB: www.hrplus.com
SIC: 7361 Placement agencies
HQ: Sterling Infosystems, Inc.
 1 State St Fl 24
 New York NY 10004
 800 899-2272

(G-12214)
GRAFTECH HOLDINGS INC
6100 Oak Tree Blvd # 300 (44131-6970)
PHONE.....................216 676-2000
Joel L Hawthorne, *CEO*
Bill McFadden, *General Mgr*
Erick R Asmussen, *Vice Pres*
John D Moran, *Vice Pres*
Mark Sullivan, *Vice Pres*
EMP: 227
SALES (est): 757.5K
SALES (corp-wide): 18B **Privately Held**
SIC: 1499 3624 Graphite mining; carbon & graphite products
HQ: Graftech International Ltd.
 982 Keynote Cir Ste 6
 Brooklyn Heights OH 44131

(G-12215)
GREAT LAKES COLD LOGISTICS
Also Called: Coldstream Logistics
6548 Brecksville Rd (44131-4800)
PHONE.....................216 520-0930
Daniel Palus, *President*
Howard Schillinger, *Vice Pres*
EMP: 50

Independence - Cuyahoga County (G-12216)

SALES (est): 2.1MM **Privately Held**
SIC: 4789 Cargo loading & unloading services

(G-12216)
HEARTLAND HOSPICE SERVICES LLC
Also Called: Heartland HM Hlth Care Hospice
4807 Rockside Rd Ste 110 (44131-2140)
PHONE..................................216 901-1464
Fax: 216 986-0081
Diane Dawson, *Manager*
Cynthia Sil, *Manager*
EMP: 100
SALES (corp-wide): 3.6B **Publicly Held**
SIC: 8082 Home health care services
HQ: Heartland Hospice Services, Llc
333 N Summit St
Toledo OH 43604

(G-12217)
HUMANA INC
6100 Oak Tree Blvd (44131-2544)
PHONE..................................216 328-2047
Larry Farmer, *Manager*
EMP: 41
SALES (corp-wide): 53.7B **Publicly Held**
SIC: 6324 Health maintenance organization (HMO), insurance only
PA: Humana Inc.
500 W Main St Ste 300
Louisville KY 40202
502 580-1000

(G-12218)
INDEPENDENCE EXCAVATING INC (PA)
5720 E Schaaf Rd (44131-1396)
PHONE..................................216 524-1700
Fax: 216 524-1701
Victor Digeronimo Sr, *CEO*
Victor Digeronimo Jr, *President*
Mike Orlando, *President*
Steve Wilk, *Superintendent*
Rick Digeronimo, *Vice Pres*
▲ EMP: 50
SQ FT: 35,000
SALES (est): 196MM **Privately Held**
WEB: www.indexc.com
SIC: 1629 1794 1611 1771 Land preparation construction; excavation work; general contractor, highway & street construction; concrete repair; demolition, buildings & other structures

(G-12219)
INDEPENDENCE LOCAL SCHOOLS
6111 Archwood Rd (44131-4901)
PHONE..................................216 642-5865
Robert Sykora, *Principal*
EMP: 29
SALES (est): 418.1K **Privately Held**
SIC: 8211 8351 Public elementary & secondary schools; child day care services
PA: Independence Local Schools
7733 Stone Rd
Independence OH 44131

(G-12220)
INTELLINEX LLC
Also Called: ACS Learning Services
6000 Fredom Sq Dr Ste 100 (44131)
PHONE..................................216 685-6000
Fax: 216 685-6997
Richard Klingshirn, *Managing Dir*
Leo Blankenship, *VP Opers*
Ted Bartlett, *Controller*
Dennis Stergar, *Manager*
EMP: 325
SQ FT: 50,000
SALES (est): 101.2MM
SALES (corp-wide): 6B **Publicly Held**
WEB: www.intellinex.com
SIC: 4813
HQ: Conduent Business Services, Llc
100 Campus Dr Ste 200
Florham Park NJ 07932
214 841-6111

(G-12221)
JAGI SPRINGHILL LLC
Also Called: Springhill Suites Independence
6060 Rockside Pl (44131-2225)
PHONE..................................216 264-4190
Michael Nanosky, *President*
EMP: 35
SALES (est): 242.5K **Privately Held**
SIC: 7011 Hotels

(G-12222)
KFORCE INC
3 Summit Park Dr Ste 550 (44131-6902)
PHONE..................................216 643-8141
Brent Heyneman, *Accounts Exec*
Jeff Farrington, *Director*
EMP: 40
SALES (corp-wide): 1.3B **Publicly Held**
SIC: 7361 Executive placement
PA: Kforce Inc.
1001 E Palm Ave
Tampa FL 33605
813 552-5000

(G-12223)
LEGEND EQUITIES CORPORATION
5755 Granger Rd Ste 910 (44131-1461)
PHONE..................................216 741-3113
Fax: 216 520-2672
Todd Stout, *Manager*
EMP: 75 **Privately Held**
SIC: 7389 Personal service agents, brokers & bureaus
PA: Legend Equities Corporation
4600 E Park Dr Ste 300
West Palm Beach FL 33410

(G-12224)
LEVEL SEVEN
Also Called: S. B. Stone & Company
4807 Rockside Rd Ste 700 (44131-2159)
PHONE..................................216 524-9055
Fax: 216 524-2594
Stuart Taylor, *CEO*
Gina Drobnick, *COO*
Larry Morris, *CFO*
Alysia Kaplan, *Mktg Coord*
Lisa Locklear, *Marketing Staff*
EMP: 75
SALES (est): 8.6MM **Privately Held**
SIC: 8742 Management consulting services

(G-12225)
LEWIS P C JACKSON
6100 Oak Tree Blvd # 400 (44131-6944)
PHONE..................................216 750-0404
Jeffrey Keiper, *Owner*
Mark Dombrowski, *CPA*
Stephen R Beiting, *Associate*
Doston B Jones, *Associate*
Corey D Tracey, *Associate*
EMP: 36
SALES (corp-wide): 340.5MM **Privately Held**
SIC: 8111 General practice attorney, lawyer
PA: Lewis P C Jackson
1133 Weschester Ave
White Plains NY 10604
914 872-8060

(G-12226)
LIFE LINE SCREENING
6150 Oak Tree Blvd # 200 (44131-2569)
PHONE..................................216 581-6556
Colin Scully, *CEO*
Timothy Phillips, *Vice Pres*
Sarah Hay, *Manager*
EMP: 100
SALES (est): 9.8MM **Privately Held**
SIC: 8011 8062 Medical centers; general medical & surgical hospitals

(G-12227)
LIFE LINE SCREENING AMER LTD (PA)
6150 Oak Tree Blvd (44131-6917)
PHONE..................................216 581-6556
Sean Schultz, *CEO*
Andy Manganaro, *Principal*
Colin Scully, *Chairman*
Don Mann, *Exec VP*
Timothy Phillips, *Exec VP*
EMP: 150
SQ FT: 25,000
SALES (est): 46.8MM **Privately Held**
WEB: www.llsaz.com
SIC: 8099 Health screening service

(G-12228)
LIGHTHOUSE INSURANCE GROUP LLC (PA)
6150 Oak Tree Blvd # 210 (44131-6976)
PHONE..................................216 503-2439
Jason Farro, *CEO*
Charles Farro, *Principal*
William Major, *Consultant*
EMP: 80
SALES (est): 16.8MM **Privately Held**
SIC: 6411 Insurance agents

(G-12229)
LOCUM MEDICAL GROUP LLC
6100 Oak Tree Blvd (44131-2544)
PHONE..................................216 464-2125
Fax: 216 464-7599
Daniel Groth, *CEO*
Nancy Taber, *President*
Daniel Burg, *Exec VP*
Betsy Rader, *Senior VP*
Judy Wills, *CFO*
EMP: 55
SQ FT: 9,600
SALES (est): 2.9MM
SALES (corp-wide): 27.4B **Privately Held**
WEB: www.locummedical.com
SIC: 7363 Medical help service
HQ: Randstad Professional Us, Lp
150 Presidential Way Fl 4
Woburn MA 01801

(G-12230)
LONGBOW RESEARCH LLC (PA)
6050 Oak Tree Blvd # 350 (44131-6931)
PHONE..................................216 986-0700
Fax: 216 986-0720
Bob Wazevich, *Vice Pres*
Brian Bollenbacher, *Research*
Jingshuang Chen, *Research*
Matthew Skowronski, *Research*
Mark Douglass, *Engineer*
EMP: 60
SQ FT: 15,000
SALES (est): 10.9MM **Privately Held**
SIC: 6282 Investment research

(G-12231)
M-A BUILDING AND MAINT CO
5515 Old Brecksville Rd (44131-1525)
PHONE..................................216 391-5577
Fax: 216 391-5577
Peter F Wamelink, *President*
Bill Thomas, *Superintendent*
Beverly Wamelink, *Corp Secy*
John Wamelink, *Vice Pres*
Scott Luthman, *Project Mgr*
EMP: 25
SQ FT: 12,000
SALES (est): 7.2MM **Privately Held**
SIC: 1542 Commercial & office buildings, renovation & repair

(G-12232)
MAT INNOVATIVE SOLUTIONS LLC
Also Called: Mattress Warehouse
153 Hayes Dr (44131-1001)
PHONE..................................216 398-8010
Kim Knopf, *President*
EMP: 28 **Privately Held**
SIC: 5021 Mattresses
PA: Innovative Mattress Solutions, Llc
11060 Winfield Rd
Winfield WV 25213

(G-12233)
MAXIM HEALTHCARE SERVICES INC
6155 Rockside Rd (44131-2200)
PHONE..................................216 606-3000
EMP: 80
SALES (corp-wide): 1.3B **Privately Held**
SIC: 8099 Blood related health services
PA: Maxim Healthcare Services, Inc.
7227 Lee Deforest Dr
Columbia MD 21046
410 910-1500

(G-12234)
MMI-CPR LLC
7100 E Pleasant Valley Rd (44131-5544)
PHONE..................................216 674-0645
Jeffrey Harcourt, *Admin Sec*

EMP: 50
SQ FT: 15,000
SALES (est): 2.7MM **Privately Held**
SIC: 7629 Telephone set repair

(G-12235)
MOLINA HEALTHCARE INC
Also Called: Molina Healthcare of Ohio
6161 Oak Tree Blvd (44131-2516)
PHONE..................................216 606-1400
EMP: 290
SALES (corp-wide): 19.8B **Publicly Held**
SIC: 8099 Childbirth preparation clinic
PA: Molina Healthcare, Inc.
200 Oceangate Ste 100
Long Beach CA 90802
562 435-3666

(G-12236)
MR ROOTER PLUMBING CORPORATION
8200 E Pleasant Valley Rd (44131-5523)
PHONE..................................419 625-4444
James Eble, *President*
Joan Mancuso, *Finance*
▲ EMP: 50
SQ FT: 4,000
SALES (est): 10.6MM **Privately Held**
SIC: 7699 Sewer cleaning & rodding

(G-12237)
NATIONAL YLLOW PAGES MEDIA LLC
Also Called: Linkmedia 360
2 Summit Park Dr Ste 630 (44131-2565)
PHONE..................................216 447-9400
Phil Smith, *Business Mgr*
Betty Brown, *COO*
Marcie Sprosty, *Senior VP*
Taylor Nagy, *Accounts Mgr*
Debbie Lamb, *Accounts Exec*
EMP: 50
SQ FT: 6,126
SALES (est): 7.2MM **Privately Held**
WEB: www.nypmedia.com
SIC: 8742 Marketing consulting services

(G-12238)
NATIONS LENDING CORPORATION
Also Called: N L C
4 Summit Park Dr Ste 200 (44131-2583)
PHONE..................................440 842-4817
Jeremy E Sopko, *CEO*
George Chapin, *President*
Leonard Ujkic, *Managing Prtnr*
Eric Roman, *Exec VP*
Frank Cimperman, *Vice Pres*
EMP: 100
SQ FT: 8,500
SALES (est): 105.2MM **Privately Held**
SIC: 6162 6163 Mortgage bankers; mortgage brokers arranging for loans, using money of others

(G-12239)
NEW YORK LIFE INSURANCE CO
6100 Oak Tree Blvd # 300 (44131-6970)
PHONE..................................216 520-1345
Fax: 216 643-8333
Jerry Fish, *Managing Dir*
Brian Furlong, *Managing Dir*
Kevin Smith, *Managing Dir*
Michael Chung, *Vice Pres*
Trish Payne, *QC Mgr*
EMP: 200
SALES (corp-wide): 27.9B **Privately Held**
WEB: www.newyorklife.com
SIC: 6411 Insurance agents & brokers
PA: New York Life Insurance Company
51 Madison Ave Bsmt 1b
New York NY 10010
212 576-7000

(G-12240)
NORTHAST SRGICAL ASSOC OF OHIO (PA)
6100 Rckside Woods Blvd N (44131-2366)
PHONE..................................216 643-2780
Keith Warner, *President*
Ashok Argekar, *Managing Dir*
Kristi French, *Business Mgr*
Michele Turner, *Sales Mgr*
Stacie Snyderburn, *Manager*

GEOGRAPHIC SECTION
Independence - Cuyahoga County (G-12264)

EMP: 43
SALES (est): 5.6MM Privately Held
SIC: 8011 Surgeon

(G-12241)
OHIO ALARM INC
Also Called: American Response Center
750 W Resource Dr Ste 200 (44131-1879)
PHONE.................................216 692-1204
James Osborne, President
Stan Nerderman, Vice Pres
Ron Price, Vice Pres
EMP: 30
SQ FT: 5,000
SALES (est): 1.6MM Privately Held
SIC: 5063 Alarm systems

(G-12242)
OLD RPBLIC TTLE NTHRN OHIO LLC
6480 Rckside Woods Blvd S (44131-2233)
PHONE.................................216 524-5700
Fax: 216 333-8825
John R Monacelli, Vice Pres
Melanie Andrews, Banking Exec
Robert A Piazza,
EMP: 627
SALES (est): 82.1MM
SALES (corp-wide): 6.2B Publicly Held
SIC: 6411 6162 6211 Insurance agents, brokers & service; mortgage bankers; underwriters, security
HQ: Old Republic National Title Insurance Company
400 2nd Ave S
Minneapolis MN 55401
612 371-1111

(G-12243)
PFG VENTURES LP (PA)
Also Called: Proforma
8800 E Pleasant Valley Rd # 1 (44131-5558)
PHONE.................................216 520-8400
Fax: 216 520-8400
Brian Smith, President
Greg Muzzillo, Principal
Vera Muzzillo, Co-CEO
Tom Rizzi, Senior VP
Dan Haar, Vice Pres
EMP: 100
SQ FT: 30,000
SALES (est): 59.2MM Privately Held
WEB: www.proforma.com
SIC: 5112 Stationery & office supplies

(G-12244)
PRECISION ENVIRONMENTAL CO (HQ)
5500 Old Brecksville Rd (44131-1508)
PHONE.................................216 642-6040
Tony Digeronimo, President
Jim Reeves, Controller
EMP: 296
SALES (est): 33.8MM
SALES (corp-wide): 47.3MM Privately Held
WEB: www.precisionprocut.com
SIC: 1799 Asbestos removal & encapsulation; lead burning
PA: Integrated Solutions, Inc.
215 S Laura St
Wichita KS 67211
316 264-7050

(G-12245)
PRECISION METALFORMING ASSN (PA)
6363 Oak Tree Blvd (44131-2556)
PHONE.................................216 241-1482
Fax: 216 901-9190
William E Gaskin, CEO
Jody Fledderman, Vice Ch Bd
Roy Hardy, President
Dana McCallum, Business Mgr
Daniel E Ellashek, Vice Pres
EMP: 41 EST: 1942
SQ FT: 20,000
SALES: 6.4MM Privately Held
SIC: 8611 2731 Trade associations; book publishing

(G-12246)
RANDSTAD TECHNOLOGIES LLC
6100 Oak Tree Blvd # 110 (44131-2544)
PHONE.................................216 520-0206
Fax: 216 520-1863
Jeff Rosen, Branch Mgr
Jeffrey Rosen, Manager
EMP: 66
SALES (corp-wide): 27.4B Privately Held
WEB: www.sapphire.com
SIC: 7361 Employment agencies
HQ: Randstad Technologies, Llc
150 Presidential Way # 300
Woburn MA 01801
781 938-1910

(G-12247)
REDWOOD LIVING INC
7510 E Pleasant Valley Rd (44131-5536)
PHONE.................................216 360-9441
Steven Kimmelman, CEO
Luke Frazier, Mktg Dir
Rose Mills, Comms Dir
Rich Batt, Manager
Doug Klar, Info Tech Dir
EMP: 201
SALES (est): 2.1MM Privately Held
SIC: 8742 Management consulting services

(G-12248)
RESOURCE TITLE NAT AGCY INC
7100 E Pleasant Valley Rd # 100 (44131-5544)
PHONE.................................216 520-0050
Leslie C Rennell, President
Anita Dembkowski, Corp Secy
Andrew W Rennell, Vice Pres
Richard J Rennell, CFO
Tim McFarland, Human Res Mgr
EMP: 64
SQ FT: 9,000
SALES (est): 26.4MM Privately Held
SIC: 6361 6531 Real estate title insurance; escrow agent, real estate

(G-12249)
RGIS LLC
4500 Rockside Rd Ste 340 (44131-2170)
PHONE.................................216 447-1744
Richard Kaimer, Branch Mgr
EMP: 79
SALES (corp-wide): 7.1B Publicly Held
SIC: 7389 Inventory computing service
HQ: Rgis, Llc
2000 Taylor Rd
Auburn Hills MI 48326
248 651-2511

(G-12250)
RJW INC (PA)
5755 Granger Rd Ste 400 (44131-1456)
PHONE.................................216 398-6090
Rick Wenham, Ch of Bd
Jeff Wenham, President
William M Bannon, Treasurer
EMP: 50
SQ FT: 3,300
SALES (est): 6.8MM Privately Held
WEB: www.bestwaysystems.com
SIC: 4213 8741 7513 Trucking, except local; administrative management; truck leasing, without drivers

(G-12251)
ROCKSIDE HOSPITALITY LLC
Also Called: Crowne Plaza Clevenland
5300 Rockside Rd (44131-2118)
PHONE.................................216 524-0700
Gloria Maciak, Controller
Cathy Ruhling, Sales Dir
Jaclyn Schneider, Manager
Tom Conran,
EMP: 81
SALES (est): 1MM Privately Held
SIC: 7011 Hotel, franchised

(G-12252)
ROE DENTAL LABORATORY INC
7165 E Pleasant Valley Rd (44131-5541)
PHONE.................................216 663-2233
Fax: 216 663-2237
Bruce Kowalski, President
Ray Woods, COO
Gregory Shreve, Vice Pres
Dana Banks, Financial Exec
Daniel Nowak, Natl Sales Mgr
EMP: 57 EST: 1930
SQ FT: 8,500
SALES (est): 6MM Privately Held
WEB: www.roedentallab.com
SIC: 8072 Crown & bridge production

(G-12253)
ROLTA ADVIZEX TECHNOLOGIES LLC (DH)
6480 S Rockside Woods (44131-2233)
PHONE.................................216 901-1818
Fax: 216 901-1447
Fred Traversi, CEO
Marc Sarazin, Exec VP
John Brier, Vice Pres
Patrick Fettuccia, Vice Pres
Mark Woelke, CFO
EMP: 39
SQ FT: 6,600
SALES (est): 186.1MM
SALES (corp-wide): 217.4MM Privately Held
WEB: www.advizex.com
SIC: 7373 Value-added resellers, computer systems; systems software development services

(G-12254)
ROSE COMMUNITY MANAGEMENT LLC (PA)
6000 Fredom Sq Dr Ste 500 (44131)
PHONE.................................917 542-3600
Angelo Pimpas, President
Jianing Zhang, General Mgr
Mike Daly,
EMP: 195
SQ FT: 11,000
SALES (est): 5MM Privately Held
SIC: 6531 Real estate managers

(G-12255)
ROSS BRITTAIN SCHONBERG LPA
6480 Rckside Woods Blvd S (44131-2233)
PHONE.................................216 447-1551
Fax: 216 447-1554
Alan Ross, President
David Andrews, Principal
Patrick Harrington, Principal
Richard Walters, Principal
Lynn Schonberg, Vice Pres
EMP: 34
SQ FT: 11,257
SALES (est): 4.4MM Privately Held
WEB: www.rbslaw.com
SIC: 8111 Labor & employment law

(G-12256)
ROYALTON 6001 LTD
Also Called: Dalad Group
6055 Rockside Woods Blvd # 100 (44131-2317)
PHONE.................................216 447-0070
Joe Balog, Senior VP
Jason Laver, Vice Pres
Keith Masters, Vice Pres
Lloyd Mazur, Vice Pres
Wynn Gerber, Controller
EMP: 40
SALES (est): 3.1MM Privately Held
SIC: 6519 Real property lessors

(G-12257)
SIRVA INC
6200 Oak Tree Blvd # 300 (44131-6934)
PHONE.................................216 606-4000
Marcy Nash, Financial Analy
Marie Henderson, Branch Mgr
Ann Callarman, Consultant
EMP: 25
SALES (corp-wide): 2B Privately Held
SIC: 7389 Relocation service
PA: Sirva, Inc.
1 Parkview Plz
Oakbrook Terrace IL 60181
630 570-3047

(G-12258)
SIRVA MORTGAGE INC
6200 Oak Tree Blvd # 300 (44131-6934)
PHONE.................................800 531-3837
Fax: 216 606-7606
Paul Klemme, President
David Drozin, Controller
Timothy Callahan, Marketing Mgr
EMP: 76
SALES: 1.7MM
SALES (corp-wide): 2B Privately Held
WEB: www.sirvamortgage.com
SIC: 6162 Mortgage bankers
HQ: Cms Holding, Llc
700 Oakmont Ln
Westmont IL

(G-12259)
SIRVA RELOCATION LLC (DH)
Also Called: Sirva Worldwide Relocation Mvg
6200 Oak Tree Blvd # 300 (44131-6934)
PHONE.................................216 606-4000
Wes W Lucas, CEO
Deborah L Balli, President
Andrew P Coolidge, COO
Thomas Oberdorf, CFO
Douglas V Gathany, Treasurer
EMP: 385 EST: 1981
SALES (est): 71.8MM
SALES (corp-wide): 2B Privately Held
WEB: www.sirvarelocation.com
SIC: 7389 Relocation service
HQ: North American Van Lines, Inc.
101 E Wa Blvd Ste 1100
Fort Wayne IN 46802
800 348-3746

(G-12260)
SKILLSOFT CORPORATION
6645 Acres Dr (44131-4962)
PHONE.................................216 524-5200
Joe Garrison, Branch Mgr
EMP: 66 Privately Held
SIC: 7372 Educational computer software
HQ: Skillsoft Corporation
300 Innovative Way # 201
Nashua NH 03062
603 324-3000

(G-12261)
SMITH PETER KALAIL CO LPA
6480 Rckside Wds Blvd S # 300 (44131-2233)
PHONE.................................216 503-5055
Scott C Peters, Managing Prtnr
Karrie M Kalail, Partner
Giselle S Johnson, Counsel
Michael E Stinn, Counsel
Eileen Zimlich, Manager
EMP: 29 EST: 2001
SALES (est): 2.9MM Privately Held
WEB: www.ohioedlaw.com
SIC: 8111 Labor & employment law

(G-12262)
STERLING INFOSYSTEMS INC
Also Called: Occupational Hlth Safety Dept
6111 Oak Tree Blvd (44131-2589)
PHONE.................................216 685-7600
Kurt Schwall, Principal
EMP: 33
SALES (corp-wide): 264.7MM Privately Held
SIC: 7381 7389 Private investigator; personal investigation service
HQ: Sterling Infosystems, Inc.
1 State St Fl 24
New York NY 10004
800 899-2272

(G-12263)
SUPPORTCARE INC
4700 Rockside Rd Ste 100 (44131-2148)
PHONE.................................216 446-2650
Regan Eveland, Administration
EMP: 215 Privately Held
SIC: 8052 Home for the mentally retarded, with health care
PA: Supportcare, Inc.
525 Metro Pl N Ste 350
Dublin OH 43017

(G-12264)
SYMANTEC CORPORATION
6100 Oak Tree Blvd (44131-2544)
PHONE.................................216 643-6700
EMP: 70
SALES (corp-wide): 4B Publicly Held
SIC: 7372 Prepackaged software

Independence - Cuyahoga County (G-12265)

PA: Symantec Corporation
350 Ellis St
Mountain View CA 94043
650 527-8000

(G-12265)
TEKSYSTEMS INC
5990 W Creek Rd Ste 175 (44131-2191)
PHONE..................................216 606-3600
Chad Colombari, *Manager*
CJ Thibault, *Tech Recruiter*
Taylor Snyder, *Recruiter*
EMP: 30
SALES (corp-wide): 4.1B **Privately Held**
WEB: www.teksystems.com
SIC: 7379 Computer related consulting services
HQ: Teksystems, Inc.
7437 Race Rd
Hanover MD 21076

(G-12266)
THERAPY IN MOTION LLC
5000 Rockside Rd Ste 500 (44131-2178)
PHONE..................................216 459-2846
Neal Polan, *CEO*
Rudy Denius,
Deb Graziani,
Melodie Roach,
EMP: 190
SQ FT: 1,500
SALES (est): 6.4MM **Privately Held**
SIC: 8049 Occupational therapist; physical therapist; speech therapist

(G-12267)
THYSSENKRUPP MATERIALS NA INC
6050 Oak Tree Blvd # 110 (44131-6927)
PHONE..................................216 883-8100
Rob Hanzie, *Regional Mgr*
Bryan Dascani, *Plant Mgr*
Todd Angelo, *Accounts Mgr*
Steve Szopo, *Sales Associate*
E M Habart, *Marketing Staff*
EMP: 87
SQ FT: 65,000
SALES (corp-wide): 48.7B **Privately Held**
SIC: 5051 3341 Steel; secondary nonferrous metals
HQ: Thyssenkrupp Materials Na, Inc.
22355 W 11 Mile Rd
Southfield MI 48033
248 233-5600

(G-12268)
TOYOTA MATERIAL HDLG OHIO INC (PA)
5667 E Schaaf Rd (44131-1305)
PHONE..................................216 328-0970
Brian Arnold, *General Mgr*
Hank Durica, *General Mgr*
Shawn Karb, *Opers Mgr*
Mike Brooks, *Parts Mgr*
Daniel Hegler, *CFO*
EMP: 98 EST: 2012
SALES (est): 37.9MM **Privately Held**
SIC: 5084 Lift trucks & parts

(G-12269)
TRANSAMERICA PREMIER LF INSUR
6480 Rockside Woods S 1 (44131-2233)
PHONE..................................216 524-1436
Florence Stan, *District Mgr*
Walter Freeman, *Manager*
EMP: 30
SALES (corp-wide): 593.2MM **Privately Held**
WEB: www.monlife.com
SIC: 6411 Life insurance agents
HQ: Transamerica Premier Life Insurance Company
4333 Edgewood Rd Ne
Cedar Rapids IA 52499
319 355-8511

(G-12270)
U S DEPT OF LABOR OCCUPATIONAL
6393 Oak Tree Blvd # 203 (44131-6973)
PHONE..................................216 447-4194
Howard Evert, *Director*
EMP: 30 EST: 2014

SALES (est): 406.4K **Privately Held**
SIC: 8631 Labor unions & similar labor organizations

(G-12271)
UNITED STATES PROTECTIVE (PA)
Also Called: U S Protective Services
750 W Resource Dr Ste 200 (44131-1879)
PHONE..................................216 475-8550
Theodore Cohen Jr, *President*
Marty Borer, *General Mgr*
Gilda Cohen, *Corp Secy*
James Wooten, *Opers Mgr*
Chuck Hayes, *Sales Dir*
EMP: 50
SQ FT: 48,000
SALES (est): 8.2MM **Privately Held**
SIC: 7382 Burglar alarm maintenance & monitoring

(G-12272)
VERIFIED PERSON INC
4511 Rockside Rd Ste 400 (44131-2156)
PHONE..................................901 767-6121
Jim Davis, *CEO*
Camille Gamble, *Vice Pres*
Josh Travis, *Technical Mgr*
John Clark, *VP Sales*
Edward Gostkowski, *VP Sales*
EMP: 45
SQ FT: 18,000
SALES (est): 2.8MM
SALES (corp-wide): 264.7MM **Privately Held**
SIC: 7363 Employee leasing service
HQ: Sterling Infosystems, Inc.
1 State St Fl 24
New York NY 10004
800 899-2272

(G-12273)
VERITIV OPERATING COMPANY
Midwest Market Area
7575 E Pleasant Valley Rd # 200 (44131-5567)
PHONE..................................216 573-7400
Fax: 216 573-7573
Steve Bartniski, *Sales/Mktg Mgr*
EMP: 35
SALES (corp-wide): 8.3B **Publicly Held**
WEB: www.unisourcelink.com
SIC: 5113 Industrial & personal service paper
HQ: Veritiv Operating Company
1000 Abernathy Rd
Atlanta GA 30328
770 391-8200

(G-12274)
VOX MOBILE
6100 Rockside Woods # 100 (44131-2355)
PHONE..................................800 536-9030
Kris Snyder, *CEO*
Dennis Lewis, *Business Mgr*
Gerald Hetrick, *COO*
Stephen Davis, *Vice Pres*
Harjot Sidhu, *Vice Pres*
EMP: 30
SALES (est): 7.3MM **Privately Held**
WEB: www.voxmobile.com
SIC: 4899 4813 Communication signal enhancement network system; telephone communication, except radio

(G-12275)
WELLINGTON GROUP LLC
6133 Rockside Rd Ste 205 (44131-2242)
PHONE..................................216 525-2200
Dean Rossiter, *Manager*
EMP: 25
SALES (est): 2.2MM **Privately Held**
WEB: www.wellingtongroup.biz
SIC: 8742 Hospital & health services consultant

(G-12276)
WESTON BRANDS LLC
7575 E Pleasant Valley Rd # 100 (44131-5568)
PHONE..................................216 901-6801
Cheryl Lowery, *Accountant*
Victor Manfredi, *Marketing Staff*
Michael Casper,
Jason Berry,
▲ EMP: 42

SQ FT: 63,000
SALES (est): 8.9MM
SALES (corp-wide): 1.1B **Publicly Held**
WEB: www.westonsupply.com
SIC: 5091 Hunting equipment & supplies; camping equipment & supplies
HQ: Hamilton Beach Brands, Inc.
4421 Waterfront Dr
Glen Allen VA 23060
804 273-9777

(G-12277)
WINE TRENDS INC
9101 E Pleasant Valley Rd (44131-5504)
PHONE..................................216 520-2626
Daniel Greathouse, *Principal*
Mary Horn, *Sales Dir*
Caitlin McKenney, *Sales Staff*
John Hopkins, *VP Mktg*
Craig Cracchiolo, *Marketing Staff*
▲ EMP: 50
SQ FT: 14,000
SALES (est): 9MM
SALES (corp-wide): 369.4MM **Privately Held**
WEB: www.winetrendsinc.com
SIC: 5182 Wine
PA: Dayton Heidelberg Distributing Co.
3601 Dryden Rd
Moraine OH 45439
937 222-8692

(G-12278)
X-S MERCHANDISE INC (PA)
7000 Granger Rd Ste 2 (44131-1462)
PHONE..................................216 524-5620
Fax: 216 524-5077
Len Stern, *Ch of Bd*
David Robbins, *President*
Todd Stern, *President*
Bill Sample, *Vice Pres*
Rick Schwartz, *Vice Pres*
◆ EMP: 25
SQ FT: 65,000
SALES (est): 25.9MM **Privately Held**
WEB: www.xsmdse.com
SIC: 5199 General merchandise, nondurable

(G-12279)
ZURICH AMERICAN INSURANCE CO
5005 Rockside Rd Ste 200 (44131-6808)
PHONE..................................216 328-9400
Fax: 216 447-4055
James Savage, *Accounts Exec*
Frank Hammers, *Branch Mgr*
Robert Louis, *Manager*
Laura Cupach, *Executive*
EMP: 40
SALES (corp-wide): 68.4B **Privately Held**
WEB: www.zurichna.com
SIC: 6411 Insurance agents
HQ: Zurich American Insurance Company
1299 Zurich Way
Schaumburg IL 60196
800 987-3373

Ironton
Lawrence County

(G-12280)
AHF OHIO INC
Also Called: Sanctuary At The Ohio Valley
2932 S 5th St (45638-2865)
PHONE..................................740 532-6188
John Haemmerle, *Ch of Bd*
Mark Haemmerle, *President*
J Michael Haemmerle, *Treasurer*
Tim Lehman, *Director*
Jim McDonough, *Director*
EMP: 68
SALES (corp-wide): 21MM **Privately Held**
SIC: 8051 Skilled nursing care facilities
PA: Ahf Ohio, Inc.
5920 Venture Dr Ste 100
Dublin OH 43017
614 760-7352

(G-12281)
BARTRAM & SONS GROCERIES
Also Called: Bartram Groceries
2407 S 6th St (45638-2632)
PHONE..................................740 532-5216
Fax: 740 532-2820
Steve Bartram, *President*
Jane Mc Connell, *Corp Secy*
EMP: 40
SQ FT: 10,500
SALES: 300K **Privately Held**
SIC: 4225 General warehousing & storage

(G-12282)
BRAYMAN CONSTRUCTION CORP
505 S 3rd St (45638-1835)
PHONE..................................740 237-0000
EMP: 40
SALES (corp-wide): 32.9MM **Privately Held**
SIC: 1521 Single-family housing construction
PA: Brayman Construction Corporation
1000 John Roebling Way
Saxonburg PA 16056
724 443-1533

(G-12283)
BRYANT HEALTH CENTER INC
Also Called: Sanctuary of The Ohio Valley
2932 S 5th St (45638-2865)
PHONE..................................740 532-6188
Robert Banasik, *President*
Todd Harding, *Purch Agent*
Rancie Hannah, *Med Doctor*
Robert Thomas, *Med Doctor*
David Apgar, *Director*
EMP: 136
SALES (est): 4.2MM
SALES (corp-wide): 9.1MM **Privately Held**
WEB: www.omnilife.net
SIC: 8059 8051 Nursing home, except skilled & intermediate care facility; skilled nursing care facilities
PA: Omnilife Health Care Systems, Inc.
50 W 5th Ave
Columbus OH 43201
614 299-3100

(G-12284)
BWC TRUCKING COMPANY INC
164 State Route 650 (45638-7919)
P.O. Box 267 (45638-0267)
PHONE..................................740 532-5188
Fax: 740 532-5188
Randy Kelley, *President*
Debbie Russell, *General Mgr*
Kathy Kelley, *Corp Secy*
Beth Pugh, *Project Dir*
Stephanie Bias, *CFO*
EMP: 50
SQ FT: 1,020
SALES (est): 12.2MM **Privately Held**
WEB: www.bwctrucking.com
SIC: 4213 Trucking, except local

(G-12285)
CARING HANDS HOME HEALTH CARE
2615 S 3rd St (45638-2759)
PHONE..................................740 532-9020
Teresa Jenkins, *President*
George Jenkins, *Administration*
EMP: 25
SALES (est): 511.1K **Privately Held**
SIC: 8082 Home health care services

(G-12286)
CLOSE TO HOME III
617 Center St (45638-1510)
PHONE..................................740 534-1100
Charles Kunkel, *Owner*
Sharon Shartwig, *Co-Owner*
EMP: 30
SALES (est): 741.8K **Privately Held**
SIC: 8361 Residential care

(G-12287)
COAL GROVE LONG TERM CARE INC
Also Called: Sunset Nursing Center
813 1/2 Marion Pike (45638-3070)
PHONE..................................740 532-0449

GEOGRAPHIC SECTION

Jackson - Jackson County (G-12312)

Fax: 740 532-7141
David Dixon, *Administration*
EMP: 60
SALES (est): 2.6MM **Privately Held**
WEB: www.sunsetnursingcare.com
SIC: 8051 Convalescent home with continuous nursing care

(G-12288)
FEECORP INDUSTRIAL SERVICES
1120 Wyanoke St (45638-2784)
P.O. Box 447, Pickerington (43147-0447)
PHONE..................740 533-1445
Karen Fee, *CEO*
EMP: 150
SALES (est): 1.2MM **Privately Held**
SIC: 7349 Building maintenance services

(G-12289)
FLAGSHIP SERVICES OF OHIO INC
82 Township Road 1331 (45638-8383)
PHONE..................740 533-1657
Keith Lewis, *President*
EMP: 55
SALES (est): 2.6MM **Privately Held**
SIC: 7538 General automotive repair shops

(G-12290)
HECLA WATER ASSOCIATION (PA)
3190 State Route 141 (45638-8486)
PHONE..................740 533-0526
Fax: 740 533-0003
Ray Howard, *CEO*
EMP: 33
SQ FT: 8,000
SALES: 4.6MM **Privately Held**
SIC: 8611 Public utility association

(G-12291)
IRONTON AND LAWRENCE COUNTY (PA)
305 N 5th St (45638-1578)
PHONE..................740 532-3534
Fax: 740 532-4763
Ralph Kline, *General Mgr*
James Ingram, *Persnl Dir*
Carol Rideout, *Human Resources*
Vinod Miriyala, *Med Doctor*
Cheryl Egnor, *Manager*
EMP: 260
SQ FT: 4,500
SALES: 20.9MM **Privately Held**
SIC: 4111 8099 8351 8331 Local & suburban transit; nutrition services; preschool center; job training & vocational rehabilitation services; primary care medical clinic; mental health clinic, outpatient

(G-12292)
IRONTON AND LAWRENCE COUNTY
Also Called: Family Guidance Center
1518 S 3rd St (45638-2140)
PHONE..................740 532-7855
Ruth Langer, *Branch Mgr*
EMP: 25
SALES (corp-wide): 20.9MM **Privately Held**
SIC: 8099 4111 Nutrition services; local & suburban transit
PA: Ironton And Lawrence County Area Community Action Organization
305 N 5th St
Ironton OH 45638
740 532-3534

(G-12293)
J & J GENERAL MAINTENANCE INC
2430 S 3rd St (45638-2637)
PHONE..................740 533-9729
Jackie Fields, *President*
Jeffery Fields, *Vice Pres*
Bobby Bradley, *Manager*
Tricia Fields, *Manager*
Tom Frazier, *Admin Mgr*
EMP: 30
SQ FT: 1,800

SALES: 11MM **Privately Held**
SIC: 1731 1711 1794 1623 General electrical contractor; plumbing, heating, air-conditioning contractors; excavation & grading, building construction; water & sewer line construction; steel building construction

(G-12294)
JEFFREY W SMITH
411 Center St (45638-1506)
PHONE..................740 532-9000
Jeffrey W Smith, *Principal*
EMP: 25
SALES (est): 1.7MM **Privately Held**
SIC: 8111 General practice attorney, lawyer

(G-12295)
JO LIN HEALTH CENTER INC
1050 Clinton St (45638-2876)
P.O. Box 329 (45638-0329)
PHONE..................740 532-0860
Fax: 740 532-6011
Jo L Heaberlin, *President*
Jo Linda Heaberlin, *President*
Richard Heaberlin, *Vice Pres*
Delores Jean Dalton, *Treasurer*
Jo Heaberlin, *Director*
EMP: 215
SQ FT: 20,000
SALES: 10.1MM **Privately Held**
SIC: 8361 8051 Rehabilitation center, residential; health care incidental; skilled nursing care facilities

(G-12296)
LAWRENCE CNTY HSTORICAL MUSEUM
506 S 6th St (45638-1825)
P.O. Box 73 (45638-0073)
PHONE..................740 532-1222
Piggy Karfhner, *President*
Naumi Beer, *Vice Pres*
Patricia Ericson, *Treasurer*
Dibbie Rogers, *Admin Sec*
EMP: 50
SQ FT: 3,798
SALES (est): 777.7K **Privately Held**
SIC: 8412 8111 Museum; legal services

(G-12297)
LUCAS BUILDING MAINENANCE LLC
323 Mastin Ave (45638-2432)
PHONE..................740 479-1800
James R Lucas,
Kathy Hughes,
EMP: 740
SALES: 200K **Privately Held**
SIC: 7349 Building cleaning service

(G-12298)
MENDED REEDS HOME
803 Vernon St (45638-1645)
PHONE..................740 533-1883
David Lambert, *Director*
EMP: 35
SALES (est): 890.4K **Privately Held**
SIC: 8361 Group foster home

(G-12299)
MI - DE - CON INC
3331 S 3rd St (45638-2863)
P.O. Box 4450 (45638-4450)
PHONE..................740 532-2277
Fax: 740 237-4152
Michael L Floyd, *President*
Dennis L Salyers, *President*
EMP: 99 **EST:** 1999
SALES (est): 31.6MM **Privately Held**
SIC: 1542 Nonresidential construction

(G-12300)
MUTH LUMBER COMPANY INC
1301 Adams Ln (45638-9004)
PHONE..................740 533-0800
Fax: 740 533-0725
Richard A Muth, *President*
J Tim Muth, *Vice Pres*
▼ **EMP:** 25 **EST:** 1965
SQ FT: 350,000
SALES (est): 8.6MM **Privately Held**
SIC: 5031 Lumber: rough, dressed & finished

(G-12301)
PATRIOT EMERGENCY MED SVCS INC
2914 S 4th St (45638-2867)
P.O. Box 4434 (45638-4434)
PHONE..................740 532-2222
Robert Blankenship, *Exec VP*
EMP: 30
SALES (est): 1MM **Privately Held**
WEB: www.patriotems.com
SIC: 4119 Ambulance service

(G-12302)
SHERMAN THOMPSON OH TC LP
275 N 3rd St (45638-1469)
PHONE..................216 520-1250
Frank Sinito, *General Ptnr*
EMP: 99
SALES (est): 789.1K **Privately Held**
SIC: 6513 Apartment building operators

(G-12303)
SOUTHERN OHIO BHVORAL HLTH LLC
2113 S 7th St (45638-2538)
P.O. Box 327 (45638-0327)
PHONE..................740 533-0055
Fax: 740 533-1511
Terri Anderson, *Office Mgr*
Kara Howard, *Executive*
Michael Dowdy,
EMP: 45
SQ FT: 1,500
SALES (est): 1MM **Privately Held**
SIC: 8093 Mental health clinic, outpatient

(G-12304)
WESBANCO INC
311 S 5th St (45638-1609)
PHONE..................740 532-0263
Mary Cronacher, *Manager*
EMP: 40
SALES (corp-wide): 421.2MM **Publicly Held**
WEB: www.oakhillbanks.com
SIC: 6022 6035 State commercial banks; federal savings banks
PA: Wesbanco, Inc.
1 Bank Plz
Wheeling WV 26003
304 234-9000

Jackson
Jackson County

(G-12305)
A J STOCKMEISTER INC (PA)
702 E Main St (45640-2131)
P.O. Box 667 (45640-0667)
PHONE..................740 286-2106
Fax: 740 286-6013
Alan Stockmeister, *Ch of Bd*
Tom Geiger, *President*
Seth Stockmeister, *Vice Pres*
Kay Howe, *CFO*
EMP: 30 **EST:** 1947
SQ FT: 5,000
SALES (est): 6.6MM **Privately Held**
SIC: 1711 Mechanical contractor

(G-12306)
ALUCHEM OF JACKSON INC
14782 Beaver Pike (45640-9661)
PHONE..................740 286-2455
Fax: 740 286-2004
Ronald P Zapletal, *President*
Edward L Butera, *Vice Pres*
Ronald L Bell, *Treasurer*
EMP: 50
SALES (est): 6.1MM **Privately Held**
SIC: 1481 Nonmetallic mineral services

(G-12307)
BRENMAR CONSTRUCTION INC
900 Morton St (45640-1089)
PHONE..................740 286-2151
Fax: 740 286-6150
Todd Ghearing, *President*
Andy Graham, *Corp Secy*
Tim Ousley, *Vice Pres*
EMP: 60

SQ FT: 5,000
SALES: 8MM **Privately Held**
WEB: www.brenmarconstruction.com
SIC: 1542 3312 Commercial & office building contractors; structural shapes & pilings, steel

(G-12308)
CECIL I WALKER MACHINERY CO
Also Called: Walker Machinery and Lift
1477 Mayhew Rd (45640-9186)
P.O. Box 981 (45640-0981)
PHONE..................740 286-7566
Fax: 740 286-6040
Bob Adkins, *Manager*
EMP: 25 **Privately Held**
WEB: www.walker-cat.com
SIC: 5084 7699 5082 7353 Industrial machinery & equipment; industrial machinery & equipment repair; contractors' materials; heavy construction equipment rental
HQ: Cecil I. Walker Machinery Co.
10001 Lyn Stn Rd Ky 40223
Louisville KY 40223
304 949-6400

(G-12309)
CHILD DEV CTR JACKSON CNTY
692 Pattonsville Rd (45640-9452)
P.O. Box 431 (45640-0431)
PHONE..................740 286-3995
Fax: 740 286-8677
Sharon Hayes, *Office Mgr*
Marlene D Ray, *Exec Dir*
EMP: 35
SQ FT: 4,000
SALES: 588.6K **Privately Held**
SIC: 8351 Group day care center

(G-12310)
COMMUNITY ACTION COMM PIKE CNT
Also Called: Valley View Health Center
14590 State Route 93 (45640-8977)
PHONE..................740 286-2826
Cheryl Tackett, *Asst Director*
EMP: 50
SALES (corp-wide): 22.3MM **Privately Held**
SIC: 8322 Family service agency
PA: The Community Action Committee Of Pike County
941 Market St
Piketon OH 45661
740 289-2371

(G-12311)
FAMILY ENTERTAINMENT SERVICES
780 Rock Run Rd (45640-8619)
PHONE..................740 286-8587
Rosetta Johnson, *CEO*
William Johnson, *General Mgr*
David Ford, *Vice Pres*
Bryan Malott, *Vice Pres*
Thomas E Smith, *Treasurer*
EMP: 70
SQ FT: 2,500
SALES (est): 2.6MM **Privately Held**
SIC: 0781 7349 1711 Landscape services; janitorial service, contract basis; plumbing, heating, air-conditioning contractors

(G-12312)
HEALTH CARE RTREMENT CORP AMER
Also Called: Heartland of Jackson
8668 State Route 93 (45640-9728)
PHONE..................740 286-5026
Debbie Lackey, *Sales Staff*
Bonnie McCain, *Administration*
EMP: 90
SALES (corp-wide): 3.6B **Publicly Held**
WEB: www.hrc-manorcare.com
SIC: 8051 Convalescent home with continuous nursing care
HQ: Health Care And Retirement Corporation Of America
333 N Summit St Ste 103
Toledo OH 43604
419 252-5500

Jackson - Jackson County (G-12313)

(G-12313)
HOLZER MEDICAL CTR - JACKSON
500 Burlington Rd (45640-9360)
PHONE 740 288-4625
Fax: 740 395-8502
Ross A Matlack, *President*
Rhonda Dailey, *Vice Pres*
Susan Moore, *CTO*
Hope Bauer, *Executive*
William Rose, *Emerg Med Spec*
EMP: 285
SALES: 28.8MM **Privately Held**
SIC: 8062 General medical & surgical hospitals

(G-12314)
HOSSER ASSISTED LIVING
101 Markham Dr (45640-8697)
PHONE 740 286-8785
Tim Hackworth, *Exec Dir*
Jami Gross, *Administration*
Mark Haner, *Administration*
EMP: 40
SQ FT: 36,000
SALES (est): 890.3K **Privately Held**
SIC: 8051 Skilled nursing care facilities

(G-12315)
JACKSON COUNTY BOARD ON AGING (PA)
Also Called: JACKSON COUNTY SENIOR CITIZENS
25 E Mound St (45640-1223)
PHONE 740 286-2909
Fax: 740 286-5191
Anglea Harrisison, *Director*
Rose Henson, *Admin Sec*
EMP: 40
SALES: 978.8K **Privately Held**
SIC: 8322 Old age assistance; referral service for personal & social problems

(G-12316)
OHIO METAL PROCESSING INC
Also Called: Steelsummit Ohio
16064 Beaver Pike (45640-9659)
PHONE 740 286-6457
John Flick, *President*
Kazuhiro Atsushi, *Chairman*
Shigeki Tanaka, *Corp Secy*
Kay Howe, *CFO*
Loren Altizer, *Natl Sales Mgr*
EMP: 48
SQ FT: 85,000
SALES: 54MM
SALES (corp-wide): 35.1B **Privately Held**
SIC: 5051 7389 Metals service centers & offices; metal slitting & shearing
HQ: Sumitomo Corporation Of Americas
300 Madison Ave Frnt 3
New York NY 10017
212 207-0700

(G-12317)
QUALITY SUPPLY & RENTAL INC (PA)
Also Called: Callahan Hardware
720 Veterans Dr (45640-2172)
PHONE 740 286-7517
Sam Brackman, *President*
Susan Barckman, *Admin Sec*
EMP: 25
SALES (est): 2.9MM **Privately Held**
SIC: 7359 Rental store, general

(G-12318)
STOCKMEISTER ENTERPRISES INC
700 E Main St (45640-2131)
P.O. Box 684 (45640-0684)
PHONE 740 286-1619
Fax: 740 286-7330
Alan Stockmeister, *CEO*
Susan Ridge, *Admin Asst*
EMP: 35
SQ FT: 5,300
SALES (est): 8.1MM **Privately Held**
SIC: 1542 Commercial & office building contractors

(G-12319)
TREPANIER DANIELS & TREPANIER
Also Called: A & A Truck Stop
80 Dixon Run Rd Ste 80 (45640-9511)
P.O. Box 966 (45640-0966)
PHONE 740 286-1288
Fax: 740 286-2340
Steve Trepanier, *President*
Alfred Daniels, *Corp Secy*
Sally Case, *Vice Pres*
EMP: 55
SALES (est): 9.6MM **Privately Held**
WEB: www.trepanierlambert.com
SIC: 5541 5812 7538 5331 Truck stops; eating places; general automotive repair shops; variety stores

(G-12320)
UNITED CHURCH HOMES INC
Also Called: Four Winds Nursing Facility
215 Seth Ave (45640-9405)
PHONE 740 286-7551
Fax: 740 286-1397
B Raeller, *Director*
John Evans, *Administration*
EMP: 78
SALES (corp-wide): 78.1MM **Privately Held**
WEB: www.altenheimcommunity.org
SIC: 8052 8051 Intermediate care facilities; skilled nursing care facilities
PA: United Church Homes Inc
170 E Center St
Marion OH 43302
740 382-4885

(G-12321)
WALMART INC
100 Walmart Dr (45640-8692)
PHONE 740 286-8203
Fax: 740 288-2708
Danny Tharpe, *Branch Mgr*
EMP: 450
SALES (corp-wide): 500.3B **Publicly Held**
WEB: www.walmartstores.com
SIC: 5311 5411 5912 5048 Department stores, discount; supermarkets, hypermarket; drug stores & proprietary stores; ophthalmic goods
PA: Walmart Inc.
702 Sw 8th St
Bentonville AR 72716
479 273-4000

Jackson Center
Shelby County

(G-12322)
EMI CORP (PA)
Also Called: E M I Plastic Equipment
801 W Pike St (45334-6037)
P.O. Box 590 (45334-0590)
PHONE 937 596-5511
Fax: 216 535-4809
James E Andraitis, *President*
Bill Bruce, *Vice Pres*
Brad Wren, *Vice Pres*
Larry Stephens, *Plant Mgr*
Deb Hereld, *Purch Agent*
▲ EMP: 85 EST: 1980
SQ FT: 80,000
SALES (est): 16.3MM **Privately Held**
WEB: www.emiplastics.com
SIC: 3544 5084 Special dies, tools, jigs & fixtures; industrial machinery & equipment

(G-12323)
M E THEATERS INC
106 W Pike St (45334-6028)
P.O. Box 477 (45334-0477)
PHONE 937 596-6424
Rodney Miller, *President*
EMP: 26
SALES (est): 461.7K **Privately Held**
SIC: 7832 Motion picture theaters, except drive-in

(G-12324)
RISING SUN EXPRESS LLC
1003 S Main St (45334-1123)
P.O. Box 610 (45334-0610)
PHONE 937 596-6167
Fax: 937 596-0649
Rick Howerton, *Parts Mgr*
Barb Howerton, *CFO*
Herman McBride, *Mng Member*
Barbara Howerton,
EMP: 90
SALES: 9.4MM **Privately Held**
SIC: 4213 4212 Trucking, except local; local trucking, without storage

(G-12325)
RSE GROUP INC
Also Called: Rising Sun Express
1003 S Main St (45334-1123)
PHONE 937 596-6167
Lynn J McBride, *President*
EMP: 90
SALES (est): 11.4MM **Privately Held**
SIC: 8742 Management consulting services

Jamestown
Greene County

(G-12326)
GREENEVIEW FOODS LLC
Also Called: Uhl's Jamestown Market
96 W Washington St (45335-2519)
PHONE 937 675-4161
Robert J Uhl, *President*
Rudy Brown, *General Mgr*
EMP: 30 EST: 2013
SALES (est): 5MM **Privately Held**
SIC: 5141 Groceries, general line

(G-12327)
LIBERTY NRSING CTR OF JMESTOWN
4960 Old Us Route 35 E (45335-1712)
PHONE 937 675-3311
Linda Black-Kurck, *President*
Linda Blackkurck, *President*
Mandy Sparkman, *Financial Exec*
Kevin Sharrett, *Director*
EMP: 70
SALES: 3.9MM **Privately Held**
SIC: 8051 Convalescent home with continuous nursing care

Jefferson
Ashtabula County

(G-12328)
ASHTABULA CNTY EDUCTL SVC CTR
4200 State Rd (44047)
PHONE 440 576-4085
Richard Crepage, *Superintendent*
Joseph P Hudok Jr, *Vice Pres*
EMP: 56
SALES: 40.3K **Privately Held**
SIC: 8211 8748 Specialty education; business consulting

(G-12329)
ASHTABULA COUNTY COMMISSIONERS
Also Called: Ashtabula County Highway Dept
186 E Satin St (44047-1419)
PHONE 440 576-2816
Fax: 440 576-3719
Randy Anslow, *Design Engr*
Timothy Martin, *Manager*
Justin Cline, *Manager*
James Donathan, *Administration*
EMP: 50
SQ FT: 250 **Privately Held**
SIC: 1611 Highway & street maintenance
PA: Ashtabula County Commissioners
25 W Jefferson St
Jefferson OH 44047
440 576-3649

(G-12330)
ASHTABULA COUNTY COMMNTY ACTN
32 E Jefferson St (44047-1112)
PHONE 440 576-6911
Diana Brook, *Manager*
EMP: 54
SALES (corp-wide): 92.1K **Privately Held**
SIC: 8399 8322 Antipoverty board; individual & family services
PA: Ashtabula County Community Action Agency Properties Corporation
6920 Austinburg Rd
Ashtabula OH 44004
440 997-1721

(G-12331)
CENTERRA CO-OP
161 E Jefferson St (44047-1113)
PHONE 800 362-9598
Fax: 440 576-4012
Jim Reader, *Manager*
EMP: 28
SALES (corp-wide): 174.6MM **Privately Held**
SIC: 5172 5261 2048 5191 Gases, liquefied petroleum (propane); fertilizer; bird food, prepared; farm supplies
PA: Centerra Co-Op
813 Clark Ave
Ashland OH 44805
419 281-2153

(G-12332)
SUNNY BORDER OHIO INC
3637 State Route 167 (44047-9463)
P.O. Box 483, Berlin CT (06037-0483)
PHONE 440 858-9660
Fax: 440 858-9666
Valerie Jo Hawkins, *President*
EMP: 60
SQ FT: 3,500
SALES (est): 1.6MM **Privately Held**
WEB: www.sunnyborderohio.com
SIC: 0181 0182 Flowers: grown under cover (e.g. greenhouse production); food crops grown under cover

Jeromesville
Ashland County

(G-12333)
MOHICAN HILLS GOLF CLUB INC
25 County Road 1950 (44840-9627)
PHONE 419 368-4700
James A Markling Jr, *President*
David Markling, *Shareholder*
Thomas Markling, *Shareholder*
Janet Markling, *Admin Sec*
EMP: 30
SALES (est): 1MM **Privately Held**
SIC: 7992 Public golf courses

(G-12334)
SCENIC RIDGE FRUIT FARMS
2031 State Route 89 (44840-9654)
PHONE 419 368-3353
James Kendel, *Owner*
Marion Bauman, *Owner*
EMP: 30
SALES (est): 551.5K **Privately Held**
SIC: 0175 Apple orchard

Johnstown
Licking County

(G-12335)
ATRIUM APPAREL CORPORATION
Also Called: Atrium Assembly Corporation
188 Commerce Blvd (43031-9011)
PHONE 612 889-0959
Fax: 740 967-2012
Douglas Tu, *President*
Dave Hirsch, *Vice Pres*
Jason Tu, *CFO*
EMP: 65
SQ FT: 80,000

GEOGRAPHIC SECTION

Kent - Portage County (G-12357)

SALES (est): 6.4MM **Privately Held**
SIC: **4226** 7363 7361 Special warehousing & storage; help supply services; employment agencies

(G-12336)
BIGMAR INC
9711 Sportsman Club Rd (43031-9141)
PHONE....................740 966-5800
John Tramontana, *CEO*
John Tramontata, *CEO*
Cynthia R May, *President*
Bernard Kramer, *COO*
Massimo Pedrani, *Exec VP*
EMP: 50
SQ FT: 8,600
SALES (est): 3.7MM **Privately Held**
SIC: **2834** 8111 Pharmaceutical preparations; legal services

(G-12337)
BLECKMANN USA LLC
188 Commerce Blvd Ste B (43031-9011)
PHONE....................740 809-2645
Patrick McGinnis, *General Mgr*
EMP: 45
SALES (est): 4.5MM **Privately Held**
SIC: **4731** Freight transportation arrangement

(G-12338)
BON SECOURS HEALTH SYSTEM
8148 Windy Hollow Rd (43031-9515)
PHONE....................740 966-3116
EMP: 46
SALES (corp-wide): 2.5B **Privately Held**
SIC: **8062** General Hospital
PA: Bon Secours Health System, Inc
    1505 Marriottsville Rd
    Marriottsville MD 21104
    410 442-5511

(G-12339)
COUNTY OF LICKING
Also Called: Water & Sewer Department
395 W Jersey St (43031-1158)
P.O. Box 457 (43031-0457)
PHONE....................740 967-5951
Michael Sharpe, *President*
Randy Ashbrook, *Manager*
Karen Wilson, *Manager*
EMP: 35 **Privately Held**
WEB: www.lcats.org
SIC: **4941** Water supply
PA: County Of Licking
    20 S 2nd St
    Newark OH 43055
    740 670-5040

(G-12340)
HEIMERL FARMS LTD
3891 Mink St (43031-9529)
PHONE....................740 967-0063
James Heimerl, *CEO*
Brad Heimerl,
Matt Heimerl,
EMP: 40
SALES (est): 1MM **Privately Held**
SIC: **0191** General farms, primarily crop

(G-12341)
HILLANDALE FARMS TRNSP
10513 Croton Rd (43031-9105)
PHONE....................740 893-2232
Fax: 740 893-2338
Jim Clark, *General Mgr*
EMP: 70
SALES (est): 5.9MM **Privately Held**
SIC: **4213** Trucking, except local

(G-12342)
SOHO DEVELOPMENT COMPANY
501 Cole Dr (43031-1088)
PHONE....................614 207-3261
Braden Nida, *Manager*
EMP: 75
SALES (est): 2.1MM **Privately Held**
SIC: **6552** Subdividers & developers

(G-12343)
TECHNICAL RUBBER COMPANY INC (PA)
Also Called: Tech International
200 E Coshocton St (43031-1083)
P.O. Box 486 (43031-0486)
PHONE....................740 967-9015
Fax: 740 967-3583
Micheal Chambers, *CEO*
Dan Layne, *President*
Robert Overs, *COO*
Gary Armstrong, *Senior VP*
Tim Grove, *Maint Spvr*
◆ EMP: 270
SQ FT: 10,000
SALES (est): 114.2MM **Privately Held**
WEB: www.techtirerepairs.com
SIC: **3011** 5014 2891 Tire sundries or tire repair materials, rubber; tire & tube repair materials; sealing compounds, synthetic rubber or plastic

(G-12344)
ZANDEX INC
Also Called: Northview Senior Living Center
267 N Main St (43031-1018)
PHONE....................740 967-1111
Fax: 740 927-6463
Karen Baltzell, *Branch Mgr*
Rowena Terry, *Nursing Dir*
EMP: 70
SALES (corp-wide): 34MM **Privately Held**
SIC: **8052** 8051 Personal care facility; skilled nursing care facilities
PA: Zandex, Inc.
    1122 Taylor St
    Zanesville OH 43701
    740 454-1400

(G-12345)
ZANDEX HEALTH CARE CORPORATION
Also Called: Northview Senior Living Center
267 N Main St (43031-1018)
PHONE....................740 454-1400
Karen Baltzell, *Manager*
EMP: 70
SALES (corp-wide): 34MM **Privately Held**
SIC: **8052** 8059 Intermediate care facilities; rest home, with health care
HQ: Zandex Health Care Corporation
    1122 Taylor St
    Zanesville OH 43701

Kalida
Putnam County

(G-12346)
TRILOGY HEALTHCARE PUTNAM LLC
755 Ottawa St (45853)
P.O. Box 388 (45853-0388)
PHONE....................419 532-2961
Randal J Bufford, *Mng Member*
Kevin Kidd, *Exec Dir*
EMP: 125 EST: 2005
SALES (est): 1.4MM
SALES (corp-wide): 151.1MM **Privately Held**
SIC: **8051** Skilled nursing care facilities
PA: Trilogy Rehab Services, Llc
    2701 Chestnut Station Ct
    Louisville KY 40299
    800 335-1060

Kansas
Seneca County

(G-12347)
LAKOTA BUS GARAGE
5186 Sandusky Cty Rd 13 (44841)
PHONE....................419 986-5558
Mike Eaglowski, *Superintendent*
EMP: 30
SALES (est): 603.8K **Privately Held**
SIC: **7538** General automotive repair shops

Kelleys Island
Erie County

(G-12348)
CAMP PATMOS INC
920 Monagan Rd (43438)
PHONE....................419 746-2214
Fax: 419 710-7005
Ed Miller, *Exec Dir*
EMP: 50 EST: 1951
SALES (est): 760K **Privately Held**
WEB: www.camppatmos.com
SIC: **7032** Summer camp, except day & sports instructional

Kensington
Columbiana County

(G-12349)
PAULA JO MOORE
10990 Myers Rd (44427-9753)
PHONE....................330 894-2910
Paula Moore, *Owner*
EMP: 30
SQ FT: 3,705
SALES (est): 540.8K **Privately Held**
SIC: **8082** Home health care services

Kent
Portage County

(G-12350)
1106 WEST MAIN INC
Also Called: Klaben Auto Group
1106 W Main St (44240-2008)
PHONE....................330 673-2122
Fax: 330 677-2810
Richard Klaben, *President*
Michael Klaben, *Vice Pres*
Tim Assaf, *Treasurer*
Albert Klaben, *Shareholder*
Joyce Calvert, *Assistant*
EMP: 40
SQ FT: 10,000
SALES (est): 9MM **Privately Held**
SIC: **5511** 7515 5012 Automobiles, new & used; passenger car leasing; automobiles & other motor vehicles

(G-12351)
ALPHAMICRON INC
1950 State Route 59 (44240-4112)
PHONE....................330 676-0648
Fax: 330 676-0649
Bahman Taheriy, *President*
Thomas Kosa, *COO*
Ysabel Hoover, *Production*
Peter Palffy, *Shareholder*
Alexis Makani, *Administration*
EMP: 40
SQ FT: 30,000
SALES (est): 5.5MM **Privately Held**
WEB: www.alphamicron.com
SIC: **8732** Research services, except laboratory

(G-12352)
AMETEK TCHNICAL INDUS PDTS INC (HQ)
Also Called: Ametek Electromechanical Group
100 E Erie St Ste 130 (44240-3587)
PHONE....................330 677-3754
Fax: 330 677-3306
Todd Schlegel, *General Mgr*
Matt French, *Vice Pres*
Dan Kirtz, *Opers Mgr*
Peter Smith, *CFO*
William D Burke, *Treasurer*
EMP: 65 EST: 2009
SALES (est): 69MM
SALES (corp-wide): 4.3B **Publicly Held**
SIC: **3621** 5063 3566 Motors, electric; motors, electric; speed changers, drives & gears
PA: Ametek, Inc.
    1100 Cassatt Rd
    Berwyn PA 19312
    610 647-2121

(G-12353)
CARE OF TREES INC
1500 N Mantua St (44240-2372)
PHONE....................800 445-8733
Shelly, *Branch Mgr*
EMP: 45
SALES (corp-wide): 38MM **Privately Held**
SIC: **0783** Surgery services, ornamental tree
PA: The Care Of Trees Inc
    2371 Foster Ave
    Wheeling IL 60090
    847 394-3903

(G-12354)
CARTER-JONES COMPANIES INC (PA)
Also Called: DO IT BEST
601 Tallmadge Rd (44240-7331)
P.O. Box 5194 (44240-5194)
PHONE....................330 673-6100
Neil Sackett, *President*
Jeffrey Donley, *CFO*
Brian Horning, *Controller*
Judy Lee, *Admin Sec*
EMP: 50
SQ FT: 60,000
SALES: 1.2B **Privately Held**
WEB: www.carterlumber.com
SIC: **5211** 5031 6552 Lumber & other building materials; lumber: rough, dressed & finished; subdividers & developers

(G-12355)
CARTER-JONES LUMBER COMPANY (HQ)
601 Tallmadge Rd (44240-7331)
PHONE....................330 673-6100
Fax: 330 678-6134
Neil Sackett, *CEO*
Jeffrey S Donley, *CFO*
Brian Horning, *Controller*
Dale Webber, *Manager*
Judy Lee, *Admin Sec*
▲ EMP: 156 EST: 1934
SQ FT: 60,000
SALES (est): 378.4MM
SALES (corp-wide): 1.2B **Privately Held**
SIC: **5211** 5031 Lumber products; lumber: rough, dressed & finished; millwork; building materials, exterior; building materials, interior
PA: Carter-Jones Companies, Inc.
    601 Tallmadge Rd
    Kent OH 44240
    330 673-6100

(G-12356)
CARTER-JONES LUMBER COMPANY
601 Tallmadge Rd (44240-7331)
PHONE....................330 673-6000
EMP: 1575
SALES (corp-wide): 1.2B **Privately Held**
SIC: **5211** 5031 Ret Lumber & Building Materials Whol Lumber
HQ: The Carter-Jones Lumber Company
    601 Tallmadge Rd
    Kent OH 44240
    330 673-6100

(G-12357)
CHILDRENS HOSP MED CTR AKRON
1951 State Route 59 Ste A (44240-8128)
PHONE....................330 676-1020
Fax: 330 678-4092
Carrie Gavriloff, *Principal*
Michele Wilmoth, *Director*
Debbi Kilmer, *Nurse*
EMP: 40
SALES (corp-wide): 747.4MM **Privately Held**
SIC: **8069** Children's hospital
PA: Childrens Hospital Medical Center Of Akron
    1 Perkins Sq
    Akron OH 44308
    330 543-1000

Kent - Portage County (G-12358)

(G-12358)
CITY OF AKRON
Also Called: Municipal Water Supply
1570 Ravenna Rd (44240-6111)
PHONE 330 678-0077
Jeff Bronowski, *Manager*
David Biasella, *Maintence Staff*
EMP: 40 **Privately Held**
SIC: 4941 Water supply
PA: City Of Akron
166 S High St Rm 502
Akron OH 44308
330 375-2720

(G-12359)
CITY OF KENT
Street & Sewer Maintenance
930 Overholt Rd (44240-7551)
PHONE 330 678-8105
Steve Hardesty, *Plant Mgr*
Gene Robert, *Exec Dir*
Gene Roberts, *Director*
Eugene Roberts, *Director*
EMP: 60 **Privately Held**
SIC: 1611 4952 9111 Highway & street maintenance; sewerage systems; executive offices
PA: City Of Kent
325 S Depeyster St
Kent OH 44240
330 676-4189

(G-12360)
COLEMAN PROFESSIONAL SVCS INC (PA)
Also Called: Coleman Data Solutions
5982 Rhodes Rd (44240-8100)
PHONE 330 673-1347
Nelson Burns, *CEO*
Diana Barone, *Vice Pres*
Donna Patterson, *Vice Pres*
Ben Dabbs, *CFO*
Andra Polasky, *Sales Executive*
EMP: 500
SALES: 43.8MM **Privately Held**
SIC: 8093 7349 7374 7371 Mental health clinic, outpatient; rehabilitation center, outpatient treatment; janitorial service, contract basis; data entry service; custom computer programming services; psychological consultant; offices & clinics of medical doctors

(G-12361)
COMMAND CARPET
1976 Tallmadge Rd (44240-6808)
PHONE 330 673-7404
Michele Sibbio, *President*
John Sibbio, *Vice Pres*
EMP: 55
SALES (est): 5.5MM **Privately Held**
SIC: 5713 1752 Floor covering stores; floor laying & floor work

(G-12362)
DAVEY RESOURCE GROUP INC
1500 N Mantua St (44240-2372)
PHONE 330 673-9511
Patrick Covey, *CEO*
Thea Sears, *Controller*
Barb Smith, *Manager*
EMP: 45
SALES (est): 1.5MM
SALES (corp-wide): 915.9MM **Privately Held**
SIC: 0783 Ornamental shrub & tree services
PA: The Davey Tree Expert Company
1500 N Mantua St
Kent OH 44240
330 673-9511

(G-12363)
DAVEY TREE EXPERT COMPANY (PA)
1500 N Mantua St (44240-2399)
P.O. Box 5193 (44240-5193)
PHONE 330 673-9511
Fax: 330 673-9843
Karl J Warnke, *Ch of Bd*
William J Ginn, *Principal*
Douglas K Hall, *Principal*
Sandra W Harbrecht, *Principal*
John E Warfel, *Principal*
EMP: 175
SALES: 915.9MM **Privately Held**
SIC: 0783 0782 0811 0181 Removal services, bush & tree; lawn care services; tree farm; nursery stock, growing of

(G-12364)
DAYTON FREIGHT LINES INC
280 Progress Blvd (44240-8015)
PHONE 330 346-0750
Fax: 330 346-0760
Robert Kantorowski, *Principal*
Bill Durstock, *Risk Mgmt Dir*
EMP: 35
SALES (corp-wide): 1B **Privately Held**
SIC: 4213 Contract haulers
PA: Dayton Freight Lines, Inc.
6450 Poe Ave Ste 311
Dayton OH 45414
937 264-4060

(G-12365)
DIAMOND HEAVY HAUL INC
123 N Water St Ste A (44240-2414)
PHONE 330 677-8061
Steven J Engel, *President*
Tonya Engel, *Vice Pres*
EMP: 25
SALES (est): 1.2MM **Privately Held**
SIC: 4213 Heavy hauling

(G-12366)
DON WARTKO CONSTRUCTION CO (PA)
Also Called: Design Concrete Surfaces
975 Tallmadge Rd (44240-6474)
PHONE 330 673-5252
Fax: 330 673-5501
Thomas Wartko, *President*
David Wartko, *Vice Pres*
Mike Wartko, *Vice Pres*
Ron Wartko, *Vice Pres*
Doris Wartko, *Admin Sec*
EMP: 60
SQ FT: 15,000
SALES (est): 18.4MM **Privately Held**
SIC: 1623 1794 3732 Oil & gas line & compressor station construction; excavation work; boat building & repairing

(G-12367)
EAST END WELDING COMPANY
357 Tallmadge Rd (44240-7201)
PHONE 330 677-6000
Fax: 330 677-6006
John E Susong, *President*
Fred Dietz, *Project Mgr*
John Marcolini, *Project Mgr*
Nate Molnar, *Project Mgr*
Tim Carr, *CFO*
▲ **EMP:** 120
SQ FT: 146,500
SALES (est): 33.1MM **Privately Held**
SIC: 3599 7692 Custom machinery; welding repair

(G-12368)
ENVIROTEST SYSTEMS CORP
1460t Fairchild Ave (44240-1818)
PHONE 330 963-4464
EMP: 34 **Privately Held**
WEB: www.il.etest.com
SIC: 7549 Emissions testing without repairs, automotive
HQ: Envirotest Systems Corp.
7 Kripes Rd
East Granby CT 06026

(G-12369)
FAIRCHILD MD LEASING CO LLC
Also Called: Kent Healthcare Center
1290 Fairchild Ave (44240-1814)
PHONE 330 678-4912
Fax: 330 678-1040
Sam Petery, *Envir Svcs Dir*
Mark Gardner, *Manager*
John Wagner, *Director*
Stephen Rosedale,
Christina Ayres, *Administration*
EMP: 150
SALES (est): 5.3MM **Privately Held**
SIC: 8051 Skilled nursing care facilities

(G-12370)
G & S TRANSFER INC
4055a Highway View Dr (44240-8010)
PHONE 330 673-3899
Fax: 330 673-1978
Shelly Begue, *Corp Secy*
Gary Begue, *Vice Pres*
EMP: 36
SALES (est): 4.2MM **Privately Held**
SIC: 4212 4213 Mail carriers, contract; dump truck haulage; contract haulers

(G-12371)
GERMAN FAMILY SOCIETY INC
Also Called: GERMAN AMERICAN FAMILY SOCIETY
3871 Ranfield Rd (44240-6760)
PHONE 330 678-8229
Joseph Geiser, *President*
Jim Armbrust, *Vice Pres*
Carl Townhauser, *Vice Pres*
Jim Resnick, *Treasurer*
Hilda Resnick, *Admin Sec*
EMP: 40
SALES: 343.4K **Privately Held**
WEB: www.germanfamilysociety.com
SIC: 7997 7299 Membership sports & recreation clubs; banquet hall facilities

(G-12372)
GFS LEASING INC (PA)
Also Called: Altercare of Ravenna
1463 Tallmadge Rd (44240-6664)
PHONE 330 296-6415
Gerald F Schroer, *President*
EMP: 80
SQ FT: 23,000
SALES (est): 2.8MM **Privately Held**
SIC: 8051 Skilled nursing care facilities

(G-12373)
HOMETOWN BANK (PA)
142 N Water St (44240-2419)
P.O. Box 310 (44240-0006)
PHONE 330 673-9827
Fax: 330 673-4310
Timothy J McFarlane, *Chairman*
Brian Bialik, *Senior VP*
Jack Schneider, *Senior VP*
Colin Boyle, *Assistant VP*
Michael A Lewis, *Vice Pres*
EMP: 27
SQ FT: 6,000
SALES: 8.6MM **Privately Held**
SIC: 6036 State savings banks, not federally chartered

(G-12374)
INDUSTRIAL TUBE AND STEEL CORP (PA)
4658 Crystal Pkwy (44240-8020)
P.O. Box 76054, Cleveland (44101-4203)
PHONE 330 474-5530
Fax: 330 474-0015
Dick Siess, *President*
Frederick H Gillen, *Principal*
H William Kranz Jr, *Principal*
Geoff Siess, *VP Opers*
Richard Moone, *Plant Mgr*
▲ **EMP:** 100 **EST:** 1956
SQ FT: 30,000
SALES (est): 104.4MM **Privately Held**
SIC: 5051 Tubing, metal; bars, metal

(G-12375)
KAISER FOUNDATION HOSPITALS
Also Called: Kent Medical Offices
2500 State Route 59 (44240-7105)
PHONE 800 524-7377
EMP: 593
SALES (corp-wide): 82.6B **Privately Held**
SIC: 8011 Offices & clinics of medical doctors
HQ: Kaiser Foundation Hospitals Inc
1 Kaiser Plz
Oakland CA 94612
510 271-6611

(G-12376)
KENT ADHESIVE PRODUCTS CO
Also Called: K A P C O
1000 Cherry St (44240-7501)
P.O. Box 626 (44240-0011)
PHONE 330 678-1626
Fax: 330 678-3922
Edward Small, *President*
Jenifer Codrea, *Vice Pres*
Philip M Zavracky, *Vice Pres*
Nate Foltz, *Purch Mgr*
Larry Nitzsche, *Engineer*
▼ **EMP:** 80 **EST:** 1974
SQ FT: 100,000
SALES (est): 38.4MM **Privately Held**
WEB: www.kapco.com
SIC: 2679 2672 2675 7389 Paper products, converted; adhesive papers, labels or tapes: from purchased material; tape, pressure sensitive: made from purchased materials; die-cut paper & board; laminating service; tape slitting

(G-12377)
KENT AUTOMOTIVE INC
Also Called: Kent Lincoln-Mercury Sales
1080 W Main St (44240-2006)
PHONE 330 678-5520
Fax: 330 678-8528
Bruce A Caudill, *President*
Heather Knapp, *Corp Secy*
Janett Caudill, *Vice Pres*
Larry Burke, *Sales Mgr*
Don Duke, *Sales Mgr*
EMP: 40
SALES: 32.9MM **Privately Held**
WEB: www.kentlm.com
SIC: 5511 5521 7538 7515 Automobiles, new & used; used car dealers; general automotive repair shops; passenger car leasing; automotive & home supply stores

(G-12378)
KENT RIDGE AT GOLDEN POND LTD
5241 Sunnybrook Rd (44240-7383)
PHONE 330 677-4040
Sandy Warner, *Managing Prtnr*
EMP: 90
SALES (est): 2.8MM **Privately Held**
SIC: 8361 Home for the aged

(G-12379)
KENT STATE UNIVERSITY
Also Called: Procurement Payments
237 Schwartz Ste 237 (44242-0001)
P.O. Box 5190
PHONE 330 672-2607
Emily Hurmon, *Branch Mgr*
Nicole Carlone, *Manager*
Eric Mansfield, *Exec Dir*
Ken Ditlevson, *Director*
Erin Nunn, *Officer*
EMP: 79
SALES (corp-wide): 474.6MM **Privately Held**
WEB: www.kenteliv.kent.edu
SIC: 8221 8721 University; payroll accounting service
PA: Kent State University
1500 Horning Rd
Kent OH 44242
330 672-3000

(G-12380)
KENT STATE UNIVERSITY
Also Called: Wksu FM Natl Public Radio
1613 E Summit St (44240-4684)
P.O. Box 5190 (44242-0001)
PHONE 330 672-3114
Fax: 330 672-4107
Ann Verwiebe, *Pub Rel Dir*
Mary E Powers, *Manager*
Sylvia Docking, *Producer*
Jon Nungesser, *Producer*
Scott Sharp, *Web Dvlpr*
EMP: 45
SALES (corp-wide): 474.6MM **Privately Held**
WEB: www.kenteliv.kent.edu
SIC: 4832 8221 Radio broadcasting stations; university
PA: Kent State University
1500 Horning Rd
Kent OH 44242
330 672-3000

(G-12381)
KLABEN FAMILY DODGE INC
1338 W Main St (44240-1940)
PHONE 330 673-9971
Michael G Klaben, *President*

GEOGRAPHIC SECTION
Kent - Portage County (G-12405)

Tim Assaf, *Corp Secy*
EMP: 50
SQ FT: 20,000
SALES (est): 8.6MM **Privately Held**
SIC: 5511 7538 7515 Automobiles, new & used; trucks, tractors & trailers: new & used; general automotive repair shops; passenger car leasing

(G-12382)
KLABEN LEASING AND SALES INC
1338 W Main St (44240-1940)
PHONE..............................330 673-9971
Fax: 330 678-3936
Albert Klaben, *President*
Dan Peters, *Sales Staff*
Jeffrey Beane, *Manager*
EMP: 65 EST: 1990
SALES (est): 6.2MM **Privately Held**
SIC: 6159 Automobile finance leasing

(G-12383)
KLABEN LINCOLN FORD INC (PA)
Also Called: Klaben Auto Group
1089 W Main St (44240-2005)
PHONE..............................330 673-3139
Fax: 330 677-2863
Albert Klaben, *President*
Richard Klaben, *Vice Pres*
Steve Perkins, *Parts Mgr*
Brian Franklin, *Finance Mgr*
Christine Klaben, *Finance Mgr*
EMP: 81
SALES (est): 59.1MM **Privately Held**
WEB: www.klaben.com
SIC: 5511 7515 5012 Automobiles, new & used; pickups, new & used; passenger car leasing; automobiles & other motor vehicles

(G-12384)
LOWES HOME CENTERS LLC
218 Nicholas Way (44240-8032)
PHONE..............................330 677-3040
Fax: 330 677-3043
Susan Sellf, *Branch Mgr*
EMP: 150
SALES (corp-wide): 68.6B **Publicly Held**
SIC: 5211 5031 5722 5064 Home centers; building materials, exterior; building materials, interior; household appliance stores; electrical appliances, television & radio
HQ: Lowe's Home Centers, Llc
1605 Curtis Bridge Rd
Wilkesboro NC 28697
336 658-4000

(G-12385)
MAAG AUTOMATIK INC
Also Called: Maag Reduction Engineering
235 Progress Blvd (44240-8055)
PHONE..............................330 677-2225
EMP: 35
SALES (corp-wide): 7.8B **Publicly Held**
SIC: 5084 3532 Industrial machinery & equipment; pulverizing & equipment; crushing, pulverizing & screening equipment; pellet mills (mining machinery)
HQ: Maag Automatik, Inc.
9401 Southern Pine Blvd Q
Charlotte NC 28273

(G-12386)
MEDIA-COM INC
Also Called: Wnir/FM
2449 State Route 59 (44240)
P.O. Box 2170, Akron (44309-2170)
PHONE..............................330 673-2323
Fax: 330 673-0301
Richard M Klaus, *President*
Robert A Klaus, *Vice Pres*
William B Klaus, *Vice Pres*
Steve Stroup, *Accounts Exec*
Debbie Hull, *Manager*
EMP: 40
SQ FT: 4,200
SALES (est): 3.6MM **Privately Held**
WEB: www.wnir.com
SIC: 4832 Radio broadcasting stations

(G-12387)
NORTHAST OHIO EYE SURGEONS INC (PA)
2013 State Route 59 (44240-4113)
PHONE..............................330 678-0201
Fax: 330 678-4272
Lawrence E Lohman, *President*
Marc Jones, *Principal*
Matthew Willett, *Principal*
April Lemaster, *Development*
Lori Durkin, *Director*
EMP: 26
SALES: 1.1MM **Privately Held**
WEB: www.neoes.net
SIC: 8011 Eyes, ears, nose & throat specialist: physician/surgeon

(G-12388)
NORTHASTERN EDUCTL TV OHIO INC
Also Called: Western Reserve Public Media
1750 W Campus Center Dr (44240-3820)
P.O. Box 5191 (44240-5191)
PHONE..............................330 677-4549
David Hunter, *Ch of Bd*
Trina Cutter, *President*
Mark Auburn, *Admin Sec*
EMP: 30
SALES (corp-wide): 4.1MM **Privately Held**
SIC: 4833 Television broadcasting stations
PA: Northeastern Educational Television Of Ohio, Inc.
1750 W Campus Center Dr
Kent OH
330 677-4549

(G-12389)
NVR INC
4034 Willow Way (44240-6888)
PHONE..............................440 584-4200
EMP: 33 **Publicly Held**
SIC: 1521 New construction, single-family houses
PA: Nvr, Inc.
11700 Plaza America Dr # 500
Reston VA 20190

(G-12390)
PALESTINE CHLD RELIEF FUND
Also Called: Pcrf, The
1340 Morris Rd (44240-4518)
PHONE..............................330 678-2645
Steve Sosebee, *CEO*
Amanda Pudloski, *Admin Asst*
EMP: 56
SALES: 7.9MM **Privately Held**
WEB: www.pcrf.net
SIC: 8099 Medical services organization

(G-12391)
PORTAGE AREA RGONAL TRNSP AUTH
Also Called: Parta
2000 Summit Rd (44240-7140)
PHONE..............................330 678-1287
Fax: 330 676-6310
Rick Bissler, *President*
Claudia Amrhein, *General Mgr*
John Drew Jr, *General Mgr*
Clayton Davis, *Opers Mgr*
Richard Fonte, *Sls & Mktg Exec*
EMP: 100
SQ FT: 41,905
SALES (est): 12.2MM **Privately Held**
WEB: www.partaonline.org
SIC: 8742 Transportation consultant

(G-12392)
PROVINCE KENT OH LLC
609 S Lincoln St Ste F (44240-5366)
PHONE..............................330 673-3808
Patty McNerney, *Mng Member*
EMP: 30
SALES (est): 1.1MM **Privately Held**
SIC: 6513 Apartment building operators

(G-12393)
RAHF IV KENT LLC
1546 S Water St (44240-4464)
PHONE..............................216 621-6060
Victoria Gousse, *Administration*
EMP: 50
SALES (est): 498.2K **Privately Held**
SIC: 6513 Apartment building operators

(G-12394)
ROBINSON HEALTH SYSTEM INC
Med Center One
1993 State Route 59 (44240-7609)
PHONE..............................330 297-0811
Fax: 330 678-6716
Wanda Carr, *Office Mgr*
Jack Monda, *Director*
EMP: 30
SALES (corp-wide): 2.3B **Privately Held**
SIC: 8062 General medical & surgical hospitals
HQ: Robinson Health System, Inc.
6847 N Chestnut St
Ravenna OH 44266
330 297-0811

(G-12395)
SCHNELLER LLC
Polyplastex International
6019 Powdermill Rd (44240-7109)
PHONE..............................330 673-1299
Tom Spseisser, *Manager*
EMP: 75
SALES (corp-wide): 3.5B **Publicly Held**
WEB: www.schneller.com
SIC: 3083 8731 3728 Laminated plastic sheets; commercial physical research; aircraft parts & equipment
HQ: Schneller Llc
6019 Powdermill Rd
Kent OH 44240
330 676-7183

(G-12396)
STOW-KENT ANIMAL HOSPITAL INC (PA)
4559 Kent Rd (44240-5298)
PHONE..............................330 673-0049
Fax: 330 673-1002
Thomas Albers Dvm, *President*
Carmella Albers, *Vice Pres*
EMP: 27
SALES (est): 2.5MM **Privately Held**
SIC: 0742 Animal hospital services, pets & other animal specialties; veterinarian, animal specialties

(G-12397)
STOW-KENT ANIMAL HOSPITAL INC
Also Called: Portage Animal Clinic
4148 State Route 43 (44240-6916)
PHONE..............................330 673-1002
EMP: 27
SALES (corp-wide): 2.5MM **Privately Held**
SIC: 0742 Animal hospital services, pets & other animal specialties
PA: Stow-Kent Animal Hospital Inc
4559 Kent Rd
Kent OH 44240
330 673-0049

(G-12398)
SYMCOX GRINDING & STEELE CO
825 Tallmadge Rd (44240-6463)
P.O. Box 156, Tallmadge (44278-0156)
PHONE..............................330 678-1080
Chuck Lewis, *President*
John Lewis, *Vice Pres*
Don Shaffer, *Treasurer*
Ron Lewis, *Admin Sec*
EMP: 32
SALES (est): 4.5MM **Privately Held**
SIC: 5051 Metals service centers & offices

(G-12399)
TALLMADGE ASPHALT & PAV CO INC
741 Tallmadge Rd (44240-7329)
PHONE..............................330 677-0000
Fax: 330 677-9851
Michael Sekulich, *President*
EMP: 60
SQ FT: 15,000
SALES (est): 9.9MM **Privately Held**
WEB: www.tallmadgeasphalt.com
SIC: 1771 Blacktop (asphalt) work

(G-12400)
TOWNHALL 2
Also Called: TOWNHALL 2 24 HOUR HELPLINE
155 N Water St (44240-2418)
PHONE..............................330 678-3006
Fax: 330 678-7558
Deana Douglas, *General Mgr*
Barbara Deakins, *Business Mgr*
Sue Whitehurst, *Exec Dir*
Barbara Folan, *Admin Asst*
EMP: 50
SALES: 22.2K **Privately Held**
WEB: www.townhall2.com
SIC: 8322 General counseling services

(G-12401)
U S DEVELOPMENT CORP (PA)
Also Called: Akro-Plastics
900 W Main St (44240-2285)
PHONE..............................330 673-6900
Fax: 330 673-4940
Jerold Ramsey, *President*
Darrell Laney, *Plant Mgr*
David Meier, *Prdtn Mgr*
EMP: 50
SQ FT: 185,000
SALES (est): 10.2MM **Privately Held**
WEB: www.rotomold.com
SIC: 3089 6512 Molding primary plastic; commercial & industrial building operation

(G-12402)
ULRICH PROFESSIONAL GROUP
401 Devon Pl Ste 215 (44240-6483)
PHONE..............................330 673-9501
Fax: 330 673-8204
Jack Monda, *President*
Kerry Simons, *Manager*
Kashif Anwar, *Family Practiti*
EMP: 25 EST: 1962
SALES (est): 1.1MM **Privately Held**
SIC: 8031 7361 Offices & clinics of osteopathic physicians; nurses' registry

(G-12403)
UNITY HEALTH NETWORK LLC
307 W Main St (44240-2400)
PHONE..............................330 678-7782
Robert A Kent Jr, *Administration*
EMP: 41
SALES (corp-wide): 14.5MM **Privately Held**
SIC: 8011 Internal medicine practitioners
PA: Unity Health Network, Llc
3033 State Rd
Cuyahoga Falls OH 44223
330 923-5899

(G-12404)
WALGREEN CO
Also Called: Walgreens
320 S Water St (44240-3528)
PHONE..............................330 677-5650
Fax: 330 677-3212
Andrew Dougt, *Manager*
Victoria Muller, *Manager*
EMP: 30
SALES (corp-wide): 118.2B **Publicly Held**
WEB: www.walgreens.com
SIC: 5912 7384 Drug stores; photofinishing laboratory
HQ: Walgreen Co.
200 Wilmot Rd
Deerfield IL 60015
847 315-2500

(G-12405)
WILBUR REALTY INC (PA)
Also Called: Century 21
548 S Water St (44240-3548)
P.O. Box 624 (44240-0011)
PHONE..............................330 673-5883
Fax: 330 673-4558
Steve Boyles, *President*
Tim Weisman, *Manager*
EMP: 40
SQ FT: 3,000
SALES (est): 2.2MM **Privately Held**
WEB: www.philmarch.com
SIC: 6531 Real estate agent, residential

Kent - Portage County (G-12406)

(G-12406)
WINE-ART OF OHIO INC
Also Called: Carlson, L D Company
463 Portage Blvd (44240-7286)
PHONE...................330 678-7733
Fax: 216 678-6686
Ronald Hartman, *CEO*
Laurence D Carlson, *Principal*
Ann Carst, *Principal*
Bruce B Laybourne, *Principal*
Judy Pauling, *Accountant*
▲ **EMP:** 45
SQ FT: 40,000
SALES (est): 17.3MM **Privately Held**
WEB: www.ldcarlson.com
SIC: 5149 Wine makers' equipment & supplies

(G-12407)
YOUNG AND ASSOCIATES INC
121 E Main St (44240-2524)
P.O. Box 711 (44240-0013)
PHONE...................330 678-0524
James Kleinfelter, *President*
Gary J Young, *Chairman*
Ryan Young, *COO*
Ivan Garrabrant, *Manager*
Robert Whitehead, *Consultant*
EMP: 38
SQ FT: 2,500
SALES (est): 3.9MM **Privately Held**
WEB: www.younginc.com
SIC: 8742 Marketing consulting services; general management consultant

Kenton
Hardin County

(G-12408)
BKP AMBULANCE DISTRICT
439 S Main St (43326-1946)
PHONE...................419 674-4574
Fax: 419 674-4574
Allen Barrett, *President*
Alan Long, *Principal*
Randy Scharf, *Principal*
EMP: 40 **EST:** 1975
SALES: 786.7K **Privately Held**
SIC: 4119 Ambulance service

(G-12409)
CITY OF KENTON (PA)
111 W Franklin St (43326-1972)
PHONE...................419 674-4850
Fax: 419 673-1721
Randy Manns, *Mayor*
EMP: 38 **Privately Held**
WEB: www.kentoncity.com
SIC: 9111 8611 Mayors' offices; business associations

(G-12410)
COUNTY OF HARDIN
Also Called: Hardin Cnty Dept Mntl Hlth Ret
705 N Ida St (43326-1060)
PHONE...................419 674-4158
Mark Kieffer, *Principal*
Amy Newland, *Office Mgr*
EMP: 42 **Privately Held**
WEB: www.kenton.com
SIC: 8331 Vocational training agency
PA: County Of Hardin
1 Court House Sq Rm 100
Kenton OH 43326
419 674-2205

(G-12411)
FREEDOM ENTERPRISES INC
11441 County Road 75 (43326-9417)
PHONE...................419 675-1192
Fax: 419 673-8382
James Michael Rose, *President*
Ryan Rose, *Opers Staff*
Lavonna S Rose, *Admin Sec*
EMP: 27
SQ FT: 5,000
SALES: 3.2MM **Privately Held**
SIC: 4731 Truck transportation brokers

(G-12412)
H & H GREEN LLC
13670 Us Highway 68 (43326-9302)
PHONE...................419 674-4152

Sherri Haushalter, *Controller*
William Hall, *Mng Member*
Mark Haushalter,
EMP: 43
SQ FT: 43,000
SALES (est): 1.7MM **Privately Held**
SIC: 5087 Service establishment equipment

(G-12413)
HARCO INDUSTRIES INC
707 N Ida St (43326-1060)
PHONE...................419 674-4159
Fax: 419 675-3274
Jason Seggerson, *CEO*
Pat Evans, *Executive*
EMP: 44
SQ FT: 7,000
SALES: 113.7K **Privately Held**
SIC: 8331 Sheltered workshop

(G-12414)
HARDIN CNTY CNCIL ON AGING INC
100 Memorial Dr (43326-2089)
PHONE...................419 673-1102
Fax: 419 673-8161
Bette Bibler, *Director*
Sandra McKinley, *Bd of Directors*
Virginia Tice, *Bd of Directors*
EMP: 30
SALES: 1.4MM **Privately Held**
SIC: 8322 Senior citizens' center or association

(G-12415)
HARDIN COUNTY ENGINEER
1040 W Franklin St (43326-8852)
PHONE...................419 673-2232
Fax: 419 673-1232
Michael Smith, *Engineer*
EMP: 35
SALES: 3MM **Privately Held**
SIC: 1611 Highway & street construction

(G-12416)
HARDIN COUNTY FAMILY YMCA
918 W Franklin St (43326-1720)
PHONE...................419 673-6131
Fax: 419 675-3492
Shawn Galvin, *Director*
EMP: 48
SALES: 568.7K **Privately Held**
WEB: www.hardincoymca.com
SIC: 8641 7991 8351 7032 Youth organizations; physical fitness facilities; child day care services; youth camps; individual & family services

(G-12417)
HARDIN COUNTY HOME
Also Called: Hardin Hills Health Center
1211 W Lima St (43326-8846)
PHONE...................419 673-0961
Fax: 419 675-2538
Debbie Lamb, *President*
Richard Kevern, *Managing Prtnr*
Mike Lawrence, *Envir Svcs Dir*
R Linzen, *Human Res Mgr*
Kathy Martino, *Executive*
EMP: 71
SALES (est): 4.4MM **Privately Held**
WEB: www.hardinhills.org
SIC: 8059 Nursing home, except skilled & intermediate care facility

(G-12418)
HARDIN MEMORIAL HOSPITAL (HQ)
Also Called: Ohiohealth
921 E Franklin St (43326-2099)
PHONE...................419 673-0761
Fax: 419 673-1097
David Blom, *CEO*
Mark Seckinger, *President*
Ron Snyder, *COO*
Michael W Louge, *Exec VP*
Janet Jones, *Facilities Mgr*
EMP: 47
SQ FT: 91,678
SALES: 26MM
SALES (corp-wide): 3.7B **Privately Held**
WEB: www.hardinmemorialhospital.com
SIC: 8062 General medical & surgical hospitals

PA: Ohiohealth Corporation
180 E Broad St
Columbus OH 43215
614 788-8860

(G-12419)
HEALTH PARTNERS WESTERN OHIO
Also Called: Kenton Community Health Center
111 W Espy St (43326-2117)
PHONE...................419 679-5994
Liza Frantz, *Director*
EMP: 30
SALES (corp-wide): 23.2MM **Privately Held**
SIC: 8099 Blood related health services
PA: Health Partners Of Western Ohio
441 E 8th St
Lima OH 45804
419 221-3072

(G-12420)
KENTON AUTO AND TRUCK WRECKING
Also Called: Kenton Motor Sales
13188 Us Highway 68 (43326-9302)
PHONE...................419 673-8234
Franklin L Roof, *Owner*
EMP: 25
SQ FT: 1,200
SALES (est): 2MM **Privately Held**
SIC: 5093 5521 5013 Automotive wrecking for scrap; automobiles, used cars only; automotive supplies & parts

(G-12421)
MID-OHIO ENERGY COOPERATIVE
Also Called: MIDOHIO ENERGY COOPERATIVE
1210 W Lima St (43326-1798)
P.O. Box 224 (43326-0224)
PHONE...................419 568-5321
John Metcalf, *President*
Karl Marshall, *Vice Pres*
Mark Terrill, *Comp Tech*
EMP: 28
SQ FT: 10,000
SALES: 21.1MM **Privately Held**
WEB: www.midohioenergy.com
SIC: 4911 Distribution, electric power

(G-12422)
MORTON BUILDINGS INC
Also Called: Morton Buildings Plant
14483 State Route 31 (43326-9055)
P.O. Box 223 (43326-0223)
PHONE...................419 675-2311
Fax: 419 675-2012
Paul Hudson, *General Mgr*
Mike Morrison, *Vice Pres*
Karen Baker, *Plant Mgr*
Jim Stevens, *Plant Mgr*
Mike Richardson, *Production*
EMP: 70
SALES (corp-wide): 492.6MM **Privately Held**
SIC: 3448 5039 2452 Farm & utility buildings; prefabricated structures; prefabricated wood buildings
PA: Morton Buildings, Inc.
252 W Adams St
Morton IL 61550
800 447-7436

(G-12423)
SCHNEIDER NATIONAL INC
808 Fontaine St (43326-2160)
PHONE...................419 673-0254
EMP: 268
SALES (corp-wide): 4.3B **Publicly Held**
SIC: 4213 Trucking, except local
PA: Schneider National, Inc.
3101 Packerland Dr
Green Bay WI 54313
920 592-2000

(G-12424)
THE LIBERTY NAT BANKOF ADA
100 E Franklin St (43326-1924)
P.O. Box 234 (43326-0234)
PHONE...................419 673-1217
William Carr, *CEO*
EMP: 25

SQ FT: 10,000
SALES (corp-wide): 13.5MM **Privately Held**
SIC: 6021 6022 National commercial banks; state commercial banks
PA: Liberty National Bankof Ada, The (Inc)
118 S Main St
Ada OH 45810
419 634-5015

(G-12425)
UNITED CHURCH RES OF KENTON
Also Called: CHAPEL HILL COMMUNITY
900 E Columbus St (43326-1758)
P.O. Box 1806, Marion (43301-1806)
PHONE...................740 382-4885
Fax: 419 673-8893
Mark Seckinger, *President*
Brian Allen, *Assistant VP*
Robert Hart, *Vice Pres*
Ronald Beach, *CFO*
Cheryl Wickersham, *Treasurer*
EMP: 60
SQ FT: 28,000
SALES: 447.5K
SALES (corp-wide): 78.1MM **Privately Held**
WEB: www.altenheimcommunity.org
SIC: 6513 Apartment building operators
PA: United Church Homes Inc
170 E Center St
Marion OH 43302
740 382-4885

Kettering
Montgomery County

(G-12426)
ADVANCED MEDICAL EQUIPMENT INC (PA)
2655 S Dixie Dr (45409-1504)
PHONE...................937 534-1080
Fax: 937 534-1081
Randy Willhelm, *Owner*
Andrew Willhelm, *Vice Pres*
Todd Wright, *Treasurer*
EMP: 37
SQ FT: 4,000
SALES (est): 10.1MM **Privately Held**
SIC: 5999 5047 Medical apparatus & supplies; medical equipment & supplies

(G-12427)
BASIN DIALYSIS LLC
Also Called: Buckeye Dialysis
3050 S Dixie Dr (45409-1516)
PHONE...................937 643-2337
James K Hilger,
Brenda Barrett, *Administration*
EMP: 41
SALES (est): 664.1K **Publicly Held**
SIC: 8092 Kidney dialysis centers
PA: Davita Inc.
2000 16th St
Denver CO 80202

(G-12428)
BUCKEYE AMBULANCE LLC
4601 Gateway Cir (45440-1713)
PHONE...................937 435-1584
Brian Hart, *Business Mgr*
Courtney Myers, *Human Resources*
Dereck Pristas,
EMP: 70 **EST:** 2011
SQ FT: 12,000
SALES (est): 2.9MM **Privately Held**
SIC: 4119 Ambulance service

(G-12429)
EFIX COMPUTER REPAIR & SVC LLC
Also Called: It Services
1389 E Stroop Rd (45429-4925)
PHONE...................937 985-4447
Edwin Kariuki, *Mng Member*
EMP: 45
SALES: 1MM **Privately Held**
SIC: 7378 Computer & data processing equipment repair/maintenance

GEOGRAPHIC SECTION

(G-12430)
KETTERING ADVENTIST HEALTHCARE
Also Called: Kettering Health Network
3533 Southern Blvd (45429-1264)
PHONE..................................937 298-3399
EMP: 90
SALES (corp-wide): 1.7B Privately Held
SIC: 8011 Physicians' office, including specialists
PA: Kettering Adventist Healthcare
  3535 Southern Blvd
  Dayton OH 45429
  937 298-4331

(G-12431)
KETTERING MEDICAL CENTER (HQ)
Also Called: Charles F Kettering Mem Hosp
3535 Southern Blvd (45429-1298)
PHONE..................................937 298-4331
Fax: 937 395-8021
Jarrod McNaughton, CEO
Fred Manchur, CEO
Roy Chew, President
Terri Day, President
J Bidell, Ch Radiology
EMP: 50 EST: 1959
SQ FT: 500,000
SALES (est): 533.9MM
SALES (corp-wide): 1.7B Privately Held
WEB: www.kmcfoundation.org
SIC: 8062 Hospital, professional nursing school; hospital, medical school affiliated with nursing & residency
PA: Kettering Adventist Healthcare
  3535 Southern Blvd
  Dayton OH 45429
  937 298-4331

(G-12432)
LADD DISTRIBUTION LLC (DH)
4849 Hempstead Station Dr (45429-5156)
PHONE..................................937 438-2646
Mark Sparling, Controller
Paul Zeiser, Accounts Mgr
Scott Leichtling, Mng Member
Grace Christiansen, Supervisor
Tony Cranfield, Director
▲ EMP: 80
SQ FT: 48,000
SALES (est): 33.4MM
SALES (corp-wide): 12.2B Privately Held
SIC: 5065 Connectors, electronic
HQ: Te Connectivity Corporation
  1050 Westlakes Dr
  Berwyn PA 19312
  610 893-9800

(G-12433)
MARXENT LABS LLC
3100 Res Blvd Ste 360 (45420)
PHONE..................................937 999-5005
Beck Desecker, CEO
Patrice Hall, Project Mgr
Ryan Roche, Design Engr
Barry Desecker, CTO
Vince Kilian, Creative Dir
EMP: 78
SALES (est): 1.8MM Privately Held
SIC: 7371 Computer software development & applications

(G-12434)
OOVOO LLC
Also Called: Krush Technology
1700 S Patterson Blvd (45409-2140)
P.O. Box 340488, Dayton (45434-0488)
PHONE..................................917 515-2074
JP Nauses, CEO
Robert Danielle, Controller
EMP: 75
SALES (est): 4.5MM Privately Held
WEB: www.oovoo.com
SIC: 4899 Data communication services

(G-12435)
REYNOLDS AND REYNOLDS COMPANY (HQ)
1 Reynolds Way (45430-1586)
PHONE..................................937 485-2000
Fax: 937 485-2787
Bob Brockman, CEO
Jeanne M Kirkland, Principal
Melinda Duvall, Business Mgr
Jeffrey Almoney, Exec VP
Frank Caccamo, Exec VP
EMP: 1000 EST: 1889
SQ FT: 60,000
SALES (est): 1.9B Privately Held
WEB: www.reyrey.com
SIC: 7373 6159 Computer integrated systems design; machinery & equipment finance leasing
PA: Universal Computer Systems, Inc.
  6700 Hollister St
  Houston TX 77040
  713 718-1800

(G-12436)
TOTAL RENAL CARE INC
Also Called: Home Dialysis of Dayton South
3030 S Dixie Dr (45409-1516)
PHONE..................................937 294-6711
James K Hilger,
EMP: 40
SQ FT: 14,095 Publicly Held
SIC: 8092 8011 Kidney dialysis centers; clinic, operated by physicians
HQ: Total Renal Care, Inc.
  2000 16th St
  Denver CO 80202
  303 405-2100

(G-12437)
VAN BUREN DENTAL ASSOCIATES
1950 S Smithville Rd (45420-1446)
PHONE..................................937 253-9115
Fax: 937 253-4990
Michael C Dahm DDS, Owner
Michael Dahm, Principal
Jo Dellon, Manager
EMP: 30
SQ FT: 2,500
SALES (est): 1.5MM Privately Held
SIC: 8021 Dentists' office

(G-12438)
WALGREEN CO
Also Called: Walgreens
4497 Far Hills Ave (45429-2405)
PHONE..................................937 396-1358
Fax: 937 396-1355
Kelly Dewald, Pharmacist
John Fawer, Manager
Eric Olmstead, Manager
EMP: 30
SALES (corp-wide): 118.2B Publicly Held
WEB: www.walgreens.com
SIC: 5912 7384 Drug stores; photofinishing laboratory
HQ: Walgreen Co.
  200 Wilmot Rd
  Deerfield IL 60015
  847 315-2500

(G-12439)
WRIGHT STATE UNIVERSITY
Also Called: Cox Institute
3525 Southern Blvd (45429-1221)
PHONE..................................937 298-4331
Amanda Dahlman, Engineer
Diane Myers, Branch Mgr
Guang Z LI, Manager
Sidney Pinkus, Exec Dir
John M Ballester, Emerg Med Spec
EMP: 45
SALES (corp-wide): 238.1MM Privately Held
WEB: www.wright.edu
SIC: 8733 8221 Medical research; university
PA: Wright State University
  3640 Colonel Glenn Hwy
  Dayton OH 45435
  937 775-3333

Kidron
Wayne County

(G-12440)
CHRISTIAN SCHOOLS INC
Also Called: Central Christian School
3970 Kidron Rd (44636)
P.O. Box 9 (44636-0009)
PHONE..................................330 857-7311
Fax: 330 857-7331
Eugene Miller, Superintendent
Patrick Helmuth, Business Mgr
Russell Miller, Maintenance Dir
Nussbaum Steve, Network Tech
Bethany Nussbaum, Director
EMP: 55
SALES (est): 4.9MM Privately Held
SIC: 8211 8351 Private combined elementary & secondary school; private senior high school; preschool center

(G-12441)
JILCO INDUSTRIES INC (PA)
Also Called: Preferred Airparts
11234 Hackett Rd (44636)
P.O. Box 12 (44636-0012)
PHONE..................................330 698-0280
Fax: 330 698-3164
Ken Stoltzfus Jr, President
Brian Stoltzfus, Corp Secy
Colby Stoltfus, Vice Pres
Nate Berky, Sales Mgr
Diana Feller, Accounts Mgr
◆ EMP: 46
SQ FT: 78,000
SALES (est): 15.5MM Privately Held
WEB: www.preferredairparts.com
SIC: 5088 5599 4522 Aircraft & parts; aircraft instruments, equipment or parts; nonscheduled charter services

(G-12442)
KIDRON AUCTION INC
4885 Kidron Rd (44636)
PHONE..................................330 857-2641
John Sprunger, President
EMP: 50
SQ FT: 60,000
SALES (est): 7.7MM Privately Held
WEB: www.kidronauction.com
SIC: 5154 Auctioning livestock

(G-12443)
KIDRON ELECTRIC INC
Also Called: Kidron Electric & Mech Contrs
5358 Kidron Rd (44636)
P.O. Box 248 (44636-0248)
PHONE..................................330 857-2871
Fax: 330 857-2831
Carrie Neuenschwander, Principal
Jon Baker, Sales Staff
Terry Wenger, Sales Staff
EMP: 30 EST: 1938
SQ FT: 50,000
SALES (est): 6.1MM Privately Held
WEB: www.kidronelectric.com
SIC: 1731 1711 General electrical contractor; warm air heating & air conditioning contractor; plumbing contractors

(G-12444)
MILLER HOMES OF KIDRON LLC
6397 Kidron Rd (44636)
P.O. Box 212 (44636-0212)
PHONE..................................330 857-0161
Roy Miller, Mng Member
EMP: 26
SALES (est): 1.1MM Privately Held
SIC: 1521 New construction, single-family houses

Killbuck
Holmes County

(G-12445)
KILLBUCK SAVINGS BANK CO INC (HQ)
165 N Main St (44637-9795)
P.O. Box 407 (44637-0407)
PHONE..................................330 276-4881
Fax: 330 276-0591
Craig Lawhead, President
Eric Roll, President
Vic Weaver, Exec VP
Marion Troyer, Senior VP
Theodore Thorpe, Assistant VP
EMP: 40
SQ FT: 12,000
SALES: 19.8MM Publicly Held
WEB: www.killbuckbank.com
SIC: 6022 State trust companies accepting deposits, commercial

Kimbolton
Guernsey County

(G-12446)
CARDIDA CORPORATION (PA)
74978 Broadhead Rd (43749-9747)
PHONE..................................740 439-4359
Fax: 740 432-7582
Carl Larue, President
Bill La Rue, Vice Pres
Bill L Rue, Marketing Staff
Dan La Rue, Admin Sec
Karen Striff, Administration
EMP: 50
SALES: 2.6MM Privately Held
WEB: www.cardidaresortgroup.com
SIC: 7011 6552 Resort hotel; land subdividers & developers, commercial

(G-12447)
SALT FORK RESORT CLUB INC
74978 Broadhead Rd (43749-9747)
PHONE..................................740 498-8116
Fax: 740 498-8157
Karl Larue, President
EMP: 1000
SALES: 1.8MM Privately Held
SIC: 7011 7997 Resort hotel; membership sports & recreation clubs

Kings Mills
Warren County

(G-12448)
KINGS ISLAND COMPANY
6300 Kings Island Dr (45034)
PHONE..................................513 754-5700
Carl Lindner, President
Jamie Gaffney, Vice Pres
Jim Newport, Buyer
Deborah Day, Accounting Mgr
Mike Koontz, Finance
▲ EMP: 220
SALES (est): 23.7MM
SALES (corp-wide): 1.3B Publicly Held
SIC: 7996 Amusement parks
PA: Cedar Fair, L.P.
  1 Cedar Point Dr
  Sandusky OH 44870
  419 626-0830

(G-12449)
KINGS ISLAND PARK LLC
6300 Kings Island Dr (45034)
P.O. Box 901 (45034-0901)
PHONE..................................513 754-5901
Fax: 513 754-5725
Chris Brayton, Facilities Mgr
Cindy Gunther, Human Res Dir
Greg Scheid, Branch Mgr
EMP: 200
SALES (corp-wide): 1.3B Publicly Held
WEB: www.cedarfair.com
SIC: 7996 Theme park, amusement
HQ: Kings Island Park Llc
  1 Cedar Point Dr
  Sandusky OH 44870
  419 626-0830

Kingston
Ross County

(G-12450)
HAROLD TATMAN & SONS ENTPS INC
Also Called: Tatman, Harold & Sons
9171 State Route 180 (45644-9547)
P.O. Box 448, Adelphi (43101-0448)
PHONE..................................740 655-2880
Fax: 740 655-2887
EMP: 30 EST: 1963
SALES (est): 4.7MM Privately Held
SIC: 5199 Whol Nondurable Goods

Kingston - Ross County (G-12451)

(G-12451)
KINGSTON NATIONAL BANK INC (PA)
2 N Main St (45644-9745)
P.O. Box 613 (45644-0613)
PHONE.....................740 642-2191
Fax: 740 642-2195
Phil Evans, *President*
Ann Blake, *Vice Pres*
Susan Hixson, *Controller*
Lisa Wiseman, *Manager*
Larry Ellinger, *Officer*
EMP: 36
SQ FT: 2,000
SALES: 11.7MM **Privately Held**
WEB: www.kingstonnationalbank.com
SIC: 6021 National commercial banks

Kinsman
Trumbull County

(G-12452)
BAYLOFF STMPED PDTS KNSMAN INC
8091 State Route 5 (44428-9628)
PHONE.....................330 876-4511
Fax: 330 876-4632
Richard Bayer, *President*
Rufus S Day Jr, *Principal*
Dixon Morgan, *Principal*
M E Newcomer, *Principal*
Dan Moore, *Vice Pres*
EMP: 80
SQ FT: 115,000
SALES (est): 14.6MM **Privately Held**
SIC: 3469 7692 3444 3315 Stamping metal for the trade; welding repair; sheet metalwork; steel wire & related products

(G-12453)
BOYDS KINSMAN HOME INC
7929 State Route 5 (44428-9727)
P.O. Box 315 (44428-0315)
PHONE.....................330 876-5581
Fax: 330 876-8804
Paula Ruby, *Administration*
EMP: 39
SQ FT: 7,200
SALES: 2.9MM **Privately Held**
SIC: 8052 8059 Home for the mentally retarded, with health care; home for the mentally retarded, exc. skilled or intermediate

(G-12454)
PITMARK SERVICES INC
7925 State Route 5 (44428-9783)
P.O. Box 176 (44428-0176)
PHONE.....................330 876-2217
Anthony J Pitoscia, *Owner*
EMP: 50
SALES (est): 3.2MM **Privately Held**
SIC: 8742 Marketing consulting services

Kirkersville
Licking County

(G-12455)
LIVIN CARE ALTER OF KIRKE INC
Also Called: Pine Kirk Nursing Home
205 E Main St (43033-7517)
P.O. Box 221 (43033-0221)
PHONE.....................740 927-3209
Fax: 740 898-1993
Thomas Rosser, *President*
Karen Rosser, *Principal*
Denver Drennen, *Director*
Rebecca Ginnery, *Director*
Alison Herges, *Director*
EMP: 35
SALES (est): 1.5MM **Privately Held**
SIC: 8051 Skilled nursing care facilities

(G-12456)
LIVING CARE ALTERNATIVES
205 E Main St (43033-7517)
P.O. Box 223 (43033-0223)
PHONE.....................740 927-3209
Thomas Rosser, *Manager*

Bruce Miller, *Director*
Wilma Moody, *Nursing Dir*
Mary Crowford, *Social Dir*
Sheena Orr, *Food Svc Dir*
EMP: 35 **Privately Held**
SIC: 8051 Skilled nursing care facilities
PA: Living Care Alternatives
855 S Sunbury Rd
Westerville OH

Kirtland
Lake County

(G-12457)
LAKE METROPARKS
Also Called: Lake Farm Park
8800 Chardon Rd (44094-9520)
PHONE.....................440 256-2122
Fax: 440 256-2147
Lawrence Elswick, *Project Mgr*
Shawn Parker, *Park Mgr*
Andrew Baker, *Manager*
Barbara Tokar, *Info Tech Mgr*
Rick Cooper, *Officer*
EMP: 80
SQ FT: 28,107 **Privately Held**
WEB: www.lakemetroparks.com
SIC: 7999 Recreation services
PA: Lake Metroparks
11211 Spear Rd
Painesville OH 44077
440 639-7275

(G-12458)
MR EXCAVATOR INC
8616 Euclid Chardon Rd (44094-9586)
PHONE.....................440 256-2008
Fax: 440 256-0036
William A Flesher, *President*
Patricia Flesher, *Principal*
Tim Flesher, *Vice Pres*
Bob Flesher, *Chief Mktg Ofcr*
Elizabeth Miranda, *Manager*
EMP: 85
SALES (est): 27.9MM **Privately Held**
WEB: www.mrexcavator.com
SIC: 1794 Excavation & grading, building construction

La Rue
Marion County

(G-12459)
STOFCHECK AMBULANCE SVC INC (PA)
220 S High St (43332-8881)
P.O. Box 333 (43332-0333)
PHONE.....................740 499-2200
Fax: 740 499-3617
Edward Stofcheck, *President*
Edward Stofcheck Sr, *President*
EMP: 30
SALES (est): 7MM **Privately Held**
SIC: 4119 Ambulance service

Lagrange
Lorain County

(G-12460)
MERCY HEALTH
105 Opportunity Way (44050-9018)
PHONE.....................440 355-4206
Cindi Keith, *Office Mgr*
EMP: 28
SALES (corp-wide): 4.2B **Privately Held**
SIC: 8011 Offices & clinics of medical doctors
PA: Mercy Health
1701 Mercy Health Pl
Cincinnati OH 45237
513 639-2800

(G-12461)
RURAL LORAIN COUNTY WATER AUTH
42401 State Route 303 (44050-9717)
P.O. Box 567 (44050-0567)
PHONE.....................440 355-5121

Fax: 440 355-6628
George Green, *President*
Tim Mahoney, *Manager*
Daniel Martin, *Exec Dir*
EMP: 60
SALES: 15.1MM **Privately Held**
WEB: www.rlcwa.com
SIC: 4941 Water supply

(G-12462)
WEST ROOFING SYSTEMS INC (PA)
121 Commerce Dr (44050-9491)
PHONE.....................800 356-5748
Fax: 440 355-8106
Jeff Johnson, *Prdtn Mgr*
Karen Swirs, *Manager*
▲ **EMP:** 39
SQ FT: 10,700
SALES (est): 8.9MM **Privately Held**
WEB: www.westroofingsystems.com
SIC: 1761 1542 Roofing contractor; commercial & office building, new construction; commercial & office buildings, renovation & repair

Lake Waynoka
Brown County

(G-12463)
LAKE WYNOKA PRPRTY OWNERS ASSN
1 Waynoka Dr (45171-9749)
PHONE.....................937 446-3774
Fax: 937 446-3253
Vickie Johnson, *Principal*
Timothy O'Farrell, *Executive*
EMP: 30
SQ FT: 1,100
SALES (est): 1.7MM **Privately Held**
WEB: www.lakewaynoka.com
SIC: 7997 Membership sports & recreation clubs

Lakeside
Ottawa County

(G-12464)
LAKESIDE ASSOCIATION
236 Walnut Ave (43440-1400)
PHONE.....................419 798-4461
Fax: 419 798-5033
Wendy Eller, *Vice Pres*
Thomas Derby, *CFO*
Becky Couch, *Manager*
Dave Geyer, *Manager*
Marian Shepard, *Manager*
EMP: 30
SQ FT: 3,500
SALES: 8.2MM **Privately Held**
WEB: www.lakesideohio.com
SIC: 8621 Professional membership organizations

(G-12465)
NORTH SHORE RETIREMENT CMNTY
Also Called: OTTERBEIN NORTH SHORE
9400 E Northshore Blvd (43440-1337)
PHONE.....................419 798-8203
Fax: 419 798-4662
Lisa Hart, *Exec Dir*
EMP: 45
SQ FT: 22,058
SALES: 1.5MM **Privately Held**
SIC: 8052 Intermediate care facilities

Lakeside Marblehead
Ottawa County

(G-12466)
SOUTH BEACH RESORT
8620 E Bayshore Rd (43440-9719)
PHONE.....................419 798-4900
Fax: 419 798-0135
Kathy Kolar, *President*
Fred Kolar, *COO*
EMP: 50

SALES (est): 1.8MM **Privately Held**
SIC: 7011 Resort hotel

Lakeview
Logan County

(G-12467)
ACRUX INVESTIGATION AGENCY (PA)
8823 Township Road 239 (43331-9321)
PHONE.....................937 842-5780
Fax: 937 599-4338
Alana Robinaugh, *Partner*
Deborah Proffrt, *Co-Owner*
Sally Robb, *Purch Mgr*
Don Proffitt, *Information Mgr*
William Maddox, *MIS Staff*
EMP: 300
SALES: 9MM **Privately Held**
SIC: 7381 Detective agency; security guard service

(G-12468)
SURMOUNT SOLUTIONS GROUP LLC
8823 Township Road 239 (43331-9321)
PHONE.....................937 842-5780
Chris Prickett, *CEO*
Deb Martin-Proffitt, *COO*
EMP: 31 **EST:** 2005
SALES: 1.1MM **Privately Held**
SIC: 7382 Security systems services

Lakewood
Cuyahoga County

(G-12469)
12000 EDGEWATER DRIVE LLC
12000 Edgewater Dr (44107-1784)
PHONE.....................216 520-1250
Frank Sinito,
EMP: 99 **EST:** 2014
SALES (est): 954.8K **Privately Held**
SIC: 6513 Apartment building operators

(G-12470)
AMERIFIRST FINANCIAL CORP
14701 Detroit Ave Ste 750 (44107-4109)
PHONE.....................216 452-5120
EMP: 89
SALES (corp-wide): 166.8MM **Privately Held**
SIC: 6162 Mortgage bankers & correspondents
PA: Amerifirst Financial Corporation
950 Trade Centre Way # 400
Portage MI 49002
269 324-4240

(G-12471)
AREA TEMPS INC
14801 Detroit Ave (44107-3909)
PHONE.....................216 227-8200
Tammy Jett, *General Mgr*
Gail Enders, *Principal*
EMP: 1383
SALES (corp-wide): 87.8MM **Privately Held**
SIC: 7363 Temporary help service
PA: Area Temps, Inc.
4511 Rockside Rd Ste 190
Independence OH 44131
216 781-5350

(G-12472)
BROWNSTONE PRIVATE CHILD CARE
18225 Sloane Ave (44107-3109)
PHONE.....................216 221-1470
Fax: 216 333-9461
Nancy Rafferty, *President*
Alice Mann, *Corp Secy*
Maggie Rafferty, *Director*
EMP: 35
SQ FT: 10,000
SALES (est): 1.7MM **Privately Held**
SIC: 8351 Preschool center

GEOGRAPHIC SECTION
Lakewood - Cuyahoga County (G-12497)

(G-12473)
CITY OF LAKEWOOD
Also Called: Senior Center West
16024 Madison Ave (44107-5616)
PHONE..................216 521-1515
Fax: 216 521-2613
Paulette McMonagle, *Director*
EMP: 25 **Privately Held**
SIC: 8322 Senior citizens' center or association
PA: City Of Lakewood
    12650 Detroit Ave
    Lakewood OH 44107
    216 521-7580

(G-12474)
CORNUCOPIA INC
Also Called: NATURES BIN
18120 Sloane Ave (44107-3108)
PHONE..................216 521-4600
Fax: 216 521-9460
David Dorosy, *Finance Mgr*
Nancy Cuttler, *Exec Dir*
Scott Duennes, *Exec Dir*
Sandy Gross, *Director*
Kenya Banks, *Executive*
EMP: 36
SQ FT: 6,000
SALES: 2.4MM **Privately Held**
SIC: 8331 5499 Vocational rehabilitation agency; health foods

(G-12475)
CRESTMONT NURSING HOME N CORP (PA)
Also Called: Crestmont North
13330 Detroit Ave (44107-2850)
PHONE..................216 228-9550
Fax: 216 521-2121
Elias J Coury, *President*
Norman Fox, *Corp Secy*
Steve Demeter, *CFO*
Jim McConnaughy, *HR Admin*
Jean Miller, *Office Mgr*
EMP: 110
SALES (est): 7.9MM **Privately Held**
SIC: 8051 Convalescent home with continuous nursing care

(G-12476)
CRESTMONT NURSING HOME N CORP
13330 Detroit Ave (44107-2850)
PHONE..................216 228-9550
Wendy Tyler, *Administration*
EMP: 100
SQ FT: 24,209
SALES (corp-wide): 7.9MM **Privately Held**
SIC: 8051 Convalescent home with continuous nursing care
PA: Crestmont Nursing Home North Corp.
    13330 Detroit Ave
    Lakewood OH 44107
    216 228-9550

(G-12477)
ETECH-SYSTEMS LLC
14600 Detroit Ave # 1500 (44107-4207)
PHONE..................216 221-6600
Walter Zaremba, *CEO*
Katherine Kearney, *Admin Asst*
Gary Biales,
Robert Steadley,
Al Sulin,
EMP: 70
SQ FT: 12,000
SALES (est): 5.3MM **Privately Held**
SIC: 1542 1522 1521 Shopping center construction; apartment building construction; new construction, single-family houses

(G-12478)
FIRST FDRAL SAV LN ASSN LKWOOD (PA)
14806 Detroit Ave (44107-3910)
PHONE..................216 221-7300
Fax: 216 226-0622
Thomas Fraser, *CEO*
W Charles Geiger III, *Ch of Bd*
Judy Platek, *Assistant VP*
Jeffrey Bechtel, *Vice Pres*
Paul Capka, *Vice Pres*
EMP: 130
SQ FT: 12,000
SALES: 60.9MM **Privately Held**
WEB: www.ffl.net
SIC: 6035 Federal savings & loan associations

(G-12479)
FORTUNEFAVORSTHE BOLD LLC
11716 Detroit Ave (44107-3002)
PHONE..................216 469-2845
Jennifer Ilgauskas, *President*
Mary Boyer, *Office Mgr*
EMP: 25
SQ FT: 6,980
SALES (est): 185.5K **Privately Held**
SIC: 8011 Offices & clinics of medical doctors

(G-12480)
HANSON SERVICES INC (PA)
17017 Madison Ave (44107-3501)
P.O. Box 771222, Cleveland (44107-0051)
PHONE..................216 226-5425
Fax: 216 226-5623
Mary Ann Hanson, *President*
Kanchan Adhikary, *CFO*
Peggy Kilroy, *Human Resources*
Amy Johnston, *Mktg Dir*
Laura Hazen, *Director*
EMP: 125 **EST:** 1996
SQ FT: 2,200
SALES (est): 8MM **Privately Held**
SIC: 8082 Visiting nurse service

(G-12481)
HEALTHSPAN INTEGRATED CARE
Also Called: Kaiser Foundation Health Plan
14600 Detroit Ave Ste 700 (44107-4219)
PHONE..................216 362-2277
Belva Denmark, *Director*
EMP: 25
SALES (corp-wide): 4.2B **Privately Held**
SIC: 6324 Hospital & medical service plans
HQ: Healthspan Integrated Care
    1001 Lakeside Ave E # 1200
    Cleveland OH 44114
    216 621-5600

(G-12482)
ICE LAND USA LAKEWOOD
14740 Lakewood Hts Blvd (44107-5901)
PHONE..................216 529-1200
Patrick Krausman, *Manager*
EMP: 26
SALES (est): 381.4K **Privately Held**
SIC: 7999 Ice skating rink operation

(G-12483)
IMCD US LLC (HQ)
14725 Detroit Ave Ste 300 (44107-4124)
PHONE..................216 228-8900
John L Mastrantoni, *President*
Loretta Storch, *Business Mgr*
Alison M Azar, *Vice Pres*
Bruce D Jarosz, *CFO*
Robin Schade, *Controller*
▲ **EMP:** 46
SALES (est): 259.3MM
SALES (corp-wide): 1.8B **Privately Held**
WEB: www.mfcachat.com
SIC: 5169 Chemicals & allied products
PA: Imcd N.V.
    Wilhelminaplein 32
    Rotterdam
    102 908-684

(G-12484)
KANSAS CITY HARDWOOD CORP
17717 Hilliard Rd (44107-5332)
PHONE..................913 621-1975
Dan Schneider, *President*
Robert Vogel, *Corp Secy*
John Hawkinson, *Vice Pres*
Windy Hargis, *Manager*
EMP: 28
SQ FT: 45,000
SALES (est): 6.3MM **Privately Held**
SIC: 5031 Hardboard

(G-12485)
L S C SERVICE CORP
14306 Detroit Ave Apt 237 (44107-4450)
PHONE..................216 521-7260
Lawrence Faulhaber, *Director*
EMP: 35
SALES (est): 532.4K **Privately Held**
SIC: 6513 Apartment hotel operation

(G-12486)
LAKEWOOD CATHOLIC ACADEMY
Also Called: Holy Family
14808 Lake Ave (44107-1352)
PHONE..................216 521-4352
Charles P Battiato, *Partner*
Brian E Powers, *Partner*
Paul Nickels, *Webmaster*
Kathleen Ogrin, *Director*
EMP: 30 **Privately Held**
SIC: 8351 Child day care services
PA: Lakewood Catholic Academy
    14808 Lake Ave
    Lakewood OH 44107

(G-12487)
LAKEWOOD CITY SCHOOL DISTRICT
Also Called: Winterhurst Ice Rink
14740 Lakewood Hts Blvd (44107-5901)
PHONE..................216 529-4400
Fax: 216 529-6884
Tim Starks, *Manager*
EMP: 50
SALES (corp-wide): 117.8MM **Privately Held**
SIC: 8211 7999 Public elementary & secondary schools; ice skating rink operation
PA: Lakewood City School District
    1470 Warren Rd
    Cleveland OH 44107
    216 529-4092

(G-12488)
LAKEWOOD CLVELAND FMLY MED CTR
16215 Madison Ave (44107-5618)
PHONE..................216 227-2162
Carl Culley MD, *Director*
Robert Colacarro, *Deputy Dir*
Joyce Booth, *Executive*
EMP: 25
SALES (est): 1.8MM **Privately Held**
SIC: 8011 Primary care medical clinic

(G-12489)
LAKEWOOD COMMUNITY CARE CENTER
2019 Woodward Ave (44107-5635)
PHONE..................216 226-0080
Fax: 216 226-8995
Pam Meade, *Exec Dir*
Gay Henrikson, *Director*
EMP: 30
SQ FT: 8,000
SALES: 639K **Privately Held**
SIC: 8351 Preschool center

(G-12490)
LAKEWOOD HEALTH CARE CENTER
Also Called: Ennis Court
13315 Detroit Ave (44107-2849)
PHONE..................216 226-3103
Fax: 216 226-8344
Patrice Campbell, *President*
Louis Klein, *Director*
EMP: 120
SQ FT: 20,000
SALES (est): 4.2MM **Privately Held**
SIC: 8051 Extended care facility

(G-12491)
LAKEWOOD HOSPITAL ASSOCIATION (HQ)
14519 Detroit Ave (44107-4383)
PHONE..................216 529-7160
Fax: 216 529-7161
Fred Degrandis, *CEO*
W C Geiger III, *Vice Pres*
Jay Justice, *Maint Spvr*
Krisin Broadben, *Med Doctor*
Rose Ketler, *Director*
EMP: 530
SQ FT: 100,000
SALES: 94MM
SALES (corp-wide): 8B **Privately Held**
SIC: 8062 General medical & surgical hospitals
PA: The Cleveland Clinic Foundation
    9500 Euclid Ave
    Cleveland OH 44195
    216 636-8335

(G-12492)
NEW YORK LIFE INSURANCE CO
14600 Detroit Ave Ste 900 (44107-4221)
PHONE..................216 221-1100
Fax: 216 221-3229
George Hewlett, *Vice Pres*
Bill Tate, *VP Finance*
Stephanie Pittman, *Manager*
David Baker, *Agent*
Calinda Stringer, *Assistant*
EMP: 60
SALES (corp-wide): 27.9B **Privately Held**
SIC: 6311 Life insurance
PA: New York Life Insurance Company
    51 Madison Ave Bsmt 1b
    New York NY 10010
    212 576-7000

(G-12493)
ON-CALL NURSING INC
15644 Madison Ave (44107-5622)
PHONE..................216 577-8890
Jennifer Fox, *President*
EMP: 99
SALES (est): 682.1K **Privately Held**
SIC: 8052 8059 8082 Intermediate care facilities; personal care facility; home for the mentally retarded, exc. skilled or intermediate; home health care services; visiting nurse service

(G-12494)
PALLET DISTRIBUTORS INC (PA)
Also Called: E-Pallet
14701 Detroit Ave Ste 610 (44107-4180)
PHONE..................888 805-9670
Greg Fronk, *President*
Sandy Riedel, *Vice Pres*
EMP: 105
SQ FT: 3,500
SALES (est): 45.6MM **Privately Held**
SIC: 5031 5085 Pallets, wood; plastic pallets

(G-12495)
PRUDENTIAL LUCIEN REALTY
Also Called: Century 21
18630 Detroit Ave (44107-3202)
PHONE..................216 226-4673
Fax: 216 331-9504
Ronald Lucien, *President*
Chris Bergin, *Broker*
Tim Cunningham, *Real Est Agnt*
Joseph Dill, *Real Est Agnt*
Eric Lowrey, *Real Est Agnt*
EMP: 50
SALES (est): 3.1MM **Privately Held**
WEB: www.lucienrealty.com
SIC: 6531 Real estate agent, residential

(G-12496)
RAD-CON INC (PA)
Also Called: Entec International Systems
13001 Athens Ave Ste 300 (44107-6246)
PHONE..................440 871-5720
Fax: 440 871-2948
David R Blackman, *President*
Christopher Messina, *President*
Michael McDonald, *Vice Pres*
Sean McGreer, *Vice Pres*
Christopher J Messina, *Vice Pres*
EMP: 26
SQ FT: 6,000
SALES: 10MM **Privately Held**
WEB: www.rad-con.com
SIC: 8711 3567 Engineering services; industrial furnaces & ovens

(G-12497)
REALTY ONE INC
1495 Warren Rd Ste 201 (44107-3931)
PHONE..................216 221-6585
Fax: 216 221-1956
Richard Barber, *Manager*

Lakewood - Cuyahoga County (G-12498)

EMP: 40
SALES (corp-wide): 67.8MM **Privately Held**
WEB: www.realty-1st.com
SIC: 6531 Real estate brokers & agents
HQ: Realty One, Inc.
  800 W Saint Clair Ave
  Cleveland OH 44113
  216 328-2500

(G-12498)
RETINA ASSOCIATE OF CLEVELAND
14725 Detroit Ave Ste 200 (44107-4125)
PHONE.....................216 221-2878
Fax: 216 221-2594
Warren Laurita, *Administration*
EMP: 35
SALES (corp-wide): 10.8MM **Privately Held**
SIC: 8011 Ophthalmologist
PA: Retina Associate of Cleveland Inc
  3401 Entp Pkwy Ste 300
  Beachwood OH 44122
  216 831-5700

(G-12499)
ROUNDSTONE MANAGEMENT LTD
15422 Detroit Ave (44107-3830)
PHONE.....................440 617-0333
Mike Schroeder, *President*
Michael Schroeder, *President*
Dave Konrad, *Vice Pres*
Jim Mohler, *Regl Sales Mgr*
Robert Pace, *Regl Sales Mgr*
EMP: 32
SALES (est): 2.7MM **Privately Held**
SIC: 8741 Business management

(G-12500)
SECURITY HUT INC (PA)
Also Called: Secura Fact
18614 Detroit Ave (44107-3202)
PHONE.....................216 226-0461
Fax: 216 226-6742
Charles Brooks, *President*
EMP: 150
SALES: 500K **Privately Held**
WEB: www.securityhut.com
SIC: 7381 7375 Private investigator; security guard service; information retrieval services

(G-12501)
ST AUGUSTINE CORPORATION
1341 Nicholson Ave (44107-2735)
PHONE.....................216 939-7600
Patrick Gareau, *President*
EMP: 400
SQ FT: 256,593
SALES: 18MM **Privately Held**
SIC: 8741 8052 8051 Nursing & personal care facility management; intermediate care facilities; skilled nursing care facilities

(G-12502)
YOUNG MNS CHRSTN ASSN CLVELAND
Also Called: Lakewood Y
16915 Detroit Ave (44107-3620)
PHONE.....................216 521-8400
Fax: 216 521-2992
Sam Kincaid, *Business Mgr*
Gary Brick, *Director*
EMP: 39
SQ FT: 21,781
SALES (corp-wide): 29.2MM **Privately Held**
SIC: 8641 7991 8351 7032 Youth organizations; physical fitness facilities; child day care services; youth camps; individual & family services
PA: Young Men's Christian Association Of Cleveland
  1801 Superior Ave E # 130
  Cleveland OH 44114
  216 781-1337

(G-12503)
ZARCAL ZANESVILLE LLC
14600 Detroit Ave # 1500 (44107-4207)
PHONE.....................216 226-2132
Edward Kiss, *Principal*

EMP: 60
SALES (est): 1.5MM **Privately Held**
SIC: 8741 Business management

(G-12504)
ZAREMBA GROUP LLC
14600 Detroit Ave (44107-4207)
PHONE.....................216 221-6600
David Zaremba, *CEO*
Alan J Bellis, *Project Mgr*
Beth Sullivan, *Project Mgr*
Marty McKrell, *Maint Spvr*
Ron Wampler, *Maint Spvr*
EMP: 110 EST: 1997
SQ FT: 12,000
SALES (est): 18.5MM **Privately Held**
WEB: www.zarembagroup.com
SIC: 6552 8111 6531 Land subdividers & developers, commercial; legal services; real estate managers; real estate agent, commercial

(G-12505)
ZAREMBA ZANESVILLE LLC
14600 Detroit Ave # 1500 (44107-4207)
PHONE.....................216 221-6600
Robert F Steadley,
EMP: 50
SALES (est): 1.7MM **Privately Held**
SIC: 6531 Real estate agents & managers

Lancaster
Fairfield County

(G-12506)
ACCURATE MECHANICAL INC
566 Mill Park Dr (43130-7744)
PHONE.....................740 654-5898
EMP: 40
SALES (corp-wide): 14.1MM **Privately Held**
SIC: 5074 5063 3499 1711 Heating equipment (hydronic); electrical supplies; aerosol valves, metal; septic system construction
PA: Accurate Mechanical, Inc.
  3001 River Rd
  Chillicothe OH
  740 775-5005

(G-12507)
ALLERGY & ASTHMA INC
2405 N Columbus St # 270 (43130-8185)
PHONE.....................740 654-8623
H C Nataraj, *Branch Mgr*
EMP: 28
SALES (corp-wide): 2.1MM **Privately Held**
SIC: 8011 Allergist
PA: Allergy & Asthma, Inc.
  5965 E Broad St Ste 320
  Columbus OH 43213
  614 864-6649

(G-12508)
ALTERNACARE HOME HEALTH INC
1566 Monmouth Dr Ste 103 (43130-8048)
PHONE.....................740 689-1589
Diane Stuckey, *President*
Shawna Martens, *Principal*
Annie Romine, *CFO*
Ashley Byers, *Human Res Dir*
Carrie Roberts, *Marketing Staff*
EMP: 43
SQ FT: 2,421
SALES (est): 2.3MM **Privately Held**
WEB: www.alternacare.biz
SIC: 8082 Visiting nurse service

(G-12509)
ARBOR VIEW FAMILY MEDICINE INC
2405 N Columbus St # 200 (43130-8185)
PHONE.....................740 687-3386
Fax: 740 687-5898
David Scoggin, *Principal*
Martha Scott, *Office Mgr*
Patrick Kobelenske, *Manager*
EMP: 33 EST: 1997
SALES (est): 3.1MM **Privately Held**
WEB: www.avfm.org
SIC: 8071 Medical laboratories

(G-12510)
BOB-BOYD FORD INC (PA)
Also Called: Bobboyd Auto Family
2840 N Columbus St (43130-8128)
P.O. Box 767 (43130-0767)
PHONE.....................614 860-0606
Robert G Dawes, *President*
Bobby Dawes, *General Mgr*
Michael D Bornstein, *Principal*
Mark Falls, *Principal*
Randy Ott, *Parts Mgr*
EMP: 60
SALES (est): 26.4MM **Privately Held**
WEB: www.bobboyd.com
SIC: 5511 7538 Automobiles, new & used; general automotive repair shops

(G-12511)
BROOKDALE SNIOR LVING CMMNTIES
Also Called: Sterling House of Lancaster
241 Whittier Dr S (43130-5717)
PHONE.....................740 681-9903
Fax: 740 681-9344
Veronica Finnefrock, *Corp Comm Staff*
Michael Weeks, *Manager*
EMP: 28
SALES (corp-wide): 4.7B **Publicly Held**
WEB: www.assisted.com
SIC: 8059 Rest home, with health care
HQ: Brookdale Senior Living Communities, Inc.
  6737 W Wa St Ste 2300
  Milwaukee WI 53214
  414 918-5000

(G-12512)
C M S ENTERPRISES INC (PA)
Also Called: ServiceMaster
664 S Columbus St (43130-4661)
PHONE.....................740 653-1940
Fax: 740 653-4958
Robert Marshall, *President*
EMP: 25
SQ FT: 8,000
SALES (est): 3.3MM **Privately Held**
SIC: 7349 1799 7217 Building maintenance services; post-disaster renovations; carpet & rug cleaning plant

(G-12513)
CARLETON REALTY INC
826 N Memorial Dr (43130-2567)
PHONE.....................740 653-5200
John Grady, *Sales Staff*
Lauren Henley, *Sales Staff*
Renee Schmelzer, *Branch Mgr*
EMP: 47
SALES (corp-wide): 2.9MM **Privately Held**
SIC: 6531 Real estate agent, residential
PA: Carleton Realty Inc
  580 W Schrock Rd
  Westerville OH 43081
  614 431-5700

(G-12514)
CARRIAGE COURT COMPANY INC
Also Called: Carriage Court Community
800 Becks Knob Rd Ofc (43130-8804)
PHONE.....................740 654-4422
Fax: 740 654-4402
Debbie Cook, *Manager*
EMP: 35 **Privately Held**
SIC: 8059 8361 8051 Personal care home, with health care; residential care; skilled nursing care facilities
PA: Carriage Court Company, Inc.
  2041 Riverside Dr Ste 100
  Columbus OH

(G-12515)
CELLCO PARTNERSHIP
Also Called: Verizon Wireless
1926 N Memorial Dr (43130-1665)
PHONE.....................740 652-9540
Fax: 740 652-9653
EMP: 71
SALES (corp-wide): 126B **Publicly Held**
SIC: 4812 Cellular telephone services
HQ: Cellco Partnership
  1 Verizon Way
  Basking Ridge NJ 07920

(G-12516)
CHEERS CHALET
Also Called: Cheers & Lakeside Chalet
1211 Coonpath Rd Nw (43130-8999)
PHONE.....................740 654-9036
Fax: 740 654-6661
Gary Krasnosky, *Partner*
EMP: 25
SALES (est): 1MM **Privately Held**
WEB: www.cheerschalet.com
SIC: 7299 5812 Banquet hall facilities; eating places

(G-12517)
CINTAS CORPORATION NO 2
2250 Commerce St (43130-9363)
PHONE.....................740 687-6230
Fax: 740 687-4668
Jason Hill, *General Mgr*
EMP: 50
SQ FT: 35,000
SALES (corp-wide): 5.3B **Publicly Held**
WEB: www.cintas-corp.com
SIC: 7213 Linen supply
HQ: Cintas Corporation No. 2
  6800 Cintas Blvd
  Mason OH 45040

(G-12518)
CITY OF LANCASTER
Also Called: Lancaster Municipal Gas
1424 Campground Rd (43130-9503)
PHONE.....................740 687-6670
Fax: 740 653-5708
Michael R Pettit, *Superintendent*
Bill Burrows, *Superintendent*
Cheryl K Lott, *Controller*
Jeff Gerken, *Manager*
Mike Courtney, *Director*
EMP: 25 **Privately Held**
WEB: www.ci.lancaster.oh.us
SIC: 1311 4924 Crude petroleum & natural gas; natural gas distribution
PA: City Of Lancaster
  104 E Main St
  Lancaster OH 43130
  740 687-6617

(G-12519)
CLAYPOOL ELECTRIC INC
Also Called: Claypool Electrical Contg
1275 Lncstr Krkrsville Rd (43130-8969)
PHONE.....................740 653-5683
Fax: 740 653-5729
Charles Claypool, *CEO*
Greg Davis, *President*
John Kern, *Superintendent*
Barbara Claypool, *Corp Secy*
Tucker Brady, *Treasurer*
EMP: 160 EST: 1955
SQ FT: 20,000
SALES (est): 31.3MM **Privately Held**
WEB: www.claypoolelectric.com
SIC: 1731 General electrical contractor

(G-12520)
CMS BUSINESS SERVICES LLC
Also Called: Servicmster Coml Clg Advantage
416 N Mount Pleasant Ave (43130-3134)
PHONE.....................740 687-0577
Teresa Marshall, *Mng Member*
Dan Marshall, *Mng Member*
Renee Stubbs, *Admin Asst*
EMP: 80 EST: 2008
SALES: 1MM **Privately Held**
SIC: 7349 Janitorial service, contract basis

(G-12521)
COMMUNITY ACTION PROGRAM COMM (PA)
Also Called: LANCASTER-FAIRFIELD COMMUNITY
1743 E Main St (43130-9838)
P.O. Box 768 (43130-0768)
PHONE.....................740 653-1711
Fax: 740 653-4462
Kellie Ailes, *Exec Dir*
Donna Fox-Moore, *Director*
Valerie Irion, *Director*
EMP: 100
SQ FT: 3,000
SALES (est): 8MM **Privately Held**
WEB: www.faircaa.org
SIC: 8322 Social service center

GEOGRAPHIC SECTION
Lancaster - Fairfield County (G-12545)

(G-12522)
COMMUNITY ASSISTED LIVING INC
500 N Pierce Ave (43130-2963)
PHONE..................740 653-2575
Cynthia A Lamb, *President*
EMP: 50
SALES (est): 2.6MM **Privately Held**
SIC: 8052 Home for the mentally retarded, with health care

(G-12523)
CORK ENTERPRISES INC
Also Called: Shaw's Inn
123 N Broad St (43130-3702)
PHONE..................740 654-1842
Fax: 740 654-7032
A Bruce Cork, *President*
David Swain, *CTO*
EMP: 50 **EST:** 1946
SALES (est): 1.7MM **Privately Held**
WEB: www.shawsinn.com
SIC: 5812 5813 7011 American restaurant; tavern (drinking places); hotels & motels

(G-12524)
CRESTVIEW MANOR NURSING HOME (PA)
Also Called: CRESTVIEW MANOR I
957 Becks Knob Rd (43130-8800)
PHONE..................740 654-2634
Fax: 740 654-9645
Winfield S Eckert, *President*
Jo Ann Eckert, *Admin Sec*
EMP: 220
SQ FT: 52,000
SALES: 17MM **Privately Held**
SIC: 8051 6513 Extended care facility; apartment building operators

(G-12525)
CRESTVIEW MANOR NURSING HOME
Also Called: Crestview Manor II
925 Becks Knob Rd (43130-8800)
PHONE..................740 654-2634
Winfield S Eckert, *President*
EMP: 110
SALES (corp-wide): 17MM **Privately Held**
SIC: 8051 Extended care facility
PA: Crestview Manor Nursing Home, Inc
   957 Becks Knob Rd
   Lancaster OH 43130
   740 654-2634

(G-12526)
DAGGER JOHNSTON MILLER (PA)
144 E Main St (43130-3712)
P.O. Box 667 (43130-0667)
PHONE..................740 653-6464
Fax: 740 653-8522
Norman J Ogilvie, *Partner*
Mark Bibler, *Partner*
J Jay Hampson, *Partner*
Randy Happeney, *Partner*
Robert E Johnston, *Partner*
EMP: 35
SQ FT: 2,200
SALES (est): 4.5MM **Privately Held**
WEB: www.daggerlaw.com
SIC: 8111 General practice attorney, lawyer

(G-12527)
DISPATCH CONSUMER SERVICES
Also Called: Bag, The
3160 W Fair Ave (43130-9568)
PHONE..................740 687-1893
Fax: 740 687-0799
Donna Holbrook, *Manager*
EMP: 70
SALES (corp-wide): 600.6MM **Privately Held**
SIC: 7319 Distribution of advertising material or sample services
HQ: Dispatch Consumer Services Inc
   5300 Crosswind Dr
   Columbus OH 43228
   740 548-5555

(G-12528)
DREW VENTURES INC (PA)
Also Called: Drew Shoe
252 Quarry Rd Se (43130-8054)
PHONE..................740 653-4271
Fax: 740 654-4979
Dennis B Tishkoff, *Ch of Bd*
Marc Tishkoff, *President*
Marc Tishoff, *COO*
Peter Struzzi, *CFO*
Susie Hannan, *Credit Mgr*
▲ **EMP:** 40 **EST:** 1875
SQ FT: 60,000
SALES (est): 15.7MM **Privately Held**
WEB: www.drewshoe.com
SIC: 5139 Shoes

(G-12529)
FAIRFIELD CNTY JOB & FMLY SVCS
239 W Main St (43130-3739)
PHONE..................800 450-8845
Michael Orlando, *Principal*
Jamie Fauble, *Principal*
EMP: 99
SALES (est): 2.2MM **Privately Held**
WEB: www.fcjfs.org
SIC: 8399 Council for social agency

(G-12530)
FAIRFIELD COMMUNITY HEALTH CTR
Also Called: Fchc
1155 E Main St (43130-4056)
PHONE..................740 277-6043
Clinton G Kuntz, *CEO*
Micheal Horn Berger, *CFO*
Daniel Fisher, *CFO*
Audrey Simpson, *Director*
Marilyn Steiner, *Director*
EMP: 39
SQ FT: 5,000
SALES (est): 3.3MM **Privately Held**
SIC: 8082 Home health care services

(G-12531)
FAIRFIELD COUNTY
Also Called: Fairfield Cnty Chld Prtctd
239 W Main St (43130-3739)
PHONE..................740 653-4060
Rich Bowlen, *Director*
EMP: 61 **Privately Held**
WEB: www.fairfieldmha.org
SIC: 8399 Council for social agency
PA: Fairfield County
   210 E Main St Rm 201
   Lancaster OH 43130
   740 652-7020

(G-12532)
FAIRFIELD DIAGNSTC IMAGING LLC
Also Called: Fairfield Medical Center
1241 River Valley Blvd (43130-1653)
PHONE..................740 654-7559
Sky Gettys, *CEO*
Tina Gillum, *General Mgr*
Tamara Scott, *Med Doctor*
Tina Gomez, *Manager*
EMP: 25 **EST:** 1998
SALES (est): 1.1MM **Privately Held**
WEB: www.fairfielddiagnosticimaging.com
SIC: 8099 Physical examination & testing services

(G-12533)
FAIRFIELD FEDERAL SAV LN ASSN (PA)
111 E Main St (43130-3713)
P.O. Box 728 (43130-0728)
PHONE..................740 653-3863
Fax: 740 653-3650
Ronald Keaton, *President*
Clara Beiter, *Assistant VP*
Cathy Glenn, *Assistant VP*
Bev Stratton, *Assistant VP*
Bruce Baughman, *Vice Pres*
EMP: 50
SQ FT: 22,500
SALES: 10.9MM **Privately Held**
WEB: www.fairfieldfederal.com
SIC: 6035 8111 Federal savings & loan associations; legal services

(G-12534)
FAIRFIELD HOMES INC (PA)
Also Called: Gorsuch Management
603 W Wheeling St (43130-3630)
P.O. Box 190 (43130-0190)
PHONE..................740 653-3583
Leonard F Gorsuch, *CEO*
Ron Edwards, *Project Mgr*
Michael Williams, *Project Mgr*
Ronald P Burson, *Treasurer*
Sherry White, *Admin Sec*
EMP: 30
SQ FT: 7,000
SALES (est): 20.4MM **Privately Held**
WEB: www.gorsuch-homes.com
SIC: 6531 1522 Real estate managers; multi-family dwelling construction

(G-12535)
FAIRFIELD HOMES INC (PA)
Also Called: Gorsuch Management
603 W Wheeling St (43130-3630)
PHONE..................740 653-3583
Leonard F Gorsuch, *President*
Jackie Evans, *Controller*
EMP: 30
SALES (est): 2.1MM **Privately Held**
SIC: 6513 Apartment building operators

(G-12536)
FAIRFIELD INSUL & DRYWALL INC
1655 Election House Rd Nw (43130-9059)
PHONE..................740 654-8811
Fax: 740 654-5913
Doug Rose, *President*
Cathy Megahey, *Accountant*
EMP: 40
SQ FT: 10,000
SALES (est): 5.6MM **Privately Held**
SIC: 1742 Drywall; insulation, buildings; acoustical & ceiling work

(G-12537)
FAIRFIELD MEDICAL CENTER (PA)
401 N Ewing St (43130-3371)
PHONE..................740 687-8000
Fax: 740 687-8115
Sky Gettys, *CEO*
Tina Gillum, *General Mgr*
Howard Sniderman, *COO*
Gerald Smidebush, *Ch Radiology*
Chuck Davis, *Buyer*
EMP: 2000 **EST:** 1914
SQ FT: 380,000
SALES: 283.9MM **Privately Held**
WEB: www.fmchealth.org
SIC: 8062 7352 5999 General medical & surgical hospitals; medical equipment rental; medical apparatus & supplies

(G-12538)
FAIRFIELD NATIONAL BANK (HQ)
143 W Main St (43130-3700)
P.O. Box 607 (43130-0607)
PHONE..................740 653-7242
Fax: 740 653-8004
Stephen Wells, *President*
Timothy Hall, *Vice Pres*
Donna Cotterman, *Accounting Mgr*
Phil Joseph, *Branch Mgr*
Cindy Moore, *Branch Mgr*
EMP: 50
SQ FT: 5,000
SALES (est): 2.3MM
SALES (corp-wide): 367MM **Publicly Held**
WEB: www.fairfieldnationalbank.com
SIC: 6021 National commercial banks
PA: Park National Corporation
   50 N 3rd St
   Newark OH 43055
   740 349-8451

(G-12539)
FAIRFLD CTR FOR DISABLTS & CER
681 E 6th Ave (43130-2602)
PHONE..................740 653-1186
Fax: 740 653-6046
Bob Bottarini, *Treasurer*
Edwin Payne, *Director*
EMP: 30

SQ FT: 10,000
SALES: 1.3MM **Privately Held**
WEB: www.fairfieldcenter.org
SIC: 8093 Specialty outpatient clinics; rehabilitation center, outpatient treatment

(G-12540)
FAIRHOPE HOSPICE AND PALLIATIV
282 Sells Rd (43130-3461)
PHONE..................740 654-7077
Denise Bauer, *CEO*
Joyce Cox, *Vice Pres*
Daryl Reynolds, *Treasurer*
Lori Householder, *Director*
Susan Foglesong, *Administration*
EMP: 100
SALES (est): 2.4MM **Privately Held**
WEB: www.hospicefairfieldco.org
SIC: 8051 8082 Skilled nursing care facilities; home health care services

(G-12541)
FAMILY YMCA OF LANCSTR&FAIRFLD
1180 E Locust St (43130-4044)
PHONE..................740 277-7373
Mike Lieber, *Branch Mgr*
EMP: 63
SALES (corp-wide): 2.4MM **Privately Held**
SIC: 8641 7991 8351 7032 Youth organizations; physical fitness facilities; child day care services; youth camps; individual & family services
PA: Family Ymca Of Lancaster And Fairfield County
   465 W 6th Ave
   Lancaster OH 43130
   740 654-0616

(G-12542)
FAMILY YMCA OF LANCSTR&FAIRFLD (PA)
Also Called: ROBERT K FOX FAMILY WIDE
465 W 6th Ave (43130-2597)
PHONE..................740 654-0616
Mike Lieber, *CEO*
Steve Murry, *CFO*
EMP: 110
SALES: 2.4MM **Privately Held**
WEB: www.ymcalancaster.org
SIC: 7991 7997 Physical fitness facilities; membership sports & recreation clubs

(G-12543)
FIRST MED URGENT & FMLY CTR
1201 River Valley Blvd (43130-1653)
PHONE..................740 756-9238
Fax: 740 687-9059
Robert Dominguez, *President*
EMP: 26
SQ FT: 11,600
SALES (est): 2.7MM **Privately Held**
SIC: 8011 Offices & clinics of medical doctors; general & family practice, physician/surgeon

(G-12544)
GHP II LLC
2893 W Fair Ave (43130-8993)
P.O. Box 600 (43130-0600)
PHONE..................740 681-6825
Fax: 740 681-6842
Tom Gilligan, *Manager*
EMP: 280
SQ FT: 1,300,000
SALES (corp-wide): 543.6MM **Privately Held**
WEB: www.anchorhocking.com
SIC: 5023 3231 China; glassware; products of purchased glass
HQ: Ghp Ii, Llc
   1115 W 5th Ave
   Lancaster OH 43130
   740 687-2500

(G-12545)
JONES COCHENOUR & CO INC (PA)
125 W Mulberry St (43130-3064)
PHONE..................740 653-9581
David Jones, *President*
Dean Cochenour, *Vice Pres*

Lancaster - Fairfield County (G-12546)

Marcia Friesner, *Accounting Mgr*
Keith Lewis, *CPA*
EMP: 50
SALES (est): 4.7MM **Privately Held**
WEB: www.jcccpa.com
SIC: 8721 Certified public accountant

(G-12546)
KUMLER COLLISION INC
Also Called: Kumler Automotive
2313 E Main St (43130-9350)
PHONE.................................740 653-4301
Fax: 740 653-7380
Dean De Rolph, *President*
Scott Landis, *General Mgr*
Cathie De Rolph, *Vice Pres*
Cathie D Rolph, *Vice Pres*
Rusty Knece, *Parts Mgr*
EMP: 34 **EST:** 1928
SQ FT: 24,000
SALES (est): 3.5MM **Privately Held**
WEB: www.kumlercollision.com
SIC: 7532 Body shop, automotive

(G-12547)
L AND M INVESTMENT CO
603 W Wheeling St (43130-3630)
P.O. Box 190 (43130-0190)
PHONE.................................740 653-3583
Leonard Gorsuch, *Principal*
EMP: 25
SQ FT: 7,000
SALES (est): 620.9K **Privately Held**
SIC: 6514 6512 Dwelling operators, except apartments; commercial & industrial building operation

(G-12548)
LANCASTER BINGO COMPANY INC (PA)
Also Called: Lancaster Bingo Company
200 Quarry Rd Se (43130-9304)
P.O. Box 668 (43130-0668)
PHONE.................................740 681-4759
Fax: 740 653-7193
Mark A Sells, *Ch of Bd*
Jonathan Smith, *President*
Steven Root, *Vice Pres*
John Claybourn, *Warehouse Mgr*
Tracey Friesner, *Buyer*
▲ **EMP:** 80
SQ FT: 2,700
SALES (est): 41.5MM **Privately Held**
WEB: www.lancasterbingo.com
SIC: 5092 Bingo games & supplies

(G-12549)
LANCASTER COUNTRY CLUB
3100 Country Club Rd Sw (43130-8937)
P.O. Box 1098 (43130-0818)
PHONE.................................740 654-3535
Fax: 740 837-0813
Jim Aranda, *Principal*
Richard Waibel,
EMP: 55 **EST:** 1909
SQ FT: 4,000
SALES (est): 3.1MM **Privately Held**
SIC: 7997 5941 5812 Swimming club, membership; tennis club, membership; golf club, membership; golf goods & equipment; eating places

(G-12550)
LANCASTER HOST LLC
Also Called: Holiday Inn
1861 Riverway Dr (43130-1494)
PHONE.................................740 654-4445
Fax: 740 654-5546
Jennifer Thieman, *General Mgr*
Laurie Emerson, *Manager*
Bill Curt,
EMP: 30
SALES (est): 1.5MM **Privately Held**
SIC: 7011 Hotels

(G-12551)
LOWES HOME CENTERS LLC
2240 Lowes Dr (43130-5700)
PHONE.................................740 681-3464
Fax: 740 681-3467
Dave Taylor, *Manager*
EMP: 150

SALES (corp-wide): 68.6B **Publicly Held**
SIC: 5211 5031 5722 5064 Home centers; building materials, exterior; building materials, interior; household appliance stores; electrical appliances, television & radio
HQ: Lowe's Home Centers, Llc
1605 Curtis Bridge Rd
Wilkesboro NC 28697
336 658-4000

(G-12552)
LUKE COLLISON
Also Called: Collison Luke Drywall Txturing
565 Rainbow Dr Nw (43130-9195)
PHONE.................................740 969-2283
Luke Collison, *Owner*
EMP: 25
SQ FT: 3,944
SALES (est): 1.1MM **Privately Held**
WEB: www.pltools.com
SIC: 1742 5085 Plastering, drywall & insulation; tools

(G-12553)
MAIN STREET TERRACE CARE CTR
1318 E Main St (43130-4004)
PHONE.................................740 653-8767
Fax: 740 653-8919
Ed Telle, *President*
Susan Luning, *Med Doctor*
John Lloyd, *Director*
Peggy S Dupler, *Admin Sec*
EMP: 56
SQ FT: 5,182
SALES (est): 2.2MM **Privately Held**
SIC: 8052 8051 Intermediate care facilities; skilled nursing care facilities

(G-12554)
MCDERMOTT INTERNATIONAL INC
2600 E Main St (43130-8490)
PHONE.................................740 687-4292
Steve Shover, *Principal*
EMP: 171
SALES (corp-wide): 2.9B **Publicly Held**
SIC: 1629 Marine construction
PA: Mcdermott International, Inc.
4424 W Sam Houston Pkwy N
Houston TX 77041
281 870-5000

(G-12555)
MEALS ON WHEELS-OLDER ADULT AL
253 Boving Rd (43130-4240)
PHONE.................................740 681-5050
Fax: 740 681-5046
Diana Bradford, *Human Res Mgr*
Phyllis Saylor, *Exec Dir*
Bill Miller, *Administration*
EMP: 50
SQ FT: 6,600
SALES (est): 2.5MM **Privately Held**
SIC: 8322 Meal delivery program

(G-12556)
MEDILL ELEMNTARY SCH OF VOLNTR
1160 Sheridan Dr (43130-1927)
PHONE.................................740 687-7352
EMP: 50
SALES (est): 461.5K **Privately Held**
SIC: 8211 8399 Elementary & secondary schools; fund raising organization, non-fee basis

(G-12557)
MICHA LTD
144 E Main St (43130-3712)
P.O. Box 667 (43130-0667)
PHONE.................................740 653-6464
Robert Johnston, *Partner*
EMP: 45
SALES (est): 2MM **Privately Held**
SIC: 8111 General practice attorney, lawyer

(G-12558)
MID-OHIO PSYCHLOGICAL SVCS INC (PA)
624 E Main St (43130-3903)
PHONE.................................740 687-0042

Fax: 740 687-0024
Kimberly Blair, *Exec Dir*
EMP: 32
SQ FT: 3,529
SALES (est): 3.7MM **Privately Held**
WEB: www.mopsohio.com
SIC: 8322 8093 General counseling services; mental health clinic, outpatient

(G-12559)
MULTI COUNTY JUVENILE DET CTR
923 Liberty Dr (43130-8045)
PHONE.................................740 652-1525
Edgar A Penrod, *Principal*
EMP: 33
SALES (est): 2MM **Privately Held**
SIC: 8361 Juvenile correctional facilities

(G-12560)
NEW HORIZON YOUTH FAMILY CTR (PA)
Also Called: Pickerngton Area Cunseling Ctr
1592 Granville Pike (43130-1076)
PHONE.................................740 687-0835
Fax: 740 687-9391
Anthony Motta, *CEO*
Larry Reeves, *General Mgr*
Patrick Fleming, *CFO*
Richard A Black, *Psychologist*
Susan Garrett, *Info Tech Dir*
EMP: 25
SALES (est): 4.6MM **Privately Held**
WEB: www.pickareacounseling.com
SIC: 8322 Family service agency

(G-12561)
NEW LIFE CHRISTIAN CENTER
2642 Clumbus Lancaster Rd (43130-8814)
P.O. Box 2239 (43130-5239)
PHONE.................................740 687-1572
Gary A Keller, *Pastor*
Amy Heston, *Director*
EMP: 27
SQ FT: 48,600
SALES (est): 762.6K **Privately Held**
SIC: 8661 8351 Pentecostal Church; child day care services

(G-12562)
NL OF KY INC
Also Called: Hampson Insurance Agency
2680 Kull Rd (43130-7707)
P.O. Box 7, Baltimore (43105-0007)
PHONE.................................740 689-9876
Timothy D Hampson, *Branch Mgr*
EMP: 30 **Privately Held**
SIC: 6411 Insurance agents, brokers & service
HQ: Nl Of Ky, Inc.
2305 River Rd
Louisville KY 40206

(G-12563)
OB GYN ASSOCIATES OF LANCASTER
1532 Wesley Way (43130-7642)
PHONE.................................740 653-5088
Laurel Santino MD, *President*
Debbie Leith, *Office Mgr*
Mary Bitzler,
EMP: 25
SALES (est): 1.4MM **Privately Held**
SIC: 8011 Physicians' office, including specialists

(G-12564)
PAYROLL SERVICES UNLIMITED
125 W Mulberry St (43130-3014)
PHONE.................................740 653-9581
Brian Long, *Partner*
EMP: 40
SALES (est): 1.3MM **Privately Held**
SIC: 8721 Payroll accounting service

(G-12565)
PRECISION PIPELINE SVCS LLC
10 Whiley Rd (43130-8147)
PHONE.................................740 652-1679
Matt Upp, *CFO*
EMP: 40 **Privately Held**
SIC: 1623 Underground utilities contractor

(G-12566)
PRO-KLEEN INDUSTRIAL SVCS INC
Also Called: Porta-Kleen
1030 Mill Park Dr (43130-9576)
PHONE.................................740 689-1886
Fax: 740 689-1778
Monte Black, *Ch of Bd*
Chad Littrell, *Sales Dir*
Steven Rafferty, *Branch Mgr*
Fran Borelli, *Asst Director*
EMP: 45
SALES (est): 8.3MM **Privately Held**
WEB: www.portakleen.com
SIC: 7359 7699 5963 3088 Portable toilet rental; septic tank cleaning service; bottled water delivery; tubs (bath, shower & laundry), plastic

(G-12567)
PROLINE ELECTRIC INC
301 Cedar Hill Rd (43130-3641)
PHONE.................................740 687-4571
Fax: 740 653-7588
Mike Shafer, *President*
Michelle Hampson, *Manager*
EMP: 25
SALES (est): 600K **Privately Held**
SIC: 1731 General electrical contractor

(G-12568)
RECOVERY CENTER
201 S Columbus St (43130-4315)
PHONE.................................740 687-4500
Traci Mason, *COO*
Don Stegman, *Financial Exec*
Jennifer Blackston, *Mktg Coord*
Joyce Matheny, *Psychologist*
Lacey Carrel, *Manager*
EMP: 28
SQ FT: 12,500
SALES: 1.9MM **Privately Held**
SIC: 8699 8093 Charitable organization; rehabilitation center, outpatient treatment

(G-12569)
RICKETTS EXCAVATING INC
230 Hamburg Rd Sw (43130-9040)
P.O. Box 912 (43130-0912)
PHONE.................................740 687-0338
Fax: 740 687-6055
Michael Ricketts, *President*
Harry H Ricketts, *Exec VP*
Della Ricketts, *Admin Sec*
EMP: 30 **EST:** 1951
SQ FT: 10,500
SALES (est): 4.2MM **Privately Held**
SIC: 1794 4212 Excavation & grading, building construction; local trucking, without storage

(G-12570)
RIVER VLY ORTHPDICS SPT MDCINE (PA)
Also Called: Ohio Orthopedic Center
2405 N Columbus St # 120 (43130-8185)
PHONE.................................740 687-3346
Fax: 740 687-1897
Stephen J Voto MD, *President*
Diane Voto, *Business Mgr*
Karma Hutchinson, *Office Mgr*
Paul Degenova, *Obstetrician*
EMP: 25
SALES (est): 3.6MM **Privately Held**
SIC: 8011 Orthopedic physician

(G-12571)
RIVERVIEW SURGERY CENTER
Also Called: River View Surgery Center
2401 N Columbus St (43130-8190)
PHONE.................................740 681-2700
Fax: 740 681-2750
Tina Barr, *Manager*
Pamela Reed,
Amanda Northrop, *Administration*
EMP: 45
SALES (est): 2.2MM **Privately Held**
SIC: 8011 Ambulatory surgical center

(G-12572)
SCHROER PROPERTIES INC
Also Called: Schroer Properties of Lanfair
1590 Chartwell St Ofc (43130-7843)
PHONE.................................740 687-5100
Sean Cleary, *Manager*

GEOGRAPHIC SECTION

Lebanon - Warren County (G-12596)

EMP: 90 **Privately Held**
SIC: 8051 Skilled nursing care facilities
PA: Schroer Properties, Inc
　339 E Maple St
　North Canton OH 44720

(G-12573)
SERVICEMASTER BY SIDWELL INC
430 E Mulberry St (43130-3167)
PHONE..................740 687-1077
Fax: 740 687-2454
Muriel S Sidwell, *President*
Todd George, *Vice Pres*
EMP: 28 EST: 1979
SQ FT: 3,200
SALES (est): 1MM **Privately Held**
SIC: 7349 Building maintenance services

(G-12574)
SLATERS INC
Also Called: Do It Best
1141 N Memorial Dr (43130-1749)
P.O. Box 489 (43130-0489)
PHONE..................740 654-2204
Fax: 740 654-2637
Lou Ann Weisenstein, *President*
Jackie Pamston, *Co-Owner*
Steve Slater, *Vice Pres*
EMP: 30 EST: 1947
SQ FT: 15,000
SALES (est): 3.6MM **Privately Held**
WEB: www.slatershardware.com
SIC: 5251 6513 Tools; apartment building operators

(G-12575)
SOUTH CENTRAL POWER COMPANY (PA)
2780 Coonpath Rd Ne (43130-9343)
P.O. Box 250 (43130-0250)
PHONE..................740 653-4422
Fax: 740 681-4488
Rick Lemonds, *President*
Chris Hall, *Superintendent*
James Evans, *Principal*
Mike Hummel, *Principal*
Richard Poling, *Principal*
▲ EMP: 110
SQ FT: 10,000
SALES: 282.1MM **Privately Held**
WEB: www.southcentralpower.com
SIC: 4911 Distribution, electric power

(G-12576)
SPECTRUM MGT HOLDG CO LLC
Also Called: Time Warner
1315 Granville Pike Ne (43130-1034)
PHONE..................740 772-7809
Todd Acker, *Manager*
EMP: 40
SALES (corp-wide): 41.5B **Publicly Held**
SIC: 4841 Cable television services
HQ: Spectrum Management Holding Company, Llc
　400 Atlantic St
　Stamford CT 06901
　203 905-7801

(G-12577)
STANDING STONE NATIONAL BANK (PA)
137 W Wheeling St (43130-3708)
P.O. Box 2610 (43130-5610)
PHONE..................740 653-5115
Fax: 740 687-7280
Barry Ritchey, *President*
Albert Horvath, *Vice Pres*
EMP: 50
SQ FT: 7,500
SALES: 4.7MM **Privately Held**
WEB: www.standingstonenationalbank.com
SIC: 6021 National commercial banks

(G-12578)
SUNBRIDGE CARE ENTERPRISES INC
Also Called: Homestead Care Rhblitation Ctr
1900 E Main St (43130-9302)
PHONE..................740 653-8630
David Perry, *Vice Pres*
Angela Mc Coy, *Branch Mgr*
Troy Edwards, *Director*
Melody Veyon, *Nursing Dir*

Deb Malone, *Food Svc Dir*
EMP: 100 **Publicly Held**
SIC: 8051 Skilled nursing care facilities
HQ: Sunbridge Care Enterprises, Inc.
　5100 Sun Ave Ne
　Albuquerque NM

(G-12579)
TAYLOR CHEVROLET INC
Also Called: Taylor Dealership
2510 N Memorial Dr (43130-1637)
P.O. Box 10 (43130-0010)
PHONE..................740 653-2091
Fax: 740 653-0632
Martin N Taylor, *President*
Milton Taylor Jr, *Vice Pres*
Stephen Bowsher, *Sales Mgr*
Tom Matthews, *Sales Mgr*
Carmella Earich, *Sales Staff*
EMP: 150
SQ FT: 40,000
SALES: 42.9MM **Privately Held**
SIC: 5511 7538 7514 Automobiles, new & used; general automotive repair shops; passenger car rental

(G-12580)
TBN ACQUISITION LLC
Also Called: Hugh White Buick
2480 N Memorial Dr (43130-1637)
P.O. Box 10 (43130-0010)
PHONE..................740 653-2091
William Thagard, *Mng Member*
Marilyn Waltz, *Manager*
EMP: 100
SALES (est): 1.1MM **Privately Held**
SIC: 7389 5511 Automobile recovery service; automobiles, new & used

(G-12581)
TIKI BOWLING LANES INC
Also Called: Tiki Lounge & Restaurant
1521 Tiki Ln (43130-8793)
PHONE..................740 654-4513
Fax: 740 654-4523
James Shaner, *President*
Greg Russell, *General Mgr*
EMP: 50
SALES (est): 2.4MM **Privately Held**
WEB: www.tikilanes.com
SIC: 7933 5812 Ten pin center; eating places

(G-12582)
V CLEW LLC
1201 River Valley Blvd (43130-1653)
PHONE..................740 687-2273
Paul Van Camp, *Principal*
EMP: 30
SALES (est): 327.4K **Privately Held**
SIC: 8051 Skilled nursing care facilities

(G-12583)
WESTERN & SOUTHERN LF INSUR CO
1583 Victor Rd Nw (43130-8039)
P.O. Box 648 (43130-0648)
PHONE..................740 653-3210
Fax: 740 653-6127
Gene Patterson, *Sales Mgr*
Greg Shaffer, *Manager*
EMP: 30 **Privately Held**
SIC: 6411 Life insurance agents
HQ: The Western & Southern Life Insurance Company
　400 Broadway St
　Cincinnati OH 45202
　513 629-1800

(G-12584)
WINDSOR COMPANIES (PA)
1430 Collins Rd Nw (43130-8815)
PHONE..................740 653-8822
Thomas W Moore, *Partner*
Melvin L Moore, *Partner*
Jeff Meiskin, *CFO*
EMP: 33 EST: 1973
SQ FT: 2,200
SALES (est): 3.4MM **Privately Held**
WEB: www.thewindsorcompanies.com
SIC: 6552 Subdividers & developers

Lebanon
Warren County

(G-12585)
A 1 JANITORIAL CLEANING SVC
Also Called: ServiceMaster
939 Old 122 Rd (45036-8636)
P.O. Box 797 (45036-0797)
PHONE..................513 932-8003
Jimmy Collins, *President*
EMP: 50
SQ FT: 4,000
SALES: 750K **Privately Held**
SIC: 7349 Building maintenance services

(G-12586)
AAA ALLIED GROUP INC
Also Called: AAA Travel Agency
603 E Main St (45036-1915)
PHONE..................513 228-0866
James Pease, *Branch Mgr*
EMP: 78
SALES (corp-wide): 143.9MM **Privately Held**
SIC: 4481 Deep sea passenger transportation, except ferry
PA: Aaa Allied Group, Inc.
　15 W Central Pkwy
　Cincinnati OH 45202
　513 762-3100

(G-12587)
ADDISONMCKEE INC (PA)
1637 Kingsview Dr (45036-8395)
PHONE..................513 228-7000
Jim Sabine, *CEO*
Lonnie McGrew, *Vice Pres*
Mike Burnett, *VP Mfg*
Claud Lessard, *CFO*
Suzanne White, *Accountant*
▲ EMP: 142
SQ FT: 78,000
SALES: 8MM **Privately Held**
WEB: www.addisonmckee.com
SIC: 3542 3599 5084 3549 Bending machines; machine shop, jobbing & repair; industrial machinery & equipment; metalworking machinery; rolling mill machinery; special dies, tools, jigs & fixtures

(G-12588)
ADVANCE CARE INC
Also Called: Lebanon Health Care Center
115 Oregonia Rd (45036-1983)
P.O. Box 376 (45036-0376)
PHONE..................513 932-1121
Fax: 513 932-7181
William E Ullum, *President*
Kelly Watson, *Corp Secy*
EMP: 100
SQ FT: 45,000
SALES (est): 2.6MM **Privately Held**
WEB: www.advancecare.com
SIC: 8051 8052 Skilled nursing care facilities; intermediate care facilities

(G-12589)
ARMCO ASSOCIATION PARK
Also Called: ARMCO PARK
1223 N State Route 741 (45036-9746)
PHONE..................513 695-3980
Fax: 513 727-3983
Tedd Wood, *President*
James Unglesby, *Vice Pres*
John Kraft, *Park Mgr*
EMP: 45 EST: 1956
SQ FT: 1,200
SALES: 29.8K **Privately Held**
WEB: www.armcopark.com
SIC: 7997 Membership sports & recreation clubs

(G-12590)
ASC OF CINCINNATI INC
4028 Binion Way (45036-9367)
P.O. Box 230, Alexandria KY (41001-0230)
PHONE..................513 886-7100
Steven Stortz, *President*
Stain Smith, *Vice Pres*
Scott Harris, *Manager*
EMP: 34
SQ FT: 3,000

SALES: 2.7MM **Privately Held**
SIC: 4841 Cable & other pay television services

(G-12591)
BEST REALTY INC
645 Columbus Ave Ste A (45036-1605)
PHONE..................513 932-3948
Ralph Blanton, *Owner*
EMP: 25 EST: 2014
SALES (est): 111.7K **Privately Held**
SIC: 6531 Real estate brokers & agents

(G-12592)
BILL DELORD AUTOCENTER INC
Also Called: Pontiac Bill Delord Autocenter
917 Columbus Ave (45036-1401)
PHONE..................513 932-3000
Fax: 513 932-9924
William Delord, *President*
Jerry Perron, *General Mgr*
Julie Spencer, *Corp Secy*
Steve Butsch, *Finance Mgr*
Scot Cassidy, *Finance*
EMP: 51
SQ FT: 21,500
SALES (est): 21.8MM **Privately Held**
WEB: www.billdelord.com
SIC: 5511 7538 Automobiles, new & used; pickups, new & used; vans, new & used; general automotive repair shops

(G-12593)
BOB PULTE CHEVROLET INC
909 Columbus Ave (45036-1401)
P.O. Box 814 (45036-0814)
PHONE..................513 932-0303
Robert Pulte, *President*
Dan Pulte, *President*
Mike McMurray, *Sales Staff*
Jim Kleiser, *Sales Associate*
Jack Landis, *Sales Associate*
EMP: 36
SQ FT: 19,000
SALES (est): 14.5MM **Privately Held**
WEB: www.bobpulte.com
SIC: 5511 7515 5551 Automobiles, new & used; passenger car leasing; boat dealers

(G-12594)
CARL E OEDER SONS SAND & GRAV
1000 Mason Morrow Rd (45036-9271)
PHONE..................513 494-1555
Carl Edward Oeder, *President*
David Oeder, *Vice Pres*
Diane Browning, *Treasurer*
Verna Rae Oeder, *Admin Sec*
EMP: 30 EST: 1955
SQ FT: 23,600
SALES (est): 2.1MM **Privately Held**
WEB: www.oeder.com
SIC: 1442 4212 7538 Sand mining; gravel mining; dump truck haulage; truck engine repair, except industrial

(G-12595)
CO OPEN OPTIONS INC
19 N Mechanic St (45036-1801)
PHONE..................513 932-0724
Patricia Evans, *Owner*
Ben Vestal, *VP Sales*
Leslie Ealy, *Manager*
EMP: 30
SALES: 1MM **Privately Held**
SIC: 8052 Personal care facility

(G-12596)
COMMUNITY MNTL HLTH CTR (PA)
Also Called: MENTAL HEALTH RECOVERY CENTERS
975 Kingsview Dr (45036-9562)
PHONE..................513 228-7800
Jane Groh, *Opers Staff*
Andrea K Baumann, *Supervisor*
Dave Lorenz, *Exec Dir*
Russell Dern, *Director*
Duane Wooton, *Officer*
EMP: 70
SQ FT: 20,000
SALES: 12.5MM **Privately Held**
SIC: 8093 Mental health clinic, outpatient

(PA)=Parent Co (HQ)=Headquarters (DH)=Div Headquarters
✪ = New Business established in last 2 years

Lebanon - Warren County (G-12597)

(G-12597)
CONGER CONSTRUCTION GROUP INC
2020 Mckinley Blvd (45036-6425)
P.O. Box 1069 (45036-5069)
PHONE..................513 932-1206
Fax: 513 932-3204
Larry Conger, *President*
Rick Roessler, *Superintendent*
Bill Varney, *Superintendent*
Joseph Litvin, *Principal*
Dennis Blake, *Adv Board Mem*
EMP: 30
SQ FT: 12,000
SALES: 28MM **Privately Held**
WEB: www.gccontracting.com
SIC: 1542 Commercial & office building, new construction

(G-12598)
COUNTY OF WARREN
Also Called: Warren Co Human Services Dept
416 S East St Unit 1 (45036-2378)
PHONE..................513 695-1420
Fax: 513 695-2940
Doris Bishop, *Branch Mgr*
Duane Stansbury, *Manager*
Susan Walther, *Director*
EMP: 40 **Privately Held**
SIC: 8322 Social service center
PA: County Of Warren
406 Justice Dr Rm 323
Lebanon OH 45036
513 695-1242

(G-12599)
COUNTY OF WARREN
Also Called: Warren County Park District
300 E Silver St Ste 5 (45036-1800)
PHONE..................513 695-1109
Fax: 513 695-2956
Larry Easterly, *Manager*
EMP: 30 **Privately Held**
SIC: 0782 Lawn care services
PA: County Of Warren
406 Justice Dr Rm 323
Lebanon OH 45036
513 695-1242

(G-12600)
COUNTY OF WARREN
Also Called: Warren County Wtr & Sewer Dept
406 Justice Dr Rm 323 (45036-2523)
P.O. Box 530 (45036-0530)
PHONE..................513 925-1377
Fax: 513 695-2995
Chris Brausch, *Manager*
EMP: 55
SQ FT: 1,940 **Privately Held**
SIC: 4941 4952 Water supply; sewerage systems
PA: County Of Warren
406 Justice Dr Rm 323
Lebanon OH 45036
513 695-1242

(G-12601)
DOMINION ENERGY TRANSM INC
1262 W State Route 122 (45036-9616)
P.O. Box 560 (45036-0560)
PHONE..................513 932-5793
Fax: 513 932-4078
Scott Ratcliff, *Manager*
EMP: 32
SALES (corp-wide): 12.5B **Publicly Held**
WEB: www.domres.com
SIC: 4922 Natural gas transmission
HQ: Dominion Energy Transmission, Inc.
120 Tredegar St
Richmond VA 23219
800 688-4673

(G-12602)
EASTSIDE NURSERY INC
2830 Greentree Rd (45036-9773)
PHONE..................513 934-1661
Fax: 513 934-1795
Cheryl Miyer, *Manager*
EMP: 50
SALES (est): 993.8K **Privately Held**
SIC: 0782 0781 Landscape contractors; landscape counseling & planning

(G-12603)
EQUIPMENT DEPOT OHIO INC
1000 Kingsview Dr (45036-9572)
PHONE..................513 934-2121
Don Pratt, *General Mgr*
Josh Baker, *Sales Mgr*
Jim Keller, *Accounts Mgr*
Neil Williams, *Manager*
Jeff Fisher, *Manager*
EMP: 45
SQ FT: 63,218
SALES (corp-wide): 7.3B **Privately Held**
WEB: www.portmanpeople.com
SIC: 5084 Industrial machinery & equipment
HQ: Equipment Depot Ohio, Inc.
4331 Rossplain Dr
Blue Ash OH 45236
513 891-0600

(G-12604)
EQUIPMENT DEPOT OHIO INC
Cleaning Division
1000 Kingsview Dr (45036-9572)
PHONE..................513 934-2121
Neil Williams, *General Mgr*
John Dierichs, *Manager*
Tim Stidham, *Manager*
EMP: 35
SALES (corp-wide): 7.3B **Privately Held**
WEB: www.portmanpeople.com
SIC: 5084 7359 Processing & packaging equipment; home cleaning & maintenance equipment rental services
HQ: Equipment Depot Ohio, Inc.
4331 Rossplain Dr
Blue Ash OH 45236
513 891-0600

(G-12605)
FAMILY DENTISTRY INC (PA)
600 Mound Ct (45036-1994)
P.O. Box 467 (45036-0467)
PHONE..................513 932-6991
Fax: 513 932-5002
David Haas DDS, *President*
David Robert Haas, *President*
Michael C Peters, *Treasurer*
EMP: 31 **EST:** 1975
SQ FT: 3,000
SALES (est): 2.6MM **Privately Held**
SIC: 8021 Dentists' office

(G-12606)
GEORGE STEEL FABRICATING INC
1207 S Us Route 42 (45036-8198)
PHONE..................513 932-2887
Fax: 513 932-2059
John George, *President*
Brad Frost, *Corp Secy*
Kevin Nickell, *Vice Pres*
Tom Bausmith, *Project Mgr*
Blake Berryman, *Project Mgr*
EMP: 35
SQ FT: 32,100
SALES (est): 7.1MM **Privately Held**
WEB: www.georgesteel.com
SIC: 7692 3441 3599 Welding repair; fabricated structural metal; machine shop, jobbing & repair

(G-12607)
GIDEONS INTERNATIONAL
8 Claridge Ct B (45036-2803)
P.O. Box 612 (45036-0612)
PHONE..................513 932-2857
Robert F Amburgy, *Admin Sec*
EMP: 30
SALES (est): 394.4K **Privately Held**
SIC: 8699 Charitable organization

(G-12608)
GOLDEN LAMB
Also Called: Golden Lamb Rest Ht & Gift Sp
27 S Broadway St (45036-1705)
PHONE..................513 932-5065
Fax: 513 934-3049
Bill Kilimnik, *General Mgr*
N Lee Comisar, *Chairman*
EMP: 125
SALES (est): 4.4MM **Privately Held**
SIC: 5812 5947 7011 Eating places; gift shop; hotels

(G-12609)
HEALTH CARE OPPORTUNITIES INC (PA)
Also Called: Cedars of Lebanon Nursing Home
102 E Silver St (45036-1812)
PHONE..................513 932-0300
Fax: 513 932-9278
Bernard Moscowitz, *President*
EMP: 35
SQ FT: 12,000
SALES (est): 2.5MM **Privately Held**
SIC: 8059 Nursing home, except skilled & intermediate care facility

(G-12610)
HEALTH CARE OPPORTUNITIES INC
Also Called: Lebanon Nursing Home
220 S Mechanic St (45036-2212)
PHONE..................513 932-4861
Fax: 513 932-4591
Terri Moore, *Branch Mgr*
EMP: 50
SALES (corp-wide): 2.5MM **Privately Held**
SIC: 8051 Skilled nursing care facilities
PA: Health Care Opportunities Inc
102 E Silver St
Lebanon OH 45036
513 932-0300

(G-12611)
HENKLE-SCHUELER & ASSOCIATES (PA)
Also Called: Henkle Schueler Realtors
3000 Henkle Dr G (45036-9258)
PHONE..................513 932-6070
Fax: 513 932-1237
Michael T Schueler, *President*
Harry Biles, *Vice Pres*
Dwain Keller, *Controller*
Connie Bennett, *Office Mgr*
Pat South, *Branch Mgr*
EMP: 50
SQ FT: 3,000
SALES (est): 5.5MM **Privately Held**
WEB: www.henkleschueler.com
SIC: 6531 6552 Real estate agent, residential; subdividers & developers

(G-12612)
INDUSTRIAL VIBRATIONS CONS (PA)
Also Called: I V C
210 S West St (45036-2163)
PHONE..................513 932-4678
Jeffrey Epperson, *Ch of Bd*
Jerry Matiyow, *President*
Pete Epperson, *President*
Peter Epperson, *President*
Nathan Bruewer, *Regional Mgr*
EMP: 75
SQ FT: 12,000
SALES (est): 10.3MM **Privately Held**
WEB: www.ivctechnologies.com
SIC: 8748 Systems analysis & engineering consulting services

(G-12613)
INTERFAITH HOSPTLTY NTWRK OF W
Also Called: IHNWC
203 E Warren St (45036-1855)
PHONE..................513 934-5250
Linda Rabolt, *Exec Dir*
EMP: 99
SALES: 590.5K **Privately Held**
SIC: 8322 Individual & family services

(G-12614)
IRONS FRUIT FARM
1640 Stubbs Mill Rd (45036-9657)
PHONE..................513 932-2853
Ron Irons, *Owner*
Carolyn House, *Executive*
EMP: 30
SALES (est): 219K **Privately Held**
WEB: www.ironsfruitfarm.com
SIC: 0175 Apple orchard

(G-12615)
KINDRED NURSING CENTERS E LLC
Also Called: Kindred Nrsing Rhbltton- Lbnon
700 Monroe Rd (45036-1409)
PHONE..................513 932-0105
Fax: 513 932-7232
EMP: 110
SALES (corp-wide): 7B **Publicly Held**
SIC: 8051 Skilled Nursing Care Facility
HQ: Kindred Nursing Centers East, L.L.C.
680 S 4th St
Louisville KY 40202
502 596-7300

(G-12616)
KINGSMASON PROPERTIES LTD
Also Called: Kings-Mason Properties,
3000 Henkle Dr Ste G (45036-9258)
PHONE..................513 932-6010
Michael Schueler, *Managing Prtnr*
Ted Gilbert, *Manager*
EMP: 35
SALES (est): 2.2MM **Privately Held**
SIC: 6512 Shopping center, property operation only

(G-12617)
KWEEN INDUSTRIES INC
Also Called: King's Electric Services
2964 S State Route 42 (45036-8887)
P.O. Box 382 (45036-0382)
PHONE..................513 932-2293
Kingsley M Wientge III, *President*
Kelly Wientge, *Admin Sec*
EMP: 50
SQ FT: 4,000
SALES (est): 11.2MM **Privately Held**
SIC: 1731 General electrical contractor

(G-12618)
LCNB NATIONAL BANK (HQ)
2 N Broadway St Lowr (45036-1795)
P.O. Box 59 (45036-0059)
PHONE..................513 932-1414
Fax: 513 939-0572
Steve Foster, *President*
Ben Jackson, *Exec VP*
Leroy F McKay, *Exec VP*
Eric J Meilstrup, *Exec VP*
Kenneth R Layer, *Senior VP*
EMP: 80
SALES: 53.6MM
SALES (corp-wide): 54.9MM **Publicly Held**
WEB: www.lcnb.com
SIC: 6021 National commercial banks
PA: Lcnb Corp.
2 N Broadway St Lowr
Lebanon OH 45036
513 932-1414

(G-12619)
LEATHER GALLERY INC
50 Farnese Ct (45036-9601)
PHONE..................513 312-1722
Curtis Jackson, *President*
Tammy Jackson, *Vice Pres*
▲ **EMP:** 30
SQ FT: 3,800
SALES (est): 2MM **Privately Held**
WEB: www.leather-gallery.com
SIC: 5948 5199 Leather goods, except luggage & shoes; leather & cut stock

(G-12620)
LEBANON CHRYSLER - PLYMTH INC
Also Called: Sweeney Chrysler Dodge Jeep
518 W Main St (45036-2097)
PHONE..................513 932-2717
Fax: 513 932-4941
Tim Sweeney, *President*
Brian Sweeney, *Vice Pres*
Rick Nelson, *Exec Dir*
EMP: 25 **EST:** 1976
SQ FT: 16,000
SALES (est): 8.9MM **Privately Held**
SIC: 5511 7538 7515 5531 Automobiles, new & used; general automotive repair shops; passenger car leasing; automotive & home supply stores; used car dealers

GEOGRAPHIC SECTION

Lebanon - Warren County (G-12647)

(G-12621)
LEBANON FORD INC
Also Called: Lebanon Ford
770 Columbus Ave (45036-1608)
P.O. Box 118 (45036-0118)
PHONE..................513 932-1010
Fax: 513 932-0632
Winston R Pittman Sr, *President*
Lisa A Cryder, *Vice Pres*
Bonnie A Kasik, *CFO*
Frank Beaver, *Sales Mgr*
Aaron Funkhouser, *Sales Staff*
EMP: 52
SQ FT: 21,000
SALES: 86.7MM **Privately Held**
WEB: www.lebanon-ford.com
SIC: **5511** 5521 7538 Automobiles, new & used; pickups, new & used; used car dealers; general automotive repair shops

(G-12622)
LEBANON NURSING & REHAB CTR
115 Oregonia Rd (45036-1983)
P.O. Box 376 (45036-0376)
PHONE..................513 932-1121
Steve Feigenbaum, *Partner*
Leo Feigenbaum, *Partner*
EMP: 65
SALES: 40MM **Privately Held**
SIC: **8051** Skilled nursing care facilities

(G-12623)
LEBANON PRESBYTERIAN CHURCH
123 N East St (45036-1881)
PHONE..................513 932-0369
Fax: 513 934-0339
Peter Larson, *Pastor*
Andrew Johnson, *Director*
Brenda Bingham, *Bd of Directors*
EMP: 30
SALES: 11.1K **Privately Held**
WEB: www.lebanonpresbyterian.org
SIC: **8661** 8351 Presbyterian Church; nursery school

(G-12624)
MARATHON PETROLEUM COMPANY LP
999 W State Route 122 (45036-9615)
PHONE..................513 932-6007
Joe Elsner, *Manager*
EMP: 34 **Publicly Held**
WEB: www.mapllc.com
SIC: **5172** Gasoline
HQ: Marathon Petroleum Company Lp
539 S Main St
Findlay OH 45840

(G-12625)
MASTERS DRUG COMPANY INC
3600 Pharma Way (45036-9479)
PHONE..................800 982-7922
Nick Loporcaro, *Principal*
Timothy Cross, *Project Mgr*
EMP: 99
SALES (est): 9.8MM **Privately Held**
SIC: **5122** Pharmaceuticals

(G-12626)
MASTERS PHARMACEUTICAL INC (PA)
3600 Pharma Way (45036-9479)
PHONE..................513 354-2690
Fax: 513 354-2007
Dennis Smith, *President*
Brian Besse, *Vice Pres*
John Edmiston, *Vice Pres*
Jennifer Seiple, *Vice Pres*
Mike Warner, *Buyer*
▲ EMP: 180
SQ FT: 40,000
SALES (est): 110.3MM **Privately Held**
WEB: www.mastersrx.com
SIC: **5122** Pharmaceuticals

(G-12627)
MASTERS PHARMACEUTICAL INC
3600 Pharma Way (45036-9479)
PHONE..................800 982-7922
Dennis Smith, *President*
EMP: 95

SALES (corp-wide): 110.3MM **Privately Held**
SIC: **5122** Pharmaceuticals
PA: Masters Pharmaceutical, Inc.
3600 Pharma Way
Lebanon OH 45036
513 354-2690

(G-12628)
MIAMI VALLEY GAMING & RACG LLC
6000 W State Route 63 (45036-7900)
PHONE..................513 934-7070
Domenic Mancini, *President*
Anthony Green, *Vice Pres*
EMP: 80
SALES (est): 7.7MM **Privately Held**
SIC: **7999** 0971 Gambling & lottery services; game services

(G-12629)
MIAMI VLY FANDOM FOR LITERACY
Also Called: Mvfl
222 S Mechanic St (45036-2212)
PHONE..................513 933-0452
Dan Ryan, *CEO*
EMP: 26
SALES (est): 477.5K **Privately Held**
WEB: www.mvfl.org
SIC: **8399** Advocacy group

(G-12630)
NEWMAN INTERNATIONAL INC
Also Called: Newman Sanitary Gasket
964 W Main St (45036-9173)
P.O. Box 222 (45036-0222)
PHONE..................513 932-7379
Thomas C Moore, *President*
David Wj Newman, *Vice Pres*
▲ EMP: 52
SALES (est): 6.3MM **Privately Held**
SIC: **5085** Gaskets

(G-12631)
NORTHSIDE BAPTST CHILD DEV CTR
Also Called: Northside Baptist Church
161 Miller Rd (45036-1233)
PHONE..................513 932-5642
Fax: 513 932-3202
Jan Watson, *Pastor*
EMP: 26
SQ FT: 26,280
SALES (est): 615.5K **Privately Held**
WEB: www.northsideonline.net
SIC: **8351** Preschool center

(G-12632)
OEDER CARL E SONS SAND & GRAV
1000 Mason Mrrow Mlgrv Rd (45036-9271)
PHONE..................513 494-1238
Carl E Oeder, *President*
EMP: 35
SALES (est): 3.5MM **Privately Held**
SIC: **4213** 1442 Trucking, except local; construction sand & gravel

(G-12633)
ON-POWER INC
3525 Grant Ave Ste A (45036-6431)
PHONE..................513 228-2100
Fax: 513 228-0111
Larry D Davis, *President*
Joe Back, *Purchasing*
Tim Quackenbush, *Electrical Engi*
Tom Mergy, *CFO*
Mark Meineke, *Info Tech Mgr*
EMP: 32
SQ FT: 41,350
SALES: 8MM **Privately Held**
WEB: www.onpowerinc.com
SIC: **3511** 8711 Gas turbines, mechanical drive; consulting engineer

(G-12634)
OTTERBEIN HOMES
Also Called: OTTERBEIN SENIOR LIFESTYLE CHO
580 N State Route 741 (45036-8839)
PHONE..................513 933-5439
Jill Hreben, *President*
Ken Allen, *Principal*
Gary Horning, *Vice Pres*

Sue Brunker, *Human Res Dir*
Marilyn Wright, *Mktg Dir*
EMP: 60
SQ FT: 36,232
SALES: 105.5MM **Privately Held**
SIC: **8361** Home for the aged

(G-12635)
OTTERBEIN LEBANON
585 N State Route 741 (45036-8840)
PHONE..................513 933-5465
Richard A Mapes, *President*
Tammy Johnston, *Manager*
Joseph J Devore, *Exec Dir*
Lisa Hart, *Exec Dir*
Thomas Keith, *Exec Dir*
EMP: 25
SALES: 22.5MM **Privately Held**
SIC: **8059** Rest home, with health care

(G-12636)
OTTERBEIN SNIOR LFSTYLE CHICES (PA)
Also Called: Otterbein St Mary's
585 N State Route 741 (45036-8840)
PHONE..................513 933-5400
Fax: 513 932-1054
Jill Hreben, *President*
Donald L Gilmore, *President*
George Phillips, *Pastor*
Soni Marker, *Assistant VP*
Tammy Cassidy, *Vice Pres*
EMP: 400
SALES (est): 43.8MM **Privately Held**
SIC: **8361** 8051 8052 1522 Home for the aged; skilled nursing care facilities; intermediate care facilities; residential construction

(G-12637)
PRODUCTION SERVICES UNLIMITED
Also Called: WARREN COUNTY OF PRODUCTION SE
575 Columbus Ave (45036-1603)
PHONE..................513 695-1658
Fax: 513 695-2934
Heather Moore, *Director*
EMP: 65 EST: 1969
SQ FT: 30,000
SALES: 712.3K **Privately Held**
SIC: **8331** Sheltered workshop

(G-12638)
QUANTUM METALS INC
3675 Taft Rd (45036-6424)
PHONE..................513 573-0144
Fax: 513 573-0944
Mark A Kolb, *President*
Cheryl Kolb, *Corp Secy*
Erica Harris, *Manager*
◆ EMP: 40
SQ FT: 100,000
SALES (est): 22.9MM **Privately Held**
WEB: www.quantummetals.com
SIC: **5093** Nonferrous metals scrap

(G-12639)
RACEWAY FOODS INC
665 N Brdway Lbnon Rceway (45036)
P.O. Box 58 (45036-0058)
PHONE..................513 932-2457
Keith Nixon, *President*
EMP: 25
SALES (est): 830K **Privately Held**
SIC: **7948** Race track operation

(G-12640)
RDE SYSTEM CORP
Also Called: Sunshine Housekeeping
986 Winzig Ln (45036-8693)
PHONE..................513 933-8000
Bob Estepp, *President*
Donna Estepp, *Corp Secy*
Ruth Estepp, *Shareholder*
EMP: 140
SQ FT: 900
SALES (est): 10.6MM **Privately Held**
SIC: **5084** 7349 5169 5087 Materials handling machinery; janitorial service, contract basis; chemicals & allied products; service establishment equipment

(G-12641)
REALM TECHNOLOGIES LLC
954 Greengate Dr (45036-7943)
PHONE..................513 297-3095
Melissa Bolton,
EMP: 28
SALES: 980K **Privately Held**
SIC: **7378** Computer & data processing equipment repair/maintenance

(G-12642)
RED APPLE PACKAGING LLC
Also Called: Eastgate Graphics
611 Norgal Dr (45036-9275)
PHONE..................513 228-5522
Fax: 513 383-1314
Thomas Ludeke, *President*
EMP: 31
SALES (est): 5.1MM **Privately Held**
SIC: **5199** Packaging materials

(G-12643)
RK FAMILY INC
1879 Deerfield Rd (45036-8602)
PHONE..................513 934-0015
Tim F Lodes, *Principal*
EMP: 219
SALES (corp-wide): 1.2B **Privately Held**
SIC: **5099** Firearms & ammunition, except sporting
PA: Rk Family, Inc.
4216 Dewitt Ave
Mattoon IL 61938
217 235-7102

(G-12644)
SCHNEDER ELC BLDNGS AMRCAS INC
1770 Masn Mrrw Millgrv Rd (45036-9688)
PHONE..................513 398-9800
James C Mocas, *Project Mgr*
Bill Korn, *Branch Mgr*
Larry Mueller, *Branch Mgr*
EMP: 80
SALES (corp-wide): 241K **Privately Held**
SIC: **1731** 3822 Electrical work; auto controls regulating residntl & coml environmt & applncs
HQ: Schneider Electric Buildings Americas, Inc.
1650 W Crosby Rd
Carrollton TX 75006
972 323-1111

(G-12645)
SHAKER RUN GOLF CLUB
1320 Golf Club Dr (45036-4069)
PHONE..................513 727-0007
Steve Lambert, *Owner*
Tyler Geswein, *Principal*
Patrick Piccioni, *Principal*
Ryan Gilley, *Sales Dir*
Joe Robertson, *Sales Dir*
EMP: 52
SALES (est): 3.2MM **Privately Held**
SIC: **7992** Public golf courses

(G-12646)
SIBCY CLINE INC
Also Called: Sibcy, Cline Realtors
103 Oregonia Rd (45036-1983)
PHONE..................513 932-6334
Fax: 513 932-7580
Amy Davis, *Manager*
EMP: 80
SALES (corp-wide): 2.1B **Privately Held**
WEB: www.sibcycline.com
SIC: **6531** Real estate agent, residential
PA: Sibcy Cline, Inc.
8044 Montgomery Rd # 300
Cincinnati OH 45236
513 984-4100

(G-12647)
SITE WORX LLC
Also Called: Siteworx
3980 Turtlecreek Rd (45036-8643)
P.O. Box 767 (45036-0767)
PHONE..................513 229-0295
Matt Smith, *President*
Joe Smith, *Vice Pres*
Shawn Swaggerty, *Foreman/Supr*
Jason Davidson, *Controller*
EMP: 95

Lebanon - Warren County (G-12648)

SALES (est): 33.4MM **Privately Held**
SIC: **1542** Commercial & office building, new construction

(G-12648)
SOFTWARE SOLUTIONS INC (PA)
420 E Main St (45036-2234)
PHONE.................................513 932-6667
Fax: 513 932-4058
John Rettig, *President*
Laura Brown, *Vice Pres*
Linda Jones, *Opers Staff*
Dave Christensen, *QC Mgr*
Al Ferguson, *VP Sls/Mktg*
EMP: 32 EST: 1978
SQ FT: 12,200
SALES (est): 4.5MM **Privately Held**
WEB: www.elocalgovernment.com
SIC: **5045** 7372 7373 Computer software; disk drives; application computer software; computer integrated systems design

(G-12649)
SOUTHERN OHIO GUN DISTRS INC
240 Harmon Ave (45036-8800)
PHONE.................................513 932-8148
Phil Flannigan, *Branch Mgr*
EMP: 43
SALES (corp-wide): 6.7MM **Privately Held**
WEB: www.southernohiogun.com
SIC: **5099** Firearms, except sporting; ammunition, except sporting
PA: Southern Ohio Gun Distributors, Inc.
 105 E Main St
 Lebanon OH 45036
 513 932-8148

(G-12650)
SPARTAN SUPPLY CO INC
942 Old 122 Rd (45036-8632)
PHONE.................................513 932-6954
Fax: 513 933-9142
Tim Carpenter, *CEO*
Robert Hill, *Ch of Bd*
Joann Hill, *Corp Secy*
EMP: 40
SQ FT: 50,000
SALES (est): 5MM **Privately Held**
WEB: www.spartanindustries.net
SIC: **7699** Pallet repair

(G-12651)
SWEENEY TEAM INC
576 Mound Ct Ste A (45036-2090)
PHONE.................................513 934-0700
Mike Walter, *Branch Mgr*
Nancy Fields, *Real Est Agnt*
EMP: 25
SALES (est): 839.2K
SALES (corp-wide): 2.7MM **Privately Held**
SIC: **6531** Real estate agent, residential
PA: Sweeney Team, Inc.
 1440 Main St
 Cincinnati OH 45202
 513 241-3400

(G-12652)
TALBERT HOUSE
Also Called: Community Correctional Center
5234 W State Route 63 (45036-8202)
PHONE.................................513 933-9304
Fax: 513 933-9305
Jennifer Burnside, *Manager*
Scott McKay, *Manager*
Troy Newman, *Manager*
EMP: 55
SALES (corp-wide): 58.6MM **Privately Held**
WEB: www.talberthouse.org
SIC: **8322** Substance abuse counseling
PA: Talbert House
 2600 Victory Pkwy
 Cincinnati OH 45206
 513 872-5863

(G-12653)
TEXAS EASTERN TRANSMISSION LP
1157 W State Route 122 (45036-9616)
PHONE.................................513 932-1816
Fax: 513 932-1101
Larry D Moody, *Enginr/R&D Mgr*
EMP: 33
SALES (corp-wide): 25.5B **Publicly Held**
SIC: **4922** Natural gas transmission
HQ: Texas Eastern Transmission, Lp
 5400 Westheimer Ct
 Houston TX 77056
 713 627-5400

(G-12654)
TRIPLE Q FOUNDATIONS CO INC
139 Harmon Ave (45036-9511)
PHONE.................................513 932-3121
Fax: 513 932-3121
John Ball, *President*
Kathleen Ball, *Vice Pres*
Dan Crosthwaite, *Opers Mgr*
EMP: 35
SALES (est): 4.4MM **Privately Held**
SIC: **1771** Concrete work

(G-12655)
TWIN CEDARS SERVICES INC
935 Old Ralph 122 (45036)
PHONE.................................513 932-0399
Fax: 513 932-0373
Jimmy Collins, *President*
Teresa Collins, *Vice Pres*
EMP: 71
SALES (est): 859.7K **Privately Held**
SIC: **7349** Janitorial service, contract basis

(G-12656)
VISIONS MATTER LLC
838 W State Route 122 (45036-9615)
PHONE.................................513 934-1934
Fax: 513 934-2934
Sandra Sebecke, *Principal*
Deidre Dyer, *Director*
EMP: 80
SALES (est): 1.7MM **Privately Held**
SIC: **8082** Home health care services

(G-12657)
WALT SWEENEY FLEET SALES
Also Called: Sweeney Chrysler Dodge Jeep
518 W Main St (45036-2048)
PHONE.................................513 932-2717
Brian Sweeney, *CEO*
Bridget Reinberger, *General Mgr*
Steve Pieper, *Sales Mgr*
EMP: 40
SALES (est): 5.3MM **Privately Held**
SIC: **5012** Automobiles & other motor vehicles

(G-12658)
WARREN COUNTY BOARD DEVLPMNTAL
42 Kings Way (45036-9593)
PHONE.................................513 925-1813
Megan Manuel, *Superintendent*
Angie Tapogna, *Pub Rel Mgr*
Michele Swearingen, *CFO*
Patrick Poteet, *Associate*
EMP: 25
SALES (est): 913.8K **Privately Held**
SIC: **8052** Home for the mentally retarded, with health care

(G-12659)
WARREN COUNTY COMMUNITY SVCS (PA)
Also Called: WCCS
570 N State Route 741 (45036-8839)
PHONE.................................513 695-2100
Fax: 513 695-2277
Dr Charles Peckham, *President*
Gregg Smith, *Controller*
James Smith, *Controller*
Tom Cox, *Manager*
Tom Salzbrun, *Exec Dir*
EMP: 175
SQ FT: 24,000
SALES (est): 9MM **Privately Held**
WEB: www.wccsinc.org
SIC: **8399** Antipoverty board

(G-12660)
YOUNG MENS CHRISTIAN
Also Called: Countryside YMCA Child Dev
1699 Deerfield Rd (45036-9215)
PHONE.................................513 932-1424
Fax: 513 933-9390
Mike Carroll, *CEO*
Phil Breeding, *Maint Spvr*
Sandra Hamilton, *QA Dir*
Renee Lay, *Financial Exec*
Nick Kneer, *Mktg Coord*
EMP: 300
SALES (corp-wide): 33.6MM **Privately Held**
WEB: www.cincinnatiymca.org
SIC: **8641** 7991 8351 7032 Youth organizations; physical fitness facilities; child day care services; youth camps; individual & family services
PA: Young Mens Christian Association Of Greater Cincinnati
 1105 Elm St
 Cincinnati OH 45202
 513 651-2100

Leetonia
Columbiana County

(G-12661)
ADVANTAGE TANK LINES INC
404 12 Pearl St (44431)
PHONE.................................330 427-1010
Fax: 330 427-1012
EMP: 180
SALES (corp-wide): 26.3MM **Privately Held**
SIC: **4213** 4212 Trucking Operator-Nonlocal Local Trucking Operator
PA: Advantage Tank Lines, Inc.
 4366 Mount Pleasant St Nw
 North Canton OH 44720
 330 491-0474

(G-12662)
S&P GLOBAL INC
41438 Kings Ct (44431-8617)
PHONE.................................330 482-9544
Nancy Marr, *Branch Mgr*
EMP: 148
SALES (corp-wide): 6B **Publicly Held**
SIC: **6282** Investment advisory service
PA: S&P Global Inc.
 55 Water St Ste Conc2
 New York NY 10041
 212 438-1000

Leipsic
Putnam County

(G-12663)
OTTERBEIN SNIOR LFSTYLE CHICES
Also Called: Oherbein Kpsic Rtirement Cmnty
901 E Main St (45856-9326)
PHONE.................................419 943-4376
Fax: 419 943-2104
Jason McClellan, *Exec Dir*
EMP: 50
SALES (corp-wide): 43.8MM **Privately Held**
SIC: **8361** Home for the aged
PA: Senior Otterbein Lifestyle Choices
 585 N State Route 741
 Lebanon OH 45036
 513 933-5400

(G-12664)
PGT TRUCKING INC
Also Called: C and D Truck Repairs
6302 Road 5 (45856-9761)
P.O. Box 107 (45856-0107)
PHONE.................................419 943-3437
Fax: 419 943-3438
Charles Kitchen, *Manager*
EMP: 50
SALES (corp-wide): 178.7MM **Privately Held**
SIC: **4213** 4212 7538 Contract haulers; local trucking, without storage; general truck repair
PA: Pgt Trucking, Inc.
 1 Pgt Way
 Monaca PA 15061
 724 728-3500

Lewis Center
Delaware County

(G-12665)
AMERICAN BUS SOLUTIONS INC
8850 Whitney Dr (43035-8297)
PHONE.................................614 888-2227
Rajeev Kumar, *President*
Manisha Dixit, *Vice Pres*
Mark Heidkamp, *CFO*
EMP: 58
SQ FT: 2,000
SALES (est): 17.5MM **Privately Held**
SIC: **7379** Computer related consulting services

(G-12666)
ANIMAL HOSPITAL POLARIS LLC
8928 S Old State Rd (43035-8401)
PHONE.................................614 888-4050
Fax: 614 547-0205
Heather Stern, *Marketing Staff*
Brittani Sell,
EMP: 45
SALES (est): 2.6MM **Privately Held**
WEB: www.animalhospitalofpolaris.com
SIC: **0742** Animal hospital services, pets & other animal specialties

(G-12667)
AT&T CORP
8601 Columbus Pike (43035-9614)
PHONE.................................740 549-4546
EMP: 82
SALES (corp-wide): 160.5B **Publicly Held**
SIC: **4813** Local & long distance telephone communications
HQ: At&T Corp.
 1 At&T Way
 Bedminster NJ 07921
 800 403-3302

(G-12668)
ATS SYSTEMS OREGON INC
425 Enterprise Dr (43035-9424)
PHONE.................................541 738-0932
Anthony Caputo, *CEO*
Maria Perrella, *President*
Mike Larkin, *Purch Mgr*
Sam Haines, *Engineer*
Michael Forgt, *Design Engr*
▲ EMP: 300
SQ FT: 85,000
SALES (est): 81.1MM
SALES (corp-wide): 769.5MM **Privately Held**
SIC: **3569** 5084 Robots, assembly line: industrial & commercial; industrial machinery & equipment
PA: Ats Automation Tooling Systems Inc
 730 Fountain St N Suite 2b
 Cambridge ON N3H 4
 519 653-6500

(G-12669)
AUNTIES ATTIC
1550 Lewis Center Rd G (43035-8232)
PHONE.................................740 548-5059
Sherry Clay, *Owner*
EMP: 35
SQ FT: 3,500
SALES (est): 1.5MM **Privately Held**
SIC: **2392** 5199 Comforters & quilts: made from purchased materials; tablecloths & table settings; towels, dishcloths & dust cloths; gifts & novelties

(G-12670)
BLENDON GARDENS INC
9590 S Old State Rd (43035-9492)
PHONE.................................614 840-0500
Fax: 614 840-0504
Loren L Brelsford, *President*
Amy Mahler, *Office Mgr*
Brian Thornton, *Info Tech Mgr*
Deidra Ross, *Administration*
EMP: 26
SQ FT: 1,979

GEOGRAPHIC SECTION
Lewis Center - Delaware County (G-12696)

SALES (est): 3.6MM **Privately Held**
WEB: www.blendongardens.com
SIC: 0781 Landscape architects

(G-12671)
BOARD OF DELAWARE COUNTY
7991 Columbus Pike (43035-9611)
PHONE.................740 201-3600
Robert R Morgan, *Superintendent*
Jared Zirillo, *Opers Staff*
Wendy Mack, *Purch Agent*
Jillian Johnson, *Office Mgr*
Debbie Sonner, *Office Mgr*
EMP: 82
SALES: 17.2MM **Privately Held**
SIC: 8322 Child related social services

(G-12672)
BOB WEBB BUILDERS INC
Also Called: Bob Webb Homes
7662 N Central Dr (43035-9400)
PHONE.................740 548-5577
Robert A Webb, *President*
Rebecca L Webb, *Treasurer*
Pete Taylor, *Admin Sec*
EMP: 30 EST: 1960
SQ FT: 5,000
SALES (est): 4.3MM **Privately Held**
SIC: 1521 New construction, single-family houses

(G-12673)
CELLCO PARTNERSHIP
Also Called: Verizon Wireless
7575 Commerce Ct (43035-9702)
PHONE.................614 560-8552
EMP: 71
SALES (corp-wide): 126B **Publicly Held**
SIC: 4812 Cellular telephone services
HQ: Cellco Partnership
  1 Verizon Way
  Basking Ridge NJ 07920

(G-12674)
CENTRAL BEVERAGE GROUP LTD
Also Called: Superior Bev Group Centl Ohio
8133 Highfield Dr (43035-9673)
PHONE.................614 294-3555
John Antonucci, *Partner*
Scott Hall, *Purch Mgr*
Kelli Decker, *Controller*
▲ EMP: 140
SQ FT: 116,000
SALES (est): 30.8MM **Privately Held**
SIC: 5181 Beer & other fermented malt liquors

(G-12675)
CHILLER LLC
8144 Highfield Dr (43035-9673)
PHONE.................740 549-0009
Jason Beebee, *Manager*
Carol Hall, *Director*
Spanhel Martin, *Director*
EMP: 40
SALES (corp-wide): 11.7MM **Privately Held**
SIC: 7999 Ice skating rink operation
PA: Chiller Llc
  7001 Dublin Park Dr
  Dublin OH 43016
  614 764-1000

(G-12676)
COLUMBUS FRKLN CNTY PK
9466 Columbus Pike (43035-9414)
PHONE.................614 846-9962
Fax: 614 846-9536
Richard Rapp, *Branch Mgr*
Jennifer Boniface, *Manager*
EMP: 27
SALES (corp-wide): 18.3MM **Privately Held**
SIC: 7996 Theme park, amusement
PA: Columbus & Franklin County Metropolitan Park District
  1069 W Main St Unit B
  Westerville OH 43081
  614 891-0700

(G-12677)
COLUMBUS SAIL AND PWR SQUADRON
8492 Cotter St (43035-7139)
PHONE.................614 384-0245
Robert L Prior, *Commander*
Thresa Nadowlson, *Treasurer*
EMP: 250
SQ FT: 1,500
SALES: 35.2K **Privately Held**
SIC: 7997 Boating club, membership

(G-12678)
COUNTY OF DELAWARE
Also Called: Title Division
8647 Columbus Pike (43035-9616)
PHONE.................740 657-3945
Jan Antonoplis, *Clerk*
EMP: 79 **Privately Held**
WEB: www.delawarecountysheriff.com
SIC: 6541 Title abstract offices
PA: County Of Delaware
  101 N Sandusky St
  Delaware OH 43015
  740 368-1800

(G-12679)
CULVER ART & FRAME CO
7890 N Central Dr (43035-9406)
P.O. Box 310 (43035-0310)
PHONE.................740 548-6868
Ronald D Lehman, *President*
Mark Lehman, *President*
David E Lehman, *Vice Pres*
▲ EMP: 40 EST: 1932
SQ FT: 42,000
SALES (est): 7.2MM **Privately Held**
WEB: www.culverframe.com
SIC: 5023 Frames & framing, picture & mirror

(G-12680)
D J- SEVE GROUP INC
Also Called: McDonald's
10030 Columbus Pike (43035-9414)
PHONE.................614 888-6600
Ron Severance, *President*
Shad Severance, *Vice Pres*
Sandy Snyder, *Controller*
EMP: 45
SALES (est): 2.3MM **Privately Held**
SIC: 5812 8741 Fast-food restaurant, chain; restaurant management

(G-12681)
DEXXXON DIGITAL STORAGE INC
7611 Green Meadows Dr (43035-9445)
PHONE.................740 548-7179
Babak Sarshar, *Ch of Bd*
Simon N Garneau, *President*
Dave Burke, *Exec VP*
Leon Rijnbeek, *Treasurer*
Gay Cordell-Smith, *Sales Staff*
▲ EMP: 45
SQ FT: 60,000
SALES (est): 28.3MM **Privately Held**
SIC: 5112 7371 Computer & photocopying supplies; custom computer programming services
PA: Dexxxon Groupe
  79 Avenue Louis Roche
  Gennevilliers 92230

(G-12682)
DIETARY SOLUTIONS INC
171 Green Meadows Dr S (43035-9458)
PHONE.................614 985-6567
Fax: 614 985-6568
Kay Lachi, *President*
Lisa McGovern, *Nutritionist*
Rebecca Hong, *Consultant*
EMP: 50
SALES (est): 1.2MM **Privately Held**
WEB: www.dietarysolutions.net
SIC: 8049 Dietician

(G-12683)
DIGITEK SOFTWARE INC
650 Radio Dr (43035-7111)
PHONE.................614 764-8875
Fax: 614 792-5840
Chetan Bhuta, *President*
Vivek Kanakia, *General Mgr*
Pankaj Oza, *General Mgr*
Art Andre, *Vice Pres*
Bharat Gandhi, *Vice Pres*
EMP: 40
SQ FT: 3,000

SALES (est): 5.6MM **Privately Held**
WEB: www.digiteksw.com
SIC: 7371 Computer software development

(G-12684)
DISPATCH PRINTING COMPANY
Also Called: Columbus Dispatch
7801 N Central Dr (43035-9407)
PHONE.................740 548-5331
Fax: 740 888-6406
Don Patton, *Branch Mgr*
EMP: 238
SALES (corp-wide): 600.6MM **Privately Held**
SIC: 2711 4833 Commercial printing & newspaper publishing combined; television broadcasting stations
PA: The Dispatch Printing Company
  62 E Broad St
  Columbus OH 43215
  614 461-5000

(G-12685)
FIRST COMMONWEALTH BANK
110 Riverbend Ave (43035)
PHONE.................740 657-7000
EMP: 166
SALES (corp-wide): 330.8MM **Publicly Held**
SIC: 6022 State trust companies accepting deposits, commercial
HQ: First Commonwealth Bank
  601 Philadelphia St
  Indiana PA 15701
  724 349-7220

(G-12686)
GLEAMING SYSTEMS LLC
2417 Charoe St (43035-7290)
PHONE.................614 348-7475
Pratik Shah, *CEO*
EMP: 30
SALES (est): 498.4K **Privately Held**
SIC: 8748 Systems engineering consultant, ex. computer or professional

(G-12687)
HE HARI INC (PA)
600 Enterprise Dr (43035-9432)
PHONE.................614 846-6600
Naresh Patel, *Principal*
EMP: 90
SALES (est): 1.8MM **Privately Held**
SIC: 7011 Hotels & motels

(G-12688)
HOMEREACH INC
Also Called: Homereach Healthcare
7708 Green Meadows Dr D (43035-1116)
PHONE.................614 566-0850
Gwen Norris, *Manager*
Ken Symanski, *Director*
EMP: 28
SALES (corp-wide): 3.7B **Privately Held**
WEB: www.homereach.net
SIC: 5047 Medical equipment & supplies
HQ: Homereach, Inc.
  404 E Wilson Bridge Rd
  Worthington OH 43085

(G-12689)
INDEPENDENT ORDER ODD FELLOWS
5230 Cypress Dr (43035-9028)
P.O. Box 333, Galena (43021-0333)
PHONE.................740 548-5038
Lorraine Saunders, *Admin Sec*
EMP: 28
SALES (est): 291K **Privately Held**
SIC: 8641 Civic social & fraternal associations

(G-12690)
JPMORGAN CHASE BANK NAT ASSN
8681 Columbus Pike (43035-9617)
PHONE.................740 657-8906
Michelle Mayberry, *Manager*
EMP: 26
SALES (corp-wide): 99.6B **Publicly Held**
WEB: www.chasebank.com
SIC: 6021 National commercial banks

HQ: Jpmorgan Chase Bank, National Association
  1111 Polaris Pkwy
  Columbus OH 43240
  614 436-3055

(G-12691)
KINDERCARE LEARNING CTRS LLC
Also Called: Polaris Kindercare
96 Neverland Dr (43035-9151)
PHONE.................740 549-0264
Fax: 740 549-1752
Deeann Goebel, *Branch Mgr*
EMP: 25
SALES (corp-wide): 1.2B **Privately Held**
WEB: www.kindercare.com
SIC: 8351 Group day care center
HQ: Kindercare Learning Centers, Llc
  650 Ne Holladay St # 1400
  Portland OR 97232
  503 872-1300

(G-12692)
LEADER TECHNOLOGIES INC (PA)
674 Enterprise Dr (43035-9434)
P.O. Box 224 (43035-0224)
PHONE.................614 890-1986
Fax: 614 864-7922
Michael T McKibben, *Ch of Bd*
James Sobwick, *COO*
Michael Mc Kibben, *Human Res Dir*
John Needham, *Natl Sales Mgr*
Douglas Clay, *Technology*
EMP: 30
SQ FT: 6,000
SALES (est): 3.3MM **Privately Held**
WEB: www.leader.com
SIC: 7371 Computer software development

(G-12693)
LUMENOMICS INC
Also Called: Inside Outfitters
8333 Green Meadows Dr N (43035-8496)
PHONE.................614 798-3500
Carlee Swihart, *Vice Pres*
Stephen Jaszek, *Sales Mgr*
Carol Foughty, *Administration*
EMP: 46 **Privately Held**
SIC: 5023 2591 2221 2211 Draperies; venetian blinds; vertical blinds; window covering parts & accessories; drapery hardware & blinds & shades; window shades; draperies & drapery fabrics, man-made fiber & silk; draperies & drapery fabrics, cotton; shades, canvas: made from purchased materials
PA: Lumenomics, Inc.
  500 Mercer St C2
  Seattle WA 98109

(G-12694)
MES INC (PA)
625 Bear Run Ln (43035-7133)
PHONE.................740 201-8112
Hiten Shah, *President*
Shraddha Patel, *Accountant*
▲ EMP: 51
SALES: 72.9MM **Privately Held**
SIC: 5051 8742 Metals service centers & offices; marketing consulting services

(G-12695)
MEYERS LDSCP SVCS & NURS INC
6081 Columbus Pike (43035-9008)
P.O. Box 697 (43035-0697)
PHONE.................614 210-1194
Michael Meyers, *President*
Charles Camphausen, *VP Opers*
Nancy Doyle, *Office Mgr*
Stephanie Lambert, *Admin Asst*
EMP: 45
SQ FT: 2,400
SALES (est): 4.7MM **Privately Held**
SIC: 0781 Landscape services

(G-12696)
MULTI-PLASTICS INC (PA)
7770 N Central Dr (43035-9404)
PHONE.................740 548-4894
Fax: 740 548-5177
John R Parsio, *President*

Lewis Center - Delaware County (G-12697)

John Parsio Jr, *Exec VP*
Wesley Hall, *Vice Pres*
Steven Parsio, *Vice Pres*
Juan Escobar, *Mfg Dir*
◆ **EMP:** 55
SQ FT: 32,000
SALES (est): 228.8MM Privately Held
WEB: www.multi-plastics.com
SIC: 5162 Plastics film

(G-12697)
NATIONWIDE MUTUAL INSURANCE CO
9243 Columbus Pike (43035-8278)
PHONE 614 430-3047
Fax: 614 840-7245
Tom Rosati, *Engineer*
Steve Falker, *Manager*
Pat Stiles, *Consultant*
Jordan Elasky, *IT/INT Sup*
EMP: 35
SQ FT: 4,032
SALES (corp-wide): 26.6B Privately Held
WEB: www.nirassn.com
SIC: 6311 Life insurance
PA: Nationwide Mutual Insurance Company
    1 Nationwide Plz
    Columbus OH 43215
    614 249-7111

(G-12698)
NSB RETAIL SYSTEMS INC
400 Venture Dr (43035-9275)
PHONE 614 840-1421
Howard Stotland, *President*
Bob Nikolajczyk, *General Mgr*
Eric Eichensehr, *Vice Pres*
EMP: 90
SQ FT: 18,000
SALES: 7.9MM
SALES (corp-wide): 164K Privately Held
SIC: 7371 Computer software development
HQ: Nsb Retail Systems Limited
    1 The Arena
    Bracknell BERKS

(G-12699)
ON SITE INSTRUMENTS LLC
403 Venture Dr (43035-9519)
P.O. Box 290 (43035-0290)
PHONE 614 846-1900
Fax: 614 846-1991
Laurie Beckley, *Comptroller*
EMP: 50
SALES (est): 3.2MM Privately Held
WEB: www.on-siteinstruments.com
SIC: 8748 Environmental consultant

(G-12700)
ORBIT SYSTEMS INC
615 Carle Ave (43035-8294)
PHONE 614 504-8011
Amit Rateria, *President*
Neelam Pandey, *Human Res Mgr*
EMP: 40
SQ FT: 1,427
SALES: 2.4MM Privately Held
SIC: 8742 Business consultant

(G-12701)
PCM INC
Also Called: Pcm Logistics
8337 Green Meadows Dr N (43035-9451)
PHONE 614 854-1399
Eric Keating, *Senior VP*
Paul Neiswinger, *Vice Pres*
Kurt Blanton, *Opers Mgr*
Michelle Umambac, *Purchasing*
Paul Kovach, *Engineer*
EMP: 41
SALES (corp-wide): 2.1B Publicly Held
SIC: 8999 Artists & artists' studios
PA: Pcm, Inc.
    1940 E Mariposa Ave
    El Segundo CA 90245
    310 354-5600

(G-12702)
PCM SALES INC
Also Called: Inacomp Computer Centers
8337 Green Meadows Dr N (43035-9451)
PHONE 740 548-2222
Todd Crites, *President*
Anthony Rodriguez, *President*
Tonya Lee, *Business Mgr*
Bob Miller, *Business Mgr*
Jon Cima, *Senior VP*
EMP: 40
SALES (corp-wide): 2.1B Publicly Held
WEB: www.sarcom.com
SIC: 5045 Computers
HQ: Pcm Sales, Inc.
    1940 E Mariposa Ave
    El Segundo CA 90245
    310 354-5600

(G-12703)
PF HOLDINGS LLC
8522 Cotter St (43035-7138)
PHONE 740 549-3558
Bob Patel, *President*
Preney Patel, *District Mgr*
EMP: 90 **EST:** 2011
SQ FT: 1,500 Privately Held
SIC: 6719 Investment holding companies, except banks

(G-12704)
POLARIS AUTOMATION INC
Also Called: Electrical Design & Engrg Svcs
8333 Green Meadows Dr N A (43035-8497)
PHONE 614 431-0170
James D Cooke, *President*
Scott Cooke, *Principal*
Susan Cooke, *Corp Secy*
Sam Zungri, *Opers Mgr*
Tony Bickel, *Engineer*
EMP: 51
SQ FT: 2,573
SALES (est): 4.7MM Privately Held
SIC: 7389 8711 Design, commercial & industrial; engineering services

(G-12705)
QUINTUS TECHNOLOGIES LLC
8270 Green Meadows Dr N (43035-9450)
PHONE 614 891-2732
Dennis Schwegel, *Manager*
Ed Williams,
EMP: 28
SALES (est): 3.7MM Privately Held
SIC: 7699 7389 3443 Industrial equipment services; industrial & commercial equipment inspection service; industrial vessels, tanks & containers

(G-12706)
SUPERIOR BEVERAGE GROUP LTD
8133 Highfield Dr (43035-9673)
PHONE 614 294-3555
Dewayne Godby, *Area Mgr*
Marty Williard, *Vice Pres*
Brian Ahern, *Opers Mgr*
Aaron Jones, *Opers Mgr*
Aaron Lowther, *Opers Mgr*
EMP: 57
SALES (corp-wide): 98.5MM Privately Held
SIC: 5149 5499 Beverages, except coffee & tea; beverage stores
PA: The Superior Beverage Group Ltd
    31031 Diamond Pkwy
    Solon OH 44139
    440 703-4580

(G-12707)
TRIPLE T TRANSPORT INC (PA)
433 Lewis Center Rd (43035-9049)
P.O. Box 649 (43035-0649)
PHONE 740 657-3244
Fax: 740 657-3352
Darin Puppel, *President*
Terry McKenzie, *Vice Pres*
David Santisi, *Vice Pres*
Wade Amelung, *CFO*
Jamie Salum, *Credit Staff*
EMP: 70
SQ FT: 12,000
SALES: 126.9MM Privately Held
WEB: www.triplettransport.com
SIC: 4731 Transportation agents & brokers

(G-12708)
TRUGREEN LIMITED PARTNERSHIP
Also Called: Tru Green-Chemlawn
461 Enterprise Dr (43035-9424)
P.O. Box 548, Westerville (43086-0548)
PHONE 614 285-3721
Fax: 614 431-0155
Scott Smith, *Sales Mgr*
Al Carow, *Branch Mgr*
Al Karow, *Branch Mgr*
EMP: 103
SALES (corp-wide): 4B Privately Held
SIC: 0782 Lawn care services
HQ: Trugreen Limited Partnership
    1790 Kirby Pkwy
    Memphis TN 38138
    901 251-4128

(G-12709)
V WESTAAR INC
6249 Westwick Pl (43035-8978)
PHONE 740 803-2803
Pam A Westerlund, *President*
Tom Westerlund, *Vice Pres*
EMP: 32
SALES (est): 1.9MM Privately Held
SIC: 8741 Restaurant management

(G-12710)
VAUGHN INDUSTRIES LLC
7749 Green Meadows Dr (43035-9445)
PHONE 740 548-7100
Alan W Rutherford, *Vice Chairman*
Kelli Kitzler, *Manager*
Daniel A Abramowicz, *Bd of Directors*
Karen E Berigan, *Bd of Directors*
Michael B Burns, *Bd of Directors*
EMP: 25
SALES (corp-wide): 158.5MM Privately Held
SIC: 1731 1711 Electrical work; mechanical contractor
PA: Vaughn Industries, Llc
    1201 E Findlay St
    Carey OH 43316
    419 396-3900

Lewisburg
Preble County

(G-12711)
JANUS HOTELS AND RESORTS INC
Also Called: Days Inn
6840 State Route 503 N (45338-9773)
PHONE 513 631-8500
Arun Patel, *Manager*
Parimal Patel, *Manager*
EMP: 25
SALES (corp-wide): 23.5MM Privately Held
WEB: www.bestwesterncambridge.com
SIC: 7011 Hotels
PA: Janus Hotels And Resorts, Inc.
    2300 Nw Corp Blvd Ste 232
    Boca Raton FL 33431
    561 997-2325

(G-12712)
M & L ELECTRIC INC
4439a New Market Banta Rd (45338-7747)
PHONE 937 833-5154
Fax: 937 833-5154
Don Myers, *President*
Mark Lehman, *Vice Pres*
Rebecca Myers, *Treasurer*
EMP: 25
SQ FT: 10,000
SALES (est): 3.1MM Privately Held
SIC: 1731 Electrical work

(G-12713)
NUTRITION TRNSP SVCS LLC
6531 State Route 503 N (45338-6713)
PHONE 937 962-2661
Andrew Willett, *Senior VP*
Carol Combs, *Human Res Mgr*
Scott Rutgers, *Mng Member*
Coulbreath Aleck, *Info Tech Mgr*
EMP: 250
SALES (est): 11.3MM
SALES (corp-wide): 109.7B Privately Held
WEB: www.vigortone.com
SIC: 4731 Freight forwarding
HQ: Provimi North America, Inc.
    10 Collective Way
    Brookville OH 45309
    937 770-2400

Lewisville
Monroe County

(G-12714)
BAKER & SONS EQUIPMENT CO
45381 State Route 145 (43754-9460)
PHONE 740 567-3317
Fax: 740 567-3337
James J Baker, *CEO*
Gregory S Baker, *President*
Steven Baker, *Vice Pres*
Rhonda Marshall, *Manager*
EMP: 25
SQ FT: 18,000
SALES (est): 16MM Privately Held
WEB: www.bakerandsons.com
SIC: 5082 5083 Logging equipment & supplies; agricultural machinery & equipment

Lexington
Richland County

(G-12715)
MEADE CONSTRUCTION INC (PA)
Also Called: Meade Construction Company
13 N Mill St (44904-1200)
PHONE 740 694-5525
Fax: 740 694-1148
Andrew Meade, *CEO*
Chris Thornton, *Corp Secy*
Chris Mortimer, *Senior VP*
Shiela Buckley, *Vice Pres*
Philip Meade, *Vice Pres*
EMP: 30
SALES (est): 8.7MM Privately Held
WEB: www.meadeconstructioninc.com
SIC: 1761 Roofing contractor

Liberty Center
Henry County

(G-12716)
YOUTH SERVICES OHIO DEPARTMENT
Also Called: Maumee Youth Center
Township Rd 1 D U 469 (43532)
PHONE 419 875-6965
Fax: 419 875-5913
Bruce Flory, *Opers Dir*
Nan Hoff, *Manager*
EMP: 145 Privately Held
SIC: 9223 8322 Prison, government; ; youth center
HQ: Department Of Youth Service, Ohio
    30 W Spring St Fl 5
    Columbus OH 43215

Liberty Township
Butler County

(G-12717)
CAPANO & ASSOCIATES LLC
8312 Alpine Aster Ct (45044-1902)
PHONE 513 403-6000
Jeffrey Capano,
Cynthia Capano,
EMP: 49
SQ FT: 2,800
SALES: 15.5MM Privately Held
WEB: www.capanoandassociates.com/
SIC: 8331 8711 Skill training center; professional engineer

(G-12718)
CHESTER WEST YMCA
6703 Yankee Rd (45044-9130)
P.O. Box 692, West Chester (45071-0692)
PHONE 513 779-3917
Fax: 513 759-5438
John Schaller, *Director*
Tom Cuticchia, *Athletic Dir*
EMP: 25

GEOGRAPHIC SECTION

Lima - Allen County (G-12743)

SALES (est): 326.9K **Privately Held**
WEB: www.westchesterrunningclub.com
SIC: 8641 Youth organizations

(G-12719)
CHILDRENS HOSPITAL MEDICAL CTR
7777 Yankee Rd (45044-3500)
PHONE..................513 803-9600
Katherine Kemme, *Research*
Mark Mumford, *CFO*
Catherine Douglas-Penn, *Director*
Beth Haberman, *Director*
Nagendra Monangi, *Director*
EMP: 1051
SALES (corp-wide): 1.6B **Privately Held**
SIC: 8062 8011 General medical & surgical hospitals; medical centers
PA: Children's Hospital Medical Center
3333 Burnet Ave
Cincinnati OH 45229
513 636-4200

(G-12720)
FOUR BRIDGES COUNTRY CLUB LTD
Also Called: Liberty Township
8300 Four Bridges Dr (45044-8489)
PHONE..................513 759-4620
Ron Townsend, *Partner*
Mark Kelley, *General Mgr*
Amanda Cicchinelli, *Director*
Connie Rosenbloom,
EMP: 100
SALES (est): 5.8MM **Privately Held**
WEB: www.fourbridges.com
SIC: 7997 Country club, membership

(G-12721)
KETTERING ADVENTIST HEALTHCARE
Also Called: Kettering Health Network
7117 Dutchland Pkwy (45044-9096)
PHONE..................513 867-3166
EMP: 30
SALES (corp-wide): 1.7B **Privately Held**
SIC: 8742 Construction project management consultant
PA: Kettering Adventist Healthcare
3535 Southern Blvd
Dayton OH 45429
937 298-4331

(G-12722)
LAKOTA LOCAL SCHOOL DISTRICT
Also Called: Bus Garage
6947 Yankee Rd (45044-9719)
PHONE..................513 777-2150
Fax: 513 777-3037
Doug Lantz, *Branch Mgr*
EMP: 230
SALES (corp-wide): 204.7MM **Privately Held**
SIC: 4151 4225 4173 School buses; general warehousing & storage; bus terminal & service facilities
PA: Lakota Local School District
5572 Princeton Rd
Liberty Twp OH 45011
513 874-5505

(G-12723)
LIBERTY CTR LODGING ASSOC LLC
Also Called: Liberty Center AC By Marriott
7505 Gibson St (45069-7517)
PHONE..................608 833-4100
Jacob Dykstra, *Controller*
CJ Raymond, *Mng Member*
EMP: 30
SQ FT: 109,457
SALES (est): 359.5K **Privately Held**
SIC: 7011 Hotels

(G-12724)
SERVICES ON DECK INC (PA)
8263 Kyles Station Rd # 1 (45044-9573)
PHONE..................513 759-2854
Fax: 513 759-2254
Daniel B Stoddard, *President*
EMP: 36
SQ FT: 5,000
SALES (est): 4MM **Privately Held**
SIC: 1521 Patio & deck construction & repair

Liberty Twp
Butler County

(G-12725)
HAMILTON LODGE 93 BENEVOLANT P
Also Called: ELKS B P O E
4444 Hmlton Middletown Rd (45011-2352)
PHONE..................513 887-4384
Richard Sullivan, *President*
EMP: 25
SQ FT: 5,000
SALES: 1.1MM **Privately Held**
SIC: 8641 Fraternal associations

(G-12726)
INDIGO GROUP
4645 Stonehaven Dr (45011-6614)
PHONE..................513 557-8794
EMP: 45
SALES: 1,000K **Privately Held**
SIC: 7371 Web Development And Consulting

(G-12727)
PHYSICIANS CHOICE INC
5130 Prnceton Glendale Rd (45011-2415)
PHONE..................513 844-1608
Fax: 513 844-1803
Tammy Gebhart, *President*
Steven Gephart, *Treasurer*
EMP: 50
SALES (est): 2.3MM **Privately Held**
WEB: www.physicianschoiceinc.com
SIC: 8082 Home health care services

(G-12728)
THE COLUMBIA OIL CO
4951 Hmlton Middletown Rd (45011-2370)
PHONE..................513 868-8700
Fax: 513 785-2100
James W Megginson II, *President*
EMP: 70 EST: 1936
SALES (est): 19.6MM **Privately Held**
WEB: www.lykinscompanies.com
SIC: 5172 5983 Gasoline; fuel oil dealers

Lima
Allen County

(G-12729)
3 B VENTURES LLC
Also Called: 4 Seasons Car Wash
980 N Eastown Rd (45807-2273)
PHONE..................419 236-9461
Kyle Benrogh, *Mng Member*
EMP: 25
SALES: 800K **Privately Held**
SIC: 7542 Washing & polishing, automotive

(G-12730)
AAA ALLIED GROUP INC
2115 Allentown Rd (45805-1749)
PHONE..................419 228-1022
Fax: 419 228-1631
Marion Bicker, *Branch Mgr*
EMP: 35
SALES (corp-wide): 143.9MM **Privately Held**
SIC: 4724 Travel agencies
PA: Aaa Allied Group, Inc.
15 W Central Pkwy
Cincinnati OH 45202
513 762-3100

(G-12731)
ADO STAFFING INC
2100 Harding Hwy (45804-3443)
PHONE..................419 222-8395
John Cavinee, *Branch Mgr*
EMP: 30
SALES (corp-wide): 24B **Privately Held**
WEB: www.adeccona.com
SIC: 7363 Temporary help service
HQ: Ado Staffing, Inc.
175 Broadhollow Rd
Melville NY 11747
631 844-7800

(G-12732)
AERCO SANDBLASTING COMPANY
429 N Jackson St (45801-4121)
PHONE..................419 224-2464
Fax: 419 224-8968
Cynthia Wallace, *President*
Norma Miller, *Corp Secy*
Pearl Miller, *Vice Pres*
EMP: 35
SQ FT: 1,296
SALES: 5.1MM **Privately Held**
SIC: 1799 Sandblasting of building exteriors

(G-12733)
ALLEN CNTY REGIONAL TRNST AUTH
Also Called: R T A
200 E High St Ste 2a (45801-4465)
PHONE..................419 222-2782
Fax: 419 224-0989
Patricia Stein, *Finance*
Scott Stemen, *Manager*
Shelia Schmitt, *Exec Dir*
Lynn Cary, *Director*
EMP: 25
SQ FT: 200,000
SALES (est): 1.6MM **Privately Held**
WEB: www.acrta.com
SIC: 4111 Bus line operations

(G-12734)
ALLEN COUNTY EDUCTL SVC CTR
1920 Slabtown Rd (45801-3309)
PHONE..................419 222-1836
Donald Smith, *Superintendent*
Dean Wittwer, *Superintendent*
Joe Dietrich, *Transptn Dir*
Karla Wireman, *Purch Dir*
Max Place, *Director*
EMP: 91
SALES (est): 1.4MM **Privately Held**
SIC: 8299 8351 Educational services; preschool center

(G-12735)
ALLEN COUNTY RECYCLERS INC
Also Called: Allen County Refuse
541 S Central Ave (45804-1305)
P.O. Box 1264 (45802-1264)
PHONE..................419 223-5010
Fax: 419 224-8387
Otis Roger Wright, *President*
Steve Byrne, *Sales Mgr*
Jennifer Wright, *Office Mgr*
EMP: 37
SQ FT: 5,500
SALES: 1.3MM **Privately Held**
SIC: 5093 Ferrous metal scrap & waste; bottles, waste; plastics scrap; waste paper

(G-12736)
ALLEN METRO HSING MGT DEV CORP
Also Called: Mat
600 S Main St (45804-1242)
PHONE..................410 228-6065
Tiffany Wright, *Principal*
Anna Schnippel, *Exec Dir*
EMP: 27
SALES (est): 981K **Privately Held**
SIC: 6531 Real estate agents & managers

(G-12737)
ALLEN METROPOLITAN HSING AUTH
Also Called: Allen Metro Tenants Councel
600 S Main St (45804-1242)
PHONE..................410 228-6065
Fax: 419 228-1018
James Christman, *Maint Spvr*
Kim Elwer, *Finance Mgr*
Kathy Hubbard, *Finance Asst*
Anna Schnippel, *Exec Dir*
Tiffany Wright, *Director*
EMP: 35

SALES (est): 1.3MM **Privately Held**
WEB: www.allenmha.org
SIC: 6513 Apartment building operators

(G-12738)
ALLIANCE FOR WOMENS HEALTH
310 S Cable Rd (45805-3110)
PHONE..................419 228-1000
Maurice Chung, *President*
Annie Metzger, *Manager*
EMP: 36
SALES (est): 5MM **Privately Held**
SIC: 8011 Obstetrician; gynecologist

(G-12739)
ALLIED ENVIRONMENTAL SVCS INC
585 Liberty Commons Pkwy (45804-1829)
PHONE..................419 227-4004
Fax: 419 229-4106
Kay E Rauch, *President*
Clyde R Rauch, *Vice Pres*
Chad Reynolds, *Sales Mgr*
Steve Carr, *Manager*
EMP: 45
SQ FT: 5,000
SALES (est): 6MM **Privately Held**
WEB: www.allied-environmental.com
SIC: 8748 1799 Environmental consultant; asbestos removal & encapsulation

(G-12740)
AMERICAN ELECTRIC POWER CO INC
369 E Oconnor Ave (45801-2935)
PHONE..................419 998-5106
Luersman Mike, *Principal*
EMP: 33
SALES (corp-wide): 15.4B **Publicly Held**
SIC: 1731 Electrical work
PA: American Electric Power Company, Inc.
1 Riverside Plz Fl 1 # 1
Columbus OH 43215
614 716-1000

(G-12741)
AMERICAN NURSING CARE INC
658 W Market St Ste 200 (45801-5611)
PHONE..................419 228-0888
Fax: 419 227-5709
Tracy Schramke, *Manager*
EMP: 100 **Privately Held**
WEB: www.americannursingcare.com
SIC: 8051 8082 Convalescent home with continuous nursing care; home health care services
HQ: American Nursing Care, Inc.
1700 Edison Dr Ste 300
Milford OH 45150
513 576-0262

(G-12742)
ASSISTED LIVING CONCEPTS LLC
Also Called: Amanda House
1070 Gloria Ave Ofc (45805-2967)
PHONE..................419 224-6327
Fax: 419 224-5554
Janelle Miller, *Manager*
EMP: 35
SALES (corp-wide): 380.5MM **Privately Held**
WEB: www.assistedlivingconcepts.com
SIC: 8361 Home for the aged
HQ: Assisted Living Concepts, Llc
330 N Wabash Ave Ste 3700
Chicago IL 60611

(G-12743)
AT&T MOBILITY LLC
2421 Elida Rd (45805-1203)
PHONE..................419 516-0602
EMP: 26
SALES (corp-wide): 160.5B **Publicly Held**
SIC: 4812 Cellular telephone services
HQ: At&T Mobility Llc
1025 Lenox Park Blvd Ne
Brookhaven GA 30319
800 331-0500

Lima - Allen County (G-12744)

(G-12744)
AUTO-OWNERS LIFE INSURANCE CO
2325 N Cole St (45801-2305)
P.O. Box 4570 (45802-4570)
PHONE..............................419 227-1452
Fax: 419 227-6686
J Fisher, *Div Sub Head*
Scott Wilder, *Manager*
Jim Kuhlman, *Manager*
EMP: 75
SALES (corp-wide): 2.4B **Privately Held**
WEB: www.sheratonlansing.com
SIC: 6411 Insurance agents; fire insurance underwriters' laboratories
HQ: Auto-Owners Life Insurance Company
6101 Anacapri Blvd
Lansing MI 48917

(G-12745)
BENJAMIN STEEL COMPANY INC
Also Called: Lima Division
3111 Saint Johns Rd (45804-4024)
PHONE..............................419 229-8045
Fax: 419 229-8010
Jerry Snyder, *Manager*
EMP: 40
SQ FT: 25,000
SALES (corp-wide): 86.5MM **Privately Held**
WEB: www.benjaminsteel.com
SIC: 5051 Steel
PA: Benjamin Steel Company, Inc.
777 Benjamin Dr
Springfield OH 45502
937 322-8600

(G-12746)
BEST ONE TIRE & SVC LIMA INC (PA)
701 E Hanthorn Rd (45804-3823)
PHONE..............................419 229-2380
David Mitchell, *President*
Sheila Mitchell, *Vice Pres*
▲ EMP: 45 EST: 1933
SQ FT: 100,000
SALES (est): 13.1MM **Privately Held**
WEB: www.eastertire.com
SIC: 7534 5531 5014 Tire recapping; automotive tires; truck tires & tubes

(G-12747)
BETTER BRAKE PARTS INC
915 Shawnee Rd (45805-3439)
PHONE..............................419 227-0685
Fax: 419 228-9092
Rosemarie Mikesell, *CEO*
Edwin F Mikesell, *CEO*
Damien Mikesell, *President*
Ronald Kimmel, *Vice Pres*
Mark Misell, *Vice Pres*
◆ EMP: 40 EST: 1981
SALES (est): 13.5MM **Privately Held**
WEB: www.betterbrake.com
SIC: 5013 Truck parts & accessories; automotive brakes

(G-12748)
BIOLIFE PLASMA SERVICES LP
4299 Elida Rd (45807-1551)
PHONE..............................419 224-0117
Fax: 419 224-2348
Deb Lauth, *Branch Mgr*
EMP: 33
SALES (corp-wide): 11.4B **Privately Held**
WEB: www.biolifeplasma.com
SIC: 8099 Blood bank
HQ: Biolife Plasma Services L.P.
1435 Lake Cook Rd
Philadelphia PA 19182
847 940-5559

(G-12749)
BROOKSIDE HOLDINGS LLC
Also Called: Brookside Trucking
3211 S Dixie Hwy (45804-3759)
PHONE..............................419 224-7019
Fax: 419 224-3590
Tim Knotts, *Manager*
EMP: 30
SALES (corp-wide): 3.8MM **Privately Held**
SIC: 4212 Light haulage & cartage, local

PA: Brookside Holdings, Llc
8022 State Route 119
Maria Stein OH 45860
419 925-4457

(G-12750)
BUCKEYE CHARTER SERVICE INC (PA)
1235 E Hanthorn Rd (45804-3996)
P.O. Box 627 (45802-0627)
PHONE..............................419 222-2455
Fax: 419 222-3817
William Harnishfeger, *President*
Frank Harnishfeger, *Corp Secy*
EMP: 40
SALES (est): 5.1MM **Privately Held**
WEB: www.buckeyecharterservice.com
SIC: 4142 Bus charter service, except local

(G-12751)
CANCER NTWK OF W CENT
Also Called: Cancer Network West Centl Ohio
2615 Fort Amanda Rd (45804-3704)
PHONE..............................419 226-9085
Sheryl Darnell, *Director*
EMP: 30
SALES: 1.6MM **Privately Held**
WEB: www.cancernetwork.com
SIC: 8093 Rehabilitation center, outpatient treatment

(G-12752)
CELLCO PARTNERSHIP
Also Called: Verizon
2465 Elida Rd (45805-1203)
PHONE..............................419 331-4644
Fax: 419 224-4912
Angie Slater, *Manager*
EMP: 25
SALES (corp-wide): 126B **Publicly Held**
SIC: 4812 Cellular telephone services
HQ: Cellco Partnership
1 Verizon Way
Basking Ridge NJ 07920

(G-12753)
CITIZENS NAT BNK OF BLUFFTON
201 N Main St (45801-4432)
P.O. Box 990 (45802-0990)
PHONE..............................419 224-0400
Fax: 419 229-2095
Chad King, *Vice Pres*
Linda Houchin, *Manager*
EMP: 30 **Privately Held**
WEB: www.cnbohio.com
SIC: 6021 National commercial banks
HQ: The Citizens National Bank Of Bluffton
102 S Main St
Bluffton OH 45817
419 358-8040

(G-12754)
CITY OF LIMA
Streets & Traffic
900 S Collett St (45804-1005)
PHONE..............................419 221-5165
Fax: 419 222-5522
Saul Allen, *Director*
EMP: 50 **Privately Held**
WEB: www.cityhall.lima.oh.us
SIC: 9621 1611 ; highway & street paving contractor
PA: City Of Lima
50 Town Sq
Lima OH 45801
419 228-5462

(G-12755)
CITY OF LIMA
Sanitary Engineer
50 Town Sq Fl 3 (45801-4948)
P.O. Box 1198 (45802-1198)
PHONE..............................419 221-5294
David Burger, *Mayor*
Sharetta Smith, *Senior Mgr*
EMP: 400 **Privately Held**
WEB: www.cityhall.lima.oh.us
SIC: 4959 Sanitary services
PA: City Of Lima
50 Town Sq
Lima OH 45801
419 228-5462

(G-12756)
CITY OF LIMA
Also Called: Utility Field Services
1405 Reservoir Rd (45802-2937)
PHONE..............................419 221-5175
Larry Huber, *Manager*
Steve Lee, *Manager*
EMP: 30
SQ FT: 624 **Privately Held**
WEB: www.cityhall.lima.oh.us
SIC: 4952 Sewerage systems
PA: City Of Lima
50 Town Sq
Lima OH 45801
419 228-5462

(G-12757)
COLUMBIA PROPERTIES LIMA LLC
Also Called: Holiday Inn
1920 Roschman Ave (45804-3444)
PHONE..............................419 222-0004
Fax: 419 222-2176
Sharron Snider, *Sales Executive*
EMP: 80
SALES (est): 1.2MM **Privately Held**
SIC: 7011 Hotels & motels

(G-12758)
COMFORT KEEPERS
Also Called: Kin Care
1726 Allentown Rd (45805-1856)
PHONE..............................419 229-1031
Fax: 419 229-1032
Peggy J Kincaid, *President*
Walter Kincaid Jr, *Vice Pres*
EMP: 46
SALES (est): 1.4MM **Privately Held**
SIC: 8082 Visiting nurse service

(G-12759)
CONTINUED CARE INC
920 W Market St Ste 202 (45805-2774)
PHONE..............................419 222-2273
Fax: 419 222-6261
Francis Oruma, *President*
Rose Cookey-Aruma, *Vice Pres*
EMP: 25
SQ FT: 1,000
SALES (est): 1.4MM **Privately Held**
SIC: 8082 Home health care services

(G-12760)
CORA HEALTH SERVICES INC (PA)
1110 Shawnee Rd (45805-3529)
P.O. Box 150 (45802-0150)
PHONE..............................419 221-3004
Fax: 419 221-3070
Dennis R Smith, *President*
Justin A Borra, *COO*
Brad C Roush, *Exec VP*
Sally Darlin, *Vice Pres*
Stephen R Krzyminski, *CFO*
▲ EMP: 40
SQ FT: 9,000
SALES (est): 43.8MM **Privately Held**
SIC: 8093 Rehabilitation center, outpatient treatment

(G-12761)
CORPORATE SUPPORT INC (PA)
750 Buckeye Rd (45804-1935)
PHONE..............................419 221-3838
Fax: 419 221-3842
Harold Breidenbach, *CEO*
Troy Breidenbach, *President*
Marc Finn, *Vice Pres*
William Schroeder, *Vice Pres*
John Whittaker, *Shareholder*
EMP: 50
SQ FT: 300,000
SALES (est): 8.2MM **Privately Held**
SIC: 7389 Packaging & labeling services

(G-12762)
COUNTY OF ALLEN
Also Called: Allen Metro Housinig Auth
600 S Main St (45804-1242)
PHONE..............................419 228-6065
Laura Johnson, *Manager*
Cindi Parr, *Exec Dir*
Cindy Ring, *Director*
EMP: 25 **Privately Held**

WEB: www.allencountyohio.com
SIC: 6531 Housing authority operator
PA: County Of Allen
301 N Main St
Lima OH 45801
419 228-3700

(G-12763)
COUNTY OF ALLEN
Also Called: Allen County Health Care Ctr
3125 Ada Rd (45801-3328)
PHONE..............................419 221-1103
Fax: 419 221-1125
Jerome O'Neal, *Administration*
Jerome Neal, *Administration*
EMP: 110 **Privately Held**
WEB: www.allencountyohio.com
SIC: 8361 8051 Home for the aged; skilled nursing care facilities
PA: County Of Allen
301 N Main St
Lima OH 45801
419 228-3700

(G-12764)
COUNTY OF ALLEN
Also Called: Information & Referral Center
1501 S Dixie Hwy (45804-1844)
P.O. Box 4506 (45802-4506)
PHONE..............................419 228-2120
Fax: 419 227-2448
Lynn Shock, *Director*
EMP: 150 **Privately Held**
WEB: www.allencountyohio.com
SIC: 8322 Social service center
PA: County Of Allen
301 N Main St
Lima OH 45801
419 228-3700

(G-12765)
COUNTY OF ALLEN
Also Called: Allen County Childrens Svcs Bd
123 W Spring St (45801-4833)
PHONE..............................419 227-8590
Fax: 419 229-2296
Mike Mullins, *Director*
Cynthia Scanland, *Director*
EMP: 40 **Privately Held**
WEB: www.allencountyohio.com
SIC: 8322 Child related social services
PA: County Of Allen
301 N Main St
Lima OH 45801
419 228-3700

(G-12766)
COUNTY OF ALLEN
Also Called: Marimor Industries
2450 Ada Rd (45801-3342)
PHONE..............................419 221-1226
Angie Herzog, *Manager*
EMP: 50 **Privately Held**
WEB: www.allencountyohio.com
SIC: 8093 Mental health clinic, outpatient
PA: County Of Allen
301 N Main St
Lima OH 45801
419 228-3700

(G-12767)
COUNTY OF ALLEN
Also Called: Bureau of Support
608 W High St (45801-4706)
P.O. Box 1589 (45802-1589)
PHONE..............................419 996-7050
Fax: 419 222-6135
Daniel Cade, *Director*
EMP: 37
SQ FT: 3,424 **Privately Held**
WEB: www.allencountyohio.com
SIC: 8322 Child related social services
PA: County Of Allen
301 N Main St
Lima OH 45801
419 228-3700

(G-12768)
CSS PUBLISHING CO INC
5450 N Dixie Hwy (45807-9559)
PHONE..............................419 227-1818
Wesley T Runk, *President*
Patti Furr, *Vice Pres*
Elen Shockey, *Treasurer*
David Runk, *VP Sales*
Alanna Pugsley, *Marketing Staff*

GEOGRAPHIC SECTION
Lima - Allen County (G-12794)

EMP: 30
SQ FT: 50,000
SALES (est): 2.6MM **Privately Held**
WEB: www.csspub.com
SIC: **2731** 5192 Books: publishing only; books

(G-12769)
CSX CORPORATION
401 E Robb Ave (45801-2952)
PHONE..........................419 225-4121
Fax: 419 228-4272
Eric Osborn, *Principal*
Tony Ferrera, *Manager*
EMP: 149
SALES (corp-wide): 11.4B **Publicly Held**
WEB: www.csx.com
SIC: **4011** Railroads, line-haul operating
PA: Csx Corporation
 500 Water St Fl 15
 Jacksonville FL 32202
 904 359-3200

(G-12770)
CUSTOM STAFFING INC (PA)
505 W Market St (45801-4717)
P.O. Box 5275 (45802-5275)
PHONE..........................419 221-3097
Mike Simmons, *General Mgr*
EMP: 39
SALES (est): 6.5MM **Privately Held**
WEB: www.customstaffing-online.com
SIC: **7363** 7361 Temporary help service; employment agencies

(G-12771)
EAST OF CHICAGO PIZZA INC (PA)
121 W High St Fl 12 (45801-4349)
PHONE..........................419 225-7116
Anthony Collins, *President*
Chuck McGee, *Vice Pres*
Darlene Thomas, *Branch Mgr*
Tony Collins, *Manager*
EMP: 29
SALES (est): 16.8MM **Privately Held**
SIC: **6794** 5812 Franchises, selling or licensing; pizzeria, chain

(G-12772)
EDGEWOOD SKATE ARENA
2170 Edgewood Dr (45805-1147)
PHONE..........................419 331-0647
Betty Ray, *President*
Jerid Ray, *President*
EMP: 25
SQ FT: 24,000
SALES: 232.8K **Privately Held**
SIC: **7999** Roller skating rink operation

(G-12773)
ELDERLY DAY CARE CENTER
225 E High St (45801-4419)
PHONE..........................419 228-2688
Diane Bishope, *Exec Dir*
EMP: 25
SALES (est): 547.9K **Privately Held**
SIC: **8351** Child day care services

(G-12774)
EXEL INC
635 N Cool Rd (45801-9707)
PHONE..........................419 996-7703
EMP: 55
SALES (corp-wide): 71.2B **Privately Held**
SIC: **4225** General warehousing
HQ: Exel Inc.
 570 Polaris Pkwy
 Westerville OH 43082
 614 865-8500

(G-12775)
EXEL INC
3875 Reservoir Rd (45801-3310)
PHONE..........................419 226-5500
Daniel King, *Manager*
John Haverstick, *Manager*
Sharon Post, *Executive*
EMP: 100
SALES (corp-wide): 71.2B **Privately Held**
WEB: www.exel-logistics.com
SIC: **4225** General warehousing
HQ: Exel Inc.
 570 Polaris Pkwy
 Westerville OH 43082
 614 865-8500

(G-12776)
FAMILY BIRTH CENTER LIMA MEM
1001 Bellefontaine Ave (45804-2800)
PHONE..........................419 998-4570
Fax: 419 998-4571
Jacque Perrin, *Exec Dir*
Kathy Davis, *Director*
EMP: 35 EST: 1998
SALES (est): 410.9K **Privately Held**
SIC: **8099** Childbirth preparation clinic

(G-12777)
FAMILY RSOURCE CTR NW OHIO INC (PA)
Also Called: Northwest Fam Svc Dda Fam Rsou
530 S Main St (45804-1240)
PHONE..........................419 222-1168
Fax: 419 222-7610
John Bindas, *President*
Mark Howe, *CFO*
Charles Powell, *Treasurer*
Alicia Cook, *Case Mgr*
Laura Brickner, *Manager*
EMP: 50
SQ FT: 23,000
SALES: 3.9MM **Privately Held**
WEB: www.frcohio.com
SIC: **8093** Mental health clinic, outpatient; drug clinic, outpatient; alcohol clinic, outpatient

(G-12778)
FARMERS EQUIPMENT INC
6008 Elida Rd (45807-9453)
PHONE..........................419 339-7000
Todd Channel, *General Mgr*
EMP: 42
SALES (est): 1.1MM
SALES (corp-wide): 12.4MM **Privately Held**
SIC: **5083** Farm implements
PA: Farmers Equipment, Inc.
 1749 E Us Highway 36 A
 Urbana OH 43078
 419 339-7000

(G-12779)
FAT JACKS PIZZA II INC (PA)
1806 N West St (45801-2631)
PHONE..........................419 227-1813
David Boyles, *President*
EMP: 25
SQ FT: 6,000
SALES: 2.1MM **Privately Held**
WEB: www.fatjackspizza.com
SIC: **5812** 5813 7999 Pizzeria, independent; drinking places; lottery tickets, sale of

(G-12780)
FEDERAL EXPRESS CORPORATION
Also Called: Fedex
3499 Saint Johns Rd (45804-4018)
PHONE..........................800 463-3339
Damond Ellison, *Manager*
EMP: 27
SALES (corp-wide): 60.3B **Publicly Held**
WEB: www.federalexpress.com
SIC: **4513** Letter delivery, private air; package delivery, private air; parcel delivery, private air
HQ: Federal Express Corporation
 3610 Hacks Cross Rd
 Memphis TN 38125
 901 369-3600

(G-12781)
FEDEX FREIGHT CORPORATION
2335 Saint Johns Rd (45804-3862)
PHONE..........................800 521-3505
Fax: 419 228-6722
Robin Lynn, *Manager*
EMP: 39
SALES (corp-wide): 60.3B **Publicly Held**
SIC: **4213** 4731 4215 Less-than-truckload (LTL) transport; freight transportation arrangement; courier services, except by air
HQ: Fedex Freight Corporation
 1715 Aaron Brenner Dr
 Memphis TN 38120

(G-12782)
GENERAL AUDIT CORP
Also Called: Keybridge Medical Revenue MGT
2348 Baton Rouge Ste A (45805-1167)
P.O. Box 1568 (45802-1568)
PHONE..........................419 993-2900
Scott G Koenig, *President*
Michael J Miller, *General Mgr*
Ned E Koenig, *Chairman*
N Jean Koenig, *Corp Secy*
Brandon Lee, *Vice Pres*
EMP: 40
SQ FT: 6,300
SALES (est): 5.3MM **Privately Held**
SIC: **8111** Collection agency, except real estate; legal services

(G-12783)
GIRL SCUTS APPLESEED RIDGE INC
1870 W Robb Ave (45805-1535)
PHONE..........................419 225-4085
Fax: 419 229-7570
Jane Krites, *CEO*
EMP: 30
SQ FT: 1,404
SALES: 1.5MM **Privately Held**
SIC: **8641** 8322 Girl Scout organization; individual & family services

(G-12784)
GOLDEN LIVING LLC
Also Called: Beverly
599 S Shawnee St (45804-1461)
PHONE..........................419 227-2154
Peggy Stewart, *Manager*
EMP: 100
SALES (corp-wide): 7.4MM **Privately Held**
SIC: **8059** 8052 8051 Convalescent home; intermediate care facilities; convalescent home with continuous nursing care
PA: Golden Living Llc
 5220 Tennyson Pkwy # 400
 Plano TX 75024
 972 372-6300

(G-12785)
GOODWILL INDUSTRIES OF LIMA (PA)
940 N Cable Rd Ste 1 (45805-1739)
PHONE..........................419 228-4821
Fax: 419 222-5269
Eugene Montycka, *President*
Amy Lutell, *President*
Evelyn E Thompson, *Admin Asst*
EMP: 86
SQ FT: 22,000
SALES (est): 2.6MM **Privately Held**
WEB: www.limagoodwill.org
SIC: **8331** Vocational rehabilitation agency

(G-12786)
GORDON FOOD SERVICE INC
Also Called: G F S Marketplace
3447 Elida Rd (45807-1627)
PHONE..........................419 225-8983
Fax: 419 225-9715
Dennis Clay, *Manager*
EMP: 25
SALES (corp-wide): 88.9MM **Privately Held**
WEB: www.gfs.com
SIC: **5149** 5142 Groceries & related products; packaged frozen goods
PA: Gordon Food Service, Inc.
 1300 Gezon Pkwy Sw
 Wyoming MI 49509
 888 437-3663

(G-12787)
GREENFIELD HTS OPER GROUP LLC ✪
1318 Chestnut St (45804-2542)
PHONE..........................312 877-1153
Josiah Mathews,
EMP: 50 EST: 2017
SALES (est): 2.3MM **Privately Held**
SIC: **5122** Pharmaceuticals

(G-12788)
GUARDIAN ELDE
Also Called: Lost Creek Health C
804 S Mumaugh Rd (45804-3569)
PHONE..........................419 225-9040
Brian Bosak, *Accounting Mgr*
Georgia Brumbrugh,
EMP: 95 EST: 2012
SALES (est): 2.4MM **Privately Held**
SIC: **8052** Intermediate care facilities

(G-12789)
GUARDSMARK LLC
209 N Main St Ste 4a (45801-4494)
PHONE..........................419 229-9300
Mark Morrissey, *Manager*
EMP: 45
SALES (corp-wide): 746.3MM **Privately Held**
WEB: www.guardsmark.com
SIC: **7381** Security guard service
HQ: Guardsmark, Llc
 1551 N Tustin Ave Ste 650
 Santa Ana CA 92705
 714 619-9700

(G-12790)
HARTER VENTURES INC
Also Called: Lima-Allen County Paramedics
3623 S Buckskin Trl (45807-2168)
PHONE..........................419 224-4075
Fax: 419 227-6847
Brad Harter, *President*
EMP: 53
SQ FT: 8,000
SALES (est): 2.8MM **Privately Held**
SIC: **8099** 4119 Medical rescue squad; ambulance service

(G-12791)
HCF MANAGEMENT INC (PA)
Also Called: Health Care Facilities
1100 Shawnee Rd (45805-3583)
PHONE..........................419 999-2010
Fax: 419 999-6284
Robert Wilson, *CEO*
Jim Unverferth, *President*
Shane Stewart, *Regional Mgr*
Dave Walsh, *Regional Mgr*
Steve Wilder, *Exec VP*
EMP: 60
SQ FT: 15,000
SALES (est): 154.8MM **Privately Held**
WEB: www.hcfinc.com
SIC: **8051** 6513 Convalescent home with continuous nursing care; apartment building operators

(G-12792)
HCF MANAGEMENT INC
Also Called: Shawnee Manor Nursing Home
2535 Fort Amanda Rd (45804-3728)
PHONE..........................419 999-2055
Fax: 419 999-5410
Kevin Kidd, *Director*
Wendy Harbarger, *Executive*
EMP: 175
SALES (corp-wide): 154.8MM **Privately Held**
WEB: www.hcfinc.com
SIC: **8361** 8051 Geriatric residential care; skilled nursing care facilities
PA: Hcf Management, Inc.
 1100 Shawnee Rd
 Lima OH 45805
 419 999-2010

(G-12793)
HCF OF LIMA INC
Also Called: Lima Manor
1100 Shawnee Rd (45805-3583)
PHONE..........................419 999-2010
EMP: 81
SALES (corp-wide): 3.2MM **Privately Held**
SIC: **8051** Skilled nursing care facilities
PA: Hcf Of Lima, Inc.
 750 Brower Rd
 Lima OH 45801
 419 227-2611

(G-12794)
HCF OF SHAWNEE INC
Also Called: Shawnee Manor
2535 Fort Amanda Rd (45804-3728)
PHONE..........................419 999-2055

David Walsh, *Vice Pres*
Renee Schmehl, *Hum Res Coord*
Brenda Bruce, *Marketing Staff*
Val Doty, *Nursing Dir*
Amy Niese, *Nursing Dir*
EMP: 99
SALES: 950K **Privately Held**
SIC: 8051 Convalescent home with continuous nursing care

(G-12795)
HEALTH PARTNERS WESTERN OHIO (PA)
Also Called: Lima Community Health Center
441 E 8th St (45804-2482)
PHONE..................................419 221-3072
Janis Sunderhaus, *Partner*
Melissa Bowman, *Finance*
Nanette Weaver, *Human Res Dir*
Micah J Swoboda, *Pharmacist*
Angela M Trent, *Pharmacist*
EMP: 92
SALES: 23.2MM **Privately Held**
WEB: www.achp.biz
SIC: 8399 Health systems agency

(G-12796)
HEALTHPRO MEDICAL BILLING INC
4132 Elida Rd (45807-1548)
PHONE..................................419 223-2717
John Stiles, *President*
Megan Rodden, *Opers Staff*
Jaime Hale, *Human Res Mgr*
Cheri Brinkman, *Manager*
Nicole Jett, *Manager*
EMP: 55 **EST:** 1981
SALES (est): 4.2MM **Privately Held**
WEB: www.healthpromedical.com
SIC: 8721 Billing & bookkeeping service

(G-12797)
HECTOR A BUCH JR MD
Also Called: Positions
750 W High St Ste 250 (45801-3959)
PHONE..................................419 227-7399
Hector Buch, *Principal*
EMP: 30 **EST:** 2001
SALES (est): 513.6K **Privately Held**
SIC: 8011 Internal medicine, physician/surgeon

(G-12798)
HERITAGE HEALTH CARE SERVICES
3748 Allentown Rd (45807-2140)
PHONE..................................419 222-2404
Fax: 419 222-2478
Pam Frese, *Manager*
Aubrey Ackles, *Executive*
EMP: 55
SALES (corp-wide): 10MM **Privately Held**
SIC: 8082 Home health care services
PA: Heritage Health Care Services, Inc
 1745 Indian Wood Cir # 252
 Maumee OH 43537
 419 867-2002

(G-12799)
HR SERVICES INC
675 W Market St Ste 200 (45801-5619)
P.O. Box 1155 (45802-1155)
PHONE..................................419 224-2462
Fax: 419 221-2687
Robert Schulte, *President*
Amy Morman, *Manager*
Drew Kimmet, *Network Enginr*
Drew Kimmett, *Network Enginr*
Jenni Roof, *Director*
EMP: 25
SQ FT: 8,500
SALES (est): 1.2MM
SALES (corp-wide): 3.1B **Publicly Held**
WEB: www.mystaffingpro.com
SIC: 7363 7361 Employee leasing service; employment agencies
PA: Paychex, Inc.
 911 Panorama Trl S
 Rochester NY 14625
 585 385-6666

(G-12800)
HUME SUPPLY INC
1359 E Hanthorn Rd (45804-3933)
PHONE..................................419 991-5751
Fax: 419 991-5751
Daven Stedke, *President*
John E Stedke, *Vice Pres*
Cory McMichael, *Project Mgr*
Brad Scarberry, *Project Mgr*
Janice Stedke, *Treasurer*
EMP: 42 **EST:** 1948
SQ FT: 15,000
SALES (est): 11.1MM **Privately Held**
WEB: www.humesupply.com
SIC: 1541 Industrial buildings, new construction

(G-12801)
HUNTINGTON NATIONAL BANK
Also Called: Home Mortgage
631 W Market St (45804-4603)
PHONE..................................419 226-8200
Fax: 419 229-6601
Rick Kortokrax, *Manager*
EMP: 50
SALES (corp-wide): 4.7B **Publicly Held**
WEB: www.huntingtonnationalbank.com
SIC: 6029 6162 6021 Commercial banks; mortgage bankers; national commercial banks
HQ: The Huntington National Bank
 17 S High St Fl 1
 Columbus OH 43215
 614 480-4293

(G-12802)
I H S SERVICES INC
3225 W Elm St Ste D (45805-2520)
PHONE..................................419 224-8811
Fax: 419 224-2393
Janet Seward, *Director*
EMP: 40 **Privately Held**
SIC: 6531 Real estate managers
PA: I H S Services Inc
 5888 Cleveland Ave # 201
 Columbus OH 43231

(G-12803)
IHEARTCOMMUNICATIONS INC
Also Called: Clear Channel
667 W Market St (45804-4603)
PHONE..................................419 223-2060
Kim Field, *General Mgr*
Matt Bell, *Sales Executive*
John Bell, *Executive*
Robin Palmer, *Executive*
EMP: 65 **Publicly Held**
SIC: 4832 2711 Radio broadcasting stations; newspapers
HQ: Iheartcommunications, Inc.
 20880 Stone Oak Pkwy
 San Antonio TX 78258
 210 822-2828

(G-12804)
INDIANA & OHIO RAIL CORP
1750 N Sugar St (45801-3138)
PHONE..................................419 229-1010
Fax: 419 222-0197
Brad Urton, *Manager*
EMP: 25
SALES (corp-wide): 2.2B **Publicly Held**
SIC: 4011 Railroads, line-haul operating
HQ: The Indiana & Ohio Rail Corp
 2856 Cypress Way
 Cincinnati OH 45212
 513 860-1000

(G-12805)
INTERDYNE CORPORATION
931 N Jefferson St (45801-4166)
PHONE..................................419 227-0015
Fax: 419 227-0015
Powell Prater, *President*
M D Basinger, *Principal*
Richard E Meredith, *Principal*
Dan Lucke, *Vice Pres*
Clint Rolland, *Vice Pres*
EMP: 35
SQ FT: 55,000
SALES (est): 9.7MM **Privately Held**
WEB: www.interdyne-transvac.com
SIC: 4959 8748 Environmental cleanup services; environmental consultant

(G-12806)
JACOBS CONSTRUCTORS INC
Also Called: Equipment Yard & Maint Div
1840 Buckeye Rd Gatew (45804-1830)
P.O. Box 5365 (45802-5365)
PHONE..................................419 226-1344
W Don Turner, *Manager*
EMP: 80
SALES (corp-wide): 10B **Publicly Held**
SIC: 1629 8711 Dams, waterways, docks & other marine construction; engineering services
HQ: Jacobs Constructors, Inc.
 4949 Essen Ln
 Baton Rouge LA 70809
 225 769-7700

(G-12807)
K M CLEMENS DDS INC
Also Called: Butts, Charles L II DDS
2115 Allentown Rd Ste C (45805-1749)
PHONE..................................419 228-4036
Kenneth M Clemens, *President*
EMP: 25
SALES: 2MM **Privately Held**
SIC: 6799 Investors

(G-12808)
KIDNEY SERVICES W CENTL OHIO
750 W High St Ste 100 (45801-3959)
PHONE..................................419 227-0918
Dodi West, *CEO*
Patty Smith, *Manager*
EMP: 50
SALES: 6.6MM **Privately Held**
SIC: 8092 Kidney dialysis centers

(G-12809)
KINDRED HEALTHCARE INC
Also Called: Scci Hospital Lima
730 W Market St (45801-4602)
PHONE..................................419 224-1888
Joe Rayman, *Purch Dir*
Gwen Taulbee, *Branch Mgr*
Cynthia Grone, *Pharmacy Dir*
EMP: 77
SALES (corp-wide): 6B **Publicly Held**
SIC: 8099 Blood related health services
PA: Kindred Healthcare, Inc.
 680 S 4th St
 Louisville KY 40202
 502 596-7300

(G-12810)
KINDRED HOSPITAL CENTRAL OHIO
730 W Market St (45801-4602)
PHONE..................................419 526-0777
Vanessa Nelson, *CEO*
EMP: 37
SALES (est): 4.4MM **Privately Held**
SIC: 8062 General medical & surgical hospitals

(G-12811)
KLEMAN SERVICES LLC
Also Called: ServiceMaster
2150 Baty Rd (45807-1957)
PHONE..................................419 339-0871
Fax: 419 339-0872
Michael C Kleman, *Mng Member*
Adam Kleman, *Manager*
EMP: 30
SQ FT: 7,500
SALES: 1MM **Privately Held**
SIC: 7349 Building maintenance services

(G-12812)
KOI SIFERD HOSSELLMAN (PA)
700 N Main St (45801-4012)
PHONE..................................419 228-1221
Andrew W Burneson, *President*
David Wesselman, *President*
EMP: 31 **EST:** 1919
SQ FT: 31,000
SALES (est): 6.6MM **Privately Held**
SIC: 5085 Industrial supplies

(G-12813)
LA KING TRUCKING INC
1516 Findlay Rd (45801-3110)
PHONE..................................419 225-9039
Russell J King, *President*
Bob Werling, *Manager*

Derrol R King, *Shareholder*
Kenneth E Lawrence, *Shareholder*
EMP: 40
SQ FT: 4,800
SALES (est): 4.3MM **Privately Held**
SIC: 4213 Contract haulers

(G-12814)
LACP ST RITAS MEDICAL CTR LLC
708 W Spring St (45801-4661)
PHONE..................................419 324-4075
David Pohlman, *Coordinator*
EMP: 60
SALES (est): 829.2K **Privately Held**
SIC: 4119 Ambulance service

(G-12815)
LANES TRANSFER INC
Also Called: Lane's Moving & Storage
245 E Murphy St (45801-4172)
PHONE..................................419 222-8692
Richard Lane, *President*
Brad A King, *Principal*
Janet Lane, *Vice Pres*
Tod Lane, *Manager*
EMP: 25
SQ FT: 20,000
SALES (est): 3.9MM **Privately Held**
SIC: 7513 Truck leasing, without drivers

(G-12816)
LIMA AUTO MALL INC
Also Called: Lima Cdllac Pntiac Olds Nissan
2200 N Cable Rd (45807-1792)
P.O. Box 1649 (45802-1649)
PHONE..................................419 993-6000
Fax: 419 993-6112
William C Timmermeister, *President*
Matt Kondik, *Business Mgr*
Susan B Timmermeister, *Corp Secy*
Rodger L Mc Clain, *Vice Pres*
Ryan Swaney, *Sales Mgr*
EMP: 100 **EST:** 1921
SQ FT: 21,000
SALES (est): 39.8MM **Privately Held**
WEB: www.limaautomall.com
SIC: 5511 7538 7532 7515 Automobiles, new & used; general automotive repair shops; top & body repair & paint shops; passenger car leasing

(G-12817)
LIMA CITY SCHOOL DISTRICT
Also Called: Lima City School Central Svcs
600 E Wayne St (45801-4182)
PHONE..................................419 996-3450
Tim Haller, *Principal*
Randy Crossley, *Manager*
EMP: 28
SALES (corp-wide): 51.8MM **Privately Held**
SIC: 8211 4151 7538 Public elementary school; school buses; general automotive repair shops
PA: Lima City School District
 755 Saint Johns Ave
 Lima OH 45804
 419 996-3400

(G-12818)
LIMA CNVLSCENT HM FNDATION INC (PA)
1650 Allentown Rd (45805-1802)
PHONE..................................419 227-5450
Fax: 419 224-2761
Randy Bond, *Finance*
Becky Morris, *Office Mgr*
Randy Cox, *Exec Dir*
Joy Reichenbach, *Exec Dir*
Amy Howard, *Director*
EMP: 60
SQ FT: 41,886
SALES: 6.1MM **Privately Held**
WEB: www.limalochhaven.com
SIC: 8059 8051 Convalescent home; personal care home, with health care; skilled nursing care facilities

(G-12819)
LIMA COMMUNICATIONS CORP
Also Called: Wlio Television-Channel 35
1424 Rice Ave (45805-1949)
PHONE..................................419 228-8835
Fax: 419 229-7091
Kevin Creamer, *President*

GEOGRAPHIC SECTION

Lima - Allen County (G-12842)

Frederick R Vobbe, *Vice Pres*
Donna Stuttler, *Warehouse Mgr*
David E Plaugher, *Treasurer*
Michael Carpenter, *Producer*
EMP: 75
SQ FT: 5,000
SALES (est): 11.1MM
SALES (corp-wide): 690.9MM Privately Held
WEB: www.wlio.com
SIC: 4833 Television broadcasting stations
PA: Block Communications, Inc.
  405 Madison Ave Ste 2100
  Toledo OH 43604
  419 724-6212

(G-12820)
LIMA DENTAL ASSOC RISOLVATO LT
2115 Allentown Rd Ste C (45805-1749)
PHONE 419 228-4036
Erik J Risolvato, *Principal*
Corey Risolvato, *Top Exec*
Brenda Kimmett, *Dental Hygenist*
Carol Mohr, *Dental Hygenist*
EMP: 25
SALES (est): 2.1MM Privately Held
SIC: 8021 Offices & clinics of dentists

(G-12821)
LIMA FAMILY YMCA (PA)
345 S Elizabeth St (45801-4805)
PHONE 419 223-6045
Clyde Raush, *Ch of Bd*
William Blewit, *President*
Terri Averesch, *Senior VP*
Julie Jordan, *Controller*
Chriss Martin, *Controller*
EMP: 39 **EST:** 1888
SQ FT: 111,000
SALES: 3.8MM Privately Held
WEB: www.limaymca.net
SIC: 8641 8351 8322 7991 Civic associations; child day care services; individual & family services; physical fitness facilities

(G-12822)
LIMA MALL INC
2400 Elida Rd Ste 166 (45805-1233)
PHONE 419 331-6255
Fax: 419 331-0502
Edward J Debartolo Sr, *Ch of Bd*
Simon Debartolo, *President*
Edward J Debartolo Jr, *President*
Chris Garlock, *Mktg Dir*
EMP: 30
SQ FT: 750,000
SALES (est): 1.8MM
SALES (corp-wide): 19.2MM Privately Held
WEB: www.shoprivercenter.com
SIC: 6512 Shopping center, property operation only
PA: Nid Corporation
  15436 N Florida Ave # 200
  Tampa FL 33613
  813 908-8400

(G-12823)
LIMA MEDICAL SUPPLIES INC
770 W North St (45801-3923)
PHONE 419 226-9581
Fax: 419 228-1233
April Enderud, *Manager*
Ron Drees, *Director*
EMP: 39 **EST:** 1964
SQ FT: 13,000
SALES (est): 330.1K
SALES (corp-wide): 4.2B Privately Held
SIC: 5047 Medical equipment & supplies
HQ: Mcauley Management Services, Inc.
  730 W Market St
  Lima OH 45801
  419 226-9684

(G-12824)
LIMA MEMORIAL HOSPITAL (HQ)
Also Called: Lima Memorial Health System
1001 Bellefontaine Ave (45804-2899)
P.O. Box 932842, Cleveland (44193-0023)
PHONE 419 228-3335
Fax: 419 226-5013
Michael Swick, *President*
Bob Armstrong, *Vice Pres*
Beth Skym, *Project Mgr*
Aubrey Cook, *Buyer*
Donna Miller, *Buyer*
EMP: 87
SALES: 184.6MM
SALES (corp-wide): 189.6MM Privately Held
SIC: 8062 General medical & surgical hospitals
PA: Lima Memorial Joint Operating Company
  1001 Belelfontaine Ave
  Lima OH 45804
  419 228-5165

(G-12825)
LIMA MEMORIAL JOINT OPER CO (PA)
1001 Belelfontaine Ave (45804)
P.O. Box 932842, Cleveland (44193-0023)
PHONE 419 228-5165
Michael Swick, *President*
Eric Pohjala, *CFO*
Sandra Young, *Director*
EMP: 1500
SALES: 189.6MM Privately Held
SIC: 8062 General medical & surgical hospitals

(G-12826)
LIMA PATHOLOGY ASSOCIATES LABS (PA)
Also Called: Findlay Laboratory Services
415 W Market St Ste B (45801-4786)
PHONE 419 226-9595
Fax: 419 224-0866
Joseph Sreenan, *President*
Anne M Gideon, *Treasurer*
EMP: 26
SQ FT: 3,200
SALES: 6MM Privately Held
WEB: www.limapathlabs.com
SIC: 8071 Pathological laboratory

(G-12827)
LIMA SHEET METAL MACHINE & MFG
1001 Bowman Rd (45804-3409)
PHONE 419 229-1161
Fax: 419 229-8538
Michael R Emerick, *President*
Ann Emerick, *Corp Secy*
Thomas Emerick, *Exec VP*
Brian Hershberger, *Project Mgr*
Steve Emerick, *Engineer*
EMP: 31 **EST:** 1974
SQ FT: 26,250
SALES (est): 6.6MM Privately Held
WEB: www.limasheetmetal.com
SIC: 3589 3599 7349 7692 Commercial cooking & foodwarming equipment; machine shop, jobbing & repair; building maintenance, except repairs; welding repair; food products machinery; sheet metalwork

(G-12828)
LIMA SUPERIOR FEDERAL CR UN (PA)
4230 Elida Rd (45807-1550)
P.O. Box 1110 (45802-1110)
PHONE 419 223-9746
Fax: 419 224-2803
Phil Buell, *President*
Matt Otto, *President*
Susan Wagner, *Senior VP*
Jeff Beining, *Vice Pres*
Stephen Oren, *Vice Pres*
EMP: 105
SQ FT: 5,200
SALES: 18.2MM Privately Held
SIC: 6061 Federal credit unions

(G-12829)
LIPPINCOTT PLUMBING-HEATING AC
872 Saint Johns Ave (45804-1567)
PHONE 419 222-0856
Fax: 419 222-2357
Michael Ray Lawrence, *President*
Rebecca Sue Lawrence, *Corp Secy*
Richard Michael Lyons, *Vice Pres*
EMP: 25
SQ FT: 2,000
SALES (est): 5.6MM Privately Held
SIC: 1731 1711 Electrical work; plumbing contractors

(G-12830)
LITTLE SQUIRT SPORTS PARK
1996 W Robb Ave (45805-1537)
P.O. Box 367587, Bonita Springs FL (34136-7587)
PHONE 419 227-6200
Fax: 419 227-6200
Victoria Strickland, *President*
Norman Greber, *Owner*
EMP: 50 **EST:** 1994
SALES (est): 1.1MM Privately Held
SIC: 7996 Kiddie park

(G-12831)
LOST CREEK COUNTRY CLUB INC
2409 Lost Creek Blvd (45804-3221)
PHONE 419 228-4399
Fax: 419 228-4399
Matt Holtsberry, *President*
EMP: 34
SQ FT: 10,000
SALES (est): 773.5K Privately Held
SIC: 7997 Golf club, membership; swimming club, membership

(G-12832)
LOWES HOME CENTERS LLC
2411 N Eastown Rd (45807-1618)
PHONE 419 331-3598
Fax: 419 331-6724
Jason Carhorn, *Manager*
Anthony Adams, *Manager*
EMP: 150
SALES (corp-wide): 68.6B Publicly Held
SIC: 5211 5031 5722 5064 Home centers; building materials, exterior; building materials, interior; household appliance stores; electrical appliances, television & radio
HQ: Lowe's Home Centers, Llc
  1605 Curtis Bridge Rd
  Wilkesboro NC 28697
  336 658-4000

(G-12833)
LUKE IMMEDIATE CARE CENTER
Also Called: Luke Medical Center
825 W Market St Ste 205 (45801-2745)
PHONE 419 227-2245
Fax: 419 229-1573
Jay W Martin, *President*
Silvia Kennis, *Treasurer*
EMP: 30
SQ FT: 4,100
SALES (est): 1.7MM Privately Held
SIC: 8011 Primary care medical clinic

(G-12834)
LUTHERAN SOCIAL
Also Called: Social Services of Allen, Augl
205 W Market St Ste 500 (45801-4868)
PHONE 419 229-2222
Fax: 419 229-2227
Dr Mychail Scheramic, *Vice Pres*
Michael Swingle, *Vice Pres*
Tammie Colon, *Manager*
EMP: 30
SALES (corp-wide): 2.1MM Privately Held
SIC: 8093 Mental health clinic, outpatient
PA: Lutheran Social Services Of Northwestern, Ohio
  2149 Collingwood Blvd
  Toledo OH 43620
  419 243-9178

(G-12835)
M & W CONSTRUCTION ENTPS LLC
1201 Crestwood Dr (45805-1669)
PHONE 419 227-2000
Fax: 419 227-3500
Steven W Roebuck, *President*
Brad Beining, *General Mgr*
Pam Roeder, *Office Mgr*
EMP: 26
SALES (est): 4.2MM Privately Held
SIC: 1541 1542 Industrial buildings & warehouses; nonresidential construction

(G-12836)
MARIMOR INDUSTRIES INC
2450 Ada Rd (45801-3342)
PHONE 419 221-1226
Amy Allen, *Finance Mgr*
Al Allender, *Human Res Mgr*
William Hodosko, *Info Tech Mgr*
Angela Herzog, *Exec Dir*
Rashawna Perry, *Exec Dir*
EMP: 200
SQ FT: 31,000
SALES: 821K Privately Held
WEB: www.acbmrdd.org
SIC: 8331 Vocational rehabilitation agency

(G-12837)
MATHEWS JOSIAH
602 E 5th St (45804-2524)
PHONE 567 204-8818
EMP: 25
SALES (est): 430K Privately Held
SIC: 7349 Janitorial Service

(G-12838)
MAVERICK MEDIA (PA)
Also Called: Wege
57 Town Sq (45801-4950)
PHONE 419 331-1600
Gary Rozynek, *President*
Phil Austin, *Opers Mgr*
Deb Klaus, *Financial Exec*
Matt Childers, *Sales Executive*
Aaron Matthews, *Program Dir*
EMP: 25
SALES (est): 2.7MM Privately Held
WEB: www.maverick-media.ws
SIC: 4832 7313 Radio broadcasting stations; radio, television, publisher representatives

(G-12839)
MERCY HEALTH
Also Called: St. Rita's Home Care
959 W North St (45805-2457)
PHONE 419 226-9064
Fax: 419 226-5281
Shannon Hatfield, *Development*
Melissa Engle, *Pharmacist*
Katie Hunt, *Director*
EMP: 35
SALES (corp-wide): 4.2B Privately Held
SIC: 8069 Specialty hospitals, except psychiatric
PA: Mercy Health
  1701 Mercy Health Pl
  Cincinnati OH 45237
  513 639-2800

(G-12840)
MID-AMERICAN CLG CONTRS INC (PA)
447 N Elizabeth St (45801-4336)
PHONE 419 229-3899
Fax: 419 224-8780
Harold Breidenbach, *CEO*
John Whittacker, *President*
Bob Foley, *Vice Pres*
Bill Thompson, *Opers Mgr*
Lora Alexander, *Site Mgr*
EMP: 100
SQ FT: 8,000
SALES (est): 19.8MM Privately Held
WEB: www.corporatesupportinc.com
SIC: 7349 Janitorial service, contract basis

(G-12841)
MISTRAS GROUP INC
3157 Harding Hwy Bldg (45804-2589)
PHONE 419 227-4100
EMP: 36 Publicly Held
SIC: 7389 Inspection & testing services
PA: Mistras Group, Inc.
  195 Clarksville Rd Ste 2
  Princeton Junction NJ 08550

(G-12842)
NELSON PACKAGING COMPANY INC
1801 Reservoir Rd (45804-3152)
PHONE 419 229-3471
Sharon Faza, *President*
Stephen L Becker, *Principal*
Issam Faza, *Corp Secy*
Tony Golding, *Human Res Dir*
Mike Hoehn, *Manager*

Lima - Allen County (G-12843)

EMP: 65 **EST:** 1980
SQ FT: 70,000
SALES (est): 10.4MM **Privately Held**
WEB: www.nelsonpackagingco.com
SIC: 7389 Packaging & labeling services

(G-12843)
NICHOLAS D STARR INC (PA)
Also Called: Master Maintenance Co
301 W Elm St (45801-4813)
P.O. Box 5092 (45802-5092)
PHONE 419 229-3192
Fax: 419 229-3622
Nicholas D Starr, *Owner*
Marty Howard, *Sales Staff*
Rocky Starr, *Sales Staff*
EMP: 120
SQ FT: 25,000
SALES (est): 6.1MM **Privately Held**
WEB: www.master-maintenance.com
SIC: 7349 Janitorial service, contract basis

(G-12844)
NORTHLAND LANES INC
721 N Cable Rd (45805-1738)
PHONE 419 224-1961
Fax: 419 224-0729
Andy Johnston, *President*
Ray Custer, *General Mgr*
Keith Callahan, *Treasurer*
EMP: 40
SQ FT: 10,000
SALES (est): 836.8K **Privately Held**
WEB: www.northlandlanes.com
SIC: 7933 5813 Ten pin center; tavern (drinking places)

(G-12845)
NORTHWESTERN OHIO SEC SYSTEMS (PA)
121 E High St (45801-4417)
P.O. Box 869 (45802-0869)
PHONE 419 227-1655
Fax: 419 227-2426
Trell Yocum, *President*
EMP: 35 **EST:** 1972
SQ FT: 36,000
SALES (est): 7.7MM **Privately Held**
SIC: 5999 1731 7382 Alarm signal systems; safety supplies & equipment; access control systems specialization; fire detection & burglar alarm systems specialization; security systems services; burglar alarm maintenance & monitoring; confinement surveillance systems maintenance & monitoring

(G-12846)
OB-GYN SPECIALISTS LIMA INC
Also Called: Ryan, Charles R MD Facog
830 W High St Ste 101 (45801-3968)
PHONE 419 227-0610
James L Kahn, *President*
Rita Myers, *Office Mgr*
Michele Wittler, *Office Mgr*
Tammy Herrick, *Obstetrician*
Charles R Ryan, *Obstetrician*
EMP: 30
SQ FT: 6,900
SALES (est): 1.2MM **Privately Held**
WEB: www.obgynspecialistsoflima.com
SIC: 8011 Gynecologist; obstetrician

(G-12847)
OHIO NORTHERN UNIVERSITY
Also Called: Ohio Nthrn Univ Legal Clinic
306 N Main St (45801-4435)
PHONE 419 227-0061
Fax: 419 228-1096
Bryan Ward, *Manager*
Jeffrey Sellick, *Technology*
EMP: 158
SALES (corp-wide): 87.6MM **Privately Held**
SIC: 8111 General practice attorney, lawyer
PA: Ohio Northern University
525 S Main St Unit 1
Ada OH 45810
419 772-2000

(G-12848)
OLD BARN OUT BACK INC
Also Called: Old Barn Out Back Restaurant
3175 W Elm St (45805-2516)
PHONE 419 999-3989
Fax: 419 991-2672
Peter J Williams, *President*
Melvin J Williams, *Vice Pres*
EMP: 60
SQ FT: 20,000
SALES (est): 2.4MM **Privately Held**
SIC: 5812 7299 Restaurant, family: independent; banquet hall facilities

(G-12849)
OMNISOURCE LLC
1610 E 4th St (45804-2712)
PHONE 419 227-3411
Jake Yessenow, *Principal*
Todd Dilbone, *Branch Mgr*
EMP: 50
SQ FT: 15,000 **Publicly Held**
WEB: www.omnisource.com
SIC: 5093 Scrap & waste materials
HQ: Omnisource, Llc
7575 W Jefferson Blvd
Fort Wayne IN 46804
260 422-5541

(G-12850)
ORTHODONTIC ASSOCIATES LLC (PA)
Also Called: Fowler, Gary J DDS Ms
260 S Eastown Rd (45807-2200)
PHONE 419 224-2514
Fax: 419 224-2514
Thomas Ahman, *President*
Jenny Wade, *Office Mgr*
EMP: 50
SALES (est): 2.8MM **Privately Held**
SIC: 8021 Orthodontist

(G-12851)
ORTHOPAEDIC INSTITUTE OHIO INC (PA)
801 Medical Dr Ste A (45804-4030)
PHONE 419 222-6622
John Duggan, *President*
Steven Calte, *Principal*
Nancy McMichael, *Principal*
Todd W Otto, *Principal*
Selvon St Clair, *Principal*
EMP: 100
SQ FT: 4,335
SALES (est): 11.9MM **Privately Held**
WEB: www.orthoohio.com
SIC: 8011 Orthopedic physician

(G-12852)
OTIS WRIGHT & SONS INC
1601 E 4th St (45804-2711)
PHONE 419 227-4400
Fax: 419 227-6036
O Roger Wright, *President*
EMP: 30 **EST:** 1940
SQ FT: 300,000
SALES (est): 2.4MM **Privately Held**
SIC: 4213 4212 Contract haulers; local trucking, without storage

(G-12853)
P-AMERICAS LLC
1750 Greely Chapel Rd (45804-4122)
PHONE 419 227-3541
Rob Rosser, *Manager*
EMP: 25
SALES (corp-wide): 63.5B **Publicly Held**
SIC: 5149 2086 Soft drinks; bottled & canned soft drinks
HQ: P-Americas Llc
1 Pepsi Way
Somers NY 10589
336 896-5740

(G-12854)
PAJKA EYE CENTER INC
855 W Market St Ste A (45805-2764)
P.O. Box 1692 (45802-1692)
PHONE 419 228-7432
John Pajka, *President*
EMP: 25
SALES (est): 2.4MM **Privately Held**
WEB: www.pajkaeyecenter.com
SIC: 8011 Ophthalmologist

(G-12855)
PAYCHEX INC
My Staffing Pro
675 W Market St (45801-4600)
PHONE 800 939-2462
Lara Soltren, *Human Resources*
Mike Mills, *Sales Staff*
Jamie Roof, *Branch Mgr*
Jennifer Brogee, *Manager*
EMP: 60
SALES (corp-wide): 3.1B **Publicly Held**
SIC: 7371 Computer software development
PA: Paychex, Inc.
911 Panorama Trl S
Rochester NY 14625
585 385-6666

(G-12856)
PEDIATRICS OF LIMA INC
830 W High St Ste 102 (45801-3972)
PHONE 419 222-4045
Fax: 419 228-5665
Cindy Beidelschies, *Manager*
Robin R Hicks, *Receptionist Se*
Jaylene Ellerbrock, *Assistant*
EMP: 30
SQ FT: 3,000
SALES (est): 5.6MM **Privately Held**
SIC: 8011 Pediatrician

(G-12857)
PERRY PRO TECH INC (PA)
545 W Market St Lowr Lowr (45801-4792)
PHONE 419 228-1360
Fax: 419 224-8128
Barry Clark, *President*
David Fikes, *General Mgr*
Dave Krites, *General Mgr*
John Rees, *General Mgr*
David Zimerle, *Exec VP*
EMP: 80
SQ FT: 45,000
SALES (est): 57.4MM **Privately Held**
SIC: 5999 5044 7378 Typewriters & business machines; office equipment; computer maintenance & repair

(G-12858)
PGIM INC
Also Called: Prudential
3435 W Elm St (45807-2226)
PHONE 419 331-6604
J P Delano, *Branch Mgr*
EMP: 50
SALES (corp-wide): 59.6B **Publicly Held**
SIC: 6162 Mortgage bankers & correspondents
HQ: Pgim, Inc.
655 Broad St
Newark NJ 07102
973 802-3654

(G-12859)
PGW AUTO GLASS LLC
Also Called: PPG Industries
2599 Ft Shawnee Ind Dr (45804-2365)
PHONE 419 993-2421
Mark Hemans, *Manager*
Jeanine Radesic, *Manager*
EMP: 50
SALES (corp-wide): 9.7B **Publicly Held**
SIC: 5013 7536 3229 Automobile glass; automotive glass replacement shops; pressed & blown glass
HQ: Pgw Auto Glass, Llc
30 Isabella St Ste 500
Pittsburgh PA 15212
888 774-2886

(G-12860)
PLUS MANAGEMENT SERVICES INC (PA)
2440 Baton Rouge Ofc C (45805-5105)
PHONE 419 225-9018
Jerome O'Neal, *President*
EMP: 112
SALES (est): 16MM **Privately Held**
SIC: 8742 8741 Hospital & health services consultant; management services

(G-12861)
POWELL COMPANY LTD (PA)
Also Called: Rightway Food Service
3255 Saint Johns Rd (45804-4022)
PHONE 419 228-3552
Fax: 419 222-7242
William Schroeder, *President*
Marc Finn, *Opers Mgr*
Jeff Moore, *Purch Dir*
Bev Bailey, *Purch Agent*
Todd Vandemark, *Buyer*
EMP: 79 **EST:** 1995
SQ FT: 30,000
SALES (est): 59.3MM **Privately Held**
WEB: www.powellcompanyltd.com
SIC: 5149 5148 5142 5087 Canned goods: fruit, vegetables, seafood, meats, etc.; fruits, fresh; vegetables, fresh; fruits, frozen; vegetables, frozen; janitors' supplies; office supplies

(G-12862)
PRIMROSE RTRMENT CMMNITIES LLC
3500 W Elm St (45807-2296)
PHONE 419 224-1200
Fax: 419 777-6503
Carla Dysert, *Exec Dir*
EMP: 40 **Privately Held**
SIC: 8361 Rest home, with health care incidental
PA: Primrose Retirement Communities Llc
815 N 2nd St
Aberdeen SD 57401

(G-12863)
PURINA ANIMAL NUTRITION LLC
1111 N Cole St (45805-2003)
PHONE 419 224-2015
Robert Geir, *Branch Mgr*
EMP: 35
SALES (corp-wide): 14.9B **Privately Held**
SIC: 5191 Feed
HQ: Purina Animal Nutrition Llc
1080 County Road F W
Shoreview MN 55126

(G-12864)
QUALITY CARRIERS INC
1586 Findlay Rd (45801-3110)
PHONE 419 222-6800
Lenny Morgan, *President*
Mike Pence, *Terminal Mgr*
Lynn Pence, *Manager*
EMP: 25
SALES (corp-wide): 974.1MM **Privately Held**
WEB: www.qualitycarriers.com
SIC: 4213 Automobiles, transport & delivery
HQ: Quality Carriers, Inc.
1208 E Kennedy Blvd
Tampa FL 33602
800 282-2031

(G-12865)
QUALITY ELECTRICAL & MECH INC
Also Called: Quality Mechanical Services
1190 N Kibby St (45804-1650)
PHONE 419 294-3591
Mark Kuss, *President*
John Reily, *Manager*
EMP: 35
SQ FT: 2,000
SALES (est): 5.4MM **Privately Held**
SIC: 1711 1761 Warm air heating & air conditioning contractor; sheet metalwork

(G-12866)
R & K GORBY LLC
Also Called: Howard Johnson Lima
1920 Roschman Ave (45804-3444)
PHONE 419 222-0004
Fax: 419 227-2221
Brittany Lee, *Accountant*
Jeff Lee, *Sales Dir*
Ron Gorby,
EMP: 44 **EST:** 1958
SALES (est): 2.5MM **Privately Held**
WEB: www.bvistmarys.com
SIC: 7011 Hotels

(G-12867)
RESIDENTIAL MANAGEMENT SYSTEMS
1555 Allentown Rd (45805-2205)
PHONE 419 222-8806
Fax: 419 222-6652
Rose Childers, *COO*
Jennifer Gast, *Director*
EMP: 41
SALES (corp-wide): 4.5MM **Privately Held**
SIC: 8361 Residential care for the handicapped

PA: Residential Management Systems, Inc
402 E Wilson Bridge Rd
Worthington OH 43085
614 880-6014

(G-12868)
REYNOLDS ELECTRIC COMPANY INC
413 Flanders Ave (45801-4117)
PHONE..................................419 228-5448
Fax: 419 222-1778
Michael A Gossard, *President*
Gregory W Schade, *CFO*
EMP: 70 **EST:** 1936
SQ FT: 17,000
SALES (est): 4.9MM **Privately Held**
WEB: www.reynoldselectric.net
SIC: 1731 General electrical contractor

(G-12869)
RKPL INC
Also Called: National Staffing Alternative
216 N Elizabeth St (45801-4303)
P.O. Box 1155 (45802-1155)
PHONE..................................419 224-2121
Robert M Shulty, *President*
EMP: 100
SALES (est): 2.6MM **Privately Held**
SIC: 7361 7363 Employment agencies; help supply services

(G-12870)
ROEDER CARTAGE COMPANY INC (PA)
1979 N Dixie Hwy (45801-3253)
PHONE..................................419 221-1600
Calvin E Roeder, *CEO*
Wanda Whitmore, *Human Res Mgr*
Joe Patterson, *Manager*
Jack Cobb, *CTO*
Mike Fay, *Maintence Staff*
EMP: 55
SQ FT: 21,000
SALES (est): 6.7MM **Privately Held**
SIC: 4213 Contract haulers

(G-12871)
ROSCHMANS RESTAURANT ADM
Also Called: Hampton Inn
1933 Roschman Ave (45804-3496)
PHONE..................................419 225-8300
Fax: 419 225-8328
Robert Roschman, *President*
EMP: 30
SALES (est): 1.6MM **Privately Held**
SIC: 7011 Hotels & motels

(G-12872)
RUSH TRUCK CENTERS OHIO INC
Also Called: Rush Truck Center, Lima
2655 Saint Johns Rd (45804-4006)
PHONE..................................419 224-6045
Fax: 419 224-2891
Todd Jordan, *Manager*
EMP: 40
SALES (corp-wide): 4.7B **Publicly Held**
SIC: 5012 7538 5531 5014 Automobiles & other motor vehicles; general automotive repair shops; automotive & home supply stores; tires & tubes; truck rental & leasing, no drivers
HQ: Rush Truck Centers Of Ohio, Inc.
11775 Highway Dr
Cincinnati OH 45241
513 733-8500

(G-12873)
SCHAAF DRUGS LLC (PA)
Also Called: Heartlight Pharmacy Services
1331 N Cole St (45801-3415)
PHONE..................................419 879-4327
Eric H Schaaf, *Owner*
Angela Rhoades, *Cert Phar Tech*
Chris McClendon, *Director*
Tony Masten, *Technician*
EMP: 35
SQ FT: 9,000
SALES: 4.4MM **Privately Held**
WEB: www.heartlightpharmacy.com
SIC: 5169 Chemicals & allied products

(G-12874)
SEARS ROEBUCK AND CO
2400 Elida Rd Ste 100 (45805-1299)
PHONE..................................419 226-4172
Fax: 419 226-4115
Ryan Betts, *Manager*
EMP: 93
SALES (corp-wide): 16.7B **Publicly Held**
SIC: 7549 Automotive maintenance services
HQ: Sears, Roebuck And Co.
3333 Beverly Rd
Hoffman Estates IL 60179
847 286-2500

(G-12875)
SENIOR CARE INC
2075 N Eastown Rd (45807-2067)
PHONE..................................419 516-4788
Suzanne Hollenbacher, *Principal*
EMP: 113 **Privately Held**
SIC: 8052 Intermediate care facilities
PA: Senior Care, Inc.
700 N Hurstbourne Pkwy # 200
Louisville KY 40222

(G-12876)
SEWER RODDING EQUIPMENT CO
Also Called: Sreco Flexible
3434 S Dixie Hwy (45804-3756)
PHONE..................................419 991-2065
Fax: 419 999-2300
Larry Drain, *Manager*
EMP: 30
SALES (corp-wide): 17.6MM **Privately Held**
SIC: 5032 3546 3423 Sewer pipe, clay; power-driven handtools; hand & edge tools
PA: Sewer Rodding Equipment Co Inc
3217 Carter Ave
Marina Del Rey CA 90292
310 301-9009

(G-12877)
SHAWNEE COUNTRY CLUB
1700 Shawnee Rd (45805-3899)
PHONE..................................419 227-7177
Fax: 419 222-0345
Elliot Burke, *Manager*
EMP: 75 **EST:** 1904
SQ FT: 37,000
SALES: 2.4MM **Privately Held**
WEB: www.shawneecountryclub.com
SIC: 7997 5812 Country club, membership; eating places

(G-12878)
SIGN SOURCE USA INC
1700 S Dixie Hwy (45804-1834)
P.O. Box 776 (45802-0776)
PHONE..................................419 224-1130
Fax: 419 224-1138
Jeff Pisel, *President*
Sompahkoun Southibounnorath, *Vice Pres*
Grant Pisel, *Production*
Karen Hoblein, *Admin Sec*
EMP: 55
SALES (est): 25MM **Privately Held**
WEB: www.signsourceusa.com
SIC: 5085 3993 Signmaker equipment & supplies; signs & advertising specialties

(G-12879)
SPALLINGER MILLWRIGHT SVC CO
Also Called: Spall Autoc Syste / US Millwr
1155 E Hanthorn Rd (45804-3929)
PHONE..................................419 225-5830
Fax: 419 225-8466
Scott Spallinger, *President*
Debbie Earl, *Manager*
▲ **EMP:** 85
SQ FT: 80,000
SALES (est): 31.7MM **Privately Held**
WEB: www.spallinger.com
SIC: 3446 1796 Stairs, staircases, stair treads: prefabricated metal; railings, prefabricated metal; machinery installation

(G-12880)
SPARTANNASH COMPANY
Also Called: Lima Distribution Center
1100 Prosperity Rd (45801-3130)
P.O. Box 510 (45802-0510)
PHONE..................................419 228-3141
Nikki Shafer, *Human Res Mgr*
Bruce Brandfon, *Manager*
Scott Warris, *Manager*
Mike Parish, *Director*
Britt Wiggins, *Director*
EMP: 350
SQ FT: 367,000
SALES (corp-wide): 8.1B **Publicly Held**
WEB: www.nashfinch.com
SIC: 5141 Food brokers
PA: Spartannash Company
850 76th St Sw
Byron Center MI 49315
616 878-2000

(G-12881)
SPARTANNASH COMPANY
1257 Neubrecht Rd (45801-3117)
PHONE..................................419 998-2562
Tina Fisher, *Marketing Staff*
Doug Herr, *Manager*
Bill Jones, *Maintence Staff*
EMP: 90
SALES (corp-wide): 8.1B **Publicly Held**
SIC: 5141 Groceries, general line
PA: Spartannash Company
850 76th St Sw
Byron Center MI 49315
616 878-2000

(G-12882)
SPHERION OF LIMA INC (PA)
216 N Elizabeth St (45801-4303)
P.O. Box 1155 (45802-1155)
PHONE..................................419 224-8367
Grace Schulte, *President*
Robert Schulte, *Vice Pres*
Bud Downing, *Regl Sales Mgr*
Sue Contini, *Manager*
Lorraine Wieging, *Technology*
EMP: 4500
SQ FT: 4,400
SALES (est): 98.4MM **Privately Held**
WEB: www.spherion-schulte.com
SIC: 7363 Temporary help service

(G-12883)
SPRINGVIEW MANOR NURSING HOME
883 W Spring St (45805-3228)
PHONE..................................419 227-3661
Fax: 419 227-6970
Josh McClellan, *Owner*
EMP: 25 **EST:** 1963
SQ FT: 20,000
SALES (est): 1MM **Privately Held**
SIC: 8051 Extended care facility

(G-12884)
ST RITAS MEDICAL CENTER
Also Called: Saint Rtas Bhavioral Hlth Svcs
730 W Market St (45801-4667)
PHONE..................................419 226-9067
Jim Reber, *President*
Will Cason, *VP Human Res*
EMP: 50
SALES (corp-wide): 4.2B **Privately Held**
SIC: 8093 8063 Mental health clinic, outpatient; psychiatric hospitals
HQ: St. Rita's Medical Center
730 W Market St
Lima OH 45801
419 227-3361

(G-12885)
ST RITAS MEDICAL CENTER (HQ)
Also Called: Putnam Cnty Amblatory Care Ctr
730 W Market St (45801-4667)
PHONE..................................419 227-3361
Fax: 419 226-9750
Steve Walter, *Ch of Bd*
John Renner, *CFO*
Gwen Taulbee, *Persnl Dir*
Kenneth E Patick MD, *Med Doctor*
Al Gay, *Director*
EMP: 1700 **EST:** 1918
SQ FT: 563,000
SALES: 408.6MM
SALES (corp-wide): 4.2B **Privately Held**
SIC: 8062 7352 General medical & surgical hospitals; medical equipment rental
PA: Mercy Health
1701 Mercy Health Pl
Cincinnati OH 45237
513 639-2800

(G-12886)
ST RITAS MEDICAL CENTER
Also Called: New Vision Medical Labs
750 W High St Ste 400 (45801-2967)
PHONE..................................419 226-9229
Dr James Conley, *Principal*
EMP: 100
SALES (corp-wide): 4.2B **Privately Held**
SIC: 8071 Medical laboratories
HQ: St. Rita's Medical Center
730 W Market St
Lima OH 45801
419 227-3361

(G-12887)
ST RITAS MEDICAL CENTER
Also Called: St Rita's Homecare
959 W North St (45805-2457)
PHONE..................................419 538-7025
Denice Cook, *Director*
Connie Rode, *Executive*
EMP: 120
SALES (corp-wide): 4.2B **Privately Held**
SIC: 8082 7361 Home health care services; nurses' registry
HQ: St. Rita's Medical Center
730 W Market St
Lima OH 45801
419 227-3361

(G-12888)
ST RITAS MEDICAL CENTER
Also Called: Putnam Cnty Amblatory Care Ctr
4357 Ottawa Rd (45801-1110)
PHONE..................................419 227-3361
Donna Konst, *Director*
EMP: 55
SALES (corp-wide): 4.2B **Privately Held**
SIC: 8011 Freestanding emergency medical center
HQ: St. Rita's Medical Center
730 W Market St
Lima OH 45801
419 227-3361

(G-12889)
ST RITAS MEDICAL CENTER
967 Bellefontaine Ave # 201 (45804-2888)
PHONE..................................419 996-5895
Melvin Monroe, *Manager*
EMP: 50
SALES (corp-wide): 4.2B **Privately Held**
SIC: 8011 Medical centers
HQ: St. Rita's Medical Center
730 W Market St
Lima OH 45801
419 227-3361

(G-12890)
ST RITAS MEDICAL CENTER
Also Called: St Ritas Work Ornted Rhbltition
830 W High St Ste 150 (45801-3980)
PHONE..................................419 228-1535
Kelley Recker, *Director*
EMP: 50
SQ FT: 2,721
SALES (corp-wide): 4.2B **Privately Held**
SIC: 8093 Rehabilitation center, outpatient treatment
HQ: St. Rita's Medical Center
730 W Market St
Lima OH 45801
419 227-3361

(G-12891)
STANLEY STEEMER INTL INC
1253 N Cole St (45801-3413)
P.O. Box 1431 (45802-1431)
PHONE..................................419 227-1212
Fax: 419 227-1213
Kris Nagley, *Principal*
EMP: 32
SALES (corp-wide): 241.9MM **Privately Held**
SIC: 7217 Carpet & furniture cleaning on location

Lima - Allen County (G-12892)

PA: Stanley Steemer International, Inc.
5800 Innovation Dr
Dublin OH 43016
614 764-2007

(G-12892)
STERLING LODGING LLC
Also Called: Holiday Inn
803 S Leonard Ave (45804-3185)
PHONE....................419 879-4000
Brad Will, *General Mgr*
Rob Hayes, *Principal*
Michele Hicks, *Sales Mgr*
Joan Knight, *Asst Mgr*
EMP: 45
SALES (est): 1.8MM **Privately Held**
SIC: 7011 Hotels & motels

(G-12893)
STOLLY INSURANCE AGENCY INC
Also Called: Stolly Financial Planning
1730 Allentown Rd (45805-1856)
P.O. Box 5067 (45802-5067)
PHONE....................419 227-2570
Fax: 419 227-8743
Mark E Stolly, *President*
Janet K Wade, *Corp Secy*
Timothy J Stolly, *Vice Pres*
William R Stolly, *Vice Pres*
Amy Dillon, *Accounts Mgr*
EMP: 27
SQ FT: 4,600
SALES (est): 7.7MM **Privately Held**
SIC: 6411 Insurance agents

(G-12894)
STOOPS OF LIMA INC
598 E Hanthorn Rd (45804-3822)
PHONE....................419 228-4334
Jeffrey Stoops, *CEO*
Trevor Cole, *General Mgr*
John Frigge, *CFO*
EMP: 200 EST: 1983
SALES (est): 24MM **Privately Held**
SIC: 5012 5511 Trucks, commercial; trucks, tractors & trailers: new & used

(G-12895)
SWARTZ ENTERPRISES INC
Also Called: Swartz Contracting
2622 Baty Rd (45807-1511)
PHONE....................419 331-1024
Fax: 419 331-9524
Paul Swartz, *President*
David Finchum, *VP Sls/Mktg*
Carol Swartz, *Treasurer*
Seth Clawson, *Sales Staff*
Tom Turner, *Sales Staff*
EMP: 25
SALES: 1.6MM **Privately Held**
SIC: 1521 1542 Single-family housing construction; general remodeling, single-family houses; commercial & office buildings, renovation & repair

(G-12896)
SWD CORPORATION
Also Called: SUPERIOR WHOLESALE DISTRIBUTOR
435 N Main St (45801-4314)
P.O. Box 340 (45802-0340)
PHONE....................419 227-2436
Carl Berger Jr, *President*
Kenneth Simmers, *Corp Secy*
David L Cockerell, *Exec VP*
Sola Curtis, *VP Opers*
Jim Schweller, *Buyer*
EMP: 50 EST: 1884
SQ FT: 85,000
SALES: 49.2MM **Privately Held**
SIC: 5194 5142 Tobacco & tobacco products; packaged frozen goods

(G-12897)
T AND D INTERIORS INCORPORATED
3626 Allentown Rd (45807-2138)
PHONE....................419 331-4372
Fax: 419 331-8243
Brad Selover, *President*
William Timothy Estes, *President*
Marsha Estes, *Treasurer*
Amy Hafer, *Office Mgr*
Randy Frankhouser, *Manager*
EMP: 40

SQ FT: 14,800
SALES (est): 6.1MM **Privately Held**
SIC: 1742 1752 Acoustical & ceiling work; floor laying & floor work

(G-12898)
T J ELLIS ENTERPRISES INC (PA)
Also Called: Hardwood Wholesalers Exporters
1505 Neubrecht Rd (45801-3123)
PHONE....................419 999-5026
Terry Ellis, *President*
Pam Ellis, *Vice Pres*
Don Hohenbrink, *CPA*
◆ **EMP:** 25
SQ FT: 3,000
SALES (est): 4.5MM **Privately Held**
SIC: 5031 Veneer; lumber: rough, dressed & finished

(G-12899)
TIME WARNER CABLE INC
3100 Elida Rd (45805-1218)
PHONE....................419 331-1111
Fax: 419 331-1573
Marge Thompson, *Branch Mgr*
EMP: 83
SALES (corp-wide): 41.5B **Publicly Held**
SIC: 4841 Cable television services
HQ: Spectrum Management Holding Company, Llc
400 Atlantic St
Stamford CT 06901
203 905-7801

(G-12900)
TIMMERMAN JOHN P HEATING AC CO (PA)
Also Called: Honeywell Authorized Dealer
4563 Elida Rd (45807-1151)
PHONE....................419 229-4015
Larry Esmonde, *President*
Darryl Sawmiller, *General Mgr*
Mike Theobalb, *Principal*
EMP: 35
SQ FT: 30,000
SALES (est): 6.8MM **Privately Held**
WEB: www.jptimmerman.com
SIC: 1711 1731 Warm air heating & air conditioning contractor; plumbing contractors; electrical work

(G-12901)
TOM AHL CHRYSLR-PLYMOUTH-DODGE
617 King Ave (45805-1793)
PHONE....................419 227-0202
Thomas W Ahl, *President*
Andrea Ahl, *Treasurer*
Mindi Ahl, *Executive*
EMP: 150
SQ FT: 4,000
SALES (est): 45.8MM **Privately Held**
SIC: 5511 7515 Automobiles, new & used; passenger car leasing

(G-12902)
TRACY REFRIGERATION INC
Also Called: Tracy Appliance
4064 Elida Rd (45807-1556)
PHONE....................419 223-4786
Jeffrey K Tracy, *President*
Dennis Scott, *Vice Pres*
Rebecca Scott, *Treasurer*
EMP: 25 EST: 1952
SQ FT: 21,000
SALES (est): 4.3MM **Privately Held**
SIC: 5722 7699 Household appliance stores; household appliance repair services

(G-12903)
TRANS VAC INC
931 N Jefferson St (45801-4166)
PHONE....................419 229-8192
Powell Prater, *Ch of Bd*
Brad Prater, *President*
Daniel Lucke, *Vice Pres*
Charlotte Prater, *Treasurer*
Lynn Bibler, *Admin Sec*
EMP: 30
SALES: 819K **Privately Held**
SIC: 4212 Hazardous waste transport

(G-12904)
TRIAD GROUP INC (PA)
855 W Market St Lowr (45805-2795)
PHONE....................419 228-8800
Paul Shin, *President*
EMP: 55 EST: 1976
SQ FT: 4,800
SALES: 4MM **Privately Held**
WEB: www.medilabinc.com
SIC: 8071 Testing laboratories

(G-12905)
TRINITY UNITED METHODIST CH
Also Called: Trinity United Methodist Ctr
301 W Market St (45801-4713)
PHONE....................419 224-2909
Christina Vorhes, *Director*
EMP: 25
SALES (corp-wide): 2.1MM **Privately Held**
SIC: 8351 Child day care services
PA: Trinity United Methodist Church
301 W Market St
Lima OH 45801
419 227-0800

(G-12906)
TRISCO SYSTEMS INCORPORATED
2000 Baty Rd (45807-1955)
PHONE....................419 339-9912
Steven W Walter, *President*
Brian U Walter, *Vice Pres*
Todd Zapp, *Project Mgr*
Kelly Wuebker, *Production*
Tom McGraw, *Controller*
EMP: 130 EST: 1990
SQ FT: 15,000
SALES (est): 26.5MM **Privately Held**
WEB: www.triscosystems.com
SIC: 1541 1542 Renovation, remodeling & repairs: industrial buildings; commercial & office buildings, renovation & repair

(G-12907)
TRUCK COUNTRY INDIANA INC
598 E Hanthorn Rd (45804-3822)
PHONE....................419 228-4334
Treavor Cole, *General Mgr*
EMP: 200
SALES (corp-wide): 531.9MM **Privately Held**
WEB: www.stoops.com
SIC: 5511 5012 Trucks, tractors & trailers: new & used; trucks, commercial
HQ: Truck Country Of Indiana, Inc.
1851 W Thompson Rd
Indianapolis IN 46217
317 788-1533

(G-12908)
TRUGREEN LIMITED PARTNERSHIP
Also Called: Tru Green-Chemlawn
2083 N Dixie Hwy (45801-3251)
P.O. Box 630 (45802-0630)
PHONE....................419 516-4200
Tim Caloahan, *Manager*
EMP: 30
SQ FT: 2,500
SALES (corp-wide): 4B **Privately Held**
SIC: 0782 Lawn care services
HQ: Trugreen Limited Partnership
1790 Kirby Pkwy
Memphis TN 38138
901 251-4128

(G-12909)
UNITED PARCEL SERVICE INC OH
Also Called: UPS
801 Industry Ave (45804-4169)
PHONE....................419 222-7399
Fax: 419 222-4851
John Smith, *Manager*
Brian Smith, *Manager*
EMP: 90
SALES (corp-wide): 65.8B **Publicly Held**
WEB: www.upsscs.com
SIC: 4215 4513 Parcel delivery, vehicular; air courier services
HQ: United Parcel Service, Inc. (Oh)
55 Glenlake Pkwy
Atlanta GA 30328
404 828-6000

(G-12910)
UNITED TELEPHONE COMPANY OHIO
122 S Elizabeth St (45801-4802)
P.O. Box 2001, Cridersville (45806-0001)
PHONE....................419 227-1660
James D Gadd, *Manager*
Claude Cliborne, *Executive*
EMP: 300
SALES (corp-wide): 17.6B **Publicly Held**
SIC: 4813 Telephone communication, except radio
HQ: United Telephone Company Of Ohio
100 Centurylink Dr
Monroe LA 71203
318 388-9000

(G-12911)
VOLUNTERS AMER CARE FACILITIES
Also Called: Lost Creek Care Center
804 S Mumaugh Rd (45804-3569)
P.O. Box 804 (45802-0804)
PHONE....................419 225-9040
Shelley Kendick, *Manager*
EMP: 120
SALES (corp-wide): 66.7MM **Privately Held**
SIC: 8051 8052 Skilled nursing care facilities; intermediate care facilities
PA: Volunteers Of America Care Facilities
7530 Market Place Dr
Eden Prairie MN 55344
952 941-0305

(G-12912)
WANNEMACHER ENTERPRISES INC (PA)
Also Called: Wannemacher Truck Lines
400 E Hanthorn Rd (45804-2460)
PHONE....................419 225-9060
Greg Wannemacher, *President*
Scott Cockerell, *Principal*
Randy Fetter, *Vice Pres*
Beth Nickles, *Vice Pres*
Andy Wannemacher, *Vice Pres*
EMP: 60
SQ FT: 1,000,450
SALES (est): 21.5MM **Privately Held**
WEB: www.wanntl.com
SIC: 4212 4213 Local trucking, without storage; trucking, except local

(G-12913)
WASTE MANAGEMENT OHIO INC
Also Called: Waste Management of Lima
1550 E 4th St (45804-2710)
PHONE....................419 221-3644
Fax: 419 221-3624
Ed Romatowski, *President*
Ginger Kaladas, *Credit Staff*
Peggy McNett, *Human Resources*
EMP: 75
SQ FT: 1,340
SALES (corp-wide): 14.4B **Publicly Held**
SIC: 4953 Garbage: collecting, destroying & processing
HQ: Waste Management Of Ohio, Inc.
1700 N Broad St
Fairborn OH 45324

(G-12914)
WASTE MANAGEMENT OHIO INC
1550 E 4th St (45804-2710)
PHONE....................419 221-2029
Ed Romatowski, *President*
Jayne Overman, *Manager*
Lee Hicks, *Contract Law*
EMP: 49
SALES (corp-wide): 14.4B **Publicly Held**
SIC: 4953 Refuse systems
HQ: Waste Management Of Ohio, Inc.
1700 N Broad St
Fairborn OH 45324

(G-12915)
WEST CENTRAL OHIO GROUP LTD
Also Called: Institute For Orthpdic Surgery
801 Medical Dr Ste B (45804-4030)
PHONE....................419 224-7586
Fax: 419 224-9769

Mark G McDonald, *CEO*
Samir Patel, *Orthopedist*
Justin Waite, *Network Enginr*
Diane Moorman, *Director*
Sally Rhodes, *Administration*
EMP: 75
SALES (est): 46.1MM **Privately Held**
SIC: 8011 Surgeon

(G-12916)
WEST CENTRAL OHIO INTERNET
Also Called: Wcoil
215 N Elizabeth St (45801-4302)
P.O. Box 5620 (45802-5620)
PHONE..............................419 229-2645
Toll Free:..............................888 -
Fax: 419 229-5278
Mike O'Connor, *President*
Rick Skilliter, *Chief*
Ken Francis, *District Mgr*
Barbara O'Connor, *Vice Pres*
Chris Cleary, *Safety Dir*
EMP: 27
SQ FT: 10,000
SALES (est): 5.4MM **Privately Held**
WEB: www.wcoil.com
SIC: 4813 ;

(G-12917)
WEST CENTRAL OHIO SURGERY & EN
770 W High St Ste 100 (45801-5900)
PHONE..............................419 226-8700
Fax: 419 226-8799
Cheryl Swenar,
Sheryl Swenar, *Administration*
EMP: 45 **EST:** 1998
SQ FT: 17,000
SALES: 1MM **Privately Held**
SIC: 8011 Ambulatory surgical center

(G-12918)
WEST OHIO CMNTY ACTION PARTNR
Also Called: Lacca
540 S Central Ave (45804-1306)
PHONE..............................419 227-2586
Jacqueline Fox, *CEO*
EMP: 116
SALES (est): 1.1MM **Privately Held**
SIC: 8322 Social service center
PA: West Ohio Community Action Partnership
540 S Central Ave
Lima OH 45804

(G-12919)
WEST OHIO CMNTY ACTION PARTNR (PA)
Also Called: Head Start
540 S Central Ave (45804-1306)
PHONE..............................419 227-2586
Fax: 419 227-7626
Susan Graymire, *Manager*
Steven Gilroy, *Asst Mgr*
Jan Terry, *Info Tech Mgr*
Jacqueline Fox, *Exec Dir*
EMP: 160
SALES: 7.6MM **Privately Held**
SIC: 8399 8322 8351 Community action agency; individual & family services; child day care services

(G-12920)
WESTGATE LANES INCORPORATED
721 N Cable Rd (45805-1738)
PHONE..............................419 229-3845
Fax: 419 229-3013
Andy Johnston, *President*
Keith Callahan, *Corp Secy*
Wes Johnston, *Vice Pres*
EMP: 42 **EST:** 1958
SQ FT: 50,000
SALES: 2MM **Privately Held**
WEB: www.westgatelanes.com
SIC: 5812 7933 Cafeteria; bowling centers

(G-12921)
WIECHART ENTERPRISES INC
Also Called: All Service Glass Company
4511 Elida Rd (45807-1151)
PHONE..............................419 227-0027
Fax: 419 227-7811
Eric Wiechart, *President*
Steffanie Atkins, *Cust Mgr*
Mike Kennedy, *Sales Executive*
Michelle Wilson, *Manager*
EMP: 30
SQ FT: 12,000
SALES (est): 8.6MM **Privately Held**
SIC: 7536 1793 Automotive glass replacement shops; glass & glazing work

(G-12922)
WRIGHT DISTRIBUTION CENTERS
1000 E Hanthorn Rd (45804-3928)
P.O. Box 817 (45802-0817)
PHONE..............................419 227-7621
Fax: 419 227-7774
Donald E Wright, *President*
Emily Snyder, *General Mgr*
Russ Ramey, *Opers Mgr*
Wendy Flook, *Manager*
Deb Seffernick, *Traffic Dir*
EMP: 28
SQ FT: 300,000
SALES (est): 5.7MM **Privately Held**
WEB: www.wrightdistribution.com
SIC: 4225 4731 General warehousing; freight transportation arrangement

(G-12923)
WRIGHTWAY FD SVC REST SUP INC
3255 Saint Johns Rd (45804-4022)
PHONE..............................419 222-7911
Karen Wright, *Vice Pres*
Robert Balyeat, *Admin Sec*
EMP: 25 **EST:** 1952
SQ FT: 40,000
SALES (est): 4.5MM **Privately Held**
WEB: www.wrightwayfoods.com
SIC: 5141 Groceries, general line

(G-12924)
WZRX
667 W Market St (45801-4603)
PHONE..............................419 223-2060
Matt Bell, *District Mgr*
Jenny Cartwright, *Mktg Dir*
Nakiya Stauffer, *Admin Asst*
EMP: 30
SALES (est): 498.8K **Privately Held**
SIC: 4832 Radio broadcasting stations

(G-12925)
YOCUM REALTY COMPANY
421 S Cable Rd (45805-3111)
PHONE..............................419 222-3040
Fax: 419 227-6108
Timothy L Stanford, *President*
John Coplen, *Sales Associate*
Jennifer Loetz, *Manager*
Bill Bible, *Real Est Agnt*
Linda Coplen, *Real Est Agnt*
EMP: 30
SQ FT: 2,240
SALES (est): 2.9MM **Privately Held**
WEB: www.yocumrealty.com
SIC: 6531 Real estate agent, residential

Lima
Auglaize County

(G-12926)
COMMUNITY HLTH PRFSSIONALS INC
Also Called: Helping Hands
3719 Shawnee Rd (45806-1618)
PHONE..............................419 991-1822
Fax: 419 999-2983
Claudia Crawford, *Director*
EMP: 30
SALES (corp-wide): 14MM **Privately Held**
SIC: 8082 Visiting nurse service
PA: Community Health Professionals, Inc.
1159 Westwood Dr
Van Wert OH 45891
419 238-9223

(G-12927)
LEARNING TREE CHILDCARE CTR
775 S Thayer Rd (45806-8205)
PHONE..............................419 229-5484
Shanda Cox, *Director*
Andrea Stout, *Director*
EMP: 27
SALES (est): 428.4K **Privately Held**
SIC: 8351 Preschool center

(G-12928)
OFFICE WORLD INC (PA)
Also Called: Virtual Pc's
3820 S Dixie Hwy (45806-1848)
PHONE..............................419 991-4694
Fax: 419 991-4329
Chuck Greeley, *President*
EMP: 41 **EST:** 1962
SQ FT: 20,000
SALES (est): 11.7MM **Privately Held**
SIC: 5045 5044 7374 5734 Computers; office equipment; copying equipment; data processing service; computer & software stores; radio & television repair; custom computer programming services

(G-12929)
REA & ASSOCIATES INC
2579 Shawnee Rd (45806-1409)
PHONE..............................419 331-1040
Dennis Gallant, *Partner*
Jan Stiles, *Director*
Lorraine Bruns, *Admin Asst*
EMP: 25
SALES (corp-wide): 32.3MM **Privately Held**
SIC: 8721 Certified public accountant
PA: Rea & Associates, Inc.
419 W High Ave
New Philadelphia OH 44663
330 339-6651

(G-12930)
SHAWNEE WEEKDAY EARLY LRNG CTR
2600 Zurmehly Rd (45806-1424)
PHONE..............................419 991-4806
James Hile, *Ch of Bd*
J Ditto, *Director*
J Leigh Ditto, *Administration*
EMP: 35 **EST:** 1969
SQ FT: 36,000
SALES (est): 1.4MM **Privately Held**
SIC: 6732 Trusts: educational, religious, etc.

Lisbon
Columbiana County

(G-12931)
ALBCO SALES INC (PA)
230 Maple St (44432-1274)
PHONE..............................330 424-9446
Fax: 330 424-7698
Joe Stafeld, *President*
Gary Staffeld, *President*
James Brewster, *Superintendent*
William Mullane Jr, *Corp Secy*
Steve Meals, *Natl Sales Mgr*
EMP: 50
SQ FT: 1,000
SALES (est): 8.5MM **Privately Held**
WEB: www.albco.com
SIC: 5051 Steel

(G-12932)
COMMUNITY ACTION COLUMBIANA CT (PA)
7880 Lincole Pl (44432-8324)
PHONE..............................330 424-7221
Personna Grimm, *COO*
Quinten Melius, *Transptn Dir*
Tizzy Butream, *Persnl Dir*
Ruth Allison, *Pub Rel Dir*
Phillip Smith, *Technical Staff*
EMP: 71
SQ FT: 12,600
SALES: 15.2MM **Privately Held**
SIC: 8399 Social change association

(G-12933)
COMMUNITY EDUCATION CTRS INC
8473 County Home Rd (44432-9418)
PHONE..............................330 424-4065
Michael L Caltabiano, *Branch Mgr*
EMP: 374
SALES (corp-wide): 2.2B **Privately Held**
SIC: 8744 Correctional facility
HQ: Community Education Centers, Inc.
621 Nw 53rd St Ste 700
Boca Raton FL 33487
973 226-2900

(G-12934)
COUNTY OF COLUMBIANA
Also Called: Community Action
7880 Lincole Pl (44432-8322)
PHONE..............................330 424-1386
Fax: 330 424-3731
Carol Bretz, *Manager*
EMP: 150 **Privately Held**
WEB: www.colcountysheriff.com
SIC: 8322 Individual & family services
PA: County Of Columbiana
105 S Market St
Lisbon OH 44432
330 424-9511

(G-12935)
D W DICKEY AND SON INC (PA)
Also Called: D W Dickey
7896 Dickey Dr (44432-9391)
P.O. Box 189 (44432-0189)
PHONE..............................330 424-1441
Fax: 330 424-7607
Gary Neville, *President*
Timothy Dickey, *President*
David Dickey, *Vice Pres*
Janet Blosser, *Admin Sec*
EMP: 47
SALES (est): 68.1MM **Privately Held**
SIC: 5169 3273 5172 Explosives; ready-mixed concrete; fuel oil

(G-12936)
EMPLOYMENT DEVELOPMENT INC
8330 County Home Rd (44432-9418)
PHONE..............................330 424-7711
Fax: 330 424-6651
Dale L Sutton, *Pastor*
Phil Carter, *Director*
EMP: 250
SQ FT: 8,000
SALES: 1.6MM **Privately Held**
SIC: 8331 Sheltered workshop

(G-12937)
FAMILY RECOVERY CENTER INC (PA)
964 N Market St (44432-9363)
P.O. Box 464 (44432-0464)
PHONE..............................330 424-1468
Fax: 330 424-9844
David Hogue, *CFO*
Millie Burton, *Manager*
Ryan Hull, *Info Tech Mgr*
Maryann Theiss, *Exec Dir*
Eloise Traina, *Director*
EMP: 38
SQ FT: 4,800
SALES: 4.9MM **Privately Held**
SIC: 8093 Substance abuse clinics (outpatient)

(G-12938)
GLOBAL-PAK INC (PA)
9636 Elkton Rd (44432-9575)
P.O. Box 89, Elkton (44415-0089)
PHONE..............................330 482-1993
Kevin Channell, *CEO*
James Foster, *President*
Adam Debonis, *Sales Staff*
Brady Webster, *Sales Staff*
▲ **EMP:** 26 **EST:** 1998
SQ FT: 75,000
SALES: 10MM **Privately Held**
WEB: www.global-pak.com
SIC: 5199 Packaging materials

Lisbon - Columbiana County (G-12939)

(G-12939)
LIONS CLUB INTERNATIONAL INC
Also Called: Lisbon Lions Club
38240 Industrial Park Rd (44432-8325)
P.O. Box 383 (44432-0383)
PHONE..................330 424-3490
Daniel Webber, *President*
EMP: 35
SALES: 93.2K **Privately Held**
SIC: 7997 Membership sports & recreation clubs

(G-12940)
MIKOUIS ENTERPRISE INC
Also Called: Sunrise Homes
38655 Saltwell Rd (44432-8348)
P.O. Box 329 (44432-0329)
PHONE..................330 424-1418
Fax: 330 424-3029
Jeannette Mikouis, *President*
Nick Mikouis, *Vice Pres*
EMP: 55
SALES: 840K **Privately Held**
WEB: www.sunrisehomes-oh.com
SIC: 8059 Nursing home, except skilled & intermediate care facility

(G-12941)
OPPORTUNITY HOMES INC
7891 State Route 45 (44432-9396)
P.O. Box 327 (44432-0327)
PHONE..................330 424-1411
Fax: 330 424-1412
Cathy Plant, *Finance Mgr*
Jim King, *Exec Dir*
Carol Mc Gaffic, *Admin Sec*
EMP: 50
SQ FT: 10,000
SALES: 2.4MM **Privately Held**
SIC: 8361 Home for the mentally retarded

(G-12942)
VISTA CENTRE
100 Vista Dr (44432-1010)
PHONE..................330 424-5852
Fax: 330 424-1030
Mary Rice, *President*
Annette Sell, *Manager*
EMP: 75
SALES (est): 3.5MM **Privately Held**
SIC: 8052 8051 Home for the mentally retarded, with health care; skilled nursing care facilities

Little Hocking
Washington County

(G-12943)
DSV SOLUTIONS LLC
251 Arrowhead Rd (45742-5394)
P.O. Box 452 (45742-0452)
PHONE..................740 989-1200
Larry Hawkins, *Office Mgr*
EMP: 74
SALES (corp-wide): 11.8B **Privately Held**
SIC: 4789 Pipeline terminal facilities, independently operated
HQ: Dsv Solutions, Llc
1100 Laval Blvd Ste 100
Lawrenceville GA 30043
678 381-0553

Lockbourne
Franklin County

(G-12944)
AMERISOURCEBERGEN CORPORATION
6305 Lasalle Dr (43137-9280)
PHONE..................614 497-3665
Frank Dicenso, *Director*
EMP: 100
SALES (corp-wide): 153.1B **Publicly Held**
SIC: 2834 5122 Pharmaceutical preparations; pharmaceuticals; druggists' sundries

PA: Amerisourcebergen Corporation
1300 Morris Dr Ste 100
Chesterbrook PA 19087
610 727-7000

(G-12945)
AMERISOURCEBERGEN DRUG CORP
Also Called: Columbus GF Division
6305 Lasalle Dr (43137-9280)
PHONE..................614 409-0741
Tom Morris, *General Mgr*
Michael Dicandilo, *Vice Pres*
David Yost, *Branch Mgr*
EMP: 66
SALES (corp-wide): 153.1B **Publicly Held**
SIC: 5122 Pharmaceuticals
HQ: Amerisourcebergen Drug Corporation
1300 Morris Dr Ste 100
Chesterbrook PA 19087
610 727-7000

(G-12946)
CATHOLIC CEMETERIES
6440 S High St (43137-9207)
PHONE..................614 491-2751
Rich Finn, *Director*
EMP: 30
SALES (est): 1.8MM **Privately Held**
SIC: 6553 Cemetery subdividers & developers

(G-12947)
CITY OF COLUMBUS
Also Called: Public Utilities- Water Div
6977 S High St (43137-9202)
PHONE..................614 645-3248
Terry Estridge, *Plant Mgr*
Jeff Hall, *Opers Mgr*
Carry Estridge, *Manager*
Rex Davis, *Technician*
EMP: 100 **Privately Held**
WEB: www.cityofcolumbus.org
SIC: 4952 9511 Sewerage systems; air, water & solid waste management;
PA: City Of Columbus
90 W Broad St Rm B33
Columbus OH 43215
614 645-7671

(G-12948)
DEALERS SUPPLY NORTH INC (HQ)
Also Called: Dsn
2315 Creekside Pkwy # 500 (43137-9313)
PHONE..................614 274-6285
Kim R Holm, *President*
Ed Wiethe, *President*
Dick Wallet, *Manager*
▲ **EMP:** 30
SQ FT: 56,000
SALES (est): 14.1MM
SALES (corp-wide): 792.9MM **Privately Held**
WEB: www.dealersnorth.com
SIC: 5023 Carpets
PA: Mannington Mills Inc.
75 Mannington Mills Rd
Salem NJ 08079
856 935-3000

(G-12949)
DHL EXPRESS (USA) INC
2315 Creekside Pkwy (43137-9312)
PHONE..................800 225-5345
Shane Rhoades, *Manager*
EMP: 31
SALES (corp-wide): 71.2B **Privately Held**
SIC: 4513 Air courier services
HQ: Dhl Express (Usa), Inc.
1210 S Pine Island Rd
Plantation FL 33324
954 888-7000

(G-12950)
DHL SUPPLY CHAIN (USA)
2750 Creekside Pkwy (43137-9271)
PHONE..................614 492-6614
Dorsey Hessler, *Branch Mgr*
EMP: 29
SALES (corp-wide): 71.2B **Privately Held**
WEB: www.exel-logistics.com
SIC: 4213 Trucking, except local

HQ: Exel Inc.
570 Polaris Pkwy
Westerville OH 43082
614 865-8500

(G-12951)
DHL SUPPLY CHAIN (USA)
Also Called: Dhl Solutions
4900 Creekside Pkwy (43137-7562)
PHONE..................614 662-9200
Paul Wills, *Finance Mgr*
Mike Detty, *Branch Mgr*
EMP: 100
SALES (corp-wide): 71.2B **Privately Held**
SIC: 4731 Freight forwarding
HQ: Exel Inc.
570 Polaris Pkwy
Westerville OH 43082
614 865-8500

(G-12952)
EXEL INC
Also Called: Dhl Supply Chain USA
2450 Creekside Pkwy (43137-7559)
PHONE..................614 670-6473
Christine Lyons, *Manager*
Mark Smolik, *Officer*
EMP: 50 **EST:** 1983
SQ FT: 425,000
SALES (est): 1.5MM **Privately Held**
SIC: 4225 General warehousing & storage

(G-12953)
EXPEDITORS INTL WASH INC
6054 Shook Rd Ste 100 (43137-9315)
PHONE..................614 492-9840
Fax: 614 492-9855
Nick Whalen, *Sales Staff*
Kelly Begley, *Manager*
EMP: 25
SALES (corp-wide): 6.9B **Publicly Held**
WEB: www.expd.com
SIC: 4731 Freight forwarding; foreign freight forwarding; domestic freight forwarding; customhouse brokers
PA: Expeditors International Of Washington, Inc.
1015 3rd Ave Fl 12
Seattle WA 98104
206 674-3400

(G-12954)
FEDEX SUPPLY CHAIN
Also Called: Genco Atc
3795 Creekside Prk Way (43137)
PHONE..................412 820-3700
Sarah White, *Manager*
EMP: 400
SALES (corp-wide): 60.3B **Publicly Held**
SIC: 4225 General warehousing & storage
HQ: Fedex Supply Chain Distribution System, Inc.
700 Cranberry Woods Dr
Cranberry Township PA 16066

(G-12955)
FEDEX SUPPLY CHAIN
Also Called: Genco
4555 Creekside Pkwy Ste A (43137-9287)
PHONE..................614 491-1518
Aaron Tyler, *Principal*
EMP: 250
SALES (corp-wide): 60.3B **Publicly Held**
SIC: 4731 Freight transportation arrangement
HQ: Fedex Supply Chain Distribution System, Inc.
700 Cranberry Woods Dr
Cranberry Township PA 16066

(G-12956)
INTELISOL INC
4555 Creekside Pkwy (43137-9287)
PHONE..................614 409-0052
Charles Huggins, *Manager*
EMP: 60
SALES (corp-wide): 5.2MM **Privately Held**
SIC: 7299 Personal shopping service
PA: Intelisol, Inc.
1001 Ne Loop 820 Ste 200
Fort Worth TX 76131
817 230-5000

(G-12957)
J A G BLACK GOLD MANAGEMENT CO
6301 S High St (43137-9723)
PHONE..................614 565-3246
EMP: 61
SALES (corp-wide): 23.8MM **Privately Held**
SIC: 8741 Management services
PA: J A G Black Gold Management Co.
2560 London Groveport Rd
Groveport OH 43125
614 409-0290

(G-12958)
J P SAND & GRAVEL COMPANY
Also Called: Marble Cliff Block & Bldrs Sup
5911 Lockbourne Rd (43137-9256)
P.O. Box 2 (43137-0002)
PHONE..................614 497-0083
Fax: 614 497-1138
Herbert Hartshorn, *Ch of Bd*
Richard A Roberts, *President*
Mike Craiglow, *Vice Pres*
Joann Roberts, *Treasurer*
EMP: 28 **EST:** 1925
SQ FT: 6,200
SALES (est): 3MM **Privately Held**
SIC: 3271 1442 Blocks, concrete or cinder: standard; construction sand mining; gravel mining

(G-12959)
NATIONAL LIME AND STONE CO
5911 Lockbourne Rd (43137-9256)
PHONE..................614 497-0083
Martin Cudoc, *Plant Mgr*
Richard Roberts, *Branch Mgr*
EMP: 25
SQ FT: 4,032
SALES (corp-wide): 3.2B **Privately Held**
WEB: www.natlime.com
SIC: 3271 1442 Blocks, concrete or cinder: standard; construction sand mining; gravel mining
PA: The National Lime And Stone Company
551 Lake Cascade Pkwy
Findlay OH 45840
419 422-4341

(G-12960)
SCHENKER INC
2525 Rohr Rd Ste C (43137-9296)
PHONE..................614 257-8365
Brian Leja, *General Mgr*
EMP: 65 **Privately Held**
SIC: 5044 Microfilm equipment
HQ: Schenker, Inc.
150 Albany Ave
Freeport NY 11520
757 821-3400

(G-12961)
STREAMLINE TECHNICAL SVCS LLC
4555 Creekside Pkwy (43137-9287)
PHONE..................614 441-7448
EMP: 80
SALES (est): 37.2K **Privately Held**
SIC: 7389 Business services

(G-12962)
WALMART INC
2525 Rohr Rd Ste A (43137-9296)
PHONE..................614 409-5500
Eduardo Herrera, *Branch Mgr*
EMP: 477
SALES (corp-wide): 500.3B **Publicly Held**
SIC: 4225 General warehousing & storage
PA: Walmart Inc.
702 Sw 8th St
Bentonville AR 72716
479 273-4000

(G-12963)
YOUNG MENS CHRISTIAN ASSOC
Also Called: YMCA
1570 Rohr Rd (43137-9251)
PHONE..................614 491-0980
Fax: 614 491-1024
Kevin Pack, *Corp Comm Staff*
Becky Atkins, *Manager*
Justin McCormick, *Technology*

GEOGRAPHIC SECTION

Logan - Hocking County (G-12985)

Heather Knoplesch, *Director*
EMP: 114
SQ FT: 864
SALES (corp-wide): 44.9MM **Privately Held**
WEB: www.ymca-columbus.com
SIC: 8641 Youth organizations
PA: Young Men's Christian Association Of Central Ohio
40 W Long St
Columbus OH 43215
614 389-4409

Lodi
Medina County

(G-12964)
LODI COMMUNITY HOSPITAL (PA)
225 Elyria St (44254-1096)
PHONE 330 948-1222
Fax: 330 948-2543
Barb Fish, *Vice Pres*
Susan Gregg, *VP Opers*
Karen Gagat, *Opers Mgr*
Keith Wertz, *Facilities Mgr*
Cindy Dennison, *CFO*
EMP: 130
SQ FT: 30,118
SALES: 17.3MM **Privately Held**
WEB: www.lodihospital.com
SIC: 8062 General medical & surgical hospitals

(G-12965)
MAPLE MOUNTAIN INDUSTRIES INC
312 Bank St (44254-1006)
PHONE 330 948-2510
Aileen McDowell, *Principal*
EMP: 122 **Privately Held**
SIC: 5084 Industrial machinery & equipment
PA: Maple Mountain Industries Inc
1820 Mulligan Hill Rd
New Florence PA 15944

(G-12966)
TRAVELCENTERS OF AMERICA LLC
Also Called: Truckstops of America
Junction Of I 71 And I 76 (44254)
P.O. Box 125, Seville (44273-0125)
PHONE 330 769-2053
Allan Buhite, *General Mgr*
EMP: 82 **Publicly Held**
WEB: www.iowa80group.com
SIC: 5541 5812 7011 5411 Gasoline service stations; eating places; hotels & motels; convenience stores, chain; general automotive repair shops; gift, novelty & souvenir shop
PA: Travelcenters Of America Llc
24601 Center Ridge Rd # 200
Westlake OH 44145

Logan
Hocking County

(G-12967)
ALCO INC
Also Called: U.S.t Environmental Contractor
36050 Smith Chapel Rd (43138-8855)
PHONE 740 527-2991
Burbridge B Cook, *President*
Molly Cook, *Principal*
EMP: 25
SALES (est): 1.1MM **Privately Held**
SIC: 8744

(G-12968)
BAZELL OIL CO INC
14371 State Route 328 (43138-9449)
P.O. Box 2 (43138-0002)
PHONE 740 385-5420
Joseph Michael Bazell, *President*
Donald D Poling, *Corp Secy*
Janet S Bazell, *Vice Pres*
EMP: 35
SQ FT: 7,500
SALES (est): 99.6MM **Privately Held**
WEB: www.bazellfuels.com
SIC: 5172 5983 Fuel oil; petroleum brokers; fuel oil dealers

(G-12969)
BRASS RING GOLF CLUB LTD
14405 Country Club Ln (43138-8638)
PHONE 740 385-8966
Fax: 740 385-0079
Mike Bazell, *Owner*
Janet Bazell,
EMP: 30 EST: 1997
SALES (est): 963.5K **Privately Held**
WEB: www.brassringgolfclub.com
SIC: 7997 Golf club, membership

(G-12970)
CITIZENS BNK OF LOGAN OHIO INC (HQ)
188 W Main St (43138-1606)
P.O. Box 591 (43138-0591)
PHONE 740 380-2561
Fax: 740 380-0621
Brayan K Starner, *President*
Kirk Amick, *Exec VP*
Robert D Hammon, *Exec VP*
Paul Harris, *Assistant VP*
Alexander M Pavluck, *Assistant VP*
EMP: 48
SQ FT: 3,600
SALES: 9.2MM **Privately Held**
SIC: 6022 State commercial banks

(G-12971)
DARFUS
1135 W Hunter St (43138-1009)
PHONE 740 380-1710
Fax: 740 380-1723
Jim Darfus, *Owner*
Lacy Demastry, *Sales Associate*
Jacqueline Miller, *Sales Associate*
Sandy Adair, *Real Est Agnt*
Eric Duemmel, *Real Est Agnt*
EMP: 50
SALES: 2MM **Privately Held**
WEB: www.darfus.com
SIC: 6519 6531 Real property lessors; real estate agents & managers

(G-12972)
FIRST COMMUNITY CHURCH
Also Called: Camp Akita
29746 Logan Horns Mill Rd (43138-9578)
PHONE 740 385-3827
Mike Young, *Maintenance Dir*
Danita Wolfe, *Property Mgr*
Bill McComb, *Manager*
Sarah Kientz, *Director*
Scot Nicoll, *Director*
EMP: 26
SALES (corp-wide): 4.7MM **Privately Held**
SIC: 8661 7032 Community church; sporting & recreational camps
PA: The First Community Church
1320 Cambridge Blvd
Columbus OH 43212
614 488-0681

(G-12973)
HEALING HANDS HOME HEALTH LTD
30605 Stage Coach Rd (43138-8857)
PHONE 740 385-0710
Fax: 740 385-0787
Jennifer Brown, *Owner*
EMP: 25
SALES: 680K **Privately Held**
SIC: 8082 Visiting nurse service

(G-12974)
HOCKING VALLEY COMMUNITY HO (PA)
601 State Route 664 N (43138-8541)
P.O. Box 966 (43138-0966)
PHONE 740 380-8336
Fax: 740 380-2932
Julie Stuck, *CEO*
Leeann Helber, *President*
Brian Bolyard, *Purchasing*
Steve Berkhouse, *CFO*
Robert Schmidt, *Personnel*
EMP: 380
SQ FT: 69,000
SALES: 36.6MM **Privately Held**
WEB: www.hvch.org
SIC: 8062 Hospital, affiliated with AMA residency

(G-12975)
HOCKING VALLEY INDUSTRIES INC
1369 E Front St (43138-9031)
P.O. Box 64 (43138-0064)
PHONE 740 385-2118
Fax: 740 385-5594
Karon Fisher, *Finance*
Janet Flanagan, *Manager*
Ron Spung, *Director*
Miranda Smathers, *Receptionist*
EMP: 100
SQ FT: 12,000
SALES: 627.4K **Privately Held**
SIC: 8331 Sheltered workshop

(G-12976)
HOCKINGTHENSPERRY CMNTY ACTION
1005 C I C Dr (43138-9245)
PHONE 740 385-6813
Dick Stevens, *Branch Mgr*
EMP: 30
SALES (est): 822.4K
SALES (corp-wide): 12MM **Privately Held**
SIC: 8322 Social service center
PA: Hocking.Athens.Perry Community Action
3 Cardaras Dr
Glouster OH 45732
740 767-4500

(G-12977)
HOPEWELL HEALTH CENTERS INC
541 State Route 664 N C (43138-8541)
P.O. Box 1145 (43138-4145)
PHONE 740 385-6594
Tom Odell, *Director*
EMP: 25
SALES (corp-wide): 33.1MM **Privately Held**
WEB: www.epilepsyservices.org
SIC: 8093 Mental health clinic, outpatient
PA: Hopewell Health Centers, Inc.
1049 Western Ave
Chillicothe OH 45601
740 773-1006

(G-12978)
INDIANA & OHIO CENTRAL RR
Also Called: Indiana & Ohio Rail
665 E Front St (43138-1719)
PHONE 740 385-3127
Fax: 740 385-6724
Rail America, *Principal*
Jon Dunn, *Associate Dir*
EMP: 120
SQ FT: 150
SALES (est): 3.9MM
SALES (corp-wide): 2.2B **Publicly Held**
SIC: 4011 Railroads, line-haul operating
HQ: The Indiana & Ohio Rail Corp
2856 Cypress Way
Cincinnati OH 45212
513 860-1000

(G-12979)
KEYNES BROS INC (PA)
1 W Front St (43138-1825)
P.O. Box 628 (43138-0628)
PHONE 740 385-6824
Fax: 740 385-9076
William W Keynes, *President*
William W Keynes Jr, *Corp Secy*
Charles H Keynes, *Vice Pres*
David Grooms, *Plant Mgr*
Jeff Brown, *QA Dir*
EMP: 37 EST: 1869
SQ FT: 13,145
SALES: 34.9MM **Privately Held**
WEB: www.keynesbros.com
SIC: 2041 5191 Flour mills, cereal (except rice); feed

(G-12980)
KILBARGER CONSTRUCTION INC
Also Called: C & L Supply
450 Gallagher Ave (43138-1893)
P.O. Box 946 (43138-0946)
PHONE 740 385-5531
Fax: 740 385-7254
Edward Kilbarger, *CEO*
Anthony Kilbarger, *Vice Pres*
James E Kilbarger, *Vice Pres*
Tony Kilbarger, *Vice Pres*
Daniel Stohs, *Opers Mgr*
EMP: 120
SQ FT: 2,500
SALES (est): 25.8MM **Privately Held**
WEB: www.kilbarger.com
SIC: 1381 Drilling oil & gas wells

(G-12981)
KINDRED NURSING CENTERS E LLC
Also Called: Kindred Transitional Care
300 Arlington Ave (43138-1708)
PHONE 502 596-7300
Jennifer Jones, *Med Doctor*
Aaron Kenedy, *Med Doctor*
Cheryl Guyman, *Manager*
Scott Ratless, *Exec Dir*
Kathie Will, *Exec Dir*
EMP: 135
SALES (corp-wide): 6B **Publicly Held**
WEB: www.salemhaven.com
SIC: 8051 8093 Convalescent home with continuous nursing care; rehabilitation center, outpatient treatment
HQ: Kindred Nursing Centers East, L.L.C.
680 S 4th St
Louisville KY 40202
502 596-7300

(G-12982)
KIWANIS INTERNATIONAL INC
13519 Lakefront Dr (43138-8509)
P.O. Box 908 (43138-0908)
PHONE 740 385-5887
Robert Lindsay, *Admin Sec*
EMP: 39
SALES (corp-wide): 22.4MM **Privately Held**
WEB: www.kfne.org
SIC: 8641 Civic associations
PA: Kiwanis International, Inc.
3636 Woodview Trce
Indianapolis IN 46268
317 875-8755

(G-12983)
LOGAN HEALTH CARE CENTER
300 Arlington Ave (43138-1797)
PHONE 740 385-2155
Fax: 740 385-1789
Scott Ratless, *Exec Dir*
Terry Wolfe, *Nursing Dir*
Clay Enflen, *Administration*
EMP: 130
SALES: 2.9MM
SALES (corp-wide): 1.1B **Privately Held**
SIC: 8051 Skilled nursing care facilities
PA: Midwest Geriatric Management, Llc
477 N Lindbergh Blvd # 310
Saint Louis MO 63141
314 631-3000

(G-12984)
LOGAN HEALTHCARE LEASING LLC
300 Arlington Ave (43138-1708)
PHONE 216 367-1214
Eli Gunzburg, *Manager*
EMP: 99
SQ FT: 42,100
SALES (est): 356.7K **Privately Held**
SIC: 8051 Mental retardation hospital

(G-12985)
LOGAN-HOCKING SCHOOL DISTRICT
Also Called: Maintenance Department
13483 Mysville William Rd (43138-8971)
PHONE 740 385-7844
Fax: 740 385-7844
Keith Brown, *Manager*
EMP: 45

Logan - Hocking County (G-12986)

SALES (corp-wide): 45.1MM **Privately Held**
SIC: 8211 7349 Public elementary school; school custodian, contract basis
PA: Logan-Hocking School District
2019 E Front St
Logan OH 43138
740 385-8517

(G-12986)
NOTOWEEGA NATION INC
38494 Mysvlle Grendale Rd (43138)
PHONE.................................740 777-1480
Marshall Dancing Elk Lucas, *Director*
EMP: 99
SALES (est): 1.1MM **Privately Held**
SIC: 7389 Business services

(G-12987)
SENECA STEEL ERECTORS INC (PA)
975 E Main St (43138-1743)
PHONE.................................740 385-0517
Fax: 740 385-6435
Dale Campbell, *President*
Kathie Campbell, *Corp Secy*
Melissa Collingsworth, *Admin Sec*
Julie Philips, *Admin Asst*
EMP: 30
SQ FT: 1,000
SALES (est): 6.9MM **Privately Held**
WEB: www.senecasteelerectors.com
SIC: 1791 Structural steel erection

(G-12988)
SOUTHSTERN OHIO RGIONAL FD CTR
1005 C I C Dr (43138-9245)
PHONE.................................740 385-6813
Dick Stevens, *Director*
EMP: 30 EST: 2000
SALES (est): 1.1MM **Privately Held**
SIC: 8322 Individual & family services

(G-12989)
TANSKY MOTORS INC (PA)
Also Called: Toyota of Logan
297 E Main St (43138-1399)
PHONE.................................650 322-7069
Fax: 740 385-4372
John Tansky, *President*
Marian Tansky, *Corp Secy*
Larry Beal, *Manager*
EMP: 28
SQ FT: 10,000
SALES (est): 7.6MM **Privately Held**
SIC: 5511 7538 7532 7515 Automobiles, new & used; general automotive repair shops; top & body repair & paint shops; passenger car leasing; automotive & home supply stores; used car dealers

(G-12990)
TRI COUNTY NITE HUNTER ASSN CI
2940 Laurel Run Rd (43138)
PHONE.................................740 385-7341
Cyde Johnson, *President*
EMP: 40
SALES (est): 433.6K **Privately Held**
SIC: 7997 Hunting club, membership

(G-12991)
TRI-COUNTY COMMUNITY ACT
Also Called: Regional Food Program
1005 C I C Dr (43138-9245)
PHONE.................................740 385-6812
Richard Stevens, *Director*
EMP: 35
SALES (corp-wide): 3.6MM **Privately Held**
WEB: www.tricountycls.com
SIC: 8399 8322 Community action agency; individual & family services
PA: Tri-County Community Action Commission For Champaign, Logan And Shelby Counties
868 Amherst Dr
Urbana OH 43078
937 593-0034

London
Madison County

(G-12992)
ARMALY LLC
Also Called: Armaly Brands
110 W 1st St (43140-1484)
PHONE.................................740 852-3621
Annmarie Armaly, *Treasurer*
▼ EMP: 40
SALES (est): 8.4MM **Privately Held**
SIC: 3089 5199 3086 Floor coverings, plastic; sponges (animal); plastics foam products
PA: Armaly Sponge Company
1900 Easy St
Commerce Township MI 48390
248 669-2100

(G-12993)
BLUEBIRD RETIREMENT COMMUNITY
2260 State Route 56 Sw (43140-9380)
PHONE.................................740 845-1880
Jane Herman, *Exec Dir*
EMP: 30
SALES (est): 898.6K **Privately Held**
SIC: 8322 Old age assistance

(G-12994)
BUILDING SYSTEMS TRNSP CO
Also Called: B S T
460 E High St (43140-9303)
PHONE.................................740 852-9700
Fax: 740 852-7111
Jerry Alcott, *President*
David Beickman, *COO*
Brian Brady, *Vice Pres*
Jim Crace, *Maintenance Dir*
Bryan Robinson, *Manager*
EMP: 170
SQ FT: 95,000
SALES (est): 40MM **Privately Held**
WEB: www.bsttrucking.com
SIC: 4213 4212 4225 Trucking, except local; local trucking, without storage; general warehousing

(G-12995)
COUGHLIN CHEVROLET INC
255 Lafayette St (43140-9071)
P.O. Box 438 (43140-0438)
PHONE.................................740 852-1122
Fax: 740 852-3270
Mike Colucci, *Sales Staff*
Todd Hardy, *Manager*
Dominic Caminiti, *Manager*
Barbara Sanford, *Director*
Derek Wilson, *Executive*
EMP: 40
SALES (corp-wide): 95.1MM **Privately Held**
WEB: www.coughlinford.com
SIC: 5511 7532 5521 5083 Automobiles, new & used; pickups, new & used; body shop, automotive; automobiles, used cars only; livestock equipment
PA: Coughlin Chevrolet, Inc.
9000 Broad St Sw
Pataskala OH 43062
740 964-9191

(G-12996)
COUNTY OF MADISON
Also Called: Madison County Engineer
825 Us Highway 42 Ne (43140-8512)
PHONE.................................740 852-9404
Fax: 740 852-9530
Jim Sabin, *Sheriff*
David Brand, *Manager*
EMP: 40 **Privately Held**
SIC: 8711 9111 Engineering services; county supervisors' & executives' offices
PA: County Of Madison
1 N Main St
London OH 43140
740 852-2972

(G-12997)
LONDON CITY ADMIN OFFICES
6 E 2nd St (43140-1205)
PHONE.................................740 852-3243
Fax: 740 852-7028

David Eades, *Mayor*
Stephen Hume, *Director*
EMP: 65
SALES (est): 2.1MM **Privately Held**
SIC: 8111 Administrative & government law

(G-12998)
LOVING CARE HOSPICE INC (PA)
56 S Oak St (43140-1024)
P.O. Box 445 (43140-0445)
PHONE.................................740 852-7755
Fax: 740 852-7762
Wendy Starr, *CEO*
Robbi Huddleston, *General Mgr*
Barb Dixon, *Human Resources*
Robby Daily, *Manager*
EMP: 25
SALES (est): 3MM **Privately Held**
SIC: 8051 Skilled nursing care facilities

(G-12999)
MADISON CNTY LNDON CY HLTH DST
306 Lafayette St Ste B (43140-9069)
PHONE.................................740 852-3065
James Canney, *Superintendent*
Bridget Lane, *Finance*
Susan Thompson, *Persnl Dir*
EMP: 25
SALES (est): 494.6K **Privately Held**
SIC: 7389 Business services

(G-13000)
MADISON FAMILY HEALTH CORP
210 N Main St (43140-1115)
PHONE.................................740 845-7000
Fred Kolb, *CEO*
EMP: 221
SALES (est): 938.9K
SALES (corp-wide): 45.1MM **Privately Held**
SIC: 8062 General medical & surgical hospitals
PA: Madison County Community Hospital
210 N Main St
London OH 43140
740 845-7000

(G-13001)
MADISON HOUSE INC
351 Keny Blvd (43140-8524)
PHONE.................................740 845-0145
Jane Herman, *Administration*
EMP: 50
SALES (est): 2.2MM **Privately Held**
SIC: 8361 Self-help group home

(G-13002)
MATCO INDUSTRIES INC
Also Called: MATCO SERVICES
204 Maple St (43140-1490)
P.O. Box 533 (43140-0533)
PHONE.................................740 852-7054
Fax: 740 852-7055
Van A Viney, *CEO*
Van Viney, *CEO*
Sharyn Koelling, *Director*
EMP: 28
SALES: 587.7K **Privately Held**
SIC: 8322 8331 Social services for the handicapped; job training & vocational rehabilitation services

(G-13003)
MENTAL HLTH SERV FOR CL & MAD
210 N Main St (43140-1115)
PHONE.................................740 852-6256
Fax: 740 852-6395
Jennifer Piccione, *COO*
Keith Heinlein, *Controller*
Anne Slanker, *Manager*
Cathy Spencer, *Manager*
Anita Zeigler, *Manager*
EMP: 30
SALES (corp-wide): 13.3MM **Privately Held**
WEB: www.mhscc.org
SIC: 8063 8093 Hospital for the mentally ill; mental health clinic, outpatient

PA: Mental Health Services For Clark And Madison Counties, Inc.
474 N Yellow Springs St
Springfield OH 45504
937 399-9500

(G-13004)
OREILLY AUTOMOTIVE INC
229 Lafayette St (43140-9364)
PHONE.................................740 845-1016
Jim Harris, *Principal*
EMP: 46 **Publicly Held**
SIC: 7538 General automotive repair shops
PA: O'reilly Automotive, Inc.
233 S Patterson Ave
Springfield MO 65802

(G-13005)
PETERS MAIN STREET PHOTOGRAPHY (PA)
314 N Main St (43140-9339)
P.O. Box 587 (43140-0587)
PHONE.................................740 852-2731
Fax: 740 852-6883
Larry Peters, *President*
Brian Jester, *Graphic Designe*
EMP: 28
SQ FT: 4,500
SALES (est): 1.6MM **Privately Held**
WEB: www.peters-photography.com
SIC: 7221 Photographer, still or video

(G-13006)
PRESBYTERIAN CHILD CENTER
211 Garfield Ave (43140-9203)
PHONE.................................740 852-3190
Fax: 740 852-1253
Cindy Clifton, *Director*
Cindy Clifton, *Director*
EMP: 31
SALES (est): 855.2K **Privately Held**
SIC: 8351 Child day care services

(G-13007)
STAPLES INC
500 E High St (43140-9303)
PHONE.................................740 845-5600
Barb Dagley, *Human Res Mgr*
Arnold Ferayna, *Manager*
EMP: 40
SALES (corp-wide): 18.2B **Privately Held**
SIC: 5943 5112 Stationery stores; stationery & office supplies
HQ: Staples, Inc.
500 Staples Dr
Framingham MA 01702
508 253-5000

(G-13008)
TRI GREEN INTERSTATE EQUIPMENT
1499 Us Highway 42 Ne (43140-1900)
PHONE.................................614 879-7731
Richard Green, *President*
Connie Ballah, *Corp Secy*
Judy Green, *Vice Pres*
EMP: 30
SQ FT: 14,000
SALES (est): 2.5MM **Privately Held**
WEB: www.trigreeneq.com
SIC: 7389 5261 Auctioneers, fee basis; lawnmowers & tractors

Long Bottom
Meigs County

(G-13009)
BARBARA GHEENS PAINTING INC
50550 Township Road 43 (45743-9001)
PHONE.................................740 949-0405
Fax: 740 843-5424
Manuel Gheen, *President*
Daniel Gheen, *Vice Pres*
Michael Gheen, *Vice Pres*
Janine Gheen, *Admin Sec*
EMP: 25
SQ FT: 1,500
SALES (est): 3.5MM **Privately Held**
SIC: 1721 Exterior commercial painting contractor

Lorain
Lorain County

(G-13010)
ABSOLUTE MACHINE TOOLS INC (PA)
7420 Industrial Pkwy Dr (44053-2064)
PHONE..............440 839-9696
Fax: 440 690-6918
Steve Ortner, *President*
Denis Tapper, *General Mgr*
Hayden Wellman, *Vice Pres*
Jason Bartosch, *Parts Mgr*
John Small, *CFO*
▲ EMP: 51
SQ FT: 18,000
SALES (est): 46.2MM **Privately Held**
SIC: 5084 Machine tools & accessories

(G-13011)
AMERICAN EAGLE MORTGAGE CO LLC (PA)
6145 Park Square Dr Ste 4 (44053-4147)
PHONE..............440 988-2900
John Schrenkel, *President*
Mark Johnston, *Vice Pres*
David Barry, *CFO*
Diane Schrenkel, *Admin Sec*
EMP: 29 EST: 2001
SALES (est): 23.2MM **Privately Held**
SIC: 6163 Mortgage brokers arranging for loans, using money of others

(G-13012)
ANCHOR LODGE NURSING HOME INC
3756 W Erie Ave Ofc (44053-1298)
PHONE..............440 244-2019
Fax: 440 244-9952
Scott Springer, *President*
Donel L Springer, *Vice Pres*
Kimberly Clark-Johns, *Chf Purch Ofc*
Michael Sprenger, *Administration*
EMP: 150 EST: 1962
SQ FT: 20,000
SALES (est): 5.3MM **Privately Held**
WEB: www.sprengerretirement.com
SIC: 8052 8051 Intermediate care facilities; skilled nursing care facilities
PA: Sprenger Enterprises, Inc.
2198 Gladstone Ct
Glendale Heights IL 60139

(G-13013)
ANTHONY DAVID SALON & SPA
6401 S Broadway (44053-3955)
PHONE..............440 233-8570
Fax: 440 233-4701
Peggy S Sinibaldi, *President*
EMP: 26
SALES (est): 506.1K **Privately Held**
SIC: 7231 Hairdressers

(G-13014)
APPLEWOOD CENTERS INC
1865 N Ridge Rd E Ste A (44055-3359)
PHONE..............440 324-1300
Mary Munn, *Branch Mgr*
EMP: 45
SALES (est): 1MM
SALES (corp-wide): 19.6MM **Privately Held**
SIC: 8322 Child related social services
PA: Applewood Centers, Inc.
10427 Detroit Ave
Cleveland OH 44102
216 696-6815

(G-13015)
AUTUMN AEGIS INC
Also Called: Assisted Living Apartments
1130 Tower Blvd Ste A (44052-5200)
PHONE..............440 282-6768
Fax: 440 960-5612
Anthony Sprenger, *President*
Itri Eren, *Director*
Ted Mitchell, *Director*
EMP: 85
SALES (est): 3MM **Privately Held**
WEB: www.autumnaegis.com
SIC: 8051 Skilled nursing care facilities

PA: Sprenger Enterprises, Inc.
2198 Gladstone Ct
Glendale Heights IL 60139

(G-13016)
BARB LINDEN
Also Called: Occupational Health Center
1800 Livingston Ave # 200 (44052-3781)
PHONE..............440 233-1068
Fax: 440 246-4560
Barbara Linden, *Principal*
Rick Svat, *Director*
Daniel J Basinski, *Physician Asst*
EMP: 30
SALES (est): 726.5K **Privately Held**
SIC: 8011 Physical medicine, physician/surgeon

(G-13017)
BAY MECHANICAL & ELEC CORP
2221 W Park Dr (44053-1158)
PHONE..............440 282-6816
Fax: 440 282-1544
Terry Burns, *Ch of Bd*
Robin Newberry, *President*
Mark Houston, *Vice Pres*
Jason Smith, *Purch Mgr*
Mary Lou Gross, *Controller*
EMP: 51 EST: 1948
SQ FT: 22,000
SALES (est): 18MM **Privately Held**
WEB: www.baymec.com
SIC: 1711 1731 7389 Plumbing contractors; electrical work; crane & aerial lift service

(G-13018)
BERKEBILE RUSSELL & ASSOCIATES
1720 Cooper Foster Park R (44053-4200)
PHONE..............440 989-4480
Lawrence G Thorley MD, *President*
Stephen Ticich MD, *Admin Sec*
Walt Blackham, *Administration*
EMP: 26
SQ FT: 4,000
SALES (est): 3.1MM **Privately Held**
SIC: 8071 X-ray laboratory, including dental

(G-13019)
BRIAN-KYLES CONSTRUCTION INC
875 N Ridge Rd E (44055-3035)
PHONE..............440 242-0298
Douglas Maurer, *President*
EMP: 25
SALES (est): 3.1MM **Privately Held**
WEB: www.briankyles.com
SIC: 0782 1521 Landscape contractors; general remodeling, single-family houses

(G-13020)
BUCKEYE COMMUNITY BANK
105 Sheffield Ctr (44055-3134)
PHONE..............440 233-8800
Fax: 440 233-8804
Bruce E Stevens, *President*
Stephen C Wright, *Principal*
Sandi Dubell, *Senior VP*
Ben Norton, *Senior VP*
Linda O'Malley, *Senior VP*
EMP: 25
SQ FT: 10,000
SALES (est): 7.9MM **Privately Held**
WEB: www.buckeyebank.com
SIC: 6022 State trust companies accepting deposits, commercial

(G-13021)
BURGE BUILDING CO INC
2626 Broadway (44052-4834)
P.O. Box 1352, Ormond Beach FL (32175-1352)
PHONE..............440 245-6871
Fax: 440 245-6873
Bruce Burge, *CEO*
Jeffry Watkins, *President*
Charlotte Burge, *Admin Sec*
EMP: 32
SQ FT: 3,600

SALES (est): 2.8MM **Privately Held**
SIC: 1521 1542 General remodeling, single-family houses; commercial & office buildings, renovation & repair

(G-13022)
CENTURY TEL OF ODON INC (HQ)
Also Called: Centurylink
203 W 9th St (44052-1906)
PHONE..............440 244-8544
Fax: 440 244-1818
Glen Post, *Ch of Bd*
Karen Pucket, *President*
Tim Kissane, *General Mgr*
Dwayne Ring, *Vice Pres*
Candace Naylor, *Project Mgr*
EMP: 250 EST: 1984
SALES (est): 31.3MM
SALES (corp-wide): 17.6B **Publicly Held**
SIC: 4812 Cellular telephone services
PA: Centurylink, Inc.
100 Centurylink Dr
Monroe LA 71203
318 388-9000

(G-13023)
CITY OF LORAIN
Also Called: Water Pollution Control
100 Alabama Ave (44052-2042)
PHONE..............440 288-0281
Alex Berki, *Maint Spvr*
EMP: 30 **Privately Held**
WEB: www.cityoflorain.org
SIC: 4941 Water supply
PA: Lorain, City Of (Inc)
200 W Erie Ave Ste 714
Lorain OH 44052
440 204-2090

(G-13024)
CITY OF LORAIN
Water Div
1106 W 1st St (44052-1434)
PHONE..............440 204-2500
Robert De Santis, *Director*
Ron Russell, *Director*
EMP: 122 **Privately Held**
WEB: www.cityoflorain.org
SIC: 4941 4952 4939 Water supply; sewerage systems; combination utilities
PA: Lorain, City Of (Inc)
200 W Erie Ave Ste 714
Lorain OH 44052
440 204-2090

(G-13025)
CLEVELAND CLINIC FOUNDATION
Cleveland Clinic Hlth Systems
1142 W 37th St (44052-5115)
PHONE..............440 282-6669
EMP: 3544
SALES (corp-wide): 8B **Privately Held**
SIC: 8062 General medical & surgical hospitals
PA: The Cleveland Clinic Foundation
9500 Euclid Ave
Cleveland OH 44195
216 636-8335

(G-13026)
CLEVELAND CLINIC FOUNDATION
Also Called: Lorain Family Hlth & RES Ctrs
5700 Cooper Foster Park R (44053-4152)
PHONE..............440 988-5651
Fax: 440 204-7397
Floyd D Loop, *Branch Mgr*
Dina Serhal, *Med Doctor*
Mandy White, *Med Doctor*
Robert Wilden, *Director*
Jason A Genin II, *Sports Medicine*
EMP: 100
SALES (corp-wide): 8B **Privately Held**
SIC: 8093 8062 Specialty outpatient clinics; general medical & surgical hospitals
PA: The Cleveland Clinic Foundation
9500 Euclid Ave
Cleveland OH 44195
216 636-8335

(G-13027)
CLEVELAND CLINIC FOUNDATION
5800 Coper Foster Pk Rd W (44053-4131)
PHONE..............440 204-7800
Blanca Gonzalez, *Manager*
EMP: 85
SALES (corp-wide): 8B **Privately Held**
SIC: 6733 Trusts
PA: The Cleveland Clinic Foundation
9500 Euclid Ave
Cleveland OH 44195
216 636-8335

(G-13028)
CMS & CO MANAGEMENT SVCS INC
Also Called: Sprenger Retirement Centers
3905 Oberlin Ave (44053-2853)
PHONE..............440 989-5200
Fax: 440 282-6857
Nita Anderson, *President*
Medina Gonzalez, *Director*
Jamie Marino-Freetage, *Director*
Audrey Moyer, *Director*
Liane Hrvatin, *Advisor*
EMP: 25
SALES (est): 3.2MM **Privately Held**
SIC: 8741 Management services

(G-13029)
COMMUNITY HEALTH PARTNERS REGI (HQ)
3700 Kolbe Rd (44053-1611)
PHONE..............440 960-4000
Edwin M Oley, *President*
Cindy Dennison, *CFO*
Jose Mendoza, *Med Doctor*
Sami Othman, *Officer*
EMP: 27
SALES: 197.5MM
SALES (corp-wide): 4.2B **Privately Held**
SIC: 8011 Medical centers
PA: Mercy Health
1701 Mercy Health Pl
Cincinnati OH 45237
513 639-2800

(G-13030)
COMMUNITY HEALTH PTNRS REG FOU (HQ)
3700 Kolbe Rd (44053-1611)
PHONE..............440 960-4000
Brian Lockwood, *President*
Heather Nickum, *Principal*
Everett Taylor, *Principal*
Francis Kearney, *Ch Radiology*
Gary Wengerd, *VP Finance*
EMP: 1520
SALES: 4.4MM
SALES (corp-wide): 4.2B **Privately Held**
SIC: 8062 General medical & surgical hospitals
PA: Mercy Health
1701 Mercy Health Pl
Cincinnati OH 45237
513 639-2800

(G-13031)
COMMUNITY HLTH PTNR REG HLTH S
3700 Kolbe Rd (44053-1611)
PHONE..............440 960-4000
Fax: 440 960-4011
EMP: 2000
SALES: 31.6MM **Privately Held**
SIC: 8062 General Hospital

(G-13032)
COMPREHENSIVE LOGISTICS CO INC
5401 Baumhart Rd (44053-2078)
PHONE..............440 934-0870
Daryl Legg, *Branch Mgr*
EMP: 50 **Privately Held**
SIC: 4225 General warehousing & storage
PA: Comprehensive Logistics Co., Inc.
4944 Belmont Ave Ste 202
Youngstown OH 44505

Lorain - Lorain County (G-13033) — GEOGRAPHIC SECTION

(G-13033)
CORNERSTONE MANAGED PRPTS LLC
2147 E 28th St (44055-1932)
PHONE 440 263-7708
Brain Burney, *Finance Dir*
Angela Decker, *Human Res Mgr*
James E Dixon Jr, *Mng Member*
EMP: 30
SALES (est): 2.7MM **Privately Held**
SIC: 6512 Nonresidential building operators

(G-13034)
COUNTY OF LORAIN
Also Called: Loraine Cnty Bd Mntal Rtrdtion
4609 Meister Rd (44053-1530)
PHONE 440 282-3074
Fax: 440 282-5346
Amber Fisher, *Superintendent*
EMP: 28 **Privately Held**
WEB: www.lcmhb.org
SIC: 8361 8052 Home for the mentally retarded; intermediate care facilities
PA: County Of Lorain
226 Middle Ave
Elyria OH 44035
440 329-5201

(G-13035)
DE LUCAS PLACE IN PARK
6075 Middle Ridge Rd (44053-3948)
PHONE 440 233-7272
Fax: 440 233-6909
Sally De Luca, *Owner*
EMP: 73 **EST:** 1925
SQ FT: 21,000
SALES (est): 1.3MM **Privately Held**
WEB: www.delucasplace.com
SIC: 5812 7299 Caterers; banquet hall facilities

(G-13036)
EASTER SEALS NOTHERN OHIO INC
2173 N Ridge Rd E Ste G (44055-3400)
PHONE 440 324-6600
Shiela Dunn, *President*
EMP: 185
SQ FT: 3,000
SALES: 2.9MM **Privately Held**
SIC: 8641 Civic associations

(G-13037)
ECHOING HILLS VILLAGE INC
Also Called: Echoing Lake Residential Home
3295 Leavitt Rd (44053-2203)
PHONE 440 989-1400
Fax: 440 989-1155
Willy Csincsak, *Office Mgr*
Standford Washington, *Manager*
EMP: 100
SALES (corp-wide): 25.3MM **Privately Held**
WEB: www.echoinghillsvillage.org
SIC: 7032 8052 8051 Sporting & recreational camps; intermediate care facilities; skilled nursing care facilities
PA: Echoing Hills Village, Inc.
36272 County Road 79
Warsaw OH 43844
740 327-2311

(G-13038)
ELECTRICAL CORP AMERICA INC
3807 W Erie Ave (44053-1239)
PHONE 440 245-3007
Fax: 440 245-1947
Mark Benco, *Manager*
EMP: 100
SALES (corp-wide): 129.4MM **Privately Held**
WEB: www.ecahq.com
SIC: 1731 General electrical contractor
PA: Electrical Corporation Of America, Inc.
7320 Arlington Ave
Raytown MO 64133
816 737-3206

(G-13039)
FIRST FDRAL SAV LN ASSN LORAIN (PA)
3721 Oberlin Ave (44053-2761)
PHONE 440 282-6188
Fax: 440 282-6164
John Malanski, *President*
Greg Fluckiger, *Assistant VP*
Zachary Kelsey, *Assistant VP*
Stephanie Musgrave, *Assistant VP*
Paul Czarney, *Vice Pres*
EMP: 75
SQ FT: 28,000
SALES: 17MM **Privately Held**
WEB: www.firstfedlorain.com
SIC: 6035 Federal savings & loan associations

(G-13040)
GOODMAN BEVERAGE CO INC
Also Called: Heidelberg Distributing Lorain
5901 Baumhart Rd (44053-2012)
PHONE 440 787-2255
Kenneth H Goodman, *President*
Lawrence Z Goodman, *Vice Pres*
Michael Goodman, *Vice Pres*
Wendy Pickett, *Manager*
▲ **EMP:** 65
SQ FT: 75,000
SALES (est): 15.7MM **Privately Held**
SIC: 5181 5182 Beer & other fermented malt liquors; ale; wine

(G-13041)
HEAD QUARTERS INC
Also Called: Head Qaurters Salon & Spa
6071 Middle Ridge Rd (44053-3948)
PHONE 440 233-8508
Ronald Bennett, *President*
EMP: 25
SALES (est): 641.6K **Privately Held**
WEB: www.hqoasis.com
SIC: 7231 7241 Beauty shops; barber shops

(G-13042)
HOSPICE OF THE WESTERN RESERVE
2173 N Ridge Rd E Ste H (44055-3400)
PHONE 440 787-2080
Jeff Zink, *Branch Mgr*
EMP: 30
SALES (corp-wide): 89.8MM **Privately Held**
SIC: 8051 Skilled nursing care facilities
PA: Hospice Of The Western Reserve, Inc
17876 Saint Clair Ave
Cleveland OH 44110
216 383-2222

(G-13043)
JIFFY PRODUCTS AMERICA INC
5401 Baumhart Rd Ste B (44053-2078)
PHONE 440 282-2818
Aarstein Knutson, *Ch of Bd*
Ornulf Sjursen, *Ch of Bd*
Daniel Schrodt, *President*
Chris Seibel, *Partner*
Siggen Brandanger, *Plant Mgr*
◆ **EMP:** 30
SQ FT: 12,000
SALES: 15.7MM
SALES (corp-wide): 122.2MM **Privately Held**
WEB: www.jiffyproducts.com
SIC: 5191 Farm supplies
HQ: Jiffy International As
Markens Gate 2a
Kristiansand S 4610
381 056-70

(G-13044)
JPMORGAN CHASE BANK NAT ASSN
1882 E 29th St (44055-1806)
PHONE 440 277-1038
EMP: 34
SALES (corp-wide): 99.6B **Publicly Held**
WEB: www.chase.com
SIC: 6029 Commercial banks
HQ: Jpmorgan Chase Bank, National Association
1111 Polaris Pkwy
Columbus OH 43240
614 436-3055

(G-13045)
KOHLMYER SPORTING GOODS INC
Also Called: Kohlmyer Sports
5000 Grove Ave (44055-3612)
PHONE 440 277-8296
Fax: 440 277-0177
Mike Molnar, *President*
Richard Boesger, *Vice Pres*
Dale Hoffman, *Vice Pres*
▲ **EMP:** 40
SQ FT: 13,000
SALES (est): 3.9MM **Privately Held**
WEB: www.kohlmyer.com
SIC: 5941 5091 Sporting goods & bicycle shops; sporting & recreation goods

(G-13046)
KOLCZUN & KOLCZUN ORTHOPEDICS
Also Called: Cleveland Clinic
5800 Coper Foster Pk Rd W (44053-4134)
PHONE 440 985-3113
Fax: 440 204-7815
Michael Kolczun Jr, *President*
Donald Blanford, *Vice Pres*
David Eastaugh, *Materials Mgr*
EMP: 40
SQ FT: 11,000
SALES (est): 5.9MM
SALES (corp-wide): 8B **Privately Held**
SIC: 8011 Orthopedic physician
PA: The Cleveland Clinic Foundation
9500 Euclid Ave
Cleveland OH 44195
216 636-8335

(G-13047)
LAKELAND GLASS CO (PA)
4994 Grove Ave (44055-3614)
PHONE 440 277-4527
Fax: 440 277-9988
Scott Kosman, *President*
Joe Gregory, *Vice Pres*
EMP: 27
SQ FT: 40,000
SALES (est): 4.4MM **Privately Held**
WEB: www.lorainglass.com
SIC: 1793 Glass & glazing work

(G-13048)
LORAIN CNTY BYS GIRLS CLB INC (PA)
4111 Pearl Ave (44055-2523)
PHONE 440 775-2582
Fax: 440 774-9736
Michael Conibear, *President*
Sonia Rodriguez, *Administration*
EMP: 30 **EST:** 1997
SALES (est): 2.2MM **Privately Held**
SIC: 8322 Youth center

(G-13049)
LORAIN CNTY ELDERLY HSING CORP
1600 Kansas Ave (44052-3366)
PHONE 440 288-1600
Clark Hamlin, *CFO*
Homer A Virden, *Exec Dir*
EMP: 99
SALES: 1.5MM **Privately Held**
SIC: 8748 Urban planning & consulting services

(G-13050)
LORAIN COUNTY ALCOHOL AND DRUG
305 W 20th St (44052-3726)
PHONE 440 246-0109
Sami Sfeir, *Owner*
EMP: 62
SALES (corp-wide): 4.4MM **Privately Held**
SIC: 8093 Substance abuse clinics (outpatient)
PA: Lorain County Alcohol And Drug Abuse Services, Inc
2115 W Park Dr
Lorain OH 44053
440 989-4900

(G-13051)
LORAIN COUNTY ALCOHOL AND DRUG (PA)
Also Called: L C A D A
2115 W Park Dr (44053-1138)
PHONE 440 989-4900
Dan Haight, *COO*
Tom Stuber, *Director*
Sharon Asimou, *Admin Asst*
EMP: 25
SQ FT: 6,000
SALES: 4.4MM **Privately Held**
WEB: www.lcada.com
SIC: 8069 8093 Drug addiction rehabilitation hospital; rehabilitation center, outpatient treatment

(G-13052)
LORAIN COUNTY COMMUNITY ACTION (PA)
Also Called: Head Start Program
936 Broadway (44052-1950)
PHONE 440 245-2009
Carla Rodriguez, *Opers Mgr*
Chris Haney, *Finance*
Mary Keuper, *Finance*
Bill Abston, *Human Res Dir*
Don Thigpen, *Human Res Dir*
EMP: 25
SQ FT: 19,116
SALES: 9.5MM **Privately Held**
WEB: www.lccaa.net
SIC: 8399 Community action agency

(G-13053)
LORAIN COUNTY COMMUNITY ACTION
Also Called: Lccaa-Hopkins Locke-Head Start
1050 Reid Ave (44052-1962)
PHONE 440 246-0480
Shauna Matelski, *Principal*
EMP: 30
SALES (est): 492.1K
SALES (corp-wide): 9.5MM **Privately Held**
SIC: 8351 Head start center, except in conjunction with school
PA: Lorain County Community Action Agency, Inc.
936 Broadway
Lorain OH 44052
440 245-2009

(G-13054)
LORAIN GLASS CO INC
1865 N Ridge Rd E Ste E (44055-3360)
PHONE 440 277-6004
Fax: 440 246-5544
Eugene Sofranko, *Ch of Bd*
Kevin Sofranko, *President*
F J Stack, *Principal*
Jack Kosman, *Vice Pres*
Diane Kosman, *Treasurer*
EMP: 55 **EST:** 1924
SQ FT: 25,000
SALES (est): 9MM **Privately Held**
WEB: www.lorainglass.com
SIC: 1793 5231 Glass & glazing work; glass

(G-13055)
LORAIN LIFE CARE AMBULANCE SVC
109 W 23rd St (44052-4801)
PHONE 440 244-6467
Kim Mason, *Branch Mgr*
EMP: 65
SALES (est): 709.7K **Privately Held**
SIC: 4119 Ambulance service

(G-13056)
LORAIN NATIONAL BANK (HQ)
457 Broadway (44052-1769)
PHONE 440 244-6000
Fax: 440 244-4133
Dan Klimas, *CEO*
James R Herrick, *Ch of Bd*
James F Kidd, *Vice Ch Bd*
Kevin W Nelson, *COO*
Kevin Ball, *Senior VP*
EMP: 125
SQ FT: 50,000
SALES: 55MM **Publicly Held**
SIC: 6021 National trust companies with deposits, commercial

▲ = Import ▼ = Export
◆ = Import/Export

GEOGRAPHIC SECTION

Lorain - Lorain County (G-13081)

(G-13057)
LORAIN PARTY CENTER
Also Called: Bill & Don's Catering
5900 S Mayflower Dr (44053-4120)
PHONE..................440 282-5599
Will Schuster, *Owner*
EMP: 37
SQ FT: 15,000
SALES: 300K **Privately Held**
SIC: 5812 7299 Caterers; banquet hall facilities

(G-13058)
LOWES HOME CENTERS LLC
7500 Oak Point Rd (44053-4149)
PHONE..................440 985-5700
Fax: 440 985-5703
Matthew Holstein, *Sales Mgr*
Dave Summers, *Branch Mgr*
Jeffrey Crabeels, *Manager*
EMP: 158
SALES (corp-wide): 68.6B **Publicly Held**
SIC: 5211 5031 5722 5064 Home centers; building materials, exterior; building materials, interior; household appliance stores; electrical appliances, television & radio
HQ: Lowe's Home Centers, Llc
1605 Curtis Bridge Rd
Wilkesboro NC 28697
336 658-4000

(G-13059)
LUCAS PLUMBING & HEATING INC
2125 W Park Dr (44053-1195)
PHONE..................440 282-4567
Fax: 440 282-6360
Frank J Lucas, *President*
Bruce Mc Cartney, *Admin Sec*
EMP: 50
SQ FT: 9,800
SALES (est): 10.2MM **Privately Held**
SIC: 1711 Process piping contractor

(G-13060)
MERCY HEALTH
Also Called: Poison & Toxic Control Center
3700 Kolbe Rd (44053-1611)
PHONE..................440 233-1000
Sally Lash, *Division Mgr*
Ed Oley, *Branch Mgr*
Dennis Dawson, *Med Doctor*
Gary Wegerd, *Med Doctor*
Gary Wengerd, *Med Doctor*
EMP: 4000
SALES (corp-wide): 4.2B **Privately Held**
SIC: 8322 8063 8062 Emergency social services; psychiatric hospitals; general medical & surgical hospitals
PA: Mercy Health
1701 Mercy Health Pl
Cincinnati OH 45237
513 639-2800

(G-13061)
MID-OHIO WINES INC
5901 Baumhart Rd (44053-2012)
PHONE..................440 989-1011
Fax: 419 663-3500
Lawrence Goodman, *President*
Michael Goodman, *Vice Pres*
▲ **EMP:** 40
SQ FT: 35,000
SALES (est): 8.4MM **Privately Held**
SIC: 5182 Wine; liquor

(G-13062)
MPW INDUSTRIAL SERVICES INC
Also Called: Industrial Cleaning
1930 E 28th St (44055-1907)
PHONE..................440 277-9072
Fax: 440 277-9103
Helen Pirl, *Office Mgr*
Tom Webb, *Manager*
EMP: 40
SALES (corp-wide): 257.9MM **Privately Held**
SIC: 7349 Building cleaning service
HQ: Mpw Industrial Services, Inc.
9711 Lancaster Rd
Hebron OH 43025
800 827-8790

(G-13063)
NATIONAL BRONZE MTLS OHIO INC
Also Called: Aviva Metals
5311 W River Rd (44055-3735)
PHONE..................440 277-1226
Michael Greathead, *President*
Norman M Lazarus, *Exec VP*
Jeff Fulton, *Purch Mgr*
Stephanie Dadante, *QC Mgr*
Tim Nielsens, *Sales Staff*
▲ **EMP:** 27
SALES (est): 14.1MM **Privately Held**
SIC: 5051 3366 3341 Metals service centers & offices; copper; copper foundries; secondary nonferrous metals
PA: Metchem Anstalt
Feger Treuunternehmen Reg.
Vaduz
237 454-5

(G-13064)
NEW LIFE HOSPICE INC
Also Called: New Life Hospice Ctr St Joseph
3500 Kolbe Rd (44053-1632)
PHONE..................440 934-1458
Tanya Anderson, *Manager*
Joan Hanson, *Exec Dir*
Cheryl Rieves, *Nursing Dir*
EMP: 30
SALES (corp-wide): 4.2B **Privately Held**
SIC: 8082 8051 Home health care services; skilled nursing care facilities
HQ: New Life Hospice Inc
5255 N Abbe Rd Ste 2
Sheffield Village OH 44035

(G-13065)
NORCARE ENTERPRISES INC (PA)
Also Called: NORTH CENTER, THE
6140 S Broadway (44053-3821)
PHONE..................440 233-7232
Amy Denger, *CEO*
Bernadek Stchick, *CFO*
Betsey Kamm, *Director*
EMP: 289
SQ FT: 55,000
SALES: 2MM **Privately Held**
SIC: 8093 Mental health clinic, outpatient

(G-13066)
NORD CENTER
6140 S Broadway (44053-3891)
PHONE..................440 233-7232
Amy Denger, *CEO*
William Richardson, *CFO*
Daniel Moehring, *Human Res Dir*
Jack Holt, *MIS Dir*
Lori Berencsi, *Director*
EMP: 32
SALES (est): 14.1MM **Privately Held**
SIC: 8093 Mental health clinic, outpatient

(G-13067)
NORD CENTER ASSOCIATES INC (HQ)
Also Called: W.G. Nord Cmnty Mntal Hlth Ctr
6140 S Broadway (44053-3891)
PHONE..................440 233-7232
Fax: 440 233-7232
Amy Denger, *CEO*
▲ **EMP:** 185
SQ FT: 46,371
SALES: 12.5MM
SALES (corp-wide): 2MM **Privately Held**
SIC: 8093 Mental health clinic, outpatient
PA: Norcare Enterprises, Inc.
6140 S Broadway
Lorain OH 44053
440 233-7232

(G-13068)
NORD CENTER ASSOCIATES INC
Also Called: Nord Rehabilitation Center
3150 Clifton Ave (44053-1553)
PHONE..................440 233-7232
Fax: 440 245-3570
Amy Denger, *Director*
Sarah Swanson, *Administration*
EMP: 26

SALES (est): 1.4MM
SALES (corp-wide): 2MM **Privately Held**
SIC: 8069 Specialty hospitals, except psychiatric
HQ: Nord Center Associates Inc
6140 S Broadway
Lorain OH 44053
440 233-7232

(G-13069)
NORTH OHIO HEART CENTER
Also Called: John W. Schaeffer, M.d
3600 Kolbe Rd Ste 127 (44053-1652)
PHONE..................440 204-4000
John W Schaeffer MD, *President*
EMP: 55
SQ FT: 2,000
SALES (est): 2.2MM **Privately Held**
SIC: 7352 Medical equipment rental

(G-13070)
NORTH OHIO HEART CENTER INC (PA)
3600 Kolbe Rd Ste 127 (44053-1652)
PHONE..................440 204-4000
Fax: 440 282-7133
John W Schaeffer, *President*
Abdul Wattar, *Med Doctor*
EMP: 50
SALES (est): 13.5MM **Privately Held**
WEB: www.nohc.com
SIC: 8011 Cardiologist & cardio-vascular specialist

(G-13071)
PERKINS MOTOR SERVICE LTD (PA)
Also Called: Standard Welding & Lift Truck
1864 E 28th St (44055-1804)
PHONE..................440 277-1256
Fax: 440 277-0970
Thomas L Shumaker,
EMP: 38
SQ FT: 10,200
SALES (est): 5.4MM **Privately Held**
SIC: 5013 5531 7692 7539 Truck parts & accessories; automotive supplies & parts; truck equipment & parts; automotive parts; automotive welding; radiator repair shop, automotive; brake repair, automotive; automotive springs, rebuilding & repair; hydraulic equipment repair

(G-13072)
R & J TRUCKING INC
5250 Baumhart Rd (44053-2046)
PHONE..................440 960-1508
Fax: 440 960-1983
Glenn Parks, *Manager*
EMP: 52 **Privately Held**
WEB: www.rjtrucking.com
SIC: 4212 Dump truck haulage
HQ: R & J Trucking, Inc.
8063 Southern Blvd
Youngstown OH 44512
800 262-9365

(G-13073)
RDF TRUCKING CORPORATION
Also Called: RDF Logistics
7425 Industrial Pkwy Dr (44053-2064)
PHONE..................440 282-9060
Fax: 440 239-3588
Rosario Boscarello, *President*
Nancy Irvine, *Corp Secy*
Dino Boscarello, *Vice Pres*
Jim Adams, *Manager*
Paul Urban, *Maintence Staff*
EMP: 70
SALES: 23MM **Privately Held**
SIC: 4731 Truck transportation brokers

(G-13074)
REBMAN RECREATION INC
5300 Oberlin Ave (44053-3438)
PHONE..................440 282-6761
Fax: 440 282-7415
Richard Rebman, *President*
Mary Rebman, *Vice Pres*
Robert Rebman, *Vice Pres*
Dominic Rebman Jr, *Shareholder*
EMP: 25
SQ FT: 28,000
SALES (est): 743.2K **Privately Held**
SIC: 7933 Ten pin center

(G-13075)
S B S TRANSIT INC
Also Called: First Student
1800 Colorado Ave (44052-3280)
PHONE..................440 288-2222
Fax: 440 949-2979
Kenneth Van Wagnen, *President*
EMP: 267
SALES (est): 10MM
SALES (corp-wide): 7B **Privately Held**
WEB: www.sbstransit.com
SIC: 4151 4142 4493 5551 School buses; bus charter service, except local; marinas; boat dealers; marine supplies; marine supplies & equipment; local bus charter service
PA: Firstgroup Plc
395 King Street
Aberdeen AB24
122 465-0100

(G-13076)
SPECIALTY MEDICAL SERVICES
Also Called: Billing Services
221 W 8th St (44052-1817)
PHONE..................440 245-8010
Walt Blackham, *President*
EMP: 25
SALES (est): 1.6MM **Privately Held**
SIC: 8721 Billing & bookkeeping service

(G-13077)
SPORTSMAN GUN & REEL CLUB INC
44165 Middle Ridge Rd (44053-3915)
PHONE..................440 233-8287
Robert Sertgent, *President*
EMP: 150
SALES: 88.9K **Privately Held**
SIC: 7997 Gun club, membership

(G-13078)
SPRENGER ENTRPRISES INC
Also Called: Nursing Home & Assisted Living
3756 W Erie Ave Apt 201 (44053-1291)
PHONE..................440 244-2019
Scott Sprenger, *President*
EMP: 100
SALES (est): 1.3MM **Privately Held**
SIC: 8051 Skilled nursing care facilities

(G-13079)
STEVENS ENGINEERS CONSTRS INC
Also Called: Martinez Construction Services
1515 E 28th St (44055-1605)
PHONE..................440 277-6207
Mike Beetler, *Manager*
EMP: 40
SALES (corp-wide): 87.3MM **Privately Held**
WEB: www.spcdmg.com
SIC: 1541 Industrial buildings, new construction
PA: Stevens Engineers & Constructors, Inc.
7850 Freeway Cir Ste 100
Cleveland OH 44130
440 234-7888

(G-13080)
SUPERIOR MEDICAL CARE INC
5172 Leavitt Rd Ste B (44053-2385)
PHONE..................440 282-7420
John Barb, *President*
Dr George Adams, *Vice Pres*
EMP: 25
SALES (est): 3.3MM **Privately Held**
SIC: 8011 8071 General & family practice, physician/surgeon; medical laboratories

(G-13081)
TERMINAL READY-MIX INC
524 Colorado Ave (44052-2198)
PHONE..................440 288-0181
Fax: 440 288-3142
Theresa Pelton, *President*
John Falbo, *Vice Pres*
Russ Rosso, *Plant Mgr*
Pete Falbo, *Treasurer*
Diane Gale, *Admin Sec*
▲ **EMP:** 45 **EST:** 1954
SQ FT: 1,000

Lorain - Lorain County (G-13082)

SALES (est): 9.6MM **Privately Held**
WEB: www.falboconstruction.com
SIC: 3273 1611 Ready-mixed concrete; highway & street paving contractor

(G-13082)
TRADEMARK GLOBAL LLC (HQ)
Also Called: Trademark Games
7951 W Erie Ave (44053-2093)
PHONE...........................440 960-6226
Daniel Sustar, *CEO*
Jim Sustar, *President*
Mark Terlecky, *Business Mgr*
Paul Hervey, *Vice Pres*
Jason Pavlik, *Senior Buyer*
▲ EMP: 95
SQ FT: 300,000
SALES (est): 47.1MM **Privately Held**
WEB: www.5starwholesale.com
SIC: 5199 General merchandise, non-durable
PA: Trademark Games Holdings, Llc
7951 W Erie Ave
Lorain OH 44053
440 960-6226

(G-13083)
UNITED STEELWORKERS
Also Called: Uswa
2501 Broadway (44052-4831)
PHONE...........................440 244-1358
Dash Sokol, *Branch Mgr*
EMP: 44
SALES (corp-wide): 61.5K **Privately Held**
WEB: www.uswa.org
SIC: 8631 7361 Labor union; labor contractors (employment agency)
PA: United Steelworkers
60 Bolevard Of The Allies
Pittsburgh PA 15222
412 562-2400

(G-13084)
VARCO LP
1807 E 28th St (44055-1803)
PHONE...........................440 277-8696
Randy Hamilton, *Branch Mgr*
Peggy Roblin, *Admin Asst*
EMP: 35
SALES (corp-wide): 7.3B **Publicly Held**
WEB: www.tuboscope.com
SIC: 1389 Running, cutting & pulling casings, tubes & rods
HQ: Varco, L.P.
2835 Holmes Rd
Houston TX 77051
713 799-5272

(G-13085)
VERTIV ENERGY SYSTEMS INC
1510 Kansas Ave (44052-3364)
PHONE...........................440 288-1122
Dennis Del Campo, *Vice Pres*
Dave Smith, *Opers Mgr*
Rick Wrye, *Opers Staff*
Bonnie Edwards, *Buyer*
James Cook, *Engineer*
◆ EMP: 800
SALES (est): 1MM **Privately Held**
SIC: 3661 3644 7629 Telephone & telegraph apparatus; noncurrent-carrying wiring services; telecommunication equipment repair (except telephones)
HQ: Vertiv Group Corporation
1050 Dearborn Dr
Columbus OH 43085
614 888-0246

Lore City
Guernsey County

(G-13086)
COUNTRYVIEW ASSISTANT LIVING
62825 County Home Rd (43755-9758)
PHONE...........................740 489-5351
Bob Lahey, *Facilities Mgr*
Teresa Yakubik, *Corp Comm Staff*
Adrian Paden, *Director*
Sandra Rainer, *Administration*
EMP: 26

SALES (est): 867.2K **Privately Held**
SIC: 8059 Rest home, with health care

(G-13087)
QES PRESSURE CONTROL LLC
64201 Wintergreen Rd (43755-9704)
PHONE...........................724 324-2391
Charles Jones, *Branch Mgr*
EMP: 25
SALES (corp-wide): 736.2MM **Privately Held**
SIC: 1381 Drilling oil & gas wells
HQ: Qes Pressure Control Llc
4500 Se 59th St
Oklahoma City OK 73135

Loudonville
Ashland County

(G-13088)
C E S CREDIT UNION INC
3030 State Route 3 (44842-9526)
PHONE...........................561 203-5443
Sandy Coffing, *Branch Mgr*
EMP: 25
SALES (corp-wide): 4MM **Privately Held**
SIC: 6062 State credit unions, not federally chartered
PA: C E S Credit Union, Inc.
1215 Yauger Rd
Mount Vernon OH 43050
740 397-1136

(G-13089)
COLONIAL MANOR HEALTH CARE CTR
747 S Mount Vernon Ave (44842-1416)
PHONE...........................419 994-4191
Fax: 419 994-4193
Jack Snowbarger, *President*
Linda Snowbarger, *Treasurer*
Nancy Moor, *Office Mgr*
Linda O'Brien, *Dietician*
Rachel Cammuse, *Manager*
EMP: 110
SQ FT: 32,000
SALES (est): 5.4MM **Privately Held**
SIC: 8051 Skilled nursing care facilities

(G-13090)
H&H CUSTOM HOMES LLC
16573 State Route 3 (44842-9735)
P.O. Box 409 (44842-0409)
PHONE...........................419 994-4070
Fax: 419 994-0307
Eddie Troyer, *Mng Member*
EMP: 25
SQ FT: 2,000
SALES (est): 161K **Privately Held**
SIC: 1521 New construction, single-family houses

(G-13091)
JAC-LIN MANOR
695 S Mount Vernon Ave (44842-1414)
PHONE...........................419 994-5700
Fax: 419 994-7100
Bert Macqueen, *Director*
Bert McQueen, *Administration*
EMP: 70
SALES (est): 3.6MM **Privately Held**
SIC: 8093 Mental health clinic, outpatient

(G-13092)
JO LYNN INC
Also Called: Gribble Foods
430 N Jefferson St (44842-1323)
PHONE...........................419 994-3204
Fax: 419 994-5521
Robert Gribble, *President*
Bonnie Gribble, *Vice Pres*
EMP: 75
SALES: 6MM **Privately Held**
SIC: 5411 7549 Supermarkets, chain; towing service, automotive

Louisville
Stark County

(G-13093)
ALTERCARE OF LOUISVILLE CENTER
7187 Saint Francis St (44641-9050)
PHONE...........................330 875-4224
Fax: 330 875-4225
Gerald Schroer, *President*
Gary Dubin, *Vice Pres*
Glenn Wickes, *Treasurer*
Kyle Blankenship, *Human Resources*
Kenneth Biros, *Director*
EMP: 107
SQ FT: 12,000
SALES (est): 4MM **Privately Held**
SIC: 8051 Skilled nursing care facilities

(G-13094)
AULTMAN HEALTH FOUNDATION
1925 Williamsburg Way Ne (44641-8781)
PHONE...........................330 875-6050
Fax: 330 875-6055
EMP: 463
SALES (corp-wide): 1.1MM **Privately Held**
SIC: 8049 Physical therapist
PA: Aultman Health Foundation
2600 6th St Sw
Canton OH 44710
330 452-9911

(G-13095)
CHAPMAN INDUSTRIAL CNSTR INC
3475 Rue Depaul St (44641-9134)
P.O. Box 356, Dover (44622-0356)
PHONE...........................330 343-1632
Michael Chapman, *President*
EMP: 80
SALES (est): 9.6MM **Privately Held**
SIC: 1541 Industrial buildings, new construction

(G-13096)
CITY OF LOUISVILLE (PA)
215 S Mill St (44641-1665)
PHONE...........................330 875-3321
Fax: 330 875-4864
Cynthia Kerchner, *Mayor*
Paula Russell, *Mayor*
Thomas Ault, *City Mgr*
Guy Guidone, *Council Mbr*
Tom McAlister, *Council Mbr*
EMP: 100
SQ FT: 50,000 **Privately Held**
WEB: www.louisvilleohio.com
SIC: 9111 8611 City & town managers' offices; ; business associations

(G-13097)
CONCORDE THERAPY GROUP INC
513 E Main St (44641-1421)
PHONE...........................330 493-4210
Morgan Aster, *Branch Mgr*
EMP: 30
SALES (est): 402.7K **Privately Held**
SIC: 8049 Physiotherapist
PA: Concorde Therapy Group Inc
4645 Belpar St Nw
Canton OH 44718

(G-13098)
COON CAULKING & SEALANTS INC
Also Called: Coon Caulking & Restoration
7349 Ravenna Ave (44641-9788)
P.O. Box 259 (44641-0259)
PHONE...........................330 875-2100
Fax: 330 875-1721
Stephen Coon, *President*
Joseph Kreinbrink, *Vice Pres*
Scott McGhee, *Vice Pres*
Matt Sibila, *Project Mgr*
Carolyn M Buckridge, *Treasurer*
EMP: 60
SQ FT: 50,000

SALES (est): 8.7MM **Privately Held**
WEB: www.coonrestoration.com
SIC: 1799 Caulking (construction); waterproofing

(G-13099)
DISABLED AMERICAN VETERANS
128 Indiana Ave (44641-1102)
PHONE...........................330 875-5795
Denise Proffitt, *Treasurer*
EMP: 34
SALES (corp-wide): 202.6MM **Privately Held**
SIC: 8641 Veterans' organization
PA: Disabled American Veterans
3725 Alexandria Pike
Cold Spring KY 41076
859 441-7300

(G-13100)
ENVIROSCAPES
7727 Paris Ave (44641-9598)
PHONE...........................330 875-0768
Todd Pugh, *President*
Denise Crawford, *Controller*
Denise Bergert, *Human Resources*
Rhonda Patrick, *Sales Staff*
Matt Courtney, *Branch Mgr*
EMP: 50
SALES (est): 3.2MM **Privately Held**
SIC: 0782 Lawn care services; landscape contractors

(G-13101)
ESLICH WRECKING COMPANY
3525 Broadway Ave (44641-8902)
PHONE...........................330 488-8300
Fax: 330 488-0820
Richard Eslich, *CEO*
John Eslich, *President*
Elizabeth Eslich, *Admin Sec*
EMP: 50 EST: 1964
SQ FT: 30,000
SALES (est): 7.8MM **Privately Held**
WEB: www.eslichwrecking.com
SIC: 1795 1794 Demolition, buildings & other structures; excavation work

(G-13102)
LOUISVILLE FRTERNAL ORDER OF E
306 W Main St (44641-1230)
PHONE...........................330 875-2113
David Fischer, *Admin Sec*
EMP: 27
SQ FT: 30,000
SALES (est): 568.3K **Privately Held**
SIC: 8641 5812 5813 Fraternal associations; restaurant, family: independent; bar (drinking places)

(G-13103)
O D MILLER ELECTRIC CO INC
1115 W Main St (44641-1109)
PHONE...........................330 875-1651
Fax: 330 875-5804
Dale Miller, *President*
Robert Ickes, *Vice Pres*
Don Miller, *Vice Pres*
EMP: 28
SQ FT: 10,000
SALES (est): 3.4MM **Privately Held**
SIC: 1731 Electrical work

(G-13104)
OAKHILL MANOR CARE CENTER
4466 Lynnhaven Ave (44641-9513)
PHONE...........................330 875-5060
Ana Schaefer, *President*
EMP: 120
SALES (est): 5.6MM **Privately Held**
SIC: 8059 Nursing home, except skilled & intermediate care facility

(G-13105)
PROGRESSIVE GREEN MEADOWS LLC
Also Called: Green Madows Hlth Wellness Ctr
7770 Columbus Rd (44641-9773)
PHONE...........................330 875-1456
Julie Esack, *Mng Member*
Julie Esackn, *Mng Member*
EMP: 180

▲ = Import ▼=Export
◆ =Import/Export

SALES (est): 6.6MM Privately Held
WEB: www.progressivequalitycare.com
SIC: 8051 Convalescent home with continuous nursing care

(G-13106)
ROMAN CTHLIC DOCESE YOUNGSTOWN
Also Called: St Joseph Care Center
2308 Reno Dr (44641-9083)
PHONE..................................330 875-5562
Fax: 330 875-8947
John Banks, Superintendent
Cynthia Carapella, Director
Lynette Brinkerhoff, Nursing Dir
Ann Kellar, Nursing Dir
Richard Fleck, Food Svc Dir
EMP: 160
SALES (corp-wide): 23.6MM Privately Held
WEB: www.stjosephmantua.com
SIC: 8361 8052 8051 Rest home, with health care incidental; intermediate care facilities; skilled nursing care facilities
PA: Roman Catholic Diocese Of Youngstown
144 W Wood St
Youngstown OH 44503
330 744-8451

(G-13107)
TODDS ENVIROSCAPES INC
7727 Paris Ave (44641-9598)
PHONE..................................330 875-0768
Fax: 330 875-0782
Todd E Pugh, President
Bill McCroskeyr, Manager
EMP: 38
SALES (est): 10.8MM Privately Held
WEB: www.enviroscapesgroup.com
SIC: 0781 Landscape services

(G-13108)
Y M C A CENTRAL STARK COUNTY
Also Called: Louisville YMCA
1421 S Nickelplate St (44641-2647)
PHONE..................................330 875-1611
Fax: 330 875-8004
Donna Kuehner, Director
EMP: 50
SALES (corp-wide): 16.5MM Privately Held
WEB: www.ymcastark.org
SIC: 8641 7991 8351 7032 Youth organizations; physical fitness facilities; child day care services; youth camps; individual & family services
PA: Y M C A Of Central Stark County
1201 30th St Nw Ste 200a
Canton OH 44709
330 491-9622

Loveland
Clermont County

(G-13109)
ADVANCED GERIATRIC EDUCATION &
9823 Tulip Tree Ct (45140-5597)
PHONE..................................888 393-9799
Phyllis Atkinson,
EMP: 40
SALES (est): 690.9K
SALES (corp-wide): 13.8MM Privately Held
SIC: 8361 Geriatric residential care
PA: Black Stone Of Cincinnati, Llc
4700 E Galbraith Rd Fl 3
Cincinnati OH 45236
513 924-1370

(G-13110)
AMS CONSTRUCTION INC (PA)
10670 Loveland Madeira Rd (45140-8964)
P.O. Box 42068, Cincinnati (45242-0068)
PHONE..................................513 794-0410
Fax: 513 794-0414
John K Stephenson, President
Brenda Stephenson, President
Karen Stephenson, Vice Pres
George Meyer, Sales Executive
EMP: 38

SALES (est): 24.4MM Privately Held
SIC: 1731 Electrical work

(G-13111)
AQUARIAN POOLS INC
631 Lveland Miamiville Rd (45140-6932)
PHONE..................................513 576-9771
Fax: 513 576-9460
Michael Iori, President
Linda Iori, Corp Secy
Rebecca Fatute, Manager
EMP: 25
SQ FT: 2,000
SALES (est): 3.6MM Privately Held
WEB: www.aquarianpools.com
SIC: 1799 Swimming pool construction

(G-13112)
CANDO PHARMACEUTICAL
100 Commerce Dr (45140-7726)
PHONE..................................513 354-2694
Dennis Smith, Owner
Jim Light, Manager
EMP: 25
SALES (est): 736.8K
SALES (corp-wide): 10.7MM Privately Held
WEB: www.mastersinhealthcare.com
SIC: 5047 Medical equipment & supplies
PA: Mhc Medical Products, Llc
11930 Kemper Springs Dr
Cincinnati OH 45240
877 358-4342

(G-13113)
CARESPRING HEALTH CARE MGT LLC (PA)
390 Wards Corner Rd (45140-6969)
PHONE..................................513 943-4000
Chris Chirumbolo, CEO
Debbie Berling, Vice Pres
Cathy Hamblen, Vice Pres
Kimberly Majick, Vice Pres
John Muller, Vice Pres
EMP: 40 EST: 2007
SALES (est): 74MM Privately Held
SIC: 8741 8099 Hospital management; nursing & personal care facility management; blood related health services

(G-13114)
CINCINNATI DENTAL SERVICES
8944 Columbia Rd Ste 300 (45140-1173)
PHONE..................................513 774-8800
Fred White V, Officer
EMP: 45
SALES (corp-wide): 5.8MM Privately Held
SIC: 8021 Dentists' office
PA: Cincinnati Dental Services Inc
121 E Mcmillan St
Cincinnati OH 45219
513 721-8888

(G-13115)
CINCINNATI VOICE AND DATA
136 Commerce Dr (45140-7726)
PHONE..................................513 683-4127
Fax: 937 683-4733
Jeffrey Black, President
Holly Black, Admin Sec
EMP: 100
SALES (est): 2.4MM Privately Held
SIC: 4899 7378 5065 1731 Communication signal enhancement network system; computer maintenance & repair; electronic parts & equipment; electrical work

(G-13116)
COLLINS SALON INC
12125 N Lebanon Rd (45140-1824)
PHONE..................................513 683-1700
Donna Collins, Owner
EMP: 30
SALES (est): 584.3K Privately Held
WEB: www.collinssalons.com
SIC: 7231 Unisex hair salons

(G-13117)
CRAPSEY & GILLIS CONTRACTORS
8887 Glendale Milford Rd (45140-8906)
PHONE..................................513 891-6333
Fax: 513 891-7866
Robert S Crapsey, President
Christopher Gillis, Vice Pres

Tony Accurso, Project Mgr
James Nutter, Project Mgr
EMP: 35
SQ FT: 3,000
SALES (est): 4.3MM Privately Held
WEB: www.crapseyandgilles.com
SIC: 1521 1542 New construction, single-family houses; commercial & office building, new construction

(G-13118)
CREEKSIDE LTD LLC
Also Called: Oasis Golf Club
902 Lveland Miamiville Rd (45140-6952)
PHONE..................................513 583-4977
Fax: 513 583-9872
Lew Rosenbloom, General Mgr
EMP: 70
SALES (est): 2.2MM Privately Held
SIC: 7992 Public golf courses
PA: Creekside, Ltd, Llc
1250 Springfield Pike # 400
Cincinnati OH 45215

(G-13119)
CUSTOM CHEMICAL SOLUTIONS
167 Commerce Dr (45140-7727)
PHONE..................................800 291-1057
EMP: 45
SALES (est): 1.3MM Privately Held
SIC: 5169 Industrial chemicals

(G-13120)
DANIEL MAURY CONSTRUCTION CO
8960 Glendale Milford Rd (45140-8908)
PHONE..................................513 984-4096
Joseph Bitzer, President
Maxine Bitzer, Vice Pres
Lisa Milyo, Controller
Maureen Merkel, Clerk
EMP: 50 EST: 1951
SQ FT: 15,000
SALES (est): 1.8MM Privately Held
SIC: 6512 Commercial & industrial building operation

(G-13121)
DECORATIVE PAVING COMPANY
39 Glendale Milford Rd (45140-8848)
PHONE..................................513 576-1222
Kevin Piers, President
Debbie Reynolds, Technology
EMP: 30
SALES (est): 5.9MM Privately Held
SIC: 1611 Highway & street paving contractor

(G-13122)
DEERFIELD CONSTRUCTION CO INC (PA)
8960 Glendale Milford Rd (45140-8900)
PHONE..................................513 984-4096
Fax: 513 984-3035
Joseph Bitzer, CEO
Steve Bitzer, President
Scott Bitzer, Vice Pres
David Knueven, Vice Pres
John Stewart, CFO
EMP: 36
SQ FT: 15,000
SALES (est): 22.5MM Privately Held
WEB: www.deerfieldconstruction.com
SIC: 1542 1541 Commercial & office building, new construction; commercial & office buildings, renovation & repair; restaurant construction; shopping center construction; industrial buildings & warehouses; warehouse construction; renovation, remodeling & repairs: industrial buildings

(G-13123)
DILL-ELAM INC
Also Called: City Service
1461 State Route 28 (45140-8778)
PHONE..................................513 575-0017
Fax: 513 575-0524
Gary Dill, President
Steve Elam, Vice Pres
EMP: 48
SALES (est): 11.2MM Privately Held
SIC: 4213 4212 Trucking, except local; local trucking, without storage

(G-13124)
ELITE AMBULANCE SERVICE LLC
1451 State Route 28 Ste B (45140-8442)
PHONE..................................888 222-1356
Jeremy Woodward, Principal
Dillon Jacobs, Manager
Jeremy L Woodward,
EMP: 25
SALES (est): 399K Privately Held
SIC: 4119 Ambulance service

(G-13125)
FISCHER PUMP & VALVE COMPANY (PA)
Also Called: Fischer Process Industries
155 Commerce Dr (45140-7727)
PHONE..................................513 583-4800
Fax: 513 583-4815
Ken Fischer, President
Ray Didonato, Vice Pres
Chuck Douglas, VP Sales
Curt Edwards, Manager
Bob Hellmann, Manager
▲ EMP: 38
SQ FT: 18,000
SALES (est): 33.1MM Privately Held
SIC: 5085 5084 Pistons & valves; pumps & pumping equipment

(G-13126)
GARRETSON FIRM RESOLUTION (PA)
Also Called: Garretson Resolution Group
6281 Tri Ridge Blvd # 300 (45140-8345)
PHONE..................................513 794-0400
Matt Garretson, CEO
Jason Wolf, President
Dan Docherty, Senior VP
Asim Ali, Vice Pres
Philip Jenkins, Vice Pres
EMP: 200
SALES (est): 25.3MM Privately Held
SIC: 8111 Bankruptcy law; debt collection law; taxation law; corporate, partnership & business law

(G-13127)
GARRETYSON FRM RESOLUTION GRP
6281 Tri Ridge Blvd # 300 (45140-8345)
PHONE..................................513 794-0400
Shawn Kocher, CEO
Thomas Bagley,
David Johnston,
John Starcevich,
EMP: 180
SALES (est): 11.5MM Privately Held
SIC: 8742 Management consulting services

(G-13128)
GL NAUSE CO INC
1971 Phoenix Dr (45140-9241)
PHONE..................................513 722-9500
Fax: 513 722-0819
Gregory L Nause, President
Mark Rosselot, General Mgr
Jeff Brewsaugh, Sales Staff
Jodie K Nause, Admin Sec
Jodie Nause, Admin Sec
EMP: 25
SQ FT: 30,000
SALES (est): 5.2MM Privately Held
WEB: www.glnause.com
SIC: 3441 3443 1791 7699 Building components, structural steel; fabricated plate work (boiler shop); structural steel erection; industrial equipment services; industrial machinery & equipment repair; architectural metalwork; sheet metalwork

(G-13129)
GODDARD SCHOOL
782 Lveland Miamiville Rd (45140-6933)
PHONE..................................513 697-9663
Fax: 513 697-9099
Sandy Joseph, Owner
EMP: 25
SALES (est): 491.5K Privately Held
SIC: 8351 Preschool center

Loveland - Clermont County (G-13130)   GEOGRAPHIC SECTION

(G-13130)
HEARTLAND PAYMENT SYSTEMS LLC
3455 Steeplechase Ln (45140-3280)
PHONE..................513 518-6125
EMP: 99
SALES (corp-wide): 3.9B Publicly Held
SIC: 7389 Credit card service
HQ: Heartland Payment Systems, Llc
 10 Glenlake Pkwy Ste 324
 Atlanta GA 30328
 609 683-3831

(G-13131)
HICKORY WOODS GOLF COURSE INC
1240 Hickory Woods Dr (45140-9488)
PHONE..................513 575-3900
Fax: 513 575-3921
Dennis Acomb, *President*
Tom Schindler, *CFO*
EMP: 40
SALES (est): 1.6MM Privately Held
WEB: www.hickorywoods.com
SIC: 7992 Public golf courses

(G-13132)
I T E LLC
424 Wards Corner Rd # 300 (45140-6967)
PHONE..................513 576-6200
Kyle Lehr, *Vice Pres*
David Mackenzie, *Vice Pres*
Adam Hensel, *Engineer*
Ancy Ebby, *Accountant*
Martha Mc Clain, *Personnel Exec*
EMP: 60
SQ FT: 9,660
SALES (est): 9.2MM Privately Held
WEB: www.ite.com
SIC: 8711 8742 8732 Electrical or electronic engineering; management consulting services; commercial nonphysical research

(G-13133)
INTERNATIONAL PAPER COMPA
6283 Tri Ridge Blvd (45140-8318)
P.O. Box 62717, Cincinnati (45262-0717)
PHONE..................513 248-6000
Fax: 513 248-6500
Don Zeitinger, *Project Mgr*
Michael Schumpp, *Manager*
Bruce Archibald, *Manager*
Jim Baumer, *Manager*
Vic Kawamura, *Manager*
EMP: 67
SALES (est): 17.7MM Privately Held
SIC: 8111 General practice attorney, lawyer

(G-13134)
J DANIEL & COMPANY INC
1975 Phoenix Dr (45140-9241)
PHONE..................513 575-3100
Fax: 513 575-5636
Price Jackson, *President*
John Tuerck, *Safety Mgr*
Robert Kearns, *Treasurer*
Doug Boden, *Manager*
Dave Woeste, *Director*
EMP: 90
SALES: 16.4MM
SALES (corp-wide): 208.3MM Privately Held
WEB: www.jdanielco.com
SIC: 1623 Underground utilities contractor
PA: Danella Companies, Inc.
 2290 Butler Pike
 Plymouth Meeting PA 19462
 610 828-6200

(G-13135)
J K MEURER CORP
33 Glendale Milford Rd (45140-8848)
PHONE..................513 831-7500
Fax: 513 248-5575
Jeffrey K Meurer, *President*
Kane Meurer, *Superintendent*
Bryan Shepherd, *Project Mgr*
Nicky Adkins, *Controller*
Christa Davenport, *Human Res Mgr*
EMP: 45
SQ FT: 3,500
SALES: 13.4MM Privately Held
SIC: 1611 Highway & street paving contractor

(G-13136)
KROSS ACQUISITION COMPANY LLC
10690 Loveland Madeira Rd (45140-8964)
PHONE..................513 554-0555
Robert D Miles,
EMP: 30
SALES (est): 4.5MM Privately Held
SIC: 8741 Business management

(G-13137)
L & I CUSTOM WALLS INC
10369 Cones Rd (45140-7211)
PHONE..................513 683-2045
Alvin Walker, *President*
Marjorie Walker, *Corp Secy*
Jack Walker, *Vice Pres*
EMP: 50
SQ FT: 1,200
SALES (est): 3.1MM Privately Held
SIC: 1771 Concrete work

(G-13138)
LIFE ENRICHING COMMUNITIES (PA)
6279 Tri Ridge Blvd # 320 (45140-8320)
PHONE..................513 719-3510
Jim Bowersox, *CFO*
Connie Kingsbury, *VP Mktg*
Nancy Hartman, *Manager*
Mark Mountel, *Info Tech Dir*
Tim Grimes, *Exec Dir*
EMP: 30
SALES (est): 5.9MM Privately Held
SIC: 8399 Community development groups

(G-13139)
LODGE CARE CENTER INC
9370 Union Cemetery Rd (45140-9577)
PHONE..................513 683-9966
Fax: 513 677-4905
Barry A Kohn, *President*
Sam Boymel, *Vice Pres*
Amanda Plavsic, *Manager*
Thaddeus Bort, *Medical Dir*
Cari Carmack, *Hlthcr Dir*
EMP: 164
SALES (est): 11MM Privately Held
WEB: www.lodgecarecenter.com
SIC: 8051 Convalescent home with continuous nursing care

(G-13140)
LONDON COMPUTER SYSTEMS INC
Also Called: Lcs
1007 Cottonwood Dr (45140-9356)
PHONE..................513 583-0840
David Hegemann, *President*
Abbie Huffman, *Business Mgr*
Brittany Christerson, *Sales Mgr*
Eva Gonzales, *Accounts Mgr*
Tawny Worth, *Accounts Mgr*
EMP: 100 EST: 1987
SQ FT: 20,000
SALES (est): 15.5MM Privately Held
WEB: www.rentmanager.com
SIC: 7379 7371 ; computer software development

(G-13141)
LOVELAND HEALTH CARE CTR LLC
Also Called: Rand Loveland
501 N 2nd St (45140-6667)
PHONE..................513 605-6000
Fax: 513 683-1936
Steve Boymel, *President*
Tamara Bell, *Accountant*
Nicole Breving, *Human Res Dir*
Lori Erdman, *Office Mgr*
EMP: 110
SQ FT: 20,000
SALES (est): 7.2MM Privately Held
SIC: 8051 Convalescent home with continuous nursing care

(G-13142)
LOWRY CONTROLS INC
273 E Kemper Rd (45140-8627)
PHONE..................513 583-0182
Fax: 513 583-8007
Kelly Barry, *President*
Kelly Lowry, *President*
EMP: 27
SALES (est): 2.9MM Privately Held
WEB: www.lowrycontrols.com
SIC: 1731 General electrical contractor

(G-13143)
MARSH & MCLENNAN AGENCY LLC
6279 Tri Ridge Blvd # 400 (45140-8320)
PHONE..................513 248-4888
Chris Schwarz, *Accounts Exec*
Dave Eveleigh, *Sales Staff*
Debbie Joffe, *Marketing Staff*
Vicky Tuten, *Branch Mgr*
Bill Clasen, *Agent*
EMP: 27
SALES (corp-wide): 14B Publicly Held
SIC: 6411 Insurance brokers
HQ: Marsh & Mclennan Agency Llc
 360 Hamilton Ave Ste 930
 White Plains NY 10601

(G-13144)
MARSHALL & ASSOCIATES INC
1537 Durango Dr (45140-2129)
P.O. Box 498428, Cincinnati (45249-7428)
PHONE..................513 683-6396
Fax: 513 683-9183
Ronald Marshall, *President*
Betty Marshall, *Corp Secy*
Linda Hunter, *Vice Pres*
EMP: 28
SALES (est): 674K Privately Held
SIC: 7381 8111 Detective agency; security guard service; legal services

(G-13145)
MCCORMICK EQUIPMENT CO INC (PA)
112 Northeast Dr (45140-7144)
PHONE..................513 677-8888
Fax: 513 677-9322
R Peter Kimener, *President*
Steve Scaggs, *Opers Mgr*
Deanda Esparza, *Opers Staff*
Bruce A Buckley, *CFO*
Dave Poissant, *VP Sales*
EMP: 33
SQ FT: 30,000
SALES (est): 37.7MM Privately Held
WEB: www.mccequip.com
SIC: 5084 Materials handling machinery

(G-13146)
MIKES CARWASH INC (PA)
100 Northeast Dr (45140-7144)
PHONE..................513 677-4700
Mike Dahm, *President*
Andrew Dowden, *COO*
Greg Reis, *Exec VP*
EMP: 250
SALES (est): 28.6MM Privately Held
SIC: 7542 Washing & polishing, automotive

(G-13147)
MMIC INC
6867 Obannon Blf (45140-6018)
PHONE..................513 697-0445
Beth McDonald, *President*
EMP: 75
SALES (est): 1.3MM Privately Held
SIC: 7699 Industrial machinery & equipment repair

(G-13148)
NESTLE USA INC
6279 Tri Ridge Blvd # 100 (45140-8396)
PHONE..................513 576-4930
Teresa Donley, *Branch Mgr*
EMP: 25
SALES (corp-wide): 88.4B Privately Held
WEB: www.nestleusa.com
SIC: 2064 5141 Candy & other confectionery products; groceries, general line
HQ: Nestle Usa, Inc.
 1812 N Moore St
 Rosslyn VA 22209
 818 549-6000

(G-13149)
NURTUR HOLDINGS LLC (PA)
6279 Tri Ridge Blvd # 250 (45140-8301)
PHONE..................614 487-3033
Fax: 513 576-0374
Alefare Thompson, *Accountant*
Collins Meg, *Human Res Mgr*
Mindi Graham, *Marketing Mgr*
Christopher Deluca,
EMP: 33
SALES (est): 4.5MM Privately Held
SIC: 7231 Cosmetology school

(G-13150)
OASIS TURF & TREE INC
8900 Glendl Milford Rd A4 (45140-8959)
PHONE..................513 697-9090
Robert A Reindl, *President*
Angela Reindl, *Vice Pres*
EMP: 25
SQ FT: 4,000
SALES (est): 3.5MM Privately Held
SIC: 0781 Landscape services

(G-13151)
OBANNON CREEK GOLF CLUB
6842 Oakland Rd (45140-9723)
PHONE..................513 683-5657
Fax: 513 683-0066
Marianne Fahms, *General Mgr*
Maryann Sahms, *General Mgr*
Marian Reid, *Manager*
EMP: 40
SQ FT: 17,000
SALES: 1.7MM Privately Held
SIC: 7997 5941 5813 5812 Golf club, membership; golf goods & equipment; bar (drinking places); grills (eating places)

(G-13152)
PARAMOUNT LAWN SERVICE INC
8900 Glendale Milford Rd A1 (45140-8959)
PHONE..................513 984-5200
Fax: 513 984-8229
Joseph Tekulve, *President*
Dennis Eppert, *Opers Mgr*
Miki Mills, *Manager*
EMP: 25
SQ FT: 3,750
SALES: 2MM Privately Held
WEB: www.paramountlandscaping.com
SIC: 0782 4959 Landscape contractors; lawn services; snowplowing

(G-13153)
PRICE WOODS PRODUCTS INC
6507 Snider Rd (45140-9588)
PHONE..................513 722-1200
Fax: 513 722-1211
Dallas Wayne Price, *Owner*
Theresa Price, *Vice Pres*
▼ EMP: 25
SALES: 3.3MM Privately Held
SIC: 5031 Lumber: rough, dressed & finished; veneer

(G-13154)
RAPID PLUMBING INC
1407 State Route 28 (45140-8777)
PHONE..................513 575-1509
Fax: 513 575-1154
Walter D Minton, *President*
Ronald Minton, *Corp Secy*
Patty Durbin, *Director*
EMP: 65
SQ FT: 4,500
SALES (est): 5.6MM Privately Held
WEB: www.rapidplumbing.net
SIC: 1711 Plumbing contractors

(G-13155)
RAY MEYER SIGN COMPANY INC
8942 Glendale Milford Rd (45140-8908)
PHONE..................513 984-5446
Fax: 513 984-5663
Ray A Meyer, *President*
Barbara A Meyer, *Corp Secy*
John A Meyer, *Vice Pres*
Michael A Meyer, *VP Sales*
EMP: 25
SQ FT: 12,000

GEOGRAPHIC SECTION
Lucasville - Scioto County (G-13179)

SALES: 1.8MM **Privately Held**
WEB: www.raymeyersigns.com
SIC: 7389 Sign painting & lettering shop

(G-13156)
RECREATIONAL GOLF INC
Also Called: Eastgate Advntres Golf G-Karts
203 Glen Lake Rd (45140-2603)
PHONE..................513 677-0347
Timothy C Jones, *President*
Mary Ellen Hofmann, *Corp Secy*
J Thomas Jones, *Vice Pres*
EMP: 25
SQ FT: 5,400
SALES (est): 506.9K **Privately Held**
SIC: 7999 Miniature golf course operation; go-cart raceway operation & rentals

(G-13157)
RVET OPERATING LLC
Also Called: Recruitmilitary
422 W Loveland Ave (45140-2322)
PHONE..................513 683-5020
Fax: 513 683-5021
Tim Best, *CEO*
Larry Slagel, *COO*
Mike Francomb, *Senior VP*
Robert Arndt, *Vice Pres*
Jordan Bohrer, *Vice Pres*
EMP: 43
SALES (est): 924.6K
SALES (corp-wide): 18.1MM **Privately Held**
SIC: 7361 7389 Executive placement; advertising, promotional & trade show services; subscription fulfillment services: magazine, newspaper, etc.
PA: Bradley-Morris Holdings, Llc
1825 Barrett Lakes Blvd N
Kennesaw GA 30144
678 819-4171

(G-13158)
SEM VILLA INC
Also Called: Sem Villa Retirement Community
6409 Small House Cir (45140-7524)
PHONE..................513 831-3262
Julie Foley, *Director*
Rosanna Stephenson, *Food Svc Dir*
EMP: 25
SQ FT: 400,000
SALES: 1.1MM **Privately Held**
SIC: 8361 Home for the aged

(G-13159)
SHAWCOR PIPE PROTECTION LLC
Also Called: Dsg Canusa
173 Commerce Dr (45140-7727)
P.O. Box 498830, Cincinnati (45249-8830)
PHONE..................513 683-7800
Fax: 513 683-7809
Jim Raussen, *Sales Staff*
Jim Huntebrinker, *Branch Mgr*
EMP: 25
SALES (corp-wide): 894.4MM **Privately Held**
WEB: www.bredero-shaw.com
SIC: 5084 Industrial machinery & equipment
HQ: Shawcor Pipe Protection Llc
3838 N Sam Houston Pkwy E # 300
Houston TX 77032

(G-13160)
SHAWNEESPRING HLTH CRE CNTR RL
390 Wards Corner Rd (45140-6969)
PHONE..................513 943-4000
Barry Bortz, *Principal*
EMP: 288
SALES (est): 171.1K
SALES (corp-wide): 74MM **Privately Held**
SIC: 8011 Offices & clinics of medical doctors
HQ: Shawneespring Health Care Center
10111 Simonson Rd
Harrison OH 45030
513 367-7780

(G-13161)
SMITH & ENGLISH II INC
12191 State Route 22 3 (45140-9355)
P.O. Box 750968, Dayton (45475-0968)
PHONE..................513 697-9300
John R Gierl, *Principal*
EMP: 45
SALES (est): 2.8MM **Privately Held**
SIC: 8748 8742 Business consulting; business consultant

(G-13162)
TALEMED LLC
6279 Tri Ridge Blvd # 110 (45140-8320)
PHONE..................513 774-7300
Randy Baker, *General Mgr*
Elizabeth Tracy, *Marketing Staff*
Barbara Annz, *Manager*
Brad Baumer, *Manager*
Kristen Bowles, *Manager*
EMP: 260
SALES (est): 12.5MM **Privately Held**
SIC: 7361 Nurses' registry

(G-13163)
WASHING SYSTEMS LLC (PA)
167 Commerce Dr (45140-7727)
PHONE..................800 272-1974
Greg Brodrick, *VP Opers*
Phil Newman, *Materials Mgr*
Leah Boyd, *Safety Mgr*
Marc Fisher, *Manager*
John Walraus, *Manager*
▼ EMP: 110
SALES: 90MM **Privately Held**
WEB: www.washingsystems.com
SIC: 5169 2841 Detergents; industrial chemicals; soap & other detergents

(G-13164)
WEST SHELL GALE SCHNETZER
748 Wards Corner Rd (45140-8740)
PHONE..................513 683-3833
Gale Schnetzer, *Partner*
EMP: 50 EST: 1999
SALES (est): 1.2MM **Privately Held**
SIC: 6531 Real estate brokers & agents

(G-13165)
WESTERN & SOUTHERN LF INSUR CO
6281 Tri Ridge Blvd # 310 (45140-8345)
PHONE..................513 891-0777
Fax: 513 794-8741
Edward Babbitt, *Vice Pres*
Robert Dennison, *Investment Ofcr*
Lawrence Sowders, *Manager*
Mary Baxter, *Manager*
EMP: 30
SQ FT: 6,473 **Privately Held**
SIC: 6411 Life insurance agents
HQ: The Western & Southern Life Insurance Company
400 Broadway St
Cincinnati OH 45202
513 629-1800

(G-13166)
WILMARED INC
Also Called: Kinker Eveleigh Insurance
6279 Tri Ridge Blvd (45140-8396)
PHONE..................513 891-6615
Fax: 513 891-6621
Sam Tuten, *President*
Vida Reith, *Vice Pres*
George Seurkamp, *Vice Pres*
Vicky Tuten, *Treasurer*
Chris Schwarz, *Accounts Exec*
EMP: 32
SQ FT: 4,100
SALES (est): 5.5MM **Privately Held**
WEB: www.ekinker.com
SIC: 6411 Insurance agents

Lowell
Washington County

(G-13167)
BURKHART EXCAVATING INC
9950 State Route 60 (45744-7577)
PHONE..................740 896-3312
William Burkhart III, *President*
Brad Mason, *Admin Sec*
EMP: 35
SALES (est): 1.3MM **Privately Held**
SIC: 1794 Excavation work

(G-13168)
BURKHART TRUCKING INC
Also Called: Burkhart Trucking & Excavating
9950 State Route 60 (45744-7577)
PHONE..................740 896-2244
Fax: 740 896-2675
William H Burkhart III, *President*
Bradley S Mason, *Corp Secy*
EMP: 30
SQ FT: 3,200
SALES: 2.5MM **Privately Held**
SIC: 4212 1521 Dump truck haulage; coal haulage, local; single-family housing construction

(G-13169)
MARIETTA TRANSFER COMPANY
Also Called: Mills Transfer
11569 State Route 60 (45744)
PHONE..................740 896-3565
Gene Davis, *President*
Dennis Davis, *Vice Pres*
EMP: 40
SALES (est): 1.1MM **Privately Held**
SIC: 4789 Transportation services

Lowellville
Mahoning County

(G-13170)
BROWNING-FERRIS INDS OF OHIO
Site L08
8100 S State Line Rd (44436-9596)
PHONE..................330 536-8013
Mike Heher, *Manager*
EMP: 60
SALES (corp-wide): 10B **Publicly Held**
SIC: 4953 Sanitary landfill operation
HQ: Browning-Ferris Industries Of Ohio Inc
3870 Hendricks Rd
Youngstown OH 44515
330 793-7676

(G-13171)
ENERTECH ELECTRICAL INC
101 Yngstown Lwllville Rd (44436-1010)
PHONE..................330 536-2131
Fax: 330 536-8889
Gregory T Haren, *CEO*
John Donofrio Jr, *President*
John A Wilaj, *Vice Pres*
James Burgy, *Purch Mgr*
Ernie Yacovone, *Engineer*
▲ EMP: 30
SQ FT: 8,000
SALES (est): 6.7MM **Privately Held**
WEB: www.enertechelectrical.com
SIC: 1731 General electrical contractor

(G-13172)
M & M WINE CELLAR INC
Also Called: L'U Vabella
259 Bedford Rd (44436-9547)
PHONE..................330 536-6450
Frank Sergi, *President*
EMP: 30
SALES: 2MM **Privately Held**
SIC: 5499 5149 5182 Juices, fruit or vegetable; juices; wine

(G-13173)
REPUBLIC SERVICES INC
8100 S State Line Rd (44436-9596)
PHONE..................330 536-8013
Fax: 330 536-5026
Mike Heher, *Branch Mgr*
EMP: 34
SALES (corp-wide): 10B **Publicly Held**
SIC: 4953 Refuse collection & disposal services
PA: Republic Services, Inc.
18500 N Allied Way # 100
Phoenix AZ 85054
480 627-2700

(G-13174)
S E T INC
235 E Water St Ste C (44436-1273)
PHONE..................330 536-6724
Fax: 330 536-8274
Douglas Susany, *President*
Moussa Bittar, *Project Mgr*
Greg Susany, *Project Mgr*
Nancy Schmall, *Controller*
Patty McNamee, *Manager*
EMP: 50
SQ FT: 3,500
SALES: 17MM **Privately Held**
WEB: www.setinc.com
SIC: 1794 Excavation work

(G-13175)
VIMAS PAINTING COMPANY INC
4328 Mccartney Rd (44436-9567)
P.O. Box 601, Campbell (44405-0601)
PHONE..................330 536-2222
Fax: 330 755-6050
Bessie Xipolitas, *President*
Nick Frangopoulos, *General Mgr*
EMP: 40
SQ FT: 2,000
SALES: 5.3MM **Privately Held**
SIC: 1721 Industrial painting; bridge painting

Lucasville
Scioto County

(G-13176)
CONSULATE MANAGEMENT CO LLC
Also Called: Edgewood Manor Lucasville II
10098 Big Bear Creek Rd (45648-9168)
PHONE..................740 259-2351
Fax: 740 259-3056
Mike Bubinsky, *Manager*
EMP: 100
SALES (corp-wide): 581.9MM **Privately Held**
WEB: www.tandemhealthcare.com
SIC: 8059 8051 Nursing home, except skilled & intermediate care facility; skilled nursing care facilities
PA: Consulate Management Company, Llc
800 Concourse Pkwy S
Maitland FL 32751
407 571-1550

(G-13177)
CONSULATE MANAGEMENT CO LLC
10098 Big Bear Creek Rd (45648-9168)
PHONE..................740 259-5536
Thomas Barr, *General Mgr*
Satonya Fields, *Human Res Dir*
Carla Naegele,
EMP: 80
SALES (est): 1.3MM **Privately Held**
SIC: 8099 Health & allied services

(G-13178)
EDGEWOOD MANOR OF LUCASVILLE
Also Called: Convalescent Center Lucasville
10098 Big Bear Creek Rd (45648-9168)
PHONE..................740 259-5536
Fax: 740 259-2531
Jennifer McGlona, *Office Mgr*
Tom Barr, *Administration*
Donald Claggett, *Administration*
EMP: 120
SALES (est): 3.3MM **Privately Held**
SIC: 8051 Skilled nursing care facilities

(G-13179)
FRIENDS OF GOOD SHEPHERD MANOR
374 Good Manor Rd (45648-9606)
PHONE..................740 289-2861
Normand Tremblay, *Systems Dir*
Helen Dovenbarger, *Associate Dir*
Susan Hutchinson, *Executive*
EMP: 92
SQ FT: 30,593
SALES: 1MM **Privately Held**
SIC: 8361 8052 Home for the mentally retarded; intermediate care facilities

Lucasville - Scioto County (G-13180)

GEOGRAPHIC SECTION

(G-13180)
HEARTLAND HOSPICE SERVICES LLC
Also Called: Heartland HM Hlth Care Hospice
205 North St (45648)
P.O. Box 400 (45648-0400)
PHONE..................................740 259-0281
Fax: 740 259-0282
Christina Williams, *Branch Mgr*
EMP: 53
SALES (corp-wide): 3.6B **Publicly Held**
SIC: 8082 Home health care services
HQ: Heartland Hospice Services, Llc
333 N Summit St
Toledo OH 43604

(G-13181)
HIGHWAY PATROL
7611 Us Highway 23 (45648-8419)
PHONE..................................740 354-2888
Fax: 740 353-7338
John Kisik, *Principal*
EMP: 30
SALES (est): 129.9K **Privately Held**
SIC: 7381 Protective services, guard

(G-13182)
SCIOTO COUNTY REGION WTR DST 1
Also Called: Water 1
326 Robert Lucas Rd (45648-9204)
P.O. Box 310 (45648-0310)
PHONE..................................740 259-2301
Fax: 740 259-3446
Johnathan King, *General Mgr*
Kathie Edwards, *Treasurer*
Kathie Martin, *Financial Exec*
EMP: 29
SALES (est): 4.2MM **Privately Held**
WEB: www.water1.org
SIC: 4941 Water supply

Luckey
Wood County

(G-13183)
HIRZEL FARMS INC
20790 Bradner Rd (43443-9727)
PHONE..................................419 837-2710
Fax: 419 837-5717
Lou Kozma, *President*
EMP: 25
SALES (est): 775.6K **Privately Held**
SIC: 0161 Tomato farm

Lynchburg
Highland County

(G-13184)
SKW MANAGEMENT LLC
3841 Panhandle Rd (45142-9449)
PHONE..................................937 382-7938
Samuel K Wilkin, *Mng Member*
EMP: 42 EST: 2009
SQ FT: 1,200
SALES: 1MM **Privately Held**
SIC: 6513 Apartment building operators

Lyons
Fulton County

(G-13185)
B W GRINDING CO
Also Called: Bw Supply Co.
15048 County Road 10 3 (43533-9713)
P.O. Box 307 (43533-0307)
PHONE..................................419 923-1376
Fax: 419 923-1381
Martin Welch, *President*
Robert Welch, *Vice Pres*
Rick Rozewicki, *Manager*
EMP: 35
SQ FT: 30,000
SALES (est): 13.2MM **Privately Held**
WEB: www.bwsupplyco.com
SIC: 5085 3324 Industrial tools; commercial investment castings, ferrous

Macedonia
Summit County

(G-13186)
AGS CUSTOM GRAPHICS INC
Also Called: A G S Ohio
8107 Bavaria Rd (44056)
PHONE..................................330 963-7770
Fax: 330 349-4771
John Green, *President*
Chuck Straka, *VP Opers*
Laura Williams, *Project Mgr*
Stephan Kolakowski, *Production*
Doug Craddock, *Purch Mgr*
EMP: 74
SQ FT: 70,000
SALES (est): 20.6MM
SALES (corp-wide): 6.9B **Publicly Held**
WEB: www.automatedgraphic.com
SIC: 2752 2721 7375 2791 Commercial printing, offset; periodicals; information retrieval services; typesetting; bookbinding & related work; commercial printing
PA: R. R. Donnelley & Sons Company
35 W Wacker Dr Ste 3650
Chicago IL 60601
312 326-8000

(G-13187)
AVATAR MANAGEMENT SERVICES (PA)
Also Called: Avatar Solutions
8157 Bavaria Dr E (44056-2252)
PHONE..................................330 963-3900
Fax: 330 963-0369
Mark G Gardner, *CEO*
Linda M Gardner, *President*
EMP: 25
SQ FT: 13,000
SALES (est): 3.5MM **Privately Held**
WEB: www.avatarms.com
SIC: 8742 Business consultant

(G-13188)
AWE HOSPITALITY GROUP LLC
9652 N Bedford Rd (44056-1008)
PHONE..................................330 888-8836
Anthony Budroe, *President*
Rochelle Budroe, *Admin Sec*
EMP: 120 EST: 2011
SALES (est): 2.4MM **Privately Held**
SIC: 7011 Hotels & motels

(G-13189)
BAKER VEHICLE SYSTEMS INC
9035 Freeway Dr (44056-1508)
PHONE..................................330 467-2250
Fax: 330 467-8308
Harland R Baker, *President*
A C Baker, *Principal*
Harland E Baker, *Principal*
Virginia M Baker, *Principal*
Richard A Baker, *Vice Pres*
EMP: 36 EST: 1940
SQ FT: 38,000
SALES (est): 16.2MM **Privately Held**
WEB: www.bakervehicle.com
SIC: 5012 7359 Automobiles & other motor vehicles; equipment rental & leasing

(G-13190)
BENNETT SUPPLY OF OHIO LLC
8170 Roll And Hold Pkwy (44056-2146)
PHONE..................................800 292-5577
Fax: 330 936-0275
David Williams, *Manager*
David Bennett III,
Richard Bowman, *Admin Sec*
Andrew C Bennett,
▼ EMP: 25
SALES: 19.6MM
SALES (corp-wide): 43.8MM **Privately Held**
SIC: 5031 Building materials, exterior
PA: Bennett Supply Co.
300 Business Center Dr
Cheswick PA 15024
724 274-1700

(G-13191)
BURNS INDUSTRIAL EQUIPMENT INC
8155 Roll And Hold Pkwy (44056-2146)
PHONE..................................330 425-2476
Fax: 330 468-4955
Chris Burns, *President*
EMP: 25
SALES (corp-wide): 62MM **Privately Held**
SIC: 5046 Commercial equipment
PA: Burns Industrial Equipment, Inc.
230 Thorn Hill Rd
Warrendale PA 15086
412 856-9253

(G-13192)
CAPITAL SENIOR LIVING CORP
9633 Valley View Rd Ofc C (44056-3017)
PHONE..................................330 748-4204
Devan Owens, *Exec Dir*
EMP: 191
SALES (corp-wide): 467MM **Publicly Held**
SIC: 8082 Home health care services
PA: Capital Senior Living Corp
14160 Dallas Pkwy Ste 300
Dallas TX 75254
972 770-5600

(G-13193)
CINEMARK USA INC
Also Called: Cinemark 15
8161 Macedonia Commons Bi (44056-1848)
PHONE..................................330 908-1005
Carrie Walker, *Manager*
EMP: 25 **Publicly Held**
SIC: 7832 Motion picture theaters, except drive-in
HQ: Cinemark Usa, Inc.
3900 Dallas Pkwy Ste 500
Plano TX 75093
972 665-1000

(G-13194)
CONSOLIDATED RAIL CORPORATION
401 Ledge Rd (44056-1020)
PHONE..................................440 786-3014
Greg Drakulic, *Branch Mgr*
EMP: 60
SALES (corp-wide): 293.9MM **Privately Held**
SIC: 7699 Railroad car customizing
HQ: Consolidated Rail Corporation
1717 Arch St Ste 1310
Philadelphia PA 19103
800 456-7509

(G-13195)
DAVEY TREE EXPERT COMPANY
837 Highland Rd E (44056-2113)
PHONE..................................330 908-0833
Kent Winterhalter, *Branch Mgr*
EMP: 40
SALES (corp-wide): 915.9MM **Privately Held**
SIC: 0783 Planting, pruning & trimming services
PA: The Davey Tree Expert Company
1500 N Mantua St
Kent OH 44240
330 673-9511

(G-13196)
DUN RITE HOME IMPROVEMENT INC
8601 Freeway Dr (44056-1535)
PHONE..................................330 650-5322
Jim Carson, *President*
Karen Scott, *Bookkeeper*
Dia Ray, *Executive*
EMP: 30
SQ FT: 5,400
SALES (est): 5.2MM **Privately Held**
WEB: www.calldunrite.com
SIC: 4959 1761 5211 1521 Snowplowing; roofing contractor; door & window products; single-family home remodeling, additions & repairs

(G-13197)
FUN N STUFF AMUSEMENTS INC
661 Highland Rd E (44056-2109)
PHONE..................................330 467-0821
Fax: 330 467-5165
Raymond Atwell, *President*
Bob Switalski, *General Mgr*
Amanda Motz, *Food Svc Dir*
Victoria Noland, *Admin Sec*
▲ EMP: 66
SQ FT: 20,000
SALES (est): 2.2MM **Privately Held**
WEB: www.fun-n-stuff.com
SIC: 7996 Theme park, amusement

(G-13198)
GENERAL CRANE RENTAL LLC
9680 Freeway Dr (44056-1035)
PHONE..................................330 908-0001
Fax: 330 908-0005
Dan Manos, *President*
Karen Harnar, *Manager*
EMP: 35
SQ FT: 10,000
SALES (est): 7.9MM **Privately Held**
WEB: www.generalcranerental.com
SIC: 7353 Cranes & aerial lift equipment, rental or leasing

(G-13199)
GIRL SCOUTS LAKE ERIE COUNCIL
1 Girl Scout Way (44056-2156)
PHONE..................................330 864-9933
Cheryl Goggans, *CEO*
Giselle L Torres, *Program Mgr*
Rufus Hudson, *Bd of Directors*
EMP: 46 EST: 1918
SQ FT: 15,000
SALES (est): 2.6MM **Privately Held**
WEB: www.gslec.org
SIC: 8641 Girl Scout organization

(G-13200)
GIRL SCOUTS NORTH EAST OHIO (PA)
1 Girl Scout Way (44056-2156)
PHONE..................................330 864-9933
Fax: 330 467-1901
Jane Christyson, *CEO*
Brittany Zaehringer, *COO*
Patrica Mishic, *Vice Pres*
John Graves, *CFO*
Kristina Markovic, *Corp Comm Staff*
EMP: 94
SQ FT: 35,000
SALES: 10.8MM **Privately Held**
SIC: 8641 Girl Scout organization

(G-13201)
HANDL-IT INC (PA)
360 Highland Rd E 2 (44056-2139)
PHONE..................................330 468-0734
Fax: 440 786-7700
John S Peters, *Ch of Bd*
Jerry Peters, *President*
Don Barry, *CFO*
Kelly Patsolic, *Sales Executive*
Bill Ambrogio, *Manager*
EMP: 125
SQ FT: 66,500
SALES (est): 9.6MM **Privately Held**
WEB: www.handlit.net
SIC: 4225 General warehousing

(G-13202)
HOWARD HANNA SMYTHE CRAMER
907 E Aurora Rd (44056-1905)
PHONE..................................330 468-6833
Fax: 330 468-6861
Karen Griffith, *Manager*
Janet M Biel, *Real Est Agnt*
Cynthia R Maciejowski, *Real Est Agnt*
Jessica M Mercurio, *Real Est Agnt*
Donna Tanno, *Real Est Agnt*
EMP: 30
SALES (corp-wide): 76.4MM **Privately Held**
WEB: www.smythecramer.com
SIC: 6531 Real estate brokers & agents

▲ = Import ▼ = Export
◆ = Import/Export

HQ: Howard Hanna Smythe Cramer
6000 Parkland Blvd
Cleveland OH 44124
216 447-4477

(G-13203)
INTER DISTR SVCS OF CLEVE
8055 Highland Pointe Pkwy (44056-2147)
PHONE.................................330 468-4949
Fax: 330 468-4950
Jack A Russo, *President*
Jeffrey Fine, *Vice Pres*
Richard Kuzma, *CFO*
EMP: 27
SQ FT: 250,000
SALES (est): 2.4MM **Privately Held**
SIC: 4225 General warehousing & storage

(G-13204)
JAEKLE GROUP INC
1410 Highland Rd E (44056-2386)
PHONE.................................330 405-9353
Greeg Jaekle, *President*
David Weldon, *Engineer*
Karen Spivak, *Office Admin*
Rick Jaekle, *Administration*
Todd Mohr, *Administration*
EMP: 25
SALES (est): 3MM **Privately Held**
SIC: 7373 Systems integration services

(G-13205)
KAMAN CORPORATION
7900 Empire Pkwy (44056-2144)
PHONE.................................330 468-1811
Fax: 216 468-2766
Andy Dalzell, *Principal*
Jerry Frank, *Accounts Mgr*
EMP: 42
SALES (corp-wide): 1.8B **Publicly Held**
WEB: www.bwrogers.com
SIC: 5085 Industrial supplies
PA: Kaman Corporation
1332 Blue Hills Ave
Bloomfield CT 06002
860 243-7100

(G-13206)
NEWTOWN NINE INC (PA)
Also Called: Ohio Materials Handling
8155 Roll And Hold Pkwy (44056-2146)
PHONE.................................440 781-0623
Fax: 330 439-5103
James P Orenga, *President*
Eric Eide, *COO*
Pat Albanese, *Controller*
Dave Wojciechowski, *Controller*
Richard Bowman, *Admin Sec*
▲ **EMP:** 57
SQ FT: 38,000
SALES (est): 40MM **Privately Held**
WEB: www.ohiomaterialshandling.com
SIC: 5084 Lift trucks & parts; materials handling machinery

(G-13207)
OHIO STATE HOME SERVICES INC (PA)
Also Called: Ohio State Waterproofing
365 Highland Rd E (44056-2103)
PHONE.................................330 467-1055
Fax: 330 468-3323
Nick Di Cello, *President*
Randy Hushour, *Purch Mgr*
Judith Garvin, *VP Finance*
Judy Garvin, *VP Finance*
Gay Schrom, *Human Res Dir*
EMP: 170
SQ FT: 15,000
SALES (est): 32.5MM **Privately Held**
WEB: www.ohiostatewaterproofing.com
SIC: 1799 Waterproofing

(G-13208)
REGENCY ROOFING COMPANIES INC (PA)
Also Called: Shakemasters
576 Highland Rd E Ste A (44056-2134)
PHONE.................................330 468-1021
Fax: 330 467-0596
John J Zivich, *President*
Barb Zivich, *Manager*
EMP: 38 **EST:** 1974
SQ FT: 8,000
SALES (est): 4.7MM **Privately Held**
WEB: www.shakemaster.com
SIC: 1761 1799 Roofing contractor; siding contractor; coating, caulking & weather, water & fireproofing

(G-13209)
SALON SUCCESS INTL LLC
420 Highland Rd E (44056-2165)
PHONE.................................330 468-0476
Keith Chandler, *Mng Member*
EMP: 25
SALES (est): 2.5MM **Privately Held**
SIC: 5087 Beauty parlor equipment & supplies

(G-13210)
SPECIALTY LUBRICANTS CORP
Also Called: SLC Custom Packaging
8300 Corporate Park Dr (44056-2300)
PHONE.................................330 425-2567
Fax: 330 425-9637
Robin Bugenske, *CEO*
Sherry Bugenske, *President*
Paul Jones, *Purch Mgr*
Kahy Urner, *Human Res Mgr*
Ken Saraniti, *Sales Staff*
EMP: 82
SQ FT: 64,000
SALES (est): 8.2MM **Privately Held**
WEB: www.slipkote.com
SIC: 7389 5172 Packaging & labeling services; lubricating oils & greases

(G-13211)
SYSTEMS PACK INC
649 Highland Rd E (44056-2109)
PHONE.................................330 467-5729
Fax: 216 468-2299
Ray Attwell, *President*
Denny Kay, *VP Sales*
John Hood, *Sales Mgr*
Sean Freeman, *Consultant*
Cindi Laing, *Consultant*
EMP: 30 **EST:** 1977
SQ FT: 62,131
SALES (est): 15.2MM **Privately Held**
WEB: www.systemspackinc.com
SIC: 5199 7389 5113 2653 Packaging materials; packaging & labeling services; shipping supplies; corrugated & solid fiber boxes

(G-13212)
THOMAS TRANSPORT DELIVERY INC
9055 Freeway Dr Unit 1 (44056-1573)
PHONE.................................330 908-3100
Fax: 330 908-3101
Jeff Thomas, *President*
Glenn Berry, *Principal*
Frank Mandato, *Principal*
Bob Seaman, *Principal*
Sean Williams, *Vice Pres*
EMP: 40
SALES (est): 12.5MM **Privately Held**
WEB: www.thomastransportdelivery.com
SIC: 4212 Delivery service, vehicular

(G-13213)
TPC WIRE & CABLE CORP (HQ)
Also Called: Hoffman Products
9600 Valley View Rd (44056-2059)
PHONE.................................800 521-7935
Fax: 216 525-4392
Jeff Crane, *President*
Marianne Culver, *Senior VP*
Joseph Daprlle, *Vice Pres*
Victor March, *CFO*
Paul M Barlak, *Asst Treas*
▲ **EMP:** 86
SALES (est): 60.9MM
SALES (corp-wide): 1.6B **Privately Held**
SIC: 5063 Electronic wire & cable
PA: Audax Group, L.P.
101 Huntington Ave # 2450
Boston MA 02199
617 859-1500

(G-13214)
TRADESMEN INTERNATIONAL LLC (PA)
9760 Shepard Rd (44056-1124)
PHONE.................................440 349-3432
Joseph O Wesley, *President*
George Brophy, *President*
Joe Yeager, *President*
Richard Alanskas, *General Mgr*
Ryan Allen, *General Mgr*
EMP: 25
SQ FT: 3,000
SALES (est): 120.1MM **Privately Held**
WEB: www.tradesmen-intl.com
SIC: 7361 Labor contractors (employment agency)

(G-13215)
TRADESMEN SERVICES LLC
Also Called: Tradesmen Services, Inc.
9760 Shepard Rd (44056-1124)
PHONE.................................440 349-3432
Joe Wesley, *President*
Elaine Kapusta, *CFO*
Patrick Flynn, *General Counsel*
EMP: 80
SALES (est): 950K **Privately Held**
WEB: www.tradesmen-intl.com
SIC: 7361 Employment agencies
PA: Tradesmen International, Llc
9760 Shepard Rd
Macedonia OH 44056

(G-13216)
VMI GROUP INC
8854 Valley View Rd (44056-2316)
PHONE.................................330 405-4146
Neille Vitale, *President*
EMP: 90
SQ FT: 800
SALES (est): 1.8MM **Privately Held**
SIC: 1791 Precast concrete structural framing or panels, placing of

(G-13217)
W W GRAINGER INC
Also Called: Grainger 165
8211 Bavaria Dr E (44056-2259)
PHONE.................................330 425-8387
Fax: 330 425-3775
Candace Gaston, *Human Res Mgr*
Bob Holzer, *Manager*
EMP: 250
SALES (corp-wide): 10.4B **Publicly Held**
WEB: www.grainger.com
SIC: 5085 5063 Industrial supplies; electrical apparatus & equipment
PA: W.W. Grainger, Inc.
100 Grainger Pkwy
Lake Forest IL 60045
847 535-1000

(G-13218)
WESTERN RSRVE GIRL SCOUT CNCIL
1 Girl Scout Way (44056-2156)
PHONE.................................330 864-9933
Fax: 330 864-5720
EMP: 30
SQ FT: 27,000
SALES: 11.7MM **Privately Held**
SIC: 8641 Girl Scout Council

(G-13219)
YOUNG MENS CHRISTIAN ASSOC
Also Called: Longwood Family YMCA
8761 Shepard Rd (44056-1990)
PHONE.................................330 467-8366
Fax: 330 650-6144
John Herman, *Director*
John Hearman, *Director*
EMP: 30
SALES (corp-wide): 16.0MM **Privately Held**
WEB: www.campynoah.com
SIC: 8641 7991 8351 7032 Youth organizations; physical fitness facilities; child day care services; youth camps; individual & family services
PA: The Young Men's Christian Association Of Akron Ohio
50 S Mn St Ste LI100
Akron OH 44308
330 376-1335

Madison
Lake County

(G-13220)
AMERICAN EAGLE HLTH CARE SVCS
Also Called: Cardinal Wds Skilled Nursing
6831 Chapel Rd (44057-2255)
PHONE.................................440 428-5103
Fax: 440 428-9003
Joyce Humphrey, *President*
Andrea Carlson, *Facilities Dir*
Brenda Johnson, *Director*
Micki King, *Director*
Arthur Molinoff, *Director*
EMP: 120
SQ FT: 2,237
SALES (est): 10.2MM **Privately Held**
SIC: 8051 Skilled nursing care facilities

(G-13221)
BRIGHTER HORIZONS RESIDENTIAL
1899 Hubbard Rd (44057-2103)
PHONE.................................440 417-1751
Kelly Richmond, *President*
EMP: 50
SALES (est): 1.9MM **Privately Held**
WEB: www.brighterhorizonsinc.com
SIC: 8361 Home for the physically handicapped

(G-13222)
DAVITA INC
6830 N Ridge Rd (44057-2637)
PHONE.................................440 251-6237
EMP: 29 **Publicly Held**
SIC: 8092 Kidney dialysis centers
PA: Davita Inc.
2000 16th St
Denver CO 80202

(G-13223)
EASTWOOD RESIDENTIAL LIVING
6261 Chapel Rd (44057-2160)
PHONE.................................440 417-0608
Louanne Busch, *Manager*
EMP: 36
SALES (est): 246.6K
SALES (corp-wide): 1.6MM **Privately Held**
SIC: 8361 Home for the mentally handicapped
PA: Eastwood Residential Living Inc
6381 N Ridge Rd
Madison OH

(G-13224)
EASTWOOD RESIDENTIAL LIVING
Also Called: Searidge
6412 N Ridge Rd (44057-2550)
PHONE.................................440 428-1588
Fax: 440 328-3450
Jim Victor, *Manager*
EMP: 40
SQ FT: 2,025
SALES (corp-wide): 1.6MM **Privately Held**
SIC: 8361 Home for the mentally retarded
PA: Eastwood Residential Living Inc
6381 N Ridge Rd
Madison OH

(G-13225)
HOWARD HANNA SMYTHE CRAMER
Also Called: Smythe-Cramer Co Madison
2757 Hubbard Rd (44057-2931)
PHONE.................................440 428-1818
Fax: 440 428-7161
Robin Tilbery, *Manager*
Janice Warren, *Real Est Agnt*
EMP: 28
SALES (corp-wide): 76.4MM **Privately Held**
WEB: www.smythecramer.com
SIC: 6531 Real estate agents & managers

Madison - Lake County (G-13226)

GEOGRAPHIC SECTION

HQ: Howard Hanna Smythe Cramer
6000 Parkland Blvd
Cleveland OH 44124
216 447-4477

(G-13226)
J P JENKS INC
4493 S Madison Rd (44057-9422)
P.O. Box 370 (44057-0370)
PHONE.................................440 428-4500
Fax: 440 428-2099
Ray Kennedy, *President*
Brad Biro, *Manager*
Ernie Camodeca, *Manager*
EMP: 40 **EST:** 1972
SQ FT: 20,000
SALES (est): 4.9MM
SALES (corp-wide): 136.8MM **Privately Held**
WEB: www.rwsidleyinc.com
SIC: 4213 4212 Contract haulers; local trucking, without storage
PA: R. W. Sidley Incorporated
436 Casement Ave
Painesville OH 44077
440 352-9343

(G-13227)
LAKE COUNTY YMCA
Also Called: East End YMCA Pre School
730 N Lake St (44057-3153)
PHONE.................................440 428-5125
Fax: 440 428-1413
Dick Bennett, *Senior Mgr*
Michele Kuester, *Director*
Julie Headings, *Program Dir*
EMP: 70
SALES (corp-wide): 8.9MM **Privately Held**
SIC: 8641 7991 8351 7032 Youth organizations; physical fitness facilities; child day care services; youth camps; individual & family services
PA: Lake County Ymca
933 Mentor Ave Fl 2
Painesville OH 44077
440 352-3303

(G-13228)
LAKE METROPARKS
Also Called: Erie Shores Golf Club
7298 Lake Rd (44057-1512)
PHONE.................................440 428-3164
Fax: 440 428-8313
John Miller, *Manager*
EMP: 25 **Privately Held**
WEB: www.lakemetroparks.com
SIC: 7992 Public golf courses
PA: Lake Metroparks
11211 Spear Rd
Painesville OH 44077
440 639-7275

(G-13229)
LCN HOLDINGS INC
Also Called: Lake County Nursery
5052 S Ridge Rd (44057-9709)
P.O. Box 122, Perry (44081-0122)
PHONE.................................440 259-5571
Fax: 440 259-3114
Jeff Hyrne, *President*
Robert Pettorin, *VP Prdtn*
Joe Zampini, *VP Sales*
EMP: 34
SQ FT: 15,000
SALES (est): 4.1MM **Privately Held**
WEB: www.lakecountynursery.com
SIC: 5193 Flowers & nursery stock

(G-13230)
MADISON CARE INC
Also Called: Madison Health Care
7600 S Ridge Rd (44057-9746)
PHONE.................................440 428-1492
Fax: 440 428-8698
Susan Knowlson, *Director*
Thomas Wysinski, *Administration*
Thomas Wyszynski, *Administration*
EMP: 100 **EST:** 1966
SQ FT: 69,000
SALES (est): 7.2MM
SALES (corp-wide): 85.7MM **Privately Held**
SIC: 8051 Extended care facility

PA: Carington Health Systems
8200 Beckett Park Dr
Hamilton OH 45011
513 682-2700

(G-13231)
MADISON LOCAL SCHOOL DISTRICT
Also Called: Memorial Complex
92 E Main St (44057-3224)
PHONE.................................440 428-5111
Maureen Fedor, *Principal*
EMP: 25
SALES (corp-wide): 31.8MM **Privately Held**
WEB: www.madisonlocalschooldistrict.com
SIC: 8351 Preschool center
PA: Madison Local School District
1956 Red Bird Rd
Madison OH 44057
440 428-2166

(G-13232)
MADISON MEDICAL CAMPUS
Also Called: Lake Hospital Systems
6270 N Ridge Rd (44057-2567)
PHONE.................................440 428-6800
Fax: 440 428-8231
Rick Kondas, *Director*
EMP: 40
SALES (est): 1.6MM **Privately Held**
WEB: www.lakehospitalsystems.com
SIC: 8062 General medical & surgical hospitals

(G-13233)
NORTH COAST PERENNIALS INC
3754 Dayton Rd (44057-9782)
PHONE.................................440 428-4036
Fax: 440 428-1277
Mark Freshour, *Owner*
EMP: 35
SALES (est): 2.5MM **Privately Held**
WEB: www.northcoastperennials.com
SIC: 5193 Nursery stock

(G-13234)
NORTH RIDGE VETERINARY HOSP
6336 N Ridge Rd (44057-2548)
PHONE.................................440 428-5166
Fax: 440 428-9009
Rw Pierce Dvm, *Owner*
Debbie Heaven, *Practice Mgr*
EMP: 30
SQ FT: 11,000
SALES (est): 1.3MM **Privately Held**
SIC: 0742 Animal hospital services, pets & other animal specialties

(G-13235)
RIDGE MANOR NUSERIES INC
Also Called: Willow Ridge Nursery
7925 N Ridge Rd (44057-3026)
PHONE.................................440 466-5781
Fax: 440 466-5854
Angelo Petitti, *President*
Jeff Kunovic, *Sales Mgr*
Joe Dawson, *Marketing Staff*
Lindsey Santore, *Manager*
John Johnson, *Info Tech Mgr*
EMP: 130
SQ FT: 200,000
SALES (est): 5.4MM
SALES (corp-wide): 11MM **Privately Held**
WEB: www.ridgemanor.com
SIC: 0181 Foliage, growing of
PA: Petitti Enterprises, Inc.
25018 Broadway Ave
Cleveland OH 44146
440 439-8636

(G-13236)
STEWART LODGE INC
7774 Warner Rd (44057-9547)
P.O. Box 520 (44057-0520)
PHONE.................................440 417-1898
Fax: 440 428-5948
Sarah Wood, *MIS Dir*
John Dalsky, *Administration*
EMP: 84
SQ FT: 7,500

SALES (est): 2.7MM **Privately Held**
WEB: www.stewartlodge.com
SIC: 8059 Home for the mentally retarded, exc. skilled or intermediate

(G-13237)
WARNER NURSERIES INC
Also Called: Warner Nursery
6190 Middle Ridge Rd (44057-2807)
PHONE.................................440 946-0880
Fax: 440 946-1886
Gail J Ruckel, *President*
Sally Ruckel, *Corp Secy*
Collin Ruckel, *Vice Pres*
EMP: 50
SQ FT: 2,500
SALES (est): 2.8MM **Privately Held**
WEB: www.warnerkingwood.com
SIC: 5193 Nursery stock

(G-13238)
WIRTZBERGER ENTERPRISES CORP
136 W Main St (44057-3128)
PHONE.................................440 428-1901
Fax: 440 428-9411
Michael Wirtzberger, *President*
Megan Herrick, *Corp Secy*
EMP: 25
SALES (est): 2.1MM **Privately Held**
WEB: www.wirtzberger.com
SIC: 1522 Residential construction

Magnolia
Stark County

(G-13239)
EAGLE INDUSTRIAL PAINTING LLC
3215 Magnolia Rd Nw (44643-9527)
PHONE.................................330 866-5965
Artemis Sklavenitis, *Office Mgr*
Steve Zoumberakis, *Mng Member*
EMP: 30 **EST:** 2013
SQ FT: 217,800
SALES (est): 6MM **Privately Held**
SIC: 1721 Industrial painting; bridge painting

Maineville
Warren County

(G-13240)
AMS CONSTRUCTION INC
Also Called: Estephenson Brenda & John
7431 Windsor Park Dr (45039-9193)
PHONE.................................513 398-6689
John K Stephenson, *Branch Mgr*
EMP: 150
SALES (est): 4.1MM **Privately Held**
SIC: 1731 Electrical work
PA: Ams Construction, Inc.
10670 Loveland Madeira Rd
Loveland OH 45140

(G-13241)
CHARLES H HAMILTON CO
5875 S State Route 48 (45039-9798)
P.O. Box 99 (45039-0099)
PHONE.................................513 683-2442
Fax: 513 683-6966
Charles H Hamilton Jr, *President*
Steve Bauer, *Controller*
Jason Davidson, *Manager*
EMP: 85 **EST:** 1964
SQ FT: 8,000
SALES (est): 13.9MM **Privately Held**
WEB: www.charleshhamiltonco.com
SIC: 1794 1623 1771 Excavation & grading, building construction; water, sewer & utility lines; curb construction

(G-13242)
DAMASCUS STAFFING LLC
2263 W Us 22 And 3 (45039-9477)
PHONE.................................513 954-8941
Todd Wurzbacher, *Principal*
EMP: 60
SALES (est): 613.1K **Privately Held**
SIC: 7361 Employment agencies

(G-13243)
E F BAVIS & ASSOCIATES INC
201 Grandin Rd (45039-9762)
PHONE.................................513 677-0500
Edward F Bavis, *CEO*
William P Sieber, *President*
Mike Brown, *VP Mfg*
Susan Overbeck, *Treasurer*
Barbara Calhoun, *Human Resources*
EMP: 35 **EST:** 1970
SQ FT: 4,000
SALES (est): 13.2MM **Privately Held**
SIC: 5084 Conveyor systems

(G-13244)
MIKE WARD LANDSCAPING INC
Also Called: Eastgate Sod
424 E Us Highway 22 And 3 (45039-9650)
PHONE.................................513 683-6436
Fax: 513 683-2128
Kenneth Michael Ward, *President*
Nancy Giles, *Human Res Mgr*
EMP: 30
SQ FT: 15,441
SALES (est): 4.6MM **Privately Held**
WEB: www.eastgatesod.com
SIC: 0181 0782 Sod farms; lawn services; lawn care services; spraying services, lawn; turf installation services, except artificial

(G-13245)
PRIME HOME CARE LLC (PA)
2775 W Us Hwy 22 3 Ste 1 (45039)
PHONE.................................513 340-4183
Okshana Aminov,
EMP: 50 **EST:** 2009
SALES (est): 1.6MM **Privately Held**
SIC: 8082 Visiting nurse service

(G-13246)
SENSATION RESEARCH
1159 Chaucer Pl (45039-9134)
PHONE.................................513 602-1611
Cynthia Ward, *Owner*
EMP: 30 **EST:** 2012
SALES (est): 650K **Privately Held**
SIC: 8734 8731 Testing laboratories; commercial physical research

(G-13247)
THORNTON LANDSCAPE INC
424 E Us Highway 22 And 3 (45039-9650)
PHONE.................................513 683-8100
Fax: 513 683-6538
Richard Doesburg, *CEO*
Andrew Doesburg, *President*
Lynn Stover, *Human Res Mgr*
Larry Henry, *Architect*
EMP: 35 **EST:** 1961
SQ FT: 12,000
SALES (est): 2.5MM **Privately Held**
WEB: www.thorntonlandscape.com
SIC: 0782 0781 Landscape contractors; landscape counseling & planning

(G-13248)
Z SNOW REMOVAL INC
8177 S State Route 48 (45039-9631)
PHONE.................................513 683-7719
Frank Ziebell, *Mng Member*
Ashley Sotarty, *Administration*
EMP: 45
SALES (est): 2.4MM **Privately Held**
WEB: www.oneworldholdings.net
SIC: 4959 Snowplowing

Malta
Morgan County

(G-13249)
EZ GROUT CORPORATION INC
Also Called: Ezg Manufacturing
1833 N Riverview Rd (43758-9303)
PHONE.................................740 962-2024
Damian Lang, *Owner*
Steve Wheeler, *Marketing Staff*
EMP: 40 **EST:** 2007
SALES (est): 13MM **Privately Held**
SIC: 5082 3499 3549 Masonry equipment & supplies; chests, fire or burglary resistive: metal; wiredrawing & fabricating machinery & equipment, ex. die

Malvern
Carroll County

(G-13250)
DR MICHAEL J HULIT
107 N Reed Ave (44644)
P.O. Box 937 (44644-0937)
PHONE..............................330 863-7173
Michael Hulit, *Owner*
EMP: 25
SALES (est): 852.3K **Privately Held**
SIC: 1522 8021 Residential construction; offices & clinics of dentists

(G-13251)
GREEN LINES TRANSPORTATION INC (PA)
7089 Alliance Rd Nw (44644-9428)
P.O. Box 377 (44644-0377)
PHONE..............................330 863-2111
Fax: 330 863-1558
Roger A Bettis, *President*
Kevin White, *General Mgr*
Michael Ragan, *Business Mgr*
Brad Yoder, *Vice Pres*
Steve Ryan, *Safety Dir*
EMP: 50
SQ FT: 17,000
SALES (est): 13.6MM **Privately Held**
WEB: www.greenlines.net
SIC: 4213 Trucking, except local

(G-13252)
HOPPES CONSTRUCTION LLC
4036 Coral Rd Nw (44644-9468)
P.O. Box 604 (44644-0604)
PHONE..............................580 310-0090
Lynn Hoppe, *Branch Mgr*
EMP: 30 **Privately Held**
SIC: 1521 Single-family housing construction
PA: Hoppe"s Construction, Llc
   12580 County Road 1538
   Ada OK 74820

(G-13253)
LAKE MHAWK PRPERTY OWNERS ASSN
1 N Mohawk Dr (44644-9556)
PHONE..............................330 863-0000
Fax: 330 863-0031
Jack Buetner, *President*
Scott Noble, *General Mgr*
Paul Lemmon, *Director*
Scott Moushey, *Director*
Dick Moyer, *Security Dir*
EMP: 36
SQ FT: 7,000
SALES (est): 1MM **Privately Held**
WEB: www.lake-mohawk.org
SIC: 8641 Homeowners' association

(G-13254)
ROGER BETTIS TRUCKING INC
7089 Alliance Rd Nw (44644-9428)
P.O. Box 396 (44644-0396)
PHONE..............................330 863-2111
Roger Bettis, *President*
Walt Downing, *Vice Pres*
Dennis Bing, *Controller*
EMP: 112
SQ FT: 14,000
SALES (est): 12MM **Privately Held**
SIC: 7513 Truck leasing, without drivers

Manchester
Adams County

(G-13255)
DAYTON POWER AND LIGHT COMPANY
14869 Us 52 (45144-9332)
PHONE..............................937 549-2641
Fax: 937 549-3159
Dave Orme, *Plant Mgr*
John Hendrix, *Project Mgr*
Linda Kirschner, *Materials Mgr*
Sandi Doyle, *Accounting Dir*
Jim Stice, *Manager*
EMP: 60
SALES (corp-wide): 10.5B **Publicly Held**
WEB: www.waytogo.com
SIC: 4931 4932 4911 Electric & other services combined; gas & other services combined;
HQ: The Dayton Power And Light Company
   1065 Woodman Dr
   Dayton OH 45432
   937 224-6000

(G-13256)
SPECIAL TOUCH HOMECARE LLC
207 Pike St (45144-1218)
PHONE..............................937 549-1843
Vickie Vivens, *Mng Member*
Conny Leonard,
EMP: 32
SALES (est): 461.3K **Privately Held**
SIC: 8082 Home health care services

Mansfield
Richland County

(G-13257)
3RD STREET COMMUNITY CLINIC
Also Called: 3rd Street Family Health Svcs
600 W 3rd St (44906-2633)
PHONE..............................419 522-6191
Fax: 419 526-7939
Robert A Bowers, *CEO*
Gerad Pollick, *President*
Suellyn George, *CFO*
Michael J Raizen, *Surgeon*
Lori Farver, *Nurse Practr*
EMP: 57
SALES: 11.8MM **Privately Held**
SIC: 8011 Primary care medical clinic

(G-13258)
ABF FREIGHT SYSTEM INC
25 S Mulberry St (44902-1907)
PHONE..............................419 525-0118
Rick Speckert, *Branch Mgr*
EMP: 200
SALES (corp-wide): 2.8B **Publicly Held**
SIC: 4731 Transportation agents & brokers
HQ: Abf Freight System, Inc.
   3801 Old Greenwood Rd
   Fort Smith AR 72903
   479 785-8700

(G-13259)
ALLEN EST MANGEMENT LTD
132 Distl Ave (44902-2125)
PHONE..............................419 526-6505
Rod Shag, *President*
Melody Shag, *Vice Pres*
Matt Schag, *Exec Dir*
EMP: 30
SALES (est): 1.2MM **Privately Held**
WEB: www.allencabinetry.com
SIC: 6531 Real estate brokers & agents

(G-13260)
ALLIED RESTAURANT SVC OHIO INC (PA)
187 Illinois Ave S (44905-2825)
PHONE..............................419 589-4759
Robert A Baxter, *President*
Terry Fisher, *Purchasing*
Betty Conley, *Manager*
Jayne Conley, *Manager*
Tim Lawhorn, *Manager*
EMP: 26
SQ FT: 9,000
SALES (est): 5.9MM **Privately Held**
SIC: 1711 Heating & air conditioning contractors

(G-13261)
AMERICAN HLTH NTWRK & FMLY PRC
Also Called: Mansfield Family Practice
248 Blymyer Ave (44903-2306)
PHONE..............................419 524-2212
Fax: 419 524-9040
Raymond J Gardner, *Principal*
Terry Weston, *Principal*
Sue Ramsey, *Manager*
EMP: 30
SALES (est): 1.4MM **Privately Held**
SIC: 8011 Physicians' office, including specialists

(G-13262)
ASHLAND RAILWAY INC
803 N Main St (44902-4205)
PHONE..............................419 525-2822
Fax: 419 522-4608
Mike Mosley, *Manager*
Steve Nielsen, *Director*
EMP: 43
SALES (corp-wide): 10.6MM **Privately Held**
SIC: 4011 4013 Railroads, line-haul operating; switching & terminal services
PA: The Ashland Railway Inc
   6055d Kellers Church Rd
   Pipersville PA 18947
   215 795-8082

(G-13263)
BAKERS CLLSION REPR SPECIALIST
595 5th Ave (44905-1946)
PHONE..............................419 524-1350
Toll Free:..............................866 -
Fax: 419 524-8855
Larry Baker, *President*
Delee Powell, *Owner*
Laura Doug, *Controller*
EMP: 30
SQ FT: 18,500
SALES (est): 4.4MM **Privately Held**
WEB: www.bakerscollision.com
SIC: 7532 Body shop, automotive

(G-13264)
BBT FLEET SERVICES LLC
549 Russell Rd (44903-1928)
P.O. Box 542, Galion (44833-0542)
PHONE..............................419 462-7722
Steve Laird, *General Mgr*
John Schmidt,
EMP: 38
SQ FT: 24,000
SALES: 2MM **Privately Held**
SIC: 7539 Trailer repair

(G-13265)
BENJAMIN STEEL COMPANY INC
15 Industrial Pkwy (44903-8800)
PHONE..............................419 522-5500
Fax: 419 522-5811
Timothy Sinclair, *Branch Mgr*
EMP: 36
SALES (est): 3.8MM
SALES (corp-wide): 86.5MM **Privately Held**
WEB: www.benjaminsteel.com
SIC: 5051 Steel
PA: Benjamin Steel Company, Inc.
   777 Benjamin Dr
   Springfield OH 45502
   937 322-8600

(G-13266)
BIO-MDCAL APPLCATIONS OHIO INC
Also Called: FMC Dalysis Svcs Richland Cnty
680 Bally Row (44906-2969)
PHONE..............................419 774-0180
Jim Barsanti, *Manager*
EMP: 25
SALES (corp-wide): 20.9B **Privately Held**
WEB: www.fresenius.org
SIC: 8092 Kidney dialysis centers
HQ: Bio-Medical Applications Of Ohio, Inc.
   920 Winter St
   Waltham MA 02451

(G-13267)
BLEVINS METAL FABRICATION INC
Also Called: Blevins Fabrication
288 Illinois Ave S (44905-2827)
PHONE..............................419 522-6082
Fax: 419 522-6092
Lloyd T Blevins, *President*
Mark Gowitzka, *Opers Mgr*
Karen Smith, *Manager*
EMP: 25 EST: 1997
SQ FT: 13,000
SALES (est): 4.7MM **Privately Held**
SIC: 7692 3446 3444 3443 Welding repair; architectural metalwork; sheet metalwork; fabricated plate work (boiler shop); fabricated structural metal

(G-13268)
BRAMARJAC INC
Also Called: Pebble Creek Golf Club
4300 Algire Rd (44904-9554)
PHONE..............................419 884-3434
Fax: 419 884-9695
George J Pidgeon, *President*
Marjorie L Pidgeon, *Corp Secy*
Bradley J Pidgeon, *Vice Pres*
EMP: 33
SQ FT: 5,000
SALES (est): 1MM **Privately Held**
WEB: www.pebblecreekgolfclub.com
SIC: 7992 5813 5941 7999 Public golf courses; cocktail lounge; golf goods & equipment; golf driving range

(G-13269)
BREITINGER COMPANY
595 Oakenwaldt St (44905-1900)
PHONE..............................419 526-4255
Fax: 419 526-1398
Milo Breitinger, *President*
Richard Bayer, *QC Mgr*
Breitinger Kim, *CFO*
Kim Breitinger, *Manager*
Nikki Williams, *Admin Asst*
EMP: 120
SQ FT: 106,000
SALES (est): 35.9MM **Privately Held**
WEB: www.breitingercompany.com
SIC: 3441 3469 7692 3444 Fabricated structural metal; metal stampings; welding repair; sheet metalwork; fabricated plate work (boiler shop)

(G-13270)
BROOKDALE SENIOR LIVING INC
Also Called: Sterling House of Mansfield
1841 Middle Bellville Rd (44904-1798)
PHONE..............................419 756-5599
Fax: 419 756-5578
Lana Mishey, *Branch Mgr*
Kim Wilson, *Hlthcr Dir*
Meredith Pasco, *Officer*
EMP: 35
SALES (corp-wide): 4.7B **Publicly Held**
SIC: 8059 Convalescent home
PA: Brookdale Senior Living
   111 Westwood Pl Ste 400
   Brentwood TN 37027
   615 221-2250

(G-13271)
BROOKDALE SNIOR LVING CMMNTIES
Also Called: Sterling House of Mansfield
1841 Middle Bellville Rd (44904-1798)
PHONE..............................419 756-5599
Lana Mishey, *Exec Dir*
Karel Freiwar, *Director*
EMP: 30
SALES (corp-wide): 4.7B **Publicly Held**
WEB: www.assisted.com
SIC: 8059 Rest home, with health care
HQ: Brookdale Senior Living Communities, Inc.
   6737 W Wa St Ste 2300
   Milwaukee WI 53214
   414 910-5000

(G-13272)
CASTO HEALTH CARE
Also Called: Lexington Court Care Center
20 N Mill St (44904-1251)
PHONE..............................419 884-6400
Fax: 419 884-6411
William Casto, *Owner*
Randy Casto, *Webmaster*
EMP: 60 EST: 2001
SALES (est): 1.3MM **Privately Held**
WEB: www.castohealthcare.com
SIC: 8051 8322 Convalescent home with continuous nursing care; individual & family services

Mansfield - Richland County (G-13273)   GEOGRAPHIC SECTION

(G-13273)
CENTAURUS FINANCIAL INC
58 W 3rd St Ste B (44902-1251)
PHONE..................................419 756-9747
Edward Klesack, *Principal*
EMP: 98 **Privately Held**
SIC: 6282 Investment advisory service
PA: Centaurus Financial, Inc.
2300 E Katella Ave # 200
Anaheim CA 92806

(G-13274)
CENTER FOR INDIVIDUAL AND FMLY (PA)
Also Called: REHABILITATION SERVICES OF NOR
741 Scholl Rd (44907-1571)
PHONE..................................419 522-4357
Veronica L Groff, *President*
Debra Panke, *Vice Pres*
Lori Hagar, *Accountant*
Tammy Link, *Manager*
Bethanie Vranekovic, *Executive*
EMP: 250
SQ FT: 30,000
SALES: 15.1MM **Privately Held**
WEB: www.cifscenter.org
SIC: 8093 8322 Mental health clinic, outpatient; individual & family services

(G-13275)
CENTRAL STAR
Also Called: Central Star Home Health Svcs
380 N Main St Ste L102 (44902-7307)
PHONE..................................419 756-9449
Steve Sternbock, *CEO*
Michelle Applegate, *Hum Res Coord*
Julie Charlton, *Administration*
EMP: 120
SALES (est): 1.9MM
SALES (corp-wide): 32.5MM **Privately Held**
SIC: 8082 Home health care services
PA: Star Multi Care Services, Inc.
115 Broadhollow Rd # 275
Melville NY 11747
631 423-6689

(G-13276)
CHILDRENS CMPRHENSIVE SVCS INC
1451 Lucas Rd (44903-8682)
P.O. Box 2226 (44905-0226)
PHONE..................................419 589-5511
Steven Covington, *Branch Mgr*
EMP: 100
SALES (corp-wide): 10.4B **Publicly Held**
WEB: www.keystoneyouth.com
SIC: 8322 8361 Individual & family services; residential care
HQ: Children's Comprehensive Services, Inc.
3401 West End Ave Ste 400
Nashville TN 37203
615 250-0000

(G-13277)
COUNTY OF RICHLAND
Also Called: Rain Tree, The
721 Scholl Rd (44907-1571)
PHONE..................................419 774-4300
Lisa Gulian, *Director*
Elaine Wamsley, *Executive*
EMP: 100 **Privately Held**
WEB: www.mrcpl.org
SIC: 8361 Home for the mentally retarded
PA: County Of Richland
50 Park Ave E Ste 3
Mansfield OH 44902
419 774-5501

(G-13278)
COUNTY OF RICHLAND
Also Called: Richland County Prosectors Off
38 Park St S Ste B (44902-1717)
PHONE..................................419 774-5676
Fax: 419 774-5589
James Mayer Jr, *Administration*
EMP: 30 **Privately Held**
WEB: www.mrcpl.org
SIC: 8651 9111 9222 Political organizations; county supervisors' & executives' offices;

PA: County Of Richland
50 Park Ave E Ste 3
Mansfield OH 44902
419 774-5501

(G-13279)
COUNTY OF RICHLAND
Also Called: Dayspring Residential Care
3220 Olivesburg Rd (44903-8243)
PHONE..................................419 774-5894
Michelle Swank, *Director*
EMP: 40 **Privately Held**
WEB: www.mrcpl.org
SIC: 8322 Old age assistance
PA: County Of Richland
50 Park Ave E Ste 3
Mansfield OH 44902
419 774-5501

(G-13280)
COUNTY OF RICHLAND
Also Called: Children Services
731 Scholl Rd (44907-1571)
PHONE..................................419 774-4100
Fax: 419 774-4103
Randy Parker, *Manager*
EMP: 133 **Privately Held**
WEB: www.mrcpl.org
SIC: 8361 9111 8322 Children's home; county supervisors' & executives' offices; individual & family services
PA: County Of Richland
50 Park Ave E Ste 3
Mansfield OH 44902
419 774-5501

(G-13281)
COUNTY OF RICHLAND
Also Called: Dept of Human Services
171 Park Ave E (44902-1829)
PHONE..................................419 774-5400
Fax: 419 526-4802
Doug Theaker, *Director*
Sharlene Neumann, *Director*
EMP: 105 **Privately Held**
WEB: www.mrcpl.org
SIC: 8322 9111 Social service center; county supervisors' & executives' offices
PA: County Of Richland
50 Park Ave E Ste 3
Mansfield OH 44902
419 774-5501

(G-13282)
COUNTY OF RICHLAND
411 S Diamond St (44902-7812)
PHONE..................................419 774-5578
Ron Sopon, *Principal*
EMP: 65 **Privately Held**
WEB: www.mrcpl.org
SIC: 8361 Juvenile correctional facilities
PA: County Of Richland
50 Park Ave E Ste 3
Mansfield OH 44902
419 774-5501

(G-13283)
COUNTY OF RICHLAND
Also Called: Richland County Engineers
77 N Mulberry St (44902-1208)
PHONE..................................419 774-5591
Fax: 419 774-5539
Tom Beck, *Engineer*
EMP: 50 **Privately Held**
WEB: www.mrcpl.org
SIC: 8711 9111 Engineering services; county supervisors' & executives' offices
PA: County Of Richland
50 Park Ave E Ste 3
Mansfield OH 44902
419 774-5501

(G-13284)
COUNTY OF RICHLAND
Also Called: New Hope Center
314 Cleveland Ave (44902-8623)
PHONE..................................419 774-4200
Constance F Ament, *Superintendent*
H M Miller, *Superintendent*
Elizabeth Prather, *Principal*
Ann Glaze, *Safety Mgr*
Dawn Trosper, *HR Admin*
EMP: 350 **Privately Held**
WEB: www.mrcpl.org

SIC: 8059 9111 Home for the mentally retarded, exc. skilled or intermediate; county supervisors' & executives' offices
PA: County Of Richland
50 Park Ave E Ste 3
Mansfield OH 44902
419 774-5501

(G-13285)
CRITICAL LIFE INC
35 Logan Rd (44907-2810)
PHONE..................................419 525-0502
Fax: 419 525-3630
Jason Dotson, *President*
Carrie Dotson, *Corp Secy*
EMP: 30
SALES (est): 896.6K **Privately Held**
WEB: www.criticallife.com
SIC: 4119 Local passenger transportation

(G-13286)
CRYSTAL CARE CENTERS INC
458 Vanderbilt Rd Unit 1 (44904-8649)
P.O. Box 3167 (44904-0167)
PHONE..................................419 747-2666
Jerry Smith, *Administration*
EMP: 45 **Privately Held**
SIC: 8051 8052 Convalescent home with continuous nursing care; intermediate care facilities
PA: Crystal Care Centers Inc
1159 Wyandotte Ave
Mansfield OH 44906

(G-13287)
CRYSTAL CARE CENTERS INC (PA)
Also Called: Crystal Care of Mansfield
1159 Wyandotte Ave (44906-1940)
PHONE..................................419 747-2666
Fax: 419 747-7291
Jerry Smith, *President*
Jason Ramirez, *Director*
Kelly Reichardt, *Director*
EMP: 90
SALES (est): 7.6MM **Privately Held**
SIC: 8051 8059 Convalescent home with continuous nursing care; rest home, with health care

(G-13288)
D & S CRTIVE CMMUNICATIONS INC (PA)
Also Called: Black River Display Group
140 Park Ave E (44902-1830)
P.O. Box 876 (44901-0876)
PHONE..................................419 524-6699
Terry Neff, *President*
Julie Campbell, *Editor*
David Whitaker, *Project Mgr*
Ed Brown, *Controller*
Chris Baldasare, *Accounting Mgr*
EMP: 65
SQ FT: 74,000
SALES: 120MM **Privately Held**
WEB: www.ds-creative.com
SIC: 7311 2752 2791 2789 Advertising agencies; commercial printing, lithographic; typesetting; bookbinding & related work

(G-13289)
D & S CRTIVE CMMUNICATIONS INC
Also Called: Black River Display
195 E 4th St (44902-1519)
PHONE..................................419 524-4312
Greg Tritt, *Branch Mgr*
Chris Shannon, *Manager*
Bob Hanes, *Info Tech Mgr*
EMP: 40
SALES (corp-wide): 120MM **Privately Held**
WEB: www.ds-creative.com
SIC: 5023 5039 Floor coverings; resilient floor coverings: tile or sheet; ceiling systems & products
PA: D & S Creative Communications, Inc.
140 Park Ave E
Mansfield OH 44902
419 524-6699

(G-13290)
DAYTON FREIGHT LINES INC
103 Cairns Rd (44903-8992)
PHONE..................................419 589-0350
Fax: 419 589-0349
Justin Sharky, *Branch Mgr*
EMP: 212
SALES (corp-wide): 1B **Privately Held**
SIC: 4789 Pipeline terminal facilities, independently operated
PA: Dayton Freight Lines, Inc.
6450 Poe Ave Ste 311
Dayton OH 45414
937 264-4060

(G-13291)
DEARMAN MOVING & STORAGE CO
961 N Main St (44903-8113)
P.O. Box 1992 (44901-1992)
PHONE..................................419 524-3456
Fax: 419 524-6144
Jeffrey L Campbell, *President*
Ruthann Campbell, *Vice Pres*
EMP: 40
SQ FT: 45,000
SALES (est): 4.7MM **Privately Held**
SIC: 4213 Household goods transport

(G-13292)
DIRECTIONS CREDIT UNION INC
777 N Main St (44902-4203)
PHONE..................................419 524-7113
Fred Brink, *Vice Pres*
Pam Nottingham, *Branch Mgr*
Brenda Schwin, *Analyst*
EMP: 40
SALES (corp-wide): 20.9MM **Privately Held**
SIC: 6062 6163 State credit unions, not federally chartered; loan brokers
PA: Directions Credit Union, Inc.
5121 Whiteford Rd
Sylvania OH 43560
419 720-4769

(G-13293)
DISABLED AMERICAN VETERANS
34 Park Ave W (44902-1603)
PHONE..................................419 526-0203
Hayne K Holstine, *Principal*
EMP: 400
SALES (corp-wide): 202.6MM **Privately Held**
SIC: 8641 Veterans' organization
PA: Disabled American Veterans
3725 Alexandria Pike
Cold Spring KY 41076
859 441-7300

(G-13294)
DISCOVERY SCHOOL
855 Millsboro Rd (44903-1997)
PHONE..................................419 756-8880
Fax: 419 756-5881
Amy Oswalt, *Principal*
Shirley Heck, *Principal*
John Miller, *Principal*
EMP: 25
SALES: 1.1MM **Privately Held**
WEB: www.discovery-school.net
SIC: 8211 8351 Private elementary school; preschool center

(G-13295)
DTE INC
110 Baird Pkwy (44903-7909)
PHONE..................................419 522-3428
Fax: 419 522-3568
Rob Nelson, *CEO*
Dean Russell, *President*
Roger Nelson, *General Mgr*
Burke Melching, *Vice Pres*
EMP: 30
SQ FT: 45,000
SALES (est): 3.8MM **Privately Held**
WEB: www.dteinc.com
SIC: 7629 3661 Telephone set repair; telephone & telegraph apparatus

GEOGRAPHIC SECTION
Mansfield - Richland County (G-13321)

(G-13296)
EDGE PLASTICS INC
Also Called: Jobs On Site
449 Newman St (44902-1123)
PHONE..............................419 522-6696
Fax: 419 522-2792
Stephanie Fackler, *Human Res Mgr*
Diana White, *Manager*
EMP: 50
SALES (corp-wide): 58.7MM **Privately Held**
SIC: 7363 Help supply services
PA: Edge Plastics, Inc.
449 Newman St
Mansfield OH 44902
419 522-6696

(G-13297)
ELITE EXCAVATING COMPANY INC
Also Called: Elite Excavating Ohio Company
4500 Snodgrass Rd (44903-8065)
P.O. Box 290, Ontario (44862-0290)
PHONE..............................419 683-4200
Fax: 419 683-1761
Micheal Scott Fulmer, *President*
Patricia Fulmer, *Vice Pres*
EMP: 28
SQ FT: 8,000
SALES (est): 5MM **Privately Held**
SIC: 1794 Excavation work

(G-13298)
ESTES EXPRESS LINES INC
792 5th Ave (44905-1421)
PHONE..............................419 522-2641
Patricia Estes, *Branch Mgr*
EMP: 59
SALES (corp-wide): 2.4B **Privately Held**
SIC: 4213 Contract haulers
PA: Estes Express Lines, Inc.
3901 W Broad St
Richmond VA 23230
804 353-1900

(G-13299)
FAMILY LIFE COUNSELING (PA)
151 Marion Ave Lowr Lvl (44903-2223)
PHONE..............................419 774-9969
Fax: 419 756-5642
John Cochran, *CFO*
Steven Burggras, *Exec Dir*
EMP: 30
SALES: 2.7MM **Privately Held**
SIC: 8322 General counseling services

(G-13300)
FEDERAL EXPRESS CORPORATION
Also Called: Fedex
65 Paragon Pkwy (44903-8074)
PHONE..............................800 463-3339
Jim Gleissmer, *Manager*
EMP: 34
SALES (corp-wide): 60.3B **Publicly Held**
WEB: www.fedex.com
SIC: 4513 Package delivery, private air
HQ: Federal Express Corporation
3610 Hacks Cross Rd
Memphis TN 38125
901 369-3600

(G-13301)
FEDEX FREIGHT CORPORATION
160 Industrial Pkwy (44903-8999)
PHONE..............................800 390-0159
Fax: 419 522-9162
Chris Leonard, *Manager*
EMP: 32
SALES (corp-wide): 60.3B **Publicly Held**
SIC: 4213 Less-than-truckload (LTL) transport
HQ: Fedex Freight Corporation
1715 Aaron Brenner Dr
Memphis TN 38120

(G-13302)
FIRST ASSEMBLY CHILD CARE
1000 Mcpherson St (44903-7145)
PHONE..............................419 529-6501
Fax: 419 529-6470
Kelly Zehner, *Manager*
Kim McCoy, *Director*
Kim Glavic, *Deputy Dir*
EMP: 30

SALES (est): 1.1MM **Privately Held**
WEB: www.mansfieldfirstassembly.org
SIC: 8351 8661 Child day care services; religious organizations

(G-13303)
FIRST CHOICE MED STAFF OF OHIO
90 W 2nd St (44902-1917)
PHONE..............................419 521-2700
Charles Slone, *Branch Mgr*
Terri Poth, *Exec Dir*
EMP: 67
SALES (corp-wide): 4.6MM **Privately Held**
SIC: 7361 Employment agencies
PA: First Choice Medical Staffing Of Ohio, Inc.
1457 W 117th St
Cleveland OH 44107
216 521-2222

(G-13304)
FRANS CHILD CARE-MANSFIELD
Also Called: YMCA
750 Scholl Rd (44907-1570)
PHONE..............................419 775-2500
Fax: 419 525-3009
Michael Kenyon, *CEO*
Mike Kenyon, *President*
Lesly Murphy, *CFO*
EMP: 150
SQ FT: 120,000
SALES (est): 3MM **Privately Held**
SIC: 8641 7991 8351 8322 Youth organizations; physical fitness facilities; child day care services; individual & family services

(G-13305)
GORDON FLESCH COMPANY INC
2756 Lexington Ave (44904-1429)
PHONE..............................419 884-2031
Larry Layne, *Branch Mgr*
Gordon Flesch, *Manager*
EMP: 25
SALES (corp-wide): 6.1MM **Privately Held**
SIC: 5044 5045 5065 7359 Photocopy machines; word processing equipment; facsimile equipment; office machine rental, except computers
PA: Gordon Flesch Company, Inc.
2675 Research Park Dr
Fitchburg WI 53711
608 271-2100

(G-13306)
GRASAN EQUIPMENT COMPANY INC
440 S Illinois Ave (44907-1809)
PHONE..............................419 526-4440
Fax: 419 524-2176
Marian L Eilenfeld, *President*
Edward Eilenfeld Jr, *Vice Pres*
Chuck Ferguson, *Engineer*
Brian Lake, *Engineer*
Aaron Niswander, *Engineer*
▼ EMP: 65 EST: 1970
SQ FT: 62,000
SALES (est): 20.2MM **Privately Held**
WEB: www.grasan.com
SIC: 4953 3532 3559 3535 Recycling, waste materials; crushers, stationary; rock crushing machinery, stationary; screeners, stationary; recycling machinery; conveyors & conveying equipment; construction machinery

(G-13307)
HEALING HRTS CUNSELING CTR INC
680 Park Ave W (44906-3706)
PHONE..............................419 528-5993
Maja-Lisa Anderson, *President*
EMP: 35
SALES (est): 155.2K **Privately Held**
SIC: 8322 Individual & family services

(G-13308)
HEART OF OH CNCL BSA (PA)
3 N Main St Ste 303 (44902-1716)
PHONE..............................419 522-8300

Fax: 419 207-8150
Matthew Smith, *President*
Lisa Whisler, *Manager*
Barry Norris, *Exec Dir*
EMP: 35
SALES: 1.6MM **Privately Held**
SIC: 8641 Boy Scout organization

(G-13309)
HORIZON MECHANICAL AND ELEC
Also Called: Buckeye Horizon
323 N Trimble Rd (44906-2539)
PHONE..............................419 529-2738
Fax: 419 884-1668
Mark Albert, *President*
Mark McClure, *Sales Staff*
Linda Albert, *Admin Sec*
EMP: 30
SALES (est): 4.8MM **Privately Held**
SIC: 1711 1731 5999 Heating & air conditioning contractors; electrical work; plumbing & heating supplies

(G-13310)
IGH II INC
Also Called: Trugreen Chemlawn
110 Industrial Dr (44904-1339)
PHONE..............................419 874-3575
Fax: 419 874-7107
Terry Korczyk, *President*
EMP: 33
SQ FT: 11,900
SALES (est): 2.9MM **Privately Held**
SIC: 0782 Lawn care services; landscape contractors

(G-13311)
IHEARTCOMMUNICATIONS INC
Also Called: Wman
1400 Radio Ln (44906-2525)
PHONE..............................419 529-2211
Diana Coon, *General Mgr*
Eric Hansen, *Opers Mgr*
EMP: 35 **Publicly Held**
SIC: 4832 Radio broadcasting stations, music format
HQ: Iheartcommunications, Inc.
20880 Stone Oak Pkwy
San Antonio TX 78258
210 822-2828

(G-13312)
INFO TRAK INCORPORATED
Also Called: Info Trak &
165 Marion Ave (44903-2223)
PHONE..............................419 747-9296
Fax: 419 747-9298
David W Satterfield, *President*
Ed Grove, *Director*
EMP: 40 EST: 1999
SQ FT: 1,700
SALES (est): 800K **Privately Held**
WEB: www.infotrakincorporated.com
SIC: 7381 Private investigator

(G-13313)
INFOCISION MANAGEMENT CORP
1404 Park Ave E (44905-2952)
PHONE..............................419 529-8685
Jill Adamescu, *Branch Mgr*
EMP: 99
SALES (corp-wide): 242.3MM **Privately Held**
WEB: www.infocision.com
SIC: 7380 Telemarketing services
PA: Infocision Management Corporation
325 Springside Dr
Akron OH 44333
330 668-1411

(G-13314)
J & B EQUIPMENT & SUPPLY INC
Also Called: J & B Classical Glass & Mirror
2750 Lexington Ave (44904-1429)
P.O. Box 3028 (44904-0028)
PHONE..............................419 884-1155
Michael Chambers, *President*
Gino Cappadonna, *Manager*
Kim Miller, *Admin Sec*
EMP: 60
SQ FT: 10,000

SALES (est): 9.1MM **Privately Held**
WEB: www.jbacoustical.com
SIC: 5032 5211 1793 1751 Drywall materials; lumber & other building materials; glass & glazing work; carpentry work

(G-13315)
J-TRAC INC
Also Called: Dearman Moving and Storage
961 N Main St (44903-8113)
P.O. Box 1992 (44901-1992)
PHONE..............................419 524-3456
Tim Cambell, *President*
Chris Cambell, *Vice Pres*
EMP: 50
SALES (est): 3.3MM **Privately Held**
SIC: 4225 4214 4213 4212 General warehousing; local trucking with storage; trucking, except local; local trucking, without storage

(G-13316)
JAMES RAY LOZIER
Also Called: TSA Inspections
84 Foxcroft Rd (44904-9705)
PHONE..............................419 884-2656
James R Lozier, *Owner*
Jim Luzier, *Owner*
EMP: 27
SALES (est): 450K **Privately Held**
SIC: 7389 Inspection & testing services

(G-13317)
JONES POTATO CHIP CO (PA)
823 Bowman St (44903-4107)
PHONE..............................419 529-9424
Fax: 419 529-6789
Robert Jones, *President*
Charles K Hellinger, *Principal*
Frederick W Jones, *Principal*
Darryl Jones, *Vice Pres*
Rick Bartram, *Prdtn Mgr*
EMP: 46
SQ FT: 50,000
SALES (est): 8.8MM **Privately Held**
WEB: www.joneschips.com
SIC: 2096 5145 Potato chips & other potato-based snacks; potato chips

(G-13318)
KADEMENOS WISEHART HINES (PA)
6 W 3rd St Ste 200 (44902-1200)
PHONE..............................419 524-6011
Fax: 419 526-1431
Troy Wisehart, *President*
Victor P Kademenos, *Vice Pres*
EMP: 40
SALES (est): 4.5MM **Privately Held**
WEB: www.ckhlaw.com
SIC: 8111 General practice law office

(G-13319)
KEY OFFICE SERVICES
1999 Leppo Rd (44903-9076)
PHONE..............................419 747-9749
Brenda Upchuch, *Owner*
EMP: 29
SALES (est): 1.4MM **Privately Held**
WEB: www.keyofficeservices.com
SIC: 8748 Business consulting

(G-13320)
KINGWOOD CENTER
900 Park Ave W (44906-2904)
PHONE..............................419 522-0211
Fax: 419 522-0211
Charles Gleabes, *Director*
Charles Gleaves, *Director*
EMP: 30
SALES (est): 1MM **Privately Held**
WEB: www.kingwoodcenter.org
SIC: 8412 Museum

(G-13321)
L A HAIR FORCE
1509 Lexington Ave (44907-2631)
PHONE..............................419 756-3101
Fax: 419 756-5065
Vicki Wittmer, *Owner*
EMP: 35
SALES (est): 416.9K **Privately Held**
SIC: 7231 Hairdressers

Mansfield - Richland County (G-13322)

(G-13322)
LABORATORY CORPORATION AMERICA
418 E Broad St (44907)
PHONE..................440 328-3275
Kathy Bruns, *Branch Mgr*
EMP: 40 **Publicly Held**
WEB: www.labcorp.com
SIC: 8071 Medical laboratories
HQ: Laboratory Corporation Of America
358 S Main St Ste 458
Burlington NC 27215
336 229-1127

(G-13323)
LEVERING MANAGEMENT INC
Also Called: Winchester Terrace
70 Winchester Rd (44907-2042)
PHONE..................419 756-4747
Fax: 419 756-4237
L Bruce Levering, *President*
Dana Andrews, *Director*
Alice Cree, *Administration*
Ben Atkins, *Maintence Staff*
EMP: 88
SALES (corp-wide): 32.8MM **Privately Held**
SIC: 8051 Convalescent home with continuous nursing care
PA: Levering Management, Inc.
201 N Main St
Mount Vernon OH 43050
740 397-3897

(G-13324)
LEXINGTON COURT CARE CENTER
Also Called: Burns International Staffing
250 Delaware Ave (44904-1215)
PHONE..................419 884-2000
Fax: 419 884-3474
Rhonda Eichorn, *Office Mgr*
Thomas Freundlich, *Director*
Rhonda Freed, *Executive*
Toni Marone, *Administration*
EMP: 98
SALES (est): 3.3MM **Privately Held**
SIC: 8052 8051 Intermediate care facilities; skilled nursing care facilities

(G-13325)
LYNNHAVEN XII LLC
Also Called: Woodlawn Nursing Home
535 Lexington Ave (44907-1502)
PHONE..................419 756-7111
Fax: 419 774-9055
Missy Faries, *Marketing Mgr*
Richard Stewart, *Manager*
Angelique Ciavarella, *Director*
Alfred Granson Jr, *Director*
Christy Kilgore, *Food Svc Dir*
EMP: 125
SALES (corp-wide): 7.8MM **Privately Held**
SIC: 8051 Convalescent home with continuous nursing care
PA: Lynnhaven Xii, Llc
206 Southgate Dr
Boone NC 28607
828 265-0080

(G-13326)
MADISON LOCAL SCHOOL DISTRICT (PA)
1379 Grace St (44905-2742)
PHONE..................419 589-2600
Jeff Meyers, *President*
Shelley Hilderbrand, *Superintendent*
Lee Kaple, *Superintendent*
Steve Crist, *Facilities Dir*
Michael Yost, *Transptn Dir*
EMP: 450
SALES (est): 26MM **Privately Held**
WEB: www.madison-lake.k12.oh.us
SIC: 8211 8351 Public elementary & secondary schools; public junior high school; public senior high school; school board; child day care services

(G-13327)
MAJOR METALS COMPANY
844 Kochheiser Rd (44904-8637)
PHONE..................419 886-4600
Fax: 419 886-4670
Jeffrey C Mason, *President*
Wayne Riffe, *Vice Pres*
Jason Dials, *Sales Mgr*
Ania Pitchco, *Manager*
EMP: 30
SQ FT: 60,000
SALES (est): 13.7MM **Privately Held**
WEB: www.majormetalscompany.com
SIC: 3312 5051 3317 Plate, sheet & strip, except coated products; iron or steel flat products; steel pipe & tubes

(G-13328)
MANFIELD LIVING CENTER LTD
Also Called: Twinoaks Living and Lrng Ctr
73 Madison Rd (44905-2830)
P.O. Box 1218 (44901-1218)
PHONE..................419 512-1711
Tracy Robertson, *Manager*
Anthony Wheaton, *Exec Dir*
EMP: 30
SALES (est): 1.2MM **Privately Held**
SIC: 8361 Home for the mentally retarded

(G-13329)
MANSFIELD AMBULANCE INC
369 Marion Ave (44903-2064)
P.O. Box 2687 (44906-0687)
PHONE..................419 525-3311
Tom Durbin, *President*
Margaret Neill, *Treasurer*
EMP: 40
SQ FT: 5,000
SALES (est): 1.9MM **Privately Held**
WEB: www.mansfieldambulance.com
SIC: 4119 Ambulance service

(G-13330)
MANSFIELD CITY BUILDING MAINT
30 N Diamond St (44902-1702)
PHONE..................419 755-9698
Fax: 419 755-9454
Todd Dilley, *COO*
EMP: 38
SALES (est): 1.3MM **Privately Held**
SIC: 5087 Cleaning & maintenance equipment & supplies

(G-13331)
MANSFIELD HOTEL PARTNERSHIP
Also Called: Knights Inn
555 N Trimble Rd (44906-2101)
PHONE..................419 529-2100
Fax: 419 529-6679
Sandy Keiser, *Manager*
EMP: 26
SALES (corp-wide): 2.5MM **Privately Held**
SIC: 7011 Hotels & motels
PA: Mansfield Hotel Partnership
500 N Trimble Rd
Mansfield OH 44906
419 529-1000

(G-13332)
MANSFIELD HOTEL PARTNERSHIP (PA)
Also Called: Quality Inn
500 N Trimble Rd (44906-2102)
PHONE..................419 529-1000
Dr When Fu Chin, *Partner*
Ronald Fewster, *Partner*
Patrick Mc Allister, *Partner*
Sandy Kiser, *Manager*
EMP: 60
SQ FT: 44,000
SALES (est): 2.5MM **Privately Held**
SIC: 7011 7991 Hotel, franchised; physical fitness facilities

(G-13333)
MANSFIELD MEMORIAL HOMES LLC (PA)
Also Called: GERIATRICS CENTER OF MANSFIELD
50 Blymyer Ave (44903-2343)
P.O. Box 966 (44901-0966)
PHONE..................419 774-5100
Fax: 419 524-6134
Dan Miller,
Seth Robert, *Administration*
Raymond Loughman,
EMP: 135 **EST:** 1953

SALES: 7.8MM **Privately Held**
WEB: www.mansfieldmh.com
SIC: 8051 8052 Convalescent home with continuous nursing care; intermediate care facilities

(G-13334)
MANSFIELD OPCO LLC
Also Called: Arbors At Mifflin
1600 Crider Rd (44903-9268)
PHONE..................502 429-8062
Robert Norcross, *CEO*
Benjamin Sparks, *Clerk*
EMP: 99
SQ FT: 60,000
SALES (est): 2.2MM **Privately Held**
SIC: 8051 Skilled nursing care facilities

(G-13335)
MANSFIELD TRUCK SALES & SVC
85 Longview Ave E (44903-4205)
P.O. Box 1516 (44901-1516)
PHONE..................419 522-9811
Fred Bollon, *President*
Jim Robinson, *General Mgr*
Rick Harbour, *Sales Executive*
EMP: 50
SALES (est): 5.4MM **Privately Held**
SIC: 5012 5511 7538 Trucks, commercial; trucks, tractors & trailers: new & used; general truck repair
PA: Truck Sales & Service, Inc.
3429 Brightwood Rd
Midvale OH 44653

(G-13336)
MCELVAIN GROUP HOME
634 Mcbride Rd (44905-2962)
PHONE..................419 589-6697
Kathy McElvain, *Partner*
Donald McElvain, *Partner*
EMP: 30 **EST:** 1988
SALES (est): 816.3K **Privately Held**
SIC: 8361 Home for the mentally handicapped

(G-13337)
MECHANICS BANK (PA)
2 S Main St (44902-2931)
PHONE..................419 524-0831
Fax: 419 522-2301
Mark Masters, *President*
Deborah Adams, *Senior VP*
Nick Gesouras, *Senior VP*
Phil McClenathan, *Assistant VP*
Martin E Campbell, *Vice Pres*
EMP: 35
SQ FT: 5,000
SALES: 21.4MM **Privately Held**
SIC: 6036 Savings & loan associations, not federally chartered

(G-13338)
MEDCENTRAL HEALTH SYSTEM
Also Called: Med Central HM Hlth & Hospice
335 Glessner Ave (44903-2269)
PHONE..................419 526-8442
Fax: 419 756-2298
Marte Alsleben, *Owner*
Marte Griffith, *Director*
EMP: 30
SALES (corp-wide): 3.7B **Privately Held**
SIC: 8062 8082 8093 General medical & surgical hospitals; home health care services; specialty outpatient clinics
HQ: Medcentral Health System
335 Glessner Ave
Mansfield OH 44903
419 526-8000

(G-13339)
MEDCENTRAL HEALTH SYSTEM (HQ)
Also Called: OHIOHEALTH MANSFIELD HOSPITAL
335 Glessner Ave (44903-2269)
PHONE..................419 526-8000
Fax: 419 526-8136
Beth Hildreth, *Vice Pres*
Brad Peffley, *Vice Pres*
Tammy Poth, *Vice Pres*
Robert Wirtz, *Vice Pres*
Mike Hildreth, *Safety Mgr*
EMP: 59
SQ FT: 300,000

SALES: 269MM
SALES (corp-wide): 3.7B **Privately Held**
SIC: 8062 General medical & surgical hospitals
PA: Ohiohealth Corporation
180 E Broad St
Columbus OH 43215
614 788-8860

(G-13340)
MEDCENTRAL HEALTH SYSTEM
770 Balgreen Dr Ste 105 (44906-4106)
PHONE..................419 526-8970
Fax: 419 526-8973
James Meyer, *Branch Mgr*
Barbara Scott, *Manager*
Velma Scott, *Manager*
Shirley Back, *Supervisor*
Tammy Reynolds, *Cashier*
EMP: 80
SALES (corp-wide): 3.7B **Privately Held**
SIC: 8062 General medical & surgical hospitals
HQ: Medcentral Health System
335 Glessner Ave
Mansfield OH 44903
419 526-8000

(G-13341)
MEDCENTRAL HEALTH SYSTEM
Also Called: Med Cntral Hlth Sys Child Care
160 S Linden Rd (44906-3028)
PHONE..................419 526-8043
Patricia Harding, *Director*
EMP: 26
SALES (corp-wide): 3.7B **Privately Held**
SIC: 8062 8351 General medical & surgical hospitals; child day care services
HQ: Medcentral Health System
335 Glessner Ave
Mansfield OH 44903
419 526-8000

(G-13342)
MEDIC RESPONSE SERVICE INC (PA)
98 S Diamond St (44902-7564)
PHONE..................419 522-1998
Thomas F Wappner, *President*
William C Wappner, *Vice Pres*
EMP: 45
SQ FT: 1,600
SALES (est): 982.1K **Privately Held**
SIC: 4119 Ambulance service

(G-13343)
METAL CONVERSIONS LTD (PA)
849 Crawford Ave N (44905-1205)
P.O. Box 787 (44901-0787)
PHONE..................419 525-0011
Fax: 419 525-0750
Steve Senser, *CEO*
Rob Care, *President*
Carl Roark, *Exec VP*
Jay Levant, *Vice Pres*
Andy Senser, *Vice Pres*
▲ **EMP:** 25
SQ FT: 16,000
SALES (est): 24.5MM **Privately Held**
SIC: 5051 Aluminum bars, rods, ingots, sheets, pipes, plates, etc.

(G-13344)
MICKIS CREATIVE OPTIONS INC
327 Park Ave W (44906-3113)
PHONE..................419 526-4254
Fax: 419 526-5683
Michele Stambaugh, *Principal*
EMP: 50
SALES (est): 1.1MM **Privately Held**
SIC: 8331 Job training & vocational rehabilitation services

(G-13345)
MID-OHIO HEART CLINIC INC
680 Park Ave W Ste 100 (44906-3723)
PHONE..................419 524-8151
Fax: 419 524-1747
William Polinsky MD, *President*
Michael Amalfitano MD, *Vice Pres*
Gregory Vigesaa MD, *Vice Pres*
Deborah Sorensen, *Financial Analy*
Mary Alton, *Med Doctor*
EMP: 40

GEOGRAPHIC SECTION

Mansfield - Richland County (G-13369)

SALES (est): 4.8MM Privately Held
SIC: 8011 Cardiologist & cardio-vascular specialist

(G-13346)
MID-OHIO PIPELINE COMPANY INC
Also Called: Mid-Ohio Pipeline Services
2270 Eckert Rd (44904-9742)
P.O. Box 3049 (44904-0049)
PHONE..................................419 884-3772
Chuck Austin, *President*
Gene F Yates, *Principal*
Jim Johnson, *Business Mgr*
Kelly Nissenbaum, *Business Mgr*
Thomas Lorenz, *Vice Pres*
EMP: 40 EST: 1970
SQ FT: 3,000
SALES (est): 20.6MM Privately Held
SIC: 1623 Oil & gas pipeline construction

(G-13347)
MILLIRON RECYCLING INC
Also Called: Milliron Iron & Metal
2384 Springmill Rd (44903-8712)
PHONE..................................419 747-6522
Brant Milliron, *President*
Donna McNeely, *Manager*
Audrey Cook, *Admin Asst*
EMP: 60
SALES (est): 14.3MM Privately Held
SIC: 4953 Recycling, waste materials

(G-13348)
MT BUSINESS TECHNOLOGIES INC (DH)
1150 National Pkwy (44906-1911)
PHONE..................................419 529-6100
Fax: 419 529-3903
Chuck Rounds, *President*
Mark E Oswald, *General Mgr*
Jake Bell, *Area Mgr*
William Forrester, *Area Mgr*
Rod Hicks, *Business Mgr*
EMP: 130 EST: 1930
SQ FT: 64,000
SALES: 60MM
SALES (corp-wide): 10.2B Publicly Held
WEB: www.mtbustech.com
SIC: 5044 7378 7379 Copying equipment; computer peripheral equipment repair & maintenance; computer related consulting services

(G-13349)
NATIONAL WEATHER SERVICE
2101 Harrington Mem Rd (44903-8052)
PHONE..................................419 522-1375
EMP: 33 Publicly Held
SIC: 8999 9611 Weather forecasting; administration of general economic programs;
HQ: National Weather Service
  1325 E West Hwy
  Silver Spring MD 20910

(G-13350)
OAK GROVE MANOR INC
1670 Crider Rd (44903-9268)
PHONE..................................419 589-6222
Fax: 419 589-2576
Chris Plantz, *Maintenance Dir*
Marlene Pachl, *Human Res Mgr*
Glenna Holley, *Manager*
Jeff Music, *Director*
Allison Deloach, *Hlthcr Dir*
EMP: 114
SALES (est): 4.4MM Privately Held
SIC: 8051 Skilled nursing care facilities

(G-13351)
OHIO CANCER SPECIALISTS (PA)
1125 Aspira Ct. (44906-4125)
PHONE..................................419 756-2122
Fax: 419 756-3530
Donald L Dewald, *Partner*
Saurabh Das, *Partner*
Shahzad Khan, *Partner*
EMP: 26
SQ FT: 6,000
SALES (est): 3.6MM Privately Held
WEB: www.ohcancer.com
SIC: 8011 Hematologist; internal medicine, physician/surgeon; oncologist

(G-13352)
R G SMITH COMPANY
Also Called: Smith, R G of Mansfield
166 W 6th St (44902-1096)
P.O. Box 1057 (44901-1057)
PHONE..................................419 524-4778
Fax: 419 524-4779
Rick Reece, *Branch Mgr*
Mike Black, *Manager*
Margo Rowen, *Manager*
EMP: 25
SALES (corp-wide): 22.8MM Privately Held
SIC: 1541 Industrial buildings, new construction
PA: R. G. Smith Company
  1249 Dueber Ave Sw
  Canton OH 44706
  330 456-3415

(G-13353)
RAMA TIKA DEVELOPERS LLC
719 Earick Rd (44903-8622)
PHONE..................................419 806-6446
Vaibhav Patel, *President*
EMP: 30
SQ FT: 85,000
SALES: 2MM Privately Held
SIC: 6552 8741 Subdividers & developers; hotel or motel management

(G-13354)
REBMAN TRUCK SERVICE INC
1004 Vanderbilt Rd (44904-8608)
PHONE..................................419 589-8161
Fax: 419 589-8774
James B Redman Jr, *President*
Denise Redman, *President*
EMP: 25
SALES (est): 2.6MM Privately Held
SIC: 7538 General truck repair

(G-13355)
RESEARCH & INVESTIGATION ASSOC
Also Called: Sonitrol Security Systems
186 Sturges Ave (44903-2313)
PHONE..................................419 526-1299
Fax: 419 524-7385
C Ray Gregory, *President*
Merle Burton, *Business Mgr*
Steve Miller, *Exec VP*
Chuck Gregory, *VP Opers*
Carol A Gregory, *Treasurer*
EMP: 26
SQ FT: 3,500
SALES: 1.4MM Privately Held
SIC: 5999 5063 1731 7382 Alarm signal systems; electric alarms & signaling equipment; alarm systems; burglar alarm systems; fire detection & burglar alarm systems specialization; burglar alarm maintenance & monitoring

(G-13356)
RICHLAND COUNTY CHILD SUPPORT
161 Park Ave E (44902-1829)
PHONE..................................419 774-5700
Fax: 419 524-1507
Robert Sparks, *Director*
Dawn Bolinger, *Admin Sec*
EMP: 42
SALES (est): 459.7K Privately Held
SIC: 8322 Child guidance agency

(G-13357)
RICHLAND MALL SHOPPING CTR
2209 Lexington Ave (44907-3027)
PHONE..................................419 529-4003
Fax: 419 529-6059
Richard E Jacobs, *Partner*
EMP: 25 EST: 1969
SQ FT: 500,000
SALES (est): 1.6MM Privately Held
SIC: 8741 6552 6531 Management services; subdividers & developers; real estate agents & managers

(G-13358)
RICHLAND NEWHOPE INDUSTRIES (PA)
150 E 4th St (44902-1520)
P.O. Box 916 (44901-0916)
PHONE..................................419 774-4400
Fax: 419 774-4409
Greg Young, *Prdtn Mgr*
Mike Bradley, *Manager*
Michele Giess, *Manager*
Elizabeth Prather, *Exec Dir*
Dave Keinath, *Director*
EMP: 250
SQ FT: 63,000
SALES: 3.4MM Privately Held
SIC: 0782 2448 7349 8331 Lawn & garden services; wood pallets & skids; building maintenance services; job training & vocational rehabilitation services; packaging & labeling services

(G-13359)
RICHLAND NEWHOPE INDUSTRIES
314 Cleveland Ave (44902-8623)
PHONE..................................419 774-4200
H M Miller, *Superintendent*
Angie Lambert, *Financial Exec*
Anthony Persky, *HR Admin*
Christina Stransky, *Human Resources*
Jim Moore, *Marketing Mgr*
EMP: 45
SALES (corp-wide): 3.4MM Privately Held
SIC: 8331 Job training & vocational rehabilitation services
PA: Richland Newhope Industries, Inc
  150 E 4th St
  Mansfield OH 44902
  419 774-4400

(G-13360)
RICHLAND NEWHOPE INDUSTRIES
985 W Longview Ave (44906-2133)
PHONE..................................419 774-4496
Marsha Madden, *Principal*
EMP: 100
SALES (corp-wide): 3.4MM Privately Held
SIC: 8331 Job training & vocational rehabilitation services
PA: Richland Newhope Industries, Inc
  150 E 4th St
  Mansfield OH 44902
  419 774-4400

(G-13361)
RICHLAND TRUST COMPANY (HQ)
3 N Main St Ste 1 (44902-1740)
P.O. Box 355 (44901-0355)
PHONE..................................419 525-8700
Fax: 419 525-3876
Timothy J Lehman, *President*
Jerrold Coon, *Corp Secy*
Ray Piar, *Vice Pres*
Garland Karen, *Human Res Dir*
Linda Curry, *Manager*
EMP: 84
SALES (est): 2.5MM
SALES (corp-wide): 367MM Publicly Held
WEB: www.richlandbank.com
SIC: 6022 8721 State trust companies accepting deposits, commercial; accounting, auditing & bookkeeping
PA: Park National Corporation
  50 N 3rd St
  Newark OH 43055
  740 349-8451

(G-13362)
SC MADISON BUS GARAGE
Also Called: Madison Local School
600 Esley Ln (44905-2718)
PHONE..................................419 589-3373
Rodger Harramam, *Superintendent*
EMP: 54
SALES (est): 1.5MM Privately Held
SIC: 4151 School buses

(G-13363)
SHAFFER POMEROY LTD
909 S Main St (44907-2037)
P.O. Box 3598 (44907-0598)
PHONE..................................419 756-7302
Keith A Amstutz,
EMP: 27
SALES: 250K Privately Held
SIC: 8711 Consulting engineer

(G-13364)
SKYBOX PACKAGING LLC
Also Called: Mr Box
1275 Pollock Pkwy (44905-1374)
P.O. Box 1567 (44901-1567)
PHONE..................................419 525-7209
Fax: 419 525-7210
Marc Miller, *President*
Rodney Robertson, *Vice Pres*
Tim Hooper, *Project Mgr*
John Olin, *Finance Mgr*
Rob Mangan, *Regl Sales Mgr*
EMP: 73
SALES (est): 15.7MM
SALES (corp-wide): 227.6MM Privately Held
SIC: 3086 5199 Packaging & shipping materials, foamed plastic; packaging materials
PA: Atlantic Packaging Products Ltd
  111 Progress Ave
  Scarborough ON M1P 2
  416 298-8101

(G-13365)
SOUTHERN TITLE OF OHIO LTD (PA)
58 W 3rd St Ste D (44902-1251)
P.O. Box 937 (44901-0937)
PHONE..................................419 525-4600
Mark Wilkinson, *President*
EMP: 27
SALES (est): 10MM Privately Held
WEB: www.southerntitleofohio.com
SIC: 6361 Title insurance

(G-13366)
SPECTRUM MGT HOLDG CO LLC
1280 Park Ave W (44906-2814)
PHONE..................................419 775-9292
EMP: 83
SALES (corp-wide): 41.5B Publicly Held
SIC: 4841 Cable television services
HQ: Spectrum Management Holding Company, Llc
  400 Atlantic St
  Stamford CT 06901
  203 905-7801

(G-13367)
SPRING MEADOW EXTENDED CARE CE
105 S Main St (44902-7901)
PHONE..................................419 866-6124
Donald D Graber, *Branch Mgr*
EMP: 65
SALES (corp-wide): 1.4MM Privately Held
SIC: 8052 Intermediate care facilities
PA: Spring Meadow Extended Care Center Facility, Inc.
  1125 Clarion Ave
  Holland OH 43528
  419 866-6124

(G-13368)
SURGICENTER OF MANSFIELD
1030 Cricket Ln (44906-4104)
PHONE..................................419 774-9410
Fax: 419 774-1072
Edroy McMillam, *Chairman*
EMP: 40
SALES (est): 2.1MM Privately Held
WEB: www.surgictr.com
SIC: 8093 Specialty outpatient clinics

(G-13369)
SYSTEMS JAY LLC NANOGATE (HQ)
150 Longview Ave E (44903-4206)
PHONE..................................419 524-3778
Ralf Zastrau, *CEO*
Michael Jung, *COO*
Daniel Seibert, *CFO*

Mansfield - Richland County (G-13370)

EMP: 930 **EST:** 2016
SALES (est): 9.5MM
SALES (corp-wide): 118.9MM **Privately Held**
SIC: 1799 Coating of concrete structures with plastic
PA: Nanogate Se
Zum Schacht 6
Quierschied 66287
682 595-910

(G-13370)
SYSTEMS JAY LLC NANOGATE
Broscho Fabricated Products
1595 W Longview Ave (44906-1806)
PHONE 419 747-4161
John Vidonish, *Maint Spvr*
Dick Young, *Mfg Staff*
Carlos Sanjur, *QC Dir*
Bruce Souder, *Engineer*
Kay Zartman, *Human Resources*
EMP: 400
SALES (corp-wide): 118.9MM **Privately Held**
WEB: www.jayindinc.com
SIC: 3499 7692 Automobile seat frames, metal; welding repair
HQ: Jay Nanogate Systems Llc
150 Longview Ave E
Mansfield OH 44903
419 524-3778

(G-13371)
SYSTEMS JAY LLC NANOGATE
Also Called: Kronis Coatings
1575 W Longview Ave (44906-1806)
PHONE 419 747-6639
Fax: 419 747-6827
Kay Zartman, *Human Res Dir*
Dick Ward, *Branch Mgr*
EMP: 45
SALES (corp-wide): 118.9MM **Privately Held**
WEB: www.jayindinc.com
SIC: 5198 Paints
HQ: Jay Nanogate Systems Llc
150 Longview Ave E
Mansfield OH 44903
419 524-3778

(G-13372)
TARA FLAHERTY
Also Called: Cuttin' It Close
1872 White Pine Dr (44904-1715)
PHONE 419 565-1334
Tara Flaherty, *Owner*
EMP: 27
SALES: 200K **Privately Held**
WEB: www.cuttinitclose.com
SIC: 7231 Beauty shops

(G-13373)
THE MAPLE CITY ICE COMPANY
Also Called: Mansfield Distributing Co Div
1245 W Longview Ave (44906-1907)
PHONE 419 747-4777
Fax: 419 747-5464
Mary Berry, *Owner*
Michael J Berry, *Branch Mgr*
EMP: 25
SQ FT: 16,463
SALES (corp-wide): 26.9MM **Privately Held**
SIC: 4225 General warehousing
PA: Maple City Ice Company, The (Inc)
371 Cleveland Rd
Norwalk OH 44857
419 668-2531

(G-13374)
THINK-ABILITY LLC
1256 Warner Ave (44905-2619)
PHONE 419 589-2238
Michael Mazak,
EMP: 28
SALES (est): 826.2K **Privately Held**
SIC: 8082 Home health care services

(G-13375)
TMS INTERNATIONAL LLC
1344 Bowman St (44903-4009)
PHONE 419 747-5500
EMP: 40 **Privately Held**
SIC: 5093 Scrap And Waste Materials

(G-13376)
TRIUMPH HOSPITAL MANSFIELD
335 Glessner Ave (44903-2269)
PHONE 419 526-0777
Fax: 419 526-0458
Russell Test, *Principal*
David Ginez, *VP Finance*
Dollie Chultz, *Human Resources*
Gail Wright, *Manager*
Joseph Stolfi, *Director*
EMP: 36
SALES (est): 3.4MM **Privately Held**
SIC: 8051 Skilled nursing care facilities

(G-13377)
TRUGREEN LIMITED PARTNERSHIP
Also Called: Tru Green-Chemlawn
110 Industrial Dr (44904-1339)
P.O. Box 3088 (44904-0088)
PHONE 419 884-3636
Fax: 419 884-1506
Jim Morris, *Manager*
EMP: 25
SALES (corp-wide): 4B **Privately Held**
SIC: 0782 Lawn care services
HQ: Trugreen Limited Partnership
1790 Kirby Pkwy
Memphis TN 38138
901 251-4128

(G-13378)
TUTTLE LANDSCAPING & GRDN CTR
1295 S Trimble Rd (44907-2699)
PHONE 419 756-7555
Fax: 419 756-7755
Charles A Tuttle, *President*
Tod Tuttle, *Vice Pres*
EMP: 25
SQ FT: 30,000
SALES: 750K **Privately Held**
SIC: 0782 5261 Landscape contractors; lawnmowers & tractors; garden supplies & tools; nursery stock, seeds & bulbs

(G-13379)
TWIN OAKS CARE CENTER INC
73 Madison Rd (44905-2830)
P.O. Box 1218 (44901-1218)
PHONE 419 524-1205
Fax: 419 522-1445
Michael Daffin, *President*
James Boyd III, *Vice Pres*
EMP: 25
SALES (est): 1.1MM **Privately Held**
SIC: 8051 8069 Skilled nursing care facilities; specialty hospitals, except psychiatric

(G-13380)
UNITED PARCEL SERVICE INC OH
Also Called: UPS
875 W Longview Ave (44906-2131)
PHONE 419 747-3080
Chuck Kastor, *Manager*
UPS Bond, *Supervisor*
EMP: 112
SALES (corp-wide): 65.8B **Publicly Held**
WEB: www.upsscs.com
SIC: 4215 Package delivery, vehicular
HQ: United Parcel Service, Inc. (Oh)
55 Glenlake Pkwy
Atlanta GA 30328
404 828-6000

(G-13381)
VISITING NRSE ASSN OF CLVELAND
Also Called: Vna of Mid Ohio
40 W 4th St (44902-1206)
P.O. Box 1742 (44901-1742)
PHONE 419 522-4969
Fax: 419 522-9590
Mary Matt, *Sales Executive*
Cortney Swihart, *Exec Dir*
Dana Traxler, *Exec Dir*
EMP: 25
SALES (est): 2MM **Privately Held**
SIC: 8082 Visiting nurse service

(G-13382)
VOLUNTERS OF AMER GREATER OHIO
921 N Main St (44903-8113)
PHONE 419 524-5013
Fax: 419 524-5021
Lyle Draper, *Branch Mgr*
EMP: 30
SALES (corp-wide): 8MM **Privately Held**
WEB: www.voa.org
SIC: 8322 Individual & family services
PA: Volunteers Of America Of Greater Ohio
1776 E Broad St
Columbus OH 43203
614 253-6100

(G-13383)
WOMENS CARE INC
500 S Trimble Rd (44906-4103)
PHONE 419 756-6000
Thomas H Croghan, *President*
Edroy L Mc Millan, *Vice Pres*
Hunter Wilson, *Vice Pres*
Virginia Brown, *Manager*
Elizabeth Chung, *Obstetrician*
EMP: 77
SQ FT: 8,500
SALES (est): 5.8MM **Privately Held**
WEB: www.wcareinc.com
SIC: 8011 Gynecologist; obstetrician

Mantua
Portage County

(G-13384)
AWL TRANSPORT INC
4626 State Route 82 (44255-9654)
PHONE 330 899-3444
Jerry W Carlton, *President*
Linda Carlton, *General Mgr*
David Wehner, *Controller*
EMP: 34
SALES (est): 11.2MM **Privately Held**
SIC: 4213 Contract haulers

(G-13385)
COLUMBIAN CORPORATION MANTUA
Also Called: KNIGHTS OF COLUMBUS #3766
11845 State Route 44 (44255-9647)
P.O. Box 52 (44255-0052)
PHONE 330 274-2576
Bob Hartman, *President*
Mark Kasubick, *President*
EMP: 30
SALES: 52.9K **Privately Held**
SIC: 6512 Nonresidential building operators

(G-13386)
COMPASS PACKAGING LLC
10585 Main St (44255-9600)
P.O. Box 739, Parkman (44080-0739)
PHONE 330 274-2001
Fax: 330 274-2004
Phil Rath, *President*
John Rath, *Vice Pres*
Debbie Palusis, *Controller*
Andy Piech, *Sales Mgr*
Wayne Brugmann, *Maintence Staff*
▲ **EMP:** 41
SQ FT: 24,000
SALES (est): 24.2MM **Privately Held**
WEB: www.compasspackaging.com
SIC: 5113 Corrugated & solid fiber boxes

(G-13387)
HATTIE LARLHAM CENTER FOR (PA)
9772 Diagonal Rd (44255-9160)
PHONE 330 274-2272
Dennis Allen, *CEO*
Darryl E Mast, *COO*
Michelle Anderson, *Vice Pres*
Dotty Grexa, *Vice Pres*
Sandy Neal, *Vice Pres*
EMP: 246
SQ FT: 120,000
SALES: 19.2MM **Privately Held**
SIC: 8361 8322 8052 Home for the mentally retarded; individual & family services; intermediate care facilities

(G-13388)
HATTIE LARLHAM CENTER FOR
9772 Diagonal Rd (44255-9160)
PHONE 330 274-2272
Dennis Allen, *CEO*
EMP: 83
SALES (corp-wide): 19.2MM **Privately Held**
SIC: 8361 Home for the mentally retarded
PA: Hattie Larlham Center For Children With Disabilities
9772 Diagonal Rd
Mantua OH 44255
330 274-2272

(G-13389)
HATTIE LARLHAM COMMUNITY SVCS
9772 Diagonal Rd (44255-9160)
PHONE 330 274-2272
Jim Felter, *Controller*
EMP: 40
SALES: 13.5MM **Privately Held**
SIC: 8082 Home health care services

(G-13390)
LAKESIDE SAND & GRAVEL INC
3498 Frost Rd (44255-9136)
PHONE 330 274-2569
Fax: 330 274-3569
Larry Kotkowski, *President*
Ronald Kotkowski, *Corp Secy*
William Ulla, *Engineer*
EMP: 25
SQ FT: 4,200
SALES: 1.6MM **Privately Held**
SIC: 1442 Construction sand mining; gravel mining

(G-13391)
LARLHAM CARE HATTIE GROUP
9772 Diagonal Rd (44255-9128)
PHONE 330 274-2272
Fax: 330 732-2497
Dennis Allen, *CEO*
Greg Relyea, *Accounting Mgr*
Elizabeth Jones, *Manager*
EMP: 53
SALES: 3.7MM **Privately Held**
SIC: 8099 Medical services organization

(G-13392)
MANTALINE CORPORATION
Also Called: Transportation Group
4754 E High St (44255-9201)
PHONE 330 274-2264
Fax: 330 995-3773
Bryan Fink, *Manager*
Jeff Watson, *Manager*
EMP: 75
SALES (corp-wide): 35.5MM **Privately Held**
WEB: www.mantaline.com
SIC: 5169 3061 Synthetic rubber; mechanical rubber goods
PA: Mantaline Corporation
4754 E High St
Mantua OH 44255
330 274-2264

(G-13393)
OTTO FALKENBERG EXCAVATING
9350 Coit Rd (44255-9139)
PHONE 330 626-4215
Otto Falkenberg, *President*
Marilyn Falkenberg, *Vice Pres*
Carol Helmling, *Admin Sec*
EMP: 30
SALES (est): 2MM **Privately Held**
SIC: 1794 Excavation & grading, building construction

(G-13394)
PIPER PLUMBING INC
2480 Bartlett Rd (44255-9417)
PHONE 330 274-0160
Fax: 330 220-3357
Irene Terry, *President*
David Terry, *Vice Pres*
John Terry, *Treasurer*
EMP: 25
SALES: 2.4MM **Privately Held**
WEB: www.terryproperties.com
SIC: 1711 Plumbing contractors

GEOGRAPHIC SECTION

(G-13395)
STAMM CONTRACTING CO INC
4566 Orchard St (44255-9701)
P.O. Box 450 (44255-0450)
PHONE...................330 274-8230
Fax: 330 274-3520
Hal Stamm, *President*
Elva Novotny, *Corp Secy*
Paul Stamm, *Vice Pres*
Jason Hielman, *Purch Agent*
Ellie Stamm, *Treasurer*
EMP: 40 EST: 1913
SQ FT: 1,500
SALES (est): 5.9MM **Privately Held**
WEB: www.stammcontracting.com
SIC: 3273 1541 1542 5211 Ready-mixed concrete; industrial buildings & warehouses; commercial & office building contractors; lumber & other building materials; brick, stone & related material; concrete work

(G-13396)
TRIPLE LADYS AGENCY INC (PA)
Also Called: T L Express
4626 State Route 82 (44255-9654)
PHONE...................330 274-1100
Fax: 330 274-5610
Gloria G Vechery, *President*
Heather L Carlton, *Vice Pres*
Linda A Carlton, *Admin Sec*
EMP: 25
SQ FT: 10,000
SALES (est): 22MM **Privately Held**
SIC: 4213 4212 4225 Trucking, except local; local trucking, without storage; general warehousing

(G-13397)
VISUAL ART GRAPHIC SERVICES
5244 Goodell Rd (44255-9746)
PHONE...................330 274-2775
George South, *President*
EMP: 30
SQ FT: 35,000
SALES (est): 3MM **Privately Held**
WEB: www.evisualarts.com
SIC: 2752 7336 Commercial printing, lithographic; commercial art & graphic design

Maple Heights
Cuyahoga County

(G-13398)
AARONS INC
5420 Northfield Rd (44137-3113)
PHONE...................216 587-2745
William Wagner, *Office Mgr*
Mark Riggetts, *Manager*
EMP: 25
SALES (corp-wide): 3.3B **Publicly Held**
WEB: www.aaronrents.com
SIC: 7359 Furniture rental
PA: Aaron's, Inc.
    400 Galleria Pkwy Se # 300
    Atlanta GA 30339
    678 402-3000

(G-13399)
AGMET LLC
5463 Dunham Rd (44137-3644)
PHONE...................216 662-6939
John Rankin, *Sales Executive*
Dave Crose, *Office Mgr*
EMP: 35
SALES (corp-wide): 21.8MM **Privately Held**
WEB: www.agmetmetals.com
SIC: 5093 Ferrous metal scrap & waste
PA: Agmet Llc
    7800 Medusa Rd
    Cleveland OH 44146
    440 439-7400

(G-13400)
AREA TEMPS INC
15689 Broadway Ave (44137-1121)
PHONE...................216 518-2000
Tom Shea, *Manager*
EMP: 2305
SALES (corp-wide): 87.8MM **Privately Held**
WEB: www.areatemps.com
SIC: 7363 Temporary help service
PA: Area Temps, Inc.
    4511 Rockside Rd Ste 190
    Independence OH 44131
    216 781-5350

(G-13401)
BROADWAY CARE CTR MPLE HTS LLC
16231 Broadway Ave (44137-2526)
PHONE...................216 662-0551
Louis Kraus,
EMP: 28
SALES (est): 2.4MM **Privately Held**
SIC: 8361 Residential care

(G-13402)
BRUDER INC
16900 Rockside Rd (44137-4333)
PHONE...................216 791-9800
Fax: 216 791-5116
Robert Bruder, *President*
Michael Bruder, *Vice Pres*
▼ EMP: 27
SQ FT: 2,000
SALES (est): 5.9MM **Privately Held**
WEB: www.bruderinc.com
SIC: 5211 5032 Brick; tile, ceramic; roofing material; aggregate

(G-13403)
CLIFTON STEEL COMPANY (PA)
16500 Rockside Rd (44137-4324)
PHONE...................216 662-6111
Fax: 216 662-6107
Herbert C Neides, *President*
Howard Feldenkris, *Vice Pres*
Bruce Goodman, *Vice Pres*
Joe Shoemaker, *Vice Pres*
Joe Tomasi, *Prdtn Mgr*
▲ EMP: 95
SQ FT: 160,000
SALES (est): 95.3MM **Privately Held**
WEB: www.cliftonsteel.com
SIC: 5051 3441 3443 3398 Steel; structural shapes, iron or steel; fabricated structural metal; metal parts; metal heat treating

(G-13404)
CUYAHOGA VENDING CO INC (PA)
Also Called: Cuyahoga Group, The
14250 Industrial Ave S # 104 (44137-3260)
PHONE...................216 663-1457
James N Variglotti, *President*
David Karley, *Vice Pres*
Ed Komoroski, *Vice Pres*
EMP: 65
SQ FT: 20,000
SALES (est): 10.9MM **Privately Held**
SIC: 7359 Vending machine rental

(G-13405)
DAYNAS HOMECARE LLC
14616 Tabor Ave (44137-3859)
PHONE...................216 323-0323
Dayna M Rasberry,
EMP: 30
SALES (est): 400K **Privately Held**
SIC: 8082 Home health care services

(G-13406)
EAST OHIO GAS COMPANY (HQ)
Also Called: Dominion Energy Ohio
19701 Libby Rd (44137-2371)
PHONE...................800 362-7557
Fax: 216 736-6247
Tom D Newland, *President*
Anne E Bomar, *Senior VP*
Brian Brakeman, *Vice Pres*
B C Klink Sr, *Vice Pres*
Ron Kovach, *Vice Pres*
EMP: 1051
SQ FT: 121,000
SALES (est): 150MM
SALES (corp-wide): 12.5B **Publicly Held**
SIC: 4923 Gas transmission & distribution
PA: Dominion Energy, Inc.
    120 Tredegar St
    Richmond VA 23219
    804 819-2000

(G-13407)
EASTSIDE MULTI CARE INC
Also Called: Sunrise Pointe
19900 Clare Ave (44137-1806)
PHONE...................216 662-3343
Motti Schonfeld, *President*
Basya Rovner, *Office Mgr*
Kamdasamy Umapathy, *Director*
Debra Price, *Hlthcr Dir*
Basya Rover, *Executive*
EMP: 135 EST: 2003
SALES (est): 7.5MM **Privately Held**
SIC: 8051 Convalescent home with continuous nursing care

(G-13408)
HOME DEPOT USA INC
Also Called: Home Depot, The
21000 Libby Rd (44137-2931)
PHONE...................216 581-6611
Fax: 216 332-2916
Randy Behm, *Manager*
EMP: 200
SALES (corp-wide): 100.9B **Publicly Held**
WEB: www.homerentalsdepot.com
SIC: 5211 7359 Home centers; tool rental
HQ: Home Depot U.S.A., Inc.
    2455 Paces Ferry Rd Se
    Atlanta GA 30339

(G-13409)
IN TERMINAL SERVICES CORP
5300 Greenhurst Ext (44137-1139)
PHONE...................216 518-8407
Bill Donahue, *Branch Mgr*
EMP: 50
SALES (corp-wide): 16.3MM **Privately Held**
SIC: 7389 Crane & aerial lift service
PA: In Terminal Services Corporation
    3111 167th St
    Hazel Crest IL 60429
    708 225-2400

(G-13410)
MAMMANA CUSTOM WOODWORKING INC
14400 Industrial Ave N (44137-3249)
PHONE...................216 581-9059
Max Mammana, *President*
EMP: 25
SQ FT: 18,000
SALES: 980K **Privately Held**
SIC: 1751 Cabinet & finish carpentry

(G-13411)
NORFOLK SOUTHERN CORPORATION
5300 Greenhurst Ext (44137-1139)
PHONE...................216 518-8407
Bill Donaghue, *Manager*
EMP: 32
SALES (corp-wide): 10.5B **Publicly Held**
WEB: www.nscorp.com
SIC: 4731 Freight forwarding
PA: Norfolk Southern Corporation
    3 Commercial Pl Ste 1a
    Norfolk VA 23510
    757 629-2680

(G-13412)
OREILLY AUTOMOTIVE INC
5489 Warrensville Ctr Rd (44137-1930)
PHONE...................213 332-0427
EMP: 58 **Privately Held**
SIC: 7389 Automobile recovery service
PA: O'reilly Automotive, Inc.
    233 S Patterson Ave
    Springfield MO 65802

(G-13413)
PECK DISTRIBUTORS INC
Also Called: Peck Food Service
17000 Rockside Rd (44137-4345)
PHONE...................216 587-6814
Fax: 216 587-6523
Stephen Peck Jr, *President*
Kenneth Peck, *Vice Pres*
Scott Peck, *Treasurer*
David Peck, *Admin Sec*
▲ EMP: 35
SQ FT: 50,000
SALES (est): 24MM **Privately Held**
WEB: www.peckfoodservice.com
SIC: 5113 5149 5142 Industrial & personal service paper; canned goods: fruit, vegetables, seafood, meats, etc.; packaged frozen goods

(G-13414)
R L LIPTON DISTRIBUTING CO
5900 Pennsylvania Ave (44137-4302)
PHONE...................216 475-4150
Fax: 216 475-6256
Steve Eisenberg, *President*
W Terry Patrick, *Vice Pres*
Dean Gerberick, *Warehouse Mgr*
W Bud Biggin, *Treasurer*
C Jack Amstutz, *Shareholder*
▲ EMP: 75
SQ FT: 70,000
SALES (est): 36.9MM **Privately Held**
SIC: 5181 5182 5149 Beer & other fermented malt liquors; wine; groceries & related products

(G-13415)
ROBERT A KAUFMANN INC
Also Called: Building Blocks Child Care Ctr
5210 Northfield Rd (44137-2466)
PHONE...................216 663-1150
Robert A Kaufmann, *President*
Mary Kaufmann, *Vice Pres*
EMP: 35
SQ FT: 3,000
SALES: 750K **Privately Held**
SIC: 8351 Child day care services

(G-13416)
SABER HEALTHCARE GROUP LLC
Also Called: Sunrise Pointe
19900 Clare Ave (44137-1806)
PHONE...................216 662-3343
Angela Hammons, *Administration*
EMP: 36
SALES (corp-wide): 68.5MM **Privately Held**
SIC: 8051 Skilled nursing care facilities
PA: Saber Healthcare Group, L.L.C.
    26691 Richmond Rd Frnt
    Bedford OH 44146
    216 292-5706

(G-13417)
SFD COMPANY LLC
Also Called: Sherwood Fd Dstrs Clveland Div
16625 Granite Rd (44137-4301)
PHONE...................216 662-8000
Jaque Mathews, *Transptn Dir*
Doug Pierce, *Credit Mgr*
Michael Montini, *Accounts Mgr*
Karen Hentemann, *Marketing Staff*
John Politowski, *Marketing Staff*
EMP: 88
SALES (corp-wide): 309.6MM **Privately Held**
SIC: 5147 5144 5146 Meats, fresh; poultry: live, dressed or frozen (unpackaged); fish, frozen, unpackaged
HQ: Sfd Company Llc
    12499 Evergreen Ave
    Detroit MI 48228
    313 659-7300

(G-13418)
SHERWOOD FOOD DISTRIBUTORS LLC
Also Called: SHERWOOD FOOD DISTRIBUTORS, L.L.C.
16625 Granite Rd (44137-4301)
PHONE...................216 662-6794
Bobby Lipson, *Exec VP*
John Killik, *Data Proc Staff*
EMP: 325
SQ FT: 350,000
SALES (corp-wide): 309.6MM **Privately Held**
WEB: www.sherwoodfoods.com
SIC: 5147 5146 5149 5141 Meats, fresh; fish & seafoods; specialty food items; groceries, general line; packaged frozen goods; meat, frozen: packaged
HQ: Sfd Company Llc
    12499 Evergreen Ave
    Detroit MI 48228
    313 659-7300

Maple Heights - Cuyahoga County (G-13419)

(G-13419)
STAR BEAUTY PLUS LLC (PA)
20900 Libby Rd (44137-2929)
PHONE..................216 662-9750
Fax: 216 662-9765
John Kim,
EMP: 40 EST: 1973
SQ FT: 13,000
SALES (est): 2.1MM Privately Held
SIC: 7231 Cosmetologist

(G-13420)
SUNTWIST CORP
Also Called: Post-Up Stand
5461 Dunham Rd (44137-3644)
PHONE..................800 935-3534
Fax: 216 332-0531
Ram Tamir, President
Alon Weimer, Vice Pres
Alon Weimer, Vice Pres
Tina Schulte, Cust Mgr
Jason Novicky, Accounts Exec
EMP: 76
SQ FT: 2,600
SALES (est): 3.5MM Privately Held
SIC: 7336 Graphic arts & related design

Marblehead
Ottawa County

(G-13421)
KELLEYS ISLE FERRY BOAT LINES
510 W Main St (43440-2250)
PHONE..................419 798-9763
Fax: 419 798-8009
Paula Moody, Manager
EMP: 25 Privately Held
WEB: www.kelleysislandferry.com
SIC: 4482 Ferries
PA: The Kelley's Island Ferry Boat Lines Inc
3203 Harvard Ave
Newburgh Heights OH 44105

(G-13422)
LAFARGE NORTH AMERICA INC
831 S Quarry Rd (43440-2576)
PHONE..................419 798-4486
Fax: 419 798-5795
Dave Baker, Safety Mgr
Allen Boros, Sales Staff
Tim Winters, Sales Executive
Jeff Grashel, Manager
EMP: 64
SALES (corp-wide): 26.4B Privately Held
WEB: www.lafargenorthamerica.com
SIC: 5032 Aggregate
HQ: Lafarge North America Inc.
8700 W Bryn Mawr Ave
Chicago IL 60631
773 372-1000

Marengo
Morrow County

(G-13423)
DEARTH MANAGEMENT COMPANY
Also Called: Bennington Glen Nursing Home
825 State Route 61 (43334-9215)
P.O. Box 10 (43334-0010)
PHONE..................419 253-0144
Toll Free:..................888 -
Jim Deel, Administration
Chris Nikerson, Administration
EMP: 110
SALES (est): 3.7MM
SALES (corp-wide): 11.7MM Privately Held
WEB: www.schoenbrunnhealthcare.com
SIC: 8051 8052 Skilled nursing care facilities; intermediate care facilities
PA: Dearth Management Company
134 Northwoods Blvd Ste C
Columbus OH 43235
614 847-1070

(G-13424)
FISHBURN TANK TRUCK SERVICE
5012 State Route 229 (43334-9634)
P.O. Box 278 (43334-0278)
PHONE..................419 253-6031
Jack Fishburn, Owner
EMP: 60
SALES (est): 2.1MM Privately Held
SIC: 1389 Haulage, oil field

(G-13425)
RINGLER FEEDLOTS LLC
461 State Route 61 (43334-9415)
PHONE..................419 253-5300
David Ringler, President
Angela Bower, Manager
EMP: 25 EST: 2007
SALES (est): 993.7K Privately Held
SIC: 4731 Brokers, shipping

(G-13426)
RINGLER INC
461 State Route 61 (43334-9415)
PHONE..................419 253-5300
Alexander N Ringler, President
EMP: 25
SALES (est): 194.8K Privately Held
SIC: 0191 General farms, primarily crop

Maria Stein
Mercer County

(G-13427)
BROOKSIDE HOLDINGS LLC (PA)
Also Called: Brookside Trucking
8022 State Route 119 (45860-8708)
P.O. Box 68 (45860-0068)
PHONE..................419 925-4457
Fax: 419 925-4390
Ricky Uppenkamp,
Steve Cook,
John D Richards,
EMP: 43
SQ FT: 9,800
SALES (est): 3.8MM Privately Held
SIC: 4212 4213 Local trucking, without storage; trucking, except local

(G-13428)
HOMAN INC
6915 Olding Rd (45860-9735)
PHONE..................419 925-4349
Fax: 419 925-5401
Roger R Homan, President
Dave Pleiman, Parts Mgr
Dale Everman, Sales Staff
Karen Boeke, Office Mgr
Jim Brackman, Manager
▲ EMP: 25
SQ FT: 13,700
SALES (est): 9.3MM Privately Held
WEB: www.homaninc.com
SIC: 1542 5999 Commercial & office building, new construction; farm machinery

(G-13429)
MOELLER TRUCKING INC
8100 Industrial Dr (45860-9544)
PHONE..................419 925-4799
Fax: 419 925-4189
Gary Moeller, President
Dan Moeller, Opers Mgr
Mike Moeller, Opers Mgr
Brenda Hamberg, Terminal Mgr
Art Moeller Jr, Treasurer
EMP: 90
SQ FT: 3,500
SALES (est): 23MM Privately Held
SIC: 4213 4212 Contract haulers; local trucking, without storage

Marietta
Washington County

(G-13430)
AMEDISYS INC
Also Called: Home Health Agency
210 N 7th St (45750-2244)
PHONE..................740 373-8549
Pamela Parr, Exec Dir
Teresa Meyer, Director
EMP: 40 Publicly Held
WEB: www.amedisys.com
SIC: 8082 8051 8049 8361 Home health care services; skilled nursing care facilities; physical therapist; occupational therapist; speech therapist; rehabilitation center, residential; health care incidental
PA: Amedisys, Inc.
3854 American Way Ste A
Baton Rouge LA 70816

(G-13431)
AMERICAN PRODUCERS SUP CO INC (PA)
119 2nd St (45750-3102)
P.O. Box 1050 (45750-6050)
PHONE..................740 373-5050
Fax: 740 373-7096
Christopher L Brunton, President
Gabe Davis, General Mgr
Rick Blizzard, Vice Pres
Joseph Wesel, Vice Pres
Vickie Richards, Buyer
▲ EMP: 54 EST: 1963
SQ FT: 50,000
SALES (est): 33.8MM Privately Held
SIC: 5082 5085 Contractors' materials; abrasives

(G-13432)
AMERICAN STAR PAINTING CO LLC
Also Called: American Star Pntg & Coatings
201 Mitchells Ln (45750-6868)
PHONE..................740 373-5634
Toll Free:..................888 -
Fax: 304 275-1174
Greg Dotson, Vice Pres
James Dunn, Treasurer
Garold Greenlees, Mng Member
Terri Lilly, Manager
Pete Saliba, Manager
EMP: 25
SALES: 1.7MM Privately Held
SIC: 1721 1799 1752 Commercial painting; coating, caulking & weather, water & fireproofing; access flooring system installation

(G-13433)
ANTERO RESOURCES CORPORATION
2335 State Route 821 (45750-5362)
PHONE..................740 760-1000
EMP: 60 Publicly Held
SIC: 8742 Business planning & organizing services
PA: Antero Resources Corporation
1615 Wynkoop St
Denver CO 80202

(G-13434)
B & L AGENCY LLC
1001 Pike St Ste 4 (45750-3516)
PHONE..................740 373-8272
Fax: 740 373-0770
Brenda Frazier, Principal
EMP: 41
SALES (est): 1.2MM Privately Held
SIC: 8082 Home health care services

(G-13435)
BD OIL GATHERING CORP
649 Mitchells Ln (45750-6865)
PHONE..................740 374-9355
Fax: 740 374-6077
Floyd Deer Sr, President
Keith Young, Opers Mgr
Sherry Young, Office Mgr
Floyd A Deer Jr, Director
Gordon J Deer, Director
EMP: 29

SALES (est): 7MM Privately Held
WEB: www.bdoil.com
SIC: 5172 Crude oil

(G-13436)
COMMUNITY ACTION PROGRAM CORP (PA)
218 Putnam St (45750-3014)
P.O. Box 144 (45750-0144)
PHONE..................740 373-3745
Fax: 740 373-6775
Cathy Rees, Finance
David E Brightbill, Exec Dir
Richard Edgington, Exec Dir
Anthony Mele, Exec Dir
Rachel Shipley, Director
EMP: 85 EST: 1967
SQ FT: 9,700
SALES: 9.9MM Privately Held
WEB: www.wmcap.org
SIC: 8399 Community action agency

(G-13437)
COMMUNITY ACTION PROGRAM CORP
Also Called: Norwood School
205 Phillips St (45750-3427)
PHONE..................740 373-6016
Rosie Foreman, Director
EMP: 30
SALES (est): 241.4K
SALES (corp-wide): 9.9MM Privately Held
WEB: www.wmcap.org
SIC: 8399 8322 Community action agency; individual & family services
PA: Community Action Program Corp
218 Putnam St
Marietta OH 45750
740 373-3745

(G-13438)
COUNTY OF WASHINGTON
Also Called: Washington Cnty Engineers Off
103 Westview Ave (45750-9403)
PHONE..................740 376-7430
Fax: 740 376-7085
Roger Wright, Engineer
EMP: 37 Privately Held
WEB: www.washingtongov.org
SIC: 8711 Engineering services
PA: County Of Washington
205 Putnam St
Marietta OH 45750
740 373-6623

(G-13439)
COUNTY OF WASHINGTON
Also Called: Washington County Home
County House Ln (45750)
PHONE..................740 373-2028
Fax: 740 373-2094
Ted Williams, Administration
EMP: 42 Privately Held
WEB: www.washingtongov.org
SIC: 8082 Home health care services
PA: County Of Washington
205 Putnam St
Marietta OH 45750
740 373-6623

(G-13440)
COUNTY OF WASHINGTON
Also Called: Department Jobs and Fmly Svcs
1115 Gilman Ave (45750-9428)
PHONE..................740 373-5513
Fax: 740 374-7692
Dave Keerps, Manager
Chuck Wise, Manager
Thomas Ballengee, Director
EMP: 55 Privately Held
SIC: 8322 Social service center
PA: County Of Washington
205 Putnam St
Marietta OH 45750
740 373-6623

(G-13441)
DAVIS PICKERING & COMPANY INC
Also Called: American Procomm
165 Enterprise Dr (45750-8051)
PHONE..................740 373-5896
Fax: 740 373-5897
Jeffrey A Williamson, CEO

▲ = Import ▼ = Export
◆ = Import/Export

GEOGRAPHIC SECTION

Marietta - Washington County (G-13466)

Dustin W Flinn, *President*
Kelly A Fisher, *Vice Pres*
Daniel M Fliehman, *Vice Pres*
Kelly Fisher, *Controller*
EMP: 100
SQ FT: 6,000
SALES (est): 33.5MM **Privately Held**
SIC: 1731 General electrical contractor

(G-13442)
DAVITA INC
Also Called: Da Vita
1019 Pike St (45750-3500)
PHONE..................740 376-2622
Scott Wagstaff, *Branch Mgr*
EMP: 29 **Publicly Held**
SIC: 8092 Kidney dialysis centers
PA: Davita Inc.
2000 16th St
Denver CO 80202

(G-13443)
E T B LTD
Also Called: John Deere Authorized Dealer
15 Acme St (45750-3305)
PHONE..................740 373-6686
John Kitts, *Sales Staff*
Chris Walters, *Branch Mgr*
EMP: 30 **Privately Held**
SIC: 7359 5082 Stores & yards equipment rental; construction & mining machinery
PA: E T B Ltd
500 Hall St
Bridgeport OH 43912

(G-13444)
EUREKA MIDSTREAM LLC
27710 State Route 7 (45750-5147)
PHONE..................740 868-1325
Chris Akers, *CEO*
EMP: 40
SALES (est): 386.8K **Privately Held**
SIC: 4922 Pipelines, natural gas

(G-13445)
FAMILY FORD LINCOLN INC
Also Called: Family Lincoln
909 Pike St (45750-5100)
P.O. Box 588 (45750-0588)
PHONE..................740 373-9127
Fax: 740 373-5304
Carl Nourse, *President*
Todd Bishop, *Sales Mgr*
EMP: 60
SALES (est): 15.7MM **Privately Held**
SIC: 5511 7538 7514 7532 Automobiles, new & used; general automotive repair shops; hearse or limousine rental, without drivers; top & body repair & paint shops

(G-13446)
FIRST SETTLEMENT ORTHOPAEDICS (PA)
Also Called: Nayak, Naresh K MD
611 2nd St Ste A (45750-2167)
PHONE..................740 373-8756
Fax: 740 373-7246
Gregory Krivchenia II, *President*
Naresh K Nayak, *Vice Pres*
Gary W Miller, *Treasurer*
Tom Billingsley, *Manager*
Doreen Grasley, *Manager*
EMP: 32
SQ FT: 17,500
SALES (est): 5.3MM **Privately Held**
SIC: 8011 8049 Sports medicine specialist, physician; physical therapist

(G-13447)
GLENWOOD COMMUNITY INC
Also Called: Pines At Glenwood
200 Timberline Dr Apt 206 (45750-9372)
PHONE..................740 376-9555
Fax: 740 376-0153
Margarine Shonard, *Exec Dir*
EMP: 45
SALES (est): 3.7MM **Privately Held**
SIC: 8361 Home for the aged

(G-13448)
GOODWILL INDS CENTL OHIO INC
1303 Colegate Dr (45750-1328)
PHONE..................740 373-1304
Fax: 740 373-1304
F Pierpoint, *Branch Mgr*
EMP: 83
SALES (corp-wide): 45.1MM **Privately Held**
SIC: 8331 Vocational rehabilitation agency
PA: Goodwill Industries Of Central Ohio, Inc.
1331 Edgehill Rd
Columbus OH 43212
614 294-5181

(G-13449)
GREENLEAF LANDSCAPES INC
414 Muskingum Dr (45750-9306)
PHONE..................740 373-1639
Fax: 740 373-1135
Albert J Lang, *President*
David Fleming, *General Mgr*
Pam McKitrick, *Regional Mgr*
Jeanne Lang, *Vice Pres*
Garrett Lang, *Sales Staff*
EMP: 63
SQ FT: 3,500
SALES: 5.7MM **Privately Held**
WEB: www.greenleaflandscapes.com
SIC: 0782 5261 Landscape contractors; nurseries & garden centers

(G-13450)
HARRISON CONSTRUCTION INC
Also Called: Harrison Contruction
1408 Colegate Dr (45750-1330)
PHONE..................740 373-7000
Fax: 740 373-3398
Daniel Harrison, *President*
Gillian Harrison, *Treasurer*
EMP: 27
SQ FT: 7,100
SALES (est): 3.6MM **Privately Held**
SIC: 1521 5722 General remodeling, single-family houses; kitchens, complete (sinks, cabinets, etc.)

(G-13451)
HAVAR INC
416 3rd St (45750-2101)
P.O. Box 1107 (45750-6107)
PHONE..................740 373-7175
Fax: 740 373-7116
Debbie Schmeiding, *Director*
EMP: 35
SALES (corp-wide): 3.6MM **Privately Held**
WEB: www.havar.com
SIC: 8051 Extended care facility
PA: Havar Inc
396 Richland Ave
Athens OH 45701
740 594-3533

(G-13452)
HEALTH CARE RTREMENT CORP AMER
Also Called: Heartland of Marietta
5001 State Route 60 (45750-5343)
PHONE..................740 373-8920
Linda Daily, *Manager*
EMP: 100
SALES (corp-wide): 3.6B **Publicly Held**
WEB: www.hrc-manorcare.com
SIC: 8051 Convalescent home with continuous nursing care
HQ: Health Care And Retirement Corporation Of America
333 N Summit St Ste 103
Toledo OH 43604
419 252-5500

(G-13453)
IDDINGS TRUCKING INC
741 Blue Knob Rd (45750-8275)
PHONE..................740 568-1780
George C Loeber, *President*
Richard Gessel, *General Mgr*
Brad Loeber, *General Mgr*
Raymond E Waters, *Principal*
Donn Kerr, *Exec VP*
EMP: 105 **EST:** 1966
SQ FT: 13,400
SALES (est): 26.6MM **Privately Held**
WEB: www.iddingstrucking.com
SIC: 4212 4213 Coal haulage, local; dump truck haulage; heavy hauling

(G-13454)
IEH AUTO PARTS LLC
Also Called: Auto Plus
123 Tennis Center Dr (45750-9765)
PHONE..................740 373-8327
Scott Reynolds, *Branch Mgr*
EMP: 27
SALES (corp-wide): 21.7B **Publicly Held**
SIC: 5013 Automotive supplies & parts
HQ: Ieh Auto Parts Llc
108 Townpark Dr Nw
Kennesaw GA 30144
770 701-5000

(G-13455)
IEH AUTO PARTS LLC
121 Tennis Center Dr (45750-9765)
PHONE..................740 373-8151
EMP: 26
SALES (corp-wide): 21.7B **Publicly Held**
SIC: 5013 Automotive supplies & parts
HQ: Ieh Auto Parts Llc
108 Townpark Dr Nw
Kennesaw GA 30144
770 701-5000

(G-13456)
INN AT MARIETTA LTD
150 Browns Rd Ofc (45750-9086)
PHONE..................740 373-9600
Fax: 740 374-3171
Charlotte Forsyth, *Partner*
Randy Wright, *Exec Dir*
Deb Patrick, *Administration*
James O Biehl,
EMP: 80 **EST:** 1996
SALES (est): 3MM **Privately Held**
SIC: 7011 8052 Inns; intermediate care facilities

(G-13457)
INTERIM HEALTHCARE SE OHIO INC
1017 Pike St (45750-3522)
PHONE..................740 373-3800
Diane Hunter, *CEO*
Bradford C Hunter, *CFO*
Diana Kirk, *Branch Mgr*
Sandy Schilling, *Manager*
Terri Strawn, *Administration*
EMP: 80
SQ FT: 2,100
SALES: 2MM **Privately Held**
SIC: 8082 Home health care services

(G-13458)
JANI-SOURCE INC
478 Bramblewood Hts Rd (45750-8501)
PHONE..................740 374-6298
Toll Free:..................877 -
Bryan Waller, *President*
Ronald Burnworth, *Opers Mgr*
Kurt Vogel, *Mktg Dir*
Judy Waller,
EMP: 30
SQ FT: 2,400
SALES (est): 1.1MM **Privately Held**
WEB: www.janisource.com
SIC: 7349 Janitorial service, contract basis

(G-13459)
JPMORGAN CHASE BANK NAT ASSN
125 Putnam St (45750-2936)
PHONE..................740 374-2263
Dawn Wilson, *Manager*
EMP: 26
SALES (corp-wide): 99.6B **Publicly Held**
WEB: www.chase.com
SIC: 6021 National commercial banks
HQ: Jpmorgan Chase Bank, National Association
1111 Polaris Pkwy
Columbus OH 43240
614 436-3055

(G-13460)
KEMRON ENVIRONMENTAL SVCS INC
2343 State Route 821 (45750-5464)
PHONE..................740 373-4071
Fax: 740 374-4835
David Vandenberg, *Branch Mgr*
Deanna Hesson, *Med Doctor*
John Wass, *CIO*
EMP: 90
SALES (corp-wide): 34.5MM **Privately Held**
WEB: www.kemron.com
SIC: 8711 8748 8731 8734 Consulting engineer; environmental consultant; commercial physical research; testing laboratories
PA: Kemron Environmental Services, Inc.
1359a Ellswrth Indus Blvd
Atlanta GA 30318
404 636-0928

(G-13461)
KOROSEAL INTERIOR PRODUCTS LLC
700 Bf Goodrich Rd (45750-7849)
PHONE..................855 753-5474
EMP: 40
SALES (corp-wide): 121MM **Privately Held**
SIC: 1541 Warehouse construction
PA: Koroseal Interior Products, Llc
3875 Embassy Pkwy Ste 110
Fairlawn OH 44333
330 668-7600

(G-13462)
LOWES HOME CENTERS LLC
842 Pike St (45750-3503)
PHONE..................740 374-2151
Fax: 740 374-3841
Paul REA, *Branch Mgr*
EMP: 150
SALES (corp-wide): 68.6B **Publicly Held**
SIC: 5211 5031 5722 5064 Home centers; building materials, exterior; building materials, interior; household appliance stores; electrical appliances, television & radio
HQ: Lowe's Home Centers, Llc
1605 Curtis Bridge Rd
Wilkesboro NC 28697
336 658-4000

(G-13463)
MARCH INVESTORS LTD
Also Called: Hampton Inn
508 Pike St (45750-3332)
PHONE..................740 373-5353
Fax: 740 373-3803
David M Archer,
EMP: 25
SALES (est): 1.4MM **Privately Held**
SIC: 7011 Hotels

(G-13464)
MARIETTA AQUATIC CENTER
233 Pennsylvania Ave (45750-1663)
PHONE..................740 373-2445
Peter Ianniciello, *Principal*
EMP: 30 **EST:** 2007
SALES (est): 233.2K **Privately Held**
SIC: 7999 Swimming pool, non-membership

(G-13465)
MARIETTA BANTAM BASEBALL LEAG
103 Chalet Ln (45750-9370)
PHONE..................740 350-9844
Lisa Weekley, *President*
EMP: 31 **EST:** 2010
SALES: 30K **Privately Held**
SIC: 7997 Membership sports & recreation clubs

(G-13466)
MARIETTA CENTER FOR HEALTH &
Also Called: Marietta Nursing and Rehab Ctr
117 Bartlett St (45750-2683)
PHONE..................740 373-1867
Fax: 740 373-3133
Randy Wright, *Director*
EMP: 150
SALES (est): 2.2MM
SALES (corp-wide): 6B **Publicly Held**
WEB: www.kindredhealthcare.com
SIC: 8093 8051 Rehabilitation center, outpatient treatment; skilled nursing care facilities

Marietta - Washington County (G-13467)

PA: Kindred Healthcare, Inc.
680 S 4th St
Louisville KY 40202
502 596-7300

(G-13467)
MARIETTA COLLEGE
Also Called: Phisical Plant
213 4th St (45750-3004)
PHONE..................740 376-4790
Fred Smith, *Manager*
Jason Mader, *Manager*
EMP: 50
SALES (est): 970.5K
SALES (corp-wide): 36.2MM **Privately Held**
WEB: www.marietta.edu
SIC: 8221 4832 4813 College, except junior; educational; long distance telephone communications
PA: Marietta College
215 5th St Dept 32
Marietta OH 45750
740 376-4643

(G-13468)
MARIETTA COUNTRY CLUB INC
705 Pike St (45750-3502)
PHONE..................740 373-7722
Fax: 740 373-7722
David Mitchem, *President*
EMP: 35 EST: 1932
SQ FT: 4,000
SALES: 823.2K **Privately Held**
WEB: www.mariettacountryclub.com
SIC: 7997 Country club, membership

(G-13469)
MARIETTA GYNECOLOGIC ASSOC
410 2nd St (45750-2115)
PHONE..................740 374-3622
Fax: 740 374-4209
Warren L Cooper MD, *President*
Curtis D White MD, *Corp Secy*
Todd Myers MD, *Vice Pres*
EMP: 55
SQ FT: 13,000
SALES (est): 4.9MM **Privately Held**
WEB: www.gynassociates.com
SIC: 8011 Gynecologist

(G-13470)
MARIETTA INDUSTRIAL ENTPS INC (PA)
Also Called: Mie
17943 State Route 7 (45750-8239)
PHONE..................740 373-2252
W Scott Elliott, *President*
Burt Elliott, *Vice Pres*
David Downing, *CFO*
Stacey Orr, *Office Mgr*
Grant Elliott, *Admin Sec*
EMP: 51 EST: 1955
SQ FT: 450,000
SALES (est): 11.1MM **Privately Held**
WEB: www.miecorp.com
SIC: 4491 4214 Marine cargo handling; local trucking with storage

(G-13471)
MARIETTA MEMORIAL HOSPITAL (PA)
401 Matthew St (45750-1699)
PHONE..................740 374-1400
Fax: 740 374-1412
Tom Tucker, *Ch of Bd*
J Stott Cantley, *President*
Diana Chapman, *General Mgr*
Inge Chenoweth, *General Mgr*
Orive E Fischer, *Vice Pres*
EMP: 900
SQ FT: 100,000
SALES: 400.4MM **Privately Held**
SIC: 8062 8069 General medical & surgical hospitals; alcoholism rehabilitation hospital

(G-13472)
MARIETTA MEMORIAL HOSPITAL
Also Called: Home Nursing Service & Hospice
210 N 7th St Ste 300 (45750-2244)
PHONE..................740 373-8549
Cindy Carpenter, *Manager*
Lee A Robinson, *Manager*
Pam Parr, *Director*
EMP: 40
SALES (corp-wide): 400.4MM **Privately Held**
SIC: 8062 8082 General medical & surgical hospitals; visiting nurse service
PA: Marietta Memorial Hospital Inc
401 Matthew St
Marietta OH 45750
740 374-1400

(G-13473)
MARIETTA SILOS LLC
2417 Waterford Rd (45750-7828)
PHONE..................740 373-2822
Dennis Blauser, *CEO*
Joe Riggs, *Business Mgr*
EMP: 50
SQ FT: 50,000
SALES (est): 9.1MM **Privately Held**
WEB: www.mariettasilos.com
SIC: 1542 Silo construction, agricultural

(G-13474)
MC ALARNEY POOL SPAS AND BILLD
Also Called: McAlarney Pols Spas Billd More
908 Pike St (45750-3505)
PHONE..................740 373-6698
Fax: 740 373-7724
Cheryl McAlarney, *President*
Wayne Mc Alarney, *Exec VP*
EMP: 25 EST: 1975
SQ FT: 6,500
SALES (est): 1.2MM **Privately Held**
WEB: www.mcalarney.com
SIC: 5091 3949 Swimming pools, equipment & supplies; spa equipment & supplies; billiard equipment & supplies; sporting & athletic goods

(G-13475)
MERCHANTS 5 STAR LTD
18192 State Route 7 (45750-8237)
P.O. Box 541 (45750-0541)
PHONE..................740 373-0313
Jeffrey A Starner, *President*
Ellen Miller, *Treasurer*
Terry Lipps, *Admin Sec*
EMP: 100
SQ FT: 4,000
SALES (est): 6.5MM **Privately Held**
SIC: 4213 Trucking, except local

(G-13476)
MID OHIO VLY BULK TRNSPT INC
16380 State Route 7 (45750-8246)
P.O. Box 734 (45750-0734)
PHONE..................740 373-2481
Fax: 740 373-2482
Mayeeta Merrill, *President*
Charles Merrill, *Corp Secy*
EMP: 30
SALES (est): 6.7MM
SALES (corp-wide): 8.6MM **Privately Held**
SIC: 4731 Freight transportation arrangement
PA: Mid-Ohio Valley Lime, Inc.
State Rt 7 S
Marietta OH 45750
740 373-1006

(G-13477)
MID-OHIO VALLEY LIME INC (PA)
State Rt 7 S (45750)
P.O. Box 734 (45750-0734)
PHONE..................740 373-1006
Fax: 740 373-7505
Mayetta Merrill, *President*
Charles Merrill, *Corp Secy*
Orville Merrill, *Vice Pres*
EMP: 32 EST: 1973
SQ FT: 10,000
SALES (est): 8.6MM **Privately Held**
WEB: www.midohiovalleylime.com
SIC: 5032 Lime, except agricultural

(G-13478)
MORRISON INC
Also Called: Honeywell Authorized Dealer
410 Colegate Dr (45750-9549)
PHONE..................740 373-5869
Fax: 740 373-6319
Kenneth Morrison, *President*
Pete Saliba, *Business Mgr*
David M Haas, *Vice Pres*
Chase Hughes, *Project Mgr*
Ben Banks, *Manager*
EMP: 35 EST: 1955
SQ FT: 6,000
SALES (est): 5.7MM **Privately Held**
WEB: www.morrisonhvac.com
SIC: 1711 5722 Refrigeration contractor; warm air heating & air conditioning contractor; ventilation & duct work contractor; electric household appliances

(G-13479)
MOTEL INVESTMENTS MARIETTA INC
Also Called: Quality Inn
700 Pike St (45750-3501)
PHONE..................740 374-8190
Thomas Dowdy, *President*
Libby Pickenn, *General Mgr*
Jane Dowdy, *Vice Pres*
Jason Dowdy, *Vice Pres*
Byron Dowdy, *Treasurer*
EMP: 32
SALES (est): 1.6MM **Privately Held**
SIC: 7011 Motels

(G-13480)
NORTHPOINT SENIOR SERVICES LLC
Also Called: Arbors At Marietta
400 N 7th St (45750-2024)
PHONE..................740 373-3597
Fax: 740 373-3597
Jill Jonas, *Manager*
Kenneth Leopold, *Director*
EMP: 117
SALES (corp-wide): 37.8MM **Privately Held**
WEB: www.extendicarehealth.com
SIC: 8051 8052 Convalescent home with continuous nursing care; intermediate care facilities
PA: Senior Northpoint Services Llc
7400 New Lagrange 100
Louisville KY 40222
502 429-8062

(G-13481)
OHIO STATE UNIVERSITY
Also Called: Ohio State University EXT
202 Davis Ave (45750-1415)
PHONE..................740 376-7431
Eric Barrett, *Ch of Bd*
EMP: 66
SALES (corp-wide): 5.5B **Privately Held**
SIC: 8732 8221 Educational research; university
PA: The Ohio State University
Student Acade Servi Bldg
Columbus OH 43210
614 292-6446

(G-13482)
ONEILL SENIOR CENTER INC (PA)
333 4th St (45750-2002)
PHONE..................740 373-3914
Fax: 740 373-8191
Jennifer Houtman, *Vice Pres*
Connie Huntsman, *Psychologist*
Terry Zdrale, *Director*
EMP: 27
SALES: 1.3MM **Privately Held**
WEB: www.oneillcenter.com
SIC: 8322 Adult day care center

(G-13483)
PAWNEE MAINTENANCE INC
101 Rathbone Rd (45750-1437)
P.O. Box 269 (45750-0269)
PHONE..................740 373-6861
Fax: 740 373-6832
Ted R Szabo, *President*
Judy Pierpont, *Manager*
EMP: 60
SQ FT: 3,000
SALES (est): 4.5MM **Privately Held**
WEB: www.pawnee.com
SIC: 1541 3272 Industrial buildings & warehouses; concrete products

(G-13484)
PEOPLES BANCORP INC (PA)
138 Putnam St (45750-2923)
P.O. Box 738 (45750-0738)
PHONE..................740 373-3155
David L Mead, *Ch of Bd*
Charles W Sulerzyski, *President*
Daniel K McGill, *Exec VP*
Kristi Beeman, *Vice Pres*
Keith Cropper, *Vice Pres*
EMP: 44
SALES: 182.1MM **Publicly Held**
WEB: www.peoplesbancorp.com
SIC: 6021 National commercial banks

(G-13485)
PEOPLES BANK (HQ)
138 Putnam St (45750-2923)
P.O. Box 738 (45750-0738)
PHONE..................740 373-3155
Fax: 740 568-2878
Chuck Sulerziski, *President*
Steve Nulter, *General Ptnr*
Thomas Greathouse, *Senior VP*
Rich Vaughan, *Senior VP*
John Autry, *Vice Pres*
EMP: 87 EST: 1914
SALES: 121.1MM
SALES (corp-wide): 182.1MM **Publicly Held**
SIC: 6035 Federal savings banks
PA: Peoples Bancorp Inc.
138 Putnam St
Marietta OH 45750
740 373-3155

(G-13486)
PEOPLES BANKING AND TRUST CO (HQ)
138 Putnam St (45750-2923)
P.O. Box 738 (45750-0738)
PHONE..................740 373-3155
Fax: 740 374-2020
Paul T Theisen, *Ch of Bd*
Wilford D Dimit, *Vice Ch Bd*
Mark Bradley, *President*
Larry E Holdren, *President*
Carroll Schneeberger, *CFO*
EMP: 225
SQ FT: 20,000
SALES: 166.9MM
SALES (corp-wide): 182.1MM **Publicly Held**
SIC: 6022 State trust companies accepting deposits, commercial
PA: Peoples Bancorp Inc.
138 Putnam St
Marietta OH 45750
740 373-3155

(G-13487)
PHYSICIANS CARE OF MARIETTA (PA)
Also Called: Physicians Care of Marrita
800 Pike St Ste 2 (45750-3507)
PHONE..................740 373-2519
Fax: 740 373-3965
Lloyd Dennis, *President*
John Riggs MD, *Treasurer*
Gregory W Balturshot MD, *Med Doctor*
Eric C Hunkele MD, *Med Doctor*
William R Kemp MD, *Med Doctor*
EMP: 75
SALES (est): 3.8MM **Privately Held**
SIC: 8011 Offices & clinics of medical doctors

(G-13488)
PIONEER PIPE INC
Also Called: Pioneer Pipe Fabricating
2021 Hanna Rd (45750-8255)
PHONE..................740 376-2400
Fax: 740 373-8964
David M Archer, *President*
Chuck Hall, *Superintendent*
Matthew Hilverding, *Corp Secy*
Arlene M Archer, *Vice Pres*
Karl Robinson, *Vice Pres*
▲ EMP: 275
SQ FT: 24,800

GEOGRAPHIC SECTION

Marietta - Washington County (G-13515)

SALES (est): 153.8MM **Privately Held**
WEB: www.pioneerpipeinc.com
SIC: 3498 1711 3443 3441 Pipe sections fabricated from purchased pipe; pipe fittings, fabricated from purchased pipe; plumbing contractors; warm air heating & air conditioning contractor; mechanical contractor; fabricated plate work (boiler shop); fabricated structural metal; blast furnaces & steel mills

(G-13489)
PITNEY BOWES INC
111 Marshall Rd (45750-1160)
PHONE..............................740 374-5535
Marcia Pawloski, *Branch Mgr*
EMP: 60
SALES (corp-wide): 3.5B **Publicly Held**
SIC: 3579 7359 Postage meters; business machine & electronic equipment rental services
PA: Pitney Bowes Inc.
  3001 Summer St Ste 3
  Stamford CT 06905
  203 356-5000

(G-13490)
POWER SYSTEM ENGINEERING INC
Also Called: Pse
2349a State Route 821 (45750-5362)
PHONE..............................740 568-9220
Douglas R Joens, *President*
Bruce Lane, *Branch Mgr*
EMP: 29
SALES (corp-wide): 9.8MM **Privately Held**
SIC: 8711 Consulting engineer
PA: Power System Engineering, Inc.
  1532 W Broadway
  Monona WI 53713
  608 268-3528

(G-13491)
PROMANCO INC
27823 State Route 7 (45750-9060)
PHONE..............................740 374-2120
Fax: 740 374-3618
Rudolph Lehman, *President*
David Hill, *Finance*
Jocelyn Adelsperger, *Info Tech Mgr*
EMP: 25 EST: 1988
SQ FT: 3,000
SALES (est): 3.2MM **Privately Held**
WEB: www.promanco.com
SIC: 1761 7349 Roofing contractor; building maintenance services

(G-13492)
R & J TRUCKING INC
14530 Sr 7 (45750)
PHONE..............................740 374-3050
Fax: 740 374-3059
Dennis Coe, *Manager*
Jeff Caltrider, *Maintence Staff*
EMP: 100 **Privately Held**
WEB: www.rjtrucking.com
SIC: 4212 4213 Dump truck haulage; heavy hauling
HQ: R & J Trucking, Inc.
  8063 Southern Blvd
  Youngstown OH 44512
  800 262-9365

(G-13493)
REHABLTTION CTR AT MRIETTA MEM
Also Called: Rohablttion Ctr At Mrtta Mmorl
401 Matthew St (45750-1635)
PHONE..............................740 374-1407
Carol McAuley, *Director*
EMP: 65
SALES (est): 1.7MM **Privately Held**
SIC: 8093 8361 Rehabilitation center, outpatient treatment; residential care

(G-13494)
REO NETWORK INC
Also Called: Century 21
203 Pike St (45750-3320)
PHONE..............................740 374-8900
Fax: 740 374-4222
Lea Ioanou, *President*
Windy Keefe, *Business Mgr*
EMP: 25

SALES (est): 1.4MM **Privately Held**
WEB: www.reonetwork.com
SIC: 6531 Real estate agent, residential

(G-13495)
RICHARDSON PRINTING CORP (PA)
Also Called: Zip Center, The-Division
201 Acme St (45750-3404)
P.O. Box 663 (45750-0663)
PHONE..............................740 373-5362
Fax: 740 373-8713
Dennis E Valentine, *President*
Candace Schwab, *Manager*
Robert Richardson Jr, *Shareholder*
Charles E Schwab, *Admin Sec*
▲ EMP: 60
SQ FT: 100,000
SALES (est): 8.5MM **Privately Held**
WEB: www.rpcprint.com
SIC: 2752 7389 Commercial printing, lithographic; commercial printing, offset; photo-offset printing; mailing & messenger services

(G-13496)
SCHWENDEMAN AGENCY INC (PA)
Also Called: Schwendeman Sigafoos Agcy
109 Putnam St (45750-2924)
PHONE..............................740 373-6793
Fax: 740 376-2979
Mark Schewndeman, *President*
Angie Lawrence, *General Mgr*
Larry Schewendeman, *Vice Pres*
Michael Schwendeman, *Vice Pres*
EMP: 30 EST: 1938
SQ FT: 5,000
SALES (est): 9.8MM **Privately Held**
WEB: www.schwendeman.com
SIC: 6411 Insurance agents

(G-13497)
SELBY GENERAL HOSPITAL
1338 Colegate Dr (45750-1329)
PHONE..............................740 568-2037
Fax: 740 568-2231
Steve Smith, *Branch Mgr*
EMP: 139
SALES (corp-wide): 48.5MM **Privately Held**
SIC: 8049 Physical therapist
PA: Selby General Hospital
  1106 Colegate Dr
  Marietta OH 45750
  740 568-2000

(G-13498)
SELBY GENERAL HOSPITAL (PA)
1106 Colegate Dr (45750-1323)
PHONE..............................740 568-2000
Fax: 740 568-2089
Thomas Tucker, *Ch of Bd*
Steve Smith, *President*
Scott Cantley, *President*
Eric Young, *CFO*
Nathan Hood, *Controller*
EMP: 250
SQ FT: 65,000
SALES: 48.5MM **Privately Held**
WEB: www.selbygeneralhospital.com
SIC: 8062 Hospital, affiliated with AMA residency

(G-13499)
SHIV HOTELS LLC
700 Pike St (45750-3501)
PHONE..............................740 374-8190
Mahesh Nichani,
EMP: 30
SALES: 3MM **Privately Held**
SIC: 7011 Hotels

(G-13500)
SMITH BROTHERS ERECTION INC
101 Industry Rd (45750-9355)
PHONE..............................740 373-3575
Robert A Gribben Jr, *President*
Robert A Gribben III, *Director*
EMP: 45 EST: 2011
SALES: 1.2MM **Privately Held**
SIC: 1791 3449 Structural steel erection; bars, concrete reinforcing; fabricated steel

(G-13501)
SPAGNAS
301 Gilman Ave (45750)
PHONE..............................740 376-9245
Fax: 740 373-2275
Kevin Whitby, *Owner*
EMP: 25
SALES (est): 495.7K **Privately Held**
SIC: 5812 7299 Italian restaurant; banquet hall facilities

(G-13502)
STRATAGRAPH NE INC
116 Ellsworth Ave (45750-8607)
P.O. Box 59, Reno (45773-0059)
PHONE..............................740 373-3091
Fax: 740 373-3091
Walt Teer, *President*
EMP: 32
SQ FT: 2,400
SALES: 700K **Privately Held**
SIC: 1389 1381 Oil field services; drilling oil & gas wells

(G-13503)
THOMAS L MILLER
Also Called: Miller Engineering
111 Strecker Hl (45750-1657)
PHONE..............................740 374-3041
Thomas L Miller, *Owner*
EMP: 77
SALES (est): 3MM **Privately Held**
SIC: 8711 Consulting engineer

(G-13504)
THOMSONS LANDSCAPING
26130 State Route 7 (45750-5113)
PHONE..............................740 374-9353
Fax: 740 374-3863
Russell Thomson, *Mng Member*
EMP: 25 EST: 1979
SQ FT: 2,500
SALES (est): 283.7K **Privately Held**
SIC: 0782 5261 Landscape contractors; lawn & garden supplies

(G-13505)
TRIAD ENERGY CORPORATION
125 Putnam St (45750-2936)
PHONE..............................740 374-2940
Kean Weaver, *President*
James R Bryden, *Vice Pres*
Brent Powell, *Safety Mgr*
Kim Arnold, *Human Res Mgr*
EMP: 26
SALES (est): 3.3MM **Privately Held**
SIC: 2992 1382 Lubricating oils & greases; oil & gas exploration services

(G-13506)
TRIAD OIL & GAS ENGINEERING
27724 State Route 7 (45750-5147)
PHONE..............................740 374-2940
Kean Weaver, *President*
Richard Farrell, *Vice Pres*
EMP: 100
SQ FT: 7,800
SALES (est): 4.1MM **Privately Held**
SIC: 8742 Industry specialist consultants

(G-13507)
TRIAD PLL
27724 State Route 7 (45750-5147)
PHONE..............................740 374-2940
James R Briden, *Partner*
EMP: 35
SALES (est): 763.3K **Privately Held**
SIC: 6531 Real estate leasing & rentals

(G-13508)
TWIN COMM INC
Also Called: Telepage Communication Systems
2349 State Route 821 (45750-5362)
PHONE..............................740 774-4701
Fax: 740 568-9199
Bruce Lane, *President*
EMP: 31
SQ FT: 6,000
SALES (est): 3.6MM **Privately Held**
WEB: www.telepagepaging.com
SIC: 4812 7389 5999 Radio pager (beeper) communication services; telephone answering service; telephone equipment & systems

(G-13509)
UBS FINANCIAL SERVICES INC
324 3rd St (45750-2901)
PHONE..............................740 336-7823
EMP: 43
SALES (corp-wide): 28B **Privately Held**
SIC: 7389 Financial services
HQ: Ubs Financial Services Inc.
  1285 Ave Of The Americas
  New York NY 10019
  212 713-2000

(G-13510)
UNITED CHURCH HOMES INC
Also Called: Harmer Place
401 Harmar St (45750-2732)
PHONE..............................740 376-5600
Fax: 740 376-5617
Kenneth Daniel, *CEO*
James Henry, *Ch of Bd*
Patti Klingel, *Director*
EMP: 72
SALES: 7.7MM **Privately Held**
SIC: 8361 8051 Home for the aged; skilled nursing care facilities

(G-13511)
UNITED PARCEL SERVICE INC OH
Also Called: UPS
105 Industry Rd (45750-9355)
PHONE..............................740 373-0772
EMP: 158
SALES (corp-wide): 65.8B **Publicly Held**
SIC: 4215 Package delivery, vehicular
HQ: United Parcel Service, Inc. (Oh)
  55 Glenlake Pkwy
  Atlanta GA 30328
  404 828-6000

(G-13512)
VADAKIN INC
110 Industry Rd (45750-9355)
P.O. Box 565 (45750-0565)
PHONE..............................740 373-7518
Fax: 740 373-2063
Sara Hooper, *President*
Mark Whiteley, *Vice Pres*
EMP: 50
SQ FT: 16,000
SALES (est): 2.7MM **Privately Held**
WEB: www.vadakininc.com
SIC: 7349 Cleaning service, industrial or commercial

(G-13513)
VALLEY HOSPITALITY INC
Also Called: Holiday Inn
701 Pike St (45750-3502)
PHONE..............................740 374-9660
Fax: 740 373-1762
Andy Benson, *President*
Rita H Stephan, *Admin Sec*
EMP: 40
SQ FT: 50,000
SALES (est): 1.6MM **Privately Held**
SIC: 7011 5812 5813 7299 Hotels; family restaurants; bars & lounges; banquet hall facilities

(G-13514)
VETERANS HEALTH ADMINISTRATION
Also Called: Marietta Community Based
418 Colegate Dr (45750-9549)
PHONE..............................740 568 0412
Fax: 740 568-0413
Dianna Dowler, *Manager*
EMP: 264 **Publicly Held**
WEB: www.veterans-ru.org
SIC: 8011 9451 Clinic, operated by physicians; psychiatric clinic;
HQ: Veterans Health Administration
  810 Vermont Ave Nw
  Washington DC 20420

(G-13515)
VIKING FABRICATORS INC
2021 Hanna Rd (45750-8255)
PHONE..............................740 374-5246
Fax: 740 374-5232
David M Archer, *President*
James S Huggins, *Principal*
Matthew Hilverding, *Corp Secy*
Arlene M Archer, *Vice Pres*

Marietta - Washington County (G-13516)

GEOGRAPHIC SECTION

EMP: 25
SQ FT: 20,000
SALES (est): 5.1MM **Privately Held**
SIC: 3441 7692 3446 3443 Fabricated structural metal; welding repair; architectural metalwork; fabricated plate work (boiler shop)

(G-13516)
WARREN BROS & SONS INC (PA)
Also Called: Warrens IGA
108b S 7th St (45750-3338)
PHONE..................740 373-1430
Fax: 740 373-8043
Kin Brewer, *President*
Lisa G Brewer, *Admin Sec*
EMP: 50
SALES (est): 5MM **Privately Held**
SIC: 8721 Accounting, auditing & bookkeeping

(G-13517)
WARREN TWNSHIP VLNTR FIRE DEPT
17305 State Route 550 (45750-8315)
PHONE..................740 373-2424
Jeff Knowlton, *Principal*
Mark Wile, *Manager*
EMP: 30
SALES (est): 1.8MM **Privately Held**
SIC: 8621 Professional membership organizations

(G-13518)
WASCO INC (PA)
340 Muskingum Dr (45750-1435)
PHONE..................740 373-3418
Fax: 740 373-3560
Joseph Faires, *CEO*
Tara Parmiter, *CFO*
Tara Meeks, *Manager*
EMP: 28
SQ FT: 22,000
SALES: 3.6MM **Privately Held**
SIC: 8331 Sheltered workshop; job training services

(G-13519)
WAYNE STREET DEVELOPMENT LLC
424 2nd St (45750-2115)
PHONE..................740 373-5455
Abraham Sellers, *Principal*
EMP: 30
SALES (est): 175.3K **Privately Held**
SIC: 8741 Management services

(G-13520)
YOUNG MENS CHRISTIAN ASSN
Also Called: MARIETTA FAMILY YMCA
300 N 7th St (45750-2243)
PHONE..................740 373-2250
Fax: 740 373-0512
Roger Pitasky, *President*
Robert Ferguson, *Vice Pres*
Dennis Cooke, *Treasurer*
Ruth Broughton, *Finance Mgr*
Suzy Zumwalde, *Exec Dir*
EMP: 65
SQ FT: 35,000
SALES: 876.6K **Privately Held**
WEB: www.mariettaymca.org
SIC: 8641 8351 Recreation association; child day care services

(G-13521)
ZIDE SPORT SHOP OF OHIO INC (PA)
Also Called: Zide Screen Printing
253 2nd St (45750-2918)
PHONE..................740 373-6446
Rodney Zide, *President*
Anita Zide, *Treasurer*
Selena Schackleford, *Manager*
John Zide, *Shareholder*
EMP: 60
SQ FT: 19,000
SALES (est): 7.4MM **Privately Held**
SIC: 5941 5091 Bicycle & bicycle parts; golf goods & equipment; skiing equipment; sporting & recreation goods

Marion
Marion County

(G-13522)
ACCENTCARE HOME HEALTH CAL INC
Also Called: Sunplus Home Health - Marion
458 E Center St (43302-4245)
PHONE..................740 387-4568
Fax: 740 387-4728
Linda Davis, *Manager*
EMP: 108
SALES (corp-wide): 379.9MM **Privately Held**
WEB: www.dhsi.com
SIC: 8082 7361 Home health care services; nurses' registry
HQ: Accentcare Home Health Of California, Inc.
17855 Dallas Pkwy
Dallas TX 75287

(G-13523)
AQUA TECH ENVMTL LABS INC (PA)
Also Called: Atel
1776 Marion Waldo Rd (43302-7428)
PHONE..................740 389-5991
Fax: 740 389-1481
Paul Crerar, *President*
Rhonda Morris, *Manager*
EMP: 29
SQ FT: 5,000
SALES (est): 4.7MM **Privately Held**
WEB: www.atel2.com
SIC: 8734 Hazardous waste testing

(G-13524)
BIO-MDICAL APPLICATIONS RI INC
Also Called: Fresenius Medical Care
1730 Marion Waldo Rd (43302-7428)
PHONE..................740 389-4111
EMP: 25
SALES (corp-wide): 20.9B **Privately Held**
SIC: 8092 8011 Kidney dialysis centers; offices & clinics of medical doctors
HQ: Bio-Medical Applications Of Rhode Island, Inc.
920 Winter St Ste A
Waltham MA 02451
781 699-9000

(G-13525)
BOISE CASCADE COMPANY
3007 Harding Hwy E (43302-2575)
PHONE..................740 382-6766
Fax: 740 382-6702
Jeff Wiska, *Branch Mgr*
EMP: 26
SALES (corp-wide): 4.4B **Publicly Held**
SIC: 5031 Building materials, exterior; building materials, interior; composite board products, woodboard; lumber: rough, dressed & finished
PA: Boise Cascade Company
1111 W Jefferson St # 300
Boise ID 83702
208 384-6161

(G-13526)
BRIDGES TO INDEPENDENCE INC
117 N Greenwood St Ste 2 (43302-3129)
PHONE..................740 375-5533
Chris Ritchie, *Manager*
Tracy Baker, *Manager*
EMP: 25
SALES (corp-wide): 4.7MM **Privately Held**
WEB: www.bridgestoindependence.com
SIC: 8051 Mental retardation hospital
PA: Bridges To Independence Inc
61 W William St
Delaware OH 43015
740 362-1996

(G-13527)
BURNS & SCALO ROOFING CO INC
2181 Innovation Dr # 101 (43302-8254)
PHONE..................740 383-4639
Jack Scalo, *Owner*
Stephen L Butcher, *Branch Mgr*
EMP: 30
SALES (corp-wide): 33.1MM **Privately Held**
SIC: 1761 Roofing contractor
PA: Burns & Scalo Roofing Company, Inc.
22 Rutgers Rd Ste 200
Pittsburgh PA 15205
412 928-3060

(G-13528)
CARLSON HOTELS LTD PARTNERSHIP
Also Called: Marion Country Inn & Suites
2091 Marion Mt Gilead Rd (43302-8990)
PHONE..................740 386-5451
Yantrini Patel, *Branch Mgr*
EMP: 60
SALES (corp-wide): 3.9B **Privately Held**
SIC: 7011 Hotels & motels
HQ: Carlson Hotels Limited Partnership
Carlson Parkway 701 Twr St Carlson Parkw
Minneapolis MN 55459
763 212-1000

(G-13529)
CENTER STREET CMNTY CLINIC INC
136 W Center St (43302-3704)
PHONE..................740 751-6380
Cliff Edwards, *CEO*
EMP: 36
SALES: 3.8MM **Privately Held**
SIC: 8059 Personal care home, with health care

(G-13530)
CIRCLE T LOGISTICS INC
617 W Center St Ste 26 (43302-3569)
P.O. Box 357 (43301-0357)
PHONE..................740 262-5096
Mark Lyon, *President*
Michelle Crast, *Manager*
EMP: 45
SQ FT: 11,000
SALES (est): 4.9MM **Privately Held**
SIC: 4214 Local trucking with storage

(G-13531)
CITY OF MARION
Also Called: Sanitation & Garage Services
981 W Center St (43302-3463)
PHONE..................740 382-1479
Bob Moats, *Manager*
Brad Norton, *IT/INT Sup*
EMP: 70 **Privately Held**
WEB: www.marionohio.org
SIC: 4212 8111 9111 Garbage collection & transport, no disposal; general practice attorney, lawyer; mayors' offices
PA: City Of Marion
233 W Center St
Marion OH 43302
740 387-2020

(G-13532)
COUNTY OF MARION
Also Called: Child Support Services
620 Leader St (43302-2230)
PHONE..................740 387-6688
Roxanne Somerlot, *Director*
EMP: 40 **Privately Held**
WEB: www.co.marion.oh.us
SIC: 8322 9111 Public welfare center; county supervisors' & executives' offices
PA: County Of Marion
222 W Center St Ste A1031
Marion OH 43302
740 223-4030

(G-13533)
COUNTY OF MARION
Also Called: East Lawn Manor
1422 Mount Vernon Ave (43302-5629)
PHONE..................740 389-4624
Fax: 740 389-1036
Barbara Balsley, *Administration*
EMP: 100
SQ FT: 550,000 **Privately Held**
WEB: www.co.marion.oh.us
SIC: 8051 Skilled nursing care facilities

PA: County Of Marion
222 W Center St Ste A1031
Marion OH 43302
740 223-4030

(G-13534)
COUNTY OF MARION
Also Called: Wadell Village Children Svcs
1680 Marion Waldo Rd (43302-7426)
PHONE..................740 389-2317
Jacqueline Ringer, *Director*
Eric Bush, *Director*
EMP: 40 **Privately Held**
WEB: www.co.marion.oh.us
SIC: 8322 9111 Child related social services; county supervisors' & executives' offices
PA: County Of Marion
222 W Center St Ste A1031
Marion OH 43302
740 223-4030

(G-13535)
COUNTY OF MARION
Also Called: Board of Mrdd
2387 Harding Hwy E (43302-8529)
PHONE..................740 387-1035
Cheryl Plaster, *Supervisor*
EMP: 95 **Privately Held**
WEB: www.co.marion.oh.us
SIC: 9111 8331 County supervisors' & executives' offices; job training & vocational rehabilitation services
PA: County Of Marion
222 W Center St Ste A1031
Marion OH 43302
740 223-4030

(G-13536)
COUNTY OF MARION
Also Called: Department of Transportation
1775 Mrn Williamsprt Rd E (43302-8512)
PHONE..................740 382-0624
Bruce Mays, *Manager*
EMP: 30 **Privately Held**
WEB: www.co.marion.oh.us
SIC: 8742 Maintenance management consultant; food & beverage consultant
PA: County Of Marion
222 W Center St Ste A1031
Marion OH 43302
740 223-4030

(G-13537)
DEARTH MANAGEMENT COMPANY
Also Called: Morning View Care Center
677 Marion Cardington Rd (43302-7317)
P.O. Box 656 (43301-0656)
PHONE..................740 389-1214
Fax: 740 389-2074
Dixie Waite, *Administration*
EMP: 25
SALES (corp-wide): 11.7MM **Privately Held**
WEB: www.schoenbrunnhealthcare.com
SIC: 8052 8051 Personal care facility; skilled nursing care facilities
PA: Dearth Management Company
134 Northwoods Blvd Ste C
Columbus OH 43235
614 847-1070

(G-13538)
EPWORTH PRESCHOOL AND DAYCARE
Also Called: Epworth United Methodist Ch
249 E Center St (43302-3814)
PHONE..................740 387-1062
Fax: 740 387-1689
Heder Mawler, *Director*
Robin Rick, *Director*
EMP: 40
SALES (est): 847.9K **Privately Held**
SIC: 8661 8351 Miscellaneous denomination church; child day care services

(G-13539)
EPWORTH UNITED METHODIST CH
249 E Center St (43302-3873)
PHONE..................740 387-1062
Jim Hering Jr, *Minister*
Max L Williams, *Pastor*
Robin Rick, *Director*

GEOGRAPHIC SECTION

Marion - Marion County (G-13563)

Marlene La Shat, *Assoc Pastor*
EMP: 86
SALES (est): 2.2MM **Privately Held**
SIC: 8661 8351 Methodist Church; group day care center; preschool center

(G-13540)
FREDERICK C SMITH CLINIC INC (PA)
Also Called: Marion Area Health Center
1040 Delaware Ave (43302-6416)
PHONE..................740 383-7000
Fax: 740 383-8084
Dalsukh Madia, *President*
Michael P Coyne, *Principal*
Ronald J Waldheger, *Principal*
J C Garvin MD, *Vice Pres*
Sanjay K Vora MD, *Med Doctor*
EMP: 400
SQ FT: 100,000
SALES (est): 32.7MM **Privately Held**
WEB: www.marionareahealth.com
SIC: 8011 Physicians' office, including specialists

(G-13541)
GRAHAM INVESTMENT CO (PA)
Also Called: Casod Industrial Properties
3007 Harding Hwy E # 203 (43302-2575)
PHONE..................740 382-0902
Ted Graham, *President*
Linda K West, *Vice Pres*
Frank Shelby, *Info Tech Mgr*
EMP: 100 **EST:** 1969
SALES (est): 6.7MM **Privately Held**
WEB: www.micwarehouse.com
SIC: 6512 4225 Commercial & industrial building operation; general warehousing & storage

(G-13542)
HEALTH & HM CARE CONCEPTS INC
Also Called: Health & Homecare Concepts
353 S State St (43302-5019)
PHONE..................740 383-4968
Fax: 740 382-1206
Thomas Veith, *President*
EMP: 45
SALES: 1.2MM **Privately Held**
SIC: 7361 Nurses' registry

(G-13543)
HOLBROOK & MANTER (PA)
181 E Center St (43302-3813)
P.O. Box 437 (43301-0437)
PHONE..................740 387-8620
Fax: 740 383-4676
Carolyn Morgan, *President*
Brad Idge, *Partner*
Thomas Kalb, *Partner*
Bradley Ridge, *CPA*
Mike Kirch, *Director*
EMP: 30
SQ FT: 6,270
SALES (est): 3.8MM **Privately Held**
SIC: 8721 Certified public accountant

(G-13544)
JPMORGAN CHASE BANK NAT ASSN
165 W Center St (43302-3742)
PHONE..................740 382-7362
Tracie Wilson, *Branch Mgr*
EMP: 34
SALES (corp-wide): 99.6B **Publicly Held**
SIC: 6029 Commercial banks
HQ: Jpmorgan Chase Bank, National Association
1111 Polaris Pkwy
Columbus OH 43240
614 436-3055

(G-13545)
KINDRED HEALTHCARE OPER INC
Also Called: Kindred Nrsing Rhbltton- Cmnty
175 Community Dr (43302-6487)
PHONE..................740 387-7537
Hollis Missi, *Accountant*
Lisa Graham, *Office Mgr*
Kyle H Oogendoorn, *Med Doctor*
Sue Fretz, *Exec Dir*
Van A Ngo, *Director*
EMP: 112

SQ FT: 28,000
SALES (corp-wide): 6B **Publicly Held**
WEB: www.salemhaven.com
SIC: 8051 8093 8049 Skilled nursing care facilities; rehabilitation center, outpatient treatment; physical therapist
HQ: Kindred Healthcare Operating, Inc.
680 S 4th St
Louisville KY 40202
502 596-7300

(G-13546)
KINGSTON HEALTHCARE COMPANY
Also Called: Kingston Residence of Marion
464 James Way Ofc (43302-7817)
PHONE..................740 389-2311
Bob Goyer, *Pub Rel Dir*
Carrie Hutchman, *Branch Mgr*
Tami Doyle, *Director*
EMP: 80
SQ FT: 47,452
SALES (corp-wide): 95.5MM **Privately Held**
WEB: www.kingstonhealthcare.com
SIC: 8361 Home for the aged
PA: Kingston Healthcare Company
1 Seagate Ste 1960
Toledo OH 43604
419 247-2880

(G-13547)
KNIGHTS OF COLUMBUS
1242 E Center St (43302-4406)
PHONE..................740 382-3671
Gray Hubbard, *President*
EMP: 60
SALES (corp-wide): 2.2B **Privately Held**
WEB: www.kofc.org
SIC: 8641 Fraternal associations
PA: Knights Of Columbus
1 Columbus Plz Ste 1700
New Haven CT 06510
203 752-4000

(G-13548)
LEVERING MANAGEMENT INC
Also Called: Marion Manor Nursing Home
195 Executive Dr (43302-6343)
PHONE..................740 387-9545
Fax: 740 382-9545
William Dunn, *Administration*
EMP: 90
SALES (corp-wide): 32.8MM **Privately Held**
SIC: 8741 8051 Management services; skilled nursing care facilities
PA: Levering Management, Inc.
201 N Main St
Mount Vernon OH 43050
740 397-3897

(G-13549)
LOWES HOME CENTERS LLC
1840 Marion Mt Gilead Rd (43302-5826)
PHONE..................740 389-9737
Fax: 740 389-3727
Rhonda Walker, *Manager*
EMP: 150
SALES (corp-wide): 68.6B **Publicly Held**
SIC: 5211 5031 5722 5064 Home centers; building materials, exterior; building materials, interior; household appliance stores; electrical appliances, television & radio
HQ: Lowe's Home Centers, Llc
1605 Curtis Bridge Rd
Wilkesboro NC 28697
336 658-4000

(G-13550)
MAPLEWOOD NURSING CENTER INC
409 Bellefontaine Ave (43302-4811)
PHONE..................740 383-2126
Fax: 740 382-3814
Paul A Granger, *President*
Mohammad Khan, *Director*
EMP: 50
SQ FT: 15,000
SALES (est): 1.8MM **Privately Held**
SIC: 8051 Convalescent home with continuous nursing care

(G-13551)
MARCA INDUSTRIES INC
2387 Harding Hwy E (43302-8531)
PHONE..................740 387-1035
Fax: 740 387-1159
Liz Owens, *Director*
EMP: 39 **EST:** 1967
SQ FT: 50,000
SALES: 658.2K **Privately Held**
SIC: 8331 Sheltered workshop

(G-13552)
MARCY INDUSTRIES COMPANY LLC
1836 Likens Rd (43302-8652)
PHONE..................740 943-2343
Fax: 740 943-3636
Dan Shew, *CEO*
Merlin Reimer, *General Mgr*
EMP: 34 **EST:** 2009
SALES (est): 6.8MM **Privately Held**
SIC: 5084 Industrial machinery & equipment

(G-13553)
MARION AREA COUNSELING CTR (PA)
320 Executive Dr (43302-6373)
PHONE..................740 387-5210
Caryn Knapp, *Human Res Mgr*
Linda Harris, *Manager*
Beverly Young, *Director*
EMP: 109
SQ FT: 2,500
SALES: 5MM **Privately Held**
WEB: www.maccsite.com
SIC: 8322 8093 General counseling services; specialty outpatient clinics

(G-13554)
MARION CNTY BD DEV DSABILITIES
Also Called: Marion County Board of Mr Dd
2387 Harding Hwy E (43302-8529)
PHONE..................740 387-1035
Lee Wedemeyer, *Superintendent*
Julie Cummins, *Director*
Judy Enders, *Director*
Jessica Trainer, *Executive*
EMP: 95 **EST:** 2001
SALES (est): 3.3MM **Privately Held**
SIC: 8331 Community service employment training program

(G-13555)
MARION COUNTRY CLUB COMPANY
Also Called: Marion Country Club, The
2415 Crissinger Rd (43302-8231)
PHONE..................740 387-0974
Fax: 740 387-0540
Bill Maybury, *General Mgr*
EMP: 25
SQ FT: 30,000
SALES (est): 940K **Privately Held**
SIC: 7997 5812 Country club, membership; golf club, membership; swimming club, membership; tennis club, membership; eating places

(G-13556)
MARION FAMILY YMCA
645 Barks Rd E (43302-6517)
PHONE..................740 725-9622
Bob Houston, *President*
Evan Shanley, *Director*
Jill Grimes, *Telecom Exec*
EMP: 60
SALES: 3.5MM **Privately Held**
WEB: www.marionymca.com
SIC: 8322 8641 Youth center; youth organizations

(G-13557)
MARION GEN SOCIAL WORK DEPT
Also Called: Marion General Hospital
1000 Mckinley Park Dr (43302-6399)
PHONE..................740 383-8788
Mary Beth Hapfield, *Director*
EMP: 25
SALES (est): 409.5K **Privately Held**
SIC: 8062 General medical & surgical hospitals

(G-13558)
MARION GENERAL HOSP HM HLTH
278 Barks Rd W (43302-7367)
PHONE..................740 383-8770
Fax: 614 383-8764
Cindy Schifer, *Principal*
Kathy Flickinger, *Manager*
Dick Martin, *Security Dir*
EMP: 31
SALES (est): 811.9K **Privately Held**
SIC: 8082 Home health care services

(G-13559)
MARION GENERAL HOSPITAL INC (HQ)
1000 Mckinley Park Dr (43302-6397)
PHONE..................740 383-8400
Fax: 740 382-2978
John Sanders, *President*
Mitch Chambers, *Plant Mgr*
Christine McCoy, *Finance Mgr*
Linda Alesi, *Human Res Dir*
Kim Frank, *Benefits Mgr*
EMP: 61 **EST:** 1955
SQ FT: 247,000
SALES: 186.9MM
SALES (corp-wide): 3.7B **Privately Held**
WEB: www.mariongeneral.com
SIC: 8062 Hospital, AMA approved residency
PA: Ohiohealth Corporation
180 E Broad St
Columbus OH 43215
614 788-8860

(G-13560)
MARION GOODWILL INDUSTRIES (PA)
340 W Fairground St (43302-1728)
PHONE..................740 387-7023
Fax: 614 382-0420
Ryan Payton, *Human Resources*
Sandra Pyles, *Manager*
Christina Wiggers, *Manager*
Bob Jordan, *Exec Dir*
EMP: 25
SQ FT: 17,500
SALES: 16.6MM **Privately Held**
SIC: 5932 8331 Furniture, secondhand; sheltered workshop

(G-13561)
MARION HEAD START CENTER
2387 Harding Hwy E (43302-8529)
PHONE..................740 382-6858
Andrew Devany, *CFO*
Jennifer Ishida, *Director*
EMP: 27
SALES (est): 300.9K **Privately Held**
SIC: 8351 Head start center, except in conjunction with school

(G-13562)
MARION MANOR
195 Executive Dr (43302-6343)
PHONE..................740 387-9545
L Bruce Levering, *President*
William L Dunn, *Treasurer*
EMP: 75
SQ FT: 30,000
SALES (est): 2.6MM **Privately Held**
SIC: 8059 8051 Nursing home, except skilled & intermediate care facility; convalescent home; skilled nursing care facilities

(G-13563)
MATHEWS DODGE CHRYSLER JEEP
1866 Marion Waldo Rd (43302-7430)
PHONE..................740 389-2341
Thurman Matthews, *President*
David Columber, *Project Mgr*
EMP: 30
SALES: 14MM **Privately Held**
SIC: 5511 7538 7515 Automobiles, new & used; general automotive repair shops; passenger car leasing

---

(PA)=Parent Co (HQ)=Headquarters (DH)=Div Headquarters
✪ = New Business established in last 2 years

(G-13564)
MATHEWS KENNEDY FORD L-M INC (PA)
Also Called: Mathews Auto Group
1155 Delaware Ave (43302-6417)
PHONE...................740 387-3673
Fax: 614 383-2192
Thurman R Mathews, *President*
Jean Mitchell, *Corp Secy*
Val Goodrich, *Sales Staff*
Thomas Mathews,
EMP: 100
SQ FT: 35,000
SALES (est): 41.9MM **Privately Held**
WEB: www.mathewsautogroup.com
SIC: 5511 7538 7532 7515 Automobiles, new & used; general automotive repair shops; top & body repair & paint shops; passenger car leasing

(G-13565)
MC DANIEL MOTOR CO (INC)
1111 Mount Vernon Ave (43302-5699)
PHONE...................740 389-2355
Fax: 740 389-6646
Michael Mc Daniel, *President*
James P Waddell, *Exec VP*
Matt Reynolds, *Info Tech Dir*
EMP: 44
SQ FT: 60,000
SALES (est): 13.1MM **Privately Held**
WEB: www.mcdanieltoyota.com
SIC: 5511 7515 Automobiles, new & used; passenger car leasing

(G-13566)
MCCOY LANDSCAPE SERVICES INC
2391 Likens Rd (43302-8541)
PHONE...................740 375-2730
Matt McCoy, *President*
Mark McCoy, *Vice Pres*
Erick Klenzman, *Controller*
James Larkins, *Branch Mgr*
EMP: 35
SALES (est): 1.5MM **Privately Held**
WEB: www.mccoylandscape.com
SIC: 0782 5999 Landscape contractors; Christmas lights & decorations

(G-13567)
NATIONAL SERVICE INFORMATION
145 Baker St (43302-4111)
P.O. Box 6293 (43301-6293)
PHONE...................740 387-6806
Fax: 740 382-1256
Cozy Lee Dixon, *President*
Kim Dixon, *Admin Sec*
EMP: 25
SQ FT: 6,700
SALES (est): 1.8MM **Privately Held**
WEB: www.nsii.net
SIC: 7338 8111 8999 Court reporting service; legal services; information bureau

(G-13568)
NEW HORIZONS SURGERY CENTER
1167 Independence Ave (43302-6360)
PHONE...................740 375-5854
Brian Hempstead, *CEO*
EMP: 26
SALES (est): 3.2MM **Privately Held**
SIC: 8011 General & family practice, physician/surgeon

(G-13569)
OHIO HRTLAND CMNTY ACTION COMM (PA)
372 E Center St (43302-4126)
PHONE...................740 387-1039
James Lavelle, *CFO*
Jennifer Villard, *CFO*
Philip Richardson, *Manager*
Andrew J Devany, *Exec Dir*
Bonita Howard, *Director*
EMP: 45
SALES: 10MM **Privately Held**
SIC: 8399 Community action agency

(G-13570)
OHIO-AMERICAN WATER CO INC (HQ)
Also Called: Marion District
365 E Center St (43302-4155)
PHONE...................740 382-3993
Fax: 740 387-1195
John E Eckart, *President*
T Wilkes Coleman, *Vice Pres*
Dwayne D Cole, *VP Opers*
Christine J Doron, *Treasurer*
Deb Rapert, *Human Res Mgr*
EMP: 45
SQ FT: 8,500
SALES (est): 25.3MM
SALES (corp-wide): 3.3B **Publicly Held**
SIC: 4941 Water supply
PA: American Water Works Company, Inc.
1025 Laurel Oak Rd
Voorhees NJ 08043
856 346-8200

(G-13571)
ORDER OF SYMPOSIARCHS AMERICA
704 Vernon Heights Blvd (43302-5380)
PHONE...................740 387-9713
James Greetham, *Treasurer*
EMP: 30
SALES (est): 940K **Privately Held**
SIC: 8641 Civic associations

(G-13572)
PERSISTENT SYSTEMS INC
145 Baker St (43302-4111)
PHONE...................727 786-0379
EMP: 33
SALES (corp-wide): 258.9MM **Privately Held**
SIC: 7371 Computer software development
HQ: Persistent Systems Inc.
2055 Laurelwood Rd # 210
Santa Clara CA 95054
408 216-7010

(G-13573)
QUALITY MASONRY COMPANY INC
Also Called: Quality Maintenance Company
1001 S Prospect St # 101 (43302-6289)
PHONE...................740 387-6720
William Bowers, *President*
Justin Bowers, *General Mgr*
Bret Bowers, *Vice Pres*
Jackie Waters, *Manager*
EMP: 30 **EST:** 1973
SQ FT: 2,000
SALES: 4.9MM **Privately Held**
WEB: www.qualitymasonryco.com
SIC: 1542 Commercial & office buildings, renovation & repair

(G-13574)
REAL ESTATE SHOWCASE
731 E Center St (43302-4346)
PHONE...................740 389-2000
Fax: 740 389-2004
Rick R Roe, *CEO*
Brenda Ulbrich-Roe, *Financial Exec*
EMP: 30
SALES (est): 1.7MM **Privately Held**
SIC: 6531 Real estate brokers & agents

(G-13575)
RESIDENTIAL HM ASSN OF MARION (PA)
Also Called: Rham
205 W Center St Ste 100 (43302-3700)
PHONE...................740 387-9999
Fax: 740 387-7639
Dottie N Bowes, *Human Res Dir*
Shirley Russell, *Director*
EMP: 106
SALES: 3.1MM **Privately Held**
SIC: 8742 8361 6531 Management consulting services; home for the mentally retarded; real estate agents & managers

(G-13576)
RIVER ROCK REHABILITATION
990 S Prospect St Ste 4 (43302-6283)
PHONE...................740 382-4035
Fax: 740 387-2922
William Reinbolt, *CEO*
Timothy Burkam, *COO*
EMP: 50
SALES (est): 1.9MM **Privately Held**
SIC: 8322 Rehabilitation services

(G-13577)
RK FAMILY INC
233 America Blvd (43302-7805)
PHONE...................740 389-2674
Tim Lodes, *Principal*
EMP: 246
SALES (corp-wide): 1.2B **Privately Held**
SIC: 5099 Firearms & ammunition, except sporting
PA: Rk Family, Inc.
4216 Dewitt Ave
Mattoon IL 61938
217 235-7102

(G-13578)
SACK N SAVE INC
Also Called: King Saver
725 Richmond Ave (43302-1935)
PHONE...................740 382-2464
David Fass, *Manager*
EMP: 30 **Privately Held**
SIC: 5411 6099 Grocery stores, chain; money order issuance
HQ: Sack 'n Save, Inc.
317 W Main Cross St
Findlay OH 45840
419 422-8090

(G-13579)
SIKA CORPORATION
1682 Mrn Williamsprt Rd E (43302-8694)
PHONE...................740 387-9224
Fax: 740 382-6454
Todd Petrie, *VP Opers*
Ray Gear, *Purch Mgr*
Scott Joehlin, *Engineer*
Doug White, *Branch Mgr*
EMP: 62
SALES (corp-wide): 5.6B **Privately Held**
WEB: www.sikacorp.com
SIC: 2899 5169 3566 Concrete curing & hardening compounds; concrete additives; speed changers, drives & gears
HQ: Sika Corporation
201 Polito Ave
Lyndhurst NJ 07071
201 933-8800

(G-13580)
SMITHFOODS ORRVILLE INC
135 Sara Ave (43302-4542)
PHONE...................740 389-4643
Mike Miley, *Manager*
EMP: 25
SALES (corp-wide): 62.3MM **Privately Held**
WEB: www.smithdairy.com
SIC: 5451 5142 0241 Dairy products stores; packaged frozen goods; milk production
HQ: Smithfoods Orrville Inc.
1381 Dairy Ln
Orrville OH 44667
330 683-8710

(G-13581)
STOFCHECK AMBULANCE INC
Also Called: Stofcheck Ambulance Service
314 W Center St (43302-3614)
PHONE...................740 383-2787
Edward Stofcheck Jr, *President*
Barbara Stofcheck, *Vice Pres*
EMP: 200
SALES (est): 3.1MM **Privately Held**
SIC: 4119 Ambulance service

(G-13582)
SUNBRDGE MARION HLTH CARE CORP
Also Called: Partners of Marion Care
524 James Way (43302-7801)
PHONE...................740 389-6306
Fax: 740 389-4042
Whitney Smith, *CFO*
Shelley Smith, *Marketing Staff*
Shannon Kellogg, *Manager*
EMP: 100 **Publicly Held**
SIC: 8051 8093 Skilled nursing care facilities; rehabilitation center, outpatient treatment
HQ: Marion Sunbridge Health Care Corp
101 Sun Ave Ne
Albuquerque NM

(G-13583)
SUPERMEDIA LLC
Also Called: Verizon
19 E Central Ave Fl 1 (43302)
PHONE...................740 369-2391
Jeff Germann, *Manager*
Lloyd L Pfahler, *Supervisor*
EMP: 80
SALES (corp-wide): 1.8B **Privately Held**
WEB: www.verizon.superpages.com
SIC: 4812 Cellular telephone services
HQ: Supermedia Llc
2200 W Airfield Dr
Dfw Airport TX 75261
972 453-7000

(G-13584)
TED GRAHAM
Also Called: G P Properties
3007 Harding Hwy E (43302-2575)
PHONE...................740 223-3509
Ted Graham, *Owner*
EMP: 50
SQ FT: 1,300
SALES (est): 1.8MM **Privately Held**
WEB: www.tedgraham.com
SIC: 6512 Commercial & industrial building operation

(G-13585)
TONKA BAY DIALYSIS LLC
Also Called: Heart of Marion Dialysis
1221 Delaware Ave (43302-6419)
PHONE...................740 375-0849
James K Hilger,
EMP: 25
SALES (est): 224.3K **Publicly Held**
SIC: 8092 Kidney dialysis centers
PA: Davita Inc.
2000 16th St
Denver CO 80202

(G-13586)
TRAFZER EXCAVATING INC
1560 Likens Rd (43302-8652)
PHONE...................740 383-2616
Fax: 740 383-3783
James E Trafzer, *President*
EMP: 30
SQ FT: 6,000
SALES (est): 3.4MM **Privately Held**
SIC: 1794 Excavation & grading, building construction

(G-13587)
TURBO PARTS LLC
1676 Cascade Dr (43302-8509)
PHONE...................740 223-1695
Tony Mitola, *Branch Mgr*
Charlie White, *Manager*
John Bell, *Director*
Frances Gossett, *Admin Sec*
EMP: 30 **Privately Held**
SIC: 5013 Automotive supplies & parts
PA: Turbo Parts, Llc
767 Pierce Rd Ste 2
Clifton Park NY 12065

(G-13588)
UNION BANK COMPANY
111 S Main St (43302-3701)
PHONE...................740 387-2265
EMP: 34
SALES (corp-wide): 24.3MM **Publicly Held**
SIC: 6022 State Commercial Bank
HQ: The Union Bank Company
100 S High St
Columbus Grove OH 45830
419 659-2141

(G-13589)
UNION TANK CAR COMPANY
939 Holland Rd W (43302-9406)
P.O. Box 1125 (43301-1125)
PHONE...................419 864-7216
Fax: 740 382-5012
Mike Nestor, *Manager*
Tom Cassady, *Analyst*
EMP: 119

SALES (corp-wide): 242.1B **Publicly Held**
WEB: www.utlx.com
SIC: **5099** Safety equipment & supplies
HQ: Union Tank Car Company
175 W Jackson Blvd # 2100
Chicago IL 60604
312 431-3111

(G-13590)
UNITE CHURC RESID OF OXFOR MIS (HQ)
Also Called: CHAPEL HILL COMMUNITY
170 E Center St (43302-3815)
P.O. Box 1806 (43301-1806)
PHONE...................................740 382-4885
Dorothy Eckert, *President*
John R Dickson, *Corp Secy*
Paul Kiewit, *Vice Pres*
Lori Martin, *Treasurer*
EMP: 25
SQ FT: 20,000
SALES: 266.8K
SALES (corp-wide): 78.1MM **Privately Held**
SIC: **6513** Apartment building operators
PA: United Church Homes Inc
170 E Center St
Marion OH 43302
740 382-4885

(G-13591)
UNITED CHURCH HOMES
170 E Center St (43302-3815)
P.O. Box 1806 (43301-1806)
PHONE...................................740 382-4885
Brian Allen, *President*
John R Dickson, *Corp Secy*
Edwin R Allen Jr, *Vice Pres*
Ronald Beach, *Vice Pres*
Richard Dible, *Vice Pres*
EMP: 60
SQ FT: 20,000
SALES: 325K
SALES (corp-wide): 78.1MM **Privately Held**
WEB: www.altenheimcommunity.org
SIC: **6513** Apartment building operators
PA: United Church Homes Inc
170 E Center St
Marion OH 43302
740 382-4885

(G-13592)
UNITED CHURCH HOMES INC (PA)
Also Called: Chapel Hill Community
170 E Center St (43302-3815)
P.O. Box 1806 (43301-1806)
PHONE...................................740 382-4885
Fax: 740 382-4884
Rev Kenneth Daniel, *CEO*
Brian S Allen, *President*
Edwin Allen, *Vice Pres*
Vincent Dent, *Vice Pres*
Timothy Hackett, *Vice Pres*
EMP: 60
SQ FT: 20,000
SALES: 78.1MM **Privately Held**
WEB: www.altenheimcommunity.org
SIC: **8051** Skilled nursing care facilities

(G-13593)
UNITED PARCEL SERVICE INC OH
Also Called: UPS
1476 Likens Rd (43302-8788)
PHONE...................................614 383-4580
EMP: 158
SALES (corp-wide): 65.8B **Publicly Held**
SIC: **4215** Parcel delivery, vehicular
HQ: United Parcel Service, Inc. (Oh)
55 Glenlake Pkwy
Atlanta GA 30328
404 828-6000

(G-13594)
VERIZON COMMUNICATIONS INC
550 Leader St (43302-2271)
PHONE...................................740 383-0527
Larry Dan, *Manager*
EMP: 113

SALES (corp-wide): 126B **Publicly Held**
WEB: www.verizon.com
SIC: **4813** Local & long distance telephone communications
PA: Verizon Communications Inc.
1095 Ave Of The Americas
New York NY 10036
212 395-1000

(G-13595)
VERIZON NEW YORK INC
100 Executive Dr (43302-6306)
P.O. Box 1804 (43301-1804)
PHONE...................................740 383-0411
Fax: 740 383-0491
Jack Kennedy, *President*
Dick Armstrong, *Administration*
EMP: 180
SALES (corp-wide): 126B **Publicly Held**
SIC: **4813** Telephone communication, except radio
HQ: Verizon New York Inc.
140 West St
New York NY 10007
212 395-1000

(G-13596)
WHIRLPOOL CORPORATION
1300 Marion Agosta Rd (43302-9577)
PHONE...................................740 383-7122
Fax: 740 383-7656
Brian Gahr, *President*
Stan Kenneth, *Vice Pres*
David Strzalka, *Mfg Dir*
Barbara Klee, *Safety Dir*
Bruce Alexander, *Plant Mgr*
EMP: 250
SALES (corp-wide): 21.2B **Publicly Held**
WEB: www.whirlpoolcorp.com
SIC: **3633 5064 3632** Laundry dryers, household or coin-operated; washing machines; household refrigerators & freezers
PA: Whirlpool Corporation
2000 N M 63
Benton Harbor MI 49022
269 923-5000

Marshallville
Wayne County

(G-13597)
MARSHALLVILLE PACKING CO INC
50 E Market St (44645-9468)
P.O. Box 276 (44645-0276)
PHONE...................................330 855-2871
Frank T Tucker, *President*
Jeannette Tucker, *Corp Secy*
Jacki Chamberlain, *Marketing Staff*
Martha Starkey, *Exec Dir*
EMP: 29 EST: 1960
SQ FT: 35,000
SALES (est): 1.9MM **Privately Held**
SIC: **5421 5147 2013 2011** Meat markets, including freezer provisioners; meats, fresh; sausages & other prepared meats; meat packing plants

(G-13598)
STOLL FARMS INC
15040 Fox Lake Rd (44645-9784)
PHONE...................................330 682-5786
Fax: 330 682-5110
Edward Stoll, *President*
Bonnie Stoll, *Admin Sec*
EMP: 35 EST: 1937
SALES: 2MM **Privately Held**
SIC: **0241** Dairy farms

Martins Ferry
Belmont County

(G-13599)
BELMONT METRO HSING AUTH (PA)
Also Called: Belmont Metro Hsing Auth A
100 S 3rd St (43935-1457)
PHONE...................................740 633-5085
Fax: 740 633-9978
Bruce Kinsel, *Owner*
EMP: 26

SQ FT: 63,000
SALES: 4.9MM **Privately Held**
SIC: **6513** Apartment building operators

(G-13600)
N F MANSUETTO & SONS INC
Also Called: Mansuetto Roofing Company
116 Wood St (43935-1710)
PHONE...................................740 633-7320
Fax: 740 633-7322
Matthew Mansuetto, *President*
Francis M Mansuetto, *Corp Secy*
Eugene Ochap, *Vice Pres*
EMP: 30
SQ FT: 10,000
SALES (est): 6.2MM **Privately Held**
SIC: **1761** Roofing contractor

(G-13601)
STONEY HOLLOW TIRE INC
1st & Hanover Sts (43935)
P.O. Box 310 (43935-0310)
PHONE...................................740 635-5200
Fax: 740 635-5204
John Seckman, *President*
Earl Buono, *Corp Secy*
Bob Beriford, *Manager*
Scott Hudson, *Manager*
Shawn Holmes, *Producer*
▲ EMP: 70
SQ FT: 80,000
SALES (est): 44.3MM **Privately Held**
WEB: www.stoneyhollowtire.com
SIC: **5014** Automobile tires & tubes; truck tires & tubes; tire & tube repair materials

(G-13602)
UNIFIED BANK (HQ)
Also Called: CITIZENS BANK
201 S 4th St (43935-1311)
P.O. Box 10 (43935-0010)
PHONE...................................740 633-0445
Fax: 740 633-2679
James W Everson, *Ch of Bd*
Scott Everson, *President*
Elmer Leeper, *Senior VP*
Michael A Lloyd, *Senior VP*
James Lodes, *Senior VP*
EMP: 40
SQ FT: 20,000
SALES: 21MM
SALES (corp-wide): 21.1MM **Publicly Held**
WEB: www.unitedbancorp.net
SIC: **6022** State commercial banks
PA: United Bancorp, Inc.
201 S 4th St
Martins Ferry OH 43935
740 633-0445

(G-13603)
UNITED STEELWORKERS
Also Called: Uswa
705 Main St (43935-1715)
PHONE...................................740 633-0899
Fax: 740 633-9552
Ken Afpenleiger, *President*
John Aubaugh, *Engineer*
Katrina Mills, *Controller*
Carmen De Stefano, *VP Finance*
Bert Colvin, *Manager*
EMP: 32
SALES (corp-wide): 61.5K **Privately Held**
WEB: www.uswa.org
SIC: **8631** Labor union
PA: United Steelworkers
60 Bolevard Of The Allies
Pittsburgh PA 15222
412 562-2400

(G-13604)
WHEELING HOSPITAL INC
Also Called: Valley Gstrnterology Endoscopy
90 N 4th St (43935-1648)
PHONE...................................740 633-4765
Ronald Violi, *CEO*
EMP: 57
SALES (corp-wide): 375.6MM **Privately Held**
SIC: **8011** Physical medicine, physician/surgeon
PA: Wheeling Hospital, Inc.
1 Medical Park
Wheeling WV 26003
304 243-3000

Marysville
Union County

(G-13605)
ACE RENTAL PLACE
Also Called: Ace Hardware
1299 W 5th St (43040-9291)
PHONE...................................937 642-2891
Fax: 937 642-4019
Dan Fitzgerald, *Owner*
Jim Fitzgerald, *Co-Owner*
EMP: 75
SALES (est): 5.6MM **Privately Held**
SIC: **7359 5251** Stores & yards equipment rental; hardware

(G-13606)
AREA ENERGY & ELECTRIC INC
19255 Smokey Rd (43040-9141)
PHONE...................................937 642-0386
Fax: 937 642-0387
Karri Fryman, *Human Res Mgr*
Joe Lachey, *Manager*
EMP: 40
SALES (est): 2.8MM
SALES (corp-wide): 99.7MM **Privately Held**
SIC: **1731** General electrical contractor
PA: Area Energy & Electric, Inc.
2001 Commerce Dr
Sidney OH 45365
937 498-4784

(G-13607)
BROOKDALE SENIOR LIVING INC
1565 London Ave Frnt (43040-6808)
PHONE...................................937 738-7342
Angela Maxwell, *Director*
EMP: 97
SALES (corp-wide): 4.7B **Publicly Held**
SIC: **7011** Inns
PA: Brookdale Senior Living
111 Westwood Pl Ste 400
Brentwood TN 37027
615 221-2250

(G-13608)
BY-LINE TRANSIT INC
17075 White Stone Rd (43040-9479)
PHONE...................................937 642-2500
Fax: 937 642-2662
Deborah Bywater, *President*
Ronald P Bywater, *Vice Pres*
EMP: 49
SQ FT: 1,600
SALES: 5MM **Privately Held**
SIC: **4213** Trucking, except local; contract haulers; refrigerated products transport

(G-13609)
CARRIAGE CRT MRYSVLLE LTD PRTN
717 S Walnut St (43040-1639)
PHONE...................................937 642-2202
Fax: 937 642-2207
Rita Orahood, *Exec Dir*
EMP: 30
SALES (est): 1.1MM **Privately Held**
SIC: **8361 8052** Home for the aged; intermediate care facilities

(G-13610)
CASSENS TRANSPORT COMPANY
24777 Honda Pkwy (43040-9189)
PHONE...................................937 644-8886
Fax: 937 642-5860
Don Trainer, *Manager*
EMP: 125
SQ FT: 14,400
SALES (corp-wide): 219.4MM **Privately Held**
SIC: **4213** Automobiles, transport & delivery
HQ: Cassens Transport Company
145 N Kansas St
Edwardsville IL 62025
618 656-3006

Marysville - Union County (G-13611)

(G-13611)
CELLCO PARTNERSHIP
Also Called: Verizon Wireless
1095 Delaware Ave (43040-9401)
PHONE..................................937 578-0022
Fax: 937 578-0075
Patricia Fisher, *Branch Mgr*
EMP: 71
SALES (corp-wide): 126B **Publicly Held**
SIC: 4812 Cellular telephone services
HQ: Cellco Partnership
   1 Verizon Way
   Basking Ridge NJ 07920

(G-13612)
COUNTY OF UNION
Also Called: Environmental Engineering Dept
128 S Main St Ste 203 (43040-1653)
PHONE..................................937 645-3018
Fax: 937 645-3161
Steve Stolte, *Principal*
EMP: 45 **Privately Held**
SIC: 8711 9111 Engineering services; county supervisors' & executives' offices
PA: County Of Union
   227 E 5th St
   Marysville OH 43040
   937 642-6279

(G-13613)
COUNTY OF UNION
Also Called: Union Cnty Board of Devlpmt
1280 Charles Ln (43040-9797)
PHONE..................................937 645-6733
Fax: 937 642-8427
Jerry L Burger, *Superintendent*
Kim Miller, *Manager*
Laura Zureich, *Manager*
EMP: 80 **Privately Held**
SIC: 9431 8322 ; social services for the handicapped
PA: County Of Union
   227 E 5th St
   Marysville OH 43040
   937 642-6279

(G-13614)
COUNTY OF UNION
Also Called: Engineer's Office
128 S Main St Ste 203 (43040-1653)
PHONE..................................937 645-4145
Amy Hamilton, *CFO*
EMP: 78 **Privately Held**
SIC: 1623 Water, sewer & utility lines
PA: County Of Union
   227 E 5th St
   Marysville OH 43040
   937 642-6279

(G-13615)
CSX TRANSPORTATION INC
19835 Johnson Rd (43040-9252)
PHONE..................................937 642-2221
Fax: 937 642-2227
Mario Morales, *Sales Executive*
Dave Schmidt, *Branch Mgr*
Sam Scott, *Manager*
John Gardner, *Administration*
Roger Pederson, *Administration*
EMP: 39
SALES (corp-wide): 11.4B **Publicly Held**
SIC: 4011 Railroads, line-haul operating
HQ: Csx Transportation, Inc.
   500 Water St
   Jacksonville FL 32202
   904 359-3100

(G-13616)
DARBY CREEK GOLF COURSE INC
19300 Orchard Rd (43040-9044)
PHONE..................................937 349-7491
Fax: 937 349-5573
Scott Hanhart, *President*
Tony Benincasa, *Vice Pres*
Ralph M La Porte, *Vice Pres*
David Hanhart, *Shareholder*
Mark Starniery, *Shareholder*
EMP: 25
SALES (est): 1.5MM **Privately Held**
WEB: www.darbycreekgolf.com
SIC: 7992 7999 5941 Public golf courses; golf driving range; golf goods & equipment

(G-13617)
FIRST STUDENT INC
1280 Charles Ln (43040-9797)
P.O. Box 49 (43040-0049)
PHONE..................................937 645-0201
Kim Scharf, *Manager*
EMP: 25
SALES (corp-wide): 7B **Privately Held**
WEB: www.leag.com
SIC: 4151 School buses
HQ: First Student, Inc.
   600 Vine St Ste 1400
   Cincinnati OH 45202

(G-13618)
FIVE COUNTY JOINT JUVENILE DET
Also Called: Central Ohio Youth Center
18100 State Route 4 (43040-8550)
PHONE..................................937 642-1015
Fax: 937 642-5900
Vicky Jordon, *Superintendent*
Travis Stillion, *Principal*
Darryl Goree, *Manager*
EMP: 40
SALES (est): 1.5MM **Privately Held**
SIC: 8361 Juvenile correctional facilities

(G-13619)
FRANKES UNLIMITED INC
825 Collins Ave (43040-1330)
PHONE..................................937 642-0706
Bill Franke, *President*
Christopher Franke, *Vice Pres*
Kevine Franke, *Vice Pres*
Michelle R Franke, *Admin Sec*
EMP: 30 EST: 1998
SALES: 3MM **Privately Held**
SIC: 7389 Field warehousing

(G-13620)
FRANKES WOOD PRODUCTS LLC
825 Collins Ave (43040-1330)
PHONE..................................937 642-0706
Fax: 937 642-3528
William Franke, *President*
Judy Franke, *Office Mgr*
Christopher S Franke, *Shareholder*
Kevin Franke, *Shareholder*
Michelle R Franke, *Shareholder*
EMP: 37
SQ FT: 93,800
SALES (est): 7MM **Privately Held**
SIC: 2448 2449 2493 3061 Cargo containers, wood; shipping cases & drums, wood: wirebound & plywood; fiberboard, other vegetable pulp; mechanical rubber goods; rubber scrap; marketing consulting services

(G-13621)
GABLES AT GREEN PASTURES
390 Gables Dr (43040-9582)
PHONE..................................937 642-3893
Fax: 937 578-2480
Kristi Eads, *Sls & Mktg Exec*
Robert Collins, *Technology*
Lorie Whittington, *Director*
Lisa Donahue, *Admin Asst*
Laurie Whittington, *Administration*
EMP: 112
SALES: 9.3MM **Privately Held**
WEB: www.gablesatgreenpastures.com
SIC: 8051 Convalescent home with continuous nursing care

(G-13622)
GEETA HOSPITALITY INC
Also Called: Hampton Inn
16610 Square Dr (43040-8558)
PHONE..................................937 642-3777
Fax: 937 642-3778
Amar Pandey, *President*
EMP: 25
SALES (est): 1.4MM **Privately Held**
SIC: 7011 7991 Hotels; physical fitness facilities

(G-13623)
HEALTH PARTNERS HEALTH CLINIC
19900 State Route 739 (43040-9256)
PHONE..................................937 645-8488
Tammy Allen, *Owner*
Robert Shadel, *Medical Dir*
Michael Dick, *Executive*
▲ EMP: 25 EST: 2000
SALES (est): 1.3MM **Privately Held**
SIC: 8093 Mental health clinic, outpatient

(G-13624)
HONDA FEDERAL CREDIT UNION
24000 Honda Pkwy (43040-9251)
PHONE..................................937 642-6000
Fax: 937 642-5184
Joe Mattera, *Branch Mgr*
EMP: 40
SALES (corp-wide): 25.7MM **Privately Held**
SIC: 6061 Federal credit unions
PA: Honda Federal Credit Union
   19701 Hamilton Ave # 130
   Torrance CA 90502
   310 217-0509

(G-13625)
HONDA NORTH AMERICA INC
24000 Honda Pkwy (43040-9251)
PHONE..................................937 642-5000
Fax: 937 644-6577
Takuji Yamada, *President*
Erik Berkman, *President*
Tomoni Kosaka, *President*
Richyard Schostek, *President*
Chitoshi Yokata, *President*
▼ EMP: 50 EST: 2014
SQ FT: 30,000
SALES (est): 58.6MM
SALES (corp-wide): 123.1B **Privately Held**
SIC: 5012 Automobiles
PA: Honda Motor Co., Ltd.
   2-1-1, Minamiaoyama
   Minato-Ku TKY 107-0
   334 231-111

(G-13626)
HONDA OF AMERICA MFG INC
Also Called: Honda Support Office
19900 State Route 739 (43040-9256)
PHONE..................................937 644-0724
Gary Mabrey, *Purch Mgr*
Nobu Hashimoto, *Purchasing*
Bob Brizendine, *CIO*
EMP: 200
SALES (corp-wide): 123.1B **Privately Held**
SIC: 3714 3711 3465 8742 Motor vehicle parts & accessories; motor vehicles & car bodies; automotive stampings; training & development consultant
HQ: Honda Of America Mfg., Inc.
   24000 Honda Pkwy
   Marysville OH 43040
   937 642-5000

(G-13627)
HONDA TRADING AMERICA CORP
19900 State Route 739 (43040-9256)
PHONE..................................937 644-8004
Fax: 937 644-8070
Dustin Hill, *Buyer*
Denise Hamilton, *Sales Staff*
Jim Honda, *Marketing Staff*
Greg Norval, *Branch Mgr*
Kotaro Fujiwara, *Manager*
EMP: 140
SALES (corp-wide): 123.1B **Privately Held**
WEB: www.htaoh.honda.com
SIC: 5013 Automotive supplies & parts
HQ: Honda Trading America Corp
   19210 Van Ness Ave
   Torrance CA 90501
   310 787-5000

(G-13628)
HOYER POURED WALLS INC
18205 Poling Rd (43040-9149)
PHONE..................................937 642-6148
Fax: 937 642-8103
Jerry Hoyer, *President*
John Dawson, *Vice Pres*
EMP: 25
SQ FT: 3,200
SALES (est): 2.6MM **Privately Held**
WEB: www.hoyerpouredwalls.com
SIC: 1771 Foundation & footing contractor

(G-13629)
J A GUY INC
Also Called: Mechanical Contractors
13116 Weaver Rd (43040-9057)
PHONE..................................937 642-3415
Fax: 614 889-5822
Barbara Guy Guess, *President*
Roger L Guess, *Vice Pres*
EMP: 30
SQ FT: 4,000
SALES: 2MM **Privately Held**
WEB: www.gregguy.com
SIC: 1711 1761 Warm air heating & air conditioning contractor; plumbing contractors; sheet metalwork

(G-13630)
KARE MEDICAL TRNSPT SVCS LLP
1002 Columbus Ave (43040-8563)
P.O. Box 110 (43040-0110)
PHONE..................................937 578-0263
Fax: 937 578-0264
Jason Keeran,
EMP: 30
SQ FT: 2,400
SALES (est): 1.2MM **Privately Held**
SIC: 4119 Ambulance service

(G-13631)
LINKS
200 Gallery Dr (43040-8347)
PHONE..................................937 644-9988
Fax: 937 324-6008
Scott Brown, *Manager*
Dennis Sammut, *Exec Dir*
Craig Allardice, *Representative*
EMP: 30
SALES (est): 1.2MM **Privately Held**
SIC: 6513 Apartment building operators

(G-13632)
LOWES HOME CENTERS LLC
15775 Us Highway 36 (43040-9484)
PHONE..................................937 578-4440
Fax: 937 578-4443
EMP: 158
SALES (corp-wide): 68.6B **Publicly Held**
SIC: 5211 5031 5722 5064 Home centers; building materials, exterior; building materials, interior; household appliance stores; electrical appliances, television & radio
HQ: Lowe's Home Centers, Llc
   1605 Curtis Bridge Rd
   Wilkesboro NC 28697
   336 658-4000

(G-13633)
MAHONEY DIALYSIS LLC
Also Called: Meadowhawk Dialysis
491 Colemans Xing (43040-7068)
PHONE..................................937 642-0676
James K Hilger,
EMP: 29
SALES (est): 238.3K **Publicly Held**
SIC: 8092 Kidney dialysis centers
PA: Davita Inc.
   2000 16th St
   Denver CO 80202

(G-13634)
MARYHAVEN INC
715 S Plum St (43040-1631)
PHONE..................................937 644-9192
Paul Coleman, *Branch Mgr*
EMP: 35
SALES (est): 779.8K
SALES (corp-wide): 21.9MM **Privately Held**
SIC: 8069 Alcoholism rehabilitation hospital
PA: Maryhaven, Inc
   1791 Alum Creek Dr
   Columbus OH 43207
   614 449-1530

(G-13635)
MARYSVILLE FOOD PANTRY
333 Ash St (43040-1543)
PHONE..................................937 644-3248
Gary Simpson, *Director*
EMP: 25
SALES: 87.4K **Privately Held**
SIC: 8699 Charitable organization

▲ = Import ▼=Export
◆ =Import/Export

GEOGRAPHIC SECTION
Mason - Warren County (G-13658)

(G-13636)
MARYSVILLE STEEL INC
323 E 8th St (43040)
P.O. Box 383 (43040-0383)
PHONE..................................937 642-5971
Fax: 937 642-1529
Steven J Clayman, *CEO*
Sheryl Blum, *Admin Asst*
EMP: 31
SQ FT: 50,000
SALES (est): 10.6MM **Privately Held**
SIC: 3441 1791 5039 Fabricated structural metal; structural steel erection; joists

(G-13637)
MARYSVLLE OBSTTRICS GYNECOLOGY (PA)
150 Morey Dr (43040-1646)
PHONE..................................937 644-1244
Fax: 937 642-7535
Frank Raymond, *President*
Norman Raymond, *Vice Pres*
EMP: 42
SQ FT: 4,000
SALES (est): 3MM **Privately Held**
SIC: 8011 Obstetrician; gynecologist

(G-13638)
MARYSVLLE OHIO SRGICAL CTR LLC (PA)
122 Professional Pkwy (43040-8053)
PHONE..................................937 642-6622
Fax: 937 642-6635
Daniel J Saale,
Jim Christie,
EMP: 69
SALES (est): 34.7MM **Privately Held**
SIC: 8062 General medical & surgical hospitals

(G-13639)
MARYSVLLE OHIO SRGICAL CTR LLC
17853 State Route 31 (43040-9609)
PHONE..................................937 578-4200
R Mark Stover, *Branch Mgr*
EMP: 637
SALES (corp-wide): 34.7MM **Privately Held**
SIC: 8011 Orthopedic physician
PA: Marysville Ohio Surgical Center, L.L.C.
122 Professional Pkwy
Marysville OH 43040
937 642-6622

(G-13640)
MEMORIAL HOSPITAL UNION COUNTY
660 London Ave (43040-1515)
PHONE..................................937 644-1001
Chip Hubbs, *Branch Mgr*
EMP: 200
SALES (corp-wide): 101.8MM **Privately Held**
SIC: 8062 General medical & surgical hospitals
PA: Memorial Hospital Of Union County
500 London Ave
Marysville OH 43040
937 644-6115

(G-13641)
MEMORIAL HOSPITAL UNION COUNTY (PA)
500 London Ave (43040-1594)
PHONE..................................937 644-6115
Fax: 937 644-3976
Olas A Hubbs, *CEO*
Dennis Stone, *Chairman*
James Taylor, *Pastor*
Spence Fisher, *Exec VP*
John R Evans, *Vice Pres*
EMP: 800
SQ FT: 132,000
SALES: 101.8MM **Privately Held**
WEB: www.memorialhosp.org
SIC: 8062 Hospital, affiliated with AMA residency

(G-13642)
NISSIN INTL TRNSPT USA INC
16940 Square Dr (43040-9616)
PHONE..................................937 644-2644
Fax: 937 644-3146

Teresa Kesterson, *Admin Asst*
EMP: 75
SALES (corp-wide): 1.7B **Privately Held**
WEB: www.nitusa.com
SIC: 4731 Freight forwarding
HQ: Nissin International Transport U.S.A., Inc.
1540 W 190th St
Torrance CA 90501
310 222-8500

(G-13643)
OHIO MEDICAL TRNSP INC
Also Called: Medical Flight 2
22758 Wilbur Rd (43040-9120)
PHONE..................................937 747-3540
Rod Crane, *Manager*
EMP: 25 **Privately Held**
WEB: www.medflight.com
SIC: 4522 Air passenger carriers, non-scheduled
PA: Ohio Medical Transportation, Inc.
2827 W Dblin Granville Rd
Columbus OH 43235

(G-13644)
PICKLESIMER TRUCKING INC
360 Palm Dr (43040-5534)
PHONE..................................937 642-1091
Fax: 937 644-8828
Charles Picklesimer, *President*
Patsy Picklesimer, *Corp Secy*
EMP: 25
SQ FT: 2,500
SALES (est): 1.7MM **Privately Held**
SIC: 4214 Local trucking with storage

(G-13645)
PRECISION COATINGS SYSTEMS
948 Columbus Ave (43040-9501)
PHONE..................................937 642-4727
Fax: 937 644-3206
Fred Myers Jr, *President*
Mark Myers, *Vice Pres*
Sherry Myers, *Vice Pres*
Wendy Myers, *Vice Pres*
Graig Bartlett, *Plant Mgr*
EMP: 30
SQ FT: 26,000
SALES (est): 2.4MM **Privately Held**
WEB: www.precisioncoatingsystems.com
SIC: 3479 7532 7549 7514 Painting of metal products; paint shop, automotive; collision shops, automotive; towing services; rent-a-car service

(G-13646)
R & D NESTLE CENTER INC
Also Called: Nestle Product Technology Ctr
809 Collins Ave (43040-1308)
PHONE..................................937 642-7015
Gillian Anantharaman, *Vice Pres*
Kenneth G Boehm, *Vice Pres*
Darren Crow, *Engineer*
John Howard, *Branch Mgr*
Ken Boehm, *Director*
EMP: 230
SALES (est): 31.5MM
SALES (corp-wide): 88.4B **Privately Held**
WEB: www.rdoh.nestle.com
SIC: 8731 Food research
PA: Nestle S.A.
Avenue Nestle 55
Vevey VD 1800
219 242-111

(G-13647)
RMI INTERNATIONAL INC
Also Called: Rodbat Security Services
24500 Honda Pwky (43040)
PHONE..................................937 642-5032
Marco Norman, *Manager*
EMP: 60
SALES (corp-wide): 25.5MM **Privately Held**
WEB: www.rmiintl.com
SIC: 7381 Guard services; protective services, guard
PA: Rmi International Inc
8125 Somerset Blvd
Paramount CA 90723
562 806-9098

(G-13648)
RYAN LOGISTICS INC
711 Clymer Rd (43040-9502)
PHONE..................................937 642-4158
Fax: 937 734-0700
Tracy Yoesting, *President*
Matt Price, *Accountant*
Tammy Yelton, *Human Resources*
Tim Luallen, *Manager*
EMP: 80
SQ FT: 1,680
SALES (est): 27.2MM **Privately Held**
WEB: www.ryanlogistics.com
SIC: 4731 Freight forwarding

(G-13649)
SCIOTO SERVICES LLC (HQ)
405 S Oak St (43040-1735)
PHONE..................................937 644-0888
Fax: 937 644-1356
Thomas C Kruse, *CEO*
Mike Jones, *Regional Mgr*
John Vogele, *Regional Mgr*
Donnie Jones, *Area Mgr*
Charles Thompson, *Area Mgr*
EMP: 42
SALES (est): 18MM
SALES (corp-wide): 681.3MM **Privately Held**
WEB: www.sciotocorp.com
SIC: 7349 1711 5085 Janitorial service, contract basis; mechanical contractor; industrial supplies
PA: Marsden Holding, L.L.C.
2124 University Ave W
Saint Paul MN 55114
651 641-1717

(G-13650)
SCOTTS COMPANY LLC (HQ)
Also Called: Scotts Miracle-Gro Products
14111 Scottslawn Rd (43040-7801)
P.O. Box 418 (43040-0418)
PHONE..................................937 644-3729
Fax: 937 644-7557
James Hagedorn, *CEO*
Ryan McClendon, *General Mgr*
David Sanborn, *Managing Dir*
Christiane Schmenk, *Managing Dir*
Mike Lukemire, *Exec VP*
◆ **EMP:** 585
SALES (est): 1.8B
SALES (corp-wide): 2.6B **Publicly Held**
WEB: www.scottscompany.com
SIC: 2873 2874 2879 0782 Fertilizers: natural (organic), except compost; phosphates; fungicides, herbicides, insecticides, agricultural or household; lawn services; mulch, wood & bark; lawn & garden equipment; lawnmowers, residential: hand or power
PA: The Scotts Miracle-Gro Company
14111 Scottslawn Rd
Marysville OH 43040
937 644-0011

(G-13651)
SCOTTS MIRACLE-GRO COMPANY (PA)
14111 Scottslawn Rd (43040-7801)
PHONE..................................937 644-0011
James Hagedorn, *Ch of Bd*
Michael C Lukemire, *President*
Denise S Stump, *Exec VP*
Thomas R Coleman, *CFO*
Ivan C Smith, *Ch Credit Ofcr*
▲ **FMP:** 277
SALES: 2.6B **Publicly Held**
WEB: www.scotts.com
SIC: 2879 3542 0782 7342 Agricultural chemicals; insecticides & pesticides; plant hormones; soil conditioners; machine tools, metal forming type; lawn & garden services; pest control services

(G-13652)
STRAIGHT 72 INC
Also Called: MAI Manufacturing
20078 State Route 4 (43040-9723)
PHONE..................................740 943-5730
Chris Vogelsang, *President*
John Haller, *General Mgr*
Linda Wolf, *Vice Pres*
Mike Thomas, *QC Mgr*
Veda Kirt, *Accountant*
EMP: 60

SALES (est): 7.6MM **Privately Held**
SIC: 8711 3544 Acoustical engineering; special dies, tools, jigs & fixtures

(G-13653)
SUMITOMO ELC WIRG SYSTEMS INC
14800 Industrial Pkwy (43040-7507)
PHONE..................................937 642-7579
EMP: 33
SALES (corp-wide): 24.7B **Privately Held**
SIC: 3714 5063 3694 Automotive wiring harness sets; wire & cable; engine electrical equipment
HQ: Sumitomo Electric Wiring Systems, Inc.
1018 Ashley St
Bowling Green KY 42103
270 782-7397

(G-13654)
SUMITOMO ELC WIRG SYSTEMS INC
Also Called: Honda Research Center
16960 Square Dr (43040-9616)
PHONE..................................937 642-7579
Mike Mirkovich, *Engineer*
Feng Xue, *Engineer*
Koji Morisada, *Branch Mgr*
Chad Boggs, *Manager*
EMP: 50
SALES (corp-wide): 24.7B **Privately Held**
WEB: www.sewsus.com
SIC: 8711 Engineering services
HQ: Sumitomo Electric Wiring Systems, Inc.
1018 Ashley St
Bowling Green KY 42103
270 782-7397

(G-13655)
THOMAS R TRUITT OD
Also Called: Truitt Thos R & Truitt Susan M
1001 W 5th St (43040-8666)
PHONE..................................937 644-8637
Fax: 937 644-8653
Thomas R Truitt, *President*
Tom R Truitt,
EMP: 25
SALES (est): 1.3MM **Privately Held**
SIC: 8042 Specialized optometrists

(G-13656)
U-CO INDUSTRIES INC
16900 Square Dr Ste 110 (43040-8948)
PHONE..................................937 644-3021
Fax: 937 644-9799
Tonya Hamby, *QC Mgr*
Teresa O'Connell, *Administration*
EMP: 71
SQ FT: 6,500
SALES: 1.2MM **Privately Held**
SIC: 8331 Sheltered workshop

(G-13657)
UNION RURAL ELECTRIC COOP INC (PA)
15461 Us Highway 36 (43040-9405)
P.O. Box 393 (43040-0393)
PHONE..................................937 642-1826
Fax: 937 644-4239
Roger Yoder, *President*
Anthony Smith, *President*
Michael Aquillo, *Vice Pres*
Mike Rose, *Controller*
Dave Speicher, *Accountant*
EMP: 39 **EST:** 1926
SQ FT: 4,000
SALES (est): 36.9MM **Privately Held**
WEB: www.ure.com
SIC: 4911 8611 Distribution, electric power; business associations

---

Mason
Warren County

(G-13658)
AERO FULFILLMENT SERVICES CORP (PA)
3900 Aero Dr (45040-8840)
PHONE..................................800 225-7145
Fax: 513 459-3950

Jon T Gimpel, *Ch of Bd*
Wendy Neuburger, *General Mgr*
Brenda Conaway, *VP Finance*
Marianne Morisson, *VP Finance*
Jeremy Shubert, *CTO*
EMP: 100
SQ FT: 125,000
SALES: 23MM **Privately Held**
WEB: www.aerofulfillment.com
SIC: 4225 7374 7331 2759 General warehousing; data processing service; mailing service; commercial printing

(G-13659)
AFIDENCE INC
309 Reading Rd (45040-1511)
PHONE 513 234-5822
Bryan Hogan, *President*
Barbara Hogan, *Vice Pres*
Andy Hickey, *Project Mgr*
Heath Boroff, *Consultant*
Jim Hanna, *Consultant*
EMP: 28
SALES (est): 3.8MM **Privately Held**
SIC: 7373 Computer integrated systems design

(G-13660)
ALTRIA GROUP DISTRIBUTION CO
4680 Parkway Dr Ste 450 (45040-7979)
PHONE 804 274-2000
Craig A Johnson, *President*
EMP: 104
SALES (corp-wide): 25.5B **Publicly Held**
SIC: 5159 Tobacco distributors & products
HQ: Altria Group Distribution Company
6601 W Broad St
Richmond VA 23230

(G-13661)
AMERICAN BUS PERSONNEL SVCS (PA)
7547 Central Parke Blvd (45040-6811)
PHONE 513 770-3300
Jim Wilson, *President*
Piotr Machon, *Regl Sales Mgr*
Chris Walton, *Manager*
Kevin Mulholland, *Software Dev*
EMP: 50
SQ FT: 3,000
SALES (est): 3.5MM **Privately Held**
SIC: 7361 Executive placement

(G-13662)
ANDRE CORPORATION
4600 N Masn Montgomery Rd (45040-9176)
PHONE 574 293-0207
David Andre, *President*
EMP: 50
SQ FT: 50,000
SALES (est): 15.6MM **Privately Held**
WEB: www.andrecorp.com
SIC: 3452 3469 5085 Washers, metal; stamping metal for the trade; fasteners, industrial: nuts, bolts, screws, etc.

(G-13663)
ANTHEM MIDWEST INC
4361 Irwin Simpson Rd (45040-9479)
PHONE 614 433-8350
Larry Glasscock, *President*
Doug Laflamme, *Vice Pres*
Stephhane Berger-Lauson, *Project Dir*
John Kaesemeyer, *Project Dir*
Gabriela Soteros, *Mktg Coord*
EMP: 550
SALES (est): 67.4MM **Privately Held**
SIC: 6411 Insurance agents, brokers & service

(G-13664)
ARTIS SENIOR LIVING
6200 Snider Rd (45040-2640)
PHONE 513 229-7450
Jerry Craft, *Manager*
Diane Klaoenne, *Director*
EMP: 40
SALES (est): 791.9K **Privately Held**
SIC: 8322 Old age assistance

(G-13665)
ATOS IT SOLUTIONS AND SVCS INC
4705 Duke Dr (45040-7645)
PHONE 513 336-1000
Brandy Wilhite, *Manager*
Maria Babilon, *Info Tech Mgr*
EMP: 451
SALES (corp-wide): 179.3MM **Privately Held**
SIC: 7379 Computer related maintenance services
HQ: Atos It Solutions And Services Inc.
2500 Westchester Ave Fl 3
Purchase NY 10577
914 881-3000

(G-13666)
BAYER & BECKER INC
Also Called: Becker & Becker
6900 Tylersville Rd Ste A (45040-1593)
PHONE 513 492-7297
Bob Garlock, *Manager*
EMP: 25
SALES (corp-wide): 5MM **Privately Held**
SIC: 8713 Surveying services
PA: Bayer & Becker, Inc.
6900 Tylersville Rd Ste A
Mason OH 45040
513 492-7401

(G-13667)
BAYER & BECKER INC (PA)
6900 Tylersville Rd Ste A (45040-1593)
PHONE 513 492-7401
Fax: 513 336-9365
Keith Becker, *President*
Matt Hoeller, *Business Mgr*
John Del Verne, *Vice Pres*
Chris Gephart, *Vice Pres*
Tim Bayer, *Project Mgr*
EMP: 36
SQ FT: 2,000
SALES: 5MM **Privately Held**
SIC: 8713 8711 Surveying services; civil engineering

(G-13668)
BROOKDALE SENIOR LIVING INC
5535 Irwin Simpson Rd (45040-8107)
PHONE 513 229-3155
EMP: 85
SALES (corp-wide): 4.7B **Publicly Held**
SIC: 8361 Home for the aged
PA: Brookdale Senior Living
111 Westwood Pl Ste 400
Brentwood TN 37027
615 221-2250

(G-13669)
BROOKSIDE EXTENDED CARE CENTER
780 Snider Rd (45040-1391)
P.O. Box 246 (45040-0246)
PHONE 513 398-1020
Fax: 513 398-5228
Mike Levenson, *CEO*
Rich Johnson, *President*
Becky Meister, *Vice Pres*
Ryan Kramer, *Controller*
Tammy Condit, *Marketing Staff*
EMP: 215
SQ FT: 37,000
SALES: 7.6MM **Privately Held**
SIC: 8059 Home for the mentally retarded, exc. skilled or intermediate

(G-13670)
CARING HEARTS HOME HEALTH CARE (PA)
6677 Summer Field Dr (45040-7332)
PHONE 513 339-1237
Fax: 513 761-6063
Gloria Hayes, *President*
Tyrone Spears, *Vice Pres*
Ronnell Spears, *CFO*
Pam Custard, *Personnel*
Diane Eichcorn, *Nursing Dir*
EMP: 275
SALES (est): 5.3MM **Privately Held**
WEB: www.caringhearts.cc
SIC: 8082 Home health care services

(G-13671)
CARROLL PROPERTIES
5589 Kings Mills Rd (45040-2539)
P.O. Box 425, Kings Mills (45034-0425)
PHONE 513 398-8075
Rick Ziegeilmeyer, *General Mgr*
EMP: 30
SALES (corp-wide): 10.4MM **Privately Held**
WEB: www.carroll-properties.com
SIC: 7011 7991 Hotels & motels; physical fitness facilities
PA: Carroll Properties
12734 Kenwood Ln Ste 35
Fort Myers FL 33907
239 278-5900

(G-13672)
CARTER MANUFACTURING CO INC
4220 State Route 42 (45040-1931)
PHONE 513 398-7303
Fax: 513 398-6231
Chris Carter, *President*
David Bullock, *Foreman/Supr*
Gordon Stewart, *Purchasing*
Kathy Valandingham, *Accounting Mgr*
EMP: 26
SALES (est): 885.7K **Privately Held**
WEB: www.cartermanufacturing.com
SIC: 3544 7692 3541 Dies & die holders for metal cutting, forming, die casting; jigs & fixtures; welding repair; machine tools, metal cutting type

(G-13673)
CDD LLC
6800 Cintas Blvd (45040-9151)
PHONE 905 829-2794
Ron L Sency, *Business Dir*
EMP: 500
SALES (est): 9.1MM **Privately Held**
SIC: 7389 Document & office record destruction

(G-13674)
CENGAGE LEARNING INC
South-Western
5191 Natorp Blvd Lowr (45040-7599)
PHONE 513 229-1000
Fax: 513 527-6979
Jennifer Castillo, *Publisher*
Diane Bowdler, *Editor*
Rob Ellington, *Editor*
Eve Lewis, *Editor*
Kristen Meere, *Editor*
EMP: 500 **Privately Held**
WEB: www.thomsonlearning.com
SIC: 7371 Custom computer programming services
PA: Cengage Learning, Inc.
20 Channel Ctr St
Boston MA 02210

(G-13675)
CHARD SNYDER & ASSOCIATES INC
Also Called: Chard Snyder
3510 Irwin Simpson Rd A (45040-9744)
PHONE 513 459-9997
Fax: 513 459-9947
Joyce Snyder, *President*
Kenneth Chard, *Vice Pres*
Barb Yearout, *VP Opers*
John Gutzwiller, *CFO*
Corrie Kline, *HR Admin*
EMP: 165
SQ FT: 24,600
SALES (est): 13.1MM **Privately Held**
SIC: 8721 Payroll accounting service

(G-13676)
CHILDRENS HOSPITAL MEDICAL CTR
Also Called: Children's Outpatient North
9560 Children Dr (45040-9362)
PHONE 513 636-6800
Fax: 513 636-6835
Char Mason, *Branch Mgr*
Jessica McClure, *Med Doctor*
David Sullivan, *Manager*
Murray Dock, *Fmly & Gen Dent*
EMP: 40
SALES (corp-wide): 1.6B **Privately Held**
WEB: www.cincinnatichildrens.org
SIC: 8733 8093 8011 8069 Medical research; specialty outpatient clinics; offices & clinics of medical doctors; children's hospital
PA: Children's Hospital Medical Center
3333 Burnet Ave
Cincinnati OH 45229
513 636-4200

(G-13677)
CINCOM SYSTEMS INC
4605 Duke Dr (45040-9410)
PHONE 513 459-1470
Thomas M Nies, *Branch Mgr*
EMP: 200
SALES (corp-wide): 121.7MM **Privately Held**
SIC: 7372 Business oriented computer software
PA: Cincom Systems, Inc.
55 Merchant St Ste 100
Cincinnati OH 45246
513 612-2300

(G-13678)
CINTAS CORPORATION NO 1 (HQ)
6800 Cintas Blvd (45040-9151)
PHONE 513 459-1200
Richard T Farmer, *Ch of Bd*
Robert Kohlhepp, *Vice Ch Bd*
Karen L Carnahan, *Vice Pres*
Michael Thompson, *Vice Pres*
William C Gale, *CFO*
EMP: 1500
SQ FT: 75,000
SALES (est): 325MM
SALES (corp-wide): 5.3B **Publicly Held**
SIC: 7213 5136 5137 7549 Uniform supply; uniforms, men's & boys'; uniforms, women's & children's; automotive maintenance services
PA: Cintas Corporation
6800 Cintas Blvd
Cincinnati OH 45262
513 459-1200

(G-13679)
CINTAS CORPORATION NO 2
5800 Cintas Blvd (45040)
P.O. Box 636525, Cincinnati (45263-6525)
PHONE 513 459-1200
EMP: 1000
SALES (corp-wide): 5.3B **Publicly Held**
SIC: 5084 Safety equipment
HQ: Cintas Corporation No. 2
6800 Cintas Blvd
Mason OH 45040

(G-13680)
CINTAS CORPORATION NO 2 (HQ)
Also Called: Cintas First Aid & Safety
6800 Cintas Blvd (45040-9151)
P.O. Box 625737, Cincinnati (45262-5737)
PHONE 513 459-1200
Scott D Farmer, *CEO*
Thomas E Frooman, *Exec VP*
Robert J Kohlhepp, *Exec VP*
Mike L Thompson, *Treasurer*
▲ **EMP:** 2000
SALES (est): 3.5B
SALES (corp-wide): 5.3B **Publicly Held**
SIC: 5084 Safety equipment
PA: Cintas Corporation
6800 Cintas Blvd
Cincinnati OH 45262
513 459-1200

(G-13681)
CINTAS CORPORATION NO 2
6800 Cintas Blvd (45040-9151)
PHONE 513 459-1200
Judith Benatar, *Manager*
EMP: 99
SALES (corp-wide): 5.3B **Publicly Held**
SIC: 5047 Medical & hospital equipment
HQ: Cintas Corporation No. 2
6800 Cintas Blvd
Mason OH 45040

GEOGRAPHIC SECTION

Mason - Warren County (G-13705)

(G-13682)
CINTAS DOCUMENT MANAGEMENT LLC (HQ)
6800 Cintas Blvd (45040-9151)
PHONE..................800 914-1960
Scott D Farmer, *CEO*
Laura Jordan, *Executive Asst*
Susan Towns,
EMP: 36
SALES (est): 4.1MM
SALES (corp-wide): 5.3B **Publicly Held**
SIC: 7299 Personal document & information services
PA: Cintas Corporation
  6800 Cintas Blvd
  Cincinnati OH 45262
  513 459-1200

(G-13683)
CINTAS-RUS LP (HQ)
6800 Cintas Blvd (45040-9151)
P.O. Box 625737, Cincinnati (45262-5737)
PHONE..................513 459-1200
Scott D Farmer, *CEO*
EMP: 27
SALES (est): 39.2MM
SALES (corp-wide): 5.3B **Publicly Held**
SIC: 7218 Industrial uniform supply
PA: Cintas Corporation
  6800 Cintas Blvd
  Cincinnati OH 45262
  513 459-1200

(G-13684)
CLEANER CARPET & JANTR INC
6516 Bluebird Ct (45040-9725)
PHONE..................513 469-2070
Lary McGuffey, *President*
Dan McGuffey, *Sales Mgr*
Brenda McGuffey, *Admin Sec*
Matthew Hochstetler, *Associate*
EMP: 50
SQ FT: 2,000
SALES (est): 1.4MM **Privately Held**
WEB: www.ccjinc.com
SIC: 7349 Janitorial service, contract basis

(G-13685)
CLEVELAND CONSTRUCTION INC
5390 Curseview Dr Ste 200 (45040)
PHONE..................440 255-8000
Fax: 513 398-8418
Jon D Small, *President*
Will L Rawdon, *Project Mgr*
Gary J Todd, *Controller*
David Kurilko, *Systems Mgr*
EMP: 30
SALES (corp-wide): 411.5MM **Privately Held**
SIC: 1542 1721 1742 1521 Commercial & office building contractors; commercial wallcovering contractor; plastering, drywall & insulation; single-family housing construction
PA: Cleveland Construction, Inc.
  8620 Tyler Blvd
  Mentor OH 44060
  440 255-8000

(G-13686)
CLOPAY CORPORATION (HQ)
8585 Duke Blvd (45040-3100)
PHONE..................800 282-2260
Gary Abyad, *President*
Eugene Colleran, *Senior VP*
Ellen Shoemaker, *Senior VP*
Vivek Jain, *Vice Pres*
John Palazzolo, *Vice Pres*
▲ EMP: 231
SQ FT: 130,587
SALES (est): 915.2MM **Publicly Held**
WEB: www.clopay.com
SIC: 3081 3442 2431 1796 Plastic film & sheet; garage doors, overhead: metal; garage doors, overhead: wood; doors, wood; power generating equipment installation

(G-13687)
COMMUNITY CONCEPTS INC (PA)
Also Called: Community Concepts & Options
6699 Tri Way Dr (45040-2604)
PHONE..................513 398-8181
Betty Davis, *President*
Deana M Davis, *Vice Pres*
Marc C Davis, *Vice Pres*
Wayne E Davis, *VP Opers*
Richard Gutierrez, *CFO*
EMP: 110
SALES (est): 8.8MM **Privately Held**
WEB: www.communityconcepts.com
SIC: 8059 8082 Home for the mentally retarded, exc. skilled or intermediate; home health care services

(G-13688)
COMPLETE SERVICES INC (PA)
Also Called: Countrtops Cabinetry By Design
6345 Castle Dr (45040-9415)
PHONE..................513 770-5575
Chris Holtz, *President*
EMP: 30
SQ FT: 5,200
SALES (est): 6.1MM **Privately Held**
SIC: 1799 Kitchen & bathroom remodeling

(G-13689)
CONNECT CALL GLOBAL LLC
7560 Central Parke Blvd (45040-6816)
P.O. Box 632 (45040-0632)
PHONE..................513 348-1800
Chris Lutts, *President*
Jason Gabis, *Vice Pres*
Tusha Gorman, *VP Opers*
EMP: 29 EST: 2010
SQ FT: 47,000
SALES (est): 3.1MM **Privately Held**
SIC: 4813 Telephone communication, except radio; data telephone communications

(G-13690)
COUNTY ANIMAL HOSPITAL
1185 Reading Rd (45040-9154)
PHONE..................513 398-8000
Fax: 513 459-7531
Gary Smith Dvm, *Owner*
Mary Wuest, *Office Mgr*
EMP: 30
SALES (est): 1MM **Privately Held**
SIC: 0742 Animal hospital services, pets & other animal specialties

(G-13691)
CRAIG AND FRANCES LINDNER CENT
Also Called: LINDER CENTER OF HOPE
4075 Old Western Row Rd (45040-3104)
PHONE..................513 536-4673
Paul E Keck Jr, *CEO*
Fred Bishop, *Principal*
Brian A Owens, *COO*
Lynn M Oswald, *Exec VP*
Jan Marhefka, *QA Dir*
EMP: 200 EST: 2006
SALES: 28.6MM **Privately Held**
SIC: 8093 Mental health clinic, outpatient

(G-13692)
CREATIVE CHILDRENS WORLD LLC (PA)
7818 S Masn Montgomery Rd (45040-9316)
PHONE..................513 336-7799
Fax: 513 336-7846
Shawna McCastro, *Mng Member*
Shawna Necastro, *Manager*
EMP: 28
SALES (est): 1.1MM **Privately Held**
SIC: 8351 Child day care services

(G-13693)
CREME DE LA CREME COLORADO INC
5324 Natorp Blvd (45040-7912)
PHONE..................513 459-4300
Fax: 513 459-2111
Gale Sarant, *Branch Mgr*
EMP: 32
SALES (corp-wide): 16.7MM **Privately Held**
SIC: 8351 Child day care services
PA: Creme De La Creme (Colorado), Inc.
  8400 E Prentice Ave # 1320
  Greenwood Village CO 80111
  303 662-9150

(G-13694)
DASSAULT SYSTEMES SIMULIA CORP
Also Called: Central Region
5181 Natorp Blvd Ste 205 (45040-7987)
PHONE..................513 275-1430
Curt Schrader, *Manager*
EMP: 33
SALES (corp-wide): 1.7B **Privately Held**
SIC: 7371 Computer software development
HQ: Dassault Systemes Simulia Corp.
  1301 Atwood Ave Ste 101w
  Johnston RI 02919
  401 531-5000

(G-13695)
DIGITAL MANAGEMENT INC
4660 Duke Dr Ste 100 (45040-8464)
PHONE..................240 223-4800
EMP: 76
SALES (corp-wide): 423MM **Privately Held**
SIC: 7379 Computer related maintenance services
PA: Digital Management, Llc
  6550 Rock Spring Dr Fl 7
  Bethesda MD 20817
  240 223-4800

(G-13696)
DIRECT EXPEDITING LLC
5311 Bentley Oak Dr (45040-8780)
P.O. Box 317 (45040-0317)
PHONE..................513 459-0100
Mike Beegle,
EMP: 35
SQ FT: 10,000
SALES: 2MM **Privately Held**
SIC: 4119 Local rental transportation

(G-13697)
DOMIN-8 ENTP SOLUTIONS INC (PA)
4660 Duke Dr Ste 210 (45040-8466)
PHONE..................513 492-5800
Tom Thistleton, *CEO*
Bill Deakin, *Vice Pres*
Don Vincent, *Vice Pres*
Ted Buettgenbach, *CFO*
Tim Hock, *Controller*
EMP: 90
SQ FT: 15,000
SALES (est): 6.3MM **Privately Held**
WEB: www.domin-8.com
SIC: 7371 Computer software development

(G-13698)
DUKE REALTY CORPORATION
Also Called: Duke Realty Investors
5181 Natorp Blvd Ste 600 (45040-5910)
PHONE..................513 651-3900
Bob Fessler, *Manager*
EMP: 60
SALES (corp-wide): 780.9MM **Privately Held**
WEB: www.dukereit.com
SIC: 6552 6531 Land subdividers & developers, commercial; real estate agents & managers
PA: Duke Realty Corporation
  600 E 96th St Ste 100
  Indianapolis IN 46240
  317 808-6000

(G-13699)
ENGISYSTEMS INC
7588 Central Parke Blvd (45040-6857)
PHONE..................513 229-8860
Gregory W Pierce, *President*
EMP: 100
SALES: 9MM **Privately Held**
SIC: 8711 Consulting engineer

(G-13700)
EVOKES LLC
8118 Corp Way Ste 212 (45040)
PHONE..................513 947-8433
Daniel Lincoln, *President*
Tony Leslie, *Office Mgr*
EMP: 50 EST: 2015
SQ FT: 900
SALES (est): 2.4MM **Privately Held**
SIC: 3822 8011 Building services monitoring controls, automatic; surgeon

(G-13701)
FOOD CONCEPTS INTL INC
5010 Deerfield Blvd (45040-2504)
PHONE..................513 336-7449
Fax: 513 336-9151
EMP: 84
SALES (corp-wide): 151.4MM **Privately Held**
SIC: 5812 7929 Mexican restaurant; entertainment service
PA: Food Concepts International, Inc.
  4401 82nd St
  Lubbock TX 79424
  806 785-8686

(G-13702)
FORD MOTOR COMPANY
4680 Parkway Dr Ste 420 (45040-8117)
PHONE..................513 573-1101
Fax: 513 573-1173
Greg Wedding, *President*
Jim Splendore, *Manager*
Michael Murphy, *Manager*
Al Walls, *Manager*
EMP: 30
SALES (corp-wide): 156.7B **Publicly Held**
WEB: www.ford.com
SIC: 6159 Automobile finance leasing
PA: Ford Motor Company
  1 American Rd
  Dearborn MI 48126
  313 322-3000

(G-13703)
FORTE INDUS EQP SYSTEMS INC
Also Called: Forte Industries
6037 Commerce Ct (45040-8819)
PHONE..................513 398-2800
Eugene A Forte, *President*
Mark Miller, *Vice Pres*
Charlie Rizzo, *Vice Pres*
Jerry Vink, *Vice Pres*
Matt Wojewuczki, *Vice Pres*
EMP: 32
SQ FT: 16,000
SALES (est): 25.3MM
SALES (corp-wide): 36.5B **Privately Held**
WEB: www.forte-industries.com
SIC: 5084 8711 3537 Materials handling machinery; consulting engineer; industrial trucks & tractors
HQ: Swisslog Holding Ag
  Webereiweg 3
  Buchs AG
  628 379-537

(G-13704)
GATESAIR INC (HQ)
5300 Kings Island Dr (45040-2353)
PHONE..................513 459-3400
Phil Argyris, *President*
Bryant Burke, *Vice Pres*
Darren Frearson, *Vice Pres*
Joe Mack, *Vice Pres*
Joseph Mack, *Vice Pres*
▲ EMP: 43
SQ FT: 30,000
SALES (est): 12.4MM
SALES (corp-wide): 6.1B **Privately Held**
SIC: 1731 3663 7371 Communications specialization; radio & TV communications equipment; computer software development & applications
PA: The Gores Group Llc
  9800 Wilshire Blvd
  Beverly Hills CA 90212
  310 209-3010

(G-13705)
GENERAL ELECTRIC COMPANY
4800 Parkway Dr Ste 100 (45040-9012)
PHONE..................513 583-3626
Joe Ferrell, *Manager*
Ivan Wood, *Manager*
EMP: 150
SALES (corp-wide): 122B **Publicly Held**
SIC: 8748 Business consulting

Mason - Warren County (G-13706)

PA: General Electric Company
41 Farnsworth St
Boston MA 02210
617 443-3000

(G-13706)
GENERAL MILLS INC
5181 Natorp Blvd Ste 540 (45040-2183)
PHONE..................513 770-0558
Peter Baruk, *Branch Mgr*
EMP: 55
SALES (corp-wide): 15.6B **Publicly Held**
WEB: www.generalmills.com
SIC: 5141 2041 Food brokers; flour mixes
PA: General Mills, Inc.
1 General Mills Blvd
Minneapolis MN 55426
763 764-7600

(G-13707)
GENERAL REVENUE CORPORATION (HQ)
Also Called: G R C
4660 Duke Dr Ste 300 (45040-8466)
PHONE..................513 469-1472
Fax: 513 469-4311
John Kane, *CEO*
Brian Hill, *President*
Michael Amstadt, *Managing Dir*
Justen Gay, *Vice Pres*
Kendra McAnear, *Vice Pres*
EMP: 480 **EST:** 1981
SQ FT: 100,000
SALES (est): 26.3MM
SALES (corp-wide): 5.1B **Publicly Held**
WEB: www.generalrevenue.com
SIC: 7322 6141 Collection agency, except real estate; personal credit institutions
PA: Navient Corporation
123 S Justison St Ste 300
Wilmington DE 19801
302 283-8000

(G-13708)
GENSUITE LLC
4680 Parkway Dr Ste 400 (45040-8108)
PHONE..................513 774-1000
Mia Vetter, *Vice Pres*
Ashleigh Schlessinger, *Opers Staff*
R Mukund, *Mng Member*
Will Baltz, *Senior Mgr*
Natasha Porter,
EMP: 95
SQ FT: 16,000
SALES: 18.9MM **Privately Held**
SIC: 7371 Computer software systems analysis & design, custom

(G-13709)
GLOBAL CNSLD HOLDINGS INC (PA)
3965 Marble Ridge Ln (45040-2892)
PHONE..................513 703-0965
Mark Cohen, *President*
EMP: 52
SQ FT: 6,000
SALES (est): 3.4MM **Privately Held**
SIC: 8742 6719 Materials mgmt. (purchasing, handling, inventory) consultant; personal holding companies, except banks

(G-13710)
GP STRATEGIES CORPORATION
4770 Duke Dr Ste 120 (45040-9376)
PHONE..................513 583-8810
Terry Donahue, *Principal*
Brian Lapthorn, *Exec Dir*
Keisha Mosley, *Admin Asst*
EMP: 35
SALES (corp-wide): 509.2MM **Publicly Held**
WEB: www.rwd.com
SIC: 7379 8742 8331 Computer related consulting services; management consulting services; job training services
PA: Gp Strategies Corporation
11000 Broken Land Pkwy # 200
Columbia MD 21044
443 367-9600

(G-13711)
GREATER CINCINNATI CREDIT UN
7948 S Masn Montgomery Rd (45040-8249)
PHONE..................513 559-1234
Ben Sawyer, *Branch Mgr*
EMP: 27
SALES (corp-wide): 5.1MM **Privately Held**
SIC: 6062 State credit unions, not federally chartered
PA: Greater Cincinnati Credit Union
7221 Montgomery Rd Ste 1
Cincinnati OH 45236
513 559-1234

(G-13712)
GRIZZLY GOLF CENTER INC
Also Called: Golf Center At Kings Island
6042 Fairway Dr (45040-2006)
PHONE..................513 398-5200
Peter Ryan, *General Mgr*
EMP: 300
SQ FT: 5,000
SALES (est): 6.5MM **Publicly Held**
WEB: www.thegolfcenter.com
SIC: 7992 5812 5941 0782 Public golf courses; eating places; golf goods & equipment; landscape contractors
HQ: Great American Insurance Company
301 E 4th St Fl 8
Cincinnati OH 45202
513 369-5000

(G-13713)
HAAG-STREIT USA INC
5500 Courseview Dr (45040-2366)
PHONE..................513 336-7255
Ernest Cavin, *CEO*
EMP: 25 **Privately Held**
SIC: 5047 Surgical equipment & supplies
HQ: Haag-Streit Usa Inc
3535 Kings Mills Rd
Mason OH 45040

(G-13714)
HAAG-STREIT USA INC (DH)
3535 Kings Mills Rd (45040-2303)
PHONE..................513 336-7255
Ernest Cavin, *CEO*
Dominik Beck, *President*
Steve Juenger, *Vice Pres*
Anthony Lanza, *Engineer*
David R Edenfield, *CFO*
EMP: 110
SQ FT: 22,988
SALES (est): 34.3MM **Privately Held**
SIC: 5047 5048 Surgical equipment & supplies; ophthalmic goods

(G-13715)
HERITAGE CLUB
6690 Heritage Club Dr (45040-4649)
PHONE..................513 459-7711
Lewis Rosenbloom, *General Mgr*
Dana Cimorell, *COO*
Luke Marts, *Maintenance Dir*
Juan Campbell, *Food Svc Dir*
Jeffrey Brown, *Executive*
EMP: 100
SQ FT: 11,600
SALES: 2.5MM **Privately Held**
WEB: www.heritageclub.com
SIC: 7997 Golf club, membership

(G-13716)
HI-FIVE DEVELOPMENT SVCS INC
202 W Main St Ste C (45040-1882)
PHONE..................513 336-9280
Fax: 513 336-0196
Mark Davis, *President*
Brian Zilch, *President*
Glen Burkhardt, *Superintendent*
Fred Hostetler, *Superintendent*
Paul Young, *Superintendent*
EMP: 27
SQ FT: 1,200
SALES (est): 4.8MM **Privately Held**
WEB: www.hifive1.com
SIC: 1542 Design & erection, combined: non-residential

(G-13717)
HI-TEK MANUFACTURING INC
Also Called: System EDM of Ohio
6050 Hi Tek Ct (45040-2602)
PHONE..................513 459-1094
Fax: 513 459-9882
Cletis Jackson, *President*
Scott Stang, *Plant Mgr*
Rich Hawk, *Maint Spvr*
Craig Enderle, *QA Dir*
George Carrington, *QC Mgr*
▲ **EMP:** 180
SQ FT: 71,000
SALES (est): 74.4MM **Privately Held**
WEB: www.hitekmfg.com
SIC: 3599 7692 3724 3714 Machine shop, jobbing & repair; welding repair; aircraft engines & engine parts; motor vehicle parts & accessories; special dies, tools, jigs & fixtures

(G-13718)
ICR INC
Also Called: Icr Engineering
4770 Duke Dr Ste 370 (45040-8460)
PHONE..................513 900-7007
Robert Dunn, *President*
EMP: 77
SALES (est): 1.1MM **Privately Held**
SIC: 7371 8711 Custom computer programming services; software programming applications; custom computer programming services; engineering services

(G-13719)
ILLUMINATION RESEARCH INC
5947 Drfield Blvd Ste 203 (45040)
PHONE..................513 774-9531
Jeff Bass, *Principal*
Kristin Bush, *Vice Pres*
Chris Breheim, *Project Dir*
Alice Moore, *Project Dir*
Kelly Legault, *Marketing Staff*
EMP: 25
SALES (est): 2.9MM **Privately Held**
SIC: 8732 8731 Business economic service; commercial physical research

(G-13720)
INTELLIGRATED SYSTEMS INC (HQ)
7901 Innovation Way (45040-9498)
PHONE..................866 936-7300
Chris Cole, *CEO*
Jim McCarthy, *President*
Gregory Cronin, *Exec VP*
Jim Sharp, *Exec VP*
John Cullen, *Senior VP*
▲ **EMP:** 800 **EST:** 1996
SQ FT: 390,000
SALES: 800MM
SALES (corp-wide): 40.5B **Publicly Held**
SIC: 3535 5084 7371 Conveyors & conveying equipment; industrial machinery & equipment; computer software development
PA: Honeywell International Inc.
115 Tabor Rd
Morris Plains NJ 07950
973 455-2000

(G-13721)
INTELLIGRATED SYSTEMS LLC
7901 Innovation Way (45040-9498)
PHONE..................513 701-7300
Chris Cole, *CEO*
Jim McCarthy, *President*
Amy Ball, *General Mgr*
James Sharp, *Exec VP*
John Cullen, *Senior VP*
EMP: 2300
SQ FT: 260,000
SALES (est): 228.8MM
SALES (corp-wide): 40.5B **Publicly Held**
SIC: 3535 5084 7371 Conveyors & conveying equipment; materials handling machinery; computer software development
HQ: Intelligrated Systems, Inc.
7901 Innovation Way
Mason OH 45040
866 936-7300

(G-13722)
INTELLIGRATED SYSTEMS OHIO LLC (DH)
7901 Innovation Way (45040-9498)
P.O. Box 60843, Charlotte NC (28260-0843)
PHONE..................513 701-7300
Jim McCarthy, *President*
Stephen Ackerman, *Exec VP*
Chuck Waddle, *Exec VP*
Stephen Causey, *Vice Pres*
Wes Goode, *Vice Pres*
◆ **EMP:** 600 **EST:** 2010
SQ FT: 332,000
SALES (est): 261.5MM
SALES (corp-wide): 40.5B **Publicly Held**
WEB: www.fkilogistex.com
SIC: 3535 5084 3537 Conveyors & conveying equipment; industrial machinery & equipment; palletizers & depalletizers
HQ: Intelligrated Systems, Inc.
7901 Innovation Way
Mason OH 45040
866 936-7300

(G-13723)
INTERSTATE CONTRACTORS LLC
Also Called: Ic Roofing
762 Reading Rd G (45040-1362)
PHONE..................513 372-5393
Joel Presar, *Vice Pres*
Young Chon Jung,
Jiah Jung,
EMP: 40
SALES (est): 2.8MM **Privately Held**
SIC: 8611 3444 Business associations; metal roofing & roof drainage equipment

(G-13724)
ISAACS COMPANY (PA)
Also Called: Isaacs Fluid Power Eqp Co
6091 Commerce Ct (45040-8819)
PHONE..................513 336-8500
Fax: 513 336-8502
Roy S Carman, *President*
Beverly Massey, *Corp Secy*
Bruce R Becknell, *Vice Pres*
Shane Howard, *Sales Staff*
Jordan Ojeda, *Sales Associate*
EMP: 28 **EST:** 1948
SQ FT: 12,000
SALES (est): 19.8MM **Privately Held**
WEB: www.isaacsfluidpower.com
SIC: 5084 Hydraulic systems equipment & supplies

(G-13725)
J AND J ENVIRONMENTAL INC
Also Called: Tele-Vac Environmental
7611 Easy St (45040-9424)
PHONE..................513 398-4521
Fax: 513 398-5628
Larry McCauley, *President*
Andy Andrews, *Project Mgr*
Pete Kellum, *Project Mgr*
Joe McCauley, *Project Mgr*
Jim Winchester, *Treasurer*
EMP: 28
SQ FT: 6,000
SALES (est): 4.9MM **Privately Held**
WEB: www.tele-vac.com
SIC: 7699 Sewer cleaning & rodding

(G-13726)
JEWISH HOME OF CINCINNATI
Also Called: Cedar Village
5467 Cedar Village Dr (45040-8693)
PHONE..................513 754-3100
Fax: 513 336-3174
Dan Fagan, *CEO*
Sally Korkin, *Development*
David A Neu, *Finance Spvr*
Gail Davis, *Med Doctor*
Connie Biederman, *Director*
EMP: 275 **EST:** 1883
SQ FT: 257,000
SALES: 25MM **Privately Held**
SIC: 8049 8051 Physical therapist; skilled nursing care facilities

GEOGRAPHIC SECTION

Mason - Warren County (G-13750)

(G-13727)
KINANE INC
Also Called: Manor Hse Bnquet Cnference Ctr
7440 S Masn Montgomery Rd (45040-9762)
PHONE...................513 459-0177
Fax: 513 459-0562
William Kinane, *President*
Michelle Bow, *Sales Mgr*
EMP: 60
SQ FT: 36,989
SALES (est): 4.5MM **Privately Held**
WEB: www.manorhouseohio.com
SIC: 7299 5812 Banquet hall facilities; eating places

(G-13728)
KINDRED HEALTHCARE INC
411 Western Row Rd (45040-1438)
PHONE...................513 336-0178
E Richard Crabtree, *Branch Mgr*
EMP: 39
SALES (corp-wide): 6B **Publicly Held**
SIC: 8099 Blood related health services
PA: Kindred Healthcare, Inc.
680 S 4th St
Louisville KY 40202
502 596-7300

(G-13729)
KRIEGER ENTERPRISES INC
Also Called: Goddard School of Landon, The
3613 Scialville Foster Rd (45040-9335)
PHONE...................513 573-9132
Fax: 513 573-0201
Karen Krieger, *President*
EMP: 25
SALES (est): 1.1MM **Privately Held**
SIC: 8351 Preschool center

(G-13730)
L-3 CMMNCATIONS NOVA ENGRG INC
4393 Digital Way (45040-7604)
P.O. Box 16850, Salt Lake City UT (84116-0850)
PHONE...................877 282-1168
Fax: 513 642-3300
Mark Fischer, *President*
Andrea West, *Accountant*
EMP: 150
SQ FT: 80,000
SALES (est): 8.7MM
SALES (corp-wide): 9.5B **Publicly Held**
WEB: www.l-3com.com
SIC: 8711 3663 Electrical or electronic engineering; carrier equipment, radio communications
PA: L3 Technologies, Inc.
600 3rd Ave Fl 34
New York NY 10016
212 697-1111

(G-13731)
LIBERTY BIBLE ACADEMY ASSN
4900 Old Irwin Simpson Rd (45040-9751)
PHONE...................513 754-1234
Fax: 513 754-1237
Dana Honerlaw, *Principal*
Ona Truesdale, *Finance Mgr*
Teresa Rynearson, *Teacher*
EMP: 33
SQ FT: 13,000
SALES (est): 1.3MM **Privately Held**
WEB: www.libertybibleacademy.org
SIC: 8351 Preschool center

(G-13732)
LIFE TIME FITNESS INC
Also Called: Lifetime
8310 Wilkens Blvd (45040-7364)
PHONE...................513 234-0660
Schuana Lynn Doyle, *Principal*
EMP: 132
SALES (corp-wide): 773.5MM **Privately Held**
SIC: 7991 Athletic club & gymnasiums, membership
HQ: Life Time Fitness, Inc.
2902 Corporate Pl
Chanhassen MN 55317

(G-13733)
LOWES HOME CENTERS LLC
9380 S Masn Montgomery Rd (45040-7665)
PHONE...................513 336-9741
Fax: 513 336-9849
Kathleen Barefield, *Branch Mgr*
EMP: 150
SALES (corp-wide): 68.6B **Publicly Held**
SIC: 5211 5031 5722 5064 Home centers; building materials, exterior; building materials, interior; household appliance stores; electrical appliances, television & radio
HQ: Lowe's Home Centers, Llc
1605 Curtis Bridge Rd
Wilkesboro NC 28697
336 658-4000

(G-13734)
MACYS CR & CUSTOMER SVCS INC (DH)
9111 Duke Blvd (45040-8999)
PHONE...................513 398-5221
Michael Gatio, *President*
Alicia Hamann, *General Mgr*
Dave Faulk, *Exec VP*
Cynthia Walker, *Vice Pres*
Felicia Williams, *Vice Pres*
EMP: 1200
SALES (est): 111.4MM
SALES (corp-wide): 24.8B **Publicly Held**
SIC: 7389 7322 6141 Credit card service; adjustment & collection services; personal credit institutions

(G-13735)
MARKETING INDUS SOLUTIONS CORP (HQ)
3965 Marble Ridge Ln (45040-2892)
PHONE...................513 703-0965
Mark Cohen, *President*
Adam Cohen, *Supervisor*
EMP: 25
SALES (est): 6.8MM **Privately Held**
SIC: 8742 Materials mgmt. (purchasing, handling, inventory) consultant

(G-13736)
MASON FAMILY RESORTS LLC
Also Called: Great Wolf Lodge
2501 Great Wolf Dr (45040-8085)
PHONE...................513 339-0141
Shannon K Kelly, *Marketing Staff*
Ryan Chewning, *Manager*
Austin Kuhn, *Manager*
Shwan Scully, *Director*
Patrick Alvaraz,
EMP: 450
SALES (est): 19.6MM
SALES (corp-wide): 3B **Privately Held**
SIC: 5812 7011 7299 Family restaurants; hotels & motels; banquet hall facilities
HQ: Great Wolf Resorts Holdings, Inc.
525 Junction Rd Ste 6000
Madison WI 53717
608 662-4700

(G-13737)
MASON HEALTH CARE CENTER
5640 Cox Smith Rd (45040-2210)
PHONE...................513 398-2881
Jamie-Lee Thompson, *Office Mgr*
John Monhollen, *Manager*
Shelley Owens, *Director*
EMP: 90
SALES (est): 2.3MM **Privately Held**
SIC: 8051 8361 Convalescent home with continuous nursing care; home for the aged

(G-13738)
MCV HEALTH CARE FACILITIES
411 Western Row Rd (45040-1438)
PHONE...................513 398-1486
Donald Sams, *President*
Roger H Schwartz, *CFO*
Angie Green, *Admin Sec*
EMP: 130
SQ FT: 79,000
SALES: 13MM **Privately Held**
SIC: 8051 8059 8052 Skilled nursing care facilities; rest home, with health care; intermediate care facilities

(G-13739)
MICROSOFT CORPORATION
4605 Duke Dr Ste 800 (45040-7627)
PHONE...................513 339-2800
John Junker, *Accounts Mgr*
Jack Lapan, *Branch Mgr*
EMP: 54
SALES (corp-wide): 89.9B **Publicly Held**
WEB: www.microsoft.com
SIC: 7372 Application computer software
PA: Microsoft Corporation
1 Microsoft Way
Redmond WA 98052
425 882-8080

(G-13740)
MILLENNIUM LEATHER LLC
Also Called: Andrew Philips Collection
4680 Parkway Dr Ste 200 (45040-8173)
PHONE...................201 541-7121
Ram Iyer, *Controller*
Fred Jagodzinski, *Manager*
Philip Kahan,
George Dobbs, *Administration*
Donna L Kahan,
▲ **EMP:** 35
SQ FT: 20,000
SALES (est): 5.4MM **Privately Held**
WEB: www.millenniumleatherllc.com
SIC: 5199 Leather, leather goods & furs

(G-13741)
MVD COMMUNICATIONS LLC (PA)
Also Called: Mvd Connect
5188 Cox Smith Rd (45040-9005)
PHONE...................513 683-4711
Hank Ramsey, *Accounts Mgr*
Joe King, *Sales Engr*
Meghan Murray, *Sales Associate*
Maureen Schaller, *Chief Mktg Ofcr*
Jeff Black, *Mng Member*
EMP: 65
SQ FT: 16,000
SALES (est): 27.6MM **Privately Held**
WEB: www.mvdcommunications.com
SIC: 4813 Data telephone communications; voice telephone communications

(G-13742)
NATORPS INC (PA)
8601 Snider Rd (45040-9273)
PHONE...................513 398-4769
Fax: 513 459-7251
Kyle Natorp, *President*
William Kenneth Natorp, *Chairman*
Craig Natorp, *Vice Pres*
Dave Lapham, *CFO*
Ralph Malaney, *Manager*
EMP: 60
SQ FT: 10,000
SALES: 7MM **Privately Held**
SIC: 5261 0781 Garden supplies & tools; landscape services

(G-13743)
NORTHEAST CINCINNATI HOTEL LLC
9664 S Masn Montgomery Rd (45040-9397)
PHONE...................513 459-9800
David Meisner, *General Mgr*
Lisa Birck, *Sls & Mktg Exec*
Amy Hill, *Human Res Mgr*
Erik Waltz,
Christopher Stone, *Assistant*
EMP: 250
SQ FT: 197,115
SALES (est): 13.2MM **Privately Held**
SIC: 6513 7011 5813 5812 Residential hotel operation; hotels & motels; drinking places; eating places

(G-13744)
P J & R J CONNECTION INC
Also Called: Goddard School, The
754 Reading Rd (45040-1362)
PHONE...................513 398-2777
Fax: 513 573-9716
Ron Herman, *President*
Paula Herman, *Vice Pres*
Kerra Dayton, *Financial Exec*
Amy Van Verth, *Director*
EMP: 28
SALES (est): 1.1MM **Privately Held**
SIC: 8351 Preschool center; group day care center

(G-13745)
PANASONIC CORP NORTH AMERICA
6402 Thornberry Ct (45040-7846)
PHONE...................513 770-9294
Michael Wilson, *Branch Mgr*
EMP: 53
SALES (corp-wide): 64.6B **Privately Held**
SIC: 5064 Electrical appliances, television & radio
HQ: Panasonic Corporation Of North America
2 Riverfront Plz Ste 200
Newark NJ 07102
201 348-7000

(G-13746)
PETSMART INC
8175 Arbor Square Dr (45040-5003)
PHONE...................513 336-0365
Rodney Cramer, *Branch Mgr*
EMP: 28
SALES (corp-wide): 12.7B **Privately Held**
WEB: www.petsmart.com
SIC: 5999 0752 Pets & pet supplies; training services, pet & animal specialties (not horses)
HQ: Petsmart, Inc.
19601 N 27th Ave
Phoenix AZ 85027
623 580-6100

(G-13747)
PIONEER CLDDING GLZING SYSTEMS (PA)
4074 Bethany Rd (45040-9047)
PHONE...................513 583-5925
Fax: 513 583-5926
Tom Heinold, *Principal*
Timothy Hoh, *Vice Pres*
Tom Koogle, *Project Mgr*
Tim Moan, *Project Mgr*
Paul Robinson, *Project Mgr*
▲ **EMP:** 90 **EST:** 1999
SQ FT: 215,000
SALES (est): 56.9MM **Privately Held**
WEB: www.pioneerglazing.com
SIC: 1793 Glass & glazing work

(G-13748)
PRASCO LLC (PA)
Also Called: Prasco Laboratories
6125 Commerce Ct (45040-6723)
PHONE...................513 204-1100
Fax: 513 618-3334
Christopher H Arington, *CEO*
Jonathan Lapps, *President*
Herman Snyder, *President*
David Vucurevich, *President*
Mike Brumfield, *Vice Pres*
▲ **EMP:** 73
SALES (est): 128.9MM **Privately Held**
WEB: www.prasco.com
SIC: 5122 Pharmaceuticals

(G-13749)
PRIMARY CR NTWRK PRMR HLTH PRT
4859 Nixon Park Dr Ste A (45040-8106)
PHONE...................513 492-5940
EMP: 48
SALES (corp-wide): 33.7MM **Privately Held**
SIC: 8011 General & family practice, physician/surgeon
PA: Primary Care Network Of Premier Health Partners
110 N Main St Ste 350
Dayton OH 45402
937 226-7085

(G-13750)
PRIMARY CR NTWRK PRMR HLTH PRT
7450 S Masn Montgomery Rd (45040-7802)
PHONE...................513 204-5785
EMP: 32
SALES (corp-wide): 33.7MM **Privately Held**
SIC: 8099 Childbirth preparation clinic

Mason - Warren County (G-13751) GEOGRAPHIC SECTION

PA: Primary Care Network Of Premier
Health Partners
110 N Main St Ste 350
Dayton OH 45402
937 226-7085

(G-13751)
PURE CONCEPT SALON INC
Also Called: Pure Concept Ecosalon & Spa
5625 Deerfield Cir (45040-1484)
PHONE.................513 770-2120
Renee Hydrich, Branch Mgr
EMP: 47 Privately Held
WEB: www.pureconceptsalon.com
SIC: 7231 Cosmetology & personal hygiene salons; manicurist, pedicurist
PA: Pure Concept Salon, Inc.
8740 Montgomery Rd Ste 7
Cincinnati OH 45236

(G-13752)
QUOTIENT TECHNOLOGY INC
5191 Natorp Blvd Ste 420 (45040-7599)
PHONE.................513 229-8659
EMP: 50
SALES (est): 2MM Publicly Held
SIC: 7389 8742 8743 Advertising, promotional & trade show services; marketing consulting services; promotion service
PA: Quotient Technology Inc.
400 Logue Ave
Mountain View CA 94043

(G-13753)
RE MIDDLETON CNSTR LLC
503 W Main St (45040-1625)
PHONE.................513 398-9255
Robert Middelton,
EMP: 25
SALES (est): 2.6MM Privately Held
SIC: 1521 Single-family housing construction

(G-13754)
REGAL CINEMAS CORPORATION
5500 Deerfield Blvd (45040-2514)
PHONE.................513 770-0713
EMP: 30
SALES (corp-wide): 982.1MM Privately Held
SIC: 7832 Motion picture theaters, except drive-in
HQ: Regal Cinemas Corporation
7132 Regal Ln
Knoxville TN 37920
865 922-1123

(G-13755)
REMTEC AUTOMATION LLC
6049 Hi Tek Ct (45040-2603)
PHONE.................877 759-8151
Keith Rosnell, President
EMP: 25
SALES (est): 220.9K
SALES (corp-wide): 12.9MM Privately Held
SIC: 8742 Automation & robotics consultant
PA: The C M Paula Company
6049 Hi Tek Ct
Mason OH 45040
513 759-7473

(G-13756)
REMTEC ENGINEERING
Also Called: Mbs Acquisition
6049 Hi Tek Ct (45040-2603)
PHONE.................513 860-4299
Keith Rosnell, CEO
Steven Mustain, Engineer
EMP: 45
SQ FT: 25,000
SALES (est): 8.2MM Privately Held
WEB: www.remtecautomation.com
SIC: 3569 5084 Assembly machines, non-metalworking; robots, assembly line: industrial & commercial; robots, industrial

(G-13757)
SEAPINE SOFTWARE INC (HQ)
6960 Cintas Blvd (45040-8922)
PHONE.................513 754-1655
Richard Riccetti, President
Richard Clyde, President
Mark Mason, General Mgr
Ashley Agar, Business Mgr
Bill Anastasia, Business Mgr
EMP: 50
SQ FT: 36,000
SALES (est): 14.8MM Privately Held
WEB: www.seapine.net
SIC: 7372 7371 Prepackaged software; operating systems computer software; business oriented computer software; application computer software; custom computer programming services

(G-13758)
SECURITY NAT AUTO ACCPTNCE LLC
6951 Cintas Blvd (45040-8923)
PHONE.................513 459-8118
Grant Skeens, CEO
Adam Catino, CFO
Adam Contino, CFO
Suzanne Rozniak, Sales Staff
Andrea Andre, Manager
EMP: 162
SQ FT: 24,000
SALES (est): 126MM Privately Held
SIC: 6141 6159 Personal credit institutions; automobile finance leasing

(G-13759)
SELECT HOTELS GROUP LLC
Also Called: Hyatt Pl Cincinnati-Northeast
5070 Natorp Blvd (45040-8263)
PHONE.................513 754-0003
Chris Larmour, Branch Mgr
EMP: 35
SALES (corp-wide): 4.6B Publicly Held
WEB: www.amerisuites.com
SIC: 7011 8741 6519 Hotels; hotel or motel management; real property lessors
HQ: Select Hotels Group, L.L.C.
71 S Wacker Dr
Chicago IL 60606
312 750-1234

(G-13760)
SHIVER SECURITY SYSTEMS INC
Also Called: Sonitrol of South West Ohio
6404 Thornberry Ct # 410 (45040-3502)
PHONE.................513 719-4000
Chip Shizer Sr, Owner
Dwayne Tackett, Opers Mgr
Monica Claxton, Manager
EMP: 40
SALES (est): 5.7MM
SALES (corp-wide): 6.1MM Privately Held
WEB: www.sonitrolsw.com
SIC: 7382 Burglar alarm maintenance & monitoring
PA: Shiver Security Systems, Inc.
15 Pinnacle Point Dr
Miamisburg OH
937 228-7301

(G-13761)
SIBCY CLINE INC
Also Called: Sibcy Cline Realtors
7395 Mason Montgomery Rd (45040-7827)
PHONE.................513 677-1830
Madeline Hoge, General Mgr
EMP: 70
SALES (corp-wide): 2.1B Privately Held
WEB: www.sibcycline.com
SIC: 6531 Real estate agent, residential
PA: Sibcy Cline, Inc.
8044 Montgomery Rd # 300
Cincinnati OH 45236
513 984-4100

(G-13762)
SKILLED CARE PHARMACY INC (PA)
6175 Hi Tek Ct (45040-2603)
PHONE.................513 459-7626
Fax: 513 459-8278
Larry Galluzzo Rph, CEO
Bill Bauza, Vice Pres
Joe Cesta, Vice Pres
Nancy Mlinarik, Vice Pres
Steve Scoby, Facilities Mgr
EMP: 220
SQ FT: 40,000
SALES (est): 66.8MM Privately Held
WEB: www.skilledcare.com
SIC: 5122 Pharmaceuticals

(G-13763)
STOHEN GROUP LLC
3965 Marble Ridge Ln (45040-2892)
PHONE.................513 448-6288
Mark Cohen,
EMP: 33 EST: 2013
SALES (est): 606.1K Privately Held
SIC: 8742 Marketing consulting services

(G-13764)
STRESS ENGINEERING SVCS INC
7030 Stress Engrg Way (45040-7386)
PHONE.................513 336-6701
Fax: 513 336-6817
Christopher Matice, Principal
Beau Loker, Business Mgr
Gary Vissing, Business Mgr
Martin Gibler, Engineer
Amanda Haynes, Marketing Staff
EMP: 60
SALES (corp-wide): 136.8MM Privately Held
WEB: www.stress.com
SIC: 8711 Consulting engineer
PA: Stress Engineering Services, Inc.
13800 Westfair East Dr
Houston TX 77041
281 955-2900

(G-13765)
SUMMIT FUNDING GROUP INC (PA)
4680 Parkway Dr Ste 300 (45040-7979)
PHONE.................513 489-1222
Fax: 513 489-1490
Richard Ross, President
Galen Busse, District Mgr
Marc Ackman, Business Mgr
Betty Duvelius, COO
Carlton Zwilling, Senior VP
EMP: 51
SQ FT: 19,395
SALES (est): 17.5MM Privately Held
WEB: www.summit-funding.com
SIC: 6159 Equipment & vehicle finance leasing companies

(G-13766)
SYNERGY HEALTH NORTH AMER INC
7086 Industrial Row Dr (45040-1363)
PHONE.................513 398-6406
Mike Vell, Manager
EMP: 75
SALES (corp-wide): 2.6B Privately Held
SIC: 3841 7213 Surgical & medical instruments; linen supply
HQ: Synergy Health North America, Inc.
3903 Northdale Blvd 100e
Tampa FL 33624
813 891-9550

(G-13767)
TELEDYNE INSTRUMENTS INC
Also Called: Teledyne Tekmar
4736 Scialville Foster Rd (45040-8265)
PHONE.................513 229-7000
Robert Mehrabian, CEO
Martin Motz, Electrical Engi
Melanie Dahlberg, Manager
Tammy Rellar, Manager
Susan Scheib, Technology
EMP: 25
SALES (corp-wide): 2.6B Publicly Held
SIC: 5049 3826 3829 3821 Laboratory equipment, except medical or dental; analytical instruments; environmental testing equipment; measuring & controlling devices; laboratory apparatus & furniture
HQ: Teledyne Instruments, Inc.
16830 Chestnut St
City Of Industry CA 91748
626 934-1500

(G-13768)
TELEDYNE TEKMAR COMPANY (HQ)
Also Called: Tekmar-Dohrmann
4736 Scialville Foster Rd (45040-8265)
PHONE.................513 229-7000
Fax: 513 229-7050
Robert Mehrabian, Ch of Bd
Ron Uchtman, Opers Mgr
Cindy Cancel, Purchasing
Roger Bardsley, Research
Stephen Proffitt, Research
EMP: 25
SQ FT: 40,000
SALES (est): 34.2MM
SALES (corp-wide): 2.6B Publicly Held
WEB: www.teledynetekmar.com
SIC: 5049 3826 3829 3821 Laboratory equipment, except medical or dental; analytical instruments; environmental testing equipment; measuring & controlling devices; laboratory apparatus & furniture
PA: Teledyne Technologies Inc
1049 Camino Dos Rios
Thousand Oaks CA 91360
805 373-4545

(G-13769)
TO SCALE SOFTWARE LLC
Also Called: Stack Constructyion Technology
6398 Thornberry Ct (45040-7816)
PHONE.................513 253-0053
Phillip Ogilby, Mng Member
Jane Baysore,
EMP: 35
SALES: 2.5MM Privately Held
SIC: 7372 Prepackaged software

(G-13770)
TOP GUN SALES PERFORMANCE INC
5155 Financial Way Ste 1 (45040-2557)
PHONE.................513 770-0870
J Steven Osborne, CEO
Barry Gorsun, President
David Kessinger, Vice Pres
Michael Wlotzko, Vice Pres
Michelle Hook, Accounting Mgr
EMP: 30
SALES (est): 5.9MM Privately Held
SIC: 7379 Computer related maintenance services

(G-13771)
TOUCHSTONE MDSE GROUP LLC (HQ)
7200 Industrial Row Dr (45040-1386)
PHONE.................513 741-0400
Fax: 513 770-3222
Derek Block, President
Bill Bok, President
Steve Pardiso, COO
Andrew Backen, Senior VP
Chris Berger, Senior VP
EMP: 64
SQ FT: 12,000
SALES (est): 18.9MM Privately Held
SIC: 7311 Advertising agencies

(G-13772)
TRAK-1 TECHNOLOGY INC
4770 Duke Dr Ste 200 (45040-9010)
PHONE.................513 204-5530
EMP: 37
SALES (corp-wide): 4MM Privately Held
SIC: 1799 Building board-up contractor
PA: Trak-1 Technology, Inc.
7131 Riverside Pkwy
Tulsa OK 74136
918 779-7000

(G-13773)
TRIHEALTH HF LLC
7423 S Mason Mntgomery (45040-7828)
PHONE.................513 398-3445
Brian Hoffman, Mng Member
EMP: 27 EST: 2012
SALES (est): 73K Privately Held
SIC: 8099 Health & allied services

(G-13774)
TRITON SERVICES INC
8162 Duke Blvd (45040-8111)
PHONE.................513 679-6800
Fax: 513 679-6808
Majid H Samarghandi, CEO
Michael E Defrank, Principal
Mike Frazier, Project Mgr
Brian Pastura, Project Mgr
Scott Royer, Project Mgr
EMP: 125
SALES (est): 37.9MM Privately Held
WEB: www.tritonservicesinc.com
SIC: 1711 Mechanical contractor

GEOGRAPHIC SECTION
Massillon - Stark County (G-13799)

(G-13775)
TRUECHOICEPACK CORP
5155 Financial Way Ste 6 (45040-0055)
PHONE...................................937 630-3832
Heena Rathore, *President*
Christopher Che, *Chairman*
Rakesh Rathore, *COO*
Alyssa Yates, *Admin Asst*
EMP: 44
SALES (est): 2MM **Privately Held**
SIC: 3089 3086 8748 7389 Blister or bubble formed packaging, plastic; packaging & shipping materials, foamed plastic; business consulting; field warehousing
PA: Che International Group, Llc
9435 Waterstone Blvd # 140
Cincinnati OH 45249
513 444-2072

(G-13776)
UC HEALTH LLC
Also Called: Uc Health Primary Care Mason
9313 S Mason Montgomery R (45040-8009)
PHONE...................................513 584-6999
Monica Hartman, *Gnrl Med Prac*
Jeffrey T Baker, *Internal Med*
Amy Hovermale, *Internal Med*
Christopher McKiernan, *Internal Med*
Garvin Nickell, *Internal Med*
EMP: 252 **Privately Held**
SIC: 8011 General & family practice, physician/surgeon
PA: Uc Health, Llc.
3200 Burnet Ave
Cincinnati OH 45229

(G-13777)
VAN DYK MORTGAGE CORPORATION
4680 Parkway Dr Ste 100 (45040-8296)
PHONE...................................513 429-2122
Todd Bitter, *Principal*
EMP: 32
SALES (corp-wide): 96.1MM **Privately Held**
SIC: 6211 Mortgages, buying & selling
PA: Van Dyk Mortgage Corporation
2449 Camelot Ct Se
Grand Rapids MI 49546
616 940-3000

(G-13778)
VET PATH SERVICES INC
Also Called: Vps, Inc.
6450 Castle Dr (45040-9412)
PHONE...................................513 469-0777
Christopher Johnson, *President*
Philip Long, *Vice Pres*
Kim Schon, *Office Mgr*
EMP: 35
SQ FT: 13,000
SALES (est): 2.2MM **Privately Held**
WEB: www.vetpathservicesinc.com
SIC: 8071 Pathological laboratory

(G-13779)
WALL2WALL SOCCER LLC
846 Reading Rd (45040-1886)
PHONE...................................513 573-9898
Fax: 513 573-9899
Donte Rainone, *Mng Member*
Pat Benedetto, *Manager*
EMP: 40
SALES (est): 975.8K **Privately Held**
WEB: www.wall2wallsoccer.com
SIC: 7941 Soccer club

Massillon
Stark County

(G-13780)
3-D SERVICE LTD (PA)
Also Called: Magnetech
800 Nave Rd Se (44646-9476)
PHONE...................................330 830-3500
Fax: 330 830-3510
Bernie Dewees, *President*
Jim Depew, *Managing Dir*
Gordon Mayer, *Controller*
Lori Oberlin, *Asst Controller*
Tracy Tucker, *Human Res Mgr*
▲ **EMP:** 120
SQ FT: 85,000
SALES (est): 7.1MM **Privately Held**
WEB: www.3-dservice.com
SIC: 7694 7699 Electric motor repair; industrial equipment services

(G-13781)
A A HAMMERSMITH INSURANCE INC (PA)
210 Erie St N (44646-8400)
P.O. Box 591 (44648-0591)
PHONE...................................330 832-7411
Fax: 330 833-5045
Herold Weatherbee, *CEO*
Robert McAfee, *President*
Phillip Fox, *Vice Pres*
John Muhlbach Jr, *Vice Pres*
Richard Snyder, *Vice Pres*
EMP: 27
SQ FT: 6,000
SALES (est): 8.7MM **Privately Held**
WEB: www.aahammersmith.com
SIC: 6411 Insurance agents

(G-13782)
A P & P DEV & CNSTR CO (PA)
2851 Lincoln Way E (44646-3769)
PHONE...................................330 833-8886
Nichkolas Maragas, *President*
Theresa Edwards, *Manager*
EMP: 70
SQ FT: 2,000
SALES (est): 13.5MM **Privately Held**
SIC: 1542 6513 Commercial & office building, new construction; apartment building operators

(G-13783)
AAUW ACTION FUND INC
8400 Milmont St Nw (44646-1761)
PHONE...................................330 833-0520
Jacqueline Woods, *Exec Dir*
EMP: 25
SALES (corp-wide): 226.2K **Privately Held**
SIC: 8621 Education & teacher association
PA: Aauw Action Fund, Inc.
1310 L St Nw Ste 1000
Washington DC 20005
202 785-7700

(G-13784)
ADVANCED INDUSTRIAL ROOFG INC
1330 Erie St S (44646-7906)
PHONE...................................330 837-1999
Fax: 330 837-7864
Fred Horner, *President*
Jeff Rupert, *Vice Pres*
Dawn Horner, *Manager*
EMP: 75
SQ FT: 12,140
SALES (est): 14.4MM **Privately Held**
WEB: www.airoofing.com
SIC: 1761 Roofing contractor

(G-13785)
AMERICOLD LOGISTICS LLC
2140 17th St Sw (44647-7525)
PHONE...................................330 834-1742
Fax: 330 834-2678
Duane Wilson, *Facilities Mgr*
Ron Lair, *Branch Mgr*
John Bair, *Manager*
EMP: 90
SALES (corp-wide): 1.5B **Privately Held**
WEB: www.americoldlogistics.com
SIC: 4222 Warehousing, cold storage or refrigerated
HQ: Americold Logistics, Llc
10 Glenlake Pkwy Ste 324
Atlanta GA 30328
678 441-1400

(G-13786)
AMVETS POST NO 6 INC
8417 Audubon St Nw (44646-7811)
PHONE...................................330 833-5935
Orran Cahoun, *Owner*
EMP: 40
SALES: 4.5K **Privately Held**
SIC: 8641 Veterans' organization

(G-13787)
AQUA OHIO INC
Water Treatment Plant
870 3rd St Nw (44647-4206)
PHONE...................................330 832-5764
James Purtz, *Principal*
EMP: 25
SALES (corp-wide): 809.5MM **Publicly Held**
SIC: 4941 Water supply
HQ: Aqua Ohio, Inc.
6650 South Ave
Youngstown OH 44512
330 726-8151

(G-13788)
AULTCOMP INC
2458 Lincoln Way E (44646-5085)
P.O. Box 4817 (44648-4817)
PHONE...................................330 830-4919
Fax: 330 830-4901
Edward J Roth, *President*
EMP: 25
SQ FT: 4,200
SALES (est): 1.2MM **Privately Held**
WEB: www.aultcomp.com
SIC: 8741 Administrative management

(G-13789)
BRINKS INCORPORATED
300 Nova Dr Se (44646-8899)
PHONE...................................330 832-6130
Fax: 330 832-6196
Scott Nichols, *Branch Mgr*
EMP: 27
SALES (corp-wide): 3.3B **Publicly Held**
WEB: www.brinksinc.com
SIC: 7381 Armored car services
HQ: Brink's, Incorporated
1801 Bayberry Ct Ste 400
Richmond VA 23226
804 289-9600

(G-13790)
BUTTERFIELD CO INC
Also Called: Finishing Touch Cleaning Svcs
401 26th St Nw (44647-5124)
PHONE...................................330 832-1282
David M Butterfield, *President*
David Butterfield, *President*
EMP: 75
SALES (est): 1.9MM **Privately Held**
SIC: 7349 Building maintenance services; cleaning service, industrial or commercial

(G-13791)
C-N-D INDUSTRIES INC
Also Called: Cnd Machine
359 State Ave Nw (44647-4269)
PHONE...................................330 478-8811
Clyde Shetler, *President*
Don Rossbach, *CFO*
Karen Hawelo, *Manager*
EMP: 42
SQ FT: 28,000
SALES (est): 8.6MM **Privately Held**
WEB: www.cndinc.com
SIC: 3441 3599 7692 3444 Fabricated structural metal; machine shop, jobbing & repair; welding repair; sheet metalwork

(G-13792)
CAMPBELL OIL COMPANY (PA)
7977 Hills & Dales Rd Ne (44646-6798)
PHONE...................................330 833-8555
Fax: 330 833-1083
Mac Campbell Jr, *CEO*
Brian D Campbell, *President*
Chris Campbell, *Owner*
Wesley S Campbell, *Owner*
Jay Weisgarber, *Project Mgr*
EMP: 58 **EST:** 1939
SQ FT: 5,000
SALES (est): 115MM **Privately Held**
SIC: 5171 Petroleum bulk stations

(G-13793)
CASE FARMS LLC
Also Called: Massillon Feed Mill
4001 Millennium Blvd Se (44646-9606)
PHONE...................................330 832-0030
Thomas R Shelton, *Branch Mgr*
Josh Carney, *Manager*
EMP: 106 **Privately Held**
SIC: 0723 Feed milling custom services
PA: Case Farms, L.L.C.
385 Pilch Rd
Troutman NC 28166

(G-13794)
CHILDS INVESTMENT CO
Also Called: Hospitality House
205 Rohr Ave Nw (44646-3671)
PHONE...................................330 837-2100
Fax: 330 837-2454
Steven Childs, *CEO*
Judy Willard, *Exec Dir*
Fritz Colleen, *Social Dir*
Trish Gruno, *Executive*
EMP: 50
SQ FT: 20,000
SALES (est): 3.2MM **Privately Held**
SIC: 8052 8051 Intermediate care facilities; skilled nursing care facilities

(G-13795)
CHRISTIAN RIVERTREE SCHOOL
Also Called: Rivertreechristian.com
7373 Portage St Nw (44646-9315)
PHONE...................................330 494-1860
Jason Lantz, *Pastor*
Roger Schuler, *Pastor*
Krista Canter, *Manager*
Pamela Clevenger, *Director*
Danielle Harper, *Director*
EMP: 46
SALES (est): 1MM **Privately Held**
WEB: www.rivertreechristian.com
SIC: 8351 Preschool center

(G-13796)
CITY OF MASSILLON
Also Called: Waste Water Treatment Plant
100 Dig Indian Dr Sw (44646)
PHONE...................................330 833-3304
Fax: 330 833-2077
Tony Ulrich, *Plant Mgr*
Joseph R Ulrich, *Manager*
EMP: 29 **Privately Held**
SIC: 4941 Water supply
PA: City Of Massillon
1 James Duncan Plz Ste 7
Massillon OH 44646
330 830-1734

(G-13797)
CLOVERLEAF COLD STORAGE CO
950 Cloverleaf St Se (44646-9647)
PHONE...................................330 833-9870
Fax: 330 833-9860
Al Harwick, *Manager*
EMP: 50
SALES (corp-wide): 57.3MM **Privately Held**
WEB: www.cloverleafco.com
SIC: 4222 Warehousing, cold storage or refrigerated
PA: Cloverleaf Cold Storage Co.
401 Douglas St Ste 406
Sioux City IA 51101
712 279-8000

(G-13798)
CONSULATE MANAGEMENT CO LLC
Also Called: Legends Care Center
2311 Nave Rd Sw (44646)
PHONE...................................330 837-1001
Fax: 330 837-1623
Tara Price, *Manager*
Aruna RAO, *Director*
EMP: 100
SALES (corp-wide): 581.9MM **Privately Held**
WEB: www.tandemhealthcare.com
SIC: 8051 Skilled nursing care facilities
PA: Consulate Management Company, Llc
800 Concourse Pkwy S
Maitland FL 32751
407 571-1550

(G-13799)
COUNTY OF STARK
Also Called: Park Dist Maintenance
798 Genoa Ave Nw (44646-3164)
PHONE...................................330 477-3609
Fax: 330 479-2150
Robert Font, *Director*

Massillon - Stark County (G-13800)

EMP: 48 **Privately Held**
WEB: www.starkadas.org
SIC: 7699 9111 Miscellaneous automotive repair services; county supervisors' & executives' offices
PA: County Of Stark
110 Central Plz S Ste 240
Canton OH 44702
330 451-7371

(G-13800)
DHSC LLC (HQ)
Also Called: Affinity Medical Center
875 8th St Ne (44646-8503)
PHONE..................................330 832-8761
Elizabeth Pruitt, *CEO*
Micheal Holt, *CFO*
Oneda Benjamin, *Administration*
Andrew Ohar, *Surg-Orthopdc*
Mouhamed R Lababidi, *Urology*
▲ **EMP:** 58
SALES: 91.8MM
SALES (corp-wide): 2B **Publicly Held**
WEB: www.chs.net
SIC: 8062 General medical & surgical hospitals
PA: Quorum Health Corporation
1573 Mallory Ln
Brentwood TN 37027
615 221-1400

(G-13801)
DOCTORS HOSP PHYSCN SVCS LLC
Also Called: Affinity Family Physicians
830 Amherst Rd Ne Ste 201 (44646-8518)
PHONE..................................330 834-4725
Ron Bierman, *CEO*
EMP: 40
SALES (est): 10.6MM
SALES (corp-wide): 2B **Publicly Held**
SIC: 8011 General & family practice, physician/surgeon
PA: Quorum Health Corporation
1573 Mallory Ln
Brentwood TN 37027
615 221-1400

(G-13802)
DUSK TO DAWN PROTECTIVE SVCS
3554 Lincoln Way E 3 (44646-8607)
PHONE..................................330 837-9992
Fax: 330 837-9994
Ralph Ury, *Owner*
EMP: 25
SALES (est): 300K **Privately Held**
SIC: 7381 Security guard service

(G-13803)
EMSCO INC (HQ)
1000 Nave Rd Ne (44646-9478)
P.O. Box 607 (44648-0607)
PHONE..................................330 830-7125
James J Dyer, *President*
Steve Otto, *General Mgr*
Greg Guggisberg, *Area Mgr*
Donald Miller, *Vice Pres*
Tom McWilliams, *Project Mgr*
▲ **EMP:** 31
SQ FT: 55,000
SALES (est): 17.4MM
SALES (corp-wide): 930.4MM **Privately Held**
WEB: www.emsco.com
SIC: 7699 Industrial machinery & equipment repair
PA: Rowan Technologies, Inc.
10 Indel Ave
Rancocas NJ 08073
609 267-9000

(G-13804)
EMSCO INC
Emsco North Division
1000 Nave Rd Ne (44646-9478)
PHONE..................................330 833-5600
Paul D Wolanski, *Division Mgr*
EMP: 25
SALES (corp-wide): 930.4MM **Privately Held**
SIC: 7699 Industrial machinery & equipment repair

HQ: Emsco, Inc.
1000 Nave Rd Se
Massillon OH 44646
330 830-7125

(G-13805)
F W ARNOLD AGENCY CO INC
Also Called: Hammer Smith Agency
210 Erie St N (44646-8450)
PHONE..................................330 832-1556
Fax: 330 832-9852
John L Muhlbach Jr, *President*
Charles Clark, *Vice Pres*
Faye Hedrick, *Treasurer*
Virginia Sorg, *Admin Sec*
EMP: 30 **EST:** 1876
SALES (est): 2.8MM **Privately Held**
WEB: www.fwarnold.com
SIC: 6411 Insurance agents

(G-13806)
FAIRPORT ENTERPRISES INC
Also Called: Laurels of Massillon, The
2000 Sherman Cir Ne (44646-5219)
PHONE..................................330 830-9988
Fax: 330 830-0039
Thomas F Franke, *Ch of Bd*
Dennis Sherman, *President*
Jason A Frutschy, *Maintenance Dir*
Lynette Mock Sherman, *Asst Treas*
Diane McKeen, *Office Mgr*
EMP: 150
SALES: 12.2MM **Privately Held**
SIC: 8051 Convalescent home with continuous nursing care
PA: Laurel Health Care Company Of North Worthtington
8181 Worthington Rd
Westerville OH 43082

(G-13807)
FARRIS PRODUCE INC
2421 Lincoln Way Nw (44647-5111)
PHONE..................................330 837-4607
Fax: 330 837-6781
Wanda Farris, *President*
Stephen Farris, *Treasurer*
EMP: 25
SQ FT: 9,996
SALES: 4.4MM **Privately Held**
WEB: www.farrisproduce.com
SIC: 5148 Fruits, fresh; vegetables

(G-13808)
FLORLINE GROUP INC
Also Called: Florline Midwest
800 Vista Ave Se (44646-7948)
PHONE..................................330 830-3380
Fax: 330 830-3381
Christopher Reynolds, *President*
Peter W Reynolds, *Principal*
Shane Reynolds, *Vice Pres*
EMP: 25
SQ FT: 11,700
SALES (est): 5.7MM **Privately Held**
SIC: 1752 5162 Floor laying & floor work; resins

(G-13809)
FORT DIALYSIS LLC
Also Called: Massillon Community Dialysis
2112 Lincoln Way E (44646-7034)
PHONE..................................330 837-7730
James K Hilger,
EMP: 33 **EST:** 2012
SALES (est): 395K **Publicly Held**
SIC: 8092 Kidney dialysis centers
PA: Davita Inc.
2000 16th St
Denver CO 80202

(G-13810)
FRESH MARK INC (PA)
Also Called: Superior's Brand Meats
1888 Southway St Se (44646)
P.O. Box 571 (44648-0571)
PHONE..................................330 834-3669
Fax: 330 430-5658
Neil Genshaft, *CEO*
David Cochenour, *President*
Tim Cranor, *President*
Lee Poludinak, *Purchasing*
Debbie Seese, *QA Dir*
◆ **EMP:** 500 **EST:** 1932
SQ FT: 80,000

SALES (est): 519.4MM **Privately Held**
WEB: www.freshmark.com
SIC: 2013 5147 2011 Prepared beef products from purchased beef; prepared pork products from purchased pork; sausages & related products, from purchased meat; meats & meat products; meat packing plants

(G-13811)
FRESH MARK INC
950 Cloverleaf St Se (44646-9647)
PHONE..................................330 833-9870
Mike Portilla, *Branch Mgr*
EMP: 254
SALES (corp-wide): 519.4MM **Privately Held**
SIC: 4222 Warehousing, cold storage or refrigerated
PA: Fresh Mark, Inc.
1888 Southway St Se
Massillon OH 44646
330 834-3669

(G-13812)
FRESH MARK INC
Also Called: Fresh Mark Sugardale
1888 Southway St Sw (44646-9429)
P.O. Box 571 (44648-0571)
PHONE..................................330 832-7491
Fax: 330 830-3174
Tim Craner, *President*
Scott Cannon, *Senior VP*
Keith Kiewall, *Senior VP*
Anthony Lacerenza, *Inv Control Mgr*
Tom Miller, *QC Mgr*
EMP: 350
SALES (corp-wide): 519.4MM **Privately Held**
WEB: www.freshmark.com
SIC: 5147 2013 Meats & meat products; sausages & other prepared meats
PA: Fresh Mark, Inc.
1888 Southway St Se
Massillon OH 44646
330 834-3669

(G-13813)
GENCO OF LEBANON INC
Also Called: Genco Marketing Place
4300 Sterilite St Se (44646-7452)
PHONE..................................330 837-0561
Marc Wittenberg, *Manager*
EMP: 2520
SALES (corp-wide): 262.7MM **Privately Held**
SIC: 1541 Warehouse construction
PA: Genco Of Lebanon, Inc.
700 Cranberry Woods Dr
Cranberry Township PA 16066
412 820-3747

(G-13814)
GREENLEAF AUTO RECYCLERS LLC
12192 Lincoln Way Nw (44647-9601)
PHONE..................................330 832-6001
Jerr Banta, *Principal*
EMP: 31
SALES (corp-wide): 9.7B **Publicly Held**
SIC: 5013 Automotive supplies & parts
HQ: Greenleaf Auto Recyclers, Llc
904 S Intrstate 45 Svc Rd
Hutchins TX

(G-13815)
GREENLEAF OHIO LLC
Also Called: Grand Central Auto Recycling
12192 Lincoln Way Nw (44647-9601)
PHONE..................................330 832-6001
Fax: 330 833-4503
Eric Bagwell, *General Mgr*
EMP: 35
SQ FT: 5,000
SALES: 1.5MM **Privately Held**
SIC: 5015 5531 Automotive parts & supplies, used; automotive parts

(G-13816)
H & W CONTRACTORS INC
1722 1st St Ne (44646-4068)
P.O. Box 876 (44648-0876)
PHONE..................................330 833-0982
Fax: 330 833-5575
Michael R Watkins, *President*
Anne Watkins, *Corp Secy*

Daniel R Watkins, *Vice Pres*
EMP: 26 **EST:** 1970
SQ FT: 7,000
SALES (est): 3.1MM **Privately Held**
SIC: 1623 Pipeline construction; water main construction; sewer line construction

(G-13817)
HANOVER HOUSE INC
435 Avis Ave Nw (44646-3599)
PHONE..................................330 837-1741
Fax: 330 837-1747
Jill Hodgson, *Office Mgr*
Kenneth Biros, *Director*
Hollis Garfield,
Albert Wiggins,
EMP: 160
SALES (est): 4MM **Privately Held**
SIC: 8051 Convalescent home with continuous nursing care

(G-13818)
HEALTH SERVICES INC
Also Called: Complete Home Care
2520 Wales Ave Nw Ste 120 (44646-2398)
PHONE..................................330 837-7678
Fax: 330 837-8068
Mervin Strine, *Ch of Bd*
James Budiscak, *President*
Richard Leffler, *Treasurer*
Allison Fischer, *Controller*
EMP: 30
SQ FT: 5,500
SALES (est): 460.4K
SALES (corp-wide): 11MM **Privately Held**
WEB: www.thehealthgroup.com
SIC: 8049 5999 Physical therapist; hospital equipment & supplies
PA: The Health Group
5425 High Mill Ave Nw
Massillon OH
330 833-3174

(G-13819)
HEARTLAND BHAVIORAL HEALTHCARE
3000 Erie St S (44646-7976)
PHONE..................................330 833-3135
Fax: 330 833-6564
Helen Stevens, *CEO*
Phyllis Adams, *Facilities Mgr*
Thomas Halter, *Facilities Mgr*
Pat Henderschot, *CFO*
Lori McCambridge, *CFO*
EMP: 320
SALES (est): 22MM **Privately Held**
SIC: 8063 Psychiatric hospitals

(G-13820)
HOMETOWN HOSPITAL HEALTH PLAN
100 Lillian Gish Blvd Sw # 301 (44647-6588)
PHONE..................................330 834-2200
Fax: 330 837-6869
William Epling, *President*
Duane E Davis, *Vice Pres*
Gennaro A Daniels, *Bd of Directors*
EMP: 175
SALES (est): 3.4MM **Privately Held**
SIC: 8062 6321 General medical & surgical hospitals; health insurance carriers

(G-13821)
HYDRO-DYNE INC
225 Wetmore Ave Se (44646-6788)
P.O. Box 318 (44648-0318)
PHONE..................................330 832-5076
Fax: 330 832-8163
Rose Ann Dare, *President*
Lynn Neel, *Vice Pres*
Jean Holiday, *Manager*
Craig McMillen, *Manager*
Sherri McMillen, *Manager*
▲ **EMP:** 30
SQ FT: 130,000
SALES (est): 8.2MM **Privately Held**
WEB: www.hydrodyneinc.com
SIC: 3585 8711 Evaporative condensers, heat transfer equipment; engineering services

GEOGRAPHIC SECTION

Massillon - Stark County (G-13845)

(G-13822)
IDENTITEK SYSTEMS INC
Also Called: Adams Signs
1100 Industrial Ave Sw (44647-7608)
P.O. Box 347 (44648-0347)
PHONE..................330 832-9844
Fax: 330 832-6999
Joseph Pugliese, *President*
EMP: 53
SQ FT: 70,000
SALES (est): 8.4MM **Privately Held**
WEB: www.adamsigns.com
SIC: 1799 3993 Sign installation & maintenance; signs & advertising specialties; electric signs

(G-13823)
IES INFRSTRCTURE SOLUTIONS LLC (HQ)
800 Nave Rd Se (44646-9476)
PHONE..................330 830-3500
Michael Rice, *President*
EMP: 30
SALES (est): 64.2MM **Publicly Held**
SIC: 1731 Electrical work

(G-13824)
INN AT UNIV VLG MGT CO LLC
2650 Ohio State Dr Se (44646-9656)
PHONE..................330 837-3000
Denise Beck, *Principal*
Karen Goodwin, *Business Dir*
EMP: 34
SALES (est): 1.7MM **Privately Held**
SIC: 8052 Personal care facility

(G-13825)
J B M CLEANING & SUPPLY CO
Also Called: Jbm Cleaning
3106 Sheila St Nw (44646-3075)
P.O. Box 23 (44648-0023)
PHONE..................330 837-8805
Fax: 330 830-6436
Patrick Leslie, *President*
Deborah Leslie, *Vice Pres*
EMP: 25
SALES: 500K **Privately Held**
WEB: www.jbmcleans.com
SIC: 7349 5999 Janitorial service, contract basis; concrete products, pre-cast

(G-13826)
JEFFREY CARR CONSTRCTION INC
4164 Erie Ave Sw (44646-9668)
P.O. Box 1051 (44648-1051)
PHONE..................330 879-5210
Jeffrey Carr, *President*
Mike Mills, *Superintendent*
Jeff Carr, *Principal*
Joel Reott, *VP Opers*
Lisa Aul, *Manager*
EMP: 50
SQ FT: 3,500
SALES: 15.9MM **Privately Held**
WEB: www.jcarrconstruction.com
SIC: 1542 Commercial & office buildings, renovation & repair

(G-13827)
KENMORE CONSTRUCTION CO INC
Also Called: American Sand & Gravel Div
9500 Forty Corners Rd Nw (44647-9309)
PHONE..................330 832-8888
Chris Scala, *Manager*
EMP: 48
SALES (corp-wide): 93MM **Privately Held**
WEB: www.kenmorecompanies.com
SIC: 1611 1442 General contractor, highway & street construction; construction sand & gravel
PA: Kenmore Construction Co., Inc.
700 Home Ave
Akron OH 44310
330 762-8936

(G-13828)
LAND OLAKES INC
8485 Navarre Rd Sw (44646-8814)
PHONE..................330 879-2158
Fax: 330 879-5804
Gary Hauenstin, *Manager*
EMP: 41
SALES (corp-wide): 14.9B **Privately Held**
WEB: www.landolakes.com
SIC: 2048 5191 2047 Livestock feeds; animal feeds; dog & cat food
PA: Land O'lakes, Inc.
4001 Lexington Ave N
Arden Hills MN 55126
651 375-2222

(G-13829)
LOWES HOME CENTERS LLC
101 Massillon Marketplace (44646-2015)
PHONE..................330 832-1901
Fax: 330 832-7537
Shelley Brucker, *Design Engr*
Yquanda Addison, *Human Resources*
Jay Millovitsch, *Marketing Staff*
Ron Vyof, *Branch Mgr*
Tommy Bowlin, *Manager*
EMP: 150
SALES (corp-wide): 68.6B **Publicly Held**
SIC: 5211 5031 5722 5064 Home centers; building materials, exterior; building materials, interior; household appliance stores; electrical appliances, television & radio
HQ: Lowe's Home Centers, Llc
1605 Curtis Bridge Rd
Wilkesboro NC 28697
336 658-4000

(G-13830)
MAGNETECH INDUSTRIAL SVCS INC (DH)
800 Nave Rd Se (44646-9476)
PHONE..................330 830-3500
Michael P Moore, *President*
Cullen Burdette, *Vice Pres*
Edward Matheny, *Vice Pres*
William Wisniewski, *Vice Pres*
Jim Depew, *QC Dir*
▲ EMP: 80
SALES (est): 36.8MM **Publicly Held**
SIC: 7629 Electrical equipment repair services
HQ: Ies Subsidiary Holdings, Inc
5433 Westheimer Rd # 500
Houston TX 77056
713 860-1500

(G-13831)
MAGNETECH INDUSTRIAL SVCS INC
800 Nave Rd Se (44646-9476)
PHONE..................330 830-3500
Mike Rice, *Branch Mgr*
Bill Muncy, *Manager*
David Tharp, *Manager*
EMP: 120 **Publicly Held**
SIC: 7694 7699 Electric motor repair; industrial equipment services
HQ: Magnetech Industrial Services, Inc.
800 Nave Rd Se
Massillon OH 44646
330 830-3500

(G-13832)
MASSILLON AUTOMOBILE CLUB
Also Called: AAA Massillon Automobile Club
1972 Wales Rd Ne Ste 1 (44646-4197)
PHONE..................330 833-1084
Fax: 330 833-5542
Jeff Bushman, *Director*
EMP: 26
SQ FT: 11,912
SALES (est): 40K **Privately Held**
SIC: 8699 Automobile owners' association

(G-13833)
MASSILLON CABLE TV INC (PA)
814 Cable Ct Nw (44647-4284)
P.O. Box 1000 (44648-1000)
PHONE..................330 833-4134
Fax: 330 833-7522
Robert B Gessner, *President*
H Chas Hess, *Principal*
Jacob F Hess, *Principal*
M P L Kirchhofer, *Principal*
Susan Gessner, *COO*
EMP: 75 EST: 1965
SQ FT: 10,000
SALES (est): 26.5MM **Privately Held**
WEB: www.massilloncabletv.com
SIC: 4841 8748 4813 Cable television services; telecommunications consultant;

(G-13834)
MASSILLON CITY SCHOOL BUS GAR
1 George Red Bird Dr Se (44646-7176)
PHONE..................330 830-1849
Fax: 330 830-1858
Ken McCune, *Superintendent*
Ken Cune, *Manager*
Therese Penland, *Manager*
Monica Shrader, *Teacher*
EMP: 30
SALES (est): 601.5K **Privately Held**
SIC: 4151 School buses

(G-13835)
MASSILLON CMNTY HOSP HLTH PLAN
Also Called: Home Town Health Network
100 Lillian Gish Blvd Sw (44647-6587)
PHONE..................330 837-6880
William Epling, *President*
Mervin F Strine, *Director*
EMP: 160
SALES (est): 50MM **Privately Held**
SIC: 6324 Health maintenance organization (HMO), insurance only

(G-13836)
MASSILLON HEALTH SYSTEM LLC
400 Austin Ave Nw (44646-3554)
PHONE..................330 837-7200
Bill Chandler, *Med Doctor*
Ranga Thalluri, *Med Doctor*
Mary Bing, *Manager*
Michael Richfeld,
EMP: 1451
SQ FT: 230,000
SALES (est): 385.6MM
SALES (corp-wide): 2B **Publicly Held**
SIC: 8062 General medical & surgical hospitals
PA: Quorum Health Corporation
1573 Mallory Ln
Brentwood TN 37027
615 221-1400

(G-13837)
MATRIX SYS AUTO FINISHES LLC
600 Nova Dr Se (44646-8884)
PHONE..................248 668-8135
W Kent Gardner, *President*
Terry Peterson, *Manager*
Sean Hook, *Director*
EMP: 100
SQ FT: 26,000
SALES (est): 37MM
SALES (corp-wide): 155.9MM **Privately Held**
WEB: www.matrixsystem.com
SIC: 5198 2851 Paints; paints & allied products
PA: Quest Specialty Chemicals, Inc.
225 Sven Farms Dr Ste 204
Charleston SC 29492
800 966-7580

(G-13838)
MEADOW WIND HLTH CARE CTR INC
300 23rd St Ne (44646-4996)
PHONE..................330 833-3026
Fax: 330 833-0548
Robert Buchanan, *President*
Anne Marie King, *Personnel*
Daniel Cannone, *Director*
John Faust, *Director*
EMP: 130
SQ FT: 32,000
SALES (est): 7.5MM **Privately Held**
SIC: 8051 Convalescent home with continuous nursing care

(G-13839)
MERCY PROFESSIONAL CARE
2859 Aaronwood Ave Ne (44646-2390)
PHONE..................330 832-2280
EMP: 40
SALES (corp-wide): 4.7MM **Privately Held**
SIC: 8011 Offices & clinics of medical doctors
PA: Mercy Professional Care
1320 Mercy Dr Nw
Canton OH 44708
330 489-1435

(G-13840)
MIDWEST HEALTH SERVICES INC
107 Tommy Henrich Dr Nw (44647-5402)
PHONE..................330 828-0779
Joseph Knetzer, *President*
Kristine Knetzer, *Hlthcr Dir*
EMP: 125
SALES (est): 7.7MM **Privately Held**
WEB: www.midwesths.com
SIC: 8361 Halfway group home, persons with social or personal problems

(G-13841)
NFM/WELDING ENGINEERS INC
1339 Duncan St Sw (44647-7843)
PHONE..................330 837-3868
Fax: 330 837-7727
Tim Boron, *Vice Pres*
John Roberson, *Vice Pres*
Bob Kirkland, *Purch Agent*
Bill Schaffer, *Purch Agent*
Phil Roberson, *Manager*
EMP: 50
SALES (corp-wide): 43.2MM **Privately Held**
WEB: www.nfmwe.com
SIC: 5084 Plastic products machinery
PA: Nfm/Welding Engineers, Inc.
577 Oberlin Ave Sw
Massillon OH 44647
330 837-3868

(G-13842)
OHIO DRILLING COMPANY (PA)
2405 Bostic Blvd Sw (44647-7686)
P.O. Box 847 (44648-0847)
PHONE..................330 832-1521
Fax: 330 832-5302
George P Mayhew, *President*
Jeff Brest, *Admin Sec*
EMP: 25 EST: 1907
SQ FT: 23,000
SALES (est): 4.2MM **Privately Held**
SIC: 1781 Water well servicing

(G-13843)
PEOPLES CARTAGE INC
8045 Navarre Rd Sw (44648)
PHONE..................330 833-8571
Fax: 330 833-2035
Joseph Chevreau, *Principal*
EMP: 35 **Privately Held**
SIC: 4225 General warehousing
HQ: People's Cartage, Inc.
2207 Kimball Rd Se
Canton OH 44707
330 453-3709

(G-13844)
POLYMER PACKAGING INC (PA)
Also Called: Polymer Protective Packaging
8333 Navarre Rd Se (44646-9652)
PHONE..................330 832-2000
Larry L Lanham, *CEO*
Ronald Reagan, *President*
William D Lanham, *Exec VP*
Chris Thomazin, *Vice Pres*
Jeffrey S Davis, *CFO*
▲ EMP: 65
SQ FT: 36,000
SALES (est): 58.1MM **Privately Held**
WEB: www.polymerpkg.com
SIC: 5113 5162 2621 2821 Paper & products, wrapping or coarse; plastics products; wrapping & packaging papers; plastics materials & resins

(G-13845)
PROGRSSIVE OLDSMOBILE CADILLAC
Also Called: Progressive Dodge
7966 Hills & Dales Rd Ne (44646-5241)
PHONE..................330 833-8585
Toll Free:..................877 -
Fax: 330 833-3728
Dan Sanders, *President*
Carol Coates, *Treasurer*
Jay Johnson, *Sales Mgr*
EMP: 48
SQ FT: 20,000

Massillon - Stark County (G-13846)

SALES (est): 14.5MM Privately Held
WEB: www.progressivedodge.com
SIC: 5511 7538 5521 Automobiles, new & used; general automotive repair shops; used car dealers

(G-13846)
PURINA ANIMAL NUTRITION LLC
8485 Navarre Rd Sw (44646-8814)
PHONE....................330 879-2158
Gary Hauenstein, Manager
EMP: 35
SALES (corp-wide): 14.9B Privately Held
SIC: 5191 Feed
HQ: Purina Animal Nutrition Llc
1080 County Road F W
Shoreview MN 55126

(G-13847)
REPUBLIC SERVICES INC
2800 Erie St S (44646-7915)
PHONE....................330 830-9050
Fax: 330 834-3769
Ronald Setterlin, Principal
Pete Gutwin, Branch Mgr
Pete Gutwein Jr, Manager
EMP: 34
SQ FT: 11,000
SALES (corp-wide): 10B Publicly Held
WEB: www.republicservices.com
SIC: 4953 Refuse collection & disposal services
PA: Republic Services, Inc.
18500 N Allied Way # 100
Phoenix AZ 85054
480 627-2700

(G-13848)
REPUBLIC SERVICES INC
2800 Erie St S (44646-7915)
PHONE....................800 247-3644
Ronald Setterlin, Branch Mgr
EMP: 34
SALES (corp-wide): 10B Publicly Held
WEB: www.republicservices.com
SIC: 4953 Refuse collection & disposal services
PA: Republic Services, Inc.
18500 N Allied Way # 100
Phoenix AZ 85054
480 627-2700

(G-13849)
ROBERT J MATTHEWS COMPANY (PA)
Also Called: P B S Animal Health
2780 Richville Dr Se (44646-8396)
PHONE....................330 834-3000
Fax: 330 830-2762
Della L Matthews, Ch of Bd
John K Cox, Principal
Robert J Matthews, Principal
J Stephen Matthews, Vice Pres
John D Matthews, Vice Pres
▲ EMP: 60
SQ FT: 40,000
SALES (est): 63MM Privately Held
WEB: www.horsehealthusa.com
SIC: 5122 Pharmaceuticals

(G-13850)
ROSE LN HLTH RHABILITATION INC
Also Called: Rose Lane Inc
5425 High Mill Ave Nw (44646-9005)
PHONE....................330 833-3174
Fax: 330 833-4216
Karren Talbot, CEO
Dennis Potts, President
Chase Tennant, Office Mgr
Blair Kingsley, Director
Aruna RAO, Director
EMP: 240
SQ FT: 34,000
SALES (est): 11MM Privately Held
WEB: www.roselane.org
SIC: 8051 Skilled nursing care facilities; extended care facility
PA: The Health Group
5425 High Mill Ave Nw
Massillon OH
330 833-3174

(G-13851)
ROUND ROOM LLC
Also Called: Unknown
3 Massillon Mrktplc Dr Sw (44646-2014)
PHONE....................330 880-0660
EMP: 44 Privately Held
SIC: 4813 Local & long distance telephone communications
PA: Round Room, Llc
525 Congressional Blvd
Carmel IN 46032

(G-13852)
SEIFERT & GROUP INC
2323 Nave Rd Se (44646-8822)
PHONE....................330 833-2700
Fax: 330 833-2793
Tim Seifert, President
Kevin Pierson, General Mgr
Michael Lee, Vice Pres
Sue Corrigan, Sales Executive
Dale Musser, Data Proc Staff
EMP: 89
SQ FT: 9,000
SALES (est): 4.5MM Privately Held
WEB: www.seifertgroup.com
SIC: 8748 8711 7375 7371 Business consulting; engineering services; information retrieval services; custom computer programming services; employment agencies

(G-13853)
SEIFERT TECHNOLOGIES INC (PA)
2323 Nave Rd Se (44646-8822)
PHONE....................330 833-2700
Timothy Seifert, President
Matthew D Ashton, Vice Pres
Richard T Kettler, Vice Pres
Neil Slabaugh, Project Engr
Angela Sterling, Accounting Mgr
EMP: 65
SQ FT: 8,900
SALES (est): 12.7MM Privately Held
WEB: www.seifert.com
SIC: 7389 Drafting service, except temporary help; design services

(G-13854)
SHADY HOLLOW CNTRY CLB CO INC
4865 Wales Ave Nw (44646-9396)
PHONE....................330 832-1581
Fax: 330 830-3350
Keith Baklarc, Manager
EMP: 100
SALES (est): 5.4MM Privately Held
SIC: 7997 7992 7991 5941 Country club, membership; public golf courses; physical fitness facilities; sporting goods & bicycle shops; eating places

(G-13855)
SHEARERS FOODS LLC (PA)
Also Called: Shearer's Snacks
100 Lincoln Way E (44646-6634)
PHONE....................330 834-4030
C J Fraleigh, CEO
Christopher Fraleigh, CEO
Dan Kessler, Business Mgr
Erik Nadig, Business Mgr
Brad Patrick, Exec VP
◆ EMP: 700 EST: 1980
SQ FT: 200,000
SALES (est): 590.9MM Privately Held
SIC: 2096 5145 Potato chips & similar snacks; snack foods

(G-13856)
STANDARDS TESTING LABS INC (PA)
1845 Harsh Ave Se (44646-7123)
P.O. Box 758 (44648-0758)
PHONE....................330 833-8548
Fax: 330 833-7902
Anthony E Efremoff, President
Darryl Fuller, President
Tina Wood, Purch Mgr
Jason Sumney, Draft/Design
Tim Flood, Chief Engr
▲ EMP: 48
SQ FT: 84,000

SALES (est): 9.8MM Privately Held
WEB: www.stllabs.com
SIC: 3829 8734 8071 Testing equipment: abrasion, shearing strength, etc.; product testing laboratory, safety or performance; automobile proving & testing ground; medical laboratories

(G-13857)
STARK MEDICAL SPECIALTIES INC (PA)
323 Marion Ave Nw Ste 200 (44646-3639)
PHONE....................330 837-1111
Fax: 330 837-1769
Seth Brown, President
Dr John Uslick, Corp Secy
Dr Wayne Gross, Vice Pres
Dr George Seese, Vice Pres
EMP: 34 EST: 1970
SQ FT: 8,400
SALES (est): 4.6MM Privately Held
SIC: 8011 Physicians' office, including specialists

(G-13858)
STEAKS & SUCH INC
Also Called: Meat Packers Outlet
244 Federal Ave Nw (44647-5469)
PHONE....................330 837-9296
Fax: 330 837-2870
William E Hemperly, President
Mary Hemperly, Treasurer
Lisa Etheridge, Admin Sec
EMP: 25
SQ FT: 2,000
SALES (est): 1.1MM Privately Held
SIC: 5421 5147 Meat markets, including freezer provisioners; meats, fresh

(G-13859)
TWELVE INC (PA)
Also Called: TWELVE OF OHIO, THE
619 Tremont Ave Sw (44647-6468)
P.O. Box 376 (44648-0376)
PHONE....................330 837-3555
Fax: 330 837-0513
Mark Huemme, President
Charles J Bendetta, Vice Pres
Linda Sirpilla, Hum Res Coord
John D Stoia, Exec Dir
Danelle Bryant, Director
EMP: 31 EST: 2002
SQ FT: 7,000
SALES: 2.4MM Privately Held
WEB: www.the12inc.org
SIC: 8361 8322 Boys' Towns; individual & family services

(G-13860)
WESTARK FAMILY SERVICES INC
42 1st St Ne (44646-8406)
PHONE....................330 832-5043
Fax: 330 830-2540
Nancy Maier, Exec Dir
EMP: 35
SALES: 713.5K Privately Held
WEB: www.westarkfamilyservices.com
SIC: 8322 Family counseling services

(G-13861)
WHISLER PLUMBING & HEATING INC
2521 Lincoln Way E (44646-5099)
PHONE....................330 833-2875
Fax: 330 833-0584
Jack Sponseller, President
Sharon Kannel, Corp Secy
Jerry Whisler, Vice Pres
Dale Taylor, Senior Buyer
EMP: 40 EST: 1930
SQ FT: 2,500
SALES (est): 8MM Privately Held
SIC: 1711 Plumbing contractors; warm air heating & air conditioning contractor

(G-13862)
Y M C A CENTRAL STARK COUNTY
Also Called: Jackson Community YMCA
7389 Caritas Cir Nw (44646-6275)
PHONE....................330 830-6275
Jean Campbell, Branch Mgr
EMP: 27

SALES (corp-wide): 16.5MM Privately Held
SIC: 8641 7991 8351 7032 Youth organizations; physical fitness facilities; child day care services; youth camps; individual & family services
PA: Y M C A Of Central Stark County
1201 30th St Nw Ste 200a
Canton OH 44709
330 491-9622

(G-13863)
YMCA OF MASSILLON (PA)
Also Called: YMCA OF WESTERN STARK COUNTY
131 Tremont Ave Se (44646-6637)
PHONE....................330 837-5116
Fax: 330 837-5119
Jim Stamford, Director
EMP: 31
SQ FT: 16,342
SALES: 2MM Privately Held
WEB: www.massillonymca.org
SIC: 8641 Civic associations

(G-13864)
YUND INC
Also Called: Yund Car Care Center
205 1st St Nw (44647-5437)
PHONE....................330 837-9358
Fax: 330 837-8772
Robert K Yund, President
Douglad Drushal, Treasurer
EMP: 28
SQ FT: 6,764
SALES (est): 1.1MM Privately Held
SIC: 7542 7549 5411 Washing & polishing, automotive; lubrication service, automotive; grocery stores

(G-13865)
ZIEGLER TIRE AND SUPPLY CO (PA)
4150 Millennium Blvd Se (44646-7449)
PHONE....................330 353-1499
Fax: 330 834-3342
Curtis A Hanner, Principal
Hommer A Ray, Principal
Oliver Ziegler, Principal
Nate Clements, COO
John Ziegler Jr, Vice Pres
EMP: 35 EST: 1919
SQ FT: 112,000
SALES (est): 78.9MM Privately Held
WEB: www.zieglertire.com
SIC: 5531 5014 Automotive tires; truck equipment & parts; truck tires & tubes

---

Masury
Trumbull County

(G-13866)
P I & I MOTOR EXPRESS INC (PA)
908 Broadway St (44438-1356)
P.O. Box 685, Sharon PA (16146-0685)
PHONE....................330 448-4035
Fax: 330 448-1379
Joseph Kerola, President
William Kerola, Exec VP
Ray Tedesco, Opers Staff
Jeanne Bortner, CFO
Jeanie Bordner, Financial Exec
EMP: 128
SQ FT: 76,000
SALES (est): 34.7MM Privately Held
WEB: www.piimx.com
SIC: 8741 4213 4212 Management services; trucking, except local; local trucking, without storage

(G-13867)
PENN-OHIO ELECTRICAL COMPANY
Also Called: Penn Ohio Electrical Contrs
1370 Sharon Hogue Rd (44438-8710)
PHONE....................330 448-1234
Fax: 330 448-0335
Chris O'Brien, President
John P O'Brien, Vice Pres
Daniel O'Brien, Treasurer
Kirt J O'Brien, Admin Sec
EMP: 30

SQ FT: 5,000
SALES (est): 8.9MM Privately Held
SIC: 1731 General electrical contractor

(G-13868)
SPECIALIZED SERVICES INC
908 Broadway St (44438-1356)
P.O. Box 62 (44438-0062)
PHONE..................330 448-4035
Joe Kerola, *President*
Bill Kerola, *Vice Pres*
EMP: 26
SALES (est): 1.3MM Privately Held
SIC: 7538 General automotive repair shops

(G-13869)
UPS GROUND FREIGHT INC
7945 3rd St (44438-1336)
PHONE..................330 448-0440
Ike Henry, *Manager*
EMP: 42
SALES (corp-wide): 65.8B Publicly Held
WEB: www.overnite.com
SIC: 4213 Trucking, except local
HQ: Ups Ground Freight, Inc.
   1000 Semmes Ave
   Richmond VA 23224
   866 372-5619

Maumee
Lucas County

(G-13870)
A THOMAS DALAGIANNIS MD
1360 Arrowhead Dr (43537-1728)
PHONE..................419 887-7000
Thomas Dalagiannis, *Partner*
Lawrence Baibak, *Partner*
Jeff Kesler, *Partner*
EMP: 25 **EST:** 2001
SALES (est): 350.9K Privately Held
SIC: 8011 Plastic surgeon

(G-13871)
ABOUTGOLF LIMITED (PA)
352 Tomahawk Dr (43537-1612)
PHONE..................419 482-9095
William Bales, *CEO*
Bill Bales, *Principal*
Paul Basmajian, *Vice Pres*
Troy Gulgin, *Engineer*
Pat Moore, *Regl Sales Mgr*
▲ **EMP:** 55
SQ FT: 20,000
SALES (est): 4.8MM Privately Held
WEB: www.aboutgolf.com
SIC: 7992 Public golf courses

(G-13872)
ACCESSRN INC
1540 S Hiland Sylvania Rd (43537)
PHONE..................419 698-1988
Joseph Pettee, *President*
Mary Pettee, *President*
Jeff Condon, *Marketing Staff*
Kay Rasmus, *Marketing Staff*
Erin McPartland, *Manager*
EMP: 99
SQ FT: 1,500
SALES (est): 8.3MM Privately Held
SIC: 8748 Business consulting

(G-13873)
AKTION ASSOCIATES INCORPORATED
1687 Woodlands Dr (43537-4018)
PHONE..................419 893-7001
Scott E Irwin, *President*
EMP: 50
SALES (corp-wide): 63.3MM Privately Held
SIC: 8731 7371 Computer (hardware) development; computer software development & applications
PA: Aktion Associates, Incorporated
   1687 Woodlands Dr
   Maumee OH 43537
   419 893-7001

(G-13874)
AMERICAN FRAME CORPORATION (PA)
400 Tomahawk Dr (43537-1695)
PHONE..................419 893-5595
Fax: 419 893-3553
Ronald J Mickel, *President*
Michael Cromly, *Vice Pres*
Larry Haddad, *Vice Pres*
Kevin Wiley, *Plant Mgr*
Dana Dunbar, *Treasurer*
▲ **EMP:** 44
SQ FT: 33,000
SALES (est): 5.6MM Privately Held
WEB: www.americanframe.com
SIC: 7699 5961 5023 3444 Picture framing, custom; mail order house; home furnishings; sheet metalwork

(G-13875)
AMERICAN HEALTH GROUP INC
570 Longbow Dr (43537-1724)
PHONE..................419 891-1212
Fax: 419 891-1280
Warren Eckles MD, *President*
Steven Bronber, *VP Opers*
Oshia Hale, *Manager*
Julie Richardson,
EMP: 70
SQ FT: 15,000
SALES: 10MM Privately Held
SIC: 8742 8748 Hospital & health services consultant; business consulting

(G-13876)
ANATRACE PRODUCTS LLC (HQ)
434 W Dussel Dr (43537-1624)
PHONE..................419 740-6600
Ben Travis, *President*
Mike Drury, *CFO*
Brian German, *VP Sales*
Judy McCormick, *Cust Mgr*
Connie Cupilary,
EMP: 34
SALES (est): 7.3MM Privately Held
SIC: 5169 3585 Detergents & soaps, except specialty cleaning; refrigeration & heating equipment

(G-13877)
ANDERSONS INC
Also Called: Retail Distribution Center
1380 Ford St (43537-1733)
P.O. Box 119 (43537-0119)
PHONE..................419 891-6479
Mike Anderson, *Manager*
Russ Kahler, *Manager*
Bill Hichcock, *Info Tech Mgr*
EMP: 120
SALES (corp-wide): 3.6B Publicly Held
WEB: www.andersonsinc.com
SIC: 4225 General warehousing
PA: The Andersons Inc
   1947 Briarfield Blvd
   Maumee OH 43537
   419 893-5050

(G-13878)
ANDERSONS INC
Also Called: Anderson's Rail Car Service
421 Illinois Ave (43537-1705)
P.O. Box 119 (43537-0119)
PHONE..................419 891-6634
Bill Kubista, *Purchasing*
Tom Waggoner, *Branch Mgr*
Gary Beale, *Manager*
Joromy Espinoza, *Admin Asst*
EMP: 38
SALES (corp-wide): 3.6B Publicly Held
SIC: 4789 Railroad maintenance & repair services
PA: The Andersons Inc
   1947 Briarfield Blvd
   Maumee OH 43537
   419 893-5050

(G-13879)
ANDERSONS INC (PA)
1947 Briarfield Blvd (43537-1690)
P.O. Box 119 (43537-0119)
PHONE..................419 893-5050
Fax: 419 891-6672
Daniel T Anderson, *President*
Patrick E Bowe, *President*
Michael S Irmen, *President*
Corbett Jorgenson, *President*
Rasesh H Shah, *President*
◆ **EMP:** 150
SQ FT: 245,000
SALES: 3.6B Publicly Held
WEB: www.andersonsinc.com
SIC: 5153 0723 5191 2874 Grain & field beans; grains; grain elevators; crop preparation services for market; cash grain crops market preparation services; farm supplies; fertilizers & agricultural chemicals; seeds & bulbs; phosphatic fertilizers; plant foods, mixed: from plants making phosphatic fertilizer; railroad car repair; rental of railroad cars

(G-13880)
ANDERSONS INC
533 Illinois Ave (43537-1707)
PHONE..................419 893-5050
Rob Hassen, *Chief Engr*
Herm Kurrelmeier, *Branch Mgr*
Christopher Schwind, *Supervisor*
EMP: 120
SALES (corp-wide): 3.6B Publicly Held
WEB: www.andersonsinc.com
SIC: 4225 General warehousing
PA: The Andersons Inc
   1947 Briarfield Blvd
   Maumee OH 43537
   419 893-5050

(G-13881)
ANDERSONS AGRICULTURE GROUP LP (HQ)
Also Called: Anderson's Farm
1947 Briarfield Blvd (43537-1690)
P.O. Box 119 (43537-0119)
PHONE..................419 893-5050
Hal Reed, *Partner*
Naran Burchinow, *Vice Pres*
Joe Needham, *Vice Pres*
Robert Petree, *Warehouse Mgr*
Dan Marsalek, *Project Engr*
◆ **EMP:** 45
SALES (est): 60.1MM
SALES (corp-wide): 3.6B Publicly Held
SIC: 5191 Fertilizer & fertilizer materials
PA: The Andersons Inc
   1947 Briarfield Blvd
   Maumee OH 43537
   419 893-5050

(G-13882)
ANDY FRAIN SERVICES INC
1715 Indian Wood Cir # 200 (43537-4055)
PHONE..................419 897-7909
Fax: 419 897-7912
Maryann Cook, *Branch Mgr*
EMP: 500
SALES (corp-wide): 244.6MM Privately Held
SIC: 7381 Security guard service
PA: Andy Frain Services, Inc.
   761 Shoreline Dr
   Aurora IL 60504
   630 820-3820

(G-13883)
APRIA HEALTHCARE LLC
Also Called: Young Medical
4062 Technology Dr (43537-9263)
PHONE..................419 471-1919
Shawn Cowell, *Branch Mgr*
Patricia Mahon, *Manager*
Cynthia Parsons, *Director*
EMP: 54
SQ FT: 22,000 Privately Held
SIC: 5047 7352 Hospital equipment & furniture; medical equipment rental
HQ: Apria Healthcare Llc
   26220 Enterprise Ct
   Lake Forest CA 92630
   949 616-2606

(G-13884)
AUXILIARY ST LUKES HOSPITAL
Also Called: St Lukes Gift Shop
5901 Monclova Rd (43537-1841)
PHONE..................419 893-5911
Iris Weirich, *President*
Richard Patt, *Chief Mktg Ofcr*
Irene Wolff, *Manager*
Ellie Kotowicz, *Nurse*
Merrie Gilson DDS, *Fmly & Gen Dent*
EMP: 50
SQ FT: 500
SALES (est): 2.1MM Privately Held
SIC: 5947 8699 Gift shop; charitable organization

(G-13885)
BARNES GROUP INC
Associated Spring Raymond
370 W Dussel Dr Ste A (43537-1604)
PHONE..................419 891-9292
Fax: 419 891-9192
Peter Korczynski, *Opers Mgr*
Erica Denton, *Purch Mgr*
Tracy Allison, *Controller*
Tyler Schroeder, *Sales Engr*
Jeffrey Finch, *Info Tech Mgr*
EMP: 30
SALES (corp-wide): 1.4B Publicly Held
WEB: www.barnesgroupinc.com
SIC: 5072 3495 Hardware; wire springs
PA: Barnes Group Inc.
   123 Main St
   Bristol CT 06010
   860 583-7070

(G-13886)
BAUER LAWN MAINTENANCE INC
6341 Monclova Rd (43537-9760)
P.O. Box 8732 (43537-8732)
PHONE..................419 893-5296
Fax: 419 893-3944
Craig Bauer, *President*
Josh Cash, *Project Mgr*
Lori Bauer, *Admin Sec*
EMP: 50
SQ FT: 2,000
SALES (est): 4MM Privately Held
WEB: www.bauerlawn.com
SIC: 0782 4959 Lawn care services; landscape contractors; snowplowing

(G-13887)
BENNETT ENTERPRISES INC
Also Called: Hampton Inn
1409 Reynolds Rd (43537-1625)
PHONE..................419 893-1004
Fax: 419 893-4613
Ken Brandt, *Manager*
EMP: 30
SQ FT: 3,613
SALES (corp-wide): 66.6MM Privately Held
WEB: www.bennett-enterprises.com
SIC: 7011 Hotels & motels
PA: Bennett Enterprises, Inc.
   27476 Holiday Ln
   Perrysburg OH 43551
   419 874-1933

(G-13888)
BPF ENTERPRISES LTD
Cold Fire Decor
1901 Middlesbrough Ct # 2 (43537-2202)
PHONE..................419 855-2545
EMP: 100
SALES (corp-wide): 3.1MM Privately Held
SIC: 7389
PA: Bpf Enterprises Ltd.
   1901 Middlesbrough Ct # 2
   Maumee OH 43537
   419 855-2545

(G-13889)
BRANDYWINE MASTER ASSN
7705 Pilgrims Lndg (43537-9571)
PHONE..................419 866-0135
Charles Zsarnay, *Treasurer*
EMP: 56
SALES (est): 588.5K Privately Held
SIC: 8641 Condominium association

(G-13890)
BRIDGEPOINT RISK MGT LLC
1440 Arrowhead Dr (43537-4016)
PHONE..................419 794-1075
Greg Jones, *Branch Mgr*
EMP: 34
SALES (corp-wide): 9.6MM Privately Held
SIC: 8741 Management services

Maumee - Lucas County (G-13891)

PA: Bridgepoint Risk Management Llc
5 Greenwich Office Park
Greenwich CT 06831
203 274-8010

(G-13891)
BRONDES ALL MAKES AUTO LEASING
1511 Reynolds Rd (43537-1601)
PHONE..............................419 887-1511
Phillip Brondes Jr, *President*
EMP: 86
SALES (corp-wide): 3.3MM **Privately Held**
SIC: 7515 Passenger car leasing
PA: Brondes All Makes Auto Leasing Inc
5545 Secor Rd
Toledo OH 43623
419 473-1411

(G-13892)
CELLCO PARTNERSHIP
Also Called: Verizon
1378 Conant St (43537-1610)
PHONE..............................419 897-9133
David Johnson, *Branch Mgr*
EMP: 71
SALES (corp-wide): 126B **Publicly Held**
SIC: 4812 5999 Cellular telephone services; telephone equipment & systems
HQ: Cellco Partnership
1 Verizon Way
Basking Ridge NJ 07920

(G-13893)
CENTAUR MAIL INC
Also Called: Centaur Associates
4064 Technology Dr Ste A (43537-9739)
PHONE..............................419 887-5857
Fax: 419 482-6563
Michael J Walters, *President*
Dennise Kamcza, *Exec VP*
Lisa Willford, *Vice Pres*
EMP: 50
SQ FT: 10,500
SALES (est): 5.9MM **Privately Held**
WEB: www.centaur-associates.com
SIC: 4215 Parcel delivery, vehicular

(G-13894)
CHECKER NOTIONS COMPANY INC (PA)
Also Called: Checker Distributors
400 W Dussel Dr Ste B (43537-1636)
PHONE..............................419 893-3636
Fax: 419 893-2422
J Robert Krieger III, *President*
Lisa Frantz, *Managing Prtnr*
Bradley Krieger, *Vice Pres*
James McDonald, *Opers Mgr*
Jim Steedman, *Opers Mgr*
▲ EMP: 89
SQ FT: 120,000
SALES (est): 78.1MM **Privately Held**
WEB: www.checkerdist.com
SIC: 5131 5199 5949 5162 Sewing supplies & notions; art goods & supplies; quilting materials & supplies; plastics basic shapes

(G-13895)
COLGAN-DAVIS INC
1682 Lance Pointe Rd (43537-1600)
PHONE..............................419 893-6116
Fax: 419 893-7977
Patrick Davis, *President*
Marlene Davis, *Corp Secy*
EMP: 25
SQ FT: 9,600
SALES: 4.9MM **Privately Held**
SIC: 1731 Electrical work

(G-13896)
COLONIAL COURIER SERVICE INC
409 Osage St (43537-1637)
PHONE..............................419 891-0922
Ken Miller, *Manager*
EMP: 29
SALES (corp-wide): 4.1MM **Privately Held**
WEB: www.forwardair.net
SIC: 4731 Truck transportation brokers

PA: Colonial Courier Service Inc
413 Osage St
Maumee OH 43537
419 891-0922

(G-13897)
COLONIAL COURIER SERVICE INC (PA)
413 Osage St (43537-1637)
PHONE..............................419 891-0922
Fax: 419 893-4616
Judith J Miller, *President*
Robert E Miller, *Vice Pres*
EMP: 30
SQ FT: 35,000
SALES (est): 4.1MM **Privately Held**
SIC: 4731 Freight forwarding

(G-13898)
COLT ENTERPRISES INC
Also Called: Right At Home
133 E John St (43537-3341)
PHONE..............................567 336-6062
John Baldwin, *Owner*
Connie Fox, *Assistant*
EMP: 30
SALES (est): 667.1K **Privately Held**
SIC: 8082 Visiting nurse service

(G-13899)
CONSULATE HEALTHCARE INC (PA)
Also Called: PARKSIDE MANOR
3231 Manley Rd (43537-9680)
PHONE..............................419 865-1248
Fax: 419 865-7524
Lynn Buchlee, *President*
Mary Huff, *Chf Purch Ofc*
Ashley Snyder, *Accounting Mgr*
Samantha Waller, *Office Mgr*
Theresa Martinez, *Manager*
EMP: 50
SALES: 5.6MM **Privately Held**
SIC: 8051 8052 Skilled nursing care facilities; intermediate care facilities

(G-13900)
CONSULATE MANAGEMENT CO LLC
Also Called: Swan Point Care Center
3600 Butz Rd (43537-9691)
PHONE..............................419 867-7926
Patrick Airson, *Administration*
EMP: 80
SALES (corp-wide): 581.9MM **Privately Held**
WEB: www.tandemhealthcare.com
SIC: 8051 Skilled nursing care facilities
PA: Consulate Management Company, Llc
800 Concourse Pkwy S
Maitland FL 32751
407 571-1550

(G-13901)
CRAIG TRANSPORTATION CO
819 Kingsbury St Ste 102 (43537-1861)
P.O. Box 1010, Perrysburg (43552-1010)
PHONE..............................419 874-7981
Fax: 419 874-3094
Lance C Craig, *Principal*
Phil Jacks, *Vice Pres*
Chris Simmons, *Vice Pres*
Gail M Craig, *CFO*
Carla Tipton, *Accountant*
EMP: 40 EST: 1929
SQ FT: 14,000
SALES (est): 22.6MM **Privately Held**
WEB: www.craigtransport.com
SIC: 4731 4213 Freight transportation arrangement; trucking, except local

(G-13902)
CROGHAN BANCSHARES INC
6465 Wheatstone Ct (43537-8610)
PHONE..............................419 794-9399
Kirby Holman, *Branch Mgr*
EMP: 90 **Publicly Held**
SIC: 6029 6021 Commercial banks; national commercial banks
PA: Croghan Bancshares, Inc.
323 Croghan St
Fremont OH 43420

(G-13903)
DANA CREDIT CORPORATION (DH)
3939 Technology Dr (43537-9194)
PHONE..............................419 887-3000
Paul J Bishop, *President*
Dennis Greenwald, *Vice Pres*
Latitia D Marth, *Vice Pres*
Dean L Wilson, *Vice Pres*
Cindy Stokes, *Info Tech Mgr*
EMP: 100
SQ FT: 55,000
SALES (est): 25.1MM **Publicly Held**
SIC: 6159 Machinery & equipment finance leasing

(G-13904)
DANBERRY CO
3555 Briarfield Blvd (43537-9383)
PHONE..............................419 866-8888
Fax: 419 868-7653
Dan McQuillen, *Branch Mgr*
Julie Wood, *Manager*
EMP: 60
SALES (corp-wide): 24MM **Privately Held**
SIC: 6531 Real estate agent, residential
PA: The Danberry Co
3242 Executive Pkwy # 203
Toledo OH 43606
419 534-6592

(G-13905)
DARI PIZZA ENTERPRISES II INC
1683 Woodlands Dr Ste A (43537-4052)
PHONE..............................419 534-3000
Suzan Dari, *President*
Omar Dari, *Principal*
MO Dari, *Vice Pres*
EMP: 150
SALES (est): 4.8MM **Privately Held**
SIC: 5812 8742 6531 Lunchrooms & cafeterias; new business start-up consultant; real estate agents & managers

(G-13906)
DEFINITIONS OF DESIGN INC
467 W Dussel Dr (43537-4210)
PHONE..............................419 891-0188
Fax: 419 891-0120
Kathline Forshe, *President*
Peggy George, *Vice Pres*
EMP: 35
SALES (est): 959.2K **Privately Held**
SIC: 7231 Beauty shops; manicurist, pedicurist; cosmetologist; facial salons

(G-13907)
EATON-AEROQUIP LLC
1660 Indian Wood Cir (43537-4004)
PHONE..............................419 891-7775
Howard Selland, *President*
Chad Achenbach, *Purchasing*
Douglas Hanlon, *Manager*
Robert Koehler, *Manager*
Lennard McMinn, *Technology*
EMP: 90 **Privately Held**
SIC: 8711 3594 3593 3561 Professional engineer; fluid power pumps & motors; fluid power cylinders & actuators; pumps & pumping equipment; fluid power valves & hose fittings; rubber & plastics hose & beltings
HQ: Eaton Aeroquip Llc
1000 Eaton Blvd
Cleveland OH 44122
216 523-5000

(G-13908)
ED SCHMIDT CHEVROLET INC
1425 Reynolds Rd (43537-1625)
P.O. Box 1180 (43537-8180)
PHONE..............................419 897-8600
Fax: 419 897-8713
Robert E Schmidt, *President*
Charles R Schmidt, *Vice Pres*
John Schmidt, *Vice Pres*
William C Wagoner, *Treasurer*
Lynn Schmidt, *Admin Sec*
EMP: 60
SQ FT: 83,000
SALES (est): 11.7MM **Privately Held**
SIC: 5511 7515 Automobiles, new & used; passenger car leasing

(G-13909)
ELIZABETH SCOTT INC
Also Called: Elizabeth Scott Mem Care Ctr
2720 Albon Rd (43537-9752)
PHONE..............................419 865-3002
Fax: 419 865-1283
Paul Bucher, *President*
Debra Bucher, *Vice Pres*
Matt Bucher, *Mktg Dir*
Patrick McSurley, *Director*
Jonathan Rohrs, *Director*
EMP: 116
SQ FT: 73,000
SALES (est): 6.2MM **Privately Held**
SIC: 8059 Nursing home, except skilled & intermediate care facility

(G-13910)
ENTELCO CORPORATION (PA)
6528 Weatherfield Ct (43537-9468)
PHONE..............................419 872-4620
Fax: 419 872-4623
Stephen Stranahan, *President*
Ann Stranahan, *Manager*
EMP: 63
SQ FT: 3,000
SALES: 66.6K **Privately Held**
WEB: www.en-tel.com
SIC: 6719 Investment holding companies, except banks

(G-13911)
EPILEPSY CNTR OF NRTHWSTRN OH
1701 Holland Rd (43537-1699)
PHONE..............................419 867-5950
Jocelyn Sugg, *Human Res Mgr*
Betty Hartman, *Office Mgr*
Roy J Cherry, *Exec Dir*
Chad Bringman, *Director*
Wendy Turner, *Director*
EMP: 56 EST: 1977
SALES: 3.2MM **Privately Held**
SIC: 8399 Health systems agency

(G-13912)
ERIE SHORES CREDIT UNION INC (PA)
1688 Woodlands Dr (43537-4069)
P.O. Box 9037 (43537-9037)
PHONE..............................419 897-8110
Ralph Kubacki, *CEO*
Jim Troknya, *Ch of Bd*
Phil Parker, *CTO*
EMP: 31
SQ FT: 8,536
SALES (est): 5.2MM **Privately Held**
SIC: 6062 State credit unions, not federally chartered

(G-13913)
FALLEN TIMBERS FMLY PHYSICIANS
Also Called: Bertka, Vicki M MD
5705 Monclova Rd (43537-1875)
PHONE..............................419 893-3321
Fax: 419 893-8395
John Croci, *Business Mgr*
Vicki Bertka, *Corp Secy*
Donna Woodson, *Vice Pres*
Brian K Miller, *Med Doctor*
Marcie Williams, *Manager*
EMP: 55
SALES (est): 4.6MM **Privately Held**
WEB: www.ftfp.net
SIC: 8011 General & family practice, physician/surgeon

(G-13914)
FASTER INC
6560 Weatherfield Ct (43537-9468)
PHONE..............................419 868-8197
Stijn Vriends, *President*
Francesco Arosio, *President*
Ted Frost, *Vice Pres*
Bill Crossen, *Sales Staff*
Tammy Montgomery, *Marketing Staff*
▲ EMP: 32
SQ FT: 16,000
SALES: 31MM
SALES (corp-wide): 352.2K **Privately Held**
WEB: www.fasterinc.com
SIC: 5085 Industrial fittings

HQ: Faster Spa
Via Ariosto 7
Rivolta D'adda CR 26027
036 337-7211

(G-13915)
FED EX ROB CARPENTER
4348 Beck Dr (43537-1804)
PHONE..................................419 260-1889
Rob Carpenter, *President*
EMP: 26
SALES: 1MM **Privately Held**
SIC: 4215 Package delivery, vehicular

(G-13916)
FELLER FINCH & ASSOCIATES INC (PA)
1683 Woodlands Dr Ste A (43537-4052)
PHONE..................................419 893-3680
Fax: 419 893-2982
Donald L Feller, *President*
Brenda Thompson, *Business Mgr*
Chris Crisenbery, *Vice Pres*
Gregory N Feller, *Vice Pres*
Dave Kuhn, *Project Mgr*
EMP: 46
SQ FT: 5,000
SALES (est): 3.2MM **Privately Held**
WEB: www.fellerfinch.com
SIC: 8713 8711 Surveying services; civil engineering

(G-13917)
FITNESS INTERNATIONAL LLC
1361 Conant St (43537-1609)
PHONE..................................419 482-7740
Joe Walker, *Opers Mgr*
EMP: 34
SALES (corp-wide): 176.8MM **Privately Held**
SIC: 7991 Physical fitness facilities
PA: Fitness International, Llc
3161 Michelson Dr Ste 600
Irvine CA 92612
949 255-7200

(G-13918)
FOCUS HEALTHCARE OF OHIO LLC
1725 Timber Line Rd (43537-4015)
PHONE..................................419 891-9333
Mark Veal, *Marketing Staff*
Loren Robby, *Manager*
Karen Green, *Nursing Dir*
Jackie Switzer, *Quality Imp Dir*
Carey Plummer,
EMP: 50
SALES (est): 2.5MM
SALES (corp-wide): 3.7MM **Privately Held**
WEB: www.focushc.com
SIC: 8063 Psychiatric hospitals
PA: Focus Healthcare Of Tennessee, Llc
7429 Shallowford Rd
Chattanooga TN 37421
423 308-2560

(G-13919)
FRITO-LAY NORTH AMERICA INC
6501 Monclova Rd (43537-9657)
PHONE..................................419 893-8171
Fax: 419 893-3556
Rick Mengel, *Human Res Dir*
Don Stupica, *Manager*
James Kirby, *Manager*
EMP: 80
SQ FT: 11,250
SALES (corp-wide): 63.5B **Publicly Held**
WEB: www.fritolay.com
SIC: 8741 5149 Management services; groceries & related products
HQ: Frito-Lay North America, Inc.
7701 Legacy Dr
Plano TX 75024

(G-13920)
GENTIVA HEALTH SERVICES INC
1745 Indian Wood Cir # 200 (43537-4342)
PHONE..................................419 887-6700
Fax: 419 887-6701
Rey Cilinsky, *Branch Mgr*
EMP: 100

SALES (corp-wide): 6B **Publicly Held**
SIC: 8059 Personal care home, with health care
HQ: Gentiva Health Services, Inc.
3350 Riverwood Pkwy Se # 1400
Atlanta GA 30339
770 951-6450

(G-13921)
GILMORE JASION MAHLER LTD (PA)
1715 Indian Wood Cir # 100 (43537-4055)
PHONE..................................419 794-2000
Kevin M Gilmore, *Managing Prtnr*
Adele Jasion, *Partner*
Andrew Mahler, *Partner*
Itzel Krauss, *Manager*
EMP: 43
SALES: 10MM **Privately Held**
WEB: www.gjmltd.com
SIC: 8721 9311 Accounting, auditing & bookkeeping; certified public accountant; taxation

(G-13922)
GLASS CITY FEDERAL CREDIT UN (PA)
1340 Arrowhead Dr (43537-1741)
PHONE..................................419 887-1000
Fax: 419 887-1099
Mark Slates, *President*
David Kramb, *Exec VP*
Mary Barris, *Credit Mgr*
David Bazeley, *Mktg Coord*
Katie Beakas, *Mktg Coord*
EMP: 25
SQ FT: 22,190
SALES: 7.5MM **Privately Held**
WEB: www.glasscityfcu.com
SIC: 6061 Federal credit unions

(G-13923)
HANSON PRODUCTIONS INC
1695 Indian Wood Cir # 200 (43537-4082)
PHONE..................................419 327-6100
Fax: 419 327-6101
Steven Hanson, *President*
Brian Garratt, *Managing Dir*
Ron Senkowski, *Vice Pres*
Bradley Perrott, *Engineer*
Jennifer Samson, *Treasurer*
EMP: 40
SQ FT: 8,000
SALES (est): 3.7MM **Privately Held**
WEB: www.hansoninc.com
SIC: 7922 Television program, including commercial producers

(G-13924)
HELM AND ASSOCIATES INC
501 W Sophia St Unit 8 (43537-1884)
PHONE..................................419 893-1480
Fax: 419 893-7592
Keith Helminski, *President*
Jerry Helminski, *Vice Pres*
Maria Iwinski, *Shareholder*
John Schrein, *Admin Sec*
EMP: 25
SQ FT: 6,900
SALES (est): 3.7MM **Privately Held**
WEB: www.helmandassociates.com
SIC: 1711 1731 1541 Warm air heating & air conditioning contractor; refrigeration contractor; plumbing contractors; electrical work; industrial buildings & warehouses

(G-13925)
HERITAGE HEALTH CARE SERVICES (PA)
1745 Indian Wood Cir # 252 (43537-4168)
PHONE..................................419 867-2002
Fax: 419 867-2714
Rich Adams, *President*
Jeff House, *Vice Pres*
Jill Besgrove, *Human Res Dir*
Liz Taylor, *Human Res Dir*
Amanda Swihart, *Human Resources*
EMP: 150
SQ FT: 2,500
SALES (est): 10MM **Privately Held**
SIC: 8082 Home health care services

(G-13926)
HIGH POINT ANIMAL HOSPITAL
6020 Manley Rd (43537-1531)
PHONE..................................419 865-3611
Fax: 419 865-4789
Thomas Mowery, *President*
EMP: 25
SALES (est): 1.8MM **Privately Held**
WEB: www.highpointanimalhospital.com
SIC: 0742 Animal hospital services, pets & other animal specialties

(G-13927)
IMAGE BY J & K LLC
1575 Henthorne Dr (43537-1372)
PHONE..................................888 667-6929
James Land IV, *Mng Member*
EMP: 400
SQ FT: 10,000
SALES (est): 51.6MM **Privately Held**
SIC: 3589 7217 7349 7342 Floor washing & polishing machines, commercial; carpet & upholstery cleaning; building & office cleaning services; service station cleaning & degreasing; air duct cleaning; rest room cleaning service

(G-13928)
INOVATIVE FACILITY SVCS LLC
1573 Henthorne Dr (43537-1372)
P.O. Box 1048, Holland (43528-1048)
PHONE..................................419 861-1710
Brett Harlett,
Betsy Beam,
Richard Werderman,
EMP: 400
SALES (est): 5.6MM
SALES (corp-wide): 673.8MM **Privately Held**
WEB: www.kbs-clean.com
SIC: 7349 Building maintenance services
PA: Kellermyer Bergensons Services, Llc
1575 Henthorne Dr
Maumee OH 43537
419 867-4300

(G-13929)
INTERNATIONAL UNION UNITED AU
Also Called: Region 2b
1691 Woodlands Dr (43537-4018)
PHONE..................................419 893-4677
Fax: 419 893-4073
Lloyd Mahaffey, *Director*
EMP: 25
SALES (corp-wide): 207.4MM **Privately Held**
SIC: 8631 Labor union
PA: International Union, United Automobile, Aerospace And Agricultural Implement Workers Of Am
8000 E Jefferson Ave
Detroit MI 48214
313 926-5000

(G-13930)
JDI GROUP INC
360 W Dussel Dr (43537-1631)
PHONE..................................419 725-7161
Fax: 419 725-7160
Timothy Fry, *President*
Matthew Davis, *Principal*
Bryan Autullo, *Project Mgr*
Bill Edens, *Engineer*
Roxanne Manger, *Engineer*
EMP: 78
SQ FT: 27,000
SALES (est): 15MM **Privately Held**
WEB: www.cmdtechnologies.net
SIC: 8712 8711 Architectural engineering; engineering services

(G-13931)
JOHNSON CNTRLS SEC SLTIONS LLC
1722 Indian Wood Cir F (43537-4044)
PHONE..................................419 243-8400
Fax: 419 891-6095
Steve Carlson, *General Mgr*
EMP: 35 **Privately Held**
WEB: www.adt.com
SIC: 7382 Burglar alarm maintenance & monitoring; fire alarm maintenance & monitoring

HQ: Johnson Controls Security Solutions Llc
4700 Exchange Ct Ste 300
Boca Raton FL 33431
561 264-2071

(G-13932)
KELLERMYER BERGENSONS SVCS LLC (PA)
1575 Henthorne Dr (43537-1372)
PHONE..................................419 867-4300
Mark Minasian, *CEO*
Cassidy Koch, *President*
Bob Thompson, *President*
David Belanger, *Regional Mgr*
Joaquin Blanco, *Regional Mgr*
EMP: 60
SQ FT: 40,000
SALES (est): 673.8MM **Privately Held**
WEB: www.kbs-clean.com
SIC: 7349 Janitorial service, contract basis

(G-13933)
KMON INC
1401 Arrowhead Dr (43537-4017)
PHONE..................................419 873-0029
Mohamed Elwerdny, *CEO*
Mohamad Elwerdny, *CEO*
EMP: 50
SALES (est): 1.9MM **Privately Held**
WEB: www.kmon.com
SIC: 8741 Restaurant management

(G-13934)
KUHLMAN CORPORATION (PA)
Also Called: Kuhlman Construction Products
1845 Indian Wood Cir (43537-4072)
P.O. Box 714, Toledo (43697-0714)
PHONE..................................419 897-6000
Fax: 419 897-6061
Timothy L Goligoski, *President*
Kenneth Kuhlman, *Vice Pres*
Larry Matuszak, *Purchasing*
Terry Schaefer, *CFO*
Vernon J Nagel, *Treasurer*
EMP: 150 **EST:** 1901
SQ FT: 18,000
SALES (est): 55.6MM **Privately Held**
WEB: www.kuhlman-corp.com
SIC: 4226 5032 3273 Special warehousing & storage; brick, stone & related material; brick, except refractory; building blocks; sewer pipe, clay; ready-mixed concrete

(G-13935)
LIFE CONNECTION OF OHIO
3661 Brrfeld Blvd Ste 105 (43537)
PHONE..................................419 893-4891
Fax: 419 893-1827
Douglas Heiney, *President*
John Emmerich, *CFO*
Kenneth Kropp, *Treasurer*
Kara Steele, *Pub Rel Dir*
James Davis, *Admin Sec*
EMP: 35
SQ FT: 52,000
SALES: 8.6MM **Privately Held**
WEB: www.lifeconnectionofohio.org
SIC: 8099 Organ bank

(G-13936)
LMT ENTERPRISES MAUMEE INC
1772 Indian Wood Cir (43537-4006)
PHONE..................................419 891-7325
Mark E Thees, *President*
Glenda L Hawley, *Director*
EMP: 45
SQ FT: 24,000
SALES (est): 3.5MM **Privately Held**
WEB: www.eventmakers.com
SIC: 6512 5812 Commercial & industrial building operation; caterers

(G-13937)
LOTT INDUSTRIES INCORPORATED
1645 Holland Rd (43537-1622)
PHONE..................................419 891-5215
Fax: 419 891-5222
Robert Stebbins, *Manager*
Patrick Cotton, *Technology*
EMP: 371

Maumee - Lucas County (G-13938)

SALES (corp-wide): 8.1MM **Privately Held**
WEB: www.lottindustries.com
SIC: 8331 Sheltered workshop
PA: Lott Industries Incorporated
3350 Hill Ave
Toledo OH 43607
419 534-4980

(G-13938)
MANNIK & SMITH GROUP INC (PA)
Also Called: M S G
1800 Indian Wood Cir (43537-4086)
PHONE..................419 891-2222
Fax: 419 891-1595
C Michael Smith, *President*
Rich Bertz, *Principal*
John Browning, *Principal*
Brian Geer, *Principal*
Mark Smoley, *Principal*
EMP: 205 EST: 1955
SQ FT: 36,500
SALES: 34.3MM **Privately Held**
WEB: www.manniksmithgroup.com
SIC: 8711 8748 Consulting engineer; civil engineering; business consulting

(G-13939)
MARBLE RESTORATION INC
Also Called: Decorative Flooring Services
6539 Weatherfield Ct (43537-9018)
PHONE..................419 865-9000
Fax: 419 865-9005
Dan Grant, *President*
Gary J Haskins, *Treasurer*
Michael McAuley, *Admin Sec*
▲ EMP: 75
SQ FT: 12,000
SALES (est): 5.3MM **Privately Held**
WEB: www.dfs-flooring.com
SIC: 1752 5713 Floor laying & floor work; carpet laying; carpets

(G-13940)
MARITZ TRAVEL COMPANY
1740 Indian Wood Cir (43537-4174)
PHONE..................660 626-1501
Janet Drummond, *Branch Mgr*
EMP: 312
SALES (corp-wide): 1.2B **Privately Held**
SIC: 4724 Travel agencies
HQ: Maritz Global Events Inc.
1395 N Highway Dr
Fenton MO 63026
636 827-4000

(G-13941)
MARITZCX RESEARCH LLC
1740 Indian Wood Cir (43537-4174)
PHONE..................419 725-4000
Fax: 419 725-4299
Mary Gomoll, *Branch Mgr*
Becky Pogorelac, *Technology*
Dolan Greene, *Software Dev*
Jon Hepner, *Director*
EMP: 443
SALES (corp-wide): 1.2B **Privately Held**
SIC: 8732 Market analysis or research
HQ: Maritzcx Research Llc
1355 N Highway Dr
Fenton MO 63026
636 827-4000

(G-13942)
MATRIX TECHNOLOGIES INC (PA)
1760 Indian Wood Cir (43537-4070)
PHONE..................419 897-7200
Fax: 419 897-7214
David L Bishop, *President*
Joe Dietz, *Regional Mgr*
David J Blaida, *Vice Pres*
Raymond A Sudheimer, *Project Mgr*
Jon Marshall, *Engineer*
EMP: 100
SQ FT: 39,000
SALES (est): 59.2MM **Privately Held**
WEB: www.matrixti.com
SIC: 7373 Systems integration services

(G-13943)
MAUMEE LODGE NO 1850 BNVLT
Also Called: ELKS OF THE UNITED STATES OF A
137 W Wayne St (43537-2150)
PHONE..................419 893-7272
Fax: 419 893-5373
Charles E Scott, *Principal*
Tom Biggs, *Principal*
Harry Crooks, *Principal*
EMP: 25
SQ FT: 18,000
SALES: 601.2K **Privately Held**
SIC: 8641 Fraternal associations; bars & restaurants, members only

(G-13944)
MAUMEE LODGING ENTERPRISES
Also Called: Knights Inn
1520 S Hiland Sylvania Rd (43537)
PHONE..................419 865-1380
Fax: 419 865-0344
Bobby Patel, *Principal*
Hiren Patel, *Manager*
EMP: 75
SQ FT: 51,552
SALES (est): 1.4MM **Privately Held**
SIC: 7011 Hotels & motels

(G-13945)
MAUMEE OB GYN ASSOC
660 Beaver Creek Cir # 200 (43537-1746)
PHONE..................419 891-6201
Fax: 419 891-6290
Christine McMahon, *Manager*
EMP: 47
SALES (est): 2.5MM **Privately Held**
WEB: www.promedical.org
SIC: 8011 Gynecologist

(G-13946)
MCNAUGHTON-MCKAY ELC OHIO INC
355 Tomahawk Dr Unit 1 (43537-1757)
PHONE..................419 891-0262
Timothy J Krucki, *Branch Mgr*
EMP: 45
SQ FT: 38,000
SALES (corp-wide): 724.3MM **Privately Held**
WEB: www.mc.mc.com
SIC: 5063 Electrical supplies
HQ: Mcnaughton-Mckay Electric Company Of Ohio, Inc.
2255 Citygate Dr
Columbus OH 43219
614 476-2800

(G-13947)
MEYER HILL LYNCH CORPORATION
1771 Indian Wood Cir (43537-4009)
PHONE..................419 897-9797
Fax: 419 897-9710
D Stuart Lovee, *President*
D Stuart Love, *President*
Robert Shick, *Vice Pres*
Chad King, *Project Mgr*
Brandon Ruiz, *Project Mgr*
▼ EMP: 40
SQ FT: 20,000
SALES (est): 28.1MM **Privately Held**
WEB: www.mhl.com
SIC: 5045 Computer peripheral equipment

(G-13948)
MOSLEY PFUNDT & GLICK INC
6455 Wheatstone Ct (43537-9403)
PHONE..................419 861-1120
Fax: 419 861-1121
Larry Mosley, *President*
Garth Tebay, *Mng Member*
Leslie Demarco, *Shareholder*
EMP: 25
SQ FT: 4,974
SALES (est): 1.9MM **Privately Held**
WEB: www.tebaymosley.com
SIC: 8721 Certified public accountant

(G-13949)
NATIONAL AMUSEMENTS INC
Also Called: Showcase Cinemas
2300 Village Dr W # 1700 (43537-7550)
PHONE..................419 215-3095
Elena Allen, *Manager*
EMP: 80
SALES (corp-wide): 13.7B **Publicly Held**
WEB: www.nationalamusements.com
SIC: 7832 Motion picture theaters, except drive-in
PA: National Amusements, Inc.
846 University Ave
Norwood MA 02062
781 461-1600

(G-13950)
NORTHWEST OHIO CHAPTER CFMA
145 Chesterfield Ln (43537-2209)
PHONE..................419 891-1040
Georgia L Martin, *Principal*
EMP: 49
SALES: 43.1K **Privately Held**
SIC: 6022 State commercial banks

(G-13951)
NURSING RESOURCES CORP
3600 Brrfeld Blvd Ste 100 (43537)
PHONE..................419 333-3000
David Venzke, *President*
Rachel Bolton, *Hum Res Coord*
Darren Horrigan, *Sales Executive*
Lori Prutton, *Director*
EMP: 200
SALES (est): 7.8MM **Privately Held**
WEB: www.nursingresources.com
SIC: 8059 8082 7363 Personal care home, with health care; home health care services; help supply services

(G-13952)
OHIOCARE AMBULATORY SURGERY
Also Called: Surgi Care Ambulatory
5959 Monclova Rd (43537-1888)
PHONE..................419 897-5501
Fax: 419 897-5502
Darcy Egan, *Financial Exec*
Dawn Lane, *Administration*
Dee Williams, *Administration*
Frank L Bartell,
Gerald Cichocki,
EMP: 30
SQ FT: 16,000
SALES (est): 4MM **Privately Held**
SIC: 8011 Ambulatory surgical center

(G-13953)
OPHTHALMOLOGY ASSOCIATES OF
Also Called: Eye Institute of Northwestern
3509 Briarfield Blvd (43537-9383)
PHONE..................419 865-3866
Carol R Kollarits MD, *President*
John Bay, *Corp Secy*
Frank Kollarits, *Vice Pres*
Ayo-Lynn Richards, *Ophthalmology*
EMP: 35
SQ FT: 8,500
SALES (est): 3.3MM **Privately Held**
SIC: 8011 Ophthalmologist

(G-13954)
ORC INTERNATIONAL INC
1900 Indian Wood Cir # 200 (43537-4039)
PHONE..................419 893-0029
Terry Reilly, *Vice Pres*
Anna Colon, *Accounting Mgr*
Jeri Piehl, *Mktg Dir*
Debi Jankowski, *Manager*
Carol Moss, *Executive*
EMP: 30 **Privately Held**
WEB: www.opinionresearch.com
SIC: 8732 Survey service: marketing, location, etc.
HQ: Orc International, Inc
902 Carnegie Ctr Ste 220
Princeton NJ 08540
609 452-5400

(G-13955)
PARAMOUNT CARE INC (DH)
Also Called: Paramount Health Care
1901 Indian Wood Cir (43537-4002)
P.O. Box 928, Toledo (43697-0928)
PHONE..................419 887-2500
Fax: 419 891-2530
John C Randolph, *President*
Mark Moser, *Vice Pres*
Richard Moore, *Opers Mgr*
Rochelle Barmash, *Finance Mgr*
Robert J Kolodgy, *Finance*
EMP: 365
SQ FT: 59,900
SALES (est): 37.8MM
SALES (corp-wide): 1.5B **Privately Held**
WEB: www.paramounthealthcare.com
SIC: 6321 Accident insurance carriers; health insurance carriers
HQ: Promedica Insurance Corp
1901 Indian Wood Cir
Maumee OH 43537
419 887-2500

(G-13956)
PARK MANAGEMENT SPECIALIST (PA)
216 W Wayne St (43537-2125)
PHONE..................419 893-4879
Dean S Skillman, *President*
EMP: 60
SQ FT: 3,500
SALES (est): 3.8MM **Privately Held**
SIC: 6515 Mobile home site operators

(G-13957)
PARKER STEEL INTERNATIONAL INC (PA)
Also Called: Parker Steel Company
1625 Indian Wood Cir (43537-4003)
P.O. Box 1508 (43537-8508)
PHONE..................419 473-2481
Fax: 419 471-2655
Paul D Goldner, *Ch of Bd*
Jerry Hidalgo, *President*
Vicki Kretz, *VP Finance*
Lori Adams, *Manager*
Sharon Goldner, *Manager*
▲ EMP: 37
SQ FT: 6,500
SALES: 17MM **Privately Held**
WEB: www.metricmetal.com
SIC: 5051 Steel; aluminum bars, rods, ingots, sheets, pipes, plates, etc.; miscellaneous nonferrous products

(G-13958)
PEOPLEFACTS LLC
135 Chesterfield Ln # 100 (43537-2259)
PHONE..................800 849-1071
Jevin Sackett, *CEO*
Bill Thompson, *COO*
Ajit Habbu, *CFO*
Michelle Lowary, *Sales Associate*
EMP: 50
SALES (est): 2.4MM
SALES (corp-wide): 36.5MM **Privately Held**
SIC: 7375 8742 Information retrieval services; human resource consulting services
PA: Sackett National Holdings, Inc.
7373 Peak Dr
Las Vegas NV 89128
702 900-1791

(G-13959)
PONTOON SOLUTIONS INC
1695 Indian Wood Cir # 200 (43537-4082)
PHONE..................855 881-1533
Meghan Loomis, *Human Res Mgr*
EMP: 75
SALES (corp-wide): 24B **Privately Held**
SIC: 7363 Temporary help service
HQ: Pontoon Solutions, Inc.
1301 Riverplace Blvd # 1000
Jacksonville FL 32207
855 881-1533

(G-13960)
PROMEDICA
1695 Indian Wood Cir # 100 (43537-4083)
PHONE..................419 291-3450
EMP: 95
SALES (est): 19MM **Privately Held**
SIC: 8011 Clinic, operated by physicians

▲ = Import ▼=Export
♦ =Import/Export

GEOGRAPHIC SECTION

Maumee - Lucas County (G-13986)

(G-13961)
PROMEDICA HEALTH SYSTEMS INC
Also Called: Promedidcal Heath Syytem
660 Beaver Creek Cir # 200 (43537-1745)
PHONE..................419 891-6201
Dawn Neuman, *Manager*
EMP: 30
SALES (corp-wide): 1.5B **Privately Held**
SIC: 8011 Offices & clinics of medical doctors
PA: Promedica Health Systems, Inc.
100 Madison Ave
Toledo OH 43604
567 585-7454

(G-13962)
PRUDENTIAL INSUR CO OF AMER
1705 Indian Wood Cir # 115 (43537-4074)
PHONE..................419 893-6227
Fax: 419 893-7215
Ronald Fleming, *Manager*
David Kondas, *Manager*
EMP: 50
SALES (corp-wide): 59.6B **Publicly Held**
SIC: 6411 Insurance agents, brokers & service
HQ: The Prudential Insurance Company Of America
751 Broad St
Newark NJ 07102
973 802-6000

(G-13963)
PSYCHIATRIC SOLUTIONS INC
1725 Timber Line Rd (43537-4015)
PHONE..................419 891-9333
Elicia Bunch, *Manager*
EMP: 137
SALES (corp-wide): 10.4B **Publicly Held**
WEB: www.intermountainhospital.com
SIC: 8011 Psychiatric clinic
HQ: Psychiatric Solutions, Inc.
6640 Carothers Pkwy # 500
Franklin TN 37067
615 312-5700

(G-13964)
PULMONARY CRTCAL CARE SPCALIST
1661 Holland Rd Ste 200 (43537-1659)
PHONE..................419 843-7800
Hany Khalil MD Fccp, *President*
EMP: 30 EST: 1997
SQ FT: 3,700
SALES (est): 3.8MM **Privately Held**
WEB: www.pccsionline.com
SIC: 8011 Pulmonary specialist, physician/surgeon

(G-13965)
QUEST QUALITY SERVICES LLC
8036 Joshua Ln (43537-9293)
PHONE..................419 704-7407
Fax: 419 482-0618
Joe Braker, *CFO*
Kim Newby, *Manager*
Stephen Bowen,
EMP: 100
SQ FT: 5,000
SALES (est): 4.2MM **Privately Held**
WEB: www.questinc.com
SIC: 7549 Automotive maintenance services

(G-13966)
RANDSTAD PROFESSIONALS US LLC
Also Called: Mergis Group, The
1745 Indian Wood Cir # 150 (43537-4042)
PHONE..................419 893-2400
Scott Gearig, *Principal*
Mike Minger, *Business Mgr*
Harmony Baird, *Accounts Mgr*
Nancy O Rammuny, *Accounts Mgr*
EMP: 39
SALES (corp-wide): 27.4B **Privately Held**
SIC: 7363 Temporary help service
HQ: Randstad Professional Us, Lp
150 Presidential Way Fl 4
Woburn MA 01801

(G-13967)
RANDY L FORK INC
Also Called: Honda East
1230 Conant St (43537-1608)
PHONE..................419 891-1230
Fax: 419 891-1218
Sheryl Fork, *Owner*
Sheryl A Fork, *Vice Pres*
Janet Brown, *Human Resources*
Harry Niner, *Sales Staff*
Gabe Miller, *Manager*
EMP: 36
SQ FT: 25,000
SALES (est): 11.7MM **Privately Held**
WEB: www.hondaeasttoledo.com
SIC: 5571 7699 Motorcycle dealers; all-terrain vehicles; motor scooters; motorcycle repair service

(G-13968)
RECYCLING SERVICES INC (PA)
Also Called: Allshred Services
3940 Technology Dr (43537-9264)
PHONE..................419 381-7762
Willie Geiser, *President*
Kevin Cole, *General Mgr*
Jarret Silagyi, *Opers Staff*
Mallory Guerrero, *Human Res Mgr*
Donald Hendershot, *Accounts Mgr*
EMP: 40
SQ FT: 47,000
SALES (est): 21MM **Privately Held**
WEB: www.allshredservices.com
SIC: 4953 Recycling, waste materials

(G-13969)
RESIDENTIAL MANAGEMENT SYSTEMS
1446 Reynolds Rd Ste 100 (43537-1634)
PHONE..................419 255-6060
Monica Schmidt, *Director*
Larry Covert, *Director*
EMP: 70
SALES (corp-wide): 4.5MM **Privately Held**
SIC: 8361 Residential care for the handicapped
PA: Residential Management Systems, Inc
402 E Wilson Bridge Rd
Worthington OH 43085
614 880-6014

(G-13970)
RESOLUTE BANK
3425 Brrfeld Blvd Ste 100 (43537)
PHONE..................419 868-1750
Fax: 419 868-1623
Kevin Rahe, *CEO*
Gary Hoyer, *Vice Pres*
G Mark Loreto, *Vice Pres*
Susan Martin, *Vice Pres*
Roxie Hill, *VP Opers*
EMP: 70
SALES (est): 17.4MM **Privately Held**
SIC: 6036 State savings banks, not federally chartered

(G-13971)
RICHARD J NELSON MD
Also Called: Toledo Ear Nose and Throat
6005 Monclova Rd Ste 320 (43537-1862)
PHONE..................419 578-7555
Richard J Nelson, *Principal*
John Gears, *Office Admin*
Megan Boyle, *Speech Therapis*
EMP: 50
SALES (est): 1.7MM **Privately Held**
SIC: 8011 Ears, nose & throat specialist: physician/surgeon

(G-13972)
RITTER & ASSOCIATES INC
Also Called: Alta360 Research
1690 Woodlands Dr Ste 103 (43537-4165)
PHONE..................419 535-5757
Stanley G Hart, *President*
Albert Hepp, *Broker*
Jennifer Niswander, *Manager*
EMP: 50
SQ FT: 5,000
SALES: 6MM **Privately Held**
SIC: 8732 Market analysis or research
PA: Brand Equity Builders Inc
31 Bailey Ave Ste 1
Ridgefield CT 06877

(G-13973)
ROBERT E KOSE
1661 Holland Rd Ste 200 (43537-1659)
PHONE..................419 843-7800
Robert E Kose, *Principal*
EMP: 30 EST: 2010
SALES (est): 464.4K **Privately Held**
SIC: 8011 Internal medicine, physician/surgeon

(G-13974)
SAR BIREN
Also Called: Baymont Inn & Suites
6425 Kit Ln (43537-8655)
PHONE..................419 865-0407
Biren Sar, *Owner*
Danny Talati, *Manager*
EMP: 29
SALES: 1,000K **Privately Held**
SIC: 7011 Inns

(G-13975)
SEYMOUR & ASSOCIATES
1760 Manley Rd (43537-9400)
PHONE..................419 517-7079
Fax: 419 893-3569
Dale Seymour, *Owner*
Angie Barney, *Business Mgr*
EMP: 35
SQ FT: 16,000
SALES (est): 4.9MM **Privately Held**
SIC: 6411 Insurance agents & brokers

(G-13976)
SHADOW VALLEY TENNIS CLUB
1661 S Hlland Sylvania Rd (43537)
PHONE..................419 865-1141
Fax: 419 865-5788
Jim Davis, *Partner*
John Murmer, *Partner*
Carol Weiner, *Partner*
EMP: 25
SALES (est): 870K **Privately Held**
SIC: 7997 Tennis club, membership

(G-13977)
SOCCER CENTRE INC
1620 Market Place Dr # 1 (43537-4318)
PHONE..................419 893-5419
Fax: 419 893-5498
Dave Hafner, *President*
Brant Smith, *Asst Mgr*
EMP: 25
SQ FT: 50,000
SALES (est): 1MM **Privately Held**
WEB: www.maumeesoccercentre.com
SIC: 7997 Soccer club, except professional & semi-professional

(G-13978)
SOCCER CENTRE OWNERS LTD
1620 Market Place Dr (43537-4318)
PHONE..................419 893-5425
Brant Smith, *President*
EMP: 30 EST: 2012
SQ FT: 300,000
SALES (est): 970.8K **Privately Held**
SIC: 3949 7999 Pads: football, basketball, soccer, lacrosse, etc.; indoor court clubs

(G-13979)
SORDYL & ASSOCIATES INC
2962 W Course Rd (43537-9624)
PHONE..................419 866-6811
Michael Sordyl, *President*
Gregg Cooper, *Network Mgr*
EMP: 25
SALES (est): 1MM **Privately Held**
SIC: 7371 8748 Custom computer programming services; business consulting

(G-13980)
ST LUKES HOSPITAL
Also Called: PROMEDICA
5901 Monclova Rd (43537-1899)
PHONE..................419 893-5911
Fax: 419 891-8079
Frank J Bartell III, *President*
Stephen Bazeley, *Vice Pres*
Don Miller, *Vice Pres*
Jill Trosin, *Vice Pres*
Cheresa Hadsell, *Facilities Mgr*
EMP: 1558 EST: 1906
SQ FT: 324,324
SALES: 177.7MM **Privately Held**
SIC: 8062 5912 Hospital, affiliated with AMA residency; drug stores

(G-13981)
SUN FEDERAL CREDIT UNION (PA)
1625 Holland Rd (43537-1622)
PHONE..................800 786-0945
Fax: 419 893-5071
Gary C Moritz, *President*
Marcia Bourdo, *Vice Pres*
Mark Deyoung, *Vice Pres*
Francesca Vogel, *Vice Pres*
Don Kruger, *VP Opers*
EMP: 40
SQ FT: 21,000
SALES: 17MM **Privately Held**
SIC: 6061 Federal credit unions

(G-13982)
SUNSHINE COMMUNITIES (PA)
Also Called: Sunshine Inc. Northwest Ohio
7223 Maumee Western Rd (43537-9755)
PHONE..................419 865-0251
Fax: 419 865-9715
Jason Abodeely, *COO*
Susan Dorrington, *Ch Admin Ofcr*
Steve Howe, *Vice Pres*
Tyson Stuckey, *Treasurer*
Amy Gibson, *Accountant*
EMP: 280 EST: 1949
SQ FT: 150,000
SALES: 250K **Privately Held**
WEB: www.sunshineincnwo.org
SIC: 8361 8052 8322 Home for the mentally retarded; intermediate care facilities; individual & family services

(G-13983)
SWAN PNTE FCLTY OPERATIONS LLC
Also Called: Addison Hts Hlth Rhblttion Ctr
3600 Butz Rd (43537-9691)
PHONE..................419 867-7926
Fax: 419 868-3515
Sherrie Banas, *Manager*
TI Brown, *Director*
Joe Conte,
Carla Naegele,
EMP: 97
SALES: 950K **Privately Held**
SIC: 8051 Skilled nursing care facilities

(G-13984)
SYLVANIA FRANCISCAN HEALTH (HQ)
1715 Indian Wood Cir # 200 (43537-4055)
PHONE..................419 882-8373
Fax: 419 882-7360
James Pope, *President*
Mary A Grzeskowiak, *Trustee*
Mary J Mike, *Trustee*
William Waters, *Treasurer*
Teri Bockstahler, *Director*
EMP: 45
SALES: 12.5MM **Privately Held**
WEB: www.fscsylvania.org
SIC: 8062 8741 General medical & surgical hospitals; management services

(G-13985)
SYSTEMS ALTERNATIVES INTL
1705 Indian Wood Cir # 100 (43537-4097)
PHONE..................419 891-1100
Fax: 419 891-1045
John W Underwood, *President*
Paul Trestan, *Vice Pres*
David A Youngman, *Vice Pres*
Brian Gribble, *CFO*
Anna Emahiser, *Controller*
EMP: 28
SQ FT: 13,000
SALES (est): 4.3MM **Privately Held**
WEB: www.sysalt.com
SIC: 7371 7378 Computer software systems analysis & design, custom; computer maintenance & repair

(G-13986)
TERMINIX INTL CO LTD PARTNR
6541 Weatherfield Ct (43537-9018)
PHONE..................419 868-8290
Fax: 419 868-8750
Clint Geog, *Manager*

Maumee - Lucas County (G-13987)

EMP: 29
SALES (corp-wide): 2.9B Publicly Held
SIC: 7342 Pest control services
HQ: The Terminix International Company
Limited Partnership
860 Ridge Lake Blvd A3-4008
Memphis TN 38120
901 766-1400

(G-13987)
TOLEDO MEDICAL EQUIPMENT CO (PA)
Also Called: Young Medical Services
4060 Technology Dr (43537-9263)
PHONE 419 866-7120
Timothy D Pontius, *President*
Kathy Mikolajczak, *Vice Pres*
Shawn Cowell, *Branch Mgr*
Teri Gonzales, *Manager*
EMP: 48
SQ FT: 20,000
SALES (est): 3.2MM Privately Held
SIC: 7352 5999 Medical equipment rental; medical apparatus & supplies

(G-13988)
TRIAD RESIDENTIAL (PA)
1605 Holland Rd Ste A4 (43537-1630)
PHONE 419 482-0711
Podd Frick, *Partner*
Margie Boon, *Exec Dir*
EMP: 28
SALES (est): 2.2MM Privately Held
WEB: www.triad-residential.com
SIC: 8052 Home for the mentally retarded, with health care

(G-13989)
UNITED COLLECTION BUREAU INC
1345 Ford St (43537-1732)
PHONE 419 866-6227
Ka W Tsui, *Branch Mgr*
Rachel Brooks, *Services*
EMP: 49
SALES (corp-wide): 66.5MM Privately Held
WEB: www.ucbinc.com
SIC: 7322 Collection agency, except real estate
PA: United Collection Bureau, Inc.
5620 Southwyck Blvd
Toledo OH 43614
419 866-6227

(G-13990)
UNITED PARCEL SERVICE INC OH
Also Called: UPS
1550 Holland Rd (43537-1657)
PHONE 419 891-6776
Mike Clark, *Branch Mgr*
Karen Park, *Manager*
Michael Fall, *Supervisor*
EMP: 4500
SALES (corp-wide): 65.8B Publicly Held
WEB: www.upsscs.com
SIC: 4215 Package delivery, vehicular; parcel delivery, vehicular
HQ: United Parcel Service, Inc. (Oh)
55 Glenlake Pkwy
Atlanta GA 30328
404 828-6000

(G-13991)
UNITED SEATING & MOBILITY LLC
Also Called: Numotion
412 W Dussel Dr (43537-1686)
PHONE 567 302-4000
Shirley Frye, *Branch Mgr*
EMP: 36
SALES (corp-wide): 123.6MM Privately Held
SIC: 5047 Medical equipment & supplies
PA: United Seating & Mobility Llc
975 Hornet Dr
Hazelwood MO 63042
314 731-7867

(G-13992)
VENATOR HOLDINGS LLC
1690 Woodlands Dr Ste 220 (43537-4045)
PHONE 248 792-9209
EMP: 65

SALES (corp-wide): 3.8MM Privately Held
SIC: 8742 Management consulting services
PA: Venator Holdings Llc
3001 W Big Beaver Rd # 220
Troy MI 48084
248 792-9209

(G-13993)
WARNOCK TANNER & ASSOC INC
Also Called: Wta Consulting
959 Illinois Ave Ste C (43537-1744)
PHONE 419 897-6999
Fax: 419 897-6994
Roger Warnock, *President*
Ken Lynch, *Exec VP*
Richard Rusgo, *CFO*
Deirdre Jones, *Accounts Exec*
Brie Hobbs, *Marketing Staff*
EMP: 26
SQ FT: 3,000
SALES (est): 4.2MM Privately Held
SIC: 7379 7373 Computer related consulting services; value-added resellers, computer systems

(G-13994)
WHITEHURST COMPANY (PA)
6325 Garden Rd (43537-1271)
P.O. Box 351869, Toledo (43635-1869)
PHONE 419 865-0799
Herb Fultz, *President*
James Mc Innis, *Vice Pres*
EMP: 43
SALES: 500K Privately Held
WEB: www.thewhitehurstcompany.com
SIC: 6531 6513 Real estate managers; apartment building operators

(G-13995)
WILLIAM VAUGHAN COMPANY
Also Called: Northwest Ohio Practice
145 Chesterfield Ln (43537-2209)
PHONE 419 891-1040
Fax: 419 891-1065
William J Horst, *President*
Gregory J Arndt, *Vice Pres*
Michelle M Clement, *Vice Pres*
Aaron D Swiggum, *Vice Pres*
Jack C Hagmeyer, *Treasurer*
EMP: 60
SQ FT: 1,600
SALES (est): 6.7MM Privately Held
WEB: www.wvco.com
SIC: 8721 Certified public accountant

(G-13996)
YOUNG MENS CHRISTIAN ASSOCIAT
716 Askin St (43537-3602)
PHONE 419 794-7304
EMP: 108
SALES (corp-wide): 29.1MM Privately Held
SIC: 8099 Blood related health services
PA: Young Men's Christian Association Of Greater Toledo
1500 N Superior St Fl 2
Toledo OH 43604
419 729-8135

(G-13997)
YOUNG MENS CHRISTIAN ASSOCIAT
2100 S Hlland Sylvania Rd (43537)
PHONE 419 866-9622
Fax: 419 866-5980
Julie Mason, *Business Mgr*
Vicki Coleman, *Manager*
Jill Morris, *Director*
EMP: 55
SALES (corp-wide): 29.1MM Privately Held
WEB: www.ymcastorercamps.org
SIC: 8641 7991 8351 7032 Youth organizations; physical fitness facilities; child day care services; youth camps; individual & family services
PA: Young Men's Christian Association Of Greater Toledo
1500 N Superior St Fl 2
Toledo OH 43604
419 729-8135

Mayfield Heights
Cuyahoga County

(G-13998)
ABA INSURANCE SERVICES INC
5910 Landerbrook Dr # 100 (44124-6534)
PHONE 800 274-5222
John N Wells, *CEO*
John Wolff, *Exec VP*
Robert J Brewer, *Vice Pres*
Alena Dreskin, *Opers Staff*
Lia Miller, *Opers Staff*
EMP: 56
SQ FT: 18,000
SALES: 17MM Privately Held
SIC: 6411 Insurance agents

(G-13999)
CLEVELAND EAR NOSE THROAT CTR
6770 Mayfield Rd Ste 210 (44124-2299)
PHONE 440 550-4179
Fax: 440 461-8221
Bert M Brown, *Branch Mgr*
EMP: 35
SALES (est): 980K
SALES (corp-wide): 4.2MM Privately Held
SIC: 8011 Ears, nose & throat specialist; physician/surgeon
PA: Cleveland Ear, Nose, Throat Center Inc
5400 Trnsp Blvd Ste 8
Cleveland OH 44125
216 662-3373

(G-14000)
DATATRAK INTERNATIONAL INC
5900 Landerbrook Dr # 170 (44124-4085)
PHONE 440 443-0082
Fax: 440 442-3482
Alex Tabatabai, *Ch of Bd*
James R Ward, *President*
Marc J Shlaes, *Vice Pres*
Osman Muhammad, *Project Mgr*
Julia Henderson, *CFO*
EMP: 47
SQ FT: 4,300
SALES: 7.5MM Privately Held
WEB: www.datatrak.net
SIC: 7374 7372 Data processing & preparation; prepackaged software

(G-14001)
DTV INC (PA)
Also Called: Danny Veghs Home Entertainment
6505 Mayfield Rd (44124-3216)
PHONE 216 226-5465
Kathy Vegh, *CEO*
Frank Plutt, *Controller*
Margaret Manzo, *Bookkeeper*
Alison Rifici, *Sales Staff*
EMP: 35
SQ FT: 26,000
SALES (est): 5.9MM Privately Held
WEB: www.dannyveghs.com
SIC: 5046 7699 5962 5091 Vending machines, coin-operated; billiard table repair; vending machine repair; merchandising machine operators; billiard equipment & supplies; furniture stores; hobby, toy & game shops

(G-14002)
ELK & ELK CO LPA (PA)
6105 Parkland Blvd # 200 (44124-4258)
PHONE 800 355-6446
Fax: 440 442-7944
David J Elk, *Partner*
Arthur M Elk, *Partner*
Marilyn Elk, *CFO*
Maria Santogrossi, *Human Res Mgr*
Brandon Roth, *Human Resources*
EMP: 53
SALES (est): 8.7MM Privately Held
SIC: 8111 General practice law office

(G-14003)
KIDDIE PARTY COMPANY LLC
1690 Lander Rd (44124-3301)
PHONE 440 273-7680
Tanisha Jamison, *Principal*

EMP: 25 EST: 2014
SALES (est): 407.7K Privately Held
SIC: 7299 Facility rental & party planning services; party planning service

(G-14004)
LITIGATION MANAGEMENT INC
6000 Parkland Blvd # 100 (44124-6120)
PHONE 440 484-2000
Elizabeth Juliano, *President*
Sonya Virant, *COO*
Karen Brooks, *Opers Staff*
Melima Craddock, *Opers Staff*
Deborah Prokay, *Opers Staff*
EMP: 452
SQ FT: 2,000
SALES (est): 48.5MM Privately Held
WEB: www.medicineforthedefense.com
SIC: 8111 Legal aid service

(G-14005)
PARK PLACE TECHNOLOGIES LLC
Also Called: AMI
5910 Landerbrook Dr # 300 (44124-6500)
PHONE 610 544-0571
EMP: 390 Privately Held
SIC: 7378 Computer maintenance & repair
PA: Park Place Technologies, Llc
5910 Landerbrook Dr # 300
Mayfield Heights OH 44124

(G-14006)
PARK PLACE TECHNOLOGIES LLC (PA)
5910 Landerbrook Dr # 300 (44124-6500)
PHONE 877 778-8707
Ed Kenty, *CEO*
Tony Susi, *President*
Chris Adams, *COO*
Mike Knightly, *Exec VP*
Hal Malstrom, *Exec VP*
EMP: 161
SQ FT: 41,000
SALES (est): 141.8MM Privately Held
WEB: www.parkplaceintl.com
SIC: 7378 Computer maintenance & repair

(G-14007)
SEAL MAYFIELD LLC
Also Called: Staybridge Suites
6103 Landerhaven Dr (44124-4189)
PHONE 440 684-4100
Monika Cepaitis, *Administration*
Sheenal Patel,
EMP: 25
SALES (est): 136.5K Privately Held
SIC: 7011 Resort hotel, franchised

(G-14008)
TMW SYSTEMS INC (HQ)
6085 Parkland Blvd (44124-4184)
PHONE 216 831-6606
Fax: 216 831-3606
David Wangler, *President*
Rod Strata, *COO*
Timothy Leonard, *Exec VP*
David Mook, *Exec VP*
Jeffrey Ritter, *Exec VP*
EMP: 125
SQ FT: 32,500
SALES (est): 79.8MM
SALES (corp-wide): 2.6B Publicly Held
WEB: www.bulktrucker.com
SIC: 7372 Business oriented computer software
PA: Trimble Inc.
935 Stewart Dr
Sunnyvale CA 94085
408 481-8000

(G-14009)
TRUE NORTH ENERGY LLC
Also Called: Truenorth Energy
6411 Mayfield Rd (44124-3214)
PHONE 440 442-0060
EMP: 34
SALES (corp-wide): 274.9MM Privately Held
SIC: 5541 1382 Filling stations, gasoline; oil & gas exploration services
PA: True North Energy, Llc
10346 Brecksville Rd
Brecksville OH 44141
877 245-9336

Mayfield Village
Cuyahoga County

(G-14010)
CENTER SCHOOL ASSOCIATION
6625 Wilson Mills Rd (44143-3406)
PHONE...................................440 995-7400
EMP: 58
SALES: 26.8K Privately Held
SIC: 8621 Professional membership organizations

(G-14011)
FIRST REALTY PROPERTY MGT LTD
6690 Beta Dr Ste 220 (44143-2359)
PHONE...................................440 720-0100
Joseph T Aveni,
Marie Abazio,
William Pender,
EMP: 40
SALES (est): 4.3MM Privately Held
SIC: 6531 Real estate managers

(G-14012)
PROGRESSIVE CASUALTY INSUR CO (HQ)
Also Called: PROGRESSIVE INSURANCE
6300 Wilson Mills Rd (44143-2109)
P.O. Box W33 (44143)
PHONE...................................440 461-5000
Glenn M Renwick, *Ch of Bd*
Jim Mauck, *COO*
Jonathan Klein, *Senior VP*
Mary B Andreano, *Vice Pres*
Jeffrey W Basch, *Vice Pres*
EMP: 3300
SALES: 6.2B
SALES (corp-wide): 26.8B Publicly Held
WEB: www.progressinsurance.com
SIC: 6331 6351 6411 6321 Fire, marine & casualty insurance; fire, marine & casualty insurance & carriers; automobile insurance; property damage insurance; surety insurance; credit & other financial responsibility insurance; insurance agents, brokers & service; insurance claim adjusters, not employed by insurance company; insurance agents & brokers; insurance agents; accident & health insurance; accident insurance carriers
PA: The Progressive Corporation
6300 Wilson Mills Rd
Mayfield Village OH 44143
440 461-5000

(G-14013)
SKODA MNTTI CRTIF PUB ACCNTNTS (HQ)
6685 Beta Dr (44143-2320)
PHONE...................................440 449-6800
Fax: 440 442-5609
Gregory Skoda, *CEO*
Michael Minotti, *President*
Patrick Carney, *Vice Pres*
Stella Metz, *Tax Mgr*
Kat Fuller, *Accountant*
EMP: 63
SALES (est): 17.7MM
SALES (corp-wide): 21.5MM Privately Held
SIC: 8721 Certified public accountant
PA: Skoda Minotti Holdings Llc
6685 Beta Dr
Cleveland OH 44143
440 449-6800

(G-14014)
WIRELESS ENVIRONMENT LLC
Also Called: Mr. Beams
600 Beta Dr Ste 100 (44143-2355)
PHONE...................................216 455-0192
David Levine, *President*
Karen Walker, *Manager*
Mike Recker, *CTO*
▲ EMP: 28
SQ FT: 1,000
SALES (est): 1.9MM Publicly Held
SIC: 1731 Lighting contractor
HQ: Ring Inc.
1523 26th St
Santa Monica CA 90404
800 656-1918

Mc Arthur
Vinton County

(G-14015)
APPALACHIA WOOD INC (PA)
Also Called: McArthur Lumber and Post
31310 State Route 93 (45651-8924)
PHONE...................................740 596-2551
Fax: 740 596-2555
EMP: 30 EST: 1951
SQ FT: 150,000
SALES: 3.6MM Privately Held
SIC: 2491 2421 5031 2411 Wood Preserving Sawmill/Planing Mill Whol Lumber/Plywd/Millwk Logging

(G-14016)
HOPEWELL HEALTH CENTERS INC
31891 State Route 93 (45651-9006)
P.O. Box 308 (45651-0308)
PHONE...................................740 596-5249
Dawn Murray Do, *Principal*
David Moore, *Family Practiti*
EMP: 25
SALES (corp-wide): 33.1MM Privately Held
SIC: 8099 8011 Medical services organization; general & family practice, physician/surgeon
PA: Hopewell Health Centers, Inc.
1049 Western Ave
Chillicothe OH 45601
740 773-1006

(G-14017)
TWIN MAPLES HOME HEALTH CARE
63044 Us Highway 50 (45651-8404)
P.O. Box 310 (45651-0310)
PHONE...................................740 596-1022
Fax: 740 596-1626
Cindy Mullins, *Director*
EMP: 35 EST: 1997
SALES (est): 794.5K Privately Held
SIC: 8082 Home health care services

(G-14018)
TWIN MAPLES NURSING HOME
31054 State Route 93 (45651-8925)
PHONE...................................740 596-5955
Fax: 740 596-2632
Virginia Ratliff, *President*
Fred Ratliff, *Corp Secy*
Crystal Ratliff, *Vice Pres*
Tonya Kennedy, *Sales Executive*
Tracy Marx, *Director*
EMP: 45 EST: 1974
SALES: 260.4MM Privately Held
SIC: 8051 8052 Skilled nursing care facilities; intermediate care facilities

(G-14019)
VINTON COUNTY NAT BNK MCARTHUR (HQ)
Also Called: VINTON CO NATIONAL BANK
112 W Main St (45651-1214)
P.O. Box 460 (45651-0460)
PHONE...................................740 596-2525
Stephen Hunter, *President*
Ron Collins, *President*
Mark Erslan, *Exec VP*
Jane Nickels, *Senior VP*
Sheila Stickel, *Site Mgr*
EMP: 43
SQ FT: 13,239
SALES: 40.5MM Privately Held
WEB: www.vintoncountybank.com
SIC: 6022 6162 State trust companies accepting deposits, commercial; mortgage bankers & correspondents
PA: Community Bancshares Inc
112 W Main St
Mc Arthur OH 45651
740 596-4561

Mc Clure
Henry County

(G-14020)
POGGEMEYER DESIGN GROUP INC
Also Called: Industrial Fluid Management
2926 Us Highway 6 (43534-9730)
PHONE...................................419 748-7438
Richard Bennett, *President*
EMP: 25
SALES (corp-wide): 36.2MM Privately Held
WEB: www.poggemeyer.com
SIC: 8713 8711 9511 Surveying services; consulting engineer; waste management agencies
PA: Poggemeyer Design Group, Inc.
1168 N Main St
Bowling Green OH 43402
419 244-8074

Mc Comb
Hancock County

(G-14021)
GRUBB CONSTRUCTION INC
896 State Route 613 (45858-9303)
P.O. Box 728 (45858-0728)
PHONE...................................419 293-2316
Norman Grubb, *President*
Nancy Grubb, *Corp Secy*
EMP: 30
SQ FT: 4,800
SALES (est): 3.1MM Privately Held
SIC: 1796 Machinery installation

Mc Connelsville
Morgan County

(G-14022)
RIVERSIDE CARE CENTER LLC
856 Riverside Dr S (43756)
PHONE...................................740 962-5303
Brian Colleran, *President*
Barbara Murrell, *Director*
EMP: 62
SALES: 380.8MM Privately Held
WEB: www.riverside-care.net
SIC: 8051 Skilled nursing care facilities

Mc Dermott
Scioto County

(G-14023)
VOIERS ENTERPRISES INC
Also Called: Rest Haven Nursing Home
2274 Mc Dermott Pond Crk (45652)
PHONE...................................740 259-2838
Fax: 740 259-4399
Deborah Akers, *CEO*
Sarah E Voiers, *President*
Steven Akers, *Principal*
Anna Clarke, *Treasurer*
Jitrendra Patel, *Director*
EMP: 35
SALES (est): 2.1MM Privately Held
SIC: 8052 Personal care facility

Mc Donald
Trumbull County

(G-14024)
PREDATOR TRUCKING COMPANY (PA)
3181 Trumbull Ave (44437-1313)
P.O. Box 315 (44437-0315)
PHONE...................................330 530-0712
Fax: 330 530-0715
Charles Haselow, *CEO*
Russell Golden, *President*
Gary Golden, *Owner*
James Golden, *Admin Sec*
EMP: 33
SQ FT: 1,000
SALES: 6.1MM Privately Held
SIC: 7513 Truck rental & leasing, no drivers

Mc Guffey
Hardin County

(G-14025)
ROHRS FARMS
810 Courtright St (45859)
P.O. Box 300 (45859-0300)
PHONE...................................419 757-0110
Jason Rohrs, *Principal*
John Rohrs,
EMP: 30
SALES (est): 8.1MM Privately Held
SIC: 0191 General farms, primarily crop

McConnelsville
Morgan County

(G-14026)
CARESERVE INC
Also Called: Genesis Health & Rehab
4114 N State Route 376 Nw (43756-9145)
PHONE...................................740 962-3761
Kelly Bosner, *Chf Purch Ofc*
Janet Slisher, *Manager*
David Davis, *Director*
Dustin Ellis, *Director*
Barbara Murrell, *Director*
EMP: 145
SALES (corp-wide): 462MM Privately Held
SIC: 8051 Skilled nursing care facilities
HQ: Careserve
2991 Maple Ave
Zanesville OH 43701
740 454-4000

(G-14027)
FINLEY FIRE EQUIPMENT CO (PA)
5255 N State Route 60 Nw (43756-9630)
PHONE...................................740 962-4328
John W Finley, *President*
Rita D Murphy, *Financial Exec*
George Owens, *Sales Mgr*
Kevin Hardwick, *Regl Sales Mgr*
Chris Antle, *Sales Staff*
EMP: 75
SQ FT: 34,000
SALES: 29.9MM Privately Held
WEB: www.finleyfire.com
SIC: 5087 Firefighting equipment

(G-14028)
MARY HMMOND ADULT ACTVTIES CTR
Also Called: Mary Hammond Center
900 S Riverside Dr Ne (43756-9102)
PHONE...................................740 962-4200
Tom Neff, *President*
Bill Baker, *Vice Pres*
Scott Roberts, *Manager*
Wally Olszewski, *Admin Sec*
EMP: 78
SQ FT: 20,000
SALES (est): 229.6K Privately Held
SIC: 8331 Work experience center

(G-14029)
MORGAN COUNTY PUBLIC TRANSIT
37 S 5th St (43756-1203)
PHONE...................................740 962-1322
Michael Reed, *Principal*
John Sampson, *Manager*
Shannon Well, *Commissioner*
Adam Shiver, *Commissioner*
Tim Zanhorn, *Commissioner*
EMP: 25
SALES: 600K Privately Held
SIC: 4119 Ambulance service

McConnelsville - Morgan County (G-14030)

GEOGRAPHIC SECTION

(G-14030)
OHIO MEDICAL TRNSP INC
975 E Airport Rd Ne (43756-9323)
PHONE..................................740 962-2055
EMP: 53 **Privately Held**
SIC: 4522 Ambulance services, air
PA: Ohio Medical Transportation, Inc.
  2827 W Dblin Granville Rd
  Columbus OH 43235

Mechanicstown
Carroll County

(G-14031)
KINGS WELDING AND FABG INC
5259 Bane Rd Ne (44651-9020)
PHONE..................................330 738-3592
Fax: 330 738-2008
Glen Richard King Sr, *President*
Diane Garrett, *Corp Secy*
Ray Wilson, *Project Mgr*
EMP: 45
SQ FT: 9,500
SALES (est): 6.1MM **Privately Held**
SIC: 3599 7692 3498 3441 Machine shop, jobbing & repair; welding repair; fabricated pipe & fittings; fabricated structural metal

Medina
Medina County

(G-14032)
ADVOCATE PROPERTY SERVIC
620 E Smith Rd (44256-2692)
PHONE..................................330 952-1313
Amanda Klein, *Principal*
Tresa Koein,
Tresa Klein,
EMP: 30 **EST:** 2010
SALES (est): 1MM **Privately Held**
SIC: 1522 Residential construction

(G-14033)
AHF OHIO INC
Also Called: Samaritan Care Center & Villa
806 E Washinton St (44256)
PHONE..................................330 725-4123
Brad Willmore, *Administration*
EMP: 64
SALES (corp-wide): 21MM **Privately Held**
SIC: 8051 8361 Skilled nursing care facilities; residential care
PA: Ahf Ohio, Inc.
  5920 Venture Dr Ste 100
  Dublin OH 43017
  614 760-7352

(G-14034)
ALICE TRAINING INSTITUTE LLC
2508 Medina Rd (44256-8144)
P.O. Box 320 (44258-0320)
PHONE..................................330 661-0106
Greg Crane, *President*
Christopher Schneider, *Principal*
Frank Griffith, *Exec VP*
Lisa Crane, *Vice Pres*
Victoria Shaw, *Project Mgr*
EMP: 80
SQ FT: 4,000
SALES (est): 5MM **Privately Held**
SIC: 8748 Safety training service

(G-14035)
ALTERNATIVE PATHS INC
246 Northland Dr Ste 200a (44256-3440)
PHONE..................................330 725-9195
Fax: 330 725-9187
Jackie Owen, *Chairman*
Philip Londrico, *Manager*
Melinda Silliman, *Manager*
Deborah Beckstett, *Exec Dir*
EMP: 30
SQ FT: 5,000
SALES: 3MM **Privately Held**
SIC: 8093 8322 Mental health clinic, outpatient; individual & family services

(G-14036)
AMF BOWLING CENTERS INC
201 Harding St (44256-1636)
PHONE..................................330 725-4548
Fax: 330 723-2101
Ryan Sibert, *Manager*
EMP: 30
SALES (corp-wide): 81.2MM **Privately Held**
WEB: www.kidsports.org
SIC: 7933 Ten pin center
HQ: Amf Bowling Centers, Inc.
  7313 Bell Creek Rd
  Mechanicsville VA 23111

(G-14037)
AT&T CORP
1088 N Court St (44256-1586)
PHONE..................................330 723-1717
Chad Dash, *Branch Mgr*
EMP: 96
SALES (corp-wide): 160.5B **Publicly Held**
SIC: 4813 Local & long distance telephone communications
HQ: At&T Corp.
  1 At&T Way
  Bedminster NJ 07921
  800 403-3302

(G-14038)
BATTERED WOMENS SHELTER
120 W Washington St 3e1 (44256-2260)
PHONE..................................330 723-3900
Fax: 330 723-1174
Kathy Henninger, *Manager*
EMP: 49
SALES (corp-wide): 2.5MM **Privately Held**
SIC: 8322 Emergency shelters
PA: Battered Women's Shelter
  974 E Market St
  Akron OH 44305
  330 374-0740

(G-14039)
BLUE HERON GOLF COURSE INC
3225 Blue Heron Trce (44256-6362)
PHONE..................................330 722-0227
Fax: 330 725-4924
Bob Hoffman, *President*
Taya Slabaugh, *Marketing Staff*
Donna Stuver, *Asst Mgr*
Jeremy Slota, *Administration*
EMP: 30
SALES (est): 692.6K **Privately Held**
SIC: 7992 Public golf courses

(G-14040)
BRIDGESHOME HEALTH CARE
Also Called: ROBERTSON BEREAVEMENT CENTER
5075 Windfall Rd (44256-8613)
PHONE..................................330 764-1000
Fax: 330 764-8000
Kathy Segatta, *Finance*
Denise Ellenbest, *Manager*
Chris Baker, *Director*
EMP: 30 **EST:** 2012
SALES: 1.7MM
SALES (corp-wide): 89.8MM **Privately Held**
SIC: 8062 8082 General medical & surgical hospitals; home health care services
HQ: Hospice Of Medina County
  5075 Windfall Rd
  Medina OH 44256

(G-14041)
BROOKDALE SENIOR LIVING INC
49 Leisure Ln A (44256-1285)
PHONE..................................330 723-5825
EMP: 66
SALES (corp-wide): 4.7B **Publicly Held**
SIC: 6513 Retirement hotel operation
PA: Brookdale Senior Living
  111 Westwood Pl Ste 400
  Brentwood TN 37027
  615 221-2250

(G-14042)
CATHOLIC CHARITIES CORPORATION
4210 N Jefferson St (44256-5639)
PHONE..................................330 723-9615
Timothy Putka, *Director*
EMP: 397 **Privately Held**
SIC: 8322 Social service center
PA: Catholic Charities Corporation
  7911 Detroit Ave
  Cleveland OH 44102

(G-14043)
CELLCO PARTNERSHIP
2736 Medina Rd (44256-9660)
PHONE..................................330 722-6622
EMP: 31
SALES (corp-wide): 126B **Publicly Held**
SIC: 5065 4812 Telephone & telegraphic equipment; cellular telephone services
HQ: Cellco Partnership
  1 Verizon Way
  Basking Ridge NJ 07920

(G-14044)
CELLCO PARTNERSHIP
Also Called: Verizon
1231 N Court St (44256-1581)
PHONE..................................330 764-7380
Fax: 330 764-7385
Rick Burke, *General Mgr*
Chris Osborne, *Accounts Exec*
Stacy Armstrong, *Branch Mgr*
EMP: 71
SALES (corp-wide): 126B **Publicly Held**
SIC: 4812 Cellular telephone services
HQ: Cellco Partnership
  1 Verizon Way
  Basking Ridge NJ 07920

(G-14045)
CHICK MASTER INCUBATOR COMPANY (PA)
945 Lafayette Rd (44256-3510)
P.O. Box 704 (44258-0704)
PHONE..................................330 722-5591
Fax: 330 723-0233
Robert Holzer, *CEO*
Brian Keiser, *COO*
Chad Daniels, *Vice Pres*
Alan Shandler, *Vice Pres*
John Milner, *Plant Mgr*
◆ **EMP:** 118
SQ FT: 100,000
SALES (est): 26.5MM **Privately Held**
WEB: www.chickmaster.com
SIC: 3523 1711 Incubators & brooders, farm; plumbing, heating, air-conditioning contractors

(G-14046)
CHILDTIME CHILDCARE INC
3550 Octagon Dr (44256-6836)
PHONE..................................330 723-8697
Chris Burkholder, *Owner*
EMP: 30
SALES (corp-wide): 281.2MM **Privately Held**
WEB: www.learninggroup.com
SIC: 8351 Preschool center
HQ: Childtime Childcare, Inc.
  21333 Haggerty Rd Ste 300
  Novi MI 48375
  248 697-9000

(G-14047)
CHU MANAGEMENT CO INC (PA)
2875 Medina Rd (44256-9672)
PHONE..................................330 725-4571
Ding-Shu Chu, *President*
EMP: 40
SQ FT: 45,000
SALES: 1.7MM **Privately Held**
SIC: 8741 Hotel or motel management

(G-14048)
CLARK BRANDS LLC
427 N Court St (44256-1869)
PHONE..................................330 723-9886
Al Carmen, *Principal*
EMP: 3098
SALES (corp-wide): 303.3MM **Privately Held**
SIC: 6794 Franchises, selling or licensing
PA: Clark Brands Llc
  4200 Commerce Ct Ste 350
  Lisle IL 60532
  630 355-8918

(G-14049)
COMMUNITY LEGAL AID SERVICES
120 W Washington St 2c (44256-2271)
PHONE..................................330 725-1231
Jennifer Dulmen, *Manager*
Sara Strattan, *Director*
EMP: 35
SALES (est): 1.5MM
SALES (corp-wide): 4.7MM **Privately Held**
SIC: 8111 Legal aid service
PA: Community Legal Aid Services, Inc
  50 S Main St Ste 800
  Akron OH 44308
  330 535-4191

(G-14050)
CONSUMER SUPPORT SERVICES INC
2575 Medina Rd A (44256-9626)
PHONE..................................330 764-4785
Fax: 330 764-4787
Barbie Knoll, *Manager*
EMP: 60
SALES (corp-wide): 26.7MM **Privately Held**
SIC: 8059 8322 Personal care home, with health care; individual & family services
PA: Consumer Support Services Inc
  2040 Cherry Valley Rd # 1
  Newark OH 43055
  740 788-8257

(G-14051)
CONTROLS INC
5204 Portside Dr (44256-5966)
P.O. Box 368, Sharon Center (44274-0368)
PHONE..................................330 239-4345
Fax: 330 239-2845
Robert Cowen, *President*
Scott Izzo, *Vice Pres*
Becky McNamara, *Manager*
EMP: 25
SALES: 1.8MM **Privately Held**
WEB: www.controlsinc.com
SIC: 3625 7389 1731 Control equipment, electric; industrial controls: push button, selector switches, pilot; design services; electronic controls installation

(G-14052)
CORRPRO COMPANIES INC (DH)
1055 W Smith Rd (44256-2444)
PHONE..................................330 723-5082
David H Kroon, *President*
Gehring George, *Exec VP*
Dorwin Hawn, *Exec VP*
Grady Joiner, *Exec VP*
Barry W Schadeck, *Exec VP*
▼ **EMP:** 50
SQ FT: 8,000
SALES (est): 216MM
SALES (corp-wide): 1.3B **Publicly Held**
WEB: www.corrpro.com
SIC: 3699 8711 Electrical equipment & supplies; engineering services
HQ: Insituform Technologies, Llc
  17988 Edison Ave
  Chesterfield MO 63005
  636 530-8000

(G-14053)
COUNTY OF MEDINA
Also Called: Medina County Home
6144 Wedgewood Rd (44256-7860)
PHONE..................................330 723-9553
Fax: 330 764-8654
Lynn Remington, *Manager*
Joyce Farmfworth, *Administration*
EMP: 27
SQ FT: 33,504 **Privately Held**
WEB: www.mcbmrdd.org
SIC: 8361 9111 Rest home, with health care incidental; county supervisors' & executives' offices
PA: County Of Medina
  144 N Brdwy St Rm 201
  Medina OH 44256
  330 722-9208

▲ = Import ▼=Export
◆ =Import/Export

GEOGRAPHIC SECTION

Medina - Medina County (G-14077)

(G-14054)
COUNTY OF MEDINA
Also Called: Medina County Health Dept
4800 Ledgewood Dr (44256-7666)
PHONE.................................330 995-5243
Fax: 330 723-9630
Daniel J Raub, *Commissioner*
Jeannie Bunch, *Supervisor*
Suzanne Kanner, *Supervisor*
Theresa Schlauch, *Supervisor*
Kristen Hildreth, *Director*
EMP: 70 **Privately Held**
WEB: www.mcbmrdd.org
SIC: 8399 9111 Health systems agency; county supervisors' & executives' offices
PA: County Of Medina
144 N Brdwy St Rm 201
Medina OH 44256
330 722-9208

(G-14055)
COUNTY OF MEDINA
Medina County Transportation
114 Bradway St (44256-1711)
PHONE.................................330 723-9670
Fax: 330 725-9169
Michael Salamon, *Director*
EMP: 25
SQ FT: 1,080 **Privately Held**
WEB: www.mcbmrdd.org
SIC: 4731 9111 Freight transportation arrangement; county supervisors' & executives' offices
PA: County Of Medina
144 N Brdwy St Rm 201
Medina OH 44256
330 722-9208

(G-14056)
CUSTOM-PAK INC
Also Called: Custompak
885 W Smith Rd (44256-2424)
PHONE.................................330 725-0800
Ronald P Camaglia, *President*
Frederick Camaglia, *Vice Pres*
Renee Cranet, *Manager*
EMP: 65
SQ FT: 55,000
SALES (est): 3.9MM
SALES (corp-wide): 28.6MM **Privately Held**
WEB: www.custompakproducts.com
SIC: 7389 Packaging & labeling services
PA: Industrial Chemical Corp.
885 W Smith Rd
Medina OH 44256
330 725-0800

(G-14057)
DAIRY FARMERS AMERICA INC
1035 Medina Rd Ste 300 (44256-5398)
PHONE.................................330 670-7800
Glenn Wallace, *Chief*
Sam Stone, *Exec VP*
Shawnon Canfield, *Opers Mgr*
EMP: 30
SALES (corp-wide): 14.6B **Privately Held**
WEB: www.dfamilk.com
SIC: 2022 2026 2021 0211 Cheese, natural & processed; fluid milk; creamery butter; beef cattle feedlots
PA: Dairy Farmers Of America, Inc.
1405 N 98th St
Kansas City KS 66111
816 801-6455

(G-14058)
DIPROINDUCA (USA) LIMITED LLC
Also Called: Diproinduca USA
2528 Medina Rd (44256-8144)
PHONE.................................330 722-4442
Efrain Riera, *President*
Mark Heuschkel, *Vice Pres*
Gerardo Ferreira, *Treasurer*
▼ **EMP:** 100
SQ FT: 4,300
SALES (est): 30.9MM **Privately Held**
SIC: 5093 8999 4959 Metal scrap & waste materials; earth science services; environmental cleanup services

(G-14059)
DISCOUNT DRUG MART INC (PA)
211 Commerce Dr (44256-1331)
PHONE.................................330 725-2340
Fax: 330 722-2990
Donald Boodjeh, *CEO*
Parviz Boodjeh, *Ch of Bd*
John Gains, *President*
Heather Ashburn, *General Mgr*
Dough Boodjeh, *COO*
▲ **EMP:** 250
SQ FT: 500,000
SALES (est): 747.4MM **Privately Held**
WEB: www.discount-drugmart.com
SIC: 5912 5331 5411 5451 Drug stores; variety stores; grocery stores; dairy products stores; pharmaceuticals; home health care services

(G-14060)
DIVERSFIED EMPLYEE SLTIONS INC
3745 Medina Rd (44256-9510)
PHONE.................................330 764-4125
Thomas L Skeen, *Principal*
Tina Brostek, *Human Res Dir*
Pamela Gojoch, *Executive*
EMP: 500
SALES (est): 27.4MM **Privately Held**
WEB: www.des4you.com
SIC: 7363 Employee leasing service

(G-14061)
DO IT BEST CORP
444 Independence Dr (44256-2407)
PHONE.................................330 725-3859
Fax: 330 723-9036
Mike Patalita, *Manager*
Dan Buckland, *Supervisor*
Jim Arthur, *Executive*
EMP: 150
SALES (corp-wide): 2.9B **Privately Held**
WEB: www.doitbestcorp.com
SIC: 5072 5211 5251 Builders' hardware; lumber & other building materials; hardware
PA: Do It Best Corp.
6502 Nelson Rd
Fort Wayne IN 46803
260 748-5300

(G-14062)
ENHANCED HOMECARE MEDINA INC
3745 Medina Rd Ste E (44256-9510)
PHONE.................................330 952-2331
Edward Swinarski, *Principal*
EMP: 50
SALES (est): 469.2K **Privately Held**
SIC: 8082 Home health care services

(G-14063)
ENVIROTEST SYSTEMS CORP
770 S Progress Dr (44256-1368)
PHONE.................................330 963-4464
EMP: 34
SQ FT: 7,400 **Privately Held**
WEB: www.il.etest.com
SIC: 7549 Emissions testing without repairs, automotive
HQ: Envirotest Systems Corp.
7 Kripes Rd
East Granby CT 06026

(G-14064)
FECHKO EXCAVATING INC
865 W Liberty St Ste 120 (44256-1332)
PHONE.................................330 722-2890
Fax: 330 722-5701
John Fechko, *President*
Matthew Honigman, *Vice Pres*
Don Damyanic, *Project Mgr*
Brad Capenter, *Controller*
Dean Fechko, *Admin Sec*
EMP: 70
SQ FT: 4,000
SALES (est): 13.5MM **Privately Held**
WEB: www.fechko.com
SIC: 1794 Excavation & grading, building construction

(G-14065)
FIORILLI CONSTRUCTION CO INC
1247 Medina Rd (44256-8135)
PHONE.................................216 696-5845
Fax: 216 696-5844
Carmen Fiorilli, *President*
Shane Hoover, *Superintendent*
Keith Roberts, *Vice Pres*
Jeff Crowl, *Finance Dir*
Barbara Nimrichter, *Accounts Mgr*
EMP: 30
SALES (est): 12MM **Privately Held**
WEB: www.fio-con.com
SIC: 1542 Commercial & office building, new construction

(G-14066)
FNB CORPORATION
3613 Medina Rd (44256-8181)
PHONE.................................330 721-7484
Fax: 330 721-7585
Marguerite Krahe, *Manager*
EMP: 73
SALES (corp-wide): 1.2B **Publicly Held**
SIC: 6162 Mortgage bankers & correspondents
PA: F.N.B. Corporation
1 N Shore Ctr
Pittsburgh PA 15212
800 555-5455

(G-14067)
FREE ENTERPRISES INCORPORATED (PA)
241 S State Rd (44256-2430)
P.O. Box 1199 (44258-1199)
PHONE.................................330 722-2031
Fax: 330 722-1577
James H Patneau Sr, *President*
Brian Fisher, *Business Mgr*
Tonia Fisher, *Vice Pres*
Annette M Patneau, *Vice Pres*
Paul Ballachino, *Sales Staff*
EMP: 84
SQ FT: 14,590
SALES (est): 32.7MM **Privately Held**
SIC: 5172 5541 Gasoline; gasoline service stations

(G-14068)
GENE TOLLIVER CORP
Also Called: All American Heating AC
6222 Norwalk Rd (44256-9454)
PHONE.................................440 324-7727
Eugene Tolliver, *President*
Keith Tolliver, *Vice Pres*
EMP: 100
SQ FT: 4,300
SALES (est): 6.4MM **Privately Held**
SIC: 1711 Warm air heating & air conditioning contractor; refrigeration contractor

(G-14069)
GENES REFRIGERATION HTG & AC
6222 Norwalk Rd (44256-9454)
PHONE.................................330 723-4104
Fax: 330 723-0154
Ralph E Tolliver, *President*
Gene Tolliver, *President*
Keith Tolliver, *President*
Emily M Berberich, *Principal*
Carolyn S Byrd, *Principal*
EMP: 43
SQ FT: 8,600
SALES (est): 8.7MM **Privately Held**
SIC: 1711 Warm air heating & air conditioning contractor; refrigeration contractor

(G-14070)
GERSPACHER COMPANIES
Also Called: Forest Meadow Villas
574 Leisure Ln (44256-1657)
PHONE.................................330 725-1596
Melvin Gerspacher, *President*
David Gerspacher, *Principal*
Diane Gerspacher, *Admin Sec*
EMP: 47
SQ FT: 22,000
SALES: 1.4MM **Privately Held**
WEB: www.camelotplace.net
SIC: 8361 Residential care

(G-14071)
GOLDEN LIVING LLC
Also Called: Beverly
555 Springbrook Dr (44256-3651)
PHONE.................................330 725-3393
Pam Haman, *Manager*
Yatish Goyal, *Director*
EMP: 100
SALES (corp-wide): 7.4MM **Privately Held**
SIC: 8059 8051 Convalescent home; skilled nursing care facilities
PA: Golden Living Llc
5220 Tennyson Pkwy # 400
Plano TX 75024
972 372-6300

(G-14072)
GRANGER TOWNSHIP
Also Called: Granger Township Fire & Rescue
3737 Ridge Rd (44256-7919)
PHONE.................................330 239-2111
Fax: 330 239-5111
John Hadam, *Chief*
EMP: 30 **Privately Held**
WEB: www.grangertwp.us
SIC: 9111 8699 City & town managers' offices; charitable organization
PA: Granger Township
3717 Ridge Rd
Medina OH 44256
330 239-3611

(G-14073)
H M T DERMATOLOGY INC
Also Called: Trillium Creek Dermatology
5783 Wooster Pike (44256-8816)
PHONE.................................330 725-0569
Helen Torok, *President*
Jim Spinelli, *Sr Corp Ofcr*
Aaron Funk, *Personnel Exec*
EMP: 30
SQ FT: 10,000
SALES (est): 3.5MM **Privately Held**
SIC: 8011 Dermatologist

(G-14074)
HASTINGS HOME HEALTH CTR INC
211 Commerce Dr (44256-1331)
PHONE.................................216 898-3300
David Ondrish, *Branch Mgr*
EMP: 34
SALES (corp-wide): 9MM **Privately Held**
SIC: 8082 Home health care services
PA: Hastings Home Health Center, Inc.
15210 Industrial Pkwy
Cleveland OH 44135
216 898-3300

(G-14075)
HELEN M TOROK MD (PA)
Also Called: H M T Dermatology
5783 Wooster Pike (44256-8816)
PHONE.................................330 722-5477
Fax: 330 725-2099
Helen M Torok, *Owner*
EMP: 29 **EST:** 1979
SALES (est): 4MM **Privately Held**
SIC: 8011 Dermatologist

(G-14076)
HINCKLEY ROOFING INC
3587 Ridge Rd (44256-7917)
P.O. Box 458, Hinckley (44233-0458)
PHONE.................................330 722-7663
Fax: 330 239-0209
Ed Walkuski, *President*
Pam Walkuski, *Treasurer*
Steve Walkuski Jr, *Admin Sec*
EMP: 25
SQ FT: 2,000
SALES (est): 2.7MM **Privately Held**
SIC: 1761 Roofing contractor

(G-14077)
HOSPICE OF THE WESTERN RESERVE
5075 Windfall Rd (44256-8613)
PHONE.................................330 800-2240
William E Finn, *CEO*
EMP: 57

Medina - Medina County (G-14078) — GEOGRAPHIC SECTION

SALES (corp-wide): 89.8MM **Privately Held**
SIC: 8082 8069 Home health care services; specialty hospitals, except psychiatric
PA: Hospice Of The Western Reserve, Inc
    17876 Saint Clair Ave
    Cleveland OH 44110
    216 383-2222

(G-14078)
HOWARD HANNA SMYTHE CRAMER
3565 Medina Rd (44256-8182)
PHONE.................330 725-4137
Fax: 330 722-2238
Bonnie Mahoney, *Broker*
Karen Thompson, *Manager*
Carol Harrington, *Real Est Agnt*
Hannah Jones, *Real Est Agnt*
EMP: 53
SALES (corp-wide): 76.4MM **Privately Held**
WEB: www.smythecramer.com
SIC: 6531 6311 6141 6361 Real estate brokers & agents; life insurance; consumer finance companies; title insurance
HQ: Howard Hanna Smythe Cramer
    6000 Parkland Blvd
    Cleveland OH 44124
    216 447-4477

(G-14079)
INDUSTRIAL CHEMICAL CORP (PA)
Also Called: Custom Pak
885 W Smith Rd (44256-2424)
PHONE.................330 725-0800
Fax: 330 722-5187
Ron Camaglia, *President*
Frederick Camaglia, *Vice Pres*
Joseph Valore, *Purch Mgr*
Renee Brandt, *Office Mgr*
▲ EMP: 50
SQ FT: 55,000
SALES (est): 28.6MM **Privately Held**
SIC: 5169 7389 Chemicals, industrial & heavy; caustic soda; packaging & labeling services

(G-14080)
INN AT MEDINA LIMITED LLC
Also Called: Inn At Medina The
100 High Point Dr Ofc (44256-4363)
PHONE.................330 723-0110
Fax: 330 723-1030
Pam Row, *Manager*
Dan Ihrig,
EMP: 70 EST: 2000
SQ FT: 60,000
SALES (est): 2.4MM **Privately Held**
SIC: 8322 Individual & family services

(G-14081)
INTEGRES GLOBAL LOGISTICS INC (DH)
Also Called: Integres Fast Forward Shipping
84 Medina Rd (44256-9616)
PHONE.................866 347-2101
R Louis Schneeberger, *President*
Jeff Hurine, *CFO*
Dave Brooks, *Bd of Directors*
EMP: 79
SQ FT: 20,954
SALES (est): 6.1MM
SALES (corp-wide): 2.8B **Publicly Held**
WEB: www.integres.com
SIC: 4213 Trucking, except local

(G-14082)
INTERACTIVE ENGINEERING CORP
884 Medina Rd (44256-9615)
PHONE.................330 239-6888
Ming Zhang, *President*
Andy Dan, *Purchasing*
Erik Stevens, *Engineer*
EMP: 25 EST: 1995
SQ FT: 200,000
SALES (est): 3.3MM **Privately Held**
SIC: 8748 3672 Systems analysis & engineering consulting services; printed circuit boards

(G-14083)
INTERVENTION FOR PEACE INC
Also Called: Peace Foundation
689 W Liberty St Ste 7 (44256-2268)
PHONE.................330 725-1298
Fax: 330 722-7755
Pattie Henighan, *Human Resources*
Rick Davidson, *Manager*
David Clardy, *Executive*
EMP: 55
SALES (est): 1.6MM **Privately Held**
WEB: www.interventionforpeace.com
SIC: 8082 Visiting nurse service

(G-14084)
JACOR LLC
1011 Lake Rd (44256-2450)
PHONE.................330 441-4182
Chester Sipsock, *CFO*
Jeremy Carter,
Robert Zufra,
EMP: 600
SQ FT: 4,100
SALES (est): 18.2MM **Privately Held**
WEB: www.gojacor.com
SIC: 7361 Executive placement

(G-14085)
JAMES B OSWALD COMPANY
Also Called: Hoffman Group The
5000 Foote Rd (44256-5396)
PHONE.................330 723-3637
Robin Hammond, *Manager*
EMP: 40
SALES (corp-wide): 179.4MM **Privately Held**
SIC: 6411 6331 6321 Insurance agents, brokers & service; fire, marine & casualty insurance; accident & health insurance
PA: The James B Oswald Company
    1100 Superior Ave E # 1500
    Cleveland OH 44114
    216 367-8787

(G-14086)
JARRELLS MOVING & TRANSPORT CO
1155 Industrial Pkwy (44256-2492)
PHONE.................330 952-1240
Robert S Zufra, *Branch Mgr*
EMP: 50
SALES (corp-wide): 10.6MM **Privately Held**
SIC: 4789 Pipeline terminal facilities, independently operated
PA: Jarrells Moving & Transport Co., Inc
    5076 Park Ave W
    Seville OH 44273
    330 764-4333

(G-14087)
JPMORGAN CHASE BANK NAT ASSN
3626 Medina Rd (44256-8100)
PHONE.................330 722-6626
Dave Cleckner, *Branch Mgr*
EMP: 26
SALES (corp-wide): 99.6B **Publicly Held**
WEB: www.chase.com
SIC: 6021 National commercial banks
HQ: Jpmorgan Chase Bank, National Association
    1111 Polaris Pkwy
    Columbus OH 43240
    614 436-3055

(G-14088)
JUSTICE & CO INC
Also Called: Architectural Justice
2462 Pearl Rd (44256-9015)
PHONE.................330 225-6000
Fax: 330 273-2448
James Justice, *President*
Laura Justice, *Vice Pres*
▲ EMP: 25
SQ FT: 10,000
SALES (est): 5.3MM **Privately Held**
SIC: 5713 5032 Floor tile; granite building stone

(G-14089)
K & M CONSTRUCTION COMPANY
230 E Smith Rd (44256-2623)
PHONE.................330 723-3681
Jerry A Schwab, *President*
David Schwab, *Vice Pres*
Mary Lynn Hites, *Treasurer*
Mary Schwab, *Treasurer*
Daryl Albright, *Manager*
EMP: 128
SQ FT: 2,000
SALES (est): 6MM
SALES (corp-wide): 29.7B **Privately Held**
SIC: 1611 1771 Resurfacing contractor; driveway, parking lot & blacktop contractors
HQ: Medina Supply Company
    230 E Smith Rd
    Medina OH 44256
    330 723-3681

(G-14090)
KAISER FOUNDATION HOSPITALS
Also Called: Medina Medical Offices
3443 Medina Rd (44256-5360)
PHONE.................800 524-7377
Marvin Baker, *Branch Mgr*
EMP: 593
SALES (corp-wide): 82.6B **Privately Held**
SIC: 8011 Offices & clinics of medical doctors
HQ: Kaiser Foundation Hospitals Inc
    1 Kaiser Plz
    Oakland CA 94612
    510 271-6611

(G-14091)
KENMAR LAWN & GRDN CARE CO LLC
Also Called: Kenmar Landscaping Company
3665 Ridge Rd (44256-7918)
P.O. Box 281 (44258-0281)
PHONE.................330 239-2924
Kenneth Bell, *Owner*
EMP: 48
SALES (est): 5.8MM **Privately Held**
SIC: 5083 Landscaping equipment

(G-14092)
KRAKOWSKI TRUCKING INC
1100 W Smith Rd (44256-3500)
PHONE.................330 722-7935
Barbara Krakowski, *President*
Lawrence C Krakowski, *President*
William Disbrow, *Vice Pres*
Jim Brooks, *Admin Sec*
EMP: 39
SQ FT: 2,146
SALES (est): 4.5MM **Privately Held**
WEB: www.ktitrucking.com
SIC: 4731 Domestic freight forwarding

(G-14093)
KTIB INC
1100 W Smith Rd (44256-2443)
PHONE.................330 722-7935
Barbara J Krakowski, *President*
William R Disbrow, *Vice Pres*
Bryan Dressler, *Opers Mgr*
EMP: 30
SALES (est): 2.8MM **Privately Held**
SIC: 4212 Local trucking, without storage

(G-14094)
MARKS CLEANING SERVICE INC
325 S Elmwood Ave (44256-2322)
PHONE.................330 725-5702
Fax: 330 723-7179
Eric Palmer, *President*
Mark Skoda, *President*
Bonnie Skoda, *Vice Pres*
Michael Gallucci, *Manager*
EMP: 37
SALES (est): 2MM **Privately Held**
WEB: www.markscleaning.com
SIC: 7217 7349 Carpet & upholstery cleaning on customer premises; janitorial service, contract basis

(G-14095)
MARVIN W MIELKE INC
Also Called: Mw Mielke
1040 Industrial Pkwy (44256-2449)
PHONE.................330 725-8845
Fax: 330 723-1995
David A Mielke, *President*
Terry Mielke, *Vice Pres*
Scott Givens, *VP Opers*
Mike Fisher, *Treasurer*
Mary Anne Mielke, *Treasurer*
EMP: 100
SQ FT: 20,000
SALES: 25MM **Privately Held**
WEB: www.mwmielke.com
SIC: 1711 Plumbing contractors; sprinkler contractors; warm air heating & air conditioning contractor

(G-14096)
MEDINA ADVANTAGE INC
Also Called: Kids Country
3550 Octagon Dr (44256-6836)
PHONE.................330 723-8697
Fax: 330 725-8638
Christine Burkholder, *President*
Rick Burkholder, *Principal*
EMP: 30
SALES (est): 779.4K **Privately Held**
SIC: 8351 Group day care center

(G-14097)
MEDINA CNTY JVNILE DTNTION CTR
655 Independence Dr (44256-3547)
PHONE.................330 764-8408
Fax: 330 764-8412
Ronald Stollar, *Superintendent*
Reva Keaton, *Manager*
EMP: 33
SALES (est): 1.6MM **Privately Held**
SIC: 8361 Juvenile correctional home

(G-14098)
MEDINA COUNTY SANITARY
791 W Smith Rd (44256-2422)
P.O. Box 542 (44258-0542)
PHONE.................330 273-3610
Fax: 330 723-9661
Jim Troike, *Manager*
EMP: 39
SALES (est): 5.4MM **Privately Held**
SIC: 8711 Sanitary engineers

(G-14099)
MEDINA CREATIVE ACCESSIBILITY
232 N Court St (44256-1925)
PHONE.................330 220-2112
Dianne De-Pasquale-Hagerty, *Principal*
EMP: 80
SALES (est): 949.4K **Privately Held**
SIC: 8322 Association for the handicapped

(G-14100)
MEDINA GLASS BLOCK INC
Also Called: GBA Architectural Pdts Svcs
1213 Medina Rd (44256-8135)
PHONE.................330 239-0239
Fax: 330 239-0230
Jeffery W Boesch, *President*
Buck Kirkpatrick, *COO*
Stephen J Boesch, *Vice Pres*
Darlene Saxon, *Controller*
John Powers, *VP Finance*
▲ EMP: 25
SQ FT: 38,000
SALES (est): 9MM **Privately Held**
WEB: www.medinaglassblock.com
SIC: 1793 5039 5231 Glass & glazing work; glass construction materials; glass

(G-14101)
MEDINA HOSPITAL
Life Support Team
1000 E Washington St (44256-2167)
PHONE.................330 723-3117
Ken Milligan, *Branch Mgr*
EMP: 30
SALES (corp-wide): 101.8MM **Privately Held**
SIC: 8062 General medical & surgical hospitals
PA: Medina Hospital
    1000 E Washington St
    Medina OH 44256
    330 725-1000

(G-14102)
MEDINA MANAGEMENT COMPANY LLC
Also Called: Medina Automall
3205 Medina Rd (44256-9631)
PHONE.................330 723-3291
Jim Brown, *Principal*

Tammy Oberaitis, *Controller*
EMP: 70
SQ FT: 30,526
SALES (est): 1.2MM **Privately Held**
SIC: 5012 Automobiles & other motor vehicles

(G-14103)
MEDINA MEADOWS
550 Miner Dr (44256-1472)
PHONE.................................330 725-1550
Sharona Grunspan, *President*
Sam Krichevsky, *Vice Pres*
Jean Bergman, *Director*
Karen Gosset, *Director*
Denise Urbanski, *Nursing Dir*
EMP: 85
SQ FT: 28,000
SALES (est): 3.8MM **Privately Held**
SIC: 8051 Convalescent home with continuous nursing care

(G-14104)
MEDINA MEDICAL INVESTORS LTD
Also Called: Life Care Center of Medina
2400 Columbia Rd (44256-9414)
PHONE.................................330 483-3131
Fax: 330 483-3132
Jim Everley, *Managing Dir*
Forrest I Preston, *General Ptnr*
Rob Berger, *Human Res Dir*
Mark O Spillman, *Exec Dir*
Mark Speelman, *Director*
EMP: 180
SQ FT: 70,000
SALES: 8.5MM **Privately Held**
SIC: 8051 8059 Convalescent home with continuous nursing care; rest home, with health care

(G-14105)
MICHAEL T LEE DVM
Also Called: Animal Medical Center Medina
1060 S Court St (44256-2885)
PHONE.................................330 722-5076
Fax: 330 723-5907
Michael T Lee Dvm, *Owner*
Kim Davey,
William Feeman,
Rebecca Prada-Smanik,
EMP: 30 **EST:** 1980
SQ FT: 1,500
SALES (est): 1.1MM **Privately Held**
WEB: www.animalmedicalcentreofmedina.com
SIC: 0742 Animal hospital services, pets & other animal specialties

(G-14106)
NEW BIRCH MANOR I ASSOC LLC
Also Called: Birch Manor Apartments I
23875 Miner Dr (44256)
PHONE.................................330 723-3404
ABC Management, *Principal*
Larry Looney, *Mng Member*
Sally Keith, *Manager*
EMP: 99
SALES: 1,000K **Privately Held**
SIC: 6513 Apartment building operators

(G-14107)
NORHTEAST OHIO MUSEUM
6807 Boneta Rd (44256-9771)
PHONE.................................330 336-7657
Wayne H Lavin, *Owner*
EMP: 27
SALES (est): 366.7K **Privately Held**
SIC: 8412 Museum

(G-14108)
NORTH GATEWAY TIRE CO INC
4001 Pearl Rd (44256-9000)
PHONE.................................330 725-8473
Fax: 330 725-8550
Robert H Dunlap, *CEO*
Darrell Hill, *President*
G E Mc Kittrick, *Corp Secy*
Jeffrey Beattie, *Comms Mgr*
Donna Napalo, *Manager*
EMP: 41
SQ FT: 40,000
SALES (est): 2MM
SALES (corp-wide): 104.7MM **Privately Held**
WEB: www.northgatewaytire.com
SIC: 5531 5014 Automotive tires; automobile tires & tubes
PA: Dunlap & Kyle Company, Inc.
280 Eureka St
Batesville MS 38606
662 563-7601

(G-14109)
NURTURY
250 N Spring Grove St (44256-1921)
PHONE.................................330 723-1800
Fax: 330 725-2236
Mary Kubasta, *President*
Kent Kubasta, *Vice Pres*
EMP: 30
SQ FT: 7,500
SALES (est): 959K **Privately Held**
WEB: www.thenurturyschool.com
SIC: 8351 Nursery school; preschool center

(G-14110)
OHIO CAMP CHERITH INC
3854 Remsen Rd (44256-7656)
PHONE.................................330 725-4202
Judy Kirsch, *President*
Gary Waldinger, *Vice Pres*
Sharon Lort, *Admin Sec*
EMP: 25
SALES: 57K **Privately Held**
SIC: 7032 Boys' camp; girls' camp; summer camp, except day & sports instructional

(G-14111)
PANTHER II TRANSPORTATION INC (DH)
84 Medina Rd (44256-9616)
PHONE.................................800 685-0657
Fax: 330 769-5835
R Louis Schneeberger, *CEO*
Edward Wadel, *COO*
Mary Lawton, *Exec VP*
David Buss, *Vice Pres*
Stpierre Jeff, *Vice Pres*
EMP: 185
SQ FT: 33,000
SALES (est): 76.9MM
SALES (corp-wide): 2.8B **Publicly Held**
WEB: www.panther2.com
SIC: 4213 4212 4522 Trucking, except local; local trucking, without storage; air transportation, nonscheduled
HQ: Panther Premium Logistics, Inc.
84 Medina Rd
Medina OH 44256
800 685-0657

(G-14112)
PANTHER PREMIUM LOGISTICS INC (HQ)
84 Medina Rd (44256-9616)
PHONE.................................800 685-0657
R Louis Schneeberger, *President*
Edward Wadel, *COO*
David Buss, *Vice Pres*
Frank Ilacqua, *Vice Pres*
Mark Pare, *Vice Pres*
EMP: 300
SQ FT: 50,000
SALES (est): 78MM
SALES (corp-wide): 2.8B **Publicly Held**
WEB: www.pantherii.com
SIC: 4213 4212 Trucking, except local; local trucking, without storage
PA: Arcbest Corporation
8401 Mcclure Dr
Fort Smith AR 72916
479 785-6000

(G-14113)
PRIME POLYMERS INC
Also Called: Engineered Polymer Systems
2600 Medina Rd (44256-8145)
P.O. Box 351, Sharon Center (44274-0351)
PHONE.................................330 662-4200
Fax: 330 662-4217
Ronnie Rotli, *President*
Brian Guccion, *Sales Mgr*
Cathy Lehecka, *Accounts Mgr*
EMP: 25
SQ FT: 80,000
SALES (est): 4.4MM **Privately Held**
WEB: www.primepolymers.com
SIC: 1771 1752 1799 1611 Concrete repair; floor laying & floor work; coating, caulking & weather, water & fireproofing; resurfacing contractor

(G-14114)
PROFESSIONAL RESTORATION SVC
Also Called: Serv Pro of Barberton/Norton
1170 Industrial Pkwy (44256-2486)
P.O. Box 22, Barberton (44203-0022)
PHONE.................................330 825-1803
Fax: 330 723-3626
Michal Fosdick, *President*
EMP: 42 **EST:** 1996
SQ FT: 36,500
SALES (est): 1.7MM **Privately Held**
WEB: www.spbarberton.com
SIC: 7349 Building component cleaning service

(G-14115)
PSYCHOLOGY CONSULTANTS INC
3591 Reserve Commons Dr # 301 (44256-5334)
PHONE.................................330 764-7916
Fax: 330 723-6399
Thomas McArthy, *President*
Daniel McArthy, *Vice Pres*
Beth Plumley, *Administration*
EMP: 40
SALES (est): 1.5MM **Privately Held**
SIC: 8999 Psychological consultant

(G-14116)
PULTE HOMES INC
387 Medina Rd Ste 1700 (44256-9679)
PHONE.................................330 239-1587
Paul Spenthoff, *Vice Pres*
Andrew Orley, *Purch Agent*
EMP: 30
SALES (est): 1.4MM **Privately Held**
SIC: 1522 Residential construction

(G-14117)
REA & ASSOCIATES INC
694 E Washington St (44256-2125)
PHONE.................................330 722-8222
Fax: 330 722-0704
Ted Klimczak, *CPA*
Vicki Cooper, *Sales Mgr*
Dan Watson, *Branch Mgr*
Thomas Kotick, *Branch Mgr*
EMP: 27
SQ FT: 6,400
SALES (corp-wide): 32.3MM **Privately Held**
WEB: www.reacpa.com
SIC: 8721 Certified public accountant
PA: Rea & Associates, Inc.
419 W High Ave
New Philadelphia OH 44663
330 339-6651

(G-14118)
REDEFINE ENTERPRISES LLC
Also Called: Rise Fitness
3839 Pearl Rd (44256-9001)
PHONE.................................330 952-2024
Andrew Hamlin, *Mng Member*
EMP: 28 **EST:** 2016
SQ FT: 12,500
SALES (est): 43.2K **Privately Held**
SIC: 7991 Physical fitness facilities

(G-14119)
REFLECTIONS HAIR STUDIO INC
3605 Medina Rd (44256-8181)
PHONE.................................330 725-5782
Fax: 330 722-8706
Lori Daso, *President*
EMP: 32
SQ FT: 3,000
SALES: 320K **Privately Held**
SIC: 7231 Hairdressers

(G-14120)
REGAL CINEMAS INC
Also Called: Huntington Street 16
200 W Reagan Pkwy (44256-1567)
PHONE.................................330 723-4416
Raymond Flato, *Manager*
EMP: 35
SALES (corp-wide): 982.1MM **Privately Held**
WEB: www.regalcinemas.com
SIC: 7832 Motion picture theaters, except drive-in
HQ: Regal Cinemas, Inc.
101 E Blount Ave Ste 100
Knoxville TN 37920
865 922-1123

(G-14121)
S&V INDUSTRIES INC (PA)
5054 Paramount Dr (44256-5363)
PHONE.................................330 666-1986
Fax: 330 253-7573
Senthil Sundarapandian, *CEO*
Senthil Kumar Sundarapandian, *CEO*
Mahesh Douglas, *President*
Joan Owens, *Vice Pres*
Karen Peel, *Manager*
▲ **EMP:** 40
SQ FT: 1,618
SALES: 50MM **Privately Held**
WEB: www.svindustries.com
SIC: 5049 3089 3312 Engineers' equipment & supplies; casting of plastic; forgings, iron & steel

(G-14122)
SAMARITAN CARE CENTER & VILLA
806 E Washington St (44256-2194)
PHONE.................................330 725-4123
Fax: 330 723-2412
Bob Banasik, *President*
Tom Slivka, *Facilities Dir*
Kunal Mitra, *Director*
Sarah Crawford, *Nursing Dir*
Sue Shrodes, *Records Dir*
EMP: 100
SALES (est): 4.7MM
SALES (corp-wide): 9.1MM **Privately Held**
WEB: www.omnilife.net
SIC: 8059 8051 8052 Nursing home, except skilled & intermediate care facility; skilled nursing care facilities; intermediate care facilities
PA: Omnilife Health Care Systems, Inc.
50 W 5th Ave
Columbus OH 43201
614 299-3100

(G-14123)
SANDRIDGE FOOD CORPORATION
Also Called: Sandridge Gourmet Salads
133 Commerce Dr (44256-1333)
PHONE.................................330 725-8883
Barry Pioski, *Manager*
EMP: 225
SALES (corp-wide): 112.3MM **Privately Held**
WEB: www.sandridge.com
SIC: 2099 5141 Salads, fresh or refrigerated; groceries, general line
PA: Sandridge Food Corporation
133 Commerce Dr
Medina OH 44256
330 725-2348

(G-14124)
SENIOR CARE INC
Also Called: Elmcroft of Medina
1046 N Jefferson St (44256-1102)
PHONE.................................330 721-2000
Dinah Lambert, *Corp Comm Staff*
Greg Kaminfki, *Branch Mgr*
Ann Haltrich, *Nursing Dir*
EMP: 66 **Privately Held**
SIC: 8052 Intermediate care facilities
PA: Senior Care, Inc.
700 N Hurstbourne Pkwy # 200
Louisville KY 40222

(G-14125)
SIMMONS BROTHERS CORPORATION
780 W Smith Rd Ste A (44256-3513)
PHONE.................................330 722-1415
Fax: 330 722-1416
Donald Simmons, *CEO*
William Simmons, *President*
Stephen Hummel, *Vice Pres*
David Simmons, *Vice Pres*
EMP: 32 **EST:** 1959

Medina - Medina County (G-14126)

SQ FT: 14,336
SALES (est): 6.4MM **Privately Held**
SIC: 1541 Industrial buildings, new construction

(G-14126)
SISLER HEATING & COOLING INC
249 S State Rd (44256-2430)
P.O. Box 308 (44258-0308)
PHONE..................330 722-7101
Fax: 330 723-6591
Dennis Sisler, *President*
Christy Meadows, *Admin Sec*
EMP: 32
SQ FT: 7,500
SALES (est): 3.7MM **Privately Held**
SIC: 1711 1794 Ventilation & duct work contractor; warm air heating & air conditioning contractor; excavation work

(G-14127)
SOCIETY HANDICAPPED CITZ MEDIN
5810 Deerview Ln (44256-8003)
PHONE..................330 722-1710
Fax: 330 722-1710
EMP: 88
SALES (corp-wide): 7.7MM **Privately Held**
SIC: 1521 New construction, single-family houses
PA: Society For Handicapped Citizens Of Medina County
4283 Paradise Rd
Seville OH 44273
330 722-1900

(G-14128)
SOUTH STAR CORP
Also Called: Number 1 Landscaping
3775 Ridge Rd (44256-7919)
PHONE..................330 239-5466
Fax: 330 239-4268
Tom Csanyi, *President*
EMP: 30 **EST**: 1987
SQ FT: 2,226
SALES (est): 2.9MM **Privately Held**
WEB: www.southstarcorp.com
SIC: 0782 Landscape contractors

(G-14129)
STEINGASS MECHANICAL CONTG
754 S Progress Dr (44256-1368)
PHONE..................330 725-6090
Fax: 330 725-0492
William Steingass, *Principal*
Linda Steingass, *Corp Secy*
Nancy Shelton, *Vice Pres*
Chad Barco, *Project Mgr*
Richard Mann, *Project Mgr*
EMP: 30
SQ FT: 12,000
SALES (est): 7.4MM **Privately Held**
WEB: www.steingassmechanical.com
SIC: 1711 1794 Plumbing contractors; warm air heating & air conditioning contractor; fire sprinkler system installation; excavation & grading, building construction

(G-14130)
SUMMA HEALTH CENTER LK MEDINA
3780 Medina Rd Ste 220 (44256-9312)
PHONE..................330 952-0014
Victoria J Meshekow, *Principal*
EMP: 47
SALES (est): 3.7MM **Privately Held**
SIC: 8082 Home health care services

(G-14131)
SUMMIT MANAGEMENT SERVICES INC
201 Northland Dr Ofc (44256-1528)
PHONE..................330 723-0864
EMP: 42
SALES (corp-wide): 6MM **Privately Held**
SIC: 6513 Apartment building operators
PA: Summit Management Services, Inc.
730 W Market St
Akron OH 44303
330 762-4011

(G-14132)
SUPER TAN
1110 N Court St (44256-1578)
PHONE..................330 722-2799
Jodie James, *Owner*
EMP: 50
SALES (est): 343.8K **Privately Held**
SIC: 7299 Tanning salon

(G-14133)
TEKNOBILITY LLC
3013 Gary Kyle Ct (44256-6854)
PHONE..................216 255-9433
Carmen Melillo, *President*
Carmen D Melillo, *Principal*
EMP: 45
SALES (est): 2.6MM **Privately Held**
SIC: 7373 Computer systems analysis & design

(G-14134)
TELCOM CONSTRUCTION SVCS INC
5067 Paramount Dr (44256-5364)
PHONE..................330 239-6900
Joe Anello, *President*
EMP: 85 **EST**: 1998
SQ FT: 5,000
SALES (est): 12.4MM **Privately Held**
WEB: www.telcomcs.com
SIC: 4899 Communication signal enhancement network system

(G-14135)
TELINX SOLUTIONS LLC
961 Mallet Hill Ct (44256-3098)
PHONE..................330 819-0657
Lola Cargill,
EMP: 25
SALES (est): 825.9K **Privately Held**
SIC: 7389 Telemarketing services; telephone solicitation service; fund raising organizations; subscription fulfillment services: magazine, newspaper, etc.

(G-14136)
VERMEER SALES & SERVICE INC (PA)
2389 Medina Rd (44256-9666)
PHONE..................330 723-8383
Fax: 330 723-4635
Frank Sklarski, *President*
Cathie Sklarski, *Corp Secy*
Joe Buchtinec, *Financial Exec*
EMP: 39
SQ FT: 6,500
SALES (est): 26.5MM **Privately Held**
SIC: 5082 7699 Contractors' materials; construction equipment repair

(G-14137)
VEXOR TECHNOLOGY INC (PA)
955 W Smith Rd (44256-2446)
PHONE..................330 721-9773
Fax: 330 721-9438
Joseph E Waters, *President*
Steven M Berry, *President*
F Phillip Stapf, *Principal*
Fred Stapf, *Vice Pres*
Mike Deluca, *Plant Mgr*
▲ EMP: 37
SQ FT: 60,800
SALES (est): 17.5MM **Privately Held**
WEB: www.vexortechnology.com
SIC: 4953 4212 Recycling, waste materials; local trucking, without storage

(G-14138)
WESTERN RSRVE MSONIC CMNTY INC
4931 Nettleton Rd # 4318 (44256-5353)
PHONE..................330 721-3000
Fax: 330 721-3375
Kelly Reed, *Office Mgr*
Jay Dettorre, *Exec Dir*
Kelly Gordon, *Director*
EMP: 150
SALES (est): 8.7MM **Privately Held**
SIC: 8059 8052 8051 Rest home, with health care; intermediate care facilities; skilled nursing care facilities
PA: Browning Mesonic Community Inc
8883 Browning Dr
Waterville OH 43566
419 878-4055

(G-14139)
WOLCOTT GROUP
1684 Medina Rd Ste 204 (44256-9316)
PHONE..................330 666-5900
Daniel P Butcher, *Principal*
EMP: 31 **EST**: 2005
SALES (est): 2.8MM **Privately Held**
SIC: 7379 Computer related consulting services

Medway
Clark County

(G-14140)
AMERICAN LINE BUILDERS APPRENT
Also Called: Albat
1900 Lake Rd (45341-1244)
P.O. Box 370 (45341-0370)
PHONE..................937 849-4177
Fax: 937 849-0592
Howard Miller, *Exec Dir*
Daniel Dade, *Director*
Danny Doss, *Asst Director*
Larry Stover, *Training Spec*
EMP: 76
SALES: 10MM **Privately Held**
SIC: 8331 Job training services

Mentor
Lake County

(G-14141)
ALLIANCE HOSPITALITY INC
Also Called: Comfort Inn
7701 Reynolds Rd (44060-5320)
PHONE..................440 951-7333
Jessica Gilbride, *Manager*
EMP: 30
SALES (corp-wide): 11.2MM **Privately Held**
SIC: 7011 7999 Hotels & motels; swimming pool, non-membership; tennis courts, outdoor/indoor: non-membership
PA: Alliance Hospitality, Inc.
600 Enterprise Dr
Lewis Center OH 43035
614 846-6600

(G-14142)
ALTERCARE OF MENTOR CENTER
9901 Johnnycake Ridge Rd (44060-6739)
PHONE..................440 953-4421
Gerald Schroer, *President*
EMP: 150
SALES (est): 1.5MM **Privately Held**
SIC: 8051 Convalescent home with continuous nursing care

(G-14143)
AMITEL MENTOR LTD PARTNERSHIP
Also Called: Residence Inn By Marriott
5660 Emerald Ct (44060-1869)
PHONE..................440 392-0800
Lauri Siclair, *General Mgr*
Lauri Sinclair, *General Mgr*
EMP: 30
SALES (est): 1.1MM **Privately Held**
SIC: 7011 Hotels & motels

(G-14144)
ANGELS IN WAITING HOME CARE
8336 Tyler Blvd (44060-4221)
PHONE..................440 946-0349
Terri Jochum, *Branch Mgr*
EMP: 32
SALES (corp-wide): 1.1MM **Privately Held**
SIC: 8082 Home health care services
PA: Angels In Waiting Home Care
38052 Euclid Ave Ste 280
Willoughby OH 44094
440 946-0347

(G-14145)
AVERY DENNISON CORPORATION
Also Called: Avery Dennison Materials Group
8080 Norton Pkwy (44060-5990)
PHONE..................440 534-6000
Fax: 440 534-6333
Tina Hart, *Vice Pres*
Donna Pruneski, *Project Mgr*
Omar Rueda, *Opers Mgr*
Scott Yopp, *Opers Mgr*
John Hussmann, *Safety Mgr*
EMP: 115
SALES (corp-wide): 6.6B **Publicly Held**
WEB: www.avery.com
SIC: 5199 7389 Packaging materials; packaging & labeling services
PA: Avery Dennison Corporation
207 N Goode Ave Fl 6
Glendale CA 91203
626 304-2000

(G-14146)
AVI FOOD SYSTEMS INC
7710 Tyler Blvd (44060-4802)
PHONE..................440 255-3468
Sam Miller, *President*
EMP: 41
SALES (corp-wide): 661.7MM **Privately Held**
SIC: 7353 Heavy construction equipment rental
PA: Avi Food Systems, Inc.
2590 Elm Rd Ne
Warren OH 44483
330 372-6000

(G-14147)
BACKTRACK INC
8850 Tyler Blvd (44060-4361)
PHONE..................440 205-8280
Fax: 440 205-8355
Robert Gandee, *President*
Susan Gurbach Cotter, *Vice Pres*
Linda Gandee, *Vice Pres*
Susan Gurbach, *Vice Pres*
John Hawkins, *Vice Pres*
EMP: 73
SQ FT: 12,000
SALES (est): 6.5MM **Privately Held**
WEB: www.backtracker.com
SIC: 7361 Executive placement
PA: General Information Solutions Llc
917 Chapin Rd
Chapin SC 29036

(G-14148)
BEACON HEALTH
9220 Mentor Ave (44060-6412)
PHONE..................440 354-9924
Fax: 440 354-9924
Spencer Kline, *CEO*
Gerry Reis, *Vice Pres*
Gary Sopnicar, *Vice Pres*
Ginger Yanchar, *Manager*
Laura Corrigan, *Technology*
EMP: 150
SQ FT: 14,000
SALES: 3.4MM **Privately Held**
WEB: www.neighboring.org
SIC: 8093 Mental health clinic, outpatient

(G-14149)
BEALL INC
7875 Johnnycake Ridge Rd (44060-5529)
PHONE..................440 974-8719
Michelle Bartoul, *Branch Mgr*
EMP: 40 **Privately Held**
SIC: 8099 Hearing testing service
PA: Beall, Inc.
11260 Chester Rd Ste 450
Cincinnati OH 45246

(G-14150)
BLACKBROOK COUNTRY CLUB INC
8900 Lake Shore Blvd (44060-1524)
PHONE..................440 951-0010
Mary Lou Colbow, *President*
Karen Hillock, *Vice Pres*
EMP: 35
SQ FT: 3,500
SALES (est): 874.9K **Privately Held**
SIC: 7992 Public golf courses

GEOGRAPHIC SECTION
Mentor - Lake County (G-14173)

(G-14151)
BURRIER SERVICE COMPANY INC
Also Called: Hvac
8669 Twinbrook Rd (44060-4340)
P.O. Box 661 (44061-0661)
PHONE.................................440 946-6019
Fax: 440 946-6019
Cary Burrier, *President*
Kevin Barry, *Vice Pres*
Maryann Intihar, *Admin Sec*
EMP: 30
SQ FT: 6,400
SALES (est): 5MM Privately Held
WEB: www.have.com
SIC: 1711 Warm air heating & air conditioning contractor; refrigeration contractor

(G-14152)
BUYERS PRODUCTS COMPANY (PA)
9049 Tyler Blvd (44060-4800)
PHONE.................................440 974-8888
Fax: 440 974-0165
Mark Saltzman, *President*
Dave Durst, *General Mgr*
Jeff Mueller, *Vice Pres*
Brian Lanican, *Mfg Dir*
Gary Kadow, *Plant Mgr*
▲ EMP: 160
SQ FT: 172,000
SALES (est): 149MM Privately Held
WEB: www.buyersproducts.com
SIC: 5013 3714 Truck parts & accessories; motor vehicle parts & accessories

(G-14153)
CARDINALCOMMERCE CORPORATION
Also Called: C C
8100 Tyler Blvd Ste 100 (44060-4887)
PHONE.................................877 352-8444
Fax: 440 352-1646
Michael A Keresman III, *CEO*
Chandra Balasubramanian, *Exec VP*
John Schick, *Exec VP*
Francis M Sherwin, *Exec VP*
Tim Sherwin, *Exec VP*
EMP: 60
SALES (est): 11.1MM Privately Held
SIC: 7361 Employment agencies

(G-14154)
CCI SUPPLY INC
8620 Tyler Blvd (44060-4300)
PHONE.................................440 953-0045
Tim Small, *President*
Ed Marko, *Vice Pres*
Jon Small, *Vice Pres*
Mark T Small, *Vice Pres*
Elaine Paradise, *Manager*
EMP: 187
SQ FT: 22,000
SALES (est): 14.6MM Privately Held
SIC: 5032 5033 5211 Brick, stone & related material; insulation materials; lumber & other building materials; insulation material, building

(G-14155)
CELLCO PARTNERSHIP
Also Called: Verizon
7685 Mentor Ave (44060-5540)
PHONE.................................440 953-1155
Terry Tindel, *Branch Mgr*
Ken Baker, *Manager*
James Sankey, *Data Proc Dir*
EMP: 25
SALES (corp-wide): 126B Publicly Held
SIC: 4812 5999 Cellular telephone services; mobile telephones & equipment
HQ: Cellco Partnership
1 Verizon Way
Basking Ridge NJ 07920

(G-14156)
CHARTER HOTEL GROUP LTD PARTNR (PA)
Also Called: Courtyard By Marriott
5966 Heisley Rd (44060-1886)
PHONE.................................216 772-4538
Patricia Treaster, *Principal*
EMP: 35
SQ FT: 2,500
SALES (est): 1.4MM Privately Held
SIC: 7011 5812 Hotels & motels; eating places

(G-14157)
CHEMSULTANTS INTERNATIONAL INC (PA)
9079 Tyler Blvd (44060-1868)
P.O. Box 1118 (44061-1118)
PHONE.................................440 974-3080
Fax: 440 352-8572
Judith Muny, *Corp Secy*
Keith Muny, *Vice Pres*
Mark Van Ness, *Prdtn Mgr*
Jennifer Muny, *Dir Ops-Prd-Mfg*
Aaron Caunter, *Director*
EMP: 25
SQ FT: 10,000
SALES (est): 5.4MM Privately Held
SIC: 3821 8734 8742 Laboratory apparatus & furniture; product testing laboratory, safety or performance; industry specialist consultants

(G-14158)
CLASSIC INTERNATIONAL INC (PA)
Also Called: Classic Lexus
8470 Tyler Blvd (44060-4230)
P.O. Box 300 (44061-0300)
PHONE.................................440 975-1222
Fax: 440 255-0326
James Brown, *President*
Alex Cooke, *General Mgr*
Matt Dietz, *General Mgr*
Rex Harrison, *General Mgr*
Ben Villines, *General Mgr*
EMP: 62
SQ FT: 18,000
SALES (est): 24.1MM Privately Held
WEB: www.classiclexus.com
SIC: 5511 7538 Automobiles, new & used; general automotive repair shops

(G-14159)
CLEVELAND CONSTRUCTION INC (PA)
Also Called: CCI
8620 Tyler Blvd (44060-4348)
PHONE.................................440 255-8000
Fax: 440 255-7443
Jon Small, *President*
Brad Erath, *Superintendent*
Scott Kershaw, *Superintendent*
James Small, *Vice Pres*
Jason Ziegler, *Vice Pres*
▲ EMP: 50
SQ FT: 42,500
SALES (est): 411.5MM Privately Held
SIC: 1542 1742 1752 Commercial & office building contractors; commercial & office building, new construction; commercial & office buildings, renovation & repair; specialized public building contractors; plastering, plain or ornamental; drywall; insulation, buildings; acoustical & ceiling work; floor laying & floor work

(G-14160)
CLS FACILITIES MGT SVCS INC
Also Called: Cls Facilities Management Svcs
8061 Tyler Blvd (44060-4809)
PHONE.................................440 602-4600
Robert A Waldrip, *President*
Bill Brodnick, *CFO*
Amanda Bachmann, *Accounts Mgr*
EMP: 37
SQ FT: 10,000
SALES (est): 15.8MM Privately Held
WEB: www.clsfacilityservices.com
SIC: 5063 1731 Lighting fixtures, commercial & industrial; lighting contractor

(G-14161)
COMMUNITY DIALYSIS CTR MENTOR
8900 Tyler Blvd (44060-2185)
PHONE.................................440 255-5999
Fax: 440 255-7581
Diane Wish, *CEO*
EMP: 40
SQ FT: 8,000
SALES (est): 992.8K Privately Held
SIC: 8092 Kidney dialysis centers

(G-14162)
CONTRACT MARKETING INC
Also Called: Sales Building Systems
9325 Progress Pkwy (44060-1855)
PHONE.................................440 639-9100
Fax: 440 350-7475
Patricia White, *CEO*
Timothy Mc Carthy, *President*
Terry Goins, *Exec VP*
Cindy Venable, *VP Sales*
Alice Mc Carthy, *Admin Sec*
EMP: 60
SQ FT: 20,000
SALES (est): 4.3MM Privately Held
WEB: www.sbsteam.com
SIC: 8742 Marketing consulting services

(G-14163)
CONVENIENT FOOD MART INC (HQ)
6078 Pinecone Dr (44060-1865)
PHONE.................................800 860-4844
John Call, *President*
Tom Lind, *COO*
EMP: 30
SQ FT: 12,000
SALES (est): 11.4MM Privately Held
SIC: 5411 5541 6794 Convenience stores, chain; filling stations, gasoline; franchises, selling or licensing

(G-14164)
COUNTY OF LAKE
Also Called: Deepwood Center
8121 Deepwood Blvd (44060-7703)
PHONE.................................440 350-5100
Fax: 440 918-5290
Elfriede Roman, *Superintendent*
Christen Sanzobrino, *Manager*
Rikke Coach, *Exec Dir*
EMP: 650 Privately Held
WEB: www.lakecountyohio.gov
SIC: 8331 Job training & vocational rehabilitation services
PA: County Of Lake
8 N State St Ste 215
Painesville OH 44077
440 350-2500

(G-14165)
CROSSROADS LAKE COUNTY ADOLE (PA)
8445 Munson Rd (44060-2410)
PHONE.................................440 255-1700
Fax: 440 205-2417
Noel Walker, *Principal*
Kenneth Iwashita, *Principal*
Christopher Butcher, *COO*
Tim Vicars, *Finance Mgr*
Suzanne Plumb, *Exec Dir*
EMP: 100
SALES (est): 7.6MM Privately Held
WEB: www.crossroads-lake.org
SIC: 8093 8322 8011 Mental health clinic, outpatient; individual & family services; offices & clinics of medical doctors

(G-14166)
CT CONSULTANTS INC (PA)
8150 Sterling Ct (44060-5698)
PHONE.................................440 951-9000
David Wiles, *President*
Wes Hall, *Vice Pres*
Benny Sugawara, *Engineer*
Jim Shumate, *Project Engr*
Jonathan Peel, *Design Engr*
EMP: 128
SQ FT: 24,000
SALES (est): 43.6MM Privately Held
WEB: www.ctconsultants.com
SIC: 8713 8711 8712 Surveying services; civil engineering; structural engineering; electrical or electronic engineering; mechanical engineering; architectural services

(G-14167)
DCR SYSTEMS LLC (PA)
Also Called: Classic Accident Repair Center
8697 Tyler Blvd (44060-4346)
PHONE.................................440 205-9900
Fax: 440 205-9929
Cheryl Boswell, *CFO*
Paula Jackson, *Office Mgr*
Mandy Tsui, *Office Mgr*
Mandy Wynn, *Manager*
Michael J Giarrizzo Jr,
EMP: 45
SALES (est): 6.3MM Privately Held
WEB: www.dcrsystems.net
SIC: 7538 General automotive repair shops

(G-14168)
DEEPWOOD INDUSTRIES INC
8121 Deepwood Blvd (44060-7703)
PHONE.................................440 350-5231
Fax: 440 255-2046
Brett Bevis, *President*
Gary Planaka, *Exec VP*
Laura Harig, *Treasurer*
Marcie Barbic, *Sales Mgr*
Scott Hill, *Manager*
EMP: 181
SALES (est): 669.5K Privately Held
WEB: www.deepwoodindustries.com
SIC: 8322 8331 7331 Settlement house; job training & vocational rehabilitation services; direct mail advertising services

(G-14169)
DELTH CORPORATION
Also Called: Rainbow Connection Day Care
6312 Center St Ste C (44060-2449)
PHONE.................................440 255-7655
Delrene Showman, *President*
EMP: 35
SALES (est): 990.9K Privately Held
SIC: 8351 Preschool center; group day care center

(G-14170)
EAST MENTOR RECREATION INC
Also Called: Scores Fun Center
65 Normandy Dr (44060)
PHONE.................................440 354-2000
Fax: 440 354-2000
George Eisenhart Jr, *President*
Jody Hainrock, *Admin Sec*
EMP: 30
SALES (est): 1.4MM Privately Held
SIC: 7933 Ten pin center

(G-14171)
ELECTRO-ANALYTICAL INC
Also Called: E A Group
7118 Industrial Park Blvd (44060-5314)
PHONE.................................440 951-3514
Fax: 440 951-3514
Patrick G Herbert, *President*
Michael Herbert, *General Mgr*
Timothy S Bowen, *Vice Pres*
Jeffrey A Herbert, *Vice Pres*
EMP: 33
SQ FT: 7,700
SALES (est): 4MM Privately Held
WEB: www.eagroup-ohio.com
SIC: 8734 Testing laboratories

(G-14172)
EUCLID FISH COMPANY
7839 Enterprise Dr (44060-5386)
P.O. Box 180 (44061-0180)
PHONE.................................440 951-6448
Fax: 440 951-6448
Charles L Young, *Ch of Bd*
John Young, *President*
Marilyn G Young, *Corp Secy*
Susan Lanese, *Manager*
EMP: 66
SQ FT: 10,000
SALES (est): 38.8MM Privately Held
WEB: www.euclidfish.com
SIC: 5141 5142 5143 5144 Food brokers; packaged frozen goods; frozen fish, meat & poultry; fish, frozen: packaged; meat, frozen: packaged; dairy products, except dried or canned; poultry & poultry products; meat & fish markets; fish & seafood markets; fruit & vegetable markets

(G-14173)
EVERSTAFF LLC
7448 Mentor Ave (44060-5406)
PHONE.................................440 992-0238
Danny Spitz, *Branch Mgr*
EMP: 33 Privately Held
SIC: 7363 Temporary help service

Mentor - Lake County (G-14174)

PA: Everstaff, Llc
6500 Rockside Rd Ste 385
Cleveland OH 44131

(G-14174)
FAITHFUL COMPANIONS INC
8500 Station St Ste 111 (44060-4963)
PHONE.....................440 255-4357
Diana K Ross, *President*
Kenneth B Ross, *Exec VP*
EMP: 25
SQ FT: 700
SALES: 158K Privately Held
WEB: www.faithfulcompanions.com
SIC: 8059 Personal care home, with health care

(G-14175)
FEDEX FREIGHT CORPORATION
7685 Saint Clair Ave (44060-5235)
PHONE.....................877 661-8956
Fax: 440 953-3141
Ken Cary, *Manager*
Ken Radford, *Manager*
EMP: 28
SALES (corp-wide): 60.3B Publicly Held
SIC: 4213 4231 Contract haulers; trucking terminal facilities
HQ: Fedex Freight Corporation
1715 Aaron Brenner Dr
Memphis TN 38120

(G-14176)
FRANTZ MEDICAL GROUP
7740 Metric Dr (44060-4862)
PHONE.....................440 974-8522
Mark Frantz, *Principal*
Jim Looker, *Maintence Staff*
EMP: 32
SALES (est): 3MM Privately Held
SIC: 5047 Medical equipment & supplies

(G-14177)
FREEDOM STEEL INC
8200 Tyler Blvd Ste G (44060-4250)
P.O. Box 391377, Solon (44139-8377)
PHONE.....................440 266-6800
Fax: 440 266-7202
Timothy Jacobs, *President*
Jeff Shriver, *Manager*
EMP: 25
SQ FT: 200,000
SALES (est): 18.7MM Privately Held
WEB: www.freedomsteel.net
SIC: 5051 Steel

(G-14178)
FREEWAY LANES BOWL GROUP LLC
7300 Palisades Pkwy (44060-5302)
PHONE.....................440 946-5131
Fax: 440 975-5145
Dan Rodia, *Manager*
Dave Patz,
EMP: 25
SQ FT: 50,000
SALES (est): 634.3K Privately Held
SIC: 7933 5812 Ten pin center; snack bar

(G-14179)
GENERAL ELECTRIC COMPANY
8696 Applewood Ct (44060-2212)
PHONE.....................440 255-0930
EMP: 119
SALES (corp-wide): 123.6B Publicly Held
SIC: 6153 Short-Term Business Credit Institution
PA: General Electric Company
41 Farnsworth St
Boston MA 02210
617 443-3000

(G-14180)
GILES MARATHON INC
8648 Tyler Blvd (44060-4348)
PHONE.....................440 974-8815
Fax: 440 946-2833
James Gils, *President*
Eric Giles, *Vice Pres*
Judy Giles, *Admin Sec*
EMP: 25
SQ FT: 3,500
SALES (est): 3.4MM Privately Held
SIC: 5541 7538 Filling stations, gasoline; general automotive repair shops

(G-14181)
GORDON FOOD SERVICE INC
Also Called: G F S Marketplace
7220 Mentor Ave (44060-7522)
PHONE.....................440 953-1785
Fax: 440 953-5936
Jay Sheldon, *Manager*
Veronica Cekada, *Manager*
EMP: 30
SALES (corp-wide): 88.9MM Privately Held
WEB: www.gfs.com
SIC: 5149 Groceries & related products
PA: Gordon Food Service, Inc.
1300 Gezon Pkwy Sw
Wyoming MI 49509
888 437-3663

(G-14182)
GOVERNORS POINTE LLC
8506 Hendricks Rd Ofc (44060-8642)
PHONE.....................440 205-1570
Fax: 440 205-1573
Christopher C Randall,
EMP: 40
SALES (est): 1.3MM Privately Held
WEB: www.randallresidence.com
SIC: 8059 Personal care home, with health care

(G-14183)
GRACE HOSPICE LLC
7314 Industrial Park Blvd (44060-5318)
PHONE.....................216 288-7413
Mark Mitchell, *Branch Mgr*
EMP: 102 Privately Held
SIC: 8052 Personal care facility
PA: Grace Hospice, Llc
500 Kirts Blvd Ste 250
Troy MI 48084

(G-14184)
GREAT LAKES HOME HLTH SVCS INC
5966 Heisley Rd Ste 100 (44060-5849)
PHONE.....................888 260-9835
William L Deary III, *CEO*
EMP: 50 Privately Held
SIC: 8082 Home health care services
PA: Great Lakes Home Health Services, Inc.
900 Cooper St
Jackson MI 49202

(G-14185)
GREAT LAKES POWER PRODUCTS INC (PA)
Also Called: John Deere Authorized Dealer
7455 Tyler Blvd (44060-8389)
PHONE.....................440 951-5111
Fax: 216 953-1052
Harry Allen Jr, *CEO*
Harry L Allen Jr, *Ch of Bd*
Richard J Pennza, *President*
David Bell, *Vice Pres*
Sam Profio, *Vice Pres*
▲ EMP: 60
SQ FT: 55,000
SALES (est): 31.9MM Privately Held
WEB: www.glpowerlift.com
SIC: 5085 5084 3566 Power transmission equipment & apparatus; materials handling machinery; speed changers (power transmission equipment), except auto

(G-14186)
GREINER DENTAL ASSOCIATION
7553 Center St (44060-6001)
PHONE.....................440 255-2600
Fax: 440 255-0162
Steve Greiner, *Partner*
Anna Visger, *Fmly & Gen Dent*
EMP: 30
SALES (est): 1.3MM Privately Held
SIC: 8621 Professional membership organizations

(G-14187)
HABCO TOOL AND DEV CO INC
7725 Metric Dr (44060-4863)
PHONE.....................440 946-5546
Fax: 440 255-8122
Steven Sanders, *President*
James Patchin, *Plant Mgr*
Kathy Fulmer, *Purchasing*
Cathy Fulmer, *Manager*
Donna Taylor, *Manager*
EMP: 46 EST: 1955
SQ FT: 24,000
SALES: 3MM Privately Held
WEB: www.habcotool.com
SIC: 3599 7692 Machine shop, jobbing & repair; welding repair

(G-14188)
HEALTH CARE RTREMENT CORP AMER
Also Called: Heartland of Mentor
8200 Mentor Hills Dr (44060-7861)
PHONE.....................440 946-1912
Fax: 440 256-4935
Elizabeth Schupp, *Manager*
Stephen Baum, *Director*
EMP: 200
SALES (corp-wide): 3.6B Publicly Held
WEB: www.hrc-manorcare.com
SIC: 8051 Skilled nursing care facilities
HQ: Health Care And Retirement Corporation Of America
333 N Summit St Ste 103
Toledo OH 43604
419 252-5500

(G-14189)
HENKEL CORPORATION
7405 Production Dr (44060-4876)
PHONE.....................440 255-8900
Traci Roe, *Business Mgr*
Tim Viskocil, *Plant Mgr*
Brian Elston, *Engineer*
Luke Jones, *Regl Sales Mgr*
Robert Kern, *Branch Mgr*
EMP: 35
SALES (corp-wide): 23.6B Privately Held
SIC: 8741 Business management
HQ: Henkel Us Operations Corporation
1 Henkel Way
Rocky Hill CT 06067
860 571-5100

(G-14190)
HERITAGE BEVERAGE COMPANY LLC
7333 Corporate Blvd (44060-4857)
PHONE.....................440 255-5550
Chris Foradas, *Business Anlyst*
Paul Insana, *Network Enginr*
Scott Siegel,
▲ EMP: 85
SQ FT: 15,000
SALES (est): 6.9MM Privately Held
SIC: 5181 Beer & other fermented malt liquors

(G-14191)
HOME DEPOT USA INC
Also Called: Home Depot, The
9615 Diamond Centre Dr (44060-1879)
PHONE.....................440 357-0428
Fax: 440 392-3416
Gregory L Loney, *Store Mgr*
Maria Pope, *Manager*
EMP: 150
SALES (corp-wide): 100.9B Publicly Held
WEB: www.homerentalsdepot.com
SIC: 5211 7359 Home centers; tool rental
HQ: Home Depot U.S.A., Inc.
2455 Paces Ferry Rd Se
Atlanta GA 30339

(G-14192)
HOSPICE OF THE WESTERN RESERVE
5786 Heisley Rd (44060-1874)
PHONE.....................440 951-8692
Fax: 440 951-8692
Kathy Maltry, *Director*
EMP: 85
SALES (corp-wide): 89.8MM Privately Held
SIC: 8051 Skilled nursing care facilities
PA: Hospice Of The Western Reserve, Inc
17876 Saint Clair Ave
Cleveland OH 44110
216 383-2222

(G-14193)
HOSPICE OF THE WESTERN RESERVE
5786 Heisley Rd (44060-1874)
PHONE.....................440 357-5833
Cathy Maltry, *Principal*
EMP: 100
SALES (corp-wide): 89.8MM Privately Held
SIC: 8059 Convalescent home
PA: Hospice Of The Western Reserve, Inc
17876 Saint Clair Ave
Cleveland OH 44110
216 383-2222

(G-14194)
HZW ENVIRONMENTAL CONS LLC (PA)
6105 Heisley Rd (44060-1837)
PHONE.....................800 804-8484
Fax: 440 951-9279
Phillip Shrout, *Ch of Bd*
Matthew D Knecht, *President*
Joan Sablar, *Safety Mgr*
Seline Griffith, *Bookkeeper*
EMP: 27
SQ FT: 4,400
SALES (est): 5MM Privately Held
WEB: www.hzwenv.com
SIC: 8748 Environmental consultant

(G-14195)
INFINITE SHARES LLC
9401 Mentor Ave 167 (44060-4519)
PHONE.....................216 317-1601
Jacob Gatewood, *Principal*
Niyoshi Williams,
EMP: 25
SALES (est): 925.8K Privately Held
SIC: 8741 Management services

(G-14196)
ISOMEDIX OPERATIONS INC (DH)
5960 Heisley Rd (44060-1834)
PHONE.....................440 354-2600
Walter Rosebrough, *CEO*
Michael J Tokich, *Vice Pres*
Karen L Burton, *Treasurer*
Jen Clemente, *Human Res Mgr*
Christopher Dodge, *Marketing Staff*
EMP: 148
SQ FT: 5,000
SALES (est): 84.1MM
SALES (corp-wide): 2.6B Privately Held
SIC: 8734 Industrial sterilization service
HQ: Steris Corporation
5960 Heisley Rd
Mentor OH 44060
440 354-2600

(G-14197)
JIM BROWN CHEVROLET INC (PA)
6877 Center St (44060-4233)
P.O. Box 300 (44061-0300)
PHONE.....................440 255-5511
Fax: 440 255-0351
James Brown, *President*
Jeff Fortuna, *Corp Secy*
Frank Lakava, *Vice Pres*
Larry Villines, *CFO*
Bob Phillips, *Controller*
EMP: 175
SQ FT: 47,000
SALES (est): 69.7MM Privately Held
WEB: www.classic.com
SIC: 5511 7515 Automobiles, new & used; passenger car leasing

(G-14198)
JIM BROWN CHEVROLET INC
Also Called: Classic Autobody
8490 Tyler Blvd (44060-4230)
P.O. Box 300 (44061-0300)
PHONE.....................440 255-5511
Fax: 440 255-1380
Dennis Macko, *Manager*
EMP: 35
SALES (corp-wide): 69.7MM Privately Held
WEB: www.classic.com
SIC: 7538 7532 General automotive repair shops; paint shop, automotive

GEOGRAPHIC SECTION
Mentor - Lake County (G-14221)

PA: Jim Brown Chevrolet Inc
6877 Center St
Mentor OH 44060
440 255-5511

(G-14199)
JJO CONSTRUCTION INC
9045 Osborne Dr (44060-4326)
P.O. Box 713 (44061-0713)
PHONE..............................440 255-1515
Fax: 440 255-4141
Joseph J Orel, *President*
Charles Simmons, *Vice Pres*
Rick Allen, *Project Mgr*
Jay Hurwitz, *Project Mgr*
Dustin Morgan, *Project Mgr*
EMP: 25
SQ FT: 7,500
SALES: 24.4MM **Privately Held**
WEB: www.jjoconstruction.com
SIC: 1542 Commercial & office building, new construction; commercial & office buildings, renovation & repair

(G-14200)
JTO CLUB CORP
Also Called: Mentor Hsley Rcquet Fitnes CLB
6011 Heisley Rd (44060-1867)
PHONE..............................440 352-1900
Maureen Osborne, *CEO*
Jerome Osborne, *President*
William Wickli, *Branch Mgr*
EMP: 60
SQ FT: 70,000
SALES (est): 1.4MM
SALES (corp-wide): 19.9MM **Privately Held**
WEB: www.mentorheisleyfitness.com
SIC: 7991 Physical fitness facilities
PA: T O J Inc
6011 Heisley Rd
Mentor OH 44060
440 352-1900

(G-14201)
KAISER FOUNDATION HOSPITALS
Also Called: Mentor Medical Offices
7695 Mentor Ave (44060-5540)
PHONE..............................800 524-7377
EMP: 593
SALES (corp-wide): 82.6B **Privately Held**
SIC: 8011 Offices & clinics of medical doctors
HQ: Kaiser Foundation Hospitals Inc
1 Kaiser Plz
Oakland CA 94612
510 271-6611

(G-14202)
LABORATORY CORPORATION AMERICA
8300 Tyler Blvd (44060-4217)
PHONE..............................440 205-8299
Kolita Benedict, *Manager*
EMP: 25 **Publicly Held**
WEB: www.labcorp.com
SIC: 8734 Testing laboratories
HQ: Laboratory Corporation Of America
358 S Main St Ste 458
Burlington NC 27215
336 229-1127

(G-14203)
LAKE COUNTY COUNCIL ON AGING (PA)
8520 East Ave (44060-4302)
PHONE..............................440 205-8111
Fax: 440 205-7055
Joseph R Tomsick, *CEO*
Maria Pope, *Opers Staff*
Patricia McAteer, *Human Res Dir*
Edgar Barnett Jr, *Exec Dir*
Lyle D Shull, *Director*
EMP: 45
SALES: 2.3MM **Privately Held**
WEB: www.lccoa.org
SIC: 8322 Senior citizens' center or association

(G-14204)
LAKE COUNTY FAMILY PRACTICE
Also Called: 7 Physcian Fmly Practice Group
9500 Mentor Ave Ste 100 (44060-8702)
PHONE..............................440 352-4880
Fax: 440 352-3629
Mark Komar, *President*
Susan Hollobaugh, *Med Doctor*
Quinn Duchon, *Manager*
Eileen Sraj, *Administration*
EMP: 35
SQ FT: 37,000
SALES (est): 3.2MM **Privately Held**
WEB: www.lcfp.net
SIC: 8011 General & family practice, physician/surgeon

(G-14205)
LAKE COUNTY LOCAL HAZMAT
8505 Garfield Rd (44060-5961)
P.O. Box 480 (44061-0480)
PHONE..............................440 350-5499
Fax: 440 953-5397
Thomas Talcott, *Chief*
Larry Greene, *Director*
Ann Myers, *Admin Asst*
Cheryl White, *Admin Asst*
EMP: 25
SALES (est): 550.1K **Privately Held**
SIC: 8631 Labor unions & similar labor organizations

(G-14206)
LAKE URGENT & FAMILY MED CTR (PA)
Also Called: Lake Urgent Care Centers
6965 Center St (44060-4952)
PHONE..............................440 255-6400
Fax: 440 255-3637
Joseph Saboca, *Director*
EMP: 40
SALES (est): 777.9K **Privately Held**
SIC: 8011 Freestanding emergency medical center; general & family practice, physician/surgeon

(G-14207)
LAND DESIGN CONSULTANTS
9025 Osborne Dr (44060-4326)
PHONE..............................440 255-8463
James R Pegoraro, *President*
Frank J Chorba, *Corp Secy*
EMP: 30
SQ FT: 5,000
SALES (est): 2.8MM **Privately Held**
WEB: www.ldcinc.net
SIC: 8711 8713 Civil engineering; surveying services

(G-14208)
LAWNFIELD PROPERTIES LLC
Also Called: Best Wstn Lawnfield Inn Suites
8434 Mentor Ave (44060-5817)
PHONE..............................440 974-3572
Fax: 440 205-8436
Nancy Zaroogian, *General Mgr*
Rob Kneen, *Manager*
EMP: 25
SQ FT: 1,375
SALES (est): 1.8MM **Privately Held**
WEB: www.lawnfield.com
SIC: 7011 Hotels & motels

(G-14209)
LIFESERVICES DEVELOPMENT CORP
Also Called: Salidawoods
7685 Lake Shore Blvd (44060-3359)
PHONE..............................440 257-3866
Karen Harrell, *General Mgr*
EMP: 47 **Privately Held**
WEB: www.lifeservicesnetwork.com
SIC: 8399 8052 Community development groups; intermediate care facilities
PA: Lifeservices Development Corporation
1625 Lowell Ave
Erie PA 16505

(G-14210)
LOWES HOME CENTERS LLC
9600 Mentor Ave (44060-4529)
PHONE..............................440 392-0027
Fax: 440 354-0409
William Carpenter, *Engineer*
David Gomez, *Sales Associate*
Brian Braunstien, *Manager*
EMP: 150
SALES (corp-wide): 68.6B **Publicly Held**
SIC: 5211 5031 5722 5064 Lumber & other building materials; building materials, exterior; building materials, interior; household appliance stores; electrical appliances, television & radio
HQ: Lowe's Home Centers, Llc
1605 Curtis Bridge Rd
Wilkesboro NC 28697
336 658-4000

(G-14211)
MC SIGN COMPANY (PA)
8959 Tyler Blvd (44060-2184)
PHONE..............................440 209-6200
Fax: 440 992-8882
Tim Eippert, *President*
Jeanne Baker-Meaney, *Accounting Mgr*
James Peake, *Sales Staff*
Erin Buehler, *Program Mgr*
Tim Fenske, *Program Mgr*
▲ **EMP:** 130 **EST:** 1995
SALES (est): 41.2MM **Privately Held**
WEB: www.mcsign.com
SIC: 3993 2752 7336 Electric signs; commercial printing, lithographic; commercial art & graphic design

(G-14212)
MENTOR EXEMPTED VLG SCHL DST
Also Called: Mentor School Service Trnsp
7060 Hopkins Rd (44060-4487)
PHONE..............................440 974-5260
Karen Gerardi, *Director*
Mike Malloy, *Director*
EMP: 150
SALES (corp-wide): 103.9MM **Privately Held**
WEB: www.mboe.org
SIC: 4151 School buses
PA: Mentor Exempted Village School District
6451 Center St
Mentor OH 44060
440 255-4444

(G-14213)
MENTOR LAGOONS YACHT CLUB INC
8365 Harbor Dr (44060-1413)
P.O. Box 574 (44061-0574)
PHONE..............................440 205-3625
Cliff Gabriel, *CEO*
Jim Capp, *Manager*
EMP: 60
SQ FT: 4,000
SALES: 54.3K **Privately Held**
SIC: 7997 Yacht club, membership

(G-14214)
MENTOR LUMBER AND SUPPLY CO (PA)
Also Called: Mentor Wholesale Lumber
7180 Center St (44060-4979)
P.O. Box 599 (44061-0599)
PHONE..............................440 255-8814
Fax: 440 255-4149
Jerome T Osborne, *Ch of Bd*
Reed H Martin, *President*
Robert Sanderson, *Senior VP*
Ray Sanderson, *Vice Pres*
Mack Stewart, *Vice Pres*
EMP: 120
SQ FT: 100,000
SALES (est): 42MM **Privately Held**
SIC: 5031 5211 Lumber: rough, dressed & finished; lumber & other building materials

(G-14215)
MENTOR SURGERY CENTER LTD
9485 Mentor Ave Ste 1 (44060-8711)
PHONE..............................440 205-5725
David Wier, *Administration*
EMP: 50
SALES (est): 5.8MM **Privately Held**
SIC: 8062 Hospital, medical school affiliated with nursing & residency

(G-14216)
MENTOR WAY NURSING & REHAB CEN
8881 Schaeffer St (44060-5035)
PHONE..............................440 255-9309
Fax: 440 205-9120
EMP: 150
SQ FT: 54,000
SALES (est): 11.4MM **Privately Held**
SIC: 8051 Skilled Nursing Care Facility

(G-14217)
MICHAELS INC
Also Called: Lamalfa Party Center
5783 Heisley Rd (44060-1883)
PHONE..............................440 357-0384
Fax: 440 357-8371
Michael Lamalfa Sr, *President*
Martin Lamalfa, *Vice Pres*
EMP: 77
SQ FT: 36,000
SALES (est): 3.3MM **Privately Held**
WEB: www.lamalfa.com
SIC: 7299 Banquet hall facilities

(G-14218)
MIKE SIKORA REALTY INC
7340 Center St (44060-5802)
PHONE..............................440 255-7777
Mike Sikora, *President*
Jean Sikora, *Vice Pres*
EMP: 33
SQ FT: 900
SALES (est): 1MM **Privately Held**
SIC: 6531 Real estate brokers & agents

(G-14219)
MILL ROSE LABORATORIES INC
7310 Corp Blvd (44060)
PHONE..............................440 974-6730
Fax: 440 255-5061
Paul M Miller, *President*
Thom Olmstead, *General Mgr*
Stephen W Kovalcheck Jr, *CFO*
Vince Ponna, *Controller*
Lawrence W Miller, *Admin Sec*
▲ **EMP:** 40 **EST:** 1977
SQ FT: 59,000
SALES (est): 6.3MM
SALES (corp-wide): 32.4MM **Privately Held**
WEB: www.millrose.com
SIC: 3991 5047 Brooms & brushes; medical equipment & supplies
PA: The Mill-Rose Company
7995 Tyler Blvd
Mentor OH 44060
440 255-9171

(G-14220)
MILL-ROSE COMPANY (PA)
7995 Tyler Blvd (44060-4896)
PHONE..............................440 255-9171
Fax: 440 255-5039
Paul M Miller, *President*
Gregory Miller, *General Mgr*
Lawrence W Miller, *Vice Pres*
Barbara Tokar, *Manager*
Diane Miller, *Admin Sec*
▲ **EMP:** 160
SQ FT: 61,000
SALES (est): 32.4MM **Privately Held**
WEB: www.millrose.com
SIC: 3841 5085 3991 3624 Surgical instruments & apparatus; industrial supplies; brushes, industrial; brushes, household or industrial; carbon & graphite products; abrasive products

(G-14221)
MJ AUTO PARTS INC (PA)
Also Called: NAPA Auto Parts
7900 Tyler Blvd (44060-4806)
PHONE..............................440 205-6272
Fax: 440 205-0811
Lindy M Adelstein, *CEO*
James Starke, *President*
Jill Grinstead, *Vice Pres*
Susan Starke, *Treasurer*
Jessica Kovac, *Manager*
◆ **EMP:** 30 **EST:** 1957
SQ FT: 12,000

Mentor - Lake County (G-14222)

SALES (est): 7.9MM **Privately Held**
SIC: 5531 5013 Automobile & truck equipment & parts; automotive supplies & parts

(G-14222)
MONODE MARKING PRODUCTS INC (PA)
Also Called: Waldorf Marking Devices Div
9200 Tyler Blvd (44060-1882)
PHONE..................................440 975-8802
Fax: 440 975-1364
Tom Mackey, *President*
Bill Vickery, *General Mgr*
Christine Lillstrung, *Plant Mgr*
Tom Rempe, *Purch Agent*
Les Szakallas, *Engineer*
EMP: 45
SQ FT: 15,000
SALES (est): 8.6MM **Privately Held**
SIC: 3542 5084 Marking machines; printing trades machinery, equipment & supplies

(G-14223)
MOVING SOLUTIONS INC
Also Called: Great Lakes Record Center
8001 Moving Way (44060-4898)
PHONE..................................440 946-9300
William Tyers, *President*
Ed Insana, *General Mgr*
Lynne Mazeika, *Vice Pres*
Don Blauman, *Opers Mgr*
Mike Simonds, *Sales Staff*
EMP: 60 EST: 1976
SQ FT: 100,000
SALES (est): 8MM **Privately Held**
WEB: www.yourmovingsolutions.com
SIC: 4214 4731 Furniture moving & storage, local; household goods moving & storage, local; freight transportation arrangement

(G-14224)
OHIO RENAL CARE GROUP LLC
Also Called: Ohio Renal Care Grp Mentor Dia
8840 Tyler Blvd (44060-4361)
PHONE..................................440 974-3459
Mary Garber,
Ron Kuerbitz,
EMP: 53 EST: 2013
SALES (est): 518K **Privately Held**
SIC: 8092 Kidney dialysis centers

(G-14225)
OMNI CART SERVICES INC
Also Called: Ohio Carts
7370 Production Dr (44060-4859)
P.O. Box 366 (44061-0366)
PHONE..................................440 205-8363
Fax: 440 205-8366
Keith Woolf, *President*
William Jacobson, *Corp Secy*
Jennifer Chuha, *Human Resources*
Marilyn Roberson, *Accounts Exec*
Patty Tosti, *Office Mgr*
EMP: 35
SQ FT: 10,000
SALES (est): 7.9MM **Privately Held**
WEB: www.ocserv.com
SIC: 7699 Shopping cart repair

(G-14226)
OSBORNE CO
7954 Reynolds Rd (44060-5334)
P.O. Box 658 (44061-0658)
PHONE..................................440 942-7000
Jerome T Osborne, *President*
Gerald J Smith, *Admin Sec*
EMP: 60
SQ FT: 4,500
SALES (est): 2.2MM **Privately Held**
SIC: 1794 Excavation work

(G-14227)
PARK PET AND PLAY LLC
7471 Tyler Blvd Ste N (44060-5413)
PHONE..................................877 907-6222
Chris Harding, *Sales Staff*
Kristen Chisler, *Mng Member*
EMP: 25
SQ FT: 5,000
SALES (est): 658.7K **Privately Held**
SIC: 0752 Animal boarding services

(G-14228)
PETSMART INC
9122 Mentor Ave (44060-6404)
PHONE..................................440 974-1100
Fax: 440 974-1100
Andrea Carlton, *Manager*
EMP: 30
SALES (corp-wide): 12.7B **Privately Held**
WEB: www.petsmart.com
SIC: 5999 0752 Pet food; animal specialty services
HQ: Petsmart, Inc.
19601 N 27th Ave
Phoenix AZ 85027
623 580-6100

(G-14229)
PLATFORM CEMENT INC
7503 Tyler Blvd (44060-5403)
PHONE..................................440 602-9750
Jason Klar, *President*
Elizabeth Bechkowiak, *Principal*
Sally Murphy, *Admin Sec*
EMP: 35
SQ FT: 1,000
SALES (est): 5.4MM **Privately Held**
SIC: 1771 Concrete work

(G-14230)
PRUDENTIAL SELECT PROPERTIES (PA)
Also Called: Century 21
7395 Center St (44060-5801)
PHONE..................................440 255-1111
Fax: 440 255-8131
Frank Kaim, *President*
Sharon Friedman, *Sales Associate*
David Perkins, *Manager*
Jane Kaim, *Admin Sec*
Mike Alley, *Real Est Agnt*
EMP: 65
SQ FT: 6,000
SALES (est): 6.3MM **Privately Held**
WEB: www.pruselectprop.com
SIC: 6531 Real estate agent, residential

(G-14231)
PRUDENTIAL WELSH REALTY
7400 Center St (44060-5848)
PHONE..................................440 974-3100
Fax: 440 974-3120
Don Welsh, *Owner*
EMP: 25
SALES (est): 690.4K **Privately Held**
SIC: 6531 Real estate agent, residential

(G-14232)
RAYMOND A GREINER DDS INC
Also Called: Greiner Dental & Associates
7553 Center St (44060-6001)
PHONE..................................440 951-6688
James N Greiner DDS, *Vice Pres*
Steven H Greiner DDS, *Vice Pres*
Marcia Tupa DDS, *Manager*
EMP: 32 EST: 1954
SQ FT: 4,000
SALES (est): 1.5MM **Privately Held**
SIC: 8021 Dentists' office

(G-14233)
RE/MAX REAL ESTATE EXPERTS
8444 Mentor Ave (44060-5817)
PHONE..................................440 255-6505
Fax: 440 255-6551
Cheryl Maggard, *Partner*
Liz Bauer, *Partner*
Mary Margaret Dacar, *Partner*
Karen Schultz, *Partner*
Kathy Thomas, *Partner*
EMP: 28
SALES (est): 1.3MM **Privately Held**
WEB: www.ohiorealestate4you.com
SIC: 6531 Real estate agent, residential

(G-14234)
REALTY ONE INC
8396 Mentor Ave (44060-5748)
PHONE..................................440 951-2123
Fax: 440 255-4290
Todd C Crockett, *Sales Mgr*
Shever McDonald, *Manager*
Mary Holtcamp, *Executive*
EMP: 120
SALES (corp-wide): 67.8MM **Privately Held**
WEB: www.realty-1st.com
SIC: 6531 Selling agent, real estate
HQ: Realty One, Inc.
800 W Saint Clair Ave
Cleveland OH 44113
216 328-2500

(G-14235)
REGISTERED CONTRACTORS INC
8425 Station St (44060-4924)
PHONE..................................440 205-0873
Fax: 440 205-0879
Edward A Krevas, *CEO*
Livio Stipcic, *President*
EMP: 40
SQ FT: 7,000
SALES (est): 5.3MM **Privately Held**
WEB: www.registeredcontractors.com
SIC: 1542 1541 1521 Commercial & office building contractors; industrial buildings & warehouses; single-family housing construction

(G-14236)
RELIABLE RNNERS CURIER SVC INC
8624 Station St (44060-4316)
PHONE..................................440 578-1011
Marc P Coben, *President*
EMP: 40
SQ FT: 2,800
SALES (est): 3.9MM **Privately Held**
WEB: www.rrunners.com
SIC: 7389 Courier or messenger service

(G-14237)
RICHCREEK BAILEY REHABILITATIO
Also Called: New Hope Vocational Services
7600 Tyler Blvd (44060-4853)
PHONE..................................440 527-8610
James Richcreek, *President*
James E Richcreek, *President*
Douglas M Bailey, *Principal*
Sherry L Richcreek, *Director*
EMP: 40
SALES (est): 42.5K **Privately Held**
SIC: 8331 Vocational rehabilitation agency

(G-14238)
RUNYON & SONS ROOFING INC
8745 Munson Rd (44060-4323)
PHONE..................................440 974-6810
Fax: 440 974-6814
Clyde Runyon Jr, *President*
Tom Runyon, *Vice Pres*
Jean Kovach, *Financial Exec*
Patrick Stenger, *Sales Staff*
Jack Deboe, *Supervisor*
EMP: 60
SALES (est): 6.4MM **Privately Held**
SIC: 1522 1542 1521 Multi-family dwelling construction; commercial & office building contractors; single-family home remodeling, additions & repairs

(G-14239)
SCHROER PROPERTIES INC
Also Called: Altercare of Mentor
9901 Johnnycake Ridge Rd (44060-6739)
PHONE..................................440 357-7900
Berry Lieberman, *Manager*
EMP: 115 **Privately Held**
SIC: 8051 Skilled nursing care facilities
PA: Schroer Properties, Inc
339 E Maple St
North Canton OH 44720

(G-14240)
SEACRIST LANDSCAPING AND CNSTR
9442 Mercantile Dr (44060-1889)
PHONE..................................440 946-2731
Fax: 440 358-9778
Charles Seacrist, *Owner*
Dale Stefancic, *Manager*
EMP: 25
SALES (est): 868.5K **Privately Held**
SIC: 0781 0782 Landscape architects; landscape contractors

(G-14241)
SHARP EDGE LLC
8855 Twinbrook Rd (44060-4334)
P.O. Box 1178 (44061-1178)
PHONE..................................440 255-5917
Robert Kennedy,
EMP: 25
SALES: 1.5MM **Privately Held**
SIC: 0782 Lawn care services

(G-14242)
SHIMA LIMOUSINE SERVICES INC
7555 Tyler Blvd Ste 12 (44060-4866)
PHONE..................................440 918-6400
Fax: 440 918-6406
George Shima, *President*
Michele Carothers, *Vice Pres*
Michele Shima, *Personnel Exec*
Barbara Shima, *Shareholder*
EMP: 34
SALES (est): 1.5MM **Privately Held**
WEB: www.shimalimo.com
SIC: 4119 Limousine rental, with driver

(G-14243)
SOCIETY FOR REHABILITATION
Also Called: Society Rehabilitation
9290 Lake Shore Blvd (44060-1664)
PHONE..................................440 209-0135
Christopher Webb, *Director*
Elizabeth Ann Dietrich, *Director*
Mary Wilson, *Admin Sec*
EMP: 28
SQ FT: 12,000
SALES: 100.3K **Privately Held**
WEB: www.societyhelps.org
SIC: 8093 8049 Rehabilitation center, outpatient treatment; physical therapist; occupational therapist; speech therapist; audiologist

(G-14244)
SOURCEONE HEALTHCARE TECH INC (HQ)
Also Called: Mxr Sourceone
8020 Tyler Blvd (44060-4825)
PHONE..................................440 701-1200
Fax: 440 740-1492
Leo Zuckerman, *CEO*
Larry Lawson, *President*
Ted Sloan, *Vice Pres*
Bob Bedwell, *Regl Sales Mgr*
Tracy Wilkson, *Office Mgr*
EMP: 150
SQ FT: 42,000
SALES (est): 87.7MM **Privately Held**
SALES (corp-wide): 164.6MM **Privately Held**
SIC: 5047 Medical laboratory equipment
PA: Merry X-Ray Chemical Corporation
4444 Viewridge Ave A
San Diego CA 92123
858 565-4472

(G-14245)
STODDARD IMPORTED CARS INC
Also Called: Audi Willoughby
8599 Market St (44060-4124)
PHONE..................................440 951-1040
Fax: 440 946-9410
Jerry Severin, *President*
Pat Dicesare, *General Mgr*
Karl Colbary, *Business Mgr*
Lisa Mullin, *Business Mgr*
Bryan Gallion, *Sales Mgr*
▲ EMP: 51 EST: 1957
SQ FT: 22,000
SALES (est): 20.4MM **Privately Held**
WEB: www.stoddard.com
SIC: 5511 5013 Automobiles, new & used; automotive supplies & parts

(G-14246)
SUMMERVILLE SENIOR LIVING INC
Also Called: Summerville At Mentor
5700 Emerald Ct (44060-1870)
PHONE..................................440 354-5499
Fax: 440 354-5422
Russell Ragland, *President*
Valerie Hayden, *Exec Dir*
EMP: 60

GEOGRAPHIC SECTION

Miamisburg - Montgomery County (G-14267)

SALES (corp-wide): 4.7B Publicly Held
SIC: 8361 Residential care
HQ: Summerville Senior Living, Inc.
3131 Elliott Ave Ste 500
Seattle WA 98121
206 298-2909

(G-14247)
T O J INC (PA)
6011 Heisley Rd (44060-1867)
PHONE..................................440 352-1900
Fax: 440 357-8900
Maureen Osborne, *President*
Jerry Osborne III, *President*
Loraine Mauk, *General Mgr*
Leong Tan, *Vice Pres*
Christine Baglione, *Safety Mgr*
EMP: 38
SQ FT: 32,000
SALES (est): 19.9MM Privately Held
WEB: www.jtoinc.com
SIC: 1542 1522 6552 4959 Commercial & office building, new construction; condominium construction; land subdividers & developers, commercial; snowplowing; health club

(G-14248)
TRANE INC
Also Called: Trane Cleveland
7567 Tyler Blvd (44060-4869)
PHONE..................................440 946-7823
EMP: 30 Privately Held
SIC: 1711 Warm air heating & air conditioning contractor; refrigeration contractor
HQ: Trane Inc.
1 Centennial Ave Ste 101
Piscataway NJ 08854
732 652-7100

(G-14249)
TRICOUNTY AMBULANCE SERVICE
7000 Spinach Dr (44060-4958)
PHONE..................................440 951-4600
Fax: 440 951-4600
Kevin Farrell, *President*
John F Farrell, *Vice Pres*
Barb Baughman, *Opers Staff*
Beth Farrell, *Admin Sec*
EMP: 55
SQ FT: 8,000
SALES (est): 2.3MM Privately Held
SIC: 4119 Ambulance service

(G-14250)
TRUGREEN LIMITED PARTNERSHIP
Also Called: Tru Green-Chemlawn
7460 Clover Ave (44060-5212)
PHONE..................................440 290-3340
Jos Byers, *Service Mgr*
George Strata, *Manager*
EMP: 30
SQ FT: 20,000
SALES (corp-wide): 4B Privately Held
SIC: 0782 Lawn care services; spraying services, lawn
HQ: Trugreen Limited Partnership
1790 Kirby Pkwy
Memphis TN 38138
901 251-4128

(G-14251)
TYLINTER INC (HQ)
8570 Tyler Blvd (44060-4232)
PHONE..................................800 321-6188
Fax: 440 255-9745
Larry Polk, *President*
Tony Bandera, *Vice Pres*
Judy Osgood, *Vice Pres*
Jeff Pope, *Manager*
◆ EMP: 65
SQ FT: 65,000
SALES (est): 19.3MM
SALES (corp-wide): 491MM Privately Held
WEB: www.wstyler.com
SIC: 5051 Metal wires, ties, cables & screening
PA: Haver & Boecker Ohg
Carl-Haver-Platz 3
Oelde 59302
252 230-0

(G-14252)
UNIVERSITY HOSPITALS CLEVELAND
Also Called: Lake Univ Ireland Cancer Ctr
9485 Mentor Ave Ste 102 (44060-8722)
PHONE..................................440 205-5755
Joel Saltzman, *Med Doctor*
Lois Teston, *Med Doctor*
Steven Waggoner, *Med Doctor*
Jeffrey Hardacre, *Surgeon*
Lizabeth Lyons, *Info Tech Mgr*
EMP: 45
SQ FT: 1,269
SALES (corp-wide): 2.3B Privately Held
SIC: 8062 8011 General medical & surgical hospitals; oncologist
HQ: University Hospitals Of Cleveland
11100 Euclid Ave
Cleveland OH 44106
216 844-1000

(G-14253)
UNIVERSITY MEDNET
9000 Mentor Ave Ste 101 (44060-4496)
PHONE..................................440 255-0800
Jackie Bickie, *Facilities Mgr*
Colleen Endemans, *Office Mgr*
Philip C Bezozowski, *Med Doctor*
Norton A Winer, *Med Doctor*
Evelyn Havrillo, *Manager*
EMP: 200
SALES (corp-wide): 11.6MM Privately Held
SIC: 8011 8093 Clinic, operated by physicians; specialty outpatient clinics
PA: University Mednet
18599 Lake Shore Blvd
Euclid OH 44119
216 383-0100

(G-14254)
VECMAR CORPORATION
Also Called: Vecmar Computer Solutions
7595 Jenther Dr (44060-4872)
PHONE..................................440 953-1119
Fax: 440 953-1119
Greg Pluscusky, *President*
Brian Dipasquale, *Vice Pres*
Philip R Pagon II, *Vice Pres*
Nick Zitnik, *Treasurer*
Laura Sirianni, *Sales Associate*
▲ EMP: 30
SQ FT: 25,000
SALES (est): 10.8MM Privately Held
WEB: www.vecmar.com
SIC: 5045 Computers

(G-14255)
VINIFERA IMPORTS LTD
7551 Clover Ave (44060-5206)
PHONE..................................440 942-9463
Matt Geisler, *Branch Mgr*
EMP: 36
SALES (corp-wide): 19MM Privately Held
SIC: 5099 Firearms & ammunition, except sporting
PA: Vinifera Imports, Ltd.
205 13th Ave
Ronkonkoma NY 11779
631 467-5907

(G-14256)
VIP ELECTRIC COMPANY
8358 Mentor Ave (44060-5748)
PHONE..................................440 255-0180
Fax: 440 255-9169
Ellie Vayo, *President*
Kevin Vayo, *Vice Pres*
Dan W Yanick, *VP Opers*
Jackie Wallace, *Manager*
Erin Vayo, *Shareholder*
EMP: 30 EST: 1997
SQ FT: 2,000
SALES (est): 4.3MM Privately Held
WEB: www.vipelectric.com
SIC: 1731 General electrical contractor

(G-14257)
VOLK OPTICAL INC
7893 Enterprise Dr (44060-5309)
PHONE..................................440 942-6161
Fax: 440 942-2257
Jyoti Gupta, *President*
Terry Cooper, *Regional Mgr*
Arlinda Vaughn, *Regional Mgr*
Steve Cech, *Vice Pres*
John Strobel, *Vice Pres*
▲ EMP: 70 EST: 1974
SQ FT: 18,000
SALES (est): 12.5MM
SALES (corp-wide): 1.2B Privately Held
SIC: 8011 3851 3827 Offices & clinics of medical doctors; lenses, ophthalmic; optical instruments & lenses
HQ: Halma Holdings Inc.
11500 Northlake Dr # 306
Cincinnati OH 45249
513 772-5501

(G-14258)
WILLOUGHBY SUPPLY COMPANY (PA)
7433 Clover Ave (44060-5211)
PHONE..................................440 942-7939
Fax: 440 602-4380
Albert Romanini, *President*
Chris Meister, *Sales Mgr*
Kevin O'Brien, *Sales Associate*
Gregory Holzapfel, *Branch Mgr*
Jeff Brown, *Programmer Anys*
EMP: 37 EST: 1983
SQ FT: 85,000
SALES (est): 117.5MM Privately Held
SIC: 5033 Roofing & siding materials

(G-14259)
WORK SOLUTIONS GROUP LLC
8324 Tyler Blvd (44060-4221)
PHONE..................................440 205-8297
Gary Jochum, *Agent*
Terry Jochum,
EMP: 30
SALES (est): 429.9K Privately Held
SIC: 7361 Employment agencies; placement agencies

(G-14260)
WORKPLACE MEDIA INC
9325 Progress Pkwy (44060-1855)
PHONE..................................440 392-2171
Stephanie Molnar, *CEO*
Pete Aranavage, *Vice Pres*
Glenn Kawasaki, *Vice Pres*
Debra Vernon, *Opers Staff*
Lori Wares, *Controller*
EMP: 34 EST: 2003
SALES (est): 6.2MM
SALES (corp-wide): 3.7B Privately Held
WEB: www.riversidecompany.com
SIC: 8742 Management consulting services
PA: Riverside Partners L.L.C.
45 Rockefeller Plz # 400
New York NY 10111
212 265-6575

Mentor On The Lake
Lake County

(G-14261)
MAIN SEQUENCE TECHNOLOGY INC (PA)
5370 Pinehill Dr (44060-1434)
PHONE..................................440 946-5214
Fax: 440 946-7659
Martin Snyder, *President*
Gretchen Kubicek, *CFO*
Patsy Lombardo, *Controller*
Bill Kubicek, *VP Sales*
Mike Owcarz, *Sales Staff*
EMP: 30
SALES (est): 6.9MM Privately Held
WEB: www.kubicek.net
SIC: 7371 Computer software development

(G-14262)
STRATEGIC CONSUMER RESEARCH
Also Called: S C R
8050 Harbor Creek Dr # 2102 (44060-2077)
PHONE..................................216 261-0308
Fax: 216 261-3546
Barry Sabol, *President*
Gerald Godic, *Vice Pres*
EMP: 35
SQ FT: 4,900
SALES (est): 2.7MM Privately Held
WEB: www.scr-research.com
SIC: 8732 Market analysis or research

Mesopotamia
Trumbull County

(G-14263)
HOPEWELL (PA)
Also Called: Hopewell Therapeutic Farm
9637 State Route 534 (44439)
P.O. Box 193 (44439-0193)
PHONE..................................440 693-4074
Fax: 440 693-4168
William Hamilton, *Principal*
Richard Karges, *Director*
EMP: 29
SQ FT: 3,600
SALES: 4.5MM Privately Held
SIC: 8361 Home for the mentally handicapped

Metamora
Fulton County

(G-14264)
AMBOY CONTRACTORS LLC
424 E Main St (43540-9753)
P.O. Box H (43540-0207)
PHONE..................................419 644-2111
Paul Hill, *Controller*
Robert Booth, *Manager*
Michael S Anderzack,
Cathy Bofer, *Admin Sec*
James R Pitzen,
EMP: 80
SALES (est): 5.3MM Privately Held
WEB: www.wecandigit.com
SIC: 1623 Underground utilities contractor

(G-14265)
ANDERZACK-PITZEN CNSTR INC
424 E Main St (43540-9753)
P.O. Box H (43540-0207)
PHONE..................................419 553-7015
Mike Anderzack, *President*
James R Pitzen, *Vice Pres*
Beth Hall, *Accounts Mgr*
Robert Booth, *Manager*
EMP: 50
SQ FT: 6,000
SALES (est): 20MM Privately Held
SIC: 1623 1794 Underground utilities contractor; excavation work

(G-14266)
TSCS INC
Also Called: Tristate Concrete
14293 State Route 64 (43540-9710)
PHONE..................................419 644-3921
John Simon, *President*
Susan Simon, *Treasurer*
EMP: 25
SALES: 1.6MM Privately Held
SIC: 1771 Concrete work

Miamisburg
Montgomery County

(G-14267)
A-1 SPRINKLER COMPANY INC
2383 Northpointe Dr (45342-2989)
PHONE..................................937 859-6198
Fax: 937 859-0651
Bill Hausmann, *CEO*
Tara Lawson, *Controller*
Kime Faine-Shaffer, *Office Mgr*
Erin Chambers, *Comp Tech*
Nick Hudgens, *Comp Tech*
EMP: 68
SQ FT: 15,000
SALES (est): 9.6MM Privately Held
WEB: www.spkr.com
SIC: 3569 5087 Firefighting apparatus & related equipment; firefighting equipment

---

(PA)=Parent Co (HQ)=Headquarters (DH)=Div Headquarters
✪ = New Business established in last 2 years

2018 Harris Ohio
Services Directory

Miamisburg - Montgomery County (G-14268)

(G-14268)
ADVANCED SERVICE TECH LLC
Also Called: AST
885 Mound Rd (45342-2591)
PHONE...................................937 435-4376
Fax: 937 435-4850
Jerry L Abner, *CEO*
Deorah Dobransky, *Vice Pres*
Brad McMartin, *Vice Pres*
David Hunt, *Technology*
Michael Keck, *Technical Staff*
EMP: 29
SALES (est): 4MM Privately Held
WEB: www.astservice.com
SIC: 1731 7373 8243 Computer installation; computer integrated systems design; office computer automation systems integration; operator training, computer; repair training, computer; software training, computer

(G-14269)
ALDRICH CHEMICAL
Also Called: Sigma-Aldrich
3858 Benner Rd (45342-4304)
PHONE...................................937 859-1808
Fax: 937 859-4878
Paul Ripplinger, *Vice Pres*
Tom Fahey, *Mfg Staff*
Tisha Micer, *Purch Agent*
John Shay, *Engineer*
Tracy Ball, *Personnel Exec*
EMP: 70
SQ FT: 30,000
SALES (corp-wide): 18B Privately Held
SIC: 2819 5084 2899 2869 Isotopes, radioactive; chemical process equipment; chemical preparations; industrial organic chemicals
HQ: Aldrich Chemical
3050 Spruce St
Saint Louis MO 63103
314 771-5765

(G-14270)
ALIEN TECHNOLOGY LLC
3001 W Tech Blvd (45342-0824)
PHONE...................................408 782-3900
Fax: 937 619-4401
Damon Bramble, *General Mgr*
Michael Mitchell, *Director*
EMP: 103 Privately Held
SIC: 7371 Computer software development
PA: Alien Technology, Llc
845 Embedded Way
San Jose CA 95138

(G-14271)
APRIA HEALTHCARE LLC
2029 Lyons Rd (45342-5453)
PHONE...................................937 291-2842
Fax: 937 312-9421
Susan Reffner-Bettinger, *Manager*
Patricia Mahon, *Manager*
Susan Reffner, *Manager*
EMP: 30 Privately Held
WEB: www.apria.com
SIC: 8082 Visiting nurse service
HQ: Apria Healthcare Llc
26220 Enterprise Ct
Lake Forest CA 92630
949 616-2606

(G-14272)
ASHFORD TRS LESSEE LLC
Also Called: Doubletree Hotel
300 Prestige Pl (45342-5300)
PHONE...................................937 436-2400
Jennifer Brown, *Manager*
EMP: 48
SALES (corp-wide): 44.6MM Privately Held
SIC: 7011 Hotels
PA: Ashford Trs Lessee Llc
14185 Dallas Pkwy # 1100
Dallas TX 75254
972 490-9600

(G-14273)
AUTO-OWNERS INSURANCE COMPANY
1 Prestige Pl Ste 280 (45342-6146)
PHONE...................................937 432-6740
Fax: 937 432-6746
Mitchel Warner, *Manager*
EMP: 58
SALES (corp-wide): 2.4B Privately Held
WEB: www.autoownersinsurancecompany.com
SIC: 6411 Insurance agents
PA: Auto-Owners Insurance Company
6101 Anacapri Blvd
Lansing MI 48917
517 323-1200

(G-14274)
BCF LLC (PA)
3160 S Tech Blvd (45342-4882)
PHONE...................................937 746-0721
Vaughan Stewart, *Facilities Mgr*
Steve Pohlman, *VP Finance*
Tammy Combs, *Accounts Mgr*
Larry Tipton, *Manager*
John Tafaro,
EMP: 45
SALES (est): 18.2MM Privately Held
WEB: www.buddyscarpet.com
SIC: 5713 5023 1752 Carpets; home furnishings; floor laying & floor work

(G-14275)
BELCAN SVCS GROUP LTD PARTNR
Also Called: Belcan Techservices
3494 Technical Dr (45342)
PHONE...................................937 859-8880
Fax: 937 859-3335
Gus Delucia, *Manager*
EMP: 60
SALES (corp-wide): 666.9MM Privately Held
SIC: 7363 Engineering help service; temporary help service
HQ: Belcan Services Group Limited Partnership
10200 Anderson Way
Blue Ash OH 45242
513 891-0972

(G-14276)
BLATCHFORD INC
Also Called: Endolite
1031 Byers Rd (45342-5487)
PHONE...................................937 291-3636
Fax: 937 291-0789
Steven Blatchford, *CEO*
Chris Nolan, *Vice Pres*
Mike Mauro, *Opers Mgr*
Chris Feighner, *Mfg Mgr*
Dave Fuls, *Materials Mgr*
▲ EMP: 60
SQ FT: 22,000
SALES (est): 14.7MM Privately Held
SIC: 5047 5999 Artificial limbs; orthopedic equipment & supplies; orthopedic & prosthesis applications

(G-14277)
BRADY WARE & SCHOENFELD INC (PA)
Also Called: Brady Ware & Company
3601 Rigby Rd Ste 400 (45342-5039)
PHONE...................................937 223-5247
Fax: 937 223-0300
James Keiser, *CEO*
Brian Carr, *President*
Samuel Agresti, *Vice Pres*
Mary Beth Blake, *Vice Pres*
Gary Brown, *Vice Pres*
EMP: 60
SQ FT: 16,000
SALES (est): 16.9MM Privately Held
SIC: 8721 Certified public accountant

(G-14278)
CANON SOLUTIONS AMERICA INC
1 Prestige Pl (45342-3794)
PHONE...................................937 260-4495
Israel Nunez, *Facilities Mgr*
Ronald Larkin, *Engineer*
Nicholas Lombardi, *Human Resources*
Stephen Holtzman, *Accounts Exec*
Kyle Rasmussen, *Accounts Exec*
EMP: 75
SALES (corp-wide): 36.4B Privately Held
SIC: 5044 5045 Copying equipment; computer software
HQ: Canon Solutions America, Inc.
1 Canon Park
Melville NY 11747
631 330-5000

(G-14279)
CB MANUFACTURING & SLS CO INC (PA)
4455 Infirmary Rd (45342-1299)
PHONE...................................937 866-5986
Fax: 937 866-6844
Charles S Biehn Jr, *CEO*
Richard Porter, *President*
Donald M Cain, *Vice Pres*
Roger Adams, *Plant Mgr*
Angie Roberts, *Purch Agent*
▲ EMP: 67
SQ FT: 90,000
SALES (est): 41.4MM Privately Held
WEB: www.cbmfg.com
SIC: 5085 3423 Knives, industrial; knives, agricultural or industrial

(G-14280)
CEC ENTERTAINMENT INC
Also Called: Chuck E. Cheese's
30 Prestige Pl (45342-5338)
PHONE...................................937 439-1108
Fax: 937 439-2370
Ralph Kick, *Branch Mgr*
EMP: 52
SQ FT: 10,200
SALES (corp-wide): 333.1K Privately Held
WEB: www.chuckecheese.com
SIC: 5812 7299 Pizzeria, chain; party planning service
HQ: Cec Entertainment, Inc.
1707 Market Pl Ste 200
Irving TX 75063
972 258-8507

(G-14281)
CESO INC (PA)
3601 Rigby Rd Ste 310 (45342-5040)
PHONE...................................937 435-8584
Fax: 937 435-3307
David Oakes, *President*
James I Weprin, *Principal*
Tina Gunter, *Human Res Dir*
Chris Broshears, *Manager*
EMP: 51
SQ FT: 30,000
SALES (est): 16.2MM Privately Held
SIC: 8711 3674 8712 Civil engineering; light emitting diodes; architectural services

(G-14282)
CHISANO MKTG CMMUNICATIONS INC
Also Called: Chisano Marketing Groups
2000 Byers Rd (45342)
PHONE...................................937 847-0607
Carolyn Chisano, *President*
Karen Borreson, *Accounts Mgr*
Jason Pennypacker, *Accounts Exec*
EMP: 45
SQ FT: 35,000
SALES (est): 7.4MM Privately Held
SIC: 7311 Advertising agencies

(G-14283)
CITY OF MIAMISBURG
Also Called: Miamisburg Pk Recreation Dept
10 N 1st St (45342-2300)
PHONE...................................937 866-4532
Fax: 937 847-6453
Jolene Walker, *Safety Mgr*
George Perrine, *Finance Dir*
Kelsey Whipp, *Director*
EMP: 25 Privately Held
WEB: www.pipestonegolf.com
SIC: 7999 Recreation center
PA: City Of Miamisburg
10 N 1st St
Miamisburg OH 45342
937 866-3303

(G-14284)
CITY OF MIAMISBURG
Also Called: Pipestone Golf Course
4344 Benner Rd (45342-4314)
PHONE...................................937 866-4653
Fax: 937 847-6427
Kyle Kuhnle, *General Mgr*
Tom Saathoff, *Principal*
Ryan L Gilley, *Marketing Staff*
EMP: 45
SQ FT: 1,464 Privately Held
WEB: www.pipestonegolf.com
SIC: 7992 Public golf courses
PA: City Of Miamisburg
10 N 1st St
Miamisburg OH 45342
937 866-3303

(G-14285)
CLICK CAMERA & VIDEO
2925 Mmsburg Cntrville Rd (45342)
PHONE...................................937 435-3072
Randy Potter, *Manager*
EMP: 30 EST: 2001
SALES (est): 1MM Privately Held
SIC: 5946 7819 7384 Camera & photographic supply stores; video tape or disk reproduction; photofinishing laboratory

(G-14286)
CONNOR GROUP A RE INV FIRM LLC
10510 Springboro Pike (45342-4956)
PHONE...................................937 434-3095
Robert Holzapfel, *CFO*
Lawrence Connor, *Mng Member*
Connie Hart,
EMP: 475 EST: 1996
SALES (est): 11.9MM Privately Held
SIC: 6531 Real estate agents & managers

(G-14287)
CORNERSTONE RESEARCH GROUP INC
Also Called: C R G
510 Earl Blvd (45342-6411)
PHONE...................................937 320-1877
Fax: 937 320-1886
Patrick J Hood, *President*
Jeffrey Bennett, *Vice Pres*
Chrysa Theodore, *Vice Pres*
Mitchell Bauer, *Engineer*
Karl Gruenberg, *Engineer*
EMP: 112
SQ FT: 20,979
SALES (est): 21.4MM Privately Held
WEB: www.crgrp.net
SIC: 8733 Scientific research agency

(G-14288)
COURTYARD BY MARRIOTT
100 Prestige Pl (45342-5340)
PHONE...................................937 433-3131
Fax: 937 433-0285
Bob Tate, *General Mgr*
Garry Kirkland, *Asst Mgr*
EMP: 80
SALES (est): 1.6MM Privately Held
SIC: 7011 Hotels & motels

(G-14289)
CRANE 1 SERVICES INC (PA)
1027 Byers Rd (45342-5487)
PHONE...................................937 704-9900
Fax: 937 704-9921
Brian Blind, *Division Mgr*
Quinton Horn, *Division Mgr*
Scott Rood, *Division Mgr*
Tom Shupe, *Division Mgr*
Steven Harris, *Vice Pres*
EMP: 40
SQ FT: 13,500
SALES: 47MM Privately Held
SIC: 7389 Crane & aerial lift service

(G-14290)
CSH GROUP
10100 Innovation Dr # 400 (45342-4966)
PHONE...................................937 226-0070
Fax: 937 226-1626
Herbert L Lemaster, *Partner*
Patty Conrad, *Controller*
Calandra James, *Tax Mgr*
Guy Nevers, *Tax Mgr*
Christine Vaughan, *Tax Mgr*
EMP: 25
SALES (corp-wide): 40.4MM Privately Held
WEB: www.cshco.com
SIC: 8721 Certified public accountant

GEOGRAPHIC SECTION
Miamisburg - Montgomery County (G-14312)

PA: Clark, Schaefer, Hackett & Co.
1 E 4th St Ste 1200
Cincinnati OH 45202
513 241-3111

(G-14291)
DANIS BUILDING CONSTRUCTION CO (PA)
3233 Newmark Dr (45342-5422)
PHONE....................937 228-1225
John Danis, *President*
Thomas P Hammelrath, *President*
Gordon Steadman, *President*
Jeff Barhorst, *Superintendent*
Jim Hall, *Superintendent*
EMP: 475
SQ FT: 29,000
SALES (est): 158.5MM **Privately Held**
SIC: 1542 1541 Commercial & office building, new construction; hospital construction; industrial buildings & warehouses

(G-14292)
DANIS INDUSTRIAL CNSTR CO
3233 Newmark Dr (45342-5422)
PHONE....................937 228-1225
John Danis, *CEO*
Jim Perkins, *Superintendent*
Steve Brown, *Project Mgr*
Jim Montgomery, *Project Mgr*
Mark McHale, *Technology*
EMP: 75
SALES (est): 7.8MM **Privately Held**
SIC: 1522 Residential construction
PA: Danis Building Construction Company
3233 Newmark Dr
Miamisburg OH 45342

(G-14293)
DAVIS H ELLIOT CNSTR CO INC
1 S Gebhart Church Rd (45342-3646)
PHONE....................937 847-8025
Fax: 937 847-8034
Eliot Davis, *Branch Mgr*
EMP: 160
SALES (corp-wide): 212.1MM **Privately Held**
SIC: 1731 Electrical work
HQ: Davis H. Elliot Construction Company, Inc.
673 Blue Sky Pkwy
Lexington KY 40509
859 263-5148

(G-14294)
DAYTON POWER AND LIGHT COMPANY
1 S Gebhart Church Rd (45342-3646)
PHONE....................937 331-3032
Fax: 937 847-1916
Madonna Nessle, *Principal*
Mark Sizemore, *Executive*
EMP: 25
SALES (corp-wide): 10.5B **Publicly Held**
WEB: www.waytogo.com
SIC: 4911 4932 4931 Generation, electric power; gas & other services combined; electric & other services combined
HQ: The Dayton Power And Light Company
1065 Woodman Dr
Dayton OH 45432
937 224-6000

(G-14295)
DEDICATED NURSING ASSOC INC
228 Byers Rd Ste 103 (45342-3675)
PHONE....................937 886-4559
EMP: 62 **Privately Held**
SIC: 7361 Nurses' registry
PA: Dedicated Nursing Associates, Inc.
6536 State Route 22
Delmont PA 15626

(G-14296)
DEL MONDE INC
2485 Belvo Rd (45342-3909)
PHONE....................859 371-7780
Alan Mc Williams, *Manager*
Williams Mc, *Manager*
EMP: 45
SALES (corp-wide): 16.8MM **Privately Held**
WEB: www.delmonde.com
SIC: 1711 Warm air heating & air conditioning contractor
PA: Del Monde, Inc.
10107 Toebben Dr Ste 100
Independence KY 41051
937 847-8711

(G-14297)
DIGITAL CONTROLS CORPORATION (PA)
444 Alexandersville Rd (45342-3658)
PHONE....................513 746-8118
Fax: 937 384-0842
Michael Denny, *CEO*
Chatles Landreville, *Senior VP*
Dan Rang, *Vice Pres*
Bob Arney, *Treasurer*
Theresa Gebhardt, *Human Res Dir*
EMP: 52 EST: 1969
SQ FT: 24,000
SALES (est): 9.1MM **Privately Held**
WEB: www.digital-controls.com
SIC: 7379 7372 5045 8742 Computer related maintenance services; prepackaged software; computers, peripherals & software; management consulting services

(G-14298)
DOUBLETREE GUEST SUITES DAYTON
300 Prestige Pl (45342-5300)
PHONE....................937 436-2400
Fax: 937 436-2886
Jennifer Brown, *General Mgr*
Kelly Brown, *Controller*
EMP: 60
SALES (est): 1.7MM **Privately Held**
SIC: 7011 Hotel, franchised

(G-14299)
ESKO-GRAPHICS INC (DH)
Also Called: Eskoartwork
8535 Gander Creek Dr (45342-5436)
PHONE....................937 454-1721
Kurt Demeuleneere, *CEO*
Jill Gehrhardt, *President*
Mark Quinlan, *President*
Tony Wiley, *President*
Gary Evers, *Vice Pres*
▲ EMP: 70
SQ FT: 27,000
SALES (est): 121.6MM
SALES (corp-wide): 106.4K **Privately Held**
SIC: 5084 7372 Printing trades machinery, equipment & supplies; prepackaged software
HQ: Esko-Graphics Bvba
Kortrijksesteenweg 1095
Gent 9051
921 692-11

(G-14300)
EUBEL BRADY SUTTMAN ASSET MGT
Also Called: Ebs Asset Management
10100 Innovation Dr # 410 (45342-4965)
PHONE....................937 291-1223
Fax: 937 291-9360
Robert J Suttman, *President*
Mark E Brady, *COO*
David K Ray, *COO*
William Hazel, *Vice Pres*
Scott Lundy, *Vice Pres*
EMP: 50
SQ FT: 12,000
SALES (est): 11.1MM **Privately Held**
WEB: www.ebs-asset.com
SIC: 6282 Investment advisory service

(G-14301)
FEDERAL EXPRESS CORPORATION
Also Called: Fedex
2578 Corporate Pl (45342-3656)
PHONE....................800 463-3339
Sam Salano, *Branch Mgr*
EMP: 100
SALES (corp-wide): 60.3B **Publicly Held**
WEB: www.federalexpress.com
SIC: 4513 4215 Air courier services; courier services, except by air
HQ: Federal Express Corporation
3610 Hacks Cross Rd
Memphis TN 38125
901 369-3600

(G-14302)
FINASTRA USA CORPORATION
8555 Gander Creek Dr (45342-5436)
PHONE....................937 435-2335
Connie Bruce, *Manager*
EMP: 49
SALES (corp-wide): 1.2B **Privately Held**
WEB: www.harlandfinancialsolutions.com
SIC: 7372 7389 Prepackaged software; personal service agents, brokers & bureaus
HQ: Finastra Usa Corporation
1320 Sw Broadway Ste 100
Portland OR 97201
407 804-6600

(G-14303)
FRONTIER SECURITY LLC
1041 Byers Rd (45342-5487)
PHONE....................937 247-2824
Holly Tsourides, *CEO*
Kelly Cain, *CFO*
Stephen Mills, *VP Finance*
EMP: 30
SQ FT: 20,000
SALES (est): 1.6MM **Privately Held**
SIC: 1731 Access control systems specialization

(G-14304)
GREENE MEMORIAL HOSP SVCS INC
1 Prestige Pl Ste 910 (45342-6105)
PHONE....................937 352-2000
EMP: 80
SALES (est): 422.6K
SALES (corp-wide): 1.7B **Privately Held**
SIC: 8062 Hospital, affiliated with AMA residency
PA: Kettering Adventist Healthcare
3535 Southern Blvd
Dayton OH 45429
937 298-4331

(G-14305)
HCL OF DAYTON INC
4000 Mmsbrg Ctrvle Rd 4 Ste (45342)
PHONE....................937 384-8300
Phillip B Douglas, *CEO*
Brad Gibson, *Safety Dir*
EMP: 103
SALES (est): 2.2MM
SALES (corp-wide): 359.5MM **Privately Held**
SIC: 8062 General medical & surgical hospitals
HQ: Lifecare Holdings, Llc
5340 Legacy Dr Ste 150
Plano TX 75024
469 241-2100

(G-14306)
HEALTH CARE RTREMENT CORP AMER
Also Called: Heartland of Oak Ridge
450 Oak Ridge Blvd (45342-3673)
PHONE....................937 866-8885
Fax: 937 866-0240
Lee M Elliott, *Manager*
M Elliott, *Administration*
EMP: 130
SQ FT: 57,139
SALES (corp-wide): 3.6B **Publicly Held**
WEB: www.hrc-manorcare.com
SIC: 8051 Convalescent home with continuous nursing care
HQ: Health Care And Retirement Corporation Of America
333 N Summit St Ste 103
Toledo OH 43604
419 252-5500

(G-14307)
INVOTEC ENGINEERING INC
10909 Industry Ln (45342-0818)
PHONE....................937 886-3232
Fax: 937 886-2131
John C Hanna, *President*
Thomas Hahn, *Principal*
Mark Dahlinghaus, *Project Mgr*
Mark Goode, *Mfg Mgr*
Karen Brunke, *Engineer*
EMP: 60
SQ FT: 63,000
SALES (est): 14.9MM **Privately Held**
WEB: www.invotec.com
SIC: 8711 3599 Machine tool design; custom machinery

(G-14308)
KETTCOR INC
Also Called: Collaborative Pharmacy Svcs
4301 Lyons Rd (45342-6446)
PHONE....................937 458-4949
Russ Weatherall, *Vice Pres*
EMP: 303
SALES (est): 10.5MM
SALES (corp-wide): 1.7B **Privately Held**
WEB: www.gvh-svh.org
SIC: 8741 Nursing & personal care facility management
PA: Kettering Adventist Healthcare
3535 Southern Blvd
Dayton OH 45429
937 298-4331

(G-14309)
KETTERING ADVENTIST HEALTHCARE
Also Called: Kettering Health Network Khn
2110 Leiter Rd (45342-3598)
PHONE....................937 395-8816
Joe Mendenhall, *President*
Pat Kenrick, *Vice Pres*
Bradley Mader, *Treasurer*
Howard D Drenth, *Branch Mgr*
Deanette Sisson, *Manager*
EMP: 70
SALES (corp-wide): 1.7B **Privately Held**
SIC: 8741 Hospital management
PA: Kettering Adventist Healthcare
3535 Southern Blvd
Dayton OH 45429
937 298-4331

(G-14310)
KETTERING MEDICAL CENTER
Also Called: Sycamore Medical Center
4000 Mmsburg Cntrville Rd (45342)
PHONE....................937 866-0551
Fax: 937 865-8780
Ray Ramono, *Purchasing*
Tim Anderson, *QA Dir*
Rick Trimbach, *Technical Mgr*
Clifton D Patten, *CFO*
Jan Wollef, *Finance*
EMP: 350
SQ FT: 110,000
SALES (corp-wide): 1.7B **Privately Held**
WEB: www.kmcfoundation.org
SIC: 8062 General medical & surgical hospitals
HQ: Kettering Medical Center
3535 Southern Blvd
Kettering OH 45429
937 298-4331

(G-14311)
KETTERING MEDICAL CENTER
Also Called: Sycamore Glen Retirement Cmnty
317 Sycamore Glen Dr Ofc (45342-5705)
PHONE....................937 866-2984
Fax: 937 866-7488
Brenda Ramont, *Manager*
Gary Van Nostrand, *Director*
EMP: 60
SALES (corp-wide): 1.7B **Privately Held**
WEB: www.kmcfoundation.org
SIC: 6513 6531 Retirement hotel operation; real estate managers
HQ: Kettering Medical Center
3535 Southern Blvd
Kettering OH 45429
937 298-4331

(G-14312)
KINGSTON HEALTHCARE COMPANY
Also Called: Kingston of Miamisburg
1120 Dunaway St (45342-3839)
PHONE....................937 866-9089
George Rumman, *President*
Crissy Carpenter, *Marketing Staff*
EMP: 115

Miamisburg - Montgomery County (G-14313)

SALES (corp-wide): 95.5MM **Privately Held**
SIC: 8051 Skilled nursing care facilities
PA: Kingston Healthcare Company
1 Seagate Ste 1960
Toledo OH 43604
419 247-2880

(G-14313)
LABORATORY CORPORATION AMERICA
415 Byers Rd Ste 100 (45342-3684)
PHONE..................937 866-8188
Fax: 937 866-0169
Rhonda Ellis, *Branch Mgr*
EMP: 25 **Publicly Held**
WEB: www.labcorp.com
SIC: 8071 Testing laboratories
HQ: Laboratory Corporation Of America
358 S Main St Ste 458
Burlington NC 27215
336 229-1127

(G-14314)
LEXISNEXIS GROUP (DH)
9443 Springboro Pike (45342-5490)
PHONE..................937 865-6800
Kurt Sanford, *CEO*
Doug Kaplan, *CEO*
Michael Lamb, *President*
Billy Last, *Managing Dir*
Mike Pilmer, *Managing Dir*
▲ EMP: 148
SALES (est): 512.6MM
SALES (corp-wide): 8.4B **Privately Held**
SIC: 7375 2741 Data base information retrieval; miscellaneous publishing
HQ: Relx Inc.
230 Park Ave Ste 700
New York NY 10169
212 309-8100

(G-14315)
MANAGED TECHNOLOGY SVCS LLC
3366 S Tech Blvd (45342-0823)
PHONE..................937 247-8915
Jesse Alexander, *Mng Member*
Chris Petrini Poli,
EMP: 55
SALES: 39MM **Privately Held**
SIC: 8742 7371 Management consulting services; software programming applications

(G-14316)
MED3000 GROUP INC
3131 Newmark Dr Ste 100 (45342-5400)
PHONE..................937 291-7850
Glenn Goodpaster, *Branch Mgr*
EMP: 25
SALES (corp-wide): 198.5B **Publicly Held**
WEB: www.hserve.com
SIC: 7376 8742 8721 Computer facilities management; hospital & health services consultant; billing & bookkeeping service
HQ: Med3000 Group, Inc.
7 Parkway Ctr Ste 400
Pittsburgh PA 15220

(G-14317)
MENARD INC
8480 Springboro Pike (45342-4407)
PHONE..................937 630-3550
Dennis Dixon, *Branch Mgr*
EMP: 118
SALES (corp-wide): 13.8B **Privately Held**
SIC: 5211 1521 Home centers; single-family home remodeling, additions & repairs
PA: Menard, Inc.
5101 Menard Dr
Eau Claire WI 54703
715 876-5911

(G-14318)
MERCHANT DATA SERVICE INC
2275 E Central Ave (45342-3628)
PHONE..................937 847-6585
Fax: 937 859-4184
Gerald Phipps, *President*
John Agmpfling, *Vice Pres*
Jerry Coleman, *Info Tech Mgr*
EMP: 120
SQ FT: 1,800
SALES (est): 6.4MM **Privately Held**
WEB: www.merchantdata.com
SIC: 7389 7374 Inventory computing service; optical scanning data service

(G-14319)
MERRILL LYNCH PIERCE FENNER
10100 Innovation Dr # 300 (45342-4966)
PHONE..................937 847-4000
Fax: 937 225-3901
John Knapke, *Accounting Dir*
Bill Anderson, *Branch Mgr*
Michael Maroni, *Manager*
Balinda Ferrara, *Manager*
Teri Engle, *Advisor*
EMP: 50
SALES (corp-wide): 100.2B **Publicly Held**
WEB: www.merlyn.com
SIC: 6211 8742 6282 6221 Security brokers & dealers; management consulting services; investment advice; commodity contracts brokers, dealers
HQ: Merrill Lynch, Pierce, Fenner & Smith Incorporated
111 8th Ave
New York NY 10011
800 637-7455

(G-14320)
METAL SHREDDERS INC
5101 Farmersville W (45342)
P.O. Box 244, Dayton (45449)
PHONE..................937 866-0777
Fax: 937 866-7420
Ken Cohen, *President*
Wilbur Cohen, *Chairman*
EMP: 30
SQ FT: 8,000
SALES (est): 3.5MM **Privately Held**
WEB: www.metalshredders.com
SIC: 7389 3341 Metal slitting & shearing; secondary nonferrous metals

(G-14321)
MIAMISBURG CITY SCHOOL DST
Also Called: Miamisburg Transportation Dept
200 N 12th St (45342-2548)
PHONE..................937 866-1283
Dan Girvin, *Branch Mgr*
EMP: 60
SALES (corp-wide): 69MM **Privately Held**
WEB: www.miamisburg.k12.oh.us
SIC: 4151 School buses
PA: Miamisburg City School District
540 Park Ave
Miamisburg OH 45342
937 866-3381

(G-14322)
MIAMISBURG FAMILY PRACTICE
Also Called: Riddle, Kevin L MD
415 Byers Rd Ste 300 (45342-3684)
PHONE..................937 866-8494
Fax: 937 866-8494
Dr David Page, *Owner*
Dr Mark Schmidt, *Officer*
Gloria Barnes, *Assistant*
Bernice Powell, *Assistant*
EMP: 50
SALES (est): 3.4MM **Privately Held**
SIC: 8011 General & family practice, physician/surgeon

(G-14323)
MOODYS OF DAYTON INC (PA)
4359 Infirmary Rd (45342-1231)
PHONE..................614 443-3898
Fax: 937 859-4522
John Wagner, *President*
Dave Upp, *Superintendent*
Jeff Spatz, *Controller*
Kathy Brazil, *Manager*
Chris Towe, *Manager*
EMP: 29
SQ FT: 12,500
SALES: 3.7MM **Privately Held**
WEB: www.moodysofdayton.com
SIC: 1781 Water well drilling

(G-14324)
MORRO DIALYSIS LLC
Also Called: Miamisburg Dialysis
290 Alexandersville Rd (45342-3611)
PHONE..................937 865-0633
James K Hilger,
EMP: 29
SALES (est): 358.8K **Publicly Held**
SIC: 8092 Kidney dialysis centers
PA: Davita Inc.
2000 16th St
Denver CO 80202

(G-14325)
NATIONAL CITY MORTGAGE INC (HQ)
3232 Newmark Dr (45342-5433)
P.O. Box 3232 (45343-3232)
PHONE..................937 910-1200
Fax: 937 436-4040
Leo E Knight Jr, *Ch of Bd*
Rick A Smalldon, *President*
Lynda Dagulo, *Regional Mgr*
Tom Taylor, *Regional Mgr*
Laura Brokas, *District Mgr*
EMP: 1600 EST: 1955
SQ FT: 500,000
SALES (est): 405.2MM
SALES (corp-wide): 18B **Publicly Held**
WEB: www.nationalcitymortgage.com
SIC: 6162 Mortgage bankers & correspondents
PA: The Pnc Financial Services Group Inc
300 5th Ave
Pittsburgh PA 15222
412 762-2000

(G-14326)
NEW LFCARE HSPITALS DAYTON LLC
4000 Mmsburg Cntrville Rd (45342)
PHONE..................937 384-8300
Fax: 937 384-8399
Phillip B Douglas, *Ch of Bd*
EMP: 379 EST: 2013
SALES (est): 19.4MM
SALES (corp-wide): 359.5MM **Privately Held**
SIC: 8062 General medical & surgical hospitals
HQ: Lifecare Holdings, Llc
5340 Legacy Dr Ste 150
Plano TX 75024
469 241-2100

(G-14327)
NURSES CARE INC (PA)
9009 Springboro Pike (45342-4418)
PHONE..................513 424-1141
Fax: 513 424-0520
Sheila Rush, *CEO*
Tammi Rush, *Financial Exec*
EMP: 100
SALES (est): 3.9MM **Privately Held**
WEB: www.nursescareinc.com
SIC: 8082 Home health care services

(G-14328)
OBERER DEVELOPMENT CO (PA)
Also Called: Oberer Companies
3445 Newmark Dr (45342-5426)
PHONE..................937 910-0851
Bruce Brun, *Division Mgr*
George R Oberer Sr, *Chairman*
Robert McCann, *COO*
Dennis Cruea, *QC Mgr*
Janie Ridd, *Marketing Staff*
EMP: 40
SALES (est): 39MM **Privately Held**
SIC: 6552 1521 1522 1542 Land subdividers & developers, commercial; single-family housing construction; residential construction; nonresidential construction; apartment building operators

(G-14329)
OBERER RESIDENTIAL CNSTR
Also Called: Gold Key Homes
3475 Newmark Dr (45342-5426)
PHONE..................937 278-0851
Fax: 937 278-6334
George Oberer Jr, *President*
Bob McCann, *COO*
Lloyd Cobble, *Vice Pres*
Jim Cramer, *Vice Pres*
Kerry Duncan, *Opers Mgr*
EMP: 150
SALES (est): 11.5MM **Privately Held**
SIC: 1521 6531 1522 New construction, single-family houses; real estate agents & managers; residential construction

(G-14330)
ONEIL & ASSOCIATES INC (PA)
495 Byers Rd (45342-3798)
PHONE..................937 865-0800
Fax: 937 865-5858
Bob Heilman, *President*
Ralph E Heyman, *Principal*
Gerald D Rapp, *Principal*
Howard N Thiele Jr, *Principal*
John Staten, *Chairman*
EMP: 200 EST: 1947
SQ FT: 75,000
SALES (est): 48.9MM **Privately Held**
WEB: www.oneil.com
SIC: 2741 8999 7336 Technical manuals: publishing only, not printed on site; technical manual preparation; commercial art & illustration

(G-14331)
PARK HOTELS & RESORTS INC
300 Prestige Pl (45342-5300)
PHONE..................937 436-2400
Jennifer Brown, *Manager*
EMP: 50
SALES (corp-wide): 2.7B **Publicly Held**
WEB: www.esirvine.com
SIC: 7011 Hotels & motels
PA: Park Hotels & Resorts Inc.
1600 Tysons Blvd Fl 10
Mc Lean VA 22102
703 584-7979

(G-14332)
PATENTED ACQUISITION CORP (PA)
Also Called: Think Patented
2490 Cross Pointe Dr (45342-3584)
PHONE..................937 353-2299
Ken McNerney, *President*
Tina Newman, *Purch Agent*
EMP: 92
SALES (est): 58.8MM **Privately Held**
WEB: www.thinkpatented.com
SIC: 7389 7331 Printers' services: folding, collating; mailing service

(G-14333)
PCM SALES INC
3020 S Tech Blvd (45342-4860)
PHONE..................937 885-6444
Fax: 937 438-8098
Joseph W Kuntz, *Vice Pres*
David Wright, *Manager*
EMP: 55
SALES (corp-wide): 2.1B **Publicly Held**
WEB: www.sarcom.com
SIC: 7379
HQ: Pcm Sales, Inc.
1940 E Mariposa Ave
El Segundo CA 90245
310 354-5600

(G-14334)
PEQ SERVICES + SOLUTIONS INC (HQ)
1 Prestige Pl Ste 900 (45342-6105)
PHONE..................937 610-4800
Jason Evans, *President*
Emily Evans, *Vice Pres*
David Senseman, *Treasurer*
Robert Butcher, *Admin Sec*
EMP: 60
SALES (est): 8.9MM
SALES (corp-wide): 80.5MM **Privately Held**
WEB: www.peqinc.com
SIC: 8748 Business consulting
PA: Buchanan Technologies, Inc.
1026 Texan Trl Ste 200
Grapevine TX 76051
972 869-3966

GEOGRAPHIC SECTION
Miamisburg - Montgomery County (G-14356)

(G-14335)
PHYSICIAN HOSPITAL ALLIANCE
10050 Innovation Dr # 240 (45342-4935)
PHONE.....................937 558-3456
Troy Tyner, *President*
EMP: 25
SALES (est): 5.1MM
SALES (corp-wide): 1.7B **Privately Held**
SIC: 8621 Medical field-related associations
PA: Kettering Adventist Healthcare
3535 Southern Blvd
Dayton OH 45429
937 298-4331

(G-14336)
PNC BANK-ATM
Also Called: Lexis Nexis
9333 Springboro Pike (45342-4424)
PHONE.....................937 865-6800
Fax: 937 865-7894
Chris Koogler, *Manager*
Andrew Loree, *Webmaster*
EMP: 35 EST: 2015
SALES (est): 21.2MM **Privately Held**
SIC: 6099 Automated teller machine (ATM) network

(G-14337)
PNC MORTGAGE COMPANY (DH)
3232 Newmark Dr Bldg 2 (45342-5433)
PHONE.....................412 762-2000
Robert Crowl, *Principal*
Mark Schwab, *Regional Mgr*
Scott Lynch, *Business Mgr*
Glenn Brunker, *Exec VP*
Steven Buisson, *Exec VP*
EMP: 102
SALES (est): 18.4MM
SALES (corp-wide): 18B **Publicly Held**
SIC: 1711 Plumbing contractors
HQ: Pnc Bank, National Association
222 Delaware Ave
Wilmington DE 19801
877 762-2000

(G-14338)
PULMONARY & MEDICINE DAYTON (PA)
4000 Miamisburg Centervil (45342-3908)
PHONE.....................937 439-3600
Fax: 937 439-3786
Ivo C Seni MD, *President*
Felipe Rubio, *Principal*
Hemant Shah, *Principal*
EMP: 32
SALES (est): 4.2MM **Privately Held**
SIC: 8011 Pulmonary specialist, physician/surgeon

(G-14339)
RELX INC
Lexis-Nexis Group
9443 Springboro Pike (45342-4425)
P.O. Box 933, Dayton (45401-0933)
PHONE.....................937 865-6800
Fax: 937 847-3090
EMP: 300
SALES (corp-wide): 9B **Privately Held**
SIC: 7375 Information Retrieval Services, Nsk
HQ: Relx Inc.
230 Park Ave
New York NY 10169
212 309-8100

(G-14340)
RELX INC
Also Called: Lexis Nexis
9443 Springboro Pike (45342-4425)
PHONE.....................937 865-6800
Fax: 937 865-1555
Elizabeth Rector, *Vice Pres*
Lewis Myers, *Senior Engr*
Kim Saldana, *Sls & Mktg Exec*
Michael Weber, *Branch Mgr*
Clemens Ceipek, *Manager*
EMP: 49
SALES (corp-wide): 8.4B **Privately Held**
WEB: www.lexis-nexis.com
SIC: 2721 2731 7389 7999 Trade journals: publishing only, not printed on site; books: publishing only; trade show arrangement; exposition operation
HQ: Relx Inc.
230 Park Ave Ste 700
New York NY 10169
212 309-8100

(G-14341)
REQ/JQH HOLDINGS INC
Also Called: Homewood Suites
3100 Contemporary Ln (45342-5399)
PHONE.....................937 432-0000
Mark Landon, *General Mgr*
EMP: 100
SALES (corp-wide): 84.3MM **Privately Held**
WEB: www.whihotels.com
SIC: 7011 Hotels & motels
PA: Req/Jqh Holdings, Inc.
4243 Hunt Rd Ste 2
Blue Ash OH 45242
513 891-1066

(G-14342)
RETALIX INC
2490 Technical Dr (45342-6136)
PHONE.....................937 384-2277
Barry Shake, *CEO*
Barry Shaked, *President*
Shelly Mandich, *Opers Mgr*
Eli Spirer, *Mfg Staff*
Tabitha Barrett, *Purchasing*
EMP: 155
SQ FT: 72,000
SALES (est): 9.6MM
SALES (corp-wide): 6.5B **Publicly Held**
SIC: 5734 7372 Software, business & non-game; prepackaged software
HQ: Ncr Global Ltd
9 Dafna
Raanana
977 666-96

(G-14343)
RETALIX USA INC
2490 Technical Dr (45342-6136)
PHONE.....................937 384-2277
Tom Mandich, *Branch Mgr*
EMP: 110
SALES (corp-wide): 6.5B **Publicly Held**
WEB: www.retalixusa.com
SIC: 7371 Computer software development
HQ: Retalix Usa, Inc.
6100 Tennyson Pkwy # 150
Plano TX 75024
469 241-8400

(G-14344)
RIVER VALLEY CREDIT UNION INC (PA)
505 Earl Blvd (45342-6411)
PHONE.....................937 859-1970
John Bowen, *CEO*
Rebecca Siciarz, *President*
Robert Delong, *Vice Pres*
Suzanne M Roush, *Vice Pres*
James Roberson Jr, *CFO*
EMP: 61
SQ FT: 10,000
SALES (est): 11MM **Privately Held**
SIC: 6061 Federal credit unions

(G-14345)
RIVERAIN TECHNOLOGIES LLC
3020 S Tech Blvd (45342-4860)
PHONE.....................937 425-6811
Fax: 937 425-6493
Steve Worrell, *CEO*
San Finkelstein, *President*
Rich Bares, *President*
Larry Cupp, *Engineer*
Dan Littman, *CFO*
EMP: 30
SALES (est): 6.5MM **Privately Held**
WEB: www.riverainmedical.com
SIC: 5047 X-ray machines & tubes

(G-14346)
SCHUSTER CARDIOLOGY
Also Called: Saini, Hari MD
4000 Miamisburg Ctr Ste (45342)
PHONE.....................937 866-0637
Fax: 937 643-9949
Benjamin Schuster MD, *Principal*
Peter Lewis, *Med Doctor*
Bruce G Hyman, *Cardiovascular*
EMP: 50
SALES (est): 3.1MM **Privately Held**
SIC: 8011 Cardiologist & cardio-vascular specialist

(G-14347)
SENIOR CARE INC
8630 Washington Church Rd (45342-3795)
PHONE.....................937 291-3211
Matthew Byerley, *Corp Comm Staff*
Sara Taylor, *Office Mgr*
Lindsey Daugherty, *Director*
EMP: 25 **Privately Held**
SIC: 8361 8059 8051 Home for the aged; convalescent home; skilled nursing care facilities
PA: Senior Care, Inc.
700 N Hurstbourne Pkwy # 200
Louisville KY 40222

(G-14348)
SENTAGE CORPORATION
Also Called: Dental Services Group
1037 Byers Rd (45342-5487)
PHONE.....................937 865-5900
Kirby Pickle, *CEO*
Babette Millard, *Accountant*
Allen Matthews, *Branch Mgr*
EMP: 35
SALES (corp-wide): 100MM **Privately Held**
WEB: www.dentalservices.net
SIC: 8072 Dental laboratories; artificial teeth production; crown & bridge production; denture production
PA: Sentage Corporation
146 2nd St N Ste 207
Saint Petersburg FL 33701
727 502-2069

(G-14349)
SGI MATRIX LLC (PA)
1041 Byers Rd (45342-5487)
PHONE.....................937 438-9033
James Young, *President*
John Gorretta, *Vice Pres*
Steven J Koranda, *Vice Pres*
Jeffrey S Young, *Vice Pres*
Rick Current, *Opers Mgr*
EMP: 68 EST: 1977
SQ FT: 12,000
SALES (est): 33.9MM **Privately Held**
WEB: www.matrixsys.com
SIC: 8711 7373 3873 Engineering services; computer integrated systems design; watches, clocks, watchcases & parts

(G-14350)
SHAWNTECH COMMUNICATIONS INC (PA)
Also Called: SCI
8521 Gander Creek Dr (45342-5436)
PHONE.....................937 898-4900
Lance Fancher, *President*
Amelia Fancher, *Treasurer*
Decerbo Dan, *Info Tech Mgr*
Winifred Labomme, *Admin Sec*
EMP: 46
SALES (est): 17.3MM **Privately Held**
WEB: www.shawntech.com
SIC: 5065 5999 1731 Mobile telephone equipment; telephone equipment; paging & signaling equipment; communication equipment; telephone equipment & systems; mobile telephones & equipment; electrical work

(G-14351)
SOGETI USA LLC (DH)
10100 Innovation Dr # 200 (45342-4966)
PHONE.....................937 291-8100
Rajnish Nath, *CEO*
Mike Pleiman, *Exec VP*
Cynthia Gibson, *Vice Pres*
Steve Hughes, *Vice Pres*
Pratosh Jhari, *Vice Pres*
EMP: 150
SQ FT: 18,332
SALES (est): 348.8MM
SALES (corp-wide): 353.3MM **Privately Held**
WEB: www.sogeti-usa.com
SIC: 7379
HQ: Capgemini North America, Inc.
79 5th Ave Frnt 3
New York NY 10003
212 314-8000

(G-14352)
SOURCELINK OHIO LLC
3303 W Tech Blvd (45342-0817)
PHONE.....................937 885-8000
Fax: 937 885-8015
Don Landrum, *CEO*
Jim Wisnionski, *President*
Mike Dolan, *COO*
Karen Clear, *Vice Pres*
Darryl K Myers, *Prdtn Mgr*
EMP: 120
SQ FT: 140,000
SALES (est): 29.9MM
SALES (corp-wide): 100.6MM **Privately Held**
SIC: 7331 7374 2752 Direct mail advertising services; data processing service; commercial printing, lithographic
PA: Sourcelink Acquisition, Llc
500 Park Blvd Ste 1425
Itasca IL 60143
866 947-6872

(G-14353)
SOUTH TOWN PAINTING INC
320 E Linden Ave (45342-2828)
PHONE.....................937 847-1600
Fax: 937 847-2365
Ronald L Elmore, *President*
James David Elmore, *Vice Pres*
EMP: 40
SQ FT: 2,000
SALES (est): 3.4MM **Privately Held**
SIC: 1721 Commercial painting; residential painting

(G-14354)
STEINER EOPTICS INC (PA)
Also Called: Sensor Technology Systems
3475 Newmark Dr (45342-5426)
PHONE.....................937 426-2341
Alan Page, *General Mgr*
Doris Byerly Anderson, *Office Mgr*
EMP: 80
SQ FT: 50,000
SALES (est): 13.9MM **Privately Held**
SIC: 8731 3851 Electronic research; ophthalmic goods

(G-14355)
TECH PRODUCTS CORPORATION (DH)
2215 Lyons Rd (45342-4465)
PHONE.....................937 438-1100
Fax: 937 438-2190
Dan Rork, *President*
Greg Kiefer, *General Mgr*
Hugh E Wall Jr, *Principal*
Peirce Wood, *Principal*
A M Zimmerman, *Principal*
EMP: 29
SQ FT: 25,000
SALES (est): 5.4MM **Privately Held**
WEB: www.tpcdayton.com
SIC: 3625 5084 3829 3651 Noise control equipment; noise control equipment; measuring & controlling devices; household audio & video equipment
HQ: Fabreeka International Holdings, Inc.
1023 Turnpike St
Stoughton MA 02072
781 341-3655

(G-14356)
TERADATA CORPORATION (PA)
10000 Innovation Dr (45342-4927)
PHONE.....................866 548-8348
Victor L Lund, *CEO*
James M Ringler, *Ch of Bd*
Jeff Amos, *President*
Karen Thomas, *President*
Robert Fair, *COO*
EMP: 277

Miamisburg - Montgomery County (G-14357)

SALES: 2.1B **Publicly Held**
WEB: www.teradata.com
SIC: **3571** 3572 7372 7371 Electronic computers; mainframe computers; minicomputers; personal computers (microcomputers); computer storage devices; disk drives, computer; prepackaged software; application computer software; software programming applications

(G-14357)
TERADATA OPERATIONS INC (HQ)
10000 Innovation Dr (45342-4927)
PHONE...................937 242-4030
John Emanuel, *President*
Michael Brown, *Vice Pres*
Elizabeth E Corley, *Vice Pres*
Keith Henry, *Vice Pres*
Kirk Johnsen, *Vice Pres*
EMP: 100
SALES (est): 428.5MM **Publicly Held**
SIC: **3571** 7379 Electronic computers; computer related consulting services

(G-14358)
THINKPATH ENGINEERING SVCS LLC (PA)
9080 Springboro Pike # 300 (45342-4670)
PHONE...................937 291-8374
Robert Trick, *President*
Kelly Hankinson, *CFO*
Steve Bishop, *Accounts Mgr*
Caleb Miller, *Comp Tech*
Christoph Rieker, *Comp Tech*
EMP: 100
SQ FT: 6,330
SALES (est): 6.3MM **Privately Held**
SIC: **8711** 7373 7361 8999 Engineering services; mechanical engineering; computer-aided engineering (CAE) systems service; executive placement; technical writing

(G-14359)
THOMPSON HINE LLP
10050 Innovation Dr # 400 (45342-4934)
P.O. Box 8801, Dayton (45401-8801)
PHONE...................937 443-6859
Fax: 937 443-6805
Jessica Sachs, *Branch Mgr*
Sherri Daley, *Technology*
Alexandra Briggs, *Associate*
Paige Connelly, *Associate*
Joseph Gabriele, *Associate*
EMP: 123
SALES (corp-wide): 98.4MM **Privately Held**
SIC: **8111** General practice attorney, lawyer
PA: Thompson Hine Llp
  127 Public Sq
  Cleveland OH 44114
  216 566-5500

(G-14360)
THYSSENKRUPP MATERIALS NA INC
Copper & Brass Sales
10100 Innovation Dr # 210 (45342-4966)
PHONE...................937 898-7400
Fax: 937 454-0235
Scot Marlin, *Vice Pres*
Paul Fairhurst, *Credit Staff*
Julie Mays, *Corp Comm Staff*
Sherry Whitaker, *Info Tech Mgr*
EMP: 25
SALES (corp-wide): 48.7B **Privately Held**
SIC: **5162** Plastics materials
HQ: Thyssenkrupp Materials Na, Inc.
  22355 W 11 Mile Rd
  Southfield MI 48033
  248 233-5600

(G-14361)
TRI-CITY INDUSTRIAL POWER INC (PA)
915 N Main St (45342-1873)
P.O. Box 576, Dayton (45449)
PHONE...................937 866-4099
Fax: 937 866-5438
Bob Tyndall, *President*
Rhonda Deweese, *Vice Pres*
Erin Chandler, *Purch Agent*
Rod Miller, *Accounts Mgr*
Rick Burton, *Branch Mgr*
EMP: 25
SQ FT: 10,000
SALES (est): 4.3MM **Privately Held**
WEB: www.tricitypower.com
SIC: **7699** 5063 Battery service & repair; storage batteries, industrial

(G-14362)
UBS FINANCIAL SERVICES INC
3601 Rigby Rd Ste 500 (45342-5039)
PHONE...................937 223-3141
Travis King, *Financial Exec*
Geoffrey Merl, *Financial Exec*
Mark Pent, *Manager*
EMP: 35
SALES (corp-wide): 28B **Privately Held**
SIC: **6211** Security brokers & dealers
HQ: Ubs Financial Services Inc.
  1285 Ave Of The Americas
  New York NY 10019
  212 713-2000

(G-14363)
ULLIMAN SCHUTTE CNSTR LLC (PA)
Also Called: U S C
9111 Springboro Pike (45342-4420)
PHONE...................937 247-0375
Fax: 937 910-9910
John Coffin, *General Mgr*
Matthew Ulliman, *General Mgr*
Jason Brown, *Superintendent*
Brian Danik, *Safety Dir*
Joe Bustamante, *Project Mgr*
EMP: 300 EST: 1998
SQ FT: 4,000
SALES: 1.9MM **Privately Held**
WEB: www.ullimanschutte.com
SIC: **1629** Waste water & sewage treatment plant construction

(G-14364)
UNITED GRINDING NORTH AMER INC (DH)
2100 United Grinding Blvd (45342-6804)
PHONE...................937 859-1975
Mr Terry Derrico, *CEO*
Rodger Pinney, *President*
Michael Martin, *Regional Mgr*
Larry Marchand, *Vice Pres*
Glen Mullins, *Senior Buyer*
▲ EMP: 66
SALES (est): 62.7MM **Privately Held**
WEB: www.grinding.com
SIC: **5084** Industrial machinery & equipment
HQ: United Grinding Gmbh
  Kurt-A.-Korber-Chaussee 8-32
  Hamburg 21033
  407 250-07

(G-14365)
VEOLIA ES TCHNCAL SLUTIONS LLC
4301 Infirmary Rd (45342-1231)
PHONE...................937 859-6101
Danny Sibert, *Plant Mgr*
Jason Sowards, *Facilities Mgr*
Sam Foster, *Research*
Bob Luzanski, *Manager*
Andrew Yadvish, *Manager*
EMP: 55
SALES (corp-wide): 572.2MM **Privately Held**
WEB: www.onyxes.com
SIC: **4953** Recycling, waste materials
HQ: Onyx Environmental Services Llc
  700 E Bttrfeld Rd Ste 201
  Lombard IL 60148
  630 218-1500

(G-14366)
WALGREEN CO
Also Called: Walgreens
1260 E Central Ave (45342-3546)
PHONE...................937 859-3879
Fax: 937 859-3258
Steve Smith, *Manager*
EMP: 40
SALES (corp-wide): 118.2B **Publicly Held**
WEB: www.walgreens.com
SIC: **5912** 7384 Drug stores; photofinishing laboratory
HQ: Walgreen Co.
  200 Wilmot Rd
  Deerfield IL 60015
  847 315-2500

(G-14367)
WALKER AUTO GROUP INC
Also Called: Walker Mitsubishi
8457 Springboro Pike (45342-4403)
PHONE...................937 433-4950
Fax: 937 493-4950
Jeff Walker, *President*
John Walker III, *President*
John V H Walker Jr, *Chairman*
Beverly Walker, *Corp Secy*
Charlie Middleton, *Controller*
EMP: 90 EST: 1950
SQ FT: 65,000
SALES (est): 37.4MM **Privately Held**
WEB: www.jackwalker.com
SIC: **5511** 7538 7532 5531 Automobiles, new & used; general automotive repair shops; top & body repair & paint shops; automotive & home supply stores; used car dealers

(G-14368)
WESTERN TRADEWINDS INC (PA)
521 Byers Rd (45342-7302)
P.O. Box 750608, Dayton (45475-0608)
PHONE...................937 859-4300
Fax: 937 439-9463
Harry Bossey, *President*
Kevin Mooney, *Admin Sec*
◆ EMP: 30
SQ FT: 10,000
SALES (est): 5.3MM **Privately Held**
WEB: www.westerntradewinds.com
SIC: **5084** 5065 5083 5013 Industrial machinery & equipment; electronic parts & equipment; farm & garden machinery; motor vehicle supplies & new parts

(G-14369)
WINSUPPLY INC
9300 Byers Rd (45342-4352)
PHONE...................937 865-0796
Jeff Porter, *Manager*
Brock Smith, *Assistant*
EMP: 30
SALES (corp-wide): 2.7B **Privately Held**
SIC: **5074** Plumbing fittings & supplies
PA: Winsupply Inc.
  3110 Kettering Blvd
  Moraine OH 45439
  937 294-5331

Miamitown
Hamilton County

(G-14370)
BRENNAN ELECTRIC LLC
6859 Cemetary Dr (45041)
P.O. Box 266 (45041-0266)
PHONE...................513 353-2229
Fax: 513 353-2719
Timothy Brennan,
Debra Brennan,
EMP: 25
SQ FT: 3,000
SALES (est): 2.7MM **Privately Held**
SIC: **1731** General electrical contractor

(G-14371)
GATEWAY CONCRETE FORMING SVCS
5938 Hamilton Cleves Rd (45041)
P.O. Box 130 (45041-0130)
PHONE...................513 353-2000
Fax: 513 353-2002
Robert Bilz, *President*
Tim Hughey, *President*
Brandon Erfman, *Vice Pres*
Jean C Hughey, *Treasurer*
J Robert Hughey, *Shareholder*
EMP: 75
SQ FT: 3,000
SALES (est): 8MM **Privately Held**
WEB: www.gatewaybuildingproducts.com
SIC: **1771** 3449 3496 3429 Foundation & footing contractor; bars, concrete reinforcing; fabricated steel; miscellaneous fabricated wire products; manufactured hardware (general)

(G-14372)
MERCHANDISE INC
Also Called: MI
5929 State Rte 128 (45041)
P.O. Box 10 (45041-0010)
PHONE...................513 353-2200
Donald W Karches, *President*
Elizabeth Ann Karches, *Vice Pres*
Beth Schwarb, *Human Res Mgr*
Mike Lockard, *Supervisor*
Jim Powell, *Director*
◆ EMP: 70
SQ FT: 50,000
SALES (est): 45.3MM **Privately Held**
WEB: www.merchandise.com
SIC: **5085** 5099 5122 5199 Industrial supplies; video & audio equipment; compact discs; tapes & cassettes, prerecorded; video cassettes, accessories & supplies; drugs, proprietaries & sundries; cosmetics; medicine cabinet sundries; general merchandise, non-durable

(G-14373)
SOUTHERN OHIO DOOR CONTRLS INC (PA)
8080 Furlong Dr (45041)
P.O. Box 331 (45041-0331)
PHONE...................513 353-4793
Fax: 513 353-4817
Pete Nicolaou, *President*
Ronald Merkt, *Principal*
Terry Mains, *Controller*
Steve Jones, *VP Sales*
Jim Meese, *Sales Staff*
EMP: 34
SQ FT: 3,000
SALES: 3.8MM **Privately Held**
SIC: **5031** 7699 Doors & windows; door & window repair

Miamiville
Clermont County

(G-14374)
AIM MRO HOLDINGS INC (PA)
Also Called: T&B Manufacturing
375 Center St 175 (45147)
PHONE...................513 831-2938
Barry F Bucher, *Chairman*
Scott Bucher, *Vice Pres*
Tom Kennard, *Vice Pres*
Jeffrey C Liesch, *Vice Pres*
Scott Wandtke, *Vice Pres*
◆ EMP: 60
SQ FT: 20,000
SALES (est): 36.2MM **Privately Held**
WEB: www.aimmro.com
SIC: **5088** Aircraft engines & engine parts

(G-14375)
D&M CARTER LLC
106 Glendale Milford Rd (45147)
P.O. Box 20 (45147-0020)
PHONE...................513 831-8843
David Carter, *Mng Member*
Mark Carter,
EMP: 30
SALES (est): 924.5K **Privately Held**
SIC: **1611** Grading; highway & street paving contractor

Middle Point
Van Wert County

(G-14376)
COUNTY OF VAN WERT
Also Called: Lincolnway Home
17872 Lincoln Hwy (45863-9700)
PHONE...................419 968-2141
Fax: 419 968-2390
Dan Qurik, *Manager*
EMP: 40 **Privately Held**

▲ = Import ▼ = Export
◆ = Import/Export

GEOGRAPHIC SECTION

Middlefield - Geauga County (G-14398)

SIC: 8051 Skilled nursing care facilities
PA: County Of Van Wert
  121 E Main St Rm 200
  Van Wert OH 45891
  419 238-7020

(G-14377)
OGLETHORPE MIDDLEPOINT LLC
Also Called: Ridgeview Hospital
17872 Lincoln Hwy (45863-9700)
PHONE..............................419 968-2950
James Coyle, *Accountant*
Shanne Davis, *Human Resources*
Randy La Fond,
EMP: 33
SALES: 12.7MM **Privately Held**
SIC: 8063 Psychiatric hospitals

Middleburg Heights
Cuyahoga County

(G-14378)
BREWER-GARRETT CO (PA)
6800 Eastland Rd (44130-2402)
PHONE..............................440 243-3535
Fax: 440 243-9993
Lou Joseph, *President*
Kayla Degeorge, *Accountant*
Mike Djordjevic, *Manager*
Jason Zorc, *Manager*
Michelle Brody, *Executive Asst*
EMP: 155 EST: 1959
SQ FT: 31,500
SALES: 22MM **Privately Held**
WEB: www.brewer-garrett.com
SIC: 1711 4961 8711 Mechanical contractor; steam & air-conditioning supply; engineering services

(G-14379)
CHEMSTEEL CONSTRUCTION COMPANY (PA)
7850 Freeway Cir Ste 110 (44130-6317)
PHONE..............................440 234-3930
Ernest Grochalski, *President*
Vicki Anderson, *Chairman*
David Morse, *Project Mgr*
Alan Tatro, *Project Mgr*
Tony Deluca, *Controller*
EMP: 25
SQ FT: 5,000
SALES: 13.9MM **Privately Held**
WEB: www.chemsteel.com
SIC: 1541 1711 1799 Industrial buildings & warehouses; mechanical contractor; coating of metal structures at construction site

(G-14380)
COMPASS HEALTH BRANDS CORP (PA)
Also Called: Roscoe Medical
6753 Engle Rd Ste A (44130-7935)
PHONE..............................800 947-1728
Fax: 440 572-4261
Paul Guth, *President*
Henry Lin, *COO*
Mike Giesken, *Vice Pres*
Tony West, *Vice Pres*
Jim Hileman, *CFO*
◆ EMP: 110
SQ FT: 20,000
SALES (est): 131.5MM **Privately Held**
SIC: 5047 Medical equipment & supplies

(G-14381)
FIDELITONE INC
17851 Englewood Dr Ste I (44130-3489)
PHONE..............................440 260-6523
EMP: 54
SALES (corp-wide): 287MM **Privately Held**
SIC: 4789 Pipeline terminal facilities, independently operated
PA: Fidelitone, Inc.
  1260 Karl Ct
  Wauconda IL 60084
  847 487-3300

(G-14382)
HAMPTON INN & SUITE INC
7074 Engle Rd (44130-3423)
PHONE..............................440 234-0206
Fax: 440 234-0208
Mark Csepll, *Manager*
Jeff Charo, *Manager*
Mark Cseplo, *Manager*
EMP: 50
SALES (est): 1.8MM **Privately Held**
SIC: 7011 Hotels

(G-14383)
OH-16 CLVLND ARPRT S PRPRTY SU
Also Called: Courtyard Cleveland Airport S
7345 Engle Rd (44130-3430)
PHONE..............................440 243-8785
Erin Severinski, *General Mgr*
Gregory Moundas, *Vice Pres*
Louisa Yeung, *Administration*
EMP: 33 EST: 2014
SALES (est): 193.8K **Privately Held**
SIC: 7011 Hotels

(G-14384)
QUADAX INC (PA)
7500 Old Oak Blvd (44130-3343)
PHONE..............................440 777-6300
Fax: 216 765-0984
Thomas Hockman, *Ch of Bd*
R Ralph Daugstrup, *President*
John Leskiw, *President*
Len Stusek, *General Mgr*
Anthony Petras, *COO*
EMP: 108
SQ FT: 2,000
SALES (est): 34.6MM **Privately Held**
WEB: www.quadax.net
SIC: 8721 Billing & bookkeeping service

(G-14385)
RICHS TOWING & SERVICE INC (PA)
20531 1st Ave (44130-2437)
PHONE..............................440 234-3435
Michael Tomasko, *President*
Sandy Saponari, *Vice Pres*
Patricia Smith, *CFO*
Richard Smith, *Human Res Mgr*
Tammy Rice, *Marketing Staff*
EMP: 50
SQ FT: 5,000
SALES (est): 7.3MM **Privately Held**
SIC: 7549 Towing service, automotive

(G-14386)
RIVALS SPORTS GRILLE LLC
6710 Smith Rd (44130-2656)
PHONE..............................216 267-0005
John Simmons,
EMP: 48
SQ FT: 4,368
SALES: 1.9MM **Privately Held**
SIC: 5812 7372 Grills (eating places); application computer software

(G-14387)
TAZMANIAN FREIGHT FWDG INC (PA)
Also Called: Tazmanian Freight Systems
6640 Engle Rd Ste A (44130-7949)
P.O. Box 811090, Cleveland (44181-1090)
PHONE..............................216 265-7881
Robert Rossbach, *CEO*
Jerry Metzo, *General Mgr*
Pat Santell, *Regional Mgr*
Rich Oblanis, *District Mgr*
Marco Aponte, *Business Mgr*
EMP: 40
SALES (est): 71.1MM **Privately Held**
WEB: www.tazmanian.com
SIC: 4731 Freight forwarding

(G-14388)
THE INTERLAKE STEAMSHIP CO
7300 Engle Rd (44130-3429)
PHONE..............................440 260-6900
Fax: 330 659-1445
Paul R Tregurtha, *Vice Ch Bd*
Mark W Barker, *President*
James R Barker, *Chairman*
Robert F Dorn, *Senior VP*
Kimberly Noe, *Buyer*
EMP: 25
SQ FT: 18,456
SALES: 108.8MM **Privately Held**
SALES (corp-wide): 108.8MM **Privately Held**
WEB: www.interlake-steamship.com
SIC: 4432 Freight transportation on the Great Lakes
PA: Interlake Holding Company
  1 Landmark Sq Ste 710
  Stamford CT 06901
  203 977-8900

(G-14389)
UNITED PARCEL SERVICE INC
Also Called: UPS
6940 Engle Rd Ste C (44130-3435)
PHONE..............................440 243-3344
Kevin Snow, *Purch Agent*
Nancy Was, *Human Res Mgr*
George Smith, *Manager*
EMP: 40
SALES (corp-wide): 65.8B **Publicly Held**
WEB: www.ups.com
SIC: 7389 Mailbox rental & related service
PA: United Parcel Service, Inc.
  55 Glenlake Pkwy
  Atlanta GA 30328
  404 828-6000

(G-14390)
VERANTIS CORPORATION (HQ)
7251 Engle Rd Ste 300 (44130-3400)
PHONE..............................440 243-0700
William Jackson, *Senior VP*
Jeffrey Edwards, *Production*
Josh Sheppard, *Finance*
Marty Molina, *Accounts Mgr*
▼ EMP: 30
SALES (est): 16.7MM **Privately Held**
SIC: 3564 5075 Air purification equipment; blowers & fans; air pollution control equipment & supplies
PA: Tanglewood Investments Inc.
  5051 Westheimer Rd # 300
  Houston TX 77056
  713 629-5525

(G-14391)
WADSWORTH SERVICE INC
7851 Freeway Cir (44130-6308)
PHONE..............................419 861-8181
EMP: 45
SALES (corp-wide): 10.6MM **Privately Held**
SIC: 1711 Refrigeration contractor
PA: Wadsworth Service, Inc.
  1500 Michael Owens Way
  Perrysburg OH 43551
  216 391-7263

(G-14392)
ZIN TECHNOLOGIES INC (PA)
6745 Engle Rd Ste 105 (44130-7993)
PHONE..............................440 625-2200
Fax: 440 625-2294
Daryl Z Laisure, *President*
Chris Sheehan, *Area Mgr*
Carlos Grodsinsky, *COO*
Brian Borowski, *Project Mgr*
Valerie Romanko, *Senior Buyer*
EMP: 128
SQ FT: 60,000
SALES: 30MM **Privately Held**
SIC: 8731 8711 7379 Engineering laboratory, except testing; consulting engineer; computer related consulting services

Middlefield
Geauga County

(G-14393)
AIRGAS INC
14943 Madison Rd (44062-8403)
PHONE..............................440 632-1758
Woodrow Burton, *President*
EMP: 264
SALES (corp-wide): 163.9MM **Privately Held**
SIC: 5169 Industrial gases
HQ: Airgas, Inc.
  259 N Radnor Chester Rd # 100
  Radnor PA 19087
  610 687-5253

(G-14394)
BRIAR HL HLTH CARE RSDENCE INC
Also Called: Briar Hill Hlth Care Residence
15950 Pierce St (44062-9577)
P.O. Box 277 (44062-0277)
PHONE..............................440 632-5241
Fax: 440 632-9362
George Ohman, *President*
Charles Ohman, *Vice Pres*
Ken Ward, *Maint Spvr*
Donald Gray, *Treasurer*
Marilyn Reckart, *Corp Comm Staff*
EMP: 95
SQ FT: 10,000
SALES (est): 8.1MM **Privately Held**
SIC: 8051 Convalescent home with continuous nursing care

(G-14395)
HANS ROTHENBUHLER & SON INC
15815 Nauvoo Rd (44062-8501)
PHONE..............................440 632-6000
John Rothenbuhler, *President*
Joyce Filla, *General Mgr*
Ann Rothenbuhler, *Controller*
Gary Schoenwald, *Marketing Staff*
▲ EMP: 40
SALES (est): 12.3MM **Privately Held**
SIC: 2022 5451 5143 2023 Natural cheese; dairy products stores; dairy products, except dried or canned; dry, condensed, evaporated dairy products

(G-14396)
KRAFTMAID TRUCKING INC (PA)
16052 Industrial Pkwy (44062-9382)
P.O. Box 1055 (44062-1055)
PHONE..............................440 632-2531
Tom Chieffe, *President*
Richard Moodie, *COO*
Sandy Allen, *Vice Pres*
Bob Hawthorne, *Plant Mgr*
Paul Graham, *Engineer*
EMP: 100
SQ FT: 12,000
SALES (est): 16.7MM **Privately Held**
SIC: 4813 2517 Telephone communication, except radio; wood television & radio cabinets

(G-14397)
LAKE HOSPITAL SYSTEM INC
15050 S Springdale Ave (44062-9211)
PHONE..............................440 632-3024
Dave Ebel, *Branch Mgr*
EMP: 1100
SALES (corp-wide): 334.1MM **Privately Held**
SIC: 8062 8011 General medical & surgical hospitals; medical centers
PA: Lake Hospital System, Inc.
  7590 Auburn Rd
  Painesville OH 44077
  440 375-8100

(G-14398)
MYERS INDUSTRIES INC
Dillen Products
15150 Madison Rd (44062-9495)
P.O. Box 738 (44062-0738)
PHONE..............................440 632-0230
Dan Nauert, *General Mgr*
Ron Ostrander, *District Mgr*
Chad Canfield, *Maint Spvr*
John Magouyrk, *Sales Mgr*
Ron Olsen, *Sales Mgr*
EMP: 90
SALES (corp-wide): 547MM **Publicly Held**
WEB: www.myersind.com
SIC: 0781 3423 Horticulture services; hand & edge tools
PA: Myers Industries, Inc.
  1293 S Main St
  Akron OH 44301
  330 253-5592

Middlefield - Geauga County

(G-14399)
NORSTAR ALUMINUM MOLDS INC
Also Called: Starwood
15986 Valpalst St (44062-9399)
PHONE..................440 632-0853
Erik Adams, *Sales Staff*
Brian Gresch, *Branch Mgr*
Ravi Mehra, *Director*
EMP: 60
SALES (corp-wide): 8MM **Privately Held**
SIC: 7011 3444 Hotels & motels; sheet metalwork
PA: Norstar Aluminum Molds, Inc.
W66622 Madison Ave
Cedarburg WI 53012
262 375-5600

(G-14400)
NORTH COAST SALES
15200 Madison Rd 101c (44062-9429)
P.O. Box 157 (44062-0157)
PHONE..................440 632-0793
Bonnie Vaughan, *Owner*
James Vaughan III, *Owner*
EMP: 50
SALES (est): 1.3MM **Privately Held**
SIC: 7349 Janitorial service, contract basis

(G-14401)
RAVENWOOD MENTAL HEALTH CENTER
16030 E High St (44062-9474)
P.O. Box 246 (44062-0246)
PHONE..................440 632-5355
Dave Boyle, *Branch Mgr*
Karen Podojil, *Manager*
EMP: 50
SALES (corp-wide): 7.4MM **Privately Held**
SIC: 8093 Mental health clinic, outpatient
PA: Ravenwood Mental Health Center, Inc.
12557 Ravenwood Dr
Chardon OH 44024
440 285-3568

(G-14402)
SANTAS HIDE AWAY HOLLOW INC
15400 Bundysburg Rd (44062-8437)
PHONE..................440 632-5000
William Dietdrle, *Exec Dir*
EMP: 47
SALES: 50.7K **Privately Held**
SIC: 8351 Child day care services

(G-14403)
THE MIDDLEFIELD BANKING CO (HQ)
15985 E High St (44062-7229)
P.O. Box 35 (44062-0035)
PHONE..................440 632-1666
Fax: 440 632-0531
Carolyn J Turk, *Ch of Bd*
Tom Caldwell, *President*
Charles O Moore, *President*
Eric P Hollinger, *Senior VP*
Tom Parker, *Assistant VP*
EMP: 25 EST: 1901
SQ FT: 2,500
SALES: 34MM
SALES (corp-wide): 48.8MM **Publicly Held**
WEB: www.middlefieldbank.com
SIC: 6022 State commercial banks
PA: Middlefield Banc Corp.
15985 E High St
Middlefield OH 44062
440 632-1666

(G-14404)
VALLEY TITLE & ESCROW AGENCY
15985 E High St Ste 203 (44062-7229)
P.O. Box 1269 (44062-1269)
PHONE..................440 632-9833
Fax: 440 632-9034
Tom Hedrick, *CFO*
EMP: 30
SALES (est): 616.6K **Privately Held**
SIC: 6541 Title & trust companies

(G-14405)
WHITFORD WOODS CO INC
16192 Bundysburg Rd (44062-8444)
P.O. Box 290, Burton (44021-0290)
PHONE..................440 693-4344
Bill Papenbrock, *President*
EMP: 35
SALES (est): 876.8K **Privately Held**
SIC: 6512 Commercial & industrial building operation

Middleport
Meigs County

(G-14406)
COUNTY OF MEIGS
Also Called: Meigs Cnty Dept Jobs Fmly Svcs
175 Race St (45760-1078)
P.O. Box 191 (45760-0191)
PHONE..................740 992-2117
Fax: 740 992-7500
Michael Swisher, *Manager*
EMP: 50 **Privately Held**
WEB: www.meigsdjfs.net
SIC: 8322 9111 Social service center; county supervisors' & executives' offices
PA: County Of Meigs
100 E 2nd St Rm 201
Pomeroy OH 45769
740 992-5290

(G-14407)
MEIGS CENTER LTD
Also Called: Overbrook Center
333 Page St (45760-1391)
PHONE..................740 992-6472
Fax: 740 992-7406
Charla Brown, *Partner*
David Snyder, *Administration*
EMP: 150
SQ FT: 36,000
SALES (est): 7.8MM **Privately Held**
SIC: 8051 8052 8093 Extended care facility; personal care facility; rehabilitation center, outpatient treatment

(G-14408)
MEIGS LOCAL SCHOOL DISTRICT
Also Called: Rutland Bus Garage
36895 State Route 124 (45760-9717)
PHONE..................740 742-2990
Paul McElroy, *Manager*
EMP: 41
SALES (corp-wide): 16MM **Privately Held**
SIC: 4173 Bus terminal & service facilities
PA: Meigs Local School District
41765 Pomeroy Pike
Pomeroy OH 45769
740 992-5650

(G-14409)
SONS OF UN VTRANS OF CIVIL WAR
600 Grant St (45760-1214)
PHONE..................740 992-6144
James Oiler, *Chief*
James Mourning, *Treasurer*
EMP: 60
SALES (est): 1.7MM **Privately Held**
SIC: 8699 Personal interest organization

Middletown
Butler County

(G-14410)
1440 CORPORATION INC
Also Called: Coldwell Banker
1440 S Breiel Blvd (45044-6791)
PHONE..................513 424-2421
Fax: 513 424-0386
Michael Combs, *President*
Ron Davis, *Vice Pres*
EMP: 34
SALES: 1.5MM **Privately Held**
WEB: www.coldwellbankeroyer.com
SIC: 6531 Real estate agent, residential

(G-14411)
ABILITIES FIRST FOUNDATION (PA)
4710 Timber Trail Dr (45044-5399)
PHONE..................513 423-9496
Fax: 513 423-1717
J Thomas Wheeler, *President*
Elaine Garver, *Vice Pres*
Ray Debrosse, *VP Finance*
Tom Wheeler, *Exec Dir*
Scott Inscho, *Exec Dir*
EMP: 106
SQ FT: 31,200
SALES: 5.5MM **Privately Held**
WEB: www.abilitiesfirst.org
SIC: 8211 8361 8049 8351 School for the retarded; home for the mentally handicapped; physical therapist; child day care services; job training & vocational rehabilitation services; employment agencies

(G-14412)
AK STEEL CORPORATION
1801 Crawford St (45044-4583)
PHONE..................513 425-6541
Fax: 513 425-2302
Bill Cro, *General Mgr*
Bill Cross, *General Mgr*
MO Reed, *General Mgr*
John W Young, *General Mgr*
Stephen W Gilby, *Managing Dir*
EMP: 148 **Publicly Held**
SIC: 8732 Commercial nonphysical research
HQ: Ak Steel Corporation
9227 Centre Pointe Dr
West Chester OH 45069
513 425-4200

(G-14413)
AMIX INC
Also Called: Pleasant Hill Golf Club
6487 Hankins Rd (45044-9712)
PHONE..................513 539-7220
Fax: 513 539-7221
Dennis Meyer, *President*
Curtis L Meyer, *Corp Secy*
Lynn Meyer, *Vice Pres*
EMP: 25
SALES: 850K **Privately Held**
SIC: 7992 Public golf courses

(G-14414)
ATRIUM MEDICAL CENTER
Also Called: Sports Medicine and Spine Ctr
105 Mcknight Dr (45044-4838)
PHONE..................513 420-5013
Ron Hoehn, *Director*
Joanne Morgan, *Pharmacy Dir*
EMP: 30
SALES (corp-wide): 354MM **Privately Held**
SIC: 8062 8049 General medical & surgical hospitals; physical therapist
HQ: Atrium Medical Center
1 Medical Center Dr
Middletown OH 45005
513 424-2111

(G-14415)
BECK DIALYSIS LLC
Also Called: Atrium Dialysis
4421 Roosevelt Blvd Ste D (45044-9024)
PHONE..................513 422-6879
James K Hilger, *-*
EMP: 41
SALES (est): 655.3K **Publicly Held**
SIC: 8092 Kidney dialysis centers
PA: Davita Inc.
2000 16th St
Denver CO 80202

(G-14416)
BELCAN LLC
Also Called: Belcan Staffing Solutions
4490 Marie Dr (45044-6248)
PHONE..................513 217-4562
Kimberly Roberts, *Branch Mgr*
EMP: 749
SALES (corp-wide): 666.9MM **Privately Held**
SIC: 7363 Engineering help service
PA: Belcan, Llc
10200 Anderson Way
Blue Ash OH 45242
513 891-0972

(G-14417)
BENCHMARK MASONRY CONTRACTORS
2924 Cincinnati Dayton Rd (45044-9313)
P.O. Box 976, Miamisburg (45343-0976)
PHONE..................937 228-1225
Fax: 513 705-9162
Stephen R Hester, *President*
Timothy Bibler, *Vice Pres*
Ken Hays, *Vice Pres*
EMP: 80
SALES: 7K **Privately Held**
WEB: www.benchmarkmasonry.com
SIC: 1741 Masonry & other stonework

(G-14418)
BERNS GRNHSE & GRDN CTR INC (PA)
Also Called: Berns Garden Center
825 Greentree Rd (45044-8919)
PHONE..................513 423-5306
Fax: 513 423-6733
Albert Berns, *Ch of Bd*
Cherie Berns, *President*
Greg Berns, *Vice Pres*
Jeff Berns, *Vice Pres*
Vickie Berns, *Vice Pres*
EMP: 25
SALES (est): 9.1MM **Privately Held**
SIC: 5261 0782 5191 Garden supplies & tools; nurseries; landscape contractors; garden supplies

(G-14419)
BROWNS RUN COUNTRY CLUB
6855 Sloebig Rd (45042-9448)
PHONE..................513 423-6291
Fax: 513 423-5510
David Baril, *General Mgr*
Becky Kemplin, *General Mgr*
Todd Dodge, *Superintendent*
Gerg Martin, *Treasurer*
Carol Hipsher, *Manager*
EMP: 52
SALES: 918.6K **Privately Held**
WEB: www.brownsruncc.com
SIC: 7997 Country club, membership

(G-14420)
CHURCH OF GOD RETIREMENT CMNTY
Also Called: Willow Knoll Nursing Center
4400 Vannest Ave (45042-2770)
PHONE..................513 422-5600
Fax: 513 422-6532
West Johnson, *COO*
Gerry Bail, *Human Resources*
Sara Marshall, *Manager*
Dee Allen, *Director*
Pamela Van Nest, *Administration*
EMP: 130
SQ FT: 28,000
SALES (est): 4.5MM **Privately Held**
SIC: 8051 8052 8361 Convalescent home with continuous nursing care; intermediate care facilities; residential care

(G-14421)
COHEN ELECTRONICS INC
Also Called: Cohen Middletown
3110 S Verity Pkwy (45044-7443)
PHONE..................513 425-6911
Amy E Brown, *Principal*
Matt Neal, *Safety Mgr*
Matt O'Shea, *Agent*
Tammy Walling, *Asst Mgr*
David Dellostritto, *Director*
EMP: 99
SALES (est): 4.3MM
SALES (corp-wide): 84.4MM **Privately Held**
SIC: 5093 Ferrous metal scrap & waste
PA: Cohen Brothers, Inc.
1723 Woodlawn Ave
Middletown OH 45044
513 422-3696

(G-14422)
COMPREHENSIVE COUNSELING SVC
1659 S Breiel Blvd Ste A (45044-6705)
PHONE..................513 424-0921
Fax: 513 424-4810
Henry Dorsman, *Director*
Deanna Proctor, *Director*

GEOGRAPHIC SECTION
Middletown - Butler County (G-14447)

EMP: 45
SALES (est): 1.3MM **Privately Held**
WEB: www.comprehensivecounselingservice.com
SIC: 8093 Mental health clinic, outpatient

(G-14423)
CSX TRANSPORTATION INC
1003 Forrer St (45044-7516)
PHONE.................513 422-2031
Fax: 513 422-1449
Pat Henry, *Branch Mgr*
Jerry Hughes, *Manager*
EMP: 25
SALES (corp-wide): 11.4B **Publicly Held**
WEB: www.csxt.com
SIC: 4011 Railroads, line-haul operating
HQ: Csx Transportation, Inc.
 500 Water St
 Jacksonville FL 32202
 904 359-3100

(G-14424)
DOMINGUEZ INC
125 Park St (45044-4025)
P.O. Box 693, Springboro (45066-0693)
PHONE.................513 425-9955
Frank Dominguez, *President*
Francisco Dominguez, *Corp Secy*
Luz M Dominguez, *Treasurer*
EMP: 30
SALES (est): 4.4MM **Privately Held**
WEB: www.dominguezinc.net
SIC: 1752 Carpet laying; ceramic floor tile installation; wood floor installation & refinishing

(G-14425)
ELLIOTT AUTO BATH INC
901 Elliott Dr (45044-6213)
PHONE.................513 422-3700
Fax: 513 422-3700
Patrice Drury, *President*
EMP: 26
SQ FT: 5,200
SALES (est): 100K **Privately Held**
SIC: 7542 Carwash, automatic

(G-14426)
GARDEN MANOR EXTENDED CARE CEN
6898 Hmlton Middletown Rd (45044-7851)
PHONE.................513 420-5972
Fax: 513 420-5489
Sam Boymel, *President*
Gidon Eldad, *Vice Pres*
Peggy Morris, *Vice Pres*
Rachel Boymel, *Treasurer*
Judy Maple, *Director*
EMP: 250
SQ FT: 10,000
SALES: 14.8MM **Privately Held**
SIC: 8051 8361 Convalescent home with continuous nursing care; residential care

(G-14427)
HART INDUSTRIES INC (PA)
Also Called: Hart Industrial Products Div
931 Jeanette St (45044-5701)
PHONE.................513 541-4278
Herman E Hart, *CEO*
Roger Hart, *President*
Daniel Sucher, *General Mgr*
Joseph Debacker, *Opers Mgr*
Christopher Hart, *Treasurer*
▲ **EMP:** 34 **EST:** 1966
SQ FT: 47,000
SALES (est): 34.8MM **Privately Held**
WEB: www.hose.com
SIC: 5085 Hose, belting & packing; rubber goods, mechanical

(G-14428)
HOSPICE OF MIDDLETOWN
3909 Central Ave (45044-5006)
PHONE.................513 424-2273
Fax: 513 424-0283
Rose Fromer, *Manager*
Amy Lindon, *Manager*
EMP: 35
SALES: 1.8MM **Privately Held**
SIC: 8069 Specialty hospitals, except psychiatric

(G-14429)
INTERSCOPE MANUFACTURING INC
2901 Carmody Blvd (45042-1761)
PHONE.................513 423-8866
Fax: 513 423-5065
John Michael Brill, *CEO*
Robert Conrad, *General Mgr*
◆ **EMP:** 50
SQ FT: 175,000
SALES (est): 6.6MM **Privately Held**
WEB: www.interscopemfg.com
SIC: 3599 7389 Custom machinery; repossession service

(G-14430)
J P TRANSPORTATION COMPANY
2518 Oxford State Rd (45044-8909)
PHONE.................513 424-6978
Fax: 513 423-8943
Kenneth Henderson, *President*
Donald Henderson, *Vice Pres*
EMP: 45
SQ FT: 3,200
SALES (est): 4.9MM **Privately Held**
SIC: 4213 4212 Contract haulers; local trucking, without storage

(G-14431)
LOWES HOME CENTERS LLC
3125 Towne Blvd (45044-6299)
PHONE.................513 727-3900
Fax: 513 727-3914
Josh Crumrine, *Manager*
EMP: 150
SALES (corp-wide): 68.6B **Publicly Held**
SIC: 5211 5031 5722 5064 Home centers; building materials, exterior; building materials, interior; household appliance stores; electrical appliances, television & radio
HQ: Lowe's Home Centers, Llc
 1605 Curtis Bridge Rd
 Wilkesboro NC 28697
 336 658-4000

(G-14432)
MAINTENANCE & REPAIR TECH INC
Also Called: M R T
408 Vanderveer St (45044-4239)
PHONE.................513 422-1198
Talbert Selby, *President*
Tal Selby, *President*
David Poe, *Vice Pres*
Roni Stasaitis, *Opers Staff*
Dawn Hail, *Controller*
EMP: 25
SQ FT: 25,000
SALES (est): 3.7MM **Privately Held**
SIC: 7699 Industrial machinery & equipment repair

(G-14433)
MARTIN GREG EXCAVATING INC
1501 S University Blvd (45044-5967)
PHONE.................513 727-9300
Fax: 513 727-8325
Gregory L Martin, *President*
Rebecca Martin, *Corp Secy*
Herbert Martin, *Vice Pres*
EMP: 36
SQ FT: 27,500
SALES (est): 5.3MM **Privately Held**
SIC: 1794 Excavation & grading, building construction

(G-14434)
MECCO INC
2100 S Main St (45044-7345)
PHONE.................513 422-3651
Fax: 513 422-8746
David T Morgan, *President*
Charles E Morgan, *Vice Pres*
Bill Perry, *Vice Pres*
Ron Price, *Vice Pres*
Stephen Rains, *Treasurer*
EMP: 45 **EST:** 1956
SQ FT: 2,000
SALES (est): 4.3MM **Privately Held**
WEB: www.meccoconcrete.com
SIC: 3273 1442 Ready-mixed concrete; construction sand mining; gravel mining

(G-14435)
MIAMI UNIVERSITY
Also Called: Miami University-Middletown
4200 E University Blvd (45042)
PHONE.................513 727-3200
Fax: 513 727-3223
Kelly Cowan, *Exec Dir*
Anthony Rose, *Professor*
Ted Light, *Assoc Prof*
Amy Weeks, *Nurse Practr*
Deborah Ulrich,
EMP: 350
SALES (corp-wide): 544.5MM **Privately Held**
WEB: www.muohio.edu
SIC: 8221 8742 8331 University; training & development consultant; job training services
PA: Miami University
 501 E High St
 Oxford OH 45056
 513 529-1809

(G-14436)
MIDDLETOWN CITY DIVISON FIRE
2300 Roosevelt Blvd (45044-4741)
PHONE.................513 425-7996
Fax: 513 425-1820
John Sauter, *Chief*
Susan Woodrome, *Financial Analy*
EMP: 84
SALES (est): 1.6MM **Privately Held**
SIC: 0851 Fire fighting services, forest

(G-14437)
MIDDLETOWN SCHOOL VHCL SVC CTR
2951 Cincinnati Dayton Rd (45044-9313)
PHONE.................513 420-4568
Thelma Hacker, *Principal*
Michael Hammond, *Manager*
EMP: 70
SALES (est): 1.4MM **Privately Held**
SIC: 4151 School buses

(G-14438)
MIDDLTOWN AREA SENIOR CITIZENS
3907 Central Ave (45044-5006)
PHONE.................513 423-1734
Ralph Conner, *President*
Alesia Childress, *President*
Basil Fleming, *President*
Alicia Chambers, *Exec Dir*
EMP: 54 **EST:** 1956
SQ FT: 22,000
SALES (est): 2.2MM **Privately Held**
WEB: www.middletownohioseniors.org
SIC: 8322 Senior citizens' center or association

(G-14439)
MIDDLTOWN CRDVSCULAR ASSOC INC
103 Mcknight Dr Ste A (45044-4891)
PHONE.................513 217-6400
Thomas D Anthony, *President*
EMP: 38
SALES (est): 6.5MM **Privately Held**
SIC: 8011 Cardiologist & cardio-vascular specialist

(G-14440)
MIDUSA CREDIT UNION (PA)
1201 Crawford St (45044-4575)
PHONE.................513 420-8640
Fax: 513 420-8834
Chris Johnson, *President*
Kelly Nugent, *Vice Pres*
EMP: 40
SQ FT: 6,000
SALES (est): 7MM **Privately Held**
WEB: www.midfirstcu.org
SIC: 6062 State credit unions, not federally chartered

(G-14441)
MOOSE INTERNATIONAL INC
Also Called: Moose Fmly Ctr 501 Middletown
3009 S Main St (45044-7418)
PHONE.................513 422-6776
Fax: 513 423-0898
Jerry Gabbard, *Administration*
EMP: 47
SALES (corp-wide): 48.4MM **Privately Held**
WEB: www.thalist.com
SIC: 8641 Fraternal associations
PA: Moose International, Incorporated
 155 S International Dr
 Mooseheart IL 60539
 630 859-2000

(G-14442)
NORTHWESTRN NATL INSUR COMPANY
709 Curtis St (45044-5812)
PHONE.................513 425-5899
Ernest J Blache Jr, *President*
John Allare, *Vice Pres*
Seitz Thomas W, *Vice Pres*
James Stephens, *Treasurer*
EMP: 26 **EST:** 1869
SALES (est): 6.1MM **Privately Held**
SIC: 6331 Fire, marine & casualty insurance: stock

(G-14443)
NORVELL LANDSCAPING INC
218 Old Oxford St Rd (45044)
PHONE.................513 423-9009
Jill South, *Manager*
EMP: 30
SALES (corp-wide): 2.7MM **Privately Held**
WEB: www.norvellslandscaping.com
SIC: 0781 5261 Landscape services; nurseries & garden centers
PA: Norvell Landscaping Inc
 218 Oxford State Rd
 Middletown OH 45044
 513 422-3533

(G-14444)
NU WAVES LTD
Also Called: Nuwaves Engineering
132 Edison Dr (45044-3269)
PHONE.................513 360-0800
Fax: 513 360-0888
Jeffrey Wells, *President*
Mike Trimble, *General Mgr*
Timothy Wurth, *Vice Pres*
Ben Thomas, *Opers Staff*
Sakada Sleng, *Production*
EMP: 64 **EST:** 2003
SQ FT: 30,200
SALES (est): 13.4MM **Privately Held**
WEB: www.nuwaves-ltd.com
SIC: 8711 Electrical or electronic engineering

(G-14445)
OHIO TRANSMISSION CORPORATION
Also Called: Otp Industrial Solutions
400 Wright Dr (45044-3263)
PHONE.................513 539-8411
Steve Nimmo, *Accounts Mgr*
Dan Acuna, *Sales Executive*
Susan Davidson, *Office Mgr*
EMP: 26 **Privately Held**
WEB: www.otpnet.com
SIC: 5084 Industrial machinery & equipment
HQ: Ohio Transmission Corporation
 1900 Jetway Blvd
 Columbus OH 43219
 614 342-6247

(G-14446)
OHIO TRANSPORT CORPORATION (PA)
5593 Hmlton Middletown Rd (45044-9703)
PHONE.................513 539-0576
William C Hill, *President*
Chad Hill, *Corp Secy*
EMP: 52
SQ FT: 3,000
SALES (est): 10.1MM **Privately Held**
SIC: 4212 Local trucking, without storage

(G-14447)
ORTHOPDIC SPT MDICINE CONS INC
275 N Breiel Blvd (45042-3807)
PHONE.................513 777-7714
Jerry B Magone MD, *President*
Ray E Kiefhaber, *Principal*
Betty Barnett, *CFO*

Middletown - Butler County (G-14448)

Alice Flinn, *Office Mgr*
M S True MD, *Med Doctor*
EMP: 30
SQ FT: 12,000
SALES (est): 5.6MM **Privately Held**
WEB: www.ortho-sportsmed.com
SIC: 8011 Orthopedic physician; surgeon

(G-14448)
PAC WORLDWIDE CORPORATION
Also Called: Pac Manufacturing
3131 Cincinnati Dayton Rd (45044-8965)
PHONE.................................800 610-9367
Fax: 513 933-9744
Bruce Johnson, *Manager*
EMP: 77 **Privately Held**
SIC: 5112 2677 Envelopes; envelopes
HQ: Pac Worldwide Corporation
15435 Ne 92nd St
Redmond WA 98052
425 202-4000

(G-14449)
PHOENIX CORPORATION
Also Called: Phoenix Metals
1211 Hook Dr (45042-1713)
PHONE.................................513 727-4763
Mike Gara, *Principal*
Chad Davis, *Supervisor*
EMP: 36
SALES (corp-wide): 9.7B **Publicly Held**
SIC: 5051 Steel
HQ: Phoenix Corporation
4685 Buford Hwy
Peachtree Corners GA 30071
770 447-4211

(G-14450)
PRECISION STRIP INC
4400 Oxford State Rd (45044-8914)
PHONE.................................513 423-4166
Fax: 513 423-1617
Darren Wolf, *Branch Mgr*
EMP: 85
SALES (corp-wide): 9.7B **Publicly Held**
WEB: www.precision-strip.com
SIC: 7389 Metal slitting & shearing
HQ: Precision Strip Inc.
86 S Ohio St
Minster OH 45865
419 628-2343

(G-14451)
PREMIER RSTRTION MECH SVCS LLC
2890 S Main St (45044-2800)
P.O. Box 8286, Franklin (45005-8286)
PHONE.................................513 420-1600
Jennifer Brown, *Principal*
EMP: 28
SALES (est): 5.5MM **Privately Held**
SIC: 1711 Mechanical contractor

(G-14452)
PREMIER SYSTEM INTEGRATORS INC
2660 Towne Blvd (45044-8986)
PHONE.................................513 217-7294
EMP: 73 **Privately Held**
SIC: 4813
PA: Premier System Integrators, Inc.
140 Weakley Ln
Smyrna TN 37167

(G-14453)
RITTENHOUSE
3000 Mcgee Ave (45044-4991)
PHONE.................................513 423-2322
Lisa Rice, *Exec Dir*
Lisa Minera, *Exec Dir*
EMP: 37
SQ FT: 4,800
SALES: 746.4K **Privately Held**
WEB: www.mcknightterrace.com
SIC: 8059 Personal care home, with health care

(G-14454)
RMB ENTERPRISES INC
2742 Oxford State Rd (45044-8911)
PHONE.................................513 539-3431
Fax: 513 539-4544
Bill Bowling, *President*
Don Bowling, *Vice Pres*

Michelle Cherry, *Purch Mgr*
EMP: 100
SALES (est): 7.6MM **Privately Held**
SIC: 4214 Local trucking with storage

(G-14455)
ROBINSON HTG AIR-CONDITIONING
1208 2nd Ave (45044-4210)
PHONE.................................513 422-6812
Fax: 513 422-3697
Stuart Robinson, *President*
Zereda Robinson, *Vice Pres*
Zereda Vega, *Technology*
EMP: 27
SQ FT: 4,000
SALES (est): 4.5MM **Privately Held**
WEB: www.robinsonheating.com
SIC: 1711 1731 Heating & air conditioning contractors; electrical work

(G-14456)
SAWYER REALTORS
1505 S Breiel Blvd (45044-6703)
PHONE.................................513 423-6521
Fax: 513 423-2388
John Sawyer, *Owner*
EMP: 27
SALES (est): 1.1MM **Privately Held**
WEB: www.sawyerrealtors.com
SIC: 6552 6531 Subdividers & developers; real estate agents & managers

(G-14457)
SEMMA ENTERPRISES INC
Also Called: Hawthorn Glenn Nursing Center
5414 Hankins Rd (45044-9782)
PHONE.................................513 863-7775
Paul Depalma, *President*
Brain Gibbony, *Vice Pres*
Jacqueline Depalma, *Admin Sec*
EMP: 150
SALES (est): 2.8MM **Privately Held**
WEB: www.hawthornglennc.com
SIC: 8051 Skilled nursing care facilities

(G-14458)
SOUTHWEST OHIO AMBLATRY SRGERY
295 N Breiel Blvd (45042-3807)
PHONE.................................513 425-0930
Fax: 513 425-0960
Eugene D Herrmann, *President*
Jerry Magone, *Vice Pres*
Gary Cobb, *Treasurer*
Jeffrey Nicolai, *Administration*
EMP: 38
SQ FT: 11,500
SALES (est): 4.7MM **Privately Held*
WEB: www.magone.com
SIC: 8011 Ambulatory surgical center

(G-14459)
SSI FABRICATED INC
2860 Cincinnati Dayton Rd (45044-8902)
PHONE.................................513 217-3535
Fax: 513 727-8338
Richard Hall, *President*
Joel K Elkin, *Principal*
Mark Franks, *Vice Pres*
Jon Cooke, *Project Mgr*
Dave Branscum, *Prdtn Mgr*
EMP: 33
SQ FT: 6,000
SALES (est): 7.5MM **Privately Held**
WEB: www.steamsystems.com
SIC: 7699 5074 Industrial equipment services; heating equipment (hydronic)

(G-14460)
STANDARD LABORATORIES INC
2601 S Verity Pkwy (45044-7482)
PHONE.................................513 422-1088
Joy Wright, *Branch Mgr*
EMP: 28
SALES (corp-wide): 68.2MM **Privately Held**
SIC: 8734 Product testing laboratories
PA: Standard Laboratories, Inc.
147 11th Ave Ste 100
South Charleston WV 25303
304 744-6800

(G-14461)
STERICYCLE INC
4495 Salzman Rd (45044-9709)
PHONE.................................513 539-6213
Mike Cavanaugh, *Principal*
EMP: 36
SALES (corp-wide): 3.5B **Publicly Held**
SIC: 4953 Medical waste disposal
PA: Stericycle, Inc.
28161 N Keith Dr
Lake Forest IL 60045
847 367-5910

(G-14462)
STEVE S TOWING AND RECOVERY
6475 Trenton Franklin Rd (45042-1749)
PHONE.................................513 422-0254
Steve Gebhradt, *Principal*
EMP: 50
SALES (est): 1MM **Privately Held**
SIC: 7549 Towing service, automotive

(G-14463)
SUNCOKE ENERGY NC
Also Called: Mto Suncoke
3353 Yankee Rd (45044-8927)
PHONE.................................513 727-5571
Frederick Fritz A Henderson, *CEO*
Dovie Majors, *Opers Mgr*
David O'Brien, *Manager*
Tracy Laxton, *Director*
EMP: 40
SALES (est): 5.4MM **Privately Held**
SIC: 1241 Coal mining services

(G-14464)
SUPER SHINE INC
1549 S Breiel Blvd Ste A (45044-6861)
P.O. Box 146 (45042-0146)
PHONE.................................513 423-8999
Fax: 513 705-8999
Marsha Giltrow, *President*
EMP: 35
SALES: 500K **Privately Held**
SIC: 7349 7363 Janitorial service, contract basis; domestic help service

(G-14465)
SWAN SALES
Also Called: Tonys Pizza Service
2910 Oxford State Rd (45044-8916)
PHONE.................................513 422-3100
Marvin Schwann, *President*
Clay Thurman, *Manager*
EMP: 50
SALES (est): 3.8MM **Privately Held**
SIC: 5149 Pizza supplies

(G-14466)
TERMINIX INTL CO LTD PARTNR
4455 Salman Rd (45044)
PHONE.................................513 539-7846
Terry Perrine, *Financial Exec*
Don Dunn, *Branch Mgr*
EMP: 29
SALES (corp-wide): 2.9B **Publicly Held**
SIC: 7342 7389 Pest control services; termite control; air pollution measuring service
HQ: The Terminix International Company Limited Partnership
860 Ridge Lake Blvd A3-4008
Memphis TN 38120
901 766-1400

(G-14467)
TERMINIX INTL COML XENIA
4455 Salzman Rd (45044-9709)
PHONE.................................513 539-7846
Kathy Fitzgerald, *Principal*
EMP: 48
SALES (est): 1.1MM **Privately Held**
SIC: 7342 Pest control in structures

(G-14468)
TOMSON STEEL COMPANY
1400 Made Industrial Dr (45044-8936)
P.O. Box 940 (45044-0940)
PHONE.................................513 420-8600
Fax: 513 420-8610
Stephen Lutz, *President*
Larry L Knapp, *Principal*
Thomas Lutz, *Vice Pres*
Steve Reynolds, *Plant Mgr*

James Strok, *VP Sales*
EMP: 25
SQ FT: 94,000
SALES (est): 22.6MM **Privately Held**
WEB: www.tomsonsteel.com
SIC: 5051 3291 Steel; abrasive metal & steel products

(G-14469)
TOPMIND/PLANEX CONSTRUCTION
831 Elliott Dr (45044-6211)
PHONE.................................248 719-0474
EMP: 35
SALES: 950K **Privately Held**
SIC: 1522 Residential Construction Contractor

(G-14470)
WELLS FARGO BANK NATIONAL ASSN
1076 Summitt Dr (45042-3400)
PHONE.................................513 424-6640
Lou Christy, *Branch Mgr*
EMP: 84
SALES (corp-wide): 97.7B **Publicly Held**
SIC: 6021 National commercial banks
HQ: Wells Fargo Bank, N.A.
101 N Phillips Ave Ste A
Sioux Falls SD 57104
605 575-6900

(G-14471)
WMVH LLC
Also Called: Weatherwax
4616 Manchester Rd (45042-3818)
PHONE.................................513 425-7886
Jim T Kraft, *Mng Member*
EMP: 60
SALES (est): 376.5K **Privately Held**
SIC: 7992 Public golf courses

Middletown
Warren County

(G-14472)
ACCESS COUNSELING SERVICES LLC
4464 S Dixie Hwy (45005-5464)
PHONE.................................513 649-8008
Deanna L Proctor,
Debra Cotter,
Judith Freeland,
Lynn Harris,
EMP: 101
SALES (est): 2.6MM **Privately Held**
SIC: 8322 General counseling services

(G-14473)
ATRIUM HEALTH SYSTEM (HQ)
1 Medical Center Dr (45005-2584)
PHONE.................................937 499-5606
Mike Uhl, *President*
EMP: 1502
SALES (est): 217.8MM
SALES (corp-wide): 354MM **Privately Held**
SIC: 8082 Home health care services
PA: Premier Health Partners
110 N Main St Ste 450
Dayton OH 45402
937 499-9596

(G-14474)
ATRIUM MEDICAL CENTER
1 Medical Center Dr (45005-1066)
PHONE.................................937 499-9596
Carol Turner, *President*
EMP: 1600
SALES: 233MM **Privately Held**
SIC: 8099 Blood related health services

(G-14475)
BARRETT PAVING MATERIALS INC
3751 Commerce Dr (45005-5234)
PHONE.................................513 271-6200
Fax: 937 279-3205
Jerry Bushelman, *Division Mgr*
Rod Russell, *Regional Mgr*
Tony Strete, *Financial Exec*
Anthony Strete, *Human Res Dir*

Janice Misch, *Human Res Mgr*
EMP: 200
SALES (corp-wide): 95.5MM **Privately Held**
WEB: www.barrettpaving.com
SIC: 5032 2951 1771 1611 Asphalt mixture; asphalt paving mixtures & blocks; driveway, parking lot & blacktop contractors; surfacing & paving; construction sand & gravel
HQ: Barrett Paving Materials Inc.
3 Becker Farm Rd Ste 307
Roseland NJ 07068
973 533-1001

(G-14476)
CBL & ASSOCIATES PRPTS INC
Also Called: Towne Mall
3461 Towne Blvd Unit 200 (45005-5533)
PHONE..........513 424-8517
Kelly Askine, *Manager*
EMP: 30 **Publicly Held**
WEB: www.yorkgalleriamall.com
SIC: 6512 Shopping center, property operation only
PA: Cbl & Associates Properties, Inc.
2030 Hamilton Place Blvd
Chattanooga TN 37421

(G-14477)
CELLCO PARTNERSHIP
Also Called: Verizon Wireless
3663 Towne Blvd (45005-5516)
PHONE..........513 422-3437
Fax: 513 422-3803
EMP: 76
SALES (corp-wide): 126B **Publicly Held**
SIC: 4812 Cellular telephone services
HQ: Cellco Partnership
1 Verizon Way
Basking Ridge NJ 07920

(G-14478)
ERMC II LP
Also Called: Towne Mall
3461 Towne Blvd Unit 250 (45005-5555)
PHONE..........513 424-8517
Emerson Russell, *Manager*
Dee Florence, *Manager*
EMP: 30 **Privately Held**
WEB: www.ermc2.com
SIC: 7349 Lighting maintenance service
PA: Ermc Ii, L.P.
1 Park Pl 6148
Chattanooga TN 37421

(G-14479)
GREAT MIAMI VALLEY YMCA
5750 Innovation Dr (45005-5172)
PHONE..........513 217-5501
Donna Keith, *Director*
EMP: 85
SALES (corp-wide): 13.3MM **Privately Held**
SIC: 8641 Youth organizations
PA: Great Miami Valley Ymca
105 N 2nd St
Hamilton OH 45011
513 887-0001

(G-14480)
HIGHTOWERS PETROLEUM COMPANY
3577 Commerce Dr (45005-5232)
PHONE..........513 423-4272
Steve Hightower Sr, *CEO*
Yudell Hightower, *Vice Pres*
Tracey Bunch, *Pub Rel Mgr*
Gary Visher, *CFO*
John Milliron, *VP Sales*
EMP: 50
SQ FT: 4,400
SALES: 308MM **Privately Held**
WEB: www.hightowerspetroleum.com
SIC: 5172 Diesel fuel; gasoline

(G-14481)
JUSTIN L PAULK
Also Called: Facility Svcs & Maint Systems
3641 Commerce Dr (45005-5215)
P.O. Box 941 (45044-0941)
PHONE..........513 422-7060
Justin L Paulk, *Owner*
David Bollinger, *Manager*
EMP: 58
SQ FT: 2,200
SALES: 500K **Privately Held**
SIC: 7349 Janitorial service, contract basis

(G-14482)
MIDUSA CREDIT UNION
3600 Towne Blvd Ste A (45005-5543)
PHONE..........513 420-8640
Christopher Johnson, *CEO*
EMP: 30
SQ FT: 56,744
SALES (corp-wide): 7MM **Privately Held**
WEB: www.midfirstcu.org
SIC: 6062 State credit unions
PA: Midusa Credit Union
1201 Crawford St
Middletown OH 45044
513 420-8640

(G-14483)
OTTERBEIN SNIOR LFSTYLE CHICES
105 Atrium Dr (45005-5166)
PHONE..........513 260-7690
EMP: 146
SALES (corp-wide): 43.8MM **Privately Held**
SIC: 8361 8059 8051 Home for the aged; nursing home, except skilled & intermediate care facility; skilled nursing care facilities
PA: Senior Otterbein Lifestyle Choices
585 N State Route 741
Lebanon OH 45036
513 933-5400

(G-14484)
PAYCHEX INC
3420 Atrium Blvd Ste 200 (45005-5186)
PHONE..........513 727-9182
Marcia Paulick, *President*
EMP: 37
SALES (corp-wide): 3.1B **Publicly Held**
SIC: 8721 Payroll accounting service
PA: Paychex, Inc.
911 Panorama Trl S
Rochester NY 14625
585 385-6666

(G-14485)
PIERSON AUTOMOTIVE INC
Also Called: Guyler Automotive
3456 S Dixie Hwy (45005-5718)
PHONE..........513 424-1881
Fax: 513 424-6186
Brenda Pierson, *President*
J Michael Guyler, *President*
Jennifer James, *VP Finance*
Bill Mues, *Sales Mgr*
EMP: 40
SQ FT: 30,000
SALES (est): 14.3MM **Privately Held**
SIC: 5511 7538 7532 Automobiles, new & used; trucks, tractors & trailers: new & used; general automotive repair shops; top & body repair & paint shops

(G-14486)
PRIMARY CR NTWRK PRMR HLTH PRT
Also Called: Anne Camm, Psy.d., Company
1 Medical Center Dr (45005-2584)
PHONE..........513 420-5233
Christopher Danis, *CEO*
EMP: 32
SALES (corp-wide): 33.7MM **Privately Held**
SIC: 8011 General & family practice, physician/surgeon
PA: Primary Care Network Of Premier Health Partners
110 N Main St Ste 350
Dayton OH 45402
937 226-7085

(G-14487)
SPRINGHILLS LLC
Also Called: Spring Hills At Middletown
3851 Towne Blvd (45005-5595)
PHONE..........513 424-9999
Toni Allen, *Financial Exec*
Charlene Himes, *Manager*
EMP: 61 **Privately Held**
SIC: 8051 Skilled nursing care facilities
PA: Springhills Llc
515 Plainfield Ave
Edison NJ 08817

(G-14488)
UCC CHILDRENS CENTER
Also Called: Y M C A
5750 Innovation Dr (45005-5172)
PHONE..........513 217-5501
Donna Keith, *Director*
EMP: 35
SALES: 400K **Privately Held**
SIC: 8641 7991 8351 7032 Youth organizations; physical fitness facilities; child day care services; youth camps; individual & family services

Midvale
Tuscarawas County

(G-14489)
AMKO SERVICE COMPANY (HQ)
Also Called: Dover Cryogenics
3211 Brightwood Rd (44653)
P.O. Box 280 (44653-0280)
PHONE..........330 364-8857
Darren Nippard, *President*
Duane R Yant, *Principal*
Tim Johnson, *Purch Mgr*
Gordon Wheating, *Purchasing*
Andrew Lee, *Manager*
▲ **EMP:** 50
SALES (est): 6.4MM
SALES (corp-wide): 11.4B **Publicly Held**
SIC: 7699 3443 7629 Tank repair & cleaning services; cryogenic tanks, for liquids & gases; electrical repair shops
PA: Praxair, Inc.
10 Riverview Dr
Danbury CT 06810
203 837-2000

(G-14490)
HYDRAULIC SPECIALISTS INC
5655 Gundy Dr (44653)
PHONE..........740 922-3343
Dale Burkholder, *President*
Laraine Burkholder, *Corp Secy*
EMP: 25
SQ FT: 15,000
SALES (est): 3.7MM **Privately Held**
SIC: 3443 7699 3593 Industrial vessels, tanks & containers; hydraulic equipment repair; fluid power cylinders & actuators

(G-14491)
TRUCK SALES LEASING INC (PA)
Also Called: Canton Truck Sales and Service
3429 Brightwood Rd (44653)
P.O. Box 262 (44653-0262)
PHONE..........330 343-5581
Fred Bollon, *President*
Herman C Bahler, *Principal*
Rodney Rafael, *Vice Pres*
Michael Murphy, *Financial Exec*
▼ **EMP:** 30
SQ FT: 2,000
SALES (est): 6.5MM **Privately Held**
SIC: 7513 Truck leasing, without drivers

Milan
Erie County

(G-14492)
BELLEVUE FOUR CNTY EMS N CENTL
Also Called: Ems Service
12513 Us Highway 250 N (44846-9546)
PHONE..........419 483-3322
Don Ballah, *Director*
EMP: 150
SALES (est): 1.9MM **Privately Held**
WEB: www.emsservice.com
SIC: 4119 Ambulance service

(G-14493)
COUNTY OF ERIE
Erie County Dept Envmtl Svcs
10102 Hoover Rd (44846-9711)
PHONE..........419 433-0617
Fax: 419 433-6214
Jack R Meyers, *Director*
EMP: 59 **Privately Held**
WEB: www.gem.org
SIC: 4953 9111 Sanitary landfill operation; county supervisors' & executives' offices
PA: County Of Erie
2900 Columbus Ave
Sandusky OH 44870
419 627-7682

(G-14494)
FREUDENBERG-NOK GENERAL PARTNR
Transtec
11617 State Re 13 (44846)
P.O. Box 556 (44846-0556)
PHONE..........419 499-2502
Fax: 419 499-2438
David B Gardner, *President*
Robert Evans, *Vice Pres*
Doug Hints, *Opers Mgr*
Karry Kirchner, *Opers Mgr*
Eric Ward, *Materials Mgr*
EMP: 300
SALES (corp-wide): 8.3B **Privately Held**
WEB: www.freudenberg-nok.com
SIC: 7389 5013 Packaging & labeling services; automotive supplies & parts
HQ: Freudenberg-Nok General Partnership
47774 W Anchor Ct
Plymouth MI 48170
734 451-0020

(G-14495)
NORWALK AREA HEALTH SERVICES
Also Called: North Central Ems
12513 State Route 250 (44846-9546)
PHONE..........419 499-2515
Fax: 440 967-2664
Lisa Wildman, *Exec Dir*
Donald Ballah, *Director*
Ashley Ballah, *Director*
Jason Maurer, *Director*
EMP: 150
SALES (corp-wide): 1.5MM **Privately Held**
SIC: 4119 Ambulance service
HQ: Norwalk Area Health Services
272 Benedict Ave
Norwalk OH 44857

(G-14496)
OLDE TOWNE WINDOWS INC
Also Called: Old Towne Windows & Doors
9501 Us Highway 250 N # 1 (44846-9377)
PHONE..........419 626-9613
Fax: 419 626-9611
Charles Hemker, *Vice Pres*
Lisa Hemker, *Treasurer*
Joyce Swint, *Admin Sec*
EMP: 40
SQ FT: 28,000
SALES (est): 6.3MM **Privately Held**
WEB: www.oldetownewindows.com
SIC: 5211 5031 5039 1761 Door & window products; windows; glass construction materials; siding contractor; patio & deck construction & repair

(G-14497)
PACKAGING & PADS R US LLC (PA)
12406 Us Highway 250 N C (44846-9382)
PHONE..........419 499-2905
Harry Perdue Jr, *President*
Lisa Brownell, *Corp Secy*
Sharon Berger, *Administration*
EMP: 30
SQ FT: 40,000
SALES: 6.6MM **Privately Held**
SIC: 5199 Packaging materials

(G-14498)
PRECISION PAVING INC
3414 State Route 113 E (44846-9426)
PHONE..........419 499-7283
Fax: 419 499-7284
Mike Kegarise, *President*
Matt Kluding, *Corp Secy*
Jeff Crecelius, *Vice Pres*
EMP: 33
SQ FT: 10,000
SALES (est): 5.4MM **Privately Held**
WEB: www.precisionpaving.com
SIC: 1611 Surfacing & paving

Milan - Erie County (G-14499)

(G-14499)
SCHLESSMAN SEED CO (PA)
11513 Us Highway 250 N (44846-9708)
PHONE.................................419 499-2572
Fax: 419 499-2574
Daryl Deering, *Ch of Bd*
David Schlessman, *CFO*
Dave Herzer, *Treasurer*
Mark Skaggs, *Controller*
Arthur Schlessman,
EMP: 25
SQ FT: 100,000
SALES (est): 23.5MM Privately Held
WEB: www.schlessman-seed.com
SIC: 5191 2075 0723 0116 Seeds: field, garden & flower; soybean oil mills; crop preparation services for market; soybeans; corn; wheat

(G-14500)
XPO LOGISTICS FREIGHT INC
12518 State Route 250 (44846-9540)
PHONE.................................419 499-8888
Fax: 419 499-9114
Jeffrey Mount, *Manager*
EMP: 50
SALES (corp-wide): 15.3B Publicly Held
WEB: www.con-way.com
SIC: 4213 Contract haulers
HQ: Xpo Logistics Freight, Inc.
2211 Old Earhart Rd # 100
Ann Arbor MI 48105
734 998-4200

Milford
Clermont County

(G-14501)
ALBRECHT INC (PA)
Also Called: Albrecht & Company
1040 Techne Center Dr (45150-2731)
PHONE.................................513 576-9900
Fax: 513 576-8517
Vera Muzzillo, *CEO*
Brian Smith, *President*
Carl Albrecht, *General Mgr*
Pam Paeltz, *Regional Mgr*
Tom Rizzi, *Senior VP*
▲ EMP: 25
SQ FT: 6,500
SALES (est): 17.3MM Privately Held
WEB: www.albrechtcompany.com
SIC: 5199 Candy making goods & supplies

(G-14502)
AMBULATORY MEDICAL CARE INC (PA)
Also Called: Doctor's Urgent Care Offices
935 State Route 28 (45150-1957)
PHONE.................................513 831-8555
Fax: 513 831-5985
Paul J Amrhein, *President*
Dean Judkins, *President*
Paul Amrhein, *Exec VP*
Tabatha Ealey, *Office Mgr*
EMP: 170
SQ FT: 6,000
SALES (est): 25.9MM Privately Held
WEB: www.amcareinc.com
SIC: 8011 Clinic, operated by physicians

(G-14503)
AMERICAN NURSING CARE INC (DH)
1700 Edison Dr Ste 300 (45150-2729)
PHONE.................................513 576-0262
Fax: 513 576-0379
Thomas J Karpinski, *President*
Mary Molnar, *Opers Staff*
Joanell Phillips, *Opers Staff*
James Graham, *Technical Mgr*
Jerry McKinney, *CFO*
EMP: 65 EST: 1976
SALES (est): 102.1MM Privately Held
WEB: www.americannursingcare.com
SIC: 8051 Convalescent home with continuous nursing care

(G-14504)
ANDY MARK INC
Also Called: Mark Andy Comco
910 Lila Ave (45150-1631)
PHONE.................................513 248-8000
Chris Mosby, *Branch Mgr*
Chuck Mullins, *Manager*
EMP: 120
SALES (corp-wide): 230.1MM Privately Held
WEB: www.comcointl.com
SIC: 8748 Business consulting
PA: Andy Mark' Inc
18081 Chstrfld Aprt Rd
Chesterfield MO 63005
636 532-4433

(G-14505)
AW FARRELL SON INC
745 Us Route 50 (45150-9510)
PHONE.................................513 334-0715
Craig Miller, *Manager*
EMP: 45
SALES (est): 1.8MM Privately Held
SIC: 1761 Roofing contractor

(G-14506)
AZTEC PLUMBING INC
Also Called: Aztec Plumbg
5989 Meijer Dr Ste 8 (45150-1544)
P.O. Box 121 (45150-0121)
PHONE.................................513 732-3320
Fax: 513 732-3446
Gerald Blanchard, *President*
Archie Adams, *Project Mgr*
Catherine Blanchard, *Treasurer*
EMP: 30
SQ FT: 1,026
SALES (est): 2.5MM Privately Held
SIC: 1711 Plumbing contractors

(G-14507)
BURKE INC
Also Called: Burke Milford
25 Whitney Dr Ste 110 (45150-8400)
PHONE.................................513 576-5700
Fax: 513 576-5777
Dick Clark, *Purchasing*
Ron Tatham, *Branch Mgr*
Phillip Poore, *IT/INT Sup*
Sharon Seitz, *MIS Staff*
David Dobelhoff, *Executive*
EMP: 100
SALES (corp-wide): 50MM Privately Held
SIC: 8732 Market analysis or research
PA: Burke, Inc.
500 W 7th St
Cincinnati OH 45203
513 241-5663

(G-14508)
BZAK LANDSCAPING INC (PA)
Also Called: Bzak Ldscpg & Maintainance
931 Round Bottom Rd (45150-9520)
PHONE.................................513 831-0907
Fax: 513 831-3260
Michael G Bieszczak, *President*
Awilda Lachtrop, *Accounts Mgr*
Linda Radcliff, *Sales Staff*
Tori Koppe, *Manager*
Mona Shaw, *Manager*
EMP: 30
SALES (est): 9MM Privately Held
SIC: 0781 0782 1521 5261 Landscape planning services; lawn care services; patio & deck construction & repair; nurseries & garden centers; farm & garden machinery

(G-14509)
CHI HEALTH AT HOME
1700 Edison Dr Ste 300 (45150-2729)
PHONE.................................513 576-0262
EMP: 66
SALES (est): 462K Privately Held
SIC: 8082 Home health care services
HQ: Chi Health At Home
1700 Edison Dr Ste 300
Milford OH 45150

(G-14510)
CHI HEALTH AT HOME (DH)
1700 Edison Dr Ste 300 (45150-2729)
PHONE.................................513 576-0262
Dan Dietz, *President*
L T Wilburn Jr, *President*
Rich Smith, *Principal*
Thomas Painter, *Vice Pres*
Roxanne Hemm, *Project Mgr*
EMP: 50

SALES (est): 103.6MM Privately Held
SIC: 7363 8093 Medical help service; specialty outpatient clinics
HQ: Bethesda, Inc.
619 Oak St 7n
Cincinnati OH 45206
513 569-6400

(G-14511)
CINTAS CORPORATION NO 2
27 Whitney Dr (45150-9784)
PHONE.................................513 965-0800
Fax: 513 965-5000
Joe Ross, *Human Res Mgr*
Scott Wolfe, *Manager*
EMP: 180
SALES (corp-wide): 5.3B Publicly Held
WEB: www.cintas-corp.com
SIC: 7218 7213 Industrial uniform supply; uniform supply
HQ: Cintas Corporation No. 2
6800 Cintas Blvd
Mason OH 45040

(G-14512)
CIVIL & ENVIRONMENTAL CONS INC
5899 Montclair Blvd (45150-3067)
PHONE.................................513 985-0226
Fax: 513 985-0228
John Imbus, *Principal*
Maxwell Bailey, *Project Mgr*
Todd Ford, *Project Mgr*
Adam Lehmann, *Project Mgr*
Steve Parker, *Manager*
EMP: 30
SALES (corp-wide): 116.9MM Privately Held
SIC: 8711 0781 Engineering services; civil engineering; landscape architects
PA: Civil & Environmental Consultants, Inc.
333 Baldwin Rd Ste 1
Pittsburgh PA 15205
412 429-2324

(G-14513)
CLERMONT CARE INC
Also Called: Clearmont Nursing Convalecent
934 State Route 28 (45150-1912)
PHONE.................................513 831-1770
Fax: 513 831-1924
Roger King, *President*
Greg Jacobs, *Maintence Staff*
EMP: 190 EST: 1966
SQ FT: 50,000
SALES (est): 6.7MM Privately Held
SIC: 8051 Convalescent home with continuous nursing care

(G-14514)
COVINGTON CAR WASH INC
5942 Creekview Dr (45150-1518)
PHONE.................................513 831-6164
Maureen Hein, *President*
Richard Hein, *Vice Pres*
EMP: 25
SALES (est): 330.5K Privately Held
SIC: 7542 Carwashes

(G-14515)
DAVEY TREE EXPERT COMPANY
Also Called: Davey Tree & Lawn Care
6065 Br Hill Guinea Pike (45150-2219)
PHONE.................................513 575-1733
Fax: 513 575-0091
Cathy Crocker, *Purch Agent*
Rick Hannah, *Manager*
EMP: 40
SQ FT: 1,376
SALES (corp-wide): 915.9MM Privately Held
SIC: 0782 Lawn services
PA: The Davey Tree Expert Company
1500 N Mantua St
Kent OH 44240
330 673-9511

(G-14516)
DELANEYS TAX ACCUNTING SVC LTD
1157b State Route 131 (45150-2717)
PHONE.................................513 248-2829
Fax: 513 248-4747
John Doughty, *Owner*

EMP: 30
SALES (est): 430K Privately Held
SIC: 7291 Tax return preparation services

(G-14517)
DNV GL HEALTHCARE USA INC
400 Techne Center Dr # 100 (45150-2792)
PHONE.................................281 396-1610
Bob Gordon, *Engng Exec*
Yehuda Dror, *Branch Mgr*
EMP: 44
SALES (corp-wide): 2.4B Privately Held
SIC: 8621 Medical field-related associations; professional standards review board
HQ: Dnv Gl Healthcare Usa, Inc.
1400 Ravello Rd
Katy TX 77449
281 396-1703

(G-14518)
FORWITH LOGISTICS LLC
6129 Guinea Pike (45150-2221)
PHONE.................................513 386-8310
Kevin Forwith, *Mng Member*
EMP: 40
SALES (est): 856K Privately Held
SIC: 8743 Public relations services

(G-14519)
FRONTLINE NATIONAL LLC
502 Techne Center Dr G (45150-8780)
PHONE.................................513 528-7823
Katherine Latham, *President*
Robert Latham, *Vice Pres*
EMP: 90
SALES (est): 4.5MM Privately Held
WEB: www.frontlinenational.com
SIC: 7363 Medical help service

(G-14520)
GB LIQUIDATING COMPANY INC
22 Whitney Dr (45150-9783)
PHONE.................................513 248-7600
Fax: 513 248-7606
Ruth Burkhard, *Editor*
Cory Sherman, *Editor*
Leon Lovette, *Regional Mgr*
Bo Sherman, *Vice Pres*
Tom Compton, *Finance Mgr*
EMP: 50
SALES (est): 7.6MM Privately Held
WEB: www.gordonbernard.com
SIC: 2752 7371 2759 2741 Commercial printing, lithographic; calendar & card printing, lithographic; custom computer programming services; commercial printing; miscellaneous publishing

(G-14521)
GEM INTERIORS INC
769 Us Route 50 (45150-9510)
PHONE.................................513 831-6535
Fax: 513 576-8172
Greg E Massie, *President*
EMP: 40
SQ FT: 8,000
SALES (est): 6.6MM Privately Held
SIC: 1542 Custom builders, non-residential

(G-14522)
GLENNY GLASS COMPANY
209 Castleberry Ct (45150-1193)
PHONE.................................513 489-2233
R Braxton Smith, *President*
April Shinkle, *Treasurer*
▲ EMP: 40
SQ FT: 48,000
SALES (est): 19.6MM Privately Held
SIC: 5039 Glass construction materials

(G-14523)
GORDON BERNARD COMPANY LLC
22 Whitney Dr (45150-9781)
PHONE.................................513 248-7600
Robert Sherman Jr, *President*
EMP: 45
SQ FT: 25,000
SALES (est): 5.6MM Privately Held
SIC: 5199 2752 2741 Calendars; commercial printing, lithographic; miscellaneous publishing

(G-14524)
HENRY P THOMPSON COMPANY (PA)
101 Main St Ste 300 (45150-1183)
PHONE..................513 248-3200
Fax: 513 248-3201
William S Cantwell, *President*
Gary R Lubin, *Vice Pres*
Michael S Macy, *Vice Pres*
Michael Macy, *Vice Pres*
Tim Shaw, *Vice Pres*
EMP: 25
SQ FT: 16,000
SALES (est): 10.9MM Privately Held
WEB: www.hpthompson.com
SIC: 5084 7699 Pumps & pumping equipment; industrial equipment services

(G-14525)
HOMETOWN URGENT CARE
1068 State Route 28 Ste C (45150-2095)
PHONE..................513 831-5900
EMP: 101
SALES (corp-wide): 73.2MM Privately Held
SIC: 8049 8011 Occupational therapist; medical centers
PA: Hometown Urgent Care
 2400 Corp Exchange Dr # 102
 Columbus OH 43231
 614 505-7633

(G-14526)
ICON ENVIRONMENTAL GROUP LLC
Also Called: Icon Property Rescue
24 Whitney Dr Ste D (45150-9521)
PHONE..................513 426-6767
Fax: 513 396-6050
Larry Hensley, *President*
Paula Hensley, *Vice Pres*
Brian Blakley, *Office Admin*
EMP: 45
SALES (est): 5.7MM Privately Held
SIC: 8748 1521 1542 7217 Environmental consultant; repairing fire damage, single-family houses; commercial & office buildings, renovation & repair; carpet & upholstery cleaning; renovation, remodeling & repairs: industrial buildings

(G-14527)
INTERNATIONAL TECHNEGROUP INC (PA)
5303 Dupont Cir (45150-2734)
PHONE..................513 576-3900
Fax: 937 576-3994
Thomas A Gregory, *CEO*
Ronald Scott, *Business Mgr*
Tom Makoski, *Sales Executive*
Margo Mohler, *Mktg Dir*
Robert Campbell, *Manager*
EMP: 100
SQ FT: 28,000
SALES (est): 27.6MM Privately Held
WEB: www.iti-oh.com
SIC: 7371 Computer software development

(G-14528)
JARVIS MECHANICAL CONSTRS INC (PA)
803 Us Route 50 (45150-9513)
PHONE..................513 831-0055
Jeffery Jarvis, *President*
Kathy Cardone, *Accounts Mgr*
Brenda Holtzman, *Admin Sec*
EMP: 30
SQ FT: 13,500
SALES (est): 7.6MM Privately Held
WEB: www.jmc-afm.com
SIC: 1711 Mechanical contractor

(G-14529)
JPMORGAN CHASE BANK NAT ASSN
967 Lila Ave (45150-1617)
PHONE..................513 985-5350
Beth Hauke, *Manager*
EMP: 26
SALES (corp-wide): 99.6B Publicly Held
WEB: www.chase.com
SIC: 6021 National commercial banks
HQ: Jpmorgan Chase Bank, National Association
 1111 Polaris Pkwy
 Columbus OH 43240
 614 436-3055

(G-14530)
LIBERTY INSULATION CO INC
5782 Deerfield Rd (45150-2657)
PHONE..................513 621-0108
Russ Smith, *Manager*
EMP: 25
SALES (corp-wide): 4.8MM Privately Held
SIC: 4225 General warehousing
PA: Liberty Insulation Co Inc
 2903 Kant Pl
 Beavercreek OH 45431
 513 621-0108

(G-14531)
LITTLE MIAMI HOME CARE INC
5371 S Milford Rd Apt 16 (45150-9502)
PHONE..................513 248-8988
Fax: 513 665-6770
Susan Flynn, *President*
EMP: 40
SALES (est): 1.2MM Privately Held
SIC: 8082 Home health care services

(G-14532)
LOWES HOME CENTERS LLC
5694 Romar Dr (45150-8505)
PHONE..................513 965-3280
Fax: 513 965-3283
EMP: 150
SALES (corp-wide): 68.6B Publicly Held
SIC: 5211 5031 5722 5064 Home centers; building materials, exterior; building materials, interior; household appliance stores; electrical appliances, television & radio
HQ: Lowe's Home Centers, Llc
 1605 Curtis Bridge Rd
 Wilkesboro NC 28697
 336 658-4000

(G-14533)
LYKINS COMPANIES INC (PA)
Also Called: Lykins Energy Solutions
5163 Wlfpn Plsnt Hl Rd (45150-9632)
P.O. Box 643875, Cincinnati (45264-3875)
PHONE..................513 831-8820
Fax: 513 831-1428
Jeff Lykins, *CEO*
Diana Brown, *Division Mgr*
Mike Schmid, *Division Mgr*
Kathy Igo, *Counsel*
Brandon Bernard, *Safety Dir*
EMP: 235
SQ FT: 10,000
SALES (est): 54.5MM Privately Held
SIC: 4213 5172 5411 Trucking, except local; gasoline; diesel fuel; fuel oil; convenience stores, chain

(G-14534)
LYKINS OIL COMPANY (HQ)
5163 Wlfpn Plsnt Hl Rd (45150-9632)
PHONE..................513 831-8820
Fax: 937 831-8820
D Jeff Lykins, *President*
Ronald Lykins, *Vice Pres*
Robert J Manning, *CFO*
Sue Grill, *Controller*
Mary U Gray, *Chief Mktg Ofcr*
EMP: 30
SQ FT: 12,000
SALES (est): 173.3MM
SALES (corp-wide): 54.5MM Privately Held
SIC: 5172 5983 Gasoline; fuel oil dealers
PA: Lykins Companies, Inc.
 5163 Wlfpn Plsnt Hl Rd
 Milford OH 45150
 513 831-8820

(G-14535)
LYKINS TRANSPORTATION INC
5163 Wlfpn Plsnt Hl Rd (45150-9632)
PHONE..................513 831-8820
Donald F Lykins, *CEO*
Jeff Lykins, *President*
Ron Lykins, *Vice Pres*
Robert J Manning, *CFO*
Lawrence Owens, *CIO*
EMP: 60 EST: 1996
SQ FT: 10,000
SALES: 12MM
SALES (corp-wide): 54.5MM Privately Held
WEB: www.lykinstransportation.com
SIC: 4213 Liquid petroleum transport, non-local
PA: Lykins Companies, Inc.
 5163 Wlfpn Plsnt Hl Rd
 Milford OH 45150
 513 831-8820

(G-14536)
MADISON TREE CARE & LDSCPG INC
636 Round Bottom Rd (45150-9568)
PHONE..................513 576-6391
Fax: 513 576-6394
Frederick J Butcher, *President*
Dora Mae Butcher, *Exec VP*
Richard L E Butcher, *Vice Pres*
John Butcher, *Treasurer*
Cingy Churchil, *Manager*
EMP: 48
SALES (est): 4.5MM Privately Held
WEB: www.mtcandl.com
SIC: 0783 Ornamental shrub & tree services

(G-14537)
MAX DIXONS EXPRESSWAY PARK
Also Called: Expressway Pk Softball Complex
689 Us Route 50 (45150-9102)
P.O. Box 402 (45150-0402)
PHONE..................513 831-2273
Fax: 513 831-4663
Bob Owens, *President*
Betty Dixon, *Vice Pres*
EMP: 25
SQ FT: 2,400
SALES (est): 848.2K Privately Held
WEB: www.expresswaypark.com
SIC: 7999 Recreation center

(G-14538)
MERCY HEALTH
201 Old Bank Rd Ste 103 (45150-2443)
PHONE..................513 248-0100
EMP: 35
SALES (corp-wide): 4.2B Privately Held
SIC: 8011 Internal medicine, physician/surgeon
PA: Mercy Health
 1701 Mercy Health Pl
 Cincinnati OH 45237
 513 639-2800

(G-14539)
MIAMI RIFLE PISTOL CLUB
P.O. Box 235 (45150-0235)
PHONE..................513 732-9943
Ken Leyor, *Owner*
Ben Laux, *Director*
EMP: 100
SALES: 274.6K Privately Held
WEB: www.miamirifle-pistol.org
SIC: 7997 Membership sports & recreation clubs

(G-14540)
MIDWEST ULTRASOUND INC (PA)
50 W Techne Center Dr D (45150-8403)
PHONE..................513 248-8885
Fax: 513 248-9045
Garth Belcher, *Ch of Bd*
Dr Peter Podore, *President*
EMP: 53
SALES (est): 1.2MM Privately Held
WEB: www.midwestultrasound.com
SIC: 8071 Medical laboratories

(G-14541)
MIKE CASTRUCCI FORD
1020 State Route 28 (45150-2002)
PHONE..................513 831-7010
Fax: 513 831-6239
Mike Castrucci, *Owner*
Greg Nicholas, *Manager*
EMP: 150 EST: 1987
SQ FT: 1,152
SALES (est): 37.2MM Privately Held
SIC: 5511 7538 7532 5521 Automobiles, new & used; general automotive repair shops; top & body repair & paint shops; used car dealers

(G-14542)
MILFORD COML CLG SVCS INC
701 Us Highway 50 Ste A (45150-9580)
P.O. Box 183 (45150-0183)
PHONE..................513 575-5678
Tim Rhea, *President*
EMP: 30
SALES (est): 1.1MM Privately Held
SIC: 7349 Cleaning service, industrial or commercial

(G-14543)
MRP INC
Also Called: Medical Radiation Physics
5632 Sugar Camp Rd (45150-9673)
PHONE..................513 965-9700
Fax: 513 965-9750
John Freshcorn, *President*
George Eckhardt, *Opers Staff*
Jonida Hale, *Office Admin*
EMP: 30
SQ FT: 6,200
SALES: 7.8MM Privately Held
WEB: www.mrpinc.com
SIC: 8011 Radiologist

(G-14544)
NATIONAL AMUSEMENTS INC
Also Called: Nam Showcase Cinemas Milford
500 Rivers Edge (45150-1490)
PHONE..................513 699-1500
James Warman, *Manager*
EMP: 41
SALES (corp-wide): 13.7B Publicly Held
WEB: www.nationalamusements.com
SIC: 7832 Motion picture theaters, except drive-in
PA: National Amusements, Inc.
 846 University Ave
 Norwood MA 02062
 781 461-1600

(G-14545)
NORTHPOINT SENIOR SERVICES LLC
Also Called: Arbors At Milfor, The
5900 Meadow Creek Dr (45150-5641)
PHONE..................513 248-1655
Fax: 513 248-0466
Kate Wagner, *Marketing Staff*
Judy Hall, *Nursing Dir*
Tim Wagstrom, *Social Dir*
Diana Kelch, *Records Dir*
Mark Johnston, *Administration*
EMP: 100
SALES (corp-wide): 37.8MM Privately Held
WEB: www.extendicarehealth.com
SIC: 8051 8052 Convalescent home with continuous nursing care; intermediate care facilities
PA: Senior Northpoint Services Llc
 7400 New Lagrange 100
 Louisville KY 40222
 502 429-8062

(G-14546)
OPTION CARE ENTERPRISES INC
50 W Techne Center Dr J (45150-9798)
PHONE..................513 576-8400
Julie Koenig, *Manager*
Sharon Niewinski, *Manager*
Kathleen Alvarez, *Director*
Marcia Hackett, *Receptionist*
EMP: 143
SALES (corp-wide): 1.7B Privately Held
SIC: 8082 Home health care services
HQ: Option Care Enterprises, Inc.
 3000 Lakeside Dr Ste 300n
 Bannockburn IL 60015

(G-14547)
OPTION CARE INFUSION SVCS INC
25 Whitney Dr Ste 114 (45150-8400)
PHONE..................513 576-8400
Ron Ferguson, *Manager*
EMP: 100

Milford - Clermont County (G-14548)

SALES (corp-wide): 1.7B Privately Held
SIC: 8082 Home health care services
HQ: Option Care Infusion Services, Inc.
3000 Lakeside Dr Ste 300n
Bannockburn IL 60015
312 940-2500

(G-14548)
PAGER PLUS ONE INC
927 Old State Rt 28 Ste G (45150)
PHONE..................513 748-3788
Roger Saddler, President
Logan A Saddler, Vice Pres
EMP: 240
SQ FT: 1,200
SALES: 356K Privately Held
SIC: 5065 Paging & signaling equipment

(G-14549)
PARKER MARKETING RESEARCH LLC
5405 Dupont Cir Ste B (45150-2798)
PHONE..................513 248-8100
Fax: 513 248-8101
Mike Brintzenhoff, President
Robert Goodwin, Senior VP
James Whalen, Research
Greg Tetzloff, CFO
Amy Bucher, Manager
EMP: 26
SALES (est): 3MM Privately Held
WEB: www.parkerresearch.com
SIC: 8742 Marketing consulting services

(G-14550)
PARKER-HANNIFIN CORPORATION
Also Called: Electromechanical North Amer
50 W Techne Center Dr H (45150-8403)
PHONE..................513 831-2340
Kenneth Sweet, Branch Mgr
Burleigh Bailey, Manager
EMP: 75
SALES (corp-wide): 12B Publicly Held
WEB: www.parker.com
SIC: 3577 7371 3575 3571 Computer peripheral equipment; computer software development; computer terminals; electronic computers
PA: Parker-Hannifin Corporation
6035 Parkland Blvd
Cleveland OH 44124
216 896-3000

(G-14551)
PAT HENRY GROUP LLC (PA)
Also Called: Phg Retail Services
6046 Bridgehaven Dr (45150-5623)
PHONE..................216 447-0831
Kennie Hopper, CFO
Judith Hominy,
EMP: 25
SQ FT: 1,000
SALES (est): 4MM Privately Held
WEB: www.pathenry.com
SIC: 8742 Marketing consulting services

(G-14552)
PATRIOT INDUS CONTG SVCS LLC
200 Olympic Dr (45150-9522)
PHONE..................513 248-8222
Pat Booth, Project Mgr
Ben Hall, Project Mgr
Mike Wilkerson,
EMP: 30
SALES (est): 5.3MM Privately Held
WEB: www.patrioticsi.com
SIC: 7699 Industrial machinery & equipment repair; welding equipment repair

(G-14553)
PETSMART INC
245 Rivers Edge (45150-2592)
PHONE..................513 248-4954
Tim Irwin, Branch Mgr
EMP: 28
SALES (corp-wide): 12.7B Privately Held
WEB: www.petsmart.com
SIC: 5999 0752 Pet supplies; training services, pet & animal specialties (not horses)

HQ: Petsmart, Inc.
19601 N 27th Ave
Phoenix AZ 85027
623 580-6100

(G-14554)
PLUS REALTY CINCINNATI INC
Also Called: Remax Results Plus
1160 State Route 28 (45150-2155)
PHONE..................513 575-4500
Richard J Hoffman, President
Thomas Hoffman, Vice Pres
EMP: 25
SALES (est): 1.6MM Privately Held
SIC: 6531 1531 Selling agent, real estate; speculative builder, single-family houses

(G-14555)
PREMIER CLEANING SERVICES INC
Also Called: Cleaning Authority
5866 Wlfpen Plasant Hl Rd (45150)
PHONE..................513 831-2492
Fax: 513 831-2753
Michael A Randall, President
EMP: 32
SQ FT: 1,200
SALES (est): 2MM Privately Held
SIC: 7699 Cleaning services

(G-14556)
PROFESSIONAL LAMINATE MLLWK INC
Also Called: Pro-Lam
1003 Tech Dr (45150-9780)
PHONE..................513 891-7858
Fax: 513 891-8080
Shannon P Bitzer, CEO
Scott W Bitzer, Vice Pres
Jason O'Brien, VP Opers
Ryan Kerrick, Engineer
Nikki Young, Office Mgr
▲ EMP: 42
SQ FT: 22,000
SALES (est): 18.8MM Privately Held
WEB: www.prolamonline.com
SIC: 5031 5712 Kitchen cabinets; customized furniture & cabinets

(G-14557)
RIVERHILLS BANK (HQ)
553 Chamber Dr (45150-1498)
P.O. Box 48, New Richmond (45157-0048)
PHONE..................513 553-6700
Fax: 513 248-4482
Charles Snyder, President
Chuck Snyder, Vice Pres
Wendy Taylor, CFO
Mike Peters, Loan Officer
Sarah Schwartz, Admin Asst
EMP: 50
SQ FT: 3,000
SALES: 8.3MM
SALES (corp-wide): 7.2MM Privately Held
SIC: 6021 National commercial banks
PA: New Richmond Bancorporation
110 Front St
New Richmond OH 45157
513 553-6700

(G-14558)
ROCKWELL AUTOMATION OHIO INC (HQ)
1700 Edison Dr (45150-2729)
PHONE..................513 576-6151
Ralph Delisio, General Mgr
Jim Fitch, Project Mgr
Tanja Bartulovic, Marketing Staff
Michael Cole, Info Tech Mgr
David Wray, Technology
EMP: 75
SALES (est): 8.6MM Publicly Held
WEB: www.entek.com
SIC: 7373 7379 Systems software development services; computer systems analysis & design; computer related consulting services

(G-14559)
SCANNER APPLICATIONS LLC
Also Called: Scanner Applications, Inc.
400 Milford Pkwy (45150-9104)
PHONE..................513 248-5588
Fax: 513 248-5888

Robert W Gibson, CEO
Jay Griffiths, General Mgr
Kim Gregory, Area Mgr
Jeffrey Gibson, Vice Pres
Jack Linberg, Vice Pres
EMP: 48
SALES (est): 3.5MM Privately Held
WEB: www.scanapps.com
SIC: 8732 Business analysis
HQ: Inmar, Inc.
635 Vine St
Winston Salem NC 27101
800 765-1277

(G-14560)
SCHUMACHER & CO INC
920 Lila Ave (45150-1641)
PHONE..................859 655-9000
Steve Contois, CEO
Roy Young, QC Mgr
Ashley Taylor, Accountant
EMP: 33
SQ FT: 22,000
SALES (est): 1.6MM
SALES (corp-wide): 32.8MM Privately Held
WEB: www.schumacherco.com
SIC: 1752 Wood floor installation & refinishing
PA: CI Investments, Inc.
1050 Skillman Dr
Cincinnati OH 45215
513 771-2345

(G-14561)
SIEMENS PLM SOFTWARE
2000 Eastman Dr (45150-2712)
PHONE..................513 576-2400
Geoff Halliday, Vice Pres
Jim Menego, Vice Pres
Miklos Magdich, Purch Dir
Ryan Dial, Sales Staff
Daniel Staresinic, Mktg Dir
EMP: 37
SALES (est): 7MM
SALES (corp-wide): 925.1MM Privately Held
SIC: 7373 Systems software development services
PA: Siemens Product Lifecycle Management Software Inc.
5800 Granite Pkwy Ste 600
Plano TX 75024
972 987-3000

(G-14562)
SIEMENS PRODUCT LIFE MGMT SFTW
2000 Eastman Dr (45150-2712)
PHONE..................513 576-2400
Tony Asfusso, President
Tom Eberle, General Mgr
Suzanne Kopcha, Vice Pres
Kenneth Lewis, Opers Mgr
Otto Terri, Sales Associate
EMP: 70
SALES (corp-wide): 925.1MM Privately Held
WEB: www.ugs.com
SIC: 7371 Computer software development
PA: Siemens Product Lifecycle Management Software Inc.
5800 Granite Pkwy Ste 600
Plano TX 75024
972 987-3000

(G-14563)
SILER EXCAVATION SERVICES
6025 Catherine Dr (45150-2203)
PHONE..................513 400-8628
Mike Siler,
EMP: 40 EST: 2007
SALES (est): 1.1MM Privately Held
SIC: 1794 1389 Excavation work; construction, repair & dismantling services

(G-14564)
SMITHPEARLMAN & CO
100 Techne Center Dr # 200 (45150-2780)
PHONE..................513 248-9210
Fax: 513 248-9327
Donald J Burkhardt, President
Judy Radloff, Business Mgr
Al Pearlman, Corp Secy
Kim Lorenzo, Accountant

Sheryl Sheshull, Accountant
EMP: 30
SALES (est): 3.1MM Privately Held
WEB: www.burkhardtcpa.com
SIC: 8721 Certified public accountant

(G-14565)
TATA AMERICA INTL CORP
Also Called: Tata Consultancy Services
1000 Summit Dr Unit 1 (45150-2724)
PHONE..................513 677-6500
Sumanta Roy, Regional Mgr
Krishnendu Datta, Manager
Brian Purvis, Manager
Khizar Mahamad, Project Leader
Monu Sharma, Consultant
EMP: 300
SALES (corp-wide): 81.3MM Privately Held
SIC: 7372 7373 7371 Prepackaged software; computer integrated systems design; custom computer programming services
HQ: Tata America International Corporation
101 Park Ave Rm 2603
New York NY 10178
212 557-8038

(G-14566)
TECHNA GLASS INC
904 State Route 28 (45150-1952)
PHONE..................513 685-3800
Joe Dills, Owner
EMP: 31 Privately Held
SIC: 7536 Automotive glass replacement shops
PA: Techna Glass, Inc.
460 W 9000 S
Sandy UT 84070

(G-14567)
TERRACE PARK COUNTRY CLUB INC
5341 S Milford Rd (45150-9744)
PHONE..................513 965-4061
Fax: 513 831-1368
Al Washvill, General Mgr
EMP: 75
SQ FT: 17,000
SALES: 2.9MM Privately Held
SIC: 7997 Country club, membership

(G-14568)
TOTAL QUALITY LOGISTICS LLC
Also Called: Tql
1701 Edison Dr (45150-2728)
PHONE..................513 831-2600
Ken Oaks, CEO
EMP: 40
SALES (corp-wide): 2.3B Privately Held
SIC: 4731 Truck transportation brokers
HQ: Total Quality Logistics, Llc
4289 Ivy Pointe Blvd
Cincinnati OH 45245

(G-14569)
TOTAL QUALITY LOGISTICS LLC
1701 Edison Dr (45150-2728)
PHONE..................513 831-2600
Kenneth G Oaks, CEO
EMP: 150
SALES (corp-wide): 2.3B Privately Held
SIC: 4731 Truck transportation brokers
HQ: Total Quality Logistics, Llc
4289 Ivy Pointe Blvd
Cincinnati OH 45245

(G-14570)
TRIPACK LLC
Also Called: Tripack Sleever
401 Milford Pkwy Ste B (45150-9119)
PHONE..................859 282-7914
Mark Tredo, Controller
Tom S Linz, Mng Member
▲ EMP: 30
SQ FT: 6,000
SALES (est): 6.6MM Privately Held
WEB: www.tripack.net
SIC: 5084 Packaging machinery & equipment

GEOGRAPHIC SECTION

(G-14571)
UNITED MERCANTILE CORPORATION
575 Chamber Dr (45150-1498)
PHONE.................................513 831-1300
Fax: 513 831-6010
Paul Spires, *Owner*
EMP: 30
SALES (est): 5MM **Privately Held**
SIC: 6794 Franchises, selling or licensing

(G-14572)
VALLEY ROOFING LLC
5293 Tech Valley Dr (45150-9762)
PHONE.................................513 831-9444
Fax: 513 831-4366
Erich Manteuffel, *Owner*
Hans Philippo, *Mng Member*
Bonnie Fath, *Manager*
Rudolf Manteuffel, *Executive*
Eric Manteuffel,
EMP: 40
SQ FT: 11,600
SALES (est): 1.9MM **Privately Held**
SIC: 1761 Roofing contractor

(G-14573)
VASCONCELLOS INC
400 Techne Center Dr # 406 (45150-2792)
PHONE.................................513 576-1250
Timothy Vasconcellos, *Owner*
EMP: 50 EST: 2008
SALES (est): 710.9K **Privately Held**
SIC: 8322 Senior citizens' center or association

(G-14574)
WESCOM SOLUTIONS INC
Also Called: Pointclickcare
300 Techne Center Dr A (45150-2795)
PHONE.................................513 831-1207
Darcy Strong, *Manager*
EMP: 45
SALES (corp-wide): 38.5MM **Privately Held**
SIC: 7373 Computer integrated systems design
HQ: Pointclickcare Technologies Inc
5570 Explorer Dr
Mississauga ON L4W 0
905 858-8885

Milford Center
Union County

(G-14575)
CHAMPAIGN PREMIUM GRN GROWERS
Also Called: Integrated AG Services
24320 Woodstock Rd (43045-8004)
P.O. Box 138 (43045-0138)
PHONE.................................937 826-3003
David Scheiderer, *Principal*
Susan Follrod, *Principal*
EMP: 38
SALES (est): 1.4MM **Privately Held**
SIC: 8731 Agricultural research

(G-14576)
FORUM MANUFACTURING INC
77 Brown St (43045-8900)
PHONE.................................937 349-8685
Fax: 937 349-8785
Nancy Kovacs, *President*
Jim J Kraus, *Principal*
Gerald Shannon, *Principal*
▲ EMP: 25
SQ FT: 19,000
SALES (est): 4.1MM **Privately Held**
SIC: 1751 Cabinet building & installation

Millbury
Wood County

(G-14577)
BEST AIRE COMPRESSOR SERVICE (DH)
3648 Rockland Cir (43447-9804)
PHONE.................................419 726-0055
Tracy D Paglary, *Principal*
Brandon Russell, *CFO*
Kyle Kayden, *Controller*
Don Cowell, *Accountant*
Michelle Payson, *Accounts Mgr*
EMP: 100
SQ FT: 37,100
SALES (est): 40.3MM
SALES (corp-wide): 2.3B **Publicly Held**
WEB: www.amsba.com
SIC: 5251 7699 5075 Pumps & pumping equipment; compressor repair; compressors, air conditioning

(G-14578)
DELVENTHAL COMPANY
3796 Rockland Cir (43447-9651)
PHONE.................................419 244-5570
Steve Delventhal, *President*
Shawn Albert, *Superintendent*
Tommy Wiggins, *Superintendent*
Sharon Delventhal, *Corp Secy*
Tom Koepfler, *Project Mgr*
EMP: 30
SQ FT: 12,000
SALES: 10MM **Privately Held**
WEB: www.thedelventhalco.com
SIC: 1541 1542 Industrial buildings, new construction; commercial & office building contractors

(G-14579)
GETGO TRANSPORTATION CO LLC
28500 Lemoyne Rd (43447-9431)
PHONE.................................419 666-6850
Fax: 419 666-6891
Anthony W Tomase,
EMP: 39 EST: 2001
SQ FT: 14,000
SALES (est): 5.9MM **Privately Held**
SIC: 4214 4225 Local trucking with storage; general warehousing

(G-14580)
MISTRAS GROUP INC
3094 Moline Martin Rd (43447-9691)
PHONE.................................419 836-5904
Mike Hoy, *District Mgr*
EMP: 58 **Publicly Held**
SIC: 8711 Engineering services
PA: Mistras Group, Inc.
195 Clarksville Rd Ste 2
Princeton Junction NJ 08550

(G-14581)
STONEY LODGE INC
Also Called: Super 8 Motel
3491 Latcha Rd (43447-9786)
P.O. Box 701004, Plymouth MI (48170-0957)
PHONE.................................419 837-6409
William Nofar, *President*
EMP: 85
SALES (est): 3.9MM **Privately Held**
SIC: 7011 Hotels & motels

Millersburg
Holmes County

(G-14582)
77 COACH SUPPLY LTD
7426 County Road 77 (44654-9279)
PHONE.................................330 674-1454
Fax: 330 359-5946
Atlee Kaufman,
EMP: 26
SALES (est): 3MM **Privately Held**
SIC: 5099 2499 Wood & wood by-products; decorative wood & woodwork

(G-14583)
A & R BUILDERS LTD
6914 County Road 672 (44654-8350)
PHONE.................................330 893-2111
Fax: 330 893-8018
Alan Yoder, *Partner*
Erma Yoder, *Partner*
EMP: 25
SALES (est): 2.4MM **Privately Held**
SIC: 1521 New construction, single-family houses; general remodeling, single-family houses

(G-14584)
ALTERCARE OF MILLERSBURG
105 Majora Ln (44654-8955)
PHONE.................................330 674-4444
Fax: 330 674-0108
Don McVay, *Maint Spvr*
Diana Jackson, *Administration*
Crystal Torrence, *Administration*
EMP: 80
SALES (est): 1.2MM **Privately Held**
SIC: 8051 Convalescent home with continuous nursing care

(G-14585)
ASAP HOMECARE INC
31 N Mad Anthony St (44654-1169)
PHONE.................................330 674-3306
EMP: 64
SALES (corp-wide): 6.9MM **Privately Held**
SIC: 8059 Personal care home, with health care
PA: Asap Homecare Inc
1 Park Centre Dr Ste 107
Wadsworth OH 44281
330 334-7027

(G-14586)
B & L TRANSPORT INC (PA)
3149 State Route 39 (44654-8805)
P.O. Box 172, Walnut Creek (44687-0172)
PHONE.................................866 848-2888
Ben Mast, *President*
Jon Mast, *Vice Pres*
Maryann Schrock, *Manager*
EMP: 28
SQ FT: 4,500
SALES (est): 4MM **Privately Held**
SIC: 4212 Local trucking, without storage

(G-14587)
BERLIN CONSTRUCTION LTD
4740 Township Road 356 (44654-8719)
PHONE.................................330 893-2003
Gideon Yoder, *Partner*
Jacob A Hershberger, *Partner*
EMP: 25
SALES: 6MM **Privately Held**
SIC: 1542 1521 Commercial & office building contractors; general remodeling, single-family houses

(G-14588)
BERLIN TRANSPORTAION LLC
7576 State Route 241 (44654-8822)
PHONE.................................330 674-3395
Fax: 330 674-5069
Thomas Wengerd,
Ken Wengard,
Marlin Wengerd,
EMP: 30
SQ FT: 6,000
SALES (est): 6.1MM **Privately Held**
WEB: www.berlintransportation.com
SIC: 4213 Trucking, except local

(G-14589)
BIRD ENTERPRISES LLC
Also Called: Millersburg Hotel
35 W Jackson St (44654-1321)
P.O. Box 127 (44654-0127)
PHONE.................................330 674-1457
Fax: 330 674-4487
Bill Robinson, *Manager*
EMP: 25
SQ FT: 20,000
SALES (corp-wide): 1.4MM **Privately Held**
SIC: 7011 5812 7929 5813 Inns; restaurant, family: independent; entertainers & entertainment groups; drinking places
PA: Bird Enterprises Llc
31 N Mad Anthony St
Millersburg OH 44654
330 674-2339

(G-14590)
BLACK DIAMOND GOLF COURSE
7500 Township Road 103 (44654-8516)
PHONE.................................330 674-6110
Fax: 330 674-6148
Walter Eppley, *President*
Jeffrey Eppley, *Vice Pres*
Debra Eppley, *Treasurer*
EMP: 25
SQ FT: 1,950
SALES (est): 1MM **Privately Held**
WEB: www.blackdiamondgolfcourse.com
SIC: 7992 Public golf courses

(G-14591)
CARTER-JONES LUMBER COMPANY
6139 State Route 39 (44654-8845)
PHONE.................................330 674-9060
EMP: 104
SALES (corp-wide): 1.2B **Privately Held**
SIC: 5031 5211 2439 2434 Lumber, plywood & millwork; lumber & other building materials; structural wood members; wood kitchen cabinets; millwork; hardwood dimension & flooring mills
HQ: The Carter-Jones Lumber Company
601 Tallmadge Rd
Kent OH 44240
330 673-6100

(G-14592)
CASTLE NURSING HOMES INC
Also Called: Sycamore Run Nursing
6180 State Route 83 (44654-9463)
PHONE.................................330 674-0015
Fax: 330 763-2225
Kirk Hartline, *Branch Mgr*
EMP: 200
SALES (corp-wide): 256.1K **Privately Held**
SIC: 8051 Skilled nursing care facilities
HQ: Castle Nursing Homes, Inc.
6967 Deer Trail Ave Ne
Canton OH 44721
440 793-2245

(G-14593)
CHRISTIAN AID MINISTRIES (PA)
Also Called: Good Samaritan, The
4464 State Route 39 (44654-9677)
P.O. Box 360, Berlin (44610-0360)
PHONE.................................330 893-2428
Fax: 330 893-2305
David N Troyer, *President*
Paul Weaver, *Principal*
Roman Mullet, *Finance Dir*
Karen Zook, *Manager*
Wendell Sommers, *Webmaster*
EMP: 50
SQ FT: 8,160
SALES: 111.1MM **Privately Held**
SIC: 8322 5999 Individual & family services; religious goods

(G-14594)
CHUCK NICHOLSON INC
Also Called: Chuck Nicholson Leasing
7190 State Route 39 (44654-9204)
P.O. Box 311 (44654-0311)
PHONE.................................330 674-4015
Fax: 330 674-2355
Charles Nicholson, *President*
Barry Nicholson, *General Mgr*
Billie Nicholson, *Corp Secy*
Mark Miller, *Senior VP*
Christi Wengerd, *VP Sls/Mktg*
EMP: 40
SQ FT: 9,000
SALES (est): 4.9MM **Privately Held**
WEB: www.chucknicholson.com
SIC: 7515 Passenger car leasing

(G-14595)
COMMERCIAL SVGS BANK MILLERSBU (HQ)
Also Called: CSB
91 N Clay St (44654-1117)
P.O. Box 232 (44654-0232)
PHONE.................................330 674-9015
Eddie Steiner, *CEO*
Paula Meiler, *Senior VP*
Lindsay Petitte,
EMP: 25
SALES: 30.7MM
SALES (corp-wide): 30.7MM **Publicly Held**
SIC: 6022 State commercial banks
PA: Csb Bancorp, Inc.
91 N Clay St
Millersburg OH 44654
330 674-9015

Millersburg - Holmes County (G-14596)

(G-14596)
COUNTY OF HOLMES
Also Called: Holmes County Fire Department
8478 State Route 39 (44654-9766)
P.O. Box 7 (44654-0007)
PHONE....................................330 674-1926
Fax: 330 674-3535
Scott Boulder, Chief
EMP: 27 Privately Held
WEB: www.district1fire.com
SIC: 9224 8322 ; emergency social services
PA: County Of Holmes
2 Court St Ste 14
Millersburg OH 44654
330 674-1896

(G-14597)
COUNTY OF HOLMES
Also Called: Holmes County Health Dept
85 N Grant St B (44654-1166)
PHONE....................................330 674-5035
Fax: 330 674-2528
Dr Maurice Mullet, Director
EMP: 25 Privately Held
WEB: www.district1fire.com
SIC: 9431 7361 ; nurses' registry
PA: County Of Holmes
2 Court St Ste 14
Millersburg OH 44654
330 674-1896

(G-14598)
COUNTY OF HOLMES
Also Called: Engineer's Office
7191 State Route 39 (44654-9204)
P.O. Box 29 (44654-0029)
PHONE....................................330 674-5076
Chris Young, Principal
EMP: 33 Privately Held
WEB: www.district1fire.com
SIC: 1611 Highway & street maintenance
PA: County Of Holmes
2 Court St Ste 14
Millersburg OH 44654
330 674-1896

(G-14599)
COUNTY OF HOLMES
Also Called: Highway Department
75 E Clinton St (44654-1283)
PHONE....................................330 674-5916
Fax: 330 674-2230
Chris Young, Finance Mgr
Robert Kasner, Manager
EMP: 38 Privately Held
WEB: www.district1fire.com
SIC: 7521 9111 Parking garage; county supervisors' & executives' offices
PA: County Of Holmes
2 Court St Ste 14
Millersburg OH 44654
330 674-1896

(G-14600)
COUNTY OF HOLMES
Also Called: Joel Pomerene Memorial Hosp
981 Wooster Rd (44654-1536)
PHONE....................................330 674-1015
Phillip W Smith, CEO
EMP: 213 Privately Held
WEB: www.district1fire.com
SIC: 8062 9111 General medical & surgical hospitals; county supervisors' & executives' offices
PA: County Of Holmes
2 Court St Ste 14
Millersburg OH 44654
330 674-1896

(G-14601)
COUNTY OF HOLMES
Also Called: Child Support Enforcement Agcy
85 N Grant St (44654-1166)
P.O. Box 72 (44654-0072)
PHONE....................................330 674-1111
Dan Jackson, Director
EMP: 42 Privately Held
WEB: www.district1fire.com
SIC: 8322 9111 8331 Individual & family services; county supervisors' & executives' offices; job training services
PA: County Of Holmes
2 Court St Ste 14
Millersburg OH 44654
330 674-1896

(G-14602)
CSB BANCORP INC (PA)
91 N Clay St (44654-1117)
P.O. Box 232 (44654-0232)
PHONE....................................330 674-9015
Fax: 330 674-4941
Robert K Baker, Ch of Bd
Eddie L Steiner, President
Christopher Delatore, Vice Pres
Julie Jones, Vice Pres
Paula J Meiler, CFO
EMP: 40
SALES: 30.7MM Publicly Held
WEB: www.csb1.com
SIC: 6022 State commercial banks

(G-14603)
GRAPHIC PUBLICATIONS INC
Also Called: Bargain Hunter
7368 County Road 623 (44654-9256)
P.O. Box 358 (44654-0358)
PHONE....................................330 674-2300
Fax: 330 674-2461
Michael Mast, President
Paul Money, Editor
Frances Mast, Corp Secy
Devlin Stermer, Credit Mgr
Damian Conkle, Accounts Mgr
▲ EMP: 45
SQ FT: 12,000
SALES (est): 5.9MM Privately Held
WEB: www.gpubs.com
SIC: 2721 7336 Periodicals: publishing only; graphic arts & related design

(G-14604)
HOLMES LUMBER & BLDG CTR INC
Also Called: Holmes Lumber & Supply
6139 Hc 39 (44654)
PHONE....................................330 674-9060
Fax: 330 674-0265
Paul Miller, President
Eric Wiedemann, Store Mgr
D Tim Yoder, Credit Mgr
Randy Smith, Sales Staff
Dan Broderick, Manager
EMP: 150 EST: 1952
SQ FT: 16,000
SALES (est): 971.4K Privately Held
WEB: www.holmeslumber.com
SIC: 5031 5211 2439 2434 Lumber, plywood & millwork; lumber & other building materials; structural wood members; wood kitchen cabinets; millwork; hardwood dimension & flooring mills

(G-14605)
HOLMES SIDING CONTRACTORS
6767 County Road 624 (44654-8840)
PHONE....................................330 674-2867
Fax: 330 674-0032
Edward Yoder, Partner
Daniel Mast, Partner
Jamin Yoder, Human Resources
EMP: 75
SQ FT: 100,000
SALES (est): 7.1MM Privately Held
SIC: 1761 Siding contractor

(G-14606)
HOLMES-WAYNE ELECTRIC COOP
6060 State Route 83 (44654-9172)
P.O. Box 112 (44654-0112)
PHONE....................................330 674-1055
Fax: 330 674-1869
Glenn Miller, President
John Porter, President
Stacy Shaw, Safety Dir
Casey Wagner, Accountant
Lisa Baker,
EMP: 42
SQ FT: 25,000
SALES: 15.3MM Privately Held
WEB: www.hwecoop.com
SIC: 4911 Distribution, electric power

(G-14607)
HONEY RUN RETREATS LLC (PA)
Also Called: Inn At Honey Run
6920 County Road 203 (44654-9018)
PHONE....................................330 674-0011
Fax: 330 674-2623
Will Marmet, Director
Jason Nies,
EMP: 35
SALES: 2.9MM Privately Held
SIC: 7011 Hotels

(G-14608)
HUNTINGTON INSURANCE INC
212 N Washington St (44654-1123)
PHONE....................................330 674-2931
Ronald D Scherer, Branch Mgr
EMP: 37
SALES (corp-wide): 4.7B Publicly Held
SIC: 6411 Insurance agents
HQ: Huntington Insurance, Inc.
519 Madison Ave
Toledo OH 43604
419 720-7900

(G-14609)
JOEL POMERENE MEMORIAL HOSP (PA)
Also Called: POMERENE HOSPITAL
981 Wooster Rd (44654-1536)
PHONE....................................330 674-1015
Fax: 330 674-3019
P W Smith Jr, CEO
Claudia Rozuk, Ch Radiology
Nicole Kolacz, VP Opers
Jason Justus, CFO
Craig Miller, Human Res Dir
EMP: 280 EST: 1937
SQ FT: 45,000
SALES: 31.9MM Privately Held
SIC: 8062 General medical & surgical hospitals

(G-14610)
LIEBEN WOOSTER LP
6834 County Road 672 # 102 (44654-8349)
PHONE....................................330 390-5722
Robert Schlabach, Partner
EMP: 25 EST: 2016
SALES (est): 150.1K Privately Held
SIC: 7011 Hotel, franchised

(G-14611)
MAST TRUCKING INC
6471 County Road 625 (44654-8833)
PHONE....................................330 674-8913
Fax: 330 674-0913
Willis Mast, President
Elsie Mast, Vice Pres
Kevin Mast, Vice Pres
Jorden Shaw, Safety Dir
Nikolas Marty, Opers Mgr
EMP: 100
SALES (est): 28MM Privately Held
SIC: 4213 Contract haulers; refrigerated products transport

(G-14612)
MILLERSBURG TIRE SERVICE INC
7375 State Route 39 (44654-8319)
PHONE....................................330 674-1085
Fax: 330 674-6598
Brad Schmuker, President
Wes Schmucker, Vice Pres
Valerie Crilow, Accountant
Bob Hanna, Sales Staff
▲ EMP: 30
SQ FT: 7,000
SALES (est): 12.1MM Privately Held
WEB: www.millersburgtireservice.com
SIC: 5014 5531 Automobile tires & tubes; truck tires & tubes; motorcycle tires & tubes; tires, used; automotive tires

(G-14613)
MULTI PRODUCTS COMPANY
7188 State Route 39 (44654-9204)
P.O. Box 1597, Gainesville TX (76241-1597)
PHONE....................................330 674-5981
Fax: 330 674-2125
Jeff Berlin, CEO
William T Baker, President
Bud Doty, Corp Secy
Greg Guthrie, Vice Pres
▲ EMP: 42
SQ FT: 30,000
SALES (est): 12.5MM Privately Held
SIC: 3533 5084 Oil field machinery & equipment; industrial machinery & equipment

(G-14614)
N SAFE SOUND SECURITY INC
5555 County Road 203 (44654-8242)
PHONE....................................888 317-7233
Ryan Torrence, President
Jerry Anderson, Director
Richard Schneider, Director
EMP: 40
SALES (est): 1.5MM Privately Held
SIC: 7389 Music & broadcasting services

(G-14615)
PINECRAFT LAND HOLDINGS LLC
6834 County Road 672 # 102 (44654-8349)
PHONE....................................330 390-5722
David Schlabach, Managing Prtnr
Robert Schlabach, Managing Prtnr
EMP: 25
SALES (est): 136.5K Privately Held
SIC: 7011 Hotels & motels

(G-14616)
PIONEER TRAILS INC
7572 State Route 241 (44654-8822)
PHONE....................................330 674-1234
Fax: 330 674-1790
David Swartzentruber, President
EMP: 35
SQ FT: 16,000
SALES (est): 2.6MM Privately Held
WEB: www.pioneertrailsbus.com
SIC: 4142 Bus charter service, except local

(G-14617)
PRECISION GEOPHYSICAL INC (PA)
2695 State Route 83 (44654-9455)
PHONE....................................330 674-2198
Fax: 330 674-1729
Steven Mc Crossin, President
EMP: 32
SALES (est): 4.8MM Privately Held
WEB: www.precisiongeophysical.com
SIC: 1382 Oil & gas exploration services

(G-14618)
REA & ASSOCIATES INC
212 N Washington St # 100 (44654-1122)
PHONE....................................330 674-6055
Fax: 330 674-3859
Jordan Miller, Accountant
Chris Roush, Branch Mgr
Dustin Raber, Senior Mgr
EMP: 25
SALES (corp-wide): 32.3MM Privately Held
WEB: www.reacpa.com
SIC: 8721 Certified public accountant
PA: Rea & Associates, Inc.
419 W High Ave
New Philadelphia OH 44663
330 339-6651

(G-14619)
ROY J MILLER
6739 State Route 241 (44654-9467)
PHONE....................................330 674-2405
Roy J Miller,
EMP: 36
SALES (est): 1.2MM Privately Held
SIC: 7389

(G-14620)
S AND R LEASING
9705 Township Rd (44654)
PHONE....................................330 276-3061
Donna Shreiner, President
David Shreiner, Vice Pres
Patrick Roche, Treasurer
EMP: 30
SALES (est): 1.2MM Privately Held
SIC: 7359 Equipment rental & leasing

(G-14621)
SAFE-N-SOUND SECURITY INC
5555 County Road 203 (44654-8242)
PHONE....................................330 491-1148
Fax: 330 491-1166

GEOGRAPHIC SECTION

Minerva - Stark County (G-14644)

Ryan Torrence, *President*
EMP: 60
SALES (est): 6.3MM **Privately Held**
WEB: www.rusafensound.com
SIC: 7382 Security systems services

(G-14622)
SKYVIEW BAPTIST RANCH INC
7241 Township Road 319 (44654-8708)
PHONE..................330 674-7511
Bill Roloff, *Exec Dir*
William E Roloff, *Director*
E Roloff, *Director*
Sarah Kidner, *Admin Sec*
EMP: 46
SALES (est): 935.5K **Privately Held**
SIC: 8322 7032 0752 Multi-service center; summer camp, except day & sports instructional; animal specialty services

(G-14623)
T & L TRANSPORT INC
4395 County Road 58 (44654-9634)
P.O. Box 441 (44654-0441)
PHONE..................330 674-0655
Fax: 330 674-9744
Thomas Klein, *President*
Theresa Loder, *Treasurer*
Brad Ringwalt, *Manager*
Larry Loder, *Admin Sec*
EMP: 38
SALES (est): 5.2MM **Privately Held**
SIC: 4213 Refrigerated products transport

(G-14624)
THREE M ASSOCIATES
7488 State Route 241 (44654-8383)
PHONE..................330 674-9646
Dean Mullet, *Partner*
Dennis Mullet, *Partner*
Jacob Mullet, *Partner*
EMP: 70 EST: 1974
SQ FT: 1,716
SALES (est): 2.7MM **Privately Held**
WEB: www.mulletcabinet.com
SIC: 6512 Nonresidential building operators

(G-14625)
TROYER CHEESE INC
Also Called: Amish Wedding Foods
6597 County Road 625 (44654-9071)
PHONE..................330 893-2479
Fax: 330 893-2375
James Troyer, *President*
Jonas A Troyer, *Chairman*
Doug Gerwig, *Purch Mgr*
Aaron Yoder, *Purch Mgr*
Steve Yoder, *Buyer*
EMP: 45
SQ FT: 59,500
SALES (est): 23.7MM **Privately Held**
WEB: www.troyercheese.com
SIC: 5149 5143 5147 2032 Specialty food items; cheese; meats, cured or smoked; ethnic foods: canned, jarred, etc.

(G-14626)
VILLAGE MOTORS INC
Also Called: Village Chrysler-Dodge
784 Wooster Rd (44654-1031)
PHONE..................330 674-2055
Fax: 330 674-5364
Thomas Green, *President*
Cory Allison, *Business Mgr*
Marc Miller, *Treasurer*
Deke Miller, *Sales Mgr*
Deb Burgess, *Sales Staff*
EMP: 67
SQ FT: 11,200
SALES (est): 25.3MM **Privately Held**
WEB: www.villagemotorsinc.com
SIC: 5511 5521 5012 Automobiles, new & used; used car dealers; automobiles & other motor vehicles

(G-14627)
WASTE PARCHMENT INC
4510 Township Road 307 (44654-9656)
PHONE..................330 674-6868
Fax: 330 674-5057
Robert Smith, *President*
Cheri Mainwaring, *Manager*
Elaine Smith, *Admin Sec*
EMP: 30
SQ FT: 80,000
SALES: 1MM **Privately Held**
SIC: 4953 2611 Recycling, waste materials; pulp mills

(G-14628)
WB SERVICES INC
6834 County Road 672 # 102 (44654-8349)
PHONE..................330 390-5722
Robert Schlabach, *President*
EMP: 72
SALES (est): 1.5MM **Privately Held**
SIC: 1522 Hotel/motel & multi-family home construction

Millersport
Fairfield County

(G-14629)
ASPLUNDH TREE EXPERT LLC
12488 Lancaster St # 94 (43046-8072)
PHONE..................740 467-1028
Debbie Tooper, *Manager*
EMP: 150
SALES (corp-wide): 4.3B **Privately Held**
WEB: www.asplundh.com
SIC: 0783 Tree trimming services for public utility lines
PA: Asplundh Tree Expert Llc
  708 Blair Mill Rd
  Willow Grove PA 19090
  215 784-4200

(G-14630)
CEDAR CREEK VTERINARY SVCS INC
12575 Lancaster St Ne (43046-8065)
PHONE..................740 467-2949
Steven Debruin, *President*
Edgar Biggie, *Vice Pres*
EMP: 25
SQ FT: 3,502
SALES (est): 1.2MM **Privately Held**
SIC: 0742 Veterinarian, animal specialties

(G-14631)
PRE-FORE INC
Also Called: Professional Refrigeration
410 Blacklick Rd (43046-9527)
P.O. Box 518 (43046-0518)
PHONE..................740 467-2206
Fax: 614 467-3297
Gary Kendrick, *President*
Keith Schooley, *Vice Pres*
John Callow Sr, *Treasurer*
EMP: 35
SALES (est): 6.4MM **Privately Held**
WEB: www.pre-fore.com
SIC: 1711 Warm air heating & air conditioning contractor; refrigeration contractor

Millfield
Athens County

(G-14632)
FAST TRAXX PROMOTIONS LLC
17575 Jacksonville Rd (45761-9006)
PHONE..................740 767-3740
Fax: 740 767-3660
Shawna Bickley,
Norman Bickley,
EMP: 50
SALES (est): 590.6K **Privately Held**
WEB: www.fasttraxxracing.com
SIC: 7948 8743 Automotive race track operation; promotion service

Mineral City
Tuscarawas County

(G-14633)
M & L LEASING CO
8999 Bay Dr Ne (44656-9015)
PHONE..................330 343-8910
Michael Morris, *Partner*
Lionel Meister, *Partner*
EMP: 41
SQ FT: 80,000
SALES (est): 1.3MM **Privately Held**
SIC: 6512 7359 Commercial & industrial building operation; equipment rental & leasing

(G-14634)
MUSKINGUM WTRSHED CNSRVNCY DST
Also Called: Atwood Lake Park
4956 Shop Rd Ne (44656-8851)
PHONE..................330 343-6780
Fax: 330 343-5454
J Anthony Luther, *Superintendent*
Tom Fisher, *Info Tech Mgr*
EMP: 30 **Privately Held**
WEB: www.muskingumfoundation.org
SIC: 7996 7033 Amusement parks; trailer parks & campsites
PA: Muskingum Watershed Conservancy District
  1319 3rd St Nw
  New Philadelphia OH 44663
  330 343-6647

Mineral Ridge
Trumbull County

(G-14635)
ADOLPH JOHNSON & SON CO
3497 Union St (44440-9009)
P.O. Box 1583, Youngstown (44501-1583)
PHONE..................330 544-8900
Paul Johnson, *President*
Warner Lawson, *Chairman*
James Johnson, *Vice Pres*
EMP: 25 EST: 1910
SQ FT: 4,300
SALES (est): 5.3MM **Privately Held**
WEB: www.adolphjohnson.com
SIC: 1542 1541 Commercial & office building, new construction; institutional building construction; industrial buildings & warehouses

(G-14636)
GLENN VIEW MANOR INC
3379 Main St Star Rt 46 (44440)
PHONE..................330 652-9901
Fax: 330 544-7541
Edward C Hood, *President*
Judy Grimes, *Admin Sec*
Joseph Ketchaver, *Administration*
EMP: 207 EST: 1964
SQ FT: 23,500
SALES (est): 4.9MM **Privately Held**
SIC: 8051 Skilled nursing care facilities

(G-14637)
L B FOSTER COMPANY
Also Called: Relay Rail Div.
1193 Salt Springs Rd (44440-9318)
PHONE..................330 652-1461
Fax: 330 652-7494
Scott Calahoun, *Manager*
EMP: 25
SQ FT: 3,000
SALES (corp-wide): 536.3MM **Publicly Held**
WEB: www.lbfoster.com
SIC: 1799 3743 Coating of metal structures at construction site; railroad equipment
PA: L. B. Foster Company
  415 Holiday Dr Ste 1
  Pittsburgh PA 15220
  412 928-3400

(G-14638)
REINNOVATIONS CONTRACTING INC
3711 Main St (44440-9791)
PHONE..................330 505-9035
Jeffrey S McElhaney, *President*
George Wrataric, *Vice Pres*
Steffeny Ohino, *Manager*
EMP: 40
SALES (est): 3.8MM **Privately Held**
SIC: 1541 Renovation, remodeling & repairs: industrial buildings

(G-14639)
ROOD TRUCKING COMPANY INC (PA)
3505 Union St (44440-9007)
PHONE..................330 652-3519
George H Rood, *President*
Diane E Rood, *Vice Pres*
Jeff Rood, *Vice Pres*
EMP: 125
SQ FT: 10,000
SALES (est): 16.4MM **Privately Held**
WEB: www.roodtrucking.com
SIC: 4212 4213 Mail carriers, contract; trucking, except local

(G-14640)
TERRE FORME ENTERPRISES INC
Also Called: Clearview Lantern Suites
3000 Austintown Warren Rd (44440-9758)
PHONE..................330 847-6800
Stephen Sandberg, *President*
Betty Crews, *Vice Pres*
Kevin Sandberg, *Vice Pres*
Ellisa Sandberg-Roden, *Treasurer*
Briana Freye, *Marketing Staff*
EMP: 32
SQ FT: 35,868
SALES (est): 1.7MM **Privately Held**
SIC: 8361 Home for the aged

Minerva
Stark County

(G-14641)
AMERIDIAL INC
102 N Market St (44657-1614)
PHONE..................330 868-2000
Fax: 330 868-6037
Shannon Phillips, *Manager*
EMP: 60
SALES (corp-wide): 40MM **Privately Held**
SIC: 7389 Telemarketing services
PA: Ameridial, Inc.
  4535 Strausser St Nw
  North Canton OH 44720
  330 497-4888

(G-14642)
C C & S AMBULANCE SERVICE INC
Also Called: Bartley Ambulance
207 W Lincolnway (44657-1414)
P.O. Box 374 (44657-0374)
PHONE..................330 868-4114
Fax: 330 868-5007
Catherine Viola, *President*
David Viola, *Treasurer*
EMP: 50
SALES (est): 1.4MM **Privately Held**
SIC: 4119 Ambulance service

(G-14643)
CONSUMERS BANCORP INC
614 E Lincolnway (44657-2009)
P.O. Box 256 (44657-0256)
PHONE..................330 868-7701
Laurie L McClellan, *Ch of Bd*
Ralph J Lober II, *President*
John P Furey, *Chairman*
Derek G Williams, *Senior VP*
Renee K Wood, *CFO*
EMP: 128
SALES: 18.8MM **Privately Held**
SIC: 6022 State commercial banks

(G-14644)
CONSUMERS NATIONAL BANK (PA)
614 E Lincolnway (44657-2096)
PHONE..................330 868-7701
Fax: 330 868-3460
Ralf Lober, *President*
Stormie Gross, *Senior VP*
Rick Baxter, *Assistant VP*
Michele Catlett, *Assistant VP*
Vicki Hall, *Assistant VP*
EMP: 45
SQ FT: 6,000

Minerva - Stark County (G-14645)

SALES: 17.9MM **Privately Held**
WEB: www.consumersbank.com
SIC: 6021 National commercial banks

(G-14645)
FAMILY MEDICINE CENTER MINERVA
Also Called: Minerva Medical Center
200 Carolyn Ct (44657-8758)
PHONE..........................330 868-4184
Fax: 330 868-5095
Joseph Khalil, *President*
EMP: 30
SQ FT: 6,000
SALES (est): 1.4MM **Privately Held**
SIC: 8011 General & family practice, physician/surgeon

(G-14646)
IMPERIAL ALUM - MINERVA LLC
217 Roosevelt St (44657-1541)
PHONE..........................330 868-7765
Fax: 330 868-4308
Mike Chenoweth, *Vice Pres*
David Riddell, *Vice Pres*
Gary Grim, *Plant Supt*
David Goss, *CFO*
Greg Donay, *Sales Staff*
EMP: 55
SALES (est): 12.7MM **Privately Held**
SIC: 3334 5093 Slabs (primary), aluminum; scrap & waste materials

(G-14647)
INTERNAL MEDICAL PHYSICIANS
1168 Alliance Rd Nw (44657-8736)
PHONE..........................330 868-3711
Claudio Deperalta, *Owner*
Jody Norris, *Office Mgr*
EMP: 27 **Privately Held**
SIC: 8011 Internal medicine, physician/surgeon
PA: Internal Medical Physicians
    1207 W State St Ste N
    Alliance OH 44601

(G-14648)
MINERVA ELDER CARE INC
Also Called: Minerva Elderly Care
1035 E Lincolnway (44657-1297)
PHONE..........................330 868-4147
Edward Martell Sr, *President*
Pat Moschgat, *Director*
Tracy Randall, *Director*
Renee Forester, *Administration*
Martha Martell, *Admin Sec*
EMP: 35 EST: 1971
SQ FT: 12,000
SALES (est): 1.4MM **Privately Held**
SIC: 8051 Extended care facility

(G-14649)
MINERVA WELDING AND FABG INC
22133 Us Route 30 (44657-9401)
P.O. Box 369 (44657-0369)
PHONE..........................330 868-7731
Fax: 330 868-3377
James A Gram, *President*
Jody Loper, *Safety Dir*
Stephen J Gram, *Treasurer*
Daniel E Gram, *Admin Sec*
Margie Wilson, *Admin Asst*
EMP: 40 EST: 1949
SQ FT: 10,000
SALES (est): 18.7MM **Privately Held**
WEB: www.minweld.com
SIC: 5084 3599 Industrial machinery & equipment; machine shop, jobbing & repair

(G-14650)
SANDY CREEK JOINT FIRE DST
505 E Lincolnway (44657-2007)
PHONE..........................330 868-5193
Rudy Evanich, *Owner*
David Detchon, *Owner*
James Kiko, *Owner*
Richard McClellan, *Owner*
Laurie Peach, *Owner*
EMP: 45
SALES (est): 810.5K **Privately Held**
SIC: 8049 Paramedic

(G-14651)
ST LUKE LUTHERAN COMMUNITY
4301 Woodale Ave Se (44657-8570)
PHONE..........................330 868-5600
Vicki Nicholson, *Principal*
EMP: 25
SALES (corp-wide): 15.5MM **Privately Held**
SIC: 8361 Home for the aged
PA: St. Luke Lutheran Community
    220 Applegrove St Ne
    Canton OH
    330 499-8341

Minford
Scioto County

(G-14652)
MINFORD RETIREMENT CENTER LLC
9641 State Route 335 (45653-8904)
P.O. Box 276 (45653-0276)
PHONE..........................740 820-2821
Fax: 740 820-8939
Kevin Kammler, *Director*
Henry Collins,
Hank Collins II, *Maintence Staff*
Jeaneta Collins,
EMP: 42
SALES (est): 1.5MM **Privately Held**
SIC: 8059 Rest home, with health care

Mingo Junction
Jefferson County

(G-14653)
BELLAS CO
Also Called: Iron City Distributing
2670 Commercial Ave (43938-1613)
P.O. Box 2399, Steubenville (43953-0399)
PHONE..........................740 598-4171
Michael C Bellas, *Ch of Bd*
Robert M Chapman, *President*
Charles D Burrier Sr, *Principal*
Diane Bellas Terzis, *Corp Secy*
Albert Bellas, *Vice Pres*
▲ EMP: 50
SQ FT: 38,000
SALES (est): 10.9MM
SALES (corp-wide): 5.3MM **Privately Held**
WEB: www.ironcitydist.com
SIC: 5181 5182 5149 Beer & other fermented malt liquors; wine; soft drinks
PA: The K M C Corporation
    2670 Commercial Ave
    Mingo Junction OH 43938
    740 598-4171

(G-14654)
CBO LLC
2680 Commercial Ave (43938-1613)
P.O. Box 2399, Steubenville (43953-0399)
PHONE..........................740 598-4121
Michael Bellas, *Mng Member*
Robert M Chapman, *Mng Member*
Nick Latousakis, *Mng Member*
Diane Bellas Terzais, *Mng Member*
EMP: 26
SALES (est): 5.2MM
SALES (corp-wide): 5.3MM **Privately Held**
WEB: www.choicebrandsofohio.com
SIC: 5181 Beer & other fermented malt liquors
PA: The K M C Corporation
    2670 Commercial Ave
    Mingo Junction OH 43938
    740 598-4171

(G-14655)
K M C CORPORATION (PA)
2670 Commercial Ave (43938-1613)
P.O. Box 2399, Steubenville (43953-0399)
PHONE..........................740 598-4171
Michael C Bellas, *President*
Dianne Bellas Terezis, *Corp Secy*
Robert M Chapman, *Senior VP*
Albert Bellas, *Vice Pres*
EMP: 50 EST: 1975
SQ FT: 10,000
SALES (est): 5.3MM **Privately Held**
SIC: 5181 5182 5194 Beer & other fermented malt liquors; wine; tobacco & tobacco products

(G-14656)
NORFOLK SOUTHERN CORPORATION
200 Wabash Ave (43938)
PHONE..........................740 535-4102
Michael Bradley, *Manager*
EMP: 100
SALES (corp-wide): 10.5B **Publicly Held**
WEB: www.nscorp.com
SIC: 4731 4013 Railroad freight agency; switching & terminal services
PA: Norfolk Southern Corporation
    3 Commercial Pl Ste 1a
    Norfolk VA 23510
    757 629-2680

(G-14657)
START-BLACK SERVICESJV LLC
797 Cool Spring Rd (43938-1611)
PHONE..........................740 598-4891
Frank Hoagland,
EMP: 65
SALES (est): 540.8K **Privately Held**
SIC: 7381 Guard services

(G-14658)
SUNRISE TELEVISION CORP
Also Called: Wtov TV 9
9 Red Donely Plz (43938)
P.O. Box 9999, Steubenville (43952-6799)
PHONE..........................740 282-9999
EMP: 70
SALES (corp-wide): 674.9MM **Publicly Held**
SIC: 7622 4833 Television repair shop; television broadcasting stations
HQ: Sunrise Television Corp.
    1 W Exchange St Ste 5a
    Providence RI

Minster
Auglaize County

(G-14659)
ALBERT FREYTAG INC
306 Executive Dr (45865)
P.O. Box 5 (45865-0005)
PHONE..........................419 628-2018
Fax: 419 628-3771
William Freytag, *President*
Joseph Freytag, *Vice Pres*
Kelli Francis, *Engineer*
Dorothy Weaver, *Controller*
EMP: 25
SQ FT: 1,200
SALES (est): 6.7MM **Privately Held**
SIC: 3441 1741 Fabricated structural metal; masonry & other stonework

(G-14660)
DORSTEN INDUSTRIES INC
146 N Main St (45865-1120)
P.O. Box 156 (45865-0156)
PHONE..........................419 628-2327
Ronald A Dorsten, *President*
Kevin Huber, *Superintendent*
Frank P Connaughton, *Principal*
H A Dersten, *Principal*
James E Weger, *Principal*
EMP: 50 EST: 1953
SQ FT: 2,500
SALES (est): 12.3MM **Privately Held**
WEB: www.hadorsteninc.com
SIC: 1541 1542 Industrial buildings, new construction; commercial & office building, new construction

(G-14661)
EMMYS BRIDAL INC
336 N Main St (45865-9561)
PHONE..........................419 628-7555
Fax: 419 628-7558
Lori Rindler, *President*
Anne Puthoff, *Vice Pres*
EMP: 25

SALES: 600K **Privately Held**
WEB: www.emmysbridal.com
SIC: 5621 7299 Bridal shops; clothing rental services

(G-14662)
GARMANN/MILLER & ASSOC INC
Also Called: Garmann Miller Architects
38 S Lincoln Dr (45865-1220)
P.O. Box 71 (45865-0071)
PHONE..........................419 628-4240
Fax: 419 628-4299
James Turissini, *Ch of Bd*
Bruce Miller, *President*
Brad Garmann, *Vice Pres*
Matthew Kremer, *Engineer*
Kevin Rinderle, *Engineer*
EMP: 38
SQ FT: 2,800
SALES: 900K **Privately Held**
WEB: www.garmannmiller.com
SIC: 8712 8711 0781 Architectural engineering; engineering services; mechanical engineering; heating & ventilation engineering; electrical or electronic engineering; landscape architects

(G-14663)
GRAHAM PACKAGING HOLDINGS CO
255 Southgate (45865-9552)
P.O. Box 123 (45865-0123)
PHONE..........................419 628-1070
Robert Andreas, *Branch Mgr*
EMP: 45 **Privately Held**
SIC: 5199 Packaging materials
HQ: Graham Packaging Holdings Co
    700 Indian Springs Dr # 100
    Lancaster PA 17601
    717 849-8500

(G-14664)
HOSKINS INTERNATIONAL LLC
Also Called: Hoskins Intl SEC Invstigations
5116 State Route 119 (45865-9404)
PHONE..........................419 628-6015
James Hoskins,
James Joyce,
EMP: 26
SQ FT: 10,000
SALES: 2MM **Privately Held**
WEB: www.hoskinsinternational.com
SIC: 8748 1731 Energy conservation consultant; energy management controls

(G-14665)
KNIGHTS OF COLUMBUS
40 N Main St (45865-1119)
P.O. Box 48 (45865-0048)
PHONE..........................419 628-2089
Kurt Hilgefort, *President*
EMP: 37
SALES (corp-wide): 2.2B **Privately Held**
WEB: www.kofc.org
SIC: 8641 Fraternal associations
PA: Knights Of Columbus
    1 Columbus Plz Ste 1700
    New Haven CT 06510
    203 752-4000

(G-14666)
MINSTER BANK (PA)
95 W 4th St (45865-1060)
P.O. Box 90 (45865-0090)
PHONE..........................419 628-2351
Fax: 419 628-2103
Mark Henschen, *CEO*
Dale Luebke, *Exec VP*
Phyllis Rose, *Senior VP*
Daniel Heitmeyer, *Vice Pres*
Kenneth Wuebker, *CFO*
EMP: 42
SQ FT: 33,000
SALES: 17.9MM **Privately Held**
WEB: www.minsterbank.com
SIC: 6022 State trust companies accepting deposits, commercial

(G-14667)
PARK ARROWHEAD GOLF CLUB INC
2211 Dirksen Rd (45865-9348)
P.O. Box 73 (45865-0073)
PHONE..........................419 628-2444

GEOGRAPHIC SECTION

Monroe - Butler County (G-14691)

Fax: 419 628-3926
Mike Griner, *President*
Bruce Bernhole, *Treasurer*
Tom Griner, *Admin Sec*
EMP: 30
SALES (est): 1MM **Privately Held**
SIC: 7992 5941 Public golf courses; golf goods & equipment

(G-14668)
PRECISION STRIP INC (HQ)
86 S Ohio St (45865-1246)
P.O. Box 104 (45865-0104)
PHONE.................................419 628-2343
Fax: 419 628-3367
Thomas A Compton, *Ch of Bd*
Joe Wolf, *President*
Don Bomhorst, *Vice Pres*
Joe Price, *Maintence Staff*
EMP: 200 **EST:** 1977
SQ FT: 300,000
SALES (est): 235.9MM
SALES (corp-wide): 9.7B **Publicly Held**
WEB: www.precision-strip.com
SIC: 7389 Metal slitting & shearing
PA: Reliance Steel & Aluminum Co.
    350 S Grand Ave Ste 5100
    Los Angeles CA 90071
    213 687-7700

Mogadore
Portage County

(G-14669)
ALFRED NICKLES BAKERY INC
3775 Mogadore Rd (44260-1232)
PHONE.................................330 628-9964
Fax: 330 628-0198
Charles Moy, *Manager*
EMP: 53
SQ FT: 14,870
SALES (corp-wide): 205MM **Privately Held**
WEB: www.nicklesbakery.com
SIC: 5149 Bakery products
PA: Alfred Nickles Bakery, Inc.
    26 Main St N
    Navarre OH 44662
    330 879-5635

(G-14670)
ASW GLOBAL LLC (PA)
3375 Gilchrist Rd (44260-1253)
PHONE.................................330 733-6291
Andre Thornton, *CEO*
George Hand, *Senior VP*
Nick Mihiylov, *Senior VP*
Carolyn Pizzuto, *Senior VP*
Marilyn Cancilla, *Vice Pres*
EMP: 70
SQ FT: 1,500,000
SALES (est): 84.5MM **Privately Held**
WEB: www.aswservices.com
SIC: 4225 General warehousing

(G-14671)
ASW GLOBAL LLC
Also Called: Asw Supply Chain Service
3325 Gilchrist Rd (44260-1253)
PHONE.................................330 798-5184
Diana Rowe, *Accounts Mgr*
Robert Sims, *Marketing Mgr*
Nick Mihiylov, *Branch Mgr*
EMP: 100
SALES (corp-wide): 84.5MM **Privately Held**
WEB: www.aswservices.com
SIC: 4225 General warehousing
PA: Asw Global, Llc
    3375 Gilchrist Rd
    Mogadore OH 44260
    330 733-6291

(G-14672)
BICO AKRON INC
Also Called: Bico Steel Service Centers
3100 Gilchrist Rd (44260-1246)
PHONE.................................330 794-1716
Fax: 330 733-7189
Thomas Fiocca, *President*
Marilyn L Tuzzio, *Principal*
Michael Ensminger, *Vice Pres*
Chad Kovitk, *Controller*
Jeff Ford, *Sales Staff*

▲ **EMP:** 65
SQ FT: 90,000
SALES (est): 35.1MM
SALES (corp-wide): 48.4MM **Privately Held**
SIC: 5051 3443 Steel; fabricated plate work (boiler shop)
HQ: Bico Michigan, Inc.
    O-99 Steele St Nw
    Grand Rapids MI 49534

(G-14673)
CORNWELL QUALITY TOOLS COMPANY
200 N Cleveland Ave (44260-1205)
PHONE.................................330 628-2627
Fax: 330 628-8496
Bill Nobley, *Branch Mgr*
Dianna Stump, *Executive*
EMP: 75
SQ FT: 3,000
SALES (est): 13.3MM
SALES (corp-wide): 151.2MM **Privately Held**
WEB: www.cornwelltools.com
SIC: 3423 5085 Hand & edge tools; industrial supplies
PA: The Cornwell Quality Tools Company
    667 Seville Rd
    Wadsworth OH 44281
    330 336-3506

(G-14674)
DAVEY TREE EXPERT COMPANY
1437 State Route 43 (44260-9604)
PHONE.................................330 628-1499
Carl Warnke, *President*
Jeff Parson, *Manager*
EMP: 25
SALES (corp-wide): 915.9MM **Privately Held**
SIC: 0782 Lawn services
PA: The Davey Tree Expert Company
    1500 N Mantua St
    Kent OH 44240
    330 673-9511

(G-14675)
DENNIS C MCCLUSKEY MD & ASSOC
754 S Cleveland Ave # 300 (44260-2210)
PHONE.................................330 628-2686
Dennis Mc Cluskey MD, *President*
Brian Cain, *Shareholder*
EMP: 42
SQ FT: 10,600
SALES (est): 1.8MM **Privately Held**
SIC: 8011 General & family practice, physician/surgeon

(G-14676)
EMPIRE ONE LLC
1532 State Route 43 (44260-8820)
PHONE.................................330 628-9310
Brian Taylor, *Principal*
EMP: 40
SALES (est): 1.7MM **Privately Held**
SIC: 7389 Water softener service

(G-14677)
H M MILLER CONSTRUCTION CO
1225 Waterloo Rd (44260-9598)
P.O. Box 131 (44260-0131)
PHONE.................................330 628-4811
Fax: 330 628-3406
John Smith, *President*
Mike Smith, *Treasurer*
Patrick Smith, *Admin Sec*
Kris Fisher, *Admin Asst*
EMP: 55 **EST:** 1972
SQ FT: 20,000
SALES (est): 12.5MM **Privately Held**
SIC: 1623 7353 Sewer line construction; water main construction; heavy construction equipment rental

(G-14678)
HENRYS KING TOURING COMPANY
1369 Burbridge Dr (44260-1601)
PHONE.................................330 628-1886
Fax: 330 628-1886
Timothy Walsh, *Principal*

EMP: 35
SALES (est): 46.4K **Privately Held**
SIC: 7929 Entertainers & entertainment groups

(G-14679)
HMS CONSTRUCTION & RENTAL CO
1225 Waterloo Rd (44260-9598)
P.O. Box 131 (44260-0131)
PHONE.................................330 628-4811
John Smith, *President*
EMP: 60
SQ FT: 1,200
SALES (est): 2.3MM **Privately Held**
SIC: 1521 New construction, single-family houses

(G-14680)
KIDS AHEAD INC
726 S Cleveland Ave (44260-2205)
PHONE.................................330 628-7404
Julie Begue, *Owner*
EMP: 35
SALES (est): 627.4K **Privately Held**
SIC: 8351 Group day care center

(G-14681)
OMEGA LABORATORIES INC
400 N Cleveland Ave (44260-1209)
PHONE.................................330 628-5748
Fax: 330 628-5803
John C Vitullo, *CEO*
Bill Corl, *CEO*
Jay Davis, *President*
Veronica Kero, *Senior Engr*
Dave Engelhar, *Director*
EMP: 61 **EST:** 2000
SQ FT: 44,709
SALES (est): 12.6MM **Privately Held**
WEB: www.omegalabs.net
SIC: 8734 Testing laboratories

(G-14682)
PARRISH TIRE COMPANY OF AKRON
Also Called: Parrish McIntyre Tire
3833 Mogadore Indus Pkwy (44260-1216)
PHONE.................................330 628-6800
Logan Jackson, *President*
Mike Everhart, *Corp Secy*
Mike McIntyre, *Vice Pres*
EMP: 36
SQ FT: 8,800
SALES (est): 3.9MM **Privately Held**
SIC: 7538 General automotive repair shops

(G-14683)
R & R SANITATION INC
1447 Martin Rd (44260-1562)
PHONE.................................330 325-2311
Lola Kennell, *President*
Greg Kennell, *Partner*
EMP: 30
SALES (est): 3MM **Privately Held**
WEB: www.rrsanitation.net
SIC: 4953 4212 Refuse systems; refuse collection & disposal services; garbage collection & transport, no disposal

(G-14684)
TAYLOR CONSTRUCTION COMPANY
1532 State Route 43 (44260-8820)
PHONE.................................330 628-9310
Fax: 330 628-9313
Brian Taylor, *Principal*
Rick Taylor, *Principal*
EMP: 30
SALES (est): 2.9MM **Privately Held**
SIC: 1794 Excavation & grading, building construction

(G-14685)
TAYLOR TELECOMMUNICATIONS INC
3470 Gilchrist Rd (44260-1215)
PHONE.................................330 628-5501
Fax: 330 628-5420
Sherry Taylor, *President*
Chris Taylor, *Vice Pres*
Joe Taylor, *Treasurer*
Tam Taylor, *Admin Sec*
EMP: 95 **EST:** 1981

SQ FT: 4,000
SALES: 14.8MM **Privately Held**
SIC: 1731 Fiber optic cable installation

(G-14686)
THOMAS L STOVER INC
754 S Cleveland Ave # 300 (44260-2210)
PHONE.................................330 665-8060
Fax: 330 665-8069
Thomas L Stover, *President*
EMP: 30
SALES (est): 1.5MM **Privately Held**
SIC: 8011 Offices & clinics of medical doctors

Monroe
Butler County

(G-14687)
ASSEMBLY CENTER
913 Lebanon St (45050-1448)
PHONE.................................800 582-1099
Lenny Wyatt, *President*
EMP: 45
SALES (est): 1.1MM **Privately Held**
SIC: 6512 7299 Auditorium & hall operation; banquet hall facilities

(G-14688)
BAKER CONCRETE CNSTR INC (PA)
900 N Garver Rd (45050-1277)
PHONE.................................513 539-4000
Fax: 513 539-4380
Daniel L Baker, *President*
Gary L Benson, *Vice Pres*
Steven A Lydy, *Vice Pres*
Stephen E Martin, *Vice Pres*
Dennis W Phillips, *Vice Pres*
◆ **EMP:** 700
SQ FT: 27,000
SALES (est): 856.9MM **Privately Held**
WEB: www.bakerconcrete.com
SIC: 1771 1611 Concrete work; concrete construction: roads, highways, sidewalks, etc.

(G-14689)
BAKER EQUIPMENT AND MTLS LTD
990 N Main St (45050)
P.O. Box 526 (45050-0526)
PHONE.................................513 422-6697
Cynthia S Baker, *Mng Member*
Diane Jones, *Manager*
EMP: 30
SALES (est): 6.6MM **Privately Held**
SIC: 7359 Equipment rental & leasing

(G-14690)
BENEDICT ENTERPRISES INC (PA)
750 Lakeview Rd (45050-1707)
P.O. Box 370 (45050-0370)
PHONE.................................513 539-9216
Arnold Benedict, *President*
Elizabeth Benedict, *Exec VP*
Lisa Benedict, *Treasurer*
June Wolfe, *Controller*
Ted Linebaugh, *Manager*
EMP: 28
SQ FT: 20,528
SALES (est): 4.7MM **Privately Held**
WEB: www.bei-benedict.com
SIC: 7513 7519 5511 7538 Truck rental, without drivers; truck leasing, without drivers; trailer rental; trucks, tractors & trailers: new & used; general truck repair

(G-14691)
BRUNK EXCAVATING INC
301 Breaden Dr (45050-1428)
PHONE.................................513 360-0308
Fax: 513 360-0380
Jason Brunk, *President*
EMP: 28
SALES (est): 4.6MM **Privately Held**
SIC: 1629 1794 1795 4959 Pond construction; excavation work; wrecking & demolition work; snowplowing

Monroe - Butler County (G-14692) GEOGRAPHIC SECTION

(G-14692)
CONTINENTAL TRANSPORT INC
Also Called: CTI
997 Platte River Blvd (45050)
P.O. Box 100, Springboro (45066-0100)
PHONE.................................513 360-2960
James R Office, *President*
Steven L Messer, *Principal*
Allison Eder, *Vice Pres*
Dan Seifring, *Manager*
EMP: 50
SALES (est): 5.4MM **Privately Held**
SIC: 4212 Local trucking, without storage

(G-14693)
DICKERSON DISTRIBUTING COMPANY
150 Lawton Ave (45050-1212)
PHONE.................................513 539-8483
Fax: 513 539-8268
John Dickerson Jr, *Ch of Bd*
Michael Dickerson, *President*
Don Schwab, *Opers Mgr*
▲ **EMP:** 60
SQ FT: 32,000
SALES (est): 24.1MM **Privately Held**
WEB: www.dickersondist.com
SIC: 5181 Beer & other fermented malt liquors

(G-14694)
EQUIPMENT DEPOT OHIO INC
Also Called: Portman Material Handling
101 Lawton Ave (45050-1211)
PHONE.................................513 539-8464
Fax: 513 539-8876
Patrick Schmetzer, *General Mgr*
Brian Anderson, *Manager*
Mark Fisher, *Manager*
EMP: 40
SQ FT: 11,000
SALES (corp-wide): 7.3B **Privately Held**
WEB: www.portmanpeople.com
SIC: 5084 Materials handling machinery
HQ: Equipment Depot Ohio, Inc.
4331 Rossplain Dr
Blue Ash OH 45236
513 891-0600

(G-14695)
FORMWORK SERVICES LLC
900 N Garver Rd (45050-1241)
PHONE.................................513 539-4000
Daniel Baker, *President*
Cheryl Sammons, *Manager*
EMP: 50
SALES (est): 2.7MM **Privately Held**
SIC: 1771 Concrete work

(G-14696)
FOUR SEASONS ENVIRONMENTAL INC (PA)
43 New Garver Rd (45050-1281)
PHONE.................................513 539-2978
Fax: 513 539-2972
Daniel Tarkington, *CEO*
Reed Tarkington, *President*
John Hedrick, *Business Mgr*
Timothy McDonald, *Business Mgr*
Ron Wyrtzen, *Vice Pres*
EMP: 350
SQ FT: 9,500
SALES (est): 46.3MM **Privately Held**
WEB: www.fseinc.net
SIC: 8744 8742 ; management consulting services

(G-14697)
HCG INC
Also Called: Zack Pack
203 N Garver Rd (45050-1235)
PHONE.................................513 539-9269
Fax: 513 539-9273
Mark Knue, *President*
Kenneth May, *Treasurer*
James R Office, *Admin Sec*
EMP: 40
SQ FT: 108,000
SALES (est): 3.8MM **Privately Held**
SIC: 4783 Packing goods for shipping

(G-14698)
HOME DEPOT USA INC
Also Called: Home Depot, The
500 Gateway Blvd (45050-1844)
PHONE.................................513 360-1100
EMP: 72
SALES (corp-wide): 100.9B **Publicly Held**
SIC: 4225 General warehousing & storage
HQ: Home Depot U.S.A., Inc.
2455 Paces Ferry Rd Se
Atlanta GA 30339

(G-14699)
J T EXPRESS INC
1200 N Main St (45050)
P.O. Box 439 (45050-0439)
PHONE.................................513 727-8185
Fax: 513 727-8007
Timothy Foister, *President*
Tim Foister, *President*
Jimmie Foister, *Principal*
EMP: 27
SQ FT: 30,000
SALES (est): 4.7MM **Privately Held**
SIC: 4213 4212 Trucking, except local; local trucking, without storage

(G-14700)
KAISER LOGISTICS LLC
201 Lawton Ave (45050-1213)
PHONE.................................937 534-0213
Dewey Weeda,
EMP: 65
SALES (est): 5.6MM
SALES (corp-wide): 16.7B **Publicly Held**
SIC: 8741 Business management
PA: Performance Food Group Company
12500 West Creek Pkwy
Richmond VA 23238
804 484-7700

(G-14701)
KASTLE ELECTRIC COMPANY
Also Called: Kastle Technologies
100 Cart Path Dr (45050-1494)
PHONE.................................513 360-2901
EMP: 40
SALES (est): 22.7MM **Privately Held**
SIC: 1731 General Electrical Contractor
PA: Kastle Electric Company
4501 Kettering Blvd
Moraine OH 45439
937 254-2681

(G-14702)
KASTLE TECHNOLOGIES CO LLC (HQ)
100 Cart Path Dr (45050-1494)
PHONE.................................513 360-2901
Dennis Quebe, *CEO*
Lyman Smith, *President*
Gregory Ross, *COO*
William Page, *CFO*
EMP: 25
SQ FT: 20,000
SALES (est): 4.8MM
SALES (corp-wide): 83.3MM **Privately Held**
SIC: 1731 Electrical work
PA: Quebe Holdings, Inc.
1985 Founders Dr
Dayton OH 45420
937 222-2290

(G-14703)
LITHKO CONTRACTING LLC
900 N Garver Rd (45050-1241)
PHONE.................................513 863-5100
Ivory-Lithko Brimelow, *Superintendent*
Jerry Spoon, *Superintendent*
Westin Jensen, *Project Mgr*
Zach Proctor, *Project Mgr*
Garret Hossfeld, *Project Engr*
EMP: 58
SALES (corp-wide): 177.7MM **Privately Held**
SIC: 1771 Concrete work; foundation & footing contractor; flooring contractor; concrete repair
PA: Lithko Contracting, Llc
2958 Crescentville Rd
West Chester OH 45069
513 564-2000

(G-14704)
LITHKO RESTORATION TECH LLC (PA)
990 N Main St (45050)
P.O. Box 569 (45050-0569)
PHONE.................................513 863-5500
Jim Dean, *Project Mgr*
Gary Huismann, *Project Mgr*
Matt Glasshagel, *Opers Mgr*
Mike Pellegrini, *CFO*
Erik Henry, *Accounts Mgr*
EMP: 80
SALES (est): 23.1MM **Privately Held**
SIC: 1771 Concrete repair

(G-14705)
MCGRAW/KOKOSING INC
101 Clark Blvd (45044-3216)
PHONE.................................614 212-5700
Daniel B Walker, *President*
Chris A Bergs, *Vice Pres*
Tim Freed, *CFO*
EMP: 500
SQ FT: 232,000
SALES (est): 131.8MM
SALES (corp-wide): 674.3MM **Privately Held**
WEB: www.mcgrawkokosing.com
SIC: 1541 Renovation, remodeling & repairs: industrial buildings
PA: Kokosing Inc.
6235 Wstrville Rd Ste 200
Westerville OH 43081
614 212-5700

(G-14706)
MONROE MECHANICAL INCORPORATED
Also Called: Monroe Heating and AC
150 Breaden Dr B (45050-1427)
PHONE.................................513 539-7555
Fax: 513 539-9555
William M Housh III, *President*
RG Bender, *Manager*
EMP: 35
SQ FT: 24,000
SALES (est): 7.5MM **Privately Held**
SIC: 1711 5075 Mechanical contractor; plumbing contractors; warm air heating & air conditioning

(G-14707)
OHIO PIZZA PRODUCTS INC (DH)
Also Called: Performnce Fodservice - Presto
201 Lawton Ave (45050-1213)
P.O. Box 549 (45050-0549)
PHONE.................................937 294-6969
Fax: 513 539-4527
Vito P Weeda, *Ch of Bd*
Jeff Schrand, *President*
Phil Weeda Sr, *Chairman*
Roberta Schrater, *Vice Pres*
Weeda Vito, *Vice Pres*
EMP: 80
SQ FT: 80,000
SALES (est): 147MM
SALES (corp-wide): 16.7B **Publicly Held**
WEB: www.prestofoods.com
SIC: 5149 Pizza supplies; specialty food items; baking supplies
HQ: Institution Food House, Inc.
543 12th Street Dr Nw
Hickory NC 28601
800 800-0434

(G-14708)
OHIO PRESBT RETIREMENT SVCS
Also Called: Ohio Presbt Retirement Vlg
225 Britton Ln (45050-1154)
PHONE.................................513 539-7391
Fax: 513 539-9463
Tim Chupka, *Persnl Dir*
Stan Kappers, *Branch Mgr*
Derek Dye, *Director*
Josh Sparks, *Director*
Dyrk Vanvalkenburg, *Director*
EMP: 250 **Privately Held**
WEB: www.nwo.oprs.org
SIC: 8361 8052 8051 Rest home, with health care incidental; intermediate care facilities; skilled nursing care facilities
PA: Ohio Living
1001 Kingsmill Pkwy
Columbus OH 43229

(G-14709)
PETERMANN
505 Yankee Rd (45050-1069)
PHONE.................................513 539-0324
Fax: 513 539-0327
Peter Settle, *Owner*
Lee A Cary, *VP Sls/Mktg*
EMP: 25
SALES (est): 660K **Privately Held**
SIC: 4151 School buses

(G-14710)
RICHTER LANDSCAPING
240 Senate Dr (45050-1715)
PHONE.................................513 539-0300
Richard Richter, *Owner*
EMP: 30
SQ FT: 19,280
SALES (est): 1.7MM **Privately Held**
SIC: 0782 Landscape contractors

(G-14711)
SENIOR INDEPENDENCE ADULT
25 Indiana Ave (45050-1146)
PHONE.................................513 681-8174
Joan Punchfleming, *Manager*
EMP: 50
SALES (corp-wide): 2.7MM **Privately Held**
SIC: 8322 Adult day care center
PA: Senior Independence Adult Day Services
717 Neil Ave
Columbus OH 43215
614 224-5344

(G-14712)
SENIOR INDEPENDENCE ADULT
27 Indiana Ave (45050-1146)
PHONE.................................513 539-2697
Joan Punch-Fleming, *Manager*
EMP: 50
SALES (corp-wide): 2.7MM **Privately Held**
SIC: 8322 8082 Adult day care center; refugee service; home health care services
PA: Senior Independence Adult Day Services
717 Neil Ave
Columbus OH 43215
614 224-5344

(G-14713)
STONEY RIDGE INN SOUTH LTD
Also Called: Stoney Ridge Truck Plaza
1250 Hmilton Lebanon Rd E (45050-1704)
P.O. Box 485, Canfield (44406-0485)
PHONE.................................513 539-9247
Fax: 513 539-7254
James Underwood, *General Ptnr*
Kathy Elkins, *Manager*
EMP: 80
SQ FT: 28,000
SALES (est): 1.2MM **Privately Held**
WEB: www.stoneyridgewinery.com
SIC: 7011 Inns

(G-14714)
TEREX UTILITIES INC
Also Called: Cincinnati Division
920 Deneen Ave (45050-1210)
PHONE.................................513 539-9770
Fax: 513 539-6971
Steve Harris, *Vice Pres*
Ron Schmittou, *Regl Sales Mgr*
Rick Girffis, *Branch Mgr*
Ruedi Vancoppenolle, *Manager*
EMP: 53
SALES (corp-wide): 4.3B **Publicly Held**
WEB: www.craneamerica.com
SIC: 3531 7629 3536 Cranes; electrical repair shops; hoists, cranes & monorails
HQ: Terex Utilities, Inc.
12805 Sw 77th Pl
Tigard OR 97223
503 620-0611

(G-14715)
TRADERS WORLD INC
601 Union Rd (45050)
PHONE.................................513 424-2052

▲ = Import ▼=Export
◆ =Import/Export

GEOGRAPHIC SECTION
Montgomery - Hamilton County (G-14735)

Fax: 513 741-7187
Jay Frick Jr, *President*
Helen Frick, *Vice Pres*
EMP: 40
SALES (est): 2.9MM **Privately Held**
SIC: 6512 7389 Commercial & industrial building operation; flea market

(G-14716)
UNIVERSAL TRANSPORTATION SYSTE
220 Senate Dr (45050-1715)
PHONE..........................513 539-9491
Fax: 513 539-9821
Lori Vogft, *Branch Mgr*
EMP: 35
SALES (corp-wide): 18.3MM **Privately Held**
WEB: www.utswct.com
SIC: 4789 4111 Cargo loading & unloading services; local & suburban transit
PA: Universal Transportation Systems Llc
5284 Winton Rd
Fairfield OH 45014
513 829-1287

(G-14717)
VALICOR ENVIRONMENTAL SVCS LLC (HQ)
1045 Reed Dr Ste A (45050-1717)
PHONE..........................513 733-4666
Fax: 513 539-9180
James Devlin, *CEO*
Dave Brown, *COO*
Jami Paul, *Sales Executive*
Bill Hinton, *Officer*
▲ EMP: 70
SQ FT: 16,000
SALES (est): 39.7MM
SALES (corp-wide): 1.4B **Privately Held**
WEB: www.unitedwastewater.com
SIC: 5039 Septic tanks
PA: Wind Point Partners, L.P.
676 N Michigan Ave # 3700
Chicago IL 60611
312 255-4800

(G-14718)
WORTHINGTON INDUSTRIES INC
Worthington Steel
350 Lawton Ave (45050-1216)
PHONE..........................513 539-9291
John Lawhorn, *Purchasing*
Rusty Alward, *QC Dir*
Dustin Lawson, *Engineer*
David Kleimeyer, *Sales/Mktg Mgr*
John Jessee, *Sales Staff*
EMP: 165
SQ FT: 120,000
SALES (corp-wide): 3B **Publicly Held**
WEB: www.worthingtonindustries.com
SIC: 3325 5051 3471 3441 Steel foundries; metals service centers & offices; plating & polishing; fabricated structural metal; blast furnaces & steel mills
PA: Worthington Industries, Inc.
200 W Old Wlson Bridge Rd
Worthington OH 43085
614 438-3210

(G-14719)
ZIEGLER TIRE AND SUPPLY CO
1100 Reed Dr (45050-1721)
PHONE..........................513 539-7574
Steve Hubicz, *Branch Mgr*
EMP: 30
SALES (corp-wide): 78.9MM **Privately Held**
SIC: 7538 General automotive repair shops
PA: The Ziegler Tire And Supply Company
4150 Millennium Blvd Se
Massillon OH 44646
330 353-1499

Monroeville
Huron County

(G-14720)
HOMAN TRANSPORTATION INC
22 Fort Monroe Pkwy (44847-9411)
PHONE..........................419 465-2626
Fax: 419 465-2869
Andrew Homan, *President*
Cameron Chandler, *Controller*
Andy Homan, *Manager*
Angela Homan, *Admin Sec*
EMP: 80
SALES (est): 14.9MM **Privately Held**
SIC: 4213 Heavy hauling

(G-14721)
JHI GROUP INC (PA)
Also Called: Janotta & Herner
309 Monroe St (44847-9406)
PHONE..........................419 465-4611
Fax: 419 465-2866
James Shelley, *Ch of Bd*
James Limbird, *President*
Steve Durbin, *Vice Pres*
Seth Herrnstein, *Vice Pres*
Jason Ott, *Vice Pres*
EMP: 165
SALES (est): 70.6MM **Privately Held**
WEB: www.janottaherner.com
SIC: 1542 Commercial & office building, new construction

(G-14722)
SHEARER FARM INC
Also Called: John Deere Authorized Dealer
13 Fort Monroe Pkwy (44847-9411)
PHONE..........................419 465-4622
Ivan Maibach, *Branch Mgr*
EMP: 35
SALES (corp-wide): 59.5MM **Privately Held**
SIC: 5046 5082 Commercial equipment; construction & mining machinery
PA: Shearer Farm, Inc
7762 Cleveland Rd
Wooster OH 44691
330 345-9023

(G-14723)
TUSING BUILDERS LTD
2596 Us Route 20 E (44847)
PHONE..........................419 465-3100
Fax: 419 465-3101
Jason Tusing, *Partner*
Todd Limpert, *Superintendent*
Jason Cleland, *Opers Mgr*
Colleen Shupe, *Controller*
EMP: 28
SALES (est): 6.7MM **Privately Held**
WEB: www.tusingbuilders.com
SIC: 1542 1521 Commercial & office building, new construction; single-family housing construction

(G-14724)
UNDERGROUND UTILITIES INC
416 Monroe St (44847-9789)
P.O. Box 428 (44847-0428)
PHONE..........................419 465-2587
Fax: 419 465-4289
John A Bores, *CEO*
Joseph Hossler, *Vice Pres*
Michael Prinatt, *Vice Pres*
Greg Schafer, *Vice Pres*
Mike Prenatt, *Project Mgr*
EMP: 96 EST: 1978
SQ FT: 12,000
SALES: 37MM **Privately Held**
SIC: 1623 Water main construction; sewer line construction

Montgomery
Hamilton County

(G-14725)
COLLIER NURSING SERVICE INC
9844 Zig Zag Rd (45242-6311)
PHONE..........................513 791-4357
Fax: 513 791-3293
Bette M Collier, *President*
EMP: 250
SALES (est): 8.5MM **Privately Held**
WEB: www.colliernursingservices.com
SIC: 7361 Nurses' registry

(G-14726)
INFORMATION BUILDERS INC
1 Financial Way Ste 307 (45242-5800)
PHONE..........................513 891-2338
Fax: 513 891-8385
James Roy, *Regional Mgr*
Rick Rohde, *Manager*
EMP: 30
SALES (corp-wide): 313.7MM **Privately Held**
WEB: www.informationbuilders.com
SIC: 5734 7377 Computer software & accessories; computer rental & leasing
PA: Information Builders, Inc.
2 Penn Plz Fl 28
New York NY 10121
212 736-4433

(G-14727)
MONTGOMERY SWIM & TENNIS CLUB
9941 Orchard Club Dr (45242-4466)
PHONE..........................513 793-6433
Fax: 513 793-6433
Mary Blood, *Manager*
EMP: 29
SQ FT: 1,963
SALES (est): 1.1MM **Privately Held**
SIC: 7997 Country club, membership

(G-14728)
O N EQUITY SALES COMPANY
Also Called: Onesco
1 Financial Way Ste 100 (45242-5800)
P.O. Box 371, Cincinnati (45201-0371)
PHONE..........................513 794-6794
Barbara Turner, *President*
Rick Picard, *COO*
Sherri Lehman, *Production*
Donna Clapp, *Administration*
EMP: 600 EST: 1968
SALES (est): 46.1MM
SALES (corp-wide): 857MM **Privately Held**
WEB: www.hummelagency.com
SIC: 6211 Security brokers & dealers
HQ: Ohio National Financial Services, Inc.
1 Financial Way Ste 100
Montgomery OH 45242
513 794-6100

(G-14729)
OHIO NAT MUTL HOLDINGS INC (PA)
1 Financial Way Ste 100 (45242-5800)
PHONE..........................513 794-6100
Fax: 513 794-7272
Gary Huffman, *Ch of Bd*
Barbara A Turner, *Exec VP*
David A Azzarito, *Senior VP*
Richard J Bodner, *Senior VP*
Christopher A Carlson, *Senior VP*
EMP: 750 EST: 1993
SALES (est): 857MM **Privately Held**
SIC: 6311 Mutual association life insurance

(G-14730)
OHIO NATIONAL FINCL SVCS INC (HQ)
1 Financial Way Ste 100 (45242-5800)
P.O. Box 237, Cincinnati (45201-0237)
PHONE..........................513 794-6100
Fax: 513 794-4508
Gary T Huffman, *President*
Howard Clark, *President*
Arthur J Roberts, *President*
Ronald Dolan, *Vice Chairman*
Gary Huffman, *Vice Chairman*
EMP: 700
SALES (est): 856.7MM
SALES (corp-wide): 857MM **Privately Held**
SIC: 6311 Mutual association life insurance
PA: Ohio National Mutual Holdings, Inc.
1 Financial Way Ste 100
Montgomery OH 45242
513 794-6100

(G-14731)
OHIO NATIONAL LIFE ASSURANCE
1 Financial Way Ste 100 (45242-5800)
P.O. Box 237, Cincinnati (45201-0237)
PHONE..........................513 794-6100
David B Omaley, *CEO*
Gates Smith, *Exec VP*
Robert Bowen, *Vice Pres*
Terry L Garrard, *Vice Pres*
Ronald J Dolan, *CFO*
EMP: 716 EST: 1979
SALES (est): 88.1MM
SALES (corp-wide): 857MM **Privately Held**
WEB: www.ohionatl.com
SIC: 6411 Insurance agents
HQ: The Ohio National Life Insurance Company
1 Financial Way Ste 100
Montgomery OH 45242

(G-14732)
OHIO NATIONAL LIFE INSUR CO (DH)
Also Called: Ohio Casualty Insurance
1 Financial Way Ste 100 (45242-5800)
P.O. Box 237, Cincinnati (45201-0237)
PHONE..........................513 794-6100
David B Omaley, *CEO*
Michael Vogel, *Vice Pres*
Danny Leach, *Manager*
Peggy Williamson, *Consultant*
Braun Kim, *Technology*
EMP: 80
SALES (est): 307MM
SALES (corp-wide): 857MM **Privately Held**
WEB: www.nslac.com
SIC: 6331 Fire, marine & casualty insurance
HQ: Ohio National Financial Services, Inc.
1 Financial Way Ste 100
Montgomery OH 45242
513 794-6100

(G-14733)
ORTHOPEDIC DIAGNSTC TRTMNT CTR
10547 Montgomery Rd 400a (45242-4418)
PHONE..........................513 791-6611
Fax: 513 791-6788
Thomas Carothers, *Branch Mgr*
James Muccio, *Med Doctor*
Edmund Schweitzer, *Med Doctor*
Donna Walters, *Assistant*
EMP: 26
SALES (corp-wide): 3MM **Privately Held**
SIC: 8011 Orthopedic physician
PA: Orthopedic Diagnostic & Treatment Center Inc
4600 Smith Rd Ste B
Cincinnati OH 45212
513 221-4848

(G-14734)
TRIHEALTH INC
Also Called: Trihealth Fitnes Hlth Pavilion
6200 Pfeiffer Rd Ste 330 (45242-5864)
PHONE..........................513 985-0900
Fax: 513 985-6751
Tom Poff, *Project Mgr*
Michael Fiore, *Accountant*
Stacey Lawson, *Human Resources*
Deb Riggs, *Branch Mgr*
Diane Kelly, *Manager*
EMP: 134 **Privately Held**
WEB: www.trihealth.com
SIC: 8741 8011 Hospital management; offices & clinics of medical doctors
HQ: Trihealth, Inc.
619 Oak St
Cincinnati OH 45206
513 569-6111

(G-14735)
TRIHEALTH OS LLC
Also Called: Trihealth Orthpd & Spine Inst
10547 Montgomery Rd 400a (45242-4418)
PHONE..........................513 791-6611
Valerie Hall, *Manager*
EMP: 60 **Privately Held**
SIC: 8069 Orthopedic hospital
HQ: Trihealth Os, Llc
8311 Montgomery Rd
Cincinnati OH 45236
513 985-3700

Montpelier
Williams County

(G-14736)
B & H INDUSTRIES INC
14020 Us Highway 20a (43543-9270)
PHONE..............................419 485-8373
Ron Dean, *CEO*
Cindy Dennis, *VP Opers*
EMP: 28
SQ FT: 4,000
SALES (est): 2.6MM
SALES (corp-wide): 16.7MM **Privately Held**
WEB: www.bryansystems.com
SIC: 4213 4212 Trucking, except local; local trucking, without storage
PA: Best Way Motor Lines, Inc.
  14020 Us Highway 20a
  Montpelier OH 43543
  419 485-8373

(G-14737)
BOB MOR INC
Also Called: Quality Inn
13508 State Route 15 (43543-9737)
PHONE..............................419 485-5555
John P Kidston, *President*
Hal R Hendricks, *Vice Pres*
EMP: 130
SQ FT: 150,000
SALES (est): 4.4MM **Privately Held**
SIC: 7011 5812 Hotels & motels; eating places

(G-14738)
BRIDGEWATER DAIRY LLC
14587 County Road 8 50 (43543-9337)
PHONE..............................419 485-8157
Nancy Weaver, *Office Mgr*
Brenda Woodroff, *Office Mgr*
Leon D Weaver,
Tim Den Dulk,
Chris Weaver,
EMP: 35 EST: 1998
SALES (est): 7.7MM **Privately Held**
SIC: 0241 Milk production

(G-14739)
BRYAN TRUCK LINE INC
Also Called: Bryan Systems
14020 Us Hwy 20 Ste A (43543)
PHONE..............................419 485-8373
Ronald W Dean, *Ch of Bd*
Larry H Dean, *President*
Cindy Dennis, *Vice Pres*
Buck Muhlford, *CFO*
EMP: 100
SQ FT: 16,000
SALES (est): 12.4MM
SALES (corp-wide): 16.7MM **Privately Held**
WEB: www.bryansystems.com
SIC: 4212 4213 Local trucking, without storage; trucking, except local
PA: Best Way Motor Lines, Inc.
  14020 Us Highway 20a
  Montpelier OH 43543
  419 485-8373

(G-14740)
COMMUNICARE HEALTH SVCS INC
Also Called: Evergreen Healthcare Center
924 Charlies Way (43543-1904)
PHONE..............................419 485-8307
Fax: 419 485-1015
Clarence Bell, *Director*
Fara Nickle, *Director*
Dee F Shoup, *Hlthcr Dir*
Terry Schollmeier, *Administration*
Robert Brailey, *Administration*
EMP: 70
SALES (corp-wide): 103.9MM **Privately Held**
WEB: www.atriumlivingcenters.com
SIC: 6531 Real estate agents & managers
PA: Communicare Health Services, Inc.
  4700 Ashwood Dr Ste 200
  Blue Ash OH 45241
  513 530-1654

(G-14741)
COMMUNITY HSPTALS WLLNESS CTRS
Also Called: Montpelier Hospital
909 E Snyder Ave (43543-1251)
PHONE..............................419 485-3154
Fax: 419 485-3833
Phil Ennen, *CEO*
Bob Hauck, *Pharmacist*
Lisa Fitzenrider, *Case Mgr*
Chris Conti, *Info Tech Mgr*
Greg Slattery, *Data Proc Exec*
EMP: 76
SALES (corp-wide): 77.2MM **Privately Held**
SIC: 8062 General medical & surgical hospitals
PA: Community Hospitals And Wellness Centers
  433 W High St
  Bryan OH 43506
  419 636-1131

(G-14742)
COUNTY OF WILLIAMS
Also Called: Williams County Health Dept
310 Lincoln Ave Ste A (43543-1274)
P.O. Box 146 (43543-0146)
PHONE..............................419 485-3141
Fax: 419 485-5420
James Watkins, *Director*
EMP: 25 **Privately Held**
SIC: 9431 8082 ; home health care services
PA: County Of Williams
  1 Courthouse Sq Ste L
  Bryan OH 43506
  419 636-2059

(G-14743)
DECORATIVE PAINT INCORPORATED
700 Randolph St (43543-1464)
PHONE..............................419 485-0632
John Simon, *President*
Greg Dirrim, *Vice Pres*
Mike Avina, *Opers Mgr*
Michael Rude, *QC Mgr*
Terri Snyder, *Controller*
EMP: 83
SALES (est): 1.2MM **Privately Held**
WEB: www.dpii.biz
SIC: 7532 Paint shop, automotive

(G-14744)
MONTPELIER AUTO AUCTION OHIO
14125 County Road M50 (43543-9233)
P.O. Box 47 (43543-0047)
PHONE..............................419 485-1691
Fax: 419 485-5103
Bob Hebergsen, *President*
Robert Hubregson, *Manager*
John Sullivan, *Director*
EMP: 150
SALES (est): 12.9MM **Privately Held**
SIC: 5012 5521 Automobile auction; automobiles, used cars only

(G-14745)
MONTPELIER SENIOR CENTER
325 N Jonesville St (43543-1009)
PHONE..............................419 485-3218
Jewel Head, *Director*
EMP: 40
SALES (est): 71.6K **Privately Held**
SIC: 8399 Community development groups

(G-14746)
NEY OIL COMPANY INC
Also Called: Exit Two Stop N Go
13441 State Route 15 (43543-9296)
PHONE..............................419 485-4009
Fax: 419 485-4009
Christie Cogswell, *Branch Mgr*
EMP: 68
SALES (corp-wide): 84.8MM **Privately Held**
WEB: www.neyoil.com
SIC: 5171 Petroleum bulk stations
PA: Ney Oil Company Inc
  145 S Water St
  Ney OH 43549
  419 658-2324

(G-14747)
NORFOLK SOUTHERN CORPORATION
701 Linden St (43543-1886)
PHONE..............................419 485-3510
S E Smith, *Manager*
EMP: 25
SALES (corp-wide): 10.5B **Publicly Held**
WEB: www.nscorp.com
SIC: 4011 Railroads, line-haul operating
PA: Norfolk Southern Corporation
  3 Commercial Pl Ste 1a
  Norfolk VA 23510
  757 629-2680

(G-14748)
STATE BANK AND TRUST COMPANY
1201 E Main St (43543-1247)
PHONE..............................419 485-5521
Misty Fritsch, *Office Mgr*
Al Fiser, *Branch Mgr*
EMP: 49
SALES (corp-wide): 49.7MM **Publicly Held**
SIC: 6022 6021 State trust companies accepting deposits, commercial; national commercial banks
HQ: The State Bank And Trust Company
  401 Clinton St
  Defiance OH 43512
  419 783-8950

Moraine
Montgomery County

(G-14749)
ANDERSON SECURITY INC (PA)
4600 S Dixie Dr (45439-2114)
PHONE..............................937 294-1478
Robert A Anderson, *President*
Gaye N Anderson, *President*
Bob Anderson, *COO*
Andrew Papanek, *VP Opers*
Linda L Papanek, *Human Res Mgr*
EMP: 80
SQ FT: 6,500
SALES (est): 2.9MM **Privately Held**
WEB: www.anderson-security.com
SIC: 7381 7382 Security guard service; security systems services

(G-14750)
ANGEL HEARTS HOME HEALTH INC
2213 Arbor Blvd (45439-1521)
P.O. Box 49383, Dayton (45449-0383)
PHONE..............................937 263-6194
Jeniffer Jones, *President*
EMP: 200
SALES (est): 7.1MM **Privately Held**
SIC: 8059 Personal care home, with health care

(G-14751)
APRIL ENTERPRISES INC
Also Called: Walnut Creek Nursing Facility
5070 Lamme Rd (45439-3266)
PHONE..............................937 293-7703
Fax: 937 293-1890
Diane Gumbert, *CFO*
CAM Swift, *Financial Exec*
Steve Wilson Jr, *Info Tech Dir*
Mileah Marion, *Nursing Dir*
Stephanie Miller, *Nursing Dir*
EMP: 319
SALES (est): 11.5MM **Privately Held**
WEB: www.wcreekoh.com
SIC: 8051 Skilled nursing care facilities

(G-14752)
BDS PACKAGING INC
3155 Elbee Rd Ste 201 (45439-2046)
PHONE..............................937 643-0530
Fax: 937 643-0866
Wendell T Bryant, *President*
Jeff Sloneker, *Vice Pres*
EMP: 58
SQ FT: 78,264
SALES (est): 11.6MM **Privately Held**
WEB: www.bdspackaging.com
SIC: 2653 3993 7389 Boxes, corrugated: made from purchased materials; displays & cutouts, window & lobby; packaging & labeling services

(G-14753)
BERRY NETWORK LLC (DH)
3100 Kettering Blvd (45439-1924)
P.O. Box 8818, Dayton (45401-8818)
PHONE..............................800 366-1264
Fax: 937 296-4863
Joni Arison, *President*
Michelle Hutchinson, *Vice Pres*
Frank McNaulty, *Vice Pres*
Tom Smith, *Vice Pres*
Kory Walton, *Vice Pres*
EMP: 196
SQ FT: 55,000
SALES (est): 21.5K
SALES (corp-wide): 1.8B **Privately Held**
WEB: www.berrynetwork.com
SIC: 7319 Distribution of advertising material or sample services
HQ: Yp Holdings Llc
  2247 Northlake Pkwy Fl 10
  Tucker GA 30084
  866 570-8863

(G-14754)
BLACK STONE CINCINNATI LLC
Also Called: Assisted Care By Black Stone
3044 Kettering Blvd (45439-1922)
PHONE..............................937 424-1370
Jordan Broome, *CFO*
Matt Cooksey, *CFO*
David Tramontana, *Branch Mgr*
Chris Doggett, *Manager*
Steve Black, *CTO*
EMP: 87
SALES (corp-wide): 13.8MM **Privately Held**
SIC: 8082 Home health care services
PA: Black Stone Of Cincinnati, Llc
  4700 E Galbraith Rd Fl 3
  Cincinnati OH 45236
  513 924-1370

(G-14755)
BOBCAT OF DAYTON INC (PA)
2850 E River Rd Unit 1 (45439-1582)
PHONE..............................937 293-3176
Fax: 937 293-7392
Ruston Pettit, *President*
Byron Pettit, *Vice Pres*
Shirley Stidham, *Office Mgr*
EMP: 30
SQ FT: 19,200
SALES (est): 10.2MM **Privately Held**
SIC: 5084 7359 Materials handling machinery; industrial truck rental

(G-14756)
BUCKEYE POWER SALES CO INC
Also Called: Lawn & Garden Equipment
5238 Cobblegate Blvd (45439-5114)
PHONE..............................937 346-8322
Jim Watson, *Branch Mgr*
EMP: 29
SALES (corp-wide): 66.4MM **Privately Held**
SIC: 5063 Generators
PA: Buckeye Power Sales Co., Inc.
  6850 Commerce Court Dr
  Blacklick OH 43004
  513 755-2323

(G-14757)
BWI NORTH AMERICA INC
Also Called: Bwi Group NA
2582 E River Rd (45439-1514)
PHONE..............................937 212-2892
Greg Bowman, *Manager*
EMP: 50 **Privately Held**
WEB: www.delphiauto.com
SIC: 8734 Product testing laboratories
HQ: Bwi North America Inc.
  3100 Res Blvd Ste 240
  Kettering OH 45420

(G-14758)
CARAUSTAR INDUSTRIES INC
2601 E River Rd (45439-1533)
PHONE..............................937 298-9969

GEOGRAPHIC SECTION — Moraine - Montgomery County (G-14779)

Bill Theado, *Manager*
EMP: 40
SALES (corp-wide): 1.4B **Privately Held**
WEB:
www.newarkpaperboardproducts.com
SIC: 4953 Recycling, waste materials
PA: Caraustar Industries, Inc.
5000 Astell Pwdr Sprng Rd
Austell GA 30106
770 948-3101

(G-14759)
CARDINAL HEALTH 414 LLC
2217 Arbor Blvd (45439-1521)
PHONE.....................937 438-1888
Gary Hoogland, *Sales/Mktg Mgr*
EMP: 30
SALES (corp-wide): 129.9B **Publicly Held**
WEB: www.syncor.com
SIC: 5122 Pharmaceuticals
HQ: Cardinal Health 414, Llc
7000 Cardinal Pl
Dublin OH 43017
614 757-5000

(G-14760)
COMMAND ROOFING CO
2485 Arbor Blvd (45439-1776)
PHONE.....................937 298-1155
Fax: 937 298-2340
Donald L Phlipot, *President*
Michael R Davis, *Vice Pres*
Gary Martin, *Project Mgr*
Dave Honious, *Maintence Staff*
EMP: 110
SQ FT: 50,000
SALES: 12MM **Privately Held**
WEB: www.commandroofing.com
SIC: 1761 1751 Roofing contractor; carpentry work

(G-14761)
COMMSYS INC
3055 Kettering Blvd # 415 (45439-1900)
PHONE.....................937 220-4990
Fax: 937 220-4919
Robert S Turner, *President*
Linda Mullins, *Financial Analy*
Jill Steele, *Finance*
Kelli Adkins, *Mktg Dir*
John Wise, *Manager*
EMP: 26
SQ FT: 4,000
SALES (est): 3.9MM **Privately Held**
WEB: www.commsys.net
SIC: 7373 7371 Systems integration services; computer software systems analysis & design, custom

(G-14762)
COMMUNICATION SVC FOR DEAF INC
Also Called: Communication Svcs For Deaf
2448 W Dorothy Ln (45439-1828)
PHONE.....................937 299-0917
Fax: 937 643-4605
Mike Lamontagne, *Manager*
EMP: 200
SALES (corp-wide): 31.5MM **Privately Held**
WEB: www.relaysd.com
SIC: 4899 Data communication services
PA: Communication Service For The Deaf, Inc.
2028 E B White 240-5250
Austin TX 78741
844 222-0002

(G-14763)
COMPUNET CLINICAL LABS LLC (HQ)
Also Called: Compunet Clinical Labs
2308 Sandridge Dr (45439-1856)
PHONE.....................937 296-0844
Fax: 937 299-7278
James Pancoast, *President*
Teresa Williams, *COO*
Joanne Denlinger, *Vice Pres*
Paul Labbe, *Vice Pres*
Kathy Mannier, *Vice Pres*
EMP: 250
SALES (est): 22.3MM
SALES (corp-wide): 354MM **Privately Held**
SIC: 8071 Medical laboratories

PA: Premier Health Partners
110 N Main St Ste 450
Dayton OH 45402
937 499-9596

(G-14764)
COUNTY OF MONTGOMERY
Also Called: Montgomery County N Incertr
2550 Sandridge Dr (45439-1851)
PHONE.....................937 781-3046
Fax: 937 454-8133
EMP: 40
SQ FT: 672 **Privately Held**
SIC: 4953 Incinerator Operation
PA: County Of Montgomery
451 W 3rd St Fl 4
Dayton OH 45422
937 225-4000

(G-14765)
CUSHMAN & WAKEFIELD INC
Also Called: Cassidy Turley
3033 Kettering Blvd # 111 (45439-1962)
PHONE.....................937 222-7884
Mark Burkhart, *President*
EMP: 48
SALES (corp-wide): 5.5B **Privately Held**
SIC: 6531 Real estate agent, commercial
HQ: Cushman & Wakefield, Inc.
225 W Wacker Dr Ste 3000
Chicago IL 60606
312 424-8000

(G-14766)
DAVIS PAUL RESTORATION DAYTON
Also Called: Paul Davis Restoration
1960 W Dorothy Ln Ste 207 (45439-1818)
PHONE.....................937 436-3411
Fax: 937 436-9961
Mark Adley, *Partner*
Scott Siens, *Project Mgr*
Gayle Garrison, *Accountant*
Mark Bradley,
EMP: 27
SQ FT: 2,400
SALES (est): 3.1MM **Privately Held**
SIC: 1521 Repairing fire damage, single-family houses

(G-14767)
DAY-MET CREDIT UNION INC (PA)
3199 S Dixie Dr (45439-2207)
P.O. Box 13087, Dayton (45413-0087)
PHONE.....................937 236-2562
Fax: 937 236-2786
Walt Helman, *CEO*
Jerry Scalf, *Ch of Bd*
Tom Keyes, *Business Mgr*
Kevin Van Bibber, *Vice Pres*
Stephanie Etienne, *Finance*
EMP: 26
SQ FT: 15,000
SALES: 2.6MM **Privately Held**
WEB: www.daymetcu.com
SIC: 6062 State credit unions, not federally chartered

(G-14768)
DAY-MONT BHVORAL HLTH CARE INC (PA)
Also Called: Day-Mont Behavioral Hlth Care
2710 Dryden Rd (45439-1614)
PHONE.....................937 222-8111
Fax: 937 222-3019
Gayle Johnson, *President*
Akil Sharif, *Vice Pres*
Marva Busby, *Exec Sec*
EMP: 100
SQ FT: 33,000
SALES: 5MM **Privately Held**
WEB: www.daymont.org
SIC: 8093 Mental health clinic, outpatient

(G-14769)
DAYTON DOG TRAINING CLUB INC
3040 E River Rd Ste 5 (45439-1436)
PHONE.....................937 293-5219
Cathy Hahn, *Director*
EMP: 30

SALES (est): 367.7K **Privately Held**
WEB: www.daytondogtraining.com
SIC: 0752 Training services, pet & animal specialties (not horses)

(G-14770)
DAYTON HEIDELBERG DISTRG CO (PA)
Also Called: Heidelberg Distributing Div
3601 Dryden Rd (45439-1411)
PHONE.....................937 222-8692
Fax: 937 220-6463
Albert W Vontz III, *CEO*
Vail Miller, *Ch of Bd*
Steve Lowrey, *President*
Michael Nolen, *District Mgr*
Sebastian Palicki, *District Mgr*
▲ EMP: 200
SQ FT: 165,000
SALES (est): 369.4MM **Privately Held**
SIC: 5181 Beer & other fermented malt liquors

(G-14771)
DAYTON HEIDELBERG DISTRG CO
3601 Dryden Rd (45439-1411)
PHONE.....................937 220-6450
EMP: 60
SALES (corp-wide): 369.4MM **Privately Held**
SIC: 5199 Advertising specialties
PA: Dayton Heidelberg Distributing Co.
3601 Dryden Rd
Moraine OH 45439
937 222-8692

(G-14772)
DAYTON HEIDELBERG DISTRG CO
Service Distributing Div
3601 Dryden Rd (45439-1411)
PHONE.....................937 220-6450
Steven Lowery, *President*
Thomas A Rouse, *Accountant*
Ken Aquila, *Sales Mgr*
EMP: 127
SALES (corp-wide): 369.4MM **Privately Held**
SIC: 5181 5182 5149 5921 Beer & other fermented malt liquors; wine; groceries & related products; beer (packaged)
PA: Dayton Heidelberg Distributing Co.
3601 Dryden Rd
Moraine OH 45439
937 222-8692

(G-14773)
DAYTON MARSHALL TIRE SALES CO
3091 S Dixie Dr (45439-2205)
PHONE.....................937 293-8330
Fax: 937 293-6747
John Marshall, *President*
Charles L Marshall II, *Corp Secy*
Tony Fiori, *Manager*
Steve Whitehead, *Manager*
EMP: 26
SQ FT: 24,000
SALES (est): 4.1MM **Privately Held**
SIC: 5531 5014 Automotive tires; automobile tires & tubes

(G-14774)
DAYTON POWER AND LIGHT COMPANY
1900 Dryden Rd (45439-1762)
P.O. Box 1247, Dayton (45401-1247)
PHONE.....................937 331-4123
Fax: 937 331-4375
Scott Michaelson, *General Mgr*
Charles F Hatfield, *Principal*
Jeff Teuscher, *Opers Mgr*
Joseph Kelly, *Engineer*
David Phillips, *Engineer*
EMP: 60
SALES (corp-wide): 10.5B **Publicly Held**
WEB: www.waytogo.com
SIC: 4931 4932 4923 4911 Electric & other services combined; gas & other services combined; gas transmission & distribution; electric services

HQ: The Dayton Power And Light Company
1065 Woodman Dr
Dayton OH 45432
937 224-6000

(G-14775)
DONNELLON MC CARTHY INC
2580 Lance Dr (45409-1512)
PHONE.....................937 299-3564
Rob Lee, *Manager*
EMP: 35
SALES (est): 1.5MM
SALES (corp-wide): 34.3MM **Privately Held**
WEB: www.dmdayton.com
SIC: 5044 Photocopy machines
PA: Donnellon Mc Carthy, Inc.
10855 Medallion Dr
Cincinnati OH 45241
513 769-7800

(G-14776)
DONNELLON MC CARTHY INC
2580 Lance Dr (45409-1512)
PHONE.....................937 299-0200
Fax: 937 299-9087
Jim Donnellon, *General Mgr*
Rob Lee, *General Mgr*
Brenda Schmidt, *Sls & Mktg Exec*
Amy Hamilton, *Marketing Staff*
Christopher Roser, *Technology*
EMP: 50
SALES (corp-wide): 34.3MM **Privately Held**
WEB: www.dmdayton.com
SIC: 5999 5065 Photocopy machines; facsimile equipment
PA: Donnellon Mc Carthy, Inc.
10855 Medallion Dr
Cincinnati OH 45241
513 769-7800

(G-14777)
E S GALLON & ASSOCIATES
Also Called: Gallon, E S Associates
2621 Dryden Rd Ste 105 (45439-1661)
PHONE.....................937 586-3100
Fax: 937 586-3200
Joseph Ebenger, *President*
David Saphire, *Treasurer*
Rebecca A Schott, *Administration*
Joann Brenner, *Admin Sec*
Pearlie Brewer,
EMP: 40 EST: 1953
SALES (est): 3.6MM **Privately Held**
WEB: www.esgallon.com
SIC: 8111 General practice law office; general practice attorney, lawyer

(G-14778)
ECG SCANNING & MEDICAL SVCS (DH)
3055 Kettering Blvd 219b (45439-1900)
PHONE.....................888 346-5837
John Nasuti, *President*
Joseph Maclean, *COO*
Amanda Hayes, *Controller*
Denise Van Tongeren-Nicolai, *Officer*
EMP: 25
SQ FT: 7,500
SALES (est): 3.2MM
SALES (corp-wide): 286.7MM **Publicly Held**
WEB: www.ecgscanning.com
SIC: 8071 Testing laboratories
HQ: Cardionet, Llc
1000 Cedar Hollow Rd
Malvern PA 19355
610 729-7000

(G-14779)
ELASTIZELL SYSTEMS INC
2475 Arbor Blvd (45439-1754)
PHONE.....................937 298-1313
Fax: 937 298-7949
Donald L Phlipot, *President*
Jeannine E Phlipot, *Treasurer*
Mike Rachford, *Manager*
EMP: 50 EST: 1972
SQ FT: 6,000
SALES (est): 5.9MM **Privately Held**
SIC: 1771 Concrete work

(PA)=Parent Co (HQ)=Headquarters (DH)=Div Headquarters
✪ = New Business established in last 2 years

Moraine - Montgomery County (G-14780)   GEOGRAPHIC SECTION

(G-14780)
ELDER-BEERMAN STORES CORP (HQ)
Also Called: El-Bee
3155 Elbee Rd Ste 201 (45439-2046)
PHONE..................937 296-2700
Fax: 937 296-2948
Byron Bergren, *President*
Raymond Clayman, *Counsel*
Leonard Peal, *Exec VP*
Charles P Shaffer, *Exec VP*
James M Zamberlan, *Exec VP*
▲ **EMP:** 1000
SQ FT: 302,570
SALES (est): 440.9MM
SALES (corp-wide): 2.6B **Publicly Held**
WEB: www.elder-beerman.com
SIC: 5311 5661 7389 Department stores, non-discount; shoe stores; credit card service
PA: The Bon-Ton Stores Inc
  2801 E Market St
  York PA 17402
  717 757-7660

(G-14781)
ENTING WATER CONDITIONING INC (PA)
Also Called: Superior Water Conditioning Co
3211 Dryden Rd Frnt Frnt (45439-1400)
PHONE..................937 294-5100
Mel Entingh, *CEO*
Dan Entingh, *President*
Yvonne Albert, *Purch Mgr*
Amber Entingh, *Purchasing*
Karen Entingh, *Treasurer*
▲ **EMP:** 31 **EST:** 1965
SQ FT: 43,440
SALES (est): 3.2MM **Privately Held**
WEB: www.enting.com
SIC: 3589 5999 5074 Water filters & softeners, household type; water purification equipment, household type; water treatment equipment, industrial; water purification equipment; water softeners

(G-14782)
EVERYBODYS INC
Also Called: Everybodys Workplace Solutions
3050 Springboro Pike (45439-1812)
PHONE..................937 293-1010
Fax: 937 293-7501
Bill Kasch, *President*
Scot Freeman, *COO*
Thomas Shafer, *Vice Pres*
Dick Counter, *VP Opers*
Kevin N Maxwell, *Sales Associate*
EMP: 50
SQ FT: 80,000
SALES (est): 13.4MM **Privately Held**
WEB: www.everybodysinc.com
SIC: 5021 7641 5023 Office furniture; furniture repair & maintenance; carpets

(G-14783)
FAMILY SERVICE ASSOCIATION
Also Called: FAMILY SERVICES AND COMMUNITY
2211 Arbor Blvd (45439-1521)
PHONE..................937 222-9481
Fax: 937 222-3710
Luisa Hocking, *Finance Mgr*
Bonnie Parrish, *Exec Dir*
Mercedes Dossa, *Director*
Heather Oborne, *Director*
Cheryl Roslund, *Director*
EMP: 50 **EST:** 1896
SQ FT: 7,700
SALES (est): 1.6MM **Privately Held**
SIC: 8322 Social service center; family service agency

(G-14784)
FEDERATED LOGISTICS
Also Called: Eletto Transfer
2260 Arbor Blvd (45439-1522)
PHONE..................937 294-3074
Fax: 937 534-4060
Mark Powell, *Manager*
EMP: 25
SALES (est): 1.9MM **Privately Held**
SIC: 5021 Furniture

(G-14785)
FIDELITY HEALTH CARE
3170 Kettering Blvd (45439-1924)
PHONE..................937 208-6400
Fax: 937 208-6471
Paula Thompson, *President*
Renee Mock, *CFO*
Sinda Jones, *Manager*
Dale Mound, *Supervisor*
Merideth Sasser, *Exec Dir*
EMP: 450
SQ FT: 30,000
SALES: 41.8MM
SALES (corp-wide): 968.3MM **Privately Held**
WEB: www.fidelityhealthcare.com
SIC: 8082 Home health care services
PA: Med America Health Systems Corporation
  1 Wyoming St
  Dayton OH 45409
  937 223-6192

(G-14786)
FIELDSTONE LIMITED PARTNERSHIP (PA)
Also Called: Fox Run Apartments
4000 Miller Valentine Ct (45439-1465)
PHONE..................937 293-0900
Dan Keller, *Principal*
Steve Ireland, *Vice Pres*
EMP: 200
SALES (est): 4.7MM **Privately Held**
SIC: 6513 Apartment building operators

(G-14787)
FLAGEL HUBER FLAGEL & CO (PA)
3400 S Dixie Dr (45439-2304)
PHONE..................937 299-3400
James R Harkwall, *Partner*
Linda Galaise, *Accountant*
Carol Tolson, *Accountant*
Randal Kuvin, *Mng Member*
Chris McCaskey, *Manager*
EMP: 50
SQ FT: 13,200
SALES (est): 5.6MM **Privately Held**
WEB: www.fhf-cpa.com
SIC: 8721 Certified public accountant

(G-14788)
GARDA CL TECHNICAL SVCS INC
2690 Lance Dr (45409-1527)
PHONE..................937 294-4099
Steve Fosnot, *Branch Mgr*
EMP: 34
SALES (corp-wide): 69.3K **Privately Held**
SIC: 7381 3578 4513 Armored car services; coin counters; air courier services
HQ: Garda Cl Technical Services, Inc.
  700 S Federal Hwy Ste 300
  Boca Raton FL 33432

(G-14789)
GLEN ARBORS LTD PARTNERSHIP
4000 Miller Valentine Ct (45439-1465)
PHONE..................937 293-0900
Miller-Valentine Apts Etc, *Partner*
Edward Blake, *Manager*
Victoria McDonald, *Assistant*
EMP: 100 **EST:** 1997
SALES (est): 5.1MM **Privately Held**
SIC: 6512 Nonresidential building operators

(G-14790)
GLOBE FOOD EQUIPMENT COMPANY
2153 Dryden Rd (45439-1739)
PHONE..................937 299-5493
Fax: 937 299-4147
Hilton Garner, *President*
Dale Smart, *Facilities Mgr*
Jeff Ott, *Production*
John Skapiak, *Purch Mgr*
Heather Dwire, *Engineer*
▲ **EMP:** 39
SALES: 50MM
SALES (corp-wide): 2.3B **Publicly Held**
WEB: www.globeslicers.com
SIC: 5046 Restaurant equipment & supplies

PA: The Middleby Corporation
  1400 Toastmaster Dr
  Elgin IL 60120
  847 741-3300

(G-14791)
GLT INC
2691 Lance Dr (45409-1515)
PHONE..................937 395-0508
Brad Labensky, *Branch Mgr*
EMP: 25
SALES (est): 891.8K
SALES (corp-wide): 11.3MM **Privately Held**
WEB: www.gltonline.com
SIC: 1796 Machinery installation
PA: Glt, Inc.
  3341 Successful Way
  Dayton OH 45414
  937 237-0055

(G-14792)
GRACE HOSPICE LLC
3033 Kettering Blvd # 220 (45439-1948)
PHONE..................937 293-1381
Fax: 937 293-1382
Janice Urke, *Administration*
EMP: 115 **Privately Held**
SIC: 8052 Personal care facility
PA: Grace Hospice, Llc
  500 Kirts Blvd Ste 250
  Troy MI 48084

(G-14793)
GROUNDSYSTEMS INC
2929 Northlawn Ave (45439-1647)
PHONE..................937 903-5325
Steve Barhorst, *Branch Mgr*
EMP: 30
SALES (corp-wide): 22.3MM **Privately Held**
SIC: 0782 Landscape contractors
PA: Groundsystems, Inc.
  11315 Williamson Rd
  Blue Ash OH 45241
  800 570-0213

(G-14794)
KASTLE ELECTRIC CO LLC
4501 Kettering Blvd (45439-2137)
PHONE..................937 254-2681
Dennis Quebe, *CEO*
K Andrew Stuhlmiller, *President*
Gregory Ross, *COO*
William Page, *CFO*
EMP: 53
SQ FT: 20,000
SALES (est): 1.8MM
SALES (corp-wide): 83.3MM **Privately Held**
SIC: 1731 General electrical contractor
PA: Quebe Holdings, Inc.
  1985 Founders Dr
  Dayton OH 45420
  937 222-2290

(G-14795)
KASTLE ELECTRIC COMPANY
4501 Kettering Blvd (45439-2137)
P.O. Box 1451, Dayton (45401-1451)
PHONE..................937 254-2681
K Andrew Stuhlmiller, *CEO*
Gregory P Brush, *President*
Jason Soderquest, *Project Mgr*
Ryan Adams, *Engineer*
William S Page, *CFO*
EMP: 120 **EST:** 1925
SALES (est): 2.4MM **Privately Held**
WEB: www.kastle-elec.com
SIC: 1731 General electrical contractor

(G-14796)
KETTERING ADVENTIST HEALTHCARE
Also Called: Kettering Hospital Youth Svcs
5350 Lamme Rd (45439-3215)
PHONE..................937 534-4651
Fax: 937 534-4609
Dorawbaugh David, *Manager*
EMP: 100
SALES (corp-wide): 1.7B **Privately Held**
SIC: 8062 General medical & surgical hospitals

PA: Kettering Adventist Healthcare
  3535 Southern Blvd
  Dayton OH 45429
  937 298-4331

(G-14797)
L M BERRY AND COMPANY (PA)
3170 Kettering Blvd (45439-1924)
PHONE..................937 296-2121
Fax: 937 296-2011
Daniel J Graham, *President*
Jack Mullins, *Engng Exec*
Carol Betts, *Sls & Mktg Exec*
Ron Huist, *Controller*
Jim Bowles, *Persnl Mgr*
EMP: 650
SQ FT: 141,000
SALES (est): 71MM **Privately Held**
WEB: www.lmberry.com
SIC: 7311 2741 Advertising agencies; miscellaneous publishing

(G-14798)
LEGRAND NORTH AMERICA LLC
Also Called: C2g
3555 Kettering Blvd (45439-2014)
PHONE..................937 224-0639
Joe Cornwall, *Area Mgr*
Andrea McDermott, *Project Mgr*
Michael Leach, *Natl Sales Mgr*
Jacqueline Carner, *Accounts Mgr*
Eric Overholser, *Accounts Mgr*
EMP: 420
SALES (corp-wide): 16.3MM **Privately Held**
SIC: 1731 5063 5045 3643 Communications specialization; cable conduit; computer peripheral equipment; current-carrying wiring devices; nonferrous wiredrawing & insulating
HQ: Legrand North America, Llc
  60 Woodlawn St
  West Hartford CT 06110
  860 233-6251

(G-14799)
MANDALAY INC
Also Called: Mandalay Banquet Center
2700 E River Rd (45439-1536)
PHONE..................937 294-6600
Fax: 937 294-9759
Donald L Phillips, *Ch of Bd*
Cay Phillips, *President*
EMP: 42
SQ FT: 72,000
SALES (est): 2.1MM **Privately Held**
WEB: www.mandalaycatering.com
SIC: 7299 Banquet hall facilities

(G-14800)
MCGOHAN/BRABENDER AGENCY INC (PA)
Also Called: McGohan Brabender
3931 S Dixie Dr (45439-2313)
PHONE..................937 293-1600
Scott McGohan, *CEO*
Patrick L McGohan, *CEO*
Tim Brabender, *President*
Beth Ferrin, *CFO*
Rodney L Miller, *CFO*
EMP: 73
SQ FT: 1,400
SALES (est): 34.2MM **Privately Held**
WEB: www.mcgohanbrabender.com
SIC: 6411 Insurance agents

(G-14801)
MDU RESOURCES GROUP INC
Also Called: Capital Electric
3150 Encrete Ln (45439-1902)
PHONE..................937 424-2550
Matthew Slasher, *Foreman/Supr*
Steve Taulbee, *Branch Mgr*
EMP: 25
SALES (corp-wide): 4.4B **Publicly Held**
SIC: 1731 General electrical contractor
PA: Mdu Resources Group, Inc.
  1200 W Century Ave
  Bismarck ND 58503
  701 530-1000

(G-14802)
MED-TRANS INC
3510 Encrete Ln (45439-1951)
PHONE..................937 293-9771

GEOGRAPHIC SECTION

Moraine - Montgomery County (G-14826)

Jim Shiverdecker, *Manager*
Michael George, *Manager*
EMP: 32
SALES (corp-wide): 18.6MM **Privately Held**
WEB: www.med-trans.com
SIC: 4119 Ambulance service
PA: Med-Trans, Inc
   714 W Columbia St
   Springfield OH 45504
   937 325-4926

(G-14803)
MEDICAL ACCOUNT SERVICES INC
3131 S Dixie Dr Ste 535 (45439-2223)
PHONE..................937 297-6072
David Ackley, *CEO*
EMP: 30
SQ FT: 8,200
SALES (est): 1.5MM
SALES (corp-wide): 70.2MM **Privately Held**
WEB: www.medacct.com
SIC: 8721 8742 Billing & bookkeeping service; management consulting services
PA: Advantedge Healthcare Solutions, Inc.
   30 Technology Dr Ste 1n
   Warren NJ 07059
   908 279-8111

(G-14804)
MEDVET ASSOCIATES INC
2714 Springboro W (45439-1710)
PHONE..................937 293-2714
Fax: 937 293-2787
EMP: 348 **Privately Held**
SIC: 0742 Veterinarian, animal specialties
PA: Medvet Associates, Inc
   300 E Wilson Bridge Rd # 100
   Worthington OH 43085

(G-14805)
MIAMI INDUSTRIAL TRUCKS INC (PA)
2830 E River Rd (45439-1500)
PHONE..................937 293-4194
Fax: 937 293-1168
Mark Jones, *CEO*
Bill Miller, *Editor*
Paul Olon, *Editor*
George Malacos, *Chairman*
Jim Shriner, *Opers Mgr*
EMP: 75
SQ FT: 43,000
SALES (est): 51.9MM **Privately Held**
WEB: www.mitlift.com
SIC: 5084 7359 7699 Materials handling machinery; equipment rental & leasing; industrial equipment services

(G-14806)
MILLER CONSOLIDATED INDUSTRIES (PA)
2221 Arbor Blvd (45439-1521)
PHONE..................937 294-2681
Fax: 937 296-7986
Larry Cartwright, *General Mgr*
Nick Miller, *Plant Mgr*
Tom Miller, *CFO*
Carl Black, *Sales Mgr*
Kelly Henderson, *Director*
EMP: 106
SQ FT: 55,000
SALES (est): 19.3MM **Privately Held**
WEB: www.millerconsolidated.com
SIC: 5051 3398 Steel; metal heat treating

(G-14807)
MILLER-VALENTINE PARTNERS
4000 Miller Valentine Ct (45439-1465)
PHONE..................937 293-0900
EMP: 200
SALES (est): 6.1MM **Privately Held**
SIC: 6512 Operator Of Commercial & Industrial Bldgs

(G-14808)
MIRACLECORP PRODUCTS (PA)
2425 W Dorothy Ln (45439-1827)
PHONE..................937 293-9994
Fax: 937 293-9995
William M Sherk Jr, *President*
Lori Fouts, *VP Sales*
Denise Williams, *Sales Staff*
Susie Lovy, *Mktg Dir*
Lori Lindsey, *Manager*
◆ **EMP:** 55
SQ FT: 11,500
SALES: 21MM **Privately Held**
WEB: www.miraclecorp.com
SIC: 3999 0752 5999 Pet supplies; animal specialty services; pet supplies

(G-14809)
MOONLIGHT SECURITY INC
2710 Dryden Rd (45439-1614)
PHONE..................937 252-1600
John Pawelski, *President*
EMP: 85
SQ FT: 13,000
SALES (est): 2.1MM **Privately Held**
SIC: 7381 Security guard service

(G-14810)
MV RESIDENTIAL DEVELOPMENT LLC
4000 Miller Valentine Ct (45439-1465)
PHONE..................937 293-0900
Michael B Green, *Mng Member*
David R Liette,
EMP: 25
SALES (est): 1.6MM **Privately Held**
SIC: 6552 Subdividers & developers

(G-14811)
NEXSTAR BROADCASTING INC
Also Called: Wdtn
4595 S Dixie Dr (45439-2111)
PHONE..................937 293-2101
Jackie Lainhart, *Manager*
Shawn Macintyre, *Manager*
EMP: 80
SALES (corp-wide): 2.4B **Publicly Held**
WEB: www.wluk.com
SIC: 4833 Television broadcasting stations
HQ: Nexstar Broadcasting, Inc.
   545 E John Carpenter Fwy # 700
   Irving TX 75062
   972 373-8800

(G-14812)
NOLAND COMPANY (HQ)
Also Called: Greenville Noland
3110 Kettering Blvd (45439-1924)
PHONE..................937 396-7980
Arjay Hoggard, *President*
Alan Thacker, *General Mgr*
James H Adcox, *COO*
John W Simmons, *COO*
Ron K Binger, *Vice Pres*
◆ **EMP:** 224 **EST:** 1915
SALES (est): 274.1MM
SALES (corp-wide): 2.7B **Privately Held**
WEB: www.noland.com
SIC: 5074 5075 5063 5085 Plumbing & hydronic heating supplies; air conditioning equipment, except room units; electrical supplies; industrial supplies
PA: Winsupply Inc.
   3110 Kettering Blvd
   Moraine OH 45439
   937 294-5331

(G-14813)
NORFOLK SOUTHERN CORPORATION
3101 Springboro Pike (45439-1970)
PHONE..................937 297-5420
Fax: 937 297-5421
Mike Fender, *Manager*
EMP: 43
SALES (corp-wide): 10.5B **Publicly Held**
WEB: www.nscorp.com
SIC: 4011 Railroads, line-haul operating
PA: Norfolk Southern Corporation
   3 Commercial Pl Ste 1a
   Norfolk VA 23510
   757 629-2680

(G-14814)
P C VPA
3033 Kettering Blvd # 319 (45439-1962)
PHONE..................937 293-2133
Blaise Gatto, *Family Practiti*
EMP: 34 **Privately Held**
SIC: 8011 Geriatric specialist, physician/surgeon
PA: P C Vpa
   500 Kirts Blvd Ste 200
   Troy MI 48084

(G-14815)
PRIME TIME PARTY RENTAL INC
5225 Springboro Pike (45439-2970)
PHONE..................937 296-9262
Fax: 937 296-9260
Bart A Nye, *President*
Dave Sercu, *General Mgr*
Frances McDonagh, *Opers Staff*
Christina Pearson, *Controller*
Christina Welsh, *Controller*
EMP: 33
SQ FT: 17,000
SALES (est): 5.7MM **Privately Held**
WEB: www.primetimepartyrental.com
SIC: 7359 Party supplies rental services

(G-14816)
PROVIDENCE HEALTH PARTNERS LLC
2912 Springboro W Ste 201 (45439-1674)
PHONE..................937 297-8999
Susan Becker, *COO*
Cheryl Burns, *Project Mgr*
EMP: 50
SALES (est): 2.7MM **Privately Held**
SIC: 8741 Business management; financial management for business; administrative management

(G-14817)
PROVIDENCE MEDICAL GROUP INC
2912 Springboro W Ste 201 (45439-1674)
PHONE..................937 297-8999
Susan Becker, *COO*
Brenden Wynn, *Opers Mgr*
Kim Hilton, *Purchasing*
Cheryl Davis, *Office Mgr*
Trisha Holbrook, *Pharmacist*
EMP: 99
SALES (est): 11.3MM **Privately Held**
SIC: 8741 Administrative management

(G-14818)
QUALITY STEELS CORP (HQ)
2221 Arbor Blvd (45439-1521)
PHONE..................937 294-4133
Fax: 937 294-0656
Thomas Miller, *President*
Alice L Miller, *Corp Secy*
Carl Black, *Manager*
Umesh Deshpande, *Manager*
Tim Shade, *Manager*
EMP: 26
SQ FT: 42,000
SALES (est): 16.8MM
SALES (corp-wide): 19.3MM **Privately Held**
WEB: www.qualitysteels.com
SIC: 5051 Steel
PA: Miller Consolidated Industries Inc
   2221 Arbor Blvd
   Moraine OH 45439
   937 294-2681

(G-14819)
R G SELLERS COMPANY (PA)
Also Called: R G Seller Co
3185 Elbee Rd (45439-1919)
PHONE..................937 299-1545
Fax: 937 299-2527
Doug Sellers, *CEO*
Barbara Sellers, *Corp Secy*
Tom Sellers, *Vice Pres*
Mary Sellers, *Treasurer*
EMP: 37
SQ FT: 10,500
SALES (est): 8.2MM **Privately Held**
SIC: 5141 Food brokers

(G-14820)
RANAC COMPUTER CORPORATION
3460 S Dixie Dr (45439-2304)
PHONE..................317 844-0141
Fax: 317 848-2269
Keith A Pitzele, *President*
Theresa Wright, *Director*
Pam Eicher, *Administration*
EMP: 26
SQ FT: 5,200
SALES (est): 2.2MM **Privately Held**
WEB: www.ranac.com
SIC: 7373 Turnkey vendors, computer systems; value-added resellers, computer systems

(G-14821)
RSM US LLP
2000 W Dorothy Ln (45439-1820)
PHONE..................937 298-0201
Charlie Foley, *Managing Prtnr*
EMP: 105
SALES (corp-wide): 1.8B **Privately Held**
SIC: 8721 Certified public accountant
PA: Rsm Us Llp
   1 S Wacker Dr Ste 800
   Chicago IL 60606
   312 384-6000

(G-14822)
SAINT JOSEPH ORPHANAGE
3131 S Dixie Dr Ste 220 (45439-2223)
PHONE..................937 643-0398
Annette Kingery, *Branch Mgr*
EMP: 76
SALES (corp-wide): 16.2MM **Privately Held**
SIC: 8361 Group foster home
PA: Saint Joseph Orphanage
   5400 Edalbert Dr
   Cincinnati OH 45239
   513 741-3100

(G-14823)
SANDYS AUTO & TRUCK SVC INC
3053 Springboro W (45439-1811)
PHONE..................937 461-4980
Fax: 937 294-6980
Ted Durig, *President*
Doug Thomas, *Vice Pres*
EMP: 60
SQ FT: 14,000
SALES (est): 4.4MM **Privately Held**
WEB: www.sandystowing.com
SIC: 7549 Towing service, automotive

(G-14824)
SANDYS TOWING (PA)
3053 Springboro W (45439-1811)
PHONE..................937 461-4980
Ted Durig, *President*
EMP: 26
SALES (est): 4.7MM **Privately Held**
SIC: 7549 Towing service, automotive

(G-14825)
SNYDER CONCRETE PRODUCTS INC (PA)
Also Called: Snyder Brick and Block
2301 W Dorothy Ln (45439-1825)
PHONE..................937 885-5176
Lee E Snyder, *CEO*
Mark Snyder, *Vice Pres*
Julie Flory, *Treasurer*
Todd Hopf, *Controller*
Joe Rohrer, *Sales Mgr*
▲ **EMP:** 25
SQ FT: 50,000
SALES (est): 13.3MM **Privately Held**
WEB: www.snyderonline.com
SIC: 5032 3271 3272 Brick, except refractory; concrete & cinder building products; blocks, concrete or cinder: standard; concrete products

(G-14826)
SOUTH COMMUNITY INC (PA)
3095 Kettering Blvd Ste 1 (45439-1983)
PHONE..................937 293-8300
Fax: 937 534-1347
Carol Smerz, *President*
Rose Combs, *Finance*
Gerre Murdock, *Human Res Dir*
Celeste Autrey, *Human Resources*
Jeni Sand, *Marketing Mgr*
EMP: 205
SQ FT: 40,883
SALES: 19MM **Privately Held**
SIC: 8093 Mental health clinic, outpatient

Moraine - Montgomery County (G-14827)

(G-14827)
SOUTHTOWN HEATING & COOLING
3024 Springboro W Unit A (45439-1707)
PHONE 937 320-9900
Joe Trame, *President*
Terri Trame, *Vice Pres*
EMP: 26
SQ FT: 3,000
SALES (est): 4.7MM **Privately Held**
WEB: www.southtownheatingcooling.com
SIC: **1711** 1731 7349 5999 Plumbing, heating, air-conditioning contractors; electrical work; air duct cleaning; plumbing & heating supplies; fireplaces & wood burning stoves; oil & gas pipeline construction

(G-14828)
SUNRISE TELEVISION CORP
Also Called: Wdtn
4595 S Dixie Dr (45439-2111)
P.O. Box 741, Dayton (45401-0741)
PHONE 937 293-2101
EMP: 105
SALES (corp-wide): 674.9MM **Publicly Held**
SIC: **4833** Television broadcasting stations
HQ: Sunrise Television Corp.
1 W Exchange St Ste 5a
Providence RI

(G-14829)
TANNER HEATING & AC INC
2238 E River Rd (45439-1520)
PHONE 937 299-2500
Fax: 937 299-2590
Robert F Tanner, *President*
David M Tanner, *Vice Pres*
Thomas Tanner, *Vice Pres*
Steve Gambrell, *Production*
Andrew Davis, *Engineer*
EMP: 45
SQ FT: 17,500
SALES (est): 7.2MM **Privately Held**
WEB: www.tannerhtg-ac.com
SIC: **1711** Warm air heating & air conditioning contractor; ventilation & duct work contractor

(G-14830)
TESTAMERICA LABORATORIES INC
2017 Springboro W (45439-1665)
PHONE 937 294-6856
Debra Lowe, *Systems Mgr*
EMP: 75
SALES (corp-wide): 609.6MM **Privately Held**
WEB: www.stl-inc.com
SIC: **5049** Analytical instruments
HQ: Testamerica Laboratories, Inc.
4101 Shuffel St Nw
North Canton OH 44720
800 456-9396

(G-14831)
TYLER TECHNOLOGIES INC
Cole Layer Trumble Company Div
4100 Miller Valentine Ct (45439-1478)
PHONE 937 276-5261
Fax: 937 278-3711
G E Griscom, *Vice Pres*
Robert Peckingpaugh, *Vice Pres*
Benjamin A Story, *Vice Pres*
Benjamin Nadola, *Assoc VP*
Mark Brown, *Controller*
EMP: 200
SALES (corp-wide): 840.6MM **Publicly Held**
WEB: www.tylertechnologies.com
SIC: **7389** Auction, appraisal & exchange services
PA: Tyler Technologies, Inc.
5101 Tennyson Pkwy
Plano TX 75024
972 713-3700

(G-14832)
VAN MAYBERRYS & STORAGE INC
1850 Cardington Rd (45409-1503)
PHONE 937 298-8800
Fax: 937 298-0413
William Mayberry Jr, *President*
James Roberts, *General Mgr*
Victoria Voehringer, *Corp Secy*
Tom Maguire, *Opers Mgr*
EMP: 35
SQ FT: 35,000
SALES (est): 5.2MM **Privately Held**
SIC: **4213** 4214 Household goods transport; local trucking with storage

(G-14833)
WAGNER INDUSTRIAL ELECTRIC INC (HQ)
Also Called: Wagner Smith Company
3178 Encrete Ln (45439-1902)
P.O. Box 55, Dayton (45401-0055)
PHONE 937 298-7481
Fax: 937 298-0268
James A Fortkamp, *President*
Don Ringwald, *Division Mgr*
Todd Frankenberg, *Area Mgr*
Thomas Cope, *Vice Pres*
Thomas E Cope, *Vice Pres*
EMP: 25
SALES (est): 12.9MM
SALES (corp-wide): 4.4B **Publicly Held**
WEB: www.wagnersmith.com
SIC: **1731** General electrical contractor
PA: Mdu Resources Group, Inc.
1200 W Century Ave
Bismarck ND 58503
701 530-1000

(G-14834)
WAKONI DIALYSIS LLC
Also Called: Dayton South Dialysis
4700 Springboro Pike A (45439-1964)
PHONE 937 294-7188
Lisa Smiley, *Administration*
EMP: 29
SALES (est): 268.4K **Publicly Held**
SIC: **8092** Kidney dialysis centers
PA: Davita Inc.
2000 16th St
Denver CO 80202

(G-14835)
WEILER WELDING COMPANY INC (PA)
2400 Sandridge Dr (45439-1849)
PHONE 937 222-8312
Fax: 937 222-2729
Herbert G Weiler Jr, *President*
Dave Radominski, *General Mgr*
Herbert G Weiler III, *Vice Pres*
James C Weiler, *Vice Pres*
Bud Weiler, *VP Opers*
EMP: 53
SQ FT: 50,125
SALES (est): 40MM **Privately Held**
SIC: **5169** 5084 Compressed gas; welding machinery & equipment

(G-14836)
WINSUPPLY INC (PA)
Also Called: Wss- Dayton
3110 Kettering Blvd (45439-1924)
P.O. Box 1127, Dayton (45401-1127)
PHONE 937 294-5331
Fax: 937 425-6720
Roland Gordon, *President*
Jason Barcel, *Managing Dir*
Julie Beach, *Managing Dir*
Richard W Schwartz, *Chairman*
Bill Summers, *Area Mgr*
EMP: 100
SQ FT: 20,000
SALES (est): 2.7B **Privately Held**
SIC: **1542** 5074 5085 Commercial & office building contractors; plumbing fittings & supplies; industrial supplies

(G-14837)
YECK BROTHERS COMPANY
2222 Arbor Blvd (45439-1522)
P.O. Box 225, Dayton (45401-0225)
PHONE 937 294-4000
Fax: 937 294-6985
Bob Yeck, *President*
Linda Maidment, *President*
Janet Archer, *Accounts Mgr*
Chris McClellan, *Accounts Mgr*
Mary Taylor, *Accounts Mgr*
EMP: 35
SQ FT: 35,000
SALES: 3.4MM **Privately Held**
WEB: www.yeck.com
SIC: **7331** 1731 Direct mail advertising services; mailing service; access control systems specialization

(G-14838)
YOWELL TRANSPORTATION SVC INC
1840 Cardington Rd (45409-1503)
PHONE 937 294-5933
Fax: 937 294-4132
Victor Yowell, *President*
Neil T Yowell III, *Principal*
Joe Ford, *Vice Pres*
EMP: 75
SQ FT: 22,000
SALES (est): 13.1MM **Privately Held**
SIC: **4213** 4214 Contract haulers; local trucking with storage

Moreland Hills
Cuyahoga County

(G-14839)
GALT ENTERPRISES INC
34555 Chagrin Blvd # 100 (44022-1068)
P.O. Box 22189, Cleveland (44122-0189)
PHONE 216 464-6744
Fax: 216 464-2669
Lee M Hoffman, *President*
Hank Rapport, *Vice Pres*
Sherry Kahn, *Accountant*
Grace Planck, *Sales Mgr*
Darryl Whitehead, *Mktg Dir*
EMP: 50 EST: 1977
SQ FT: 5,000
SALES: 6.1MM **Privately Held**
WEB: www.galtenterprises.com
SIC: **6411** Insurance agents

Morral
Marion County

(G-14840)
FETTER AND SON LLC
Also Called: Fetter and Son Farms
2421 Mrral Krkptrick Rd W (43337-9314)
P.O. Box 38 (43337-0038)
PHONE 740 465-2961
Panny Robert, *Accounts Mgr*
Steven Fetter,
EMP: 39
SQ FT: 5,000
SALES: 5.3MM **Privately Held**
SIC: **4213** Contract haulers

(G-14841)
FETTER SON FARMS LTD LBLTY CO
2421 Mrral Krkptrick Rd W (43337-9314)
P.O. Box 38 (43337-0038)
PHONE 740 465-2961
Steven K Fetter, *Principal*
T Jane Fetter, *Principal*
Steven Fetter, *Mng Member*
Penny Roberts, *Admin Sec*
EMP: 35
SALES (est): 3.1MM **Privately Held**
SIC: **4213** Contract haulers

(G-14842)
MORRAL COMPANIES LLC (HQ)
132 Postle Ave (43337-7505)
P.O. Box 26 (43337-0026)
PHONE 740 465-3251
Fax: 740 465-9781
Daryl Gates, *CEO*
Sandy Wampler, *Senior VP*
Jay Hildreth, *Plant Mgr*
Bill Corthers, *Safety Mgr*
John Hartshorn, *QC Mgr*
EMP: 46
SQ FT: 15,000
SALES (est): 25.4MM **Privately Held**
WEB: www.morralcompanies.com
SIC: **4783** 5191 Packing & crating; fertilizer & fertilizer materials

Morrow
Warren County

(G-14843)
BEL-WOOD COUNTRY CLUB INC
5873 Ludlum Rd (45152-8364)
P.O. Box 195 (45152-0195)
PHONE 513 899-3361
Fax: 513 899-3365
Michelle Rooney, *General Mgr*
Jeff Bab, *Accounts Mgr*
EMP: 60
SQ FT: 12,052
SALES (est): 3.4MM **Privately Held**
SIC: **7997** 5812 Country club, membership; eating places

(G-14844)
BROWNING-FERRIS INDUSTRIES INC
Also Called: Site L10
2420 Mason Morrow Millgro (45152-9605)
PHONE 513 899-2942
Fax: 513 899-3369
Rob Dolder, *Manager*
EMP: 38
SQ FT: 5,896
SALES (corp-wide): 10B **Publicly Held**
WEB: www.alliedwaste.com
SIC: **4953** Sanitary landfill operation
HQ: Browning-Ferris Industries, Llc
18500 N Allied Way # 100
Phoenix AZ 85054
480 627-2700

(G-14845)
CONGREGATE LIVING OF AMERICA (PA)
463 E Pike St (45152-1221)
PHONE 513 899-2801
Oscar Jarnicki, *President*
Cynthia Jarnicki, *Treasurer*
Sherline Tennix, *Office Mgr*
Mike Harrison, *Administration*
EMP: 60
SALES (est): 4.4MM **Privately Held**
SIC: **8051** 8052 Skilled nursing care facilities; intermediate care facilities

(G-14846)
OPERATION THANK YOU
2467 Ford Rd (45152-8425)
PHONE 513 899-3134
Carol Alexander, *Director*
EMP: 25
SALES: 55.4K **Privately Held**
SIC: **8322** Individual & family services

(G-14847)
VALLEY MACHINE TOOL CO INC
9773 Morrow Cozaddale Rd (45152-8589)
PHONE 513 899-2737
Fax: 513 899-2390
Larry R Wilson, *President*
Douglas Wilson, *Corp Secy*
Ralph Wilson, *Vice Pres*
Charlotte Lyttle, *Office Mgr*
Roger J Wilson, *Manager*
EMP: 40
SQ FT: 11,000
SALES (est): 6.5MM **Privately Held**
SIC: **3599** 7692 Machine shop, jobbing & repair; welding repair

(G-14848)
WORKSHOPS OF DAVID T SMITH
3600 Shawhan Rd (45152-9555)
PHONE 513 932-2472
Fax: 513 932-3233
David Smith, *Owner*
Julie Smith, *Managing Dir*
Lora Smith, *Corp Secy*
EMP: 50
SALES (est): 10MM **Privately Held**
WEB: www.davidtsmith.com
SIC: **5021** 5712 5023 5719 Furniture; furniture stores; pottery; pottery

(G-14849)
YOCKEY GROUP INC
6344 E Us Hwy 22 And 3 (45152-9417)
PHONE.................................513 899-2188
Jim Yockey, *President*
EMP: 45 **EST:** 1997
SALES (est): 4.5MM **Privately Held**
SIC: 7359 Equipment rental & leasing

Mount Eaton
Wayne County

(G-14850)
QUALITY BLOCK & SUPPLY INC (DH)
Rr 250 (44659)
PHONE.................................330 364-4411
Jerry A Schwab, *President*
David Schwab, *Vice Pres*
Donna Schwab, *Admin Sec*
EMP: 27
SQ FT: 4,000
SALES (est): 2.2MM
SALES (corp-wide): 29.7B **Privately Held**
SIC: 3271 3273 5032 Blocks, concrete or cinder: standard; ready-mixed concrete; concrete & cinder block
HQ: Schwab Industries, Inc.
 2301 Progress St
 Dover OH 44622
 330 364-4411

Mount Gilead
Morrow County

(G-14851)
ANGELS HOME CARE LLC
4440 State Route 61 (43338-9781)
PHONE.................................419 947-9373
Mary Eckard, *Mng Member*
EMP: 38
SALES: 900K **Privately Held**
SIC: 8082 Oxygen tent service

(G-14852)
CONSOLIDATED ELECTRIC COOP INC
5255 State Route 95 (43338-9763)
P.O. Box 111 (43338-0111)
PHONE.................................419 947-3055
Fax: 419 949-2961
Richard Carter, *Ch of Bd*
Brian Newton, *President*
Nancy Salyer, *Vice Pres*
Jedidiah Markley, *Engineer*
Wes Reinhardt, *CFO*
EMP: 55 **EST:** 1936
SQ FT: 18,000
SALES: 46.2MM **Privately Held**
WEB: www.conelec.com
SIC: 4911 8611 Distribution, electric power; business associations

(G-14853)
COUNTY OF MORROW
Also Called: Morrow Co Ed Service Center
27 W High St (43338-1251)
PHONE.................................419 946-2618
Fax: 419 946-7080
Tom Wiston, *Mayor*
Thomas Ash, *Manager*
Kevin Carney, *Exec Dir*
Michele Hall, *Exec Dir*
EMP: 38 **Privately Held**
WEB: www.morrowcountyhealth.org
SIC: 8741 Administrative management
PA: County Of Morrow
 80 N Walnut St
 Mount Gilead OH 43338
 419 947-7535

(G-14854)
JPMORGAN CHASE BANK NAT ASSN
16 N Main St (43338-1344)
PHONE.................................419 946-3015
Allen Cooper, *Manager*
EMP: 50
SALES (corp-wide): 99.6B **Publicly Held**
WEB: www.chase.com
SIC: 6021 National commercial banks
HQ: Jpmorgan Chase Bank, National Association
 1111 Polaris Pkwy
 Columbus OH 43240
 614 436-3055

(G-14855)
MARYHAVEN INC
245 Neal Ave Ste A (43338-9372)
PHONE.................................419 946-6734
Fax: 419 946-6952
Mike Durham, *Branch Mgr*
EMP: 31
SALES (corp-wide): 21.9MM **Privately Held**
SIC: 8093 Alcohol clinic, outpatient
PA: Maryhaven, Inc
 1791 Alum Creek Dr
 Columbus OH 43207
 614 449-1530

(G-14856)
MORROW CNTY FIRE FIGHTER
Also Called: Morrow County Emergency Squad
140 S Main St (43338-1408)
PHONE.................................419 946-7976
Fax: 419 946-1307
Jeff Sparks, *Controller*
EMP: 100
SALES (est): 2.2MM **Privately Held**
SIC: 4119 Ambulance service

(G-14857)
MORROW COUNTY CHILD CARE CTR
406 Bank St (43338-1300)
PHONE.................................419 946-5007
Fax: 419 947-1187
Terry Grieble, *President*
Lori Walters, *Director*
EMP: 60
SALES (est): 401.2K **Privately Held**
SIC: 8351 Group day care center

(G-14858)
MORROW COUNTY COUNCIL ON DRUGS
Also Called: McCad
950 Meadow Dr (43338-1389)
PHONE.................................419 947-4055
Fax: 419 947-4285
Eric Preuss, *Director*
EMP: 26
SALES (est): 950K **Privately Held**
SIC: 8069 Alcoholism rehabilitation hospital

(G-14859)
MORROW COUNTY HOSPITAL
Also Called: Morrow County Hospital MCH At
651 W Marion Rd (43338-1096)
PHONE.................................419 949-3085
Fax: 419 362-6034
Christopher Truax, *President*
EMP: 300
SALES (corp-wide): 27.8MM **Privately Held**
SIC: 8062 General medical & surgical hospitals
PA: Morrow County Hospital
 651 W Marion Rd
 Mount Gilead OH 43338
 419 947-9127

(G-14860)
MORROW COUNTY HOSPITAL (PA)
Also Called: MORROW COUNTY HOSPITAL HOME HE
651 W Marion Rd (43338-1096)
PHONE.................................419 947-9127
Fax: 419 947-8956
Christopher Truax, *CEO*
Joseph Schuler, *Controller*
Conni McChesney, *Finance Mgr*
Laura Morris, *Pharmacist*
Michael Patterson, *Manager*
EMP: 320
SQ FT: 89,702
SALES: 27.8MM **Privately Held**
WEB: www.morrowcountyhospital.com
SIC: 8062 General medical & surgical hospitals

(G-14861)
PAM JOHNSONIDENT
Also Called: McDonald's
535 W Marion Rd (43338-1025)
PHONE.................................419 946-4551
Fax: 419 946-4551
Pam Johnson, *President*
EMP: 60 **EST:** 1994
SALES (est): 1.2MM **Privately Held**
SIC: 5812 7221 Fast-food restaurant, chain; photographic studios, portrait

(G-14862)
PLANE DETAIL LLC
5707 State Route 61 (43338-1192)
PHONE.................................614 734-1201
Steve Rotermund, *President*
Amy Lenhart, *Human Res Mgr*
Stephen H Dodd,
EMP: 35
SALES (est): 4.7MM **Privately Held**
SIC: 4581 Aircraft cleaning & janitorial service

(G-14863)
PUBLIC SAFETY OHIO DEPARTMENT
3980 County Road 172 (43338-9529)
PHONE.................................419 768-3955
Fax: 419 768-2078
C McGinty, *Branch Mgr*
EMP: 25 **Privately Held**
SIC: 7381 Protective services, guard
HQ: Ohio Department Of Public Safety
 1970 W Broad St Fl 5
 Columbus OH 43223

(G-14864)
WHETSTONE INDUSTRIES INC
Also Called: WHETSTONE SCHOOL
440 Douglas St (43338-1019)
PHONE.................................419 947-9222
Fax: 419 947-8195
Dr Richard A Kohler, *Principal*
Barb Gentille Green, *Director*
Anne Stock, *Director*
Kim Taber, *Director*
EMP: 30 **EST:** 1975
SALES: 99.7K **Privately Held**
WEB: www.whetstoneserves.com
SIC: 8211 8322 School for the retarded; social services for the handicapped

(G-14865)
WOODSIDE VILLAGE CARE CENTER
841 W Marion Rd (43338-1094)
PHONE.................................419 947-2015
Fax: 419 947-9589
William Casto, *Partner*
Gary Casto, *Partner*
William R Casto, *Partner*
Cathy Rox, *Administration*
EMP: 95
SQ FT: 28,000
SALES (est): 3.8MM **Privately Held**
SIC: 8052 8051 Intermediate care facilities; skilled nursing care facilities

Mount Hope
Holmes County

(G-14866)
MT HOPE AUCTION INC (PA)
Also Called: Farmers Produce Auction
8076 State Rte 241 (44660)
P.O. Box 82 (44660-0082)
PHONE.................................330 674-6188
Fax: 330 674-3748
Steven Mullett, *President*
Jim Mullet, *Manager*
EMP: 30
SALES (est): 16.2MM **Privately Held**
WEB: www.mthopeauction.com
SIC: 5154 7389 Auctioning livestock; auctioneers, fee basis

Mount Orab
Brown County

(G-14867)
CHILD FOCUS INC
710 N High St (45154-8349)
PHONE.................................937 444-1613
Jim Carter, *President*
Linda Hickman, *Manager*
EMP: 55
SALES (corp-wide): 15.7MM **Privately Held**
WEB: www.child-focus.org
SIC: 8322 8351 Child related social services; child day care services
PA: Child Focus, Inc.
 4629 Aicholtz Rd Ste 2
 Cincinnati OH 45244
 513 752-1555

(G-14868)
EVERYDAY HOMECARE
711 S High St (45154-8947)
PHONE.................................937 444-1672
Vicky Cirley, *Owner*
EMP: 35
SALES (est): 930K **Privately Held**
SIC: 8082 Home health care services

(G-14869)
HOSPICE OF HOPE INC
215 Hughes Blvd (45154-8356)
PHONE.................................937 444-4900
Fax: 937 444-4966
Kavin Cartmell, *Branch Mgr*
Lisa Grierson, *Manager*
EMP: 98 **Privately Held**
SIC: 8052 Personal care facility
PA: Hospice Of Hope, Inc.
 909 Kenton Station Dr B
 Maysville KY 41056

(G-14870)
MT ORAB FIRE DEPARTMENT INC
Also Called: Mount Orab Ems
113 Spice St (45154-8932)
P.O. Box 454 (45154-0454)
PHONE.................................937 444-3945
Lisa Reeves, *Chief*
EMP: 27 **Privately Held**
WEB: www.mtorabfire.com
SIC: 4119 Ambulance service
PA: Mt Orab Fire Department Inc
 105 Spice St
 Mount Orab OH 45154
 937 446-2379

Mount Saint Joseph
Hamilton County

(G-14871)
SISTERS OF CHARITY OF CINC (HQ)
5900 Delhi Rd (45051-1500)
PHONE.................................513 347-5200
Fax: 513 347-5228
Sister Bjoan Cook, *President*
Louise Grundish, *Editor*
Tim Moller, *CFO*
Vicki Humphrey, *VP Finance*
Linda Robertson, *Human Resources*
EMP: 80
SQ FT: 60,000
SALES (est): 16.9MM **Privately Held**
SIC: 8051 8661 Skilled nursing care facilities; non-church religious organizations

(G-14872)
SISTERS OF CHARITY OF CINC
Also Called: Sisters Charity Mother House
5900 Delhi Rd (45051-1500)
PHONE.................................513 347-5436
Barbara Hegidorn, *President*
Ron Swiech, *Persnl Mgr*
EMP: 200 **Privately Held**
SIC: 8051 Extended care facility

Mount Sterling - Madison County (G-14873)

HQ: Sisters Of Charity Of Cincinnati, Ohio
5900 Delhi Rd
Mount Saint Joseph OH 45051
513 347-5200

Mount Sterling
Madison County

(G-14873)
KEIHIN THERMAL TECH AMER INC
10500 Oday Harrison Rd (43143-9474)
PHONE..................740 869-3000
Tatsuhiko Arai, *President*
Scott Mortimer, *General Mgr*
Scott Amortimer, *Vice Pres*
Robert Feltz, *Safety Mgr*
Steve Shonk, *Purchasing*
◆ **EMP:** 475
SALES (est): 133.1MM
SALES (corp-wide): 2.8B **Privately Held**
SIC: 5013 3714 Automotive engines & engine parts; motor vehicle engines & parts
PA: Keihin Corporation
1-26-2, Nishishinjuku
Shinjuku-Ku TKY 160-0
333 453-411

(G-14874)
OHIO DEPT NATURAL RESOURCES
Also Called: Deer Creek State Park
20635 State Park Road 20 (43143-9541)
PHONE..................740 869-3124
Fax: 740 869-3608
Mark Hoffhines, *Manager*
Sonya Lindsey, *Manager*
EMP: 50 **Privately Held**
WEB: www.ohiostateparks.com
SIC: 9512 7999 Land, mineral & wildlife conservation; ; beach & water sports equipment rental & services
HQ: Ohio Department Of Natural Resources
2045 Morse Rd Bldg D-3
Columbus OH 43229

(G-14875)
STERLING JOINT AMBULANCE DST
24 S London St (43143-1133)
P.O. Box 51 (43143-0051)
PHONE..................740 869-3006
Chief John McCalland, *Principal*
John McCalland, *Chief*
EMP: 40
SALES (est): 955.7K **Privately Held**
SIC: 4119 Ambulance service

(G-14876)
XANTERRA PARKS & RESORTS INC
Also Called: Deer Creek Rsort Confrence Ctr
22300 State Park 20 Rd (43143-9569)
P.O. Box 125 (43143-0125)
PHONE..................740 869-2020
Fax: 740 869-4059
Tammy Dick, *Division Mgr*
Bill Brown, *General Mgr*
Chris Morris, *Chief Engr*
Ken Bales, *Controller*
Markee Armentrout, *Human Res Mgr*
EMP: 106
SALES (corp-wide): 414.9MM **Privately Held**
SIC: 7011 Resort hotel
HQ: Parks Xanterra & Resorts Inc
6312 S Fiddlers Green Cir 600n
Greenwood Village CO 80111
303 600-3400

Mount Vernon
Knox County

(G-14877)
A TOUCH OF GRACE INC (PA)
809 Coshocton Ave Ste B (43050-1900)
PHONE..................740 397-7971
Carolyn Crow, *President*
Donna J Steele, *President*
Tammy Guillory, *Pharmacy Dir*
EMP: 100
SALES (est): 2.1MM **Privately Held**
SIC: 8082 Visiting nurse service

(G-14878)
BELCAN LLC
Also Called: Belcan Engineering Services
105 N Sandusky St (43050-2447)
PHONE..................740 393-8888
Brenda Pek, *General Mgr*
Joseph Wierda, *General Mgr*
Bryan Riss, *Vice Pres*
Lindsay Covington, *Marketing Mgr*
Paul Comper, *Manager*
EMP: 749
SALES (corp-wide): 666.9MM **Privately Held**
SIC: 7363 Engineering help service
PA: Belcan, Llc
10200 Anderson Way
Blue Ash OH 45242
513 891-0972

(G-14879)
BRENNEMAN LUMBER CO
51 Parrott St (43050-4570)
P.O. Box 951 (43050-0951)
PHONE..................740 397-0573
Fax: 740 392-9498
Charles Brenneman, *President*
Douglas J Brenneman Jr, *CFO*
▼ **EMP:** 36 **EST:** 1932
SQ FT: 20,000
SALES (est): 12.1MM **Privately Held**
WEB: www.brennemanlumber.com
SIC: 5031 Lumber: rough, dressed & finished

(G-14880)
C E S CREDIT UNION INC (PA)
1215 Yauger Rd (43050-9233)
P.O. Box 631 (43050-0631)
PHONE..................740 397-1136
Fax: 740 397-4248
James Depue, *President*
Kelly Schermerhorn, *Vice Pres*
Michael Copley, *VP Opers*
Brittany Hahler, *CFO*
Tami Karcher, *Finance Mgr*
EMP: 45
SQ FT: 7,800
SALES: 4MM **Privately Held**
WEB: www.cescu.com
SIC: 6062 State credit unions, not federally chartered

(G-14881)
CELLCO PARTNERSHIP
Also Called: Verizon
1002 Coshocton Ave 3 (43050-1550)
PHONE..................740 397-6609
Fax: 740 397-6425
John Tipton, *Branch Mgr*
EMP: 25
SALES (corp-wide): 126B **Publicly Held**
SIC: 4812 5999 5731 Cellular telephone services; mobile telephones & equipment; radio, television & electronic stores
HQ: Cellco Partnership
1 Verizon Way
Basking Ridge NJ 07920

(G-14882)
CENTRAL OHIO CUSTOM CONTG LLC
10541 New Delaware Rd (43050-9144)
PHONE..................614 579-4971
Kelly Kelley, *Principal*
EMP: 25
SALES: 300K **Privately Held**
SIC: 1799 Special trade contractors

(G-14883)
COLONIAL SALES INC (PA)
Also Called: Colonial Terrace
8927 Columbus Rd Ste A (43050-4440)
PHONE..................740 397-4970
Larry D Cordial, *President*
Betty J Cordial, *Vice Pres*
Cynthia Cordial, *Vice Pres*
EMP: 28
SQ FT: 14,000
SALES: 4.5MM **Privately Held**
WEB: www.colonialsales.com
SIC: 5064 5271 Electric household appliances; mobile homes

(G-14884)
COLUMBIA GAS TRANSMISSION LLC
Columbia Energy
8484 Columbus Rd (43050-9366)
PHONE..................740 397-8242
Fax: 740 392-4357
R E Davidson, *Branch Mgr*
Richard Jacobs, *Manager*
EMP: 41
SALES (corp-wide): 9.2B **Privately Held**
SIC: 4922 Pipelines, natural gas
HQ: Columbia Gas Transmission, Llc
200 Cizzic Ctr Dr
Columbus OH 43216
614 460-6000

(G-14885)
CONCEPTS IN COMMUNITY LIVING (PA)
700 Wooster Rd (43050-1488)
PHONE..................740 393-0055
Karen Hendley, *President*
EMP: 25
SQ FT: 6,800
SALES (est): 1.8MM **Privately Held**
SIC: 8361 Home for the mentally retarded

(G-14886)
COUNTRY CLUB CENTER II LTD
Also Called: Country Club Retirement Campus
1350 Yauger Rd (43050-9233)
PHONE..................740 397-2350
Fax: 740 393-1197
John Holland, *Partner*
Tonia Ressing, *Partner*
Ann Turner, *Director*
Carri Rejonis, *Asst Director*
EMP: 150
SQ FT: 50,000
SALES (est): 6.1MM **Privately Held**
SIC: 8051 8052 Convalescent home with continuous nursing care; intermediate care facilities

(G-14887)
COUNTRY COURT LTD
Also Called: Country Court Nursing Home
1076 Coshocton Ave (43050-1474)
PHONE..................740 397-4125
Fax: 740 392-1533
L Bruce Levering, *Partner*
William Elder, *Director*
EMP: 136
SQ FT: 30,000
SALES: 5.4MM
SALES (corp-wide): 32.8MM **Privately Held**
SIC: 8051 Convalescent home with continuous nursing care
PA: Levering Management, Inc.
201 N Main St
Mount Vernon OH 43050
740 397-3897

(G-14888)
COUNTY OF KNOX
Also Called: Knox County Health Department
11660 Upper Gilchrist Rd (43050-9084)
PHONE..................740 392-2200
Fax: 740 392-9613
Dennis Murray, *Manager*
Joan Stringfellow, *Manager*
Stacey Robinson, *Director*
EMP: 49 **Privately Held**
WEB: www.knoxhealth.com
SIC: 9431 8082 ; home health care services
PA: Knox County
117 E High St Rm 161
Mount Vernon OH 43050
740 393-6703

(G-14889)
COYNE GRAPHIC FINISHING INC
1301 Newark Rd (43050-4730)
PHONE..................740 397-6232
Fax: 740 392-9119
Kevin Coyne, *President*
Robert Coyne, *Chairman*
Alice Ann Coyne, *Corp Secy*
Valerie Price, *Accounts Mgr*
EMP: 28 **EST:** 1926
SQ FT: 57,000
SALES: 3MM **Privately Held**
WEB: www.coynefinishing.com
SIC: 7336 Graphic arts & related design

(G-14890)
CREATIVE FOUNDATIONS INC
127 S Main St (43050-3323)
PHONE..................614 832-2121
EMP: 26
SALES (corp-wide): 9.9MM **Privately Held**
SIC: 8051 Mental retardation hospital
PA: Creative Foundations, Inc.
57 N Sandusky St
Delaware OH 43015
740 362-5102

(G-14891)
DAILY SERVICES LLC
12 E Gambier St (43050-3316)
PHONE..................740 326-6130
Ryan Mason, *Branch Mgr*
EMP: 199
SALES (corp-wide): 22.3MM **Privately Held**
SIC: 8999 Artists & artists' studios
PA: Daily Services Llc
1110 Morse Rd Ste B1
Columbus OH 43229
614 431-5100

(G-14892)
DECOSKY MOTOR HOLDINGS INC
Also Called: Decosky GM Center
510 Harcourt Rd 550 (43050-3920)
P.O. Box 351 (43050-0351)
PHONE..................740 397-9122
Fax: 740 397-9122
John Decosky, *President*
Jason Decosky, *General Mgr*
John Descosky, *Executive*
EMP: 35 **EST:** 1956
SALES: 21.4MM **Privately Held**
SIC: 5511 7538 Automobiles, new & used; general automotive repair shops

(G-14893)
DIVERSIFIED PRODUCTS & SVCS
1250 Vernonview Dr (43050-1447)
PHONE..................740 393-6202
Louis Ohara, *Director*
EMP: 118
SALES (est): 6.6MM **Privately Held**
SIC: 5199 2541 2511 Packaging materials; wood partitions & fixtures; wood household furniture

(G-14894)
EMMETT DAN HOUSE LTD PARTNR
Also Called: Amerihost Mt. Vernon
150 Howard St (43050-3596)
PHONE..................740 392-6886
Fax: 740 392-3194
Tom Metcalf, *Managing Prtnr*
Colleen Mc Peek, *Manager*
EMP: 30
SQ FT: 50,000
SALES (est): 538.7K **Privately Held**
SIC: 7011 6512 5812 Bed & breakfast inn; nonresidential building operators; eating places

(G-14895)
EUROLINK INC
106 W Ohio Ave (43050-2442)
PHONE..................740 392-1549
Mark Hauberg, *President*
Brad Shuff, *Opers Mgr*
Elaine Hauberg, *Treasurer*
Paul Schoellman, *VP Sales*
▲ **EMP:** 30
SALES (est): 955.4K **Privately Held**
SIC: 5084 Machine tools & accessories

GEOGRAPHIC SECTION

Mount Vernon - Knox County (G-14920)

(G-14896)
FAST EDDYS GROUNDS MAINT LLC
19280 Coshocton Rd (43050-8274)
PHONE.................740 599-2955
Sandy Burd, *Manager*
Ed Stewart,
EMP: 30
SALES (est): 1.3MM **Privately Held**
SIC: 0782 Lawn & garden services

(G-14897)
FIRST-KNOX NATIONAL BANK (HQ)
Also Called: First-Knox National Division
1 S Main St (43050-3223)
PHONE.................740 399-5500
Fax: 740 399-5175
Gordon E Yance, *President*
David L Trautman, *Chairman*
Douglas W Leonard, *Finance Dir*
Barbara Barry, *CPA*
Rachelle Hartman, *Branch Mgr*
EMP: 140
SQ FT: 58,000
SALES (est): 3.6MM
SALES (corp-wide): 367MM **Publicly Held**
WEB: www.farmersandsavings.com
SIC: 6021 8721 National trust companies with deposits, commercial; accounting, auditing & bookkeeping
PA: Park National Corporation
50 N 3rd St
Newark OH 43055
740 349-8451

(G-14898)
HOME INSTEAD SENIOR CARE
Also Called: Senior Help Solutions
400 W High St (43050-2325)
PHONE.................740 393-2500
Richard L Shoemaker, *President*
EMP: 32
SALES: 500K **Privately Held**
SIC: 8082 Home health care services

(G-14899)
HOSPICE OF KNOX COUNTY
17700 Coshocton Rd (43050-9218)
PHONE.................740 397-5188
Fax: 740 397-5189
Kim Giffin, *Finance*
Austin Swallow, *Director*
EMP: 36
SQ FT: 2,300
SALES: 6.9K **Privately Held**
WEB: www.hospiceofknox.org
SIC: 8082 8322 Home health care services; individual & family services

(G-14900)
INN AT HILLENVALE LTD
1615 Yauger Rd Ste B26 (43050-8342)
PHONE.................740 392-8245
Fax: 740 392-8246
Chris Wolfard, *Director*
EMP: 67
SALES (est): 1.6MM **Privately Held**
SIC: 8059 Rest home, with health care

(G-14901)
JADA INC
Also Called: Rose Garden Nursing Home
303 N Main St (43050-2045)
PHONE.................419 512-1713
Fax: 740 393-5140
Michael L Dafin, *President*
EMP: 30
SALES: 736.4K **Privately Held**
SIC: 8051 Skilled nursing care facilities

(G-14902)
KNOX AREA TRANSIT
Also Called: Knox Area Transit Kat
25 Columbus Rd (43050-4050)
PHONE.................740 392-7433
Martin McAvoy, *Administration*
EMP: 42
SALES: 2MM **Privately Held**
SIC: 4121 Taxicabs

(G-14903)
KNOX COMMUNITY HOSP FOUNDATION
1330 Coshocton Ave (43050-1440)
PHONE.................740 393-9814
Jeff Scott, *President*
Sandy Kollar, *Vice Pres*
Danielle O'Brien, *VP Finance*
Jessica Beeman, *Human Res Mgr*
Carole Wagner, *Marketing Staff*
EMP: 49
SALES: 542.9K **Privately Held**
SIC: 8699 Charitable organization

(G-14904)
KNOX COMMUNITY HOSPITAL
1330 Coshocton Ave (43050-1495)
PHONE.................740 393-9000
Fax: 740 392-5695
Bruce White, *CEO*
Sheila Cochran, *CEO*
Michael Ambrosiani, *CFO*
Tom Beekman, *Accountant*
Darcy Bussard, *Accountant*
EMP: 628
SQ FT: 160,000
SALES: 149.6MM **Privately Held**
SIC: 8062 General medical & surgical hospitals

(G-14905)
KNOX COUNTY ENGINEER
422 Columbus Rd (43050-4499)
PHONE.................740 397-1590
Jim Henry, *Principal*
EMP: 37
SALES (est): 9MM **Privately Held**
SIC: 8711 Engineering services

(G-14906)
KNOX COUNTY HEAD START INC (PA)
11700 Upper Gilchrist Rd B (43050-9232)
P.O. Box 1225 (43050-8225)
PHONE.................740 397-1344
Fax: 740 393-6981
Ada Jacobs, *Human Resources*
Margaret Tazewell, *Exec Dir*
EMP: 33
SQ FT: 4,000
SALES: 4.6MM **Privately Held**
SIC: 8351 Head start center, except in conjunction with school

(G-14907)
KNOX NEW HOPE INDUSTRIES INC
1375 Newark Rd (43050-4779)
PHONE.................740 397-4601
Fax: 740 392-5669
Angie Wise, *Business Mgr*
Bill Bryant, *Transptn Dir*
Bill Kershner, *Prdtn Mgr*
Patricia Hissong, *Manager*
Melissa Oxenford, *Manager*
EMP: 150
SQ FT: 30,000
SALES: 1.8MM **Privately Held**
SIC: 8331 Sheltered workshop

(G-14908)
LABELLE HMHEALTH CARE SVCS LLC
314 S Main St Ste B (43050-3333)
PHONE.................740 392-1405
Eva Ingram, *Manager*
EMP: 85
SALES (corp-wide): 2.4MM **Privately Held**
SIC: 8082 Home health care services
PA: Labelle Homehealth Care Services Llc
1653 Brice Rd
Reynoldsburg OH 43068
614 367-0881

(G-14909)
LICKING-KNOX GOODWILL INDS INC
60 Parrott St (43050-4571)
PHONE.................740 397-0051
Timothy J Young, *President*
EMP: 57

SALES (corp-wide): 8.8MM **Privately Held**
SIC: 7361 Employment agencies
PA: Licking-Knox Goodwill Industries, Inc.
65 S 5th St
Newark OH 43055
740 345-9861

(G-14910)
LOWES HOME CENTERS LLC
1010 Coshocton Ave (43050-1411)
PHONE.................740 393-5350
Fax: 740 393-5351
Eben Plank, *Sales Executive*
Ken Kaiser, *Manager*
EMP: 150
SALES (corp-wide): 68.6B **Publicly Held**
SIC: 5211 5031 5722 5064 Home centers; building materials, exterior; building materials, interior; household appliance stores; electrical appliances, television & radio
HQ: Lowe's Home Centers, Llc
1605 Curtis Bridge Rd
Wilkesboro NC 28697
336 658-4000

(G-14911)
MAUSER USA LLC
219 Commerce Dr (43050-4645)
PHONE.................740 397-1762
Lynn Lemons, *Office Mgr*
Stefania Maschio, *Director*
EMP: 34
SALES (corp-wide): 8.5B **Privately Held**
WEB: www.mausergroup.com
SIC: 5093 Scrap & waste materials
HQ: Mauser Usa, Llc
2 Tower Center Blvd 20-1
East Brunswick NJ 08816
732 353-7100

(G-14912)
MAUSER USA LLC
219 Commerce Dr (43050-4645)
PHONE.................740 397-1762
Scott Colgan, *Engineer*
Chuck Sesco, *Manager*
James Beach, *Manager*
Kerri Yaegel, *Manager*
EMP: 35
SALES (corp-wide): 8.5B **Privately Held**
WEB: www.mausergroup.com
SIC: 5085 Packing, industrial
HQ: Mauser Usa, Llc
2 Tower Center Blvd 20-1
East Brunswick NJ 08816
732 353-7100

(G-14913)
MOUNDBUILDERS GUIDANCE CTR INC
8402 Blackjack Rd (43050-9193)
PHONE.................740 397-0442
Fax: 740 392-1814
Tom Cline, *Plant Mgr*
Karen Nadolson, *Child Psychlgy*
Paul Wissinger, *MIS Dir*
Luke Mickley, *IT/INT Sup*
Francis Deutschle, *Director*
EMP: 40
SALES (corp-wide): 10MM **Privately Held**
SIC: 8093 Mental health clinic, outpatient
PA: Behavorial Healthcare Partners Of Central Ohio, Inc.
66 Moccimor Dr
Newark OH 43055
740 522-8477

(G-14914)
MOUNT VERNON NH LLC
Also Called: Mount Vrnon Hlth Rhbltition Ctr
1135 Gambier Rd (43050-3839)
PHONE.................740 392-1099
Mordecai Rosenberg, *President*
Ronald Swartz, *CFO*
Lisa Schwartz, *Admin Sec*
EMP: 49 **EST:** 2015
SALES (est): 344.4K **Privately Held**
SIC: 8051 Skilled nursing care facilities

(G-14915)
MOVERS AND SHUCKERS LLC
11275 Lovers Ln (43050-9615)
PHONE.................740 263-2164

Jeremy Freer, *Mng Member*
Michael Niggard, *Manager*
Shanda Thompson, *Admin Asst*
EMP: 29
SQ FT: 15,000
SALES (est): 3.5MM **Privately Held**
SIC: 4789 1794 0761 1541 Cargo loading & unloading services; excavation & grading, building construction; farm labor contractors; grain elevator construction; grain drying services; pea & bean farms (legumes)

(G-14916)
OAK HEALTH CARE INVESTORS
Also Called: Laurels of Mt Vernon
13 Avalon Rd (43050-1403)
PHONE.................740 397-3200
Fax: 740 397-4326
Dennis Sherman, *CEO*
Regina Cheuvront, *Purchasing*
Fredrick Carroll, *Director*
Kenneth Doolittle II, *Director*
Truely Moore, *Director*
EMP: 60 **Privately Held**
WEB: www.laurelhealth.com
SIC: 8051 8052 Convalescent home with continuous nursing care; intermediate care facilities
HQ: Oak Health Care Investors Of Mt Vernon, Inc
8181 Worthington Rd
Westerville OH 43082

(G-14917)
OHIO EASTERN STAR HOME
1451 Gambier Rd Ofc (43050-9299)
PHONE.................740 397-1706
Fax: 740 392-1662
Wendy Hiett, *Controller*
Barbara Tier, *Human Resources*
Laura Paalvast, *Manager*
Jason Bostic, *Info Tech Mgr*
Linda Lamson, *Exec Dir*
EMP: 150
SQ FT: 60,000
SALES: 7.8MM **Privately Held**
WEB: www.oeshome.org
SIC: 8052 6513 8051 Intermediate care facilities; apartment building operators; skilled nursing care facilities

(G-14918)
RANDS TRUCKING INC
1201 Gambier Rd (43050-3844)
PHONE.................740 397-1144
EMP: 33
SALES (corp-wide): 32MM **Privately Held**
SIC: 4212 Local trucking, without storage
PA: Rands Trucking, Inc.
W8527 Gokey Rd
Ladysmith WI 54848
800 268-3933

(G-14919)
REVLOCAL INC
895 Harcourt Rd Ste C (43050-4325)
P.O. Box 511 (43050-0511)
PHONE.................740 392-9246
Fax: 740 392-5775
Patrick Dichter, *Business Mgr*
Amy Merithew, *Business Mgr*
David Robinson, *Business Mgr*
Aj Shull, *Business Mgr*
Kelly W Wick, *Business Mgr*
EMP: 82
SALES (est): 15.9MM **Privately Held**
SIC: 8742 Marketing consulting services

(G-14920)
RICHARD WOLFE TRUCKING INC
7299 Newark Rd (43050-9552)
PHONE.................740 392-2445
Fax: 740 392-9974
Richard J Wolfe, *President*
Heather McNamara, *General Mgr*
EMP: 41
SALES (est): 9.9MM **Privately Held**
SIC: 4213 Heavy hauling

Mount Vernon - Knox County (G-14921)

(G-14921)
S AND S GILARDI INC
Also Called: Lannings Foods
1033 Newark Rd (43050-4640)
PHONE..................................740 397-2751
Fax: 740 392-1771
Sam Gilardi, *President*
Brenda Giraldi, *Vice Pres*
Steve Gilardi, *Treasurer*
Zach Phillippi, *Cust Mgr*
Cindy Smith, *Sales Executive*
EMP: 90
SQ FT: 20,000
SALES (est): 30.1MM **Privately Held**
WEB: www.lannings.com
SIC: 5147 5421 5451 5143 Meats, fresh; meat markets, including freezer provisioners; dairy products stores; dairy products, except dried or canned

(G-14922)
SANOH AMERICA INC
7905 Industrial Park Dr (43050-2776)
PHONE..................................740 392-9200
Eric Carroll, *Principal*
Barbara Biffath, *Administration*
Clay Hooper, *Maintence Staff*
EMP: 220
SALES (corp-wide): 1.1B **Privately Held**
WEB: www.sanoh-america.com
SIC: 7539 3714 Automotive repair shops; motor vehicle parts & accessories
HQ: Sanoh America, Inc.
1849 Industrial Dr
Findlay OH 45840
419 425-2600

(G-14923)
SIEMENS ENERGY INC
105 N Sandusky St (43050-2447)
PHONE..................................740 393-8897
EMP: 252
SALES (corp-wide): 97.7B **Privately Held**
SIC: 1629 1731 3511 Power plant construction; energy management controls; turbines & turbine generator sets
HQ: Siemens Energy, Inc.
4400 N Alafaya Trl
Orlando FL 32826
407 736-2000

(G-14924)
W M V O 1300 AM
Also Called: Branch Clear Chan San Antonio
17421 Coshocton Rd (43050-9256)
PHONE..................................740 397-1000
Curtis Newland, *General Mgr*
Adam Klein, *General Mgr*
Jeff Neidert, *Manager*
Shar Shingler, *Manager*
EMP: 25
SALES (est): 754.8K **Privately Held**
SIC: 4832 Radio broadcasting stations

(G-14925)
WHISPERING HILLS CARE CENTER
416 Wooster Rd (43050-1216)
PHONE..................................740 392-3982
Fax: 740 392-3727
Jessica Link, *Exec Dir*
Frederick Carroll, *Director*
Brent Nimeth, *Director*
EMP: 30
SALES (est): 1.4MM **Privately Held**
SIC: 8059 Convalescent home

(G-14926)
WQIO 93Q REQUEST
17421 Coshocton Rd (43050-9256)
PHONE..................................740 392-9370
Tom Klein, *CEO*
Jim Lorenzen, *President*
EMP: 50
SALES (est): 613.3K **Privately Held**
SIC: 4832 Radio broadcasting stations

(G-14927)
YOUNG MENS CHRISTIAN MT VERNON
Also Called: YMCA
103 N Main St (43050-2407)
PHONE..................................740 392-9622
Fax: 740 392-9627
Elizabeth Toledo, *Human Res Mgr*
Wayne Uhrig, *Director*
Cameo Curry, *Director*
Denise Patrick, *Education*
EMP: 60
SQ FT: 53,000
SALES: 1MM **Privately Held**
SIC: 8641 7991 8351 7032 Youth organizations; physical fitness facilities; child day care services; youth camps; individual & family services

(G-14928)
YOUNG MNS CHRSTN ASSN GRTER NY
Also Called: Young Mens Christian Assn
103 N Main St (43050-2407)
PHONE..................................740 392-9622
Wayne Urhig, *Exec Dir*
EMP: 55
SALES (corp-wide): 187.7MM **Privately Held**
SIC: 8641 7991 8351 7032 Youth organizations; physical fitness facilities; child day care services; youth camps; individual & family services
PA: Young Men's Christian Association Of Greater New York
5 W 63rd St Fl 6
New York NY 10023
212 630-9600

Mount Victory
Hardin County

(G-14929)
OHIO FRESH EGGS LLC
20449 County Road 245 (43340-9710)
P.O. Box 118 (43340-0118)
PHONE..................................937 354-2233
Brian Kinter, *Manager*
EMP: 30
SALES (est): 1.5MM
SALES (corp-wide): 24.3MM **Privately Held**
SIC: 5144 2015 0252 Eggs; poultry slaughtering & processing; chicken eggs
PA: Ohio Fresh Eggs, Llc
11212 Croton Rd
Croton OH 43013
740 893-7200

(G-14930)
PLAZA INN FOODS INC
Also Called: Plaza Inn Restaurant
491 S Main St (43340-8869)
P.O. Box 257 (43340-0257)
PHONE..................................937 354-2181
Fax: 937 354-2971
Joan Wagner, *President*
Traci Rader, *Manager*
EMP: 50
SQ FT: 9,600
SALES (est): 1.7MM **Privately Held**
SIC: 5812 7011 Caterers; inns

Munroe Falls
Summit County

(G-14931)
KYOCERA SGS PRECISION TOOLS (PA)
55 S Main St (44262-1635)
P.O. Box 187 (44262-0187)
PHONE..................................330 688-6667
Fax: 330 686-4111
Thomas Haag, *President*
Ernest Garza, *Regional Mgr*
Rick Dawson, *Plant Mgr*
Ronald Rushnok, *Purch Agent*
Sara Yakubik, *Purch Agent*
▲ EMP: 50 EST: 1961
SQ FT: 45,000
SALES: 78.5MM **Privately Held**
WEB: www.sgstool.com
SIC: 3545 5084 Cutting tools for machine tools; industrial machinery & equipment

(G-14932)
MULBERRY GARDEN A L S
395 S Main St Apt 210 (44262-1671)
PHONE..................................330 630-3980
Maryann Ervin, *Administration*
EMP: 40
SALES (est): 1.3MM **Privately Held**
SIC: 6513 8361 Retirement hotel operation; residential care

(G-14933)
THOMPSON ELECTRIC INC
49 Northmoreland Ave (44262-1717)
PHONE..................................330 686-2300
Fax: 330 686-2362
Larry Thompson, *President*
Scott Manby, *Division Mgr*
Robert Mileski, *Division Mgr*
Bill Anderson, *Vice Pres*
Denny Rhodes, *Vice Pres*
EMP: 250
SQ FT: 33,000
SALES: 73MM **Privately Held**
SIC: 1731 General electrical contractor

Napoleon
Henry County

(G-14934)
CLOVERLEAF COLD STORAGE CO
1165 Independence Dr (43545-9718)
PHONE..................................419 599-5015
Tony Castle, *Branch Mgr*
EMP: 150
SALES (corp-wide): 57.3MM **Privately Held**
WEB: www.cloverleafco.com
SIC: 4225 4222 General warehousing; refrigerated warehousing & storage
PA: Cloverleaf Cold Storage Co.
401 Douglas St Ste 406
Sioux City IA 51101
712 279-8000

(G-14935)
CLOVERLEAF TRANSPORT CO
1165 Independence Dr (43545-9718)
PHONE..................................419 599-5015
Dale Lilleholm, *General Mgr*
EMP: 50
SALES (corp-wide): 3.8MM **Privately Held**
SIC: 4119 Local passenger transportation
PA: Cloverleaf Transport Co
2800 Cloverleaf Ct
Sioux City IA 51111
712 279-8044

(G-14936)
COMUNIBANC CORP (PA)
122 E Washington St (43545-1646)
P.O. Box 72 (43545-0072)
PHONE..................................419 599-1065
William Wendt, *Principal*
Paul K Chamberlin, *Bd of Directors*
EMP: 56 **Privately Held**
SIC: 6712 Bank holding companies

(G-14937)
COUNTY OF HENRY
Country View Haven
R858 County Road 15 (43545-7968)
PHONE..................................419 592-8075
Fax: 419 592-6620
Sue Meister, *Manager*
EMP: 30 **Privately Held**
WEB: www.henrycoelections.com
SIC: 8059 Nursing home, except skilled & intermediate care facility
PA: County Of Henry
660 N Perry St Ste 101
Napoleon OH 43545
419 592-1956

(G-14938)
FILLING MEMORIAL HOME OF MERCY (PA)
N160 State Route 108 (43545-9278)
PHONE..................................419 592-6451
Fax: 419 599-5178
Paul E Oehrtman, *Principal*
Nancy Wiechers, *Human Res Dir*
Paul Oehrtman, *Administration*
EMP: 350
SQ FT: 53,000
SALES: 10.2MM **Privately Held**
WEB: www.fillinghome.org
SIC: 8052 Intermediate care facilities

(G-14939)
FIRST CALL FOR HELP INC
600 Freedom Dr (43545-9038)
PHONE..................................419 599-1660
Fax: 419 592-8336
Joe Dildine, *CEO*
Lynda Sheets, *CFO*
Jenny Hoeffel, *Director*
EMP: 50
SQ FT: 10,000
SALES: 1.1MM **Privately Held**
WEB: www.fcfhnwo.org
SIC: 8093 Biofeedback center

(G-14940)
GERMAN MUTUAL INSURANCE CO
1000 Westmoreland Ave (43545-1257)
P.O. Box 191 (43545-0191)
PHONE..................................419 599-3993
Fax: 419 599-0109
Philip Menzel, *President*
Louis Knapp, *Vice Pres*
Rupert Knape, *VP Systems*
Jim Nafziger, *VP Systems*
EMP: 42
SALES (est): 7.5MM **Privately Held**
WEB: www.heartland-ins.com
SIC: 6411 Insurance agents

(G-14941)
GOLDEN LIVING LLC
Also Called: Beverly
240 Northcrest Dr (43545-7737)
PHONE..................................419 599-4070
Larry Cathcart, *Exec Dir*
EMP: 97
SALES (corp-wide): 7.4MM **Privately Held**
SIC: 8059 8051 Convalescent home; skilled nursing care facilities
PA: Golden Living Llc
5220 Tennyson Pkwy # 400
Plano TX 75024
972 372-6300

(G-14942)
HENRY COUNTY BANK (HQ)
122 E Washington St (43545-1646)
P.O. Box 72 (43545-0072)
PHONE..................................419 599-1065
Fax: 419 599-4357
William L Wendt, *President*
Anthony B Grieser, *Exec VP*
Kevin Yarnell, *Senior VP*
J Kevin Yarnell, *Vice Pres*
Timothy Okuley, *Broker*
EMP: 39
SALES: 10MM **Privately Held**
WEB: www.thehenrycountybank.com
SIC: 6022 6163 State commercial banks; loan brokers

(G-14943)
HENRY COUNTY HOSPITAL INC
1600 E Riverview Ave Frnt (43545-9399)
PHONE..................................419 592-4015
Fax: 419 592-4017
Kim Bordenkircher, *CEO*
Jerry Erven, *Safety Dir*
Marie Clapp, *Controller*
Ed Ledden, *Med Doctor*
Debra Bspharm, *Manager*
EMP: 308
SQ FT: 100,000
SALES: 28MM **Privately Held**
SIC: 8062 General medical & surgical hospitals

(G-14944)
LEADERS FAMILY FARMS
0064 County Rd 16 (43545)
PHONE..................................419 599-1570
EMP: 30
SALES (est): 346.3K **Privately Held**
SIC: 7999 Amusement/Recreation Services

(G-14945)
MEL LANZER CO
2266 Scott St (43545-1064)
PHONE..................................419 592-2801

GEOGRAPHIC SECTION

Fax: 419 599-2861
Charlotte Zgela, *President*
Cheryl Huffman, *Vice Pres*
Matthew Lanzer, *Vice Pres*
Dan Follett, *Treasurer*
Margaret Lanzer, *Admin Sec*
EMP: 33 **EST:** 1950
SQ FT: 5,000
SALES: 15.1MM **Privately Held**
WEB: www.mellanzer.com
SIC: 1541 1542 Industrial buildings, new construction; commercial & office building contractors; religious building construction

(G-14946)
MWA ENTERPRISES LTD
900 American Rd (43545-6498)
PHONE.................................419 599-3835
Michael Adams, *Principal*
Jake Adams, *CFO*
EMP: 28
SALES (est): 721.1K **Privately Held**
SIC: 6519 Landholding office

(G-14947)
NAPOLEON WASH-N-FILL INC (PA)
485 N Perry St (43545-1706)
PHONE.................................419 592-0851
Fax: 419 592-1009
Mike Synder, *President*
Leo D Snyder Jr, *President*
Chauncey I Moore, *Corp Secy*
Michael Snyder, *Vice Pres*
EMP: 90 **EST:** 1969
SQ FT: 3,000
SALES (est): 859K **Privately Held**
SIC: 7542 5541 Carwashes; filling stations, gasoline

(G-14948)
NCOP LLC
Also Called: Orcha of North Livin & Rehab C
240 Northcrest Dr (43545-7737)
PHONE.................................419 599-4070
Andrew Fishman, *CEO*
Jeniffer Rohrs, *Exec Dir*
EMP: 99
SALES (est): 1.5MM **Privately Held**
SIC: 8051 Skilled nursing care facilities

(G-14949)
ROYAL ARCH MASONS OF OHIO
Also Called: Haly Chapter 136
109 E School St (43545-9217)
PHONE.................................419 762-5565
Dallas Andrew, *Admin Sec*
EMP: 30 **EST:** 1999
SALES (est): 337.6K **Privately Held**
SIC: 8699 Charitable organization

(G-14950)
SAFETY GROOVING & GRINDING LP
13226 County Road R (43545-5966)
P.O. Box 675, Abingdon MD (21009-0675)
PHONE.................................419 592-8666
Fax: 419 592-8665
Rex Parker, *Partner*
Tom Parker, *Partner*
Russell C Swank III, *General Ptnr*
Sueann Thomas, *Manager*
EMP: 40
SALES (est): 3.8MM
SALES (corp-wide): 33.4MM **Privately Held**
WEB: www.cwankoo.com
SIC: 1799 Diamond drilling & sawing
PA: Swank Construction Company, Llc
632 Hunt Valley Cir
New Kensington PA 15068
724 727-3497

Nashport
Muskingum County

(G-14951)
HANBY FARMS INC
10790 Newark Rd (43830-9066)
P.O. Box 97 (43830-0097)
PHONE.................................740 763-3554
Fax: 740 828-3621
Ralph F Hanby, *President*
David R Hanby, *President*
Ron Seitez, *Plant Mgr*
Doug Hanby, *CFO*
Carol Hanby, *Admin Sec*
EMP: 34
SQ FT: 10,000
SALES (est): 7.8MM **Privately Held**
SIC: 2048 5153 5191 Livestock feeds; corn; soybeans; fertilizer & fertilizer materials

(G-14952)
NEWARK DRYWALL INC
Also Called: A1 Drywall Supply
18122 Nashport Rd (43830-9629)
PHONE.................................740 763-3572
Fax: 740 345-1097
Rick Frenton, *President*
Jeffrey Frenton, *Principal*
Michael Frenton, *Principal*
EMP: 45 **EST:** 1977
SALES (est): 3MM **Privately Held**
SIC: 1742 Drywall

(G-14953)
OHIO OIL GATHERING CORPORATION (DH)
9320 Blackrun Rd (43830-9434)
P.O. Box 430, Frazeysburg (43822-0430)
PHONE.................................740 828-2892
Fax: 740 828-3660
Michael A Mayers, *President*
Michael McKee, *Vice Pres*
Mark Sterling, *Manager*
Robert Bumpus, *Asst Sec*
EMP: 25
SQ FT: 1,000
SALES (est): 5.2MM **Publicly Held**
WEB: www.ohiooil.com
SIC: 4213 4612 4212 Liquid petroleum transport, non-local; crude petroleum pipelines; local trucking, without storage
HQ: Clearfield Energy Inc
5 Radnor Corp Ctr Ste 400
Radnor PA 19087
610 293-0410

Navarre
Stark County

(G-14954)
CARMEN STEERING COMMITTEE
8074 Goodrich Rd Sw (44662-9436)
PHONE.................................330 756-2066
Edward V Smith Jr, *Principal*
EMP: 32
SALES (est): 470.8K **Privately Held**
SIC: 8699 Personal interest organization

(G-14955)
MDS FOODS INC (PA)
4676 Erie Ave Sw Ste A (44662-9658)
PHONE.................................330 879-9780
James Straughn, *President*
Pete Effinger, *Exec VP*
Misty D Lewis, *Vice Pres*
Lisa Straughn, *Vice Pres*
Scott Ward, *Maint Spvr*
EMP: 50
SQ FT: 40,000
SALES (est): 31.8MM **Privately Held**
WEB: www.mdsfoods.com
SIC: 5143 Cheese

(G-14956)
ROBERT G OWEN TRUCKING INC (PA)
9260 Erie Ave Sw (44662-9448)
P.O. Box 187 (44662-0187)
PHONE.................................330 756-1013
Fax: 330 879-9014
Steven Owen, *President*
Christopher Owen, *Vice Pres*
Rob Emmert, *Sales Executive*
Patricia Owen, *Admin Sec*
Owen Patricia, *Admin Sec*
EMP: 33
SQ FT: 8,000
SALES (est): 4.7MM **Privately Held**
SIC: 4213 Contract haulers

(G-14957)
YMCA OF MASSILLON
1226 Market St Ne (44662-8576)
PHONE.................................330 879-0800
Jim Stanford, *Manager*
EMP: 25
SALES (corp-wide): 2MM **Privately Held**
SIC: 8641 7991 8351 7032 Youth organizations; physical fitness facilities; child day care services; youth camps; individual & family services
PA: Ymca Of Massillon
131 Tremont Ave Se
Massillon OH 44646
330 837-5116

Negley
Columbiana County

(G-14958)
A M & O TOWING INC
11341 State Route 170 (44441-9713)
PHONE.................................330 385-0639
Mary Price, *President*
EMP: 40
SALES (est): 2.9MM **Privately Held**
SIC: 4492 Towing & tugboat service

(G-14959)
CHERISHED CHILDRENS EARLY
Also Called: Cherished Children's Ecdc
47677 Tomahawk Dr (44441-9778)
PHONE.................................330 424-4402
Fax: 330 420-9939
Angie Serrao,
EMP: 49
SALES: 1.9MM **Privately Held**
SIC: 8351 Preschool center

Nelsonville
Athens County

(G-14960)
CORRECTONS COMM STHASTERN OHIO
16677 Riverside Dr (45764-9528)
PHONE.................................740 753-4060
Jeremy Tolson, *Chairman*
EMP: 60
SALES (est): 3.6MM **Privately Held**
WEB: www.seorj.com
SIC: 8744 Jails, privately operated

(G-14961)
DOCTORS HOSPITAL CLEVELAND INC
Also Called: Ohio Health
11 John Lloyd Evns Mem Dr (45764-2523)
PHONE.................................740 753-7300
Fax: 740 753-2197
Steve Swart, *President*
Lemar Wyse, *President*
Sandra Rudawsky, *Vice Pres*
Diane Plamer, *Purchasing*
Stephanie Clelland, *QA Dir*
EMP: 185
SQ FT: 15,000
SALES (est): 21.6MM **Privately Held**
SIC: 8051 8062 Skilled nursing care facilities; general medical & surgical hospitals

(G-14962)
ED MAP INC
296 S Harper St Ste 1 (45764-1600)
PHONE.................................740 753-3439
Fax: 740 753-9402
Michael Mark, *CEO*
Kerry Stoessel Pigman, *President*
Andrew J Herd, *Vice Pres*
Kelby Kostival, *Vice Pres*
Sarah Riddlebarger, *Vice Pres*
EMP: 83
SQ FT: 7,000
SALES (est): 83MM **Privately Held**
WEB: www.edmap.biz
SIC: 5192 Books

(G-14963)
FIRST NAT BNK OF NELSONVILLE (PA)
11 Public Sq (45764-1132)
P.O. Box 149 (45764-0149)
PHONE.................................740 753-1941
Fax: 740 753-1334
Steven Cox, *President*
Mary Jane Lax, *Senior VP*
Eric Courtney, *Vice Pres*
Suzie Witmann, *Treasurer*
Gary Sayers, *Loan Officer*
EMP: 32
SALES: 3.1MM **Privately Held**
WEB: www.fnbnelsonville.com
SIC: 6021 National commercial banks

(G-14964)
GEORGIA BOOT LLC
39 E Canal St (45764-1247)
PHONE.................................740 753-1951
Gerald M Cohn, *CEO*
Thomas R Morrison, *President*
Jim McDonald, *CFO*
Ken Furlong, *Controller*
Kevin Lyle, *Controller*
EMP: 100
SALES (est): 19.1MM
SALES (corp-wide): 253.2MM **Publicly Held**
WEB: www.durangoboot.com
SIC: 5139 3144 3143 3021 Shoes; women's footwear, except athletic; men's footwear, except athletic; rubber & plastics footwear
HQ: Ej Footwear Llc
381 Riverside Dr Ste 300
Franklin TN

(G-14965)
LEHIGH OUTFITTERS LLC (HQ)
Also Called: Slipgrips
39 E Canal St (45764-1247)
PHONE.................................740 753-1951
Joseph J Sebes, *President*
Ken Furlong, *Controller*
Lisa Johnson, *Marketing Staff*
Richard Simms, *Mng Member*
Joe Hanning, *Director*
◆ **EMP:** 200
SQ FT: 24,000
SALES (est): 120.4MM
SALES (corp-wide): 253.2MM **Publicly Held**
SIC: 5661 5139 Men's shoes; women's shoes; shoes
PA: Rocky Brands, Inc.
39 E Canal St
Nelsonville OH 45764
740 753-1951

(G-14966)
PINE HILLS CONTINUING CARE CTR
1950 Mount Saint Marys Dr # 2 (45764-1280)
PHONE.................................740 753-1931
Lorina Harkless, *Director*
Steven Fwartz, *Administration*
EMP: 50
SALES (est): 578.7K **Privately Held**
SIC: 8051 Skilled nursing care facilities

(G-14967)
S & B ENTERPRISES LLC
Also Called: Sanborn Vending
668 Poplar St (45764-1420)
PHONE.................................740 753-2646
Bill Wend,
EMP: 28 **EST:** 1940
SQ FT: 5,000
SALES (est): 413.8K **Privately Held**
SIC: 7993 5962 Amusement machine rental, coin-operated; merchandising machine operators

(G-14968)
SECHKAR COMPANY
4831 2nd St (45764-9568)
PHONE.................................740 385-8900
Dan Sechkar, *Owner*
EMP: 42
SALES (est): 1.2MM **Privately Held**
SIC: 8322 Social services for the handicapped

Nevada
Wyandot County

(G-14969)
PHILLIP MC GUIRE
Also Called: H & R Block
1585 County Highway 62 (44849-9798)
PHONE 740 482-2701
Phillip Mc Guire, *Owner*
Charlene McGuire, *Co-Owner*
EMP: 50
SALES (est): 750.1K **Privately Held**
SIC: 7291 Tax return preparation services

New Albany
Franklin County

(G-14970)
ABERCROMBIE & FITCH TRADING CO (DH)
6301 Fitch Path (43054-9269)
PHONE 614 283-6500
Fran Horowitz, *CEO*
Seth Johnson, *COO*
Michael Kramer, *CFO*
Wesley S McDonald, *CFO*
Caroline Gonzalez, *Human Res Dir*
▼ EMP: 50 EST: 2000
SALES (est): 365.2MM
SALES (corp-wide): 3.4B **Publicly Held**
SIC: 5136 5137 5641 5621 Men's & boys' clothing; women's & children's clothing; children's & infants' wear stores; women's clothing stores; men's & boys' clothing stores

(G-14971)
ACCEL INC
9000 Smiths Mill Rd (43054-6647)
PHONE 614 656-1100
Fax: 614 549-4199
Tara Abraham, *CEO*
David Abraham, *President*
Margaetta Keel, *Manager*
Jason Schroder, *Director*
EMP: 200
SQ FT: 305,000
SALES (est): 28.3MM **Privately Held**
SIC: 7389 Packaging & labeling services

(G-14972)
AETNA HEALTH CALIFORNIA INC
7400 W Campus Rd Ste 100 (43054-8723)
PHONE 614 933-6000
Barb Hard, *Branch Mgr*
EMP: 50 **Publicly Held**
SIC: 6324 Health maintenance organization (HMO), insurance only
HQ: Aetna Health Of California, Inc.
2409 Camino Ramon
San Ramon CA 94583
925 543-9000

(G-14973)
ALLSTARS TRAVEL GROUP INC
Also Called: Troilo & Associates
7775 Walton Pkwy Ste 100 (43054-8202)
PHONE 614 901-4100
Torsten Krings, *President*
Tammy Troilo, *Vice Pres*
Jennifer Apple, *Manager*
Colin Busse, *Manager*
Leah Lawson, *Manager*
EMP: 120
SALES (est): 30.6MM **Privately Held**
WEB: www.ts24.com
SIC: 4724 Tourist agency arranging transport, lodging & car rental

(G-14974)
BEST PLUMBING LIMITED
5791 Zarley St Ste A (43054-7091)
PHONE 614 855-1919
Fax: 614 855-4027
Jim Mullins,
Joe Electric,
EMP: 50 EST: 1995
SQ FT: 3,000
SALES (est): 6.1MM **Privately Held**
SIC: 1711 Plumbing contractors

(G-14975)
BRIGHTVIEW LANDSCAPES LLC
Also Called: Brickman Facility Services
6530 W Campus Oval # 300 (43054-8726)
PHONE 614 741-8233
Scott Brickman, *CEO*
Jeff Iles, *Opers Mgr*
Chad Marshall, *Opers Staff*
Mark Gsp, *Director*
EMP: 56
SALES (corp-wide): 914MM **Privately Held**
SIC: 0781 0782 Landscape services; landscape contractors
HQ: Brightview Landscapes, Llc
401 Plymouth Rd Ste 500
Plymouth Meeting PA 19462
484 567-7204

(G-14976)
BRODHEAD VILLAGE LTD (PA)
Also Called: Wallick Company, The
160 W Main St (43054-1188)
PHONE 614 863-4640
Layne Hurst, *President*
Thomas A Feusse, *Partner*
Jerry Bowen, *General Mgr*
Victoria Taylor, *Regional Mgr*
William Hinga, *Senior VP*
EMP: 60
SQ FT: 13,000
SALES (est): 5.6MM **Privately Held**
SIC: 6513 Apartment building operators

(G-14977)
CAMPBELL FAMILY CHILDCARE INC
Also Called: Goddard School of New Albany
5351 New Albany Rd W (43054-8853)
PHONE 614 855-4780
Jeffrey Campbell, *Director*
Coleen Barber, *Director*
EMP: 26
SALES (est): 1MM **Privately Held**
SIC: 8351 Preschool center

(G-14978)
CAPITAL CITY ELECTRIC LLC
9798 Karmar Ct Ste B (43054-8210)
PHONE 614 933-8700
Danita Kessler, *Principal*
Blaze Bishop, *Project Engr*
Eric Baker, *Accounts Mgr*
EMP: 45
SQ FT: 4,500
SALES (est): 8.3MM **Privately Held**
WEB: www.capcityelectric.com
SIC: 1731 General electrical contractor

(G-14979)
CAROL SCUDERE
Also Called: Domestic Connection
6912 Keesee Cir (43054-8876)
PHONE 614 839-4357
Carol Scudere, *Owner*
EMP: 28
SALES (est): 1.7MM **Privately Held**
WEB: www.pdspdi.com
SIC: 8742 8351 7363 7349 Industry specialist consultants; child day care services; domestic help service; maid services, contract or fee basis; babysitting bureau

(G-14980)
CASAGRANDE MASONRY INC
13530 Morse Rd Sw (43054-7792)
P.O. Box 1540, Pataskala (43062-1540)
PHONE 740 964-0781
Anthony A Casagrande, *President*
EMP: 50
SALES: 5MM **Privately Held**
SIC: 1741 Stone masonry

(G-14981)
COLUMBUS CTR FOR HUMN SVCS INC
6227 Harlem Rd (43054-9707)
PHONE 614 245-8180
Rebecca Sharp, *CEO*
EMP: 37
SALES (corp-wide): 7.7MM **Privately Held**
SIC: 8059 Home for the mentally retarded, exc. skilled or intermediate
PA: Columbus Center For Human Services, Inc.
540 Industrial Mile Rd
Columbus OH 43228
614 641-2904

(G-14982)
COMMUNICATION OPTIONS INC (HQ)
4689 Reynoldsburg New Alb (43054-9585)
PHONE 614 901-7095
Jeff Swenson, *CEO*
Scott Halliday, *President*
John E Oberfield, *Principal*
Steve Vogelmeier, *Principal*
EMP: 27
SQ FT: 12,000
SALES: 5MM
SALES (corp-wide): 8.3MM **Privately Held**
WEB: www.coi.net
SIC: 4813 Local & long distance telephone communications
PA: Communications Iii, Inc
921 Eastwind Dr Ste 104
Westerville OH 43081
614 901-7720

(G-14983)
DFS CORPORATE SERVICES LLC
Also Called: Discover Financial Services
6500 New Albany Rd E (43054-8730)
PHONE 614 283-2499
Don Probst, *Manager*
EMP: 30
SALES (corp-wide): 11.5B **Publicly Held**
WEB: www.discovercard.com
SIC: 6141 Consumer finance companies
HQ: Dfs Corporate Services Llc
2500 Lake Cook Rd 2
Riverwoods IL 60015
224 405-0900

(G-14984)
EVANS MECHWART HAM (PA)
Also Called: E M H & T
5500 New Albany Rd (43054-8703)
PHONE 614 775-4500
Nelson Kohman, *President*
David Faulkner, *COO*
Craig A Bohnin, *Vice Pres*
Craig Bohning, *Vice Pres*
Gregory Comfort, *Vice Pres*
EMP: 285 EST: 1925
SQ FT: 13,200
SALES (est): 57.5MM **Privately Held**
WEB: www.emht.com
SIC: 8713 8711 Surveying services; consulting engineer

(G-14985)
EXHIBITPRO INC
8900 Smiths Mill Rd (43054-1281)
P.O. Box 537 (43054-0537)
PHONE 614 885-9541
Fax: 614 885-5347
Lori Miller, *CEO*
Lori J Miller, *CEO*
Edward Miller, *President*
Greg Lindsey, *Vice Pres*
Gavin Duckwall, *Opers Mgr*
EMP: 30
SQ FT: 15,000
SALES (est): 4.8MM **Privately Held**
WEB: www.exhibitpro.net
SIC: 7336 7389 Commercial art & graphic design; trade show arrangement

(G-14986)
FRANKLIN CMPT SVCS GROUP INC
6650 Walnut St (43054-9138)
PHONE 614 431-3327
Mike Castrodale, *President*
Gail Gmelko, *Admin Sec*
EMP: 45
SALES (est): 1.7MM **Privately Held**
WEB: www.fcsg.com
SIC: 7379 Computer related consulting services;

(G-14987)
GOLF CLUB CO
4522 Kitzmiller Rd (43054-9565)
P.O. Box 369 (43054-0369)
PHONE 614 855-7326
Grant Marrow, *Ch of Bd*
George McElroy, *Ch of Bd*
C T Rice, *President*
EMP: 35
SQ FT: 5,000
SALES: 3.2MM **Privately Held**
WEB: www.thegolfclub.com
SIC: 7997 Golf club, membership

(G-14988)
HIGHLAND VILLAGE LTD PARTNR
Also Called: Wallick Co.
160 W Main St (43054-1188)
PHONE 614 863-4640
Kevin Allmandinger, *Partner*
EMP: 60
SALES (est): 2MM **Privately Held**
SIC: 6512 6513 Nonresidential building operators; apartment building operators

(G-14989)
JD EQUIPMENT INC (PA)
Also Called: John Deere Authorized Dealer
5850 Zarley St (43054-9700)
PHONE 614 527-8800
Fax: 614 879-5767
Jeff Mitchell, *CEO*
Don K Mitchell Jr, *President*
Maxine Mitchell, *Vice Pres*
Nick Trostle, *Opers Mgr*
Luke Harbage, *Store Mgr*
▼ EMP: 75
SQ FT: 25,000
SALES (est): 147.6MM **Privately Held**
SIC: 5999 5083 Farm equipment & supplies; agricultural machinery & equipment

(G-14990)
JOINT IMPLANT SURGEONS INC
Also Called: Ortholink Physicians
7727 Smiths Mill Rd 200 (43054-7568)
PHONE 614 221-6331
Fax: 614 221-6301
Adolph V Lombardi Jr, *President*
Thomas H Mallory MD, *President*
Rebecca Dunaway, *Office Mgr*
Joanne Adams, *Director*
EMP: 35
SQ FT: 2,500
SALES (est): 6.6MM **Privately Held**
WEB: www.jointimplantsurgeons.com
SIC: 8011 Orthopedic physician

(G-14991)
LOFT SERVICES LLC
Also Called: Home Helpers and Direct Link
8010 Morse Rd (43054-8518)
PHONE 614 855-2452
Paige Loft, *Mng Member*
EMP: 40
SALES (est): 349.1K **Privately Held**
SIC: 8082 Home health care services

(G-14992)
MISSION ESSNTIAL PERSONNEL LLC (PA)
6525 W Campus Oval # 101 (43054-8831)
PHONE 614 416-2345
Fax: 614 416-2346
Jim Begley, *Vice Pres*
Steve Frith, *Vice Pres*
Mark Halbig, *Vice Pres*
David Larocca, *Vice Pres*
Charlie Miller, *Vice Pres*
EMP: 150
SQ FT: 8,000
SALES (est): 64.4MM **Privately Held**
WEB: www.aegismep.com
SIC: 7389 8748 Translation services; safety training service

(G-14993)
MOUNT CARMEL HEALTH
55 N High St Ste A (43054-7098)
PHONE 614 855-4878
Fax: 614 939-0612
Diane Beggs, *Branch Mgr*
EMP: 25

GEOGRAPHIC SECTION

New Bremen - Auglaize County (G-15017)

SALES (corp-wide): 16.3B **Privately Held**
SIC: 8031 Offices & clinics of osteopathic physicians
HQ: Mount Carmel Health
793 W State St
Columbus OH 43222
614 234-5000

(G-14994)
MOUNT CARMEL HEALTH SYSTEM
7333 Smiths Mill Rd (43054-9291)
PHONE.................................614 775-6600
Dick Denbeau, *CEO*
Amanda Parker, *Pharmacist*
Dawn Buck, *Manager*
Donna Hutchinson, *Director*
Lynda Yonker, *Ch Nursing Ofcr*
EMP: 36
SALES (corp-wide): 16.3B **Privately Held**
SIC: 8062 General medical & surgical hospitals
HQ: Mount Carmel Health System
6150 E Broad St
Columbus OH 43213
614 234-6000

(G-14995)
MXD GROUP INC (HQ)
Also Called: Mxd Group, Inc.
7795 Walton Pkwy (43054-0001)
PHONE.................................866 711-3129
Fax: 614 865-8503
Terry Solvedt, *CEO*
David Vieira, *President*
Peter Elmasri, *General Mgr*
Sam Marshall, *General Mgr*
Allison Ramer, *General Mgr*
◆ EMP: 70
SALES (est): 389.4MM **Privately Held**
SIC: 4214 4213 Local trucking with storage; household goods transport

(G-14996)
NEW ALBANY ATHC BOOSTER CLB
7600 Fodor Rd (43054-8738)
PHONE.................................614 413-8325
Tim Cline, *President*
EMP: 50
SALES (est): 834.2K **Privately Held**
SIC: 7997 Membership sports & recreation clubs

(G-14997)
NEW ALBANY CLEANING SERVICES
108 N High St Ste B (43054-8993)
P.O. Box 452 (43054-0452)
PHONE.................................614 855-9990
Fax: 614 855-9991
Greg Stanley, *President*
Jennifer Stanley, *Vice Pres*
Jennifer Standley, *Technology*
Andrew Roeth, *Assistant*
EMP: 30
SALES (est): 1.4MM **Privately Held**
SIC: 7217 7349 Carpet & upholstery cleaning; cleaning service, industrial or commercial

(G-14998)
NEW ALBANY COUNTRY CLUB COMM A
1 Club Ln (43054-9377)
PHONE.................................614 939-8500
Fax: 614 939-8525
Leslie Wexner, *President*
Tony Shill, *General Mgr*
Ted B Hipsher, *Principal*
Ann Dinda, *Controller*
Debbie Smith, *Controller*
EMP: 150
SQ FT: 55,000
SALES (est): 14.6MM **Privately Held**
WEB: www.nacc.org
SIC: 7997 Country club, membership

(G-14999)
NEW ALBANY LINKS DEV CO LTD
7100 New Albany Links Dr (43054-8194)
PHONE.................................614 939-5914
Fax: 614 939-0507
T Bruce Oldendick, *President*

Thomas Bruce Oldendick, *President*
Glenn Hay, *Superintendent*
Matt Reeves, *Director*
Jessica Mahr, *Assistant*
EMP: 70
SQ FT: 1,932
SALES (est): 2.4MM **Privately Held**
SIC: 7997 Golf club, membership

(G-15000)
NEW ALBANY PLAIN LOC SC TRANSP
55 N High St Ste A (43054-7098)
PHONE.................................614 855-2033
Fax: 614 855-4030
Philip Vice, *Transportation*
Carol Mulbay, *Manager*
EMP: 35
SQ FT: 1,516
SALES: 1.5MM **Privately Held**
SIC: 4151 School buses

(G-15001)
NEW ALBANY SURGERY CENTER LLC
5040 Forest Dr Ste 100 (43054-9187)
PHONE.................................614 775-1616
Fax: 614 507-5073
Jacqueline A Primeau, *Principal*
Dick D'Enbeau, *Manager*
Cindyrd Williams, *Info Tech Mgr*
Matt Myers, *Technology*
EMP: 175
SQ FT: 95,000
SALES (est): 25.5MM
SALES (corp-wide): 16.3B **Privately Held**
SIC: 8062 General medical & surgical hospitals
HQ: Mount Carmel Health
793 W State St
Columbus OH 43222
614 234-5000

(G-15002)
NORM SHARLOTTE INC
Also Called: N. S. Farrington & Co.
5101 Forest Dr Ste C (43054-8226)
PHONE.................................336 788-7705
Fax: 336 788-7729
John Erskine, *President*
Ken Farrington, *Vice Pres*
Earl Gardner, *Vice Pres*
Christopher Thomas, *Sales Staff*
Dennis Mitchell, *Marketing Staff*
▲ EMP: 30
SQ FT: 30,000
SALES (est): 9.7MM **Privately Held**
WEB: www.nsfarrington.com
SIC: 5087 Laundry & dry cleaning equipment & supplies

(G-15003)
QWAIDE ENTERPRISES LLC
Also Called: Gng Music Instruction
6044 Phar Lap Dr (43054-8106)
PHONE.................................614 209-0551
Gregory N Gould, *Owner*
EMP: 30 EST: 2008
SALES (est): 488.7K **Privately Held**
SIC: 8748 Business consulting

(G-15004)
RE/MAX CONSULTANT GROUP
6650 Walnut St (43054-9138)
PHONE.................................614 855-2822
Fax: 614 855-2823
Mora Ackermann, *CEO*
Lauren Fladung, *Broker*
Philip Hicks, *Broker*
Jim Paepeghem, *Real Est Agnt*
Sandy Sanders, *Real Est Agnt*
EMP: 70
SQ FT: 10,000
SALES: 300MM **Privately Held**
SIC: 6531 Real estate agent, residential

(G-15005)
READY SET GROW
5200 New Albany Rd (43054-8836)
PHONE.................................614 855-5100
Fax: 614 855-5135
Steve Lefkovitz, *Owner*
Michelle Rosser, *Co-Owner*
EMP: 30
SALES (est): 677.9K **Privately Held**
SIC: 8351 Preschool center

(G-15006)
ROSSMAN
Also Called: P C B
7795 Walton Pkwy (43054-0001)
P.O. Box 2051 (43054-2051)
PHONE.................................614 523-4150
Brad Rossman, *Principal*
Kevin Rossman, *Financial Exec*
Tom Harrington, *Sales Executive*
EMP: 30 EST: 2010
SALES: 4.7MM **Privately Held**
SIC: 7322 Collection agency, except real estate

(G-15007)
SHREMSHOCK ARCHITECTS INC (PA)
Also Called: S A I
7400 W Campus Rd Ste 150 (43054-8739)
PHONE.................................614 545-4550
Fax: 614 545-4555
Gerald Shremshock, *President*
EMP: 100
SQ FT: 18,000
SALES: 4.4MM **Privately Held**
WEB: www.shremshock.com
SIC: 8712 Architectural services

(G-15008)
STATE FARM MUTL AUTO INSUR CO
Also Called: State Farm Insurance
5400 New Albany Rd (43054-8861)
PHONE.................................614 775-2001
Jason McCrory, *Principal*
EMP: 750
SALES (corp-wide): 39.5MM **Privately Held**
WEB: www.statefarm.com
SIC: 6411 6321 6311 Insurance agents & brokers; accident & health insurance; life insurance
PA: State Farm Mutual Automobile Insurance Company
1 State Farm Plz
Bloomington IL 61710
309 766-2311

(G-15009)
WALLICK ENTERPRISES INC
Also Called: Wallick Companies Cnstr Prpts
160 W Main St (43054-1188)
PHONE.................................614 863-4640
Sanford Goldston, *Ch of Bd*
Bob Dayne, *President*
EMP: 60
SQ FT: 13,000
SALES (est): 3.7MM **Privately Held**
SIC: 6552 Subdividers & developers

(G-15010)
WALLICK PROPERTIES MIDWEST LLC (PA)
160 W Main St Ste 200 (43054-1189)
P.O. Box 1023, Columbus (43216-1023)
PHONE.................................614 863-4640
Fax: 614 863-5649
Howard Wallick, *Mng Member*
Amie Flibordnick, *Manager*
Lynn Hayes, *Executive Asst*
Tom Feusse,
Dave Hendy,
EMP: 650 EST: 1966
SQ FT: 32,000
SALES (est): 46MM **Privately Held**
WEB: www.wallickcos.com
SIC: 6531 Real estate managers

New Boston
Scioto County

(G-15011)
HERITAGE PROFESSIONAL SERVICES
Also Called: Heritage Square New Boston
3304 Rhodes Ave (45662-4914)
PHONE.................................740 456-8245
Fax: 740 456-5164
Gilbert E Lawson, *President*
Irene Leadingham, *Admin Sec*
EMP: 25

SALES (est): 1.6MM **Privately Held**
WEB: www.heritagesquareonline.com
SIC: 8052 Intermediate care facilities; personal care facility

(G-15012)
NEW BOSTON AERIE 2271 FOE
Also Called: New Boston Eagles
3200 Rhodes Ave (45662-4912)
PHONE.................................740 456-0171
Oral Gulley, *President*
Jeff Gulley, *Vice Pres*
William David Jones, *Treasurer*
Scott Shope, *Admin Sec*
Don Cox,
EMP: 33
SALES (est): 477.1K **Privately Held**
SIC: 8641 Fraternal associations

(G-15013)
SCIOTO COUNTY OHIO
Also Called: Scioto County Child Services
3940 Gallia St (45662-4925)
PHONE.................................740 456-4164
Lisa Wiltshire, *Director*
EMP: 31 **Privately Held**
WEB: www.sciotocountychildrenservices.com
SIC: 8322 9111 Children's aid society; county supervisors' & executives' offices
PA: Scioto County Ohio
602 7th St Rm 1
Portsmouth OH 45662
740 355-8313

(G-15014)
SOUTH CENTRAL OHIO EDUCTL CTR
522 Glenwood Ave (45662-5505)
PHONE.................................740 456-0517
Darren Jenkins, *Superintendent*
Sandy Mers, *Superintendent*
Scott Holstein, *Asst Supt*
Andrew Riehl, *Treasurer*
Tom Hoggard, *Finance Other*
EMP: 109
SALES (est): 3.8MM **Privately Held**
SIC: 8299 8748 Arts & crafts schools; testing services

(G-15015)
SUPERIOR KRAFT HOMES LLC
3404 Rhodes Ave (45662-4916)
PHONE.................................740 947-7710
Linda Fetty, *Manager*
Jeffrey Keller,
Gary Parsley,
EMP: 61
SALES (est): 3.8MM **Privately Held**
SIC: 1522 Condominium construction; apartment building construction; hotel/motel, new construction

---

New Bremen
Auglaize County

(G-15016)
BROOKSIDE LABORATORIES INC
200 White Mountain Dr (45869-8603)
PHONE.................................419 977-2766
Fax: 419 753-2949
Thomas Menke, *Ch of Bd*
Mark Fluck, *President*
Allen Metzger, *CFO*
Kari Long, *Director*
EMP: 34
SQ FT: 25,000
SALES: 4.2MM **Privately Held**
WEB: www.blinc.com
SIC: 8734 Soil analysis

(G-15017)
COUNTY OF AUGLAIZE
Also Called: Auglaize County Board of Mr/Dd
20 E 1st St (45869-1165)
PHONE.................................419 629-2419
Fax: 419 629-3806
Alvin Willis, *Superintendent*
Rick Bice, *Manager*
EMP: 70 **Privately Held**
WEB: www.augmrdd.org

New Bremen - Auglaize County (G-15018) — GEOGRAPHIC SECTION

SIC: 8361 9111 Home for the mentally handicapped; county supervisors' & executives' offices
PA: County Of Auglaize
209 S Blackhoof St # 201
Wapakoneta OH 45895
419 739-6710

(G-15018)
CROWN EQUIPMENT CORPORATION (PA)
Also Called: Crown Lift Trucks
44 S Washington St (45869-1288)
P.O. Box 97 (45869-0097)
PHONE..................................419 629-2311
Fax: 419 629-2900
James F Dicke II, *Ch of Bd*
James F Dicke III, *President*
David J Besser, *Senior VP*
James R Mozer, *Senior VP*
Timothy S Quellhorst, *Senior VP*
◆ EMP: 3480
SQ FT: 25,000
SALES: 2.9B Privately Held
WEB: www.crown.com
SIC: 5084 Lift trucks & parts

(G-15019)
CROWN EQUIPMENT CORPORATION
40 S Washington St (45869-1247)
PHONE..................................419 629-2311
EMP: 65
SALES (corp-wide): 1.3B Privately Held
SIC: 5084 3537 Whol Industrial Equipment Mfg Industrial Trucks/Tractors
PA: Crown Equipment Corporation
44 S Washington St
New Bremen OH 45869
419 629-2311

New Carlisle
Clark County

(G-15020)
BMNH INC
Also Called: Belle Manor Nursing Home
1885 N Dayton Lakeview Rd (45344-9101)
PHONE..................................937 845-3561
Fax: 937 845-3339
Sanford R Gerber, *President*
EMP: 125
SQ FT: 50,000
SALES (est): 4.9MM Privately Held
WEB: www.bellemanor.com
SIC: 8051 8059 Skilled nursing care facilities; convalescent home

(G-15021)
CHAMBER COMMERCE NEW CARLISLE
131 S Main St (45344-1952)
PHONE..................................937 845-3911
Linda Campbell, *President*
EMP: 47
SALES (est): 619.7K Privately Held
SIC: 8611 Chamber of Commerce

(G-15022)
ELM VALLEY FISHING CLUB
5118 S Dayton Brandt Rd (45344-9611)
PHONE..................................937 845-0584
Bill Hammonds, *Principal*
EMP: 100
SQ FT: 2,646
SALES (est): 1.1MM Privately Held
SIC: 7997 Hunting club, membership

(G-15023)
FAMILY VIDEO MOVIE CLUB INC
401 N Main St (45344-1428)
PHONE..................................937 846-1021
Tracey Turner, *Branch Mgr*
EMP: 26
SALES (corp-wide): 234.2MM Privately Held
SIC: 7841 Video disk/tape rental to the general public
HQ: Family Video Movie Club Inc.
2500 Lehigh Mt Ave
Glenview IL 60026
847 904-9000

(G-15024)
INTEGRITY INFORMATION TECH INC
Also Called: Integrity It
2742 N Dayton Lakeview Rd (45344-8503)
PHONE..................................937 846-1769
Mark Debreceni, *President*
Sara E Debreceni, *Owner*
John Simkins, *Principal*
John Sines, *Technology*
EMP: 25
SALES: 3.3MM Privately Held
WEB: www.integrity-it.com
SIC: 7379

(G-15025)
KAFFENBARGER TRUCK EQP CO (PA)
10100 Ballentine Pike (45344-9534)
PHONE..................................937 845-3804
Fax: 937 857-9068
Larry Kaffenbarger, *President*
Edward W Dunn, *Principal*
Everett L Kaffenbarger, *Principal*
Timothy Schuler, *Controller*
Denise Miller, *Accountant*
◆ EMP: 180
SQ FT: 30,000
SALES (est): 68MM Privately Held
WEB: www.kaffenbarger.com
SIC: 3713 5013 Truck bodies (motor vehicles); truck parts & accessories

(G-15026)
LOUDERBACK FMLY INVSTMENTS INC
Also Called: Professional Property Maint
3545 S Dayton Lakeview Rd (45344-2345)
P.O. Box 24383, Dayton (45424-0383)
PHONE..................................937 845-1762
Kevin Louderback, *President*
Don Louderback, *General Mgr*
Brad Mittlestead, *Opers Staff*
Matt Mundey, *Sales Mgr*
Amy Neace, *Manager*
EMP: 35
SQ FT: 6,000
SALES (est): 1.3MM Privately Held
SIC: 7349 0781 Building maintenance, except repairs; landscape services

(G-15027)
MARTIN CHEVROLET INC
2135 S Dayton Lakeview Rd (45344-2314)
PHONE..................................937 849-1381
Cornelius Martin, *President*
EMP: 45
SQ FT: 50,000
SALES (est): 9.3MM Privately Held
SIC: 5511 7538 Automobiles, new & used; pickups, new & used; general automotive repair shops

(G-15028)
MIGRANT HEAD START
476 N Dayton Lakeview Rd (45344-2109)
PHONE..................................937 846-0699
George Hardy, *Owner*
Elizabeth Ray, *Administration*
EMP: 45
SALES (est): 62K Privately Held
SIC: 8351 Head start center, except in conjunction with school

(G-15029)
NEW CARLISLE SPT & FITNES CTR
524 N Dayton Lakeview Rd (45344-2111)
PHONE..................................937 846-1000
Vijaya Devatha, *Owner*
EMP: 35
SALES (est): 716.2K Privately Held
SIC: 8099 7991 Nutrition services; health club

(G-15030)
ROOFING BY INSULATION INC
1727 Dalton Dr (45344-2309)
PHONE..................................937 315-5024
Dave Dick, *President*
EMP: 27
SALES: 1.2MM Privately Held
SIC: 1761 1742 Roofing contractor; insulation, buildings

(G-15031)
SCARFFS NURSERY INC
411 N Dayton Lakeview Rd (45344-2149)
PHONE..................................937 845-3130
Fax: 937 845-9731
Peter Scarff, *President*
William N Scarff Sr, *Chairman*
Bill Duff, *Sales Staff*
John Kinsella, *Sales Staff*
Jeremy Wal, *Sales Staff*
EMP: 125
SQ FT: 8,000
SALES: 6MM Privately Held
WEB: www.scarffs.com
SIC: 0181 5992 0781 5261 Nursery stock, growing of; flowers, fresh; plants, potted; landscape architects; nurseries & garden centers; flowers & florists' supplies

(G-15032)
STUDEBAKER NURSERIES INC
Also Called: Studebaker Wholesale Nurseries
11140 Milton Carlisle Rd (45344-9298)
PHONE..................................800 845-0584
Fax: 937 845-1935
William Studebaker, *President*
Richard Obermeyer, *Vice Pres*
Dan W Studebaker, *Vice Pres*
Hope Leeds, *Buyer*
Karla Hicks, *Controller*
EMP: 80
SQ FT: 2,500
SALES (est): 8.5MM Privately Held
WEB: www.studebakernurseries.com
SIC: 0181 Nursery stock, growing of

(G-15033)
WENCO INC
1807 Dalton Dr (45344-2305)
PHONE..................................937 849-6002
Fax: 937 845-9221
EMP: 125
SQ FT: 12,000
SALES (est): 35.1MM Privately Held
SIC: 1542 1541 Nonresidential Construction Industrial Building Construction

New Concord
Muskingum County

(G-15034)
GUERNSY-MUSKINGUM ELC COOP INC (PA)
17 S Liberty St (43762-1230)
PHONE..................................740 826-7661
Fax: 740 826-7171
Shirley Stutz, *President*
Brian Hill, *President*
John Enos, *Corp Secy*
EMP: 44
SQ FT: 15,000
SALES: 34.4MM Privately Held
WEB: www.gmenergy.com
SIC: 4911 Distribution, electric power

(G-15035)
MUSKINGUM VLY SYMPHONIC WINDS
163 Stormont St (43762-1118)
PHONE..................................740 826-8095
David Turrill, *CEO*
Kathy Brown, *Principal*
EMP: 25
SALES (est): 300.6K Privately Held
SIC: 7929 Entertainers & entertainment groups

(G-15036)
NEW CONCORD HEALTH CENTER
1280 Friendship Dr (43762-1024)
PHONE..................................740 826-4135
Mark Richards, *Manager*
EMP: 137
SALES (est): 5MM Privately Held
WEB: www.zandex.com
SIC: 8059 Nursing home, except skilled & intermediate care facility

(G-15037)
SOUTHEASTERN OHIO SYMPHONY ORC
163 Stormont St (43762-1118)
P.O. Box 42 (43762-0042)
PHONE..................................740 826-8197
Chris Stotler, *President*
Erin France, *Vice Pres*
EMP: 50
SALES: 52K Privately Held
SIC: 7929 Symphony orchestras

(G-15038)
TK GAS SERVICES INC
2303 John Glenn Hwy (43762-9310)
PHONE..................................740 826-0303
Ted Korte, *President*
Jill Pattison, *Corp Secy*
Kylee Foraker, *Human Resources*
EMP: 50
SQ FT: 4,000
SALES (est): 6.6MM Privately Held
SIC: 1389 Oil field services

(G-15039)
TRIPLETT & ADAMS ENTPS INC
Also Called: Triad Data Processing
140 S Friendship Dr (43762-9453)
PHONE..................................816 221-1024
R Gregory Adams, *CEO*
Lawrence Triplett, *President*
Kelly Cale, *Managing Dir*
Cindy Rhodes, *Managing Dir*
Nancy Maynard, *Opers Mgr*
EMP: 76
SQ FT: 14,500
SALES (est): 6MM Privately Held
WEB: www.resourcesystem.com
SIC: 7372 7371 Home entertainment computer software; custom computer programming services

(G-15040)
ZANDEX INC
Also Called: Beckett House
1280 Friendship Dr (43762-1024)
PHONE..................................740 872-0809
Fax: 740 826-7363
Tiffany Houston, *Purch Agent*
Donna Devers, *Personnel Exec*
Mark Richards, *Manager*
Kara Maroot, *Manager*
EMP: 120
SALES (corp-wide): 34MM Privately Held
SIC: 8052 8051 Intermediate care facilities; skilled nursing care facilities
PA: Zandex, Inc.
1122 Taylor St
Zanesville OH 43701
740 454-1400

(G-15041)
ZANDEX HEALTH CARE CORPORATION
Also Called: Beckett House At New Concord
1280 Friendship Dr (43762-1024)
PHONE..................................740 454-1400
Margarett Richard, *Manager*
Kevin Candabovich, *Director*
William Shade, *Director*
EMP: 140
SALES (corp-wide): 34MM Privately Held
SIC: 8052 8051 8361 Intermediate care facilities; skilled nursing care facilities; residential care
HQ: Zandex Health Care Corporation
1122 Taylor St
Zanesville OH 43701

New Franklin
Summit County

(G-15042)
CLINTON ALUMINUM DIST INC (PA)
6270 Van Buren Rd (44216-9743)
PHONE..................................330 882-6743
Robert Krieger, *President*
Tom Dagenback, *Vice Pres*
Gregory Ertle, *Vice Pres*
Mark Jodon, *Manager*

▲ = Import ▼ = Export
◆ = Import/Export

Amanda Morris, *Info Tech Mgr*
▲ **EMP:** 106
SQ FT: 165,000
SALES (est): 78.6MM **Privately Held**
SIC: 5051 Steel

(G-15043)
CONCEPT FREIGHT SERVICE INC
4386 Point Comfort Dr (44319-4076)
PHONE....................330 784-1134
Fax: 330 724-2729
Thomas L Cook, *President*
Jody Hamilton, *Corp Secy*
Jeffrey L Cook, *Vice Pres*
Allen Klever, *Vice Pres*
Jan Good, *Manager*
EMP: 40
SQ FT: 9,600
SALES (est): 6.1MM **Privately Held**
WEB: www.conceptfreightinc.com
SIC: 4213 Trucking, except local

(G-15044)
EAST OHIO GAS COMPANY
Also Called: Dominion Energy Ohio
6500 Hampsher Rd (44216-8905)
PHONE....................330 266-2169
Greg Theril, *Manager*
EMP: 296
SALES (corp-wide): 12.5B **Publicly Held**
SIC: 4923 Gas transmission & distribution
HQ: The East Ohio Gas Company
19701 Libby Rd
Maple Heights OH 44137
800 362-7557

(G-15045)
JPMORGAN CHASE BANK NAT ASSN
5638 Manchester Rd (44319-4213)
PHONE....................330 972-1735
Fax: 330 882-6222
Connie Nagy, *Principal*
EMP: 26
SALES (corp-wide): 99.6B **Publicly Held**
SIC: 6021 National commercial banks
HQ: Jpmorgan Chase Bank, National Association
1111 Polaris Pkwy
Columbus OH 43240
614 436-3055

(G-15046)
OCCASIONS PARTY CENTRE
6800 Manchester Rd (44216-9491)
PHONE....................330 882-5113
Fax: 330 882-9727
Lisa Masey, *Owner*
EMP: 50
SQ FT: 30,471
SALES (est): 1.1MM **Privately Held**
WEB: www.occasionspartycentre.com
SIC: 7299 Banquet hall facilities

(G-15047)
SPRING HILLS GOLF CLUB
6571 Clvland Massillon Rd (44216-9342)
PHONE....................330 825-2439
Gary Kendron, *General Mgr*
EMP: 25
SALES (est): 900K **Privately Held**
SIC: 7992 Public golf courses

(G-15048)
ST LUKE LUTHERAN COMMUNITY
615 Latham Ln (44319-4338)
PHONE....................330 644-3914
John L Spieler, *President*
Ron Derry, *CFO*
Richard Pitts, *Director*
Karen Hardlica, *Administration*
EMP: 60
SQ FT: 4,000
SALES (est): 2.9MM **Privately Held**
SIC: 8052 Personal care facility

(G-15049)
ST LUKE LUTHERAN COMMUNITY
615 Latham Ln (44319-4338)
PHONE....................330 644-3914
Fax: 330 245-7328
Rev L W Lautenschlager, *Branch Mgr*

EMP: 80
SQ FT: 19,346
SALES (corp-wide): 15.5MM **Privately Held**
WEB: www.stlukelutherancommunity.org
SIC: 8052 Personal care facility
PA: St. Luke Lutheran Community
220 Applegrove St Ne
Canton OH
330 499-8341

(G-15050)
SUMMIT CLAIM SERVICES LLC
5511 Manchester Rd C (44319-4210)
PHONE....................330 706-9898
Ron Costa,
EMP: 100 **EST:** 2008
SALES (est): 9.4MM **Privately Held**
SIC: 6411 7389 Insurance adjusters; auction, appraisal & exchange services

New Haven
Huron County

(G-15051)
NEW HAVEN ESTATES INC (PA)
2744 E State Highway 224 (44850)
PHONE....................419 933-2181
Fax: 419 933-2348
Thomas M Saas, *President*
David F Roberts, *Vice Pres*
Sheila Urie, *Vice Pres*
Ann W Von Saas, *Admin Sec*
EMP: 28
SQ FT: 38,000
SALES (est): 8.2MM **Privately Held**
WEB: www.newhavensupply.com
SIC: 5063 5085 5074 Electrical apparatus & equipment; industrial supplies; plumbing & hydronic heating supplies

New Knoxville
Auglaize County

(G-15052)
HOGE LUMBER COMPANY (PA)
Also Called: Hoge Brush
701 S Main St State (45871)
PHONE....................419 753-2263
Fax: 419 753-2611
John H Hoge, *President*
Jack R Hoge, *Exec VP*
Clark T Froning, *Vice Pres*
Bruce L Hoge, *Vice Pres*
▲ **EMP:** 35
SQ FT: 400,000
SALES (est): 6.8MM **Privately Held**
WEB: www.hoge.com
SIC: 3448 1521 2521 Prefabricated metal buildings; new construction, single-family houses; cabinets, office: wood

New Lexington
Perry County

(G-15053)
COUNTY OF PERRY
445 W Broadway St Ste C (43764-1097)
PHONE....................740 342-0416
Robin Demattia, *Branch Mgr*
EMP: 37 **Privately Held**
SIC: 9199 8051 7997 ; mental retardation hospital; country club; membership
PA: County Of Perry
121 W Brown St D
New Lexington OH 43764
740 342-2045

(G-15054)
COUNTY OF PERRY
Also Called: Perry County Engineer
2645 Old Somerset Rd (43764-9547)
PHONE....................740 342-2191
Fax: 740 342-5502
Kenton C Cannon, *Director*
EMP: 35 **Privately Held**
SIC: 8711 Engineering services

PA: County Of Perry
121 W Brown St D
New Lexington OH 43764
740 342-2045

(G-15055)
LORI HOLDING CO (PA)
Also Called: Siemer Distributing
1400 Commerce Dr (43764-9500)
PHONE....................740 342-3230
Fax: 740 342-9813
Joseph A Siemer III, *President*
Dolores Siemer, *Admin Sec*
EMP: 30
SALES (est): 10.8MM **Privately Held**
SIC: 5147 5143 5199 5142 Meats, fresh; cheese; ice, manufactured or natural; packaged frozen goods; manufactured ice

(G-15056)
MOUNT ALOYSIUS CORP
5375 Tile Plant Rd Se (43764-9801)
P.O. Box 598 (43764-0598)
PHONE....................740 342-3343
Fax: 740 342-4805
William Shimp, *Ch of Bd*
Jean Ann Arbaugh, *President*
George Fisher, *Vice Pres*
EMP: 135 **EST:** 1969
SALES (est): 11.4MM **Privately Held**
SIC: 8361 8052 Home for the mentally retarded; intermediate care facilities

(G-15057)
NEW LEXINGTON CITY OF
Also Called: New Lexington Mncpl Water Plnt
215 S Main St (43764-1370)
PHONE....................740 342-1633
Fax: 740 342-1075
Mark Cooper, *Superintendent*
EMP: 50
SALES (est): 7.4MM **Privately Held**
SIC: 4952 4941 Sewerage systems; water supply

(G-15058)
NEWLEX CLASSIC RIDERS INC
810 N Main St (43764-1042)
P.O. Box 27 (43764-0027)
PHONE....................740 342-3885
Randy Altier, *President*
Ted Johnson, *Vice Pres*
EMP: 55
SALES (est): 824.5K **Privately Held**
WEB: www.newlexclassicriders.com
SIC: 7997 Membership sports & recreation clubs

(G-15059)
OXFORD MINING COMPANY INC
Also Called: Tunnell Hill Reclamation
2500 Township Rd 205 (43764)
PHONE....................740 342-7666
Jeff Williams, *Superintendent*
EMP: 58
SALES (corp-wide): 1.3B **Publicly Held**
SIC: 1221 Strip mining, bituminous
HQ: Oxford Mining Company, Inc.
544 Chestnut St
Coshocton OH 43812
740 622-6302

(G-15060)
PEOPLES NAT BNK OF NEW LXNGTON (PA)
110 N Main St (43764-1261)
P.O. Box 111 (43764-0111)
PHONE....................740 342-5111
Fax: 740 342-3206
G Courtney Haning, *CEO*
Tony L Davis, *President*
Brenda Wright, *Exec VP*
Bill Barnett, *Vice Pres*
EMP: 40
SALES: 5.5MM **Privately Held**
WEB: www.peoplesnational.com
SIC: 6021 National trust companies with deposits, commercial

(G-15061)
PERCO INC
2235 State Route 13 Ne (43764-9707)
PHONE....................740 342-5156
Fax: 740 342-3255
Ron Spung, *Principal*
Jessica Stroup, *Human Res Mgr*

Janet Taylor, *Office Mgr*
Vanessa Orsborne, *Program Mgr*
Johnna Nash, *Supervisor*
EMP: 85
SQ FT: 14,000
SALES: 422.9K **Privately Held**
SIC: 8331 Vocational rehabilitation agency

(G-15062)
RESIDENTIAL INC
226 S Main St (43764-1369)
P.O. Box 101 (43764-0101)
PHONE....................740 342-4158
Fax: 740 342-4218
Gretchen Brown, *Manager*
Linda Stonebrook, *Director*
EMP: 50
SQ FT: 1,000
SALES: 1.5MM **Privately Held**
SIC: 8361 Home for the mentally retarded

(G-15063)
SIEMER DISTRIBUTING COMPANY
1400 Commerce Dr (43764-9500)
PHONE....................740 342-3230
Joseph A Siemer III, *President*
Mandie Goins, *Accountant*
Veronica Rodgers, *Director*
Dolores Siemer, *Admin Sec*
EMP: 30
SQ FT: 3,000
SALES (est): 2.7MM
SALES (corp-wide): 10.8MM **Privately Held**
WEB: www.siemerdistributingcompany.com
SIC: 5147 5143 5199 Meats, fresh; cheese; ice, manufactured or natural
PA: Lori Holding Co.
1400 Commerce Dr
New Lexington OH 43764
740 342-3230

(G-15064)
SUNBRIDGE HEALTHCARE LLC
Also Called: New Lxngton Care Rhblttion Ctr
920 S Main St (43764-1552)
P.O. Box 507 (43764-0507)
PHONE....................740 342-5161
Fax: 740 342-2226
Tammy Corp, *Facilities Dir*
Rhonda Ours, *Financial Exec*
Rhonda Wood, *Office Mgr*
Andy Iekies, *Manager*
Bradley Wilson, *Director*
EMP: 112 **Publicly Held**
WEB: www.innoventurehealthcare.com
SIC: 8052 8051 Intermediate care facilities; skilled nursing care facilities
HQ: Sunbridge Healthcare, Llc
101 Sun Ave Ne
Albuquerque NM 87109
505 821-3355

New London
Huron County

(G-15065)
204 W MAIN STREET OPER CO LLC
Also Called: Rehab Nursing Ctr At Firelands
204 W Main St (44851-1070)
PHONE....................419 929-1563
Trace Patner, *Manager*
Dena Mc Killips, *Nursing Dir*
Amy Donaldson, *Administration*
EMP: 85
SALES (est): 2.7MM **Privately Held**
WEB: www.hazelstreet.com
SIC: 8051 Skilled nursing care facilities

(G-15066)
CLARE-MAR CAMP INC
Also Called: Clare-Mar Lakes Rv Sales
47571 New Lndon Eastrn Rd (44851)
P.O. Box 229, Wellington (44090-0229)
PHONE....................440 647-3318
Fax: 440 647-6182
Donald B Sears, *President*
Barbara J Sears, *Treasurer*
EMP: 27

New London - Huron County (G-15067)

SALES (est): 1.3MM **Privately Held**
SIC: 7033 5561 Campgrounds; recreational vehicle dealers

(G-15067)
FIRELANDS AMBULANCE SERVICE
25 James St (44851-1211)
PHONE..................419 929-1487
Paul Lortcher, *President*
Jeffrey Vanderpool,
EMP: 35
SQ FT: 500
SALES: 200K **Privately Held**
SIC: 4119 Ambulance service

(G-15068)
NEW LONDON AREA HISTORICAL SOC
210 E Main St (44851-1154)
PHONE..................419 929-3674
Thomas Neel, *President*
Martha Sturges, *Vice Pres*
Vaughn Neel, *Treasurer*
Jean Myers, *Admin Sec*
EMP: 81 EST: 1985
SALES: 11.5K **Privately Held**
SIC: 8412 Historical society

(G-15069)
PACE INTERNATIONAL UNION
100 New London Ave (44851-1186)
PHONE..................419 929-1335
David Harlan, *Treasurer*
EMP: 45
SALES (corp-wide): 26.9MM **Privately Held**
SIC: 8631 Labor unions & similar labor organizations
PA: Pace International Union
5 Gateway Ctr
Pittsburgh PA 15222
412 562-2400

(G-15070)
PRIMETALS TECHNOLOGIES USA LLC
81 E Washburn St (44851-1247)
PHONE..................419 929-1554
John Bailey, *Manager*
EMP: 50
SALES (corp-wide): 34.4B **Privately Held**
WEB: www.srt-ar.com
SIC: 7699 5084 Industrial equipment services; industrial machinery & equipment
HQ: Primetals Technologies Usa Llc
5895 Windward Pkwy Fl 2
Alpharetta GA 30005
770 740-3800

(G-15071)
U-HAUL NEIGHBORHOOD DEALER -CE
1005 Us Highway 250 S (44851-9110)
PHONE..................419 929-3724
EMP: 25 EST: 2010
SALES (est): 336.5K **Privately Held**
SIC: 7519 7513 5099 4212 Utility trailer rental; truck rental & leasing, no drivers; durable goods; local trucking, without storage

New Madison
Darke County

(G-15072)
LUDY GREENHOUSE MFG CORP (PA)
122 Railroad St (45346-5016)
P.O. Box 141 (45346-0141)
PHONE..................800 255-5839
Fax: 937 996-8031
Stephan A Scantland, *President*
Deborah Scantland, *Vice Pres*
Brian Munchel, *Engineer*
Leann Wiford, *Human Resources*
Becky Yount, *Regl Sales Mgr*
EMP: 62
SQ FT: 2,500
SALES (est): 18.3MM **Privately Held**
SIC: 1542 3448 Greenhouse construction; greenhouses: prefabricated metal

(G-15073)
TRI VILLAGE RESCUE SERVICE
Also Called: Tri Village Joint Ambulance
320 N Main St (45346-9794)
P.O. Box 247 (45346-0247)
PHONE..................937 996-3155
Fax: 937 996-4600
Eric Burns, *Chief*
EMP: 30
SALES: 300.9K **Privately Held**
SIC: 4119 Ambulance service

New Middletown
Mahoning County

(G-15074)
VENEZIA TRANSPORT SERVICE INC
Also Called: Venezia Hauling
6017 E Calla Rd (44442-9725)
P.O. Box 26, Bessemer PA (16112-0026)
PHONE..................330 542-9735
Fax: 330 542-9736
Ted Habuda, *Manager*
EMP: 30
SALES (est): 1.5MM **Privately Held**
WEB: www.veneziainc.com
SIC: 4213 Contract haulers
PA: Venezia Transport Service, Inc.
86 Airport Rd
Pottstown PA 19464

New Paris
Preble County

(G-15075)
BLUE BEACON USA LP II
Also Called: Blue Beacon Truck Wash
9787 Us Route 40 W (45347-1521)
PHONE..................937 437-5533
Fax: 937 437-3724
Jody Cochrain, *Manager*
EMP: 35
SALES (corp-wide): 88.4MM **Privately Held**
WEB: www.bluebeacon.com
SIC: 7542 Truck wash
PA: Blue Beacon U.S.A., L.P. Ii
500 Graves Blvd
Salina KS 67401
785 825-2221

(G-15076)
CREATIVE LEARNING WORKSHOP
146 N Washington St (45347-1152)
PHONE..................937 437-0146
Vincent E Fisher, *Manager*
EMP: 25
SALES (corp-wide): 7.2MM **Privately Held**
SIC: 8331 Vocational rehabilitation agency
PA: The Creative Learning Workshop
2460 Elm Rd Ne Ste 500
Warren OH 44483
330 393-5929

(G-15077)
FOUNDATIONS
Also Called: Cedar Springs
7739 Us Route 40 (45347-9048)
PHONE..................937 437-2311
Tracey Ross, *Administration*
EMP: 75
SALES (est): 1.5MM **Privately Held**
SIC: 8052 Home for the mentally retarded, with health care

(G-15078)
HERITAGE PARK REHABILITA
Also Called: Cedar Springs Care Center
7739 Us Route 40 (45347-9048)
PHONE..................937 437-2311
Suw Watts, *Manager*
EMP: 30
SALES (corp-wide): 249.5MM **Privately Held**
WEB: www.eldercareofwv.com
SIC: 8051 8052 Extended care facility; intermediate care facilities
HQ: Heritage Park Rehabilitation And Healthcare Center, Llc
5565 Bankers Ave
Baton Rouge LA 70808

(G-15079)
NORTHWEST FIRE AMBULANCE
135 N Washington St (45347-1151)
P.O. Box 66 (45347-0066)
PHONE..................937 437-8354
Paul Cones, *Chief*
Brad Simpson, *Asst Chief*
EMP: 27
SALES (est): 607.9K **Privately Held**
SIC: 4119 Ambulance service

New Philadelphia
Tuscarawas County

(G-15080)
ALLSTATE TRK SLS OF ESTRN OH
Also Called: Alstate-Peterbilt-Trucks
327 Stonecreek Rd Nw (44663-6902)
PHONE..................330 339-5555
Fax: 330 339-6698
Jesse Smitley, *Manager*
Glen Evan, *Manager*
EMP: 33
SALES (corp-wide): 6.4MM **Privately Held**
SIC: 5511 5531 7538 Automobiles, new & used; automobile & truck equipment & parts; general truck repair
PA: Allstate Truck Sales Of Eastern Ohio, Llc
10700 Lyndale Ave S
Minneapolis MN 55420
952 703-3444

(G-15081)
AMBERWOOD MANOR
245 S Broadway St (44663-3842)
PHONE..................330 339-2151
Tasha Cox, *Principal*
Earl Romig, *Principal*
Cynthia Dutton, *Administration*
EMP: 54
SALES (est): 1.5MM
SALES (corp-wide): 68.5MM **Privately Held**
SIC: 8051 Convalescent home with continuous nursing care
PA: Saber Healthcare Group, L.L.C.
26691 Richmond Rd Frnt
Bedford OH 44146
216 292-5706

(G-15082)
AMERIDIAL INC
521 W High Ave (44663-2053)
PHONE..................330 339-7222
Fax: 330 339-7222
Cathy McGee, *Branch Mgr*
EMP: 65
SALES (corp-wide): 40MM **Privately Held**
SIC: 7389 Telemarketing services
PA: Ameridial, Inc.
4535 Strausser St Nw
North Canton OH 44720
330 497-4888

(G-15083)
BULK CARRIER TRNSP EQP CO
2743 Brightwood Rd Se (44663-6773)
PHONE..................330 339-3333
Fax: 330 339-6606
Richard S Hartrick, *President*
Jim Everett, *Exec VP*
Marcia Hartrick, *Vice Pres*
Nick Pace, *CFO*
EMP: 26
SALES (est): 4.4MM **Privately Held**
WEB: www.bcte.com
SIC: 5012 2519 Trailers for trucks, new & used; household furniture, except wood or metal: upholstered

(G-15084)
CELLCO PARTNERSHIP
Also Called: Verizon Wireless
507 Mill Ave Se (44663-3864)
PHONE..................330 308-0549
Fax: 330 339-7537
EMP: 57
SALES (corp-wide): 126B **Publicly Held**
SIC: 4899 Data communication services
HQ: Cellco Partnership
1 Verizon Way
Basking Ridge NJ 07920

(G-15085)
CHILDRENS HOSP MED CTR AKRON
1045 W High Ave (44663-2071)
PHONE..................330 308-5432
Susan Karitides, *Branch Mgr*
John Fargo, *Director*
EMP: 732
SALES (corp-wide): 747.4MM **Privately Held**
SIC: 8069 8062 Children's hospital; general medical & surgical hospitals
PA: Childrens Hospital Medical Center Of Akron
1 Perkins Sq
Akron OH 44308
330 543-1000

(G-15086)
CITY OF NEW PHILADELPHIA
Also Called: New Philadelphia General Svcs
1234 Commercial Ave Se (44663-2355)
PHONE..................330 339-2121
Fax: 330 308-9435
Fred Neff, *Superintendent*
EMP: 35
SQ FT: 2,301 **Privately Held**
WEB: www.newphilaoh.com
SIC: 7521 9111 Automobile parking; automobile storage garage; mayors' offices
PA: City Of New Philadelphia
150 E High Ave Ste 15
New Philadelphia OH 44663
330 364-4491

(G-15087)
COPLEY OHIO NEWSPAPERS INC
Also Called: Times Reporter/Midwest Offset
629 Wabash Ave Nw (44663-4145)
P.O. Box 667 (44663-0667)
PHONE..................330 364-5577
Fax: 330 364-1364
Kevin Kampman, *Publisher*
Mike Starn, *Publisher*
Gene Cush, *Manager*
Travis Fisher, *Manager*
Mike Gorfich, *Manager*
EMP: 245
SALES (corp-wide): 1.3B **Publicly Held**
WEB: www.timesreporter.com
SIC: 2711 2752 7313 2791 Commercial printing & newspaper publishing combined; commercial printing, offset; newspaper advertising representative; typesetting; bookbinding & related work
HQ: Copley Ohio Newspapers Inc
500 Market Ave S
Canton OH 44702
585 598-0030

(G-15088)
CORNERSTONE SUPPORT SERVICES (PA)
Also Called: Southeast
344 W High Ave (44663-2152)
PHONE..................330 339-7850
Fax: 330 339-7844
Beth Powell, *Exec Dir*
Sandra Stevenson, *Director*
Carrie Baker, *Director*
Joe Wilson, *Director*
EMP: 75
SQ FT: 2,856
SALES (est): 2MM **Privately Held**
SIC: 8093 Mental health clinic, outpatient

(G-15089)
CORPORATION FOR OH APPALACHIAN
1260 Monroe St Nw Ste 39s (44663-4147)
PHONE..................330 364-8882

GEOGRAPHIC SECTION
New Philadelphia - Tuscarawas County (G-15113)

Sherri Guthrie, *Branch Mgr*
EMP: 29
SALES (corp-wide): 25.3MM **Privately Held**
SIC: 8351 Head start center, except in conjunction with school
PA: Corporation For Ohio Appalachian Development
1 Pinchot Pl
Athens OH 45701
740 594-8499

(G-15090)
COUNTY OF TUSCARAWAS
Also Called: Child Support
154 2nd St Ne (44663-2854)
PHONE.....................330 343-0099
Fax: 330 364-4854
Linda Warner, *Director*
Michael Colbert, *Director*
Bill Alderman, *Officer*
EMP: 45
SQ FT: 8,868 **Privately Held**
WEB: www.neohiotravel.com
SIC: 8322 9111 Child related social services; county supervisors' & executives' offices
PA: County Of Tuscarawas
125 E High Ave
New Philadelphia OH 44663
330 364-8811

(G-15091)
COUNTY OF TUSCARAWAS
Also Called: Tuscarawas Cnty Job Fmly Svcs
389 16th St Sw (44663-6401)
PHONE.....................330 339-7791
Fax: 330 339-6388
Lynn Angellzzi, *Manager*
EMP: 80 **Privately Held**
WEB: www.neohiotravel.com
SIC: 8322 9199 Probation office; adoption services; child related social services;
PA: County Of Tuscarawas
125 E High Ave
New Philadelphia OH 44663
330 364-8811

(G-15092)
DEARTH MANAGEMENT COMPANY
Also Called: Moring View Care Center
2594 E High Ave (44663-6737)
PHONE.....................330 339-3595
Fax: 330 339-7155
Denise La Creta, *Persnl Dir*
Loraine Lady, *Director*
EMP: 150
SALES (est): 2.3MM
SALES (corp-wide): 11.7MM **Privately Held**
WEB: www.schoenbrunnhealthcare.com
SIC: 8052 8051 Personal care facility; skilled nursing care facilities
PA: Dearth Management Company
134 Northwoods Blvd Ste C
Columbus OH 43235
614 847-1070

(G-15093)
DISABLED AMERICAN VETERANS
824 Hardesty Ave Nw (44663-1132)
PHONE.....................330 364-1204
George Phillips, *President*
Donald Thomas, *Treasurer*
EMP: 330
SALES (corp-wide): 202.6MM **Privately Held**
SIC: 8641 Veterans' organization
PA: Disabled American Veterans
3725 Alexandria Pike
Cold Spring KY 41076
859 441-7300

(G-15094)
FENTON BROS ELECTRIC CO
Also Called: Fenton's Festival of Lights
235 Ray Ave Ne (44663-2813)
P.O. Box 996 (44663-0996)
PHONE.....................330 343-0093
Fax: 330 343-6874
Tom Fenton, *President*
Dennis Fenton, *Vice Pres*
Brian Fenton, *Treasurer*
Warren Toland, *Human Res Dir*
Dale E Fenton, *Shareholder*
EMP: 30 EST: 1947
SQ FT: 37,000
SALES (est): 23.4MM **Privately Held**
WEB: www.fentonbros.com
SIC: 5063 7694 Electrical supplies; electric motor repair

(G-15095)
GOODWILL IDSTRS GRTR CLVLND L
260 Bluebell Dr Nw (44663-9676)
PHONE.....................330 339-5746
EMP: 33
SALES (corp-wide): 27.6MM **Privately Held**
SIC: 8999 Actuarial consultant
PA: Goodwill Industries Of Greater Cleveland And East Central Ohio, Inc.
408 9th St Sw
Canton OH 44707
330 454-9461

(G-15096)
HARBOR HOUSE INC
349 E High Ave (44663-2535)
P.O. Box 435 (44663-0435)
PHONE.....................740 498-7213
Fax: 330 343-7415
Starlene Lewis, *Exec Dir*
Connie Cheslock, *Exec Dir*
EMP: 25
SALES: 540K **Privately Held**
SIC: 8322 Emergency shelters

(G-15097)
HARCATUS TRI-COUNTY COMMUNITY (PA)
225 Fair Ave Ne (44663-2837)
PHONE.....................740 922-0933
Fax: 740 922-4128
Charles Lorenz II, *Exec Dir*
Charles E Lorenz, *Exec Dir*
Michele Lucas, *Exec Dir*
Chris Grill, *Director*
Kris Grill, *Director*
EMP: 46
SQ FT: 1,500
SALES: 7.5MM **Privately Held**
SIC: 8322 Social service center; referral service for personal & social problems; emergency social services; meal delivery program

(G-15098)
HARCATUS TRI-COUNTY COMMUNITY
504 Bowers Ave Nw (44663-4107)
PHONE.....................330 602-5442
EMP: 76
SALES (corp-wide): 7.5MM **Privately Held**
SIC: 8351 Head start center, except in conjunction with school
PA: Harcatus Tri-County Community Action Organization
225 Fair Ave Ne
New Philadelphia OH 44663
740 922-0933

(G-15099)
HARIBOL HARIBOL INC (PA)
Also Called: Holiday Inn
145 Bluebell Dr Sw (44663-9660)
PHONE.....................330 339-7731
Fax: 330 339-1555
Naresh Patel, *President*
EMP: 30
SALES (est): 1.2MM **Privately Held**
SIC: 7011 7299 Hotels; banquet hall facilities

(G-15100)
HICKS ROOFING INC
Also Called: Hicks Industrial Roofing
2162 Pleasant Vly Rd Ne (44663-8079)
PHONE.....................330 364-7737
Fax: 330 343-1393
Michael Hicks, *President*
Tad Schull, *General Mgr*
Beth Hicks, *Vice Pres*
Bob Pryse, *Technical Mgr*
Ben Reynolds, *Technical Mgr*
EMP: 40
SQ FT: 14,600
SALES (est): 5.7MM **Privately Held**
WEB: www.hicksroofing.com
SIC: 1761 Roofing contractor

(G-15101)
HOSPICE TUSCARAWAS COUNTY INC (PA)
Also Called: COMMUNITY HOSPICE
716 Commercial Ave Sw (44663-9367)
PHONE.....................330 343-7605
Fax: 330 343-3542
Norman Mast, *President*
Nicholas Reynolds, *Vice Pres*
Janie Jones, *Exec Dir*
Bob Phipps, *Director*
Sue Ott, *Executive*
EMP: 100
SQ FT: 22,500
SALES: 16.4MM **Privately Held**
WEB: www.hospiceoftusc.org
SIC: 8059 Nursing home, except skilled & intermediate care facility

(G-15102)
HYDRAULIC PARTS STORE INC
145 1st Dr Ne (44663-2663)
P.O. Box 808 (44663-0808)
PHONE.....................330 364-6667
Fax: 330 364-1601
Robert M Henning Sr, *President*
EMP: 30
SQ FT: 25,000
SALES (est): 14.6MM **Privately Held**
SIC: 5084 3594 3593 3492 Hydraulic systems equipment & supplies; fluid power pumps & motors; fluid power cylinders & actuators; fluid power valves & hose fittings

(G-15103)
J & D MINING INC
3497 University Dr Ne (44663-6711)
PHONE.....................330 339-4935
Fax: 330 866-4511
John R Demuth, *President*
James R Demuth, *Vice Pres*
EMP: 38
SQ FT: 1,000
SALES (est): 4.8MM **Privately Held**
SIC: 1221 Bituminous coal surface mining

(G-15104)
JPMORGAN CHASE BANK NAT ASSN
Also Called: Chase Bank and Atm
141 E High Ave (44663-2539)
PHONE.....................330 364-7242
Patricia Hile, *Principal*
EMP: 26
SALES (corp-wide): 99.6B **Publicly Held**
SIC: 6021 National commercial banks
HQ: Jpmorgan Chase Bank, National Association
1111 Polaris Pkwy
Columbus OH 43240
614 436-3055

(G-15105)
KRUGLIAK WILKINS GRIFIYHD &
158 N Broadway St (44663-2628)
PHONE.....................330 364-3472
Terry Moore, *Branch Mgr*
Dean Swift, *Director*
Ian Hoke, *Senior Editor*
John Schomer,
Matthew Duney, *Associate*
EMP: 36
SALES (corp-wide): 11.2MM **Privately Held**
SIC: 8111 General practice attorney, lawyer
PA: Krugliak, Wilkins, Griffiths And Dougherty Co Lpa
4775 Munson St Nw
Canton OH 44718
330 497-0700

(G-15106)
LANDSCPING RCLMTION SPCIALISTS
3497 University Dr Ne (44663-6711)
PHONE.....................330 339-4900
John R Demuth, *President*
EMP: 50
SQ FT: 3,000
SALES (est): 2.9MM **Privately Held**
SIC: 1629 Land clearing contractor

(G-15107)
LOWES HOME CENTERS LLC
495 Mill Rd (44663)
PHONE.....................330 339-1936
Fax: 330 339-4682
Ken Kaiser, *Branch Mgr*
EMP: 150
SALES (corp-wide): 68.6B **Publicly Held**
SIC: 5211 5031 5722 5064 Home centers; building materials, exterior; building materials, interior; household appliance stores; electrical appliances, television & radio
HQ: Lowe's Home Centers, Llc
1605 Curtis Bridge Rd
Wilkesboro NC 28697
336 658-4000

(G-15108)
MARATHON MFG & SUP CO
5165 Main St Ne (44663-8802)
P.O. Box 701 (44663-0701)
PHONE.....................330 343-2656
Emory Brumit, *President*
Peggy Brumit, *Treasurer*
EMP: 60 EST: 1969
SALES (est): 5MM **Privately Held**
SIC: 5199 3953 Advertising specialties; screens, textile printing

(G-15109)
MARK LUIKART INC
715 Cookson Ave Se (44663-6800)
PHONE.....................330 339-9141
Fax: 330 308-5157
Mark Luikart, *President*
EMP: 50
SQ FT: 6,400
SALES (est): 1.1MM **Privately Held**
WEB: www.marksplace.net
SIC: 7231 7299 5999 Beauty shops; manicurist, pedicurist; massage parlor; hair care products

(G-15110)
N P MOTEL SYSTEM INC
Also Called: Holiday Inn
145 Bluebell Dr Sw (44663-9660)
PHONE.....................330 339-7731
Naresh Patel, *Principal*
EMP: 30
SALES (est): 667.2K **Privately Held**
WEB: www.radhe.net
SIC: 7011 Hotels & motels

(G-15111)
PERSONAL & FMLY COUNSELING SVC
1433 5th St Nw (44663-1223)
PHONE.....................330 343-8171
Pamela Trimmer, *Director*
William Buchwald, *Social Worker*
EMP: 38
SALES: 1.9MM **Privately Held**
SIC: 8322 Social service center

(G-15112)
REA & ASSOCIATES INC (PA)
419 W High Ave (44663-3621)
P.O. Box 1020 (44663-5120)
PHONE.....................330 339-6651
Leman G Beall, *President*
Clayton Rose, *Partner*
Jeremiah Senften, *Principal*
Debi Gellenbeck, *Corp Secy*
Tara Lengler, *Opers Staff*
EMP: 58
SQ FT: 680
SALES: 32.3MM **Privately Held**
WEB: www.reacpa.com
SIC: 8721 Certified public accountant

(G-15113)
REA & ASSOCIATES INC
122 4th St Nw (44663-1938)
P.O. Box 1020 (44663-5120)
PHONE.....................440 266-0077
Fax: 330 339-4837
Ryan Dumermuth, *CPA*
Greg R Goodie, *CPA*
Jeff Tucker, *Branch Mgr*
Morgan Helmick, *Supervisor*

New Philadelphia - Tuscarawas County (G-15114)

Joe Welker, *Network Mgr*
EMP: 55
SALES (corp-wide): 32.3MM **Privately Held**
WEB: www.reacpa.com
SIC: 8721 Certified public accountant
PA: Rea & Associates, Inc.
  419 W High Ave
  New Philadelphia OH 44663
  330 339-6651

(G-15114)
SCHOENBRUNN HEALTHCARE
2594 E High Ave (44663-6737)
PHONE..................330 339-3595
Shaul Flank, *Owner*
Susan Emhoff, *Director*
Paul McFadden, *Director*
Corey Moner, *Administration*
Joel Sausen, *Administration*
EMP: 100 **EST:** 2008
SALES (est): 1MM
SALES (corp-wide): 59MM **Privately Held**
SIC: 8059 8051 8011 Nursing home, except skilled & intermediate care facility; skilled nursing care facilities; clinic, operated by physicians
PA: Progressive Quality Care Inc
  5553 Broadview Rd
  Parma OH 44134
  216 661-6800

(G-15115)
STALEY TECHNOLOGIES INC (PA)
1035 Front Ave Sw (44663-2077)
PHONE..................330 339-2898
Fax: 330 339-6362
Timothy Staley, *President*
Edgar Vanhoose, *Sales Dir*
Ron Dumermuth, *Accounts Mgr*
Chris Staley, *Accounts Mgr*
Rich Ewing, *Manager*
EMP: 45
SQ FT: 3,000
SALES (est): 7.1MM **Privately Held**
SIC: 5731 7622 Radios, two-way, citizens' band, weather, short-wave, etc.; radio repair shop

(G-15116)
STARLIGHT ENTERPRISES INC
Also Called: S.E.I.
400 E High Ave (44663-2549)
P.O. Box 1054 (44663-5154)
PHONE..................330 339-3020
Fax: 330 339-7357
Cassie Elvin, *Director*
Eleanor Scott, *Admin Sec*
Charlotte Lynch, *Assistant*
EMP: 175
SQ FT: 27,300
SALES (est): 719K **Privately Held**
WEB: www.starlightenterprises.com
SIC: 8331 7349 Sheltered workshop; janitorial service, contract basis

(G-15117)
TANK LEASING CORP
Also Called: Bulk Carriers and Tank Leasing
2743 Brightwood Rd Se (44663-6773)
PHONE..................330 339-3333
Marcia Hartrick, *President*
Richard Hartrick, *Vice Pres*
Debbie Hanni, *Executive Asst*
Jennifer Hartrick, *Receptionist*
EMP: 25
SQ FT: 1,800
SALES (est): 5.6MM **Privately Held**
SIC: 5084 Tanks, storage

(G-15118)
TUCSON INC
3497 University Dr Ne (44663-6711)
PHONE..................330 339-4935
James R Demuth, *President*
Ed Wilson, *Project Mgr*
Peggy Billow, *Controller*
Becky Sharp, *Admin Asst*
EMP: 41 **EST:** 2001
SQ FT: 2,250
SALES (est): 7.4MM **Privately Held**
WEB: www.tucson.com
SIC: 1611 General contractor, highway & street construction

(G-15119)
TUSCARAWAS COUNTY HELP ME GROW
1433 5th St Nw (44663-1223)
PHONE..................330 339-3493
Marilyn Henry, *Exec Dir*
Lisa Crites, *Director*
EMP: 50
SALES (est): 427.7K **Privately Held**
WEB: www.pfcs1.org
SIC: 8322 General counseling services

(G-15120)
UNITED PARCEL SERVICE INC OH
Also Called: UPS
241 8th Street Ext Sw (44663-2027)
PHONE..................330 339-6281
Matt Walker, *Manager*
Bob Karl, *Manager*
EMP: 150
SALES (corp-wide): 65.8B **Publicly Held**
WEB: www.upsscs.com
SIC: 4215 4513 Parcel delivery, vehicular; air courier services
HQ: United Parcel Service, Inc. (Oh)
  55 Glenlake Pkwy
  Atlanta GA 30328
  404 828-6000

(G-15121)
VERIZON NORTH INC
1121 Tuscarawas Ave Nw (44663-1019)
PHONE..................330 339-7733
Gerald H Landis, *Branch Mgr*
EMP: 50
SALES (corp-wide): 126B **Publicly Held**
SIC: 4813 Local telephone communications
HQ: Verizon North Inc
  140 West St
  New York NY 10007
  212 395-1000

(G-15122)
W E QUICKSALL AND ASSOC INC (PA)
554 W High Ave (44663-2006)
P.O. Box 646 (44663-0646)
PHONE..................330 339-6676
Fax: 330 339-2227
David R Quicksall, *CEO*
Donald R Quicksall, *President*
Zack Deems, *Vice Pres*
Nathan Quicksall, *Opers Mgr*
John Snyder, *Engineer*
EMP: 25 **EST:** 1959
SQ FT: 10,400
SALES (est): 2.3MM **Privately Held**
WEB: www.wequicksall.com
SIC: 8711 Consulting engineer

(G-15123)
WOOD ELECTRIC INC
210 11th St Nw (44663-1510)
PHONE..................330 339-7002
Fax: 330 339-3917
Larry Wood, *President*
Lisa Wood, *Vice Pres*
Al Ledrich, *Project Mgr*
Buck Ickes, *Manager*
EMP: 85
SQ FT: 8,000
SALES (est): 11.6MM **Privately Held**
SIC: 1731 General electrical contractor

New Richmond
Clermont County

(G-15124)
ANGEL ABOVE BYOND HM HLTH SVCS
1041 Old Us Highway 52 (45157-8536)
PHONE..................513 553-9955
Fax: 513 553-1089
Scott Wolf, *President*
Nicholas Wolf, *Corp Secy*
Edna Burns, *Admin Asst*
EMP: 40
SALES (est): 1.6MM **Privately Held**
SIC: 8082 Home health care services

(G-15125)
DAVE & BARB ENTERPRISES INC
Also Called: Janitec Building Service
Address Unknonwn (45157)
P.O. Box 242 (45157-0242)
PHONE..................513 553-0050
Barbara Henry, *President*
Dave Henry, *Vice Pres*
EMP: 53
SQ FT: 2,000
SALES (est): 700K **Privately Held**
SIC: 7349 Janitorial service, contract basis

(G-15126)
DOBBINS NURSING HOME INC
400 Main St (45157-1129)
P.O. Box 54923, Cincinnati (45254-0923)
PHONE..................513 553-4139
Fax: 513 553-1060
Howard Meeker, *President*
Steven Meeker, *Vice Pres*
Patricia A Meeker, *Treasurer*
Jyoti Mehta, *Director*
EMP: 125 **EST:** 1950
SALES (est): 3.2MM
SALES (corp-wide): 4.7MM **Privately Held**
SIC: 8059 Nursing home, except skilled & intermediate care facility
PA: Locust Ridge Nursing Home Inc
  12745 Elm Corner Rd
  Williamsburg OH 45176
  937 444-2920

(G-15127)
DUKE ENERGY OHIO INC
Also Called: Beckjord Power Station
757 Us 52 (45157-9709)
PHONE..................513 467-5000
Anya Lieb, *Engineer*
Jim Cumbow, *Manager*
Alan Burck, *Manager*
EMP: 195
SALES (corp-wide): 23.5B **Publicly Held**
SIC: 4911 Electric services
HQ: Duke Energy Ohio, Inc.
  139 E 4th St
  Cincinnati OH 45202
  704 382-3853

(G-15128)
JKL CONSTRUCTION INC
620 Hamilton St (45157-1267)
PHONE..................513 553-3333
Fax: 513 553-3333
Guy Montgomery, *President*
EMP: 25
SQ FT: 1,500
SALES (est): 2.4MM **Privately Held**
SIC: 1542 Commercial & office building, new construction; commercial & office buildings, renovation & repair

New Springfield
Mahoning County

(G-15129)
ED WILSON & SON TRUCKING INC
14766 Woodworth Rd (44443-9738)
P.O. Box 2208 (44443-2208)
PHONE..................330 549-9287
Edward Wilson, *President*
Gloria Wilson, *Vice Pres*
EMP: 25
SALES (est): 3MM **Privately Held**
SIC: 4212 Local trucking, without storage

(G-15130)
RURITAN
Also Called: Raritan National
3814 Columbiana Rd (44443-9776)
PHONE..................330 542-2308
Francis Gebhardt, *Director*
EMP: 40
SALES (est): 282.3K **Privately Held**
WEB: www.ruritan.com
SIC: 8699 Charitable organization

(G-15131)
SNYDERS ANTIQUE AUTO PARTS INC
12925 Woodworth Rd (44443-8722)
PHONE..................330 549-5313
Fax: 330 549-2211
Donald Snyder III, *President*
Donald Snyder Jr, *Vice Pres*
John Yeagle, *Director*
▲ **EMP:** 30
SALES (est): 5.5MM **Privately Held**
WEB: www.snydersantiqueauto.com
SIC: 5531 5013 Automotive parts; automotive supplies & parts

New Vienna
Clinton County

(G-15132)
SNOW HILL COUNTRY CLUB INC
11093 State Route 73 (45159-9638)
PHONE..................937 987-2491
Fax: 937 987-2492
Jennifer Hodge, *Superintendent*
Nick Brunotte, *Manager*
Bradley Taylor, *Manager*
Joe Bischoff, *Administration*
EMP: 25 **EST:** 1924
SALES (est): 680K **Privately Held**
SIC: 7997 Country club, membership

New Washington
Crawford County

(G-15133)
BUCYRUS COMMUNITY PHYSICIANS
120 W Main St (44854-9431)
PHONE..................419 492-2200
Tom Klitzka, *Principal*
EMP: 61 **EST:** 2010
SALES (est): 1.4MM
SALES (corp-wide): 22.9MM **Privately Held**
SIC: 8011 Physical medicine, physician/surgeon
PA: Avita Health System
  269 Portland Way S
  Galion OH 44833
  419 468-4841

(G-15134)
CREST BENDING INC
108 John St (44854-9702)
P.O. Box 458 (44854-0458)
PHONE..................419 492-2108
Fax: 419 492-2546
Robert E Studer, *President*
EMP: 45 **EST:** 1966
SQ FT: 50,000
SALES (est): 8.8MM **Privately Held**
WEB: www.crestbending.com
SIC: 3312 7692 3498 3317 Tubes, steel & iron; welding repair; fabricated pipe & fittings; steel pipe & tubes

(G-15135)
MERCY HEALTH
202 W Mansfield St (44854-9532)
P.O. Box 397 (44854-0397)
PHONE..................419 492-1300
EMP: 35
SALES (corp-wide): 4.2B **Privately Held**
SIC: 8011 General & family practice, physician/surgeon
PA: Mercy Health
  1701 Mercy Health Pl
  Cincinnati OH 45237
  513 639-2800

(G-15136)
STUDER-OBRINGER INC
525 S Kibler St (44854-9524)
P.O. Box 278 (44854-0278)
PHONE..................419 492-2121
Fax: 419 492-2033
Kenneth Falter, *President*
John Cronau, *Exec VP*
Jim Alt, *Vice Pres*
Ashley Dallas, *Manager*

GEOGRAPHIC SECTION

Newark - Licking County (G-15157)

Mike Obringer, *Manager*
EMP: 40
SQ FT: 1,500
SALES (est): 8.8MM Privately Held
SIC: 1542 1541 Commercial & office building, new construction; industrial buildings & warehouses

---

New Waterford
Columbiana County

(G-15137)
DYNAMIC STRUCTURES INC (PA)
3790 State Route 7 Ste B (44445-9784)
PHONE.................................330 892-0164
Fax: 330 426-9362
Scott McCrea, *President*
Carol Henry, *Manager*
Jes McCrea, *Manager*
EMP: 25
SQ FT: 4,500
SALES (est): 7.2MM Privately Held
SIC: 1751 1542 1541 Framing contractor; lightweight steel framing (metal stud) installation; nonresidential construction; industrial buildings & warehouses

(G-15138)
MAJESTIC MANUFACTURING INC
4536 State Route 7 (44445-9785)
P.O. Box 128 (44445-0128)
PHONE.................................330 457-2447
Fax: 330 457-7490
Paul Kudler, *President*
Jeff Kudler, *Vice Pres*
Rick Steed, *Purch Agent*
Vincent Kudler, *Treasurer*
Candy Hawkins, *Executive*
▲ **EMP:** 45
SQ FT: 68,000
SALES (est): 8MM Privately Held
WEB: www.majesticrides.com
SIC: 3599 5087 Carnival machines & equipment, amusement park; carnival & amusement park equipment

(G-15139)
NEW WATERFORD FIREMAN
3766 E Main St (44445)
PHONE.................................330 457-2363
Fax: 330 457-1128
Harry Wilson, *Principal*
Bryland Henderson, *Chief*
Chief Bryland Henderson, *Chief*
EMP: 28
SALES: 33K Privately Held
SIC: 8611 Trade associations

New Weston
Darke County

(G-15140)
ELDORA ENTERPRISES INC
Also Called: Eldora Speedway
13929 State Route 118 (45348-9726)
PHONE.................................937 338-3815
Earl H Baltes, *President*
Roger Slack, *General Mgr*
Starr Smith Myer, *Corp Secy*
Bernice Baltes, *Vice Pres*
Sherry Evans, *Manager*
EMP: 48
SALES (est): 2.5MM Privately Held
WEB: www.eldoraspeedway.com
SIC: 7948 7911 Automotive race track operation; dance hall or ballroom operation

---

Newark
Licking County

(G-15141)
ALLTEL COMMUNICATIONS CORP (DH)
66 N 4th St (43055-5000)
P.O. Box 3005 (43058-3005)
PHONE.................................740 349-8551
Fax: 740 349-8862
Dennis Mervis, *President*
Richard Mc Clain, *Area Mgr*
Ken Blake, *Vice Pres*
Giulio Freda, *Treasurer*
Hugh Hindman, *Manager*
EMP: 60
SQ FT: 38,716
SALES (est): 108.8MM
SALES (corp-wide): 160.5B Publicly Held
SIC: 4813 4812 Local telephone communications; long distance telephone communications; radio telephone communication
HQ: Alltel Corporation
1001 Technology Dr
Little Rock AR 72223
866 255-8357

(G-15142)
ALPHA NURSING HOMES INC
Also Called: Autumn Health Care
17 Forry St (43055-4004)
PHONE.................................740 345-9197
Fax: 740 345-9289
Bob Huffman, *Manager*
Thomas Petryk, *Director*
Joyce Smith, *Nursing Dir*
Kalina Tapealava, *Records Dir*
Tracy Imhoff, *Administration*
EMP: 60
SQ FT: 1,400
SALES (corp-wide): 3.1MM Privately Held
WEB: www.alphanursingservice.com
SIC: 8052 8051 Intermediate care facilities; skilled nursing care facilities
PA: Alpha Nursing Homes, Inc
419 E Main St
Lancaster OH

(G-15143)
ARLINGTON CARE CTR
Also Called: CHS Ohio Valley Inc
98 S 30th St (43055-1940)
PHONE.................................740 344-0303
Fax: 740 344-3303
Edward L Byington Sr, *President*
Michael Campolo, *Director*
Terri Sidle, *Director*
Cindy Warthen, *Director*
Betsy Mc Pherson, *Hlthcr Dir*
EMP: 200
SQ FT: 50,000
SALES (est): 5MM
SALES (corp-wide): 85.7MM Privately Held
SIC: 8051 8052 Skilled nursing care facilities; intermediate care facilities
PA: Carington Health Systems
8200 Beckett Park Dr
Hamilton OH 45011
513 682-2700

(G-15144)
ARMSTRONG STEEL ERECTORS INC
50 S 4th St (43055-5436)
P.O. Box 577 (43058-0577)
PHONE.................................740 345-4503
Fax: 740 345-4505
Diane M Reed, *President*
Roy Mc Intosh, *Vice Pres*
Roy McIntosh, *Vice Pres*
EMP: 50 **EST:** 1954
SQ FT: 20,000
SALES (est): 9.9MM Privately Held
WEB: www.armstrongsteelerectors.com
SIC: 1622 Bridge construction; highway construction, elevated

(G-15145)
AUTUMN HEALTH CARE INC
23 Forry St (43055-4057)
PHONE.................................740 366-2321
Bonnie Stepanian, *Director*
EMP: 25
SALES (corp-wide): 535.3K Privately Held
SIC: 8361 Rest home, with health care incidental
PA: Autumn Health Care, Inc
23 Forry St
Newark OH 43055
740 345-9198

(G-15146)
BEHAVORIAL HEALTHCARE (PA)
65 Messimer Dr (43055-1874)
PHONE.................................740 522-8477
Kathryn E Saylor, *CEO*
Patty Devlin, *Administration*
EMP: 175
SQ FT: 15,000
SALES: 10MM Privately Held
SIC: 8093 Mental health clinic, outpatient

(G-15147)
BOEING COMPANY
801 Irving Wick Dr W (43056-1199)
PHONE.................................740 788-4000
Fax: 740 788-6414
Brian McGuire, *Vice Pres*
Anthony J Panella, *Project Dir*
Tony Hensley, *QC Mgr*
Jeremy Addy, *Engineer*
Daryl Dickerson, *Engineer*
EMP: 700
SALES (corp-wide): 93.3B Publicly Held
SIC: 3761 4581 Guided missiles & space vehicles; airports, flying fields & services
PA: The Boeing Company
100 N Riverside Plz
Chicago IL 60606
312 544-2000

(G-15148)
BOEING COMPANY
801 Irving Wick Dr W (43056-1199)
PHONE.................................740 788-4000
Daniel Acassidy, *Branch Mgr*
Dan Cassidy, *MIS Mgr*
EMP: 25
SALES (corp-wide): 93.3B Publicly Held
SIC: 7629 3812 Electrical repair shops; search & navigation equipment
PA: The Boeing Company
100 N Riverside Plz
Chicago IL 60606
312 544-2000

(G-15149)
BROOKDALE SNIOR LVING CMMNTIES
Also Called: Sterling House of Newark
331 Goosepond Rd (43055-3184)
PHONE.................................740 366-0005
Fax: 740 366-0797
Marge Shawger, *Manager*
EMP: 30
SALES (corp-wide): 4.7B Publicly Held
WEB: www.assisted.com
SIC: 8059 Rest home, with health care
HQ: Brookdale Senior Living Communities, Inc.
6737 W Wa St Ste 2300
Milwaukee WI 53214
414 918-5000

(G-15150)
BROTHERHOOD OF LOCOMOTIVE ENGI
Also Called: Brothrhood Lcomotive Engineers
745 Sherman Ave (43055-6928)
PHONE.................................740 345-0978
Dave Moorhead, *Chairman*
EMP: 26
SALES (corp-wide): 20.9MM Privately Held
SIC: 8631 Labor union
PA: Brotherhood Of Locomotive Engineers & Trainmen
7061 E Pleasant Valley Rd
Independence OH 44131
216 241-2630

(G-15151)
BROWN DISTRIBUTING INC
51 Swans Rd Ne (43055-8809)
PHONE.................................740 349-7999
Fax: 740 345-7546
Richard L Brown, *President*
▲ **EMP:** 51
SALES (est): 11.9MM Privately Held
SIC: 5181 Beer & other fermented malt liquors

(G-15152)
BUCKEYE LINEN SERVICE INC
76 Jefferson St (43055-4936)
P.O. Box 159 (43058-0159)
PHONE.................................740 345-4046
Fax: 740 345-4047
Donald Struminger, *President*
Michael Perez, *General Mgr*
David Struminger, *Exec VP*
Nancy P Alley, *Vice Pres*
John Crockford, *Vice Pres*
EMP: 70
SQ FT: 20,000
SALES (est): 4.1MM
SALES (corp-wide): 21.7MM Privately Held
WEB: www.mohenis.com
SIC: 7213 Uniform supply
PA: Mohenis Services, Inc.
875 E Bank St
Petersburg VA 23803
800 879-3315

(G-15153)
BURDENS MACHINE & WELDING
94 S 5th St (43055-5302)
P.O. Box 177 (43058-0177)
PHONE.................................740 345-9246
Fax: 740 345-9247
Donald Burden Sr, *President*
Robert Burden, *Corp Secy*
Darrell Burden, *Vice Pres*
Donald Burden Jr, *Vice Pres*
EMP: 26
SQ FT: 4,400
SALES: 1.9MM Privately Held
SIC: 1799 3599 Welding on site; machine shop, jobbing & repair

(G-15154)
CAMPOLO MICHAEL MD
1930 Tamarack Rd (43055-2303)
PHONE.................................740 522-7600
Michael Campolo, *President*
EMP: 50
SALES (est): 821.5K Privately Held
SIC: 8011 General & family practice, physician/surgeon

(G-15155)
CELLCO PARTNERSHIP
Also Called: Verizon
668 Hebron Rd (43056-1348)
P.O. Box 2266 (43058-0266)
PHONE.................................740 522-6446
Fax: 740 778-9228
Maggie Hallett, *Branch Mgr*
EMP: 25
SALES (corp-wide): 126B Publicly Held
SIC: 4812 5999 Cellular telephone services; mobile telephones & equipment
HQ: Cellco Partnership
1 Verizon Way
Basking Ridge NJ 07920

(G-15156)
CHERRY VALLEY LODGE
Also Called: Cherry Valley Lodge and Coco
2299 Cherry Valley Rd Se (43055-9393)
P.O. Box 771207, Houston TX (77215-1207)
PHONE.................................740 788-1200
Fax: 740 788-8800
Steve Hsu, *President*
Larry Murphy, *General Mgr*
Sherry Sorrell, *Sales Staff*
Bernadette Vinning, *Sales Staff*
Paulette George, *Manager*
EMP: 45
SALES (est): 3.8MM Privately Held
SIC: 7011 5812 5091 Hotels; restaurant, family: independent; water slides (recreation park)

(G-15157)
COMMERCIAL ELECTRONICS INC
1294 N 21st St (43055-3061)
PHONE.................................740 281-0180
Chris Cover, *President*
EMP: 25
SALES (est): 1.7MM Privately Held
SIC: 5065 5999 Communication equipment; mobile telephones & equipment

Newark - Licking County (G-15158)

(G-15158)
CONSUMER SUPPORT SERVICES INC (PA)
2040 Cherry Valley Rd # 1 (43055-1197)
PHONE.................740 788-8257
Fax: 740 788-8266
Daniel F Swickard, *President*
Randall C Nipps, *CFO*
Melanie Gallop, *Director*
EMP: 500
SQ FT: 5,000
SALES (est): 26.7MM **Privately Held**
SIC: 8059 8322 8082 Home for the mentally retarded, exc. skilled or intermediate; individual & family services; home health care services

(G-15159)
CONSUMER SUPPORT SERVICES INC
640 Industrial Pkwy (43056-1528)
PHONE.................740 522-5464
EMP: 91
SALES (corp-wide): 26.7MM **Privately Held**
SIC: 8322 Social service center
PA: Consumer Support Services Inc
2040 Cherry Valley Rd # 1
Newark OH 43055
740 788-8257

(G-15160)
CONSUMER SUPPORT SERVICES INC
100 James St (43055-3931)
PHONE.................740 344-3600
Lisa Cline, *Branch Mgr*
EMP: 73
SALES (corp-wide): 26.7MM **Privately Held**
SIC: 8322 Adult day care center
PA: Consumer Support Services Inc
2040 Cherry Valley Rd # 1
Newark OH 43055
740 788-8257

(G-15161)
CORPORATE HEALTH BENEFITS
1915 Tamarack Rd (43055-1300)
PHONE.................740 348-1401
Bob Kamps, *President*
EMP: 34
SALES: 371.6K **Privately Held**
SIC: 6411 Insurance agents, brokers & service
PA: Licking Memorial Health Systems
1320 W Main St
Newark OH 43055

(G-15162)
COUGHLIN CHEVROLET TOYOTA INC
Also Called: Coughlin Automotive
1850 N 21st St (43055-3186)
P.O. Box 749, Pataskala (43062-0749)
PHONE.................740 366-1381
Fax: 740 366-4607
Al Coughlin, *President*
Brent Harbold, *General Mgr*
Al Coughlin Jr, *Corp Secy*
Bill Vina, *Vice Pres*
Max Forster, *CFO*
EMP: 90
SQ FT: 50,000
SALES (est): 26.5MM
SALES (corp-wide): 95.1MM **Privately Held**
WEB: www.coughlinford.com
SIC: 5511 7532 5531 5521 Automobiles, new & used; top & body repair & paint shops; automotive & home supply stores; used car dealers
PA: Coughlin Chevrolet, Inc.
9000 Broad St Sw
Pataskala OH 43062
740 964-9191

(G-15163)
COURTESY AMBULANCE INC
1890 W Main St (43055-1134)
PHONE.................740 522-8588
Fax: 740 522-3031
Lois Griggs, *President*
Clair Griggs, *Chairman*
Michael Hardway, *Opers Mgr*
EMP: 37
SQ FT: 1,000
SALES (est): 1.9MM **Privately Held**
SIC: 4119 Ambulance service

(G-15164)
DAWES ARBORETUM
7770 Jacksontown Rd (43056-9380)
PHONE.................740 323-2355
Fax: 740 323-4058
Richard Larson, *Manager*
Peter Lowe, *Manager*
Gregory Payton, *Manager*
Luke Messinger, *Director*
Shana Byrd, *Director*
EMP: 38
SALES: 1.8MM **Privately Held**
WEB: www.dawesarb.org
SIC: 8422 5261 Arboretum; nurseries & garden centers

(G-15165)
ENVIRONMENTAL SPECIALISTS INC
55 Builders Dr (43055-1343)
PHONE.................740 788-8134
Ken Walls, *Branch Mgr*
EMP: 44 **Privately Held**
SIC: 8744
PA: Environmental Specialists, Inc.
1000 Andrews Ave
Youngstown OH 44505

(G-15166)
FIRST FDRAL SAV LN ASSN NEWARK (PA)
2 N 2nd St (43055-5610)
P.O. Box 4460 (43058-4460)
PHONE.................740 345-3494
Paul M Thompson, *President*
Sarah R Wallace, *Chairman*
Charity McFarland, *Assistant VP*
Jennie Hall, *Vice Pres*
Brian Murray, *Vice Pres*
EMP: 50
SQ FT: 5,000
SALES: 8.4MM **Privately Held**
SIC: 6035 Federal savings & loan associations

(G-15167)
FLYING COLORS PUBLIC PRESCHOOL
119 Union St (43055-3937)
PHONE.................740 349-1629
Fax: 740 349-1644
Davelyn Ross, *Director*
EMP: 50
SALES (est): 765.5K **Privately Held**
WEB: www.flyingcolorspreschool.com
SIC: 8351 8211 Preschool center; elementary & secondary schools

(G-15168)
GENERATION HEALTH & REHAB CNTR
Also Called: Flint Ridge Nursing & Rehab
1450 W Main St (43055-1825)
PHONE.................740 344-9465
Fax: 740 344-4453
Karen Moss, *CFO*
Kim Mason, *Personnel*
John R Huges,
Ed Renicker, *Maintence Staff*
EMP: 92
SALES (est): 7.9MM **Privately Held**
SIC: 8052 8051 Intermediate care facilities; skilled nursing care facilities

(G-15169)
GEORGE W ARENSBERG PHRM INC
Also Called: Arensberg Home Health
1272 W Main St (43055-2053)
PHONE.................740 344-2195
Fax: 740 344-8371
Jeff Read, *Manager*
EMP: 50
SALES (corp-wide): 7.4MM **Privately Held**
SIC: 5912 8049 Drug stores; nutritionist
PA: The George W Arensberg Pharmacy Inc
176 Hudson Ave
Newark OH 43055
740 345-9761

(G-15170)
GOLF GALAXY GOLFWORKS INC
Also Called: Golfworks, The
4820 Jacksontown Rd (43056-9377)
P.O. Box 3008 (43058-3008)
PHONE.................740 328-4193
Fax: 740 328-4213
Mark McCormick, *CEO*
Richard C Nordvoid, *Principal*
Mark Wilson, *Vice Pres*
Pete Calloway, *Research*
Jerry Datz, *CFO*
▲ **EMP:** 150 **EST:** 1974
SQ FT: 80,000
SALES (est): 58.7MM
SALES (corp-wide): 8.5B **Publicly Held**
WEB: www.golfworks.com
SIC: 5091 2731 3949 5941 Golf equipment; books: publishing only; golf equipment; shafts, golf club; golf, tennis & ski shops
HQ: Golf Galaxy, Inc.
345 Court St
Coraopolis PA 15108

(G-15171)
GOODIN ELECTRIC INC
605 Garfield Ave Ste A (43055-6889)
PHONE.................740 522-3113
Fax: 740 522-3116
John A Goodin, *CEO*
Howard Goodin, *Vice Pres*
EMP: 25
SQ FT: 10,000
SALES (est): 2.7MM **Privately Held**
SIC: 1731 General electrical contractor

(G-15172)
GW BUSINESS SOLUTIONS LLC
65 S 5th St (43055-5404)
PHONE.................740 645-9861
EMP: 148 **EST:** 2013
SQ FT: 9,000
SALES (est): 3.9MM **Privately Held**
SIC: 8331 5932 Job Training/Related Services Ret Used Merchandise

(G-15173)
HEATH NURSING CARE CENTER
717 S 30th St (43056-1294)
PHONE.................740 522-1171
Fax: 740 522-5313
Robert Lehman, *President*
Mike Campolo, *Director*
Luke Sutherland, *Administration*
EMP: 180
SALES: 10.5MM **Privately Held**
WEB: www.carington.com
SIC: 8051 8059 Skilled nursing care facilities; convalescent home

(G-15174)
HOPEWELL DENTAL CARE
572 Industrial Pkwy Ste B (43056-1638)
PHONE.................740 522-5000
Orest Kowalsky, *President*
EMP: 25 **EST:** 1981
SALES (est): 2MM **Privately Held**
WEB: www.hopewelldentalcare.com
SIC: 8021 Dentists' office

(G-15175)
HOSPICE OF CENTRAL OHIO (PA)
Also Called: Palliative Care of Ohio
2269 Cherry Valley Rd Se (43055-9323)
PHONE.................740 344-0311
Kerry Hamilton, *CEO*
Calvin Robinson, *Principal*
Lisa Maurer, *Vice Pres*
Stacy Thompson, *Vice Pres*
Barbara Ford, *Project Mgr*
EMP: 130
SALES: 18.9MM **Privately Held**
WEB: www.hospiceofcentralohio.org
SIC: 8069 Specialty hospitals, except psychiatric

(G-15176)
HOUSTON DICK PLBG & HTG INC
Also Called: Houston Plumbing & Heating
724 Montgomery Rd Ne (43055-9461)
PHONE.................740 763-3961
Fax: 740 763-4397
Richard F Houston, *President*
Patricia Houston, *Vice Pres*
Beverly Dodson, *Treasurer*
Beth L Cramer, *Admin Sec*
EMP: 40
SQ FT: 8,000
SALES: 5MM **Privately Held**
WEB: www.houstonplumbingheating.com
SIC: 1711 Plumbing contractors; warm air heating & air conditioning contractor

(G-15177)
INTERIM HALTHCARE COLUMBUS INC
Also Called: Interim Services
900 Sharon Valley Rd (43055-2804)
PHONE.................740 349-8700
Fax: 740 366-0191
Susan Hamann, *Branch Mgr*
EMP: 743
SALES (corp-wide): 24.4MM **Privately Held**
SIC: 7363 Temporary help service
HQ: Interim Healthcare Of Columbus, Inc.
784 Morrison Rd
Gahanna OH 43230
614 888-3130

(G-15178)
JOBES HENDERSON & ASSOC INC
59 Grant St (43055-3939)
PHONE.................740 344-5451
Fax: 740 344-5746
Jim Roberts, *President*
Joseph Rutherford, *COO*
Jeremy Van Ostran, *Senior VP*
Gary Love, *CFO*
EMP: 40
SQ FT: 9,000
SALES (est): 4.8MM
SALES (corp-wide): 39.8MM **Privately Held**
WEB: www.jobeshenderson.com
SIC: 8713 8711 Surveying services; engineering services
PA: Hull & Associates, Inc.
6397 Emerald Pkwy Ste 200
Dublin OH 43016
614 793-8777

(G-15179)
KINDRED NURSING CENTERS E LLC
Also Called: Kindred Transitional
75 Mcmillen Dr (43055-1808)
PHONE.................740 344-0357
Lori Bishop, *Human Res Mgr*
Erin Kennedy, *Manager*
Sheri Webb, *Manager*
Beth Mueller, *Director*
Michelle Hudak, *Hlthcr Dir*
EMP: 128
SALES (corp-wide): 6B **Publicly Held**
WEB: www.salemhaven.com
SIC: 8051 Skilled nursing care facilities
HQ: Kindred Nursing Centers East, L.L.C.
680 S 4th St
Louisville KY 40202
502 596-7300

(G-15180)
KRIBHA LLC
Also Called: Hampton Inn-Newark/Heath
1008 Hebron Rd (43056-1121)
PHONE.................740 788-8991
Dennis O'Neill, *General Mgr*
Ashok Patel, *Mng Member*
Jeffery Daniels, *Manager*
Vimal Patel,
EMP: 25
SALES (est): 1.6MM **Privately Held**
SIC: 7011 Hotels

GEOGRAPHIC SECTION
Newark - Licking County (G-15205)

(G-15181)
LABORATORY CORPORATION AMERICA
95 S Terrace Ave (43055-1355)
PHONE..................740 522-2034
Diane Noland, *Branch Mgr*
EMP: 25 **Publicly Held**
WEB: www.labcorp.com
SIC: 8071 Testing laboratories
HQ: Laboratory Corporation Of America
  358 S Main St Ste 458
  Burlington NC 27215
  336 229-1127

(G-15182)
LAYTON INC (PA)
169 Dayton Rd Ne (43055-8879)
PHONE..................740 349-7101
Fax: 740 349-7102
Gerard Layton, *President*
Steve Carson, *Corp Secy*
EMP: 36
SQ FT: 9,200
SALES (est): 7.6MM **Privately Held**
SIC: 1794 Excavation work

(G-15183)
LAYTON TRUCKING INC
Also Called: Layton Services
1384 E Main St (43055-1199)
P.O. Box 723 (43058-0723)
PHONE..................740 366-1447
Fax: 740 366-1775
Diane L Layton, *President*
EMP: 25
SALES (est): 4.7MM **Privately Held**
SIC: 1794 Excavation work

(G-15184)
LEADS INC (PA)
Also Called: LEADS COMMUNITY ACTION AGENCY
159 Wilson St (43055-4921)
PHONE..................740 349-8606
Fax: 740 345-2380
Ken Kempton, *CEO*
Terry Boehm, *General Mgr*
Doug Pearl, *Prdtn Mgr*
Jessica Gosselin, *Hum Res Coord*
Amy Mason, *Officer*
EMP: 25
SQ FT: 8,180
SALES: 9.1MM **Privately Held**
WEB: www.leadscaa.org
SIC: 8399 8322 Community action agency; individual & family services

(G-15185)
LICCO INC
600 Industrial Pkwy (43056-1594)
P.O. Box 4008 (43058-4008)
PHONE..................740 522-8345
Fax: 740 522-8340
Gary Smith, *Business Mgr*
Linda Swank, *Business Mgr*
Leland Lescalleet, *Sales Mgr*
Brett McClintock, *Sales Staff*
Lynne Bowman, *Sales Executive*
EMP: 250 **EST:** 1963
SQ FT: 32,000
SALES: 1.5MM **Privately Held**
WEB: www.liccoinc.com
SIC: 8331 8322 Sheltered workshop; individual & family services

(G-15186)
LICKING CNTY ALCOHOLISM PRVNTN
Also Called: Alcohlism Chem Dpndncy Program
62 E Stevens St (43055-5969)
PHONE..................740 281-3639
Fax: 740 366-7404
Jim Takacs, *Exec Dir*
EMP: 42
SALES: 1.5MM **Privately Held**
SIC: 8322 Alcoholism counseling, nontreatment

(G-15187)
LICKING COUNTY AGING PROGRAM
1058 E Main St (43055-6940)
PHONE..................740 345-0821
Fax: 740 349-8003
Martine Fuller, *General Mgr*
David Bibler, *Director*
Janis Clark, *Director*
Bonnie Morton, *Director*
Marti Hartz, *Associate Dir*
EMP: 85
SQ FT: 11,930
SALES: 5.2MM **Privately Held**
WEB: www.lcap.org
SIC: 8322 8399 Meal delivery program; old age assistance; general counseling services; health systems agency

(G-15188)
LICKING COUNTY BOARD OF MRDD
Also Called: Community Employment Services
116 N 22nd St (43055-2755)
PHONE..................740 349-6588
Fax: 740 349-6595
Nancy Neely, *Superintendent*
Beth Riggs, *Admin Asst*
EMP: 200
SALES (est): 6.3MM **Privately Held**
WEB: www.lcbmrdd.org
SIC: 8322 Social services for the handicapped
PA: County Of Licking
  20 S 2nd St
  Newark OH 43055
  740 670-5040

(G-15189)
LICKING COUNTY PLAYERS INC
131 W Main St (43055-5007)
PHONE..................740 349-2287
Christina Barth, *President*
Willy Wonka, *Prdtn Dir*
EMP: 25
SALES: 59.7K **Privately Held**
SIC: 7922 Community theater production

(G-15190)
LICKING KNOX LABOR COUNCIL
34 N 4th St (43055-5010)
PHONE..................740 345-1765
Dave McFortsh, *President*
EMP: 65
SALES (est): 212.5K **Privately Held**
SIC: 8631 Labor union

(G-15191)
LICKING MEMORIAL HLTH SYSTEMS (PA)
1320 W Main St (43055-1822)
PHONE..................220 564-4000
Robert Montagnese, *President*
Sallie Arnett, *Vice Pres*
Rob Montagnese, *CFO*
Kim D Fleming, *Treasurer*
David Claypool, *Controller*
EMP: 990
SALES: 209.7MM **Privately Held**
SIC: 8741 6411 Hospital management; insurance agents, brokers & service

(G-15192)
LICKING MEMORIAL HOSPITAL (HQ)
Also Called: LICKING MEMORIAL HEALTH SYSTEMS
1320 W Main St (43055-3699)
PHONE..................740 348-4137
Fax: 740 348-1555
Robert A Montagnese, *President*
Sallie Arnett, *Vice Pres*
Craig Cairns, *Vice Pres*
Ann Hubbuch, *Vice Pres*
Veronica Link, *Vice Pres*
EMP: 1143 **EST:** 1898
SQ FT: 394,784
SALES: 213.7MM **Privately Held**
SIC: 8062 General medical & surgical hospitals

(G-15193)
LICKING MUSKINGUM CMNTY CORREC
20 S 2nd St (43055-5602)
PHONE..................740 349-6980
Fax: 740 670-5354
Jim Thissen, *Manager*
Marian Skeen, *Director*
EMP: 35
SALES (est): 1.4MM **Privately Held**
SIC: 8744 Correctional facility

(G-15194)
LICKING RHABILITATION SVCS INC
11177 Lambs Ln (43055-9779)
PHONE..................740 345-2837
Fax: 740 763-0475
Cathy Konkler, *President*
Jeff Konkler, *Vice Pres*
Connie Bess, *Opers Staff*
Paul Kaple, *Director*
Julie Bay,
EMP: 25
SALES (est): 1.8MM **Privately Held**
SIC: 8049 Physical therapist; speech therapist; occupational therapist

(G-15195)
LICKING VALLEY LIONS CLUB
Also Called: International Assn Lions Clubs
3187 Licking Valley Rd (43055-9107)
PHONE..................740 763-3733
Don Devault, *President*
EMP: 121
SALES: 24.2K **Privately Held**
SIC: 8699 Charitable organization

(G-15196)
LICKING-KNOX GOODWILL INDS INC (PA)
65 S 5th St (43055-5404)
P.O. Box 828 (43058-0828)
PHONE..................740 345-9861
Timothy J Young, *CEO*
Vicki M Osborn, *CFO*
Lynn Fawcett, *VP Finance*
Lisa Baker, *Comms Dir*
Mari Church, *Office Mgr*
EMP: 60
SQ FT: 17,000
SALES: 8.8MM **Privately Held**
SIC: 8331 8741 5932 Community service employment training program; sheltered workshop; vocational training agency; management services; used merchandise stores

(G-15197)
LONGABERGER COMPANY
Also Called: Inn On The Square
50 N 2nd St (43055-5622)
PHONE..................740 349-8411
Mike Bennett, *Vice Pres*
Rachel Schmidt, *Vice Pres*
Cindy Hovey, *Systems Staff*
EMP: 64
SALES (corp-wide): 119.9MM **Publicly Held**
WEB: www.longaberger.com
SIC: 7011 8611 Hotels; business associations
HQ: The Longaberger Company
  5563 Raiders Rd
  Frazeysburg OH 43822
  740 828-4000

(G-15198)
LORY DIALYSIS LLC
Also Called: Premiere Kidney Center Newark
65 S Terrace Ave (43055-1355)
PHONE..................740 522-2955
Jim Hilger, *Principal*
EMP: 25
SALES (est): 541.6K **Publicly Held**
SIC: 8092 Kidney dialysis centers
PA: Davita Inc.
  2000 16th St
  Denver CO 80202

(G-15199)
LOWES HOME CENTERS LLC
888 Hebron Rd (43056-1399)
PHONE..................740 522-0003
Fax: 740 522-0158
Jason Altemose, *Store Mgr*
John Armstrong, *Manager*
EMP: 150
SALES (corp-wide): 68.6B **Publicly Held**
SIC: 5211 5031 5722 5064 Home centers; building materials, exterior; building materials, interior; household appliance stores; electrical appliances, television & radio
HQ: Lowe's Home Centers, Llc
  1605 Curtis Bridge Rd
  Wilkesboro NC 28697
  336 658-4000

(G-15200)
MAIN PLACE INC (PA)
112 S 3rd St (43055-5335)
PHONE..................740 345-6246
Fax: 740 345-3697
James W Williams, *Vice Pres*
Kathy Vanwy, *Bookkeeper*
Janice Miller, *Case Mgr*
Kellen Rafferty, *Case Mgr*
Farrah Shoemaker, *Case Mgr*
EMP: 27 **EST:** 2008
SALES: 1.2MM **Privately Held**
SIC: 8093 Mental health clinic, outpatient

(G-15201)
MATESICH DISTRIBUTING CO
1190 E Main St (43055-8803)
PHONE..................740 349-8686
Fax: 740 349-3830
John C Matesich III, *CEO*
Pam Ferick, *General Mgr*
James M Matesich, *Corp Secy*
Pam Firich, *Controller*
Garrett Oliver, *Accounts Mgr*
▲ **EMP:** 91
SQ FT: 103,000
SALES (est): 38.7MM **Privately Held**
SIC: 5181 Beer & other fermented malt liquors

(G-15202)
MATHEWS FORD INC
500 Hebron Rd (43056-1435)
P.O. Box 4220 (43058-4220)
PHONE..................740 522-2181
Fax: 740 522-2835
Thurman Mathews, *President*
Doug Moore, *General Mgr*
Sue Alfrey, *Treasurer*
John Hankinson, *Sales Staff*
Stephen Hegele, *Sales Staff*
EMP: 77
SALES (est): 29.2MM **Privately Held**
SIC: 5511 7538 Automobiles, new & used; general automotive repair shops

(G-15203)
MC MAHON REALESTATE CO (PA)
Also Called: Coldwell Banker
591 Country Club Dr (43055-2102)
PHONE..................740 344-2250
Fax: 740 344-8097
Joseph Mc Mahon, *Owner*
Ryan Paxton, *Sales Staff*
Carol Marr, *Sales Associate*
Carol Sherman, *Sales Associate*
Jerry Furniss, *Manager*
EMP: 40
SALES (est): 2.6MM **Privately Held**
SIC: 6531 Real estate agent, residential

(G-15204)
MEDICAL BENEFITS MUTL LF INSUR (PA)
Also Called: Medben Companies
1975 Tamarack Rd (43055-1300)
P.O. Box 1009 (43058-1009)
PHONE..................740 522-8425
Fax: 740 522-5002
C Arthur Morrow, *Ch of Bd*
Douglas Freeman, *President*
Kurt Harden, *Senior VP*
Lori Kane, *VP Admin*
James Weisent, *Vice Pres*
EMP: 150
SQ FT: 32,000
SALES: 16.4MM **Privately Held**
SIC: 6321 Health insurance carriers

(G-15205)
MEDICAL BNFITS ADMNSTRTORS INC
Also Called: MEDBEN COMPANIES
1975 Tamarack Rd (43055-1300)
P.O. Box 1009 (43058-1009)
PHONE..................740 522-8425
C Arthur Morrow, *Ch of Bd*
Douglas Freeman, *President*
Charlie Krajacic, *Corp Secy*

Newark - Licking County (G-15206)

Kurt Hardin, *Senior VP*
Cara Delcher, *Vice Pres*
EMP: 70
SQ FT: 32,000
SALES: 9.9MM
SALES (corp-wide): 16.4MM **Privately Held**
SIC: 6321 Accident & health insurance
PA: Medical Benefits Mutual Life Insurance Co
1975 Tamarack Rd
Newark OH 43055
740 522-8425

(G-15206)
MEDICAL SURGICAL ASSOCIATES
1930 Tamarack Rd (43055-2303)
PHONE................................740 522-7600
Michael Campolo, *Family Practiti*
EMP: 50
SALES (est): 4.2MM **Privately Held**
SIC: 8031 Offices & clinics of osteopathic physicians

(G-15207)
MIDWAY GARAGE INC
140 Everett Ave (43055-5702)
P.O. Box 750 (43058-0750)
PHONE................................740 345-0699
Fax: 740 345-9704
J Wine Gardner, *President*
EMP: 40
SQ FT: 26,000
SALES (est): 1.6MM **Privately Held**
WEB: www.midwaytt.com
SIC: 7538 Truck engine repair, except industrial

(G-15208)
MILESTONE VENTURES LLC
1776 Tamarack Rd (43055-1359)
PHONE................................317 908-2093
Dittmar Schaefer, *Branch Mgr*
EMP: 25 **Privately Held**
SIC: 5031 Veneer
PA: Milestone Ventures, Llc
2924 Hallie Ln
Granville OH 43023

(G-15209)
MODERN WELDING CO OHIO INC
1 Modern Way (43055-3921)
P.O. Box 4430 (43058-4430)
PHONE................................740 344-9425
John W Jones, *President*
Doug Routher, *General Mgr*
Bob Weidner, *COO*
James M Ruth, *Exec VP*
Doug Rothert, *Vice Pres*
EMP: 30
SQ FT: 52,000
SALES (est): 8.1MM
SALES (corp-wide): 83.4MM **Privately Held**
WEB: www.modweldco.net
SIC: 3443 5051 Tanks, lined: metal plate; metals service centers & offices
PA: Modern Welding Company, Inc.
2880 New Hartford Rd
Owensboro KY 42303
270 685-4400

(G-15210)
MONACO PALACE INC
Also Called: Monacos Place Bnquet Spcalists
4869 Rock Haven Rd (43055-8121)
PHONE................................614 475-4817
Fax: 614 475-0825
George Norris, *President*
Wynn Wiksell, *President*
John Howard, *Accountant*
Kevin Luzader, *Executive*
EMP: 37
SQ FT: 16,000
SALES: 200K **Privately Held**
WEB: www.monacoscatering.com
SIC: 7299 5812 Banquet hall facilities; eating places

(G-15211)
MONTESSORI COMMUNITY SCHOOL
621 Country Club Dr (43055-1601)
PHONE................................740 344-9411
Fax: 740 344-6060
Helen M Moore, *President*
Lynn Bandley, *COO*
Elizabeth Wells, *Director*
EMP: 34
SALES (est): 1.1MM **Privately Held**
WEB: www.montessorinewark.com
SIC: 8351 8211 Nursery school; preschool center; Montessori child development center; kindergarten

(G-15212)
MOUND BUILDERS GUIDANCE CENTER
65 Messimer Dr Unit 2 (43055-1879)
PHONE................................740 522-2828
Francis Deutshle, *Exec Dir*
Laura Maxwell, *Director*
EMP: 99
SALES: 1MM **Privately Held**
SIC: 8322 Individual & family services

(G-15213)
MOUNDBUILDERS COUNTRY CLUB CO
125 N 33rd St (43055-2014)
PHONE................................740 344-4500
Fax: 740 344-4122
Joseph Moore, *General Mgr*
Rosanne Nethers, *Bookkeeper*
Joe Renaud,
EMP: 55
SQ FT: 50,000
SALES: 1.8MM **Privately Held**
WEB: www.moundbuilderscc.com
SIC: 7997 5812 7992 5941 Country club, membership; golf club, membership; swimming club, membership; tennis club, membership; restaurant, family: independent; public golf courses; sporting goods & bicycle shops

(G-15214)
MPW INDUSTRIAL SERVICES INC
150 S 29th St (43055-1964)
PHONE................................740 345-2431
Fax: 740 344-7715
Tony Donnadio, *Engineer*
Jared Black, *Branch Mgr*
Tom Thompson, *Manager*
EMP: 30
SALES (corp-wide): 257.9MM **Privately Held**
SIC: 8734 Water testing laboratory
HQ: Mpw Industrial Services, Inc.
9711 Lancaster Rd
Hebron OH 43025
800 827-8790

(G-15215)
MY PLACE CHILD CARE
1335 E Main St (43055-8848)
P.O. Box 4218 (43058-4218)
PHONE................................740 349-3505
Fax: 740 349-3567
Shaun Linton,
EMP: 33
SALES: 1MM **Privately Held**
SIC: 8351 Child day care services

(G-15216)
NATIONAL GAS & OIL CORPORATION (HQ)
Also Called: Permian Oil & Gas Division
1500 Granville Rd (43055-1500)
P.O. Box 4970 (43058-4970)
PHONE................................740 344-2102
Fax: 740 344-2054
William Sullivan Jr, *Ch of Bd*
Patrick J Mc Gonagle, *President*
Gordon M King, *Vice Pres*
Todd P Ware, *Vice Pres*
EMP: 96
SQ FT: 10,000
SALES: 37.1MM
SALES (corp-wide): 72.4MM **Privately Held**
WEB: www.theenergycoop.com
SIC: 4922 4924 4932 4911 Natural gas transmission; natural gas distribution; gas & other services combined; electric services; industrial gases
PA: National Gas & Oil Company Inc
1500 Granville Rd
Newark OH 43055
740 344-2102

(G-15217)
NATIONAL YOUTH ADVOCATE PROGRA
15 N 3rd St Fl 3 (43055-5550)
PHONE................................740 349-7511
Ken Larimore, *Branch Mgr*
EMP: 33
SALES (corp-wide): 53.3MM **Privately Held**
SIC: 8322 Child related social services
PA: National Youth Advocate Program, Inc.
1801 Watermark Dr Ste 200
Columbus OH 43215
614 487-8758

(G-15218)
NEW WORLD ENERGY RESOURCES (PA)
1500 Granville Rd (43055-1536)
PHONE................................740 344-4087
John Manczak, *CEO*
EMP: 488
SALES (est): 18.8MM **Privately Held**
SIC: 1382 Geological exploration, oil & gas field

(G-15219)
NEWARK CARE CENTER LLC
Also Called: Price Rd Hlth Rhbilitation Ctr
151 Price Rd (43055-3317)
PHONE................................740 366-2321
Mordecai Rosenberg, *President*
Ronald Swartz, *CFO*
Lisa Schwartz, *Admin Sec*
EMP: 99
SALES (est): 522.2K **Privately Held**
SIC: 8051 Convalescent home with continuous nursing care

(G-15220)
NEWARK MANAGEMENT PARTNERS LLC
Also Called: Newark Metropolitan Hotel
50 N 2nd St (43055-5622)
PHONE................................740 322-6455
Martin Schrader,
Jane Simmons,
EMP: 80
SALES (est): 3.1MM **Privately Held**
SIC: 7011 Hotel, franchised

(G-15221)
NEWARK NH LLC
Also Called: Newark Hlls Hlth Rhbltion Ctr
17 Forry St (43055-4004)
PHONE................................740 345-9197
Mordecai Rosenberg, *President*
Ronald Swartz, *CFO*
Lisa Schwartz, *Admin Sec*
EMP: 74 **EST:** 2015
SALES (est): 369.7K **Privately Held**
SIC: 8051 Skilled nursing care facilities

(G-15222)
NEWARK RESIDENT HOMES INC
15 W Saint Clair St Apt C (43055-5732)
PHONE................................740 345-7231
Fax: 740 345-9397
Dave Cook, *Exec Dir*
Julie Burely, *Exec Dir*
Julie Burley, *Exec Dir*
EMP: 75
SALES: 1.3MM **Privately Held**
SIC: 8361 Residential care

(G-15223)
NEWARK SLEEP DIAGNOSTIC CENTER
1900 Tamarack Rd Ste 1908 (43055-2303)
PHONE................................740 522-9499
Gautam Samadder, *President*
EMP: 50
SALES (est): 563.2K **Privately Held**
SIC: 8069 Specialty hospitals, except psychiatric

(G-15224)
NOAHS ARK CREATIVE CARE
1255 Nadine Dr (43056-9234)
PHONE................................740 323-3664
Fax: 740 323-2706
Jennifer Cominsky, *Owner*
Brett Cominsky, *Co-Owner*
EMP: 35 **EST:** 1999
SALES (est): 759.2K **Privately Held**
SIC: 8351 Preschool center

(G-15225)
PARK NATIONAL BANK (HQ)
50 N 3rd St (43055-5548)
P.O. Box 3500 (43058-3500)
PHONE................................740 349-8451
Fax: 740 345-9239
David Trautman, *President*
Dan Delawder, *Chairman*
Thomas J Button, *Senior VP*
Cheryl Snyder, *Senior VP*
John W Kozak, *CFO*
EMP: 150
SALES: 339.5MM
SALES (corp-wide): 367MM **Publicly Held**
WEB: www.parknationalbank.com
SIC: 6021 National commercial banks
PA: Park National Corporation
50 N 3rd St
Newark OH 43055
740 349-8451

(G-15226)
PARK NATIONAL BANK
21 S 1st St Ste Front (43055-5634)
P.O. Box 3500 (43058-3500)
PHONE................................740 349-8451
David C Bowers, *Manager*
Nathan Cook, *Admin Mgr*
Larry Bailey, *Technology*
Brad Gard, *Technology*
David Armstrong, *Analyst*
EMP: 133
SALES (corp-wide): 367MM **Publicly Held**
WEB: www.parknationalbank.com
SIC: 6022 State commercial banks
HQ: The Park National Bank
50 N 3rd St
Newark OH 43055
740 349-8451

(G-15227)
PATHWAYS OF CENTRAL OHIO
1627 Bryn Mawr Dr (43055-1505)
PHONE................................740 345-6166
Maureen Barnes, *CFO*
Kristin McCloud, *Exec Dir*
Carla Kiernan, *Teacher*
EMP: 28
SQ FT: 7,000
SALES: 1.1MM **Privately Held**
WEB: www.pathwayslc.org
SIC: 8322 Social service center; crisis center

(G-15228)
PNC BANK NATIONAL ASSOCIATION
Also Called: National City Bank
68 W Church St Fl 1 (43055-5050)
PHONE................................740 349-8431
Fax: 740 345-2903
Tom Decker, *Branch Mgr*
EMP: 30
SALES (corp-wide): 18B **Publicly Held**
WEB: www.allegiantbank.com
SIC: 6021 National commercial banks
HQ: Pnc Bank, National Association
222 Delaware Ave
Wilmington DE 19801
877 762-2000

(G-15229)
PRIDE -N- JOY PRESCHOOL INC
1319 W Main St (43055-1821)
PHONE................................740 522-3338
Mark Nutter, *President*
Vonnie Nutter, *Vice Pres*
EMP: 25
SQ FT: 3,000

GEOGRAPHIC SECTION
Newburgh Heights - Cuyahoga County (G-15252)

SALES: 1MM Privately Held
SIC: 8351 Preschool center

(G-15230)
R & R PIPELINE INC (PA)
155 Dayton Rd Ne (43055-8879)
P.O. Box 37 (43058-0037)
PHONE..................740 345-3692
Fax: 740 349-1987
Rick Reed, *President*
Jim Shepherd, *General Mgr*
Jeff Emery, *Vice Pres*
Rick Green, *Safety Dir*
Cody Thoman, *Safety Dir*
EMP: 55
SQ FT: 7,400
SALES (est): 11.1MM Privately Held
WEB: www.rrpipelineinc.com
SIC: 1623 Pipeline construction

(G-15231)
REESE PYLE DRAKE & MEYER (PA)
36 N 2nd St (43055-5610)
P.O. Box 919 (43058-0919)
PHONE..................740 345-3431
Fax: 740 345-7302
J Andrew Crawford, *Partner*
Ann Munro Kennedy, *Partner*
William Douglas Lowe, *Partner*
David W Wenger, *Partner*
Robert Abdalla, *Corp Counsel*
EMP: 44 EST: 1904
SQ FT: 12,000
SALES (est): 6.5MM Privately Held
WEB: www.rpdm.com
SIC: 8111 General practice attorney, lawyer

(G-15232)
RICHARDSON GLASS SERVICE INC (PA)
Also Called: RICHARDSON GLASS SERVICE INC DBA LEE'S GLASS SERVICE
1165 Mount Vernon Rd (43055-3032)
PHONE..................740 366-5090
Toll Free:..................888 -
Fax: 740 366-3299
Mark W McPeek, *President*
Steve Davis, *Principal*
John P Johnson II, *Principal*
Laura McPeek, *Vice Pres*
Gary Watson, *Project Mgr*
EMP: 62
SQ FT: 21,480
SALES (est): 10.4MM Privately Held
WEB: www.richardsonglass.com
SIC: 1793 Glass & glazing work

(G-15233)
SECURITY NATIONAL BANK & TR CO (HQ)
50 N 3rd St (43055-5523)
P.O. Box 1726, Springfield (45501-1726)
PHONE..................740 426-6384
Fax: 937 324-6816
William C Fralick, *President*
Daniel M O'Keefe, *Vice Pres*
J William Stapleton, *CFO*
William J Stapleton, *CFO*
Jeff Sanders, *Manager*
EMP: 120 EST: 1903
SQ FT: 40,000
SALES (est): 3.8MM
SALES (corp-wide): 367MM Publicly Held
WEB: www.securitynationalbank.com
SIC: 6021 National trust companies with deposits, commercial
PA: Park National Corporation
    50 N 3rd St
    Newark OH 43055
    740 349-8451

(G-15234)
SOUTHGATE CORP
1499 W Main St (43055-1988)
P.O. Box 397 (43058-0397)
PHONE..................740 522-2151
Robert O'Neill, *President*
Robert O Neill, *President*
Russ Boren, *Project Mgr*
Mark Schillig, *Sales Dir*
Tim Ryan, *Sales Mgr*
EMP: 26

SALES (est): 3.6MM Privately Held
SIC: 6552 Land subdividers & developers, commercial

(G-15235)
STATE FARM GENERAL INSUR CO
Also Called: State Farm Insurance
1440 Granville Rd (43055-1538)
PHONE..................740 364-5000
Fax: 740 349-5044
Lee Baumann, *Vice Pres*
EMP: 89
SALES (corp-wide): 39.5MM Privately Held
SIC: 6411 Insurance agents & brokers
HQ: State Farm General Insurance Co Inc
    1 State Farm Plz
    Bloomington IL 61701
    309 766-2311

(G-15236)
STATE FARM MUTL AUTO INSUR CO
Also Called: State Farm Insurance
1440 Granville Rd (43055-1538)
PHONE..................740 364-5000
Lee Baumann, *Vice Pres*
Paula Olson, *Broker*
Kendra Hill, *Underwriter*
Thad Camp, *Manager*
Joe Campbell, *Manager*
EMP: 2000
SALES (corp-wide): 39.5MM Privately Held
WEB: www.statefarm.com
SIC: 6411 Insurance agents & brokers
PA: State Farm Mutual Automobile Insurance Company
    1 State Farm Plz
    Bloomington IL 61710
    309 766-2311

(G-15237)
SURGICENTER LTD
Also Called: Speacialty Care Vision
1651 W Main St (43055-1345)
PHONE..................740 522-3937
Leroy Bloomberg, *Principal*
Shahin Shahinfar, *Director*
EMP: 35
SALES (est): 1MM Privately Held
SIC: 8011 Eyes, ears, nose & throat specialist: physician/surgeon

(G-15238)
TH SERVICES
12151 Bolen Rd Ne (43055-8875)
PHONE..................740 258-9054
Troy Hartman, *Principal*
EMP: 42
SALES (est): 1,000K Privately Held
SIC: 8748 Business consulting

(G-15239)
THERATRUST
23 Forry St (43055-4057)
PHONE..................740 345-7688
Fax: 740 345-7737
Steve Hitchens, *Owner*
Mike McCoy, *Manager*
EMP: 50
SALES (est): 1.6MM Privately Held
WEB: www.theratrust.net
SIC: 8093 Rehabilitation center, outpatient treatment

(G-15240)
TIME WARNER CABLE INC
111 N 11th St (43055-4262)
PHONE..................740 345-4329
Eric Lauvray, *Manager*
EMP: 83
SALES (corp-wide): 41.5B Publicly Held
SIC: 4841 Cable television services
HQ: Spectrum Management Holding Company, Llc
    400 Atlantic St
    Stamford CT 06901
    203 905-7801

(G-15241)
TRUE CORE FEDERAL CREDIT UNION
215 Deo Dr (43055-3051)
PHONE..................740 345-6608
Fred Longstreth, *President*
Shani Smith, *Exec VP*
Tyler Crall, *Vice Pres*
Dorothy Ridenbaugh, *Vice Pres*
Beth Sheets, *Marketing Staff*
EMP: 45
SALES: 5.6MM Privately Held
WEB: www.fiberglas.org
SIC: 6061 Federal credit unions

(G-15242)
UNITED STEELWORKERS
Also Called: Uswa
2100 James Pkwy (43056-1031)
PHONE..................740 928-0157
Gary Sities, *President*
EMP: 240
SALES (corp-wide): 61.5K Privately Held
WEB: www.uswa.org
SIC: 8631 Labor union
PA: United Steelworkers
    60 Bolevard Of The Allies
    Pittsburgh PA 15222
    412 562-2400

(G-15243)
UNIVERSAL VENEER MILL CORP
1776 Tamarack Rd (43055-1384)
PHONE..................740 522-1147
Fax: 740 522-6144
Klaus Krajewski, *President*
William Cooper, *CFO*
Aundrea Antritt, *Controller*
EMP: 180
SQ FT: 75,000
SALES (est): 9.7MM Privately Held
SIC: 6512 Commercial & industrial building operation

(G-15244)
WASHINGTON SQUARE APARTMENTS
340 Eastern Ave Ofc (43055-6580)
PHONE..................740 349-8353
Fax: 740 349-8354
Charles W Nobel, *President*
Sandy Henderson, *Director*
EMP: 28
SALES (est): 1.7MM Privately Held
SIC: 6513 6531 Apartment hotel operation; real estate agents & managers

(G-15245)
WASTE MANAGEMENT OHIO INC
100 Ecology Row (43055-8894)
PHONE..................740 345-1212
Fred Harmon, *District Mgr*
Ginger Kaladas, *Credit Staff*
Tim Giardina, *Manager*
Lee Hicks, *Contract Law*
EMP: 100
SALES (corp-wide): 14.4B Publicly Held
WEB: www.wm.com
SIC: 4953 Refuse systems
HQ: Waste Management Of Ohio, Inc.
    1700 N Broad St
    Fairborn OH 45324

(G-15246)
WILSON SHANNON & SNOW INC
10 W Locust St (43055-5508)
PHONE..................740 345-6611
Philip Z Shannon, *President*
Noble B Snow III, *Corp Secy*
William W Weidaw, *Vice Pres*
Leila Doup, *CPA*
Peggy Evans, *CPA*
EMP: 28
SQ FT: 4,500
SALES (est): 2.8MM Privately Held
WEB: www.wssinc.net
SIC: 8721 Certified public accountant

(G-15247)
WILSONS HILLVIEW FARM INC
Also Called: Wilson's Garden Center
10923 Lambs Ln (43055-8897)
PHONE..................740 763-2873
Fax: 740 763-2874
Ned Wilson, *President*
Brian Wilson, *General Mgr*
Mitzie Wilson, *Corp Secy*
Harry Wilson, *Vice Pres*
EMP: 40
SQ FT: 80,000
SALES: 2MM Privately Held
WEB: www.great-gardeners.com
SIC: 0181 5992 Shrubberies grown under cover (e.g. greenhouse production); flowers: grown under cover (e.g. greenhouse production); florists

(G-15248)
WOODLNDS SRVING CENTL OHIO INC
Also Called: Family Counseling Services
68 W Church St Ste 318 (43055-5050)
PHONE..................740 349-7051
Fax: 740 345-6028
Ann Rudrauf, *Branch Mgr*
EMP: 30
SALES (corp-wide): 1.2MM Privately Held
WEB: www.thewoodland.org
SIC: 8322 Social service center
PA: The Woodlands Serving Central Ohio Inc
    195 Union St Ste B1
    Newark OH 43055
    740 349-7066

(G-15249)
YEATER ALENE K MD
Also Called: Govana Hospital
15 Messimer Dr (43055-1841)
PHONE..................740 348-4694
Alene Yeater, *Owner*
EMP: 40
SALES (est): 128.2K Privately Held
SIC: 8011 Offices & clinics of medical doctors

Newburgh Heights
Cuyahoga County

(G-15250)
ALL INDUSTRIAL GROUP INC (PA)
1555 1/2 Harvard Ave (44105-3064)
PHONE..................216 441-2000
Fax: 216 441-2211
Donald W Martinez, *President*
Rick Martinez, *Treasurer*
EMP: 33
SQ FT: 20,000
SALES (est): 6MM Privately Held
SIC: 4213 Contract haulers

(G-15251)
HOWMET CORPORATION (DH)
Also Called: Alcoa Power & Propulsion
1616 Harvard Ave (44105-3040)
PHONE..................800 242-9898
David L Squier, *President*
Marklin Lasker, *Senior VP*
James R Stanley, *Senior VP*
Roland A Paul, *Vice Pres*
B Dennis Albrechtsen, *VP Mfg*
◆ EMP: 30
SQ FT: 10,000
SALES (est): 2B
SALES (corp-wide): 12.9B Publicly Held
WEB: www.alcoa.com
SIC: 3324 3542 5051 3479 Commercial investment castings, ferrous; machine tools, metal forming type; ferroalloys; ingots; coating of metals & formed products
HQ: Howmet Holdings Corporation
    1 Misco Dr
    Whitehall MI 49461
    231 894-5686

(G-15252)
HUNT PRODUCTS INC
3982 E 42nd St (44105-3165)
PHONE..................440 667-2457

Fax: 216 281-1128
Jo Ann Hunt, *President*
Laura Hunt, *Vice Pres*
Albert Styer, *Manager*
Sandra Jones, *Receptionist*
EMP: 35 EST: 1970
SQ FT: 30,000
SALES (est): 2.2MM **Privately Held**
SIC: 7389 3544 3053 2675 Packaging & labeling services; special dies, tools, jigs & fixtures; gaskets, packing & sealing devices; die-cut paper & board; packaging paper & plastics film, coated & laminated; automotive & apparel trimmings

Newbury
Geauga County

(G-15253)
ADVANCED TENTING SOLUTIONS
10750 Music St (44065-9559)
PHONE 216 291-3300
Fax: 440 564-1138
Kim Goodrick, *Partner*
EMP: 30
SALES (est): 2MM **Privately Held**
SIC: 7359 Tent & tarpaulin rental

(G-15254)
ANDOVER FLOOR COVERING
9950 Belleflower Cir (44065-9159)
PHONE 440 293-5339
Fax: 440 293-8049
Diana Hammer, *Owner*
EMP: 29
SQ FT: 1,000
SALES (est): 2.1MM **Privately Held**
SIC: 5713 1752 Carpets; floor laying & floor work

(G-15255)
CREATIVE MOLD AND MACHINE INC
10385 Kinsman Rd (44065-9701)
P.O. Box 323 (44065-0323)
PHONE 440 338-5146
Fax: 440 338-1647
Ray Lyons, *President*
Greg Davis, *Vice Pres*
Mishal Dedeck, *Vice Pres*
Kimberly Simcak, *Accountant*
EMP: 25
SQ FT: 39,000
SALES (est): 4.3MM **Privately Held**
SIC: 7692 3599 Welding repair; machine shop, jobbing & repair

(G-15256)
FAIRMONT NURSING HOME INC
Also Called: Holly Hill Nursing Home
10190 Fairmount Rd (44065-9531)
P.O. Box 337 (44065-0337)
PHONE 440 338-8220
Fax: 440 338-5778
George Ohman, *President*
Ron Durkee, *Maint Spvr*
Amy Grubbs, *Human Res Dir*
Jamie Linstra, *Office Mgr*
Catherine Dahlem, *Nursing Dir*
EMP: 95
SQ FT: 28,000
SALES (est): 6.3MM **Privately Held**
SIC: 8052 8051 Intermediate care facilities; skilled nursing care facilities

(G-15257)
GEAUGA SAVINGS BANK (PA)
10800 Kinsman Rd (44065-8701)
PHONE 440 564-9441
Fax: 440 564-9185
James Kleinfelter, *President*
Tracy Dragolich, *COO*
Dell Duncan, *Exec VP*
Joan Lamarca, *Exec VP*
Robert Breslow, *Vice Pres*
EMP: 31
SALES (est): 12.9MM **Privately Held**
WEB: www.geaugasavings.com
SIC: 6036 Savings & loan associations, not federally chartered

(G-15258)
KUHNLE BROTHERS INC
Also Called: Kuhnle Bros Trucking
14905 Cross Creek Pkwy (44065-9788)
P.O. Box 375 (44065-0375)
PHONE 440 564-7168
Fax: 440 338-1427
Kim Taylor Kuhnle, *CEO*
Robert Russell, *Treasurer*
Thomas Kuhnle, *Admin Sec*
EMP: 150 EST: 1963
SQ FT: 20,000
SALES: 270MM **Privately Held**
SIC: 4213 4212 Trucking, except local; local trucking, without storage

(G-15259)
MULLETT COMPANY
14980 Cross Creek Pkwy (44065-9788)
P.O. Box 5000 (44065-0509)
PHONE 440 564-9000
Fax: 440 564-9003
Owen A Mullett, *President*
Steve Mullett, *General Mgr*
Daniel Gingerich, *Vice Pres*
Mike Lucarelli, *Project Mgr*
Dale Nelson, *Project Mgr*
EMP: 25
SQ FT: 6,800
SALES: 8MM **Privately Held**
WEB: www.mullettco.com
SIC: 1541 1542 Industrial buildings, new construction; renovation, remodeling & repairs: industrial buildings; commercial & office building, new construction; commercial & office buildings, renovation & repair

(G-15260)
PRECIOUS CARGO TRANSPORTATION
15050 Cross Creek Pkwy (44065-9726)
P.O. Box 23617, Chagrin Falls (44023-0617)
PHONE 440 564-8039
Fax: 440 564-8064
Richard Wervey, *President*
EMP: 30
SQ FT: 10,000
SALES: 500K **Privately Held**
SIC: 4141 4119 4131 Local bus charter service; limousine rental, with driver; intercity & rural bus transportation

(G-15261)
SCOT BURTON CONTRACTORS LLC
11330 Kinsman Rd (44065-9666)
PHONE 440 564-1011
Fax: 440 564-1088
Carol Nemeth, *Controller*
David Paulitsch,
Scot Paulitsch,
EMP: 40
SQ FT: 6,000
SALES (est): 7.8MM **Privately Held**
SIC: 1611 Highway & street paving contractor

(G-15262)
TW RECREATIONAL SERVICES INC
Also Called: Punderson Manor Resort
11755 Kinsman Rd (44065-9691)
P.O. Box 224 (44065-0224)
PHONE 440 564-9144
James Adamson, *President*
John Muller, *General Mgr*
Kate Patterson, *Financial Exec*
Mia Bell, *Manager*
Peter Donnelly, *Manager*
EMP: 40
SALES (est): 1.3MM **Privately Held**
WEB: www.pundersonmanorresort.com
SIC: 7011 Tourist camps, cabins, cottages & courts

(G-15263)
VAN NESS STONE INC
10500 Kinsman Rd (44065-9803)
P.O. Box 1000 (44065-0199)
PHONE 440 564-1111
Fax: 440 564-5172
Fred Van Ness, *President*
EMP: 28 EST: 1969
SQ FT: 9,120
SALES (est): 2.9MM **Privately Held**
WEB: www.vannesstone.com
SIC: 1741 Stone masonry

(G-15264)
WICKED WOODS GULF CLUB INC
Also Called: Wicked Woods Golf Club
14085 Ravenna Rd (44065-9511)
PHONE 440 564-7960
Fax: 440 564-9237
Edith Zimerman, *President*
Sam Zimerman, *Vice Pres*
EMP: 40
SALES (est): 909.3K **Privately Held**
SIC: 7992 Public golf courses

(G-15265)
XANTERRA PARKS & RESORTS INC
Also Called: Punderson Manor State Park
11755 Kinsman Rd (44065-9691)
P.O. Box 224 (44065-0224)
PHONE 440 564-9144
Mia Bell, *Branch Mgr*
EMP: 87
SALES (corp-wide): 414.9MM **Privately Held**
WEB: www.amfac.com
SIC: 7011 Resort hotel
HQ: Parks Xanterra & Resorts Inc
6312 S Fiddlers Green Cir 600n
Greenwood Village CO 80111
303 600-3400

Newcomerstown
Tuscarawas County

(G-15266)
DAVID BARBER CIVIC CENTER
1066 E State St (43832-1550)
P.O. Box 29 (43832-0029)
PHONE 740 498-4383
Heather Wells, *President*
EMP: 25
SALES (est): 380.1K **Privately Held**
SIC: 7999 Bingo hall

(G-15267)
EAGLE HARDWOODS INC
6138 Stonecreek Rd (43832-9162)
P.O. Box 96, Stone Creek (43840-0096)
PHONE 330 339-8838
Fax: 330 339-8838
Ronald D Furbay, *President*
Todd Luburgh, *General Mgr*
Loy E Wiggins Jr, *Vice Pres*
Jenny King, *Manager*
▼ **EMP:** 40
SQ FT: 1,344
SALES (est): 12.3MM **Privately Held**
SIC: 5031 Lumber: rough, dressed & finished

(G-15268)
EXPRESS PACKAGING OHIO INC (PA)
301 Enterprise Dr (43832-9240)
PHONE 740 498-4700
Fax: 740 498-6983
Pam Hartzler, *CEO*
Fred Hartzler, *Owner*
Donald Faulhaber, *Principal*
Dan Crone, *Project Mgr*
Janet Earley, *Traffic Mgr*
EMP: 520
SQ FT: 240,000
SALES (est): 93MM **Privately Held**
SIC: 7389 Packaging & labeling services

(G-15269)
GEORGE DARR
Also Called: Darr Farms
21284 Township Road 257 (43832-9660)
PHONE 740 498-5400
George Darr, *Owner*
Beverly Darr, *Co-Owner*
Michelle Patterson, *Sales Staff*
EMP: 40

SALES (est): 4.3MM **Privately Held**
SIC: 0161 0175 0116 0115 Vegetables & melons; deciduous tree fruits; soybeans; corn

(G-15270)
NEWCOMERSTOWN DEVELOPMENT INC
Also Called: Riverside Mnor Nrsing Rhab Ctr
1100 E State Rd (43832-9446)
PHONE 740 498-5165
Dwayne Shepherd, *Administration*
EMP: 125
SQ FT: 40,000
SALES: 6.5MM **Privately Held**
SIC: 6552 Subdividers & developers

(G-15271)
NEWCOMERSTOWN PROGRESS CORP
Also Called: Riverside Manor
1100 E State Rd (43832-9446)
PHONE 740 498-5165
Fax: 740 498-8064
Terry Overholser, *President*
Roger Bambeck, *Corp Secy*
Wayne Mortine, *Vice Pres*
Dwayne Shepherd, *Administration*
EMP: 130 EST: 1973
SQ FT: 35,000
SALES: 3.4MM **Privately Held**
WEB: www.riversidemanor.com
SIC: 8051 8049 Convalescent home with continuous nursing care; physical therapist

Newton Falls
Trumbull County

(G-15272)
AMERICAN LEGION POST
2025 E River Rd (44444)
PHONE 330 872-5475
Tom Greathouse, *Principal*
EMP: 25
SALES: 196.2K **Privately Held**
SIC: 8611 Business associations

(G-15273)
CADLE COMPANY II INC
100 N Center St (44444-1380)
PHONE 330 872-0918
Daniel C Cadle, *President*
Ruth Cadle, *Principal*
Greg Cadle, *Officer*
Marc Giampapa, *Officer*
Pam Hudy, *Officer*
EMP: 120
SQ FT: 5,000
SALES (est): 14MM **Privately Held**
SIC: 6211 Investment bankers

(G-15274)
HOOBERRY ASSOCIATES INC
Also Called: Laurie Ann Nursing Home
2200 Milton Blvd (44444-8746)
PHONE 330 872-1991
Fax: 330 872-1983
Doris Hooberry, *President*
Frank Veres, *Director*
Sharon Jones, *Admin Sec*
EMP: 60
SQ FT: 15,415
SALES: 3.8MM **Privately Held**
SIC: 8051 Convalescent home with continuous nursing care

(G-15275)
LAURIE ANN HOME HEALTH CARE
2200 Milton Blvd (44444-8746)
PHONE 330 872-7512
Katherine Kolesar, *Owner*
EMP: 38
SALES (est): 1MM **Privately Held**
SIC: 8082 Home health care services

(G-15276)
LEES ROBY INC
Also Called: Roby Lees Restaurant & Catrg
425 Ridge Rd (44444-1246)
PHONE 330 872-0983
Fax: 330 872-0983

GEOGRAPHIC SECTION

Niles - Trumbull County (G-15302)

Robert J Lee, *President*
Carolyn Lee, *Admin Sec*
EMP: 30
SALES (est): 1.1MM **Privately Held**
WEB: www.robylees.com
SIC: 5812 7299 Restaurant, family: independent; banquet hall facilities

(G-15277)
LIBERTY ASHTABULA HOLDINGS
Also Called: Holiday Inn
4185 State Route 5 (44444-9566)
PHONE..........................330 872-6000
Ketki Shah, *President*
Raxit Shah, *Corp Secy*
EMP: 25 **EST:** 1998
SALES (est): 1.1MM **Privately Held**
WEB: www.libertyg.com
SIC: 7011 Hotels & motels

(G-15278)
THE CADLE COMPANY (PA)
100 N Center St (44444-1380)
PHONE..........................330 872-0918
Daniel Cadle, *President*
Maria Hunt, *Managing Dir*
Victor Buente Jr, *Director*
Ruth Cadle, *Admin Sec*
EMP: 136
SQ FT: 25,000
SALES (est): 38MM **Privately Held**
SIC: 6211 6282 Mortgages, buying & selling; investment advice

(G-15279)
VENTURE PLASTICS INC
4325 Warren Ravenna Rd (44444-8736)
PHONE..........................330 872-6262
EMP: 25
SALES (corp-wide): 37.5MM **Privately Held**
SIC: 7389 Automobile recovery service
PA: Venture Plastics, Inc.
4000 Warren Rd
Newton Falls OH 44444
330 872-5774

Niles
Trumbull County

(G-15280)
ALTOBELLI REALESTATE (PA)
304 Vienna Ave (44446-2628)
PHONE..........................330 652-0200
Fax: 330 652-2484
Jerry Altobelli, *Owner*
EMP: 33
SALES (est): 1.6MM **Privately Held**
SIC: 6531 Real estate brokers & agents

(G-15281)
AMERICAN TITLE SERVICES INC
700 Youngstown Warren Rd (44446-3552)
PHONE..........................330 652-1609
Ralph Zuzolo Sr, *President*
Renee Zuzolo, *Vice Pres*
Ralph Zuzolo Jr, *Treasurer*
Christopher Zuzolo, *Admin Sec*
Ralph Susalow Sr,
EMP: 34 **EST:** 1975
SALES (est): 1.1MM **Privately Held**
WEB: www.americantitleservices.com
SIC: 6541 8111 6531 Title abstract offices; legal services; real estate agents & managers

(G-15282)
AT&T CORP
5412 Youngstown Warren Rd (44446-4910)
PHONE..........................330 505-4200
EMP: 46
SALES (corp-wide): 160.5B **Publicly Held**
SIC: 5065 4812 Telephone & telegraphic equipment; cellular telephone services
HQ: At&T Corp.
1 At&T Way
Bedminster NJ 07921
800 403-3302

(G-15283)
AUTUMN HILLS CARE CENTER INC
2565 Niles Vienna Rd (44446-4400)
PHONE..........................330 652-2053
Fax: 330 652-0112
Michael J Coats, *President*
Dr Carl R Gillette, *Vice Pres*
Bill Barth, *Purch Dir*
Bahaa Awadalla, *Director*
Jennifer Schiraldi, *Food Svc Dir*
EMP: 200
SQ FT: 37,000
SALES (est): 10MM **Privately Held**
WEB: www.autumnhills.com
SIC: 8051 Convalescent home with continuous nursing care

(G-15284)
BECDEL CONTROLS INCORPORATED
1869 Warren Ave (44446-1143)
PHONE..........................330 652-1386
Kerry Beck, *President*
John Schell III, *Vice Pres*
Maigen Wild, *Office Mgr*
EMP: 32
SALES (est): 3.2MM **Privately Held**
SIC: 1731 General electrical contractor

(G-15285)
C R G HEALTH CARE SYSTEMS
Also Called: Manor, The
2567 Niles Vienna Rd Ofc (44446-5406)
PHONE..........................330 498-8107
Cynthia Woodford, *Director*
EMP: 35
SALES (est): 1.1MM **Privately Held**
WEB: www.manoratautumnhills.com
SIC: 8082 8052 Home health care services; intermediate care facilities

(G-15286)
CAFARO CO
Also Called: Eastwood Mall Kids Club
5555 Youngstown Warren Rd (44446-4804)
PHONE..........................330 652-6980
Ken Koler, *Manager*
EMP: 25
SALES (est): 591.7K **Privately Held**
SIC: 8641 Youth organizations

(G-15287)
CARARO CO INC
Also Called: Eastwood Mall
492 Eastwood Mall (44446)
PHONE..........................330 652-6980
William M Cafaro, *Ch of Bd*
Ken Kollar, *President*
Anthony M Cafaro, *Vice Pres*
Patty Wiltrout, *Opers Mgr*
Joseph Nohra, *Treasurer*
EMP: 42
SALES (est): 2.6MM **Privately Held**
SIC: 6512 Commercial & industrial building operation

(G-15288)
CLEVELAND CLINIC FOUNDATION
650 Youngstown Warren Rd (44446-4356)
PHONE..........................330 505-2280
Guiyun Wu, *Manager*
EMP: 85
SALES (corp-wide): 8B **Privately Held**
SIC: 6733 Trusts
PA: The Cleveland Clinic Foundation
9500 Euclid Ave
Cleveland OH 44195
216 636-8335

(G-15289)
COATES CAR CARE INC
59 Youngstown Warren Rd (44446-4592)
PHONE..........................330 652-4180
Fax: 330 652-4191
James M Coates Sr, *President*
Jamie Williams, *Corp Secy*
James M Coates Jr, *Vice Pres*
EMP: 35
SQ FT: 38,000
SALES (est): 2.7MM **Privately Held**
SIC: 7539 7542 7549 Automotive repair shops; carwash, self-service; lubrication service, automotive; automotive customizing services, non-factory basis

(G-15290)
CONSUMER SUPPORT SERVICES INC
1254 Yngstwn Wrrn Rd B (44446)
PHONE..........................330 652-8800
Fax: 330 652-8883
Patty Beckley, *Exec Dir*
EMP: 146
SALES (corp-wide): 26.7MM **Privately Held**
SIC: 8082 Home health care services
PA: Consumer Support Services Inc
2040 Cherry Valley Rd # 1
Newark OH 43055
740 788-8257

(G-15291)
FAIRHAVEN SHELTERED WORKSHOP
6000 Youngstown Warren Rd (44446-4624)
PHONE..........................330 652-1116
Rocco Maiorca, *Branch Mgr*
EMP: 178
SALES (corp-wide): 4.5MM **Privately Held**
SIC: 8331 Sheltered workshop
PA: Fairhaven Sheltered Workshop
45 North Rd
Niles OH 44446
330 505-3644

(G-15292)
FAIRHAVEN SHELTERED WORKSHOP (PA)
45 North Rd (44446-1918)
PHONE..........................330 505-3644
Douglas Burkhardt, *Principal*
EMP: 205
SALES (est): 4.5MM **Privately Held**
SIC: 8331 Sheltered workshop

(G-15293)
FARMERS NATIONAL BANK
51 S Main St (44446-5011)
PHONE..........................330 544-7447
Fax: 330 530-4342
Frank Padenk, *President*
Kerry Pizzulo, *Financial Exec*
Desirae Monaco, *Branch Mgr*
EMP: 67
SALES (corp-wide): 104.5MM **Publicly Held**
SIC: 6021 6022 National commercial banks; state commercial banks
HQ: The Farmers National Bank Of Canfield
20 S Broad St
Canfield OH 44406
330 533-3341

(G-15294)
HOMES FOR KIDS OF OHIO INC
165 E Park Ave (44446-2352)
P.O. Box 683 (44446-0683)
PHONE..........................330 544-8005
Fax: 330 544-9379
Debra Wilson, *President*
EMP: 50
SALES: 4.6MM **Privately Held**
SIC: 8322 Children's aid society

(G-15295)
MARION PLAZA INC
Also Called: Eastwood Mall
5577 Youngstown Warren Rd (44446-4803)
P.O. Box 2186, Youngstown (44504-0186)
PHONE..........................330 747-2661
Vincent Morgione, *CEO*
John Sinclair, *Accountant*
Thom Sharp, *Manager*
EMP: 60
SALES: 950K **Privately Held**
SIC: 6531 Real estate managers

(G-15296)
MIENCORP INC
706 Robbins Ave (44446-2416)
P.O. Box 8726, Warren (44484-0726)
PHONE..........................330 978-8511
Greg Mientkiewicz, *President*
Steve Hareg, *Project Mgr*
EMP: 50
SALES: 6MM **Privately Held**
SIC: 1541 7389 Renovation, remodeling & repairs: industrial buildings; ; estimating service, construction

(G-15297)
MIKE COATES CNSTR CO INC
800 Summit Ave (44446-3695)
PHONE..........................330 652-0190
Fax: 330 652-3463
Michael J Coates Sr, *President*
Michael J Coates Jr, *Vice Pres*
Jim Huffman, *Project Mgr*
Joanne Coates, *Admin Sec*
EMP: 150
SQ FT: 15,000
SALES (est): 40.2MM **Privately Held**
SIC: 1541 1542 Institutional building construction; commercial & office building contractors; industrial buildings & warehouses

(G-15298)
NATIONAL VETERINARY ASSOC INC
1007 Youngstown Warren Rd (44446-4620)
PHONE..........................330 652-0055
Fax: 330 652-1932
EMP: 58
SALES (corp-wide): 756.2MM **Privately Held**
SIC: 0742 Animal hospital services, pets & other animal specialties
PA: National Veterinary Associates, Inc.
29229 Canwood St Ste 100
Agoura Hills CA 91301
805 777-7722

(G-15299)
NILES HISTORICAL SOCIETY
503 Brown St (44446-1443)
P.O. Box 368 (44446-0368)
PHONE..........................330 544-2143
Jessie Scott, *President*
Fred Kubli, *President*
Ann Townley, *President*
EMP: 51
SQ FT: 3,909
SALES: 27.7K **Privately Held**
SIC: 8699 Historical club

(G-15300)
NILES IRON & METAL COMPANY LLC (PA)
Also Called: Niles Scrap Iron & Metal Co
700 S Main St (44446-1372)
P.O. Box 166 (44446-0166)
PHONE..........................330 652-2262
Fax: 330 652-1240
Joel Clayman, *Vice Pres*
Sharna Larson, *Controller*
Gary Clayman, *Mng Member*
Michael Clayman, *Mng Member*
EMP: 50
SQ FT: 2,000
SALES (est): 33.4MM **Privately Held**
SIC: 5093 Ferrous metal scrap & waste

(G-15301)
NRG POWER MIDWEST LP
Also Called: Niles Generating Station
1047 Belmont Ave (44446-1356)
PHONE..........................330 505-4327
Rocky Tondo, *Branch Mgr*
EMP: 54 **Publicly Held**
SIC: 4911 Generation, electric power
HQ: Nrg Power Midwest Lp
1000 Main St
Houston TX 77002

(G-15302)
PALISDES BSBAL A CAL LTD PRTNR
Also Called: Mahoning Valley Scrappers
111 Eastwood Mall Blvd (44446-4841)
PHONE..........................330 505-0000

Niles - Trumbull County (G-15303)

Alan Levin, *Partner*
Andy Milovich, *General Mgr*
Duncan Matt, *COO*
Stephanie Fife, *Store Mgr*
Chris Sumner, *Accounts Exec*
EMP: 175 **EST:** 1994
SALES (est): 197.6K **Privately Held**
WEB: www.palisadesbaseball.com
SIC: 7941 Baseball club, professional & semi-professional

(G-15303)
PETSMART INC
5812 Youngstown Warren Rd (44446-4706)
PHONE..................330 544-1499
Fax: 330 544-1968
Jim Moroco, *Manager*
EMP: 30
SALES (corp-wide): 12.7B **Privately Held**
WEB: www.petsmart.com
SIC: 5999 0752 Pet food; animal specialty services
HQ: Petsmart, Inc.
19601 N 27th Ave
Phoenix AZ 85027
623 580-6100

(G-15304)
SEARS ROEBUCK AND CO
Also Called: Sears Auto Center
5555 Youngstown Warren Rd # 120 (44446-4899)
PHONE..................330 652-5128
Fax: 330 652-9630
Kathy Baca-Stehnach, *General Mgr*
EMP: 150
SALES (corp-wide): 16.7B **Publicly Held**
SIC: 7549 Automotive maintenance services
HQ: Sears, Roebuck And Co.
3333 Beverly Rd
Hoffman Estates IL 60179
847 286-2500

(G-15305)
SELECT STEEL INC
1825 Hunter Ave (44446-1672)
PHONE..................330 652-1756
Jeffrey A Gotthardt, *President*
Glenn E Gotthardt, *Corp Secy*
Danielle Tenney, *Manager*
EMP: 40
SQ FT: 76,000
SALES (est): 20.8MM **Privately Held**
WEB: www.selectstl.com
SIC: 5051 Steel

(G-15306)
SOUTHSIDE ENVMTL GROUP LLC
1806 Warren Ave (44446-1144)
P.O. Box 372 (44446-0372)
PHONE..................330 299-0027
Matthew J Schimley, *Principal*
EMP: 30
SALES (est): 3.8MM **Privately Held**
SIC: 8744 0781 ; landscape services

(G-15307)
TRAICHAL CONSTRUCTION COMPANY (PA)
Also Called: Warren Door
332 Plant St (44446-1895)
P.O. Box 70 (44446-0070)
PHONE..................800 255-3667
Fax: 330 652-6899
Edward Traichal, *President*
Nick Gorcheff, *Vice Pres*
Vince Roberts, *Purchasing*
Mike Lisko, *Controller*
Alfonso Roberts, *VP Sales*
EMP: 30
SQ FT: 15,000
SALES (est): 7.8MM **Privately Held**
WEB: www.plantia.com
SIC: 3442 1751 5199 5031 Metal doors; rolling doors for industrial buildings or warehouses, metal; window & door installation & erection; advertising specialties; doors & windows

(G-15308)
VERIZON BUSINESS GLOBAL LLC
5185 Youngstown Warren Rd (44446-4906)
PHONE..................330 505-2368
Carolyn Smolko, *Principal*
EMP: 49
SALES (corp-wide): 126B **Publicly Held**
SIC: 4813 Long distance telephone communications
HQ: Verizon Business Global Llc
22001 Loudoun County Pkwy
Ashburn VA 20147
703 886-5600

(G-15309)
W T C S A HEADSTART NILES CTR
Also Called: Casaro Headstart
309 N Rhodes Ave (44446-3821)
PHONE..................330 652-0338
Fax: 330 652-0805
James W Abicht, *President*
Jeanne Wall, *Director*
EMP: 40
SALES (est): 442.9K **Privately Held**
SIC: 8299 8399 Educational services; social services

(G-15310)
WEST CORPORATION
5185 Youngstown Warren Rd (44446-4906)
PHONE..................330 574-0510
Fax: 330 574-0533
James Evans, *Branch Mgr*
EMP: 269
SALES (corp-wide): 2.2B **Privately Held**
SIC: 7389 Automobile recovery service
HQ: West Corporation
11808 Miracle Hills Dr
Omaha NE 68154

(G-15311)
WESTERN RESERVE MECHANICAL INC
3041 S Main St (44446-1313)
PHONE..................330 652-3888
Fax: 330 652-6365
Linda Leger, *President*
Mark Leger, *President*
Larry Moore, *Vice Pres*
Bill Williams, *Project Engr*
Mike Jewell, *Manager*
EMP: 50
SALES (est): 8.9MM **Privately Held**
WEB: www.wrmech.com
SIC: 1711 Mechanical contractor

North Baltimore
Wood County

(G-15312)
CSX TRANSPORTATION INC
17000 Deshler Rd (45872-8719)
PHONE..................419 257-1225
Jaime Reyes, *Business Anlyst*
Steven M Loewengart, *Branch Mgr*
Brendan Slattery, *Manager*
EMP: 36
SALES (corp-wide): 11.4B **Publicly Held**
SIC: 4011 Railroads, line-haul operating
HQ: Csx Transportation, Inc.
500 Water St
Jacksonville FL 32202
904 359-3100

(G-15313)
HANCOCK-WOOD ELECTRIC COOP INC (PA)
1399 Business Park Dr S (45872-8716)
P.O. Box 190 (45872-0190)
PHONE..................419 257-3241
Fax: 419 257-3024
George Walton, *President*
William Barnhart, *VP Opers*
Marcia Jones, *VP Finance*
Ryan Marquette, *Info Tech Mgr*
EMP: 35
SALES: 44.3MM **Privately Held**
WEB: www.hwelectric.com
SIC: 4911 Electric services

(G-15314)
HPJ INDUSTRIES INC (PA)
510 W Broadway St (45872-9521)
P.O. Box 860, Bowling Green (43402-0860)
PHONE..................419 278-1000
Chris Beck, *CEO*
Scott M Rothweiler, *President*
Megan Willing, *Controller*
Tosha Kern, *Sales Mgr*
EMP: 90
SALES (est): 14.1MM **Privately Held**
SIC: 4953 Recycling, waste materials

(G-15315)
POLYONE CORPORATION
733 E Water St (45872-1434)
P.O. Box 247 (45872-0247)
PHONE..................440 930-1000
Pete Jacob, *Vice Pres*
Peter Jacobs, *Plant Mgr*
Pete Laughlin, *Purchasing*
Mike Brandenburg, *Sales Staff*
Charles Geicher, *Info Tech Mgr*
EMP: 80 **Publicly Held**
WEB: www.polyone.com
SIC: 2821 5169 3087 Vinyl resins; synthetic resins, rubber & plastic materials; custom compound purchased resins
PA: Polyone Corporation
33587 Walker Rd
Avon Lake OH 44012

(G-15316)
USIC LOCATING SERVICES LLC
12769 Eagleville Rd B (45872-9656)
PHONE..................419 874-9988
Fax: 419 874-9988
EMP: 36 **Privately Held**
SIC: 1623 Water/Sewer/Utility Construction
HQ: Usic Locating Services, Llc
9045 River Rd Ste 300
Indianapolis IN 46240
317 575-7800

North Bend
Hamilton County

(G-15317)
ASTON OAKS GOLF CLUB
1 Aston Oaks Dr (45052-9621)
PHONE..................513 467-0070
Fax: 513 941-8148
Andrew Macke, *Vice Pres*
EMP: 40
SALES (est): 1.3MM **Privately Held**
WEB: www.astonoaks.com
SIC: 7992 Public golf courses

(G-15318)
DYNEGY INC
11021 Brower Rd (45052-9755)
PHONE..................513 467-4900
Chris Osterbrink, *General Mgr*
Jeff Foglesong, *Technical Mgr*
Tim Thiemann, *Manager*
Josh Gooding, *Manager*
Phil Williamson, *Manager*
EMP: 205
SALES (corp-wide): 4.8B **Publicly Held**
SIC: 4911
PA: Dynegy Inc.
601 Travis St Ste 1400
Houston TX 77002
713 507-6400

(G-15319)
MARTIN MARIETTA MATERIALS INC
Martin Marietta Aggregates
10905 Us 50 (45052-9730)
PHONE..................513 353-1400
Bernie Jelen, *Branch Mgr*
EMP: 55 **Publicly Held**
WEB: www.martinmarietta.com
SIC: 1422 Crushed & broken limestone
PA: Martin Marietta Materials Inc
2710 Wycliff Rd
Raleigh NC 27607

North Canton
Stark County

(G-15320)
ADVANTAGE HOME HEALTH SVCS INC
7951 Pittsburg Ave Nw (44720-5669)
PHONE..................330 491-8161
Kun Woo Nam, *President*
Maria N Swisher, *Vice Pres*
EMP: 32
SALES (est): 2.8MM **Privately Held**
SIC: 8082 Home health care services

(G-15321)
ADVANTAGE TANK LINES INC (HQ)
4366 Mount Pleasant St Nw (44720-5446)
PHONE..................330 491-0474
Dennis Nash, *President*
Dave Michelsky, *General Mgr*
Douglas Allen, *COO*
Bill Downey, *Exec VP*
Robert Schurer, *Exec VP*
EMP: 35
SALES (est): 29.6MM
SALES (corp-wide): 2.7B **Privately Held**
WEB: www.advantagemgmtgroup.com
SIC: 4213 Trucking, except local
PA: The Kenan Advantage Group Inc
4366 Mount Pleasant St Nw
North Canton OH 44720
877 999-2524

(G-15322)
AKRON-CANTON REGIONAL AIRPORT
Also Called: Akron Canton Airport
5400 Lauby Rd Ste 9 (44720-1598)
PHONE..................330 499-4059
Fax: 330 499-5176
Richard McQueen, *President*
Kristie Vanauken, *Senior VP*
Kristie Van Auken, *Mktg Dir*
Kevin Ripple, *Manager*
Linda Decker, *Executive Asst*
EMP: 48
SQ FT: 150,000
SALES (est): 9MM **Privately Held**
WEB: www.akroncantonairport.com
SIC: 4581 8721 Airport; accounting, auditing & bookkeeping

(G-15323)
ALL ABOUT KIDS DAYCARE N
6199 Frank Ave Nw (44720-7225)
PHONE..................330 494-8700
Melvin Clark, *President*
Julie Lenox, *Principal*
EMP: 26
SALES (est): 436.2K **Privately Held**
SIC: 8351 Child day care services

(G-15324)
AMERIDIAL INC
4535 Strausser St Nw (44720-6979)
PHONE..................330 479-8044
James McGeorge, *Branch Mgr*
EMP: 70
SALES (corp-wide): 40MM **Privately Held**
SIC: 7389 Telemarketing services
PA: Ameridial, Inc.
4535 Strausser St Nw
North Canton OH 44720
330 497-4888

(G-15325)
AMERIDIAL INC (PA)
4535 Strausser St Nw (44720-6979)
PHONE..................330 497-4888
Fax: 330 497-9518
James McGeorge, *President*
Matt McGeorge, *Exec VP*
Michael McCarthy, *Vice Pres*
Terri Peterman, *Vice Pres*
Topaz Tolloti, *Vice Pres*
EMP: 429
SQ FT: 3,000
SALES: 40MM **Privately Held**
WEB: www.ameridial.com
SIC: 7389 Telemarketing services

GEOGRAPHIC SECTION
North Canton - Stark County (G-15348)

(G-15326)
ARTHUR MIDDLETON CAPITAL HOLDN (PA)
8000 Freedom Ave Nw (44720-6912)
PHONE.................330 966-9000
Rodney L Napier, *Ch of Bd*
Dean Petersen, *Vice Pres*
Dan Calvo, *Project Mgr*
Deborah Algeri, *Treasurer*
Dean Peterson, *Controller*
EMP: 47
SALES (est): 63.2MM **Privately Held**
SIC: 8111 8721 8741 Legal services; accounting, auditing & bookkeeping; administrative management

(G-15327)
AWP INC (PA)
Also Called: Area Wide Protective
4244 Mount Pleasant St Nw # 100 (44720-5469)
PHONE.................330 677-7401
Fax: 330 644-0027
William A Fink, *President*
John Sypek, *President*
Jack Peak, *Exec VP*
Doug Naeding, *Vice Pres*
James Patton, *Opers Mgr*
EMP: 600
SQ FT: 5,500
SALES (est): 188.3MM **Privately Held**
SIC: 7381 Security guard service

(G-15328)
CAVENEY INC
Also Called: SERVPRO
7801 Cleveland Ave Nw (44720-5657)
PHONE.................330 497-4600
Fax: 330 497-1732
John Caveney, *President*
Linda L Caveney, *Treasurer*
Lori Colen, *Executive*
EMP: 85
SQ FT: 5,200
SALES (est): 3.1MM **Privately Held**
SIC: 7349 Building maintenance services

(G-15329)
CPI - CNSTR POLYMERS INC (PA)
7576 Freedom Ave Nw (44720-6902)
PHONE.................330 861-5200
Dirk Benthien, *CEO*
Jack Demita, *COO*
▲ **EMP:** 27
SQ FT: 35,000
SALES (est): 4.3MM **Privately Held**
WEB: www.cpifoam.com
SIC: 5084 Industrial machinery & equipment

(G-15330)
CPX CANTON AIRPORT LLC
Also Called: Embassy Stes Akrn-Canton Arprt
7883 Freedom Ave Nw (44720-6907)
PHONE.................330 305-0500
Gordon Snyder, *President*
EMP: 110 **EST:** 2015
SQ FT: 129,291
SALES (est): 1MM **Privately Held**
SIC: 7011 Hotels

(G-15331)
CUTLER REAL ESTATE
203 Applegrove St Nw (44720-1613)
PHONE.................330 499-9922
Richard Motts, *Branch Mgr*
EMP: 63 **Privately Held**
SIC: 6531 Real estate agents & managers
PA: Cutler Real Estate
  4618 Dressler Rd Nw
  Canton OH 44718

(G-15332)
DESIGN RSTRTION RECONSTRUCTION
4305 Mount Pleasant St Nw # 103 (44720-5429)
PHONE.................330 563-0010
Ray Santiago, *President*
Greg Campbell, *Vice Pres*
Mike Rankin, *Treasurer*
Randa Tettar, *Manager*
Don Schultz, *Shareholder*
EMP: 38
SQ FT: 9,000
SALES: 3MM **Privately Held**
WEB: www.designrestoration.net
SIC: 1799 Post-disaster renovations

(G-15333)
DOCUMENT CONCEPTS INC
Also Called: Office Furniture Solution
607 S Main St A (44720-3065)
PHONE.................330 575-5685
Fax: 330 471-3109
Tim Barr, *President*
Terry A Moore, *Admin Sec*
EMP: 30
SQ FT: 15,000
SALES (est): 3.9MM **Privately Held**
WEB: www.document-concepts.com
SIC: 7389 Printers' services: folding, collating

(G-15334)
EMERGENCY MEDICAL TRANSPORT
Also Called: Emt Ambulance
7100 Whipple Ave Nw Ste A (44720-7167)
PHONE.................330 484-4000
Kenneth J Joseph, *President*
William Swoyer, *Manager*
Bill Soplata, *Technology*
EMP: 88
SQ FT: 5,000
SALES (est): 4.9MM **Privately Held**
WEB: www.emtambulance.com
SIC: 4119 8621 Ambulance service; professional membership organizations

(G-15335)
EMLAB P&K LLC (DH)
Also Called: Test America
4101 Shuffel St Nw # 200 (44720-6900)
PHONE.................330 497-9396
Fax: 650 829-5852
Rachel Brydon Jannetta, *President*
Heather Collins Villemaire, *CFO*
Sicilia Bertoldi, *Controller*
Michael Berg, *Director*
Jenny L Stewart, *Admin Sec*
EMP: 69
SALES (est): 9.3MM
SALES (corp-wide): 609.6MM **Privately Held**
WEB: www.emlabpk.com
SIC: 8734 Testing laboratories
HQ: Testamerica Holdings, Inc.
  4101 Shuffel St Nw
  North Canton OH 44720
  330 497-9396

(G-15336)
EYE CENTERS OF OHIO INC
6407 Frank Ave Nw (44720-7263)
PHONE.................330 966-1111
John Malik, *Manager*
EMP: 50
SALES (est): 3.2MM
SALES (corp-wide): 4.7MM **Privately Held**
WEB: www.eyecentersofohio.com
SIC: 8011 Ophthalmologist
PA: Eye Centers Of Ohio Inc
  1330 Mercy Dr Nw Ste 310
  Canton OH 44708
  330 489-1441

(G-15337)
FISHER FOODS MARKETING INC (PA)
4855 Frank Ave Nw (44720-7425)
PHONE.................330 497-3000
Jeffrey A Fisher, *President*
Jack B Fisher, *Vice Pres*
Debbie Grasse, *Buyer*
Joe Pileggi, *Buyer*
Melanie Veigel, *Accounting Mgr*
EMP: 200
SQ FT: 100,000
SALES (est): 106.5MM **Privately Held**
WEB: www.fisherfoods.com
SIC: 5411 8741 Supermarkets, independent; management services

(G-15338)
FRED OLIVIERI CONSTRUCTION CO (PA)
6315 Promway Ave Nw (44720-7695)
PHONE.................330 494-1007
Alfred A Olivieri, *CEO*
Dean L Olivieri, *President*
Jim Segrest, *Superintendent*
Edward French, *Vice Pres*
Virginia C Olivieri, *Vice Pres*
▲ **EMP:** 153
SQ FT: 12,600
SALES (est): 87.5MM **Privately Held**
WEB: www.fredolivieri.com
SIC: 1542 Commercial & office building, new construction

(G-15339)
GBS CORP (PA)
Also Called: GBS Printech Solutions
7233 Freedom Ave Nw (44720-7123)
P.O. Box 2340, Canton (44720-0340)
PHONE.................330 494-5330
Fax: 330 497-6943
Eugene Calabria, *President*
Ryan Hamsher, *General Mgr*
Steve Hoy, *Managing Dir*
Laurence Merriman, *Chairman*
Jackie Davison, *Vice Pres*
▲ **EMP:** 150 **EST:** 1971
SQ FT: 115,000
SALES (est): 72.8MM **Privately Held**
WEB: www.gbscorp.com
SIC: 5045 5112 2675 2672 Computers, peripherals & software; business forms; folders, filing, die-cut: made from purchased materials; labels (unprinted), gummed: made from purchased materials; tape, pressure sensitive: made from purchased materials; manifold business forms; commercial printing

(G-15340)
GRAPHIC ENTERPRISES INC
3874 Highland Park Nw (44720-4538)
PHONE.................800 553-6616
Fax: 330 494-5481
Brian Frank, *President*
Michael Brigner, *VP Opers*
Rick Plant, *Facilities Mgr*
Kim Allen, *Purch Dir*
Yvonne Brown, *CFO*
▲ **EMP:** 54 **EST:** 2003
SQ FT: 10,000
SALES (est): 31.8MM
SALES (corp-wide): 52.8MM **Privately Held**
WEB: www.geiohio.com
SIC: 5044 Photocopy machines
PA: Visual Edge Technology, Inc.
  3874 Highland Park Nw
  Canton OH 44720
  330 494-9694

(G-15341)
GRAPHIC ENTPS OFF SLUTIONS INC
3874 Highland Park Nw (44720-4538)
PHONE.................800 553-6616
Austin Vanchieri, *CEO*
Brian Frank, *President*
Yvonne Brown, *CFO*
Debra Pyles, *Human Resources*
Debra Yeles, *Human Resources*
EMP: 75
SALES (est): 17.9MM **Privately Held**
SIC: 5044 Copying equipment

(G-15342)
HABEGGER CORPORATION
7580 Whipple Ave Nw (44720-6922)
PHONE.................330 499-4328
EMP: 31
SALES (corp-wide): 91.9MM **Privately Held**
SIC: 5074 Plumbing & hydronic heating supplies
PA: The Habegger Corporation
  4995 Winton Rd
  Cincinnati OH 45232
  513 853-6644

(G-15343)
HAINES & COMPANY INC (PA)
Also Called: Criss Cross Directories
8050 Freedom Ave Nw (44720-6985)
P.O. Box 2117 (44720-0117)
PHONE.................330 494-9111
Fax: 330 497-5507
William K Haines Jr, *Ch of Bd*
Leonard W Haines, *Principal*
Harriett E Jones, *Principal*
Delores Ball, *Treasurer*
Kerry Keen, *Broker*
▲ **EMP:** 130 **EST:** 1932
SQ FT: 20,000
SALES (est): 34MM **Privately Held**
WEB: www.haines.com
SIC: 2741 7331 2752 2759 Directories: publishing & printing; mailing list compilers; commercial printing, lithographic; commercial printing

(G-15344)
HOME SAVINGS BANK
600 S Main St (44720-3031)
PHONE.................330 499-1900
Rick Hull, *Manager*
EMP: 77
SALES (corp-wide): 118.7MM **Publicly Held**
SIC: 6036 Savings & loan associations, not federally chartered
HQ: Home Savings Bank
  275 W Federal St
  Youngstown OH 44503
  330 742-0500

(G-15345)
INDIAN NATION INC
1051 Skyline Cir Se (44709-1154)
PHONE.................740 532-6143
Ron Brammer, *Principal*
EMP: 50
SALES (est): 2.9MM **Privately Held**
SIC: 1794 7353 Excavation work; heavy construction equipment rental

(G-15346)
J & C AMBULANCE SERVICES INC (PA)
Also Called: Life Care Medical Services
7100 Whipple Ave Nw Ste G (44720-7167)
PHONE.................330 899-0022
James Caplinger, *President*
Tracy Kalmar, *Opers Mgr*
Rick Reed, *Opers Staff*
Michelle Skinner, *Manager*
Gary Lawrence, *Officer*
EMP: 180 **EST:** 1999
SQ FT: 4,500
SALES: 10.9MM **Privately Held**
SIC: 4119 Ambulance service

(G-15347)
KAISER FOUNDATION HOSPITALS
Also Called: North Canton Medical Offices
4914 Portage Rd (44720)
PHONE.................800 524-7377
EMP: 593
SALES (corp-wide): 82.6B **Privately Held**
SIC: 8011 Offices & clinics of medical doctors
HQ: Kaiser Foundation Hospitals Inc
  1 Kaiser Plz
  Oakland CA 94612
  510 271-6611

(G-15348)
KARCHER GROUP INC
5590 Lauby Rd Ste 8 (44720-1500)
PHONE.................330 493-6141
Fax: 330 493-5756
Geoff Karcher, *President*
James Golden, *Vice Pres*
Todd Whetstone, *Controller*
Aaron Lehman, *Marketing Staff*
Leanne Wicks, *Marketing Staff*
EMP: 42
SALES (est): 5MM **Privately Held**
WEB: www.tkg.com
SIC: 7374 Computer graphics service

North Canton - Stark County

(G-15349)
KENAN ADVANTAGE GROUP INC (PA)
4366 Mount Pleasant St Nw (44720-5446)
PHONE...................877 999-2524
Dennis Nash, *CEO*
Bruce Blaise, *President*
Calvin Kniffin, *General Mgr*
Tony Moenich, *Regional Mgr*
Bill Wilson, *Regional Mgr*
EMP: 114
SQ FT: 86,500
SALES (est): 2.7B **Privately Held**
SIC: 4213 4212 Trucking, except local; liquid petroleum transport, non-local; local trucking, without storage; petroleum haulage, local

(G-15350)
KIRK KEY INTERLOCK COMPANY LLC
9048 Meridian Cir Nw (44720-8387)
PHONE...................330 833-8223
Fax: 330 833-1528
Scott Life, *President*
Jim Pettigrew, *Prdtn Mgr*
Tom Baer, *Production*
Matt Define, *Sales Mgr*
Greg Wise, *Sales Staff*
▲ **EMP:** 47
SQ FT: 26,000
SALES (est): 13.4MM
SALES (corp-wide): 1.2B **Privately Held**
WEB: www.kirkkey.com
SIC: 3429 5063 Keys, locks & related hardware; electrical apparatus & equipment
PA: Halma Public Limited Company
   Misbourne Court
   Amersham BUCKS HP7 0
   149 472-1111

(G-15351)
LEMMON & LEMMON INC
1201 S Main St Ste 200 (44720-4283)
PHONE...................330 497-8686
Fax: 330 497-8899
William J Lemmon, *President*
Stephen Lemmon, *Vice Pres*
Molly Johanning, *Manager*
EMP: 160
SQ FT: 9,600
SALES (est): 15.3MM **Privately Held**
WEB: www.lemmonandlemmon.com
SIC: 1521 1522 New construction, single-family houses; apartment building construction; condominium construction

(G-15352)
MEDICAL TRANSPORT SYSTEMS INC
Also Called: Stark Summit Ambulance
909 Las Olas Blvd Nw (44720-6130)
PHONE...................330 837-9818
Ronald Cordray, *President*
Karla McClaskey, *Vice Pres*
Jeffrey Finkelstein, *Treasurer*
Arthur Leb, *Admin Sec*
EMP: 100 **EST:** 1978
SALES (est): 4.8MM **Privately Held**
WEB: www.starksummit.com
SIC: 4119 Local passenger transportation; ambulance service

(G-15353)
MICROPLEX INC
7568 Whipple Ave Nw (44720-6922)
PHONE...................330 498-0600
Fax: 330 498-0433
Valerie Walters, *President*
Peter Dankowski, *Vice Pres*
John Walters, *Vice Pres*
Jo A Schwenning, *Purch Agent*
April Harsha, *Buyer*
EMP: 30
SQ FT: 12,000
SALES (est): 6.2MM **Privately Held**
WEB: www.microplex.com
SIC: 3496 3679 5045 Cable, uninsulated wire; made from purchased wire; harness assemblies for electronic use: wire or cable; computer peripheral equipment

(G-15354)
MIDWEST COMMUNICATIONS INC
Also Called: Group Midwest
4721 Eagle St Nw (44720-7083)
PHONE...................800 229-4756
Fax: 330 244-2413
George K Dixon, *CEO*
Brian Stimer, *President*
Tom Lyon, *Vice Pres*
EMP: 92
SQ FT: 160,000
SALES (est): 10.2MM **Privately Held**
WEB: www.groupmidwest.com
SIC: 5065 Telephone equipment

(G-15355)
MIDWEST DIGITAL INC
4721 Eagle St Nw (44720-7083)
PHONE...................330 966-4744
Brian Stimer, *President*
EMP: 65
SALES: 19MM **Privately Held**
SIC: 5065 Communication equipment

(G-15356)
MISTRAS GROUP INC
413 Applegrove St Nw (44720-1617)
PHONE...................330 244-1541
EMP: 54 **Publicly Held**
SIC: 8711 Engineering services
PA: Mistras Group, Inc.
   195 Clarksville Rd Ste 2
   Princeton Junction NJ 08550

(G-15357)
NEXTEL PARTNERS OPERATING CORP
Also Called: Sprint
6791 Strip Ave Nw (44720-7093)
PHONE...................330 305-1365
EMP: 30
SALES (corp-wide): 78.3B **Publicly Held**
WEB: www.nymobilellc.com
SIC: 4812 Cellular telephone services
HQ: Nextel Partners Operating Corp.
   6200 Sprint Pkwy
   Overland Park KS 66251
   800 829-0965

(G-15358)
NORTHSTAR ASPHALT INC
7345 Sunset Strip Ave Nw (44720-7040)
P.O. Box 2646 (44720-0646)
PHONE...................330 497-0936
Howard J Wenger, *President*
EMP: 45
SQ FT: 10,000
SALES (est): 4.2MM **Privately Held**
SIC: 1771 1611 Blacktop (asphalt) work; highway & street construction

(G-15359)
ORCHARD PHRM SVCS LLC
7835 Freedom Ave Nw (44720-6907)
PHONE...................330 491-4200
Bruce Scott, *President*
John Baker Sr, *Vice Pres*
Ray Hesketh, *Controller*
Martin Mount, *Asst Controller*
John Sedlak, *Info Tech Dir*
EMP: 112
SALES (est): 53.8MM **Privately Held**
SIC: 5122 Pharmaceuticals

(G-15360)
OREILLY AUTOMOTIVE INC
1233 N Main St (44720-1925)
PHONE...................330 494-0042
Phillip Oreilly, *Branch Mgr*
EMP: 69 **Publicly Held**
SIC: 5531 5013 Batteries, automotive & truck; automotive supplies & parts
PA: O'reilly Automotive, Inc.
   233 S Patterson Ave
   Springfield MO 65802

(G-15361)
PRIME PRODATA INC
800 N Main St (44720-2011)
PHONE...................330 497-2578
Susan Caghan, *President*
EMP: 30

SALES (est): 4.3MM **Privately Held**
SIC: 7379 Computer related consulting services

(G-15362)
PROVANTAGE LLC
7576 Freedom Ave Nw (44720-6902)
PHONE...................330 494-3781
Arno Zirngibl, *CEO*
Alison Carey, *General Mgr*
Scott Dibattista, *COO*
Leda Zamilski, *Purch Dir*
Carol Baker, *Purch Mgr*
▼ **EMP:** 60
SQ FT: 30,000
SALES: 225MM **Privately Held**
WEB: www.provantage.com
SIC: 5961 5719 5734 5045 Computer software, mail order; computers & peripheral equipment, mail order; housewares; computer software & accessories; computers, peripherals & software

(G-15363)
QUESTAR SOLUTIONS LLC
Also Called: Questar, Inc.
7948 Freedom Ave Nw (44720-6910)
PHONE...................330 966-2070
Fax: 330 966-9503
Kevin Gray, *General Mgr*
Andy Good, *Opers Mgr*
Taneal Eddy, *Sales Associate*
Nate Clark, *Manager*
Ed Devine, *Manager*
▼ **EMP:** 26
SQ FT: 20,000
SALES (est): 26.7MM
SALES (corp-wide): 1.8B **Privately Held**
WEB: www.questarusa.com
SIC: 5199 5084 Packaging materials; pollution control equipment, air (environmental); safety equipment
HQ: Industrial Container Services Llc
   2400 Maitland Center Pkwy
   Maitland FL 32751
   800 273-3786

(G-15364)
REPUBLIC TELCOM WORLDWIDE LLC
8000 Freedom Ave Nw (44720-6912)
PHONE...................330 244-8285
Monica Wallace, *Branch Mgr*
EMP: 52 **Privately Held**
SIC: 7389 Telephone services
HQ: Republic Telcom Worldwide, Llc
   3939 Everhard Rd Nw
   Canton OH 44709

(G-15365)
SCHROER PROPERTIES INC (PA)
Also Called: Altercare of Navarre
339 E Maple St (44720-2593)
P.O. Box 2279 (44720-0279)
PHONE...................330 498-8200
Gerald F Schroer, *President*
Dennis Conley, *COO*
Suzanne F Schroer, *Treasurer*
INA Lauer, *Program Dir*
Denise Stargen, *Assistant*
EMP: 76
SQ FT: 30,000
SALES (est): 11.9MM **Privately Held**
SIC: 8051 Skilled nursing care facilities

(G-15366)
SCI DIRECT LLC
7800 Whipple Ave Nw (44720-6928)
PHONE...................330 494-5504
EMP: 570 **EST:** 1968
SQ FT: 170,000
SALES (est): 13.5MM **Privately Held**
SIC: 8742 Management Consulting Services

(G-15367)
SPECTRUM ORTHPEDICS INC CANTON (PA)
7442 Frank Ave Nw (44720-7022)
PHONE...................330 455-5367
Mark Shepard, *President*
Dr Robert Manns, *Corp Secy*
P W Welch, *Vice Pres*
Steven Coss, *Orthopedist*

James T Viole, *Orthopedist*
EMP: 45
SQ FT: 6,000
SALES (est): 6.4MM **Privately Held**
WEB: www.spectrumortho.com
SIC: 8011 Orthopedic physician; surgeon

(G-15368)
STARK INDUSTRIAL LLC
5103 Stoneham Rd (44720-1540)
P.O. Box 3030 (44720-8030)
PHONE...................330 493-9773
Beth Miller, *Purch Agent*
Drew Prine, *Technical Mgr*
Ed Ginther, *Engineer*
Jonathan Wilkof, *Design Engr*
Rosetta Wilkof, *CFO*
▼ **EMP:** 40
SQ FT: 25,000
SALES (est): 24.2MM **Privately Held**
WEB: www.starkindustrial.com
SIC: 5085 3545 Industrial supplies; machine tool accessories

(G-15369)
STOLLE MACHINERY COMPANY LLC
4337 Excel St (44720-6995)
PHONE...................330 453-2015
Jim McClung, *Branch Mgr*
EMP: 58
SALES (corp-wide): 262.3MM **Privately Held**
SIC: 5084 Industrial machinery & equipment
PA: Stolle Machinery Company, Llc
   6949 S Potomac St
   Centennial CO 80112
   303 708-9044

(G-15370)
SUNPRO INC (HQ)
Also Called: Enviroserve
7640 Whipple Ave Nw (44720-6924)
PHONE...................330 966-0910
Fax: 330 966-1954
M James Kozak, *President*
Kenneth G Kozak, *Vice Pres*
Jack E Lewis, *Vice Pres*
Michael Davrd, *Project Mgr*
Matt Mendenha, *Opers Mgr*
EMP: 57
SQ FT: 7,200
SALES: 14.7MM
SALES (corp-wide): 1B **Privately Held**
WEB: www.sunproservices.com
SIC: 8748 1731 8744 Environmental consultant; electrical work;
PA: Savage Companies
   901 W Legacy Center Way
   Midvale UT 84047
   801 944-6600

(G-15371)
SURGERE INC
5399 Lauby Rd Ste 200 (44720-1554)
PHONE...................330 526-7971
William J Wappler, *President*
David Hampton, *Vice Pres*
Timothy Nickel, *Vice Pres*
Michael Wappler, *Manager*
Michael Curran, *Sr Software Eng*
EMP: 26
SQ FT: 3,000
SALES (est): 3.7MM **Privately Held**
SIC: 8742 Management consulting services

(G-15372)
TESTAMERICA LABORATORIES INC (DH)
4101 Shuffel St Nw (44720-6900)
P.O. Box 2912 (44720-0912)
PHONE...................800 456-9396
Rachel Brydon Jannetta, *CEO*
Chris Oprandi, *General Mgr*
Patrick Omeara, *Project Mgr*
Heather Collins Villemaire, *CFO*
Dorothy Moser, *Controller*
EMP: 139
SALES (est): 495.1MM
SALES (corp-wide): 609.6MM **Privately Held**
WEB: www.stl-inc.com
SIC: 8734 Soil analysis

HQ: Testamerica Holdings, Inc.
4101 Shuffel St Nw
North Canton OH 44720
330 497-9396

(G-15373)
TIGER 2010 LLC (PA)
6929 Portage St Nw (44720-6535)
PHONE...................................330 236-5100
Anthony T Ferrante,
Debra L Ferrante,
EMP: 31 EST: 2010
SQ FT: 2,400
SALES (est): 1.4MM **Privately Held**
WEB: www.homesaroundohio.com
SIC: 6531 Real estate agent, residential

(G-15374)
TIMKEN CORPORATION (DH)
4500 Mount Pleasant St Nw (44720-5450)
P.O. Box 477905, Broadview Heights (44147-7905)
PHONE...................................330 471-3378
Fax: 330 471-3810
Richard G Kyle, *CEO*
Nancy Noeske, *President*
William R Burkhart, *Exec VP*
Christopher A Coughlin, *Exec VP*
Ronald J Myers, *Vice Pres*
◆ **EMP:** 50
SALES (est): 232MM
SALES (corp-wide): 3B **Publicly Held**
WEB: www.timken.com
SIC: 5085 5051 Bearings, bushings, wheels & gears; aluminum bars, rods, ingots, sheets, pipes, plates, etc.
HQ: Timken Us Llc
336 Mechanic St
Lebanon NH 03766
603 443-5217

(G-15375)
TRI-STATE AMBLNCE PRAMEDIC SVC
7100 Whipple Ave Nw Ste C (44720-7167)
PHONE...................................304 233-2331
Fax: 304 233-2647
Robert Ritner, *Director*
EMP: 30
SQ FT: 3,000
SALES (est): 860.3K **Privately Held**
SIC: 4119 Ambulance service

(G-15376)
TSG RESOURCES INC
339 E Maple St Ste 110 (44720-2593)
PHONE...................................330 498-8200
Dennis Conley, *CEO*
EMP: 3609
SALES (est): 5.6MM **Privately Held**
SIC: 8742 Business planning & organizing services

(G-15377)
ULTIMATE JETCHARTERS LLC
Also Called: Ultimate Air Center
6061 W Airport Dr (44720-1447)
PHONE...................................330 497-3344
John Gordon, *CEO*
Jeff Moneypenny, *Vice Pres*
Dave Parsons, *Opers Staff*
Les Kuglics, *Buyer*
Michael Degirolamo, *CFO*
EMP: 98
SQ FT: 30,000
SALES (est): 22MM **Privately Held**
WEB: www.ultimatejetcharters.com
SIC: 4581 Airport; airport terminal services

(G-15378)
UNITED ARCHITECTURAL MTLS INC
7830 Cleveland Ave Nw (44720-5658)
PHONE...................................330 433-9220
Shelly Nesbitt, *President*
Robert W Eckinger, *Principal*
Greg Reed, *Plant Mgr*
Maria Liossis, *Controller*
Michelle Smith, *Senior Mgr*
EMP: 36
SALES (est): 9.5MM **Privately Held**
SIC: 8712 Architectural services

(G-15379)
WILLIAMS PARTNERS LP
7235 Whipple Ave Nw (44720-7137)
PHONE...................................330 966-3674
EMP: 245 **Publicly Held**
SIC: 1311 Crude Petroleum/Natural Gas Production
PA: Williams Partners L.P.
1 Williams Ctr
Tulsa OK 74172

North Fairfield
Huron County

(G-15380)
DOUGLAS WALCHER FARMS
Also Called: Drw Packing
866 State Route 162 E (44855-9687)
PHONE...................................419 744-2427
Fax: 419 744-2010
Kevin Holphouse, *Treasurer*
Ken Holphouse,
Kirk Holphouse,
Steve Holphouse,
EMP: 100
SALES (est): 4.1MM **Privately Held**
SIC: 0161 0119 Vegetables & melons; pea & bean farms (legumes)

North Jackson
Mahoning County

(G-15381)
HILLTRUX TANK LINES INC
200 Rosemont Rd (44451-9631)
P.O. Box 696 (44451-0696)
PHONE...................................330 538-3700
Brad Hille, *President*
Jim Prather, *Vice Pres*
Marvin Carroll, *Safety Dir*
CJ Woodring, *Office Mgr*
Lori Rupert, *Administration*
EMP: 50
SALES (est): 2.5MM **Privately Held**
SIC: 4213 Contract haulers

(G-15382)
JS PARIS EXCAVATING INC
12240 Commissioner Rd (44451-9641)
P.O. Box 219 (44451-0219)
PHONE...................................330 538-3048
Fax: 330 538-3112
James S Paris Jr, *President*
James S Paris Sr, *Corp Secy*
Jason A Paris, *Vice Pres*
Rick Basista, *Project Mgr*
John Haifley, *Project Mgr*
EMP: 50
SQ FT: 80,000
SALES (est): 11.1MM **Privately Held**
SIC: 1794 1795 Excavation & grading, building construction; demolition, buildings & other structures

(G-15383)
LIBERTY STEEL PRODUCTS INC (PA)
11650 Mahoning Ave (44451-9688)
P.O. Box 175 (44451-0175)
PHONE...................................330 538-2236
Fax: 330 538-0833
Andrew J Weller Jr, *CEO*
James T Weller Sr, *Ch of Bd*
James M Grasso, *Principal*
Joe Dubaj, *VP Mfg*
Rick Phillips, *Plant Mgr*
◆ **EMP:** 40
SQ FT: 110,000
SALES: 74MM **Privately Held**
SIC: 5051 Steel

(G-15384)
NILCO LLC
489 Rosemont Rd (44451-9717)
PHONE...................................330 538-3386
Fax: 330 538-2277
Kieran Kavanagh, *Purchasing*
Scott Honthy, *Branch Mgr*
EMP: 30

SALES (corp-wide): 800MM **Privately Held**
SIC: 5031 Lumber: rough, dressed & finished; building materials, exterior
HQ: Nilco, Llc
1221 W Maple St Ste 100
Hartville OH 44632
888 248-5151

(G-15385)
PAM TRANSPORTATION SVCS INC
12274 Mahoning Ave (44451-9617)
PHONE...................................330 270-7900
Fax: 330 270-7927
Glenn J Schwartz, *Branch Mgr*
EMP: 652
SALES (corp-wide): 437.8MM **Publicly Held**
SIC: 4789 Pipeline terminal facilities, independently operated
PA: P.A.M. Transportation Services, Inc.
297 W Henri De Tonti Blvd
Tontitown AR 72770
479 361-9111

(G-15386)
PMC SYSTEMS LIMITED
12155 Commissioner Dr (44451-9640)
P.O. Box 486 (44451-0486)
PHONE...................................330 538-2268
John Frano, *President*
Randy G Yakubek, *President*
Paul Graff, *Vice Pres*
Kim Hoffman, *Manager*
EMP: 30
SQ FT: 3,000
SALES (est): 5.7MM **Privately Held**
SIC: 3625 8711 Electric controls & control accessories, industrial; electrical or electronic engineering

(G-15387)
RAILWORKS CORPORATION
Also Called: Railwork Track Services
1550 N Bailey Rd (44451-8601)
P.O. Box 555, Sewell NJ (08080-0555)
PHONE...................................330 538-2261
Fax: 513 538-2223
Ray List, *CEO*
EMP: 300
SALES (corp-wide): 1.4B **Privately Held**
WEB: www.rwksrs.com
SIC: 1629 Railroad & railway roadbed construction
HQ: Railworks Corporation
5 Penn Plz
New York NY 10001
212 502-7900

(G-15388)
TRANSPORT CORP AMERICA INC
1951 N Bailey Rd (44451-9621)
PHONE...................................330 538-3328
Fax: 330 538-2953
Marc Slettedahl, *Opers Mgr*
Marjorie Plant, *Manager*
Chad Campbell, *Manager*
Jason Gagnon, *Manager*
Ed A Paul, *Manager*
EMP: 31
SQ FT: 2,378
SALES (corp-wide): 2.7B **Privately Held**
WEB: www.transportamerica.com
SIC: 4213 Contract haulers
HQ: Transport Corporation Of America, Inc.
1715 Yankee Doodle Rd # 100
Eagan MN 55121
651 686-2500

(G-15389)
TRI COUNTY TOWER SERVICE
8900 Mahoning Ave (44451-9750)
PHONE...................................330 538-9874
Fax: 330 538-9879
Frank Kovach, *Partner*
Doug Henry, *Partner*
Dale Williams, *Warehouse Mgr*
▼ **EMP:** 28
SALES (est): 4.3MM **Privately Held**
SIC: 1623 7389 Transmitting tower (telecommunication) construction;

(G-15390)
WASTE MANAGEMENT OHIO INC
12201 Council Dr (44451-9650)
P.O. Box 368 (44451-0368)
PHONE...................................866 797-9018
Fax: 330 538-3699
James Judge, *Principal*
Ginger Kaladas, *Credit Staff*
Lee Hicks, *Contract Law*
EMP: 50
SALES (corp-wide): 14.4B **Publicly Held**
WEB: www.wm.com
SIC: 4953 Refuse systems
HQ: Waste Management Of Ohio, Inc.
1700 N Broad St
Fairborn OH 45324

North Kingsville
Ashtabula County

(G-15391)
GREG FORD SWEET INC
Also Called: Greg Sweet Ford
4011 E Center St (44068)
P.O. Box 659 (44068-0659)
PHONE...................................440 593-7714
Fax: 440 593-1559
Gregory Sweet, *President*
Michael Kelly, *Finance Mgr*
EMP: 35
SQ FT: 25,000
SALES: 9MM **Privately Held**
SIC: 5511 7538 Automobiles, new & used; trucks, tractors & trailers: new & used; general automotive repair shops; general truck repair

North Lawrence
Stark County

(G-15392)
ELMS COUNTRY CLUB INC
1608 Manchester Ave Sw (44666-9432)
PHONE...................................330 833-2668
Fax: 330 833-8456
Mark Sweany, *President*
Lance Manion, *General Mgr*
EMP: 40
SALES (est): 1.2MM **Privately Held**
WEB: www.elmscc.com
SIC: 7997 5812 5813 Country club, membership; American restaurant; bar (drinking places)

(G-15393)
ELMS OF MASSILLON INC
Also Called: Elms Country Club
1608 Manchester Ave Sw (44666-9432)
P.O. Box 846, Massillon (44648-0846)
PHONE...................................330 833-2668
Johnny Lambada, *President*
EMP: 29
SALES: 39.3K **Privately Held**
SIC: 7997 Country club, membership

(G-15394)
US TUBULAR PRODUCTS INC
Also Called: Benmit Division
14852 Lincoln Way W (44666)
PHONE...................................330 832-1734
Fax: 330 832-8284
Jeffrey J Cunningham, *President*
Connye Cunningham, *Corp Secy*
Brian Cunningham, *Vice Pres*
Chris Siffrin, *QC Mgr*
Hank Sims, *QC Mgr*
EMP: 60 EST: 1973
SQ FT: 100,000
SALES (est): 9.2MM **Privately Held**
SIC: 8734 3498 Hydrostatic testing laboratory; tube fabricating (contract bending & shaping)

North Lima
Mahoning County

(G-15395)
ABF FREIGHT SYSTEM INC
11000 Market St (44452-9775)
PHONE..................................330 549-3800
Fax: 330 549-0621
James Rimstidt, *Opers Spvr*
Cliff Willoughby, *Manager*
David McKiban, *Supervisor*
EMP: 50
SALES (corp-wide): 2.8B **Publicly Held**
WEB: www.abfs.com
SIC: 4213 Contract haulers
HQ: Abf Freight System, Inc.
3801 Old Greenwood Rd
Fort Smith AR 72903
479 785-8700

(G-15396)
ARMSTRONG UTILITIES INC
Also Called: Armstrong Cable Services
9328 Woodworth Rd (44452-9712)
PHONE..................................330 758-6411
Fax: 330 726-0117
Dan McGahagan, *General Mgr*
Paul Wachtel, *Manager*
EMP: 40 **Privately Held**
SIC: 4841 Cable & other pay television services
HQ: Armstrong Utilities, Inc.
1 Armstrong Pl
Butler PA 16001
724 283-0925

(G-15397)
ASSOCIATED PAPER STOCK INC (PA)
11510 South Ave (44452-9527)
P.O. Box 470 (44452-0470)
PHONE..................................330 549-5311
Fax: 330 549-0111
Thomas Yanko, *President*
Michael Aey, *Sales Executive*
Dan Betz, *Admin Sec*
EMP: 35
SQ FT: 10,000
SALES (est): 9.4MM **Privately Held**
WEB: www.associatedpaperstock.com
SIC: 5093 Scrap & waste materials; waste paper; metal scrap & waste materials

(G-15398)
ASSUMPTION VILLAGE
Also Called: Marian Living Center
9800 Market St (44452-9560)
PHONE..................................330 549-2434
Fax: 330 549-0701
Jenna Anness, *Manager*
William Eddy, *Director*
Mary Luke, *Administration*
Joe Molocea, *Executive Asst*
EMP: 200 **EST:** 1974
SQ FT: 7,440
SALES: 13.7MM **Privately Held**
SIC: 8051 Skilled nursing care facilities

(G-15399)
B & T EXPRESS INC (PA)
400 Miley Rd (44452-8545)
P.O. Box 468 (44452-0468)
PHONE..................................330 549-0000
Breen O'Malley, *President*
Tom Cook, *Vice Pres*
Bill Rypcinski, *VP Opers*
John Redmon, *Office Mgr*
Rus Bray, *Manager*
EMP: 74
SQ FT: 25,000
SALES (est): 13.3MM **Privately Held**
WEB: www.btair.com
SIC: 4213 Heavy hauling

(G-15400)
CAPRICE HEALTH CARE INC
Also Called: Caprice Health Care Center
9184 Market St (44452-9558)
PHONE..................................330 965-9200
Fax: 330 965-9547
Celeste Hawkins, *Office Mgr*
Joe Cilone, *Info Tech Mgr*
Marcia Kirker, *Director*
Ravinder Nath, *Director*
Jeniffer See, *Administration*
EMP: 150 **EST:** 1998
SALES (est): 9.4MM **Privately Held**
SIC: 8051 8093 8082 8052 Skilled nursing care facilities; specialty outpatient clinics; home health care services; intermediate care facilities

(G-15401)
DART TRUCKING COMPANY INC (PA)
11017 Market St (44452-9782)
P.O. Box 157 (44452-0157)
PHONE..................................330 549-0994
John Polli, *President*
James Pazzanita, *Vice Pres*
David Lynch, *CFO*
EMP: 25
SQ FT: 12,000
SALES (est): 1.8MM **Privately Held**
SIC: 4213 Trucking, except local

(G-15402)
GUARDIAN ELDER CARE LLC
Also Called: Rolling Acres Care Center
9625 Market St (44452-8564)
PHONE..................................330 549-0898
Fax: 330 549-9434
Laurie Ference, *Branch Mgr*
Adil Jaffers, *Director*
EMP: 120 **Privately Held**
SIC: 8051 Convalescent home with continuous nursing care
PA: Guardian Elder Care, Llc
8796 Route 219
Brockway PA 15824

(G-15403)
JOE DICKEY ELECTRIC INC
180 W South Range Rd (44452-9578)
P.O. Box 158 (44452-0158)
PHONE..................................330 549-3976
Fax: 330 549-0324
Joseph Dickey Jr, *CEO*
David A Dickey, *President*
Brian Crumbacher, *Superintendent*
Eric Carlson, *Vice Pres*
Joseph Dickey III, *Vice Pres*
EMP: 80
SALES (est): 20.4MM **Privately Held**
WEB: www.dickeyelectric.com
SIC: 1731 General electrical contractor

(G-15404)
LAKESIDE MANOR INC
Also Called: Glenellen
9661 Market St (44452-8564)
PHONE..................................330 549-2545
Fax: 330 549-2170
James E McMurray, *President*
Roger F Herrmann, *Vice Pres*
Belinda Grace, *Administration*
EMP: 31
SALES (est): 1.9MM **Privately Held**
SIC: 8361 8052 Home for the aged; rehabilitation center, residential: health care incidental; rest home, with health care incidental; self-help group home; intermediate care facilities

(G-15405)
MKM DISTRIBUTION SERVICES INC
100 Eastgate Dr (44452-8563)
PHONE..................................330 549-9670
EMP: 60
SALES (corp-wide): 50.5MM **Privately Held**
SIC: 4789 Transportation Services
PA: Mkm Distribution Services Inc
8256 Zionsville Rd
Indianapolis IN 46268
317 334-7900

(G-15406)
NORTH LIMA DAIRY QUEEN INC (PA)
10067 Market St (44452-8560)
P.O. Box 125 (44452-0125)
PHONE..................................330 549-3220
Fax: 330 549-0555
Dean Rapp, *Owner*
Rick Firestone, *Corp Secy*
Randy Rapp, *Vice Pres*
EMP: 38 **EST:** 1961
SQ FT: 24,713
SALES (est): 1.2MM **Privately Held**
SIC: 5812 7542 Ice cream stands or dairy bars; carwash, automatic

(G-15407)
R T VERNAL PAVING INC
11299 South Ave (44452-9731)
P.O. Box 519 (44452-0519)
PHONE..................................330 549-3189
Richard Vernal, *President*
Jo Anne Vernal, *Corp Secy*
EMP: 40
SALES (est): 1.4MM **Privately Held**
SIC: 1794 1611 Excavation & grading, building construction; highway & street paving contractor

(G-15408)
USF HOLLAND LLC
Also Called: USFreightways
10855 Market St (44452-9562)
PHONE..................................330 549-2917
Vince Secarro, *Manager*
EMP: 150
SALES (corp-wide): 4.8B **Publicly Held**
WEB: www.usfc.com
SIC: 4213 Less-than-truckload (LTL) transport
HQ: Usf Holland Llc
700 S Waverly Rd
Holland MI 49423
616 395-5000

North Olmsted
Cuyahoga County

(G-15409)
AFFILIATED FM INSURANCE CO
25050 Country Club Blvd # 400 (44070-5356)
PHONE..................................216 362-4820
Patti Hutsko, *Vice Pres*
Brian Nyquist, *Branch Mgr*
Tim Hester, *Branch Mgr*
Anne Horvath, *Assistant*
EMP: 26
SALES (corp-wide): 4B **Privately Held**
SIC: 6331 Fire, marine & casualty insurance
HQ: Affiliated Fm Insurance Company
270 Central Ave
Johnston RI 02919
401 275-3000

(G-15410)
AFFORDABLE CARS & FINANCE INC (PA)
Also Called: Halleen Kia
27932 Lorain Rd (44070-4024)
PHONE..................................440 777-2424
Fax: 440 777-9129
Carl Halleen, *President*
Eric Halleen, *Vice Pres*
Ronald Kula, *Admin Sec*
EMP: 30
SQ FT: 3,200
SALES (est): 8.4MM **Privately Held**
WEB: www.halleenkia.com
SIC: 5511 6141 Automobiles, new & used; financing: automobiles, furniture, etc., not a deposit bank

(G-15411)
CARGILL INCORPORATED
24950 Country Club Blvd # 450 (44070-5333)
PHONE..................................440 716-4664
Fax: 440 716-4748
Toni Payne, *Marketing Staff*
Dale Sehrenbach, *Manager*
Karen Gorsuch, *Manager*
EMP: 75
SALES (corp-wide): 109.7B **Privately Held**
WEB: www.cargill.com
SIC: 5169 Industrial salts & polishes
PA: Cargill, Incorporated
15407 Mcginty Rd W
Wayzata MN 55391
952 742-7575

(G-15412)
CELLCO PARTNERSHIP
Also Called: Verizon Wireless
24121 Lorain Rd (44070-2163)
PHONE..................................440 779-1313
Fax: 440 779-0101
Larry Shiever, *General Mgr*
EMP: 25
SALES (corp-wide): 126B **Publicly Held**
SIC: 7629 5065 5999 Telephone set repair; mobile telephone equipment; telephone & communication equipment
HQ: Cellco Partnership
1 Verizon Way
Basking Ridge NJ 07920

(G-15413)
CHAMPLAIN ENTERPRISES LLC (PA)
Also Called: Commutair
24950 Country Club Blvd # 300 (44070-5333)
PHONE..................................440 779-4588
Subodh Karnik, *CEO*
John A Sullivan, *Ch of Bd*
Marval July, *General Mgr*
Joel Raymond, *COO*
Lon Ziegler, *Vice Pres*
EMP: 900
SQ FT: 41,000
SALES (est): 91.1MM **Privately Held**
WEB: www.commutair.com
SIC: 4512 Air passenger carrier, scheduled

(G-15414)
CHEMICAL BANK
25000 Country Club Blvd # 200 (44070-5344)
PHONE..................................440 779-0807
Fax: 440 779-0883
Timothy Atkinson, *Senior VP*
Kathy Shaw, *Vice Pres*
EMP: 36
SALES (corp-wide): 776.1MM **Publicly Held**
SIC: 6035 Federal savings & loan associations
HQ: Chemical Bank
333 E Main St
Midland MI 48640
989 631-9200

(G-15415)
CITY OF NORTH OLMSTED
Also Called: Commission On Partransit
5200 Dover Center Rd (44070-3129)
PHONE..................................440 777-8000
A E Boessneck, *Branch Mgr*
EMP: 27 **Privately Held**
SIC: 4111 Local & suburban transit
PA: City Of North Olmsted
5200 Dover Center Rd
North Olmsted OH 44070
440 716-4171

(G-15416)
CITY OF NORTH OLMSTED
Also Called: Olmsted Parks and Recreation
26000 Lorain Rd (44070-2738)
PHONE..................................440 734-8200
Fax: 440 734-3550
Ted Disalvo, *Manager*
Ted Disaldo, *Commissioner*
EMP: 53 **Privately Held**
WEB: www.north-olmsted.com
SIC: 7999 Recreation center; swimming pool, non-membership; tennis club, non-membership; tennis courts, outdoor/indoor: non-membership
PA: City Of North Olmsted
5200 Dover Center Rd
North Olmsted OH 44070
440 716-4171

(G-15417)
CITY OF NORTH OLMSTED
Also Called: Springvale Golf Crse Ballroom
5873 Canterbury Rd (44070-4522)
PHONE..................................440 777-0678
Fax: 440 777-4653
Marty Young, *Branch Mgr*
EMP: 50 **Privately Held**
WEB: www.north-olmsted.com
SIC: 7389 Convention & show services

GEOGRAPHIC SECTION
North Olmsted - Cuyahoga County (G-15441)

PA: City Of North Olmsted
5200 Dover Center Rd
North Olmsted OH 44070
440 716-4171

(G-15418)
CONSTRUCTION BIDDINGCOM LLC
31269 Bradley Rd (44070-3875)
PHONE.................440 716-4087
EMP: 50
SALES (est): 5.1MM **Privately Held**
SIC: 4813 Telephone Communications

(G-15419)
DAVID SCOTT SALON
107a Great Northern Mall (44070-3301)
PHONE.................440 734-7595
Fax: 440 734-7597
David Petrella, *Partner*
Scott Stettin, *Partner*
EMP: 30 **EST:** 1999
SALES (est): 841.7K **Privately Held**
SIC: 7231 Hairdressers

(G-15420)
ENT AND ALLERGY HEALTH SVCS (PA)
25761 Lorain Rd Fl 3 (44070-3369)
PHONE.................440 779-1112
Jeffrey E Binder Do, *President*
Mark Mehle, *Vice Pres*
Anita Burgess, *Office Mgr*
Joyce A Lender, *Med Doctor*
▲ **EMP:** 48
SQ FT: 5,000
SALES (est): 6.8MM **Privately Held**
WEB: www.enthealth.com
SIC: 8011 Ears, nose & throat specialist: physician/surgeon

(G-15421)
FACTORY MUTUAL INSURANCE CO
Also Called: FM Global
25050 Country Club Blvd # 400 (44070-5356)
PHONE.................440 779-0651
Joseph Gall, *Vice Pres*
Maralee Rodgers, *Human Resources*
Angela Edwards, *Admin Asst*
EMP: 120
SALES (corp-wide): 4B **Privately Held**
SIC: 6331 Property damage insurance
PA: Factory Mutual Insurance Co
270 Central Ave
Johnston RI 02919
401 275-3000

(G-15422)
FORTNEY & WEYGANDT INC
31269 Bradley Rd (44070-3875)
PHONE.................440 716-4000
Robert L Fortney, *President*
Greg Freeh, *Corp Secy*
Ruth Fortney, *Vice Pres*
Donna Straka, *Office Mgr*
Hanson Mike, *Executive*
EMP: 50
SQ FT: 21,000
SALES: 84.1MM **Privately Held**
WEB: www.fwprojects.com
SIC: 1541 1542 Industrial buildings, new construction; commercial & office building, new construction
PA: R. L. Fortney Management, Inc.
31269 Bradley Rd
North Olmsted OH 44070
440 716-4000

(G-15423)
FOUNDATIONS HLTH SOLUTIONS INC
Also Called: Provider Services
25000 Country Club Blvd (44070-5344)
PHONE.................440 793-0200
Daniel Parker, *President*
EMP: 78

SALES (est): 15.6MM **Privately Held**
SIC: 8721 8361 8322 8052 Certified public accountant; accounting services, except auditing; rehabilitation center, residential: health care incidental; home for the mentally handicapped; old age assistance; intermediate care facilities; personal care facility; health maintenance organization

(G-15424)
GRAND HERITAGE HOTEL PORTLAND
Also Called: Hampton Inn Cleveland
25105 Country Club Blvd (44070-5312)
PHONE.................440 734-4477
Fax: 440 734-0836
Meghan Carruthers, *General Mgr*
EMP: 45
SALES (est): 1.1MM
SALES (corp-wide): 6.1MM **Privately Held**
SIC: 7011 Hotels
PA: Grand Heritage Hotel Portland
39 Bay Dr
Annapolis MD 21403
410 280-9800

(G-15425)
HIGH-TECH POOLS INC
31330 Industrial Pkwy (44070-4787)
PHONE.................440 979-5070
Fax: 440 979-5076
Jeff Hammerschmidt, *President*
Frank Duale, *Project Mgr*
Terry Brennan, *Marketing Staff*
Trish Buddner, *Office Mgr*
Richard Ryan, *Manager*
▲ **EMP:** 30
SQ FT: 7,800
SALES (est): 5.5MM **Privately Held**
WEB: www.hightechpools.com
SIC: 1799 Swimming pool construction

(G-15426)
HORIZON EDUCATION CENTERS (PA)
29510 Lorain Rd (44070-3909)
PHONE.................440 779-1930
Fax: 440 779-6324
Judy Woehrman, *Finance Dir*
David Smith, *Exec Dir*
Dawn Marflake, *Director*
EMP: 115
SALES: 6.1MM **Privately Held**
SIC: 8351 Preschool center

(G-15427)
INTERNTONAL ALIANCE THEA STAGE
Also Called: Local 883
4689 Georgette Ave (44070-3735)
PHONE.................440 734-4883
Diane M Burke, *Principal*
EMP: 30
SALES (est): 406.3K **Privately Held**
SIC: 7922 Theatrical producers & services

(G-15428)
JOHN ATWOOD INC
Also Called: Aquasonic Auto & Van Wash
28800 Lorain Rd (44070-4012)
PHONE.................440 777-4147
Fax: 440 777-4147
John Atwood Jr, *President*
Jim Capone, *Vice Pres*
Cindy Shalala, *Vice Pres*
EMP: 50
SALES (est): 747.8K **Privately Held**
SIC: 7542 Washing & polishing, automotive

(G-15429)
LAKETEC COMMUNICATIONS INC
27881 Lorain Rd (44070-4023)
PHONE.................440 892-2001
Fax: 440 892-2094
Joseph Little, *President*
Joseph J Little, *General Mgr*
Ron Siebert, *Vice Pres*
Ron Kovach, *Opers Mgr*
Ryan Bir, *Accounts Exec*
EMP: 25
SQ FT: 10,000

SALES (est): 6.7MM **Privately Held**
WEB: www.laketec.net
SIC: 7379 Computer related maintenance services

(G-15430)
MANOR CARE OF AMERICA INC
23225 Lorain Rd (44070-1624)
PHONE.................440 779-6900
Fax: 440 779-1859
Geri Roetzel, *Facilities Dir*
Beverly S Baum, *Chf Purch Ofc*
Dian Zawadzki, *Manager*
Nitin Govani, *Director*
Darleen Perry, *Hlthcr Dir*
EMP: 200
SALES (corp-wide): 3.6B **Publicly Held**
WEB: www.trisunhealthcare.com
SIC: 8051 Convalescent home with continuous nursing care
HQ: Manor Care Of America, Inc.
333 N Summit St Ste 103
Toledo OH 43604
419 252-5500

(G-15431)
MARRIOTT INTERNATIONAL INC
Also Called: Courtyard By Marriott
24901 Country Club Blvd (44070-5308)
PHONE.................440 716-9977
Fax: 440 716-1995
Erica Todhunter, *General Mgr*
Nancy Conner, *General Mgr*
EMP: 28
SALES (corp-wide): 22.8B **Publicly Held**
SIC: 7011 Hotels & motels
PA: Marriott International, Inc.
10400 Fernwood Rd
Bethesda MD 20817
301 380-3000

(G-15432)
MORRIS CADILLAC BUICK GMC (PA)
26100 Lorain Rd (44070-2740)
PHONE.................440 327-4181
Fax: 440 327-5860
Robert Morris III, *President*
Dale Freeman, *Sales Mgr*
Steve Bansek, *Marketing Mgr*
Shawn Belles, *Manager*
EMP: 55
SQ FT: 20,000
SALES (est): 19.7MM **Privately Held**
SIC: 5511 7538 Automobiles, new & used; pickups, new & used; general automotive repair shops

(G-15433)
MOTORISTS MUTUAL INSURANCE CO
28111 Lorain Rd (44070-4027)
PHONE.................440 779-8900
Fax: 440 779-4017
Robert Hart, *Branch Mgr*
EMP: 30
SQ FT: 9,696
SALES (corp-wide): 494.7MM **Privately Held**
SIC: 6331 6411 Fire, marine & casualty insurance: mutual; insurance agents
PA: Motorists Mutual Insurance Company
471 E Broad St Ste 200
Columbus OH 43215
614 225-8211

(G-15434)
NEW YORK COMMUNITY BANK
4800 Great Northern Blvd (44070-3444)
PHONE.................440 734-7040
Chris Cinmisenick, *Manager*
EMP: 31 **Publicly Held**
WEB: www.amtrustinvest.com
SIC: 6035 Federal savings & loan associations
HQ: New York Community Bank
615 Merrick Ave
Westbury NY 11590
516 203-0010

(G-15435)
OLMSTED LANES INC
Also Called: Buckeye Lanes
24488 Lorain Rd (44070-2167)
PHONE.................440 777-6363
Fax: 440 777-2701
Jim Carney Jr, *President*
Jackie Dotson, *Financial Exec*
Carole Sutherland, *Manager*
EMP: 30
SQ FT: 60,000
SALES (est): 1.3MM **Privately Held**
SIC: 7933 Ten pin center

(G-15436)
OLMSTED MANOR NURSING HOME
27500 Mill Rd (44070-3197)
PHONE.................440 250-4080
Fax: 440 777-5796
John Coury, *Owner*
David Day, *Envir Svcs Dir*
Verna Horwedel, *Data Proc Staff*
Jill Kazmer, *Administration*
EMP: 130 **EST:** 1967
SQ FT: 25,000
SALES (est): 4.2MM **Privately Held**
WEB: www.olmstedmanor.com
SIC: 8051 8052 Skilled nursing care facilities; intermediate care facilities

(G-15437)
OLMSTED MNOR RTRMENT CMNTY LTD
27420 Mill Rd (44070-3190)
PHONE.................440 779-8886
Fax: 440 779-9569
Katherine Mossrbruger, *Administration*
EMP: 35
SQ FT: 17,690
SALES (est): 1.6MM **Privately Held**
SIC: 6513 8051 Retirement hotel operation; skilled nursing care facilities

(G-15438)
PALMER HOLLAND INC
25000 Country Club Blvd # 444 (44070-5331)
PHONE.................440 686-2300
Fax: 440 686-2180
Bryn Irvine, *CEO*
C Bradley Steven, *President*
Bert D Bradley, *Principal*
Fred H Palmer III, *Principal*
Dorothy Waldern, *Principal*
▲ **EMP:** 95 **EST:** 1925
SALES (est): 119.5MM **Privately Held**
SIC: 5169 Industrial chemicals

(G-15439)
PROFESSIONAL TRAVEL INC (PA)
25000 Country Club Blvd # 170 (44070-5338)
PHONE.................440 734-8800
Fax: 440 734-1241
Bob Sturm, *CEO*
Rob Turk, *Exec VP*
Robert Turk, *Exec VP*
Marilyn Abruzzino, *Vice Pres*
Lauri Curtis, *Vice Pres*
EMP: 75
SQ FT: 6,000
SALES (est): 24.4MM **Privately Held**
WEB: www.protrav.com
SIC: 4724 Travel agencies

(G-15440)
PROLINE XPRESS INC
24371 Lorain Rd Ste 206 (44070-2108)
PHONE.................440 777-8120
Fax: 440 777-8193
Charlene Penn, *President*
EMP: 25
SQ FT: 2,500
SALES (est): 3.8MM **Privately Held**
SIC: 4212 Local trucking, without storage

(G-15441)
R L FORTNEY MANAGEMENT INC (PA)
Also Called: Fortney & Weygandt
31269 Bradley Rd (44070-3875)
PHONE.................440 716-4000
Fax: 440 716-4010

North Olmsted - Cuyahoga County (G-15442)

Ruth Fortney, *President*
Matthew McBride, *Project Mgr*
Kristen Martin, *Accounts Mgr*
EMP: 101
SALES: 84.1MM **Privately Held**
SIC: 1542 Commercial & office building, new construction

(G-15442)
RADISSON HOTEL CLEVE
25070 Country Club Blvd (44070-5309)
PHONE 440 734-5060
Syed M Zaman, *Partner*
Cathy Stocker, *Controller*
Michael Kliman, *Financial Exec*
Carol Diegidio, *Sales Mgr*
EMP: 38
SALES: 950K **Privately Held**
SIC: 7011 Hotels

(G-15443)
SCHIRMER CONSTRUCTION CO
31350 Industrial Pkwy (44070-4787)
PHONE 440 716-4900
Fax: 440 716-4907
Fred Schirmer, *CEO*
James A Yungman, *CEO*
Nick Iafigliola, *President*
Frederick Schirmer, *Exec VP*
John M Roche, *Vice Pres*
EMP: 45
SQ FT: 38,500
SALES (est): 15.1MM **Privately Held**
SIC: 1541 1542 Industrial buildings, new construction; renovation, remodeling & repairs: industrial buildings; commercial & office building, new construction; commercial & office buildings, renovation & repair; institutional building construction

(G-15444)
SMART (PA)
Also Called: Smart - Transportation Div
24950 Country Club Blvd # 340 (44070-5333)
PHONE 216 228-9400
John Previsich, *President*
Joe Shivak, *President*
C F Lane, *Principal*
Charles Luna, *Principal*
Dan Johnson, *Treasurer*
◆ **EMP:** 120
SQ FT: 50,000
SALES: 27.7MM **Privately Held**
SIC: 8631 6411 Labor union; insurance agents, brokers & service

(G-15445)
SPRINT SPECTRUM LP
25363 Lorain Rd (44070-2061)
PHONE 440 686-2600
Fax: 440 777-7479
David Latto, *Manager*
EMP: 30
SALES (corp-wide): 78.3B **Publicly Held**
WEB: www.sprintpcs.com
SIC: 4813 Local & long distance telephone communications
HQ: Sprint Spectrum L.P.
6800 Sprint Pkwy
Overland Park KS 66251

(G-15446)
SUNNYSIDE TOYOTA INC
27000 Lorain Rd (44070-3212)
PHONE 440 777-9911
Fax: 440 777-8954
Kirt Frye, *President*
Jordon Baker, *Finance Mgr*
Brian Harris, *Finance Mgr*
Eric Sonnie, *Sales Mgr*
Matt Stolarski, *Sales Mgr*
EMP: 100
SALES (est): 31.7MM **Privately Held**
SIC: 5511 7538 7532 7515 Automobiles, new & used; general automotive repair shops; top & body repair & paint shops; passenger car leasing; automotive & home supply stores; used car dealers

(G-15447)
SUNSET MEMORIAL PARK ASSN
6265 Columbia Rd (44070-4620)
P.O. Box 729 (44070-0729)
PHONE 440 777-0450
Fax: 440 777-5763

Bryn Baracskai, *President*
Thomas Baracskai, *Vice Pres*
Edward Shubeck Jr, *Vice Pres*
EMP: 50
SQ FT: 3,000
SALES: 6.7MM **Privately Held**
SIC: 6553 Cemeteries, real estate operation; cemetery association; mausoleum operation

(G-15448)
THIRD FEDERAL SAVINGS
26949 Lorain Rd (44070-3211)
PHONE 440 716-1865
Fax: 440 734-5977
Liz M Robinson, *Manager*
Diana Kincaid, *Manager*
EMP: 25
SALES (corp-wide): 834.2MM **Publicly Held**
SIC: 6035 Federal savings & loan associations
HQ: Third Federal Savings And Loan Association Of Cleveland
7007 Broadway Ave
Cleveland OH 44105
800 844-7333

(G-15449)
UNITED STEELWORKERS
Also Called: Uswa
24371 Lorain Rd Ste 207 (44070-2108)
PHONE 440 979-1050
John Majorek, *Manager*
EMP: 44
SALES (corp-wide): 61.5K **Privately Held**
SIC: 8631 Labor union
PA: United Steelworkers
60 Bolevard Of The Allies
Pittsburgh PA 15222
412 562-2400

(G-15450)
WELLINGTON PLACE LLC
4800 Clague Rd Apt 108 (44070-6209)
PHONE 440 734-9933
Fax: 440 716-5424
Marge Siedlecki, *Manager*
John O'Neill,
John O Neill,
EMP: 65
SQ FT: 24,480
SALES (est): 5MM **Privately Held**
WEB: www.wellingtonplace.net
SIC: 8052 Intermediate care facilities

(G-15451)
XPO CNW INC
5498 Dorothy Dr (44070-4263)
PHONE 440 716-8971
Daniel Conway, *Principal*
EMP: 155
SALES (corp-wide): 15.3B **Publicly Held**
WEB: www.cnf.com
SIC: 4213 Trucking, except local
HQ: Xpo Cnw, Inc.
2211 Old Earhart Rd
Ann Arbor MI 48105
734 757-1444

North Ridgeville
Lorain County

(G-15452)
0714 INC
32648 Center Ridge Rd (44039-2457)
PHONE 440 327-2123
Fax: 440 327-6401
Adrian Frederick, *President*
Linda Blackstone, *Sales Staff*
Stacey Hruska, *Sales Staff*
Barbara McCarthy, *Sales Staff*
Patricia Frederick, *Agent*
EMP: 44
SQ FT: 2,229
SALES (est): 2.9MM **Privately Held**
SIC: 8742 6531 Real estate consultant; construction project management consultant; real estate agents & managers

(G-15453)
ALL AMERICAN SPORTS CORP (HQ)
Also Called: Riddell All American Sport
7501 Performance Ln (44039-2765)
PHONE 440 366-8225
Fax: 440 365-9629
Don Gleisner, *President*
Joe Antczak, *Plant Supt*
Linda Walsh, *Credit Staff*
Scott Nunez, *Sales Staff*
Gary Boevers, *Marketing Staff*
▲ **EMP:** 1000
SALES: 5MM **Privately Held**
SIC: 7699 Recreational sporting equipment repair services

(G-15454)
ALTERCARE INC (PA)
Also Called: Northridge Health Center
35990 Westminister Ave (44039-1399)
PHONE 440 327-5285
Fax: 440 327-8798
Robert A Wickes, *President*
Dennis Conley, *CFO*
Itri Eren, *Director*
Teresa Brown, *Nursing Dir*
Hazel Singer, *Executive*
EMP: 42
SQ FT: 30,000
SALES (est): 10.6MM **Privately Held**
SIC: 8051 Skilled nursing care facilities

(G-15455)
BOB SCHMITT HOMES INC
9095 Gapaston Rd (44039)
PHONE 440 327-9495
Fax: 440 327-7540
Michael Schmitt, *CEO*
Edward A Schmitt, *Ch of Bd*
Joseph D Molnar, *Assistant VP*
Scott Kubit, *Vice Pres*
EMP: 67 EST: 1946
SQ FT: 10,000
SALES (est): 7.4MM **Privately Held**
WEB: www.bshinc.com
SIC: 1521 1522 6552 New construction, single-family houses; townhouse construction; condominium construction; land subdividers & developers, residential

(G-15456)
BOWLMOR AMF CORP
Also Called: Brunswick Center Ridge Lanes
38931 Center Ridge Rd (44039-2753)
PHONE 440 327-1190
Fax: 440 327-7196
Matt Schneider, *Manager*
EMP: 32
SQ FT: 432
SALES (corp-wide): 354.5MM **Privately Held**
SIC: 7933 Ten pin center
PA: Bowlmor Amf Corp.
222 W 44th St
New York NY 10036
212 777-2214

(G-15457)
CASTLE CARE
Also Called: Castle Care Landscaping
6043 Oakwood Cir (44039-2661)
PHONE 440 327-3700
Fax: 440 327-2363
John Krakowski, *Owner*
Lori Krakowski, *Manager*
EMP: 25
SALES: 500K **Privately Held**
SIC: 0782 Landscape contractors

(G-15458)
CENTER RIDGE NURSING HOME INC
38600 Center Ridge Rd (44039-2837)
PHONE 440 327-1295
Fax: 440 353-0177
John T O'Neil, *President*
Barbara McGrady, *Exec Dir*
Niraj Mistry, *Director*
EMP: 200
SQ FT: 45,000

SALES (est): 4.5MM **Privately Held**
WEB: www.centerridgenursinghome.com
SIC: 8059 8052 8051 Nursing home, except skilled & intermediate care facility; intermediate care facilities; skilled nursing care facilities

(G-15459)
CHAPIN LOGISTICS INC
Also Called: Chapin Leasing
39111 Center Ridge Rd (44039-2744)
P.O. Box 1317, Elyria (44036-1317)
PHONE 440 327-1360
Timothy J Watson, *President*
Barry Jirousek, *Mktg Dir*
EMP: 25
SALES (est): 3.1MM **Privately Held**
WEB: www.chapinlogistics.com
SIC: 4212 Local trucking, without storage

(G-15460)
CITY OF NORTH RIDGEVILLE
Also Called: Dept of Streets
35010 Bainbridge Rd (44039-4072)
PHONE 440 327-8326
Fax: 440 353-0052
Chris Rangus, *Branch Mgr*
EMP: 33 **Privately Held**
SIC: 1611 Highway & street maintenance
PA: City Of North Ridgeville
7307 Avon Belden Rd
North Ridgeville OH 44039
440 353-0819

(G-15461)
CLEVELAND CLINIC FOUNDATION
Also Called: Cleveland Clinic Health System
35105 Center Ridge Rd (44039-3081)
PHONE 440 327-1050
EMP: 2554
SALES (corp-wide): 8B **Privately Held**
SIC: 8062 General medical & surgical hospitals
PA: The Cleveland Clinic Foundation
9500 Euclid Ave
Cleveland OH 44195
216 636-8335

(G-15462)
DAVITA HEALTHCARE PARTNERS INC
35143 Center Ridge Rd (44039-3089)
PHONE 440 353-0114
Gregory Beattie, *Branch Mgr*
EMP: 27 **Publicly Held**
SIC: 8092 Kidney dialysis centers
PA: Davita Inc.
2000 16th St
Denver CO 80202

(G-15463)
ESTES EXPRESS LINES INC
38495 Center Ridge Rd (44039-2833)
PHONE 440 327-3884
Fax: 440 327-3191
Hill Shirley, *VP Sales*
Ron Jordan, *Mktg Dir*
Tom Lamb, *Manager*
Chuck Davison, *Manager*
Maggie Hales, *Executive*
EMP: 75
SALES (corp-wide): 2.4B **Privately Held**
WEB: www.estes-express.com
SIC: 4213 Heavy hauling
PA: Estes Express Lines, Inc.
3901 W Broad St
Richmond VA 23230
804 353-1900

(G-15464)
FOREVERGREEN LAWN CARE
38601 Sugar Ridge Rd (44039-3526)
PHONE 440 327-8987
Fax: 440 366-8987
Michael J Babet, *President*
Pam Karkoff, *Manager*
Debbie M Babet,
EMP: 35
SALES: 1MM **Privately Held**
SIC: 0782 0783 Lawn care services; planting, pruning & trimming services

▲ = Import ▼=Export
◆ =Import/Export

North Royalton - Cuyahoga County

(G-15465)
JIMS ELECTRIC INC
39221 Center Ridge Rd (44039-2747)
PHONE..................440 327-8800
Fax: 440 327-8801
James Tweardy, *President*
Kim Tweardy, *Corp Secy*
EMP: 40
SQ FT: 14,000
SALES (est): 5.2MM **Privately Held**
SIC: 1731 General electrical contractor

(G-15466)
KIDDIE KOLLEGE INC
33169 Center Ridge Rd (44039-2566)
PHONE..................440 327-5435
Fax: 440 327-5493
Joanne Mollel, *Branch Mgr*
EMP: 25 **Privately Held**
SIC: 8351 Group day care center
PA: Kiddie Kollege Inc
  660 Dover Center Rd Ste 2
  Bay Village OH 44140

(G-15467)
LASER CRAFT INC
38900 Taylor Pkwy (44035-6259)
PHONE..................440 327-4300
Fax: 440 327-4141
Greg Claycomb, *President*
William Flickinger, *Vice Pres*
Joe Schmitt, *Vice Pres*
Leonard J Sikora, *Vice Pres*
Carol Mucha, *Controller*
EMP: 25
SALES (est): 4MM **Privately Held**
WEB: www.lasercraftusa.com
SIC: 7389 Metal slitting & shearing

(G-15468)
LIFESTYLE LANDSCAPING INC
34613 Center Ridge Rd (44039-3157)
PHONE..................440 353-0333
Fax: 440 327-0398
Donald Hoffman, *CEO*
David Hoffman, *President*
Karen Hoffman, *Corp Secy*
EMP: 25
SALES (est): 2.3MM **Privately Held**
WEB: www.lifestylelandscaping.com
SIC: 0781 Landscape planning services

(G-15469)
MERCY HEALTH
6115 Emerald St (44039-2047)
PHONE..................440 327-7372
EMP: 28
SALES (corp-wide): 4.2B **Privately Held**
SIC: 8011 Offices & clinics of medical doctors
PA: Mercy Health
  1701 Mercy Health Pl
  Cincinnati OH 45237
  513 639-2800

(G-15470)
MERCY HEALTH
39263 Center Ridge Rd (44039-2759)
PHONE..................440 366-5577
Fax: 440 365-0367
EMP: 42
SALES (corp-wide): 4.2B **Privately Held**
SIC: 8011 Primary care medical clinic; occupational & industrial specialist, physician/surgeon
PA: Mercy Health
  1701 Mercy Health Pl
  Cincinnati OH 45237
  513 639-2800

(G-15471)
MILLS CREEK ASSOCIATION
5175 Mills Creek Ln (44039-2332)
P.O. Box 39084 (44039-0084)
PHONE..................440 327-5336
Warren Blakely, *President*
Art Hubble, *Vice Pres*
Richard Bartels, *Treasurer*
Janice Kennard, *Admin Sec*
EMP: 28
SALES: 280K **Privately Held**
WEB: www.millscreek.org
SIC: 8641 Homeowners' association

(G-15472)
NEUTRAL TELECOM CORPORATION
6472 Monroe Ln Ste 200 (44039-5306)
PHONE..................440 377-4700
Beth Ellen Davis, *President*
EMP: 40
SQ FT: 40,000
SALES: 10MM **Privately Held**
SIC: 8748 Telecommunications consultant

(G-15473)
PETRO-COM CORP (PA)
32523 Lorain Rd (44039-3423)
PHONE..................440 327-6900
Manny Sclimenti Sr, *President*
Sharon Sclimenti, *Vice Pres*
Teresa Curtis, *Manager*
EMP: 29
SQ FT: 10,000
SALES (est): 3.6MM **Privately Held**
WEB: www.petrocomcorp.com
SIC: 7699 Service station equipment repair

(G-15474)
POPPEES POPCORN INC
38727 Taylor Pkwy (44035-6275)
PHONE..................440 327-0775
Tim McGuir, *President*
Jennifer McGuire, *Vice Pres*
Tom McGuire, *Sales Staff*
Jesscia Puresutto, *Manager*
EMP: 32 **EST:** 1948
SQ FT: 20,000
SALES (est): 13.3MM **Privately Held**
SIC: 5145 Popcorn & supplies

(G-15475)
RHENIUM ALLOYS INC (PA)
38683 Taylor Pkwy (44035-6200)
P.O. Box 245, Elyria (44036-0245)
PHONE..................440 365-7388
Fax: 440 366-9831
Mike Prokop, *President*
Todd Leonhardt, *Vice Pres*
Randall Mohr, *Buyer*
Timothy Carlson, *Engineer*
Carol Pilan, *Sls & Mktg Exec*
▲ **EMP:** 60 **EST:** 1994
SQ FT: 35,500
SALES (est): 14.2MM **Privately Held**
WEB: www.rhenium.com
SIC: 3313 3356 3498 3339 Electrometallurgical products; tungsten, basic shapes; fabricated pipe & fittings; primary nonferrous metals; chemical preparations; ferroalloy ores, except vanadium

(G-15476)
RIDDELL INC
7501 Performance Ln (44039-2765)
PHONE..................440 366-8225
Robert Kelly, *Manager*
EMP: 25 **Privately Held**
WEB: www.riddellsports.com
SIC: 5091 Athletic goods
HQ: Riddell, Inc.
  1700 E Higgins Rd Ste 500
  Des Plaines IL 60018
  847 292-1472

(G-15477)
SCHILL LANDSCAPING AND LAWN CA (PA)
Also Called: Schill Grounds Management
5000 Mills Indus Pkwy (44039-1971)
PHONE..................440 327-3030
Fax: 440 949-6087
Joseph H Schill, *President*
Gerald J Schill Jr, *Vice Pres*
James Schill, *Vice Pres*
EMP: 63
SQ FT: 10,000
SALES (est): 11.5MM **Privately Held**
WEB: www.schilllandscaping.com
SIC: 0781 0782 4959 Landscape architects; lawn services; snowplowing

(G-15478)
UNITED STTES BOWL CONGRESS INC
38931 Center Ridge Rd (44039-2753)
PHONE..................440 327-0102
EMP: 51
SALES (corp-wide): 32.9MM **Privately Held**
SIC: 8699 Athletic organizations
PA: United States Bowling Congress, Inc.
  621 Six Flags Dr
  Arlington TX 76011
  817 385-8200

North Royalton
Cuyahoga County

(G-15479)
AARON LANDSCAPE INC
Also Called: Accucut
14900 York Rd (44133-4526)
PHONE..................440 838-8875
Fax: 440 838-8663
Aaron Zaremba, *President*
Tom Fritsch, *Manager*
EMP: 30 **EST:** 1993
SALES (est): 3.8MM **Privately Held**
WEB: www.aaronlandscaping.com
SIC: 0781 Landscape services

(G-15480)
ABC FIRE INC
10250 Royalton Rd (44133-4429)
PHONE..................440 237-6677
Fax: 440 237-6670
Richard W Watson, *President*
John Leitch, *General Mgr*
Joe Watson, *Sales Mgr*
Dan Jindra, *Sales Associate*
Eric Cathcart, *Manager*
EMP: 25
SQ FT: 13,500
SALES (est): 10.2MM **Privately Held**
WEB: www.abcfireinc.net
SIC: 5099 1731 1711 8748 Safety equipment & supplies; fire detection & burglar alarm systems specialization; fire sprinkler system installation; safety training service; fire alarm maintenance & monitoring

(G-15481)
B & D AUTO & TOWING INC
14290 State Rd Ste 1 (44133-5129)
PHONE..................440 237-3737
David Quinn, *President*
EMP: 30
SQ FT: 87,120
SALES (est): 179.6K **Privately Held**
SIC: 7549 Towing service, automotive

(G-15482)
BERARDIS FRESH ROAST INC
12029 Abbey Rd (44133-2637)
PHONE..................440 582-4303
Fax: 440 582-4359
Patrick Leneghan, *CEO*
Brian Leneghan, *Vice Pres*
Tim Allington, *Purchasing*
Angela Caruso, *Manager*
EMP: 40
SQ FT: 17,000
SALES (est): 8.3MM **Privately Held**
WEB: www.berardiscoffee.com
SIC: 5149 Coffee, green or roasted; tea; cocoa

(G-15483)
CHILDRENS FOREVER HAVEN INC (PA)
Also Called: Haven Hill Home
10983 Abbey Rd (44133-2537)
PHONE..................440 652-6749
Fax: 440 526-6615
Elizabeth Hernandez, *Opers Staff*
Avedon Lawrence, *QA Dir*
Kelly Simmons, *Accounting Mgr*
Sharon Curlett, *Human Res Mgr*
Ijaz Qureshi, *Program Mgr*
EMP: 47
SQ FT: 9,000
SALES: 96.1K **Privately Held**
SIC: 8052 Personal care facility

(G-15484)
CLASSROOM ANTICS INC
10143 Royalton Rd Ste G (44133-4468)
PHONE..................800 595-3776
Marjorie Andrews, *Business Mgr*
Tara Foote, *Director*
Toby Foote, *Director*
EMP: 30
SQ FT: 1,800
SALES (est): 534.3K **Privately Held**
SIC: 7032 Summer camp, except day & sports instructional

(G-15485)
D C TRANSPORTATION SERVICE
Also Called: Commercial Drivers
5740 Royalwood Rd Ste C (44133-3936)
PHONE..................440 237-0900
Fax: 440 237-7360
Thomas Fink, *President*
Leigh Cromleigh, *General Mgr*
Liz Krauth, *Accounting Mgr*
EMP: 190 **EST:** 1976
SALES (est): 5.4MM **Privately Held**
SIC: 7363 Employee leasing service

(G-15486)
DAVE COMMERCIAL GROUND MGT
9956 Akins Rd (44133-4547)
PHONE..................440 237-5394
Vito Montelbone, *Branch Mgr*
EMP: 28
SALES (est): 3.3MM **Privately Held**
SIC: 8741 Management services

(G-15487)
DIGIOIA/SUBURBAN EXCVTG LLC
11293 Royalton Rd (44133-4409)
PHONE..................440 237-1978
Gail Martinez, *Manager*
Nick Di Gioia Jr,
Terry Monnolly,
EMP: 85 **EST:** 1976
SQ FT: 23,000
SALES (est): 20.5MM **Privately Held**
SIC: 1623 1794 Water main construction; sewer line construction; excavation work

(G-15488)
EMPIRE MASONRY COMPANY INC
Also Called: Empire Poured Walls
12359 Abbey Rd Ste B (44133-2642)
PHONE..................440 230-2800
Fax: 440 230-4800
Bernard Nofel, *President*
Kathlene Nofel, *Manager*
EMP: 70
SQ FT: 2,000
SALES (est): 4MM **Privately Held**
SIC: 1741 Masonry & other stonework

(G-15489)
EPILOGUE INC
Also Called: Ltc Nursing
12333 Ridge Rd Ste E (44133-3700)
PHONE..................440 582-5555
Fax: 440 582-2758
Richard Buesch, *President*
Andrea Wisniewski, *Nurse*
EMP: 56
SALES (est): 3.2MM **Privately Held**
SIC: 7361 Nurses' registry

(G-15490)
GRABER METAL WORKS INC
9664 Akins Rd Ste 1 (44133-4595)
PHONE..................440 237-8422
Fax: 440 237-0135
Steve M Graber Sr, *President*
Michael R Horvath, *Vice Pres*
Katherine Graber, *Treasurer*
Richard Graber, *Office Mgr*
EMP: 30 **EST:** 1965
SQ FT: 25,000
SALES (est): 3MM **Privately Held**
WEB: www.grabermetal.com
SIC: 3599 5051 3446 3444 Machine shop, jobbing & repair; tubing, flexible metallic; metals service centers & offices; architectural metalwork; sheet metalwork; fabricated plate work (boiler shop); fabricated structural metal

North Royalton - Cuyahoga County (G-15491)

(G-15491)
H & D STEEL SERVICE INC
Also Called: H & D Steel Service Center
9960 York Alpha Dr (44133-3588)
PHONE.................................440 237-3390
Fax: 440 237-4540
Raymond Gary Schreiber, *Ch of Bd*
Joseph Bubba, *President*
Joseph A Cachat, *Principal*
R M Jones, *Principal*
R G Schreiber, *Principal*
▲ **EMP:** 50
SQ FT: 125,000
SALES (est): 53.9MM **Privately Held**
WEB: www.hdsteel.com
SIC: 5051 3541 5085 Iron or steel flat products; sheets, metal; tubing, metal; bars, metal; home workshop machine tools, metalworking; industrial tools

(G-15492)
HANNA HOLDINGS INC
Also Called: Howard Hanna RE & Mrtg Svcs
9485 W Sprague Rd (44133-1210)
PHONE.................................440 971-5600
Stacy Nickels, *Branch Mgr*
Ron Casella, *Executive*
EMP: 50
SALES (corp-wide): 76.4MM **Privately Held**
SIC: 6531 6111 Real estate brokers & agents; Federal Home Loan Mortgage Corporation
PA: Hanna Holdings, Inc.
1090 Freeport Rd Ste 1a
Pittsburgh PA 15238
412 967-9000

(G-15493)
HARMONY HOME CARE INC
12608 State Rd Ste 1a (44133-3281)
PHONE.................................440 243-1332
Fax: 440 243-1664
Christine Tharp, *President*
EMP: 50
SALES (est): 1.5MM **Privately Held**
SIC: 8361 Residential care

(G-15494)
HCR MANORCARE MED SVCS FLA LLC
Also Called: Arden Courts of Parma
9205 W Sprague Rd (44133-1286)
PHONE.................................440 887-1442
Meredith Pasco, *Manager*
Stephanie Chambers, *Director*
April Suva, *Hlthcr Dir*
EMP: 65
SALES (corp-wide): 3.6B **Publicly Held**
WEB: www.manorcare.com
SIC: 8322 8051 Old age assistance; skilled nursing care facilities
HQ: Hcr Manorcare Medical Services Of Florida, Llc
333 N Summit St Ste 100
Toledo OH 43604
419 252-5500

(G-15495)
HOWARD HANNA SMYTHE CRAMER
5730 Wallings Rd (44133-3015)
PHONE.................................440 237-8888
Joesephine Calabro, *Manager*
Regina Deininger, *Manager*
Diane Joeright, *Real Est Agnt*
EMP: 30
SALES (corp-wide): 76.4MM **Privately Held**
SIC: 6531 Real estate brokers & agents
HQ: Howard Hanna Smythe Cramer
6000 Parkland Blvd
Cleveland OH 44124
216 447-4477

(G-15496)
MANOR CARE OF AMERICA INC
9055 W Sprague Rd (44133-1285)
PHONE.................................440 345-9300
Fax: 440 888-6853
Hans Larsen, *Branch Mgr*
Sara Fielding-Russe, *Administration*
EMP: 200
SALES (corp-wide): 3.6B **Publicly Held**
SIC: 8051 Convalescent home with continuous nursing care
HQ: Manor Care Of America, Inc.
333 N Summit St Ste 103
Toledo OH 43604
419 252-5500

(G-15497)
OAK BROOK GARDENS
Also Called: Oak Brook Garden Apartments
13911 Oakbrook Dr Apt 205 (44133-4641)
PHONE.................................440 237-3613
Fax: 440 237-0706
Harley Gross, *President*
Gary Gross, *Partner*
Morton J Gross, *Partner*
EMP: 90
SQ FT: 500
SALES (est): 3.6MM **Privately Held**
SIC: 6513 6531 Apartment building operators; real estate agents & managers

(G-15498)
PREMIER ASPHALT PAVING CO INC
10519 Royalton Rd (44133-4401)
PHONE.................................440 237-6600
Fax: 440 237-1545
Ronald Fabricius Sr, *President*
Ronald Fabricius Jr, *Vice Pres*
Troy Fabricius, *Vice Pres*
James Finley, *Opers Mgr*
EMP: 25
SQ FT: 7,000
SALES (est): 5.6MM **Privately Held**
WEB: www.premierasphaltpaving.com
SIC: 1611 1771 Highway & street paving contractor; blacktop (asphalt) work

(G-15499)
REALTY ONE INC
9225 W Sprague Rd (44133-1208)
PHONE.................................440 888-8600
Stacy Nickles, *Branch Mgr*
Lauren Martinez, *Real Est Agnt*
EMP: 60
SALES (corp-wide): 67.8MM **Privately Held**
WEB: www.realty-1st.com
SIC: 6531 Real estate agent, residential
HQ: Realty One, Inc.
800 W Saint Clair Ave
Cleveland OH 44113
216 328-2500

(G-15500)
ROUND ROOM LLC
9253 W Sprague Rd (44133-1208)
PHONE.................................440 888-0322
EMP: 44 **Privately Held**
SIC: 4812 Cellular telephone services
PA: Round Room, Llc
525 Congressional Blvd
Carmel IN 46032

(G-15501)
ROYALTON SENIOR LIVING INC
Also Called: Royalton Woods
14277 State Rd (44133-5130)
PHONE.................................440 582-4111
Fax: 440 230-2974
Linda Arduina, *CFO*
Linda Arduini, *Director*
Monica Ferrante, *Director*
EMP: 44
SQ FT: 18,407
SALES (est): 2MM **Privately Held**
SIC: 8059 Rest home, with health care

(G-15502)
SHEARER FARM INC
Also Called: John Deere Authorized Dealer
11204 Royalton Rd (44133-4417)
PHONE.................................440 237-4806
EMP: 35
SALES (corp-wide): 59.5MM **Privately Held**
SIC: 5261 5084 5083 Lawnmowers & tractors; industrial machinery & equipment; tractors, agricultural
PA: Shearer Farm, Inc
7762 Cleveland Rd
Wooster OH 44691
330 345-9023

(G-15503)
SUBURBAN MAINT & CNSTR INC
16330 York Rd Ste 2 (44133-5551)
P.O. Box 33009, Cleveland (44133-0009)
PHONE.................................440 237-7765
Brian Stucky, *President*
EMP: 35
SQ FT: 12,000
SALES (est): 3.8MM **Privately Held**
SIC: 1799 1771 Waterproofing; concrete repair

(G-15504)
SUBURBAN MAINT CONTRS INC
16330 York Rd (44133-5551)
PHONE.................................440 237-7765
Fax: 440 237-7897
Donna Gallo, *Principal*
EMP: 25
SALES (est): 1.5MM **Privately Held**
SIC: 7349 Building maintenance services

(G-15505)
VERIZON BUSINESS GLOBAL LLC
12300 Ridge Rd (44133-3745)
PHONE.................................440 457-4049
Jeff Ferringer, *Branch Mgr*
Behan Tom, *IT/INT Sup*
EMP: 49
SALES (corp-wide): 126B **Publicly Held**
WEB: www.mccmt.com
SIC: 4813 Local & long distance telephone communications
HQ: Verizon Business Global Llc
22001 Loudoun County Pkwy
Ashburn VA 20147
703 886-5600

(G-15506)
VERIZON SELECT SERVICES INC
12300 Ridge Rd (44133-3745)
PHONE.................................908 559-2054
Linda Fischer, *Branch Mgr*
EMP: 30 **Privately Held**
SIC: 4822 Telegraph & other communications
PA: Verizon Select Services Inc.
4255 Patriot Dr Ste 400
Grapevine TX 76051

(G-15507)
YOUNG MNS CHRSTN ASSN CLVELAND
Also Called: Ridgewood YMCA
11409 State Rd (44133-3262)
PHONE.................................440 842-5200
Fax: 440 842-1166
Cindy Tomascewski, *Manager*
Steven Crone, *Exec Dir*
Gary Guzy, *Director*
EMP: 75
SQ FT: 18,462
SALES (corp-wide): 29.2MM **Privately Held**
SIC: 8641 7991 8351 7032 Youth organizations; physical fitness facilities; child day care services; youth camps; individual & family services
PA: Young Men's Christian Association Of Cleveland
1801 Superior Ave E # 130
Cleveland OH 44114
216 781-1337

Northfield
Summit County

(G-15508)
ADESA-OHIO LLC
Also Called: Adesa Cleveland
210 E Twinsburg Rd (44067-2848)
PHONE.................................330 467-8280
Fax: 330 467-2278
Jim Hellet, *Ch of Bd*
Don Harris, *COO*
Frank Birkas, *Opers Mgr*
William Stackhouse, *CFO*
John Hogsette, *VP Sales*
EMP: 200
SQ FT: 150,000
SALES (est): 30MM **Publicly Held**
WEB: www.adesa.com
SIC: 5012 Automobile auction
HQ: Adesa Corporation, Llc
13085 Hamilton Crossing B
Carmel IN 46032

(G-15509)
BALANCED CARE CORPORATION
Also Called: Outlook Pointe
997 W Aurora Rd (44067-1605)
PHONE.................................330 908-1166
Pete Szigeti, *Principal*
Toni Montgomery, *Director*
EMP: 50 **Privately Held**
SIC: 8741 8051 8621 Nursing & personal care facility management; skilled nursing care facilities; professional membership organizations
PA: Balanced Care Corporation
5000 Ritter Rd Ste 202
Mechanicsburg PA 17055

(G-15510)
BAVAN & ASSOCIATES
Also Called: Bevan and Associates Lpa
10360 Northfield Rd (44067-1445)
PHONE.................................330 650-0088
Fax: 330 467-4493
Keith Bavan, *President*
Dale S Economus, *Partner*
Dwight Motsco, *Financial Exec*
Raymond M Powell,
Charlene Gedeon, *Legal Staff*
EMP: 30
SQ FT: 7,000
SALES (est): 2.3MM **Privately Held**
WEB: www.bevanlaw.com
SIC: 8111 General practice attorney, lawyer

(G-15511)
BRENTWOOD LIFE CARE COMPANY
Also Called: Brentwood Health Care Center
907 W Aurora Rd (44067-1605)
PHONE.................................330 468-2273
Fax: 330 468-0455
Brent Classen, *Owner*
Autumn Richmond, *Director*
Pam Hustosky, *Social Worker*
EMP: 135
SQ FT: 38,700
SALES (est): 8MM **Privately Held**
SIC: 8051 Convalescent home with continuous nursing care

(G-15512)
CLEVELND CLNC HLTH SYSTM EAST
Also Called: Sagamore Hills Medical Center
863 W Aurora Rd (44067-1603)
PHONE.................................330 468-0190
Fax: 330 467-2283
Jennifer Simmons, *Branch Mgr*
EMP: 40
SALES (corp-wide): 8B **Privately Held**
SIC: 8062 8093 General medical & surgical hospitals; specialty outpatient clinics
HQ: Cleveland Clinic Health System-East Region
6803 Mayfield Rd Ste 500
Cleveland OH 44124
440 312-6010

(G-15513)
DENNIS & CAROL LIEDERBACH
8651 Wood Hollow Rd (44067-1852)
PHONE.................................256 582-6200
David Lienback, *General Mgr*
EMP: 35
SALES (est): 1.8MM **Privately Held**
SIC: 7389 Business services

(G-15514)
ESSENTIAL FREIGHT SYSTEMS INC (PA)
201 E Twinsburg Rd (44067-2847)
P.O. Box 118, Twinsburg (44087-0118)
PHONE.................................330 468-5898
Dale Hug, *President*
Cynthia Hug, *Treasurer*
Fred Coon, *Manager*

GEOGRAPHIC SECTION
Northwood - Wood County (G-15537)

EMP: 55
SALES (est): 4.5MM **Privately Held**
WEB: www.essentialfreight.com
SIC: 4214 Local trucking with storage

(G-15515)
FARMERS GROUP INC
Also Called: Farmers Insurance
500 W Aurora Rd Ste 115 (44067-2166)
PHONE..................................330 467-6575
Jose Quiles, *Branch Mgr*
Jeffrey Sindelar, *Agent*
EMP: 25
SALES (corp-wide): 68.4B **Privately Held**
SIC: 6411 Insurance agents, brokers & service
HQ: Farmers Group, Inc.
6301 Owensmouth Ave
Woodland Hills CA 91367
323 932-3200

(G-15516)
FERFOLIA FUNERAL HOMES INC
356 W Aurora Rd (44067-2104)
PHONE..................................216 663-4222
Fax: 330 467-5416
Donald Berfolia, *President*
Donald L Berfolia, *President*
Alice Ferfolia, *Treasurer*
Theresa Ferfolia, *Admin Sec*
EMP: 36
SQ FT: 15,000
SALES (est): 3.7MM **Privately Held**
WEB: www.ferfolia.com
SIC: 7261 Funeral home

(G-15517)
INNOVATIVE LOGISTICS SVCS INC
201 E Twinsburg Rd (44067-2847)
P.O. Box 560206, Macedonia (44056-0206)
PHONE..................................330 468-6422
Fax: 330 468-6442
Dale Hug, *President*
Cynthia Hug, *Corp Secy*
Fred Coon, *Opers Mgr*
Tony Hug, *Manager*
EMP: 55
SQ FT: 8,000
SALES (est): 8.8MM **Privately Held**
WEB: www.innlogistics.com
SIC: 4212 Local trucking, without storage

(G-15518)
JACKSON COMFORT SYSTEMS INC
Also Called: Jackson Comfort Htg Coolg Sys
499 E Twinsburg Rd (44067-2851)
PHONE..................................330 468-3111
Paul Jackson, *President*
Mark Jackson, *Vice Pres*
Matt Rhodes, *Vice Pres*
Gary Jackson, *Treasurer*
Keith McCann, *Sales Mgr*
EMP: 30
SQ FT: 13,000
SALES (est): 5.6MM **Privately Held**
WEB: www.jacksoncomfort.com
SIC: 1711 Hydronics heating contractor; warm air heating & air conditioning contractor; refrigeration contractor

(G-15519)
LOWES HOME CENTERS LLC
8224 Golden Link Blvd (44067-2067)
PHONE..................................330 908-2750
Fax: 330 908-2751
Al Rito, *Office Mgr*
Dave Rhodes, *Manager*
EMP: 150
SALES (corp-wide): 68.6B **Publicly Held**
SIC: 5211 5031 5722 5064 Home centers; building materials, exterior; building materials, interior; household appliance stores; electrical appliances, television & radio
HQ: Lowe's Home Centers, Llc
1605 Curtis Bridge Rd
Wilkesboro NC 28697
336 658-4000

(G-15520)
MENTAL HEALTH AND ADDI SERV
Also Called: Northcast Bhvral Halthcare Sys
1756 Sagamore Rd (44067-1086)
PHONE..................................330 467-7131
Fax: 330 467-3183
Douglas Kern, *CEO*
Tim Higgenbothem, *Safety Dir*
Eula Burrell, *Materials Mgr*
William Alt, *CFO*
Karl Donenwirth, *Director*
EMP: 300 **Privately Held**
SIC: 8063 9431 Psychiatric hospitals; mental health agency administration, government;
HQ: Ohio Department Of Mental Health And Addiction Services
30 E Broad St Fl 8
Columbus OH 43215

(G-15521)
NORTHFIELD PRESBT CH DAY CARE
7755 S Boyden Rd (44067-2452)
PHONE..................................330 467-4411
Maryellen Noss, *Director*
Bob Scott, *Director*
EMP: 33
SALES (est): 415.5K **Privately Held**
SIC: 8351 Child day care services

(G-15522)
NORTHFIELD PRESBT DAY CARE CTR
7755 S Boyden Rd (44067-2452)
PHONE..................................330 467-4411
Ann Kujawski, *Administration*
EMP: 40
SALES (est): 826.9K **Privately Held**
SIC: 8351 Child day care services

(G-15523)
REVILLE TIRE CO (PA)
Also Called: Reville Wholesale Distributing
8044 Olde 8 Rd (44067-2830)
PHONE..................................330 468-1900
Fax: 216 468-2396
Robert J Reville, *President*
James S Bidlake, *Principal*
Michael Reville, *Vice Pres*
Raymond L Reville III, *Vice Pres*
Richard H Reville, *Vice Pres*
EMP: 65 **EST:** 1970
SQ FT: 30,000
SALES (est): 44.6MM **Privately Held**
WEB: www.revillewhs.com
SIC: 5014 Automobile tires & tubes

(G-15524)
SPITZER CHEVROLET INC
333 E Aurora Rd (44067-2022)
PHONE..................................330 467-4141
Fax: 330 650-4973
Alan Spitzer, *Ch of Bd*
Janet May, *Treasurer*
Gary Blanchard, *Admin Sec*
EMP: 70
SQ FT: 45,000
SALES (est): 20.5MM **Privately Held**
SIC: 5511 7539 7538 5521 Automobiles, new & used; automotive repair shops; general automotive repair shops; used car dealers

(G-15525)
THOMAS E ANDERSON DDS INC
147 E Aurora Rd (44067-2084)
PHONE..................................330 467-6466
Thomas E Anderson, *President*
EMP: 25
SALES (est): 717.9K **Privately Held**
SIC: 8021 Dentists' office

Northwood
Wood County

(G-15526)
A E D INC
Also Called: Interstate Coml GL & Door
2845 Crane Way (43619-1098)
PHONE..................................419 661-9999
Fax: 419 661-9912
Daniel Erickson, *President*
Walter Erickson, *Vice Pres*
Karen Gurtveweilier, *Bookkeeper*
Pamela Erickson, *Admin Sec*
EMP: 33
SQ FT: 11,500
SALES (est): 7.2MM **Privately Held**
WEB: www.icgad.com
SIC: 1793 Glass & glazing work

(G-15527)
BRIDGESTONE RET OPERATIONS LLC
Also Called: Michel Tires Plus 227574
3311 Woodville Rd (43619-1527)
PHONE..................................419 691-7111
Melissa Goodman, *Manager*
EMP: 30
SALES (corp-wide): 32.5B **Privately Held**
WEB: www.tiresplus.com
SIC: 7534 Tire retreading & repair shops
HQ: Bridgestone Retail Operations, Llc
333 E Lake St Ste 300
Bloomingdale IL 60108
630 259-9000

(G-15528)
BUCKEYE TELESYSTEM INC
2700 Oregon Rd (43619-1057)
P.O. Box 1116, Holland (43528-1116)
PHONE..................................419 724-9898
Fax: 419 724-3814
Thomas K Dawson, *Vice Pres*
Kirk Dombek, *Vice Pres*
John E Martin, *Vice Pres*
Doug Ward, *Vice Pres*
Harry Kuebler, *Technical Mgr*
EMP: 60
SALES (est): 9.8MM
SALES (corp-wide): 690.9MM **Privately Held**
WEB: www.blockcommunications.com
SIC: 4813
PA: Block Communications, Inc.
405 Madison Ave Ste 2100
Toledo OH 43604
419 724-6212

(G-15529)
CAMPBELL INC (PA)
Also Called: Total Solutions
2875 Crane Way (43619-1098)
PHONE..................................419 476-4444
K Keith Campbell, *President*
Robert A Eaton, *Vice Pres*
Peter J Vavrinek, *CFO*
Paul Suda, *Sales Engr*
Dan Feasby, *Sales Staff*
EMP: 61 **EST:** 1968
SQ FT: 14,650
SALES (est): 10.7MM **Privately Held**
WEB: www.campbellinc.com
SIC: 1711 Mechanical contractor

(G-15530)
EMI ENTERPRISES INC
Also Called: Envelope Mart
2639 Tracy Rd (43619-1006)
P.O. Box 307, Toledo (43697-0307)
PHONE..................................419 666-0012
Fax: 419 666-8885
Norman Shapiro, *President*
Gregory Shapiro, *Vice Pres*
Myron Shapiro, *Vice Pres*
Grace Schumacher, *CFO*
Nicole Norwalk, *Sales Executive*
EMP: 45
SQ FT: 15,000
SALES (est): 13.5MM **Privately Held**
WEB: www.envelopemart.com
SIC: 5112 Envelopes

(G-15531)
FEDERAL EXPRESS CORPORATION
Also Called: Fedex
7600 Caple Blvd (43619-1091)
PHONE..................................800 463-3339
Ken Davison, *Manager*
EMP: 109
SALES (corp-wide): 60.3B **Publicly Held**
WEB: www.federalexpress.com
SIC: 4513 Package delivery, private air
HQ: Federal Express Corporation
3610 Hacks Cross Rd
Memphis TN 38125
901 369-3600

(G-15532)
FEDEX FREIGHT CORPORATION
7779 Arbor Dr (43619-7506)
PHONE..................................800 728-8190
Fax: 419 727-1687
Thil Harper, *Branch Mgr*
EMP: 150
SQ FT: 62,424
SALES (corp-wide): 60.3B **Publicly Held**
SIC: 4213 4731 Less-than-truckload (LTL) transport; freight transportation arrangement
HQ: Fedex Freight Corporation
1715 Aaron Brenner Dr
Memphis TN 38120

(G-15533)
HIRZEL CANNING COMPANY (PA)
Also Called: Dei Fratelli
411 Lemoyne Rd (43619-1699)
PHONE..................................419 693-0531
Fax: 419 693-4859
Karl A Hirzel Jr, *President*
Eric Hirzel, *General Mgr*
Lou Kozma, *General Mgr*
Emily Neuenschwander, *QA Dir*
Michael Rudin, *QC Mgr*
▲ EMP: 100 **EST:** 1923
SQ FT: 250,000
SALES (est): 29.6MM **Privately Held**
WEB: www.hirzel.com
SIC: 2033 8611 2034 Tomato products: packaged in cans, jars, etc.; tomato juice: packaged in cans, jars, etc.; tomato paste: packaged in cans, jars, etc.; tomato purees: packaged in cans, jars, etc.; business associations; dehydrated fruits, vegetables, soups

(G-15534)
INSTALLED BUILDING PDTS LLC
Also Called: Royalty Mooney & Moses
6412 Fairfield Dr Ste A (43619-7514)
PHONE..................................419 662-4524
Fax: 419 662-4530
Joe Loch, *Principal*
EMP: 40
SALES (est): 1.6MM **Privately Held**
SIC: 1742 5211 Insulation, buildings; insulation material, building; bathroom fixtures, equipment & supplies

(G-15535)
LAKEWOOD GREENHOUSE INC
909 Lemoyne Rd (43619-1817)
PHONE..................................419 691-3541
Fax: 419 691-4313
Walter F Krueger Jr, *President*
Mary M Krueger, *Corp Secy*
Mary Ann Franke, *Manager*
▲ EMP: 45
SQ FT: 20,000
SALES (est): 4.1MM **Privately Held**
SIC: 0181 Flowers: grown under cover (e.g. greenhouse production)

(G-15536)
MACOMB GROUP INC
Also Called: Macomb Group Toledo Division
2830 Crane Way (43619-1095)
PHONE..................................419 666-6899
Mark D Calzolano, *Vice Pres*
Kenny Miller, *Purch Agent*
Tom Samson, *Sales Engr*
Mike Pavelich, *Sales Staff*
Kelly Brisbin, *Sales Associate*
EMP: 30
SALES (corp-wide): 166.9MM **Privately Held**
SIC: 5074 Pipes & fittings, plastic
PA: The Macomb Group Inc
6600 15 Mile Rd
Sterling Heights MI 48312
586 274-4100

(G-15537)
MOTOR CARRIER SERVICE INC
815 Lemoyne Rd (43619-1815)
PHONE..................................419 693-6207
Fax: 419 693-2510

Northwood - Wood County (G-15538)

Keith A Tuttle, *President*
John Fritziuf, *General Mgr*
Sara Wood, *Opers Staff*
Ronda Sherrer, *Purch Dir*
David Slesinski, *Controller*
EMP: 110
SQ FT: 10,000
SALES (est): 31MM **Privately Held**
SIC: 4213 Contract haulers

(G-15538)
NATIONAL ASSN LTR CARRIERS
Also Called: N A L C
4437 Woodville Rd (43619-1859)
PHONE...................................419 693-8392
Robert T Newbold, *President*
EMP: 53
SALES (corp-wide): 1.4B **Privately Held**
WEB: www.nalc.org
SIC: 8631 Labor union
PA: National Association Of Letter Carriers
100 Indana Ave Nw Ste 709
Washington DC 20001
202 393-4695

(G-15539)
NORTH AMERCN SCIENCE ASSOC INC (PA)
Also Called: Namsa
6750 Wales Rd (43619-1012)
PHONE...................................419 666-9455
Fax: 419 662-4386
John J Gorski, *President*
An Liu, *General Mgr*
Elizabeth Kempen, *COO*
John Amat, *Vice Pres*
Jane A Kervin, *Vice Pres*
EMP: 250
SQ FT: 135,000
SALES (est): 156.2MM **Privately Held**
WEB: www.namsa.com
SIC: 8731 8734 Medical research, commercial; testing laboratories

(G-15540)
NORTH AMERCN SCIENCE ASSOC INC
Also Called: Namsa Sterilization Products
2261 Tracy Rd (43619-1397)
PHONE...................................419 666-9455
Fax: 419 666-2954
Richard Wallin, *Branch Mgr*
EMP: 142
SALES (corp-wide): 156.2MM **Privately Held**
SIC: 8731 Medical research, commercial
PA: North American Science Associates, Inc.
6750 Wales Rd
Northwood OH 43619
419 666-9455

(G-15541)
NWO BEVERAGE INC
Also Called: N W O
6700 Wales Rd (43619-1012)
PHONE...................................419 725-2162
Pj Sullivan, *Vice Pres*
Joe Schetz, *Vice Pres*
Chris Moses, *Manager*
EMP: 48
SALES (est): 18.6MM **Privately Held**
SIC: 5181 Beer & other fermented malt liquors

(G-15542)
OH ST TRANS DIST 02 OUTPOST
200 Lemoyne Rd (43619-1630)
PHONE...................................419 693-8870
Herman Munn, *Manager*
Craig Schneiderbauer, *Manager*
EMP: 30
SALES (est): 920.5K **Privately Held**
SIC: 4789 Transportation services

(G-15543)
PRESCRIPTION SUPPLY INC
2233 Tracy Rd (43619-1302)
PHONE...................................419 661-6600
Fax: 419 661-6617
Thomas Schoen, *President*
Jacquelyn J Harbauer, *Corp Secy*
Candace Harbauer, *Vice Pres*
Randy Buck, *Controller*
Julie A Lewandowski, *Controller*
EMP: 54
SQ FT: 30,000
SALES: 78.3MM **Privately Held**
WEB: www.prescriptionsupply.com
SIC: 5122 Pharmaceuticals

(G-15544)
SATTLERPEARSON INC
Also Called: Wright Harvey House, The
3055 E Plaza Blvd (43619-2037)
PHONE...................................419 698-3822
Fax: 419 698-3855
Patricia Pearson, *President*
Jenny Bucher, *Mktg Dir*
Chris Mills, *Office Mgr*
Natalie Tousley, *Director*
Paula Cluckey, *Food Svc Dir*
EMP: 26
SALES: 800K **Privately Held**
WEB: www.wrightharvey.com
SIC: 8361 Geriatric residential care

(G-15545)
THYSSENKRUPP LOGISTICS INC (DH)
Also Called: Copper and Brass Sales Div
8001 Thyssenkrupp Pkwy (43619-2082)
PHONE...................................419 662-1800
Joachim Limberg, *Chairman*
James Baber, *Vice Pres*
EMP: 62
SALES (est): 22.3MM
SALES (corp-wide): 48.7B **Privately Held**
SIC: 4213 Trucking, except local
HQ: Thyssenkrupp Materials Na, Inc.
22355 W 11 Mile Rd
Southfield MI 48033
248 233-5600

(G-15546)
TKX LOGISTICS
Also Called: Thyssen Krupp Logistics
8001 Thyssenkrupp Pkwy (43619-2082)
PHONE...................................419 662-1800
Fax: 419 662-6563
Joachim Limberg, *Chairman*
Jim Baber, *Vice Pres*
EMP: 43
SALES (est): 9.9MM **Privately Held**
SIC: 4213 Trucking, except local

(G-15547)
TL INDUSTRIES INC (PA)
2541 Tracy Rd (43619-1097)
PHONE...................................419 666-8144
Fax: 419 666-6534
Richard Blausey, *President*
Joseph Young, *Vice Pres*
Theodore Stetschulte, *Vice Pres*
Paul Rodgers, *Prdtn Mgr*
Keith Kogler, *Purch Agent*
EMP: 200
SQ FT: 36,000
SALES (est): 30.7MM **Privately Held**
SIC: 8711 3444 3629 3679 Electrical or electronic engineering; sheet metalwork; battery chargers, rectifying or nonrotating; loads, electronic

(G-15548)
TOWLIFT INC
2860 Crane Way (43619-1095)
PHONE...................................419 666-1333
Fax: 419 666-3608
Brent Cannon, *Manager*
EMP: 50
SALES (corp-wide): 106.6MM **Privately Held**
SIC: 5084 7353 7699 Materials handling machinery; heavy construction equipment rental; industrial equipment services
PA: Towlift, Inc.
1395 Valley Belt Rd
Brooklyn Heights OH 44131
216 749-6800

(G-15549)
TREU HOUSE OF MUNCH INC
8000 Arbor Dr (43619-7505)
PHONE...................................419 666-7770
Fax: 419 666-5712
Richard G Esser, *President*
Todd Esser, *Vice Pres*
Rick Niehaus, *Vice Pres*
James Layman, *Treasurer*
Greg Hipp, *Human Res Dir*
EMP: 100 **EST:** 1875
SQ FT: 120,000
SALES (est): 29.1MM **Privately Held**
WEB: www.treuhouse.com
SIC: 5181 Beer & other fermented malt liquors

(G-15550)
WASTE MANAGEMENT OHIO INC
Also Called: Waste Management Ohio NW
6525 Wales Rd (43619-1330)
PHONE...................................866 409-4671
Ginger Kaladas, *Credit Staff*
John Stark, *Manager*
Lee Hicks, *Contract Law*
EMP: 65
SALES (corp-wide): 14.4B **Publicly Held**
SIC: 4953 Rubbish collection & disposal
HQ: Waste Management Of Ohio, Inc.
1700 N Broad St
Fairborn OH 45324

(G-15551)
WESCO DISTRIBUTION INC
6519 Fairfield Dr (43619-7507)
PHONE...................................419 666-1670
Chad Marrison, *Branch Mgr*
EMP: 28 **Publicly Held**
SIC: 5085 3699 Industrial supplies; electrical equipment & supplies
HQ: Wesco Distribution, Inc.
225 W Station Square Dr # 700
Pittsburgh PA 15219

(G-15552)
WOJOS HEATING & AC INC
5523 Woodville Rd (43619-2209)
PHONE...................................419 693-3220
Fax: 419 698-0587
Thomas Wojo Ciehowfki, *President*
Chuck Westenbarger, *Opers Mgr*
Robert Shamy, *Sales Mgr*
Leann St Johns, *Manager*
EMP: 25
SALES (est): 2.8MM **Privately Held**
SIC: 1711 Warm air heating & air conditioning contractor

(G-15553)
YANFENG US AUTOMOTIVE
Also Called: Johnson Contrls Authorized Dlr
7560 Arbor Dr (43619-7500)
PHONE...................................419 662-4905
Fax: 419 662-4977
Keith Wandell, *President*
Jeffrey Peterson, *Engineer*
Justin Shupp, *Manager*
EMP: 96 **Privately Held**
SIC: 2531 5075 Public building & related furniture; warm air heating & air conditioning
HQ: Yanfeng Us Automotive Interior Systems I Llc
41935 W 12 Mile Rd
Novi MI 48377
248 319-7333

Norton
Summit County

(G-15554)
BARBERTON TREE SERVICE INC
3307 Clark Mill Rd (44203-1027)
PHONE...................................330 848-2344
Fax: 330 848-9474
Keith Luck, *President*
EMP: 50 **EST:** 1978
SQ FT: 5,000
SALES (est): 7MM **Privately Held**
WEB: www.barbertontree.com
SIC: 0783 Pruning services, ornamental tree; removal services, bush & tree; surgery services, ornamental tree

(G-15555)
COMPASS SYSTEMS & SALES LLC
5185 New Haven Cir (44203-4672)
PHONE...................................330 733-2111
Fax: 330 733-2161
Robert S Sherrod, *President*
Mark Rubin, *Vice Pres*
Steve Sherrod, *Opers Mgr*
Bob Gannon, *Project Engr*
Brenda Pavlantos, *Treasurer*
▼ **EMP:** 56
SQ FT: 43,500
SALES (est): 14.6MM **Privately Held**
SIC: 3542 0724 Mechanical (pneumatic or hydraulic) metal forming machines; cotton ginning

(G-15556)
NARAGON COMPANIES INC
2197 Wadsworth Rd (44203-5328)
PHONE...................................330 745-7700
Fax: 330 745-4786
Michael Naragon, *President*
Jeff Naragon, *Vice Pres*
EMP: 30
SQ FT: 1,780
SALES (est): 5.1MM **Privately Held**
SIC: 1711 5261 Irrigation sprinkler system installation; hydroponic equipment & supplies

(G-15557)
NELSEN CORPORATION (PA)
3250 Barber Rd (44203-1012)
P.O. Box 1028 (44203-9428)
PHONE...................................330 745-6000
Fax: 330 745-8635
Ronald E Nelsen, *CEO*
David Nelsen, *President*
Jeanette Nelsen, *Corp Secy*
Kim Bell, *Vice Pres*
Calvin Washechek, *Sales Associate*
▲ **EMP:** 50
SQ FT: 33,000
SALES (est): 34MM **Privately Held**
WEB: www.nelsencorp.com
SIC: 5074 Water purification equipment

(G-15558)
PARAMOUNT PLUMBING INC (PA)
3080 S Medina Line Rd (44203-7900)
PHONE...................................330 336-1096
James Reynolds, *President*
Kim Reynolds, *Corp Secy*
Kelly Good, *Office Mgr*
EMP: 39
SALES (est): 4.3MM **Privately Held**
SIC: 1711 Plumbing contractors

(G-15559)
ROMASTER CORP
3013 Wadsworth Rd (44203-5310)
PHONE...................................330 825-1945
Valentin Roman, *President*
EMP: 65
SALES (est): 1.7MM **Privately Held**
SIC: 7349 Janitorial service, contract basis

(G-15560)
WILLIAMS CONCRETE CNSTR CO INC
2959 Barber Rd Ste 100 (44203-1005)
PHONE...................................330 745-6388
Nancy C Williams, *President*
EMP: 36
SQ FT: 4,000
SALES (est): 4.4MM **Privately Held**
SIC: 1771 Concrete pumping

Norwalk
Huron County

(G-15561)
ADVANCED CMPT CONNECTIONS LLC
Also Called: Wireless Connections
166 Milan Ave (44857-1146)
PHONE...................................419 668-4080
Fax: 419 668-4077
Michael Cowan, *President*
Terry Wilson, *Editor*
Sabu Krishnan, *COO*
David Hatala, *Vice Pres*
Bill Waters, *Vice Pres*
EMP: 32
SQ FT: 28,000

GEOGRAPHIC SECTION

Norwalk - Huron County (G-15586)

SALES (est): 21MM **Privately Held**
WEB: www.acc-corp.net
SIC: 5045 4813 Computer peripheral equipment; computer software;

(G-15562)
BACKOFFICE ASSOCIATES LLC
16 Executive Dr Ste 200 (44857-2486)
PHONE..........................419 660-4600
Nick Woolaver, *Branch Mgr*
EMP: 65 **Privately Held**
SIC: 8742 Management consulting services
HQ: Backoffice Associates, Llc
    75 Perseverance Way 201a
    Hyannis MA 02601

(G-15563)
CITY OF NORWALK
Also Called: Street Deparment
42 Woodlawn Ave (44857-2257)
PHONE..........................419 663-6715
Fax: 419 663-6716
Richard Moore, *Superintendent*
EMP: 27
SQ FT: 1,224 **Privately Held**
SIC: 1611 9111 Highway & street paving contractor; mayors' offices
PA: City Of Norwalk
    38 Whittlesey Ave
    Norwalk OH 44857
    419 663-6700

(G-15564)
CIVISTA BANK
16 Executive Dr (44857-2486)
P.O. Box 5016, Sandusky (44871-5016)
PHONE..........................419 744-3100
Fax: 419 668-1630
William Heitman, *Vice Pres*
Dennis Shaffer, *Vice Pres*
EMP: 35 **Publicly Held**
SIC: 6022 6021 State commercial banks; national commercial banks
HQ: Civista Bank
    100 E Water St
    Sandusky OH 44870
    419 625-4121

(G-15565)
CLE TRANSPORTATION COMPANY
203 Republic St (44857-1157)
PHONE..........................567 805-4008
Igor Stankic, *President*
Daniela Stankic, *Vice Pres*
EMP: 62 EST: 2016
SALES (est): 8MM **Privately Held**
SIC: 4213 Trucking, except local

(G-15566)
CLI INCORPORATED
306 S Norwalk Rd W (44857-9529)
PHONE..........................419 668-8840
John Schwartz, *President*
EMP: 125 EST: 1976
SQ FT: 20,000
SALES (est): 764.3K **Privately Held**
SIC: 8331 Sheltered workshop

(G-15567)
COUNSELING CENTER HURON COUNTY
Also Called: Fireland Hospital
292 Benedict Ave (44857-2374)
PHONE..........................419 663-3737
Fax: 419 663-5096
Bruce Kijowski, *Manager*
Renee Jerome, *Manager*
EMP: 31
SALES (est): 728.3K **Privately Held**
SIC: 8093 8322 Mental health clinic, outpatient; emergency social services

(G-15568)
COUNTY OF HURON
Also Called: Job and Family Services
185 Shady Lane Dr (44857-2397)
PHONE..........................419 668-8126
Jill Eversol Nolan, *Director*
Joe Nolan, *Director*
Lenora Minor, *Administration*
EMP: 95
SQ FT: 25,000 **Privately Held**
WEB: www.huroncountyema.com

SIC: 8322 9111 7361 Public welfare center; children's aid society; county supervisors' & executives' offices; employment agencies
PA: County Of Huron
    180 Milan Ave Ste 7
    Norwalk OH 44857
    419 668-3092

(G-15569)
COUNTY OF HURON
Also Called: Children Service Unit
185 Shady Lane Dr (44857-2397)
PHONE..........................419 663-5437
Fax: 419 668-4738
David Broehl, *Manager*
Elayne Siegfried, *Manager*
Judy Fegen, *Director*
EMP: 90 **Privately Held**
WEB: www.huroncountyema.com
SIC: 8322 9111 Child related social services; county supervisors' & executives' offices
PA: County Of Huron
    180 Milan Ave Ste 7
    Norwalk OH 44857
    419 668-3092

(G-15570)
DON TESTER FORD LINCOLN INC
2800 Route 250 S (44857)
PHONE..........................419 668-8233
Scott Tester, *President*
Pete Lepley, *General Mgr*
EMP: 50
SALES (est): 3MM **Privately Held**
SIC: 5511 7532 Automobiles, new & used; body shop, automotive

(G-15571)
DURABLE CORPORATION
75 N Pleasant St (44857-1218)
P.O. Box 290 (44857-0290)
PHONE..........................800 537-1603
Fax: 419 668-8068
Jon M Anderson, *CEO*
Tom Secor, *President*
Marcia Norris, *Principal*
Michael Croskey, *Plant Mgr*
Tom Phillips, *Production*
◆ EMP: 60
SQ FT: 3,000
SALES (est): 12.6MM **Privately Held**
WEB: www.durablecorp.com
SIC: 3069 2273 5013 Mats or matting, rubber; molded rubber products; rubber automotive products; mats & matting; bumpers

(G-15572)
ERIE HURON CAC HEADSTART INC
11 E League St (44857-1378)
PHONE..........................419 663-2623
Janice Alexander, *Director*
EMP: 25
SALES (est): 251.1K **Privately Held**
SIC: 8351 Child day care services

(G-15573)
FIRELANDS REGIONAL HEALTH SYS
Also Called: Firelnds Cnsling Recovery Svcs
292 Benedict Ave (44857-2374)
PHONE..........................419 663-3737
Renee Gerome, *Manager*
EMP: 28
SALES (corp-wide): 15.5K **Privately Held**
SIC: 8093 8322 Alcohol clinic, outpatient; emergency social services
PA: Firelands Regional Health System
    1111 Hayes Ave
    Sandusky OH 44870
    419 557-7400

(G-15574)
FISHER-TITUS MEDICAL CENTER
Also Called: Carriage House
175 Shady Lane Dr Off (44857-2387)
PHONE..........................419 668-4228
Fax: 419 668-6026
Terri William, *Administration*
EMP: 25

SALES (est): 870.6K
SALES (corp-wide): 130.8MM **Privately Held**
WEB: www.fisher-titus.com
SIC: 8052 Intermediate care facilities
PA: Fisher-Titus Medical Center
    272 Benedict Ave
    Norwalk OH 44857
    419 668-8101

(G-15575)
FISHER-TITUS MEDICAL CENTER (PA)
272 Benedict Ave (44857-2374)
PHONE..........................419 668-8101
Fax: 419 663-6036
Robert Andrews, *Ch of Bd*
Virginia Poling, *Vice Ch Bd*
Patrick J Martin, *President*
Matthew Gutowicz, *Ch Radiology*
Duane Woods, *Vice Pres*
▲ EMP: 850
SQ FT: 83,000
SALES: 130.8MM **Privately Held**
WEB: www.fisher-titus.com
SIC: 8052 8062 Intermediate care facilities; general medical & surgical hospitals

(G-15576)
GAYMONT NURSING HOMES INC
Also Called: Gaymont Nursing Center
66 Norwood Ave (44857-2385)
PHONE..........................419 668-8258
William C Dotson, *President*
James Gottfried, *Director*
Theresa Porter, *Director*
Tami Taft, *Hlthcr Dir*
Pat Peschke, *Records Dir*
EMP: 95
SQ FT: 34,500
SALES (est): 6.6MM **Privately Held**
SIC: 8051 8052 Convalescent home with continuous nursing care; intermediate care facilities

(G-15577)
KAISER-WELLS INC
Also Called: Kaiser Wells Pharmacy
251 Benedict Ave (44857-2346)
PHONE..........................419 668-7651
Fax: 419 663-5837
John G Kaiser Jr, *President*
Donald A Baur, *Vice Pres*
Lisa R Nestor, *Vice Pres*
EMP: 30
SQ FT: 8,000
SALES (est): 5.9MM **Privately Held**
SIC: 5912 8082 Drug stores; home health care services

(G-15578)
LAKE ERIE CONSTRUCTION CO
25 S Norwalk Rd E (44857-9259)
P.O. Box 777 (44857-0777)
PHONE..........................419 668-3302
Fax: 419 663-4324
David P Bleile, *President*
Raymond Chapin, *Vice Pres*
Michael Bleile, *Treasurer*
Rebecca Ames, *Manager*
Kenneth Bleile, *Admin Sec*
EMP: 200
SQ FT: 6,000
SALES (est): 31MM **Privately Held**
WEB: www.lec-co.com
SIC: 1611 Guardrail construction, highways; highway & street sign installation

(G-15579)
LAKE ERIE HOME REPAIR
257 Milan Ave (44857-1123)
PHONE..........................419 871-0687
John Jackson, *Principal*
Darell Williams, *Manager*
EMP: 25
SALES: 950K **Privately Held**
SIC: 1522 Residential construction

(G-15580)
MC FADDEN CONSTRUCTION INC
4426 Old State Rd N (44857-9139)
P.O. Box 463 (44857-0463)
PHONE..........................419 668-4165
Marvin Smith, *President*
Michael F McFadden, *Superintendent*

Neil E McFadden, *Principal*
EMP: 30
SALES (est): 1.3MM **Privately Held**
SIC: 1799 Exterior cleaning, including sandblasting

(G-15581)
NEWCOMER CONCRETE SERVICES INC (PA)
646 Townline Road 151 (44857-9255)
P.O. Box 672 (44857-0672)
PHONE..........................419 668-2789
Fax: 419 663-3441
Jeffery Newcomer, *CEO*
David Newcomer, *CFO*
Linda Newcomer Holmer, *Admin Sec*
EMP: 64
SQ FT: 13,000
SALES (est): 9.1MM **Privately Held**
WEB: www.newcomerconcrete.com
SIC: 1771 1794 Concrete pumping; excavation & grading, building construction

(G-15582)
NORTHERN OHIO RURAL WATER
2205 Us Highway 20 E (44857-9521)
P.O. Box 96, Collins (44826-0096)
PHONE..........................419 668-7213
Fax: 419 668-7617
Jim Ruggles, *Bookkeeper*
Thomas Reese, *Director*
EMP: 35
SALES: 6.7MM **Privately Held**
SIC: 4941 Water supply

(G-15583)
NORWALK AREA HEALTH SERVICES (HQ)
272 Benedict Ave (44857-2374)
PHONE..........................419 668-8101
Patrick Martin, *President*
Paul Douglas, *VP Finance*
EMP: 150
SALES: 7.5MM
SALES (corp-wide): 1.5MM **Privately Held**
SIC: 4119 Ambulance service
PA: Norwalk Area Health Systems, Inc.
    272 Benedict Ave
    Norwalk OH 44857
    419 668-8101

(G-15584)
NORWALK AREA HLTH SYSTEMS INC (PA)
272 Benedict Ave (44857-2374)
PHONE..........................419 668-8101
Patrick J Martin, *President*
Duane Woods, *Vice Pres*
David Wilson, *Controller*
Lisa Demcho, *Associate*
EMP: 800
SQ FT: 200,000
SALES: 1.5MM **Privately Held**
WEB: www.ftmc.com
SIC: 8062 8051 General medical & surgical hospitals; skilled nursing care facilities

(G-15585)
NORWALK CLINIC INC
257 Benedict Ave Ste C1 (44857-2391)
PHONE..........................419 668-4851
Fax: 419 663-5146
James A Gottfried, *President*
Marcia Ceil, *Financial Exec*
EMP: 30 EST: 1962
SQ FT: 4,000
SALES (est): 2.1MM **Privately Held**
SIC: 8011 Clinic, operated by physicians

(G-15586)
NORWALK GOLF PROPERTIES INC
Also Called: Eagle Creek Golf Club
2406 New State Rd (44857-7100)
PHONE..........................419 668-8535
Fax: 419 668-9087
Robert Bleile, *President*
Marc Schaffer, *Vice Pres*
Jeff Rosengarten, *Treasurer*
Gary Wilkins, *Treasurer*
Becky Carpenter, *Manager*
EMP: 30
SQ FT: 100

Norwalk - Huron County (G-15587)

SALES (est): 1.4MM **Privately Held**
WEB: www.eaglecreekgolf.com
SIC: **7992** 6514 Public golf courses; dwelling operators, except apartments

(G-15587)
PALAZZO BROTHERS ELECTRIC INC
2811 State Route 18 (44857-8829)
PHONE..........................419 668-1100
Joseph M Palazzo, *President*
Doug Stang, *Opers Mgr*
EMP: 32
SQ FT: 2,674
SALES (est): 7.4MM **Privately Held**
SIC: **1731** 1799 General electrical contractor; sign installation & maintenance

(G-15588)
PAYNE NICKLES & CO CPA (PA)
Also Called: Furlong, Lawrence P CPA
257 Benedict Ave Ste D (44857-2715)
PHONE..........................419 668-2552
Fax: 419 663-3637
Carl McGookey, *President*
John Payne, *President*
Dave Brink, *Vice Pres*
Ennis Camp, *Vice Pres*
Allen Nickles, *Vice Pres*
EMP: 28
SALES (est): 4MM **Privately Held**
SIC: **8721** Certified public accountant

(G-15589)
R & L TRANSFER INC
Also Called: R & L Carriers
1403 State Route 18 (44857-9519)
PHONE..........................216 531-3324
Fax: 419 668-6629
Chris Biock, *General Mgr*
Chris Viock, *Branch Mgr*
Jim Ronde, *Manager*
EMP: 225 **Privately Held**
WEB: www.robertsarena.com
SIC: **4213** 4212 Trucking, except local; local trucking, without storage
HQ: R & L Transfer, Inc.
600 Gilliam Rd
Wilmington OH 45177
937 382-1494

(G-15590)
RENAISSANCE HOUSE INC
48 Executive Dr Ste 1 (44857-2492)
PHONE..........................419 663-1316
Fax: 419 663-6307
Joan Tommas, *Manager*
Joni Tommas, *Manager*
EMP: 35
SALES (corp-wide): 4.4MM **Privately Held**
WEB: www.renaissancehouseinc.com
SIC: **8361** Home for the mentally retarded
PA: Renaissance House Inc
103 N Washington St
Tiffin OH 44883
419 447-7901

(G-15591)
RON JOHNSON PLUMBING AND HTG
14805 Shawmill Rd (44857-9633)
PHONE..........................419 433-5365
Fax: 419 433-5426
Sandra S Johnson, *President*
Scott Johnson, *Corp Secy*
Mylinda Johnson, *Manager*
EMP: 25
SQ FT: 22,000
SALES (est): 3.1MM **Privately Held**
WEB: www.johnsonphe.com
SIC: **1711** Plumbing contractors; warm air heating & air conditioning contractor

(G-15592)
SCHAFFER MARK EXCVTG & TRCKING
1623 Old State Rd N (44857-9377)
PHONE..........................419 663-0984
Fax: 419 663-0984
Mark Schaffer, *President*
Mary Jo Moyer, *Vice Pres*
Diane Schaffer, *Admin Sec*
EMP: 55
SQ FT: 100,000
SALES (est): 11.9MM **Privately Held**
SIC: **1794** 1623 1795 Excavation & grading, building construction; water, sewer & utility lines; wrecking & demolition work

(G-15593)
STEIN HOSPICE SERVICES INC
150 Milan Ave (44857-2620)
PHONE..........................419 663-3222
Annabelle Stewart, *Manager*
EMP: 89
SALES (corp-wide): 28.8MM **Privately Held**
SIC: **8069** 8052 Chronic disease hospital; personal care facility
PA: Stein Hospice Services, Inc.
1200 Sycamore Line
Sandusky OH 44870
800 625-5269

(G-15594)
THE MAPLE CITY ICE COMPANY (PA)
371 Cleveland Rd (44857-9027)
PHONE..........................419 668-2531
Fax: 419 668-5291
Patricia Hipp, *President*
John Hipp, *Vice Pres*
Jeff Hipp, *Treasurer*
Donn Eddy, *Manager*
Gerard Hipp, *Admin Sec*
EMP: 41
SQ FT: 57,000
SALES (est): 26.9MM **Privately Held**
SIC: **5181** Beer & other fermented malt liquors

(G-15595)
TWILIGHT GARDENS HEALTHCARE
196 W Main St (44857-1915)
PHONE..........................419 668-2086
Fax: 419 668-9365
Carol Starkey, *President*
Kenneth Corby Starkey, *Vice Pres*
Kermit Starkey Jr, *Vice Pres*
Cindy Starkey, *Treasurer*
Mark Bigler, *Director*
EMP: 40 EST: 1960
SQ FT: 5,500
SALES (est): 2.6MM
SALES (corp-wide): 68.5MM **Privately Held**
SIC: **8051** 8052 Skilled nursing care facilities; intermediate care facilities
PA: Saber Healthcare Group, L.L.C.
26691 Richmond Rd Frnt
Bedford OH 44146
216 292-5706

(G-15596)
WASINIAK CONSTRUCTION INC
2519 State Route 61 (44857-9181)
PHONE..........................419 668-8624
Fax: 419 668-0338
John Wasiniak, *President*
James Wasiniak, *Vice Pres*
Edward Will, *Vice Pres*
Jakie Crane, *Manager*
EMP: 60
SQ FT: 1,000
SALES (est): 6.8MM **Privately Held**
SIC: **1741** 1771 Masonry & other stonework; concrete work

(G-15597)
ZEITER TRUCKING INC
Also Called: Zeiter Leasing
2590 State Route 18 (44857-8831)
PHONE..........................419 668-2229
Richard D Zeiter, *President*
Mark Zeiter, *Vice Pres*
Steven Zeiter, *Vice Pres*
Carol C Zeiter, *Director*
Kim Zieter, *Admin Sec*
EMP: 45 EST: 1963
SALES: 6MM **Privately Held**
SIC: **4212** Dump truck haulage

Norwood
Hamilton County

(G-15598)
CUSHMAN & WAKEFIELD INC
Also Called: Cassidy Turley
4600 Montgomery Rd (45212-2697)
PHONE..........................513 631-1121
Rick Sickinger, *Accountant*
EMP: 44
SALES (corp-wide): 5.5B **Privately Held**
SIC: **6531** Real estate agents & managers
HQ: Cushman & Wakefield, Inc.
225 W Wacker Dr Ste 3000
Chicago IL 60606
312 424-8000

(G-15599)
EMD MILLIPORE CORPORATION
2909 Highland Ave (45212-2411)
PHONE..........................513 631-0445
Michael Mulligan, *Prdtn Mgr*
Bob Wileczek, *Prdtn Mgr*
Rob Highley, *Safety Mgr*
Lisa Morris, *Purch Mgr*
Kevin Drews, *Purch Agent*
EMP: 150
SQ FT: 100,000
SALES (corp-wide): 18B **Privately Held**
WEB: www.emdchemicals.com
SIC: **8731** 3295 2899 2842 Biotechnical research, commercial; minerals, ground or treated; chemical preparations; specialty cleaning, polishes & sanitation goods; biological products, except diagnostic
HQ: Emd Millipore Corporation
400 Summit Dr
Burlington MA 01803
781 533-6000

(G-15600)
TEXO INTERNATIONAL INC
2828 Highland Ave (45212-2410)
PHONE..........................513 731-6350
Robert W Fisher, *President*
Craig Berkhart, *Principal*
Michael A Fisher, *Exec VP*
Greg Brodrick, *Vice Pres*
Jack Forrester, *Vice Pres*
EMP: 80
SALES (est): 7.8MM **Privately Held**
SIC: **5169** Specialty cleaning & sanitation preparations

Novelty
Geauga County

(G-15601)
ASM INTERNATIONAL
9639 Kinsman Rd (44073-0002)
PHONE..........................440 338-5151
Fax: 440 338-4634
Thomas Dudley, *CEO*
William Mahoney, *Managing Dir*
Ed Kubel, *Editor*
Steve Lampman, *Editor*
Joanne Miller, *Prdtn Mgr*
▲ EMP: 80 EST: 1913
SQ FT: 55,000
SALES: 12.8MM **Privately Held**
WEB: www.aeromat.com
SIC: **2731** 2721 7389 7999 Books: publishing only; periodicals: publishing only; advertising, promotional & trade show services; promoters of shows & exhibitions; trade show arrangement; exhibition operation

(G-15602)
O C I CONSTRUCTION CO INC
8560 Pekin Rd (44072-9717)
PHONE..........................440 338-3166
Fax: 440 338-3160
Robert Wantz, *President*
Daniel Wantz, *Vice Pres*
EMP: 30
SQ FT: 3,000
SALES (est): 4.6MM **Privately Held**
SIC: **1623** Telephone & communication line construction

(G-15603)
PATTIE GROUP INC (PA)
Also Called: Pattie's Landscaping
15533 Chillicothe Rd (44072-9646)
PHONE..........................440 338-1288
Fax: 440 338-3519
Steve Pattie, *President*
Matt Matisko, *Project Dir*
Danielle Beausoleil, *Project Mgr*
William Pattie, *Treasurer*
Nicole Morreale, *Finance Mgr*
EMP: 95
SQ FT: 2,000
SALES (est): 13.9MM **Privately Held**
WEB: www.pattiegroup.com
SIC: **0781** Landscape services

(G-15604)
WIEGANDS LAKE PARK INC
9390 Kinsman Rd (44072-9633)
PHONE..........................440 338-5795
William B Frantz, *President*
Wendy Wiegand, *Vice Pres*
EMP: 45
SALES (est): 1MM **Privately Held**
WEB: www.wiegandslakepark.com
SIC: **7999** 7389 Picnic ground operation; convention & show services

Oak Harbor
Ottawa County

(G-15605)
BENTON-CARROLL-SALEM
Also Called: Benton School Bus Garage
601 N Benton St (43449-1009)
PHONE..........................419 898-6214
Ginger Staymancho, *Principal*
EMP: 30
SALES (corp-wide): 15.9MM **Privately Held**
SIC: **4151** School buses
PA: Benton Carroll Salem Local School District
11685 W State Route 163
Oak Harbor OH 43449
419 898-6210

(G-15606)
COUNTY OF OTTAWA
275 N Toussaint South Rd (43449-9086)
PHONE..........................419 898-7433
Fax: 419 732-6572
Bill Lowe, *Director*
EMP: 37
SALES (est): 743.5K **Privately Held**
WEB: www.ottawacocpcourt.com
SIC: **4119** 9111 Local passenger transportation; county supervisors' & executives' offices
PA: County Of Ottawa
315 Madison St Ste 201
Port Clinton OH 43452
419 734-6700

(G-15607)
COUNTY OF OTTAWA
Also Called: Ottawa Cnty Sr Healthcare
8180 W State Route 163 (43449-8855)
PHONE..........................419 898-6459
Fax: 419 898-9501
Megan Knecht, *Director*
Jean Marquette, *Nursing Dir*
John Ambrosecchia, *Administration*
Kendra German, *Administration*
EMP: 200
SQ FT: 20,000 **Privately Held**
WEB: www.ottawacocpcourt.com
SIC: **8051** 9111 8111 Convalescent home with continuous nursing care; county supervisors' & executives' offices; general practice attorney, lawyer
PA: County Of Ottawa
315 Madison St Ste 201
Port Clinton OH 43452
419 734-6700

GEOGRAPHIC SECTION

Oakwood Village - Cuyahoga County (G-15631)

(G-15608)
COUNTY OF OTTAWA
Also Called: Ottawa County Dept Human Svcs
8444 W State Route 163 # 102 (43449-8884)
PHONE..................419 898-2089
Fax: 419 898-2436
Jim Adkins, *Manager*
Juan Cortez, *Web Proj Mgr*
Doris James, *Director*
EMP: 50
SALES (est): 1.3MM **Privately Held**
WEB: www.ottawacocpcourt.com
SIC: 8322 9111 8111 Individual & family services; county supervisors' & executives' offices; general practice attorney, lawyer
PA: County Of Ottawa
 315 Madison St Ste 201
 Port Clinton OH 43452
 419 734-6700

(G-15609)
DURBIN TRUCKING INC
10044 Scott St (43449-9359)
PHONE..................419 334-2422
Fax: 419 334-5548
Joseph J Durbin, *President*
EMP: 30
SALES (est): 2MM **Privately Held**
SIC: 4213 Contract haulers

(G-15610)
GIVING TREE INC (HQ)
11969 W State Route 105 (43449-9168)
PHONE..................419 898-0077
Fax: 419 898-0177
David Mariann, *Director*
EMP: 35
SQ FT: 1,200
SALES (est): 1MM
SALES (corp-wide): 15.5K **Privately Held**
WEB: www.givingtreecounseling.com
SIC: 8093 Mental health clinic, outpatient
PA: Firelands Regional Health System
 1111 Hayes Ave
 Sandusky OH 44870
 419 557-7400

(G-15611)
JERSEY CENTRAL PWR & LIGHT CO
Also Called: Firstenergy
5501 N State Route 2 (43449-9752)
PHONE..................419 321-7207
James Black, *Engineer*
Howard Bergendahl, *Manager*
EMP: 35 **Publicly Held**
WEB: www.jersey-central-power-light.monmouth.n
SIC: 7629 Telecommunication equipment repair (except telephones)
HQ: Jersey Central Power & Light Company
 76 S Main St
 Akron OH 44308
 800 736-3402

(G-15612)
MID COUNTY EMS
222 W Washington St (43449-1148)
P.O. Box 88 (43449-0088)
PHONE..................419 898-9366
Fax: 419 898-0010
Marcia Eehlmer, *Chief*
EMP: 30
SALES (est): 608.9K **Privately Held**
SIC: 4119 Ambulance service

(G-15613)
OAK HARBOR LIONS CLUB
101 S Brookside Dr (43449-1276)
P.O. Box 144 (43449-0144)
PHONE..................419 898-3828
Ron Buehler, *President*
EMP: 34
SALES (est): 17.1K **Privately Held**
SIC: 8611 Community affairs & services

(G-15614)
OTTAWA COUNTY BOARD M R D D
Also Called: Services & Support ADM
235 N Toussaint St (43449-1246)
PHONE..................419 734-6650
Ronald S Green, *Director*
Luann Monak, *Bd of Directors*
Bobbi Beck, *Exec Sec*
EMP: 50
SQ FT: 5,000
SALES (est): 1.1MM **Privately Held**
SIC: 8699 Charitable organization

(G-15615)
OTTAWA COUNTY TRANSIT BOARD
275 N Toussaint South Rd (43449-9086)
PHONE..................419 898-7433
Bill Lowe, *Exec Dir*
EMP: 29
SALES: 950K **Privately Held**
SIC: 4173 Bus terminal & service facilities

(G-15616)
RIVERVIEW INDUSTRIES INC
8380 W State Route 163 (43449-8859)
PHONE..................419 898-5250
Fax: 419 898-1141
Mark Yost, *Business Mgr*
Cortney Key, *Manager*
Brenda Smith, *Director*
Michelle Ish, *Executive*
Robin Marsh, *Lic Prac Nurse*
EMP: 180
SALES (est): 4.4MM **Privately Held**
SIC: 8331 Manpower training

(G-15617)
TOLEDO EDISON COMPANY
Also Called: Davis Beese Nuclear Power Stn
5501 N State Route 2 (43449-9752)
PHONE..................419 321-8488
Fax: 419 249-2342
Jon Hook, *Engineer*
James J Powers, *Engineer*
Connie Moore, *Supervisor*
EMP: 50 **Publicly Held**
SIC: 4911 Generation, electric power
HQ: The Toledo Edison Company
 76 S Main St Bsmt
 Akron OH 44308
 800 447-3333

Oak Hill
Jackson County

(G-15618)
H & H RETREADING INC
5400 State Route 93 (45656-9361)
P.O. Box 236 (45656-0236)
PHONE..................740 682-7721
Fax: 740 682-7475
Noah Hickman, *President*
Joel Hickman Jr, *Corp Secy*
EMP: 74 EST: 1970
SQ FT: 2,000
SALES (est): 4.2MM **Privately Held**
SIC: 7534 Tire recapping

(G-15619)
LEGRAND SERVICES INC
Also Called: Fantastic Sams
230 W Hill St (15666 1012)
PHONE..................740 682-6046
Don Legrand, *President*
EMP: 42 EST: 1987
SALES (est): 655.3K **Privately Held**
SIC: 7231 Unisex hair salons

Oakwood
Montgomery County

(G-15620)
BROOKDALE SENIOR LIVING INC
1701 Far Hills Ave (45419-2532)
PHONE..................937 294-1772
Omer Jack, *Branch Mgr*
Ellen Rice, *Hlthcr Dir*
EMP: 160
SALES (corp-wide): 4.7B **Publicly Held**
SIC: 8051 Convalescent home with continuous nursing care
PA: Brookdale Senior Living
 111 Westwood Pl Ste 400
 Brentwood TN 37027
 615 221-2250

(G-15621)
KUNESH EYE CENTER INC
Also Called: Oakwood Optical
2601 Far Hills Ave Ste 2 (45419-1634)
PHONE..................937 298-1703
Fax: 937 298-6344
Kristine K Part MD, *President*
Kristine Kunesh-Part MD, *President*
Michael T Kunesh, *Vice Pres*
John Kunesh, *Admin Sec*
Lucy Helmers, *Administration*
EMP: 35
SALES (est): 5.1MM **Privately Held**
SIC: 8011 Ophthalmologist

(G-15622)
OHIO EYECARE SPECIALISTS INC (PA)
105 Sugar Camp Cir # 200 (45409-1977)
PHONE..................937 222-3937
Edward R Thomas MD, *President*
Richard Carlile, *Treasurer*
Donna C Smear, *Manager*
Majid Moshirfar, *Director*
EMP: 35
SQ FT: 6,346
SALES (est): 3.6MM **Privately Held**
WEB: www.oheyecare.com
SIC: 8011 Ophthalmologist

Oakwood
Paulding County

(G-15623)
COOPER HATCHERY INC (PA)
Also Called: Cooper Farms
22348 Road 140 (45873-9303)
PHONE..................419 594-3325
Fax: 419 594-3372
James R Cooper, *President*
Gary A Cooper, *COO*
Neil Diller, *Vice Pres*
Karl Koenig, *Facilities Dir*
Dale Hart, *Opers Staff*
EMP: 225 EST: 1934
SQ FT: 47,000
SALES (est): 256.7MM **Privately Held**
WEB: www.cooperfarm.com
SIC: 0254 0253 2015 5153 Poultry hatcheries; turkey farm; turkey, processed; grains; prepared feeds

(G-15624)
STONECO INC
13762 Road 179 (45873-9012)
PHONE..................419 393-2555
Fax: 419 393-2455
Rick Welch, *Superintendent*
Dale Mathew, *Sales Mgr*
Scott Rychener, *Sales Staff*
EMP: 25
SALES (corp-wide): 29.7B **Privately Held**
WEB: www.stoneco.net
SIC: 1422 2951 Crushed & broken limestone; asphalt paving mixtures & blocks
HQ: Stoneco, Inc.
 1700 Fostoria Ave Ste 200
 Findlay OH 45840
 419 422-8854

Oakwood Village
Cuyahoga County

(G-15625)
AIRGAS USA LLC
7600 Oak Leaf Rd (44146-5554)
PHONE..................440 786-2864
John Mazzola, *Branch Mgr*
EMP: 100
SALES (corp-wide): 163.9MM **Privately Held**
WEB: www.us.linde-gas.com
SIC: 5169 Industrial gases
HQ: Airgas Usa, Llc
 259 N Radnor Chester Rd # 100
 Radnor PA 19087
 610 687-5253

(G-15626)
BRIGHTVIEW LANDSCAPES LLC
25072 Broadway Ave (44146-6309)
PHONE..................216 398-1289
David Frisbee, *Accounts Mgr*
Brad McBride, *Branch Mgr*
EMP: 38
SALES (corp-wide): 914MM **Privately Held**
SIC: 0781 Landscape services
HQ: Brightview Landscapes, Llc
 401 Plymouth Rd Ste 500
 Plymouth Meeting PA 19462
 484 567-7204

(G-15627)
BUILDING INTEGRATED SVCS LLC
7777 First Pl (44146-6733)
PHONE..................330 733-9191
Scott K Jordan,
EMP: 60
SALES (est): 1.4MM **Privately Held**
SIC: 1711 Plumbing, heating, air-conditioning contractors

(G-15628)
CRYSTAL CLEAR BLDG SVCS INC
26118 Broadway Ave Ste B (44146-6530)
PHONE..................440 439-2288
Jim Lesko, *President*
Stephen M Lesko, *Principal*
EMP: 90 EST: 1997
SALES (est): 3.2MM **Privately Held**
SIC: 7349 Janitorial service, contract basis

(G-15629)
FLOWERLAND GARDEN CENTERS (PA)
Also Called: Petitti Garden Centers
25018 Broadway Ave (44146-6309)
PHONE..................440 439-8636
Angelo Petitti, *President*
Brent Cherkala, *Controller*
▲ EMP: 29
SALES: 30MM **Privately Held**
SIC: 5193 Flowers & florists' supplies

(G-15630)
MEDICAL SPECIALTIES DISTRS LLC
26350 Broadway Ave (44146-6517)
PHONE..................440 232-0320
Carl Farago, *Branch Mgr*
Philip Russo, *Supervisor*
EMP: 37
SALES (corp-wide): 474.2MM **Privately Held**
WEB: www.msdistributors.com
SIC: 7352 Medical equipment rental
PA: Medical Specialties Distributors, Llc
 800 Technology Center Dr # 3
 Stoughton MA 02072
 781 344-6000

(G-15631)
MID-CONTINENT CONSTRUCTION CO
7235 Free Ave Ste A (44146-5461)
PHONE..................440 439-6100
Thomas McDonald, *CEO*
Darryl Wilkins, *CEO*
William Schmid, *Vice Pres*
Chad Jurisch, *Vice Pres*
Ray Krankowski, *Vice Pres*
EMP: 25
SQ FT: 8,000
SALES (est): 6.3MM **Privately Held**
SIC: 1542 1541 Commercial & office building, new construction; industrial buildings, new construction

Oakwood Village - Cuyahoga County (G-15632)

(G-15632)
PERFORMANCE PAINTING LLC
7603 First Pl (44146-6703)
PHONE...................440 735-3340
Keith Donaldson,
Tim Wilson,
EMP: 25
SALES (est): 1.2MM **Privately Held**
SIC: 1721 Painting & paper hanging

(G-15633)
ROCK HOUSE ENTRMT GROUP INC
7809 First Pl (44146-6707)
PHONE...................440 232-7625
Fax: 440 232-7626
Matt Radicelli, *President*
Jeremy Guffin, *Project Mgr*
Ben Allison, *Prdtn Mgr*
Jeff Kutz, *Mktg Dir*
Amy Van Duyne, *Manager*
▲ **EMP:** 120
SALES (est): 732K **Privately Held**
WEB: www.rockthehousedj.net
SIC: 7929 Disc jockey service; entertainment service

(G-15634)
SWIFT FILTERS INC (PA)
24040 Forbes Rd (44146-5650)
PHONE...................440 735-0995
Edwin C Swift Jr, *President*
Edwin Swift, *General Mgr*
Charles C Swift, *Vice Pres*
Mat Fleischer, *Plant Mgr*
Michelle Pacino, *Purchasing*
EMP: 38
SQ FT: 6,000
SALES: 6.9MM **Privately Held**
WEB: www.swiftfilters.com
SIC: 3569 5075 Filters; air filters

(G-15635)
THERMO FISHER SCIENTIFIC INC
Also Called: Remel Products
1 Thermo Fisher Way (44146-6536)
PHONE...................800 871-8909
Debra Dicillo, *Manager*
Harold Liepert, *Project Leader*
EMP: 150
SALES (corp-wide): 20.9B **Publicly Held**
SIC: 5047 2835 3841 Diagnostic equipment, medical; in vitro & in vivo diagnostic substances; surgical & medical instruments
PA: Thermo Fisher Scientific Inc.
168 3rd Ave
Waltham MA 02451
781 622-1000

(G-15636)
VIEWRAY INCORPORATED
2 Thermo Fisher Way (44146-6536)
PHONE...................440 703-3210
Chris A Raanes, *President*
Bela Vajko, *Managing Dir*
Doug Keare, *COO*
Peter Sullivan, *Exec VP*
Robert Bea, *Senior VP*
▲ **EMP:** 70
SALES: 34MM **Privately Held**
SIC: 3845 5047 Electromedical equipment; therapy equipment

Oberlin
Lorain County

(G-15637)
AGRINOMIX LLC
300 Creekside Dr (44074-1272)
PHONE...................440 774-2981
Fax: 440 775-2104
Charlie Kirschner, *Vice Pres*
Joe Smith, *VP Mfg*
George Andulics, *Engineer*
Neil Mabrouk, *Engineer*
Norman T Baxter, *Controller*
▲ **EMP:** 36
SQ FT: 74,800
SALES: 14MM **Privately Held**
WEB: www.agrinomix.com
SIC: 5083 5084 Planting machinery & equipment; materials handling machinery

(G-15638)
ALLEN MEDICAL CENTER
200 W Lorain St (44074-1026)
PHONE...................440 986-4000
Fax: 440 775-9147
Edwin Oley, *CEO*
Maggie Monter, *Accounting Mgr*
Wendy Simmons, *Med Doctor*
Mercy Centers, *Manager*
Ed Oley, *Administration*
▲ **EMP:** 250
SQ FT: 77,460
SALES: 212.3K **Privately Held**
SIC: 8062 8051 General medical & surgical hospitals; skilled nursing care facilities

(G-15639)
ALLIED WASTE INDUSTRIES LLC
Also Called: Site R24
43502 Oberlin Elyria Rd (44074-9591)
PHONE...................440 774-3100
David Matthews, *General Mgr*
Debra Slusser, *Sales Associate*
Keith Cordesman, *Manager*
EMP: 30
SALES (corp-wide): 10B **Publicly Held**
SIC: 4953 Recycling, waste materials; sanitary landfill operation
HQ: Allied Waste Industries, Llc
18500 N Allied Way # 100
Phoenix AZ 85054
480 627-2700

(G-15640)
CITY OF OBERLIN (PA)
Also Called: OBERLIN MUNICIPAL LIGHT & POWE
85 S Main St (44074-1603)
PHONE...................440 775-1531
Fax: 440 775-7208
Ron Rimbert, *President*
Dennis Cuthbertson, *Superintendent*
Eric Norenberg, *Principal*
Linda Slocum, *Vice Pres*
Sharon Soucy, *Vice Pres*
EMP: 47
SQ FT: 10,000 **Privately Held**
WEB: www.oberlinpd.com
SIC: 9111 8611 City & town managers' offices; business associations

(G-15641)
CUSTOM CLEANING SERVICE LLC
305 Artino St Unit A (44074-1277)
PHONE...................440 774-1222
Stacy Fenderson,
EMP: 46
SALES (est): 936.1K **Privately Held**
SIC: 7349 Janitorial service, contract basis

(G-15642)
DOVIN DAIRY FARMS LLC
Also Called: Dovin Land Company
15967 State Route 58 (44074-9581)
PHONE...................440 653-7009
Billie Jo Dovin, *Mng Member*
John M Dovin,
Lisa Gilbert,
EMP: 28
SALES (est): 5.3MM **Privately Held**
SIC: 0241 Milk production

(G-15643)
EXPRESS SEED COMPANY
51051 Us Highway 20 (44074-1253)
PHONE...................440 774-2259
Fax: 440 774-2728
John Van Wingerden, *Owner*
Charles Dressler, *General Mgr*
Norm Baxter, *Controller*
Dawn Van Wingerden, *Admin Sec*
▲ **EMP:** 60 **EST:** 1982
SQ FT: 30,000
SALES (est): 11.9MM **Privately Held**
SIC: 5193 5191 Plants, potted; flower & field bulbs

(G-15644)
GREEN CIRCLE GROWERS INC (PA)
51051 Us Highway 20 (44074-9637)
PHONE...................440 775-1411
John Van Wingerden, *President*
Dawn Van Wingerden, *Vice Pres*
Dan Reed, *Opers Mgr*
Norman Daxter, *CFO*
David Martin, *Human Resources*
◆ **EMP:** 130
SQ FT: 2,500
SALES (est): 98.3MM **Privately Held**
WEB: www.greencirclehome.com
SIC: 0181 Flowers: grown under cover (e.g. greenhouse production); plants, potted; growing of

(G-15645)
GREEN CIRCLE GROWERS INC
15650 State Route 511 (44074-9699)
PHONE...................440 775-1411
Fax: 440 774-1465
Peggy Tallman, *Human Res Dir*
Van Wingerden John, *Branch Mgr*
Mark Sheldon, *Maintence Staff*
EMP: 470
SALES (corp-wide): 98.3MM **Privately Held**
SIC: 0181 Flowers: grown under cover (e.g. greenhouse production); plants, potted; growing of
PA: Green Circle Growers, Inc.
51051 Us Highway 20
Oberlin OH 44074
440 775-1411

(G-15646)
INDICO LLC (HQ)
528 E Lorain St (44074-1238)
PHONE...................440 775-7777
Fax: 440 774-1335
Rene Yang, *Vice Pres*
Terry Schubert, *Purch Agent*
Lori Smith, *Buyer*
Dan Bramwell, *Engineer*
Frank Sulen, *VP Finance*
EMP: 85
SQ FT: 162,000
SALES (est): 16.3MM
SALES (corp-wide): 33.6MM **Privately Held**
WEB: www.nacscorp.com
SIC: 5045 5192 Computer software; books
PA: National Association Of College Stores, Inc.
500 E Lorain St
Oberlin OH 44074
207 287-3531

(G-15647)
KENDAL AT OBERLIN
600 Kendal Dr (44074-1900)
PHONE...................440 775-0094
Fax: 440 775-9820
Barbara Thomas, *CEO*
George Bent, *President*
Judy Miller, *Accountant*
Rebecca Butler, *Human Resources*
Ann M Oalley, *Manager*
EMP: 222
SALES: 17.2MM **Privately Held**
WEB: www.kao.kendal.org
SIC: 8051 8052 Skilled nursing care facilities; intermediate care facilities

(G-15648)
LOCKES GARDEN CENTER INC
461 E Lorain St (44074-1217)
PHONE...................440 774-6981
Charles H Annable, *President*
EMP: 46
SQ FT: 5,000
SALES: 250K **Privately Held**
SIC: 0782 5261 Landscape contractors; nurseries

(G-15649)
MCCONNELL EXCAVATING LTD
15804 State Route 58 (44074-9580)
PHONE...................440 774-4578
Fax: 440 774-2604
Eric McConnell, *General Ptnr*
Dave Sustar, *VP Finance*
Sandy Camp, *Manager*
Bruce Jones, *Manager*
Sandy Gmerek, *Admin Asst*
EMP: 47
SALES (est): 15.1MM **Privately Held**
SIC: 1794 7389 Excavation & grading, building construction;

(G-15650)
MERCY HEALTH
319 W Lorain St (44074-1027)
PHONE...................440 775-1881
EMP: 42
SALES (corp-wide): 4.2B **Privately Held**
SIC: 8011 Offices & clinics of medical doctors
PA: Mercy Health
1701 Mercy Health Pl
Cincinnati OH 45237
513 639-2800

(G-15651)
MERCY HEALTH
200 W Lorain St (44074-1026)
PHONE...................440 775-1211
Fax: 440 774-3191
Stacie Whitacre, *Telecomm Dir*
Thomas K Wu, *Diag Radio*
Lora Jones, *Receptionist Se*
Linda K Novak, *Receptionist Se*
Dawn Rogers, *Receptionist Se*
EMP: 48
SALES (corp-wide): 4.2B **Privately Held**
SIC: 4119 Ambulance service
PA: Mercy Health
1701 Mercy Health Pl
Cincinnati OH 45237
513 639-2800

(G-15652)
MERCY HEALTH
Also Called: Mercy Allen Hospital
200 W Lorain St (44074-1026)
PHONE...................440 774-6800
Fax: 440 774-8014
Mark Kellam, *Emerg Med Spec*
EMP: 104
SALES (corp-wide): 4.2B **Privately Held**
SIC: 8049 Physical therapist
PA: Mercy Health
1701 Mercy Health Pl
Cincinnati OH 45237
513 639-2800

(G-15653)
OBERLIN CLINIC INC
224 W Lorain St Ste P (44074-1042)
PHONE...................440 774-7337
Toll Free:...................866 -
Jim Schaum, *President*
Donna Moyers, *Admin Sec*
EMP: 150
SQ FT: 24,000
SALES (est): 5.4MM **Privately Held**
SIC: 8011 Clinic, operated by physicians

(G-15654)
OBERLIN COLLEGE
Also Called: Oberlin College Recreation Ctr
200 Woodland St (44074-1051)
PHONE...................440 775-8519
Amy Eckhart, *HR Admin*
David Knapp, *HR Admin*
Betsy Bruce, *Manager*
Brant Fairchild, *Director*
Creg Jantz, *Associate Dir*
EMP: 125
SALES (corp-wide): 184.7MM **Privately Held**
WEB: www.oberlin.edu
SIC: 8221 7997 7999 College, except junior; membership sports & recreation clubs; recreation center
PA: Oberlin College
173 W Lorain St
Oberlin OH 44074
440 775-8121

(G-15655)
OBERLIN COLLEGE
Also Called: Athletic Dept
200 Woodland St (44074-1051)
PHONE...................440 775-8500
Gayle Boyer, *Opers Mgr*
Richard Wood, *Facilities Mgr*
Heidi Pycraft, *Controller*
Calvin Frye, *Technology*

▲ = Import ▼ = Export
◆ = Import/Export

Victor Lananna, *Director*
EMP: 41
SALES (corp-wide): 184.7MM **Privately Held**
WEB: www.oberlin.edu
SIC: 8221 8699 University; athletic organizations
PA: Oberlin College
173 W Lorain St
Oberlin OH 44074
440 775-8121

(G-15656)
OBERLIN COLLEGE
Also Called: Oberlin Inn
10 E College St (44074-1613)
PHONE.................................440 935-1475
Mary Lane, *Sales Mgr*
Rex Angle, *Manager*
Liz Hui, *Director*
Dana Hamdan, *Asst Director*
EMP: 75
SALES (corp-wide): 184.7MM **Privately Held**
WEB: www.oberlin.edu
SIC: 5812 7011 American restaurant; hotels
PA: Oberlin College
173 W Lorain St
Oberlin OH 44074
440 775-8121

(G-15657)
OBERLIN EARLY CHILDHOOD CENTER
317 E College St (44074-1316)
PHONE.................................440 774-8193
Fax: 440 774-5307
Carrie Fiala, *Exec Dir*
Nancy Sabath, *Director*
EMP: 30
SQ FT: 16,000
SALES: 977.6K **Privately Held**
SIC: 8351 Group day care center

(G-15658)
PHYSICIANS IN FAMILY PRACTICE
319 W Lorain St (44074-1027)
PHONE.................................440 775-1881
Fax: 440 774-5707
John M Jonesco, *President*
Jane Jonesco, *Vice Pres*
Frances Smith, *Manager*
Mika Johnson, *Director*
EMP: 25
SQ FT: 1,800
SALES (est): 858.2K **Privately Held**
SIC: 8031 8011 Offices & clinics of osteopathic physicians; offices & clinics of medical doctors

(G-15659)
REPUBLIC SERVICES INC
Also Called: Lorain County Landfill
43502 Oberlin Elyria Rd (44074-9591)
PHONE.................................440 774-4060
EMP: 34
SALES (corp-wide): 10B **Publicly Held**
SIC: 4953 Refuse collection & disposal services
PA: Republic Services, Inc.
18500 N Allied Way # 100
Phoenix AZ 85054
480 627-2700

(G-15660)
RIDGE MURRAY PROD CTR OBERLIN
285 Artino St (44074-1207)
PHONE.................................440 774-7400
Fax: 440 774-5804
Kristine Johnson, *Manager*
Edgar Barnett, *Director*
EMP: 39
SALES (est): 1.7MM **Privately Held**
SIC: 8051 8331 Mental retardation hospital; job training & vocational rehabilitation services

(G-15661)
SUPERS LANDSCAPING INC
48211 State Route 511 (44074-9205)
PHONE.................................440 775-0027
Fax: 440 775-0601

Greg Supers, *Exec VP*
EMP: 30
SQ FT: 10,000
SALES: 800K **Privately Held**
WEB: www.superslandscape.com
SIC: 0782 4959 5261 7699 Landscape contractors; lawn services; snowplowing; lawn & garden equipment; lawn mower repair shop

(G-15662)
WESSELL GENERATIONS INC
Also Called: Welcome Nursing Home
417 S Main St (44074-1749)
PHONE.................................440 775-1491
Fax: 440 774-3378
Jill Herron, *President*
Heidi Freas, *Vice Pres*
Feite Hofman, *Director*
Terrie Rader, *Nursing Dir*
Kelly Wessell, *Admin Sec*
EMP: 140
SQ FT: 40,766
SALES (est): 8.4MM **Privately Held**
SIC: 8051 Convalescent home with continuous nursing care

Obetz
Franklin County

(G-15663)
AUCTION SERVICES INC
4700 Groveport Rd (43207-5217)
PHONE.................................614 497-2000
Fax: 614 497-1711
Alexis A Jacobs, *President*
Brett Vanmeter, *Principal*
Leslie Ivery, *Human Res Mgr*
Rodney Chenos, *Sales Staff*
Mark Thomas, *Sales Staff*
EMP: 700
SQ FT: 60,000
SALES: 64.7K **Privately Held**
SIC: 7389 Auctioneers, fee basis

(G-15664)
CAPITOL CITY TRAILERS INC
3960 Groveport Rd (43207-5127)
PHONE.................................614 491-2616
Fax: 614 491-2665
Buck Stewart, *President*
Scott Brown, *Vice Pres*
Dante Holland, *Vice Pres*
Tim Stewart, *Vice Pres*
Jeff Steen, *Sales Engr*
EMP: 58
SQ FT: 20,000
SALES (est): 10.8MM **Privately Held**
WEB: www.capitolcitytrailers.net
SIC: 7539 3792 Trailer repair; travel trailers & campers

(G-15665)
CARDINAL HEALTH INC
2320 Mcgaw Rd (43207-4805)
PHONE.................................614 497-9552
Kelly Byrd, *Branch Mgr*
Joe Bowman, *Manager*
Keely Kellner, *Assistant*
EMP: 74
SALES (corp-wide): 129.9B **Publicly Held**
SIC: 5122 5047 8741 Pharmaceuticals; biologicals & allied products; druggists' sundries; blood plasma; surgical equipment & supplies; hospital equipment & supplies; management services
PA: Cardinal Health, Inc.
7000 Cardinal Pl
Dublin OH 43017
614 757-5000

(G-15666)
COLUMBUS FAIR AUTO AUCTION INC
Also Called: Wednesday Auto Auction
4700 Groveport Rd (43207-5217)
P.O. Box 32490, Columbus (43232-0490)
PHONE.................................614 497-2000
Keith Whann, *CEO*
Harold Varvel, *General Mgr*
Jeff Baerga, *Vice Pres*
Chuck Dearing, *Opers Mgr*

Debbie Fleshman, *Facilities Mgr*
EMP: 1240
SQ FT: 60,000
SALES (est): 221.8MM **Privately Held**
SIC: 5012 5521 Automobile auction; used car dealers

(G-15667)
HUTTIG BUILDING PRODUCTS INC
Also Called: Huttig Sash & Door Co
2160 Mcgaw Rd (43207-4801)
PHONE.................................614 492-8248
Dave McCormick, *General Mgr*
Ellen Marshall, *Office Mgr*
Dave McCormack, *Branch Mgr*
EMP: 50
SQ FT: 100,000
SALES (corp-wide): 753.2MM **Publicly Held**
WEB: www.huttig.com
SIC: 5031 Door frames, all materials
PA: Huttig Building Products, Inc.
555 Maryville University
Saint Louis MO 63141
314 216-2600

(G-15668)
JACOBSON WAREHOUSE COMPANY INC
Also Called: Xpo Logistics
3880 Groveport Rd (43207-5125)
PHONE.................................614 314-1091
EMP: 142
SALES (corp-wide): 15.3B **Publicly Held**
SIC: 4226 Special warehousing & storage
HQ: Jacobson Warehouse Company, Inc.
3811 Dixon St
Des Moines IA 50313
515 265-6171

(G-15669)
PAR INTERNATIONAL INC
2160 Mcgaw Rd (43207-4801)
PHONE.................................614 529-1300
Fax: 614 529-1052
Eli Goldach, *President*
Dan Stergiou, *Exec VP*
Dan Goldach, *Vice Pres*
▼ EMP: 30
SQ FT: 300,000
SALES (est): 10MM **Privately Held**
WEB: www.parinternational.com
SIC: 5013 5199 Automotive supplies & parts; gifts & novelties

(G-15670)
S P RICHARDS COMPANY
2410 Mcgaw Rd (43207-4513)
PHONE.................................614 497-2270
Fax: 614 497-1433
Dennis Reid, *General Mgr*
EMP: 50
SALES (corp-wide): 16.3B **Publicly Held**
WEB: www.sprichards.com
SIC: 5112 5021 Stationery & office supplies; office furniture
HQ: S. P. Richards Company
6300 Highlands Pkwy Se
Smyrna GA 30082
770 434-4571

(G-15671)
SYNERGY HOTELS LLC
Also Called: Holiday Inn
4870 Old Rathmell Ct (43207-4580)
PHONE.................................614 492-9000
Mike Duncan, *General Mgr*
Stephen Berger, *Manager*
James Blevins, *Manager*
EMP: 30
SALES: 500K **Privately Held**
SIC: 7011 7991 Hotels; physical fitness facilities

(G-15672)
UNITED PARCEL SERVICE INC OH
Also Called: UPS
2450 Rathmell Rd (43207-4591)
P.O. Box 557, Holland (43528-0557)
PHONE.................................614 272-8500
Paul Stotridge, *Manager*
EMP: 158

SALES (corp-wide): 65.8B **Publicly Held**
SIC: 4215 Parcel delivery, vehicular
HQ: United Parcel Service, Inc. (Oh)
55 Glenlake Pkwy
Atlanta GA 30328
404 828-6000

Olmsted Falls
Cuyahoga County

(G-15673)
DOVER INVESTMENTS INC
7989 Columbia Rd (44138-2019)
P.O. Box 450739, Westlake (44145-0615)
PHONE.................................440 235-5511
EMP: 45 **Privately Held**
SIC: 5082 Ladders
PA: Dover Investments Inc
694 Dover Center Rd
Westlake OH 44145

(G-15674)
KIDS FIRST LEARNING CENTERS
26184 Bagley Rd (44138-1812)
PHONE.................................440 235-2500
Fax: 440 235-3148
Coleen Siss, *Exec Dir*
EMP: 60
SALES (est): 882.2K **Privately Held**
SIC: 8351 Preschool center

Olmsted Twp
Cuyahoga County

(G-15675)
E J LINKS CO THE INC
Also Called: Links At The Renaissance
26111 John Rd (44138-1223)
PHONE.................................440 235-0501
Fax: 440 235-5161
EMP: 40
SALES: 500K
SALES (corp-wide): 4.4MM **Privately Held**
SIC: 7992 Public Golf Course
HQ: The Eliza Jennings Home Inc
10603 Detroit Ave
Cleveland OH 44102
216 226-0282

(G-15676)
JENNINGS ELIZA SENIOR CARE (PA)
26376 John Rd Ofc C (44138-1283)
PHONE.................................216 226-5000
Deborah Hiller, *CEO*
Jim Rogerson, *COO*
Patricia Scanlon, *Trustee*
Colleen De De Boer, *Human Resources*
Toby Mileta, *Manager*
EMP: 600
SALES: 3.8MM **Privately Held**
WEB: www.therapypartnersohio.com
SIC: 8051 Skilled nursing care facilities

(G-15677)
LENAU PARK
Also Called: Donauschwaben's Grmnamrcn Cltr
7370 Columbia Rd (44138-1502)
P.O. Box 38160, Olmsted Falls (44138-0160)
PHONE.................................440 235-2646
Fax: 440 235-2671
Frank Rimps, *President*
Anita Kalkhof, *Vice Pres*
Rudy Koch, *Vice Pres*
John Szeltner, *Vice Pres*
EMP: 40
SQ FT: 32,075
SALES: 562.2K **Privately Held**
SIC: 7997 8641 Country club, membership; civic social & fraternal associations

(G-15678)
LINK & RENEISSANCE INC
Also Called: Links Golf Course
26111 John Rd (44138-1223)
PHONE.................................440 235-0501

Olmsted Twp - Cuyahoga County (G-15679)   **GEOGRAPHIC SECTION**

Jim Rogerson, *President*
John Garus, *General Mgr*
EMP: 30
SALES (est): 1.2MM **Privately Held**
WEB: www.linksgolfcourse.com
SIC: 7992 Public golf courses

(G-15679)
OLMSTED HEALTH AND SVC CORP
Also Called: Health Center At Renaissance
26376 John Rd Ofc (44138-1283)
PHONE..................................440 235-7100
Leeann Youshak, *Finance Other*
Ms Leeann Youshak, *Finance*
Elizabeth Bartelme, *Exec Dir*
George Khuri, *Director*
Pat Stanovic, *Director*
EMP: 300
SQ FT: 256,000
SALES: 6.8MM **Privately Held**
SIC: 8051 Skilled nursing care facilities

(G-15680)
OLMSTED RESIDENCE CORPORATION
Also Called: Renaissance, The
26376 John Rd Ofc (44138-1283)
PHONE..................................440 235-7100
Fax: 440 235-7115
Deborah Hiller, *CEO*
Bill Murphy, *Maint Spvr*
Joan Lampe, *CFO*
Kara Serger, *Human Res Dir*
EMP: 200
SQ FT: 256,000
SALES: 6.6MM **Privately Held**
WEB: www.therapypartnersohio.com
SIC: 8322 6531 Senior citizens' center or association; real estate managers
PA: Jennings, Eliza Senior Care Network
26376 John Rd Ofc C
Olmsted Twp OH 44138

(G-15681)
STRIKE ZONE INC
Also Called: Swings N Things Family Fun Pk
8501 Stearns Rd (44138-1738)
PHONE..................................440 235-4420
Fax: 440 235-4469
Tim Sorge, *President*
Steve Bonham, *General Mgr*
Helen Burko, *Financial Exec*
EMP: 85 **EST:** 1982
SQ FT: 24,000
SALES (est): 1.1MM **Privately Held**
WEB: www.swings-n-things.com
SIC: 7999 7993 5812 Recreation services; baseball batting cage; miniature golf course operation; go-cart raceway operation & rentals; video game arcade; ice cream stands or dairy bars

Ontario
Richland County

(G-15682)
ADENA CORPORATION
1310 W 4th St (44906-1828)
PHONE..................................419 529-4456
Fax: 419 529-5387
Randy A Payne, *President*
Dave Heyl, *Superintendent*
Dwight Farmer, *Vice Pres*
Brad Geissman, *Vice Pres*
Josh Darling, *Project Mgr*
EMP: 160
SQ FT: 7,000
SALES: 65MM **Privately Held**
WEB: www.adenacorporation.com
SIC: 1541 1542 Industrial buildings, new construction; nonresidential construction

(G-15683)
ADVANTAGE CREDIT UNION INC (PA)
700 Stumbo Rd (44906-1279)
P.O. Box 2674, Mansfield (44906-0674)
PHONE..................................419 529-5603
Fax: 419 529-5068
Wesley P Volz, *President*
Becky Hasenzahl, *Loan Officer*
EMP: 30

SALES: 1.1MM **Privately Held**
SIC: 6062 State credit unions, not federally chartered

(G-15684)
ALL AMERICAN TRNSP SVCS LLC
575 Beer Rd (44906-1214)
PHONE..................................419 589-7433
James Blevins, *General Mgr*
EMP: 35
SALES (est): 105.9K **Privately Held**
SIC: 4789 Cargo loading & unloading services

(G-15685)
CINEMARK USA INC
2355 Walker Lake Rd (44903-6529)
PHONE..................................419 589-7300
Yolanda Hubbard, *Branch Mgr*
EMP: 34 **Publicly Held**
SIC: 7832 Motion picture theaters, except drive-in
HQ: Cinemark Usa, Inc.
3900 Dallas Pkwy Ste 500
Plano TX 75093
972 665-1000

(G-15686)
DIVERSICARE OF MANSFIELD LLC
Also Called: Ontario Commons
2124 Park Ave W (44906-3807)
PHONE..................................419 529-6447
Kelly Gill, *President*
EMP: 60 **EST:** 2014
SALES (est): 2.1MM
SALES (corp-wide): 574.7MM **Publicly Held**
SIC: 8051 Skilled nursing care facilities
PA: Diversicare Healthcare Services, Inc.
1621 Galleria Blvd
Brentwood TN 37027
615 771-7575

(G-15687)
DTA INC
Also Called: Arnold's Landscaping
3128 Park Ave W (44906-1051)
PHONE..................................419 529-2920
Darrell Arnold, *President*
EMP: 30
SQ FT: 4,000
SALES (est): 6.8MM **Privately Held**
WEB: www.stone-creations.net
SIC: 5083 0782 Landscaping equipment; landscape contractors

(G-15688)
EXECUTIVE MANAGEMENT SERVICES
1225 Home Rd N (44906-1407)
PHONE..................................419 529-8800
Lawrence Grin, *President*
Mark Reed, *Controller*
Jam Fisher, *Administration*
EMP: 250
SALES (est): 4.3MM
SALES (corp-wide): 307MM **Privately Held**
WEB: www.outsourcepartners.net
SIC: 7349 Janitorial service, contract basis
HQ: U.S. Security Holdings, Inc.
200 Mansell Ct E Ste 500
Roswell GA 30076
770 625-1400

(G-15689)
GORDON FOOD SERVICE INC
Also Called: G F S Marketplace
1310 N Lexngtn Sprngmill (44906-1127)
PHONE..................................419 747-1212
Jeff White, *Manager*
EMP: 25
SALES (corp-wide): 88.9MM **Privately Held**
WEB: www.gfs.com
SIC: 5149 5142 Groceries & related products; packaged frozen goods
PA: Gordon Food Service, Inc.
1300 Gezon Pkwy Sw
Wyoming MI 49509
888 437-3663

(G-15690)
GRAHAM CHEVROLET-CADILLAC CO (PA)
Also Called: Ford
1515 W 4th St (44906-1857)
P.O. Box 340, Zanesville (43702-0340)
PHONE..................................419 989-4012
James Graham, *President*
Joel Foss, *General Mgr*
Ken Williams, *Vice Pres*
Clay Graham, *Treasurer*
Rick Hammond, *Controller*
EMP: 82
SQ FT: 44,000
SALES (est): 64.1MM **Privately Held**
WEB: www.grahamjeep.com
SIC: 5511 7515 7513 5521 Automobiles, new & used; passenger car leasing; truck rental & leasing, no drivers; used car dealers; automobiles & other motor vehicles

(G-15691)
HOME DEPOT USA INC
Also Called: Home Depot, The
2000 August Dr (44906-3350)
PHONE..................................419 529-0015
Rob Haner, *Manager*
EMP: 200
SALES (corp-wide): 100.9B **Publicly Held**
WEB: www.homerentalsdepot.com
SIC: 5211 7359 Home centers; tool rental
HQ: Home Depot U.S.A., Inc.
2455 Paces Ferry Rd Se
Atlanta GA 30339

(G-15692)
HOSPICE OF NORTH CENTRAL OHIO
2131 Park Ave W (44906-1226)
PHONE..................................419 524-9200
Anne Shelley, *CEO*
EMP: 34
SALES (est): 514.1K **Privately Held**
SIC: 8082 Home health care services

(G-15693)
INTERCITY AMATEUR RDO CLB INC
Also Called: Iarc
120 Homewood Rd (44906-1324)
PHONE..................................419 989-3429
Derrick Martin, *Principal*
EMP: 40
SALES (est): 353K **Privately Held**
SIC: 8641 Civic social & fraternal associations

(G-15694)
INTERSTATE OPTICAL CO (DH)
680 Lindaire Ln E (44906-1760)
P.O. Box 308, Mansfield (44901-0308)
PHONE..................................419 529-6800
Fax: 419 529-6801
John Art, *President*
Robert Art, *Vice Pres*
Deborah L Art, *Treasurer*
Tom Arnold, *Sales Associate*
▲ **EMP:** 61
SQ FT: 14,000
SALES (est): 34.5MM **Privately Held**
WEB: www.interstateoptical.com
SIC: 5048 Ophthalmic goods
HQ: Essilor Laboratories Of America Holding Co., Inc.
13555 N Stemmons Fwy
Dallas TX 75234
214 496-4141

(G-15695)
JOHNNY APPLESEED BROADCASTING
Also Called: Wvno-FM
2900 Park Ave W (44906-1062)
PHONE..................................419 529-5900
Fax: 419 529-2319
Gunther S Meisse, *President*
Gunther S Meie, *Marketing Staff*
Glenn Cheesman, *Advt Staff*
Albert Allen, *Director*
EMP: 42
SQ FT: 17,000

SALES (est): 4.1MM **Privately Held**
WEB: www.wmfd.com
SIC: 4832 4833 Radio broadcasting stations; television broadcasting stations

(G-15696)
JOYCE BUICK INC
Also Called: Joyce Buick GMC of Mansfield
1400 Park Ave W (44906-2799)
PHONE..................................419 529-3211
Fax: 419 529-2813
William F Joyce, *President*
Brian M Joyce, *Vice Pres*
Heather Figley, *Executive*
EMP: 37
SQ FT: 32,000
SALES (est): 15.7MM **Privately Held**
WEB: www.saturnofmansfield.com
SIC: 5511 7532 Automobiles, new & used; body shop, automotive

(G-15697)
LAKE ERIE ELECTRIC INC
Also Called: Charnan Div
539 Home Rd N (44906-2325)
P.O. Box 2539, Mansfield (44906-0539)
PHONE..................................419 529-4611
Keith Rowland, *General Mgr*
Larry Mooney, *Manager*
EMP: 25
SALES (corp-wide): 137.9MM **Privately Held**
SIC: 1731 General electrical contractor
PA: Erie Lake Electric Inc
25730 1st St
Westlake OH 44145
440 835-5565

(G-15698)
LOWES HOME CENTERS LLC
940 N Lexington Spring Rd (44906-1119)
PHONE..................................419 747-1920
Fax: 419 747-1940
Joe Lynn, *Branch Mgr*
Dan Messord, *Manager*
EMP: 150
SALES (corp-wide): 68.6B **Publicly Held**
SIC: 5211 5031 5722 5064 Home centers; building materials, exterior; building materials, interior; household appliance stores; electrical appliances, television & radio
HQ: Lowe's Home Centers, Llc
1605 Curtis Bridge Rd
Wilkesboro NC 28697
336 658-4000

(G-15699)
MANSFIELD WHSNG & DIST INC (HQ)
Also Called: Mansfield Express
222 Tappan Dr N (44906-1333)
P.O. Box 2685, Mansfield (44906-0685)
PHONE..................................419 522-3510
Fax: 419 522-3512
Stuart Lichter, *Ch of Bd*
Brian Glowaski, *President*
Dawn Stevenson, *General Mgr*
Paul Kistner, *Senior VP*
Chris Swearingen, *Facilities Mgr*
EMP: 130
SQ FT: 1,500,000
SALES (est): 12.6MM
SALES (corp-wide): 32.2MM **Privately Held**
SIC: 4225 4213 General warehousing; trucking, except local
PA: Mwd Logistics Inc
245 E 4th St
Mansfield OH 44902
419 522-3510

(G-15700)
MARCO PHOTO SERVICE INC
1655 Nussbaum Pkwy (44906-2300)
PHONE..................................419 529-9010
Fax: 419 529-3110
Rick Casey, *President*
Dave Elick, *COO*
Jay Allred, *Vice Pres*
Dan Berick, *VP Opers*
Sandra Griefenstine, *Human Resources*
EMP: 75 **EST:** 1965
SQ FT: 45,000

GEOGRAPHIC SECTION

Oregon - Lucas County (G-15724)

SALES (est): 10.2MM Privately Held
WEB: www.marcophotoservice.com
SIC: 7384 Film developing & printing

(G-15701)
MEDCENTRAL HEALTH SYSTEM
Also Called: Medcentral Hlth Sys Spt Mdcine
1750 W 4th St Ste 1 (44906-1796)
PHONE............................419 526-8900
Fax: 419 526-8151
Tye Christy, Network Tech
Brian Brickner, Director
Brady Groves, Executive
Albert Timperman,
EMP: 25
SALES (corp-wide): 3.7B Privately Held
SIC: 8062 8011 General medical & surgical hospitals; occupational & industrial specialist, physician/surgeon
HQ: Medcentral Health System
335 Glessner Ave
Mansfield OH 44903
419 526-8000

(G-15702)
MEDCENTRAL WORKABLE
1750 W 4th St Ste 5 (44906-1796)
PHONE............................419 526-8444
Fax: 419 529-6278
Marcia Rice, Manager
EMP: 25
SALES (est): 698.6K Privately Held
SIC: 8071 Medical laboratories

(G-15703)
MID OHIO EMPLOYMENT SERVICES (PA)
2282 Village Mall Dr # 2 (44906-1151)
PHONE............................419 747-5466
Beth Delaney, President
Ashle Finley, Area Mgr
Ann Smith, VP Opers
Jan Horn, Treasurer
Melissa Delaney, Manager
EMP: 25
SALES (est): 2.2MM Privately Held
SIC: 7361 Employment agencies

(G-15704)
MID OHIO HOME HEALTH LTD
1332 W 4th St (44906-1828)
PHONE............................419 529-3883
Fax: 419 529-0725
Kelly Purvis, CEO
Tony Ianni, Manager
EMP: 40
SALES (est): 1.6MM Privately Held
SIC: 8082 Home health care services

(G-15705)
MWD LOGISTICS INC
222 Tappan Dr N (44906-1333)
P.O. Box 2698, Mansfield (44906-0698)
PHONE............................419 522-3510
Brian Glowaski, President
EMP: 67
SALES (corp-wide): 32.2MM Privately Held
SIC: 4789 Pipeline terminal facilities, independently operated
PA: Mwd Logistics Inc
245 E 4th St
Mansfield OH 44902
419 522-3510

(G-15706)
NORFOLK SOUTHERN CORPORATION
2586 Park Ave W (44906-1235)
PHONE............................419 529-4574
Fax: 419 529-4659
Julius Chirumbolo, Principal
EMP: 43
SALES (corp-wide): 10.5B Publicly Held
SIC: 4011 Railroads, line-haul operating
PA: Norfolk Southern Corporation
3 Commercial Pl Ste 1a
Norfolk VA 23510
757 629-2680

(G-15707)
OHIO DISTRICT 5 AREA
2131 Park Ave W (44906-1226)
PHONE............................419 522-5612
Fax: 419 522-9482
Duana Patton, CEO

James Hairston, COO
EMP: 123
SALES: 40.7MM Privately Held
WEB: www.agingnorthcentralohio.org
SIC: 8322 Senior citizens' center or association

(G-15708)
ONTARIO LOCAL SCHOOL DISTRICT
Also Called: Transportation Department
3644 Pearl St (44906-1066)
PHONE............................419 529-3814
Tom Wolf, Superintendent
Pat Duffner, Director
EMP: 33 Privately Held
SIC: 4151 School buses
PA: Ontario Local School District
457 Shelby Ontario Rd
Ontario OH 44906

(G-15709)
ONTARIO MECHANICAL LLC
2880 Park Ave W (44906-1026)
PHONE............................419 529-2578
Dave Baker, Vice Pres
Kenneth Earhart, Mng Member
Margaret Pauley, Info Tech Mgr
EMP: 30 EST: 2012
SALES (est): 6.8MM Privately Held
SIC: 3449 1761 1791 Custom roll formed products; sheet metalwork; structural steel erection

(G-15710)
P R MACHINE WORKS INC
1825 Nussbaum Pkwy (44906-2360)
PHONE............................419 529-5748
Fax: 419 529-9052
Mark Romanchuk, President
Mark J Romanchuk, President
Craig Franklin, Business Mgr
Jerry Schwall, Vice Pres
Mike Strench, Purch Mgr
▲ EMP: 75
SQ FT: 14,100
SALES (est): 9.5MM Privately Held
WEB: www.prmachineworks.com
SIC: 3599 1531 Machine shop, jobbing & repair;

(G-15711)
PETSMART INC
2275 Walker Lake Rd (44903-6519)
PHONE............................419 747-4544
Fax: 419 747-4140
Mike Pupa, Manager
EMP: 32
SALES (corp-wide): 12.7B Privately Held
SIC: 0752 Grooming services, pet & animal specialties
HQ: Petsmart, Inc.
19601 N 27th Ave
Phoenix AZ 85027
623 580-6100

(G-15712)
SHEARER FARM INC
Also Called: John Deere Authorized Dealer
2715 W 4th St (44906-1212)
PHONE............................419 529-6160
Fax: 419 529-4838
Jeff S Clair, Finance Mgr
Lucy Hofacre, Financial Exec
Ivan Maibach, Manager
EMP: 25
SALES (corp-wide): 59.5MM Privately Held
WEB: www.shearerequipment.com
SIC: 5083 5999 Farm implements; farm machinery
PA: Shearer Farm, Inc
7762 Cleveland Rd
Wooster OH 44691
330 345-9023

(G-15713)
SHELLY AND SANDS INC
Mansfield Saphalt Paving
1300 W 4th St Rear (44906-1828)
P.O. Box 1321, Mansfield (44901-1321)
PHONE............................419 529-8455
Fax: 419 529-8157
Tom Ellis, Manager
EMP: 75
SQ FT: 5,000

SALES (corp-wide): 260.8MM Privately Held
WEB: www.shellyandsands.com
SIC: 1611 Highway & street paving contractor
PA: Shelly And Sands, Inc.
3570 S River Rd
Zanesville OH 43701
740 453-0721

(G-15714)
SLICK AUTOMATED SOLUTIONS INC
1825 Nussbaum Pkwy (44906-2360)
PHONE............................567 247-1080
Zoi Romanchuk, President
Mark Romanchuk, Vice Pres
Mike Wilgus, Project Mgr
Jeff Blanchard, Engineer
EMP: 26
SALES (est): 4.9MM Privately Held
SIC: 8711 Engineering services

(G-15715)
SOUTHERN CARE INC
41 Briggs Dr (44906-3805)
PHONE............................419 774-0555
Fax: 419 774-0155
Michael Pardy, Branch Mgr
EMP: 50 Privately Held
SIC: 8082 Home health care services
PA: Southern Care, Inc
1000 Urban Center Dr # 115
Vestavia AL 35242

(G-15716)
SPITZER MOTOR CITY INC
Also Called: Spitzer Motors of Mansfield
1777 W 4th St (44906-1704)
PHONE............................567 307-7119
EMP: 26
SALES (corp-wide): 9.3MM Privately Held
SIC: 7538 General Auto Repair
PA: Spitzer Motor City, Inc.
13001 Brookpark Rd
Cleveland OH 44142
216 267-2100

(G-15717)
STARTEK INC
850 W 4th St (44906-2534)
PHONE............................419 528-7801
Brenda Young, Branch Mgr
EMP: 137
SALES (corp-wide): 292.6MM Publicly Held
WEB: www.startek.com
SIC: 7389 Telemarketing services
PA: Startek, Inc.
8200 E Maplewood Ave # 100
Greenwood Village CO 80111
303 262-4500

(G-15718)
UNIVERSAL ENTERPRISES INC (PA)
Also Called: Universal Refrigeration Div
545 Beer Rd (44906-1214)
PHONE............................419 529-3500
Fax: 419 529-4570
Ralph Ridenour, President
George Reece, Owner
Todd Kiger, Vice Pres
Rob Ridenour, Vice Pres
Dolores Moody, Office Mgr
EMP: 180 EST: 1952
SALES (est): 34.8MM Privately Held
WEB: www.universalrefrigeration.com
SIC: 1711 7374 Warm air heating & air conditioning contractor; computer graphics service

(G-15719)
WALLOWA DIALYSIS LLC
Also Called: Mid Ohio Dialysis
2148 W 4th St (44906-1200)
PHONE............................419 747-4039
James K Hilger,
EMP: 29 EST: 2013
SALES (est): 324K Publicly Held
SIC: 8092 Kidney dialysis centers
PA: Davita Inc.
2000 16th St
Denver CO 80202

(G-15720)
WESTERN & SOUTHERN LF INSUR CO
Also Called: Western Southern Life Insur
1989 W 4th St (44906-1708)
PHONE............................419 524-1800
Fax: 419 525-0709
Vicky Brand, Marketing Staff
Barry Danko, Manager
EMP: 40 Privately Held
SIC: 6311 Life insurance
HQ: The Western & Southern Life Insurance Company
400 Broadway St
Cincinnati OH 45202
513 629-1800

Oregon
Lucas County

(G-15721)
AA BOOS & SONS INC
2015 Pickle Rd (43616-3155)
PHONE............................419 691-2329
Fax: 419 691-2057
Robert Boos, CEO
Robert D Boos, CEO
James Cousino, President
Bret Boos, Vice Pres
Kevin Skotynsky, Project Mgr
EMP: 80 EST: 1948
SQ FT: 6,000
SALES: 33.5MM Privately Held
WEB: www.aaboos.com
SIC: 1541 1542 Industrial buildings, new construction; renovation, remodeling & repairs: industrial buildings; commercial & office building, new construction; commercial & office buildings, renovation & repair

(G-15722)
ABC APPLIANCE INC
3012 Navarre Ave (43616-3308)
PHONE............................419 693-4414
Fax: 419 693-4142
J R Pruss, Manager
EMP: 30
SALES (corp-wide): 358.3MM Privately Held
WEB: www.abcwarehouse.com
SIC: 3639 5722 5731 5065 Major kitchen appliances, except refrigerators & stoves; vacuum cleaners; high fidelity stereo equipment; telephone equipment; photocopy machines
PA: Abc Appliance, Inc.
1 W Silverdome Indus Park
Pontiac MI 48342
248 335-4222

(G-15723)
AECOM ENERGY & CNSTR INC
Also Called: Washington Group
4001 Cedar Point Rd (43616-1310)
P.O. Box 696, Toledo (43697-0696)
PHONE............................419 698-6277
EMP: 125
SALES (corp-wide): 18.2B Publicly Held
WEB: www.wgint.com
SIC: 1542 2911 Nonresidential construction; petroleum refining
HQ: Aecom Energy & Construction, Inc.
1999 Avenue Of The Stars
Los Angeles CA 90067
213 593-8100

(G-15724)
ASSOCTED CTRACT LASER SURGEONS
Also Called: Center For Prgressive Eye Care
2740 Navarre Ave (43616-3216)
PHONE............................419 693-4444
Fax: 419 693-4915
William G Martin MD, President
Robert G Wiley MD, Vice Pres
EMP: 25
SQ FT: 4,500
SALES (est): 824.6K Privately Held
SIC: 8011 Ophthalmologist

Oregon - Lucas County (G-15725)   GEOGRAPHIC SECTION

(G-15725)
BAY PARK COMMUNITY HOSPITAL (HQ)
Also Called: PROMEDICA
2801 Bay Park Dr (43616-4920)
PHONE...................................419 690-7900
Fax: 419 697-6713
Bill Mueller, *President*
Jonathan Nadaud, *Ch Radiology*
Cristy McNalley, *Finance*
Bernice Chisholm, *Human Resources*
Jeannette Rohr, *Med Doctor*
EMP: 85 EST: 1998
SQ FT: 270,000
SALES: 70.7MM
SALES (corp-wide): 1.5B **Privately Held**
SIC: **8062** General medical & surgical hospitals
PA: Promedica Health Systems, Inc.
   100 Madison Ave
   Toledo OH 43604
   567 585-7454

(G-15726)
BUCKEYE PIPE LINE SERVICES CO
3321 York St (43616-1215)
P.O. Box 167567 (43616-7567)
PHONE...................................419 698-8770
Fax: 419 698-8151
Bob McDowel, *Manager*
EMP: 28
SALES (corp-wide): 3.6B **Publicly Held**
SIC: **4613** Refined petroleum pipelines
HQ: Buckeye Pipe Line Services Company
   5002 Buckeye Rd
   Emmaus PA 18049
   484 232-4000

(G-15727)
C & W TANK CLEANING COMPANY
50 N Lallendorf Rd (43616-1847)
PHONE...................................419 691-1995
Fax: 419 691-1997
James C Parker, *President*
Ben Patterson, *Safety Dir*
Brian Francis, *Opers Mgr*
Brent Tank, *Opers Mgr*
Christy Schramm, *Human Res Mgr*
EMP: 65
SQ FT: 6,000
SALES (est): 9.3MM **Privately Held**
WEB: www.nk.com
SIC: **7699** Tank & boiler cleaning service

(G-15728)
CHARLES MERCY HLTH-ST HOSPITA (PA)
2600 Navarre Ave (43616-3207)
PHONE...................................419 696-7200
Fax: 419 696-7347
Jeffrey Dempseyn, *CEO*
Jacalyn Liebowitz, *President*
John M Starcher, *Principal*
F J Gallagher, *Principal*
Joseph W Rossler, *Principal*
EMP: 83
SQ FT: 515,000
SALES: 133.5MM **Privately Held**
SIC: **8062** General medical & surgical hospitals

(G-15729)
CSX TRANSPORTATION INC
600 Millard Ave (43616-1201)
PHONE...................................419 697-2323
Paul Lecomtte, *Manager*
EMP: 75
SALES (corp-wide): 11.4B **Publicly Held**
WEB: www.csxt.com
SIC: **4011** Railroads, line-haul operating
HQ: Csx Transportation, Inc.
   500 Water St
   Jacksonville FL 32202
   904 359-3100

(G-15730)
DAVITA INC
3310 Dustin Rd (43616-3302)
PHONE...................................419 697-2191
Anil Mehta, *Branch Mgr*
EMP: 33 **Publicly Held**
SIC: **8092** Kidney dialysis centers
PA: Davita Inc.
   2000 16th St
   Denver CO 80202

(G-15731)
DESOTO DIALYSIS LLC
Also Called: Lucas County Home Training
2702 Navarre Ave Ste 203 (43616-3224)
PHONE...................................419 691-1514
James K Hilger,
EMP: 33
SALES (est): 507.3K **Publicly Held**
SIC: **8092** Kidney dialysis centers
PA: Davita Inc.
   2000 16th St
   Denver CO 80202

(G-15732)
DURE INVESTMENTS LLC
Also Called: Sleep Inn
1761 Meijers Cir (43616-4923)
PHONE...................................419 697-7800
Fax: 419 697-7810
Darrell Ducat,
Rudolph Eckert III,
EMP: 25
SQ FT: 42,478
SALES (est): 1MM **Privately Held**
SIC: **7011** Hotels & motels

(G-15733)
E S WAGNER COMPANY
Also Called: Esw
840 Patchen Rd (43616-3132)
PHONE...................................419 691-8651
Fax: 419 691-0429
Lewis John Wagner, *CEO*
Scott Boyle, *Superintendent*
Jim Pilewski, *Vice Pres*
John C Wagner, *Vice Pres*
Brandon Jordan, *Project Mgr*
EMP: 60 EST: 1949
SQ FT: 8,500
SALES (est): 30.7MM **Privately Held**
WEB: www.eswagner.com
SIC: **1794** 1622 1611 1623 Excavation & grading, building construction; bridge construction; concrete construction: roads, highways, sidewalks, etc.; sewer line construction; railroad & subway construction

(G-15734)
EASTERN MUMEE BAY ARTS COUNCIL
595 Sylvandale Ave (43616-2721)
PHONE...................................419 690-5718
Martin Danekind, *President*
Vernon Pattont, *Vice Pres*
Steve Sheskey, *Treasurer*
Claudia Winn, *Admin Sec*
EMP: 50
SALES (est): 274.3K **Privately Held**
WEB: www.maumeebay.org
SIC: **8699** Art council

(G-15735)
ENVIROSAFE SERVICES OF OHIO (DH)
876 Otter Creek Rd (43616-1243)
PHONE...................................419 698-3500
Fax: 419 698-8663
Doug Roberts, *President*
Scott Brummett, *Purchasing*
John Nienius, *Sales Mgr*
Corey Heenan, *Accounts Mgr*
John Heenan, *Accounts Mgr*
EMP: 48
SALES (est): 24.3MM **Privately Held**
WEB: www.envirosafeservices.com
SIC: **4953** Hazardous waste collection & disposal
HQ: Tms International Corporation
   12 Monongahela Ave
   Glassport PA 15045
   412 678-6141

(G-15736)
FRESENIUS USA INC
555 Blue Heron Dr (43616-1849)
PHONE...................................419 691-2475
Gary Heleman, *Manager*
EMP: 28
SQ FT: 58,000
SALES (corp-wide): 20.9B **Privately Held**
WEB: www.fresenius.org
SIC: **5047** Medical equipment & supplies
HQ: Fresenius Usa, Inc.
   4040 Nelson Ave
   Concord CA 94520
   925 288-4218

(G-15737)
GREAT EASTERN THEATRE COMPANY
4500 Navarre Ave (43616-3520)
PHONE...................................419 691-9668
Kevin Christy, *Branch Mgr*
EMP: 73
SALES (corp-wide): 4.7MM **Privately Held**
SIC: **7832** Motion picture theaters, except drive-in
PA: Great Eastern Theatre Company
   3361 Executive Pkwy # 300
   Toledo OH 43606
   419 537-9682

(G-15738)
HCR MANORCARE MED SVCS FLA LLC
Also Called: Heartland of Oregon
3953 Navarre Ave (43616-3437)
PHONE...................................419 691-3088
Fax: 419 693-8199
Abby Taylor, *Manager*
Cindy Amorelli, *Director*
Irshad Hasan, *Director*
Michelle Cline, *Executive*
EMP: 110
SQ FT: 30,158
SALES (corp-wide): 3.6B **Publicly Held**
WEB: www.manorcare.com
SIC: **8051** Convalescent home with continuous nursing care
HQ: Hcr Manorcare Medical Services Of Florida, Llc
   333 N Summit St Ste 100
   Toledo OH 43604
   419 252-5500

(G-15739)
HOLIDAY INN
3154 Navarre Ave (43616-3310)
PHONE...................................419 691-8800
Fax: 419 691-8072
Christine Shallal, *Manager*
Saad Roumaya,
Frank Shallal,
EMP: 26
SQ FT: 5,694
SALES (est): 2MM **Privately Held**
SIC: **7011** Hotels & motels

(G-15740)
JEFFERS CRANE SERVICE INC (HQ)
5421 Navarre Ave (43616-3551)
P.O. Box 167789 (43616-7789)
PHONE...................................419 693-0421
Toll Free:..................................888 -
Fax: 419 693-0210
Michael C Liptak Jr, *President*
David E Bucher, *General Mgr*
Butch Butcher, *General Mgr*
Lawrence Liptak, *Treasurer*
Marty Bowman, *Sales Staff*
EMP: 56
SQ FT: 20,000
SALES (est): 9.5MM
SALES (corp-wide): 100.5MM **Privately Held**
SIC: **7353** Cranes & aerial lift equipment, rental or leasing
PA: All Erection' & Crane Rental Corp
   4700 Acorn Dr
   Cleveland OH 44131
   234 524-6550

(G-15741)
MERCY HEALTH - ST
Also Called: St Charles Child Dev Center
2600 Navarre Ave (43616-3207)
PHONE...................................419 696-7465
Bobbie Kehlmeier, *Exec Dir*
Christina Cassaubon, *Director*
Adnan A Al-Khaleefa, *Oncology*
EMP: 30
SALES (corp-wide): 133.5MM **Privately Held**
SIC: **8062** 8322 General medical & surgical hospitals; child guidance agency
PA: Mercy Health - St. Charles Hospital Llc
   2600 Navarre Ave
   Oregon OH 43616
   419 696-7200

(G-15742)
NORTHTOWN SQUARE LTD PARTNR
Also Called: Comfort Inn
2930 Navarre Ave (43616-3373)
PHONE...................................419 691-8911
Fax: 419 691-2107
Darrell Ducat, *General Ptnr*
Erwin Hollander, *CPA*
Karen Magnone, *Manager*
EMP: 30
SQ FT: 36,000
SALES (est): 1.5MM **Privately Held**
SIC: **7011** Hotels & motels

(G-15743)
OPTIVUE INC
Also Called: Ohio Vision of Toledo Inc Opt
2740 Navarre Ave (43616-3216)
PHONE...................................419 891-1391
Fax: 419 891-1397
Mary Martin, *President*
William Martin, *Principal*
Connie Richards, *COO*
Kathleen Harrison, *Controller*
EMP: 126
SALES (est): 14.3MM **Privately Held**
SIC: **8011** 8042 Ophthalmologist; specialized optometrists

(G-15744)
ORCHARD VILLA INC
2841 Munding Dr (43616-3290)
PHONE...................................419 697-4100
Fax: 419 697-4101
Bruce Daskal, *Owner*
Rey Nevarez, *Director*
EMP: 200
SALES (est): 6.2MM **Privately Held**
SIC: **8059** 8052 8051 Nursing home, except skilled & intermediate care facility; intermediate care facilities; skilled nursing care facilities

(G-15745)
OREGON CLEAN ENERGY CENTER
816 N Lallendorf Rd (43616-1339)
PHONE...................................419 566-9466
Moe Collins, *Principal*
EMP: 25
SALES (est): 41.9K **Privately Held**
SIC: **7699** Cleaning services

(G-15746)
OREGON FORD INC
Also Called: Mathews Ford-Oregon
2811 Navarre Ave (43616-3397)
PHONE...................................419 698-4444
Fax: 419 691-5077
Timothy W Mathews, *President*
Lauren Jarzeboski, *Sales Staff*
Alan Robinson, *Sales Staff*
EMP: 110
SQ FT: 33,000
SALES (est): 46MM **Privately Held**
SIC: **5511** 7538 7532 7515 Automobiles, new & used; trucks, tractors & trailers: new & used; general automotive repair shops; top & body repair & paint shops; passenger car leasing

(G-15747)
OTTIVUE (PA)
Also Called: Optio-Vision By Kahn & Diehl
2740 Navarre Ave (43616-3216)
PHONE...................................419 693-4444
Connie Richards, *CEO*
EMP: 100
SALES (est): 1.8MM **Privately Held**
WEB: www.optivue.com
SIC: **8042** Specialized optometrists

(G-15748)
RBM ENVIRONMENTAL AND CNSTR
4526 Bayshore Rd (43616-1035)
PHONE...................................419 693-5840
Fax: 419 693-8746
Bob J Petty, *President*

Mike S Petty, *Vice Pres*
EMP: 40
SALES (est): 4.9MM **Privately Held**
SIC: **1794** 7699 7692 3498 Excavation work; tank & boiler cleaning service; welding repair; fabricated pipe & fittings; fabricated structural metal

(G-15749)
SISTERS OF LITTLE
Also Called: Scared Heart Nursing Home
930 S Wynn Rd (43616-3530)
PHONE.................................419 698-4331
Fax: 419 698-8601
Laurie Ferguson, *Nursing Dir*
Mother Contance, *Administration*
Martha Dunn, *Administration*
Cecilia Sartorius, *Administration*
EMP: 120
SALES (corp-wide): 3.5MM **Privately Held**
SIC: **8051** Skilled nursing care facilities
PA: Little Sisters Of The Poor, Baltimore, Inc.
   601 Maiden Choice Ln
   Baltimore MD 21228
   410 744-9367

(G-15750)
SISTERS OF MERCY AMER REG COMM
Also Called: Mercy Ctr For Hlth Promtn St
1001 Isaac Streets Dr (43616-3205)
PHONE.................................419 696-7203
Fax: 419 696-7639
Rick Gray, *Director*
EMP: 75
SALES (corp-wide): 17.4MM **Privately Held**
SIC: **8049** Nurses, registered & practical
PA: Sisters Of Mercy Of The Union In The United States Of America
   2335 Grandview Ave Fl 5
   Cincinnati OH 45206
   513 475-6700

(G-15751)
TESCO-TRANSPORTION EQP SLS
6401 Seaman Rd (43616-4223)
P.O. Box 167230 (43616-7230)
PHONE.................................419 836-2835
Noel E Graham Jr, *President*
EMP: 50 EST: 2007
SALES (est): 1.6MM **Privately Held**
SIC: **4142** 5012 Bus charter service, except local; buses

(G-15752)
TOLEDO REFINING COMPANY LLC (DH)
1819 Woodville Rd (43616-3159)
PHONE.................................419 698-6600
Fax: 419 698-6627
Tom Nimbley, *CEO*
Michael D Gayda, *President*
Jeffrey Dill, *Senior VP*
Matthew C Lucey, *Senior VP*
Paul Davis, *Vice Pres*
EMP: 147
SALES (est): 198.1MM
SALES (corp-wide): 21.7B **Publicly Held**
SIC: **1629** Oil refinery construction

(G-15753)
TOLEDO SWISS SINGERS
3860 Starr Ave (43616-2438)
PHONE.................................419 693-4110
Charles Justus, *President*
Ernie Bollinger, *Principal*
John Murr, *Vice Pres*
EMP: 40
SALES (est): 301K **Privately Held**
SIC: **7929** Musicians

(G-15754)
TW RECREATIONAL SERVICES
Also Called: Maumee Bay Golf Course
1750 State Park Rd 2 (43616-5800)
PHONE.................................419 836-1466
Don Karns, *Principal*
Paul Noel, *Controller*
EMP: 25
SQ FT: 1,800

SALES (est): 680.8K **Privately Held**
SIC: **7992** Public golf courses

(G-15755)
XANTERRA PARKS & RESORTS INC
Also Called: Maumee Bay State Park Resort
1750 State Park Rd 2 (43616-5800)
PHONE.................................419 836-1466
Fax: 419 836-2438
Patrick Czarny, *General Mgr*
Paul Noel, *Controller*
Kristy Valleroy, *Human Res Mgr*
EMP: 200
SALES (corp-wide): 414.9MM **Privately Held**
WEB: www.amfac.com
SIC: **7011** Resort hotel
HQ: Parks Xanterra & Resorts Inc
   6312 S Fiddlers Green Cir 600n
   Greenwood Village CO 80111
   303 600-3400

(G-15756)
YOUNG MENS CHRISTIAN ASSOCIAT
Also Called: Eastern Community YMCA
2960 Pickle Rd (43616-4051)
PHONE.................................419 691-3523
Fax: 419 691-2409
Tracy Adams, *Director*
EMP: 80
SALES (corp-wide): 29.1MM **Privately Held**
WEB: www.ymcastorercamps.org
SIC: **8641** 7991 8351 7032 Youth organizations; physical fitness facilities; child day care services; youth camps; individual & family services
PA: Young Men's Christian Association Of Greater Toledo
   1500 N Superior St Fl 2
   Toledo OH 43604
   419 729-8135

Oregonia
Warren County

(G-15757)
DAYTON SOCIETY NATURAL HISTORY
Also Called: Fort Ancient State Memorial
6123 State Route 350 (45054-9708)
PHONE.................................513 932-4421
Jack Blosser, *Branch Mgr*
EMP: 43
SQ FT: 20,526
SALES (est): 604.2K
SALES (corp-wide): 5MM **Privately Held**
SIC: **8412** 8699 Museum; historical club
PA: Dayton Society Of Natural History
   2600 Deweese Pkwy
   Dayton OH 45414
   937 275-7431

(G-15758)
ROGER SHAWN HOUCK
Also Called: Prengers
7887 Wilmington Rd (45054-9448)
PHONE.................................513 933-0563
Roger S Houck, *Partner*
EMP: 45
SALES (est): 2.8MM **Privately Held**
SIC: **5083** Dairy machinery & equipment

(G-15759)
YOUNG MENS CHRISTIAN ASSOC
Also Called: Dayton YMCA Camp Kern
5291 State Route 350 (45054-9746)
PHONE.................................513 932-3756
Fax: 513 932-8607
C Addison, *Exec Dir*
Tim Short, *Exec Dir*
Devin Carr, *Director*
EMP: 90
SALES (est): 1.6MM
SALES (corp-wide): 26.1MM **Privately Held**
WEB: www.daytonymca.org
SIC: **8641** 7032 Youth organizations; summer camp, except day & sports instructional

PA: Young Men's Christian Association Of Greater Dayton
   118 W St Ste 300
   Dayton OH 45402
   937 223-5201

Orient
Pickaway County

(G-15760)
EITEL TOWING SERVICE INC
Also Called: Eitels Amrcas Towing Trnsp Svc
7111 Stahl Rd (43146-9601)
PHONE.................................614 877-4139
Fax: 614 877-4601
Stacy L Wills, *President*
Larry Cyrus, *Administration*
EMP: 30
SQ FT: 10,000
SALES (est): 3.9MM **Privately Held**
WEB: www.eitelstowing.com
SIC: **7549** Towing service, automotive

(G-15761)
KMJ LEASING LTD
Also Called: B & B Industries
7001 Harrisburg Pike (43146-9468)
PHONE.................................614 871-3883
Kenneth A Harwood,
Mary A Harwood,
EMP: 38 EST: 1971
SQ FT: 5,000
SALES (est): 6.6MM **Privately Held**
WEB: www.bandbindustriesinc.com
SIC: **4213** 3799 Contract haulers; golf carts, powered

(G-15762)
SPLIT ROCK GOLF CLUB INC
10210 Scioto Darby Rd (43146-9016)
PHONE.................................614 877-9755
Fax: 614 877-9956
Glen B Gulick, *President*
Lucinda Gulick, *Corp Secy*
EMP: 30
SALES (est): 1MM **Privately Held**
SIC: **7992** Public golf courses

Orrville
Wayne County

(G-15763)
AMTRAC OF OHIO INC
Also Called: Amtrac Railroad Contrs Ohio
11842 Lincoln Way E (44667-9597)
PHONE.................................330 683-7206
Fax: 330 683-3243
Rickey J Geib, *President*
Lynn Lawson, *President*
Mary A Shank, *Corp Secy*
Brian L Lawson, *Vice Pres*
Mary Shank, *Manager*
EMP: 55
SQ FT: 10,000
SALES (est): 8.4MM **Privately Held**
WEB: www.amtracohio.com
SIC: **1629** Railroad & railway roadbed construction

(G-15764)
ASPIRE ENERGY OF OHIO LLC (HQ)
300 Tracy Bridge Rd (44667-9384)
PHONE.................................330 682-7726
Fax: 330 498-9557
Tony Kovacevich, *President*
Ralph Knoll, *Vice Pres*
EMP: 39
SQ FT: 11,446
SALES (est): 20.2MM
SALES (corp-wide): 617.5MM **Publicly Held**
WEB: www.gatherco.com
SIC: **4923** Gas transmission & distribution
PA: Chesapeake Utilities Corporation
   909 Silver Lake Blvd
   Dover DE 19904
   302 734-6799

(G-15765)
AULTMAN HEALTH FOUNDATION
832 S Main St (44667-2208)
PHONE.................................330 682-3010
Jessica Immel, *Office Mgr*
Timothy K Cooley, *Emerg Med Spec*
John P Robinson, *Emerg Med Spec*
Paul Stephens, *Emerg Med Spec*
Ronald R Usnak, *Emerg Med Spec*
EMP: 2315
SALES (corp-wide): 1.1MM **Privately Held**
SIC: **8742** Management consulting services
PA: Aultman Health Foundation
   2600 6th St Sw
   Canton OH 44710
   330 452-9911

(G-15766)
BEN D IMHOFF INC
Also Called: Imhoff Construction
315 E Market St (44667-1805)
PHONE.................................330 683-4498
Fax: 330 683-1952
Scott Imhoff, *President*
Lisle Liston, *Vice Pres*
Audrey Franklin, *Controller*
Tom Miller, *Shareholder*
EMP: 40
SQ FT: 9,000
SALES (est): 10.4MM **Privately Held**
WEB: www.imhoffinc.com
SIC: **1542** 1541 Institutional building construction; commercial & office building, new construction; commercial & office buildings, renovation & repair; industrial buildings, new construction; renovation, remodeling & repairs: industrial buildings

(G-15767)
BRENN FIELD NURSING CENTER
1980 Lynn Dr (44667-2337)
PHONE.................................330 683-4075
Fax: 330 683-4414
Jeanne Stepfield, *President*
Sandy Brockman, *Corp Secy*
Tom Brockman, *Vice Pres*
EMP: 116
SQ FT: 30,000
SALES (est): 5.3MM **Privately Held**
WEB: www.brenn-field.com
SIC: **8051** 8322 Convalescent home with continuous nursing care; individual & family services

(G-15768)
CONSUMERS GAS COOPERATIVE
298 Tracy Bridge Rd (44667-9383)
PHONE.................................330 682-4144
Anthony Kovakevich, *President*
Lance Jones, *Marketing Staff*
Dave Tennant, *Marketing Staff*
Dan Burkhart, *Executive*
EMP: 45
SALES: 1.6MM **Privately Held**
SIC: **4922** Natural gas transmission

(G-15769)
DUNLAP FAMILY PHYSICIANS INC (PA)
830 S Main St Ste Rear (44667-2218)
PHONE.................................330 684-2015
Fax: 330 684-2075
Larry Sander, *President*
Brenda Kamp, *Project Mgr*
Edward Dunham, *Network Mgr*
EMP: 34
SALES (est): 4.5MM **Privately Held**
SIC: **8011** General & family practice, physician/surgeon

(G-15770)
FAMILY PRACTICE CENTER INC
365 S Crown Hill Rd (44667-9598)
PHONE.................................330 682-3075
Fax: 330 682-7454
Oliver Eshenaur Do, *President*
Dr Charles D Milligan, *Corp Secy*
Dr Douglas R Brown, *Vice Pres*
EMP: 31
SQ FT: 10,300

Orrville - Wayne County (G-15771)

SALES (est): 1.8MM **Privately Held**
SIC: 8031 Offices & clinics of osteopathic physicians

(G-15771)
FARMERS NATIONAL BANK
112 W Market St (44667-1847)
PHONE..................................330 682-1010
Keri Litman, *Executive Asst*
EMP: 122
SALES (corp-wide): 104.5MM **Publicly Held**
SIC: 6021 National commercial banks
HQ: The Farmers National Bank Of Canfield
20 S Broad St
Canfield OH 44406
330 533-3341

(G-15772)
FARMERS NATIONAL BANK
1444 N Main St (44667-9169)
P.O. Box 57 (44667-0057)
PHONE..................................330 682-1030
Jim Griffith, *Manager*
EMP: 54
SALES (corp-wide): 104.5MM **Publicly Held**
WEB: www.fnborrville.com
SIC: 6021 National commercial banks
HQ: The Farmers National Bank Of Canfield
20 S Broad St
Canfield OH 44406
330 533-3341

(G-15773)
GENERAL BUILDING MAINTENANCE
500 Jefferson Ave (44667-1811)
PHONE..................................330 682-2238
Fax: 330 682-4930
James M Corbett, *President*
Lavinia Corbett, *Vice Pres*
Tim Corbett, *Accounts Mgr*
EMP: 80
SQ FT: 140
SALES (est): 2.4MM **Privately Held**
SIC: 7349 Janitorial service, contract basis

(G-15774)
HUMMEL GROUP INC
461 Wadsworth Rd (44667-9215)
P.O. Box 3 (44667-0003)
PHONE..................................330 683-1050
Tony Rohrer, *Branch Mgr*
EMP: 30
SALES (corp-wide): 21.4MM **Privately Held**
SIC: 6411 Insurance agents
PA: Hummel Group, Inc.
4585 State Rt 39
Berlin OH
330 893-2600

(G-15775)
JARRETT LOGISTICS SYSTEMS INC
1347 N Main St (44667-9761)
PHONE..................................330 682-0099
Fax: 330 682-0271
Michael Jarrett, *President*
Matt Angell, *Vice Pres*
Robert Churgovich, *Hum Res Coord*
Ellen Wood, *Hum Res Coord*
Josh Becker, *Sales Staff*
EMP: 150
SQ FT: 73,000
SALES: 100MM **Privately Held**
WEB: www.jarrettlogistics.com
SIC: 8742 4731 Transportation consultant; freight transportation arrangement

(G-15776)
ORRVILLA INC
333 E Sassafras St (44667-2250)
PHONE..................................330 683-4455
Morris Stutcman, *Chairman*
George Bixler, *Director*
EMP: 25
SALES: 1.3MM **Privately Held**
WEB: www.orrvilla.com
SIC: 6513 Retirement hotel operation

(G-15777)
ORRVILLA RETIREMENT COMMUNITY
Also Called: Manor 1
333 E Sassafras St (44667-2250)
PHONE..................................330 683-4455
Fax: 330 683-7375
George Bixler, *Director*
EMP: 35
SALES (est): 1.2MM **Privately Held**
SIC: 8361 Home for the aged

(G-15778)
ORRVILLE BOYS AND GIRLS CLUB
820 N Ella St (44667-1155)
P.O. Box 17 (44667-0017)
PHONE..................................330 683-4888
Fax: 330 683-3119
Frederick Maibach, *Vice Pres*
Steven McCumber, *Vice Pres*
Kevin Platz, *Exec Dir*
EMP: 32
SALES: 876.8K **Privately Held**
WEB: www.oabgc.org
SIC: 8641 Youth organizations

(G-15779)
ORRVILLE HOSPITAL FOUNDATION
Also Called: AULTMAN ORRVILLE HOSPITAL
832 S Main St (44667-2208)
PHONE..................................330 684-4700
Marchelle Suppan, *CEO*
Janice Oberly, *Facilities Mgr*
Kim Gossard, *Human Resources*
Daniel D Lynch, *Anesthesiology*
Laura Brelin, *Obstetrician*
EMP: 240
SQ FT: 90,000
SALES: 25.2MM **Privately Held**
SIC: 8062 General medical & surgical hospitals

(G-15780)
ORRVILLE TRUCKING & GRADING CO (PA)
475 Orr St (44667-9764)
P.O. Box 220 (44667-0220)
PHONE..................................330 682-4010
Fax: 330 682-4457
Auvil Richmond, *President*
Tim Fnyter, *General Mgr*
John H Wilson, *Treasurer*
EMP: 50
SQ FT: 15,000
SALES (est): 7.4MM **Privately Held**
SIC: 3273 3272 5031 Ready-mixed concrete; concrete products; building materials, exterior; building materials, interior

(G-15781)
ORVILLE PET SPA & RESORT
1669 N Main St (44667-9171)
PHONE..................................330 683-3335
Anne Kollier, *Office Mgr*
Anne Weiser, *Manager*
EMP: 25
SALES (est): 515K **Privately Held**
SIC: 0752 Boarding services, kennels

(G-15782)
PACKSHIP USA INC (PA)
1347 N Main St (44667-9761)
PHONE..................................330 682-7225
Fax: 330 682-7447
W Michael Jarrett, *President*
Diane Jarrett, *Vice Pres*
Greg Gaither, *Opers Mgr*
Jacob Davenport, *Info Tech Dir*
Dan Auxter, *Business Dir*
EMP: 56
SQ FT: 15,000
SALES (est): 7.3MM **Privately Held**
WEB: www.packshipusa.com
SIC: 7389 4783 4731 Packaging & labeling services; packing & crating; freight transportation arrangement

(G-15783)
PINES GOLF CLUB
1319 N Millborne Rd (44667-9500)
P.O. Box 308 (44667-0308)
PHONE..................................330 684-1414
Fax: 330 684-1020
Glen Miller, *Partner*
Ron Contini, *Partner*
Gary Ertle, *Partner*
Glenn Miller, *Partner*
Howard Wenger, *Partner*
EMP: 25
SALES (est): 1.3MM **Privately Held**
SIC: 7992 5812 7299 5941 Public golf courses; eating places; banquet hall facilities; sporting goods & bicycle shops

(G-15784)
PURINA ANIMAL NUTRITION LLC
635 Collins Blvd (44667-9796)
PHONE..................................330 682-1951
Ken Schwarvrock, *Manager*
EMP: 35
SALES (corp-wide): 14.9B **Privately Held**
SIC: 5191 Feed
HQ: Purina Animal Nutrition Llc
1080 County Road F W
Shoreview MN 55126

(G-15785)
REGENCY PARK
230 S Crown Hill Rd (44667-1328)
PHONE..................................330 682-2273
Robert Kline, *President*
Harvey Rickert Sr, *President*
Harvey Rickert Jr, *Vice Pres*
Kathy Sowards, *Executive*
Lauren Fiser, *Administration*
EMP: 80
SALES (est): 1.1MM **Privately Held**
SIC: 8059 Nursing home, except skilled & intermediate care facility

(G-15786)
REGENCY PARK NURSING & REHAB
230 S Crown Hill Rd (44667-1328)
PHONE..................................330 682-2273
Robert Klein, *President*
Alan Jaffa, *Treasurer*
EMP: 55
SALES: 2.1MM **Privately Held**
SIC: 8059 Nursing home, except skilled & intermediate care facility

(G-15787)
SIDLE TRANSIT SERVICE INC
5454 N Crown Hill Rd (44667-9134)
PHONE..................................330 683-2807
Fax: 330 682-2802
Dennis I Sidle, *President*
Duane B Sidle, *Corp Secy*
Judith Sidle, *Manager*
Richard Sidle, *Manager*
EMP: 35
SALES (est): 3.3MM **Privately Held**
SIC: 4212 Liquid haulage, local

(G-15788)
SMITHFOODS TRUCKING INC
1201 Sterling Ave (44667-1054)
P.O. Box 28 (44667-0028)
PHONE..................................330 684-6502
Daniel Brimm, *President*
EMP: 30
SALES (est): 572.7K **Privately Held**
SALES (corp-wide): 62.3MM **Privately Held**
SIC: 4214 Local trucking with storage
PA: Smithfoods Inc.
1381 Dairy Ln
Orrville OH 44667
330 683-8710

(G-15789)
WILL-BURT COMPANY (PA)
169 S Main St (44667-1801)
P.O. Box 900 (44667-0900)
PHONE..................................330 682-7015
Fax: 330 684-1190
Jeffrey Evans, *President*
John Stroia, *General Mgr*
John Glenn, *Regional Mgr*
Eric Dubendorfer, *Business Mgr*
Thomas Howard, *Business Mgr*
▲ **EMP:** 275 **EST:** 1918
SQ FT: 170,000
SALES: 63.8MM **Privately Held**
WEB: www.willburt.com
SIC: 3599 5039 3443 3449 Machine shop, jobbing & repair; prefabricated structures; fabricated plate work (boiler shop); miscellaneous metalwork; lighting equipment; sheet metalwork

(G-15790)
WILL-BURT COMPANY
312 Collins Blvd (44667-9727)
P.O. Box 900 (44667-0900)
PHONE..................................330 682-7015
Vicki Oravec, *Purch Agent*
Mike Ohlsen, *Engineer*
Andrew Wasson, *Engineer*
Deborah Malta, *Human Res Dir*
Jeffrey O Evans, *Manager*
EMP: 37
SALES (corp-wide): 63.8MM **Privately Held**
WEB: www.willburt.com
SIC: 3443 3449 3599 5039 Fabricated plate work (boiler shop); miscellaneous metalwork; machine shop, jobbing & repair; prefabricated structures
PA: The Will-Burt Company
169 S Main St
Orrville OH 44667
330 682-7015

Osgood
Darke County

(G-15791)
DYNAMIC WELD CORPORATION
242 N St (45351)
P.O. Box 127 (45351-0127)
PHONE..................................419 582-2900
Fax: 419 582-2105
Harry Heitkamp, *President*
Greg Heitkamp, *Engineer*
Sue Heitkamp, *Finance Mgr*
Lois Poeppelman, *Manager*
EMP: 44
SQ FT: 35,000
SALES (est): 11.8MM **Privately Held**
WEB: www.dynamicweld.com
SIC: 3444 7692 Sheet metalwork; welding repair

(G-15792)
OSGOOD STATE BANK (INC) (PA)
275 W Main St (45351)
P.O. Box 69 (45351-0069)
PHONE..................................419 582-2681
Fax: 419 582-2017
Jon Alexander, *Chairman*
Sandra Hoehne, *CFO*
Sheila Tumbusch, *Loan Officer*
Kelly Rose, *Mktg Dir*
Nancy Mueller, *Office Mgr*
EMP: 40 **EST:** 1915
SQ FT: 4,500
SALES: 9.6MM **Privately Held**
SIC: 6022 6163 State trust companies accepting deposits, commercial; loan brokers

Ostrander
Delaware County

(G-15793)
MILL CREEK GOLF COURSE CORP
Also Called: Mill Creek Golf Club
7259 Penn Rd (43061-9430)
PHONE..................................740 666-7711
Fax: 740 666-1110
Jeanne Bash, *President*
Janice E Curtis, *Treasurer*
Nancy Plant, *Admin Sec*
EMP: 35
SQ FT: 1,700
SALES: 1MM **Privately Held**
WEB: www.millcreekgolfclub.com
SIC: 7992 7997 Public golf courses; golf club, membership

GEOGRAPHIC SECTION

(G-15794)
SHELLY MATERIALS INC
8328 Watkins Rd (43061-9311)
PHONE 740 666-5841
Keith Siler, *Vice Pres*
EMP: 25
SALES (corp-wide): 29.7B Privately Held
SIC: 2951 1611 3274 1422 Asphalt & asphaltic paving mixtures (not from refineries); surfacing & paving; lime; crushed & broken limestone
HQ: Shelly Materials, Inc.
  80 Park Dr
  Thornville OH 43076
  740 246-6315

(G-15795)
T & B ELECTRIC LTD
7464 Watkins Rd (43061-9309)
PHONE 740 881-5696
Fax: 740 881-9999
Lynn Vara,
Thomas Beshara,
EMP: 40
SQ FT: 3,600
SALES (est): 4.9MM Privately Held
SIC: 1731 Electrical work

Ottawa
Putnam County

(G-15796)
BROOKHILL CENTER INDUSTRIES
7989 State Route 108 (45875-9678)
PHONE 419 876-3932
Fax: 419 876-3931
Bill Unterbink, *President*
Terry Leopold, *Superintendent*
EMP: 115
SQ FT: 16,000
SALES: 753K Privately Held
SIC: 8331 2448 Sheltered workshop; wood pallets & skids

(G-15797)
CROYS MOWING LLC
440 N Maple St (45875-1331)
PHONE 419 523-5884
Fax: 419 523-5884
Lyle Croy, *Accounts Mgr*
Donald Croy,
EMP: 25
SALES (est): 1.5MM Privately Held
SIC: 0782 Mowing services, lawn

(G-15798)
HOVEST CONSTRUCTION
4997 Old State Route 224 (45875-9763)
PHONE 419 456-3426
Fax: 419 456-3416
Ed Hovest Jr, *President*
Charles Hovest, *Corp Secy*
EMP: 30
SALES (est): 1.8MM Privately Held
WEB: www.hovestconstruction.com
SIC: 1741 1791 1771 Masonry & other stonework; structural steel erection; concrete work

(G-15799)
NELSON MANUFACTURING COMPANY
6448 State Route 224 (45875-9789)
PHONE 419 523-5321
Fax: 419 523-6247
Anthony Niese, *President*
Chad Stall, *Vice Pres*
Dan Liebrecht, *Project Mgr*
Patricia Taylor, *Treasurer*
Tony Niese, *Sales Executive*
▼ **EMP:** 80 EST: 1947
SQ FT: 46,000
SALES: 17.6MM Privately Held
WEB: www.nelsontrailer.com
SIC: 3715 7539 Semitrailers for truck tractors; trailer repair

(G-15800)
NIESE TRANSPORT INC
Also Called: Niese Leasing
418 N Agner St (45875-1537)
P.O. Box 226 (45875-0226)
PHONE 419 523-3840
Fax: 419 523-3840
Jerry Niese, *President*
Kevin Niese, *Vice Pres*
Sam Langhals, *Manager*
EMP: 30
SALES (est): 1.7MM Privately Held
SIC: 4789 Transportation services

(G-15801)
ORTHODONTIC ASSOCIATION
1020 N Perry St (45875-1158)
PHONE 419 523-4014
Thomas Ahman, *Mng Member*
EMP: 50
SALES (est): 407.2K Privately Held
SIC: 8621 Professional membership organizations

(G-15802)
PANDORA MANUFACTURING LLC (PA)
157 W Main St (45875-1721)
PHONE 419 384-3241
Ralph Whetsel, *Vice Pres*
Dave Roper, *Mng Member*
Patrick Parks,
EMP: 51
SQ FT: 113,000
SALES (est): 6.7MM Privately Held
WEB: www.pandoramfg.com
SIC: 7389 Packaging & labeling services; filling pressure containers

(G-15803)
PIKE RUN GOLF CLUB INC
10807 Road H (45875-9655)
PHONE 419 538-7000
Fax: 419 523-4531
Charles Miller, *President*
Steve Radcliff, *General Mgr*
Kenneth Pester, *Vice Pres*
James Hattery, *Treasurer*
Robert Buckland, *Admin Sec*
EMP: 27
SQ FT: 4,100
SALES (est): 704.4K Privately Held
SIC: 7997 5813 5812 Golf club, membership; cocktail lounge; eating places

(G-15804)
R K INDUSTRIES INC
725 N Locust St (45875-1466)
P.O. Box 306 (45875-0306)
PHONE 419 523-5001
Fax: 419 523-5187
Ann Woodyard, *President*
Joe Maag, *Vice Pres*
Dennis Siefker, *VP Mfg*
Barry Woodyard, *Manager*
Kimberly French, *Admin Sec*
▲ **EMP:** 85
SQ FT: 45,000
SALES (est): 8.8MM Privately Held
WEB: www.rkindustries.org
SIC: 7692 3465 Automotive welding; automotive stampings

(G-15805)
YOUNG MENS CHRISTIAN ASSOC
Also Called: Putnam County Y M C A
101 Putnam Pkwy (45875-8657)
PHONE 419 523-5233
Lynn Watchnan, *Manager*
Doug Klima, *Director*
EMP: 84
SALES (corp-wide): 16.8MM Privately Held
WEB: www.campynoah.com
SIC: 8641 8351 Recreation association; child day care services
PA: The Young Men's Christian Association
  Of Akron Ohio
  50 S Mn St Ste Ll100
  Akron OH 44308
  330 376-1335

Ottawa Hills
Lucas County

(G-15806)
OTTAWA HILLS MEMORIAL PARK
4210 W Central Ave Ste 1 (43606-2270)
PHONE 419 539-0218
Fax: 419 539-6290
Jay M Brammer, *President*
Judith Koester, *Manager*
EMP: 35
SQ FT: 1,350
SALES (est): 1.5MM Privately Held
SIC: 6553 Cemeteries, real estate operation; mausoleum operation

(G-15807)
SUNSET RTRMENT COMMUNITIES INC (PA)
4040 Indian Rd (43606-2266)
PHONE 419 724-1200
Fax: 419 724-1201
Vicky Bartlett, *CEO*
Cynthia Williams, *Trustee*
Christine Gladieux, *CFO*
Judy Bishop-Pierce, *Exec Dir*
Judy Pierce, *Exec Dir*
EMP: 100
SALES (est): 15.9MM Privately Held
SIC: 6513 8361 Retirement hotel operation; home for the aged

Ottoville
Putnam County

(G-15808)
MILLER CONTRACTING GROUP INC
17359 S Rt E 66 (45876)
P.O. Box 162 (45876-0162)
PHONE 419 453-3825
Fax: 419 453-3025
Alan J Miller, *President*
Chuck Daniels, *Business Mgr*
Patrick Miller, *Vice Pres*
Candy Lammers, *Manager*
EMP: 44
SALES (est): 12.9MM Privately Held
WEB: www.millercontractinggroup.com
SIC: 1542 1521 Commercial & office building, new construction; single-family housing construction

Owensville
Clermont County

(G-15809)
DEVELOPMENTAL DISABILITIES
Also Called: Thomas A Wildey School
204 State Rte Hwy 50ben (45160)
P.O. Box 8 (45160-0008)
PHONE 513 732-7015
Fax: 513 732-4950
Jay Williams, *Principal*
EMP: 100
SALES (corp-wide): 7.1MM Privately Held
WEB: www.comrdd.org
SIC: 8322 Individual & family services
PA: Clermont County Board Of Developmental Disabilities
  2040 Us Highway 50
  Batavia OH 45103
  513 732-7000

Oxford
Butler County

(G-15810)
ALEXANDER HOUSE INC
Also Called: Governor's Room
118 Hilltop Rd (45056-1521)
PHONE 513 523-4569
Fax: 513 523-3696
Steve Friede, *President*
EMP: 25
SALES (est): 599.9K Privately Held
SIC: 7011 Bed & breakfast inn

(G-15811)
BETA THETA PI FRATERNITY (PA)
5134 Bonham Rd (45056-1429)
P.O. Box 6277 (45056-6067)
PHONE 513 523-7591
Fax: 513 523-2381
Clark Crabell, *Financial Exec*
Clark V Carbioo, *Finance*
Reece Quesnel, *Consultant*
Noah Reetz, *Consultant*
Raheem Kareem, *Senior Mgr*
EMP: 30
SQ FT: 18,000
SALES: 6.3MM Privately Held
SIC: 8641 University club

(G-15812)
BUTLER RURAL ELECTRIC COOP
3888 Stillwell Beckett Rd (45056-9115)
PHONE 513 867-4400
Thomas Mc Quiston, *President*
Michael Sims, *General Mgr*
Michael L Sims, *Principal*
Mary Beth Dorrel, *Corp Secy*
Sam Woodruff, *Vice Pres*
EMP: 38
SQ FT: 27,000
SALES: 32.1MM Privately Held
WEB: www.butlerrural.coop
SIC: 4911 Distribution, electric power

(G-15813)
CAPITOL VARSITY SPORTS INC
6723 Ringwood Rd (45056-9709)
P.O. Box 669 (45056-0669)
PHONE 513 523-4126
Fax: 513 523-0426
Bob Fawley, *President*
Scott Trostel, *Marketing Staff*
Bruce Gray, *Manager*
EMP: 30
SQ FT: 22,000
SALES: 4.9MM Privately Held
WEB: www.capitolvarsitysports.com
SIC: 5941 7699 Specialty sport supplies; team sports equipment; football equipment; baseball equipment; recreational sporting equipment repair services

(G-15814)
CASH FLOW SOLUTIONS INC
5166 College Corner Pike (45056-1004)
PHONE 513 524-2320
Fax: 513 524-5889
Kasey Princell, *President*
Annette Higgins, *Vice Pres*
EMP: 51
SQ FT: 6,000
SALES (est): 22.5MM Privately Held
SIC: 8748 Business consulting

(G-15815)
FIRST MIAMI STUDENT CREDIT UN
117 Shriver Ctr (45056)
PHONE 513 529-1251
Randi M Thomas, *Chairman*
EMP: 50
SALES: 28.9K Privately Held
SIC: 6061 Federal credit unions

(G-15816)
INDIAN RIDGE GOLF CLUB L L C
2600 Oxford Millville Rd (45056-9415)
PHONE 513 524-4653
Fax: 513 524-9603
Jim Robefon,
Tim Derickson,
Dale Leirman,
Jim Rohr,
EMP: 40
SALES (est): 1.9MM Privately Held
WEB: www.theindianridgegolfclub.com
SIC: 7992 Public golf courses

Oxford - Butler County (G-15817)

(G-15817)
MAPLE KNOLL COMMUNITIES INC
6727 Contreras Rd (45056-8769)
PHONE 513 524-7990
Lina Mares, *Exec Dir*
EMP: 30
SALES (est): 566.9K
SALES (corp-wide): 44.7MM **Privately Held**
SIC: **8051** 8361 Convalescent home with continuous nursing care; residential care
PA: Knoll Maple Communities Inc
11100 Springfield Pike
Cincinnati OH 45246
513 782-2400

(G-15818)
MCCULLOUGH-HYDE MEM HOSP INC (PA)
110 N Poplar St (45056-1204)
PHONE 513 523-2111
Fax: 513 524-5665
Bryan D Hehemann, *President*
Richard Norman, *Chairman*
Alan D Oak, *Corp Secy*
John Svirbely, *Ch Pathology*
Sharon Klein, *Project Mgr*
EMP: 43
SQ FT: 115,000
SALES: 23.2MM **Privately Held**
SIC: **8062** General medical & surgical hospitals

(G-15819)
MIAMI UNIVERSITY
801 S Patterson Ave (45056-3404)
PHONE 513 529-2232
Fax: 513 529-6555
Robert Wicks, *Principal*
Tanmay Mathur, *Research*
EMP: 144
SALES (corp-wide): 544.5MM **Privately Held**
SIC: **8412** Museum
PA: Miami University
501 E High St
Oxford OH 45056
513 529-1809

(G-15820)
MIAMI UNIVERSITY
410 E Spring St (45056-1859)
PHONE 513 529-8380
Paul Urayama, *Branch Mgr*
EMP: 115
SALES (corp-wide): 544.5MM **Privately Held**
SIC: **8412** Museum
PA: Miami University
501 E High St
Oxford OH 45056
513 529-1809

(G-15821)
MIAMI UNIVERSITY
Also Called: Marcum Conference Center
Fisher Dr (45056)
PHONE 513 529-6911
Fax: 513 529-5700
Leni Marshall, *Editor*
Cornch Waite, *Manager*
Amy Poppel, *Director*
EMP: 75
SALES (corp-wide): 544.5MM **Privately Held**
WEB: www.muohio.edu
SIC: **8221** 7389 University; convention & show services
PA: Miami University
501 E High St
Oxford OH 45056
513 529-1809

(G-15822)
MIAMI UNIVERSITY
First Miami University Student
701 E Spring St Ste 117 (45056-2801)
PHONE 513 529-1251
Fax: 513 529-1988
Willard Hopkins, *Manager*
Susan Mosley-Howard, *Professor*
EMP: 50

SALES (corp-wide): 544.5MM **Privately Held**
WEB: www.muohio.edu
SIC: **6061** 8221 Federal credit unions; university
PA: Miami University
501 E High St
Oxford OH 45056
513 529-1809

(G-15823)
MIAMI UNIVERSITY
Also Called: Office of Divisional Support
725 E Chestnut St (45056-3450)
PHONE 513 529-1230
Jane Whitehead, *Vice Pres*
Emily Berry, *Director*
Heidi Bortel, *Director*
Jennifer Clark, *Director*
Erika Dockery, *Director*
EMP: 80
SQ FT: 2,001
SALES (corp-wide): 544.5MM **Privately Held**
WEB: www.muohio.edu
SIC: **7389** 8221 Fund raising organizations; university
PA: Miami University
501 E High St
Oxford OH 45056
513 529-1809

(G-15824)
MILLER BROTHERS CNSTR DEM LLC
3685 Oxford Millville Rd (45056-9038)
PHONE 513 257-1082
Frederick Click,
Mitch Stevenson,
Steve Stevenson II,
EMP: 35
SQ FT: 2,000
SALES (est): 1.9MM **Privately Held**
SIC: **1795** Demolition, buildings & other structures

(G-15825)
MINI UNIVERSITY INC
401 Western College Dr (45056-1902)
PHONE 513 275-5184
Ruth Williamson, *Director*
Molly Herre, *Teacher*
EMP: 69
SALES (corp-wide): 1MM **Privately Held**
SIC: **8351** Child day care services
PA: Mini University Inc
115 Harbert Dr Ste A
Beavercreek OH 45440
937 426-1414

(G-15826)
MOON CO-OP SERVICES
1 Oakhill Dr (45056-2700)
PHONE 513 523-3990
Bernadette Unger, *Principal*
EMP: 99
SALES (est): 926.1K **Privately Held**
SIC: **8999** Services

(G-15827)
OXFORD COUNTRY CLUB INC
6200 Contreras Rd (45056-9736)
P.O. Box 229 (45056-0229)
PHONE 513 524-0801
Reed Maltbie, *President*
Jeff McDonald, *Vice Pres*
Jack Cotter, *Treasurer*
Thomas Fyffe, *Manager*
Jj Slager, *Admin Sec*
EMP: 28
SALES (est): 1.4MM **Privately Held**
SIC: **7997** Country club, membership; golf club, membership; swimming club, membership; tennis club, membership

(G-15828)
OXFORD HOSPITALITY GROUP INC
Also Called: Comfort Inn
5056 College Corner Pike (45056-1103)
PHONE 513 524-0114
Dennis Day, *President*
EMP: 25
SALES (est): 914.2K **Privately Held**
SIC: **7011** Hotels & motels

(G-15829)
RDI CORPORATION
110 S Locust St Ste A (45056-1751)
PHONE 513 524-3320
George Trebbi, *President*
Matt Dowd, *General Mgr*
EMP: 100
SALES (est): 2.7MM
SALES (corp-wide): 94.5MM **Privately Held**
SIC: **7389** Telemarketing services
PA: The Rdi Corporation
4350 Glendale Milford Rd # 250
Blue Ash OH 45242
513 984-5927

(G-15830)
RED BRICK PROPERTY MGT LLC
21 N Poplar St (45056-1254)
PHONE 513 524-9340
Fax: 513 524-9345
Matt Rodro, *President*
Sarah Rodbro, *Managing Prtnr*
EMP: 50
SQ FT: 1,938
SALES (est): 3.4MM **Privately Held**
WEB: www.redbrickproperty.com
SIC: **6531** Real estate managers

(G-15831)
TIME WARNER CABLE INC
114 S Locust St (45056-1717)
PHONE 513 523-6333
Danny Schiffer, *Manager*
EMP: 83
SALES (corp-wide): 41.5B **Publicly Held**
SIC: **4841** Cable television services
HQ: Spectrum Management Holding Company, Llc
400 Atlantic St
Stamford CT 06901
203 905-7801

Painesville
Lake County

(G-15832)
ABLE CONTRACTING GROUP INC (PA)
Also Called: Able Fence & Guard Rail Co
11117 Caddie Ln (44077-8939)
PHONE 440 951-0880
Donna Richards, *President*
Douglas J Richards, *COO*
Marianne Richards, *Treasurer*
Pamela Richards, *Treasurer*
Sania Richards, *Manager*
EMP: 25 EST: 1971
SQ FT: 12,500
SALES (est): 3MM **Privately Held**
WEB: www.ablefence.com
SIC: **1611** 0782 5211 Highway & street maintenance; guardrail construction, highways; highway & street sign installation; highway lawn & garden maintenance services; fencing

(G-15833)
AEROCONTROLEX GROUP INC (DH)
313 Gillett St (44077-2918)
PHONE 440 352-6182
Fax: 440 354-2912
Raymond Laubenthal, *President*
John Distler, *General Mgr*
Robert Henderson, *Exec VP*
Gene Mack, *Materials Mgr*
John Kuss, *Opers Staff*
EMP: 99
SQ FT: 55,000
SALES (est): 18.7MM
SALES (corp-wide): 3.5B **Publicly Held**
WEB: www.aerocontrolex.com
SIC: **3492** 5084 3594 Valves, hydraulic, aircraft; industrial machinery & equipment; fluid power pumps & motors

(G-15834)
ANESTHESIA ASSOCIATES INC
7757 Auburn Rd Ste 15 (44077-9604)
PHONE 440 350-0832
James Donohue, *President*

John R Gingrich, *Med Doctor*
John Hagopian, *Anesthesiology*
Anne Meyers, *Anesthesiology*
Mark Myers, *Anesthesiology*
EMP: 30
SQ FT: 1,000
SALES (est): 3.3MM **Privately Held**
SIC: **8011** Anesthesiologist

(G-15835)
AROUND CLOCK HOME CARE
7757 Auburn Rd Ste 6 (44077-9604)
PHONE 440 350-2547
Fax: 440 350-2548
Carmen Ettinger, *Director*
Connie Sinkovich, *Admin Sec*
EMP: 75
SALES: 1MM **Privately Held**
WEB: www.lcghd.org
SIC: **8049** 8082 Nurses, registered & practical; home health care services

(G-15836)
BENEVOLENT/PROTECTV ORDER ELKS
Also Called: ELKS LODGE 549
723 Liberty St (44077-3623)
PHONE 440 357-6943
Fax: 440 357-6995
Dave Larsen, *Principal*
EMP: 27 EST: 1972
SALES: 310.3K **Privately Held**
SIC: **8641** Civic associations

(G-15837)
BURGESS & NIPLE INC
100 W Erie St (44077-3203)
PHONE 440 354-9700
Fax: 440 352-8373
Peggy Garrison, *CFO*
Charles J Zibbel, *Manager*
EMP: 75
SALES (corp-wide): 122.1MM **Privately Held**
WEB: www.burgessniple.com
SIC: **8711** 8712 Consulting engineer; architectural services
PA: Burgess & Niple, Inc.
5085 Reed Rd
Columbus OH 43220
502 254-2344

(G-15838)
C & M EXPRESS LOGISTICS INC
342 Blackbrook Rd (44077-1217)
PHONE 440 350-0802
Michael Pettrey, *President*
EMP: 25
SQ FT: 6,000
SALES: 7MM **Privately Held**
SIC: **4731** Freight forwarding

(G-15839)
CINTAS CORPORATION NO 2
800 Renaissance Pkwy (44077-1287)
PHONE 440 352-4003
Fax: 440 354-6588
Richard Farmer, *Branch Mgr*
EMP: 98
SALES (corp-wide): 5.3B **Publicly Held**
WEB: www.cintas-corp.com
SIC: **7213** Uniform supply
HQ: Cintas Corporation No. 2
6800 Cintas Blvd
Mason OH 45040

(G-15840)
CITY OF PAINESVILLE
Also Called: Painesville Municipal Electric
325 Richmond St (44077-3262)
P.O. Box 601 (44077-0601)
PHONE 440 392-5954
Fax: 440 392-5938
Paul Morton, *General Mgr*
Thomas A Green, *Superintendent*
Ken Newton, *Manager*
EMP: 43 **Privately Held**
WEB: www.pmcourt.com
SIC: **4911** ; distribution, electric power; transmission, electric power
PA: City Of Painesville
7 Richmond St
Painesville OH 44077
440 352-9301

GEOGRAPHIC SECTION

Painesville - Lake County (G-15864)

(G-15841)
CITY OF PAINESVILLE
Also Called: Utilities Dept
7 Richmond St (44077-3222)
P.O. Box 601 (44077-0601)
PHONE..................440 392-5795
Fax: 440 392-0111
Timothy Petric, *Director*
Barbara Monacelli, *Admin Asst*
EMP: 294 **Privately Held**
WEB: www.pmcourt.com
SIC: 4939 Combination utilities
PA: City Of Painesville
7 Richmond St
Painesville OH 44077
440 352-9301

(G-15842)
CLASSIC BUICK OLDS CADILLAC
Also Called: Classic Oldsmobile
1700 Mentor Ave (44077-1438)
PHONE..................440 639-4500
Fax: 440 639-4523
Ralph W Wilson, *President*
Deborah Anderson, *Business Mgr*
Allison Leone, *Business Mgr*
Chris Gragg, *Finance Mgr*
Mark Carroll, *Sales Mgr*
EMP: 75
SQ FT: 35,000
SALES (est): 22.8MM **Privately Held**
WEB: www.classicoldsmobile.com
SIC: 5511 7515 Automobiles, new & used; passenger car leasing

(G-15843)
CLEVELAND ELC ILLUMINATING CO
7755 Auburn Rd (44077-9177)
PHONE..................440 953-7650
Tom McGonnell, *Manager*
EMP: 70 **Publicly Held**
SIC: 4911 Distribution, electric power
HQ: The Cleveland Electric Illuminating Company
76 S Main St
Akron OH 44308
800 589-3101

(G-15844)
COMFORT KEEPERS
368 Blackbrook Rd (44077-1285)
P.O. Box 1000 (44077-8280)
PHONE..................440 721-0100
Dale Gassor, *Owner*
EMP: 45
SALES (est): 782.9K **Privately Held**
SIC: 8082 Visiting nurse service

(G-15845)
CONCORD BIOSCIENCES LLC
10845 Wellness Way (44077-9041)
PHONE..................440 357-3200
Fax: 440 354-6276
Clifford W Croley, *CEO*
Lisa Bernard, *Sr Corp Ofcr*
Michael W Martell, *Exec VP*
Michael Dougherty, *Vice Pres*
James Szabo, *Vice Pres*
EMP: 94
SQ FT: 260,000
SALES (est): 37.6MM **Privately Held**
WEB: www.ricerca.com
SIC: 8731 Medical research, commercial

(G-15846)
CONSULTNTS IN GASTROENTEROLOGY
7530 Fredle Dr (44077-9406)
PHONE..................440 386-2250
Davivd Gottesman, *President*
Fred Kessler, *Principal*
Peter Yang, *Principal*
Don Brinberg, *Vice Pres*
Miriam Vishny, *Admin Sec*
EMP: 30
SALES (est): 1.8MM **Privately Held**
SIC: 8011 Gastronomist

(G-15847)
COUNTY OF LAKE
Also Called: Lake County Job and Fmly Svcs
177 Main St (44077-3402)
PHONE..................440 350-4000
Fax: 440 918-4399
Debra Wernick, *Director*
EMP: 43 **Privately Held**
WEB: www.lakecountyohio.gov
SIC: 8322 Child related social services
PA: County Of Lake
8 N State St Ste 215
Painesville OH 44077
440 350-2500

(G-15848)
CROSSROADS LAKE COUNTY ADOLE
Also Called: Cross Roads Head Start
1083 Mentor Ave (44077-1829)
PHONE..................440 358-7370
Fax: 440 358-7373
Susan Walsh, *Manager*
EMP: 25
SALES (corp-wide): 7.6MM **Privately Held**
WEB: www.crossroads-lake.org
SIC: 8351 Head start center, except in conjunction with school
PA: Crossroads Lake County Adolescent Counseling Service
8445 Munson Rd
Mentor OH 44060
440 255-1700

(G-15849)
D B BENTLEY INC
Also Called: Bentley Excavating
2649 Narrows Rd (44077-4908)
PHONE..................440 352-8495
Fax: 440 352-1403
Mike Bentley, *President*
Dennis R Bentley, *Vice Pres*
Dennis B Bentley, *Treasurer*
EMP: 25 EST: 1976
SALES: 5MM **Privately Held**
WEB: www.bentleyexc.com
SIC: 1611 1794 General contractor, highway & street construction; excavation work

(G-15850)
DE NORA TECH LLC (DH)
7590 Discovery Ln (44077-9190)
PHONE..................440 710-5300
Paolo Dellacha, *CEO*
Takashi Oishi, *General Mgr*
Charlotte Valencic, *General Mgr*
Michele Sponchiado, *Business Mgr*
Frank J McGorty, *COO*
◆ EMP: 80 EST: 1982
SQ FT: 20,000
SALES (est): 38.3MM **Privately Held**
WEB: www.eltechsystems.com
SIC: 3624 3589 7359 Electrodes, thermal & electrolytic uses: carbon, graphite; sewage & water treatment equipment; equipment rental & leasing
HQ: Industrie De Nora Spa
Via Leonardo Bistolfi 35
Milano MI 20134
022 129-1

(G-15851)
DIZER CORP (PA)
1912 Mentor Ave (44077-1325)
PHONE..................440 368-0200
Jagdish Medarametla, *President*
Sagar Ghimire, *Engineer*
Ajay Kumar, *Human Res Mgr*
Waseem Shareef, *Sales Staff*
Shravan Bandi, *Technology*
EMP: 27
SQ FT: 2,300
SALES (est): 7.9MM **Privately Held**
WEB: www.dizercorp.com
SIC: 7371 8711 Computer software development; engineering services

(G-15852)
DOLBEY SYSTEMS INC (PA)
7280 Auburn Rd (44077-9724)
PHONE..................440 392-9900
Fax: 440 392-9901
Kris Wilson, *President*
Bob Leslie, *Senior VP*
Chris Casto, *Vice Pres*
Dennis Dorr, *Vice Pres*
Carrie Labondano, *Buyer*
EMP: 37
SQ FT: 26,000
SALES (est): 7.2MM **Privately Held**
SIC: 5045 Computer software

(G-15853)
DWORKEN & BERNSTEIN CO LPA
60 S Park Pl Fl 2 (44077-3417)
PHONE..................440 352-3391
Toll Free:..................877 -
Fax: 440 352-3469
Howard Rebb, *Manager*
EMP: 40
SALES (corp-wide): 4.6MM **Privately Held**
WEB: www.dworken-bernstein.com
SIC: 8111 General practice attorney, lawyer
PA: Dworken & Bernstein Co Lpa
1468 W 9th St Ste 135
Cleveland OH 44113
216 861-4211

(G-15854)
EMILY MANAGEMENT INC
Also Called: Quality Plus
10280 Pinecrest Rd (44077-9795)
PHONE..................440 354-6713
Elizabeth Bauer, *President*
Debbie Jasic, *Manager*
EMP: 60
SALES (est): 1.4MM **Privately Held**
SIC: 7363 Temporary help service

(G-15855)
ENVIROTEST SYSTEMS CORP
Also Called: Ohio E Check
1755 N Ridge Rd (44077-4811)
PHONE..................330 963-4464
Mike Hensley, *Manager*
EMP: 25 **Privately Held**
SIC: 7549 Emissions testing without repairs, automotive
HQ: Envirotest Systems Corp.
7 Kripes Rd
East Granby CT 06026

(G-15856)
FAMILY PLNNING ASSOC OF NE (PA)
54 S State St Ste 203 (44077-3445)
PHONE..................440 352-0608
Mary Wynn Peasetane, *Exec Dir*
EMP: 25
SQ FT: 5,250
SALES: 1.5MM **Privately Held**
WEB: www.fpaneo.org
SIC: 8093 Family planning clinic

(G-15857)
FIRST FRANCIS COMPANY INC (HQ)
Also Called: Federal Hose Manufacturing
25 Florence Ave (44077-1103)
PHONE..................440 352-8927
Ron George, *President*
Jim McLain, *Vice Pres*
Beverly Gladson, *Opers Staff*
John Lally, *Controller*
Debbie Middleton, *Accounting Mgr*
EMP: 28
SALES (est): 9.3MM
SALES (corp-wide): 23.8MM **Publicly Held**
WEB: www.federalhose.com
SIC: 5085 3599 3444 3429 Hose, belting & packing; hose, flexible metallic; sheet metalwork; manufactured hardware (general)
PA: Hickok Incorporated
10514 Dupont Ave
Cleveland OH 44108
216 541-8060

(G-15858)
JERSEY CENTRAL PWR & LIGHT CO
Also Called: Firstenergy
7755 Auburn Rd (44077-9177)
PHONE..................440 953-7651
Heintz Limer, *Manager*
EMP: 100 **Publicly Held**
WEB: www.jersey-central-power-light.monmouth.n
SIC: 4911 Electric services
HQ: Jersey Central Power & Light Company
76 S Main St
Akron OH 44308
800 736-3402

(G-15859)
JPMORGAN CHASE BANK NAT ASSN
30 S Park Pl Ste 100 (44077-3467)
PHONE..................440 352-5969
Janet Cummings, *Manager*
EMP: 500
SALES (corp-wide): 99.6B **Publicly Held**
WEB: www.chase.com
SIC: 6021 National commercial banks
HQ: Jpmorgan Chase Bank, National Association
1111 Polaris Pkwy
Columbus OH 43240
614 436-3055

(G-15860)
LAKE COUNTY YMCA (PA)
933 Mentor Ave Fl 2 (44077-2519)
PHONE..................440 352-3303
Fax: 440 354-2076
Richard Bennett, *CEO*
Janet Storer, *Business Mgr*
Bob Diak, *COO*
Lori Franceschini, *Human Resources*
Don Elliott, *Property Mgr*
EMP: 575
SQ FT: 80,000
SALES: 8.9MM **Privately Held**
SIC: 8641 7991 8351 7032 Youth organizations; physical fitness facilities; child day care services; youth camps; individual & family services

(G-15861)
LAKE HOSPITAL SYSTEM INC (PA)
Also Called: Tripoint Medical Center
7590 Auburn Rd (44077-9176)
PHONE..................440 375-8100
Fax: 440 354-1994
Cynthia Moore-Hardy, *President*
Richard Cicero, *Senior VP*
Michael R Goler, *Senior VP*
Steven R Karns, *Senior VP*
Mary L Ogrinc, *Senior VP*
EMP: 1200
SQ FT: 150,000
SALES: 334.1MM **Privately Held**
WEB: www.lakehospitalsystem.com
SIC: 8062 Hospital, affiliated with AMA residency

(G-15862)
LAKETRAN
555 Lakeshore Blvd (44077-1121)
P.O. Box 158, Grand River (44045-0158)
PHONE..................440 350-1000
Fax: 440 350-1032
Ray Jurkowski, *CEO*
Andrew Alpenweg, *General Mgr*
John Redmond, *Vice Pres*
EMP: 210
SQ FT: 150,000
SALES: 2.2MM **Privately Held**
WEB: www.laketran.com
SIC: 4111 Local & suburban transit; subway operation

(G-15863)
LEROY TWP FIRE DEPT
13028 Leroy Center Rd (44077-9317)
PHONE..................440 254-4124
Franklin Huffman, *Chief*
EMP: 30 **Privately Held**
SIC: 9224 8099 Fire department, volunteer; medical rescue squad

(G-15864)
MADISON ROUTE 20 LLC
Also Called: Little Mountain Country Club
7667 Hermitage Rd (44077-9770)
PHONE..................440 358-7888
Fax: 440 358-7889
Brian Intenhar, *General Mgr*
Brian Intihar, *Manager*
Richard M Osbourne Sr,
Steven A Calabrese,
EMP: 50

Painesville - Lake County (G-15865)

SALES: 2MM **Privately Held**
SIC: 7997 7992 5941 5813 Golf club, membership; public golf courses; sporting goods & bicycle shops; drinking places; eating places

(G-15865)
MC NEAL INDUSTRIES INC
835 Richmond Rd (44077-1143)
PHONE...........................440 721-0400
Randall McNeil, *President*
Randall J Mc Neil, *President*
Justine McNeil, *Vice Pres*
EMP: 30
SALES (est): 5.6MM **Privately Held**
SIC: 5085 Seals, industrial

(G-15866)
MCNEIL INDUSTRIES INC
835 Richmond Rd (44077-1143)
PHONE...........................440 951-7756
Fax: 440 721-0401
Randall J McNeil, *President*
Robert Madden, *Vice Pres*
Mark Boskovic, *Project Mgr*
Jim Cammerata, *Engineer*
Keith Webster, *Project Engr*
▲ EMP: 30
SQ FT: 18,000
SALES (est): 8.4MM **Privately Held**
WEB: www.mcneilindustries.com
SIC: 3366 5085 Bushings & bearings; seals, industrial

(G-15867)
MULTI-CARE INC
Also Called: Homestead II
60 Wood St (44077-3332)
PHONE...........................440 352-0788
Morton J Weisburg, *Manager*
P K K Yakkundi, *Director*
Roberta Fields, *Social Dir*
Tracy Huber, *Administration*
John Spisak, *Maintence Staff*
EMP: 100
SALES (corp-wide): 6.1MM **Privately Held**
WEB: www.nursehome.com
SIC: 8051 Skilled nursing care facilities
PA: Multi-Care, Inc
    26691 Richmond Rd Frnt
    Bedford OH 44146
    216 292-5706

(G-15868)
NVR INC
408 Greenfield Ln (44077-6149)
PHONE...........................440 639-0525
EMP: 33 **Publicly Held**
SIC: 1521 New construction, single-family houses
PA: Nvr, Inc.
    11700 Plaza America Dr # 500
    Reston VA 20190

(G-15869)
OLON RICERCA BIOSCIENCE LLC ✪
7528 Auburn Rd (44077-9176)
PHONE...........................440 357-3300
Paolo Tubertini, *CEO*
EMP: 99 EST: 2017
SALES (est): 87.2K **Privately Held**
SIC: 8731 Commercial physical research
HQ: Olon Spa
    Strada Provinciale Rivoltana 6/7
    Rodano MI 20090
    029 523-1

(G-15870)
OMEGA SEA LLC
1000 Bacon Rd (44077-4637)
PHONE...........................440 639-2372
Jim Randall, *Vice Pres*
Joe Ruvolo, *Plant Mgr*
Jennifer Boles, *Sales Staff*
Brian Moore, *Sales Staff*
Dennis Crews,
◆ EMP: 40 EST: 2010
SALES (est): 8.8MM **Privately Held**
SIC: 5146 Fish & seafoods

(G-15871)
OMEGASEA LTD LIABILITY CO
1000 Bacon Rd (44077-4637)
PHONE...........................440 639-2372
Dan Crews, *Sales Mgr*
Suzy Allman, *Manager*
Kelly Crews, *Director*
James Randall,
Dennis Crews,
EMP: 50
SALES (est): 3.6MM **Privately Held**
SIC: 5146 Fish & seafoods

(G-15872)
PAINESVILLE DENTAL GROUP INC (PA)
128 Mentor Ave (44077-3232)
PHONE...........................440 354-2183
Fax: 440 354-0811
Donald Brekholder, *President*
Liz Jackway, *Manager*
Joseph Gurley, *Director*
EMP: 30
SALES (est): 2.6MM **Privately Held**
WEB: www.painesville.com
SIC: 8021 Dentists' office; orthodontist

(G-15873)
PERSONACARE OF OHIO INC
Also Called: Kindred Transitional Care and
70 Normandy Dr (44077-1616)
PHONE...........................440 357-1311
Fax: 440 352-9977
Vesta Jones, *Administration*
EMP: 150
SALES (corp-wide): 6B **Publicly Held**
SIC: 8052 Intermediate care facilities
HQ: Personacare Of Ohio Inc
    1801 Macy Dr
    Roswell GA 30076

(G-15874)
QUAIL HOLLOW MANAGEMENT INC
Also Called: Quail Hollow Resort Cntry CLB
11295 Quail Hollow Dr (44077-9036)
PHONE...........................440 354-0498
Fax: 440 354-3822
Eric Affeldt, *President*
Tom Delozier, *General Mgr*
Dan Decrow, *Manager*
EMP: 80 EST: 1972
SQ FT: 17,000
SALES (est): 2.7MM
SALES (corp-wide): 433.7MM **Privately Held**
SIC: 7997 5812 7992 7011 Golf club, membership; eating places; public golf courses; hotels & motels; sporting goods & bicycle shops; drinking places
HQ: Clubcorp Usa, Inc.
    3030 Lyndon B Johnson Fwy
    Dallas TX 75234
    972 243-6191

(G-15875)
R W SIDLEY INCORPORATED (PA)
436 Casement Ave (44077-3817)
P.O. Box 150 (44077-0150)
PHONE...........................440 352-9343
Fax: 440 354-3822
Robert C Sidley, *Ch of Bd*
Robert J Buescher, *President*
Brad Busher, *General Mgr*
Iola Black, *Principal*
R H Bostick, *Principal*
▲ EMP: 30
SQ FT: 10,000
SALES (est): 136.8MM **Privately Held**
WEB: www.rwsidleyinc.com
SIC: 1771 3299 Concrete work; blocks & brick, sand lime

(G-15876)
R W SIDLEY INCORPORATED
Mining & Materials Division
436 Casement Ave (44077-3817)
P.O. Box 150 (44077-0150)
PHONE...........................440 352-9343
Bob Buscher, *President*
EMP: 30
SALES (corp-wide): 136.8MM **Privately Held**
WEB: www.rwsidleyinc.com
SIC: 1422 Cement rock, crushed & broken-quarrying

PA: R. W. Sidley Incorporated
    436 Casement Ave
    Painesville OH 44077
    440 352-9343

(G-15877)
REAL LIVING TITLE AGENCY LTD
7470b Auburn Rd (44077-9703)
PHONE...........................440 974-7810
Fax: 440 974-1629
Barbara Reynolds, *Branch Mgr*
EMP: 35
SALES (corp-wide): 24.2MM **Privately Held**
SIC: 6531 Real estate brokers & agents
PA: Real Living Title Agency Ltd
    77 E Nationwide Blvd
    Columbus OH 43215
    614 459-7400

(G-15878)
RIDERS 1812 INN
792 Mentor Ave (44077-2516)
PHONE...........................440 354-0922
Fax: 440 350-9385
Elaine Crane, *Owner*
Gary Herman, *Co-Owner*
EMP: 25
SALES (est): 453.4K **Privately Held**
SIC: 5812 7011 Eating places; bed & breakfast inn

(G-15879)
SINES INC
1744 N Ridge Rd (44077-4812)
PHONE...........................440 352-6572
Suanne Sines, *President*
Raymond Sines, *Treasurer*
Pam Schlaugh, *Shareholder*
EMP: 30
SQ FT: 1,800
SALES (est): 15.2MM **Privately Held**
WEB: www.sines.com
SIC: 5172 5541 5531 Fuel oil; filling stations, gasoline; automotive tires

(G-15880)
STAFAST PRODUCTS INC (PA)
Also Called: Stafast West
505 Lakeshore Blvd (44077-1197)
PHONE...........................440 357-5546
Fax: 440 357-7137
Donald S Selle, *President*
Elmer T Elbrecht, *Principal*
John G Roberts, *Principal*
Joan Selle, *Corp Secy*
Stephen Selle, *Production*
▲ EMP: 40
SQ FT: 20,600
SALES (est): 27.3MM **Privately Held**
WEB: www.stafast.com
SIC: 5085 3452 Fasteners, industrial: nuts, bolts, screws, etc.; bolts, nuts, rivets & washers

(G-15881)
STERILTEK INC (PA)
11910 Briarwyck Woods Dr (44077-9392)
PHONE...........................615 627-0241
William O'Riordian, *CEO*
William Aamonth, *Vice Pres*
William L Aamoth, *Treasurer*
Jon Backholm, *VP Finance*
Shirley Walsh, *Manager*
EMP: 35
SQ FT: 15,000
SALES (est): 4.5MM **Privately Held**
WEB: www.steriltek.com
SIC: 7389 Product sterilization service

(G-15882)
TRANSCRIPTIONGEAR INC
Also Called: Transcriptiongear.com
7280 Auburn Rd (44077-9724)
PHONE...........................888 834-2392
Kris Wilson, *President*
Jerry Dolbey, *Corp Secy*
EMP: 45
SALES: 6MM **Privately Held**
SIC: 5045 Computer software

(G-15883)
TRIPOINT MEDICAL CENTER
Also Called: Lake Health
7590 Auburn Rd (44077-9176)
PHONE...........................440 375-8100
Donna M Kuta, *Manager*
Domenic Clemente, *Director*
EMP: 825
SQ FT: 300,000
SALES: 324.4MM **Privately Held**
SIC: 8062 General medical & surgical hospitals

(G-15884)
UNITED REST HOMES INC
Also Called: Ivy House Care Center
308 S State St (44077-3532)
PHONE...........................440 354-2131
Fax: 440 354-2068
Marie Swaim, *President*
EMP: 30
SALES (est): 1.2MM **Privately Held**
SIC: 8059 Personal care home, with health care

(G-15885)
UNITED STEELWORKERS
Also Called: Uswa
50 Branch Ave (44077-3819)
PHONE...........................440 354-2328
John Gombos, *Branch Mgr*
EMP: 50
SALES (corp-wide): 61.5K **Privately Held**
WEB: www.uswa.org
SIC: 8631 Labor union
PA: United Steelworkers
    60 Bolevard Of The Allies
    Pittsburgh PA 15222
    412 562-2400

(G-15886)
WEINSTEIN DONALD JAY PHD
Also Called: Weinstein and Associates
54 S State St (44077-3445)
PHONE...........................216 831-1040
Donald Weinstein, *President*
EMP: 25
SALES (corp-wide): 1.4MM **Privately Held**
WEB: www.djweinstein.com
SIC: 8049 Clinical psychologist
PA: Weinstein, Donald Jay Phd, Inc
    25700 Science Park Dr # 200
    Beachwood OH 44122
    216 831-1040

(G-15887)
WILLIAM R MORSE
Also Called: Morse Van Line
83 S State St (44077-3405)
PHONE...........................440 352-2600
Fax: 440 352-4258
William R Morse, *Owner*
EMP: 25
SALES (est): 3.2MM **Privately Held**
SIC: 4731 4213 4214 Freight transportation arrangement; trucking, except local; local trucking with storage

(G-15888)
YARDMASTER INC (PA)
1447 N Ridge Rd (44077-4494)
PHONE...........................440 357-8400
Fax: 440 357-1624
Kurt Kluznik, *CEO*
Jerry Kunco, *General Mgr*
Ed Gallagher, *COO*
Rick Colwell, *Vice Pres*
Cyndi Paskell, *Controller*
EMP: 100
SQ FT: 6,000
SALES: 15MM **Privately Held**
WEB: www.yardmaster.com
SIC: 0782 Landscape contractors

Pandora
Putnam County

(G-15889)
DRC HOLDINGS INC
Also Called: Shirleys Gourmet Popcorn Co
17623 Road 4 (45877-8714)
P.O. Box 131, Bluffton (45817-0131)
PHONE..................................419 230-0188
J Peter Suter, *President*
Kimberly Suter, *Vice Pres*
EMP: 40
SALES: 850K **Privately Held**
SIC: 5441 7832 Popcorn, including caramel corn; motion picture theaters, except drive-in

(G-15890)
FIRST NATIONAL BANK OF PANDORA (DH)
102 E Main St (45877-8706)
P.O. Box 329 (45877-0329)
PHONE..................................419 384-3221
Fax: 419 384-7404
Todd Monson, *President*
Doug Shaneyfelt, *Assistant VP*
Sally Burris, *Opers Staff*
Alison Hovest, *Opers Staff*
Jim Downhower, *CFO*
EMP: 28
SQ FT: 10,000
SALES: 7.6MM
SALES (corp-wide): 7.3MM **Privately Held**
WEB: www.e-fnb.com
SIC: 6021 National commercial banks
HQ: Pandora Bancshares, Incorporated
    102 E Main St
    Pandora OH 45877
    419 384-3221

(G-15891)
HILTY CHILD CARE CENTER
304 Hilty Dr (45877-9476)
P.O. Box 359 (45877-0359)
PHONE..................................419 384-3220
Fax: 419 384-3217
Heather Sanchez, *Director*
EMP: 50
SALES (est): 226.9K **Privately Held**
SIC: 8351 Group day care center

(G-15892)
HILTY MEMORIAL HOME INC
304 Hilty Dr (45877-9476)
P.O. Box 359 (45877-0359)
PHONE..................................419 384-3218
Laura Both, *CEO*
Randy Bond, *Office Mgr*
Jason Cox, *Exec Dir*
EMP: 157
SQ FT: 25,707
SALES: 5.8MM **Privately Held**
SIC: 8051 8322 8049 Convalescent home with continuous nursing care; old age assistance; physical therapist; speech therapist

(G-15893)
PANDORA BANCSHARES INC (HQ)
102 E Main St (45877-8706)
P.O. Box 329 (45877-0329)
PHONE..................................419 384-3221
Todd A Mason, *President*
James Downhower, *CFO*
EMP: 34
SQ FT: 15,000
SALES: 5.6MM
SALES (corp-wide): 7.3MM **Privately Held**
SIC: 6021 National commercial banks
PA: Pandora Banchares Inc
    102 E Main St
    Pandora OH 45877
    419 384-3221

(G-15894)
SUTER PRODUCE INC
12200 Pandora Rd (45877-9501)
PHONE..................................419 384-3665
Jerry Suter, *President*
EMP: 80 **EST:** 1977
SALES (est): 4.4MM **Privately Held**
SIC: 0191 0171 0161 General farms, primarily crop; strawberry farm; corn farm, sweet

Paris
Stark County

(G-15895)
D L BELKNAP TRUCKING INC
3526 Baird Ave Se (44669-9732)
PHONE..................................330 868-7766
Fax: 330 868-3729
Denver Belknap, *President*
Norma Belknap, *Treasurer*
EMP: 84
SQ FT: 30,000
SALES (est): 9.5MM **Privately Held**
SIC: 4213 Contract haulers

(G-15896)
STALLION OILFIELD CNSTR LLC
3361 Baird Ave Se (44669-9769)
PHONE..................................330 868-2083
Fax: 330 868-2084
Chrysta Dansby, *Branch Mgr*
EMP: 25 **Privately Held**
SIC: 5082 Oil field equipment
PA: Stallion Oilfield Construction, Llc
    950 Corbindale Rd Ste 300
    Houston TX 77024

Parma
Cuyahoga County

(G-15897)
3G OPERATING COMPANY LLC
Also Called: Wickliffe Country Place
12380 Plaza Dr (44130-1043)
PHONE..................................440 944-9400
Bruce Daskal,
EMP: 330 **EST:** 2007
SALES (est): 4.2MM **Privately Held**
SIC: 8051 Convalescent home with continuous nursing care

(G-15898)
ADVANCED GRAPHITE MACHINING US ✪
12300 Snow Rd (44130-1001)
PHONE..................................216 658-6521
Baker Kearney, *CEO*
Karthi Gounden, *COO*
Hunter Kearney, *Sales Staff*
Keith Kearney,
EMP: 25 **EST:** 2017
SQ FT: 430,702
SALES: 12MM **Privately Held**
SIC: 5051 Metals service centers & offices

(G-15899)
AMERICAN NATIONAL RED CROSS
5585 Pearl Rd (44129-2544)
PHONE..................................216 303-5476
EMP: 95
SALES (corp-wide): 2.5B **Privately Held**
SIC: 8322 Individual & family services
PA: The American National Red Cross
    430 17th St Nw
    Washington DC 20006
    202 737-8300

(G-15900)
BROADVIEW NURSING HOME INC
Also Called: Broadview Multi-Care Center
5520 Broadview Rd (44134-1699)
PHONE..................................216 661-5084
Harold Shachter, *President*
Mike Flank, *Vice Pres*
Erna Laufer, *Admin Sec*
EMP: 250
SQ FT: 68,000
SALES (est): 12.5MM **Privately Held**
WEB: www.broadviewmulticare.com
SIC: 8051 Extended care facility

(G-15901)
CELLCO PARTNERSHIP
Also Called: Verizon Wireless
7779 Day Dr (44129-5604)
PHONE..................................440 886-5461
Fax: 440 887-0831
Michael Haney, *Branch Mgr*
EMP: 71
SALES (corp-wide): 126B **Publicly Held**
SIC: 4812 Cellular telephone services
HQ: Cellco Partnership
    1 Verizon Way
    Basking Ridge NJ 07920

(G-15902)
COMPREHENSIVE LOGISTICS CO INC
5520 Chevrolet Blvd (44130-1476)
PHONE..................................330 233-0805
Eric Williams, *Branch Mgr*
EMP: 25 **Privately Held**
SIC: 4225 General warehousing & storage
PA: Comprehensive Logistics Co., Inc.
    4944 Belmont Ave Ste 202
    Youngstown OH 44505

(G-15903)
COX COMMUNICATIONS INC
12221 Plaza Dr (44130-1059)
PHONE..................................216 712-4500
Todd Smith, *Director*
EMP: 86
SALES (corp-wide): 33B **Privately Held**
SIC: 4841 Cable television services
HQ: Cox Communications, Inc.
    6205 B Pchtree Dunwody Ne
    Atlanta GA 30328

(G-15904)
COX OHIO TELCOM LLC
12221 Plaza Dr (44130-1059)
PHONE..................................216 535-3500
Tom Hamilton, *Principal*
Patrick Conner, *Controller*
Nelson Newbank, *VP Finance*
Chris Koenigshos, *Human Resources*
Jerry Debato, *IT/INT Sup*
EMP: 76
SALES (corp-wide): 33B **Privately Held**
SIC: 4813 Telephone communication, except radio
HQ: Cox Ohio Telcom, L.L.C.
    1400 Lake Hearn Dr Ne
    Brookhaven GA 30319

(G-15905)
DEDICATED NURSING ASSOC INC
1339a Rockside Rd (44134-2776)
PHONE..................................877 547-9144
EMP: 41 **Privately Held**
SIC: 7361 7363 8051 Nurses' registry; medical help service; skilled nursing care facilities
PA: Dedicated Nursing Associates, Inc.
    6536 State Route 22
    Delmont PA 15626

(G-15906)
ELECTRA SOUND INC (PA)
Also Called: Electrasound TV & Appl Svc
5260 Commerce Pkwy W (44130-1271)
PHONE..................................216 433-9600
Robert C Masa Jr, *CEO*
Charles C Masa, *President*
Patricia Masa, *Vice Pres*
Nancy Reschke, *Opers Mgr*
Charles Masa, *CFO*
EMP: 70
SQ FT: 28,000
SALES (est): 31MM **Privately Held**
WEB: www.electrasound.com
SIC: 3694 7622 5065 5731 Automotive electrical equipment; television repair shop; radio repair shop; video repair; sound equipment, electronic; sound equipment, automotive

(G-15907)
FDC MACHINE REPAIR INC
5585 Venture Dr (44130-9300)
PHONE..................................216 362-1082
Fax: 216 362-1811
Fred Di Censo, *President*
Ferdinando Di Censo, *President*
Maria Di Censo, *Vice Pres*
EMP: 30
SQ FT: 32,000
SALES (est): 4.9MM **Privately Held**
SIC: 7699 Mechanical instrument repair

(G-15908)
GES GRAPHITE INC (PA)
Also Called: G E S
12300 Snow Rd (44130-1001)
PHONE..................................205 838-0820
Keith Kearney, *CEO*
Baker Kearney, *President*
Makism Belski, *Purchasing*
Hunter Kearney, *Treasurer*
Karthi Gouden, *Controller*
▲ **EMP:** 45
SQ FT: 30,000
SALES (est): 11.7MM **Privately Held**
WEB: www.geselectrodes.com
SIC: 5085 Industrial supplies

(G-15909)
HOLY FAMILY HOSPICE
Also Called: Holy Family Home
6707 State Rd (44134-4595)
PHONE..................................440 888-7722
Peggy Rossi, *Mktg Dir*
Kristin Graham, *Director*
Michael Debs, *Director*
EMP: 75
SALES (est): 1.7MM **Privately Held**
SIC: 8082 Home health care services

(G-15910)
METROPOLITAN POOL SERVICE CO
Also Called: Metropolitan Pools
3427 Brookpark Rd (44134-1298)
PHONE..................................216 741-9451
Fax: 216 741-1809
Robert Matney, *CEO*
Todd Whitlock, *President*
Matt Spring, *Director*
EMP: 50 **EST:** 1961
SQ FT: 6,000
SALES (est): 5.1MM **Privately Held**
WEB: www.metropools.com
SIC: 1799 5999 5091 7389 Swimming pool construction; swimming pool chemicals, equipment & supplies; swimming pools, equipment & supplies; swimming pool & hot tub service & maintenance; lifeguard service

(G-15911)
NATIONWIDE HEALTH MGT LLC
5700 Chevrolet Blvd (44130-1412)
PHONE..................................440 888-8888
Chanthou Phay,
EMP: 75
SALES (est): 195.5K **Privately Held**
SIC: 8082 Home health care services

(G-15912)
PARMA COMMUNITY GENERAL HOSP (PA)
7007 Powers Blvd (44129-5437)
P.O. Box 73270n, Cleveland (44193-0001)
PHONE..................................440 743-3000
Fax: 440 843-4386
Patricia A Ruflin, *President*
Kathy Aseff, *General Mgr*
Robert Jacobson, *Ch Radiology*
Terrance Deis, *Vice Pres*
Richard Jacobs, *Vice Pres*
EMP: 2000
SQ FT: 415,000
SALES: 179.1MM **Privately Held**
SIC: 8062 General medical & surgical hospitals

(G-15913)
PARMA COMMUNITY GENERAL HOSP
7007 Powers Blvd (44129-5437)
PHONE..................................440 743-4280
Jeffrey E Brown, *Materials Mgr*
Tim Mosley, *Facilities Mgr*
M Furgeson, *Exec Dir*
EMP: 293
SALES (corp-wide): 179.1MM **Privately Held**
SIC: 8699 Charitable organization

Parma - Cuyahoga County (G-15914)

PA: Parma Community General Hospital
7007 Powers Blvd
Parma OH 44129
440 743-3000

(G-15914)
PROGRESSIVE QUALITY CARE INC (PA)
5553 Broadview Rd (44134-1604)
PHONE..................................216 661-6800
Mike Flank, *President*
Eitan Flank, *CFO*
Dan Shiller, *Manager*
Carl Holbrook, *Senior Mgr*
EMP: 33
SQ FT: 500,000
SALES (est): 59MM **Privately Held**
SIC: 7389 Personal service agents, brokers & bureaus

(G-15915)
SEBESTA INC
2802 Tuxedo Ave (44134-1329)
PHONE..................................216 351-7621
Mark Banas, *Principal*
EMP: 25
SALES (corp-wide): 333MM **Publicly Held**
SIC: 8711 Consulting engineer
HQ: Sebesta, Inc.
1450 Energy Park Dr # 300
Saint Paul MN 55108

(G-15916)
TRADESOURCE INC
5504 State Rd (44134-2250)
PHONE..................................216 801-4944
EMP: 112 **Privately Held**
SIC: 7361 Employment agencies
PA: Tradesource, Inc.
205 Hallene Rd Unit 211
Warwick RI 02886

(G-15917)
UNIVERSITY HOSPITALS
Also Called: University Hospitals Parma
7007 Powers Blvd (44129-5437)
PHONE..................................440 743-3000
Suzanne Hoover, *Purch Dir*
Meghan Ramic, *QA Dir*
Susan Longville, *Manager*
James McAlarney, *Director*
Matthew Wolbert, *Director*
EMP: 2000
SALES (corp-wide): 2.3B **Privately Held**
SIC: 8062 8011 8741 General medical & surgical hospitals; offices & clinics of medical doctors; hospital management; nursing & personal care facility management
PA: University Hospitals Health System, Inc.
3605 Warrensville Ctr Rd
Shaker Heights OH 44122
216 767-8900

(G-15918)
VALA HOLDINGS LTD
Also Called: Giant Eagle
1825 Snow Rd Ste 1 (44134-2778)
PHONE..................................216 398-2980
John C Gillombardo, *Partner*
Charles J Gillombardo, *Partner*
Louis J Gillombardo, *Partner*
Haifa Hurley, *Mng Member*
EMP: 110 **Privately Held**
SIC: 6719 Investment holding companies, except banks

(G-15919)
XPO LOGISTICS FREIGHT INC
12901 Snow Rd (44130-1004)
PHONE..................................216 433-1000
Gene Carson, *Branch Mgr*
EMP: 140
SALES (corp-wide): 15.3B **Publicly Held**
WEB: www.con-way.com
SIC: 4213 4212 Contract haulers; local trucking, without storage
HQ: Xpo Logistics Freight, Inc.
2211 Old Earhart Rd # 100
Ann Arbor MI 48105
734 998-4200

Pataskala
Licking County

(G-15920)
ALLEN REFRACTORIES COMPANY
131 Shackelford Rd (43062-9106)
PHONE..................................740 927-8000
Fax: 740 927-9404
James A Shackelford, *President*
Margaret O'Connor Shackelford, *Exec VP*
James Gibson, *Vice Pres*
Patrick Casey, *Accountant*
William Patton, *Sales Staff*
EMP: 245
SQ FT: 32,000
SALES (est): 39.2MM **Privately Held**
WEB: www.allenrefractories.com
SIC: 1741 5085 Refractory or acid brick masonry; refractory material

(G-15921)
CONTRACT LUMBER INC (PA)
3245 Sr 310 (43062)
PHONE..................................740 964-3147
Fax: 740 927-7344
Richard Hiegel, *President*
Harold T Bieser, *Chairman*
Thomas S Wymore, *Vice Pres*
James Holloway, *CFO*
EMP: 120
SQ FT: 35,000
SALES (est): 63.9MM **Privately Held**
SIC: 1751 1761 5211 Carpentry work; roofing contractor; lumber & other building materials

(G-15922)
COUGHLIN CHEVROLET INC (PA)
Also Called: Coughlin Automotive Group
9000 Broad St Sw (43062-7879)
P.O. Box 1480 (43062-1480)
PHONE..................................740 964-9191
Al Coughlin, *President*
Dan Turner, *General Mgr*
Frederick J Simon, *Principal*
Michael Coughlin, *Vice Pres*
Todd Adcock, *CFO*
EMP: 100
SALES (est): 95.1MM **Privately Held**
WEB: www.coughlinford.com
SIC: 5511 5012 7538 7532 Automobiles, new & used; automobiles & other motor vehicles; general automotive repair shops; top & body repair & paint shops; automotive & home supply stores

(G-15923)
DYNAMIC CONSTRUCTION INC
172 Coors Blvd (43062-7313)
PHONE..................................740 927-8898
Fax: 740 927-8855
Mark S Gray, *President*
Adam Messerall, *Project Mgr*
Lisa Wynd, *Admin Sec*
Amy Bost, *Admin Asst*
Jason Hall, *Technician*
EMP: 60
SQ FT: 1,200
SALES (est): 14.1MM **Privately Held**
SIC: 1623 Transmitting tower (telecommunication) construction

(G-15924)
NURSING CARE MGT AMER INC
Also Called: Pataskala Oaks Care Center
144 E Broad St (43062-7536)
PHONE..................................740 927-9888
Fax: 740 927-4220
Butch Wright, *Maintenance Dir*
Cynthia Craner, *Manager*
Teresa Roberts, *Manager*
Jennifer May, *Director*
Teresa Bowman, *Director*
EMP: 100
SALES (corp-wide): 26.1MM **Privately Held**
WEB: www.nursinghomeinfo.org
SIC: 8741 8051 8059 Nursing & personal care facility management; skilled nursing care facilities; nursing home, except skilled & intermediate care facility

PA: Nursing Care Management Of America, Inc.
7265 Kenwood Rd Ste 300
Cincinnati OH 45236
513 793-8804

(G-15925)
SALO INCORPORATED
350 S Main St B (43062-9626)
PHONE..................................740 964-2904
EMP: 2599
SALES (corp-wide): 24.4MM **Privately Held**
SIC: 8099 Childbirth preparation clinic
PA: Salo, Inc.
960 Checkrein Ave Ste A
Columbus OH 43229
614 436-9404

Patriot
Gallia County

(G-15926)
BUCKEYE RURAL ELC COOP INC
4848 State Route 325 (45658-8960)
P.O. Box 200, Rio Grande (45674-0200)
PHONE..................................740 379-2025
Fax: 740 379-2048
David Lester, *Ch of Bd*
Tonda Meadows, *Exec VP*
Tedd Mollohon, *Vice Pres*
Maggie M Rucker, *CFO*
EMP: 45 **EST:** 1938
SALES: 40.8MM **Privately Held**
WEB: www.aceinter.net
SIC: 4911 Distribution, electric power

Paulding
Paulding County

(G-15927)
ALEX PRODUCTS INC
810 W Gasser Rd (45879-8770)
PHONE..................................419 399-4500
Fax: 419 399-9023
Dave Dondeylon, *Manager*
Jade Crossland, *Executive*
EMP: 110
SALES (corp-wide): 110.3MM **Privately Held**
WEB: www.alexproducts.com
SIC: 3499 5013 3714 Automobile seat frames, metal; automotive supplies & parts; motor vehicle parts & accessories
PA: Alex Products, Inc.
19911 County Rd T
Ridgeville Corners OH 43555
419 267-5240

(G-15928)
COMMUNITY HLTH PRFSSIONALS INC
Also Called: Paulding Area Visiting Nurses
250 Dooley Dr Ste A (45879-8846)
PHONE..................................419 399-4708
Peggy Carnhan, *Manager*
EMP: 33
SALES (corp-wide): 14MM **Privately Held**
SIC: 8082 Visiting nurse service
PA: Community Health Professionals, Inc.
1159 Westwood Dr
Van Wert OH 45891
419 238-9223

(G-15929)
COUNTY OF CUYAHOGA
112 N Williams St (45879-1281)
PHONE..................................419 399-8260
Anna Campbell, *Branch Mgr*
EMP: 650 **Privately Held**
SIC: 8322 Probation office
PA: County Of Cuyahoga
1215 W 3rd St
Cleveland OH 44113
216 443-7022

(G-15930)
COUNTY OF PAULDING
Also Called: Westwood Bhvioural Hlth Centre
501 Mc Donald Pike (45879-9239)
PHONE..................................419 399-3636
Tom Stricker, *Director*
EMP: 30 **Privately Held**
WEB: www.pauldingcountycourt.com
SIC: 9431 8322 8063 Mental health agency administration, government; family counseling services; hospital for the mentally ill
PA: County Of Paulding
115 N Williams St
Paulding OH 45879
419 399-8280

(G-15931)
HERBERT E ORR COMPANY
335 W Wall St (45879-1163)
P.O. Box 209 (45879-0209)
PHONE..................................419 399-4866
Fax: 419 399-3862
Greg Johnson, *President*
Michael Murnane, *QC Mgr*
Steven Mayer, *Engineer*
Shawn Hull, *Plant Engr*
Bruce Whitman, *Supervisor*
EMP: 125
SQ FT: 48,000
SALES (est): 46.1MM **Privately Held**
WEB: www.heorr.com
SIC: 5013 3479 Wheels, motor vehicle; painting of metal products

(G-15932)
P C WORKSHOP INC
900 W Caroline St (45879-1381)
P.O. Box 390 (45879-0390)
PHONE..................................419 399-4805
Fax: 419 399-3897
Megan Sierra, *CEO*
Brenda Miller, *Director*
EMP: 100
SALES: 424.2K **Privately Held**
WEB: www.pcworkshop.com
SIC: 7389 3711 Document & office record destruction; automobile assembly, including specialty automobiles

(G-15933)
PAULDING COUNTY HOSPITAL
1035 W Wayne St (45879-9235)
PHONE..................................419 399-4080
Fax: 419 399-2462
Gary Adkins, *CEO*
Randy Ruge, *CEO*
Michael Winans, *Ch of Bd*
Ron Etzler, *Corp Secy*
Kelly Ferrell, *Ch Radiology*
EMP: 213
SQ FT: 36,000
SALES: 21.3MM **Privately Held**
WEB: www.pauldingcountyhospital.com
SIC: 8062 Hospital, affiliated with AMA residency

(G-15934)
PAULDING EXEMPTED VLG SCHL DST (PA)
405 N Water St (45879-1251)
PHONE..................................419 594-3309
Fax: 419 399-2404
Greg Reinhart, *President*
John Baysinger, *Superintendent*
Ken Amstutz, *Superintendent*
Nancy Ruhe, *Psychologist*
Kelly Agler, *Manager*
EMP: 230
SALES: 19.6MM **Privately Held**
SIC: 8351 8211 Preschool center; elementary & secondary schools

(G-15935)
PAULDING-PUTNAM ELECTRIC COOP (PA)
Also Called: PAULDING PUTNAM ELECTRIC COOPE
401 Mc Donald Pike (45879-9270)
PHONE..................................419 399-5015
Fax: 419 399-3026
George Carter, *President*
Alan Kohart, *Engineer*
Renee Boss, *Human Resources*
Erika Willitzer, *Marketing Staff*

GEOGRAPHIC SECTION

EMP: 34 EST: 1935
SALES: 38.7MM Privately Held
SIC: 4911 Distribution, electric power

(G-15936)
SHAFER CONFESSION
411 E Jackson St (45879-1229)
PHONE..................419 399-4662
Terry J Shafer, Owner
EMP: 45
SALES (est): 546.2K Privately Held
SIC: 8399 Social services

Pedro
Lawrence County

(G-15937)
NECCO CENTER
115 Private Road 977 (45659-8608)
PHONE..................740 534-1386
Dr J Kulkari, President
EMP: 65
SALES (est): 3MM Privately Held
SIC: 8361 Children's home

Peebles
Adams County

(G-15938)
GENERAL ELECTRIC COMPANY
1200 Jaybird Rd (45660-9550)
PHONE..................937 587-2631
Fax: 937 587-3466
Terry Craig, Senior Engr
Dean Schultz, Manager
Dane Clark, Manager
Kevin Hunter, Senior Mgr
Sam Young, Senior Mgr
EMP: 200
SALES (corp-wide): 122B Publicly Held
SIC: 8734 Testing laboratories
PA: General Electric Company
 41 Farnsworth St
 Boston MA 02210
 617 443-3000

(G-15939)
HANSON AGGREGATES EAST LLC
Plum Run Stone Division
848 Plum Run Rd (45660-9706)
PHONE..................937 587-2671
Fax: 937 587-2674
Karrion Bragg, Office Mgr
Terry Lauderback, Manager
Terry Louderback, Manager
EMP: 50
SALES (corp-wide): 16B Privately Held
SIC: 1422 3274 3273 Crushed & broken limestone; lime; ready-mixed concrete
HQ: Hanson Aggregates East Llc
 3131 Rdu Center Dr
 Morrisville NC 27560
 919 380-2500

(G-15940)
J MCCOY LUMBER CO LTD (PA)
6 N Main St (45660-1243)
P.O. Box 306 (45660-0306)
PHONE..................937 587-3423
Fax: 937 587-3931
Jack McCoy, Owner
Sue Burns, Manager
EMP: 40
SQ FT: 2,400
SALES (est): 4.4MM Privately Held
SIC: 5031 2426 2431 Lumber: rough, dressed & finished; dimension, hardwood; moldings, wood: unfinished & prefinished

Pemberville
Wood County

(G-15941)
HIRZEL TRANSFER CO
115 Columbus St (43450-7029)
P.O. Box A (43450-0428)
PHONE..................419 287-3288
Joseph Hirzel, President
William Hirzel, Treasurer
Karl Hirzel Jr, Admin Sec
EMP: 35
SALES: 500K
SALES (corp-wide): 29.6MM Privately Held
WEB: www.hirzel.com
SIC: 4212 Truck rental with drivers
PA: Hirzel Canning Company
 411 Lemoyne Rd
 Northwood OH 43619
 419 693-0531

(G-15942)
NORTH BRANCH NURSERY INC
3359 Kesson Rd (43450-9204)
P.O. Box 353 (43450-0353)
PHONE..................419 287-4679
Fax: 419 287-4161
Thomas Oberhouse, President
Lynnette Oberhouse, Vice Pres
Craig Baldauf, Human Res Dir
Sara Schleicher, Sales Staff
Arianna Wilcox, Sales Staff
EMP: 50
SQ FT: 3,200
SALES (est): 3.5MM Privately Held
WEB: www.northbranchnursery.com
SIC: 0782 5261 5193 1521 Landscape contractors; nurseries & garden centers; flowers & florists' supplies; patio & deck construction & repair; flowers: grown under cover (e.g. greenhouse production)

(G-15943)
OTTERBEIN PORTAGE VALLEY INC
Also Called: OTTERBEIN ST MARY'S
20311 Pemberville Rd Ofc (43450-9411)
PHONE..................888 749-4950
Toll Free:..................888 -
Fax: 419 833-5763
Thomas Keith, Director
Cheri Diller, Director
EMP: 150
SQ FT: 96,000
SALES: 5.3MM
SALES (corp-wide): 43.8MM Privately Held
SIC: 8051 8052 6513 Skilled nursing care facilities; intermediate care facilities; apartment building operators
PA: Senior Otterbein Lifestyle Choices
 585 N State Route 741
 Lebanon OH 45036
 513 933-5400

(G-15944)
SOCIETY PLASTICS ENGINEERS INC
15520 S River Rd (43450-9303)
PHONE..................419 287-4898
Jamie Prybylski, Treasurer
EMP: 150
SALES (corp-wide): 4.3MM Privately Held
WEB: www.4spe.org
SIC: 8621 8711 Engineering association; engineering services
PA: Society Of Plastics Engineers, Incorporated
 6 Berkshire Blvd Ste 306
 Bethel CT 06801
 203 740-5422

(G-15945)
TIRE CENTERS LLC
Also Called: TCI 214
4004 State Route 105 (43450-9704)
P.O. Box 717 (43450-0717)
PHONE..................419 287-3227
Steve Messer, Manager
EMP: 40
SALES (corp-wide): 568.4MM Privately Held
WEB: www.tirecenters.com
SIC: 5531 7534 Automotive tires; tire retreading & repair shops
HQ: Tire Centers, Llc
 310 Inglesby Pkwy
 Duncan SC 29334
 864 329-2700

Peninsula
Summit County

(G-15946)
A & C WELDING INC
80 Cuyahoga Fls Indus Pkwy (44264-9568)
PHONE..................330 762-4777
Fax: 330 762-8562
Carl Lamancusa, President
Michael Lamancusa, Vice Pres
Carl Erney, Purch Agent
Chad Moles, Engineer
Timothy Gorbach, Treasurer
EMP: 25
SALES (est): 5.9MM Privately Held
SIC: 3444 7692 Sheet metalwork; welding repair

(G-15947)
BELFOR USA GROUP INC
79 Cuyahoga Fls Indus Par (44264-9567)
PHONE..................330 916-6468
Matt Carr, Purch Agent
Heather L Dodson, Sales Staff
Brandon Carr, Manager
EMP: 25
SALES (corp-wide): 1B Privately Held
SIC: 1521 1541 1542 Repairing fire damage, single-family houses; renovation, remodeling & repairs: industrial buildings; commercial & office buildings, renovation & repair
HQ: Belfor Usa Group Inc.
 185 Oakland Ave Ste 150
 Birmingham MI 48009

(G-15948)
BRANDYWINE COUNTRY CLUB INC
Also Called: Brandywine Golf Course
5555 Akron Peninsula Rd (44264-9528)
PHONE..................330 657-2525
Fax: 330 657-2362
Brett Yesberger, President
Scott Yesberger, President
EMP: 25 EST: 1963
SQ FT: 1,500
SALES (est): 1MM Privately Held
SIC: 7992 5812 Public golf courses; eating places

(G-15949)
CONSERV FOR CYHG VLLY NAT PRK
Also Called: CVNPA
1403 W Hines Hill Rd (44264-9646)
PHONE..................330 657-2909
Fax: 330 657-2328
Deb Yandala, CEO
Barb Greene, Principal
Mary K Holmes, Principal
Mary Doorley, Opers Mgr
Kara Kracker, Store Mgr
EMP: 55
SALES: 3.8MM Privately Held
WEB: www.cvnpa.org
SIC: 8699 Charitable organization

(G-15950)
ROADRUNNER TRNSP SYSTEMS INC
89 Cuyahoga Fls Indus Pkwy (44264-9567)
PHONE..................330 920-4101
Dan Arnold, President
EMP: 29
SALES (corp-wide): 2B Publicly Held
SIC: 4731 Freight forwarding
PA: Roadrunner Transportation Systems, Inc.
 4900 S Pennsylvania Ave
 Cudahy WI 53110
 414 615-1500

(G-15951)
SUNCREST GARDENS INC
5157 Akron Cleveland Rd (44264-9515)
PHONE..................330 650-4969
Richard Haury, President
Barb Heffelman, Financial Exec
Robert Gray, Manager
Kolin Atkinson, Director
EMP: 125 EST: 1976
SQ FT: 1,000
SALES (est): 17.8MM Privately Held
WEB: www.suncrestgardens.com
SIC: 0781 0782 Landscape services; lawn & garden services

(G-15952)
WAYSIDE FARMS INC
Also Called: Wayside Farms Nursing
4557 Quick Rd (44264-9708)
PHONE..................330 666-7716
Fax: 330 923-1201
Rebecca K Pool, President
Dr Loren Pool, Vice Pres
Bruce Greenwood, Personnel
Jan Baggett, Director
Lori Hamilton, Food Svc Dir
EMP: 95
SQ FT: 14,000
SALES: 6.6MM Privately Held
WEB: www.waysidefarms.com
SIC: 8051 Skilled nursing care facilities

(G-15953)
WHOLECYCLE INC
Also Called: State 8 Motorcycle & Atv
100 Cyhoga Fls Indus Pkwy (44264-9569)
PHONE..................330 929-8123
Fax: 330 929-8310
R Kirk Compton, President
Brett H Huff, Business Mgr
Gar Compton, Corp Secy
Paul Compton, Vice Pres
Scott Garner, CFO
▼EMP: 40
SQ FT: 25,000
SALES (est): 13.9MM Privately Held
SIC: 5012 5571 3799 Motorcycles; motorcycles; all terrain vehicles (ATV)

(G-15954)
WINKING LIZARD INC
1615 Main St (44264-9754)
PHONE..................330 467-1002
Fax: 330 467-8669
Carla Wauscoe, Manager
Greg Bartlow, Manager
EMP: 75
SALES (corp-wide): 101.4MM Privately Held
SIC: 7299 5812 Banquet hall facilities; caterers
PA: Winking Lizard, Inc.
 25380 Miles Rd
 Bedford OH 44146
 216 831-0022

Pepper Pike
Cuyahoga County

(G-15955)
FRANK SANTO LLC
Also Called: Santo Salon & Spa
31100 Pinetree Rd (44124-5963)
PHONE..................216 831-9374
Fax: 216 360-8755
Frank Santo Schiciano,
EMP: 29
SALES: 1.4MM Privately Held
SIC: 7231 Hairdressers

(G-15956)
HOWARD HANNA SMYTHE CRAMER
Also Called: Howard Hanna Real Estate Svcs
3550 Lander Rd Ste 300 (44124-5727)
PHONE..................216 831-9310
Fax: 216 831-4982
Barbara Reynolds, Manager
Pam Poling, Asst Broker
Paul Blumberg, Real Est Agnt
Cici Riley, Real Est Agnt
EMP: 100
SALES (corp-wide): 76.4MM Privately Held
SIC: 6531 Real estate brokers & agents
HQ: Howard Hanna Smythe Cramer
 6000 Parkland Blvd
 Cleveland OH 44124
 216 447-4477

Pepper Pike - Cuyahoga County (G-15957)

GEOGRAPHIC SECTION

(G-15957)
JEWISH DAY SCHL ASSOC GRTR CLV (PA)
Also Called: Schechter, Gross Day School
27601 Fairmount Blvd (44124-4614)
PHONE..................216 763-1400
Rabbi Jim Rogozen, *Headmaster*
Mindy Slade, *Finance Dir*
Kim Martorana, *Human Resources*
Mary A Donovan, *Office Mgr*
Joel Faulkner, *Librarian*
EMP: 56
SQ FT: 59,000
SALES: 3.5MM **Privately Held**
WEB: www.grossschechter.org
SIC: **8211** 8351 Private elementary & secondary schools; group day care center

Perry
Lake County

(G-15958)
C M BROWN NURSERIES INC
4906 Middle Ridge Rd (44081-8700)
PHONE..................440 259-5403
Fax: 440 259-4965
Shane S Brown, *President*
Mary Jane Brown, *Treasurer*
Karen Madrigal, *Admin Sec*
EMP: 30
SALES (est): 2.7MM **Privately Held**
WEB: www.cmbrown.com
SIC: **5193** Nursery stock

(G-15959)
CAR PARTS WAREHOUSE INC
3382 N Ridge Rd (44081-9530)
PHONE..................440 259-2991
Tony Difiore, *President*
EMP: 40
SALES (corp-wide): 91.4MM **Privately Held**
SIC: **5013** Automotive supplies & parts
PA: Car Parts Warehouse, Inc.
    5200 W 130th St
    Brookpark OH 44142
    216 281-4500

(G-15960)
COTTAGE GARDENS INC
4992 Middle Ridge Rd (44081-8700)
PHONE..................440 259-2900
Fax: 440 259-3154
Thomas Varcak, *Branch Mgr*
EMP: 90
SQ FT: 3,640
SALES (corp-wide): 61.2MM **Privately Held**
WEB: www.cottagegardensinc.com
SIC: **0181** 5193 Nursery stock, growing of; flowers & florists' supplies
PA: The Cottage Gardens Inc
    2611 S Waverly Hwy
    Lansing MI 48911
    517 882-5728

(G-15961)
JPMORGAN CHASE BANK NAT ASSN
2772 N Ridge Rd (44081-9553)
PHONE..................440 352-5491
Fax: 440 354-0559
Charles Fay, *Principal*
EMP: 26
SALES (corp-wide): 99.6B **Publicly Held**
SIC: **6021** National commercial banks
HQ: Jpmorgan Chase Bank, National Association
    1111 Polaris Pkwy
    Columbus OH 43240
    614 436-3055

(G-15962)
LAKE COUNTY YMCA
Also Called: Outdoor Family Center
4540 River Rd (44081-8613)
PHONE..................440 259-2724
Fax: 440 259-2491
Richard Bennett, *Director*
EMP: 40

SALES (est): 807.7K
SALES (corp-wide): 8.9MM **Privately Held**
SIC: **8641** 7991 8351 7032 Youth organizations; physical fitness facilities; child day care services; youth camps; individual & family services
PA: Lake County Ymca
    933 Mentor Ave Fl 2
    Painesville OH 44077
    440 352-3303

(G-15963)
MAC KENZIE NURSERY SUPPLY INC
3891 Shepard Rd (44081-9633)
P.O. Box 322 (44081-0322)
PHONE..................440 259-3517
Fax: 440 259-3004
Douglas Mackenzie, *President*
Wilson J Burr, *Treasurer*
Amy Burr, *Admin Sec*
▲ EMP: 35 EST: 1977
SQ FT: 5,000
SALES (est): 3.4MM **Privately Held**
WEB: www.mackenzie-nsy-supply.com
SIC: **5193** 5191 Flowers & nursery stock; greenhouse equipment & supplies

(G-15964)
MCCALLISTERS LANDSCAPING & SUP
2519 N Ridge Rd (44081)
PHONE..................440 259-3348
Fax: 440 352-8629
James McCallister, *President*
Carla McCallister, *Vice Pres*
EMP: 29
SALES (est): 961.5K **Privately Held**
SIC: **0782** 5261 Landscape contractors; lawn & garden supplies

(G-15965)
MID-WEST MATERIALS INC
3687 Shepard Rd (44081-9694)
P.O. Box 345 (44081-0345)
PHONE..................440 259-5200
Fax: 440 259-5204
Noreen Goldstein, *President*
Brian D Robbins, *Principal*
Mark Chabot, *Plant Mgr*
Lynn Clark, *Purch Mgr*
David Goldstein, *Inv Control Mgr*
EMP: 49
SQ FT: 220,000
SALES: 45.9MM **Privately Held**
WEB: www.mid-westmaterials.com
SIC: **5051** Steel

(G-15966)
PERRY TRANSPORTATION DEPT
3829 Main St (44081-8502)
PHONE..................440 259-3005
Michael Sawyers, *Superintendent*
EMP: 35
SALES (est): 1.2MM **Privately Held**
SIC: **4151** School buses

(G-15967)
SOUTH SHORE CONTROLS INC
4485 N Ridge Rd (44081-9760)
PHONE..................440 259-2500
Rick Stark, *President*
Bob Weber, *General Mgr*
George Strekal, *Vice Pres*
Mike Shaffer, *Plant Mgr*
Jason McKinney, *Project Mgr*
EMP: 45
SQ FT: 22,000
SALES: 7MM **Privately Held**
WEB: www.southshorecontrols.com
SIC: **3549** 5084 Metalworking machinery; instruments & control equipment

(G-15968)
WILLOWBEND NURSERIES LLC
4654 Davis Rd (44081-9667)
PHONE..................440 259-3121
Fax: 440 259-3299
Brent Cherkala, *CFO*
Peggy Norris, *Manager*
Angelo Petitti,
▲ EMP: 150
SALES (est): 14.1MM **Privately Held**
SIC: **0181** Nursery stock, growing of; shrubberies grown in field nurseries

(G-15969)
XZAMCORP
4119 Logans Way (44081-8654)
PHONE..................330 629-2218
Craig Zamary, *Principal*
Carol Michaels, *Client Mgr*
EMP: 25
SALES (est): 1.5MM **Privately Held**
WEB: www.xzamcorp.com
SIC: **8742** General management consultant

Perrysburg
Wood County

(G-15970)
A RENEWED MIND
Also Called: CITY OF COMPASSION
885 Commerce Dr Ste C (43551-5268)
PHONE..................419 214-0606
Matthew Rizzo, *CEO*
Cheri Gorajewski, *CFO*
Martha Campbell, *Psychologist*
Steve Kaighin, *Administration*
EMP: 90
SALES: 7.8MM **Privately Held**
SIC: **8322** Rehabilitation services

(G-15971)
ABC DETROIT/TOLEDO AUTO AUCTN
9797 Fremont Pike 3 (43551-4221)
PHONE..................419 872-0872
Michael Hockett, *President*
EMP: 50
SQ FT: 9,600
SALES (est): 6.5MM
SALES (corp-wide): 72.6MM **Privately Held**
SIC: **5012** Automobile auction
PA: Auction Broadcasting Company Llc
    1919 S Post Rd
    Indianapolis IN 46239
    317 862-7325

(G-15972)
AUCTION BROADCASTING CO LLC
Also Called: ABC Detroit/Toledo
9797 Fremont Pike (43551-4221)
PHONE..................419 872-0872
Mary Haller, *Branch Mgr*
EMP: 140
SALES (corp-wide): 72.6MM **Privately Held**
SIC: **5012** Automobile auction
PA: Auction Broadcasting Company Llc
    1919 S Post Rd
    Indianapolis IN 46239
    317 862-7325

(G-15973)
AUTOMATION & CONTROL TECH LTD
28210 Cedar Park Blvd (43551-4865)
PHONE..................419 661-6400
Dan Pfouts, *General Mgr*
Kathy Dominiak, *Purch Mgr*
Kellie Melchert, *Asst Controller*
Nancy Jamoski, *Bookkeeper*
Chris Farrar, *Sales Dir*
▲ EMP: 27
SQ FT: 8,500
SALES (est): 5.7MM **Privately Held**
SIC: **7629** Electronic equipment repair

(G-15974)
AZG INC
Also Called: Augustine Zeller Group
423 E 2nd St (43551-2108)
PHONE..................419 724-3000
Fax: 419 353-1511
John Augustine, *President*
Vicki Foard, *Project Mgr*
EMP: 95
SALES (est): 5.5MM **Privately Held**
WEB: www.azgresearch.com
SIC: **8732** Market analysis or research

(G-15975)
BAYES INC
7414 Ponderosa Rd (43551-4857)
PHONE..................419 661-3933
Fax: 419 661-3733
Christopher Bayes, *President*
Kevin Carpenter, *Warehouse Mgr*
Joan E Bayes, *CFO*
EMP: 25
SQ FT: 13,800
SALES (est): 5.9MM **Privately Held**
WEB: www.bayesinc.com
SIC: **1711** Mechanical contractor

(G-15976)
BEHAVRAL CNNCTIONS WD CNTY INC
27072 Carronade Dr Ste A (43551-5363)
PHONE..................419 872-2419
Mark Haskin, *Director*
EMP: 26
SALES (corp-wide): 4.8MM **Privately Held**
SIC: **8093** 8322 Alcohol clinic, outpatient; individual & family services
PA: Behavioral Connections Of Wood County, Inc.
    280 S Main St
    Bowling Green OH 43402
    419 352-5387

(G-15977)
BELMONT COUNTRY CLUB
29601 Bates Rd (43551-3899)
PHONE..................419 666-1472
Fax: 419 666-3773
Bill Ammann, *President*
Gary Kovach, *General Mgr*
Barb Muir, *Vice Pres*
EMP: 75
SALES: 1.7MM **Privately Held**
SIC: **7997** Country club, membership; golf club, membership

(G-15978)
BENNETT ENTERPRISES INC
Also Called: Holiday Inn
10630 Fremont Pike (43551-3354)
P.O. Box 268 (43552-0268)
PHONE..................419 874-3111
Fax: 419 874-0198
Gerrie Hayes, *General Mgr*
Carol Sattler, *Manager*
Alberta Pace, *Manager*
EMP: 350
SALES (corp-wide): 66.6MM **Privately Held**
WEB: www.bennett-enterprises.com
SIC: **7011** 5812 5947 7991 Hotels; restaurant, family: chain; gift shop; physical fitness facilities
PA: Bennett Enterprises, Inc.
    27476 Holiday Ln
    Perrysburg OH 43551
    419 874-1933

(G-15979)
BIO-MDCAL APPLCATIONS OHIO INC
Also Called: Fresenius Med Care Perrysburg
701 Commerce Dr (43551-5271)
PHONE..................419 874-3447
Jacque Cady, *Principal*
Mary Garber, *Manager*
EMP: 31
SALES (corp-wide): 20.9B **Privately Held**
SIC: **8092** Kidney dialysis centers
HQ: Bio-Medical Applications Of Ohio, Inc.
    920 Winter St
    Waltham MA 02451

(G-15980)
BRAND TECHNOLOGIES INC
Also Called: Bluefin Media
2262 Levis Commons Blvd (43551-7142)
PHONE..................419 873-6600
Brad Mandell, *CEO*
Steven L Mandell, *President*
Sarah Kofoid, *Principal*
Mike Lavalette, *Senior VP*
Zack Mandell, *Senior VP*
EMP: 50
SALES (est): 2.3MM **Privately Held**
SIC: **4899** Data communication services

▲ = Import ▼ = Export
◆ = Import/Export

GEOGRAPHIC SECTION
Perrysburg - Wood County (G-16003)

(G-15981)
BROWN & BROWN OF OHIO LLC
360 3 Meadows Dr (43551-3197)
P.O. Box 428 (43552-0428)
PHONE..............................419 874-1974
James K Mc Whinnie, *CEO*
Daniel E Dumbauld, *COO*
Jack N Conley, *Vice Pres*
Mark Patterson, *Controller*
EMP: 102
SQ FT: 20,000
SALES (est): 553.7K **Privately Held**
SIC: 6411 Insurance agents, brokers & service

(G-15982)
BURKETT AND SONS INC
Also Called: Burkett Restaurant Equipment
28740 Glenwood Rd (43551-3014)
P.O. Box 984, Toledo (43697-0984)
PHONE..............................419 242-7377
Jameel Burkett, *President*
Rachel Miller, *Principal*
Emily Grosswiler, *Accountant*
Jerrard Michael, *Manager*
Erica Cline, *Representative*
▼ **EMP:** 50
SQ FT: 95,000
SALES (est): 44.3MM **Privately Held**
SIC: 5046 Restaurant equipment & supplies

(G-15983)
CAPITAL SENIOR LIVING CORP
7100 S Wilkinson Way (43551-2590)
PHONE..............................419 874-2564
EMP: 169
SALES (corp-wide): 467MM **Publicly Held**
SIC: 8361 Residential care
PA: Capital Senior Living Corp
  14160 Dallas Pkwy Ste 300
  Dallas TX 75254
  972 770-5600

(G-15984)
CARGOTEC SERVICES USA INC
12233 Williams Rd (43551-6802)
PHONE..............................419 482-6866
Lennart Brelin, *President*
James Anasticio, *Senior VP*
Trevor Lockyer, *Purch Agent*
Howard Case, *CFO*
Jeff Rosenberg, *Adv Dir*
EMP: 62
SALES (est): 2.5MM
SALES (corp-wide): 4B **Privately Held**
WEB: www.cargotecservices.com
SIC: 8741 Management services
PA: Cargotec Oyj
  Porkkalankatu 5
  Helsinki 00180
  207 774-000

(G-15985)
CAVINS TRUCKING & GARAGE LLC (PA)
100 J St C (43551-4418)
PHONE..............................419 661-9947
Rocky Cavins, *Mng Member*
Belinda Cavin,
EMP: 30
SALES: 1.2MM **Privately Held**
SIC: 4213 Contract haulers

(G-15986)
CINTAS CORPORATION NO 2
28140 Cedar Park Blvd (43551-4872)
PHONE..............................419 661-8714
Fax: 419 661-9714
Paul Dorsey, *General Mgr*
EMP: 200
SALES (corp-wide): 5.3B **Publicly Held**
WEB: www.cintas-corp.com
SIC: 7213 Uniform supply
HQ: Cintas Corporation No. 2
  6800 Cintas Blvd
  Mason OH 45040

(G-15987)
CITY OF PERRYSBURG
Also Called: Bureau of Sanitation
11980 Route Roached Rd (43551)
PHONE..............................419 872-8020
Fax: 419 872-8024
Jon Eckeo, *Manager*
EMP: 30
SQ FT: 1,664 **Privately Held**
WEB: www.perrysburgcourt.com
SIC: 4953 9111 Refuse systems; mayors' offices
PA: City Of Perrysburg
  201 W Indiana Ave
  Perrysburg OH 43551
  419 873-6225

(G-15988)
COMMERCIAL COMFORT SYSTEMS INC
26610 Eckel Rd Ste 3a (43551-1254)
P.O. Box 8792, Maumee (43537-8792)
PHONE..............................419 481-4444
Francis Lanciaux, *President*
Laurel Lanzio, *Treasurer*
EMP: 34
SQ FT: 25,300
SALES (est): 6.5MM **Privately Held**
WEB: www.commercialcomfort.com
SIC: 1711 Warm air heating & air conditioning contractor

(G-15989)
CORRIGAN MOVING SYSTEMS-ANN AR
12377 Williams Rd (43551-1981)
PHONE..............................419 874-2900
William Axel, *General Mgr*
EMP: 25
SALES (corp-wide): 12.7MM **Privately Held**
SIC: 4213 4214 4212 Household goods transport; household goods moving & storage, local; moving services
HQ: Corrigan Moving Systems-Ann Arbor, Inc.
  23923 Research Dr
  Farmington Hills MI 48335
  248 471-4000

(G-15990)
CRAWFORD GROUP INC
12611 Eckel Junction Rd (43551-1304)
PHONE..............................419 873-7360
Andy Bouza, *Branch Mgr*
EMP: 54
SALES (corp-wide): 6.1B **Privately Held**
SIC: 7514 Rent-a-car service
PA: The Crawford Group Inc
  600 Corporate Park Dr
  Saint Louis MO 63105
  314 512-5000

(G-15991)
CRITICAL BUSINESS ANALYSIS INC
Also Called: CBA
133 W 2nd St Ste 1 (43551-1479)
PHONE..............................419 874-0800
Fax: 419 874-2219
John Gordon, *CEO*
Donald Monteleone, *President*
Bob Ferris, *Senior VP*
Paul Deraedt, *Mktg Dir*
Linda Rich, *Manager*
EMP: 48
SQ FT: 5,000
SALES: 3.1MM **Privately Held**
WEB: www.cbainc.com
SIC: 8243 7371 8742 8741 Software training, computer; custom computer programming services; construction project management consultant; business consultant; financial management for business; construction management

(G-15992)
CUTTING EDGE COUNTERTOPS INC
1300 Flagship Dr (43551-1375)
PHONE..............................419 873-9500
Fax: 419 873-9600
Brad Burns, *President*
Jon Cousino, *Principal*
Rob Loughridge, *Principal*
Jeff Erickson, *COO*
Brian Burns, *Vice Pres*
▼ **EMP:** 32
SQ FT: 24,000
SALES (est): 6.1MM **Privately Held**
WEB: www.cectops.com
SIC: 3281 1743 Granite, cut & shaped; marble installation, interior

(G-15993)
DAYTON FREIGHT LINES INC
28240 Oregon Rd (43551-4739)
PHONE..............................419 661-8600
Bill Nieset, *Manager*
EMP: 50
SALES (corp-wide): 1B **Privately Held**
SIC: 4213 Trucking, except local
PA: Dayton Freight Lines, Inc.
  6450 Poe Ave Ste 311
  Dayton OH 45414
  937 264-4060

(G-15994)
DAYTON HEIDELBERG DISTRG CO
Also Called: Burman Wine
912 3rd St (43551-4356)
PHONE..............................419 666-9783
Tom McHugh, *Manager*
EMP: 150
SALES (corp-wide): 369.4MM **Privately Held**
SIC: 4225 5182 5181 General warehousing & storage; wine & distilled beverages; beer & ale
PA: Dayton Heidelberg Distributing Co.
  3601 Dryden Rd
  Moraine OH 45439
  937 222-8692

(G-15995)
DAYTON HEIDELBERG DISTRG CO
912 3rd St (43551-4356)
PHONE..............................419 666-9783
Fax: 419 661-5983
Logan Bravard, *District Mgr*
Kevin Knight, *Vice Pres*
Jim Cameron, *Accounting Mgr*
Teresa Budinsky, *Sales Mgr*
Dj Homan, *Sales Mgr*
EMP: 90
SALES (corp-wide): 369.4MM **Privately Held**
SIC: 5182 Wine
PA: Dayton Heidelberg Distributing Co.
  3601 Dryden Rd
  Moraine OH 45439
  937 222-8692

(G-15996)
DCO LLC (HQ)
Also Called: Dana Companies, LLC
900 E Boundary St Ste 8a (43551-2406)
PHONE..............................419 931-9086
Michael L Debacker, *President*
Doris Brown, *Vice Pres*
Anthony Trigona, *Maint Spvr*
Mark Neidert, *Engineer*
Bricy Stringham,
◆ **EMP:** 265 **EST:** 1904
SALES (est): 2.3MM
SALES (corp-wide): 38.5MM **Privately Held**
WEB: www.dana.com
SIC: 3751 8741 Motor scooters & parts; financial management for business
PA: Enstar Holdings (Us) Llc
  150 2nd Ave N Fl 3
  Saint Petersburg FL 33701
  727 217-2900

(G-15997)
DEACONIS ASSOCATION INC
Also Called: Deaconis Association
27062 Oakmead Dr (43551-2657)
PHONE..............................419 874-9008
Fax: 419 874-9888
Felicia Evans, *Exec Dir*
Marlene Burke, *Administration*
EMP: 75
SALES (est): 722K **Privately Held**
SIC: 8621 Professional membership organizations

(G-15998)
DILLIN ENGINEERED SYSTEMS CORP
8030 Broadstone Rd (43551-4856)
PHONE..............................419 666-6789
David A Smith, *President*
Chic Coleman, *Engineer*
Kathy McCormick, *Finance*
Chris Mc Ilroy, *Manager*
Marty Shaffer, *Data Proc Dir*
EMP: 50
SQ FT: 40,000
SALES (est): 10.9MM **Privately Held**
SIC: 8711 3535 Mechanical engineering; conveyors & conveying equipment

(G-15999)
DOLD HOMES INC (PA)
26610 Eckel Rd (43551-1247)
PHONE..............................419 874-2535
Fax: 419 872-2476
William H Dold, *President*
Eric Roof, *Controller*
Darcey McKinley, *Manager*
Edward Cluekey, *Exec Dir*
Mary Lou Dold, *Admin Sec*
EMP: 45 **EST:** 1976
SQ FT: 16,000
SALES (est): 14MM **Privately Held**
WEB: www.doldhomes.com
SIC: 1521 1531 New construction, single-family houses; speculative builder, single-family houses

(G-16000)
E H SCHMIDT EXECUTIVE
26785 Dixie Hwy (43551-1714)
P.O. Box 111 (43552-0111)
PHONE..............................419 874-4331
Thomas G Schmidt, *President*
Darin Moughler, *Vice Pres*
Edward H Schmidt, *Vice Pres*
Craig Jenkins, *Opers Staff*
Eric Scott, *Parts Mgr*
EMP: 100
SALES (est): 3.3MM **Privately Held**
SIC: 7513 7515 Truck rental & leasing, no drivers; passenger car leasing

(G-16001)
ED SCHMIDT AUTO INC
26875 Dixie Hwy (43551-1716)
PHONE..............................419 874-4331
Fax: 419 872-4405
Thomas G Schmidt, *President*
Adam Stockburger, *Business Mgr*
Matt Urbaniak, *Business Mgr*
Nick Ort, *Sales Mgr*
Eric Kudas, *Sales Staff*
EMP: 250
SQ FT: 55,000
SALES (est): 71.8MM **Privately Held**
SIC: 5511 5521 5012 7538 Automobiles, new & used; pickups, new & used; vans, new & used; used car dealers; automobiles & other motor vehicles; general automotive repair shops; top & body repair & paint shops; automotive & home supply stores

(G-16002)
ENVIRCARE LAWN LANDSCACAPE LLC
24112 Lime City Rd (43551-9043)
PHONE..............................419 874-6779
Fax: 419 872-6202
Jeffrey D Eberly, *President*
EMP: 30 **EST:** 1993
SALES (est): 2.7MM **Privately Held**
WEB: www.envirocarelawn.com
SIC: 0782 Lawn care services

(G-16003)
FIRST 2 MARKET PRODUCTS LLC
25671 Fort Meigs Rd Ste A (43551-1191)
PHONE..............................419 874-5444
Dan Sackett, *Vice Pres*
Danny Sackett,
▲ **EMP:** 32
SQ FT: 20,000
SALES (est): 2.6MM **Privately Held**
SIC: 5199 Packaging materials

Perrysburg - Wood County (G-16004)

(G-16004)
FLUX A SALON BY HAZELTON
131 W Indiana Ave (43551-1578)
PHONE..........................419 841-5100
Greg Hazelton, *Owner*
EMP: 35
SALES (est): 188.8K **Privately Held**
WEB: www.fluxasalon.com
SIC: 7231 Beauty shops

(G-16005)
FRAM GROUP OPERATIONS LLC
Also Called: Honeywell
28399 Cedar Park Blvd (43551-4864)
P.O. Box 981729, El Paso TX (79998-1729)
PHONE..........................419 661-6700
Jerry Bolser, *Principal*
Lee Bennet, *VP Opers*
Lee Bennett, *Branch Mgr*
James Romer, *Planning Mgr*
Steven Powell, *Manager*
EMP: 100 **Privately Held**
WEB: www.honeywell.com
SIC: 3714 3694 8734 8731 Motor vehicle engines & parts; filters: oil, fuel & air, motor vehicle; spark plugs for internal combustion engines; testing laboratories; commercial physical research
HQ: Fram Group Operations Llc
   1900 W Field Ct
   Lake Forest IL 60045

(G-16006)
GENOX TRANSPORTATION INC
25750 Oregon Rd (43551-9778)
PHONE..........................419 837-2023
Kevin Matthews, *President*
Lisa Mathews, *CFO*
EMP: 50
SALES (est): 138.6K **Privately Held**
SIC: 4789 Transportation services

(G-16007)
GLOW INDUSTRIES INC (PA)
12962 Eckel Junction Rd (43551-1309)
PHONE..........................419 872-4772
Fax: 419 872-4773
David P Glowacki, *President*
Jason Glowacki, *Vice Pres*
Brian Nupp, *Sales Mgr*
◆ **EMP:** 58
SQ FT: 40,000
SALES (est): 15.4MM **Privately Held**
SIC: 5199 5331 Variety store merchandise; variety stores

(G-16008)
HCF OF PERRYSBURG INC
Also Called: Manor At Perrysburg, The
250 Manor Dr (43551-3118)
PHONE..........................419 874-0306
Kenneth Zeilinski, *Manager*
EMP: 99
SALES (est): 993.1K
SALES (corp-wide): 154.8MM **Privately Held**
SIC: 8051 Skilled nursing care facilities
PA: Hcf Management, Inc.
   1100 Shawnee Rd
   Lima OH 45805
   419 999-2010

(G-16009)
HEALTH CARE RTREMENT CORP AMER
10540 Fremont Pike (43551-3356)
PHONE..........................419 874-3578
Sara Louk, *Branch Mgr*
EMP: 113
SALES (corp-wide): 3.6B **Publicly Held**
WEB: www.hrc-manorcare.com
SIC: 8051 Skilled nursing care facilities
HQ: Health Care And Retirement Corporation Of America
   333 N Summit St Ste 103
   Toledo OH 43604
   419 252-5500

(G-16010)
HEARTLAND HOSPICE SERVICES LLC
Also Called: Heartland HM Hlth Care Hospice
28555 Starbright Blvd E (43551-5662)
PHONE..........................419 531-0440
Fax: 419 531-0437
Amy Marino, *Manager*
Jessica Clark, *Executive*
EMP: 56
SALES (corp-wide): 3.6B **Publicly Held**
SIC: 8082 Home health care services
HQ: Heartland Hospice Services, Llc
   333 N Summit St
   Toledo OH 43604

(G-16011)
HERB THYME FARMS INC
8600 S Wilkinson Way G (43551-2598)
PHONE..........................866 386-0854
Howard Roeder, *President*
Maria Yepez, *Human Resources*
EMP: 500 EST: 2000
SALES (est): 12MM **Privately Held**
SIC: 0191 General farms, primarily crop

(G-16012)
HIAB USA INC (HQ)
12233 Williams Rd (43551-6802)
PHONE..........................419 482-6000
Roland Sunden, *President*
Lennart Brelin, *President*
David Gardner, *Managing Dir*
Mike Splettstosser, *Area Mgr*
Robert Nichols, *Plant Mgr*
◆ **EMP:** 70 EST: 1991
SQ FT: 56,000
SALES (est): 78.1MM
SALES (corp-wide): 4B **Privately Held**
SIC: 5084 3536 Cranes, industrial; hoists; cranes, industrial plant; hoists
PA: Cargotec Oyj
   Porkkalankatu 5
   Helsinki 00180
   207 774-000

(G-16013)
HOSPICE OF NORTHWEST OHIO (PA)
30000 E River Rd (43551-3429)
PHONE..........................419 661-4001
Fax: 419 661-4015
Mark English, *Pastor*
Michelle Katz, *Human Resources*
John McGreevey, *Med Doctor*
Angie Baltzell, *Manager*
Susan Smith, *Senior Mgr*
EMP: 450
SQ FT: 48,000
SALES (est): 31.2MM **Privately Held**
SIC: 8099 Medical services organization

(G-16014)
HOSTER HOTELS LLC
5995 Levis Commons Blvd (43551)
PHONE..........................419 931-8900
Robert Volker, *Mng Member*
EMP: 30
SALES (est): 137.8K **Privately Held**
SIC: 7011 Hotels

(G-16015)
IMCO CARBIDE TOOL INC
Also Called: Toledo Cutting Tools
28170 Cedar Park Blvd (43551-4872)
PHONE..........................419 661-6313
Fax: 419 661-6314
Perry L Osburn, *Ch of Bd*
Matthew S Osburn, *Vice Pres*
Patrick Clewis, *Sales Staff*
Julie Whitlow, *Admin Sec*
Lesley Shawbriggs, *Admin Asst*
EMP: 90 EST: 1977
SQ FT: 25,000
SALES (est): 27.1MM **Privately Held**
WEB: www.imcousa.com
SIC: 3545 5084 Machine tool accessories; tools & accessories for machine tools; machine tools & accessories

(G-16016)
INDEPENDENT EVALUATORS INC
27457 Holiday Ln Ste B (43551-5364)
PHONE..........................419 872-5650
Fax: 419 872-5654
Charles Burke, *President*
Dawn N Schmidt, *Administration*
EMP: 100
SALES (est): 6MM **Privately Held**
WEB: www.independentevaluators.com
SIC: 8742 Compensation & benefits planning consultant

(G-16017)
INGRAM ENTRMT HOLDINGS INC
668 1st St (43551-4480)
PHONE..........................419 662-3132
EMP: 41
SALES (corp-wide): 400MM **Privately Held**
SIC: 7929 Entertainers & entertainment groups
PA: Ingram Entertainment Holdings Inc.
   2 Ingram Blvd
   La Vergne TN 37089
   615 287-4000

(G-16018)
INVESTEK MANAGEMENT SVCS F/C
1090 W South Boundary St # 100 (43551-5234)
PHONE..........................419 873-1236
John Aubry, *Owner*
Anne Weilgopolski, *Manager*
EMP: 26 EST: 2011
SALES (est): 2.7MM **Privately Held**
SIC: 8741 Management services

(G-16019)
INVESTEK REALTY LLC
1090 W South Boundary St # 100 (43551-5285)
PHONE..........................419 873-1236
Fax: 419 873-1239
John Anbury,
EMP: 25 EST: 2001
SALES (est): 1.9MM **Privately Held**
SIC: 6531 Real estate agents & managers

(G-16020)
JERL MACHINE INC
11140 Avenue Rd (43551-2825)
PHONE..........................419 873-0270
Fax: 419 873-0276
Robert L Brossia, *CEO*
Carol Coe, *President*
Eileen Brossia, *Vice Pres*
Jason Coy, *VP Mfg*
William Peters, *Opers Mgr*
EMP: 61
SQ FT: 76,000
SALES (est): 10.6MM **Privately Held**
WEB: www.jerl.com
SIC: 7692 3599 Welding repair; machine shop, jobbing & repair

(G-16021)
JON R DVORAK MD
Also Called: Weeber-Morse, Carmen MD
1090 W South Boundary St # 5 (43551-5234)
PHONE..........................419 872-7700
Jon R Dvorak MD, *Med Doctor*
Morse C Weeber, *Med Doctor*
EMP: 25
SALES (est): 1MM **Privately Held**
SIC: 8011 Pediatrician

(G-16022)
K WEST GROUP LLC
8305 Fremont Pike (43551-9427)
PHONE..........................972 722-3874
Martha Kwest, *Principal*
Dave Grafitti, *Project Mgr*
Mark Troilo, *Project Mgr*
EMP: 116
SALES (corp-wide): 36.4MM **Privately Held**
SIC: 1611 General contractor, highway & street construction
PA: K. West Group, Llc
   8305 Fremont Pike
   Perrysburg OH 43551
   419 874-4284

(G-16023)
KENS FLOWER SHOP INC
140 W South Boundary St (43551-1754)
PHONE..........................419 841-9590
Art Balk, *Manager*
EMP: 28
SQ FT: 3,000
SALES (corp-wide): 12.1MM **Privately Held**
WEB: www.kensflowers.com
SIC: 5992 5193 Flowers, fresh; flowers, fresh
PA: Ken's Flower Shop, Inc
   140 W South Boundary St
   Perrysburg OH 43551
   419 874-1333

(G-16024)
KIEMLE-HANKINS COMPANY (PA)
94 H St (43551-4497)
P.O. Box 507, Toledo (43697-0507)
PHONE..........................419 661-2430
Fax: 419 666-3096
Tim Martindale, *President*
Charles Dill, *Division Mgr*
Kevin Napierala, *Division Mgr*
Stephen Martindale, *Chairman*
Josh Brown, *Opers Mgr*
EMP: 50
SQ FT: 50,000
SALES: 20MM **Privately Held**
WEB: www.kiemlehankins.com
SIC: 7694 7629 3699 Electric motor repair; electrical equipment repair services; electrical equipment & supplies

(G-16025)
KINGSTON RSDNCE PERRYSBURG LLC
345 E Boundary St (43551-2760)
PHONE..........................419 872-6200
Fax: 419 872-6209
Cheryl Hartman, *Exec Dir*
William Nichols, *Director*
Diana Oreck, *Director*
EMP: 53
SALES (est): 3.6MM
SALES (corp-wide): 95.5MM **Privately Held**
WEB: www.kingstonhealthcare.com
SIC: 8322 8051 Rehabilitation services; skilled nursing care facilities
PA: Kingston Healthcare Company
   1 Seagate Ste 1960
   Toledo OH 43604
   419 247-2880

(G-16026)
LAND ART INC (PA)
7728 Ponderosa Rd (43551-4851)
P.O. Box 879 (43552-0879)
PHONE..........................419 666-5296
Fax: 419 666-3653
Martin W Strassner Jr, *President*
EMP: 30 EST: 1974
SQ FT: 12,000
SALES (est): 3MM **Privately Held**
SIC: 0783 0782 Spraying services, ornamental tree; fertilizing services, lawn

(G-16027)
LEVIS COMMONS HOTEL LLC
Also Called: Hilton Garden Inn Perrysburg
6165 Levis Commons Blvd (43551-7269)
PHONE..........................419 873-3573
Fax: 419 873-0701
Izzet Sozeri, *General Mgr*
Cynthia Dixon, *Accounts Mgr*
Izzet Sueri, *Manager*
Jenny McCord, *Manager*
Ron Degregorio, *Teacher*
EMP: 98
SALES (est): 6MM
SALES (corp-wide): 7.4MM **Privately Held**
WEB: www.ghghotels.net
SIC: 7011 Hotels
PA: Gateway Hospitality Group Inc
   8921 Canyon Falls Blvd # 140
   Twinsburg OH 44087
   330 405-9800

(G-16028)
LOVES TRAVEL STOPS
26530 Baker Dr (43551-8847)
PHONE..........................419 837-0071
Josh Shaffer, *Branch Mgr*
EMP: 55
SALES (corp-wide): 5.5B **Privately Held**
SIC: 8699 Travel club

GEOGRAPHIC SECTION
Perrysburg - Wood County (G-16054)

PA: Love's Travel Stops & Country Stores, Inc.
10601 N Pennsylvania Ave
Oklahoma City OK 73120
405 302-6500

(G-16029)
LOWER GREAT LAKES KENWORTH INC
Also Called: Whiteford Kenworth
12650 Eckel Junction Rd (43551-1303)
P.O. Box 387 (43552-0387)
PHONE..................................419 874-3511
Roger Euler, *Manager*
Bob Holland, *Manager*
Diana Payne, *Receptionist*
EMP: 33
SQ FT: 10,000
SALES (corp-wide): 76.9MM **Privately Held**
WEB: www.lglk.com
SIC: 5012 7538 5013 Trucks, commercial; general automotive repair shops; motor vehicle supplies & new parts
PA: Lower Great Lakes Kenworth, Inc.
4625 W Western Ave
South Bend IN 46619
574 234-9007

(G-16030)
LOWES HOME CENTERS LLC
10295 Fremont Pike (43551-3334)
PHONE..................................419 874-6758
Fax: 419 874-7186
Darcy Mueller, *Branch Mgr*
EMP: 150
SALES (corp-wide): 68.6B **Publicly Held**
SIC: 5211 5031 5722 5064 Home centers; building materials, exterior; building materials, interior; household appliance stores; electrical appliances, television & radio
HQ: Lowe's Home Centers, Llc
1605 Curtis Bridge Rd
Wilkesboro NC 28697
336 658-4000

(G-16031)
MAUMEE PLUMBING & HTG SUP INC (PA)
Also Called: Waterhouse Bath and Kit Studio
12860 Eckel Junction Rd (43551-1307)
P.O. Box 309 (43552-0309)
PHONE..................................419 874-7991
Fax: 419 874-3758
Douglas Williams, *President*
Greg Williams, *Vice Pres*
Scott Williams, *Opers Mgr*
Tony Cannon, *Purch Agent*
Frank Mata, *Purch Agent*
EMP: 25
SQ FT: 48,000
SALES (est): 13.4MM **Privately Held**
WEB: www.maumeesupply.com
SIC: 5074 Plumbing fittings & supplies

(G-16032)
MERRILL LYNCH PIERCE FENNER
3292 Levis Commons Blvd (43551-7144)
PHONE..................................419 891-2091
Fax: 419 469-4493
Alan Lynch, *Branch Mgr*
Maher Majdalani, *Advisor*
EMP: 27
SALES (corp-wide): 100.2B **Publicly Held**
WEB: www.ml.com
SIC: 6211 Stock brokers & dealers
HQ: Merrill Lynch, Pierce, Fenner & Smith Incorporated
111 8th Ave
New York NY 10011
800 637-7455

(G-16033)
MIDWEST CHURCH CNSTR LTD
634 Eckel Rd Ste A (43551-6031)
PHONE..................................419 874-0838
Fax: 419 874-2295
Ken Miller,
EMP: 28
SALES (est): 4.9MM **Privately Held**
WEB: www.midwestchurch.com
SIC: 1542 Religious building construction

(G-16034)
MIDWEST ENVIRONMENTAL INC
28757 Glenwood Rd (43551-3004)
PHONE..................................419 382-9200
Dale Bruhl, *President*
EMP: 30 **EST:** 2014
SALES (est): 2.2MM **Privately Held**
SIC: 8744

(G-16035)
OHIO & MICHIGAN PAPER COMPANY
350 4th St (43551-4338)
P.O. Box 621, Toledo (43697-0621)
PHONE..................................419 666-1500
Fax: 419 666-3768
Alan Leininger, *President*
Kevin Leininger, *General Mgr*
Robert Steve Fronk, *Corp Secy*
Phillip Christensen, *Vice Pres*
Steve Fronk, *Financial Exec*
EMP: 25 **EST:** 1868
SQ FT: 75,000
SALES (est): 17.4MM **Privately Held**
SIC: 5113 5111 5112 Industrial & personal service paper; printing paper; stationery

(G-16036)
OHIO MACHINERY CO
Also Called: Caterpillar Authorized Dealer
25970 Dixie Hwy (43551-1701)
PHONE..................................419 874-7975
Fax: 419 873-8253
Randy McCabe, *Manager*
Donna Blanco, *Manager*
EMP: 101
SQ FT: 19,000
SALES (corp-wide): 222.7MM **Privately Held**
WEB: www.enginesnow.com
SIC: 5082 7359 General construction machinery & equipment; equipment rental & leasing
PA: Ohio Machinery Co.
3993 E Royalton Rd
Broadview Heights OH 44147
440 526-6200

(G-16037)
OHIOANS HOME HEALTH CARE INC
28315 Kensington Ln (43551-4177)
PHONE..................................419 843-4422
Josh Adams, *President*
Christa Firsdon, *Human Res Dir*
Kim Schmeltz, *Manager*
Ken Eisenbach, *Lic Prac Nurse*
Mary Kmic, *Receptionist*
EMP: 95
SQ FT: 3,500
SALES (est): 4.1MM **Privately Held**
SIC: 8082 Visiting nurse service

(G-16038)
PEAK TRANSPORTATION INC
26624 Glenwood Rd (43551-4846)
P.O. Box 150 (43552-0150)
PHONE..................................419 874-5201
Fax: 419 872-8162
Milton F Knight, *President*
Brad Hart, *CFO*
Kathy Horvath, *Accountant*
Ryan Knight, *Marketing Staff*
Kathy Burk, *Office Mgr*
EMP: 66
SQ FT: 20,000
SALES: 3.5MM **Privately Held**
SIC: 4212 4213 Local trucking, without storage; trucking, except local

(G-16039)
PENSKE TRUCK LEASING CO LP
12222 Williams Rd (43551-6803)
PHONE..................................419 873-8611
Fax: 419 873-1903
Mike Pritchard, *Manager*
EMP: 40
SALES (corp-wide): 2.9B **Privately Held**
WEB: www.pensketruckleasing.com
SIC: 7513 Truck leasing, without drivers

PA: Penske Truck Leasing Co., L.P.
2675 Morgantown Rd
Reading PA 19607
610 775-6000

(G-16040)
PERRY PRO TECH INC
1270 Flagship Dr (43551-1381)
PHONE..................................419 475-9030
Fax: 419 472-7335
Courtney King, *Accounts Mgr*
John Rees, *Manager*
EMP: 30
SALES (corp-wide): 57.4MM **Privately Held**
SIC: 5044 Office equipment
PA: Perry Pro Tech, Inc.
545 W Market St Lowr Lowr
Lima OH 45801
419 228-1360

(G-16041)
PERRYSBURG BOARD OF EDUCATION
Also Called: Perrysburg Bus Garage
25715 Fort Meigs Rd (43551-1138)
PHONE..................................419 874-3127
Fax: 419 872-6473
Michael Cline, *Manager*
Rick Gilts, *Traffic Dir*
EMP: 30
SALES (corp-wide): 17.1MM **Privately Held**
SIC: 4151 School buses
PA: Perrysburg Board Of Education Inc
140 E Indiana Ave
Perrysburg OH 43551
419 874-9131

(G-16042)
PERRYSBURG PEDIATRICS
1601 Brigham Dr Ste 200 (43551-7117)
PHONE..................................419 872-7700
Fax: 419 874-0196
Kenneth Turk, *Principal*
EMP: 25
SALES (est): 928.2K **Privately Held**
SIC: 8011 Pediatrician

(G-16043)
PERRYSBURG RSDNTIAL SEAL CTING
26651 Eckel Rd (43551-1209)
P.O. Box 170 (43552-0170)
PHONE..................................419 872-7325
Richard Jambor, *Owner*
EMP: 30
SALES (est): 1.5MM **Privately Held**
SIC: 1799 Coating of concrete structures with plastic

(G-16044)
PRECISION STRIP INC
7401 Ponderosa Rd (43551-4858)
PHONE..................................419 661-1100
Tracy Drees, *Controller*
Greg Bergman, *Manager*
EMP: 70
SALES (corp-wide): 9.7B **Publicly Held**
WEB: www.precision-strip.com
SIC: 7389 Metal slitting & shearing
HQ: Precision Strip Inc.
86 S Ohio St
Minster OH 45865
419 628-2343

(G-16045)
PROHEALTH PARTNERS INC
12661 Eckel Junction Rd (43551)
PHONE..................................419 491-7150
Rich Adam, *President*
Josh Kaiser, *Controller*
EMP: 50
SALES (est): 1.8MM **Privately Held**
SIC: 8049 Physical therapist

(G-16046)
PRUETER ENTERPRISES LTD
Also Called: Great Lakes Medical Staffing
25660 Dixie Hwy Ste 2 (43551-2167)
PHONE..................................419 872-5343
E Kyle Prueter, *President*
Ann M Prueter, *Vice Pres*
EMP: 212
SQ FT: 2,400

SALES (est): 5.8MM **Privately Held**
SIC: 7363 Employee leasing service

(G-16047)
PUPS PARADISE
12615 Roachton Rd (43551-1349)
PHONE..................................419 873-6115
Ron Deleeuw, *Owner*
EMP: 25
SALES (est): 195.2K **Privately Held**
SIC: 0752 Boarding services, kennels

(G-16048)
QUINCY AMUSEMENTS INC
2005 Hollenbeck Dr (43551-7137)
PHONE..................................419 874-2154
Elena Allen, *Principal*
EMP: 50
SALES (est): 397.5K **Privately Held**
SIC: 7832 Motion picture theaters, except drive-in

(G-16049)
R & J TRUCKING INC
3423 Genoa Rd (43551-9703)
PHONE..................................419 837-9937
Mike Schnider, *Manager*
EMP: 30 **Privately Held**
WEB: www.rjtrucking.com
SIC: 4212 Dump truck haulage
HQ: R & J Trucking, Inc.
8063 Southern Blvd
Youngstown OH 44512
800 262-9365

(G-16050)
R & L CARRIERS INC
134 W South Boundary St (43551-1763)
PHONE..................................419 874-5976
EMP: 27 **Privately Held**
SIC: 4213 Contract haulers
PA: R & L Carriers, Inc.
600 Gilliam Rd
Wilmington OH 45177

(G-16051)
RENHILL STFFING SRVCES-AMERICA (HQ)
28315 Kensington Ln Ste B (43551-4177)
PHONE..................................419 254-2800
Joseph T Braden, *President*
Monte Bandeen, *Recruiter*
EMP: 25
SQ FT: 6,000
SALES (est): 3.9MM
SALES (corp-wide): 8.4MM **Privately Held**
SIC: 7363 Employee leasing service
PA: Renhill Group Inc
28315 Kensington Ln Ste B
Perrysburg OH 43551
419 254-2800

(G-16052)
RIVER ROAD FAMILY PHYSICIANS
1601 Brigham Dr Ste 250 (43551-7115)
PHONE..................................419 872-7745
Jason Evans, *Owner*
EMP: 25
SALES (est): 940K **Privately Held**
SIC: 8011 General & family practice, physician/surgeon

(G-16053)
RRP PACKAGING
327 5th St (43551-4919)
PHONE..................................419 666-6119
Jeff Freiburger, *Principal*
Robert Hinkle, *Vice Pres*
EMP: 50 **EST:** 2008
SALES (est): 3.4MM **Privately Held**
SIC: 5199 Packaging materials

(G-16054)
RYDER TRUCK RENTAL INC
1380 4th St (43551-4365)
PHONE..................................419 666-9833
Fax: 419 666-6724
Jon Rodgers, *Site Mgr*
Henry Alexander, *Manager*
EMP: 50
SALES (corp-wide): 7.3B **Publicly Held**
SIC: 7513 Truck rental, without drivers

Perrysburg - Wood County (G-16055)

HQ: Ryder Truck Rental, Inc.
11690 Nw 105th St
Medley FL 33178
305 500-3726

(G-16055)
SALON HAZELTON
131 W Indiana Ave (43551-1578)
PHONE..................................419 874-9404
Fax: 419 872-0493
Greg Hazelton, *Owner*
Kimberly Michalak, *Marketing Staff*
EMP: 26
SQ FT: 1,420
SALES (est): 836.1K **Privately Held**
WEB: www.salonhazelton.com
SIC: 7231 5999 Cosmetologist; hair care products

(G-16056)
SARO TRUCK DISPATCH INC
26180 Glenwood Rd (43551-4822)
PHONE..................................419 873-1358
Fax: 419 873-1362
Sandra Ankney, *President*
Jeff Mc Coy, *Vice Pres*
EMP: 42
SALES (est): 5.2MM **Privately Held**
SIC: 4213 Heavy hauling

(G-16057)
SCHMIDT DAILY RENTAL INC
Also Called: Ed Schmidt Chevrolet
26875 Dixie Hwy (43551-1716)
PHONE..................................419 874-4331
Thomas Schmidt, *President*
EMP: 61
SALES: 44.6MM **Privately Held**
SIC: 7514 Passenger car rental

(G-16058)
SHAMAS LTD
102 W Indiana Ave (43551-1577)
PHONE..................................419 872-9908
Fax: 419 872-3655
Rhonda Broadway, *Partner*
Tony Shamas, *Partner*
EMP: 40
SALES (est): 1.2MM **Privately Held**
WEB: www.shamas.com
SIC: 7231 Hairdressers

(G-16059)
SIGMA TECHNOLOGIES LTD
27096 Oakmead Dr (43551-2657)
PHONE..................................419 874-9262
Fax: 419 873-0747
Tony Valentino, *Managing Dir*
Jay Carpenter, *Opers Mgr*
Hannah Balge, *Engineer*
Matthew Zalaiskalns, *Engineer*
Philip Mathieu, *Accountant*
EMP: 45
SALES (est): 8.8MM **Privately Held**
WEB: www.teamsigma.com
SIC: 8711 Consulting engineer

(G-16060)
SOTO SALON & SPA
580 Craig Dr Ste 6 (43551-1776)
PHONE..................................419 872-5555
Fax: 419 872-5554
Denise Soto, *Owner*
Jan Fridrich, *CFO*
EMP: 28
SALES (est): 870K **Privately Held**
WEB: www.salonsoto.com
SIC: 7231 Cosmetologist

(G-16061)
SOUTHERN GRAPHIC SYSTEMS INC
9648 Grassy Creek Dr (43551-3544)
PHONE..................................419 662-9873
Christine Wood, *Manager*
EMP: 415
SALES (corp-wide): 303.4MM **Privately Held**
SIC: 7389 Personal service agents, brokers & bureaus
HQ: Southern Graphic Systems, Llc
626 W Main St Ste 500
Louisville KY 40202
502 637-5443

(G-16062)
SPIEKER COMPANY
8350 Fremont Pike (43551-9427)
PHONE..................................419 872-7000
Fax: 419 872-7010
Norman T White, *President*
Dennis Hoodlebrink, *Superintendent*
Matt Berg, *Vice Pres*
Matthew Berg, *Vice Pres*
Babette Burnett, *Safety Dir*
EMP: 50 EST: 1977
SQ FT: 22,000
SALES (est): 22.2MM **Privately Held**
WEB: www.spiekercompany.com
SIC: 1542 1541 1611 Commercial & office building, new construction; industrial buildings, new construction; general contractor, highway & street construction

(G-16063)
STATE FARM MUTL AUTO INSUR CO
Also Called: State Farm Insurance
13001 Roachton Rd (43551-1357)
PHONE..................................419 873-0100
Fax: 419 693-1974
Keith Kirkpatrick, *Branch Mgr*
Patrici Kirkpatrick, *Agent*
Barry Hoozen, *Real Est Agnt*
EMP: 89
SALES (corp-wide): 39.5MM **Privately Held**
SIC: 6411 Insurance agents & brokers
PA: State Farm Mutual Automobile Insurance Company
1 State Farm Plz
Bloomington IL 61710
309 766-2311

(G-16064)
TMT INC
Also Called: Tmt Logistics
655 D St (43551-4908)
P.O. Box 408 (43552-0408)
PHONE..................................419 592-1041
Tony Marks, *President*
EMP: 250
SALES (est): 9.6MM **Privately Held**
SIC: 4789 3999 Railroad maintenance & repair services; dock equipment & supplies, industrial

(G-16065)
TRT MANAGEMENT CORPORATION (PA)
Also Called: Kenakore Solutions
487 J St (43551-4303)
PHONE..................................419 661-1233
Fax: 419 661-1251
Bruce Gonring, *CEO*
Chris Huver, *President*
Carol Jansen, *Controller*
EMP: 37 EST: 2015
SQ FT: 128,000
SALES: 1.1MM **Privately Held**
SIC: 4225 General warehousing

(G-16066)
UNITED PARCEL SERVICE INC OH
Also Called: UPS
12171 Eckel Rd (43551-1241)
PHONE..................................419 872-0211
Gene Magam, *Manager*
Carey Hudson, *Supervisor*
EMP: 128
SALES (corp-wide): 65.8B **Publicly Held**
WEB: www.upsscs.com
SIC: 4215 7538 Courier services, except by air; general automotive repair shops; general truck repair
HQ: United Parcel Service, Inc. (Oh)
55 Glenlake Pkwy
Atlanta GA 30328
404 828-6000

(G-16067)
UNITED RENTALS NORTH AMER INC
620 Eckel Rd (43551-1202)
P.O. Box 240 (43552-0240)
PHONE..................................800 877-3687
Mike Scorziell, *Foreman/Supr*
Brad Taylor, *Natl Sales Mgr*
Kelly Milligan, *Accounts Mgr*
Mike Lowell, *Branch Mgr*
EMP: 25
SALES (corp-wide): 6.6B **Publicly Held**
WEB: www.ur.com
SIC: 7353 7359 Cranes & aerial lift equipment, rental or leasing; equipment rental & leasing
HQ: United Rentals (North America), Inc.
100 Frederick St 700
Stamford CT 06902
203 622-3131

(G-16068)
VAN TASSEL CONSTRUCTION CORP
25591 Fort Meigs Rd Ste A (43551-1394)
P.O. Box 698, Sylvania (43560-0698)
PHONE..................................419 873-0188
Fax: 419 873-0190
Kipp Van Tassel, *President*
EMP: 30
SQ FT: 20,000
SALES (est): 2.8MM **Privately Held**
WEB: www.vantasselconstruction.com
SIC: 1541 1542 Renovation, remodeling & repairs: industrial buildings; commercial & office building, new construction

(G-16069)
VERIZON COMMUNICATIONS INC
1130 Levis Commons Blvd (43551-7125)
PHONE..................................419 874-3933
Fax: 419 874-2516
Stephen Imes, *Branch Mgr*
EMP: 165
SALES (corp-wide): 126B **Publicly Held**
WEB: www.verizon.com
SIC: 4899 Data communication services
PA: Verizon Communications Inc.
1095 Ave Of The Americas
New York NY 10036
212 395-1000

(G-16070)
W W WILLIAMS COMPANY LLC
3325 Libbey Rd (43551-9740)
P.O. Box 427, Lemoyne (43441-0427)
PHONE..................................419 837-5067
Alan Gatlin, *President*
Dave Obrock, *VP Mktg*
John M Stephenson, *Branch Mgr*
Led McIntyre, *Manager*
Dorian Norstrom, *Administration*
EMP: 25
SALES (corp-wide): 2.1B **Privately Held**
WEB: www.williamsdistribution.com
SIC: 7538 5013 5084 5063 Diesel engine repair: automotive; automotive supplies & parts; industrial machinery & equipment; electrical apparatus & equipment
HQ: The W W Williams Company Llc
835 Goodale Blvd
Columbus OH 43212
614 228-5000

(G-16071)
W W WILLIAMS COMPANY LLC
3325 Libbey Rd (43551-9740)
PHONE..................................419 837-5067
W Williams, *Branch Mgr*
EMP: 67
SALES (corp-wide): 2.1B **Privately Held**
SIC: 5013 Truck parts & accessories
HQ: The W W Williams Company Llc
835 Goodale Blvd
Columbus OH 43212
614 228-5000

(G-16072)
WADSWORTH-SLAWSON INC
Also Called: Wadsworth Solutions Northeast
1500 Michael Owens Way (43551-2975)
PHONE..................................216 391-7263
Brit R Wadsworth, *CEO*
Thomas H McClave, *President*
Gary L McClave, *Vice Pres*
David Sommer, *Vice Pres*
Jared Cowan, *Opers Staff*
EMP: 32
SALES (est): 18.3MM **Privately Held**
SIC: 5075 Warm air heating & air conditioning

(G-16073)
WESTHAVEN SERVICES CO LLC
Also Called: Omnicare of Northwest Ohio
7643 Ponderosa Rd (43551-4862)
P.O. Box 1030 (43552-1030)
PHONE..................................419 661-2200
Fax: 419 661-2228
Sue Neuber, *Exec VP*
Rolf Schrader, *Regional VP*
Chrissy Sarns, *Manager*
EMP: 300
SALES (est): 57.8MM
SALES (corp-wide): 184.7B **Publicly Held**
SIC: 5122 Pharmaceuticals
HQ: Neighborcare Pharmacy Services, Inc.
201 E 4th St Ste 900
Cincinnati OH 45202

(G-16074)
WHELCO INDUSTRIAL LTD
28210 Cedar Park Blvd (43551-4865)
PHONE..................................419 873-6134
Mike Farar, *Branch Mgr*
EMP: 36
SALES (corp-wide): 5.1MM **Privately Held**
WEB: www.whelco.com
SIC: 7694 Electric motor repair
PA: Whelco Industrial, Ltd
28210 Cedar Park Blvd
Perrysburg OH 43551
419 385-4627

(G-16075)
XPO LOGISTICS FREIGHT INC
28291 Glenwood Rd (43551-4809)
PHONE..................................419 666-3022
Fax: 419 666-7144
Robert Bull, *Manager*
EMP: 60
SALES (corp-wide): 15.3B **Publicly Held**
WEB: www.con-way.com
SIC: 4213 Contract haulers
HQ: Xpo Logistics Freight, Inc.
2211 Old Earhart Rd # 100
Ann Arbor MI 48105
734 998-4200

(G-16076)
YOUNG MENS CHRISTIAN ASSOCIAT
Also Called: YMCA of Greater Toledo
13415 Eckel Junction Rd (43551-1320)
PHONE..................................419 251-9622
Fax: 419 251-0970
Joe Hillrich, *Principal*
Glen King, *Vice Pres*
EMP: 216
SALES (corp-wide): 29.1MM **Privately Held**
SIC: 7997 Membership sports & recreation clubs
PA: Young Men's Christian Association Of Greater Toledo
1500 N Superior St Fl 2
Toledo OH 43604
419 729-8135

Perrysville
Ashland County

(G-16077)
AYERS FARMS INC
820 State Route 39 (44864-9539)
PHONE..................................419 938-7707
Carl Ayers, *President*
Steve Ayers, *Vice Pres*
EMP: 25
SALES: 500K **Privately Held**
SIC: 0119 0241 0211 Pea & bean farms (legumes); milk production; beef cattle feedlots

(G-16078)
COWEN TRUCK LINE INC
2697 State Route 39 (44864-9535)
P.O. Box 480 (44864-0480)
PHONE..................................419 938-3401
Fax: 419 938-5046
Tim Cowen, *President*
Marianne Cowell, *COO*

Cindy Newcomer, *Human Resources*
Dean Ulery, *Sales Mgr*
Tara Mitchell, *Sales Staff*
EMP: 85
SQ FT: 20,000
SALES (est): 17MM **Privately Held**
WEB: www.cowentruckline.com
SIC: 4213 4212 Contract haulers; local trucking, without storage

(G-16079)
MANSFIELD PLUMBING PDTS LLC (HQ)
150 E 1st St (44864-9421)
P.O. Box 620 (44864-0620)
PHONE..........................419 938-5211
Fax: 419 938-6234
Jim Morando, *President*
Paul Stover, *Vice Pres*
Keith Hughes, *Safety Dir*
Jerry Dudte, *Mfg Spvr*
William Suarez, *Opers Staff*
◆ **EMP:** 600
SQ FT: 700,000
SALES (est): 181MM **Privately Held**
SIC: 3261 3463 3088 3431 Vitreous plumbing fixtures; plumbing fixture forgings, nonferrous; plastics plumbing fixtures; bathtubs: enameled iron, cast iron or pressed metal; shower stalls, metal; plumbing fixture fittings & trim; plumbing fittings & supplies

(G-16080)
NATURAL RESOURCES OHIO DEPT
Also Called: Mohican State Park Lodge & Con
1098 Ashlnd Cnty Rd 300 Ste 3006 (44864)
PHONE..........................419 938-5411
Fax: 419 938-7504
Laura Weirick, *Manager*
Larry Stephens, *Manager*
EMP: 100 **Privately Held**
WEB: www.ohiostateparks.com
SIC: 7011 9512 5813 5812 Hotels; land, mineral & wildlife conservation; ; drinking places; eating places
HQ: Ohio Department Of Natural Resources
2045 Morse Rd Bldg D-3
Columbus OH 43229

Petersburg
Mahoning County

(G-16081)
DAVE SUGAR EXCAVATING LLC
11640 S State Line Rd (44454-9705)
P.O. Box 459, New Middletown (44442-0459)
PHONE..........................330 542-1100
Dave Sugar,
EMP: 35
SALES (est): 2.7MM **Privately Held**
SIC: 1794 1795 1623 Excavation work; wrecking & demolition work; water, sewer & utility lines

Pettisville
Fulton County

(G-16082)
P T I INC
421 Commercial (43553)
PHONE..........................419 445-2800
Fax: 419 445-9400
Charles J Lantz, *President*
Charles F Lantz, *President*
▲ **EMP:** 40
SALES (est): 2.8MM **Privately Held**
WEB: www.inplastech.com
SIC: 1521 New construction, single-family houses

Pickerington
Fairfield County

(G-16083)
AMERICAN MOTORCYCLE ASSN (PA)
Also Called: AMERICAN MOTORCYCLIST ASSOCIAT
13515 Yarmouth Dr (43147-8273)
PHONE..........................614 856-1900
Fax: 614 856-1920
Robert M Dingman, *President*
Joel Moor, *COO*
Gary Sweet, *Vice Pres*
Steve Morehead, *Opers Mgr*
Darcel Higgins, *CFO*
EMP: 85 **EST:** 1952
SQ FT: 30,000
SALES (est): 12.6MM **Privately Held**
WEB: www.americanmotorcyclist.com
SIC: 8699 Automobile owners' association

(G-16084)
ANOTHER CHANCE INC
9866 Haverford Pl (43147-9544)
PHONE..........................614 868-3541
Robert Scott, *President*
EMP: 33
SALES (est): 26.1K **Privately Held**
WEB: www.anotherchance.com
SIC: 7389 Personal service agents, brokers & bureaus

(G-16085)
ANTIOCH CNNCTION CANTON MI LLC
799 Windmiller Dr (43147-8199)
PHONE..........................614 531-9285
Gary Smelser, *Mng Member*
EMP: 50 **EST:** 2013
SQ FT: 86,000
SALES (est): 167.7K **Privately Held**
SIC: 8059 Nursing home, except skilled & intermediate care facility

(G-16086)
ANTIOCH SALEM FIELDS FREDERICK
799 Windmiller Dr (43147-8199)
PHONE..........................614 531-9285
Gary Smelser, *Mng Member*
EMP: 50
SQ FT: 90,000
SALES (est): 167.7K **Privately Held**
SIC: 8059 Nursing home, except skilled & intermediate care facility

(G-16087)
BUCKEYE COMMERCIAL CLEANING
12936 Stonecreek Dr Ste F (43147-8846)
PHONE..........................614 866-4700
David Myers, *President*
Logan Myers, *Marketing Staff*
EMP: 42
SALES (est): 1.2MM **Privately Held**
SIC: 7349 Janitorial service, contract basis

(G-16088)
BUREAU WORKERS COMPENSATION
Also Called: Safety and Hygiene
13430 Yarmouth Dr (43147-8310)
PHONE..........................614 466-5109
Mark Garver, *Superintendent*
Victoria Congrove, *Manager*
Linda O'Brien, *Executive*
EMP: 45
SALES (est): 2.3MM **Privately Held**
SIC: 7382 Security systems services

(G-16089)
CITY OF PICKERINGTON
Also Called: Municipal Golf Course
1145 Clubhouse Ln (43147-8715)
PHONE..........................614 645-8474
Fax: 614 322-0588
Scott Jones, *Manager*
EMP: 50 **Privately Held**
SIC: 7992 Public golf courses

PA: City Of Pickerington
100 Lockville Rd
Pickerington OH 43147
614 833-2289

(G-16090)
COLDWELL BANKER KING THOMPSON
176 Clint Dr (43147-7994)
PHONE..........................614 759-0808
Kevin Strait, *Owner*
Marianne Hall, *Sales Staff*
Brenda Cessna, *Real Est Agnt*
Diane Cheatham, *Real Est Agnt*
Joyce Clark, *Real Est Agnt*
EMP: 60
SALES (est): 2.2MM **Privately Held**
SIC: 6531 Real estate agent, residential

(G-16091)
COLONIAL HEATING & COOLING CO
Also Called: Honeywell Authorized Dealer
671 Windmiller Dr (43147-8192)
PHONE..........................614 837-6100
Fax: 614 837-6202
Robert L Posey Jr, *President*
Rob Elkins, *Vice Pres*
Lora Posey, *Treasurer*
Mary Posey, *Admin Sec*
EMP: 50
SQ FT: 12,000
SALES (est): 7.6MM **Privately Held**
WEB: www.colonialheating.com
SIC: 1711 Warm air heating & air conditioning contractor

(G-16092)
COMO INC
8670 Hill Rd S (43147-8536)
PHONE..........................614 830-2666
Robert Hart, *President*
EMP: 28
SQ FT: 1,970
SALES (est): 1.3MM **Privately Held**
SIC: 0782 Landscape contractors

(G-16093)
COOKIE CUTTERS HAIRCUTTERS
1726 Hill Rd N (43147-8880)
PHONE..........................614 522-0220
Alison Celento, *Owner*
EMP: 30
SALES (est): 233.3K **Privately Held**
SIC: 7231 Unisex hair salons

(G-16094)
DONLEY CONCRETE CUTTING
151 W Borland St (43147-1206)
PHONE..........................614 834-0300
Fax: 614 834-8844
David Donley, *Branch Mgr*
EMP: 60
SALES (corp-wide): 660.3K **Privately Held**
SIC: 1771 Concrete work
PA: Donley Concrete Cutting
1441 Gest St
Cincinnati OH 45203
513 421-1950

(G-16095)
HER INC
1450 Tussing Rd (43147-9499)
PHONE..........................614 864-7400
Michael Kocher, *Partner*
Ed Caldwell, *Manager*
EMP: 100
SALES (corp-wide): 14.3MM **Privately Held**
WEB: www.eassent.com
SIC: 6531 Real estate agents & managers
PA: Her, Inc
4261 Morse Rd
Columbus OH 43230
614 221-7400

(G-16096)
HOME ECHO CLUB INC
Also Called: Echo Manor Extended Care Ctr
10270 Blacklick Eastrn Rd (43147)
PHONE..........................614 864-1718
Fax: 614 864-2313
William T Johnson, *President*

Paul Grandenetti, *Director*
Gary Brand, *Administration*
EMP: 107
SQ FT: 66,000
SALES (est): 5MM **Privately Held**
SIC: 8052 8051 Intermediate care facilities; skilled nursing care facilities

(G-16097)
HUNTINGTON HLLS RECREATION CLB
6600 Springbrook Dr (43147-9142)
P.O. Box 75 (43147-0075)
PHONE..........................614 837-0293
Jon Hanna, *President*
Paul Sherry, *Human Resources*
EMP: 30
SALES: 114.3K **Privately Held**
SIC: 7999 Swimming pool, non-membership

(G-16098)
JPMORGAN CHASE BANK NAT ASSN
7915 Refugee Rd (43147-9428)
PHONE..........................614 834-3120
Sheila Williamslee, *Branch Mgr*
EMP: 26
SALES (corp-wide): 99.6B **Publicly Held**
WEB: www.chase.com
SIC: 6021 National commercial banks
HQ: Jpmorgan Chase Bank, National Association
1111 Polaris Pkwy
Columbus OH 43240
614 436-3055

(G-16099)
KINDRED NURSING CENTERS E LLC
Also Called: Kindred Transitional Care
1300 Hill Rd N (43147-8986)
PHONE..........................314 631-3000
Judy Dennis, *Facilities Mgr*
Brian Newman, *Branch Mgr*
EMP: 121
SALES (corp-wide): 6B **Publicly Held**
WEB: www.salemhaven.com
SIC: 8051 Convalescent home with continuous nursing care
HQ: Kindred Nursing Centers East, L.L.C.
680 S 4th St
Louisville KY 40202
502 596-7300

(G-16100)
LBS INTERNATIONAL INC
Also Called: Friendly Care Agency
12920 Sheffield Dr (43147-7706)
PHONE..........................614 866-3688
Sam I Lantsman, *President*
Larisa B Lantsman, *Exec VP*
EMP: 100
SALES: 1MM **Privately Held**
SIC: 8082 Home health care services

(G-16101)
MARCUS THEATRES CORPORATION
Also Called: Pickerington Marcus Cinemas
1776 Hill Rd N (43147-8880)
PHONE..........................614 759-6500
Alan Zetting, *Manager*
EMP: 41
SALES (corp-wide): 622.7MM **Publicly Held**
SIC: 7832 Motion picture theaters, except drive-in
HQ: Marcus Theatres Corporation
100 E Wisconsin Ave
Milwaukee WI 53202
414 905-1500

(G-16102)
NATIONWIDE CHILDRENS HOSPITAL
1310 Hill Rd N (43147-7814)
PHONE..........................614 864-9216
Junxin Shi, *Research*
Elizabeth Allen, *Director*
Antoinette Eaton, *Professor*
EMP: 830
SALES (corp-wide): 1.3B **Privately Held**
SIC: 8069 Children's hospital

Pickerington - Fairfield County (G-16103) — GEOGRAPHIC SECTION

PA: Nationwide Children's Hospital
700 Childrens Dr
Columbus OH 43205
614 722-2000

(G-16103)
PROVENITFINANCE LLC
195 Fox Glen Dr W (43147-8097)
PHONE..................888 958-1060
Craig Hollenbeck, *Partner*
William Miller, *Mng Member*
Nicholas Reade, *Consultant*
EMP: 25
SALES: 5MM Privately Held
SIC: 8742 Management consulting services

(G-16104)
RAINBOW STATION DAY CARE INC (PA)
226 Durand St (43147-7941)
PHONE..................614 759-8667
Bonnie Gibbs, *President*
EMP: 36
SQ FT: 7,000
SALES: 2.5MM Privately Held
WEB: www.rainbowstation.com
SIC: 8351 Group day care center

(G-16105)
RG BARRY CORPORATION (HQ)
13405 Yarmouth Rd Nw (43147)
PHONE..................614 864-6400
Fax: 614 866-9787
Bob Mullaney, *President*
Jerry Hemphill, *President*
Garry Bincoski, *COO*
Yvonne E Kalucis, *Senior VP*
Thomas J Z Konecki, *Senior VP*
▲ EMP: 77 EST: 1947
SQ FT: 55,000
SALES (est): 85.6MM
SALES (corp-wide): 84.5MM Privately Held
WEB: www.rgbarry.com
SIC: 5139 5136 5137 Footwear; slippers, house; shoe accessories; men's & boys' furnishings; handbags
PA: Mrgb Hold Co.
382 Greenwich Ave Apt 1
Greenwich CT 06830
203 987-3500

(G-16106)
SPORTS MEDICINE GRANT INC
417 Hill Rd N Ste 401 (43147-1310)
PHONE..................614 461-8199
Raymond J Tesner, *Principal*
EMP: 26
SALES (corp-wide): 6.5MM Privately Held
SIC: 8099 Childbirth preparation clinic
PA: Sports Medicine Grant Inc
323 E Town St Ste 100
Columbus OH 43215
614 461-8174

(G-16107)
VOLUNTEER ENERGY SERVICES INC (PA)
790 Windmiller Dr Ste A (43147-6879)
PHONE..................614 856-3128
Richard Curnutte Sr, *President*
Marc Runck, *CFO*
Mike Boudreau, *VP Finance*
Rick Pyles, *Sales Mgr*
Chris Munn, *Accounts Mgr*
EMP: 50
SQ FT: 8,000
SALES (est): 26.4MM Privately Held
WEB: www.volunteerenergy.com
SIC: 4924 Natural gas distribution

Piketon
Pike County

(G-16108)
ACORD RK LUMBER COMPANY
125 W 4th St (45661-9650)
PHONE..................740 289-3761
Fax: 740 493-2816
Randy Acord, *Owner*
EMP: 29

SALES (est): 2.1MM Privately Held
SIC: 5031 Lumber: rough, dressed & finished

(G-16109)
ATOMIC CREDIT UNION INC (PA)
711 Beaver Creek Rd (45661-9140)
PHONE..................740 289-5060
Fax: 740 947-1094
Thomas Griffith, *President*
Katrina Slark, *President*
Aaron Michael, *COO*
Aaron C Mihael, *COO*
Sandy Swindler, *VP Opers*
EMP: 25
SALES: 10.5MM Privately Held
WEB: www.2mycu.com
SIC: 6062 State credit unions, not federally chartered

(G-16110)
CDM SMITH INC
3930 Us Rte 23 S (45661)
PHONE..................740 897-2937
EMP: 50
SALES (corp-wide): 1.2B Privately Held
SIC: 8711 Engineering Services
PA: Smith Cdm Inc
75 State St Ste 701
Boston MA 02109
617 452-6000

(G-16111)
CENTRUS ENERGY CORP
Also Called: American Centrifuge Plant
3930 Us Rt 23 S (45661)
PHONE..................740 897-2457
Dale Bauer, *General Mgr*
James Schoettler, *Counsel*
Angie Duduit, *Manager*
James Vogelsang, *Director*
Dennis Scott, *General Counsel*
EMP: 200
SALES (corp-wide): 218.4MM Publicly Held
SIC: 1094 Uranium ore mining
PA: Centrus Energy Corp.
6901 Rockledge Dr Ste 800
Bethesda MD 20817
301 564-3200

(G-16112)
COMMUNITY ACTION COMM PIKE CNT (PA)
941 Market St (45661-9757)
P.O. Box 799 (45661-0799)
PHONE..................740 289-2371
Fax: 740 289-4229
Rebecca Adkins, *CFO*
Barb Crabtree, *Marketing Staff*
Gary Roberts, *Exec Dir*
Cindy Balzer, *Director*
Rita Moore, *Director*
EMP: 115
SQ FT: 21,360
SALES: 22.3MM Privately Held
SIC: 8322 Family service agency

(G-16113)
DKM CONSTRUCTION INC
W Perimeter Rd (45661)
PHONE..................740 289-3006
Fax: 740 289-4867
Dennis Martin, *President*
Debbie Martin, *Corp Secy*
William Martin, *Vice Pres*
Stephanie Wiseman, *Manager*
EMP: 35
SQ FT: 2,400
SALES: 10.6MM Privately Held
SIC: 1541 1542 Industrial buildings & warehouses; commercial & office building, new construction

(G-16114)
FIRST NATIONAL BANK OF WAVERLY
13256 State Route 124 (45661-9013)
PHONE..................740 493-3372
Fax: 740 493-3593
Kimberly Davis, *Manager*
EMP: 28

SALES (corp-wide): 6.2MM Privately Held
WEB: www.thefirstnational.com
SIC: 6021 National commercial banks
PA: The First National Bank Of Waverly
107 N Market St
Waverly OH 45690
740 947-2136

(G-16115)
FLUOR-BWXT PORTSMOUTH LLC
1862 Shyville Rd Ste 216 (45661-9749)
P.O. Box 548 (45661-0548)
PHONE..................866 706-6992
Tracy Heidelberg, *CFO*
Mark Ashby, *Mng Member*
Pam Hensley, *Manager*
Rick Holbrook, *Manager*
Joseph Moss, *Manager*
EMP: 1200
SALES (est): 158.5MM
SALES (corp-wide): 19.5B Publicly Held
SIC: 1795 Wrecking & demolition work
PA: Fluor Corporation
6700 Las Colinas Blvd
Irving TX 75039
469 398-7000

(G-16116)
H C F INC
Also Called: Pleasant Hl Otptent Thrapy Ctr
7143 Us Rte 23 (45661)
PHONE..................740 289-2528
Fax: 740 289-4406
Jim Unverferth, *President*
David Roddy, *Director*
EMP: 220
SALES (est): 3MM Privately Held
SIC: 8059 Nursing home, except skilled & intermediate care facility

(G-16117)
HCF MANAGEMENT INC
7143 Us Highway 23 (45661-9527)
PHONE..................740 289-2394
Abby Walls, *Human Res Dir*
Amy Clemons, *Administration*
EMP: 170
SALES (corp-wide): 154.8MM Privately Held
SIC: 8051 8322 Skilled nursing care facilities; rehabilitation services
PA: Hcf Management, Inc.
1100 Shawnee Rd
Lima OH 45805
419 999-2010

(G-16118)
INNOVTIVE SLTONS UNLIMITED LLC (PA)
1862 Shyville Rd (45661-9749)
PHONE..................740 289-3282
Fax: 740 820-5451
Kristen Preston, *Human Res Mgr*
Jennifer Barbarits, *Mng Member*
Frank Barbarits,
EMP: 37
SQ FT: 3,000
SALES (est): 14.5MM Privately Held
WEB: www.insolves.com
SIC: 8711 7363 Engineering services; employee leasing service

(G-16119)
INNOVTIVE SLTONS UNLIMITED LLC
1862 Shyville Rd (45661-9749)
PHONE..................740 289-3282
Richard Warner, *Business Mgr*
Donnie Locke, *Engineer*
Angela Stuart, *Engineer*
Steven Barbarits, *Personnel Exec*
Brent McGinnis, *Sr Associate*
EMP: 100
SALES (est): 16.2MM Privately Held
WEB: www.insolves.com
SIC: 8711 7363 Engineering services; help supply services
PA: Innovative Solutions Unlimited, Llc
1862 Shyville Rd
Piketon OH 45661

(G-16120)
OHIO DEPARTMENT OF EDUCATION
Also Called: South Central Ohio Cmpt Assn
175 Beaver Creek Rd (45661-9114)
P.O. Box 577 (45661-0577)
PHONE..................740 289-2908
Philip E Satterfield, *Superintendent*
Sandra Benson, *CFO*
David Brown, *Data Proc Staff*
Shawn Clemmons, *Exec Dir*
Jackie Taylor, *Teacher*
EMP: 40 Privately Held
WEB: www.osd.oh.gov
SIC: 9411 8741 Administration of educational programs; ; management services
HQ: Department Of Education Ohio
25 S Front St
Columbus OH 43215

(G-16121)
OHIO VALLEY ELECTRIC CORP (PA)
Also Called: OVEC
3932 Us Rte 23 (45661)
P.O. Box 468 (45661-0468)
PHONE..................740 289-7200
Fax: 740 289-7284
Nicholas Akins, *President*
John Brodt, *Corp Secy*
Mark Piefer, *Vice Pres*
David E Jons, *VP Opers*
Andy Ashbury, *Maint Spvr*
EMP: 93
SQ FT: 100,000
SALES: 451.3MM Privately Held
SIC: 4911 Generation, electric power; transmission, electric power; distribution, electric power

(G-16122)
OHIO VALLEY ELECTRIC CORP
Also Called: Power Scheduling Group
3932 Us Rt 23 (45661)
P.O. Box 468 (45661-0468)
PHONE..................740 289-7225
Scott Cunningham, *Engineer*
Ann A Huff, *Human Res Mgr*
David Jones, *Branch Mgr*
Edward McGovern, *Manager*
John Campbell, *Director*
EMP: 83
SALES (corp-wide): 451.3MM Privately Held
SIC: 4911
PA: Ohio Valley Electric Corporation
3932 Us Rte 23
Piketon OH 45661
740 289-7200

(G-16123)
PACE INTERNATIONAL UNION
Also Called: Local 5-689
2288 Wakefield Mound Rd (45661-9660)
P.O. Box 467 (45661-0467)
PHONE..................740 289-2368
Fax: 740 289-2126
Daniel Mintor, *President*
EMP: 33
SALES (corp-wide): 26.9MM Privately Held
SIC: 8631 Labor unions & similar labor organizations
PA: Pace International Union
5 Gateway Ctr
Pittsburgh PA 15222
412 562-2400

(G-16124)
PIKE COUNTY HEAD START INC
941 Market St (45661-9757)
P.O. Box 799 (45661-0799)
PHONE..................740 289-2371
Chris Ervin, *CTO*
Raymond Roberts, *Exec Dir*
Barb Tackett, *Director*
Barb Davis, *Director*
EMP: 60
SALES (est): 958.6K Privately Held
SIC: 8351 Head start center, except in conjunction with school

GEOGRAPHIC SECTION
Piqua - Miami County (G-16146)

(G-16125)
PIKETON NURSING CENTER INC
300 Overlook Dr (45661-9760)
PHONE..................740 289-4074
Fax: 740 289-4581
James Renacci, *President*
EMP: 65
SALES (est): 2.8MM
SALES (corp-wide): 581.9MM **Privately Held**
WEB: www.tandemhealthcare.com
SIC: 8051 Convalescent home with continuous nursing care
PA: Consulate Management Company, Llc
800 Concourse Pkwy S
Maitland FL 32751
407 571-1550

(G-16126)
PLEASANT HILL LEASING LLC
Also Called: Pleasant Hill Manor
7143 Us Rte 23 S (45661)
PHONE..................740 289-2394
Fax: 740 289-2231
Eli Gunzburg,
Jody Kupchak, *Executive Asst*
EMP: 130 EST: 2016
SALES (est): 147.7K **Privately Held**
SIC: 8051 Mental retardation hospital

(G-16127)
RITCHIES FOOD DISTRIBUTORS INC
527 S West St (45661-8042)
PHONE..................740 443-6303
Fax: 740 289-4375
James P Ritchie, *President*
Nancy Ritchie, *Corp Secy*
Joyce Lightle, *Vice Pres*
Twyla Suter, *Vice Pres*
Joyce Vitel, *Vice Pres*
EMP: 31
SALES (est): 14MM **Privately Held**
SIC: 5146 5147 5142 5149 Seafoods; meats, fresh; packaged frozen goods; canned goods: fruit, vegetables, seafood, meats, etc.

(G-16128)
UNITED STATES ENRICHMENT CORP
Also Called: Usec
3930 Us Highway 23 Anx (45661-9113)
P.O. Box 628 (45661-0628)
PHONE..................740 897-2331
Fax: 740 897-2972
Ralph Donnelly, *Branch Mgr*
James Anzelmo, *Manager*
Gary Hairston, *Manager*
Chris Harper, *Manager*
Martin Karr, *Manager*
EMP: 1200
SALES (corp-wide): 218.4MM **Publicly Held**
WEB: www.portslab.com
SIC: 8742 Public utilities consultant
HQ: United States Enrichment Corporation
6903 Rockledge Dr
Bethesda MD 20817
301 564-3200

(G-16129)
UNITED STATES ENRICHMENT CORP
3930 Us Rte 23 S (45661)
PHONE..................740 897-2457
Ray Jordan, *Manager*
EMP: 1100
SALES (corp-wide): 218.4MM **Publicly Held**
WEB: www.portslab.com
SIC: 8742 8351 Public utilities consultant; child day care services
HQ: United States Enrichment Corporation
6903 Rockledge Dr
Bethesda MD 20817
301 564-3200

(G-16130)
URANIUM DISPOSITION SVCS LLC
3930 Us Highway 23 Anx (45661-9113)
PHONE..................740 289-3620
Paul Kreitz, *Branch Mgr*
EMP: 156

SALES (corp-wide): 33.7MM **Privately Held**
SIC: 1629 Waste disposal plant construction
PA: Uranium Disposition Services, Llc
1020 Monarch St Ste 100
Lexington KY 40513
859 296-0023

(G-16131)
WASTREN - ENERGX MISSION
Also Called: Wems
1571 Shyville Rd (45661-9201)
P.O. Box 307 (45661-0307)
PHONE..................740 897-3724
Steven Moore, *CEO*
Glenn Henderson, *COO*
Jim Gardner, *Vice Pres*
Keith Tucker, *Vice Pres*
Damon Detillion, *Project Mgr*
EMP: 170
SALES (est): 23.2MM **Privately Held**
SIC: 8744 Facilities support services
PA: Wastren Advantage, Inc.
1571 Shyville Rd
Piketon OH 45661

(G-16132)
WASTREN ADVANTAGE INC (PA)
1571 Shyville Rd (45661-9201)
PHONE..................970 254-1277
Fax: 740 443-7979
Steve Moore, *President*
Charlie Anderson, *General Mgr*
John Essman, *General Mgr*
Glenn Henderson, *COO*
Jim Gardner, *Exec VP*
EMP: 30
SALES: 105MM **Privately Held**
SIC: 4959 8744 8711 Sanitary services; facilities support services; engineering services

Piqua
Miami County

(G-16133)
A M LEONARD INC
Also Called: Gardeners Edge
241 Fox Dr (45356-9265)
P.O. Box 816 (45356-0816)
PHONE..................937 773-2694
Fax: 937 773-9959
Betty L Ziegler, *President*
Jill Oldiges, *Project Mgr*
Emily Burnside, *Buyer*
Angie Mayse, *Buyer*
Marcia Cavender, *Purchasing*
◆ EMP: 90 EST: 1885
SQ FT: 120,000
SALES (est): 43.4MM **Privately Held**
WEB: www.amleo.com
SIC: 5072 5191 Garden tools, hand; farm supplies; garden supplies

(G-16134)
AARONS INC
1305 E Ash St (45356-4108)
PHONE..................937 778-3577
Fax: 937 492-3123
Matthew Bradley, *Branch Mgr*
EMP: 25
SALES (corp-wide): 3.3B **Publicly Held**
WEB: www.aaronrents.com
SIC: 7359 Furniture rental
PA: Aaron's, Inc.
400 Galleria Pkwy Se # 300
Atlanta GA 30339
678 402-3000

(G-16135)
B D TRANSPORTATION INC
9590 Looney Rd (45356-2584)
PHONE..................937 773-9280
Fax: 937 773-9284
John Douglas, *President*
Teresa Douglas, *Vice Pres*
Phil Douglas, *Manager*
EMP: 30
SQ FT: 1,000

SALES (est): 7.1MM **Privately Held**
WEB: www.bdtransport.com
SIC: 4213 4212 Contract haulers; local trucking, without storage

(G-16136)
BLACK STONE CINCINNATI LLC
Also Called: Home Care By Black Stone
106 W Ash St Ste 504 (45356-2343)
PHONE..................937 773-8573
Regina Carroll, *Branch Mgr*
EMP: 27
SALES (corp-wide): 13.8MM **Privately Held**
SIC: 8099 Blood related health services
PA: Black Stone Of Cincinnati, Llc
4700 E Galbraith Rd Fl 3
Cincinnati OH 45236
513 924-1370

(G-16137)
BROOKDALE SNIOR LVING CMMNTIES
Also Called: Sterling House of Piqua
1744 W High St Ofc (45356-8333)
PHONE..................937 773-0500
Fax: 937 773-8521
Ida Hecht, *General Mgr*
Anne Murphy, *Exec Dir*
EMP: 25
SALES (corp-wide): 4.7B **Publicly Held**
WEB: www.assisted.com
SIC: 8059 Rest home, with health care
HQ: Brookdale Senior Living Communities, Inc.
6737 W Wa St Ste 2300
Milwaukee WI 53214
414 918-5000

(G-16138)
BUCKEYE STATE MUTUAL INSUR CO (PA)
1 Heritage Pl (45356-4148)
PHONE..................937 778-5000
Fax: 937 778-5021
R Douglas Haines, *President*
Rob Bornhorst, *Senior VP*
Steve Moeller, *Vice Pres*
Amy C Hanes, *Research*
Doug Nickemp, *Accountant*
EMP: 70
SQ FT: 17,000
SALES (est): 30.6MM **Privately Held**
SIC: 6331 Fire, marine & casualty insurance & carriers

(G-16139)
COILPLUS INC
Also Called: Coilplus Berwick
100 Steelway Dr (45356-7530)
PHONE..................937 778-8884
Fax: 937 778-1708
Larry Apple, *QC Mgr*
Terry Harold, *Manager*
Larry Wood, *Maintence Staff*
EMP: 51
SALES (corp-wide): 56.5B **Privately Held**
SIC: 5051 Steel
HQ: Coilplus, Inc.
6250 N River Rd Ste 6050
Rosemont IL 60018
847 384-3000

(G-16140)
COUNCIL ON RUR SVC PRGRAMS INC (PA)
201 Robert M Davis Pkwy B (45356-8342)
PHONE..................937 778-5220
Daniel Schwanitz, *Exec Dir*
Matt Boley, *Director*
EMP: 40
SALES: 14.7MM **Privately Held**
WEB: www.corsp.org
SIC: 8399 Community action agency

(G-16141)
COUNCIL ON RUR SVC PRGRAMS INC
Also Called: Beary Land
285 Robert M Davis Pkwy (45356-8342)
PHONE..................937 773-0773
Mark Schlater, *COO*
Shirley Hathaway, *Director*
EMP: 40

SALES (corp-wide): 14.7MM **Privately Held**
WEB: www.corsp.org
SIC: 8399 8351 8322 Community action agency; child day care services; individual & family services
PA: Council On Rural Service Programs, Inc.
201 Robert M Davis Pkwy B
Piqua OH 45356
937 778-5220

(G-16142)
CRANE PUMPS & SYSTEMS INC
Also Called: Pacific Valve
420 3rd St (45356-3918)
PHONE..................937 773-2442
Peter Kendall, *Vice Pres*
Joe Jochim, *VP Opers*
Tim Grierson, *Finance Dir*
Richard Perez, *Finance Dir*
Nancy Scanlon, *Human Res Dir*
EMP: 280
SALES (corp-wide): 2.7B **Publicly Held**
SIC: 5085 3494 Valves & fittings; valves & pipe fittings
HQ: Crane Pumps & Systems, Inc.
420 3rd St
Piqua OH 45356
937 773-2442

(G-16143)
EXPERT TECHNICAL CONSULTANTS
1268 E Ash St (45356-4160)
PHONE..................614 430-9113
Ana L Keck, *President*
Linda Schwieterman, *Vice Pres*
Pam Miller, *Office Mgr*
EMP: 35
SALES (est): 2.4MM **Privately Held**
WEB: www.etci.net
SIC: 7371 Computer software development

(G-16144)
FIRST ACCEPTANCE CORPORATION
987 E Ash St (45356-4133)
PHONE..................937 778-8888
Shela Schipper, *Principal*
EMP: 31
SALES (corp-wide): 347.5MM **Publicly Held**
SIC: 6411 Insurance agents, brokers & service
PA: First Acceptance Corporation
3813 Green Hills Vlg Dr
Nashville TN 37215
615 844-2800

(G-16145)
GARBRY RIDGE ASSISTED LIVING
1567 Garbry Rd (45356-8238)
PHONE..................937 778-9385
Fax: 937 778-9530
Debbie Adkins, *Exec Dir*
Rhonda McConnaughey, *Director*
EMP: 35
SQ FT: 2,234
SALES (est): 1.2MM **Privately Held**
WEB: www.garbryridge.com
SIC: 8052 Intermediate care facilities

(G-16146)
HARTZELL HARDWOODS INC (PA)
1025 S Roosevelt Ave (45356-3713)
P.O. Box 919 (45356-0919)
PHONE..................937 773-7054
Fax: 937 773-7436
Jeffery Bannister, *CEO*
James Robert Hartzell, *Ch of Bd*
Kelly Hostetter, *President*
Josiah McKamey, *Sales Associate*
Jane Osborn, *Admin Sec*
▼ EMP: 90
SQ FT: 275,000
SALES (est): 30.1MM **Privately Held**
WEB: www.hartzellhardwoods.com
SIC: 5031 2421 2426 Lumber: rough, dressed & finished; sawmills & planing mills, general; hardwood dimension & flooring mills

Piqua - Miami County (G-16147)

(G-16147)
HCF OF PIQUA INC
Also Called: Piqua Manor
1840 W High St (45356-9399)
PHONE.................937 773-0040
Fax: 937 773-4836
James Unberferth, *President*
Cassie Vanoss, *Manager*
Donald Luna, *Director*
Garth Hoellrich, *Phys Thrpy Dir*
EMP: 99
SQ FT: 41,920
SALES (est): 3.5MM
SALES (corp-wide): 154.8MM **Privately Held**
SIC: 8051 Convalescent home with continuous nursing care
PA: Hcf Management, Inc.
1100 Shawnee Rd
Lima OH 45805
419 999-2010

(G-16148)
HEALTH CARE RTREMENT CORP AMER
Also Called: Heartland of Piqua
275 Kienle Dr (45356-4119)
PHONE.................937 773-9346
Stacie Atherton, *Branch Mgr*
Scott Swabb, *Director*
Angela Shuff, *Executive*
EMP: 92
SQ FT: 27,568
SALES (corp-wide): 3.6B **Publicly Held**
WEB: www.hrc-manorcare.com
SIC: 8051 Convalescent home with continuous nursing care
HQ: Health Care And Retirement Corporation Of America
333 N Summit St Ste 103
Toledo OH 43604
419 252-5500

(G-16149)
HOME AND FARM INSURANCE CO
Also Called: Buckeye Insurance
1 Heritage Pl (45356-4148)
PHONE.................937 778-5000
Doug Haynes, *President*
Steve Moeller, *Assoc VP*
Lisa Wesner, *Human Resources*
Brian Minnich, *Information Mgr*
Shelley Johnson, *Executive Asst*
EMP: 60 EST: 1985
SQ FT: 500
SALES (est): 11.1MM
SALES (corp-wide): 30.6MM **Privately Held**
WEB: www.buckeye-ins.com
SIC: 6411 6331 Insurance agents; fire, marine & casualty insurance
PA: The Buckeye State Mutual Insurance Company
1 Heritage Pl
Piqua OH 45356
937 778-5000

(G-16150)
INDUSTRY PRODUCTS CO (PA)
500 W Statler Rd (45356-8281)
PHONE.................937 778-0585
Fax: 937 778-9613
Linda Cleveland, *President*
David Brown, *Vice Pres*
Tom Craft, *Mfg Dir*
Gerry Hamby, *Plant Mgr*
Todd Guenther, *Project Mgr*
▲ EMP: 366 EST: 1966
SQ FT: 335,000
SALES: 76MM **Privately Held**
WEB: www.industryproductsco.com
SIC: 7692 3053 3714 3544 Automotive welding; gaskets, all materials; motor vehicle parts & accessories; motor vehicle body components & frame; special dies, tools, jigs & fixtures; unsupported plastics film & sheet

(G-16151)
M&C HOTEL INTERESTS INC
Also Called: Comfort Inn
987 E Ash St Ste 171 (45356-4198)
PHONE.................937 778-8100
Fax: 937 778-9573
Jessalyn Younce, *General Mgr*
Larry Chester, *Manager*
EMP: 30 **Privately Held**
WEB: www.richfield.com
SIC: 7011 Hotels & motels
HQ: M&C Hotel Interests, Inc.
6560 Greenwood Plaza Blvd # 300
Greenwood Village CO 80111

(G-16152)
MIAMI CO YMCA CHILD CARE
325 W Ash St (45356-2203)
PHONE.................937 778-5241
James McMaken, *Exec Dir*
EMP: 30
SALES (est): 105.2K **Privately Held**
SIC: 8641 Youth organizations

(G-16153)
MIAMI VALLEY STEEL SERVICE INC
201 Fox Dr (45356-9265)
PHONE.................937 773-7127
Fax: 937 773-1615
Louis Moran, *CEO*
Guy House, *Vice Pres*
Chip Lamoreaux, *Plant Mgr*
Brian Layne, *Maint Mgr*
Joe Prenger, *Purch Dir*
▼ EMP: 140
SQ FT: 320,000
SALES (est): 149.7MM **Privately Held**
SIC: 5051 Steel

(G-16154)
MURRAY WLLS WNDELN RBNSON CPAS (PA)
Also Called: Murray Wells Wendeln & Robinsn
326 N Wayne St (45356-2230)
P.O. Box 613 (45356-0613)
PHONE.................937 773-6373
Fax: 937 773-8224
Tony Wendeln, *CEO*
Samuel Robinson, *President*
Douglas Murray, *Trustee*
Karen Benanzer, *Bd of Directors*
EMP: 26
SQ FT: 5,000
SALES (est): 2.7MM **Privately Held**
SIC: 8721 Certified public accountant

(G-16155)
PIONEER RURAL ELECTRIC COOP (PA)
344 W Us Route 36 (45356-9255)
PHONE.................800 762-0997
Fax: 937 773-7549
Ronald Salyer, *President*
Matthew Orient, *Engineer*
Aaron Stalling, *CFO*
Debbie Ridder,
EMP: 62 EST: 1936
SQ FT: 32,000
SALES: 67.9MM **Privately Held**
WEB: www.pioneerec.com
SIC: 4911 Distribution, electric power

(G-16156)
PIQUA COUNTRY CLUB HOLDING CO
Also Called: PIQUA COUNTRY CLUB POOL
9812 Country Club Rd (45356-9594)
PHONE.................937 773-7744
Fax: 937 773-1010
Don Goettpmoeller, *Treasurer*
Don Grieshop, *Treasurer*
Sharon Asbury, *Office Mgr*
Leanne Smith, *Relations*
EMP: 40
SQ FT: 9,000
SALES: 1.4MM **Privately Held**
SIC: 7997 5812 7911 Country club, membership; golf club, membership; swimming club, membership; eating places; dance hall or ballroom operation

(G-16157)
PIQUA INDUSTRIAL CUT & SEW
727 E Ash St (45356-2411)
P.O. Box 1657 (45356-4657)
PHONE.................937 773-7397
Fax: 937 773-1109
Yvonne Mc Greevy, *President*
EMP: 35
SQ FT: 4,800
SALES: 750K **Privately Held**
SIC: 7389 Sewing contractor

(G-16158)
PIQUA MATERIALS INC
Also Called: Piqua Mineral Division
1750 W Statler Rd (45356-9264)
PHONE.................937 773-0791
Fax: 937 773-4824
Brent Phillips, *Safety Mgr*
John Harris, *Branch Mgr*
EMP: 30
SQ FT: 16,808
SALES (corp-wide): 16.3MM **Privately Held**
SIC: 1422 3274 Limestones, ground; lime
PA: Piqua Materials Inc
11641 Mosteller Rd Ste 1
Cincinnati OH 45241
513 771-0820

(G-16159)
PIQUA STEEL CO
Also Called: PSC Crane & Rigging
4243 W Us Route 36 (45356-9334)
PHONE.................937 773-3632
Fax: 937 778-8136
James R Sever, *President*
Earl F Sever III, *Chairman*
Randy Sever, *Exec VP*
Brian Fogle, *Project Mgr*
James Weston, *Project Mgr*
EMP: 75 EST: 1933
SQ FT: 30,000
SALES: 31.9MM **Privately Held**
WEB: www.piquasteel.com
SIC: 4225 7353 1796 7359 General warehousing; cranes & aerial lift equipment, rental or leasing; machine moving & rigging; equipment rental & leasing

(G-16160)
PIQUA TRANSFER & STORAGE CO
9782 Looney Rd (45356-2587)
P.O. Box 823 (45356-0823)
PHONE.................937 773-3743
Fax: 937 773-8769
John D Laughman, *President*
Damita Hoblit, *Corp Secy*
H L Lane, *Vice Pres*
John Basye, *Safety Mgr*
Steve Nash, *Accounting Mgr*
EMP: 86 EST: 1904
SQ FT: 24,000
SALES (est): 11.8MM **Privately Held**
SIC: 4213 4214 Contract haulers; local trucking with storage

(G-16161)
PLASTIC RECYCLING TECH INC (PA)
Also Called: Prt
9054 N County Road 25a (45356-7522)
PHONE.................937 615-9286
Fax: 937 615-9256
Matthew Kreigel, *President*
Stephen Larger, *Vice Pres*
Brian E Voisard, *Plant Mgr*
Mark Miller, *Treasurer*
Lorri Anster, *Manager*
EMP: 30
SALES (est): 45.2MM **Privately Held**
SIC: 4953 Recycling, waste materials

(G-16162)
PRO CARE JANITOR SUPPLY
317 N Main St (45356-2315)
P.O. Box 1748 (45356-4748)
PHONE.................937 778-2275
Fax: 937 778-2275
Mark Miller, *Owner*
Connie Miller, *Manager*
EMP: 50
SQ FT: 1,800
SALES (est): 1.1MM **Privately Held**
SIC: 7349 Janitorial service, contract basis

(G-16163)
R C HEMM GLASS SHOPS INC (PA)
514 S Main St (45356-3942)
PHONE.................937 773-5591
Fax: 937 773-6054
Jeff Hemm, *President*
Michelle Baker, *Project Mgr*
Casey Brooks, *Project Mgr*
Josh Hesse, *Project Mgr*
Audrey Morse, *Project Mgr*
EMP: 48 EST: 1948
SQ FT: 20,000
SALES (est): 18.2MM **Privately Held**
WEB: www.hemmglass.com
SIC: 1793 5231 Glass & glazing work; glass

(G-16164)
R K HYDRO-VAC INC (PA)
322 Wyndham Way (45356-9267)
P.O. Box 915 (45356-0915)
PHONE.................937 773-8600
Fax: 937 773-8676
Rusty D Kimmel, *Principal*
Tricia Alsip, *Vice Pres*
Randy Kimmel, *Vice Pres*
Don Borchers, *VP Opers*
EMP: 50
SALES (est): 10.9MM **Privately Held**
SIC: 7349 Cleaning service, industrial or commercial

(G-16165)
S & H RISNER INC
Also Called: Hr Associates Personnel Svc
314 N Wayne St (45356-2230)
PHONE.................937 778-8563
Fax: 937 778-8569
Heather Risner, *CEO*
Michelle Horner, *Office Mgr*
EMP: 63
SALES (est): 3.2MM **Privately Held**
SIC: 7361 Executive placement

(G-16166)
SPECTRUM MGT HOLDG CO LLC
Time Warner
614 N Main St (45356-2347)
PHONE.................937 306-6082
Charlotte Small,
EMP: 83
SQ FT: 3,608
SALES (corp-wide): 41.5B **Publicly Held**
SIC: 4841 Cable television services
HQ: Spectrum Management Holding Company, Llc
400 Atlantic St
Stamford CT 06901
203 905-7801

(G-16167)
SUNRISE COOPERATIVE INC
215 Looney Rd (45356-4147)
P.O. Box 870, Fremont (43420-0870)
PHONE.................937 575-6780
Erin Cole, *Consultant*
EMP: 450
SALES (corp-wide): 56.3MM **Privately Held**
SIC: 5153 5191 Grains; farm supplies
PA: Sunrise Cooperative, Inc.
2025 W State St Ste A
Fremont OH 43420
419 332-6468

(G-16168)
TK HOLDINGS INC
Also Called: T K Holdings
1401 Innovation Pkwy (45356-7524)
PHONE.................937 778-9713
Monica Baughn, *Plant Mgr*
Monica Bauthn, *Manager*
EMP: 25 **Privately Held**
SIC: 2399 5013 Seat belts, automobile & aircraft; motor vehicle supplies & new parts
HQ: Tk Holdings Inc.
4611 Wiseman Blvd
San Antonio TX 78251
210 509-0762

(G-16169)
TRUPOINTE COOPERATIVE INC
215 Looney Rd (45356-4147)
P.O. Box 870 (45356)
PHONE.................937 575-6780
John Waymire, *CEO*
Larry Hammond, *President*
Jeff Goodbar, *Business Mgr*
Gordon Wallace, *COO*
Gailyn Thomsen, *VP Admin*

EMP: 450
SALES (est): 8.6MM **Privately Held**
SIC: 5153 5191 Grains; farm supplies

(G-16170)
UNITED PARCEL SERVICE INC OH
Also Called: UPS
8460 Industry Park Dr (45356-8538)
PHONE.....................937 773-4762
Paul Francis, *Branch Mgr*
EMP: 110
SALES (corp-wide): 65.8B **Publicly Held**
WEB: www.upsscs.com
SIC: 4215 Parcel delivery, vehicular
HQ: United Parcel Service, Inc. (Oh)
55 Glenlake Pkwy
Atlanta GA 30328
404 828-6000

(G-16171)
UNITY NATIONAL BANK (HQ)
Also Called: Third Savings
215 N Wayne St (45356-2227)
P.O. Box 913 (45356-0913)
PHONE.....................937 773-0752
Fax: 937 773-1059
Scott Rasor, *President*
Scott Gabriel, *President*
Steve Vallo, *Manager*
EMP: 42 EST: 1884
SQ FT: 6,000
SALES (est): 982.3K
SALES (corp-wide): 367MM **Publicly Held**
WEB: www.unitynationalbk.com
SIC: 6035 Federal savings & loan associations
PA: Park National Corporation
50 N 3rd St
Newark OH 43055
740 349-8451

(G-16172)
UPPER VALLEY FAMILY CARE
200 Kienle Dr (45356-4120)
PHONE.....................937 339-5355
Fax: 937 773-9810
James S Burkhardt Do, *Principal*
Beth Burroughs, *Project Mgr*
Joni Walker, *Admin Asst*
EMP: 45
SALES (est): 1.2MM **Privately Held**
WEB: www.uvfc.com
SIC: 8011 General & family practice, physician/surgeon

(G-16173)
USI CABLE CORP
102 Fox Dr (45356-9269)
P.O. Box 820 (45356-0820)
PHONE.....................937 606-2636
Carol Gaston, *President*
John Gaston, *Manager*
EMP: 30
SALES (est): 2.3MM **Privately Held**
SIC: 4841 Cable television services

(G-16174)
VALLEY REGIONAL SURGERY CENTER
Also Called: Sydney ASC
283 Looney Rd (45356-4147)
P.O. Box 914 (45356-0914)
PHONE.....................877 858-5029
Fax: 937 778-3853
Randall Welsh, *Partner*
Robert MoDcvitt, *Partner*
Anita Couchot, *Administration*
EMP: 25
SQ FT: 6,700
SALES (est): 4.6MM **Privately Held**
SIC: 8011 Ambulatory surgical center

(G-16175)
WEST OHIO CONFERENCE OF
Also Called: Drop In Babysitting Service
415 W Greene St (45356-2113)
PHONE.....................937 773-5313
Fax: 937 773-5397
Debbie Fraser, *Manager*
Kent Amey, *Director*
Zane Baumann, *Director*
Jeff Jackson, *Director*
EMP: 30

SALES (corp-wide): 5.6MM **Privately Held**
WEB: www.cliftonumc.com
SIC: 8661 8351 Methodist Church; child day care services
PA: The West Ohio Conference Of United Methodist Church
32 Wesley Blvd
Worthington OH 43085
614 844-6200

(G-16176)
WESTERN & SOUTHERN LF INSUR CO
1255 E Ash St Ste 2 (45356-4141)
PHONE.....................937 773-5303
Fax: 937 773-5475
Terry Bosworth, *District Mgr*
EMP: 30 **Privately Held**
SIC: 6411 Life insurance agents
HQ: The Western & Southern Life Insurance Company
400 Broadway St
Cincinnati OH 45202
513 629-1800

(G-16177)
WILLIAMS BROS ROOFG & SIDING
3600 Valley Pike (45356)
PHONE.....................937 434-3838
Greg Oldiges, *Partner*
EMP: 25
SALES (est): 866.7K **Privately Held**
SIC: 1761 Roofing, siding & sheet metal work

Plain City
Madison County

(G-16178)
A-1 ADVANCED PLUMBING INC
8299 Memorial Dr (43064-8623)
PHONE.....................614 873-0548
Fax: 614 873-0551
Wesley Zimmer, *President*
Eearl Sagraves, *Exec VP*
EMP: 30
SQ FT: 4,500
SALES (est): 3.4MM **Privately Held**
SIC: 1711 Plumbing contractors

(G-16179)
A2Z FIELD SERVICES LLC
7450 Industrial Pkwy # 105 (43064-8789)
P.O. Box 3215, Dublin (43016-0100)
PHONE.....................614 873-0211
William McMullen III, *CEO*
Amie Sparks, *Senior VP*
Paige Pellegrino, *QA Dir*
Louis Burwell, *Controller*
Justin Ault, *Accountant*
EMP: 130
SQ FT: 6,000
SALES: 23.5MM **Privately Held**
SIC: 7389 Building inspection service

(G-16180)
ABBRUZZESE BROTHERS INC (PA)
7775 Smith Calhoun Rd (43064-9192)
P.O. Box 215, Hilliard (43026-0215)
PHONE.....................614 873-1550
Fax: 614 873-1370
Jim Abbruzzese, *President*
John Abbruzzese, *Vice Pres*
Brian Roudabush, *Production*
Joe Abbruzzese, *CFO*
EMP: 31
SQ FT: 7,200
SALES (est): 3.8MM **Privately Held**
WEB: www.abbzinc.com
SIC: 0782 Lawn care services; landscape contractors

(G-16181)
AMERICAN COATINGS CORPORATION
Also Called: Americoat
7510 Montgomery Rd (43064-8611)
PHONE.....................614 335-1000
Philip Freedman, *President*

Erin Friedman, *Human Resources*
EMP: 30
SALES (est): 3.7MM **Privately Held**
WEB: www.americoat.net
SIC: 1771 Driveway contractor

(G-16182)
ARCHITECTURAL SYSTEMS INC
Also Called: A S I
8633 Memorial Dr (43064-8608)
PHONE.....................614 873-2057
Fax: 614 873-2078
David Phillips, *President*
Becky Row, *Office Mgr*
EMP: 55
SQ FT: 6,000
SALES (est): 9.2MM **Privately Held**
SIC: 1761 Roofing contractor

(G-16183)
BENCHMARK LANDSCAPE CNSTR INC
9600 Industrial Pkwy (43064-9426)
PHONE.....................614 873-8080
Fax: 614 873-8060
Roy Ed Veley, *President*
Mark Chamberlain, *Vice Pres*
Matt Hecht, *Mng Member*
Doug Heindel, *Mng Member*
Devon Stanley, *Mng Member*
EMP: 38
SQ FT: 1,900
SALES (est): 3.8MM **Privately Held**
WEB: www.benchmarkohio.com
SIC: 0782 Landscape contractors

(G-16184)
BINDERY & SPC PRESSWORKS INC
351 W Bigelow Ave (43064-1152)
PHONE.....................614 873-4623
Fax: 614 873-4625
Dick Izzard, *President*
Betty Izzard, *Vice Pres*
Doug Izzard, *Vice Pres*
Mark Izzard, *Vice Pres*
Rodney Owens, *Manager*
EMP: 74
SQ FT: 42,000
SALES (est): 18.1MM **Privately Held**
SIC: 2791 2759 2752 2789 Typesetting; commercial printing; commercial printing, offset; bookbinding & related work; mailing service

(G-16185)
BULK TRANSIT CORPORATION (PA)
7177 Indl Pkwy (43064)
PHONE.....................614 873-4632
Fax: 614 873-3393
Ronald De Wolf, *President*
Paul F Beery, *Principal*
John Hornbeck, *Safety Dir*
Danny Cottrell, *Terminal Mgr*
Laura Boyles, *Office Mgr*
EMP: 40
SQ FT: 5,000
SALES (est): 26.7MM **Privately Held**
WEB: www.bulktransit.com
SIC: 4213 Contract haulers

(G-16186)
CSI COMPLETE INC
8080 Corporate Blvd (43064-9220)
PHONE.....................800 343-0641
Doug Webb, *CEO*
EMP: 50
SALES (est): 802.8K **Privately Held**
SIC: 7374 Data processing service
PA: Douglas Webb & Associates, Inc
8080 Corporate Blvd
Plain City OH 43064

(G-16187)
DKMP CONSULTING INC
8000 Corporate Blvd (43064-9220)
PHONE.....................614 733-0979
Fax: 614 733-0639
Mark Patel, *President*
Matthew S Patel, *President*
Daniel Koczur, *Vice Pres*
Jeff Lanthron, *Purchasing*
EMP: 105

SQ FT: 33,000
SALES: 18MM **Privately Held**
WEB: www.pkcontrols.com
SIC: 8711 Engineering services
HQ: Ohio Transmission Corporation
1900 Jetway Blvd
Columbus OH 43219
614 342-6247

(G-16188)
DOUGLAS WEBB & ASSOCIATES (PA)
Also Called: Csi Complete
8080 Corporate Blvd (43064-9220)
PHONE.....................614 873-9830
Fax: 614 873-9834
Doug Webb, *CEO*
John Webb, *President*
Eric Keller, *VP Sales*
Jake Boyd, *Sales Mgr*
Mary Howard, *Cust Mgr*
EMP: 60
SQ FT: 6,000
SALES (est): 4.9MM **Privately Held**
WEB: www.csicomplete.com
SIC: 8732 7389 Market analysis or research; telemarketing services

(G-16189)
DUTCHMAN HOSPITALITY GROUP INC
Also Called: Der Dutchman's Restaurant
445 S Jefferson Ave (43064-1166)
PHONE.....................614 873-3414
Fax: 740 873-3478
Dan Yoder, *Branch Mgr*
Cindy Miller, *Executive*
EMP: 200
SALES (corp-wide): 47.5MM **Privately Held**
SIC: 5812 5947 5149 Italian restaurant; gift shop; bakery products
PA: Dutchman Hospitality Group, Inc.
4985 State Rte 515
Walnut Creek OH 44687
330 893-2926

(G-16190)
ENVIRONMENTAL MGT SVCS INC (PA)
8220 Industrial Pkwy (43064-9371)
P.O. Box 175, Dublin (43017-0175)
PHONE.....................614 876-9988
Mark Wehinger, *President*
Gregory C Farell, *Principal*
Brandon Gepper, *Project Mgr*
Tanya Adams, *Controller*
Lynn Dulgamore, *Manager*
EMP: 40
SALES (est): 9.8MM **Privately Held**
SIC: 0782 Landscape contractors

(G-16191)
EVOLUTION AG LLC
Also Called: Kubota Authorized Dealer
13275 Us Highway 42 N (43064-8748)
PHONE.....................740 363-1341
James R Henkel, *Ch of Bd*
Thomas M Hill, *President*
Nick Crist, *Parts Mgr*
Zach Dennis, *Parts Mgr*
Rob Zeid, *CFO*
EMP: 36
SALES: 24.5MM **Privately Held**
SIC: 5083 Farm implements

(G-16192)
FAIRFIELD HOMES INC
Also Called: Madison Square Apartments
445 Fairfield Dr Ofc (43064-1274)
PHONE.....................614 873-3533
Leonard F Gorsuch, *Branch Mgr*
EMP: 200
SALES (corp-wide): 20.4MM **Privately Held**
WEB: www.gorsuch-homes.com
SIC: 6513 1522 6531 1542 Apartment building operators; residential construction; real estate agents & managers; nonresidential construction; nonresidential building operators
PA: Fairfield Homes Inc.
603 W Wheeling St
Lancaster OH 43130
740 653-3583

Plain City - Madison County (G-16193)

(G-16193)
HERITAGE EQUIPMENT COMPANY
9000 Heritage Dr (43064-8744)
PHONE............................614 873-3941
Fax: 614 873-3549
Louis Cascelli, *CEO*
Eric J Zwirner, *President*
Carl Hubbard, *Vice Pres*
Don Behan, *CFO*
Don Behna, *Financial Exec*
▲ **EMP:** 30 **EST:** 1982
SQ FT: 10,000
SALES (est): 18.6MM **Privately Held**
WEB: www.heritage-equipment.com
SIC: 5084 Dairy products manufacturing machinery; food product manufacturing machinery

(G-16194)
INTEGRITY GYMNSTICS CHRLEADING
8185 Business Way (43064-9216)
PHONE............................614 733-0818
Les Hood, *Mng Member*
John Brooks, *Manager*
Randy Cline, *Manager*
Anna Loescher, *Manager*
Karen Isabella, *Director*
EMP: 34
SALES (est): 1.1MM **Privately Held**
SIC: 7999 Instruction schools, camps & services; gymnastic instruction, non-membership

(G-16195)
K AMALIA ENTERPRISES INC
Also Called: Mjr Sales
8025 Corporate Blvd (43064-9208)
PHONE............................614 733-3800
Jeff Bradshaw, *President*
Mark Laufersweiler, *Vice Pres*
Michael Cacchio, *CFO*
▲ **EMP:** 90
SQ FT: 53,000
SALES (est): 8MM **Privately Held**
WEB: www.kamalia.com
SIC: 5699 5136 Designers, apparel; men's & boys' clothing

(G-16196)
LITHKO CONTRACTING LLC
8065 Corporate Blvd (43064-9208)
PHONE............................614 733-0300
Fax: 614 733-0301
Randy Doss, *Manager*
EMP: 125
SALES (corp-wide): 177.7MM **Privately Held**
SIC: 1771 Foundation & footing contractor
PA: Lithko Contracting, Llc
2958 Crescentville Rd
West Chester OH 45069
513 564-2000

(G-16197)
MADE FROM SCRATCH INC (PA)
Also Called: Celebrations
7500 Montgomery Rd (43064-8611)
PHONE............................614 873-3344
Fax: 740 873-1965
Larry G Clark, *President*
Bill Moler, *CFO*
Lisa Dubley, *Sales Executive*
EMP: 31
SQ FT: 12,000
SALES (est): 3.9MM **Privately Held**
WEB: www.made-from-scratch.com
SIC: 7359 5812 5149 5992 Party supplies rental services; caterers; bakery products; florists

(G-16198)
MAZA INC
7635 Commerce Pl (43064-9223)
PHONE............................614 760-0003
Fax: 614 873-8173
Chris Watson, *President*
Bryon Warner, *Opers Mgr*
Barb Muncie, *Financial Exec*
Brooke Steinke, *Accounts Mgr*
▲ **EMP:** 50
SQ FT: 15,400

SALES (est): 8.1MM
SALES (corp-wide): 68.6B **Publicly Held**
WEB: www.mgworks.com
SIC: 5211 5999 5032 Masonry materials & supplies; monuments & tombstones; marble building stone
PA: Lowe's Companies, Inc.
1000 Lowes Blvd
Mooresville NC 28117
704 758-1000

(G-16199)
MEDIA SOURCE INC (PA)
7858 Industrial Pkwy (43064-9468)
PHONE............................614 873-7635
Steve Zales, *CEO*
Victor F Ganzi, *Ch of Bd*
Randall J Asmo, *President*
Ian Singer, *Publisher*
Kathy Ishizuka, *Editor*
EMP: 60
SQ FT: 4,800
SALES (est): 31.6MM **Privately Held**
WEB: www.juniorlibraryguild.com
SIC: 5192 Books

(G-16200)
MJ DESIGN ASSOCIATES INC
8463 Estates Ct (43064-8015)
PHONE............................614 873-7333
Fax: 614 760-9883
Joel John, *President*
Molly John, *Vice Pres*
Liz Foutt, *Executive Asst*
EMP: 25
SALES (est): 2.2MM **Privately Held**
WEB: www.mjdesignassociates.com
SIC: 0782 Landscape contractors

(G-16201)
MOBILE ANALYTICAL SERVICES
8426 Industrial Pkwy (43064-9364)
PHONE............................614 873-1710
Dwane Hartzler, *Manager*
EMP: 40
SALES (corp-wide): 5.3MM **Privately Held**
WEB: www.masilabs.com
SIC: 8734 Water testing laboratory
PA: Mobile Analytical Services Inc
7940 Memorial Dr
Plain City OH 43064
614 873-4654

(G-16202)
NO CAGES HARLEY-DAVIDSON
7610 Commerce Pl (43064-9222)
PHONE............................614 764-2453
Lynn Loomis, *Partner*
EMP: 25
SALES (est): 178.8K **Privately Held**
SIC: 7699 Motorcycle repair service

(G-16203)
PAINTING COMPANY
6969 Industrial Pkwy (43064-8799)
PHONE............................614 873-1334
Fax: 614 873-1809
David Asman, *Vice Pres*
Terry Asman, *Vice Pres*
Sandra Contorno-Milne, *Manager*
Jeffery D Sammons, *Incorporator*
Shelly Ambose, *Administration*
EMP: 105
SALES: 10MM **Privately Held**
WEB: www.thepaintingcompany.com
SIC: 1721 Commercial painting; industrial painting; wallcovering contractors

(G-16204)
SCHEIDERER TRANSPORT INC
8520 State Route 161 E (43064-9101)
PHONE............................614 873-5103
Fax: 614 873-5517
Roger C Scheiderer, *President*
EMP: 55
SQ FT: 10,000
SALES: 6.5MM **Privately Held**
SIC: 4213 Contract haulers

(G-16205)
SHALOM MINISTRIES INTL INC
Also Called: Discovering The Jewish Jesus
9018 Heritage Dr (43064-9493)
P.O. Box 777, Blissfield MI (49228-0077)
PHONE............................614 504-6052

Kirt A Schneider, *President*
Cynthia Schneider, *Human Resources*
EMP: 35
SALES: 7MM **Privately Held**
SIC: 7812 Motion picture & video production

(G-16206)
SHARRON GROUP INC (PA)
Also Called: Buckeye Western Star
7605 Commerce Pl (43064-9223)
PHONE............................614 873-5856
Fax: 614 873-6826
Thomas A Ewers, *President*
Gil Sears, *Controller*
Cody Martindale, *Sales Staff*
Linda Ewers, *Manager*
Amanda Harris, *Admin Asst*
EMP: 25
SALES (est): 9.6MM **Privately Held**
WEB: www.buckeyewesternstar.com
SIC: 5012 7699 Commercial vehicles; industrial truck repair

(G-16207)
STALEY INC
8040 Corporate Blvd (43064-9220)
PHONE............................614 552-2333
Fax: 614 552-2349
Sean Hall, *Principal*
Jim Hlywiak, *Project Mgr*
EMP: 30
SALES (corp-wide): 84.2MM **Privately Held**
WEB: www.staleyinc.com
SIC: 1731 Computer installation
PA: Staley, Inc.
8101 Fourche Rd
Little Rock AR 72209
501 565-3006

(G-16208)
STOVER EXCAVATING INC
7500 Industrial Pkwy (43064-9005)
PHONE............................614 873-5865
Anthony Stover, *President*
Pat Kalinkiewicz, *Project Mgr*
Chad Turner, *Project Mgr*
Karen Swartz, *Office Mgr*
Vickie Watson, *Office Mgr*
EMP: 28 **EST:** 2006
SALES (est): 4MM **Privately Held**
SIC: 1794 Excavation & grading, building construction

(G-16209)
TOMITA USA INC (HQ)
7801 Corp Blvd Unit G (43064)
PHONE............................614 873-6509
Kaoru Tomita, *President*
Masahiko Yatsuyanagi, *Corp Secy*
Sayaka Suzuki, *Accounts Mgr*
Brinda Raymond, *Manager*
▲ **EMP:** 50
SQ FT: 6,000
SALES (est): 14.5MM
SALES (corp-wide): 192.8MM **Privately Held**
SIC: 5084 Pneumatic tools & equipment
PA: Tomita Co., Ltd.
1-18-16, Omorinaka
Ota-Ku TKY 143-0
337 651-219

(G-16210)
TRADESMEN GROUP INC
8465 Rausch Dr (43064-8064)
PHONE............................614 799-0889
Fax: 614 799-1690
Melissa West, *President*
Chris Blike, *Vice Pres*
Jack Graw, *Sales Staff*
Judy Gregory, *Manager*
Karen Suvak, *Manager*
EMP: 40
SQ FT: 12,000
SALES: 4MM **Privately Held**
WEB: www.tradesmengroup.com
SIC: 1541 Renovation, remodeling & repairs: industrial buildings

(G-16211)
VELOCYS INC
7950 Corporate Blvd (43064-9230)
PHONE............................614 733-3300
Fax: 614 733-3301

David Pummell, *CEO*
Jeff McDaniel, *General Mgr*
Laura Silva, *General Mgr*
Dr Paul F Schubert, *COO*
Don Kirkham, *Facilities Mgr*
EMP: 60
SQ FT: 26,800
SALES (est): 10.3MM
SALES (corp-wide): 1.7MM **Privately Held**
WEB: www.velocys.com
SIC: 8731 3559 Commercial physical research; refinery, chemical processing & similar machinery
PA: Velocys Plc
115e-115h Olympic Avenue
Abingdon OXON OX14

(G-16212)
WRIGHT NUTRITION INC
8000 Memorial Dr (43064-9007)
PHONE............................614 873-0418
Michael Halls, *Branch Mgr*
EMP: 30
SALES (est): 999.2K
SALES (corp-wide): 2.4MM **Privately Held**
SIC: 8099 Nutrition services
PA: Wright Nutrition Inc
6428 Airport Rd
Crowley LA 70526
614 886-8075

Pleasant City
Guernsey County

(G-16213)
TIMOTHY SINFIELD
54962 Marietta Rd (43772-9601)
PHONE............................740 685-3684
Timothy Sinfield, *Director*
EMP: 47
SALES (est): 1MM **Privately Held**
SIC: 1389 Oil & gas field services

Pleasant Plain
Warren County

(G-16214)
ENDEAVOR CONSTRUCTION LTD
6801 Long Spurling Rd (45162-9742)
PHONE............................513 469-1900
David Beiersdorfer, *President*
Valerie Webster, *Vice Pres*
Lee Doratey, *Accountant*
EMP: 50
SQ FT: 3,000
SALES (est): 5.3MM **Privately Held**
SIC: 1522 1521 Residential construction; single-family housing construction

(G-16215)
MID-WESTERN CHILDRENS HOME
Also Called: Village Christian Schools
4585 Long Spurling Rd (45162-9790)
P.O. Box 48 (45162-0048)
PHONE............................513 877-2141
Fax: 513 877-2015
James Frampton, *President*
Cotton Blakely, *Vice Pres*
Ron Hartman, *Treasurer*
Sarah Mitsui, *Case Mgr*
Barry Boverie, *Administration*
EMP: 38
SQ FT: 68,283
SALES: 1.7MM **Privately Held**
WEB: www.village-christian.com
SIC: 8361 Children's home

Plymouth
Huron County

(G-16216)
BESTWAY TRANSPORT CO (PA)
2040 Sandusky St (44865-9412)
PHONE............................419 687-2000

GEOGRAPHIC SECTION
Port Clinton - Ottawa County (G-16241)

Fax: 419 687-2004
Rich M Myers, *President*
Beverly Tuttle, *Corp Secy*
EMP: 30
SQ FT: 5,300
SALES (est): 3.2MM **Privately Held**
WEB: www.bestwaytransport.com
SIC: 4213 Trucking, except local

(G-16217)
JOHN F STAMBAUGH & CO
5063 Bevier Rd (44865)
PHONE 419 687-6833
Fax: 419 687-8243
Charles F Hanline, *President*
Foster William, *Sales Executive*
Deborah Hanline, *Admin Sec*
EMP: 35
SQ FT: 1,332
SALES (est): 3.5MM **Privately Held**
SIC: 0161 0134 Onion farm; Irish potatoes

Point Pleasant
Clermont County

(G-16218)
CENTRAL REPAIR SERVICE INC
1606 Locust St (45153-9784)
PHONE 513 943-0500
Garrett Sloane, *President*
EMP: 25 **EST:** 1997
SALES (est): 1.2MM **Privately Held**
WEB: www.centralrepairservice.com
SIC: 5963 7629 Appliance sales, house-to-house; clothing sales, house-to-house; electrical household appliance repair

Poland
Mahoning County

(G-16219)
ACME COMPANY
9495 Harvard Blvd (44514-3369)
PHONE 330 758-2313
Carmine Zarlenga Jr, *President*
Adam Lonardo, *Opers Mgr*
Marianne Mancuso, *Manager*
Martin Suarez, *Manager*
John M Newman, *Incorporator*
EMP: 60 **EST:** 1934
SQ FT: 10,000
SALES (est): 13.3MM **Privately Held**
SIC: 5032 3423 1422 3295 Sand, construction; stone, crushed or broken; gravel; hand & edge tools; crushed & broken limestone; minerals, ground or treated

(G-16220)
ALPHA SECURITY LLC
87 W Mckinley Way Ste 1 (44514-1975)
PHONE 330 406-2181
Steven Liller,
EMP: 100
SALES (est): 1MM **Privately Held**
SIC: 7381 Security guard service

(G-16221)
C-Z TRUCKING CO
Also Called: C-Z Trckng Co
9495 Harvard Blvd (44514-3369)
PHONE 330 758-2313
Dan Zarlingo, *President*
Daniel Zarlenga, *Vice Pres*
Carmine Zarlingo Jr, *Treasurer*
Martha Zarlingo, *Admin Sec*
EMP: 65
SQ FT: 1,000
SALES (est): 3MM **Privately Held**
SIC: 4212 Local trucking, without storage

(G-16222)
CHEMICAL BANK
2 S Main St (44514-1914)
PHONE 330 314-1395
EMP: 36
SALES (corp-wide): 776.1MM **Publicly Held**
SIC: 6035 Federal savings & loan associations

HQ: Chemical Bank
333 E Main St
Midland MI 48640
989 631-9200

(G-16223)
COLDWELL BANKER FIRST PLACE RE
1275 Boardman Poland Rd # 1 (44514-3911)
PHONE 330 726-8161
Eric Caspray, *Principal*
Eunice Duff, *Info Tech Mgr*
EMP: 100
SALES (est): 4.1MM **Privately Held**
SIC: 6531 Real estate agent, residential

(G-16224)
HAMPTON WOODS NURSING CTR INC
Also Called: Woodlands At Hampton
1525 E Western Reserve Rd (44514-3254)
PHONE 330 707-1400
Kathy Prasad, *Principal*
EMP: 32
SALES (est): 3.3MM **Privately Held**
SIC: 8051 8059 Convalescent home with continuous nursing care; nursing & personal care

(G-16225)
HANNA HOLDINGS INC
100 W Mckinley Way (44514-1954)
PHONE 330 707-1000
Ann Delacroix, *Manager*
EMP: 70
SALES (corp-wide): 76.4MM **Privately Held**
WEB: www.howardhanna.com
SIC: 6531 Real estate brokers & agents
PA: Hanna Holdings, Inc.
1090 Freeport Rd Ste 1a
Pittsburgh PA 15238
412 967-9000

(G-16226)
SHANE SECURITY SERVICES INC
7217 Pennsylvania Ave (44514-1652)
P.O. Box 5366 (44514-0366)
PHONE 330 757-4001
Fax: 330 757-9143
Conrad Childers, *President*
Geraldine Childers, *President*
EMP: 75 **EST:** 1976
SALES (est): 1.1MM **Privately Held**
SIC: 7381 6211 Protective services, guard; detective services; security brokers & dealers

(G-16227)
SHEPHERD OF THE VALLEY LUTHERA
Also Called: Shepards Meadows
301 W Western Reserve Rd (44514-3527)
PHONE 330 726-7110
Fax: 330 726-2517
Kelly Stansloski, *Director*
EMP: 45
SALES (corp-wide): 31.6MM **Privately Held**
WEB: www.shepherdofthevalley.com
SIC: 6513 Retirement hotel operation
PA: Shepherd Of The Valley Lutheran Retirement Services, Inc.
5525 Silica Rd
Youngstown OH 44515
330 530-4038

(G-16228)
SUNRISE SENIOR LIVING LLC
Also Called: Sunrise of Poland
335 W Mckinley Way (44514-1681)
PHONE 330 707-1313
Fax: 330 707-1411
Nicole Lagata, *Branch Mgr*
EMP: 50
SALES (corp-wide): 4.3B **Publicly Held**
WEB: www.sunrise.com
SIC: 8361 Residential care
HQ: Sunrise Senior Living, Llc
7902 Westpark Dr
Mc Lean VA 22102

(G-16229)
TRUGREEN-CHEM LAWN
8529 South Ave (44514-3699)
P.O. Box 5070 (44514-0070)
PHONE 330 533-2839
Dave Slott, *President*
EMP: 60
SALES (est): 1.6MM **Privately Held**
SIC: 0782 Lawn care services

Polk
Ashland County

(G-16230)
FALLING STAR FARM LTD
Also Called: Dairy Farm
626 State Route 89 (44866-9712)
PHONE 419 945-2651
Fax: 419 945-9841
Karen Meyer, *Owner*
Dewey Meyer, *Principal*
Jess Brushaber, *Marketing Staff*
Tama Taber, *Manager*
EMP: 25
SALES (est): 2.9MM **Privately Held**
WEB: www.meyerhatchery.com
SIC: 0241 Dairy farms

Pomeroy
Meigs County

(G-16231)
COUNTY OF MEIGS
Also Called: Meigs County Emrgncy Med Svcs
Mulburry Heights Stn 11 (45769)
P.O. Box 748 (45769-0748)
PHONE 740 992-6617
Patsy Warner, *Director*
EMP: 35
SQ FT: 2,000 **Privately Held**
WEB: www.meigsdjfs.net
SIC: 4119 Ambulance service
PA: County Of Meigs
100 E 2nd St Rm 201
Pomeroy OH 45769
740 992-5290

(G-16232)
FARMERS BANK & SAVINGS CO INC (PA)
211 W 2nd St (45769-1037)
PHONE 740 992-0088
Fax: 740 992-7583
Paul Reed, *President*
Mark Groves, *COO*
Randall Hays, *Assistant VP*
Edna Weber, *Assistant VP*
Roger Hysell, *Vice Pres*
EMP: 45
SALES (est): 14.7MM **Privately Held**
WEB: www.fbsc.com
SIC: 6022 State trust companies accepting deposits, commercial

(G-16233)
MEIGS COUNTY COUNCIL ON AGING
112 E Memorial Dr Fl 1 (45769-9569)
P.O. Box 722 (45769-0722)
PHONE 740 992-2161
Debbie Jones, *Corp Comm Staff*
Beth Shaver, *Exec Dir*
Diana Coats, *Director*
EMP: 50
SALES (est): 1MM **Privately Held**
WEB: www.meigsseniors.com
SIC: 8322 Old age assistance

(G-16234)
PDK CONSTRUCTION INC
34070 Crew Rd (45769-9715)
P.O. Box 683 (45769-0683)
PHONE 740 992-6451
Fax: 740 992-3074
Phillip R Harrison, *President*
Donald Roush, *Vice Pres*
EMP: 45
SQ FT: 4,080

SALES (est): 7.8MM **Privately Held**
SIC: 1611 Guardrail construction, highways; highway & street sign installation

(G-16235)
SYRACUSE WATER DEPT
2581 3rd St (45769)
P.O. Box 323, Syracuse (45779-0323)
PHONE 740 992-7777
Gordon Winerenner, *President*
Allen Gran, *Bd of Directors*
Dencil Hudson, *Bd of Directors*
EMP: 26
SALES (est): 955.5K **Privately Held**
SIC: 4941 Water supply

(G-16236)
TAYLORS STAFFING
37817 State Route 124 (45769-9302)
PHONE 740 446-3305
Frances Taylor, *Owner*
EMP: 83
SALES (est): 100K **Privately Held**
SIC: 7361 7363 Nurses' registry; help supply services

Port Clinton
Ottawa County

(G-16237)
ANIMAL MGT SVCS OHIO INC
Also Called: African Safari Wildlife Park
267 S Lightner Rd (43452-3851)
PHONE 248 398-6533
Fax: 419 734-1919
Jon Mikosz, *Principal*
EMP: 35 **Privately Held**
WEB: www.animalmanagementservices.com
SIC: 8422 Zoological garden, noncommercial
PA: Animal Management Services Of Ohio Inc.
25600 Woodward Ave Ste 11
Royal Oak MI 48067

(G-16238)
BROWN CONTRACTING & DEV LLC
318 Madison St (43452-1921)
PHONE 419 341-3939
William A Brown, *Principal*
EMP: 27
SALES (est): 2.1MM **Privately Held**
SIC: 1799 Special trade contractors

(G-16239)
CATAWBA-CLEVELAND DEV CORP (PA)
Also Called: Catawba Island Marina
4235 E Beachclub Rd (43452-3009)
PHONE 419 797-4424
Fax: 419 797-2493
James V Stouffer, *CEO*
Event Inquiries, *General Mgr*
Jack Madison, *General Mgr*
Sherri Marshall, *Personnel*
Michael Schenk, *Manager*
EMP: 99
SQ FT: 4,500
SALES (est): 8.1MM **Privately Held**
WEB: www.cicclub.com
SIC: 7997 4493 6519 Country club, membership; marinas; real property lessors

(G-16240)
COMMODORE PRRY INNS SUITES LLC
255 W Lakeshore Dr (43452-9477)
PHONE 419 732-2645
Edward R Fitzgerald,
EMP: 80
SALES (est): 2.2MM **Privately Held**
SIC: 7011 5812 Hotels; eating places

(G-16241)
COMMODORE RESORTS INC
Also Called: Commodore Motel
255 W Lakeshore Dr (43452-9477)
PHONE 419 285-3101
Fax: 419 285-1301
Edward Fitzgerald, *President*
EMP: 30 **EST:** 1967

Port Clinton - Ottawa County (G-16242)

SALES (est): 1.3MM **Privately Held**
WEB: www.commodoreresorts.com
SIC: 7011 Motels

(G-16242)
COVENANT CARE OHIO INC
Also Called: Edgewood Manor Nursing Center
1330 Fulton St (43452-9297)
PHONE..............................419 898-5506
Fax: 419 734-2384
Denise Day, *Branch Mgr*
Bev Norton, *Director*
Thomas Rowe, *Director*
EMP: 94 **Privately Held**
WEB: www.villagegeorgetown.com
SIC: 8051 Convalescent home with continuous nursing care
HQ: Covenant Care Ohio, Inc.
    27071 Aliso Creek Rd # 100
    Aliso Viejo CA 92656
    949 349-1200

(G-16243)
D & G FOCHT CONSTRUCTION CO
2040 E State Rd (43452-2525)
P.O. Box 446 (43452-0446)
PHONE..............................419 732-2412
Fax: 419 732-8315
Douglas Focht, *President*
Joy Taylor, *General Mgr*
Jeanette Focht, *Corp Secy*
EMP: 35 **EST:** 1975
SQ FT: 5,000
SALES (est): 6.8MM **Privately Held**
WEB: www.fochtconstruction.com
SIC: 1541 1542 Industrial buildings, new construction; commercial & office building, new construction; institutional building construction

(G-16244)
DUBLIN COML PROPERTY SVCS INC
127 Madison St (43452-1103)
PHONE..............................419 732-6732
Fax: 419 732-6733
James E McKinney, *President*
Judith McKinney, *Vice Pres*
Gregory A Staib, *Vice Pres*
EMP: 25
SQ FT: 3,000
SALES (est): 1MM **Privately Held**
WEB: www.dublincps.com
SIC: 7349 Janitorial service, contract basis

(G-16245)
GOOFY GOLF II INC
Also Called: Monsoon Lagoon Water Park
1530 S Danbury Rd (43452-3920)
PHONE..............................419 732-6671
Fax: 419 734-1289
John Heilman, *President*
Patricia Heilman, *Corp Secy*
EMP: 65
SQ FT: 5,000
SALES (est): 1.5MM **Privately Held**
WEB: www.monsoonlagoonwaterpark.com
SIC: 7999 Miniature golf course operation

(G-16246)
GUNDLACH SHEET METAL WORKS INC
Also Called: Shilling AC Heating & Plumbing
2439 E Gill Rd (43452-2555)
PHONE..............................419 734-7351
Fax: 419 734-9230
Roger Gundlach, *President*
EMP: 40
SALES (est): 1.6MM
SALES (corp-wide): 18.7MM **Privately Held**
WEB: www.gundlach-hvac.com
SIC: 1711 Warm air heating & air conditioning contractor
PA: Gundlach Sheet Metal Works, Inc.
    910 Columbus Ave
    Sandusky OH 44870
    419 626-4525

(G-16247)
H B MAGRUDER MEMORIAL HOSPITAL
611 Fulton St (43452-2008)
PHONE..............................419 734-4539
EMP: 365
SALES (corp-wide): 48.9MM **Privately Held**
SIC: 8099 Blood related health services
PA: H B Magruder Memorial Hospital
    615 Fulton St
    Port Clinton OH 43452
    419 734-3131

(G-16248)
ISLAND HOUSE INC
Also Called: Island House Inn
102 Madison St (43452-1104)
PHONE..............................419 734-0100
Fax: 419 734-5333
Dave Walerie, *President*
Jim Zibert, *General Mgr*
EMP: 40 **EST:** 1990
SALES (est): 1.4MM **Privately Held**
SIC: 5812 7011 5813 Restaurant, family: chain; cafe; hotels; tavern (drinking places)

(G-16249)
KUEHNE + NAGEL INC
Erie Industrial Park # 2 (43452-9412)
PHONE..............................419 635-4051
Jeffrey Crosby, *Manager*
EMP: 50
SALES (corp-wide): 18.8B **Privately Held**
WEB: www.kuehnenagel.com
SIC: 4225 General warehousing & storage
HQ: Kuehne + Nagel Inc.
    10 Exchange Pl Fl 19
    Jersey City NJ 07302
    201 413-5500

(G-16250)
LODGING INDUSTRY INC
Also Called: Quality Inn
1723 E Perry St (43452-1425)
PHONE..............................419 732-2929
Fax: 419 732-2929
Jacqueline Seibold, *General Mgr*
EMP: 31
SALES (corp-wide): 1.5MM **Privately Held**
SIC: 7011 Hotels & motels
PA: Lodging Industry Inc
    910 Lorain Blvd Ste N
    Elyria OH
    440 323-9820

(G-16251)
PORT CLNTON BPO ELKS LDGE 1718
Also Called: ELKS LODGE # 1718
231 Buckeye Blvd (43452-1421)
PHONE..............................419 734-1900
Fax: 419 732-8155
Heath Krupp, *President*
Luis Catania, *General Mgr*
Jeff Davis, *Manager*
EMP: 25
SALES (est): 228K **Privately Held**
SIC: 8641 Fraternal associations

(G-16252)
REPUBLIC SERVICES INC
530 N Camp Rd (43452-9599)
PHONE..............................419 635-2367
EMP: 34
SALES (corp-wide): 10B **Publicly Held**
SIC: 4953 Refuse collection & disposal services
PA: Republic Services, Inc.
    18500 N Allied Way # 100
    Phoenix AZ 85054
    480 627-2700

(G-16253)
RJ RUNGE COMPANY INC
3539 Ne Catawba Rd (43452-9609)
P.O. Box 977 (43452-0977)
PHONE..............................419 740-5781
Richard J Runge, *CEO*
Amy Runge, *President*
Joe Christ, *Project Mgr*
EMP: 30
SQ FT: 3,000
SALES (est): 4.8MM **Privately Held**
WEB: www.rjrunge.com
SIC: 8741 1731 8748 Construction management; electrical work; business consulting

(G-16254)
RL TRUCKING INC
62 Grande Lake Dr (43452-1450)
P.O. Box 458 (43452-0458)
PHONE..............................419 732-4177
Linda Burke, *CEO*
Roland Burke, *President*
EMP: 145
SQ FT: 1,000
SALES (est): 12.5MM **Privately Held**
SIC: 4213 Trucking, except local

(G-16255)
SHIP SHAPE MARINE INC
410 W Perry St (43452-1048)
P.O. Box 387 (43452-0387)
PHONE..............................419 734-1554
Fax: 419 734-7237
Kevin Leneghan, *President*
Michelle Miller, *Corp Secy*
Brian Holly, *Vice Pres*
Jenna Sandvick, *Manager*
EMP: 25
SALES (est): 2.2MM **Privately Held**
SIC: 4499 4226 Boat cleaning; special warehousing & storage

(G-16256)
SPECTRUM MGT HOLDG CO LLC
Also Called: Time Warner
2853 East Harbor Rd Ste A (43452-2679)
PHONE..............................419 386-0040
Kathryn Warner, *Branch Mgr*
EMP: 83
SALES (corp-wide): 41.5B **Publicly Held**
SIC: 4841 Cable television services
HQ: Spectrum Management Holding Company, Llc
    400 Atlantic St
    Stamford CT 06901
    203 905-7801

(G-16257)
TACK-ANEW INC
Also Called: Brands' Marina
451 W Lakeshore Dr (43452-9478)
PHONE..............................419 734-4212
Fax: 419 734-5854
Dalton Brand, *President*
Darrell A Brand, *President*
Elisabeth Brand, *Editor*
EMP: 26
SQ FT: 15,000
SALES (est): 2MM **Privately Held**
WEB: www.brandsmarina.com
SIC: 4493 3731 Boat yards, storage & incidental repair; shipbuilding & repairing

(G-16258)
VERIZON NORTH INC
1971 E State Rd (43452-2522)
PHONE..............................419 734-5000
John Carlson, *Manager*
EMP: 50
SALES (corp-wide): 126B **Publicly Held**
SIC: 4813 Local telephone communications
HQ: Verizon North Inc
    140 West St
    New York NY 10007
    212 395-1000

(G-16259)
ZINK CALLS
30 Park Dr (43452-2075)
PHONE..............................419 732-6171
Dawn Zink, *Principal*
▲ EMP: 32
SALES (est): 1.3MM **Privately Held**
SIC: 7929 Entertainment service

Port Washington
Tuscarawas County

(G-16260)
BATES METAL PRODUCTS INC
403 E Mn St (43837)
P.O. Box 68 (43837-0068)
PHONE..............................740 498-8371
Fax: 614 498-6315
James A Bates, *President*
Betty Bates, *Corp Secy*
Terry L Bates, *Vice Pres*
Kathy Huston, *Purch Mgr*
Justin Dichler, *Purchasing*
EMP: 60 **EST:** 1956
SQ FT: 106,500
SALES (est): 15.4MM **Privately Held**
WEB: www.batesmetal.com
SIC: 4783 2542 3993 3469 Packing & crating; racks, merchandise display or storage: except wood; signs & advertising specialties; metal stampings; automotive & apparel trimmings

Portage
Wood County

(G-16261)
COUNTY OF WOOD
Also Called: Portage Group Werner Home
351 W Main St (43451-9802)
PHONE..............................419 686-6951
Cathy Miller, *Manager*
EMP: 350 **Privately Held**
WEB: www.woodmrdd.org
SIC: 8059 8052 Home for the mentally retarded, exc. skilled or intermediate; intermediate care facilities
PA: Wood County Ohio
    1 Court House Sq
    Bowling Green OH 43402
    419 354-9100

Portsmouth
Scioto County

(G-16262)
AAA SOUTH CENTRAL OHIO INC
1414 12th St (45662-4206)
PHONE..............................740 354-5614
Robert L Morton, *President*
Micheal Morgan, *President*
EMP: 40
SALES (est): 771.1K **Privately Held**
SIC: 8699 Automobile owners' association

(G-16263)
ADVANTAGE HOME HEALTH CARE
1656 Coles Blvd (45662-2632)
PHONE..............................800 636-2330
Kathy Pierrion, *President*
Kathy Pierrion, *Vice Pres*
EMP: 80
SALES (est): 1.5MM **Privately Held**
SIC: 8082 Visiting nurse service

(G-16264)
AMERICAN SAVINGS BANK (PA)
Also Called: AMERICAN SAVINGS BANK F S B
503 Chillicothe St (45662-4015)
P.O. Box 1583 (45662-1583)
PHONE..............................740 354-3177
Fax: 740 354-3170
Robert Smith, *President*
Roberts Beth, *Vice Pres*
Betsy Rossi, *Vice Pres*
Jack Stephenson, *Vice Pres*
Robyn Cheek, *Opers Staff*
EMP: 25
SQ FT: 6,000
SALES: 17.1MM **Privately Held**
WEB: www.asbportsmouth.com
SIC: 6035 Federal savings & loan associations

GEOGRAPHIC SECTION
Portsmouth - Scioto County (G-16289)

(G-16265)
BIG SANDY FURNITURE INC
Also Called: Big Sandy Furniture Store 5
730 10th St (45662-4033)
PHONE..................740 354-3193
Fax: 740 353-4823
Tyler Conley, Branch Mgr
EMP: 30 Privately Held
WEB: www.bigsandyfurniture.com
SIC: 4225 5722 5712 General warehousing & storage; gas household appliances; furniture stores
HQ: Big Sandy Furniture, Inc.
8375 Gallia Pike
Franklin Furnace OH 45629
740 574-2113

(G-16266)
BOONE COLEMAN CONSTRUCTION INC
32 State Route 239 (45663-8929)
PHONE..................740 858-6661
Fax: 740 858-5251
Timothy Coleman, President
Cathy Coleman, Office Mgr
EMP: 35
SQ FT: 500
SALES (est): 5.5MM Privately Held
SIC: 1623 Water, sewer & utility lines

(G-16267)
CANTER INN INC (HQ)
Also Called: Ramada Inn
711 2nd St (45662-4001)
PHONE..................740 354-7711
Fax: 740 353-1539
Jeff Albrecht, President
Gary Albrecht, Corp Secy
EMP: 26
SQ FT: 38,000
SALES (est): 1.2MM
SALES (corp-wide): 1.6MM Privately Held
WEB: www.ramadaportsmouth.com
SIC: 7011 7991 5812 Hotels & motels; physical fitness facilities; eating places
PA: Albrechts Ohio Inn
711 2nd St Ste 35
Portsmouth OH 45662
740 354-7711

(G-16268)
CITY OF PORTSMOUTH
Also Called: Portsmouth Health Department
605 Washington St (45662-3919)
PHONE..................740 353-5153
Fax: 740 353-3638
Don Walden, Manager
Celeste Tucker, Officer
EMP: 37 Privately Held
WEB: www.pmcourt.org
SIC: 8399 Health systems agency; health & welfare council
PA: City Of Portsmouth
728 2nd St Rm 1
Portsmouth OH 45662
740 354-8807

(G-16269)
CITY OF PORTSMOUTH
Also Called: Public Service Dept
55 Mary Ann St (45662-4647)
PHONE..................740 353-5419
Bill Beaumont, Director
Christopher Murphy, Director
Teresa Harmon, Clerk
EMP: 34 Privately Held
WEB: www.pmcourt.org
SIC: 1611 9111 Highway & street maintenance; mayors' offices
PA: City Of Portsmouth
728 2nd St Rm 1
Portsmouth OH 45662
740 354-8807

(G-16270)
CITY OF PORTSMOUTH
Also Called: City Garage
55 Mary Ann St (45662-4647)
PHONE..................740 353-3459
Christopher Murphy, Manager
EMP: 40 Privately Held
WEB: www.pmcourt.org
SIC: 7521 Parking garage

PA: City Of Portsmouth
728 2nd St Rm 1
Portsmouth OH 45662
740 354-8807

(G-16271)
COMMUNITY ACTION (PA)
433 3rd St (45662-3811)
P.O. Box 1525 (45662-1525)
PHONE..................740 354-7541
Fax: 740 354-3933
Tami Wellman, Manager
Carolyn Powell, Info Tech Mgr
Steve Sturgill, Exec Dir
EMP: 50
SQ FT: 6,000
SALES (est): 2.3MM Privately Held
SIC: 8322 8331 Social service center; community service employment training program

(G-16272)
COMMUNITY ACTION COMM PIKE CNT
Also Called: Valley View Health Center
621 Broadway St (45662-4788)
PHONE..................740 961-4011
Cheryl Tackett, Asst Director
EMP: 50
SALES (corp-wide): 22.3MM Privately Held
SIC: 8322 Family service agency
PA: The Community Action Committee Of Pike County
941 Market St
Piketon OH 45661
740 289-2371

(G-16273)
COMPASS COMMUNITY HEALTH
1634 11th St (45662-4526)
PHONE..................740 355-7102
Ed Hughes, CEO
Kevin Blevins, General Mgr
Lora Gampp, CFO
Erin Trapp, Director
EMP: 40 EST: 2012
SALES: 2.9MM Privately Held
SIC: 8011 8093 Offices & clinics of medical doctors; mental health clinic, outpatient

(G-16274)
CRYSTAL CARE CTR OF PORTSMOUTH
1319 Spring St (45662-2675)
P.O. Box 439 (45662-0439)
PHONE..................740 354-6619
Fax: 740 353-6770
George Esham, Director
Kim Nye, Administration
EMP: 30
SQ FT: 7,900
SALES: 950K Privately Held
WEB: www.crystalcarecenters.com
SIC: 8051 Convalescent home with continuous nursing care

(G-16275)
DESCO FEDERAL CREDIT UNION (PA)
401 Chillicothe St (45662-4013)
P.O. Box 1546 (45662-1546)
PHONE..................740 354-7791
Fax: 740 351-1483
Richard Powell, President
Chris Hamilton, Assistant VP
Lou Bennett, Vice Pres
Joyce Myers, Vice Pres
Kara Tieman, CFO
EMP: 85 EST: 1963
SQ FT: 10,000
SALES: 9.9MM Privately Held
SIC: 6061 Federal credit unions

(G-16276)
DIALYSIS CLINIC INC
1207 17th St (45662-3573)
PHONE..................740 351-0596
Darrel Allmon, Technical Mgr
Naga G Yadlapalli, Med Doctor
Andrew Mazon, Manager
Tonda Bussa, Manager
EMP: 25

SALES (corp-wide): 736.2MM Privately Held
WEB: www.dciinc.org
SIC: 8092 Kidney dialysis centers
PA: Dialysis Clinic, Inc.
1633 Church St Ste 500
Nashville TN 37203
615 327-3061

(G-16277)
EARL TWINAM
550 Field Rd (45662-8919)
PHONE..................740 820-2654
Earl Twinam, General Mgr
EMP: 25
SALES (est): 1.5MM Privately Held
SIC: 8711 Engineering services

(G-16278)
GENESIS RESPIRATORY SVCS INC (PA)
Also Called: Genesis Oxygen & Home Med Eqp
4132 Gallia St (45662-5511)
PHONE..................740 354-4363
Fax: 740 353-1938
Rosalie Kay Williams, President
Dawn Barker, Business Mgr
James Blair, Vice Pres
Steve Mefford, Safety Mgr
Don Baker, Manager
EMP: 43 EST: 1977
SQ FT: 8,000
SALES: 14MM Privately Held
SIC: 5999 8093 Medical apparatus & supplies; respiratory therapy clinic

(G-16279)
GEORGE P PETTIT MD INC
Also Called: Dr Darren Adams Dr Grge Pettit
1729 27th St Bldg G (45662-2638)
PHONE..................740 354-1434
Fax: 740 353-8811
George P Pettit MD, President
EMP: 40
SALES (est): 4.1MM Privately Held
SIC: 8011 Gynecologist; obstetrician; physicians' office, including specialists

(G-16280)
GLENNCO SYSTEMS INC
928 16th St (45662-2901)
PHONE..................740 353-4328
Fax: 740 353-0379
Dan Glenn, President
Sue Glenn, Vice Pres
Anne Riffe, Accountant
EMP: 25
SQ FT: 2,000
SALES: 2.5MM Privately Held
SIC: 1711 Plumbing contractors

(G-16281)
GOODWILL INDS OF SOUTHERN OHIO (PA)
324 Chillicothe St (45662-4012)
PHONE..................740 353-4394
Lenore Mason, CEO
Opal Spears, Director
EMP: 26
SQ FT: 16,000
SALES: 2MM Privately Held
SIC: 8742 Retail trade consultant

(G-16282)
GRACIE PLUM INVESTMENTS INC
609 2nd St Unit 2 (45662-3974)
PHONE..................740 355-9029
Fax: 740 354-1170
Francesca G Hartop, CEO
Clayton Johnson, Software Engr
EMP: 27
SQ FT: 3,150
SALES: 4.3MM Privately Held
WEB: www.yostengineering.com
SIC: 7372 7374 7371 Application computer software; data processing & preparation; custom computer programming services

(G-16283)
HCR MANORCARE MED SVCS FLA LLC
35 Bierly Rd Ste 2 (45662-8503)
PHONE..................419 252-5500
Criag Thurston, CEO
EMP: 105
SALES (corp-wide): 3.6B Publicly Held
SIC: 8051 Convalescent home with continuous nursing care
HQ: Hcr Manorcare Medical Services Of Florida, Llc
333 N Summit St Ste 100
Toledo OH 43604
419 252-5500

(G-16284)
HEALTH CARE RTREMENT CORP AMER
Also Called: Heartland of Portsmouth
20 Easter Dr (45662-8659)
PHONE..................740 354-4505
Lois Clay, Administration
EMP: 126
SALES (corp-wide): 3.6B Publicly Held
WEB: www.hrc-manorcare.com
SIC: 8051 Skilled nursing care facilities
HQ: Health Care And Retirement Corporation Of America
333 N Summit St Ste 103
Toledo OH 43604
419 252-5500

(G-16285)
HEARTLAND HOSPICE SERVICES LLC
35 Bierly Rd Ste 2 (45662-8503)
PHONE..................740 351-0575
EMP: 100
SALES (corp-wide): 3.8B Publicly Held
SIC: 8082 Home Health Care Service
HQ: Heartland Hospice Services, Llc
333 N Summit St
Toledo OH 43604

(G-16286)
HEMPSTEAD MANOR
727 8th St (45662-4020)
PHONE..................740 354-8150
Linda Purek, President
Gary Curtis, Vice Pres
Melissa Adkins, Personnel Exec
Jitendra Patel, Director
Linda Hanley, Administration
EMP: 130
SQ FT: 80,000
SALES (est): 4.6MM Privately Held
SIC: 8051 8052 Convalescent home with continuous nursing care; intermediate care facilities

(G-16287)
HILL VIEW RETIREMENT CENTER
1610 28th St (45662-2641)
PHONE..................740 354-3135
Fax: 740 353-5511
John Prose, President
Mike Hodge, Purch Agent
Jim Harness, Controller
Suzanne Bonzo, Director
Juanita Robinson, Director
EMP: 174
SQ FT: 14,500
SALES: 14.1MM Privately Held
WEB: www.hillviewretirement.org
SIC: 8051 Skilled nursing care facilities

(G-16288)
HORIZON HOUSE APARTMENTS LLC
700 2nd St (45662-4064)
PHONE..................740 354-6393
Michelle Hert,
EMP: 55
SALES: 320K Privately Held
SIC: 6513 Apartment building operators

(G-16289)
HOSPICE OF SOUTHERN OHIO
Also Called: Somc Hospice
2201 25th St (45662-3259)
PHONE..................740 356-2567
Fax: 740 356-6109

Portsmouth - Scioto County (G-16290)

Teresa Ruby, *Director*
EMP: 80
SALES (est): 4MM **Privately Held**
SIC: 8741 Hospital management

(G-16290)
INFRA-METALS CO
1 Sturgill Way (45662-5179)
PHONE 740 353-1350
Oak Williams, *Branch Mgr*
EMP: 25
SALES (corp-wide): 9.7B **Publicly Held**
SIC: 5051 Structural shapes, iron or steel
HQ: Infra-Metals Co.
580 Middletown Blvd D100
Langhorne PA 19047
215 741-1000

(G-16291)
INTERIM HEALTHCARE (PA)
4130 Gallia St (45662-5511)
PHONE 740 354-5550
Fax: 740 354-5670
Donna Southworth, *President*
Kelly Conklin, *Human Res Dir*
Lawrence Conn, *Technology*
Melissa Williams, *Administration*
EMP: 82
SALES (est): 3.8MM **Privately Held**
SIC: 8082 Home health care services

(G-16292)
J&H RNFRCING STRL ERECTORS INC
Also Called: J & H Erectors
55 River Ave (45662-4712)
P.O. Box 60 (45662-0060)
PHONE 740 355-0141
Fax: 740 355-3513
Donald Hadsell, *President*
Lisa Hadsell, *Corp Secy*
EMP: 150
SQ FT: 30,000
SALES (est): 33.3MM **Privately Held**
WEB: www.jherectors.com
SIC: 1542 1791 Commercial & office building contractors; iron work, structural

(G-16293)
KENTUCKY HEART INSTITUTE INC
2001 Scioto Trl Ste 200 (45662-2845)
PHONE 740 353-8100
Debbie Bell, *Principal*
EMP: 41
SALES (corp-wide): 92.7K **Privately Held**
SIC: 8011 Offices & clinics of medical doctors
PA: Kentucky Heart Institute, Inc
613 23rd St
Ashland KY 41101
606 329-1997

(G-16294)
LUTE SUPPLY INC (PA)
3920 Us Highway 23 (45662-6468)
P.O. Box 721 (45662-0721)
PHONE 740 353-1447
Fax: 740 353-7638
Christopher H Lute, *President*
Dave Fleming, *Vice Pres*
Brian Hancock, *Vice Pres*
Dan McManus, *Purch Mgr*
Jason C Lute, *Treasurer*
EMP: 25 **EST:** 1952
SALES (est): 78.5MM **Privately Held**
WEB: www.lutesupply.com
SIC: 5074 5075 5031 5087 Plumbing fittings & supplies; air conditioning & ventilation equipment & supplies; kitchen cabinets; service establishment equipment; tools

(G-16295)
MECHANICAL CONSTRUCTION CO
Also Called: McCo
2302 8th St (45662-4798)
PHONE 740 353-5668
Fax: 740 353-4208
Darrell Stapleton, *President*
Jackie Enz, *Corp Secy*
W Michael Stapleton, *Vice Pres*
Tony Dingus, *Project Mgr*
EMP: 50 **EST:** 1957
SQ FT: 10,000
SALES (est): 10.7MM **Privately Held**
SIC: 1711 1761 Plumbing contractors; warm air heating & air conditioning contractor; sheet metalwork

(G-16296)
NORFOLK SOUTHERN CORPORATION
2435 8th St (45662-4781)
PHONE 740 353-4529
Dianne Ravizee, *Manager*
EMP: 54
SALES (corp-wide): 10.5B **Publicly Held**
WEB: www.nscorp.com
SIC: 4011 Railroads, line-haul operating
PA: Norfolk Southern Corporation
3 Commercial Pl Ste 1a
Norfolk VA 23510
757 629-2680

(G-16297)
PAINTERS LOCAL UNION 555
2101 7th St (45662-4726)
PHONE 740 353-1431
Joe Crytser, *Manager*
EMP: 65 **EST:** 1932
SQ FT: 2,800
SALES (est): 1.2MM **Privately Held**
SIC: 8631 Trade union

(G-16298)
PORTSMOUTH AMBULANCE
2796 Gallia St (45662-4807)
PHONE 740 289-2932
Fax: 740 354-1276
Sherri Fannin, *Owner*
EMP: 180
SALES (est): 2.3MM **Privately Held**
SIC: 4119 Ambulance service

(G-16299)
PORTSMOUTH LODGE 154 B P O E (PA)
Also Called: Elks
544 4th St (45662-3838)
P.O. Box 871 (45662-0871)
PHONE 740 353-1013
Clark Thompson, *Director*
Gary Plant, *Director*
EMP: 50
SALES (est): 1.1MM **Privately Held**
SIC: 8641 Fraternal associations

(G-16300)
PORTSMOUTH METRO HSING AUTH (PA)
Also Called: Section 8 Housing Assistance
410 Court St (45662-3949)
PHONE 740 354-4547
Fax: 740 353-3677
Paul Downey, *Purch Dir*
Peggy Rice, *Finance*
Teresa Everett, *Finance*
Stephanie Sands, *Manager*
Paul Blaine, *Director*
EMP: 45
SALES (est): 4.1MM **Privately Held**
WEB: www.pmha.us
SIC: 8322 Individual & family services

(G-16301)
PORTSMOUTH RACEWAY PARK INC
Highway 52 (45662)
PHONE 740 354-3278
Jennie Coleman, *President*
EMP: 50
SALES (est): 965.1K **Privately Held**
SIC: 7948 Automotive race track operation

(G-16302)
PORTSMUTH EMRGNCY AMBLANCE SVC
2796 Gallia St (45662-4807)
PHONE 740 354-3122
Fax: 740 353-2086
Michael L Adkins, *President*
Trina Adkins, *Vice Pres*
Rachael Estep, *Treasurer*
Michael R Adkins, *Admin Sec*
EMP: 500
SQ FT: 11,000
SALES (est): 9.4MM **Privately Held**
SIC: 4119 Ambulance service

(G-16303)
REHABCARE GROUP MGT SVCS INC
Also Called: Somc Speech and Hearing Svcs
1202 18th St (45662-2922)
PHONE 740 356-6160
Fax: 740 353-1238
Kevin Staimpert, *Director*
Kristie Thaker, *Otolaryngology*
EMP: 68
SALES (corp-wide): 6B **Publicly Held**
WEB: www.rehabcare.com
SIC: 8093 Rehabilitation center, outpatient treatment
HQ: Rehabcare Group Mgt Svcs Inc
680 S 4th St
Louisville KY 40202
502 596-7300

(G-16304)
REYNOLDS & CO INC
Also Called: Reynolds & Company Cpa's
839 Gallia St (45662-4137)
P.O. Box 1364 (45662-1364)
PHONE 740 353-1040
Fax: 740 353-3668
Greg Brown, *Principal*
Ronald F Champan, *Treasurer*
Christopher Allen, *Accountant*
Amanda Caldwell, *Accountant*
Debra Coburn, *Accountant*
EMP: 35
SQ FT: 6,000
SALES (est): 2.5MM **Privately Held**
WEB: www.reynolds-cpa.com
SIC: 8721 Certified public accountant

(G-16305)
ROYCE LEASING CO LLC
Also Called: Bridgeport Healthcare Center
2125 Royce St (45662-4714)
PHONE 740 354-1240
Colleen Cullison, *Administration*
EMP: 99
SALES (est): 3.3MM
SALES (corp-wide): 103.9MM **Privately Held**
SIC: 8051 Skilled nursing care facilities
HQ: Health Care Facility Management, Llc
4700 Ashwood Dr Ste 200
Blue Ash OH 45241

(G-16306)
SCIOTO COUNTY C A O HEADSTART
Also Called: Highland Ctr Early Head Start
1511 Hutchins St (45662-3615)
P.O. Box 1525 (45662-1525)
PHONE 740 354-3333
Fax: 740 354-1245
Robert Walton, *Exec Dir*
Mary Parker, *Director*
EMP: 33
SALES (est): 950K **Privately Held**
SIC: 8351 Head start center, except in conjunction with school

(G-16307)
SCIOTO COUNTY COUNSELING CTR (PA)
Also Called: COUNSELING CENTER, THE
1634 11th St (45662-4526)
PHONE 740 354-6685
Fax: 740 354-5061
Melanie Colmer, *CFO*
Ed Hughes, *Exec Dir*
Rick Calvin, *Director*
Andrea Davis, *Hlthcr Dir*
Andrea Queen, *Hlthcr Dir*
EMP: 59
SALES (est): 11.9MM **Privately Held**
SIC: 8322 Alcoholism counseling, nontreatment; drug abuse counselor, nontreatment; family counseling services

(G-16308)
SCIOTO RESIDENTIAL SERVICES
2333 Vinton Ave (45662-3741)
PHONE 740 353-0288
Lisa Francis, *Principal*
EMP: 27
SALES (corp-wide): 5MM **Privately Held**
SIC: 8399 Advocacy group
PA: Scioto Residential Services, Inc
9 Plaza Dr
Portsmouth OH 45662
740 354-7958

(G-16309)
SHAWNEE ANIMAL CLINIC INC
101 Bierly Rd (45662-8805)
PHONE 740 353-5758
Fax: 740 353-5438
Gail Counts Dvm, *President*
EMP: 25
SALES (est): 2MM **Privately Held**
SIC: 0742 Animal hospital services, pets & other animal specialties

(G-16310)
SOMC FOUNDATION INC
1805 27th St (45662-2686)
PHONE 740 356-5000
Stewart Yes, *President*
Brande Charles, *Office Mgr*
EMP: 60
SALES (est): 1.2K **Privately Held**
SIC: 8011 Physicians' office, including specialists

(G-16311)
SOUTHERN OHIO MEDICAL CENTER (PA)
Also Called: SCIOTO MEMORIAL HOSPITAL CAMPU
1805 27th St (45662-2640)
PHONE 740 354-5000
Fax: 740 353-2981
Robert E Dever, *Ch of Bd*
Randal M Arnett, *President*
Claudia Burchett, *Vice Pres*
Harold Bise, *Plant Mgr*
Peter Keller, *Safety Mgr*
▲ **EMP:** 2100 **EST:** 1954
SALES: 365.4MM **Privately Held**
SIC: 8062 General medical & surgical hospitals

(G-16312)
SOUTHERN OHIO MEDICAL CENTER
Also Called: Somc Urgent Care Ctr Prtsmouth
1248 Kinneys Ln (45662-2927)
PHONE 740 356-5000
Jackie Lowder, *Project Mgr*
Diane Applegate, *Manager*
Ted Stidham, *Manager*
Greg Gilliland, *Director*
Mary K Dilts, *Hlthcr Dir*
EMP: 30
SALES (corp-wide): 365.4MM **Privately Held**
SIC: 8742 Materials mgmt. (purchasing, handling, inventory) consultant
PA: Southern Ohio Medical Center
1805 27th St
Portsmouth OH 45662
740 354-5000

(G-16313)
SOUTHERN OHIO MEDICAL CENTER
Also Called: Somc
1805 27th St (45662-2640)
PHONE 740 354-5000
Fax: 740 858-9140
Karen Rickey, *Facilities Mgr*
Emily Van Loon, *CFO*
Sara Bender, *VP Human Res*
Linda Horner, *Nursing Mgr*
Paul Rase, *Nursing Mgr*
EMP: 2000
SALES (corp-wide): 365.4MM **Privately Held**
SIC: 8322 Community center
PA: Southern Ohio Medical Center
1805 27th St
Portsmouth OH 45662
740 354-5000

(G-16314)
STAR INC
2625 Gallia St (45662-4805)
PHONE 740 354-1517
Fax: 740 353-7236
John Kantz, *President*
John Burke, *Vice Pres*
Nancy Bays, *Office Mgr*

Patricia Rase, *Manager*
Karren Griffith, *Exec Dir*
EMP: 150
SQ FT: 32,000
SALES: 1.7MM **Privately Held**
SIC: 8331 7349 Job training services; vocational rehabilitation agency; building maintenance services

(G-16315)
UNITED PARCEL SERVICE INC OH
Also Called: UPS
21 Gingersnap Rd (45662-8825)
PHONE............................740 962-7971
EMP: 316
SALES (corp-wide): 65.8B **Publicly Held**
SIC: 7389 Personal service agents, brokers & bureaus
HQ: United Parcel Service, Inc. (Oh)
55 Glenlake Pkwy
Atlanta GA 30328
404 828-6000

(G-16316)
UNITED SCOTO SENIOR ACTIVITIES (PA)
Also Called: SENIOR CITIZENS CENTER
117 Market St 119 (45662)
P.O. Box 597 (45662-0597)
PHONE............................740 354-6672
Fax: 740 354-1891
Chester Neff, *President*
Laurna Garlinger, *Principal*
Renee Ellis, *Director*
EMP: 32
SALES: 648.9K **Privately Held**
SIC: 8322 8111 7349 5812 Senior citizens' center or association; legal services; building maintenance services; eating places; local passenger transportation; local & suburban transit

(G-16317)
UNITY I HOME HEALTHCARE LLC
221 Market St (45662-3831)
PHONE............................740 351-0500
Fax: 740 351-0550
Patricia Powell, *Manager*
Trish Larkin,
EMP: 30
SQ FT: 1,926
SALES (est): 1.3MM **Privately Held**
SIC: 8099 Medical services organization

(G-16318)
US BANK NATIONAL ASSOCIATION
Also Called: US Bank
602 Chillicothe St Frnt (45662-4095)
P.O. Box 1151 (45662-1151)
PHONE............................740 353-4151
James Barrett, *Manager*
EMP: 25
SALES (corp-wide): 22.7B **Publicly Held**
WEB: www.firstar.com
SIC: 6021 National commercial banks
HQ: U.S. Bank National Association
425 Walnut St Fl 1
Cincinnati OH 45202
513 632-4234

(G-16319)
USSA INC
Also Called: Golden Buckeye Program
117 119 Market St (45662)
P.O. Box 597 (45662-0597)
PHONE............................740 354-6672
Lorna Garlinger, *Principal*
Renee Ellis, *Exec Dir*
EMP: 34
SALES (est): 1.3MM **Privately Held**
SIC: 8322 8082 7299 Social service center; home health care services; personal appearance services

(G-16320)
VALLEY WHOLESALE FOODS INC (PA)
Also Called: V F
415 Market St (45662-3834)
P.O. Box 1281 (45662-1281)
PHONE............................740 354-5216
Fax: 740 354-6147
Ernest J Vastine Sr, *President*
Jay Vastine, *Principal*
Jim Vastine, *Principal*
Zack Vastine, *Principal*
Kristi Vastine-Mckenzie, *Principal*
EMP: 35
SQ FT: 40,000
SALES (est): 17.1MM **Privately Held**
SIC: 5141 Food brokers

(G-16321)
VERIZON SOUTH INC
1121 Robinson Ave (45662-3589)
PHONE............................740 354-0544
Ron Stanko, *Manager*
EMP: 60
SALES (corp-wide): 126B **Publicly Held**
SIC: 4813 Local & long distance telephone communications
HQ: Verizon South Inc.
600 Hidden Rdg
Irving TX 75038
972 718-5600

(G-16322)
WESTERN & SOUTHERN LF INSUR CO
35 Bierly Rd Ste 1 (45662-8503)
PHONE............................740 354-2848
Fax: 740 354-4743
David Carle, *Manager*
EMP: 32 **Privately Held**
SIC: 6411 Life insurance agents
HQ: The Western & Southern Life Insurance Company
400 Broadway St
Cincinnati OH 45202
513 629-1800

Powell
Delaware County

(G-16323)
ADVOCATE RADIOLOGY BIL
10567 Swmill Pkwy Ste 100 (43065)
PHONE............................614 210-1885
Kirk Reinitz, *President*
Samuel J Merandi, *Principal*
Todd Kohl, *COO*
Beth Myers, *Opers Mgr*
Michael Murphy, *CFO*
EMP: 169
SALES (est): 16.4MM **Privately Held**
SIC: 8011 Radiologist

(G-16324)
ARMADA LTD
23 Clairedan Dr (43065-8064)
PHONE............................614 505-7256
Thomas Foos, *President*
Marilyn Podracky, *Office Mgr*
Josh Rock, *Manager*
Fred Alverson, *Executive*
Jeff Podracky, *Admin Sec*
EMP: 70
SALES (est): 6.1MM **Privately Held**
WEB: www.armadausa.com
SIC: 8742 Management consulting services

(G-16325)
AT&T CORP
10654 Brettridge Dr (43065-7860)
PHONE............................614 271-8911
EMP: 105
SALES (corp-wide): 160.5B **Publicly Held**
SIC: 4813 Telephone communication, except radio
HQ: At&T Corp.
1 At&T Way
Bedminster NJ 07921
800 403-3302

(G-16326)
BOENNING & SCATTERGOOD INC
9922 Brewster Ln (43065-7571)
PHONE............................614 336-8851
Cortney Hart, *Manager*
EMP: 43
SALES (corp-wide): 64.9MM **Privately Held**
SIC: 8742 Financial consultant
PA: Boenning & Scattergood Inc.
200 Barr Harbor Dr # 300
Conshohocken PA 19428
610 832-1212

(G-16327)
BROADVIEW MORTGAGE COMPANY (PA)
3982 Powell Rd Ste 230 (43065-7662)
PHONE............................614 854-7000
Steve Schenck, *President*
Steven K Hartzler, *Chairman*
Rebecca Hill, *Exec VP*
John C Rosenberger, *Admin Sec*
EMP: 26
SQ FT: 10,000
SALES (est): 6.1MM **Privately Held**
WEB: www.aemc.cc
SIC: 6162 Mortgage bankers

(G-16328)
CLICK4CARE INC
50 S Liberty St Ste 200 (43065-4006)
PHONE............................614 431-3700
Fax: 614 431-3721
Rob Gillette, *CEO*
Keith Dayton, *Exec VP*
Kim Ingram, *Vice Pres*
David Smith, *VP Sales*
Becky Darche, *Manager*
EMP: 65
SQ FT: 10,000
SALES (est): 7MM
SALES (corp-wide): 26.6MM **Privately Held**
WEB: www.click4care.com
SIC: 7371 Computer software systems analysis & design, custom
PA: Healthedge Software, Inc.
30 Corporate Dr Ste 150
Burlington MA 01803
781 285-1300

(G-16329)
COCHRAN ELECTRIC INC
Also Called: Cochran W R Industrial Elc
90 Grace Dr (43065-9331)
PHONE............................614 847-0035
Fax: 614 847-1227
Donna E Cochran, *President*
Carol Cameron, *COO*
William R Cochran, *Vice Pres*
Dan Walker, *Project Mgr*
EMP: 25
SQ FT: 10,000
SALES (est): 3.7MM **Privately Held**
SIC: 1731 General electrical contractor

(G-16330)
COLUMBUS ZOOLOGICAL PARK ASSN (PA)
Also Called: COLUMBUS ZOO AND AQUARIUM
5220 Powell Rd (43065-7288)
P.O. Box 400 (43065-0400)
PHONE............................614 645-3400
Fax: 614 645-3465
Tom Stalf, *President*
Juli Shultz, *General Mgr*
John Gannon, *Senior VP*
Lewis Greene, *Senior VP*
Terri Kepes, *Senior VP*
EMP: 200
SQ FT: 25,000
SALES (est): 77.9MM **Privately Held**
WEB: www.czda.org
SIC: 8422 5947 7992 Zoological garden, noncommercial; gift shop; public golf courses

(G-16331)
COMPREHENSIVE MED DATA MGT LLC
Also Called: Cmdm
9980 Brewster Ln Ste 100 (43065-7278)
PHONE............................614 717-9840
Dan Crocker, *Owner*
Kirk Reinitz, *Principal*
EMP: 65
SQ FT: 22,000
SALES (est): 2.4MM **Privately Held**
WEB: www.cmdm.com
SIC: 8721 Billing & bookkeeping service

(G-16332)
CONTINENTAL GL SLS & INV GROUP
Also Called: Continental Group
315 Ashmoore Ct (43065-7486)
P.O. Box 1764 (43065-1764)
PHONE............................614 679-1201
Sean Snyder, *Partner*
Chris Snyder, *Partner*
Mark McClain, *Vice Pres*
▲ **EMP:** 400
SQ FT: 100,000
SALES (est): 33.7MM **Privately Held**
SIC: 3441 7011 3211 Fabricated structural metal; hotels; structural glass

(G-16333)
CTV MEDIA INC (PA)
1490 Manning Pkwy (43065-9171)
PHONE............................614 848-5800
Fax: 614 848-4099
Kathryn C Dixon, *President*
Abigail Levi, *Buyer*
Kevin McCrady, *Buyer*
Emil Stackpoole, *Buyer*
Laura Huber, *Research*
EMP: 40 **EST:** 1980
SQ FT: 20,000
SALES (est): 7.2MM **Privately Held**
WEB: www.ctvmedia.com
SIC: 7313 7319 Electronic media advertising representatives; media buying service

(G-16334)
FH TCH
4541 Powell Rd Ste H (43065-8757)
PHONE............................614 781-1645
Cullen Stackpole, *General Mgr*
Cody Hearn, *Comptroller*
EMP: 40
SQ FT: 63,000
SALES (est): 162.6K **Privately Held**
SIC: 7011 Resort hotel, franchised

(G-16335)
FIRST COMMONWEALTH BANK
10149 Brewster Ln (43065-7571)
PHONE............................614 336-2280
Fred Fowler, *Branch Mgr*
EMP: 27
SALES (corp-wide): 330.8MM **Publicly Held**
SIC: 6022 State trust companies accepting deposits, commercial
HQ: First Commonwealth Bank
601 Philadelphia St
Indiana PA 15701
724 349-7220

(G-16336)
GANZHORN SUITES INC
10272 Sawmill Pkwy (43065-9189)
PHONE............................614 356-9810
Eleanor Alvarez, *President*
EMP: 65
SALES (est): 1.8MM **Privately Held**
SIC: 8322 Old age assistance

(G-16337)
GS OHIO INC
Also Called: Maple Lee Greenhouse
8573 Owenfield Dr (43065-9835)
PHONE............................614 885-5350
Fax: 614 885-4194
George S Davis, *Ch of Bd*
Charles Davis, *President*
Steven Davis, *Vice Pres*
Leza Cutforth, *Treasurer*
Sherrie Robinson, *Admin Sec*
EMP: 90
SQ FT: 17,000
SALES (est): 3MM **Privately Held**
SIC: 5992 5947 5193 5261 Flowers, fresh; gift shop; flowers, fresh; florists' supplies; nurseries & garden centers

(G-16338)
IMPROVEDGE LLC
9878 Brewster Ln 210 (43065-7980)
PHONE............................614 793-1738
Karen H Majidzadeh,
Christy Fryman, *Administration*
EMP: 25
SALES (est): 1.4MM **Privately Held**
WEB: www.improvedge.com
SIC: 8748 7389 Business consulting;

Powell - Delaware County (G-16339)

(G-16339)
JBENTLEY STUDIO & SPA LLC
8882 Moreland St (43065-6678)
PHONE..............................614 790-8828
Kendra Cook, *COO*
John Paton,
Kelsey Mason, *Graphic Designe*
EMP: 55
SQ FT: 7,500
SALES (est): 1.2MM **Privately Held**
SIC: 7231 7991 Unisex hair salons; spas

(G-16340)
JPMORGAN CHASE BANK NAT ASSN
4066 Powell Rd (43065-7898)
PHONE..............................614 248-3315
Elaine Borling, *Branch Mgr*
EMP: 26
SALES (corp-wide): 99.6B **Publicly Held**
WEB: www.chasebank.com
SIC: 6021 National commercial banks
HQ: Jpmorgan Chase Bank, National Association
1111 Polaris Pkwy
Columbus OH 43240
614 436-3055

(G-16341)
KAISER CONSULTING LLC
818 Riverbend Ave (43065-7067)
PHONE..............................614 378-5361
Cassie Chun, *Project Mgr*
Lori Kaiser, *Mng Member*
Elizabeth Grzelak, *Consultant*
Tracey Cozzolino, *Advisor*
EMP: 50
SALES (est): 1.8MM **Privately Held**
SIC: 8721 8742 Accounting, auditing & bookkeeping; financial consultant

(G-16342)
KF EXPRESS LLC
10440 Delwood Pl (43065-7896)
PHONE..............................614 258-8858
Fax: 614 258-8935
Kevin Flaherty, *President*
Chris Henneforth, *Mng Member*
Shelly Johnson, *Manager*
EMP: 35
SQ FT: 6,500
SALES (est): 6MM **Privately Held**
SIC: 4212 4213 Local trucking, without storage; trucking, except local

(G-16343)
KINSALE GOLF & FITNES CLB LLC
3737 Village Club Dr (43065-8196)
PHONE..............................740 881-6500
Fax: 740 881-6565
Alan McCarrell, *General Mgr*
Richard Smith, *General Mgr*
Brian French, *Asst Supt*
Raed Yaish, *Controller*
Randy Allen, *Accounts Mgr*
EMP: 189
SQ FT: 1,537
SALES (est): 12.1MM **Privately Held**
WEB: www.golfkinsale.com
SIC: 7992 7991 Public golf courses; health club

(G-16344)
NEW PATH INTERNATIONAL LLC
1476 Manning Pkwy Ste A (43065-7295)
PHONE..............................614 410-3974
Henry Todd, *Financial Exec*
Richard S Baum, *VP Mktg*
Damon Canfield, *Mng Member*
Aaron Carter, *Administration*
Neil Macivor,
▲ **EMP:** 50
SQ FT: 13,000
SALES (est): 8.1MM **Privately Held**
WEB: www.npi.com
SIC: 3639 7389 8711 Major kitchen appliances, except refrigerators & stoves; design, commercial & industrial; engineering services

(G-16345)
NEW PROS COMMUNICATIONS INC
155 Hidden Ravines Dr (43065-8739)
PHONE..............................740 201-0410
Fax: 614 201-0411
J Alan Dyer, *President*
Andy Smith, *COO*
Alan Dyer, *Human Res Mgr*
Vanita Thomas, *Human Res Mgr*
Kenneth Molihan, *Sales Dir*
EMP: 90
SQ FT: 15,000
SALES (est): 10.4MM **Privately Held**
WEB: www.newpros.com
SIC: 7331 7374 Mailing list brokers; data processing & preparation

(G-16346)
PRIMROSE SCHOOL AT GOLF VLG
8771 Moreland St (43065-7177)
PHONE..............................740 881-5830
CAM Struck, *Owner*
Julie Esker, *Director*
Deanna Brown, *Asst Director*
Tami Cheslock, *Teacher*
Jade Christiansen, *Teacher*
EMP: 30
SALES (est): 774.1K **Privately Held**
SIC: 8351 Preschool center

(G-16347)
REAL LIVING INC
379 W Olentangy St (43065-8719)
PHONE..............................614 560-9942
Linda Whiting, *Principal*
Thomas Holcombe, *Executive*
EMP: 60
SALES (corp-wide): 67.8MM **Privately Held**
SIC: 6519 6531 Real property lessors; real estate agents & managers
PA: Real Living Inc
77 E Nationwide Blvd
Columbus OH 43215
614 221-7400

(G-16348)
ROLLS REALTY
6706 Harriott Rd (43065-8408)
PHONE..............................614 792-5662
Fax: 614 766-8166
Christopher Gregory, *President*
EMP: 35
SALES (est): 1.8MM **Privately Held**
SIC: 6531 Real estate agent, residential

(G-16349)
SCIOTO RESERVE INC (PA)
Also Called: Scioto Reserve Golf & Athc CLB
7383 Scioto Pkwy (43065-7956)
PHONE..............................740 881-9082
Fax: 740 881-4052
Joe Bush, *General Mgr*
Regan Koivesto, *Principal*
Jeff Olson, *Principal*
Andy Montgomery, *Opers Staff*
Reagan Koivesto, *Manager*
EMP: 81 EST: 1990
SALES (est): 7.3MM **Privately Held**
WEB: www.sciotoreserve.com
SIC: 7992 7997 7991 Public golf courses; membership sports & recreation clubs; physical fitness facilities

(G-16350)
SCIOTO RESERVE INC
Also Called: Scioto Reserve Country Club
3982 Powell Rd Ste 332 (43065-7662)
PHONE..............................740 881-6500
EMP: 79
SALES (corp-wide): 7.3MM **Privately Held**
SIC: 7992 Public golf courses
PA: Scioto Reserve, Inc.
7383 Scioto Pkwy
Powell OH 43065
740 881-9082

(G-16351)
SEARCH 2 CLOSE COLUMBUS LTD (PA)
10254 Sawmill Pkwy (43065-9189)
PHONE..............................614 389-5353
Fax: 614 212-5325
Emily Owens, *Corp Counsel*
Rebekah Haskin, *Manager*
Kevin Alexander,
Brooke Munekata,
EMP: 25
SQ FT: 6,000
SALES (est): 12.2MM **Privately Held**
WEB: www.search2close.com
SIC: 6361 Real estate title insurance

(G-16352)
SMOKY ROW CHILDRENS CENTER
8615 Smoky Row Rd (43065-9201)
PHONE..............................614 766-2122
Fax: 614 888-3599
Judy Chosy, *Owner*
EMP: 30
SALES (est): 1MM **Privately Held**
SIC: 8351 Preschool center

(G-16353)
W R SHEPHERD INC (PA)
390 W Olentangy St (43065-8716)
PHONE..............................614 889-2896
Fax: 614 766-5835
William R Shepherd, *President*
Sharon Shepherd, *Corp Secy*
Brad Shepperd, *Vice Pres*
EMP: 50
SQ FT: 4,000
SALES (est): 2.3MM **Privately Held**
SIC: 1752 Floor laying & floor work

(G-16354)
WEDGEWOOD GOLF & COUNTRY CLUB
9600 Wedgewood Blvd (43065-8788)
PHONE..............................614 793-9600
Fax: 614 793-2588
James Simonton, *President*
Pat Dugan, *Vice Pres*
Steve Jackson, *Vice Pres*
Lee Slone, *Facilities Mgr*
Robert Baker, *Treasurer*
EMP: 140
SQ FT: 43,500
SALES (est): 7.4MM **Privately Held**
SIC: 7997 Country club, membership

(G-16355)
YOUNG MENS CHRISTIAN ASSOC
Also Called: YMCA
7798 Liberty Rd N (43065-9707)
PHONE..............................740 881-1058
Steve Gorman, *Branch Mgr*
Jodye Carman, *Director*
EMP: 200
SALES (corp-wide): 44.9MM **Privately Held**
WEB: www.ymca-columbus.com
SIC: 8641 7991 8351 7032 Youth organizations; physical fitness facilities; child day care services; youth camps; individual & family services
PA: Young Men's Christian Association Of Central Ohio
40 W Long St
Columbus OH 43215
614 389-4409

Powhatan Point
Belmont County

(G-16356)
COAL SERVICES INC
Also Called: Coal Services Group
155 Highway 7 S (43942-1033)
PHONE..............................740 795-5220
Don Gentry, *President*
Michael O McKown, *Principal*
Robert Moore, *Principal*
Barb Boyce, *Manager*
Bonnie Froehlich, *Manager*
EMP: 90
SALES (est): 12MM
SALES (corp-wide): 4.8B **Publicly Held**
WEB: www.coalservices.com
SIC: 8741 8711 1231 1222 Management services; engineering services; anthracite mining; bituminous coal-underground mining; bituminous coal & lignite-surface mining; coal mining services
HQ: The American Coal Company
9085 Highway 34 N
Galatia IL 62935
618 268-6311

Proctorville
Lawrence County

(G-16357)
A&L HOME CARE & TRAINING CTR
6101 County Road 107 (45669-5022)
P.O. Box 1010 (45669-1010)
PHONE..............................740 886-7623
Fax: 740 886-7625
Dawnetta Abbett, *Owner*
Mike Cross, *Manager*
EMP: 160
SALES (est): 2.2MM **Privately Held**
SIC: 8361 Residential care

(G-16358)
FORTHS FOODS INC
Also Called: Procterville Food Fair
7604 County Road 107 (45669-8173)
PHONE..............................740 886-9769
Fax: 740 886-9990
Don Plybon, *Manager*
EMP: 48
SALES (corp-wide): 99.8MM **Privately Held**
WEB: www.foodfairmarkets.com
SIC: 5141 5411 Groceries, general line; grocery stores
PA: Forth's Foods, Inc.
3090 Woodville Dr
Huntington WV 25701
304 525-3293

(G-16359)
HOLZER CLINIC LLC
Also Called: Holzer Clinic Lawrence County
98 State St (45669-8163)
P.O. Box 646 (45669-0646)
PHONE..............................740 886-9403
Fax: 740 446-5153
Nathan Miller, *Manager*
Tammy Duffild, *Manager*
Amanda L Cheshire, *Neurology*
Pam Mathews, *Receptionist*
EMP: 26
SALES (corp-wide): 323.8MM **Privately Held**
WEB: www.holzerclinic.com
SIC: 8011 8049 General & family practice, physician/surgeon; physical therapist
HQ: Holzer Clinic Llc
90 Jackson Pike
Gallipolis OH 45631
740 446-5411

(G-16360)
KINDER KARE DAY NURSERY
627 County Road 411 (45669-9407)
PHONE..............................740 886-6905
Fax: 740 886-6907
Aimee Sites, *Director*
Amiee Sites, *Director*
EMP: 25
SALES (est): 393K **Privately Held**
SIC: 8351 Group day care center

(G-16361)
SUPERIOR MARINE WAYS INC
5852 County Rd 1 Suoth Pt (45669)
P.O. Box 519 (45669-0519)
PHONE..............................740 894-6224
Dale Manns, *Manager*
EMP: 120
SALES (corp-wide): 16.3MM **Privately Held**
WEB: www.superiormarine.on.ca
SIC: 3731 7699 Barges, building & repairing; boat repair

PA: Superior Marine Ways, Inc.
5852 County Road 1
South Point OH 45680
740 894-6224

(G-16362)
THERMAL SOLUTIONS INC
9329 County Road 107 (45669-8732)
P.O. Box 661 (45669-0661)
PHONE..................................740 886-2861
Fax: 740 886-2911
John Stevens, *President*
David Vance, *Regional Mgr*
Tommy Crank, *Project Mgr*
John Browning, *CFO*
Barry Kelley, *Manager*
EMP: 100
SQ FT: 1,200
SALES (est): 14.6MM **Privately Held**
SIC: 1742 1799 Insulation, buildings; fire-proofing buildings

Prospect
Marion County

(G-16363)
CUMMINS BUILDING MAINT INC
5202 Marion Waldo Rd (43342-9758)
P.O. Box 350, Waldo (43356-0350)
PHONE..................................740 726-9800
Fax: 740 726-9880
Ronald H Cummins, *CEO*
Jill Frey, *Senior VP*
Myra Cummins, *CFO*
Sheila Piser, *Office Mgr*
EMP: 70
SALES (est): 1.5MM **Privately Held**
WEB: www.cumminsmaint.com
SIC: 7349 1721 Janitorial service, contract basis; painting & paper hanging

(G-16364)
CUMMINS FACILITY SERVICES LLC
5202 Marion Waldo Rd (43342-9758)
P.O. Box 350, Waldo (43356-0350)
PHONE..................................740 726-9800
Bob Tieche, *Regional Mgr*
Alicia Hill, *Business Mgr*
Missy Haas, *VP Admin*
Vanessa Schetter, *Accounts Mgr*
Kelly Dehn, *Marketing Staff*
EMP: 350
SALES (est): 6.4MM **Privately Held**
SIC: 7349 Cleaning service, industrial or commercial

(G-16365)
FLEMING CONSTRUCTION CO
Also Called: Scioto Sand & Gravel
5298 Marion Marysville Rd (43342-9342)
P.O. Box 31, Marion (43301-0031)
PHONE..................................740 494-2177
Fax: 614 494-2177
Gerald E Fleming, *President*
Sonya Fleming, *Vice Pres*
Butch Jones, *Manager*
EMP: 35
SQ FT: 2,400
SALES (est): 6.7MM **Privately Held**
SIC: 1542 1541 1623 1442 Commercial & office building, new construction; industrial buildings, new construction; sewer line construction; gravel mining; excavation & grading, building construction

Put In Bay
Ottawa County

(G-16366)
CAPITAL CITY INDUS SYSTEMS LLC
1494 Langram Rd (43456-6721)
PHONE..................................614 519-5047
Dennis Bryant, *President*
EMP: 25
SALES (est): 697.2K **Privately Held**
SIC: 8748 Business consulting

(G-16367)
ISLAND BIKE RENTAL INC
2071 Langram Rd (43456)
PHONE..................................419 285-2016
Fax: 419 285-3318
Charles Duggan, *President*
Mike Steidl, *Manager*
EMP: 25
SALES (est): 1MM **Privately Held**
WEB: www.islandbikerental.com
SIC: 7999 Bicycle rental

(G-16368)
ISLAND SERVICE COMPANY
Also Called: Middle Bass Ferry Company, The
341 Bayview Ave (43456-5503)
P.O. Box 360 (43456-0360)
PHONE..................................419 285-3695
Marvin Booker, *CEO*
Pat Thwaite, *Treasurer*
EMP: 130
SQ FT: 250,000
SALES (est): 4.8MM **Privately Held**
WEB: www.the-boardwalk.com
SIC: 5812 5541 7997 4493 Eating places; marine service station; boating club, membership; marinas; cocktail lounge; management services

(G-16369)
MILLER BOAT LINE INC (PA)
Also Called: ISLAND VIEW GIFTS
535 Bayview Ave (43456-6524)
PHONE..................................419 285-2421
Fax: 419 285-2032
William C Market, *President*
Mary Ann Market, *Vice Pres*
Scott E Market, *VP Opers*
Julene Marie Market, *Treasurer*
Lorine Miller, *Manager*
▲ EMP: 57
SQ FT: 1,800
SALES: 10.1MM **Privately Held**
WEB: www.millerferry.com
SIC: 4482 5947 Ferries; gift, novelty & souvenir shop

(G-16370)
PUT IN BAY TRANSPORTATION
2009 Langram Rd (43456-6734)
P.O. Box 190 (43456-0190)
PHONE..................................419 285-4855
Charles Duggan, *President*
Dianne Duggan, *Principal*
EMP: 25
SALES (est): 1MM **Privately Held**
WEB: www.put-in-bay-trans.com
SIC: 4142 Bus charter service, except local

Racine
Meigs County

(G-16371)
J D DRILLING CO
107 S 3rd St (45771-9552)
P.O. Box 369 (45771-0369)
PHONE..................................740 949-2512
Fax: 740 949-2018
James E Diddle, *President*
EMP: 25
SQ FT: 6,000
SALES (est): 3.8MM **Privately Held**
SIC: 1381 Drilling oil & gas wells

Randolph
Portage County

(G-16372)
EAST MANUFACTURING CORPORATION (PA)
1871 State Rte 44 (44265)
P.O. Box 277 (44265-0277)
PHONE..................................330 325-9921
Fax: 330 325-7851
Howard D Booher, *CEO*
David De Poincy, *President*
Mark T Tate, *Corp Secy*
Robert J Bruce, *Vice Pres*
Joseph F Coletti, *Vice Pres*
▼ EMP: 267
SQ FT: 350,000
SALES (est): 68.3MM **Privately Held**
WEB: www.eastmfg.com
SIC: 3715 5013 7539 Trailer bodies; truck parts & accessories; automotive repair shops

(G-16373)
JPMORGAN CHASE BANK NAT ASSN
4000 Waterloo Rd (44265)
P.O. Box 186 (44265-0186)
PHONE..................................330 325-7855
Peggy Tyrakowski, *Manager*
EMP: 26
SALES (corp-wide): 99.6B **Publicly Held**
WEB: www.chase.com
SIC: 6021 National commercial banks
HQ: Jpmorgan Chase Bank, National Association
1111 Polaris Pkwy
Columbus OH 43240
614 436-3055

Ravenna
Portage County

(G-16374)
BUCKEYE RSDNTIAL SOLUTIONS LLC
320 E Main St Ste 301 (44266-3102)
PHONE..................................330 235-9183
Chad Konkle, *CEO*
Matthew Ferrell, *CFO*
Paul Lynn, *Officer*
EMP: 75 EST: 2012
SQ FT: 12,000
SALES (est): 215K **Privately Held**
SIC: 8082 Home health care services

(G-16375)
CARDIOLOGY SPECIALISTS INC
6847 N Chestnut St # 100 (44266-3929)
PHONE..................................330 297-6110
A R Tsai MD, *President*
Leslie Tobias, *Vice Pres*
EMP: 32
SALES (est): 1.6MM **Privately Held**
SIC: 8011 Cardiologist & cardio-vascular specialist

(G-16376)
CHEMICAL BANK
999 E Main St (44266-3325)
PHONE..................................330 298-0510
Lisa Lee, *Manager*
Kandy Hricik, *Manager*
EMP: 70
SALES (corp-wide): 776.1MM **Publicly Held**
WEB: www.dlkbank.com
SIC: 6035 Federal savings & loan associations; federal savings banks
HQ: Chemical Bank
333 E Main St
Midland MI 48640
989 631-9200

(G-16377)
COLEMAN PROFESSIONAL SVCS INC
3920 Lovers Ln (44266-4200)
PHONE..................................330 296-8313
Nelson Burns, *CEO*
EMP: 70
SALES (est): 1.1MM
SALES (corp-wide): 43.8MM **Privately Held**
SIC: 8093 8049 Mental health clinic, out-patient; clinical psychologist
PA: Coleman Professional Services, Inc.
5982 Rhodes Rd
Kent OH 44240
330 673-1347

(G-16378)
COMPETITIVE INTERIORS INC
625 Enterprise Pkwy (44266-8058)
PHONE..................................330 297-1281
Fax: 330 297-1282
Paul Cunningham, *President*
Nancy Cunningham, *Vice Pres*
Erik Cunningham, *Project Mgr*
Kevin McConnell, *Project Mgr*
Ryan Metze, *Project Mgr*
EMP: 120
SQ FT: 5,104
SALES (est): 13.1MM **Privately Held**
WEB: www.competitiveinteriors.com
SIC: 1751 1742 Carpentry work; drywall

(G-16379)
COUNTY OF PORTAGE
Also Called: Portage County Engineer Office
5000 Newton Falls Rd (44266-9602)
PHONE..................................330 296-6411
Fax: 330 296-2303
Don Van Metre, *Superintendent*
David Doak, *Sheriff*
Glenn Cooper, *Production*
Tom Medzie, *Purch Mgr*
Heather Ripley, *Project Engr*
EMP: 65 **Privately Held**
WEB: www.portageprosecutor.com
SIC: 8711 1611 0782 Engineering services; highway & street construction; lawn & garden services
PA: County Of Portage
449 S Meridian St Fl 7
Ravenna OH 44266
330 297-3561

(G-16380)
COUNTY OF PORTAGE
Sanitary Engineer
449 S Meridian St Fl 3 (44266-2914)
P.O. Box 1217 (44266-1217)
PHONE..................................330 297-3670
John Vence, *Design Engr*
Amy Kuss, *Office Admin*
Harold G Huff, *Director*
EMP: 40 **Privately Held**
WEB: www.portageprosecutor.com
SIC: 4953 Refuse systems
PA: County Of Portage
449 S Meridian St Fl 7
Ravenna OH 44266
330 297-3561

(G-16381)
COUNTY OF PORTAGE
Prosecuting Attorney's Office
466 S Chestnut St (44266-3006)
PHONE..................................330 297-3850
Victor Valuchi, *Principal*
Jennifer E Redman,
EMP: 40 **Privately Held**
WEB: www.portageprosecutor.com
SIC: 9222 8111 Public prosecutors' offices; legal services
PA: County Of Portage
449 S Meridian St Fl 7
Ravenna OH 44266
330 297-3561

(G-16382)
CROWE MASONRY
Also Called: Crowe Enterprises
4699 Loomis Pkwy (44266-9114)
PHONE..................................330 296-5539
Fax: 330 296-5567
Donald Crowe, *President*
Debbie Crowe, *Admin Sec*
◆ EMP: 50 EST: 1993
SQ FT: 2,293
SALES (est): 3.9MM **Privately Held**
SIC: 1741 Masonry & other stonework

(G-16383)
CUTLER REAL ESTATE
525 N Scranton St (44266-1429)
PHONE..................................330 733-7575
EMP: 60
SALES (corp-wide): 6.9MM **Privately Held**
SIC: 6531 Real estate brokers & agents
PA: Cutler Real Estate
2800 W Market St
Fairlawn OH 44333
330 836-9141

(G-16384)
ECLIPSE BLIND SYSTEMS INC
7154 State Route 88 (44266-9189)
PHONE..................................330 296-0112
James W Watson, *President*

Ravenna - Portage County (G-16385) — GEOGRAPHIC SECTION

Dave Cline, *Plant Mgr*
Lucky Monroe, *Plant Mgr*
Mike Skidmore, *Plant Mgr*
Dennis Miller, *Purchasing*
EMP: 165
SQ FT: 110,000
SALES (est): 15.2MM Privately Held
SIC: 3089 7371 Extruded finished plastic products; custom computer programming services
HQ: Turnils (Uk) Limited
10 Fountain Crescent
Renfrew PA4 9
141 812-3322

(G-16385)
FAMILY CMNTY SVCS PORTAGE CNTY
Also Called: FAMILIES THAT WORK
705 Oakwood St (44266-2191)
PHONE..................................330 297-0078
Greg Musci, *Finance Dir*
Mark Srisone, *Exec Dir*
Mark Frisone, *Exec Dir*
Tom Albanese, *Associate Dir*
EMP: 110
SQ FT: 800
SALES: 8.1MM Privately Held
SIC: 8322 Individual & family services

(G-16386)
GOLDEN LIVING LLC
Also Called: Beverly
565 Bryn Mawr St (44266-9696)
PHONE..................................330 297-5781
Debbie Shrieve, *Director*
EMP: 150
SALES (corp-wide): 7.4MM Privately Held
SIC: 8059 8052 8051 Convalescent home; intermediate care facilities; skilled nursing care facilities
PA: Golden Living Llc
5220 Tennyson Pkwy # 400
Plano TX 75024
972 372-6300

(G-16387)
HAASZ AUTOMALL LLC
4886 State Route 59 (44266-8838)
PHONE..................................330 296-2866
Kevin Haasz, *President*
Tyler Kline, *General Mgr*
Heather Mayle, *Business Mgr*
Mary Scott, *Finance Mgr*
Greg Baxter, *Financial Exec*
EMP: 38
SALES (est): 5.6MM Privately Held
SIC: 5531 7539 Automotive parts; automotive repair shops

(G-16388)
HUMMEL CONSTRUCTION COMPANY
127 E Main St (44266-3103)
PHONE..................................330 274-8584
Fax: 330 296-7780
Eric W Hummel, *President*
Marty Snode, *Vice Pres*
Ronald Ayers, *Controller*
A Bing, *Manager*
EMP: 40 **EST:** 1971
SQ FT: 5,000
SALES (est): 9.2MM Privately Held
WEB: www.hummelconstruction.com
SIC: 1541 Industrial buildings, new construction

(G-16389)
INDEPENDENCE FOUNDATION INC
161 E Main St (44266-3129)
PHONE..................................330 296-2851
Anna Barrett, *Exec Dir*
EMP: 134
SALES: 123.8K
SALES (corp-wide): 4.3MM Privately Held
SIC: 8641 Civic social & fraternal associations
PA: Independence Of Portage County Inc
161 E Main St
Ravenna OH 44266
330 296-2851

(G-16390)
INDEPENDENCE OF PORTAGE COUNTY (PA)
161 E Main St (44266-3129)
PHONE..................................330 296-2851
Fax: 330 296-8631
Taren Morrow, *Finance Mgr*
William Ullman, *Finance*
Bill Hixon, *Technology*
Anna Barrett, *Exec Dir*
EMP: 180
SQ FT: 4,000
SALES: 4.3MM Privately Held
WEB: www.independenceofportage.org
SIC: 8361 8744 8052 Home for the mentally handicapped; facilities support services; intermediate care facilities

(G-16391)
KENMORE RESEARCH COMPANY
935 N Freedom St (44266-2496)
PHONE..................................330 297-1407
Gave Moorehouse, *Branch Mgr*
Rick Hood, *Admin Asst*
Tom Cichon, *Administration*
Richard Weber, *Administration*
EMP: 100
SALES (corp-wide): 1.1B Privately Held
SIC: 8731 8734 Commercial physical research; testing laboratories
HQ: Kenmore Research Company
29500 Solon Rd
Cleveland OH 44139
440 248-4600

(G-16392)
LONGMEADOW CARE CENTER INC
565 Bryn Mawr St (44266-9696)
PHONE..................................330 297-5781
Fax: 330 297-7445
Dave Cruser, *Principal*
Sherry Stano, *Business Mgr*
EMP: 120
SALES (est): 5.5MM Privately Held
SIC: 8052 Intermediate care facilities

(G-16393)
NEIGHBORHOOD DEVELOPMENT SVCS
Also Called: Nds
120 E Main St (44266-3104)
PHONE..................................330 296-2003
Fax: 330 297-1633
William Hale, *CEO*
David Vauthan, *President*
Michael Bogo, *President*
Stacy Brown, *President*
Kelley Palone, *Manager*
EMP: 30
SQ FT: 1,500
SALES: 5.7MM Privately Held
SIC: 8399 8742 8641 Community development groups; financial consultant; civic social & fraternal associations

(G-16394)
NON EMERGENCY AMBULANCE SVC
4830 Harding Ave (44266-8813)
PHONE..................................330 296-4541
Fax: 330 296-4985
Robert Turley, *President*
EMP: 25
SALES (est): 730K Privately Held
SIC: 4119 Ambulance service

(G-16395)
PARIS CLEANERS INC
Also Called: Paris Healthcare Linen
650 Enterprise Pkwy (44266-8054)
PHONE..................................330 296-3300
Fax: 330 296-7692
Bob Lattimer, *Chief Engr*
Sean Flanders, *Branch Mgr*
Janet Bland, *Supervisor*
EMP: 150
SALES (corp-wide): 67.2MM Privately Held
WEB: www.parisco.com
SIC: 7213 Uniform supply

PA: Paris Cleaners, Inc.
67 Hoover Ave
Du Bois PA 15801
814 375-9700

(G-16396)
PORTAGE BANCSHARES INC (PA)
Also Called: Portage Community Bank
1311 E Main St (44266-3329)
PHONE..................................330 296-8090
Richard Coe, *President*
Connie Bennett, *President*
Jill Conard, *President*
Kevin Lewis, *Officer*
EMP: 85
SQ FT: 10,000 Privately Held
WEB: www.pcbbank.com
SIC: 6712 Bank holding companies

(G-16397)
PORTAGE COMMUNITY BANK INC (HQ)
1311 E Main St (44266-3329)
PHONE..................................330 296-8090
Fax: 330 296-6082
Donald Herman, *CEO*
Richard Coe, *President*
Connie Bennett, *COO*
John Forberg, *COO*
Deb Bish, *Vice Pres*
EMP: 55
SALES: 13.9MM Privately Held
WEB: www.portagecommunitybank.com
SIC: 6022 State commercial banks
PA: Portage Bancshares Inc
1311 E Main St
Ravenna OH 44266
330 296-8090

(G-16398)
PORTAGE COUNTY BOARD
Also Called: Happy Day School
2500 Brady Lake Rd (44266-1610)
PHONE..................................330 678-2400
Fax: 330 673-3714
Gail McAlister, *Principal*
Mim Cherrie, *Tech/Comp Coord*
EMP: 80
SALES (corp-wide): 21.5MM Privately Held
SIC: 8322 Social services for the handicapped
PA: Portage County Board Of Developmental Disabilities
2606 Brady Lake Rd
Ravenna OH 44266
330 297-6209

(G-16399)
PORTAGE COUNTY BOARD (PA)
2606 Brady Lake Rd (44266-1604)
PHONE..................................330 297-6209
Fax: 330 297-1202
Omar Nagi, *Superintendent*
Dennis Coble, *Principal*
Lynn Leslie, *Human Res Dir*
Tim Torch, *HR Admin*
Patrick Macke, *Manager*
EMP: 34
SALES: 21.5MM Privately Held
SIC: 8361 Home for the mentally handicapped

(G-16400)
PORTAGE INDUSTRIES INC
7008 State Route 88 (44266-9134)
PHONE..................................330 296-2839
Fax: 330 296-8875
Philip Miller, *President*
Jim Bobek, *Manager*
Jaime Nichols, *Manager*
Gary Smith, *Manager*
John Snyder, *Manager*
EMP: 200
SQ FT: 48,000
SALES: 1.7MM Privately Held
WEB: www.portageind.org
SIC: 8331 Sheltered workshop

(G-16401)
PORTAGE PEDIATRICS
6847 N Chestnut St # 200 (44266-3929)
PHONE..................................330 297-8824
Cheryl Kemerer, *Principal*
EMP: 40

SALES (est): 1.2MM Privately Held
SIC: 8011 Pediatrician

(G-16402)
PORTAGE PHYSICAL THERAPISTS (PA)
Also Called: Allied Health Rehab Centers
771 N Freedom St (44266-2470)
PHONE..................................330 297-9020
Fax: 330 297-9094
Don Marsjall, *CEO*
Mark Hussing, *President*
Amy Faust, *Vice Pres*
Cheryl Hyde, *Supervisor*
Paul Ferrara, *Shareholder*
EMP: 58 **EST:** 1965
SALES (est): 4.3MM Privately Held
WEB: www.portagept.com
SIC: 8093 Rehabilitation center, outpatient treatment

(G-16403)
PORTAGE PRIVATE INDUSTRY
Also Called: PORTAGE LEARNING CENTERS
145 N Chestnut St Lowr (44266-4008)
PHONE..................................330 297-7795
Fax: 330 297-3469
James Tinnin, *Chairman*
Josie Carlton, *Opers Staff*
Suzanne Livinggood, *Exec Dir*
Karen Johnson, *Director*
Rebecca Gorczyca, *Admin Sec*
EMP: 70
SALES: 3.3MM Privately Held
SIC: 8351 8331 Head start center, except in conjunction with school; job training services

(G-16404)
RAVENNA ASSEMBLY OF GOD INC
6401 State Route 14 (44266-9692)
PHONE..................................330 297-1493
Gary Beck, *Pastor*
EMP: 39
SQ FT: 25,000
SALES: 800K Privately Held
WEB: www.ravennaag.com
SIC: 8661 8211 8351 Pentecostal Church; elementary & secondary schools; child day care services

(G-16405)
REHAB CENTER
Also Called: Rehabcenter
6847 N Chestnut St (44266-3929)
P.O. Box 1204 (44266-1204)
PHONE..................................330 297-2770
Stephen Colecchi, *CEO*
David Baldwin, *Principal*
Richard E Clough, *COO*
Linda Breedlove, *Vice Pres*
EMP: 28
SALES (est): 735.4K Privately Held
WEB: www.rmh2.org
SIC: 8049 8093 Physical therapist; rehabilitation center, outpatient treatment

(G-16406)
ROBINSON HEALTH SYSTEM INC
Also Called: Robinson Surgery Center
6847 N Chestnut St (44266-3929)
PHONE..................................330 678-4100
Fax: 330 678-5949
Janis Barnes, *Director*
EMP: 25
SALES (corp-wide): 2.3B Privately Held
SIC: 8062 8093 General medical & surgical hospitals; specialty outpatient clinics
HQ: Robinson Health System, Inc.
6847 N Chestnut St
Ravenna OH 44266
330 297-0811

(G-16407)
ROBINSON HEALTH SYSTEM INC (HQ)
Also Called: University Hosp Prtage Med Ctr
6847 N Chestnut St (44266-3929)
P.O. Box 1204 (44266-1204)
PHONE..................................330 297-0811
Fax: 330 297-2949
Stephen Colecchi, *President*

GEOGRAPHIC SECTION

Reynoldsburg - Franklin County (G-16429)

Bradley Raum, *President*
David Frase, *Business Mgr*
Norman Sandvoss, *Trustee*
Larry Wright, *Trustee*
EMP: 1200
SQ FT: 307,000
SALES: 160.5MM
SALES (corp-wide): 2.3B Privately Held
SIC: 8062 8011 General medical & surgical hospitals; offices & clinics of medical doctors
PA: University Hospitals Health System, Inc.
3605 Warrensville Ctr Rd
Shaker Heights OH 44122
216 767-8900

(G-16408)
ROBINSON VISITN NRS ASOC/HOSPC
6847 N Chestnut St (44266-3929)
PHONE................330 297-8899
Fax: 330 297-8823
Patty Clain, *COO*
Bill Kahl, *Exec Dir*
EMP: 50
SALES (est): 1.1MM Privately Held
SIC: 8082 Visiting nurse service

(G-16409)
ROOTSTOWN TOWNSHIP
4268 Sandy Lake Rd (44266-9324)
PHONE................330 296-8240
Bonnie Howe, *Trustee*
Diane Dillon, *Trustee*
Bret Howe, *Trustee*
Joann Townend, *Finance*
EMP: 40
SALES (est): 2.5MM Privately Held
WEB: www.rootstowntwp.com
SIC: 6512 Auditorium & hall operation

(G-16410)
SABER HEALTHCARE GROUP LLC
Also Called: Woodlands At Robinson, The
6831 N Chestnut St (44266-3929)
PHONE................330 297-4564
Fax: 330 298-4530
Haithem Azem, *Director*
EMP: 40
SALES (corp-wide): 68.5MM Privately Held
WEB: www.portageprosecutor.com
SIC: 8051 Skilled nursing care facilities
PA: Saber Healthcare Group, L.L.C.
26691 Richmond Rd Frnt
Bedford OH 44146
216 292-5706

(G-16411)
SIRNA & SONS INC (PA)
Also Called: Sirna's Market & Deli
7176 State Route 88 (44266-9189)
PHONE................330 298-2222
Fax: 330 298-9733
Joseph Sirna, *CEO*
Tom Sirna, *President*
Serena Wagner, *Corp Secy*
Vince Sirna, *Vice Pres*
Troy Bennington, *Opers Mgr*
EMP: 150
SQ FT: 20,000
SALES (est): 104.3MM Privately Held
WEB: www.sirnaandsonsproduce.com
SIC: 5148 Fruits, fresh; vegetables, fresh

(G-16412)
SIX C FABRICATION INC
5245 S Prospect St (44266-9032)
PHONE................330 296-5594
EMP: 60
SQ FT: 400,000
SALES (est): 2.3MM Privately Held
SIC: 1799 1623 5039 Trade Contractor Water/Sewer/Utility Construction Whol Construction Materials

(G-16413)
SMITHERS RAPRA INC
Also Called: Compliance Testing
1150 N Freedom St (44266-2457)
PHONE................330 297-1495
Fax: 330 297-0038
Tom Cerjak, *General Mgr*
Cindy White, *Admin Asst*

Dave Schwarz, *Administration*
EMP: 25
SQ FT: 30,000
SALES (corp-wide): 63.6MM Privately Held
WEB: www.smithersconsulting.com
SIC: 8734 Product testing laboratories
HQ: Smithers Rapra Inc.
425 W Market St
Akron OH 44303
330 762-7441

(G-16414)
TSK ASSISTED LIVING SERVICES
Also Called: Visiting Angels
240 W Riddle Ave (44266-2949)
PHONE................330 297-2000
Steven W Kastenhuber, *President*
EMP: 35
SALES (est): 1.1MM Privately Held
SIC: 8082 Home health care services

(G-16415)
W POL CONTRACTING INC
4188 Ohio 14 (44266)
PHONE................330 325-7177
Fax: 330 325-0263
Wade Pol, *President*
Christine Pol, *Treasurer*
EMP: 26
SQ FT: 6,640
SALES: 6.5MM Privately Held
SIC: 1629 Oil refinery construction

(G-16416)
WALL ST RECYCLING LLC
Also Called: Wall Street Recycling
6751 Wall St (44266-1734)
P.O. Box 526, Medina (44258-0526)
PHONE................330 296-8657
Fax: 330 296-8658
Jason Weigel, *Purch Agent*
Dan Hereda, *Buyer*
Barbara Joseph, *Controller*
Sam Pilato, *Controller*
Mike Ambrose, *Mng Member*
EMP: 25
SQ FT: 5,000
SALES (est): 6.3MM Privately Held
SIC: 5093 Ferrous metal scrap & waste

Rayland
Jefferson County

(G-16417)
HEAVENLY HOME HEALTH
1800 Old State Route 7 (43943-7962)
PHONE................740 859-4735
Colin Goff, *Owner*
Karen Dowell, *Co-Owner*
EMP: 30
SALES: 350K Privately Held
SIC: 8082 Home health care services

(G-16418)
SHELLY AND SANDS INC
Also Called: Tri-State Asphalt Co
1731 Old State Route 7 (43943-7962)
P.O. Box 66 (43943-0066)
PHONE................740 859-2104
Fax: 740 859-2134
Mark Haverty, *General Mgr*
EMP: 60
SALES (corp-wide): 260.8MM Privately Held
WEB: www.shellyandsands.com
SIC: 2951 1542 Asphalt paving mixtures & blocks; nonresidential construction
PA: Shelly And Sands, Inc.
3570 S River Rd
Zanesville OH 43701
740 453-0721

(G-16419)
VALLEY HOSPICE INC (PA)
10686 State Route 150 (43943-7847)
PHONE................740 859-5041
Fax: 740 284-4478
Karen Nicols, *President*
Cindy Knox, *Reverend*
EMP: 55

SALES: 14.4MM Privately Held
WEB: www.valleyhospice.com
SIC: 8051 Skilled nursing care facilities

Raymond
Union County

(G-16420)
HONDA R&D AMERICAS INC
Also Called: Honda Marysville Location
21001 State Route 739 (43067-9705)
PHONE................937 644-0439
Andrew Wagner, *Facilities Mgr*
Lance Anthony, *Production*
Bill Chamblin, *Purch Mgr*
Scott Forsythe, *Buyer*
Chip Maurer, *Buyer*
EMP: 25
SALES (corp-wide): 123.1B Privately Held
WEB: www.hra.com
SIC: 8732 Market analysis or research
HQ: Honda R&D Americas, Inc.
1900 Harpers Way
Torrance CA 90501
310 781-5500

Reno
Washington County

(G-16421)
BUCKEYE HILLS-HCK VLY REG DEV
Also Called: Area Agency On Aging
P.O. Box 368 (45773-0368)
PHONE................740 373-6400
Fax: 740 373-1594
Pat Palmer, *Branch Mgr*
Jamie Lewis, *Manager*
Karen A Pawloski, *Manager*
Dru Sexton, *Advisor*
EMP: 27
SALES (corp-wide): 223.9K Privately Held
WEB: www.buckeyehills.org
SIC: 8082 Home health care services
HQ: Buckeye Hills Hocking Valley Regional Development District
1400 Pike St
Marietta OH 45750
740 373-0087

(G-16422)
MONDO POLYMER TECHNOLOGIES INC
27620 State Rte 7 (45773)
P.O. Box 250 (45773-0250)
PHONE................740 376-9396
Mark Mondo, *President*
Maggie Ellis, *General Mgr*
Judy Mondo, *Vice Pres*
Rick Hockenberry, *Opers Mgr*
Tony Carver, *Production*
EMP: 40
SQ FT: 3,200
SALES (est): 15.2MM Privately Held
WEB: www.mondopolymer.com
SIC: 4953 2822 Recycling, waste materials; synthetic rubber

Reynoldsburg
Franklin County

(G-16423)
ABACUS CORPORATION
1676 Brice Rd (43068-2704)
PHONE................614 367-7000
April Calausi, *Branch Mgr*
EMP: 445
SALES (corp-wide): 234.6MM Privately Held
SIC: 7361 Executive placement
PA: Abacus Corporation
610 Gusryan St
Baltimore MD 21224
410 633-1900

(G-16424)
ACCURATE ELECTRIC CNSTR INC
6901 Americana Pkwy (43068-4116)
PHONE................614 863-1844
Robert S Beal, *President*
Bill Roche, *Superintendent*
Ralph Stout, *Vice Pres*
Dan Nussbaum, *Project Mgr*
Kevin Ledy, *Human Res Dir*
EMP: 160
SQ FT: 10,000
SALES (est): 31.6MM Privately Held
WEB: www.aecohio.com
SIC: 1731 General electrical contractor

(G-16425)
ALLIANCE DATA SYSTEMS CORP
6939 Americana Pkwy (43068-4171)
PHONE................614 729-5800
Fax: 614 729-5840
Peg Hansel, *Manager*
Matthew Lazzaro, *Manager*
Angela Risacher, *Manager*
Paul Strosnyder, *Software Dev*
Kelly Kroskie, *Director*
EMP: 160 Publicly Held
WEB: www.alliancedatasystems.com
SIC: 7389 Credit card service
PA: Alliance Data Systems Corporation
7500 Dallas Pkwy Ste 700
Plano TX 75024

(G-16426)
AMERICAN CRANE INC
Also Called: American Crane & Lift Trck Svc
7791 Taylor Rd Sw Ste A (43068-9632)
PHONE................614 496-2268
Fax: 614 863-1509
Richard W Palmer Jr, *President*
Scott Hughes, *Vice Pres*
Lisa Edwards, *Controller*
Steve Cole, *Marketing Staff*
Bryan McAfee, *Manager*
EMP: 34
SQ FT: 25,000
SALES (est): 4.9MM Privately Held
WEB: www.americancraneinc.com
SIC: 7389 7353 5082 Crane & aerial lift service; cranes & aerial lift equipment, rental or leasing; cranes, construction

(G-16427)
AMERICAN JERSEY CATTLE ASSN (PA)
6486 E Main St (43068-2349)
PHONE................614 861-3636
Fax: 614 861-8040
Neal Smith, *CEO*
Vickie White, *Treasurer*
EMP: 35 EST: 1868
SQ FT: 9,000
SALES: 3.8MM Privately Held
WEB: www.infojersey.com
SIC: 8611 Trade associations

(G-16428)
AMERICAN KENDA RBR INDUS LTD (HQ)
Also Called: Kenda USA
7095 Americana Pkwy (43068-4118)
PHONE................866 536-3287
Fax: 614 866-9805
CHI-Jen Yang, *President*
Jeff Pizzola, *CFO*
Ching-Huey Yang, *Treasurer*
Robin Kamal, *Controller*
Hank Chang, *Manager*
▲ EMP: 45
SQ FT: 100,000
SALES (est): 30.2MM
SALES (corp-wide): 921.5MM Privately Held
SIC: 5014 Tires & tubes
PA: Kenda Rubber Ind. Co., Ltd.
146, Chung Shan Rd., Sec. 1,
Yuanlin City CHA 51064
483 451-71

(G-16429)
ARMOR PAVING & SEALING
6900 Americana Pkwy (43068-4115)
PHONE................614 751-6900
Fax: 614 751-6939

Reynoldsburg - Franklin County (G-16430)

Donald S Trasin, *President*
EMP: 25
SALES (est): 4.1MM **Privately Held**
WEB: www.armorpavingandsealing.com
SIC: 1611 Highway & street paving contractor

(G-16430)
BILLING CONNECTION INC
6422 E Main St Ste 202 (43068-2302)
PHONE..................740 964-0043
Willis Wolf, *President*
Britney Hickey, *Admin Asst*
EMP: 26
SALES (est): 1.9MM **Privately Held**
SIC: 8721 Billing & bookkeeping service

(G-16431)
BREATHING AIR SYSTEMS INC
8855 E Broad St (43068-9602)
PHONE..................614 864-1235
Mark Schuster, *President*
Lou Howard, *Treasurer*
EMP: 32
SALES (est): 5.4MM **Privately Held**
SIC: 5084 Compressors, except air conditioning

(G-16432)
BRICE HOTEL INC
Also Called: Days Inn
2100 Brice Rd (43068-3446)
PHONE..................614 864-1280
Fax: 614 866-2221
Juijer Lin, *President*
Matthew Hwang, *General Mgr*
Joyce Robinson, *General Mgr*
Yong Hwang, *Manager*
EMP: 70
SALES (est): 850K **Privately Held**
SIC: 7011 Hotels & motels

(G-16433)
BUSINESS ADMNSTRATORS CONS INC (PA)
6331 E Livingston Ave (43068-2756)
P.O. Box 107 (43068-0107)
PHONE..................614 863-8780
Fax: 614 863-9137
Richard Raup, *President*
Edmund Finley Jr, *Vice Pres*
Linda Flynn, *Controller*
Nannette J Richardson, *Sales Dir*
Tim Carlson, *Sales Staff*
EMP: 47
SQ FT: 4,600
SALES: 6.3MM **Privately Held**
WEB: www.bactpa.com
SIC: 6411 Insurance information & consulting services

(G-16434)
CELLCO PARTNERSHIP
Also Called: Verizon
2406 Taylor Park Dr (43068-8036)
PHONE..................614 759-4400
Fax: 614 751-2298
Tom Martinelli, *Principal*
EMP: 25
SALES (corp-wide): 126B **Publicly Held**
SIC: 4812 Cellular telephone services
HQ: Cellco Partnership
1 Verizon Way
Basking Ridge NJ 07920

(G-16435)
CENTIMARK CORPORATION
7077 Americana Pkwy (43068-4118)
PHONE..................614 536-1960
Steve Caudill, *Branch Mgr*
EMP: 45
SALES (corp-wide): 625.8MM **Privately Held**
SIC: 1761 Roof repair
PA: Centimark Corporation
12 Grandview Cir
Canonsburg PA 15317
724 514-8700

(G-16436)
CENTRAL CREDIT CORP
2040 Brice Rd Ste 200 (43068-3460)
PHONE..................614 856-5840
Fax: 614 856-0859
Rhett Ricart, *President*
Mary Yarbrough, *Controller*
Ben Stefanovski, *Credit Mgr*
Stephanie Bragg, *Human Res Mgr*
George Coles, *Marketing Staff*
EMP: 55
SALES (est): 9.3MM **Privately Held**
WEB: www.centralcreditcorp.com
SIC: 6141 Automobile loans, including insurance

(G-16437)
CENTRAL OHIO PRIMARY CARE
6488 E Main St Ste C (43068-7310)
PHONE..................614 552-2300
Fax: 614 552-2305
Randolph O Schultz, *Gnrl Med Prac*
EMP: 56 **Privately Held**
SIC: 8099 Childbirth preparation clinic
PA: Central Ohio Primary Care Physicians, Inc.
570 Polaris Pkwy Ste 250
Westerville OH 43082

(G-16438)
CHARDON LABORATORIES INC
7300 Tussing Rd (43068-4111)
PHONE..................614 860-1000
Fax: 614 759-2558
Robert S Butt, *CEO*
Chris Mace, *Engineer*
Mark Davenport, *CFO*
Cynthia King, *Human Res Mgr*
Mike Chaffee, *Sales Engr*
EMP: 50
SQ FT: 10,000
SALES: 7.5MM **Privately Held**
WEB: www.chardonlabs.com
SIC: 7389 Water softener service

(G-16439)
COLUMBUS DIESEL SUPPLY CO INC
3100 Delta Marine Dr (43068-3992)
PHONE..................614 445-8391
Fax: 614 445-8104
Brad Fry, *General Mgr*
Susan Boone, *Office Mgr*
EMP: 25
SALES (corp-wide): 13.6MM **Privately Held**
WEB: www.columbusdieselsupply.com
SIC: 7538 5013 Diesel engine repair: automotive; automotive supplies & parts; automotive supplies
PA: Columbus Diesel Supply Co Inc
4710 Allmond Ave
Louisville KY 40209
502 361-1181

(G-16440)
COLUMBUS FRKLN CNTY PK
Also Called: Blacklick Wods Mtro Golf Crses
7309 E Livingston Ave (43068-3019)
P.O. Box 3 (43068-0003)
PHONE..................614 861-3193
Fax: 614 861-8051
Chuck Doran, *Manager*
EMP: 28
SALES (corp-wide): 18.3MM **Privately Held**
WEB: www.metroparks.net
SIC: 7992 Public golf courses
PA: Columbus & Franklin County Metropolitan Park District
1069 W Main St Unit B
Westerville OH 43081
614 891-0700

(G-16441)
CONTRACT FREIGHTERS INC
945 Mahle Dr (43068-6797)
PHONE..................614 577-0447
EMP: 625
SALES (corp-wide): 2.7B **Privately Held**
SIC: 4213 Trucking, except local
HQ: Contract Freighters, Inc.
4701 E 32nd St
Joplin MO 64804
417 623-5229

(G-16442)
DA VINCI GROUP INC
7815 Pembrook Dr (43068-3129)
PHONE..................614 419-2393
Jeff Porter, *President*
◆ **EMP:** 30
SALES (est): 2.2MM **Privately Held**
SIC: 1542 Commercial & office building contractors

(G-16443)
DAIFUKU AMERICA CORPORATION (HQ)
Also Called: Daifuku Co
6700 Tussing Rd (43068-5083)
PHONE..................614 863-1888
Fax: 614 863-9977
Nobo Morita, *President*
Mike Conner, *President*
Ken Hamel, *President*
Akihiko Nishimura, *President*
Tetsuya Hibi, *Corp Secy*
▲ **EMP:** 150
SQ FT: 70,000
SALES (est): 373.3MM
SALES (corp-wide): 2.8B **Privately Held**
WEB: www.daifukuamerica.com
SIC: 5084 Conveyor systems
PA: Daifuku Co., Ltd.
3-2-11, Mitejima, Nishiyodogawa-Ku
Osaka OSK 555-0
664 721-261

(G-16444)
DATACOMM TECH
Also Called: Techdisposal
6606 Tussing Rd Ste B (43068-4174)
PHONE..................614 755-5100
Sepehr Rajaie, *President*
Mandy Prifogle, *Manager*
EMP: 40
SQ FT: 60,000
SALES (est): 3.5MM **Privately Held**
WEB: www.techdisposal.com
SIC: 7379 Computer related consulting services

(G-16445)
DENTAL SERVICS OF OHIO DANIEL
6323 Tussing Rd (43068-3984)
P.O. Box 11568, Overland Park KS (66207-4268)
PHONE..................614 863-2222
EMP: 99
SQ FT: 1,500
SALES (est): 1.8MM **Privately Held**
SIC: 8021 Dentist's Office

(G-16446)
DIEWALD & POPE INC
245 Connell Ct (43068-4307)
PHONE..................614 861-6160
Joseph Pope, *President*
Jesse Pope, *Treasurer*
EMP: 25 **EST:** 1974
SQ FT: 3,000
SALES (est): 1.4MM **Privately Held**
SIC: 1711 Plumbing contractors; heating & air conditioning contractors

(G-16447)
DIMENSIONAL METALS INC (PA)
Also Called: D M I
58 Klema Dr N (43068-9691)
PHONE..................740 927-3633
Fax: 740 927-3319
Stephen C Wissman, *CEO*
Phillip Gastaldo, *President*
Dan Begley, *Managing Dir*
Steven Gastaldo, *Vice Pres*
Shawn Walters, *Prdtn Mgr*
EMP: 52
SQ FT: 34,000
SALES (est): 12.7MM **Privately Held**
WEB: www.dmimetals.com
SIC: 1761 3444 3531 Sheet metalwork; sheet metalwork; roofing equipment

(G-16448)
DREIER & MALLER INC (PA)
6508 Taylor Rd Sw (43068-9633)
PHONE..................614 575-0065
Fax: 614 575-0765
Stewart Dreier, *President*
Bruce Stevenson, *Business Mgr*
Steve Maller, *Corp Secy*
Amanda Madrigrano, *Admin Asst*
EMP: 28
SALES (est): 11.1MM **Privately Held**
WEB: www.dreierandmaller.com
SIC: 5084 7389 7699 Industrial machinery & equipment; measuring & testing equipment, electrical; pipeline & power line inspection service; sewer cleaning & rodding

(G-16449)
DUCKWORTH ENTERPRISES LLC
Also Called: Scwashtan
2020 Brice Rd Ste 210 (43068-3457)
PHONE..................614 575-2900
Daniel Duckworth, *General Mgr*
Kelly Kal, *Controller*
Thomas M Duckworth, *Mng Member*
EMP: 25 **EST:** 2001
SALES (est): 1.5MM **Privately Held**
SIC: 7218 Industrial launderers

(G-16450)
ECHO 24 INC (PA)
167 Cypress St Sw Ste A (43068-9692)
PHONE..................740 964-7081
Anthony J Gunter, *President*
Ryan Sagraves, *Opers Mgr*
Lisa L Gunter, *CPA*
Dean Kehres, *Sales Engr*
Debbie Spicer, *Office Mgr*
EMP: 40
SQ FT: 2,000
SALES: 6MM **Privately Held**
SIC: 4813 Telephone communication, except radio

(G-16451)
ENTERPRISE HOLDINGS INC
6501 Tussing Rd (43068-3990)
PHONE..................614 866-1480
EMP: 53
SALES (corp-wide): 6.1B **Privately Held**
SIC: 7514 Rent-a-car service
HQ: Enterprise Holdings, Inc.
600 Corporate Park Dr
Saint Louis MO 63105
314 512-5000

(G-16452)
FIRST HOSPITALITY COMPANY LLC
Also Called: Fairfield Inn
2826 Taylor Road Ext (43068-9555)
PHONE..................614 864-4555
Fax: 614 864-4777
Amar Pandey, *Partner*
Rey Harrison, *General Mgr*
EMP: 50
SALES (est): 2.8MM **Privately Held**
SIC: 7011 Hotels & motels

(G-16453)
FIRST HOTEL MANAGEMENT LLC
Also Called: Days Inn Stes Columbus E Arprt
2100 Brice Rd (43068-3446)
PHONE..................614 864-1280
Axia Zhang, *Mng Member*
EMP: 25 **EST:** 2015
SALES (est): 60.1K **Privately Held**
SIC: 7011 Hotels & motels

(G-16454)
GLOBAL TRANSPORTATION SERVICES
7139 Americana Pkwy (43068-4120)
PHONE..................614 409-0770
EMP: 29
SALES (corp-wide): 171.7MM **Privately Held**
SIC: 4731 Freight forwarding; customhouse brokers
HQ: Global Transportation Services, Inc
18209 80th Ave S Ste A
Kent WA 98032
425 207-1500

(G-16455)
GOLIATH CONTRACTING LTD
405 Waggoner Rd (43068-9729)
PHONE..................614 568-7878
Steve Hatton, *President*
Beth Gosiewski, *Administration*
EMP: 25
SQ FT: 2,500

▲ = Import ▼ = Export
◆ = Import/Export

GEOGRAPHIC SECTION

Reynoldsburg - Franklin County (G-16480)

SALES: 4MM **Privately Held**
SIC: **1751** 1542 Store fixture installation; commercial & office building contractors

(G-16456)
GPAX LTD
555 Lancaster Ave (43068-1128)
PHONE.....................614 501-7622
Fax: 614 501-7626
Gary James, *Partner*
William Mahoney, *VP Mktg*
Mike Schneider, *Manager*
EMP: 50
SALES (est): 4.1MM
SALES (corp-wide): 59.5MM **Privately Held**
WEB: www.gpax.com
SIC: 5199 Packaging materials
PA: Dynalab, Inc.
    555 Lancaster Ave
    Reynoldsburg OH 43068
    614 866-9999

(G-16457)
GREEN KING COMPANY INC
9562 Taylor Rd Sw (43068-3228)
PHONE.....................614 861-4132
Fax: 614 861-1964
Adam T High, *President*
Erik High, *Vice Pres*
Pichen Hill, *Controller*
EMP: 30
SQ FT: 4,000
SALES (est): 2.2MM **Privately Held**
SIC: 0782 Landscape contractors

(G-16458)
HOME DEPOT USA INC
Also Called: Home Depot, The
2480 Brice Rd (43068-5431)
PHONE.....................614 577-1601
Fax: 614 868-7416
Chris Howard, *Sales Executive*
Mark Smith, *Manager*
EMP: 160
SALES (corp-wide): 100.9B **Publicly Held**
WEB: www.homerentalsdepot.com
SIC: **5211** 7359 Home centers; tool rental
HQ: Home Depot U.S.A., Inc.
    2455 Paces Ferry Rd Se
    Atlanta GA 30339

(G-16459)
J & D HOME IMPROVEMENT INC (PA)
Also Called: J & D Basement Sytems
13659 E Main St (43068)
PHONE.....................740 927-0722
Fax: 513 927-1271
Tom Johnston, *President*
Ronald Greenbaum, *Vice Pres*
EMP: 65
SQ FT: 13,000
SALES (est): 13.7MM **Privately Held**
WEB: www.crawlspacemaintenance.com
SIC: **1799** 1771 1521 1741 Waterproofing; foundation & footing contractor; general remodeling, single-family houses; foundation building; plumbing contractors

(G-16460)
JPMORGAN CHASE BANK NAT ASSN
8445 E Main St (43068-4707)
PHONE.....................614 759-8955
Carissa Davis, *Branch Mgr*
EMP: 34
SALES (corp-wide): 99.6B **Publicly Held**
SIC: **6029** 6022 6021 Commercial banks; state commercial banks; national commercial banks
HQ: Jpmorgan Chase Bank, National Association
    1111 Polaris Pkwy
    Columbus OH 43240
    614 436-3055

(G-16461)
JPMORGAN CHASE BANK NAT ASSN
2025 Brice Rd (43068-3447)
P.O. Box 1651 (43068-6651)
PHONE.....................614 248-2410
Fax: 614 248-2361
E C Carter, *Principal*
EMP: 26
SALES (corp-wide): 99.6B **Publicly Held**
SIC: 6021 National commercial banks
HQ: Jpmorgan Chase Bank, National Association
    1111 Polaris Pkwy
    Columbus OH 43240
    614 436-3055

(G-16462)
KARST & SONS INC
6496 Taylor Rd Sw (43068-9633)
PHONE.....................614 501-9530
Fax: 614 501-9533
John G Karst, *President*
EMP: 45
SALES (est): 1.1MM **Privately Held**
SIC: 1741 Masonry & other stonework

(G-16463)
KINDERCARE LEARNING CTRS LLC
Also Called: Reynoldsburg Kindercare
6601 Bartlett Rd (43068-2382)
PHONE.....................614 866-4446
Fax: 614 863-9011
Debi Standiford, *Branch Mgr*
EMP: 25
SALES (corp-wide): 1.2B **Privately Held**
WEB: www.kindercare.com
SIC: 8351 Group day care center
HQ: Kindercare Learning Centers, Llc
    650 Ne Holladay St # 1400
    Portland OR 97232
    503 872-1300

(G-16464)
KRISTI BRITTON
Also Called: Comtron Professional Cons
6400 E Main St Ste 203 (43068-2348)
PHONE.....................614 868-7612
Fax: 614 868-7613
Kristi Britton, *Owner*
EMP: 30 EST: 1978
SQ FT: 1,000
SALES (est): 1.3MM **Privately Held**
SIC: 7379 Computer related consulting services

(G-16465)
LIFE CENTER ADULT DAY CARE
Also Called: LIFE CENTER AT WESLEY RIDGE
2225 State Route 256 (43068)
PHONE.....................614 866-7212
Fax: 614 863-4200
Elizabeth Vogt, *Director*
EMP: 30
SALES: 238.1K **Privately Held**
SIC: **8322** 8351 Adult day care center; child day care services

(G-16466)
LOWES HOME CENTERS LLC
8231 E Broad St (43068-9732)
PHONE.....................614 769-9940
Fax: 614 769-9943
Jeff Fetters, *Branch Mgr*
Becky Boudreaux, *Admin Asst*
EMP: 150
SALES (corp-wide): 68.6B **Publicly Held**
SIC: **5211** 5031 5722 5064 Home centers; building materials, exterior; building materials, interior; household appliance stores; electrical appliances, television & radio
HQ: Lowe's Home Centers, Llc
    1605 Curtis Bridge Rd
    Wilkesboro NC 28697
    336 658-4000

(G-16467)
LQ MANAGEMENT LLC
Also Called: La Quinta Inn
2447 Brice Rd (43068-3455)
PHONE.....................614 866-6456
Fax: 614 866-4522
Ed Sosa, *General Mgr*
Riley Doublday, *Manager*
EMP: 30
SQ FT: 27,145
SALES (corp-wide): 980.6MM **Publicly Held**
WEB: www.neubayern.net
SIC: 7011 Hotels
HQ: Lq Management L.L.C.
    909 Hidden Rdg Ste 600
    Irving TX 75038
    214 492-6600

(G-16468)
MAST INDUSTRIES INC
Also Called: Mast Global Fashions
8655 E Broad St (43068-9715)
PHONE.....................614 856-6000
Richard Paul, *President*
Joe Bozzi, *Technical Staff*
Craig Hoffman, *Plan/Corp Dev D*
EMP: 52
SALES (corp-wide): 12.6B **Publicly Held**
SIC: **5137** 5136 Women's & children's clothing; men's & boys' clothing
HQ: Mast Industries, Inc.
    2 Limited Pkwy
    Columbus OH 43230
    614 415-7000

(G-16469)
METROPOLITAN FAMILY CARE INC
Also Called: Metropolitan Family Care
7094 E Main St (43068-2010)
PHONE.....................614 237-1067
Fax: 614 237-2655
Andrew J Pultz MD, *President*
Diana Max, *Manager*
EMP: 25
SALES (est): 2.9MM **Privately Held**
SIC: 8011 General & family practice, physician/surgeon

(G-16470)
NATIONAL ALL-JERSEY INC (PA)
6486 E Main St (43068-2349)
PHONE.....................614 861-3636
Neal Smith, *CEO*
Eric Metzger, *General Mgr*
Vickie J White, *Treasurer*
EMP: 40 EST: 1957
SQ FT: 1,350
SALES: 939K **Privately Held**
WEB: www.usjersey.com
SIC: 0241 Dairy farms

(G-16471)
OAKWOOD MANAGEMENT COMPANY (PA)
6950 Americana Pkwy Ste A (43068-4126)
PHONE.....................614 866-8702
Fax: 614 866-6824
John D Wymer, *President*
Donald W Kelley, *Vice Pres*
Dana L Moore, *Vice Pres*
Patrick J Kelley, *Treasurer*
Holly Ellis, *Manager*
EMP: 45
SQ FT: 10,000
SALES: 4.3MM **Privately Held**
WEB: www.oakwoodmgmt.com
SIC: 6531 Real estate managers

(G-16472)
OHIO FEDERATION OF SOIL AND WA
Also Called: OFSWCD
8995 E Main St (43068-3342)
PHONE.....................614 784-1900
Melinda Bankey, *CEO*
Kris Swartz, *President*
Jack Hazelbaker, *Corp Secy*
Harold Neuenschwander, *Vice Pres*
Bob Short, *Vice Pres*
EMP: 40
SALES: 1MM **Privately Held**
SIC: 8699 Charitable organization

(G-16473)
PXP OHIO
6800 Tussing Rd (43068-7044)
PHONE.....................614 575-4242
Fax: 614 575-4252
Greg Scott, *Owner*
Linda Scott, *Co-Owner*
Tony Allbaugh, *Foreman/Supr*
Tom Kirtis, *Controller*
Mayrna Ayyoub, *Accountant*
EMP: 31
SQ FT: 15,688
SALES (est): 2.9MM **Privately Held**
SIC: 7389 Printing broker

(G-16474)
REM-OHIO INC
Also Called: REM Ohio Waivered Services
6402 E Main St Ste 103 (43068-2356)
PHONE.....................614 367-1370
Fax: 614 367-9751
Theresa Setser, *Director*
EMP: 80
SALES (est): 2MM
SALES (corp-wide): 2.8MM **Privately Held**
WEB: www.remohio.com
SIC: 8361 Home for the mentally retarded
PA: Rem-Ohio, Inc
    6921 York Ave S
    Minneapolis MN 55435
    952 925-5067

(G-16475)
REYNOLDSBURG CITY SCHOOLS
Also Called: School Bus Garage
7932 E Main St (43068-1239)
PHONE.....................614 501-1041
Mike Rosenberger, *Director*
EMP: 45
SQ FT: 8,640
SALES (corp-wide): 93.4MM **Privately Held**
SIC: 4173 Maintenance facilities, buses
PA: Reynoldsburg City Schools
    7244 E Main St
    Reynoldsburg OH 43068
    614 501-1020

(G-16476)
REYNOLDSBURG SWIM CLUB INC
7215 E Main St (43068-2000)
PHONE.....................614 866-3211
Fax: 614 866-5270
EMP: 30
SQ FT: 4,000
SALES (est): 901.4K **Privately Held**
SIC: 7997 Membership Sport/Recreation Club

(G-16477)
RGIS LLC
6488 E Main St Ste B (43068-7310)
PHONE.....................248 651-2511
Art Alexander, *Manager*
EMP: 65
SALES (corp-wide): 7.1B **Publicly Held**
WEB: www.rgisinv.com
SIC: **7389** 7374 Inventory computing service; data processing & preparation
HQ: Rgis, Llc
    2000 Taylor Rd
    Auburn Hills MI 48326
    248 651-2511

(G-16478)
RITE RUG CO
6574 E Broadstreet (43068)
PHONE.....................614 552-1190
Michael Goldberg, *President*
EMP: 35
SALES (corp-wide): 82.2MM **Privately Held**
SIC: 1743 Tile installation, ceramic
PA: Rite Rug Co.
    4450 Poth Rd Ste A
    Columbus OH 43213
    614 261-6060

(G-16479)
RIVERSIDE COMMONS LTD PARTNR
6880 Tussing Rd (43068-4101)
PHONE.....................614 863-4640
Sandsord Goldston, *CEO*
Sandy Goldston, *Chairman*
Timothy M West, *Human Res Dir*
Judy Bassinger, *Manager*
Jo A Haden, *Manager*
EMP: 60
SQ FT: 17,000
SALES (est): 2.8MM **Privately Held**
SIC: 6513 Apartment building operators

(G-16480)
ROSE TRANSPORT INC
6747 Taylor Rd Sw (43068-9674)
PHONE.....................614 864-4004

Reynoldsburg - Franklin County (G-16481) GEOGRAPHIC SECTION

John W Spencer, *President*
Ralph Spencer, *Vice Pres*
John Schetzsle, *Marketing Staff*
EMP: 25
SQ FT: 14,000
SALES (est): 3.8MM
SALES (corp-wide): 44.9MM **Privately Held**
WEB: www.mulchmfg.com
SIC: 4213 Trucking, except local
PA: Mulch Manufacturing, Inc.
  6747 Taylor Rd Sw
  Reynoldsburg OH 43068
  614 864-4004

(G-16481)
SATCOM SERVICE LLC
7052 Americana Pkwy (43068-4117)
PHONE 614 863-6470
Steve Farber, *President*
Ken Farber, *CFO*
Patty Jackson, *Manager*
EMP: 60
SQ FT: 50,000
SALES (est): 1.8MM **Privately Held**
SIC: 4841 Direct broadcast satellite services (DBS)

(G-16482)
TENDER NURSING CARE
7668 Slate Ridge Blvd (43068-8160)
PHONE 614 856-3508
Fax: 614 367-1929
Maria Thacker, *Principal*
EMP: 25
SALES (est): 1.3MM **Privately Held**
SIC: 8051 Skilled nursing care facilities

(G-16483)
THAYER PWR COMM LINE CNSTR LLC (PA)
Also Called: Thayer Power & Comm Line
117 Cypress St Sw (43068-9692)
PHONE 814 474-1174
Fax: 814 474-3474
Timothy Luden, *Mng Member*
Sean Peebles, *Manager*
Dennis Rachocki, *Manager*
Jackie Foster, *Receptionist*
EMP: 40
SQ FT: 16,000
SALES (est): 71.3MM **Privately Held**
SIC: 1623 Water, sewer & utility lines; communication line & transmission tower construction; electric power line construction; telephone & communication line construction

(G-16484)
TM WALLICK RSDNTL PRPTS I LTD
6880 Tussing Rd (43068-4101)
PHONE 614 863-4640
Amber Spohn, *Mng Member*
Park Lawrence,
EMP: 83
SALES: 950K **Privately Held**
SIC: 6513 Apartment building operators

(G-16485)
TOYS R US INC
2686 Taylor Road Ext (43068-9553)
PHONE 614 759-7744
EMP: 50
SALES (corp-wide): 11.5B **Privately Held**
SIC: 5137 Baby goods
PA: Toys "r" Us, Inc.
  1 Geoffrey Way
  Wayne NJ 07470
  973 617-3500

(G-16486)
TS TECH AMERICAS INC (HQ)
8458 E Broad St (43068-9749)
PHONE 614 575-4100
Minoru Maeda, *President*
Jason MA, *Exec VP*
Takayuki Maegawa, *Senior VP*
Kazuhisa Saito, *Vice Pres*
Rosalba Perez, *Opers Staff*
▲ **EMP:** 350 **EST:** 2013
SALES (est): 984.7MM
SALES (corp-wide): 3.7B **Privately Held**
SIC: 5099 Child restraint seats, automotive

PA: Ts Tech Co., Ltd.
  3-7-27, Sakaecho
  Asaka STM 351-0
  484 621-121

(G-16487)
UNIVERSAL GREEN ENERGY SOLUTIO
2086 Belltree Dr (43068-3505)
PHONE 844 723-7768
Kerry E Fletcher, *President*
EMP: 25
SQ FT: 1,700
SALES (est): 851.8K **Privately Held**
SIC: 4939 7382 Combination utilities; security systems services

(G-16488)
VALMER LAND TITLE AGENCY (PA)
2227 State Route 256 B (43068-9326)
PHONE 614 860-0005
Fax: 614 860-0010
Valerie Lambert, *President*
Monica Merriman, *Vice Pres*
Monica Merryman, *Vice Pres*
Chris Borgan, *Sales Mgr*
EMP: 25
SALES (est): 20MM **Privately Held**
SIC: 6361 Real estate title insurance

(G-16489)
WESLEY RIDGE INC
Also Called: Methodist Elder Care Services
2225 Taylor Park Dr (43068-8053)
PHONE 614 759-0023
Fax: 614 501-1399
Robert L Rouse, *CEO*
Kenya George, *Pub Rel Dir*
Dinah Cason, *Exec Dir*
Christopher Nichols, *Exec Dir*
Wesley Ridge, *Exec Dir*
EMP: 126 **EST:** 1996
SALES (est): 6.1MM **Privately Held**
WEB: www.wesleyridge.com
SIC: 8059 8052 Personal care home, with health care; intermediate care facilities

(G-16490)
WHITE BARN CANDLE CO
7 Limited Pkwy E (43068-5300)
PHONE 614 856-6000
Diane Neal, *CEO*
EMP: 1000
SALES (est): 140.1MM
SALES (corp-wide): 12.6B **Publicly Held**
WEB: www.limited.com
SIC: 5199 Candles
PA: L Brands, Inc.
  3 Limited Pkwy
  Columbus OH 43230
  614 415-7000

(G-16491)
WOODWARD EXCAVATING CO
7340 Tussing Rd (43068-4111)
PHONE 614 866-4384
John Woodward, *President*
Clay Woodward, *Corp Secy*
Brad Woodward, *Vice Pres*
EMP: 25
SQ FT: 7,200
SALES: 1.9MM **Privately Held**
SIC: 1623 Underground utilities contractor; sewer line construction; water main construction

(G-16492)
XTREME CONTRACTING LTD
7600 Asden Ct (43068-9757)
PHONE 614 568-7030
Steven Hatton, *President*
Beth Gosiwski, *Office Mgr*
EMP: 25
SQ FT: 2,500
SALES: 4MM **Privately Held**
SIC: 5211 1542 Bathroom fixtures, equipment & supplies; commercial & office building contractors

Richfield
Summit County

(G-16493)
AETNA LIFE INSURANCE COMPANY
4059 Kinros Lake Pkwy # 300 (44286-9253)
PHONE 330 659-8000
Fax: 330 464-2723
Scott Ushkowitz, *Branch Mgr*
Karen Keberle, *Manager*
EMP: 50 **Publicly Held**
SIC: 6324 Health maintenance organization (HMO), insurance only
HQ: Aetna Life Insurance Company Inc
  151 Farmington Ave
  Hartford CT 06156
  860 273-0123

(G-16494)
ALL AERIALS LLC
4945 Brecksville Rd (44286-9244)
PHONE 330 659-9600
Fax: 330 659-0894
Danille Sinnons, *Human Res Mgr*
Kimberly Kasparek, *Manager*
Brian Miller, *Manager*
Susi Motz,
EMP: 25
SALES (est): 5.9MM **Privately Held**
WEB: www.allaerials.com
SIC: 7353 Cranes & aerial lift equipment, rental or leasing

(G-16495)
AMERICAN ENVMTL GROUP LTD
3600 Brecksville Rd # 100 (44286-9668)
PHONE 330 659-5930
Fax: 330 659-5931
Carl Apicella, *President*
Ronald Zunker, *General Mgr*
Roy McMasters, *Superintendent*
Kevin Shull, *Superintendent*
Gerald E Hersh, *Business Mgr*
▲ **EMP:** 450
SALES (est): 57.6MM
SALES (corp-wide): 2.7B **Publicly Held**
WEB: www.aegl.net
SIC: 1382 Oil & gas exploration services
PA: Tetra Tech, Inc.
  3475 E Foothill Blvd
  Pasadena CA 91107
  626 351-4664

(G-16496)
AMERICAN HIGHWAYS INSUR AGCY
3250 Interstate Dr (44286-9000)
PHONE 330 659-8900
Fax: 330 659-8912
Alan Spachman, *Principal*
Terri Johnson, *Vice Pres*
Rob Divine, *Regl Sales Mgr*
Donna Schultz, *Office Mgr*
Angelo Fortunato, *Senior Mgr*
EMP: 101
SALES (est): 10.1MM **Publicly Held**
WEB: www.nationalinterstate.com
SIC: 6411 Insurance agents
HQ: National Interstate Corporation
  3250 Interstate Dr
  Richfield OH 44286
  330 659-8900

(G-16497)
AMERICAN ROADWAY LOGISTICS INC
3920 Congress Pkwy (44286-9745)
PHONE 330 659-2003
Heidi Claxton, *President*
Jonathon Claxton, *Vice Pres*
Harold Schaffer, *CFO*
Tina Sutton, *Payroll Mgr*
EMP: 30
SALES (est): 5.9MM **Privately Held**
SIC: 7359 Work zone traffic equipment (flags, cones, barrels, etc.)

(G-16498)
BRECKSVILLE LEASING CO LLC
Also Called: Pine Valley Care Center
4360 Brecksville Rd (44286-9457)
PHONE 330 659-6166
Fax: 330 659-2944
Stephen Rosedale,
EMP: 140
SALES (est): 5.7MM **Privately Held**
SIC: 8051 Convalescent home with continuous nursing care

(G-16499)
CARRARA COMPANIES INC
3774 Congress Pkwy (44286-9041)
PHONE 330 659-2800
Toll Free: .... 888 -
Fax: 330 659-0683
Justin Sucato, *President*
Maggie Luth, *Business Mgr*
Julie Sucato, *Corp Secy*
Jim Hlas, *Marketing Staff*
Mike Moore, *Manager*
EMP: 58 **EST:** 1996
SQ FT: 16,000
SALES: 10.4MM **Privately Held**
WEB: www.steamaticneo.com
SIC: 7349 6331 Cleaning service, industrial or commercial; property damage insurance

(G-16500)
CHARLES SCHWAB & CO INC
4150 Kinross Lakes Pkwy (44286-9369)
P.O. Box 5050 (44286-5050)
PHONE 330 908-4478
Rick Haseltine, *General Mgr*
Brian Bender, *Vice Pres*
Nancy Morris, *Property Mgr*
Walter Bettinger II, *Manager*
Gabriel Hanselman, *Manager*
EMP: 50
SALES (corp-wide): 8.6B **Publicly Held**
WEB: www.schwabrt.com
SIC: 6211 Brokers, security
HQ: Charles Schwab & Co., Inc.
  211 Main St Fl 17
  San Francisco CA 94105
  415 636-7000

(G-16501)
CISCO SYSTEMS INC
4125 Highlander Pkwy (44286-9085)
PHONE 330 523-2000
Dan Cusick, *Business Mgr*
Michael Chmura, *Engineer*
John Coxn, *Engineer*
Craig Hyps, *Engineer*
Jeff Klaas, *Engineer*
EMP: 239
SALES (corp-wide): 48B **Publicly Held**
WEB: www.cisco.com
SIC: 7373 Local area network (LAN) systems integrator
PA: Cisco Systems, Inc.
  170 W Tasman Dr
  San Jose CA 95134
  408 526-4000

(G-16502)
COLUMBUS EQUIPMENT COMPANY
3942 Brecksville Rd (44286-9627)
PHONE 330 659-6681
Fax: 330 659-4760
Ron Duperow, *Sales Staff*
Jeff Thornburg, *Branch Mgr*
Jeff Badner, *Asst Mgr*
EMP: 30
SQ FT: 20,000
SALES (corp-wide): 84.2MM **Privately Held**
WEB: www.colsequipment.com
SIC: 5082 General construction machinery & equipment
PA: The Columbus Equipment Company
  2323 Performance Way
  Columbus OH 43207
  614 437-0352

(G-16503)
DAWSON COMPANIES
3900 Kinross Lakes Pkwy (44286-9381)
PHONE 440 333-9000

GEOGRAPHIC SECTION
Richfield - Summit County (G-16527)

Rob Odney, *Principal*
Rick Cote, *Exec VP*
Darren Faye, *Exec VP*
Bob Grevey, *Exec VP*
Jack Suber, *Senior VP*
EMP: 79
SALES (est): 57.3MM **Privately Held**
SIC: 6321 Health insurance carriers

(G-16504)
DENTAL CERAMICS INC
3404 Brecksville Rd (44286-9662)
PHONE..................330 523-5240
Fax: 216 518-8225
John Lavicka, *President*
EMP: 37
SALES (est): 4.3MM **Privately Held**
WEB: www.dentalceramics.net
SIC: 8072 3843 Crown & bridge production; dental equipment & supplies

(G-16505)
EMPACO EQUIPMENT CORPORATION (PA)
Also Called: Emil Pawuk & Associates
2958 Brecksville Rd (44286-9747)
P.O. Box 535 (44286-0535)
PHONE..................330 659-9393
Fax: 330 659-4772
Emil M Pawuk Sr, *President*
L R Gaiduk, *Principal*
C B Wheeler, *Principal*
Emil M Pawuk Jr, *Vice Pres*
Paul Backo, *Project Mgr*
EMP: 40
SQ FT: 11,280
SALES (est): 11.6MM **Privately Held**
WEB: www.empacoequipment.com
SIC: 1799 Service station equipment installation & maintenance

(G-16506)
ESTES EXPRESS LINES INC
2755 Brecksville Rd (44286-9735)
PHONE..................330 659-9750
EMP: 28
SALES (corp-wide): 2.4B **Privately Held**
SIC: 4731 Freight transportation arrangement
PA: Estes Express Lines, Inc.
3901 W Broad St
Richmond VA 23230
804 353-1900

(G-16507)
EXPLORER RV INSURANCE AGCY INC
Also Called: GMAC Insurance
3250 Interstate Dr (44286-9000)
P.O. Box 568 (44286-0568)
PHONE..................330 659-8900
Alan R Spachman, *Principal*
Benjamin Weiss, *Accountant*
Bill Tuttle, *Manager*
EMP: 121
SALES (est): 10.6MM **Publicly Held**
WEB: www.explorerv.com
SIC: 6411 Insurance agents
HQ: National Interstate Corporation
3250 Interstate Dr
Richfield OH 44286
330 659-8900

(G-16508)
FEDEX GROUND PACKAGE SYS INC
3245 Henry Rd (44286-9701)
PHONE..................800 463-3339
Kyle Ryan, *Branch Mgr*
Chad Fogle, *Manager*
EMP: 34
SALES (corp-wide): 60.3B **Publicly Held**
WEB: www.fedex.com
SIC: 4513 Letter delivery, private air; parcel delivery, private air
HQ: Fedex Ground Package System, Inc.
1000 Fed Ex Dr
Coraopolis PA 15108
412 269-1000

(G-16509)
FEDEX GROUND PACKAGE SYS INC
3201 Columbia Rd (44286-9622)
PHONE..................800 463-3339

Paul Sojda, *Branch Mgr*
EMP: 200
SALES (corp-wide): 60.3B **Publicly Held**
SIC: 4215 Package delivery, vehicular; parcel delivery, vehicular
HQ: Fedex Ground Package System, Inc.
1000 Fed Ex Dr
Coraopolis PA 15108
412 269-1000

(G-16510)
FRONTIER TANK CENTER INC
3800 Congress Pkwy (44286-9745)
P.O. Box 460 (44286-0460)
PHONE..................330 659-9410
Fax: 216 519-3888
James S Hollabaugh, *President*
Ed Vincenzi, *Finance Dir*
Erica AM, *Admin Sec*
Mary Hollabaugh, *Admin Sec*
EMP: 25
SQ FT: 25,000
SALES (est): 3.2MM **Privately Held**
WEB: www.frontiertrailer.com
SIC: 7699 5013 3714 Tank repair; trailer parts & accessories; motor vehicle body components & frame

(G-16511)
GROUP MANAGEMENT SERVICES INC (PA)
3750 Timberlake Dr (44286-9187)
PHONE..................330 659-0100
Fax: 330 659-0150
Mike Kahoe, *President*
Pam Amacciato, *Assistant VP*
Mark Watkins, *Vice Pres*
Matt Dalakas, *Opers Mgr*
Rosalie McCarthy, *Accounting Mgr*
EMP: 30
SQ FT: 6,000
SALES (est): 5.9MM **Privately Held**
WEB: www.groupmgmt.com
SIC: 8742 Compensation & benefits planning consultant

(G-16512)
I-TRAN INC
Also Called: Low Country Metal
4100 Congress Pkwy W (44286-9732)
PHONE..................330 659-0801
Ryan Macallister, *President*
Melissa Mayavess, *Controller*
◆ **EMP:** 25 **EST:** 2007
SALES (est): 4.4MM **Privately Held**
SIC: 5093 Metal scrap & waste materials

(G-16513)
IRG REALTY ADVISORS LLC (PA)
4020 Kinross Lakes Pkwy (44286-9084)
PHONE..................330 659-4060
Tracy C Green, *President*
Donald McKnight, *General Mgr*
Jessica Hunsinger, *Vice Pres*
Jon Cundiff, *Project Mgr*
Sam Maj, *Project Mgr*
EMP: 30
SQ FT: 1,200
SALES (est): 44.6MM **Privately Held**
WEB: www.ohiorealtyadvisors.com
SIC: 6531 Real estate managers

(G-16514)
MAS INC (PA)
2718 Brecksville Rd (44286-9735)
P.O. Box 526 (44286-0526)
PHONE..................330 659-3333
Fax: 330 659-0928
C Edwin Howard, *Ch of Bd*
Brian T Parsell, *President*
Ken E Weegar, *Exec VP*
Dave Hyne, *Manager*
Tami Roth, *Manager*
◆ **EMP:** 41
SQ FT: 80,000
SALES (est): 35.7MM **Privately Held**
WEB: www.masdist.com
SIC: 5064 5092 Electrical appliances, television & radio; electrical entertainment equipment; electrical appliances, major; video games

(G-16515)
NATIONAL INTERSTATE CORP (HQ)
3250 Interstate Dr (44286-9000)
PHONE..................330 659-8900
Fax: 330 595-8901
Anthony J Mercurio, *President*
Arthur J Gonzales, *Senior VP*
Terry E Phillips, *Senior VP*
Michelle Wiltgen, *Assistant VP*
Donald Davis, *Vice Pres*
EMP: 79
SQ FT: 143,000
SALES (est): 625.7MM **Publicly Held**
WEB: www.nationalinterstate.com
SIC: 6331 6411 Fire, marine & casualty insurance; property & casualty insurance agent

(G-16516)
NATIONAL INTERSTATE INSUR CO (DH)
3250 Interstate Dr (44286-9000)
PHONE..................330 659-8900
David W Michelson, *President*
Keith Boyle, *General Mgr*
Alan R Spachman, *Chairman*
Terry Phillips, *Senior VP*
George Skuggen, *Senior VP*
EMP: 200
SQ FT: 22,000
SALES (est): 268.9MM **Publicly Held**
SIC: 6331 Fire, marine & casualty insurance
HQ: National Interstate Corporation
3250 Interstate Dr
Richfield OH 44286
330 659-8900

(G-16517)
NEWARK CORPORATION
Newark Electronics Div
4180 Highlander Pkwy (44286-9352)
PHONE..................330 523-4457
Vicky Villicana, *General Mgr*
Steve Webb, *Vice Pres*
Rafael Castanos, *Engineer*
Antony Thomas, *Accountant*
Allison Root, *Sales Staff*
EMP: 300 **Privately Held**
WEB: www.newarkinone.com
SIC: 5065 Electronic parts
HQ: Newark Corporation
300 S Riverside Plz # 2200
Chicago IL 60606
773 784-5100

(G-16518)
NEWARK ELECTRONICS CORPORATION
4180 Highlander Pkwy (44286-9352)
PHONE..................330 523-4912
Tim Smith, *Branch Mgr*
EMP: 150 **Privately Held**
SIC: 5065 5063 Electronic parts; electrical apparatus & equipment
HQ: Newark Electronics Corporation
300 S Riverside Plz
Chicago IL 60606
773 784-5100

(G-16519)
OECONNECTION LLC
4205 Highlander Pkwy (44286-9077)
PHONE..................888 776-5792
Fax: 330 523-1700
Terry Cummins, *Exec VP*
Philip Firrell, *Exec VP*
Ike Herman, *Exec VP*
Jon Palazzo, *Vice Pres*
Walter Hayes, *QA Dir*
EMP: 175
SALES (est): 38.1MM **Privately Held**
WEB: www.oeconnection.com
SIC: 7371 Computer software systems analysis & design, custom

(G-16520)
OHIO ASSN PUB SCHL EMPLOYEES
3380 Brecksville Rd # 101 (44286-9801)
PHONE..................330 659-7335
Marc Beallor, *Manager*
EMP: 55

SALES (corp-wide): 9.2MM **Privately Held**
SIC: 8631 Labor union
PA: Ohio Association Of Public School Employees
6805 Oak Creek Dr Ste 1
Columbus OH 43229
614 890-4770

(G-16521)
OHIO TOOL SYSTEMS INC (PA)
3863 Congress Pkwy (44286-9797)
PHONE..................330 659-4181
Fax: 330 659-6991
Greg Grace, *President*
Jack Grace, *Corp Secy*
Eric Grace, *Vice Pres*
EMP: 55 **EST:** 1974
SQ FT: 16,000
SALES (est): 40.7MM **Privately Held**
WEB: www.ohiotool.com
SIC: 5084 Machine tools & accessories

(G-16522)
OLDER WISER LIFE SERVICES LLC
4028 Broadview Rd Ste 1 (44286-9231)
PHONE..................330 659-2111
Cheryl M Bass,
EMP: 30 **EST:** 2014
SALES (est): 95.3K **Privately Held**
SIC: 8322 Senior citizens' center or association

(G-16523)
QUALITY PLANT PRODUCTIONS INC
4586 Newton Rd (44286-9609)
PHONE..................440 526-8711
Fax: 440 526-8719
Cheryl Aschenbener, *Office Mgr*
EMP: 30
SQ FT: 1,600
SALES (est): 1.3MM **Privately Held**
WEB: www.qualityplantinc.com
SIC: 0181 0175 Shrubberies grown in field nurseries; deciduous tree fruits

(G-16524)
QUILALEA CORPORATION
3861 Sawbridge Dr (44286-9679)
PHONE..................330 487-0777
Mark Sinreich, *President*
EMP: 40
SALES (est): 6.9MM **Privately Held**
WEB: www.avid-tech.com
SIC: 8711 5045 Consulting engineer; computer software

(G-16525)
RECEIVABLE MGT SVCS CORP
4836 Brecksville Rd (44286-9177)
PHONE..................330 659-1000
Dan Leo Montenaro, *Branch Mgr*
EMP: 65 **Privately Held**
SIC: 7322 Collection agency, except real estate
HQ: The Receivable Management Services Corporation
240 Emery St
Bethlehem PA 18015
484 242-4000

(G-16526)
RICHFIELD BANQUET & CONFER
Also Called: Quality Inn
4742 Brecksville Rd (44286-9619)
PHONE..................330 659-6151
Sandip Tharkar,
EMP: 43
SALES (est): 2.6MM **Privately Held**
SIC: 7011 Hotels & motels

(G-16527)
RICOH USA INC
Also Called: American Business Machines
4125 Highlander Pkwy # 175 (44286-8903)
PHONE..................330 523-3900
Rex Swartz, *Branch Mgr*
John Cannon, *Manager*
EMP: 80
SALES (corp-wide): 17.8B **Privately Held**
WEB: www.ikon.com
SIC: 5044 Photocopy machines

Richfield - Summit County (G-16528)

HQ: Ricoh Usa, Inc.
70 Valley Stream Pkwy
Malvern PA 19355
610 296-8000

(G-16528)
SAIA MOTOR FREIGHT LINE LLC
2920 Brecksville Rd Ste B (44286-9265)
PHONE.................................330 659-4277
Fax: 330 362-1114
M Pawuk, *Branch Mgr*
EMP: 31
SALES (corp-wide): 1.3B Publicly Held
WEB: www.saia.com
SIC: 4213 Contract haulers
HQ: Saia Motor Freight Line, Llc
11465 Johns Creek Pkwy # 400
Duluth GA 30097
770 232-5067

(G-16529)
SCHNEIDER ELECTRIC USA INC
Also Called: Schneider Electric 324
3623 Brecksville Rd Ste A (44286-9264)
PHONE.................................440 526-9070
Bill McHenry, *Manager*
Dawn Barrett, *Coordinator*
EMP: 25
SALES (corp-wide): 241K Privately Held
WEB: www.squared.com
SIC: 5063 Electrical supplies
HQ: Schneider Electric Usa, Inc.
800 Federal St
Andover MA 01810
978 975-9600

(G-16530)
THORSON BAKER & ASSOC INC (PA)
3030 W Streetsboro Rd (44286-9632)
PHONE.................................330 659-6688
Fax: 330 659-6675
Michael Thorson, *President*
Gordon Baker, *Vice Pres*
Michael Cochran, *Project Mgr*
Patricia Fellenstein, *Project Mgr*
Jeff Graham, *Project Mgr*
EMP: 121
SQ FT: 48,000
SALES (est): 17.5MM Privately Held
WEB: www.thorsonbaker.com
SIC: 8711 Professional engineer

(G-16531)
UPS GROUND FREIGHT INC
3495 Brecksville Rd (44286-9663)
PHONE.................................330 659-6693
Jerry Ruediger, *Manager*
EMP: 200
SQ FT: 3,500
SALES (corp-wide): 65.8B Publicly Held
WEB: www.overnite.com
SIC: 4213 4212 Contract haulers; local trucking, without storage
HQ: Ups Ground Freight, Inc.
1000 Semmes Ave
Richmond VA 23224
866 372-5619

(G-16532)
WARD TRUCKING LLC
2800 Brecksville Rd (44286-9740)
PHONE.................................330 659-6658
Fax: 330 659-6789
Robert Kane, *Manager*
EMP: 50
SALES (corp-wide): 153.4MM Privately Held
SIC: 4213 Contract haulers
PA: Ward Trucking, Llc
1436 Ward Trucking Dr
Altoona PA 16602
814 944-0803

(G-16533)
WMK INC
Also Called: MOBILITY WORKS FOUNDATION, THE
4199 Kinross Lakes Pkwy (44286-9010)
PHONE.................................630 782-1900
William M Koeblitz, *Principal*
Shaun Dye, *Parts Mgr*
Charles Gibson, *Regl Sales Mgr*
Jim Cermak, *Marketing Staff*
Diane Brush, *Manager*

EMP: 29
SALES: 377.1K Privately Held
SIC: 4789 Cargo loading & unloading services

(G-16534)
YRC INC
Also Called: Yellow Transportation
5250 Brecksville Rd (44286-9461)
PHONE.................................330 659-4151
Fax: 330 659-1250
Joel Campbell, *Manager*
EMP: 52
SQ FT: 800
SALES (corp-wide): 4.8B Publicly Held
WEB: www.roadway.com
SIC: 4213 4212 Contract haulers; local trucking, without storage
HQ: Yrc Inc.
10990 Roe Ave
Overland Park KS 66211
913 696-6100

Richmond
Jefferson County

(G-16535)
SIGN AMERICA INCORPORATED
3887 State Route 43 (43944-7912)
P.O. Box 396 (43944-0396)
PHONE.................................740 765-5555
Fax: 740 765-5631
Judith A Hilty, *President*
Scott Hilty Jr, *Vice Pres*
John Bray, *Admin Sec*
EMP: 40
SQ FT: 6,000
SALES (est): 9.6MM Privately Held
WEB: www.signamericainc.com
SIC: 5046 3993 Signs, electrical; neon signs; signs & advertising specialties

Richmond Heights
Cuyahoga County

(G-16536)
CAPITAL SENIOR LIVING CORP
261 Richmond Rd (44143-4422)
PHONE.................................216 289-9800
Fax: 216 289-9801
EMP: 214
SALES (corp-wide): 467MM Publicly Held
SIC: 8361 Residential care
PA: Capital Senior Living Corp
14160 Dallas Pkwy Ste 300
Dallas TX 75254
972 770-5600

(G-16537)
FLIGHT OPTIONS INC (PA)
26180 Curtiss Wright Pkwy (44143-1453)
PHONE.................................216 261-3880
Michael J Silvestro, *CEO*
Darnell H Martens, *President*
Robert Pinkas, *President*
David H Davies, *Principal*
Kenneth Ricci, *Chairman*
EMP: 500
SQ FT: 30,000
SALES (est): 91.1MM Privately Held
SIC: 4581 Aircraft maintenance & repair services

(G-16538)
FLIGHT OPTIONS INTL INC (HQ)
355 Richmond Rd (44143-4405)
PHONE.................................216 261-3500
Ed Mc Donald, *President*
EMP: 33
SQ FT: 15,000
SALES (est): 14.4MM
SALES (corp-wide): 91.1MM Privately Held
SIC: 4581 Aircraft maintenance & repair services
PA: Flight Options, Inc.
26180 Curtiss Wright Pkwy
Richmond Heights OH 44143
216 261-3880

(G-16539)
INTEX SUPPLY COMPANY
26301 Curtiss Wright Pkwy (44143-4413)
PHONE.................................216 535-4300
Ken Vuylsteke, *President*
Tom Friedl, *CFO*
Dan Soukup, *Controller*
Patrick Fitz Maurice, *Finance Dir*
Deena Bugara, *Payroll Mgr*
▼ EMP: 50
SQ FT: 12,500
SALES (est): 10.5MM Privately Held
SIC: 5093 Waste rags; waste paper

(G-16540)
PK MANAGEMENT LLC (PA)
26301 Curtiss Wright Pkwy (44143-4413)
PHONE.................................216 472-1870
Denis Fortier, *Regional Mgr*
Penny Higgins, *Regional Mgr*
Amarie Land, *Regional Mgr*
Wendy Messer, *Regional Mgr*
Amy Nutter, *Area Mgr*
EMP: 106
SALES: 52.1MM Privately Held
SIC: 8741 Management services

(G-16541)
REGAL CINEMAS CORPORATION
631 Richmond Rd (44143-2915)
PHONE.................................440 720-0500
EMP: 30
SALES (corp-wide): 982.1MM Privately Held
SIC: 7832 Motion picture theaters, except drive-in
HQ: Regal Cinemas Corporation
7132 Regal Ln
Knoxville TN 37920
865 922-1123

(G-16542)
RICHMOND MEDICAL CENTER (PA)
27100 Chardon Rd (44143-1116)
PHONE.................................440 585-6500
Laurie Delgado, *President*
Dianne Frate, *Manager*
Daniel Rzepka, *Obstetrician*
Naushad Banani, *Podiatrist*
Amy A Barko, *Podiatrist*
EMP: 400 EST: 1996
SALES (est): 17.1MM Privately Held
SIC: 8062 8011 General medical & surgical hospitals; medical centers

(G-16543)
YOUTH MNTRNG & AT RSK INTRVNTN
2092 Washington Dr (44143-1357)
PHONE.................................216 324-2451
Willie L Gary, *Exec Dir*
EMP: 50
SALES: 75K Privately Held
SIC: 8322 Individual & family services

Richwood
Union County

(G-16544)
RICHWOOD BANKING CO (PA)
28 N Franklin St (43344-1027)
PHONE.................................740 943-2317
Fax: 740 943-3563
Nancy K Hoffman, *President*
Chad Hoffman, *Vice Pres*
Seth Taylor, *CFO*
Brian Gehres, *Ch Credit Ofcr*
Greg Roy, *Loan Officer*
EMP: 27
SALES: 21.6MM Privately Held
WEB: www.richwoodbank.com
SIC: 6022 State trust companies accepting deposits, commercial

Ridgeville Corners
Henry County

(G-16545)
RIDGEVILLE COMMUNITY CHOIR
633 First St (43555)
PHONE.................................419 267-3820
Pat Basselman, *Treasurer*
Steven Basselman, *Director*
EMP: 40 EST: 2010
SALES (est): 303.2K Privately Held
SIC: 8699 Charitable organization

Rio Grande
Gallia County

(G-16546)
AREA AGENCY ON AGING DST 7 INC (PA)
160 Dorsey Dr (45674-7517)
P.O. Box 500 (45674-0500)
PHONE.................................800 582-7277
Becky Simon, *General Mgr*
Donna Saunders, *Finance Dir*
Kristy Bowman, *Human Resources*
Vicky Abdella, *Pub Rel Dir*
Jenni Dovyak-Lewis, *Comms Mgr*
EMP: 130
SALES: 61MM Privately Held
SIC: 8322 Senior citizens' center or association

Ripley
Brown County

(G-16547)
LEGACY INDUSTRIAL SERVICES LLC
9272 Scoffield Rd (45167-9627)
PHONE.................................606 584-8953
Phillip Truesdell,
EMP: 25
SALES (est): 759.7K Privately Held
SIC: 1791 7389 Structural steel erection;

(G-16548)
OHIO VALLEY MANOR INC
5280 Us Highway 62 And 68 (45167-8650)
PHONE.................................937 392-4318
Fax: 937 392-4599
Dave Seesholtz, *President*
Evelyn Seesholtz, *President*
George Balz, *Vice Pres*
Gary Seesholtz, *Treasurer*
Dale G Wilson, *Admin Sec*
EMP: 230
SQ FT: 72,000
SALES: 11.7MM Privately Held
SIC: 8059 8052 8051 Convalescent home; intermediate care facilities; skilled nursing care facilities

(G-16549)
OVM INVESTMENT GROUP LLC
5280 Us Hwy 62 & 88 (45167)
PHONE.................................937 392-0145
Steven Boymel, *President*
Allan Acheson, *CFO*
EMP: 220
SQ FT: 150,000
SALES (est): 574.2K Privately Held
SIC: 8051 Skilled nursing care facilities

Rittman
Wayne County

(G-16550)
APOSTOLIC CHRISTIAN HOME INC
10680 Steiner Rd (44270-9518)
PHONE.................................330 927-1010
Fax: 330 927-1020
Bruce Maibach, *Envir Svcs Dir*

GEOGRAPHIC SECTION

Rocky River - Cuyahoga County (G-16575)

Eugene Petrilla, *Director*
Jeannie Stoller, *Director*
Dave Maletich, *Administration*
EMP: 90
SQ FT: 23,000
SALES: 5.6MM **Privately Held**
SIC: 8059 8052 8051 Nursing home, except skilled & intermediate care facility; intermediate care facilities; skilled nursing care facilities

(G-16551)
BAUMAN ORCHARDS INC
161 Rittman Ave (44270-1253)
PHONE.................330 925-6861
Fax: 330 925-5676
Marion E Bauman, *President*
William Bauman, *Corp Secy*
Doug Bauman, *Vice Pres*
Lisa Meese, *Office Mgr*
EMP: 43
SQ FT: 13,500
SALES (est): 3.3MM **Privately Held**
WEB: www.baumanorchards.com
SIC: 0175 Peach orchard

(G-16552)
EMBASSY AUTUMNWOOD MGT LLC
275 E Sunset Dr (44270-1165)
PHONE.................330 927-2060
Darla Handler, *COO*
Jill Hoffman, *Finance Dir*
EMP: 99
SALES (est): 356.7K **Privately Held**
SIC: 8051 Skilled nursing care facilities

(G-16553)
LARIA CHEVROLET-BUICK INC
112 E Ohio Ave (44270-1537)
PHONE.................330 925-2015
Toll Free:.................866 -
John W Laria, *President*
Jessica Foster, *Business Mgr*
Jennifer Laria, *Manager*
EMP: 40 **EST:** 1934
SALES (est): 17.3MM **Privately Held**
WEB: www.lariachevybuick.com
SIC: 5511 5521 5012 Automobiles, new & used; used car dealers; automobiles & other motor vehicles

(G-16554)
MORTON SALT INC
151 Industrial Ave (44270-1593)
PHONE.................330 925-3015
Fax: 330 927-1070
Tim Declerck, *Plant Mgr*
Robert Hileman, *Purchasing*
Eric Shirk, *QC Dir*
Rick Blakeslee, *Engineer*
J Schamback, *Plant Engr*
EMP: 150
SALES (corp-wide): 4.2B **Privately Held**
WEB: www.mortonintl.com
SIC: 5149 2899 Salt, edible; chemical preparations
HQ: Morton Salt, Inc.
444 W Lake St Ste 3000
Chicago IL 60606

(G-16555)
RITTMAN CITY OF INC
Also Called: Ems Station
25 N State St (44270-1584)
PHONE.................330 925-2065
Larry Boggs, *Manager*
EMP: 35 **Privately Held**
SIC: 4119 Ambulance service
PA: Rittman, City Of Inc
30 N Main St
Rittman OH 44270
330 925-2045

(G-16556)
RITTMAN INC
Also Called: Mull Iron
10 Mull Dr (44270-9777)
PHONE.................330 927-6855
Chester Mull Jr, *President*
Robert A O'Neil, *Principal*
Richard J Wendelken, *Principal*
Beth Mull, *Corp Secy*
William Mull, *Vice Pres*
EMP: 60
SQ FT: 34,000
SALES (est): 15.8MM **Privately Held**
SIC: 3441 1791 Fabricated structural metal; structural steel erection

(G-16557)
U SAVE AUTO RENTAL
Also Called: U-Save Auto Rental
112 E Ohio Ave (44270-1537)
PHONE.................330 925-2015
John Laria, *Owner*
Jessica Foster, *Manager*
Rick Mumaw, *Manager*
EMP: 50
SALES (est): 1.1MM **Privately Held**
SIC: 7514 Rent-a-car service

Rock Creek
Ashtabula County

(G-16558)
GLENBEIGH HEALTH SOURCES INC (PA)
2863 State Route 45 N (44084-9352)
P.O. Box 298 (44084-0298)
PHONE.................440 951-7000
Patricia Weston-Hall, *CEO*
Michelle Manthey, *Info Tech Dir*
Tom Dailey, *Director*
Barbara Enstrom, *Director*
Kathy Gasier, *Director*
EMP: 180
SALES (est): 28.2MM **Privately Held**
SIC: 8069 Drug addiction rehabilitation hospital

(G-16559)
GLENBEIGH HOSPITAL (PA)
Also Called: Rock Creek Medical Center
2863 State Route 45 N (44084-9352)
P.O. Box 298 (44084-0298)
PHONE.................440 563-3400
Pat Weston-Hall, *CEO*
Joseph Vendel, *Chairman*
Robert Keaton, *Med Doctor*
Kathy Defazio, *Manager*
Carol Krotzer, *Manager*
EMP: 40
SALES (est): 7.4MM **Privately Held**
SIC: 8069 Drug addiction rehabilitation hospital

Rockbridge
Hocking County

(G-16560)
GLENLAUREL INC
Also Called: Glenlurel-A Scottish Cntry Inn
14940 Mount Olive Rd (43149-9736)
PHONE.................740 385-4070
Fax: 740 385-9669
Greg Leonard, *President*
Rick Brown, *Opers Mgr*
EMP: 25
SQ FT: 20,000
SALES (est): 630K **Privately Held**
WEB: www.glenlaurelinn.com
SIC: 5812 7011 Eating places; inns

Rockford
Mercer County

(G-16561)
ECO GLOBAL CORP
10803 Erastus Durbin Rd (45882-9654)
PHONE.................419 363-2681
Lloyd Linton, *Principal*
EMP: 37
SALES (est): 827.5K **Privately Held**
SIC: 4953 Recycling, waste materials

(G-16562)
GLM TRANSPORT INC (PA)
12806 State Route 118 (45882-9354)
PHONE.................419 363-2041
Daniel Ruhe, *President*
Tyson Bailey, *Vice Pres*
Ty Conrad, *Vice Pres*
Edward Ruhe, *Vice Pres*
Carolyn Moore, *Manager*
EMP: 30
SALES (est): 11.4MM **Privately Held**
SIC: 4212 4213 Local trucking, without storage; trucking, except local

(G-16563)
HEALTHCARE MANAGEMENT CONS
Also Called: Colonial Nursing Home
201 Buckeye St (45882-9266)
PHONE.................419 363-2193
Fax: 419 363-3807
Paul Bergener, *President*
Paul Kalogerou, *Director*
Jan Hoblet, *Nursing Dir*
Dennis Trimboli, *Administration*
EMP: 32 **EST:** 1949
SQ FT: 3,500
SALES (est): 2.1MM **Privately Held**
WEB: www.colonialnursingcenter.com
SIC: 8741 8052 Nursing & personal care facility management; intermediate care facilities

(G-16564)
TIRE WASTE TRANSPORT INC
10803 Erastus Durbin Rd (45882-9654)
PHONE.................419 363-2681
Lloyd Linton, *CEO*
EMP: 320
SQ FT: 13,000
SALES (est): 19.4MM **Privately Held**
SIC: 5014 Tires & tubes

(G-16565)
TSM LOGISTICS LLC
4567 Old Town Run Rd (45882-9331)
PHONE.................419 234-6074
Steve Marks, *Branch Mgr*
EMP: 45
SALES (est): 1.6MM
SALES (corp-wide): 600K **Privately Held**
SIC: 4212 Local trucking, without storage
PA: Tsm Logistics, Llc
2421 S Nappanee St
Elkhart IN 46517
419 363-2041

Rocky Ridge
Ottawa County

(G-16566)
BLATT TRUCKING CO INC (PA)
1205 Main St (43458)
P.O. Box 100 (43458-0100)
PHONE.................419 898-0002
Fax: 419 898-1780
Russell Blatt, *President*
Virginia Hopple, *Manager*
EMP: 40
SALES (est): 4.8MM **Privately Held**
SIC: 4213 4212 Contract haulers; local trucking, without storage

Rocky River
Cuyahoga County

(G-16567)
A W S INC
Also Called: S A W - Rocky River Adult Trai
20120 Detroit Rd (44116-2421)
PHONE.................440 333-1791
Katherine L Johnson, *Branch Mgr*
EMP: 200
SALES (corp-wide): 7.8MM **Privately Held**
SIC: 8331 7331 Vocational training agency; direct mail advertising services
PA: A W S Inc
1275 Lakeside Ave E
Cleveland OH 44114
216 861-0250

(G-16568)
ACE HARDWARE CORPORATION
20200 Detroit Rd (44116-2422)
PHONE.................440 333-4223
EMP: 139
SALES (corp-wide): 5.3B **Privately Held**
SIC: 5251 5072 Hardware; hardware
PA: Ace Hardware Corporation
2200 Kensington Ct
Oak Brook IL 60523
866 681-1836

(G-16569)
AMERICAN MULTI-CINEMA INC
Also Called: AMC
21653 Center Ridge Rd (44116-3917)
PHONE.................440 331-2826
Eric Supple, *President*
EMP: 30 **Publicly Held**
WEB: www.arrowheadtowncenter.com
SIC: 7832 Motion picture theaters, except drive-in
HQ: American Multi-Cinema, Inc.
1 Amc Way
Leawood KS 66211
913 213-2000

(G-16570)
AUTOMOTIVE EVENTS INC
19111 Detroit Rd Ste 306 (44116-1740)
PHONE.................440 356-1383
John Thorne, *President*
Iain Dobson, *President*
Charles E Wern Jr, *Principal*
Mike Foss, *Controller*
Lorynn Godfrey, *Manager*
EMP: 25
SQ FT: 3,000
SALES (est): 4.6MM **Privately Held**
WEB: www.automotive-events.com
SIC: 8743 8742 Sales promotion; training & development consultant

(G-16571)
BOUNDLESS FLIGHT INC (PA)
20226 Detroit Rd (44116-2422)
P.O. Box 360109, Strongsville (44136-0002)
PHONE.................440 610-3683
Gary Baney, *CEO*
Joanna Orloff, *Principal*
Dave Brumbaugh, *Technology*
EMP: 25
SALES (est): 3.5MM **Privately Held**
WEB: www.boundlessflight.com
SIC: 7371 Computer software writers, free-lance

(G-16572)
CAPITAL SENIOR LIVING (PA)
Also Called: Harbor Court
22900 Center Ridge Rd (44116-3000)
PHONE.................440 356-5444
Fax: 440 356-2744
Xen Zapis, *Partner*
Lisa Lukehart, *Accountant*
EMP: 50
SQ FT: 19,064
SALES (est): 4.3MM **Privately Held**
WEB: www.theharborcourt.com
SIC: 8059 6531 Rest home, with health care; real estate agents & managers

(G-16573)
CHILD & ELDER CARE INSIGHTS
18500 Lake Rd Ste 200 (44116-1746)
PHONE.................440 356-2900
Fax: 440 356-2919
Elisabeth Bryenton, *CEO*
EMP: 27
SQ FT: 2,500
SALES (est): 602.5K **Privately Held**
WEB: www.carereports.com
SIC: 7299 Information services, consumer

(G-16574)
CLEVELAND PHLHRMONIC ORCHESTRA
1158 Bates Rd (44116-2173)
PHONE.................216 556-1800
Lisa Wilson, *Exec Dir*
Amy Griger, *Admin Sec*
EMP: 90
SALES: 48.2K **Privately Held**
SIC: 7929 Orchestras or bands

(G-16575)
COWEN AND COMPANY LLC
20006 Detroit Rd Ste 100 (44116-2406)
PHONE.................440 331-3531
Allen Gerard, *Managing Dir*

Rocky River - Cuyahoga County (G-16576)

Diane Davenport, *Director*
Michael J Mulvaney, *Director*
Brooks Hulett, *Analyst*
EMP: 50 **Publicly Held**
SIC: 6211 Securities flotation companies
HQ: Cowen And Company, Llc
  599 Lexington Ave Fl 19
  New York NY 10022
  646 562-1000

(G-16576)
DAVITA INC
19133 Hilliard Blvd (44116-2907)
PHONE 216 712-4700
Fax: 216 712-4702
EMP: 27 **Publicly Held**
SIC: 8092 Kidney dialysis centers
PA: Davita Inc.
  2000 16th St
  Denver CO 80202

(G-16577)
EARNEST MACHINE PRODUCTS CO (PA)
1250 Linda St Ste 301 (44116-1854)
PHONE 440 895-8400
Fax: 216 362-1694
Kirk P Zehnder, *President*
Paul Zehnder, *Principal*
Victor Zehnder, *Principal*
John P Zehnder, *Co-President*
Timothy D Weber, *Vice Pres*
▲ **EMP:** 50 **EST:** 1951
SQ FT: 68,000
SALES (est): 32.4MM **Privately Held**
SIC: 5085 Fasteners, industrial: nuts, bolts, screws, etc.

(G-16578)
FITWORKS HOLDING LLC
20001 Center Ridge Rd (44116-3659)
PHONE 440 333-4630
Fax: 440 333-4141
Max Stillwagon, *Manager*
EMP: 40 **Privately Held**
SIC: 7991 7997 Health club; membership sports & recreation clubs
PA: Fitworks Holding, Llc
  849 Brainard Rd
  Cleveland OH 44143

(G-16579)
GOLDWOOD PRIMARY SCHOOL PTA
Also Called: GOLDWOOD PTA
21600 Center Ridge Rd (44116-3918)
PHONE 440 356-6720
Fax: 440 356-6044
Chris Albano, *President*
EMP: 37
SALES: 10.6K **Privately Held**
SIC: 8211 8641 Elementary school; civic social & fraternal associations

(G-16580)
HERITAGE HOME HEALTH CARE
20800 Center Ridge Rd # 401 (44116-4312)
PHONE 440 333-1925
Fax: 440 333-2223
Ray Cancelliere, *Director*
EMP: 40
SALES (est): 762.7K **Privately Held**
WEB: www.heritagehomehealthcare.com
SIC: 8082 Home health care services

(G-16581)
HOWARD HANNA SMYTHE CRAMER
19204 Detroit Rd (44116-1706)
PHONE 440 333-6500
Fax: 440 333-2883
Caroline Angelilli, *Broker*
Norma Archer, *Broker*
Kristina Bailey, *Broker*
Joseph Bridges, *Broker*
Loni Choltco, *Broker*
EMP: 45
SQ FT: 576
SALES (corp-wide): 76.4MM **Privately Held**
WEB: www.smythecramer.com
SIC: 6531 Real estate agent, residential

HQ: Howard Hanna Smythe Cramer
  6000 Parkland Blvd
  Cleveland OH 44124
  216 447-4477

(G-16582)
JAG HEALTHCARE INC
220 Buckingham Rd (44116-1623)
PHONE 440 385-4370
James Griffiths, *President*
Richard Gebhard, *Vice Pres*
William Soroka, *Vice Pres*
Miriam Walters, *Vice Pres*
David Cooley, *CFO*
EMP: 650
SALES (est): 14MM **Privately Held**
SIC: 8082 Home health care services

(G-16583)
JP RECOVERY SERVICES INC
Also Called: Patient Financial Services
20220 Center Ridge Rd # 370 (44116-3501)
PHONE 440 356-5048
John Beirne, *President*
Steven Little, *Vice Pres*
John Murray, *Vice Pres*
Teresa Busser, *Bookkeeper*
Angela Anthos, *Human Res Mgr*
EMP: 90
SQ FT: 7,000
SALES (est): 10.3MM **Privately Held**
WEB: www.jprecovery.com
SIC: 7322 Collection agency, except real estate

(G-16584)
KAISER FOUNDATION HOSPITALS
Also Called: Rocky River Medical Offices
20575 Ctr Ridgerd Ste 500 (44116)
PHONE 216 524-7377
EMP: 593
SALES (corp-wide): 19.1B **Privately Held**
SIC: 8011 Medical Doctor's Office
PA: Kaiser Foundation Hospitals Inc
  1 Kaiser Plz Ste 2600
  Oakland CA 94612
  510 271-5800

(G-16585)
LOWES HOME CENTERS LLC
20639 Center Ridge Rd (44116-3449)
PHONE 440 331-1027
Fax: 440 331-1073
Lorie Thomas, *Branch Mgr*
EMP: 150
SALES (corp-wide): 68.6B **Publicly Held**
SIC: 5211 5031 5722 5064 Home centers; building materials, exterior; building materials, interior; household appliance stores; electrical appliances, television & radio
HQ: Lowe's Home Centers, Llc
  1605 Curtis Bridge Rd
  Wilkesboro NC 28697
  336 658-4000

(G-16586)
MSAB PARK CREEK LLC
Also Called: Park Creek Center
20375 Center Ridge Rd # 204 (44116-3561)
PHONE 440 842-5100
Mary Thomas, *Corp Counsel*
David A Farkas, *Mng Member*
Valerie Farkas,
EMP: 38
SALES (est): 1.5MM **Privately Held**
WEB: www.parkcreekretirement.com
SIC: 8059 Personal care home, with health care

(G-16587)
NL OF KY INC
Also Called: Neace Lukens
1340 Depot St Ste 300 (44116-1741)
PHONE 216 643-7100
Kimberly Elko, *Controller*
Skip Vogelsberger, *Manager*
EMP: 30 **Privately Held**
SIC: 6411 Insurance agents & brokers
HQ: Nl Of Ky, Inc.
  2305 River Rd
  Louisville KY 40206

(G-16588)
NORMANDY MANOR OF ROCKY RIVER
22709 Lake Rd (44116-1021)
PHONE 440 333-5401
Fax: 440 356-8923
David Orlean, *Partner*
Debra Sue Orlean, *Partner*
Susan Orlean, *Partner*
Stephanie Johnson, *Purch Agent*
Amanda Argabrite, *Office Mgr*
EMP: 150 **EST:** 1988
SALES (est): 15.1MM **Privately Held**
WEB: www.normandyretirement.com
SIC: 8051 Convalescent home with continuous nursing care

(G-16589)
PRODUCER GROUP LLC (PA)
Also Called: Todd Organization, The
19111 Detroit Rd Ste 304 (44116-1740)
PHONE 440 871-7700
William Holton, *Vice Pres*
B W Garber, *Consultant*
Leslie Wood, *Consultant*
Michael Powers, *Exec Dir*
Bill Holton, *Executive*
EMP: 26
SQ FT: 25,000
SALES (est): 4.6MM **Privately Held**
SIC: 6411 8742 Pension & retirement plan consultants; franchising consultant

(G-16590)
REALTY ONE INC
20800 Center Ridge Rd # 203 (44116-4310)
PHONE 440 333-8700
Fax: 440 333-8704
Jim Poulos, *Branch Mgr*
EMP: 36
SALES (corp-wide): 67.8MM **Privately Held**
SIC: 6531 6519 Real estate agents & managers; real property lessors
HQ: Realty One, Inc.
  800 W Saint Clair Ave
  Cleveland OH 44113
  216 328-2500

(G-16591)
RUFFING MONTESSORI SCHOOL
1285 Orchard Park Dr (44116-2045)
PHONE 440 333-2250
Fax: 440 333-2540
Debra Mitchell, *Finance*
John McNamara, *Director*
Barbara Geiger, *Admin Asst*
Lori Coticchia, *Administration*
EMP: 26
SQ FT: 34,727
SALES: 3MM **Privately Held**
WEB: www.ruffingmontessori.org
SIC: 8211 8351 Private elementary & secondary schools; Montessori child development center

(G-16592)
SQUIRES CONSTRUCTION COMPANY
Also Called: Squires Roofing Company
20800 Center Ridge Rd Ll15 (44116-4317)
PHONE 216 252-0300
Fax: 330 467-1721
Chris Koehler, *President*
Don Caiola, *Controller*
EMP: 30
SQ FT: 12,000
SALES (est): 3MM **Privately Held**
SIC: 1761 5211 1521 Roofing contractor; windows, storm: wood or metal; general remodeling, single-family houses

(G-16593)
SUNRISE SENIOR LIVING INC
Also Called: Sunrise of Rocky River
21600 Detroit Rd (44116-2218)
PHONE 440 895-2383
Fax: 440 356-9997
Natalie Antosh, *Manager*
Crystal Parrish, *Director*
EMP: 58

SALES (corp-wide): 4.3B **Publicly Held**
WEB: www.sunrise.com
SIC: 8051 8361 Skilled nursing care facilities; home for the aged
HQ: Sunrise Senior Living, Llc
  7902 Westpark Dr
  Mc Lean VA 22102

(G-16594)
VER-A-FAST CORP
20545 Center Ridge Rd # 300 (44116-3423)
PHONE 440 331-0250
Fax: 440 331-2701
Robert Bensman, *President*
Cathleen Soprano, *CFO*
Diane Missirlis, *Prgrmr*
EMP: 45
SQ FT: 13,000
SALES (est): 6.3MM **Privately Held**
WEB: www.verafast.com
SIC: 8743 Public relations & publicity

(G-16595)
WESTWOOD COUNTRY CLUB COMPANY
22625 Detroit Rd (44116-2024)
P.O. Box 16459 (44116-0459)
PHONE 440 331-3016
Fax: 440 331-0294
Richard McClure, *President*
Thomas M Cawley, *Vice Pres*
Robert J Koepke, *Treasurer*
Jamie Kearney, *Controller*
Alice R Alexander, *Admin Sec*
EMP: 75
SQ FT: 53,000
SALES: 6.2MM **Privately Held**
WEB: www.westwoodcountryclub.org
SIC: 7997 Country club, membership

(G-16596)
WOMENS WELSH CLUBS OF AMERICA
Also Called: WELSH HOME FOR THE AGED
22199 Center Ridge Rd (44116-3925)
PHONE 440 331-0420
Fax: 440 331-3810
Chasity Smith, *Bookkeeper*
Lauren Teschner, *Marketing Staff*
Chris Parent, *Director*
Sarah Cook, *Administration*
Marilyn Davis, *Administration*
EMP: 100
SQ FT: 31,206
SALES: 8.8MM **Privately Held*
SIC: 8361 8051 Home for the aged; rest home, with health care incidental; skilled nursing care facilities

Rootstown
Portage County

(G-16597)
JET RUBBER COMPANY
4457 Tallmadge Rd (44272-9610)
PHONE 330 325-1821
Fax: 330 325-2876
Franklin R Brubaker, *Principal*
Karen Crooks, *Corp Secy*
Gail Tarsinos, *Vice Pres*
Robert Geinitz, *Research*
Sherri Zalewski, *Accountant*
EMP: 43 **EST:** 1954
SQ FT: 20,000
SALES (est): 8.5MM **Privately Held**
WEB: www.jetrubber.com
SIC: 3069 3053 3533 5085 Molded rubber products; gaskets, packing & sealing devices; gaskets & sealing devices; gas field machinery & equipment; oil field machinery & equipment; rubber goods, mechanical

(G-16598)
MILLER TRANSFER AND RIGGING CO (HQ)
3833 State Route 183 (44272-9799)
P.O. Box 453 (44272-0453)
PHONE 330 325-2521
Jim Unger, *President*
Norman Hartline, *President*
Mike Raus, *Regional Mgr*

GEOGRAPHIC SECTION

Kenneth H Rusinoff, *Corp Secy*
David Cochran, *Vice Pres*
EMP: 50
SQ FT: 10,000
SALES (est): 59.1MM
SALES (corp-wide): 62.2MM **Privately Held**
WEB: www.millertransfer.com
SIC: 4213 Heavy machinery transport
PA: United Transport Industries, Inc
1310 N King St
Wilmington DE 19801
302 888-6500

(G-16599)
NOAHS ARK CHILD CARE INC (PA)
Also Called: Noah's Ark After School Care
4524 Lynn Rd (44272-9710)
P.O. Box 59 (44272-0059)
PHONE..................................330 325-7236
Fax: 330 325-0161
Brenda Kelsey, *President*
EMP: 31
SALES (est): 771.4K **Privately Held**
SIC: 8351 Preschool center

Roseville
Muskingum County

(G-16600)
ACCCO INC
451 Gordon St (43777-1110)
P.O. Box 35 (43777-0035)
PHONE..................................740 697-2005
Fax: 740 697-2500
Peter Petratsaf, *President*
Rick Emmert, *Vice Pres*
▲ **EMP:** 50
SQ FT: 50,000
SALES (est): 11.7MM **Privately Held**
WEB: www.accco-inc.com
SIC: 5032 Ceramic wall & floor tile

(G-16601)
CLAY BURLEY PRODUCTS CO (PA)
455 Gordon St (43777-1110)
P.O. Box 35 (43777-0035)
PHONE..................................740 452-3633
Fax: 740 697-0246
Peter Petratsas, *President*
Bobbi Bennett, *Sales Executive*
▲ **EMP:** 50
SQ FT: 180,000
SALES (est): 8.3MM **Privately Held**
WEB: www.burleyclay.com
SIC: 3269 5032 Stoneware pottery products; art & ornamental ware, pottery; ceramic wall & floor tile

(G-16602)
RMX FREIGHT SYSTEMS INC (PA)
Also Called: R M X
4550 Roseville Rd (43777-9720)
P.O. Box 185, White Cottage (43791-0185)
PHONE..................................740 849-2374
Jeff Moore, *President*
Dan Knox, *Vice Pres*
Robert Sowers, *Vice Pres*
Rosemary Baker, *Cust Mgr*
Derek Dunn, *Traffic Dir*
EMP: 25 **EST:** 1917
SQ FT: 10,000
SALES (est): 6MM **Privately Held**
SIC: 4212 Local trucking, without storage

Ross
Butler County

(G-16603)
GUENTHER & SONS INC
2578 Long St (45061)
P.O. Box 28 (45061-0028)
PHONE..................................513 738-1448
James Guenther, *President*
Steve Guenther, *Vice Pres*
Gary Guenther, *Treasurer*
Dorris Focht, *Manager*

Glenn Guenther, *Admin Sec*
EMP: 42
SQ FT: 6,280
SALES: 1.5MM **Privately Held**
SIC: 4213 Contract haulers

Rossburg
Darke County

(G-16604)
CAL-MAINE FOODS INC
3078 Washington Rd (45362-9500)
PHONE..................................937 337-9576
Fax: 937 337-6535
Leonard Kropp, *General Mgr*
Brian Clum, *Manager*
Leonard Cropp, *Manager*
EMP: 43
SALES (corp-wide): 1B **Publicly Held**
WEB: www.calmainefoods.com
SIC: 0252 2015 Chicken eggs; poultry slaughtering & processing
PA: Cal-Maine Foods, Inc.
3320 W Woodrow Wilson Ave
Jackson MS 39209
601 948-6813

(G-16605)
COOPER FRMS SPRING MADOW FARMS
13243 Cochran Rd (45362-9753)
PHONE..................................419 375-4119
Marvin Lefeld, *CFO*
EMP: 35
SALES (est): 1.7MM **Privately Held**
SIC: 5144 Eggs

Rossford
Wood County

(G-16606)
ALLIEDBARTON SECURITY SVCS LLC
Also Called: Allied Barton Security Svcs
1001 Dixie Hwy Ste F (43460-1389)
PHONE..................................419 874-9005
Fax: 419 874-9014
Timothy Dotson, *Manager*
EMP: 50
SALES (corp-wide): 2.6B **Privately Held**
WEB: www.alliedsecurity.com
SIC: 7381 Security guard service
HQ: Alliedbarton Security Services Llc
8 Tower Bridge 161 Wshgtn
Conshohocken PA 19428
610 239-1100

(G-16607)
COURTYARD BY MARRIOTT ROSSFORD
9789 Clark Dr (43460-1700)
PHONE..................................419 872-5636
Arne Sorenson's, *President*
Andrew Groom, *Info Tech Mgr*
EMP: 25
SALES: 1.1MM **Privately Held**
SIC: 7011 Hotels & motels

(G-16608)
INDUSTRIAL POWER SYSTEMS INC
Also Called: I P S
146 Dixie Hwy (43460-1215)
PHONE..................................419 531-3121
Fax: 419 531-5320
Kevin Gray, *President*
Terri Never, *Business Mgr*
John Gray, *Vice Pres*
Jeremiah Johnson, *Vice Pres*
William Norris, *Safety Dir*
EMP: 250
SQ FT: 20,000
SALES: 67.2MM **Privately Held**
WEB: www.indpowsys.com
SIC: 1711 1796 1731 Mechanical contractor; machinery installation; electrical work

(G-16609)
INTERSTATE LANES OF OHIO LTD
819 Lime City Rd (43460-1613)
PHONE..................................419 666-2695
Fax: 419 666-7540
Nicholas Veronica, *Partner*
Barbara Golbinec, *Partner*
Howard Teifke, *Partner*
Sue Penske, *Manager*
Sue Pinski, *Webmaster*
EMP: 28 **EST:** 1981
SQ FT: 30,000
SALES (est): 1MM **Privately Held**
WEB: www.interstatelanes.com
SIC: 7933 5813 Ten pin center; cocktail lounge

(G-16610)
OBR COOLING TOWERS INC
9665 S Compass Dr (43460-1740)
PHONE..................................419 243-3443
Fax: 419 244-2157
Peter Poll, *President*
Matt Pinkelman, *General Mgr*
John Hall, *Exec VP*
Philip Poll, *Treasurer*
Adrain Hill, *Manager*
EMP: 45
SQ FT: 6,000
SALES (est): 7.7MM **Privately Held**
WEB: www.obrcoolingtowers.com
SIC: 7699 3444 Industrial equipment services; cooling towers, sheet metal

(G-16611)
ROSSFORD HOSPITALITY GROUP INC
Also Called: Hampton Inn
9753 Clark Dr (43460-1700)
PHONE..................................419 874-2345
Fax: 419 662-8900
Thomas Shoemaker, *Owner*
Mary Helge, *General Mgr*
Douglas Steinke, *Manager*
Marlene Ambos, *Director*
EMP: 25
SALES: 950K **Privately Held**
SIC: 7011 Hotels & motels

(G-16612)
TOLEDO ELEC JINT APPRNTICESHIP
Also Called: ELECTRICAL TRAINING CENTER
803 Lime City Rd (43460-1613)
PHONE..................................419 666-8088
Fax: 419 666-0336
Dave Wellington, *Director*
James Hamel, *Instructor*
Ray Sruffolino, *Education*
EMP: 45
SALES: 4.1MM **Privately Held**
WEB: www.tejatc.org
SIC: 8611 Business associations

Rushville
Fairfield County

(G-16613)
RICHLAND TOWNSHIP FIRE DEPT
3150 Market St (43150-9750)
PHONE..................................740 536-7313
Fax: 740 536-7313
Kenneth Rookard, *Chief*
Scott Baker, *Chief*
EMP: 35 **Privately Held**
SIC: 9224 8999 Fire department, volunteer; search & rescue service

Russia
Shelby County

(G-16614)
FRANCIS-SCHULZE CO
3880 Rangeline Rd (45363-9711)
P.O. Box 245 (45363-0245)
PHONE..................................937 295-3941
Fax: 937 295-3706

Ralph Schulze, *President*
Ken Francis, *Engineer*
Rita Schulze, *Treasurer*
John Francis, *Financial Exec*
Luke Boerger, *Sales Staff*
EMP: 45 **EST:** 1943
SQ FT: 50,000
SALES (est): 7.8MM **Privately Held**
WEB: www.francisschulze.com
SIC: 3442 5031 Metal doors; building materials, exterior

Sabina
Clinton County

(G-16615)
EARLEY & ROSS LTD
Also Called: Autumn Years Nursing Center
580 E Washington St (45169-1253)
PHONE..................................740 634-3301
Fax: 937 584-2508
Tim Ross, *Partner*
Marty Knapp, *Human Res Mgr*
Dirk Juschka, *Director*
EMP: 62 **EST:** 1973
SALES (est): 4.7MM **Privately Held**
SIC: 8052 Intermediate care facilities

Saint Clairsville
Belmont County

(G-16616)
ALTERNATIVE RESIDENCES TWO (PA)
Also Called: Wiley Avenue Group Home
67051 Executive Dr (43950-8473)
PHONE..................................740 526-0514
Shirley M Johnson, *Chairman*
Lavelle Lloyd, *Corp Secy*
Wendy Mankin, *Manager*
EMP: 150
SALES: 5K **Privately Held**
SIC: 8361 8052 Home for the mentally handicapped; home for the mentally retarded; intermediate care facilities

(G-16617)
BELCO WORKS INC
340 Fox Shannon Pl (43950-8753)
PHONE..................................740 695-0500
Fax: 740 695-5910
Sandra Elson, *Business Mgr*
Sally Traversa, *Finance Mgr*
Debbie Alexander, *HR Admin*
Kim Cain, *Manager*
Sherri Marlin, *Manager*
EMP: 350
SQ FT: 5,000
SALES: 2.2MM **Privately Held**
WEB: www.belcoworks.com
SIC: 8331 3993 3931 2448 Sheltered workshop; signs & advertising specialties; musical instruments; wood pallets & skids

(G-16618)
BELLMONT COUNTY
Also Called: Sargus Juvenille Center
210 Fox Shannon Pl (43950-8752)
PHONE..................................740 695-9750
Fax: 740 695-6001
Beth Oprisch, *Exec Dir*
EMP: 32
SALES (est): 1MM **Privately Held**
SIC: 8361 Juvenile correctional facilities

(G-16619)
BELMONT & MONROE LODGE 6 OF
72200 Gun Club Rd (43950-9632)
P.O. Box 621 (43950-0621)
PHONE..................................740 695-2121
Stanley Galownia, *Vice Pres*
EMP: 38
SALES (est): 514.3K **Privately Held**
SIC: 8641 Fraternal associations

Saint Clairsville - Belmont County (G-16620)

GEOGRAPHIC SECTION

(G-16620)
BELMONT COUNTY HOME
Also Called: Park Health Center
100 Pine Ave (43950-9738)
PHONE..................740 695-4925
Fax: 740 695-4915
Pam Neff, *Persnl Dir*
Gordy Longshaw, *Commissioner*
Chuck Probst, *Commissioner*
Mark Thomas, *Commissioner*
Mike Maistros, *Director*
EMP: 100
SALES (est): 2.7MM **Privately Held**
SIC: 8051 Skilled nursing care facilities
PA: Belmont County Of Ohio
  101 W Main St
  Saint Clairsville OH 43950
  740 695-2121

(G-16621)
BELMONT COUNTY OF OHIO
Also Called: Animal Shelter Blemont CN
45244 National Rd (43950-8707)
PHONE..................740 695-4708
Verna Painter, *Branch Mgr*
EMP: 27
SQ FT: 2,532 **Privately Held**
WEB: www.belmontsheriff.com
SIC: 8699 Animal humane society
PA: Belmont County Of Ohio
  101 W Main St
  Saint Clairsville OH 43950
  740 695-2121

(G-16622)
BELMONT COUNTY OF OHIO
Also Called: Belmont County Sani Sewer Dst
68325 Bannock Rd (43950-8792)
P.O. Box 457 (43950-0457)
PHONE..................740 695-3144
Mark Esposito, *Director*
EMP: 27 **Privately Held**
WEB: www.belmontsheriff.com
SIC: 4941 4952 Water supply; sewerage systems
PA: Belmont County Of Ohio
  101 W Main St
  Saint Clairsville OH 43950
  740 695-2121

(G-16623)
BELMONT COUNTY OF OHIO
Also Called: Belmont County Children Svcs
101 N Market St Ste A (43950-1270)
PHONE..................740 695-3813
Jeff Felton, *Partner*
EMP: 29 **Privately Held**
WEB: www.belmontsheriff.com
SIC: 8322 Public welfare center
PA: Belmont County Of Ohio
  101 W Main St
  Saint Clairsville OH 43950
  740 695-2121

(G-16624)
BELMONT COUNTY OF OHIO
68421 Hammond Rd (43950-8783)
PHONE..................740 695-0460
Jamie Bauman, *Principal*
EMP: 100 **Privately Held**
SIC: 8211 8322 Public special education school; individual & family services
PA: Belmont County Of Ohio
  101 W Main St
  Saint Clairsville OH 43950
  740 695-2121

(G-16625)
BELMONT COUNTY OF OHIO
Also Called: Belmont County Engineering
101 W Maint St (43950)
PHONE..................740 695-1580
Fax: 740 695-8894
Dave Sloan, *Superintendent*
EMP: 50 **Privately Held**
WEB: www.belmontsheriff.com
SIC: 1611 Highway & street maintenance
PA: Belmont County Of Ohio
  101 W Main St
  Saint Clairsville OH 43950
  740 695-2121

(G-16626)
BELMONT HILLS COUNTRY CLUB
47080 National Rd W (43950-8711)
PHONE..................740 695-2181
Fax: 740 695-3310
Thomas Dowler, *President*
Joan Jones, *Controller*
Andy Porier, *Manager*
EMP: 75
SQ FT: 30,000
SALES: 1.5MM **Privately Held**
SIC: 7997 Country club, membership; golf club, membership; swimming club, membership; tennis club, membership

(G-16627)
BELMONT SAVINGS BANK
215 W Main St (43950-1141)
P.O. Box 71 (43950-0071)
PHONE..................740 695-0140
Fax: 740 695-2234
Nick Rocchio, *Manager*
EMP: 31
SALES (corp-wide): 14.3MM **Privately Held**
SIC: 6036 State savings banks, not federally chartered
PA: Belmont Savings Bank
  3301 Guernsey St
  Bellaire OH 43906
  740 676-1165

(G-16628)
BHC FOX RUN HOSPITAL INC
Also Called: Fox Run Cntr For Chldrn & Adol
67670 Traco Dr (43950-9375)
PHONE..................740 695-2131
Fax: 740 695-7158
Karen Maxwell, *CEO*
William Hale, *Senior VP*
Joe Smith, *CFO*
Amy Cupp, *Director*
Ali Melhem, *Director*
EMP: 146
SQ FT: 8,200
SALES (est): 11MM **Privately Held**
WEB: www.foxrunhospital.com
SIC: 8063 8093 Psychiatric hospitals; mental health clinic, outpatient

(G-16629)
BORDAS & BORDAS PLLC
106 E Main St (43950-1526)
PHONE..................740 695-8141
Fax: 740 695-6999
Terri A Phillips, *Mktg Dir*
Michelle Marinacci, *Executive*
Jay Stoneking, *Executive*
Linda Bordas,
Scott Blass,
EMP: 26
SALES (est): 1.2MM
SALES (corp-wide): 13.2MM **Privately Held**
SIC: 8111 General practice attorney, lawyer
PA: Bordas & Bordas Pllc
  1358 National Rd
  Wheeling WV 26003
  304 242-8410

(G-16630)
BRYAN ELECTRIC INC
46139 National Rd W (43950-8715)
PHONE..................740 695-9834
Fax: 740 695-7247
Joseph Dallison, *President*
EMP: 30
SQ FT: 12,000
SALES (est): 3.6MM **Privately Held**
SIC: 1731 General electrical contractor

(G-16631)
CELLCO PARTNERSHIP
Also Called: Verizon Wireless
50641 Valley Plaza Dr (43950-1750)
PHONE..................740 695-3600
EMP: 71
SALES (corp-wide): 126B **Publicly Held**
SIC: 4812 Cellular telephone services
HQ: Cellco Partnership
  1 Verizon Way
  Basking Ridge NJ 07920

(G-16632)
COMMUNITY ACTION COMSN BELMONT (PA)
Also Called: Community Action Comm Blmont C
153 1/2 W Main St (43950-1224)
PHONE..................740 695-0293
Fax: 740 695-9255
Gary Obloy, *Exec Dir*
Shirley Mallory, *Admin Director*
EMP: 30 EST: 1965
SQ FT: 3,600
SALES: 3.9MM **Privately Held**
WEB: www.cacbelmont.org
SIC: 8322 8351 1742 Social service center; referral service for personal & social problems; head start center, except in conjunction with school; insulation, buildings

(G-16633)
COMMUNITY MENTAL HEALTH SVC (PA)
Also Called: Community Mental Health Svcs
68353 Bannock Rd (43950-9736)
PHONE..................740 695-9344
Fax: 740 695-7777
Jack Stephens, *Treasurer*
Mary Denoble, *Exec Dir*
Katherine Whinnery, *Admin Sec*
EMP: 61 EST: 1970
SQ FT: 6,000
SALES (est): 3.5MM **Privately Held**
WEB: www.cmhs.net
SIC: 8011 Clinic, operated by physicians; specialty outpatient clinics

(G-16634)
CRESTVIEW HEALTH CARE CENTER
Also Called: Crestview Nursing Home
68637 Bannock Rd (43950-9736)
PHONE..................740 695-2500
Fax: 740 695-5969
Thomas D Nordquist, *President*
Ryan Erdos, *Administration*
EMP: 100
SALES (est): 2.7MM **Privately Held**
SIC: 8361 8092 8051 Rehabilitation center, residential; health care incidental; kidney dialysis centers; skilled nursing care facilities

(G-16635)
DAYS INN
52601 Holiday Dr (43950-9313)
PHONE..................740 695-0100
Fax: 740 695-4135
Rajendra Patel, *President*
Debbie Britton, *General Mgr*
EMP: 28
SQ FT: 5,000
SALES (est): 1.6MM **Privately Held**
SIC: 7011 Hotels & motels

(G-16636)
GULFPORT ENERGY CORPORATION
67185 Executive Dr (43950-8494)
PHONE..................740 251-0407
William Sowards, *Facilities Mgr*
Justin Lindsey, *Buyer*
Jen Masters, *Engineer*
Cindy Gray, *Branch Mgr*
Kevin Hitt, *Consultant*
EMP: 40
SALES (corp-wide): 1.3B **Publicly Held**
SIC: 1311 Crude petroleum production
PA: Gulfport Energy Corporation
  3001 Quail Springs Pkwy
  Oklahoma City OK 73134
  405 848-8807

(G-16637)
HARRISON COUNTY COAL COMPANY (PA)
46226 National Rd (43950-8742)
PHONE..................740 338-3100
Jason D Witt, *Manager*
EMP: 60
SALES (est): 19.4MM **Privately Held**
SIC: 1241 Coal mining services

(G-16638)
HUNTINGTON NATIONAL BANK
154 W Main St (43950-1225)
P.O. Box 249 (43950-0249)
PHONE..................740 695-3323
Fax: 740 699-4014
Susan Neal, *Site Mgr*
Carol Debonis, *Branch Mgr*
Will Heskett, *Manager*
EMP: 50
SALES (corp-wide): 4.7B **Publicly Held**
WEB: www.huntingtonnationalbank.com
SIC: 6029 6022 Commercial banks; state commercial banks
HQ: The Huntington National Bank
  17 S High St Fl 1
  Columbus OH 43215
  614 480-4293

(G-16639)
LAMAR ADVERTISING COMPANY
52610 Holiday Dr (43950-9313)
PHONE..................740 699-0000
Fax: 740 699-0100
Shane Walters, *Manager*
EMP: 48 **Publicly Held**
WEB: www.lamar.com
SIC: 7312 Outdoor advertising services
PA: Lamar Advertising Company
  5321 Corporate Blvd
  Baton Rouge LA 70808

(G-16640)
LANCIA NURSING HOME INC
Also Called: Belmont Manor Nursing Home
51999 Guirino Dr (43950-8314)
PHONE..................740 695-4404
Fax: 740 695-7495
Karen Layman, *Manager*
EMP: 50
SALES (corp-wide): 8MM **Privately Held**
SIC: 8051 Convalescent home with continuous nursing care
PA: Lancia Nursing Home Inc
  1852 Sinclair Ave
  Steubenville OH 43953
  740 264-7101

(G-16641)
LM CONSTRCTION TRRY LVRINI INC
67682 Clark Rd (43950-9257)
P.O. Box 339 (43950-0339)
PHONE..................740 695-9604
Terry Lavorini, *President*
Lisa Lavorini, *Vice Pres*
Jennifer Maier, *Manager*
Mickey Mickler, *Admin Sec*
EMP: 50
SQ FT: 10,000
SALES (est): 13.3MM **Privately Held**
SIC: 1542 1742 1541 Commercial & office building, new construction; commercial & office buildings, renovation & repair; plastering, plain or ornamental; industrial buildings & warehouses

(G-16642)
LOWES HOME CENTERS LLC
50421 Valley Plaza Dr (43950-1749)
PHONE..................740 699-3000
Fax: 740 699-3018
Jennifer Rogers, *Office Mgr*
Cary Johnson, *Manager*
Terry Grierson, *Manager*
EMP: 150
SALES (corp-wide): 68.6B **Publicly Held**
SIC: 5211 5031 5722 5064 Home centers; building materials, exterior; building materials, interior; household appliance stores; electrical appliances, television & radio
HQ: Lowe's Home Centers, Llc
  1605 Curtis Bridge Rd
  Wilkesboro NC 28697
  336 658-4000

(G-16643)
MARIETTA COAL CO (PA)
67705 Friends Church Rd (43950-9500)
PHONE..................740 695-2197
Fax: 740 695-8055
Paul Gill, *President*
George Nicolozakes, *Chairman*

John Nicolozakes, *Vice Pres*
EMP: 50 EST: 1946
SQ FT: 4,300
SALES (est): 8.2MM **Privately Held**
WEB: www.mcatee.biz
SIC: 1221 Surface mining, bituminous

(G-16644)
MCKEEN SECURITY INC
69100 Bayberry Dr Ste 200 (43950-9194)
P.O. Box 740 (43950-0740)
PHONE....................740 699-1301
David McKeen, *President*
EMP: 100
SALES (est): 2MM **Privately Held**
SIC: 7381 Security guard service

(G-16645)
MURRAY AMERICAN ENERGY INC
46226 National Rd (43950-8742)
PHONE....................740 338-3100
Robert E Murray, *President*
Robert D Moore, *Vice Pres*
Michael D Loiacono, *Treasurer*
Penny Elliott, *Manager*
Jason D Witt, *Admin Sec*
EMP: 2667 EST: 2013
SALES (est): 443.4K
SALES (corp-wide): 4.8B **Publicly Held**
SIC: 1221 Bituminous coal surface mining
PA: Murray Energy Corporation
    46226 National Rd
    Saint Clairsville OH 43950
    740 338-3100

(G-16646)
MURRAY KENTUCKY ENERGY INC (HQ)
46226 National Rd (43950-8742)
PHONE....................740 338-3100
Robert E Murray, *President*
EMP: 400
SALES (est): 3.7MM
SALES (corp-wide): 4.8B **Publicly Held**
SIC: 1222 Bituminous coal-underground mining
PA: Murray Energy Corporation
    46226 National Rd
    Saint Clairsville OH 43950
    740 338-3100

(G-16647)
OHIO POWER COMPANY
47687 National Rd (43950-8714)
P.O. Box 99 (43950-0099)
PHONE....................740 695-7800
Fax: 740 695-7838
Phil Lewis, *Manager*
EMP: 100
SALES (corp-wide): 15.4B **Publicly Held**
SIC: 4911 Electric services
HQ: Ohio Power Company
    1 Riverside Plz
    Columbus OH 43215
    614 716-1000

(G-16648)
OHIO VALLEY COAL COMPANY (DH)
46226 National Rd (43950-8742)
PHONE....................740 926-1351
Fax: 740 926-1615
Robert E Murray, *CEO*
Ryan M Murray, *President*
John R Forrelli, *Senior VP*
Michael O McKown, *Senior VP*
Robert D Moore, *Vice Pres*
EMP: 395
SQ FT: 40,380
SALES (est): 243MM
SALES (corp-wide): 4.8B **Publicly Held**
SIC: 1241 Bituminous coal mining services, contract basis
HQ: Ohio Valley Resources, Inc.
    29325 Chagrin Blvd # 300
    Beachwood OH 44122
    216 765-1240

(G-16649)
OHIO VALLEY RESOURCES INC
Also Called: Ohio Valley Coal
46226 National Rd (43950-8742)
PHONE....................740 795-5220
Robert E Murray, *CEO*

Mike Yates, *General Mgr*
McKown Michael, *Senior VP*
Rick Taylor, *Plant Mgr*
Ryan Ross, *Warehouse Mgr*
EMP: 30
SALES (corp-wide): 4.8B **Publicly Held**
SIC: 1241 Coal mining services
HQ: Ohio Valley Resources, Inc.
    29325 Chagrin Blvd # 300
    Beachwood OH 44122
    216 765-1240

(G-16650)
OHIO VALLEY TRANSLOADING CO
46226 National Rd (43950-8742)
PHONE....................740 795-4967
Fax: 740 795-5265
Robert Murray, *CEO*
Mark Hurst, *Manager*
EMP: 2566
SALES (est): 57.6MM
SALES (corp-wide): 4.8B **Publicly Held**
SIC: 1241 Bituminous coal mining services, contract basis
HQ: Ohio Valley Resources, Inc.
    29325 Chagrin Blvd # 300
    Beachwood OH 44122
    216 765-1240

(G-16651)
PARAMOUNT SUPPORT SERVICE
252 W Main St Ste H (43950-1065)
P.O. Box 543 (43950-0543)
PHONE....................740 526-0540
Brent Kovalski, *President*
Sharon Porter, *Manager*
Lorinda Cunningham, *Supervisor*
Jay Van Horn, *Supervisor*
Cheryl Howells, *Representative*
EMP: 86
SALES (est): 1.5MM **Privately Held**
SIC: 8082 Home health care services

(G-16652)
PATTERSON-UTI DRILLING CO LLC
67090 Executive Dr (43950-8473)
PHONE....................724 239-2812
Ron Swegheimer, *General Mgr*
EMP: 26
SALES (est): 4.1MM **Privately Held**
SIC: 1781 Water well drilling

(G-16653)
PSYCHIATRIC SOLUTIONS INC
67670 Traco Dr (43950-9375)
PHONE....................740 695-2131
Karen Maxwell, *CEO*
EMP: 137
SALES (corp-wide): 10.4B **Publicly Held**
WEB: www.intermountainhospital.com
SIC: 8011 Psychiatric clinic
HQ: Psychiatric Solutions, Inc.
    6640 Carothers Pkwy # 500
    Franklin TN 37067
    615 312-5700

(G-16654)
RED ROOF INNS INC
68301 Red Roof Ln (43950-1706)
PHONE....................740 695-4057
Fax: 740 695-6956
Chris Bolt, *Manager*
EMP: 30 **Privately Held**
WEB: www.redroof.com
SIC: 7011 Hotels & motels
HQ: Red Roof Inns, Inc.
    605 S Front St Ste 150
    Columbus OH 43215
    614 744-2600

(G-16655)
RES-CARE INC
66387 Airport Rd (43950-9421)
PHONE....................740 526-0285
Tonya Bartyzel, *Branch Mgr*
EMP: 48
SALES (corp-wide): 24.5B **Privately Held**
SIC: 8052 Home for the mentally retarded, with health care

HQ: Res-Care, Inc.
    9901 Linn Station Rd
    Louisville KY 40223
    502 394-2100

(G-16656)
SOMNUS CORPORATION
Also Called: Hampton Inn
51130 National Rd (43950-9118)
PHONE....................740 695-3961
Edward Hitchman, *President*
Christopher Chesebrough, *General Mgr*
Debbie Kennedy, *Manager*
Dalto Mark, *Manager*
EMP: 35
SALES (est): 2.1MM **Privately Held**
SIC: 7011 Hotels & motels

(G-16657)
TRI COUNTY HELP CENTER INC (PA)
104 1/2 N Marietta St (43950-1255)
P.O. Box 494 (43950-0494)
PHONE....................740 695-5441
Fax: 740 695-6747
Karen Scott, *Exec Dir*
EMP: 43
SQ FT: 2,021
SALES: 1.5MM **Privately Held**
SIC: 8322 Emergency shelters; alcoholism counseling, nontreatment; drug abuse counselor, nontreatment

(G-16658)
UNITED PARCEL SERVICE INC OH
Also Called: UPS
44191 Lafferty Rd (43950-9743)
PHONE....................740 968-3508
James Stickradt, *Manager*
EMP: 50
SALES (corp-wide): 65.8B **Publicly Held**
WEB: www.upsscs.com
SIC: 4215 Parcel delivery, vehicular
HQ: United Parcel Service, Inc. (Oh)
    55 Glenlake Pkwy
    Atlanta GA 30328
    404 828-6000

(G-16659)
VETERANS HEALTH ADMINISTRATION
Also Called: St Clairsville V A Primary
103 Plaza Dr Ste A (43950-7729)
PHONE....................740 695-9321
Fax: 740 695-9420
Misty Reynolds, *Manager*
Zita Lee, *Manager*
EMP: 264 **Publicly Held**
WEB: www.veterans-ru.org
SIC: 8011 9451 Clinic, operated by physicians; psychiatric clinic;
HQ: Veterans Health Administration
    810 Vermont Ave Nw
    Washington DC 20420

(G-16660)
WESTERN KY COAL RESOURCES LLC
46226 National Rd (43950-8742)
PHONE....................740 338-3100
Robert E Murray, *President*
EMP: 400
SALES (est): 3.7MM
SALES (corp-wide): 4.8B **Publicly Held**
SIC: 1222 Bituminous coal-underground mining
HQ: Murray Kentucky Energy, Inc.
    46226 National Rd
    Saint Clairsville OH 43950
    740 338-3100

(G-16661)
WHEELING HOSPITAL INC
107 Plaza Dr Ste D (43950-8735)
PHONE....................740 695-2090
EMP: 57
SALES (corp-wide): 375.6MM **Privately Held**
SIC: 8011 General & family practice, physician/surgeon
PA: Wheeling Hospital, Inc.
    1 Medical Park
    Wheeling WV 26003
    304 243-3000

(G-16662)
ZANDEX INC
Also Called: Beacon House, The
100 Reservoir Rd Ofc 2 (43950-1033)
PHONE....................740 695-3281
Cathy Kocher, *Manager*
Sherry Kuhn, *Manager*
Daphne Berry, *Data Proc Exec*
Heather Borkoski, *Executive*
EMP: 34
SALES (corp-wide): 34MM **Privately Held**
SIC: 8052 Intermediate care facilities
PA: Zandex, Inc.
    1122 Taylor St
    Zanesville OH 43701
    740 454-1400

(G-16663)
ZANDEX INC
Also Called: Forest Hill Care Center
100 Reservoir Rd Ofc 1 (43950-1063)
PHONE....................740 695-7233
Heather Borkoski, *Administration*
EMP: 150
SALES (corp-wide): 34MM **Privately Held**
SIC: 8052 8051 Intermediate care facilities; skilled nursing care facilities
PA: Zandex, Inc.
    1122 Taylor St
    Zanesville OH 43701
    740 454-1400

(G-16664)
ZANDEX HEALTH CARE CORPORATION
Also Called: Forest Hill Retirement Cmnty
100 Reservoir Rd (43950-1064)
PHONE....................740 695-7233
Fax: 740 695-2499
Heather Borkoski, *Manager*
Eileen Kanzic, *Nursing Dir*
Carol Stewart, *Social Dir*
EMP: 150
SQ FT: 1,920
SALES (corp-wide): 34MM **Privately Held**
SIC: 8052 8051 8059 Personal care facility; skilled nursing care facilities; nursing home, except skilled & intermediate care facility
HQ: Zandex Health Care Corporation
    1122 Taylor St
    Zanesville OH 43701

Saint Henry
Mercer County

(G-16665)
BRUNS BUILDING & DEV CORP INC
Also Called: Ohio and Indiana Roofing Co
1429 Cranberry Rd (45883-9749)
PHONE....................419 925-4095
Fax: 419 925-5902
Robert E Bruns, *CEO*
Mike Bruns, *President*
Dave Bruns, *Exec VP*
Dan Bruns, *Vice Pres*
Steve Elston, *Project Mgr*
▲ EMP: 86
SQ FT: 10,000
SALES (est): 33.8MM **Privately Held**
WEB: www.brunsbuilding.com
SIC: 1542 Commercial & office building, new construction

(G-16666)
LCS INC
411 Stachler Dr (45883-9581)
P.O. Box 414 (45883-0414)
PHONE....................419 678-8600
Dan Lennartz, *President*
Theresa Lennartz, *Corp Secy*
EMP: 35
SQ FT: 4,000
SALES: 2.8MM **Privately Held**
SIC: 1541 Industrial buildings & warehouses

(G-16667)
STACHLER CONCRETE INC
431 Stachler Dr (45883-9581)
PHONE.................................419 678-3867
Fax: 419 678-8179
Andy Stockwood, *President*
Janice Ridler, *Office Mgr*
EMP: 28
SQ FT: 1,200
SALES: 4MM **Privately Held**
SIC: 1799 Erection & dismantling of forms for poured concrete

Saint Louisville
Licking County

(G-16668)
HOUSE OF NEW HOPE
8135 Mount Vernon Rd (43071-9670)
PHONE.................................740 345-5437
Fax: 740 745-3429
Edward Sharp, *President*
Shirley Sharp, *Vice Pres*
Samantha Powers, *Human Res Dir*
Jeffrey Greene PHD, *Exec Dir*
Jenny Weiss, *Director*
EMP: 35
SQ FT: 18,000
SALES: 3.6MM **Privately Held**
SIC: 8322 Child related social services

(G-16669)
LAW EXCAVATING INC
9128 Mount Vernon Rd (43071-9637)
PHONE.................................740 745-3420
Tom Law, *President*
Veronica Edwards, *Corp Secy*
Nick Edwards, *Vice Pres*
Mark Cherubini, *Director*
EMP: 45
SQ FT: 120
SALES (est): 3.6MM **Privately Held**
SIC: 1794 Excavation work

Saint Marys
Auglaize County

(G-16670)
CAPABILITIES INC (PA)
124 S Front St (45885-2301)
PHONE.................................419 394-0003
Fax: 419 394-2853
Karen Blumhorst, *CEO*
William Blumhorst, *CFO*
Bill Blumhorst, *Sales Executive*
Belinda Bockrath, *Manager*
Gary Loach, *Manager*
EMP: 45
SQ FT: 2,720
SALES (est): 3.2MM **Privately Held**
SIC: 8331 Sheltered workshop; vocational rehabilitation agency

(G-16671)
CLASSIC DELIGHT INC
310 S Park Dr (45885-9688)
P.O. Box 367 (45885-0367)
PHONE.................................419 394-7955
Fax: 419 394-3199
Darl Harkleroad, *Owner*
Joni Harkleroad, *Vice Pres*
Matt Harkleroad, *Safety Mgr*
Michele Laughman, *Production*
K Mickelson, *Manager*
EMP: 50
SQ FT: 18,800
SALES (est): 16.6MM **Privately Held**
WEB: www.classicdelight.com
SIC: 5149 Specialty food items

(G-16672)
COMMUNICARE HEALTH SVCS INC
Also Called: Saint Marys Living Center
1209 Indiana Ave (45885-1310)
PHONE.................................419 394-7611
Fax: 419 394-7882
Jane Fiely, *Director*
James Luedeke, *Director*
EMP: 75
SALES (corp-wide): 103.9MM **Privately Held**
WEB: www.atriumlivingcenters.com
SIC: 6531 8052 8051 Real estate agents & managers; intermediate care facilities; skilled nursing care facilities
PA: Communicare Health Services, Inc.
4700 Ashwood Dr Ste 200
Blue Ash OH 45241
513 530-1654

(G-16673)
CONAG INC
Also Called: Con-AG
16672 County Road 66a (45885-9212)
PHONE.................................419 394-8870
Fax: 419 394-6329
Robert Hirschfeld, *President*
John Hirschfeld, *President*
Lee Kuck, *Corp Secy*
Barbara Koenig, *Finance Mgr*
EMP: 35
SALES (est): 3.5MM **Privately Held**
WEB: www.conag.com
SIC: 1422 Limestones, ground

(G-16674)
GOLDEN LIVING LLC
Also Called: Beverly
1140 S Knoxville Ave (45885-2609)
PHONE.................................419 394-3308
Joe Austin, *Manager*
EMP: 90
SALES (corp-wide): 7.4MM **Privately Held**
SIC: 8059 8052 8051 Convalescent home; intermediate care facilities; skilled nursing care facilities
PA: Golden Living Llc
5220 Tennyson Pkwy # 400
Plano TX 75024
972 372-6300

(G-16675)
JOINT TOWNSHIP DST MEM HOSP
Also Called: Grand Lake Primary Care
1040 Hager St (45885-2421)
PHONE.................................419 394-9959
Fax: 419 394-0255
Jeffrey W Vossler, *Vice Pres*
EMP: 60
SALES (est): 705.6K
SALES (corp-wide): 71.6MM **Privately Held**
SIC: 8011 Internal medicine practitioners
PA: Joint Township District Memorial Hospital
200 Saint Clair Ave
Saint Marys OH 45885
419 394-3335

(G-16676)
JOINT TOWNSHIP DST MEM HOSP (PA)
Also Called: GRAND LAKE HEALTH SYSTEM
200 Saint Clair Ave (45885-2494)
PHONE.................................419 394-3335
Fax: 419 394-5186
Kevin W Harlan, *CEO*
Joann Hegemier, *Facilities Mgr*
Jeffrey Vassler, *CFO*
Jeff Vossler, *Treasurer*
David Mitchell, *Obstetrician*
EMP: 400
SQ FT: 170,000
SALES: 71.6MM **Privately Held**
WEB: www.jtdmh.org
SIC: 8062 8051 General medical & surgical hospitals; skilled nursing care facilities

(G-16677)
JOINT TOWNSHIP DST MEM HOSP
975 Hager St (45885-2420)
PHONE.................................419 394-9992
Fax: 419 394-9629
Bridget Heckler, *Branch Mgr*
EMP: 60
SALES (corp-wide): 71.6MM **Privately Held**
SIC: 8322 Individual & family services
PA: Joint Township District Memorial Hospital
200 Saint Clair Ave
Saint Marys OH 45885
419 394-3335

(G-16678)
JPMORGAN CHASE BANK NAT ASSN
125 W Spring St (45885-2313)
PHONE.................................419 394-2358
Larry Gautschi, *Principal*
EMP: 26
SALES (corp-wide): 99.6B **Publicly Held**
SIC: 6021 National commercial banks
HQ: Jpmorgan Chase Bank, National Association
1111 Polaris Pkwy
Columbus OH 43240
614 436-3055

(G-16679)
JTD HEALTH SYSTEMS INC
Also Called: Speech Center
200 Saint Clair Ave (45885-2400)
PHONE.................................419 394-3335
Jeff Vossler, *Treasurer*
Kevin W Harlan, *Administration*
Jill Dickman, *Admin Sec*
EMP: 600
SQ FT: 150,000
SALES: 90MM **Privately Held**
SIC: 8741 Hospital management

(G-16680)
NATURAL RESOURCES OHIO DEPT
Also Called: Division of Parks
834 Edgewater Dr (45885-1132)
PHONE.................................419 394-3611
Brian Miller, *Manager*
EMP: 30 **Privately Held**
WEB: www.ohiostateparks.com
SIC: 9512 7033 Land, mineral & wildlife conservation; ; trailer parks & campsites
HQ: Ohio Department Of Natural Resources
2045 Morse Rd Bldg D-3
Columbus OH 43229

(G-16681)
OMNISOURCE LLC
04575 County Road 33a (45885-9655)
PHONE.................................419 394-3351
Fax: 419 394-3833
Mlike Starkey, *Branch Mgr*
EMP: 25 **Publicly Held**
WEB: www.omnisource.com
SIC: 5093 Ferrous metal scrap & waste
HQ: Omnisource, Llc
7575 W Jefferson Blvd
Fort Wayne IN 46804
260 422-5541

(G-16682)
OTTERBEIN SNIOR LFSTYLE CHICES
Also Called: Otterbein St Marys Retrmnt
11230 State Route 364 (45885-9534)
PHONE.................................419 394-2366
Fax: 419 394-2367
Ed Bray, *Trustee*
Scott Beach, *Finance*
Fred Wiswell, *Manager*
Tiffany Burden, *Director*
Alfredo Paguirigan, *Director*
EMP: 120
SALES (corp-wide): 43.8MM **Privately Held**
SIC: 8322 8361 8051 Geriatric social service; residential care; skilled nursing care facilities
PA: Senior Otterbein Lifestyle Choices
585 N State Route 741
Lebanon OH 45036
513 933-5400

(G-16683)
PET FOOD HOLDINGS INC (HQ)
1601 Mckinley Rd (45885-1864)
PHONE.................................419 394-3374
Jim Wiegmann, *President*
EMP: 93
SALES (corp-wide): 109.7B **Privately Held**
SIC: 6719 Investment holding companies, except banks
PA: Cargill, Incorporated
15407 Mcginty Rd W
Wayzata MN 55391
952 742-7575

(G-16684)
ST MARYS CITY BOARD EDUCATION
Also Called: Saint Marys Cy Schools-Bus Gar
1445 Celina Rd (45885-1210)
PHONE.................................419 394-1116
Mary Riepenhoff, *Superintendent*
Kurt Kuffner, *Manager*
EMP: 25
SALES (corp-wide): 10.7MM **Privately Held**
WEB: www.smriders.net
SIC: 8211 7699 Public elementary & secondary schools; miscellaneous automotive repair services
PA: St Marys City Board Of Education
100 W Spring St
Saint Marys OH 45885
419 394-4312

(G-16685)
ST MARYS CITY BOARD EDUCATION
Also Called: East Elementary School
650 Armstrong St (45885-1840)
PHONE.................................419 394-2616
Fax: 419 394-1149
Susan Sherman, *Principal*
EMP: 60
SALES (corp-wide): 10.7MM **Privately Held**
WEB: www.smriders.net
SIC: 8211 8351 Public elementary & secondary schools; child day care services
PA: St Marys City Board Of Education
100 W Spring St
Saint Marys OH 45885
419 394-4312

Saint Paris
Champaign County

(G-16686)
THE FIRST CENTRAL NATIONAL BNK (PA)
103 S Springfield St (43072-7704)
P.O. Box 730 (43072-0730)
PHONE.................................937 663-4186
Fax: 937 663-5395
Jeff McCulla, *President*
Jeffrey McCulla, *Financial Exec*
EMP: 25 EST: 1880
SALES: 3.5MM **Privately Held**
WEB: www.firststparis.com
SIC: 6021 National commercial banks

Salem
Columbiana County

(G-16687)
AT&T CORP
1098 E State St Ste A (44460-2212)
PHONE.................................330 337-3505
EMP: 69
SALES (corp-wide): 146.8B **Publicly Held**
SIC: 4813 Telephone Communications
HQ: At&T Corp.
1 At&T Way
Bedminster NJ 07921
800 403-3302

(G-16688)
BENTLEY LEASING CO LLC
Also Called: Salem West Healthcare Center
2511 Bentley Dr (44460-2503)
PHONE.................................330 337-9503
Charles Stoltz, *CEO*
Steve Rosedale, *COO*
Isaac Rosedale, *CFO*
EMP: 3830

GEOGRAPHIC SECTION

Salem - Columbiana County (G-16712)

SALES (est): 2.7MM Privately Held
SIC: 8051 Skilled nursing care facilities

(G-16689)
BFI WASTE SERVICES LLC
1717 Pennsylvania Ave (44460-2781)
PHONE...................800 437-1123
Fax: 330 337-2260
John Carlson, Branch Mgr
EMP: 48
SALES (corp-wide): 10B Publicly Held
SIC: 4212 4953 Garbage collection & transport, no disposal; refuse collection & disposal services
HQ: Bfi Waste Services, Llc
   18500 N Allied Way # 100
   Phoenix AZ 85054
   480 627-2700

(G-16690)
BLOSSOM NURSING & REHAB CENTER
Also Called: Blossom Nrsing Rhblitation Ctr
109 Blossom Ln (44460-4284)
PHONE...................330 337-3033
Fax: 330 337-0916
Robin Bates, Med Doctor
David Keast, Director
Walter Dombroski, Director
Joseph Pilla, Director
EMP: 110
SALES (est): 5MM Privately Held
SIC: 8071 8051 Medical laboratories; skilled nursing care facilities

(G-16691)
BOC WATER HYDRAULICS INC
12024 Salem Warren Rd (44460-7649)
P.O. Box 1028 (44460-8028)
PHONE...................330 332-4444
Fax: 330 332-1650
Todd Olson, President
Donald Olson, Vice Pres
Brian Frederick, Controller
Bea Olson, Office Mgr
EMP: 44
SQ FT: 14,000
SALES: 8.2MM Privately Held
SIC: 7699 Hydraulic equipment repair

(G-16692)
COUNTRY SAW AND KNIFE INC
1375 W State St (44460-1952)
P.O. Box 887 (44460-0887)
PHONE...................330 332-1611
Stanley Glista, President
Daniel Glista, Vice Pres
Anthony Glista, Treasurer
Richard Mercer, Admin Sec
▲ EMP: 40
SQ FT: 4,800
SALES (est): 4.3MM Privately Held
WEB: www.countrysaw.com
SIC: 7699 5072 Knife, saw & tool sharpening & repair; saw blades

(G-16693)
CTM INTEGRATION INCORPORATED
1318 Quaker Cir (44460-1051)
P.O. Box 589 (44460-0589)
PHONE...................330 332-1800
Fax: 330 332-2144
Thomas C Rumsey, President
Dan Mc Laughlin, Exec VP
Dan McLaughlin, Exec VP
Vera Sobotka, Purchasing
Mike Kennedy, Engineer
EMP: 36
SQ FT: 30,000
SALES (est): 10.9MM Privately Held
WEB: www.ctmint.com
SIC: 3565 5084 3549 Packaging machinery; industrial machinery & equipment; metalworking machinery

(G-16694)
DONNELL FORD-LINCOLN
152 Continental Dr (44460-2506)
P.O. Box 765 (44460-0765)
PHONE...................330 332-0031
Fax: 330 332-7031
Tim Loudon, CEO
Hank Loudon Jr, President
Jason Murdock, Sales Associate
EMP: 40

SALES (est): 8.6MM Privately Held
WEB: www.loudonford.com
SIC: 5511 5521 7538 7532 Automobiles, new & used; used car dealers; general automotive repair shops; top & body repair & paint shops

(G-16695)
FAMILY PRACTICE CTR SALEM INC
2370 Southeast Blvd (44460-3498)
PHONE...................330 332-9961
Richard Banning, President
Richard Fawcett, Med Doctor
EMP: 25
SALES (est): 2.7MM Privately Held
SIC: 8011 General & family practice, physician/surgeon

(G-16696)
FRENCOR INC
Also Called: Visiting Angels
409 E 2nd St Ste 6 (44460-2862)
P.O. Box 67 (44460-0067)
PHONE...................330 332-1203
Fax: 330 332-2940
Mark Frenger, President
Susan Frenger, Vice Pres
Susan Jennin, Manager
EMP: 60
SALES (est): 1.6MM Privately Held
SIC: 8082 Home health care services

(G-16697)
GORDON BROTHERS INC (PA)
Also Called: Gordon Bros Water
776 N Ellsworth Ave (44460-1600)
P.O. Box 358 (44460-0358)
PHONE...................800 331-7611
Fax: 330 337-5907
Bruce Gordon, Ch of Bd
Ned Jones, President
Joan Harvey, COO
Scott P Jones, Vice Pres
Crish Wood, Manager
EMP: 39
SQ FT: 4,500
SALES (est): 4.7MM Privately Held
WEB: www.gordonbros.com
SIC: 7359 5999 5078 5074 Equipment rental & leasing; water purification equipment; refrigeration equipment & supplies; plumbing & hydronic heating supplies

(G-16698)
HICKEY METAL FABRICATION ROOFG
873 Georgetown Rd (44460-9710)
PHONE...................330 337-9329
Fax: 330 337-1400
Bob Hickey, President
Harry Koons, General Mgr
Robert R Hickey, Principal
Leo Hickey, Vice Pres
Nick Peters, Vice Pres
▲ EMP: 30
SALES (est): 6.9MM Privately Held
WEB: www.hickeymetal.com
SIC: 1761 Sheet metalwork

(G-16699)
HOME CARE ADVANTAGE
718 E 3rd St Ste C (44460-2915)
PHONE...................330 337-4663
Fax: 330 337-0481
Carolyn Crookston, Principal
Cynthia Kenst, Principal
EMP: 60
SALES (est): 1.5MM Privately Held
SIC: 8082 Visiting nurse service

(G-16700)
HUNTINGTON INSURANCE INC
542 E State St (44460-2933)
PHONE...................330 337-9933
David B Hazen, Branch Mgr
EMP: 37
SALES (corp-wide): 4.7B Publicly Held
WEB: www.skyinsure.com
SIC: 6411 Insurance agents, brokers & service
HQ: Huntington Insurance, Inc.
   519 Madison Ave
   Toledo OH 43604
   419 720-7900

(G-16701)
INTEGRATED PRJ RESOURCES LLC
600 E 2nd St (44460-2916)
PHONE...................330 272-0998
Emma Wetzl, Managing Dir
Tina Hertzel, Mng Member
John Hertzel,
EMP: 28
SQ FT: 2,500
SALES: 3MM Privately Held
WEB: www.iprglobal.net
SIC: 8742 Management consulting services

(G-16702)
L B BRUNK & SONS INC
Also Called: Brunk's Stoves
10460 Salem Warren Rd (44460-9666)
PHONE...................330 332-0359
Fax: 330 332-9768
Lawrence B Brunk, President
Joseph Brunk, Treasurer
Dave Waggoner, Controller
Gary Saunders, Sales Mgr
EMP: 35
SQ FT: 2,000
SALES (est): 7.1MM Privately Held
WEB: www.brunks.com
SIC: 5074 5561 Fireplaces, prefabricated; stoves, wood burning; recreational vehicle dealers

(G-16703)
LAKE FRONT II INC
Also Called: Salem Hills Golf and Cntry CLB
12688 Salem Warren Rd (44460-9668)
PHONE...................330 337-8033
Fax: 330 337-8023
Clement L Ross, President
EMP: 30
SQ FT: 12,000
SALES (est): 1.2MM Privately Held
SIC: 7997 Country club, membership

(G-16704)
MAC MANUFACTURING INC
1453 Allen Rd (44460-1004)
PHONE...................330 829-1680
David Sandor, VP Opers
Tony Sparks, Sales Staff
Brian Whitlatch, Sales Staff
Kenny Butler, Sales Associate
Kristi Rummel, Marketing Mgr
EMP: 104
SALES (est): 36.2MM Privately Held
SIC: 3715 5012 Truck trailers; trailers for trucks, new & used; truck bodies
PA: Mac Manufacturing, Inc.
   14599 Commerce St Ne
   Alliance OH 44601

(G-16705)
MOBILE MEALS OF SALEM INC
1995 E State St (44460-2423)
PHONE...................330 332-2160
Jeff Goll, President
Barb Plummer, Vice Pres
Laura Todd, Treasurer
Joanna Bosel, Manager
Marilyn McBride, Admin Sec
EMP: 45
SALES (est): 1.7MM Privately Held
SIC: 8322 Individual & family services

(G-16706)
POLLOCK RESEARCH & DESIGN INC
Simmers Crane Design & Svc Co
1134 Salem Pkwy (44460-1063)
PHONE...................330 332-3300
Fax: 330 332-3322
Peter Evans, Vice Pres
Mark Kastner, Vice Pres
Randall Gross, Treasurer
John Adkins, Branch Mgr
Randy L Stull, Manager
EMP: 45

SALES (est): 12.6MM
SALES (corp-wide): 34.3MM Privately Held
SIC: 8711 7389 7353 3537 Civil engineering; mechanical engineering; structural engineering; crane & aerial lift service; heavy construction equipment rental; industrial trucks & tractors
PA: Pollock Research & Design, Inc.
   11 Vanguard Dr
   Reading PA 19606
   610 582-7203

(G-16707)
QUALITY FABRICATED METALS INC
14000 W Middletown Rd (44460-9184)
PHONE...................330 332-7008
Fax: 330 332-9140
Danny Beegle, President
Kay Tuttle, Manager
EMP: 25
SQ FT: 42,000
SALES (est): 5.3MM Privately Held
WEB: www.gtd-qfm.com
SIC: 3469 1799 Metal stampings; welding on site

(G-16708)
QUALITY TRAILERS OF OH INC
1664 Salem Pkwy W (44460-1083)
PHONE...................330 332-9630
Fax: 330 332-2436
Robb Kaufman, President
Lori Reiser, Vice Pres
Mary Lambeth, Manager
Veda Kaufman, Admin Sec
EMP: 25
SALES (est): 4.9MM Privately Held
SIC: 5084 Trailers, industrial

(G-16709)
R K CAMPF CORP
Also Called: R-K-Campf Transport
465 Newgarden Ave (44460-3042)
PHONE...................330 332-7089
Rob Campf, President
Karrin Campf, Vice Pres
Jack Carr, Manager
Raquel Ceballos, Manager
EMP: 50 EST: 1993
SALES (est): 4.3MM Privately Held
WEB: www.rkcampf.com
SIC: 4213 4214 Contract haulers; local trucking with storage

(G-16710)
RENT-A-CENTER INC
2870 E State St Ste 500 (44460-9335)
PHONE...................330 337-1107
Fax: 330 337-0917
Anthony Dieudenil, Manager
EMP: 56
SALES (corp-wide): 2.7B Publicly Held
WEB: www.rentacenter.com
SIC: 7359 Appliance rental; furniture rental; home entertainment equipment rental; television rental
PA: Rent-A-Center, Inc.
   5501 Headquarters Dr
   Plano TX 75024
   972 801-1100

(G-16711)
SALEM AREA VSITING NURSE ASSOC
718 E 3rd St Ste A (44460-2915)
PHONE...................330 332-9986
Fax: 330 332-8899
Susan K Yoder, Exec Dir
EMP: 50
SQ FT: 9,000
SALES: 2.2MM Privately Held
WEB: www.salemohiovna.com
SIC: 8082 Visiting nurse service

(G-16712)
SALEM COMMUNITY CENTER INC
1098 N Ellsworth Ave (44460-1536)
PHONE...................330 332-5885
Caroline Stone, Exec Dir
Heather Young, Director
Shane Harding-Cpo, Director
Cory Wonner, Director

Salem - Columbiana County (G-16713) GEOGRAPHIC SECTION

EMP: 75
SALES: 2.5MM **Privately Held**
SIC: 8322 Community center

(G-16713)
SALEM COMMUNITY HOSPITAL (PA)
Also Called: SALEM HOME MEDICAL
1995 E State St (44460-2400)
PHONE.................................330 332-1551
Fax: 330 332-7592
Anita Hackstedde MD, *CEO*
Mark Talbott, *Maintenance Dir*
Sue Suarez, *Facilities Mgr*
Michael Giangardella, *CFO*
Michele Hoffmeister, *Pub Rel Dir*
EMP: 1000
SQ FT: 300,000
SALES: 105.5MM **Privately Held**
WEB: www.salemhosp.com
SIC: 8062 8051 General medical & surgical hospitals; skilled nursing care facilities

(G-16714)
SALEM HEALTHCARE MGT LLC
1985 E Pershing St (44460-3411)
PHONE.................................330 332-1588
Martha Reed, *Facilities Dir*
Tammy Hubbard, *Human Res Dir*
Cheryl Hess, *Office Mgr*
Alan Schwartz, *Mng Member*
George Wilson, *Director*
EMP: 40
SALES (est): 3.8MM **Privately Held**
SIC: 8741 Nursing & personal care facility management

(G-16715)
SALEM HISTORICAL SOC MUSEUM
208 S Broadway Ave (44460-3004)
PHONE.................................330 337-6733
David Stratton, *Director*
EMP: 25
SALES: 1.7MM **Privately Held**
SIC: 8412 Museum

(G-16716)
SALEM INTERNAL MEDICINE ASSOC
564 E 2nd St (44460-2914)
PHONE.................................330 332-5232
Fax: 330 332-4771
Dr Michael A Lileas Do, *President*
Steven M De Mailo Do, *Corp Secy*
Thomas R Timko MD, *Vice Pres*
Eileen McCombs, *Project Mgr*
Denis Lunne MD, *Treasurer*
EMP: 32
SQ FT: 2,400
SALES (est): 1.8MM **Privately Held**
SIC: 8011 Internal medicine, physician/surgeon

(G-16717)
TFI TRANSPORTATION INC
10370 W South Range Rd (44460-9621)
P.O. Box 310 (44460-0310)
PHONE.................................330 332-4655
Fax: 330 332-2330
Verona Lippiatt, *President*
Sam Lippiatt, *Vice Pres*
Bill Sinclair, *Vice Pres*
Sue Sinclair, *Treasurer*
Mary McLaughlin, *Admin Sec*
EMP: 35
SALES (est): 3.4MM **Privately Held**
SIC: 4213 Heavy machinery transport; building materials transport

(G-16718)
VENTRA SALEM LLC
800 Pennsylvania Ave (44460-2783)
PHONE.................................330 337-8002
Scott Tuel, *General Mgr*
Darlene Hart, *Controller*
Jim Zebok, *Finance*
Timothy F Graham, *Manager*
Shahid Khan,
▲ EMP: 750
SQ FT: 400,000
SALES (est): 221.8MM
SALES (corp-wide): 3.4B **Privately Held**
WEB: www.flex-n-gate.com
SIC: 5013 Automotive supplies & parts

PA: Flex-N-Gate Corporation
1306 E University Ave
Urbana IL 61802
217 384-6600

(G-16719)
WITMERS INC
39821 Salem Unity Rd (44460-9696)
P.O. Box 368, Columbiana (44408-0368)
PHONE.................................330 427-2147
Fax: 330 427-2611
Ralph Witmer, *CEO*
Nelson Witmer, *President*
Grace Styer, *Corp Secy*
EMP: 30
SQ FT: 20,000
SALES (est): 5.9MM **Privately Held**
SIC: 5999 1542 7699 Farm equipment & supplies; agricultural building contractors; commercial & office building, new construction; farm machinery repair

Salesville
Guernsey County

(G-16720)
SOUTHEASTERN REHABILITATION
62222 Frankfort Rd (43778-9638)
PHONE.................................740 679-2111
Fax: 740 679-3288
Renee Nelson, *Owner*
Sheri Vandyne, *Admin Sec*
EMP: 35
SALES (est): 635.8K **Privately Held**
SIC: 8322 Rehabilitation services

(G-16721)
WAMPUM HARDWARE CO
60711 Dynamite Rd (43778-9756)
PHONE.................................740 685-2585
Fax: 740 685-6268
Bob Wright, *Manager*
EMP: 45
SALES (corp-wide): 37.9MM **Privately Held**
WEB: www.wampumhardware.com
SIC: 5169 Chemicals & allied products
PA: Wampum Hardware Co.
636 Paden Rd
New Galilee PA 16141
724 336-4501

Salineville
Columbiana County

(G-16722)
CIRCLE J HOME HEALTH CARE (PA)
412 State Route 164 (43945-7701)
PHONE.................................330 482-0877
Betty Johnson, *President*
EMP: 67
SALES (est): 1.5MM **Privately Held**
SIC: 8082 Home health care services

Sandusky
Erie County

(G-16723)
ABILITY WORKS INC
Also Called: Mrdd
3920 Columbus Ave (44870-5791)
PHONE.................................419 626-1048
Lisa Moore, *General Mgr*
Laura Lagodney, *COO*
Kevin Furback, *Safety Dir*
Larry Stein, *Mfg Staff*
Celeste Hillman, *Manager*
EMP: 125
SALES (est): 2.1MM **Privately Held**
WEB: www.doublejind.com
SIC: 8331 8322 7389 Sheltered workshop; individual & family services;

(G-16724)
AKIL INCORPORATED
Also Called: Akil Industrial Cleaning
2525 W Monroe St (44870-1902)
PHONE.................................419 625-0857
Fax: 419 627-8182
William A Mason, *Ch of Bd*
Charles Stovall, *President*
Yvonne Mason, *Treasurer*
Josephine Stovall, *Admin Sec*
EMP: 40
SQ FT: 33,000
SALES (est): 1.4MM **Privately Held**
SIC: 7699 1622 1611 Cleaning services; bridge construction; highway construction, elevated; highway & street paving contractor

(G-16725)
ALL PHASE POWER AND LTG INC
Also Called: Insight Technical Services
2122 Campbell St (44870-4816)
P.O. Box 2515 (44871-2515)
PHONE.................................419 624-9640
Fax: 419 626-0500
William Tunnell, *President*
Frank Kath, *President*
Steve Hill, *General Mgr*
Jude Poggiali, *Vice Pres*
Dave Stein, *Vice Pres*
EMP: 35
SQ FT: 6,400
SALES: 6.7MM **Privately Held**
WEB: www.4-insight.com
SIC: 1731 General electrical contractor; switchgear & related devices installation

(G-16726)
AMERICAS BEST VALUE INN
Also Called: Ramada Inn
5608 Milan Rd (44870-5879)
PHONE.................................419 626-9890
EMP: 35
SALES (est): 618.8K **Privately Held**
SIC: 7011 6512 5812 Hotel/Motel Operation Nonresidential Building Operator Eating Place

(G-16727)
AUGUST CORSO SONS INC
Also Called: Corso's Flower & Garden Center
3404 Milan Rd (44870-5678)
P.O. Box 1575 (44871-1575)
PHONE.................................419 626-0765
Fax: 419 626-0367
August J Corso, *CEO*
Chad Corso, *President*
Brad Corso, *Vice Pres*
John Corso, *Vice Pres*
▲ EMP: 120
SQ FT: 8,000
SALES: 43.4MM **Privately Held**
WEB: www.corsos.com
SIC: 5193 5261 Flowers & nursery stock; nurseries & garden centers

(G-16728)
BAYSHORE COUNSELING SERVICE (PA)
1218 Cleveland Rd Ste 3 (44870-4200)
PHONE.................................419 626-9156
Fax: 419 621-0099
Tim Naughton, *Exec Dir*
EMP: 35
SQ FT: 3,700
SALES: 1.5MM **Privately Held**
SIC: 8093 Mental health clinic, outpatient

(G-16729)
BROOK PLUM COUNTRY CLUB
3712 Galloway Rd (44870-6021)
PHONE.................................419 625-5394
Fax: 419 625-5486
Dan Moncher, *President*
Craig Wood, *Vice Pres*
Mark Kling, *Manager*
EMP: 100
SQ FT: 33,469
SALES: 2.2MM **Privately Held**
WEB: www.pbcc.net
SIC: 7997 Country club, membership

(G-16730)
BUDERER DRUG COMPANY INC (PA)
633 Hancock St (44870-3603)
PHONE.................................419 627-2800
James Buderer, *President*
Matthew Buderer, *Vice Pres*
Suzanne Fomich, *Pharmacist*
EMP: 34 EST: 2014
SQ FT: 5,000
SALES (est): 4.7MM **Privately Held**
SIC: 5122 2834 Drugs & drug proprietaries; animal medicines; proprietary (patent) medicines; proprietary drug products

(G-16731)
CAFARO PEACHCREEK CO LTD
Also Called: Clarion Hotel
1119 Sandusky Mall Blvd (44870-5849)
PHONE.................................419 625-6280
Fax: 419 625-9080
Mary Sartor, *Manager*
EMP: 60
SALES (corp-wide): 4.1MM **Privately Held**
WEB: www.millcreekmall.net
SIC: 7011 Hotels & motels
PA: Cafaro Peachcreek Co Ltd
5577 Youngstown Warren Rd
Niles OH 44446
330 747-2661

(G-16732)
CANTON S-GROUP LTD
4000 Columbus Ave (44870-7325)
PHONE.................................419 625-7003
John Stock, *Partner*
Becky Stock, *Partner*
Tim Wade, *Partner*
David Volz, *Controller*
Gloria Canode, *Persnl Mgr*
EMP: 400
SALES (est): 11.5MM **Privately Held**
SIC: 7389 Personal service agents, brokers & bureaus

(G-16733)
CARE & SHARE OF ERIE COUNT
241 Jackson St (44870-2608)
PHONE.................................419 624-1411
Louise Moos, *Treasurer*
L M More, *Exec Dir*
Linda Miller More, *Exec Dir*
EMP: 100
SALES: 149.8K **Privately Held**
SIC: 8322 Senior citizens' center or association

(G-16734)
CEDAR FAIR LP (PA)
1 Cedar Point Dr (44870-5259)
PHONE.................................419 626-0830
Fax: 419 627-2260
Matthew A Ouimet, *CEO*
Richard A Zimmerman, *President*
Jacob Falfas, *COO*
Tim Fisher, *COO*
H Philip Bender, *Exec VP*
▲ EMP: 600
SALES: 1.3B **Publicly Held**
WEB: www.cedarfair.com
SIC: 7996 Theme park, amusement

(G-16735)
CEDAR POINT PARK LLC
Also Called: Castaway Bay
2001 Cleveland Rd (44870-4403)
PHONE.................................419 627-2500
Robert Gigliotti, *Manager*
EMP: 100
SALES (corp-wide): 1.3B **Publicly Held**
WEB: www.cedarfair.com
SIC: 7996 7011 Theme park, amusement; resort hotel
HQ: Cedar Point Park Llc
1 Cedar Point Dr
Sandusky OH 44870
419 626-0830

(G-16736)
CELLCO PARTNERSHIP
Also Called: Verizon
4816 Milan Rd Ste F (44870-5886)
PHONE.................................419 625-7900
Fax: 419 625-7961

GEOGRAPHIC SECTION
Sandusky - Erie County (G-16758)

Mike Dohar, *Branch Mgr*
EMP: 71
SALES (corp-wide): 126B **Publicly Held**
SIC: 4812 Cellular telephone services
HQ: Cellco Partnership
1 Verizon Way
Basking Ridge NJ 07920

(G-16737)
CITY OF SANDUSKY
Also Called: Water Pollution Control
304 Harrison St (44870-2149)
PHONE.....................419 627-5906
Gary Retzke, *Superintendent*
EMP: 30 **Privately Held**
SIC: 4952 Sewerage systems
PA: City Of Sandusky
222 Meigs St
Sandusky OH 44870
419 627-5844

(G-16738)
CITY OF SANDUSKY
Engineering Department
222 Meigs St (44870-2835)
PHONE.....................419 627-5829
Fax: 419 609-1147
Luella Knight, *Manager*
Debbie Leslie, *Manager*
Erich Obrien, *Manager*
Kris Wood, *Manager*
Kathryn McKillips, *Director*
EMP: 61 **Privately Held**
SIC: 8711 Engineering services
PA: City Of Sandusky
222 Meigs St
Sandusky OH 44870
419 627-5844

(G-16739)
CITY OF SANDUSKY
Also Called: Sewer Department
304 Harrison St (44870-2149)
PHONE.....................419 627-5907
Fax: 419 627-5800
Jeff Meinert, *Manager*
EMP: 30 **Privately Held**
SIC: 4952 9111 Sewerage systems; mayors' offices
PA: City Of Sandusky
222 Meigs St
Sandusky OH 44870
419 627-5844

(G-16740)
CIVISTA BANK (HQ)
100 E Water St (44870-2524)
P.O. Box 5016 (44871-5016)
PHONE.....................419 625-4121
Fax: 419 627-0103
James O Miller, *CEO*
David A Voight, *Ch of Bd*
John O Bacon, *President*
Thomas Lloyd, *President*
Richard Dutton, *COO*
EMP: 100 **EST:** 1898
SQ FT: 23,000
SALES: 69.6MM **Publicly Held**
WEB: www.citizensbankco.com
SIC: 6022 State trust companies accepting deposits, commercial

(G-16741)
CLP GW SANDUSKY TENANT LP
Also Called: Great Wolf Lodge
4600 Milan Rd (44870-5840)
PHONE.....................419 609-6000
Jim Calder, *Partner*
Alex Lombardo, *Partner*
Jan Kinkopf, *Manager*
Abby Pearson, *Manager*
Beth Schwiefert, *Manager*
EMP: 354
SQ FT: 300,000
SALES (est): 10.4MM **Privately Held**
SIC: 7011 Resort hotel
PA: Cnl Lifestyle Properties, Inc.
450 S Orange Ave
Orlando FL 32801

(G-16742)
COACHS SPORTS CORNER INC
1130 Cleveland Rd (44870-4036)
PHONE.....................419 609-3737
Fax: 419 625-5403
James E Fischer, *President*
Greg Fischer, *Vice Pres*
Emily J Fischer, *Treasurer*
EMP: 32
SQ FT: 7,250
SALES (est): 3.6MM **Privately Held**
WEB: www.csc1st.com
SIC: 5091 5941 Sporting & recreation goods; sporting goods & bicycle shops

(G-16743)
COMMODORE DENIG POST NO 83
3615 Hayes Ave (44870-5324)
P.O. Box 2101 (44871-2101)
PHONE.....................419 625-3274
Jim Caldwell, *Commander*
EMP: 40
SALES: 305.8K **Privately Held**
SIC: 8641 Veterans' organization

(G-16744)
COMMONS OF PROVIDENCE
Also Called: PROVIDENCE CARE CENTERS
5000 Providence Dr Ste 1 (44870-1415)
PHONE.....................419 624-1171
Fax: 419 624-1175
Rick Ryan, *CEO*
Jane Windisch, *Mktg Dir*
Wendy Dolyk, *Exec Dir*
Angel Wadsworth, *Director*
Rick Didomenici, *Administration*
EMP: 75 **EST:** 1997
SALES: 4.8MM **Privately Held**
SIC: 8361 6513 8052 Group foster home; apartment building operators; intermediate care facilities

(G-16745)
COMMUNITY ACTION COMMISSION (PA)
908 Seavers Way (44870-4659)
P.O. Box 2500 (44871-2500)
PHONE.....................419 626-6540
Emma Moore, *Treasurer*
Jeanette Colbert, *Finance Dir*
Kim Newman, *Comptroller*
Janice W Warner, *Exec Dir*
Pervis D Brown, *Admin Sec*
EMP: 100
SQ FT: 10,934
SALES: 4.4MM **Privately Held**
WEB: www.ehcac.com
SIC: 8322 Family service agency

(G-16746)
CONCORD HEALTH CARE INC
Also Called: Briarfield of Sandusky
620 W Strub Rd (44870-5779)
PHONE.....................419 626-5373
Richard Keller, *Director*
Dianne McFarlyn, *Administration*
EMP: 50 **Privately Held**
SIC: 8052 Intermediate care facilities
PA: Concord Health Care Inc
202 Churchill Hubbard Rd
Youngstown OH 44505

(G-16747)
COOPER/T SMITH CORPORATION
2705 W Monroe St (44870-1831)
P.O. Box 2647 (44871-2647)
PHONE.....................419 626-0801
Fax: 419 626-8248
Ron House, *Manager*
EMP: 37
SALES (corp-wide): 534MM **Privately Held**
SIC: 4491 Docks, piers & terminals
PA: Smith Cooper/T Corporation
118 N Royal St Ste 1000
Mobile AL 36602
251 431-6100

(G-16748)
COUNTY OF ERIE
Also Called: Child Support Enforcement Agcy
221 W Parish St (44870-4877)
PHONE.....................419 626-6781
Fax: 419 624-6387
Judith K Englehart, *Director*
Karen Balconi-Ghezzi, *Director*
K Englehart, *Director*
EMP: 125 **Privately Held**
WEB: www.gem.org
SIC: 8322 9111 Probation office; county supervisors' & executives' offices
PA: County Of Erie
2900 Columbus Ave
Sandusky OH 44870
419 627-7682

(G-16749)
COUNTY OF ERIE
Also Called: Erie County Hwy Dept
2700 Columbus Ave (44870-5551)
PHONE.....................419 627-7710
John Farschman, *Principal*
EMP: 33 **Privately Held**
WEB: www.gem.org
SIC: 8711 9111 Engineering services; county supervisors' & executives' offices
PA: County Of Erie
2900 Columbus Ave
Sandusky OH 44870
419 627-7682

(G-16750)
ECONO LODGE
1904 Cleveland Rd (44870-4307)
PHONE.....................419 627-8000
Fax: 419 627-8944
George Spadaro, *President*
EMP: 70
SALES (est): 1.4MM **Privately Held**
SIC: 7011 Motels

(G-16751)
ERIE BLACKTOP INC
4507 Tiffin Ave (44870-9646)
P.O. Box 2308 (44871-2308)
PHONE.....................419 625-7374
Fax: 419 625-5751
Dean Wikel, *President*
Chris Schaeffer, *Vice Pres*
Bob Boehk, *Safety Mgr*
Dan White, *QC Dir*
James Kromer, *CFO*
EMP: 30
SQ FT: 560
SALES (est): 6.3MM
SALES (corp-wide): 45.6MM **Privately Held**
WEB: www.erieblacktop.com
SIC: 1611 Highway & street paving contractor
PA: Erie Materials, Inc.
4507 Tiffin Ave
Sandusky OH 44870
419 625-7374

(G-16752)
ERIE CONSTRUCTION GROUP INC
4507 Tiffin Ave (44870-9646)
P.O. Box 2308 (44871-2308)
PHONE.....................419 625-7374
Dean Wikel, *President*
Chris Schaffer, *Vice Pres*
Chris Walters, *Treasurer*
EMP: 50
SALES: 1.4MM
SALES (corp-wide): 45.6MM **Privately Held**
WEB: www.eriematerials.com
SIC: 1611 Highway & street construction; general contractor, highway & street construction; highway & street maintenance; highway & street paving contractor
PA: Erie Materials, Inc.
4507 Tiffin Ave
Sandusky OH 44870
419 625-7374

(G-16753)
ERIE COUNTY CABLEVISION INC
Also Called: Cable System, The
409 E Market St (44870-2814)
PHONE.....................419 627-0800
Fax: 419 627-0180
David Huey, *President*
Patrick L Deville, *Vice Pres*
Ken Lewis, *Project Mgr*
Gloria Duncan, *Exec Sec*
EMP: 33
SQ FT: 8,600
SALES (est): 4MM
SALES (corp-wide): 690.9MM **Privately Held**
WEB: www.blockcommunications.com
SIC: 4841 Cable television services
PA: Block Communications, Inc.
405 Madison Ave Ste 2100
Toledo OH 43604
419 724-6212

(G-16754)
ERIE RESIDENTIAL LIVING INC
Also Called: ERIE RESIDENTIAL LIVING HOME I
706 E Park St (44870-3301)
PHONE.....................419 625-0060
Fax: 419 626-8825
Donna Frost, *Exec Dir*
EMP: 30 **EST:** 1976
SALES: 918.4K **Privately Held**
SIC: 8361 Home for the mentally handicapped

(G-16755)
ERIE TRUCKING INC
4507 Tiffin Ave (44870-9646)
P.O. Box 2308 (44871-2308)
PHONE.....................419 625-7374
Dean Wikel, *President*
Chris Walters, *Corp Secy*
Chris Schaeffer, *Vice Pres*
Tyler Wasserman, *Project Mgr*
Ned Wikel, *Manager*
EMP: 30 **EST:** 1927
SQ FT: 1,000
SALES (est): 3.3MM
SALES (corp-wide): 45.6MM **Privately Held**
WEB: www.eriematerials.com
SIC: 4213 Contract haulers
PA: Erie Materials, Inc.
4507 Tiffin Ave
Sandusky OH 44870
419 625-7374

(G-16756)
FEICK CONTRACTORS INC
224 E Water St (44870-2545)
PHONE.....................419 625-3241
John A Feick, *President*
Carl M Feick, *Vice Pres*
Edward Feick, *Manager*
EMP: 30
SQ FT: 4,000
SALES: 783.7K **Privately Held**
SIC: 1542 Commercial & office building, new construction

(G-16757)
FIRELANDS REGIONAL HEALTH SYS (PA)
Also Called: FIRELANDS REGIONAL MEDICAL CEN
1111 Hayes Ave (44870-3323)
PHONE.....................419 557-7400
Fax: 419 557-7025
Martin E Tursky, *CEO*
Robert Aryes, *COO*
Mike Canfield, *Vice Pres*
Marsha O Mruk, *Vice Pres*
Bud Seville, *Materials Mgr*
EMP: 1300
SQ FT: 320,000
SALES: 15.5K **Privately Held**
SIC: 8062 General medical & surgical hospitals

(G-16758)
FIRELANDS REGIONAL HEALTH SYS
Also Called: Out Patient
1101 Decatur St (44870-3364)
PHONE.....................419 626-7400
Tina Monarch, *Purchasing*
Ron Parthemore, *VP Mktg*
Steven Ayres, *Manager*
Phyllis Osby, *Manager*
Dennis Sokel, *Exec Dir*
EMP: 150
SALES (corp-wide): 15.5K **Privately Held**
SIC: 6324 Hospital & medical service plans
PA: Firelands Regional Health System
1111 Hayes Ave
Sandusky OH 44870
419 557-7400

Sandusky - Erie County (G-16759) GEOGRAPHIC SECTION

(G-16759)
FIRELANDS SECURITY SERVICES
1210 Sycamore Line (44870-4029)
P.O. Box 2587 (44871-2587)
PHONE..................419 627-0562
Fax: 419 627-9110
Brian Dietrich, *President*
EMP: 30
SQ FT: 400
SALES (est): 601.6K Privately Held
WEB: www.firelandssecurityservices.com
SIC: 7381 4215 Security guard service; private investigator; lie detection service; courier services, except by air

(G-16760)
FIRST AMERICAN TITLE INSUR CO
143 E Water St (44870-2525)
PHONE..................419 625-8505
Sally Lucius, *Manager*
EMP: 25 Publicly Held
WEB: www.firstam.com
SIC: 6361 Real estate title insurance
HQ: First American Title Insurance Company
    1 First American Way
    Santa Ana CA 92707
    800 854-3643

(G-16761)
FIRST CHOICE MEDICAL STAFFING
1164 Cleveland Rd (44870-4036)
PHONE..................419 626-9740
Fax: 419 626-6116
Charles Slone, *President*
Lavinda Ross, *Manager*
Carol Spicer, *Manager*
EMP: 38
SALES (corp-wide): 4.6MM Privately Held
WEB: www.rxprn.com
SIC: 8742 Hospital & health services consultant
PA: First Choice Medical Staffing Of Ohio, Inc.
    1457 W 117th St
    Cleveland OH 44107
    216 521-2222

(G-16762)
GILBERT HEATING & AC
Also Called: Gilbert Heating AC & Plumb
2121 Cleveland Rd Ste A (44870-4493)
PHONE..................419 625-8875
Fax: 419 625-5430
Thomas Runkle, *President*
Jim Stookey, *Vice Pres*
Sandy Sandres, *Manager*
EMP: 30
SQ FT: 8,500
SALES: 2MM Privately Held
SIC: 1711 Warm air heating & air conditioning contractor; plumbing contractors

(G-16763)
GOODWILL INDUSTRIES OF ERIE (PA)
Also Called: Goodw Indus of Erie, Huron, Ot
419 W Market St (44870-2411)
PHONE..................419 625-4744
Fax: 419 625-4692
Eric Kochendoerfer, *CEO*
Robert Talcott, *President*
Mark Stratton, *CFO*
Don Hanck, *Treasurer*
Jason Stout, *VP Finance*
EMP: 50
SQ FT: 30,000
SALES: 8.9MM Privately Held
SIC: 8322 5932 Individual & family services; clothing, secondhand

(G-16764)
GOOFY GOLF INC
3020 Milan Rd (44870-5676)
PHONE..................419 625-1308
Roger Andrews, *President*
Diane Andrews, *Principal*
Dianne Andrews, *Vice Pres*
EMP: 38

SALES (est): 1.1MM Privately Held
SIC: 7999 5599 Recreation center; go-carts

(G-16765)
GREAT BEAR LODGE SANDUSKY LLC
Also Called: Great Wolf Lodge
4600 Milan Rd (44870-5840)
PHONE..................419 609-6000
Fax: 419 609-6001
John Emery, *CEO*
Jim Calder, *CFO*
Alex Lombardo, *Treasurer*
Elan Blutinger, *Director*
Randy Churchey, *Director*
EMP: 300
SALES (est): 4MM Privately Held
SIC: 7011 Resort hotel

(G-16766)
GUNDLACH SHEET METAL WORKS INC (PA)
Also Called: Honeywell Authorized Dealer
910 Columbus Ave (44870-3594)
PHONE..................419 626-4525
Fax: 419 626-9365
Roger M Gundlach, *President*
Terry W Gundlach, *Chairman*
Richard Hohler, *Vice Pres*
Terry Kette, *Vice Pres*
Andrew Gundluch, *Admin Sec*
EMP: 76
SQ FT: 17,000
SALES (est): 18.7MM Privately Held
WEB: www.gundlach-hvac.com
SIC: 1711 3444 Warm air heating & air conditioning contractor; sheet metalwork

(G-16767)
HEAP HOME ENERGY ASSISTANCE
908 Seavers Way (44870-4659)
PHONE..................419 626-6540
Janice Alexander, *Exec Dir*
EMP: 85
SALES (est): 685.7K Privately Held
SIC: 8322 Individual & family services

(G-16768)
HOME DEPOT USA INC
Also Called: Home Depot, The
715 Crossings Rd (44870-8903)
PHONE..................419 626-6493
Fax: 419 609-7413
Matt Carey, *Exec VP*
Marvin Ellison, *Exec VP*
Craig Menear, *Exec VP*
Mark Holifield, *Senior VP*
Cara Kinzey, *Senior VP*
EMP: 120
SALES (corp-wide): 100.9B Publicly Held
WEB: www.homerentalsdepot.com
SIC: 5211 7359 Home centers; tool rental
HQ: Home Depot U.S.A., Inc.
    2455 Paces Ferry Rd Se
    Atlanta GA 30339

(G-16769)
HOTY ENTERPRISES INC (PA)
5500 Milan Rd Ste 220 (44870-7804)
PHONE..................419 609-7000
John M Hoty, *President*
Mac Lehrer, *Counsel*
Todd Hart, *Vice Pres*
Angelo Hoty, *Vice Pres*
Zack Hoty, *Vice Pres*
EMP: 28
SQ FT: 6,000
SALES (est): 4.2MM Privately Held
WEB: www.hoty.com
SIC: 6512 Commercial & industrial building operation

(G-16770)
IHEARTCOMMUNICATIONS INC
Also Called: Wmjk FM
1640 Cleveland Rd (44870-4357)
PHONE..................419 625-1010
Fax: 419 625-1348
Adam Klein, *Manager*
Paul Mize, *Manager*
EMP: 30 Publicly Held
SIC: 4832 Radio broadcasting stations

HQ: Iheartcommunications, Inc.
    20880 Stone Oak Pkwy
    San Antonio TX 78258
    210 822-2828

(G-16771)
JERSEY CENTRAL PWR & LIGHT CO
Also Called: Firstenergy
2508 W Perkins Ave (44870-1917)
PHONE..................419 366-2915
Jim Gill, *Manager*
EMP: 60 Publicly Held
WEB: www.jersey-central-power-light.monmouth.n
SIC: 4911 Electric services
HQ: Jersey Central Power & Light Company
    76 S Main St
    Akron OH 44308
    800 736-3402

(G-16772)
K & K INTERIORS INC
2230 Superior St (44870-1843)
PHONE..................419 627-0039
Kyle Camp, *President*
Mark Wall, *Vice Pres*
Sue Sowden, *Human Res Mgr*
Beverly Wilson, *Manager*
◆ EMP: 53 EST: 1996
SQ FT: 125,000
SALES (est): 21.6MM Privately Held
WEB: www.kkinteriors.com
SIC: 5092 Arts & crafts equipment & supplies

(G-16773)
KIDDLE KORRAL
Also Called: Kiddie Korral
315 W Follett St (44870-4881)
PHONE..................419 626-9082
Diedre Bartemes, *Exec Dir*
EMP: 45
SALES (est): 789.3K Privately Held
SIC: 8351 Preschool center

(G-16774)
KOCH ALUMINUM MFG INC
1615 E Perkins Ave (44870-5199)
PHONE..................419 625-5956
Fax: 419 625-4953
Randall G Koch, *President*
Dan Lawrence, *Manager*
EMP: 30 EST: 1952
SQ FT: 25,000
SALES (est): 9.5MM Privately Held
WEB: www.kochdoorsandwindows.com
SIC: 5031 5211 Building materials, exterior; building materials, interior; doors, wood or metal, except storm

(G-16775)
LMN DEVELOPMENT LLC (PA)
Also Called: Kalahari Resort
7000 Kalahari Dr (44870-8628)
PHONE..................419 433-7200
Todd Nelson, *President*
Brian Shanle, *General Mgr*
Mary Bonte-Stath, *CFO*
Carri Corwin, *Human Res Dir*
Terry Wex, *Corp Counsel*
EMP: 95
SALES (est): 67.3MM Privately Held
SIC: 7011 7996 5091 Resort hotel; amusement parks; water slides (recreation park)

(G-16776)
LODGING INDUSTRY INC
Also Called: Super 8 Motel
7704 Milan Rd (44870-8356)
PHONE..................440 323-7488
Michael Ruta, *Owner*
EMP: 31
SALES (corp-wide): 1.5MM Privately Held
SIC: 7011 5813 Hotels & motels; drinking places
PA: Lodging Industry Inc
    910 Lorain Blvd Ste N
    Elyria OH
    440 323-9820

(G-16777)
LOWES HOME CENTERS LLC
5500 Milan Rd Ste 304 (44870-7805)
PHONE..................419 624-6000
Fax: 419 624-4490
Fred Schlick, *Branch Mgr*
EMP: 150
SALES (corp-wide): 68.6B Publicly Held
SIC: 5211 5031 5722 5064 Home centers; building materials, exterior; building materials, interior; household appliance stores; electrical appliances, television & radio
HQ: Lowe's Home Centers, Llc
    1605 Curtis Bridge Rd
    Wilkesboro NC 28697
    336 658-4000

(G-16778)
MAGNUM MANAGEMENT CORPORATION
1 Cedar Point Dr (44870-5259)
PHONE..................419 627-2334
Richard L Kinzel, *CEO*
Duffield E Milkie, *Vice Pres*
Jim Rein, *Vice Pres*
Charles M Paul, *Controller*
Lois A Lawrence, *Office Mgr*
EMP: 800
SQ FT: 6,000
SALES (est): 91.1MM
SALES (corp-wide): 1.3B Publicly Held
WEB: www.cedarpointresorts.com
SIC: 4785 6552 7996 Toll bridge operation; subdividers & developers; amusement parks
PA: Cedar Fair, L.P.
    1 Cedar Point Dr
    Sandusky OH 44870
    419 626-0830

(G-16779)
MURRAY & MURRAY CO LPA (PA)
111 E Shoreline Dr Ste 2 (44870-2579)
PHONE..................419 624-3000
Fax: 419 624-0707
John Murray, *President*
Charles Murray, *President*
Dennis E Murray Sr, *President*
Dennis E Murray Jr, *President*
James Murray, *President*
EMP: 36
SQ FT: 33,000
SALES (est): 5.9MM Privately Held
WEB: www.murrayandmurray.com
SIC: 8111 General practice attorney, lawyer

(G-16780)
MV TRANSPORTATION INC
1230 N Depot St (44870-3165)
PHONE..................419 627-0740
Peter Carey, *Branch Mgr*
EMP: 76
SALES (corp-wide): 2.1B Privately Held
SIC: 4111 Local & suburban transit
PA: Mv Transportation, Inc.
    2711 N Haskell Ave
    Dallas TX 75204
    214 265-3400

(G-16781)
NORFOLK SOUTHERN CORPORATION
2234 Tiffin Ave (44870-1940)
P.O. Box 759 (44871-0759)
PHONE..................419 626-4323
Corey Plunkett, *Purch Mgr*
D A Hill, *Manager*
EMP: 30
SALES (corp-wide): 10.5B Publicly Held
WEB: www.nscorp.com
SIC: 4011 Railroads, line-haul operating
PA: Norfolk Southern Corporation
    3 Commercial Pl Ste 1a
    Norfolk VA 23510
    757 629-2680

(G-16782)
NORTH COAST PROF CO LLC
Also Called: Firelands Physicians Group
1031 Pierce St (44870-4669)
PHONE..................419 557-5541
Martin Tursky, *CEO*

Shawn Biggins, *Accountant*
EMP: 191
SALES (est): 19.4MM **Privately Held**
SIC: 8011 Primary care medical clinic

(G-16783)
NORTHERN OHIO MED SPCLISTS LLC
Also Called: Bayshore Obgyn
2500 W Strub Rd Ste 210 (44870-5390)
PHONE 419 625-2841
McLaughlin, *Branch Mgr*
Rick A Visci, *Med Doctor*
EMP: 29
SALES (corp-wide): 35.2MM **Privately Held**
WEB: www.nomsdrs.com
SIC: 8011 Cardiologist & cardio-vascular specialist
PA: Northern Ohio Medical Specialists Llc
3004 Hayes Ave
Sandusky OH 44870
419 626-6161

(G-16784)
O E MEYER CO (PA)
3303 Tiffin Ave (44870-9752)
P.O. Box 479 (44871-0479)
PHONE 419 625-1256
Fax: 419 625-3999
Rodney S Belden, *CEO*
David Belden, *President*
Craig A Wood, *President*
Eric Wood, *President*
Jim Frederick, *Division Mgr*
▲ **EMP:** 95
SQ FT: 46,000
SALES (est): 55.7MM **Privately Held**
WEB: www.oemeyer.com
SIC: 5084 5047 Welding machinery & equipment; medical & hospital equipment

(G-16785)
PNC BANK NATIONAL ASSOCIATION
Also Called: National City Bank
129 W Perkins Ave (44870-4802)
PHONE 419 621-2930
Fax: 419 621-2999
Josephine Angelo, *Vice Pres*
Robert Johns, *Branch Mgr*
EMP: 25
SALES (corp-wide): 18B **Publicly Held**
WEB: www.allegiantbank.com
SIC: 6021 National commercial banks
HQ: Pnc Bank, National Association
222 Delaware Ave
Wilmington DE 19801
877 762-2000

(G-16786)
PROVIDENCE CARE CENTER
2025 Hayes Ave (44870-4739)
PHONE 419 627-2273
Fax: 419 627-0092
Shannon Agee, *Director*
Jessica Burkhart, *Director*
Shirl Felder, *Social Dir*
Donna Novak, *Executive*
Denice Day, *Administration*
EMP: 160
SALES: 13.1MM **Privately Held**
WEB: www.providencecenters.org
SIC: 8062 Hospital, affiliated with AMA residency

(G-16787)
RENAISSANCE HOUSE INC
158 E Market St Ste 805 (44870-2556)
PHONE 419 626-1110
Fax: 419 626-3375
Robert Weinhardt, *Director*
EMP: 55
SALES (corp-wide): 4.4MM **Privately Held**
WEB: www.renaissancehouseinc.com
SIC: 8741 8052 Hospital management; nursing & personal care facility management; intermediate care facilities
PA: Renaissance House Inc
103 N Washington St
Tiffin OH 44883
419 447-7901

(G-16788)
REPUBLIC SERVICES INC
4005 Tiffin Ave (44870-9689)
PHONE 419 626-2454
Neil Carlson, *Branch Mgr*
EMP: 34
SALES (corp-wide): 10B **Publicly Held**
SIC: 4953 Refuse collection & disposal services
PA: Republic Services, Inc.
18500 N Allied Way # 100
Phoenix AZ 85054
480 627-2700

(G-16789)
REXEL USA INC
Also Called: Brohl & Appell
140 Lane St (44870-3560)
PHONE 419 625-6761
Mary Ebert, *Regional Mgr*
Mike W Dresser, *Vice Pres*
Lisa Corfman, *Credit Mgr*
Darrell Schneider, *Sales Mgr*
Tom Hartman, *Accounts Mgr*
EMP: 29
SALES (corp-wide): 3MM **Privately Held**
SIC: 5063 5074 Electrical supplies; plumbing & hydronic heating supplies
HQ: Rexel Usa, Inc.
14951 Dallas Pkwy
Dallas TX 75254

(G-16790)
SANDUSKY AREA YMCA FOUNDATION
Also Called: Sandusky YMCA
2101 W Perkins Ave (44870-2043)
PHONE 419 621-9622
Donald Yontz, *President*
William Parker, *Vice Pres*
John Bacon, *Treasurer*
Paul Mc Callister, *Exec Dir*
Bjorn Wiberg, *Director*
EMP: 29 **EST:** 1960
SQ FT: 39,000
SALES: 882K **Privately Held**
SIC: 8641 8351 Youth organizations; child day care services

(G-16791)
SANDUSKY HARBOR MARINA INC
Also Called: Sandusky Harbour Marina
1 Huron St (44870-1805)
PHONE 419 627-1201
Fax: 419 627-2055
Jerry Parsons, *Manager*
EMP: 37
SALES: 4MM **Privately Held**
WEB: www.sanduskyharbor.com
SIC: 4493 Boat yards, storage & incidental repair

(G-16792)
SANDUSKY NEWSPAPERS INC (PA)
314 W Market St (44870-2410)
PHONE 419 625-5500
Fax: 419 625-1137
Dudley A White Jr, *Ch of Bd*
David A Rau, *President*
Jane Righi, *Manager*
Susan E White, *Admin Sec*
EMP: 140
SQ FT: 45,000
SALES (est): 89.7MM **Privately Held**
WEB: www.sanduskyregister.com
SIC: 4832 2711 2752 Radio broadcasting stations; newspapers; commercial printing, lithographic

(G-16793)
SANDUSKY REGISTER
314 W Market St (44870-2410)
P.O. Box 5071 (44871-5071)
PHONE 419 625-5500
Fax: 419 625-3007
Tim Kelly, *President*
Dudley White, *Principal*
Bri Haller, *Editor*
Matt Westerhold, *Editor*
Richard Kimble, *Production*
EMP: 26

SALES (est): 2.8MM **Privately Held**
SIC: 7313 5994 Newspaper advertising representative; newsstand

(G-16794)
SANDUSKY YACHT CLUB INC
529 E Water St (44870-2875)
PHONE 419 625-6567
Fax: 419 621-9416
Mike Thuemmler, *General Mgr*
David Dunn, *General Mgr*
EMP: 80 **EST:** 1894
SQ FT: 25,000
SALES: 1.8MM **Privately Held**
WEB: www.sanduskyyachtclub.com
SIC: 7997 Boating club, membership; yacht club, membership

(G-16795)
SMILE BRANDS INC
Also Called: Bright Dental
1313 W Bogart Rd Ste D (44870-5704)
PHONE 419 627-1255
Jeana Janik, *Branch Mgr*
EMP: 30
SALES (corp-wide): 599MM **Privately Held**
WEB: www.monarchdental.com
SIC: 8021 Dental clinic
HQ: Smile Brands Inc.
100 Spectrum Center Dr # 1
Irvine CA 92618
714 668-1300

(G-16796)
SORTINO MANAGEMENT & DEV CO
Also Called: Greentree Inn
1935 Cleveland Rd (44870-4308)
PHONE 419 626-6761
Fax: 419 624-1204
EMP: 50
SQ FT: 80,000
SALES (corp-wide): 7.3MM **Privately Held**
SIC: 7011 5812 7933 Hotel/Motel Operation Eating Place Bowling Center
PA: Sortino Management & Development Co
1210 Sycamore Line
Sandusky OH 44870
419 625-0362

(G-16797)
ST STEPHEN UNITED CHURCH CHRST
905 E Perkins Ave (44870-5067)
PHONE 419 624-1814
Fax: 419 626-1617
Robert C Patton, *Pastor*
Kenneth L Heintzelman, *Pastor*
EMP: 30
SALES (est): 858.2K **Privately Held**
SIC: 8661 8351 Church of Christ; child day care services

(G-16798)
STEIN HOSPICE SERVICES INC
1200 Sycamore Line (44870-4029)
P.O. Box Camore Lin (44870)
PHONE 419 447-0475
Carl Stein, *Branch Mgr*
EMP: 89
SALES (corp-wide): 28.8MM **Privately Held**
SIC: 8069 Specialty hospitals, except psychiatric
PA: Stein Hospice Services, Inc.
1200 Sycamore Line
Sandusky OH 44870
800 625-5269

(G-16799)
STEIN HOSPICE SERVICES INC
126 Columbus Ave (44870-2502)
PHONE 419 502-0019
Gail Shatzer, *Branch Mgr*
EMP: 71
SALES (corp-wide): 28.8MM **Privately Held**
SIC: 8069 Specialty hospitals, except psychiatric
PA: Stein Hospice Services, Inc.
1200 Sycamore Line
Sandusky OH 44870
800 625-5269

(G-16800)
STEIN HOSPICE SERVICES INC (PA)
1200 Sycamore Line (44870-4029)
PHONE 800 625-5269
Fax: 419 625-5761
Jan Bucholz, *CEO*
David Clarke, *Pastor*
Jonathan McCabe, *Info Tech Dir*
Robin Ringley, *Info Tech Dir*
Larry Robinson, *Director*
▲ **EMP:** 370
SALES (est): 28.8MM **Privately Held**
WEB: www.steinhospice.com
SIC: 8069 Chronic disease hospital

(G-16801)
STERLING HEIGHTS GSA PRPTS LTD
5500 Milan Rd Ste 220 (44870-7804)
PHONE 419 609-7000
John M Hoty,
Lucy Spencer,
EMP: 37
SALES: 175K **Privately Held**
SIC: 6531 Real estate agents & managers

(G-16802)
TRADESMEN INTERNATIONAL LLC
2419 E Perkins Ave (44870-7998)
PHONE 419 502-9140
EMP: 153 **Privately Held**
SIC: 8741 Construction management
PA: Tradesmen International, Llc
9760 Shepard Rd
Macedonia OH 44056

(G-16803)
UBS FINANCIAL SERVICES INC
111 E Shoreline Dr Ste 3 (44870-2579)
PHONE 419 624-6800
Tim Vansimaeys, *Branch Mgr*
EMP: 43
SALES (corp-wide): 28B **Privately Held**
SIC: 7389 Financial services
HQ: Ubs Financial Services Inc.
1285 Ave Of The Americas
New York NY 10019
212 713-2000

(G-16804)
ULTA BEAUTY INC
4020 Milan Rd Unit 915 (44870-5871)
PHONE 419 621-1345
EMP: 99
SALES (corp-wide): 4.8B **Publicly Held**
SIC: 7241 Barber shops
PA: Ulta Beauty, Inc.
1000 Remington Blvd # 120
Bolingbrook IL 60440
630 410-4800

(G-16805)
UNITED CHURCH HOMES INC
Also Called: Parkview Health Care
3800 Boardwalk Blvd (44870-7044)
PHONE 419 621-1900
Fax: 419 621-1121
Timothy Hackett, *Vice Pres*
Pamela White, *Vice Pres*
Cheryl Wickersham, *Vice Pres*
Bill Coleman, *Safety Dir*
Ken Keller, *Administration*
EMP: 150
SALES (corp-wide): 78.1MM **Privately Held**
WEB: www.altenheimcommunity.org
SIC: 8051 Skilled nursing care facilities
PA: United Church Homes Inc
170 E Center St
Marion OH 43302
740 382-4885

(G-16806)
UNITED STATES DEPT AGRICULTURE
2900 Columbus Ave (44870-5574)
PHONE 419 626-8439
Valarie Grahl, *Branch Mgr*
EMP: 81 **Publicly Held**
WEB: www.usda.gov
SIC: 9641 5191 Agriculture fair board, government; farm supplies

Sandusky - Erie County (G-16807)

HQ: United States Department Of Agriculture
1400 Independence Ave Sw
Washington DC 20250
202 720-3631

(G-16807)
US TSUBAKI POWER TRANSM LLC
Also Called: Engineering Chain Div
1010 Edgewater Ave (44870-1601)
PHONE..................................419 626-4560
Fax: 419 626-5194
Myron Timmer, *Vice Pres*
Steve Funni, *Mfg Staff*
Frank Bobel, *Sales/Mktg Mgr*
Roger Frey, *Controller*
Charles Rosenbalm, *Human Res Dir*
EMP: 180
SALES (corp-wide): 1.7B **Privately Held**
SIC: **5049** 3568 3714 3462 Engineers' equipment & supplies; chain, power transmission; motor vehicle parts & accessories; iron & steel forgings
HQ: U.S. Tsubaki Power Transmission Llc
301 E Marquardt Dr
Wheeling IL 60090
847 459-9500

(G-16808)
VACATIONLAND FEDERAL CREDIT UN
2911 Hayes Ave (44870-7206)
PHONE..................................440 967-5155
Kevin Ralofsky, *CEO*
Barbara Yost, *Vice Pres*
Mary Jackson, *Officer*
Derek Callin, *Tech/Comp Coord*
EMP: 25
SALES (corp-wide): 8MM **Privately Held**
SIC: **6061** Federal credit unions
PA: Vacationland Federal Credit Union
2409 E Perkins Ave
Sandusky OH 44870
419 625-9025

(G-16809)
WAGNER QUARRIES COMPANY
Also Called: Hanson Aggregates
4203 Milan Rd (44870-5880)
PHONE..................................419 625-8141
Fax: 419 625-7150
Norman Jacobs, *Plant Mgr*
Chris Kinner, *Plant Mgr*
Bill Hoelzer, *Marketing Staff*
Chuck Cashan, *Manager*
Andrew Harper, *Manager*
EMP: 48
SQ FT: 2,400
SALES (est): 4.5MM **Privately Held**
SIC: **1422** Limestones, ground

(G-16810)
WOLFF BROS SUPPLY INC
2800 W Strub Rd (44870-5368)
PHONE..................................330 400-5990
Fax: 419 626-1994
Jim Fitzgerald, *Sales Associate*
Bill Rutherford, *Marketing Staff*
Pete Doyle, *Manager*
EMP: 32
SALES (corp-wide): 114.4MM **Privately Held**
WEB: www.wolffbros.com
SIC: **5063** Electrical supplies
PA: Wolff Bros. Supply, Inc
6078 Wolff Rd
Medina OH 44256
330 725-3451

(G-16811)
YMCA OF SANDUSKY OHIO INC
Also Called: International MGT Counsel
2101 W Perkins Ave (44870-2057)
PHONE..................................419 621-9622
Fax: 419 625-6166
John Bacon, *Treasurer*
Kevin Holloway, *Office Mgr*
Jared Williams, *Exec Dir*
Steve Snyder, *Exec Dir*
Bjorn Wiberg, *Director*
EMP: 45
SALES (est): 1MM **Privately Held**
SIC: **8641** Youth organizations; recreation association

Sardinia
Brown County

(G-16812)
CORNERSTONE CONCRETE CNSTR INC
3166 State Route 321 (45171-8236)
PHONE..................................937 442-2805
Harold Dorsey, *President*
Vicky Dorsey, *Office Mgr*
EMP: 25
SQ FT: 6,500
SALES (est): 4MM **Privately Held**
SIC: **1771** Concrete work

(G-16813)
G & D ALTERNATIVE LIVING INC
Also Called: Pinewood Home
121 Charles St (45171-9338)
P.O. Box 341 (45171-0341)
PHONE..................................937 446-2803
Fax: 937 446-4078
Gordon L Fitzpatrick, *President*
Keith Crothers, *Director*
Diana Fitzpatrick, *Administration*
EMP: 35
SQ FT: 6,400
SALES (est): 1.2MM **Privately Held**
SIC: **8361** Home for the mentally handicapped

(G-16814)
SARDINIA LIFE SQUAD
159 Winchester St (45171-9326)
P.O. Box 380 (45171-0380)
PHONE..................................937 446-2178
Capt Bernard Haynes, *Principal*
Darcy Hamm, *Treasurer*
EMP: 29
SALES: 127.4K **Privately Held**
WEB: www.sardinialifesquad.com
SIC: **4119** Ambulance service

Sardis
Monroe County

(G-16815)
SLAY TRANSPORTATION CO INC
Rr 7 Box 34684 (43946)
PHONE..................................740 865-2910
Gary Slay, *President*
EMP: 110
SALES (corp-wide): 142.9MM **Privately Held**
SIC: **4213** 4231 4212 Trucking, except local; trucking terminal facilities; local trucking, without storage
HQ: Slay Transportation Co., Inc.
1441 Hampton Ave
Saint Louis MO 63139
800 852-7529

Scio
Harrison County

(G-16816)
BHF INCORPORATED
Also Called: Bhfi
147 E College St (43988-8732)
PHONE..................................740 945-6410
James W Anderson III, *CEO*
EMP: 35
SALES (est): 1.3MM **Privately Held**
SIC: **8711** Engineering services

(G-16817)
TAPPAN LAKE MARINA INC
Also Called: Tappan Marina
33315 Cadiz Dennison Rd (43988-9724)
PHONE..................................740 269-2031
Fax: 740 269-8002
Dick Henry, *President*
Sandra Henry, *Partner*
Cathrine Cramblett, *Vice Pres*
EMP: 36
SALES (est): 49.8K **Privately Held**
SIC: **5812** 4493 Ethnic food restaurants; marinas

Seaman
Adams County

(G-16818)
ADAMS COUNTY REGIONAL MED CTR
230 Medical Center Dr (45679-8002)
PHONE..................................937 386-3001
Fax: 937 386-3019
Bill May, *CEO*
Sharon Ashley, *QC Dir*
Pete Dagenbach, *CFO*
Danny Urban, *CFO*
Radah Brown, *Manager*
EMP: 250
SQ FT: 94,600
SALES: 23.5MM **Privately Held**
SIC: **8062** General medical & surgical hospitals

(G-16819)
ADAMS COUNTY REGIONAL MED CTR
230 Medical Center Dr (45679-8002)
PHONE..................................937 386-3400
Bill May, *CEO*
Marsha Dunbar, *Principal*
John McCormick, *Purch Mgr*
Scott Smith, *CFO*
Linda Thorpe, *CFO*
EMP: 80
SALES (est): 340.9K **Privately Held**
SIC: **8062** General medical & surgical hospitals

Sebring
Mahoning County

(G-16820)
COPELAND OAKS
715 S Johnson Rd (44672-1709)
PHONE..................................330 938-1050
Bill Williams, *Vice Pres*
Jerry Thomas, *Manager*
Sue Bleggi, *Director*
Tom Gant, *Director*
To Mdrakulich, *Director*
EMP: 397
SALES (corp-wide): 14.7MM **Privately Held**
SIC: **6513** Retirement hotel operation
PA: Copeland Oaks
800 S 15th St
Sebring OH 44672
330 938-6126

(G-16821)
COPELAND OAKS (PA)
800 S 15th St (44672-2099)
PHONE..................................330 938-6126
Fax: 330 938-7406
Phillip Braisted, *CEO*
Dave Mannion, *CFO*
Lisa Hines, *Manager*
Trudi Whayley, *Manager*
Anthony Nemes, *Consultant*
EMP: 500
SQ FT: 383,672
SALES: 14.7MM **Privately Held**
WEB: www.copelandoaks.com
SIC: **8361** Rest home, with health care incidental

(G-16822)
FAMOUS ENTERPRISES INC
350 Courtney Rd (44672-1337)
PHONE..................................330 938-6350
Tanja Kozul, *Branch Mgr*
EMP: 29 **Privately Held**
WEB: www.jfgood.com
SIC: **5074** Plumbing fittings & supplies
PA: Famous Enterprises, Inc.
2620 Ridgewood Rd Ste 200
Akron OH 44313

Senecaville
Guernsey County

(G-16823)
DEEPWELL ENERGY SERVICES LLC
14764 Clay Pike Rd (43780-9701)
PHONE..................................740 685-2253
Daniel Smith, *CEO*
EMP: 126
SALES (corp-wide): 210.6MM **Privately Held**
SIC: **4911** Distribution, electric power
PA: Deepwell Energy Services, Llc
4025 Highway 35 N
Columbia MS 39429
800 477-2855

(G-16824)
MUSKINGUM WTRSHED CNSRVNCY DST
Also Called: Seneca Lake Park
22172 Park Rd (43780-9613)
PHONE..................................740 685-6013
Fax: 740 685-6013
Gary Perrish, *Superintendent*
EMP: 40
SALES (est): 806.4K **Privately Held**
WEB: www.muskingumfoundation.org
SIC: **7996** Amusement parks
PA: Muskingum Watershed Conservancy District
1319 3rd St Nw
New Philadelphia OH 44663
330 343-6647

Seven Hills
Cuyahoga County

(G-16825)
ALEX N SILL COMPANY (PA)
6000 Lombardo Ctr Ste 600 (44131-6911)
PHONE..................................216 524-9999
Fax: 216 524-8152
Michael Perlmuter, *President*
Dean Harclerode, *Vice Pres*
Michael Hickle, *Vice Pres*
Preston Hoopes, *Vice Pres*
Jeffrey O'Connor, *Vice Pres*
EMP: 35
SQ FT: 7,500
SALES (est): 13.9MM **Privately Held**
WEB: www.sill.com
SIC: **6411** Policyholders' consulting service

(G-16826)
ANTHEM INSURANCE COMPANIES INC
Also Called: Blue Cross
6000 Lombardo Ctr Lowr 3 (44131-6905)
P.O. Box 2709, Youngstown (44507-0709)
PHONE..................................330 783-9800
Fax: 330 783-3802
Lisa Angelo, *Marketing Staff*
Barbara D'Alesandro, *Manager*
Anthony Firmstone, *Exec Dir*
EMP: 182
SALES (corp-wide): 90B **Publicly Held**
WEB: www.anthem-inc.com
SIC: **6324** Group hospitalization plans
HQ: Anthem Insurance Companies, Inc.
120 Monument Cir Ste 200
Indianapolis IN 46204
317 488-6000

(G-16827)
BLUE CHIP CONSULTING GROUP LLC
6000 Lombardo Ctr Ste 650 (44131-6916)
PHONE..................................216 503-6001
James Filicko, *Mng Member*
Jim Peelman
EMP: 28
SQ FT: 14,000
SALES (est): 4MM **Privately Held**
SIC: **7379**

GEOGRAPHIC SECTION

(G-16828)
CITY OF SEVEN HILLS
7777 Summitview Dr (44131-4441)
PHONE...................216 524-6262
Jennifer Burger, *Chief*
EMP: 116 Privately Held
SIC: 7999 Recreation center
PA: City Of Seven Hills
7325 Summitview Dr
Seven Hills OH 44131
216 524-4421

(G-16829)
EQUITY CONSULTANTS LLC
5800 Lombardo Ctr Ste 202 (44131-2588)
PHONE...................330 659-7600
Brooke Dudas, *Manager*
Goran Marich,
Ryko Marich,
EMP: 60
SQ FT: 10,000
SALES (est): 3.7MM Privately Held
WEB: www.equityconsultants.org
SIC: 6163 Mortgage brokers arranging for loans, using money of others

(G-16830)
EXPERIS FINANCE US LLC
6000 Lombardo Ctr Ste 400 (44131-6926)
PHONE...................216 621-0200
Edward Primisoch, *Director*
EMP: 35 Publicly Held
SIC: 8721 Accounting, auditing & bookkeeping
HQ: Experis Finance Us, Llc
100 W Manpower Pl
Milwaukee WI 53212

(G-16831)
JPMORGAN CHASE BANK NAT ASSN
7703 Broadview Rd (44131-5724)
PHONE...................216 524-0600
Jim Henderson, *Manager*
EMP: 26
SQ FT: 2,631
SALES (corp-wide): 99.6B Publicly Held
WEB: www.chase.com
SIC: 6021 National commercial banks
HQ: Jpmorgan Chase Bank, National Association
1111 Polaris Pkwy
Columbus OH 43240
614 436-3055

(G-16832)
KA INC
Also Called: Ka Architecture
6000 Lombardo Ctr Ste 500 (44131-6910)
PHONE...................216 781-9144
Fax: 216 781-6566
James B Heller, *President*
Thomas M Milanich, *COO*
Craig Wasserman, *Exec VP*
Todd Wolfgang, *Project Mgr*
Carl Frey, *Research*
EMP: 108 EST: 1960
SQ FT: 30,000
SALES (est): 16.4MM Privately Held
WEB: www.kainc.com
SIC: 8712 Architectural services

(G-16833)
OHIO EDUCATIONAL CREDIT UNION (PA)
4141 Rockside Rd Ste 400 (44131-2537)
P.O. Box 93079, Cleveland (44101-5079)
PHONE...................216 621-6296
Fax: 216 621-4801
Jerome R Valco, *CEO*
Richard Gore, *President*
Art Boehm, *CFO*
Patricia Gardner, *Branch Mgr*
Evan Holgan, *Manager*
EMP: 38 EST: 1933
SQ FT: 27,000
SALES: 3.8MM Privately Held
WEB: www.ohioedcu.com
SIC: 6062 State credit unions, not federally chartered

(G-16834)
OHIO KEPRO INC
5700 Lombardo Ctr Ste 100 (44131-2542)
PHONE...................216 447-9604
Fax: 216 447-7925
Joe Dougher, *CEO*
Donald Harrop, *Ch of Bd*
Samir Gautam, *Managing Dir*
Susan Garlando, *Marketing Staff*
Linda Greel, *Office Mgr*
EMP: 48
SQ FT: 12,000
SALES (est): 2.8MM
SALES (corp-wide): 68.4MM Privately Held
WEB: www.ohiokepro.com
SIC: 8099 Medical services organization
PA: Keystone Peer Review Organization, Inc.
777 E Park Dr
Harrisburg PA 17111
717 564-8288

(G-16835)
OREILLY AUTOMOTIVE INC
7621 Broadview Rd (44131-5723)
PHONE...................216 642-7591
EMP: 69 Publicly Held
SIC: 7389 Automobile recovery service
PA: O'reilly Automotive, Inc.
233 S Patterson Ave
Springfield MO 65802

(G-16836)
SEVEN HILLS FIREMAN ASSN
7195 Broadview Rd (44131-4210)
PHONE...................216 524-3321
Fax: 216 524-4262
Charles Osta, *President*
EMP: 35
SALES (est): 634.8K Privately Held
SIC: 8641 6331 Civic social & fraternal associations; workers' compensation insurance

Seville
Medina County

(G-16837)
BENCHMARK CRAFTSMAN INC
Also Called: Benchmark Craftsmen
4700 Greenwich Rd (44273-8848)
PHONE...................330 975-4214
Nathan Sublett, *President*
Denise Trouten, *Controller*
Denise Trouton, *Accountant*
EMP: 30
SALES (est): 4.1MM Privately Held
WEB: www.benchmarkcraftsmen.com
SIC: 7389 3993 Exhibit construction by industrial contractors; displays & cutouts, window & lobby

(G-16838)
BLEACHTECH LLC
320 Ryan Rd (44273-9109)
PHONE...................216 921-1980
Joseph Traylinek, *Maintenance Dir*
William Schaad, *Plant Mgr*
Richard Immerman, *Mng Member*
Benjamin Calkins,
EMP: 25
SALES (est): 2MM Privately Held
SIC: 7349 5169 2819 Chemical cleaning services; chemicals & allied products; bleaching powder, lime bleaching compounds

(G-16839)
ELITE TRANSPORTATION SVCS LLC
Also Called: Elite Logistics Worldwide
4940 Enterprise Pkwy (44273-8929)
PHONE...................330 769-5830
Maggie Petrush, *Administration*
EMP: 30
SALES (est): 3.7MM
SALES (corp-wide): 2.8B Publicly Held
WEB: www.elitepdx.com
SIC: 4731 Foreign freight forwarding; freight forwarding
HQ: Panther Ii Transportation, Inc.
84 Medina Rd
Medina OH 44256

(G-16840)
ENCORE HEALTHCARE LLC
Also Called: Meadowview Care Center
83 High St (44273-9308)
PHONE...................330 769-2015
Fax: 330 769-3790
EMP: 120
SALES (corp-wide): 24MM Privately Held
SIC: 8059 8051 Nursing/Personal Care Skilled Nursing Care Facility
PA: Encore Healthcare, Llc
7150 Columbia Gateway Dr A
Columbia MD 21046
443 539-2350

(G-16841)
JARRELLS MOVING & TRANSPORT CO (PA)
Also Called: J M T Freight Specialists
5076 Park Ave W (44273-8916)
PHONE...................330 764-4333
Fax: 330 764-4533
Robert S Zufra, *CEO*
David J Jarrell, *Exec VP*
Randy J Jarrell, *Exec VP*
Chester A Sipsock, *CFO*
Teresa Johnson, *Controller*
EMP: 70 EST: 1997
SQ FT: 8,200
SALES (est): 10.6MM Privately Held
WEB: www.gojmt.com
SIC: 4213 Trucking, except local

(G-16842)
PROFESSIONAL SALES ASSOCIATES
5045 Park Ave W Ste 1b (44273-8963)
PHONE...................330 299-7343
Richard Reinhardt, *Ch of Bd*
James McGonigal, *President*
Mary Hayes, *Asst Sec*
EMP: 34
SALES (est): 4.8MM Privately Held
WEB: www.profsales.com
SIC: 5047 Dental equipment & supplies

(G-16843)
RAWIGA COUNTRY CLUB INC
10353 Rawiga Rd (44273-9700)
PHONE...................330 336-2220
Fax: 330 336-9222
Larry Mills, *Superintendent*
Jeanne Pritchard, *Principal*
Robert Hermann, *Receiver*
Barb Sullivan, *Bookkeeper*
EMP: 75
SQ FT: 19,000
SALES (est): 1.2MM Privately Held
SIC: 7997 Country club, membership

(G-16844)
SOCIETY HANDICAPPED CITZ MEDIN (PA)
4283 Paradise Rd (44273-9353)
PHONE...................330 722-1900
Fax: 330 723-6695
Roger Ware, *Maintenance Dir*
Will McMahan, *Opers Mgr*
Michael Beh, *Finance*
Jessica Hazelkorn, *Manager*
Melanie Kasten-Krause, *Exec Dir*
EMP: 35
SQ FT: 4,800
SALES: 7.7MM Privately Held
WEB: www.shc-medina.org
SIC: 8361 8052 Home for the mentally handicapped; home for the physically handicapped; intermediate care facilities

(G-16845)
SOCIEY FOR HANDICAPPED CITIZEN
Also Called: Camp Paradise
4283 Paradise Rd (44273-9353)
PHONE...................330 725-7041
Dana Henderson, *Manager*
Janine Dalton, *Exec Dir*
EMP: 180
SALES (est): 1.5MM Privately Held
SIC: 8361 8052 Home for the mentally handicapped; intermediate care facilities

(G-16846)
SON-RISE HOTELS INC
Also Called: Comfort Inn
4949 Park Ave W (44273-9313)
PHONE...................330 769-4949
Fax: 330 769-4964
Fateme Shaikary, *President*
Abbas Shaikary MD, *Vice Pres*
Jackie Albright, *Manager*
EMP: 28
SALES (est): 1MM Privately Held
SIC: 7011 Hotels & motels

(G-16847)
STELLAR SRKG ACQUISITION LLC
Also Called: Stellar Automotive Group
4935 Enterprise Pkwy (44273-8930)
PHONE...................330 769-8484
Nora Howsare, *Controller*
Pam Riffle, *Manager*
Abbie Eichel, *Office Admin*
Justin Archer,
▲ **EMP: 33**
SQ FT: 40,000
SALES (est): 12.7MM Privately Held
WEB: www.stellargroup.com
SIC: 5013 Automotive supplies & parts

(G-16848)
WORLD TRCK TOWING RECOVERY INC
4970 Park Ave W (44273-9376)
PHONE...................330 723-1116
Fax: 330 722-6691
Mike Schoen, *Principal*
EMP: 29
SALES (est): 6.4MM Privately Held
SIC: 7549 4789 5521 Towing services; cargo loading & unloading services; trucks, tractors & trailers: used

Shadyside
Belmont County

(G-16849)
H L C TRUCKING INC
57245 Ferry Landing Rd (43947-9701)
P.O. Box 127, Powhatan Point (43942-0127)
PHONE...................740 676-6181
Fax: 740 671-0594
Dennis Hendershot, *President*
Roger Lewis, *Business Mgr*
Dennis Winkler, *Vice Pres*
Donald Hendershot, *Treasurer*
Robin Burkhart, *Human Res Dir*
EMP: 62
SALES (est): 7.2MM Privately Held
WEB: www.hlctrucking.com
SIC: 4212 Local trucking, without storage

(G-16850)
LYNDCO INC
56805 Ferry Landing Rd 8a (43947-8769)
PHONE...................740 671-9098
Lynda Hendershot, *President*
Tammy Helman, *Admin Asst*
EMP: 50
SQ FT: 10,000
SALES (est): 6.8MM Privately Held
SIC: 1611 Surfacing & paving

(G-16851)
OHIO EDISON COMPANY
Also Called: Burger Plant
57246 Ferry Landing Rd (43947-9701)
P.O. Box 8 (43947-0008)
PHONE...................740 671-2900
Fax: 740 671-2916
Peter Robinson, *Manager*
EMP: 140 Publicly Held
SIC: 4911 4939 Generation, electric power; combination utilities
HQ: Ohio Edison Company
76 S Main St Bsmt
Akron OH 44308
800 736-3402

Shadyside - Belmont County (G-16852)

(G-16852)
VIRGINIA OHIO-WEST EXCVTG CO
Also Called: Owv Exc
56461 Ferry Landing Rd (43947-9705)
P.O. Box 128, Powhatan Point (43942-0128)
PHONE.................................740 676-7464
Dennis Hendershot, *CEO*
Roger Lewis, *President*
Brian Hendershot, *Vice Pres*
Daniel Rhome, *Project Mgr*
Dennie Winkler, *Sales Executive*
EMP: 120
SQ FT: 2,800
SALES: 37MM **Privately Held**
WEB: www.owvexcavating.com
SIC: 1611 1541 General contractor, highway & street construction; renovation, remodeling & repairs; industrial buildings

(G-16853)
WHEELING HOSPITAL INC
Also Called: Shadyside Health Center
3801 Lincoln Ave (43947-1320)
PHONE.................................740 671-0850
Fax: 740 671-9739
Ronald L Violi, *CEO*
EMP: 86
SALES (corp-wide): 375.6MM **Privately Held**
SIC: 8099 Childbirth preparation clinic
PA: Wheeling Hospital, Inc.
   1 Medical Park
   Wheeling WV 26003
   304 243-3000

(G-16854)
ZANDEX INC
Also Called: Shadyside Care Center
60583 State Route 7 (43947-9704)
PHONE.................................740 676-8381
Fax: 740 676-3979
Ruth Fowkes, *Purch Agent*
Susan Schmelich, *Personnel Exec*
Joni Fox, *Manager*
Roxanne Tharp, *Manager*
EMP: 125
SALES (corp-wide): 34MM **Privately Held**
SIC: 8051 Convalescent home with continuous nursing care
PA: Zandex, Inc.
   1122 Taylor St
   Zanesville OH 43701
   740 454-1400

Shaker Heights
Cuyahoga County

(G-16855)
1ST ALL FILE RECOVERY USA
Also Called: Data Recovery
3570 Warrensville Ctr Rd (44122-5288)
PHONE.................................800 399-7150
Dmitry Belkin, *CEO*
Peter Irace, *Manager*
EMP: 40
SALES (est): 2.8MM **Privately Held**
WEB: www.dataretrieval.com
SIC: 7374 Data processing service

(G-16856)
BELLEFAIRE JEWISH CHLD BUR (PA)
22001 Fairmount Blvd (44118-4819)
PHONE.................................216 932-2800
Fax: 440 247-3359
Ryan Davis, *Managing Dir*
Betty Schieferstein, *Human Res Dir*
Jennifer Blumhagen, *Pub Rel Dir*
Pamela Budak, *Pub Rel Dir*
Cynthia Hartz, *Marketing Staff*
EMP: 400
SQ FT: 102,000
SALES: 47.9MM **Privately Held**
WEB: www.bellefairejcb.org
SIC: 8361 8322 Home for the emotionally disturbed; individual & family services

(G-16857)
CELLULAR TECHNOLOGY LIMITED
Also Called: Ctl Analyzers
20521 Chagrin Blvd # 200 (44122-5350)
PHONE.................................216 791-5084
Fax: 216 791-8814
Barbara Staron, *Manager*
Magdelian Tary-Lehmann, *Security Dir*
Paul V Lehmann,
EMP: 40
SQ FT: 30,000
SALES (est): 6MM **Privately Held**
SIC: 8071 3821 Medical laboratories; clinical laboratory instruments, except medical & dental

(G-16858)
CENTERS FOR DIALYSIS CARE INC (PA)
18720 Chagrin Blvd (44122-4855)
PHONE.................................216 295-7000
Cheryl Winterich, *Vice Pres*
Alan Zarach, *Technical Mgr*
David Oppenland, *CFO*
David M Oppenlander, *CFO*
Sylvia Young, *Human Res Mgr*
EMP: 25
SQ FT: 25,000
SALES (est): 3.2MM **Privately Held**
SIC: 8011 8092 Clinic, operated by physicians; kidney dialysis centers

(G-16859)
DURABLE SLATE CO
3530 Warrensville Ctr Rd (44122-5278)
PHONE.................................216 751-0151
Cleveland Slate, *Branch Mgr*
EMP: 30
SALES (corp-wide): 21.5MM **Privately Held**
SIC: 1761 Gutter & downspout contractor
PA: The Durable Slate Co
   3933 Groves Rd
   Columbus OH 43232
   614 299-5522

(G-16860)
EQUITY ENGINEERING GROUP INC (PA)
20600 Chagrin Blvd # 1200 (44122-5342)
PHONE.................................216 283-9519
David A Osage, *President*
Michael Coach, *Engineer*
Joel Andreani, *Treasurer*
Joseph Simari, *Admin Sec*
Ryan Jones,
EMP: 60
SQ FT: 27,000
SALES (est): 13.7MM **Privately Held**
WEB: www.equityeng.com
SIC: 8748 Systems engineering consultant, ex. computer or professional

(G-16861)
HANNA PERKINS SCHOOL
Also Called: HANNA PERKIN CENTER
19910 Malvern Rd (44122-2823)
PHONE.................................216 991-4472
Fax: 216 991-5472
Karen Baer, *CEO*
Zach France, *Treasurer*
Barbara Streeter, *Director*
Thomas F Barrett PHD, *Director*
Burt Griffin, *Bd of Directors*
EMP: 25
SQ FT: 33,000
SALES: 1.1MM **Privately Held**
SIC: 8351 8211 Preschool center; kindergarten

(G-16862)
J CHERIE LLC
3645 Norwood Rd (44122-4911)
PHONE.................................216 453-1051
Cherie McElroy-Burch, *General Mgr*
EMP: 30
SALES (est): 1.1MM **Privately Held**
SIC: 5621 7389 Women's clothing stores; business services

(G-16863)
MFF SOMERSET LLC
Also Called: Shaker Grdns Nursing Rehab Ctr
3550 Northfield Rd (44122-5253)
PHONE.................................216 752-5600
Michael F Flanagan, *Principal*
EMP: 36
SALES (est): 2.7MM **Privately Held**
SIC: 8051 Skilled nursing care facilities

(G-16864)
MYCITY TRANSPORATATION CO
16781 Shgrin Blvd Ste 283 (44120)
PHONE.................................216 591-1900
James R Crosby, *CEO*
EMP: 45
SQ FT: 4,500
SALES: 2.5MM **Privately Held**
SIC: 4119 Local passenger transportation

(G-16865)
SHAKER HEIGHTS COUNTRY CLUB CO
3300 Courtland Blvd (44122-2810)
PHONE.................................216 991-3324
Fax: 216 991-7771
Phil Boova, *CEO*
Gerald Breen, *President*
D H Tilden, *Principal*
Allen Waddle, *Vice Pres*
Michael Abdalian, *Treasurer*
EMP: 225
SQ FT: 62,000
SALES: 4.8MM **Privately Held**
WEB: www.shakerheightscc.org
SIC: 7997 Country club, membership

(G-16866)
SOFTWARE SUPPORT GROUP INC
Also Called: Ssg
22211 Westchester Rd (44122-2968)
PHONE.................................216 566-0555
David Rosenblatt, *Ch of Bd*
Drew Sellers, *President*
Michael S Goodman, *Managing Dir*
Matthew P Karlson, *Managing Dir*
Scott Victor, *Managing Dir*
EMP: 62
SQ FT: 4,000
SALES (est): 3.7MM **Privately Held**
WEB: www.ssgcom.com
SIC: 8748 Business consulting

(G-16867)
SPECIALIZED ALTERNATIVES FOR F
Also Called: Safy of Cleveland
20600 Chagrin Blvd # 900 (44122-5327)
PHONE.................................216 295-7239
Fax: 216 295-7240
Dru Whitaker, *Principal*
EMP: 202
SALES (corp-wide): 18.8MM **Privately Held**
SIC: 8322 Individual & family services; child related social services; adoption services; social service center
PA: Specialized Alternatives For Families And Youth Of Ohio, Inc.
   10100 Elida Rd
   Delphos OH 45833
   419 695-8010

(G-16868)
SUPERIOR STREET PARTNERS LLC
19010 Shaker Blvd (44122-2544)
PHONE.................................216 862-0058
Jon Herbst, *President*
Samir D Desai, *Advisor*
EMP: 100
SALES (est): 4.5MM **Privately Held**
SIC: 6799 Investors

(G-16869)
UNIVERSITY HOSPITALS (PA)
3605 Warrensville Ctr Rd (44122-5203)
PHONE.................................216 767-8900
Thomas S Zenty, *CEO*
Janet L Miller, *Senior VP*
Elizabeth Novak, *Vice Pres*
Michael Szubski, *CFO*
Bradley Bond, *Treasurer*
▲ EMP: 950
SALES: 2.3B **Privately Held**
SIC: 8062 8011 8741 General medical & surgical hospitals; offices & clinics of medical doctors; hospital management; nursing & personal care facility management

(G-16870)
UNIVERSITY HOSPITALS CLEVELAND
3605 Warrensville Ctr Rd (44122-5203)
PHONE.................................216 844-3323
Harlin Adelman, *Vice Pres*
David Gillum, *Finance Mgr*
Marcelle Hood, *Auditing Mgr*
Elliott Kellman, *Human Res Dir*
Loretta Dawson, *Human Resources*
EMP: 607
SALES (corp-wide): 2.3B **Privately Held**
SIC: 8062 General medical & surgical hospitals
HQ: University Hospitals Of Cleveland
   11100 Euclid Ave
   Cleveland OH 44106
   216 844-1000

(G-16871)
VIGILANT GLOBAL TRADE SVCS LLC (PA)
3140 Courtland Blvd # 3400 (44122-2808)
PHONE.................................260 417-1825
David Moore, *President*
Derek Abramovitch,
EMP: 25
SALES: 2.2MM **Privately Held**
SIC: 8611 7389 Trade associations;

(G-16872)
WINGSPAN CARE GROUP (PA)
22001 Fairmount Blvd (44118-4819)
PHONE.................................216 932-2800
Adam G Jacobs PHD, *President*
Pramik Pam, *Accountant*
Kelli Michaud, *Human Res Dir*
Nicholas Barcelo, *Manager*
Raymond Fink, *Info Tech Dir*
EMP: 41
SALES: 7.3MM **Privately Held**
SIC: 8621 Medical field-related associations

Shandon
Butler County

(G-16873)
R & B CONTRACTORS LLC
Also Called: Robert McConnell
3730 Schloss Ln (45063)
PHONE.................................513 738-0954
Fax: 513 738-2452
Robert R McConnell, *Owner*
Kim McConnell, *Manager*
EMP: 35
SALES (est): 3.2MM **Privately Held**
SIC: 1761 Roofing contractor

Sharon Center
Medina County

(G-16874)
HOLLAND MANAGEMENT INC (PA)
1383 Sharon Copley Rd (44274)
PHONE.................................330 239-4474
John E Holland Jr, *President*
Teresa Holland, *Admin Sec*
EMP: 300
SALES (est): 18.1MM **Privately Held**
SIC: 6513 6512 Apartment building operators; nonresidential building operators

(G-16875)
HOLLAND PROFESSIONAL GROUP
Also Called: Holand Management
1343 Sharon Copley (44274)
PHONE.................................330 239-4474
John E Holland Jr, *President*
John Houghton, *Architect*
EMP: 65 EST: 1972

SQ FT: 2,000
SALES (est): 4.1MM Privately Held
SIC: 8712 Architectural services

(G-16876)
MIRIFEX SYSTEMS LLC (PA)
1383 Sharon Copley Rd (44274)
P.O. Box 328 (44274-0328)
PHONE..................440 891-1210
William Nemeth,
Frank Desimone, *Administration*
Chris Brinkman,
Dennis Langdon,
EMP: 200
SQ FT: 6,522
SALES (est): 10.5MM Privately Held
WEB: www.mirifex.com
SIC: 7371 7375 Computer software development; remote data base information retrieval

(G-16877)
RUHLIN COMPANY (PA)
6931 Ridge Rd (44274)
PHONE..................330 239-2800
Fax: 330 239-1828
James L Ruhlin, *President*
Thomas Huff, *Superintendent*
Jennifer Watson, *COO*
Mike Ciammaichella, *Vice Pres*
Michael Deiwert, *Vice Pres*
EMP: 151 **EST:** 1915
SQ FT: 16,500
SALES (est): 109.6MM Privately Held
WEB: www.ruhlin.com
SIC: 1542 1541 1622 1611 Commercial & office building, new construction; industrial buildings, new construction; bridge construction; general contractor, highway & street construction

(G-16878)
SHARON TWNSHIP FRFIGHTERS ASSN
1274 Sharon Copley Rd (44274)
P.O. Box 310 (44274-0310)
PHONE..................330 239-4992
Fax: 330 239-1280
Michael George, *President*
Valerie Mravepc, *Admin Sec*
Bill Spalin,
EMP: 35
SALES (est): 35.6K Privately Held
SIC: 8399 Fund raising organization, non-fee basis

(G-16879)
SOUTHEAST SECURITY CORPORATION
1385 Wolf Creek Trl (44274)
P.O. Box 326 (44274-0326)
PHONE..................330 239-4600
Fax: 330 239-4660
Matt Lentine, *President*
David Brown, *General Mgr*
Thomas Cutlip, *Project Mgr*
Mike Kelly, *Project Mgr*
Denice Lentine, *Accounts Mgr*
EMP: 40
SQ FT: 8,000
SALES (est): 9.2MM Privately Held
WEB: www.southeastsecurity.com
SIC: 1731 Fire detection & burglar alarm systems specialization

(G-16880)
VELOTTA COMPANY
6740 Ridge Rd (44274)
P.O. Box 157 (44274-0157)
PHONE..................330 239-1211
Fax: 330 239-1195
Robert P Velotta, *President*
Carolann V Stercula, *Vice Pres*
Michael Velotta, *Vice Pres*
Thomas F Velotta, *Vice Pres*
Bob Velotta, *Manager*
EMP: 50
SQ FT: 4,500
SALES (est): 14.4MM Privately Held
WEB: www.velottacompany.com
SIC: 1611 1622 General contractor, highway & street construction; bridge construction; highway construction, elevated

Sharonville
Hamilton County

(G-16881)
DCP HOLDING COMPANY
Also Called: DENTAL CARE PLUS GROUP (DCPG)
100 Crowne Point Pl (45241-5427)
PHONE..................513 554-1100
Stephen T Schuler, *Ch of Bd*
Anthony A Cook, *President*
Jodi M Fronczek, *COO*
Robert C Hodgkins Jr, *CFO*
EMP: 77
SALES: 108.1MM Privately Held
SIC: 6324 Hospital & medical service plans; dental insurance; health maintenance organization (HMO), insurance only

(G-16882)
INNOMARK COMMUNICATIONS LLC
12080 Mosteller Rd (45241-5510)
PHONE..................937 425-6152
Gary P Boens,
EMP: 30
SALES (corp-wide): 126.2MM Privately Held
SIC: 7319 Display advertising service
PA: Innomark Communications Llc
420 Distribution Cir
Fairfield OH 45014
937 427-6100

Sheffield Village
Lorain County

(G-16883)
ADVANCED DESIGN INDUSTRIES INC
Also Called: ADI
4686 French Creek Rd (44054-2716)
PHONE..................440 277-4141
Fax: 440 277-4257
Jerome Winiasz, *President*
R G Brooks Jr, *Principal*
Edward J Winiasz, *Principal*
Thomas Winiasz, *Corp Secy*
▲ **EMP:** 25
SQ FT: 27,000
SALES (est): 7.3MM Privately Held
SIC: 3569 3599 8711 Robots, assembly line: industrial & commercial; machine shop, jobbing & repair; designing: ship, boat, machine & product

(G-16884)
BRENTWOOD GOLF CLUB INC
4456 Abbe Rd (44054-2910)
PHONE..................440 322-9254
Fax: 440 458-4537
Walter Jalowiec Jr, *President*
John Jalowiec, *General Mgr*
Henry Jalowiec, *Principal*
EMP: 30
SQ FT: 5,000
SALES (est): 1.2MM Privately Held
WEB: www.golfwillow.com
SIC: 7992 Public golf courses

(G-16885)
CABBAGE INC (PA)
5050 Waterford Dr (44035-1497)
P.O. Box 890, Vermilion (44089-0890)
PHONE..................440 899-9171
Fax: 440 899-3261
David Hille, *President*
Randy Marcum, *President*
EMP: 26
SQ FT: 3,800
SALES (est): 18.6MM Privately Held
WEB: www.cabbageinc.com
SIC: 5148 Vegetables, fresh

(G-16886)
GREEN IMPRESSIONS LLC
842 Abbe Rd (44054-2302)
PHONE..................440 240-8508
Joseph Schill, *President*
James P Louth, *Vice Pres*
Maureen Loewe, *Office Mgr*
EMP: 45
SALES: 3.3MM Privately Held
SIC: 0781 4959 7349 Landscape services; snowplowing; building maintenance services

(G-16887)
J E DAVIS CORPORATION
5187 Smith Ct Ste 100 (44054-2470)
PHONE..................440 377-4700
Doug Davis, *President*
EMP: 37
SQ FT: 2,500
SALES (est): 4.9MM Privately Held
SIC: 4813 Telephone communications broker

(G-16888)
JACK COOPER TRANSPORT CO INC
5211 Oster Rd (44054-1568)
PHONE..................440 949-2044
Larry Suscha, *Branch Mgr*
EMP: 131
SALES (corp-wide): 667.8MM Privately Held
SIC: 4213 Automobiles, transport & delivery
HQ: Jack Cooper Transport Company, Inc.
1100 Walnut St Ste 2400
Kansas City MO 64106
816 983-4000

(G-16889)
JOSEPH A GIRGIS MD INC (PA)
Also Called: Superior Medical Care
5334 Meadow Lane Ct (44035-1469)
PHONE..................440 930-6095
Joseph A Girgis, *President*
Deborah Lamp, *Office Mgr*
EMP: 39
SALES (est): 6.1MM Privately Held
SIC: 8011 5912 Medical centers; drug stores

(G-16890)
LUXURY HEATING CO
Also Called: L & H Wholesale & Supply
5327 Ford Rd (44035-1349)
PHONE..................440 366-0971
Fax: 440 365-9988
William Samek, *President*
Garry Weich, *General Mgr*
Paul Samek, *COO*
Michael Samek, *Vice Pres*
Jodie Reynolds, *Office Mgr*
EMP: 65 **EST:** 1947
SALES: 7MM Privately Held
SIC: 1711 5075 Warm air heating & air conditioning contractor; warm air heating & air conditioning

(G-16891)
MERCY HEALTH
5054 Waterford Dr (44035-1497)
PHONE..................440 934-8344
EMP: 48
SALES (corp-wide): 4.2B Privately Held
SIC: 8011 Offices & clinics of medical doctors
PA: Mercy Health
1701 Mercy Health Pl
Cincinnati OH 45237
513 639-2800

(G-16892)
MONTROSE SHEFFIELD LLC
5033 Detroit Rd (44054-2810)
PHONE..................440 934-6699
Doug Beasley, *Parts Mgr*
Michael Thompson, *Mng Member*
Carla Swope, *Supervisor*
Christopher Mills,
Joseph M Stefanini,
EMP: 36
SALES (est): 2.4MM Privately Held
SIC: 7539 5511 Automotive repair shops; automobiles, new & used

(G-16893)
NEW LIFE HOSPICE INC (DH)
5255 N Abbe Rd Ste 2 (44035-1451)
PHONE..................440 934-1458
Fax: 440 934-1567
Daniel C Zaworski, *Med Doctor*
Jon Hanson, *Director*
Chris Tolley, *Admin Sec*
EMP: 60
SQ FT: 21,000
SALES (corp-wide): 4.2B Privately Held
SIC: 8082 8051 Home health care services; skilled nursing care facilities
HQ: Community Health Partners Regional Foundation
3700 Kolbe Rd
Lorain OH 44053
440 960-4000

(G-16894)
NICHOLAS CARNEY-MC INC
Also Called: Carney McNicholas
2931 Abbe Rd (44054-2424)
PHONE..................440 243-8560
Fax: 440 243-8562
Tim Carney, *Manager*
Cory Srebnik, *Technology*
EMP: 30
SALES (est): 2.3MM
SALES (corp-wide): 2.2MM Privately Held
WEB: www.cmcn.com
SIC: 4213 Household goods transport
PA: Nicholas Carney-Mc Inc
100 Victoria Rd
Youngstown OH 44515
330 792-5460

(G-16895)
TRUENORTH CULTURAL ARTS
4530 Colorado Ave (44054-2606)
PHONE..................440 949-5200
Rick Fortney, *President*
Richard Fortney, *President*
EMP: 25
SALES: 179.7K Privately Held
SIC: 8733 7911 Noncommercial social research organization; dance studio & school

(G-16896)
WESTSHORE PRMRY CARE ASSOC INC
5323 Meadow Lane Ct (44035-1469)
PHONE..................440 934-0276
Fax: 440 934-0272
Ellen Egan, *Branch Mgr*
EMP: 95
SALES (corp-wide): 6.8MM Privately Held
SIC: 8011 General & family practice, physician/surgeon
PA: Westshore Primary Care Associates, Inc.
26908 Detroit Rd Ste 201
Westlake OH 44145
440 808-1283

Shelby
Richland County

(G-16897)
CENTRAL OHIO ASSOCIATES LTD
Central Oh Ind 18 (44875)
P.O. Box 646 (44875-0646)
PHONE..................419 342-2045
Stephen Rosen, *Partner*
Uehuda Mendelson, *Partner*
Benjamin Rosen, *Partner*
Holly Copley, *Admin Asst*
EMP: 33
SQ FT: 2,500,000
SALES (est): 3.2MM Privately Held
SIC: 6512 Nonresidential building operators

(G-16898)
CORNELL COMPANIES INC
Also Called: Abraxas Foundation of Ohio
2775 State Route 39 (44875-9466)
PHONE..................419 747-3322
Fax: 419 747-3504
Erich Dumbeck, *Administration*
EMP: 110

Shelby - Richland County (G-16899)

GEOGRAPHIC SECTION

SALES (corp-wide): 2.2B *Privately Held*
WEB: www.cornellcorrections.com
SIC: 8069 8361 Substance abuse hospitals; residential care
HQ: Cornell Companies, Inc.
621 Nw 53rd St Ste 700
Boca Raton FL 33487

(G-16899)
DECOATING INC
3955 Industrial Pkwy (44875-9259)
P.O. Box 5100 (44875-5100)
PHONE..................................419 347-9191
Dave Wagner, *President*
David Wagner, *President*
Pearl Biller, *Finance Mgr*
EMP: 25
SQ FT: 10,000
SALES: 750K *Privately Held*
WEB: www.decoating.com
SIC: 1799 Paint & wallpaper stripping

(G-16900)
GLEN SURPLUS SALES INC (PA)
14 E Smiley Ave (44875-1080)
PHONE..................................419 347-1212
Fax: 419 347-1885
Glen H Arms, *President*
Bobby Arms, *Vice Pres*
James Arms, *Vice Pres*
Jennifer Arms, *Vice Pres*
Chad Crider, *Finance*
EMP: 25
SQ FT: 109,000
SALES (est): 3MM *Privately Held*
SIC: 5399 5199 Surplus & salvage goods; variety store merchandise

(G-16901)
MEDCENTRAL HEALTH SYSTEM
199 W Main St (44875-1490)
PHONE..................................419 342-5015
Fax: 419 522-2240
Deb Ruckman, *Supervisor*
Ronald Distl, *Director*
Judy Carrocci, *Nursing Dir*
Monica Cirata, *Nursing Dir*
Heidi Them, *Lab Dir*
EMP: 200
SALES (corp-wide): 3.7B *Privately Held*
SIC: 8062 8049 General medical & surgical hospitals; physical therapist
HQ: Medcentral Health System
335 Glessner Ave
Mansfield OH 44903
419 526-8000

(G-16902)
PHILLIPS MFG AND TOWER CO (PA)
Also Called: Shelby Welded Tube Div
5578 State Route 61 N (44875-9564)
P.O. Box 125 (44875-0125)
PHONE..................................419 347-1720
Fax: 419 347-5231
Angela Phillip, *CEO*
Theresa Wallace, *CFO*
Ben Willman, *Sales Mgr*
EMP: 85
SQ FT: 90,000
SALES (est): 29.3MM *Privately Held*
WEB: www.shelbytube.com
SIC: 3312 3498 3317 7692 Tubes, steel & iron; fabricated pipe & fittings; steel pipe & tubes; welding repair

(G-16903)
R & J TRUCKING INC
147 Curtis Dr (44875-9501)
PHONE..................................330 758-0841
EMP: 56 *Privately Held*
SIC: 4212 Dump truck haulage
HQ: R & J Trucking, Inc.
8063 Southern Blvd
Youngstown OH 44512
800 262-9365

(G-16904)
YOUNG MENS CHRISTN ASSN SHELBY
Also Called: Y M C A
111 W Smiley Ave (44875-2112)
PHONE..................................419 347-1312
Fax: 419 347-1629

Jeff Ream, *President*
Joyce Douglas, *Business Mgr*
Kevin Herring, *Treasurer*
Rich Haight, *Exec Dir*
EMP: 60
SALES: 439.2K *Privately Held*
SIC: 8641 7997 7991 Youth organizations; membership sports & recreation clubs; physical fitness facilities

Sherrodsville
Carroll County

(G-16905)
ATWOOD YACHT CLUB INC
2637 Lodge Rd Sw (44675-9719)
P.O. Box 165 (44675-0165)
PHONE..................................330 735-2135
Fax: 330 735-2726
Joseph Montero, *Principal*
Norma Campbell, *Manager*
Tony Rozler, *Exec Dir*
Todd Davis, *Director*
Phil Eberhart,
EMP: 25
SQ FT: 7,719
SALES: 407.1K *Privately Held*
WEB: www.atwoodyc.com
SIC: 7997 Yacht club, membership

(G-16906)
RADIUS HOSPITALITY MGT LLC
Atwood Lake Resort & Golf CLB
2650 Lodge Rd Sw (44675-9718)
PHONE..................................330 735-2211
Fax: 330 735-2562
Brad Cass, *General Mgr*
EMP: 75
SALES (corp-wide): 6.8MM *Privately Held*
SIC: 7011 7997 Resort hotel; golf club, membership
PA: Radius Hospitality Management Llc
405 Rothrock Rd Ste 102
Copley OH 44321
330 526-5000

Shreve
Wayne County

(G-16907)
CRW INC
3716 S Elyria Rd (44676-9529)
PHONE..................................330 264-3785
Fax: 330 264-8050
Chris Wood, *President*
Charles R Wood, *Vice Pres*
EMP: 52
SQ FT: 9,800
SALES (est): 9.5MM *Privately Held*
SIC: 4213 Contract haulers

(G-16908)
QUALITY CLEANING SYSTEMS LLC
7945 Shreve Rd (44676-9565)
PHONE..................................330 567-2050
Steven Pogue,
EMP: 47
SALES (est): 846.9K *Privately Held*
SIC: 7349 Janitorial service, contract basis

Sidney
Shelby County

(G-16909)
1157 DESIGN CONCEPTS LLC
171 S Lester Ave (45365-7044)
PHONE..................................937 497-1157
Evelyn Flock, *President*
Dan Naas, *Accountant*
Tria Keene, *Marketing Staff*
EMP: 25
SALES (est): 3.4MM *Privately Held*
SIC: 7699 Customizing services

(G-16910)
AAA SHELBY COUNTY MOTOR CLUB
Also Called: World Wide Travel Service
920 Wapakoneta Ave (45365-1471)
PHONE..................................937 492-3167
Fax: 937 492-7297
Debra Barga, *CEO*
Keith Putman, *President*
Gary Elsass, *Manager*
EMP: 25
SQ FT: 10,400
SALES (est): 4MM *Privately Held*
WEB: www.shelbycounty.aaa.com
SIC: 4724 Travel agencies

(G-16911)
AG TRUCKING INC
798 S Vandemark Rd (45365-8139)
PHONE..................................937 497-7770
Fax: 937 497-7397
Katie Stamp, *Manager*
EMP: 28
SALES (corp-wide): 34MM *Privately Held*
WEB: www.ag-trucking.com
SIC: 4213 4212 Contract haulers; local trucking, without storage
PA: Ag Trucking Inc
2430 Lincolnway E
Goshen IN 46526
574 642-3351

(G-16912)
AMOS MEDIA COMPANY (PA)
Also Called: Coin World
911 S Vandemark Rd (45365-8974)
P.O. Box 4129 (45365-4129)
PHONE..................................937 498-2111
Fax: 937 498-0888
John O Amos, *Ch of Bd*
Bruce Boyd, *President*
Jeff Starck, *Editor*
Robert Bryan, *Purch Dir*
Jane Volland, *CFO*
▲ **EMP:** 300 **EST:** 1876
SQ FT: 90,000
SALES (est): 39.1MM *Privately Held*
SIC: 2721 2711 2796 7389 Magazines: publishing only, not printed on site; newspapers, publishing & printing; platemaking services; appraisers, except real estate; miscellaneous publishing

(G-16913)
AREA ENERGY & ELECTRIC INC (PA)
Also Called: Honeywell Authorized Dealer
2001 Commerce Dr (45365-9393)
PHONE..................................937 498-4784
Fax: 937 492-3911
Nathan Perry, *Superintendent*
Kenneth Schlater, *Principal*
Jon Ranly, *Business Mgr*
Joe Lachey, *Vice Pres*
Marc Larger, *Project Mgr*
EMP: 219
SQ FT: 20,000
SALES (est): 99.7MM *Privately Held*
SIC: 1731 1711 General electrical contractor; heating & air conditioning contractors

(G-16914)
BAUMFOLDER CORPORATION
1660 Campbell Rd (45365-2480)
PHONE..................................937 492-1281
Fax: 937 492-7280
Ulrik Nygaard, *President*
Jason Muldoon, *President*
Sesha RAO, *Managing Dir*
Janice Benanzer, *Corp Secy*
Carl Fullenkamp, *Vice Pres*
▲ **EMP:** 100 **EST:** 1917
SQ FT: 125,000
SALES (est): 24.2MM
SALES (corp-wide): 2.6B *Privately Held*
WEB: www.baumfolder.com
SIC: 3554 3579 7389 Paper industries machinery; folding machines, paper; cutting machines, paper; binding machines, plastic & adhesive; packaging & labeling services
HQ: Heidelberg Americas Inc
1000 Gutenberg Dr Nw
Kennesaw GA 30144

(G-16915)
BELL HENSLEY INC
Also Called: AMS
804 W Parkwood St (45365-3626)
PHONE..................................937 498-1718
Fax: 937 498-0766
Darrell Hensley, *Vice Pres*
EMP: 35
SALES (est): 3.2MM *Privately Held*
WEB: www.alternative-maintenance.com
SIC: 1541 Industrial buildings & warehouses

(G-16916)
BELTING COMPANY OF CINCINNATI
Also Called: Cbt Company
301 Stolle Ave (45365-7807)
PHONE..................................937 498-2104
James E Stahl Jr, *President*
EMP: 28
SALES (corp-wide): 198.2MM *Privately Held*
SIC: 5063 Electrical apparatus & equipment
PA: The Belting Company Of Cincinnati
5500 Ridge Ave
Cincinnati OH 45213
513 621-9050

(G-16917)
BULK TRANSIT CORPORATION
1377 Riverside Dr (45365-9197)
PHONE..................................937 497-9573
Fax: 937 497-9603
Scott Woods, *Manager*
Pat McClintock, *Manager*
EMP: 30
SALES (corp-wide): 26.7MM *Privately Held*
WEB: www.bulktransit.com
SIC: 4213 Contract haulers
PA: Bulk Transit Corporation
7177 Indl Pkwy
Plain City OH 43064
614 873-4632

(G-16918)
CELLCO PARTNERSHIP
Also Called: Verizon
2400 Michigan St (45365-9080)
PHONE..................................937 498-2371
Kenneth Wysong, *Manager*
EMP: 230
SALES (corp-wide): 126B *Publicly Held*
SIC: 4813 Telephone communication, except radio
HQ: Cellco Partnership
1 Verizon Way
Basking Ridge NJ 07920

(G-16919)
CHOICE ONE ENGINEERING CORP
440 E Hoewisher Rd (45365-8450)
PHONE..................................937 497-0200
Fax: 937 497-0300
Anthony Schroeder, *Owner*
Brian Barhorst, *Owner*
Steven E Bowersox, *Owner*
Thomas Coverstone, *Owner*
Jeffery M Kunk, *Owner*
EMP: 25
SALES (est): 3.6MM *Privately Held*
WEB: www.choiceoneengineering.com
SIC: 8711 8713 Consulting engineer; surveying services

(G-16920)
CHS MIAMI VALLEY INC
Also Called: Sidney Care Center
510 Buckeye Ave (45365-1214)
PHONE..................................330 204-1040
Fax: 937 492-3781
Edward L Byington, *President*
EMP: 50 **EST:** 2002
SALES: 3.4MM *Privately Held*
SIC: 8051 Convalescent home with continuous nursing care

(G-16921)
CLEAN ALL SERVICES INC
324 Adams St Bldg 1 (45365-2328)
P.O. Box 4127 (45365-4127)
PHONE..................................937 498-4146

GEOGRAPHIC SECTION **Sidney - Shelby County (G-16943)**

Fax: 937 498-4919
Steve Shuchat, *President*
Gary Shuchat, *Chairman*
John Cianciolo, *Business Mgr*
Jim Smith, *Opers Mgr*
Sarah Wesbecher, *Human Res Mgr*
EMP: 203
SQ FT: 6,000
SALES (est): 7.3MM Privately Held
SIC: 7349 Janitorial service, contract basis

(G-16922)
CONTINENTAL EXPRESS INC
10450 State Route 47 W (45365-9009)
PHONE 937 497-2100
Fax: 937 498-2155
Russell L Gottemoeller, *President*
Rene Gottemoeller, *Vice Pres*
Daniel Subler, *Opers Mgr*
Bill Maurer, *Safety Mgr*
John Hulecki, *Sls & Mktg Exec*
EMP: 350
SQ FT: 31,000
SALES: 82.8MM Privately Held
SIC: 4213 4212 Refrigerated products transport; local trucking, without storage

(G-16923)
COPELAND ACCESS + INC
1675 Campbell Rd (45365-2479)
P.O. Box 669 (45365-0669)
PHONE 937 498-3802
Fax: 937 498-3334
Clinton Clay, *Principal*
David Dunbar, *COO*
Jan Burns, *Assistant VP*
Shyam Maladkar, *Engineer*
Julie Sharp, *Accountant*
▲ **EMP:** 31
SALES (est): 25.6MM
SALES (corp-wide): 15.2B Publicly Held
WEB: www.copeland-corp.com
SIC: 5075 Warm air heating & air conditioning
HQ: Emerson Climate Technologies, Inc.
1675 Campbell Rd
Sidney OH 45365
937 498-3011

(G-16924)
COUNCIL ON RUR SVC PRGRAMS INC
Also Called: Shelby County Child Care
1502 N Main Ave (45365-1761)
PHONE 937 492-8787
Brenda Lillicrap, *Manager*
EMP: 34
SALES (corp-wide): 14.7MM Privately Held
WEB: www.corsp.org
SIC: 8399 8351 Community action agency; head start center, except in conjunction with school
PA: Council On Rural Service Programs, Inc.
201 Robert M Davis Pkwy B
Piqua OH 45356
937 778-5220

(G-16925)
COUNTY OF SHELBY
Also Called: Shelby County Highway Dept
500 Gearhart Rd (45365-9404)
PHONE 937 498-7244
Fax: 937 492-8411
Robert Geuy, *Manager*
EMP: 32
SQ FT: 3,200 Privately Held
WEB: www.shelbycountyauditors.com
SIC: 1611 Highway & street construction
PA: County Of Shelby
129 E Court St
Sidney OH 45365
937 498-7226

(G-16926)
COUNTY OF SHELBY
Also Called: Fair Haven Shelby County Home
2901 Fair Rd (45365-9534)
PHONE 937 492-6900
Fax: 937 492-8826
Melissa Malone, *Site Mgr*
Judy McCorkle, *Human Res Dir*
Miguel Topolov, *Director*
Anita Miller, *Administration*
EMP: 150 Privately Held

WEB: www.shelbycountyauditors.com
SIC: 8059 8052 8051 Nursing home, except skilled & intermediate care facility; intermediate care facilities; skilled nursing care facilities
PA: County Of Shelby
129 E Court St
Sidney OH 45365
937 498-7226

(G-16927)
COVER CROP SHOP LLC
Also Called: Center Seeds
739 S Vandemark Rd (45365-8959)
PHONE 937 417-3972
Eric L Belcher, *Mng Member*
EMP: 78
SALES (corp-wide): 5.3MM Privately Held
SIC: 0182 Food crops grown under cover
PA: Cover Crop Shop, Llc
40 W 4th St
Minster OH 45865
937 417-3972

(G-16928)
DICKMAN SUPPLY INC (PA)
1991 St Marys Ave (45365)
P.O. Box 569 (45365-0569)
PHONE 937 492-6166
Tim Geise, *President*
Timothy Geise, *President*
Adam Barhorst, *Division Mgr*
Marla Geise, *Corp Secy*
Chris Geise, *Vice Pres*
EMP: 110
SQ FT: 28,000
SALES (est): 114MM Privately Held
WEB: www.electro-controls.com
SIC: 5063 5084 Electrical apparatus & equipment; drilling bits; paper, sawmill & woodworking machinery

(G-16929)
DICKMAN SUPPLY INC
Also Called: Electro Controls
1991 St Mary Ave (45365)
P.O. Box 569 (45365-0569)
PHONE 937 492-6166
Linda Silverthorn, *Plant Mgr*
Dara Inman, *Buyer*
Chris Geise, *Manager*
EMP: 50
SALES (est): 6.9MM
SALES (corp-wide): 114MM Privately Held
WEB: www.electro-controls.com
SIC: 5063 Electrical supplies
PA: Dickman Supply, Inc.
1991 St Marys Ave
Sidney OH 45365
937 492-6166

(G-16930)
EAGLE BRIDGE CO
800 S Vandemark Rd (45365-8139)
P.O. Box 59 (45365-0059)
PHONE 937 492-5654
Richard Franz, *President*
Thomas Frantz, *Vice Pres*
EMP: 80
SALES (est): 17.2MM Privately Held
WEB: www.eaglebridge.net
SIC: 1622 Bridge construction

(G-16931)
ELITE ENCLOSURE COMPANY LLC
2349 Industrial Dr (45365-8100)
P.O. Box 916 (45365-0916)
PHONE 937 492-3548
Fax: 937 295-3582
Michael Trempe, *President*
Karen Trempe, *Corp Secy*
Sherry Pottorf, *Controller*
EMP: 35
SQ FT: 63,000
SALES: 6MM
SALES (corp-wide): 5.1MM Privately Held
WEB: www.eliteenclosure.com
SIC: 3499 7389 Machine bases, metal; design, commercial & industrial

PA: Mk Trempe Corporation
2349 Industrial Dr
Sidney OH 45365
937 492-3548

(G-16932)
FAULKNER GRMHSEN KEISTER SHENK (PA)
100 S Main Ave (45365-2771)
PHONE 937 492-1271
Fax: 937 498-1306
Ralph F Keister, *Partner*
Ralph Keister, *Partner*
James R Shenk,
Justin Spillers, *Associate*
EMP: 28
SALES (est): 3.9MM Privately Held
WEB: www.fgks-law.com
SIC: 8111 General practice law office

(G-16933)
FERGUSON CONSTRUCTION COMPANY (PA)
400 Canal St (45365-2312)
P.O. Box 726 (45365-0726)
PHONE 937 498-2381
Fax: 937 498-1796
Martin Given, *President*
Benjamin Lindsay, *General Mgr*
Jeff Lindbom, *Superintendent*
Thomas Pleiman, *Corp Secy*
Douglas Fortkamp, *Exec VP*
EMP: 150
SQ FT: 40,000
SALES (est): 128.4MM Privately Held
WEB: www.ferguson-construction.com
SIC: 1541 1542 Industrial buildings, new construction; commercial & office building, new construction

(G-16934)
FOOT & ANKLE CARE CENTER
1000 Michigan St (45365-2404)
PHONE 937 492-1211
Fax: 419 492-6557
Eric Polanski DPM, *President*
EMP: 30
SALES (est): 472.6K Privately Held
SIC: 8011 Specialized medical practitioners, except internal

(G-16935)
FREISTHLER PAVING INC
2323 Campbell Rd (45365-9529)
PHONE 937 498-4802
Fax: 937 492-8009
Michael J Freisthler, *President*
Janet Freisthler, *Corp Secy*
Chad Moos, *Exec VP*
Melanie Hina, *Manager*
EMP: 48
SQ FT: 14,000
SALES (est): 3MM Privately Held
SIC: 1771 Blacktop (asphalt) work

(G-16936)
FRESHWAY FOODS INC (PA)
Also Called: Fresh and Limited
601 Stolle Ave (45365-8895)
PHONE 937 498-4664
Fax: 937 498-1529
Frank Gilardi Jr, *Ch of Bd*
Phil Gilardi, *President*
Devon Beer, *CFO*
Mike Koon, *Controller*
Janice Snider, *Accounting Mgr*
EMP: 147
SQ FT: 90,000
SALES: 109MM Privately Held
SIC: 5148 2099 Vegetables, fresh; food preparations

(G-16937)
FRESHWAY FOODS INC
601 Stolle Ave (45365-8895)
PHONE 937 498-4664
Devon Beer, *Branch Mgr*
EMP: 241
SALES (corp-wide): 109MM Privately Held
SIC: 4731 Transportation agents & brokers
PA: Freshway Foods, Inc.
601 Stolle Ave
Sidney OH 45365
937 498-4664

(G-16938)
HEIDELBERG USA INC
Also Called: Baum USA
1660 Campbell Rd (45365-2480)
PHONE 937 492-1281
Micheal Gravel, *Branch Mgr*
EMP: 30
SALES (corp-wide): 2.6B Privately Held
SIC: 5084 Printing trades machinery, equipment & supplies
HQ: Heidelberg Usa, Inc.
1000 Gutenberg Dr Nw
Kennesaw GA 30144
770 419-6500

(G-16939)
KIRK NATIONALEASE CO (PA)
3885 Michigan St (45365-8623)
P.O. Box 4369 (45365-4369)
PHONE 937 498-1151
Fax: 937 498-9920
Jeff Phlitot, *President*
Jeff Phlipot, *COO*
James R Harvey, *Vice Pres*
Deb Hovestreybt, *Vice Pres*
Tom Menker, *CFO*
EMP: 40 EST: 1920
SQ FT: 20,000
SALES (est): 44.6MM Privately Held
WEB: www.knl.cc
SIC: 7513 7538 Truck leasing, without drivers; truck rental, without drivers; truck engine repair, except industrial

(G-16940)
LOCHARD INC
Also Called: Do It Best
903 Wapakoneta Ave (45365-1409)
PHONE 937 492-8811
Fax: 937 492-5640
Michael Lochard, *President*
Donald W Lochard, *Vice Pres*
Tim Kleptz, *VP Opers*
Chris Hutson, *Accountant*
Ray Shaw, *Sales Mgr*
EMP: 58 EST: 1945
SQ FT: 44,500
SALES: 7MM Privately Held
WEB: www.lochard-inc.com
SIC: 1711 5251 Mechanical contractor; hardware

(G-16941)
LOWES HOME CENTERS LLC
2700 W Michigan St (45365-9007)
PHONE 937 498-8400
Fax: 937 498-8403
Mike Herrera, *Manager*
Anastasia Paine, *Executive*
EMP: 150
SALES (corp-wide): 68.6B Publicly Held
SIC: 5211 5031 5722 5064 Home centers; building materials, exterior; building materials, interior; household appliance stores; electrical appliances, television & radio
HQ: Lowe's Home Centers, Llc
1605 Curtis Bridge Rd
Wilkesboro NC 28697
336 658-4000

(G-16942)
MCCRATE DELAET & CO
Also Called: McCrate Delaet & Co Cpa's
100 S Main Ave Ste 203 (45365-2771)
P.O. Box 339 (45365-0339)
PHONE 937 492-3161
Fax: 937 492-8050
Dale Schwieterman, *President*
Richard Rihm, *CPA*
Sarah Stammen, *Manager*
Travis Wilges, *Manager*
Donald Goettemoeller, *Advisor*
EMP: 25
SALES (est): 2.2MM Privately Held
SIC: 8721 Certified public accountant

(G-16943)
NK PARTS INDUSTRIES INC
Also Called: Nkp West
2640 Campbell Rd (45365-8836)
PHONE 937 493-4651
Fax: 937 498-4865
Tammy Eilerman, *Manager*
EMP: 30

Sidney - Shelby County (G-16944)

SALES (corp-wide): 1.5B Privately Held
SIC: 5013 5015 Motor vehicle supplies & new parts; motor vehicle parts, used
HQ: Nk Parts Industries, Inc.
777 S Kuther Rd
Sidney OH 45365
937 498-4651

(G-16944)
OCCUPATIONAL HEALTH SERVICES
Also Called: Wilson Mem Hosp Occptnal Clnic
915 Michigan St (45365-2401)
PHONE..................................937 492-7296
Cindy Bay, *Manager*
EMP: 25
SALES (est): 541.4K Privately Held
SIC: 8011 8748 8049 Internal medicine, physician/surgeon; business consulting; offices of health practitioner

(G-16945)
OHIO PRESBT RETIREMENT SVCS
Also Called: Dorothy Love Retirement Cmnty
3003 Cisco Rd (45365-9343)
PHONE..................................937 498-2391
Fax: 937 492-3544
Anne Roller, *Principal*
Kelly Foster, *Maintenance Dir*
Deb Cromes, *Chf Purch Ofc*
Cathy Koverman, *Human Res Dir*
Lou Ann Presser, *Marketing Staff*
EMP: 300 Privately Held
WEB: www.nwo.oprs.org
SIC: 8059 8051 8052 Rest home, with health care; skilled nursing care facilities; intermediate care facilities
PA: Ohio Living
1001 Kingsmill Pkwy
Columbus OH 43229

(G-16946)
OHIO VALLEY INTEGRATION SVCS
2005 Commerce Dr (45365-9393)
PHONE..................................937 492-0008
Fax: 937 492-9688
John M Garmhausen, *President*
EMP: 35
SALES (est): 4MM
SALES (corp-wide): 99.7MM Privately Held
WEB: www.ohiovalleyintegration.com
SIC: 7382 Burglar alarm maintenance & monitoring
PA: Area Energy & Electric, Inc.
2001 Commerce Dr
Sidney OH 45365
937 498-4784

(G-16947)
PEOPLES FEDERAL SAV & LN ASSN (HQ)
101 E Court St (45365-3021)
P.O. Box 727 (45365-0727)
PHONE..................................937 492-6129
Fax: 937 498-4554
Douglas Stewart, *President*
David Fogt, *COO*
Gary N Fullenkamp, *Vice Pres*
Debra Geuy, *CFO*
Richard T Martin, *Accountant*
EMP: 31
SALES: 4.4MM
SALES (corp-wide): 7.7MM Publicly Held
SIC: 6035 Federal savings & loan associations
PA: Peoples-Sidney Financial Corporation
101 E Court St
Sidney OH 45365
937 492-6129

(G-16948)
PRIMARY EYECARE ASSOCIATES (PA)
1086 Fairington Dr (45365-8913)
PHONE..................................937 492-2351
Fax: 937 492-7865
Jeffery Ahrns, *CEO*
Shelley Vanskiver, *Med Doctor*
EMP: 25

SALES (est): 2.9MM Privately Held
WEB: www.primaryeyecare.org
SIC: 8042 8011 Offices & clinics of optometrists; offices & clinics of medical doctors

(G-16949)
REGAL PLUMBING & HEATING CO
9303 State Route 29 W (45365)
PHONE..................................937 492-2894
Fax: 937 498-4127
Gary Thoma, *President*
Phil Wyen, *Shareholder*
Sandy Bruns, *Admin Sec*
EMP: 45
SQ FT: 21,000
SALES (est): 11.5MM Privately Held
WEB: www.regalplbg-htg.com
SIC: 1711 Mechanical contractor

(G-16950)
REPUBLIC SERVICES INC
1600 Riverside Dr (45365-9156)
PHONE..................................937 492-3470
EMP: 34
SALES (corp-wide): 8.1B Publicly Held
SIC: 4953 Refuse System
PA: Republic Services, Inc.
18500 N Allied Way # 100
Phoenix AZ 85054
480 627-2700

(G-16951)
ROE TRANSPORT INC
Also Called: R-3 Enterprises
3680 Michigan St (45365-9086)
PHONE..................................937 497-7161
Shane Roe, *President*
Chad Roe, *Vice Pres*
EMP: 25
SALES (est): 7.9MM Privately Held
SIC: 4731 5088 Freight transportation arrangement; transportation equipment & supplies

(G-16952)
SHELBY COUNTY MEM HOSP ASSN (PA)
Also Called: Wilson Health
915 Michigan St (45365-2401)
PHONE..................................937 498-2311
Fax: 937 498-4669
Mark Dooley, *President*
Cindy Cable, *President*
Craig Lannoye, *COO*
Greg Long, *COO*
Linda Maurer, *Vice Pres*
EMP: 679
SQ FT: 116,000
SALES: 102.5MM Privately Held
SIC: 8062 General medical & surgical hospitals

(G-16953)
SHELBY COUNTY MEM HOSP ASSN
Also Called: The Pavilion
705 Fulton St (45365-3203)
PHONE..................................937 492-9591
Karen Gillette, *Office Mgr*
Marianne Wildermuth, *Manager*
Gail Kohler, *Director*
Peggy Wolfe, *Director*
Linda Wiley, *Nursing Dir*
EMP: 80
SALES (corp-wide): 102.5MM Privately Held
SIC: 8051 8062 Skilled nursing care facilities; general medical & surgical hospitals
PA: Shelby County Memorial Hospital Association
915 Michigan St
Sidney OH 45365
937 498-2311

(G-16954)
SIDNEY ELECTRIC COMPANY (PA)
840 S Vandemark Rd (45365-8139)
PHONE..................................419 222-1109
Fax: 937 498-1178
John S Frantz, *President*
Mike Ellett, *Vice Pres*
Ted Michel, *Project Mgr*

Brad Baxter, *Human Resources*
Lino Rivera, *Supervisor*
EMP: 59
SQ FT: 20,000
SALES (est): 15.2MM Privately Held
SIC: 1731 General electrical contractor

(G-16955)
SIDNEY-SHELBY COUNTY YMCA (PA)
300 E Parkwood St (45365-1642)
PHONE..................................937 492-9134
Fax: 937 492-4705
Ed Thomas, *CEO*
Jack Weiss, *Property Mgr*
Dennis Ruble, *Exec Dir*
Michele Dotson, *Director*
EMP: 35
SALES: 126.2K Privately Held
WEB: www.sidney-ymca.org
SIC: 8641 8661 8322 Youth organizations; religious organizations; individual & family services

(G-16956)
SLAGLE MECHANICAL CONTRACTORS
877 W Russell Rd (45365-8633)
P.O. Box 823 (45365-0823)
PHONE..................................937 492-4151
Fax: 937 492-7318
Jerry Kingseed, *President*
Gary Smith, *Vice Pres*
Bob Snarr, *Vice Pres*
Rick Williams, *Project Mgr*
Rick Baker, *Engineer*
EMP: 45
SQ FT: 32,000
SALES (est): 13.6MM Privately Held
WEB: www.slaglemech.com
SIC: 1711 1761 Plumbing contractors; warm air heating & air conditioning contractor; ventilation & duct work contractor; mechanical contractor; sheet metalwork

(G-16957)
TIME WARNER CABLE INC
1602 Wapakoneta Ave (45365-1434)
PHONE..................................937 492-4145
Jerry Degrazia, *Branch Mgr*
EMP: 83
SALES (corp-wide): 41.5B Publicly Held
SIC: 4841 Cable television services
HQ: Spectrum Management Holding Company, Llc
400 Atlantic St
Stamford CT 06901
203 905-7801

(G-16958)
US BANK NATIONAL ASSOCIATION
Also Called: US Bank
115 E Court St (45365-3021)
PHONE..................................937 498-1131
Susan Kaser, *Branch Mgr*
Perrica Short, *Branch Mgr*
Jamie Wurstner, *Manager*
EMP: 43
SALES (corp-wide): 22.7B Publicly Held
WEB: www.firstar.com
SIC: 6021 National commercial banks
HQ: U.S. Bank National Association
425 Walnut St Fl 1
Cincinnati OH 45202
513 632-4234

(G-16959)
VICTORY MACHINE AND FAB
920 S Vandemark Rd (45365-8140)
PHONE..................................937 693-3171
Hannah Wilcox, *Principal*
EMP: 25
SALES (est): 2.8MM Privately Held
SIC: 7699 Industrial machinery & equipment repair

(G-16960)
WAPPOO WOOD PRODUCTS INC
Also Called: Interntnal Pckg Pallets Crates
12877 Kirkwood Rd (45365-8102)
PHONE..................................937 492-1166
Fax: 937 492-3441
Thomas G Baker, *Ch of Bd*

T Adam Baker, *President*
Gary O'Connor, *Principal*
Matthew Baker, *Office Mgr*
Timm Flinn, *Director*
EMP: 40
SQ FT: 21,800
SALES (est): 19.1MM Privately Held
WEB: www.wappoowood.com
SIC: 5031 2435 2436 2421 Lumber: rough, dressed & finished; hardwood veneer & plywood; softwood veneer & plywood; sawmills & planing mills, general; hardwood dimension & flooring mills

(G-16961)
XPO LOGISTICS FREIGHT INC
2021 Campbell Rd (45365-2474)
PHONE..................................937 492-3899
Fax: 937 492-4015
Jeff Farrell, *Manager*
Greg Byers, *Manager*
EMP: 30
SALES (corp-wide): 15.3B Publicly Held
WEB: www.con-way.com
SIC: 4213 Contract haulers
HQ: Xpo Logistics Freight, Inc.
2211 Old Earhart Rd # 100
Ann Arbor MI 48105
734 998-4200

Silver Lake
Summit County

(G-16962)
F B AND S MASONRY INC
Also Called: Brown, Frank R & Sons
3021 Harriet Rd (44224-3811)
PHONE..................................330 608-3442
Fax: 330 688-7478
Thomas Earl Brown, *President*
Paula Brown, *Vice Pres*
EMP: 30
SQ FT: 3,000
SALES (est): 2.5MM Privately Held
SIC: 1741 Masonry & other stonework

(G-16963)
S P S & ASSOCIATES INC
2926 Ivanhoe Rd (44224-3012)
PHONE..................................330 283-4267
Sterling Paul Shand, *President*
▲ **EMP:** 30
SALES (est): 2MM Privately Held
WEB: www.spsassociates.com
SIC: 1741 Stone masonry

(G-16964)
SILVER LAKE COUNTRY CLUB
1325 Graham Rd (44224-2999)
PHONE..................................330 688-6066
Fax: 330 688-2479
Bob Dedman Jr, *Ch of Bd*
Mike Stevens, *General Mgr*
Doug Koepnick, *Chairman*
EMP: 65 EST: 1957
SQ FT: 15,000
SALES (est): 2.7MM Privately Held
WEB: www.teemonline.com
SIC: 7997 7992 5941 5812 Country club, membership; public golf courses; sporting goods & bicycle shops; eating places

(G-16965)
SILVER LAKE MANAGEMENT CORP
Also Called: Sliver Lake Country Club
1325 Graham Rd (44224-2940)
PHONE..................................330 688-6066
Doug Koepnick, *General Mgr*
EMP: 120
SQ FT: 15,000
SALES (est): 2MM
SALES (corp-wide): 433.7MM Privately Held
WEB: www.remington-gc.com
SIC: 7997 Country club, membership
HQ: Clubcorp Usa, Inc.
3030 Lyndon B Johnson Fwy
Dallas TX 75234
972 243-6191

Smithville
Wayne County

(G-16966)
METRO HEALTH SYSTEM
6022 N Honeytown Rd (44677-9563)
PHONE..................................330 669-2249
Kenneth Kirby, *Manager*
Sara Albrecht, *Nurse*
Michelle Querry, *Nurse*
EMP: 69
SALES (est): 1.5MM **Privately Held**
SIC: 8099 8031 8011 Health & allied services; offices & clinics of osteopathic physicians; offices & clinics of medical doctors

Solon
Cuyahoga County

(G-16967)
1 EDI SOURCE INC
31875 Solon Rd (44139-3553)
P.O. Box 391466 (44139-8466)
PHONE..................................440 519-7800
John Onysko, *CEO*
David Lowman, *President*
Correen Brown, *Finance*
Brittany Rohner, *Human Res Mgr*
Jesse Hudson, *Client Mgr*
EMP: 105
SQ FT: 30,000
SALES (est): 18.6MM **Privately Held**
WEB: www.1edisource.com
SIC: 7379 7371 Computer related consulting services; software programming applications

(G-16968)
ABSOLUTE CLEANING SERVICES
5349 Harper Rd (44139-1517)
PHONE..................................440 542-1742
Mikheil Kavtaradze, *President*
EMP: 89
SALES: 1,000K **Privately Held**
SIC: 7349 Building maintenance services

(G-16969)
ACLARA TECHNOLOGIES LLC
30400 Solon Rd (44139-3416)
PHONE..................................440 528-7200
Jeff Conrad, *Project Mgr*
John Bennington, *Engineer*
Patti Gavorski, *Human Resources*
Gary Moore, *Branch Mgr*
Mark Deehr, *Manager*
EMP: 120
SALES (corp-wide): 3.6B **Publicly Held**
SIC: 3824 3825 3829 7371 Mechanical & electromechanical counters & devices; instruments to measure electricity; measuring & controlling devices; custom computer programming services; computer integrated systems design
HQ: Aclara Technologies Llc
77 West Port Plz Ste 500
Saint Louis MO 63146
314 895-6400

(G-16970)
ACOSTA INC
30600 Aurora Rd Ste 100 (44139-2761)
PHONE..................................440 490-7370
Tim McShane, *Branch Mgr*
EMP: 61
SALES (corp-wide): 8.7B **Privately Held**
WEB: www.acosta.com
SIC: 5141 Food brokers
PA: Acosta Inc.
6600 Corporate Ctr Pkwy
Jacksonville FL 32216
904 332-7986

(G-16971)
AGILYSYS INC
Also Called: Solon Branch
6521 Davis Indus Pkwy (44139-3549)
PHONE..................................440 519-6262
Robert Mungary, *Sales Engr*
Frank Petsock, *Manager*
Roberta A Gerz, *Admin Asst*
Aida Douglas, *Contractor*
EMP: 30
SALES (corp-wide): 127.6MM **Publicly Held**
SIC: 5065 5045 Electronic parts & equipment; computers, peripherals & software
PA: Agilysys, Inc.
1000 Windward Concourse # 250
Alpharetta GA 30005
770 810-7800

(G-16972)
AHERN RENTALS INC
29001 Solon Rd Ste 17 (44139-3468)
PHONE..................................440 498-0869
Scott Mellenger, *Principal*
EMP: 38
SALES (corp-wide): 599.8MM **Privately Held**
SIC: 7353 Heavy construction equipment rental
PA: Ahern Rentals, Inc.
1401 Mineral Ave
Las Vegas NV 89106
702 362-0623

(G-16973)
AIR VENTURI LTD
5135 Naiman Pkwy (44139-1003)
PHONE..................................216 292-2570
Joshua Unger, *CEO*
Valentin Gamerman, *President*
EMP: 54
SQ FT: 70,000
SALES (est): 5MM **Privately Held**
SIC: 5091 Sporting & recreation goods
PA: Pyramyd Air Ltd.
5135 Naiman Pkwy
Solon OH 44139

(G-16974)
ALL PRO CLEANING SERVICES INC
6001 Cochran Rd Ste 103 (44139-3325)
P.O. Box 391711, Cleveland (44139-8711)
PHONE..................................440 519-0055
Steven Altman, *President*
EMP: 75
SQ FT: 2,000
SALES (est): 1.8MM **Privately Held**
SIC: 7349 Janitorial service, contract basis

(G-16975)
AMG MARKETING RESOURCES INC
Also Called: AMG Advertising & PR
30670 Bnbridge Rd Ste 200 (44139)
PHONE..................................216 621-1835
Fax: 216 621-2061
Anthony Fatica, *President*
Marilyn Clark, *Corp Secy*
Kip Botirius, *Vice Pres*
Annette Fatica, *Vice Pres*
Debra Records, *Prdtn Mgr*
EMP: 25
SQ FT: 7,500
SALES: 1.2MM **Privately Held**
WEB: www.amgadvertising.com
SIC: 7311 Advertising consultant

(G-16976)
ARCO HEATING & AC CO (PA)
5325 Naiman Pkwy Ste J (44139-1019)
PHONE..................................216 663-3211
Brian Friedman, *President*
Jim Fisher, *Opers Mgr*
Bill Dodd, *Manager*
EMP: 50
SQ FT: 50,000
SALES (est): 5.2MM **Privately Held**
WEB: www.arcohvac.com
SIC: 1711 Warm air heating & air conditioning contractor

(G-16977)
ARROW ELECTRONICS INC
Power & Signal Group
5440 Naiman Pkwy (44139-1010)
PHONE..................................440 498-3617
Donald Akery, *President*
David Cluggish, *Manager*
Tony Vitello, *Consultant*
Jim Hawersaat, *Director*
Nathaniel Wright, *Training Spec*
EMP: 87
SALES (corp-wide): 26.8B **Publicly Held**
WEB: www.arrow.com
SIC: 5065 Electronic parts & equipment
PA: Arrow Electronics, Inc.
9201 E Dry Creek Rd
Centennial CO 80112
303 824-4000

(G-16978)
ARROW ELECTRONICS INC
6675 Parkland Blvd (44139-4345)
PHONE..................................440 498-6400
Bradley Stark, *Opers Mgr*
Katrina Kinnaman, *Engineer*
Kristin Bedford, *Sales Staff*
Nicholas Zebrowski, *Sales Associate*
Susan Kato, *Marketing Mgr*
EMP: 53
SALES (corp-wide): 26.8B **Publicly Held**
SIC: 7379 Computer related maintenance services
PA: Arrow Electronics, Inc.
9201 E Dry Creek Rd
Centennial CO 80112
303 824-4000

(G-16979)
ATS GROUP LLC
5845 Harper Rd (44139-1832)
P.O. Box 391202 (44139-8202)
PHONE..................................216 744-5757
Maryna Svilovich, *President*
EMP: 176
SALES (est): 2.4MM **Privately Held**
SIC: 7349 Building maintenance services

(G-16980)
AURORA WHOLESALERS LLC (PA)
Also Called: Mazel Company, The
31000 Aurora Rd (44139-2769)
PHONE..................................440 248-5200
Fax: 440 349-1931
Kara A Velotta, *Vice Pres*
Larry Hulkama, *CFO*
Rich Reedy, *Human Resources*
Richard Goroff, *Marketing Mgr*
Bob Kaiser, *Marketing Mgr*
◆ **EMP:** 76
SQ FT: 1,000,000
SALES (est): 70.3MM **Privately Held**
WEB: www.mazelcompany.com
SIC: 5199 General merchandise, nondurable

(G-16981)
B D G WRAP-TITE INC
6200 Cochran Rd (44139-3308)
PHONE..................................440 349-5400
Suresh Bafna, *CEO*
Sunil Daga, *President*
Bob Magyaros, *Business Mgr*
Chirag Patel, *Office Mgr*
Rebecca Tousey, *Manager*
◆ **EMP:** 80
SQ FT: 89,000
SALES (est): 10MM **Privately Held**
WEB: www.jainco.com
SIC: 3069 5199 Film, rubber; leather goods, except footwear, gloves, luggage, belting

(G-16982)
BALSARA ENTERPRISE LTD
Also Called: Learning Trails School
6545 Som Center Rd (44139-4201)
PHONE..................................330 497-7000
Jaideep Balsara, *Vice Pres*
Mary Mucklow, *Financial Exec*
Kristin Kamenash, *Director*
EMP: 45
SALES (est): 1.7MM **Privately Held**
SIC: 8351 Preschool center

(G-16983)
BELCAN CORPORATION
Also Called: Specialty Equipment Engrg Div
28999 Aurora Rd (44139-1840)
PHONE..................................513 891-0972
Fax: 440 349-3286
Robert Brehm, *Project Mgr*
Angela Noyes, *Project Mgr*
Robert McCoy, *Opers Mgr*
Kieron Powell, *Opers Mgr*
Neil Davis, *Engineer*
EMP: 85
SALES (corp-wide): 666.9MM **Privately Held**
SIC: 7363 Engineering help service
PA: Belcan, Llc
10200 Anderson Way
Blue Ash OH 45242
513 891-0972

(G-16984)
BREEZY POINT LTD PARTNERSHIP (PA)
Also Called: Heritage Development
30575 Bnbridge Rd Ste 100 (44139)
PHONE..................................440 247-3363
Don Pepin, *VP Opers*
James A Schoff,
John Mc Gill,
Bert Wolstein,
Scott Wolstein,
EMP: 130
SQ FT: 6,000
SALES (est): 11.8MM **Privately Held**
SIC: 6552 7997 Land subdividers & developers, residential; golf club, membership

(G-16985)
BRENNAN INDUSTRIES INC
30205 Solon Rd (44139-3411)
PHONE..................................440 248-7088
Fax: 440 248-9375
David Carr, *President*
Bill Jarrell, *Vice Pres*
Ted Moyer, *Vice Pres*
EMP: 30
SALES (corp-wide): 40.1MM **Privately Held**
WEB: www.brennaninc.com
SIC: 5085 Valves & fittings
PA: Brennan Industries, Inc.
6701 Cochran Rd
Cleveland OH 44139
440 248-1880

(G-16986)
BROWNING-FERRIS INDUSTRIES LLC
Also Called: Republic Services
30300 Pettibone Rd (44139-5414)
PHONE..................................440 786-9390
Fax: 440 786-9690
Dave Matthews, *Branch Mgr*
EMP: 38
SALES (corp-wide): 10B **Publicly Held**
SIC: 4953 Refuse collection & disposal services
HQ: Browning-Ferris Industries, Llc
18500 N Allied Way # 100
Phoenix AZ 85054
480 627-2700

(G-16987)
CARNEGIE COMPANIES INC
6190 Cochran Rd Ste A (44139-3323)
PHONE..................................440 232-2300
Paul Pesses, *President*
Peter Meisel, *Exec VP*
Caryn Weinberg, *Controller*
Lucy Vila, *Asst Controller*
Cole Pesses, *Marketing Staff*
EMP: 50
SQ FT: 20,000
SALES (est): 4.8MM **Privately Held**
WEB: www.carnegiecos.com
SIC: 6531 Real estate agent, commercial; real estate agent, residential

(G-16908)
CARTEMP USA INC (PA)
29100 Aurora Rd (44139-1855)
PHONE..................................440 715-1000
Fax: 216 715-1000
Ed Hammer, *General Ptnr*
Snappy Funding Corp, *General Ptnr*
EMP: 250
SALES (est): 4MM **Privately Held**
SIC: 7514 Rent-a-car service

(G-16989)
CASTLE HEATING & AIR INC
30355 Solon Indus Pkwy (44139-4325)
PHONE..................................216 696-3940
Fax: 216 696-3942
Mark Boucher, *President*
Marybeth Gavak, *Controller*
Bridget Herron, *Finance Mgr*
EMP: 25

Solon - Cuyahoga County (G-16990)

SQ FT: 14,000
SALES (est): 4.4MM **Privately Held**
WEB: www.castlehvac.net
SIC: **1711** Warm air heating & air conditioning contractor

(G-16990)
CELLCO PARTNERSHIP
Also Called: Verizon Wireless
6440 Som Center Rd Ste C (44139-6806)
PHONE.................................440 542-9631
Fax: 440 542-9636
Antonio Martin, *Manager*
EMP: 71
SALES (corp-wide): 126B **Publicly Held**
SIC: **4812** Cellular telephone services
HQ: Cellco Partnership
1 Verizon Way
Basking Ridge NJ 07920

(G-16991)
CINCINNATI EQUITABLE INSUR CO
Also Called: Equitable Life Assurance
5910 Harper Rd Ste 100 (44139-1886)
PHONE.................................440 349-2210
Ken Uveges, *President*
John Lohrman, *Sales Mgr*
Gary Uveges, *Admin Sec*
EMP: 27 **Privately Held**
WEB: www.1826.com
SIC: **6411** Insurance agents, brokers & service
HQ: Cincinnati Equitable Insurance Company
525 Vine St Ste 1925
Cincinnati OH 45202
513 621-1826

(G-16992)
CITY OF SOLON
Also Called: Solon Fire Department
34025 Bainbridge Rd (44139-3002)
PHONE.................................440 248-6939
William Shaw, *Chief*
EMP: 50 **Privately Held**
SIC: **7389** Fire protection service other than forestry or public
PA: City Of Solon
34200 Bainbridge Rd
Solon OH 44139
440 248-1155

(G-16993)
CLEVELAND HARBOR BELT RR LLC
Also Called: Chb
29930 Pettibone Rd (44139-5407)
PHONE.................................440 746-0801
William D Brown, *Administration*
EMP: 26
SALES (est): 863K
SALES (corp-wide): 4.7MM **Privately Held**
SIC: **4011** Railroads, line-haul operating
PA: Cleveland Commercial Railroad Company, Llc
29930 Pettibone Rd
Solon OH 44139
440 746-0801

(G-16994)
CORE-MARK OHIO
30300 Emerald Valley Pkwy (44139-4394)
PHONE.................................650 589-9445
Tom Perkins, *CEO*
EMP: 150 **EST:** 2014
SQ FT: 179,000
SALES (est): 100.6MM **Privately Held**
SIC: **5194** Cigarettes

(G-16995)
CORPORATE PLANS INC
Also Called: CPI-Hr
6830 Cochran Rd (44139-3966)
PHONE.................................440 542-7800
Fax: 440 542-7801
James Hopkins, *CEO*
Brian Meharry, *President*
Elaine Ferretti, *Vice Pres*
Mike Grinnell, *Vice Pres*
Kirsten Tudman, *Vice Pres*
EMP: 35
SQ FT: 3,000
SALES (est): 4.3MM **Privately Held**
WEB: www.cpihr.com
SIC: **8742 6411** Compensation & benefits planning consultant; insurance agents, brokers & service

(G-16996)
COSMAX USA INC COSMAX USA CORP
30701 Carter St (44139-3515)
PHONE.................................440 600-5738
Howard Lim, *Principal*
Kent Puthoff, *Purch Mgr*
Barbara Hach, *QC Mgr*
Alyssa Kim, *Research*
Kerri Yarbrough, *Hum Res Coord*
▲ EMP: 50
SALES (est): 46.4MM
SALES (corp-wide): 19.7MM **Privately Held**
SIC: **5122** Cosmetics
PA: Cosmax Bti, Inc.
Rm F-801 Pangyo Innovalley
Seongnam 13486
823 178-9330

(G-16997)
CREATIVE PLAYROOM
Also Called: Solon Creative Playroom Center
32750 Solon Rd Ste 3 (44139-2865)
PHONE.................................440 248-3100
Fax: 440 248-3410
Joan Wenk, *Owner*
Kathleen Milliken, *Exec Dir*
EMP: 35
SALES (corp-wide): 1.8MM **Privately Held**
SIC: **8351** Montessori child development center
PA: Creative Playroom
16574 Broadway Ave
Cleveland OH 44137
216 475-6464

(G-16998)
CREATIVE PLAYROOMS INC (PA)
32750 Solon Rd Ste 3 (44139-2865)
PHONE.................................440 349-9111
Joan P Wenk, *President*
Debbie Pack, *Director*
EMP: 25
SQ FT: 5,440
SALES (est): 3.7MM **Privately Held**
SIC: **8351** Child day care services

(G-16999)
CUSTOM PRODUCTS CORPORATION (PA)
7100 Cochran Rd (44139-4306)
PHONE.................................440 528-7100
Fax: 440 528-0140
Timothy Stepanek, *President*
John Stepanek, *Vice Pres*
William Stepanek Jr, *Vice Pres*
Christopher Stepanek, *Project Mgr*
Ashley Cross, *Buyer*
EMP: 78 **EST:** 1974
SQ FT: 82,000
SALES (est): 14.6MM **Privately Held**
WEB: www.customproducts.net
SIC: **7389 5131 5199 2761** Packaging & labeling services; labels; packaging materials; manifold business forms; commercial printing; packaging paper & plastics film, coated & laminated

(G-17000)
DATASCAN FIELD SERVICES LLC
30600 Aurora Rd Ste 180 (44139-2761)
PHONE.................................440 914-7300
Colin Brown, *CEO*
April Maynard, *Controller*
Lamicca Blackwell, *Accountant*
Brian Koprowski,
EMP: 25
SQ FT: 10,500
SALES (est): 4.2MM **Privately Held**
WEB: www.datascantech.com
SIC: **7373** Systems integration services

(G-17001)
EFFICIENT COLLABORATIVE RETAIL (PA)
Also Called: Ecrm
27070 Miles Rd Ste A (44139-1162)
PHONE.................................440 498-0500
Fax: 440 498-0900
Greg Farrar, *CEO*
Wayne Bennett, *Senior VP*
Brian Nelson, *CFO*
Cameron Rosenstrach, *Sales Mgr*
Kelsee Haight, *Accounts Mgr*
EMP: 56
SQ FT: 6,000
SALES (est): 34.2MM **Privately Held**
WEB: www.ecrm-epps.com
SIC: **8742** Marketing consulting services

(G-17002)
EMERGENCY RESPONSE & TRNNG
Also Called: Erts
6001 Cochran Rd (44139-3310)
P.O. Box 72333, Cleveland (44192-0002)
PHONE.................................440 349-2700
Clay Richter, *President*
Ed Ballash, *Vice Pres*
Nate Walden, *VP Opers*
Philip Blashford, *Project Mgr*
Brian Clukey, *Project Mgr*
EMP: 50
SALES (est): 1.9MM
SALES (corp-wide): 367.3MM **Privately Held**
WEB: www.ertsonline.com
SIC: **8748** Environmental consultant
PA: Hepaco, Llc
2711 Burch Dr
Charlotte NC 28269
704 598-9787

(G-17003)
ENTERPRISE CONSTRUCTION INC
30505 Bnbridge Rd Ste 200 (44139)
PHONE.................................440 349-3443
David Jezek, *President*
EMP: 25
SALES (est): 3.3MM **Privately Held**
SIC: **1521 1542** New construction, single-family houses; commercial & office building, new construction

(G-17004)
ENVIROCHEMICAL INC
29325 Aurora Rd (44139-1848)
PHONE.................................440 287-2200
Brian Fox, *President*
A Richard Valore, *Principal*
Keith Karakul, *Vice Pres*
Robin Burns, *Manager*
Turner Tom, *Director*
EMP: 35
SALES (est): 9MM **Privately Held**
WEB: www.envirochemical.net
SIC: **5087** Janitors' supplies

(G-17005)
F I L US INC (HQ)
Also Called: Baldwin International
30403 Bruce Indus Pkwy (44139-3941)
PHONE.................................440 248-9500
Fax: 440 248-9500
Edward Webber, *CEO*
G W Goertz, *President*
Edward Weber, *COO*
J D Sherwood, *Vice Pres*
▲ EMP: 25
SQ FT: 44,500
SALES (est): 6.8MM
SALES (corp-wide): 1.9B **Privately Held**
WEB: www.filus.com
SIC: **5051** Steel
PA: Russel Metals Inc
6600 Financial Dr
Mississauga ON L5N 7
905 819-7777

(G-17006)
FAK GROUP INC
Also Called: Raf Automation
6750 Arnold Miller Pkwy (44139-4363)
PHONE.................................440 498-8465
Fax: 440 498-8475
Thomas J Koly, *President*
Willard E Frissell, *Corp Secy*
EMP: 28 **EST:** 1953
SQ FT: 22,000
SALES (est): 6.8MM
SALES (corp-wide): 76.9MM **Privately Held**
WEB: www.raffluidpower.com
SIC: **7629** Electrical equipment repair services
PA: Electro-Matic Ventures, Inc.
23409 Industrial Park Ct
Farmington Hills MI 48335
248 478-1182

(G-17007)
FINDAWAY WORLD LLC
31999 Aurora Rd (44139-2853)
PHONE.................................440 893-0808
Mitch Kroll, *CEO*
Howard Alston, *Sales Mgr*
Andrew Goldstein, *Manager*
Jon Sustar, *Manager*
Lauren Spilman,
▲ EMP: 100
SALES (est): 15.4MM **Privately Held**
WEB: www.playawaydigital.com
SIC: **5999 8331 3669 5192** Audio-visual equipment & supplies; job training & vocational rehabilitation services; visual communication systems; periodicals

(G-17008)
GARDINER SERVICE COMPANY (PA)
31200 Bainbridge Rd Ste 1 (44139-2298)
P.O. Box 39280 (44139-0280)
PHONE.................................440 248-3400
Fax: 440 349-6980
Robert M Case, *CEO*
William H Gardiner, *Ch of Bd*
Todd Barnhart, *President*
Michael R Reder, *Treasurer*
Richard Reder, *Controller*
EMP: 160
SQ FT: 32,000
SALES (est): 64.2MM **Privately Held**
WEB: www.gardinertrane.com
SIC: **5075 1711 7623** Air conditioning & ventilation equipment & supplies; plumbing, heating, air-conditioning contractors; refrigeration service & repair; air conditioning repair

(G-17009)
GLAVIN INDUSTRIES INC
Also Called: Glavin Specialty Co
6835 Cochran Rd Ste A (44139-3927)
P.O. Box 391316 (44139-8316)
PHONE.................................440 349-0049
Fax: 440 786-7446
Julia S Glavin, *CEO*
David H Glavin, *President*
Jody Kapsandy, *General Mgr*
EMP: 25
SQ FT: 23,000
SALES (est): 15.6MM **Privately Held**
SIC: **5084 3993 2759** Industrial machinery & equipment; signs & advertising specialties; screen printing

(G-17010)
GLAZERS DISTRIBUTORS OHIO INC
7800 Cochran Rd (44139-4342)
PHONE.................................440 542-7000
EMP: 25
SALES (corp-wide): 5.8B **Privately Held**
SIC: **5181 5182** Beer & ale; wine & distilled beverages
HQ: Southern Glazer's Distributors Of Ohio, Llc
4800 Poth Rd
Columbus OH 43213

(G-17011)
GORBETT ENTERPRISES OF SOLON (PA)
Also Called: Great Lakes Cold Storage
6531 Cochran Rd (44139-3959)
PHONE.................................440 248-3950
Patrick J Gorbett, *President*
Michael Calko, *Plant Supt*
John Grill, *Controller*
Harry Zegeiler, *Manager*
David Lowden,
EMP: 30

Solon - Cuyahoga County

SQ FT: 240,000
SALES (est): 14.2MM **Privately Held**
SIC: 4222 Warehousing, cold storage or refrigerated

(G-17012)
GREAT LAKES TEXTILES INC (PA)
Also Called: Glt Products
6810 Cochran Rd (44139-3908)
PHONE..................440 439-1300
Steven Wake, *President*
Joel Hammer, *Vice Pres*
Patrick Burch, *Plant Mgr*
Marinko Milos, *CFO*
Julie Mecone, *Controller*
◆ **EMP:** 47
SQ FT: 117,000
SALES (est): 15.6MM **Privately Held**
WEB: www.gltproducts.com
SIC: 2821 5033 5131 5085 Polyvinylidene chloride resins; insulation materials; tape, textile; industrial supplies

(G-17013)
GRL ENGINEERS INC (PA)
30725 Aurora Rd (44139-2735)
PHONE..................216 831-6131
Patrick Hannigan, *President*
Jamie Dhondt, *General Mgr*
Mohamad Hussein, *Vice Pres*
Mark Rawlings, *Site Mgr*
Karen Webster, *Site Mgr*
EMP: 30 **EST:** 1976
SALES (est): 5.4MM **Privately Held**
SIC: 8734 Testing laboratories

(G-17014)
HD SUPPLY FACILITIES MAINT LTD
30311 Emerald Valley Pkwy (44139-4339)
PHONE..................440 542-9188
Steve Yaney, *Manager*
Jim Angelo, *Manager*
Jim Deangelo, *Manager*
Cantrell Johnson, *Manager*
EMP: 40 **Publicly Held**
SIC: 5087 5072 5085 Cleaning & maintenance equipment & supplies; hardware; industrial supplies
HQ: Hd Supply Facilities Maintenance, Ltd.
3100 Cumberland Blvd Se # 1700
Atlanta GA 30339
770 852-9000

(G-17015)
HOWARD HANNA SMYTHE CRAMER
6240 Som Center Rd # 100 (44139-2950)
PHONE..................440 248-3000
EMP: 50
SALES (corp-wide): 76.4MM **Privately Held**
SIC: 6531 Real estate brokers & agents
HQ: Howard Hanna Smythe Cramer
6000 Parkland Blvd
Cleveland OH 44124
216 447-4477

(G-17016)
HUNTER DEFENSE TECH INC (PA)
Also Called: Hdt Engineered Technologies
30500 Aurora Rd Ste 100 (44139-2776)
PHONE..................216 438-6111
Sean Bond, *President*
Mike Hoffman, *Managing Prtnr*
Dilucente Anthony, *Exec VP*
Greg Miller, *Senior VP*
Carl Pates, *Senior VP*
▲ **EMP:** 50
SQ FT: 26,000
SALES (est): 241.4MM **Privately Held**
SIC: 3433 3569 3822 8331 Room & wall heaters, including radiators; filters; auto controls regulating residntl & coml environmt & applncs; sheltered workshop; engineering services; assembly machines, including robotic

(G-17017)
IMPERIAL HEATING AND COOLG INC (PA)
30685 Solon Industrial Pk (44139-4388)
PHONE..................440 498-1788
Fax: 440 498-1388
Todd Rickard Ozanich, *President*
Mark Harris, *Accounts Mgr*
Bob Campus, *Technology*
EMP: 54
SQ FT: 19,000
SALES (est): 12.8MM **Privately Held**
WEB: www.imperialhvac.com
SIC: 1711 Warm air heating & air conditioning contractor

(G-17018)
INTERDESIGN INC
Also Called: Swiss Tech Products
30725 Solon Indus Pkwy (44139-4380)
P.O. Box 39606 (44139-0606)
PHONE..................440 248-0136
Fax: 440 248-0178
Chris Quinn, *CEO*
Robert Immerman, *President*
Chris Banning, *Exec VP*
Joyce Libman, *Vice Pres*
Jason Shefrin, *Vice Pres*
◆ **EMP:** 280 **EST:** 1974
SQ FT: 178,096
SALES (est): 178MM **Privately Held**
WEB: www.interdesignusa.com
SIC: 5023 Home furnishings

(G-17019)
IRON MOUNTAIN INFO MGT LLC
5101 Naiman Pkwy Ste B (44139-1018)
PHONE..................440 248-0999
Travis Glasper, *Manager*
Meg Caddick, *Director*
EMP: 101
SALES (corp-wide): 3.8B **Publicly Held**
SIC: 4226 8742 Document & office records storage; management consulting services
HQ: Iron Mountain Information Management, Llc
1 Federal St
Boston MA 02110
800 899-4766

(G-17020)
JAINCO INTERNATIONAL INC
Also Called: Jaincotech
30405 Solon Rd Ste 9 (44139-3477)
PHONE..................440 519-0100
Suresh Bafna, *CEO*
Jasvinder Mandair, *President*
Vijay Sharma, *CFO*
Vaishali Gala, *Marketing Staff*
▲ **EMP:** 250
SQ FT: 30,000
SALES (est): 20.4MM **Privately Held**
SIC: 5032 Granite building stone

(G-17021)
KEITHLEY INSTRUMENTS LLC (DH)
28775 Aurora Rd (44139-1891)
PHONE..................440 248-0400
Fax: 440 248-6168
Joseph P Keithley, *President*
Steve Greer, *Business Mgr*
Linda C Rae, *COO*
Philip R Etsler, *Vice Pres*
Alan S Gaffney, *Vice Pres*
▲ **EMP:** 124 **EST:** 1946
SQ FT: 125,000
SALES: 92.3MM
SALES (corp-wide): 6.6B **Publicly Held**
SIC: 3825 3823 7371 Instruments to measure electricity; test equipment for electronic & electric measurement; multimeters; semiconductor test equipment; computer interface equipment for industrial process control; computer software development
HQ: Tektronix, Inc.
14150 Sw Karl Braun Dr
Beaverton OR 97005
800 833-9200

(G-17022)
KINDERCARE LEARNING CTRS LLC
Also Called: Kindercare Child Care Network
6140 Kruse Dr (44139-2374)
PHONE..................440 248-5437
Fax: 440 519-1106
Julie Felder, *Manager*
EMP: 25
SALES (corp-wide): 1.2B **Privately Held**
WEB: www.kindercare.com
SIC: 8351 Nursery school
HQ: Kindercare Learning Centers, Llc
650 Ne Holladay St # 1400
Portland OR 97232
503 872-1300

(G-17023)
LUTHERAN MEDICAL CENTER (HQ)
Also Called: Lutheran Hospital
33001 Solon Rd Ste 112 (44139-2864)
PHONE..................216 696-4300
Fax: 216 696-7407
David Pesre MD, *CEO*
Christopher Winters, *CFO*
Elizabeth Winter, *Human Res Dir*
Virginia R Tipton, *Office Mgr*
Leslie J Gilbert MD, *Med Doctor*
EMP: 320
SQ FT: 350,000
SALES: 111MM
SALES (corp-wide): 8B **Privately Held**
SIC: 8062 8011 8069 General medical & surgical hospitals; offices & clinics of medical doctors; specialty hospitals, except psychiatric
PA: The Cleveland Clinic Foundation
9500 Euclid Ave
Cleveland OH 44195
216 636-8335

(G-17024)
M & A DISTRIBUTING CO INC (PA)
Also Called: M & A Distribution
31031 Diamond Pkwy (44139-5463)
PHONE..................440 703-4580
John M Antonucci, *President*
Jason Edwards, *Director*
EMP: 37
SQ FT: 12,000
SALES (est): 53.7MM **Privately Held**
SIC: 5182 5181 Wine & distilled beverages; beer & other fermented malt liquors

(G-17025)
MAJESTIC TOOL AND MACHINE INC
30700 Carter St Ste C (44139-3585)
PHONE..................440 248-5058
Fax: 440 786-2622
Walter Krueger, *President*
Kurt Krueger, *Vice Pres*
Todd Krueger, *Vice Pres*
EMP: 32
SQ FT: 30,000
SALES: 2.5MM **Privately Held**
SIC: 3599 7692 3544 Machine shop, jobbing & repair; welding repair; special dies, tools, jigs & fixtures

(G-17026)
MARRIOTT
31225 Bainbridge Rd Ste A (44139-2293)
PHONE..................440 542-2375
Amy Oblinger, *Owner*
Charles Kirkland, *Human Res Dir*
EMP: 30
SALES (est): 1.6MM **Privately Held**
SIC: 7011 Hotels & motels

(G-17027)
MILES FARMERS MARKET INC
28560 Miles Rd (44139-1184)
PHONE..................440 248-5222
Fax: 440 248-5222
Frank Cangemi, *President*
Joseph Degaetano, *Vice Pres*
Dave Rondini, *Vice Pres*
Debbie Slak, *Office Mgr*
Bill Papczun, *Manager*
EMP: 150
SQ FT: 50,000
SALES (est): 14.9MM **Privately Held**
WEB: www.milesfarmersmarket.com
SIC: 5431 5148 Fruit stands or markets; fruits, fresh

(G-17028)
MILLWOOD INC
30311 Emerald Valley Pkwu (44139)
PHONE..................440 914-0540
Fax: 440 914-0543
Vern Walker, *Branch Mgr*
Carla Cotter, *Director*
EMP: 115 **Privately Held**
SIC: 5031 Pallets, wood
PA: Millwood, Inc.
3708 International Blvd
Vienna OH 44473

(G-17029)
MP BIOMEDICALS LLC
29525 Fountain Pkwy (44139-4351)
PHONE..................440 337-1200
Fax: 330 337-1180
Samson Chen, *General Mgr*
Nebojsa Pesic, *Vice Pres*
Rhonda Gilmartin, *Opers Staff*
Avenir Liu, *Human Res Mgr*
Dana Hummel, *Cust Mgr*
EMP: 130
SALES (corp-wide): 370.7MM **Privately Held**
WEB: www.mpbio.com
SIC: 8731 2869 2834 8071 Biological research; enzymes; pharmaceutical preparations; medical laboratories; medical research
HQ: Mp Biomedicals, Llc
3 Hutton Centre Dr # 100
Santa Ana CA 92707
949 833-2500

(G-17030)
MRI SOFTWARE LLC (PA)
28925 Fountain Pkwy (44139-4356)
PHONE..................800 327-8770
Patrick Ghilani, *CEO*
John Ensign, *Exec VP*
David Carner, *Vice Pres*
Nick Constantino, *Vice Pres*
Marc Dicapua, *Vice Pres*
EMP: 101
SQ FT: 44,000
SALES (est): 138.3MM **Privately Held**
WEB: www.mrisoftware.com
SIC: 7374 7371 6531 Data processing & preparation; computer software development; real estate agents & managers; real estate managers

(G-17031)
MUSTARD SEED HEALTH FD MKT INC
6025 Kruse Dr Ste 100 (44139-2378)
PHONE..................440 519-3663
Fax: 440 519-0623
Margaret Kanfer-Nabors, *Ch of Bd*
Bill Goodwin, *Financial Exec*
Ann Vojta, *Human Res Mgr*
Greg James, *Info Tech Mgr*
EMP: 35
SALES (corp-wide): 59.5MM **Privately Held**
WEB: www.mustardseedmarket.com
SIC: 5499 7299 5812 2051 Gourmet food stores; banquet hall facilities; caterers; bread, cake & related products
PA: Mustard Seed Health Food Market, Inc.
3885 Medina Rd
Akron OH 44333
330 666-7333

(G-17032)
NATIONAL ENTP SYSTEMS INC (PA)
Also Called: Nes
29125 Solon Rd (44139-3442)
PHONE..................440 542-1360
Fax: 440 542-1380
Ernest Pollak, *President*
Chris Pollak, *General Mgr*
Bob Deter, *Vice Pres*
Ellen Pollak, *Vice Pres*
Jeff Pollak, *Vice Pres*
EMP: 350 **EST:** 1987
SQ FT: 48,000
SALES (est): 45.6MM **Privately Held**
WEB: www.nes1.com
SIC: 7322 Collection agency, except real estate

(G-17033)
NETSMART TECHNOLOGIES INC
Also Called: Trend Consulting Services
30775 Bnbridge Rd Ste 200 (44139)
PHONE..................440 942-4040

Solon - Cuyahoga County (G-17034)

Michael Valentine, *CEO*
Michelle Walters, *Manager*
Shana Chapman, *Consultant*
Adrian Stovall, *Software Dev*
John Gohman, *Director*
EMP: 39 **Privately Held**
SIC: 7379 7372 Computer related consulting services; business oriented computer software
PA: Netsmart Technologies, Inc.
4950 College Blvd
Overland Park KS 66211

(G-17034) NOBLE-DAVIS CONSULTING INC
6190 Cochran Rd Ste D (44139-3323)
PHONE.................................440 519-0850
Fax: 440 498-9566
Pamela Noble, *President*
Jan L Davis, *Vice Pres*
Jesica Wilfong, *Manager*
James Abrams, *Consultant*
EMP: 25
SQ FT: 7,200
SALES (est): 4.5MM **Privately Held**
WEB: www.noblepension.com
SIC: 6411 Pension & retirement plan consultants

(G-17035) NOCO COMPANY
30339 Diamond Pkwy # 102 (44139-5473)
PHONE.................................216 464-8131
Fax: 216 464-8131
William K Nook, *President*
Luke Case, *Vice Pres*
Kevin Tucker, *CFO*
John Nook, *VP Sales*
▲ **EMP:** 500 EST: 1914
SQ FT: 100,000
SALES (est): 29.3MM **Privately Held**
WEB: www.noco-usa.com
SIC: 3694 3714 3315 2899 Battery cable wiring sets for internal combustion engines; booster (jump-start) cables, automotive; filters: oil, fuel & air, motor vehicle; steel wire & related products; chemical preparations; wire & cable; power tools & accessories

(G-17036) ON SEARCH PARTNERS LLC
6240 Som Center Rd # 230 (44139-2950)
PHONE.................................440 318-1006
Joshua Nathanson, *Partner*
Kristin Barnes, *Vice Pres*
Kaycey Bruhn, *Project Mgr*
Greg Kleeh CPA, *CFO*
Jennifer Bodovetz, *Office Mgr*
EMP: 27
SALES (est): 1.5MM **Privately Held**
SIC: 7361 Executive placement

(G-17037) P K WADSWORTH HEATING & COOLG
34280 Solon Rd Frnt (44139-2668)
PHONE.................................440 248-4821
Fax: 440 248-2110
Paul K Wadsworth Jr, *President*
Tyler Wadsworth, *Design Engr*
Craig Hoffman, *Controller*
Bonnie Wargis, *Controller*
Dan Benes, *Manager*
EMP: 45
SQ FT: 6,000
SALES (est): 8.9MM **Privately Held**
WEB: www.pkwadsworth.com
SIC: 1711 Warm air heating & air conditioning contractor

(G-17038) PAUL MOSS LLC
Also Called: Moss Affiliate Marketing
5895 Harper Rd (44139-1832)
PHONE.................................216 765-1580
Kate Budd, *Senior VP*
David Scott, *Opers Mgr*
Brock Thompson, *Marketing Mgr*
Jason Pasciak, *CTO*
Paul Moss,
EMP: 35 EST: 2009
SALES (est): 3.5MM **Privately Held**
SIC: 6411 Insurance information & consulting services

(G-17039) PHYSICIAN STAFFING INC
Also Called: Martin Healthcare Group, The
30680 Bainbridge Rd Lowr (44139-2268)
PHONE.................................440 542-1950
John S Martin III, *President*
David Martin, *Vice Pres*
John H Elffers, *VP Mktg*
Leopoldo Alvarado, *Med Doctor*
Martin David, *CIO*
EMP: 365
SQ FT: 10,000
SALES (est): 21.3MM **Privately Held**
WEB: www.physicianstaffing.com
SIC: 7363 Medical help service

(G-17040) PIPELINE PACKAGING CORPORATION (HQ)
30310 Emerald Valley Pkwy (44139-4394)
PHONE.................................440 349-3200
Fax: 330 405-9688
Christopher I Page, *Ch of Bd*
Christopher Nelson, *President*
Josh Stewart, *Business Mgr*
Rosie Jenkins, *Purchasing*
Daniel Herbert, *CFO*
▲ **EMP:** 30
SQ FT: 85,000
SALES (est): 114.3MM
SALES (corp-wide): 132MM **Privately Held**
SIC: 5099 Containers: glass, metal or plastic
PA: Cleveland Steel Container Corporation
30310 Emerald Valley Pkwy
Solon OH 44139
440 349-8000

(G-17041) PRIORITY DISPATCH INC
5385 Naiman Pkwy (44139-1007)
PHONE.................................216 332-9852
Dan Walter, *Branch Mgr*
EMP: 25
SALES (corp-wide): 16.1MM **Privately Held**
SIC: 4212 4215 Delivery service, vehicular; courier services, except by air
PA: Priority Dispatch, Inc.
4665 Malsbary Rd
Blue Ash OH 45242
513 791-3900

(G-17042) PTMJ ENTERPRISES
32000 Aurora Rd (44139-2875)
P.O. Box 391437 (44139-8437)
PHONE.................................440 543-8000
Fax: 440 543-7077
Peter Joyce, *President*
Joe Miller, *Opers Staff*
Kimberly Greer, *Office Mgr*
▲ **EMP:** 180
SALES (est): 34.4MM **Privately Held**
WEB: www.signum-inc.com
SIC: 2541 1799 Display fixtures, wood; closet organizers, installation & design

(G-17043) PYRAMYD AIR LTD (PA)
5135 Naiman Pkwy (44139-1003)
PHONE.................................216 896-0893
Val Gamerman, *Partner*
Joshua Ungier, *General Ptnr*
Tom Chandler, *Business Mgr*
Nicole Mendelsohn, *Vice Pres*
Todd Bahr, *Warehouse Mgr*
▲ **EMP:** 40
SQ FT: 22,500
SALES (est): 9.7MM **Privately Held**
WEB: www.pyramydair.com
SIC: 5941 5092 Firearms; toys

(G-17044) R L MORRISSEY & ASSOC INC (PA)
Also Called: American Ring & Tool Co
30450 Bruce Indus Pkwy (44139-3940)
P.O. Box 75510, Cleveland (44101-4200)
PHONE.................................440 498-3730
Fax: 440 498-2432
James N Morrissey, *President*
William F Chinnock, *Principal*
Robert H Morrissey, *Corp Secy*
Jack Morrissey, *Vice Pres*
▲ **EMP:** 40
SQ FT: 28,000
SALES (est): 26MM **Privately Held**
SIC: 5085 5051 5013 Fasteners, industrial: nuts, bolts, screws, etc.; stampings, metal; automotive supplies & parts

(G-17045) REIMER LAW CO
30455 Solon Rd Ste 1 (44139-3435)
PHONE.................................440 600-5500
Fax: 330 425-2155
Dennis Reimer, *President*
Michael Lorber, *Vice Pres*
Jill Cohn, *Human Res Dir*
Jeannie Mocny, *Manager*
Nicole Alling, *Business Dir*
EMP: 150
SALES (est): 7.1MM **Privately Held**
WEB: www.reimerlaw.com
SIC: 8111 General practice attorney, lawyer

(G-17046) RELAM INC
Also Called: Railway Equipment Lsg & Maint
7695 Bond St (44139-5350)
PHONE.................................440 232-3354
Carl Eberhardt, *President*
Linda Ertel, *Corp Secy*
David Horth, *Shareholder*
EMP: 35
SQ FT: 4,800
SALES (est): 10.4MM **Privately Held**
SIC: 7353 Heavy construction equipment rental

(G-17047) REXEL USA INC
2699 Solon Sales 30310 (44139)
PHONE.................................440 248-3800
Robert A Shupp, *Assistant VP*
Orman Malkes, *Accounts Mgr*
Mark Shenker, *Sales Staff*
Dave Gerding, *Branch Mgr*
Richard Kinkopf, *Director*
EMP: 70
SQ FT: 5,000
SALES (corp-wide): 3MM **Privately Held**
WEB: www.rexelusa.com
SIC: 5063 Electrical supplies
HQ: Rexel Usa, Inc.
14951 Dallas Pkwy
Dallas TX 75254

(G-17048) ROTO-ROOTER SERVICES COMPANY
5375 Naiman Pkwy (44139-1007)
PHONE.................................216 429-1928
Rick Beechy, *Manager*
EMP: 40
SALES (corp-wide): 1.6BB **Publicly Held**
SIC: 7699 Sewer cleaning & rodding
HQ: Roto-Rooter Services Company
255 E 5th St Ste 2500
Cincinnati OH 45202
513 762-6690

(G-17049) SCHWEBEL BAKING COMPANY
Also Called: Schwebel Baking Co-Solon Bky
6250 Camp Industrial Rd (44139-2750)
PHONE.................................440 248-1500
Dave Gulau, *Plant Engr*
Grant West, *Manager*
EMP: 150
SALES (corp-wide): 170MM **Privately Held**
WEB: www.schwebels.com
SIC: 5461 5149 2051 Bread; groceries & related products; bread, cake & related products
PA: Schwebel Baking Company
965 E Midlothian Blvd
Youngstown OH 44502
330 783-2860

(G-17050) SERVICELINK FIELD SERVICES LLC
30825 Aurora Rd Ste 140 (44139-2733)
PHONE.................................440 424-0058
Robert J Caruso, *President*
EMP: 709
SALES (est): 28.4MM
SALES (corp-wide): 7.6B **Publicly Held**
SIC: 7389 Inspection & testing services
HQ: Black Knight Infoserv, Llc
601 Riverside Ave
Jacksonville FL 32204

(G-17051) SIGNUM LLC
32000 Aurora Rd Ste C (44139-2849)
PHONE.................................440 248-2233
Todd McCuaig,
EMP: 100
SALES (est): 12MM **Privately Held**
SIC: 7319 Sample distribution

(G-17052) SNF WADSWORTH LLC
Also Called: Golden Leaf
5625 Emerald Ridge Pkwy (44139-1860)
PHONE.................................330 336-3472
Melissa Nelson, *Mng Member*
EMP: 80
SALES (est): 672.3K **Privately Held**
SIC: 8051 Skilled nursing care facilities

(G-17053) SOLON LODGING ASSOCIATES LLC
Also Called: Springhill Suites
30100 Aurora Rd (44139-2730)
PHONE.................................440 248-9600
Fax: 440 248-9120
Brent Fountain, *General Mgr*
Bridget Graff, *General Mgr*
Pamela Keeven, *General Mgr*
Jeannie Ventura, *Sales Dir*
Ron Kindall,
EMP: 26
SALES (est): 2.3MM
SALES (corp-wide): 22.8B **Publicly Held**
WEB: www.buffalolodging.com
SIC: 7011 Hotels & motels
PA: Marriott International, Inc.
10400 Fernwood Rd
Bethesda MD 20817
301 380-3000

(G-17054) SOLON PNTE AT EMRALD RIDGE LLC
5625 Emerald Ridge Pkwy (44139-1860)
PHONE.................................440 498-3000
Mark P McGrievy,
EMP: 40
SALES (est): 4.1MM **Privately Held**
SIC: 8051 Convalescent home with continuous nursing care

(G-17055) SOURCE DIAGNOSTICS LLC (PA)
5275 Naiman Pkwy Ste E (44139-1033)
PHONE.................................440 542-9481
Mike Yarwood, *Regional Mgr*
Kathy Barry, *COO*
Ed Salyers, *Technical Mgr*
Keith Marchand, *Mng Member*
David Burns,
EMP: 95
SALES (est): 1.8MM **Privately Held**
WEB: www.sourcediagnostics.com
SIC: 8082 Home health care services

(G-17056) STRATFORD COMMONS INC
7000 Cochran Rd (44139-4304)
PHONE.................................440 914-0900
Fax: 440 914-7494
Maureen Moffatte, *President*
William Altman, *Vice Pres*
Joseph Landenwich, *Vice Pres*
Gregory Miller, *Vice Pres*
Elizabeth Jaworski, *Human Res Dir*
EMP: 179
SALES (est): 8MM **Privately Held**
WEB: www.stratfordcommons.com
SIC: 8059 8052 Nursing home, except skilled & intermediate care facility; intermediate care facilities

GEOGRAPHIC SECTION

South Charleston - Clark County (G-17077)

(G-17057)
SUPERIOR BEVERAGE COMPANY INC
31031 Diamond Pkwy (44139-5463)
PHONE................440 703-4580
John R Antonucci, *President*
John Fleming, *Vice Pres*
David Robinson, *Vice Pres*
EMP: 70
SQ FT: 42,000
SALES (est): 20.2MM **Privately Held**
SIC: 5181 5182 Beer & other fermented malt liquors; wine

(G-17058)
SUPERIOR BEVERAGE GROUP LTD (PA)
31031 Diamond Pkwy (44139-5463)
PHONE................440 703-4580
Fax: 440 232-0673
Mike Caffrey, *Partner*
John W Fleming, *Partner*
Tom Hennes, *Area Mgr*
Chris Sharpe, *Area Mgr*
Joe McHenry, *Exec VP*
▲ EMP: 101
SALES (est): 98.5MM **Privately Held**
SIC: 5149 5499 Beverages, except coffee & tea; beverage stores

(G-17059)
SWAGELOK COMPANY
31400 Aurora Rd (44139-2764)
PHONE................440 349-5934
Fax: 440 349-5934
Jake Boland, *Sales Staff*
Sue Rooth, *Marketing Staff*
Nick Lubar, *Manager*
Linda Fall, *Manager*
Mark Labelle, *Manager*
EMP: 100
SALES (corp-wide): 1.1B **Privately Held**
WEB: www.swagelok.com
SIC: 5051 3593 3498 3494 Tubing, metal; fluid power cylinders & actuators; fabricated pipe & fittings; valves & pipe fittings; fabricated plate work (boiler shop)
PA: Swagelok Company
 29500 Solon Rd
 Solon OH 44139
 440 248-4600

(G-17060)
SYLVANIA LIGHTING SVCS CORP
35405 Spatterdock Ln (44139-6500)
PHONE................440 742-8208
EMP: 25
SALES (corp-wide): 4.8B **Privately Held**
SIC: 7349 Lighting maintenance service
HQ: Sylvania Lighting Services Corp.
 200 Ballardvale St
 Wilmington MA 01887
 978 570-3000

(G-17061)
TTI FLOOR CARE NORTH AMER INC (DH)
Also Called: Royal Appliance Manufacturing
7005 Cochran Rd (44139-4303)
PHONE................440 996-2000
Fax: 440 996-2027
Chris Gurreri, *President*
Dave Chaney, *President*
Mike Ferris, *President*
Scott Jackson, *General Mgr*
Stacy E Cordier, *Vice Pres*
▲ EMP: 350
SQ FT: 450,000
SALES (est): 209MM
SALES (corp-wide): 6B **Privately Held**
SIC: 5072 3825 Power tools & accessories; power measuring equipment, electrical
HQ: Royal Appliance Mfg. Co.
 7005 Cochran Rd
 Cleveland OH 44139
 440 996-2000

(G-17062)
ULTA BEAUTY INC
6025 Kruse Dr (44139-2377)
PHONE................440 248-5618
Brenva Bowser, *Principal*
EMP: 173
SALES (corp-wide): 4.8B **Publicly Held**
SIC: 7231 Beauty shops
PA: Ulta Beauty, Inc.
 1000 Remington Blvd # 120
 Bolingbrook IL 60440
 630 410-4800

(G-17063)
ULYSSES CAREMARK HOLDING CORP
29100 Aurora Rd (44139-1855)
PHONE................440 542-4214
Kenneth Kramer, *VP Opers*
Martha Villalva, *Accountant*
Wendy Brantley, *Branch Mgr*
Steve Kammer, *Director*
EMP: 158
SALES (corp-wide): 374.8MM **Privately Held**
SIC: 6311 Life insurance
PA: Ulysses Caremark Holding Corp
 44 S Broadway Fl 12f
 White Plains NY 10601
 914 934-5200

(G-17064)
VAN DYNE-CROTTY CO
Also Called: Spirit Services
30400 Bruce Indus Pkwy (44139-3929)
PHONE................440 248-6935
Fax: 440 248-6935
Jeff Brewer, *Manager*
EMP: 47
SQ FT: 41,454
SALES (est): 713.6K
SALES (corp-wide): 39MM **Privately Held**
WEB: www.getspirit.com
SIC: 7218 7213 Industrial uniform supply; linen supply
PA: Van Dyne-Crotty Co.
 2150 Fairwood Ave
 Columbus OH 43207
 614 684-0048

(G-17065)
VINCENT LTG SYSTEMS CO INC (PA)
6161 Cochran Rd Ste D (44139-3324)
PHONE................216 475-7600
Paul Vincent, *President*
Patrick Spicuzza, *COO*
Laura Andrado, *Vice Pres*
Christopher Shick, *Vice Pres*
Walter Weber, *Vice Pres*
EMP: 29
SALES (est): 18.1MM **Privately Held**
SIC: 5063 7359 5999 Lighting fixtures; equipment rental & leasing; theatrical equipment & supplies

(G-17066)
WASTE MANAGEMENT OHIO INC
6705 Richmond Rd (44139-2130)
PHONE................440 201-1235
Mark Houser, *Opers Mgr*
Ginger Kaladas, *Credit Staff*
Bobbie J Nahra, *Human Res Mgr*
Paul Pispomo, *Manager*
Colleen Davidson, *Manager*
EMP: 100
SALES (corp-wide): 14.4B **Publicly Held**
WEB: www.wm.com
SIC: 4953 4212 Refuse systems; local trucking, without storage
HQ: Waste Management Of Ohio, Inc.
 1700 N Broad St
 Fairborn OH 45324

(G-17067)
WEYMOUTH VALLEY INC
Also Called: Signature Solon Golf Course
39000 Signature Dr (44139-5266)
PHONE................440 498-8888
Gary Cramer, *CEO*
Jim Repeta, *General Mgr*
Jammi Santamari, *Manager*
Alex Hall, *Executive*
EMP: 31
SQ FT: 5,734
SALES (est): 2MM **Privately Held**
WEB: www.pgmi.net
SIC: 7997 5813 5812 Country club, membership; drinking places; eating places

(G-17068)
WINNCOM TECHNOLOGIES CORP (DH)
28900 Ftn Pkwy Unit B (44139)
PHONE................440 498-9510
Fax: 440 498-9511
Gregory Raskin, *President*
Adriana Chavarro, *Regional Mgr*
Igor Kurochkin, *Vice Pres*
Igor Dovgun, *Project Mgr*
Vlad Furman, *Warehouse Mgr*
◆ EMP: 47
SQ FT: 16,000
SALES (est): 55.2MM **Privately Held**
WEB: www.winncom.com
SIC: 5065 Communication equipment; radio & television equipment & parts; radio parts & accessories

(G-17069)
WORKSPEED MANAGEMENT LLC
28925 Fountain Pkwy (44139-4356)
PHONE................917 369-9025
Derrick Chen, *CEO*
Marcella P Mazzucca, *Chief Mktg Ofcr*
Shaul Halevi, *Director*
EMP: 25
SALES (est): 1.8MM **Privately Held**
WEB: www.workspeed.com
SIC: 7372 Business oriented computer software

Somerset
Perry County

(G-17070)
SOMERSET NH LLC
Also Called: Somerset Hlth Rhbilitation Ctr
411 S Columbus St (43783-9415)
PHONE................740 743-2924
Mordecai Rosenberg, *President*
Ronald Swartz, *CFO*
Dawn Wozniak, *Exec Dir*
Lisa Schwartz, *Admin Sec*
EMP: 79
SALES (est): 383.9K **Privately Held**
SIC: 8051 Skilled nursing care facilities

Somerville
Butler County

(G-17071)
TRI TECH SERVICE SYSTEMS INC
9501 Pleasant Valley Rd (45064-9329)
PHONE................937 787-4664
Fax: 513 423-1612
Justin Paulk, *President*
Paul Coyner, *Manager*
EMP: 200
SALES (est): 4.3MM **Privately Held**
WEB: www.tritechservicesystems.com
SIC: 7349 Building maintenance services

(G-17072)
WOODLAND COUNTRY MANOR INC
4166 Somerville Rd (45064-9707)
PHONE................513 523-4449
Fax: 513 523-7900
Ealeta Dingeldine, *President*
James Thomson, *Director*
Lori Auer, *Administration*
EMP: 35
SQ FT: 1,401
SALES (est): 5.2MM **Privately Held**
SIC: 8051 Convalescent home with continuous nursing care

South Amherst
Lorain County

(G-17073)
ECHOING HILLS VILLAGE INC
Also Called: Echoing Lake/Renouard Home
235 W Main St (44001-2925)
PHONE................440 986-3085
Pat McCraken, *Manager*
EMP: 56
SQ FT: 3,682
SALES (corp-wide): 25.3MM **Privately Held**
WEB: www.echoinghillsvillage.org
SIC: 7032 8059 Sporting & recreational camps; home for the mentally retarded, exc. skilled or intermediate
PA: Echoing Hills Village, Inc.
 36272 County Road 79
 Warsaw OH 43844
 740 327-2311

(G-17074)
REM-OHIO INC
214 W Main St (44001-2926)
PHONE................440 986-3337
Fax: 440 986-2813
Mary Ziccardi, *Exec Dir*
Carla Parker, *Director*
EMP: 25
SALES (corp-wide): 2.8MM **Privately Held**
WEB: www.remohio.com
SIC: 8399 Community development groups
PA: Rem-Ohio, Inc
 6921 York Ave S
 Minneapolis MN 55435
 952 925-5067

South Charleston
Clark County

(G-17075)
BW ENTERPRISES INC
Also Called: National Golf Links
276 Clubhouse Dr (45368-8767)
PHONE................937 568-9660
Fax: 937 568-9520
Robert W Whitmer, *President*
Patsy L Whitmer, *Admin Sec*
EMP: 28
SQ FT: 5,000
SALES: 500K **Privately Held**
SIC: 7992 Public golf courses

(G-17076)
GARICK LLC
Also Called: Paygro
11000 Huntington Rd B (45368-8800)
PHONE................937 462-8350
Fax: 937 462-7101
Rick Mahoney, *Vice Pres*
EMP: 30
SALES (corp-wide): 59.3MM **Privately Held**
WEB: www.garick.com
SIC: 5261 5031 Lawn & garden supplies; lumber, plywood & millwork
PA: Garick, Llc
 13600 Broadway Ave Ste 1
 Cleveland OH 44125
 216 581-0100

(G-17077)
SUNRISE COOPERATIVE INC
149 N Chillicothe St (45368-9744)
P.O. Box R (45368-0818)
PHONE................937 462-8341
Fax: 937 575-6780
Michael Taylor, *Manager*
EMP: 26
SALES (corp-wide): 56.3MM **Privately Held**
SIC: 5191 Feed
PA: Sunrise Cooperative, Inc.
 2025 W State St Ste A
 Fremont OH 43420
 419 332-6468

South Lebanon
Warren County

(G-17078)
LOWES HOME CENTERS LLC
575 Corwin Nixon Blvd (45065-1199)
PHONE..................513 445-1000
Fax: 513 445-1003
Bill Goodlick, *Branch Mgr*
EMP: 158
SALES (corp-wide): 68.6B **Publicly Held**
SIC: 5211 5031 5722 5064 Home centers; building materials, exterior; building materials, interior; household appliance stores; electrical appliances, television & radio
HQ: Lowe's Home Centers, Llc
1605 Curtis Bridge Rd
Wilkesboro NC 28697
336 658-4000

(G-17079)
NVR INC
5153 Riverview Dr (45065-8782)
PHONE..................513 494-0167
Ryan McCarthy, *Branch Mgr*
EMP: 33 **Publicly Held**
SIC: 1521 New construction, single-family houses
PA: Nvr, Inc.
11700 Plaza America Dr # 500
Reston VA 20190

South Point
Lawrence County

(G-17080)
ARMSTRONG UTILITIES INC
9651 County Road 1 (45680-8447)
PHONE..................740 894-3886
D Johnson, *Manager*
EMP: 30 **Privately Held**
SIC: 4899 4813 Television antenna construction & rental;
HQ: Armstrong Utilities, Inc.
1 Armstrong Pl
Butler PA 16001
724 283-0925

(G-17081)
CHATHAM STEEL CORPORATION
235 Commerce Dr (45680-8465)
PHONE..................740 377-9310
EMP: 25
SALES (corp-wide): 8.4B **Publicly Held**
SIC: 5051 Metal Service Center
HQ: Chatham Steel Corporation
501 W Boundary St
Savannah GA 31401
912 233-4182

(G-17082)
DBI SERVICES LLC
2393 County Road 1 (45680-8462)
PHONE..................410 590-4181
Paul D Deangelo, *President*
EMP: 30 **Privately Held**
SIC: 0783 Ornamental shrub & tree services
PA: Dbi Services, Llc
100 N Conahan Dr
Hazleton PA 18201

(G-17083)
DICKSON INDUSTRIAL PARK INC
Also Called: General Refrigeration
719 County Road 1 (45680-8881)
P.O. Box 617 (45680-0617)
PHONE..................740 377-9162
John M Smith, *President*
Mike E Clagg, *Vice Pres*
Aubrey Richardson, *Treasurer*
EMP: 25
SALES (est): 4.5MM **Privately Held**
WEB: www.refrigind.com
SIC: 1711 7623 Refrigeration contractor; refrigeration repair service

(G-17084)
DOLIN SUPPLY CO
702 Solida Rd (45680-8953)
PHONE..................304 529-4171
Marc Cocchiola, *Opers Staff*
Scott Brennen, *Accounts Exec*
Andy Griffin, *Branch Mgr*
Mark Sparks,
Chad Garrison,
EMP: 45
SQ FT: 83,000
SALES (est): 6MM **Publicly Held**
WEB: www.mscdirect.com
SIC: 5085 7353 7694 3496 Industrial supplies; heavy construction equipment rental; armature rewinding shops; miscellaneous fabricated wire products
PA: Msc Industrial Direct Co., Inc.
75 Maxess Rd
Melville NY 11747

(G-17085)
EARLY CONSTRUCTION CO
Also Called: Early Construction Company
307 County Road 120 S (45680-7807)
P.O. Box 551, Huntington WV (25710-0551)
PHONE..................740 894-5150
Jack W Tolliver, *President*
Cindy Marshall, *Bookkeeper*
EMP: 25 EST: 1982
SQ FT: 6,000
SALES (est): 5.9MM **Privately Held**
WEB: www.earlycc.com
SIC: 1799 8711 1542 Construction site cleanup; engineering services; commercial & office building contractors

(G-17086)
GRAND VIEW INN INC
Also Called: Grandview Inn
154 County Road 450 (45680-8853)
PHONE..................740 377-4388
Fax: 740 377-0132
Victor Hardan, *President*
Mark Wittner, *Manager*
EMP: 61
SALES (est): 2.8MM **Privately Held**
SIC: 7011 Hotels

(G-17087)
H & W HOLDINGS LLC
Also Called: Trucking and Logistics
341 County Road 120 S (45680-7807)
P.O. Box 679 (45680-0679)
PHONE..................800 826-3560
Fax: 740 894-0617
Mike Herman, *Owner*
EMP: 50 **Privately Held**
WEB: www.hwtruck.com
SIC: 4212 Local trucking, without storage
HQ: H & W Holdings, Llc
829 Graves St
Kernersville NC 27284
336 992-0288

(G-17088)
HEALTH CARE RTREMENT CORP AMER
Also Called: Heartland of Riverview
7743 County Road 1 (45680-7822)
PHONE..................740 894-3287
Fax: 740 894-4737
Lois Clay, *Branch Mgr*
EMP: 100
SALES (corp-wide): 3.6B **Publicly Held**
WEB: www.hrc-manorcare.com
SIC: 8051 Convalescent home with continuous nursing care
HQ: Health Care And Retirement Corporation Of America
333 N Summit St Ste 103
Toledo OH 43604
419 252-5500

(G-17089)
HEARTLND-RIVERVIEW S PT OH LLC
Also Called: Heartland of Riverview 4148
7743 County Road 1 (45680-7822)
PHONE..................740 894-3287
Mark Stewart, *Administration*
EMP: 110
SALES: 8.9MM
SALES (corp-wide): 3.6B **Publicly Held**
SIC: 8051 8093 Convalescent home with continuous nursing care; rehabilitation center, outpatient treatment
HQ: Manor Care, Inc.
333 N Summit St Ste 103
Toledo OH 43604

(G-17090)
LAWRENCE CNTY BD DEV DSBLITIES
Also Called: Lawrence Cnty Early Chldhd Ctr
1749 County Road 1 (45680-8850)
PHONE..................740 377-2356
Fax: 740 377-2498
Sue Canderhoof, *Director*
EMP: 50 **Privately Held**
SIC: 8322 8351 Child related social services; child day care services
PA: Lawrence County Board Of Dev Disabilities
604 Carlton Davidson Ln
Coal Grove OH 45638
740 532-7401

(G-17091)
LOWES HOME CENTERS LLC
294 County Road 120 S (45680)
PHONE..................740 894-7120
Fax: 740 894-6144
Edgel Castle, *Manager*
EMP: 190
SALES (corp-wide): 68.6B **Publicly Held**
SIC: 5211 5031 5722 5064 Home centers; building materials, exterior; building materials, interior; household appliance stores; electrical appliances, television & radio
HQ: Lowe's Home Centers, Llc
1605 Curtis Bridge Rd
Wilkesboro NC 28697
336 658-4000

(G-17092)
MCGINNIS INC (HQ)
502 2nd St E (45680-9446)
P.O. Box 534 (45680-0534)
PHONE..................740 377-4391
Fax: 740 377-9541
Bruce D McGinnis, *CEO*
Rickey Lee Griffith, *President*
Bill Jessie, *Corp Secy*
D Dwaine Stephens, *Vice Pres*
EMP: 193
SQ FT: 5,000
SALES (est): 43.9MM
SALES (corp-wide): 152.4MM **Privately Held**
WEB: www.mcginnisinc.com
SIC: 4491 3731 Marine cargo handling; barges, building & repairing
PA: Mcnational, Inc.
502 2nd St E
South Point OH 45680
740 377-4391

(G-17093)
MCNATIONAL INC (PA)
502 2nd St E (45680-9446)
P.O. Box 534 (45680-0534)
PHONE..................740 377-4391
Bruce D McGinnis, *CEO*
Rick Griffith, *President*
C Barry Gipson, *Principal*
William Jessie, *Manager*
C Clayton Johnson, *Admin Sec*
EMP: 26
SQ FT: 5,000
SALES (est): 152.4MM **Privately Held**
SIC: 3731 7699 4491 Barges, building & repairing; cargo vessels, building & repairing; aircraft & heavy equipment repair services; marine cargo handling

(G-17094)
MERCIERS INCORPORATED
Also Called: Mercier's Tree Experts
2393 County Road 1 (45680-8462)
PHONE..................410 590-4181
Craig Mercier, *President*
EMP: 110
SQ FT: 2,500
SALES: 15MM **Privately Held**
WEB: www.merciers.com
SIC: 0783 Ornamental shrub & tree services

(G-17095)
MIKE ENYART & SONS INC
Also Called: Mesi
77 Private Drive 615 (45680-1259)
P.O. Box 9 (45680-0009)
PHONE..................740 523-0235
Michael Enyart, *President*
Tommy Enyart, *Vice Pres*
Kristen Enyart, *Office Mgr*
Kim Ward, *Administration*
EMP: 85
SALES (est): 16.9MM **Privately Held**
SIC: 1623 1794 Sewer line construction; excavation work

(G-17096)
QUALITY CARE NURSING SVC INC
Also Called: Ultimate Health Care
501 Washington St Ste 13 (45680-9606)
PHONE..................740 377-9095
Fax: 740 377-9591
Douglas Freeman, *CEO*
James Carver, *Vice Pres*
Cheryl Freeman, *Manager*
Mike Gannon, *Manager*
Amy Johnson, *Manager*
EMP: 300
SQ FT: 5,500
SALES (est): 5.9MM **Privately Held**
WEB: www.qcnservices.com
SIC: 8082 8049 8051 Home health care services; physical therapist; skilled nursing care facilities

(G-17097)
RIVERS BEND HEALTH CARE LLC
335 Township Road 1026 (45680-7842)
P.O. Box 947 (45680-0947)
PHONE..................740 894-3476
David Apgar, *Director*
Ronald Lyons,
EMP: 100
SQ FT: 27,341
SALES: 5MM **Privately Held**
SIC: 8051 8052 Convalescent home with continuous nursing care; intermediate care facilities

(G-17098)
TRIBUTE CONTRACTING & CONS LLC
2125 County Road 1 (45680-5001)
PHONE..................740 451-1010
Todd Harrah, *Manager*
Tom Enyart,
EMP: 26
SALES (est): 147.7K **Privately Held**
SIC: 8748 1623 Business consulting; water, sewer & utility lines; water & sewer line construction; manhole construction; pumping station construction

(G-17099)
XPO LOGISTICS FREIGHT INC
96 Private Drive 339 (45680-8919)
PHONE..................740 894-3859
Fax: 740 894-3496
Andrew Sikes, *Manager*
EMP: 27
SALES (corp-wide): 15.3B **Publicly Held**
WEB: www.con-way.com
SIC: 4213 Contract haulers
HQ: Xpo Logistics Freight, Inc.
2211 Old Earhart Rd # 100
Ann Arbor MI 48105
734 998-4200

South Vienna
Clark County

(G-17100)
OHIO ENTERTAINMENT SECURITY
3749 Mahar Rd (45369-9728)
PHONE..................937 325-7216

GEOGRAPHIC SECTION

Springboro - Warren County (G-17121)

Fax: 937 325-3923
Gregory Powell, *President*
Wilford Potter, *Vice Pres*
Carter Feltner, *Treasurer*
EMP: 99
SALES (est): 1.3MM **Privately Held**
WEB: www.ohioentertainmentsecurity.com
SIC: 7381 Security guard service

(G-17101)
VIENNA ENTERPRISES INC
Also Called: Sharonview Nursing Home
125 E National Rd (45369-9742)
P.O. Box 339 (45369-0339)
PHONE..................................937 568-4524
Fax: 937 568-4333
Helen Diener, *CEO*
Donald H Diener, *President*
Pierre Sweeney, *Administration*
EMP: 40 EST: 1953
SQ FT: 5,000
SALES (est): 1.2MM **Privately Held**
SIC: 8059 8051 8052 Convalescent home; nursing home, except skilled & intermediate care facility; skilled nursing care facilities; intermediate care facilities

South Webster
Scioto County

(G-17102)
ALLARD EXCAVATION LLC
8336 Bennett Schl Hse Rd (45682-9029)
PHONE..................................740 778-2242
Fax: 740 778-2222
Margaret Allard, *Mng Member*
Mark Allard,
EMP: 68
SALES (est): 3.3MM **Privately Held**
SIC: 1794 Excavation work

South Zanesville
Muskingum County

(G-17103)
FIRST AMERICAN TITLE INSUR CO
961 Linden Ave (43701-3049)
PHONE..................................740 450-0006
Wendy Mallett, *Branch Mgr*
EMP: 25 **Publicly Held**
WEB: www.firstam.com
SIC: 6361 Real estate title insurance
HQ: First American Title Insurance Company
1 First American Way
Santa Ana CA 92707
800 854-3643

Southington
Trumbull County

(G-17104)
AMERICAN LEGION POST
4200 Herner Cnty Line Rd (44470-9562)
PHONE..................................330 393-9858
Norman Doyen, *Principal*
EMP: 70
SALES (est): 349.7K **Privately Held**
SIC: 8641 Veterans' organization

Spencer
Medina County

(G-17105)
ENVIROTEST SYSTEMS CORP
408 E Main St (44275-9564)
PHONE..................................330 963-4464
EMP: 34
SQ FT: 5,601 **Privately Held**
WEB: www.il.etest.com
SIC: 7549 Emissions testing without repairs, automotive

HQ: Envirotest Systems Corp.
7 Kripes Rd
East Granby CT 06026

(G-17106)
FARMERS SAVINGS BANK (PA)
111 W Main St (44275-9565)
P.O. Box 38 (44275-0038)
PHONE..................................330 648-2441
Fax: 330 648-2024
Thomas W Lee, *CEO*
John W Donley, *Vice Pres*
Chris Vanfleet, *Marketing Staff*
James F Ketchum, *Director*
Jacqueline K Simmons, *Admin Sec*
EMP: 29
SQ FT: 13,802
SALES: 9.7MM **Privately Held**
SIC: 6036 State savings banks, not federally chartered

Spencerville
Allen County

(G-17107)
CHARLES RIVER LABORATORIES INC
Also Called: Pre-Clinical Services
640 N Elizabeth St (45887-1064)
PHONE..................................419 647-4196
Krista Richardson, *Engineer*
Malcolm Blair PHD, *Manager*
Becky Lucke, *Manager*
EMP: 135
SALES (corp-wide): 1.8B **Publicly Held**
WEB: www.criver.com
SIC: 8731 Biotechnical research, commercial
HQ: Charles River Laboratories, Inc.
251 Ballardvale St
Wilmington MA 01887
978 658-6000

(G-17108)
HCF OF ROSELAWN INC
420 E 4th St (45887-1210)
PHONE..................................419 647-4115
David Walsh, *Vice Pres*
EMP: 167
SALES (est): 177.8K
SALES (corp-wide): 154.8MM **Privately Held**
SIC: 8051 8322 8093 Convalescent home with continuous nursing care; rehabilitation services; rehabilitation center, outpatient treatment
PA: Hcf Management, Inc.
1100 Shawnee Rd
Lima OH 45805
419 999-2010

Spring Valley
Greene County

(G-17109)
CENTURY 21 ELITE PERFORMANCE
2905 River Edge Cir (45370-9797)
PHONE..................................937 438-8221
Thomas Fitzgibbons, *President*
Sandy Yount, *Admin Sec*
EMP: 25
SQ FT: 2,160
SALES (est): 1.5MM **Privately Held**
WEB: www.century21ep.com
SIC: 6531 Real estate agent, residential

(G-17110)
DAYS OF DISCOVERY
3195 Clear Springs Rd (45370-7731)
PHONE..................................937 862-4465
Janine Speck, *Owner*
Jeff Baxter, *Executive*
EMP: 45
SALES (est): 434.6K **Privately Held**
SIC: 8351 Child day care services

(G-17111)
TIM MUNDY
Also Called: My Lawn Ldscp & Irrigation Co
3159 State Route 42 (45370-9736)
P.O. Box 249 (45370-0249)
PHONE..................................937 862-8686
Tim Mundy, *Owner*
Ed Blair, *Finance Mgr*
EMP: 25
SALES (est): 1.4MM **Privately Held**
SIC: 0781 0782 7389 Landscape services; lawn & garden services;

Springboro
Warren County

(G-17112)
AAA HOME REPAIR SERVICES
535 S Main St (45066-1419)
P.O. Box 1001 (45066-2001)
PHONE..................................937 748-9988
Rob Sturgill, *Owner*
David Jackson, *Owner*
EMP: 50
SALES: 1MM **Privately Held**
SIC: 1521 General remodeling, single-family houses

(G-17113)
ADVANCED ENGRG SOLUTIONS INC
Also Called: Aesi
250 Advanced Dr (45066-1802)
PHONE..................................937 743-6900
Fax: 513 743-6901
Khang Do, *President*
Thomas J Harrington, *Principal*
Marty Luers, *Plant Mgr*
Pat Croskey, *Program Mgr*
Teressa Bush, *Manager*
EMP: 70
SQ FT: 44,000
SALES (est): 11.7MM **Privately Held**
SIC: 8711 3544 Consulting engineer; special dies, tools, jigs & fixtures

(G-17114)
ALFONS HAAR INC
150 Advanced Dr (45066-1800)
PHONE..................................937 560-2031
Fax: 937 560-2032
Thomas Haar, *President*
John Dunn, *General Mgr*
Douglas Werner, *Engineer*
Bill Schrand, *Design Engr*
Bernd Haar, *Treasurer*
▲ EMP: 31
SQ FT: 5,000
SALES (est): 8MM
SALES (corp-wide): 50MM **Privately Held**
WEB: www.alfonshaar.com
SIC: 5084 3599 8711 Packaging machinery & equipment; custom machinery; engineering services
PA: Alfons Haar Maschinenbau Gmbh & Co. Kg
Fangdieckstr. 67
Hamburg 22547
408 339-10

(G-17115)
AST ENVIRONMENTAL INC
70 Commercial Way (45066-3080)
PHONE..................................937 743-0002
Fax: 937 743-0121
Robert Welsh, *President*
Duane Guifoil, *Vice Pres*
Duane Guilfoil, *Vice Pres*
William Guilfoil, *Vice Pres*
Sharon Thomas, *Accountant*
EMP: 27
SQ FT: 6,000
SALES (est): 10.9MM **Privately Held**
WEB: www.astenvironmental.com
SIC: 4959 Environmental cleanup services

(G-17116)
BRIGHT BEGINNINGS
60 E North St (45066-1367)
PHONE..................................937 748-2612
Susan Stalcup, *President*
Suzanne Allen, *Pastor*

Kim Crosen, *Director*
Kim Criosen, *Director*
EMP: 35
SALES (est): 300K **Privately Held**
SIC: 8351 Preschool center

(G-17117)
BROTHERS TRADING CO INC (PA)
Also Called: Victory Wholesale Grocery
400 Victory Ln (45066-3046)
P.O. Box 216 (45066-0216)
PHONE..................................937 746-1010
Fax: 513 746-2318
David Kantor, *President*
Steve Messer, *Sr Corp Ofcr*
Richard Kantor, *Vice Pres*
Scott Mattis, *Vice Pres*
Ian Pinales, *Sales Staff*
◆ EMP: 150
SQ FT: 25,000
SALES (est): 302.1MM **Privately Held**
SIC: 5141 5122 5149 Groceries, general line; drugs, proprietaries & sundries; groceries & related products

(G-17118)
CHILDVINE INC
Also Called: Kids 'r' Kids 3 OH
790 N Main St (45066-8944)
PHONE..................................937 748-1260
Edward Doczy, *President*
Bonnie Doczy, *Vice Pres*
EMP: 45
SQ FT: 15,000
SALES (est): 1.8MM **Privately Held**
SIC: 8351 Preschool center

(G-17119)
COLDWELL BNKR HRITG RLTORS LLC
535 N Main St (45066-9555)
PHONE..................................937 748-5500
Carol Moore, *Broker*
Karen Powell, *Manager*
Jenny Knott, *Manager*
Kristin Hoch, *Real Est Agnt*
Patricia McDonald, *Real Est Agnt*
EMP: 29
SALES (corp-wide): 7.5MM **Privately Held**
SIC: 6531 Real estate agent, residential
PA: Coldwell Banker Heritage Realtors Llc
2000 Hewitt Ave
Dayton OH 45440
937 434-7600

(G-17120)
GRAPHIC SYSTEMS SERVICES INC
Also Called: G S S
400 S Pioneer Blvd (45066-3001)
PHONE..................................937 746-0708
Fax: 937 746-0783
Kenneth J Green, *Ch of Bd*
Daniel L Green, *President*
James Copeland, *Corp Secy*
John Sillies, *Exec VP*
John Fillies, *Opers Mgr*
EMP: 41
SQ FT: 100,000
SALES: 6.6MM **Privately Held**
WEB: www.gsspress.com
SIC: 7699 3555 Industrial equipment services; printing presses

(G-17121)
HARDY DIAGNOSTICS
Also Called: Quickslide
429 S Pioneer Blvd (45066-3002)
PHONE..................................937 550-2768
Shelly Austin, *Manager*
EMP: 75
SALES (corp-wide): 45MM **Privately Held**
SIC: 8711 Machine tool design
PA: Hardy Diagnostics
1430 W Mccoy Ln
Santa Maria CA 93455
805 346-2766

Springboro - Warren County (G-17122) — GEOGRAPHIC SECTION

(G-17122)
HEATHERWOODE GOLF COURSE
88 Heatherwoode Blvd (45066-1577)
PHONE...................937 748-3222
Fax: 513 748-3224
Steve Marino, *Manager*
Ken Hultz, *Manager*
EMP: 131
SALES (est): 1.8MM Privately Held
SIC: 7992 7299 Public golf courses; banquet hall facilities

(G-17123)
HILLSPRING HEALTH CARE CENTER
325 E Central Ave (45066-8553)
PHONE...................937 748-1100
Fax: 513 748-8100
Barry Dortz, *CEO*
Peggy Karacia, *Chf Purch Ofc*
Greg Weaver, *Branch Mgr*
Molly Thumann, *Administration*
EMP: 40 EST: 1997
SQ FT: 55,611
SALES (est): 3.3MM
SALES (corp-wide): 74MM Privately Held
SIC: 8051 Convalescent home with continuous nursing care
PA: Carespring Health Care Management, Llc
390 Wards Corner Rd
Loveland OH 45140
513 943-4000

(G-17124)
HUFFY CORPORATION
Also Called: Huffy Bicycle Company
901 Pleasant Valley Dr (45066-1162)
PHONE...................937 743-5011
Beth Brooks, *Branch Mgr*
EMP: 65
SALES (corp-wide): 48.7MM Privately Held
WEB: www.huffy.com
SIC: 3751 3949 3423 3799 Bicycles & related parts; basketball equipment & supplies, general; garden & farm tools, including shovels; shovels, spades (hand tools); wheelbarrows; bicycle repair shop; lawn mower repair shop; inventory computing service
PA: Huffy Corporation
8877 Gander Creek Dr
Miamisburg OH 45342
937 865-2800

(G-17125)
KELCHNER INC (DH)
50 Advanced Dr (45066-1805)
PHONE...................937 704-9890
Todd Kelchner, *CEO*
Troy Norvell, *President*
Jeff Kelchner, *Vice Pres*
Kevin Weckel, *Vice Pres*
Jeremy White, *Project Mgr*
EMP: 126 EST: 1948
SQ FT: 8,600
SALES: 93MM
SALES (corp-wide): 4.1B Privately Held
SIC: 1794 1389 Excavation work; mud service, oil field drilling; bailing wells
HQ: Wood Group Uk Limited
Wellheads Place
Aberdeen AB21
122 450-0402

(G-17126)
KIDS R KIDS SCHOOLS QULTY LRNG
790 N Main St (45066-8944)
PHONE...................937 748-1260
Fax: 937 748-1329
Edward Doczy, *Principal*
Bonnie Doczy, *Vice Pres*
EMP: 32
SALES (est): 688.2K Privately Held
SIC: 8351 Preschool center

(G-17127)
M J J B LTD
Also Called: Day Academy
505 N Main St (45066-9555)
PHONE...................937 748-4414
Fax: 513 748-3644
Jill S Brown, *President*
Shayna Donley, *Director*
Deborah Mickey, *Director*
EMP: 28
SQ FT: 20,374
SALES (est): 725.1K Privately Held
SIC: 8351 Group day care center

(G-17128)
MIAMI-LUKEN INC (PA)
Also Called: Paramount Confection Co
265 S Pioneer Blvd (45066-3307)
PHONE...................937 743-7775
Tony Rattini, *CEO*
Joseph Mastandrea, *Ch of Bd*
Anthony V Rattini, *Principal*
Vickie Staley, *Human Res Dir*
Diane Sheltrown, *Human Resources*
EMP: 64
SQ FT: 60,000
SALES (est): 247.4MM Privately Held
WEB: www.miamiluken.com
SIC: 5122 Drugs, proprietaries & sundries

(G-17129)
MIDWEST SEAFOOD INC (PA)
475 Victory Ln (45066-3047)
PHONE...................937 746-8856
William Easton, *President*
Joseph Perry, *Vice Pres*
Sandy Curtis, *Controller*
EMP: 70
SQ FT: 10,000
SALES (est): 12.2MM Privately Held
SIC: 5146 Fish, fresh; fish, frozen, unpackaged

(G-17130)
MONRO MUFFLER BRAKE INC
4 Remick Blvd (45066-9168)
PHONE...................937 999-3202
Fax: 937 885-4607
EMP: 70
SALES (corp-wide): 1B Publicly Held
SIC: 7539 Brake services
PA: Monro, Inc.
200 Holleder Pkwy
Rochester NY 14615
585 647-6400

(G-17131)
MOUND TECHNOLOGIES INC
25 Mound Park Dr (45066-2402)
PHONE...................937 748-2937
Thomas Miller, *President*
John Barger, *Vice Pres*
Luke Brongersma, *Project Mgr*
Troy Stevens, *Project Mgr*
Carl Kinnunen, *Sales Staff*
EMP: 45
SQ FT: 40,000
SALES: 20.9MM
SALES (corp-wide): 37.2MM Privately Held
WEB: www.moundtechnologies.com
SIC: 3441 1791 3446 Building components, structural steel; structural steel erection; gates, ornamental metal; grillwork, ornamental metal
PA: Heartland, Inc.
1005 N 19th St
Middlesboro KY 40965
606 248-7323

(G-17132)
NATIONS ROOF OF OHIO LLC
Also Called: Affiliate of Nations Roof
275 S Pioneer Blvd (45066-1180)
PHONE...................937 439-4160
Fax: 937 439-4260
Chuck Painter, *President*
Andrew Strauser, *Vice Pres*
Sue Kimble, *Controller*
Jennifer Dunaway, *Sales Mgr*
Karen Wagner, *Office Mgr*
EMP: 50
SALES: 87.4MM Privately Held
SIC: 1761 Roofing contractor; siding contractor

(G-17133)
PDI COMMUNICATION SYSTEMS INC (PA)
Also Called: P D I
40 Greenwood Ln (45066-3033)
PHONE...................937 743-6010
Fax: 513 743-5664
Lou Vilardo, *Owner*
Chuck Stout, *QC Dir*
Eric Johnson, *Design Engr*
Kent Carver, *CFO*
Catherine Saettel, *Marketing Mgr*
▲ EMP: 60 EST: 1976
SQ FT: 78,000
SALES (est): 19.7MM Privately Held
WEB: www.pdiarm.com
SIC: 3663 3599 5047 5064 Television broadcasting & communications equipment; machine shop, jobbing & repair; hospital equipment & furniture; electrical appliances, television & radio

(G-17134)
PEOPLES BANK
95 Edgebrooke Dr (45066-1036)
P.O. Box 338 (45066-0338)
PHONE...................937 748-0067
Steven Harding, *Manager*
EMP: 30
SALES (corp-wide): 182.1MM Publicly Held
SIC: 6021 National commercial banks
HQ: Peoples Bank
138 Putnam St
Marietta OH 45750
740 373-3155

(G-17135)
PHOENIX GROUP HOLDING CO
4 Sycamore Creek Dr Ste A (45066-2311)
PHONE...................937 704-9850
Fax: 937 539-4476
George Coates, *CEO*
Bob Gray, *General Mgr*
Robert D Gray, *CFO*
Ben Dykes, *Sales Staff*
Kirk Wiley, *Director*
EMP: 140
SQ FT: 1,200
SALES (est): 10.2MM Privately Held
WEB: www.phoenixgrouphc.com
SIC: 8711 Consulting engineer; machine tool design

(G-17136)
PIONEER AUTOMOTIVE TECH INC (DH)
100 S Pioneer Blvd (45066-1177)
PHONE...................937 746-2293
Fax: 937 746-2293
Steven Moerner, *President*
Mike Honda, *Treasurer*
Shigeyoshi Okubo, *Treasurer*
Debbie Lee, *Accounting Mgr*
Yoshio Natsume, *Branch Mgr*
▲ EMP: 175
SQ FT: 155,000
SALES (est): 78.5MM
SALES (corp-wide): 3.4B Privately Held
SIC: 5013 3714 3651 Motor vehicle supplies & new parts; motor vehicle parts & accessories; household audio & video equipment
HQ: Pioneer North America, Inc.
2265 E 220th St
Long Beach CA 90810
213 746-6337

(G-17137)
RIGHT AT HOME
Also Called: Health Right
15 Dinsley Pl (45066-7422)
PHONE...................937 291-2244
Fax: 937 291-2525
Michael Manes, *Mng Member*
EMP: 60
SALES (est): 1.2MM Privately Held
WEB: www.rightathomedayton.com
SIC: 8082 Home health care services

(G-17138)
SPRINGBORO SERVICE CENTER
Also Called: City Springsboro Public Works
220 E Mill St (45066-1430)
PHONE...................937 748-0020
Fax: 513 748-3216
Barry Conway, *Director*
EMP: 30
SALES (est): 2.4MM Privately Held
SIC: 1611 Highway & street maintenance

(G-17139)
SYCAMORE CREEK COUNTRY CLUB
8300 Country Club Ln (45066-8436)
PHONE...................937 748-0791
Fax: 513 748-2926
David Gagner, *President*
Bradley Polkek, *COO*
Bradley Pollak, *COO*
Karen Murton, *Accounting Mgr*
EMP: 120 EST: 1959
SALES: 3.1MM Privately Held
SIC: 7997 Country club, membership

(G-17140)
TRUGREEN LIMITED PARTNERSHIP
Also Called: Tru Green-Chemlawn
760 Pleasant Valley Dr (45066-1157)
PHONE...................937 557-0060
Edmund Mackey, *Branch Mgr*
EMP: 50
SALES (corp-wide): 4B Privately Held
SIC: 0782 Lawn care services
HQ: Trugreen Limited Partnership
1790 Kirby Pkwy
Memphis TN 38138
901 251-4128

(G-17141)
WATKINS MECHANICAL INC (PA)
Also Called: Watkins Mechanical Services
10 Parker Dr (45066-1334)
PHONE...................937 748-0220
Fax: 513 748-3095
David Watkins, *President*
Lisa Watkins, *General Mgr*
Brad Michaels, *Manager*
Jason Redmon, *Manager*
EMP: 25
SALES (est): 4.4MM Privately Held
WEB: www.watkinsheating.com
SIC: 1711 Warm air heating & air conditioning contractor

(G-17142)
WILLOW AND CANE LLC
Also Called: Willow & Cane
1110 Lakemont Dr (45066-8185)
PHONE...................609 280-1150
Christopher Meyer,
EMP: 25
SALES (est): 2.2MM Privately Held
SIC: 5091 Sporting & recreation goods

(G-17143)
WOODHULL LLC (PA)
125 Commercial Way (45066-3079)
PHONE...................937 294-5311
Fax: 937 294-5017
Susan S Woodhull, *Owner*
Bill Kilker, *CFO*
Paul Tarango, *Info Tech Mgr*
Lance A Gildner,
EMP: 33
SQ FT: 6,500
SALES (est): 9.2MM Privately Held
WEB: www.woodhullusa.com
SIC: 5999 7699 Photocopy machines; photocopy machine repair

(G-17144)
YOUNG MENS CHRISTIAN ASSOC
Also Called: Coffman Branch
88 Remick Blvd (45066-9168)
PHONE...................937 223-5201
Britney Hensel, *Hum Res Coord*
Dale Brunner, *Director*
EMP: 120
SQ FT: 2,512

GEOGRAPHIC SECTION

Springfield - Clark County (G-17168)

SALES (corp-wide): 26.1MM **Privately Held**
WEB: www.daytonymca.org
SIC: **8641** 8351 7997 7991 Youth organizations; child day care services; membership sports & recreation clubs; physical fitness facilities; individual & family services
PA: Young Men's Christian Association Of Greater Dayton
118 W St Ste 300
Dayton OH 45402
937 223-5201

Springfield
Clark County

(G-17145)
56 PLUS MANAGEMENT LLC
Also Called: First Diversity MGT Group
560 E High St (45505-1010)
PHONE..................937 323-4114
Miguel Ten, *President*
Bruce Smith, *Exec VP*
EMP: 50
SALES (est): 2.1MM **Privately Held**
SIC: **7361** Placement agencies

(G-17146)
AETNA BUILDING MAINTENANCE INC
525 N Yellow Springs St (45504-2462)
P.O. Box 1985 (45501-1985)
PHONE..................937 324-5711
Fax: 937 324-5882
Julian Greenland, *Principal*
EMP: 96
SALES (corp-wide): 17.6MM **Privately Held**
SIC: **7349** Window cleaning
HQ: Aetna Building Maintenance, Inc.
646 Parsons Ave
Columbus OH 43206
614 476-1818

(G-17147)
AMERICAN SECURITY INSURANCE CO
1 Assurant Way (45505-4717)
PHONE..................937 327-7700
Michael Lawson, *Principal*
Alan R Moak, *COO*
EMP: 26
SALES (corp-wide): 6.4B **Publicly Held**
WEB: www.assurantsolutions.com
SIC: **6411** Insurance agents
HQ: American Security Insurance Company
260 Interstate N Cir Se
Atlanta GA 30339
770 763-1000

(G-17148)
ARCHDIOCESE OF CINCINNATI
Also Called: Second Harvest Food Bank
701 E Columbia St (45503-4404)
PHONE..................937 323-6507
Fax: 937 327-0516
Bill Leaver, *Manager*
EMP: 25
SALES (corp-wide): 229.4MM **Privately Held**
WEB: www.catholiccincinnati.org
SIC: **8322** Individual & family services
PA: Archdiocese Of Cincinnati
100 E 8th St Fl 8
Cincinnati OH 45202
513 421-3131

(G-17149)
ARCTECH FABRICATING INC (PA)
1317 Lagonda Ave (45503-4001)
P.O. Box 1447 (45501-1447)
PHONE..................937 525-9353
Fax: 937 322-0200
Leonard McConnaghey, *CEO*
James C Roberts II, *President*
Len McConnaughey, *Vice Pres*
Kim Williams, *Buyer*
Mark Stoltz, *Engineer*
EMP: 29
SQ FT: 13,200
SALES (est): 5MM **Privately Held**
WEB: www.arctechfabricating.com
SIC: **7692** 3441 Welding repair; fabricated structural metal

(G-17150)
BENJAMIN STEEL COMPANY INC
777 Benjamin Dr (45502-8846)
PHONE..................937 233-1212
Fax: 937 233-5704
Vincent Demana, *Owner*
Nick Demana, *General Mgr*
Shawn Taylor, *Branch Mgr*
Tim Halloran, *Branch Mgr*
EMP: 40
SQ FT: 36,000
SALES (est): 3.9MM
SALES (corp-wide): 86.5MM **Privately Held**
WEB: www.benjaminsteel.com
SIC: **5051** 3498 3334 3317 Steel; tube fabricating (contract bending & shaping); primary aluminum; steel pipe & tubes; cold finishing of steel shapes; blast furnaces & steel mills
PA: Benjamin Steel Company, Inc.
777 Benjamin Dr
Springfield OH 45502
937 322-8600

(G-17151)
BOARD OF DIR OF WITTENBE
134 W Ward St (45504-2118)
PHONE..................937 327-6231
Carol Young, *Publisher*
Chuck Dominick, *Vice Pres*
Ken Irwin, *Librarian*
Gary Luthman, *Manager*
Luther Hill, *Info Tech Dir*
EMP: 74
SQ FT: 3,636
SALES (corp-wide): 70MM **Privately Held**
SIC: **7389** Fund raising organizations
PA: The Board Of Directors Of Wittenberg College
200 W Ward St
Springfield OH 45504
937 327-6231

(G-17152)
BOARD OF DIR OF WITTENBE
Also Called: Wittenberg University
225 N Fountain Ave (45504-2534)
P.O. Box 720 (45501-0720)
PHONE..................937 327-6310
Mary Jo Darr, *Branch Mgr*
A G Anderson, *Assoc Prof*
EMP: 26
SALES (corp-wide): 70MM **Privately Held**
WEB: www.wittenberg.edu
SIC: **8221** 6163 University; loan brokers
PA: The Board Of Directors Of Wittenberg College
200 W Ward St
Springfield OH 45504
937 327-6231

(G-17153)
BROOKDALE LVING CMMUNITIES INC
Also Called: Cardinal Retirement Village
2981 Vester Ave (45503-1565)
PHONE..................937 399-1216
Fax: 937 399-7093
Katherine Hitchcock, *Manager*
EMP: 36
SALES (corp-wide): 4.7B **Publicly Held**
WEB: www.parkplace-spokane.com
SIC: **8059** Rest home, with health care
HQ: Brookdale Living Communities, Inc.
515 N State St Ste 1750
Chicago IL 60654

(G-17154)
C W A LOCAL 4326
240 Ludlow Ave (45505-1210)
PHONE..................937 322-2227
Paul Storms, *President*
Harold Oster, *Vice Pres*
EMP: 50
SALES (est): 1MM **Privately Held**
SIC: **8631** Labor unions & similar labor organizations

(G-17155)
CANUS HOSPITALITY LLC
383 E Leffel Ln (45505-4746)
PHONE..................937 323-8631
Andy Mullick, *Manager*
Jeremy L Trahan,
EMP: 40
SQ FT: 200
SALES: 1.6MM **Privately Held**
SIC: **7011** Hotels

(G-17156)
CARDIOLOGIST OF CLARK & CHAMP
1911 E High St (45505-1227)
PHONE..................937 323-1404
Fax: 937 323-1407
Bonnie Davis, *Manager*
Akber A Mohammed, *Cardiology*
EMP: 26
SALES (est): 1.9MM **Privately Held**
WEB: www.cambridgewhoswho.com
SIC: **8011** Internal medicine practitioners

(G-17157)
CATHOLIC CHARITIES OF SOUTHWST
701 E Columbia St (45503-4404)
PHONE..................937 325-8715
Kathleen Donnellan, *Exec Dir*
EMP: 99
SALES: 10.2MM **Privately Held**
SIC: **8322** Social service center

(G-17158)
CENTRAL FIRE PROTECTION CO INC
583 Selma Rd (45505-2071)
P.O. Box 1448 (45501-1448)
PHONE..................937 322-0713
Fax: 937 322-0710
Gary Adkins, *President*
Helen Gifford, *Vice Pres*
Karla Brown, *Plant Mgr*
Doug Gifford, *Project Mgr*
Jack Kaney, *Project Mgr*
EMP: 34
SALES: 700MM **Privately Held**
SIC: **1799** Coating, caulking & weather, water & fireproofing

(G-17159)
CHI OMEGA SORORITY
2 Ferncliff Pl (45504-2512)
PHONE..................937 325-9323
Louise Smockey, *President*
Mary Poland, *Manager*
EMP: 50
SALES (est): 411.8K **Privately Held**
SIC: **7041** Sorority residential house

(G-17160)
CLARK SCHAEFER HACKETT & CO
14 E Main St Ste 500 (45502-1364)
PHONE..................937 399-2000
John McKinnon, *Principal*
Brian Lawrence, *Accountant*
Devesh Kamal, *Shareholder*
EMP: 40
SALES (corp-wide): 40.4MM **Privately Held**
WEB: www.cshco.com
SIC: **8721** Certified public accountant
PA: Clark, Schaefer, Hackett & Co.
1 E 4th St Ste 1200
Cincinnati OH 45202
513 241-3111

(G-17161)
CLARK COUNTY BOARD OF DEVELOPM (PA)
Also Called: Town & Country School
2527 Kenton St (45505-3352)
PHONE..................937 328-2675
Fax: 937 328-4526
Jennifer Rousculp-Miller, *Superintendent*
Ravi Shankar, *Comptroller*
Robert Bender, *Director*
EMP: 28
SQ FT: 15,000
SALES: 32MM **Privately Held**
SIC: **8322** Rehabilitation services

(G-17162)
CLARK COUNTY BOARD OF DEVELOPM
Also Called: Clark County Mrdd Trnsp
50 W Leffel Ln (45506-3520)
PHONE..................937 328-5240
Elmer M Beard, *Director*
EMP: 53
SQ FT: 1,270
SALES (corp-wide): 32MM **Privately Held**
SIC: **4119** Local passenger transportation
PA: Clark County Board Of Developmental Disabilities
2527 Kenton St
Springfield OH 45505
937 328-2675

(G-17163)
CLARK COUNTY BOARD OF DEVELOPM
110 W Leffel Ln (45506-3522)
PHONE..................937 328-5200
Mary Brandstetter, *Director*
EMP: 236
SALES (corp-wide): 32MM **Privately Held**
SIC: **8361** Home for the mentally retarded
PA: Clark County Board Of Developmental Disabilities
2527 Kenton St
Springfield OH 45505
937 328-2675

(G-17164)
CLARK MEMORIAL HOME ASSN
106 Kewbury Rd (45504-1199)
PHONE..................937 399-4262
Fax: 937 399-4267
Sylvia Rosenlieb, *Director*
EMP: 27
SALES: 689.5K **Privately Held**
SIC: **8361** Home for the aged

(G-17165)
CLARK SHAWNEE SCHL TRANSPRTN
725 E Leffel Ln (45505-4753)
PHONE..................937 328-5382
Debbie Finkes, *Superintendent*
Wayne Leis, *Principal*
EMP: 30
SALES: 830K **Privately Held**
SIC: **4151** School buses

(G-17166)
CLEANERS EXTRAORDINAIRE INC
128 Eagle City Rd (45502-9502)
PHONE..................937 324-8488
Jeff Clouse, *Manager*
EMP: 70
SALES: 2MM **Privately Held**
SIC: **8322** Helping hand service (Big Brother, etc.)

(G-17167)
COILPLUS INC
Coilplus Ohio
4801 Gateway Blvd (45502-8866)
PHONE..................937 322-4455
Fax: 859 322-2727
James Ralston, *Division Pres*
Toby Schofield, *Manager*
EMP: 42
SALES (corp-wide): 56.5B **Privately Held**
WEB: www.coilplusohio.com
SIC: **5051** Steel
HQ: Coilplus, Inc.
6250 N River Rd Ste 6050
Rosemont IL 60018
847 384-3000

(G-17168)
COLUMBIA GAS TRANSMISSION LLC
Also Called: Columbia Energy
2101 W Main St (45504-3017)
PHONE..................937 327-7108
Lorie Sexton, *Safety Mgr*
David Carter, *Manager*
EMP: 36
SQ FT: 384

Springfield - Clark County (G-17169)

SALES (corp-wide): 9.2B **Privately Held**
SIC: 4924 Natural gas distribution
HQ: Columbia Gas Transmission, Llc
200 Cizzic Ctr Dr
Columbus OH 43216
614 460-6000

(G-17169)
COMFORT KEEPERS INC
101 N Fountain Ave (45502-1118)
PHONE.....................937 322-6288
Cris Clum, *President*
EMP: 50
SALES (corp-wide): 139.1MM **Privately Held**
WEB: www.comfortkeepers.com
SIC: 8082 Visiting nurse service
HQ: Comfort Keepers, Inc.
6640 Poe Ave Ste 200
Dayton OH 45414
937 832-2454

(G-17170)
COMMUNICARE HEALTH SVCS INC
Also Called: Homestead Healthcare Center
2317 E Home Rd (45503-2520)
PHONE.....................937 399-9217
Fax: 937 399-8567
Siva Vemana, *Director*
Maryanne Strauk, *Administration*
Missy Severt, *Administration*
EMP: 137
SALES (corp-wide): 103.9MM **Privately Held**
WEB: www.atriumlivingcenters.com
SIC: 8051 Convalescent home with continuous nursing care
PA: Communicare Health Services, Inc.
4700 Ashwood Dr Ste 200
Blue Ash OH 45241
513 530-1654

(G-17171)
COMMUNITY HOSPITAL SPRINGFIELD (PA)
Also Called: Community Hosp Schl Nursing
100 Medical Center Dr (45504-2687)
PHONE.....................937 325-0531
Fax: 937 328-8668
Mark Wiener, *President*
Dick Schillhahn, *Purch Mgr*
David Davis, *Purch Agent*
Dana Engle, *CFO*
Vince Riano, *Pharmacist*
EMP: 1300
SALES (est): 41.8MM **Privately Held**
SIC: 8062 8051 General medical & surgical hospitals; skilled nursing care facilities

(G-17172)
COMMUNITY MERCY FOUNDATION
Also Called: Oakwood Village
1500 Villa Rd (45503-1656)
PHONE.....................937 390-9000
Fax: 937 390-9333
Shannon Mitchel, *Personnel*
Jamie Halsman, *Manager*
Richard Giles, *Info Tech Dir*
Matt Loges, *Executive*
EMP: 120
SQ FT: 250,000
SALES (corp-wide): 4.2B **Privately Held**
SIC: 6513 8059 Retirement hotel operation; nursing home, except skilled & intermediate care facility
HQ: The Community Mercy Foundation
1 S Limestone St Ste 700
Springfield OH 45502

(G-17173)
COMMUNITY MERCY FOUNDATION
Also Called: Community Mercy Hlth Partners
1 S Limestone St Ste 700 (45502-1249)
P.O. Box 1380 (45501-1380)
PHONE.....................937 328-8134
Kevin Griggs, *President*
Ward Allen, *Director*
D Jerry Haley, *Director*
Jerry D Haley, *Director*
Michael Vogel, *Recruiter*
EMP: 100

SALES (corp-wide): 4.2B **Privately Held**
SIC: 5999 8741 Hospital equipment & supplies; management services
HQ: The Community Mercy Foundation
1 S Limestone St Ste 700
Springfield OH 45502

(G-17174)
COMMUNITY MERCY FOUNDATION (HQ)
1 S Limestone St Ste 700 (45502-1249)
P.O. Box 688 (45501-0688)
PHONE.....................937 328-7000
Fax: 937 328-7038
Paul Hiltz Interim, *President*
James Roediger, *Chairman*
Gary A Hagens, *COO*
John Dempsey, *Vice Pres*
Kristy McCready, *Exec Dir*
EMP: 100
SALES: 3.2MM
SALES (corp-wide): 4.2B **Privately Held**
SIC: 8641 Civic social & fraternal associations
PA: Mercy Health
1701 Mercy Health Pl
Cincinnati OH 45237
513 639-2800

(G-17175)
COMMUNITY MERCY HLTH PARTNERS (DH)
Also Called: Springfield Regional Med Ctr
100 Medical Center Dr (45504-2687)
PHONE.....................937 523-6670
Paul Hiltz, *CEO*
Gary A Hagens, *COO*
Terry Boys, *Vice Pres*
Ron Connovich, *Vice Pres*
Katrina English, *Vice Pres*
EMP: 43
SALES: 223.8MM
SALES (corp-wide): 4.2B **Privately Held**
SIC: 8062 General medical & surgical hospitals

(G-17176)
COMPUNET CLINICAL LABS LLC
2100 Emmanuel Way Ste C (45502-7218)
PHONE.....................937 342-0015
Melissa Williams, *Branch Mgr*
EMP: 61
SALES (corp-wide): 354MM **Privately Held**
SIC: 8071 Medical laboratories
HQ: Compunet Clinical Laboratories, Llc
2308 Sandridge Dr
Moraine OH 45439
937 296-0844

(G-17177)
CORROTEC INC
1125 W North St (45504-2713)
PHONE.....................937 325-3585
Fax: 937 325-9456
David A Stratton, *CEO*
Aristides G Gianakopoulos, *President*
Walter A Wildman, *Principal*
John C Stratton, *Vice Pres*
Walt Newman, *Safety Mgr*
EMP: 35 **EST:** 1981
SQ FT: 28,500
SALES (est): 9.2MM **Privately Held**
WEB: www.corrotec.com
SIC: 3559 7699 3479 3625 Electroplating machinery & equipment; tank repair; coating of metals with plastic or resins; electric controls & control accessories, industrial

(G-17178)
COUNTY OF CLARK
Also Called: Environmental Health Dept
529 E Home Rd (45503-2710)
PHONE.....................937 390-5600
Fax: 937 390-5625
Charles Patterson, *Commissioner*
EMP: 75 **Privately Held**
WEB: www.ccpl.lib.oh.us
SIC: 8099 Health screening service
PA: County Of Clark
50 E Columbia St Fl 5
Springfield OH 45502
937 521-2005

(G-17179)
COUNTY OF CLARK
Also Called: Clark County Human Services
1345 Lagonda Ave (45503-4001)
PHONE.....................937 327-1700
Fax: 937 327-1996
Robert Suver, *Branch Mgr*
EMP: 250 **Privately Held**
WEB: www.ccpl.lib.oh.us
SIC: 8322 Public welfare center
PA: County Of Clark
50 E Columbia St Fl 5
Springfield OH 45502
937 521-2005

(G-17180)
COUNTY OF CLARK
Nursing Division
529 E Home Rd (45503-2710)
PHONE.....................937 390-5615
Fax: 937 390-5626
Charles Patterson, *Commissioner*
EMP: 70 **Privately Held**
WEB: www.ccpl.lib.oh.us
SIC: 9431 8069 ; specialty hospitals, except psychiatric
PA: County Of Clark
50 E Columbia St Fl 5
Springfield OH 45502
937 521-2005

(G-17181)
COUNTY OF CLARK
Clark County Job & Family Svc
1346 Lagonda Ave (45503-4041)
PHONE.....................937 327-1700
Robert B Suver, *Branch Mgr*
EMP: 290 **Privately Held**
WEB: www.ccpl.lib.oh.us
SIC: 8322 Individual & family services; child related social services; family counseling services
PA: County Of Clark
50 E Columbia St Fl 5
Springfield OH 45502
937 521-2005

(G-17182)
COUNTY OF CLARK
Also Called: Child Support
1345 Lagonda Ave (45503-4001)
PHONE.....................937 327-1700
Nancy Zimmerman, *Manager*
EMP: 300 **Privately Held**
WEB: www.ccpl.lib.oh.us
SIC: 8322 Child related social services
PA: County Of Clark
50 E Columbia St Fl 5
Springfield OH 45502
937 521-2005

(G-17183)
COVENANT CARE OHIO INC
Also Called: Villa Springfield
701 Villa Rd (45503-1330)
PHONE.....................937 399-5551
Fax: 937 399-0737
Rhonda Nissley, *Branch Mgr*
Dawn Cavins, *Data Proc Staff*
Vitul Patel, *Director*
Missy Young, *Nursing Dir*
Gretta Gaines, *Hlthcr Dir*
EMP: 90 **Privately Held**
WEB: www.villageorgetown.com
SIC: 8051 Skilled nursing care facilities
HQ: Covenant Care Ohio, Inc.
27071 Aliso Creek Rd # 100
Aliso Viejo CA 92656
949 349-1200

(G-17184)
CREFIII WARAMAUG
Also Called: Courtyard Springfield Downtown
100 S Fountain Ave (45502-1208)
PHONE.....................937 322-3600
Becky Krieger, *General Mgr*
Craig Nussbaum, *Vice Pres*
EMP: 60
SALES (est): 992.9K **Privately Held**
SIC: 5812 7011 American restaurant; resort hotel

(G-17185)
CROWNING FOOD COMPANY
Also Called: Wober Muster
1966 Commerce Cir (45504-2012)
P.O. Box 388 (45501-0388)
PHONE.....................937 323-4699
Fax: 937 323-1679
Ray Woeber, *Owner*
Jean Lewis, *Vice Pres*
Dick Wober, *Vice Pres*
◆ **EMP:** 85
SALES (est): 10.6MM **Privately Held**
SIC: 5149 Sauces

(G-17186)
D C MINNICK CONTRACTING LTD (PA)
Also Called: D.C.minnick Heating and AC
328 Ravenwood Dr (45504-3367)
PHONE.....................937 322-1012
David Minnick, *CEO*
Mike L Cole, *Shareholder*
Darlene R Minnick, *Shareholder*
EMP: 26
SQ FT: 10,800
SALES: 5.3MM **Privately Held**
SIC: 1711 1731 Plumbing, heating, air-conditioning contractors; plumbing contractors; general electrical contractor

(G-17187)
DAVIS 5 STAR HOLDINGS LLC (PA)
14 E Main St Ste 300 (45502-1358)
PHONE.....................954 470-8456
Derek Davis Sr, *CEO*
Terrel Carlson, *COO*
EMP: 25
SQ FT: 12,500
SALES: 50MM **Privately Held**
SIC: 8742 Marketing consulting services

(G-17188)
DEMMY CONSTRUCTION INC
4324 Fairfield Pike (45502-9705)
PHONE.....................937 325-9429
Fax: 937 323-5016
Daniel E Demmy, *President*
Anne Demmy, *Vice Pres*
EMP: 25 **EST:** 1973
SQ FT: 3,500
SALES (est): 2.7MM **Privately Held**
SIC: 1794 Excavation & grading, building construction

(G-17189)
DEMMY SAND AND GRAVEL LLC
4324 Fairfield Pike (45502-9707)
PHONE.....................937 325-8840
Fax: 937 325-9482
Amy Demmy, *General Mgr*
Woodrow Demmy,
EMP: 25 **EST:** 1944
SALES (est): 2.2MM **Privately Held**
SIC: 1442 0115 0119 0111 Common sand mining; gravel mining; corn; bean (dry field & seed) farm; wheat

(G-17190)
DOLE FRESH VEGETABLES INC
600 Benjamin Dr (45502-8860)
PHONE.....................937 525-4300
Fax: 937 525-4353
Phillip Mansour, *Maint Spvr*
Lenny Pelifian, *Branch Mgr*
Leonard Davis, *Manager*
Michael Mendoza, *Manager*
Aaron Schneider, *Supervisor*
EMP: 190
SALES (corp-wide): 11.7B **Privately Held**
SIC: 5148 2099 Fruits, fresh; food preparations
HQ: Dole Fresh Vegetables, Inc.
2959 Salinas Hwy
Monterey CA 93940
831 422-8871

(G-17191)
EAGLEWOOD CARE CENTER
2000 Villa Rd (45503-1761)
PHONE.....................937 399-7195
Fax: 937 399-1474
Babur Khaan, *Administration*
Mark Lewis, *Administration*
EMP: 160

GEOGRAPHIC SECTION

Springfield - Clark County (G-17216)

SQ FT: 29,000
SALES (est): 7.7MM **Privately Held**
SIC: 8051 6513 Convalescent home with continuous nursing care; apartment building operators

(G-17192)
EBY-BROWN COMPANY LLC
1982 Commerce Cir (45504-2012)
PHONE..................937 324-1036
Rich Haen, *Sales Dir*
Tom Oktavec, *Marketing Staff*
Jeff Bundy, *Info Tech Mgr*
EMP: 225 **Privately Held**
WEB: www.eby-brown.com
SIC: 5194 5145 5141 5122 Cigarettes; cigars; snuff; confectionery; groceries, general line; drugs, proprietaries & sundries; groceries & related products
PA: Eby-Brown Company, Llc
   1415 W Diehl Rd Ste 300
   Naperville IL 60563

(G-17193)
ELDERLY UNITED OF SPRINGFIELD (PA)
Also Called: United Senior Services
125 W Main St (45502-1311)
PHONE..................937 323-4948
Fax: 937 324-9005
Treva Howell, *Bookkeeper*
Lisa McDonough, *Cust Mgr*
Maureen Fagans, *Exec Dir*
Stephanie Clark, *Director*
Joyce Ware, *Asst Director*
EMP: 99
SQ FT: 24,000
SALES (est): 4.6MM **Privately Held**
WEB: www.elderlyunited.org
SIC: 8322 Senior citizens' center or association

(G-17194)
ENCOMPASS HEALTH CORPORATION
Also Called: HealthSouth
2685 E High St (45505-1412)
PHONE..................205 970-4869
Melissa Halley, *Administration*
EMP: 28
SALES (corp-wide): 3.9B **Publicly Held**
WEB: www.healthsouth.com
SIC: 8062 General medical & surgical hospitals
PA: Encompass Health Corporation
   3660 Grandview Pkwy
   Birmingham AL 35243
   205 967-7116

(G-17195)
F H BONN
Also Called: F H Bonn Company
4300 Gateway Blvd (45502-8819)
PHONE..................937 323-7024
Neal Bonn, *Owner*
EMP: 45
SALES (est): 1.7MM **Privately Held**
SIC: 6512 Commercial & industrial building operation

(G-17196)
FAMILY PRACTICE & ASSOCIATES
2701 Moorefield Rd (45502-8207)
PHONE..................937 399-6650
Fax: 937 399-8558
Sally Abbott MD, *Partner*
Richard Gordon MD, *Partner*
Sangita A Padmalwar, *Physician Asst*
EMP: 25
SALES (est): 2.2MM **Privately Held**
SIC: 8011 General & family practice, physician/surgeon

(G-17197)
FDC ENTERPRISES INC
5470 Ballentine Pike (45502-9011)
P.O. Box 189, New Albany (43054-0189)
PHONE..................614 774-9182
Fred D Circle, *President*
Kevin L Mason, *Opers Staff*
Tom Schwartz, *Marketing Mgr*
Doug Bensman, *Manager*
Liz Hammond, *Manager*
EMP: 26

SQ FT: 2,000
SALES (est): 2.3MM **Privately Held**
WEB: www.fdcenterprises.com
SIC: 0783 Removal services, bush & tree

(G-17198)
FIRST DIVERSITY STAFFING GROUP
560 E High St (45505-1010)
PHONE..................937 323-4114
George Ten, *President*
Ten Geroge, *President*
Bruce Smith, *Business Mgr*
Eric Collins, *Vice Pres*
Geroge Ten, *Vice Pres*
EMP: 500 EST: 2008
SQ FT: 6,000
SALES (est): 27.2MM **Privately Held**
SIC: 7361 Executive placement

(G-17199)
FIRST OHIO HOME FINANCE INC
1021 N Limestone St (45503-3613)
PHONE..................937 322-3396
Anthony Coplen, *President*
Nick Cruz, *Vice Pres*
EMP: 25
SALES (est): 1.6MM **Privately Held**
SIC: 6162 Mortgage bankers & correspondents

(G-17200)
FRATERNAL ORDER OF EAGLES
Also Called: Champion Aerie 397
1802 Selma Rd (45505-4242)
PHONE..................937 323-0671
Fax: 937 323-1656
Matt Garst, *President*
Robert Miller, *President*
Charlie Heinz, *Trustee*
Louim WER, *Treasurer*
Margie Wheeler, *Office Mgr*
EMP: 40
SALES (est): 499.7K **Privately Held**
SIC: 8641 Fraternal associations

(G-17201)
GAMMA PHI BETA SORORITY ALPHA
628 Woodlawn Ave (45504-2124)
PHONE..................937 324-3436
Alexa Berklin, *President*
EMP: 72
SQ FT: 5,048
SALES: 58.2K **Privately Held**
SIC: 8641 University club

(G-17202)
GOOD SHEPARD VILLAGE LLC
422 N Burnett Rd (45503-4821)
PHONE..................937 322-1911
Fax: 937 322-8606
Curtis Springer,
EMP: 70
SALES (est): 4.4MM **Privately Held**
SIC: 8051 Convalescent home with continuous nursing care

(G-17203)
GRANDVIEW HT LTD PARTNR OHIO
Also Called: Holiday Inn
383 E Leffel Ln (45505-4746)
PHONE..................937 766-5519
Fax: 937 323-5389
Mark Russell, *Sales Executive*
Nancy Bloomingdale, *Manager*
EMP: 73
SALES (corp-wide): 8.7MM **Privately Held**
SIC: 7011 5812 7299 7991 Hotels & motels; eating places; banquet hall facilities; physical fitness facilities; drinking places
PA: Grandview Hotel Limited Partnership Of Ohio
   740 Centre View Blvd
   Crestview Hills KY

(G-17204)
HEALTH CARE RTREMENT CORP AMER
Also Called: Heartland of Springfield
2615 Derr Rd (45503-2445)
PHONE..................937 390-0005

Karen Simms, *Human Res Dir*
Kelly Meckstroch, *Branch Mgr*
EMP: 110
SALES (corp-wide): 3.6B **Publicly Held**
WEB: www.hrc-manorcare.com
SIC: 8051 Convalescent home with continuous nursing care
HQ: Health Care And Retirement Corporation Of America
   333 N Summit St Ste 103
   Toledo OH 43604
   419 252-5500

(G-17205)
HOME CITY FEDERAL SAVINGS BANK (HQ)
2454 N Limestone St (45503-1110)
P.O. Box 1288 (45501-1288)
PHONE..................937 390-0470
Fax: 937 390-0876
J William Stapleton, *CEO*
John Conroy, *Ch of Bd*
William Stapleton, *COO*
Margaret A Detty, *Vice Pres*
Peter E Duffey, *Vice Pres*
EMP: 30 EST: 1925
SQ FT: 3,500
SALES: 7.8MM
SALES (corp-wide): 6.9MM **Publicly Held**
SIC: 6035 Federal savings & loan associations
PA: Home City Financial Corp
   2454 N Limestone St
   Springfield OH 45503
   937 390-0470

(G-17206)
HOMETOWN URGENT CARE
1200 Vester Ave (45503-1304)
PHONE..................937 342-9520
Toni Rogers, *Branch Mgr*
EMP: 202
SALES (corp-wide): 73.2MM **Privately Held**
SIC: 8062 8049 8011 General medical & surgical hospitals; occupational therapist; medical centers
PA: Hometown Urgent Care
   2400 Corp Exchange Dr # 102
   Columbus OH 43231
   614 505-7633

(G-17207)
HOMETOWN URGENT CARE
1301 W 1st St (45504-1920)
PHONE..................937 322-6222
EMP: 126
SALES (corp-wide): 73.2MM **Privately Held**
SIC: 8011 Primary care medical clinic
PA: Hometown Urgent Care
   2400 Corp Exchange Dr # 102
   Columbus OH 43231
   614 505-7633

(G-17208)
HORNER INDUSTRIAL SERVICES INC
Also Called: Scherer Industrial Group
5330 Prosperity Dr (45502-9074)
PHONE..................937 390-6667
Fax: 937 390-7493
Mike Harper, *Manager*
Michael Harper, *Director*
EMP: 25
SALES (corp-wide): 46.7MM **Privately Held**
SIC: 5063 7694 Motors, electric; electric motor repair
PA: Horner Industrial Services, Inc.
   1521 E Washington St
   Indianapolis IN 46201
   317 639-4261

(G-17209)
HUSTEAD EMERGENCY MEDICAL SVC
6215 Springfield Xenia Rd (45502-8142)
PHONE..................937 324-3031
Heather Kaufman, *Chief*
EMP: 25
SALES (est): 630.3K **Privately Held**
SIC: 4119 Ambulance service

(G-17210)
IMPERIAL EXPRESS INC
202 N Limestone St # 300 (45503-4246)
P.O. Box 1607 (45501-1607)
PHONE..................937 399-9400
Charles Crabill, *President*
Dale Briggs, *Vice Pres*
Cindy Frey, *Office Mgr*
Bryan Valentine, *Executive*
James Valentine, *Admin Sec*
EMP: 44
SQ FT: 4,000
SALES: 6MM **Privately Held**
SIC: 4212 Local trucking, without storage

(G-17211)
INDEPENDENT LIVING OF OHIO
530 S Burnett Rd (45505-2720)
PHONE..................937 323-8400
Fax: 937 325-3518
Deborah Ackley, *President*
EMP: 45
SQ FT: 4,500
SALES (est): 1.1MM **Privately Held**
SIC: 8082 Home health care services

(G-17212)
INSIDE OUT (PA)
Also Called: Inside Out Child Care
501 S Wittenberg Ave (45506-2101)
PHONE..................937 525-7880
William R Stout, *President*
Diana Skinny, *Admin Asst*
EMP: 75
SQ FT: 60,000
SALES: 761.1K **Privately Held**
SIC: 8322 Social service center

(G-17213)
INTEGRATED YOUTH SERVICES INC
1055 E High St (45505-1157)
PHONE..................937 427-3837
Dave Nuscher, *CEO*
Dave Nusher, *CEO*
Michael King, *Manager*
EMP: 45
SALES: 2MM **Privately Held**
SIC: 8093 Mental health clinic, outpatient

(G-17214)
INTERNATIONAL TRUCK & ENG CORP
6125 Urbana Rd (45502-9279)
PHONE..................937 390-4045
Fax: 937 390-5834
John R Horne, *CEO*
Mr Daniel Ustian, *Ch of Bd*
Bob Baker, *Principal*
Robert A Boardman, *Senior VP*
Donald Kohs, *Vice Pres*
EMP: 1500 EST: 1999
SALES (est): 71.9MM **Privately Held**
SIC: 4212 Local trucking, without storage

(G-17215)
IOOF HOME OF OHIO INC (PA)
404 E Mccreight Ave (45503-3690)
PHONE..................937 399-8631
Fax: 937 399-8876
David Taylor, *Administration*
EMP: 30 EST: 1987
SALES (est): 3.5MM **Privately Held**
SIC: 8051 Skilled nursing care facilities

(G-17216)
JERSEY CENTRAL PWR & LIGHT CO
Also Called: Firstenergy
420 York St (45505-2143)
PHONE..................937 327-1218
Tom Clark, *Manager*
EMP: 80 **Publicly Held**
WEB: www.jersey-central-power-light.monmouth.n
SIC: 4911 Generation, electric power
HQ: Jersey Central Power & Light Company
   76 S Main St
   Akron OH 44308
   800 736-3402

Springfield - Clark County (G-17217) — GEOGRAPHIC SECTION

(G-17217)
JKL DEVELOPMENT COMPANY (PA)
Also Called: Splish Splash Auto Bath
2101 E Home Rd (45503-2516)
PHONE.................937 390-0358
Fax: 937 390-0359
Jack Sayers, *President*
EMP: 30
SALES (est): 2.2MM **Privately Held**
SIC: 7542 Carwash, automatic

(G-17218)
K - O - I WAREHOUSE INC
622 W Main St (45504-2637)
PHONE.................937 323-5585
Bob Curry, *Branch Mgr*
EMP: 25
SALES (corp-wide): 626MM **Privately Held**
WEB: www.koiwarehouse.com
SIC: 5013 5531 Automotive supplies & parts; automotive parts
HQ: K - O - I Warehouse, Inc.
2701 Spring Grove Ave
Cincinnati OH 45225
513 357-2400

(G-17219)
KAPP CONSTRUCTION INC
329 Mount Vernon Ave (45503-4143)
P.O. Box 629 (45501-0629)
PHONE.................937 324-0134
Fax: 937 324-3406
Randy Kapp, *President*
Cheryl Dalhamer, *VP Opers*
Sam Melish, *Project Mgr*
Michael R Hamilton, *Controller*
Marilyn McKenzie, *Human Res Dir*
EMP: 45
SALES (est): 15.3MM **Privately Held**
WEB: www.kappconstruction.com
SIC: 1542 1541 Commercial & office building, new construction; commercial & office buildings, renovation & repair; industrial buildings & warehouses; renovation, remodeling & repairs: industrial buildings

(G-17220)
LATEEF ELMIN MHAMMAD INV GROUP
Also Called: Imam WD Mohammed Comm Devt
524 W Liberty St (45506-2024)
PHONE.................937 450-3388
Jihad Muhammad, *CEO*
Robert Rhinehardt, *Principal*
Olenthia Rhinehart, *Vice Pres*
Yahya R El Amin, *CFO*
Lori El Amin, *Treasurer*
EMP: 56
SALES: 950K **Privately Held**
SIC: 8748 Business consulting

(G-17221)
LINEAGE LOGISTICS LLC
1985 Airpark Dr (45502-7976)
PHONE.................937 328-3349
EMP: 40
SALES (corp-wide): 1.4B **Privately Held**
SIC: 8741 Administrative management
HQ: Lineage Logistics, Llc
46500 Humboldt Dr
Novi MI 48377
248 863-4400

(G-17222)
LINKS AT WINDY KNOLL LLC
Also Called: Windy Knoll Golf Club
500 Roscommon Dr (45503-7133)
PHONE.................937 631-3744
Fax: 937 390-8860
Gary Price, *Superintendent*
Dan D'Arrigo, *Mng Member*
EMP: 65
SQ FT: 4,900
SALES (est): 2MM **Privately Held**
SIC: 7992 5941 Public golf courses; golf goods & equipment

(G-17223)
LOBBY SHOPPES INC (PA)
Also Called: Lobby Shoppes Inc-Springfield
200 N Murray St (45503-4297)
P.O. Box 1200 (45501-1200)
PHONE.................937 324-0002
Fax: 937 325-1100
Michael H Chakeres, *President*
Tony Taylor, *Sales Associate*
EMP: 200
SQ FT: 15,000
SALES (est): 4.5MM **Privately Held**
SIC: 5812 5145 Concessionaire; confectionery

(G-17224)
LOCUST HILLS GOLF INC
Also Called: Locust Hills Golf Course
5575 N River Rd (45502-6324)
PHONE.................937 265-5152
Fax: 937 265-5071
John Lee Kitchen, *President*
Carol Kitchen, *Principal*
Joann Kitchen, *Principal*
Richard Lee Kitchen, *Vice Pres*
EMP: 45
SQ FT: 5,232
SALES: 1MM **Privately Held**
WEB: www.locusthillsgc.com
SIC: 7992 Public golf courses

(G-17225)
LOVES TRAVEL STOPS
Also Called: Loves Trvl Stops Cntry Stores
4725 S Charleston Pike (45502-9345)
PHONE.................937 325-2961
EMP: 25
SALES (corp-wide): 5.5B **Privately Held**
SIC: 8699 Travel club
PA: Love's Travel Stops & Country Stores, Inc.
10601 N Pennsylvania Ave
Oklahoma City OK 73120
405 302-6500

(G-17226)
LOWES HOME CENTERS LLC
1601 N Bechtle Ave (45504-1576)
PHONE.................937 327-6000
Fax: 937 327-6018
Mark Sprague, *Manager*
Jeremy Givens, *Manager*
Dave Tanner, *Manager*
EMP: 120
SALES (corp-wide): 68.6B **Publicly Held**
SIC: 5211 5031 5722 5064 Home centers; building materials, exterior; building materials, interior; household appliance stores; electrical appliances, television & radio
HQ: Lowe's Home Centers, Llc
1605 Curtis Bridge Rd
Wilkesboro NC 28697
336 658-4000

(G-17227)
M & R AMUSEMENT SERVICES INC (PA)
Also Called: Ooh Ooh Drive Thru
1100 Lagonda Ave (45503-4303)
P.O. Box 1247 (45501-1247)
PHONE.................937 525-0404
Fax: 937 323-0606
Robert Mowell, *President*
Julie Knisley, *Vice Pres*
Julie Van Beder, *Treasurer*
Mary Mowell, *Admin Sec*
EMP: 35
SALES: 2MM **Privately Held**
SIC: 5963 5993 7999 Coffee, soda, beer, etc: house-to-house sales; cigarette store; tourist attractions, amusement park concessions & rides

(G-17228)
MAINES COLLISION REPR & BDY SP
Also Called: Maines Towing & Recovery Svc
1717 E Pleasant St (45505-3313)
P.O. Box 1045 (45501-1045)
PHONE.................937 322-4618
Fred E Maine, *President*
John Hawke Jr, *Senior VP*
Scott Hennigan, *Vice Pres*
Stacy Pavalatos, *Treasurer*
Mike Catanzaro, *Admin Sec*
EMP: 60
SQ FT: 20,000
SALES (est): 6.8MM **Privately Held**
WEB: www.mainescr.com
SIC: 7532 7549 4213 7538 Body shop, automotive; towing service, automotive; trucking, except local; heavy machinery transport; truck engine repair, except industrial

(G-17229)
MASONIC HEALTHCARE INC
3 Masonic Dr (45504-3658)
PHONE.................937 525-3001
Fax: 937 525-3085
Marion Leeman, *President*
Nancy Archabold, *Principal*
Greg Holm, *COO*
Jerry Guess, *Vice Pres*
David Stacy, *CFO*
EMP: 500 EST: 1995
SALES (est): 7.4MM **Privately Held**
WEB: www.masonichealthcare.com
SIC: 8051 Convalescent home with continuous nursing care

(G-17230)
MCKINLEY HALL INC
2624 Lexington Ave (45505-2607)
PHONE.................937 328-5300
Fax: 937 322-4900
Wendy Doolittle, *CEO*
Daniel Barksdale, *Administration*
EMP: 50
SQ FT: 3,482
SALES: 4.1MM **Privately Held**
SIC: 8069 8093 8051 Alcoholism rehabilitation hospital; drug addiction rehabilitation hospital; specialty outpatient clinics; skilled nursing care facilities

(G-17231)
MED-TRANS INC (PA)
714 W Columbia St (45504-2734)
P.O. Box 1048 (45501-1048)
PHONE.................937 325-4926
William George, *Ch of Bd*
Luanne George, *President*
Edward G Bailey, *Vice Pres*
Tyler Osborne, *Supervisor*
David Devore, *Telecom Exec*
EMP: 100
SQ FT: 7,600
SALES (est): 18.6MM **Privately Held**
WEB: www.med-trans.com
SIC: 4119 Ambulance service

(G-17232)
MENTAL HEALTH SERVICE
474 N Yellow Springs St (45504-2463)
PHONE.................937 399-9500
Curt Gillespie, *CEO*
Jo Marenberg, *Human Res Dir*
David Wolverton, *CIO*
James Gibfried, *Director*
Deb Padgett, *Nursing Dir*
EMP: 28
SALES (est): 2.2MM **Privately Held**
SIC: 8052 Home for the mentally retarded, with health care

(G-17233)
MENTAL HLTH SERV FOR CL & MAD
1086 Mound St (45505-1298)
PHONE.................937 390-7980
Jim Wade, *Manager*
Amanda I Rush, *Nurse Practr*
EMP: 50
SALES (corp-wide): 13.3MM **Privately Held**
WEB: www.mhscc.com
SIC: 8063 8322 Hospital for the mentally ill; social worker
PA: Mental Health Services For Clark And Madison Counties, Inc.
474 N Yellow Springs St
Springfield OH 45504
937 399-9500

(G-17234)
MENTAL HLTH SERV FOR CL & MAD (PA)
474 N Yellow Springs St (45504-2463)
PHONE.................937 399-9500
Fax: 937 342-4255
Jeff Hughes, *Vice Ch Bd*
James P Perry PHD, *President*
Jeff Darding, *Vice Pres*
Mary B Taylor, *CFO*
Dave Willverton, *CIO*
EMP: 219
SQ FT: 30,000
SALES: 13.3MM **Privately Held**
WEB: www.mhscc.com
SIC: 8063 Hospital for the mentally ill

(G-17235)
MERCY HEALTH
160 Tuttle Rd (45503-5234)
PHONE.................937 323-4585
EMP: 35
SALES (corp-wide): 4.2B **Privately Held**
SIC: 8099 Childbirth preparation clinic
PA: Mercy Health
1701 Mercy Health Pl
Cincinnati OH 45237
513 639-2800

(G-17236)
MERCY HEALTH
211 Northparke Dr Ste 101 (45503-1117)
PHONE.................937 390-1700
Fax: 937 390-2471
EMP: 62
SALES (corp-wide): 4.2B **Privately Held**
SIC: 8011 Internal medicine, physician/surgeon
PA: Mercy Health
1701 Mercy Health Pl
Cincinnati OH 45237
513 639-2800

(G-17237)
MERCY HEALTH
100 W Mccreight Ave # 400 (45504-1885)
P.O. Box 1380 (45501-1380)
PHONE.................937 390-9665
Fax: 937 390-2363
EMP: 138
SALES (corp-wide): 4.2B **Privately Held**
SIC: 8052 Personal care facility
PA: Mercy Health
1701 Mercy Health Pl
Cincinnati OH 45237
513 639-2800

(G-17238)
MERCY HEALTH
Also Called: Catholic Healthcare Par...
2615 E High St (45505-1412)
PHONE.................937 390-5515
Krist Kohl-Mccready, *Branch Mgr*
EMP: 28
SALES (corp-wide): 4.2B **Privately Held**
SIC: 8049 Nutrition specialist
PA: Mercy Health
1701 Mercy Health Pl
Cincinnati OH 45237
513 639-2800

(G-17239)
MERCY HEALTH
Also Called: Commun Mer OCC Healh & Medici
2501 E High St (45505-1410)
PHONE.................937 328-8700
Linda Neal, *Manager*
EMP: 62
SALES (corp-wide): 4.2B **Privately Held**
SIC: 8049 Acupuncturist
PA: Mercy Health
1701 Mercy Health Pl
Cincinnati OH 45237
513 639-2800

(G-17240)
MERCY HEALTH
2600 N Limestone St (45503-1114)
PHONE.................937 390-5075
Fax: 937 390-5091
Judy Snyder, *Opers Mgr*
Sue Balek, *Purch Mgr*
Allan Mingus, *Technology*
Brian C Dethloff, *Director*
Rod E Hayhurst, *Director*
EMP: 35
SALES (corp-wide): 4.2B **Privately Held**
SIC: 8049 Physical therapist

GEOGRAPHIC SECTION

Springfield - Clark County (G-17264)

PA: Mercy Health
1701 Mercy Health Pl
Cincinnati OH 45237
513 639-2800

(G-17241)
MERCY HEALTH - SPRINGFIELD C
Also Called: Springfeld Rgnal Cncer Ctr LLC
148 W North St (45504-2547)
PHONE..................937 323-5001
Fax: 937 323-5413
Paul Hiltz, CEO
EMP: 35 EST: 2011
SALES (est): 2.3MM
SALES (corp-wide): 4.2B Privately Held
SIC: 8069 Cancer hospital
HQ: Community Mercy Health Partners
100 Medical Center Dr
Springfield OH 45504

(G-17242)
MERCY MEDICAL CENTER
1343 N Fountain Blvd (45504-1499)
P.O. Box 688 (45501-0688)
PHONE..................937 390-5000
Andrew McCulloch, President
Marion Purdue, COO
Freddy Katai, Ch Radiology
Cindy Glassford, Purchasing
Cheryl P Williams, Med Doctor
EMP: 868
SQ FT: 25,160
SALES (est): 44.1MM Privately Held
SIC: 8062 General medical & surgical hospitals

(G-17243)
MERRILL LYNCH PIERCE FENNER
1155 Scanlon Ln (45503-6666)
PHONE..................614 225-3197
EMP: 27
SALES (corp-wide): 100.2B Publicly Held
SIC: 6211 Security brokers & dealers
HQ: Merrill Lynch, Pierce, Fenner & Smith Incorporated
111 8th Ave
New York NY 10011
800 637-7455

(G-17244)
METACARTA INCORPORATED
250 Veronia Dr Ste 300 (45505-1681)
PHONE..................937 458-0345
Steve Baldwin, President
John Donnelley, Vice Pres
Steve Egan, Engineer
Roy Marvin, Manager
EMP: 25
SALES (est): 1.1MM
SALES (corp-wide): 28.9MM Privately Held
WEB: www.metacarta.com
SIC: 7371 Computer software development
PA: Qbase, Llc
3725 Pentagon Blvd # 100
Beavercreek OH 45431
888 458-0345

(G-17245)
METALS USA CRBN FLAT RLLED INC
5750 Lower Valley Pike (45502-9101)
PHONE..................937 882-6354
Ruth Workman, Purch Mgr
Jeff Taugh, Manager
David Grimm, Manager
EMP: 54
SALES (corp-wide): 9.7B Publicly Held
SIC: 5051 3312 Steel; blast furnaces & steel mills
HQ: Metals Usa Carbon Flat Rolled, Inc.
1070 W Liberty St
Wooster OH 44691
330 264-8416

(G-17246)
MIAMI VLY CHILD DEV CTRS INC
Also Called: Clark County Office
1450 S Yellow Springs St (45506-2545)
PHONE..................937 325-2559
Fax: 937 328-7211
Diane Johnson, Manager
EMP: 106
SALES (corp-wide): 32MM Privately Held
WEB: www.mvcdc.org
SIC: 8351 Preschool center
PA: Miami Valley Child Development Centers, Inc.
215 Horace St
Dayton OH 45402
937 226-5664

(G-17247)
MID-OHIO HARLEY-DAVIDSON INC
2100 Quality Ln (45505-3623)
PHONE..................937 322-3590
Fax: 937 322-5154
Roland Ude, President
Melody Ude, Corp Secy
Brian Cubbage, Vice Pres
EMP: 25
SQ FT: 19,000
SALES (est): 6.1MM Privately Held
WEB: www.midohiohd.com
SIC: 5571 7699 Motorcycles; motorcycle parts & accessories; motorcycle repair service

(G-17248)
MIDWEST REINFORCING CONTRS
1839 N Fountain Blvd (45504-1406)
P.O. Box 2060 (45501-2060)
PHONE..................937 390-8998
Fax: 937 399-9452
Katherine A Heinzen, President
Scott Heinzen, Vice Pres
EMP: 25
SALES: 1.1MM Privately Held
SIC: 1791 Concrete reinforcement, placing of

(G-17249)
MILLERS TEXTILE SERVICES INC
540 E Columbia St (45503-4200)
PHONE..................614 262-1206
Fax: 937 323-4400
Jim Bode, Branch Mgr
John Engle, Manager
EMP: 25
SALES (corp-wide): 21.9MM Privately Held
WEB: www.millerstextile.com
SIC: 7213 Uniform supply
PA: Miller's Textile Services, Inc.
520 Commerce Rd
Wapakoneta OH
419 738-3551

(G-17250)
NAVISTAR INTL TRNSP CORP
5975 Urbana Rd (45502-9537)
PHONE..................937 390-4242
Fax: 937 390-4140
Tom Tullis, President
Brian Powell, Engineer
Kerwin Waugh, Engineer
Ed Ho, Technology
EMP: 200
SALES (est): 15.1MM Privately Held
SIC: 7538 General truck repair

(G-17251)
NEW NGHBORS RSDENTIAL SVCS INC
4230 E National Rd (45505-1759)
PHONE..................937 717-5731
Brenda McAlexander, CEO
EMP: 35
SALES: 1.3MM Privately Held
SIC: 8361 Home for the mentally handicapped

(G-17252)
NIGHTINGALE MONTESSORI INC
Also Called: NIGHTINGALE MONTESSORI SCHOOL
1106 E High St (45505-1122)
PHONE..................937 324-0336
Fax: 937 398-0086
Sheila Brown, Corp Secy
Ray Eckhardt, Comp Tech
Nancy Schwab, Administration
Maria Taylor, Administration
EMP: 34
SALES: 1.2MM Privately Held
SIC: 8211 8351 Private elementary & secondary schools; private elementary school; Montessori child development center

(G-17253)
NORTHWEST COLUMBUS UROLOGY
Also Called: Springfield Urology
1164 E Home Rd Ste J (45503-2726)
PHONE..................937 342-9260
Tina Stuart, Office Mgr
Karen Baumgardner, Office Mgr
Asha B Shah, Urology
EMP: 25 Privately Held
SIC: 8011 Urologist
PA: Northwest Columbus Urology
551 W Central Ave Ste 102
Delaware OH 43015

(G-17254)
OESTERLEN-SERVICES FOR YOUTH
Also Called: SOCIAL MINISTRY ORGANIZATION
1918 Mechanicsburg Rd (45503-3147)
PHONE..................937 399-6101
Fax: 937 399-6609
Lucy Yu, Accountant
Kathryn Murphy, Finance
Kiley Outram, Personnel Exec
Debbie Henderson, Human Resources
Mark Derr, Marketing Staff
EMP: 150
SQ FT: 10,204
SALES: 5.7MM Privately Held
WEB: www.oesterlen.org
SIC: 8211 8661 8361 Private special education school; community church; residential care

(G-17255)
OHIO INSTITUTE OF CARDIAC CARE (PA)
Also Called: Oicc
2200 N Limestone St # 100 (45503-2692)
PHONE..................937 322-1700
Fax: 937 322-8070
Salim O Dahdah MD, President
Cindy Dahdah, Vice Pres
Jen Webster, Office Mgr
Pam Gothard, Manager
Tammy Spiers, Manager
EMP: 32
SALES (est): 12MM Privately Held
WEB: www.ohiohealthchoice.com
SIC: 8011 Cardiologist & cardio-vascular specialist

(G-17256)
OHIO MASONIC RETIREMENT VLG
4 Masonic Dr (45504-3695)
PHONE..................937 525-1743
John Nofsinger, President
EMP: 65
SALES (est): 913.7K Privately Held
SIC: 8641 Civic associations

(G-17257)
OHIO VALLEY MEDICAL CENTER LLC
100 E Main St (45502-1308)
PHONE..................937 521-3900
James Cromwell, Ch of Bd
Steve Eisentrager, President
Ajay Mangal, Principal
Ronny Shumaker, COO
Dean Stoughton, Plant Mgr
EMP: 66
SALES (est): 34.4MM Privately Held
SIC: 8011 Ambulatory surgical center

(G-17258)
PARK NATIONAL BANK
40 S Limestone St (45502-1222)
PHONE..................937 324-6800
H Egger, Principal
EMP: 30
SALES (corp-wide): 367MM Publicly Held
SIC: 6022 State commercial banks
HQ: The Park National Bank
50 N 3rd St
Newark OH 43055
740 349-8451

(G-17259)
PEDIATRIC ASSOC OF SPRINGFIELD
1640 N Limestone St (45503-2652)
PHONE..................937 328-2320
Raymond Cooper MD, President
EMP: 58
SALES (est): 5.4MM Privately Held
SIC: 8011 Pediatrician

(G-17260)
PENTAFLEX INC
4981 Gateway Blvd (45502-8867)
PHONE..................937 325-5551
Fax: 937 325-2620
Dave Arndt, President
Ross McGregor, Vice Pres
Rodney Phipps, Vice Pres
Phil Dafforn, Materials Mgr
Bob Mayberry, Engineer
◆ EMP: 110
SQ FT: 146,000
SALES (est): 28.2MM Privately Held
WEB: www.pentaflex.com
SIC: 3469 7692 Stamping metal for the trade; welding repair

(G-17261)
PHYSICIANS SURGEONS FOR WOMEN
1821 E High St (45505-1225)
PHONE..................937 323-7340
Fax: 937 323-3363
David R Billing MD, Partner
Lisa M Delong MD, Partner
Veronica S Bishop, Office Mgr
Christy L Campbell, Obstetrician
EMP: 25
SQ FT: 6,000
SALES (est): 2.8MM Privately Held
WEB: www.cpso.on.ca
SIC: 8011 Gynecologist; obstetrician

(G-17262)
R&M MATERIALS HANDLING INC
Also Called: R & M
4501 Gateway Blvd (45502-8863)
PHONE..................937 328-5100
Fax: 937 325-5319
Jim Vandegrift, President
Todd Worley, Vice Pres
Troy Post, Opers-Prdtn-Mfg
Steve Mayes, Treasurer
Lisa M Roth, Treasurer
▼ EMP: 41
SQ FT: 110,000
SALES (est): 18.3MM
SALES (corp-wide): 2.2B Privately Held
WEB: www.rmhoist.com
SIC: 5084 Materials handling machinery; hoists
HQ: Kci Holding Usa Inc.
4401 Gateway Blvd
Springfield OH 45502

(G-17263)
REAL ESTATE II INC
1140 E Home Rd (45503-2726)
PHONE..................937 390-3119
Sue Smedley, President
Charlene Roberge, Broker
Janet Anderson, Sales Staff
Charlene McAllister, Manager
EMP: 26
SQ FT: 2,000
SALES: 21MM Privately Held
SIC: 6531 Real estate agent, residential

(G-17264)
ROBINSON INSULATION CO INC
Also Called: Ohio Gypsum Supply
4715 Urbana Rd (45502-9503)
PHONE..................937 323-9599
Fax: 937 323-8310
Garth S Robinson, President
Ryan J Robinson, Vice Pres

Springfield - Clark County (G-17265) — GEOGRAPHIC SECTION

Jennifer Robinson, *Treasurer*
EMP: 35 **EST:** 1975
SQ FT: 8,000
SALES (est): 4.9MM **Privately Held**
SIC: 1742 5032 Insulation, buildings; drywall materials

(G-17265)
ROCKING HORSE CHLD HLTH CTR (PA)
651 S Limestone St (45505-1965)
PHONE..................937 328-7266
James Duffy, *Partner*
Shonda Wallace, *Finance*
Stacy Lee, *Office Mgr*
Cindy Jennings,
Shelley Robbins,
EMP: 28
SALES: 13.1MM **Privately Held**
WEB: www.rockinghorsecenter.org
SIC: 8011 8322 Pediatrician; individual & family services

(G-17266)
ROEDIGER REALTY INC
331 Mount Vernon Ave (45503-4143)
PHONE..................937 322-0352
Fax: 937 322-5280
James Roediger, *President*
Diane Ericksen, *Sales Associate*
EMP: 30
SALES (est): 1.5MM **Privately Held**
WEB: www.roedigerrealty.com
SIC: 6531 Real estate agent, residential

(G-17267)
ROLLINS MOVING AND STORAGE INC
1050 Wheel St (45503-3545)
PHONE..................937 525-4013
Clyde Depuy, *Branch Mgr*
Paul Depuy, *Director*
EMP: 30
SALES (corp-wide): 21.4MM **Privately Held**
WEB: www.rollins3pl.com
SIC: 4214 4213 Household goods moving & storage, local; household goods transport
PA: Rollins Moving And Storage, Inc.
1900 E Leffel Ln
Springfield OH 45505
937 325-2484

(G-17268)
ROSE CITY MANUFACTURING INC
900 W Leffel Ln (45506-3538)
P.O. Box 1103 (45501-1103)
PHONE..................937 325-5561
Fax: 937 324-0590
Daniel McGregor, *President*
Hugh Barnett, *Principal*
Dane A Belden, *Principal*
Grant Shearer, *Data Proc Dir*
▲ **EMP:** 60
SQ FT: 44,000
SALES (est): 8.9MM **Privately Held**
WEB: www.rosecitymfg.com
SIC: 7692 Automotive welding

(G-17269)
SAGAR SATYAVOLU MD
1911 E High St (45505-1227)
PHONE..................937 323-1404
Sagar Satyavolu, *Principal*
EMP: 40 **EST:** 2001
SALES (est): 476.4K **Privately Held**
SIC: 8011 Cardiologist & cardio-vascular specialist

(G-17270)
SAWMILL ROAD MANAGEMENT CO LLC (PA)
1990 Kingsgate Rd Ste A (45502-8225)
PHONE..................937 342-9071
Judy Ross, *Mng Member*
EMP: 30
SALES (est): 1.9MM **Privately Held**
SIC: 6531 2421 Buying agent, real estate; sawmills & planing mills, general

(G-17271)
SDX HOME CARE OPERATIONS LLC
Also Called: Comfort Keepers
101 N Fountain Ave (45502-1118)
PHONE..................877 692-0345
Kristina Butler, *President*
Carol McGowan, *General Mgr*
EMP: 99
SALES (est): 2.2MM **Privately Held**
SIC: 8082 Home health care services

(G-17272)
SECURITY NATIONAL BANK & TR CO
40 S Limestone St (45502-1222)
PHONE..................937 324-6800
Fax: 937 324-3966
William Fralick, *President*
Connie Heironimus, *COO*
Gerry Tomka, *Senior VP*
Tom Keehner, *Assistant VP*
Mark Robertson, *Assistant VP*
EMP: 210
SALES (corp-wide): 367MM **Publicly Held**
WEB: www.securitynationalbank.com
SIC: 6021 6141 National trust companies with deposits, commercial; consumer finance companies
HQ: The Security National Bank And Trust Co
50 N 3rd St
Newark OH 43055
740 426-6384

(G-17273)
SELF RELIANCE INC
3674 E National Rd Ste 3 (45505-1545)
PHONE..................937 525-0809
Fax: 937 525-9027
William Smith, *President*
Jay Crawford, *Vice Pres*
EMP: 32
SALES (est): 1.6MM **Privately Held**
SIC: 8322 Social services for the handicapped

(G-17274)
SERVICE EXPERTS HTG & AC LLC
2600 S Limestone St (45505-4940)
PHONE..................937 426-3444
Mark Weaver, *General Mgr*
EMP: 30
SALES (corp-wide): 736.6MM **Privately Held**
SIC: 1711 Plumbing, heating, air-conditioning contractors
HQ: Service Experts Heating & Air Conditioning Llc
3820 American Dr Ste 200
Plano TX 75075
972 535-3800

(G-17275)
SOUTHBROOK HEALTH CARE CTR INC
Also Called: Southbrook Care Center
2299 S Yellow Springs St (45506-3368)
PHONE..................937 322-3436
Harold Sosna, *President*
Kristie Rolfsen, *Director*
Nikki Lee, *Pat Nrsg Dir*
EMP: 110
SALES: 4.4MM **Privately Held**
SIC: 8051 Skilled nursing care facilities

(G-17276)
SPECTRUM MGT HOLDG CO LLC
Also Called: Time Warner
75 W Main St (45502-1309)
PHONE..................937 552-5760
Cindy Ohagan, *Vice Pres*
EMP: 83
SALES (corp-wide): 41.5B **Publicly Held**
SIC: 4841 Cable television services; subscription television services
HQ: Spectrum Management Holding Company, Llc
400 Atlantic St
Stamford CT 06901
203 905-7801

(G-17277)
SPRINGFELD RGNAL OTPATIENT CTR
2610 N Limestone St (45503-1114)
PHONE..................937 390-8310
Cindy Morgan, *Director*
EMP: 30
SALES (est): 527.6K **Privately Held**
SIC: 8093 Specialty outpatient clinics

(G-17278)
SPRINGFELD UNFRM-LINEN SUP INC
Also Called: Miller's Textiles
141 N Murray St (45503-4321)
PHONE..................937 323-5544
Robert Hager, *President*
Jim Bode, *General Mgr*
Jim Romaker, *Corp Secy*
EMP: 68
SQ FT: 12,000
SALES (est): 896.6K
SALES (corp-wide): 21.9MM **Privately Held**
WEB: www.millerstextile.com
SIC: 7213 7219 7218 7217 Linen supply; laundry, except power & coin-operated; industrial launderers; carpet & upholstery cleaning
PA: Miller's Textile Services, Inc.
520 Commerce Rd
Wapakoneta OH
419 738-3551

(G-17279)
SPRINGFIELD BUSINESS EQP CO (PA)
3783 W National Rd (45504-3516)
PHONE..................937 322-3828
Fax: 937 322-1804
J D Lindeman, *President*
Lisa Lindeman, *Corp Secy*
Robert Brennan, *Sales Mgr*
Scott Lozan, *Sales Mgr*
Bethany Anderson, *Accounts Mgr*
EMP: 31 **EST:** 1970
SALES (est): 18.4MM **Privately Held**
SIC: 5044 5021 Office equipment; office furniture

(G-17280)
SPRINGFIELD COUNTRY CLUB CO
2315 Signal Hill Rd (45504-1042)
P.O. Box 1642 (45501-1642)
PHONE..................937 399-4215
Fax: 937 399-4317
Craig Taylor, *General Mgr*
EMP: 50 **EST:** 1896
SQ FT: 28,000
SALES: 1.9MM **Privately Held**
SIC: 7997 5812 5813 5941 Country club, membership; golf club, membership; swimming club, membership; tennis club, membership; eating places; bar (drinking places); sporting goods & bicycle shops

(G-17281)
SPRINGFIELD FAMILY Y M C A
300 S Limestone St (45505-1071)
PHONE..................937 323-3781
Chris Snyder, *Vice Pres*
Teresa Rose, *Human Res Dir*
Paul Hanus, *Director*
EMP: 85
SQ FT: 47,125
SALES: 1.5MM **Privately Held**
SIC: 8641 7991 8351 7032 Youth organizations; physical fitness facilities; child day care services; youth camps; individual & family services

(G-17282)
SUE SMEDLEY
417 Wildwood Dr (45504-1052)
PHONE..................937 399-5155
Sue Smedley, *Partner*
EMP: 50
SALES (est): 1.6MM **Privately Held**
SIC: 6531 Real estate agent, residential

(G-17283)
SUN VALLEY INFOSYS LLC
1750 N Fountain Blvd (45504-1466)
PHONE..................937 267-6435
Jude Stanley, *Mng Member*
Jessie Behl,
Marshall Behl,
WEI Cao,
EMP: 52
SQ FT: 2,000
SALES (est): 3.3MM **Privately Held**
SIC: 8742 Management consulting services

(G-17284)
SUNRISE COOPERATIVE INC
821 N Belmont Ave (45503-3515)
PHONE..................937 323-7536
Tom Waddle, *Manager*
EMP: 25
SALES (corp-wide): 56.3MM **Privately Held**
SIC: 5191 Fertilizer & fertilizer materials
PA: Sunrise Cooperative, Inc.
2025 W State St Ste A
Fremont OH 43420
419 332-6468

(G-17285)
TAC INDUSTRIES INC (PA)
Also Called: TAC Enterprises
2160 Old Selma Rd (45505-4600)
PHONE..................937 328-5200
Fax: 937 328-5233
Mary Brandstetter, *CEO*
James Neer, *Editor*
Andre Currier, *Mfg Staff*
Steve Demeter, *Engineer*
Michael Ahern, *CFO*
EMP: 280
SQ FT: 52,800
SALES: 5.2MM **Privately Held**
WEB: www.tacind.com
SIC: 8331 8741 Job training & vocational rehabilitation services; work experience center; management services

(G-17286)
TAC INDUSTRIES INC
Also Called: Town & Country Adult Services
2160 Old Selma Rd (45505-4600)
PHONE..................937 328-5200
Greg Gearhart, *VP Sales*
W K Hoke, *Branch Mgr*
Mary Brandstetter, *Exec Dir*
EMP: 218
SALES (corp-wide): 5.2MM **Privately Held**
WEB: www.tacind.com
SIC: 8331 Job training & vocational rehabilitation services
PA: Tac Industries, Inc.
2160 Old Selma Rd
Springfield OH 45505
937 328-5200

(G-17287)
TEREX UTILITIES INC
4401 Gateway Blvd (45502-9339)
PHONE..................937 293-6526
EMP: 104
SALES (corp-wide): 4.3B **Publicly Held**
SIC: 7699 Aircraft & heavy equipment repair services
HQ: Terex Utilities, Inc.
12805 Sw 77th Pl
Tigard OR 97223
503 620-0611

(G-17288)
TIER ONE DISTRIBUTION LLC
Also Called: Tri State Forest Products
2105 Sheridan Ave (45505-2419)
PHONE..................937 323-6325
Tom Berghouse, *Mng Member*
EMP: 60
SALES (est): 7MM **Privately Held**
SIC: 4731 Freight forwarding

(G-17289)
TRI-STATE FOREST PRODUCTS INC (PA)
2105 Sheridan Ave (45505-2419)
PHONE..................937 323-6325
Tom Latham, *CEO*
Becky Siderits, *COO*
Rob Latham, *Vice Pres*
Lloyd Glydewell, *Opers Mgr*
Tom Clossin, *Purchasing*
▲ **EMP:** 44

GEOGRAPHIC SECTION
Steubenville - Jefferson County (G-17313)

SQ FT: 68,000
SALES (est): 75.9MM Privately Held
WEB: www.tsfpi.com
SIC: 5031 Lumber: rough, dressed & finished

(G-17290)
TRIEC ELECTRICAL SERVICES INC
1630 Progress Rd (45505-4467)
PHONE.................................937 323-3721
Fax: 937 323-8627
Scott Yeazell, President
Michael Cain, Vice Pres
Mike Cain, Vice Pres
Jeff Anders, Project Mgr
Will Blauvelt, Project Mgr
EMP: 35
SQ FT: 10,500
SALES: 6.7MM Privately Held
WEB: www.triec.com
SIC: 1731 General electrical contractor

(G-17291)
U S XPRESS INC
825 W Leffel Ln (45506-3535)
PHONE.................................937 328-4100
Richard Schaefer, Branch Mgr
EMP: 50 Privately Held
SIC: 4213 Contract haulers
HQ: U. S. Xpress, Inc.
4080 Jenkins Rd
Chattanooga TN 37421
866 266-7270

(G-17292)
VICTORY LANES INC
1906 Commerce Cir (45504-2012)
PHONE.................................937 323-8684
Fax: 937 323-6263
Jim Zabakos, President
Ann Klein, President
Pearl Romanoff, President
Charles Kerney, Treasurer
EMP: 35
SQ FT: 40,000
SALES (est): 783.4K Privately Held
SIC: 7933 5813 Ten pin center; cocktail lounge

(G-17293)
W2005/FARGO HOTELS (POOL C)
Also Called: Country Suites By Carlson
1751 W 1st St (45504-1925)
PHONE.................................937 322-2200
Stephanie Beedy, General Mgr
EMP: 25
SALES (corp-wide): 16.5MM Privately Held
WEB: www.daytonraiders.com
SIC: 7011 Hotels & motels
HQ: W2005/Fargo Hotels (Pool C) Realty, L.P.
5851 Legacy Cir Ste 400
Plano TX 75024

(G-17294)
WALLACE & TURNER INSURANCE INC
30 Warder St Ste 200 (45504-2581)
P.O. Box 209 (45501-0209)
PHONE.................................937 324-8492
Gerald Simonton, President
Michael Trempe, Partner
Patrick Field, Principal
David McLaughlin, Principal
Lisa Miller, Marketing Staff
EMP: 25
SQ FT: 6,500
SALES (est): 3.9MM Privately Held
WEB: www.wtins.com
SIC: 6411 Insurance agents

(G-17295)
WALLICK CONSTRUCTION CO
Also Called: Eaglewood Villa
3001 Middle Urbana Rd (45502-9284)
PHONE.................................937 399-7009
Fax: 937 390-8253
Wendy Archer, Mktg Dir
Kay Dotson, Systems Mgr
Nancy Lacey, Hlthcr Dir
EMP: 27

SALES (corp-wide): 64.6MM Privately Held
WEB: www.eaglewoodvillage.com
SIC: 6513 8361 Retirement hotel operation; residential care
PA: Wallick Construction Co.
6880 Tussing Rd
Reynoldsburg OH 43068
614 863-4640

(G-17296)
WALMART INC
2100 N Bechtle Ave (45504-1575)
PHONE.................................937 399-0370
Fax: 937 324-9845
Heather Price, Manager
EMP: 200
SALES (corp-wide): 500.3B Publicly Held
WEB: www.walmartstores.com
SIC: 5311 5411 7231 Department stores, discount; supermarkets, hypermarket; manicurist, pedicurist
PA: Walmart Inc.
702 Sw 8th St
Bentonville AR 72716
479 273-4000

(G-17297)
WERNER ENTERPRISES INC
4395 Laybourne Rd (45505-3619)
PHONE.................................937 325-5403
Fax: 937 325-5480
Donovan Knight, Manager
EMP: 70
SALES (corp-wide): 2.1B Publicly Held
WEB: www.werner.com
SIC: 4213 Contract haulers
PA: Werner Enterprises, Inc
14507 Frontier Rd
Omaha NE 68138
402 895-6640

(G-17298)
WESTERN & SOUTHERN LF INSUR CO
30 Warder St Ste 130 (45504-2579)
PHONE.................................937 399-7696
EMP: 26 Privately Held
SIC: 6411 Life Insurance Agency
HQ: The Western & Southern Life Insurance Company
400 Broadway St
Cincinnati OH 45202
513 629-1800

(G-17299)
WESTFIELD STEEL INC
Also Called: Remington Steel
1120 S Burnett Rd (45505-3408)
PHONE.................................937 322-2414
Fax: 937 322-1654
Fritz Prine, President
Harry Osborne, Vice Pres
Debbie Funderburg, Treasurer
Cynthia Austin, Sales Associate
Frank Bair, Branch Mgr
EMP: 60
SALES (est): 11.5MM
SALES (corp-wide): 74.4MM Privately Held
SIC: 5051 3714 Steel; clutches, motor vehicle
PA: Westfield Steel Inc
530 W State Road 32
Westfield IN 46074
317 896-4449

(G-17300)
WOODROW MANUFACTURING CO
4300 River Rd (45502-7517)
P.O. Box 1567 (45501-1567)
PHONE.................................937 399-9333
Fax: 937 399-0464
John K Woodrow, President
Ron Deere, Prdtn Mgr
Patrick T McAtee, Treasurer
Lou Kiernan, Sales Mgr
Sandy Justice, Manager
EMP: 40
SQ FT: 26,000

SALES (est): 5MM Privately Held
WEB: www.woodrowcorp.com
SIC: 7336 3479 2752 2396 Silk screen design; etching on metals; commercial printing, lithographic; automotive & apparel trimmings

(G-17301)
WOODRUFF ENTERPRISES INC
4951 Gateway Blvd (45502-8867)
PHONE.................................937 399-9300
Todd Woodruff, President
Rob Butler, Manager
EMP: 43
SALES (est): 8.2MM Privately Held
WEB: www.woodruffenterprises.net
SIC: 4222 4789 Refrigerated warehousing & storage; pipeline terminal facilities, independently operated

Steubenville
Jefferson County

(G-17302)
ACUITY HEALTHCARE LP
Acuityhealthcare,
380 Summit Ave Fl 3 (43952-2667)
PHONE.................................740 283-7499
Fax: 740 283-7181
Judy Weaver, CEO
Richard Cassady, Senior VP
Edward Cooper, Branch Mgr
EMP: 88
SALES (corp-wide): 49.9MM Privately Held
SIC: 8741 8742 Hospital management; hospital & health services consultant
PA: Acuity Healthcare, Lp
10200 Mallard Creek Rd # 300
Charlotte NC 28262
877 228-4893

(G-17303)
BARRINGTON DIALYSIS LLC
Also Called: Steubenville Home Training
1799 Sinclair Ave Ste 2 (43953-3373)
PHONE.................................740 346-2740
Bob Badal, Principal
EMP: 41
SALES (est): 1MM Publicly Held
SIC: 8092 Kidney dialysis centers
PA: Davita Inc.
2000 16th St
Denver CO 80202

(G-17304)
BLUEFOOT INDUSTRIAL LLC
Also Called: Bluefoot Energy Services
224 N 3rd St (43952-2121)
PHONE.................................740 314-5299
Clyde Larsen,
Peter Urie,
EMP: 25
SQ FT: 7,000
SALES (est): 4MM Privately Held
SIC: 7353 2899 7359 1623 Heavy construction equipment rental; fluxes: brazing, soldering, galvanizing & welding; industrial truck rental; oil & gas pipeline construction; crude petroleum pipelines

(G-17305)
CAPITAL HEALTH HOMECARE
201 Luray Dr 2a (43953-3973)
P.O. Box 2615, Wintersville (43953-0615)
PHONE.................................740 264-8815
Fax: 740 264-8825
Shari Jo Watkins, Administration
EMP: 30
SALES (est): 1.1MM Privately Held
SIC: 8082 Home health care services

(G-17306)
CARMIKE CINEMAS INC
100 Mall Dr Unit C20 (43952-3093)
PHONE.................................740 264-1680
Ross Paino, Manager
EMP: 28 Publicly Held
WEB: www.carmike.com
SIC: 7832 Exhibitors, itinerant: motion picture

HQ: Carmike Cinemas, Llc
11500 Ash St
Leawood KS 66211
913 213-2000

(G-17307)
CARRIAGE HOUSE ASSISTED LIVING
63102 Saint Charles Dr (43952)
PHONE.................................740 264-7667
Fax: 740 264-3682
Robert Huff, President
Megan Green, Manager
EMP: 45
SALES (est): 1MM Privately Held
SIC: 8051 Skilled nursing care facilities

(G-17308)
CARRIAGE INN OF STEUBENVILLE
3102 Saint Charles Dr (43952-3556)
PHONE.................................740 264-7161
Fax: 740 264-7116
Stephen Kuruc, Director
Brad Conto, Administration
EMP: 130
SALES (corp-wide): 8.9MM Privately Held
SIC: 8051 Skilled nursing care facilities
PA: Carriage Inn Of Steubenville, Inc
5020 Philadelphia Dr C
Dayton OH 45415
740 264-7161

(G-17309)
CATHERINES CARE CENTER INC
717 N 6th Ave (43952-1832)
PHONE.................................740 282-3605
Fax: 740 282-2003
Steven Kuruc, Director
Steve Bolger, Administration
EMP: 65
SALES (est): 1.7MM Privately Held
SIC: 8051 Convalescent home with continuous nursing care

(G-17310)
CHARITY HOSPICE INC
500 Luray Dr (43953-3972)
P.O. Box 2483, Wintersville (43953-0483)
PHONE.................................740 264-2280
Cathy Marie Cich, Owner
EMP: 25
SALES: 1.2MM Privately Held
SIC: 8069 Specialty hospitals, except psychiatric

(G-17311)
COLUMBIA GAS OF OHIO INC
300 Luray Dr (43953-3901)
P.O. Box 2160 (43953-0160)
PHONE.................................740 264-5577
Clair M Colburn Jr, Branch Mgr
EMP: 46
SALES (corp-wide): 4.8B Publicly Held
WEB: www.meterrepairshop.com
SIC: 4922 Natural gas transmission
HQ: Columbia Gas Of Ohio, Inc.
290 W Nationwide Blvd # 114
Columbus OH 43215
614 460-6000

(G-17312)
COMCAST CBLE CMMUNICATIONS LLC
100 Welday Ave Ste A (43953-3779)
PHONE.................................503 372-9144
Heather Cipriani, Branch Mgr
EMP: 101
SALES (corp-wide): 84.5B Publicly Held
SIC: 4841 Cable television services
HQ: Comcast Cable Communications, Llc
1701 John Fk Blvd
Philadelphia PA 19103

(G-17313)
COMMUNICARE HEALTH SVCS INC
Also Called: Dixon Health Care Center
135 Reichart Ave (43953-4050)
PHONE.................................740 264-1155
Fax: 740 264-1704
James Burke, Office Mgr
Donna Hennis, Food Svc Dir

Steubenville - Jefferson County (G-17314)

Tammy Sagun, *Hlthcr Dir*
EMP: 100
SALES (corp-wide): 103.9MM **Privately Held**
WEB: www.atriumlivingcenters.com
SIC: 8059 Nursing home, except skilled & intermediate care facility
PA: Communicare Health Services, Inc.
4700 Ashwood Dr Ste 200
Blue Ash OH 45241
513 530-1654

(G-17314)
DIALYSIS CLINIC INC
4227 Mall Dr (43952-3011)
PHONE....................740 264-6687
Ruth Ann Blackburn, *Manager*
EMP: 25
SALES (corp-wide): 736.2MM **Privately Held**
WEB: www.dciinc.org
SIC: 8092 Kidney dialysis centers
PA: Dialysis Clinic, Inc.
1633 Church St Ste 500
Nashville TN 37203
615 327-3061

(G-17315)
DLC TRANSPORT INC
320 N 5th St (43952-2016)
PHONE....................740 282-1763
Donna Colalella, *President*
Tim Elson, *Manager*
EMP: 40
SQ FT: 43,000
SALES: 2.3MM **Privately Held**
SIC: 4213 Contract haulers

(G-17316)
FAYETTE PARTS SERVICE INC
1512 Sunset Blvd (43952-1303)
PHONE....................740 282-4547
EMP: 138
SALES (corp-wide): 58MM **Privately Held**
SIC: 5013 Automotive supplies & parts
PA: Fayette Parts Service, Inc.
325 E Main St
Uniontown PA
724 785-2506

(G-17317)
FEDEX GROUND PACKAGE SYS INC
103 Anart St (43953-7262)
PHONE....................412 859-2653
EMP: 152
SALES (corp-wide): 47.4B **Publicly Held**
SIC: 4212 Local Trucking Operator
HQ: Fedex Ground Package System, Inc.
1000 Fed Ex Dr
Coraopolis PA 15108
412 269-1000

(G-17318)
GOODMAN PROPERTIES INC
Also Called: Fort Steuben Mall
100 Mall Dr Ofc Ofc (43952-3012)
PHONE....................740 264-7781
Steph McVicker, *Mktg Dir*
Michael Glenn, *Manager*
EMP: 25
SALES (corp-wide): 11MM **Privately Held**
WEB: www.ftsteubenmall.com
SIC: 6552 6512 Land subdividers & developers, commercial; shopping center, property operation only
PA: Goodman Properties, Inc.
777 S Flagler Dr Ste 1101
West Palm Beach FL 33401
561 833-3777

(G-17319)
GOODWILL INDS RHBILITATION CTR
131 Main St (43953-3733)
PHONE....................740 264-6000
EMP: 121
SALES (corp-wide): 8MM **Privately Held**
SIC: 8322 Rehabilitation services
PA: Goodwill Industries Rehabilitation Center, Inc
408 9th St Sw
Canton OH 44707
330 454-9461

(G-17320)
GPC CONTRACTING COMPANY
500 E Church St Ste 3 (43953-3701)
P.O. Box 4372 (43952-8372)
PHONE....................740 264-6060
Gary E Speece Sr, *President*
EMP: 30 **EST:** 2009
SALES (est): 339K **Privately Held**
SIC: 1721 Industrial painting

(G-17321)
GRAE-CON CONSTRUCTION INC (PA)
Also Called: Grae-Con Contructions
880 Kingsdale Rd (43952-4361)
P.O. Box 1778 (43952-7778)
PHONE....................740 282-6830
Fax: 740 282-6849
Robert A Gribben Jr, *President*
Shirley Gribben, *Corp Secy*
Robert A Gribben III, *Vice Pres*
John A Humpe III, *Vice Pres*
EMP: 80
SQ FT: 23,000
SALES (est): 39.1MM **Privately Held**
WEB: www.graecon.com
SIC: 1542 Commercial & office building, new construction; commercial & office buildings, renovation & repair

(G-17322)
JACQUELINE KUMI-SAKYI
Also Called: Auntie Jacque Childcare
1609 Moreland Dr (43952-2545)
PHONE....................740 282-5955
Jacqueline Kumi-Sakyi, *Owner*
EMP: 57 **Privately Held**
SIC: 9411 7389 Administration of educational programs;

(G-17323)
JEFFERSON INVSTGTORS SCURITIES
1439 Sunset Blvd (43952-1521)
PHONE....................740 283-3681
Robert J D'Anniballe, *President*
Linda Ribar, *Office Mgr*
Robert Herceg, *Manager*
EMP: 60
SALES (est): 1.1MM **Privately Held**
WEB: www.danniballe.com
SIC: 7381 Private investigator; security guard service

(G-17324)
LABELLE NEWS AGENCY INC
814 University Blvd (43952-1794)
PHONE....................740 282-9731
Fax: 740 282-2402
Thomas Pentes, *President*
Arthur D'Anniballe, *Treasurer*
Andy Pentes, *Admin Sec*
EMP: 25
SQ FT: 17,200
SALES (est): 4.4MM **Privately Held**
WEB: www.labellenews.com
SIC: 5199 Anatomical specimens & research material

(G-17325)
LANCIA NURSING HOME INC (PA)
Also Called: Lancia Villa Royal
1852 Sinclair Ave (43953-3328)
PHONE....................740 264-7101
Fax: 740 264-7104
Joseph Lancia, *President*
Linda Lancia, *Vice Pres*
Barbara Newlin, *Manager*
Giusseppe Lancia, *Administration*
EMP: 60
SQ FT: 5,000
SALES (est): 8MM **Privately Held**
SIC: 8059 Nursing home, except skilled & intermediate care facility

(G-17326)
LAUREL HEALTH CARE COMPANY
Also Called: Laurels of Steubenville, The
500 Stanton Blvd (43952-3706)
PHONE....................740 264-5042
Steve Welhorsky, *Branch Mgr*
Melissa Ross-Merkel, *Director*
EMP: 100 **Privately Held**
SIC: 8059 Nursing home, except skilled & intermediate care facility
HQ: Laurel Health Care Company
8181 Worthington Rd Uppr
Westerville OH 43082

(G-17327)
LOWES HOME CENTERS LLC
4115 Mall Dr (43952-3007)
PHONE....................740 266-3500
Fax: 740 266-3525
Kevin Santon, *General Mgr*
EMP: 180
SALES (corp-wide): 68.6B **Publicly Held**
SIC: 5211 5031 5722 5064 Home centers; building materials, exterior; building materials, interior; household appliance stores; electrical appliances, television & radio
HQ: Lowe's Home Centers, Llc
1605 Curtis Bridge Rd
Wilkesboro NC 28697
336 658-4000

(G-17328)
LTAC INVESTORS LLC
Also Called: Lifeline Hospital
200 School St (43953-9610)
PHONE....................740 346-2600
Susan Tournay Colpo, *CEO*
Vincent Stonebraker,
Satbir Singh,
EMP: 150
SALES: 11.3MM **Privately Held**
SIC: 8062 General medical & surgical hospitals

(G-17329)
MEDI HOME HEALTH AGENCY INC (HQ)
Also Called: Medi-Home Care
105 Main St (43953-3733)
PHONE....................740 266-3977
Fax: 740 264-1577
Ronnie L Young, *President*
James Hardman, *Vice Pres*
John Keim, *CFO*
Mary Craver, *Director*
Donna Parrish, *Administration*
EMP: 50
SALES (est): 6.3MM
SALES (corp-wide): 193.8MM **Privately Held**
SIC: 8082 7361 5169 Home health care services; nurses' registry; oxygen
PA: Medical Services Of America, Inc.
171 Monroe Ln
Lexington SC 29072
803 957-0500

(G-17330)
MEDICAL GROUP ASSOCIATES INC
114 Brady Cir E (43952-1478)
PHONE....................740 283-4773
Stephen G Kuruc, *President*
Ruth Jarvis, *Manager*
Sue Pevac, *Asst Admin*
EMP: 29 **EST:** 1979
SQ FT: 16,400
SALES (est): 1.5MM **Privately Held**
SIC: 8011 Physicians' office, including specialists; gastronomist; hematologist; oncologist

(G-17331)
MOUGIANIS INDUSTRIES INC
Also Called: Alexander Great Distributing
1626 Cadiz Rd (43953-7630)
P.O. Box 2100 (43953-0100)
PHONE....................740 264-6372
Fax: 740 282-7707
Anthony N Mougianis, *President*
EMP: 60
SQ FT: 8,000
SALES (est): 2.6MM **Privately Held**
SIC: 7349 5087 Janitorial service, contract basis; cleaning & maintenance equipment & supplies

(G-17332)
NATIONAL COLLOID COMPANY
906 Adams St (43952-2709)
P.O. Box 309 (43952-5309)
PHONE....................740 282-1171
Fax: 740 282-3874
Michael Barber Jr, *President*
Becky Panebianco, *President*
Jami Wedlake, *Manager*
Julie Zamana, *Admin Asst*
▲ **EMP:** 25 **EST:** 1938
SQ FT: 45,000
SALES (est): 11.3MM **Privately Held**
WEB: www.natcoll.com
SIC: 2869 5169 2899 2842 Industrial organic chemicals; caustic soda; calcium chloride; chemical preparations; specialty cleaning, polishes & sanitation goods; industrial inorganic chemicals; alkalies & chlorine

(G-17333)
PHILIP ICUSS JR
Also Called: Legal Hair and Day Spa
2311 Sunset Blvd (43952-2433)
PHONE....................740 264-4647
Fax: 740 264-7999
Philip Icuss Jr, *Owner*
EMP: 40
SQ FT: 6,000
SALES (est): 841.3K **Privately Held**
SIC: 7231 Hairdressers

(G-17334)
STATE PARK MOTORS INC
766 Canton Rd (43953-4108)
P.O. Box 2328 (43953-0328)
PHONE....................740 264-3113
Fax: 740 264-0644
Sam Davis, *President*
Willard L Davis, *Vice Pres*
Norman Davis, *Treasurer*
Terry Galey, *Sales Staff*
Devon Taylor, *Sales Staff*
EMP: 25
SALES (est): 6MM **Privately Held**
WEB: www.stateparkmotors.com
SIC: 5012 Vans, commercial; automotive brokers

(G-17335)
STEUBENVILLE COUNTRY CLB MANOR
575 Lovers Ln (43953-3311)
PHONE....................740 266-6118
Fax: 740 266-2405
James Bolger, *President*
Rena Bolger, *Vice Pres*
Denise Boyle, *Treasurer*
Amy Elson, *Nursing Dir*
Stephen Bolger, *Admin Sec*
EMP: 70
SALES (est): 2.9MM **Privately Held**
WEB: www.bolgerhealthcare.com
SIC: 8059 Nursing home, except skilled & intermediate care facility

(G-17336)
STEUBENVILLE COUNTRY CLUB INC
413 Lovers Ln (43953-3309)
PHONE....................740 264-0521
Fax: 740 266-2975
Robert Chapman, *President*
Anthony Sheposh, *Vice Pres*
EMP: 75
SQ FT: 5,000
SALES: 803K **Privately Held**
WEB: www.steubenvillecountryclub.com
SIC: 7997 Country club, membership

(G-17337)
STEUBENVILLE TRUCK CENTER INC
620 South St (43952-2802)
P.O. Box 1741 (43952-7741)
PHONE....................740 282-2711
Fax: 740 282-7707
Larry A Remp, *President*
Mary Stead, *Corp Secy*
Marney Remp, *Vice Pres*
Paul Firn, *Executive*
EMP: 25
SQ FT: 7,500
SALES (est): 5.7MM **Privately Held**
WEB: www.ohiovolvo.com
SIC: 7538 5511 7692 Truck engine repair, except industrial; trucks, tractors & trailers: new & used; welding repair

GEOGRAPHIC SECTION
Stow - Summit County (G-17359)

(G-17338)
TRANSMERICA SVCS TECHNICAL SUP
Also Called: Hanna Chevrolet Cadillac
4404 Scioto Dr (43953-3320)
P.O. Box 38 (43952-5038)
PHONE..................740 282-3695
Fax: 740 282-7009
Makram A Hanna, *President*
Doreen M Deleonardis, *Principal*
D A Frazee, *Principal*
Peter S Olivito, *Principal*
Mary Hanna, *Corp Secy*
EMP: 28 EST: 1956
SQ FT: 15,000
SALES (est): 6MM **Privately Held**
SIC: 5511 4212 Automobiles, new & used; local trucking, without storage

(G-17339)
TRINITY HEALTH SYSTEM
Also Called: Radiology Department
380 Summit Ave (43952-2667)
PHONE..................740 283-7848
Fred Bowers, *President*
Tom Kiger, *CIO*
EMP: 219 **Privately Held**
SIC: 8741 Hospital management; nursing & personal care facility management
HQ: Trinity Health System
380 Summit Ave
Steubenville OH 43952

(G-17340)
TRINITY HEALTH SYSTEM
Also Called: Trinity Health West
4000 Johnson Rd Fl 1 (43952-2300)
PHONE..................740 264-8000
Fax: 740 264-8658
Fred Brower, *President*
Margaret Franklin, *Opers Staff*
Rachel Butler, *Cert Phar Tech*
Nancy Crites, *Cert Phar Tech*
Cindy Dahlem, *Cert Phar Tech*
EMP: 625 **Privately Held**
SIC: 8741 8062 Hospital management; general medical & surgical hospitals
HQ: Trinity Health System
380 Summit Ave
Steubenville OH 43952

(G-17341)
TRINITY HEALTH SYSTEM
Also Called: Medical Records
4000 Johnson Rd Fl 1 (43952-2300)
PHONE..................740 264-8101
Louis Musso, *Human Res Dir*
Mohammed Rahman, *Med Doctor*
Kim Dudich, *Manager*
Abdullah Kalla, *Anesthesiology*
Tom Kaiger, *Info Tech Dir*
EMP: 30 **Privately Held**
SIC: 8741 8062 Hospital management; general medical & surgical hospitals
HQ: Trinity Health System
380 Summit Ave
Steubenville OH 43952

(G-17342)
TRINITY HEALTH SYSTEM (DH)
Also Called: Trinity Medical Center East
380 Summit Ave (43952-2667)
PHONE..................740 283-7000
Fax: 740 283-7461
Fred Brower, *CEO*
Mike Hibbard, *Vice Pres*
Debrah Schaller, *Purch Mgr*
Elizabeth Allen, *CFO*
Melissa Friebis, *Manager*
EMP: 300
SQ FT: 1,004,854
SALES: 256MM **Privately Held**
SIC: 8062 8011 General medical & surgical hospitals; hospital, AMA approved residency; offices & clinics of medical doctors
HQ: Sylvania Franciscan Health
1715 Indian Wood Cir # 200
Maumee OH 43537
419 882-8373

(G-17343)
TRINITY HOSPITAL HOLDING CO (DH)
Also Called: Trinity Medical Center East
380 Summit Ave (43952-2667)
PHONE..................740 264-8000
Fax: 740 283-7367
Clyde Metzger MD, *Ch of Bd*
Fred B Bower, *President*
Albert Pavlik, *Admin Sec*
EMP: 600
SALES: 231.4MM **Privately Held**
SIC: 8062 8741 General medical & surgical hospitals; management services

(G-17344)
TRINITY WEST
4000 Johnson Rd Fl 1 (43952-2300)
PHONE..................740 264-8000
Fax: 740 266-2258
Fred B Brower, *President*
Chuck Rine, *Human Resources*
Lisa Ragland-Tyus, *Cert Phar Tech*
Stephanie Smith, *Manager*
Thomas Kiger, *MIS Dir*
EMP: 1640
SQ FT: 600,000
SALES (est): 69.8MM **Privately Held**
SIC: 8062 General medical & surgical hospitals
HQ: Trinity Hospital Holding Company
380 Summit Ave
Steubenville OH 43952
740 264-8000

(G-17345)
TRUEBLUE INC
Also Called: Labor Ready
2125 Sunset Blvd (43952-2469)
PHONE..................740 282-1079
Fax: 740 282-1056
Jason Callihan, *Manager*
EMP: 26
SALES (corp-wide): 2.5B **Publicly Held**
WEB: www.laborready.com
SIC: 7363 Temporary help service
PA: Trueblue, Inc.
1015 A St
Tacoma WA 98402
253 383-9101

Stockport
Morgan County

(G-17346)
STOCKPORT MILL COUNTRY INN INC
Also Called: Restaurant On The Dam
1995 Broadway St (43787-9120)
PHONE..................740 559-2822
Toll Free:..................877 -
Fax: 740 559-2236
Laura Smith, *President*
Randy Smith, *Vice Pres*
EMP: 40
SALES (est): 1.2MM **Privately Held**
SIC: 7011 5812 7999 4931 Inns; American restaurant; beach & water sports equipment rental & services; electric & other services combined

Stony Ridge
Wood County

(G-17347)
JTI TRANSPORTATION INC
5601 Cherry St (43463)
P.O. Box 187 (43463-0187)
PHONE..................419 661-9360
Jim Jacobs, *Principal*
EMP: 40
SALES (est): 621.6K **Privately Held**
SIC: 4789 Transportation services

(G-17348)
NOLLENBERGER TRUCK CENTER (PA)
5320 Fremont Pike (43463)
PHONE..................419 837-5996
Fax: 419 837-5244
Virginia M Nollenberger, *President*
George Mitchell, *Vice Pres*
Krystal Shubarga, *Admin Sec*
EMP: 41
SQ FT: 10,000
SALES (est): 6.3MM **Privately Held**
WEB: www.inttrucks.com
SIC: 5012 5511 Trucks, commercial; new & used car dealers

Stoutsville
Fairfield County

(G-17349)
CLEARCREEK CONSTRUCTION
11050 16th Rd Sw (43154-9592)
PHONE..................740 420-3568
John E Hite, *Owner*
Melisa Hite, *Co-Owner*
Tara Lamp, *Office Mgr*
EMP: 25
SQ FT: 7,000
SALES (est): 3.2MM **Privately Held**
SIC: 1711 Mechanical contractor

Stow
Summit County

(G-17350)
AKRON METROPOLITAN HSING AUTH
500 Hardman Dr (44224-4883)
PHONE..................330 920-1652
Fax: 330 922-5943
EMP: 149 **Privately Held**
SIC: 9531 8211 7299 6513 Housing authority, non-operating: government; kindergarten; apartment locating service; apartment building operators
PA: Akron Metropolitan Housing Authority
100 W Cedar St Ste 100 # 100
Akron OH 44307
330 762-9631

(G-17351)
ALL AROUND CHILDREN MONTESSORI
Also Called: Stow Montessori Center
4117 Bridgewater Pkwy (44224-6191)
PHONE..................330 928-1444
Fax: 330 945-4820
Joan Wenk, *Owner*
Ashley Peterson, *Director*
EMP: 25
SALES (est): 450K **Privately Held**
WEB: www.creativeplayrooms.com
SIC: 8351 Montessori child development center

(G-17352)
ALSTOM GRID LLC
778 Mccauley Rd Unit 110 (44224-1067)
PHONE..................330 688-4061
Noreen Menendez, *Accountant*
Edward Matheny, *Branch Mgr*
EMP: 60
SALES (corp-wide): 122B **Publicly Held**
SIC: 8711 Construction & civil engineering
HQ: Alstom Grid Llc
130 3rd St Nw
Canton OH 44702
330 452-8428

(G-17353)
AUDIO-TECHNICA US INC (HQ)
1221 Commerce Dr (44224-1760)
PHONE..................330 686-2600
Fax: 330 688-3752
K Matsushita, *Ch of Bd*
Philip Cajka, *President*
Marc Lee Shannon, *Vice Pres*
Richard Sprunlgle, *Vice Pres*
Rich Sprungle, *VP Opers*
▲ EMP: 85
SQ FT: 70,000
SALES: 79.2MM
SALES (corp-wide): 282.3MM **Privately Held**
WEB: www.atus.com
SIC: 5065 5731 Sound equipment, electronic; consumer electronic equipment
PA: Audio-Technica Corporation
2-46-1, Nishinaruse
Machida TKY 194-0
427 399-111

(G-17354)
BRIARWOOD LTD
Also Called: Briarwood Healthcare Center
3700 Englewood Dr (44224-3223)
PHONE..................330 688-1828
Fax: 330 688-2071
John Trimble, *Partner*
Erin Fromwiller, *Administration*
EMP: 100
SQ FT: 37,000
SALES (est): 6.2MM **Privately Held**
SIC: 8059 8051 Rest home, with health care; convalescent home with continuous nursing care

(G-17355)
CELLCO PARTNERSHIP
Also Called: Verizon
3490 Hudson Dr Ste 2 (44224-6962)
PHONE..................330 922-5997
Jeff Russel, *President*
Robert Lister, *VP Finance*
EMP: 25
SALES (corp-wide): 126B **Publicly Held**
SIC: 4813 Local & long distance telephone communications
HQ: Cellco Partnership
1 Verizon Way
Basking Ridge NJ 07920

(G-17356)
CENTIMARK CORPORATION
Also Called: Questmark
4665 Allen Rd Ste C (44224-1055)
PHONE..................330 920-3560
EMP: 120
SALES (corp-wide): 540.7MM **Privately Held**
SIC: 1761 1752 Roofing/Siding Contractor Floor Laying Contractor
PA: Centimark Corporation
12 Grandview Cir
Canonsburg PA 15317
724 743-7777

(G-17357)
CHEMIMAGE FILTER TECH LLC
1100 Campus Dr Ste 500 (44224-1767)
PHONE..................330 686-2829
George Ventouris, *Principal*
EMP: 47
SALES (corp-wide): 4.6MM **Privately Held**
SIC: 8731 Commercial physical research
PA: Chemimage Filter Technologies, Llc
7301 Penn Ave
Pittsburgh PA 15208
412 241-7335

(G-17358)
CUSTOM MOVERS SERVICES INC
Also Called: CMS
3290 Kent Rd (44224-4512)
PHONE..................330 564-0507
Dean Barker, *President*
Amy Nilson, *Natl Sales Mgr*
Krishna Dasika, *Prgrmr*
Brian Havran, *Prgrmr*
Brendon Broadhurst, *Traffic Dir*
EMP: 30
SALES (est): 3.8MM **Privately Held**
WEB: www.custommoversservices.com
SIC: 4212 Moving services

(G-17359)
CUTLER AND ASSOCIATES INC
3653 Darrow Rd Ste 1 (44224-4012)
PHONE..................330 688-2100
June Harvey, *Manager*
EMP: 35
SALES (corp-wide): 9.3MM **Privately Held**
WEB: www.cutlerhomes.com
SIC: 6531 Real estate agents & managers
PA: Cutler And Associates, Inc
4618 Dressler Rd Nw
Canton OH 44718
330 493-9323

Stow - Summit County (G-17360)

(G-17360)
CUTLER REAL ESTATE
3653 Darrow Rd (44224-4012)
PHONE..................330 688-2100
Shirley Chimento, *Manager*
EMP: 35 **Privately Held**
SIC: 6531 Real estate agents & managers
PA: Cutler Real Estate
4618 Dressler Rd Nw
Canton OH 44718

(G-17361)
DAVEY TREE EXPERT COMPANY
Also Called: Davey Tree & Lawn Care
4576 Allen Rd (44224-1036)
PHONE..................330 928-4911
Fax: 330 928-9382
John Martin, *Sales Staff*
Scott Heim, *Manager*
EMP: 25
SALES (corp-wide): 915.9MM **Privately Held**
SIC: 0782 0783 Lawn services; ornamental shrub & tree services
PA: The Davey Tree Expert Company
1500 N Mantua St
Kent OH 44240
330 673-9511

(G-17362)
ELECTRONIC PRINTING PDTS INC
Also Called: Laser Label Technologies
4560 Darrow Rd (44224-1888)
PHONE..................330 689-3930
James Peruzzi, *President*
Jerry S Krempa, *President*
Sheri H Edison, *Vice Pres*
Ted F Unton, *Treasurer*
Janet Page, *Sales Mgr*
EMP: 32
SQ FT: 30,000
SALES: 12MM
SALES (corp-wide): 1.8B **Privately Held**
WEB: www.lltproducts.com
SIC: 5131 5112 Labels; laserjet supplies
HQ: Morgan Adhesives Company, Llc
4560 Darrow Rd
Stow OH 44224
330 688-1111

(G-17363)
EMERITUS CORPORATION
Also Called: Emeritus At Stow
5511 Fishcreek Rd (44224-1435)
PHONE..................330 342-0934
Fax: 330 342-0937
Kelli Phillips, *Branch Mgr*
EMP: 44
SALES (corp-wide): 4.7B **Publicly Held**
SIC: 8052 Personal care facility
HQ: Emeritus Corporation
3131 Elliott Ave Ste 500
Milwaukee WI 53214

(G-17364)
ENVIROSCIENCE INC (PA)
5070 Stow Rd (44224-1530)
PHONE..................330 688-0111
Fax: 330 688-3781
Daniel G Dunstan, *CEO*
Martin A Hilovsky, *President*
James Krejsa, *Vice Pres*
Gregory F Zimmerman, *Vice Pres*
Jamie Turner, *Marketing Staff*
EMP: 55
SQ FT: 24,000
SALES (est): 13.3MM **Privately Held**
WEB: www.enviroscienceinc.com
SIC: 8734 8748 Water testing laboratory; business consulting

(G-17365)
EVANT (PA)
4500 Hudson Dr (44224-1702)
PHONE..................330 920-1517
Fax: 330 920-1016
Robert Breznai, *Finance*
Mary Corall, *Finance*
Renee Richardson, *Human Res Dir*
Peter Spadafino, *Sales Executive*
Sherry D Gedeon, *Exec Dir*
EMP: 36
SQ FT: 7,300
SALES: 9.4MM **Privately Held**
WEB: www.evant.com
SIC: 8361 Home for the mentally handicapped

(G-17366)
FISH CREEK PLAZA LTD
Also Called: Lawrence Saltis Plaza
3000 Graham Rd Unit Ofc (44224-3623)
PHONE..................330 688-0450
Walter Grund, *Partner*
Jennifer Hardee, *Principal*
Leeann Morein, *Principal*
EMP: 99
SALES (est): 3.4MM **Privately Held**
SIC: 6513 Apartment building operators

(G-17367)
FITWORKS HOLDING LLC
4301 Kent Rd Ste 26 (44224-4364)
PHONE..................330 688-2329
Chuck Ortiz, *Manager*
Linda Ortiz, *Manager*
EMP: 32 **Privately Held**
SIC: 7991 Health club
PA: Fitworks Holding, Llc
849 Brainard Rd
Cleveland OH 44143

(G-17368)
FOX DEN FAIRWAYS INC
Also Called: Fox Den Golf Course
2770 Call Rd (44224-1510)
PHONE..................330 678-6792
Fax: 330 673-4579
Herb Rake, *President*
Dennis Whalen, *President*
Jay Drennan, *Vice Pres*
Tom Mc Kinney, *Manager*
Mark Paxton, *Asst Mgr*
EMP: 46
SQ FT: 3,500
SALES: 1.2MM **Privately Held**
WEB: www.foxdengolf.com
SIC: 7992 5812 5941 Public golf courses; eating places; golf goods & equipment

(G-17369)
FUTURE ADVANTAGE INC
Also Called: Kids Country
4923 Hudson Dr (44224-1726)
PHONE..................330 686-7707
Fax: 330 686-1770
Chris Burkholder, *President*
EMP: 35
SALES (est): 666.6K **Privately Held**
WEB: www.futureadvantage.com
SIC: 8351 Group day care center

(G-17370)
GENEVA CHERVENIC REALTY INC
3589 Darrow Rd (44224-4000)
PHONE..................330 686-8400
Fax: 330 686-1363
David Chervenic, *President*
EMP: 65
SQ FT: 2,500
SALES (est): 4.9MM **Privately Held**
WEB: www.chervenicrealty.com
SIC: 6531 Real estate agent, residential

(G-17371)
HOBBY LOBBY STORES INC
4332 Kent Rd Ste 3 (44224-4394)
PHONE..................330 686-1508
EMP: 30
SALES (corp-wide): 4.5B **Privately Held**
SIC: 5945 5023 Arts & crafts supplies; frames & framing, picture & mirror
PA: Hobby Lobby Stores, Inc.
7707 Sw 44th St
Oklahoma City OK 73179
405 745-1100

(G-17372)
HOPE HOMES INC
2044 Bryn Mawr Dr (44224-2616)
PHONE..................330 688-4935
Fax: 330 688-4935
Dayna Worthy, *Branch Mgr*
EMP: 35
SALES (corp-wide): 5.6MM **Privately Held**
SIC: 8082 Home health care services
PA: Hope Homes, Inc
2300 Call Rd
Stow OH 44224
330 686-5342

(G-17373)
HOTEL STOW LP
Also Called: Courtyard By Marriott
4047 Bridgewater Pkwy (44224-6306)
PHONE..................330 945-9722
Fax: 330 945-9822
Jason Jackson, *General Mgr*
EMP: 25 EST: 2008
SALES (est): 1.2MM **Privately Held**
SIC: 7011 Hotels & motels

(G-17374)
HOWARD HANNA SMYTHE CRAMER
3925 Darrow Rd Ste 101 (44224-2600)
PHONE..................330 686-1166
Fax: 330 686-9471
Julie Domenick, *Manager*
Jacque Brittain, *Manager*
Peggy Gray, *Manager*
Bill McCloud, *Manager*
Brian Veppert, *Manager*
EMP: 50
SALES (corp-wide): 76.4MM **Privately Held**
WEB: www.smythecramer.com
SIC: 6531 Real estate brokers & agents
HQ: Howard Hanna Smythe Cramer
6000 Parkland Blvd
Cleveland OH 44124
216 447-4477

(G-17375)
INSTANTWHIP FOODS INC
4870 Hudson Dr (44224-1708)
PHONE..................330 688-8825
Fax: 330 688-8629
Dave Owen, *Manager*
EMP: 35
SQ FT: 16,905
SALES (corp-wide): 44.3MM **Privately Held**
WEB: www.instantwhip.com
SIC: 5143 5142 Dairy products, except dried or canned; packaged frozen goods
PA: Instantwhip Foods, Inc.
2200 Cardigan Ave
Columbus OH 43215
614 488-2536

(G-17376)
INSTANTWHIP-AKRON INC
4870 Hudson Dr (44224-1708)
Drawer Cardigan, Columbus (43215)
PHONE..................614 488-2536
Fred Smith, *President*
G Frederick Smith, *President*
Kevin Sheaffer, *General Mgr*
Thomas Michaelides, *Treasurer*
EMP: 40
SALES (est): 13.3MM **Privately Held**
SIC: 5143 Dairy products, except dried or canned; milk & cream, fluid; frozen dairy desserts

(G-17377)
INTERCHEZ LGISTICS SYSTEMS INC
600 Alpha Pkwy (44224-1065)
P.O. Box 2115 (44224-0115)
PHONE..................330 923-5080
Fax: 330 923-5901
Sharlene Chesnes, *President*
Cassie McClellan, *COO*
EMP: 36
SQ FT: 10,000
SALES (est): 7.9MM **Privately Held**
WEB: www.interchez.com
SIC: 8742 Transportation consultant

(G-17378)
KELLER WILLIAMS RLTY M WALKER
3589 Darrow Rd (44224-4008)
PHONE..................330 571-2020
Latonya Keths, *Principal*
Louis Mascolo, *Manager*
Sue Thomas, *Real Est Agnt*
EMP: 45 EST: 2011
SALES (est): 1.4MM **Privately Held**
SIC: 6531 Real estate agent, residential

(G-17379)
LABORATORY CORPORATION AMERICA
4482 Darrow Rd (44224-1885)
PHONE..................330 686-0194
Fax: 330 686-0545
Advancecom Technolog, *Branch Mgr*
EMP: 25 **Publicly Held**
WEB: www.labcorp.com
SIC: 8071 Testing laboratories
HQ: Laboratory Corporation Of America
358 S Main St Ste 458
Burlington NC 27215
336 229-1127

(G-17380)
LAW OFFICES OF JOHN D CLUNK C
4500 Courthouse Blvd # 400 (44224-6839)
PHONE..................330 436-0300
John D Clunk, *Owner*
Andrew Paisley, *Exec VP*
Hrm M Lacefield, *Human Res Mgr*
EMP: 55 EST: 1999
SALES (est): 6.6MM **Privately Held**
WEB: www.johndclunk.com
SIC: 8111 Bankruptcy law

(G-17381)
LOWES HOME CENTERS LLC
3570 Hudson Dr (44224-2907)
PHONE..................330 920-9280
Fax: 330 920-9067
Mike Herrera, *Office Mgr*
EMP: 150
SQ FT: 134,995
SALES (corp-wide): 68.6B **Publicly Held**
SIC: 5211 5031 5722 5064 Home centers; building materials, exterior; building materials, interior; household appliance stores; electrical appliances, television & radio
HQ: Lowe's Home Centers, Llc
1605 Curtis Bridge Rd
Wilkesboro NC 28697
336 658-4000

(G-17382)
MATCO TOOLS CORPORATION (HQ)
4403 Allen Rd (44224-1096)
PHONE..................330 929-4949
Fax: 330 929-3827
Timothy J Gilmore, *President*
Rich McKenna, *Regional Mgr*
Josh Jenkins, *District Mgr*
Mike McCaleb, *District Mgr*
David Miller, *District Mgr*
▲ EMP: 400
SALES (est): 167.4MM
SALES (corp-wide): 6.6B **Publicly Held**
WEB: www.matcotools.com
SIC: 5251 5072 3469 3423 Hardware; hardware; metal stampings; hand & edge tools; tools & equipment, automotive
PA: Fortive Corporation
6920 Seaway Blvd
Everett WA 98203
425 446-5000

(G-17383)
MOISTURE GUARD CORPORATION
4370 Allen Rd (44224-1032)
PHONE..................330 928-7200
Fax: 330 928-9991
Matthew Kuhn, *President*
Nancy J Kuhn, *Vice Pres*
Rick Hein, *Project Mgr*
Marianne Marullo, *Office Mgr*
EMP: 30
SQ FT: 3,000
SALES (est): 3.5MM **Privately Held**
WEB: www.moisture-guard.com
SIC: 1761 Roofing contractor

(G-17384)
OMEGA TITLE AGENCY LLC
4500 Courthouse Blvd # 100 (44224-6835)
PHONE..................330 436-0600
John Clunk, *Marketing Staff*
Martin Gilliland, *Manager*

GEOGRAPHIC SECTION

Streetsboro - Portage County (G-17409)

Shannon Moore, *Manager*
Paula Ivars, *Director*
Kimberly Clunk,
EMP: 53
SALES (est): 14.7MM **Privately Held**
SIC: 6361 Title insurance

(G-17385)
P3 INFRASTRUCTURE INC
3105 Preakness Dr (44224-6243)
PHONE..................................330 686-1129
Puneet Singh, *Principal*
EMP: 1811
SALES (est): 38.4MM **Privately Held**
SIC: 7389

(G-17386)
PRECISION ENDOSCOPY AMER INC (PA)
4575 Hudson Dr (44224-1725)
PHONE..................................410 527-9598
John Thormann, *CEO*
Christian Mills, *President*
Ted Honeywell, *Vice Pres*
Natalie Amonica, *Manager*
EMP: 30
SQ FT: 13,000
SALES (est): 2MM **Privately Held**
SIC: 7699 Medical equipment repair, non-electric

(G-17387)
PRUSA INC
Also Called: Lawnmark
1049 Mccauley Rd (44224-1009)
PHONE..................................330 688-8500
John Prusa, *President*
EMP: 43
SALES (est): 6.5MM **Privately Held**
SIC: 0782 Lawn care services

(G-17388)
QUALITY CLEANERS OF OHIO INC
3773 Darrow Rd (44224-4035)
PHONE..................................330 688-5616
Fax: 330 688-3883
James Croyle, *President*
EMP: 40
SQ FT: 8,300
SALES (est): 1MM **Privately Held**
SIC: 7216 7219 Drycleaning plants, except rugs; garment alteration & repair shop

(G-17389)
REALTY ONE INC
Also Called: Realty One Stowe Fall
3925 Darrow Rd Ste 101 (44224-2600)
PHONE..................................330 686-1166
Fax: 330 929-6521
Marc Hustec, *Manager*
EMP: 35
SALES (corp-wide): 67.8MM **Privately Held**
WEB: www.realty-1st.com
SIC: 6531 Real estate brokers & agents
HQ: Realty One, Inc.
 800 W Saint Clair Ave
 Cleveland OH 44113
 216 328-2500

(G-17390)
ROCE GROUP LLC
Also Called: Fairfield Inn
4170 Steels Pointe (44224-6808)
PHONE..................................330 969-2627
Bharat Patel, *Manager*
Arvind Patel,
Kishore Patel,
Leena Patel,
EMP: 30 **EST:** 2015
SQ FT: 49,043
SALES (est): 244.2K **Privately Held**
SIC: 7011 Inns

(G-17391)
RON MARHOFER COLLISION CENTER
1585 Commerce Dr (44224-1711)
PHONE..................................330 686-2262
Fax: 330 686-4830
Ron Marhofer, *CEO*
Son Spalding, *Manager*
EMP: 30

SALES (est): 968.9K **Privately Held**
SIC: 7532 Body shop, automotive

(G-17392)
SHOTSTOP BALLISTICS LLC
4319 Lorwood Dr Ste 102 (44224-2734)
P.O. Box 1393 (44224-0393)
PHONE..................................330 686-0020
Pepa Iliev, *Vice Pres*
Vall Iliev,
EMP: 26
SALES (est): 330.8K **Privately Held**
SIC: 8742 8748 8711 7389 Management engineering; systems engineering consultant, ex. computer or professional; mechanical engineering;

(G-17393)
STOW DENTAL GROUP INC
Also Called: Schlosser, David W DDS
3506 Darrow Rd (44224-4098)
PHONE..................................330 688-6456
Fax: 330 688-4178
David Wiedie DDS, *President*
Dr Mark Iati, *Vice Pres*
Dr Eric Schikowski, *Vice Pres*
Dr David Scholsser, *Treasurer*
Chris Ramano, *Office Mgr*
EMP: 39
SQ FT: 3,500
SALES (est): 3.7MM **Privately Held**
SIC: 8021 Dental clinic

(G-17394)
STOW OPCO LLC
Also Called: Arbors At Stow
2910 Lermitage Pl (44224-5219)
PHONE..................................502 429-8062
Robert Norcross, *CEO*
Tracey Cugini, *Hlthcr Dir*
Benjamin Sparks, *Clerk*
EMP: 99
SQ FT: 60,000
SALES (est): 1.7MM **Privately Held**
SIC: 8051 Skilled nursing care facilities

(G-17395)
SUMMA HEALTH
Also Called: Lab Care
3869 Darrow Rd Ste 208 (44224-2677)
PHONE..................................330 688-4531
Carla Davenport, *Branch Mgr*
EMP: 45
SALES (corp-wide): 1B **Privately Held**
WEB: www.barbhosp.com
SIC: 8062 8071 General medical & surgical hospitals; medical laboratories
PA: Summa Health System
 525 E Market St
 Akron OH 44304
 330 375-3000

(G-17396)
TERSIGNI CARGILL ENTPS LLC
Also Called: Amber Gardens
4315 Hudson Dr (44224-2216)
PHONE..................................330 351-0942
Fax: 330 945-6663
Michael J Tercini,
Kurt Cargill,
EMP: 35
SQ FT: 8,000
SALES: 1.7MM **Privately Held**
WEB: www.ambergardens.com
SIC: 5261 0782 Lawn & garden supplies; lawn services

(G-17397)
TRAXIUM LLC
Also Called: Printing Concepts
4246 Hudson Dr (44224-2251)
PHONE..................................330 572-8200
Fax: 330 572-8201
George Schmutz, *President*
Karen Black, *General Mgr*
Brent M Evans, *Vice Pres*
Tiffani Gerber, *Opers Mgr*
Craig Grant, *Facilities Mgr*
EMP: 49
SQ FT: 45,000
SALES (est): 6.6MM **Privately Held**
WEB: www.printingconcepts.com
SIC: 2759 2752 7331 2789 Letterpress printing; commercial printing, offset; direct mail advertising services; bookbinding & related work

(G-17398)
TWIN PINES RETREAT CARE CENTER
456 Seasons Rd (44224-1020)
PHONE..................................330 688-5553
Fax: 330 688-1081
Scott Phillips, *President*
Robert Roma, *VP Mktg*
Ric Kislin, *Nursing Dir*
Lisa Mansour, *Administration*
EMP: 47
SQ FT: 13,500
SALES (est): 1.8MM **Privately Held**
WEB: www.twinpinesretreatcarecenter.cc
SIC: 8052 Intermediate care facilities

(G-17399)
VIZMEG LANDSCAPE INC
778 Mccauley Rd Unit 100 (44224-1067)
PHONE..................................330 686-0901
Fax: 330 686-7866
George Vizmeg, *Principal*
Karen Ridder, *Admin Asst*
EMP: 25
SALES (est): 4.3MM **Privately Held**
WEB: www.vizmeglandscape.com
SIC: 0782 Landscape contractors; lawn care services

(G-17400)
WHEATON & SPRAGUE ENGINEERING (PA)
Also Called: Wheaton Sprague Bldg Envelope
1151 Campus Dr Ste 100 (44224-1762)
PHONE..................................330 923-5560
John L Wheaton, *President*
Richard Sprague, *Vice Pres*
Debra Parker, *Office Mgr*
EMP: 28
SQ FT: 3,000
SALES (est): 2.1MM **Privately Held**
WEB: www.wheatonsprague.com
SIC: 8711 Professional engineer

Strasburg
Tuscarawas County

(G-17401)
TUSCO IMAA CHAPTER NO 602
Also Called: Tusco RC Club
6607 Cherry Run Rd Nw (44680-9026)
PHONE..................................330 878-7369
David Dessecker, *President*
Darlinda Scwartz, *Treasurer*
EMP: 27 **EST:** 1997
SALES (est): 311.2K **Privately Held**
SIC: 8641 Social club, membership

(G-17402)
VILLAGE OF STRASBURG
Village Clerk
358 5th St Sw (44680-1254)
PHONE..................................330 878-7115
Ron Lambert, *Administration*
EMP: 29
SQ FT: 592 **Privately Held**
SIC: 8111 Administrative & government law
PA: Village Of Strasburg
 358 5th St Sw
 Strasburg OH 44680
 330 878-7115

Stratton
Jefferson County

(G-17403)
JERSEY CENTRAL PWR & LIGHT CO
Also Called: Firstenergy
29503 State Route 7 (43961)
PHONE..................................740 537-6308
Frank Ludich, *Plant Mgr*
David Foltz, *Buyer*
Daniel Carman, *Engineer*
John Kreptowski, *Manager*
Pete Zelinka, *Manager*
EMP: 200 **Publicly Held**
WEB: www.jersey-central-power-light.monmouth.n

SIC: 4911 Electric services
HQ: Jersey Central Power & Light Company
 76 S Main St
 Akron OH 44308
 800 736-3402

Streetsboro
Portage County

(G-17404)
A DUIE PYLE INC
10225 Philipp Pkwy (44241-4040)
PHONE..................................330 342-7750
Fax: 330 342-7752
Dan Stopera, *Business Mgr*
Rich Gadus, *Branch Mgr*
EMP: 63
SALES (corp-wide): 334.2MM **Privately Held**
SIC: 4225 7519 General warehousing; trailer rental
PA: A. Duie Pyle Inc.
 650 Westtown Rd
 West Chester PA 19382
 610 696-5800

(G-17405)
AERO-MARK INC
10423 Danner Dr (44241-5071)
PHONE..................................330 995-0100
Fax: 330 995-0101
Mike Krenn, *President*
Curt Huffman, *Vice Pres*
EMP: 40
SQ FT: 3,600
SALES (est): 5.3MM **Privately Held**
SIC: 1721 Pavement marking contractor

(G-17406)
AGRATRONIX LLC
10375 State Route 43 (44241-4992)
PHONE..................................330 562-2222
Randy Beck, *Purch Mgr*
Trent McElhaney, *Engineer*
Dawn Decker, *Human Res Mgr*
Vicky Rickey, *Human Res Mgr*
Roberts Deidra, *VP Mktg*
▲ **EMP:** 30
SALES (est): 10.2MM **Privately Held**
WEB: www.agratronix.com
SIC: 5039 3699 3446 Wire fence, gates & accessories; electric fence chargers; fences, gates, posts & flagpoles

(G-17407)
ARTS AND EXHIBITIONS INTL LLC
10145 Philipp Pkwy D (44241-4706)
PHONE..................................330 995-9300
Andres Numhauser, *Exec VP*
Jennifer Larock, *Opers Staff*
Curt Bechdel, *VP Finance*
Jaclyn Pyatt, *Director*
John Norman,
EMP: 75
SQ FT: 1,000
SALES (est): 1.4MM **Privately Held**
WEB: www.artsandexhibitions.com
SIC: 8412 Museums & art galleries

(G-17408)
CELLCO PARTNERSHIP
Also Called: Verizon Wireless
9315 State Route 14 (44241-3800)
PHONE..................................330 626-0524
Fax: 330 422-1565
EMP: 71
SALES (corp-wide): 126B **Publicly Held**
SIC: 4812 Cellular telephone services
HQ: Cellco Partnership
 1 Verizon Way
 Basking Ridge NJ 07920

(G-17409)
CER HOTELS LLC
Also Called: TownePlace Suites By Marriott
795 Mondial Pkwy (44241-4574)
PHONE..................................330 422-1855
Fax: 330 422-1450
Maninder S Chhabra, *Mng Member*
EMP: 50

Streetsboro - Portage County (G-17410)

SALES (est): 158.8K Privately Held
SIC: 7011 Hotel, franchised

(G-17410)
CITY OF STREETSBORO
Also Called: Service Dept
2094 State Route 303 (44241-1707)
PHONE..................330 626-2856
Fax: 330 626-4032
Bill Miller, Director
EMP: 25
SQ FT: 2,312 Privately Held
WEB: www.cityofstreetsboro.com
SIC: 1611 Highway & street maintenance
PA: City Of Streetsboro
    9184 State Route 43
    Streetsboro OH 44241
    330 626-4942

(G-17411)
CORPORATE IMAGEWORKS LLC
10375 State Route 43 (44241-4992)
PHONE..................216 292-8800
Stafford Worley,
Gerald Stephens,
▲ EMP: 30
SALES (est): 3.6MM Privately Held
WEB: www.corporateimageworks.com
SIC: 5199 Advertising specialties

(G-17412)
GARDENS WESTERN RESERVE INC (PA)
9975 Greentree Pkwy (44241-4328)
PHONE..................330 342-9100
Fax: 330 342-9393
Richard Piekarski, Owner
EMP: 75
SALES (est): 4.4MM Privately Held
WEB: www.gardensofwesternreserve.com
SIC: 8059 8322 Rest home, with health care; adult day care center

(G-17413)
GEIS CONSTRUCTION INC
Also Called: Geis Companies
10020 Aurora Hudson Rd (44241-1621)
PHONE..................330 528-3500
Fax: 330 528-0008
Jeff Martin, President
Chris Adamonis, Superintendent
Jim Flauraud, Superintendent
Dave Hostetler, Superintendent
Rich Kramcsak, Superintendent
EMP: 56
SQ FT: 10,000
SALES (est): 54.4MM Privately Held
SIC: 1541 Industrial buildings, new construction

(G-17414)
GORELL ENTERPRISES INC (PA)
Also Called: Gorell Windows & Doors
10250 Philipp Pkwy (44241-4765)
PHONE..................724 465-1800
Wayne C Gorell, Ch of Bd
Brian Zimmerman, President
Michael A Rempel, Vice Pres
Tyson Schwartz, Vice Pres
Amy Romeo, Safety Mgr
EMP: 370
SQ FT: 240,000
SALES (est): 35.7MM Privately Held
WEB: www.gorell.com
SIC: 3089 5031 Plastic hardware & building products; doors & windows

(G-17415)
HAMPTON INNS LLC
800 Mondial Pkwy (44241-4540)
PHONE..................330 422-0500
Rose Mills, Branch Mgr
EMP: 29
SALES (corp-wide): 9.1B Publicly Held
WEB: www.premierhotels.us
SIC: 7011 Hotels & motels
HQ: Hampton Inns, Llc
    755 Crossover Ln
    Memphis TN 38117
    901 374-5000

(G-17416)
HIGHLAND SOM DEVELOPMENT (PA)
Also Called: Geis Company
10020 Aurora Hudson Rd (44241-1621)
PHONE..................330 528-3500
Erwin Geis, Partner
Phil Kaminski, Project Mgr
Brandon Kline, Project Mgr
Joseph Schapel, CFO
EMP: 32
SALES (est): 20.1MM Privately Held
WEB: www.geis-companies.com
SIC: 6552 Land subdividers & developers, commercial

(G-17417)
IS ACQUISITION INC (HQ)
Also Called: Integrity Stainless
3000 Crane Centre Dr (44241-5035)
PHONE..................440 287-0150
Jerry Gideon, General Mgr
Andy Markowitz, Principal
Lori K Rinehart, Controller
Felecia Qamar, Accountant
▲ EMP: 45
SALES (est): 51.1MM
SALES (corp-wide): 1.3B Publicly Held
WEB: www.integritystainless.com
SIC: 5051 Steel
PA: Olympic Steel, Inc.
    22901 Millcreek Blvd # 650
    Cleveland OH 44122
    216 292-3800

(G-17418)
JOSEPH INDUSTRIES INC
Also Called: BUCKEYE FASTENERS COMPANY
10039 Aurora Hudson Rd (44241-1600)
PHONE..................330 528-0091
Fax: 330 342-3895
Patrick Finnegan, President
Linda Kerekes, Corp Secy
Dan Eiermann, Project Mgr
Terry Davenport, Warehouse Mgr
Wendy Lovejoy, Purch Mgr
▲ EMP: 52
SQ FT: 76,260
SALES: 10.9MM
SALES (corp-wide): 42.3MM Privately Held
WEB: www.joseph.com
SIC: 3714 5084 3713 3566 Motor vehicle parts & accessories; lift trucks & parts; truck & bus bodies; speed changers, drives & gears
PA: Fastener Industries, Inc.
    1 Berea Commons Ste 209
    Berea OH 44017
    440 243-0034

(G-17419)
LOWES HOME CENTERS LLC
1210 State Route 303 (44241-4591)
PHONE..................330 626-2980
Fax: 330 626-4357
Tim Mercer, Branch Mgr
EMP: 150
SALES (corp-wide): 68.6B Publicly Held
SIC: 5211 5031 5722 5064 Home centers; building materials, exterior; building materials, interior; household appliance stores; electrical appliances, television & radio
HQ: Lowe's Home Centers, Llc
    1605 Curtis Bridge Rd
    Wilkesboro NC 28697
    336 658-4000

(G-17420)
MEANDER HSPTALITY GROUP II LLC
Also Called: Hampton Inn
800 Mondial Pkwy (44241-4540)
PHONE..................330 422-0600
Fax: 330 422-0600
Amber Muslusky, Vice Pres
Celine Kovas,
Bill Kovas,
EMP: 25
SQ FT: 1,232
SALES (est): 1.4MM Privately Held
SIC: 7011 Hotels & motels

(G-17421)
MED CENTER ONE STREETSBORO
9318 State Route 14 (44241-5224)
PHONE..................330 626-3455
Fax: 330 626-4189
Jack Mondo, Administration
EMP: 50 EST: 1997
SALES (est): 1.9MM Privately Held
SIC: 8011 Medical centers

(G-17422)
MONDELEZ GLOBAL LLC
Also Called: Nabisco
545 Mondial Pkwy (44241-4510)
P.O. Box 340, Meadow Lands PA (15347-0340)
PHONE..................330 626-6500
Mitch Hebda, Opers Mgr
Phil Crabbe, Opers Staff
Ellen Miles, Sales Mgr
Nick Perambeau, Sales Staff
Richard Regelski, Sales Staff
EMP: 60 Publicly Held
SIC: 5149 Crackers, cookies & bakery products
HQ: Mondelez Global Llc
    3 Parkway North Blvd # 300
    Deerfield IL 60015
    847 943-4000

(G-17423)
OLYMPIC STEEL INC
Also Called: Integrity Stainless
3000 Crane Centre Dr (44241-5035)
PHONE..................440 287-0150
Andy Markowitz, Division Pres
EMP: 35
SALES (corp-wide): 1.3B Publicly Held
SIC: 5051 Steel
PA: Olympic Steel, Inc.
    22901 Millcreek Blvd # 650
    Cleveland OH 44122
    216 292-3800

(G-17424)
ONEX CONSTRUCTION INC
1430 Miller Pkwy (44241-4640)
PHONE..................330 995-9015
Fax: 330 995-4297
Ken Finnerty, President
Paul Marshall, Vice Pres
Aaron Smigelski, Controller
Paul Marshal, Shareholder
▲ EMP: 40 EST: 1996
SQ FT: 20,000
SALES: 20MM Privately Held
WEB: www.onexconstruction.com
SIC: 1741 Refractory or acid brick masonry

(G-17425)
PENSKE LOGISTICS LLC
9777 Mopar Dr (44241-5220)
PHONE..................330 626-7623
EMP: 59
SALES (corp-wide): 2.9B Privately Held
WEB: www.penskelogistics.com
SIC: 4213 Trucking, except local
HQ: Penske Logistics Llc
    Green Hls Rr 10
    Reading PA 19603
    800 529-6531

(G-17426)
PORTAGE FAMILY MEDICINE
9480 Rosemont Dr (44241-4569)
PHONE..................330 626-5566
Fax: 330 626-2042
Philip Kennedy MD, President
Lora Haver, Office Mgr
EMP: 25
SALES (est): 2.1MM Privately Held
SIC: 8011 General & family practice, physician/surgeon

(G-17427)
R & H SERVICE INC
Also Called: Americas Best Value Inn
9420 State Route 14 (44241-5226)
PHONE..................330 626-2888
Rajni S Patel, President
Hema R Patel, Manager
EMP: 25
SALES (est): 1MM Privately Held
WEB: www.rhservice.com
SIC: 7011 Inns

(G-17428)
ROBINSON MEMORIAL HOSPITAL
Also Called: Robinson Hlth Affl Med Ctr One
9424 State Route 14 (44241-5226)
PHONE..................330 626-3455
Marcy Burch, Principal
EMP: 30
SALES (corp-wide): 2.3B Privately Held
SIC: 8062 8011 General medical & surgical hospitals; primary care medical clinic
HQ: Robinson Health System, Inc.
    6847 N Chestnut St
    Ravenna OH 44266
    330 297-0811

(G-17429)
SOJOURN LODGING INC
Also Called: TownePlace Suites By Marriott
795 Mondial Pkwy (44241-4574)
PHONE..................330 422-1855
Christine Zebris, Manager
EMP: 25
SALES (corp-wide): 5MM Privately Held
SIC: 7011 Hotel, franchised
PA: Sojourn Lodging, Inc.
    265 Kings Grant Rd # 106
    Virginia Beach VA 23452
    757 463-1907

(G-17430)
SOUTHERN GLAZERS WINE AND SP
Also Called: 55 Degrees
9450 Rosemont Dr (44241-4563)
PHONE..................330 422-9463
Fax: 330 422-4727
Tim Hammer, Human Res Dir
Diane Dubin, Manager
Connie Dickerson, Admin Asst
EMP: 67
SALES (corp-wide): 5.8B Privately Held
SIC: 5182 5181 Wine; beer & ale
HQ: Southern Glazer's Wine And Spirits Of Texas, Llc
    2001 Diplomat Dr
    Farmers Branch TX 75234
    972 277-2000

(G-17431)
ST LAWRENCE STEEL CORPORATION
2500 Crane Centre Dr (44241-5072)
P.O. Box 2490 (44241-0490)
PHONE..................330 562-9000
Fax: 330 562-1100
Henry W Beechler, President
Ed Ponter, Plant Mgr
Russ Milburn, Maint Spvr
David H Harvanek, Purch Mgr
Dan Spirka, Engineer
◆ EMP: 34 EST: 1955
SQ FT: 60,000
SALES (est): 29.6MM Privately Held
WEB: www.stlawrencesteel.com
SIC: 5051 3443 3441 Steel; iron & steel (ferrous) products; fabricated plate work (boiler shop); fabricated structural metal

(G-17432)
STREETSBORO BOARD EDUCATION
Also Called: Streetsboro Bus Garage
1901 Annalane Dr (44241-1730)
PHONE..................330 626-4909
Sharon Deyoung, Director
Lori Thomson, Teacher
Megan Holtz, Education
EMP: 30
SALES (corp-wide): 25.8MM Privately Held
WEB: www.rock889.com
SIC: 4151 School buses
PA: Streetsboro Board Of Education
    9000 Kirby Ln
    Streetsboro OH 44241
    330 626-4900

(G-17433)
STREETSBORO OPCO LLC
Also Called: Arbors At Streetsboro
1645 Maplewood Dr (44241-5662)
PHONE..................502 429-8062
Robert Norcross, CEO
Benjamin Sparks, Agent

EMP: 99
SALES (est): 2.3MM Privately Held
SIC: 8051 Skilled nursing care facilities

(G-17434)
TECHNOLOGY HOUSE LTD (PA)
Also Called: North Cape Manufacturing
10036 Aurora Hudson Rd (44241-1640)
PHONE..................................440 248-3025
Hazel Taylor, *Facilities Mgr*
Greg Cebular, *Manager*
Chip Gear,
Pamela Gear,
EMP: 46
SQ FT: 14,000
SALES (est): 18.8MM Privately Held
SIC: 8711 3544 3369 Industrial engineers; machine tool design; mechanical engineering; special dies, tools, jigs & fixtures; nonferrous foundries

(G-17435)
UNITY HEALTH NETWORK LLC
9150 Market Square Dr (44241-4571)
PHONE..................................330 626-0549
Terry Kingery, *Branch Mgr*
EMP: 34
SALES (corp-wide): 14.5MM Privately Held
SIC: 8043 8011 5999 Offices & clinics of podiatrists; orthopedic physician; orthopedic & prosthesis applications
PA: Unity Health Network, Llc
3033 State Rd
Cuyahoga Falls OH 44223
330 923-5899

(G-17436)
WESTERN RESERVE RACQUET CLUB
11013 Aurora Hudson Rd (44241-1630)
PHONE..................................330 653-3103
Fax: 330 656-2089
Terry Travies, *General Mgr*
Rick Began, *Director*
Sebastien Glinzler, *Director*
EMP: 30
SQ FT: 80,000
SALES (est): 1.2MM Privately Held
WEB: www.wrrfc.com
SIC: 7997 Racquetball club, membership

Strongsville
Cuyahoga County

(G-17437)
A-ROO COMPANY LLC (HQ)
22360 Royalton Rd (44149-3826)
P.O. Box 360050 (44136-0001)
PHONE..................................440 238-8850
Fax: 440 238-2212
Bill Harshbarger, *Plant Mgr*
Ronda Orick, *Safety Mgr*
Tim Schuette, *Purch Mgr*
Michael Poretsky, *Sales Mgr*
Kevin Shuman, *Sales Mgr*
▲ EMP: 55
SQ FT: 50,000
SALES (est): 25.5MM Privately Held
SIC: 5199 Packaging materials
PA: Professional Packaging Company Inc
22360 Royalton Rd
Strongsville OH 44149
440 238-8850

(G-17438)
ACCESS CATALOG COMPANY LLC
21848 Commerce Pkwy # 100 (44149-5559)
PHONE..................................440 572-5377
Jim Vangieson, *Manager*
EMP: 33
SALES (corp-wide): 205.6MM Privately Held
WEB: www.courtesyproducts.com
SIC: 5065 5046 Electronic parts & equipment; coffee brewing equipment & supplies
HQ: Access Catalog Company, L.L.C.
10880 Linpage Pl
Saint Louis MO 63132
314 301-3300

(G-17439)
ACUATIVE CORPORATION
8237 Dow Cir (44136-1761)
PHONE..................................440 202-4500
Susan Pirzchalski, *President*
Tom Roman, *Business Mgr*
Robert Cain, *VP Opers*
William Lytle, *VP Opers*
Michael Sobochan, *Project Mgr*
EMP: 60
SALES (corp-wide): 112.4MM Privately Held
SIC: 5065 Telephone & telegraphic equipment
PA: Acuative Corporation
695 Rte 46 W Ste 305
Fairfield NJ 07004
862 926-5600

(G-17440)
ADT SECURITY
13022 Pearl Rd (44136-3442)
PHONE..................................440 397-5751
EMP: 57 Privately Held
SIC: 9229 9224 9221 7382 Public order & safety; fire protection; police protection; security systems services

(G-17441)
ALL FOILS INC
16100 Imperial Pkwy (44149-0600)
PHONE..................................440 572-3645
Fax: 440 378-0161
Kevin C Foos, *President*
Kathy Patterson, *Purch Mgr*
Robert F Gesing, *Treasurer*
Karen Mittman, *Controller*
Honie Latak, *Sales Mgr*
◆ EMP: 79
SQ FT: 140,000
SALES (est): 45.8MM Privately Held
WEB: www.allfoils.com
SIC: 5051 Steel

(G-17442)
ALTENHEIM FOUNDATION INC
18627 Shurmer Rd (44136-6150)
PHONE..................................440 238-3361
Fax: 440 238-3205
Greg McDaniels, *President*
Josh Shivak, *Technology*
Larry Zwegat, *Web Dvlpr*
Traci Gerchak, *Director*
William Smucker, *Director*
EMP: 49
SALES: 291.1K Privately Held
WEB: www.altenheim.com
SIC: 8051 Convalescent home with continuous nursing care

(G-17443)
APPLIED MINT SUPS SLUTIONS LLC (HQ)
14790 Foltz Pkwy (44149-4723)
PHONE..................................216 456-3600
Fax: 216 881-2611
Robert Onorato, *Vice Pres*
Michael Murray, *Finance*
Jeff Jarrett, *Sales Mgr*
Wendy Poole, *Sales Mgr*
Susan Kravec, *Cust Mgr*
EMP: 50
SQ FT: 102,850
SALES (est): 79MM
SALES (corp-wide): 2.5B Publicly Held
SIC: 5085 Industrial supplies
PA: Applied Industrial Technologies, Inc.
1 Applied Plz
Cleveland OH 44115
216 426-4000

(G-17444)
ARCHWAY MARKETING SERVICES INC
20770 Westwood Dr (44149-3907)
P.O. Box 360450, Cleveland (44136-0041)
PHONE..................................440 572-0725
Lawrence Zimmering, *CEO*
Brandy Squire, *Purchasing*
Sarah Kohut, *Accounts Mgr*
Teri Morrison, *Accounts Mgr*
Ryan McCarbery, *Supervisor*
EMP: 200 Privately Held
SIC: 8742 Marketing consulting services
HQ: Archway Marketing Services, Inc.
19850 S Diamond Lake Rd
Rogers MN 55374

(G-17445)
AT&T MOBILITY LLC
17970 Royalton Rd (44136-5149)
PHONE..................................440 846-3232
Anita Carile, *Branch Mgr*
EMP: 26
SALES (corp-wide): 160.5B Publicly Held
SIC: 4812 Cellular telephone services
HQ: At&T Mobility Llc
1025 Lenox Park Blvd Ne
Brookhaven GA 30319
800 331-0500

(G-17446)
BEARING & DRIVE SYSTEMS INC (PA)
14888 Foltz Pkwy (44149-4725)
PHONE..................................440 846-9700
Fax: 440 846-5560
Steve Sivo, *President*
Mike Luciano, *Vice Pres*
Bryan Muzie, *Warehouse Mgr*
Joletta Hannibal, *Controller*
Tammy Seff, *Human Res Mgr*
▲ EMP: 100
SQ FT: 35,000
SALES (est): 35.5MM Privately Held
WEB: www.bdsbearing.com
SIC: 5085 5063 Bearings; power transmission equipment, electric

(G-17447)
BRIGHTON-BEST INTL INC
16065 Imperial Pkwy (44149-0700)
PHONE..................................440 238-1350
Steve Andrasik, *Regional Mgr*
Kimberly Arnold, *Branch Mgr*
EMP: 40
SALES (corp-wide): 315.4MM Privately Held
SIC: 5072 Screws
HQ: Brighton-Best International, Inc.
5855 Obispo Ave
Long Beach CA 90805
562 808-8000

(G-17448)
CELLCO PARTNERSHIP
Also Called: Verizon
17290 Royalton Rd (44136-4400)
PHONE..................................440 846-8881
Scott Goodrich, *Manager*
EMP: 25
SALES (corp-wide): 126B Publicly Held
SIC: 4812 5999 Cellular telephone services; mobile telephones & equipment
HQ: Cellco Partnership
1 Verizon Way
Basking Ridge NJ 07920

(G-17449)
CINTAS CORPORATION NO 2
8221 Dow Cir (44136-1761)
PHONE..................................440 238-5565
Fax: 440 238-3920
Nick Blevins, *Plant Mgr*
John Miller, *Manager*
EMP: 100
SQ FT: 68,133
SALES (corp-wide): 5.3B Publicly Held
WEB: www.cintas-corp.com
SIC: 7213 7218 7216 Uniform supply; industrial launderers; drycleaning plants, except rugs
HQ: Cintas Corporation No 2
6800 Cintas Blvd
Mason OH 45040

(G-17450)
CLERAC LLC (DH)
Also Called: National Car Rental
8249 Mohawk Dr (44136-1795)
PHONE..................................440 345-3999
Kevin Keene, *Vice Pres*
Karla Conti, *Hum Res Coord*
Chryssa Thompson, *Human Resources*
Chris Heinzmann, *Sales Staff*
Justin Dyer, *Manager*
EMP: 50
SQ FT: 11,894
SALES (est): 24.2MM
SALES (corp-wide): 6.1B Privately Held
SIC: 7515 7514 Passenger car leasing; rent-a-car service
HQ: Enterprise Holdings, Inc.
600 Corporate Park Dr
Saint Louis MO 63105
314 512-5000

(G-17451)
CLEVELAND METROPARKS
9485 Eastland Rd (44149-1418)
PHONE..................................216 739-6040
Fax: 440 234-3740
Steve Dice, *Manager*
EMP: 450
SALES (corp-wide): 57.3MM Privately Held
WEB: www.clemetparks.com
SIC: 7999 Recreation services
PA: Cleveland Metroparks
4101 Fulton Pkwy
Cleveland OH 44144
216 635-3200

(G-17452)
CLEVELAND METROPARKS
Also Called: Chalet
16200 Valley Pkwy (44149)
PHONE..................................440 572-9990
Rob Muntz, *Manager*
Melissa Tirpak, *Manager*
EMP: 30
SALES (corp-wide): 57.3MM Privately Held
WEB: www.clemetparks.com
SIC: 7999 Recreation services; astrologer
PA: Cleveland Metroparks
4101 Fulton Pkwy
Cleveland OH 44144
216 635-3200

(G-17453)
CREATIVE PLAYROOMS INC
16000 Foltz Pkwy (44149-5502)
PHONE..................................440 572-9365
Fax: 440 572-1864
Debbie Kaltner, *Exec Dir*
Lisa Roff, *Director*
EMP: 30
SQ FT: 16,532
SALES (corp-wide): 3.7MM Privately Held
SIC: 8351 Child day care services
PA: Creative Playrooms, Inc.
32750 Solon Rd Ste 3
Solon OH 44139
440 349-9111

(G-17454)
CUYAHOGA LANDMARK INC (PA)
21079 Westwood Dr (44149-2901)
P.O. Box 361189 (44136-0020)
PHONE..................................440 238-3900
Gary Smith, *President*
Tony Fischiettl, *CFO*
EMP: 40 EST: 1934
SQ FT: 25,640
SALES (est): 22.1MM Privately Held
WEB: www.cfgh.hbocvan.com
SIC: 5172 5541 5983 Gasoline; fuel oil; filling stations, gasoline, fuel oil dealers

(G-17455)
DANIELS BOARDING KENNELS
21782 Royalton Rd (44149-3816)
PHONE..................................440 238-7179
Fax: 440 846-0260
James Strachen, *Partner*
Denes Pal, *Partner*
Rosalie Strachen, *Partner*
EMP: 25 EST: 2001
SQ FT: 6,100
SALES (est): 576.3K Privately Held
WEB: www.drdenespal.com
SIC: 0742 Veterinarian, animal specialties

(G-17456)
DARICE INC (DH)
Also Called: Pat Catan's Craft Centers
13000 Darice Pkwy 82 (44149-3800)
PHONE..................................440 238-9150
Michael Catanzarite, *President*
Debbie Colon, *General Mgr*
David Herbers, *General Mgr*

Strongsville - Cuyahoga County (G-17457)

Kevin Kilbane, *VP Opers*
Zachary Gryzlo, *Project Mgr*
◆ **EMP:** 150
SQ FT: 100,000
SALES (est): 193.9MM
SALES (corp-wide): 5.2B **Publicly Held**
SIC: 5945 5193 5999 Arts & crafts supplies; flowers & florists' supplies; picture frames, ready made
HQ: Michaels Stores, Inc.
8000 Bent Branch Dr
Irving TX 75063
972 409-1300

(G-17457)
DWA MRKTING PRMTIONAL PDTS LLC
Also Called: Art Wall
17000 Foltz Pkwy (44149-5522)
PHONE..........................216 476-0635
David Aheimer, *CEO*
David Khieu, *President*
Brandy Martini, *Admin Asst*
EMP: 32
SALES: 2MM **Privately Held**
SIC: 5023 5091 5141 5092 Decorative home furnishings & supplies; sporting & recreation goods; groceries, general line; toys & hobby goods & supplies; gifts & novelties

(G-17458)
EARTHBOUND HOLDING LLC
500 Southpark Ctr (44136-9320)
PHONE..........................972 248-0228
Luciana Fleitas, *Principal*
EMP: 41
SALES (corp-wide): 309.2MM **Privately Held**
SIC: 5199 Art goods & supplies
PA: Earthbound Holding, Llc
4051 Freport Pkwy Ste 400
Grapevine TX 76051
972 248-0228

(G-17459)
EDRICH SUPPLY CO
22700 Royalton Rd (44149-3838)
PHONE..........................440 238-9440
Richard A Puzzitiello, *President*
EMP: 50
SQ FT: 1,500
SALES (est): 3.3MM **Privately Held**
SIC: 1521 5031 General remodeling, single-family houses; lumber, plywood & millwork

(G-17460)
EMSCO (PA)
Also Called: Emsco Distributors
22350 Royalton Rd (44149-3826)
P.O. Box 360660 (44136-0011)
PHONE..........................440 238-2100
Mark Stoyanoff, *President*
Richard Laneve, *Vice Pres*
Eric Stoyanoff, *VP Opers*
Dave Siria, *Opers Mgr*
Sharee Justices, *Treasurer*
◆ **EMP:** 30
SQ FT: 195,000
SALES: 41MM **Privately Held**
WEB: www.emscocorp.com
SIC: 5091 Swimming pools, equipment & supplies

(G-17461)
ENABLING PARTNERS LLC
13862 Basswood Cir (44136-2693)
PHONE..........................440 878-9418
John Ice, *Principal*
EMP: 25
SQ FT: 10,000
SALES (est): 767K **Privately Held**
WEB: www.enablingpartners.com
SIC: 8742 Business consultant; productivity improvement consultant

(G-17462)
EUTHENICS INC (PA)
8235 Mohawk Dr (44136-1795)
PHONE..........................440 260-1555
Fax: 440 260-1544
Ron Bender, *President*
Richard S Wasosky, *Vice Pres*
Edward Piatak, *Project Mgr*
Vince Bobkovich, *Manager*
Dan Bender, *Comp Tech*
EMP: 34
SQ FT: 8,000
SALES (est): 4.1MM **Privately Held**
WEB: www.euthenics-inc.com
SIC: 8711 Civil engineering

(G-17463)
FALLING LEASING CO LLC
Also Called: Falling Water Healthcare Ctr
18840 Falling Water Rd (44136-4200)
PHONE..........................440 238-1100
Fax: 440 238-9575
Stephen L Rosedale, *Chairman*
Charles R Stoltz, *Exec VP*
Ronald S Wilheim, *Exec VP*
David W Trimble, *CPA*
Mark Morley, *Director*
EMP: 202
SQ FT: 60,000
SALES: 1.5MM **Privately Held**
SIC: 8051 Convalescent home with continuous nursing care

(G-17464)
FAY INDUSTRIES INC
17200 Foltz Pkwy (44149-5526)
P.O. Box 360947, Cleveland (44136-0016)
PHONE..........................440 572-5030
Fax: 440 572-5614
Richard Schnaterbeck, *President*
Jack Notarianni, *Vice Pres*
Brad Notarianni, *Purchasing*
John A Notarianni II, *Controller*
▲ **EMP:** 59 **EST:** 1974
SQ FT: 60,000
SALES (est): 63MM **Publicly Held**
SIC: 5051 Steel
PA: Ryerson Holding Corporation
227 W Monroe St Fl 27
Chicago IL 60606

(G-17465)
FOUNDATION SOFTWARE INC
17999 Foltz Pkwy (44149-5565)
PHONE..........................330 220-8383
Fax: 330 220-1443
Fred Ode, *CEO*
Steve Antill, *Vice Pres*
Michael J Basil, *VP Opers*
Stacey Kazarovich, *Project Mgr*
Lori Adamczyk, *QA Dir*
EMP: 92
SQ FT: 16,000
SALES (est): 15.6MM **Privately Held**
SIC: 7372 7371 Prepackaged software; software programming applications; custom computer programming services

(G-17466)
GOING HOME MEDICAL HOLDING CO
15830 Foltz Pkwy (44149-4745)
PHONE..........................305 340-1034
Ryan Hawley, *President*
EMP: 25 **EST:** 2016 **Privately Held**
SIC: 6719 Holding companies

(G-17467)
GOODWILL IDSTRS GRTR CLVLND L
16160 Pearl Rd (44136-6036)
PHONE..........................440 783-1168
EMP: 27
SALES (corp-wide): 27.6MM **Privately Held**
SIC: 8331 Job training & vocational rehabilitation services
PA: Goodwill Industries Of Greater Cleveland And East Central Ohio, Inc.
408 9th St Sw
Canton OH 44707
330 454-9461

(G-17468)
HEALTHCARE CIRCLE INC
18149 Williamsburg Oval (44136-7091)
PHONE..........................440 331-7347
Fax: 440 331-7342
Tammy Haseley, *President*
EMP: 75
SALES (est): 1MM **Privately Held**
SIC: 8082 Home health care services

(G-17469)
HEWLETTCO INC
Also Called: Goddard School
13590 Falling Water Rd (44136-4319)
PHONE..........................440 238-4600
Fax: 440 238-5254
Robyn T Hewlett, *President*
Craig Bach, *Principal*
Tracy Swanson, *Principal*
L Dale Todd, *Vice Pres*
Maragaret Todd, *Admin Sec*
EMP: 25
SQ FT: 10,000
SALES (est): 963.7K **Privately Held**
SIC: 8351 Preschool center

(G-17470)
HIRTS GREENHOUSE INC
Also Called: Hirts Greenhouse and Flowers
14407 Pearl Rd (44136-8797)
PHONE..........................440 238-8200
Fax: 440 238-4384
Claire Hirt, *President*
EMP: 35
SQ FT: 20,000
SALES (est): 1.8MM **Privately Held**
SIC: 0181 5992 Nursery stock, growing of; flowers, fresh

(G-17471)
HOME DEPOT USA INC
Also Called: Home Depot, The
8199 Pearl Rd (44136-1633)
PHONE..........................440 826-9092
Fax: 440 239-7416
Ron Salizar, *Manager*
EMP: 150
SALES (corp-wide): 100.9B **Publicly Held**
WEB: www.homerentalsdepot.com
SIC: 5211 7359 Home centers; tool rental
HQ: Home Depot U.S.A., Inc.
2455 Paces Ferry Rd Se
Atlanta GA 30339

(G-17472)
HONEYWELL INTERNATIONAL INC
8370 Dow Cir Ste 5 (44136-1778)
PHONE..........................440 243-8877
Fax: 440 243-1954
David Bowman, *Manager*
EMP: 75
SQ FT: 6,000
SALES (corp-wide): 40.5B **Publicly Held**
WEB: www.honeywell.com
SIC: 7629 Aircraft electrical equipment repair; electrical equipment repair, high voltage; electronic equipment repair
PA: Honeywell International Inc.
115 Tabor Rd
Morris Plains NJ 07950
973 455-2000

(G-17473)
HUGHES CORPORATION (PA)
Also Called: Weschler Instruments
16900 Foltz Pkwy (44149-5520)
PHONE..........................440 238-2550
Fax: 440 238-0660
David E Hughes, *President*
Esther Carpenter, *Principal*
Michael F Dorman, *Exec VP*
Douglas Hughes, *Vice Pres*
Gerald Lucak, *Vice Pres*
EMP: 30
SQ FT: 11,500
SALES (est): 32MM **Privately Held**
WEB: www.weschler.com
SIC: 5063 3825 Electrical apparatus & equipment; instruments to measure electricity

(G-17474)
HUGHES CORPORATION
Also Called: Mac Group, The
16900 Foltz Pkwy (44149-5520)
PHONE..........................440 238-2550
David Hughes, *CEO*
EMP: 25
SALES (corp-wide): 32MM **Privately Held**
WEB: www.weschler.com
SIC: 5065 Electronic parts & equipment

PA: Hughes Corporation
16900 Foltz Pkwy
Strongsville OH 44149
440 238-2550

(G-17475)
ICE LAND USA LTD
15381 Royalton Rd (44136-5440)
PHONE..........................440 268-2800
William Neiheiser, *President*
Tony Miletti, *General Mgr*
Katie Nieheiser, *Vice Pres*
EMP: 80
SQ FT: 97,000
SALES (est): 3.3MM **Privately Held**
SIC: 7999 5812 Ice skating rink operation; eating places

(G-17476)
ILEAD LLC
Also Called: Ilead Marketing
20376 Kelsey Ln (44149-0965)
PHONE..........................440 846-2346
Scott Flanagan,
EMP: 30
SALES (est): 2.6MM **Privately Held**
SIC: 8742 Marketing consulting services

(G-17477)
INTRALOT INC
13500 Darice Pkwy Ste C (44149-3840)
PHONE..........................440 268-2900
Dennis Karras, *Opers Mgr*
Javier Birriel, *Network Mgr*
EMP: 25
SALES (corp-wide): 78.8MM **Privately Held**
SIC: 7379
HQ: Intralot, Inc.
11360 Technology Cir
Duluth GA 30097
678 473-7200

(G-17478)
JOHNSON CONTROLS
17295 Foltz Pkwy Ste G (44149-5568)
PHONE..........................440 268-1160
Fax: 440 783-0302
Al Gray, *Sales Mgr*
Anthony Warner, *Branch Mgr*
James Selig, *Payroll Mgr*
Pierre St Arnaud, *Manager*
Sean Cromwell, *Technology*
EMP: 112 **Privately Held**
WEB: www.simplexgrinnell.com
SIC: 1711 Sprinkler contractors
HQ: Johnson Controls Fire Protection Lp
4700 Exchange Ct Ste 300
Boca Raton FL 33431
561 988-7200

(G-17479)
KAISER FOUNDATION HOSPITALS
Also Called: Strongsville Medical Offices
17406 Royalton Rd (44136-5151)
PHONE..........................216 524-7377
EMP: 593
SALES (corp-wide): 82.6B **Privately Held**
SIC: 8011 Offices & clinics of medical doctors
HQ: Kaiser Foundation Hospitals Inc
1 Kaiser Plz
Oakland CA 94612
510 271-6611

(G-17480)
KEMPER COMPANY
Also Called: Kemper House of Strongsville
10890 Prospect Rd (44149-2256)
PHONE..........................440 846-1100
Fax: 440 846-1113
John Kemper, *Branch Mgr*
Kathy Busch, *Nursing Mgr*
EMP: 85
SALES (corp-wide): 24.5MM **Privately Held**
SIC: 8748 Business consulting
PA: The Kemper Company
10307 Detroit Ave # 101
Cleveland OH 44102
216 472-4200

GEOGRAPHIC SECTION
Strongsville - Cuyahoga County (G-17503)

(G-17481)
KENNEDY GROUP ENTERPRISES INC
13370 Prospect Rd 2c (44149-3854)
PHONE..............................440 879-0078
Fax: 440 879-0084
Ronald J Kennedy, *Owner*
Jennifer Wirth, *Exec VP*
Christa Lilley, *Vice Pres*
Craig D Kennedy, *Admin Sec*
EMP: 30
SQ FT: 3,500
SALES (est): 2.1MM **Privately Held**
SIC: 8721 8742 8748 Billing & bookkeeping service; management information systems consultant; business consulting

(G-17482)
LAMRITE WEST INC (HQ)
Also Called: Darice
14225 Pearl Rd (44136-8711)
PHONE..............................440 238-7318
Fax: 440 238-1337
Michael Catanzarite, *President*
David Catanzarite, *Vice Pres*
Joe Rudolph, *CFO*
Pat Ramos, *Cust Mgr*
Randall Boring, *Asst Mgr*
▲ **EMP:** 200
SQ FT: 125,000
SALES (est): 62.3MM
SALES (corp-wide): 5.2B **Publicly Held**
WEB: www.darice.com
SIC: 5999 5199 5092 Artists' supplies & materials; artificial flowers; art goods & supplies; toys & hobby goods & supplies
PA: The Michaels Companies Inc
8000 Bent Branch Dr
Irving TX 75063
972 409-1300

(G-17483)
LAMRITE WEST INC
Also Called: A C Supply
17647 Foltz Pkwy (44149-5535)
PHONE..............................440 572-9946
Fax: 440 572-9954
Rocco Catan, *Manager*
EMP: 25
SALES (corp-wide): 5.2B **Publicly Held**
WEB: www.darice.com
SIC: 5199 Art goods & supplies
HQ: Lamrite West, Inc.
14225 Pearl Rd
Strongsville OH 44136
440 238-7318

(G-17484)
LAMRITE WEST INC
Also Called: Pat Catan's
14225 Pearl Rd (44136-8711)
PHONE..............................440 268-0634
Greg Alberty, *Manager*
Pat Catan, *Manager*
EMP: 43
SQ FT: 77,530
SALES (corp-wide): 5.2B **Publicly Held**
WEB: www.darice.com
SIC: 5092 Arts & crafts equipment & supplies
HQ: Lamrite West, Inc.
14225 Pearl Rd
Strongsville OH 44136
440 238-7318

(G-17485)
LOWES HOME CENTERS LLC
9149 Pearl Rd (44136-1414)
PHONE..............................440 239-2630
Fax: 440 239-2633
Dennis Honkala, *Department Mgr*
John Lerch, *Manager*
EMP: 150
SALES (corp-wide): 68.6B **Publicly Held**
SIC: 5211 5031 5722 5064 Home centers; building materials, exterior; building materials, interior; household appliance stores; electrical appliances, television & radio
HQ: Lowe's Home Centers, Llc
1605 Curtis Bridge Rd
Wilkesboro NC 28697
336 658-4000

(G-17486)
MAINTENANCE UNLIMITED INC
12351 Prospect Rd (44149-2941)
PHONE..............................440 238-1162
Fax: 440 238-7975
Joseph Friscone, *President*
Beth Raiter, *Manager*
EMP: 50
SQ FT: 10,000
SALES (est): 6.6MM **Privately Held**
WEB: www.maintenanceunlimited.com
SIC: 1623 1541 1629 1794 Sewer line construction; oil & gas pipeline construction; renovation, remodeling & repairs: industrial buildings; trenching contractor; excavation & grading, building construction

(G-17487)
MANCAN INC
13500 Pearl Rd Ste 109 (44136-3428)
PHONE..............................440 884-9675
EMP: 1050
SALES (corp-wide): 137.7MM **Privately Held**
SIC: 8742 7361 Industrial & labor consulting services; employment agencies
PA: Mancan, Inc.
48 1st St Nw
Massillon OH 44647
330 832-4595

(G-17488)
MANHATTAN ASSOCIATES INC
10153 S Bexley Cir (44136-2565)
PHONE..............................440 878-0771
Raymond Bernard, *Branch Mgr*
EMP: 90 **Publicly Held**
SIC: 7371 Software programming applications
PA: Manhattan Associates, Inc.
2300 Windy Ridge Pkwy Se 1000n
Atlanta GA 30339

(G-17489)
MARIA GARDENS INC (PA)
20465 Royalton Rd (44149-4967)
P.O. Box 360256, Cleveland (44136-0005)
PHONE..............................440 238-7637
Fax: 440 238-0210
David Stopper, *President*
Dave Stopper Sr, *Principal*
Rosemary Stopper, *Vice Pres*
EMP: 44
SQ FT: 85,000
SALES (est): 4.8MM **Privately Held**
SIC: 0181 5193 5992 Flowers: grown under cover (e.g. greenhouse production); plants, potted; plants, potted

(G-17490)
MASSAGE ENVY
Also Called: Dhr
6 Southpark Ctr (44136-9334)
PHONE..............................440 878-0500
Kim Lau, *Sales Mgr*
Sarah Zarife, *Manager*
Corinne Scurec, *Manager*
EMP: 25 **EST:** 2008
SALES (est): 305.9K **Privately Held**
SIC: 7299 Massage parlor

(G-17491)
MEDICAL MUTUAL OF OHIO
15885 W Sprague Rd (44136-1772)
PHONE..............................440 878-4800
Jerry Patrick, *Exec VP*
Jan Santoli, *Vice Pres*
Brian Berman, *Engineer*
Robert Klubert, *VP Sales*
Abby O'Brien, *Sales Staff*
EMP: 85
SALES (corp-wide): 1.4B **Privately Held**
SIC: 6411 Insurance agents
PA: Medical Mutual Of Ohio
2060 E 9th St Frnt Ste
Cleveland OH 44115
216 687-7000

(G-17492)
MEDICAL MUTUAL SERVICES LLC (HQ)
Also Called: Antares Management Solutions
17800 Royalton Rd (44136-5149)
PHONE..............................440 878-4800
Jeff Perry, *Exec VP*
Tom Stepec, *Vice Pres*
Jim Ebsch, *Engineer*
Lisa Yanchar, *Human Res Mgr*
Kevin Gill, *Natl Sales Mgr*
EMP: 250
SQ FT: 15,000
SALES (est): 34.5MM
SALES (corp-wide): 1.4B **Privately Held**
WEB: www.antaressolutions.com
SIC: 7374 7375 Data processing & preparation; information retrieval services
PA: Medical Mutual Of Ohio
2060 E 9th St Frnt Ste
Cleveland OH 44115
216 687-7000

(G-17493)
MEDINA WORLD CARS INC
11800 Pearl Rd (44136-3329)
PHONE..............................330 725-4901
Paul Hrnchar, *President*
Steve Karg, *Vice Pres*
EMP: 40
SQ FT: 16,000
SALES (est): 2.5MM **Privately Held**
WEB: www.4worldcars.com
SIC: 7532 5511 7538 7515 Body shop, automotive; automobiles, new & used; general automotive repair shops; passenger car leasing; automotive & home supply stores

(G-17494)
MERRICK CHEVROLET CO
15303 Royalton Rd (44136-5440)
PHONE..............................440 878-6700
Fax: 440 238-2585
Robert Serpentini Jr, *President*
Jeanine Hine, *General Mgr*
Paul Serpentini, *Corp Secy*
Mary Jo Root, *Human Res Mgr*
Sandy West, *Admin Asst*
EMP: 80
SQ FT: 18,000
SALES (est): 20.3MM **Privately Held**
SIC: 5511 7515 Automobiles, new & used; pickups, new & used; trucks, tractors & trailers: new & used; passenger car leasing

(G-17495)
MOHAWK RE-BAR SERVICES INC
15110 Foltz Pkwy Ste 106 (44149-4765)
P.O. Box 8468, Canton (44711-8468)
PHONE..............................440 268-0780
Jerry T Abrantes, *President*
EMP: 30
SQ FT: 1,500
SALES (est): 2.1MM **Privately Held**
WEB: www.mohawksoftware.com
SIC: 1791 Structural steel erection

(G-17496)
MUELLER ART COVER & BINDING CO
12005 Alameda Dr (44149-3016)
P.O. Box 360829 (44136-0014)
PHONE..............................440 238-3303
Toll Free:..........................888   -
Fax: 440 238-5574
Edmond Mueller, *President*
Bob Mueller, *COO*
Daniel Mack, *Vice Pres*
Jack Kelly, *Purchasing*
Robert Mueller, *Manager*
EMP: 45
SQ FT: 38,000
SALES (est): 6.4MM **Privately Held**
WEB: www.muellerartcover.com
SIC: 2782 7336 Looseleaf binders & devices; graphic arts & related design; silk screen design

(G-17497)
NATIONAL AUTO EXPERTS LLC
8370 Dow Cir Ste 100 (44136-1797)
PHONE..............................440 274-5114
Kelly Price, *Principal*
David Neuenschwander, *Vice Pres*
Cliff Childers, *Accounts Exec*
David Tralongo, *Accounts Exec*
Aaron Rausch, *Supervisor*
EMP: 35
SALES (est): 6.6MM **Privately Held**
SIC: 7538 General automotive repair shops

(G-17498)
OPTIONS FOR FAMILY & YOUTH
11351 Pearl Rd Ste 103 (44136-3331)
PHONE..............................216 267-7070
Fax: 216 267-7075
Michael Rush, *President*
Stephen Young, *Vice Pres*
Ginger Heyneman, *Asst Director*
EMP: 40
SALES (est): 1.7MM **Privately Held**
SIC: 8322 Adoption services

(G-17499)
PARK GROUP CO OF AMERICA INC
22700 Royalton Rd (44149-3838)
PHONE..............................440 238-9440
Richard Puzzitello Jr, *President*
Chris Bender, *Senior VP*
EMP: 50
SQ FT: 1,000
SALES (est): 3.5MM **Privately Held**
SIC: 1521 New construction, single-family houses

(G-17500)
PPG ARCHITECTURAL FINISHES INC
Glidden Professional Paint Ctr
16651 W Sprague Rd (44136-1757)
PHONE..............................440 826-5100
Patricia Starrett, *Manager*
William Hosmer, *Project Leader*
Ron Castelein, *Info Tech Mgr*
Monica Wilson, *Technology*
Randolph Glau, *Director*
EMP: 300
SALES (corp-wide): 14.7B **Publicly Held**
WEB: www.gliddenpaint.com
SIC: 8731 Commercial research laboratory
HQ: Ppg Architectural Finishes, Inc.
1 Ppg Pl
Pittsburgh PA 15272
412 434-3131

(G-17501)
RADEBAUGH-FETZER COMPANY
Also Called: Gill Podiatry Supply Co
22400 Ascoa Ct (44149-4766)
PHONE..............................440 878-4700
Eric Boggs, *President*
Gerald E Johnson, *Principal*
Dave Adriano, *Purch Dir*
Jim Rief, *Sales Staff*
Brian Murphy, *Marketing Staff*
EMP: 30
SQ FT: 22,975
SALES (est): 14.6MM **Privately Held**
WEB: www.gillpodiatry.com
SIC: 5047 Physician equipment & supplies; surgical equipment & supplies; orthopedic equipment & supplies; hospital equipment & supplies

(G-17502)
RITE RUG CO
20036 Progress Dr (44149-3214)
PHONE..............................440 945-4100
EMP: 43
SALES (corp-wide): 82.2MM **Privately Held**
SIC: 5023 Rugs
PA: Rite Rug Co.
4450 Poth Rd Ste A
Columbus OH 43213
614 261-6060

(G-17503)
ROBERT E MCGRATH INC
Also Called: Olympia Candies
11606 Pearl Rd (44136-3320)
PHONE..............................440 572-7747
Fax: 440 572-1819
Robert McGrath, *President*
Celia McGrath, *Vice Pres*
EMP: 25
SQ FT: 15,000

Strongsville - Cuyahoga County (G-17504)

SALES: 750K **Privately Held**
WEB: www.olympiacandy.com
SIC: 5145 5441 2096 2066 Candy; candy; potato chips & similar snacks; chocolate & cocoa products; ice cream & frozen desserts

(G-17504)
SCHOLASTIC BOOK FAIRS INC
12850 Darice Pkwy Ste A (44149-3827)
PHONE 440 572-4880
Fax: 440 572-8522
Robin Perjon-Mack, *General Mgr*
Tom Vollman, *Vice Pres*
Sue Carton, *Project Mgr*
Mike Bertsch, *Opers Mgr*
Sheri McCullough, *Prdtn Mgr*
EMP: 70
SALES (corp-wide): 1.7B **Publicly Held**
WEB: www.scholasticbookfairs.com
SIC: 5192 Books, periodicals & newspapers
HQ: Scholastic Book Fairs, Inc.
   1080 Greenwood Blvd
   Lake Mary FL 32746
   407 829-7300

(G-17505)
SEVEN SECURED INC
15830 Foltz Pkwy (44149-4745)
PHONE 281 362-2887
Peter Martin, *President*
Todd McCullough, *Vice Pres*
EMP: 25
SALES (est): 344.7K **Privately Held**
SIC: 7381 Detective & armored car services

(G-17506)
SGL CARBON TECHNIC LLC
21945 Drake Rd (44149-6608)
PHONE 440 572-3600
Fax: 440 572-9570
Scott Carlton, *President*
George Hronec, *Draft/Design*
Jay Tumuluri, *Finance Mgr*
Karl Schmidt, *Manager*
▲ **EMP:** 28
SQ FT: 46,004
SALES (est): 14.1MM
SALES (corp-wide): 1B **Privately Held**
SIC: 5084 Heat exchange equipment, industrial
PA: Sgl Carbon Se
   Sohnleinstr. 8
   Wiesbaden 65201
   611 602-90

(G-17507)
SHORELINE EXPRESS INC
20137 Progress Dr (44149-3215)
P.O. Box 360341 (44136-0006)
PHONE 440 878-3750
Fax: 440 878-3731
Don Sparks, *Principal*
EMP: 30
SALES (est): 5MM **Privately Held**
SIC: 4214 Local trucking with storage

(G-17508)
SHORELINE TRANSPORTATION INC
Also Called: Shoreline Company
20137 Progress Dr (44149-3215)
PHONE 440 878-2000
Janeen Mazzeo-Sparks, *President*
Donald Sparks, *Vice Pres*
EMP: 240
SQ FT: 35,000
SALES (est): 26.4MM **Privately Held**
WEB: www.shorelinetransportation.com
SIC: 4212 4213 4731 Local trucking, without storage; trucking, except local; transportation agents & brokers

(G-17509)
SHURMER PLACE AT ALTENHEIM
18821 Shurmer Rd (44136-6100)
PHONE 440 238-9001
Fax: 440 238-9157
Barb Capadona, *Personnel*
Paul Pasota, *Exec Dir*
Paul Pasotam, *Exec Dir*
William Smucker, *Director*
EMP: 50 **EST:** 2000
SALES (est): 2.2MM **Privately Held**
SIC: 8361 Residential care

(G-17510)
SOUTHWEST GENERAL HEALTH CTR
18181 Pearl Rd Ste B104 (44136-6950)
PHONE 440 816-4900
Jessica Aubin, *Med Doctor*
Barb Stec, *Manager*
Deborah Traine, *Manager*
Olga Kovacevic, *Obstetrician*
EMP: 110
SALES (corp-wide): 315.6MM **Privately Held**
SIC: 8062 8011 General medical & surgical hospitals; medical centers
PA: Southwest General Health Center
   18697 Bagley Rd
   Cleveland OH 44130
   440 816-8000

(G-17511)
STATE AUTO PRPERTY CSLTY INSUR
Also Called: State Auto Insurance Co
14843 W Sprague Rd Ste F (44136-6602)
PHONE 440 842-6200
Fax: 440 842-5277
Don Spickler, *Principal*
EMP: 40
SQ FT: 7,584
SALES (corp-wide): 570MM **Publicly Held**
SIC: 6331 6411 Fire, marine & casualty insurance & carriers; insurance agents
HQ: State Auto Property And Casualty Insurance Company
   518 E Broad St
   Columbus OH
   614 464-5000

(G-17512)
STRONGSVILLE LODGING ASSOC 1
Also Called: Holiday Inn
15471 Royalton Rd (44136-5441)
PHONE 440 238-8800
Fax: 440 238-0273
Robert Cole, *Partner*
Robert Flanders, *Partner*
Strongsville Lodging Associate, *Partner*
Jay Molitor, *General Mgr*
Renee Gala, *Controller*
EMP: 175
SQ FT: 65,414
SALES (est): 7.5MM **Privately Held**
SIC: 7011 Hotels

(G-17513)
STRONGVILLE RECREATION COMPLEX
18688 Royalton Rd (44136-5127)
PHONE 440 580-3230
David Sems, *Comms Dir*
Colleen Grady, *Branch Mgr*
Frank Pientka, *Executive*
Ronald Stolz, *Executive*
Tiffany CMC, *Asst Clerk*
EMP: 203
SALES (corp-wide): 5MM **Privately Held**
SIC: 7996 Theme park, amusement
PA: Strongville Recreation Complex
   18100 Royalton Rd
   Cleveland OH 44136
   440 878-6000

(G-17514)
SUMITOMO DEMAG PLSTC MACHINERY
11792 Alameda Dr (44149-3011)
PHONE 440 876-8960
Bastian Gutermuth, *Counsel*
John Martich, *Vice Pres*
Mike Miner, *Vice Pres*
Thomas Schnauffer, *Project Mgr*
David Jersak, *Engineer*
EMP: 25
SALES (corp-wide): 5.9B **Privately Held**
SIC: 5084 Plastic products machinery
HQ: Sumitomo (Shi) Demag Plastics Machinery North America, Inc.
   1266 Oakbrook Dr
   Norcross GA 30093

(G-17515)
TELETRONIC SERVICES INC (PA)
Also Called: Teletronics Communications
22550 Ascoa Ct (44149-4700)
PHONE 216 778-6500
Gale Kenney, *CEO*
Thomas Ursem, *President*
Gary Reffert, *Vice Pres*
EMP: 33
SQ FT: 12,000
SALES (est): 17.3MM **Privately Held**
SIC: 5065 Telephone equipment

(G-17516)
TERSHER CORPORATION
Also Called: Shamrock Moving & Storage Co
17000 Foltz Pkwy (44149-5522)
PHONE 440 439-8383
Sharon Mc Gee, *President*
Robert Struck, *Vice Pres*
▲ **EMP:** 100
SQ FT: 40,000
SALES (est): 6.8MM **Privately Held**
SIC: 4213 4731 4214 Household goods transport; agents, shipping; household goods moving & storage, local

(G-17517)
UNION HOME MORTGAGE CORP (PA)
Also Called: Vloan
8241 Dow Cir (44136-1761)
PHONE 440 234-4300
Fax: 440 234-2744
Bill Cosgrove, *CEO*
C William Cosgrove, *President*
John Racicot, *Regional Mgr*
Randa Triggs, *Area Mgr*
Jim Cmb, *Vice Pres*
EMP: 35
SQ FT: 15,000
SALES (est): 26.9MM **Privately Held**
WEB: www.unmco.com
SIC: 6162 Mortgage bankers

(G-17518)
UNITED AMERICAN INSURANCE CO
10749 Pearl Rd Ste D (44136-3347)
PHONE 440 265-9200
Fax: 216 265-0973
Karen E Dolan, *Sales & Mktg St*
Pat G Giachetti, *Branch Mgr*
EMP: 25
SALES (corp-wide): 4.1B **Publicly Held**
WEB: www.unitedamerican.com
SIC: 6411 6311 Life insurance agents; insurance agents; life insurance carriers
HQ: United American Insurance Company
   3700 S Stonebridge Dr
   Mckinney TX 75070
   800 331-2512

(G-17519)
UNITED PARCEL SERVICE INC
Also Called: UPS
13500 Pearl Rd Ste 139 (44136-3428)
PHONE 440 846-6000
Fax: 440 846-6012
Mark Munoz, *Owner*
EMP: 38
SALES (corp-wide): 65.8B **Publicly Held**
SIC: 4215 Package delivery, vehicular
PA: United Parcel Service, Inc.
   55 Glenlake Pkwy
   Atlanta GA 30328
   404 828-6000

(G-17520)
UNIVAR USA INC
21600 Drake Rd (44149-6615)
PHONE 440 238-8550
Al Bernhardt, *Manager*
Deborah Fernandez, *Director*
EMP: 80
SALES (corp-wide): 8.2B **Publicly Held**
SIC: 5169 Industrial chemicals
HQ: Univar Usa Inc.
   17411 Ne Union Hill Rd
   Redmond WA 98052
   425 889-3400

(G-17521)
VAN MILLS LINES INC
14675 Foltz Pkwy (44149-4720)
PHONE 440 846-0200
Fax: 440 846-1831
Donald Mills II, *President*
Michael McGill, *Vice Pres*
Robert Mills, *Vice Pres*
Robert Simmon, *CFO*
EMP: 110
SQ FT: 160,000
SALES (est): 17.3MM **Privately Held**
SIC: 4213 4214 4212 Household goods transport; local trucking with storage; local trucking, without storage

(G-17522)
VITAMIN SHOPPE INC
17893 Southpark Ctr (44136-9332)
PHONE 440 238-5987
EMP: 25 **Publicly Held**
SIC: 6324 5122 2834 Hospital & medical service plans; vitamins & minerals; vitamin preparations
PA: Vitamin Shoppe, Inc.
   300 Harmon Meadow Blvd # 2
   Secaucus NJ 07094

(G-17523)
WALLOVER ENTERPRISES INC (DH)
21845 Drake Rd (44149-6610)
PHONE 440 238-9250
George M Marquis, *President*
William C Cutri, *Vice Pres*
Debbie Depompei, *Admin Asst*
EMP: 30
SQ FT: 28,000
SALES (est): 25.1MM **Privately Held**
SIC: 2992 8734 Oils & greases, blending & compounding; re-refining lubricating oils & greases; product testing laboratories
HQ: Houghton International Inc.
   945 Madison Ave
   Norristown PA 19403
   610 666-4000

(G-17524)
WEST SIDE DTSCHER FRUEN VEREIN
18627 Shurmer Rd (44136-6150)
PHONE 440 238-3361
Gregory Mc Danels, *Principal*
EMP: 29
SALES: 14.9MM **Privately Held**
SIC: 8051 Skilled nursing care facilities

(G-17525)
WOODPECKERS INC
13700 Prospect Rd (44149-3862)
PHONE 440 238-1824
Rich Hummel, *Principal*
Brittany Allen, *Cust Mgr*
Will Kanzeg, *Graphic Designe*
EMP: 26
SALES (est): 5.7MM **Privately Held**
SIC: 2499 1751 Decorative wood & woodwork; carpentry work

Struthers
Mahoning County

(G-17526)
ASTRO ALUMINUM ENTERPRISES INC
65 Main St (44471-1942)
P.O. Box 208 (44471-0208)
PHONE 330 755-1414
Paul Cene, *President*
James Dibacco, *Exec VP*
Kristina Rule, *Purch Mgr*
Rick Pursifull, *Finance Mgr*
Tim Stein, *Credit Mgr*
EMP: 50
SALES (est): 2.5MM **Privately Held**
SIC: 8741 Management services

(G-17527)
CASEY EQUIPMENT CORPORATION
15 Union St Bldg 1 (44471-2901)
PHONE 330 750-1005

GEOGRAPHIC SECTION

Sunbury - Delaware County (G-17550)

Fax: 330 750-1009
Dave Sinkovach, *General Mgr*
Tammy Whitehouse, *Purch Mgr*
Mary Beatty, *Office Mgr*
James Rugh, *Branch Mgr*
Paul Ulam, *Manager*
EMP: 40
SALES (corp-wide): 9.9MM **Privately Held**
WEB: www.caseyusa.com
SIC: 7629 Electrical equipment repair, high voltage
PA: Casey Equipment Corporation
275 Kappa Dr
Pittsburgh PA 15238
412 963-1111

(G-17528)
CLEMENTE-MC KAY AMBULANCE INC (PA)
700 5th St Ste 1 (44471-1772)
PHONE 330 755-1401
EMP: 50
SQ FT: 10,200
SALES (est): 4MM **Privately Held**
SIC: 4119 Transportation Services

(G-17529)
CRED-KAP INC
Also Called: Maple Crest Nrsing HM For Aged
400 Sexton St (44471-1141)
P.O. Box 5185, Poland, (44514-0185)
PHONE 330 755-1466
Fax: 330 755-1463
Christopher Daprile, *President*
Lisa Daprile, *Vice Pres*
Santuccio Ricciardi, *Director*
EMP: 55 EST: 1960
SALES (est): 4.2MM **Privately Held**
SIC: 8052 Personal care facility

(G-17530)
DAVIDSON BECKER INC
11 Spring St (44471-1745)
PHONE 330 755-2111
Fax: 330 750-1049
Kelly Becker, *President*
Daniel Becker, *President*
Margaret L Becker, *Vice Pres*
EMP: 25
SALES (est): 1.5MM **Privately Held**
SIC: 7261 Funeral home

(G-17531)
GOLD CROSS LIMOUSINE SERVICE
26 Sexton St (44471-1773)
PHONE 330 757-3053
Fax: 330 750-0661
Grant Williams, *Manager*
EMP: 50
SALES (est): 1.3MM **Privately Held**
WEB: www.goldcrosslimo.com
SIC: 4119 Limousine rental, with driver

(G-17532)
JS BOVA EXCAVATING LLC
235 State St (44471-1958)
P.O. Box 296 (44471-0296)
PHONE 234 254-4040
Louis J Bova, *Mng Member*
Sherri Bova,
EMP: 36
SQ FT: 2,100
SALES: 8.5MM **Privately Held**
SIC: 1794 1623 Excavation work; underground utilities contractor

(G-17533)
L B INDUSTRIES INC
Also Called: Lally Pipe & Tube
534 Lowellville Rd (44471-2077)
P.O. Box 69 (44471-0069)
PHONE 330 750-1002
Fax: 330 750-1535
Josh Ball, *Asst Controller*
Jamie Disibio, *Sales Associate*
James Mocker, *Branch Mgr*
Debbie Donattlei, *Manager*
EMP: 36
SALES (corp-wide): 110MM **Privately Held**
WEB: www.lallypipe.com
SIC: 5051 7692 Pipe & tubing, steel; steel; welding repair

PA: L B Industries, Inc.
8770 Railroad Dr
Taylor Mill KY 41015
859 431-8300

(G-17534)
RUDZIK EXCAVATING INC
401 Lowellville Rd (44471-2076)
P.O. Box 206 (44471-0206)
PHONE 330 755-1540
Fax: 330 750-1330
Jeffrey A Rudzik, *Owner*
Bonnie L Rudzik, *Corp Secy*
Ricky Basista, *Manager*
EMP: 45 EST: 1998
SQ FT: 3,000
SALES (est): 9.7MM **Privately Held**
WEB: www.rudzikexcavating.com
SIC: 1794 1799 Excavation & grading, building construction; building site preparation

(G-17535)
TINY TOTS DAY NURSERY
310 Argonne St (44471-1671)
PHONE 330 755-6473
Fax: 330 755-0562
D Fontez, *Owner*
EMP: 28
SALES (est): 540.4K **Privately Held**
WEB: www.tinytotsdaynursery.com
SIC: 8351 Child day care services

Stryker
Williams County

(G-17536)
CORRECTION COMMISSION NW OHIO
3151 County Road 2425 (43557-9418)
PHONE 419 428-3800
Denny Stantz, *Maint Spvr*
Jim Dennis, *Exec Dir*
EMP: 187
SQ FT: 189,000
SALES: 15MM **Privately Held**
WEB: www.ccnoregionaljail.org
SIC: 8744 Correctional facility

(G-17537)
QUADCO REHABILITATION CENTER (PA)
Also Called: NORTHWEST PRODUCTS
427 N Defiance St (43557-9472)
PHONE 419 682-1011
Fax: 419 682-6097
Chuck Merriman, *Purch Mgr*
Terry Fruth, *CFO*
Jackie Porter, *Finance Asst*
Peggy Keith, *Manager*
Bruce Abell, *Exec Dir*
EMP: 287
SQ FT: 24,000
SALES (est): 247.7K **Privately Held**
SIC: 8331 2448 2441 Vocational rehabilitation agency; wood pallets & skids; nailed wood boxes & shook

(G-17538)
R & S LINES INC
102 Ellis St (43557-9333)
P.O. Box 410 (43557-0410)
PHONE 419 682-7807
Fax: 419 682-9006
Robert Liechty, *President*
Sharon Liechty, *Vice Pres*
EMP: 25
SQ FT: 12,000
SALES (est): 3.1MM **Privately Held**
SIC: 4213 Trucking, except local

(G-17539)
WOOLACE ELECTRIC CORP
1978 County Road 22a (43557-9778)
PHONE 419 428-3161
Fax: 419 428-2017
William D Woolace, *President*
Benjamin Woolace, *Corp Secy*
Eric Woolace, *Vice Pres*
John Schlatter, *Safety Dir*
Doug Fuhrman, *Project Mgr*
EMP: 35
SQ FT: 2,600

SALES (est): 6.1MM **Privately Held**
SIC: 1731 General electrical contractor

Sugar Grove
Fairfield County

(G-17540)
COLUMBIA GULF TRANSMISSION LLC
Also Called: Columbia Energy
6175 Old Logan Rd (43155-9795)
PHONE 740 746-9105
Tim Burton, *Safety Mgr*
Mike Milbaugh, *Plant Engr*
Larry Brown, *Branch Mgr*
Wilson Fernando, *Manager*
EMP: 30
SALES (corp-wide): 9.2B **Privately Held**
WEB: www.columbiagastrans.com
SIC: 4923 Gas transmission & distribution
HQ: Columbia Gulf Transmission, Llc
5151 San Felipe St # 2500
Houston TX 77056
713 386-3701

(G-17541)
HIDE-A-WAY HILLS CLUB
29042 Hide Away Hills Rd (43155-9607)
PHONE 740 746-9589
Rogers Childers, *President*
Jim Palmer, *General Mgr*
John Vanderbuilt, *Treasurer*
James Lloyd, *Manager*
EMP: 30
SQ FT: 2,000
SALES (est): 1.8MM **Privately Held**
WEB: www.hide-a-wayhillsclub.com
SIC: 8641 7011 Social club, membership; resort hotel

(G-17542)
POWERS EQUIPMENT
7265 Sugar Grove Rd (43155-9785)
P.O. Box 43 (43155-0043)
PHONE 740 746-8220
Mark Powers, *Owner*
EMP: 32
SQ FT: 2,189
SALES (est): 1.6MM **Privately Held**
SIC: 4212 Local trucking, without storage

Sugarcreek
Tuscarawas County

(G-17543)
ANDREAS FURNITURE COMPANY
580 Belden Pkwy Ne (44681-7695)
PHONE 330 852-2494
Matt Yoder, *Warehouse Mgr*
Chevelle Swartz, *Sales Associate*
Stephanie Saulnier, *Mktg Coord*
Tim Sisler, *Branch Mgr*
EMP: 46
SALES (corp-wide): 15.4MM **Privately Held**
WEB: www.andreasfurniture.com
SIC: 4226 Household goods & furniture storage
PA: Andreas Furniture Company
114 Dover Rd Ne
Sugarcreek OH 44681
330 852-2494

(G-17544)
DRASC ENTERPRISES INC
Also Called: Gordon Milk Transport
9060 Bollman Rd Sw (44681-8008)
P.O. Box 707 (44681-0707)
PHONE 330 852-3254
Fax: 330 852-3271
Rodney Gordon, *President*
Peggy Trushel, *Accountant*
EMP: 50 EST: 2001
SQ FT: 1,600
SALES (est): 5.7MM **Privately Held**
SIC: 4212 4213 Liquid haulage, local; trucking, except local

(G-17545)
DUTCH CREEK FOODS INC
1411 Old Route 39 Ne (44681-7400)
PHONE 330 852-2631
Mike Palmer, *President*
Dan Kane, *General Mgr*
Lynn Dessecker, *Opers Mgr*
Doug Myers, *Sales Associate*
Linda Mont, *Manager*
EMP: 27
SQ FT: 25,000
SALES (est): 13.9MM
SALES (corp-wide): 47.5MM **Privately Held**
WEB: www.dutchcreekfoods.com
SIC: 5147 Meats, fresh
PA: Dutchman Hospitality Group, Inc.
4985 State Rte 515
Walnut Creek OH 44687
330 893-2926

(G-17546)
PROVIA HOLDINGS INC (PA)
Also Called: Provia - Heritage Stone
2150 State Route 39 (44681-9201)
PHONE 330 852-4711
Brian Miller, *President*
Jeff Yoder, *General Mgr*
Bill Mullet, *Principal*
Willis Schlabach, *Principal*
Phil Wengerd, *Vice Pres*
EMP: 180
SQ FT: 280,000
SALES: 140.5MM **Privately Held**
WEB: www.precisionentry.com
SIC: 3442 5031 Metal doors; door frames, all materials

(G-17547)
RUBIN ERB
Also Called: Sugar Valley Meats
2149 Dutch Valley Dr Nw (44681-7922)
PHONE 330 852-4423
Rubin Erb, *Owner*
EMP: 25
SALES (est): 1.2MM **Privately Held**
SIC: 5421 0751 Meat markets, including freezer provisioners; slaughtering; custom livestock services

(G-17548)
YODER DRILLING AND GEOTHERMAL
997 State Route 93 Nw (44681-7728)
PHONE 330 852-4342
Fax: 330 852-4437
Daniel Yoder, *President*
Timothy Yoder, *Vice Pres*
Elaine Beech, *Admin Sec*
EMP: 34
SALES (est): 6.7MM **Privately Held**
WEB: www.yodergeothermal.com
SIC: 5082 Wellpoints (drilling equipment); bailey bridges; blades for graders, scrapers, dozers & snow plows

Sunbury
Delaware County

(G-17549)
AMERICAN SHOWA INC
677 W Cherry St (43074-9803)
PHONE 740 965-4040
Creg Cockerel, *Branch Mgr*
Brenda Cox, *Planning*
EMP: 30
SALES (corp-wide): 2.2B **Privately Held**
SIC: 8731 Commercial research laboratory
HQ: American Showa, Inc.
707 W Cherry St
Sunbury OH 43074
740 965-1133

(G-17550)
BLACKSTAR DRYWALL INC
9821 E State Route 37 (43074-9635)
P.O. Box 550, Westerville (43086-0550)
PHONE 614 242-4242
Fax: 740 965-9747
Jim Williams, *President*
Bobby Porter Jr, *Vice Pres*
EMP: 25
SQ FT: 1,100

Sunbury - Delaware County (G-17551)

SALES (est): 1.7MM **Privately Held**
SIC: **1742** Drywall

(G-17551)
BST & G JOINT FIRE DISTRICT
350 W Cherry St (43074-7508)
PHONE.................................740 965-3841
Jeff Wilson, *Chief*
EMP: 32
SALES (est): 2MM **Privately Held**
SIC: **7389** Fire protection service other than forestry or public

(G-17552)
CHAMPIONSHIP MANAGEMENT CO
Also Called: North Star Golf Club
1150 Wilson Rd (43074-9633)
PHONE.................................740 524-4653
Robert Weiler, *President*
Alisha Howell, *Food Svc Dir*
Carolyn Moore, *Assistant*
EMP: 75
SALES: 3MM **Privately Held**
SIC: **7992** Public golf courses

(G-17553)
COUNTRYVIEW OF SUNBURY
Also Called: Country View of Sunbury
14961 N Old 3c Rd (43074-9716)
PHONE.................................740 965-3984
Fax: 740 965-5674
Brian Colleran, *President*
Dionne Nicol, *Manager*
Connie Purdy, *Director*
EMP: 62
SALES (est): 9MM **Privately Held**
SIC: **8051** Skilled nursing care facilities

(G-17554)
DBP ENTERPRISES LLC
Also Called: Holiday Inn
7301 E State Route 37 (43074-9210)
PHONE.................................740 513-2399
Fax: 740 363-7376
Daxa Patel, *Mng Member*
Cassie Woolfrom, *Manager*
EMP: 30
SALES (est): 1.4MM **Privately Held**
SIC: **7011** Hotels & motels

(G-17555)
FACEMYER BACKHOE AND DOZER SVC
Also Called: FM Earth
72 Holmes St (43074)
P.O. Box 304 (43074-0304)
PHONE.................................740 965-1137
Fax: 740 965-4562
Cameron L Facemyer, *President*
Tina Hannahs, *Accounting Mgr*
Ada Facemyer, *Office Mgr*
Joyce Facemyer, *Office Mgr*
EMP: 25
SQ FT: 1,312
SALES (est): 2.9MM **Privately Held**
SIC: **1794** Excavation & grading, building construction

(G-17556)
FIRE GUARD LLC
35 E Granville St (43074-9130)
P.O. Box 730, Centerburg (43011-0730)
PHONE.................................740 625-5181
Nick McGovern, *President*
Bethann Hedges, *Manager*
EMP: 50
SALES (est): 2.9MM **Privately Held**
SIC: **1711** Fire sprinkler system installation

(G-17557)
J & J ENTPS WESTERVILLE INC
Also Called: Arrow Industrial Supply
660 Kintner Pkwy (43074-8038)
PHONE.................................614 898-5997
Colleen Jordan, *President*
Kurt Campagna, *Vice Pres*
Jeffery Jordan, *Vice Pres*
Zena Trout, *CFO*
EMP: 25
SQ FT: 8,000
SALES: 3MM **Privately Held**
WEB: www.arrowindustrialsupply.com
SIC: **5085** Fasteners, industrial: nuts, bolts, screws, etc.

(G-17558)
MINE EQUIPMENT SERVICES LLC (PA)
Also Called: Mes
3958 State Route 3 (43074-9660)
P.O. Box 120 (43074-0120)
PHONE.................................740 936-5427
Christopher Wagner,
Tony Schiavi,
EMP: 25 EST: 2012
SQ FT: 10,000
SALES: 3.4MM **Privately Held**
SIC: **5084 3535 7699** Industrial machinery & equipment; belt conveyor systems, general industrial use; construction equipment repair; pumps & pumping equipment repair; industrial equipment services; industrial machinery & equipment repair

(G-17559)
NOAHS ARK LEARNING CENTER
100 Tippett Ct Ste 103 (43074-8572)
PHONE.................................740 965-1668
Fax: 740 965-6437
Kim Low, *Owner*
Jeff Low, *Co-Owner*
EMP: 25
SALES (est): 801.5K **Privately Held**
SIC: **8351** Preschool center

(G-17560)
OHASHI TECHNICA USA INC (HQ)
111 Burrer Dr (43074-9323)
PHONE.................................740 965-5115
Hikaru Tateiwa, *President*
Mamoru Shibasaki, *Principal*
Trish Burnside, *Treasurer*
Kazuhiro Maeda, *Accountant*
Cole Croft, *Manager*
▲ EMP: 50
SQ FT: 110,000
SALES: 90MM
SALES (corp-wide): 330MM **Privately Held**
SIC: **5013 5072 3452** Automotive supplies & parts; automotive supplies; hardware; bolts, nuts, rivets & washers
PA: Ohashi Technica Inc.
4-3-13, Toranomon
Minato-Ku TKY 105-0
354 044-411

(G-17561)
RESTAURANT SPECIALTIES INC
Also Called: RSI Construction
801 W Cherry St Ste 200 (43074-8598)
PHONE.................................614 885-9707
Fax: 614 885-4575
Paul Tanzillo, *President*
Gregory Hunt, *Vice Pres*
Deborah Meyer, *Treasurer*
Robert Craven, *Manager*
Don Kubiak, *Manager*
EMP: 32
SQ FT: 4,000
SALES: 31.5MM **Privately Held**
WEB: www.rsibuilds4u.com
SIC: **1542** Restaurant construction; commercial & office buildings, renovation & repair

---

Swanton
Fulton County

(G-17562)
CESSNA AIRCRAFT COMPANY
Also Called: Cessna Toledo Citation Svc Ctr
11591 W Airport Service R (43558-9618)
PHONE.................................419 866-6761
EMP: 82
SQ FT: 42,358
SALES (corp-wide): 12.1B **Publicly Held**
SIC: **4581** Airport/Airport Services
HQ: The Cessna Aircraft Company
1 Cessna Blvd
Wichita KS 67215
316 517-6000

(G-17563)
EAGLE INDUSTRIAL TRUCK MFG LLC
Also Called: Eagle Tugs
1 Air Cargo Pkwy E (43558-9490)
PHONE.................................734 442-1000
Mark Iddon, *President*
Ed Vasicek, *Vice Pres*
Gary Spoering, *Opers Staff*
Tresa Faustman, *Parts Mgr*
Connie Sroufe, *Mktg Dir*
◆ EMP: 30 EST: 2000
SQ FT: 70,000
SALES (est): 19.5MM
SALES (corp-wide): 7B **Privately Held**
WEB: www.eaglegse.com
SIC: **5085 3537** Industrial supplies; industrial trucks & tractors
HQ: Tronair, Inc.
1740 Eber Rd Ste E
Holland OH 43528
419 866-6301

(G-17564)
FOUNDATION STEEL LLC
12525 Airport Hwy (43558-9613)
P.O. Box 210 (43558-0210)
PHONE.................................419 402-4241
Charlotte A Dymarkowski, *President*
Lori Siler, *Office Mgr*
Jim Starr, *Manager*
Jerry Vitanza, *Manager*
Kevin Martin, *Administration*
EMP: 90
SALES (est): 12.8MM **Privately Held**
SIC: **1791 1622** Iron work, structural; bridge, tunnel & elevated highway

(G-17565)
GENICON INC
12150 Monclova Rd (43558-8706)
PHONE.................................419 491-4478
Jason Byrd, *President*
EMP: 45
SQ FT: 1,500
SALES (est): 1.7MM **Privately Held**
SIC: **7549 5511** Towing service, automotive; new & used car dealers

(G-17566)
HARBORSIDE HEALTHCARE CORP
Also Called: Swanton Vly Care Rhbltion Ctr
401 W Airport Hwy (43558-1447)
PHONE.................................419 825-1111
Steven Dood, *Branch Mgr*
Karen Cline, *Nursing Dir*
Jennifer Ducat, *Social Dir*
EMP: 125 **Publicly Held**
SIC: **8051** Skilled nursing care facilities
HQ: Harborside Healthcare Corporation
5100 Sun Ave Ne
Albuquerque NM

(G-17567)
MAPLEVIEW FARMS INC (PA)
2425 S Fulton Lucas Rd (43558-9658)
PHONE.................................419 826-3671
William J Schmidt, *President*
Allen J Schmidt, *Vice Pres*
Joseph L Schmidt, *Vice Pres*
Lawrence H Schmidt, *Treasurer*
Robert V Schmidt, *Admin Sec*
EMP: 35
SQ FT: 33,100
SALES: 3.7MM **Privately Held**
WEB: www.mapleviewfarm.com
SIC: **6519 7359** Farm land leasing; equipment rental & leasing

(G-17568)
NATIONAL FLIGHT SERVICES INC (HQ)
10971 E Airport Svc Rd (43558)
PHONE.................................419 865-2311
Fax: 419 866-8322
Tom Wiles, *President*
Larry Lowry, *Vice Pres*
Emmanuel Diakonis, *Maintenance Dir*
Larry Mates, *Opers Mgr*
Rob Freeman, *Purchasing*
EMP: 75
SQ FT: 49,000
SALES (est): 18.2MM **Privately Held**
WEB: www.nationalflight.com
SIC: **4581** Aircraft servicing & repairing

(G-17569)
OHIO TPK & INFRASTRUCTURE COMM
Also Called: Swanton Maintenance Building
8891 County Road 1 (43558-8678)
PHONE.................................419 826-4831
EMP: 38 **Privately Held**
SIC: **1611 0782 9621** Highway/Street Construction Lawn/Garden Services
HQ: Ohio Turnpike And Infrastructure Commission
682 Prospect St
Berea OH 44017
440 234-2081

(G-17570)
SCHENKER INC
2 Air Cargo Pkwy E (43558-9312)
PHONE.................................419 491-1055
EMP: 30 **Privately Held**
WEB: www.schenkerlogisticsusa.com
SIC: **7349** Cleaning service, industrial or commercial
HQ: Schenker, Inc.
150 Albany Ave
Freeport NY 11520
757 821-3400

(G-17571)
SCHMIDT BROS INC
420 N Hallett Ave (43558)
PHONE.................................419 826-3671
Fax: 419 826-8696
Lawrence Schmidt, *President*
Robert V Schmidt, *President*
Allen J Schmidt, *Vice Pres*
William J Schmidt, *Vice Pres*
Michael P Schmidt, *Treasurer*
▲ EMP: 30
SQ FT: 610,000
SALES (est): 3.1MM
SALES (corp-wide): 3.7MM **Privately Held**
WEB: www.schmidtbrosinc.com
SIC: **0181 5193** Bedding plants, growing of; flowers & florists' supplies
PA: Mapleview Farms, Inc
2425 S Fulton Lucas Rd
Swanton OH 43558
419 826-3671

(G-17572)
SWANTON HLTH CARE RTREMENT CTR
214 S Munson Rd (43558-1210)
PHONE.................................419 825-1145
Fax: 419 825-1658
Lisa Mitchell, *President*
Scott Mitchell, *Vice Pres*
Gina Root, *Human Resources*
Amber Bachelder, *Sales Staff*
Ruth Williams, *Nursing Dir*
EMP: 90
SQ FT: 19,000
SALES: 5.1MM **Privately Held**
WEB: www.swantonhealthcare.com
SIC: **8051 8052** Convalescent home with continuous nursing care; intermediate care facilities

(G-17573)
TOLEDO-LUCAS COUNTY PORT AUTH
Also Called: Toledo Express Airport
11013 Airport Hwy Ste 11 (43558-9403)
PHONE.................................419 865-2351
Fax: 419 867-6243
Paul L Toht Jr, *Director*
EMP: 25
SALES (corp-wide): 12MM **Privately Held**
SIC: **4491** Marine cargo handling
PA: Toledo-Lucas County Port Authority
1 Maritime Plz Ste 701
Toledo OH 43604
419 243-8251

(G-17574)
VALLEYWOOD GOLF CLUB INC
13501 Airport Hwy (43558)
PHONE.................................419 826-3991

GEOGRAPHIC SECTION

Sylvania - Lucas County (G-17598)

Fax: 419 825-3386
Ron Dickson, *President*
Louie Carson, *Treasurer*
Neil Toeppe, *Admin Sec*
EMP: 45
SQ FT: 6,500
SALES (est): 1.6MM **Privately Held**
SIC: 7997 Golf club, membership

Sylvania
Lucas County

(G-17575)
ABILITY CTR OF GREATER TOLEDO (PA)
5605 Monroe St (43560-2702)
PHONE......................419 517-7123
Fax: 419 882-4813
Susan Golden, *Ch of Bd*
Timothy Harrington, *President*
Richard Gunden, *President*
Richard R Brown, *Treasurer*
Nancy Watts, *Financial Exec*
EMP: 43
SQ FT: 13,000
SALES: 4MM **Privately Held**
WEB: www.abilitycenter.org
SIC: 8361 Residential care for the handicapped

(G-17576)
BOBBART INDUSTRIES INC
Also Called: American Custom Industries
5035 Alexis Rd Ste 1 (43560-1637)
PHONE......................419 350-5477
Fax: 419 885-5161
Bart Lea, *President*
Laura Lea, *Corp Secy*
EMP: 25
SQ FT: 45,000
SALES: 1.7MM **Privately Held**
WEB: www.acivette.com
SIC: 3711 3082 7532 3714 Motor vehicles & car bodies; unsupported plastics profile shapes; top & body repair & paint shops; motor vehicle parts & accessories; plastics plumbing fixtures

(G-17577)
BUCKEYE LAUNDERER AND CLRS LLC
4930 N Holland Sylvania (43560-2178)
PHONE......................419 592-2941
Fax: 419 599-9978
Patrick Jackson, *Mng Member*
EMP: 85
SALES (est): 3.9MM **Privately Held**
SIC: 7211 Power laundries, family & commercial

(G-17578)
CENTENNIAL TERRACE & QUARRY
5773 Centennial Rd (43560-9846)
PHONE......................419 885-7106
Ken Katafias, *Director*
EMP: 30
SALES (est): 521K **Privately Held**
SIC: 7999 Swimming pool, non-membership

(G-17579)
CITY OF SYLVANIA
Also Called: Tam-O-Shanter Sports Complex
7060 Sylvania Ave (43560-3000)
PHONE......................419 885-1167
Tom Cline, *Manager*
EMP: 25
SQ FT: 3,775 **Privately Held**
WEB: www.cityofsylvania.com
SIC: 7999 7997 Ice skating rink operation; membership sports & recreation clubs
PA: City Of Sylvania
  6730 Monroe St Ste 201
  Sylvania OH 43560
  419 885-8930

(G-17580)
CREATIVE MARKETING ENTERPRISES
6711 Monroe St Ste 4c (43560-1968)
PHONE......................419 867-4444
Lynn P Brown, *President*
Martha L Brown, *Corp Secy*
B Joyce Clevenger, *Exec VP*
Keith Brown, *CTO*
EMP: 80
SQ FT: 11,000
SALES (est): 3.3MM **Privately Held**
WEB: www.cmeinet.com
SIC: 8732 Market analysis or research

(G-17581)
DAVE WHITE CHEVROLET INC
Also Called: White Cars
5880 Monroe St (43560-2200)
PHONE......................419 885-4444
Fax: 419 824-7602
Hugh David White, *CEO*
Hugh David White Jr, *President*
James F White Jr, *Vice Pres*
Steven R Justinger, *CFO*
EMP: 110
SQ FT: 30,000
SALES (est): 41.9MM **Privately Held**
SIC: 5511 5521 7538 7532 Automobiles, new & used; used car dealers; general automotive repair shops; top & body repair & paint shops; passenger car leasing

(G-17582)
DI SALLE REAL ESTATE CO
4904 Holland Sylvania Rd (43560-2119)
PHONE......................419 885-4475
Fax: 419 882-7237
Thomas Dull, *Manager*
EMP: 25
SALES (corp-wide): 6.8MM **Privately Held**
SIC: 6531 Real estate brokers & agents
PA: Di Salle Real Estate Co
  1909 River Rd
  Maumee OH 43537
  419 893-0751

(G-17583)
DIRECTIONS CREDIT UNION INC (PA)
5121 Whiteford Rd (43560-2987)
PHONE......................419 720-4769
Barry Shaner, *President*
Diane Harris, *President*
Katherine Martin, *President*
Ron Patton, *Senior VP*
Joan Newbury, *Assistant VP*
EMP: 57
SQ FT: 15,000
SALES: 20.9MM **Privately Held**
SIC: 6062 State credit unions, not federally chartered

(G-17584)
DRESCH TOLSON DENTAL LABS
8730 Resource Park Dr (43560-8939)
PHONE......................419 842-6730
Fax: 419 842-6731
Joseph Gerace, *Owner*
EMP: 90
SALES (est): 2MM **Privately Held**
SIC: 8072 3843 Crown & bridge production; dental equipment & supplies

(G-17585)
EBONY CONSTRUCTION CO
3510 Centennial Rd (43560-9739)
PHONE......................419 841-3455
Fax: 419 841-7845
Amy Hall, *President*
Michael Bass, *Vice Pres*
Chad Hartman, *Project Mgr*
Leefa Kidwell, *Sls & Mktg Exec*
Johnetta Gant, *Treasurer*
EMP: 35
SQ FT: 2,200
SALES (est): 6.7MM **Privately Held**
WEB: www.ebonyco.com
SIC: 1611 5082 Highway & street paving contractor; construction & mining machinery

(G-17586)
ENDOSCOPY CENTER
5700 Monroe St Unit 102 (43560-2779)
PHONE......................419 843-7993
Fax: 419 841-7789
Kevin K Koffel MD, *President*
Gregory Slee, *Gastroenterlgy*
EMP: 25
SQ FT: 4,800
SALES (est): 1.3MM **Privately Held**
SIC: 8011 Ambulatory surgical center

(G-17587)
FLOWER HOSPITAL
Also Called: Lake Park At Flower Hospital
5100 Harroun Rd (43560-2110)
PHONE......................419 824-1000
Fax: 419 824-1773
Pam Clark, *Office Mgr*
Mark Mullahy, *Manager*
John Debruyne, *Manager*
Kerri Murphy, *Director*
Maureen Weis, *Director*
EMP: 350
SALES (corp-wide): 1.5B **Privately Held**
WEB: www.flowerhospital.com
SIC: 8051 8052 Skilled nursing care facilities; intermediate care facilities
HQ: Flower Hospital
  5200 Harroun Rd
  Sylvania OH 43560
  419 824-1444

(G-17588)
FLOWER HOSPITAL (HQ)
5200 Harroun Rd (43560-2196)
PHONE......................419 824-1444
Fax: 419 824-1762
Kevin Webb, *President*
Scott Fought, *Finance Dir*
Carol Stormer, *Accountant*
Daniel A Welt MD, *Med Doctor*
Cathy Shirley, *Director*
EMP: 889 **EST:** 1910
SALES: 219.1MM
SALES (corp-wide): 1.5B **Privately Held**
WEB: www.flowerhospital.com
SIC: 8062 General medical & surgical hospitals
PA: Promedica Health Systems, Inc.
  100 Madison Ave
  Toledo OH 43604
  567 585-7454

(G-17589)
GRENADA STAMPING ASSEMBLY INC (HQ)
3810 Herr Rd (43560-8925)
PHONE......................419 842-3600
Jeffrey Snavely, *Principal*
EMP: 36
SALES (est): 28MM
SALES (corp-wide): 100MM **Privately Held**
SIC: 8999 Art related services
PA: Ice Industries, Inc.
  3810 Herr Rd
  Sylvania OH 43560
  419 842-3612

(G-17590)
GUARDIAN ANGLS HOME HLTH SVCS
Also Called: Guardian Angels Senior HM Svc
8553 Sylvania Metamora Rd (43560-9629)
PHONE......................419 517-7797
Sharee Youssef, *President*
EMP: 70
SQ FT: 2,000
SALES (est): 116.6K **Privately Held**
SIC: 8082 Home health care services

(G-17591)
HANGER INC
5551 Monroe St (43560-2539)
PHONE......................419 841-9852
EMP: 30
SALES (corp-wide): 1B **Publicly Held**
SIC: 8099 Childbirth preparation clinic
PA: Hanger, Inc.
  10910 Domain Dr Ste 300
  Austin TX 78758
  512 777-3800

(G-17592)
HARBORSIDE SYLVANIA LLC
Also Called: Sylvania Center
5757 Whiteford Rd (43560-1632)
PHONE......................419 882-1875
Fax: 419 885-1272
Stephen Guillard, *Ch of Bd*
Joseph Peyton, *Director*
Dawn Ahrens, *Nursing Dir*
Jenny Wright, *Receptionist*
EMP: 70
SQ FT: 5,000
SALES (est): 2.7MM **Publicly Held**
WEB: www.harborsideuniversity.com
SIC: 8052 8051 Intermediate care facilities; skilled nursing care facilities
HQ: Genesis Healthcare Corporation
  101 E State St
  Kennett Square PA 19348
  610 444-6350

(G-17593)
HICKMAN CANCER CENTER
5200 Harroun Rd (43560-2168)
PHONE......................419 824-1952
Kevin Webb, *Principal*
EMP: 80
SALES (est): 1MM **Privately Held**
SIC: 8011 Internal medicine, physician/surgeon

(G-17594)
HUNT CLUB LLC
5600 Alexis Rd (43560-2342)
PHONE......................419 885-4647
Flecia Sobzaka, *Property Mgr*
Joe Goodell,
Gary Van Cleef,
EMP: 25
SALES (est): 1.3MM **Privately Held**
WEB: www.huntclub.com
SIC: 6531 Real estate agents & managers

(G-17595)
JDRM ENGINEERING INC
5604 Main St Ste 200 (43560-1950)
PHONE......................419 824-2400
Fax: 419 824-2409
Steve Morris, *President*
Roger Debelly, *Senior Partner*
Daniel Rosenberger, *Corp Secy*
Darren T Keil, *Vice Pres*
Ryan Brown, *Engineer*
EMP: 44
SQ FT: 8,500
SALES (est): 7.3MM **Privately Held**
WEB: www.jdrm.com
SIC: 8711 Mechanical engineering; designing: ship, boat, machine & product

(G-17596)
JEFF CREQUE FARMS INC
Also Called: Creque's Greenhouse
9700 Sylvania Ave (43560-9662)
PHONE......................419 829-2941
Jeffery L Creque, *President*
Eileen Creque, *Corp Secy*
EMP: 44
SALES: 800K **Privately Held**
SIC: 0181 0191 Flowers: grown under cover (e.g. greenhouse production); general farms, primarily crop

(G-17597)
JEWISH CMNTY CTR OF TOLEDO
Also Called: Jcc
6465 Sylvania Ave (43560-3916)
PHONE......................419 885-4485
Eric Goldstein, *Exec Dir*
Sarah Otis, *Exec Dir*
Debbie Frison, *Director*
EMP: 60
SQ FT: 50,000
SALES: 68.5K **Privately Held**
SIC: 8322 Community center

(G-17598)
KINGSTON HEALTHCARE COMPANY
4125 King Rd (43560-4445)
PHONE......................419 824-4200
Fax: 419 824-0048
Don Ferguson, *Branch Mgr*
Amy Peters, *Exec Dir*
EMP: 83
SALES (corp-wide): 95.5MM **Privately Held**
SIC: 8361 8052 Residential care; intermediate care facilities
PA: Kingston Healthcare Company
  1 Seagate Ste 1960
  Toledo OH 43604
  419 247-2880

Sylvania - Lucas County (G-17599)   GEOGRAPHIC SECTION

(G-17599)
LEISURE SPORTS INC
Also Called: Cottonwd Crk At Spytn-Dyvl
9501 Central Ave (43560-9787)
PHONE 419 829-2891
Fax: 419 829-4505
Gary Shaneck, *President*
Susan Shaneck, *Vice Pres*
EMP: 30
SQ FT: 3,600
SALES (est): 1.8MM **Privately Held**
SIC: 7997 Golf club, membership

(G-17600)
MARK FELDSTEIN & ASSOC INC
6703 Monroe St (43560-1962)
PHONE 419 867-9500
Fax: 419 867-9210
Mark S Feldstein, *President*
Gary Mohr, *Controller*
Howard Feldstein, *Mktg Dir*
◆ **EMP:** 25
SQ FT: 30,000
SALES (est): 7.6MM **Privately Held**
WEB: www.mfagifts.com
SIC: 5199 5065 Gifts & novelties; electronic parts & equipment

(G-17601)
NORTHERN OHIO INVESTMENT CO
Also Called: Noic
6444 Monroe St Ste 6 (43560-1455)
P.O. Box 787 (43560-0787)
PHONE 419 885-8300
Fax: 419 885-8306
Ralph D Vinciguerra, *President*
Jim Nassar, *General Mgr*
April Soss, *Senior VP*
Pauline Schnell, *Assistant VP*
Marty Vihn, *Vice Pres*
EMP: 53 **EST:** 1926
SQ FT: 5,000
SALES (est): 14.1MM **Privately Held**
WEB: www.noic.com
SIC: 6162 Mortgage bankers

(G-17602)
NORTHWEST OHIO ORTHOPEDICS
6444 Monroe St Ste 1 (43560-1455)
PHONE 419 885-2553
Fax: 419 885-7070
Robert Hartwig, *President*
Jackie Oehlers, *General Mgr*
EMP: 30 **EST:** 1948
SALES (est): 1.6MM **Privately Held**
WEB: www.nwo-ortho.com
SIC: 8011 Orthopedic physician

(G-17603)
OHIO CON SAWING & DRLG INC (PA)
8534 Central Ave (43560-9748)
PHONE 419 841-1330
Fax: 419 843-6203
James R Aston, *President*
Thomas A Lenix, *Vice Pres*
Alex Frank, *Sales Staff*
Jim Hempy, *Sales Staff*
Sam Farmer, *Manager*
EMP: 29
SALES (est): 14.5MM **Privately Held**
WEB: www.gp-radar.com
SIC: 1771 Concrete repair

(G-17604)
OPTIMAL LIFE INTGRTVE MDCNE PA
4103 Stonehenge Dr (43560-3426)
PHONE 419 474-3657
Lora Lee Thaxton, *Principal*
EMP: 25
SALES (est): 1.3MM **Privately Held**
SIC: 8742 Hospital & health services consultant

(G-17605)
OVERCASHIER AND HORST HTG & AC
3745 Centennial Rd (43560-9734)
PHONE 419 841-3333
Fax: 419 843-3988
Duane Horst, *President*
Mike Horst, *Consultant*
Angie Goin, *Traffic Dir*
EMP: 45
SQ FT: 9,000
SALES (est): 7.1MM **Privately Held**
WEB: www.ohcomfort.com
SIC: 1711 Warm air heating & air conditioning contractor

(G-17606)
PROFESSNAL GLFERS ASSN OF AMER
5201 Corey Rd (43560-2202)
PHONE 419 882-3197
Jason Stuller, *Principal*
EMP: 36 **EST:** 2010
SALES (est): 217.7K
SALES (corp-wide): 7.5MM **Privately Held**
SIC: 8699 Athletic organizations
PA: Jason Stuller Pro Shop, Llc
  5201 Corey Rd
  Sylvania OH 43560
  419 882-3197

(G-17607)
PROME CONTI CARE SERV CORPO
Also Called: PROMEDICA HOME HEALTH CARE
5855 Monroe St Ste 200 (43560-2270)
PHONE 419 885-1715
Randy Oostra, *CEO*
Daniel Murtagh, *Vice Pres*
Jennifer Gruber, *Sls & Mktg Exec*
Martin Dansack, *VP Finance*
Penny White, *Cert Phar Tech*
EMP: 520
SALES: 50.6MM
SALES (corp-wide): 1.5B **Privately Held**
SIC: 8082 Home health care services
PA: Promedica Health Systems, Inc.
  100 Madison Ave
  Toledo OH 43604
  567 585-7454

(G-17608)
PROMEDICA PHYSCN CNTINUUM SVCS
Also Called: PROMEDICA PHYSICIAN GROUP
5855 Monroe St Fl 1 (43560-2270)
PHONE 419 824-7200
Fax: 419 885-3545
Lee Hammerling MD, *President*
Ann Hainen, *VP Opers*
Kevin Harrington, *Financial Exec*
Jackie Giles, *Mktg Dir*
Eric Perron, *Director*
EMP: 101
SALES: 39.4MM
SALES (corp-wide): 1.5B **Privately Held**
SIC: 8741 7361 8721 Management services; employment agencies; accounting, auditing & bookkeeping
PA: Promedica Health Systems, Inc.
  100 Madison Ave
  Toledo OH 43604
  567 585-7454

(G-17609)
REGENCY HOSPITAL TOLEDO LLC
5220 Alexis Rd (43560-2504)
PHONE 419 318-5700
Laura Van Liere, *Facilities Mgr*
Shar Pedersen, *QA Dir*
Rosemary R Munoz, *Human Resources*
Rod Laughlin, *Mng Member*
Peggy Montgomery, *Manager*
EMP: 30
SALES: 17.2MM
SALES (corp-wide): 3.7B **Publicly Held**
SIC: 8062 Hospital, medical school affiliated with nursing & residency
HQ: Select Medical Corporation
  4714 Gettysburg Rd
  Mechanicsburg PA 17055
  717 972-1100

(G-17610)
REVERSE CENTER CLINIC
Also Called: Toledo Ctr For Eting Disorders
5465 Main St (43560-2155)
PHONE 419 885-8800
David M Garner, *Owner*
EMP: 30
SALES (est): 523K **Privately Held**
WEB: www.eatingdisorders-toledo.com
SIC: 8049 Clinical psychologist

(G-17611)
REVES SALON & SPA
5633 Main St (43560-1929)
PHONE 419 885-1140
Fax: 419 885-7125
Carmen Gauer-Wigma, *Owner*
EMP: 50
SQ FT: 1,200
SALES (est): 1.2MM **Privately Held**
SIC: 7231 Manicurist, pedicurist

(G-17612)
ROOT INC (PA)
Also Called: Root Map Module
5470 Main St Ste 100 (43560-2164)
PHONE 419 874-0077
Jim Haudan, *CEO*
Arden Brion, *Managing Dir*
Nate Butki, *Managing Dir*
Kurt Cumming, *Managing Dir*
Eric Flasck, *Managing Dir*
EMP: 58
SQ FT: 17,000
SALES (est): 26MM **Privately Held**
WEB: www.rootlearning.com
SIC: 8748 8742 Business consulting; test development & evaluation service; employee programs administration; business consultant

(G-17613)
ROSARY CARE CENTER
6832 Convent Blvd (43560-4805)
PHONE 419 824-3600
Fax: 419 824-3931
Hilary Nunnari, *Asst Director*
Cheryl King, *Administration*
EMP: 80
SALES: 4.6MM **Privately Held**
WEB: www.rosarycare.org
SIC: 8051 Skilled nursing care facilities

(G-17614)
S A STORER AND SONS COMPANY
3135 Centennial Rd (43560-9689)
PHONE 419 843-3133
Fax: 419 843-7273
Jeffery R Storer, *President*
Robert W Dixon, *Vice Pres*
EMP: 60
SALES (est): 4.2MM **Privately Held**
SIC: 1741 Masonry & other stonework

(G-17615)
SMILE DEVELOPMENT INC
Also Called: Syvania Pediatric Dental Care
5860 Alexis Rd Ste 1 (43560-2347)
PHONE 419 882-7187
Rodney W Owen, *President*
Joe Inman, *Vice Pres*
Wanda Fisher, *CFO*
Philip Sprague,
EMP: 30
SQ FT: 14,376
SALES (est): 2.4MM **Privately Held**
SIC: 8021 Orthodontist; dental clinic

(G-17616)
SMITH TRUCKING INC
3775 Centennial Rd (43560-9734)
P.O. Box 9, Blissfield MI (49228-0009)
PHONE 419 841-8676
Fax: 419 841-7537
Henry Smith, *President*
EMP: 35
SALES (est): 3.4MM **Privately Held**
SIC: 4213 Trucking, except local

(G-17617)
STANSLEY MINERAL RESOURCES INC (PA)
3793 Silica Rd B (43560-9814)
PHONE 419 843-2813
Rick Stansley, *CEO*
Richard Stansley Jr, *Corp Secy*
Jeff Stansley, *COO*
Mandy Billau, *Manager*
EMP: 35
SQ FT: 10,000
SALES (est): 12.4MM **Privately Held**
SIC: 1442 Gravel mining

(G-17618)
SYLVANIA COMMUNITY SVCS CTR
4747 N Hlland Sylvania Rd (43560)
PHONE 419 885-2451
Fax: 419 882-1639
Beth Russeau, *Office Admin*
Claire A Proctor, *Exec Dir*
Claire Proctor, *Exec Dir*
Desiree Thompson, *Director*
Lisa Ames, *Assistant*
EMP: 35
SALES (est): 1.6MM **Privately Held**
WEB: www.scsonline.org
SIC: 8322 8351 Child related social services; child day care services

(G-17619)
SYLVANIA COUNTRY CLUB
5201 Corey Rd (43560-2202)
PHONE 419 392-0530
Fax: 419 885-1343
Shawne Lnd, *President*
Joe Furko, *General Mgr*
Joanne Furko, *Manager*
Kristi Weimer, *Manager*
EMP: 60 **EST:** 1916
SALES: 1.9MM **Privately Held**
SIC: 7997 Country club, membership

(G-17620)
SYLVANIA VETERINARY HOSPITAL (PA)
4801 N Hlland Sylvania Rd (43560)
PHONE 419 885-4421
Robert B Esplin, *President*
Carol Esplin, *Vice Pres*
EMP: 43 **EST:** 1974
SQ FT: 2,250
SALES (est): 3.6MM **Privately Held**
WEB: www.sylvaniavet.com
SIC: 0742 Animal hospital services, pets & other animal specialties

(G-17621)
SYLVESTER MATERIALS CO
7901 Sylvania Ave (43560-9732)
PHONE 419 841-3874
Charles Stansley, *President*
Richard B Stansley Jr, *Corp Secy*
Frank Mihalik, *Vice Pres*
EMP: 120
SQ FT: 10,000
SALES (est): 6.7MM **Privately Held**
SIC: 4212 5032 Local trucking, without storage; sand, construction

(G-17622)
TOLEDO DISTRICT NURSES ASSN
Also Called: Visiting Nurses Association
5520 Monroe St (43560-2538)
PHONE 419 255-0983
Fax: 419 259-9794
Judy E Rogers, *Director*
Andy J Hoehn, *Officer*
Jane Huth, *Receptionist*
Jane Hugh, *Clerk*
EMP: 170 **EST:** 1901
SQ FT: 16,700
SALES: 3.9MM **Privately Held**
SIC: 8049 8082 Nurses, registered & practical; home health care services

(G-17623)
TOLEDO HOSPITAL
Caring Services
5520 Monroe St (43560-2538)
PHONE 419 291-2273
Debbie Turner, *Finance*
Laura Bachmann, *Pharmacist*
Judy Rogers, *Exec Dir*
Carrol Scholtz, *Director*
Michelle Jones,
EMP: 250
SALES (corp-wide): 1.5B **Privately Held**
SIC: 8361 8082 Rehabilitation center, residential; health care incidental; home health care services

HQ: The Toledo Hospital
2142 N Cove Blvd
Toledo OH 43606
419 291-4000

(G-17624)
TOLEDO MEMORIAL PK & MAUSOLEUM
6382 Monroe St (43560-1428)
PHONE.................................419 882-7151
Fax: 419 882-6883
Jeffrey Clegg, *President*
Josette Snyder, *Admin Asst*
EMP: 25
SQ FT: 7,000
SALES: 3.1MM Privately Held
WEB: www.toledomemorialpark.com
SIC: 6553 0782 Cemetery association; mausoleum operation; lawn & garden services

(G-17625)
UBS FINANCIAL SERVICES INC
5757 Monroe St (43560-2739)
PHONE.................................419 318-5525
Fax: 419 318-5131
Dennis P Seffernick, *Vice Pres*
James Porea, *Branch Mgr*
Timothy Van Simaeys, *Manager*
Jeff Catlin, *Manager*
Judy Wietrzykowski, *Executive*
EMP: 60
SALES (corp-wide): 28B Privately Held
SIC: 6211 Stock brokers & dealers
HQ: Ubs Financial Services Inc.
1285 Ave Of The Americas
New York NY 10019
212 713-2000

(G-17626)
VIN DEVERS (PA)
5570 Monroe St (43560-2560)
PHONE.................................888 847-9535
Fax: 419 885-5790
Jason Perry, *General Mgr*
Erin McCarthy, *Business Mgr*
Clark Blackford, *Parts Mgr*
Roger Cordray, *Parts Mgr*
Linda Cymbola, *Controller*
EMP: 120
SQ FT: 40,000
SALES (est): 47.7MM Privately Held
WEB: www.vindevers.com
SIC: 5511 5521 7538 7515 Automobiles, new & used; used car dealers; general automotive repair shops; passenger car leasing; truck rental & leasing, no drivers; local trucking, without storage

(G-17627)
WEBER OBRIEN LTD
Also Called: Webert & Co
5580 Monroe St Ste 210 (43560-2561)
PHONE.................................419 885-8338
James F Weber, *Owner*
R David O'Brien, *Partner*
Steven Weber, *Partner*
Steve M Weber, *Principal*
EMP: 45
SALES (est): 4.3MM Privately Held
WEB: www.weberobrien.com
SIC: 8721 8742 8748 Certified public accountant; accounting services, except auditing; financial consultant; business consulting

(G-17628)
WHITE FAMILY COLLISION CENTER
5328 Alexis Rd (43560-2432)
P.O. Box 196 (43560-0196)
PHONE.................................419 885-8885
Fax: 419 882-6392
David White Sr, *Owner*
Dave White Jr, *General Mgr*
EMP: 26
SALES (est): 987.2K Privately Held
SIC: 7532 Body shop, automotive

Symmes Twp
Hamilton County

(G-17629)
NPC GROUP INC
8500 Governors Hill Dr (45249-1384)
PHONE.................................312 627-6000
Charles D Drucker, *CEO*
Peggy Thornton, *Accounts Mgr*
EMP: 2493 EST: 2013
SALES (est): 30.6MM
SALES (corp-wide): 4B Publicly Held
SIC: 7389 Credit card service
PA: Worldpay, Inc.
8500 Governors Hill Dr
Symmes Twp OH 45249
513 900-5250

(G-17630)
VANTIV LLC (DH)
8500 Governors Hill Dr (45249-1384)
PHONE.................................877 713-5964
Fax: 513 534-8448
Charles Drucker, *President*
George A Schafer Jr, *President*
Kevin McKeon, *Senior VP*
Deedra Scheller, *Assistant VP*
Samuel Adams, *Vice Pres*
EMP: 350
SALES (est): 891.1MM
SALES (corp-wide): 4B Publicly Held
SIC: 7374 Data processing service
HQ: Vantiv Holding, Llc
8500 Governors Hill Dr
Symmes Twp OH 45249
513 358-6192

(G-17631)
WORLDPAY INC (PA)
8500 Governors Hill Dr (45249-1384)
PHONE.................................513 900-5250
Jeffrey Stiefler, *Ch of Bd*
Charles D Drucker, *President*
Royal Cole, *President*
Matthew Taylor, *President*
Mark Heimbouch, *COO*
EMP: 148
SALES: 4B Publicly Held
SIC: 7389 Credit card service

Syracuse
Meigs County

(G-17632)
MEIGS INDUSTRIES INC
Also Called: CARLETON SCHOOL
1310 Carleton St (45779)
P.O. Box 307 (45779-0307)
PHONE.................................740 992-6681
Fax: 740 992-6438
Kay Davis, *Director*
EMP: 40
SALES: 533.1K Privately Held
SIC: 8331 Sheltered workshop

Tallmadge
Summit County

(G-17633)
BUSINESS DATA SYSTEMS INC
1267 Southeast Ave Ste 5 (44278-3148)
PHONE.................................330 633-1221
Fax: 330 633-6298
James Coffelt, *President*
Haydn Thomas, *General Mgr*
Melissa Gould, *Manager*
EMP: 34
SQ FT: 2,500
SALES: 4.5MM Privately Held
WEB: www.businessdatasystems.net
SIC: 5045 5046 5044 Terminals, computer; computer software; commercial cooking & food service equipment; cash registers

(G-17634)
CHILDRENS HOSP MED CTR AKRON
Also Called: Family Child Learning Center
143 Northwest Ave Bldg A (44278-1806)
PHONE.................................330 633-2055
Fax: 330 633-2658
Marilyn Espeshrewindt, *Director*
EMP: 27
SALES (corp-wide): 747.4MM Privately Held
WEB: www.cincinnatichildrens.org
SIC: 8733 8322 Medical research; child related social services
PA: Childrens Hospital Medical Center Of Akron
1 Perkins Sq
Akron OH 44308
330 543-1000

(G-17635)
COMMUNICARE HEALTH SVCS INC
Also Called: Colony Healthcare Center, The
563 Colony Park Dr (44278-2859)
PHONE.................................330 630-9780
Fax: 330 630-2390
Dawn Koma, *Principal*
Mark Smith, *Director*
Cathlene Champlain, *Administration*
EMP: 92
SALES (corp-wide): 103.9MM Privately Held
WEB: www.atriumlivingcenters.com
SIC: 6531 8051 Real estate agents & managers; skilled nursing care facilities
PA: Communicare Health Services, Inc.
4700 Ashwood Dr Ste 200
Blue Ash OH 45241
513 530-1654

(G-17636)
COUNTY OF SUMMIT
Also Called: Developmental Disabilities Bd
89 E Howe Rd (44278-1003)
PHONE.................................330 634-8193
Tina Overturf, *Project Mgr*
Gary Peters, *Project Mgr*
Thomas Jacobs, *Opers Staff*
Tricia Perduk, *Comms Mgr*
Thomas Armstrong, *Manager*
EMP: 600 Privately Held
WEB: www.cpcourt.summitoh.net
SIC: 9431 8322 ; individual & family services
PA: County Of Summit
650 Dan St
Akron OH 44310
330 643-2500

(G-17637)
DERMAMED COATINGS COMPANY LLC
381 Geneva Ave (44278-2732)
PHONE.................................330 634-9449
Laura Prexta, *Technical Mgr*
Phil Brady, *Mng Member*
Scott Brady, *Manager*
Steve Collins,
Brian Leek,
▲ EMP: 40
SQ FT: 10,000
SALES (est): 10.9MM Privately Held
WEB: www.dermamed.net
SIC: 5047 Medical & hospital equipment

(G-17638)
HANGER PROSTHETICS & (DH)
33 North Ave Ste 101 (44278-1900)
PHONE.................................330 633-9807
Vinit K Asar, *CEO*
Samuel M Liang, *President*
Bobbie Gross, *Director*
Shanie Scott, *Director*
EMP: 34
SALES (est): 21.3MM
SALES (corp-wide): 1B Publicly Held
SIC: 5999 8741 Orthopedic & prosthesis applications; management services
HQ: Hanger Prosthetics & Orthotics, Inc.
10910 Domain Dr Ste 300
Austin TX 78758
512 777-3800

(G-17639)
HEATHER KNOLL RETIREMENT VLG
Also Called: Heather Knoll Nursing Center
1134 North Ave (44278-1065)
PHONE.................................330 688-8600
Fax: 330 688-8495
Lisa Slomovitz, *President*
Teresa Seger, *Office Mgr*
Deanne Nemec, *Nursing Dir*
Lisa Wright, *Admin Sec*
EMP: 160
SALES: 6MM Privately Held
SIC: 8051 Skilled nursing care facilities

(G-17640)
HEAVEN BOUND ASCENSIONS
Also Called: Fun Makers
66 N Village View Rd (44278-2040)
PHONE.................................330 633-3288
Fax: 330 633-5792
Dennis Wellser, *President*
EMP: 30
SALES: 400K Privately Held
WEB: www.fun-makers.com
SIC: 5945 7999 Toys & games; tennis services & professionals

(G-17641)
J D WILLIAMSON CNSTR CO INC
441 Geneva Ave (44278-2704)
P.O. Box 113 (44278-0113)
PHONE.................................330 633-1258
Fax: 330 633-1398
Joel D Williamson, *President*
John Englehart, *Vice Pres*
Veronica Williamson, *Vice Pres*
EMP: 99
SQ FT: 3,000
SALES (est): 17.8MM Privately Held
SIC: 1794 Excavation & grading, building construction

(G-17642)
J RUSSELL CONSTRUCTION
180 Southwest Ave (44278-2231)
PHONE.................................330 633-6462
Fax: 330 633-3124
James Russell Wilson, *Owner*
Kim Miller, *Office Mgr*
EMP: 45
SQ FT: 4,500
SALES (est): 4.7MM Privately Held
SIC: 1521 General remodeling, single-family houses

(G-17643)
LEPPO INC (PA)
Also Called: LEPPO EQUIPMENT
176 West Ave (44278-2145)
P.O. Box 154 (44278-0154)
PHONE.................................330 633-3999
Fax: 330 633-3486
Dale Leppo, *CEO*
Glenn Leppo, *President*
Michael Leppo, *General Mgr*
John Dovala, *Parts Mgr*
Brian Ulman, *Parts Mgr*
EMP: 128 EST: 1945
SQ FT: 44,000
SALES: 70.6MM Privately Held
WEB: www.leppos.com
SIC: 5082 7353 7629 General construction machinery & equipment; heavy construction equipment rental; business machine repair, electric

(G-17644)
LIVING ASSISTANCE SERVICES
Also Called: Visiting Angels
22 Northwest Ave (44278-1808)
PHONE.................................330 733-1532
Jodi Wood, *President*
EMP: 65
SALES (est): 2.3MM Privately Held
SIC: 8082 Home health care services

(G-17645)
NORTHEAST FAMILY HEALTH CARE
Also Called: Dorman, Regina MD
65 Community Rd Ste C (44278-2358)
PHONE.................................330 630-2332
Mark Meyers Do, *President*
EMP: 35

Tallmadge - Summit County (G-17646)

GEOGRAPHIC SECTION

SQ FT: 3,500
SALES (est): 2.3MM **Privately Held**
SIC: 8011 Physicians' office, including specialists

(G-17646)
NOVUS CLINIC
518 West Ave (44278-2117)
PHONE.................................330 630-9699
Donald C Stephens MD, *Principal*
EMP: 29
SALES (est): 2.3MM **Privately Held**
WEB: www.novusclinic.com
SIC: 8099 Health & allied services

(G-17647)
PIONEER PHYSICIANS NETWORKING
Also Called: North East Family Healthcare
65 Community Rd Ste C (44278-2358)
PHONE.................................330 633-6601
Fax: 330 630-2941
Kathy Ray, *Site Mgr*
EMP: 30 **Privately Held**
WEB: www.pioneerphysicians.com
SIC: 8721 8011 Billing & bookkeeping service; physicians' office, including specialists
PA: Pioneer Physicians Networking, Inc
3515 Massillon Rd Ste 150
Uniontown OH 44685

(G-17648)
S D MYERS INC
180 South Ave (44278-2864)
PHONE.................................330 630-7000
Fax: 330 633-0756
Scott Myers, *Ch of Bd*
Dale Bissonette, *President*
Allan Ross, *Vice Pres*
David Myers, *Admin Sec*
Cheryl Gidley, *Education*
EMP: 230
SQ FT: 220,000
SALES (est): 36.3MM **Privately Held**
SIC: 8734 7629 Testing laboratories; electrical equipment repair services

(G-17649)
SD MYERS LLC
180 South Ave (44278-2864)
PHONE.................................330 630-7000
Dale Bissonette, *President*
Scott Myers, *Principal*
Beth Raies, *Admin Sec*
Sindi Harrison,
EMP: 99
SQ FT: 300,000
SALES (est): 3.7MM **Privately Held**
SIC: 8734 Testing laboratories

(G-17650)
SPEELMAN ELECTRIC INC
358 Commerce St (44278-2139)
PHONE.................................330 633-1410
Fax: 330 633-4244
Richard Speelman, *President*
Christeen Parsons, *CFO*
Alan Blake, *Supervisor*
EMP: 80
SQ FT: 7,000
SALES (est): 43.5MM **Privately Held**
WEB: www.speelmanelectric.com
SIC: 3825 1731 Test equipment for electronic & electric measurement; general electrical contractor

(G-17651)
SUMMA HEALTH SYSTEM
Also Called: Summa Physicians
182 East Ave (44278-2311)
PHONE.................................330 630-9726
Jeffrey Bachtel, *Branch Mgr*
EMP: 25
SALES (corp-wide): 1B **Privately Held**
SIC: 8011 General & family practice, physician/surgeon
PA: Summa Health System
525 E Market St
Akron OH 44304
330 375-3000

(G-17652)
SUMMIT FACILITY OPERATIONS LLC
Also Called: Summit Villa Care Center
330 Southwest Ave (44278-2235)
PHONE.................................330 633-0555
Fax: 330 633-5012
James Renacci, *President*
C Douglas Warner, *Vice Pres*
Ann J Warner, *Treasurer*
Rhonda Ellis, *Info Tech Dir*
Doug Pearson, *Exec Dir*
EMP: 94
SALES (est): 3.7MM
SALES (corp-wide): 581.9MM **Privately Held**
WEB: www.tandemhealthcare.com
SIC: 8051 8052 Skilled nursing care facilities; intermediate care facilities
PA: Consulate Management Company, Llc
800 Concourse Pkwy S
Maitland FL 32751
407 571-1550

(G-17653)
SYSTEM OPTICS CSMT SRGCAL ARTS
518 West Ave (44278-2117)
PHONE.................................330 630-9699
Fax: 330 630-2173
Todd L Beyer Do, *President*
Scott Weekly, *Administration*
EMP: 50
SQ FT: 11,378
SALES (est): 4.2MM **Privately Held**
WEB: www.glassline.com
SIC: 8011 Ophthalmologist

(G-17654)
SYSTEM OPTICS LASER VISION CTR
518 West Ave (44278-2117)
PHONE.................................330 630-2451
Kim Hoch, *COO*
Scott Weekly, *Administration*
EMP: 52
SALES (est): 3.4MM **Privately Held**
SIC: 8011 Eyes, ears, nose & throat specialist: physician/surgeon

(G-17655)
SYSTEMS TEMOPTICS COOP OPT UN
518 West Ave (44278-2117)
PHONE.................................330 633-4321
Todd Beyer, *President*
EMP: 40
SALES (est): 574.6K **Privately Held**
SIC: 8042 Offices & clinics of optometrists

(G-17656)
TALLMADGE BOARD OF EDUCATION
Also Called: Tallmadge Schools Bus Garage
89 W Overdale Dr (44278-1935)
PHONE.................................330 633-2215
Fax: 330 630-5980
Bev Alestock, *Branch Mgr*
John Rinehart, *Manager*
EMP: 45
SALES (corp-wide): 10.8MM **Privately Held**
SIC: 7538 General automotive repair shops
PA: Tallmadge Board Of Education
486 East Ave
Tallmadge OH 44278
330 633-3291

(G-17657)
TALLMADGE COLLISION CENTER (PA)
195 Northeast Ave (44278-1450)
P.O. Box 458 (44278-0458)
PHONE.................................330 630-2188
Fax: 330 630-3855
Kenneth Dixon, *CEO*
Robert Black III, *President*
Derek Richards, *Manager*
EMP: 40
SQ FT: 11,000
SALES (est): 5.5MM **Privately Held**
WEB: www.tallmadgecollision.com
SIC: 7532 Collision shops, automotive

(G-17658)
TWO HAPPY FROGS INCORPORATED
165 Northeast Ave (44278-1450)
P.O. Box 516 (44278-0516)
PHONE.................................330 633-1666
Fax: 330 633-1807
Bobbie Tilton, *President*
David Pape, *Vice Pres*
EMP: 35 **EST:** 1980
SQ FT: 32,000
SALES (est): 8.7MM **Privately Held**
SIC: 5199 Rubber, crude

(G-17659)
UNITY HEALTH NETWORK LLC
116 East Ave (44278-2300)
PHONE.................................330 633-7782
Robert A Kent, *Administration*
EMP: 47
SALES (corp-wide): 14.5MM **Privately Held**
SIC: 8099 Blood related health services
PA: Unity Health Network, Llc
3033 State Rd
Cuyahoga Falls OH 44223
330 923-5899

(G-17660)
WARREN GUILLARD BRICKLAYERS
Also Called: Warren Guillard Brick Layers
107 Potomac Ave (44278-2754)
PHONE.................................330 633-3855
Fax: 330 633-1448
Warren Guillard, *President*
Gene Guillard, *Treasurer*
EMP: 45
SQ FT: 2,000
SALES (est): 4MM **Privately Held**
SIC: 1741 Masonry & other stonework

(G-17661)
WEAVER INDUSTRIES INC
Also Called: Southern Center
89 E Howe Rd (44278-1003)
PHONE.................................330 733-2431
Richard Makruski, *General Mgr*
EMP: 181
SALES (corp-wide): 5.4MM **Privately Held**
SIC: 7389 8331 Packaging & labeling services; job training & vocational rehabilitation services
PA: Weaver Industries Inc.
520 S Main St Ste 2441
Akron OH 44311
330 379-3660

Terrace Park
Hamilton County

(G-17662)
ST THOMAS EPISCOPAL CHURCH
Also Called: St Thomas Nursery School
100 Miami Ave (45174-1175)
PHONE.................................513 831-6908
Becky Peharry, *Director*
EMP: 25 **Privately Held**
WEB: www.stthomasepiscopal.org
SIC: 8351 Child day care services
PA: St Thomas Episcopal Church
100 Miami Ave
Terrace Park OH 45174

(G-17663)
WILKRIS COMPANY
411 Terrace Pl (45174-1164)
P.O. Box 230 (45174-0230)
PHONE.................................513 271-9344
William J Van EE, *President*
Bonnie Van EE, *Corp Secy*
Russ Darrow, *Marketing Staff*
Jim Beauregard, *Business Dir*
EMP: 50
SALES (est): 2.6MM **Privately Held**
SIC: 8711 5084 Engineering services; industrial machinery & equipment

The Plains
Athens County

(G-17664)
ATHENS COUNTY EMRGNCY MED SVCS
36 N Plains Rd Ste 2 (45780-2003)
PHONE.................................740 797-9560
Rick Ballebes, *Director*
EMP: 54
SALES (est): 514K **Privately Held**
SIC: 4119 Ambulance service

(G-17665)
LINDLEY INN
Also Called: Athens Health Partners
9000 Hocking Hills Dr (45780-1209)
PHONE.................................740 797-9701
Fax: 740 797-2088
Roger Benson, *President*
EMP: 50
SALES (est): 2.3MM **Privately Held**
WEB: www.lindley.cc
SIC: 8361 Geriatric residential care

Thornville
Perry County

(G-17666)
BOWMAN ORGANIC FARMS LTD
Also Called: Bowman Agricultural RES Ctr
8100 Blackbird Ln (43076-9625)
P.O. Box 29 (43076-0029)
PHONE.................................740 246-3936
Brian Bowman, *Principal*
EMP: 47
SALES (est): 1.3MM **Privately Held**
SIC: 5148 Fresh fruits & vegetables

(G-17667)
ENGLEFIELD INC
10636 Jacksontown Rd (43076-8865)
PHONE.................................740 323-2077
EMP: 67
SALES (corp-wide): 503.4MM **Privately Held**
SIC: 7231 Unisex hair salons
PA: Englefield, Inc.
447 James Pkwy
Heath OH 43056
740 928-8215

(G-17668)
SHELLY MATERIALS INC (DH)
Also Called: Shelly Company, The
80 Park Dr (43076-9397)
P.O. Box 266 (43076-0266)
PHONE.................................740 246-6315
John Power, *President*
Ted Lemon, *Vice Pres*
Doug Radabaugh, *Treasurer*
John Mahon, *Controller*
Charlie West, *Manager*
EMP: 100 **EST:** 1938
SALES (est): 809.6MM
SALES (corp-wide): 29.7B **Privately Held**
SIC: 1422 1442 2951 4492 Crushed & broken limestone; construction sand & gravel; concrete, asphaltic (not from refineries); tugboat service
HQ: Shelly Company
80 Park Dr
Thornville OH 43076
740 246-6315

(G-17669)
THORNVILLE NH LLC
Also Called: Thornvlle Hlth Rhblitation Ctr
14100 Zion Rd (43076-9408)
PHONE.................................740 246-5253
Mordecai Rosenberg, *President*
Ronald Swartz, *CFO*
Dawn Wozniak, *Exec Sec*
Lisa Schwartz, *Admin Sec*
EMP: 73
SALES (est): 443.8K **Privately Held**
SIC: 8051 Skilled nursing care facilities

Thurman
Gallia County

(G-17670)
DOT SMITH LLC
3607 Garners Ford Rd (45685-9301)
PHONE.................................740 245-5105
John Smith, *Principal*
EMP: 25 EST: 2013
SALES: 692.5K **Privately Held**
SIC: 4212 Local trucking, without storage

Tiffin
Seneca County

(G-17671)
ATLAS INDUSTRIES INC
401 Wall St (44883-1369)
PHONE.................................419 637-2117
Fax: 419 637-7751
Ted Beavers, *Plant Mgr*
Donald Rickard, *Manager*
Dave Hanthorn, *Manager*
Layne Leemaster, *Maintence Staff*
EMP: 302
SALES (corp-wide): 165.3MM **Privately Held**
WEB: www.atlasindustries.com
SIC: 3599 5013 3714 Crankshafts & camshafts, machining; automotive supplies & parts; motor vehicle parts & accessories
PA: Atlas Industries, Inc.
1750 E State St
Fremont OH 43420
419 355-1000

(G-17672)
BALLREICH BROS INC
Also Called: Ballreichs Potato Chips Snacks
186 Ohio Ave (44883-1746)
PHONE.................................419 447-1814
Fax: 419 447-5635
Brian Reis, *President*
Steve Hoover, *Site Mgr*
Ann Dean, *Production*
Joseph Weininger, *Controller*
Kelly Philips, *Accountant*
EMP: 105
SQ FT: 48,000
SALES (est): 10.2MM **Privately Held**
WEB: www.ballreich.com
SIC: 2096 2099 4226 Potato chips & other potato-based snacks; food preparations; special warehousing & storage

(G-17673)
CONCORDNCE HLTHCARE SLTONS LLC (PA)
Also Called: Seneca Medical
85 Shaffer Park Dr (44883-9290)
PHONE.................................419 455-2153
Roger Benz, *Co-President*
Tom Harris, *Co-President*
Jaysen Stevenson, *COO*
Todd Howell, *CFO*
EMP: 90
SALES (est): 886.9MM **Privately Held**
SIC: 5047 Medical & hospital equipment

(G-17674)
COUNTY OF SENECA
Also Called: Seneca County Highway Dept
3210 S State Route 100 (44883-8869)
PHONE.................................419 447-3863
Fax: 419 447-1304
Joe Rumschlag, *Manager*
EMP: 25 **Privately Held**
WEB: www.senecapros.org
SIC: 1611 Highway & street maintenance
PA: County Of Seneca
111 Madison St
Tiffin OH 44883
419 447-4550

(G-17675)
COUNTY OF SENECA
Also Called: Seneca County Human Services
3362 S Township Rd (44883)
PHONE.................................419 447-5011
Fax: 419 447-5345
Kathy Oliver, *Manager*
EMP: 90 **Privately Held**
WEB: www.senecapros.org
SIC: 6371 Welfare pensions
PA: County Of Seneca
111 Madison St
Tiffin OH 44883
419 447-4550

(G-17676)
CUSTOM MACHINE INC
3315 W Township Road 158 (44883-9453)
PHONE.................................419 986-5122
Fax: 419 986-5204
David Hammer, *President*
Jeffery Hammer, *Vice Pres*
Phyllis Hammer, *Treasurer*
EMP: 30
SQ FT: 19,200
SALES: 3MM **Privately Held**
WEB: www.custom-machine-inc.com
SIC: 3544 3599 7692 Special dies & tools; machine shop, jobbing & repair; welding repair

(G-17677)
ELMWOOD CENTER INC
Also Called: Elmwood At Shawhan
54 S Washington St (44883-2377)
PHONE.................................419 447-6885
Fax: 419 447-6886
Teresa Jones, *Manager*
EMP: 60
SALES (corp-wide): 9.2MM **Privately Held**
WEB: www.elmwoodassistedliving.com
SIC: 8052 Home for the mentally retarded, with health care
PA: Elmwood Center Inc
441 N Broadway St
Green Springs OH 44836
419 639-2581

(G-17678)
FAMILY LRNG CTR AT SENTINEL
797 E Township Road 201 (44883-8861)
PHONE.................................419 448-5079
Fax: 419 448-5082
Heather Justen, *Director*
EMP: 50
SALES (est): 639.4K **Privately Held**
SIC: 8351 Preschool center

(G-17679)
FIRELANDS REGIONAL HEALTH SYS
Also Called: Firelands Counseling Recovery
76 Ashwood Dr (44883-1908)
PHONE.................................419 448-9440
Fax: 419 448-5155
Pattie Abrahamson, *Med Doctor*
Robin Reeves, *Manager*
Thomas Kapelka, *Data Proc Staff*
Annette Stahl, *Admin Sec*
EMP: 50
SALES (corp-wide): 15.5K **Privately Held**
SIC: 8361 Home for the mentally handicapped
PA: Firelands Regional Health System
1111 Hayes Ave
Sandusky OH 44870
419 557-7400

(G-17680)
FRIEDMAN VLG RETIREMENT CMNTY
Also Called: Heart & HM Assistant Friedman
175 Saint Francis Ave (44883-3457)
PHONE.................................419 443-1540
Kim Henry, *Vice Pres*
EMP: 25
SALES (est): 301.2K **Privately Held**
SIC: 8361 Residential care

(G-17681)
INSTITUTIONICAL CARE PHARMACY (PA)
1815 W County Road 54 (44883-7723)
PHONE.................................419 447-6216
Fax: 419 447-1878
James W Unverferth, *President*
Dick Sandilands, *Vice Pres*
Lori Adkins, *Marketing Mgr*
Chad Orr, *Pharmacist*
Sue Hawkins, *Info Tech Mgr*
EMP: 101 EST: 1985
SQ FT: 22,000
SALES (est): 59.8MM **Privately Held**
WEB: www.icp.com
SIC: 5122 5047 5912 Patent medicines; medical & hospital equipment; drug stores & proprietary stores

(G-17682)
LOWES HOME CENTERS LLC
1025 W Market St (44883-2541)
PHONE.................................419 447-4101
Fax: 419 447-4107
Jean Lowe, *Branch Mgr*
EMP: 158
SALES (corp-wide): 68.6B **Publicly Held**
SIC: 5211 5031 5722 5064 Home centers; building materials, exterior; building materials, interior; household appliance stores; electrical appliances, television & radio
HQ: Lowe's Home Centers, Llc
1605 Curtis Bridge Rd
Wilkesboro NC 28697
336 658-4000

(G-17683)
M G Q INC
Also Called: Maple Grove Companies
1525 W County Road 42 (44883-8457)
P.O. Box 130, Old Fort (44861-0130)
PHONE.................................419 992-4236
Lynn Radabaugh, *President*
Tim Bell, *President*
Bruce Chubb, *Principal*
Nicole Davis, *Principal*
Jeff Murphy, *Principal*
EMP: 45
SALES (est): 3.5MM **Privately Held**
WEB: www.mgq.com
SIC: 4214 1481 Local trucking with storage; mine & quarry services, nonmetallic minerals

(G-17684)
MCPAUL CORP
Also Called: Quality Inn
981 S Morgan St (44883-2535)
PHONE.................................419 447-6313
George Paul, *President*
Charlie Mc Carthy, *Principal*
Dana O'Quinn, *Manager*
EMP: 25
SQ FT: 30,000
SALES (est): 1.1MM **Privately Held**
WEB: www.mcpaul.com
SIC: 7011 5812 5813 Hotels; eating places; cocktail lounge

(G-17685)
MERCY HOSPITAL TIFFIN OHIO
Also Called: Mercy Health Tiffin Center
40 Fair Ln (44883-2543)
PHONE.................................419 455-8101
EMP: 347
SALES (corp-wide): 70.9MM **Privately Held**
SIC: 8011 Oncologist
PA: Mercy Hospital Of Tiffin, Ohio
45 St Lawrence Dr
Tiffin OH 44883
419 455-7000

(G-17686)
MERCY HOSPITAL TIFFIN OHIO (PA)
45 St Lawrence Dr (44883-8310)
PHONE.................................419 455-7000
Fax: 419 448-3181
Lynn Detterman, *President*
Renu Soni, *Med Doctor*
Dave Recker, *Manager*
Becky Wickham, *Manager*
Bankim Dalal, *Director*
EMP: 430
SQ FT: 241,000
SALES: 70.9MM **Privately Held**
SIC: 8062 General medical & surgical hospitals

(G-17687)
MOHAWK GOLF CLUB
4399 S State Route 231 (44883-9308)
P.O. Box 506 (44883-0506)
PHONE.................................419 447-5876
Fax: 419 447-3927
Robert Durbin, *President*
Robert Sankey, *Vice Pres*
EMP: 33
SALES: 570.4K **Privately Held**
SIC: 7997 5812 5813 Golf club, membership; eating places; bar (drinking places)

(G-17688)
MOLYET CROP PRODUCTION INC
546 E County Road 51 (44883-9609)
PHONE.................................419 992-4288
Bernard Molyet, *President*
Gregory Molyet, *Partner*
Jeffery Molyet, *Partner*
Michael Molyet, *Partner*
Ruth Molyet, *Partner*
EMP: 40
SALES (est): 2.3MM **Privately Held**
SIC: 0111 0115 0116 0161 Wheat; corn; soybeans; vegetables & melons

(G-17689)
NYE F A & SONS ENTERPRISES
7443 N Township Road 70 (44883-9454)
P.O. Box 398, Bettsville (44815-0398)
PHONE.................................419 986-5400
Fax: 419 986-5600
Gary Nye, *President*
Joanne Nye, *Corp Secy*
Franklin Nye, *Vice Pres*
Patty Nye, *Office Mgr*
EMP: 26
SALES (est): 1.3MM **Privately Held**
SIC: 4789 Cargo loading & unloading services

(G-17690)
OHIO DEPARTMENT OF HEALTH
Also Called: Tiffin Developmental Center
600 N River Rd (44883-1173)
PHONE.................................419 447-1450
Fax: 419 447-5829
Patricia Davis, *Treasurer*
Peggy S Bockey, *Manager*
Matt Glick, *Manager*
EMP: 400 **Privately Held**
WEB: www.jchealth.com
SIC: 9431 8361 Administration of public health programs; ; home for the mentally handicapped
HQ: Department Of Health Ohio
246 N High St
Columbus OH 43215

(G-17691)
OHIO POWER COMPANY
2622 S State Route 100 (44883-8972)
PHONE.................................419 443-4634
Carl McCue, *Branch Mgr*
EMP: 30
SALES (corp-wide): 15.4B **Publicly Held**
SIC: 1731 Electrical work
HQ: Ohio Power Company
1 Riverside Plz
Columbus OH 43215
614 716-1000

(G-17692)
OLD FORT BANKING COMPANY
Also Called: Invest
33 E Market St (44883-2829)
P.O. Box 627 (44883-0627)
PHONE.................................419 447-4790
Fax: 419 447-4925
Kathy Johnson, *Assistant VP*
Scott Kromer, *Assistant VP*
Eric Ding, *Assoc VP*
Sandy Rau, *Manager*
Brian Lehner, *Manager*
EMP: 59
SALES (corp-wide): 19.4MM **Privately Held**
WEB: www.oldfortbank.com
SIC: 6022 State trust companies accepting deposits, commercial
HQ: The Old Fort Banking Company
8034 Main St
Old Fort OH 44861
419 447-6150

(G-17693)
PIASANS MILL INC
255 Riverside Dr (44883-1609)
PHONE.................................419 448-0100

Tiffin - Seneca County (G-17694)

Scott Lyons, *President*
EMP: 35
SALES: 950K **Privately Held**
SIC: 8742 Management consulting services

(G-17694)
QUICK TAB II INC (PA)
241 Heritage Dr (44883-9504)
P.O. Box 723 (44883-0723)
PHONE.................................419 448-6622
Fax: 419 448-6627
Chuck Daughenbaugh, *CEO*
Mike Daughenbaugh, *Vice Pres*
Jim Hayes, *Opers Mgr*
Marty Ward, *Traffic Mgr*
Brad Distel, *Design Engr*
▼ **EMP:** 64
SQ FT: 30,000
SALES (est): 12.1MM **Privately Held**
WEB: www.qt2.com
SIC: 2752 5112 2791 2789 Business forms, lithographed; stationery & office supplies; typesetting; bookbinding & related work

(G-17695)
RK FAMILY INC
2300 W Market St (44883-8877)
PHONE.................................419 443-1663
Tim F Lode, *Principal*
EMP: 110
SALES (corp-wide): 1.2B **Privately Held**
SIC: 0191 General farms, primarily crop
PA: Rk Family, Inc.
4216 Dewitt Ave
Mattoon IL 61938
217 235-7102

(G-17696)
RUFFING CARE INC
Also Called: Ruffing Family Care Ctr Tiffin
2320 W County Road 6 (44883-9112)
PHONE.................................419 447-4662
Diana L Ruffing, *President*
Diana Ruffing, *President*
Dennis Ruffing, *Corp Secy*
Pat Schwab, *Facilities Dir*
Andrew Gase, *Director*
EMP: 80 **EST:** 1983
SQ FT: 7,000
SALES (est): 4.4MM **Privately Held**
SIC: 8051 Extended care facility

(G-17697)
SALVATION ARMY
505 E Market St (44883-1767)
P.O. Box 341 (44883-0341)
PHONE.................................419 447-2252
Fax: 419 447-2252
Matthew J Shriver, *CPA*
George Polariek, *Branch Mgr*
EMP: 91
SQ FT: 86,946
SALES (corp-wide): 4.3B **Privately Held**
WEB: www.salvationarmy-usaeast.org
SIC: 5932 8741 8641 Used merchandise stores; management services; civic social & fraternal associations
HQ: The Salvation Army
440 W Nyack Rd Ofc
West Nyack NY 10994
845 620-7200

(G-17698)
SENECA COUNTY EMS
126 Hopewell Ave (44883-2636)
PHONE.................................419 447-0266
Dan Stahl, *Manager*
Ken Majors,
EMP: 140
SALES: 300K **Privately Held**
SIC: 8099 Health & allied services

(G-17699)
SENECA COUNTY FIREMENS ASSN
1070 S County Road 17 (44883-9408)
PHONE.................................419 447-7909
Dennis Wilkinson, *Corp Secy*
EMP: 99
SALES (est): 834.1K **Privately Held**
SIC: 8641 Civic social & fraternal associations

(G-17700)
SENECA DIALYSIS LLC
Also Called: Seneca County Dialysis
10 St Lawrence Dr (44883-8310)
PHONE.................................419 443-1051
Bob Badal, *Principal*
Jess Wagner, *Administration*
EMP: 50
SALES (est): 1.6MM **Publicly Held**
WEB: www.davita.com
SIC: 8092 Kidney dialysis centers
PA: Davita Inc.
2000 16th St
Denver CO 80202

(G-17701)
SENECA MEDICAL LLC (HQ)
85 Shaffer Park Dr (44883-9290)
P.O. Box 399 (44883-0399)
PHONE.................................419 447-0236
Fax: 419 447-7201
Roger Benz, *CEO*
Buddy Wert, *President*
Todd Howell, *CFO*
Dave Myers, *Ch Credit Ofcr*
Michelle Clouse, *Marketing Staff*
▲ **EMP:** 235
SALES (est): 515.4MM
SALES (corp-wide): 886.9MM **Privately Held**
WEB: www.senecamedical.com
SIC: 5047 Medical equipment & supplies; surgical equipment & supplies
PA: Concordance Healthcare Solutions Llc
85 Shaffer Park Dr
Tiffin OH 44883
419 455-2153

(G-17702)
SENECA-CRAWFORD AREA TRNSP (PA)
Also Called: S C A T
3446 S Township Road 151 (44883-9499)
P.O. Box 922 (44883-0922)
PHONE.................................419 937-2428
Fax: 419 448-8484
Mary Habig, *CEO*
EMP: 35
SALES (est): 1MM **Privately Held**
SIC: 4119 Vanpool operation

(G-17703)
TECTA AMERICA CORP
Also Called: JB Roofing
1480 S County Road 594 (44883-2677)
PHONE.................................419 447-1716
Fax: 419 448-4400
Bob Swartzmiller, *Representative*
EMP: 60
SALES (corp-wide): 922.9MM **Privately Held**
SIC: 1761 Roofing contractor
PA: Tecta America Corp.
9450 Bryn Mawr Ave
Rosemont IL 60018
847 581-3888

(G-17704)
TIFFIN CMNTY YMCA RCRATION CTR (PA)
180 Summit St (44883-3168)
PHONE.................................419 447-8711
Fax: 419 447-8704
Kathy Jentgen, *President*
John Aragon, *Manager*
Francine Neal, *Program Dir*
Charles Chapman, *Master*
EMP: 80
SQ FT: 70,000
SALES (est): 1.8MM **Privately Held**
SIC: 7997 8641 Membership sports & recreation clubs; community membership club

(G-17705)
TIFFIN LOADER CRANE COMPANY
4151 W State Route 18 (44883-8997)
PHONE.................................419 448-8156
Mark Woody, *President*
Ed Gerken, *General Mgr*
Luke Kelly, *General Mgr*
Ryan Kramb, *Purch Agent*
Tony Reser, *Controller*
EMP: 55
SQ FT: 60,000
SALES (est): 22.9MM **Privately Held**
SIC: 5084 Cranes, industrial
HQ: Palfinger Ag
LamprechtshausenerBundesstraBe 8
Bergheim 5101
662 228-10

(G-17706)
TIFFIN PAPER COMPANY (PA)
Also Called: TPC Food Service
265 6th Ave (44883-1083)
P.O. Box 129 (44883-0129)
PHONE.................................419 447-2121
Fax: 419 447-7646
Thomas M Maiberger, *President*
Tony Paulus, *Vice Pres*
Angie Kimmet, *Purchasing*
Scott Maiberger, *Accountant*
Jeannie Little, *Human Resources*
EMP: 45
SQ FT: 40,000
SALES (est): 38.9MM **Privately Held**
WEB: www.tpcfoodservice.com
SIC: 5113 5149 5145 Paper & products, wrapping or coarse; groceries & related products; confectionery

(G-17707)
TRINITY HEALTH CORPORATION
485 W Market St (44883-2611)
PHONE.................................419 448-3124
Dave McBicker, *Director*
EMP: 30
SALES (corp-wide): 16.3B **Privately Held**
WEB: www.trinity-health.com
SIC: 8742 Management consulting services
PA: Trinity Health Corporation
20555 Victor Pkwy
Livonia MI 48152
734 343-1000

(G-17708)
VOLUNTERS AMER CARE FACILITIES
Also Called: Volunteer of Amer Autemwood CA
670 E State Route 18 (44883-1856)
PHONE.................................419 447-7151
Fax: 419 447-9701
Sally Turner, *Branch Mgr*
Gina Porter, *Nursing Dir*
Cindy Setliff, *Hlthcr Dir*
Mary L Creeger, *Administration*
Ron Guild, *Maintence Staff*
EMP: 130
SALES (corp-wide): 66.7MM **Privately Held**
SIC: 8051 Convalescent home with continuous nursing care
PA: Volunteers Of America Care Facilities
7530 Market Place Dr
Eden Prairie MN 55344
952 941-0305

(G-17709)
WORK CONNECTIONS INTL LLC
525 Wall St Ste A (44883-1370)
PHONE.................................419 448-4655
Fax: 419 448-5025
Ryan Shultz, *Principal*
Megan Reinhart, *Office Spvr*
EMP: 25
SALES (est): 3.5MM **Privately Held**
SIC: 8731 Natural resource research

Tipp City
Miami County

(G-17710)
AFFORD-A-CAR INC
8973 State 201 (45371)
PHONE.................................937 235-2700
Don Gilliam, *President*
EMP: 25
SALES (est): 2MM **Privately Held**
SIC: 5521 7514 Automobiles, used cars only; trucks, tractors & trailers: used; passenger car rental

(G-17711)
CALVARY CONTRACTING INC
4125 Gibson Dr (45371-9064)
PHONE.................................937 754-0300
John C Moon, *President*
Denise Moon, *Vice Pres*
Cliff Dech, *Project Mgr*
Sterling Williams, *Project Mgr*
Kim Rector, *Controller*
EMP: 27
SQ FT: 3,600
SALES (est): 7.9MM **Privately Held**
WEB: www.calvarycontracting.com
SIC: 1542 Commercial & office building, new construction; commercial & office buildings, renovation & repair

(G-17712)
CHARLES C SMITH DDS INC
Also Called: Saleh, Hady DMD
110 S Tippecanoe Dr Ste A (45371-3109)
PHONE.................................937 667-2417
Charles C Smith DDS, *President*
EMP: 30
SQ FT: 10,176
SALES (est): 1.4MM **Privately Held**
SIC: 8021 Dentists' office

(G-17713)
CHILD & ADOLESCENT SPECIALITY
1483 W Main St (45371-2803)
PHONE.................................937 667-7711
Kevin Horvath MD, *President*
EMP: 30
SALES (est): 4MM **Privately Held**
SIC: 8011 Pediatrician

(G-17714)
COMMUNITY SERVICES INC
3 E Main St (45371-1925)
P.O. Box 242 (45371-0242)
PHONE.................................937 667-8631
Kathy Taylor, *Director*
EMP: 100
SALES: 375.2K **Privately Held**
WEB: www.tmcomservices.org
SIC: 8322 7032 Community center; sporting & recreational camps

(G-17715)
DAIHEN INC (HQ)
Also Called: Advanced Welding Division
1400 Blauser Dr (45371-2471)
PHONE.................................937 667-0800
Masanobu Uchida, *President*
Todd Griffieth, *Opers Mgr*
Bill Guest, *VP Sls/Mktg*
Brandy Spencer, *Accountant*
Jeff Subler, *Human Res Mgr*
▲ **EMP:** 37 **EST:** 1979
SQ FT: 45,000
SALES: 26.8MM
SALES (corp-wide): 1.1B **Privately Held**
SIC: 5084 Welding machinery & equipment
PA: Daihen Corporation
2-1-11, Tagawa, Yodogawa-Ku
Osaka OSK 532-0
663 011-212

(G-17716)
ENVIRONMENT CTRL OF MIAMI CNTY
7939 S County Road 25a A (45371-9107)
P.O. Box 877 (45371-0877)
PHONE.................................937 669-9900
Ted Pauling, *President*
Sheryl Pauling, *Corp Secy*
William Schneider, *Shareholder*
EMP: 65
SQ FT: 3,000
SALES (est): 2.4MM **Privately Held**
SIC: 7349 Janitorial service, contract basis

(G-17717)
HIGH POWER INC
15 Industry Park Ct (45371-3060)
P.O. Box 533 (45371-0533)
PHONE.................................937 667-1772
Brent Black, *President*
EMP: 25
SQ FT: 10,000
SALES (est): 742.4K **Privately Held**
SIC: 7349 Building maintenance services

GEOGRAPHIC SECTION

(G-17718)
HIGH-TEC INDUSTRIAL SERVICES
15 Industry Park Ct (45371-3060)
P.O. Box 533 (45371-0533)
PHONE..................937 667-1772
Brent Black, *President*
William E Oldham, *President*
Christopher Taylor, *Vice Pres*
Matt Davis, *Project Mgr*
Paul Leverette, *Opers Mgr*
EMP: 139
SQ FT: 18,000
SALES (est): 25.3MM **Privately Held**
WEB: www.hightecindustrial.com
SIC: 3589 7349 Commercial cooking & foodwarming equipment; building & office cleaning services

(G-17719)
HOMESTEAD GOLF COURSE INC
5327 Worley Rd (45371-9681)
PHONE..................937 698-4876
Fax: 937 698-9052
David Knife, *President*
Ester Knife, *Corp Secy*
Karen Knife, *Vice Pres*
EMP: 39
SQ FT: 5,000
SALES (est): 1.4MM **Privately Held**
WEB: www.homesteadgolfcourse.com
SIC: 7992 Public golf courses

(G-17720)
JASON WILSON
5575 Ross Rd (45371-9710)
PHONE..................937 604-8209
Fax: 937 506-2257
Jason Wilson, *Mng Member*
Mark Nelson,
EMP: 27
SALES: 1.5MM **Privately Held**
SIC: 3663 7389 3229 Radio & TV communications equipment; ; fiber optics strands

(G-17721)
KOENIG EQUIPMENT INC
Also Called: John Deere Authorized Dealer
5695 S County Road 25a (45371-2411)
PHONE..................937 877-1920
Fax: 937 877-1238
Jeff Holthaus,
EMP: 72
SALES (corp-wide): 200MM **Privately Held**
SIC: 5046 5082 Commercial equipment; construction & mining machinery
PA: Koenig Equipment, Inc.
15213 State Route 274
Botkins OH 45306
937 693-5000

(G-17722)
MILLER PIPELINE LLC
11990 Peters Rd (45371-9669)
PHONE..................937 506-8837
Jim Wilson, *Manager*
EMP: 400
SALES (corp-wide): 2.6B **Publicly Held**
WEB: www.millerpipeline.com
SIC: 1623 Pipeline construction
HQ: Miller Pipeline, Llc
8850 Crawfordsville Rd
Indianapolis IN 46234
317 293-0278

(G-17723)
OHIO WINDOW CLEANING INC
Also Called: Kentucky Window Cleaning
4582 Us Route 40 (45371-9025)
P.O. Box 24026, Dayton (45424-0026)
PHONE..................937 877-0832
Toll Free:..................888 -
Fax: 937 667-4644
H Bernard Wilson, *President*
Brad Wilson, *General Mgr*
Brian Brabson, *Area Mgr*
Lisa Joiner, *Office Mgr*
Zach Wilson, *Manager*
EMP: 54
SALES (est): 1.9MM **Privately Held**
SIC: 7349 Window cleaning

(G-17724)
POLYMERSHAPES LLC
1480 Blauser Dr (45371-2471)
PHONE..................937 877-1903
Ken Turner, *Purch Mgr*
Nick Roach, *Cust Svc Mgr*
Patrick Welsh, *Maintence Staff*
EMP: 30
SALES (corp-wide): 182MM **Privately Held**
WEB: www.sabic-ip.com
SIC: 5162 Plastics materials & basic shapes
PA: Polymershapes Llc
10130 Perimeter Pkwy # 500
Charlotte NC 28216
866 333-0651

(G-17725)
PRECISION STRIP INC
315 Park Ave (45371-1887)
PHONE..................937 667-6255
Jerry Huber, *Manager*
EMP: 52
SQ FT: 3,080
SALES (corp-wide): 9.7B **Publicly Held**
WEB: www.precision-strip.com
SIC: 7389 3312 Metal cutting services; blast furnaces & steel mills
HQ: Precision Strip Inc.
86 S Ohio St
Minster OH 45865
419 628-2343

(G-17726)
SAFTEK INDUSTRIAL SERVICE INC
Also Called: High TEC Industrial Services
15 Industry Park Ct (45371-3060)
P.O. Box 533 (45371-0533)
PHONE..................937 667-1772
Fax: 937 667-5907
Brent Black, *President*
EMP: 25
SALES (est): 690K **Privately Held**
SIC: 7349 Janitorial service, contract basis

(G-17727)
TIME WARNER CABLE INC
1440 Commerce Park Dr (45371-2845)
PHONE..................937 667-8302
Lois Kerns, *Principal*
EMP: 83
SQ FT: 693
SALES (corp-wide): 41.5B **Publicly Held**
SIC: 4841 Cable television services
HQ: Spectrum Management Holding Company, Llc
400 Atlantic St
Stamford CT 06901
203 905-7801

(G-17728)
TIPP CITY VETERINARY HOSP INC
4900 S County Road 25a (45371-2912)
PHONE..................937 667-8489
Fax: 937 669-4443
James Mathias, *President*
Ben Spinks, *Treasurer*
Jennie Accuntius, *Department Mgr*
Shannon Sullenberger, *Manager*
EMP: 61
SALES (est): 2MM **Privately Held**
WEB: www.tippvet.com
SIC: 0742 Animal hospital services, pets & other animal specialties

(G-17729)
TIPP-MONROE COMMUNITY SVCS INC
3 E Main St (45371-1925)
P.O. Box 242 (45371-0242)
PHONE..................937 667-8631
Denise Gross, *President*
Deb Jackson, *Treasurer*
Kathy Taylor, *Exec Dir*
Carol English, *Admin Asst*
EMP: 49
SALES: 475.3K **Privately Held**
SIC: 8399 Community development groups; community action agency

(G-17730)
TOOL TESTING LAB INC
11601 N Dixie Dr (45371-9108)
PHONE..................937 898-5696
Ted Bowden, *President*
Katelyn Berbach, *Human Resources*
Robb Thomas, *Lab Dir*
Mark Miller, *Technician*
EMP: 35 **Privately Held**
SIC: 8734 5251 Product certification, safety or performance; tools
PA: Tool Testing Lab, Inc
11180 N Dixie Dr
Vandalia OH 45377

(G-17731)
UVMC NURSING CARE INC
Also Called: Springmeade
4375 S County Road 25a (45371-2956)
PHONE..................937 667-7500
Judith Nickras, *Director*
Tom Nick, *Administration*
EMP: 150
SALES (corp-wide): 20.3MM **Privately Held**
WEB: www.koesterpavilion.com
SIC: 8361 8051 Home for the aged; skilled nursing care facilities
PA: Uvmc Nursing Care, Inc.
3130 N County Road 25a
Troy OH 45373
937 440-4000

Toledo
Lucas County

(G-17732)
21ST CENTURY HEALTH SPA INC (PA)
343 New Towne Square Dr (43612-4626)
PHONE..................419 476-5585
Ronald R Hemelgarn, *Owner*
EMP: 50
SQ FT: 10,000
SALES (est): 2.9MM **Privately Held**
SIC: 5091 Fitness equipment & supplies

(G-17733)
A & K RAILROAD MATERIALS INC
2750 Hill Ave (43607-2926)
PHONE..................419 537-9470
Fax: 419 537-1987
Joe Shinsky, *Manager*
EMP: 25
SQ FT: 10,868
SALES (corp-wide): 150.1MM **Privately Held**
WEB: www.akrailroad.com
SIC: 5088 Railroad equipment & supplies
PA: A & K Railroad Materials, Inc.
1505 S Redwood Rd
Salt Lake City UT 84104
801 974-5484

(G-17734)
A AND S VENTURES INC
Also Called: Winter Drive In Theater
4311 Garden Estates Dr (43623-3414)
PHONE..................419 376-3934
Anthony J Arite, *President*
EMP: 35 **Privately Held**
SIC: 6719 Personal holding companies, except banks

(G-17735)
A R E A TITLE AGENCY INC (PA)
5450 Monroe St Ste 2 (43623-2879)
PHONE..................419 242-5485
Fax: 419 242-8920
Michael D Repass, *President*
Jim Harpen, *Vice Pres*
Erika Olsen, *Vice Pres*
Bill Gilsdorf, *Broker*
Beverly Fischer, *Financial Exec*
EMP: 25
SALES (est): 4.9MM **Privately Held**
WEB: www.areatitle.com
SIC: 6541 6361 Title & trust companies; title insurance

(G-17736)
AAA CLUB ALLIANCE INC (PA)
Also Called: AAA Mid-Atlantic
3201 Meijer Dr (43617)
PHONE..................419 843-1200
Fax: 419 843-1249
Karl Halbedl, *President*
Rich Kirsch, *Accountant*
Karen Ward, *Human Res Mgr*
Patty Hicks, *Manager*
Ester Mosley, *Manager*
EMP: 83
SQ FT: 24,000
SALES (est): 16.2MM **Privately Held**
SIC: 8699 Automobile owners' association

(G-17737)
AAA STANDARD SERVICES INC
4117 South Ave (43615-6231)
PHONE..................419 535-0274
Fax: 419 534-5503
Steven Johnson, *President*
Dale Johnson Sr, *Principal*
Jerry Pryor, *Opers Mgr*
Dee Dee Thorsby, *Manager*
Kim Tilley, *Administration*
EMP: 60
SQ FT: 24,500
SALES: 4MM **Privately Held**
WEB: www.aaastandardservices.com
SIC: 7349 1521 Janitorial service, contract basis; window cleaning; repairing fire damage, single-family houses

(G-17738)
ABBOTT TOOL INC
Also Called: ATI
405 Dura Ave (43612-2619)
PHONE..................419 476-6742
Fax: 419 476-4411
Arthur V Stange, *President*
Kevin Webb, *General Mgr*
Leonard Livecchi, *Vice Pres*
Steve Rogers, *Accountant*
Carl Stange, *Manager*
EMP: 27
SQ FT: 12,000
SALES (est): 5.4MM **Privately Held**
SIC: 3469 7692 Machine parts, stamped or pressed metal; welding repair

(G-17739)
ABCO CONTRACTING LLC
947 Belmont Ave (43607-4244)
PHONE..................419 973-4772
Floyd W Abercrombie Jr,
EMP: 37
SQ FT: 100
SALES: 200K **Privately Held**
SIC: 1522 1542 4214 6531 Apartment building construction; commercial & office building contractors; local trucking with storage; real estate agents & managers

(G-17740)
ACCURATE NURSE STAFFING
4165 Monroe St (43606-2009)
PHONE..................419 475-2424
Donna Martin, *Principal*
EMP: 50
SALES (est): 525.6K **Privately Held**
SIC: 8049 Nurses, registered & practical

(G-17741)
ADECCO USA INC
336 N Superior St 200 (43604-1422)
PHONE..................419 720-0111
Ken Davis, *Branch Mgr*
EMP: 30
SALES (corp-wide): 24B **Privately Held**
WEB: www.usadecco.com
SIC: 7361 Placement agencies
HQ: Adecco Usa, Inc.
10151 Deerwood Park Blvd
Jacksonville FL 32256
940 360-2000

(G-17742)
ADVANCED INDUSTRIAL SVCS LLC
123 Oakdale Ave (43605-3322)
PHONE..................800 846-9094
Christopher J Welsh, *Branch Mgr*
EMP: 100 **Privately Held**
WEB: www.advancedspecialtycontractors.com

Toledo - Lucas County (G-17743) GEOGRAPHIC SECTION

SIC: 5082 General construction machinery & equipment
HQ: Advanced Industrial Services Llc
123 Oakdale Ave
Toledo OH 43605

(G-17743)
ADVANCED INDUSTRIAL SVCS LLC (DH)
123 Oakdale Ave (43605-3322)
PHONE..............................419 661-8522
Fax: 419 661-8825
Bryan J Pieh, *President*
Tom Elkins, *Business Mgr*
Jason Dodd, *Treasurer*
Karen Drevyanko, *Accounts Mgr*
EMP: 100
SALES: 41.9MM **Privately Held**
SIC: 1799 Insulation of pipes & boilers; asbestos removal & encapsulation
HQ: Irex Corporation
120 N Lime St
Lancaster PA 17602
717 397-3633

(G-17744)
ADVOCTES FOR BSIC LGAL EQALITY (PA)
Also Called: Able
525 Jefferson Ave (43604-1094)
PHONE..............................419 255-0814
Fax: 419 259-2880
Betty Franks, *Controller*
Dorothy Hill, *Human Res Dir*
Will Shryock, *Info Tech Mgr*
Jose Trujillo, *Technology*
Susan Frantz, *Web Dvlpr*
EMP: 50 **EST:** 1969
SALES: 6.3MM **Privately Held**
SIC: 8111 Legal aid service

(G-17745)
AL PEAKE & SONS INC
4949 Stickney Ave (43612-3716)
PHONE..............................419 243-9284
Fax: 419 242-3308
Philip Peake, *President*
Jack Gilkerson, *Warehouse Mgr*
Mike He, *Buyer*
Joe Deeb, *Sales Mgr*
Ann Beck, *Sales Staff*
EMP: 30
SQ FT: 57,408
SALES (est): 18.3MM **Privately Held**
WEB: www.alpeake.com
SIC: 5148 Fruits, fresh

(G-17746)
ALBRING VENDING COMPANY
702 Galena St (43611-3709)
PHONE..............................419 726-8059
Bob Albring, *President*
EMP: 30
SQ FT: 2,000
SALES (corp-wide): 2.9MM **Privately Held**
SIC: 4225 General warehousing
PA: Albring Vending Company
13570 Wayne Rd
Livonia MI 48150
419 726-8059

(G-17747)
ALRO STEEL CORPORATION
3003 Airport Hwy (43609-1405)
P.O. Box 964 (43697-0964)
PHONE..............................419 720-5300
Fax: 419 720-5301
Adam Cristek, *Manager*
Donald Schlatter, *Manager*
EMP: 40
SALES (corp-wide): 1.6B **Privately Held**
WEB: www.alro.com
SIC: 5051 5085 5162 3444 Steel; aluminum bars, rods, ingots, sheets, pipes, plates, etc.; nonferrous metal sheets, bars, rods, etc.; industrial supplies; plastics materials; sheet metalwork
PA: Alro Steel Corporation
3100 E High St
Jackson MI 49203
517 787-5500

(G-17748)
AMERICAN BROADBAND TELECOM CO
1 Seagate Ste 10 (43604-1563)
PHONE..............................419 824-5800
Jeff Ansted, *President*
Rob Enos, *Sales Dir*
EMP: 36
SQ FT: 5,500
SALES (est): 5MM **Privately Held**
SIC: 8748 Telecommunications consultant

(G-17749)
AMERICAN MARITIME OFFICERS
1 Maritime Plz Fl 2 (43604-1885)
PHONE..............................419 255-3940
Fax: 419 255-2350
Michael Mc Kay, *President*
EMP: 25
SALES (est): 1.4MM **Privately Held**
SIC: 6512 Commercial & industrial building operation

(G-17750)
AMERICAN NATIONAL RED CROSS
1111 Research Dr (43614-2798)
PHONE..............................419 382-2707
Fax: 419 321-1746
Arkia Blackman, *Materials Mgr*
Mary Rietzke, *Manager*
EMP: 170
SALES (corp-wide): 2.5B **Privately Held**
WEB: www.redcross.org
SIC: 8322 Social service center; disaster service
PA: The American National Red Cross
430 17th St Nw
Washington DC 20006
202 737-8300

(G-17751)
AMERICAN POSTS LLC
810 Chicago St (43611-3609)
PHONE..............................419 720-0652
David Feniger, *Mng Member*
Andrew Spoering, *Supervisor*
EMP: 30
SALES (est): 7.8MM **Privately Held**
WEB: www.americanposts.com
SIC: 3312 5051 Rods, iron & steel: made in steel mills; steel

(G-17752)
ANN ARBOR RAILROAD INC
4058 Chrysler Dr (43608-4100)
P.O. Box 5128 (43611-0128)
PHONE..............................419 726-4181
Fax: 419 726-2250
EMP: 30
SALES (corp-wide): 8.5MM **Privately Held**
SIC: 4011 Railroad Company
HQ: Ann Arbor Railroad Inc
121 S Walnut St
Howell MI
517 548-3930

(G-17753)
ANSPACH MEEKS ELLENBERGER LLP (PA)
300 Madison Ave Ste 1600 (43604-2633)
PHONE..............................419 447-6181
Fax: 419 321-6979
Julie Busdicker, *President*
Tami Lang, *President*
Deanna Whitley, *President*
Robert M Anspach, *Partner*
Richard F Ellenberg, *Partner*
EMP: 36
SQ FT: 9,000
SALES (est): 10.1MM **Privately Held**
SIC: 8111 General practice attorney, lawyer

(G-17754)
ANTONIO SOFO SON IMPORTING CO (PA)
Also Called: Sofo Importing Company
253 Waggoner Blvd (43612-1952)
PHONE..............................419 476-4211
Fax: 419 478-6104
Antonio J Sofo, *CEO*
Mike Sofo, *President*
Paul Peer, *Principal*
Joseph J Sofo Jr, *Principal*
Wilma Jean Sofo, *Principal*
▲ **EMP:** 206 **EST:** 1940
SQ FT: 180,000
SALES (est): 63.6MM **Privately Held**
WEB: www.sofofoods.com
SIC: 5499 5149 Gourmet food stores; specialty food items

(G-17755)
APPLE TREE NURSERY SCHOOL INC
2801 W Bancroft St 280 (43606-3328)
PHONE..............................419 530-1070
Renee Myers, *Accounts Mgr*
Sherry Roush, *Director*
EMP: 25
SALES (est): 1.1MM **Privately Held**
SIC: 8351 Child day care services

(G-17756)
APS MEDICAL BILLING
Also Called: A P S Medical Billing
5620 Southwyck Blvd (43614-1501)
PHONE..............................419 866-1804
Fax: 419 866-5130
Nancy Condon, *President*
Harold S Rickard, *Principal*
Margaret Rickard, *Treasurer*
Judy Udell, *Admin Sec*
EMP: 65
SALES (est): 7.9MM
SALES (corp-wide): 66.5MM **Privately Held**
WEB: www.apsmedicalbilling.com
SIC: 8721 Billing & bookkeeping service
PA: United Collection Bureau, Inc.
5620 Southwyck Blvd
Toledo OH 43614
419 866-6227

(G-17757)
ARCADIS US INC
1 Seagate Ste 700 (43604-4508)
PHONE..............................419 473-1121
David M Oberle, *Electrical Engi*
Matt Vick, *Electrical Engi*
Bob Casaletta, *Branch Mgr*
EMP: 87
SALES (corp-wide): 2.6B **Privately Held**
WEB: www.arcadis-us.com
SIC: 8748 Environmental consultant
HQ: Arcadis U.S., Inc.
630 Plaza Dr Ste 200
Highlands Ranch CO 80129
720 344-3500

(G-17758)
AREA OFFICE ON AGING OF NWSTRN
2155 Arlington Ave (43609-1997)
PHONE..............................419 382-0624
Fax: 419 382-4560
Jayne Wagner, *Project Mgr*
Monica Henry, *Manager*
Scherry Secoy, *Manager*
Velvet Ellis, *Supervisor*
John Alderman, *Technology*
EMP: 96
SALES: 35.4MM **Privately Held**
WEB: www.areaofficeonaging.com
SIC: 8322 8082 Senior citizens' center or association; home health care services

(G-17759)
ARNOLDS HOME IMPROVEMENT LLC
1770 Premainsville (43613)
PHONE..............................734 847-9600
Jason Arnold, *Owner*
EMP: 30
SALES (corp-wide): 1.9MM **Privately Held**
SIC: 1542 1521 Commercial & office buildings, renovation & repair; general remodeling, single-family houses
PA: Arnold's Home Improvement Llc
1770 Tremainsville Rd
Toledo OH 43613
419 354-7663

(G-17760)
ASSOCIATED IMAGING CORPORATION
Also Called: M R I Center
3830 Woodley Rd Ste A (43606-1176)
PHONE..............................419 517-0500
Fax: 419 472-4467
Tom Thompson, *President*
Marty Connors, *Treasurer*
Diane Moreno, *Manager*
EMP: 30
SQ FT: 5,000
SALES: 11.2K **Privately Held**
SIC: 8071 Medical laboratories; X-ray laboratory, including dental

(G-17761)
AUTO WAREHOUSING CO INC
4405 Chrysler Dr (43608-4050)
PHONE..............................419 727-1534
Fax: 419 727-1545
Carlos Sanchez, *General Mgr*
Jose Lopez, *Manager*
EMP: 33
SALES (corp-wide): 153.3MM **Privately Held**
SIC: 4226 Automobile dead storage
PA: Auto Warehousing Co., Inc.
2810 Marshall Ave Ste B
Tacoma WA 98421
253 719-1700

(G-17762)
BAGEL PLACE INC (PA)
Also Called: Barry Bagel's Place
3715 King Rd (43617-1417)
PHONE..............................419 885-1000
Fax: 419 885-5400
Mark Greenblatt, *President*
Judie A Greenblatt, *Vice Pres*
Ted Smith, *Manager*
EMP: 50
SQ FT: 10,000
SALES (est): 30.2MM **Privately Held**
SIC: 5461 5411 5812 5149 Bagels; delicatessens; caterers; bakery products

(G-17763)
BARRINGTON TOLEDO LLC
Also Called: W N W O
300 S Byrne Rd (43615-6217)
PHONE..............................419 535-0024
Chris Popf, *General Mgr*
Victoria Scott, *Business Mgr*
George Markle, *Manager*
EMP: 50
SALES (est): 1.7MM
SALES (corp-wide): 143.8MM **Privately Held**
WEB: www.barringtontv.com
SIC: 4833 Television broadcasting stations
HQ: Barrington Broadcasting Group Llc
1270 Ave Of The Amer Fl 9
New York NY 10020
847 884-1877

(G-17764)
BAYVIEW RETIREES GOLF COURSE
3900 N Summit St (43611-3042)
PHONE..............................419 726-8081
Harold Rodgers, *Director*
EMP: 70
SALES (est): 2.1MM **Privately Held**
SIC: 7992 Public golf courses

(G-17765)
BEACON OF LIGHT LTD
Also Called: Beacon of Light Health Agency
360 S Reynolds Rd Ste A (43615-5976)
PHONE..............................419 531-9060
Shirley Foster, *Mng Member*
Lamont Love, *Manager*
Calandra Strong,
EMP: 35 **EST:** 2007
SQ FT: 4,500
SALES (est): 2.1MM **Privately Held**
SIC: 8051 8742 Convalescent home with continuous nursing care; hospital & health services consultant

(G-17766)
BEAUTY BAR LLC
2919 W Central Ave (43606-3027)
PHONE..............................419 537-5400

GEOGRAPHIC SECTION
Toledo - Lucas County (G-17788)

Fax: 419 536-4816
Randy Greben, *CFO*
Sara Buckner, *Accountant*
Sue Spallino, *Sales Executive*
Sara Stallino,
EMP: 40
SQ FT: 5,170
SALES (est): 969.4K **Privately Held**
SIC: 7231 Cosmetology & personal hygiene salons

(G-17767)
BEBLEY ENTERPRISES INC (PA)
Also Called: A Clean Sweep
2801 W Bancroft St (43606-3328)
P.O. Box 2847 (43606-0847)
PHONE 419 389-9424
Thomas M Bebley, *President*
Genamarie White, *Manager*
EMP: 40
SQ FT: 4,000
SALES (est): 1.2MM **Privately Held**
WEB: www.bebleyenterprises.com
SIC: 7349 Janitorial service, contract basis; maid services, contract or fee basis

(G-17768)
BELLE TIRE DISTRIBUTORS INC
5253 Secor Rd (43623-2401)
PHONE 419 473-1393
Fax: 419 473-1025
Carl Kandel, *Sales Staff*
James Stevenson, *Manager*
Dawn Miksys, *Director*
EMP: 50
SALES (corp-wide): 530.3MM **Privately Held**
WEB: www.belletire.com
SIC: 5014 Automobile tires & tubes
PA: Belle Tire Distributors, Inc.
1000 Enterprise Dr
Allen Park MI 48101
888 462-3553

(G-17769)
BENCHMARK TECHNOLOGIES CORP
3161 N Republic Blvd (43615-1507)
PHONE 419 843-6691
Fax: 419 843-7218
Gary A Cooper, *Ch of Bd*
Rand Palmer, *Manager*
EMP: 30
SQ FT: 17,000
SALES: 3.4MM **Privately Held**
WEB: www.benchmark-usa.com
SIC: 8741 8748 7699 8742 Management services; business management; financial management for business; construction management; test development & evaluation service; caliper, gauge & other machinists' instrument repair; management consulting services

(G-17770)
BERNER TRUCKING
4310 Lagrange St (43612-1413)
P.O. Box 660, Dover (44622-0660)
PHONE 419 476-0207
Fax: 419 364-2935
Jim Kniesly, *President*
Vernon Hochstetler, *Sales Dir*
Kimberly Hobart, *Office Mgr*
EMP: 25
SALES (est): 1.6MM **Privately Held**
SIC: 4212 Dump truck haulage

(G-17771)
BINKELMAN CORPORATION (PA)
2601 Hill Ave (43607-2922)
PHONE 419 537-9333
Dan Kazmierczak, *President*
Brad Fitzgerald, *General Mgr*
Dave Grana, *Vice Pres*
Clay Grieffendorf, *Vice Pres*
Brian Elsner, *Accounts Mgr*
EMP: 33
SQ FT: 30,000
SALES (est): 36.2MM **Privately Held**
SIC: 5085 Power transmission equipment & apparatus; bearings; hose, belting & packing

(G-17772)
BIOMAT USA INC
3217 Dorr St Ste B (43607-2716)
PHONE 419 531-3332
Nate Ringenberg, *Manager*
EMP: 38
SALES (corp-wide): 548.5MM **Privately Held**
SIC: 8322 Individual & family services
HQ: Biomat Usa, Inc.
2410 Lillyvale Ave
Los Angeles CA 90032
323 225-2221

(G-17773)
BIONIX SAFETY TECHNOLOGIES (HQ)
Also Called: National Safety Tech LLC
5154 Enterprise Blvd (43612-3807)
PHONE 419 727-0552
Andrew Milligan, *President*
John J Skreenock, *General Mgr*
Dr James Huttner, *Vice Pres*
James Vehslage, *Controller*
Paul Czerniakowski, *Sales Mgr*
EMP: 41
SALES (est): 3MM
SALES (corp-wide): 12.3MM **Privately Held**
WEB: www.nst-usa.com
SIC: 3825 3826 5084 3829 Test equipment for electronic & electric measurement; analytical instruments; gas testing apparatus; industrial machinery & equipment; measuring & controlling devices
PA: Bionix Development Corporation
315 Matzinger Rd
Toledo OH 43612
419 727-8421

(G-17774)
BOHL CRANE INC (PA)
534 W Laskey Rd (43612-3207)
PHONE 419 476-7525
Douglas E Bohl, *President*
Steven C Bohl, *Vice Pres*
Jonathon Balduf, *Project Mgr*
Sean Crayne, *Foreman/Supr*
Josh Champion, *Engineer*
EMP: 75
SQ FT: 16,400
SALES: 16.1MM **Privately Held**
WEB: www.bohlcrane.com
SIC: 5084 Materials handling machinery

(G-17775)
BOHL EQUIPMENT COMPANY (PA)
534 W Laskey Rd (43612-3299)
PHONE 419 476-7525
Fax: 419 476-0558
Robert D Bohl, *President*
Steven Bohl, *Vice Pres*
Dave Klopping, *Project Mgr*
Ron Demars, *Parts Mgr*
Douglas E Bohl, *Treasurer*
▲ **EMP:** 75
SQ FT: 11,300
SALES: 22.4MM **Privately Held**
WEB: www.bohlco.com
SIC: 5084 Materials handling machinery

(G-17776)
BOLLIN & SONS INC
Also Called: Bollin Label Systems
6001 Brent Dr (43611-1090)
PHONE 419 093-0573
Fax: 419 697-1682
Mark D Bollin, *President*
Chris Younkman, *Vice Pres*
Kathleen Schneider, *Accounts Mgr*
EMP: 40
SQ FT: 21,000
SALES (est): 15.1MM **Privately Held**
WEB: www.bollin.com
SIC: 2672 5084 7389 2851 Coated & laminated paper; adhesive papers, labels or tapes: from purchased material; labels (unprinted), gummed: made from purchased materials; packaging machinery & equipment; design services; paints & allied products; commercial printing; packaging paper & plastics film, coated & laminated

(G-17777)
BOLT EXPRESS LLC (PA)
Also Called: Strike Logistics
7255 Crossleigh Ct # 108 (43617-1556)
P.O. Box 759 (43697-0759)
PHONE 419 729-6698
Guy Sanderson, *CEO*
Chuck King, *COO*
Stephanie Doak, *Project Mgr*
Michael Cloncs, *Opers Mgr*
Debby Hamernik, *Opers Mgr*
EMP: 234
SQ FT: 5,000
SALES: 80MM **Privately Held**
WEB: www.bolt-express.com
SIC: 4731 Transportation agents & brokers

(G-17778)
BOSTWICK-BRAUN COMPANY (PA)
7349 Crossleigh Ct (43617-3108)
PHONE 419 259-3600
Fax: 419 259-3959
Chris Beach, *Principal*
George Thiel, *Vice Pres*
Paul Rang, *Buyer*
Matt Skrzynieckijj, *Buyer*
Mike Dastoli, *CFO*
▲ **EMP:** 55
SQ FT: 23,000
SALES (est): 161.1MM **Privately Held**
SIC: 5072 5084 5063 5083 Builders' hardware; industrial machinery & equipment; electrical apparatus & equipment; lawn & garden machinery & equipment; home furnishings

(G-17779)
BOWSER-MORNER INC
Also Called: Bowser Morner and Associates
1419 Miami St (43605-3314)
P.O. Box 838 (43697-0838)
PHONE 419 691-4800
Fax: 419 691-4805
Elon Bugyi, *Office Mgr*
Dick Hoppenjans, *Manager*
EMP: 50
SALES (corp-wide): 21.1MM **Privately Held**
WEB: www.bowser-morner.com
SIC: 8734 Testing laboratories; metallurgical testing laboratory; soil analysis; water testing laboratory
PA: Bowser-Morner, Inc.
4518 Taylorsville Rd
Dayton OH 45424
937 236-8805

(G-17780)
BOYS & GIRLS CLUB OF TOLEDO (PA)
Also Called: Boys Club Camp Association
2250 N Detroit Ave (43606-4690)
PHONE 419 241-4258
Fax: 419 241-1828
Chris Prince, *Manager*
Dave Wehrmeister, *Exec Dir*
Tonya Ford, *Director*
John Benzing, *Officer*
EMP: 32 **EST:** 1892
SQ FT: 35,000
SALES: 129.7K **Privately Held**
WEB: www.bgctoledo.org
SIC: 8641 Boy Scout organization

(G-17781)
BRAND ENERGY & INFRASTRUCTURE
Also Called: Empire Refractory Services
2961 South Ave (43609-1327)
PHONE 419 324-1305
David Varanese, *Branch Mgr*
EMP: 30
SALES (corp-wide): 8.5B **Privately Held**
SIC: 5085 Industrial supplies
HQ: Brand Industrial Services, Inc.
1325 Cobb Intl Dr Nw A1
Kennesaw GA 30152
678 285-1400

(G-17782)
BRENT INDUSTRIES INC
2922 South Ave (43609-1328)
PHONE 419 382-8693
Fax: 419 382-4747
Royse Willie, *Branch Mgr*
EMP: 30
SQ FT: 42,000
SALES (corp-wide): 9.5MM **Privately Held**
WEB: www.brentind.com
SIC: 7218 Safety glove supply
PA: Brent Industries, Inc.
10501 Highway 5
Brent AL 35034
205 926-4801

(G-17783)
BROADBAND EXPRESS LLC
1915 Nebraska Ave (43607-3800)
PHONE 419 536-9127
Mike Common, *District Mgr*
EMP: 52
SALES (corp-wide): 3B **Publicly Held**
WEB: www.broadbandexpress.net
SIC: 1731 1623 Cable television installation; communication line & transmission tower construction
HQ: Broadband Express, Llc
374 Westdale Ave Ste B
Westerville OH 43082
614 823-6464

(G-17784)
BROOKESIDE AMBULANCE SERVICES
Also Called: Rumpf Ambulance
640 Phillips Ave (43612-1370)
PHONE 419 476-7442
Fax: 419 476-9936
Donald Kish, *President*
Deborah Kish, *Admin Sec*
EMP: 38
SQ FT: 3,800
SALES: 1.4MM **Privately Held**
WEB: www.rumpfambulance.com
SIC: 4119 Ambulance service

(G-17785)
BROWN MOTOR SALES CO (PA)
Also Called: Brown Motors
5625 W Central Ave (43615-1505)
PHONE 419 531-0151
Fax: 419 536-1318
Rob Brown Jr, *President*
Robert W Brown Jr, *Exec VP*
Jane Singler, *Human Resources*
EMP: 39
SQ FT: 46,000
SALES (est): 37.8MM **Privately Held**
WEB: www.brownpontiac.com
SIC: 7538 7532 7515 5531 General automotive repair shops; top & body repair & paint shops; passenger car leasing; automotive & home supply stores; used car dealers

(G-17786)
BRUCE KLINGER
Also Called: Northwestern Mutual Inv Svcs
3950 Sunforest Ct Ste 200 (43623-4522)
PHONE 419 473-2270
Fax: 419 471-0274
Bruce Klinger, *Owner*
Nathan Danziger, *Agent*
Wayne Crowther, *Advisor*
Douglas Steinhauser, *Advisor*
Thomas Tillander, *Advisor*
EMP: 40
SALES (est): 9.4MM **Privately Held**
SIC: 6411 Insurance agents

(G-17787)
BUCKEYE CABLE SYSTEMS INC
4212 South Ave (43615-6234)
PHONE 419 724-2539
Ron Durham, *President*
EMP: 30
SALES (est): 1.5MM **Privately Held**
SIC: 1799 1731 Cable splicing service; electrical work

(G-17788)
BURBANK INC
Also Called: Seagate Roofg & Waterproofing
623 Burbank Dr (43607-3234)
PHONE 419 698-3434
Fax: 419 536-2757
Thomas K Elder, *President*
EMP: 40
SQ FT: 10,000

Toledo - Lucas County (G-17789)

SALES (est): 5.1MM **Privately Held**
WEB: www.seagateroofing.com
SIC: 1761 1799 1751 Roofing contractor; siding contractor; waterproofing; window & door (prefabricated) installation

(G-17789)
C & B BUCK BROS ASP MAINT LLC
2742 Victory Ave (43607-3272)
P.O. Box 735, Holland (43528-0735)
PHONE.................................419 536-7325
Fax: 419 536-5116
Gwen Gregory, *Office Mgr*
Ched Buck,
Brad Buck,
EMP: 25
SQ FT: 2,560
SALES (est): 1.1MM **Privately Held**
SIC: 0782 1629 4959 5032 Landscape contractors; tennis court construction; snowplowing; building stone

(G-17790)
CAPITAL TIRE INC (PA)
Also Called: Wholesale Tire Division
1001 Cherry St (43608-2995)
PHONE.................................419 241-5111
Fax: 419 241-7902
Thomas B Geiger, *Ch of Bd*
Thomas B Geiger Jr, *President*
Brian Haas, *Senior VP*
Carl J EBY, *Vice Pres*
Robert J Scheick, *Vice Pres*
▲ **EMP:** 40 **EST:** 1920
SQ FT: 100,000
SALES (est): 95.9MM **Privately Held**
WEB: www.capitaltire.com
SIC: 5014 Automobile tires & tubes; truck tires & tubes

(G-17791)
CAPITAL TIRE INC
Also Called: Wholesale Tire Division
2220 S Reynolds Rd (43614-1413)
PHONE.................................419 865-7151
EMP: 32
SALES (corp-wide): 95.9MM **Privately Held**
SIC: 5014 Automobile tires & tubes
PA: Capital Tire, Inc.
   1001 Cherry St
   Toledo OH 43608
   419 241-5111

(G-17792)
CARLISLE FLUID TECH INC
Also Called: Devilbiss Auto Refinishing
320 Phillips Ave (43612-1467)
PHONE.................................419 825-5186
Hans Horstik, *Branch Mgr*
EMP: 25
SALES (corp-wide): 4B **Publicly Held**
SIC: 5198 Paints, varnishes & supplies
HQ: Carlisle Fluid Technologies, Inc.
   16430 N Scottsdale Rd
   Scottsdale AZ 85254
   480 781-5250

(G-17793)
CAROL BURTON MANAGEMENT LLC
Also Called: Econo Lodge
1800 Miami St (43605-3318)
PHONE.................................419 666-5120
Fax: 419 666-4298
Laurel Dray, *Opers Mgr*
Denny Jirjis, *Manager*
T J Zebary, *Manager*
EMP: 35
SALES (corp-wide): 7.6MM **Privately Held**
SIC: 7011 Hotels
PA: Burton Carol Management
   4832 Richmond Rd Ste 200
   Cleveland OH 44128
   216 464-5130

(G-17794)
CASSENS TRANSPORT COMPANY
633 Matzinger Rd (43612-2630)
PHONE.................................419 727-0520
Fax: 419 727-3269
Greg Foster, *Site Mgr*
EMP: 130
SQ FT: 28,432
SALES (corp-wide): 219.4MM **Privately Held**
SIC: 4213 Automobiles, transport & delivery
HQ: Cassens Transport Company
   145 N Kansas St
   Edwardsville IL 62025
   618 656-3006

(G-17795)
CELLCO PARTNERSHIP
Also Called: Verizon Wireless
1260 S Reynolds Rd (43615-6962)
PHONE.................................419 381-1726
Fax: 419 381-1935
EMP: 74
SALES (corp-wide): 126B **Publicly Held**
SIC: 4812 Cellular telephone services
HQ: Cellco Partnership
   1 Verizon Way
   Basking Ridge NJ 07920

(G-17796)
CELLCO PARTNERSHIP
Also Called: Verizon
6710 W Central Ave Ste 20 (43617-1149)
PHONE.................................419 843-2995
Fax: 419 841-3687
Dave Johnson, *Manager*
EMP: 35
SALES (corp-wide): 126B **Publicly Held**
SIC: 4812 5999 Cellular telephone services; telephone & communication equipment
HQ: Cellco Partnership
   1 Verizon Way
   Basking Ridge NJ 07920

(G-17797)
CENTER FOR SPINAL DISORDERS
3000 Arlington Ave (43614-2595)
PHONE.................................419 383-4878
Beth Fields, *Principal*
Toni Welter, *Administration*
EMP: 35
SALES (est): 1.5MM **Privately Held**
WEB: www.centerforspinaldisorders.com
SIC: 8062 General medical & surgical hospitals

(G-17798)
CENTRAL COCA-COLA BTLG CO INC
3970 Catawba St (43612-1404)
PHONE.................................419 476-6622
Paul Kenny, *Manager*
EMP: 110
SALES (corp-wide): 35.4B **Publicly Held**
WEB: www.colasic.net
SIC: 2086 2087 5149 Carbonated beverages, nonalcoholic: bottled & canned; soft drinks: packaged in cans, bottles, etc.; fruit drinks (less than 100% juice): packaged in cans, etc.; syrups, drink; concentrates, drink; groceries & related products
HQ: Central Coca-Cola Bottling Company, Inc.
   555 Taxter Rd Ste 550
   Elmsford NY 10523
   914 789-1100

(G-17799)
CENTRAL TRAVEL & TICKET INC (PA)
Also Called: Central 'travel
4540 Heatherdowns Blvd # 2 (43614-3155)
PHONE.................................419 897-2070
Janie Miller, *CEO*
Richard Westmeyer, *President*
Jani Miller, *Principal*
John Miller, *Treasurer*
Mary Gillingham, *Consultant*
EMP: 25
SQ FT: 4,700
SALES (est): 7.8MM **Privately Held**
WEB: www.centraltravel.com
SIC: 4724 Tourist agency arranging transport, lodging & car rental

(G-17800)
CENTURY EQUIPMENT INC (PA)
5959 Angola Rd (43615-6332)
P.O. Box 352889 (43635-2889)
PHONE.................................419 865-7400
Fax: 419 865-8215
Robert E O'Brien, *Ch of Bd*
Martin O'Brien, *President*
Randy Rausch, *Store Mgr*
Rhonda Boggs, *Opers Staff*
Rick Puffenberger, *CFO*
EMP: 35 **EST:** 1950
SQ FT: 42,000
SALES (est): 41.7MM **Privately Held**
WEB: www.centuryequip.com
SIC: 5083 5088 Mowers, power; lawn machinery & equipment; garden machinery & equipment; irrigation equipment; golf carts

(G-17801)
CHAMBERS LEASING SYSTEMS CORP (PA)
3100 N Summit St (43611-3250)
P.O. Box 5337 (43611-0337)
PHONE.................................419 726-9747
Fax: 419 726-8986
James Chambers, *President*
H L Edman III, *Vice Pres*
Edman Lee, *Vice Pres*
EMP: 34
SQ FT: 6,200
SALES: 9MM **Privately Held**
SIC: 4212 Local trucking, without storage

(G-17802)
CHARIOTT FOODS INC
6163 Valley Park Dr (43623-2555)
PHONE.................................419 243-1101
Fax: 419 243-4425
Michael Okdie, *President*
Shirley Okdie, *Technology*
EMP: 34
SQ FT: 40,000
SALES (est): 8MM **Privately Held**
SIC: 5148 Fruits, fresh; vegetables, fresh

(G-17803)
CHELMSFORD APARTMENTS LTD
Also Called: Glendale, The
5020 Ryan Rd (43614-2065)
PHONE.................................419 389-0800
Fax: 419 389-0819
Dr Thomas Sollas, *Managing Prtnr*
Pete Olina, *Maintenance Dir*
Ellen Matteson, *Facilities Dir*
Jodi Kimball, *Director*
Keith Stroder, *Nursing Dir*
EMP: 25
SQ FT: 33,000
SALES (est): 2.2MM **Privately Held**
WEB: www.chelmsfordapartments.com
SIC: 6513 8052 Apartment building operators; intermediate care facilities

(G-17804)
CHERRY ST MISSION MINISTRIES (PA)
105 17th St (43604-6785)
PHONE.................................419 242-5141
Fax: 419 321-1831
Cuauhtemoc Valdiviez, *CEO*
Dan Rogers, *President*
Linda Cunning, *Vice Pres*
Max Lambdin, *Vice Pres*
Jerry Siler, *Maintenance Dir*
EMP: 43 **EST:** 1947
SQ FT: 120,000
SALES (est): 4.3MM **Privately Held**
WEB: www.cherrystreetmission.org
SIC: 8361 Rehabilitation center, residential: health care incidental

(G-17805)
CHRISTEN & SONS COMPANY (PA)
Also Called: Christen Detroit
714 George St (43608-2914)
P.O. Box 547 (43697-0547)
PHONE.................................419 243-4161
Frederick R Christen, *President*
Marlene Christen, *Corp Secy*
Bill Kaiser, *CFO*
EMP: 50
SQ FT: 60,000
SALES (est): 7.6MM **Privately Held**
SIC: 1761 Roofing, siding & sheet metal work

(G-17806)
CITIGROUP GLOBAL MARKETS INC
Also Called: Smith Barney
7124 W Central Ave (43617-1117)
PHONE.................................419 842-5383
Fax: 419 842-5370
Jeffrey Botruba, *Manager*
EMP: 50
SALES (corp-wide): 71.4B **Publicly Held**
WEB: www.salomonsmithbarney.com
SIC: 6211 Security brokers & dealers
HQ: Citigroup Global Markets Inc.
   388 Greenwich St Fl 18
   New York NY 10013
   212 816-6000

(G-17807)
CITY OF TOLEDO
Also Called: Utilities Department
420 Madison Ave Ste 100 (43604-1219)
PHONE.................................419 245-1800
Fax: 419 245-1853
Robert C Stevenson, *Principal*
Scott Sibley, *Administration*
EMP: 90 **Privately Held**
WEB: www.ci.toledo.oh.us
SIC: 4941 9111 4952 4924 Water supply; mayors' offices; sewerage systems; natural gas distribution; electric services
PA: City Of Toledo
   1 Government Ctr Ste 2050
   Toledo OH 43604
   419 245-1050

(G-17808)
CITY OF TOLEDO
Also Called: Municipal Government
1 Government Ctr Ste 2200 (43604-2295)
PHONE.................................419 245-1001
Fax: 419 245-1370
Sullivan Nicholls, *General Mgr*
Clinton Wallace, *General Mgr*
Mike Bell, *Mayor*
Steve Pecsenye, *Project Mgr*
Thomas Crothers, *CFO*
EMP: 2800 **Privately Held**
WEB: www.ci.toledo.oh.us
SIC: 8611 9111 Business associations; mayors' offices
PA: City Of Toledo
   1 Government Ctr Ste 2050
   Toledo OH 43604
   419 245-1050

(G-17809)
CITY OF TOLEDO
Also Called: Toledo City Parks
2201 Ottawa Dr (43606-4338)
PHONE.................................419 936-2875
Fax: 419 936-2899
Tom Crothers, *Branch Mgr*
Lisa Ward, *Commissioner*
Chelsey Labadie, *Director*
EMP: 30 **Privately Held**
WEB: www.ci.toledo.oh.us
SIC: 8999 9221 Natural resource preservation service; police protection
PA: City Of Toledo
   1 Government Ctr Ste 2050
   Toledo OH 43604
   419 245-1050

(G-17810)
CITY OF TOLEDO
Also Called: Sewer & Drainage Services
4032 Creekside Ave (43612-1478)
PHONE.................................419 936-2924
Fax: 419 936-2925
Adam Zolciak, *Senior Engr*
Kelly O'Brien, *Manager*
EMP: 129
SQ FT: 102,840 **Privately Held**
WEB: www.ci.toledo.oh.us
SIC: 4952 9111 4959 Sewerage systems; mayors' offices; sanitary services
PA: City Of Toledo
   1 Government Ctr Ste 2050
   Toledo OH 43604
   419 245-1050

GEOGRAPHIC SECTION

Toledo - Lucas County (G-17834)

(G-17811)
CITY OF TOLEDO
Also Called: Dept of Neighborhoods
1 Government Ctr Ste 1800 (43604-2275)
PHONE.....................................419 245-1400
Fax: 419 245-1413
Jerry German, *COO*
Tom Carouthers, *Branch Mgr*
EMP: 70 **Privately Held**
WEB: www.ci.toledo.oh.us
SIC: 9531 8611 Housing programs, planning & development: government; business associations
PA: City Of Toledo
1 Government Ctr Ste 2050
Toledo OH 43604
419 245-1050

(G-17812)
CITY OF TOLEDO
Also Called: Fleet Operations
555 N Expressway Dr (43608-1512)
PHONE.....................................419 936-2507
Fax: 419 245-1019
Ken Naeidert, *Manager*
Sherman R Moshe, *Administration*
EMP: 80 **Privately Held**
WEB: www.ci.toledo.oh.us
SIC: 7538 General truck repair
PA: City Of Toledo
1 Government Ctr Ste 2050
Toledo OH 43604
419 245-1050

(G-17813)
CITY OF TOLEDO
600 Jefferson Ave Ste 300 (43604-1012)
PHONE.....................................419 936-2275
Mike Elling, *Engineer*
Warian E Henry, *Commissioner*
EMP: 60 **Privately Held**
WEB: www.ci.toledo.oh.us
SIC: 8711 Engineering services
PA: City Of Toledo
1 Government Ctr Ste 2050
Toledo OH 43604
419 245-1050

(G-17814)
CLARK SCHAEFER HACKETT & CO
3166 N Republic Blvd (43615-1507)
PHONE.....................................419 243-0218
Clayton Holt, *Principal*
John R Moster, *Principal*
Neil O'Connor, *CPA*
David L Sanders, *CPA*
Brenda Collins, *Mktg Dir*
EMP: 100
SALES (corp-wide): 40.4MM **Privately Held**
WEB: www.cshco.com
SIC: 8721 Certified public accountant
PA: Clark, Schaefer, Hackett & Co.
1 E 4th St Ste 1200
Cincinnati OH 45202
513 241-3111

(G-17815)
CLEAN CARE INC
511 Phillips Ave (43612-1328)
PHONE.....................................419 725-2100
Fax: 419 725-2045
Jon Steingass, *President*
Joel Groober, *Vice Pres*
Tim Steingass, *Cust Mgr*
Bob Schoch, *Manager*
Joel Groover, *Director*
EMP: 150
SQ FT: 6,500
SALES (est): 3.9MM **Privately Held**
SIC: 7349 Janitorial service, contract basis

(G-17816)
CLEAR VISION ENGINEERING LLC
Also Called: Palmer Associates
4401 Jackman Rd (43612-1529)
PHONE.....................................419 478-7151
Fax: 419 478-3947
Tariq Alkhairy, *CEO*
Greg Barnhart, *Engineer*
Lorie Watson, *Office Mgr*
Gayle Mosley, *Technology*
EMP: 30
SQ FT: 12,000
SALES: 5MM **Privately Held**
WEB: www.palmerassoc.com
SIC: 8711 8742 Consulting engineer; mechanical engineering; electrical or electronic engineering; designing: ship, boat, machine & product; automation & robotics consultant

(G-17817)
CLIFTONLARSONALLEN LLP
1 Seagate Ste 2650 (43604-1522)
PHONE.....................................419 244-3711
Kevin B Rohrs, *Tax Mgr*
Donna Dawson, *Branch Mgr*
Todd Deindoerfer, *Mng Member*
EMP: 25
SALES (corp-wide): 755.1MM **Privately Held**
WEB: www.cliftoncpa.com
SIC: 8721 Certified public accountant
PA: Cliftonlarsonallen Llp
220 S 6th St Ste 300
Minneapolis MN 55402
612 376-4500

(G-17818)
COACT ASSOCIATES LTD
2748 Centennial Rd (43617-1829)
PHONE.....................................866 646-4400
Mark Frasco, *President*
Jennifer Mietz, *Opers Staff*
EMP: 30
SQ FT: 10,000
SALES: 2.5MM **Privately Held**
SIC: 8748 Environmental consultant

(G-17819)
COLLABORATIVE INC
1 Seagate Park Level 118 (43604)
PHONE.....................................419 242-7405
Fax: 419 242-7400
Paul Hollenbeck, *Chairman*
Dan J Tabor, *Corp Secy*
Michael Dinardo, *Vice Pres*
Rich Pace, *Project Mgr*
Dave Serra, *Engineer*
EMP: 50 EST: 1973
SQ FT: 12,000
SALES (est): 8.8MM **Privately Held**
WEB: www.thecollaborativeinc.com
SIC: 8712 0781 7389 5021 Architectural engineering; landscape architects; interior designer; office & public building furniture; office equipment

(G-17820)
COLUMBIA GAS OF OHIO INC
2901 E Manhattan Blvd (43611-1713)
PHONE.....................................419 539-6046
Jack Klein, *Branch Mgr*
EMP: 100
SQ FT: 80,340
SALES (corp-wide): 4.8B **Publicly Held**
WEB: www.meterrepairshop.com
SIC: 4932 Gas & other services combined
HQ: Columbia Gas Of Ohio, Inc.
290 W Nationwide Blvd # 114
Columbus OH 43215
614 460-6000

(G-17821)
COMMERCE PAPER COMPANY
302 S Byrne Rd Bldg 200 (43615-6208)
P.O. Box 1747 (43603-1747)
PHONE.....................................419 241-9101
Fax: 419 241-3906
Craig D Roberts, *President*
Jeffrey M Roberts, *Vice Pres*
Chas L Smith Et Al, *Incorporator*
George E Kirk, *Incorporator*
Morgan Levi, *Incorporator*
EMP: 45
SQ FT: 100,000
SALES (est): 26.9MM **Privately Held**
WEB: www.commercepaper.com
SIC: 5111 Printing paper

(G-17822)
COMMUNI CARE INC
Also Called: Advanced Health Care Center
955 Garden Lake Pkwy (43614-2777)
PHONE.....................................419 382-2200
Fax: 419 381-0188
Linda Hudson, *Purch Mgr*
Ramzieh Shousher, *Exec Dir*
EMP: 50
SALES (est): 72.1K **Privately Held**
SIC: 8051 Convalescent home with continuous nursing care

(G-17823)
COMMUNICA INC (PA)
31 N Erie St (43604-6942)
PHONE.....................................419 244-7766
Fax: 419 244-7765
Jeff Kimble, *CEO*
Debra Monagan, *President*
John Edwards, *Principal*
Julie Pompa, *Vice Pres*
Chris Perry, *Buyer*
EMP: 26
SQ FT: 8,500
SALES (est): 6.5MM **Privately Held**
WEB: www.communica-usa.com
SIC: 8742 Marketing consulting services

(G-17824)
COMMUNITY ISP INC
3035 Moffat Rd (43615-1836)
PHONE.....................................419 867-6060
Fax: 419 867-6913
Jeffrey Klingshirn, *CEO*
Dustin Wade, *President*
Kimberly Grear, *Controller*
EMP: 35
SQ FT: 42,000
SALES (est): 6.2MM **Privately Held**
WEB: www.cisp.com
SIC: 4813 7375 ; information retrieval services

(G-17825)
COMPASS CORP FOR RECOVERY SVCS
Also Called: Sasi
2005 Ashland Ave (43620-1163)
PHONE.....................................419 241-8827
Robert Stokes, *President*
Ross Chaban, *Vice Pres*
Jim Schultz, *Vice Pres*
Dave Rainsberger, *Manager*
EMP: 100
SALES: 3.7MM **Privately Held**
SIC: 8069 Drug addiction rehabilitation hospital

(G-17826)
COMPREHENSIVE ADDICTION SVC SY
Also Called: Compass
2005 Ashland Ave (43620-1703)
PHONE.....................................419 241-8827
Fax: 419 321-6834
Bill Sanford, *Sr Corp Ofcr*
Danny Witcher, *Facilities Mgr*
Jim Coressel, *Opers Staff*
Richard Faist, *Treasurer*
Vikkijean Mixon, *Personnel Exec*
EMP: 63
SQ FT: 68,000
SALES (est): 2.7MM **Privately Held**
WEB: www.ccrscompass.org
SIC: 8361 8093 Rehabilitation center, residential: health care incidental; specialty outpatient clinics

(G-17827)
COMPRHNSIVE CARE ORTHPDICS INC
4126 N Hlland Sylvania Rd (43623)
PHONE.....................................419 473-9500
Dr Stacey Bowen, *President*
EMP: 25
SALES (est): 1.6MM **Privately Held**
SIC: 8011 Orthopedic physician

(G-17828)
CONCEPT REHAB INC (PA)
7150 Granite Cir Ste 200 (43617-3114)
PHONE.....................................419 843-6002
Joan E Bayer, *CEO*
Kim Saylor, *President*
Martha Shaker, *President*
Marianne Hassen, *Senior VP*
Phil Niklowicz, *Opers Staff*
EMP: 71
SQ FT: 3,000
SALES (est): 29.5MM **Privately Held**
WEB: www.conceptrehab.com
SIC: 8093 Rehabilitation center, outpatient treatment

(G-17829)
CONCORD CARE CENTER OF TOLEDO
Also Called: BRIARFIELD AT GLANZMAN ROAD
3121 Glanzman Rd (43614-3802)
PHONE.....................................419 385-6616
Fax: 419 389-5101
Debra A Ifft, *CEO*
Cassandra Mosley, *Chf Purch Ofc*
Randy Climo, *Director*
Fran Johnson, *Nursing Dir*
Maria Laubenthal, *Food Svc Dir*
EMP: 90
SALES (est): 4.4MM **Privately Held**
SIC: 8059 Nursing home, except skilled & intermediate care facility

(G-17830)
CONSULTANTS LABORATORY MEDICI
3170 W Central Ave (43606-2945)
PHONE.....................................419 535-9629
F Michael Walsh, *Principal*
EMP: 44
SALES (est): 210.8K **Privately Held**
SIC: 8071 Pathological laboratory
HQ: Aurora Diagnostics, Llc
11025 Rca Center Dr # 300
Palm Beach Gardens FL 33410

(G-17831)
CONTAINER GRAPHICS CORP
305 Ryder Rd (43607-3105)
PHONE.....................................419 531-5133
Fax: 419 534-6174
Bill Beaker, *Branch Mgr*
Roger Passuello, *Manager*
EMP: 100
SQ FT: 24,200
SALES (corp-wide): 3MM **Privately Held**
WEB: www.containergraphics.com
SIC: 7336 3545 3944 Graphic arts & related design; cutting tools for machine tools; dice & dice cups
PA: Container Graphics Corp.
114 Ednbrgh S Dr Ste 104
Cary NC 27511
919 481-4200

(G-17832)
COOPER-SMITH ADVERTISING LLC
3500 Granite Cir (43617-1172)
PHONE.....................................419 470-5900
James D Cooper, *CEO*
Brad Rieger, *COO*
Michele Hall, *Senior VP*
Michael Jacob, *Vice Pres*
Michelle Hall, *Buyer*
EMP: 40
SQ FT: 11,000
SALES (est): 9.8MM **Privately Held**
WEB: www.cooper-smith.com
SIC: 7311 Advertising consultant

(G-17833)
COUNTY OF LUCAS
Also Called: Child Support Enforcement Agcy
701 Adams St (43604-6623)
PHONE.....................................419 213-3000
Fax: 419 259-3033
Thomas Bartlett, *Sls & Mktg Exec*
Mary Carol Torsok, *Director*
EMP: 170 **Privately Held**
WEB: www.lucascountyoh.gov
SIC: 8322 9111 Individual & family services; county supervisors' & executives' offices
PA: County Of Lucas
1 Government Ctr Ste 600
Toledo OH 43604
419 213-4406

(G-17834)
COUNTY OF LUCAS
Also Called: Lucas County Prosecution
700 Adams St Ste 150 (43604-5661)
PHONE.....................................419 213-4700
Fax: 419 213-4595

Toledo - Lucas County (G-17835) — GEOGRAPHIC SECTION

Gene Atkins, *Branch Mgr*
EMP: 114 **Privately Held**
WEB: www.lucascountyoh.gov
SIC: 8111 9111 Specialized law offices, attorneys; county supervisors' & executives' offices
PA: County Of Lucas
1 Government Ctr Ste 600
Toledo OH 43604
419 213-4406

(G-17835)
COUNTY OF LUCAS
Also Called: Job and Family Services Dept
3210 Monroe St (43606-7738)
P.O. Box 10007 (43699-0007)
PHONE.................................419 213-8999
Issacc Palmer, *Director*
Michelle Niedermier, *Director*
EMP: 400 **Privately Held**
WEB: www.lucascountyoh.gov
SIC: 8322 9111 Individual & family services; county supervisors' & executives' offices
PA: County Of Lucas
1 Government Ctr Ste 600
Toledo OH 43604
419 213-4406

(G-17836)
COUNTY OF LUCAS
Also Called: Lucas County Regional Hlth Dst
635 N Erie St (43604-5317)
PHONE.................................419 213-4018
Fax: 419 213-4624
Linda Dipierro, *Purchasing*
David L Grossman, *Med Doctor*
David Grossman, *Med Doctor*
Ionel Welt, *Med Doctor*
Jason Gears, *Manager*
EMP: 120 **Privately Held**
WEB: www.lucascountyoh.gov
SIC: 8011 Health maintenance organization
PA: County Of Lucas
1 Government Ctr Ste 600
Toledo OH 43604
419 213-4406

(G-17837)
COUNTY OF LUCAS
Also Called: Board Lucas Cnty Commissioners
1 Government Ctr Ste 800 (43604-2259)
PHONE.................................419 213-4500
Fax: 419 213-4299
Celeste Hasselbach, *Manager*
Michael Beazley, *Administration*
EMP: 45 **Privately Held**
WEB: www.lucascountyoh.gov
SIC: 9121 8721 ; accounting, auditing & bookkeeping
PA: County Of Lucas
1 Government Ctr Ste 600
Toledo OH 43604
419 213-4406

(G-17838)
COUNTY OF LUCAS
1154 Larc Ln (43614-2768)
PHONE.................................419 385-6021
John Trunk, *Manager*
EMP: 51 **Privately Held**
SIC: 9411 8051 ; skilled nursing care facilities
PA: County Of Lucas
1 Government Ctr Ste 600
Toledo OH 43604
419 213-4406

(G-17839)
COUSINS WASTE CONTROL LLC (PA)
1701 E Matzinger Rd (43612-3841)
PHONE.................................419 726-1500
Fax: 419 729-8501
Brian Recatto, *Mng Member*
EMP: 64
SQ FT: 4,000
SALES (est): 3.7MM **Privately Held**
SIC: 4212 4959 Hazardous waste transport; oil spill cleanup

(G-17840)
COVENANT CARE OHIO INC
Also Called: Fairview Skilled Nursing & Reh
4420 South Ave (43615-6417)
PHONE.................................419 531-4201
Jim Framsted, *Manager*
EMP: 90 **Privately Held**
WEB: www.villagegeorgetown.com
SIC: 8051 Skilled nursing care facilities
HQ: Covenant Care Ohio, Inc.
27071 Aliso Creek Rd # 100
Aliso Viejo CA 92656
949 349-1200

(G-17841)
CROWNE PLAZA TOLEDO
444 N Summit St (43604-1514)
PHONE.................................419 241-1411
Andy Kim, *Owner*
Tony Vetter, *Principal*
EMP: 80
SALES: 5MM **Privately Held**
SIC: 7011 Hotels

(G-17842)
CUMULUS MEDIA INC
Also Called: Wxkr
3225 Arlington Ave (43614-2427)
PHONE.................................419 725-5700
Andy Stuart, *Manager*
EMP: 60
SALES (corp-wide): 1.1B **Publicly Held**
WEB: www.cumulusmedia.com
SIC: 4832 Radio broadcasting stations
PA: Cumulus Media Inc.
3280 Peachtree Rd Ne # 2300
Atlanta GA 30305
404 949-0700

(G-17843)
CUMULUS MEDIA INC
Also Called: K 100 Radio Station
3225 Arlington Ave (43614-2427)
PHONE.................................419 240-1000
Fax: 419 725-5814
John Dickie, *President*
EMP: 93
SALES (corp-wide): 1.1B **Publicly Held**
WEB: www.cumulusmedia.com
SIC: 4832 Radio broadcasting stations
PA: Cumulus Media Inc.
3280 Peachtree Rd Ne # 2300
Atlanta GA 30305
404 949-0700

(G-17844)
DAVID LEE GROSSMAN MD
Also Called: Alexis Medical Center
1000 Regency Ct Ste 102 (43623-3074)
PHONE.................................419 843-8150
Fax: 419 479-2579
David Lee Grossman-Md, *Principal*
Grossman David, *Manager*
Patty Madrowsky, *Manager*
Timothy Hacker, *Gnrl Med Prac*
EMP: 32
SALES (est): 1.2MM **Privately Held**
SIC: 8011 Internal medicine practitioners

(G-17845)
DAYTON HCRI PLACE DENVER
4500 Dorr St (43615-4040)
PHONE.................................419 247-2800
Mary Ellen Pisanelli, *Principal*
Kevin Kirn, *Vice Pres*
Mario Gonzalez, *Director*
Zachary Zmuda, *Advisor*
EMP: 27
SALES (est): 2.7MM **Privately Held**
SIC: 6512 Nonresidential building operators

(G-17846)
DAYTON-DIXIE MUFFLERS INC (PA)
Also Called: Midas Muffler
1101 Monroe St (43604-5811)
PHONE.................................419 243-7281
Fax: 419 243-1626
Calvin Katz, *President*
Arthur Katz, *Treasurer*
EMP: 25 EST: 1970
SALES (est): 1.9MM **Privately Held**
SIC: 7533 Muffler shop, sale or repair & installation

(G-17847)
DEALER SUPPLY AND EQP LTD
1549 Campbell St (43607-4321)
PHONE.................................419 724-8473
Thomas W Heintschel, *President*
EMP: 30
SALES (est): 666.3K **Privately Held**
SIC: 7549 Automotive maintenance services

(G-17848)
DECAHEALTH INC
7071 W Central Ave Ste C (43617-2700)
PHONE.................................866 908-3514
Michael S McGowan, *President*
William James, *President*
Chad Graham, *CFO*
Rashelle Sorosiak, *Supervisor*
Lisa Seel, *Business Dir*
EMP: 80
SALES: 4.8MM **Privately Held**
SIC: 8082 Home health care services

(G-17849)
DENNIS TOP SOIL & LANDSCAPING
Also Called: Gardenland
6340 Dorr St (43615-4310)
PHONE.................................419 865-5656
Fax: 419 865-2615
Robert T Dennis, *President*
EMP: 40 EST: 1960
SQ FT: 7,270
SALES (est): 2.2MM **Privately Held**
SIC: 0782 5261 5193 Landscape contractors; nursery stock, seeds & bulbs; garden supplies & tools; nursery stock

(G-17850)
DENVER WHOLESALE FLORISTS CO
Also Called: D W F
14 N Erie St (43604-6940)
PHONE.................................419 241-7241
John Smith, *Branch Mgr*
EMP: 25
SALES (corp-wide): 100.1MM **Privately Held**
WEB: www.dwfwholesale.com
SIC: 5193 Flowers, fresh; florists' supplies; plants, potted
PA: Denver Wholesale Florists Company
4800 Dahlia St Ste A
Denver CO 80216
303 399-0970

(G-17851)
DEVELPMNTAL DSBLTIES OHIO DEPT
Also Called: Northwest Ohio Dvlopmental Ctr
1101 S Detroit Ave (43614-2704)
PHONE.................................419 385-0231
Fax: 419 382-0719
Ruth Rittchier, *Persnl Dir*
Dan Housepian, *Manager*
Janet Burtch, *Director*
Veronica Ross, *Officer*
EMP: 340 **Privately Held**
SIC: 9431 8361 Administration of public health programs; ; home for the mentally retarded
HQ: Ohio Department Of Developmental Disabilities
30 E Broad St Fl 13
Columbus OH 43215

(G-17852)
DHL SUPPLY CHAIN (USA)
1717 E Matzinger Rd (43612-3841)
PHONE.................................419 727-4318
Fax: 419 727-9605
Rory Hammerstrom, *General Mgr*
John Shadler, *Safety Mgr*
Tom Zahniser, *Engineer*
Don Bolles, *Branch Mgr*
EMP: 30
SALES (corp-wide): 71.2B **Privately Held**
WEB: www.exel-logistics.com
SIC: 4225 8741 4214 General warehousing; management services; local trucking with storage
HQ: Exel Inc.
570 Polaris Pkwy
Westerville OH 43082
614 865-8500

(G-17853)
DIMECH SERVICES INC
5505 Enterprise Blvd (43612-3858)
PHONE.................................419 727-0111
Fax: 419 727-0145
Janice Sheahan, *President*
James E Sheahan, *President*
Josh Quinlivan, *Vice Pres*
Ronald Sheahan, *Vice Pres*
Roger Sheahan, *Treasurer*
EMP: 30
SQ FT: 12,700
SALES: 11.7MM **Privately Held**
WEB: www.dimech.com
SIC: 1711 Mechanical contractor

(G-17854)
DIOCESE OF TOLEDO
Also Called: Catholic Club
1601 Jefferson Ave (43604-5724)
PHONE.................................419 243-7255
Fax: 419 243-6337
Steven Flagg, *Treasurer*
Mark Schissler, *Human Res Dir*
Frank Beier, *Info Tech Mgr*
Hope Bland, *Director*
EMP: 47
SALES (corp-wide): 89.6MM **Privately Held**
SIC: 8351 Child day care services
PA: Roman Catholic Diocese Of Toledo
1933 Spielbusch Ave
Toledo OH 43604
419 244-6711

(G-17855)
DMC TECHNOLOGY GROUP
Also Called: DMC Consulting
7657 Kings Pointe Rd (43617-1514)
PHONE.................................419 535-2900
Fax: 419 535-2901
J Patrick Sheehan, *President*
Jenny Becker, *Accounting Mgr*
Dick Coveney, *Personnel Exec*
Tim Taylor, *Sales Executive*
Darwin D Coveney, *Manager*
EMP: 30
SQ FT: 13,000
SALES (est): 7.8MM **Privately Held**
SIC: 7379 7371 5045 7378 Computer related consulting services; custom computer programming services; computers, peripherals & software; computer maintenance & repair

(G-17856)
DRS RAVIN BIRNDORF RAVIN INC
3000 Regency Ct Ste 100 (43623-3081)
PHONE.................................877 852-8463
James Ravin, *President*
Donna Hostetler, *Administration*
EMP: 40
SQ FT: 8,500
SALES (est): 3.2MM **Privately Held**
SIC: 8011 Ophthalmologist

(G-17857)
DSC LOGISTICS INC
1260 W Laskey Rd (43612-2909)
PHONE.................................847 390-6800
Fax: 419 269-3118
Ed Labo, *Facilities Mgr*
Jennifer Hatcher, *Human Resources*
Dean Whitacre, *Manager*
Martin Schemenauer, *Manager*
EMP: 59
SALES (corp-wide): 355MM **Privately Held**
SIC: 4225 General warehousing & storage
PA: Dsc Logistics, Inc.
1750 S Wolf Rd
Des Plaines IL 60018
847 390-6800

(G-17858)
DUMOUCHELLE ART GALLERIES
409 Jefferson Ave (43604-1005)
PHONE.................................419 255-7606
Lawrence Dumouchelle, *Principal*
EMP: 30
SALES (est): 225.2K **Privately Held**
SIC: 8412 Art gallery

GEOGRAPHIC SECTION

Toledo - Lucas County (G-17881)

(G-17859)
DUNBAR MECHANICAL INC (PA)
2806 N Reynolds Rd (43615-2034)
P.O. Box 352350 (43635-2350)
PHONE...................................734 856-6601
Fax: 419 537-8840
Stephen E Dunbar, *President*
Jean Elkins, *General Mgr*
Bill Bailey, *Superintendent*
Dale R Dunbar, *Principal*
Delbert R Dunbar, *Principal*
EMP: 65 EST: 1956
SQ FT: 115,000
SALES (est): 341.1MM **Privately Held**
WEB: www.dunbarmechanical.com
SIC: 1711 Mechanical contractor

(G-17860)
E N T TOLEDO INC
2865 N Reynolds Rd # 260 (43615-2070)
PHONE...................................419 578-7555
Peter Vander Meer, *President*
Mary Sullivan, *Supervisor*
EMP: 45 EST: 2001
SALES (est): 922.3K **Privately Held**
WEB: www.toledoent.com
SIC: 8011 Ears, nose & throat specialist: physician/surgeon

(G-17861)
EAST TOLEDO FAMILY CENTER (PA)
1020 Varland Ave (43605-3299)
PHONE...................................419 691-1429
Fax: 419 691-1884
Ruth Baker, *Finance*
Brenda Young, *Finance*
Staci Cook, *Supervisor*
Kim Partin, *Director*
Tracy Garufos, *Admin Asst*
EMP: 75
SQ FT: 23,755
SALES (est): 2.2MM **Privately Held**
SIC: 8322 Community center

(G-17862)
EASTMAN & SMITH LTD
1 Seagate Ste 2400 (43604-1576)
P.O. Box 10032 (43699-0032)
PHONE...................................419 241-6000
Fax: 419 247-1777
Laura Pinardo, *President*
Julie Wortketter, *President*
Mark C Abramson, *Partner*
Richard E Antonini, *Partner*
Kenneth C Baker, *Partner*
EMP: 150 EST: 1844
SQ FT: 48,000
SALES: 7.8K **Privately Held**
WEB: www.eastmansmith.com
SIC: 8111 General practice attorney, lawyer

(G-17863)
ELECTRO PRIME GROUP LLC (PA)
4510 Lint Ave Ste B (43612-2658)
PHONE...................................419 476-0100
Fax: 419 476-9161
Jim Vellequette, *Plant Mgr*
Paul Kamenca, *Production*
Don Lublin, *QC Mgr*
Chad Reinbolt, *CFO*
John Goldman, *Accounts Exec*
▲ EMP: 70
SQ FT: 20,100
SALES (est): 20MM **Privately Held**
WEB: www.electroprime.com
SIC: 3471 5169 Plating & polishing; anti-corrosion products

(G-17864)
ELLIS RICHARD CB REICHLE KLEIN
Also Called: CB Richard Ellis
1 Seagate Fl 26 (43604-1527)
PHONE...................................419 861-1100
Daniel M Klein, *President*
Harlan E Reichle, *Vice Pres*
EMP: 35
SQ FT: 6,000
SALES (est): 3.6MM **Privately Held**
SIC: 6531 Real estate agent, commercial

(G-17865)
EMERGENCY MEDICAL GROUP INC
5620 Southwyck Blvd 2 (43614-1501)
PHONE...................................419 866-6009
Nancy Condon, *President*
Jody Michalak, *Manager*
EMP: 50
SALES (est): 2.6MM **Privately Held**
WEB: www.emergencymedicalgroup.com
SIC: 8011 Offices & clinics of medical doctors

(G-17866)
EMPOWERED FOR EXCELLENCE
3222 W Central Ave (43606-2929)
PHONE...................................567 316-7253
Jonathan James, *CEO*
EMP: 25
SALES (est): 556.6K **Privately Held**
SIC: 8093 Mental health clinic, outpatient

(G-17867)
ENDEVIS LLC (PA)
7643 Kings Pointe Rd # 100 (43617-1514)
PHONE...................................419 482-4848
Mark Melfi, *Mng Member*
Melissa Shumay, *Business Dir*
Mick Fecko,
Ron Walters,
EMP: 25
SQ FT: 3,500
SALES: 12MM **Privately Held**
WEB: www.staffingmaster.com
SIC: 7361 Executive placement

(G-17868)
ENTERPRISE SYSTEMS SFTWR LLC
Also Called: Esd
4352 W Sylvania Ave Ste M (43623-3441)
PHONE...................................419 841-3179
Joseph M Torti, *President*
Bingfu Yue, *General Mgr*
Jospeh M Torti, *Mng Member*
Ashley Clifton, *Consultant*
Jean Dumas, *Consultant*
EMP: 76
SQ FT: 2,500
SALES (est): 8MM **Privately Held**
WEB: www.bootycallsystems.com
SIC: 7379 Computer related consulting services

(G-17869)
ERIE CONSTRUCTION MIDWEST INC (PA)
4271 Monroe St (43606-1968)
P.O. Box 2698 (43606-0698)
PHONE...................................419 472-4200
Patrick J Trompeter, *CEO*
Philip C Davis, *Principal*
Jeff Borucki, *Sales Mgr*
Kyle Masney, *Sales Mgr*
Tony Teresi, *Sales Mgr*
EMP: 45
SQ FT: 14,000
SALES (est): 40.4MM **Privately Held**
SIC: 1751 1761 Window & door (prefabricated) installation; siding contractor

(G-17870)
ERNST & YOUNG LLP
Also Called: Ey
1 Seagate Ste 2510 (43604-1591)
PHONE...................................419 244-8000
Fax: 419 244-8000
Thomas F Eagan, *Principal*
Randy M Kummer, *Principal*
Andrew Davis, *Marketing Staff*
Christine L Mabrey, *Manager*
Howard Altshuler, *Manager*
EMP: 150
SALES (corp-wide): 5.3B **Privately Held**
WEB: www.ey.com
SIC: 8721 Certified public accountant
PA: Ernst & Young Llp
5 Times Sq Fl Conlv1
New York NY 10036
212 773-3000

(G-17871)
ESTES EXPRESS LINES INC
Also Called: Estes Express Lines 92
5330 Angola Rd Ste B (43615-6379)
PHONE...................................419 531-1500
Fax: 419 531-8106
Bruce Roberts, *Manager*
EMP: 50
SALES (corp-wide): 2.4B **Privately Held**
WEB: www.estes-express.com
SIC: 4213 Less-than-truckload (LTL) transport
PA: Estes Express Lines, Inc.
3901 W Broad St
Richmond VA 23230
804 353-1900

(G-17872)
EXPRESSO CAR WASH SYSTEMS INC
5440 W Central Ave (43615-1502)
PHONE...................................419 536-7540
Scott Beck, *President*
EMP: 60
SALES (corp-wide): 2.5MM **Privately Held**
WEB: www.expressocarwash.com
SIC: 7542 Washing & polishing, automotive
PA: Expresso Car Wash Systems Inc
201 Illinois Ave
Maumee OH 43537
419 893-1406

(G-17873)
EXPRESSO CAR WASH SYSTEMS INC
Also Called: Expresso Car Wash 5
1750 S Reynolds Rd (43614-1404)
PHONE...................................419 866-7099
Jason Ikenburg, *Branch Mgr*
Kevin Martin, *Manager*
EMP: 35
SALES (corp-wide): 2.5MM **Privately Held**
WEB: www.expressocarwash.com
SIC: 7542 Carwash, automatic
PA: Expresso Car Wash Systems Inc
201 Illinois Ave
Maumee OH 43537
419 893-1406

(G-17874)
EXTREME DETAIL CLG CNSTR SVCS
1724 Barrows St (43613-4618)
P.O. Box 140743 (43614-0743)
PHONE...................................419 392-3243
Julie Lake, *Partner*
Melissa Leeper, *Partner*
EMP: 34
SALES: 950K **Privately Held**
SIC: 1799 7349 Construction site cleanup; janitorial service, contract basis

(G-17875)
EYE INST OF NORTHWESTERN OH IN
5555 Airport Hwy (43615-7380)
PHONE...................................419 865-3866
Fax: 419 865-3451
Carol R Kollarits MD, *President*
Frank Kollarits, *Vice Pres*
Rick Mlcek, *Treasurer*
EMP: 25
SQ FT: 9,000
SALES (est): 1MM **Privately Held**
SIC: 8011 Medical centers; ophthalmologist

(G-17876)
FAMILY & CHILD ABUSE (PA)
2460 Cherry St (43608-2667)
PHONE...................................419 244-3053
Fax: 419 244-1100
Christie Jenkins, *CEO*
Lori Kocol, *Office Mgr*
Darla McCarty, *Office Mgr*
Christie Jenkins, *Manager*
Joanne Carson, *Supervisor*
EMP: 30
SQ FT: 3,000
SALES: 1.3MM **Privately Held**
SIC: 8322 Child related social services

(G-17877)
FAMILY HEALTH PLAN INC
2200 Jefferson Ave Fl 6 (43604-7102)
PHONE...................................419 241-6501
Fax: 419 241-5441
Tom Beaty, *President*
Lauri Oakes, *Vice Pres*
Randy Hoffman, *CFO*
Mark Lanciano, *Human Resources*
Stan Golec, *Director*
EMP: 170
SQ FT: 20,000
SALES: 108MM
SALES (corp-wide): 4.2B **Privately Held**
WEB: www.fhpl.net
SIC: 6324 8011 Health maintenance organization (HMO), insurance only; offices & clinics of medical doctors
PA: Mercy Health
1701 Mercy Health Pl
Cincinnati OH 45237
513 639-2800

(G-17878)
FAMILY SERVICE OF NW OHIO (PA)
701 Jefferson Ave Ste 301 (43604-6957)
P.O. Box 1010 (43697-1010)
PHONE...................................419 321-6455
Tim Yenrick, *President*
Linda Condit, *VP Finance*
Augustine Abbott, *Supervisor*
Stuart Feldman, *Info Tech Mgr*
Judy Czarnecki, *Exec Dir*
EMP: 83
SQ FT: 12,000
SALES: 6.1MM **Privately Held**
SIC: 8322 8082 Social service center; home health care services

(G-17879)
FAMOUS ENTERPRISES INC
Also Called: Johnson Contrls Authorized Dlr
220 Matzinger Rd (43612-2625)
PHONE...................................419 478-0343
Fax: 419 478-6841
Therese Stambaugh, *Manager*
EMP: 30
SQ FT: 59,155 **Privately Held**
WEB: www.jfgood.com
SIC: 5211 5075 Lumber & other building materials; warm air heating & air conditioning
PA: Famous Enterprises, Inc.
2620 Ridgewood Rd Ste 200
Akron OH 44313

(G-17880)
FAURECIA EXHAUST SYSTEMS LLC (DH)
543 Matzinger Rd (43612-2638)
P.O. Box 64010 (43612-0010)
PHONE...................................419 727-5000
Fax: 419 727-5025
David Degraaf, *President*
Robert Parmann, *Vice Pres*
Kevin Lammers, *VP Finance*
Mike Dewitt, *Director*
Christophe Schmidt,
▲ EMP: 130
SQ FT: 40,000
SALES (est): 1.7B
SALES (corp-wide): 319.5MM **Privately Held**
WEB: www.franklin.faurecia.com
SIC: 3714 5013 Mufflers (exhaust), motor vehicle; motor vehicle supplies & new parts

(G-17881)
FCA US LLC
Also Called: Toledo Assembly Complex
4400 Chrysler Dr (43608-4000)
PHONE...................................419 727-2800
Fax: 419 727-2804
Robert Seabolt, *Principal*
EMP: 32
SALES (corp-wide): 117.3B **Privately Held**
SIC: 7538 General automotive repair shops
HQ: Fca Us Llc
1000 Chrysler Dr
Auburn Hills MI 48326

Toledo - Lucas County (G-17882)

(G-17882)
FCA US LLC
Also Called: Trucking Division
5925 Hagman Rd (43612-3919)
PHONE..................419 729-5959
Fred Prenal, *Branch Mgr*
EMP: 100
SALES (corp-wide): 117.3B **Privately Held**
SIC: 4731 Freight transportation arrangement
HQ: Fca Us Llc
1000 Chrysler Dr
Auburn Hills MI 48326

(G-17883)
FEDEX FREIGHT CORPORATION
5657 Enterprise Blvd (43612-3816)
PHONE..................419 729-1755
EMP: 50
SQ FT: 7,000
SALES (corp-wide): 47.4B **Publicly Held**
SIC: 4213 Trucking Operator-Nonlocal
HQ: Fedex Freight Corporation
1715 Aaron Brenner Dr
Memphis TN 38120
901 434-3100

(G-17884)
FEDEX GROUND PACKAGE SYS INC
650 S Reynolds Rd (43615-6345)
PHONE..................800 463-3339
Kevin Koken, *Manager*
EMP: 400
SALES (corp-wide): 60.3B **Publicly Held**
SIC: 4212 4215 Delivery service, vehicular; courier services, except by air
HQ: Fedex Ground Package System, Inc.
1000 Fed Ex Dr
Coraopolis PA 15108
412 269-1000

(G-17885)
FEED LUCAS COUNTY CHILDREN INC
Also Called: FLCC MEALS
1501 Monroe St Ste 27 (43604-5760)
P.O. Box 9363 (43697-9363)
PHONE..................419 260-1556
Pat Howard, *Opers Mgr*
Anne Hefner, *Office Admin*
Tony Siebeneck, *Director*
Robin Myers, *Food Svc Dir*
EMP: 52
SQ FT: 3,852
SALES: 973.8K **Privately Held**
WEB: www.feedlucaschildren.org
SIC: 8322 Children's aid society

(G-17886)
FIFTH THIRD BANK
606 Madison Ave Fl 8 (43604-1120)
PHONE..................419 259-7820
Fax: 419 259-7862
John Schinharl, *Senior VP*
Marilyn Monroe, *Assistant VP*
Lou Lajoe, *Vice Pres*
Bob McLair, *Sales/Mktg Mgr*
Sarah Berndt, *Invest Mgr*
EMP: 25
SQ FT: 750
SALES (corp-wide): 7.7B **Publicly Held**
WEB: www.53rd.com
SIC: 6022 State trust companies accepting deposits, commercial
HQ: The Fifth Third Bank
38 Fountain Square Plz
Cincinnati OH 45202
513 579-5203

(G-17887)
FIFTH THIRD BANK OF NW OHIO
1 Seagate Ste 2200 (43604-1525)
P.O. Box 1868 (43603-1868)
PHONE..................419 259-7820
Fax: 419 259-7169
Robert Laclair, *President*
Christopher Nance, *Controller*
Kelly Davidson, *Office Mgr*
EMP: 300
SALES (est): 127.5MM
SALES (corp-wide): 7.7B **Publicly Held**
WEB: www.53.com
SIC: 6021 National commercial banks

PA: Fifth Third Bancorp
38 Fountain Square Plz
Cincinnati OH 45202
800 972-3030

(G-17888)
FINANCE SYSTEM OF TOLEDO INC (PA)
2821 N Holland Sylvania R (43615-1871)
P.O. Box 351297 (43635-1297)
PHONE..................419 578-4300
Fax: 419 578-4330
Randall Parker, *President*
EMP: 25
SQ FT: 5,000
SALES (est): 2.2MM **Privately Held**
SIC: 7322 Collection agency, except real estate

(G-17889)
FINANCIAL DESIGN GROUP INC (PA)
3230 Central Park W # 100 (43617-1019)
PHONE..................419 843-4737
Fax: 419 843-2623
James Strasser, *President*
Robert Daney Jr, *Consultant*
Vincent Waln, *Agent*
Chris Benson, *Advisor*
Bill Cerynik, *Advisor*
EMP: 25 EST: 1994
SALES (est): 6.8MM **Privately Held**
WEB: www.fdgonline.com
SIC: 6411 8742 Insurance agents, brokers & service; management consulting services

(G-17890)
FINDLEY DAVIES INC (PA)
1 Seagate Ste 2050 (43604-1558)
PHONE..................419 255-1360
John M Weber, *President*
Kyle Pifher, *Vice Pres*
Robert J Rogers, *Vice Pres*
Marc Stockwell, *Vice Pres*
Lisa Kay, *Marketing Mgr*
EMP: 75
SQ FT: 15,000
SALES (est): 19.7MM **Privately Held**
WEB: www.findleydavies.com
SIC: 8742 Compensation & benefits planning consultant

(G-17891)
FIRST APOSTOLIC CHURCH
Also Called: Apostolic Christian Academy
5701 W Sylvania Ave (43623-3308)
PHONE..................419 885-4888
Fax: 419 885-3857
Brandon Buford, *Principal*
Gary Grzcinski, *Principal*
Ryan Jordan, *Principal*
Gary Trzcinski, *Principal*
J Mark Jordan, *Pastor*
EMP: 40
SQ FT: 47,957
SALES: 31.7K **Privately Held**
WEB: www.factoledo.com
SIC: 8661 8211 8351 Apostolic Church; private elementary & secondary schools; child day care services

(G-17892)
FIRST CHOICE MEDICAL STAFFING
5445 Sthwyck Blvd Ste 208 (43614)
PHONE..................419 861-2722
Christopher Sterben, *Branch Mgr*
EMP: 57
SALES (corp-wide): 4.6MM **Privately Held**
SIC: 7361 Nurses' registry
PA: First Choice Medical Staffing Of Ohio, Inc.
1457 W 117th St
Cleveland OH 44107
216 521-2222

(G-17893)
FIRST LOUISVILLE ARDEN LLC (DH)
333 N Summit St (43604-1531)
PHONE..................419 252-5500
Paul A Ormond, *CEO*
EMP: 40

SALES (est): 2.4MM
SALES (corp-wide): 3.6B **Publicly Held**
SIC: 8051 Skilled nursing care facilities
HQ: Manor Care Of America, Inc.
333 N Summit St Ste 103
Toledo OH 43604
419 252-5500

(G-17894)
FIRST STUDENT INC
419 N Westwood Ave (43607-3347)
PHONE..................419 382-9915
Inez Evans, *Manager*
EMP: 45
SALES (corp-wide): 7B **Privately Held**
WEB: www.leag.com
SIC: 4151 School buses
HQ: First Student, Inc.
600 Vine St Ste 1400
Cincinnati OH 45202

(G-17895)
FLEETPRIDE WEST INC
200 Indiana Ave (43604-8220)
PHONE..................419 243-3161
Joe Gears, *Branch Mgr*
EMP: 30
SALES (corp-wide): 1.2B **Privately Held**
SIC: 7539 Automotive repair shops
HQ: Fleetpride West, Inc.
600 E Las Colli Blvd Ste
Irving TX 75014
469 249-7500

(G-17896)
FLEX REALTY
Also Called: Flex Property Management
5763 Talmadge Rd Ste C2 (43623-1555)
PHONE..................419 841-6208
Jim Moody, *Partner*
EMP: 30
SALES (est): 2.9MM **Privately Held**
WEB: www.flexrealty.com
SIC: 6531 Real estate brokers & agents

(G-17897)
FLORALANDSCAPE INC
130 Elmdale Rd (43607-2914)
PHONE..................419 536-7640
Fax: 419 536-6270
Douglas J Bettinger, *CEO*
Craig Stambaugh, *Manager*
EMP: 65
SQ FT: 6,480
SALES (est): 2.9MM **Privately Held**
WEB: www.floralandscape.com
SIC: 0782 0781 Lawn care services; landscape planning services

(G-17898)
FLOYD P BUCHER & SON INC
5743 Larkhall Dr (43614-1136)
PHONE..................419 867-8792
Dan Bucher, *President*
Roger Bucher, *Corp Secy*
Verl Frazier, *Exec VP*
EMP: 50 EST: 1947
SQ FT: 10,000
SALES (est): 8.8MM **Privately Held**
WEB: www.floydpbucherandsoninc.com
SIC: 1541 1542 Industrial buildings, new construction; commercial & office building, new construction

(G-17899)
FRANCISCAN CARE CTR SYLVANIA
4111 N Hlland Sylvania Rd (43623)
PHONE..................419 882-2087
Shawn T Litton, *CEO*
Cathy Longacre, *Comptroller*
Deb Waldron, *Manager*
Allen Markowicz, *Director*
Teresa Martinez, *Nursing Dir*
EMP: 130
SQ FT: 25,712
SALES: 10.1MM **Privately Held**
WEB: www.fccsylvania.org
SIC: 8051 Skilled nursing care facilities
HQ: Sylvania Franciscan Health
1715 Indian Wood Cir # 200
Maumee OH 43537
419 882-8373

(G-17900)
FRED CHRISTEN & SONS COMPANY (PA)
714 George St (43608-2914)
P.O. Box 547 (43697-0547)
PHONE..................419 243-4161
Fax: 419 243-1292
Fredrick R Christen, *President*
Marlene P Christen, *Corp Secy*
Michael Schreiber, *Director*
EMP: 60 EST: 1929
SQ FT: 32,000
SALES (est): 21MM **Privately Held**
WEB: www.fredchristenandsons.com
SIC: 1761 Roofing contractor; sheet metalwork

(G-17901)
FULLER & HENRY LTD (PA)
1 Seagate Ste 1700 (43604-1504)
P.O. Box 2633 (43606-0633)
PHONE..................419 247-2500
Fax: 419 247-2665
Stephen J Stanford, *Partner*
David R Bainbridge, *Partner*
Michael E Born, *Partner*
Alan C Boyd, *Partner*
Martin D Carrigan, *Partner*
EMP: 50
SQ FT: 15,000
SALES (est): 5MM **Privately Held**
SIC: 8111 General practice attorney, lawyer

(G-17902)
FURNEY GROUP HOME
4656 Glendale Ave (43614-1965)
PHONE..................419 389-0152
Carlina Moore, *Director*
EMP: 35
SALES (est): 289.1K **Privately Held**
SIC: 8361 8052 Residential care; intermediate care facilities

(G-17903)
G G MARCK & ASSOCIATES INC (PA)
300 Phillips Ave (43612-1470)
PHONE..................419 478-0900
Fax: 419 478-6440
Gary Marck, *President*
Mike Whitescarver, *QC Mgr*
Christopher Miller, *CFO*
Sue Mitchel, *Controller*
Nick Arnold, *Natl Sales Mgr*
▲ **EMP:** 45
SQ FT: 300,000
SALES: 30MM **Privately Held**
WEB: www.marckassoc.com
SIC: 5023 Kitchenware

(G-17904)
G STEPHENS INC
104 N Summit St Ste 102 (43604-2306)
PHONE..................419 241-5188
Alexander Mavrides, *Branch Mgr*
EMP: 31 **Privately Held**
WEB: www.gstephensinc.com
SIC: 8742 1521 1542 Construction project management consultant; single-family housing construction; nonresidential construction
PA: G. Stephens, Inc.
133 N Summit St
Akron OH 44304

(G-17905)
GA BUSINESS PURCHASER LLC
Also Called: Guardian Alarm
1810 Jefferson Ave (43604-6729)
PHONE..................419 255-8400
Fax: 419 243-7258
Cris Zielinski, *Branch Mgr*
EMP: 60
SQ FT: 2,476
SALES (corp-wide): 55.3MM **Privately Held**
SIC: 1731 5063 7382 Fire detection & burglar alarm systems specialization; burglar alarm systems; security systems services
PA: Ga Business Purchaser Llc
20800 Southfield Rd
Southfield MI 48075
248 423-1000

GEOGRAPHIC SECTION

Toledo - Lucas County (G-17929)

(G-17906)
GALLON TAKACS BOISSONEAULT & S (PA)
3516 Granite Cir (43617-1172)
P.O. Box 352018 (43635-2018)
PHONE 419 843-2001
Jack E Gallon, *President*
Stephanie Keith, *President*
John Roca, *Publisher*
William E Takacs, *Vice Pres*
Jeffrey Julius, *Treasurer*
EMP: 100
SQ FT: 30,728
SALES (est): 15.7MM **Privately Held**
WEB: www.gallonlaw.com
SIC: 8111 General practice law office

(G-17907)
GARDA CL GREAT LAKES INC
Also Called: Metropolitan Armored Car
3635 Marine Rd (43609-1019)
PHONE 419 385-2411
Fax: 419 385-5144
Michael Odunn, *Manager*
EMP: 25
SQ FT: 500
SALES (corp-wide): 69.3K **Privately Held**
WEB: www.gocashlink.com
SIC: 7381 Armored car services
HQ: Garda Cl Technical Services, Inc.
    700 S Federal Hwy Ste 300
    Boca Raton FL 33432

(G-17908)
GARDEN II LEASING CO LLC
Also Called: Advanced Specialty Hosp Toledo
1015 Garden Lake Pkwy (43614-2779)
PHONE 419 381-0037
Fax: 419 381-3990
Robert Desotelle, *CEO*
Lauren Avigdor, *Human Res Dir*
Tine Hacker, *Human Res Mgr*
EMP: 100
SALES (est): 12.4MM
SALES (corp-wide): 103.9MM **Privately Held**
SIC: 8062 General medical & surgical hospitals
PA: Communicare Health Services, Inc.
    4700 Ashwood Dr Ste 200
    Blue Ash OH 45241
    513 530-1654

(G-17909)
GARDNER CEMENT CONTRACTORS
821 Warehouse Rd (43615-6472)
PHONE 419 389-0768
Fax: 419 382-8921
Robert W Gardner, *President*
Lynn A Gardner, *Corp Secy*
EMP: 75
SQ FT: 6,200
SALES (est): 6.5MM **Privately Held**
SIC: 1771 Concrete work

(G-17910)
GEDDIS PAVING & EXCAVATING
1019 Wamba Ave (43607-3256)
PHONE 419 536-8501
Fax: 419 536-0551
Robert J Geddis Jr, *President*
Steve Oliver, *Vice Pres*
Stella Ellerbrock, *Safety Dir*
Richard Crace, *Project Mgr*
Benjamin Geddis, *Treasurer*
EMP: 26 EST: 1949
SQ FT: 4,200
SALES (est): 4.4MM **Privately Held**
WEB: www.geddispaving.com
SIC: 1794 1771 Excavation work; blacktop (asphalt) work

(G-17911)
GEMINI PROPERTIES
Also Called: West Park Place
3501 Executive Pkwy Ofc (43606-1369)
PHONE 419 531-9211
Fax: 419 531-4103
Kristen Pickle, *Director*
EMP: 50
SALES (corp-wide): 6.2MM **Privately Held**
WEB: www.geminiproperties.com
SIC: 6513 Retirement hotel operation

PA: Gemini Properties
    1516 S Boston Ave Ste 301
    Tulsa OK 74119
    918 592-4400

(G-17912)
GEO GRADEL CO
3135 Front St (43605-1009)
P.O. Box 8337 (43605-0337)
PHONE 419 691-7123
Fax: 419 691-0877
John F Gradel, *President*
Frederick T Sander, *Vice Pres*
Alan Raven, *Treasurer*
Randall Hilkens, *Manager*
David J Pe, *Manager*
EMP: 65 EST: 1903
SQ FT: 12,200
SALES (est): 22.4MM **Privately Held**
SIC: 1794 Excavation & grading, building construction

(G-17913)
GEORGE P BALLAS BUICK GMC TRCK (PA)
Also Called: Budget Rent-A-Car
5715 W Central Ave (43615-1401)
P.O. Box 352470 (43635-2470)
PHONE 419 535-1000
Fax: 419 535-7731
George P Ballas, *President*
Robert Fowler, *Vice Pres*
Richard Farrar, *Admin Sec*
EMP: 58
SQ FT: 55,000
SALES (est): 13MM **Privately Held**
SIC: 5511 7514 7532 5521 Automobiles, new & used; rent-a-car service; top & body repair & paint shops; used car dealers; automobiles & other motor vehicles

(G-17914)
GIAMMARCO PROPERTIES LLC
5252 Monroe St (43623-3140)
PHONE 419 885-4844
Pasquale Giammarco, *President*
EMP: 30
SALES (est): 1.6MM **Privately Held**
SIC: 6531 Real estate agent, commercial

(G-17915)
GIANT INDUSTRIES INC
900 N Westwood Ave (43607-3261)
PHONE 419 531-4600
Fax: 419 531-6836
Raymond Simon, *CEO*
Edward Simon, *President*
Debbie Harrison, *Controller*
Rachel Wiles, *Marketing Staff*
Daniel Pietrowski, *Manager*
▲ EMP: 40
SQ FT: 83,000
SALES (est): 9.5MM **Privately Held**
WEB: www.giantpumps.com
SIC: 3581 3589 5084 3594 Automatic vending machines; car washing machinery; pumps & pumping equipment; fluid power pumps & motors; pumps & pumping equipment; sanitary paper products

(G-17916)
GIRL SCUTS WSTN OHIO TLEDO DIV (PA)
2244 Collingwood Blvd (43620-1147)
PHONE 419 243-8216
Fax: 419 245-5357
Patricia J Robb, *Manager*
Laura Boworman, *Director*
EMP: 38 EST: 1917
SQ FT: 22,000
SALES (est): 1.2MM **Privately Held**
WEB: www.mvgsc.org
SIC: 8641 Girl Scout organization

(G-17917)
GLOBE TRUCKING INC
5261 Stickney Ave (43612-3722)
PHONE 419 727-8307
Fax: 419 726-1103
David L Drago, *President*
EMP: 56
SQ FT: 9,000
SALES (est): 7.6MM **Privately Held**
WEB: www.globetrucking.com
SIC: 4213 Contract haulers

(G-17918)
GOODREMONTS
1017 W Sylvania Ave (43612-1701)
P.O. Box 1728, Mansfield (44901-1728)
PHONE 419 476-1492
Fax: 419 476-6419
Mark K Goodremont, *President*
EMP: 28
SQ FT: 17,000
SALES (est): 3.1MM **Privately Held**
WEB: www.goodremonts.com
SIC: 5044 Photocopy machines; dictating machines; duplicating machines; mailing machines

(G-17919)
GOODWILL INDS NW OHIO INC (PA)
1120 Madison Ave (43604-7538)
P.O. Box 336 (43697-0336)
PHONE 419 255-0070
Fax: 419 255-8152
Robert Huber, *President*
Bob Huber, *Vice Pres*
Amy Wachob, *Vice Pres*
Susan Frederick, *Plant Mgr*
Sarah Semer, *Opers Mgr*
EMP: 100
SQ FT: 66,000
SALES (est): 19.9MM **Privately Held**
WEB: www.goodwillnwohio.com
SIC: 5932 8331 Clothing, secondhand; vocational rehabilitation agency

(G-17920)
GRAY TELEVISION GROUP INC
Also Called: Wtvg-TV
4247 Dorr St (43607-2134)
PHONE 419 531-1313
Fax: 419 531-1399
Peter Veto, *Vice Pres*
EMP: 54
SALES (corp-wide): 882.7MM **Publicly Held**
SIC: 4833 Television translator station
HQ: Gray Television Group, Inc.
    4370 Peachtree Rd Ne # 500
    Brookhaven GA 30319
    404 266-8333

(G-17921)
GREAT LAKES HOME HLTH SVCS INC
3425 Executive Pkwy # 206 (43606-1334)
PHONE 888 260-9835
Adam D Nielsen, *President*
EMP: 50 **Privately Held**
SIC: 8082 Home health care services
PA: Great Lakes Home Health Services, Inc.
    900 Cooper St
    Jackson MI 49202

(G-17922)
GREAT LAKES MKTG ASSOC INC
3361 Executive Pkwy # 201 (43606-1337)
PHONE 419 534-4700
Fax: 419 531-8950
Lori Dixon, *President*
EMP: 35
SQ FT: 5,151
SALES (est): 3.8MM **Privately Held**
WEB: www.greatlakesmarketing.com
SIC: 8732 Market analysis or research

(G-17923)
GREENFIELD HEALTH SYSTEMS CORP (PA)
Also Called: Dialysis Partners of NW Ohio
3401 Glendale Ave Ste 110 (43614-2490)
PHONE 419 389-9681
Fax: 419 389-9196
Deanna Shaffer, *President*
Nathalie Lake, *Manager*
Suzee Schuler, *Manager*
Debra Tucker, *Manager*
Eva Costilla, *Admin Sec*
EMP: 48
SQ FT: 10,000
SALES (est): 4.2MM **Privately Held**
SIC: 8092 Kidney dialysis centers

(G-17924)
GROGANS TOWNE CHRYSLER INC (PA)
6100 Telegraph Rd (43612-4575)
PHONE 419 476-0761
Fax: 419 476-4877
Mark Floyd, *President*
Dennis Amrhein, *General Mgr*
Denny Amrhiem, *Vice Pres*
Ed J Lishewski, *Treasurer*
Kevin Kirkwood, *Finance Mgr*
▼ EMP: 105
SQ FT: 50,000
SALES (est): 39.9MM **Privately Held**
SIC: 5511 7515 7513 7538 Automobiles, new & used; passenger car leasing; truck leasing, without drivers; general automotive repair shops; top & body repair & paint shops; used car dealers

(G-17925)
GROSS ELECTRIC INC (PA)
2807 N Reynolds Rd (43615-2080)
P.O. Box 352377 (43635-2377)
PHONE 419 537-1818
Fax: 419 537-6627
Richard J Gross, *Ch of Bd*
Laurie Gross, *President*
Joseph Gross, *Vice Pres*
Jessica Inwood, *Store Mgr*
Jamie Dugai, *Warehouse Mgr*
EMP: 35 EST: 1910
SQ FT: 36,000
SALES (est): 44.4MM **Privately Held**
WEB: www.grosselectric.com
SIC: 5063 5719 Electrical supplies; lighting fixtures

(G-17926)
GROUND PENETRATING RADAR SYS (PA)
Also Called: Gprs
7540 New West Rd (43617-4200)
PHONE 419 843-9804
Matt Aston, *President*
Ron Anderson, *Regional Mgr*
Jordan Bradish, *Regional Mgr*
Thaddeus Bullock, *Regional Mgr*
Jeff Dehart, *Regional Mgr*
EMP: 41
SALES (est): 10.3MM **Privately Held**
SIC: 1799 8713 Building site preparation; surveying services

(G-17927)
GRUNWELL-CASHERO CO
5212 Tractor Rd (43612-3440)
PHONE 419 476-2426
Fax: 419 476-2439
Anthony Serra, *Branch Mgr*
EMP: 25
SQ FT: 3,880
SALES (corp-wide): 18MM **Privately Held**
WEB: www.grunwell-cashero.com
SIC: 1541 Renovation, remodeling & repairs: industrial buildings
PA: Grunwell-Cashero Co.
    1041 Major St
    Detroit MI 48217
    313 843-8440

(G-17928)
GW SUTHERLAND MD
2865 N Reynolds Rd # 160 (43615-2068)
PHONE 419 578 7200
Gw Sutherland, *Principal*
EMP: 25 EST: 2001
SALES (est): 378.1K **Privately Held**
SIC: 8011 Offices & clinics of medical doctors

(G-17929)
H C R CORP
Also Called: Heartland Holly Glen Care Ctr
4293 Monroe St (43606-1943)
PHONE 419 472-0076
Fax: 419 475-1946
Becky Abbey, *President*
Robert G Mason, *President*
La Donna Mason, *Corp Secy*
EMP: 80 EST: 1967
SALES (est): 2.1MM **Privately Held**
SIC: 8059 Nursing home, except skilled & intermediate care facility

Toledo - Lucas County (G-17930)

(G-17930)
HANDY HUBBY
2010 N Reynolds Rd (43615-3512)
PHONE..................................419 754-1150
Fax: 419 754-1157
John Bothe, *Owner*
EMP: 25
SQ FT: 958
SALES (est): 870K **Privately Held**
WEB: www.handyhubbyhomeimprovement.com
SIC: 7299 Handyman service

(G-17931)
HANSEN-MUELLER CO
1800 N Water St (43611)
P.O. Box 50497 (43605-0497)
PHONE..................................419 729-5535
Fax: 419 729-5510
Mike Burget, *Manager*
EMP: 26
SALES (corp-wide): 85.6MM **Privately Held**
WEB: www.hmgrain.com
SIC: 5153 2041 Grains; flour & other grain mill products
PA: Hansen-Mueller Co.
  12231 Emmet St Ste 1
  Omaha NE 68164
  402 491-3385

(G-17932)
HARBOR (PA)
6629 W Central Ave Ste 1 (43617-1098)
P.O. Box 8970 (43623-0970)
PHONE..................................419 479-3233
Dale Shreve, *CEO*
Steve Benjamin, *Vice Pres*
Cuneyd Tolek, *Vice Pres*
Susan Partridge, *Human Res Mgr*
EMP: 90 EST: 1941
SQ FT: 22,400
SALES: 43MM **Privately Held**
WEB: www.harbor.org
SIC: 8093 Mental health clinic, outpatient

(G-17933)
HARBOR
123 22nd St Ste 1 (43604-2706)
PHONE..................................419 241-6191
Fax: 419 255-5623
Dale Shreve, *Branch Mgr*
EMP: 100
SALES (corp-wide): 43MM **Privately Held**
WEB: www.harbor.org
SIC: 8093 8361 Mental health clinic, outpatient; rehabilitation center, residential: health care incidental
PA: Harbor
  6629 W Central Ave Ste 1
  Toledo OH 43617
  419 479-3233

(G-17934)
HARBOR
Also Called: Mayfair School
5331 Bennett Rd (43612-3403)
PHONE..................................800 444-3353
Fax: 419 478-1671
Rachel Holland, *Manager*
EMP: 40
SALES (corp-wide): 43MM **Privately Held**
WEB: www.harbor.org
SIC: 8093 8052 Mental health clinic, outpatient; home for the mentally retarded, with health care
PA: Harbor
  6629 W Central Ave Ste 1
  Toledo OH 43617
  419 479-3233

(G-17935)
HARBORSIDE POINTE PLACE LLC
Also Called: Point Place
6101 N Summit St (43611-1242)
PHONE..................................419 727-7870
George V Hager Jr, *Principal*
Mark Grieselding, *Principal*
Joseph Peyton, *Director*
Ronda Saffle, *Food Svc Dir*
Angelia Schlegel, *Hlthcr Dir*
EMP: 101
SALES: 1,000K **Privately Held**
SIC: 8051 Skilled nursing care facilities

(G-17936)
HART ASSOCIATES INC
811 Madison Ave (43604-5684)
PHONE..................................419 893-9600
Fax: 419 893-9070
Michael K Hart, *President*
Marc Paulenich, *Senior VP*
Mike Bell, *Vice Pres*
James Calhoun, *Vice Pres*
Susan Degens, *Vice Pres*
EMP: 55
SQ FT: 13,000
SALES (est): 13.3MM **Privately Held**
WEB: www.hartinc.com
SIC: 7311 Advertising consultant

(G-17937)
HARVEST FACILITY HOLDINGS LP
Also Called: Alexis Gardens
4560 W Alexis Rd Apt 9 (43623-1082)
PHONE..................................419 472-7115
Fax: 419 472-7115
Bob Allen, *Manager*
Duncan Campbell, *Manager*
EMP: 25
SALES (corp-wide): 1.1B **Privately Held**
WEB: www.holidaytouch.com
SIC: 6513 Retirement hotel operation
HQ: Harvest Facility Holdings Lp
  5885 Meadows Rd Ste 500
  Lake Oswego OR 97035
  503 370-7070

(G-17938)
HCR MANOR CARE SVC FLA III INC (DH)
Also Called: Heartland Hospice Services
333 N Summit St (43604-1531)
PHONE..................................419 252-5500
Michael John Reed, *President*
EMP: 34
SALES (est): 4MM
SALES (corp-wide): 3.6B **Publicly Held**
SIC: 8051 Skilled nursing care facilities

(G-17939)
HCR MANORCARE MED SVCS FLA LLC
Also Called: Heartland Care Partners 3555
3450 W Central Ave # 230 (43606-1416)
P.O. Box 10086 (43699-0086)
PHONE..................................419 531-2127
Barry A Lazarus, *Branch Mgr*
EMP: 105
SALES (corp-wide): 3.6B **Publicly Held**
SIC: 8051 Convalescent home with continuous nursing care
HQ: Hcr Manorcare Medical Services Of Florida, Llc
  333 N Summit St Ste 100
  Toledo OH 43604
  419 252-5500

(G-17940)
HCR MANORCARE MED SVCS FLA LLC (DH)
Also Called: Manor Care
333 N Summit St Ste 100 (43604-2617)
P.O. Box 10086 (43699-0086)
PHONE..................................419 252-5500
Paul Ormond, *Ch of Bd*
Stephen L Guillard, *COO*
Keith Weikel, *COO*
R Jeffrey Bixler, *Vice Pres*
Praveen Dayanithi, *Engng Exec*
EMP: 200
SQ FT: 210,000
SALES (est): 96.2MM
SALES (corp-wide): 3.6B **Publicly Held**
WEB: www.manorcare.com
SIC: 8051 Convalescent home with continuous nursing care
HQ: Manor Care Of America, Inc.
  333 N Summit St Ste 103
  Toledo OH 43604
  419 252-5500

(G-17941)
HEALTH CARE RETIREMENT CORP
333 N Summit St Ste 100 (43604-2615)
P.O. Box 10086 (43699-0086)
PHONE..................................419 252-5500
Fax: 419 252-5564
Paul A Ormond, *President*
Ben Stevens, *Vice Pres*
Michael Keith Weikel, *Vice Pres*
Spencer Molen, *Treasurer*
Jeff Bixler, *Admin Sec*
EMP: 500
SQ FT: 10,000
SALES (est): 12.8MM
SALES (corp-wide): 3.6B **Publicly Held**
WEB: www.hrc-manorcare.com
SIC: 8051 Skilled nursing care facilities
HQ: Health Care And Retirement Corporation Of America
  333 N Summit St Ste 103
  Toledo OH 43604
  419 252-5500

(G-17942)
HEALTH CARE RTREMENT CORP AMER (DH)
333 N Summit St Ste 103 (43604-2617)
P.O. Box 10086 (43699-0086)
PHONE..................................419 252-5500
Paul A Ormond, *Ch of Bd*
Stephen Guillard, *Senior VP*
Spence C Moler, *Vice Pres*
Richard Parr, *Vice Pres*
Steven Cavanaugh, *CFO*
EMP: 243
SALES (est): 45.2MM
SALES (corp-wide): 3.6B **Publicly Held**
WEB: www.hrc-manorcare.com
SIC: 8051 Convalescent home with continuous nursing care

(G-17943)
HEALTH CARE RTREMENT CORP AMER
Also Called: Heartland - Holly Glen
4293 Monroe St (43606-1943)
PHONE..................................419 474-6021
Kelly Lindeman, *Administration*
EMP: 100
SALES (corp-wide): 3.6B **Publicly Held**
WEB: www.hrc-manorcare.com
SIC: 8051 Skilled nursing care facilities
HQ: Health Care And Retirement Corporation Of America
  333 N Summit St Ste 103
  Toledo OH 43604
  419 252-5500

(G-17944)
HEALTHCARE FACILITY MGT LLC
Also Called: Advanced Healtcare Center
955 Garden Lake Pkwy (43614-2777)
PHONE..................................419 382-2200
Linda Hudson, *Purch Mgr*
Elaine Hetherwick, *Manager*
EMP: 90
SALES (corp-wide): 103.9MM **Privately Held**
WEB: www.communicarehealth.com
SIC: 8051 Skilled nursing care facilities
PA: Communicare Health Services, Inc.
  4700 Ashwood Dr Ste 200
  Blue Ash OH 45241
  513 530-1654

(G-17945)
HEARTLAND EMPLOYMENT SVCS LLC
333 N Summit St Ste 103 (43604-2617)
PHONE..................................419 252-5500
Bruce M Helberg, *Principal*
EMP: 715
SALES (est): 83.9K
SALES (corp-wide): 3.6B **Publicly Held**
SIC: 7363 Medical help service
HQ: Manor Care, Inc.
  333 N Summit St Ste 103
  Toledo OH 43604

(G-17946)
HEARTLAND FORT MYERS FL LLC (DH)
333 N Summit St (43604-1531)
PHONE..................................419 252-5500
Michael G Meyer, *Treasurer*
EMP: 37
SALES (est): 2.9MM
SALES (corp-wide): 3.6B **Publicly Held**
SIC: 8051 Skilled nursing care facilities

(G-17947)
HEARTLAND HEALTHCARE SVCS LLC (PA)
4755 South Ave (43615-6422)
PHONE..................................419 535-8435
Fax: 419 535-5682
Jerry Krbec, *General Mgr*
Cheryl Paxton, *Safety Dir*
Jeffrey Cremean, *CFO*
Dorothy Kuhl, *CFO*
Daniel Feyes Jr, *Pharmacist*
EMP: 200
SQ FT: 72,000
SALES: 204.4MM **Privately Held**
WEB: www.hhstol.com
SIC: 5122 Pharmaceuticals

(G-17948)
HEARTLAND HOME CARE LLC (DH)
333 N Summit St (43604-1531)
PHONE..................................419 252-5500
Stephen M Cavanaugh, *Vice Pres*
EMP: 53
SALES (est): 5.3MM
SALES (corp-wide): 3.6B **Publicly Held**
SIC: 8059 Personal care home, with health care
HQ: Heartland Rehabilitation Services, Inc.
  3425 Executive Pkwy # 128
  Toledo OH 43606
  419 537-0764

(G-17949)
HEARTLAND RHBLITATION SVCS INC (DH)
3425 Executive Pkwy # 128 (43606-1326)
PHONE..................................419 537-0764
Fax: 419 537-0948
Pat Smith, *Principal*
Todd Hanneman, *Marketing Mgr*
Merlin Linzy, *Manager*
Jon Turner, *Exec Dir*
EMP: 75
SALES (est): 15MM
SALES (corp-wide): 3.6B **Publicly Held**
WEB: www.hrs-contracts.com
SIC: 8093 Rehabilitation center, outpatient treatment

(G-17950)
HECKS DIRECT MAIL & PRTG SVC (PA)
417 Main St (43605-2057)
PHONE..................................419 697-3505
Fax: 419 691-0752
Edward Heck, *CEO*
EMP: 40 EST: 1943
SQ FT: 30,000
SALES (est): 4.4MM **Privately Held**
WEB: www.hecksprinting.com
SIC: 7331 2752 2791 2789 Addressing service; commercial printing, offset; typesetting; bookbinding & related work; commercial printing

(G-17951)
HECKS DIRECT MAIL & PRTG SVC
Also Called: Heck's Diamond Printing
202 W Florence Ave (43605-3304)
P.O. Box 8266 (43605-0266)
PHONE..................................419 661-6028
Fax: 419 661-6036
Cosino Trina, *Vice Pres*
EMP: 25
SALES (corp-wide): 4.4MM **Privately Held**
WEB: www.hecksprinting.com
SIC: 2752 7331 5192 Offset & photolithographic printing; direct mail advertising services; books, periodicals & newspapers

GEOGRAPHIC SECTION

Toledo - Lucas County (G-17974)

PA: Heck's Direct Mail & Printing Service Inc
417 Main St
Toledo OH 43605
419 697-3505

(G-17952)
HEIDTMAN STEEL PRODUCTS
2401 Front St (43605-1199)
PHONE.....................419 691-4646
EMP: 800
SALES (est): 53.4MM Privately Held
SIC: 5051 Metals Service Center

(G-17953)
HENRY GURTZWEILER INC
921 Galena St (43611-3717)
PHONE.....................419 729-3955
Fax: 419 729-5500
William H Myers, President
Greg Myers, Vice Pres
Craig Wymer, Opers Staff
Robert Thomason, CFO
Carol Allen, Administration
EMP: 75
SQ FT: 15,000
SALES (est): 14.4MM Privately Held
WEB: www.henrygurtzweiler.com
SIC: 1791 Structural steel erection; precast concrete structural framing or panels, placing of

(G-17954)
HERITAGE ENVMTL SVCS LLC
Also Called: Crystal Clean Parts Washer Svc
5451 Enterprise Blvd (43612-3812)
PHONE.....................419 729-1321
Fax: 419 729-1325
Bill Cedoz, Business Mgr
Adam Hoy, Manager
EMP: 50
SALES (corp-wide): 210.8MM Privately Held
WEB: www.heritage-enviro.com
SIC: 5093 Oil, waste
HQ: Heritage Environmental Services, Llc
7901 W Morris St
Indianapolis IN 46231
317 243-0811

(G-17955)
HGCC OF ALLENTOWN INC
333 N Summit St (43604-1531)
PHONE.....................419 252-5500
Paul A Ormond, Principal
EMP: 96
SALES (est): 439.9K
SALES (corp-wide): 3.6B Publicly Held
SIC: 8051 Skilled nursing care facilities
HQ: Health Care And Retirement Corporation Of America
333 N Summit St Ste 103
Toledo OH 43604
419 252-5500

(G-17956)
HOLLYWOOD CASINO TOLEDO
1968 Miami St (43605-3359)
PHONE.....................419 661-5200
Chris Wilson, Principal
EMP: 61
SALES (est): 5.3MM Privately Held
SIC: 7011 Casino hotel

(G-17957)
HOME DEPOT USA INC
Also Called: Home Depot, The
1035 W Alexis Rd (43612-4201)
PHONE.....................419 476-4573
Fax: 419 269-3416
Darcy Miller, Manager
EMP: 200
SQ FT: 9,900
SALES (corp-wide): 100.9B Publicly Held
WEB: www.homerentalsdepot.com
SIC: 5211 7359 Home centers; tool rental
HQ: Home Depot U.S.A., Inc.
2455 Paces Ferry Rd Se
Atlanta GA 30339

(G-17958)
HOME DEPOT USA INC
Also Called: Home Depot, The
3200 Secor Rd (43606-1515)
PHONE.....................419 537-1920
Fax: 419 537-5416
Don Mandabille, Manager
EMP: 140
SALES (corp-wide): 100.9B Publicly Held
WEB: www.homerentalsdepot.com
SIC: 5211 7359 Home centers; tool rental
HQ: Home Depot U.S.A., Inc.
2455 Paces Ferry Rd Se
Atlanta GA 30339

(G-17959)
HOOVER & WELLS INC
2011 Seaman St (43605-1908)
PHONE.....................419 691-9220
Fax: 419 691-8318
Margaret Hoover, Ch of Bd
Barbara Corsini, President
John Corsini, Vice Pres
James Mc Collum, Vice Pres
Nichole Simon, Vice Pres
EMP: 120
SQ FT: 23,448
SALES: 23.5MM Privately Held
WEB: www.hooverwells.com
SIC: 1752 2891 2851 Wood floor installation & refinishing; adhesives & sealants; paints & allied products

(G-17960)
HORIZONS EMPLOYMENT SVCS LLC
Also Called: Apple A Day Healthcare Svcs
2024 W Terrace View St (43607-1063)
PHONE.....................419 254-9644
Jerome A Parker, Mng Member
Patricia A Parker, Exec Dir
EMP: 300
SQ FT: 1,300
SALES: 3.5MM Privately Held
SIC: 7361 Employment agencies

(G-17961)
HOSPICE OF NORTHWEST OHIO
800 S Detroit Ave (43609-1910)
PHONE.....................419 661-4001
Judy Seibenick, Branch Mgr
Kathy Gerace, Senior Mgr
Bruce Kane, Director
Cheryl Minton,
EMP: 94
SALES (corp-wide): 31.2MM Privately Held
WEB: www.hospicenwo.org
SIC: 8069 Specialty hospitals, except psychiatric
PA: Hospice Of Northwest Ohio
30000 E River Rd
Perrysburg OH 43551
419 661-4001

(G-17962)
HOUSEHOLD CENTRALIZED SVC INC
2052 W Sylvania Ave (43613-4527)
PHONE.....................419 474-5754
Fax: 419 472-7654
David Tobian, President
Richard Chase, Vice Pres
Tamara Tobian, Admin Sec
EMP: 26
SQ FT: 10,000
SALES (est): 3MM Privately Held
WEB: www.householdcentralizedservice.com
SIC: 7629 7622 Electrical household appliance repair; television repair shop; stereophonic equipment repair; video repair; radio repair shop

(G-17963)
HS EXPRESS LLC
6003 Benore Rd (43612-3905)
PHONE.....................419 729-2400
Houston Vaughn, CEO
Larry Hall, President
EMP: 85
SQ FT: 3,000
SALES (est): 1.6MM
SALES (corp-wide): 204MM Privately Held
SIC: 4213 Trucking, except local

(G-17964)
HUB CITY TERMINALS INC
811 Madison Ave Ste 601 (43604-5684)
PHONE.....................419 217-5200
Fax: 419 867-4110
Darla Mruzek, Financial Exec
EMP: 47
SALES (corp-wide): 4B Publicly Held
WEB: www.hubgroup.com
SIC: 4731 Freight transportation arrangement
HQ: Hub City Terminals, Inc.
2000 Clearwater Dr
Oak Brook IL 60523
630 271-3600

(G-17965)
HULL & ASSOCIATES INC
219 S Erie St (43604-8607)
PHONE.....................419 385-2018
John Hull, President
EMP: 40
SALES (est): 1.4MM
SALES (corp-wide): 39.8MM Privately Held
WEB: www.hullinc.com
SIC: 8711 Consulting engineer
PA: Hull & Associates, Inc.
6397 Emerald Pkwy Ste 200
Dublin OH 43016
614 793-8777

(G-17966)
HUNTINGTON INSURANCE INC (DH)
519 Madison Ave (43604-1206)
PHONE.....................419 720-7900
Fax: 419 249-3329
Paul Baldwin, President
Mary Beth Sullivan, President
Kristopher Gerken, Business Mgr
Robert C Hawker Cpcu Arm, Senior VP
William N Fether, Senior VP
EMP: 150 EST: 1898
SALES (est): 96.1MM
SALES (corp-wide): 4.7B Publicly Held
WEB: www.skyinsure.com
SIC: 6411 Insurance agents
HQ: The Huntington National Bank
17 S High St Fl 1
Columbus OH 43215
614 480-4293

(G-17967)
HYLANT ADMINISTRATIVE SERVICES (PA)
811 Madison Ave Fl 11 (43604-5626)
P.O. Box 2083 (43603-2083)
PHONE.....................419 255-1020
Joe Seay, President
Michael Uglijesa, President
Dennis Michel, Vice Pres
Bill Petro, Vice Pres
Becky Stewart, Vice Pres
EMP: 31 EST: 1994
SALES (est): 17MM Privately Held
WEB: www.ohioplan.com
SIC: 6311 Life insurance

(G-17968)
HYLANT GROUP INC (PA)
811 Madison Ave Fl 11 (43604-5626)
P.O. Box 1687 (43603-1687)
PHONE.....................419 255-1020
Fax: 419 255-7557
Michael Hylant, CEO
Patrick Hylant, Ch of Bd
Todd Belden, President
William F Buckley, President
John W Chaney, President
EMP: 180
SQ FT: 80,000
SALES: 122MM Privately Held
WEB: www.hylant.com
SIC: 6411 Insurance agents

(G-17969)
IET INC
3539 Glendale Ave Ste C (43614-3457)
PHONE.....................419 385-1233
Timothy C Stansfield, President

PA: Ps Logistics, Llc
1810 Avenue C
Birmingham AL 35218
205 788-4000

Ronda Massey, Vice Pres
Wisdom Aiyelabowo, Engineer
Amaraja Dalvi, Engineer
Dan Holman, Engineer
EMP: 40
SQ FT: 14,000
SALES (est): 6.3MM Privately Held
WEB: www.ieteng.com
SIC: 8711 Consulting engineer

(G-17970)
ILLINOIS CENTRAL RAILROAD CO
4820 Schwartz Rd (43611-1726)
PHONE.....................419 726-6028
EMP: 50
SALES (corp-wide): 10.2B Privately Held
SIC: 4011 Interurban railways
HQ: Illinois Central Railroad Company
17641 Ashland Ave
Homewood IL 60430
708 332-3500

(G-17971)
IMPACT PRODUCTS LLC (DH)
2840 Centennial Rd (43617-1898)
PHONE.....................419 841-2891
Fax: 800 333-1531
Terry Neal, CEO
John Peggs, Business Mgr
Dennis Knapp, Research
Jeff Beery, CFO
John Dsachner, Sales Mgr
▲ EMP: 140 EST: 2001
SQ FT: 155,000
SALES: 120MM
SALES (corp-wide): 16.3B Publicly Held
WEB: www.impact-products.com
SIC: 5084 5087 2392 3089 Safety equipment; janitors' supplies; mops, floor & dust; buckets, plastic; tissue dispensers, plastic
HQ: S. P. Richards Company
6300 Highlands Pkwy Se
Smyrna GA 30082
770 434-4571

(G-17972)
IN HOME HEALTH LLC
Also Called: Heartland HM Hlth Care Hospice
3450 W Central Ave # 132 (43606-1416)
PHONE.....................419 531-0440
Fax: 419 531-0437
EMP: 50
SALES (corp-wide): 3.8B Publicly Held
SIC: 8082 Home Health Care Services
HQ: In Home Health, Llc
333 N Summit St
Toledo OH 43604
419 252-5500

(G-17973)
INFINITE SEC SOLUTIONS LLC
663 Gawil Ave (43609-1115)
PHONE.....................419 720-5678
Lawrence Leizerman, Principal
EMP: 25
SALES (est): 341.2K Privately Held
SIC: 7381 Detective & armored car services

(G-17974)
INNOVATIVE CONTROLS CORP
1354 E Broadway St (43605-3667)
PHONE.....................419 691-6684
Fax: 419 691-0170
Louis M Soltis, President
Anson F Schultz, Vice Pres
Ken Metzger, Mfg Staff
Susan Marsh, Purch Mgr
Mark Benton, Engineer
EMP: 63
SQ FT: 20,000
SALES (est): 14.1MM Privately Held
WEB: www.innovativecontrolscorp.com
SIC: 3613 3535 8711 3823 Control panels, electric; conveyors & conveying equipment; engineering services; industrial instrmnts msrmnt display/control process variable; relays & industrial controls; food products machinery

Toledo - Lucas County (G-17975)

GEOGRAPHIC SECTION

(G-17975)
INNOVATIVE DIALYSIS OF TOLEDO
3829 Woodley Rd Ste 12 (43606-1173)
PHONE.................................419 473-9900
Fax: 419 473-9050
Shannon C Weills, *CEO*
Stephen Pirri, *President*
Lisa Stewart, *Business Mgr*
EMP: 25
SALES (est): 1.3MM **Privately Held**
SIC: 8092 Kidney dialysis centers

(G-17976)
INTEGRITY WALL & CEILING INC
5242 Angola Rd Ste 180 (43615-6336)
PHONE.................................419 381-1855
Fax: 419 381-0850
Mario Dominguez, *President*
Pam Howard, *Office Mgr*
EMP: 30
SQ FT: 7,200
SALES (est): 2.8MM **Privately Held**
WEB: www.iwctoledo.com
SIC: 1742 Drywall

(G-17977)
INTERTEC CORPORATION
3400 Executive Pkwy (43606-1396)
PHONE.................................419 537-9711
George B Seifried, *President*
Scott A Slater, *Vice Pres*
Darrel G Howard, *Admin Sec*
◆ **EMP:** 300 **EST:** 1978
SQ FT: 1,000
SALES (est): 855.3K **Privately Held**
WEB: www.mspro.com
SIC: 3559 1796 3523 Glass making machinery: blowing, molding, forming, etc.; machinery installation; farm machinery & equipment

(G-17978)
INVERNESS CLUB
4601 Dorr St Ste 1 (43615-4038)
PHONE.................................419 578-9000
Fax: 419 536-4284
E C Benington, *President*
James Castle, *Executive*
EMP: 52
SALES (est): 4.7MM **Privately Held**
SIC: 7997 Country club, membership

(G-17979)
J & B LEASING INC OF OHIO
435 Dura Ave (43612-2619)
PHONE.................................419 269-1440
Fax: 419 269-1540
James M Bashore, *President*
EMP: 40
SQ FT: 6,240
SALES (est): 6.7MM **Privately Held**
SIC: 4213 Trucking, except local; refrigerated products transport

(G-17980)
J & S INDUSTRIAL MCH PDTS INC
123 Oakdale Ave (43605-3322)
PHONE.................................419 691-1380
Fax: 419 691-0339
Nancy Colyer, *Principal*
Elton E Bowland, *Principal*
George Bowland, *Principal*
John Sehr, *Principal*
Donald R Colyer, *Vice Pres*
EMP: 70 **EST:** 1946
SQ FT: 32,000
SALES (est): 9.2MM **Privately Held**
WEB: www.jsindustrialmachine.com
SIC: 3559 7692 Glass making machinery: blowing, molding, forming, etc.; welding repair

(G-17981)
J SCHOEN ENTERPRISES INC (PA)
Also Called: Cleaner & Dryer Restoration
5056 Angola Rd (43615-6415)
PHONE.................................419 536-0970
Fax: 419 382-5326
Jon Schoen, *President*
Angie Adam, *Project Mgr*
Eric Pidcock, *Accountant*
Tom Johnson, *Marketing Staff*
Kelli Klickman, *Manager*
EMP: 26
SQ FT: 5,000
SALES (est): 4.2MM **Privately Held**
SIC: 7389 Fire protection service other than forestry or public

(G-17982)
JAMES C SASS ATTY
3230 Central Park W # 200 (43617-1019)
PHONE.................................419 843-3545
James Sass, *Principal*
EMP: 29
SALES (est): 1.4MM **Privately Held**
SIC: 8111 General practice attorney, lawyer

(G-17983)
JB MANAGEMENT INC
6540 W Central Ave Ste A (43617-1095)
PHONE.................................419 841-2596
William Beck, *President*
Joe Janicki, *Vice Pres*
EMP: 90
SALES (est): 400K **Privately Held**
SIC: 7363 Employee leasing service

(G-17984)
JENNITE CO
4694 W Bancroft St (43615-3946)
PHONE.................................419 531-1791
Fax: 419 531-7591
Robert Wheeler Jr, *President*
Thomas Wheeler, *Corp Secy*
Debra Saam, *Manager*
EMP: 40
SQ FT: 2,800
SALES (est): 5.3MM **Privately Held**
WEB: www.jennite.com
SIC: 1771 Blacktop (asphalt) work

(G-17985)
JOB 1 USA (HQ)
701 Jefferson Ave Ste 202 (43604-6957)
P.O. Box 1480 (43603-1480)
PHONE.................................419 255-5005
Bruce F Rumpf, *President*
Ray Kasparian, *Area Mgr*
Charles Reedy, *Area Mgr*
Sue Daniels, *Vice Pres*
Eloise Huston, *Vice Pres*
EMP: 90
SQ FT: 35,000
SALES (est): 32.4MM
SALES (corp-wide): 33.4MM **Privately Held**
WEB: www.joboneusa.com
SIC: 7381 7363 7361 Security guard service; protective services, guard; temporary help service; medical help service; employment agencies; executive placement
PA: The Rumpf Corporation
701 Jefferson Ave Ste 201
Toledo OH 43604
419 255-5005

(G-17986)
JONES & HENRY ENGINEERS LTD (PA)
3103 Executive Pkwy # 300 (43606-1372)
PHONE.................................419 473-9611
Fax: 419 473-8924
Fraur Morsches, *Principal*
Raymond Holliday, *Plant Mgr*
Gary Bauer, *Engineer*
Troy Brehmer, *Engineer*
Jeff Landers, *Engineer*
EMP: 60 **EST:** 1926
SALES (est): 12.6MM **Privately Held**
WEB: www.jheng.com
SIC: 8711 Consulting engineer

(G-17987)
JOSINA LOTT FOUNDATION
Also Called: JOSINA LOTT RESIDENTIAL HOME
120 S Holland Sylvania Rd (43615-5622)
P.O. Box 352049 (43635-2049)
PHONE.................................419 866-9013
Fax: 419 866-8428
Rosino James, *Treasurer*
Debbie Berezowski, *Human Res Mgr*
Michael Malone, *Director*
Patty Schlosser, *Associate Dir*
EMP: 50
SQ FT: 23,600
SALES (est): 104.1K **Privately Held**
WEB: www.josinalott.org
SIC: 8361 Home for the mentally handicapped

(G-17988)
K-LIMITED CARRIER LTD (PA)
131 Matzinger Rd (43612-2623)
PHONE.................................419 269-0002
Fax: 419 269-0018
Dean Kaplan, *CEO*
Kim Kaplan, *President*
John Spurling, *Vice Pres*
Jeremy Bires, *Opers Mgr*
Dennis Perna, *CFO*
EMP: 110
SQ FT: 8,200
SALES (est): 22.6MM **Privately Held**
WEB: www.k-ltd.com
SIC: 4213 Contract haulers

(G-17989)
KA BERGQUIST INC (PA)
1100 King Rd (43617-2002)
P.O. Box 351330 (43635-1330)
PHONE.................................419 865-4196
Robert Barry, *President*
Hilda C Bergquist, *Principal*
Karl Bergquist, *Principal*
Charles E Ide Jr, *Principal*
Larry Hinkley, *Chairman*
▼ **EMP:** 30
SQ FT: 30,000
SALES (est): 43MM **Privately Held**
WEB: www.bergquistinc.com
SIC: 5084 1711 Propane conversion equipment; plumbing, heating, air-conditioning contractors

(G-17990)
KACE LOGISTICS LLC
1515 Matzinger Rd (43612-3828)
PHONE.................................419 273-3388
Joe Parin, *Mng Member*
Cameron Jamison,
Troy Schmersal,
EMP: 55
SALES (est): 2.2MM **Privately Held**
WEB: www.kacelogistics.com
SIC: 4212 Local trucking, without storage

(G-17991)
KATHLEEN K KAROL MD
2865 N Reynolds Rd # 170 (43615-2076)
PHONE.................................419 878-7992
Richard Torchia, *President*
Kathleen Karol, *Manager*
EMP: 60 **EST:** 2001
SALES (est): 820.4K **Privately Held**
SIC: 8011 Ophthalmologist

(G-17992)
KELLI WOODS MANAGEMENT INC
Also Called: Advance Cleaning Contractors
4708 Angola Rd (43615-6409)
PHONE.................................419 478-1200
Fax: 419 478-0232
Robert F Swan, *President*
Josh Carmody, *General Mgr*
Thomas Woods, *Vice Pres*
Janice Porter, *Admin Sec*
EMP: 140
SQ FT: 7,000
SALES (est): 3.8MM **Privately Held**
SIC: 7349 Janitorial service, contract basis

(G-17993)
KEYSTONE FOODS LLC
M & M Restaurant Supply Div
4763 High Oaks Blvd (43623-1087)
PHONE.................................419 843-3009
Fax: 419 729-3476
Ronald Enser, *Manager*
EMP: 120
SQ FT: 80,000 **Privately Held**
WEB: www.keystonefoods.com
SIC: 5141 5113 Food brokers; industrial & personal service paper
HQ: Keystone Foods LLC
905 Airport Rd Ste 400
West Chester PA 19380
610 667-6700

(G-17994)
KIMBERLY WILLIFORD ATTORNEY
900 Adams St (43604-5505)
PHONE.................................419 241-1220
Kimberly Williford, *Principal*
EMP: 35
SALES (est): 1.8MM **Privately Held**
SIC: 8111 General practice attorney, lawyer

(G-17995)
KINGSTON HEALTHCARE COMPANY (PA)
Also Called: Kingston Residence
1 Seagate Ste 1960 (43604-1592)
PHONE.................................419 247-2880
Fax: 419 247-2872
M George Rumman, *President*
Beth Connors, *Regional Mgr*
Licata Joe, *Regional Mgr*
Jeanne Niklis, *Business Mgr*
Kent Libbe, *Vice Pres*
EMP: 50
SQ FT: 3,000
SALES (est): 95.5MM **Privately Held**
WEB: www.kingstonhealthcare.com
SIC: 8059 8741 Nursing home, except skilled & intermediate care facility; nursing & personal care facility management

(G-17996)
KNIGHT CROCKETT MILLER INS
Also Called: K C M Consulting
22 N Erie St Ste A (43604-2723)
PHONE.................................419 254-2400
Fax: 419 321-5280
Kenneth P Knight, *Principal*
Sam Hammons, *Principal*
Tom Hart, *Principal*
Diane Roe, *Principal*
Carrie Christie, *Accounts Mgr*
EMP: 25
SQ FT: 2,000
SALES (est): 7.3MM **Privately Held**
WEB: www.knightinsurance.com
SIC: 6411 Insurance agents

(G-17997)
KWIK PARKING
709 Madison Ave Ste 205 (43604-6624)
PHONE.................................419 246-0454
George Jones, *President*
Jim Kiniep, *Vice Pres*
Michael Miller, *Opers Mgr*
EMP: 50
SQ FT: 1,110
SALES (est): 1.5MM **Privately Held**
WEB: www.kwikparking.com
SIC: 7521 6531 Parking garage; real estate agents & managers

(G-17998)
L A KING TRUCKING INC
434 Matzinger Rd (43612-2628)
PHONE.................................419 727-9398
Russell King, *CEO*
EMP: 50
SALES (est): 3.2MM **Privately Held**
SIC: 4213 Trucking, except local

(G-17999)
LAIBE ELECTRIC CO
404 N Byrne Rd (43607-2609)
PHONE.................................419 724-8200
Fax: 419 531-5809
Gerald Deaton, *CEO*
Jim Deaton, *President*
Joe Perkins, *General Mgr*
Lauren Dzierwa, *Corp Secy*
Joseph P Deaton, *Vice Pres*
EMP: 85 **EST:** 1930
SQ FT: 7,200
SALES (est): 19.1MM **Privately Held**
WEB: www.laibe.com
SIC: 1731 General electrical contractor

(G-18000)
LAKEFRONT LINES INC
Also Called: Lakefront Trailways
3152 Hill Ave (43607-2933)
PHONE.................................419 537-0677
Fax: 419 357-9791
Mike Schmul, *Manager*
Kate Henke, *Manager*

▲ = Import ▼ = Export
◆ = Import/Export

GEOGRAPHIC SECTION

Toledo - Lucas County (G-18024)

EMP: 50
SQ FT: 8,944
SALES (corp-wide): 4.9B **Privately Held**
WEB: www.lakefrontlines.com
SIC: **4119** 4142 Limousine rental, with driver; bus charter service, except local
HQ: Lakefront Lines, Inc.
   13315 Brookpark Rd
   Brookpark OH 44142
   216 267-8810

(G-18001)
LATHROP COMPANY INC (DH)
28 N Saint Clair St (43604-1001)
PHONE.................................419 893-7000
Fax: 419 893-1741
Steven M Johnson, *President*
Joseph R Kovaleski, *Vice Pres*
Douglas F Martin, *Vice Pres*
Consie Taylor, *Purch Agent*
Mark T Kusner, *Treasurer*
EMP: 50
SQ FT: 20,000
SALES (est): 26.9MM
SALES (corp-wide): 1.5B **Privately Held**
SIC: **1542** 8741 1541 Commercial & office building, new construction; construction management; industrial buildings & warehouses
HQ: Turner Construction Company Inc
   375 Hudson St Fl 6
   New York NY 10014
   212 229-6000

(G-18002)
LEADER NURING & REHABILITATION (DH)
Also Called: Hcr Manor Care
333 N Summit St (43604-1531)
P.O. Box 10086 (43699-0086)
PHONE.................................419 252-5718
Fax: 419 252-5554
Paul A Ormond, *President*
Steven Guillard, *COO*
Bruce Schroeder, *COO*
Chad Meyer, *Production*
Phil Carroll, *Engineer*
EMP: 150
SALES (est): 19.1MM
SALES (corp-wide): 3.6B **Publicly Held**
SIC: **8051** Skilled nursing care facilities
HQ: Hcr Manorcare Medical Services Of Florida, Llc
   333 N Summit St Ste 100
   Toledo OH 43604
   419 252-5500

(G-18003)
LEGAL AID WESTERN OHIO INC
Also Called: Lawo
525 Jefferson Ave 400 (43604-1094)
PHONE.................................419 724-0030
Kevin Mulder, *Director*
Sally Rumbaugh, *Admin Asst*
Meg Bowers, *Legal Staff*
Cathie Patterson, *Legal Staff*
EMP: 60
SALES: 5.6MM **Privately Held**
SIC: **8111** Legal aid service

(G-18004)
LEXAMED
705 Front St (43605-2107)
PHONE.................................419 693-5307
James Kulla, *Senior VP*
Jerome Bell, *Vice Pres*
Kelly Fahrbach, *Project Mgr*
Erin Huber, *Project Mgr*
Jemma Williams, *Opers Staff*
EMP: 40
SALES (est): 5.5MM **Privately Held**
SIC: **8071** Biological laboratory

(G-18005)
LIFESTAR AMBULANCE INC
1402 Lagrange St (43608-2928)
PHONE.................................419 245-6210
Fax: 419 251-7006
William Sutton, *President*
Kent Applehans, *Executive*
EMP: 200
SALES (est): 5MM **Privately Held**
SIC: **4119** Ambulance service

(G-18006)
LIGHTING MAINT HARMON SIGN
7844 W Central Ave (43617-1530)
PHONE.................................419 841-6658
Dan Kasper, *President*
EMP: 60
SALES (est): 1.9MM **Privately Held**
SIC: **1799** Sign installation & maintenance

(G-18007)
LOGISTICS INC
6010 Skyview Dr (43612-4715)
PHONE.................................419 478-1514
Aaron Alberts, *Branch Mgr*
EMP: 50
SALES (corp-wide): 21.1MM **Privately Held**
WEB: www.metrorush.com
SIC: **7389** Courier or messenger service
PA: Logistics Inc.
   21450 Trolley Indus Dr
   Taylor MI 48180
   734 641-1600

(G-18008)
LOTT INDUSTRIES INCORPORATED
5500 Telegraph Rd (43612-3631)
PHONE.................................419 476-2516
Fax: 419 478-8263
John Roberts, *Manager*
EMP: 400
SALES (est): 1.1MM
SALES (corp-wide): 8.1MM **Privately Held**
WEB: www.lottindustries.com
SIC: **8331** Sheltered workshop
PA: Lott Industries Incorporated
   3350 Hill Ave
   Toledo OH 43607
   419 534-4980

(G-18009)
LOTT INDUSTRIES INCORPORATED
3350 Hill Ave (43607-2937)
PHONE.................................419 534-4980
Laura Odiari, *Manager*
EMP: 480
SALES (corp-wide): 8.1MM **Privately Held**
WEB: www.lottindustries.com
SIC: **8331** Sheltered workshop
PA: Lott Industries Incorporated
   3350 Hill Ave
   Toledo OH 43607
   419 534-4980

(G-18010)
LOUIEVILLE TITLE AGNCY FOR NRT
626 Madison Ave Ste 100 (43604-1106)
PHONE.................................419 248-4611
John Martin, *President*
Vicky Feze, *Vice Pres*
William Harlet, *Vice Pres*
James Lenzey, *Vice Pres*
William Wise, *Vice Pres*
EMP: 65
SALES (est): 4.3MM **Privately Held**
SIC: **6411** Insurance agents

(G-18011)
LOUISVLLE TITLE AGCY FOR NW OH (PA)
626 Madison Ave Ste 100 (43604-1106)
PHONE.................................419 248-4611
Fax: 419 841-1040
John W Martin, *President*
Deb Tussing, *Prdtn Mgr*
Kelsey Cardell, *Sales Staff*
Esther Johnson, *Marketing Staff*
Andrea Marchal, *Banking Exec*
EMP: 91 EST: 1948
SQ FT: 20,000
SALES (est): 23.2MM **Privately Held**
WEB: www.louisvilletitle.com
SIC: **6411**

(G-18012)
LOVING FAMILY HOME CARE INC
2600 N Reynolds Rd 101a (43615-2067)
PHONE.................................888 469-2178
Solarix Fireheart, *CEO*
Suzanne Hakeos, *Sls & Mktg Exec*
EMP: 60
SQ FT: 1,400
SALES: 1.3MM **Privately Held**
SIC: **8082** Visiting nurse service

(G-18013)
LOWES HOME CENTERS LLC
5501 Airport Hwy (43615-7303)
PHONE.................................419 389-9464
Fax: 419 389-9485
Salam Hawry, *Branch Mgr*
EMP: 150
SALES (corp-wide): 68.6B **Publicly Held**
SIC: **5211** 5031 5722 5064 Home centers; building materials, exterior; building materials, interior; household appliance stores; electrical appliances, television & radio
HQ: Lowe's Home Centers, Llc
   1605 Curtis Bridge Rd
   Wilkesboro NC 28697
   336 658-4000

(G-18014)
LOWES HOME CENTERS LLC
7000 W Central Ave (43617-1115)
PHONE.................................419 843-9758
Fax: 419 843-2439
Jim Weirick, *Manager*
EMP: 150
SALES (corp-wide): 68.6B **Publicly Held**
SIC: **5211** 5031 5722 5064 Home centers; building materials, exterior; building materials, interior; household appliance stores; electrical appliances, television & radio
HQ: Lowe's Home Centers, Llc
   1605 Curtis Bridge Rd
   Wilkesboro NC 28697
   336 658-4000

(G-18015)
LOWES HOME CENTERS LLC
1136 W Alexis Rd (43612-4204)
PHONE.................................419 470-2491
Fax: 419 470-2494
John Swisher, *Department Mgr*
Randy Kitts, *Manager*
EMP: 150
SALES (corp-wide): 68.6B **Publicly Held**
SIC: **5211** 5031 5722 5064 Home centers; building materials, exterior; building materials, interior; household appliance stores; electrical appliances, television & radio
HQ: Lowe's Home Centers, Llc
   1605 Curtis Bridge Rd
   Wilkesboro NC 28697
   336 658-4000

(G-18016)
LUCAS COUNTY ASPHALT INC
Also Called: Buckeye Asphalt Paving Co
7540 Hollow Creek Dr (43617-1652)
P.O. Box 353094 (43635-3094)
PHONE.................................419 476-0705
Fax: 419 476-0700
Stephen A Dolgin, *President*
EMP: 25
SQ FT: 4,800
SALES (est): 1.7MM **Privately Held**
WEB: www.buckeyepaving.com
SIC: **1771** 2951 Blacktop (asphalt) work; asphalt & asphaltic paving mixtures (not from refineries)

(G-18017)
LUCAS COUNTY BOARD OF DEVELOPM
1154 Larc Ln (43614-2768)
PHONE.................................419 380-4000
Deb Yenrick, *Superintendent*
EMP: 100
SALES (est): 2.7MM **Privately Held**
SIC: **8052** Home for the mentally retarded, with health care

(G-18018)
LUCAS METROPOLITAN HSING AUTH
Also Called: Parkwood Apartments
435 Nebraska Ave (43604-8539)
PHONE.................................419 259-9457
Pamela Gilbert, *Human Res Dir*
Lawrence Gaster, *Branch Mgr*
Diana Drew, *Property Mgr*
Matthew Sutter, *Manager*
EMP: 100 **Privately Held**
SIC: **7241** Barber shops
PA: Lucas Metropolitan Housing Authority
   435 Nebraska Ave
   Toledo OH 43604
   419 259-9400

(G-18019)
LUTHERAN HOME
131 N Wheeling St Ofc (43605-1545)
PHONE.................................419 724-1414
Fax: 419 693-0751
Thomas Keith, *President*
David Roberts, *Director*
Tina Sherer, *Director*
Julie Kurtz, *Admin Asst*
Fancy Moreland, *Assistant*
EMP: 70 EST: 1997
SQ FT: 2,979
SALES: 8.6MM **Privately Held**
SIC: **8361** Halfway group home, persons with social or personal problems

(G-18020)
LUTHERAN HOUSING SERVICES INC
2021 N Mccord Rd Ste B (43615-3030)
PHONE.................................419 861-4990
David Roberts, *Director*
EMP: 30
SALES: 499.9K **Privately Held**
SIC: **8741** Management services

(G-18021)
LUTHERAN MEMORIAL HOME INC
2021 N Mccord Rd (43615-3030)
PHONE.................................419 502-5700
Fax: 419 625-0821
Renee Beck, *Manager*
Jason Bennett, *Exec Dir*
Brian Baxter, *Director*
EMP: 80
SQ FT: 44,000
SALES: 3.9MM **Privately Held**
SIC: **8052** 8059 Personal care facility; rest home, with health care

(G-18022)
LYDEN COMPANY
Also Called: True North Trucking
310 S Reynolds Rd Ste A (43615-5972)
PHONE.................................419 868-6800
Fax: 419 868-1458
Geoffrey W Lyden III, *CEO*
Mark Lyden, *President*
Char Salmons, *General Mgr*
John Belak, *District Mgr*
Brad Hayden, *District Mgr*
EMP: 32
SQ FT: 14,000
SALES (est): 8.4MM **Privately Held**
SIC: **4213** Contract haulers

(G-18023)
LYMAN W LIGGINS URBAN AFFAIRS
Also Called: Nutrition Program
2155 Arlington Ave (43609-1903)
PHONE.................................419 385-2532
Lisa Thompson, *Manager*
Lisa Hughley, *Director*
EMP: 100
SALES (est): 1.4MM **Privately Held**
SIC: **8322** Individual & family services; senior citizens' center or association

(G-18024)
M&M HEATING & COOLING INC
Also Called: M & M Heating & Cooling
1515 Washington St (43604-5705)
PHONE.................................419 243-3005
Fax: 419 243-0754
Mark Janowiecki, *President*
Mike Janowiecki, *Corp Secy*
EMP: 61
SQ FT: 18,000
SALES (est): 10.2MM **Privately Held**
WEB: www.m-mhvac.com
SIC: **1711** Warm air heating & air conditioning contractor

Toledo - Lucas County (G-18025) — GEOGRAPHIC SECTION

(G-18025)
MACMILLAN SOBANSKI & TODD LLC (PA)
1 Maritime Plz Fl 5 (43604-1879)
PHONE.............................419 255-5900
Thomas Brainard, *Counsel*
Catherine B Martineau, *Prdtn Dir*
Richard Mac Millan,
Chad Robinson, *Admin Asst*
Kristina Zapata, *Admin Asst*
EMP: 38
SQ FT: 8,000
SALES (est): 5.8MM **Privately Held**
WEB: www.mstfirm.com
SIC: **8111** Patent, trademark & copyright law

(G-18026)
MADISON AVENUE MKTG GROUP INC
1600 Madison Ave (43604-5464)
PHONE.............................419 473-9000
Gerald R Brown Jr, *President*
Steve Timofeev, *Opers Mgr*
Sara Ramsey, *Financial Exec*
Christa Kessler, *Accounts Mgr*
Lisa Oswald, *Sales Staff*
EMP: 25
SQ FT: 7,000
SALES (est): 2.8MM **Privately Held**
WEB: www.businessvoice.com
SIC: **7313** 8999 7311 7812 Electronic media advertising representatives; advertising copy writing; advertising agencies; advertising consultant; video production; music video production; marketing consulting services

(G-18027)
MAIL IT CORP
380 S Erie St (43604-4634)
P.O. Box 768 (43697-0768)
PHONE.............................419 249-4848
Fax: 419 249-4847
Karen Smith, *President*
Marion Howard, *Vice Pres*
Ken Yohn, *Prdtn Mgr*
H Russell Troyan, *Treasurer*
Russell H Troyan, *Treasurer*
EMP: 50
SALES (est): 6.8MM **Privately Held**
WEB: www.mailitcorp.com
SIC: **7331** Mailing service

(G-18028)
MANOR CARE INC (HQ)
333 N Summit St Ste 103 (43604-2617)
P.O. Box 10086 (43699-0086)
PHONE.............................419 252-5500
Fax: 419 252-5510
Paul A Ormond, *President*
Doug Mock, *Regional Mgr*
Stephen L Guillard, *COO*
Nancy A Edwards, *Vice Pres*
John K Graham, *Vice Pres*
EMP: 66
SALES (est): 918.2MM
SALES (corp-wide): 3.6B **Publicly Held**
WEB: www.hcr-manorcare.com
SIC: **8051** 8082 8062 Extended care facility; home health care services; general medical & surgical hospitals
PA: The Carlyle Group L P
1001 Pennsylvania Ave Nw 220s
Washington DC 20004
202 729-5626

(G-18029)
MANOR CARE NURSING CENTER (DH)
333 N Summit St Ste 100 (43604-2617)
PHONE.............................419 252-5500
Mark H Boss, *Principal*
Joseph Buckley, *Senior VP*
EMP: 26
SALES (est): 3.2MM
SALES (corp-wide): 3.6B **Publicly Held**
SIC: **8051** Skilled nursing care facilities

(G-18030)
MANOR CARE OF BOYNTON BEACH (DH)
333 N Summit St Ste 103 (43604-2617)
PHONE.............................419 252-5500
Paul A Ormond, *Chairman*
Steve Cavanaugh, *CFO*
EMP: 200
SALES (est): 10.2MM
SALES (corp-wide): 3.6B **Publicly Held**
WEB: www.manorcare.com
SIC: **8051** Skilled nursing care facilities
HQ: Hcr Manorcare Medical Services Of Florida, Llc
333 N Summit St Ste 100
Toledo OH 43604
419 252-5500

(G-18031)
MANOR CARE OF KANSAS INC (DH)
333 N Summit St Ste 100 (43604-2617)
PHONE.............................419 252-5500
Stewart Bainum Jr, *Director*
Deb Houke, *Administration*
EMP: 100
SQ FT: 43,000
SALES (est): 11.5MM
SALES (corp-wide): 3.6B **Publicly Held**
SIC: **8051** 8093 Skilled nursing care facilities; rehabilitation center, outpatient treatment
HQ: Hcr Manorcare Medical Services Of Florida, Llc
333 N Summit St Ste 100
Toledo OH 43604
419 252-5500

(G-18032)
MANOR CARE OF NORTH OLMSTED
333 N Summit St Ste 100 (43604-2617)
P.O. Box 10086 (43699-0086)
PHONE.............................419 252-5500
Paul Ormond, *President*
Stewart Bainum Jr, *President*
Donald C Tomasso, *President*
James A Maccutcheon, *Vice Pres*
EMP: 385
SQ FT: 47,000
SALES (est): 3.4MM
SALES (corp-wide): 3.6B **Publicly Held**
WEB: www.manorcare.com
SIC: **8051** Skilled nursing care facilities
HQ: Hcr Manorcare Medical Services Of Florida, Llc
333 N Summit St Ste 100
Toledo OH 43604
419 252-5500

(G-18033)
MANOR CARE OF PLANTATION INC
333 N Summit St Ste 100 (43604-2617)
PHONE.............................419 252-5500
Stewart Bainum Jr, *Ch of Bd*
Stewart Bainum Sr, *Vice Ch Bd*
Nadja Papillon, *President*
Gilda Anderson, *President*
EMP: 120
SQ FT: 48,670
SALES (est): 1.1MM
SALES (corp-wide): 3.6B **Publicly Held**
WEB: www.manorcare.com
SIC: **8051** Skilled nursing care facilities
HQ: Hcr Manorcare Medical Services Of Florida, Llc
333 N Summit St Ste 100
Toledo OH 43604
419 252-5500

(G-18034)
MANOR CARE OF YORK NORTH INC
Also Called: Manor Care-North
333 N Summit St Ste 100 (43604-2617)
PHONE.............................419 252-5500
Criag Thurston, *President*
Marion Bittner, *Principal*
James H Rempe, *Vice Pres*
Kim Rocheleau, *Administration*
EMP: 160
SQ FT: 47,000
SALES (est): 1.9MM
SALES (corp-wide): 3.6B **Publicly Held**
WEB: www.manorcare.com
SIC: **8051** Skilled nursing care facilities

HQ: Hcr Manorcare Medical Services Of Florida, Llc
333 N Summit St Ste 100
Toledo OH 43604
419 252-5500

(G-18035)
MANOR CARE WILMINGTON INC (DH)
333 N Summit St Ste 100 (43604-2617)
PHONE.............................419 252-5500
Stewart Bainum Jr, *Ch of Bd*
EMP: 42
SALES (est): 2.7MM
SALES (corp-wide): 3.6B **Publicly Held**
SIC: **8051** Skilled nursing care facilities
HQ: Hcr Manorcare Medical Services Of Florida, Llc
333 N Summit St Ste 100
Toledo OH 43604
419 252-5500

(G-18036)
MANOR CARE YORK (SOUTH) INC
333 N Summit St Ste 100 (43604-2617)
PHONE.............................419 252-5500
Paul A Ormond, *CEO*
Tami Burger Rn, *Nursing Dir*
Marilyn Alberti, *Art Dir*
Leroy Miller, *Administration*
EMP: 200
SALES (est): 2.2MM
SALES (corp-wide): 3.6B **Publicly Held**
WEB: www.manorcare.com
SIC: **8051** Skilled nursing care facilities
HQ: Hcr Manorcare Medical Services Of Florida, Llc
333 N Summit St Ste 100
Toledo OH 43604
419 252-5500

(G-18037)
MANOR CR-MPRIAL RCHMND VA LLC (DH)
333 N Summit St (43604-1531)
PHONE.............................419 252-5000
Hcr IV Healthcare, *Mng Member*
EMP: 55
SALES (est): 10.2MM
SALES (corp-wide): 3.6B **Publicly Held**
SIC: **8051** Skilled nursing care facilities
HQ: Hcr Manor Care, Inc.
333 N Summit St Ste 103
Toledo OH 43604
419 252-5743

(G-18038)
MANORCARE HEALTH SERVICES LLC (DH)
333 N Summit St Ste 100 (43604-2617)
PHONE.............................419 252-5500
Barry A Lazarus, *Principal*
Kelly Miller, *Recruiter*
EMP: 42
SALES (est): 4.4MM
SALES (corp-wide): 3.6B **Publicly Held**
SIC: **8051** Skilled nursing care facilities

(G-18039)
MANORCARE HEALTH SVCS VA INC (DH)
333 N Summit St Ste 100 (43604-2617)
P.O. Box 10086 (43699-0086)
PHONE.............................419 252-5500
Paul Ormond, *CEO*
James A Maccutcheon, *Senior VP*
James H Rempe, *Vice Pres*
Reggie Fox, *Facilities Mgr*
Steve Cavanaugh, *CFO*
EMP: 61
SALES (est): 5.2MM
SALES (corp-wide): 3.6B **Publicly Held**
SIC: **8051** Skilled nursing care facilities
HQ: Hcr Manorcare Medical Services Of Florida, Llc
333 N Summit St Ste 100
Toledo OH 43604
419 252-5500

(G-18040)
MANORCARE OF KINGSTON COURT
333 N Summit St Ste 100 (43604-2617)
PHONE.............................419 252-5500
Deb Slemmons, *Administration*
Deb Slemons, *Administration*
EMP: 135
SQ FT: 35,570
SALES (est): 1.3MM
SALES (corp-wide): 3.6B **Publicly Held**
WEB: www.manorcare.com
SIC: **8051** Skilled nursing care facilities
HQ: Hcr Manorcare Medical Services Of Florida, Llc
333 N Summit St Ste 100
Toledo OH 43604
419 252-5500

(G-18041)
MANORCARE OF WILLOUGHBY INC
333 N Summit St Ste 100 (43604-2617)
P.O. Box 10086 (43699-0086)
PHONE.............................419 252-5500
Paul Ormond, *President*
Keith Weikel, *COO*
Jeff Meyers, *CFO*
EMP: 183
SALES (est): 2.4MM
SALES (corp-wide): 3.6B **Publicly Held**
WEB: www.manorcare.com
SIC: **8051** 8052 Skilled nursing care facilities; intermediate care facilities
HQ: Hcr Manorcare Medical Services Of Florida, Llc
333 N Summit St Ste 100
Toledo OH 43604
419 252-5500

(G-18042)
MARCOS INC
Also Called: Marco's Pizza
5252 Monroe St (43623-3140)
PHONE.............................419 885-4844
Fax: 419 885-5215
Pasquale Giammarco, *President*
Sean Chowdary, *Vice Pres*
Anne Giammarco, *Vice Pres*
Pete Difilippo, *Opers Staff*
Madalyn Barajas, *Manager*
EMP: 250
SQ FT: 1,000
SALES (est): 5.9MM **Privately Held**
SIC: **5812** 6794 Pizzeria, chain; franchises, selling or licensing

(G-18043)
MARSHALL & MELHORN LLC
4 Seagate Ste 800 (43604-1599)
PHONE.............................419 249-7100
Fax: 419 249-7151
Kassi Billick, *President*
Justice G Johnson Jr, *Partner*
Marshall A Bennett Jr, *Partner*
Jennifer J Dawson, *Partner*
Lori W Decker, *Partner*
EMP: 90
SQ FT: 21,270
SALES (est): 12.7MM **Privately Held**
WEB: www.bennettlex.com
SIC: **8111** General practice law office; patent solicitor

(G-18044)
MARTIN + WD APPRISAL GROUP LTD
43 S Saint Clair St (43604-8735)
PHONE.............................419 241-4998
Kenneth Wood, *President*
Jonas Westrin, *Vice Pres*
Denise Hahn, *Office Mgr*
EMP: 30
SQ FT: 3,000
SALES (est): 3.1MM **Privately Held**
WEB: www.martinwoodappraisal.com
SIC: **6531** Appraiser, real estate

(G-18045)
MARTIN TRNSP SYSTEMS INC
320 Matzinger Rd (43612-2627)
PHONE.............................419 726-1348
June Brown, *Branch Mgr*
EMP: 85
SALES (est): 3.1MM
SALES (corp-wide): 91.1MM **Privately Held**
SIC: **4212** 4213 Local trucking, without storage; trucking, except local

PA: Martin Transportation Systems Inc.
7300 Clyde Park Ave Sw
Byron Center MI 49315
616 455-8850

(G-18046)
MCNERNEY & SON INC
1 Maritime Plz Uppr (43604-1853)
PHONE..................................419 666-0200
John H Mc Nerney, *President*
Allan L Kessler, *Principal*
F A Messerschmidt, *Principal*
N James McNerney, *Treasurer*
Terri Cochran, *Office Mgr*
EMP: 25 EST: 1900
SQ FT: 4,000
SALES (est): 6.5MM Privately Held
WEB: www.mcnerneyson.com
SIC: 1542 5021 1541 Commercial & office building, new construction; furniture; industrial buildings, new construction; warehouse construction

(G-18047)
MEDCORP INC (PA)
745 Medcorp Dr (43608-1376)
PHONE..................................419 727-7000
Fax: 419 727-0752
Fred Isch, *President*
Sandra Forest, *Human Res Mgr*
Jeff Schneiderman, *Director*
EMP: 92
SQ FT: 5,000
SALES (est): 10.9MM Privately Held
SIC: 8082 4119 Home health care services; ambulance service

(G-18048)
MEDICAL COLLEGE OF OHIO
Also Called: University Toledo Physicians
3355 Glendale Ave Fl 3 (43614-2426)
PHONE..................................419 383-7100
Diana Anaya, *Office Mgr*
Barbara Bondy, *Manager*
Mark R Bonnell, *Surgeon*
Gerard L Otten,
Thomas A Schwann, *Thoracic Surgeo*
EMP: 38
SALES (est): 7.1MM Privately Held
SIC: 8011 Physical medicine, physician/surgeon

(G-18049)
MEDICAL MUTUAL OF OHIO
3737 W Sylvania Ave (43623-4482)
P.O. Box 943 (43697-0943)
PHONE..................................419 473-7100
Fax: 419 473-7053
Joel Mercer, *Principal*
Michele Weimer, *HR Admin*
Dave Dearth, *Director*
Kathy Emery, *Director*
Carol Farmer, *Director*
EMP: 500
SALES (corp-wide): 1.4B Privately Held
SIC: 6324 Hospital & medical service plans
PA: Medical Mutual Of Ohio
2060 E 9th St Frnt Ste
Cleveland OH 44115
216 687-7000

(G-18050)
MENARDS CONTRACTOR SALES
1415 E Alexis Rd (43612-3978)
PHONE..................................419 726-4029
John Menard, *Owner*
EMP: 25
SALES (est): 2MM Privately Held
SIC: 5072 Hardware

(G-18051)
MENTAL HEALTH AND ADDI SERV
Also Called: Northcoast Behavior Healthcare
930 S Detroit Ave (43614-2701)
PHONE..................................419 381-1881
Fax: 419 389-1361
Kathy Anthony, *Director*
Chpln W Moore, *Director*
Mike Willeman, *Director*
Siba Yechoor, *Director*
Lee Lawrence, *Security Dir*
EMP: 250 Privately Held

SIC: 8063 9431 Psychiatric hospitals; mental health agency administration, government;
HQ: Ohio Department Of Mental Health And Addiction Services
30 E Broad St Fl 8
Columbus OH 43215

(G-18052)
MERCY HEALTH
2213 Cherry St (43608-2603)
PHONE..................................419 251-2393
Fax: 419 251-2659
Deb Stiemann, *Vice Pres*
Craig Morse, *Safety Dir*
Susan Woolner, *Manager*
EMP: 111
SALES (corp-wide): 4.2B Privately Held
SIC: 8011 Offices & clinics of medical doctors
PA: Mercy Health
1701 Mercy Health Pl
Cincinnati OH 45237
513 639-2800

(G-18053)
MERCY HEALTH
3930 Sunforest Ct Ste 100 (43623-4441)
PHONE..................................419 407-3990
EMP: 55
SALES (corp-wide): 4.2B Privately Held
SIC: 7299 Personal appearance services
PA: Mercy Health
1701 Mercy Health Pl
Cincinnati OH 45237
513 639-2800

(G-18054)
MERCY HEALTH
3425 Executive Pkwy 200nw (43606-1326)
PHONE..................................419 475-4666
EMP: 55
SALES (corp-wide): 4.2B Privately Held
SIC: 8011 Offices & clinics of medical doctors
PA: Mercy Health
1701 Mercy Health Pl
Cincinnati OH 45237
513 639-2800

(G-18055)
MERCY HEALTH
723 Phillips Ave Ste 201 (43612-1351)
PHONE..................................419 476-2124
EMP: 28
SALES (corp-wide): 4.2B Privately Held
SIC: 8011 Offices & clinics of medical doctors
PA: Mercy Health
1701 Mercy Health Pl
Cincinnati OH 45237
513 639-2800

(G-18056)
MERCY HEALTH SYS - NTHRN REG (HQ)
2200 Jefferson Ave (43604-7101)
PHONE..................................419 251-1359
Fax: 419 251-0722
Steven Mickus, *President*
Christine Browning, *President*
Kathleen A Osborne, *President*
Joseph Sober, *Vice Pres*
Ron Henley, *Facilities Dir*
EMP: 500
SQ FT: 4,000
SALES (est): 226.9MM
SALES (corp-wide): 4.2B Privately Held
SIC: 8062 General medical & surgical hospitals
PA: Mercy Health
1701 Mercy Health Pl
Cincinnati OH 45237
513 639-2800

(G-18057)
MERCY HLTH ST VINCENT MED LLC (PA)
Also Called: ST. VINCENT HOSPITAL AND MEDIA
2213 Cherry St (43608-2603)
PHONE..................................419 251-3232
Fax: 419 251-3845
Beverly J McBride, *Ch of Bd*
Tim Koder, *President*
Steven Mickus, *President*

Jeffrey Peterson, *President*
Craig Morse, *Safety Dir*
EMP: 3600 EST: 1875
SQ FT: 634,165
SALES: 478.7MM Privately Held
SIC: 8062 General medical & surgical hospitals

(G-18058)
MERCY HLTH ST VINCENT MED LLC
Also Called: Mercy Clinic
2200 Jefferson Ave (43604-7101)
PHONE..................................419 251-0580
Fax: 419 251-0506
Steven L Mickus, *Principal*
EMP: 812
SALES (corp-wide): 478.7MM Privately Held
SIC: 8011 Clinic, operated by physicians
PA: Mercy Health St Vincent Med Llc
2213 Cherry St
Toledo OH 43608
419 251-3232

(G-18059)
MERIT HOUSE LLC
4645 Lewis Ave (43612-2336)
PHONE..................................419 478-5131
John Stone, *President*
Donna Lawson, *Office Mgr*
EMP: 150
SALES (est): 3MM Privately Held
SIC: 8051 Skilled nursing care facilities

(G-18060)
MICHAELS GOURMET CATERING
Also Called: Michael's Cafe & Bakery
101 Main St Ste 7 (43605-2076)
PHONE..................................419 698-2988
Fax: 419 698-1880
Michael F Armstrong, *President*
Michael Armstrong, *President*
Laura Armstrong, *Vice Pres*
Wistinghausen Sue, *Sales Executive*
Sue Wistinghausen, *Sales Executive*
EMP: 30
SALES (est): 1.2MM Privately Held
WEB: www.michaelsoftoledo.com
SIC: 5812 5149 Caterers; cafe; bakery products

(G-18061)
MIDWEST INDUSTRIAL SUPPLY INC
1929 E Manhattan Blvd (43608-1534)
PHONE..................................800 321-0699
EMP: 26
SALES (corp-wide): 14.6MM Privately Held
SIC: 1799 5169 Coating, caulking & weather, water & fireproofing; specialty cleaning & sanitation preparations
PA: Midwest Industrial Supply, Inc.,
1101 3rd St Se
Canton OH 44707
330 456-3121

(G-18062)
MIDWEST MOSAIC INC
Also Called: Mw Mosaic
2268 Robinwood Ave (43620-1019)
PHONE..................................419 377-3894
Malcolm Campbell, *Owner*
EMP: 50
SALES: 2.5MM Privately Held
SIC: 1743 Mosaic work; tile installation, ceramic

(G-18063)
MIDWEST OPTOELECTRONICS LLC
2801 W Bancroft St 230 (43606-3328)
PHONE..................................419 724-0565
Liwei Xu, *General Mgr*
Karen Hunton, *Accounting Mgr*
Stanley Rubini,
EMP: 200
SALES (est): 7.4MM Privately Held
SIC: 8731 Commercial physical research

(G-18064)
MIDWEST TRMNALS TLEDO INTL INC
3518 Saint Lawrence Dr (43605-1079)
PHONE..................................419 698-8171
Doug Struvle, *Branch Mgr*
EMP: 50
SALES (corp-wide): 19.2MM Privately Held
SIC: 4789 4225 Cargo loading & unloading services; general warehousing & storage
PA: Midwest Terminals Of Toledo, International, Inc.
383 W Dussel Dr
Maumee OH 43537
419 897-6868

(G-18065)
MIZAR MOTORS INC (HQ)
Also Called: Great Lakes Western Star
6003 Benore Rd (43612-3905)
PHONE..................................419 729-2400
Fax: 419 729-2046
Rudy Vogel, *President*
Linda K Shinkle, *Principal*
John C Bates, *Chairman*
Simon Les, *Chairman*
Mark Ridenour, *Corp Secy*
EMP: 60
SQ FT: 60,000
SALES (est): 8.7MM
SALES (corp-wide): 299.5MM Privately Held
WEB: www.freightlineroftoledo.com
SIC: 4213 7538 5511 Heavy hauling; truck engine repair, except industrial; trucks, tractors & trailers: new & used
PA: Centaur, Inc.
2401 Front St
Toledo OH 43605
419 469-8000

(G-18066)
MJ-6 LLC
2621 Liverpool Ct (43617-2327)
PHONE..................................419 517-7725
Juana Barrow, *General Mgr*
Matthew Barrow,
EMP: 25
SALES: 6.1MM Privately Held
SIC: 7361 Labor contractors (employment agency)

(G-18067)
MOBILE CARDIAC IMAGING LLC
2409 Cherry St Ste 100 (43608-2670)
PHONE..................................419 251-3711
Amir Kabour,
Thomas Welch,
EMP: 25
SALES (est): 601.6K Privately Held
SIC: 8011 Cardiologist & cardio-vascular specialist

(G-18068)
MODERN BUILDERS SUPPLY INC
3500 Phillips Ave (43608-1070)
P.O. Box 80025 (43608-0025)
PHONE..................................419 241-3961
Fax: 419 254-4847
Jeff Laumann, *President*
Michael Graham, *Vice Pres*
Julie Leggett, *Vice Pres*
Scott Helms, *Opers Mgr*
Steve Holmes, *Opers Mgr*
EMP: 50
SQ FT: 69,625
SALES (corp-wide): 437.3MM Privately Held
WEB: www.polaristechnologies.com
SIC: 5032 Brick, stone & related material
PA: Modern Builders Supply, Inc.
302 Mcclurg Rd
Youngstown OH 44512
330 729-2690

(G-18069)
MOORE TRNSPT TULSA LTD LBLTY
4015 Stickney Ave (43612-2687)
PHONE..................................419 726-4499
George Wofford, *Branch Mgr*
EMP: 88

Toledo - Lucas County (G-18070) — GEOGRAPHIC SECTION

SALES (corp-wide): 42.9MM **Privately Held**
SIC: 4789 Pipeline terminal facilities, independently operated
PA: Moore Transport Of Tulsa, Llc
661 N Plano Rd Ste 319
Richardson TX 75081
972 907-3688

(G-18070)
MORGAN SERVICES INC
34 10th St (43604-6912)
PHONE..................419 243-2214
Fax: 419 243-6609
Mark Leonard, *Sales Staff*
Jennifer McHugh, *Sales Staff*
Pat Wheeler, *Branch Mgr*
EMP: 50
SALES (corp-wide): 38.6MM **Privately Held**
WEB: www.morganservices.com
SIC: 7213 7218 Linen supply; industrial launderers
PA: Morgan Services, Inc.
323 N Michigan Ave
Chicago IL 60601
312 346-3181

(G-18071)
MRC GLOBAL (US) INC
3110 Frenchmens Rd (43607-2917)
P.O. Box 352918 (43635-2918)
PHONE..................419 324-0039
Wendy Wilkins, *Manager*
EMP: 25 **Publicly Held**
SIC: 5085 Industrial supplies; valves & fittings
HQ: Mrc Global (Us) Inc.
1301 Mckinney St Ste 2300
Houston TX 77010
877 294-7574

(G-18072)
MSSTAFF LLC
5950 Airport Hwy Ste 12 (43615-7362)
PHONE..................419 868-8536
Kim Grabill, *Manager*
EMP: 200
SALES (corp-wide): 865MM **Publicly Held**
SIC: 7363 8049 Medical help service; nurses & other medical assistants
HQ: Msstaff, Llc
901 Nw 51st St Ste 110
Boca Raton FL 33431

(G-18073)
NATIONAL BLANKING LLC
135 N Fearing Blvd (43607-3604)
PHONE..................419 385-0636
Matt McCaffrey,
EMP: 25
SALES (est): 3MM **Privately Held**
SIC: 1761 Sheet metalwork

(G-18074)
NATIONAL EXCHANGE CLUB
3050 W Central Ave (43606-1700)
P.O. Box 1034, Fremont (43420-8034)
PHONE..................419 535-3232
Tracey Edwards, *Exec VP*
Kristie Lindau, *Comms Dir*
Mary Skeldon, *Comms Dir*
Julie Pardee, *Comms Mgr*
EMP: 25 **EST:** 1918
SALES: 1.9MM **Privately Held**
SIC: 7997 Membership sports & recreation clubs

(G-18075)
NATIONAL EXCHANGE CLUB FOUNDAT
Also Called: National Service Club
3050 W Central Ave (43606-1757)
PHONE..................419 535-3232
Chris Rice, *Exec VP*
Russ Finney, *Vice Pres*
Elizabeth Grantham, *Vice Pres*
Tom Karnes, *Vice Pres*
EMP: 25 **EST:** 1911
SQ FT: 22,500
SALES: 476.6K **Privately Held**
SIC: 8322 Individual & family services; child related social services

(G-18076)
NATIONAL HERITG ACADEMIES INC
Also Called: Bennett Venture Academy
5130 Bennett Rd (43612-3422)
PHONE..................419 269-2247
Xavier Owens, *Branch Mgr*
EMP: 54 **Privately Held**
SIC: 8741 Management services
PA: National Heritage Academies, Inc.
3850 Broadmoor Ave Se # 201
Grand Rapids MI 49512

(G-18077)
NATIONAL HERITG ACADEMIES INC
Also Called: Winterfield Venture Academy
305 Wenz Rd (43615-6244)
PHONE..................419 531-3285
Nate Preston, *Branch Mgr*
EMP: 54 **Privately Held**
SIC: 8741 Management services
PA: National Heritage Academies, Inc.
3850 Broadmoor Ave Se # 201
Grand Rapids MI 49512

(G-18078)
NATIONAL RAILROAD PASS CORP
Also Called: Amtrak
415 Emerald Ave (43604-8817)
PHONE..................419 246-0159
Fax: 419 244-6786
Ted Craig, *Manager*
EMP: 50 **Publicly Held**
WEB: www.amtrak.com
SIC: 9621 4013 ; switching & terminal services
HQ: National Railroad Passenger Corporation
1 Massachusetts Ave Nw
Washington DC 20001
202 906-3741

(G-18079)
NATURAL FOODS INC (PA)
Also Called: Bulkfoods.com
3040 Hill Ave (43607-2983)
PHONE..................419 537-1713
Fax: 419 531-6887
Frank Dietrich, *President*
Richard A Cohen, *Principal*
Rita Jester, *Treasurer*
Rosalie Dezandt, *Admin Sec*
▼ **EMP:** 31 **EST:** 1938
SQ FT: 424,845
SALES (est): 13.6MM **Privately Held**
WEB: www.bulkfoods.com
SIC: 5149 Health foods; natural & organic foods

(G-18080)
NEIGHBORHOOD HEALTH ASSO (PA)
Also Called: Toledo Family Health Center
313 Jefferson Ave (43604-1004)
PHONE..................419 720-7883
Fax: 419 259-4503
Doni Miller, *CEO*
Ellen Carroll, *Vice Pres*
Miranda Hoffman, *CFO*
Larry Leyland, *CFO*
Donald Perryman, *Treasurer*
EMP: 70
SQ FT: 9,000
SALES: 6.3MM **Privately Held**
SIC: 8093 Specialty outpatient clinics

(G-18081)
NEIGHBORHOOD HSG SERVS TOLEDO
Also Called: NHS WEATHERIZATION PROGRAM
704 2nd St (43605-2113)
P.O. Box 8125 (43605-0125)
PHONE..................419 691-2900
Fax: 419 691-2980
Michael Sachs, *General Mgr*
Nancy Dey, *Finance*
Pamela Campey, *Sales Executive*
William E Farnsel, *Exec Dir*
EMP: 36
SQ FT: 2,500

SALES: 4.6MM **Privately Held**
WEB: www.nhstoledo.org
SIC: 8399 Neighborhood development group

(G-18082)
NEIGHBORHOOD PROPERTIES INC
2753 W Central Ave (43606-3439)
PHONE..................419 473-2604
John Hoover, *President*
Parl Mortensen, *Sales Executive*
Lori Tyler, *Manager*
EMP: 50
SALES: 7.4MM **Privately Held**
WEB: www.neighborhoodproperties.org
SIC: 6513 6531 Retirement hotel operation; real estate agents & managers

(G-18083)
NEUROSURGICAL NETWORK INC
3909 Woodley Rd Ste 600 (43606-1179)
P.O. Box 824 (43697-0824)
PHONE..................419 251-1155
Fax: 419 251-3841
Edmont P Lawrence, *President*
Scott Dull, *Principal*
Sean Logan, *Principal*
Leo J P Clark, *Vice Pres*
Michael Healey, *Treasurer*
EMP: 43
SQ FT: 10,000
SALES (est): 3.8MM **Privately Held**
WEB: www.neurosurgical-network.com
SIC: 8011 Surgeon; neurologist

(G-18084)
NEW TECHNOLOGY STEEL LLC
135 N Fearing Blvd (43607-3604)
PHONE..................419 385-0636
EMP: 100
SQ FT: 63,404
SALES (corp-wide): 15.3MM **Privately Held**
SIC: 5051 Steel Service Center
PA: New Technology Steel, Llc
2401 Front St
Toledo OH 43605
419 385-0636

(G-18085)
NEW TECHNOLOGY STEEL LLC (PA)
2401 Front St (43605-1145)
PHONE..................419 385-0636
▲ **EMP:** 42
SQ FT: 153,000
SALES (est): 15.3MM **Privately Held**
SIC: 5051 Metals Service Center

(G-18086)
NEXTEL PARTNERS OPERATING CORP
Also Called: Sprint
5350 Airport Hwy Ste 110 (43615-6813)
PHONE..................419 380-2000
Fax: 419 380-8299
Jeff Bradish, *Branch Mgr*
EMP: 30
SALES (corp-wide): 78.3B **Publicly Held**
WEB: www.nymobilellc.com
SIC: 4812 Cellular telephone services
HQ: Nextel Partners Operating Corp.
6200 Sprint Pkwy
Overland Park KS 66251
800 829-0965

(G-18087)
NHS - TOTCO INC
704 2nd St (43605-2113)
PHONE..................419 691-2900
William Farnsel, *Exec Dir*
EMP: 40
SQ FT: 10,000
SALES (est): 1.9MM **Privately Held**
SIC: 1521 Single-family housing construction

(G-18088)
NONEMAN REAL ESTATE COMPANY
3519 Secor Rd (43606-1504)
PHONE..................419 531-4020
Dennis J Noneman, *President*

Tony Rable, *Maint Spvr*
Tyson Batdorf, *Controller*
Hillary Wagner, *Property Mgr*
EMP: 30
SQ FT: 3,200
SALES (est): 2.8MM **Privately Held**
WEB: www.noneman.com
SIC: 6531 Real estate brokers & agents

(G-18089)
NORDMANN ROOFING CO INC
1722 Starr Ave (43605-2461)
PHONE..................419 691-5737
Fax: 419 691-9521
Robert Mac Kinnon, *President*
Neil A Mac Kinnon Jr, *Chairman*
Robert R Carns, *Vice Pres*
Debbie Phillips, *Personnel Exec*
Steven N Saum, *Admin Sec*
EMP: 40 **EST:** 1931
SQ FT: 10,000
SALES (est): 11.1MM **Privately Held**
WEB: www.nordmannroofing.com
SIC: 1542 1761 Nonresidential construction; roofing contractor; sheet metalwork

(G-18090)
NORFOLK SOUTHERN CORPORATION
2101 Hill Ave (43607-3621)
PHONE..................419 381-5505
McLain Ryan, *Foreman/Supr*
EMP: 44
SALES (corp-wide): 10.5B **Publicly Held**
SIC: 4011 Railroads, line-haul operating
PA: Norfolk Southern Corporation
3 Commercial Pl Ste 1a
Norfolk VA 23510
757 629-2680

(G-18091)
NORFOLK SOUTHERN CORPORATION
341 Emerald Ave (43604-3815)
PHONE..................419 254-1562
Fax: 419 254-1552
Doug Williams, *Manager*
EMP: 75
SALES (corp-wide): 10.5B **Publicly Held**
WEB: www.nscorp.com
SIC: 4011 Railroads, line-haul operating
PA: Norfolk Southern Corporation
3 Commercial Pl Ste 1a
Norfolk VA 23510
757 629-2680

(G-18092)
NORON INC
Also Called: Honeywell Authorized Dealer
5465 Enterprise Blvd (43612-3812)
PHONE..................419 726-2677
Fax: 419 726-6651
Kevin Boeke, *President*
Vickie Jennings, *Manager*
EMP: 35
SQ FT: 15,000
SALES (est): 5.5MM **Privately Held**
WEB: www.noroninc.com
SIC: 1711 Warm air heating & air conditioning contractor

(G-18093)
NORTHWEST FIRESTOP INC
328 21st St (43604-5037)
PHONE..................419 517-4777
James House, *President*
Mike Esser, *Project Engr*
Martha Brewis, *Finance*
Betsy Blume, *Administration*
EMP: 25
SQ FT: 8,000
SALES (est): 3.9MM **Privately Held**
SIC: 1799 Fireproofing buildings

(G-18094)
NORTHWEST OHIO CARDIOLOGY CONS (PA)
2121 Hughes Dr Ste 850 (43606-5135)
PHONE..................419 842-3000
Everett M Bush MD, *President*
James Bingle, *Vice Pres*
John Letcher, *Research*
Sandy Judson, *Bookkeeper*
Thomas G Bartlett, *Med Doctor*
EMP: 70

SQ FT: 5,000
SALES (est): 6MM Privately Held
SIC: 8011 Cardiologist & cardio-vascular specialist

(G-18095)
NORTHWEST OHIO URGENT CARE INC
1421 S Reynolds Rd (43615-7413)
PHONE.................................419 720-7363
Dr Arshad Husain, *President*
EMP: 50
SALES (corp-wide): 3.4MM Privately Held
SIC: 8011 Medical centers
PA: Northwest Ohio Urgent Care, Inc.
  1015 Conant St
  Maumee OH 43537
  419 891-0525

(G-18096)
NORTHWEST TTL AGY OF OH MI IN (PA)
328 N Erie St (43604-6601)
PHONE.................................419 241-8195
Fax: 419 241-9302
EMP: 55
SALES (est): 6.2MM Privately Held
SIC: 6361 8111 Title Insurance Carrier Legal Services Office

(G-18097)
NUCENTURY TEXTILE SERVICES LLC (PA)
1 Southard Ave (43604-5215)
P.O. Box 20130 (43610-0130)
PHONE.................................419 241-2267
Jim Pacitti, *Owner*
Cheri Nopp-Hahn, *Administration*
EMP: 91
SQ FT: 1,000
SALES (est): 9.4MM Privately Held
SIC: 7389 Textile & apparel services

(G-18098)
NURSING CARE MGT AMER INC
Also Called: Foundation Park Care Center
1621 S Byrne Rd (43614-3456)
PHONE.................................419 385-3958
Fax: 419 385-0061
Stephen Bazeley, *Director*
Eric Valuckas, *Administration*
EMP: 150
SALES (est): 11MM
SALES (corp-wide): 26.1MM Privately Held
WEB: www.nursinghomeinfo.org
SIC: 8741 Nursing & personal care facility management
PA: Nursing Care Management Of America, Inc.
  7265 Kenwood Rd Ste 300
  Cincinnati OH 45236
  513 793-8804

(G-18099)
NWO GASTROENTEROLOGY ASSOC INC
4841 Monroe St Ste 110 (43623-4390)
PHONE.................................419 471-1317
Peter Reilly, *President*
EMP: 30
SALES (est): 1MM Privately Held
SIC: 8011 Gastronomist

(G-18100)
NZR RETAIL OF TOLEDO INC
4820 Monroe St (43623-4310)
PHONE.................................419 724-0005
Nick Hasan, *CEO*
Yazeed Qaimari, *Principal*
EMP: 85
SQ FT: 2,000,000
SALES (est): 110MM Privately Held
SIC: 5172 Gasoline

(G-18101)
OAKLEAF TOLEDO LTD PARTNERSHIP
Also Called: Oakleaf Village
4220 N Hllnd Sylvnia Ofc (43623)
PHONE.................................419 885-3934
Fax: 419 882-2012
Sanford Goldston, *General Ptnr*
Deborah Kelsik, *Mktg Dir*

Christopher Heban, *Food Svc Dir*
EMP: 50
SQ FT: 106,000
SALES (est): 3.3MM Privately Held
SIC: 8361 6513 Home for the aged; retirement hotel operation

(G-18102)
OEM PARTS OUTLET
1815 W Sylvania Ave (43613-4637)
PHONE.................................419 472-2237
Fax: 419 472-3704
Julie O'Donnell, *Owner*
EMP: 25
SALES (est): 1MM Privately Held
WEB: www.oempartsoutlet.com
SIC: 5075 Warm air heating equipment & supplies

(G-18103)
OHIO SKATE INC (PA)
5735 Opportunity Dr (43612-2902)
PHONE.................................419 476-2808
Joseph Yambor, *President*
EMP: 50
SQ FT: 24,000
SALES: 120K Privately Held
WEB: www.ohioskate.com
SIC: 7999 5941 Roller skating rink operation; skating rink operation services; skating equipment

(G-18104)
OLD DOMINION FREIGHT LINE INC
5950 Stickney Ave (43612-3946)
PHONE.................................419 726-4032
Fax: 419 726-1855
Robert Bolin, *Branch Mgr*
Tim Bach, *Manager*
Dick Wheeler, *Manager*
EMP: 48
SALES (corp-wide): 3.3B Publicly Held
WEB: www.odfl.com
SIC: 4213 Less-than-truckload (LTL) transport
PA: Old Dominion Freight Line Inc
  500 Old Dominion Way
  Thomasville NC 27360
  336 889-5000

(G-18105)
OLIVER HOUSE REST COMPLEX
27 Broadway St Ste A (43604-8701)
PHONE.................................419 243-1302
Fax: 419 243-9256
Patricia Appold, *President*
Neal Kovacik, *General Mgr*
James Appold, *Vice Pres*
EMP: 70
SQ FT: 70,000
SALES (est): 5MM Privately Held
SIC: 1522 1542 6513 6512 Remodeling, multi-family dwellings; commercial & office buildings, renovation & repair; apartment building operators; commercial & industrial building operation

(G-18106)
OMI TRANSPORTATION INC
1600 Water St (43604-1862)
P.O. Box 944 (43697-0944)
PHONE.................................419 241-8711
Fax: 419 241-9136
James Snyder, *President*
Kem Perkins, *Manager*
EMP: 30
SQ FT: 1,000
SALES (est): 5.2MM Privately Held
WEB: www.omitransportation.com
SIC: 4213 Trucking, except local

(G-18107)
OMNISOURCE LLC
2453 Hill Ave (43607-3610)
PHONE.................................419 537-1631
Fax: 419 423-8505
Jan McNeely, *Purchasing*
Anthony Wright, *Human Res Dir*
Jon Kinsman, *Branch Mgr*
Rick Blewett, *Systems Mgr*
EMP: 68 Publicly Held
WEB: www.omnisource.com
SIC: 5093 Ferrous metal scrap & waste

HQ: Omnisource, Llc
  7575 W Jefferson Blvd
  Fort Wayne IN 46804
  260 422-5541

(G-18108)
OMNISOURCE LLC
5130 N Detroit Ave (43612-3515)
PHONE.................................419 537-9400
Art Cheloff, *Branch Mgr*
Eugene Niuh, *Manager*
Michael Yashura, *Planning*
EMP: 218 Publicly Held
WEB: www.omnisource.com
SIC: 5093 Ferrous metal scrap & waste
HQ: Omnisource, Llc
  7575 W Jefferson Blvd
  Fort Wayne IN 46804
  260 422-5541

(G-18109)
ONLINE MEGA SELLERS CORP (PA)
Also Called: Distinct Advantage Cabinetry
4236 W Alexis Rd (43623-1255)
PHONE.................................888 384-6468
Timothy Baker, *President*
Craig Poupard, *Vice Pres*
EMP: 53
SQ FT: 250,000
SALES (est): 7.2MM Privately Held
SIC: 2434 7371 7373 Wood kitchen cabinets; computer software systems analysis & design, custom; computer software development; systems software development services

(G-18110)
ORAL & MAXILLOFACIAL SURGEONS (PA)
1850 Eastgate Rd Ste A (43614-3024)
PHONE.................................419 385-5743
Fax: 419 385-8835
Patrick McCabe, *President*
Howard I Feig DDS, *President*
Thomas Sydlowski, *Med Doctor*
EMP: 50
SQ FT: 3,354
SALES (est): 3.4MM Privately Held
WEB: www.oralmaxsurgeons.com
SIC: 8021 8093 Dental surgeon; specialty outpatient clinics

(G-18111)
ORAL & MAXILLOFACIAL SURGEONS
4646 Nantuckett Dr Ste A (43623-3194)
PHONE.................................419 471-0300
Shelby Snyder, *Accountant*
Carmen Beste, *Office Mgr*
Connie Smith, *Manager*
EMP: 42
SALES (est): 6.1MM
SALES (corp-wide): 3.4MM Privately Held
SIC: 8011 Surgeon
PA: Oral & Maxillofacial Surgeons Inc
  1850 Eastgate Rd Ste A
  Toledo OH 43614
  419 385-5743

(G-18112)
OREILLY AUTOMOTIVE INC
7417 W Central Ave (43617-1122)
PHONE.................................419 324-2077
EMP: 46 Publicly Held
SIC: 7538 General automotive repair shops
PA: O'reilly Automotive, Inc.
  233 S Patterson Ave
  Springfield MO 65802

(G-18113)
OVERHEAD INC (PA)
Also Called: Overhead Door Co of Toledo
340 New Towne Square Dr (43612-4606)
PHONE.................................419 476-7811
Fax: 419 476-7817
Lee J Huss, *President*
Michael Huss, *President*
Moody Telb, *General Mgr*
Diane Huss, *Vice Pres*
EMP: 40
SQ FT: 27,000

SALES (est): 12.4MM Privately Held
WEB: www.overheadinc.com
SIC: 1751 5211 5719 Garage door, installation or erection; garage doors, sale & installation; windows, storm: wood or metal; fireplaces & wood burning stoves

(G-18114)
OWENS CORNING SALES LLC (HQ)
1 Owens Corning Pkwy (43659-0001)
PHONE.................................419 248-8000
Michael H Thaman, *Ch of Bd*
Rhonda L Brooks, *President*
Carl B Hedlund, *President*
George E Kiemle, *President*
William E Lebaron, *President*
◆ **EMP:** 1000 **EST:** 2006
SQ FT: 400,000
SALES (est): 3.1B Publicly Held
WEB: www.owenscorning.com
SIC: 3296 2952 3229 3089 Fiberglass insulation; insulation: rock wool, slag & silica minerals; acoustical board & tile, mineral wool; roofing mats, mineral wool; asphalt felts & coatings; glass fibers, textile; yarn, fiberglass; windows, plastic; roofing, siding & sheet metal work

(G-18115)
P & W PAINTING CONTRACTORS INC
3031 Front St (43605-1007)
PHONE.................................419 698-2209
Fax: 419 698-4866
Paul Branstutter, *President*
Virginia Branstutter, *Corp Secy*
EMP: 50
SQ FT: 2,500
SALES (est): 5.1MM Privately Held
SIC: 1721 Industrial painting

(G-18116)
PARADISE HOSPITALITY INC
Also Called: Crowne Plaza Toledo
2 Seagate (43604-1443)
PHONE.................................419 255-6190
Andy Dae Kim, *President*
Jane In Kim, *Vice Pres*
Darshana Parekh, *Controller*
EMP: 120
SALES (est): 4.1MM Privately Held
WEB: www.paradisehospitality.com
SIC: 7011 Hotels & motels

(G-18117)
PARK INN
101 N Summit St (43604-1033)
PHONE.................................419 241-3000
Michael Sapara, *Principal*
Andrew Marshall, *Opers Staff*
Manuela Hasni, *Sales Dir*
EMP: 33 **EST:** 2008
SALES (est): 2.7MM Privately Held
SIC: 7011 Hotels & motels

(G-18118)
PARKCLIFFE DEVELOPMENT
4226 Parkcliff Ln (43615-7113)
PHONE.................................419 381-9447
Fax: 419 389-5002
Wayne Bucher, *Partner*
Tom Butler, *Partner*
Jenny Bucher, *Mktg Coord*
Faith Stiger, *Manager*
Charlene Sutton, *Program Dir*
EMP: 65
SALES (est): 3.8MM Privately Held
WEB: www.parkcliffe.com
SIC: 8051 8361 Skilled nursing care facilities; residential care

(G-18119)
PARKVIEW MANOR INC
Also Called: Liberty West Nursing Center
2051 Collingwood Blvd (43620-1649)
PHONE.................................419 243-5191
Amanda Gibson, *Manager*
Freda Cerny, *Administration*
EMP: 170
SALES (corp-wide): 3.1MM Privately Held
SIC: 8051 Convalescent home with continuous nursing care

Toledo - Lucas County (G-18120)

PA: Parkview Manor Inc
425 Lauricella Ct
Englewood OH 45322
937 296-1550

(G-18120)
PARKWAY SURGERY CENTER INC
2120 W Central Ave (43606-3834)
PHONE.....................419 531-7860
Richard Tapper MD, *President*
EMP: 55
SQ FT: 29,655
SALES (est): 4.7MM **Privately Held**
SIC: 8011 Urologist

(G-18121)
PATHOLOGY LABORATORIES INC (DH)
Also Called: Pathlabs
1946 N 13th St Ste 301 (43604-7264)
PHONE.....................419 255-4600
Fax: 419 255-4630
Marian C McVicker, *President*
Vicki Hite, *Vice Pres*
Miguel Every, *Controller*
Shelley Hughes, *Accounts Exec*
John Ihens, *Accounts Exec*
EMP: 160
SQ FT: 18,000
SALES (est): 14.5MM **Privately Held**
SIC: 8071 Pathological laboratory

(G-18122)
PATHWAY INC
Also Called: EOPA
505 Hamilton St (43604-8520)
PHONE.....................419 242-7304
Fax: 419 242-8263
Cheryl Grice, *CEO*
Robert Jordan, *CFO*
Mitchell Gorsha, *MIS Dir*
Eric Slack, *Plan/Corp Dev D*
EMP: 30
SQ FT: 13,000
SALES: 6MM **Privately Held**
WEB: www.eopa.org
SIC: 8322 7361 Social service center; employment agencies

(G-18123)
PHANTOM PHOTOGRAPHY LLC
1630 Avondale Ave Ste 1 (43607-3908)
PHONE.....................419 215-8060
Dennis Smith,
EMP: 30
SQ FT: 15,000
SALES (est): 935.6K **Privately Held**
SIC: 7335 Commercial photography

(G-18124)
PHILIO INC
Also Called: New Concepts
5301 Reynolds Rd (43615)
P.O. Box 20068 (43610-0068)
PHONE.....................419 531-5544
Janice Edwards, *Exec Dir*
EMP: 35 EST: 2012
SALES (est): 241.3K **Privately Held**
SIC: 8093 Substance abuse clinics (outpatient); mental health clinic, outpatient

(G-18125)
PINEWOOD PLACE APARTMENTS
1210 Collingwood Blvd (43604-8112)
PHONE.....................419 243-1413
Leean Morein, *Partner*
Jennifer Hardee, *Manager*
EMP: 3900
SALES (est): 43.4MM **Privately Held**
SIC: 6513 Apartment building operators

(G-18126)
PITT-OHIO EXPRESS LLC
5200 Stickney Ave (43612-3723)
PHONE.....................419 726-6523
Fax: 419 729-2894
Robert Divel, *General Mgr*
Shelley Hart, *Opers Spvr*
Dean Miller, *Opers Spvr*
Ron Brown, *Manager*
Jim Brywczynski,
EMP: 109

SALES (corp-wide): 507.8MM **Privately Held**
SIC: 4213 Contract haulers
PA: Pitt-Ohio Express, Llc
15 27th St
Pittsburgh PA 15222
412 232-3015

(G-18127)
PITT-OHIO EXPRESS LLC
5200 Stickney Ave (43612-3723)
PHONE.....................419 729-8173
Robert Divel, *Manager*
EMP: 80
SALES (corp-wide): 507.8MM **Privately Held**
SIC: 4212 Local trucking, without storage
PA: Pitt-Ohio Express, Llc
15 27th St
Pittsburgh PA 15222
412 232-3015

(G-18128)
PLANNED PARENTHOOD NW OHIO INC
1301 Jefferson Ave (43604-5850)
PHONE.....................419 255-1115
Lee Itson, *Opers Staff*
William H Eywood, *Treasurer*
Scott Hamner, *Treasurer*
Heidi Rogols, *Manager*
Johnetta McCollough, *Exec Dir*
EMP: 33 EST: 1937
SQ FT: 11,600
SALES: 1.7MM **Privately Held**
WEB: www.ppnwo.org
SIC: 8093 Family planning clinic

(G-18129)
PNC BANK NATIONAL ASSOCIATION
Also Called: National City Bank
405 Madison Ave Ste 4 (43604-1263)
P.O. Box 1688 (43603-1688)
PHONE.....................419 259-5466
Fax: 419 259-6601
Robert Schowalter, *Div Sub Head*
Douglas Box, *Senior VP*
Scot Masell, *Branch Mgr*
EMP: 350
SALES (corp-wide): 18B **Publicly Held**
WEB: www.allegiantbank.com
SIC: 6021 National commercial banks
HQ: Pnc Bank, National Association
222 Delaware Ave
Wilmington DE 19801
877 762-2000

(G-18130)
PORT LAWRENCE TITLE AND TR CO (DH)
4 Seagate Ste 101 (43604-1173)
PHONE.....................419 244-4605
Fax: 419 244-3414
Marggretta Laskey, *President*
Victor Crouch, *Vice Pres*
Steve Sczesny, *Vice Pres*
Gerald Stewart, *Vice Pres*
Pat Lammon, *Director*
EMP: 40
SQ FT: 16,200
SALES (est): 29.6MM **Publicly Held**
SIC: 6361 6531 Real estate title insurance; guarantee of titles; real estate agents & managers
HQ: First American Title Insurance Company
1 First American Way
Santa Ana CA 92707
800 854-3643

(G-18131)
POTTER TECHNOLOGIES LLC
843 Warehouse Rd (43615-6472)
PHONE.....................419 380-8404
Michael Teadt,
Jeffrey Potter,
EMP: 83 EST: 2010
SALES (est): 6.8MM **Privately Held**
SIC: 8731 Commercial physical research

(G-18132)
PRECISION STEEL SERVICES INC (PA)
31 E Sylvania Ave (43612-1474)
PHONE.....................419 476-5702
Fax: 419 476-4981
David L Kelley, *President*
Greg Forrester, *Vice Pres*
Ramin Kalaty, *Vice Pres*
Kathy Zolciak, *Vice Pres*
Jordan Demchyna, *Opers Mgr*
EMP: 60 EST: 1975
SQ FT: 35,000
SALES (est): 62.4MM **Privately Held**
WEB: www.precision-steel.com
SIC: 5051 3441 3444 Steel; fabricated structural metal; sheet metalwork

(G-18133)
PREMIUM TRNSP LOGISTICS LLC (PA)
5445 Sthwyck Blvd Ste 210 (43614)
PHONE.....................419 861-3430
Fax: 419 861-3526
Debbie Olilla, *Finance*
David L Swartz,
EMP: 45
SALES (est): 16.9MM **Privately Held**
SIC: 4213 Trucking, except local

(G-18134)
PRESIDIO INFRASTRUCTURE
20 N Saint Clair St (43604-1074)
PHONE.....................419 241-8303
Kirsten Smith, *Branch Mgr*
EMP: 51
SALES (corp-wide): 1.1B **Publicly Held**
SIC: 7373 Office computer automation systems integration
HQ: Presidio Infrastructure Solutions Llc
6355 E Paris Ave Se
Caledonia MI 49316
616 871-1500

(G-18135)
PRICEWATERHOUSECOOPERS LLP
406 Washington St Ste 200 (43604-1046)
PHONE.....................419 254-2500
Fax: 419 254-2550
Pam Schlosser, *Branch Mgr*
Tim Donnelly, *Manager*
Molly McCartney, *Admin Sec*
EMP: 40
SQ FT: 2,500
SALES (corp-wide): 5.6B **Privately Held**
WEB: www.pwcglobal.com
SIC: 8721 Certified public accountant
PA: Pricewaterhousecoopers Llp
300 Madison Ave Fl 24
New York NY 10017
646 471-4000

(G-18136)
PRIME HOME CARE LLC
3454 Oak Alley Ct Ste 304 (43606-1365)
PHONE.....................419 535-1414
Nataliya Romanova, *Branch Mgr*
EMP: 31
SALES (corp-wide): 1.6MM **Privately Held**
SIC: 8059 8082 Personal care home, with health care; home health care services
PA: Prime Home Care Llc
2775 W Us Hwy 22 3 Ste 1
Maineville OH 45039
513 340-4183

(G-18137)
PROFESSIONAL ELECTRIC PDTS CO
Also Called: Pepco
501 Phillips Ave (43612-1328)
P.O. Box 12020 (43612-0020)
PHONE.....................419 269-3790
Fax: 419 470-5596
Rhys Petee, *Business Mgr*
Glen McNeil, *Opers Mgr*
Jim Deraedt, *Branch Mgr*
Bill Logan, *Technology*
EMP: 30
SQ FT: 24,394

SALES (corp-wide): 90.8MM **Privately Held**
WEB: www.pepconet.com
SIC: 5063 Electrical apparatus & equipment; motors, electric; motor controls, starters & relays; electric
PA: Professional Electric Products Co Inc
33210 Lakeland Blvd
Eastlake OH 44095
440 946-3790

(G-18138)
PROGRSSIVE SWEEPING CONTRS INC (PA)
5202 Enterprise Blvd (43612-3809)
PHONE.....................419 464-0130
Fax: 419 464-0136
Michael R Lucht, *President*
Karen S Lucht, *Corp Secy*
Carol Gittus, *Manager*
EMP: 25
SQ FT: 4,800
SALES (est): 20.2MM **Privately Held**
SIC: 4959 Sweeping service: road, airport, parking lot, etc.

(G-18139)
PROMEDICA GI PHYSICIANS LLC
Also Called: Digestive Health Gastrologist
3439 Granite Cir (43617-1161)
PHONE.....................419 843-7996
Fax: 419 843-7725
Anita Eurner, *Office Mgr*
EMP: 30 EST: 2010
SALES (est): 722.7K **Privately Held**
SIC: 8011 Gastronomist

(G-18140)
PROMEDICA GNT-URINARY SURGEONS (PA)
3500 Executive Pkwy (43606-1319)
PHONE.....................419 531-8558
Fax: 419 531-8798
Gregor K Emmert MD, *President*
Mayer Waynestein MD, *Vice Pres*
Tapper Richard I, *Treasurer*
Daniel S Murtagh MD, *Admin Sec*
EMP: 30
SQ FT: 7,000
SALES (est): 3.5MM **Privately Held**
WEB: www.parkwaysc.org
SIC: 8011 Urologist

(G-18141)
PROMEDICA HEALTH SYSTEMS INC (PA)
100 Madison Ave (43604-1516)
PHONE.....................567 585-7454
Alan W Brass, *CEO*
Tom Dellaflora, *Exec VP*
Terri McLain, *Exec VP*
Tom Borer, *Vice Pres*
Mike Ruhlen, *Vice Pres*
EMP: 4500
SALES (est): 1.5B **Privately Held**
SIC: 8062 6324 8351 8741 General medical & surgical hospitals; health maintenance organization (HMO), insurance only; child day care services; management services

(G-18142)
PTI QLITY CNTNMENT SLTIONS LLC
5655 Opportunity Dr Ste 4 (43612-2934)
PHONE.....................313 304-8677
Rodney Yates, *Director*
EMP: 54
SALES (corp-wide): 32.9MM **Privately Held**
SIC: 4785 Inspection services connected with transportation
PA: Pti Quality Containment Solutions Llc
18615 Sherwood St
Detroit MI 48234
313 365-3999

(G-18143)
PTX FLOORING INC
2701 128th St (43611-2204)
PHONE.....................419 726-1775
Fax: 419 243-6370
Omar Sadin, *President*
EMP: 28

GEOGRAPHIC SECTION
Toledo - Lucas County (G-18166)

SQ FT: 17,000
SALES (est): 2.7MM **Privately Held**
SIC: **1752** 5023 Floor laying & floor work; floor coverings

(G-18144)
PUBLIC BROADCASTING FOUND NW (PA)
Also Called: WGTE-TV-FM
1270 S Detroit Ave (43614-2794)
PHONE.....................419 380-4600
Fax: 419 380-4710
Marlon P Kiser, *President*
Ron Harrison, *Finance*
Christian Fritz, *Marketing Staff*
Reed Steele, *Program Mgr*
Marcia Fetter, *Manager*
EMP: 60
SQ FT: 45,000
SALES: 4MM **Privately Held**
WEB: www.wgte.pbs.org
SIC: **4833** 4832 Television broadcasting stations; radio broadcasting stations

(G-18145)
R I D INC
Also Called: Mahajan Tita & Katra
2222 Cherry St Ste 1400 (43608-2669)
PHONE.....................419 251-4790
James Tita, *President*
EMP: 25
SALES (est): 1.7MM **Privately Held**
SIC: **8011** 8031 Offices & clinics of medical doctors; offices & clinics of osteopathic physicians

(G-18146)
REGENCY PARK EYE ASSOCIATES (PA)
Also Called: Associated Eye Care
1000 Regency Ct Ste 100 (43623-3074)
PHONE.....................419 882-0588
Fax: 419 885-3070
Richard H Koop MD, *President*
Tammy Falzone, *CFO*
Kathryn Koop, *Treasurer*
EMP: 45 EST: 1970
SALES (est): 5.1MM **Privately Held**
SIC: **8011** Ophthalmologist

(G-18147)
REGENT ELECTRIC INC
5235 Tractor Rd (43612-3439)
PHONE.....................419 476-8333
Fax: 419 476-0179
Kevin Mc Carthy, *President*
Chas Slates, *Principal*
Gail Taylor, *Principal*
James Tice, *Principal*
Brian Mc Carthy, *Vice Pres*
EMP: 75
SQ FT: 10,000
SALES (est): 10.2MM **Privately Held**
SIC: **1731** General electrical contractor

(G-18148)
REHABILITATION AQUATICS
Also Called: Central Pk W Rhabilitation Ctr
3130 Central Park W Ste A (43617-1088)
PHONE.....................419 843-2500
Fax: 419 843-8288
Leonard O Greninger, *President*
Suzette Book, *Director*
EMP: 25
SQ FT: 10,000
SALES (est): 1.4MM **Privately Held**
WEB: www.cpwrehab.com
SIC: **8049** Physical therapist

(G-18149)
REHMANN LLC
7124 W Central Ave (43617-1117)
PHONE.....................419 865-8118
Donna Simmons, *Tax Mgr*
Ryan Cassette, *Auditor*
John Hills, *Branch Mgr*
Nancy Kukielka, *Admin Asst*
EMP: 60
SALES (corp-wide): 103.9MM **Privately Held**
SIC: **8721** Certified public accountant
PA: Rehmann, Llc
1500 W Big Beaver Rd
Macomb MI 48044
866 799-9580

(G-18150)
REMINGER CO LPA
405 Madison Ave Ste 2300 (43604-1212)
PHONE.....................419 254-1311
Laurie Avery, *Partner*
EMP: 71
SALES (corp-wide): 59.8MM **Privately Held**
SIC: **8111** Specialized law offices, attorneys
PA: Reminger Co., L.P.A.
101 W Prospect Ave # 1400
Cleveland OH 44115
216 687-1311

(G-18151)
RENT-A-CENTER INC
3418 Glendale Ave (43614-2428)
PHONE.....................419 382-8585
Fax: 419 382-0473
Rodney Rodriguez, *Branch Mgr*
EMP: 64
SALES (corp-wide): 2.7B **Publicly Held**
WEB: www.rentacenter.com
SIC: **7359** Appliance rental; furniture rental; home entertainment equipment rental; television rental
PA: Rent-A-Center, Inc.
5501 Headquarters Dr
Plano TX 75024
972 801-1100

(G-18152)
REPUBLIC SERVICES INC
6196 Hagman Rd (43612-3922)
PHONE.....................419 726-9465
John Stark, *Opers Mgr*
EMP: 34
SALES (corp-wide): 10B **Publicly Held**
SIC: **4953** Rubbish collection & disposal
PA: Republic Services, Inc.
18500 N Allied Way # 100
Phoenix AZ 85054
480 627-2700

(G-18153)
RESCUE INCORPORATED
3350 Collingwood Blvd # 2 (43610-1173)
PHONE.....................419 255-9585
Fax: 419 255-2801
John Debruyne, *CEO*
Jeff Earle, *Project Mgr*
Kul Gupta, *Director*
Jan Eppard, *Nursing Dir*
Winona Robinson, *Lic Prac Nurse*
EMP: 150
SQ FT: 13,500
SALES: 7.8MM **Privately Held**
WEB: www.rescuemhs.com
SIC: **8063** 8361 8093 Hospital for the mentally ill; residential care; specialty outpatient clinics

(G-18154)
RETINA VITREOUS ASSOCIATES (PA)
6591 W Central Ave # 202 (43617-1097)
PHONE.....................419 517-6599
Fax: 419 224-7488
Ira Orgel, *Partner*
Dr Charles K Dabbs, *Partner*
Juan Lebron, *Partner*
Dr Samuel R Pesin, *Partner*
Larry Maluski, *Software Dev*
EMP: 50
SQ FT: 5,000
SALES (est): 8.8MM **Privately Held**
WFR: www.rvaonlinc.com
SIC: **8011** Ophthalmologist

(G-18155)
REUBEN CO (PA)
24 S Huron St (43604-8706)
PHONE.....................419 241-3400
Fax: 419 242-3896
George S Wade Sr, *Ch of Bd*
Penny Celestino, *Finance*
EMP: 42
SQ FT: 1,000
SALES (est): 2.7MM **Privately Held**
SIC: **6531** Real estate managers; real estate agent, commercial; real estate agent, residential

(G-18156)
REYNOLDS ROAD SURGICAL CTR LLC
Also Called: WILDWOOD SURGICAL CENTER
2865 N Reynolds Rd # 190 (43615-2068)
PHONE.....................419 578-7500
Fax: 419 539-6320
Casey Johnson, *Business Mgr*
Kelly Shirer, *Finance*
Mandy Phillips, *Manager*
EMP: 53
SALES: 7.8MM **Privately Held**
WEB: www.wildwoodsurgical.com
SIC: **8093** Specialty outpatient clinics

(G-18157)
RIVERSIDE MARINE INDS INC
Also Called: H Hansen Industries
2824 N Summit St (43611-3425)
PHONE.....................419 729-1621
Fax: 419 729-0715
Tony La Mantia, *President*
Jerry Norton, *Corp Secy*
Larry Ansler, *Vice Pres*
Bonnie Lamanpia, *Manager*
Bonnie Lamantia, *Manager*
EMP: 60
SQ FT: 30,000
SALES (est): 10.6MM **Privately Held**
SIC: **7699** Nautical repair services

(G-18158)
RLM FABRICATING INC
4801 Bennett Rd (43612-2531)
PHONE.....................419 729-6130
Michael Reser, *President*
Patrick Copeland, *President*
Trudy Turner, *Manager*
EMP: 30
SALES (est): 6.2MM **Privately Held**
SIC: **5099** Cork products, fabricated

(G-18159)
RMF NOOTER INC
915 Matzinger Rd (43612-3820)
PHONE.....................419 727-1970
Fax: 419 727-1898
Jimmy Nelson, *President*
Karl Zacharias, *Superintendent*
Don Majchrowski, *Vice Pres*
Mike Pollans, *Vice Pres*
Roger Sheidler, *Vice Pres*
EMP: 100
SALES (est): 21MM
SALES (corp-wide): 683.2MM **Privately Held**
WEB: www.nooter.com
SIC: **7699** 1711 1731 Boiler & heating repair services; mechanical contractor; electrical work
HQ: Nooter Construction Company
1500 S 2nd St
Saint Louis MO 63104
314 621-6000

(G-18160)
ROBERT C VERBON INC
Also Called: Embers
4964 Forest Hill Dr (43623-1039)
PHONE.....................419 867-6868
Robert C Verbon, *President*
EMP: 30
SQ FT: 11,000
SALES (est): 1.8MM **Privately Held**
SIC: **1521** 6552 5812 New construction, single-family houses; subdividers & developers; American restaurant

(G-18161)
ROBERT F LINDSAY CO (PA)
4268 Rose Garden Dr (43623-3457)
PHONE.....................419 476-6221
Fax: 419 476-0600
Thomas Lindsay, *President*
Marge Czarnecki, *Vice Pres*
Timothy O'Leary, *Vice Pres*
Ann Veasey, *Vice Pres*
Margaret M Lindsay, *Admin Sec*
EMP: 60
SQ FT: 2,500
SALES (est): 2.5MM **Privately Held**
WEB: www.rflindsay.com
SIC: **6531** Real estate brokers & agents

(G-18162)
ROBERT STOUGH VENTURES CORP
Also Called: Whitewater Car & Van Wash Co
5409 Monroe St (43623-2817)
PHONE.....................419 882-4073
Robert A Stough, *President*
Jeff Dheel, *Manager*
EMP: 50
SQ FT: 3,400
SALES (est): 1MM **Privately Held**
SIC: **7542** Carwash, automatic

(G-18163)
ROEMER LAND INVESTMENT CO
3912 Sunforest Ct Ste A (43623-4486)
PHONE.....................419 475-5151
Wellington F Roemer I, *President*
Wayne Shawaker, *Vice Pres*
EMP: 45 EST: 1942
SQ FT: 9,500
SALES (est): 2.3MM **Privately Held**
SIC: **6512** Commercial & industrial building operation

(G-18164)
ROMANOFF ELECTRIC CO LLC
5570 Enterprise Blvd (43612-3860)
PHONE.....................419 726-2627
Fax: 419 726-5406
Dennis Quebe, *CEO*
Roger Van Der Horst, *President*
Dana Hostdelar, *President*
Diane Frank, *Manager*
EMP: 200 EST: 1927
SQ FT: 21,000
SALES (est): 22.2MM
SALES (corp-wide): 83.3MM **Privately Held**
WEB: www.romanoffelectric.com
SIC: **1731** General electrical contractor
PA: Quebe Holdings, Inc.
1985 Founders Dr
Dayton OH 45420
937 222-2290

(G-18165)
ROMANOFF ELECTRIC CO LLC
5570 Enterprise Blvd (43612-3860)
PHONE.....................937 640-7925
Brian Carthy, *Vice Pres*
Dave Clunk, *Manager*
Dennis Quebe,
Roger Vanderhorst,
Dave Wozniak,
EMP: 100
SQ FT: 30,000
SALES (est): 4.9MM
SALES (corp-wide): 83.3MM **Privately Held**
WEB: www.quebe.com
SIC: **1731** General electrical contractor
PA: Quebe Holdings, Inc.
1985 Founders Dr
Dayton OH 45420
937 222-2290

(G-18166)
RUBINI ENTERPRISES INC
Also Called: Toledo Springs Service
5015 Enterprise Blvd (43612-3839)
P.O. Box 80039 (43608-0039)
PHONE.....................419 729-7010
Fax: 419 729-7019
Mark Rubini, *President*
Tom McNary, *Manager*
EMP: 30
SALES (corp-wide): 1.7MM **Privately Held**
SIC: **5013** 7538 7539 Automotive supplies & parts; truck engine repair, except industrial; electrical services; frame & front end repair services; wheel alignment, automotive
PA: Rubini Enterprises, Inc.
5015 Enterprise Blvd
Toledo OH
419 729-7010

Toledo - Lucas County (G-18167)

GEOGRAPHIC SECTION

(G-18167)
RUMPF CORPORATION (PA)
Also Called: Job1usa
701 Jefferson Ave Ste 201 (43604-6957)
P.O. Box 1480 (43603-1480)
PHONE..................................419 255-5005
Fax: 419 244-1870
Bruce F Rumpf, *CEO*
Robert Knowles, *Vice Pres*
Tamela Ledford, *Director*
Elizabeth B Rumpf, *Admin Sec*
EMP: 40
SQ FT: 35,000
SALES (est): 33.4MM **Privately Held**
SIC: 7361 7363 7381 Employment agencies; temporary help service; employee leasing service; security guard service; protective services, guard

(G-18168)
RUSK INDUSTRIES INC
Also Called: Everdry Waterproofing Toledo
2930 Centennial Rd (43617-1833)
PHONE..................................419 841-6055
Fax: 419 841-8267
Kenneth Rusk, *President*
Jerry Jacobiak, *QC Mgr*
Gil Ramirez, *Sales Dir*
Jessica Wilkens, *Office Mgr*
Dawn Curtis, *Admin Sec*
EMP: 60
SQ FT: 9,000
SALES (est): 7.4MM **Privately Held**
WEB: www.everdrytoledo.com
SIC: 1799 Waterproofing

(G-18169)
SABCO INDUSTRIES INC
4511 South Ave (43615-6418)
PHONE..................................419 531-5347
Robert Sulier, *President*
John Pershing, *Vice Pres*
CB M Ash, *Treasurer*
Dan Sulier, *Sales Mgr*
▲ EMP: 28 EST: 1961
SQ FT: 35,000
SALES (est): 3.2MM **Privately Held**
WEB: www.kegs.com
SIC: 7699 5085 3993 3412 Tank repair & cleaning services; barrels, new or reconditioned; signs & advertising specialties; metal barrels, drums & pails

(G-18170)
SAIA MOTOR FREIGHT LINE LLC
1919 E Manhattan Blvd (43608-1534)
PHONE..................................419 726-9761
Jim Bryan, *Branch Mgr*
EMP: 31
SALES (corp-wide): 1.3B **Publicly Held**
WEB: www.saia.com
SIC: 4213 Contract haulers
HQ: Saia Motor Freight Line, Llc
11465 Johns Creek Pkwy # 400
Duluth GA 30097
770 232-5067

(G-18171)
SAMUEL SON & CO INC
Doral Steel
1500 Coining Dr (43612-2905)
PHONE..................................419 470-7070
Fax: 419 470-7040
Gary Rowe, *Plant Supt*
Michelle Armbruster, *Credit Mgr*
Pat Connor, *Sales Mgr*
Tammy Schulte, *Sales Mgr*
Craig Biden, *Sales Associate*
EMP: 80
SALES (corp-wide): 975.8MM **Privately Held**
SIC: 5051 Steel
HQ: Samuel Son & Co. Inc.
4334 Walden Ave
Lancaster NY 14086

(G-18172)
SAR ENTERPRISES LLC
Also Called: Home Instead Senior Care
2631 W Central Ave (43606-3548)
PHONE..................................419 472-8181
Mark McPherson, *Manager*
Scott Rozanski,
Lisa Rozanski,
EMP: 80 EST: 2000
SALES (est): 2.5MM **Privately Held**
SIC: 8082 Home health care services

(G-18173)
SATURN OF TOLEDO INC
6141 W Central Ave (43615-1805)
PHONE..................................419 841-9070
Fax: 419 841-5979
Frank Kisler, *President*
Rhonda Keezer, *Controller*
Connie Reinhart, *Manager*
EMP: 28
SALES (est): 5.2MM **Privately Held**
SIC: 5511 7515 Automobiles, new & used; passenger car leasing

(G-18174)
SAVAGE AND ASSOCIATES INC (PA)
4427 Talmadge Rd Bldg 2 (43623-3523)
PHONE..................................419 475-8665
Fax: 419 475-8240
Ralph E Toland III, *President*
Phil Johnson, *Owner*
Mark Smigelski, *Owner*
Russell Karban, *Vice Pres*
Nick Camp, *CFO*
EMP: 61 EST: 1960
SQ FT: 30,000
SALES: 73.9K **Privately Held**
WEB: www.savagefinancial.com
SIC: 6411 Life insurance agents; pension & retirement plan consultants

(G-18175)
SCHROEDER COMPANY (PA)
4668 Talmadge Rd (43623-3007)
PHONE..................................419 473-3139
Edward J Schroeder Jr, *President*
◆ EMP: 40
SQ FT: 1,500
SALES (est): 5.3MM **Privately Held**
SIC: 1522 6531 Apartment building construction; real estate managers

(G-18176)
SCOTTS TOWING CO
Also Called: Scotts Commercial Truck Svcs
5930 Benore Rd (43612-3955)
PHONE..................................419 729-7888
Fax: 419 729-7880
Ronald L Scott, *President*
Mark Scott, *Corp Secy*
Dona Scott, *Vice Pres*
EMP: 25
SQ FT: 5,000
SALES (est): 3.4MM **Privately Held**
WEB: www.scott-truck.com
SIC: 7549 7538 5078 Towing services; truck engine repair, except industrial; refrigeration units, motor vehicles

(G-18177)
SEAWAY SPONGE & CHAMOIS CO (PA)
Also Called: Seaway Building Services
458 2nd St (43605-2006)
P.O. Box 8037 (43605-0037)
PHONE..................................419 691-4694
Terry Vandervlucht, *President*
EMP: 45
SALES (est): 750K **Privately Held**
SIC: 7349 5087 Building & office cleaning services; janitors' supplies

(G-18178)
SENIOR CARE MANAGEMENT INC
3501 Executive Pkwy # 219 (43606-1321)
PHONE..................................419 578-7000
Fax: 419 578-2824
Kathy Brentlinger, *Principal*
EMP: 73
SALES (est): 1.5MM **Privately Held**
WEB: www.seniorcaremanagement.com
SIC: 8082 Home health care services

(G-18179)
SENTINEL FLUID CONTROLS LLC (DH)
5702 Opportunity Dr (43612-2903)
PHONE..................................419 478-9086
Amy Sweet, *Human Resources*
Larry Peterson, *Mng Member*
Terry Moore,
EMP: 50
SALES (est): 40.1MM
SALES (corp-wide): 2.5B **Publicly Held**
WEB: www.sentinelfluidcontrols.com
SIC: 5084 Food industry machinery

(G-18180)
SERVICE CORPS RETIRED EXECS
Also Called: S C O R E
2200 Jefferson Ave Fl 1 (43604-7101)
PHONE..................................419 259-7598
Larry King, *Chairman*
EMP: 30
SALES (corp-wide): 13.1MM **Privately Held**
WEB: www.score199.mv.com
SIC: 8611 Business associations
PA: Service Corps Of Retired Executives Association
1175 Herndon Pkwy Ste 900
Herndon VA 20170
703 487-3612

(G-18181)
SFC GRAPHICS INC
110 E Woodruff Ave (43604-5226)
PHONE..................................419 255-1283
Fax: 419 255-5558
Tom Clark, *CEO*
Gary Crider, *Principal*
Deb Truscinski, *Exec VP*
Scott Flom, *Vice Pres*
Steve Macy, *Controller*
EMP: 45
SALES (est): 7.4MM **Privately Held**
SIC: 7336 Commercial art & graphic design

(G-18182)
SFN GROUP INC
Also Called: Spherion Outsourcing Group
1212 E Alexis Rd (43612-3974)
PHONE..................................419 727-4104
Peter Rogowski, *Manager*
EMP: 33
SALES (corp-wide): 27.4B **Privately Held**
SIC: 7363 Temporary help service
HQ: Sfn Group, Inc.
2050 Spectrum Blvd
Fort Lauderdale FL 33309
954 308-7600

(G-18183)
SHADOW VALLEY TENNIS & FITNESS
1661 N Hlland Sylvania Rd (43615)
PHONE..................................419 861-3986
Carol Weiner, *President*
Jim Davis, *Vice Pres*
EMP: 25
SQ FT: 85,768
SALES (est): 338.7K **Privately Held**
SIC: 7991 Athletic club & gymnasiums, membership

(G-18184)
SHINDLER NEFF HOLMES SCHLAG
300 Madison Ave Ste 1200 (43604-1567)
PHONE..................................419 243-6281
Fax: 419 243-0129
Daniel A Worline, *Partner*
Charles K Boxell, *Partner*
Paul S Goldberg, *Partner*
Martin J Holmes, *Partner*
Mark E Lupe, *Partner*
EMP: 45
SALES (est): 5.1MM **Privately Held**
WEB: www.snhslaw.com
SIC: 8111 General practice attorney, lawyer

(G-18185)
SHORT FREIGHT LINES INC
6180 Benore Rd (43612-4801)
PHONE..................................419 729-1691
Fax: 419 729-1692
Dee Palmerton, *Manager*
EMP: 40
SALES (corp-wide): 9.5MM **Privately Held**
SIC: 4213 4231 Trucking, except local; trucking terminal facilities
PA: Short Freight Lines, Inc.
459 S River Rd
Bay City MI
989 893-3505

(G-18186)
SHRADER TIRE & OIL INC (PA)
2045 W Sylvania Ave # 51 (43613-4588)
P.O. Box 5407 (43613-0407)
PHONE..................................419 472-2128
Fax: 419 471-2534
James W Shrader Jr, *Ch of Bd*
Joseph W Schrader, *President*
Zach Park, *Business Mgr*
Jim McCabe, *Vice Pres*
John Shrader, *Vice Pres*
▲ EMP: 35 EST: 1948
SQ FT: 26,000
SALES: 54.1MM **Privately Held**
WEB: www.shradertireandoil.com
SIC: 5014 5172 5013 Tires & tubes; petroleum products; lubricating oils & greases; motor vehicle supplies & new parts

(G-18187)
SHUMAKER LOOP & KENDRICK LLP (PA)
1000 Jackson St (43604-5573)
PHONE..................................419 241-9000
Fax: 419 241-6894
David F Waterman, *Managing Prtnr*
Kenneth Crooks, *COO*
Paul Favorite, *COO*
Paul W Favorite, *COO*
David Wicklund, *Technical Mgr*
EMP: 210
SQ FT: 110,000
SALES (est): 66.6MM **Privately Held**
SIC: 8111 General practice law office

(G-18188)
SIGNATURE ASSOCIATES INC
Also Called: Signature Assoc-A Cushman
4 Seagate Ste 608 (43604-2612)
PHONE..................................419 244-7505
Ken Marciniak, *Principal*
Sam Zyndorf, *Senior VP*
Janet Collins, *Personnel Exec*
Douglas Dietz, *Manager*
EMP: 25
SALES (corp-wide): 18.5MM **Privately Held**
WEB: www.signatureassociates.com
SIC: 8742 6531 6552 Real estate consultant; real estate agent, commercial; real estate managers; subdividers & developers
PA: Signature Associates, Inc.
1 Towne Sq Ste 1200
Southfield MI 48076
248 948-9000

(G-18189)
SISTERS OF NOTRE D
Also Called: Maria Child Care
3912 Sunforest Ct Ste B (43623-4486)
PHONE..................................419 471-0170
Fax: 419 479-3057
Carrie Craun, *Administration*
EMP: 25
SALES (corp-wide): 8.4MM **Privately Held**
WEB: www.stjamesvalley.org
SIC: 8351 Child day care services
PA: Sisters Of Notre Dame Of Toledo Ohio, The (Inc)
3837 Secor Rd
Toledo OH 43623
419 474-5485

(G-18190)
SLEEP NETWORK INC (PA)
3450 W Central Ave # 118 (43606-1421)
PHONE..................................419 535-9282
Fax: 419 535-9443
Terry Shiffer, *President*
Joseph I Shaffer, *President*
Bob Drager, *Vice Pres*
Terry Shaffer, *Admin Sec*
EMP: 46
SQ FT: 3,000
SALES (est): 9MM **Privately Held**
WEB: www.sleepnetwork.com
SIC: 8741 Management services

GEOGRAPHIC SECTION

Toledo - Lucas County (G-18218)

(G-18191)
SMB CONSTRUCTION CO INC (PA)
5120 Jackman Rd (43613-2923)
PHONE................................419 269-1473
Fax: 419 269-1485
Jim Mossing, *President*
Rob Keel, *Vice Pres*
Jeff Mossing, *Vice Pres*
Debbie Early, *Manager*
EMP: 47
SQ FT: 33,000
SALES (est): 7.5MM **Privately Held**
WEB: www.smbconstruction.com
SIC: 1521 6513 1542 Repairing fire damage, single-family houses; apartment building operators; commercial & office buildings, renovation & repair

(G-18192)
SOLOMON LEI & ASSOCIATES INC
Also Called: Solomon, Lei & Associates
947 Belmont Ave (43607-4244)
PHONE................................419 246-6931
Floyd Abercrombie, *CEO*
EMP: 27
SALES (est): 477.7K **Privately Held**
SIC: 7389

(G-18193)
SPA FITNESS CENTERS INC (PA)
Also Called: Utah Spas
343 New Towne Square Dr (43612-4626)
PHONE................................419 476-6018
Robert Rice, *President*
Kenneth Melby, *Vice Pres*
EMP: 50
SQ FT: 1,200
SALES (est): 4.6MM **Privately Held**
SIC: 7991 Spas

(G-18194)
SPARTAN CONSTRUCTION CO INC
3001 South Ave (43609-1333)
P.O. Box 141179 (43614-9113)
PHONE................................419 389-1854
Fax: 419 389-1855
Peter Vandenberg, *President*
Peter J Vandenberg, *President*
EMP: 35
SQ FT: 12,000
SALES (est): 3.7MM **Privately Held**
SIC: 1521 Single-family housing construction

(G-18195)
SPENGLER NATHANSON PLL
4 Seagate Ste 400 (43604-2622)
PHONE................................419 241-2201
Richard Wolff, *Managing Prtnr*
B Gary Mc Bride, *Managing Prtnr*
B G McBride, *Managing Prtnr*
James C Anderson, *Partner*
Michael W Bragg, *Partner*
EMP: 55
SQ FT: 26,000
SALES (est): 7.5MM **Privately Held**
SIC: 8111 General practice attorney, lawyer

(G-18196)
SPORTS CARE REHABILITATION
2865 N Reynolds Rd # 110 (43615-2069)
PHONE................................419 578-7530
Fax: 419 539-0288
Mike Heifferon, *Director*
Jeanne-Marie Sinnott, *Sports Medicine*
EMP: 40
SALES (est): 1.1MM **Privately Held**
WEB: www.sportscarept.com
SIC: 8011 Sports medicine specialist, physician

(G-18197)
SPRINT COMMUNICATIONS CO LP
1708 W Alexis Rd (43613-2349)
PHONE................................419 725-2444
EMP: 39
SALES (corp-wide): 78.3B **Publicly Held**
SIC: 4813 Local & long distance telephone communications
HQ: Sprint Communications Company L.P.
6391 Sprint Pkwy
Overland Park KS 66251
800 829-0965

(G-18198)
SPRYANCE INC
3101 Executive Pkwy # 600 (43606-5301)
PHONE................................678 808-0600
EMP: 34
SALES (est): 639K
SALES (corp-wide): 1.9B **Publicly Held**
SIC: 8099 Health And Allied Services, Nec, Nsk
HQ: Transcend Services, Inc.
1 Glenlake Pkwy Ste 800
Atlanta GA 30328
800 205-7047

(G-18199)
ST ANNE MERCY HOSPITAL
3404 W Sylvania Ave (43623-4480)
PHONE................................419 407-2663
Fax: 419 407-3870
Richard Evans, *CEO*
Mahjabeen M Islam MD, *Principal*
Agha Shahid MD, *Principal*
EMP: 39
SALES: 113.2MM **Privately Held**
SIC: 8062 General medical & surgical hospitals

(G-18200)
ST PAULS COMMUNITY CENTER
230 13th St (43604-5443)
P.O. Box 9564 (43697-9564)
PHONE................................419 255-5520
Fax: 419 259-4609
Ruth Arden, *Exec Dir*
EMP: 51
SQ FT: 9,464
SALES: 2.4MM **Privately Held**
SIC: 8322 Community center; temporary relief service; emergency shelters

(G-18201)
STEPHEN R SADDEMI MD
Also Called: Medical College of Ohio
2865 N Reynolds Rd # 160 (43615-2076)
PHONE................................419 578-7200
Stephen R Saddemi, *Owner*
EMP: 25
SALES (est): 359.4K **Privately Held**
SIC: 8049 Offices of health practitioner

(G-18202)
STERICYCLE INC
1301 E Alexis Rd (43612-3977)
PHONE................................419 729-1934
John Ertle, *Manager*
EMP: 36
SALES (corp-wide): 3.5B **Publicly Held**
WEB: www.stericycle.com
SIC: 4953 Hazardous waste collection & disposal
PA: Stericycle, Inc.
28161 N Keith Dr
Lake Forest IL 60045
847 367-5910

(G-18203)
STORK STUDIOS INC
Also Called: Sylvania Ultrasound Institute
3830 Woodley Rd Ste A (43606-1176)
PHONE................................419 841-7766
Rose Gozdowski, *President*
Marsha Owen, *Office Mgr*
EMP: 27
SALES (est): 1.9MM **Privately Held**
SIC: 8071 Ultrasound laboratory

(G-18204)
STRANAHAN THEATRE TRUST
Also Called: Stranahan Theatre & Great Hall
4645 Heatherdowns Blvd # 2 (43614-3192)
PHONE................................419 381-8851
Ward Whiting, *Manager*
EMP: 55
SQ FT: 50,000
SALES: 2.2MM **Privately Held**
WEB: www.stranahantheater.com
SIC: 6512 7922 6519 5812 Auditorium & hall operation; theatrical producers & services; real property lessors; eating places

(G-18205)
STS RESTAURANT MANAGEMENT INC
Also Called: STS Management
420 Madison Ave Ste 103 (43604-1209)
PHONE................................419 246-0730
David Ball, *President*
EMP: 65
SQ FT: 144,000
SALES (est): 6.1MM **Privately Held**
SIC: 6531 Real estate managers

(G-18206)
SUBSTANCE ABUSE SERVICES INC
Also Called: Sasi
2005 Ashland Ave (43620-1703)
PHONE................................419 243-7274
Dave Rainsberger, *Manager*
Carroll Parks, *Exec Dir*
Eal Word, *Director*
EMP: 45 **EST:** 1981
SQ FT: 8,700
SALES (est): 896.9K **Privately Held**
SIC: 8322 Self-help organization

(G-18207)
SUN FEDERAL CREDIT UNION
3341 Executive Pkwy (43606-1316)
PHONE................................419 537-0200
Rick Cherry, *President*
Brian Hughes, *CFO*
Melissa Gregg, *Corp Comm Staff*
Adam Wood, *Branch Mgr*
Diane Kuenzel, *Director*
EMP: 100 **EST:** 1936
SQ FT: 5,000
SALES (est): 10MM **Privately Held**
SIC: 6062 6061 State credit unions, not federally chartered; federal credit unions

(G-18208)
SUNFOREST OB GYN ASSOCIATES
Also Called: Promedica Physician
3740 W Sylvania Ave # 103 (43623-4461)
PHONE................................419 473-6622
Fax: 419 473-6627
Mary Kerr, *Manager*
Linda Whittington, *Manager*
Debra Easterwood, *Admin Asst*
EMP: 26
SQ FT: 9,200
SALES (est): 5.2MM **Privately Held**
SIC: 8011 Gynecologist

(G-18209)
SUNRISE TELEVISION CORP
Also Called: W U P W
4 Seagate Ste 101 (43604-1520)
PHONE................................419 244-2197
Fax: 419 244-8842
EMP: 50
SALES (corp-wide): 674.9MM **Publicly Held**
SIC: 4832 4833 Radio broadcasting stations; television broadcasting stations
HQ: Sunrise Television Corp.
1 W Exchange St Ste 5a
Providence RI

(G-18210)
SUNSET HOUSE INC
Also Called: Woodlands At Sunset House
4020 Indian Rd (43606-2292)
PHONE................................419 536-4645
Fax: 419 536-8972
Vickie Bartlett, *CEO*
Judy Bishop, *Opers Staff*
Marcia Kert, *Office Mgr*
Carol Jones, *Manager*
Cletus Iwuagwu, *Director*
EMP: 170 **EST:** 1873
SQ FT: 1,800
SALES (est): 17.5MM **Privately Held**
SIC: 8361 8052 Home for the aged; intermediate care facilities

(G-18211)
SUPERIOR PACKAGING TOLEDO LLC
2970 Airport Hwy (43609-1404)
PHONE................................419 380-3335
Steve Kovar, *President*
Jennifer Moore, *Vice Pres*
EMP: 40 **EST:** 2007
SALES (est): 5MM **Privately Held**
SIC: 5199 Packaging materials

(G-18212)
SUPREME COURT UNITED STATES
Also Called: US Probation
1946 N 13th St Ste 292 (43604-7264)
PHONE................................419 213-5800
Fax: 419 213-5799
Eric Corns, *Branch Mgr*
EMP: 27 **Publicly Held**
WEB: www.ao.uscourts.gov
SIC: 8322 9211 Probation office; courts;
HQ: Supreme Court, United States
1 1st St Ne
Washington DC 20543
202 479-3000

(G-18213)
TAMARON GOLF LLC
Also Called: Tamaron Country Club
2162 W Alexis Rd (43613-2216)
PHONE................................419 474-5067
Fax: 419 474-2652
Tony Fuhrman, *President*
Anthony A Fuhrman,
EMP: 58
SALES (est): 2.8MM **Privately Held**
SIC: 7992 Public golf courses

(G-18214)
TASC OF NORTHWEST OHIO INC (PA)
Also Called: Lucas County Tasc
701 Jefferson Ave Ste 101 (43604-6956)
PHONE................................419 242-9955
Fax: 419 242-8855
Larry Leyland, *General Mgr*
Johnetta McCollough, *Exec Dir*
EMP: 30
SALES (est): 1.7MM **Privately Held**
SIC: 8322 Social service center

(G-18215)
TELEPHONE & CMPT CONTRS INC
5560 308th St (43611-2354)
PHONE................................419 726-8142
Fax: 419 729-3811
Patricia Futrell, *President*
Dennis M Futrell, *Vice Pres*
EMP: 25
SQ FT: 15,000
SALES: 2.3MM **Privately Held**
WEB: www.tccontractor.com
SIC: 1731 Communications specialization

(G-18216)
TEMBEC BTLSR INC
2112 Sylvan Ave (43606-4767)
P.O. Box 2570 (43606-0570)
PHONE................................419 244-5856
Fax: 419 244-9206
James M Lopez, *President*
Lawrence Rowley, *General Mgr*
Dan Wozniak, *Admin Sec*
▲ **EMP:** 32
SQ FT: 84,000
SALES (est): 8.6MM **Privately Held**
WEB: www.btlresins.com
SIC: 2821 5169 Plastics materials & resins; industrial chemicals
HQ: Tembec Inc
4 Place Ville-Marie Bureau 100
Montreal QC H3B 2
514 871-0137

(G-18217)
THOS A LUPICA
608 Madison Ave Ste 1000 (43604-1169)
PHONE................................419 252-6298
Thomas Lupica, *Owner*
EMP: 70
SALES (est): 1.8MM **Privately Held**
SIC: 8111 General practice attorney, lawyer

(G-18218)
THREAD INFORMATION DESIGN INC
Also Called: Thread Marketing Group
4635 W Alexis Rd (43623-1005)
PHONE................................419 887-6801

Toledo - Lucas County (G-18219)

GEOGRAPHIC SECTION

Fax: 419 887-6802
Judy McFarland, *CEO*
Mark Luetke, *President*
Joe Sharp, *Principal*
Holly Goldstein, *Exec VP*
Tim Langhorst, *Exec VP*
EMP: 35
SQ FT: 11,000
SALES (est): 5.6MM **Privately Held**
WEB: www.threadgroup.com
SIC: 7311 Advertising agencies

(G-18219)
TJ METZGERS INC
207 Arco Dr (43607-2906)
PHONE.............................419 861-8611
Thomas H Metzger, *CEO*
Caitlin Meyers, *Sales Staff*
EMP: 100
SQ FT: 63,146
SALES (est): 26.7MM **Privately Held**
WEB: www.metzgers.com
SIC: 2752 2759 2789 2791 Commercial printing, offset; commercial printing; bookbinding & related work; photocomposition, for the printing trade; color separation, photographic & movie film

(G-18220)
TK HOMECARE LLC
Also Called: Visiting Angels
7110 W Central Ave Ste A (43617-3118)
PHONE.............................419 517-7000
Tamera Riggs, *President*
EMP: 132
SALES (est): 700.4K **Privately Held**
SIC: 8082 Home health care services

(G-18221)
TKY ASSOCIATES LLC
Also Called: Comfort Keepers
2451 N Reynolds Rd (43615-2840)
PHONE.............................419 535-7777
Fax: 419 535-7120
Julie Kuney, *General Mgr*
Todd A Kuney, *Mng Member*
EMP: 85 **EST:** 2011
SQ FT: 1,600
SALES (est): 4.1MM **Privately Held**
SIC: 8082 8049 Visiting nurse service; nurses & other medical assistants

(G-18222)
TLC EYECARE
3000 Regency Ct Ste 100 (43623-3081)
PHONE.............................419 882-2020
Sue Demott, *President*
EMP: 30 **EST:** 2001
SALES (est): 730.3K **Privately Held**
SIC: 8011 Ophthalmologist

(G-18223)
TLEVAY INC
Also Called: Foundation Pk Alzheimers Care
1621 S Byrne Rd (43614-3456)
PHONE.............................419 385-3958
James L Farley, *Principal*
Michael J Scharfenberger, *Principal*
Mandy Evola, *Manager*
Jason Benett, *Administration*
EMP: 140
SALES (est): 2.4MM
SALES (corp-wide): 26.1MM **Privately Held**
SIC: 8051 Skilled nursing care facilities
PA: Nursing Care Management Of America, Inc.
7265 Kenwood Rd Ste 300
Cincinnati OH 45236
513 793-8804

(G-18224)
TODD ALSPAUGH & ASSOCIATES
415 E State Line Rd (43612-4795)
PHONE.............................419 476-8126
Todd Alspaugh, *President*
Curt Asplaugh, *Vice Pres*
EMP: 45
SQ FT: 4,000
SALES: 4.5MM **Privately Held**
SIC: 1629 1794 1623 Land preparation construction; excavation work; sewer line construction

(G-18225)
TOLCO CORPORATION
1920 Linwood Ave (43604-5293)
PHONE.............................419 241-1113
Fax: 419 241-3035
George L Notarianni, *President*
Al Carver, *Division Mgr*
James Reising, *Regional Mgr*
Ted Denker, *Purchasing*
Tricia Thomas, *Design Engr*
▲ **EMP:** 75
SQ FT: 30,000
SALES (est): 32.6MM **Privately Held**
WEB: www.tolco.com
SIC: 5085 3563 3586 3561 Bottler supplies; spraying outfits: metals, paints & chemicals (compressor); vacuum pumps, except laboratory; measuring & dispensing pumps; pumps & pumping equipment; specialty cleaning, polishes & sanitation goods

(G-18226)
TOLEDO AREA INSULATOR WKRS JAC
Also Called: Heat and Frost Insulators Jatc
4535 Hill Ave (43615-5301)
PHONE.............................419 531-5911
Lynette Jones, *Principal*
EMP: 85
SALES (est): 4.2MM **Privately Held**
SIC: 1799 Special trade contractors

(G-18227)
TOLEDO AREA RGIONAL TRNST AUTH (PA)
Also Called: Tarta
1127 W Central Ave (43610-1062)
P.O. Box 792 (43697-0792)
PHONE.............................419 243-7433
Fax: 419 243-8588
James K Gee, *General Mgr*
Tim Rowe, *Maintenance Dir*
Larry Hyttenhove, *Maint Spvr*
Jim Gee, *Manager*
Daniel Hunt, *Manager*
EMP: 73 **EST:** 1971
SQ FT: 8,000
SALES (est): 22.5MM **Privately Held**
WEB: www.tarta.com
SIC: 4111 Bus line operations

(G-18228)
TOLEDO BUILDING SERVICES CO
2121 Adams St (43604-5088)
P.O. Box 2223 (43603-2223)
PHONE.............................419 241-3101
Fax: 419 241-7010
Joel B Friedman, *Ch of Bd*
Lawrence M Friedman, *President*
Ward Whiting, *Vice Pres*
Judith Friedman, *Admin Sec*
EMP: 940
SQ FT: 20,000
SALES (est): 19.3MM **Privately Held**
WEB: www.toledobuildingservices.com
SIC: 7349 Cleaning service, industrial or commercial

(G-18229)
TOLEDO CARDIOLOGY CONS INC (PA)
2409 Cherry St Ste 100 (43608-2670)
PHONE.............................419 251-6183
Thomas G Welch MD, *President*
Ameer Kabour MD, *Vice Pres*
Terry Zmuda, *Controller*
Mohammed Alo, *Med Doctor*
EMP: 56
SQ FT: 8,000
SALES (est): 7.2MM **Privately Held**
SIC: 8011 Cardiologist & cardio-vascular specialist

(G-18230)
TOLEDO CARDIOLOGY INC
Also Called: Nahhas, Ahed T MD
4235 Secor Rd (43623-4231)
PHONE.............................419 479-5690
Fax: 419 479-5700
Richard A Fell, *President*
EMP: 25
SALES (est): 1.2MM **Privately Held**
SIC: 8011 Cardiologist & cardio-vascular specialist

(G-18231)
TOLEDO CHILDRENS HOSP FDN
2142 N Cove Blvd (43606-3895)
PHONE.............................419 824-9072
Fax: 419 291-2013
Ronald Wachsman, *Principal*
Cassie Basting, *Phys Thrpy Dir*
Bobbi Miller, *Radiology Dir*
Frank Horton, *Internal Med*
EMP: 35
SALES (est): 3.6MM **Privately Held**
SIC: 8069 Children's hospital

(G-18232)
TOLEDO CLINIC INC (PA)
4235 Secor Rd (43623-4299)
PHONE.............................419 473-3561
Fax: 419 473-2049
Ian S Elliot, *President*
E L Doermann, *Principal*
Edward G Seybold, *Principal*
Barbara Stewart, *Business Mgr*
Timothy Husted, *Corp Secy*
▲ **EMP:** 500
SQ FT: 14,600
SALES (est): 119.2MM **Privately Held**
SIC: 8011 Physicians' office, including specialists

(G-18233)
TOLEDO CLINIC INC
1414 S Byrne Rd (43614-2363)
PHONE.............................419 381-9977
Jessica Makowski, *Branch Mgr*
EMP: 103
SALES (corp-wide): 119.2MM **Privately Held**
SIC: 8043 Offices & clinics of podiatrists
PA: Toledo Clinic, Inc.
4235 Secor Rd
Toledo OH 43623
419 473-3561

(G-18234)
TOLEDO CLUB
235 14th St (43604-5475)
PHONE.............................419 243-2200
Fax: 419 321-6876
Ronald Paerson, *President*
Roosh Turner, *Accounting Mgr*
Theresa Carroll, *Manager*
James Retschler, *Manager*
EMP: 78 **EST:** 1889
SQ FT: 20,000
SALES: 5MM **Privately Held**
SIC: 7997 8641 Country club, membership; social club, membership

(G-18235)
TOLEDO CY PUB UTLTY WTR DISTR
Also Called: City of Toledo Div Wtr Dist
401 S Erie St (43604-4611)
PHONE.............................419 936-2506
Fax: 419 936-2828
Terry Russeau, *Manager*
Sherman Mosser, *Commissioner*
Michael Konwinski, *Supervisor*
EMP: 155
SALES (est): 5.7MM **Privately Held**
SIC: 4941 Water supply

(G-18236)
TOLEDO FAMILY HEALTH CENTER
Also Called: Mildred Byer Clnic For Hmeless
313 Jefferson Ave (43604-1004)
PHONE.............................419 241-1554
Fax: 419 241-3034
Doni Miller, *Exec Dir*
EMP: 52 **EST:** 1969
SQ FT: 2,100
SALES: 4.9MM **Privately Held**
WEB: www.nhainc.org
SIC: 8011 Clinic, operated by physicians

(G-18237)
TOLEDO GLASS LLC (PA)
Also Called: Toledo Mirror & Glass
103 Avondale Ave (43604-8207)
PHONE.............................419 241-3151
Fax: 419 241-3122
James P Nicholson, *Mng Member*
Tina Trout, *Manager*
EMP: 32 **EST:** 1918
SQ FT: 40,000
SALES (est): 5.4MM **Privately Held**
SIC: 1793 Glass & glazing work

(G-18238)
TOLEDO HOSPITAL (HQ)
Also Called: Promedica Toledo Hospital
2142 N Cove Blvd (43606-3896)
PHONE.............................419 291-4000
Fax: 419 479-6000
Alan Brass, *CEO*
Barbara Steele, *President*
Kevin Webb, *President*
Heather Baumgartner, *Purchasing*
Cathy Hanley, *CFO*
EMP: 4900 **EST:** 1876
SALES: 745.4MM
SALES (corp-wide): 1.5B **Privately Held**
SIC: 8011 8062 Medical centers; hospital, professional nursing school with AMA residency
PA: Promedica Health Systems, Inc.
100 Madison Ave
Toledo OH 43604
567 585-7454

(G-18239)
TOLEDO HOSPITAL
Also Called: Promedica
2150 W Central Ave Ste A (43606-3859)
PHONE.............................419 291-8701
Fax: 419 479-3298
Kathy Jaworski, *Manager*
EMP: 100
SALES (corp-wide): 1.5B **Privately Held**
SIC: 8062 General medical & surgical hospitals
HQ: The Toledo Hospital
2142 N Cove Blvd
Toledo OH 43606
419 291-4000

(G-18240)
TOLEDO JEWELERS SUPPLY CO
245 23rd St (43604-6519)
PHONE.............................419 241-4181
Fax: 419 241-4594
David Perlmutter, *President*
Steven Perlmutter, *Vice Pres*
James Kersten, *Controller*
Perry Gardai, *CTO*
EMP: 27
SQ FT: 19,000
SALES (est): 5.3MM
SALES (corp-wide): 13MM **Privately Held**
SIC: 5094 Watches & parts; jewelry
PA: Peoples Jewelry Company Inc
245 23rd St
Toledo OH
419 241-4181

(G-18241)
TOLEDO LEGAL AID SOCIETY
520 Madison Ave Ste 640 (43604-1307)
PHONE.............................419 720-3048
Fax: 419 321-1582
Robert Comes, *Exec Dir*
EMP: 28
SQ FT: 5,800
SALES: 1.5MM **Privately Held**
SIC: 8111 Legal aid service

(G-18242)
TOLEDO METRO AREA CNCL GVRNMNT
300 M Luther King Jr Dr (43604)
P.O. Box 9508 (43697-9508)
PHONE.............................419 241-9155
Fax: 419 241-9116
Anthony L Reams, *President*
Linda Lowe, *General Mgr*
William Best, *Info Tech Mgr*
Christine Connell, *Admin Asst*
Jennifer Allen, *Exec Sec*
EMP: 27
SQ FT: 12,200
SALES: 792.6K **Privately Held**
WEB: www.tmacog.org
SIC: 8748 City planning

GEOGRAPHIC SECTION

Toledo - Lucas County (G-18266)

(G-18243)
TOLEDO MUD HENS BASBAL CLB INC
406 Washington St Fl 5 (43604-1046)
PHONE 419 725-4367
Fax: 419 725-4368
Michael Miller, *Owner*
Joe Napoli, *General Mgr*
Charles Bracken, *Corp Secy*
Ed Larson, *Vice Pres*
Tammy Collins, *Mktg Coord*
EMP: 85
SALES (est): 8.5MM **Privately Held**
WEB: www.mudhens.com
SIC: 7941 Baseball club, professional & semi-professional

(G-18244)
TOLEDO MUSEUM OF ART (PA)
2445 Monroe St (43620-1500)
P.O. Box 1013 (43697-1013)
PHONE 419 255-8000
Fax: 419 244-2217
Brian Kennedy, *President*
Carol Bintz, *COO*
Vivian Fitzgerald, *Purch Agent*
Mary K Siefke, *CFO*
Tim Szymanski, *Controller*
▲ **EMP:** 215
SQ FT: 200,000
SALES: 23MM **Privately Held**
WEB: www.toledomuseum.org
SIC: 8412 Museum

(G-18245)
TOLEDO OPCO LLC
Also Called: ARBORS AT SYLVANIA
7120 Port Sylvania Dr (43617-1158)
PHONE 502 429-8062
Robert Norcross, *CEO*
Benjamin Sparks, *Clerk*
EMP: 99
SQ FT: 60,000
SALES: 5.1MM **Privately Held**
SIC: 8051 Skilled nursing care facilities

(G-18246)
TOLEDO OPTICAL LABORATORY INC
1201 Jefferson Ave (43604-5836)
P.O. Box 2028 (43603-2028)
PHONE 419 248-3384
Fax: 419 321-6361
Irland Tashima, *President*
Robert Lommerse, *General Mgr*
Jeffrey Seymenski, *Vice Pres*
Paula Jahns, *Personnel Exec*
Mary Johnson, *Manager*
EMP: 52
SQ FT: 10,000
SALES (est): 8.1MM **Privately Held**
SIC: 3851 5048 Eyeglasses, lenses & frames; lenses, ophthalmic; frames, ophthalmic

(G-18247)
TOLEDO PUBLIC SCHOOLS
Also Called: Toledo Maintance Center
130 S Hawley St (43609-2318)
PHONE 419 243-6422
Gary Sautter, *Director*
EMP: 62
SALES (corp-wide): 454.8MM **Privately Held**
WEB: www.tps.org
SIC: 7349 School custodian, contract basis
PA: Toledo Public Schools
1609 N Summit St
Toledo OH 43604
419 729-8200

(G-18248)
TOLEDO SCIENCE CENTER
Also Called: IMAGINATION STATION
1 Discovery Way (43604-1579)
PHONE 419 244-2674
Fax: 419 255-2674
Chip Hambro, *COO*
Anna Kolin, *Pub Rel Mgr*
Daniel Frick, *CFO*
George Mergen, *Marketing Staff*
Julie Bolfa, *Manager*
EMP: 50
SQ FT: 100,000

SALES: 4.6MM **Privately Held**
SIC: 8412 Museum

(G-18249)
TOLEDO SHREDDING LLC
275 Millard Ave Bldg 3 (43605-1071)
PHONE 419 698-1153
Mike Valentine, *General Mgr*
Peter Paris, *Financial Exec*
Mel Rukin,
EMP: 30
SQ FT: 11,360
SALES (est): 4.7MM **Privately Held**
SIC: 7389 Scrap steel cutting
PA: Protrade Steel Company, Ltd.
5700 Darrow Rd Ste 114
Hudson OH 44236

(G-18250)
TOLEDO SIGN COMPANY INC (PA)
2021 Adams St (43604-5431)
PHONE 419 244-4444
Fax: 419 244-6546
Brad Heil, *President*
Brian Heil Jr, *Vice Pres*
Daniel Fink, *Engineer*
Windy Jones, *Controller*
Michael Kiefer, *Technology*
EMP: 25
SQ FT: 34,000
SALES (est): 3MM **Privately Held**
SIC: 7389 Sign painting & lettering shop

(G-18251)
TOLEDO SPORTS CENTER INC
1516 Starr Ave (43605-2472)
PHONE 419 693-0687
Fax: 419 698-1017
Andy Vasko, *President*
Bruce E Davis, *President*
James E Walter, *Vice Pres*
Thomas A Davis, *Treasurer*
Ivadelle Davis, *Admin Sec*
EMP: 25
SQ FT: 34,500
SALES (est): 829.8K **Privately Held**
WEB: www.toledokaraoke.com
SIC: 7933 Bowling centers

(G-18252)
TOLEDO TELEVISION INVESTORS LP
Also Called: Wnwo-TV
300 S Byrne Rd (43615-6217)
PHONE 419 535-0024
Fax: 419 535-0202
Brett Cornwell, *President*
John B Nizamis, *General Mgr*
Ralph E Becker, *Chairman*
Harold Thompson, *Chief Engr*
Jon Skorburg, *Director*
EMP: 56
SQ FT: 12,000
SALES (est): 3.2MM **Privately Held**
SIC: 4833 Television broadcasting stations

(G-18253)
TOLEDO ZOO
2700 Broadway St (43609-3100)
PHONE 419 385-5721
Fax: 419 385-6935
Lorie Wittler, *Director*
Mary Fedderke, *Director*
Jeff Sailer, *Director*
Harry Prentice, *Asst Director*
EMP: 33
SALES (est): 3.4MM **Privately Held**
SIC: 8422 Animal & reptile exhibit

(G-18254)
TOLEDO ZOOLOGICAL SOCIETY (PA)
2 Hippo Way (43609-4100)
P.O. Box 140130 (43614-0130)
PHONE 419 385-4040
Lamont Thurston, *President*
Anne Baker, *Director*
EMP: 450
SALES: 34.3MM **Privately Held**
WEB: www.toledozoo.org
SIC: 8422 Zoological garden, noncommercial

(G-18255)
TOLEDO-LUCAS COUNTY PORT AUTH (PA)
Also Called: Seaport Division
1 Maritime Plz Ste 701 (43604-1853)
PHONE 419 243-8251
Paul L Toth Jr, *CEO*
Teresa Snyder, *Business Mgr*
Matthew A Sapara, *COO*
Clarence Washington, *Project Mgr*
Anthony Schumaker, *Project Engr*
EMP: 25
SQ FT: 6,000
SALES (est): 12MM **Privately Held**
SIC: 4491 Marine cargo handling

(G-18256)
TOLSON ENTERPRISES INC
Also Called: Tolson Investment Property
6591 W Central Ave # 100 (43617-1097)
PHONE 419 843-6465
Fax: 419 841-4391
Harvey Tolson, *President*
Stephanie Lucio, *Bookkeeper*
Karen Renard, *Bookkeeper*
Brandi Bedard, *Manager*
Christina Dull, *Admin Asst*
EMP: 26
SALES (est): 1.6MM **Privately Held**
SIC: 6531 Real estate managers

(G-18257)
TONY PACKOS TOLEDO LLC (PA)
Also Called: Tony Packo's Food Company
1902 Front St (43605-1226)
PHONE 419 691-6054
Fax: 419 691-4865
Tony Packo, *CEO*
Emily Bennett, *Owner*
Brian Smith, *General Mgr*
Anthony Packo III, *Vice Pres*
Erica Adamski, *Controller*
EMP: 60
SQ FT: 7,500
SALES (est): 7.7MM **Privately Held**
WEB: www.tonypacko.com
SIC: 5812 5149 Carry-out only (except pizza) restaurant; pickles, preserves, jellies & jams

(G-18258)
TOWLIFT INC
Also Called: Forklift of Toledo
140 N Byrne Rd (43607-2603)
PHONE 419 531-6110
Dave Bongorno, *VP Finance*
James Schuller, *Branch Mgr*
EMP: 33
SQ FT: 14,408
SALES (corp-wide): 106.6MM **Privately Held**
SIC: 5084 Lift trucks & parts
PA: Towlift, Inc.
1395 Valley Belt Rd
Brooklyn Heights OH 44131
216 749-6800

(G-18259)
TRANSCO RAILWAY PRODUCTS INC
4800 Schwartz Rd (43611-1726)
P.O. Box 5009 (43611-0009)
PHONE 419 726-3383
Fax: 419 726-3562
Antwan Smith, *Branch Mgr*
EMP: 30
SALES (corp-wide): 96.7MM **Privately Held**
SIC: 3537 7699 Industrial trucks & tractors; railroad car customizing
HQ: Transco Railway Products Inc.
200 N La Salle St # 1550
Chicago IL 60601
312 427-2818

(G-18260)
TRANSTAR ELECTRIC INC
767 Warehouse Rd Ste B (43615-6491)
PHONE 419 385-7573
Daniel L Bollin, *President*
Scott Bollin, *COO*
Jerry Buchhop, *Vice Pres*
Chris Siburt, *Project Mgr*
Bob Turpening, *Project Mgr*

EMP: 60
SQ FT: 7,000
SALES (est): 15.3MM **Privately Held**
SIC: 1731 General electrical contractor

(G-18261)
TRI-STATE ALUMINIUM INC (HQ)
1663 Tracy St (43605-3463)
PHONE 419 666-0100
Marc A Schupan, *President*
Mike Eisenhark, *General Mgr*
Steve Lindback, *Accountant*
Heather Rodriguez, *Director*
EMP: 25
SQ FT: 28,000
SALES (est): 10.6MM
SALES (corp-wide): 94.1MM **Privately Held**
WEB: www.tristate-aluminum.com
SIC: 5051 Aluminum bars, rods, ingots, sheets, pipes, plates, etc.; steel
PA: Schupan & Sons, Inc.
2619 Miller Rd
Kalamazoo MI 49001
269 382-0000

(G-18262)
TSL LTD (PA)
5217 Monroe St Ste A1 (43623-4604)
P.O. Box 23100 (43623-0100)
PHONE 419 843-3200
Fax: 419 843-1072
Donald J Finnegan, *President*
Anne Marlow, *Admin Sec*
EMP: 2495
SQ FT: 3,600
SALES (est): 35MM **Privately Held**
WEB: www.tsl1.com
SIC: 7363 Truck driver services

(G-18263)
TTL ASSOCIATES INC (PA)
1915 N 12th St (43604-5305)
PHONE 419 241-4556
Thomas R Uhler, *President*
Chuck Edwards, *Superintendent*
Charles Chambers, *VP Admin*
Jeffrey Elliot, *Vice Pres*
Timothy Pedro, *Vice Pres*
EMP: 110
SQ FT: 40,000
SALES: 13MM **Privately Held**
WEB: www.ttlassoc.com
SIC: 8711 8748 8741 Consulting engineer; environmental consultant; construction management

(G-18264)
TUFFY ASSOCIATES CORP (PA)
Also Called: Tuffy Auto Service Centers
7150 Granite Cir Ste 100 (43617-3114)
PHONE 419 865-6900
Fax: 419 865-7343
Adina Harel, *Ch of Bd*
Yoav Navon, *Vice Ch Bd*
Roger Hill, *President*
Greg Mahlstedt, *District Mgr*
Warren Swenson, *District Mgr*
EMP: 50
SQ FT: 5,000
SALES (est): 94.4MM **Privately Held**
WEB: www.tuffy.com
SIC: 6794 7533 7539 Franchises, selling or licensing; muffler shop, sale or repair & installation; brake repair, automotive

(G-18265)
TWO MEN & TRUCK INC
Also Called: Two Men and A Truck
2800 Tremainsville Rd A (43613-3583)
P.O. Box 258, Van Buren (45889-0258)
PHONE 419 882-1002
Fax: 419 475-3862
Duane Sell, *President*
Luann Wendeo, *Financial Exec*
EMP: 28
SQ FT: 7,000
SALES (est): 2.2MM **Privately Held**
SIC: 4212 Moving services

(G-18266)
U HAUL CO OF NORTHWESTERN OHIO (DH)
Also Called: U-Haul
50 W Alexis Rd (43612-3692)
PHONE 419 478-1101

Toledo - Lucas County (G-18267)

Fax: 419 729-4662
Lonnie Enderle, *President*
Ali Gillentine, *President*
Pamela D Davis, *Corp Secy*
Christopher Johnson, *Vice Pres*
Pamela D Avis, *Treasurer*
EMP: 40
SQ FT: 14,000
SALES (est): 5.6MM
SALES (corp-wide): 3.4B **Publicly Held**
SIC: 7513 7519 7359 Truck rental & leasing, no drivers; trailer rental; equipment rental & leasing
HQ: U-Haul International, Inc.
2727 N Central Ave
Phoenix AZ 85004
602 263-6011

(G-18267)
UNISON BEHAVIORAL HEALTH GROUP (PA)
544 E Woodruff Ave (43604-5367)
P.O. Box 10015 (43699-0015)
PHONE.................................419 242-9577
Fax: 419 481-3814
Courtney Weiss, *COO*
Larry Hamme, *COO*
Jamie Haack, *Human Resources*
Derek Vargo, *Case Mgr*
Erika Jay, *Program Mgr*
EMP: 75
SQ FT: 17,100
SALES: 20.7MM **Privately Held**
WEB: www.unisonbhg.org
SIC: 8093 Mental health clinic, outpatient

(G-18268)
UNISON BEHAVIORAL HEALTH GROUP
Also Called: East Center
1425 Starr Ave (43605-2456)
P.O. Box 10015 (43699-0015)
PHONE.................................419 693-0631
Fax: 419 693-0768
Rick Dutridge, *Facilities Mgr*
Marisa Tebbe, *Accountant*
Holly Gilsdorf, *Program Mgr*
Trina Hecklinger, *Senior Mgr*
Larry Hamme MD, *Director*
EMP: 200
SALES (corp-wide): 20.7MM **Privately Held**
WEB: www.unisonbhg.org
SIC: 8093 Mental health clinic, outpatient
PA: Unison Behavioral Health Group Inc
544 E Woodruff Ave
Toledo OH 43604
419 242-9577

(G-18269)
UNITED COLLECTION BUREAU INC (PA)
Also Called: Ucb
5620 Southwyck Blvd (43614-1501)
PHONE.................................419 866-6227
Harold Sam Rickard, *Ch of Bd*
Moira Lechtenberg, *President*
Harold S Rickard III, *President*
Sanju Sharma, *President*
Michael R Kaosas, *COO*
EMP: 165
SQ FT: 3,500
SALES (est): 66.5MM **Privately Held**
WEB: www.ucbinc.com
SIC: 7322 Collection agency, except real estate

(G-18270)
UNITED INSURANCE COMPANY AMER
1650 N Reynolds Rd (43615-3600)
PHONE.................................419 531-4289
Fax: 419 531-0435
Anthony Powell, *Branch Mgr*
EMP: 27
SQ FT: 2,550
SALES (corp-wide): 2.7B **Publicly Held**
WEB: www.unitedinsure.com
SIC: 6411 Insurance agents, brokers & service
HQ: United Insurance Company Of America
12115 Lackland Rd
Saint Louis MO 63146
314 819-4300

(G-18271)
UNITED PARCEL SERVICE INC OH
Also Called: UPS
1212 E Alexis Rd (43612-3974)
PHONE.................................419 891-6841
Dave Bardram, *Site Mgr*
EMP: 70
SALES (corp-wide): 65.8B **Publicly Held**
WEB: www.upsscs.com
SIC: 4215 Package delivery, vehicular
HQ: United Parcel Service, Inc. (Oh)
55 Glenlake Pkwy
Atlanta GA 30328
404 828-6000

(G-18272)
UNITED ROAD SERVICES INC
Also Called: Mpg Transport
27400 Luckey Rd (43605)
PHONE.................................419 837-2703
Fax: 419 837-2717
Joseph Mell, *General Mgr*
EMP: 56
SALES (corp-wide): 321.4MM **Privately Held**
WEB: www.unitedroad.com
SIC: 4213 Automobiles, transport & delivery
PA: United Road Services, Inc.
10701 Middlebelt Rd
Romulus MI 48174
734 946-3232

(G-18273)
UNITED STTES BOWL CONGRESS INC
5062 Dorr St (43615-3852)
PHONE.................................419 531-4058
Robert Huss Jr, *Branch Mgr*
EMP: 51
SALES (corp-wide): 32.9MM **Privately Held**
SIC: 8699 Bowling club
PA: United States Bowling Congress, Inc.
621 Six Flags Dr
Arlington TX 76011
817 385-8200

(G-18274)
UNITED WAY OF GREATER TOLEDO (PA)
424 Jackson St (43604-1495)
PHONE.................................419 254-4742
Bill Kitson, *CEO*
Kathleen Doty, *COO*
Karen Mathison, *COO*
Jane Moore, *Vice Pres*
Kim Sidwell, *Vice Pres*
EMP: 60 **EST:** 1918
SQ FT: 25,000
SALES: 12.5MM **Privately Held**
WEB: www.namitoledo.org
SIC: 8322 Individual & family services

(G-18275)
UNIVERSAL MARKETING GROUP LLC
5454 Airport Hwy (43615-7302)
PHONE.................................419 720-9696
Steven Horst, *Managing Prtnr*
Jason Birch, *CFO*
EMP: 99
SALES (est): 2.7MM **Privately Held**
SIC: 8742 5963 Marketing consulting services; direct sales, telemarketing

(G-18276)
UNIVERSITY OF TLEDO FOUNDATION
2801 W Bancroft St 1002 (43606-3398)
PHONE.................................419 530-7730
Brenda Lee, *President*
EMP: 40
SQ FT: 2,336
SALES: 37.7MM **Privately Held**
SIC: 8399 Community development groups

(G-18277)
UNIVERSITY OF TOLEDO
Also Called: Hsc Dept of Psychiatry
3120 Glendale Ave Ste 79 (43614-5811)
PHONE.................................419 534-3770
Dr Marijo Tamburriono, *Principal*
Sherri Napolski, *Manager*
Stephen J Andrews, *Obstetrician*
Sandy Nuzum, *Obstetrician*
Sue Sommer, *Obstetrician*
EMP: 60
SALES (corp-wide): 753.6MM **Privately Held**
WEB: www.utoledo.edu
SIC: 8011 8221 Psychiatrist; university
PA: The University Of Toledo
2801 W Bancroft St
Toledo OH 43606
419 530-4636

(G-18278)
UNIVERSITY OF TOLEDO
Also Called: University Toledo Medical Ctr
4430 N Hllnd Sylvnia Rd Apt 7101 (43623)
PHONE.................................419 383-3556
Samir Fahed, *Manager*
EMP: 33
SALES (corp-wide): 753.6MM **Privately Held**
WEB: www.utoledo.edu
SIC: 8011 8221 Offices & clinics of medical doctors; university
PA: The University Of Toledo
2801 W Bancroft St
Toledo OH 43606
419 530-4636

(G-18279)
UNIVERSITY OF TOLEDO
Also Called: University of Toledo Med Ctr
3000 Arlington Ave (43614-2598)
PHONE.................................419 383-4000
EMP: 3200
SALES (corp-wide): 753.6MM **Privately Held**
SIC: 8062 8221 Hospital, affiliated with AMA residency; college, except junior
PA: The University Of Toledo
2801 W Bancroft St
Toledo OH 43606
419 530-4636

(G-18280)
UNIVERSITY OF TOLEDO
Also Called: Health Science Campus
3000 Arlington Ave (43614-2598)
PHONE.................................419 383-5322
Jeffrey Gold, *President*
Kathy Goans, *Opers Mgr*
Fernando T Mariz, *Med Doctor*
Ansley Abrams, *Manager*
Johan Gottgens, *Manager*
EMP: 33
SALES (corp-wide): 753.6MM **Privately Held**
WEB: www.utoledo.edu
SIC: 8011 8221 Radiologist; university
PA: The University Of Toledo
2801 W Bancroft St
Toledo OH 43606
419 530-4636

(G-18281)
UNIVERSITY OF TOLEDO
Health Science Campus
3000 Arlington Ave (43614-2598)
PHONE.................................419 383-3759
Dr Lloyd Jacobs, *Principal*
Sharon Kling, *Cert Phar Tech*
Robert Hopperton, *Professor*
EMP: 3579
SALES (corp-wide): 753.6MM **Privately Held**
WEB: www.utoledo.edu
SIC: 8062 8221 Hospital, affiliated with AMA residency; college, except junior
PA: The University Of Toledo
2801 W Bancroft St
Toledo OH 43606
419 530-4636

(G-18282)
UNIVERSITY OF TOLEDO
Also Called: Health Science Campus
3000 Arlington Ave (43614-2598)
PHONE.................................419 383-4229
Lloyd Jacobs, *President*
EMP: 322
SALES (corp-wide): 753.6MM **Privately Held**
WEB: www.utoledo.edu
SIC: 8221 8062 University; hospital, medical school affiliation
PA: The University Of Toledo
2801 W Bancroft St
Toledo OH 43606
419 530-4636

(G-18283)
URSULINE CONVENT SACRED HEART
Also Called: Ursuline Center
4035 Indian Rd (43606-2226)
PHONE.................................419 531-8990
Fax: 419 536-3398
Kathleen Voyles, *Administration*
EMP: 47
SALES (corp-wide): 2.5MM **Privately Held**
SIC: 8361 8661 Rest home, with health care incidental; convent
PA: The Ursuline Convent Of The Sacred Heart
4045 Indian Rd
Toledo OH
419 536-9587

(G-18284)
USI INC
1120 Madison Ave (43604-7538)
PHONE.................................419 243-1191
Ben Brown, *Vice Pres*
EMP: 90 **Privately Held**
SIC: 6411 Insurance agents
PA: Usi, Inc.
200 Summit Lake Dr # 350
Valhalla NY 10595

(G-18285)
V M SYSTEMS INC
3125 Hill Ave (43607-2987)
PHONE.................................419 535-1044
Fax: 419 535-8644
Craig Gabel, *President*
Ronald H Gabel, *President*
Trent Bloomfield, *Vice Pres*
Nicole Snyder, *Manager*
Kenneth J Gabel, *Admin Sec*
EMP: 100
SQ FT: 24,000
SALES (est): 26MM **Privately Held**
WEB: www.vmsystemsinc.com
SIC: 1711 3444 Warm air heating & air conditioning contractor; ventilation & duct work contractor; sheet metalwork

(G-18286)
VAN STEVENS LINES INC
64 N Fearing Blvd (43607-3601)
PHONE.................................419 729-8871
Robert Croci, *Credit Mgr*
Rich Evasius, *Manager*
EMP: 25
SALES (corp-wide): 72.7MM **Privately Held**
WEB: www.stevensworldwide.com
SIC: 4213 4214 Household goods transport; local trucking with storage
HQ: Van Stevens Lines Inc
527 W Morley Dr
Saginaw MI 48601
989 755-3000

(G-18287)
VANCE PROPERTY MANAGEMENT LLC
4200 South Ave (43615-6254)
P.O. Box 365, Maumee (43537-0365)
PHONE.................................419 467-9548
Winston Vance, *Branch Mgr*
EMP: 56
SALES (est): 1.2MM **Privately Held**
SIC: 0781 4214 Landscape services; household goods moving & storage, local
PA: Vance Property Management Llc
4200 South Ave
Toledo OH 43615

GEOGRAPHIC SECTION
Toledo - Lucas County (G-18314)

(G-18288)
VANCE PROPERTY MANAGEMENT LLC (PA)
4200 South Ave (43615-6254)
P.O. Box 365, Maumee (43537-0365)
PHONE.....................419 887-1878
Winston Vance, *Mng Member*
James W Nightingale,
EMP: 67
SQ FT: 7,500
SALES: 1.4MM Privately Held
SIC: 8741 Management services

(G-18289)
VERITIV OPERATING COMPANY
Also Called: International Paper
1320 Locust St (43608-2938)
P.O. Box 567 (43697-0567)
PHONE.....................419 243-6100
Bruce E Lang, *Branch Mgr*
EMP: 49
SALES (corp-wide): 8.3B Publicly Held
WEB: www.internationalpaper.com
SIC: 5111 5943 Printing & writing paper; office forms & supplies
HQ: Veritiv Operating Company
1000 Abernathy Rd
Atlanta GA 30328
770 391-8200

(G-18290)
VETERANS HEALTH ADMINISTRATION
Also Called: Toledo V A Outpatient Clinic
3333 Glendale Ave (43614-2426)
PHONE.....................419 259-2000
Fax: 419 259-2008
Jennifer Sherman, *Manager*
EMP: 70 Publicly Held
WEB: www.veterans-ru.org
SIC: 8011 9451 Clinic, operated by physicians; psychiatric clinic;
HQ: Veterans Health Administration
810 Vermont Ave Nw
Washington DC 20420

(G-18291)
VIDEO WORKS
336 Hayes Rd (43615-4902)
PHONE.....................419 865-6800
Ed Pohlman, *Owner*
Ron Malish, *Partner*
EMP: 70
SQ FT: 840
SALES (est): 2.6MM Privately Held
WEB: www.videoworks.com
SIC: 7812 Audio-visual program production

(G-18292)
VISION ASSOCIATES INC (PA)
Also Called: Ofori, Jason MD
2865 N Reynolds Rd # 170 (43615-2076)
PHONE.....................419 578-7598
Fax: 419 539-6323
Rodney McCarthy, *Principal*
Michelle Treloar, *Opers Mgr*
J G Rosenthal MD, *Bd of Directors*
EMP: 51
SALES (est): 9MM Privately Held
SIC: 8011 Ophthalmologist

(G-18293)
VOLUNTEERS OF AMERICA NW OHIO
701 Jefferson Ave Ste 203 (43604-6957)
PHONE.....................419 248-3733
Fax: 419 248-1571
Sue Reamsnyder, *President*
EMP: 50
SALES (est): 2.5MM Privately Held
WEB: www.voa.org
SIC: 8699 8322 Personal interest organization; individual & family services

(G-18294)
W DAVID MAUPIN INC
Also Called: Royal Building Cleaning Svcs
3564 Marine Rd (43609-1018)
P.O. Box 903 (43697-0903)
PHONE.....................419 389-0458
W David Maupin, *President*
EMP: 28
SQ FT: 13,000
SALES (est): 330K Privately Held
SIC: 7349 Building cleaning service

(G-18295)
W S O S COMMUNITY A
1500 N Superior St # 303 (43604-2157)
PHONE.....................419 729-8035
EMP: 45
SALES (corp-wide): 33.3MM Privately Held
SIC: 8351 Head start center, except in conjunction with school
PA: W. S. O. S. Community Action Commission, Inc.
109 S Front St
Fremont OH 43420
419 333-6068

(G-18296)
W W W M
3225 Arlington Ave (43614-2427)
PHONE.....................419 240-1055
Loulew Dickey, *President*
Paul Smith, *Principal*
EMP: 37
SALES (est): 1.7MM Privately Held
SIC: 5064 Radios

(G-18297)
WABE MAQUAW HOLDINGS INC
17 Corey Creek Rd (43623-1183)
PHONE.....................419 243-1191
Fax: 419 255-5928
Dennis G Johnson, *President*
Paul Johnson, *Principal*
Jim Stengle, *Senior VP*
Kevin Brennan, *Vice Pres*
Ben Brown, *Vice Pres*
EMP: 90
SQ FT: 20,000
SALES (est): 3MM Privately Held
WEB: www.brooksinsurance.com
SIC: 6411 Insurance agents

(G-18298)
WALMAN OPTICAL COMPANY
1201 Jefferson Ave (43604-5836)
PHONE.....................419 248-3384
EMP: 372
SALES (corp-wide): 381.3MM Privately Held
SIC: 5048 Optometric equipment & supplies
PA: The Walman Optical Company
801 12th Ave N Ste 1
Minneapolis MN 55411
612 520-6000

(G-18299)
WASHINGTON LOCAL SCHOOLS
Also Called: Bus Garage & Maintenance Dept
5201 Douglas Rd (43613-2640)
PHONE.....................419 473-8356
John Bettis, *Manager*
EMP: 75
SALES (corp-wide): 93.8MM Privately Held
SIC: 4173 4151 Maintenance facilities for motor vehicle passenger transport; school buses
PA: Washington Local Schools
3505 W Lincolnshr Blvd Of Ofc
Toledo OH 43606
419 473-8224

(G-18300)
WELLES BOWEN REALTY INC
2460 N Reynolds Rd (43615-2884)
PHONE.....................419 535-0011
David Browning, *President*
Kevin Smith, *Vice Pres*
Tom Dull, *Sales Associate*
Nancy Kabat, *Sales Associate*
Melissa Sargent, *Office Mgr*
EMP: 65
SALES (est): 5.1MM Privately Held
WEB: www.wellesbowen.com
SIC: 6531 6163 Real estate agent, residential; mortgage brokers arranging for loans, using money of others

(G-18301)
WELLINGTON F ROEMER INSURANCE
3912 Sunforest Ct Ste A (43623-4486)
P.O. Box 8730 (43623-0730)
PHONE.....................419 473-0258
Fax: 419 475-8750
Wellington F Roemer II, *Ch of Bd*
Wellington F Roemer III, *President*
Roy Burgoon, *Senior VP*
R Dennis Schwartz, *Senior VP*
W Thomas Roemer, *Vice Pres*
EMP: 50
SQ FT: 9,000
SALES (est): 12.3MM Privately Held
SIC: 6411 Insurance brokers; life insurance agents; property & casualty insurance agent

(G-18302)
WELLS FARGO CLEARING SVCS LLC
Also Called: Wells Fargo Advisors
3450 W Central Ave # 130 (43606-1416)
PHONE.....................419 356-3272
Fax: 419 531-9039
Linda Zachel, *Senior VP*
Gerald L Sliemers, *Manager*
EMP: 26
SQ FT: 750
SALES (corp-wide): 97.7B Publicly Held
SIC: 6211 Stock brokers & dealers
HQ: Wells Fargo Clearing Services, Llc
1 N Jefferson Ave
Saint Louis MO 63103
314 955-3000

(G-18303)
WELLS FARGO CLEARING SVCS LLC
Also Called: Wells Fargo Advisors
7335 Crossleigh Ct # 100 (43617-3124)
PHONE.....................419 720-9700
EMP: 33
SALES (corp-wide): 97.7B Publicly Held
SIC: 6211 Stock brokers & dealers
HQ: Wells Fargo Clearing Services, Llc
1 N Jefferson Ave
Saint Louis MO 63103
314 955-3000

(G-18304)
WELLTOWER INC (PA)
4500 Dorr St (43615-4040)
PHONE.....................419 247-2800
Fax: 419 247-2826
Thomas J Derosa, *CEO*
Jeffrey H Donahue, *Ch of Bd*
Lisa Schmaltz, *President*
Cheryl O'Connor, *Counsel*
Erin Ibele, *Exec VP*
▲ **EMP:** 67
SALES: 4.3B Publicly Held
WEB: www.hcreit.com
SIC: 6798 Realty investment trusts

(G-18305)
WEST PARK FAMILY PHYSICIAN
Also Called: West Park Health Partners
3425 Executive Pkwy # 100 (43606-1326)
PHONE.....................419 472-1124
Fax: 419 486-8857
Mark D Hillard, *Partner*
EMP: 30
SALES (est): 1.2MM Privately Held
SIC: 8011 Offices & clinics of medical doctors

(G-18306)
WEST SIDE MONTESSORI
7115 W Bancroft St (43615-3010)
PHONE.....................419 866-1931
Fax: 419 866-4310
Lynn Fisher, *President*
Joseph Stockdalc, *Trustee*
Dawn Weating, *Opers Staff*
Lyn Cooke, *Director*
Dawn Weating-Wsmc, *Director*
EMP: 85 **EST:** 1975
SQ FT: 22,700
SALES: 5.1MM Privately Held
WEB: www.wsmctoledo.org
SIC: 8211 8351 Private elementary school; Montessori child development center

(G-18307)
WESTGATE LIMITED PARTNERSHIP
Also Called: Ramada Hotel & Conference Ctr
457 S Reynolds Rd (43615-5953)
PHONE.....................419 535-7070
Ken Maclaren, *Partner*
Ken McLaren, *Partner*
Stephen Swigart, *Partner*
EMP: 150
SQ FT: 216,000
SALES (est): 7.5MM Privately Held
WEB: www.clariontoledo.com
SIC: 7011 6513 5813 Hotels; residential hotel operation; drinking places

(G-18308)
WHITEFORD GREENHOUSE
4554 Whiteford Rd (43623-2759)
PHONE.....................419 882-4110
Fax: 419 841-6972
Roger F Barrow, *Owner*
EMP: 50
SQ FT: 58,000
SALES (est): 2.4MM Privately Held
SIC: 0181 Bedding plants, growing of; flowers: grown under cover (e.g. greenhouse production)

(G-18309)
WILEY HOMES INC
4011 Angola Rd (43615-6509)
P.O. Box 351688 (43635-1688)
PHONE.....................419 535-3988
Fax: 419 389-0840
Stephanie C Wiley, *President*
EMP: 80
SALES (est): 1.9MM Privately Held
SIC: 8361 Home for the mentally retarded

(G-18310)
WILLIAMS HOMES LLC
1841 Eastgate Rd (43614-3034)
PHONE.....................419 472-1005
Brian Williams, *Mng Member*
EMP: 25
SALES (est): 356.8K Privately Held
SIC: 6531 Real estate brokers & agents

(G-18311)
WILLIS DAY MANAGEMENT INC (PA)
4100 Bennett Rd Ste 1 (43612-1970)
P.O. Box 676 (43697-0676)
PHONE.....................419 476-8000
Jeffrey K Day, *President*
Stephen Day, *Vice Pres*
Willis Day IV, *Admin Sec*
EMP: 25
SQ FT: 60,000
SALES (est): 1.8MM Privately Held
SIC: 6512 5084 4214 4225 Commercial & industrial building operation; materials handling machinery; local trucking with storage; general warehousing

(G-18312)
WILLIS DAY STORAGE CO (HQ)
4100 Bennett Rd Ste 1 (43612-1970)
P.O. Box 676 (43697-0676)
PHONE.....................419 470-6255
Willis Day IV, *President*
Jeffrey K Day, *Treasurer*
EMP: 25 **EST:** 1929
SQ FT: 800,000
SALES: 2.6MM
SALES (corp-wide): 1.8MM Privately Held
WEB: www.willisday.com
SIC: 4225 6512 General warehousing; commercial & industrial building operation
PA: Day Willis Management Inc
4100 Bennett Rd Ste 1
Toledo OI I 43612
419 476-8000

(G-18313)
WOLVES CLUB INC
5930 Dalton Rd (43612-4210)
PHONE.....................419 476-4418
Joe Brescol, *CEO*
EMP: 42
SQ FT: 960
SALES (est): 1.4MM Privately Held
SIC: 8641 Civic social & fraternal associations

(G-18314)
WORLD TABLEWARE INC (DH)
300 Madison Ave Fl 4 (43604-1567)
P.O. Box 10060 (43699-0060)
PHONE.....................419 325-2608
Fax: 419 325-2749

Toledo - Lucas County (G-18315)

John Myer, *CEO*
Mark Fort, *Credit Mgr*
John Pranckun, *Manager*
Heidi Moilanen, *Executive*
Jose Uresti, *Executive*
▲ **EMP:** 100
SALES (est): 37.8MM **Publicly Held**
SIC: 5023 Kitchenware
HQ: Libbey Glass Inc.
300 Madison Ave Fl 4
Toledo OH 43604
419 325-2100

(G-18315)
WRWK 1065
Also Called: 94 5 Xkr Rdo Stn Bus & Sls Off
3225 Arlington Ave (43614-2427)
PHONE.................................419 725-5700
Fax: 419 389-5172
Andy Stuart, *Manager*
Wally Londo, *Program Dir*
EMP: 50
SALES (est): 555.4K **Privately Held**
SIC: 4832 Radio broadcasting stations

(G-18316)
WUPW LLC
730 N Summit St (43604-1808)
PHONE.................................419 244-3600
Traci Grimm, *Accountant*
EMP: 50
SALES (est): 1.2MM **Privately Held**
SIC: 4833 Television broadcasting stations

(G-18317)
WURTEC INCORPORATED (PA)
6200 Brent Dr (43611-1081)
PHONE.................................419 726-1066
Fax: 419 729-5764
Steven P Wurth, *President*
Rob Wurth, *President*
Jane A Wurth, *Corp Secy*
Jeff Wagenhauser, *Mfg Mgr*
Todd Keel, *Controller*
◆ **EMP:** 62
SQ FT: 43,000
SALES (est): 27.3MM **Privately Held**
SIC: 5084 5065 Industrial machinery & equipment; elevators; telephone & telegraphic equipment

(G-18318)
XEROX CORPORATION
600 Jefferson Ave Ste 200 (43604-1012)
PHONE.................................419 418-6500
Fax: 419 418-6510
Jeffrey Wenger, *Owner*
EMP: 50
SALES (corp-wide): 10.2B **Publicly Held**
WEB: www.xerox.com
SIC: 7699 Photocopy machine repair
PA: Xerox Corporation
201 Merritt 7
Norwalk CT 06851
203 968-3000

(G-18319)
YARK AUTOMOTIVE GROUP INC (PA)
Also Called: Yark Subaru
6019 W Central Ave (43615-1803)
P.O. Box 352137 (43635-2137)
PHONE.................................419 841-7771
Fax: 419 841-7525
Douglas Kearns, *CEO*
John W Yark, *President*
Dj Yark, *General Mgr*
Jim Yark, *Principal*
Shane Madison, *Foreman/Supr*
EMP: 120
SQ FT: 40,000
SALES (est): 144.2MM **Privately Held**
WEB: www.yarkbmw.net
SIC: 5511 7515 Automobiles, new & used; passenger car leasing

(G-18320)
YOUNG MENS CHRISTIAN ASSOCIAT (PA)
Also Called: YMCA of Greater Toledo
1500 N Superior St Fl 2 (43604-2149)
PHONE.................................419 729-8135
Fax: 419 729-8114
Todd Tibbits, *President*
Casey Holck, *COO*
Stephanie Dames, *Vice Pres*
Wilma Dimanna, *Vice Pres*
Christy Gordon, *Vice Pres*
EMP: 50 **EST:** 1865
SQ FT: 2,500
SALES: 29.1MM **Privately Held**
WEB: www.ymcastorercamps.org
SIC: 8641 7991 8351 7032 Youth organizations; physical fitness facilities; child day care services; youth camps; individual & family services

(G-18321)
YOUNG MENS CHRISTIAN ASSOCIAT
2110 Tremainsville Rd (43613-3409)
PHONE.................................419 475-3496
Fax: 419 475-8837
Jason Trame, *Exec Dir*
Christy Gordon, *Exec Dir*
EMP: 252
SALES (corp-wide): 29.1MM **Privately Held**
SIC: 8641 Youth organizations
PA: Young Men's Christian Association Of Greater Toledo
1500 N Superior St Fl 2
Toledo OH 43604
419 729-8135

(G-18322)
YOUNG MENS CHRISTIAN ASSOCIAT
1500 N Superior St Fl 2 (43604-2149)
PHONE.................................419 474-3995
Regina Carter, *Principal*
Brian Keel, *Senior VP*
Mae Miller, *Technology*
EMP: 45
SALES (corp-wide): 29.1MM **Privately Held**
WEB: www.ymcastorercamps.org
SIC: 8641 7991 8351 7032 Youth organizations; physical fitness facilities; child day care services; youth camps; individual & family services
PA: Young Men's Christian Association Of Greater Toledo
1500 N Superior St Fl 2
Toledo OH 43604
419 729-8135

(G-18323)
YOUNG MENS CHRISTIAN ASSOCIAT
Also Called: Y M C A
2020 Tremainsville Rd (43613)
PHONE.................................419 475-3496
Fax: 419 475-8837
EMP: 120
SALES (corp-wide): 29.4MM **Privately Held**
SIC: 8641 7991 8351 7032 Civic/Social Association Physical Fitness Faclty Child Day Care Services Sport/Recreation Camp Individual/Family Svcs
PA: Young Men's Christian Association Of Greater Toledo
1500 N Superior St Fl 2
Toledo OH 43604
419 729-8135

(G-18324)
YOUNG SERVICES INC (PA)
Also Called: Toddler's School
806 Starr Ave (43605-2362)
PHONE.................................419 704-2009
Fax: 419 697-3939
Michael Tersigni, *President*
EMP: 25
SALES (est): 5.5MM **Privately Held**
SIC: 8351 8211 Group day care center; elementary & secondary schools

(G-18325)
YOUNG WOMENS CHRISTIAN
1018 Jefferson Ave (43604-5941)
PHONE.................................419 241-3235
Taryn Payne, *Principal*
Shelly Ulrich, *Principal*
Jack Tibbets, *Opers Staff*
Tona Rouser, *Finance Dir*
Deanna Pickett, *Finance Asst*
EMP: 70 **EST:** 1891
SQ FT: 82,470
SALES: 3.8MM **Privately Held**
SIC: 8322 8351 7032 Individual & family services; emergency shelters; crisis center; child related social services; child day care services; youth camps

(G-18326)
YOUNG WOMNS CHRSTN ASSC LIMA
Also Called: YWCA
1018 Jefferson Ave (43604-5941)
PHONE.................................419 241-3230
Fax: 419 229-4881
Carol Simons, *President*
Stephanie Hood, *CFO*
Imelda Bonilla, *Payroll Mgr*
Cristina Velez, *Manager*
Alla Voznyuk, *Manager*
EMP: 45
SQ FT: 5,156
SALES: 2MM **Privately Held**
SIC: 8641 Youth organizations

(G-18327)
YRC INC
Also Called: Roadway Express
4431 South Ave (43615-6416)
PHONE.................................419 729-0631
Fax: 419 726-7870
John McAbier, *General Mgr*
John Mc Aber, *Manager*
Grant Garvin, *Manager*
William Breen, *Director*
EMP: 300
SALES (corp-wide): 4.8B **Publicly Held**
WEB: www.roadway.com
SIC: 4213 4212 Contract haulers; local trucking, without storage
HQ: Yrc Inc.
10990 Roe Ave
Overland Park KS 66211
913 696-6100

(G-18328)
ZEPF CENTER
905 Nebraska Ave (43607-4222)
PHONE.................................419 255-4050
Jennifer Moses, *CEO*
EMP: 40
SALES (corp-wide): 37.8MM **Privately Held**
SIC: 8093 Mental health clinic, outpatient
PA: Zepf Center
6605 W Central Ave # 100
Toledo OH 43617
419 841-7701

(G-18329)
ZEPF CENTER (PA)
6605 W Central Ave # 100 (43617-1000)
PHONE.................................419 841-7701
Fax: 419 843-6431
Jennifer Moses, *CEO*
Deb Flores, *COO*
Kathleen Cesen, *CFO*
Patty Evans, *Accountant*
Nancy Paige, *Office Mgr*
EMP: 70
SQ FT: 25,000
SALES: 37.8MM **Privately Held**
WEB: www.zepfcom.com
SIC: 8093 Mental health clinic, outpatient

(G-18330)
ZEPF CENTER
Network
6605 W Central Ave # 100 (43617-1000)
PHONE.................................419 213-5627
Jennifer Moses, *Branch Mgr*
EMP: 30
SALES (corp-wide): 37.8MM **Privately Held**
WEB: www.zepfcom.com
SIC: 8093 8331 Mental health clinic, outpatient; job training & vocational rehabilitation services
PA: Zepf Center
6605 W Central Ave # 100
Toledo OH 43617
419 841-7701

(G-18331)
ZEPF CENTER
525 Hamilton St Ste 101a (43604-8547)
PHONE.................................419 255-4050
Fax: 419 255-1625
Frank Ayers, *Principal*
James Babcock, *IT/INT Sup*
Jan Cook, *Nursing Dir*
Nancy G Page, *Receptionist Se*
EMP: 30
SALES (corp-wide): 37.8MM **Privately Held**
WEB: www.zepfcom.com
SIC: 8093 8011 Mental health clinic, outpatient; clinic, operated by physicians
PA: Zepf Center
6605 W Central Ave # 100
Toledo OH 43617
419 841-7701

(G-18332)
ZEPF CENTER
Network
1301 Monroe St (43604-5815)
PHONE.................................419 213-5627
Jennifer Moses, *Branch Mgr*
EMP: 30
SALES (corp-wide): 37.8MM **Privately Held**
WEB: www.zepfcom.com
SIC: 8093 Mental health clinic, outpatient
PA: Zepf Center
6605 W Central Ave # 100
Toledo OH 43617
419 841-7701

(G-18333)
ZEPF HOUSING CORP ONE INC
Also Called: Ottawa House
5310 Hill Ave (43615-5805)
PHONE.................................419 531-0019
Kendell Alexander, *Exec Dir*
EMP: 125
SALES: 86.2K
SALES (corp-wide): 37.8MM **Privately Held**
WEB: www.zepfcom.com
SIC: 6513 Apartment building operators
PA: Zepf Center
6605 W Central Ave # 100
Toledo OH 43617
419 841-7701

Toronto
Jefferson County

(G-18334)
BUCKEYE MECHANICAL CONTG INC
2325 Township Road 370 (43964-7992)
PHONE.................................740 282-0089
Fax: 740 282-0089
Robert Hickle, *Principal*
Earla Hickle, *Corp Secy*
Roberta Glasure, *Office Mgr*
EMP: 46
SALES: 5.6MM **Privately Held**
SIC: 1711 Mechanical contractor

(G-18335)
CARL MILLS
1005 Franklin St (43964-1153)
PHONE.................................740 282-2382
Carl Mills, *Owner*
EMP: 100 **EST:** 1991
SALES (est): 891.1K **Privately Held**
SIC: 8082 Home health care services

(G-18336)
CATTRELL COMPANIES INC
906 Franklin St (43964-1152)
P.O. Box 367 (43964-0367)
PHONE.................................740 537-2481
Fax: 740 537-1528
Christine Hargrave, *President*
George R Cattrell, *Corp Secy*
Thomas L Wilson, *Vice Pres*
Brad Burkhead, *Project Mgr*
Tom Schiffer, *Project Mgr*
EMP: 52 **EST:** 1939
SQ FT: 4,000
SALES: 16MM **Privately Held**
WEB: www.cattrell.com
SIC: 1711 1731 1542 Mechanical contractor; general electrical contractor; commercial & office building contractors

GEOGRAPHIC SECTION

Troy - Miami County (G-18359)

(G-18337)
EXPRESS ENERGY SVCS OPER LP
1515 Franklin St (43964-1029)
PHONE...................740 337-4530
EMP: 42
SALES (corp-wide): 825.2MM **Privately Held**
SIC: **1389** Pipe testing, oil field service
PA: Express Energy Services Operating, Lp
9800 Richmond Ave Ste 500
Houston TX 77042
713 625-7400

(G-18338)
SHADCO INC
Also Called: Trans World Alloys
100 Titanium Way (43964-1990)
PHONE...................310 217-8777
Marc Donegan, *CEO*
Liz Fritzinger, *Treasurer*
Alice Melamed, *Credit Mgr*
▲ EMP: 26
SQ FT: 5,400
SALES (est): 7.8MM
SALES (corp-wide): 242.1B **Publicly Held**
SIC: **5051** Nonferrous metal sheets, bars, rods, etc.; aluminum bars, rods, ingots, sheets, pipes, plates, etc.; iron & steel (ferrous) products
HQ: Precision Castparts Corp.
4650 Sw Mcdam Ave Ste 300
Portland OR 97239
503 946-4800

(G-18339)
TORONTO EMERGENCY MEDICAL SVC
Also Called: Tems
201 S 4th St (43964-1369)
P.O. Box 307 (43964-0307)
PHONE...................740 537-3891
Fax: 740 537-2178
John Olesky, *President*
EMP: 27
SALES (est): 578.2K **Privately Held**
SIC: **4119** Ambulance service

Trenton
Butler County

(G-18340)
CAL CRIM INC
Also Called: Business Consultants Limited
384 Deer Run Dr (45067-1653)
PHONE...................513 563-5500
Claude Hinds, *Ch of Bd*
Gregg E Hollenbaugh, *President*
Tony Novakov, *Business Mgr*
Gerald W Cornelius, *Opers Mgr*
Nancy S Baker, *Treasurer*
EMP: 130
SQ FT: 2,250
SALES (est): 3.2MM **Privately Held**
WEB: www.calcrim.net
SIC: **7381** Protective services, guard; security guard service; private investigator

(G-18341)
LESAINT LOGISTICS LLC
5564 Alan B Shepherd St (45067-9401)
PHONE...................513 988-0101
Delbert Murphy, *Manager*
Kevin Rhymer, *Manager*
Steve Wormus, *Director*
EMP: 80
SALES (corp-wide): 94MM **Privately Held**
WEB: www.intrupa.com
SIC: **4731** 4225 8742 Freight transportation arrangement; general warehousing & storage; materials mgmt. (purchasing, handling, inventory) consultant
PA: Lesaint Logistics, Llc
868 W Crossroads Pkwy
Romeoville IL 60446
630 243-5950

(G-18342)
NOAHS ARK CHILD DEV CTR
3259 Wayne Madison Rd (45067-9532)
P.O. Box 138 (45067-0138)
PHONE...................513 988-0921
Fax: 513 988-1429
Rebecca Ncey, *Director*
Jeff Marshall, *Director*
Rocky Chasteen, *Administration*
EMP: 34
SALES (est): 892.1K **Privately Held**
SIC: **8351** Child day care services

(G-18343)
PROCESS PUMP & SEAL INC
2993 Woodsdale Rd (45067-9754)
PHONE...................513 988-7000
Daniel Quenneville, *Principal*
Aaron Satterfield, *Sales Staff*
EMP: 28
SQ FT: 12,000
SALES: 10MM **Privately Held**
WEB: www.processpumpandseal.com
SIC: **5085** 5084 Packing, industrial; seals, industrial; pumps & pumping equipment

Trotwood
Montgomery County

(G-18344)
BIO-MDCAL APPLCATIONS OHIO INC
Also Called: Fresenius Med Care Dayton W
4100 Salem Ave (45416)
PHONE...................937 279-3120
Ron Kuerbitz, *CEO*
Mary Garber, *Manager*
EMP: 30
SALES (est): 880K **Privately Held**
SIC: **8092** Kidney dialysis centers

(G-18345)
CARRIAGE INN OF TROTWOOD INC
Also Called: SHILOH SPRINGS CARE CENTER
3500 Shiloh Springs Rd (45426-2260)
PHONE...................937 854-1180
Fax: 937 854-0209
Ken Bernsen, *President*
Betty Zeller, *Finance*
Cheryl Kaylor, *Nurse*
EMP: 104
SQ FT: 6,500
SALES: 6.1MM **Privately Held**
SIC: **8051** Convalescent home with continuous nursing care

(G-18346)
E T FINANCIAL SERVICE INC
Also Called: Jackson Hewitt Tax Service
4550 Salem Ave (45416-1700)
PHONE...................937 716-1726
Emmanuel Umoren, *President*
Theo Adegdoruwa, *Vice Pres*
Theo Adegboruwa, *Manager*
EMP: 40
SQ FT: 1,800
SALES (est): 871.4K **Privately Held**
SIC: **7291** 8721 7389 Tax return preparation services; billing & bookkeeping services; financial services

Troy
Miami County

(G-18347)
ARC ABRASIVES INC
Also Called: A R C
2131 Corporate Dr (45373-1067)
P.O. Box 10 (45373-0010)
PHONE...................800 888-4885
Fax: 937 339-4969
Anthony H Stayman, *CEO*
Anthony Stayman, *President*
Erin Marquis, *Purch Agent*
Carlin Temper, *Human Res Mgr*
▲ EMP: 76 EST: 1960

SALES (est): 71.6MM **Privately Held**
WEB: www.arcabrasives.com
SIC: **5085** 3291 2296 Abrasives; abrasive products; tire cord & fabrics

(G-18348)
ARETT SALES CORP
1261 Brukner Dr (45373-3843)
PHONE...................937 552-2005
David McCarthy, *Branch Mgr*
EMP: 65
SALES (corp-wide): 129.7MM **Privately Held**
WEB: www.arett.com
SIC: **4225** General warehousing
PA: Arett Sales Corporation
9285 Commerce Hwy
Pennsauken NJ 08110
856 751-1224

(G-18349)
BIGELOW CORPORATION (PA)
Also Called: Troy Bowl
1530 Mckaig Ave (45373-2641)
PHONE...................937 339-3315
Fax: 937 339-3873
Rex Bigelow, *President*
Jan Bigelow, *Treasurer*
EMP: 30
SQ FT: 7,500
SALES (est): 1.2MM **Privately Held**
SIC: **7933** 5941 Ten pin center; sporting goods & bicycle shops

(G-18350)
BRACKETT BUILDERS INC (PA)
185 Marybill Dr S (45373-1074)
PHONE...................937 339-7505
Fax: 937 335-4201
Eric Stahl, *President*
Andy Middendorf, *Superintendent*
Dan Pierce, *Superintendent*
Janet Hieatt, *Corp Secy*
Thomas Hoying, *Vice Pres*
EMP: 27
SQ FT: 9,200
SALES: 42.2MM **Privately Held**
WEB: www.brackettbuilders.com
SIC: **1542** Commercial & office buildings, renovation & repair

(G-18351)
CITY OF TROY
Also Called: Troy City Water Distribution
1400 Experiment Farm Rd (45373-8788)
PHONE...................937 335-1914
Fax: 937 339-0006
Rosaleen Rayman, *Branch Mgr*
Larry Lewis, *Manager*
EMP: 40
SQ FT: 23,760 **Privately Held**
WEB: www.troyohio.gov
SIC: **4941** Water supply
PA: City Of Troy
100 S Market St Ste 1
Troy OH 45373
937 335-2224

(G-18352)
COUNTY OF MIAMI
Also Called: Miami Co Highway Dept
2100 N County Road 25a (45373-1333)
PHONE...................937 335-1314
Jeff Vore, *Foreman/Supr*
Jerry Jackson, *Manager*
Sandy Curtis, *Admin Sec*
EMP: 30 **Privately Held**
WEB: www.co.miami.oh.us
SIC: **8744** Base maintenance (providing personnel on continuing basis)
PA: County Of Miami
201 W Main St
Troy OH 45373
937 440-5900

(G-18353)
EARHART PETROLEUM INC (PA)
1494 Lytle Rd (45373-8925)
P.O. Box 39 (45373-0039)
PHONE...................937 335-2928
Jeffrey W Earhart, *President*
Lisa Sargent, *Vice Pres*
Jason Reynolds, *VP Opers*
Michael W Earhart, *Treasurer*
Tina Fuller, *Human Resources*

EMP: 40
SQ FT: 21,000
SALES (est): 80.3MM **Privately Held**
WEB: www.earhartpetroleum.com
SIC: **5172** 5541 5983 Fuel oil; filling stations, gasoline; fuel oil dealers

(G-18354)
FTECH R&D NORTH AMERICA INC (HQ)
1191 Horizon West Ct (45373-7560)
PHONE...................937 339-2777
Sooyoung Ji, *General Mgr*
Bing Liu, *COO*
Donald Bauer, *Administration*
EMP: 56
SQ FT: 50,000
SALES (est): 7.6MM
SALES (corp-wide): 1.6B **Privately Held**
SIC: **8731** 3714 Commercial physical research; motor vehicle parts & accessories
PA: F-Tech Inc.
19, Showanuma, Shobucho
Kuki STM 346-0
480 855-211

(G-18355)
GREENTECH CORPORATION
Also Called: Greentech Lawn and Irrigation
1405 S County Road 25a (45373-4243)
P.O. Box 679 (45373-0679)
PHONE...................937 339-4758
Fax: 937 339-6936
Larry Smith, *President*
EMP: 35
SQ FT: 2,400
SALES (est): 4.2MM **Privately Held**
SIC: **0782** Lawn care services; lawn services

(G-18356)
HARBORSIDE TROY LLC
Also Called: Troy Center
512 Crescent Dr (45373-2718)
PHONE...................937 335-7161
Rick Edwards, *Treasurer*
EMP: 99
SALES (est): 294.8K **Privately Held**
SIC: **8051** Skilled nursing care facilities

(G-18357)
HOBART BROS STICK ELECTRODE
101 Trade Sq E (45373-2476)
PHONE...................937 332-5375
Steve Knostman, *Owner*
EMP: 109
SALES (est): 3.2MM **Privately Held**
SIC: **7692** Welding repair

(G-18358)
HOSPICE OF MIAMI COUNTY INC
550 Summit Ave Ste 101 (45373-3047)
P.O. Box 502 (45373-0502)
PHONE...................937 335-5191
Fax: 937 335-8841
Jill Demmitt, *Pub Rel Dir*
Susan Hemm, *Marketing Staff*
Nancy Magel, *Exec Dir*
Joanel Rurode, *Director*
Steven R Rosen, *Psychiatry*
EMP: 50
SALES: 6MM **Privately Held**
WEB: www.homc.org
SIC: **8082** Home health care services

(G-18359)
ITW FOOD EQUIPMENT GROUP LLC (HQ)
Also Called: Hobart
701 S Ridge Ave (45374-0001)
PHONE...................937 332-2396
Fax: 937 332-2582
Tom Szafranski, *President*
Chris O Herlihy, *Exec VP*
Gary Duench, *Plant Mgr*
Steve Peditte, *Purchasing*
Ron Grise, *Engineer*
◆ EMP: 1100
SALES (est): 422.6MM
SALES (corp-wide): 14.3B **Publicly Held**
SIC: **5046** 3556 Restaurant equipment & supplies; food products machinery

Troy - Miami County (G-18360)

PA: Illinois Tool Works Inc.
155 Harlem Ave
Glenview IL 60025
847 724-7500

(G-18360)
KEY II SECURITY INC
110 W Main St (45373-3214)
P.O. Box 434, Tipp City (45371-0434)
PHONE.................................937 339-8530
Fax: 937 339-9899
Jack D Cheaddle, *President*
EMP: 50
SALES (est): 955K **Privately Held**
SIC: 7381 Detective agency

(G-18361)
LEOS LA PIAZZA INC
Also Called: La Piazza Pasta & Grill
2 N Market St (45373-3216)
PHONE.................................937 339-5553
Fax: 937 339-6892
Leo Anticoli, *President*
Peggy Anticoli, *Vice Pres*
Mike Anticoli, *Treasurer*
Emily Goodin, *Manager*
EMP: 40
SQ FT: 3,000
SALES (est): 1.5MM **Privately Held**
SIC: 5812 7299 Italian restaurant; banquet hall facilities

(G-18362)
LOWES HOME CENTERS LLC
2000 W Main St (45373-1019)
PHONE.................................937 339-2544
Fax: 937 339-2774
Mike Haehl, *Store Mgr*
Jerry Breger, *Manager*
EMP: 155
SALES (corp-wide): 68.6B **Publicly Held**
SIC: 5211 5031 5722 5064 Home centers; building materials, exterior; building materials, interior; household appliance stores; electrical appliances, television & radio
HQ: Lowe's Home Centers, Llc
1605 Curtis Bridge Rd
Wilkesboro NC 28697
336 658-4000

(G-18363)
MIAMI CNTY CMNTY ACTION CUNCIL
Also Called: Miami Metropolitan Hsing Auth
1695 Troy Sidney Rd (45373-9794)
PHONE.................................937 335-7921
Jack Baird, *Director*
EMP: 35 EST: 1966
SQ FT: 11,000
SALES: 881K **Privately Held**
SIC: 8399 6513 Community action agency; apartment building operators

(G-18364)
MIAMI COUNTY CHILDRENS SVCS BD
510 W Water St Ste 210 (45373-2982)
PHONE.................................937 335-4103
June Cannon, *Exec Dir*
EMP: 32
SALES (est): 599.9K **Privately Held**
SIC: 8322 Child related social services; substance abuse counseling

(G-18365)
MIAMI COUNTY PARK DISTRICT
2645 E State Route 41 (45373-9692)
PHONE.................................937 335-6273
J Myers, *Exec Dir*
Jerry Eldred, *Director*
Jessie Rankinen, *Relations*
EMP: 40
SALES (est): 1.4MM **Privately Held**
WEB: www.miamicountyparks.com
SIC: 8999 8641 Natural resource preservation service; civic social & fraternal associations

(G-18366)
MILCON CONCRETE INC
1360 S County Road 25a 25 A (45373)
PHONE.................................937 339-6274
Mark Miller, *President*
Deborah Collins, *Manager*
EMP: 25
SALES (est): 3.6MM **Privately Held**
WEB: www.millmark-inc.com
SIC: 1771 Concrete work
PA: Millmark Construction, Inc
1360 S County Rd 25a
Troy OH

(G-18367)
NATIONWIDE TRUCK BROKERS INC
3355 S County Road 25a (45373-9384)
PHONE.................................937 335-9229
Fax: 937 335-0259
Mike Wilcox, *Branch Mgr*
EMP: 25
SALES (corp-wide): 44.8MM **Privately Held**
SIC: 4213 Contract haulers
PA: Nationwide Truck Brokers, Inc.
4203 R B Chaffee Mem Dr
Wyoming MI 49548
616 878-5554

(G-18368)
OHIO & INDIANA ROOFING
17 S Market St (45373-3217)
PHONE.................................937 339-8768
Michael Bruns, *Principal*
EMP: 25
SALES (est): 109K **Privately Held**
SIC: 1761 Roof repair

(G-18369)
OHIO INNS INC
Also Called: Residence Inn By Marriott
87 Troy Town Dr (45373-2327)
PHONE.................................937 440-9303
Fax: 937 440-9403
Frank Crisofia, *President*
EMP: 30
SALES (est): 1.4MM **Privately Held**
WEB: www.ohioinns.com
SIC: 7011 Hotels & motels

(G-18370)
OHIO MACHINERY CO
Also Called: Caterpillar
1281 Brukner Dr (45373-3843)
PHONE.................................937 335-7660
Toll Free:.................................888 -
John Fiedler, *Sales Staff*
Tj Perkins, *Marketing Staff*
Greg Hallaway, *Manager*
Ralph Miller, *Manager*
Nathan Nichols, *Admin Sec*
EMP: 57
SALES (corp-wide): 222.7MM **Privately Held**
WEB: www.enginesnow.com
SIC: 5082 General construction machinery & equipment
PA: Ohio Machinery Co.
3993 E Royalton Rd
Broadview Heights OH 44147
440 526-6200

(G-18371)
PANASONIC CORP NORTH AMERICA
America Matsushita Electronic
1400 W Market St (45373-3889)
PHONE.................................201 392-6872
Fax: 937 440-6149
Seiji Kasamatsu, *President*
Adam Yamamoto, *QC Dir*
EMP: 25
SALES (corp-wide): 64.6B **Privately Held**
WEB: www.panasonic.com
SIC: 5064 Electrical appliances, television & radio
HQ: Panasonic Corporation Of North America
2 Riverfront Plz Ste 200
Newark NJ 07102
201 348-7000

(G-18372)
PUBLIC SAFETY OHIO DEPARTMENT
Also Called: Testing and Inspection Fcilty
1275 Experiment Farm Rd (45373-1065)
PHONE.................................937 335-6209
EMP: 32 **Privately Held**

SIC: 9221 8011 5399 State highway patrol; physicians' office, including specialists; surplus & salvage goods
HQ: Ohio Department Of Public Safety
1970 W Broad St Fl 5
Columbus OH 43223

(G-18373)
R P L CORPORATION
Also Called: Motel 6
1375 W Market St (45373-3858)
PHONE.................................937 335-0021
William A Roll MD, *President*
Juan M Palomar MD, *Treasurer*
Dean Retterer, *Controller*
Frank Scott, *Admin Sec*
EMP: 105
SQ FT: 200,000
SALES (est): 2.1MM **Privately Held**
SIC: 7011 5812 5813 Motels; family restaurants; cocktail lounge

(G-18374)
R T INDUSTRIES INC (PA)
Also Called: CHAMPION INDUSTRIES DIV
110 Foss Way (45373-1430)
PHONE.................................937 335-5784
Fax: 937 339-6978
Ann Hinkle, *Superintendent*
Karen Mayer, *Superintendent*
Ashley Brocious, *Manager*
Blair Brubaker, *CIO*
Ald Pease, *CTO*
EMP: 146
SQ FT: 18,000
SALES: 3.4MM **Privately Held**
SIC: 3579 8331 7349 2789 Paper cutters, trimmers & punches; sheltered workshop; janitorial service, contract basis; bookbinding & related work; home for the mentally handicapped

(G-18375)
R T INDUSTRIES INC
Also Called: Riverside of Miami County
1625 Troy Sidney Rd (45373-9794)
PHONE.................................937 339-8313
Fax: 937 335-6907
Brian Green, *Superintendent*
Karen Mayer, *Branch Mgr*
Helen Willis, *Manager*
Greg Green, *Administration*
EMP: 140
SALES (corp-wide): 3.4MM **Privately Held**
SIC: 8331 9111 Sheltered workshop; county supervisors' & executives' offices
PA: R T Industries Inc
110 Foss Way
Troy OH 45373
937 335-5784

(G-18376)
REM-OHIO INC
721 Lincoln Ave (45373-3176)
PHONE.................................937 335-8267
EMP: 40
SALES (corp-wide): 2.8MM **Privately Held**
SIC: 8361 Home for the mentally retarded
PA: Rem-Ohio, Inc
6921 York Ave S
Minneapolis MN 55435
952 925-5067

(G-18377)
REMEDI SENIORCARE OF OHIO LLC (HQ)
962 S Dorset Rd (45373-4705)
PHONE.................................800 232-4239
Rene Deller, *General Mgr*
Pete Cheadle, *Controller*
Darla Metz, *Human Res Dir*
Eugene McCormick, *Manager*
Dustina Monnier, *Asst Mgr*
EMP: 41
SQ FT: 20,000
SALES (est): 143.4MM **Privately Held**
SIC: 5122 Pharmaceuticals

(G-18378)
S P S INC
Also Called: Hampton Inn
45 Troy Town Dr (45373-2327)
PHONE.................................937 339-7801
Fax: 937 335-7979

Thomas J Schippel, *President*
Sheila Patel, *Manager*
Raman Patel, *Admin Sec*
EMP: 30
SALES (est): 2.1MM **Privately Held**
SIC: 7011 7991 5813 Hotels; physical fitness facilities; drinking places

(G-18379)
TIME WARNER CABLE INC
1450 Experiment Farm Rd (45373-8788)
PHONE.................................937 483-5152
Fax: 937 773-6795
Danny Schiffer, *Branch Mgr*
EMP: 50
SQ FT: 12,900
SALES (corp-wide): 41.5B **Publicly Held**
SIC: 4841 Cable television services
HQ: Spectrum Management Holding Company, Llc
400 Atlantic St
Stamford CT 06901
203 905-7801

(G-18380)
TONI & MARIE BADER
831 E Main St (45373-3420)
PHONE.................................937 339-3621
Toni O Bader, *Agent*
O Bader, *Agent*
EMP: 30
SALES (est): 1MM **Privately Held**
SIC: 8742 Real estate consultant

(G-18381)
TRANSFREIGHT INC
3355 S County Road 25a B (45373-9384)
PHONE.................................937 332-0366
Fax: 937 332-1867
Darrell Dewberry, *Manager*
EMP: 32
SALES (corp-wide): 2.9B **Privately Held**
SIC: 4731 Freight forwarding
HQ: Penske Logistics Canada Ltd
3065 King St E
Kitchener ON N2A 1
519 650-0123

(G-18382)
TROY CHRISTIAN SCHOOL
1586 Mckaig Rd (45373-2670)
PHONE.................................937 339-5692
Fax: 937 335-1271
Gary Wilber, *Superintendent*
Scott Smith, *Media Spec*
EMP: 60
SQ FT: 32,000
SALES: 6.4MM **Privately Held**
SIC: 8211 8351 Catholic combined elementary & secondary school; kindergarten; private elementary school; child day care services

(G-18383)
TROY COUNTRY CLUB INC
1830 Peters Rd (45373-3868)
P.O. Box 459 (45373-0459)
PHONE.................................937 335-5691
Fax: 937 335-2788
Philip Zwierzchowski, *Manager*
Nathan Combs, *Manager*
Todd Uhlir, *Executive*
EMP: 50 EST: 1922
SQ FT: 5,000
SALES: 1MM **Privately Held**
WEB: www.troycountryclub.com
SIC: 7997 Country club, membership

(G-18384)
US BANK NATIONAL ASSOCIATION
Also Called: US Bank
910 W Main St (45373-2846)
PHONE.................................937 335-8351
Fax: 937 332-1766
Pete Bardonaro, *District Mgr*
Thomas Atkinson, *Branch Mgr*
Deborah Wildermuth, *Executive*
EMP: 40
SALES (corp-wide): 22.7B **Publicly Held**
WEB: www.firstar.com
SIC: 6021 National commercial banks
HQ: U.S. Bank National Association
425 Walnut St Fl 1
Cincinnati OH 45202
513 632-4234

GEOGRAPHIC SECTION

Twinsburg - Summit County (G-18407)

(G-18385)
UVMC MANAGEMENT CORPORATION (HQ)
3130 N County Road 25a (45373-1309)
PHONE.................................937 440-4000
Michael Maiberger, *President*
Diane Ruhenkamp, *Controller*
Diane Ruhenkent, *Accountant*
EMP: 66
SQ FT: 169,000
SALES (est): 25.6MM
SALES (corp-wide): 354MM **Privately Held**
SIC: 8051 8062 Skilled nursing care facilities; general medical & surgical hospitals
PA: Premier Health Partners
110 N Main St Ste 450
Dayton OH 45402
937 499-9596

(G-18386)
UVMC NURSING CARE INC
Also Called: Koester Pavilion Nursing Home
3232 N County Road 25a (45373-1338)
PHONE.................................937 440-7663
Fax: 937 335-0095
Jessica Suba, *Corp Comm Staff*
Pat Meyer, *Manager*
Kristi Capper, *Director*
Joseph Hughes, *Director*
Carolyn Newhouse, *Director*
EMP: 200
SQ FT: 57,216
SALES (corp-wide): 20.3MM **Privately Held**
WEB: www.koesterpavilion.com
SIC: 8051 Skilled nursing care facilities
PA: Uvmc Nursing Care, Inc.
3130 N County Road 25a
Troy OH 45373
937 440-4000

(G-18387)
VULCAN FEG
750 Lincoln Ave (45373-3137)
PHONE.................................937 332-2763
Sharon Holloman, *Controller*
EMP: 80
SQ FT: 1,250,000
SALES (est): 5.3MM **Privately Held**
SIC: 5046 Commercial cooking & food service equipment

(G-18388)
ZEBO PRODUCTIONS
1875 Barnhart Rd (45373-9589)
PHONE.................................937 339-0397
Mike Fischer, *President*
EMP: 55
SALES (est): 310.8K **Privately Held**
SIC: 7822 Motion picture & tape distribution

Twinsburg
Summit County

(G-18389)
ADVANTAGE WAYPOINT LLC
9458 Ravenna Rd (44087-2104)
PHONE.................................248 919-3144
Marylou Wethington, *Admin Mgr*
EMP: 28
SALES (corp-wide): 200MM **Privately Held**
SIC: 5141 Food brokers
PA: Advantage Waypoint Llc
13521 Prestige Pl
Tampa FL 33635
813 358-5900

(G-18390)
AMERICAN ROCK MECHANICS INC
9241 Ravenna Rd Ste 6 (44087-2451)
PHONE.................................330 963-0550
Edward J Walter Jr, *President*
EMP: 27
SQ FT: 5,500
SALES: 3MM **Privately Held**
SIC: 8711 Engineering services

(G-18391)
ANDERSEN & ASSOCIATES INC
1960 Summit Commerce Park (44087-2372)
PHONE.................................330 425-8500
Tom Forrester, *Vice Pres*
Thomas Forestek, *Vice Pres*
EMP: 50
SALES (est): 4.1MM
SALES (corp-wide): 86.6MM **Privately Held**
SIC: 5084 Materials handling machinery
PA: Andersen & Associates, Inc.
30575 Anderson Ct
Wixom MI 48393
248 960-6800

(G-18392)
APPLE GATE OPERATING CO INC
Also Called: Hilton Garden Inn Twinsburg
8971 Wilcox Dr (44087-1945)
PHONE.................................330 405-4488
Fax: 330 405-4499
Robert Voelker, *President*
Ron Hutcheson, *CFO*
Kevin Walsh, *Controller*
Connie Maleck, *Human Res Mgr*
Roger Greene, *Manager*
EMP: 40
SALES (est): 2.4MM **Privately Held**
SIC: 7011 Hotels

(G-18393)
ASSURAMED INC (HQ)
1810 Summit Commerce Park (44087-2300)
PHONE.................................330 963-6998
Michael B Petras Jr, *CEO*
Kurt Packer, *COO*
Andy Hinkle, *Vice Pres*
Chris Lindroth, *Vice Pres*
Mark Wells, *Vice Pres*
EMP: 39
SALES (est): 76.4MM
SALES (corp-wide): 129.9B **Publicly Held**
SIC: 5047 Medical & hospital equipment
PA: Cardinal Health, Inc.
7000 Cardinal Pl
Dublin OH 43017
614 757-5000

(G-18394)
ATLAS STEEL PRODUCTS CO (PA)
Also Called: AB Tube Company
7990 Bavaria Rd (44087-2252)
PHONE.................................330 425-1600
Fax: 330 963-0020
John Adams, *President*
Fred Barrera, *COO*
Jim Fisher, *Vice Pres*
Claude Bianchi, *Opers Mgr*
Victoria Widmor, *Finance Mgr*
◆ **EMP:** 80 EST: 1957
SQ FT: 120,000
SALES (est): 61.3MM **Privately Held**
WEB: www.atlassteel.com
SIC: 5051 Sheets, metal

(G-18395)
AVID TECHNOLOGIES INC
2112 Case Pkwy Ste 1 (44087-2378)
P.O. Box 468 (44087-0468)
PHONE.................................330 487-0770
Fax: 330 487-0770
David Shen, *CEO*
Arnie Grever, *President*
Joseph R Daprile, *Vice Pres*
Paul M Barlak, *Treasurer*
Laura Radtke, *Office Mgr*
EMP: 45 EST: 2014
SQ FT: 12,000
SALES: 10.4MM **Privately Held**
SIC: 8711 5045 Consulting engineer; computer software
HQ: Premier Farnell Corp.
4180 Highlander Pkwy
Richfield OH 44286
216 525-4300

(G-18396)
BASEMENT SYSTEMS OHIO INC
8295 Darrow Rd (44087-2307)
PHONE.................................330 423-4430
Michael Rusk, *President*
Joseph Rusk, *Vice Pres*
EMP: 105
SQ FT: 65,000
SALES (est): 7.6MM **Privately Held**
WEB: www.basementsystemsohio.com
SIC: 1799 Waterproofing

(G-18397)
BEACON SALES ACQUISITION INC
Also Called: North Coast Coml Roofg Systems
2440 Edison Blvd (44087-2340)
PHONE.................................330 425-3359
Fax: 330 425-3391
Buddy Harris, *Opers Mgr*
Todd Selstad, *Safety Mgr*
Kevin Freyhauf, *Purch Mgr*
Britt Cherry, *Engineer*
Laura Cejna, *Human Res Mgr*
EMP: 200
SALES (corp-wide): 4.3B **Publicly Held**
SIC: 5033 Roofing, asphalt & sheet metal
HQ: Beacon Sales Acquisition, Inc.
50 Webster Ave
Somerville MA 02143
877 645-7663

(G-18398)
CELLCO PARTNERSHIP
8957 Canyon Falls Blvd (44087-1976)
PHONE.................................330 486-1005
Vincetta Crombie, *Principal*
EMP: 71
SALES (corp-wide): 126B **Publicly Held**
SIC: 4812 Cellular telephone services
HQ: Cellco Partnership
1 Verizon Way
Basking Ridge NJ 07920

(G-18399)
CEM-BASE INC
Also Called: Trimor
8530 N Boyle Pkwy (44087-2267)
PHONE.................................330 963-3101
John R Morris III, *President*
Steve Taylor, *Vice Pres*
Eryn Artrit, *Office Mgr*
Diana Huston, *Admin Sec*
EMP: 25
SALES (est): 2.9MM **Privately Held**
SIC: 1771 Concrete work

(G-18400)
CHILDRENS HOSP MED CTR AKRON
8054 Darrow Rd (44087-2381)
PHONE.................................330 425-3344
Fax: 330 425-8847
Alicia Lamancusa, *Controller*
Jeanne Fenton, *Branch Mgr*
Jane Messemer, *Med Doctor*
Susan Shah, *Med Doctor*
Kimberly Masterson, *Pediatrics*
EMP: 732
SALES (corp-wide): 747.4MM **Privately Held**
SIC: 8069 Children's hospital
PA: Childrens Hospital Medical Center Of Akron
1 Perkins Sq
Akron OH 44308
330 543-1000

(G-18401)
CLEVELAND ELECTRIC LABS CO (PA)
1776 Enterprise Pkwy (44087-2246)
PHONE.................................800 447-2207
Fax: 330 425-7209
Jack Allan Lieske, *President*
C M Lemmon, *Principal*
Val Jean Lieske, *Vice Pres*
Don Lieske, *Production*
John Bernier, *Purchasing*
EMP: 50
SQ FT: 30,000
SALES (est): 10.1MM **Privately Held**
WEB: www.clevelandelectriclabs.com
SIC: 3823 7699 Thermocouples, industrial process type; industrial machinery & equipment repair

(G-18402)
CLEVELAND PUMP REPR & SVCS LLC
Also Called: C P R
1761 Highland Rd (44087-2220)
PHONE.................................330 963-3100
James Durkin, *General Mgr*
Susan Knirsch, *Bookkeeper*
Tony Dailey, *
EMP: 25
SQ FT: 23,000
SALES (est): 6.7MM **Privately Held**
WEB: www.clevelandpumprepair.com
SIC: 7699 Industrial machinery & equipment repair

(G-18403)
CME ACQUISITIONS LLC
Also Called: Cleveland Metal Exchange
1900 Case Pkwy S (44087-2358)
PHONE.................................216 464-4480
Fax: 216 464-1190
Jeff Haas, *President*
Ron Glazer, *CFO*
Rick Matousek, *Sales Staff*
Kenneth Detmayer, *Manager*
Glenn Beauchamp, *
▲ **EMP:** 35
SALES: 3MM **Privately Held**
WEB: www.clevelandmetal.com
SIC: 5051 Steel

(G-18404)
CONTRACTORS STEEL COMPANY
8383 Boyle Pkwy (44087-2236)
PHONE.................................330 425-3050
Fax: 330 425-8580
Mitch Kubasek, *Manager*
EMP: 49
SQ FT: 58,000
SALES (corp-wide): 213.9MM **Privately Held**
WEB: www.contractorssteel.com
SIC: 5051 3498 3312 Steel; plates, metal; sheets, metal; strip, metal; fabricated pipe & fittings; blast furnaces & steel mills
PA: Contractors Steel Company
36555 Amrhein Rd
Livonia MI 48150
734 464-4000

(G-18405)
COWAN SYSTEMS LLC
1882 Highland Rd (44087-2223)
PHONE.................................330 963-8483
Fax: 330 487-1839
Dave Feder, *Branch Mgr*
EMP: 48 **Privately Held**
SIC: 4213 Automobiles, transport & delivery
PA: Cowan Systems, Llc
4555 Hollins Ferry Rd
Baltimore MD 21227

(G-18406)
DMD MANAGEMENT INC
Also Called: Legacy Place
2463 Sussex Blvd (44087-2442)
PHONE.................................330 405-6040
Fax: 330 405-6041
Amy Kraynak, *Branch Mgr*
EMP: 45
SQ FT: 41,918 **Privately Held**
SIC: 8051 Convalescent home with continuous nursing care
PA: Dmd Management, Inc.
12380 Plaza Dr
Cleveland OH 44130

(G-18407)
EARLE M JORGENSEN COMPANY
Also Called: EMJ Cleveland
2060 Enterprise Pkwy (44087-2210)
PHONE.................................330 425-1500
Fax: 330 963-8188
Joanna Janic, *Human Res Mgr*
John Weber, *Sales Mgr*

Ed King, *Branch Mgr*
EMP: 100
SQ FT: 75,000
SALES (corp-wide): 9.7B **Publicly Held**
WEB: www.emjmetals.com
SIC: 5051 Pipe & tubing, steel; bars, metal
HQ: Earle M. Jorgensen Company
10650 Alameda St
Lynwood CA 90262
323 567-1122

(G-18408)
ENVIRONMENT CTRL BEACHWOOD INC
1897 E Aurora Rd (44087-1917)
PHONE 330 405-6201
Fax: 440 405-6205
James Hennessy, *President*
Laura Hart, *Area Mgr*
EMP: 70
SQ FT: 4,000
SALES (est): 1.8MM **Privately Held**
SIC: 7349 Cleaning service, industrial or commercial

(G-18409)
ENVIROTEST SYSTEMS CORP
2180 Pinnacle Pkwy (44087-2379)
PHONE 330 963-4464
Steve Peterson, *Manager*
EMP: 25 **Privately Held**
SIC: 7549 Emissions testing without repairs, automotive
HQ: Envirotest Systems Corp.
7 Kripes Rd
East Granby CT 06026

(G-18410)
ENVIROTEST SYSTEMS CORP
2180 Pinnacle Pkwy (44087-2379)
PHONE 330 963-4464
Steve Peterson, *Branch Mgr*
EMP: 34 **Privately Held**
WEB: www.il.etest.com
SIC: 7549 Emissions testing without repairs, automotive
HQ: Envirotest Systems Corp.
7 Kripes Rd
East Granby CT 06026

(G-18411)
ENVISION PHRM SVCS LLC
Also Called: Envision Rx Options
2181 E Aurora Rd Ste 201 (44087-1974)
PHONE 330 405-8080
Frank Sheehy, *CEO*
Matt Gibbs, *General Mgr*
Nakul Kapadia, *Vice Pres*
Susan Richards, *Accountant*
Taylor Benjamin, *Accounts Mgr*
EMP: 320
SALES (est): 76.9MM
SALES (corp-wide): 32.8B **Publicly Held**
WEB: www.envisionrx.com
SIC: 6411 Insurance claim processing, except medical
PA: Rite Aid Corporation
30 Hunter Ln
Camp Hill PA 17011
717 761-2633

(G-18412)
ESSENDANT CO
2100 Highland Rd (44087-2229)
PHONE 330 425-4001
Fax: 216 425-4020
Janine Eterovich, *Human Res Mgr*
Dave Martin, *Manager*
Renee Starr, *Director*
EMP: 126
SALES (corp-wide): 5B **Publicly Held**
WEB: www.ussco.com
SIC: 5112 5044 Office supplies; office equipment
HQ: Essendant Co.
1 Parkway North Blvd # 100
Deerfield IL 60015
847 627-7000

(G-18413)
ESSENDANT INC
Also Called: United Stationers
2100 Highland Rd (44087-2229)
PHONE 330 425-4001
David Martin, *Opers Staff*
Sue Wickerham, *Persnl Mgr*
John Watson, *Sales Executive*
Dean Gifford, *Branch Mgr*
EMP: 85
SALES (corp-wide): 5B **Publicly Held**
SIC: 5112 Stationery & office supplies
PA: Essendant Inc.
1 Parkway North Blvd # 100
Deerfield IL 60015
847 627-7000

(G-18414)
FACIL NORTH AMERICA INC (HQ)
Also Called: Streetsboro Operations
2242 Pinnacle Pkwy # 100 (44087-5301)
PHONE 330 487-2500
Fax: 330 626-8155
Rene Achten, *CEO*
Michael REA, *Purch Mgr*
Daniel Michiels, *CFO*
Ray Ardente, *Finance Dir*
◆ **EMP:** 210
SQ FT: 150,000
SALES (est): 158.4MM
SALES (corp-wide): 5.6MM **Privately Held**
WEB: www.flexalloy.com
SIC: 5072 3452 5085 Nuts (hardware); bolts; screws; nuts, metal; fasteners, industrial: nuts, bolts, screws, etc.
PA: Facil Corporate Bvba
Geleenlaan 20
Genk 3600
894 104-50

(G-18415)
FILING SCALE COMPANY INC
1500 Enterprise Pkwy (44087-2240)
PHONE 330 425-3092
Kenneth J Filing Sr, *CEO*
Kenneth J Filing Jr, *President*
Linda Filing, *Vice Pres*
Rosemarie Filing, *Admin Sec*
EMP: 35
SQ FT: 12,000
SALES (est): 7.8MM **Privately Held**
WEB: www.filing-lts.com
SIC: 5046 7359 7699 Scales, except laboratory; equipment rental & leasing; scale repair service

(G-18416)
FNB CORPORATION
10071 Darrow Rd (44087-1409)
PHONE 330 425-1818
Jamie Williams, *Branch Mgr*
EMP: 59
SALES (corp-wide): 1.2B **Publicly Held**
SIC: 7389 6162 6029 6021 Financial services; mortgage bankers & correspondents; commercial banks; national commercial banks
PA: F.N.B. Corporation
1 N Shore Ctr
Pittsburgh PA 15212
800 555-5455

(G-18417)
FOREST CITY ERECTORS INC
Also Called: Cleveland Crane Rental
8200 Boyle Pkwy Ste 1 (44087-2248)
PHONE 330 425-2345
Fax: 330 425-8728
Denise M Beers, *President*
James Mirgliotta, *Vice Pres*
Mark Phipps, *Vice Pres*
William Dean, *Safety Mgr*
Carol Safier, *Controller*
EMP: 100
SQ FT: 6,000
SALES: 27.6MM **Privately Held**
WEB: www.forestcityerectors.com
SIC: 1791 Iron work, structural

(G-18418)
FRENCH COMPANY LLC
Also Called: Facility Connect
8289 Darrow Rd (44087-2307)
PHONE 330 963-4344
Fax: 330 963-4562
Scott Dahl, *CEO*
John Durkey, *President*
Troy Batchelor, *Business Mgr*
Christine Callahan, *Vice Pres*
David Mechenbier, *VP Finance*
EMP: 75
SALES: 7.4MM
SALES (corp-wide): 1.1MM **Privately Held**
WEB: www.thefrenchcompany.com
SIC: 7699 8741 Cleaning services; management services
HQ: Technibilt, Ltd.
700 Technibilt Dr
Newton NC 28658
828 464-7388

(G-18419)
FUCHS LUBRICANTS CO
Also Called: Fuchs Franklin Div
8036 Bavaria Rd (44087-2262)
PHONE 330 963-0400
Fax: 330 963-2995
Kipp Kofsky, *Branch Mgr*
Hendrik Noth, *Manager*
Eve Haupt, *Programmer Anys*
EMP: 25
SALES (corp-wide): 2.9B **Privately Held**
WEB: www.fuchs.com
SIC: 4225 2992 2899 2851 General warehousing & storage; lubricating oils & greases; chemical preparations; paints & allied products; specialty cleaning, polishes & sanitation goods
HQ: Fuchs Lubricants Co.
17050 Lathrop Ave
Harvey IL 60426
708 333-8901

(G-18420)
GATEWAY HOSPITALITY GROUP INC (PA)
8921 Canyon Falls Blvd # 140 (44087-3900)
PHONE 330 405-9800
Bob F Voelker, *CEO*
Ronald Dearman, *CFO*
Ron Hutcheson, *CFO*
Katie Kohlman, *Accounting Mgr*
Mayra Santiago, *Accounting Mgr*
EMP: 110
SQ FT: 2,000
SALES (est): 7.4MM **Privately Held**
WEB: www.ghghotels.net
SIC: 7011 Hotels

(G-18421)
GED HOLDINGS INC
9280 Dutton Dr (44087-1967)
PHONE 330 963-5401
William Weaver, *President*
Dave Lewis, *Research*
Steve Lang, *CFO*
EMP: 141 **EST:** 2000
SALES (est): 16.5MM **Privately Held**
SIC: 3559 3549 5084 Glass making machinery: blowing, molding, forming, etc.; cutting & slitting machinery; industrial machinery & equipment

(G-18422)
GENERAL ELECTRIC INTL INC
8941 Dutton Dr (44087-1939)
PHONE 330 963-2066
Fax: 330 425-0900
Jeffrey Pack, *Manager*
EMP: 30
SALES (corp-wide): 122B **Publicly Held**
SIC: 5084 3561 Compressors, except air conditioning; pumps, oil well & field
HQ: General Electric International, Inc.
191 Rosa Parks St
Cincinnati OH 45202
617 443-3000

(G-18423)
GIESECKE & DEVRIENT AMER INC
Also Called: G & D Twinsburg
2020 Enterprise Pkwy (44087-2210)
PHONE 330 425-1515
Flamarion Pirtouscheg, *Managing Dir*
Tina Atwell, *VP Admin*
Randy Gurganus, *Vice Pres*
Ralf Wintergerst, *Vice Pres*
Dale Ridel, *Plant Mgr*
EMP: 120
SALES (corp-wide): 308.9K **Privately Held**
SIC: 2672 5044 Coated & laminated paper; office equipment
HQ: Giesecke+Devrient Currency Technology America, Inc.
45925 Horseshoe Dr # 100
Dulles VA 20166
703 480-2000

(G-18424)
GODDARD SCHOOL OF TWINSBURG
2608 Glenwood Dr (44087-2835)
PHONE 330 487-0394
Fax: 330 487-0698
Randy Lindley, *Manager*
Jim Lindley, *Director*
EMP: 30
SALES (est): 424.3K **Privately Held**
SIC: 8351 Preschool center

(G-18425)
GREAT LAKES FASTENERS INC
2204 E Enterprise Pkwy (44087-2356)
PHONE 330 425-4488
Kevin Weidinger, *President*
Tim Umberger, *Vice Pres*
Jeff McConnell, *Buyer*
Chris Paschal, *QC Mgr*
Justin Taylor, *Regl Sales Mgr*
▲ **EMP:** 25
SQ FT: 20,000
SALES: 2MM **Privately Held**
SIC: 5085 Fasteners, industrial: nuts, bolts, screws, etc.

(G-18426)
HAHS FACTORY OUTLET
1993 Case Pkwy (44087-4328)
PHONE 330 405-4227
Gerry Haas, *Owner*
EMP: 50
SALES (est): 3.5MM **Privately Held**
SIC: 1081 Test boring, metal mining

(G-18427)
HATTIE LARLHAM COMMUNITY SVCS
Also Called: Larlham Center For Children
7996 Darrow Rd Ste 10 (44087-6822)
PHONE 330 274-2272
Kayla Bindus, *HR Admin*
Kayla Ferroni, *Manager*
Dennis Allen, *Exec Dir*
EMP: 50
SALES: 2.9MM
SALES (corp-wide): 5.2MM **Privately Held**
SIC: 8322 Association for the handicapped
PA: Hattie Larlham Community Living
7996 Darrow Rd
Twinsburg OH 44087
330 274-2272

(G-18428)
HEALTHSPAN INTEGRATED CARE
Also Called: Kaiser Foundation Health Plan
8920 Canyon Falls Blvd (44087-1990)
PHONE 330 486-2800
Patricia Kennedy Scott, *Manager*
EMP: 29
SALES (corp-wide): 4.2B **Privately Held**
SIC: 6324 Hospital & medical service plans
HQ: Healthspan Integrated Care
1001 Lakeside Ave E # 1200
Cleveland OH 44114
216 621-5600

(G-18429)
HITACHI HLTHCARE AMERICAS CORP
Also Called: Hitachi Medical Systems Amer
1959 Summit Commerce Park (44087-2371)
PHONE 330 425-1313
Donald Broomfield, *President*
Vickie Campbell, *Regional Mgr*
William Bishop, *Vice Pres*
Xiaodong Che, *Vice Pres*
James Confer, *Vice Pres*
▲ **EMP:** 370
SQ FT: 54,000
SALES (est): 196.8MM
SALES (corp-wide): 80.6B **Privately Held**
WEB: www.hitachimed.com
SIC: 5047 Diagnostic equipment, medical

GEOGRAPHIC SECTION

Twinsburg - Summit County (G-18452)

HQ: Hitachi Healthcare Manufacturing, Ltd.
2-1, Shintoyofuta
Kashiwa CHI 277-0
471 314-336

(G-18430)
HOLLAND ROOFING INC
9221 Ravenna Rd (44087-2472)
PHONE..............................330 963-0237
Joe Arway, *Branch Mgr*
EMP: 44
SALES (corp-wide): 46.6MM Privately Held
SIC: 1761 Roof repair
PA: Holland Roofing, Inc.
7450 Industrial Rd
Florence KY 41042
859 525-0887

(G-18431)
ICM DISTRIBUTING COMPANY INC
Also Called: Inventory Controlled Mdsg
1755 Entp Pkwy Ste 200 (44087)
PHONE..............................234 212-3030
Harry Singer, *President*
Phillip B Singer, *Vice Pres*
Dan Cohen, *Senior Buyer*
Gary Hawvermale, *Controller*
▼ EMP: 35
SQ FT: 80,000
SALES (est): 27.1MM
SALES (corp-wide): 31.2MM Privately Held
SIC: 5122 5049 5199 5092 Hair preparations; cosmetics; school supplies; general merchandise, non-durable; toys
PA: Sandusco, Inc.
1755 Entp Pkwy Ste 200
Twinsburg OH 44087
440 357-5964

(G-18432)
INTEGRTED PRCISION SYSTEMS INC
9321 Ravenna Rd Ste C (44087-2461)
PHONE..............................330 963-0064
Fax: 330 963-0065
James Butkovic, *President*
Greg Ponchak, *Vice Pres*
Karen Ponchak, *Controller*
Tyler Jewel, *Marketing Staff*
Valerie Fink, *Office Admin*
EMP: 25
SQ FT: 4,000
SALES (est): 5.3MM Privately Held
WEB: www.ipsid.com
SIC: 7373 Systems integration services

(G-18433)
JADE INVESTMENTS
2300 E Aurora Rd (44087-1928)
P.O. Box 1090 (44087-9090)
PHONE..............................330 425-3141
William Lieberman, *Partner*
Russell Garron, *Partner*
Gary Bauman, *Ltd Ptnr*
EMP: 50
SALES (est): 2.1MM Privately Held
WEB: www.jadeinvestments.com
SIC: 6512 Commercial & industrial building operation

(G-18434)
JADE-STERLING STEEL CO INC (PA)
2300 E Aurora Rd (44087-1987)
P.O. Box 1090 (44087-9090)
PHONE..............................330 425-3141
Fax: 330 425-3056
Howard Fertel, *CEO*
Scott Herman, *President*
Lisa Krolikowski, *General Mgr*
Bill Lieberman, *Chairman*
Dean Musarra, *Vice Pres*
▲ EMP: 45 EST: 1965
SQ FT: 375,000
SALES (est): 54.4MM Privately Held
WEB: www.jadesterling.com
SIC: 5051 Steel

(G-18435)
K & M INTERNATIONAL INC (PA)
Also Called: Wild Republic
1955 Midway Dr Ste A (44087-1961)
PHONE..............................330 425-2550
Fax: 330 425-3777
Gopala B Pillai, *President*
Mike Grasela, *Business Mgr*
Joe Onderko, *COO*
Kamala Pillai, *Vice Pres*
Vinod Kumar, *Production*
▲ EMP: 76
SQ FT: 100,000
SALES (est): 30.9MM Privately Held
WEB: www.kmtoys.com
SIC: 5092 5199 Toys; gifts & novelties; bags, baskets & cases; art goods

(G-18436)
KAISER FOUNDATION HOSPITALS
Also Called: Twinsburg Medical Offices
8920 Canyon Falls Blvd (44087-1990)
PHONE..............................330 486-2800
EMP: 593
SALES (corp-wide): 82.6B Privately Held
SIC: 8011 Offices & clinics of medical doctors
HQ: Kaiser Foundation Hospitals Inc
1 Kaiser Plz
Oakland CA 94612
510 271-6611

(G-18437)
KIMBLE COMPANIES INC
8500 Chamberlin Rd (44087-2096)
PHONE..............................330 963-5493
Fax: 330 963-0495
Denny Kijek, *Opers Mgr*
Peter Gutwein, *Branch Mgr*
EMP: 67
SALES (est): 3MM Privately Held
SIC: 4953 Garbage: collecting, destroying & processing
PA: Kimble Companies Inc.
3596 State Route 39 Nw
Dover OH 44622

(G-18438)
KINDERCARE EDUCATION LLC
Also Called: Childrens World Learning Ctr
2572 Glenwood Dr (44087-2698)
PHONE..............................330 405-5556
Fax: 330 405-2826
Jill Gay, *Director*
EMP: 27
SALES (corp-wide): 1.2B Privately Held
WEB: www.knowledgelearning.com
SIC: 8351 Group day care center
PA: Kindercare Education Llc
650 Ne Holladay St # 1400
Portland OR 97232
503 872-1300

(G-18439)
LAUDAN PROPERTIES LLC
2204 E Enterprise Pkwy (44087-2356)
PHONE..............................234 212-3225
Kevin Weidinger, *President*
Keith O'Donnell, *Vice Pres*
Blake Seal, *Accountant*
Todd Heroux, *Manager*
Lisa Murphy, *Supervisor*
EMP: 29
SQ FT: 3,000
SALES (est): 14.6MM Privately Held
SIC: 6512 Nonresidential building operators

(G-18440)
LEIDOS INC
8866 Commons Blvd Ste 201 (44087-2177)
PHONE..............................330 405-9810
Laura Obloy, *VP Opers*
Steven Visocky, *Branch Mgr*
Jeffrey Dick, *Manager*
EMP: 30
SALES (corp-wide): 10.1B Publicly Held
WEB: www.saic.com
SIC: 8731 Commercial physical research
HQ: Leidos, Inc.
11951 Freedom Dr Ste 500
Reston VA 20190
571 526-6000

(G-18441)
LEIDOS ENGINEERING LLC
8866 Commons Blvd Ste 201 (44087-2177)
PHONE..............................330 405-9810
Fax: 330 405-9811
Robin Giles, *HR Admin*
Steven Visocky, *Branch Mgr*
EMP: 54
SALES (corp-wide): 10.1B Publicly Held
SIC: 8711 Consulting engineer
HQ: Leidos Engineering, Llc
11951 Freedom Dr
Reston VA 20190
571 526-6000

(G-18442)
LIGHTING SERVICES INC
9001 Dutton Dr (44087-1930)
PHONE..............................330 405-4879
Fax: 330 963-4482
Kim Allerman, *President*
Darcy Gilbert, *General Mgr*
Bob Shostek, *Business Mgr*
Kurt Allerman, *Vice Pres*
Tom Petrey, *Project Mgr*
EMP: 30
SQ FT: 5,000
SALES: 6.3MM Privately Held
SIC: 1731 Lighting contractor

(G-18443)
LOU RITENOUR DECORATORS INC
Also Called: Ritenour Industrial
2066 Case Pkwy S (44087-2360)
PHONE..............................330 425-3232
Fax: 330 963-7123
Michael Ritenour, *President*
Aldo Sainato, *Project Mgr*
Tracey Smartt, *Project Mgr*
Karen Ritenour, *Treasurer*
EMP: 100
SQ FT: 8,000
SALES (est): 10.8MM Privately Held
SIC: 1721 Interior commercial painting contractor

(G-18444)
MARSAM METALFAB INC
1870 Enterprise Pkwy (44087-2206)
PHONE..............................330 405-1520
Fax: 330 405-1532
Mark Brownfield, *President*
EMP: 25
SQ FT: 30,000
SALES (est): 3.9MM Privately Held
SIC: 1799 3441 7692 3444 Welding on site; fabricated structural metal; welding repair; sheet metalwork

(G-18445)
MAVAL INDUSTRIES LLC
Also Called: Maval Manufacturing
1555 Enterprise Pkwy (44087-2239)
PHONE..............................330 405-1600
Fax: 330 425-4854
John Dougherty, *President*
Dale Lumby, *Vice Pres*
Steve Summerville, *Plant Mgr*
Meri Vaughn, *Finance*
Jim Stackpole, *Supervisor*
▲ EMP: 203
SQ FT: 88,000
SALES: 30MM
SALES (corp-wide): 9.8B Publicly Held
WEB: www.mavalgear.com
SIC: 3714 8711 Power steering equipment, motor vehicle; consulting engineer
HQ: Borgwarner Pds (Indiana) Inc.
600 Corporation Dr
Pendleton IN 46064
800 372-3555

(G-18446)
MEDE AMERICA OF OHIO LLC
2045 Midway Dr (44087-1933)
PHONE..............................330 425-3241
Fax: 330 963-7726
Denise Ceule, *Manager*
Wade McKenzie, *Manager*
Charles Mele, *Director*
EMP: 681
SALES (est): 163.8K
SALES (corp-wide): 1.9B Privately Held
SIC: 7371 Computer software development
HQ: Change Healthcare Operations, Llc
3055 Lebanon Pike # 1000
Nashville TN 37214

(G-18447)
MEDIA COLLECTIONS INC
Also Called: Joseph, Mann & Creed
8948 Canyon Falls Blvd # 200 (44087-1900)
P.O. Box 22253, Beachwood (44122-0253)
PHONE..............................216 831-5626
Fax: 216 831-5616
Perry Creed, *President*
Jeff Ritner, *Director*
Bill Mann, *Admin Sec*
EMP: 63
SQ FT: 10,000
SALES (est): 7.5MM Privately Held
WEB: www.jmcbiz.com
SIC: 7322 Collection agency, except real estate

(G-18448)
MERC ACQUISITIONS INC
Also Called: Electric Sweeper Service Co
1933 Highland Rd (44087-2224)
PHONE..............................216 925-5918
Robert Merckle, *President*
Gale Merckle, *Vice Pres*
Don Siegrist, *Executive*
▲ EMP: 28 EST: 1924
SQ FT: 27,000
SALES (est): 25.2MM Privately Held
SIC: 5064 Appliance parts, household; vacuum cleaners, household

(G-18449)
MIRKA USA INC
2375 Edison Blvd (44087-2376)
PHONE..............................330 963-6421
Fax: 330 963-6762
Mark Kush, *President*
Mats Sundell, *Research*
Todd Moskowitz, *Controller*
David Walker, *Sales Mgr*
Bobby Hurst, *Regl Sales Mgr*
▲ EMP: 80
SQ FT: 24,000
SALES: 36.6MM
SALES (corp-wide): 1.9MM Privately Held
WEB: www.mirkausa.com
SIC: 5085 Abrasives
HQ: Mirka Oy
Pensalantie 210
Jepua 66850
207 602-111

(G-18450)
NATIONAL TRNSP SOLUTIONS INC
1831 Highland Rd (44087-2222)
PHONE..............................330 405-2660
Larry Musarra, *President*
Ron Glazer, *CFO*
EMP: 55
SQ FT: 140,000
SALES: 14MM Privately Held
SIC: 4213 4212 Trucking, except local; local trucking, without storage

(G-18451)
NEXEO SOLUTIONS LLC
Also Called: Ashland Distribution
1842 Enterprise Pkwy (44087-2206)
PHONE..............................330 405-0461
David Newhart, *Branch Mgr*
EMP: 27
SALES (corp-wide): 3.6B Publicly Held
WEB: www.ashland.com
SIC: 5169 Industrial chemicals
HQ: Nexeo Solutions, Llc
3 Waterway Square Pl # 1000
The Woodlands TX 77380

(G-18452)
PEPPERL + FUCHS INC (HQ)
1600 Enterprise Pkwy (44087-2245)
PHONE..............................330 425-3555
Fax: 330 425-4607
Wolfgang Mueller, *President*
Hermann Best, *Managing Dir*

(PA)=Parent Co (HQ)=Headquarters (DH)=Div Headquarters
✪ = New Business established in last 2 years

2018 Harris Ohio
Services Directory

Twinsburg - Summit County (G-18453)

Michael Fuchs, *Managing Dir*
Seitz Juergen, *Managing Dir*
Claus Michael, *Managing Dir*
▲ **EMP:** 130
SQ FT: 55,050
SALES (est): 94.4MM
SALES (corp-wide): 585.6MM **Privately Held**
WEB: www.pepperlfuchs.com
SIC: 5065 3625 3822 3674 Electronic parts & equipment; relays & industrial controls; auto controls regulating residntl & coml environmt & applncs; semiconductors & related devices
PA: Pepperl + Fuchs Gmbh
Lilienthalstr. 200
Mannheim 68307
621 776-0

(G-18453)
PEPSI-COLA METRO BTLG CO INC
1999 Enterprise Pkwy (44087-2253)
PHONE 330 963-0426
Fax: 330 425-4715
Robert Oswald, *Opers Mgr*
Richard Gajewski, *Plant Engr*
Charlie Powers, *Manager*
Frank O'Neill, *Manager*
Fran Strazar, *Manager*
EMP: 500
SALES (corp-wide): 63.5B **Publicly Held**
WEB: www.joy-of-cola.com
SIC: 2086 5149 Bottled & canned soft drinks; groceries & related products
HQ: Pepsi-Cola Metropolitan Bottling Company, Inc.
1111 Westchester Ave
White Plains NY 10604
914 767-6000

(G-18454)
PHARMERICA LONG-TERM CARE INC
Also Called: Ltc Pharmacy
1750 Highland Rd Ste F (44087-2275)
PHONE 330 425-4450
Rob Koch, *Branch Mgr*
EMP: 25
SALES (corp-wide): 129MM **Privately Held**
WEB: www.pharmerica.com
SIC: 7352 Invalid supplies rental
HQ: Pharmerica Long-Term Care, Llc
3625 Queen Palm Dr
Tampa FL 33619
877 975-2273

(G-18455)
PRECISION FUNDING CORP
2132 Case Pkwy Ste A (44087-2383)
PHONE 330 405-1313
Fax: 330 486-0925
Dominic Di Franco, *President*
EMP: 32
SQ FT: 12,800
SALES: 2.5MM **Privately Held**
SIC: 6162 6163 Mortgage bankers & correspondents; loan brokers

(G-18456)
PRESTIGE INTERIORS INC
2239 E Enterprise Pkwy (44087-2347)
PHONE 330 425-1690
Fax: 330 650-1414
David Maag, *President*
EMP: 35
SQ FT: 2,500
SALES: 2.5MM **Privately Held**
WEB: www.prestigeinteriorsinc.com
SIC: 1542 Commercial & office building, new construction; commercial & office buildings, renovation & repair

(G-18457)
PSI ASSOCIATES INC
2112 Case Pkwy Ste 10 (44087-2378)
P.O. Box 468 (44087-0468)
PHONE 330 425-8474
Fax: 330 425-2905
Steve Rosenberg, *President*
Dr Colleen Lorberl, *COO*
Shyma Sumesh, *Engineer*
Cyndie Nicholl, *Manager*
Barbara Taylor-Ross, *Manager*
EMP: 300

SQ FT: 1,500
SALES (est): 16.3MM **Privately Held**
SIC: 7361 8049 Employment agencies; clinical psychologist

(G-18458)
QSR PARENT CO
1700 Highland Rd (44087-2221)
PHONE 330 425-8472
Randy Ross, *CEO*
Rich Jones, *Accountant*
EMP: 914
SALES (corp-wide): 1.7B **Privately Held**
SIC: 6719 Investment holding companies, except banks
HQ: Q Holding Company
1700 Highland Rd
Twinsburg OH 44087
330 425-8472

(G-18459)
REGENCY WINDOWS CORPORATION
2288 E Aurora Rd (44087-1926)
P.O. Box 6743, Cleveland (44101-1743)
PHONE 330 963-4077
Fax: 330 963-4092
David Gordon, *CEO*
Kim Gaebelein, *Vice Pres*
Joe Tripi Jr, *Vice Pres*
Bruce Gorrell, *CFO*
EMP: 65
SQ FT: 17,000
SALES (est): 9.4MM **Privately Held**
WEB: www.regencywindow.com
SIC: 5211 5713 1761 1751 Siding; carpets; siding contractor; window & door (prefabricated) installation

(G-18460)
RESERVE FTL LLC
Also Called: Reserve Management Group
1831 Highland Rd (44087-2222)
PHONE 440 519-1768
James Rumler, *Opers Mgr*
Robert Evenhouse, *Branch Mgr*
EMP: 30 **Privately Held**
WEB: www.reservemarine.com
SIC: 4491 Marine terminals
PA: Reserve Ftl, Llc
11600 S Burley Ave
Chicago IL 60617

(G-18461)
RIGHTWAY INVESTMENTS LLC
1959 Edgewood Dr (44087-1637)
P.O. Box 27211, Cleveland (44127-0211)
PHONE 216 854-7697
Bernard Motley, *Mng Member*
EMP: 50
SALES: 950K **Privately Held**
SIC: 6799 Investors

(G-18462)
ROGER ZATKOFF COMPANY
Also Called: Zatkoff Seals & Packings
2475 Edison Blvd (44087-2340)
PHONE 248 478-2400
Fax: 330 405-8701
Brian Gilboy, *Manager*
EMP: 25
SALES (corp-wide): 126.3MM **Privately Held**
WEB: www.zatkoff.com
SIC: 5085 Seals, industrial
PA: Roger Zatkoff Company
23230 Industrial Park Dr
Farmington Hills MI 48335
248 478-2400

(G-18463)
RSR PARTNERS LLC
Also Called: Regency Technologies
1831 Highland Rd (44087-2222)
PHONE 440 519-1768
Jim Levine, *General Mgr*
Julius Hess, *Vice Pres*
Mike Mannion, *Opers Mgr*
Brian Murphy, *Facilities Mgr*
Chris Pinchot, *Facilities Mgr*
▼ **EMP:** 300 **EST:** 2006
SALES (est): 81MM **Privately Held**
SIC: 5084 Recycling machinery & equipment

(G-18464)
RX OPTIONS LLC (HQ)
Also Called: Envision Pharmaceutical Svcs
2181 E Aurora Rd Ste 101 (44087-1962)
PHONE 330 405-8080
Barry Katz, *President*
William M Toomajian, *Principal*
James Mandella, *Chairman*
Nick Vasilopoulos, *Senior VP*
Michael Mindala, *Vice Pres*
EMP: 75
SQ FT: 2,500
SALES (est): 31.5MM
SALES (corp-wide): 40.1MM **Privately Held**
SIC: 8742 Compensation & benefits planning consultant
PA: Envision Pharmaceutical Holdings Llc
2181 E Aurora Rd Ste 201
Twinsburg OH 44087
800 361-4542

(G-18465)
S & E ELECTRIC INC
1521 Highland Rd (44087-2254)
PHONE 330 425-7866
Fax: 330 425-2745
Tony K Sasala, *President*
D J Sasala, *Chairman*
Kristine M Sasala, *Admin Sec*
EMP: 30
SQ FT: 20,000
SALES: 4.1MM **Privately Held**
SIC: 1731 General electrical contractor

(G-18466)
SAFRAN POWER USA LLC
8380 Darrow Rd (44087-2329)
PHONE 330 487-2000
Chris Plumb, *President*
Terry McGlothlin, *Engineer*
Kevin Rice, *Engineer*
Edward Tompkin, *Project Engr*
Bruce Rusnak, *Senior Engr*
EMP: 140
SALES (est): 28.4MM
SALES (corp-wide): 555.1MM **Privately Held**
SIC: 8711 8741 Engineering services; business management
HQ: Safran Usa, Inc.
700 S Washington St # 320
Alexandria VA 22314
703 351-9898

(G-18467)
SAMUEL STEEL PICKLING COMPANY (PA)
1400 Enterprise Pkwy (44087-2242)
PHONE 330 963-3777
Fax: 330 963-0770
Rick Morris, *General Mgr*
Rick Snyder, *Principal*
Michael Evelyn, *Vice Pres*
William Vason, *Opers Mgr*
Lynda Petrilli, *Accountant*
EMP: 70
SQ FT: 115,000
SALES: 15MM **Privately Held**
SIC: 7389 5051 3471 3398 Metal slitting & shearing; metals service centers & offices; plating & polishing; metal heat treating; blast furnaces & steel mills

(G-18468)
SCHUSTER ELECTRONICS INC
Also Called: Schuster/Cleveland
2057d E Aurora Rd (44087-1921)
PHONE 330 425-8134
Fax: 330 425-1863
Anne Bailey, *Branch Mgr*
EMP: 26
SALES (corp-wide): 8.6MM **Privately Held**
WEB: www.schusterusa.com
SIC: 5065 5088 Electronic parts; transportation equipment & supplies
PA: Schuster Electronics, Inc.
11320 Grooms Rd
Blue Ash OH 45242
513 489-1400

(G-18469)
SHELLY COMPANY
8920 Canyon Falls Blvd # 3 (44087-1990)
PHONE 330 425-7861

Eric A Gul, *Opers Mgr*
Doug Rauh, *Branch Mgr*
EMP: 50
SALES (corp-wide): 29.7B **Privately Held**
SIC: 1611 Highway & street construction
HQ: Shelly Company
80 Park Dr
Thornville OH 43076
740 246-6315

(G-18470)
SODEXO INC
2333 Sandalwood Dr (44087-1383)
PHONE 330 425-0709
EMP: 39
SALES (corp-wide): 145.8MM **Privately Held**
SIC: 8742 Management Consulting Services
HQ: Sodexo, Inc.
9801 Washingtonian Blvd # 1
Gaithersburg MD 20878
301 987-4000

(G-18471)
SOLUPAY CONSULTING INC
1900 Entp Pkwy Ste A (44087)
PHONE 216 535-9016
Joe Musitano Jr, *Managing Prtnr*
Jayme Moss, *Managing Prtnr*
EMP: 97
SQ FT: 4,000
SALES: 4.5MM **Privately Held**
SIC: 7389 Credit card service

(G-18472)
SSP FITTINGS CORP (PA)
8250 Boyle Pkwy (44087-2200)
PHONE 330 425-4250
Jeffrey E King, *CEO*
F B Douglas, *Principal*
O F Douglas, *Principal*
H M Hunter, *Principal*
Betsy S King, *Corp Secy*
▲ **EMP:** 100 **EST:** 1926
SQ FT: 165,000
SALES (est): 25.6MM **Privately Held**
WEB: www.sspfittings.com
SIC: 3494 5085 3498 3492 Pipe fittings; industrial supplies; fabricated pipe & fittings; fluid power valves & hose fittings

(G-18473)
STEEL PLATE LLC
8333 Boyle Pkwy (44087-2236)
PHONE 888 894-8818
Fax: 330 376-8835
Joe Curry, *Vice Pres*
Ray Kenney, *Vice Pres*
Chris Frasier, *Opers Staff*
John Faverty, *Natl Sales Mgr*
Ken Stubitsch, *Accounts Exec*
EMP: 25 **Privately Held**
SIC: 5051 Steel
PA: Steel Plate, L.L.C.
140 S Holland Dr
Pendergrass GA 30567

(G-18474)
STONEMOR PARTNERS LP
Also Called: Crown Hill Cemetery
8592 Darrow Rd (44087-2128)
PHONE 330 425-8128
Fax: 330 425-8898
Tony Cusma, *Manager*
EMP: 26
SQ FT: 2,768
SALES (corp-wide): 326.2MM **Publicly Held**
WEB: www.stonemor.com
SIC: 6553 Cemeteries, real estate operation
PA: Stonemor Partners L.P.
3600 Horizon Blvd Ste 100
Trevose PA 19053
215 826-2800

(G-18475)
THE MAU-SHERWOOD SUPPLY CO (PA)
Also Called: M S
8400 Darrow Rd Ste 1 (44087-2375)
PHONE 330 405-1200
Fax: 330 951-1180
JC Rexroth, *President*
Mg McAleenan, *Principal*

GEOGRAPHIC SECTION

WD Turner, *Principal*
▼ **EMP:** 25 **EST:** 1908
SQ FT: 11,000
SALES (est): 11.9MM **Privately Held**
WEB: www.mausherwood.com
SIC: 5085 5169 5072 Valves & fittings; chemicals & allied products; hardware

(G-18476)
TIMEWARE INC
9329 Ravenna Rd Ste D (44087-2457)
PHONE 330 963-2700
Fax: 330 963-2704
Michael Farhat, *President*
Rebecca Farhat, *Vice Pres*
EMP: 30
SQ FT: 1,782
SALES (est): 1.8MM **Privately Held**
WEB: www.timeware.net
SIC: 7371 Computer software development

(G-18477)
TRI COUNTY CONCRETE INC (PA)
9423 Darrow Rd (44087-1415)
P.O. Box 665 (44087-0665)
PHONE 330 425-4464
Fax: 330 405-3122
Tony Farenacci, *President*
Fred Farenacci, *Vice Pres*
Tony Farecci, *Manager*
Joyce Negrette, *Manager*
EMP: 30
SQ FT: 62,000
SALES (est): 4.8MM **Privately Held**
SIC: 3273 3272 1442 Ready-mixed concrete; concrete products; construction sand & gravel

(G-18478)
TRI-MOR CORP
Also Called: Trimor
8530 N Boyle Pkwy (44087-2267)
PHONE 330 963-3101
John R Morris III, *President*
Rich Desgee, *Principal*
Neille Morris, *Credit Mgr*
Diane Huston, *Human Res Mgr*
Mike Aikey, *Manager*
EMP: 120
SALES (est): 21.2MM **Privately Held**
WEB: www.trimor.com
SIC: 1771 Blacktop (asphalt) work

(G-18479)
TURFSCAPE INC
8490 Tower Dr (44087-2000)
PHONE 330 405-0741
Fax: 330 405-7179
George M Hohman Jr, *President*
Brandon Kugler, *Opers Mgr*
Jen Roberts, *Opers Staff*
Christopher White, *Opers Staff*
Marysue Hohman, *Treasurer*
EMP: 110
SALES (est): 11.9MM **Privately Held**
WEB: www.turfscapeohio.com
SIC: 0782 Landscape contractors

(G-18480)
TWIN HAVEN RECEPTION HALL
10439 Ravenna Rd (44087-1726)
PHONE 330 425-1616
Robert Friedo, *Pastor*
Andrea Zelenka, *Manager*
EMP: 25
SALES (est): 404K **Privately Held**
SIC: 5812 7299 Caterers; banquet hall facilities

(G-18481)
U S A WATERPROOFING INC
1632 Enterprise Pkwy (44087-2282)
PHONE 330 425-2440
Fax: 330 425-4051
Steven Rusk, *President*
James Rusk, *Vice Pres*
EMP: 40
SQ FT: 8,000
SALES (est): 3.3MM **Privately Held**
SIC: 1799 Waterproofing

(G-18482)
UNIVAR USA INC
1686 Highland Rd (44087-2219)
PHONE 330 425-4330
Gregory T Hereda, *Sales Mgr*
Nancy Reddy, *Marketing Staff*
Michael Sebenoler, *Branch Mgr*
Linda Mandusky, *Assistant*
EMP: 40
SALES (corp-wide): 8.2B **Publicly Held**
SIC: 5169 Industrial chemicals
HQ: Univar Usa Inc.
17411 Ne Union Hill Rd
Redmond WA 98052
425 889-3400

(G-18483)
US FOODS INC
8000 Bavaria Rd (44087-2262)
PHONE 330 963-6789
Fax: 330 963-5050
Larry Burkhart, *Transptn Dir*
Meech Boyd, *Warehouse Mgr*
Lori Sciannameo, *Marketing Mgr*
Tony Morell, *Marketing Staff*
Steve Preston, *Branch Mgr*
EMP: 250 **Publicly Held**
WEB: www.usfoodservice.com
SIC: 5141 5149 Food brokers; groceries & related products
HQ: Us Foods, Inc.
9399 W Higgins Rd Ste 500
Rosemont IL 60018

(G-18484)
VERIZON WIRELESS
2000 Highland Rd (44087-2227)
PHONE 330 963-1300
Jeffrey Gardner, *CFO*
James Andres, *Manager*
Douglas Dever, *Manager*
Todd Martin, *Network Enginr*
David Reed, *Associate Dir*
EMP: 26
SALES (est): 1.9MM
SALES (corp-wide): 9.6MM **Privately Held**
SIC: 4813 Local telephone communications
PA: Verizon Wireless
15505 Sand Canyon Ave
Irvine CA 92618
949 286-7000

(G-18485)
WEBMD HEALTH CORP
2045 Midway Dr (44087-1933)
PHONE 330 425-3241
Tom Apker, *COO*
Frank Failla, *Vice Pres*
Eric Bursack, *Project Mgr*
Mike Mc Manus, *Branch Mgr*
Wade McKenzie, *Manager*
EMP: 30
SALES (corp-wide): 705MM **Privately Held**
WEB: www.wellmed.com
SIC: 7375 Information retrieval services
HQ: Webmd Health Corp.
395 Hudson St Fl 3
New York NY 10014
212 624-3700

(G-18486)
YOUNG CHEMICAL CO LLC (HQ)
1755 Entp Pkwy Ste 400 (44087)
PHONE 330 486-4210
Brian McCue, *President*
Mike Leighty, *CFO*
Nick Lamagna, *VP Sales*
EMP: 32
SALES (est): 7.3MM
SALES (corp-wide): 85.3MM **Privately Held**
SIC: 5169 Industrial chemicals
PA: Paro Services Co.
1755 Entp Pkwy Ste 100
Twinsburg OH 44087
330 467-1300

Uhrichsville
Tuscarawas County

(G-18487)
BARBOUR PUBLISHING INC (PA)
Also Called: Heartsong Presents
1810 Barbour Dr Se (44683-1084)
P.O. Box 719 (44683-0719)
PHONE 740 922-1321
Tim Martins, *CEO*
Mary Burns, *President*
Rebecca Germany, *Editor*
George Kourkounakis, *Exec VP*
William Westfall, *Vice Pres*
◆ **EMP:** 47
SQ FT: 74,000
SALES (est): 8.9MM **Privately Held**
WEB: www.barbourbooks.com
SIC: 5942 5192 Book stores; books

(G-18488)
EMBER COMPLETE CARE (PA)
1800 N Water Street Ext (44683-1044)
P.O. Box 369 (44683-0369)
PHONE 740 922-6888
Fax: 740 922-6689
Lois Ann Grandison, *President*
Dennis Jock Grandison, *Vice Pres*
Amy Roth, *Executive*
EMP: 150
SALES (est): 5.7MM **Privately Held**
SIC: 8082 Visiting nurse service

(G-18489)
EMBER HOME CARE
730 N Water St (44683-1456)
PHONE 740 922-6968
Dennis Grandison, *Owner*
Jock Grandison, *Owner*
EMP: 300
SALES (est): 5.2MM **Privately Held**
SIC: 8082 Home health care services

(G-18490)
IMCO RECYCLING OF OHIO LLC
7335 Newport Rd Se (44683-6368)
PHONE 740 922-2373
Fax: 740 922-2377
Sean M Stack, *CEO*
Robert R Holian, *Vice Pres*
Mark Mantooth, *Manager*
▲ **EMP:** 164
SALES (est): 20.3MM **Privately Held**
WEB: www.imcorecycling.com
SIC: 3341 4953 Aluminum smelting & refining (secondary); recycling, waste materials
HQ: Aleris Rolled Products, Inc.
25825 Science Park Dr # 400
Beachwood OH 44122
216 910-3400

(G-18491)
ROSEBUD MINING COMPANY
5600 Pleasant Vly Rd Se (44683-9502)
PHONE 740 922-9122
Greg Blainer, *Branch Mgr*
EMP: 33
SALES (corp-wide): 672.6MM **Privately Held**
WEB: www.rosebudmining.com
SIC: 1222 1221 Bituminous coal-underground mining; strip mining, bituminous
PA: Rosebud Mining Company
301 Market St
Kittanning PA 16201
724 545-6222

(G-18492)
SUPERIOR CLAY CORP
6566 Superior Rd Se (44683-7487)
P.O. Box 352 (44683-0352)
PHONE 740 922-4122
Fax: 740 922-6626
Elmer W McClave III, *President*
Joe Berni, *Corp Secy*
Todd M Clave, *Vice Pres*
Tyler McClave, *Vice Pres*
William Johnson, *Purchasing*
◆ **EMP:** 75 **EST:** 1936
SQ FT: 190,000
SALES (est): 9.9MM **Privately Held**
WEB: www.superiorclay.com
SIC: 3259 8611 Sewer pipe or fittings, clay; flue lining, clay; wall coping, clay; stove lining, clay; business associations

(G-18493)
U S ARMY CORPS OF ENGINEERS
86801 Eslick Rd (44683-9614)
PHONE 740 269-2681
Jerry Herman, *Branch Mgr*
EMP: 65 **Publicly Held**
SIC: 8711 Engineering services
HQ: U S Army Corps Of Engineers
441 G St Nw
Washington DC 20314
202 761-0001

(G-18494)
UHRICHSVILLE HEALTH CARE CTR
Also Called: Beacon Point Rehab
5166 Spanson Dr Se (44683-1346)
PHONE 740 922-2208
Brian Colleran, *President*
EMP: 83 **EST:** 1981
SQ FT: 25,000
SALES (est): 4.6MM **Privately Held**
SIC: 8051 Convalescent home with continuous nursing care

(G-18495)
UNITED STTES BOWL CONGRESS INC
710 Gorley St (44683-1626)
PHONE 740 922-3120
EMP: 51
SALES (corp-wide): 32.9MM **Privately Held**
SIC: 8699 Bowling club
PA: United States Bowling Congress, Inc.
621 Six Flags Dr
Arlington TX 76011
817 385-8200

(G-18496)
VISION EXPRESS INC
801 W 1st St (44683-2205)
PHONE 740 922-8848
Fax: 740 922-8845
Todd Evans, *President*
Randy Jones, *Director*
EMP: 35
SQ FT: 10,000
SALES: 4MM **Privately Held**
SIC: 4212 4213 Local trucking, without storage; contract haulers

(G-18497)
XPO LOGISTICS FREIGHT INC
2401 N Water Street Ext (44683-2400)
PHONE 740 922-5614
Fax: 740 922-6580
Michael Hodgson, *Sales Executive*
Larry McCraken, *Branch Mgr*
EMP: 30
SALES (corp-wide): 15.3B **Publicly Held**
WEB: www.con-way.com
SIC: 4212 Local trucking, without storage
HQ: Xpo Logistics Freight, Inc.
2211 Old Earhart Rd # 100
Ann Arbor MI 48105
734 998-4200

Union
Montgomery County

(G-18498)
DILLARD ELECTRIC INC
106 Quinter Farm Rd (45322-9705)
PHONE 937 836-5381
John Dillard, *President*
EMP: 30
SALES (est): 2.7MM **Privately Held**
WEB: www.dillardelectric.net
SIC: 1731 General electrical contractor

Union City
Darke County

(G-18499)
PROCTER & GAMBLE DISTRG LLC
1800 Union Park Blvd (45377)
P.O. Box 2628, Burlington NC (27216-2628)
PHONE..................937 387-5189
Robert Fix, *General Mgr*
EMP: 178
SALES (corp-wide): 65B **Publicly Held**
SIC: 5169 Detergents
HQ: Procter & Gamble Distributing Llc
   1 Procter And Gamble Plz
   Cincinnati OH 45202
   513 983-1100

(G-18500)
CAL-MAINE FOODS INC
1039 Zumbrum Rd (45390-8646)
PHONE..................937 968-4874
Fax: 937 968-6586
Chuck Jenkins, *Branch Mgr*
EMP: 35
SALES (corp-wide): 1B **Publicly Held**
WEB: www.calmainefoods.com
SIC: 0252 2015 Chicken eggs; eggs, processed; frozen
PA: Cal-Maine Foods, Inc.
   3320 W Woodrow Wilson Ave
   Jackson MS 39209
   601 948-6813

(G-18501)
CAST METALS TECHNOLOGY INC
305 Se Deerfield Rd (45390-9072)
PHONE..................937 968-5460
Ryan Olney, *Owner*
EMP: 47 **Privately Held**
SIC: 8731 Commercial physical research
PA: Cast Metals Technology, Inc.
   550 Liberty Rd
   Delaware OH 43015

(G-18502)
CROTINGER NURSING HOME INC
Also Called: Center of Hope
907 E Central St (45390-1605)
PHONE..................937 968-5284
Fax: 937 968-7634
Meta Sue Livingston, *President*
Jamie Livingston, *Vice Pres*
Eric Hiatt, *Treasurer*
Phil Crawford, *Administration*
EMP: 70
SQ FT: 16,000
SALES (est): 1.8MM **Privately Held**
WEB: www.centerofhope.com
SIC: 8051 Skilled nursing care facilities

(G-18503)
RL PAINTING AND MFG INC
Also Called: Livingston Painting
10001 Oh In State Line (45390-9050)
P.O. Box 145 (45377-0145)
PHONE..................937 968-5526
Fax: 937 968-7866
Richard Livingston, *President*
Jack Meinerding, *Sales Executive*
L Mastrogany, *Info Tech Mgr*
EMP: 30
SALES (est): 2.7MM **Privately Held**
SIC: 1721 Exterior residential painting contractor; commercial painting; industrial painting

(G-18504)
U C M RESIDENTIAL SERVICES
400 Gade Ave (45390)
PHONE..................937 643-3757
Robert Thompson, *Owner*
Cheryl Juhl, *Administration*
EMP: 70
SALES (est): 886.6K **Privately Held**
SIC: 8051 Skilled nursing care facilities

(G-18505)
UNION CHRISTEL MANOR INC
Also Called: Union City Crystal Manor
400 S Melvin Eley Ave (45390-8611)
PHONE..................937 968-6265
Fax: 937 968-6883
Robert Thompson III, *President*
Cheryl Juhl, *Admin Sec*
EMP: 75
SALES (est): 2.5MM **Privately Held**
SIC: 8051 Mental retardation hospital

Uniontown
Stark County

(G-18506)
AEROTEK INC
1559 Corporate Woods Pkwy # 10 (44685-7872)
PHONE..................330 517-7330
Pat Hoyle, *Director*
EMP: 27
SALES (corp-wide): 11.5B **Privately Held**
SIC: 7363 Temporary help service
HQ: Aerotek, Inc.
   7301 Parkway Dr
   Hanover MD 21076
   410 694-5100

(G-18507)
BIO-MDCAL APPLCATIONS OHIO INC
Also Called: Akron Canton Kidney Center
1575 Corp Woods Pkwy # 100 (44685-7842)
PHONE..................330 896-6311
Jacqueline Powers, *Manager*
Rob Watson, *Manager*
EMP: 30
SALES (corp-wide): 20.9B **Privately Held**
WEB: www.fresenius.org
SIC: 8092 Kidney dialysis centers
HQ: Bio-Medical Applications Of Ohio, Inc.
   920 Winter St
   Waltham MA 02451

(G-18508)
BONTRAGER EXCAVATING CO INC
11087 Cleveland Ave Nw (44685-8677)
PHONE..................330 499-8775
Fax: 330 499-3013
Brian Bontrager, *President*
Helen Bontrager, *Corp Secy*
Eric Bontrager, *Vice Pres*
EMP: 27 EST: 1972
SALES (est): 4.5MM **Privately Held**
SIC: 1794 Excavation work

(G-18509)
BUSINESS ALTERNATIVES INC
3458 Massillon Rd (44685-9501)
P.O. Box 908, Akron (44309-0908)
PHONE..................724 325-2777
Lucy Garrighan, *President*
Darlene Landstorser, *Finance*
EMP: 30
SQ FT: 12,000
SALES: 5.3MM **Privately Held**
SIC: 5999 5044 Business machines & equipment; office equipment

(G-18510)
CAHILL CORPORATION
3951 Creek Wood Ln (44685-7786)
PHONE..................330 724-1224
Fax: 330 724-7523
Edwin A Huth Jr, *President*
Lori Martin, *Principal*
Gina Waligura, *Manager*
EMP: 25 EST: 1907
SQ FT: 5,000
SALES: 9.8MM **Privately Held**
WEB: www.cahillcorp.com
SIC: 1711 Mechanical contractor; process piping contractor

(G-18511)
CAMBRIA GREEN MANAGEMENT LLC
Also Called: Cambria Stes Akrn-Canton Arprt
1787 Thorn Dr (44685-9573)
PHONE..................330 899-1263
Fax: 330 899-1991
Chris Bitikofer, *General Mgr*
Laura Groves, *Manager*
Karen Friedt, *Executive*
EMP: 34 EST: 2006
SALES (est): 1.1MM **Privately Held**
SIC: 7011 Hotels

(G-18512)
CBIZ INC
13680 Cleveland Ave Nw (44685-8098)
PHONE..................330 644-2044
Michael Stickard, *Manager*
EMP: 77 **Publicly Held**
SIC: 8748 6411 Business consulting; pension & retirement plan consultants
PA: Cbiz, Inc.
   6050 Oak Tree Blvd # 500
   Cleveland OH 44131

(G-18513)
CBORD GROUP INC
3800 Tabs Dr (44685-9564)
PHONE..................330 498-2702
Matthew Irwin, *Marketing Mgr*
John Stroia, *Branch Mgr*
Paul Admundson, *MIS Mgr*
EMP: 200
SQ FT: 17,000
SALES (corp-wide): 4.6B **Publicly Held**
WEB: www.cbord.com
SIC: 7699 Automated teller machine (ATM) repair
HQ: The Cbord Group Inc
   950 Danby Rd Ste 100c
   Ithaca NY 14850
   607 257-2410

(G-18514)
COMDOC INC (DH)
3458 Massillon Rd (44685-9503)
P.O. Box 908, Akron (44309-0908)
PHONE..................330 896-2346
Fax: 330 896-3904
Riley Lochridge, *Ch of Bd*
Gordy Opitz, *President*
Frank Pacetta, *Regional Mgr*
Chuck Moorman, *Area Mgr*
Larry Frank, *COO*
EMP: 125 EST: 1955
SQ FT: 60,000
SALES (est): 82.7MM
SALES (corp-wide): 10.2B **Publicly Held**
SIC: 7699 5044 7359 Photocopy machine repair; office equipment; business machine & electronic equipment rental services

(G-18515)
CORPORATE LADDER SEARCH
1549 Boettler Rd Ste D (44685-7766)
PHONE..................330 776-4390
Kristen Babbin, *President*
Heidi Hopkins, *Vice Pres*
Christine Hall, *Manager*
Kelsey Kloss, *Manager*
Kelsey Smith, *Manager*
EMP: 25
SALES (est): 95.6K **Privately Held**
SIC: 8748 7361 Business consulting; employment agencies

(G-18516)
CROWN HEATING & COOLING INC
Also Called: Honeywell Authorized Dealer
11197 Cleveland Ave Nw (44685-9401)
P.O. Box 1030 (44685-1030)
PHONE..................330 499-4988
Eugene Seifert, *President*
Arlene Seifert, *Vice Pres*
Keith Nickas, *Manager*
Bill Campian, *Consultant*
Tim Earnsberger, *Consultant*
EMP: 70
SQ FT: 43,054
SALES (est): 12.1MM **Privately Held**
SIC: 1711 Warm air heating & air conditioning contractor

(G-18517)
DIRECTION HOME AKRON CANTON AR (PA)
1550 Corporate Woods Pkwy (44685-8730)
PHONE..................330 896-9172
Fax: 330 896-6647
Gary Cook, *COO*
Abigail Morgan, *Vice Pres*
Sheri Mozea, *Vice Pres*
Matt Reed, *Vice Pres*
Barbara Kallenbach, *CFO*
EMP: 135
SQ FT: 19,502
SALES: 47.8MM **Privately Held**
SIC: 8322 Senior citizens' center or association

(G-18518)
DREES COMPANY
3906 Kenway Blvd (44685-6230)
PHONE..................330 899-9554
Hailey Collier, *Manager*
EMP: 27
SALES (corp-wide): 722.6MM **Privately Held**
SIC: 1521 New construction, single-family houses
PA: The Drees Company
   211 Grandview Dr Ste 300
   Fort Mitchell KY 41017
   859 578-4200

(G-18519)
FEDEX CUSTOM CRITICAL INC (HQ)
1475 Boettler Rd (44685-9584)
P.O. Box 5000, Green (44232-5000)
PHONE..................234 310-4090
Fax: 234 310-4152
Virginia Albanese, *CEO*
Alan B Graf Jr, *Ch of Bd*
Claude Colombo, *Regional Mgr*
Virginia C Albanese, *Vice Pres*
Jim Snider, *Vice Pres*
EMP: 500
SQ FT: 103,000
SALES (est): 109.7MM
SALES (corp-wide): 60.3B **Publicly Held**
SIC: 4213 Trucking, except local
PA: Fedex Corporation
   942 Shady Grove Rd S
   Memphis TN 38120
   901 818-7500

(G-18520)
FEDEX TRUCKLOAD BROKERAGE INC
1475 Boettler Rd (44685-9584)
P.O. Box 5000, Green (44232-5000)
PHONE..................234 310-4090
Virginia Albanese, *President*
Bob Cohen, *Engineer*
Elaine Gray, *Accounting Mgr*
ABI Jones, *Human Resources*
Megan Hershberger, *Manager*
EMP: 123
SALES (est): 37.5MM
SALES (corp-wide): 60.3B **Publicly Held**
WEB: www.FedEx.com
SIC: 4731 Freight transportation arrangement
HQ: Fedex Custom Critical, Inc.
   1475 Boettler Rd
   Uniontown OH 44685
   234 310-4090

(G-18521)
FIRST UNION BANC CORP
1559 Corporate Woods Pkwy (44685-7872)
PHONE..................330 896-1222
Beth Mosley, *President*
EMP: 31
SALES (est): 3.2MM **Privately Held**
SIC: 6162 Mortgage bankers

(G-18522)
GREENTOWN VLNTR FIRE DEPT INC
10100 Cleveland Ave Nw (44685-9413)
PHONE..................330 494-3002
Vincent Harris, *CEO*
Aaron Baker, *President*
Thomas Radomski-Bomba, *Vice Pres*

GEOGRAPHIC SECTION

Uniontown - Stark County (G-18545)

Nicholas Nicholson, *Treasurer*
Paul Weigand, *Admin Sec*
EMP: 38
SALES: 1MM **Privately Held**
SIC: 7389 Fire protection service other than forestry or public

(G-18523)
HANKOOK TIRE AMERICA CORP
Also Called: Hankook Tire Akron Office
3535 Forest Lake Dr (44685-8105)
PHONE..................................330 896-6199
Fax: 330 896-6597
Alex Hwang, *General Mgr*
Tony Lee, *Managing Dir*
Michael McMinn, *Engineer*
Alan Shirley, *Engineer*
Yaswanth Siramdasu, *Engineer*
EMP: 40
SALES (corp-wide): 76.5MM **Privately Held**
WEB: www.hankook-atc.com
SIC: 5014 5013 Automobile tires & tubes; truck tires & tubes; automotive batteries; wheels, motor vehicle
HQ: Hankook Tire America Corporation
    333 Commerce St Ste 600
    Nashville TN 37201
    615 432-0700

(G-18524)
HOWARD HANNA SMYTHE CRAMER
Also Called: Smythe Cramer Co
3700 Massillon Rd Ste 300 (44685-9558)
PHONE..................................330 896-3333
Fax: 330 896-9825
Bruce Heath, *Manager*
EMP: 40
SALES (corp-wide): 76.4MM **Privately Held**
WEB: www.smythecramer.com
SIC: 6531 Real estate brokers & agents
HQ: Howard Hanna Smythe Cramer
    6000 Parkland Blvd
    Cleveland OH 44124
    216 447-4477

(G-18525)
KIDS COUNTRY
1801 Town Park Blvd (44685-7963)
PHONE..................................330 899-0909
Fax: 330 899-0610
Christine Burkholder, *Owner*
Joni Giorvas-Weiglin, *Director*
Aimee Coia, *Asst Director*
EMP: 25
SALES (est): 636.2K **Privately Held**
SIC: 8351 Group day care center

(G-18526)
KIDS-PLAY INC
Also Called: Kids Play Green
1651 Boettler Rd (44685-7705)
PHONE..................................330 896-2400
Fax: 330 896-2464
Stephanie Shriver, *Director*
Laurie Schoblocher, *Associate Dir*
EMP: 30
SQ FT: 15,500
SALES (corp-wide): 4.8MM **Privately Held**
SIC: 8351 Group day care center; pre-school center
PA: Kids-Play Inc
    388 S Main St Ste 100
    Akron OH 44311
    330 253-2373

(G-18527)
LOUISVILLE CHILD CARE CENTER
Also Called: Marilyn Wagner
3477 Elmhurst Cir (44685-8143)
PHONE..................................330 875-4303
Fax: 330 875-9144
EMP: 25
SQ FT: 4,980
SALES (est): 550K **Privately Held**
SIC: 8351 Child Day Care Services

(G-18528)
MAYFAIR COUNTRY CLUB INC
2229 Raber Rd (44685-8844)
PHONE..................................330 699-2209
Fax: 330 699-2209

David Springer, *President*
Jeannie Springer, *Vice Pres*
EMP: 55
SQ FT: 15,582
SALES: 1.3MM **Privately Held**
WEB: www.mayfaircountryclub.com
SIC: 7992 Public golf courses

(G-18529)
MOTORISTS MUTUAL INSURANCE CO
3532 Massillon Rd (44685-7859)
P.O. Box 7647, Akron (44306-0697)
PHONE..................................330 896-9311
Tony King, *Business Mgr*
Randy McKinney, *Branch Mgr*
EMP: 28
SALES (corp-wide): 494.7MM **Privately Held**
SIC: 6331 Fire, marine & casualty insurance
PA: Motorists Mutual Insurance Company
    471 E Broad St Ste 200
    Columbus OH 43215
    614 225-8211

(G-18530)
NEW INNOVATIONS INC
3540 Forest Lake Dr (44685-8105)
PHONE..................................330 899-9954
Fax: 330 899-9855
Stephen C Reed, *CEO*
Jeanne Brooks, *Project Mgr*
Denise M Reed, *CFO*
Lee Neal, *Finance Asst*
Stephanie Husmann, *Web Dvlpr*
EMP: 31
SQ FT: 7,500
SALES (est): 3.8MM **Privately Held**
WEB: www.new-innov.com
SIC: 7371 Computer software development

(G-18531)
NEW NV CO LLC
3777 Boettler Oaks Dr (44685-7733)
PHONE..................................330 896-7611
David Logsdon, *Mng Member*
Kim Hamrick,
EMP: 140
SALES (est): 5.4MM **Privately Held**
SIC: 1521 Single-family housing construction

(G-18532)
PHIL WAGLER CONSTRUCTION INC
Also Called: Wagler Homes
3710 Tabs Dr (44685)
PHONE..................................330 899-0316
Philip E Wagler, *Ch of Bd*
Phil E Wagler, *President*
EMP: 40
SQ FT: 9,000
SALES (est): 3.4MM **Privately Held**
SIC: 1521 1531 New construction, single-family houses; speculative builder, single-family houses

(G-18533)
PRUDENTIAL INSUR CO OF AMER
3515 Massillon Rd Ste 200 (44685-6113)
PHONE..................................330 896-7200
Fax: 330 896-5511
Ed Twele, *General Mgr*
James F Ruttenberg, *Manager*
EMP: 45
SALES (corp-wide): 59.6B **Publicly Held**
SIC: 6411 Insurance agents, brokers & service
HQ: The Prudential Insurance Company Of America
    751 Broad St
    Newark NJ 07102
    973 802-6000

(G-18534)
RAINTREE COUNTRY CLUB INC
4350 Mayfair Rd (44685-8137)
PHONE..................................330 699-3232
Fax: 330 699-3238
John Rainieri Sr, *President*
John Rainieri Jr, *Vice Pres*
Melinda Haynes, *Admin Sec*

EMP: 40
SQ FT: 10,000
SALES (est): 2.1MM **Privately Held**
WEB: www.raintreegc.com
SIC: 7997 Country club, membership

(G-18535)
REALTY ONE INC
4016 Massillon Rd Ste A (44685-7818)
PHONE..................................330 896-5225
Fax: 330 896-5235
Sue Prieto, *Manager*
Ellen Jones, *Real Est Agnt*
EMP: 45
SALES (corp-wide): 67.8MM **Privately Held**
WEB: www.realty-1st.com
SIC: 6531 Real estate brokers & agents
HQ: Realty One, Inc.
    800 W Saint Clair Ave
    Cleveland OH 44113
    216 328-2500

(G-18536)
RESOURCE AMERICA INC
3500 Massillon Rd Ste 100 (44685-9575)
PHONE..................................330 896-8510
Nancy McGurk, *Manager*
EMP: 30
SALES (corp-wide): 138.8MM **Privately Held**
SIC: 1382 1311 Oil & gas exploration services; crude petroleum & natural gas
HQ: Resource America, Inc.
    1 Crescent Dr Ste 203
    Philadelphia PA 19112
    215 546-5005

(G-18537)
RESOURCE ENERGY INC
3500 Massillon Rd Ste 100 (44685-9575)
PHONE..................................330 896-8510
Michael L Staines, *President*
Jeffrey C Simons, *Exec VP*
Nancy J McGurk, *Treasurer*
EMP: 70
SALES (est): 5.6MM
SALES (corp-wide): 138.8MM **Privately Held**
WEB: www.resourceamerica.com
SIC: 1382 1311 Oil & gas exploration services; crude petroleum production; natural gas production
HQ: Resource America, Inc.
    1 Crescent Dr Ste 203
    Philadelphia PA 19112
    215 546-5005

(G-18538)
SCHEESER BUCKLEY MAYFIELD LLC
1540 Corporate Woods Pkwy (44685-8730)
PHONE..................................330 896-4664
Fax: 330 896-9180
Chad Montgomery, *President*
Jake Copley, *Engineer*
Kevin Nobce, *Engineer*
Ron Radabaugh, *Project Engr*
Lou Begue, *Electrical Engi*
EMP: 43
SALES (est): 2MM **Privately Held**
SIC: 8711 Consulting engineer

(G-18539)
SECURITAS ELECTRONIC SEC INC (DH)
3800 Tabs Dr (44685-9564)
PHONE..................................855 331-0359
Santiago Galaz, *CEO*
Tony Byerly, *President*
Frederick W London, *Vice Pres*
Thomas C Cantlon, *Treasurer*
Shawn Matheny, *Finance*
EMP: 75
SALES (est): 100.8MM
SALES (corp-wide): 9.5B **Privately Held**
SIC: 7382 Protective devices, security
HQ: Securitas Security Services Usa, Inc.
    9 Campus Dr
    Parsippany NJ 07054
    973 267-5300

(G-18540)
SYNERGY CONSULTING GROUP INC
3700 Massillon Rd Ste 300 (44685-9558)
PHONE..................................330 899-9301
Craig Mueller, *President*
Chrisy Berkshire, *Manager*
EMP: 30
SALES (est): 3.1MM **Privately Held**
SIC: 8742 Human resource consulting services

(G-18541)
TOTAL LOOP INC
1790 Town Park Blvd Ste A (44685-7972)
PHONE..................................888 614-5667
Vincenzo Rubino, *President*
EMP: 100 EST: 2012
SALES: 2.2MM **Privately Held**
SIC: 5045 Computer software

(G-18542)
VCA GREEN ANIMAL MEDICAL CTR
Also Called: VCA Green Animal Hospital
1620 Corporate Woods Cir (44685-7819)
PHONE..................................330 896-4040
Fax: 330 896-4055
Terry White, *General Mgr*
EMP: 30
SALES (est): 679.3K **Privately Held**
SIC: 0742 Veterinarian, animal specialties

(G-18543)
WH MIDWEST LLC (PA)
Also Called: Wayne Homes
3777 Boettler Oaks Dr (44685-7733)
PHONE..................................330 896-7611
Fax: 330 896-7622
William A Post, *COO*
Keith Anstine, *Vice Pres*
Joel Cardinal, *Vice Pres*
Vicki Timmons, *Opers Staff*
David E Logsdon, *Mng Member*
EMP: 120
SQ FT: 16,000
SALES (est): 22.7MM **Privately Held**
WEB: www.waynehomes.com
SIC: 1521 New construction, single-family houses

(G-18544)
XPO LOGISTICS FREIGHT INC
3733 Massillon Rd (44685-7730)
PHONE..................................330 896-7300
Fax: 330 896-4013
Jeff Teague, *Manager*
EMP: 82
SALES (corp-wide): 15.3B **Publicly Held**
WEB: www.con-way.com
SIC: 4213 4231 4212 Contract haulers; trucking terminal facilities; local trucking, without storage
HQ: Xpo Logistics Freight, Inc.
    2211 Old Earhart Rd # 100
    Ann Arbor MI 48105
    734 998-4200

(G-18545)
Y M C A CENTRAL STARK COUNTY
Also Called: YMCA
11928 King Church Ave Nw (44685-8220)
PHONE..................................330 877-8933
Linda Phillips, *Branch Mgr*
EMP: 27
SALES (corp-wide): 16.5MM **Privately Held**
SIC: 8641 7991 8351 7032 Youth organizations; physical fitness facilities; child day care services; youth camps; individual & family services
PA: Y M C A Of Central Stark County
    1201 30th St Nw Ste 200a
    Canton OH 44709
    330 491-9622

(PA)=Parent Co (HQ)=Headquarters (DH)=Div Headquarters
✪ = New Business established in last 2 years

Upper Arlington
Franklin County

(G-18546)
AMERICAS URGENT CARE
4661 Sawmill Rd Ste 101 (43220-6123)
PHONE..........................614 929-2721
Fax: 614 583-1138
EMP: 26 Privately Held
SIC: 4119 Ambulance service
PA: America's Urgent Care
6525 W Campus Oval # 150
New Albany OH 43054

(G-18547)
ARLINGTON COURT NURSING (PA)
Also Called: Arlington Court Skilled
1605 Nw Prof Plz (43220-3866)
PHONE..........................614 545-5502
Allan Vrable, *President*
Linda Vrable, *Vice Pres*
James Merrill, *CFO*
Johnson Blu, *Administration*
EMP: 126
SQ FT: 50,000
SALES (est): 5.7MM Privately Held
SIC: 8052 8051 Intermediate care facilities; extended care facility

(G-18548)
AUTO DES SYS INC
3518 Riverside Dr (43221-1735)
PHONE..........................614 488-7984
Fax: 614 488-0848
Chris Yessios, *President*
David Kropp, *Vice Pres*
Mathew Holwiski, *Engineer*
Alexandra Yessios, *VP Sales*
Harold Gebel, *Sales Mgr*
EMP: 30
SQ FT: 2,000
SALES (est): 3MM Privately Held
WEB: www.autodessys.com
SIC: 7371 7372 Computer software development; prepackaged software

(G-18549)
DELTA GAMMA FRATERNITY (PA)
Also Called: ANCHOR TRADER
3250 Riverside Dr (43221-1725)
P.O. Box 21397, Columbus (43221-0397)
PHONE..........................614 481-8169
Betsy Fouss, *Exec Dir*
Heather Daverio, *Exec Dir*
EMP: 45
SQ FT: 22,000
SALES: 5MM Privately Held
SIC: 8641 Fraternal associations

(G-18550)
DELTA GAMMA FRATERNITY
3220 Riverside Dr Ste A2 (43221-1736)
PHONE..........................614 487-5599
Nancy Brittle, *Principal*
EMP: 38
SALES (corp-wide): 5MM Privately Held
SIC: 8641 University club
PA: Delta Gamma Fraternity
3250 Riverside Dr
Upper Arlington OH 43221
614 481-8169

(G-18551)
HOME INSTEAD SENIOR CARE
3220 Riverside Dr Ste C4 (43221-1736)
PHONE..........................614 432-8524
Nancy S Barrett-Paschke, *President*
Nancy Barrett Paschke, *Owner*
Ralph B Samson, *Treasurer*
EMP: 53
SQ FT: 1,200
SALES (est): 1.3MM Privately Held
SIC: 8082 Home health care services

(G-18552)
KAPPA HOUSE CORP OF DELTA
3220 Riverside Dr Ste A2 (43221-1736)
PHONE..........................614 487-9461
Beth Koukol, *Director*
EMP: 39
SALES: 409.7K Privately Held
SIC: 8741 Management services

(G-18553)
KENEXIS CONSULTING CORPORATION
3366 Riverside Dr Ste 200 (43221-1734)
PHONE..........................614 451-7031
Edward Marszal, *President*
Edward M Marszal, *President*
Lily Glick, *Engineer*
Ellen Phillips, *Controller*
James McGlone, *Chief Mktg Ofcr*
EMP: 25
SALES: 2.5MM Privately Held
SIC: 8748 Business consulting

(G-18554)
LOVELAND & BROSIUS LLC
3300 Riverside Dr Ste 125 (43221-1765)
PHONE..........................614 488-4092
Richard L Loveland, *Partner*
Phoebe Hauser, *Administration*
Calvin T Johnson,
EMP: 50
SALES (est): 3.7MM Privately Held
SIC: 8111 General practice attorney, lawyer

(G-18555)
MANIFEST SOLUTIONS CORP
Also Called: Manifest Software
2035 Riverside Dr (43221-4012)
PHONE..........................614 930-2800
Fax: 614 930-2890
Nancy Matijasich, *President*
Douglas Deken, *Opers Staff*
Mohamad Ettefagh, *Marketing Staff*
Michael Falanga, *Manager*
Scott Freshour, *Manager*
EMP: 65
SALES (est): 7.3MM Privately Held
WEB: www.manifest-solutions.com
SIC: 7371 7373 Computer software systems analysis & design, custom; local area network (LAN) systems integrator

(G-18556)
SUNRISE SENIOR LIVING INC
Also Called: Sunrise On The Scioto
3500 Riverside Dr (43221-1753)
PHONE..........................614 457-3500
Fax: 614 457-4300
Suzanne Johns, *Manager*
EMP: 70
SALES (corp-wide): 4.3B Publicly Held
WEB: www.sunrise.com
SIC: 8059 8051 Rest home, with health care; skilled nursing care facilities
HQ: Sunrise Senior Living, Llc
7902 Westpark Dr
Mc Lean VA 22102

Upper Sandusky
Wyandot County

(G-18557)
ANGELINE INDUSTRIES INC
11028 County Highway 44 (43351-9056)
PHONE..........................419 294-4488
Todd Dilley, *Director*
EMP: 70
SALES: 522.8K Privately Held
WEB: www.angeline.com
SIC: 8331 Sheltered workshop

(G-18558)
COUNTY OF WYANDOT
Also Called: Wyandot County Home
7830 State Highway 199 (43351-9333)
PHONE..........................419 294-1714
Fax: 419 294-6411
David Oucid, *Owner*
Curtis O'Neal, *Administration*
EMP: 92 Privately Held
WEB: www.co.wyandot.oh.us
SIC: 8059 Nursing home, except skilled & intermediate care facility
PA: County Of Wyandot
109 S Sandusky Ave Rm 10
Upper Sandusky OH 43351
419 294-6436

(G-18559)
CUSTOM AGRI SYSTEMS INC
1289 N Warpole St (43351-9381)
PHONE..........................419 209-0940
Fax: 419 209-0946
Rick Storch, *President*
EMP: 30
SALES (corp-wide): 57.1MM Privately Held
SIC: 0723 Grain drying services
PA: Custom Agri Systems, Inc.
255 County Road R
Napoleon OH 43545
419 599-5180

(G-18560)
FAIRBORN EQUIPMENT COMPANY INC (PA)
225 Tarhe Trl (43351-8700)
P.O. Box 123 (43351-0123)
PHONE..........................419 209-0760
Fax: 419 209-0762
Mark Dillon, *President*
John H Elgin, *Principal*
Jeff Shreve, *Project Mgr*
Josh Dayton, *Accountant*
Bob Hare, *VP Sales*
EMP: 60 EST: 1991
SQ FT: 55,000
SALES (est): 51.6MM Privately Held
WEB: www.fairbornequipment.com
SIC: 5084 Materials handling machinery

(G-18561)
FIRST CITIZENS NAT BNK INC (PA)
100 N Sandusky Ave (43351-1270)
P.O. Box 299 (43351-0299)
PHONE..........................419 294-2351
Fax: 419 294-2351
Mark Johnson, *President*
Robert McClure, *Exec VP*
Jevon Reile, *Senior VP*
Bonnie Shaw, *Assistant VP*
Calvin Gebhart, *Vice Pres*
EMP: 40
SALES: 10.1MM Privately Held
SIC: 6021 National commercial banks

(G-18562)
JPMORGAN CHASE BANK NAT ASSN
335 N Sandusky Ave (43351-1139)
PHONE..........................419 294-4944
Fax: 419 294-5416
Karen Kline, *Principal*
EMP: 26
SALES (corp-wide): 99.6B Publicly Held
SIC: 6021 National commercial banks
HQ: Jpmorgan Chase Bank, National Association
1111 Polaris Pkwy
Columbus OH 43240
614 436-3055

(G-18563)
KALMBACH PORK FINISHING LLC
7148 State Highway 199 (43351-9346)
PHONE..........................419 294-3838
Paul M Kalmbach, *President*
Dick Regnier, *Controller*
EMP: 100
SALES (est): 14.9MM Privately Held
WEB: www.kalmbachfeeds.com
SIC: 5154 Hogs

(G-18564)
KIMMEL CLEANERS INC (PA)
225 N Sandusky Ave (43351-1233)
P.O. Box 98 (43351-0098)
PHONE..........................419 294-1959
Kurt Kimmel, *President*
Debbie Amos, *Corp Secy*
Mark Kimmel, *Vice Pres*
Jim Karg, *Manager*
Brian Kimmel, *Manager*
EMP: 58
SQ FT: 30,000
SALES (est): 3.2MM Privately Held
WEB: www.kimmelcleaners.com
SIC: 7213 7216 7218 Linen supply; towel supply; linen supply, clothing; drycleaning plants, except rugs; laundered mat & rug supply; industrial uniform supply

(G-18565)
SAVAGE AND ASSOCIATES INC
104 E Wyandot Ave (43351-1430)
P.O. Box 465 (43351-0465)
PHONE..........................419 731-4441
EMP: 68
SALES (corp-wide): 73.9K Privately Held
SIC: 8742 Financial consultant
PA: Savage And Associates, Inc.
4427 Talmadge Rd Bldg 2
Toledo OH 43623
419 475-8665

(G-18566)
SCHMIDT MACHINE COMPANY
Also Called: S M C
7013 State Highway 199 (43351-9347)
PHONE..........................419 294-3814
Fax: 419 294-2607
Bill, *President*
Randy F Schmidt, *President*
Dorothy M Schmidt, *Principal*
Kevin Schmidt, *Vice Pres*
Darlene Mooney, *Treasurer*
EMP: 50 EST: 1935
SQ FT: 2,500
SALES: 19.4MM Privately Held
WEB: www.schmidtmachine.com
SIC: 5083 3599 7692 Farm & garden machinery; machine shop, jobbing & repair; welding repair

(G-18567)
STS LOGISTICS INC
13863 County Highway 119 (43351-9413)
PHONE..........................419 294-1498
Stephen T Smith, *President*
EMP: 25
SALES (est): 1.8MM Privately Held
SIC: 4231 Trucking terminal facilities

(G-18568)
UNITED CHURCH HOMES INC
Also Called: Fairhaven Community
850 Marseilles Ave (43351-1648)
PHONE..........................419 294-4973
Fax: 419 294-4975
Mary Curtis, *Pastor*
John Stoner, *Vice Pres*
Lindsey Henderson, *Human Res Dir*
Robert L Weisbrodt, *MIS Dir*
Daniel Miller, *Director*
EMP: 180
SALES (corp-wide): 78.1MM Privately Held
WEB: www.altenheimcommunity.org
SIC: 8059 8661 8052 Personal care home, with health care; religious organizations; intermediate care facilities
PA: United Church Homes Inc
170 E Center St
Marion OH 43302
740 382-4885

(G-18569)
WYANDOT COUNTY AG SOC
Also Called: Wyandot County Fair
10171 State Highway 53 N (43351-9272)
P.O. Box 3 (43351-0003)
PHONE..........................419 294-4320
Philip Kin, *President*
Nick Derr, *Vice Pres*
Bonnie Miller, *Admin Sec*
EMP: 25
SALES (est): 604.4K Privately Held
SIC: 7999 Agricultural fair

(G-18570)
WYANDOT MEMORIAL HOSPITAL
885 N Sandusky Ave (43351-1098)
PHONE..........................419 294-4991
Fax: 419 294-2233
Joseph D'Ettorre, *CEO*
J Craig Bowman, *Chairman*
Ty Shaull, *COO*
John Caldwell, *Materials Dir*
Abel Walton, *Opers Staff*
EMP: 200
SQ FT: 68,000
SALES: 43.4MM Privately Held
WEB: www.wyandotmemorial.com
SIC: 8062 General medical & surgical hospitals

GEOGRAPHIC SECTION

(G-18571)
WYANDOT TRACTOR & IMPLEMENT CO
Also Called: John Deere Authorized Dealer
10264 County Highway 121 (43351-9798)
P.O. Box 147 (43351-0217)
PHONE..............................419 294-2349
Fax: 419 294-5200
Bruce Kuenzli, *President*
Martha Mosser, *Corp Secy*
EMP: 28
SQ FT: 10,000
SALES (est): 4.8MM **Privately Held**
SIC: 5083 Agricultural machinery & equipment

(G-18572)
XPO LOGISTICS FREIGHT INC
1850 E Wyandot Ave (43351-9652)
PHONE..............................419 294-5728
Fax: 419 294-2916
Paul Masano, *Manager*
EMP: 25
SALES (corp-wide): 15.3B **Publicly Held**
WEB: www.con-way.com
SIC: 4213 Contract haulers
HQ: Xpo Logistics Freight, Inc.
2211 Old Earhart Rd # 100
Ann Arbor MI 48105
734 998-4200

Urbana
Champaign County

(G-18573)
BEN EL CHILD DEVELOPMENT CTR
1150 Scioto St Ste 200 (43078-2291)
P.O. Box 755 (43078-0755)
PHONE..............................937 465-0010
Fax: 937 652-4945
Vicki Casey, *Manager*
Douglas Stiner, *Director*
Douglas Steiner, *Director*
EMP: 30
SALES: 1MM **Privately Held**
SIC: 8322 General counseling services

(G-18574)
C T WIRELESS
Also Called: C T Communication
731 Scioto St (43078-2147)
PHONE..............................937 653-2208
Fax: 937 652-1952
Michael Conrad, *President*
EMP: 56
SALES (est): 1.1MM **Privately Held**
SIC: 4813 4841 5999 ; cable & other pay television services; telephone equipment & systems

(G-18575)
CARDIOLOGIST CLARK & CHAMPAIGN
900 E Court St (43078-1887)
PHONE..............................937 653-8897
Fax: 937 653-7261
Akber Mohammed, *President*
EMP: 28
SALES (est): 506.6K **Privately Held**
SIC: 8011 Cardiologist & cardio-vascular specialist

(G-18576)
CHAMPAIGN CNTY BOARD OF DD
Also Called: Champaign County Board of Mrdd
1250 E Us Highway 36 (43078-8002)
PHONE..............................937 653-5217
Jeanne Bowman, *President*
Developmental Disabilities, *Superintendent*
Max Coates, *Vice Pres*
Jennifer Bradford, *Manager*
Jeff Coaty, *Manager*
EMP: 172
SALES (est): 1.4MM **Privately Held**
SIC: 8322 9431 Individual & family services; child health program administration, government

PA: County Of Champaign
1250 E State Rte 29 Ste 3
Urbana OH 43078
937 653-5217

(G-18577)
CHAMPAIGN LANDMARK INC (PA)
304 Bloomfield Ave (43078-1206)
P.O. Box 828 (43078-0828)
PHONE..............................937 652-2135
Fax: 937 653-8082
Dean Terrill, *Ch of Bd*
John T Dunbar, *President*
Doug Mueting, *Treasurer*
Joyce Thronton, *Manager*
Zimmerman Brent, *Admin Sec*
EMP: 40 **EST:** 1923
SQ FT: 32,400
SALES (est): 26.6MM **Privately Held**
WEB: www.champaignlandmark.com
SIC: 5153 5191 5172 Grains; farm supplies; fertilizer & fertilizer materials; seeds: field, garden & flower; petroleum products

(G-18578)
CHAMPAIGN RESIDENTIAL SVCS INC (PA)
1150 Scioto St Ste 201 (43078-2292)
P.O. Box 29 (43078-0029)
PHONE..............................937 653-1320
Fax: 937 653-1320
Than Johnson, *CEO*
Ed Corwin, *Chairman*
Martin Fagans, *COO*
Phil Edwards, *Trustee*
Richard Anderson, *Materials Mgr*
EMP: 1200
SQ FT: 40,000
SALES: 36.2MM **Privately Held**
WEB: www.crsi-oh.com
SIC: 8361 Home for the mentally retarded

(G-18579)
CHAMPAIGN TELEPHONE COMPANY (PA)
Also Called: CT Communications
126 Scioto St (43078-2199)
PHONE..............................937 653-4000
Fax: 937 652-2329
Michael Conrad, *President*
Cynthia J Huffman, *Treasurer*
Brian Strunk, *Marketing Staff*
Richard Dwyner,
EMP: 25
SQ FT: 5,000
SALES (est): 13.4MM **Privately Held**
WEB: www.ctcn.net
SIC: 4813 Local telephone communications; long distance telephone communications

(G-18580)
CITIZENS NAT BNK URBANA OHIO (HQ)
1 Monument Sq (43078-9918)
PHONE..............................937 653-1200
Fax: 937 652-3184
James Wilson, *President*
Timothy Bunnell, *Vice Pres*
Judy Markinavp, *Human Resources*
EMP: 45
SQ FT: 8,000
SALES (est): 859.5K
SALES (corp-wide): 367MM **Publicly Held**
WEB: www.citnatbk.com
SIC: 6021 National commercial banks
PA: Park National Corporation
50 N 3rd St
Newark OH 43055
740 349-8451

(G-18581)
CMBB LLC
Also Called: Bundy Baking Solutions
417 E Water St (43078-2367)
P.O. Box 150 (43078-0150)
PHONE..............................937 652-2151
William McCoy, *Principal*
Elizabeth A Bundy, *Corp Secy*
Michael Miller, *Controller*
Russell T Bundy, *Mng Member*
EMP: 170

SQ FT: 55,800
SALES (est): 4.8MM **Privately Held**
SIC: 5046 7699 Bakery equipment & supplies; baking pan glazing & cleaning

(G-18582)
COMMUNITY MERCY FOUNDATION
904 Scioto St (43078-2226)
PHONE..............................937 652-3645
Fax: 937 484-3211
Freddy Katai, *Ch Radiology*
William Pryor, *Senior VP*
Steven Crichton, *Vice Pres*
Kim Weadock, *Project Mgr*
Shannon Hatfield, *Development*
EMP: 260
SQ FT: 1,196
SALES (corp-wide): 4.2B **Privately Held**
SIC: 6733 8011 Trusts; offices & clinics of medical doctors
HQ: The Community Mercy Foundation
1 S Limestone St Ste 700
Springfield OH 45502

(G-18583)
COMMUNITY MERCY HLTH PARTNERS
Also Called: Mercy McAuley Center
906 Scioto St (43078-2226)
PHONE..............................937 653-5432
Fax: 937 652-2072
Robin Cornett, *Director*
Teresita Young, *Director*
Karen Smith, *Records Dir*
Linda Walden, *Records Dir*
EMP: 250
SALES (corp-wide): 4.2B **Privately Held**
SIC: 8741 8051 Hospital management; skilled nursing care facilities
HQ: Community Mercy Health Partners
100 Medical Center Dr
Springfield OH 45504

(G-18584)
COUNTY OF CHAMPAIGN
Also Called: Champaign County Engineer
428 Beech St (43078-1920)
P.O. Box 669 (43078-0669)
PHONE..............................937 653-4848
Fax: 937 653-3172
Stephen McCall, *Manager*
EMP: 31 **Privately Held**
SIC: 8711 Consulting engineer
PA: County Of Champaign
1250 E State Rte 29 Ste 3
Urbana OH 43078
937 653-5217

(G-18585)
DINGLEDINE TRUCKING COMPANY
1000 Phoenix Dr (43078-9387)
PHONE..............................937 652-3454
Fax: 937 652-3531
Kim S Damewood, *President*
Betty Sherman, *Corp Secy*
Brad Damewood, *Vice Pres*
Gerald W Damewood, *Vice Pres*
EMP: 40 **EST:** 1918
SQ FT: 8,700
SALES (est): 7.9MM **Privately Held**
SIC: 4213 4212 Contract haulers; local trucking, without storage

(G-18586)
FARMERS EQUIPMENT INC (PA)
Also Called: Kubota Authorized Dealer
1749 E Us Highway 36 A (43078-9698)
PHONE..............................419 339-7000
Todd Channel, *General Mgr*
Brad Blymyer, *Store Mgr*
Judy McClorey, *Accounts Mgr*
Brian Baxter, *Marketing Staff*
Doris Frieszell, *Office Mgr*
EMP: 42
SALES (est): 12.4MM **Privately Held**
WEB: www.farmersequipment.com
SIC: 5083 Farm implements

(G-18587)
FIRST TRANSIT INC
2200 S Us Highway 68 (43078-9470)
PHONE..............................937 652-4175
Pam Hoffner, *Branch Mgr*

EMP: 54
SALES (corp-wide): 7B **Privately Held**
SIC: 4111 Bus transportation
HQ: First Transit, Inc.
600 Vine St Ste 1400
Cincinnati OH 45202
513 241-2200

(G-18588)
FUTURA BANC CORP (PA)
Also Called: Champagne National Bank
601 Scioto St (43078-2134)
PHONE..............................937 653-1167
Fax: 937 653-1161
Michael J Lamping, *President*
Lee Jordan, *Vice Pres*
Robert Gantzer, *CFO*
C Hire, *Credit Staff*
Patricia Cromwell, *VP Human Res*
EMP: 75
SQ FT: 8,000
SALES: 21.2MM **Privately Held**
SIC: 6021 National commercial banks

(G-18589)
GRACE BAPTIST CHURCH (PA)
Also Called: Grace Baptist Preschool
960 Childrens Home Rd (43078-9132)
PHONE..............................937 652-1133
Fax: 937 653-8377
George Riddell, *Pastor*
Joseph Fortna, *Pastor*
Steven Smith, *Pastor*
EMP: 25
SQ FT: 6,300
SALES (est): 955.2K **Privately Held**
SIC: 8661 8211 8351 Baptist Church; elementary & secondary schools; child day care services

(G-18590)
GRIMES AEROSPACE COMPANY
Also Called: Honeywell
550 State Route 55 (43078-9482)
PHONE..............................937 484-2001
Rusty Chamberlain, *Materials Mgr*
Bruce Blagg, *Branch Mgr*
Linda Reese, *Executive Asst*
EMP: 300
SALES (corp-wide): 40.5B **Publicly Held**
SIC: 5088 7699 3812 3769 Aircraft & parts; aircraft & heavy equipment repair services; search & navigation equipment; guided missile & space vehicle parts & auxiliary equipment; vehicular lighting equipment
HQ: Grimes Aerospace Company
550 State Route 55
Urbana OH 43078
937 484-2000

(G-18591)
HONEYWELL INTERNATIONAL INC
550 State Route 55 (43078-9482)
PHONE..............................937 484-2261
Mark Anglin, *President*
Joe Holmes, *Director*
Randal Macintosh, *Director*
EMP: 68
SALES (corp-wide): 40.5B **Publicly Held**
SIC: 8711 Aviation &/or aeronautical engineering
PA: Honeywell International Inc.
115 Tabor Rd
Morris Plains NJ 07950
973 455-2000

(G-18592)
J & J SCHLAEGEL INC
1250 E Us Highway 36 (43078-8002)
PHONE..............................937 652-2045
Fax: 937 652-2046
Jerry Schlaegel, *President*
Jeff Schlaegel, *Vice Pres*
EMP: 25
SQ FT: 625
SALES (est): 5.1MM **Privately Held**
SIC: 1622 Bridge construction

(G-18593)
LAWNVIEW INDUSTRIES INC
1250 E Us Highway 36 (43078-8002)
P.O. Box 38147 (43078-8147)
PHONE..............................937 653-5217
Fax: 937 653-7516

Urbana - Champaign County (G-18594)

Micheal Misler, *Director*
EMP: 175
SQ FT: 6,000
SALES: 48K **Privately Held**
SIC: 3999 3914 2392 2499 Plaques, picture, laminated; trophies; towels, fabric & nonwoven: made from purchased materials; surveyors' stakes, wood; packaging & labeling services; carwashes

(G-18594)
MC AULEY CENTER
906 Scioto St (43078-2299)
PHONE 937 653-5432
J Tollefson, *Exec Dir*
Jennifer Tollefson, *Exec Dir*
EMP: 125
SALES (est): 4.2MM **Privately Held**
SIC: 8051 Skilled nursing care facilities

(G-18595)
MERCY HEALTH
1300 S Us Highway 68 (43078-8409)
PHONE 937 653-3445
EMP: 55
SALES (corp-wide): 4.2B **Privately Held**
SIC: 8099 Childbirth preparation clinic
PA: Mercy Health
1701 Mercy Health Pl
Cincinnati OH 45237
513 639-2800

(G-18596)
MERCY MEM HOSP URBANA OHIO
Also Called: McAuley Center
904 Scioto St (43078-2226)
PHONE 937 653-5231
Fax: 937 652-1754
Paul Hiltz, *President*
Gary A Hagens, *COO*
Sherry Nelson, *Vice Pres*
Marianne Potina, *Vice Pres*
Shannon Hatfield, *Development*
EMP: 297 **EST:** 1971
SQ FT: 90,000
SALES: 33MM **Privately Held**
SIC: 8062 General medical & surgical hospitals

(G-18597)
MESILLA DIALYSIS LLC
Also Called: Midwest Urbana Dialysis
1430 E Us Highway 36 (43078-9112)
PHONE 937 484-4600
Jeffrey Spiers, *Principal*
Dianne Baumgardner, *Administration*
EMP: 37
SALES (est): 550.9K **Publicly Held**
SIC: 8092 Kidney dialysis centers
PA: Davita Inc.
2000 16th St
Denver CO 80202

(G-18598)
OHIO HI POINT CAREER CENTER
412 N Main St (43078-1608)
PHONE 937 599-3010
Sharon Halter, *President*
EMP: 25
SALES (corp-wide): 16.9MM **Privately Held**
SIC: 8049 Physical therapist
PA: Ohio Hi Point Career Center
2280 State Route 540
Bellefontaine OH 43311
937 599-3010

(G-18599)
RICHARD H FREYHOF (PA)
Also Called: Champaign Realty
1071 S Main St (43078-2578)
P.O. Box 284 (43078-0284)
PHONE 937 653-5837
Fax: 937 652-0047
Richard H Freyhof, *Owner*
EMP: 26
SALES (est): 1MM **Privately Held**
SIC: 6531 Selling agent, real estate

(G-18600)
RUSSELL T BUNDY ASSOCIATES INC (PA)
Also Called: Pan-Glo of St Louis
417 E Water St Ste 1 (43078-2154)
P.O. Box 150 (43078-0150)
PHONE 937 652-2151
Fax: 937 653-3546
Russell T Bundy, *Principal*
Elizabeth A Bundy, *Corp Secy*
Douglas H Geiser, *Vice Pres*
Scott Mouton, *VP Opers*
Cliff Trunick, *Purch Agent*
◆ **EMP:** 55
SQ FT: 55,800
SALES (est): 62MM **Privately Held**
SIC: 5046 7699 Bakery equipment & supplies; baking pan glazing & cleaning

(G-18601)
THE PEOPLES SAVINGS AND LN CO (PA)
10 Monument Sq (43078-2001)
PHONE 937 653-1600
L Richard Kadel, *Ch of Bd*
Brice L Kadel, *President*
Brian Nicol, *Senior VP*
Beth Ropp, *Assistant VP*
Cindy Cushman, *Vice Pres*
EMP: 30 **EST:** 1892
SALES: 4.8MM **Privately Held**
SIC: 6036 6163 Savings & loan associations, not federally chartered; loan brokers

(G-18602)
WHITES SERVICE CENTER INC
Also Called: White' S Ford
1246 N Main St (43078-5000)
P.O. Box 38129 (43078-8129)
PHONE 937 653-5279
Fax: 937 653-7111
Jeffrey White, *President*
Shannen R Michael, *General Mgr*
James Donahue, *Vice Pres*
James White, *Treasurer*
Leah Timmons, *Finance Mgr*
EMP: 32 **EST:** 1948
SQ FT: 18,000
SALES (est): 13.9MM **Privately Held**
SIC: 5511 5013 5012 Automobiles, new & used; automotive supplies & parts; trucks, commercial

(G-18603)
YMCA
191 Community Dr (43078-6001)
PHONE 937 653-9622
Paul Waldsmith, *CEO*
Kathy Finney, *Director*
EMP: 100
SALES (est): 1.2MM **Privately Held**
SIC: 7999 8322 7991 Recreation center; individual & family services; physical fitness facilities

Urbancrest
Franklin County

(G-18604)
DECISIONONE CORPORATION
3425 Urbancrest Indus Dr (43123-1775)
PHONE 614 883-0228
Fax: 614 883-0050
Mike Barnett, *Business Mgr*
John Tennyson, *Business Mgr*
Darin Holtz, *Engineer*
Nicholas Mack, *Engineer*
Liz Fravel, *Financial Exec*
EMP: 50
SALES (corp-wide): 44.6MM **Privately Held**
WEB: www.decisionone.com
SIC: 7378 7374 Computer & data processing equipment repair/maintenance; data processing service
HQ: Decisionone Corporation
640 Lee Rd
Wayne PA 19087
610 296-6000

(G-18605)
IRON MOUNTAIN INCORPORATED
3250 Urbancrest Indus Dr (43123-1768)
PHONE 614 801-0151
Roxann Mc Naughton, *Branch Mgr*
EMP: 51
SALES (corp-wide): 3.8B **Publicly Held**
SIC: 4226 Household goods & furniture storage
PA: Iron Mountain Incorporated
1 Federal St Fl 7
Boston MA 02110
617 535-4766

(G-18606)
MCKESSON MEDICAL-SURGICAL INC
3500 Centerpoint Dr (43123-1495)
PHONE 614 539-2600
Steve Robenolt, *Vice Pres*
Tony McCoy, *Opers Spvr*
Paul Julian, *Human Res Mgr*
Krista Carter, *Office Mgr*
Bill Heiser, *Branch Mgr*
EMP: 200
SALES (corp-wide): 198.5B **Publicly Held**
WEB: www.gmholdings.com
SIC: 5047 Medical & hospital equipment; medical equipment & supplies; medical laboratory equipment; surgical equipment & supplies
HQ: Mckesson Medical-Surgical Inc.
9954 Mayland Dr Ste 4000
Richmond VA 23233
804 264-7500

(G-18607)
PALMER-DONAVIN MFG CO
3210 Centerpoint Dr (43123-1464)
PHONE 614 277-2777
Fax: 614 277-2790
David Zimmerman, *Vice Pres*
EMP: 81
SALES (corp-wide): 220MM **Privately Held**
WEB: www.palmerdonavin.com
SIC: 5031 Building materials, exterior
PA: The Palmer-Donavin Manufacturing Company
3210 Centerpoint Dr
Columbus OH 43212
614 486-0975

(G-18608)
UNITED PARCEL SERVICE INC OH
Also Called: UPS
3500 Centerpoint Dr (43123-1495)
PHONE 614 277-3300
EMP: 316
SALES (corp-wide): 65.8B **Publicly Held**
SIC: 7389 Mailbox rental & related service
HQ: United Parcel Service, Inc. (Oh)
55 Glenlake Pkwy
Atlanta GA 30328
404 828-6000

(G-18609)
YOUNG MENS CHRISTIAN ASSOC
Also Called: Southwest Community Center
3500 1st Ave (43123-1390)
PHONE 614 539-1770
Fax: 614 539-3380
Linda Day-Mackessy, *Vice Pres*
Kim Jordan, *Branch Mgr*
Scott Debney, *Software Dev*
Nancy Brody, *Director*
Marty Delamatre, *Director*
EMP: 30
SALES (corp-wide): 44.9MM **Privately Held**
WEB: www.ymca-columbus.com
SIC: 8641 7991 8351 7032 Youth organizations; physical fitness facilities; child day care services; youth camps; individual & family services
PA: Young Men's Christian Association Of Central Ohio
40 W Long St
Columbus OH 43215
614 389-4409

Utica
Licking County

(G-18610)
C E S CREDIT UNION INC
8 N Main St (43080-7706)
PHONE 740 892-3323
Kathy Robinson, *Manager*
EMP: 25
SALES (corp-wide): 4MM **Privately Held**
SIC: 6062 State credit unions, not federally chartered
PA: C E S Credit Union, Inc.
1215 Yauger Rd
Mount Vernon OH 43050
740 397-1136

(G-18611)
CROUSE IMPLEMENT
14149 North St (43080-9437)
PHONE 740 892-2086
Richard Crouse, *Owner*
EMP: 25
SALES (est): 2.7MM **Privately Held**
SIC: 5083 Farm implements

(G-18612)
LICKING RURAL ELECTRIFICATION (PA)
11339 Mount Vernon Rd (43080-7703)
P.O. Box 455 (43080-0455)
PHONE 740 892-2071
Fax: 740 892-2429
Charles Manning, *President*
Dave Mussard, *Chairman*
Arland K Rogers, *Corp Secy*
George Charles Manning, *COO*
Neil Buxton, *Vice Pres*
EMP: 58
SQ FT: 20,000
SALES (est): 57.2MM **Privately Held**
SIC: 4911 Distribution, electric power

(G-18613)
LIVING CARE ALTRNTVES OF UTICA
Also Called: Utica Nursing Home
233 N Main St (43080-7705)
P.O. Box 518 (43080-0518)
PHONE 740 892-3414
Fax: 740 892-4683
Thomas J Rosser, *President*
Cathy Egan, *Manager*
Bruce Miller, *Director*
Jean Brown, *Administration*
EMP: 50 **EST:** 1960
SQ FT: 7,500
SALES (est): 1.8MM **Privately Held**
SIC: 8052 Personal care facility

Valley City
Medina County

(G-18614)
CHGC INC
Also Called: Cherokee Hills Golf Club
5740 Center Rd (44280-9746)
PHONE 330 225-6122
Ed Haddad, *President*
Marcia Haddad, *Treasurer*
Mark Haddad, *Admin Sec*
EMP: 85
SQ FT: 20,000
SALES (est): 3.5MM **Privately Held**
WEB: www.cherokeehillsgolf.com
SIC: 7992 5812 Public golf courses; eating places

(G-18615)
DAVIS TREE FARM & NURSERY INC
6126 Neff Rd (44280-9530)
PHONE 330 483-3324
Michael Davis, *President*
Karen Haas, *Office Mgr*
Keith Broadsword, *Manager*
Tammy Cassady,
EMP: 40 **EST:** 1989
SALES (est): 1.2MM **Privately Held**
SIC: 5193 Nursery stock

GEOGRAPHIC SECTION
Van Wert - Van Wert County (G-18637)

(G-18616)
DUNLOP AND JOHNSTON INC
5498 Innovation Dr (44280-9352)
PHONE..................................330 220-2700
Fax: 330 220-2771
William H Spencer, *CEO*
Randolph B Spencer, *President*
EMP: 30
SQ FT: 15,000
SALES (est): 10.5MM **Privately Held**
WEB: www.dunlopandjohnston.com
SIC: **1542** 1541 Commercial & office building, new construction; industrial buildings & warehouses

(G-18617)
EMH INC (PA)
Also Called: Engineered Material Handling
550 Crane Dr (44280-9361)
PHONE..................................330 220-8600
Fax: 330 220-0204
Edis Hazne, *President*
Dave Comiono, *Vice Pres*
Greg Meyer, *Purch Mgr*
Chris Denison, *Accounts Mgr*
Don Fenton, *Regl Sales Mgr*
◆ EMP: 40
SQ FT: 65,000
SALES (est): 10MM **Privately Held**
WEB: www.emh-inc.com
SIC: **3536** 8711 3441 Cranes & monorail systems; hoists; engineering services; fabricated structural metal

(G-18618)
INDEPENDENT STEEL COMPANY LLC
615 Liverpool Dr (44280-9717)
P.O. Box 472 (44280-0472)
PHONE..................................330 225-7741
Fax: 330 273-6265
Mark Schwertner, *President*
Mark A Schwertner, *Vice Pres*
Esther Stacey, *Controller*
John F Krupinski, *Mng Member*
Kirsten Alonso, *Manager*
▲ EMP: 50 EST: 1957
SQ FT: 110,000
SALES (est): 25.4MM **Privately Held**
WEB: www.independentsteel.com
SIC: **5051** 7389 3316 Steel; metal cutting services; cold finishing of steel shapes
PA: Esmark Steel Group, Llc
2500 Euclid Ave
Chicago Heights IL 60411

(G-18619)
LIFE CARE CENTERS AMERICA INC
Also Called: Life Care Centers of Medina
2400 Columbia Rd (44280)
PHONE..................................330 483-3131
Rob Berger, *Human Res Dir*
Marcial Ingal, *Office Mgr*
Steve Wolf, *Manager*
Yatish Goyal, *Director*
Janet Harst, *Director*
EMP: 200
SALES (corp-wide): 101MM **Privately Held**
SIC: **8051** 8052 Skilled nursing care facilities; intermediate care facilities
PA: Life Care Centers Of America, Inc.
3570 Keith St Nw
Cleveland TN 37312
423 472-9585

(G-18620)
LUK-AFTERMARKET SERVICE INC
Also Called: As Automotive Systems
5370 Wegman Dr (44280-9700)
PHONE..................................330 273-4383
Fax: 330 273-3522
Gerald Hinderhan, *President*
Pam Giguere, *HR Admin*
Dave Gunther, *Info Tech Dir*
Thomas Miller, *Info Tech Mgr*
Ruth Wilhelm, *Info Tech Mgr*
◆ EMP: 65 EST: 1996
SQ FT: 100,000
SALES (est): 11.2MM
SALES (corp-wide): 56.7B **Privately Held**
WEB: www.lukclutch.com
SIC: **5013** Motor vehicle supplies & new parts
HQ: Iho Holding Gmbh & Co. Kg
Industriestr. 1-3
Herzogenaurach
913 282-0

(G-18621)
MTD ACCEPTANCE CORP INC
5965 Grafton Rd (44280-9329)
PHONE..................................330 225-2600
Curt Moll, *CEO*
Dieter Kaesgen, *President*
Jim Milinski, *Treasurer*
David Hessler, *Admin Sec*
EMP: 300
SQ FT: 5,000
SALES (est): 23MM **Privately Held**
WEB: www.mtdproducts.com
SIC: **6159** Loan institutions, general & industrial

(G-18622)
MTD HOLDINGS INC (PA)
5965 Grafton Rd (44280-9329)
P.O. Box 368022, Cleveland (44136-9722)
PHONE..................................330 225-2600
Curtis E Moll, *Ch of Bd*
Jason Belsito, *Opers Mgr*
Jeff Deuch, *Treasurer*
Donald Holka, *Manager*
Connie Buzek, *Administration*
▼ EMP: 500
SALES (est): 2.5B **Privately Held**
SIC: **3524** 3544 3469 6141 Lawn & garden equipment; lawnmowers, residential: hand or power; special dies & tools; metal stampings; financing: automobiles, furniture, etc., not a deposit bank

(G-18623)
RUSTY OAK NURSERY LTD
1547 Marks Rd (44280-9779)
P.O. Box 436 (44280-0436)
PHONE..................................330 225-7704
Fax: 330 273-3834
Charlie Bailey, *Foreman/Supr*
Chad Cekada, *Supervisor*
Kirk Cekada, *Supervisor*
Joe Vasel, *Supervisor*
Mario Cekada,
EMP: 30
SQ FT: 8,000
SALES (est): 2.4MM **Privately Held**
SIC: **5193** Nursery stock

(G-18624)
SHILOH MANUFACTURING LLC (HQ)
880 Steel Dr (44280-9736)
PHONE..................................330 558-2693
Ramzi Hermiz, *CEO*
Thomas Dugan, *President*
EMP: 29
SALES (est): 47.2MM **Publicly Held**
SIC: **5013** Automotive supplies & parts

(G-18625)
THREE D METALS INC (PA)
5462 Innovation Dr (44280-9352)
PHONE..................................330 220-0451
David Dickens Sr, *CEO*
David D Dickens Jr, *President*
Jeff Cox, *Vice Pres*
Rosemarie Dejohn, *Vice Pres*
Jeremy Storrow, *Plant Mgr*
▲ EMP: 72
SQ FT: 146,000
SALES (est): 56.7MM **Privately Held**
WEB: www.threedmetals.com
SIC: **5051** Strip, metal

Van Wert
Van Wert County

(G-18626)
ALEXANDER AND BEBOUT INC
10098 Lincoln Hwy (45891-9351)
PHONE..................................419 238-9567
Thomas Alexander, *President*
T J Staude, *Vice Pres*
Charlie Salway, *Project Mgr*
Lori Dasher, *Treasurer*
Sylvia Alexander, *Admin Sec*
EMP: 62 EST: 1965
SQ FT: 9,500
SALES (est): 10.1MM **Privately Held**
WEB: www.alexanderbebout.com
SIC: **1521** Single-family housing construction

(G-18627)
ALL AMERICA INSURANCE COMPANY (HQ)
Also Called: CENTRAL INSURANCE COMPANIES
800 S Washington St (45891-2357)
PHONE..................................419 238-1010
Francis W Purmort III, *President*
Jon A Rhoades, *Principal*
Karl Waite, *Principal*
Jeffrey L Hanson, *Vice Pres*
Michael Thompson, *Vice Pres*
EMP: 350
SQ FT: 200,000
SALES: 101.9MM
SALES (corp-wide): 535.3MM **Privately Held**
SIC: **6411** Insurance agents, brokers & service
PA: Central Mutual Insurance Company
800 S Washington St
Van Wert OH 45891
419 238-1010

(G-18628)
AYERS-STERRETT INC
222 N Market St (45891-1245)
PHONE..................................419 238-5480
Fax: 419 238-5442
Stan Ayers Jr, *President*
Kim Ayers, *Corp Secy*
Jeannie Mathews, *Controller*
EMP: 25
SALES (est): 2.5MM **Privately Held**
WEB: www.ayers-sterrett.com
SIC: **1711** Mechanical contractor

(G-18629)
CENTRAL MUTUAL INSURANCE CO (PA)
Also Called: CENTRAL INSURANCE COMPANIES
800 S Washington St (45891-2357)
PHONE..................................419 238-1010
Fax: 419 238-7626
Francis W Purmort III, *Ch of Bd*
Jason Brown, *Vice Pres*
Jeff Hanson, *Vice Pres*
William Purmort, *Vice Pres*
Jan White, *Vice Pres*
EMP: 385
SQ FT: 200,000
SALES: 535.3MM **Privately Held**
WEB: www.central-insurance.com
SIC: **6331** Fire, marine & casualty insurance

(G-18630)
COMMUNITY HLTH PRFSSIONALS INC (PA)
Also Called: CELINA AREA VISITING NURSES AS
1159 Westwood Dr (45891-2464)
PHONE..................................419 238-9223
Brent Tow, *President*
Shelly Berett, *Vice Pres*
Sally Osborn,
EMP: 140
SQ FT: 13,500
SALES: 14MM **Privately Held**
SIC: **8082** 7361 Visiting nurse service; nurses' registry

(G-18631)
COMPREHENSIVE HEALTH CARE INC
140 Fox Rd Ste 402 (45891-3406)
PHONE..................................419 238-7777
Fax: 419 238-7979
Paul Kalogerou, *President*
Judy Kalogerou, *Treasurer*
Byron Kalogerou, *Admin Sec*
EMP: 25
SALES (est): 1.3MM **Privately Held**
WEB: www.chc-mso.com
SIC: **8011** Internal medicine, physician/surgeon

(G-18632)
ELMCO ENGINEERING OH INC
1171 Grill Rd (45891-9386)
P.O. Box 705 (45891-0705)
PHONE..................................419 238-1100
Fax: 419 232-2083
John Metzger, *President*
David Lilly, *Corp Secy*
Robert Beherns, *Vice Pres*
EMP: 25
SQ FT: 3,200
SALES (est): 5.3MM **Privately Held**
WEB: www.elmco-press.com
SIC: **7699** Industrial machinery & equipment repair; industrial tool grinding

(G-18633)
GKN FREIGHT SERVICES INC (DH)
1202 Industrial Dr Ste 1 (45891-2483)
PHONE..................................419 232-5623
Fax: 419 232-3143
Kareen Brown, *General Mgr*
Russell Davies, *Managing Dir*
Terry Brooks, *Vice Pres*
Peter Cook, *Vice Pres*
Juan Perez, *Vice Pres*
EMP: 34
SQ FT: 40,000
SALES (est): 25.1MM
SALES (corp-wide): 10.8B **Privately Held**
WEB: www.gknfreightservices.com
SIC: **4731** Freight forwarding
HQ: Gkn America Corp.
2715 Davey Rd Ste 300
Woodridge IL 60517
630 972-9300

(G-18634)
HCF OF VAN WERT INC
Also Called: Van Wert Manor
160 Fox Rd (45891-2440)
PHONE..................................419 999-2010
Fax: 419 238-9215
James Unberferth, *President*
Mary Trice, *CFO*
Tina Hulbert, *Financial Exec*
Meghan Dicke, *Pub Rel Dir*
Cassie Vanoss, *Manager*
EMP: 95
SALES: 950K
SALES (corp-wide): 154.8MM **Privately Held**
SIC: **8051** Convalescent home with continuous nursing care
PA: Hcf Management, Inc.
1100 Shawnee Rd
Lima OH 45805
419 999-2010

(G-18635)
HOSPICE CARING WAY
1159 Westwood Dr (45891-2464)
PHONE..................................419 238-9223
Brent Tow, *President*
Linda Boggs, *Vice Pres*
EMP: 99
SALES: 950K **Privately Held**
SIC: **8082** Visiting nurse service

(G-18636)
JOHNSON ADAMS & PROTROUSKI
1178 Professional Dr (45891-2461)
PHONE..................................419 238-6251
Fax: 419 238-1652
Robert Adams MD, *Partner*
Terrence Johnson MD, *Partner*
EMP: 40
SALES (est): 1.7MM **Privately Held**
SIC: **8011** General & family practice, physician/surgeon

(G-18637)
LIFE STAR RESCUE INC
1171 Production Dr (45891-9390)
PHONE..................................419 238-2507
Fax: 419 238-1479
Jim Dondlinger, *President*
Tim Lankenau, *General Mgr*
Dond Linger, *Principal*

Van Wert - Van Wert County (G-18638)

Jim Snyder, *Principal*
Lyle Halstead, *Vice Pres*
EMP: 25
SQ FT: 50,000
SALES (est): 7.8MM
SALES (corp-wide): 1.7B **Privately Held**
WEB: www.holmanenterprises.com
SIC: 5521 5012 3713 Pickups & vans, used; ambulances; ambulance bodies
PA: Holman Enterprises Inc.
244 E Kings Hwy
Maple Shade NJ 08052
856 663-5200

(G-18638)
LINCOLNVIEW LOCAL SCHOOLS (PA)
15945 Middle Point Rd (45891-9769)
PHONE.................419 968-2226
Fax: 419 968-2227
Doug Fries, *Superintendent*
Troy Bowersock, *Treasurer*
Greg Leeth, *Athletic Dir*
EMP: 125 **EST:** 1960
SALES (est): 6.5MM **Privately Held**
SIC: 8211 8741 Public elementary school; public senior high school; management services

(G-18639)
MARSH FOUNDATION
1229 Lincoln Hwy (45891-1877)
P.O. Box 150 (45891-0150)
PHONE.................419 238-1695
Fax: 419 238-3986
Gary Corcoran, *Trustee*
James E Price, *Treasurer*
Jeff Grothouse, *Exec Dir*
Tom Mayes, *Teacher*
EMP: 50 **EST:** 1925
SALES: 3MM **Privately Held**
WEB: www.marshfoundation.org
SIC: 8211 8322 Boarding school; individual & family services

(G-18640)
OPTIMIST INTERNATIONAL
1008 Woodland Ave (45891-1433)
PHONE.................419 238-5086
Jane Moss, *President*
EMP: 61
SALES: 93.8K **Privately Held**
WEB: www.optimistinternational.com
SIC: 8641 Social associations

(G-18641)
PLASTIC RECYCLING TECH INC
7600 Us Route 127 (45891-9363)
PHONE.................419 238-9395
Scott Bacik, *Plant Mgr*
Mike Ballinger, *Plant Mgr*
Matt Kreigel, *Branch Mgr*
EMP: 50
SALES (corp-wide): 45.2MM **Privately Held**
SIC: 4953 Recycling, waste materials
PA: Plastic Recycling Technology, Inc.
9054 N County Road 25a
Piqua OH 45356
937 615-9286

(G-18642)
PRIVATE DUTY SERVICES INC
1157 Westwood Dr (45891-2464)
PHONE.................419 238-3714
Brent Tow, *President*
Fawn Burley, *Accountant*
EMP: 200
SQ FT: 5,000
SALES: 2.7MM **Privately Held**
SIC: 8082 8322 Visiting nurse service; individual & family services

(G-18643)
SCHUMM RICHARD A PLBG & HTG
Also Called: Schumm Plumbing & Heating
9883 Liberty Union Rd (45891-9142)
PHONE.................419 238-4994
Fax: 419 238-2161
Richard A Schumm, *President*
Phyllis A Schumm, *Corp Secy*
Erna W Schumm, *Vice Pres*
EMP: 28
SQ FT: 10,000
SALES (est): 3.2MM **Privately Held**
SIC: 1711 1794 Warm air heating & air conditioning contractor; excavation work

(G-18644)
STORE & HAUL INC
Also Called: Store & Haul Trucking
1165 Grill Rd (45891-9386)
PHONE.................419 238-4284
Fax: 419 238-3740
Curt Rager, *President*
Jerry Rager, *Vice Pres*
William Rager, *Treasurer*
Eric K Cook, *Accounting Mgr*
Bill Rager, *Admin Sec*
EMP: 38
SQ FT: 13,000
SALES (est): 5MM **Privately Held**
SIC: 4212 Animal & farm product transportation services

(G-18645)
UNITED STEELWORKERS
Also Called: Uswa
351 Pleasant St Ste 1 (45891-1923)
PHONE.................419 238-7980
Patrick Herman, *Manager*
EMP: 25
SALES (corp-wide): 61.5K **Privately Held**
WEB: www.uswa.org
SIC: 8631 Labor union
PA: United Steelworkers
60 Bolevard Of The Allies
Pittsburgh PA 15222
412 562-2400

(G-18646)
VAN RUE INCORPORATED
Also Called: Vancrest Health Care Center
10357 Van Wert Decatur Rd (45891-8425)
PHONE.................419 238-0715
Fax: 419 238-1387
Mark A White, *President*
Steve White, *Corp Secy*
Connie Elder, *Purch Mgr*
Tammy Gregory, *Human Res Dir*
Carol White, *Shareholder*
EMP: 250
SQ FT: 90,000
SALES (est): 12.5MM **Privately Held**
SIC: 8051 Convalescent home with continuous nursing care

(G-18647)
VAN WERT COUNTY DAY CARE INC
Also Called: Wee Care Learning Center
10485 Van Wert Decatur Rd (45891-9209)
P.O. Box 107 (45891-0107)
PHONE.................419 238-9918
Faith Fadian, *Director*
EMP: 39
SALES: 698.1K **Privately Held**
SIC: 8351 Group day care center

(G-18648)
VAN WERT COUNTY ENGINEERS
1192 Grill Rd (45891-9389)
PHONE.................419 238-0210
Fax: 419 238-6372
Kyle Wendel, *Engineer*
Tracey Allenbaugh, *Admin Asst*
EMP: 35
SALES (est): 2.2MM **Privately Held**
SIC: 7549 Road service, automotive

(G-18649)
VAN WERT COUNTY HOSPITAL ASSN (PA)
1250 S Washington St (45891-2551)
PHONE.................419 238-2390
Fax: 419 238-9390
Mark Minick, *President*
Angela Snyder, *Principal*
Jon Bagley, *Chairman*
Sheila Brokenshire, *Vice Pres*
Elizabeth Haines, *Vice Pres*
EMP: 90 **EST:** 1905
SQ FT: 80,000
SALES: 38.8MM **Privately Held**
SIC: 8062 General medical & surgical hospitals

(G-18650)
VAN WERT COUNTY HOSPITAL ASSN
140 Fox Rd Ste 201 (45891-2492)
PHONE.................419 232-2077
Nick Spoonmore, *Branch Mgr*
Chris R Ulrich, *Nurse Practr*
EMP: 114
SALES (corp-wide): 38.8MM **Privately Held**
SIC: 8011 General & family practice, physician/surgeon
PA: The Van Wert County Hospital Association
1250 S Washington St
Van Wert OH 45891
419 238-2390

(G-18651)
VAN WERT MEDICAL SERVICES LTD
140 Fox Rd Ste 105 (45891-2490)
PHONE.................419 238-7727
Mark Minick, *President*
Julie Figley, *Office Mgr*
Brett Taylor, *Manager*
EMP: 266
SALES (est): 2.2MM
SALES (corp-wide): 38.8MM **Privately Held**
SIC: 8062 General medical & surgical hospitals
PA: The Van Wert County Hospital Association
1250 S Washington St
Van Wert OH 45891
419 238-2390

(G-18652)
WESTWOOD BEHAVIORAL HEALTH CTR
1158 Westwood Dr (45891-2449)
P.O. Box 601 (45891-0601)
PHONE.................419 238-3434
Bryna Davidow, *Marketing Staff*
Meghan Diamon, *Manager*
Hope Rochefort, *Manager*
Jan Schwartz, *Manager*
Mary Leonard, *Senior Mgr*
EMP: 25
SQ FT: 6,245
SALES: 3.5MM **Privately Held**
SIC: 8093 Mental health clinic, outpatient

(G-18653)
YOUNG MENS CHRISTIAN ASSN
Also Called: YMCA
241 W Main St (45891-1673)
PHONE.................419 238-0443
Fax: 419 238-0221
Heather Tribolet, *Office Mgr*
Shad Robeson, *Exec Dir*
Brad Perrot, *Director*
Kevin Morrison, *Director*
Clint Myers, *Director*
EMP: 32
SALES: 1.2MM **Privately Held**
SIC: 8641 7991 8351 7032 Youth organizations; physical fitness facilities; child day care services; youth camps; individual & family services

(G-18654)
YOUNG WOMENS CHRISTIAN
Also Called: YWCA
408 E Main St (45891-1809)
PHONE.................419 238-6639
Fax: 419 232-3008
Jennifer Jackson, *Principal*
EMP: 30
SALES (corp-wide): 7.3MM **Privately Held**
SIC: 8641 7991 8351 7032 Youth organizations; physical fitness facilities; child day care services; youth camps; individual & family services
PA: The Young Women's Christian Association Of The City Of New York
52 Broadway
New York NY 10004
212 755-4500

Vandalia
Montgomery County

(G-18655)
A M COMMUNICATIONS LTD
4431 Old Springfield Rd (45377-9739)
PHONE.................419 528-3051
George Mathenia, *Opers Staff*
Tim Roberson, *Opers Staff*
Alan Miller, *Branch Mgr*
EMP: 81
SALES (corp-wide): 22.2MM **Privately Held**
SIC: 4899 Data communication services
PA: A M Communications, Ltd.
5707 State Route 309
Galion OH 44833
419 528-3051

(G-18656)
AMERICAN AIRLINES INC
Also Called: US Airways
10398 Freight Dr (45377-3304)
PHONE.................937 454-7472
Dave Loving, *Branch Mgr*
EMP: 100
SALES (corp-wide): 42.2B **Publicly Held**
WEB: www.usair.com
SIC: 4581 Airport terminal services
HQ: American Airlines, Inc.
4333 Amon Carter Blvd
Fort Worth TX 76155
817 963-1234

(G-18657)
AMERICAN AIRLINES INC
3600 Terminal Rd Ste 1 (45377-1079)
PHONE.................937 890-6668
Cyrus Spaulding, *General Mgr*
EMP: 40
SALES (corp-wide): 42.2B **Publicly Held**
WEB: www.aa.com
SIC: 4512 Air passenger carrier, scheduled
HQ: American Airlines, Inc.
4333 Amon Carter Blvd
Fort Worth TX 76155
817 963-1234

(G-18658)
AMERICAN WAY VAN AND STOR INC
Also Called: American Way Van & Storage
1001 S Brown School Rd (45377-9632)
P.O. Box 547 (45377-0547)
PHONE.................937 898-7294
Fax: 937 898-7264
Robert G Vann, *President*
Diana Vann, *Vice Pres*
Wanda Lacey, *Accountant*
James Larson, *Manager*
Melinda Newport, *Consultant*
EMP: 30
SQ FT: 30,000
SALES: 4.4MM **Privately Held**
WEB: www.awvs.com
SIC: 4213 Household goods transport

(G-18659)
ASET CORPORATION (PA)
407 Corporate Center Dr (45377-1176)
P.O. Box 247 (45377-0247)
PHONE.................937 890-8881
Teresa Lucas, *Vice Pres*
Charles Carroll, *Sales Executive*
EMP: 25
SALES (est): 3.8MM **Privately Held**
SIC: 8299 7381 Educational services; detective & armored car services; detective services

(G-18660)
AVIS ADMINISTRATION
3300 Valet Dr (45377-1000)
PHONE.................937 898-2581
Robert Salerno, *President*
Cindy Rose, *Manager*
Kris Skinner, *Manager*
EMP: 99
SALES (est): 2.4MM **Privately Held**
SIC: 7514 Rent-a-car service

GEOGRAPHIC SECTION
Vandalia - Montgomery County (G-18682)

(G-18661)
BALANCING COMPANY INC (PA)
898 Center Dr (45377-3130)
PHONE 937 898-9111
Fax: 937 898-6145
Donald K Belcher, *President*
Michael W Belcher, *President*
Jack Boeke, *Vice Pres*
Jack Broadwater, *Supervisor*
Charlene Beetley, *Admin Sec*
EMP: 31 **EST:** 1967
SQ FT: 53,000
SALES (est): 6.5MM **Privately Held**
WEB: www.balco.com
SIC: 3599 8734 3544 Machine shop, jobbing & repair; testing laboratories; special dies, tools, jigs & fixtures

(G-18662)
BASIC DRUGS INC
Also Called: Basic Vitamins
300 Corporate Center Dr (45377-1162)
P.O. Box 412 (45377-0412)
PHONE 937 898-4010
Fax: 937 898-0500
Doris Fischer Lamb, *Ch of Bd*
Nancy Green, *President*
Robert F Fischer Jr, *Corp Secy*
Sharon Erbaugh, *VP Opers*
John Fischer, *Manager*
EMP: 36 **EST:** 1970
SQ FT: 12,200
SALES (est): 9.1MM **Privately Held**
WEB: www.basicvitamins.com
SIC: 5122 Vitamins & minerals

(G-18663)
BND RENTALS INC
Also Called: Vandalia Rental
950 Engle Rd (45377-9690)
P.O. Box 160 (45377-0160)
PHONE 937 898-5061
Fax: 937 898-4412
Randy Barney, *President*
Jack W Barney, *Principal*
Carl B Nickel, *Principal*
Kathy Barney, *Corp Secy*
Kurtis Barney, *Vice Pres*
EMP: 32
SQ FT: 25,000
SALES (est): 7MM **Privately Held**
WEB: www.vandaliarental.com
SIC: 7359 Tool rental

(G-18664)
BUDGET RENT A CAR SYSTEM INC
Also Called: Budget Rent-A-Car
3300 Valet Dr (45377-1072)
PHONE 937 898-1396
Fax: 937 293-7116
Dick Hagopian, *General Mgr*
EMP: 50
SALES (corp-wide): 8.8B **Publicly Held**
WEB: www.blackdogventures.com
SIC: 7515 7514 Passenger car leasing; passenger car rental
HQ: Budget Rent A Car System, Inc.
6 Sylvan Way Ste 1
Parsippany NJ 07054
973 496-3500

(G-18665)
BUILDERS FIRSTSOURCE INC
4173 Old Springfield Rd (45377-9574)
PHONE 937 898-1358
Denny Edwards, *Branch Mgr*
EMP: 30
SQ FT: 11,250
SALES (corp-wide): 7B **Publicly Held**
WEB: www.hopelumber.com
SIC: 5031 1751 Lumber, plywood & millwork; cabinet & finish carpentry
PA: Builders Firstsource, Inc.
2001 Bryan St Ste 1600
Dallas TX 75201
214 880-3500

(G-18666)
BUTLER ASPHALT CO LLC
7500 Johnson Station Rd (45377-9465)
PHONE 937 890-1141
Fax: 937 890-0143
Jamie Voisard, *Accountant*
David A Poynter,
EMP: 37

SQ FT: 3,000
SALES (est): 5.1MM
SALES (corp-wide): 84.9MM **Privately Held**
WEB: www.jrjnet.com
SIC: 1611 Highway & street paving contractor
PA: John R. Jurgensen Co.
11641 Mosteller Rd
Cincinnati OH 45241
513 771-0820

(G-18667)
CAREY ELECTRIC CO
3925 Vanco Ln (45377-9743)
PHONE 937 669-3399
Rick O'Cull, *President*
Anita Bernard, *Vice Pres*
Jerry Harter, *Project Mgr*
Ryan O'Cull, *Project Mgr*
Doug Dunham, *Foreman/Supr*
EMP: 40
SQ FT: 3,500
SALES: 7.3MM **Privately Held**
WEB: www.careyelectric.com
SIC: 1731 General electrical contractor

(G-18668)
CENTRAL EQUITY INVESTMENTS INC
Also Called: Central Warehouse Dayton
1280 Industrial Park Dr (45377-3161)
PHONE 937 454-1270
Fax: 937 454-1266
Vince Sweet, *Manager*
EMP: 25
SALES (est): 1.5MM
SALES (corp-wide): 5MM **Privately Held**
SIC: 4225 General warehousing
PA: Central Equity Investments, Inc.
2520 Schuette Rd
Midland MI 48642
989 752-4191

(G-18669)
CHARTER VANS INC
Also Called: Charter Vans Tours
303 Corporate Center Dr # 100 (45377-1178)
P.O. Box 90035, Dayton (45490-0035)
PHONE 937 898-4043
Fax: 937 898-5951
Marianne Smith, *General Mgr*
Beverly J Mc Kiban, *Corp Secy*
Gregory Mc Kiban, *Vice Pres*
EMP: 33
SALES (est): 2MM **Privately Held**
WEB: www.chartervans.com
SIC: 4111 4141 Airport transportation; local bus charter service

(G-18670)
CINTAS CORPORATION NO 2
850 Center Dr (45377-3151)
PHONE 937 401-0098
Fax: 937 890-5560
Gary Ralston, *General Mgr*
James Lillies, *Manager*
EMP: 100
SALES (corp-wide): 5.3B **Publicly Held**
WEB: www.cintas-corp.com
SIC: 5137 7213 Uniforms, women's & children's; uniform supply
HQ: Cintas Corporation No. 2
6800 Cintas Blvd
Mason OH 45040

(G-18671)
CIRCUITS & CABLES INC
Also Called: C & C Industries
815 S Brown School Rd (45377-9632)
PHONE 937 415-2070
Fax: 937 415-2075
Michael Seibert, *President*
Brian Fletcher, *General Mgr*
Cindy Seibert, *Vice Pres*
Jerriann Doll, *Electrical Engi*
L Y Sluimer-Borsboo, *Human Res Mgr*
EMP: 40
SQ FT: 40,000
SALES (est): 11.3MM **Privately Held**
WEB: www.circuitsandcables.com
SIC: 8711 Consulting engineer

(G-18672)
CITY OF DAYTON
Also Called: Aviation, Department of
3600 Terminal Rd Ste 300 (45377-3313)
PHONE 937 454-8200
Fax: 937 454-8284
Bruce Bales, *Fire Chief*
Frederick Stovall, *Safety Dir*
Michael Brading, *Supervisor*
Terrence Slaybaugh, *Director*
Shawn Little, *Officer*
EMP: 135
SQ FT: 672 **Privately Held**
WEB: www.daytonconventioncenter.com
SIC: 4581 4512 Airport; air transportation, scheduled
PA: City Of Dayton
101 W 3rd St
Dayton OH 45402
937 333-3333

(G-18673)
CITY OF DAYTON
Also Called: Department of Aviation
3848 Wright Dr (45377-1004)
PHONE 937 454-8231
Joseph Homan, *Finance Mgr*
Dan France, *Branch Mgr*
Gilbert Turner, *Manager*
Michael Etter, *Senior Mgr*
Mark Kowalski, *Supervisor*
EMP: 40 **Privately Held**
WEB: www.daytonconventioncenter.com
SIC: 4581 Airport
PA: City Of Dayton
101 W 3rd St
Dayton OH 45402
937 333-3333

(G-18674)
CITY OF VANDALIA
Also Called: Cassel Hills Golf Course
201 Clubhouse Way (45377-9693)
PHONE 937 890-1300
Fax: 937 890-9133
Douglas Knight, *Chief*
John Marchi, *Manager*
Darren Davey, *Info Tech Mgr*
Ben Lickliter, *Director*
EMP: 35 **Privately Held**
WEB: www.vandaliaohio.net
SIC: 7992 7299 Public golf courses; banquet hall facilities
PA: City Of Vandalia
333 James Bohanan Dr # 3
Vandalia OH 45377
937 898-5891

(G-18675)
COLDWELL BNKR HRITG RLTORS LLC
356 N Dixie Dr Ste 1 (45377-2063)
PHONE 937 890-2200
Lynn Warren, *Financial Exec*
Dottie Heilgeist, *Sales Associate*
Bryan J Spring, *Sales Associate*
Linda Gabbard, *Manager*
Janey Hicks, *Asst Broker*
EMP: 39
SALES (corp-wide): 7.5MM **Privately Held**
WEB: www.coldwellbankerdayton.com
SIC: 6531 Real estate agent, residential
PA: Coldwell Banker Heritage Realtors Llc
2000 Hewitt Ave
Dayton OH 45440
937 434-7600

(G-18676)
DATWYLER SLING SLTIONS USA INC
Also Called: Columbia
875 Center Dr (45377-3129)
PHONE 937 387-2800
Mark Bueltel, *Accountant*
Denise Bagaieh, *Human Res Mgr*
Brian Bueltel, *Sales Staff*
◆ **EMP:** 67
SQ FT: 100,000
SALES (est): 22MM
SALES (corp-wide): 1.3B **Privately Held**
WEB: www.columbiaerd.com
SIC: 5085 3069 3061 Seals, industrial; gaskets; molded rubber products; mechanical rubber goods

HQ: Keystone Holdings, Inc.
875 Center Dr
Vandalia OH 45377

(G-18677)
DOOR FABRICATION SERVICES INC
3250 Old Springfield Rd # 1 (45377-9599)
PHONE 937 454-9207
Fax: 937 454-9310
Brian Hakers, *Manager*
▲ **EMP:** 45
SALES (est): 4.8MM
SALES (corp-wide): 2B **Publicly Held**
WEB: www.masonite.com
SIC: 5046 2431 Partitions; millwork
PA: Masonite International Corporation
201 N Franklin St Ste 300
Tampa FL 33602
813 877-2726

(G-18678)
FAR OAKS ORTHOPEDISTS INC
55 Elva Ct Ste 100 (45377-1875)
PHONE 937 298-0452
Dan Morris, *Manager*
Vivekanand A Manocha, *Pain Mangement*
EMP: 50
SALES (corp-wide): 6.5MM **Privately Held**
SIC: 8011 Offices & clinics of medical doctors
PA: Far Oaks Orthopedists, Inc.
6490 Centervl Bus Pkwy
Dayton OH 45459
937 433-5309

(G-18679)
FEDERAL EXPRESS CORPORATION
Also Called: Fedex
3605 Concorde Dr (45377-3310)
PHONE 800 463-3339
Lorie Thompson, *Branch Mgr*
EMP: 75
SALES (corp-wide): 60.3B **Publicly Held**
WEB: www.federalexpress.com
SIC: 4513 Letter delivery, private air; package delivery, private air; parcel delivery, private air
HQ: Federal Express Corporation
3610 Hacks Cross Rd
Memphis TN 38125
901 369-3600

(G-18680)
FEDERAL EXPRESS CORPORATION
Also Called: Fedex
10340 Freight Dr (45377-1033)
PHONE 937 898-3474
EMP: 80
SALES (corp-wide): 47.4B **Publicly Held**
SIC: 4513 4215 Air Courier Services Courier Service
HQ: Federal Express Corporation
3610 Hacks Cross Rd
Memphis TN 38125
901 369-3600

(G-18681)
GE AVIATION SYSTEMS LLC
740 E National Rd (45377-3062)
PHONE 937 898-5881
Victor Bonneau, *Branch Mgr*
John Macneil, *Manager*
Gerald Fahringer, *Director*
EMP: 300
SALES (corp-wide): 122B **Publicly Held**
SIC: 8711 3643 3625 3624 Aviation &/or aeronautical engineering; current-carrying wiring devices; relays & industrial controls; carbon & graphite products; motors & generators
HQ: Ge Aviation Systems Llc
1 Neumann Way
Cincinnati OH 45215
937 898-9600

(G-18682)
HERAEUS PRECIOUS METALS NORTH
970 Industrial Park Dr (45377-3116)
PHONE 937 264-1000
Jrgen Heraeus, *Chairman*

Vandalia - Montgomery County (G-18683)

Don Peterson, *Facilities Mgr*
Paul Ripplingler, *Controller*
Kayleigh Hahan, *Office Mgr*
Tom Banks, *Manager*
▲ **EMP:** 31
SQ FT: 28,000
SALES (est): 8.8MM **Privately Held**
SIC: 2869 2819 8731 Industrial organic chemicals; chemicals, high purity: refined from technical grade; chemical laboratory, except testing
HQ: Heraeus Holding Gesellschaft Mit Beschrankter Haftung
Heraeusstr. 12-14
Hanau 63450
618 135-0

(G-18683)
HERTZ CORPORATION
James Cox Intrl Arpt (45377)
PHONE..................937 890-2721
Wm Noble, *Branch Mgr*
EMP: 30
SQ FT: 6,500
SALES (corp-wide): 8.8B **Publicly Held**
WEB: www.hertz.com
SIC: 7514 5521 Rent-a-car service; automobiles, used cars only
HQ: The Hertz Corporation
8501 Williams Rd
Estero FL 33928
239 301-7000

(G-18684)
HERTZ CORPORATION
3350 S Valet Cir (45377-1068)
PHONE..................937 898-5806
Grant Funk, *Site Mgr*
Jeff Waple, *Manager*
EMP: 80
SALES (corp-wide): 8.8B **Publicly Held**
WEB: www.hertz.com
SIC: 7514 Rent-a-car service
HQ: The Hertz Corporation
8501 Williams Rd
Estero FL 33928
239 301-7000

(G-18685)
HESTER MASONRY CO INC
10867 Engle Rd (45377-9439)
PHONE..................937 890-2283
Stan Hester, *President*
EMP: 35
SQ FT: 8,400
SALES: 2MM **Privately Held**
SIC: 1741 Masonry & other stonework

(G-18686)
HORIZON HOME HEALTH CARE
410 Corporate Center Dr (45377-1164)
PHONE..................937 264-3155
Nicole Hardin, *Owner*
Sarah Potts, *Human Resources*
Ruth Waske, *Manager*
John Taylor, *Administration*
EMP: 35
SALES (est): 2.6MM **Privately Held**
SIC: 8099 Blood related health services

(G-18687)
KOORSEN FIRE & SECURITY INC
3577 Concorde Dr (45377-3308)
PHONE..................937 324-9405
Lowell Fredrickson, *Principal*
EMP: 25
SALES (corp-wide): 264.3MM **Privately Held**
WEB: www.koorsen.com
SIC: 7389 7382 1731 5999 Fire extinguisher servicing; fire alarm maintenance & monitoring; fire detection & burglar alarm systems specialization; fire extinguishers
PA: Koorsen Fire & Security, Inc.
2719 N Arlington Ave
Indianapolis IN 46218
317 542-1800

(G-18688)
MANUFACTURED ASSEMBLIES CORP
7482 Webster St (45277)
PHONE..................937 898-2060
EMP: 70

SALES (corp-wide): 51MM **Privately Held**
SIC: 5063 Whol Electrical Equipment
PA: Manufactured Assemblies Corporation
1625 Fieldstone Way
Vandalia OH 45377
937 454-0722

(G-18689)
MIAMI VALLEY HOSPITAL
211 Kenbrook Dr (45377-2400)
PHONE..................937 208-7065
Fax: 937 208-7075
Bill Quilter, *Manager*
EMP: 814
SALES (corp-wide): 968.3MM **Privately Held**
SIC: 8062 General medical & surgical hospitals
HQ: Miami Valley Hospital
1 Wyoming St
Dayton OH 45409
937 208-8000

(G-18690)
NATIONAL RENTAL (US) INC
Also Called: National Rent A Car
3600 Terminal Rd (45377-3312)
PHONE..................937 890-0100
Fax: 937 890-6945
Mike Belcure, *Sales Mgr*
Kurt Zorss, *Manager*
Charles Allio, *Manager*
EMP: 45
SALES (corp-wide): 6.1B **Privately Held**
WEB: www.specialtyrentals.com
SIC: 7514 Rent-a-car service
HQ: National Rental (Us) Inc.
6929 N Lakewood Ave # 100
Tulsa OK 74117

(G-18691)
OHIO ASSN PUB TREASURERS
333 James Bohanan Dr (45377-2319)
PHONE..................937 415-2237
William Loy, *Mayor*
EMP: 135
SALES (est): 1.6MM **Privately Held**
WEB: www.airshowvandalia.com
SIC: 8611 Business associations

(G-18692)
PARK-N-GO INC
Also Called: Park-N-Go Airport Parking
1140 W National Rd (45377)
P.O. Box 13542, Dayton (45413-0542)
PHONE..................937 890-7275
Fax: 937 890-5432
Brian West, *President*
Carla Jones, *Manager*
EMP: 40
SALES (est): 2.2MM **Privately Held**
SIC: 4111 7521 4581 Airport transportation; parking garage; airport

(G-18693)
PRIMARY CR NTWRK PRMR HLTH PRT
900 S Dixie Dr Ste 40 (45377-2656)
PHONE..................937 890-6644
EMP: 41
SALES (corp-wide): 33.7MM **Privately Held**
SIC: 8011 Physical medicine, physician/surgeon
PA: Primary Care Network Of Premier Health Partners
110 N Main St Ste 350
Dayton OH 45402
937 226-7085

(G-18694)
PSA AIRLINES INC
3634 Cargo Rd (45377-1008)
PHONE..................937 454-9338
Keith Houk, *President*
EMP: 77
SALES (corp-wide): 42.2B **Publicly Held**
SIC: 4512 Air passenger carrier, scheduled
HQ: Psa Airlines, Inc.
3400 Terminal Rd
Vandalia OH 45377
937 454-1116

(G-18695)
PSA AIRLINES INC (HQ)
Also Called: US Airways Express
3400 Terminal Rd (45377-1041)
PHONE..................937 454-1116
Fax: 937 264-3911
Keith D Houk, *President*
Kevin Reinhalter, *Vice Pres*
James Schear, *Vice Pres*
Timothy Keuscher, *VP Opers*
Mark Zweidinger, *VP Opers*
EMP: 250
SQ FT: 18,600
SALES (est): 136.5K
SALES (corp-wide): 42.2B **Publicly Held**
SIC: 4512 Air passenger carrier, scheduled
PA: American Airlines Group Inc.
4333 Amon Carter Blvd
Fort Worth TX 76155
817 963-1234

(G-18696)
R B JERGENS CONTRACTORS INC
11418 N Dixie Dr (45377-9736)
PHONE..................937 669-9799
William Jergens, *President*
Kevin Harshberger, *Vice Pres*
Victor Roberts, *Vice Pres*
Randy Hubley, *Project Mgr*
David King, *Project Mgr*
EMP: 99
SALES (est): 27.7MM **Privately Held**
SIC: 1611 General contractor, highway & street construction; highway & street paving contractor; concrete construction: roads, highways, sidewalks, etc.

(G-18697)
R D JERGENS CONTRACTORS INC (PA)
11418 N Dixie Dr (45377-9736)
P.O. Box 309 (45377-0309)
PHONE..................937 669-9799
William Jergens, *President*
Kevin Harshberger, *Vice Pres*
Dave Tennery, *Vice Pres*
Randy Hubley, *Project Mgr*
Ruth Jergens, *Treasurer*
EMP: 100
SQ FT: 14,000
SALES (est): 29.4MM **Privately Held**
SIC: 1611 1623 Highway & street construction; underground utilities contractor

(G-18698)
REPUBLIC PARKING SYSTEM INC
3600 Terminal Rd (45377-3312)
PHONE..................937 415-0016
EMP: 46
SALES (corp-wide): 400MM **Privately Held**
SIC: 7521 Automobile Parking
PA: Republic Parking System, Inc.
633 Chestnut St Ste 2000
Chattanooga TN 37450
423 756-2771

(G-18699)
STEVENS AVIATION INC
3500 Hangar Dr (45377-1055)
P.O. Box 399 (45377-0399)
PHONE..................937 890-0189
Fax: 937 454-3414
Clint Harvey, *Parts Mgr*
Thomas D Grunbeck, *VP Sales*
Ron Tennyson, *Branch Mgr*
Mick Waltz, *Manager*
Susan Hendricks, *Supervisor*
EMP: 60
SALES (corp-wide): 117.6MM **Privately Held**
WEB: www.stevensaviation.com
SIC: 4581 Airport terminal services
PA: Stevens Aviation, Inc.
600 Delaware St
Greenville SC 29605
864 678-6000

(G-18700)
SUPREME COURT OF OHIO
Also Called: Vandalia Municipal Court
245 James Bohanan Dr (45377-2375)
P.O. Box 428 (45377-0428)
PHONE..................937 898-3996
Fax: 937 898-6648
Jerry Kaylor, *Principal*
EMP: 30
SQ FT: 5,461 **Privately Held**
WEB: www.judicialstudies.com
SIC: 9211 8111 State courts; ; legal services
HQ: The Supreme Court Of Ohio
65 S Front St Fl 1
Columbus OH 43215
614 387-9000

(G-18701)
TRIAD TECHNOLOGIES LLC (PA)
985 Falls Creek Dr (45377-9686)
PHONE..................937 832-2861
Doug Wissman, *CEO*
Tom Eyer, *CFO*
Todd Baumgartner, *Sales Mgr*
Mark Mosher, *Sales Staff*
Lew Daly, *Info Tech Dir*
EMP: 29
SALES: 43.6MM **Privately Held**
WEB: www.triadtechnologies.com
SIC: 5084 Hydraulic systems equipment & supplies

(G-18702)
TRUGREEN LIMITED PARTNERSHIP
Also Called: Tru Green-Chemlawn
800 Center Dr (45377-3130)
P.O. Box 578 (45377-0578)
PHONE..................937 410-4055
Fax: 937 454-0851
Bruce Hochwalt, *Opers Mgr*
Joan Thorton, *Manager*
Greg Lane, *Supervisor*
EMP: 75
SALES (corp-wide): 4B **Privately Held**
SIC: 0782 Lawn care services
HQ: Trugreen Limited Partnership
1790 Kirby Pkwy
Memphis TN 38138
901 251-4128

(G-18703)
UNITED AIRLINES INC
Also Called: Continental Airlines
3600 Terminal Rd Ste 213 (45377-1093)
PHONE..................937 454-2009
Jerry Jamison, *Branch Mgr*
Robert Hall, *Manager*
EMP: 35
SALES (corp-wide): 37.7B **Publicly Held**
WEB: www.continental.com
SIC: 4512 Air passenger carrier, scheduled
HQ: United Airlines, Inc.
233 S Wacker Dr Ste 710
Chicago IL 60606
872 825-4000

(G-18704)
US EXPEDITING LOGISTICS LLC
4311 Old Springfield Rd (45377-9576)
PHONE..................937 235-1014
Joel Timmons,
EMP: 32
SALES (est): 4.2MM **Privately Held**
SIC: 4213 Trucking, except local

(G-18705)
US SECURITY ASSOCIATES INC
69 N Dixie Dr Ste F (45377-2060)
PHONE..................937 454-9035
Fax: 937 454-9039
Greg Reynolds, *General Mgr*
Victor Lay, *Director*
Dan Bacon, *Asst Director*
EMP: 113 **Privately Held**
SIC: 7381 Security guard service
PA: U.S. Security Associates, Inc.
200 Mansell Ct E Ste 500
Roswell GA 30076

(G-18706)
VANCARE INC
Also Called: Vandalia Park
208 N Cassel Rd (45377-2926)
PHONE..................937 898-4202

Fax: 937 898-4075
Mark Schertzinger, *Administration*
Deb Thompson, *Receptionist*
EMP: 250 **EST:** 1996
SQ FT: 10,000
SALES (est): 5.4MM **Privately Held**
SIC: 8051 8052 Skilled nursing care facilities; intermediate care facilities

(G-18707)
WRIGHT BROTHERS AERO INC (PA)
3700 Mccauley Dr Ste C (45377-1069)
PHONE 937 890-8900
Kevin Keeley, *President*
Emerson R Keck, *Principal*
Gerald L Turner, *Principal*
Sharon S Keeley, *Chairman*
Kocher Randall, *COO*
EMP: 57
SQ FT: 47,000
SALES (est): 8.1MM **Privately Held**
WEB: www.wrightbrosaero.com
SIC: 4581 Airport terminal services

Vermilion
Erie County

(G-18708)
ELDEN MOTELS LP (PA)
Also Called: Holiday Inn
15008 Holiday Dr Ste A (44089-9291)
PHONE 440 967-8770
Kim Estep, *General Mgr*
EMP: 60
SQ FT: 40,000
SALES (est): 1.3MM **Privately Held**
SIC: 7011 Hotels & motels

(G-18709)
ELDEN PROPERTIES LTD PARTNR
Also Called: Elden & Strauss
15008 Holiday Dr Ste A (44089-9291)
PHONE 440 967-0521
John A Elden Jr, *Partner*
Carol Elden, *Partner*
Dan Strauss, *Partner*
EMP: 30
SALES (est): 1.5MM **Privately Held**
SIC: 6531 Real estate agents & managers

(G-18710)
HULL BUILDERS SUPPLY INC
685 Main St (44089-1311)
P.O. Box 432 (44089-0432)
PHONE 440 967-3159
Fax: 440 967-8823
Steve Holovacs, *President*
Ernie Johnson, *Manager*
EMP: 28
SALES: 1,000K **Privately Held**
SIC: 5032 3273 5211 Limestone; ready-mixed concrete; lumber & other building materials

(G-18711)
IRG OPERATING LLC
Also Called: Cleveland Quarries
850 W River Rd (44089-1530)
PHONE 440 963-4008
Fax: 440 963-4011
Laureen Ramsire, *Office Mgr*
Zach Carpenter, *Mng Member*
EMP: 36
SALES: 3.6MM **Privately Held**
SIC: 1411 Sandstone, dimension-quarrying

(G-18712)
KINGSTON HEALTHCARE COMPANY
Also Called: Kingston of Vermilion
4210 Telegraph Ln (44089-3748)
PHONE 440 967-1800
Fax: 440 967-2216
Kent Libbe, *CFO*
Heather Shirley, *Branch Mgr*
Itri Eren, *Director*
Elizabeth Ewers, *Administration*
EMP: 110

SALES (corp-wide): 95.5MM **Privately Held**
WEB: www.kingstonhealthcare.com
SIC: 8051 8059 Skilled nursing care facilities; home for the mentally retarded, exc. skilled or intermediate
PA: Kingston Healthcare Company
1 Seagate Ste 1960
Toledo OH 43604
419 247-2880

(G-18713)
LINWOOD PARK COMPANY
4920 Liberty Ave (44089-1434)
PHONE 440 963-0481
Fax: 440 967-4237
Anne Peters, *President*
EMP: 30
SALES (est): 993.2K **Privately Held**
SIC: 7996 Theme park, amusement

(G-18714)
MERCY HEALTH
1607 State Route 50 Ste 6 (44089)
PHONE 440 967-8713
EMP: 42
SALES (corp-wide): 4.2B **Privately Held**
SIC: 8011 Offices & clinics of medical doctors
PA: Mercy Health
1701 Mercy Health Pl
Cincinnati OH 45237
513 639-2800

(G-18715)
MILL MANOR NURSING HOME INC
983 Exchange St (44089-1256)
PHONE 440 967-6614
Fax: 440 967-1968
Ted Dush, *President*
Edie Dush, *Vice Pres*
Mary Ellen Smith, *Bookkeeper*
EMP: 39
SQ FT: 8,000
SALES (est): 1.8MM **Privately Held**
SIC: 8051 8052 Convalescent home with continuous nursing care; intermediate care facilities

(G-18716)
SHARPNACK CHEVROLET CO (PA)
5401 Portage Dr (44089-1432)
PHONE 440 967-3144
Joseph Sharpnack Jr, *President*
Thomas C Sharpnack, *Vice Pres*
Janet S Sharpnack, *Treasurer*
Storm Bowling, *Sales Staff*
Karen Bors, *Manager*
EMP: 35
SQ FT: 20,800
SALES (est): 23.5MM **Privately Held**
WEB: www.sharpnack.com
SIC: 5511 7538 7532 7515 Automobiles, new & used; general automotive repair shops; top & body repair & paint shops; passenger car leasing; used car dealers; automobiles & other motor vehicles

(G-18717)
STEP BY STEP EMPLYMENT TRINING
664 Exchange St (44089-1301)
P.O. Box 551 (44089-0551)
PHONE 440 967-9042
Fax: 440 967-9199
Susan Fischer, *President*
EMP: 35
SALES (est): 688.1K **Privately Held**
SIC: 8331 Job training services

(G-18718)
VERMILION BOARD OF EDUCATION
Also Called: Vermilion School Bus Garage
1065 Decatur St (44089-1167)
PHONE 440 204-1700
Fax: 440 967-4238
George Harizal, *Principal*
Linda Griffin, *Branch Mgr*
EMP: 50
SALES (corp-wide): 26.3MM **Privately Held**
SIC: 4151 School buses

PA: Vermilion Board Of Education
1250 Sanford St
Vermilion OH 44089
440 204-1700

(G-18719)
VERMILION BOAT CLUB INC
5416 Liberty Ave (44089-1334)
PHONE 440 967-6634
Fax: 440 967-6634
Karen Mathews, *Principal*
Rj Hickey, *Commodore*
George Vegotis, *Rear Commodore*
Roger McCoy, *Treasurer*
Sullivan Kimberly, *Manager*
EMP: 25
SQ FT: 9,200
SALES: 1MM **Privately Held**
WEB: www.vermilionboatclub.com
SIC: 7997 5812 4493 Boating club, membership; eating places; marinas

(G-18720)
VERMILION FAMILY YMCA
320 Aldrich Rd (44089-2286)
PHONE 440 967-4208
Jim Turton, *President*
Kevin Holloway, *Business Mgr*
Anne Stock, *Vice Pres*
Don Lebeau, *Treasurer*
W Robert Johnston II, *Director*
EMP: 40
SQ FT: 37,000
SALES: 678.4K **Privately Held**
SIC: 8351 8641 7991 7997 Child day care services; youth organizations; physical fitness facilities; membership sports & recreation clubs; individual & family services

(G-18721)
VERMILION FARM MARKET
2901 Liberty Ave (44089-2534)
PHONE 440 967-9666
Fax: 440 967-5620
Thomas Rottel, *President*
EMP: 43
SQ FT: 19,000
SALES (est): 2.6MM **Privately Held**
WEB: www.vermilionfarmmarket.com
SIC: 5431 5148 Fruit stands or markets; fresh fruits & vegetables

Versailles
Darke County

(G-18722)
A L SMITH TRUCKING INC
8984 Murphy Rd (45380-9752)
PHONE 937 526-3651
Fax: 937 526-3668
Dave Fullenkamp, *President*
Chad Kelch, *Manager*
EMP: 38 **EST:** 1956
SQ FT: 9,600
SALES (est): 7.2MM **Privately Held**
WEB: www.alsmithtrucking.com
SIC: 4213 4212 Contract haulers; local trucking, without storage

(G-18723)
BNSF LOGISTICS LLC
Also Called: T E S - East
611 Marker Rd (45380-9334)
P.O. Box 176 (45380-0176)
PHONE 937 526-3141
Chuck Borchers, *Branch Mgr*
Shannon Boyd, *Director*
EMP: 40
SALES (corp-wide): 242.1B **Publicly Held**
WEB: www.bnsflogistics.com
SIC: 4731 Transportation agents & brokers
HQ: Bnsf Logistics, Llc
2710 S 48th St
Springdale AR 72762
479 927-5570

(G-18724)
CLASSIC CARRIERS INC (PA)
151 Industrial Pkwy (45380-9756)
P.O. Box 295 (45380-0295)
PHONE 937 604-8118
Fax: 937 526-5169

Jim Subler, *President*
Randy Forbes, *General Mgr*
Ed Ruhe, *Vice Pres*
Lucas Subler, *Opers Mgr*
Randy French, *Opers Staff*
EMP: 50
SALES (est): 17.4MM **Privately Held**
WEB: www.classiccarrier.com
SIC: 4213 Contract haulers

(G-18725)
COUNTY OF DARKE
Also Called: Y M C A
10242 Versailles Se Rd (45380-9583)
PHONE 937 526-4488
Fax: 937 526-3425
Heather Glass, *Exec Dir*
Amy Wagner, *Director*
EMP: 40 **Privately Held**
WEB: www.darkecountyfair.com
SIC: 8641 8322 Youth organizations; individual & family services
PA: County Of Darke
520 S Broadway St
Greenville OH 45331
937 547-7370

(G-18726)
COVENANT CARE OHIO INC
Also Called: Versailles Health Care Center
200 Marker Rd (45380-9494)
PHONE 937 526-5570
Fax: 937 526-9630
Marilyn Barga, *Branch Mgr*
Tammy Hartzell, *Director*
Lisa Johnson, *Director*
Donald Pohlman, *Director*
Phyllis Grewe, *Food Svc Dir*
EMP: 85 **Privately Held**
WEB: www.villagegeorgetown.com
SIC: 8051 8011 Convalescent home with continuous nursing care; offices & clinics of medical doctors
HQ: Covenant Care Ohio, Inc.
27071 Aliso Creek Rd # 100
Aliso Viejo CA 92656
949 349-1200

(G-18727)
PHELAN INSURANCE AGENCY INC (PA)
863 E Main St (45380-1533)
P.O. Box 1 (45380-0001)
PHONE 800 843-3069
Fax: 937 548-0294
James B Phelan, *Ch of Bd*
Tim P Grow, *President*
Brent J Phelan, *COO*
Jeff Francis, *Exec VP*
Pat R Custenborder, *Vice Pres*
EMP: 31
SQ FT: 10,000
SALES: 1MM **Privately Held**
WEB: www.phelanins.com
SIC: 6411 Insurance agents

(G-18728)
PREMIER HEALTH PARTNERS
Also Called: Still Water Family Care
471 Marker Rd (45380-9324)
PHONE 937 526-3235
Fax: 937 526-9446
Daniel Elshoff MD, *President*
Robert Klamar, *Med Doctor*
EMP: 70
SALES (corp-wide): 354MM **Privately Held**
SIC: 8011 General & family practice, physician/surgeon
PA: Premier Health Partners
110 N Main St Ste 450
Dayton OH 45402
937 499-9596

(G-18729)
RENAISSANCE CORPORATION (PA)
Also Called: Inn, The
21 W Main St (45380-1215)
PHONE 937 526-3672
Fax: 937 275-5603
Ann Eiting Klumar, *President*
Frank Shimko, *Research*
Michael R Houp, *Treasurer*
Salim Hasan, *Asst Director*
Kristen Isham, *Quality Imp Dir*

Versailles - Darke County (G-18730)

EMP: 50
SALES (est): 2.5MM **Privately Held**
SIC: 7011 5812 Inns; eating places

(G-18730)
VILLAGE OF VERSAILLES
Also Called: Versailles Util Dept
177 N Center St (45380-1206)
P.O. Box 288 (45380-0288)
PHONE..................................937 526-4191
Fax: 937 526-4476
Randy Gump, *Director*
EMP: 30 **Privately Held**
SIC: 8611 Public utility association
PA: Village Of Versailles
177 N Center St
Versailles OH 45380
937 526-3294

(G-18731)
WEAVER BROS INC (PA)
Also Called: Tri County Eggs
895 E Main St (45380-1533)
P.O. Box 333 (45380-0333)
PHONE..................................937 526-3907
Fax: 937 526-4824
Timothy John Weaver, *President*
Audrey Weaver, *Principal*
Geo L Weaver, *Principal*
John D Weaver, *Principal*
Kreg Kohli, *Vice Pres*
▲ **EMP:** 60 **EST:** 1931
SQ FT: 20,000
SALES (est): 61.1MM **Privately Held**
SIC: 0252 5143 2015 Chicken eggs; dairy products, except dried or canned; cheese; butter; poultry slaughtering & processing

(G-18732)
WEAVER BROS INC
Also Called: Weaver Brothers Farm
10638 State Route 47 (45380-9743)
PHONE..................................937 526-4777
Fax: 937 526-9523
Phil Borchers, *General Mgr*
EMP: 25
SALES (corp-wide): 61.1MM **Privately Held**
SIC: 0252 Chicken eggs
PA: Weaver Bros., Inc.
895 E Main St
Versailles OH 45380
937 526-3907

Vickery
Sandusky County

(G-18733)
SR IMPROVEMENTS SERVICES LLC
1485 County Road 268 (43464-9701)
PHONE..................................567 207-6488
Ron Wilson, *General Ptnr*
Ronald E Wilson,
EMP: 40
SALES (est): 583.1K **Privately Held**
SIC: 7299 7349 Handyman service; building maintenance services

(G-18734)
WASTE MANAGEMENT OHIO INC
3956 State Route 412 (43464-9791)
PHONE..................................419 547-7791
Fax: 419 547-6144
Ginger Kaladas, *Credit Staff*
Fred Nicar, *Sales Mgr*
Steve Lonneman, *Branch Mgr*
EMP: 28
SALES (corp-wide): 14.4B **Publicly Held**
WEB: www.wm.com
SIC: 4953 Hazardous waste collection & disposal
HQ: Waste Management Of Ohio, Inc.
1700 N Broad St
Fairborn OH 45324

Vienna
Trumbull County

(G-18735)
AVALON GOLF & COUNTRY CLUB
761 Youngstown Kingsvlle (44473-8615)
PHONE..................................330 539-5008
Fax: 330 539-0200
Christine Bell, *General Mgr*
EMP: 68 **EST:** 1922
SQ FT: 10,000
SALES (est): 1.5MM **Privately Held**
SIC: 7997 7992 Country club, membership; public golf courses

(G-18736)
COLE SELBY FUNERAL INC
3966 Warren Sharon Rd (44473-9524)
PHONE..................................330 856-4695
Fax: 330 856-5253
Bob Moses, *President*
EMP: 25
SALES (est): 562.5K **Privately Held**
SIC: 7261 Funeral home

(G-18737)
GLOWE-SMITH INDUSTRIAL INC
Also Called: G. S. I.
812 Youngstwn Kgsvl Rd Se (44473)
P.O. Box 625, Cortland (44410-0625)
PHONE..................................330 638-5088
Fax: 330 539-9308
Donald Glowe, *President*
EMP: 136
SQ FT: 2,600
SALES (est): 4.6MM **Privately Held**
SIC: 8711 8734 Consulting engineer; designing; ship, boat, machine & product; product testing laboratories

(G-18738)
LATROBE SPCIALTY MTLS DIST INC (HQ)
1551 Vienna Pkwy (44473-8703)
PHONE..................................330 609-5137
Gregory A Pratt, *Ch of Bd*
Timothy R Armstrong, *Vice Pres*
Thomas F Cramsey, *Vice Pres*
James D Dee, *Vice Pres*
Matthew S Enoch, *Vice Pres*
◆ **EMP:** 80
SQ FT: 189,000
SALES (est): 69.2MM
SALES (corp-wide): 1.8B **Publicly Held**
SIC: 5051 3312 Steel; stainless steel
PA: Carpenter Technology Corporation
1735 Market St Fl 15
Philadelphia PA 19103
610 208-2000

(G-18739)
LITCO INTERNATIONAL INC (PA)
1 Litco Dr (44473-9600)
P.O. Box 150 (44473-0150)
PHONE..................................330 539-5433
Fax: 330 539-5388
Lionel F Trebilcock, *CEO*
Gary L Trebilcock, *President*
Sharyn McCurdy, *General Mgr*
Bill Smith, *General Mgr*
Gary Sharon, *Vice Pres*
◆ **EMP:** 30
SQ FT: 13,000
SALES (est): 7.3MM **Privately Held**
WEB: www.litco.com
SIC: 2448 5031 Pallets, wood; particleboard

(G-18740)
MILLWOOD INC (PA)
3708 International Blvd (44473-9796)
PHONE..................................330 393-4400
Steven J Miller, *President*
Lionel W Trebilcock, *President*
Gene Gearlds, *Pastor*
Ronald C Ringness, *Exec VP*
Brad Arnold, *VP Opers*
◆ **EMP:** 30
SQ FT: 20,000
SALES (est): 387.2MM **Privately Held**
WEB: www.millwoodinc.com
SIC: 3565 4731 Packaging machinery; freight transportation arrangement

(G-18741)
MILLWOOD NATURAL LLC
3708 International Blvd (44473-9796)
PHONE..................................330 393-4400
Lionel Trebilcock, *Partner*
EMP: 115
SALES (est): 11.6MM **Privately Held**
SIC: 3565 4731 Packaging machinery; freight transportation arrangement
PA: Millwood, Inc.
3708 International Blvd
Vienna OH 44473

(G-18742)
WINNER AVIATION CORPORATION
1453 Youngstown Kingsvill (44473-9788)
PHONE..................................330 856-5000
Fax: 330 856-7961
Rick Hale, *CEO*
Charles R Hale, *President*
Karen Hale, *Vice Pres*
Lee McCracken, *CFO*
Jeffrey A McCandless, *Treasurer*
EMP: 75
SQ FT: 5,000
SALES (est): 18.3MM **Privately Held**
WEB: www.winneraviation.com
SIC: 4581 5172 7359 Hangars & other aircraft storage facilities; aircraft fueling services; equipment rental & leasing

Vincent
Washington County

(G-18743)
DECKER DRILLING INC
11565 State Route 676 (45784-5636)
PHONE..................................740 749-3939
Dean Decker, *President*
Pat Decker, *Vice Pres*
Loretta Decker, *Administration*
EMP: 42
SALES (est): 6.6MM **Privately Held**
WEB: www.deandecker.com
SIC: 1381 Redrilling oil & gas wells

Vinton
Gallia County

(G-18744)
STEELIAL WLDG MET FBRCTION INC
Also Called: Steelial Cnstr Met Fabrication
70764 State Route 124 (45686-8545)
PHONE..................................740 669-5300
Fax: 740 669-4205
Larry Allen Hedrick Jr, *President*
Deb Karns, *Bookkeeper*
Krista Hedrick, *Manager*
Krista Lynnete Hedrick, *Admin Sec*
EMP: 32 **EST:** 1998
SQ FT: 40,000
SALES (est): 11MM **Privately Held**
WEB: www.steelial.com
SIC: 1623 3441 3444 Pipe laying construction; fabricated structural metal; sheet metalwork

Wadsworth
Medina County

(G-18745)
AKRON INN LIMITED PARTNERSHIP
Also Called: Ramada Inn
5 Park Centre Dr (44281-9431)
PHONE..................................330 336-7692
Shawn Leattherman, *Owner*
Kim Outritch, *Principal*
Rosemary Knepp, *Manager*
EMP: 25
SALES (est): 919.8K **Privately Held**
SIC: 7011 Hotels & motels

(G-18746)
ALTERCARE INC
Also Called: Altercare of Wadsworth
147 Garfield St (44281-1431)
PHONE..................................330 335-2555
Fax: 330 336-7220
Michelle Smith, *President*
Bob Tvdrik, *Maint Spvr*
Diana Jackson, *Manager*
Deb Loughee, *Administration*
EMP: 120
SALES (corp-wide): 10.6MM **Privately Held**
SIC: 8051 8052 Skilled nursing care facilities; intermediate care facilities
PA: Altercare, Inc.
35990 Westminister Ave
North Ridgeville OH 44039
440 327-5285

(G-18747)
AMERICAN HOSPITALITY GROUP INC (HQ)
Also Called: A H G
200 Smokerise Dr (44281-7401)
PHONE..................................330 336-6684
Robert Leatherman Sr, *Ch of Bd*
Robert Leatherman Jr, *President*
Rosemary Knepp, *General Mgr*
Dean Rump, *General Mgr*
Phyllis Leatherman, *Corp Secy*
EMP: 384
SQ FT: 20,000
SALES: 39.4MM
SALES (corp-wide): 21.8MM **Privately Held**
SIC: 8741 Hotel or motel management
PA: Leatherman Nursing Centers Corporation
200 Smokerise Dr Ste 300
Wadsworth OH 44281
330 336-6684

(G-18748)
ASAP HOMECARE INC (PA)
1 Park Centre Dr Ste 107 (44281-9482)
PHONE..................................330 334-7027
Fax: 330 334-2186
Luke Harmon, *CEO*
Dayna Harmon, *Principal*
EMP: 35
SALES (est): 6.9MM **Privately Held**
WEB: www.asaphomecare.com
SIC: 8082 Home health care services

(G-18749)
CITY OF WADSWORTH
Also Called: Electrical Service Dept
120 Maple St (44281-1865)
PHONE..................................330 334-1581
Fax: 330 335-2893
Peter A Giacomo, *Superintendent*
EMP: 30 **Privately Held**
SIC: 7629 9111 Electrical repair shops; mayors' offices
PA: City Of Wadsworth
120 Maple St Uppr
Wadsworth OH 44281
330 335-1521

(G-18750)
COMMUNITY CAREGIVERS
230 Quadral Dr Ste D (44281-8375)
PHONE..................................330 725-9800
Michael T Nemeth, *Branch Mgr*
EMP: 36
SALES (corp-wide): 2.2MM **Privately Held**
SIC: 8082 Home health care services
PA: Community Caregivers
66 S Miller Rd Ste 200
Fairlawn OH 44333
330 836-8585

(G-18751)
CORNWELL QUALITY TOOLS COMPANY
Also Called: Distribution Service Company
635 Seville Rd (44281-1077)
PHONE..................................330 335-2933
Bill S Nobley, *COO*
William Stemple, *Vice Pres*
Craig Croley, *VP Opers*

GEOGRAPHIC SECTION
Wakeman - Huron County (G-18774)

Dal Ringler, *Manager*
Eileen Moeller, *Director*
EMP: 46
SALES (corp-wide): 151.2MM **Privately Held**
WEB: www.cornwelltools.com
SIC: 5013 5085 Tools & equipment, automotive; industrial supplies
PA: The Cornwell Quality Tools Company
667 Seville Rd
Wadsworth OH 44281
330 336-3506

(G-18752)
DAVITA INC
195 Wadsworth Rd (44281-9504)
PHONE 330 335-2300
Julie Zubek, *Branch Mgr*
EMP: 26 **Publicly Held**
SIC: 8092 Kidney dialysis centers
PA: Davita Inc.
2000 16th St
Denver CO 80202

(G-18753)
GOLDEN LIVING LLC
Also Called: Beverly
365 Johnson Rd (44281-8609)
PHONE 330 335-1558
Fax: 330 336-6803
Rick Michell, *General Mgr*
EMP: 75
SQ FT: 28,324
SALES (corp-wide): 7.4MM **Privately Held**
SIC: 8059 8052 8051 Convalescent home; intermediate care facilities; skilled nursing care facilities
PA: Golden Living Llc
5220 Tennyson Pkwy # 400
Plano TX 75024
972 372-6300

(G-18754)
HEALTHSPAN INTEGRATED CARE
Also Called: Kaiser Foundation Health Plan
120 High St (44281-1855)
PHONE 330 334-1549
Sue Cieslack, *Branch Mgr*
EMP: 29
SALES (corp-wide): 4.2B **Privately Held**
SIC: 6324 Hospital & medical service plans
HQ: Healthspan Integrated Care
1001 Lakeside Ave E # 1200
Cleveland OH 44114
216 621-5600

(G-18755)
HEART TO HEART HOME HEALTH
250 Smokerise Dr Apt 302 (44281-8263)
PHONE 330 335-9999
Sean Leatherman, *Vice Pres*
Jake Friedt, *Manager*
Nancy Kirby, *Administration*
Phyllis Leatherman, *Admin Sec*
EMP: 40 **EST:** 1999
SALES (est): 1.2MM **Privately Held**
WEB: www.h2hhomehealth.com
SIC: 8082 8071 Home health care services; medical laboratories

(G-18756)
HOME INSTEAD SENIOR CARE
1 Park Centre Dr Ste 15 (44281-9452)
PHONE 330 334-4664
Fax: 330 334-3969
Pam Myers, *President*
EMP: 100 **EST:** 1970
SALES (est): 2.5MM **Privately Held**
SIC: 8082 8322 Home health care services; individual & family services

(G-18757)
HUBBELL POWER SYSTEMS INC
Ohio Brass
8711 Wadsworth Rd (44281-8438)
PHONE 330 335-2361
Patrick Clemente, *President*
Dennis Lenk, *Engineer*
Chris Davis, *Branch Mgr*
Steve Holler, *Director*
EMP: 75
SALES (corp-wide): 3.6B **Publicly Held**
SIC: 5065 Electronic parts
HQ: Hubbell Power Systems, Inc.
200 Center Point Cir # 200
Columbia SC 29210
803 216-2600

(G-18758)
JERSEY CENTRAL PWR & LIGHT CO
9681 Silvercreek Rd (44281-9008)
PHONE 330 336-9884
Anthony Alexander, *Branch Mgr*
EMP: 67 **Publicly Held**
WEB: www.jersey-central-power-light.monmouth.n
SIC: 4911 Electric services
HQ: Jersey Central Power & Light Company
76 S Main St
Akron OH 44308
800 736-3402

(G-18759)
LEATHERMAN NURSING CTRS CORP (PA)
200 Smokerise Dr Ste 300 (44281-9499)
PHONE 330 336-6684
Robert Leatherman, *President*
Phyllis Leatherman, *Corp Secy*
Karen Friedt, *Manager*
Sean Leatherman, *Administration*
EMP: 550
SQ FT: 20,000
SALES (est): 21.8MM **Privately Held**
SIC: 8741 Management services

(G-18760)
LIBERTY RESIDENCE II
1054 Freedom Dr Apt 115 (44281-7900)
PHONE 330 334-3262
Fax: 330 334-9713
Michelle Crinich, *Manager*
EMP: 38 **EST:** 2001
SALES (est): 1.3MM **Privately Held**
SIC: 8052 Intermediate care facilities

(G-18761)
LIFECARE HOSPICE
Also Called: Lifecare Palliative Medicine
102 Main St (44281-1453)
PHONE 330 336-6595
Fax: 330 336-1925
Greg Tesniarz, *Principal*
EMP: 90 **Privately Held**
SIC: 8322 Individual & family services
PA: Lifecare Hospice
1900 Akron Rd
Wooster OH 44691

(G-18762)
LOUIS PERRY & ASSOCIATES INC
165 Smokerise Dr (44281-8702)
PHONE 330 334-1585
Fax: 330 334-1658
Louis B Perry, *President*
James Calderone, *Senior VP*
Thomas R Payne, *Senior VP*
Thomas Payne, *Senior VP*
James T Calderone, *Vice Pres*
EMP: 135
SQ FT: 31,000
SALES: 11.9MM
SALES (corp-wide): 1.1B **Privately Held**
WEB: www.louisperry.com
SIC: 8711 8712 Consulting engineer; building construction consultant; architectural services
PA: Cdm Smith Inc
75 State St Ste 701
Boston MA 02109
617 452-6000

(G-18763)
LOWES HOME CENTERS LLC
1065 Williams Reserve Blvd (44281-9316)
PHONE 330 335-1900
Fax: 330 335-1903
Dave Labuda, *Manager*
EMP: 150
SQ FT: 137,480
SALES (corp-wide): 68.6B **Publicly Held**
SIC: 5211 5031 5722 5064 Home centers; building materials, exterior; building materials, interior; household appliance stores; electrical appliances, television & radio
HQ: Lowe's Home Centers, Llc
1605 Curtis Bridge Rd
Wilkesboro NC 28697
336 658-4000

(G-18764)
MASTERS AGENCY INC
Also Called: American Benefits Management
1108 Ledgestone Dr (44281-8113)
PHONE 330 805-5985
Fax: 330 966-5506
Paul Cantwell, *President*
EMP: 42
SQ FT: 10,000
SALES (est): 6.3MM **Privately Held**
WEB: www.americanbenefits.org
SIC: 6411 Insurance agents, brokers & service

(G-18765)
MEDINA COUNTY SHELTERED INDS
Also Called: WINDFALL INDUSTRIES
150 Quadral Dr Ste D (44281-8352)
PHONE 330 334-4491
Fax: 330 334-4492
Amanda Fulton, *Controller*
Wendy Bassak, *Accountant*
Jim Brown, *Exec Dir*
EMP: 315
SQ FT: 40,000
SALES: 2.9MM **Privately Held**
SIC: 8331 Sheltered workshop

(G-18766)
OHIO EDISON COMPANY
9681 Silvercreek Rd (44281-9008)
PHONE 330 336-9880
Bruce J Busse, *Branch Mgr*
Bruse Busse, *Director*
Kenneth Wirt, *Director*
EMP: 120 **Publicly Held**
SIC: 4911 Electric services
HQ: Ohio Edison Company
76 S Main St Bsmt
Akron OH 44308
800 736-3402

(G-18767)
PEPSI-COLA METRO BTLG CO INC
904 Seville Rd (44281-8316)
PHONE 330 336-3553
Fax: 330 336-0100
Scott Sutkaytis, *Regional Mgr*
Don Cooper, *Branch Mgr*
EMP: 50
SALES (corp-wide): 63.5B **Publicly Held**
WEB: www.joy-of-cola.com
SIC: 4225 5149 General warehousing & storage; soft drinks
HQ: Pepsi-Cola Metropolitan Bottling Company, Inc.
1111 Westchester Ave
White Plains NY 10604
914 767-6000

(G-18768)
PERRAM ELECTRIC INC
6882 Ridge Rd (44281-9706)
PHONE 330 239-2661
Fax: 330 239-2642
Zoltan J Kovacs, *President*
Dale B Perram, *Chairman*
Dave Powell, *Vice Pres*
Lori A Stanley, *Vice Pres*
Maureen Hoch, *Purch Agent*
EMP: 40
SQ FT: 2,500
SALES: 14.3MM **Privately Held**
WEB: www.perramelectric.com
SIC: 1731 General electrical contractor

(G-18769)
RELIABLE POLYMER SERVICES LP
300 1st St (44281-2084)
PHONE 800 321-0954
Michael Fagan, *President*
Jim Talarico, *CFO*
EMP: 39
SALES (est): 1.8MM **Privately Held**
SIC: 7389

(G-18770)
RETAIL RENOVATIONS INC (PA)
7530 State Rd (44281-9794)
PHONE 330 334-4501
Gary Williams, *CEO*
Frank Northcutt, *President*
Kelly Ostruh, *Vice Pres*
Ryan Wilson, *Project Mgr*
Rhonda Williams, *Treasurer*
EMP: 36
SALES (est): 7.4MM **Privately Held**
WEB: www.retailrenovations.com
SIC: 1542 Commercial & office building, new construction

(G-18771)
SUMMA HEALTH SYSTEM
195 Wadsworth Rd (44281-9504)
PHONE 330 334-1504
Hollie Kozak, *Manager*
EMP: 520
SALES (corp-wide): 1B **Privately Held**
SIC: 8062 General medical & surgical hospitals
PA: Summa Health System
525 E Market St
Akron OH 44304
330 375-3000

(G-18772)
VERIZON COMMUNICATIONS INC
1114 Williams Reserve (44281-9318)
PHONE 330 334-1268
Kevin Fruth, *Branch Mgr*
EMP: 107
SALES (corp-wide): 126B **Publicly Held**
SIC: 4813 4812 Local & long distance telephone communications; cellular telephone services
PA: Verizon Communications Inc.
1095 Ave Of The Americas
New York NY 10036
212 395-1000

(G-18773)
WADSWORTH GALAXY REST INC
201 Park Centre Dr (44281-7106)
PHONE 330 334-3663
Fax: 330 334-1471
Robert Leatherman, *President*
Phyllis Leatherman, *Corp Secy*
Robert Leatherman Jr, *Vice Pres*
Neil Winger, *Vice Pres*
Robin Winger, *Vice Pres*
EMP: 80
SALES (est): 196.8K **Privately Held**
WEB: www.galaxyrestaurant.com
SIC: 8741 5812 Restaurant management; eating places

Wakeman
Huron County

(G-18774)
BETTCHER INDUSTRIES INC (PA)
6801 State Route 60 (44889-8509)
P.O. Box 336, Vermilion (44089-0336)
PHONE 440 965-4422
Fax: 440 965-4900
Don Esch, *President*
Terry Blaine, *Regional Mgr*
Dallas Watson, *Regional Mgr*
Marty Tansey, *Mfg Dir*
Wes Mahon, *Prdtn Mgr*
▲ **EMP:** 165 **EST:** 1944
SQ FT: 65,000
SALES: 2.2MM **Privately Held**
WEB: www.bettcher.com
SIC: 5084 Food product manufacturing machinery; counterbores

Walbridge
Wood County

(G-18775)
GEM INDUSTRIAL INC (HQ)
Also Called: RUDOLPH/LIBBE
6842 Commodore Dr (43465-9793)
P.O. Box 716, Toledo (43697-0716)
PHONE...............................419 467-3287
Fax: 419 666-7004
Hussien Shousher, *President*
Bill Rudolph, *Chairman*
Brandon Gartee, *Business Mgr*
Douglas R Heyman, *Corp Secy*
Jeff Sneider, *Project Mgr*
EMP: 100
SQ FT: 33,000
SALES (est): 53.7MM
SALES (corp-wide): 502.6MM **Privately Held**
WEB: www.gemindustrial.com
SIC: **1711** 1731 1796 Mechanical contractor; boiler maintenance contractor; general electrical contractor; machinery installation
PA: The Rudolph/Libbe Companies Inc
6494 Latcha Rd
Walbridge OH 43465
419 241-5000

(G-18776)
PROFESSIONAL TRANSPORTATION
Also Called: P T I
30801 Drouillard Rd (43465-1037)
PHONE...............................419 661-0576
Fax: 419 661-1884
Justin Purkey, *Branch Mgr*
EMP: 109 **Privately Held**
SIC: **4119** 7363 Local passenger transportation; help supply services
PA: Professional Transportation Inc
3700 E Morgan Ave
Evansville IN 47715

(G-18777)
RUDOLPH LIBBE INC (HQ)
Also Called: RUDOLPH/LIBBE
6494 Latcha Rd (43465-9788)
PHONE...............................419 241-5000
Fax: 419 837-9373
Timothy Alter, *President*
Dave Boyer, *General Mgr*
Tammy Euler, *Superintendent*
Mark Murray, *Superintendent*
William Rudolph, *Chairman*
EMP: 500
SQ FT: 50,000
SALES: 300.5MM
SALES (corp-wide): 502.6MM **Privately Held**
WEB: www.rlcos.com
SIC: **1541** 1542 Industrial buildings, new construction; nonresidential construction
PA: The Rudolph/Libbe Companies Inc
6494 Latcha Rd
Walbridge OH 43465
419 241-5000

(G-18778)
RUDOLPH/LIBBE COMPANIES INC (PA)
6494 Latcha Rd (43465-9788)
PHONE...............................419 241-5000
Allan J Libbe, *President*
Frederick W Rudolph, *President*
Philip J Rudolph, *President*
Bill Rudolph, *Chairman*
Brad Delventhal, *Business Mgr*
EMP: 600
SQ FT: 40,000
SALES: 502.6MM **Privately Held**
SIC: **1541** 1542 Industrial buildings & warehouses; commercial & office building contractors

(G-18779)
UNIVAR USA INC
30450 Tracy Rd (43465-9775)
PHONE...............................419 666-7880
Scott Post, *Research*
EMP: 44
SALES (corp-wide): 8.2B **Publicly Held**
SIC: **5169** Industrial chemicals
HQ: Univar Usa Inc.
17411 Ne Union Hill Rd
Redmond WA 98052
425 889-3400

(G-18780)
WESTERN STATES ENVELOPE CO
Also Called: Western States Envelope Label
6859 Commodore Dr (43465-9765)
PHONE...............................419 666-7480
Fax: 419 666-8402
Shelly Hinkle, *Manager*
Jim Johnson, *Manager*
EMP: 70
SALES (corp-wide): 207.3MM **Privately Held**
WEB: www.westernstatesenvelope.com
SIC: **5112** 2677 Envelopes; envelopes
PA: Western States Envelope Company
4480 N 132nd St
Butler WI 53007
262 781-5540

(G-18781)
WOLFES ROOFING INC
6568 State Route 795 (43465-9760)
PHONE...............................419 666-6233
Fax: 419 666-9402
David A Wolfe, *President*
David Wolfe, *Project Mgr*
Becky Petrusky, *Bookkeeper*
Frank Wright, *Manager*
EMP: 40
SALES (est): 4.8MM **Privately Held**
SIC: **1761** Roofing contractor

Waldo
Marion County

(G-18782)
COLUMBUS DISTRIBUTING COMPANY
Delmar Distributing
6829 Waldo Delaware Rd (43356-9115)
PHONE...............................740 726-2211
Fax: 740 726-2860
Tom Wallsmith, *Manager*
EMP: 50
SALES (corp-wide): 96.7MM **Privately Held**
WEB: www.delmardistributing.com
SIC: **5181** Beer & other fermented malt liquors
PA: The Columbus Distributing Company
4949 Freeway Dr E
Columbus OH 43229
614 846-1000

(G-18783)
OHIGRO INC (PA)
6720 Gillette Rd (43356-9105)
P.O. Box 196 (43356-0196)
PHONE...............................740 726-2429
Fax: 740 726-2574
Jerry Ward, *President*
Jerry A Ward, *President*
James H Ward, *Vice Pres*
David Fierbaugh, *Plant Mgr*
Jeffrey Ward, *Treasurer*
EMP: 36
SQ FT: 9,600
SALES: 14.8MM **Privately Held**
WEB: www.ohigro.com
SIC: **5191** 5261 2875 0723 Fertilizer & fertilizer materials; fertilizer; fertilizers, mixing only; crop preparation services for market

Walnut Creek
Holmes County

(G-18784)
COBLENTZ DISTRIBUTING INC
Also Called: Walnut Creek Foods
2641 State R 39 39 R (44687)
P.O. Box 240 (44687-0240)
PHONE...............................330 852-2888
Fax: 330 852-2363
Dennis Schladach, *Branch Mgr*
EMP: 110
SALES (est): 15.7MM
SALES (corp-wide): 176.8MM **Privately Held**
SIC: **5143** Cheese
PA: Coblentz Distributing, Inc.
3850 State Route 39
Millersburg OH 44654
800 543-6848

(G-18785)
WALNUT CREEK CHOCOLATE COMPANY
Also Called: Coblentz Chocolate Co
4917 State Rte 515 (44687)
PHONE...............................330 893-2995
Fax: 330 893-3913
Jason Coblentz, *President*
Orpha Miller, *Store Mgr*
EMP: 25
SQ FT: 2,000
SALES (est): 4.6MM **Privately Held**
SIC: **2064** 2066 5149 5441 Chocolate covered dates; fruit, chocolate covered (except dates); chocolate candy, solid; chocolate; candy

(G-18786)
WALNUT HILLS INC
4748 Olde Pump St (44687)
P.O. Box 127 (44687-0127)
PHONE...............................330 852-2457
Fax: 330 893-3908
Levi Troyer, *CEO*
David Miller, *President*
Paula Miller, *Sls & Mktg Exec*
Kim Boyd, *Director*
Rachel Gerber, *Social Dir*
EMP: 150
SQ FT: 36,000
SALES (est): 5.7MM **Privately Held**
WEB: www.walnuthillsliving.com
SIC: **8052** 8051 Intermediate care facilities; skilled nursing care facilities

Walnut Hills
Hamilton County

(G-18787)
GREATER CINCINNATI BEHAVIORAL (PA)
1501 Madison Rd (45206-1706)
PHONE...............................513 354-7000
Fax: 513 354-7115
Jeff O'Neil, *CEO*
David Meek, *Business Mgr*
Steve Goldsberry, *Vice Pres*
Roger Rosenberger, *VP Opers*
Tawnya Dunn, *CFO*
EMP: 325
SQ FT: 25,000
SALES: 28.2MM **Privately Held**
WEB: www.gcbhs.com
SIC: **8322** Social service center

(G-18788)
GREATER CINCINNATI BEHAVIORAL
1501 Madison Rd Fl 1 (45206-1706)
PHONE...............................513 755-2203
Roy Hardison, *Finance*
Jeff O'Neil, *Branch Mgr*
EMP: 98
SALES (corp-wide): 28.2MM **Privately Held**
WEB: www.gcbhs.com
SIC: **8322** Social service center
PA: Greater Cincinnati Behavioral Health Services
1501 Madison Rd
Walnut Hills OH 45206
513 354-7000

Walton Hills
Cuyahoga County

(G-18789)
GOODYEAR TIRE & RUBBER COMPANY
7230 Northfield Rd (44146-6157)
PHONE...............................440 735-9910
Fax: 440 735-9913
Chad Nelson, *Branch Mgr*
EMP: 25
SALES (corp-wide): 15.3B **Publicly Held**
WEB: www.wingfootct.com
SIC: **7534** Tire retreading & repair shops
PA: The Goodyear Tire & Rubber Company
200 E Innovation Way
Akron OH 44316
330 796-2121

(G-18790)
MASON STRUCTURAL STEEL INC
Also Called: Mason Steel
7500 Northfield Rd (44146-6187)
PHONE...............................440 439-1040
Fax: 440 439-1077
Leonard N Polster, *CEO*
Keith Polster, *President*
J Moldaver, *Principal*
Joseph Patchan, *Principal*
Sol W Wyman, *Principal*
EMP: 100 EST: 1958
SQ FT: 75,000
SALES (est): 30.1MM **Privately Held**
WEB: www.masonsteel.com
SIC: **3441** 5031 5074 Fabricated structural metal; doors & windows; window frames, all materials; fireplaces, prefabricated

(G-18791)
SMITH & OBY COMPANY
7676 Northfield Rd (44146-5519)
PHONE...............................440 735-5333
Michael A Brandt, *CEO*
Ronald Vranich, *President*
Gary Y Klie, *Chairman*
Charles E Caye, *Exec VP*
Matthew P Kittelberger, *Vice Pres*
EMP: 80 EST: 1898
SQ FT: 6,500
SALES (est): 21MM **Privately Held**
WEB: www.smithandoby.com
SIC: **1711** Warm air heating & air conditioning contractor; ventilation & duct work contractor; plumbing contractors

Wapakoneta
Auglaize County

(G-18792)
COM NET INC
13888 County Road 25a (45895-8316)
PHONE...............................419 739-3100
Fax: 419 739-3154
Tim Berelsman, *CEO*
Nathan Zehringer, *Project Mgr*
Andrew McNeal, *Purchasing*
David Frey, *CFO*
Eric Damman, *Treasurer*
EMP: 60
SALES: 14.8MM **Privately Held**
WEB: www.cniteam.com
SIC: **4813** 7375 ; information retrieval services

(G-18793)
COUNTY OF AUGLAIZE
Auglaize Acres Nursing Home
13093 Infirmary Rd (45895-9325)
PHONE...............................419 738-3816
Fax: 419 738-6684
Kim Sudhoff, *Business Mgr*
Tina Reynolds, *QA Dir*
Robert Coverstone, *Financial Exec*
Bob Coverstone, *Manager*
Sandi Coiner, *Food Svc Dir*
EMP: 125 **Privately Held**
WEB: www.augmrdd.org

GEOGRAPHIC SECTION

SIC: **8059** 9121 Nursing home, except skilled & intermediate care facility; legislative bodies
PA: County Of Auglaize
209 S Blackhoof St # 201
Wapakoneta OH 45895
419 739-6710

(G-18794)
CY SCHWIETERMAN INC
10097 Kohler Rd (45895-8232)
PHONE.....................................419 753-2566
Michael Schwieterman, *President*
EMP: 40
SALES (est): **1.4MM** Privately Held
SIC: **1521** 1522 Single-family housing construction; residential construction

(G-18795)
FRATERNAL ORDER EAGLES INC
Also Called: Foe 691
25 E Auglaize St (45895-1503)
P.O. Box 1977 (45895-0977)
PHONE.....................................419 738-2582
Fax: 419 738-6121
Jack Piercefield, *Manager*
Jack Peircefield, *Manager*
EMP: 26
SALES (corp-wide): **11MM** Privately Held
WEB: www.fraternalorderofeagles.tribe.net
SIC: **8641** Fraternal associations
HQ: Fraternal Order Of Eagles Inc.
1623 Gateway Cir
Grove City OH 43123
614 883-2200

(G-18796)
FROST ROOFING INC
2 Broadway St (45895-2056)
PHONE.....................................419 739-2701
Jj Smithey, *President*
Chad Dunlap, *Business Mgr*
Marty Borchers, *Administration*
EMP: 65
SQ FT: 200,000
SALES (est): **8MM** Privately Held
WEB: www.frost-roofing.com
SIC: **1761** Roofing contractor

(G-18797)
GARDENS AT WAPAKONETA
Also Called: Trans Healthcare
505 Walnut St (45895-1868)
PHONE.....................................419 738-0725
Fax: 419 738-0724
Debbie McElroy, *Director*
EMP: 31 EST: 1999
SALES (est): **1.4MM** Privately Held
SIC: **8051** Convalescent home with continuous nursing care

(G-18798)
HCF OF WAPAKONETA INC
Also Called: Wapakoneta Manor
1010 Lincoln Hwy (45895-9347)
PHONE.....................................419 738-3711
Fax: 419 738-5688
Josiah Osborn, *Financial Exec*
Elaine Steinke, *Persnl Dir*
Josiah Meyer, *Manager*
Amy Shilling, *Director*
Amy Johnson, *Nursing Dir*
EMP: 99
SALES (est): **2.6MM** Privately Held
SIC: **8051** Convalescent home with continuous nursing care

(G-18799)
HELP ME GROW
214 S Wagner Ave (45895-1714)
PHONE.....................................419 738-4773
Charlotte Axe, *Director*
EMP: 28
SALES (est): **331.4K** Privately Held
SIC: **8322** Youth self-help agency

(G-18800)
JPMORGAN CHASE BANK NAT ASSN
801 Defiance St (45895-1020)
PHONE.....................................419 739-3600
Rob Armentrout, *Branch Mgr*
Sandy Truesdale, *Branch Mgr*
EMP: 26
SALES (corp-wide): **99.6B** Publicly Held
WEB: www.chase.com
SIC: **6021** National commercial banks
HQ: Jpmorgan Chase Bank, National Association
1111 Polaris Pkwy
Columbus OH 43240
614 436-3055

(G-18801)
LIMA MEMORIAL HOSPITAL LA
1251 Lincoln Hwy (45895-7356)
PHONE.....................................419 738-5151
Joy Brown, *Branch Mgr*
EMP: 380
SALES (est): **270.4K**
SALES (corp-wide): **189.6MM** Privately Held
SIC: **8062** General medical & surgical hospitals
HQ: Lima Memorial Hospital
1001 Bellefontaine Ave
Lima OH 45804
419 228-3335

(G-18802)
LIMA SUPERIOR FEDERAL CR UN
Also Called: Superior Financial Services
202 Willipie St (45895-1919)
PHONE.....................................419 738-4512
Fax: 419 738-4514
Steve Boroff, *VP Opers*
Phil Buell, *Branch Mgr*
EMP: 50
SALES (est): **2.7MM**
SALES (corp-wide): **18.2MM** Privately Held
WEB: www.limasuperiorfederalcreditunion.com
SIC: **6062** State credit unions, not federally chartered
PA: Lima Superior Federal Credit Union
4230 Elida Rd
Lima OH 45807
419 223-9746

(G-18803)
LOWES HOME CENTERS LLC
1340 Bellefontaine St (45895-9776)
PHONE.....................................419 739-1300
Fax: 419 739-1303
Rich Phillips, *Branch Mgr*
EMP: 158
SALES (corp-wide): **68.6B** Publicly Held
SIC: **5211** 5031 5722 5064 Lumber & other building materials; building materials, exterior; building materials, interior; household appliance stores; electrical appliances, television & radio
HQ: Lowe's Home Centers, Llc
1605 Curtis Bridge Rd
Wilkesboro NC 28697
336 658-4000

(G-18804)
MILLERS TEXTILE SERVICES INC
1002 Bellefontaine St (45895-9701)
P.O. Box 239 (45895-0239)
PHONE.....................................419 738-3552
Fax: 419 738-4075
Bob Hager, *Branch Mgr*
EMP: 68
SALES (corp-wide): **21.9MM** Privately Held
WEB: www.millerstextile.com
SIC: **7213** 5113 Uniform supply; patterns, paper
PA: Miller's Textile Services, Inc.
520 Commerce Rd
Wapakoneta OH
419 738-3551

(G-18805)
OHIO DEPARTMENT TRANSPORTATION
Also Called: Hwy Garage
511 Converse Dr (45895)
PHONE.....................................419 738-4214
Fax: 419 497-6981
Ted Hemleben, *Manager*
Ted Hemlaven, *Manager*
EMP: 25 Privately Held
SIC: **9621** 1611 Regulation, administration of transportation; ; highway & street maintenance
HQ: Ohio Department Of Transportation
1980 W Broad St
Columbus OH 43223

(G-18806)
PETERSON CONSTRUCTION COMPANY
18817 State Route 501 (45895-9392)
P.O. Box 2058 (45895-0558)
PHONE.....................................419 941-2233
Fax: 419 941-2244
Donald J Bergfeld, *President*
Douglas J Crusey, *Vice Pres*
Ty Bergfeld, *Project Mgr*
EMP: 150
SQ FT: 5,000
SALES (est): **83.9MM** Privately Held
SIC: **1542** 1629 Commercial & office building, new construction; institutional building construction; school building construction; waste water & sewage treatment plant construction

(G-18807)
S & S MANAGEMENT INC
Also Called: Holiday Inn
1510 Saturn Dr (45895-9782)
PHONE.....................................567 356-4151
Philip M Valentine, *President*
EMP: 30
SALES (est): **1MM**
SALES (corp-wide): **8.6MM** Privately Held
SIC: **7011** 5812 7999 Hotels; eating places; pool parlor
PA: S & S Management Inc
550 Folkerth Ave 100
Sidney OH 45365
937 498-9645

(G-18808)
TED RUCK CO INC
101 N Wood St (45895-1661)
P.O. Box 1327, Hilliard (43026-6327)
PHONE.....................................419 738-2613
Fax: 419 738-3611
Todd Ruck, *President*
Mike Ruck, *General Mgr*
EMP: 50
SQ FT: 2,000
SALES (est): **3.1MM** Privately Held
SIC: **4212** 7538 Mail carriers, contract; general truck repair

(G-18809)
TRI COUNTY VISITNG NRS PRVT
803 Brewfield Dr (45895-9394)
PHONE.....................................419 738-7430
Donna Grimm, *Owner*
EMP: 30
SALES (est): **505.5K** Privately Held
WEB: www.comhealthpro.org
SIC: **8082** Visiting nurse service

(G-18810)
TSC COMMUNICATIONS INC
Also Called: Telephone Service Company
2 Willipie St (45895-1969)
P.O. Box 408 (45895-0408)
PHONE.....................................419 739-2200
Lonnie D Pedersen, *President*
EMP: 49
SQ FT: 40,000
SALES: **20MM**
SALES (corp-wide): **15.5MM** Privately Held
WEB: www.brighthosting.net
SIC: **4813** 4812 7375 ; paging services; information retrieval services
PA: Telephone Service Company
2 Willipie St
Wapakoneta OH 45895
419 739-2200

(G-18811)
TSC TELEVISION INC
2 Willipie St (45895-1969)
P.O. Box 408 (45895-0408)
PHONE.....................................419 941-6001
Terrance Schwieterman, *CEO*
Lonnie Pederson, *President*
Clint Conover, *Vice Pres*
Tim Tremer, *Admin Sec*
EMP: 56 EST: 1996
SALES (est): **2.3MM** Privately Held
SIC: **4841** 4813 Cable television services; telephone communication, except radio

(G-18812)
WAPAKONETA YMCA
1100 Defiance St (45895-1022)
PHONE.....................................419 739-9622
Fax: 419 739-9623
Joshua Little, *CEO*
Lisa Atkins, *Director*
Sarah Finkelmeier, *Program Dir*
EMP: 55
SALES (est): **540.7K** Privately Held
WEB: www.wapakymca.org
SIC: **8641** 8661 Youth organizations; religious organizations

Warren
Trumbull County

(G-18813)
ACUTE CARE HOMENURSING SERVICE
Also Called: A C Homenursing
1577 Woodland St Ne (44483-5301)
PHONE.....................................216 271-9100
Fax: 216 429-9343
Dave Miller, *Director*
EMP: 32 Privately Held
SIC: **8082** Visiting nurse service
PA: Acute Care Homenursing Service Inc
5266 State Route 45
Rome OH 44085

(G-18814)
AIR MANAGEMENT GROUP LLC
Also Called: Avalon Inn and Resort
1 American Way Ne 20 (44485-5531)
PHONE.....................................330 856-1900
Fax: 330 856-2248
Merry H Pieper, *Principal*
John Kouvas, *Principal*
Klareen Sebbio, *Admin Sec*
EMP: 75
SALES (est): **3.7MM** Privately Held
SIC: **7011** Hotels

(G-18815)
AJAX TOCCO MAGNETHERMIC CORP (HQ)
1745 Overland Ave Ne (44483-2860)
PHONE.....................................330 372-8511
Fax: 330 372-8644
Thomas Illencik, *President*
Keith Anderson, *General Mgr*
Gary Andrews, *General Mgr*
John Caruso, *General Mgr*
Chun Lee, *General Mgr*
◆ EMP: 200
SQ FT: 200,000
SALES (est): **18.8MM**
SALES (corp-wide): **1.4B** Publicly Held
WEB: www.ajaxtocco.com
SIC: **3567** 7699 3612 Metal melting furnaces, industrial: electric; industrial machinery & equipment repair; electric furnace transformers
PA: Park-Ohio Holdings Corp.
6065 Parkland Blvd Ste 1
Cleveland OH 44124
440 947-2000

(G-18816)
AMERICAN WASTE MGT SVCS INC
Also Called: Awms
1 American Way Ne (44484-5531)
PHONE.....................................330 856-8800
Kenneth McMahon, *President*
Mark Cawthorne, *Vice Pres*
Tim Coxson, *Treasurer*
Bunny Bronson, *Credit Staff*
John Pichi, *Sales Mgr*
EMP: 25
SQ FT: 3,000
SALES (est): **6.3MM**
SALES (corp-wide): **55.8MM** Publicly Held
WEB: www.awmsi.com
SIC: **4212** Hazardous waste transport

Warren - Trumbull County (G-18817)
GEOGRAPHIC SECTION

PA: Avalon Holdings Corporation
1 American Way Ne
Warren OH 44484
330 856-8800

(G-18817)
ANDERSON AND DUBOSE INC (PA)
Also Called: ANDERSON-DUBOSE CO, THE
5300 Tod Ave Sw (44481-9767)
PHONE.................440 248-8800
Fax: 440 248-6208
Warren Anderson, *President*
Larry Burkhart, *Transptn Dir*
Terry Love, *Transptn Dir*
John Dettorre, *Opers Staff*
Sylvia Miller, *Accountant*
EMP: 70
SQ FT: 55,000
SALES: 518.2MM **Privately Held**
WEB: www.anderson-dubose.com
SIC: 5142 5141 Packaged frozen goods; groceries, general line

(G-18818)
ATLAS RECYCLING INC
1420 Burton St Se (44484-5129)
P.O. Box 2037 (44484-0037)
PHONE.................800 837-1520
Martin L Wilhelm, *President*
Scott A Wilhelm, *Corp Secy*
Candy Wilhelm, *Purch Mgr*
EMP: 40
SQ FT: 6,200
SALES (est): 7.3MM
SALES (corp-wide): 476MM **Privately Held**
WEB: www.atlasrecycling.com
SIC: 5051 Metals service centers & offices
PA: Metalico, Inc.
135 Dermody St
Cranford NJ 07016
908 497-9610

(G-18819)
ATTITUDES NEW INC
1543 Westview Dr Ne (44483-5254)
PHONE.................330 856-1143
Deneen Genaro, *President*
EMP: 26
SQ FT: 3,567
SALES (est): 770K **Privately Held**
SIC: 7231 Manicurist, pedicurist

(G-18820)
AUTO WAREHOUSING CO INC
1950 Halloock Young (44481)
P.O. Box 757, North Jackson (44451-0757)
PHONE.................330 824-5149
Jim Zdanczewski, *General Mgr*
EMP: 50
SALES (corp-wide): 153.3MM **Privately Held**
SIC: 7549 Automotive maintenance services
PA: Auto Warehousing Co., Inc.
2810 Marshall Ave Ste B
Tacoma WA 98421
253 719-1700

(G-18821)
AUTUMN INDUSTRIES INC (PA)
518 Perkins Jones Rd Ne (44483-1849)
PHONE.................330 372-5002
Fax: 330 372-3699
Sandra N Clark, *President*
Michael T Carney, *Senior VP*
Tammy Birch, *Credit Staff*
Amy Sailor, *Info Tech Mgr*
EMP: 47
SQ FT: 20,000
SALES: 11.5MM **Privately Held**
SIC: 4213 4212 Liquid petroleum transport, non-local; liquid haulage, local

(G-18822)
AVALON GOLF AND CNTRY CLB INC
1 American Way Ne (44484-5531)
PHONE.................330 856-8898
Ronald E Klingle, *Principal*
Avalon Club,
EMP: 75

SALES (est): 2.5MM
SALES (corp-wide): 55.8MM **Publicly Held**
SIC: 7997 Golf club, membership
PA: Avalon Holdings Corporation
1 American Way Ne
Warren OH 44484
330 856-8800

(G-18823)
AVALON HOLDINGS CORPORATION (PA)
1 American Way Ne (44484-5531)
PHONE.................330 856-8800
Ronald E Klingle, *Ch of Bd*
Kenneth J McMahon, *President*
Bryan P Saksa, *CFO*
Clifford P Davis, *CTO*
Frances R Klingle, *Officer*
EMP: 55
SQ FT: 37,000
SALES: 55.8MM **Publicly Held**
WEB: www.avalonholdings.com
SIC: 4953 7999 7991 4724 Hazardous waste collection & disposal; golf services & professionals; golf, pitch-n-putt; physical fitness facilities; travel agencies

(G-18824)
AVALON INN SERVICES INC
9519 E Market St (44484-5599)
PHONE.................330 856-1900
Fax: 330 856-2488
Thomas Keegan, *President*
John Kouvas, *Manager*
EMP: 154
SALES (est): 2.9MM **Privately Held**
WEB: www.avaloninn.com
SIC: 7011 5813 Hotel, franchised; cocktail lounge

(G-18825)
AVALON LAKES GOLF INC (HQ)
Also Called: Avalon Lakes Pro Shop
1 American Way Ne (44484-5531)
PHONE.................330 856-8898
Fax: 330 856-8482
Jeff Shaffer, *President*
Mike Ferry, *Opers Staff*
EMP: 36
SALES (est): 5.4MM
SALES (corp-wide): 55.8MM **Publicly Held**
WEB: www.avalonlakesgolf.com
SIC: 7992 Public golf courses
PA: Avalon Holdings Corporation
1 American Way Ne
Warren OH 44484
330 856-8800

(G-18826)
AVALON RESORT AND SPA LLC
9519 E Market St (44484-5511)
PHONE.................330 856-1900
Bryan Saksa, *CFO*
Bunny Bronson, *Credit Mgr*
EMP: 99
SQ FT: 50,000
SALES (est): 441.1K
SALES (corp-wide): 55.8MM **Publicly Held**
SIC: 7011 Hotels & motels
PA: Avalon Holdings Corporation
1 American Way Ne
Warren OH 44484
330 856-8800

(G-18827)
AVI FOOD SYSTEMS INC (PA)
2590 Elm Rd Ne (44483-2997)
PHONE.................330 372-6000
Fax: 330 372-6485
Anthony J Payiavlas, *CEO*
John Payiavlas, *Ch of Bd*
Patrice Kouvas, *President*
Bill Parker, *President*
Robert A Sunday, *President*
EMP: 120
SQ FT: 11,000
SALES (est): 661.7MM **Privately Held**
WEB: www.avifoodsystems.com
SIC: 5962 5812 8742 Merchandising machine operators; caterers; food & beverage consultant

(G-18828)
BARRISTERS OF OHIO LLC
223 Niles Cortland Rd Se # 1 (44484-5720)
PHONE.................330 898-5600
Alfred R Corsi Jr, *Branch Mgr*
EMP: 25
SALES (corp-wide): 5MM **Privately Held**
SIC: 6361 Title insurance
PA: Barristers Of Ohio, Llc
6000 Parkland Blvd Fl 2
Cleveland OH 44124
216 986-7600

(G-18829)
BERK ENTERPRISES INC (PA)
Also Called: Berk Paper & Supply
1554 Thomas Rd Se (44484-5119)
P.O. Box 2187 (44484-0187)
PHONE.................330 369-1192
Fax: 330 369-6279
Robert A Berk, *President*
Franks Valley, *CFO*
Regina Perry, *Controller*
Mike Ricci, *Administration*
▲ **EMP:** 81 **EST:** 1976
SQ FT: 240,000
SALES (est): 61.5MM **Privately Held**
WEB: www.berkleysquare.net
SIC: 5113 Bags, paper & disposable plastic

(G-18830)
BIG BLUE TRUCKING INC
518 Perkins Jones Rd Ne (44483-1849)
PHONE.................330 372-1421
Sandra N Clark, *President*
EMP: 47
SALES (est): 7.7MM **Privately Held**
SIC: 4212 Local trucking, without storage

(G-18831)
BROTHERS AUTO TRANSPORT LLC
2188 Lyntz Townline Rd Sw (44481-8702)
PHONE.................330 824-0082
Dan Carney, *CEO*
EMP: 50 **Privately Held**
SIC: 4789 Pipeline terminal facilities, independently operated
PA: Brothers Auto Transport, Llc
593 Male Rd
Wind Gap PA 18091

(G-18832)
BROWNING-FERRIS INDUSTRIES LLC
1901 Pine Ave Se (44483-6541)
PHONE.................330 393-0385
Paul Stacharczyk, *Manager*
EMP: 53
SALES (corp-wide): 10B **Publicly Held**
WEB: www.alliedwaste.com
SIC: 4953 4212 Medical waste disposal; local trucking, without storage
HQ: Browning-Ferris Industries, Llc
18500 N Allied Way # 100
Phoenix AZ 85054
480 627-2700

(G-18833)
CHILDRENS REHABILITATION CTR
885 Howland Wilson Rd Ne (44484-2100)
PHONE.................330 856-2107
Fax: 330 856-2107
Robert C Foster, *Director*
EMP: 38
SQ FT: 14,000
SALES: 1MM **Privately Held**
SIC: 8093 8351 Rehabilitation center, outpatient treatment; child day care services

(G-18834)
CLEAN BREAK INC
300 Muirwood Dr Ne (44484-4110)
PHONE.................330 638-5648
David Eppley, *President*
EMP: 35
SALES: 750K **Privately Held**
SIC: 7349 Janitorial service, contract basis

(G-18835)
COLE-VALLEY MOTOR CO (PA)
4111 Elm Rd Ne (44483)
P.O. Box 1500 (44482-1500)
PHONE.................330 372-1665
David Cole, *Partner*
Tom Cole, *Partner*
William Cowin, *Financial Exec*
EMP: 62
SQ FT: 25,000
SALES (est): 29.1MM **Privately Held**
WEB: www.colecars.com
SIC: 5511 5531 7538 Automobiles, new & used; automotive parts; automotive accessories; general automotive repair shops

(G-18836)
COMMUNITY HEALTH SYSTEMS INC
Also Called: Valley Care Health System
1350 E Market St (44483-6608)
PHONE.................330 841-9011
Cindy Burns, *Principal*
Justin Snyder, *Pharmacist*
Jenny Yiu, *Manager*
Teresa Wilson, *Director*
Briana Esteban,
EMP: 85
SALES (est): 6.6MM **Privately Held**
SIC: 8082 Home health care services

(G-18837)
COMMUNITY SKILLED HEALTH CARE
1320 Mahoning Ave Nw (44483-2002)
PHONE.................330 373-1160
Fax: 330 392-3644
Pam Liposky, *CFO*
Kathy Hartwiger, *Human Res Dir*
Boone Christ, *Manager*
Tony Kulisc, *CIO*
Leslie Terry, *Director*
EMP: 200
SQ FT: 42,000
SALES: 9.4MM **Privately Held**
WEB: www.communityskilled.com
SIC: 8051 Convalescent home with continuous nursing care

(G-18838)
COMMUNITY SOLUTIONS ASSN
320 High St Ne (44481-1222)
PHONE.................330 394-9090
Fax: 330 394-8160
Amy Bugos, *Accounts Mgr*
Ken Lloyd, *Director*
EMP: 40 **EST:** 2000
SALES: 1.3MM **Privately Held**
WEB: www.commissioners.co.trumbull.oh.us
SIC: 8093 8322 Mental health clinic, outpatient; substance abuse clinics (outpatient); individual & family services

(G-18839)
COUNTRYSIDE VETERINARY SERVICE
Also Called: R L Baugher, Dvm
4680 Mahoning Ave Nw (44483-1419)
PHONE.................330 847-7337
Fax: 330 847-8538
R L Baugher, *Treasurer*
EMP: 30
SALES (corp-wide): 6.6MM **Privately Held**
SIC: 0742 Veterinarian, animal specialties
PA: Countryside Veterinary Service
8004 State Route 7
Kinsman OH 44428
330 876-5555

(G-18840)
COUNTY OF TRUMBULL
Also Called: Trumbull County Engineers
650 N River Rd Nw (44483-2255)
PHONE.................330 675-2640
Randy Smith, *Engineer*
John Latell, *Director*
EMP: 74 **Privately Held**
WEB: www.co.trumbull.oh.us
SIC: 1611 9111 Highway & street maintenance; county supervisors' & executives' offices

▲ = Import ▼=Export
◆ =Import/Export

GEOGRAPHIC SECTION

Warren - Trumbull County (G-18867)

PA: County Of Trumbull
160 High St Nw
Warren OH 44481
330 675-2420

(G-18841)
COV-RO INC
3900 E Market St Ste 1 (44484-4708)
PHONE..................330 856-3176
Albert Covelli, *President*
Rebecca Palcisco, *Office Mgr*
Michael Marando, *Admin Sec*
EMP: 40 **EST:** 1964
SQ FT: 16,000
SALES: 536K **Privately Held**
SIC: 7699 7623 5661 Restaurant equipment repair; air conditioning repair; refrigeration repair service; men's shoes; women's shoes

(G-18842)
COVELLI FAMILY LTD PARTNERSHIP (PA)
Also Called: Panera Bread
3900 E Market St (44484-4708)
PHONE..................330 856-3176
Kevin Ricci, *Managing Prtnr*
EMP: 38
SALES (est): 28.2MM **Privately Held**
SIC: 5812 5461 6794 Cafe; bread; franchises, selling or licensing

(G-18843)
CRAWFORD & COMPANY
6752 Brookhollow Dr Sw (44481-8645)
PHONE..................330 652-3296
EMP: 38
SALES (corp-wide): 1.1B **Privately Held**
WEB: www.crawfordandcompany.com
SIC: 8741 Management services
PA: Crawford & Company
5335 Triangle Pkwy Ofc C
Peachtree Corners GA 30092
404 300-1000

(G-18844)
CREATIVE LEARNING WORKSHOP (PA)
2460 Elm Rd Ne Ste 500 (44483-2949)
PHONE..................330 393-5929
Jeanne Flaviani, *Bookkeeper*
Joanne Vila, *Nursing Dir*
Caren Painter,
EMP: 43
SALES (est): 7.2MM **Privately Held**
SIC: 8331 Vocational rehabilitation agency

(G-18845)
CUSTOM PKG & INSPECTING INC
5232 Tod Ave Sw Ste 3 (44481-9729)
PHONE..................330 399-8961
Fax: 330 395-2990
Christopher Harrison, *President*
EMP: 40
SQ FT: 8,000
SALES (est): 1.6MM **Privately Held**
SIC: 7389 Packaging & labeling services

(G-18846)
DACAS NURSING SYSTEMS INC
Also Called: Forum At Homes
8747 Squires Ln Ne (44484-1649)
PHONE..................330 884-2530
Fax: 330 841-5483
Walter J Pishkur, *President*
Michael Steelman, *Exec Dir*
Michael Seelman, *Director*
EMP: 200
SALES: 19.1K **Privately Held**
SIC: 8082 Home health care services

(G-18847)
DAWN INCORPORATED (PA)
106 E Market St Ste 505 (44481-1103)
PHONE..................330 652-7711
Dawn Ochman, *President*
Masood Hamid, *Mktg Dir*
Niloufer Patel, *Director*
EMP: 25
SQ FT: 2,500
SALES: 8MM **Privately Held**
SIC: 1541 Industrial buildings & warehouses

(G-18848)
DELPHI AUTOMOTIVE SYSTEMS LLC
Also Called: Delphi Packard Electrical
1265 N River Rd Ne (44483-2352)
PHONE..................248 724-5953
Stephanie Pennel, *Branch Mgr*
EMP: 25 **Privately Held**
SIC: 7549 8712 Automotive maintenance services; architectural services
HQ: Delphi Automotive Systems, Llc
5725 Delphi Dr
Troy MI 48098

(G-18849)
DIAMOND ROOFING SYSTEMS LLP
8031 E Market St Ste 6 (44484-2200)
PHONE..................330 856-2500
Amanda Marsco, *Director*
EMP: 30 **EST:** 2013
SQ FT: 2,000
SALES: 5MM **Privately Held**
SIC: 1761 Roofing contractor

(G-18850)
DIANE SAUER CHEVROLET INC
700 Niles Rd Se (44483-5951)
PHONE..................330 373-1600
Diane Sauer, *President*
Bill Rutledge, *General Mgr*
Brian Grischow, *Business Mgr*
John Maze, *Sales Mgr*
Matthew Sauer, *Sales Associate*
EMP: 80
SALES (est): 25MM **Privately Held**
WEB: www.dianesauerchevy.com
SIC: 5511 7513 7359 Automobiles, new & used; truck leasing, without drivers; business machine & electronic equipment rental services

(G-18851)
DO CUT SALES & SERVICE INC
Also Called: Do-Cut True Value
3375 Youngstown Rd Se (44484-5299)
PHONE..................330 533-9878
Fax: 330 533-2901
Dante Terzigni, *Manager*
EMP: 30
SQ FT: 17,000
SALES (corp-wide): 7.5MM **Privately Held**
WEB: www.docut.com
SIC: 5072 5191 5251 5261 Hardware; garden supplies; hardware; lawnmowers & tractors
PA: Do Cut Sales & Service Inc
3375 Youngstown Rd Se
Warren OH 44484
330 369-2345

(G-18852)
E AND P WAREHOUSE SERVICES LTD
1666 Mcmyler St Nw (44485-2703)
PHONE..................330 898-4800
George Halkias,
Anna Halkias,
EMP: 25
SQ FT: 35,000
SALES: 200K **Privately Held**
SIC: 4225 General warehousing & storage

(G-18853)
EASTERN MEDICAL EQUIPMENT CO
Also Called: E M S Medical Equipment
523 E Market St (44481-1211)
PHONE..................330 394-5555
David Logero, *President*
Kristy Motter, *Manager*
EMP: 30 **EST:** 1976
SALES (est): 4.6MM **Privately Held**
SIC: 5047 7699 Hospital equipment & furniture; hospital equipment repair services

(G-18854)
EASTERN OHIO P-16
4314 Mahoning Ave Nw (44483-1931)
PHONE..................330 675-7623
Anthony Paglia, *Principal*
Stephanie L Shaw, *Exec Dir*
EMP: 50

SALES (est): 4.4MM **Privately Held**
SIC: 6021 National commercial banks

(G-18855)
EATON GROUP GMAC REAL ESTATE
Also Called: GMAC Realestate
382 Niles Cortland Rd Ne (44484-1940)
PHONE..................330 726-9999
Mary Lou Maloy, *President*
Pamela Dubaj, *Purch Agent*
Neal Eaton, *Manager*
EMP: 31
SALES (est): 1.5MM **Privately Held**
WEB: www.janetswhite.com
SIC: 6531 Real estate agents & managers

(G-18856)
ERIE ISLAND RESORT AND MARINA
150 E Market St Ste 300 (44481-1141)
PHONE..................419 734-9117
John Gronvall,
EMP: 50
SALES (est): 3.5MM **Privately Held**
WEB: www.erieislandsresort.com
SIC: 4493 Boat yards, storage & incidental repair

(G-18857)
FAIRHAVEN SHELTERED WORKSHOP
455 Educational Hwy Nw (44483-1967)
PHONE..................330 847-7275
Fax: 330 847-6009
Rick Mistovich, *Manager*
David Sekerak, *Manager*
EMP: 150
SALES (corp-wide): 4.5MM **Privately Held**
SIC: 8331 Sheltered workshop
PA: Fairhaven Sheltered Workshop
45 North Rd
Niles OH 44446
330 505-3644

(G-18858)
FOUR SEASON CAR WASH
Also Called: Four Seasons Car Wash
437 Trumbull Ave Se (44483-6338)
PHONE..................330 372-4163
Fax: 330 372-4932
Jack Harned, *President*
Jeff Bell, *Principal*
EMP: 35
SQ FT: 6,400
SALES: 620K **Privately Held**
SIC: 7542 Carwashes

(G-18859)
GILLETTE ASSOCIATES LP
3310 Elm Rd Ne (44483-2614)
PHONE..................330 372-1960
Nadile Stein, *Partner*
Charles E Stein, *General Ptnr*
EMP: 90
SQ FT: 27,947
SALES (est): 4.1MM **Privately Held**
SIC: 8059 Nursing home, except skilled & intermediate care facility

(G-18860)
GILLETTE NURSING HOME INC
3310 Elm Rd Ne (44483-2662)
PHONE..................330 372-1960
Fax: 330 372-6132
Charles E Stein, *President*
Janet L Stein, *Vice Pres*
Nazim Jaffer, *Director*
Patty Currignton, *Hlthcr Dir*
EMP: 95
SQ FT: 42,000
SALES (est): 5.7MM **Privately Held**
SIC: 8052 8051 Intermediate care facilities; skilled nursing care facilities

(G-18861)
HAYS ENTERPRISES INC
Also Called: Carts of America
1901 Ellsworth Bailey Rd (44481-9283)
PHONE..................330 299-8639
Fax: 330 824-3776
Doris Hays, *President*
Jay Hays, *Exec VP*
Brian Maloy, *Sales Mgr*

EMP: 25
SQ FT: 22,000
SALES: 1.9MM **Privately Held**
WEB: www.haysenterprises.com
SIC: 7699 5199 Shopping cart repair; general merchandise, non-durable

(G-18862)
HOMETOWN URGENT CARE
1997 Niles Cortland Rd Se (44484-3037)
PHONE..................330 505-9400
Tammy Russell, *President*
EMP: 125
SALES (corp-wide): 73.2MM **Privately Held**
SIC: 8011 Medical centers
PA: Hometown Urgent Care
2400 Corp Exchange Dr # 102
Columbus OH 43231
614 505-7633

(G-18863)
HOPE CTR FOR CNCER CARE WARREN
1745 Niles Crtlnd Rd Ne Ste 5 (44484)
PHONE..................330 856-8600
Bruce Giambattifta, *Principal*
Terry Piperata, *Administration*
EMP: 60
SALES (est): 253.5K **Privately Held**
SIC: 8011 8093 Oncologist; specialty outpatient clinics

(G-18864)
HOWLAND CORNERS TWN & CTRY VET
Also Called: Towne & Country Vet Clinic
8000 E Market St (44484-2228)
PHONE..................330 856-1862
Fax: 330 856-6585
Rufus Sparks, *President*
Charles Moxley, *Vice Pres*
EMP: 30 **EST:** 1975
SALES (est): 1.6MM **Privately Held**
SIC: 0742 0741 Veterinarian, animal specialties; animal hospital services, livestock

(G-18865)
INTERNATIONAL STEEL GROUP
2234 Main Street Ext Sw (44481-9602)
PHONE..................330 841-2800
Rodney Mott, *President*
Jeff Foster, *General Mgr*
EMP: 135
SALES (est): 16.8MM **Privately Held**
WEB: www.internationalsteelgroup.com
SIC: 3312 1011 Blast furnaces & steel mills; iron ores
HQ: Arcelormittal Usa Llc
1 S Dearborn St Ste 1800
Chicago IL 60603
312 346-0300

(G-18866)
J V HANSEL INC
Also Called: Institutional Foods
6055 Louise Ct Nw (44481-9006)
PHONE..................330 716-0806
Fax: 330 373-0736
John J Hansel, *President*
Connie Radich, *Admin Sec*
EMP: 26
SQ FT: 26,000
SALES (est): 5MM **Privately Held**
SIC: 5113 5411 5141 5451 Industrial & personal service paper; grocery stores; groceries, general line; dairy products stores; party favors

(G-18867)
JACK GIBSON CONSTRUCTION CO
2460 Parkman Rd Nw (44485-1757)
PHONE..................330 394-5280
Fax: 330 393-6515
John C Gibson Jr, *CEO*
E James Breese, *President*
John C Gibson Sr, *Chairman*
Marilyn E Hughes, *Corp Secy*
Bill Butch, *Vice Pres*
EMP: 100
SQ FT: 27,000

Warren - Trumbull County (G-18868)

SALES: 15.4MM **Privately Held**
WEB: www.jackgibsonconstruction.com
SIC: 1542 1629 8741 1541 School building construction; industrial plant construction; construction management; industrial buildings & warehouses

(G-18868)
JARO TRANSPORTATION SVCS INC (PA)
975 Post Rd Nw (44483-2083)
P.O. Box 1890 (44482-1890)
PHONE..................330 393-5659
James S Ffy, *CEO*
Terry Fiorina, *Corp Secy*
Rick Pompeo, *Vice Pres*
Tom Halula, *Maintenance Dir*
Tammy Steele, *Controller*
EMP: 79
SQ FT: 5,000
SALES: 39.4MM **Privately Held**
WEB: www.jarotrans.com
SIC: 4213 Trucking, except local

(G-18869)
KIDZ BY RIVERSIDE INC
421 Main Ave Sw (44481-1015)
PHONE..................330 392-0700
Crystal Anderson, *Administration*
EMP: 26
SALES (est): 1MM **Privately Held**
SIC: 8351 Child day care services

(G-18870)
KING COLLISION INC
2000 N River Rd Ne (44483-2530)
PHONE..................330 372-3242
Fax: 330 372-0063
Douglas Fenstermaker, *President*
EMP: 25
SALES (est): 1.6MM **Privately Held**
WEB: www.kingcollision.net
SIC: 7532 Body shop, automotive

(G-18871)
KMART CORPORATION
541 Perkins Jones Rd Ne (44483-1848)
PHONE..................330 372-6688
Fax: 330 372-3400
Rich Shafer, *Manager*
EMP: 556
SALES (corp-wide): 16.7B **Publicly Held**
WEB: www.kmart.com
SIC: 4225 General warehousing & storage
HQ: Kmart Corporation
3333 Beverly Rd
Hoffman Estates IL 60179
847 286-2500

(G-18872)
LAFARGE NORTH AMERICA INC
Also Called: Lordstown Cnstr Recovery
6205 Newton Fls Bailey Rd (44481-9763)
PHONE..................330 393-5656
Fax: 330 399-6731
Tim Wirtz, *Plant Mgr*
EMP: 35
SALES (corp-wide): 26.4B **Privately Held**
WEB: www.lafargenorthamerica.com
SIC: 4953 Non-hazardous waste disposal sites
HQ: Lafarge North America Inc.
8700 W Bryn Mawr Ave
Chicago IL 60631
773 372-1000

(G-18873)
LANDMARK AMERICA INC (PA)
1268 N River Rd Ne Ste 1 (44483-2371)
P.O. Box 4302 (44482-4302)
PHONE..................330 372-6800
Rokki Rogan, *CEO*
Robert Delisio, *President*
Scott Baird,
EMP: 32
SALES (est): 2.3MM **Privately Held**
SIC: 7389 Financial services

(G-18874)
LEEDA SERVICES INC (PA)
1441 Parkman Rd Nw (44485-2156)
PHONE..................330 392-6006
Winifred Hosking, *President*
EMP: 30

SALES (est): 4.6MM **Privately Held**
SIC: 8052 Home for the mentally retarded, with health care

(G-18875)
LEWIS PRICE REALTY CO
8031 E Market St (44484-2200)
PHONE..................330 856-1911
Dennis Lewis, *Partner*
Patricia Potts, *Partner*
Gordon Price, *Partner*
EMP: 25
SALES (est): 1.2MM **Privately Held**
WEB: www.noas.com
SIC: 6512 6531 Commercial & industrial building operation; shopping center, property operation only; real estate brokers & agents

(G-18876)
LOWES HOME CENTERS LLC
940 Niles Cortland Rd Se (44484-2537)
PHONE..................330 609-8000
Fax: 330 609-8018
Tom Markovich, *Human Res Dir*
Jack Swedzo, *Manager*
Richard Forsman, *Manager*
EMP: 150
SQ FT: 1,315
SALES (corp-wide): 68.6B **Publicly Held**
SIC: 5211 5031 5722 5064 Home centers; building materials, exterior; building materials, interior; household appliance stores; electrical appliances, television & radio
HQ: Lowe's Home Centers, Llc
1605 Curtis Bridge Rd
Wilkesboro NC 28697
336 658-4000

(G-18877)
MAIN LITE ELECTRIC CO INC
3000 Sferra Ave Nw (44483-2266)
P.O. Box 828 (44482-0828)
PHONE..................330 369-8333
Toni M Harnar, *President*
Colleen Beil, *Vice Pres*
Kevin D Beil, *CFO*
Tracy Raschilla, *Office Mgr*
John H Harnar, *Admin Sec*
EMP: 43
SQ FT: 13,000
SALES (est): 4.9MM **Privately Held**
SIC: 1731 1623 General electrical contractor; electric power line construction

(G-18878)
MASTERPIECE PAINTING COMPANY
546 Washington St Ne (44483-4933)
PHONE..................330 395-9900
Fax: 330 395-1415
John Handerhan, *CEO*
Elaine Gustovich, *Manager*
EMP: 25
SQ FT: 3,305
SALES (est): 1.6MM **Privately Held**
WEB: www.masterpiecepaintingcompany.com
SIC: 1721 Interior commercial painting contractor; exterior commercial painting contractor; industrial painting

(G-18879)
MED STAR EMGNCY MDCL SRV (PA)
Also Called: Med Star Ems
1600 Youngstown Rd Se (44484-4251)
P.O. Box 2156 (44484-0156)
PHONE..................330 394-6611
Fax: 330 369-8026
Joseph W Robinson, *President*
EMP: 35
SQ FT: 4,800
SALES (est): 1.5MM **Privately Held**
SIC: 4119 Ambulance service

(G-18880)
MERCY HEALTH
8600 E Market St Ste 5 (44484-2375)
PHONE..................330 841-4406
Fax: 330 505-0090
EMP: 48
SALES (corp-wide): 4.2B **Privately Held**
SIC: 8734 Testing laboratories

PA: Mercy Health
1701 Mercy Health Pl
Cincinnati OH 45237
513 639-2800

(G-18881)
MERCY HEALTH YOUNGSTOWN LLC
Also Called: St. Joseph Warren Hospital
667 Eastland Ave Se (44484-4503)
PHONE..................330 841-4000
Fax: 330 841-4482
Kathy Cook, *President*
Steve Pavlak, *Manager*
EMP: 900
SALES (corp-wide): 4.2B **Privately Held**
SIC: 8062 Hospital, affiliated with AMA residency
HQ: Mercy Health Youngstown Llc
1044 Belmont Ave
Youngstown OH 44504

(G-18882)
MOCHA HOUSE INC (PA)
467 High St Ne (44481-1226)
PHONE..................330 392-3020
Fax: 330 394-8809
George N Liakaris, *President*
Nick G Liakaris, *Vice Pres*
Bill M Axiotis, *Treasurer*
EMP: 35
SQ FT: 10,000
SALES (est): 1.1MM **Privately Held**
WEB: www.mochahouse.com
SIC: 5812 5461 7299 Coffee shop; delicatessen (eating places); bakeries; banquet hall facilities

(G-18883)
MSSL CONSOLIDATED INC
8640 E Market St (44484-2346)
PHONE..................330 766-5510
Vc Sehgal, *Chairman*
Sukant Gupta, *Vice Pres*
Laksh V Sehgal, *Director*
EMP: 409
SALES: 202MM
SALES (corp-wide): 1B **Privately Held**
SIC: 6719 Investment holding companies, except banks
PA: Motherson Sumi Systems Limited
Sector-127, Plot No.1, 11th Floor
Noida UP 20130
120 667-9500

(G-18884)
NATIONAL MENTOR HOLDINGS INC
4451 Mahoning Ave Nw (44483-1977)
PHONE..................234 806-5361
EMP: 1278
SALES (corp-wide): 741.5MM **Privately Held**
SIC: 8082 Home health care services
PA: National Mentor Holdings, Inc.
313 Congress St Fl 5
Boston MA 02210
617 790-4800

(G-18885)
NEOCAP/CBCF
Also Called: Northeast Ohio Community Alter
411 Pine Ave Se (44483-5706)
PHONE..................330 675-2669
Rachel Defazio, *Opers Mgr*
Sierra Bowman, *Case Mgr*
Kenya Garner, *Case Mgr*
Jeigh Maynard, *Case Mgr*
Antonette Washington, *Case Mgr*
EMP: 35 EST: 1998
SALES: 3.7MM **Privately Held**
SIC: 8744 Correctional facility

(G-18886)
NORTH WOOD REALTY
Also Called: Century 21
1985 Niles Cortland Rd Se (44484-3037)
PHONE..................330 856-3915
Marlin Palich, *Manager*
Bernice Marino, *Real Est Agnt*
EMP: 40
SALES (corp-wide): 5.5MM **Privately Held**
WEB: www.mikeshomecenter.com
SIC: 6531 Real estate agent, residential

PA: North Wood Realty
1315 Boardman Poland Rd # 7
Youngstown OH 44514
330 423-0837

(G-18887)
NORTHEAST OHIO ADOPTION SVCS
5000 E Market St Ste 26 (44484-2259)
PHONE..................330 856-5582
John Hostetler, *QA Dir*
Beth Ward, *Controller*
Cynthia Deal, *Exec Dir*
Cary Sanders, *Planning*
Jamie Hetrick, *Recruiter*
EMP: 25
SALES: 1.3MM **Privately Held**
SIC: 8322 Adoption services

(G-18888)
NORTHEAST OHIO COMMUNIC
Also Called: Neocom
2910 Youngstown Rd Se (44484-5259)
PHONE..................330 399-2700
Eric Tobin, *CEO*
Linda Money, *President*
EMP: 60
SQ FT: 12,000
SALES (est): 2.5MM **Privately Held**
WEB: www.rooms-r-us.com
SIC: 8748 Communications consulting

(G-18889)
NORTHEAST OHIO DUKES
4289 N Park Ave (44483-1531)
PHONE..................330 360-0968
Raymond Kohn, *Principal*
EMP: 40 EST: 2010
SALES (est): 168.9K **Privately Held**
SIC: 7929 Entertainers & entertainment groups

(G-18890)
NORTHEAST OHIO ORTHOPEDICS
1552 North Rd Se Ste 101 (44484-2957)
PHONE..................330 856-1070
Kenneth Jones, *Principal*
Paula Robertson, *Persnl Mgr*
Brittany Simon, *Receptionist Se*
EMP: 25
SALES (est): 1.2MM **Privately Held**
SIC: 8099 Medical services organization

(G-18891)
PSY-CARE INC
8577 E Market St (44484-2390)
PHONE..................330 856-6663
Fax: 330 856-1581
Douglas Darnall, *CEO*
Ronald Yendrek, *Med Doctor*
Terrence Heltzel, *Director*
EMP: 30
SALES (est): 1.9MM **Privately Held**
SIC: 8093 8011 Mental health clinic, outpatient; psychiatric clinic

(G-18892)
PTI QLITY CNTNMENT SLTIONS LLC
Also Called: Pti Qcs
5232 Tod Ave Sw (44481-8727)
PHONE..................330 306-0125
Dee Mitchell, *Branch Mgr*
EMP: 37
SALES (corp-wide): 32.9MM **Privately Held**
SIC: 4785 Inspection services connected with transportation
PA: Pti Quality Containment Solutions Llc
18615 Sherwood St
Detroit MI 48234
313 365-3999

(G-18893)
REM ELECTRONICS SUPPLY CO INC (PA)
525 S Park Ave (44483-5731)
P.O. Box 831 (44482-0831)
PHONE..................330 373-1300
Fax: 330 392-1810
Robert E Miller Sr, *CEO*
Randall Miller, *President*
Richard Cowin, *Vice Pres*
Cesar Alviar, *Sales Staff*

EMP: 25
SQ FT: 30,000
SALES (est): 9.6MM Privately Held
SIC: 5065 Electronic parts

(G-18894)
SABER HEALTHCARE GROUP LLC
Also Called: White Oak Manor
1926 Ridge Ave Se (44484-2821)
PHONE..................330 369-4672
Fax: 330 369-2367
Tina Rush, Branch Mgr
EMP: 36
SALES (corp-wide): 68.5MM Privately Held
SIC: 8051 Skilled nursing care facilities
PA: Saber Healthcare Group, L.L.C.
  26691 Richmond Rd Frnt
  Bedford OH 44146
  216 292-5706

(G-18895)
SANESE SERVICES INC (PA)
2590 Elm Rd Ne (44483-2904)
P.O. Box 110 (44482-0110)
PHONE..................614 436-1234
Fax: 614 436-1592
Ralph Sanese, President
Robert A Sunday, President
Doris Sanese, Principal
Scott Church, District Mgr
Nathan Cristino, District Mgr
EMP: 300
SQ FT: 100,000
SALES (est): 118.9MM Privately Held
WEB: www.sanese.com
SIC: 5962 5812 7389 Food vending machines; eating places; cafeteria; caterers; coffee service

(G-18896)
SANFREY FREIGHT SERVICES INC
695 Summit St Nw Ste 1 (44485-2800)
P.O. Box 1770 (44482-1770)
PHONE..................330 372-1883
William Sanfrey, President
EMP: 25
SALES (corp-wide): 3.3MM Privately Held
SIC: 4213 4212 Trucking, except local; contract haulers; local trucking, without storage
PA: Sanfrey Freight Services Inc
  1256 Elm Rd Ne
  Warren OH 44483
  330 372-1883

(G-18897)
SEVEN SEVENTEEN CREDIT UN INC (PA)
3181 Larchmont Ave Ne (44483-2498)
PHONE..................330 372-8100
Fax: 330 372-5526
Gary L Soukenik, CEO
Jerome J McGee, CFO
Karen De Salvo, VP Mktg
George Barcikoski, Manager
Camile Farve, Manager
EMP: 250
SQ FT: 40,000
SALES: 40.1MM Privately Held
SIC: 6163 6062 Loan brokers; state credit unions, not federally chartered

(G-18898)
SEVEN SEVENTEEN CREDIT UN INC
100 Brewster Dr Se (44484-2462)
PHONE..................330 372-8100
Andy Wollam, Branch Mgr
EMP: 25
SALES (corp-wide): 40.1MM Privately Held
SIC: 6163 6062 Loan brokers; state credit unions, not federally chartered
PA: Seven Seventeen Credit Union, Inc.
  3181 Larchmont Ave Ne
  Warren OH 44483
  330 372-8100

(G-18899)
SIGNATURE HEALTHCARE LLC
2473 North Rd Ne (44483-3054)
PHONE..................330 372-1977
Crys Blankenship, Branch Mgr
EMP: 102 Privately Held
SIC: 8099 Blood related health services
PA: Signature Healthcare, Llc
  12201 Bluegrass Pkwy
  Louisville KY 40299

(G-18900)
SIMS BUICK-G M C TRUCK INC
Also Called: Sims GMC Trucks
3100 Elm Rd Ne (44483-2698)
PHONE..................330 372-3500
Fax: 330 372-6636
William Sims, President
Jason Wells, Business Mgr
Kenneth Sims, Corp Secy
Vito Maggio, Sales Mgr
Greg Clear, Sales Staff
EMP: 54
SQ FT: 36,000
SALES (est): 20.5MM Privately Held
WEB: www.simsnissan.com
SIC: 5511 5012 Automobiles, new & used; trucks, tractors & trailers: new & used; automobiles & other motor vehicles

(G-18901)
SPECTRUM MGT HOLDG CO LLC
Also Called: Time Warner
8600 E Market St Ste 4 (44484-2375)
PHONE..................330 856-2343
Daryl Morrison, General Mgr
Shawn Sturgeon, Sales Engr
Dan Beblo, Manager
EMP: 83
SALES (corp-wide): 41.5B Publicly Held
SIC: 4841 Cable television services
HQ: Spectrum Management Holding Company, Llc
  400 Atlantic St
  Stamford CT 06901
  203 905-7801

(G-18902)
STEEL VALLEY CONSTRUCTION CO
135 Pine Ave Se Ste 203 (44481-1249)
PHONE..................330 392-8391
Lois Shockey, President
David Shay, Vice Pres
Victor Shockey, Admin Sec
EMP: 25
SQ FT: 1,800
SALES (est): 2.4MM Privately Held
WEB: www.steelvalley.org
SIC: 1521 1711 New construction, single-family houses; general remodeling, single-family houses; plumbing contractors

(G-18903)
STERICYCLE INC
1901 Pine Ave Se (44483-6541)
PHONE..................330 393-0370
Steve Pantano, Manager
EMP: 75
SALES (corp-wide): 3.5B Publicly Held
WEB: www.stericycle.com
SIC: 4953 Medical waste disposal
PA: Stericycle, Inc.
  28161 N Keith Dr
  Lake Forest IL 60045
  847 367-5910

(G-18904)
STEWARD TRUMBULL MEM HOSP INC
1350 E Market St (44483-6608)
P.O. Box 1269 (44482-1269)
PHONE..................330 841-9011
Fax: 330 841-9315
Ronald Bierman, President
Shawn Dilmore, COO
Steven Snyder, CFO
Robert Leon, Pharmacist
William Reeves, Med Doctor
EMP: 1000 EST: 1984
SQ FT: 600,000
SALES: 130.5MM
SALES (corp-wide): 2.3B Privately Held
SIC: 8062 8049 General medical & surgical hospitals; physical therapist
PA: Steward Health Care System Llc
  111 Huntington Ave # 1800
  Boston MA 02199
  617 419-4700

(G-18905)
SU-JON ENTERPRISES
2448 Weir Rd Ne (44483-2516)
P.O. Box 1190 (44482-1190)
PHONE..................330 372-1100
John Bellando, Co-Owner
Billie Sue Bellando, Co-Owner
EMP: 28
SALES (est): 2MM Privately Held
SIC: 4212 Local trucking, without storage

(G-18906)
SURGERY CENTER HOWLAND LTD
1934 Niles Cortland Rd Ne (44484-1055)
PHONE..................330 609-7874
Fax: 330 609-6616
Theresa Turgeon, Manager
Raymundo A Castillejo, Anesthesiology
Kathy Cook, Administration
EMP: 27
SALES (est): 1.3MM Privately Held
SIC: 8011 Ambulatory surgical center

(G-18907)
TRUE2FORM COLLISION REPAIR CTR (PA)
3924 Youngstown Rd Se (44484-2839)
PHONE..................330 399-6659
Fax: 330 399-5428
Rex Dunn, President
Clark Plucinski, Exec VP
Rick Paukstitus, Vice Pres
John Sanders, Vice Pres
Gary Erculiani, Site Mgr
EMP: 29
SALES (est): 13.9MM Privately Held
WEB: www.true2form.com
SIC: 7532 Collision shops, automotive

(G-18908)
TRUMBALL CNTY FIRE CHIEFS ASSN
Also Called: Trumball Cnty Hzardous Mtl Bur
640 N River Rd Nw (44483-2255)
PHONE..................330 675-6602
Fred Youngbluth, President
Rick Bauman, Vice Pres
EMP: 60
SALES (est): 2.3MM Privately Held
SIC: 8322 Emergency social services

(G-18909)
TRUMBULL CMNTY ACTION PROGRAM (PA)
1230 Palmyra Rd Sw (44485-3730)
PHONE..................330 393-2507
Fax: 330 393-4197
Van Nelson, Vice Pres
Wanda Nelson, Program Dir
Ms Mamie C Hunt, Bd of Directors
Henry Angelo, Bd of Directors
Phyllis Cayson, Bd of Directors
EMP: 48
SALES (est): 7.1MM Privately Held
SIC: 8331 Work experience center

(G-18910)
TRUMBULL COUNTY ENGINEERING (PA)
650 N River Rd Nw (44483-2255)
PHONE..................330 675-2640
Fax: 330 675-2642
Randy Smith, Principal
Dan Elston, Technology
Jennifer Bindas, Executive Asst
Jennifer Drummond, Admin Sec
Heather Richard, Admin Sec
EMP: 60
SALES (est): 7.6MM Privately Held
SIC: 8711 Engineering services

(G-18911)
TRUMBULL COUNTY ONE STOP
280 N Park Ave (44481-1123)
PHONE..................330 675-2000
Fax: 330 399-7824
William Turner, Principal
EMP: 99
SALES (est): 1.6MM Privately Held
SIC: 8322 Social service center

(G-18912)
TRUMBULL HOUSING DEV CORP
4076 Youngstown Rd Se # 101 (44484-3367)
PHONE..................330 369-1533
Heidi Scanlon, Manager
Donald Emerson, Director
EMP: 75
SALES (est): 601K Privately Held
SIC: 8748 9531 Urban planning & consulting services; housing programs

(G-18913)
TRUMBULL INDUSTRIES INC
850 Bronze Rd Ne (44483-2759)
PHONE..................330 393-6624
Jason Crawford, MIS Dir
EMP: 34
SALES (corp-wide): 136.6MM Privately Held
SIC: 5074 Plumbing & hydronic heating supplies
PA: Trumbull Industries, Inc.
  400 Dietz Rd Ne
  Warren OH 44483
  330 393-6624

(G-18914)
TRUMBULL MANUFACTURING INC
400 Dietz Rd Ne (44483-2749)
P.O. Box 30 (44482-0030)
PHONE..................330 393-6624
Murray Miller, President
Dennis Parks, General Mgr
Julian Lehman, Treasurer
Dennis Sabol, VP Human Res
Chick Haering, VP Sales
▲ EMP: 89
SQ FT: 16,000
SALES (est): 14.8MM Privately Held
SIC: 3432 3433 5074 Plumbing fixture fittings & trim; heating equipment, except electric; plumbing & hydronic heating supplies

(G-18915)
TRUMBULL MEM HOSP FOUNDATION
Also Called: Mahoning Vly Hmtology Oncology
1350 E Market St (44483-6608)
PHONE..................330 841-9376
Fax: 330 841-9911
Charles Johns, President
Henry Sebold, CFO
EMP: 3000
SALES (est): 725.3K Privately Held
SIC: 8011 Hematologist

(G-18916)
TRUMBULL SPECIAL COURIER INC
346 Willard Ave Se (44483-6238)
PHONE..................330 841-0074
Mike Quinlan, President
Mike Quilin, Manager
EMP: 30
SALES (est): 1.4MM Privately Held
SIC: 7389 Courier or messenger service

(G-18917)
TURN AROUND GROUP INC
Also Called: Sunrise Industries Harps Jantr
1512 Phoenix Rd Ne (44483-2855)
PHONE..................330 372-0064
Jeff Swogger, President
Randy Swogger, Vice Pres
EMP: 80
SALES: 1.6MM Privately Held
WEB: www.tagdn.com
SIC: 7349 Janitorial service, contract basis

Warren - Trumbull County

(G-18918)
ULTIMATE BUILDING MAINTENANCE
3229 Youngstown Rd Se (44484-5265)
P.O. Box 4313 (44482-4313)
PHONE...................330 369-9771
James Dobson, *CEO*
EMP: 100
SALES (est): 1.4MM **Privately Held**
WEB: www.ultimatemaintenance.com
SIC: 7349 Building maintenance services

(G-18919)
US SAFETYGEAR INC (PA)
5001 Enterprise Dr Nw (44481-8713)
P.O. Box 309, Leavittsburg (44430-0309)
PHONE...................330 898-1344
Tarry A Alberini, *President*
Jeremy Krol, *Buyer*
John C Conley, *CFO*
Dave Sherock, *Sales Staff*
Jason Russo, *Web Dvlpr*
EMP: 40
SQ FT: 102,000
SALES (est): 21.9MM **Privately Held**
WEB: www.ohioglove.com
SIC: 5084 5199 Safety equipment; packaging materials

(G-18920)
VALLEY TITLE & ESCRO AGENCY
2833 Elm Rd Ne (44483-2603)
PHONE...................330 392-6171
Fax: 330 394-5507
Gilbert L Rieger, *President*
EMP: 30
SALES (est): 1.2MM **Privately Held**
SIC: 6512 Nonresidential building operators

(G-18921)
VIBRA HEALTHCARE LLC
1350 E Market St (44483-6608)
PHONE...................330 675-5555
EMP: 71
SALES (corp-wide): 320.2MM **Privately Held**
SIC: 8062 General medical & surgical hospitals
PA: Vibra Healthcare, Llc
4600 Lena Dr
Mechanicsburg PA 17055
717 591-5700

(G-18922)
VWC LIQUIDATION COMPANY LLC
1701 Henn Pkwy Sw (44481-8656)
PHONE...................330 372-6776
Ron Mascarella, *Vice Pres*
Jamie Mallery, *Project Mgr*
Justin Best, *Controller*
James E Collins Sr, *Mng Member*
Daniel J McCarthy,
EMP: 130
SQ FT: 50,000
SALES (est): 23.4MM **Privately Held**
WEB: www.vistawindowco.com
SIC: 1799 5031 Window treatment installation; lumber, plywood & millwork

(G-18923)
WARREN CITY BOARD EDUCATION
Also Called: Transportation Center
600 Roanoke Ave Sw (44483-6473)
PHONE...................330 841-2265
Phyllis Linderman, *Principal*
EMP: 42
SALES (corp-wide): 88.8MM **Privately Held**
SIC: 4226 Special warehousing & storage
PA: Warren City Board Of Education
105 High St Ne
Warren OH 44481
330 841-2321

(G-18924)
WARREN DRMATOLOGY ALLERGIES PC
Also Called: Warren Dermatology and Allergy
735 Niles Cortland Rd Se (44484-2475)
PHONE...................330 856-6365
Fax: 330 609-5088
Kristen Lynch, *President*
EMP: 25
SALES (est): 1.8MM **Privately Held**
SIC: 8011 Dermatologist

(G-18925)
WARREN HOUSING DEVELOPMENT
4076 Youngstown Rd Se # 101 (44484-3367)
PHONE...................330 369-1533
Donald Emerson, *Director*
EMP: 80
SALES (est): 2.7MM **Privately Held**
SIC: 6552 Subdividers & developers

(G-18926)
WEE CARE DAYCARE
Also Called: Lads and Lasses
1145 Niles Cortland Rd Se (44484-2542)
PHONE...................330 856-1313
Fax: 330 856-5364
Donna McGrach, *Owner*
Sheri Baily, *Director*
EMP: 25
SALES (est): 318.1K **Privately Held**
WEB: www.ladsandlasses.com
SIC: 8351 Preschool center

(G-18927)
WILLIAM ZAMARELLI REALTORS
Also Called: Zamarelli William Relators
8700 E Market St Ste 6 (44484-2340)
PHONE...................330 856-2299
Fax: 330 856-9596
William Zamarelli, *President*
EMP: 31
SALES (est): 1.8MM **Privately Held**
WEB: www.williamzamarelli.com
SIC: 6531 Real estate agent, residential

(G-18928)
WJ SERVICE CO INC (PA)
Also Called: W J Alarm Service
2592 Elm Rd Ne (44483-2904)
PHONE...................330 372-5040
Fax: 330 372-7104
James Paylavlas, *President*
Tony Paylavlas, *Corp Secy*
Nicholas Paylavlas, *Vice Pres*
EMP: 45
SQ FT: 29,704
SALES (est): 5MM **Privately Held**
WEB: www.osscompanies.com
SIC: 7349 7382 Janitorial service, contract basis; security systems services

(G-18929)
WSB REHABILITATION SVCS INC
4329 Mahoning Ave Nw B (44483-1974)
PHONE...................330 847-7819
Kelly Jenkins, *Branch Mgr*
EMP: 540
SALES (corp-wide): 26.6MM **Privately Held**
SIC: 8093 Rehabilitation center, outpatient treatment
PA: Wsb Rehabilitation Services, Inc.
510 W Main St Ste B
Canfield OH 44406
330 533-1338

(G-18930)
XPO LOGISTICS FREIGHT INC
6700 Muth Rd Sw (44481-9276)
PHONE...................330 824-2242
Farris Scott, *Manager*
EMP: 150
SALES (corp-wide): 15.3B **Publicly Held**
WEB: www.con-way.com
SIC: 4213 Contract haulers
HQ: Xpo Logistics Freight, Inc.
2211 Old Earhart Rd # 100
Ann Arbor MI 48105
734 998-4200

Warrensville Heights
Cuyahoga County

(G-18931)
ARSLANIAN BROS CRPT RUG CLG CO
Also Called: Arslanian Brothers Company
19499 Miles Rd (44128-4109)
PHONE...................216 271-6888
Fax: 216 271-5520
Ted Arslanian, *President*
Henry Arslanian, *Vice Pres*
Armen Arslanian, *Admin Sec*
EMP: 25
SQ FT: 6,000
SALES (est): 2.2MM **Privately Held**
WEB: www.arslanianblind.com
SIC: 7217 Carpet & furniture cleaning on location

(G-18932)
DIVAL INC (PA)
Also Called: W.F. Hann & Sons
26401 Miles Rd (44128-5930)
PHONE...................216 831-4200
Fax: 216 464-2523
Karen Johnson, *President*
Fred Disanto, *Shareholder*
Carl Grassi, *Shareholder*
Jerry Schafer, *Commercial*
EMP: 60
SQ FT: 12,500
SALES (est): 11.9MM **Privately Held**
SIC: 1711 Plumbing contractors; warm air heating & air conditioning contractor; refrigeration contractor

(G-18933)
GRACE HOSPITAL
20000 Harvard Ave (44122-6805)
PHONE...................216 687-1500
EMP: 55
SALES (corp-wide): 17.4MM **Privately Held**
SIC: 8062 Hospital, affiliated with AMA residency
PA: Grace Hospital
2307 W 14th St
Cleveland OH 44113
216 687-1500

(G-18934)
SISTERS OF LITTLE
Also Called: St Mary & Joseph Home
4291 Richmond Rd (44122-6103)
PHONE...................216 464-1222
Fax: 216 591-9255
Anne Donnelly, *President*
Mary Sylvia, *Administration*
EMP: 150
SALES (est): 3.5MM **Privately Held**
SIC: 8051 8052 Skilled nursing care facilities; intermediate care facilities
PA: Little Sisters Of The Poor, Baltimore, Inc.
601 Maiden Choice Ln
Baltimore MD 21228
410 744-9367

(G-18935)
TRICKERATION INC
Also Called: Donegal Bay
26055 Emery Rd Ste E (44128-6211)
PHONE...................216 360-9966
Timothy Hewitt, *President*
Mike Volchko, *Controller*
EMP: 26
SQ FT: 40,000
SALES (est): 4.3MM
SALES (corp-wide): 1.4B **Publicly Held**
WEB: www.pkoh.com.cn
SIC: 5122 Drugs, proprietaries & sundries
HQ: Park-Ohio Industries, Inc.
6065 Parkland Blvd Ste 1
Cleveland OH 44124
440 947-2000

Warsaw
Coshocton County

(G-18936)
ECHOING HILLS VILLAGE INC (PA)
Also Called: Echoing Ridge Residential Ctr
36272 County Road 79 (43844-9770)
PHONE...................740 327-2311
Fax: 740 327-6371
Buddy Busch, *CEO*
Harry C Busch, *President*
John Swanson, *Exec VP*
Dan Wallenhurst, *Purchasing*
Jane Jarrett, *Broker*
EMP: 515
SQ FT: 2,500
SALES (est): 25.3MM **Privately Held**
WEB: www.echoinghillsvillage.org
SIC: 7032 8051 8361 8322 Sporting & recreational camps; mental retardation hospital; residential care; individual & family services; real estate agents & managers

Washington Court Hou
Fayette County

(G-18937)
NB TRUCKING INC
Also Called: Nickle Bakery
1659 Rte 22 E (43160)
PHONE...................740 335-9331
Fax: 740 335-1506
Nickle Bakery, *Owner*
Gary Zingary, *Manager*
EMP: 40
SALES (corp-wide): 205MM **Privately Held**
SIC: 4212 Local trucking, without storage
HQ: Nb Trucking Inc
26 Main St N
Navarre OH 44662

Washington Township
Montgomery County

(G-18938)
L A FITNESS INTL LLC
45 W Alex Bell Rd (45459-3007)
PHONE...................937 439-2795
EMP: 29
SALES (corp-wide): 117.3MM **Privately Held**
SIC: 7991 Physical Fitness Facility
PA: L. A. Fitness International, Llc
3021 Michelson Dr
Irvine CA 92612
949 255-7200

Waterford
Washington County

(G-18939)
LANG MASONRY CONTRACTORS INC
405 Watertown Rd (45786-5248)
PHONE...................740 749-3512
Fax: 740 749-0602
Damian Lang, *President*
Tom Kern, *Project Mgr*
Doug Taylor, *CFO*
Greg Adams, *Manager*
EMP: 70
SALES (est): 12.2MM **Privately Held**
WEB: www.langmasonry.com
SIC: 1741 Stone masonry

(G-18940)
WATERTOWN STEEL COMPANY LLC
405 Watertown Rd (45786-5248)
PHONE...................740 749-3512
Joe Campbell, *Opers Mgr*
Doug Taylor, *Controller*

Ken Funk,
Ed Ewing,
Damien Lang,
EMP: 25
SALES: 2.5MM **Privately Held**
SIC: 1542 Commercial & office building contractors

Waterville
Lucas County

(G-18941)
BROWNING MESONIC COMMUNITY (PA)
8883 Browning Dr (43566-9757)
PHONE..................419 878-4055
Dave Subleski, *Director*
EMP: 35
SQ FT: 350,000
SALES (est): 8.7MM **Privately Held**
SIC: 8361 Home for the aged

(G-18942)
HEALTH CARE RTREMENT CORP AMER
Also Called: Heartland of Waterville
8885 Browning Dr (43566-9701)
PHONE..................419 878-8523
Pat Schumski, *Facilities Dir*
Pam Younglove, *Personnel*
Stephen Bazeley, *Director*
Conni Steffen, *Nursing Dir*
Vivian Kiraly, *Administration*
EMP: 160
SALES (corp-wide): 3.6B **Publicly Held**
WEB: www.hrc-manorcare.com
SIC: 8051 Convalescent home with continuous nursing care
HQ: Health Care And Retirement Corporation Of America
333 N Summit St Ste 103
Toledo OH 43604
419 252-5500

(G-18943)
PARKER-HANNIFIN CORPORATION
Also Called: Fluid Connector Group
1290 Wtrville Monclova Rd (43566-1066)
PHONE..................419 878-7000
Fax: 419 878-7001
Tom Boyer, *Branch Mgr*
Steve Dezort, *Manager*
Katherine Frigmanski, *Supervisor*
EMP: 55
SQ FT: 46,642
SALES (corp-wide): 12B **Publicly Held**
WEB: www.parker.com
SIC: 4225 General warehousing
PA: Parker-Hannifin Corporation
6035 Parkland Blvd
Cleveland OH 44124
216 896-3000

(G-18944)
PER DIEM NURSE STAFFING LLT
18 N 3rd St Lowr (43566-1532)
PHONE..................419 878-8880
Brenda Michalski, *Partner*
EMP: 40
SALES: 1MM **Privately Held**
SIC: 7361 Labor contractors (employment agency)

(G-18945)
SOMETHING SPECIAL LRNG CTR INC (PA)
8251 Wterville Swanton Rd (43566-9725)
PHONE..................419 878-4190
Fax: 419 878-4109
Mary Wolfe, *President*
EMP: 28
SQ FT: 5,000
SALES (est): 2.9MM **Privately Held**
SIC: 8351 Group day care center; nursery school

(G-18946)
SURFACE COMBUSTION INC
1270 Wtrville Monclova Rd (43566-1066)
PHONE..................419 878-8444
Fax: 419 878-0551
Doev Joelson, *Buyer*
Jeff Valuck, *Sales Dir*
Dennis Wolke, *Branch Mgr*
Jerry Wiznewski, *Manager*
EMP: 30
SALES (est): 2MM
SALES (corp-wide): 23.8MM **Privately Held**
WEB: www.surfacecombustion.com
SIC: 4225 General warehousing
PA: Surface Combustion, Inc.
1700 Indian Wood Cir
Maumee OH 43537
419 891-7150

(G-18947)
WATERVILLE CARE LLC
Also Called: ARBORS AT WATERVILLE
555 Anthony Wayne Trl (43566-1516)
PHONE..................419 878-3901
Fax: 419 878-4772
Erin Montag, *Administration*
Elyse Aasen,
EMP: 90
SALES: 4.6MM **Privately Held**
SIC: 8051 Skilled nursing care facilities

Wauseon
Fulton County

(G-18948)
ALANO CLUB INC
Also Called: Fulton County Alano Club
222 S Brunell St (43567-1360)
P.O. Box 1 (43567-0001)
PHONE..................419 335-6211
Fax: 419 335-6211
Kent Bacon, *President*
EMP: 65
SALES: 11.8K **Privately Held**
SIC: 7997 Membership sports & recreation clubs

(G-18949)
COUNTY OF FULTON
Fulton County Engineers
9120 County Road 14 (43567-9669)
PHONE..................419 335-3816
Fax: 419 335-1901
Paul Bieber, *Foreman/Supr*
Frank T Onweller, *Director*
EMP: 25 **Privately Held**
WEB: www.fultoncountyoh.com
SIC: 8711 Engineering services
PA: County Of Fulton
152 S Fulton St Ste 270
Wauseon OH 43567
419 337-9214

(G-18950)
DAVES SAND & STONE INC
Also Called: Greiser Transportation
19230 County Road F (43567-9481)
PHONE..................419 445-9256
Fax: 419 445-1280
David A Grieser, *President*
Jason Grieser, *Vice Pres*
Kathleen Grieser, *Admin Sec*
EMP: 35 **EST:** 1978
SQ FT: 18,000
SALES: 4MM **Privately Held**
SIC: 4212 4213 Dump truck haulage; trucking, except local

(G-18951)
DONS AUTOMOTIVE GROUP LLC
720 N Shoop Ave (43567-1838)
P.O. Box 208 (43567-0208)
PHONE..................419 337-3010
Fax: 419 337-4002
Larry Roush, *Transptn Dir*
Nikki Henry, *Sales Mgr*
Rick Beatty, *Manager*
Jeff Harman, *Manager*
Don Hayati,
EMP: 35
SALES (est): 11.8MM **Privately Held**
SIC: 5511 5521 5012 Automobiles, new & used; used car dealers; automobiles & other motor vehicles

(G-18952)
FOUR COUNTY FAMILY CENTER
7320 State Route 108 A (43567-8200)
PHONE..................800 693-6000
Fax: 419 335-3462
Jeanne Karmol, *Financial Exec*
Linda Condit, *Human Res Mgr*
Robin Foy, *Med Doctor*
Kathy Short, *Exec Dir*
EMP: 30
SALES (est): 1.2MM **Privately Held**
SIC: 8322 Social worker

(G-18953)
FULTON COUNTY HEALTH CENTER
Also Called: Fulton Manor Nursing Home
725 S Shoop Ave (43567-1701)
PHONE..................419 330-2714
Fax: 419 330-2714
Patricia Finn, *CEO*
Larry Heflinger, *Director*
EMP: 111
SALES (corp-wide): 83.7MM **Privately Held**
WEB: www.fulhealth.org
SIC: 8062 8051 General medical & surgical hospitals; skilled nursing care facilities
PA: Fulton County Health Center
725 S Shoop Ave
Wauseon OH 43567
419 335-2015

(G-18954)
FULTON COUNTY HEALTH CENTER
Also Called: Fulton Stress Unit
725 S Shoop Ave (43567-1701)
PHONE..................419 337-8661
Fax: 419 330-2776
EMP: 50
SALES (est): 1.8MM **Privately Held**
SIC: 8093 Specialty Outpatient Clinic

(G-18955)
FULTON COUNTY HEALTH CENTER (PA)
725 S Shoop Ave (43567-1701)
PHONE..................419 335-2015
Fax: 419 330-2602
Patti Finn, *CEO*
Carl Hill, *President*
Jenee Seibert, *Principal*
Bill Nicely, *Materials Dir*
Mike Hurd, *Facilities Mgr*
EMP: 652
SQ FT: 164,276
SALES: 83.7MM **Privately Held**
WEB: www.fulhealth.org
SIC: 8062 General medical & surgical hospitals

(G-18956)
FULTON COUNTY HEALTH DEPT
606 S Shoop Ave (43567-1712)
PHONE..................419 337-6979
Fax: 419 337-0561
Sandy Heising, *Principal*
Michael Oricko, *Commissioner*
Joan Laidlaw, *Exec Dir*
Kim Cupp, *Director*
Harry Murdiff, *Director*
EMP: 40
SALES (est): 2.4MM **Privately Held**
SIC: 9431 8093 Administration of public health programs; ; family planning clinic

(G-18957)
FULTON COUNTY SENIOR CENTER
240 Clinton St (43567-1109)
PHONE..................419 337-9299
Fax: 419 337-9289
Sandra Griggs, *Director*
Sheri Rychener, *Director*
EMP: 50
SALES (est): 1.7MM **Privately Held**
SIC: 8322 Social service center

(G-18958)
HEALTH CARE RTREMENT CORP AMER
Also Called: Heartland of Wauseon
303 W Leggett St (43567-1341)
PHONE..................419 337-3050
Fax: 419 335-1338
Eric Lehman, *Director*
Bill McDaniel, *Administration*
EMP: 50
SALES (corp-wide): 3.6B **Publicly Held**
WEB: www.hrc-manorcare.com
SIC: 8051 Skilled nursing care facilities
HQ: Health Care And Retirement Corporation Of America
333 N Summit St Ste 103
Toledo OH 43604
419 252-5500

(G-18959)
MRS DENNIS POTATO FARM INC
15370 County Road K (43567-8891)
PHONE..................419 335-2778
Fax: 419 335-2793
Suzanne Dennis, *President*
Timothy Dennis, *Corp Secy*
EMP: 30
SQ FT: 27,000
SALES (est): 16.9MM **Privately Held**
SIC: 5148 Potatoes, fresh

(G-18960)
NOFZIGER DOOR SALES INC (PA)
Also Called: Haas Doors
320 Sycamore St (43567-1100)
PHONE..................419 337-9900
Fax: 419 337-5973
Edward L Nofziger, *President*
Carol Nofziger, *Corp Secy*
Dawn Haas, *Vice Pres*
Marty Haas, *Sales Executive*
Ray Rondini, *Manager*
▼ **EMP:** 173
SQ FT: 200,000
SALES (est): 35.1MM **Privately Held**
WEB: www.haasdoor.com
SIC: 3442 1751 5211 Metal doors; garage doors, overhead: metal; garage door, installation or erection; doors, wood or metal, except storm

(G-18961)
QUALITY CLG SVC OF NW OHIO
861 N Fulton St (43567-1054)
P.O. Box 142 (43567-0142)
PHONE..................419 335-9105
Michael Draper, *President*
Linda Draper, *Treasurer*
EMP: 60
SQ FT: 400
SALES (est): 1.9MM **Privately Held**
SIC: 7349 Building cleaning service; building maintenance, except repairs

(G-18962)
SARAS GARDEN
620 W Leggett St (43567-1348)
P.O. Box 150 (43567-0150)
PHONE..................419 335-7272
Fax: 419 335-5564
Bill Frank, *President*
William Frank, *Principal*
Amy Murphy, *Principal*
Matthew Rychener, *Principal*
David Burkholder, *Vice Pres*
EMP: 66
SALES: 3.1MM **Privately Held**
SIC: 8011 Medical centers

(G-18963)
WAUSEON DIALYSIS LLC
721 S Shoop Ave (43567-1729)
PHONE..................419 335-0695
James K Hilger,
EMP: 29
SALES (est): 395.5K **Publicly Held**
WEB: www.davita.com
SIC: 8092 Kidney dialysis centers
PA: Davita Inc.
2000 16th St
Denver CO 80202

Wauseon - Fulton County (G-18964)

(G-18964)
WAUSEON MACHINE & MFG INC (PA)
995 Enterprise Ave (43567-9333)
PHONE.............................419 337-0940
Fax: 419 335-1640
Russell P Dominique, *CEO*
Eric Patty, *President*
Douglas A Weddelman, *Principal*
Cindy Baker, *Purch Agent*
Kelly Markins, *Purchasing*
▲ EMP: 75 EST: 1985
SQ FT: 24,000
SALES (est): 18.4MM **Privately Held**
WEB: www.wauseonmachine.com
SIC: 3599 3441 3559 7629 Machine shop, jobbing & repair; fabricated structural metal; automotive related machinery; electrical repair shops; rolling mill machinery; special dies, tools, jigs & fixtures

Waverly
Pike County

(G-18965)
ALOMIE DIALYSIS LLC
Also Called: Pike County Dialysis
609 W Emmitt Ave (45690-1013)
PHONE.............................740 941-1688
James K Hilger,
EMP: 33 EST: 2014
SALES (est): 348.8K **Publicly Held**
SIC: 8092 Kidney dialysis centers
PA: Davita Inc.
    2000 16th St
    Denver CO 80202

(G-18966)
BRISTOL VILLAGE HOMES
660 E 5th St (45690-1551)
PHONE.............................740 947-2118
Tanya Kim Hahn, *President*
Bob Scaggs, *Exec Dir*
EMP: 29
SALES: 5MM
SALES (corp-wide): 44.4MM **Privately Held**
SIC: 8059 Nursing home, except skilled & intermediate care facility
PA: National Church Residences
    2335 N Bank Dr
    Columbus OH 43220
    614 451-2151

(G-18967)
BUCKEYE COMMUNITY SERVICES INC
Also Called: Grandview Avenue Home
207 Remy Ct (45690-2000)
PHONE.............................740 941-1639
Jeff Adkins, *Director*
EMP: 193
SALES (corp-wide): 10.7MM **Privately Held**
SIC: 8059 Home for the mentally retarded, exc. skilled or intermediate
PA: Buckeye Community Services, Incorporated
    220 Morton St
    Jackson OH 45640
    740 286-5039

(G-18968)
CDM CONSTRUCTORS INC
301 E Emmitt Ave (45690-1339)
PHONE.............................740 947-7500
Thomas G McNeice, *CEO*
Paul R Shea, *President*
Susan Maul, *Principal*
EMP: 99
SALES: 950K **Privately Held**
SIC: 1629 Heavy construction

(G-18969)
CLEARFIELD OHIO HOLDINGS INC
300 E 2nd St (45690-1323)
PHONE.............................740 947-5121
Brian Jonard, *Branch Mgr*
EMP: 67
SALES (corp-wide): 11.4MM **Privately Held**
SIC: 1389 Gas field services
PA: Clearfield Ohio Holdings Inc
    Radnor Corp Ctr Bdg5 40
    Radnor PA 19087
    610 293-0410

(G-18970)
COMMUNITY ACTION COMM PIKE CNT
Also Called: Beaver Clinic
227 Valley View Dr (45690-9135)
PHONE.............................740 947-7726
Fax: 740 947-9354
Gary Roberts, *Exec Dir*
Cheryl Tackett, *Asst Director*
EMP: 36
SALES (corp-wide): 22.3MM **Privately Held**
SIC: 8011 Clinic, operated by physicians
PA: The Community Action Committee Of Pike County
    941 Market St
    Piketon OH 45661
    740 289-2371

(G-18971)
FIRST NATIONAL BANK OF WAVERLY (PA)
107 N Market St (45690-1354)
P.O. Box 147 (45690-0147)
PHONE.............................740 947-2136
Fax: 740 947-8124
Robert E Foster, *President*
Dwight A Massie, *Vice Pres*
Peggy Smith, *Vice Pres*
Lisa Clemmons, *Sales Staff*
Marcia Speedy, *Office Mgr*
EMP: 50 EST: 1901
SQ FT: 17,000
SALES: 6.2MM **Privately Held**
WEB: www.thefirstnational.com
SIC: 6021 National commercial banks

(G-18972)
PIKE CNTY ADULT ACTIVITIES CTR
301 Clough St (45690-1112)
PHONE.............................740 947-7503
Tracy Noble, *Exec Dir*
EMP: 25
SALES: 1.6MM **Privately Held**
SIC: 8399 Health systems agency

(G-18973)
PIKE CNTY RECOVERY COUNCIL INC (PA)
218 E North St (45690-1148)
PHONE.............................740 835-8437
Fax: 740 947-5774
Veronica Black, *Finance Dir*
Pam Johnson, *Exec Dir*
EMP: 38
SALES: 3.1MM **Privately Held**
SIC: 8069 Drug addiction rehabilitation hospital

(G-18974)
PIKE COUNTY YMCA
400 Pride Dr (45690-8979)
PHONE.............................740 947-8862
Fax: 740 947-5616
Tim Conley, *CEO*
John Pennington, *Exec Dir*
Arlie Adams, *Director*
Sharon Christopher, *Director*
Donna Dutcher, *Director*
EMP: 25
SALES: 716.3K **Privately Held**
WEB: www.pikecountyymca.org
SIC: 8641 7991 8351 7032 Youth organizations; physical fitness facilities; child day care services; youth camps; individual & family services

(G-18975)
RES-CARE INC
Also Called: RES Care
212 Saint Anns Ln (45690-1039)
PHONE.............................740 941-1178
EMP: 47
SALES (corp-wide): 24.5B **Privately Held**
SIC: 8052 Home for the mentally retarded, with health care
HQ: Res-Care, Inc.
    9901 Linn Station Rd
    Louisville KY 40223
    502 394-2100

(G-18976)
WAVERLY CARE CENTER INC
Also Called: National Ch Rsdnces Brstol Vlg
444 Cherry St Frnt (45690-1276)
PHONE.............................740 947-2113
Tanya Kim Hahn, *CEO*
Vickie J Nickell, *Executive*
Kay J Smallwood, *Administration*
EMP: 33
SALES (est): 5.7MM
SALES (corp-wide): 44.4MM **Privately Held**
SIC: 8051 Skilled nursing care facilities
PA: National Church Residences
    2335 N Bank Dr
    Columbus OH 43220
    614 451-2151

Wayne
Wood County

(G-18977)
C & G TRANSPORTATION INC
11100 Wayne Rd (43466-9846)
PHONE.............................419 288-2653
Fax: 419 288-1000
Gary Harrison, *President*
Cathy Harrison, *Vice Pres*
EMP: 50
SALES (est): 6.7MM **Privately Held**
SIC: 4212 Local trucking, without storage

(G-18978)
S & D APPLICATION LLC (PA)
158 Church St (43466-9783)
PHONE.............................419 288-3660
Fax: 419 288-3325
Elizabeth Starkey, *Manager*
Doug Miller,
EMP: 36 EST: 1997
SQ FT: 15,000
SALES (est): 13.2MM **Privately Held**
SIC: 0711 5191 Fertilizer application services; fertilizer & fertilizer materials

Waynesburg
Stark County

(G-18979)
ACE ASSEMBLY PACKAGING INC
133 N Mill St (44688-9124)
P.O. Box 55 (44688-0055)
PHONE.............................330 866-9117
Fax: 330 866-9118
Dency S Cilona, *President*
EMP: 30
SALES (est): 2.4MM **Privately Held**
SIC: 7389 3999 Packaging & labeling services; manufacturing industries

(G-18980)
AMERICAN LANDFILL INC
Also Called: Waste Management
7916 Chapel St Se (44688-9700)
PHONE.............................330 866-3265
Fax: 330 866-3709
A Maurice Myers, *Ch of Bd*
Chad Able, *Vice Pres*
Ginger Kaladas, *Credit Staff*
Mike Glenn, *Manager*
Fred Harmon, *Manager*
EMP: 25
SQ FT: 26,000
SALES (est): 3.7MM
SALES (corp-wide): 14.4B **Publicly Held**
WEB: www.americanlandfill.com
SIC: 4953 Sanitary landfill operation
HQ: Waste Management Holdings Inc
    1001 Fannin St Ste 4000
    Houston TX 77002
    713 512-6200

(G-18981)
QUAD AMBULANCE DISTRICT
6930 Minerva Rd Se (44688-9320)
P.O. Box 33 (44688-0033)
PHONE.............................330 866-9847
Fax: 330 866-2310
Steven Van Meter, *Chief*
Steven Vanmeter, *Chief*
EMP: 30
SQ FT: 1,200
SALES: 686.7K **Privately Held**
SIC: 4119 Ambulance service

Waynesville
Warren County

(G-18982)
GRANDMAS GARDENS INC
8107 State Route 48 (45068-8732)
PHONE.............................937 885-2973
Fax: 937 885-6261
Douglas B Rhinehart, *President*
Pat Rhinehart, *Corp Secy*
James B Rhinehart, *Vice Pres*
Donna Trent, *Purch Mgr*
Vicky Meek, *Manager*
EMP: 40
SQ FT: 2,500
SALES (est): 6MM **Privately Held**
SIC: 5261 0782 Nursery stock, seeds & bulbs; landscape contractors

(G-18983)
HOME THE FRIENDS INC
Also Called: Friends Boarding Home
514 High St (45068-9784)
P.O. Box 677 (45068-0677)
PHONE.............................513 897-6050
Fax: 513 897-4872
Sherry Lamb, *Manager*
Woodie Davis, *Director*
Wendy Waters, *Administration*
Wendy Waters-Connell, *Administration*
EMP: 105
SQ FT: 35,000
SALES: 6.7MM **Privately Held**
SIC: 8051 Skilled nursing care facilities

(G-18984)
INTERNATIONAL UNION UNITED AU
8137 Lytle Trails Rd (45068-9231)
PHONE.............................513 897-4939
EMP: 100
SALES (corp-wide): 207.4MM **Privately Held**
SIC: 8631 Labor union
PA: International Union, United Automobile, Aerospace And Agricultural Implement Workers Of Am
    8000 E Jefferson Ave
    Detroit MI 48214
    313 926-5000

(G-18985)
MBI TREE SERVICE LLC
872 Franklin Rd (45068-9504)
PHONE.............................513 926-9857
Luis Paez, *Principal*
EMP: 29
SALES (est): 267.3K **Privately Held**
SIC: 0783 Ornamental shrub & tree services; planting, pruning & trimming services

(G-18986)
QUAKER HEIGHTS NURSING HM INC
Also Called: Quaker Heights Care Community
514 High St (45068-9784)
PHONE.............................513 897-6050
Barry Robbins, *Vice Pres*
Wendy Waters Connell, *Exec Dir*
Paul Opsahl, *Director*
Bruce Hartman, *Social Dir*
Amanda Yauger, *Administration*
EMP: 99
SALES (est): 3.8MM **Privately Held**
SIC: 8051 Convalescent home with continuous nursing care

GEOGRAPHIC SECTION
West Carrollton - Montgomery County (G-19010)

(G-18987)
SYNTHETIC STUCCO CORPORATION
4571 Isaac Ct (45068-8113)
PHONE.....................513 897-9227
Fax: 513 897-5415
Gary W Bentley, *President*
Pamela S Bentley, *Corp Secy*
EMP: 30
SALES (est): 1.6MM **Privately Held**
SIC: 1742 Plastering, plain or ornamental

(G-18988)
VERIZON BUS NETWRK SVCS INC
9073 Lytle Ferry Rd (45068-9494)
PHONE.....................513 897-1501
David Estell, *Manager*
EMP: 25
SQ FT: 81,086
SALES (corp-wide): 126B **Publicly Held**
WEB: www.gtl.net
SIC: 4813 Telephone communication, except radio
HQ: Verizon Business Network Services Inc.
1 Verizon Way
Basking Ridge NJ 07920
908 559-2000

Wellington
Lorain County

(G-18989)
COUNTY OF LORAIN
Also Called: South Lrrain Cnty Amblance Dst
179 E Herrick Ave (44090-1302)
PHONE.....................440 647-5803
Pat Wilkinson, *Manager*
EMP: 25 **Privately Held**
WEB: www.lcmhb.org
SIC: 4119 Ambulance service
PA: County Of Lorain
226 Middle Ave
Elyria OH 44035
440 329-5201

(G-18990)
EDWARD W DANIEL LLC
46950 State Route 18 S (44090-9791)
PHONE.....................440 647-1960
Fax: 216 295-9744
Ken Wrona, *CFO*
Robert Oriti,
Stuart W Cordell,
EMP: 36 EST: 1922
SQ FT: 75,000
SALES (est): 5.8MM **Privately Held**
WEB: www.ewdaniel.com
SIC: 3429 5085 3494 3463 Manufactured hardware (general); industrial supplies; valves & pipe fittings; nonferrous forgings; iron & steel forgings; bolts, nuts, rivets & washers

(G-18991)
ELMS RETIREMENT VILLAGE INC
136 S Main St Rear (44090-3301)
PHONE.....................440 647-2414
Fax: 440 647-9004
Anthony Sprenger, *President*
Michael Springer, *President*
Donel Sprenger, *Vice Pres*
Itri Eren, *Director*
Mark Sprenger, *Admin Sec*
EMP: 80 EST: 1968
SQ FT: 21,000
SALES (est): 3.3MM **Privately Held**
WEB: www.smithvillewestern.com
SIC: 8052 8059 8051 Intermediate care facilities; convalescent home; skilled nursing care facilities
PA: Sprenger Enterprises, Inc.
2198 Gladstone Ct
Glendale Heights IL 60139

(G-18992)
GRACE CONSULTING INC (PA)
510 Dickson St Lowr (44090-1502)
P.O. Box 58 (44090-0058)
PHONE.....................440 647-6672
Fax: 440 647-6673
Carl Vineyard, *CEO*
Scott Teague, *President*
Hal Stiles, *Vice Pres*
Frank Whitt, *Vice Pres*
Darryl Christy, *Mktg Dir*
EMP: 25
SALES: 10MM **Privately Held**
WEB: www.graceconsultinginc.com
SIC: 8748 8734 Environmental consultant; pollution testing

(G-18993)
KRYSTOWSKI TRACTOR SALES INC
Also Called: Krystowski Ford Tractor Sales
47117 State Route 18 (44090-9264)
PHONE.....................440 647-2015
Fax: 440 647-6593
Jill Sheparovich, *President*
Lawrence Krystowski, *Vice Pres*
Richard Krystowski, *Treasurer*
Michael Sheparovich, *Manager*
Ronald Krystowski, *Admin Sec*
EMP: 25 EST: 1945
SQ FT: 15,000
SALES: 6MM **Privately Held**
WEB: www.krystowskitractor.com
SIC: 5999 5083 Farm equipment & supplies; farm & garden machinery

(G-18994)
MODERN POURED WALLS INC
41807 State Route 18 (44090-9677)
P.O. Box 598, Lagrange (44050-0598)
PHONE.....................440 647-6661
Fax: 440 647-7601
W S Smith, *President*
EMP: 100 EST: 1976
SQ FT: 2,500
SALES (est): 12.7MM **Privately Held**
SIC: 1771 1794 Foundation & footing contractor; excavation work

(G-18995)
MPW CONSTRUCTION SERVICES
41807 State Route 18 (44090-9677)
P.O. Box 598, Lagrange (44050-0598)
PHONE.....................440 647-6661
Scott Smith, *President*
EMP: 50
SALES (est): 3.4MM **Privately Held**
SIC: 1521 Single-family housing construction

(G-18996)
WEBER HEALTH CARE CENTER INC
214 E Herrick Ave (44090-1315)
P.O. Box 386 (44090-0386)
PHONE.....................440 647-2088
Fax: 440 647-6303
Adelbert Weber, *President*
EMP: 140 EST: 1957
SQ FT: 20,000
SALES (est): 4.1MM **Privately Held**
SIC: 8051 8052 Extended care facility; intermediate care facilities

Wellston
Jackson County

(G-18997)
AMERICAN ELECTRIC POWER CO INC
3 W 13th St (45692-9505)
PHONE.....................740 384-7981
EMP: 37
SALES (corp-wide): 15.4B **Publicly Held**
SIC: 4911 Distribution, electric power
PA: American Electric Power Company, Inc.
1 Riverside Plz Fl 1 # 1
Columbus OH 43215
614 716-1000

(G-18998)
CITY OF WELLSTON
Also Called: Wellston Auditor's Office
203 E Broadway St (45692-1521)
PHONE.....................740 384-2428
Fax: 740 384-3357
Chris Dupree, *Auditor*
EMP: 60 **Privately Held**
SIC: 9111 8721 City & town managers' offices; auditing services
PA: City Of Wellston
203 E Broadway St
Wellston OH 45692
740 384-2720

(G-18999)
EDGEWOOD MANOR OF WELLSTON
Also Called: Consulate Healthcare
405 N Park Ave (45692)
PHONE.....................740 384-5611
Fax: 740 384-5613
Jeff Jellerson, *President*
Robert Hess, *Director*
EMP: 50
SALES (est): 2.4MM **Privately Held**
SIC: 8052 Intermediate care facilities

(G-19000)
J-VAC INDUSTRIES INC
202 S Pennsylvania Ave (45692-1797)
PHONE.....................740 384-2155
Frank Declemente, *President*
Richard Moore, *Director*
Ann Ogletree, *Director*
EMP: 74
SQ FT: 8,300
SALES: 28.4K **Privately Held**
SIC: 8331 3269 Sheltered workshop; art & ornamental ware, pottery

(G-19001)
JACKSON CO BD OF DD
202 S Pennsylvania Ave (45692-1719)
PHONE.....................740 384-7938
EMP: 51 **Privately Held**
SIC: 9111 8399 Mayors' offices; social services

(G-19002)
JACKSON COUNTY HLTH FACILITIES
Also Called: JENKINS MEMORIAL HEALTH FACILI
142 Jenkins Memorial Rd (45692-9561)
PHONE.....................740 384-0722
Fax: 740 446-5703
David Nichols, *CFO*
Theresa Womeldorf, *Administration*
EMP: 97
SALES: 4.9MM **Privately Held**
SIC: 8051 Skilled nursing care facilities

(G-19003)
JACKSON-VINTON CMNTY ACTION (PA)
Also Called: JACKSON VINTON COMMUNITY ACTIO
118 S New York Ave (45692-1540)
PHONE.....................740 384-3722
Debbie Jones, *Transptn Dir*
Michelle Green, *Manager*
Tammy Riegel, *Manager*
Cheryl Thiessen, *Exec Dir*
Pamela Pittenger, *Director*
EMP: 30
SQ FT: 12,000
SALES: 4MM **Privately Held**
SIC: 8399 9111 Community action agency; county supervisors' & executives' offices

(G-19004)
MONTGOMERY TRUCKING COMPANY
103 E 13th St (45692-2305)
P.O. Box 21 (45692-0021)
PHONE.....................740 384-2138
Fax: 740 384-6796
Phillip Fain, *President*
Mary B Casteel, *Corp Secy*
Jeffrey Fain, *Purch Agent*
Betsy Fain, *Human Res Mgr*
EMP: 50
SQ FT: 7,200
SALES (est): 5.5MM **Privately Held**
WEB: www.mgotrucking.com
SIC: 4212 4213 Light haulage & cartage, local; refrigerated products transport; household goods transport

(G-19005)
PEOPLES BANK
101 E A St (45692-1211)
PHONE.....................740 286-6773
Chuck Sulerzyski, *President*
EMP: 35
SALES (corp-wide): 182.1MM **Publicly Held**
SIC: 6021 National commercial banks
HQ: Peoples Bank
138 Putnam St
Marietta OH 45750
740 373-3155

Wellsville
Columbiana County

(G-19006)
DESHLER AMUSEMENTS INC
1894 Campground Rd (43968-1766)
PHONE.....................330 532-2922
Richard E Deshler, *President*
Carolyn Deshler, *Corp Secy*
EMP: 30
SALES (est): 1.2MM **Privately Held**
SIC: 7999 Carnival operation

West Alexandria
Preble County

(G-19007)
COUNTY OF PREBLE
1251 State Route 503 N (45381-9733)
PHONE.....................937 839-5845
EMP: 40 **Privately Held**
SIC: 6733 Trusts
PA: County Of Preble
101 E Main St
Eaton OH 45320
937 456-8143

(G-19008)
D & D RV AND AUTO LLC
3376 Us Route 35 E (45381-9361)
PHONE.....................937 839-4555
Fax: 937 839-0405
Lisa Clark, *Financial Exec*
Jim Overbey, *Manager*
Johnnie D Clark,
Darlene Clark,
EMP: 25
SQ FT: 15,000
SALES (est): 6.1MM **Privately Held**
SIC: 5521 5561 7519 Automobiles, used cars only; recreational vehicle dealers; recreational vehicle rental

West Carrollton
Montgomery County

(G-19009)
RECOVERY WORKS HEALING CTR LLC
100 Elmwood Park Dr (45449-5402)
PHONE.....................937 384-0580
EMP: 38
SALES (est): 297.2K **Privately Held**
SIC: 8069 Drug addiction rehabilitation hospital

(G-19010)
UNITED PARCEL SERVICE INC
Also Called: UPS
225 S Alex Rd (45449-1910)
PHONE.....................937 859-2314
Mick Tasso, *Branch Mgr*
EMP: 86
SALES (corp-wide): 65.8B **Publicly Held**
SIC: 4215 Package delivery, vehicular
PA: United Parcel Service, Inc.
55 Glenlake Pkwy
Atlanta GA 30328
404 828-6000

West Chester
Butler County

(G-19011)
ABF FREIGHT SYSTEM INC
6290 Allen Rd (45069-3854)
P.O. Box 1063 (45071-1063)
PHONE.................513 779-7888
Mike Hinterlong, *Opers Staff*
Jon Koopman, *Sales Mgr*
Matthew Godfrey, *Branch Mgr*
EMP: 50
SALES (corp-wide): 2.8B **Publicly Held**
WEB: www.abfs.com
SIC: 4213 Contract haulers
HQ: Abf Freight System, Inc.
3801 Old Greenwood Rd
Fort Smith AR 72903
479 785-8700

(G-19012)
ADVANTAGE RN LLC (PA)
Also Called: Advantage Local
9021 Meridian Way (45069-6539)
PHONE.................866 301-4045
Dee Kilfoyle, *Regional Mgr*
Dan Gutierrez, *Vice Pres*
Marianne Heatherly, *VP Opers*
Dionne Advantagern, *Design Engr*
Jeff Klank, *CFO*
EMP: 100
SQ FT: 8,400
SALES (est): 42.3MM **Privately Held**
WEB: www.advantagern.com
SIC: 7361 Placement agencies

(G-19013)
ADVANTAGE TECHNOLOGY GROUP (PA)
7723 Tylers Place Blvd # 132 (45069-4684)
PHONE.................513 563-3560
Douglas W Lantz, *President*
EMP: 26
SQ FT: 2,000
SALES (est): 1.8MM **Privately Held**
WEB: www.advtechgroup.com
SIC: 7371 7379 Computer software development & applications; computer related consulting services

(G-19014)
AERO FULFILLMENT SERVICES CORP
6023 Un Centre Blvd Steb (45069)
PHONE.................513 874-4112
Jon T Gimpel, *Branch Mgr*
EMP: 75
SQ FT: 264,000
SALES (corp-wide): 23MM **Privately Held**
SIC: 4225 General warehousing
PA: Aero Fulfillment Services Corporation
3900 Aero Dr
Mason OH 45040
800 225-7145

(G-19015)
AFFILIATES IN ORAL & MAXLOFCL
7795 Discovery Dr Ste C (45069-2903)
PHONE.................513 829-8080
Fax: 513 779-9009
Michelle Maupin, *Manager*
EMP: 30
SALES (est): 1MM
SALES (corp-wide): 3.5MM **Privately Held**
SIC: 8069 8021 8011 Specialty hospitals, except psychiatric; specialized dental practitioners; surgeon
PA: Affiliates In Oral & Maxilliofacial Surgery Inc
5188 Winton Rd
Fairfield OH 45014
513 829-8080

(G-19016)
ALL GONE TERMITE & PEST CTRL
9037 Sutton Pl (45011-9316)
PHONE.................513 874-7500
Tony White, *President*
Sandy Nellon, *Office Mgr*
EMP: 32 **EST:** 1997
SALES (est): 2.5MM **Privately Held**
SIC: 7342 Pest control in structures

(G-19017)
ALS SERVICES USA CORP
8961 Steeplechase Way (45069-5874)
PHONE.................513 582-8277
Kenneth Parks, *Branch Mgr*
EMP: 59
SALES (corp-wide): 975.4MM **Privately Held**
SIC: 8734 Testing laboratories
HQ: Als Services Usa, Corp.
10450 Stncliff Rd Ste 210
Houston TX 77099
281 530-5656

(G-19018)
ALT & WITZIG ENGINEERING INC
6205 Schumacher Park Dr (45069-4806)
PHONE.................513 777-9890
Fax: 513 777-9070
Ashley Garmany, *Engineer*
Mark Conroy, *Manager*
EMP: 30
SALES (corp-wide): 30.1MM **Privately Held**
WEB: www.altwitzig.com
SIC: 8711 Consulting engineer
PA: Alt & Witzig Engineering Inc
4105 W 99th St
Carmel IN 46032
317 875-7000

(G-19019)
AMERIMED INC
9961 Cincinnati Dayton Rd (45069-3823)
PHONE.................513 942-3670
Dan Deitz, *CEO*
Dan Dietz, *CEO*
David Newman, *Manager*
EMP: 25
SQ FT: 6,300
SALES (est): 3.4MM **Privately Held**
WEB: www.americannursingcare.com
SIC: 5999 7363 5047 Medical apparatus & supplies; help supply services; medical & hospital equipment
HQ: American Nursing Care, Inc.
1700 Edison Dr Ste 300
Milford OH 45150
513 576-0262

(G-19020)
AMICA MUTUAL INSURANCE COMPANY
9277 Centre Pointe Dr # 230 (45069-4844)
PHONE.................866 942-6422
R Daily, *Branch Mgr*
EMP: 48
SALES (corp-wide): 1.8B **Privately Held**
WEB: www.amica.com
SIC: 6331 Fire, marine & casualty insurance: mutual
PA: Amica Mutual Insurance Company
100 Amica Way
Lincoln RI 02865
800 992-6422

(G-19021)
ANIXTER INC
4440 Muhlhauser Rd # 200 (45011-9767)
PHONE.................513 881-4600
John Teller, *Engineer*
Dave Wallace, *Manager*
Angela Slaton, *Manager*
Sean Bethel, *CTO*
EMP: 30
SALES (corp-wide): 7.9B **Publicly Held**
SIC: 5087 Locksmith equipment & supplies
HQ: Anixter Inc.
2301 Patriot Blvd
Glenview IL 60026
800 323-8167

(G-19022)
ASD SPECIALTY HEALTHCARE LLC
Also Called: Besse Medical
9075 Centre Pointe Dr (45069-4890)
PHONE.................513 682-3600
Jamie Knighet, *General Mgr*
Harold Roberts, *General Mgr*
Susan Coldren, *Principal*
Sandy Brewer, *Vice Pres*
Becky Howe, *QA Dir*
EMP: 98
SALES (corp-wide): 153.1B **Publicly Held**
HQ: Asd Specialty Healthcare, Llc
3101 Gaylord Pkwy Fl 3
Frisco TX 75034
469 365-8000

(G-19023)
BAKEMARK USA LLC
Bakemark Cincinnati
9401 Le Saint Dr (45014-5447)
PHONE.................513 870-0880
Doug Townsend, *Branch Mgr*
EMP: 100
SALES (corp-wide): 620.6MM **Privately Held**
SIC: 5149 5046 Baking supplies; commercial equipment
PA: Bakemark Usa Llc
7351 Crider Ave
Pico Rivera CA 90660
562 949-1054

(G-19024)
BECKETT RIDGE COUNTRY CLUB
5595 Beckett Ridge Blvd # 2 (45069-1897)
PHONE.................513 874-2710
Fax: 513 874-0633
Jeff Galkin, *Manager*
EMP: 65
SQ FT: 1,800
SALES (est): 6.3MM **Privately Held**
SIC: 5941 7992 Golf goods & equipment; public golf courses

(G-19025)
BECKETT SPRINGS LLC (PA)
Also Called: Beckett Springs Hospital
8614 Shepherd Farm Dr (45069-1128)
PHONE.................513 942-9500
Stacey D Banks, *President*
EMP: 28 **EST:** 2013
SALES: 9.9MM **Privately Held**
SIC: 8062 General medical & surgical hospitals

(G-19026)
BELCAN LLC
9100 Centre Pointe Dr (45069-4846)
PHONE.................513 645-1509
Lance Kwasniewski, *Branch Mgr*
EMP: 749
SALES (corp-wide): 666.9MM **Privately Held**
SIC: 7363 Engineering help service
PA: Belcan, Llc
10200 Anderson Way
Blue Ash OH 45242
513 891-0972

(G-19027)
BH GROUP LLC (PA)
Also Called: H Wz Contracting-Cinti
4730 Ashley Dr (45011-9704)
PHONE.................513 671-3300
Bradley Hardig, *President*
Russell Davis, *Sales Staff*
Pat Adams, *Office Mgr*
Pat Goffena, *Manager*
EMP: 64
SALES (est): 30.7MM **Privately Held**
SIC: 1771 Concrete work

(G-19028)
BH GROUP LLC
4730 Ashley Dr (45011-9704)
PHONE.................513 671-3300
EMP: 61
SALES (est): 1.7MM
SALES (corp-wide): 30.7MM **Privately Held**
SIC: 1761 Roofing contractor
PA: Bh Group, Llc
4730 Ashley Dr
West Chester OH 45011
513 671-3300

(G-19029)
BHATTI ENTERPRISES INC
8045 Vegas Cir (45069-9291)
PHONE.................513 886-6000
Santokh S Bhatti, *President*
EMP: 50
SQ FT: 4,000
SALES (est): 2.7MM **Privately Held**
SIC: 8111 Corporate, partnership & business law

(G-19030)
BOBCAT ENTERPRISES INC (PA)
9605 Prnceton Glendale Rd (45011-8802)
P.O. Box 46345, Cincinnati (45246-0345)
PHONE.................513 874-8945
Fax: 513 874-4227
Thomas L Trapp, *CEO*
Arlen Swenson, *General Mgr*
Mark Couto, *Inv Control Mgr*
Anthony Evans, *Controller*
Missie Jackson, *Credit Mgr*
▲ **EMP:** 145
SQ FT: 15,000
SALES (est): 74.9MM **Privately Held**
SIC: 5082 7353 Contractors' materials; cranes, construction; heavy construction equipment rental; cranes & aerial lift equipment, rental or leasing

(G-19031)
BRANDS INSURANCE AGENCY INC
6449 Allen Rd Ste 1 (45069-3803)
P.O. Box 62267, Cincinnati (45262-0267)
PHONE.................513 777-7775
Alfred T Brands, *President*
Mat Brands, *President*
Steven Murry, *COO*
Emily Kinser, *Vice Pres*
Allison Brands, *Treasurer*
EMP: 30 **EST:** 1967
SQ FT: 4,400
SALES (est): 7.4MM **Privately Held**
SIC: 6411 Insurance agents

(G-19032)
CAMEO SOLUTIONS INC
Also Called: Bcbd
9078 Union Centre Blvd # 200 (45069-4992)
PHONE.................513 645-4220
Mark Handermann, *President*
Kish Jha, *President*
John Leonhardt, *President*
Benjamin R Stockton, *Chairman*
Greg Paulson, *Exec VP*
EMP: 40
SQ FT: 6,800
SALES: 8.2MM **Privately Held**
SIC: 7373 Value-added resellers, computer systems
PA: Cameo Global, Inc.
4695 Chabot Dr Ste 101
Pleasanton CA 94588

(G-19033)
CECO CONCRETE CNSTR DEL LLC
4535 Port Union Rd (45011-9766)
PHONE.................513 874-6953
Ronald D Worth, *Sales & Mktg St*
Rick Cevasco, *Manager*
EMP: 100 **Privately Held**
WEB: www.cecoconcrete.com
SIC: 1799 1771 Erection & dismantling of forms for poured concrete; concrete work
HQ: Ceco Concrete Construction Delaware, L.L.C.
10100 N Ambassador Dr
Kansas City MO 64153

(G-19034)
CECO CONCRETE CNSTR DEL LLC
4535 Port Union Rd Ste A (45011-9766)
PHONE.................734 455-3535
Rick Cevasco, *Manager*
EMP: 28 **Privately Held**
SIC: 1771 1799 Concrete work; erection & dismantling of forms for poured concrete

GEOGRAPHIC SECTION
West Chester - Butler County (G-19057)

HQ: Ceco Concrete Construction Delaware, L.L.C.
10100 N Ambassador Dr
Kansas City MO 64153

(G-19035)
CELLCO PARTNERSHIP
Also Called: Verizon Wireless
7606 Trailside Dr (45069-7588)
PHONE..................513 755-1666
Fax: 513 759-2140
EMP: 76
SALES (corp-wide): 126B Publicly Held
SIC: 4812 Cellular telephone services
HQ: Cellco Partnership
1 Verizon Way
Basking Ridge NJ 07920

(G-19036)
CHESTER WEST DENTAL GROUP INC
5900 W Chester Rd Ste A (45069-2951)
PHONE..................513 942-8181
Sanjeev Goel, President
Jayne McAfee, Office Mgr
Lynn Yvonne, Manager
Edward Maag DDS, Fmly & Gen Dent
EMP: 50
SALES (est): 4MM Privately Held
SIC: 8021 Group & corporate practice dentists

(G-19037)
CHESTER WEST MEDICAL CENTER
Also Called: West Chester Hospital
7700 University Dr (45069-2505)
PHONE..................513 298-3000
Gina Witko, Manager
Dana Lovell, Obstetrician
Paula Hawk, Director
Frederick Zeller, Director
Chip Washienko, Business Dir
EMP: 1200
SALES (est): 37.6MM Privately Held
SIC: 8062 General medical & surgical hospitals
PA: Uc Health, Llc.
3200 Burnet Ave
Cincinnati OH 45229

(G-19038)
CHRIST HOSPITAL
7589 Tylers Place Blvd (45069-6308)
PHONE..................513 755-4700
EMP: 140
SALES (corp-wide): 929.7MM Privately Held
SIC: 8011 Health maintenance organization
PA: The Christ Hospital
2139 Auburn Ave
Cincinnati OH 45219
513 585-2000

(G-19039)
CINCINNATI HYDRAULIC SVC INC
9431 Sutton Pl (45011-9705)
PHONE..................513 874-0540
Fax: 513 874-2561
Tom Hook, President
Robin Simpson, Manager
EMP: 30
SQ FT: 20,000
SALES (est): 1.7MM Privately Held
WEB: www.cinhyd.com
SIC: 7699 Aircraft & heavy equipment repair services; hydraulic equipment repair

(G-19040)
CINMAR LLC (DH)
Also Called: Frontgate Catalog
5566 W Chester Rd (45069-2914)
P.O. Box 8167 (45069-8167)
PHONE..................513 603-1000
Fax: 513 603-1020
Andrew Daniel, Vice Pres
Joni Wilson, Project Mgr
Edward Holweger, Opers Staff
James Bishop, Buyer
Claudia Saber, Buyer
◆ EMP: 120
SQ FT: 131,000
SALES (est): 48.7MM Publicly Held
SIC: 5961 5023 5712 Catalog sales; rugs; bedding & bedsprings

(G-19041)
CIP INTERNATIONAL INC
Also Called: Commercial Interior Products
9575 Le Saint Dr (45014-5447)
PHONE..................513 874-9925
Fax: 513 874-6246
Thomas Huff, Ch of Bd
Kathleen Huff, President
Mark Elmlinger, Vice Pres
Philip Huff, Vice Pres
Brian Hubbard, Project Dir
EMP: 83 EST: 1975
SQ FT: 140,000
SALES: 33MM Privately Held
WEB: www.cipinternational.net
SIC: 7389 2541 Interior designer; lettering & sign painting services; store fixtures, wood; cabinets, except refrigerated: show, display, etc.: wood

(G-19042)
CL ZIMMERMAN DELAWARE LLC
Also Called: G M Z
5115 Excello Ct (45069-3091)
PHONE..................513 860-9300
Tom Wells, President
Craig Nelson, Regional Mgr
Tim Hawley, Accounts Mgr
Michael McQuade, Accounts Mgr
Tammi Waak, Cust Mgr
▲ EMP: 30
SQ FT: 70,000
SALES (est): 38.3MM Privately Held
SIC: 5169 Industrial chemicals
HQ: Azelis Americas, Llc
262 Harbor Dr
Stamford CT 06902
203 274-8691

(G-19043)
CLARK THEDERS INSURANCE AGENCY
9938 Crescent Park Dr (45069-3895)
PHONE..................513 779-2800
Richard R Theders, CEO
Jonathan Theders, President
Jason M Randolph, CFO
Becky Oliver, Real Est Agnt
EMP: 28
SQ FT: 6,000
SALES (est): 6.2MM Privately Held
WEB: www.ctia.com
SIC: 6411 Insurance agents

(G-19044)
CLARKDIETRICH ENGINEERING SERV
9100 Centre Pointe Dr (45069-4846)
PHONE..................513 870-1100
William Courtney, CEO
Greg Ralph, Exec VP
Cheryl Hickerson, Supervisor
Keith Harr, Admin Sec
EMP: 58
SALES (est): 1.2MM
SALES (corp-wide): 15.8B Privately Held
SIC: 8711 Consulting engineer
HQ: Clarkwestern Dietrich Building Systems Llc
9050 Centre Pointe Dr
West Chester OH 45069

(G-19045)
CLARKE CONTRACTORS CORP
4475 Muhlhauser Rd (45011-9788)
PHONE..................513 285-7844
Fax: 513 874-3998
Matt Clarke, President
Peter Chadwick, Project Mgr
Jason Clarke, Project Mgr
Jeanette Hannon, Finance
Steve Isaacs, Applctn Conslt
EMP: 30
SQ FT: 4,000
SALES (est): 5.5MM Privately Held
WEB: www.clarkecontractors.com
SIC: 1799 Post-disaster renovations

(G-19046)
COLDWELL BANKER WEST SHELL
9106 W Chester Towne Ctr (45069-3102)
PHONE..................513 829-4000
Charlie Gaw, Real Est Agnt
Denise Gifford, Real Est Agnt
Mary Hoffman, Real Est Agnt
Lisa Morales, Real Est Agnt
Mary Schneider, Real Est Agnt
EMP: 46
SALES (corp-wide): 15.3MM Privately Held
SIC: 6531 Real estate agent, residential
PA: Coldwell Banker West Shell
9321 Montgomery Rd Ste C
Cincinnati OH 45242
513 794-9494

(G-19047)
COLDWELL BANKER WEST SHELL
7311 Tylers Corner Pl (45069-6344)
PHONE..................513 777-7900
Fax: 513 755-5498
Barbara Sondgerath, Vice Pres
Tom Sturm, Vice Pres
Gayle Tipp, Vice Pres
Kim Henry, Broker
Julia Wesselkamper, VP Sales
EMP: 75
SALES (corp-wide): 15.3MM Privately Held
WEB: www.coldwellbankerwestshell.com
SIC: 6531 Real estate agent, residential
PA: Coldwell Banker West Shell
9321 Montgomery Rd Ste C
Cincinnati OH 45242
513 794-9494

(G-19048)
COMFORCARE SENIOR SERVICES INC
7419 Kingsgate Way (45069-6517)
PHONE..................513 777-4860
Glenn Capri, Principal
EMP: 49 Privately Held
SIC: 8322 Geriatric social service
PA: Senior Comforcare Services Inc
2520 S Telegraph Rd # 201
Bloomfield Hills MI 48302

(G-19049)
CONTAINERPORT GROUP INC
Also Called: CONTAINERPORT GROUP, INC.
2700 Crescentville Rd (45069-4828)
PHONE..................513 771-0275
Fax: 513 772-5612
Ken Kraus, Manager
EMP: 40
SQ FT: 750
SALES (corp-wide): 241.2MM Privately Held
WEB: www.containerport.com
SIC: 4493 Boat yards, storage & incidental repair
HQ: Containerport Group, Inc.
1340 Depot St Fl 2
Cleveland OH 44116
440 333-1330

(G-19050)
CONTECH TRCKG & LOGISTICS LLC
9025 Centre Pointe Dr # 400 (45069-9700)
PHONE..................513 645-7000
Frank H Miller, Exec VP
Mark McCormick, Senior VP
Steve Kerls, Treasurer
Don Taylor, Finance
Rick Gaynorr, Mng Member
EMP: 74
SALES (est): 12.7MM Privately Held
SIC: 4731 Freight forwarding
HQ: Contech Engineered Solutions Llc
9025 Centre Pointe Dr # 400
West Chester OH 45069
513 645-7000

(G-19051)
CONTROL CONCEPTS & DESIGN INC
Also Called: E Technologies Group
5530 Union Centre Dr (45069-4821)
PHONE..................513 771-7271
Douglas Fagaly, President
Craig Carr, Project Mgr
Tom Coyner, Purchasing
Chris Beard, Engineer
Nick Hasselbeck, Engineer
EMP: 100
SQ FT: 7,000
SALES (est): 19.3MM Privately Held
WEB: www.etech-group.com
SIC: 8711 Consulting engineer

(G-19052)
CORNERSTONE BRANDS INC (DH)
5568 W Chester Rd (45069-2914)
P.O. Box 1308 (45071-1308)
PHONE..................513 603-1000
Fax: 513 603-1124
Judy A Schmeling, President
Bill Daly, General Mgr
Lisa Barnes, Vice Pres
Bill Johnson, Vice Pres
Matthew Smith, Vice Pres
◆ EMP: 1000
SQ FT: 55,000
SALES (est): 1.4B Publicly Held
SIC: 5021 Furniture

(G-19053)
CORNERSTONE BRANDS GROUP INC
5568 W Chester Rd (45069-2914)
PHONE..................513 603-1000
▼ EMP: 918
SQ FT: 1,000,000
SALES (est): 376.2K Publicly Held
SIC: 5961 8742 Catalog & mail-order houses; marketing consulting services
HQ: Cornerstone Brands, Inc.
5568 W Chester Rd
West Chester OH 45069
513 603-1000

(G-19054)
CORT BUSINESS SERVICES CORP
Also Called: Cort Furniture Rental
7400 Squire Ct (45069-2313)
PHONE..................513 759-8181
Fax: 513 777-0232
Jerry Cox, Sales Executive
Mark Robertson, Manager
Rebekah Vazquez, Executive
EMP: 60
SQ FT: 30,000
SALES (corp-wide): 242.1B Publicly Held
SIC: 7359 5932 Furniture rental; furniture, secondhand
HQ: Cort Business Services Corporation
15000 Conference
Chantilly VA 20151
703 968-8500

(G-19055)
COURTYARD BY MARRIOTT
6250 Muhlhauser Rd (45069-4988)
PHONE..................513 341-4140
Fax: 513 874-2415
John Sukula, General Mgr
Dustin Riggs, Asst Mgr
EMP: 30
SALES (est): 1.7MM Privately Held
SIC: 7011 Hotels & motels

(G-19056)
COWAN SYSTEMS LLC
2751 Crescentville Rd (45069-3816)
PHONE..................513 721-6444
EMP: 129 Privately Held
SIC: 4213 Trucking, except local
PA: Cowan Systems, Llc
4555 Hollins Ferry Rd
Baltimore MD 21227

(G-19057)
COX AUTOMOTIVE INC
4969 Muhlhauser Rd (45011-9789)
PHONE..................513 874-9310

West Chester - Butler County (G-19058) — GEOGRAPHIC SECTION

Ryan Edwards, *Manager*
Tracy Testut, *Manager*
EMP: 150
SALES (corp-wide): 33B **Privately Held**
WEB: www.manheim.com
SIC: 5012 Automobile auction
HQ: Cox Automotive, Inc.
6205-A Pchtree Dnwoody Rd
Atlanta GA 30328
404 843-5000

(G-19058)
CR BRANDS INC (DH)
8790 Beckett Rd (45069-2904)
PHONE 513 860-5039
Richard Owen, *CEO*
Mark Winterholder, *Vice Pres*
Vickie Bridges, *Senior Buyer*
Tamra Yelton, *Senior Buyer*
John Samoya, *CFO*
EMP: 82
SQ FT: 5,000
SALES (est): 27.5MM **Publicly Held**
WEB: www.redoxbrands.com
SIC: 2841 5169 3999 Soap & other detergents; detergents & soaps, except specialty cleaning; atomizers, toiletry

(G-19059)
CRESCENT PARK CORPORATION (PA)
9817 Crescent Park Dr (45069-3867)
PHONE 513 759-7000
Fax: 513 759-7001
Chris Taylor, *CEO*
David E Taylor Sr, *Ch of Bd*
Tom Schwallie, *Exec VP*
David Combs, *CFO*
Pam Maffey, *Supervisor*
EMP: 160
SQ FT: 700,000
SALES (est): 53MM **Privately Held**
SIC: 4213 4222 4225 7389 Trucking, except local; refrigerated warehousing & storage; general warehousing; packaging & labeling services; management services; packing & crating

(G-19060)
DEDICATED LOGISTICS INC
6019 Union Centre Blvd (45014-2290)
PHONE 513 275-1135
Ryan Usher, *Branch Mgr*
EMP: 99
SALES (corp-wide): 71.8MM **Privately Held**
SIC: 4213 4212 4225 Trucking, except local; local trucking, without storage; general warehousing & storage
HQ: Dedicated Logistics, Inc.
2900 Granada Ln N
Oakdale MN 55128

(G-19061)
DIALYSIS CLINIC INC
7650 University Dr (45069)
PHONE 513 777-0855
Fax: 513 777-8797
Roy Dansro, *Administration*
EMP: 25
SQ FT: 51,052
SALES (corp-wide): 736.2MM **Privately Held**
WEB: www.dciinc.org
SIC: 8092 Kidney dialysis centers
PA: Dialysis Clinic, Inc.
1633 Church St Ste 500
Nashville TN 37203
615 327-3061

(G-19062)
DILLON HOLDINGS LLC
Also Called: Visiting Angels Lvng Asst
8050 Beckett Center Dr # 103 (45069-5017)
PHONE 513 942-5600
Tabatha Dillon, *Marketing Staff*
Tom Dillon,
Debbie Dillon,
EMP: 105
SQ FT: 1,200
SALES (est): 2MM **Privately Held**
SIC: 8082 Home health care services

(G-19063)
DIMENSIONMARK LTD
2909 Crescentville Rd (45069-3883)
PHONE 513 305-3525
Rob S Clawson, *Controller*
Todd Parnell, *Mng Member*
EMP: 25
SALES: 6.5MM **Privately Held**
SIC: 8741 Business management

(G-19064)
DIRECT OPTIONS INC
9565 Cncnnati Columbus Rd (45069-4242)
PHONE 513 779-4416
Fax: 513 779-7335
Jan S Moore, *President*
Paul Wiehe, *Vice Pres*
Peter Nolan, *Business Dir*
EMP: 28
SQ FT: 10,000
SALES: 7MM **Privately Held**
WEB: www.directoptions.com
SIC: 8742 Marketing consulting services

(G-19065)
DITTMAN-ADAMS COMPANY
4946 Rialto Rd (45069-2927)
PHONE 513 870-7530
Fax: 513 870-7535
Garry Adams, *President*
John Ewald, *Vice Pres*
Ryan Smith, *Vice Pres*
Kathy Peterson, *Credit Mgr*
Marco Mikesell, *Accountant*
EMP: 43
SQ FT: 60,000
SALES (est): 22.8MM **Privately Held**
WEB: www.dittman-adams.com
SIC: 5194 Cigarettes; cigars; chewing tobacco; smoking tobacco

(G-19066)
DIXON BUILDERS & DEVELOPERS
8050 Beckett Center Dr # 213 (45069-5018)
PHONE 513 887-6400
Brian Byington, *President*
James M Dixon, *Founder*
Greg Thorpe, *Safety Dir*
Jeffrey L Nelson, *CFO*
Mark Schraffenberger, *Admin Sec*
EMP: 100
SQ FT: 4,000
SALES (est): 6.2MM **Privately Held**
WEB: www.dixonbuilders.com
SIC: 1521 1522 1531 New construction, single-family houses; condominium construction; operative builders

(G-19067)
DYNCORP
9266 Meridian Way (45069-6521)
PHONE 513 942-6500
Fax: 513 881-7769
Duncan Dawkins, *Manager*
EMP: 200
SALES (corp-wide): 16.3B **Privately Held**
WEB: www.dyncorp.com
SIC: 7373 Systems integration services
PA: Dyncorp Llc
1700 Old Meadow Rd
Mc Lean VA 22102
571 722-0210

(G-19068)
ENSAFE INC
8187 Fox Knoll Dr (45069-2898)
PHONE 513 621-7233
Robert Goodman, *Branch Mgr*
EMP: 25
SALES (corp-wide): 56MM **Privately Held**
SIC: 8731 Commercial physical research
PA: Ensafe Inc.
5724 Summer Trees Dr
Memphis TN 38134
901 372-7962

(G-19069)
ENTERTRAINMENT INC
Also Called: Entertainment Junction
7379 Squire Ct (45069-2314)
PHONE 513 898-8000
Donald Oeters, *President*
Sue Anne Allen, *Accounts Mgr*
Katie Schumacher, *Manager*
Lindsay Thompson, *Supervisor*
Michelle Oeters, *Advisor*
EMP: 30
SALES (est): 2MM **Privately Held**
SIC: 7993 Amusement arcade

(G-19070)
ESTES EXPRESS LINES INC
6459 Allen Rd (45069-3848)
PHONE 513 779-9581
Fax: 513 779-9765
John Flynn, *Branch Mgr*
EMP: 70
SALES (corp-wide): 2.4B **Privately Held**
WEB: www.estes-express.com
SIC: 4213 Contract haulers
PA: Estes Express Lines, Inc.
3901 W Broad St
Richmond VA 23230
804 353-1900

(G-19071)
F B WRIGHT CO CINCINNATI (PA)
Also Called: FB Wright of Cincinnati
4689 Ashley Dr (45011-9706)
PHONE 513 874-9100
Fax: 513 874-0235
Jack Doerr, *CEO*
William Reno, *President*
Arthur Colburn, *President*
Charles Johnson, *Safety Mgr*
EMP: 27
SQ FT: 18,000
SALES (est): 11.8MM **Privately Held**
WEB: www.fbw-cincy.com
SIC: 5085 5162 Hose, belting & packing; plastics products

(G-19072)
FASTEMS LLC
9850 Windisch Rd (45069-3806)
PHONE 513 779-4614
Pekka Tuhkanen, *Managing Dir*
Pekka Lammassaari, *Project Mgr*
Jana Landrum, *Controller*
Robert Humphreys, *VP Sales*
Jonathan Chomicz, *Sales Mgr*
EMP: 35
SALES (est): 5.4MM **Privately Held**
SIC: 7371 Computer software development

(G-19073)
FERGUSON ENTERPRISES INC
Also Called: Ferguson Integrated Services
2945 Crescentville Rd (45069-3883)
P.O. Box 2940, Newport News VA (23609-0940)
PHONE 513 771-6566
Fax: 513 771-6512
Theresa Bell, *Project Mgr*
Beth Francis, *Project Mgr*
Mary McDonald, *Purchasing*
Andy Norkey, *Branch Mgr*
Matthew Richey, *Manager*
EMP: 50
SALES (corp-wide): 19.2B **Privately Held**
WEB: www.ferguson.com
SIC: 5074 Plumbing & hydronic heating supplies
HQ: Ferguson Enterprises, Inc.
12500 Jefferson Ave
Newport News VA 23602
757 874-7795

(G-19074)
FITNESS INTERNATIONAL LLC
Also Called: La Fitness West Chester
7730 Dudley Dr (45069-2400)
PHONE 513 298-0134
Caitlin Waters, *Branch Mgr*
EMP: 30
SALES (corp-wide): 176.8MM **Privately Held**
SIC: 7991 Physical fitness facilities
PA: Fitness International, Llc
3161 Michelson Dr Ste 600
Irvine CA 92612
949 255-7200

(G-19075)
FOCUS ON YOUTH INC
8904 Brookside Ave (45069-3139)
PHONE 513 644-1030
Fax: 513 644-1025
Penny Dugan, *Finance Mgr*
Penny Dougan, *Finance*
Christina Kappn, *Program Mgr*
Kim Brown, *Supervisor*
Leah Weimer, *Supervisor*
EMP: 30
SQ FT: 6,200
SALES: 2.7MM **Privately Held**
SIC: 8322 Youth center

(G-19076)
FREDRICS CORPORATION (PA)
7664 Voice Of America Ctr (45069-2794)
PHONE 513 874-2226
Frederic Holzberger, *President*
Gary J Trame, *CFO*
▲ **EMP:** 140
SQ FT: 35,000
SALES (est): 16.7MM **Privately Held**
WEB: www.puregiving.com
SIC: 5087 5122 Barber shop equipment & supplies; drugs, proprietaries & sundries

(G-19077)
FUSION INTERIOR SERVICES LTD (PA)
9823 Cincinnati Dayton Rd (45069-3825)
PHONE 513 759-4100
John Planes, *President*
Heath Carrier, *Vice Pres*
▲ **EMP:** 33
SALES (est): 1.6MM **Privately Held**
SIC: 7699 Office equipment & accessory customizing

(G-19078)
G R B INC (PA)
Also Called: Triangle Label
6392 Gano Rd (45069-4869)
PHONE 800 628-9195
Fax: 513 755-7855
Roger Neiheisel, *President*
Loren Monroe, *COO*
Allen Backscheider, *Vice Pres*
Dean Backscheider, *Vice Pres*
Gary McDougle, *Opers Mgr*
▲ **EMP:** 75
SQ FT: 225,000
SALES (est): 86.4MM **Privately Held**
WEB: www.bgrinc.com
SIC: 5113 Shipping supplies

(G-19079)
GE AVIATION SYSTEMS LLC
7831 Ashford Glen Ct (45069-1614)
PHONE 513 786-4555
Keith Lesch, *Engineer*
EMP: 300
SALES (corp-wide): 122B **Publicly Held**
SIC: 4581 Airports, flying fields & services
HQ: Ge Aviation Systems Llc
1 Neumann Way
Cincinnati OH 45215
937 898-9600

(G-19080)
GENERAL MOTORS LLC
9287 Meridian Way (45069-6523)
PHONE 513 874-0535
Gene Lauer, *Plant Mgr*
Lisa Veneziano, *Manager*
EMP: 190 **Publicly Held**
SIC: 4225 5013 General warehousing & storage; motor vehicle supplies & new parts
HQ: General Motors Llc
300 Renaissance Ctr L1
Detroit MI 48243

(G-19081)
GENERAL MOTORS LLC
8752 Jacquemin Dr (45069-4859)
PHONE 513 603-6600
Lisa Veneziano, *Manager*
Gene Lauer, *Manager*
EMP: 185 **Publicly Held**
SIC: 5015 5013 4226 Motor vehicle parts, used; motor vehicle supplies & new parts; special warehousing & storage
HQ: General Motors Llc
300 Renaissance Ctr L1
Detroit MI 48243

▲ = Import ▼ = Export
◆ = Import/Export

GEOGRAPHIC SECTION
West Chester - Butler County (G-19105)

(G-19082)
GLOBAL WORKPLACE SOLUTIONS LLC
Also Called: G W S
9823 Cincinnati Dayton Rd (45069-3825)
PHONE................................513 759-6000
John Sabatalo, *President*
Kyle Skeldon, *President*
Jeff Ankenbauer, *Senior VP*
Stephen Sabatalo, *Vice Pres*
Susan Bates, *Project Mgr*
EMP: 69
SALES (est): 18MM **Privately Held**
SIC: 4213 Trucking, except local

(G-19083)
GRAPHEL CORPORATION
Also Called: Carbon Products
6115 Centre Park Dr (45069-3869)
P.O. Box 369 (45071-0369)
PHONE................................513 779-6166
Fax: 513 777-8959
Cliff Kersker, *President*
Jaime Portillo, *President*
Mark Grammer, *CFO*
David Miller, *Finance Other*
Melody West, *Sales Staff*
EMP: 140 **EST:** 1965
SQ FT: 35,000
SALES (est): 64.2MM **Privately Held**
WEB: www.graphel.com
SIC: 5052 3599 3624 Coal & other minerals & ores; machine shop, jobbing & repair; electrodes, thermal & electrolytic uses: carbon, graphite
PA: Graphite Metallizing Corp
    1050 Nepperhan Ave
    Yonkers NY 10703
    914 968-8400

(G-19084)
GREAT TRADITIONS HOMES
7267 Hamilton Mason Rd (45069)
PHONE................................513 759-7444
Tom Humes, *President*
EMP: 30
SALES (est): 1MM **Privately Held**
SIC: 1521 Single-family housing construction

(G-19085)
GUARDIAN PROTECTION SVCS INC
Also Called: Honeywell Authorized Dealer
9852 Windisch Rd (45069-3806)
PHONE................................513 422-5319
Fax: 513 759-1861
Larry Weaver, *Sales Staff*
Gerry Deehan, *Manager*
EMP: 60 **Privately Held**
WEB: www.guardianprotection.com
SIC: 7382 Burglar alarm maintenance & monitoring
HQ: Guardian Protection Services, Inc.
    174 Thorn Hill Rd
    Warrendale PA 15086
    412 788-2580

(G-19086)
GUARDIAN SAVINGS BANK (PA)
Also Called: FEDERAL SAVINGS BANK
6100 W Chester Rd (45069-2943)
PHONE................................513 942-3535
Fax: 513 923-4460
Louis Beck, *Ch of Bd*
Richard L Burkhart, *President*
Paul Warner, *Senior VP*
Eileen Cameron, *Vice Pres*
Greg Capannari, *Vice Pres*
EMP: 45
SQ FT: 4,000
SALES: 42.4MM **Privately Held**
WEB: www.guardiansavingsbank.com
SIC: 6163 6035 Loan brokers; federal savings banks

(G-19087)
HAIRY CACTUS SALON INC
Also Called: Salon Spa & Wellness Center
9437 Civic Centre Blvd B (45069-7118)
PHONE................................513 771-9335
Sharon Hargis, *President*
Sandra Reader, *Corp Secy*
Sandy Reder, *Vice Pres*
EMP: 43

SQ FT: 3,100
SALES (est): 837.3K **Privately Held**
SIC: 7231 Hairdressers

(G-19088)
HAMMACHER SCHLEMMER & CO INC
9180 La Saint Dr (45069)
PHONE................................513 860-4570
Don Rogers, *Branch Mgr*
EMP: 200
SALES (est): 10MM
SALES (corp-wide): 71.8MM **Privately Held**
WEB: www.hammacher.com
SIC: 5199 General merchandise, nondurable
PA: Hammacher, Schlemmer & Co., Inc.
    9307 N Milwaukee Ave
    Niles IL 60714
    847 581-8600

(G-19089)
HARMON INC
4290 Port Union Rd (45011-9713)
PHONE................................513 645-1550
Roger Matthews, *Branch Mgr*
Nathan Burger, *Manager*
Debbie Mullett, *Officer*
EMP: 41
SALES (corp-wide): 1.1B **Publicly Held**
WEB: www.harmoninc.com
SIC: 5039 Glass construction materials
HQ: Harmon, Inc.
    7900 Xerxes Ave S # 1800
    Bloomington MN 55431
    952 944-5700

(G-19090)
HILLANDALE HEALTHCARE INC
8073 Tylersville Rd (45069-2589)
PHONE................................513 777-1400
Greg Dixon, *President*
Don Dixon, *Vice Pres*
Steve Dixon, *Treasurer*
Faith Smith, *Human Resources*
Rex Richardson, *Mktg Dir*
EMP: 80
SQ FT: 12,000
SALES (est): 4.3MM **Privately Held**
SIC: 8051 Skilled nursing care facilities

(G-19091)
HOME2 BY HILTON
7145 Liberty Centre Dr (45069-2585)
PHONE................................513 422-3454
Jed Sherman, *Partner*
Michelle Noble, *Partner*
EMP: 30
SALES (est): 201.8K **Privately Held**
SIC: 7011 Resort hotel

(G-19092)
INDUSTRIAL CONTROLS DISTRS LLC
9407 Meridian Way (45069-6525)
PHONE................................513 733-5200
Dave Cunningham, *Warehouse Mgr*
Michael McNaught, *Engineer*
Bruce Barlow, *Sales Mgr*
Russell Hatch, *Accounts Mgr*
Chuck Kudy, *Accounts Mgr*
EMP: 32 **Privately Held**
WEB: www.industrialcontrolsonline.com
SIC: 5074 5075 Heating equipment (hydronic); air conditioning equipment, except room units
HQ: Industrial Controls Distributors, Llc
    17 Christopher Way
    Eatontown NJ 07724
    732 918-9000

(G-19093)
INET INTERACTIVE LLC
9100 W Chester Towne Ctr # 200 (45069-3108)
PHONE................................513 322-5600
Fax: 937 531-6603
Troy Augustine, *President*
Nicole Henderson, *Editor*
Kelly Kleiner-Kocher, *Vice Pres*
Kelly Kocher, *Vice Pres*
Kevin Normandeau, *Vice Pres*
EMP: 35

SALES (est): 4.2MM **Privately Held**
WEB: www.inetinteractive.com
SIC: 7371 4899 Computer software development; data communication services
HQ: Penton Media, Inc.
    1166 Avenue Of The Americ
    New York NY 10036
    212 204-4200

(G-19094)
IRON MOUNTAIN INCORPORATED
9247 Meridian Way (45069-6523)
PHONE................................513 874-3535
Debbie Davis, *Manager*
EMP: 51
SALES (corp-wide): 3.8B **Publicly Held**
SIC: 4226 Document & office records storage
PA: Iron Mountain Incorporated
    1 Federal St Fl 7
    Boston MA 02110
    617 535-4766

(G-19095)
IRON MOUNTAIN INFO MGT LLC
9247 Meridian Way (45069-6523)
PHONE................................513 297-1906
Fax: 513 682-6083
Don Garza, *Manager*
EMP: 38
SALES (corp-wide): 3.8B **Publicly Held**
SIC: 4226 Special warehousing & storage
HQ: Iron Mountain Information Management, Llc
    1 Federal St
    Boston MA 02110
    800 899-4766

(G-19096)
J&B STEEL ERECTORS INC
Also Called: J&B Steel Contractors
9430 Sutton Pl (45011-9698)
PHONE................................513 874-1722
Toya Estes, *President*
Kirsten Monson, *Administration*
EMP: 107
SQ FT: 32,000
SALES: 15MM **Privately Held**
SIC: 1611 General contractor, highway & street construction

(G-19097)
JLS ENTERPRISES INC
Also Called: Jimmy's Limousine Service
8167 Regal Ln Ste A (45069-3548)
PHONE................................513 769-1888
Danielle Little, *President*
James W Barnes, *Vice Pres*
EMP: 30
SQ FT: 8,000
SALES (est): 1MM **Privately Held**
SIC: 4119 Limousine rental, with driver

(G-19098)
JOHNSON CONTROLS
9685 Cincinnati Dayton Rd (45069-3829)
PHONE................................513 874-1227
Pat Markey, *Sales Mgr*
Tom Goyer, *Branch Mgr*
Dan Thieken, *Manager*
Bernie Weiss, *Manager*
Frederick Shivadecker, *Supervisor*
EMP: 60 **Privately Held**
WEB: www.simplexgrinnell.com
SIC: 1711 Fire sprinkler system installation
HQ: Johnson Controls Fire Protection Lp
    4700 Exchange Ct Ste 300
    Boca Raton FL 33431
    561 988-7200

(G-19099)
JP FLOORING SYSTEMS INC
9097 Union Centre Blvd (45069-4861)
PHONE................................513 346-4300
Phil Shrimper, *President*
Scott M Slovin, *Principal*
Kenneth Robert Thompson II, *Principal*
Linda B Woodrow, *Principal*
John Dickhaus, *Vice Pres*
EMP: 50
SQ FT: 100,000

SALES (est): 26.7MM **Privately Held**
WEB: www.jpflooring.com
SIC: 5023 5713 Wood flooring; resilient floor coverings: tile or sheet; carpets; floor tile; carpets

(G-19100)
KEMBA CREDIT UNION INC (PA)
8763 Union Centre Blvd # 101 (45069-1207)
PHONE................................513 762-5070
Stephen Behler, *President*
Daniel Sutton, *Exec VP*
Duane Stacklin, *Vice Pres*
Brian Strasser, *Vice Pres*
Brett Salsberry, *Auditing Mgr*
EMP: 199
SQ FT: 34,000
SALES: 22MM **Privately Held**
SIC: 6062 State credit unions, not federally chartered

(G-19101)
KGBO HOLDINGS INC
8630 Jacquemin Dr (45069-4852)
PHONE................................800 580-3101
Larry Shepherd, *Branch Mgr*
EMP: 50
SALES (corp-wide): 2.3B **Privately Held**
SIC: 4731 Brokers, shipping
PA: Kgbo Holdings, Inc
    4289 Ivy Pointe Blvd
    Cincinnati OH 45245
    513 831-2600

(G-19102)
KIDS R KIDS 2 OHIO
9077 Union Centre Blvd (45069-4861)
PHONE................................513 860-3197
Fax: 513 942-8608
Emily Grabit, *General Mgr*
Debbie Even, *Administration*
EMP: 48
SALES (est): 244.5K **Privately Held**
SIC: 8351 Preschool center

(G-19103)
KLEINGERS GROUP INC (PA)
6305 Centre Park Dr (45069-3863)
PHONE................................513 779-7851
Fax: 513 779-7852
Jim Kleingers Pe PS, *CEO*
Steve Korte Pe, *Vice Pres*
Troy Messer, *Manager*
Lary Rhoach, *Manager*
Jay S Aicp, *Director*
EMP: 55
SQ FT: 15,000
SALES (est): 14.7MM **Privately Held**
WEB: www.kleingers.com
SIC: 8711 8713 0781 Consulting engineer; surveying services; landscape architects

(G-19104)
KONECRANES INC
Also Called: Crane Pro Services
9879 Crescent Park Dr (45069-3867)
PHONE................................513 755-2800
Fax: 513 755-2879
Tom Kirk, *Manager*
Barb Rothert, *Administration*
Nancy Simpson, *Admin Asst*
EMP: 30
SALES (corp-wide): 2.2B **Privately Held**
WEB: www.kciusa.com
SIC: 7699 Industrial machinery & equipment repair
HQ: Konecranes, Inc.
    4401 Gateway Blvd
    Springfield OH 45502

(G-19105)
LESAINT LOGISTICS INC
4487 Le Saint Ct (45014-2229)
PHONE................................513 874-3900
Jeff Pennington, *President*
Steve Wormus, *Controller*
Scott Riddle, *Director*
EMP: 232
SQ FT: 900,000

West Chester - Butler County (G-19106)

SALES (est): 33.9MM
SALES (corp-wide): 94MM **Privately Held**
WEB: www.lesaint.com
SIC: **4225** 4212 General warehousing & storage; local trucking, without storage
PA: Lesaint Logistics, Llc
    868 W Crossroads Pkwy
    Romeoville IL 60446
    630 243-5950

(G-19106)
LESAINT LOGISTICS LLC
4487 Le Saint Ct (45014-2229)
P.O. Box 960522, Cincinnati (45296-0001)
PHONE.................513 874-3900
Dan Harmon, *Manager*
EMP: 50
SALES (corp-wide): 94MM **Privately Held**
WEB: www.lesaint.com
SIC: **4225** General warehousing
PA: Lesaint Logistics, Llc
    868 W Crossroads Pkwy
    Romeoville IL 60446
    630 243-5950

(G-19107)
LEVEL 3 TELECOM LLC
Also Called: Time Warner Telecom
9490 Meridian Way (45069-6527)
PHONE.................513 682-7806
Fax: 513 644-8915
Thomas Cloud, *Principal*
EMP: 29
SALES (corp-wide): 17.6B **Publicly Held**
SIC: **4813** Telephone communication, except radio
HQ: Level 3 Telecom, Llc
    10475 Park Meadows Dr
    Lone Tree CO 80124
    303 566-1000

(G-19108)
LEVEL 3 TELECOM LLC
Also Called: Time Warner Telecom
9490 Meridian Way (45069-6527)
PHONE.................513 682-7806
Thomas Cloud, *Branch Mgr*
EMP: 29
SALES (corp-wide): 17.6B **Publicly Held**
SIC: **4813** Telephone communication, except radio
HQ: Level 3 Telecom, Llc
    10475 Park Meadows Dr
    Lone Tree CO 80124
    303 566-1000

(G-19109)
LEVEL 3 TELECOM LLC
Also Called: Time Warner Telecom
9490 Meridian Way (45069-6527)
PHONE.................513 682-7806
Thomas Cloud, *Branch Mgr*
EMP: 29
SALES (corp-wide): 17.6B **Publicly Held**
SIC: **4813** Telephone communication, except radio
HQ: Level 3 Telecom, Llc
    10475 Park Meadows Dr
    Lone Tree CO 80124
    303 566-1000

(G-19110)
LITHKO CONTRACTING LLC (PA)
2958 Crescentville Rd (45069-4827)
PHONE.................513 564-2000
Fax: 513 863-7913
Robert Strobel, *President*
Perry Hausfeld, *Vice Pres*
Andy Zimmerman, *Safety Dir*
Filles Comtez, *Manager*
Phyllis Mejia, *Admin Mgr*
EMP: 150 EST: 1994
SQ FT: 10,000
SALES (est): 177.7MM **Privately Held**
SIC: **1771** Concrete work; foundation & footing contractor; flooring contractor; concrete repair

(G-19111)
LONG-STANTON MFG COMPANY
9388 Sutton Pl (45011-9702)
PHONE.................513 874-8020
Fax: 513 874-4242
Daniel B Cunningham, *President*
Tom Kachovec, *COO*
Tim Hershey, *CFO*
Lisa Wetterich, *Human Res Mgr*
Michael Gallagher, *Sales Dir*
▲ EMP: 50
SQ FT: 66,000
SALES (est): 11.7MM **Privately Held**
WEB: www.longstanton.com
SIC: **3444** 7692 3469 3544 Sheet metalwork; welding repair; metal stampings; special dies, tools, jigs & fixtures; fabricated plate work (boiler shop)

(G-19112)
LONGWORTH ENTERPRISES INC
8050 Beckett Center Dr (45069-5017)
PHONE.................513 738-4663
Marc Longworth II, *CEO*
EMP: 300 EST: 2009
SALES (est): 2.8MM **Privately Held**
SIC: **7299** Home improvement & renovation contractor agency

(G-19113)
LOWES HOME CENTERS LLC
7975 Tylersville Sq Rd (45069-4691)
PHONE.................513 755-4300
Fax: 513 755-4303
EMP: 150
SALES (corp-wide): 68.6B **Publicly Held**
SIC: **5211** 5031 5722 5064 Home centers; building materials, exterior; building materials, interior; household appliance stores; electrical appliances, television & radio
HQ: Lowe's Home Centers, Llc
    1605 Curtis Bridge Rd
    Wilkesboro NC 28697
    336 658-4000

(G-19114)
MACYS CR & CUSTOMER SVCS INC
9249 Meridian Way (45069-6523)
PHONE.................513 881-9950
Tom Schneider, *Manager*
Becky Fellerhoff, *Director*
EMP: 100
SALES (corp-wide): 24.8B **Publicly Held**
SIC: **7389** 7331 Credit card service; mailing service
HQ: Macy's Credit And Customer Services, Inc.
    9111 Duke Blvd
    Mason OH 45040

(G-19115)
MAILENDER INC
9500 Glades Dr (45011-9400)
PHONE.................513 942-5453
Fax: 513 942-6070
Ken Mailender, *CEO*
Andrew Abel, *President*
Chris Ward, *Vice Pres*
Jim Fleissner Jr, *Warehouse Mgr*
Chris Hardiman, *Purchasing*
▲ EMP: 62
SQ FT: 65,000
SALES (est): 42.5MM **Privately Held**
WEB: www.mailender.com
SIC: **5113** Paper & products, wrapping or coarse

(G-19116)
MARKETVISION RESEARCH INC
5426 W Chester Rd (45069-2950)
PHONE.................513 603-6340
Fax: 513 870-4888
Tina Rucker, *Vice Pres*
Dawn Hoskins, *Branch Mgr*
Kelly Farmer, *Manager*
EMP: 40
SALES (corp-wide): 15.2MM **Privately Held**
WEB: www.copyvision.com
SIC: **8732** Market analysis or research
PA: Marketvision Research, Inc.
    5151 Pfeiffer Rd Ste 300
    Blue Ash OH 45242
    513 791-3100

(G-19117)
MARTIN MARIETTA MATERIALS INC
Also Called: Martin Marietta Aggregate
9277 Centre Pointe Dr # 250 (45069-4844)
P.O. Box 30013, Raleigh NC (27622-0013)
PHONE.................513 701-1140
Harry Charles, *Manager*
EMP: 40 **Publicly Held**
WEB: www.martinmarietta.com
SIC: **1423** 1422 3295 3297 Crushed & broken granite; crushed & broken limestone; magnesite, crude: ground, calcined or dead-burned; nonclay refractories; construction sand & gravel
PA: Martin Marietta Materials Inc
    2710 Wycliff Rd
    Raleigh NC 27607

(G-19118)
MARTIN-BROWER COMPANY LLC
Also Called: Distribution Center
4260 Port Union Rd (45011-9768)
PHONE.................513 773-2301
Ryan Rozen, *General Mgr*
Jeanne Malone, *Manager*
EMP: 275 **Privately Held**
SIC: **2013** 2015 5087 Frozen meats from purchased meat; poultry, processed: frozen; restaurant supplies
HQ: The Martin-Brower Company L L C
    6250 N River Rd Ste 9000
    Rosemont IL 60018
    847 227-6500

(G-19119)
MIDWEST TRAILER SALES & SVC
Also Called: Mike's Truck & Trailer
3000 Crescentville Rd (45069-3887)
PHONE.................513 772-2818
Fax: 513 672-8152
Dan McCabe, *President*
EMP: 25
SALES (est): 1.4MM
SALES (corp-wide): 24.7MM **Privately Held**
WEB: www.eeienv.com
SIC: **7538** General truck repair
PA: Environmental Enterprises Inc
    10163 Cncinnati Dayton Rd
    Cincinnati OH 45241
    513 772-2818

(G-19120)
MISA METALS INC (DH)
Also Called: J R Metals
9050 Centre Pointe Dr (45069-4874)
PHONE.................212 660-6000
Takeshi Mitomi, *CEO*
John Hritz, *Vice Pres*
Jason Jamieson, *Vice Pres*
David Pratt, *Vice Pres*
Ronald P Roemer, *Vice Pres*
▲ EMP: 59
SQ FT: 20,000
SALES (est): 48MM
SALES (corp-wide): 15.8B **Privately Held**
WEB: www.misametals.com
SIC: **5051** Steel; structural shapes, iron or steel
HQ: Marubeni-Itochu Steel America Inc.
    150 E 42nd St Fl 7
    New York NY 10017
    212 660-6000

(G-19121)
MITCHELLS SALON & DAY SPA
7795 University Ct Ste A (45069)
PHONE.................513 793-0900
Sherry Williams, *Branch Mgr*
EMP: 195
SALES (corp-wide): 5.3MM **Privately Held**
SIC: **7299** Personal appearance services
PA: Mitchell's Salon & Day Spa Inc
    5901 E Galbraith Rd # 230
    Cincinnati OH 45236
    513 793-0900

(G-19122)
MITEL (DELAWARE) INC
Also Called: Inter Tel
9100 W Chester Towne Ctr (45069-3106)
PHONE.................513 733-8000
John J Catalano, *Vice Pres*
Dan Ziezerink, *Branch Mgr*
EMP: 25
SALES (corp-wide): 987.6MM **Privately Held**
WEB: www.inter-tel.com
SIC: **3661** 5045 4813 5065 Telephone & telegraph apparatus; computer software; long distance telephone communications; telephone equipment; telephone & telephone equipment installation; equipment rental & leasing
HQ: Mitel (Delaware). Inc.
    1146 N Alma School Rd
    Mesa AZ 85201
    480 449-8900

(G-19123)
MOLLETT SEAMLESS GUTTER CO
Also Called: Cincinnati Gutter Supply
9345 Prnceton Glendale Rd (45011-9707)
PHONE.................513 825-0500
Radford Mollett, *President*
EMP: 25
SQ FT: 18,000
SALES (est): 1.7MM **Privately Held**
SIC: **1761** 1629 Gutter & downspout contractor; trenching contractor

(G-19124)
OHIO AUTOMOBILE CLUB
8210 Highland Pointe Dr (45069-4520)
PHONE.................513 870-0951
EMP: 36
SALES (corp-wide): 55.9MM **Privately Held**
SIC: **7997** Membership sports & recreation clubs
PA: The Ohio Automobile Club
    90 E Wilson Bridge Rd # 1
    Worthington OH 43085
    614 431-7901

(G-19125)
OLD DOMINION FREIGHT LINE INC
6431 Centre Park Dr (45069-4801)
PHONE.................513 771-1486
Fax: 513 942-6025
Brian Houser, *Manager*
EMP: 48
SALES (corp-wide): 3.3B **Publicly Held**
WEB: www.odfl.com
SIC: **4213** Less-than-truckload (LTL) transport
PA: Old Dominion Freight Line Inc
    500 Old Dominion Way
    Thomasville NC 27360
    336 889-5000

(G-19126)
OMNI FIREPROOFING CO LLC
9305 Le Saint Dr (45014-5447)
PHONE.................513 870-9115
Fax: 513 870-9312
Thomas Hochhausler, *Mng Member*
Ken Brosnan,
Greg Shields,
EMP: 55
SQ FT: 15,000
SALES (est): 6.1MM **Privately Held**
WEB: www.omnifp.com
SIC: **1799** 1742 Fireproofing buildings; acoustical & insulation work

(G-19127)
OVERHEAD DOOR CO-CINCINNATI
9345 Prnceton Glendale Rd (45011-9707)
P.O. Box 8187 (45069-8187)
PHONE.................513 346-4000
Fred S Klipsch, *Vice Ch Bd*
Terry Sarbinoff, *President*
Charlie Lanham, *Treasurer*
Karen Scalf, *Manager*
EMP: 145
SQ FT: 70,000

West Chester - Butler County (G-19150)

SALES (est): 17.4MM
SALES (corp-wide): 58.3MM Privately Held
SIC: 5211 1761 1751 1742 Garage doors, sale & installation; roofing, siding & sheet metal work; carpentry work; plastering, drywall & insulation
PA: Garage Door Systems, Llc
8811 Bash St
Indianapolis IN 46256
317 842-7444

(G-19128)
PIVOTEK LLC
8910 Le Saint Dr (45014-2291)
PHONE.............................513 372-6205
Kent Hodson, *President*
Jeff Burke, *Purch Dir*
Laura Poe, *Admin Asst*
James Foley,
Tracy Snyder,
◆ **EMP:** 35
SALES (est): 7.8MM Privately Held
SIC: 1542 1522 Commercial & office building contractors; residential construction

(G-19129)
PLANES MOVING & STORAGE INC (PA)
Also Called: Planes Companies
9823 Cincinnati Dayton Rd (45069-3825)
PHONE.............................513 759-6000
Fax: 513 759-3699
John J Planes, *CEO*
Greg Hallas, *President*
Darren S Montgomery, *President*
John Sabatalo, *President*
Dan Wurzelbacher, *Managing Prtnr*
EMP: 217 **EST:** 1928
SQ FT: 250,000
SALES (est): 72.8MM Privately Held
SIC: 4214 4213 Household goods moving & storage, local; trucking, except local

(G-19130)
PREMIERE SERVICE MORTGAGE CORP (PA)
6266 Centre Park Dr (45069-3865)
PHONE.............................513 546-9895
Fax: 513 779-6440
Gerald Matyow, *President*
Graham Strong, *Vice Pres*
Steve Fried, *Shareholder*
Rob Uebel, *Shareholder*
EMP: 40
SALES (est): 5MM Privately Held
SIC: 6163 Mortgage brokers arranging for loans, using money of others

(G-19131)
PRESTIGE TECHNICAL SVCS INC (PA)
7908 Cincinnati Dayton Rd T (45069-3382)
PHONE.............................513 779-6800
Joan Mears, *President*
Jeff H Rph, *Director*
EMP: 32
SQ FT: 2,700
SALES (est): 5.7MM Privately Held
WEB: www.prestigetechnical.com
SIC: 7363 Engineering help service

(G-19132)
PRIMETECH COMMUNICATIONS INC
4505 Muhlhauser Rd (45011-9788)
P.O. Box 531730, Cincinnati (45253-1730)
PHONE.............................513 942-6000
Brad Shoemaker, *President*
Eric Biehle, *Business Mgr*
Marcia Shoemaker, *Vice Pres*
Dave Schmuelling, *Project Mgr*
Stacey Smith, *Administration*
EMP: 60
SQ FT: 17,000
SALES (est): 8.8MM Privately Held
SIC: 1731 Cable television installation; fiber optic cable installation

(G-19133)
PROSCAN IMAGING LLC
Also Called: First Scan Imaging
7307 Tylers Corner Pl (45069-6344)
PHONE.............................513 759-7350
Fax: 513 759-7351
Stephen Pomeranz, *CEO*
Jenn Malone, *Office Mgr*
EMP: 34
SALES (corp-wide): 37.6MM Privately Held
SIC: 8071 X-ray laboratory, including dental
PA: Proscan Imaging, Llc
5400 Kennedy Ave Ste 1
Cincinnati OH 45213
513 281-3400

(G-19134)
PTS PRFSSNAL TECHNICAL SVC INC (PA)
Also Called: Est Analytical
503 Commercial Dr (45014-7594)
PHONE.............................513 642-0111
James R Murphy, *CEO*
Justin Murphy, *President*
Lindsey Pyron, *Vice Pres*
Doug Meece, *Research*
Scott Bornemann, *Controller*
EMP: 52
SQ FT: 12,000
SALES (est): 15.6MM Privately Held
WEB: www.ptsltd.com
SIC: 5049 Analytical instruments

(G-19135)
QUASONIX INC (PA)
6025 Schumacher Park Dr (45069-4812)
PHONE.............................513 942-1287
Terrance Hill, *President*
Norman Eichenberger, *Engineer*
Tim O'Connell, *Engineer*
Tim Oconnell, *Engineer*
Sean Wilson, *Engineer*
EMP: 25
SQ FT: 15,000
SALES: 15MM Privately Held
WEB: www.quasonix.com
SIC: 5065 3663 3812 3669 Communication equipment; airborne radio communications equipment; antennas, radar or communications; intercommunication systems, electric

(G-19136)
QUEEN CITY POLYMERS INC (PA)
6101 Schumacher Park Dr (45069-3818)
PHONE.............................513 779-0990
Fax: 513 779-0993
James M Powers, *President*
James L Powers, *Principal*
Kelli Alder, *Controller*
Greg Hendren, *Director*
EMP: 42
SQ FT: 33,000
SALES (est): 11.2MM Privately Held
WEB: www.qcpinc.net
SIC: 3089 5162 Injection molding of plastics; plastics products

(G-19137)
RAM CONSTRUCTION SERVICES OF
4710 Ashley Dr (45011-9704)
PHONE.............................513 297-1857
Fax: 513 671-0931
Bob Mazur, *President*
Kurt Luckow, *Regional Mgr*
John Mazur, *Vice Pres*
Kevin Houle, *CFO*
EMP: 60
SALES (est): 4.5MM
SALES (corp-wide): 107.9MM Privately Held
SIC: 1799 1541 1542 Waterproofing; renovation, remodeling & repairs: industrial buildings; commercial & office buildings, renovation & repair
PA: Ram Construction Services Of Michigan, Inc.
13800 Eckles Rd
Livonia MI 48150
734 464-3800

(G-19138)
REPS RESOURCE LLC
9120 Union Centre Blvd # 300 (45069-4896)
PHONE.............................513 874-0500
Fax: 513 874-7656
Daryl Fultz, *Principal*
Erik Murphy, *Opers Staff*
Bill Schoultheis, *Senior Engr*
Barbara Fisher, *Accountant*
Shelly Rubi, *Manager*
EMP: 30
SALES: 3MM Privately Held
WEB: www.reps-resource.com
SIC: 8711 Aviation &/or aeronautical engineering

(G-19139)
RES-CARE INC
7908 Cincinnati Dayton Rd (45069-6608)
PHONE.............................513 858-4550
Angie Mick, *Branch Mgr*
EMP: 48
SALES (corp-wide): 24.5B Privately Held
SIC: 8052 Home for the mentally retarded, with health care
HQ: Res-Care, Inc.
9901 Linn Station Rd
Louisville KY 40223
502 394-2100

(G-19140)
RICKERIER AND ECKLER
9277 Centre Pointe Dr # 100 (45069-4844)
PHONE.............................513 870-6565
Mark Engel, *Partner*
EMP: 25
SALES (est): 757.9K Privately Held
SIC: 8111 General practice attorney, lawyer

(G-19141)
RIVER CITY FURNITURE LLC (PA)
Also Called: Rcf Group
6454 Centre Park Dr (45069-4800)
PHONE.............................513 612-7303
Fax: 513 612-7313
Mike Keeney, *General Mgr*
Dana Barnard, *HR Admin*
Jim Wilson, *Sales Associate*
Jim Bracken, *Marketing Staff*
Becky Bass, *Manager*
EMP: 53
SQ FT: 7,500
SALES (est): 68.9MM Privately Held
WEB: www.r-c-f.com
SIC: 7389 5712 1752 0782 Interior design services; office furniture; resilient floor laying; mowing services, lawn; furniture moving, local: without storage; furniture moving & storage, local

(G-19142)
RIVERFRONT DIVERSIFIED INC
Also Called: Ever Dry of Cincinnati
9814 Harwood Ct (45014-7589)
PHONE.............................513 874-7200
Fax: 513 870-6159
James Gielty, *President*
Charles Begley, *General Mgr*
Nick Penegas, *Accountant*
Dorothy Hay, *Financial Exec*
Connie Fahmy, *Manager*
EMP: 70
SQ FT: 12,000
SALES (est): 7.9MM Privately Held
SIC: 1799 Waterproofing

(G-19143)
RRR EXPRESS LLC
Also Called: Rrr Logistics
6432 Centre Park Dr (45069-4800)
PHONE.............................800 723-3424
Steven D Hall, *Mng Member*
James Molloy, *Manager*
Lee Scheven,
EMP: 120
SQ FT: 31,000
SALES (est): 23MM Privately Held
WEB: www.rrrexpress.com
SIC: 4213 Trucking, except local

(G-19144)
SAFWAY SERVICES LLC
9536 Glades Dr (45011-9400)
PHONE.............................513 860-2626
Tim Debolt, *Branch Mgr*
Cheryl Clark, *Manager*
EMP: 50
SALES (corp-wide): 8.5B Privately Held
WEB: www.safway.com
SIC: 5082 Scaffolding
HQ: Safway Services, Llc
N19w24200 Riverwood Dr # 200
Waukesha WI 53188

(G-19145)
SCHNEIDER ELECTRIC USA INC
9870 Crescent Park Dr (45069-3800)
PHONE.............................513 755-5000
John Blaylock, *General Mgr*
Jerry Earl, *Plant Mgr*
Angela Fay, *Purch Mgr*
Ryan Back, *Senior Buyer*
Ashley Gerver, *Human Res Mgr*
EMP: 75
SALES (corp-wide): 241K Privately Held
WEB: www.squared.com
SIC: 3613 3643 3612 3823 Switchgear & switchboard apparatus; bus bars (electrical conductors); power transformers, electric; controllers for process variables, all types; relays & industrial controls; electrical apparatus & equipment
HQ: Schneider Electric Usa, Inc.
800 Federal St
Andover MA 01810
978 975-9600

(G-19146)
SCHOLASTIC BOOK FAIRS INC
5459 W Chester Rd Ste C (45069-2915)
PHONE.............................513 714-1000
Cindy Herman, *Sales Staff*
Anthony Hopkins, *Manager*
EMP: 60
SALES (corp-wide): 1.7B Publicly Held
WEB: www.scholasticbookfairs.com
SIC: 5192 5199 Books; posters
HQ: Scholastic Book Fairs, Inc.
1080 Greenwood Blvd
Lake Mary FL 32746
407 829-7300

(G-19147)
SCHRUDDER PRFMCE GROUP LLC
7723 Tylers Place Blvd (45069-4684)
PHONE.............................513 652-7675
Loprete Joe, *Terminal Mgr*
Tony Fearmonti, *Psychologist*
Tom Rucci, *Senior Mgr*
Jack Best, *Executive*
Mitchell R Schrudder,
EMP: 50
SALES (est): 12MM Privately Held
WEB: www.schrudderperformance.com
SIC: 8742 Management consulting services

(G-19148)
SCOTT D PHILLIPS
9277 Centre Pointe Dr (45069-4844)
PHONE.............................513 870-8200
Scott D Phillips, *Principal*
EMP: 30
SALES (est): 708.7K Privately Held
SIC: 8111 Legal services

(G-19149)
SELECT STAFFING
Also Called: Remedy Intelligent Staffing
7682 Overglen Dr (45069-9214)
PHONE.............................513 247-9772
Jason Guyler, *Manager*
EMP: 71
SALES (corp-wide): 547.8MM Privately Held
SIC: 7363 Temporary help service
HQ: Select Staffing
3820 State St Ste A
Santa Barbara CA 93105

(G-19150)
SENIOR LIFESTYLE CORPORATION
Also Called: West Chester, Barrington of
7222 Heritagespring Dr (45069-6589)
PHONE.............................513 777-4457
Stephanie Weihrman, *Director*
EMP: 55
SALES (corp-wide): 342.7MM Privately Held
SIC: 8361 8059 8011 6513 Home for the aged; convalescent home; clinic, operated by physicians; retirement hotel operation

West Chester - Butler County (G-19151)

PA: Senior Lifestyle Corporation
303 E Wacker Dr Ste 2400
Chicago IL 60601
312 673-4333

(G-19151)
SHETLER MOVING & STOR OF OHIO
Also Called: Shelter Moving & Storage
9917 Charter Park Dr (45069-3890)
PHONE................513 755-0700
Fax: 513 755-5583
Thomas J Shetler Sr, *President*
Thomas J Shetler Jr, *President*
Robert O Shetler, *General Mgr*
EMP: 30
SQ FT: 25,000
SALES (est): 4.4MM **Privately Held**
SIC: 4213 4214 Household goods transport; furniture moving & storage, local

(G-19152)
SIBCY CLINE INC
Also Called: Sibcy Cline Realtors
7677 Voice Of Amer Ctr Dr (45069-2795)
PHONE................513 777-8100
Fax: 513 777-4226
Vinit Kohli, *Vice Pres*
Patty Letzler, *Manager*
EMP: 90
SALES (corp-wide): 2.1B **Privately Held**
WEB: www.sibcycline.com
SIC: 6531 6162 Real estate brokers & agents; mortgage bankers
PA: Sibcy Cline, Inc.
8044 Montgomery Rd # 300
Cincinnati OH 45236
513 984-4100

(G-19153)
SIGHT RESOURCE CORPORATION (PA)
8100 Beckett Center Dr (45069-5015)
PHONE................513 942-4423
E Dean Butler, *Ch of Bd*
Carene S Kunkler, *President*
Duane Kimble, *Exec VP*
Sandra K Likes, *Vice Pres*
Donald L Radcliff, *CFO*
EMP: 60
SQ FT: 7,500
SALES (est): 20.9MM **Privately Held**
SIC: 8042 5048 Group & corporate practice optometrists; optometric equipment & supplies

(G-19154)
SIMPLEX TIME RECORDER LLC
8910 Beckett Rd (45069-7054)
PHONE................800 746-7539
Daniel Thiecen, *Branch Mgr*
EMP: 30 **Privately Held**
WEB: www.comtec-alaska.com
SIC: 1731 Fire detection & burglar alarm systems specialization
HQ: Simplex Time Recorder Llc
50 Technology Dr
Westminster MA 01441
978 731-2500

(G-19155)
SKATE TOWN U S A
8730 N Pavillion (45069-4894)
PHONE................513 874-9855
Fax: 513 894-3949
Ken Roesel, *Managing Prtnr*
EMP: 30
SALES (est): 688.6K **Privately Held**
SIC: 7999 Roller skating rink operation

(G-19156)
SKIDMORE SALES & DISTRG CO INC (PA)
9889 Cincinnati Dayton Rd (45069-3825)
PHONE................513 755-4200
Fax: 513 759-4270
Douglas S Skidmore, *CEO*
Jim McCarthy, *President*
Gerald Skidmore, *Chairman*
Mark Overbeck, *Vice Pres*
Eric Eldridge, *Purch Mgr*
▲ EMP: 36 EST: 1963
SQ FT: 150,000
SALES (est): 73.1MM **Privately Held**
WEB: www.foodingr.com
SIC: 5149 5169 Groceries & related products; chemicals & allied products

(G-19157)
SMYTH AUTOMOTIVE INC
Also Called: Parts Plus
8868 Cincinnati Columbus (45069-3516)
PHONE................513 777-6400
Fax: 513 777-1929
Bob Smyth, *Branch Mgr*
EMP: 33
SALES (corp-wide): 160.2MM **Privately Held**
WEB: www.smythautomotive.com
SIC: 5013 Automotive supplies & parts
PA: Smyth Automotive, Inc.
4275 Mt Carmel Tobasco Rd
Cincinnati OH 45244
513 528-2800

(G-19158)
SPRANDEL ENTERPRISES INC
Also Called: Quality Towing
6467 Gano Rd (45069-4830)
P.O. Box 1873 (45071-1873)
PHONE................513 777-6622
Fax: 513 777-1837
Michael Sprandel, *President*
Steve Kirby, *General Mgr*
Edward Sprandel, *Sr Corp Ofcr*
Jodi A Sprandel, *Manager*
Steve Bauer, *Administration*
EMP: 25
SALES (est): 3.3MM **Privately Held**
SIC: 7549 Towing service, automotive; road service, automotive

(G-19159)
STAR ONE HOLDINGS INC
6875 Fountains Blvd Ste A (45069-5149)
PHONE................513 779-9500
Fax: 513 779-9568
Steve Speed, *Sales Staff*
Sandi Cornett, *Sales Associate*
Cynthia Massey, *Sales Associate*
Mark Meinhardt, *Manager*
Elizabeth Lautner,
EMP: 35
SALES (corp-wide): 8.8MM **Privately Held**
WEB: www.nkybuilders.com
SIC: 6531 Real estate agent, residential
PA: Star One Holdings, Inc.
3895 Woodridge Blvd
Fairfield OH 45014
513 870-9100

(G-19160)
STERLING LAND TITLE AGENCY
7594 Cox Ln (45069-6519)
PHONE................513 755-3700
Pam Felino, *President*
EMP: 25
SALES (est): 2.5MM **Privately Held**
SIC: 6361 Title insurance

(G-19161)
SUNESIS CONSTRUCTION COMPANY
2610 Crescentville Rd (45069-3819)
PHONE................513 326-6000
Fax: 513 326-6001
Rick Jones, *President*
Albert C Eiselein Jr, *Principal*
Richard Jones, *Principal*
Steve Abernathy, *Vice Pres*
Chris Hertzel, *Vice Pres*
EMP: 125
SQ FT: 3,000
SALES: 40MM **Privately Held**
WEB: www.sunesisconstruction.com
SIC: 1623 1622 1611 Water, sewer & utility lines; bridge construction; general contractor, highway & street construction

(G-19162)
THYSSENKRUPP BILSTEIN AMER INC
4440 Muhlhauser Rd (45011-9767)
PHONE................513 881-7600
Jimmy Brentle, *Manager*
EMP: 25
SALES (corp-wide): 48.7B **Privately Held**
SIC: 5013 3714 Automotive supplies & parts; motor vehicle parts & accessories
HQ: Thyssenkrupp Bilstein Of America, Inc.
8685 Bilstein Blvd
Hamilton OH 45015
513 881-7600

(G-19163)
TITAN TRANSFER INC
6432 Centre Park Dr (45069-4800)
PHONE................513 458-4233
Greg Hall, *Branch Mgr*
EMP: 68
SALES (corp-wide): 56.6MM **Privately Held**
SIC: 4213 Contract haulers
PA: Titan Transfer, Inc.
1200 Stanley Blvd
Shelbyville TN 37160
931 684-0255

(G-19164)
TOYOTA INDUSTRIES N AMER INC
Also Called: Prolift Industrial Equipment
9890 Charter Park Dr (45069-4803)
PHONE................513 779-7500
Fax: 513 779-7879
Keith Ingels, *Branch Mgr*
EMP: 50
SALES (corp-wide): 19.8B **Privately Held**
SIC: 5084 Materials handling machinery
HQ: Toyota Industries North America, Inc.
3030 Barker Dr
Columbus IN 47201
812 341-3810

(G-19165)
TRANSFORCE INC
8080 Beckett Center Dr # 202 (45069-5047)
PHONE................513 860-4402
EMP: 47 **Privately Held**
SIC: 7699 Industrial equipment services
PA: Transforce, Inc.
5520 Cherokee Ave Ste 200
Alexandria VA 22312

(G-19166)
TSS TECHNOLOGIES INC (PA)
Also Called: TSS Medical
8800 Global Way (45069-7070)
PHONE................513 772-7000
Brent Nichols, *President*
Kriss Cloninger, *Managing Dir*
Leila B Nichols, *Principal*
Charles P Taft, *Principal*
Ruth Zimmerman, *Principal*
▲ EMP: 400
SQ FT: 75,000
SALES (est): 104.6MM **Privately Held**
WEB: www.tss.com
SIC: 3599 8711 Machine shop, jobbing & repair; mechanical engineering

(G-19167)
UC HEALTH LLC
7700 University Ct # 1800 (45069-7202)
PHONE................513 475-7458
Ron Rohlfing, *VP Opers*
Patrick Nunan, *Med Doctor*
Brenda Bridges, *Manager*
Rhonada Brown, *Manager*
Linda Jamison, *Infect Cntl Dir*
EMP: 505 **Privately Held**
SIC: 8011 Radiologist
PA: Uc Health, Llc.
3200 Burnet Ave
Cincinnati OH 45229

(G-19168)
UC HEALTH LLC
Also Called: U C Health Dermatology
7690 Discovery Dr # 1700 (45069-6551)
PHONE................513 475-7630
Fax: 513 475-8271
Kyle Kaufman, *Pediatrics*
EMP: 1325 **Privately Held**
SIC: 8748 Business consulting
PA: Uc Health, Llc.
3200 Burnet Ave
Cincinnati OH 45229

(G-19169)
UC HEALTH LLC
7700 University Ct (45069-7202)
PHONE................513 475-8881
EMP: 505 **Privately Held**
SIC: 8011 Surgeon
PA: Uc Health, Llc.
3200 Burnet Ave
Cincinnati OH 45229

(G-19170)
UC HEALTH LLC
7798 Discovery Dr Ste F (45069-7747)
PHONE................513 298-3000
Paula Hawk, *Director*
EMP: 210 **Privately Held**
SIC: 8741 Management services; hospital management
PA: Uc Health, Llc.
3200 Burnet Ave
Cincinnati OH 45229

(G-19171)
UC HEALTH LLC
7710 University Ct (45069)
PHONE................513 475-7777
Loraine Henderson, *Manager*
EMP: 189 **Privately Held**
WEB: www.precisionradiotherapy.com
SIC: 8011 Medical centers
PA: Uc Health, Llc.
3200 Burnet Ave
Cincinnati OH 45229

(G-19172)
UC HEALTH LLC
7798 Discovery Dr Ste E (45069-7747)
PHONE................513 475-7500
Fax: 513 475-7501
EMP: 505 **Privately Held**
SIC: 8011 Medical centers
PA: Uc Health, Llc.
3200 Burnet Ave
Cincinnati OH 45229

(G-19173)
UNION CENTRE HOTEL LLC
Also Called: Marriott
6189 Muhlhauser Rd (45069-4842)
PHONE................513 874-7335
Fax: 513 874-7336
Brian Perkins, *General Mgr*
Jerry Rigney, *Sales Dir*
EMP: 167
SALES (est): 5.7MM **Privately Held**
SIC: 7011 Hotels & motels

(G-19174)
UNIVERSITY MOVING & STORAGE CO
Also Called: North American Van Lines
8735 Rite Track Way (45069-7361)
PHONE................248 615-7000
Mark Bruns, *Manager*
Diana West, *Agent*
EMP: 35
SALES (est): 2.1MM
SALES (corp-wide): 22.3MM **Privately Held**
SIC: 4214 Household goods moving & storage, local
PA: University Moving & Storage Company
23305 Commerce Dr
Farmington Hills MI 48335
248 615-7000

(G-19175)
UNIVERSITY OF CINCINNATI PHYS
Also Called: Uc Physicians At Univ Pointe
7700 University Ct # 1800 (45069-7202)
PHONE................513 475-8000
Allen Arthur, *Dean*
Lori Mackey, *COO*
Robert Maue, *CFO*
Tonya Askren, *Psychologist*
Srilakshmi Murthy, *Med Doctor*
EMP: 40 **Privately Held**
SIC: 8011 Offices & clinics of medical doctors
PA: University Of Cincinnati Physicians, Inc.
222 Piedmont Ave Ste 2200
Cincinnati OH 45219

West Chester - Hamilton County

(G-19176)
UNIVERSTY OF CINCINNTI MEDCL C
7690 Discovery Dr # 3000 (45069-6542)
PHONE.................513 475-8300
John Tew Jr, *Branch Mgr*
EMP: 1241
SALES (corp-wide): 913.1MM **Privately Held**
SIC: 8011 Offices & clinics of medical doctors
PA: University Of Cincinnati Medical Center, Llc
234 Goodman St
Cincinnati OH 45219
513 584-1000

(G-19177)
VALLEN DISTRIBUTION INC
Also Called: Innosource
9407 Meridian Way (45069-6525)
PHONE.................513 942-9100
Fax: 513 942-9171
Brian Ramstetter, *Opers Staff*
Sandra Henry, *Buyer*
Don Cole, *Sales Mgr*
Jeff Spencer, *Sales Staff*
Blake Woelfel, *Marketing Staff*
EMP: 60
SALES (corp-wide): 10MM **Privately Held**
WEB: www.idgventures.com
SIC: 5085 Mill supplies
HQ: Vallen Distribution, Inc.
2100 The Oaks Pkwy
Belmont NC 28012

(G-19178)
VARO ENGINEERS INC
6039 Schumacher Park Dr (45069-4812)
PHONE.................513 729-9313
Tim Burnham, *CEO*
EMP: 60
SALES (corp-wide): 27.4MM **Privately Held**
SIC: 8711 Engineering services
PA: Varo Engineers, Inc.
2751 Tuller Pkwy
Dublin OH 43017
614 459-0424

(G-19179)
VENDORS SUPPLY INC
Also Called: Vendor Supply of Ohio
6448 Gano Rd (45069-4829)
P.O. Box 62883, Cincinnati (45262-0883)
PHONE.................513 755-2111
Fax: 513 755-4046
Ken Morgan, *Manager*
Sarah McGuire, *Receptionist*
EMP: 30
SALES (corp-wide): 159.4MM **Privately Held**
SIC: 5141 Food brokers
PA: Vendors Supply, Inc.
201 Saluda River Rd
Columbia SC 29210
803 772-6390

(G-19180)
VIGILANT DEFENSE
Also Called: Vigilant Technology Solutions
8366 Princeton Glendale (45069-5935)
PHONE.................513 309-0672
Chris Nyhuis, *Owner*
Katherine Nyhuis, *CFO*
EMP: 40 **EST:** 2009
SALES (est): 4.4MM **Privately Held**
SIC: 7382 Security systems services

(G-19181)
VIKING OFFICE PRODUCTS INC
4700 Muhlhauser Rd (45011-9796)
PHONE.................513 881-7200
Fax: 513 874-1728
Michael Ocran, *Opers Staff*
Bruce Harris, *Branch Mgr*
EMP: 400
SALES (corp-wide): 10.2B **Publicly Held**
SIC: 5943 5044 Office forms & supplies; office equipment
HQ: Viking Office Products, Inc.
3366 E Willow St
Signal Hill CA 90755
562 490-1000

(G-19182)
VITRAN EXPRESS INC
2789 Crescentville Rd (45069-3816)
PHONE.................513 771-4894
Mike Scott, *Manager*
EMP: 30
SALES (corp-wide): 109.4MM **Privately Held**
SIC: 4213 Less-than-truckload (LTL) transport
PA: Vitran Express, Inc.
12225 Stephens Rd
Warren MI 48089
317 803-4000

(G-19183)
WARSTEINER IMPORTERS AGENCY
Also Called: Warsteiner USA
9359 Allen Rd (45069-3846)
PHONE.................513 942-9872
Fax: 513 942-9874
Geoffery Westapher, *President*
Kevin Berning, *Controller*
Steve Montano, *VP Sales*
Rich Hamilton, *Sales Mgr*
Ben Brearley, *Regl Sales Mgr*
▲ **EMP:** 50
SQ FT: 10,000
SALES: 24.5MM **Privately Held**
WEB: www.warsteiner-usa.com
SIC: 5181 Beer & other fermented malt liquors
PA: Warsteiner International Kg
Domring 4-10
Warstein
290 280-220

(G-19184)
WEST CHESTER CHRSTN CHLD
7951 Tylersville Rd (45069-2508)
PHONE.................513 777-6300
Kathleen Wiseman, *Director*
EMP: 25
SALES: 394.8K **Privately Held**
SIC: 8351 Group day care center

(G-19185)
WETHERNGTON GOLF CNTRY CLB INC (PA)
7337 Country Club Ln (45069-1598)
PHONE.................513 755-2582
Fax: 513 755-0502
Michael Purich, *Principal*
Dana Cimorell, *COO*
Riverview B Church, *Pastor*
Donna Kiessling, *Asst Controller*
Charlotte Jarvis, *Office Mgr*
EMP: 65
SALES: 913.5K **Privately Held**
WEB: www.wetheringtongcc.com
SIC: 7997 Country club, membership

(G-19186)
WINDWOOD SWIM & TENNIS CLUB
6649 N Windwood Dr (45069-4329)
P.O. Box 8037 (45069-8037)
PHONE.................513 777-2552
Barb Russell, *President*
EMP: 25
SALES: 181.3K **Privately Held**
SIC: 7941 Sports clubs, managers & promoters

(G-19187)
WINELCO INC
6141 Centre Park Dr (45069-3869)
PHONE.................513 755-8050
Fax: 513 755-8029
Michael Ullman, *President*
Pat Stouder, *Office Mgr*
Mary Holsinger, *Manager*
David Leverage, *Manager*
EMP: 40
SQ FT: 17,000
SALES (est): 8.2MM **Privately Held**
WEB: www.winelco.com
SIC: 7699 5084 Industrial equipment services; industrial machinery & equipment

West Chester
Hamilton County

(G-19188)
A-T CONTROLS INC (PA)
9955 International Blvd (45246-4853)
PHONE.................513 530-5175
Fax: 513 247-5462
Brian Wright, *President*
Brad Mueller, *Principal*
Doug Manning, *Regional Mgr*
Jeremy Pitzel, *Regional Mgr*
Frank Spray, *Regional Mgr*
▲ **EMP:** 32
SQ FT: 17,500
SALES (est): 19.9MM **Privately Held**
WEB: www.atcontrols.com
SIC: 5085 Valves & fittings; valves, pistons & fittings

(G-19189)
ACCURATE HEALTHCARE INC
4681 Interstate Dr (45246-1109)
PHONE.................513 208-6988
James Hobbs, *President*
EMP: 49 **EST:** 2016
SQ FT: 8,000
SALES (est): 165.7K **Privately Held**
SIC: 8059 Nursing home, except skilled & intermediate care facility

(G-19190)
ATLAS MACHINE AND SUPPLY INC
4985 Provident Dr (45246-1020)
PHONE.................502 584-7262
Fax: 513 874-4263
Kurt Colwell, *Div Sub Head*
Sonny Welker, *Manager*
EMP: 32
SALES (corp-wide): 45.8MM **Privately Held**
WEB: www.atlasmachine.com
SIC: 5084 3599 Compressors, except air conditioning; machine shop, jobbing & repair
PA: Atlas Machine And Supply, Inc.
7000 Global Dr
Louisville KY 40258
502 584-7262

(G-19191)
BEIERSDORF INC
5232 E Provident Dr (45246-1040)
PHONE.................513 682-7300
Fax: 513 682-5351
Gayle Gao, *President*
Dan Heil, *Opers Mgr*
John Parrish, *Maint Spvr*
Melanie Peck, *Human Res Mgr*
Catherine Greaves, *Human Resources*
EMP: 168
SALES (corp-wide): 10.6B **Privately Held**
WEB: www.bdfusa.com
SIC: 2844 5122 3842 2841 Face creams or lotions; antiseptics; bandages & dressings; stockinette, surgical; soap; granulated, liquid, cake, flaked or chip; tape, pressure sensitive: made from purchased materials
HQ: Beiersdorf, Inc.
45 Danbury Rd
Wilton CT 06897
203 563-5800

(G-19192)
BELFOR USA GROUP INC
4710 Interstate Dr Ste L (45246-1144)
PHONE.................513 860-3111
Beth Goodhart, *Manager*
EMP: 45
SALES (corp-wide): 1B **Privately Held**
SIC: 1799 7349 Post-disaster renovations; building maintenance services
HQ: Belfor Usa Group Inc.
185 Oakland Ave Ste 150
Birmingham MI 48009

(G-19193)
BRIDGE LOGISTICS INC
5 Circle Freeway Dr (45246-1201)
PHONE.................513 874-7444
Fax: 513 874-4161

James Campbell, *CEO*
William P Lanham, *Vice Pres*
Tony Campbell, *Opers Staff*
Megan Vanover, *Opers Staff*
Paul Lanham, *VP Accounting*
EMP: 30
SQ FT: 10,000
SALES: 15MM **Privately Held**
WEB: www.bridgelogisticsinc.com
SIC: 4214 Local trucking with storage

(G-19194)
BRIGHTVIEW LANDSCAPES LLC
10139 Transportation Way (45246-1317)
PHONE.................513 874-6484
Mark McClanahan, *General Mgr*
EMP: 56
SALES (corp-wide): 914MM **Privately Held**
SIC: 0781 Landscape services
HQ: Brightview Landscapes, Llc
401 Plymouth Rd Ste 500
Plymouth Meeting PA 19462
484 567-7204

(G-19195)
E S I INC (DH)
4696 Devitt Dr (45246-1104)
PHONE.................513 454-3741
Fax: 513 454-0259
Tom Schrout, *President*
Cahrley Hartshorn, *Vice Pres*
Douglas Hurley, *Vice Pres*
Gary Laidman, *Vice Pres*
Nick Behnken, *Project Mgr*
EMP: 100
SQ FT: 9,000
SALES (est): 35.7MM
SALES (corp-wide): 4.4B **Publicly Held**
WEB: www.esielectrical.com
SIC: 1731 General electrical contractor
HQ: Mdu Construction Services Group, Inc.
1150 W Century Ave
Bismarck ND 58503
701 530-1000

(G-19196)
EMPIRE PACKING COMPANY LP
Also Called: Cincinnatti Processing
113 Circle Freeway Dr (45246-1203)
PHONE.................513 942-5400
Fax: 513 870-6068
Dennis Hioghmas, *General Mgr*
EMP: 60
SALES (corp-wide): 106.1MM **Privately Held**
WEB: www.ledbetterfoods.com
SIC: 5147 2013 2011 Meats, fresh; sausages & other prepared meats; meat packing plants
PA: Empire Packing Company, L.P.
1837 Harbor Ave
Memphis TN 38113
901 948-4788

(G-19197)
ESSENDANT CO
9775 International Blvd (45246-4855)
PHONE.................513 942-1354
Glynn Magness, *Branch Mgr*
EMP: 96
SALES (corp-wide): 5B **Publicly Held**
WEB: www.ussco.com
SIC: 5112 Office supplies
HQ: Essendant Co.
1 Parkway North Blvd # 100
Deerfield IL 60015
847 627-7000

(G-19198)
ESSIG RESEARCH INC
497 Circle Freeway Dr # 236 (45246-1257)
PHONE.................513 942-7100
Fax: 513 942-7103
Joseph P Daly, *President*
Mark Ridge, *Project Mgr*
Tiffany Spencer, *Engineer*
Bruce Akin, *Admin Asst*
EMP: 28
SQ FT: 5,000
SALES (est): 4.7MM **Privately Held**
SIC: 8711 Consulting engineer

West Chester - Hamilton County (G-19199)

GEOGRAPHIC SECTION

(G-19199)
EXPRESS TWING RECOVERY SVC INC
9772 Prnceton Glendale Rd (45246-1022)
PHONE....................513 881-1900
Mark Groteke, *President*
Jeff Steel, *General Mgr*
EMP: 44
SQ FT: 3,000
SALES (est): 4.7MM **Privately Held**
WEB: www.expressautotransport.com
SIC: **4213** Automobiles, transport & delivery

(G-19200)
FEDEX GROUND PACKAGE SYS INC
9667 Inter Ocean Dr (45246-1029)
PHONE....................513 942-4330
EMP: 100
SALES (corp-wide): 47.4B **Publicly Held**
SIC: **4213** 4212 Trucking Delivery Services
HQ: Fedex Ground Package System, Inc.
1000 Fed Ex Dr
Coraopolis PA 15108
412 269-1000

(G-19201)
FILTERFRESH COFFEE SERVICE INC
4890 Duff Dr Ste D (45246-1100)
PHONE....................513 681-8911
Fax: 513 521-5113
Yasna Hood, *Manager*
EMP: 25 **Publicly Held**
SIC: **7389** Coffee service
HQ: Filterfresh Coffee Service Inc.
1101 Market St Fl 7
Philadelphia PA 19107

(G-19202)
FRITO-LAY NORTH AMERICA INC
4696 Devitt Dr (45246-1104)
PHONE....................513 874-0112
Russell White, *Branch Mgr*
EMP: 61
SQ FT: 12,500
SALES (corp-wide): 63.5B **Publicly Held**
WEB: www.fritolay.com
SIC: **5145** Snack foods
HQ: Frito-Lay North America, Inc.
7701 Legacy Dr
Plano TX 75024

(G-19203)
FULFILLMENT TECHNOLOGIES LLC
Also Called: Filltek Fulfillment Services
5389 E Provident Dr (45246-1044)
PHONE....................513 346-3100
Fax: 513 346-3103
Steven Messer, *General Mgr*
Tom Hartman, *Vice Pres*
Vin Desalvo, *Opers Staff*
Dawn Adams, *Accountant*
Jena S Satchell, *Persnl Dir*
EMP: 150 EST: 2000
SQ FT: 304,000
SALES (est): 13.3MM **Privately Held**
WEB: www.filltek.com
SIC: **4225** 4841 Warehousing, self-storage; multipoint distribution systems services (MDS)

(G-19204)
GARAGE DOOR SYSTEMS LLC
Overhead Door of Cincinnati
858 E Crescentville Rd A (45246-4843)
PHONE....................513 321-9600
Fax: 513 346-4010
Noulis Theofylaktos, *Manager*
EMP: 115
SALES (corp-wide): 58.3MM **Privately Held**
SIC: **1751** 5211 Garage door, installation or erection; door & window products
PA: Garage Door Systems, Llc
8811 Bash St
Indianapolis IN 46256
317 842-7444

(G-19205)
GSF NORTH AMERICAN JANTR SVC
9850 Prnceton Glendale Rd (45246-1034)
PHONE....................513 733-1451
Fax: 513 733-0431
Tim Rupard, *President*
EMP: 199
SALES (corp-wide): 72.4MM **Privately Held**
SIC: **7349** Janitorial service, contract basis
HQ: Gsf North American Janitorial Service Inc
107 S Penn St Ste 300
Indianapolis IN 46204
317 262-1133

(G-19206)
HELPING HANDS HEALTH CARE INC
9692 Cncnnati Columbus Rd (45241-1071)
PHONE....................513 755-4181
Fax: 513 777-0680
Chris Ellis, *CEO*
EMP: 160 EST: 1999
SALES (est): 5.8MM **Privately Held**
WEB: www.helpinghandshealthcare.com
SIC: **8082** Home health care services

(G-19207)
HILLMAN GROUP INC
Also Called: Hargis Industries
9950 Prnceton Glendale Rd (45246-1116)
PHONE....................513 874-5905
David Quehl, *Manager*
EMP: 35
SALES (corp-wide): 838.3MM **Privately Held**
WEB: www.sealtite.com
SIC: **7319** Aerial advertising services
HQ: The Hillman Group Inc
10590 Hamilton Ave
Cincinnati OH 45231
513 851-4900

(G-19208)
HOME CARE PHARMACY LLC (DH)
Also Called: Omnicare of Cincinnati
5549 Spellmire Dr (45246-4841)
PHONE....................513 874-0009
Fax: 513 874-2136
Mike Arnold, *COO*
Beth Boone, *Assistant VP*
Connie Pinkley, *Vice Pres*
Caleb Burdette, *Manager*
Dave West,
EMP: 150
SQ FT: 20,000
SALES (corp-wide): 184.7B **Publicly Held**
SIC: **5122** Drugs, proprietaries & sundries
HQ: Omnicare Holding Company
1105 Market St Ste 1300
Cincinnati OH 45215
513 719-2600

(G-19209)
HWZ DISTRIBUTION GROUP LLC (HQ)
Also Called: Nexgen Building Supply
40 W Crescentville Rd (45246-1238)
PHONE....................513 618-0300
Fax: 513 618-0301
Robert Hoge, *CEO*
Richard Wolgemuth, *President*
Bruce Fhaey, *CFO*
EMP: 30
SALES (est): 133.8MM
SALES (corp-wide): 160.7MM **Privately Held**
WEB: www.nexgenbuildingsupply.com
SIC: **5032** Drywall materials
PA: Nexgen Enterprises, Inc.
3274 Spring Grove Ave
Cincinnati OH 45225
513 618-0300

(G-19210)
INTELLIGENT INFORMATION INC
4838 Duff Dr Ste C (45246-1143)
PHONE....................513 860-4233
Fax: 513 771-4366
George Wagenheim, *President*
Colleen Cavanaugh, *Opers Mgr*
EMP: 25
SALES (est): 1.5MM **Privately Held**
SIC: **7378** Computer maintenance & repair

(G-19211)
INTERNASH GLOBAL SVC GROUP LLC
4621 Interstate Dr (45246-1109)
PHONE....................513 772-0430
Jennifer Campos, *Branch Mgr*
EMP: 55
SALES (corp-wide): 18.1MM **Privately Held**
SIC: **7629** Electrical equipment repair services
PA: Internash Global Services, Llc
10305 Round Up Ln Ste 400
Houston TX 77064
713 722-0320

(G-19212)
LEIDOS TECHNICAL SERVICES INC
Also Called: Lockheed Martin
497 Circle Freeway Dr # 236 (45246-1257)
PHONE....................513 672-8400
Fax: 513 674-5798
EMP: 60
SALES (corp-wide): 7B **Publicly Held**
SIC: **8731** Research & Development Of Space Launch Vehicles
HQ: Leidos Technical Services, Inc.
700 N Frederick Ave
Gaithersburg MD 20879
301 240-7000

(G-19213)
LOUIS TRAUTH DAIRY LLC (HQ)
9991 Commerce Park Dr (45246-1331)
P.O. Box 721770, Newport KY (41072-1770)
PHONE....................859 431-7553
Greg Engles, *CEO*
Rachael A Gonzalez, *Principal*
Steven J Kemps, *Principal*
Gary Sparks, *Senior VP*
Dan Smith, *Vice Pres*
EMP: 260 EST: 1920
SQ FT: 160,000
SALES (est): 39.6MM **Publicly Held**
WEB: www.trauthdairy.com
SIC: **5143** 5149 2033 2026 Dairy products, except dried or canned; milk & cream, fluid; ice cream & ices; butter; beverages, except coffee & tea; mineral or spring water bottling; tea; canned fruits & specialties; fluid milk; ice cream & frozen desserts

(G-19214)
MCCC SPORTSWEAR INC
9944 Prnceton Glendale Rd (45246-1116)
PHONE....................513 583-9210
Fax: 513 583-0874
Marta Callahan, *President*
Sue Kollstedt, *Vice Pres*
Jennifer Snyder, *Marketing Staff*
Max Cole, *Manager*
Robert Seyfried, *Manager*
▲ EMP: 30
SQ FT: 45,000
SALES: 8MM **Privately Held**
WEB: www.mccc-sportswear.com
SIC: **5137** 2395 5136 Women's & children's clothing; embroidery & art needlework; men's & boys' clothing

(G-19215)
MID-AMERICA GUTTERS INC (PA)
862 E Crescentville Rd (45246-4843)
PHONE....................513 671-4000
Fax: 513 671-3575
Lee J Brown, *President*
EMP: 48
SQ FT: 37,000
SALES (est): 3.6MM **Privately Held**
SIC: **1761** Gutter & downspout contractor

(G-19216)
MIDWEST MFG SOLUTIONS LLC
Also Called: Definity Partners
5474 Spellmire Dr (45246-4842)
P.O. Box 28, Pleasant Plain (45162-0028)
PHONE....................513 381-7200
Diana Luhmann, *Human Res Mgr*
Ray Attiyah, *Administration*
Paul Hanson, *Administration*
Jay Kuhn,
EMP: 30
SALES (est): 3.5MM **Privately Held**
SIC: **8742** Manufacturing management consultant

(G-19217)
MILLIKEN MILLWORK INC
Also Called: Mmi II
400 Circle Freeway Dr (45246-1214)
PHONE....................513 874-6771
Fax: 513 870-0242
Rick Carlson, *General Mgr*
Ila Brown, *Finance Mgr*
Debbie Olding, *Human Res Dir*
EMP: 100 **Publicly Held**
WEB: www.millikenmillwork.com
SIC: **5031** Lumber, plywood & millwork; millwork; door frames, all materials; doors
HQ: Milliken Millwork, Inc.
6361 Sterling Dr N
Sterling Heights MI 48312
586 264-0950

(G-19218)
NETRADA NORTH AMERICA LLC
Also Called: Tradeglobal
5389 E Provident Dr (45246-1044)
PHONE....................866 345-5835
Dave Rice, *CEO*
Dave Eckley, *President*
Ryan Calvin, *Business Mgr*
Blake Vaughn, *COO*
Russ Carter, *Vice Pres*
EMP: 44
SALES (est): 12.1MM **Privately Held**
SIC: **7371** 7389 Computer software development; financial services

(G-19219)
ORS NASCO INC
9901 Princeton Glendale (45246-1115)
PHONE....................918 781-5300
Greg Hawkins, *Branch Mgr*
EMP: 43
SALES (corp-wide): 5B **Publicly Held**
SIC: **5085** 1541 Fasteners & fastening equipment; industrial buildings & warehouses
HQ: Ors Nasco, Inc.
907 S Detroit Ave Ste 400
Tulsa OK 74120
918 781-5300

(G-19220)
PITNEY BOWES PRESORT SVCS INC
10085 International Blvd (45246-4845)
PHONE....................513 860-3607
David Overley, *President*
David Bush, *General Mgr*
EMP: 84
SALES (corp-wide): 3.5B **Publicly Held**
WEB: www.psigroupinc.com
SIC: **7389** Presorted mail service
HQ: Pitney Bowes Presort Services, Inc.
10110 I St
Omaha NE 68127

(G-19221)
PITT-OHIO EXPRESS LLC
5000 Duff Dr (45246-1309)
PHONE....................513 860-3424
Fax: 513 771-3477
Brent Acton, *Business Mgr*
Brant Actin, *Manager*
EMP: 100
SALES (corp-wide): 507.8MM **Privately Held**
SIC: **4213** 4212 Contract haulers; local trucking, without storage
PA: Pitt-Ohio Express, Llc
15 27th St
Pittsburgh PA 15222
412 232-3015

(G-19222)
PUTMAN JANITORIAL SERVICE INC
4836 Duff Dr Ste D (45246-1194)
PHONE....................513 942-1900
James Putman, *President*
EMP: 36

▲ = Import ▼ = Export
◆ = Import/Export

SQ FT: 1,800
SALES (est): 1MM **Privately Held**
SIC: 7349 Building maintenance services

(G-19223)
READING ROCK RESIDENTIAL LLC
Also Called: Installed Products & Services
4677 Devitt Dr (45246-1103)
P.O. Box 46387, Cincinnati (45246-0387)
PHONE.................................513 874-4770
Michael Hausfeld, *General Mgr*
Eric Morefield, *Technical Mgr*
Tyler Hausfeld, *Executive*
Gordan Rich,
Richard Butcher,
▼ EMP: 36
SALES (est): 6.4MM **Privately Held**
WEB: www.installps.com
SIC: 5074 1791 Fireplaces, prefabricated; structural steel erection

(G-19224)
RECKER AND BOERGER INC
Also Called: Recker & Boerger Appliances
10115 Transportation Way (45246-1317)
PHONE.................................513 942-9663
Allen Boerger, *CEO*
Steven A Boerger, *President*
Jim Recker, *Vice Pres*
Stan Carlson, *Controller*
Stanley Carlson, *Accounts Mgr*
▲ EMP: 100 EST: 1962
SALES (est): 19.9MM **Privately Held**
WEB: www.reckerandboerger.com
SIC: 5722 1711 Electric household appliances, major; warm air heating & air conditioning contractor

(G-19225)
RITE RUG CO
9974 International Blvd (45246-4852)
PHONE.................................513 942-0010
Fax: 513 942-0090
Mickey Goldberg, *Manager*
EMP: 25
SALES (corp-wide): 82.2MM **Privately Held**
WEB: www.riterug.com
SIC: 1752 Floor laying & floor work
PA: Rite Rug Co.
  4450 Poth Rd Ste A
  Columbus OH 43213
  614 261-6060

(G-19226)
ROYAL PAPER STOCK COMPANY INC
339 Circle Freeway Dr (45246-1207)
PHONE.................................513 870-5780
Fax: 513 870-5783
Rich Dahn, *Vice Pres*
Dan Price, *Manager*
EMP: 25
SALES (corp-wide): 52.9MM **Privately Held**
WEB: www.royalpaperstock.com
SIC: 4953 Recycling, waste materials
PA: Royal Paper Stock Company Inc
  1300 Norton Rd
  Columbus OH 43228
  614 851-4714

(G-19227)
SALON ALEXANDRE INC
9755 Cncnnati Columbus Rd (45241-1074)
PHONE.................................513 207-8406
Alexandre Zinovieve, *President*
EMP: 33
SALES (est): 406.2K **Privately Held**
SIC: 7231 Beauty shops

(G-19228)
SEXTON INDUSTRIAL INC
366 Circle Freeway Dr (45246-1208)
PHONE.................................513 530-5555
Abbe Sexton, *President*
Dan Towne, *Corp Secy*
Ron Sexton, *Vice Pres*
Vikie Masnith, *Office Mgr*
EMP: 150
SQ FT: 85,000
SALES (est): 43.5MM **Privately Held**
WEB: www.artisanmechanical.com
SIC: 1711 3443 Mechanical contractor; industrial vessels, tanks & containers

(G-19229)
SIMPLEX TIME RECORDER LLC
Also Called: Simplex Time Recorder 514
10182 International Blvd (45246-4846)
PHONE.................................513 874-1227
Fax: 513 874-1246
Dan Thieken, *Branch Mgr*
EMP: 30 **Privately Held**
WEB: www.comtec-alaska.com
SIC: 1731 5063 Safety & security specialization; electrical apparatus & equipment
HQ: Simplex Time Recorder Llc
  50 Technology Dr
  Westminster MA 01441
  978 731-2500

(G-19230)
SLUSH PUPPIE
44 Carnegie Way (45246-1224)
PHONE.................................513 771-0940
Will Radcliff, *Ch of Bd*
Dan Keating, *President*
Dennis Harney, *Vice Pres*
Mike Kornbluth, *Sales Mgr*
Diane Menzer, *Marketing Staff*
EMP: 90
SQ FT: 40,000
SALES (est): 7.6MM **Privately Held**
WEB: www.slushpuppie.net
SIC: 2087 5078 Syrups, drink; cocktail mixes, nonalcoholic; soda fountain equipment, refrigerated

(G-19231)
STAR DIST & MANUFACTURRING LLC
9818 Prncton Glendale Rd (45246-1017)
PHONE.................................513 860-3573
Mario Listo, *President*
Rick Hancock, *Principal*
Brenda Butler, *Bookkeeper*
Maribeth Cash, *Cust Mgr*
Paul Thompson, *Supervisor*
EMP: 57
SALES (est): 12.7MM **Privately Held**
SIC: 1731 7629 Electrical work; electrical repair shops

(G-19232)
STOROPACK INC (DH)
Also Called: Foam Pac Materials Company
4758 Devitt Dr (45246-1106)
PHONE.................................513 874-0314
Fax: 513 874-2955
Hans Reichenecker, *Ch of Bd*
Daniel Wachter, *President*
Brigitte Vanhoorne, *General Mgr*
Thomas G Eckel, *Vice Pres*
Joe Lagrasta, *Vice Pres*
▲ EMP: 50
SQ FT: 35,000
SALES: 110MM
SALES (corp-wide): 447.2MM **Privately Held**
WEB: www.storopack.com
SIC: 5199 3086 2671 Packaging materials; packaging & shipping materials, foamed plastic; packaging paper & plastics film, coated & laminated
HQ: Storopack Deutschland Gmbh + Co. Kg
  Untere Rietstr. 30
  Metzingen 72555
  712 316-40

(G-19233)
SUPERIOR BULK LOGISTICS INC
Also Called: Superior Carriers
4963 Provident Dr (45246-1020)
PHONE.................................513 874-3440
Fax: 513 874-3361
Robert P Foltz, *Manager*
EMP: 30
SALES (corp-wide): 502.2MM **Privately Held**
WEB: www.superiorbulklogistics.com
SIC: 4213 Contract haulers
PA: Superior Bulk Logistics, Inc.
  711 Jorie Blvd Ste 101n
  Oak Brook IL 60523
  630 573-2555

(G-19234)
SUPERIOR ENVMTL SLTONS SES INC
Also Called: S E S
9976 Joseph James Dr (45246-1340)
PHONE.................................513 874-6910
Chester Yeager, *Branch Mgr*
EMP: 280
SALES (corp-wide): 34.5MM **Privately Held**
SIC: 8999 Earth science services
PA: Superior Environmental Solutions Llc
  9996 Joseph James Dr
  West Chester OH 45246
  513 874-8355

(G-19235)
SUPERIOR ENVMTL SOLUTIONS LLC (PA)
Also Called: S E S
9996 Joseph James Dr (45246-1340)
PHONE.................................513 874-8355
Fax: 513 874-8555
Dean Wallace, *President*
Chester Yeager, *Vice Pres*
Michael Malone, *Safety Dir*
Brian Runion, *Safety Mgr*
Dean Walls, *Executive*
EMP: 385
SQ FT: 10,000
SALES: 34.5MM **Privately Held**
SIC: 4959 Environmental cleanup services

(G-19236)
T&T ENTERPRISES OF OHIO INC
5100 Duff Dr (45246-1311)
PHONE.................................513 942-1141
Fax: 513 942-6141
Eric O Trautman Sr, *CEO*
EMP: 42
SQ FT: 8,500
SALES (est): 7.3MM **Privately Held**
SIC: 4212 Mail carriers, contract

(G-19237)
TRI-STATE TRAILER SALES INC
5230 Duff Dr (45246-1313)
PHONE.................................412 747-7777
Walter Gowsell, *Sales Executive*
Naomi Carr, *Manager*
EMP: 25
SALES (corp-wide): 51.4MM **Privately Held**
WEB: www.tristatetrailer.com
SIC: 5012 Trucks, commercial
PA: Tri-State Trailer Sales, Inc.
  3111 Grand Ave
  Pittsburgh PA 15225
  412 747-7777

(G-19238)
UNITED GROUP SERVICES INC (PA)
9740 Near Dr (45246-1013)
PHONE.................................800 633-9690
Daniel Freese, *President*
Kevin Sell, *Vice Pres*
Matt Mofield, *Project Mgr*
Ron Williams, *Safety Mgr*
Bob Erhart, *Purchasing*
EMP: 200
SQ FT: 45,500
SALES: 50.4MM **Privately Held**
WEB: www.united-gs.com
SIC: 3498 1711 Fabricated pipe & fittings, process piping contractor; mechanical contractor

(G-19239)
UNIVAR USA INC
4600 Dues Dr (45246-1009)
PHONE.................................513 714-5264
Vicki Turner, *Personnel Exec*
Charles Miller, *Accounts Mgr*
Gary Southern, *Branch Mgr*
Rob Couch, *Manager*
EMP: 150
SQ FT: 129,100
SALES (corp-wide): 8.2B **Publicly Held**
SIC: 5169 2819 2869 2899 Industrial chemicals; industrial inorganic chemicals; industrial organic chemicals; chemical preparations; specialty cleaning, polishes & sanitation goods
HQ: Univar Usa Inc.
  17411 Ne Union Hill Rd
  Redmond WA 98052
  425 889-3400

(G-19240)
US FOODS INC
5445 Spellmire Dr (45246-4842)
PHONE.................................614 539-7993
Fax: 513 874-5188
June Collett, *Sales Mgr*
Ron Jordon, *Manager*
Neil Hoover, *Director*
EMP: 3300 **Publicly Held**
WEB: www.usfoodservice.com
SIC: 5141 5149 5148 5143 Food brokers; groceries & related products; fresh fruits & vegetables; dairy products, except dried or canned; packaged frozen goods
HQ: Us Foods, Inc.
  9399 W Higgins Rd Ste 500
  Rosemont IL 60018

(G-19241)
USF HOLLAND LLC
Also Called: USFreightways
10074 Prncton Glendale Rd (45246-1210)
PHONE.................................513 874-8960
Dave Botos, *Branch Mgr*
Vivian Hurley, *Clerk*
EMP: 128
SALES (corp-wide): 4.8B **Publicly Held**
WEB: www.usfc.com
SIC: 4213 4212 Less-than-truckload (LTL) transport; local trucking, without storage
HQ: Usf Holland Llc
  700 S Waverly Rd
  Holland MI 49423
  616 395-5000

(G-19242)
W W WILLIAMS COMPANY LLC
4806 Interstate Dr (45246-1114)
PHONE.................................800 336-6651
EMP: 67
SALES (corp-wide): 2.1B **Privately Held**
SIC: 5084 Engines & parts, diesel
HQ: The W W Williams Company Llc
  835 Goodale Blvd
  Columbus OH 43212
  614 228-5000

(G-19243)
WACHTER INC
10186 International Blvd (45246-4846)
PHONE.................................513 777-0701
Doug Hacker, *Project Mgr*
Ken Hennings, *Branch Mgr*
EMP: 175
SALES (corp-wide): 232.7MM **Privately Held**
SIC: 1731 1623 General electrical contractor; voice, data & video wiring contractor; cable laying construction
PA: Wachter, Inc.
  16001 W 99th St
  Lenexa KS 66219
  913 541-2500

(G-19244)
XPO LOGISTICS FREIGHT INC
5289 Duff Dr (45246-1330)
PHONE.................................513 870-0044
Donald Gallam, *Manager*
EMP: 230
SALES (corp-wide): 15.3B **Publicly Held**
WEB: www.con-way.com
SIC: 4213 4212 Contract haulers; local trucking, without storage
HQ: Xpo Logistics Freight, Inc.
  2211 Old Earhart Rd # 100
  Ann Arbor MI 48105
  734 998-4200

(G-19245)
YRC INC
Also Called: Yellow Transportation
10074 Prncton Glendale Rd (45246-1210)
PHONE.................................513 874-9320
Fax: 513 874-1942
Bill Irvin, *Managing Dir*
Bob Braun, *Materials Mgr*
Jeff Carpenter, *Terminal Mgr*
Donald Smith, *Terminal Mgr*
David Rodis, *Accounts Mgr*
EMP: 200

West Farmington - Trumbull County (G-19246)

GEOGRAPHIC SECTION

SALES (corp-wide): 4.8B Publicly Held
WEB: www.roadway.com
SIC: 4213 Less-than-truckload (LTL) transport
HQ: Yrc Inc.
10990 Roe Ave
Overland Park KS 66211
913 696-6100

West Farmington
Trumbull County

(G-19246)
REYNOLDS INDUSTRIES INC
380 W Main St (44491)
P.O. Box 6 (44491-0006)
PHONE..................................330 889-9466
Fax: 330 889-9466
Gregory A Reynolds, *President*
EMP: 25
SQ FT: 3,500
SALES (est): 2.6MM Privately Held
SIC: 3069 4783 Rubber hardware; packing goods for shipping

West Jefferson
Madison County

(G-19247)
ARBORS WEST LLC
Also Called: ARBORS WEST SUBACUTE & REHABIL
375 W Main St (43162-1298)
PHONE..................................614 879-7661
Fax: 614 879-7604
Joe Knapton, *Director*
Tina Smith, *Hlthcr Dir*
Alison Morris, *Administration*
Tony Valentine, *Administration*
Ronald White, *Administration*
EMP: 100
SQ FT: 50,000
SALES: 7.2MM Privately Held
SIC: 8059 8051 Nursing home, except skilled & intermediate care facility; skilled nursing care facilities

(G-19248)
BATTELLE MEMORIAL INSTITUTE
Hc 142 (43162)
PHONE..................................614 424-5435
Holmes Rick, *Research*
Greg Kastner, *Branch Mgr*
Mark Cloran, *Manager*
EMP: 299
SALES (corp-wide): 4.8B Privately Held
WEB: www.battelle.org
SIC: 8731 Commercial physical research
PA: Battelle Memorial Institute Inc
505 King Ave
Columbus OH 43201
614 424-6424

(G-19249)
BATTELLE MEMORIAL INSTITUTE
Also Called: Battelle W Jfferson Operations
1425 State Route 142 Ne (43162-9647)
PHONE..................................614 424-5435
Darren Smith, *Project Mgr*
Stephen J Coleman, *Research*
Brian Blackstone, *Engineer*
Gary Carlin, *Human Resources*
Greg Enwen, *Manager*
EMP: 230
SALES (corp-wide): 4.8B Privately Held
WEB: www.battelle.org
SIC: 8731 Commercial physical research; medical research, commercial; environmental research; electronic research
PA: Battelle Memorial Institute Inc
505 King Ave
Columbus OH 43201
614 424-6424

(G-19250)
DENNIS TODD PAINTING INC
6055 Us Highway 40 (43162-9789)
PHONE..................................614 879-7952
Fax: 614 879-9378
Dennis Todd, *President*
EMP: 30
SALES (est): 1.9MM Privately Held
SIC: 1721 Commercial painting; commercial wallcovering contractor

(G-19251)
FEDEX FREIGHT CORPORATION
10 Commerce Pkwy (43162-9419)
PHONE..................................800 344-6448
Greg Binning, *Manager*
EMP: 80
SQ FT: 8,405
SALES (corp-wide): 60.3B Publicly Held
SIC: 4213 Trucking, except local
HQ: Fedex Freight Corporation
1715 Aaron Brenner Dr
Memphis TN 38120

(G-19252)
FORREST TRUCKING COMPANY
540 Taylor Blair Rd (43162-9718)
PHONE..................................614 879-8642
Fax: 614 879-9859
Ace Forrest, *Branch Mgr*
EMP: 38
SALES (corp-wide): 2.8MM Privately Held
SIC: 4212 Dump truck haulage
PA: Forrest Trucking Company
7 E 1st St
London OH 43140
614 879-7347

(G-19253)
M H EBY INC
4435 State Route 29 (43162-9544)
P.O. Box 137 (43162-0137)
PHONE..................................614 879-6901
Fax: 614 879-6904
EMP: 50 Privately Held
SIC: 5012 3444 Whol Autos/Motor Vehicles Mfg Sheet Metalwork

(G-19254)
MADISON TREE & LANDSCAPE CO
3180 Glade Run Rd (43162-9530)
P.O. Box 71 (43162-0071)
PHONE..................................614 207-5422
Fax: 614 852-5595
David Spegal, *Owner*
EMP: 36 EST: 1986
SALES (est): 2.4MM Privately Held
SIC: 0781 Landscape services

(G-19255)
TARGET CORPORATION
1 Walker Way (43162-9406)
PHONE..................................614 801-6700
Fax: 614 801-6896
Gerri Commodore, *General Mgr*
EMP: 344
SALES (corp-wide): 71.8B Publicly Held
WEB: www.target.com
SIC: 4226 Special warehousing & storage
PA: Target Corporation
1000 Nicollet Mall
Minneapolis MN 55403
612 304-6073

(G-19256)
WEST JEFFERSON PLUMBING HTG
Also Called: West Jefferson Plbg Htg Coolin
174 E Main St (43162-1248)
PHONE..................................614 879-9606
Fax: 614 879-9337
Ivan Mast Jr, *President*
James Schrock, *Vice Pres*
Wayne Yoder, *Vice Pres*
Bob Savarese, *Manager*
EMP: 32
SQ FT: 8,800
SALES (est): 5MM Privately Held
SIC: 1711 Plumbing contractors; warm air heating & air conditioning contractor

West Lafayette
Coshocton County

(G-19257)
JONES METAL PRODUCTS COMPANY
Jones-Zylon Company
305 N Center St (43845-1001)
PHONE..................................740 545-6341
Todd Kohl, *Manager*
EMP: 40
SALES (est): 2.3MM
SALES (corp-wide): 9.5MM Privately Held
WEB: www.joneszylon.com
SIC: 5047 3842 Hospital equipment & supplies; surgical appliances & supplies
PA: Jones Metal Products Company
200 N Center St
West Lafayette OH 43845
740 545-6381

(G-19258)
KINDRED HEALTHCARE OPER INC
Also Called: West Lafytt Rehabltion
620 E Main St (43845-1267)
PHONE..................................740 545-6355
Fax: 740 545-6763
Ira C Gross, *Principal*
Connie Lahna, *Sales Staff*
Rami Sawyer, *Office Mgr*
Gary Carver, *Director*
Jackie Wolgamott, *Administration*
EMP: 68
SALES (corp-wide): 6B Publicly Held
WEB: www.salemhaven.com
SIC: 8051 8093 8052 Skilled nursing care facilities; rehabilitation center, outpatient treatment; intermediate care facilities
HQ: Kindred Healthcare Operating, Inc.
680 S 4th St
Louisville KY 40202
502 596-7300

(G-19259)
RIVER GREENS GOLF COURSE INC
22749 State Route 751 (43845-9737)
PHONE..................................740 545-7817
Fax: 740 545-7112
Doug Davis, *President*
Lee Russell, *Corp Secy*
Lynn Russell, *Vice Pres*
EMP: 30
SQ FT: 3,000
SALES (est): 1.2MM Privately Held
WEB: www.rivergreens.com
SIC: 7992 Public golf courses

West Liberty
Logan County

(G-19260)
ADRIEL SCHOOL INC (PA)
414 N Detroit St (43357-9690)
P.O. Box 188 (43357-0188)
PHONE..................................937 465-0010
Fax: 937 465-8690
Michael Mullins, *CEO*
Van Williams, *Facilities Mgr*
Simon Schlabach, *Finance Mgr*
Jacquie Linville, *Director*
Terri McGarry, *Director*
EMP: 100 EST: 1896
SQ FT: 60,000
SALES: 8.4MM Privately Held
SIC: 8361 8063 8211 Home for the emotionally disturbed; group foster home; hospital for the mentally ill; private special education school

(G-19261)
CONSOLIDATED CARE INC
501 W Baird St (43357-9796)
P.O. Box 817 (43357-0817)
PHONE..................................937 465-8065
Randell Reminder, *President*
Sally J Willolby, *Vice Pres*
EMP: 50

SALES: 5.2MM Privately Held
WEB: www.lightofheartsvilla.org
SIC: 8322 Family counseling services

(G-19262)
CONSOLIDATED CARE INC (PA)
1521 N Detroit St (43357-9794)
P.O. Box 817 (43357-0817)
PHONE..................................937 465-8065
Jennifer Dempster, *President*
EMP: 30
SQ FT: 3,000
SALES: 4.5MM Privately Held
WEB: www.ccibhp.com
SIC: 8322 8093 8049 8011 Family counseling services; mental health clinic, outpatient; psychiatric social worker; psychiatrists & psychoanalysts

(G-19263)
OAKHILL MEDICAL ASSOCIATES
4879 Us Highway 68 S (43357-9525)
PHONE..................................937 599-1411
Fax: 937 465-9945
Roger Kauffman, *President*
Charles Kratz MD, *Principal*
Kenneth Miller MD, *Principal*
John Wenger Do, *Principal*
EMP: 35
SALES (est): 4.4MM Privately Held
SIC: 8011 General & family practice, physician/surgeon

(G-19264)
WEST LIBERTY CARE CENTER INC
Also Called: Green Hills
6557 Us Highway 68 S (43357-9536)
PHONE..................................937 465-5065
Fax: 937 465-4390
Mike Ray, *President*
Cheryl Siegenthaler, *Pastor*
Stephanie Christopher, *CFO*
Stacie Cingle, *Human Res Dir*
Jennifer Wren, *Pub Rel Dir*
EMP: 170
SQ FT: 47,346
SALES: 10.1MM Privately Held
SIC: 8051 8052 8351 Skilled nursing care facilities; intermediate care facilities; child day care services

West Manchester
Preble County

(G-19265)
BIRCHWOOD GENETICS INC (PA)
465 Stephens Rd (45382-9716)
P.O. Box 137 (45382-0137)
PHONE..................................937 678-9313
Fax: 937 678-9323
Dave Flory, *President*
Pamela Flory, *Vice Pres*
Mindy Barden, *Opers Mgr*
Curt Wagoner, *Treasurer*
Griff Tomlin, *Manager*
EMP: 30
SQ FT: 1,000
SALES: 12.6MM Privately Held
SIC: 0752 Animal breeding services

West Mansfield
Logan County

(G-19266)
HEARTLAND QUALITY EGG FARM
Also Called: Dufresh Farms
9800 County Road 26 (43358-9552)
PHONE..................................937 355-5103
Fax: 937 355-4565
Tim Weaver, *Owner*
Phil Ross, *Manager*
▲ EMP: 40
SALES (est): 1.3MM Privately Held
SIC: 0252 Chicken eggs

GEOGRAPHIC SECTION

(G-19267)
HERITAGE COOPERATIVE INC (PA)
11177 Township Road 133 (43358-9709)
P.O. Box 68 (43358-0068)
PHONE..............................419 294-2371
Fax: 937 355-0005
Eric N Parthemore, *CEO*
Derek Fauber, *Area Mgr*
John T Dunbar, *COO*
Wade Bahan, *Opers Mgr*
Lou Baughman, *Sls & Mktg Exec*
EMP: 85
SQ FT: 7,000
SALES (est): 500.1MM **Privately Held**
SIC: 5153 5261 4925 4932 Grains; fertilizer; liquefied petroleum gas, distribution through mains; gas & other services combined

West Milton
Miami County

(G-19268)
BRUMBAUGH ENGRG SURVEYING LLC
1105 S Miami St Ste 1 (45383-1260)
PHONE..............................937 698-3000
Fax: 937 698-3928
John Brumbaugh, *Mng Member*
Kathy Goodman, *Manager*
Barbara Brumbaugh,
Philip C Brumbaugh,
Steve Brumbaugh,
EMP: 35
SQ FT: 1,000
SALES (est): 1MM **Privately Held**
SIC: 8711 Civil engineering

(G-19269)
TOWE & ASSOCIATES INC
Also Called: Towe and Associates
415 S Miami St Ste 415 (45383-1558)
PHONE..............................937 275-0900
Carl Towe, *President*
Kathy Daughtry, *Tax Mgr*
Donald Carter, *Auditor*
Timothy Walsh, *Consultant*
Shawna Towe, *Info Tech Dir*
EMP: 26
SQ FT: 3,972
SALES (est): 2.2MM **Privately Held**
SIC: 8748 Business consulting

West Salem
Wayne County

(G-19270)
JOHNSON BROS RUBBER CO INC (PA)
42 W Buckeye St (44287-9747)
P.O. Box 812 (44287-0812)
PHONE..............................419 853-4122
Fax: 419 853-4062
Lawrence G Cooke, *President*
Eric Vail, *Vice Pres*
Michelle Green, *Materials Mgr*
Larry Adkins, *Engineer*
Marji Daugherty, *CFO*
▲ EMP: 100 EST: 1947
SQ FT: 70,000
SALES (est): 54.4MM **Privately Held**
SIC: 5199 3061 Foams & rubber; mechanical rubber goods

West Union
Adams County

(G-19271)
ADAMS CNTY /OHIO VLY SCHL DST
Also Called: West Union Elementary School
555 Lloyd Rd (45693-9654)
PHONE..............................937 544-2951
Rodney Wallace, *Superintendent*
EMP: 90
SALES (corp-wide): 51MM **Privately Held**
SIC: 8211 8351 High school, junior or senior; preschool center
PA: Adams County /Ohio Valley School District
141 Lloyd Rd
West Union OH 45693
937 544-5586

(G-19272)
ADAMS COUNTY MANOR
10856 State Route 41 (45693-9671)
PHONE..............................937 544-2205
Fax: 937 544-4229
John Houser, *President*
Ben Houser, *Vice Pres*
Ralph Houser, *Manager*
Stacey Dick, *Exec Dir*
Sabir Qurishi, *Director*
EMP: 60
SQ FT: 6,700
SALES (est): 2.6MM **Privately Held**
SIC: 8052 8051 Personal care facility; skilled nursing care facilities

(G-19273)
ADAMS COUNTY SENIOR CITIZENS
10835 State Route 41 (45693-9671)
PHONE..............................937 544-7459
Fax: 937 544-7149
Melody Stapleton, *Director*
EMP: 30
SALES (est): 819.5K **Privately Held**
SIC: 8399 8322 Council for social agency; geriatric social service

(G-19274)
ADAMS RURAL ELECTRIC COOP INC
4800 State Route 125 (45693-9329)
P.O. Box 247 (45693-0247)
PHONE..............................937 544-2305
Fax: 937 544-3877
Gary Kennedy, *President*
Chris Koenig, *Manager*
Alice Baird,
EMP: 33 EST: 1940
SQ FT: 11,400
SALES (est): 16.6MM **Privately Held**
WEB: www.adamsrec.com
SIC: 4911 Distribution, electric power

(G-19275)
BRUSH CREEK MOTORSPORTS
720 E Main St (45693-1109)
PHONE..............................937 515-1353
Tom Partin, *Owner*
EMP: 30
SALES (est): 95K **Privately Held**
SIC: 7948 Motor vehicle racing & drivers

(G-19276)
CLAYTON RAILROAD CNSTR LLC
500 Lane Rd (45693-9440)
PHONE..............................937 549-2952
Jim McAdams, *President*
Jim McAdams Jr, *Superintendent*
Bob Staun, *Accountant*
Sharon McAdams, *Manager*
EMP: 40
SQ FT: 1,000
SALES (est): 7.9MM **Privately Held**
SIC: 1622 Bridge, tunnel & elevated highway

(G-19277)
COUNTY OF ADAMS
Also Called: Children Services
300 N Wilson Dr (45693-1157)
PHONE..............................937 544-5067
Fax: 937 544-9724
Sonya Evans, *Supervisor*
Alpheus Lewis, *Supervisor*
Jill Wright, *Director*
Tina Gordley, *Admin Asst*
EMP: 30 **Privately Held**
SIC: 8322 Child related social services
PA: County Of Adams
11260 State Route 41
West Union OH 45693
937 544-3286

(G-19278)
EAGLE CREEK NURSING CENTER
141 Spruce Ln (45693-8807)
PHONE..............................937 544-5531
Fax: 937 544-3478
Sabir Quarishi, *Director*
Doug Himes, *Executive*
Greg Stout, *Administration*
EMP: 40
SQ FT: 15,551
SALES (est): 2.3MM
SALES (corp-wide): 68.5MM **Privately Held**
SIC: 8051 8052 Skilled nursing care facilities; intermediate care facilities
PA: Saber Healthcare Group, L.L.C.
26691 Richmond Rd Frnt
Bedford OH 44146
216 292-5706

(G-19279)
VENTURE PRODUCTIONS INC
11516 State Route 41 (45693-9434)
PHONE..............................937 544-2823
Fax: 937 544-2823
Liz Lafferty, *Director*
EMP: 60
SALES: 262K **Privately Held**
SIC: 7922 Television program, including commercial producers

West Unity
Williams County

(G-19280)
CONVERSION TECH INTL INC
700 Oak St (43570-9457)
P.O. Box 707 (43570-0707)
PHONE..............................419 924-5566
Chester Cromwell, *President*
Jason Cromwell, *Principal*
Linda Johnston, *Manager*
▲ EMP: 33
SQ FT: 130,000
SALES (est): 8.9MM **Privately Held**
WEB: www.conversiontechnologies.com
SIC: 2891 7389 Adhesives; laminating service

(G-19281)
THREE-D TRANSPORT INC
14237 Us Highway 127 (43570-9799)
PHONE..............................419 924-5368
Daniel Meyers, *President*
Debra Meyers, *Treasurer*
EMP: 40
SQ FT: 15,200
SALES (est): 8.3MM **Privately Held**
SIC: 4213 Trucking, except local

Westerville
Delaware County

(G-19282)
ABB INC
Also Called: ABB Industrial Systems
579 Executive Campus Dr (43082-9801)
PHONE..............................614 818-6300
Fax: 614 818-6570
Dave Doerschuk, *Engineer*
Roger Billy, *Branch Mgr*
Tom Sweet, *Manager*
Ken Hagy, *Info Tech Mgr*
EMP: 160
SALES (corp-wide): 33.8B **Privately Held**
WEB: www.elsterelectricity.com
SIC: 5063 Power transmission equipment, electric
HQ: Abb Inc.
305 Gregson Dr
Cary NC 27511

(G-19283)
AHV DEVELOPMENT LLC
Also Called: Ahv Construction
592 Office Pkwy (43082-7985)
PHONE..............................614 890-1440
Greg Filbrun, *Mng Member*
EMP: 52
SQ FT: 4,000
SALES: 8MM **Privately Held**
SIC: 1522 Residential construction; apartment building construction; remodeling, multi-family dwellings

(G-19284)
AMERICAN CERAMIC SOCIETY (PA)
Also Called: POTTERY MAKING ILLUSTRATE
600 N Cleveland Ave # 210 (43082-6921)
PHONE..............................614 890-4700
Fax: 614 899-6109
Marcus Bailey, *Publisher*
Pat Janeway, *Editor*
Bill Jones, *Editor*
Paul Holbrook, *COO*
Lora Saiber, *Treasurer*
EMP: 35
SQ FT: 10,126
SALES: 7.6MM **Privately Held**
WEB: www.ceramics.org
SIC: 8621 2721 Medical field-related associations; engineering association; scientific membership association; periodicals: publishing & printing

(G-19285)
ARCHER-MEEK-WEILER AGENCY INC
440 Polaris Pkwy Ste 400 (43082-7229)
PHONE..............................614 212-1009
Fax: 614 221-3414
Steven Weiler, *President*
Alan R Weiler, *Chairman*
Charles Schaeffer, *Vice Pres*
Shirley A Blades, *Admin Sec*
EMP: 37
SQ FT: 5,000
SALES (est): 4.4MM **Privately Held**
WEB: www.archer-meek.com
SIC: 6411 Insurance agents

(G-19286)
BAKERWELL INC
6295 Maxtown Rd Ste 300 (43082-8885)
P.O. Box 1678 (43086-1678)
PHONE..............................614 898-7590
Fax: 614 898-0053
Rex Baker, *President*
Jeff Baker, *Corp Secy*
EMP: 51 EST: 1981
SALES (est): 2.9MM **Privately Held**
WEB: www.bakerwell.com
SIC: 1382 Oil & gas exploration services

(G-19287)
BANC AMER PRCTICE SLUTIONS INC
600 N Cleveland Ave # 300 (43082-6920)
PHONE..............................614 794-8247
Roy Best, *Principal*
John Fiore, *Senior VP*
Charlee Rocha, *Senior VP*
Daniel J Kirwin, *Vice Pres*
Daniel Kirwin, *Vice Pres*
EMP: 250
SQ FT: 115,000
SALES (est): 9.2MM
SALES (corp-wide): 100.2B **Publicly Held**
SIC: 8742 Banking & finance consultant
PA: Bank Of America Corporation
100 N Tryon St Ste 220
Charlotte NC 28202
704 386-5681

(G-19288)
BROADBAND EXPRESS INC
374 Westdale Ave Ste B (43082-6069)
PHONE..............................614 823-6464
John Herbst, *VP Opers*
John Kuhn,
EMP: 30
SQ FT: 36,000
SALES (est): 2.2MM
SALES (corp-wide): 3B **Publicly Held**
SIC: 1731 Cable television installation
HQ: Cable Express Holding Company
374 Westdale Ave Ste B
Westerville OH 43082

Westerville - Delaware County (G-19289)

GEOGRAPHIC SECTION

(G-19289)
CENTER FOR SRGCAL DRMTLOGY INC
428 County Line Rd W (43082-7294)
PHONE.................614 847-4100
Ronald J Siegle, *President*
Peter C Seline, *Vice Pres*
Brian P Biernat, *Treasurer*
Melissa Childress, *Manager*
David C Arlisle, *Dermatology*
EMP: 60
SQ FT: 19,200
SALES (est): 6.7MM **Privately Held**
SIC: 8011 Dermatologist

(G-19290)
CENTRAL OHIO PRIMARY CARE
507 Executive Campus Dr # 160 (43082-9838)
PHONE.................614 891-9505
Katrina Tansky, *Branch Mgr*
EMP: 37 **Privately Held**
SIC: 8011 Pediatrician
PA: Central Ohio Primary Care Physicians, Inc.
570 Polaris Pkwy Ste 250
Westerville OH 43082

(G-19291)
CENTRAL OHIO PRIMARY CARE (PA)
570 Polaris Pkwy Ste 250 (43082-7923)
PHONE.................614 326-2672
J William Wulf, *CEO*
Jeffrey L Hunter Do, *President*
Michael Ashanin, *COO*
Lee Budin MD, *Vice Pres*
Paul Westfall, *Purchasing*
EMP: 60
SALES (est): 133MM **Privately Held**
WEB: www.copcp.com
SIC: 8011 Internal medicine, physician/surgeon

(G-19292)
CENTRAL OHIO SLEEP MEDICINE
Also Called: Central Ohio Pulmonary Disease
484 County Line Rd W # 130 (43082-7246)
PHONE.................614 475-6700
Fax: 614 475-6800
Sherri Whalen, *Director*
EMP: 30
SALES (est): 647.6K **Privately Held**
SIC: 8049 Offices of health practitioner

(G-19293)
CENTURY SURETY COMPANY (DH)
465 N Cleveland Ave (43082-8095)
P.O. Box 163340, Columbus (43216-3340)
PHONE.................614 895-2000
John Mazzara, *President*
Arthur I Vorys, *Principal*
Philip W Stichter, *Principal*
Larry L Thiel, *Principal*
Robert J Thiel, *Principal*
EMP: 32
SQ FT: 30,000
SALES (est): 68MM
SALES (corp-wide): 10.7B **Privately Held**
WEB: www.centurysurety.com
SIC: 6331 Property damage insurance; fire, marine & casualty insurance & carriers
HQ: Procentury Corporation
550 Polaris Pkwy Ste 300
Westerville OH 43082
614 895-2000

(G-19294)
CSC INSURANCE AGENCY INC
Also Called: Pro Century
550 Polaris Pkwy Ste 300 (43082-7113)
P.O. Box 163340, Columbus (43216-3340)
PHONE.................614 895-2000
Chrisopher J Timm, *CEO*
Rav Ravindran, *Technology*
EMP: 100
SQ FT: 16,000
SALES (est): 11.5MM
SALES (corp-wide): 10.7B **Privately Held**
WEB: www.centurysurety.com
SIC: 6411 Insurance agents, brokers & service

HQ: Century Surety Company
465 N Cleveland Ave
Westerville OH 43082
614 895-2000

(G-19295)
CSX TRANSPORTATION INC
426 Landings Loop E (43082-7421)
PHONE.................614 898-3651
Kim Sherman, *Branch Mgr*
EMP: 42
SALES (corp-wide): 11.4B **Publicly Held**
SIC: 4011 Interurban railways
HQ: Csx Transportation, Inc.
500 Water St
Jacksonville FL 32202
904 359-3100

(G-19296)
D L RYAN COMPANIES LLC
Also Called: Ryan Partnership
440 Polaris Pkwy Ste 350 (43082-7262)
PHONE.................614 436-6558
Fax: 614 436-6640
Peter Tarnapoll, *Principal*
Jody Jasser, *Human Resources*
EMP: 32 **Publicly Held**
SIC: 8743 8742 Sales promotion; marketing consulting services
HQ: D. L. Ryan Companies, Llc
10 Westport Rd Unit 10 # 10
Wilton CT 06897
203 210-3000

(G-19297)
DHL EXPRESS (USA) INC
570 Polaris Pkwy Ste 110 (43082-7902)
PHONE.................614 865-8325
Nick Kaufman, *Branch Mgr*
EMP: 31
SALES (corp-wide): 71.2B **Privately Held**
SIC: 4513 Air courier services
HQ: Dhl Express (Usa), Inc.
1210 S Pine Island Rd
Plantation FL 33324
954 888-7000

(G-19298)
DHL SUPPLY CHAIN (USA)
570 Polaris Pkwy Ste 170 (43082-7932)
PHONE.................229 888-0699
Fax: 229 888-2703
Ray Jewell, *Branch Mgr*
Mark Bryan, *Manager*
EMP: 80
SALES (corp-wide): 71.2B **Privately Held**
WEB: www.venturelogistics.com
SIC: 8741 Management services
HQ: Exel Inc.
570 Polaris Pkwy
Westerville OH 43082
614 865-8500

(G-19299)
DHL SUPPLY CHAIN (USA)
Also Called: Sam's Distribution Center
570 Polaris Pkwy Ste 110 (43082-7902)
PHONE.................614 895-1959
John Hummel, *Manager*
Shawn Murphy, *Manager*
EMP: 55
SALES (corp-wide): 71.2B **Privately Held**
WEB: www.exel-logistics.com
SIC: 4225 General warehousing & storage
HQ: Exel Inc.
570 Polaris Pkwy
Westerville OH 43082
614 865-8500

(G-19300)
DONALD R KENNEY & COMPANY (PA)
Also Called: Triangle Commercial Properties
470 Olde Worthington Rd # 101 (43082-8986)
PHONE.................614 540-2404
Fax: 614 540-2406
Donald R Kenney, *Owner*
Jennifer Cook, *Accountant*
Evan Fracasso, *Sales Staff*
Perry Smith, *Sales Staff*
Kathrine Kasas, *Property Mgr*
EMP: 50 **EST:** 1968
SQ FT: 5,000

SALES (est): 20MM **Privately Held**
WEB: www.drkrealtors.com
SIC: 1522 Apartment building construction

(G-19301)
DOOR SHOP & SERVICE INC
7385 State Route 3 Ste 52 (43082-8654)
PHONE.................614 423-8043
EMP: 35
SQ FT: 3,000
SALES: 2.5MM **Privately Held**
SIC: 1751 Carpentry Contractor

(G-19302)
EXCEPTIONAL INNOVATION INC
480 Olde Worthington Rd # 350 (43082-7067)
PHONE.................614 901-8899
Seale Moorer, *CEO*
Dinesh Chitrala, *Managing Dir*
Hal Watts, *Managing Dir*
Neil Shubert, *Senior VP*
Jon Chapman, *Vice Pres*
EMP: 79
SALES: 30MM **Privately Held**
WEB: www.exceptionalinnovation.com
SIC: 7371 Computer software development
HQ: Exceptional Innovation B.V.
Victorialaan 15
's-Hertogenbosch
736 286-677

(G-19303)
EXEL HOLDINGS (USA) INC (DH)
570 Polaris Pkwy Ste 110 (43082-7902)
PHONE.................614 865-8500
Scott Sureddin, *CEO*
Jose Fernando Nava, *CEO*
Jose Nava, *CEO*
Lynn Anderson, *Vice Pres*
Tim Sprosty, *Vice Pres*
EMP: 200
SALES (est): 7.4B
SALES (corp-wide): 71.2B **Privately Held**
SIC: 4226 4213 Special warehousing & storage; household goods transport
HQ: Exel Limited
Ocean House
Bracknell BERKS RG12
134 430-2000

(G-19304)
EXEL INC
Also Called: Genesis Logistics
570 Polaris Pkwy Ste 110 (43082-7902)
PHONE.................614 865-8294
Brian Locasto, *Branch Mgr*
EMP: 30
SALES (corp-wide): 71.2B **Privately Held**
WEB: www.exel-logistics.com
SIC: 4225 General warehousing
HQ: Exel Inc.
570 Polaris Pkwy
Westerville OH 43082
614 865-8500

(G-19305)
EXEL INC (DH)
Also Called: Dhl Supply Chain USA
570 Polaris Pkwy (43082-7900)
P.O. Box 1590 (43086-1590)
PHONE.................614 865-8500
Fax: 614 865-8875
Scott Sureddin, *CEO*
Scott Cubbler, *President*
Luis Eraa, *President*
Jim Gehr, *President*
Joe Kaplewicz, *President*
EMP: 500
SALES (est): 7.4B
SALES (corp-wide): 71.2B **Privately Held**
WEB: www.exel-logistics.com
SIC: 4213 4225 4581 Trucking, except local; general warehousing; air freight handling at airports
HQ: Exel Holdings (Usa) Inc.
570 Polaris Pkwy Ste 110
Westerville OH 43082
614 865-8500

(G-19306)
FEAZEL ROOFING COMPANY
5855 Chandler Ct (43082-9050)
PHONE.................614 898-7663
Fax: 614 898-7622

Leo Ruberto, *President*
Todd Feazel, *Vice Pres*
Karen Turner, *Accountant*
Robert Thomas, *Mktg Dir*
Jess Hellmich, *Marketing Mgr*
EMP: 46
SQ FT: 9,000
SALES: 30MM **Privately Held**
WEB: www.feazelroofingcompany.com
SIC: 1761 Roofing contractor; roofing & gutter work; siding contractor

(G-19307)
FERIDEAN COMMONS LLC
6885 Freeman Rd (43082-9113)
PHONE.................614 898-7488
Fax: 614 890-0953
Fred H Powrie III, *Mng Member*
Judy Pyle, *Manager*
Lori Coufal, *Program Dir*
Gale Koehler, *Social Dir*
EMP: 40
SQ FT: 1,748
SALES (est): 2.9MM **Privately Held**
SIC: 8051 Skilled nursing care facilities

(G-19308)
FERIDEAN GROUP INC
6885 Freeman Rd (43082-9113)
PHONE.................614 898-7488
Frederick H Powrie, *President*
Ron Pyle, *Vice Pres*
EMP: 40
SALES (est): 1.2MM **Privately Held**
SIC: 6517 Railroad property lessors

(G-19309)
FUSION ALLIANCE LLC
440 Polaris Pkwy Ste 500 (43082-6083)
PHONE.................614 852-8000
Vince Nelson, *Branch Mgr*
EMP: 40
SALES (corp-wide): 59.5MM **Privately Held**
SIC: 8742 Management information systems consultant
HQ: Fusion Alliance, Llc
301 Pennsylvania Pkwy 2
Carmel IN 46032
317 955-1300

(G-19310)
GRACE BRTHREN CH COLUMBUS OHIO (PA)
Also Called: Grace Polaris Church
8724 Olde Worthington Rd (43082-8840)
P.O. Box 1650 (43086-1650)
PHONE.................614 888-7733
Fax: 614 888-1258
Tom Anglea, *Principal*
Michael L Yoder, *Pastor*
Jonathan Wiley, *Pastor*
James S Kanzeg, *Finance Dir*
Jim Kanzeg, *Finance*
EMP: 27
SALES: 8.2MM **Privately Held**
SIC: 8661 8351 Brethren Church; child day care services

(G-19311)
HARRIS MACKESSY & BRENNAN
Also Called: Hmb Information Sys Developers
570 Polaris Pkwy Ste 125 (43082-7924)
PHONE.................614 221-6831
Fax: 614 221-6856
Thomas Harris, *President*
Tom Harris, *President*
Patrick Brennan, *Vice Pres*
Mark Buchy, *Vice Pres*
Owen Myers, *Project Mgr*
EMP: 150
SQ FT: 9,000
SALES (est): 36.4MM **Privately Held**
WEB: www.hmbnet.com
SIC: 8742 3577 Management consulting services; decoders, computer peripheral equipment

(G-19312)
HEITMEYER GROUP LLC
140 Commerce Park Dr C (43082-7811)
PHONE.................614 573-5571
Kim Dickinson, *Business Mgr*
Norm Heitmeyer,
EMP: 300

GEOGRAPHIC SECTION
Westerville - Delaware County (G-19336)

SQ FT: 1,500
SALES (est): 12MM **Privately Held**
SIC: 7361 Employment agencies

(G-19313)
HER INC
Also Called: H E R
413 N State St (43082-8276)
PHONE..................614 890-7400
Fax: 614 890-5909
Gloria Raul, *General Mgr*
Barbara March, *Admin Asst*
EMP: 106
SALES (corp-wide): 14.3MM **Privately Held**
WEB: www.eassent.com
SIC: 6531 Real estate agents & managers
PA: Her, Inc
    4261 Morse Rd
    Columbus OH 43230
    614 221-7400

(G-19314)
HUMAN RESOURCES SERVICES
465 Buckstone Pl (43082-8281)
PHONE..................740 587-3484
Keith Jenkins, *Principal*
EMP: 45
SALES (est): 1.3MM **Privately Held**
SIC: 7361 Employment agencies

(G-19315)
HUNTSEY CORPORATION
Also Called: Synergy Homecare
470 Olde Worthington Rd (43082-8985)
PHONE..................614 568-5030
Barbara Hawley, *President*
EMP: 30 EST: 2008
SALES (est): 512.1K **Privately Held**
SIC: 8082 Home health care services

(G-19316)
INSPECTION GROUP INCORPORATED
440 Polaris Pkwy Ste 170 (43082-7987)
PHONE..................614 891-3606
Fax: 614 891-4626
Saul Himelstein, *President*
Robert Gardier, *COO*
Clarence Buck, *Vice Pres*
Keith Lavrar, *Vice Pres*
Matt Lavrar, *Vice Pres*
EMP: 50
SQ FT: 2,500
SALES (est): 3.7MM **Privately Held**
WEB: www.theinspectiongroup.com
SIC: 7389 Building inspection service

(G-19317)
JEAN R WAGNER
470 Olde Worthington Rd (43082-8985)
PHONE..................614 430-0065
Jean R Wagner, *Owner*
EMP: 57 EST: 2016
SALES: 5MM **Privately Held**
SIC: 7389 Financial services

(G-19318)
JULIAN & GRUBE INC
Also Called: Trimble & Julian
333 County Line Rd W A (43082-6908)
PHONE..................614 846-1899
Steven Julian, *Ch of Bd*
Julian Sfeve, *President*
Mark Grube, *Partner*
EMP: 35
SQ FT: 4,000
SALES (est): 3.2MM **Privately Held**
WEB: www.tjginc.com
SIC: 8721 Certified public accountant

(G-19319)
KLEINGERS GROUP INC
350 Worthington Rd Ste B (43082-8327)
PHONE..................614 882-4311
Renee Stayton, *Controller*
Steven R Korte, *Manager*
Troy Messer, *Manager*
EMP: 85 **Privately Held**
WEB: www.kleingers.com
SIC: 8711 Consulting engineer
PA: The Kleingers Group Inc
    6305 Centre Park Dr
    West Chester OH 45069

(G-19320)
LAKES GOLF & COUNTRY CLUB INC
6740 Worthington Rd (43082-9491)
PHONE..................614 882-2582
Fax: 614 899-3096
Tod Ortlip, *President*
Jim Spragg, *COO*
Leigh Allen, *Trustee*
Jay Ortlip, *Trustee*
James Decker, *Purch Agent*
EMP: 50
SQ FT: 40,000
SALES (est): 7.1MM **Privately Held**
SIC: 7997 Country club, membership

(G-19321)
LAUREL DEVELOPMENT CORPORATION
8181 Worthington Rd (43082-8067)
PHONE..................614 794-8800
Dennis Sherman, *President*
Thomas Franke, *Chairman*
Jack Alcott, *Vice Pres*
Kevin Belew, *Vice Pres*
James Franke, *Vice Pres*
EMP: 25
SALES (est): 1.9MM **Privately Held**
SIC: 6552 Land subdividers & developers, commercial
PA: Laurel Health Care Company Of North Worthington
    8181 Worthington Rd
    Westerville OH 43082

(G-19322)
LAUREL HEALTH CARE COMPANY (HQ)
8181 Worthington Rd Uppr (43082-8071)
PHONE..................614 794-8800
Fax: 614 794-8805
Bradford Payne, *President*
Jack Alcott, *Vice Pres*
Carol Bailey, *Vice Pres*
Barbara Lombardi, *Vice Pres*
Timothy Patton, *Vice Pres*
EMP: 144
SALES (est): 76.7MM **Privately Held**
WEB: www.laurelsofnorworth.com
SIC: 8741 Nursing & personal care facility management

(G-19323)
LAUREL HLTH CARE BATTLE CREEK (HQ)
Also Called: Laurels of Bedford, The
8181 Worthington Rd (43082-8067)
PHONE..................614 794-8800
Dennis Sherman, *President*
Thomas Franke, *Owner*
Jack Alcott, *Vice Pres*
Kevin Belew, *Vice Pres*
James Franke, *Vice Pres*
EMP: 40
SALES (est): 2.9MM **Privately Held**
WEB: www.laurelsofbedford.com
SIC: 8051 Skilled nursing care facilities

(G-19324)
LAUREL HLTH CARE OF MT PLASANT (HQ)
Also Called: Laurels of Mt Pleasant
8181 Worthington Rd # 2 (43082-8067)
PHONE..................614 794-8800
Dennis Sherman, *President*
Thomas Franke, *Chairman*
Jack Alcott, *Vice Pres*
Kevin Belew, *Vice Pres*
James Franke, *Vice Pres*
EMP: 63 EST: 1962
SALES (est): 3.2MM **Privately Held**
WEB: www.laurelsofmtpleasant.com
SIC: 8051 Skilled nursing care facilities

(G-19325)
LIBERTY MUTUAL INSURANCE CO
440 Polaris Pkwy Ste 150 (43082-7261)
PHONE..................614 855-6193
Fax: 614 855-7110
Graham Powers, *Branch Mgr*
EMP: 35
SALES (corp-wide): 38.3B **Privately Held**
WEB: www.libertymutual.com
SIC: 6331 6321 Fire, marine & casualty insurance; workers' compensation insurance; automobile insurance; burglary & theft insurance; accident insurance carriers; health insurance carriers; reinsurance carriers, accident & health
HQ: Liberty Mutual Insurance Company
    175 Berkeley St
    Boston MA 02116
    617 357-9500

(G-19326)
LIEBERT FIELD SERVICES INC
Also Called: Vertiv
610 Executive Campus Dr (43082-8870)
PHONE..................614 841-5763
Lauri Turevon, *VP Sales*
Lisa Hunt, *Manager*
R P Bauer, *Director*
Edward Feeney, *Director*
EMP: 28 EST: 2001
SALES (est): 5.6MM **Privately Held**
SIC: 7379 Computer related services
HQ: Liebert Corporation
    1050 Dearborn Dr
    Columbus OH 43085
    614 888-0246

(G-19327)
MARK HUMRICHOUSER
Also Called: Jae Co 2
6295 Maxtown Rd Ste 100 (43082-8883)
PHONE..................614 324-5231
Mark Humrichouser, *Owner*
Chris Rudy, *Manager*
EMP: 45
SALES: 5.2MM **Privately Held**
SIC: 5722 5087 Kitchens, complete (sinks, cabinets, etc.); service establishment equipment

(G-19328)
MEDALLION CLUB (PA)
5000 Club Dr (43082-9551)
PHONE..................614 794-6999
Fax: 614 809-5958
Tateo Tanigawa, *President*
Steve Clark, *President*
Kris Miller, *Director*
Chris Ramsay, *Director*
Pablo Russo, *Director*
EMP: 105
SQ FT: 57,000
SALES (est): 8.3MM **Privately Held**
WEB: www.medallionclub.com
SIC: 7997 7991 5941 5813 Country club, membership; physical fitness facilities; sporting goods & bicycle shops; drinking places; eating places

(G-19329)
MODERN MEDICAL INC
250 Progressive Way (43082-9615)
P.O. Box 549, Lewis Center (43035-0549)
PHONE..................800 547-3330
Fax: 740 657-3337
Joseph G Favazzo, *President*
Thomas Falzone Jr, *Assistant VP*
Raymond Black, *Vice Pres*
Michael Wharton, *Facilities Mgr*
Heather Henneke, *Opers Staff*
EMP: 130
SQ FT: 40,000
SALES (est): 14.8MM
SALES (corp-wide): 201.1B **Publicly Held**
SIC: 5999 5912 5047 Medical apparatus & supplies; drug stores & proprietary stores; medical & hospital equipment
HQ: Healthcare Solutions, Inc.
    2736 Meadow Church Rd # 300
    Duluth GA 30097

(G-19330)
NATIONAL AUTO CARE CORPORATION
440 Polaris Pkwy Ste 250 (43082-6082)
PHONE..................800 548-1875
Christina Schrank, *President*
Paul Leary, *Exec VP*
Steven Juresich, *Senior VP*
Angie Hatfield, *Opers Mgr*
Kristi Turner, *Opers Staff*
EMP: 53

SQ FT: 15,000
SALES (est): 14.3MM
SALES (corp-wide): 31.5MM **Privately Held**
WEB: www.natlauto.com
SIC: 6411 Insurance agents
PA: Trivest Partners, L.P.
    550 S Dixie Hwy Ste 300
    Coral Gables FL 33146
    305 858-2200

(G-19331)
NATIONWIDE CHILDRENS HOSPITAL
Also Called: Close To Home Health Care Ctr
433 N Cleveland Ave (43082-8095)
PHONE..................614 355-8300
Fax: 614 355-8300
Christy Stocker, *Manager*
Larry Long, *Director*
EMP: 50
SALES (corp-wide): 1.3B **Privately Held**
SIC: 8069 8082 Children's hospital; home health care services
PA: Nationwide Children's Hospital
    700 Childrens Dr
    Columbus OH 43205
    614 722-2000

(G-19332)
NATIONWIDE MUTUAL INSURANCE CO
955 County Line Rd W (43082-7237)
PHONE..................614 948-4153
EMP: 40
SALES (corp-wide): 15.9B **Privately Held**
SIC: 6411 Insurance Agent/Broker
PA: Nationwide Mutual Insurance Company
    1 Nationwide Plz
    Columbus OH 43215
    614 249-7111

(G-19333)
NORTHEAST CONCRETE & CNSTR
7243 Saddlewood Dr (43082-9372)
PHONE..................614 898-5728
Thomas R Gehrlich, *President*
Samuel E Gehrlich, *Vice Pres*
Tracy Stamper, *Manager*
EMP: 85
SQ FT: 1,500
SALES: 12.5MM **Privately Held**
WEB: www.neconcreteconstruction.com
SIC: 1771 Concrete work

(G-19334)
OAK HEALTH CARE INVESTOR (DH)
8181 Worthington Rd (43082-8067)
PHONE..................614 794-8800
Dennis Sherman, *President*
Tom Franke, *Principal*
EMP: 49
SALES (est): 3.4MM **Privately Held**
SIC: 6512 Nonresidential building operators

(G-19335)
OAK HEALTH CARE INVESTORS (HQ)
Also Called: Laurels of Defiance, The
8181 Worthington Rd (43082-8067)
PHONE..................614 794-8800
Dennis Sherman, *President*
Thomas Franke, *Chairman*
Jack Alcott, *Vice Pres*
Kevin Belew, *Vice Pres*
James Franke, *Vice Pres*
EMP: 30
SALES (est): 2.1MM **Privately Held**
SIC: 8051 Skilled nursing care facilities

(G-19336)
OHIO BUILDERS RESOURCES LLC
Also Called: Ohio Resources
5901 Chandler Ct Ste D (43082-9149)
PHONE..................614 865-0306
Fax: 614 865-0312
Richard Mely, *President*
Scott Hoff, *General Mgr*
Sally Mealey, *Corp Secy*
Liz Mealey, *Marketing Mgr*
EMP: 26

Westerville - Delaware County (G-19337)

SALES (est): 2.5MM **Privately Held**
WEB: www.ohio-resources.com
SIC: 1521 1751 Single-family home remodeling, additions & repairs; carpentry work

(G-19337)
OHIO CIVIL SERVICE EMPLOYEES A
Also Called: O.C.S.E.a
390 Worthington Rd Ste A (43082-8329)
PHONE 614 865-4700
Fax: 614 865-4777
Ron Alexander, *President*
Kathleen M Stewart, *Corp Secy*
Cathy Deck, *Vice Pres*
Scott Dye, *Vice Pres*
Eddie L Parks, *Vice Pres*
EMP: 92
SQ FT: 40,000
SALES (est): 10.5MM **Privately Held**
WEB: www.ocsea.org
SIC: 8631 8611 Labor union; business associations

(G-19338)
OPTUMRX INC
250 Progressive Way (43082-9615)
PHONE 614 794-3300
EMP: 530
SALES (corp-wide): 201.1B **Publicly Held**
SIC: 6411 Medical insurance claim processing, contract or fee basis
HQ: Optumrx, Inc.
2300 Main St
Irvine CA 92614

(G-19339)
ORTON EDWARD JR CRMIC FNDATION
6991 S Old 3c Hwy (43082-9026)
P.O. Box 2760 (43086-2760)
PHONE 614 895-2663
Jonathan Hinton, *Ch of Bd*
J Gary Childress, *General Mgr*
James Litzinger, *Business Mgr*
Dr Stephen Freiman, *Trustee*
Dr John Morral, *Trustee*
▼ EMP: 31
SQ FT: 34,260
SALES: 5MM **Privately Held**
WEB: www.ortonceramic.com
SIC: 3269 3826 3825 8748 Cones, pyrometric: earthenware; analytical instruments; instruments to measure electricity; testing services

(G-19340)
PERMEDION INC
350 Worthington Rd Ste H (43082-8327)
PHONE 614 895-9900
William Lucia, *President*
Thomas A Schultz, *Vice Pres*
Sue Butterfield, *Marketing Mgr*
Jim Dompierre, *MIS Dir*
Scott Sickle, *Info Tech Dir*
EMP: 60
SQ FT: 25,000
SALES (est): 3.3MM
SALES (corp-wide): 521.2MM **Publicly Held**
WEB: www.hmsy.com
SIC: 8741 Hospital management
HQ: Health Management Systems Inc
5615 High Point Dr # 100
Irving TX 75038
214 453-3000

(G-19341)
POLARIS INNKEEPERS INC
Also Called: Fairfield Inn
9000 Worthington Rd (43082-8851)
PHONE 614 568-0770
Kezia Cromer, *Manager*
EMP: 25
SALES (est): 622.4K **Privately Held**
SIC: 7011 Hotels & motels

(G-19342)
POWELL ENTERPRISES INC
Also Called: Goddard School, The
8750 Olde Worthington Rd (43082-8853)
PHONE 614 882-0111
Fax: 614 540-0112
Steve Powell, *President*
Marykay Weite, *Director*
EMP: 25
SALES: 1MM **Privately Held**
SIC: 8351 Group day care center

(G-19343)
PRECISION BROADBND INSTALLATNS
7642 Red Bank Rd (43082-8210)
PHONE 614 523-2917
Frederick P Steininger, *CEO*
Chris Steininger, *President*
Alex Steininger, *Safety Mgr*
Laura Caraway, *Office Mgr*
Tyler Caraway, *Manager*
EMP: 140
SALES (est): 23.4MM **Privately Held**
SIC: 1731 Cable television installation

(G-19344)
PREFERRED RE INVESTMENTS LLC
Also Called: Preferred Living
470 Olde Worthington Rd # 470 (43082-8985)
PHONE 614 901-2400
Michael J Kenney, *President*
Wayne S Chang, *CFO*
Barclay Hallowell, *Manager*
Nick King, *Manager*
Amy Long, *Manager*
EMP: 30
SALES (est): 5.9MM **Privately Held**
SIC: 6531 Real estate managers

(G-19345)
PRIMROSE SCHOOL AT POLARIS
561 Westar Blvd (43082-7806)
PHONE 614 899-2588
Ashley Clement, *Owner*
Sarah McManus, *Opers Staff*
EMP: 30
SALES (est): 524.1K **Privately Held**
SIC: 8351 Preschool center

(G-19346)
PROGRESSIVE ENTPS HOLDINGS INC
250 Progressive Way (43082-9615)
PHONE 614 794-3300
Fax: 614 794-9582
Andrew Lewis, *Vice Pres*
Helen Bradburn, *QC Mgr*
Kristin Wordell, *Human Res Mgr*
Thomas Ash, *VP Sales*
Dionne Lacey-Artis, *VP Sales*
EMP: 531
SALES (est): 17.7MM **Privately Held**
SIC: 8742 Compensation & benefits planning consultant

(G-19347)
QUICK SOLUTIONS INC
440 Polaris Pkwy Ste 500 (43082-6083)
PHONE 614 825-8000
Fax: 614 825-8006
Tom Campbell, *CEO*
Rick Mariotti, *President*
Pam Hagely, *Controller*
Melissa Lewis, *Controller*
Doug Drescher, *Sales Mgr*
EMP: 200
SQ FT: 22,000
SALES (est): 27.6MM
SALES (corp-wide): 59.5MM **Privately Held**
WEB: www.quicksolutions.net
SIC: 8742 Management consulting services
PA: Fusion Alliance Holdings, Inc.
301 Pennsylvania Pkwy
Indianapolis IN 46280
317 955-1300

(G-19348)
R & E JOINT VENTURE INC
6843 Regency Dr (43082-8480)
PHONE 614 891-9404
Richard Hames, *President*
EMP: 30
SALES (est): 1.5MM **Privately Held**
SIC: 7212 Pickup station, laundry & drycleaning

(G-19349)
REVOLUTION GROUP INC
600 N Cleveland Ave # 110 (43082-6921)
PHONE 614 212-1111
Richard Snide, *President*
Polly Clavijo, *Vice Pres*
Greg Huddleston, *Vice Pres*
Firas Alnemer, *Engineer*
Cindy Snide, *Mktg Dir*
EMP: 80
SALES (est): 6.9MM **Privately Held**
SIC: 7379 7372 4813 8741 Computer related consulting services; prepackaged software; ; ; management services

(G-19350)
RITE RUG CO
6083 Chandler Ct (43082-9050)
PHONE 614 882-4322
Vita Green, *Manager*
EMP: 26
SALES (corp-wide): 82.2MM **Privately Held**
SIC: 1752 Floor laying & floor work
PA: Rite Rug Co.
4450 Poth Rd Ste A
Columbus OH 43213
614 261-6060

(G-19351)
RWC INC
6210 Frost Rd (43082-9027)
PHONE 614 890-0600
Fax: 614 890-1799
Wesley Osburn, *CEO*
EMP: 25
SALES (corp-wide): 8.8MM **Privately Held**
SIC: 5169 0782 Industrial chemicals; lawn & garden services
PA: Rwc, Inc.
248 Lockhouse Rd
Westfield MA 01085
614 890-0600

(G-19352)
SHAMROCK TOWING INC (PA)
6333 Frost Rd (43082-9027)
PHONE 614 882-3555
Fax: 614 882-3569
Charles N Duffey, *CEO*
Tim Duffey, *President*
Mike Nelson, *Corp Secy*
David T Duffey, *Executive*
EMP: 30 EST: 1952
SALES (est): 2.9MM **Privately Held**
WEB: www.shamrocktowinginc.com
SIC: 7549 Towing service, automotive

(G-19353)
SOGETI USA LLC
579 Executive Campus Dr # 300 (43082-9801)
PHONE 614 847-4477
Fax: 614 430-4367
David Dewees, *Manager*
Thomas Wesseling, *Manager*
Mike Pasquale, *Consultant*
Eric Lyon, *Applctn Conslt*
Kevin Cheesman, *Director*
EMP: 50
SALES (corp-wide): 353.3MM **Privately Held**
WEB: www.sogeti-usa.com
SIC: 7379 7373 ; computer integrated systems design
HQ: Sogeti Usa Llc
10100 Innovation Dr # 200
Miamisburg OH 45342
937 291-8100

(G-19354)
STATUS SOLUTIONS LLC
999 County Line Rd W A (43082-7237)
PHONE 866 846-7272
Michael Macleod, *Manager*
EMP: 37
SALES (corp-wide): 12.1MM **Privately Held**
SIC: 8748 Business consulting
PA: Status Solutions, Llc
1180 Seminole Trl Ste 440
Charlottesville VA 22901
434 296-1789

(G-19355)
TALON TITLE AGENCY LLC (PA)
570 Polaris Pkwy Ste 140 (43082-7902)
PHONE 614 818-0500
William L Robinson Jr, *CEO*
Joseph J Barone, *President*
EMP: 40 EST: 2012
SALES (est): 2.5MM **Privately Held**
SIC: 6541 Title & trust companies

(G-19356)
TRG MAINTENANCE LLC
514 N State St Ste B (43082-9073)
PHONE 614 891-4850
Kristy McGrath, *Principal*
EMP: 899
SALES (est): 13.2MM **Privately Held**
SIC: 7349 Building maintenance services
PA: Titan Restaurant Group, Llc
514 N State St Ste B
Westerville OH 43082

(G-19357)
VILLAGE COMMUNITIES LLC
470 Olde Worthington Rd # 100 (43082-8986)
PHONE 614 540-2400
Tre Giller, *Principal*
Joe Thomas, *Vice Pres*
Steve Godek, *Project Mgr*
Tim Snyder, *Project Mgr*
Anita Wallace, *Production*
EMP: 113
SALES (est): 15MM **Privately Held**
SIC: 6531 Rental agent, real estate

(G-19358)
WEDGEWOOD ESTATES
Also Called: Casto Health Care
730 N Spring Rd Unit 356 (43082-1812)
PHONE 419 756-7400
Fax: 419 756-5891
William Casto, *Owner*
Lori Casto, *Sales Executive*
EMP: 30 EST: 1997
SALES (est): 1.6MM **Privately Held**
WEB: www.wedgewoodestates.com
SIC: 8059 8052 Convalescent home; intermediate care facilities

(G-19359)
ZINK FOODSERVICE GROUP
Also Called: Zink Commercial
420 Westdale Ave (43082-8724)
PHONE 800 492-7400
Fax: 614 899-9797
Steve Castle, *President*
Tim Riordan, *President*
Jim Zink, *Principal*
Chad Burstein, *Business Mgr*
Matt Swift, *Vice Pres*
▲ EMP: 40
SQ FT: 10,000
SALES: 22.1MM **Privately Held**
WEB: www.zinkmarketing.com
SIC: 5046 Restaurant equipment & supplies

Westerville
Franklin County

(G-19360)
AFFINION GROUP LLC
300 W Schrock Rd (43081-1189)
PHONE 614 895-1803
Tim Feeser, *Project Mgr*
Peg Ayers, *Branch Mgr*
William Low, *MIS Dir*
EMP: 800
SALES (corp-wide): 953.1MM **Privately Held**
SIC: 8699 Personal interest organization
HQ: Affinion Group, Inc.
6 High Ridge Park Bldg A
Stamford CT 06905
203 956-1000

(G-19361)
ALADDINS ENTERPRISES INC
Also Called: Aladdin Limousines
3408 E Dblin Granville Rd (43081-9722)
PHONE 614 891-3440
Fax: 614 898-5067

GEOGRAPHIC SECTION

Westerville - Franklin County (G-19385)

Archie Synder, *President*
Janice Snyder, *Vice Pres*
EMP: 25
SQ FT: 1,000
SALES (est): 5.6MM **Privately Held**
SIC: 5511 4119 Automobiles, new & used; limousine rental, with driver

(G-19362)
ALLIANCE DATA SYSTEMS CORP
220 W Schrock Rd (43081-2873)
PHONE 614 729-5000
Fax: 614 729-5168
Stacey Smith, *Human Resources*
Jason McDonnell, *Sales Mgr*
John Cowan, *Manager*
Brian Keeling, *Manager*
Michael Tasker, *Manager*
EMP: 263 **Publicly Held**
WEB: www.alliancedatasystems.com
SIC: 7389 Credit card service
PA: Alliance Data Systems Corporation
 7500 Dallas Pkwy Ste 700
 Plano TX 75024

(G-19363)
ANNEHURST VETERINARY HOSPITAL
25 Collegeview Rd (43081-1463)
PHONE 614 818-4221
Fax: 614 882-1611
Mark Harris, *Owner*
Adam Ballard, *Manager*
EMP: 30
SQ FT: 2,000
SALES (est): 1.7MM **Privately Held**
WEB: www.reprovet.com
SIC: 0742 0752 Animal hospital services, pets & other animal specialties; animal boarding services

(G-19364)
AQUA PENNSYLVANIA INC
5481 Buenos Aires Blvd (43081-4203)
PHONE 614 882-6586
EMP: 45
SALES (corp-wide): 809.5MM **Publicly Held**
SIC: 4941 Water supply
HQ: Aqua Pennsylvania, Inc.
 762 W Lancaster Ave
 Bryn Mawr PA 19010
 610 525-1400

(G-19365)
ASSOC DVLPMTLY DISABLED (PA)
Also Called: A D D
769 Brooksedge Blvd (43081-2821)
PHONE 614 486-4361
Robert L Archer, *CEO*
J Clifford Wilcox, *President*
Paul Cain, *Vice Chairman*
Rebecca Baird, *Vice Pres*
Carla Schmitter, *Vice Pres*
EMP: 38
SQ FT: 10,000
SALES: 18.7MM **Privately Held**
WEB: www.add1.com
SIC: 8361 8322 Home for the mentally handicapped; individual & family services

(G-19366)
ASSOCIATION FOR MIDDLE LVL EDU
4151 Executive Pkwy # 300 (43081-3867)
PHONE 614 895-4730
Jeff La Roux, *President*
Nancy Polinseo, *President*
Ryan Madson, *Managing Dir*
Jeff Ward, *CFO*
William Waidelich, *Exec Dir*
EMP: 27
SALES: 2.9MM **Privately Held**
WEB: www.nmsa.org
SIC: 8621 Education & teacher association

(G-19367)
AT&T CORP
814 Green Crest Dr (43081-2839)
PHONE 614 223-5318
Don Hamilton, *Branch Mgr*
Michael Peoples, *Manager*
EMP: 69

SALES (corp-wide): 160.5B **Publicly Held**
SIC: 4813 Telephone communication, except radio
HQ: At&T Corp.
 1 At&T Way
 Bedminster NJ 07921
 800 403-3302

(G-19368)
AT&T DATACOMM LLC
814 Green Crest Dr (43081-2839)
PHONE 614 223-5799
Don Hamilton, *Branch Mgr*
EMP: 25
SALES (corp-wide): 160.5B **Publicly Held**
SIC: 4813 Data telephone communications
HQ: At&t Datacomm, Llc
 175 E Houston St Ste 100
 San Antonio TX 78205
 210 821-4105

(G-19369)
AUTO ADDITIONS INC
6001 Westerville Rd (43081-4055)
PHONE 614 899-9100
Fax: 614 899-9585
Kenneth R Morris, *President*
Vicki S Morris, *Corp Secy*
Josh Poulson, *Manager*
EMP: 31 **EST:** 1974
SQ FT: 5,000
SALES (est): 4.1MM
SALES (corp-wide): 1.2B **Privately Held**
WEB: www.autoadditions.net
SIC: 7532 Customizing services, non-factory basis
HQ: Aep North America
 3433 E Wood St
 Phoenix AZ 85040

(G-19370)
AUTOMATIC DATA PROCESSING INC
Also Called: ADP
713 Brooksedge Plaza Dr (43081-4913)
PHONE 614 212-4831
Fax: 614 901-7531
Mike Glassmacher, *Facilities Mgr*
Joe Taylor, *Facilities Mgr*
Matthew Banks, *Sales Mgr*
Bob Capace, *Sales Mgr*
Tesa Funyak, *Sales Staff*
EMP: 190
SALES (corp-wide): 12.3B **Publicly Held**
SIC: 7374 Data processing service
PA: Automatic Data Processing, Inc.
 1 Adp Blvd Ste 1 # 1
 Roseland NJ 07068
 973 974-5000

(G-19371)
BON APPETIT MANAGEMENT CO
100 W Home St (43081-1408)
PHONE 614 823-1880
Bill Taylor, *General Mgr*
EMP: 40
SALES (corp-wide): 28.9B **Privately Held**
WEB: www.cafebonappetit.com
SIC: 8741 Restaurant management
HQ: Bon Appetit Management Co.
 100 Hamilton Ave Ste 400
 Palo Alto CA 94301
 650 798-8000

(G-19372)
BROOKDALE SENIOR LIVING INC
690 Cooper Rd Apt 514 (43081-8756)
PHONE 614 794-2499
Fax: 614 794-2611
EMP: 103
SALES (corp-wide): 4.7B **Publicly Held**
SIC: 8361 Home for the aged
PA: Brookdale Senior Living
 111 Westwood Pl Ste 400
 Brentwood TN 37027
 615 221-2250

(G-19373)
BUCKEYE HOME HEALTHCARE INC
635 Park Madow Rd Ste 110 (43081)
PHONE 614 776-3372
Kinzi Farah, *President*
EMP: 25
SALES (est): 1.4MM **Privately Held**
SIC: 8082 Home health care services

(G-19374)
BUFFALO ABRASIVES INC
1093 Smoke Burr Dr (43081-4542)
PHONE 614 891-6450
Timothy J Wagner, *Principal*
EMP: 45
SALES (corp-wide): 14.1MM **Privately Held**
SIC: 5085 Abrasives
PA: Buffalo Abrasives, Inc.
 960 Erie Ave
 North Tonawanda NY 14120
 716 693-3856

(G-19375)
CANNON GROUP INC
Also Called: Pdi Plastics
5037 Pine Creek Dr (43081-4849)
PHONE 614 890-0343
Fax: 614 890-0467
Frank T Cannon Jr, *President*
Terrence A Grady, *Principal*
John Reiser, *Exec VP*
Chris Mahaffey, *Vice Pres*
Michael Walters, *Vice Pres*
▲ **EMP:** 25
SQ FT: 6,800
SALES (est): 12.6MM **Privately Held**
WEB: www.pdisaneck.com
SIC: 5113 5162 Bags, paper & disposable plastic; plastics resins

(G-19376)
CEIBA ENTERPRISES INCORPORATED
Also Called: Gracor Language Services
159 Baranof W (43081-6205)
PHONE 614 818-3220
Fax: 614 899-0733
Rosario Hubbard, *President*
Thomas Hubbard Jr, *Vice Pres*
EMP: 102
SALES: 1.1MM **Privately Held**
WEB: www.gracor.com
SIC: 7389 Translation services

(G-19377)
CENTRAL BNFITS ADMNSTRTORS INC
5150 E Dublin Grnvlle 3 (43081-8701)
PHONE 614 797-5200
Fax: 614 797-5268
John B Reinhardt Jr, *Ch of Bd*
Ted M Georges, *Vice Pres*
Scott M Vandergriff, *Vice Pres*
Joseph H Hoffman, *CFO*
David P Tague, *Accounts Mgr*
EMP: 100
SALES (est): 15MM **Privately Held**
SIC: 6411 Medical insurance claim processing, contract or fee basis

(G-19378)
CENTRAL OHIO NRLGICAL SURGEONS
955 Eastwind Dr Ste B (43081-3376)
PHONE 614 268-9561
David Yashon MD, *President*
Robert J Gewirtz MD, *Med Doctor*
Bradford B Mullin MD, *Med Doctor*
Gregory M Figg, *Anesthesiology*
Lisa L Choung, *Physical Med*
EMP: 52
SALES (est): 5.1MM **Privately Held**
SIC: 8011 Neurosurgeon

(G-19379)
CENTRAL OHIO PRIMARY CARE
285 W Schrock Rd (43081-2874)
PHONE 614 818-9550
Fax: 614 818-9556
EMP: 68 **Privately Held**
SIC: 8049 8011 Acupuncturist; offices & clinics of medical doctors

PA: Central Ohio Primary Care Physicians, Inc.
 570 Polaris Pkwy Ste 250
 Westerville OH 43082

(G-19380)
CENTRAL OHIO PRIMARY CARE
Also Called: Columbus Infectious Disease
615 Cpland Mill Rd Ste 2d (43081)
PHONE 614 508-0110
EMP: 56 **Privately Held**
SIC: 8011 Infectious disease specialist, physician/surgeon
PA: Central Ohio Primary Care Physicians, Inc.
 570 Polaris Pkwy Ste 250
 Westerville OH 43082

(G-19381)
CENTRAL OHIO PRIMARY CARE
Also Called: Northside Internal Medicine
555 W Schrock Rd Ste 110 (43081-8739)
PHONE 614 882-0708
Fax: 614 882-2878
EMP: 43 **Privately Held**
SIC: 8011 8999 Internal medicine practitioners; physics consultant
PA: Central Ohio Primary Care Physicians, Inc.
 570 Polaris Pkwy Ste 250
 Westerville OH 43082

(G-19382)
CITY OF WESTERVILLE
Also Called: Public Services Department
350 Park Meadow Dr (43081-2894)
PHONE 614 901-6500
Shari Sistek, *Engineer*
John Vance, *Engineer*
Frank Wiseman, *Branch Mgr*
Jody Stowers, *Director*
EMP: 45 **Privately Held**
SIC: 4941 9631 4971 4952 Water supply; public service commission, except transportation: government; irrigation systems; sewerage systems; highway & street construction
PA: City Of Westerville
 21 S State St
 Westerville OH 43081
 614 901-6406

(G-19383)
CITY OF WESTERVILLE
Also Called: Electric Division
139 E Broadway Ave (43081-1507)
PHONE 614 901-6700
Fax: 614 901-6731
Andy Boatwright, *General Mgr*
Stephen Garnick, *Opers Mgr*
Richard A Bell, *Engineer*
David E Flowers, *Engineer*
Guy Precht, *Engineer*
EMP: 37 **Privately Held**
SIC: 4911 Electric services
PA: City Of Westerville
 21 S State St
 Westerville OH 43081
 614 901-6406

(G-19384)
COLS HEALTH & WELLNESS TESTING
5050 Pine Creek Dr Ste B (43081-4852)
PHONE 614 839-2781
Fax: 614 839-2784
Marty Luxeder, *Owner*
Charles Flowers, *Director*
Edward Rauen, *Director*
Pamela Schuellerman, *Director*
Jennifer Taylor, *Director*
EMP: 35
SALES (est): 662.3K **Privately Held**
WEB: www.appsparamedical.com
SIC: 8099 8071 Health screening service; blood analysis laboratory

(G-19385)
COLUMBUS CLNY FOR ELDERLY CARE
Also Called: Columbus Colony Elderly Care
1150 Colony Dr (43081-3624)
PHONE 614 891-5055
Fax: 614 794-7461
Richard Huebner, *President*
Howard Snyder, *Treasurer*

Westerville - Franklin County (G-19386) GEOGRAPHIC SECTION

Jim Westlake, *Bookkeeper*
Rich Stepp, *Financial Exec*
Linda Briggle, *Administration*
EMP: 180 **EST:** 1977
SQ FT: 50,000
SALES: 9.1MM **Privately Held**
SIC: 8051 Convalescent home with continuous nursing care

(G-19386)
COLUMBUS FRKLN CNTY PK
Also Called: Blendonwoods Metro Park
4265 E Dblin Granville Rd (43081-4478)
PHONE.................614 895-6219
Fax: 614 895-6350
Dan Bissonette, *General Mgr*
EMP: 30
SALES (corp-wide): 18.3MM **Privately Held**
SIC: 7996 Amusement parks
PA: Columbus & Franklin County Metropolitan Park District
1069 W Main St Unit B
Westerville OH 43081
614 891-0700

(G-19387)
COLUMBUS FRKLN CNTY PK (PA)
Also Called: Metro Parks
1069 W Main St Unit B (43081-1186)
PHONE.................614 891-0700
Fax: 614 895-6359
Renee Telfer, *Human Res Dir*
Matthew Thompson, *Park Mgr*
Culek Ann, *Manager*
Bruce Dudley, *Manager*
Scott Felker, *Manager*
EMP: 50
SALES (est): 18.3MM **Privately Held**
WEB: www.metroparks.net
SIC: 7999 Recreation services

(G-19388)
COLUMBUS FRKLN CNTY PK
Also Called: District Office
1069 W Main St (43081-1181)
PHONE.................614 891-0700
John Omeara, *Branch Mgr*
EMP: 25
SALES (corp-wide): 18.3MM **Privately Held**
WEB: www.metroparks.net
SIC: 7032 Sporting & recreational camps
PA: Columbus & Franklin County Metropolitan Park District
1069 W Main St Unit B
Westerville OH 43081
614 891-0700

(G-19389)
COLUMBUS PRESCR PHRMS INC
975 Eastwind Dr Ste 155 (43081-3344)
PHONE.................614 294-1600
Mark A Witchey, *President*
Nick T Kalogeras, *Vice Pres*
Jack A Witchey, *Vice Pres*
Peggy Rankin, *Manager*
EMP: 113
SQ FT: 15,000
SALES (est): 19.5MM **Privately Held**
SIC: 5047 5912 Surgical equipment & supplies; drug stores

(G-19390)
COMMUNICATIONS III INC (PA)
921 Eastwind Dr Ste 104 (43081-5316)
PHONE.................614 901-7720
Scott Halliday, *President*
Hugh Cathey, *Chairman*
Peter Halliday, *Shareholder*
Steve Vogelmeier, *Admin Sec*
EMP: 27
SQ FT: 12,000
SALES (est): 8.3MM **Privately Held**
WEB: www.comiii.com
SIC: 5065 8748 Communication equipment; telecommunications consultant

(G-19391)
CONCORD
Also Called: CONCORD COUNSELING SERVICES
700 Brooksedge Blvd (43081-2820)
PHONE.................614 882-9338

Todd Schirtzinger, *Marketing Staff*
Mary Sommer, *Exec Dir*
Neil Edgar, *Director*
EMP: 50
SQ FT: 4,300
SALES: 5.2MM **Privately Held**
SIC: 8399 8322 Health & welfare council; individual & family services

(G-19392)
CORNA KOKOSING CONSTRUCTION CO
6235 Westerville Rd (43081-4041)
PHONE.................614 901-8844
Fax: 614 212-5599
Mark Corna, *President*
Jim Negron, *Exec VP*
Josh Corna, *Senior VP*
Kevin Kerr, *Project Mgr*
James Graves, *Treasurer*
▲ **EMP:** 200 **EST:** 1995
SQ FT: 23,000
SALES (est): 108.6MM **Privately Held**
WEB: www.corna.com
SIC: 1541 1542 Industrial buildings & warehouses; nonresidential construction

(G-19393)
DELIASS ASSETS CORP
780 Brooksedge Plaza Dr (43081-4914)
P.O. Box 6143 (43086-6143)
PHONE.................614 891-0101
EMP: 75
SALES (corp-wide): 136.6MM **Publicly Held**
SIC: 4813 Customer Communciation Service
HQ: Delias's Assets Corp
50 W 23rd St Rear 10
New York NY
212 807-9060

(G-19394)
DIVERSIFIED SYSTEMS INC
100 Dorchester Sq N # 103 (43081-7304)
PHONE.................614 476-9939
Archie D Williamson Jr, *President*
Nathan Paige, *Managing Prtnr*
Mike Beard, *Exec VP*
Sandy Riedl, *Office Mgr*
Kristina Mallorca, *Manager*
EMP: 35
SQ FT: 3,000
SALES: 12.9MM **Privately Held**
WEB: www.diversifiedsystems.com
SIC: 7379 8742 7371 Data processing consultant; management consulting services; computer software systems analysis & design, custom

(G-19395)
DOME DIALYSIS LLC
Also Called: Park Side Dialysis
241 W Schrock Rd (43081-2874)
PHONE.................614 882-1734
Jim Hilger, *Principal*
EMP: 37
SALES (est): 548.5K **Publicly Held**
SIC: 8092 Kidney dialysis centers
PA: Davita Inc.
2000 16th St
Denver CO 80202

(G-19396)
EATON PLUMBING INC
Also Called: Plumbing Contractor
5600 E Walnut St (43081-8229)
PHONE.................614 891-7005
Fax: 614 891-2321
John F Eaton, *President*
Max Eaton, *Vice Pres*
EMP: 36 **EST:** 1974
SQ FT: 3,200
SALES (est): 5.3MM **Privately Held**
WEB: www.eatonplumbing.com
SIC: 1711 Plumbing contractors

(G-19397)
ELECTRIC CONNECTION INC
5441 Westerville Rd (43081-8940)
PHONE.................614 436-1121
Fax: 614 436-1691
Judson G Voorhees, *President*
Michelle Maddigan, *Corp Secy*
Randy L Harmon, *Vice Pres*
Chad Moore, *Financial Exec*

EMP: 100
SQ FT: 7,000
SALES (est): 13MM **Privately Held**
SIC: 1731 General electrical contractor

(G-19398)
EXEL N AMERCN LOGISTICS INC (DH)
570 Players Pkwy (43081)
PHONE.................800 272-1052
Randy Briggs, *President*
Hugh Evans, *Vice Pres*
Catherine Hulse, *Controller*
Johnathan McCaman, *VP Finance*
Michael Steen, *VP Sales*
EMP: 125
SQ FT: 100,000
SALES (est): 100.4MM
SALES (corp-wide): 71.2B **Privately Held**
SIC: 4731 Freight forwarding

(G-19399)
FAMILY PHYSICIAN ASSOCIATES
291 W Schrock Rd (43081-2895)
PHONE.................614 901-2273
Jeffrey Hunter, *President*
John E Verhoff MD, *President*
Mary J Welker MD, *Vice Pres*
EMP: 41
SQ FT: 2,500
SALES (est): 761.7K **Privately Held**
SIC: 8011 General & family practice, physician/surgeon

(G-19400)
FEDEX OFFICE & PRINT SVCS INC
604 W Schrock Rd (43081-8996)
PHONE.................614 898-0000
Rob Heinz, *Manager*
Eric Baker, *Manager*
EMP: 40
SALES (corp-wide): 60.3B **Publicly Held**
WEB: www.kinkos.com
SIC: 7334 2759 2396 Photocopying & duplicating services; commercial printing; automotive & apparel trimmings
HQ: Fedex Office And Print Services, Inc.
7900 Legacy Dr
Plano TX 75024
214 550-7000

(G-19401)
FIDELITY NATIONAL FINCL INC
4111 Executive Pkwy # 304 (43081-3869)
PHONE.................614 865-1562
Fax: 614 865-1565
Mark Sinkhorn, *General Mgr*
EMP: 25
SALES (corp-wide): 7.6B **Publicly Held**
SIC: 6361 Real estate title insurance
PA: Fidelity National Financial, Inc.
601 Riverside Ave Fl 4
Jacksonville FL 32204
904 854-8100

(G-19402)
GANNETT FLEMING INC
Also Called: Gannet Fleming Engr & Archt
4151 Executive Pkwy # 350 (43081-3863)
PHONE.................614 794-9424
Fax: 614 794-9442
Joseph Rikk, *Branch Mgr*
EMP: 32
SALES (corp-wide): 386MM **Privately Held**
WEB: www.gfnet.com
SIC: 8711 Consulting engineer
HQ: Fleming Gannett Inc
207 Senate Ave
Camp Hill PA 17011
717 763-7211

(G-19403)
GENERAL ELECTRIC COMPANY
4151 Executive Pkwy # 110 (43081-3867)
PHONE.................614 899-8923
Mark Hamm, *Manager*
EMP: 26
SALES (corp-wide): 122B **Publicly Held**
SIC: 5065 Electronic parts

PA: General Electric Company
41 Farnsworth St
Boston MA 02210
617 443-3000

(G-19404)
GOOD NIGHT MEDICAL OHIO LLC
975 Eastwind Dr Ste 165 (43081-3398)
PHONE.................614 384-7433
Alan Rudy, *CEO*
Larry Pliskin, *Senior VP*
EMP: 30
SALES (est): 1.1MM **Privately Held**
SIC: 8099 Medical services organization

(G-19405)
HALLEY CONSULTING GROUP LLC
1224 Oak Bluff Ct (43081-3222)
P.O. Box 118 (43086-0118)
PHONE.................614 899-7325
Marc D Halley, *CEO*
Michael J Ferry, *President*
Jennifer Snider, *Vice Pres*
Karen Bridges, *CFO*
EMP: 25
SALES: 6MM **Privately Held**
SIC: 8748 8742 Business consulting; management consulting services; marketing consulting services

(G-19406)
HARRINGTON HEALTH SERVICES INC (DH)
Also Called: Fiserv Health
780 Brooksedge Plaza Dr (43081-4914)
PHONE.................614 212-7000
Fax: 937 226-8629
Jeff Mills, *President*
Patricia Keplinger, *Vice Pres*
Mary Morrill, *Project Mgr*
Terry Moore, *CFO*
Elena Bloomer, *Accountant*
EMP: 130 **EST:** 2000
SQ FT: 24,000
SALES (est): 116.5MM
SALES (corp-wide): 201.1B **Publicly Held**
WEB: www.harringtonbenefits.com
SIC: 6411 Insurance claim processing, except medical
HQ: Umr, Inc.
11 Scott St
Wausau WI 54403
800 826-9781

(G-19407)
HCR MANORCARE MED SVCS FLA LLC
Also Called: Manorcare Hlth Svcs Wsterville
140 Old County Line Rd (43081-1002)
PHONE.................614 882-1511
Beth Huey, *Facilities Dir*
Cara Aranette, *Director*
Kurt Conway, *Hlthcr Dir*
Emily Russing, *Hlthcr Dir*
Greg Ford, *Maintence Staff*
EMP: 160
SALES (corp-wide): 3.6B **Publicly Held**
WEB: www.manorcare.com
SIC: 8051 8069 Convalescent home with continuous nursing care; specialty hospitals, except psychiatric
HQ: Hcr Manorcare Medical Services Of Florida, Llc
333 N Summit St Ste 100
Toledo OH 43604
419 252-5500

(G-19408)
HEALTH CARE RTREMENT CORP AMER
Also Called: Village At Wstrvlle Retiremnt
215 Huber Village Blvd (43081-3339)
PHONE.................614 882-3782
Fax: 614 882-1107
Beverly Cabb, *Manager*
EMP: 75
SQ FT: 59,241
SALES (corp-wide): 3.6B **Publicly Held**
WEB: www.hrc-manorcare.com
SIC: 8051 Convalescent home with continuous nursing care

GEOGRAPHIC SECTION
Westerville - Franklin County (G-19429)

HQ: Health Care And Retirement Corporation Of America
333 N Summit St Ste 103
Toledo OH 43604
419 252-5500

(G-19409)
HEALTHSCOPE BENEFITS INC
5150 E Dublin Granvll 3 (43081-8701)
PHONE..................614 797-5200
Robert Gracy, *Vice Pres*
Paula Thompson, *Vice Pres*
George Forby, *Business Anlyst*
Dave Tague, *Branch Mgr*
Rwanda Elmore, *Manager*
EMP: 38 **Privately Held**
WEB: www.healthscopebenefits.com
SIC: 8741 Hospital management; nursing & personal care facility management
PA: Healthscope Benefits, Inc.
27 Corporate Hill Dr
Little Rock AR 72205

(G-19410)
IFS FINANCIAL SERVICES INC (DH)
370 S Cleveland Ave (43081-8917)
PHONE..................513 362-8000
Fax: 513 362-8086
Jill T McGruder, *President*
Mark E Caner, *President*
Brian Hirsch, *Vice Pres*
Connie Hartig, *Director*
Todd Henderson, *Business Dir*
EMP: 35
SQ FT: 2,000
SALES (est): 23.9MM **Privately Held**
SIC: 6211 6282 Security brokers & dealers; investment advice
HQ: The Western & Southern Life Insurance Company
400 Broadway St
Cincinnati OH 45202
513 629-1800

(G-19411)
IMMEDIATE HEALTH ASSOCIATES
Also Called: Wedgewood Urgent Care
575 Cpland Mill Rd Ste 1d (43081)
PHONE..................614 794-0481
Fax: 614 794-3711
Frank Orth Do, *President*
Edward Boudreau Do, *Vice Pres*
Patricia Robitaille, *Vice Pres*
Arlene Kent, *Manager*
EMP: 30
SALES (est): 6.1MM **Privately Held**
WEB: www.ihainc.org
SIC: 8011 Freestanding emergency medical center

(G-19412)
JOHNSON CONTROLS INC
835 Green Crest Dr (43081-2838)
PHONE..................614 895-6600
Stephen Carter, *Branch Mgr*
EMP: 72 **Privately Held**
SIC: 1711 Heating & air conditioning contractors
HQ: Johnson Controls, Inc.
5757 N Green Bay Ave
Milwaukee WI 53209
414 524-1200

(G-19413)
JPMORGAN CHASE BANK NAT ASSN
340 S Cleveland Ave (43081-8017)
PHONE..................614 794-7398
Kali Robinson, *Vice Pres*
Carolyn Martin, *Manager*
EMP: 50
SALES (corp-wide): 99.6B **Publicly Held**
WEB: www.chase.com
SIC: 6021 National commercial banks
HQ: Jpmorgan Chase Bank, National Association
1111 Polaris Pkwy
Columbus OH 43240
614 436-3055

(G-19414)
JPMORGAN CHASE BANK NAT ASSN
275 W Schrock Rd (43081-2874)
P.O. Box 711038, Columbus (43271-0001)
PHONE..................614 248-5800
Jim Merriman, *Manager*
EMP: 65
SALES (corp-wide): 99.6B **Publicly Held**
WEB: www.chase.com
SIC: 6021 National commercial banks
HQ: Jpmorgan Chase Bank, National Association
1111 Polaris Pkwy
Columbus OH 43240
614 436-3055

(G-19415)
JPMORGAN CHASE BANK NAT ASSN
713 Brooksedge Plaza Dr (43081-4913)
PHONE..................614 248-7505
Jeff Benton, *Branch Mgr*
EMP: 26
SALES (corp-wide): 99.6B **Publicly Held**
WEB: www.chase.com
SIC: 6021 National commercial banks
HQ: Jpmorgan Chase Bank, National Association
1111 Polaris Pkwy
Columbus OH 43240
614 436-3055

(G-19416)
JPMORGAN CHASE BANK NAT ASSN
800 Brooksedge Blvd (43081-2822)
PHONE..................614 248-5800
Robert Johnson, *Persnl Dir*
Randy Lightbpdy, *Manager*
Michael Johns, *Info Tech Mgr*
Julie Miller, *Assistant*
EMP: 250
SALES (corp-wide): 99.6B **Publicly Held**
WEB: www.chase.com
SIC: 6021 National commercial banks
HQ: Jpmorgan Chase Bank, National Association
1111 Polaris Pkwy
Columbus OH 43240
614 436-3055

(G-19417)
KOKOSING INC (PA)
6235 Wstrville Rd Ste 200 (43081)
PHONE..................614 212-5700
Dan Compston, *President*
William B Burgett, *Principal*
Tom Muraski, *Principal*
Dan Walker, *Principal*
Ryan Bodenhorn, *Controller*
EMP: 100
SALES (est): 674.3MM **Privately Held**
SIC: 1611 General contractor, highway & street construction; highway & street paving contractor

(G-19418)
KOKOSING INDUSTRIAL INC (HQ)
6235 Westerville Rd (43081-4041)
PHONE..................614 212-5700
W Brian Burgett, *CEO*
EMP: 400
SALES (est): 29.3MM
SALES (corp-wide): 674.3MM **Privately Held**
SIC: 1623 1629 Water, sewer & utility lines; dams, waterways, docks & other marine construction
PA: Kokosing Inc.
6235 Wstrville Rd Ste 200
Westerville OH 43081
614 212-5700

(G-19419)
KROGER CO
4111 Executive Pkwy # 100 (43081-3800)
PHONE..................614 898-3200
Fax: 614 898-3210
Mark Hrabcak, *Vice Pres*
David Daniels, *Personnel*
Merritt Henderson, *Manager*
Mark Driver, *Manager*
Eric Taylor, *Manager*
EMP: 300
SQ FT: 27,252
SALES (corp-wide): 122.6B **Publicly Held**
WEB: www.kroger.com
SIC: 5411 5122 Supermarkets, chain; pharmaceuticals
PA: The Kroger Co
1014 Vine St Ste 1000
Cincinnati OH 45202
513 762-4000

(G-19420)
LOS ALAMOS TECHNICAL ASSOC INC
Also Called: Lata
756 Park Meadow Rd (43081-2871)
PHONE..................614 508-1200
Rees Lattimer, *Vice Pres*
Joseph Towarnicky, *Vice Pres*
Rob Pfendler, *Branch Mgr*
Jason M Brydges, *Program Mgr*
Todd Struttmann, *Senior Mgr*
EMP: 30
SALES (corp-wide): 39.9MM **Privately Held**
SIC: 8711 4959 Industrial engineers; environmental cleanup services
PA: Los Alamos Technical Associates, Inc.
6501 Americas Pkwy Ne # 200
Albuquerque NM 87110
505 884-3800

(G-19421)
M CONSULTANTS LLC
Also Called: M-Engineering
750 Brooksedge Blvd (43081-2820)
PHONE..................614 839-4639
Fax: 614 818-1931
Jacqueline Durst, *Assoc VP*
Randy Ison, *Project Mgr*
Eric Berggren, *Engineer*
Katie Evans, *Engineer*
Brent McClure, *Engineer*
EMP: 57
SALES (est): 6.8MM **Privately Held**
SIC: 8711 Consulting engineer

(G-19422)
M RETAIL ENGINEERING INC
750 Brooksedge Blvd (43081-2820)
PHONE..................614 818-2323
Fax: 614 818-2337
Dan Gilmore, *President*
Dave Gonzollaz, *President*
David Gonzalez, *Vice Pres*
Ron Koons, *Vice Pres*
Shigeyoshi A Mori, *Vice Pres*
EMP: 45
SQ FT: 10,000
SALES (est): 2.8MM **Privately Held**
SIC: 8711 Consulting engineer

(G-19423)
M-E COMPANIES INC (HQ)
Also Called: Me/Ibi Group
635 Brooksedge Blvd (43081-2817)
PHONE..................614 818-4900
Tim Foley, *CEO*
Kevin Wood, *Vice Pres*
Randy Stoll, *Project Mgr*
Bob Foley, *Financial Exec*
Ed Orsi, *Human Res Mgr*
EMP: 65
SALES (est): 13MM
SALES (corp-wide): 261.9MM **Privately Held**
SIC: 8711 6700 Consulting engineer; real estate investors, except property operators
PA: Ibi Group Inc
55 St Clair Ave W Suite 700
Toronto ON M4V 2
416 596-1930

(G-19424)
MICRO INDUSTRIES CORPORATION (PA)
8399 Green Meadows Dr N (43081)
PHONE..................740 548-7878
Fax: 614 882-6357
John Curran, *CEO*
Michael Curran, *President*
Amanda Curran, *Vice Pres*
William Jackson, *Vice Pres*
Jeffrey Price, *Mfg Staff*

▲ **EMP:** 78
SQ FT: 52,000
SALES (est): 8.7MM **Privately Held**
WEB: www.microindustries.com
SIC: 8711 3674 Engineering services; semiconductor circuit networks; microcircuits, integrated (semiconductor)

(G-19425)
MID-OHIO PDIATRICS ADOLESCENTS
595 Cpland Mill Rd Ste 2a (43081)
PHONE..................614 899-0000
Fax: 614 899-0524
Richard Anthony Petrella, *President*
EMP: 31
SQ FT: 5,200
SALES (est): 4.8MM **Privately Held**
SIC: 8011 Pediatrician

(G-19426)
MODERN OFFICE METHODS INC
929 Eastwind Dr Ste 220 (43081-3362)
PHONE..................614 891-3693
Fax: 614 891-5089
Dan Vail, *Vice Pres*
Pamela Sacco, *Branch Mgr*
Dale Schwartzmiller, *Manager*
EMP: 40
SALES (corp-wide): 28.8MM **Privately Held**
WEB: www.momnet.com
SIC: 5999 7629 Business machines & equipment; business machine repair, electric
PA: Modern Office Methods, Inc.
4747 Lake Forest Dr # 200
Blue Ash OH 45242
513 791-0909

(G-19427)
MOUNT CARMEL HEALTH
Also Called: Mount Carmel Home Care
501 W Schrock Rd Ste 350 (43081-7155)
PHONE..................614 234-0100
Fax: 614 234-0185
Erin Denholm, *CEO*
David Sabgir, *Med Doctor*
Cindy Salvator, *Director*
Barbara Sears, *Associate*
EMP: 80
SALES (corp-wide): 16.3B **Privately Held**
SIC: 8082 Home health care services
HQ: Mount Carmel Health
793 W State St
Columbus OH 43222
614 234-5000

(G-19428)
MOUNT CARMEL HEALTH SYSTEM
500 S Cleveland Ave (43081-8971)
PHONE..................614 898-4000
Fax: 614 898-4350
Kirk Hummer, *COO*
Craig Pratt, *Vice Pres*
Lisa Wallschlaeger, *Project Mgr*
Lisa Everson, *Human Res Dir*
Debbie Drone, *Office Mgr*
EMP: 45
SALES (corp-wide): 16.3B **Privately Held**
SIC: 8621 Professional membership organizations
HQ: Mount Carmel Health System
6150 E Broad St
Columbus OH 43213
614 234-6000

(G-19429)
NATIONAL GROUND WATER ASSN INC
Also Called: NGWA
601 Dempsey Rd (43081-8978)
PHONE..................614 898-7791
Fax: 614 898-7786
Kevin B McCray, *CEO*
Richard Thron, *President*
Jeffrey Williams, *Vice Pres*
Paul Humes, *CFO*
Vickie Wiles, *Sales Staff*
EMP: 34
SQ FT: 13,600

Westerville - Franklin County (G-19430)

SALES: 5.4MM **Privately Held**
WEB: www.ngwa.org
SIC: 8621 Professional membership organizations

(G-19430)
NEW RIVER ELECTRICAL CORP
6005 Westerville Rd (43081-4055)
PHONE..................................614 891-1142
Jake Miller, *Vice Pres*
Tom Wolden, *Manager*
EMP: 25
SALES (corp-wide): 283.2MM **Privately Held**
WEB: www.newriverelectrical.com
SIC: 1731 General electrical contractor
PA: New River Electrical Corporation
15 Cloverdale Pl
Cloverdale VA 24077
540 966-1650

(G-19431)
OFFICEMAX NORTH AMERICA INC
87 Huber Village Blvd (43081-3311)
PHONE..................................614 899-6186
Fax: 614 823-5414
Ron Pierce, *Manager*
EMP: 26
SALES (corp-wide): 10.2B **Publicly Held**
WEB: www.copymax.net
SIC: 7641 5943 Reupholstery & furniture repair; office forms & supplies
HQ: Officemax North America, Inc.
263 Shuman Blvd
Naperville IL 60563
630 717-0791

(G-19432)
OHIO LBRERS FRNGE BNEFT PRGRAM
800 Hillsdowne Rd (43081-3302)
PHONE..................................614 898-9006
Mathew Archer, *President*
Denise Sikes, *Benefits Mgr*
Will Brown, *Manager*
Charlene Denny, *Tech/Comp Coord*
EMP: 30
SALES: 8.2MM **Privately Held**
WEB: www.olfbp.com
SIC: 8631 Labor union

(G-19433)
OPTIMUM SYSTEM PRODUCTS INC (PA)
Also Called: Optimum Graphics
921 Eastwind Dr Ste 133 (43081-3363)
PHONE..................................614 885-4464
Fax: 614 885-4454
John Martin, *CEO*
Dorothy Martin, *President*
Anthony Danna, *Senior Buyer*
Phil Osborn, *Marketing Staff*
Anita Pasco, *Marketing Staff*
EMP: 40
SQ FT: 75,000
SALES (est): 10.5MM **Privately Held**
WEB: www.optimumsystem.com
SIC: 2752 5112 Business form & card printing, lithographic; business forms

(G-19434)
ORTHONEURO (PA)
Also Called: Ortho Neuro
70 S Cleveland Ave (43081-1397)
PHONE..................................614 890-6555
Fax: 614 890-6663
Francis O Donnell, *President*
Jeffrey Gittins, *Vice Pres*
Chris Paige, *Financial Exec*
Gene Steffen, *Finance*
Rachel Conwell, *Human Res Mgr*
EMP: 30
SQ FT: 20,000
SALES (est): 19.3MM **Privately Held**
SIC: 8011 Orthopedic physician; neurologist; neurosurgeon

(G-19435)
OURDAY AT MESSIAH PRESCHOOL
51 N State St (43081-2123)
PHONE..................................614 882-4416
Charity Monroe, *Director*
EMP: 32 **EST:** 1979

SALES (est): 502.7K **Privately Held**
SIC: 8351 Preschool center

(G-19436)
PATROL URBAN SERVICES LLC
4563 E Walnut St (43081-9693)
PHONE..................................614 620-4672
Robert S Urban, *President*
EMP: 35
SALES: 1.3MM **Privately Held**
SIC: 7381 Security guard service; private investigator

(G-19437)
PORTER DRYWALL INC
297 Old County Line Rd (43081-1602)
P.O. Box 550 (43086-0550)
PHONE..................................614 890-2111
Fax: 614 890-0375
Robert E Porter, *President*
EMP: 100
SQ FT: 10,000
SALES (est): 7.5MM **Privately Held**
WEB: www.porterdrywall.com
SIC: 1742 Drywall

(G-19438)
QUADAX INC
4151 Executive Pkwy # 360 (43081-3820)
PHONE..................................614 882-1200
Fax: 614 882-7133
EMP: 25
SALES (corp-wide): 26MM **Privately Held**
SIC: 8721 7374 Accounting, Auditing, And Bookkeeping
PA: Quadax, Inc.
7500 Old Oak Blvd
Middleburg Heights OH 44130
216 765-1144

(G-19439)
QUANDEL CONSTRUCTION GROUP INC
Also Called: Quandel Group Main Office
774 Park Meadow Rd (43081-2871)
PHONE..................................717 657-0909
Fax: 614 865-9001
Mark Massman, *Vice Pres*
Richard Krisch, *Project Mgr*
Paul Dawson, *Comms Dir*
Roland Tokarski, *Manager*
Chris Bushey, *Officer*
EMP: 50
SALES (corp-wide): 149.4MM **Privately Held**
WEB: www.quandel-ohio.com
SIC: 1542 8741 Commercial & office building contractors; institutional building construction; construction management
HQ: The Quandel Construction Group Inc
3003 N Front St Ste 203
Harrisburg PA 17110
717 657-0909

(G-19440)
RAISIN RACK INC (PA)
Also Called: Raisin Rack Natural Food Mkt
2545 W Schrock Rd (43081-8956)
PHONE..................................614 882-5886
Toll Free:..............................888 -
Donald L Caster, *President*
Matt Patchin, *Opers Mgr*
Bill Kerekes, *Buyer*
John Marulli, *VP Mktg*
Roger Bair, *Manager*
EMP: 42 **EST:** 1978
SQ FT: 6,500
SALES (est): 3.6MM **Privately Held**
WEB: www.wholesomelife.com
SIC: 5499 5112 Health foods; vitamins & minerals

(G-19441)
ROMANELLI & HUGHES BUILDING CO
Also Called: Romanelli & Hughes Contractors
148 W Schrock Rd (43081-4915)
PHONE..................................614 891-2042
Fax: 614 891-2045
David Hughes, *President*
Darrel R Miller, *Corp Secy*
Vincent Romanelli, *Vice Pres*
EMP: 42
SQ FT: 5,000

SALES (est): 7.4MM **Privately Held**
WEB: www.rh-homes.com
SIC: 1521 1542 New construction, single-family houses; commercial & office building, new construction

(G-19442)
ROUSH EQUIPMENT INC (PA)
Also Called: Roush Honda
100 W Schrock Rd (43081-2832)
PHONE..................................614 882-1535
Fax: 614 895-5732
Jeffrey A Brindley, *President*
Kandy Lazarrus, *Purch Dir*
Mark Vanbenschoten, *CFO*
Tracy Williams, *Human Res Mgr*
Leigh Daniels, *Sales Staff*
EMP: 129
SQ FT: 16,000
SALES (est): 58.9MM **Privately Held**
WEB: www.roushhonda.com
SIC: 5511 7538 7532 7515 Automobiles, new & used; general automotive repair shops; top & body repair & paint shops; passenger car leasing; truck rental & leasing, no drivers; used car dealers

(G-19443)
SECURITY INVESTMENTS LLC
4807 Smoketalk Ln (43081-7833)
PHONE..................................614 441-4601
William Marks,
EMP: 65
SQ FT: 12,000
SALES (est): 3.2MM **Privately Held**
SIC: 7382 7373 Protective devices, security; office computer automation systems integration

(G-19444)
THOMAS ROSSER
Also Called: Financial Perspective Company
855 S Sunbury Rd (43081-9553)
PHONE..................................614 890-2900
Thomas Rosser, *Owner*
EMP: 125
SQ FT: 1,000
SALES (est): 4.6MM **Privately Held**
SIC: 8741 8721 Administrative management; financial management for business; accounting, auditing & bookkeeping

(G-19445)
THYSSENKRUPP ELEVATOR CORP
929 Eastwind Dr Ste 218 (43081-3362)
PHONE..................................614 895-8930
Marc Beyerlein, *Sales Staff*
Mike Zwick, *Branch Mgr*
Dan Eisert, *Manager*
Glen Steel, *Commissioner*
EMP: 50
SALES (corp-wide): 48.7B **Privately Held**
WEB: www.tyssenkrupp.com
SIC: 1796 7699 5084 Elevator installation & conversion; elevators: inspection, service & repair; elevators
HQ: Thyssenkrupp Elevator Corporation
11605 Haynes Bridge Rd # 650
Alpharetta GA 30009
678 319-3240

(G-19446)
TURTLE GOLF MANAGEMENT LTD (HQ)
Also Called: Little Turtle Golf Club
5400 Little Turtle Way W (43081-7821)
PHONE..................................614 882-5920
Fax: 614 882-7943
David P McDonald, *Office Mgr*
Garth Walker,
David S Hett, *Admin Sec*
Michael Hill,
EMP: 26
SQ FT: 23,000
SALES (est): 2.4MM **Privately Held**
SIC: 8742 7997 General management consultant; country club, membership

(G-19447)
UNITED STATES TROTTING ASSN (PA)
6130 S Sunbury Rd (43081-9309)
PHONE..................................614 224-2291
Fax: 614 224-4575

Michael Panner, *CEO*
Daniel Rakieten, *General Mgr*
David Carr, *Research*
Dennis Fisher, *CFO*
Jane Gray, *Treasurer*
EMP: 60
SQ FT: 20,000
SALES: 7.9MM **Privately Held**
WEB: www.ustrotting.com
SIC: 8611 Trade associations

(G-19448)
WESTERVILLE DERMATOLOGY INC
235 W Schrock Rd (43081-2874)
PHONE..................................614 895-0400
Fax: 614 895-2911
Kevin B Karikomi Do, *President*
Joyce Miller, *Manager*
Shana Beeson, *Assistant*
EMP: 25
SQ FT: 1,882
SALES (est): 1.7MM **Privately Held**
WEB: www.westervilledermatology.com
SIC: 8011 Dermatologist

(G-19449)
WESTERVILLE-WORTHINGTON LEARNI
149 Charring Cross Dr S (43081-2860)
PHONE..................................614 891-4105
Debra Jennings, *Owner*
EMP: 30
SALES (est): 378.1K **Privately Held**
SIC: 8351 Child day care services

(G-19450)
WHEELER CLEANING LLC
159 Drakewood Rd (43081-3023)
PHONE..................................614 818-0981
Daniel Patrick Wheeler, *Administration*
EMP: 32
SALES (est): 38.6K **Privately Held**
SIC: 7349 Building maintenance services

Westfield Center
Medina County

(G-19451)
AMERICAN SELECT INSURANCE CO
1 Park Cir (44251-9700)
P.O. Box 5001 (44251-5001)
PHONE..................................330 887-0101
Robert Kiraty, *Treasurer*
Wayne Hartzler, *Info Tech Mgr*
EMP: 1500 **EST:** 1850
SQ FT: 100,000
SALES (est): 234.4MM
SALES (corp-wide): 1.6B **Privately Held**
WEB: www.westfieldgrp.com
SIC: 6331 Fire, marine & casualty insurance
PA: Ohio Farmers Insurance Company
1 Park Cir
Westfield Center OH 44251
800 243-0210

(G-19452)
OHIO FARMERS INSURANCE COMPANY (PA)
Also Called: Westfield Group
1 Park Cir (44251-9700)
P.O. Box 5001 (44251-5001)
PHONE..................................800 243-0210
Fax: 330 887-0840
Edward J Largent III, *CEO*
Ed Largent, *President*
Tara Martin, *General Mgr*
Alex Mosyjowski, *General Mgr*
Ken Sterba, *General Mgr*
EMP: 1753
SQ FT: 200,000
SALES (est): 1.6B **Privately Held**
WEB: www.westfieldgrp.com
SIC: 6411 6331 Property & casualty insurance agent; fire, marine & casualty insurance

GEOGRAPHIC SECTION

Westlake - Cuyahoga County (G-19475)

(G-19453)
WESTFIELD BANK FSB (HQ)
2 Park Cir (44251-9744)
P.O. Box 5002 (44251-5002)
PHONE..................800 368-8930
Fax: 330 887-6430
Jon Park, *CEO*
Timothy E Phillips, *President*
Gary Clark, *COO*
Matthew Berthold, *Exec VP*
Glenn McClelland, *Senior VP*
EMP: 40
SALES: 48.9MM **Privately Held**
SIC: 6029 Commercial banks

Westlake
Cuyahoga County

(G-19454)
ACHIEVEMENT CTRS FOR CHILDREN
24211 Center Ridge Rd (44145-4211)
PHONE..................440 250-2520
Fax: 216 292-9721
Scott Peplin, *Manager*
EMP: 30
SALES (corp-wide): 8.2MM **Privately Held**
WEB: www.achievementcenters.org
SIC: 8322 Individual & family services
PA: Achievement Centers For Children
4255 Northfield Rd
Cleveland OH 44128
216 292-9700

(G-19455)
ADVANCED TRANSLATION/CNSLTNG
Also Called: Spanish Portugese Translation
3751 Willow Run (44145-5720)
PHONE..................440 716-0820
Hugo R Urizar, *Owner*
EMP: 30
SALES (est): 1.4MM **Privately Held**
SIC: 7389 2791 Translation services; typesetting

(G-19456)
ALL METAL SALES INC
29260 Clemens Rd Ste 3 (44145-1020)
PHONE..................440 617-1234
Thomas Klocker, *President*
Alison Klocker, *Vice Pres*
Jim Vandevelde, *Sales Associate*
Tom Klocker, *Manager*
Steve Scalf, *Manager*
▲ EMP: 26
SQ FT: 69,000
SALES (est): 22.3MM **Privately Held**
WEB: www.allmetalsalesinc.com
SIC: 5051 Ferrous metals; nonferrous metal sheets, bars, rods, etc.

(G-19457)
ALLIED ENTERPRISES INC (PA)
26021 Center Ridge Rd (44145-4013)
PHONE..................440 808-8760
Fax: 440 808-8761
Eric Pfaff, *President*
Puzant Mikikian, *Division Mgr*
Julius Berith, *Business Mgr*
Mark Pfaff, *Vice Pres*
Celine Sandevoir, *Sls & Mktg Exec*
▲ EMP: 25 EST: 1954
SALES (est): 6.9MM **Privately Held**
WEB: www.alliedenterprisesinc.com
SIC: 5065 Electronic parts

(G-19458)
ALTA PARTNERS LLC
902 Westpoint Pkwy # 320 (44145-1534)
PHONE..................440 808-3654
Fax: 440 808-3674
Ann Hanzel, *Opers Staff*
Jennifer Peregord, *Finance Mgr*
Ed Rand, *Consultant*
Lacy Sharratt, *Consultant*
Jennifer Dalton, *Senior Mgr*
EMP: 30
SALES (est): 3.6MM **Privately Held**
WEB: www.altapartnersllc.com
SIC: 8011 General & family practice, physician/surgeon

(G-19459)
ALUMINUM LINE PRODUCTS COMPANY (PA)
Also Called: Alpco
24460 Sperry Cir (44145-1591)
PHONE..................440 835-8880
Fax: 440 835-8879
Edward Murray, *Principal*
Chris Harrington, *Vice Pres*
Guy Martin, *Vice Pres*
Vicki Black, *Purchasing*
Pat Wessel, *Purchasing*
▲ EMP: 100 EST: 1960
SQ FT: 100,000
SALES: 100MM **Privately Held**
WEB: www.aluminumline.com
SIC: 5051 3365 3999 Metals service centers & offices; aluminum foundries; barber & beauty shop equipment

(G-19460)
APPLIED MARKETING SERVICES
Also Called: Ibeda Inc Sprflash Gas Equip
28825 Ranney Pkwy (44145-1173)
PHONE..................440 716-9962
David J Marquard, *President*
C V Guggenviller, *CFO*
Jane Binzer, *Sales Staff*
Laura Frederick, *Manager*
Bob McQuown, *Manager*
▲ EMP: 28
SQ FT: 20,000
SALES (est): 9.6MM **Privately Held**
WEB: www.applied-inc.com
SIC: 3569 8742 Gas producers, generators & other gas related equipment; marketing consulting services; new products & services consultants

(G-19461)
ARDMORE POWER LOGISTICS LLC
Also Called: Ardmore Logistics
24610 Detroit Rd Ste 1200 (44145-2561)
PHONE..................216 502-0640
David Cottenden, *Chairman*
Scott Dolan, *Opers Mgr*
Debbie Suhy, *Human Res Mgr*
Greg Giuliano, *Accounts Mgr*
Mark Majewski, *Accounts Mgr*
EMP: 29
SQ FT: 6,000
SALES (est): 7.9MM **Privately Held**
WEB: www.ardmorelogistics.com
SIC: 8742 4731 Transportation consultant; domestic freight forwarding

(G-19462)
ASSOCIATES IN DERMATOLOGY INC (PA)
26908 Detroit Rd Ste 103 (44145-2399)
PHONE..................440 249-0274
Fax: 216 228-1709
Paul G Hazen, *President*
John Jay Stewart, *Assistant VP*
Conley W Engstrom, *Vice Pres*
Karen Turgeon, *Treasurer*
Larson Turgeon, *Treasurer*
EMP: 32
SQ FT: 5,000
SALES (est): 4.8MM **Privately Held**
SIC: 8011 Dermatologist

(G-19463)
BAY FURNACE SHEET METAL CO
Also Called: Bay Heating & Air Conditioning
24530 Sperry Dr (44145-1578)
PHONE..................440 871-3777
Fax: 440 871-3899
Lynn Robinson, *President*
Kori Robinson, *Treasurer*
Korie Szabo, *Financial Exec*
Paul Dooney, *Sales Executive*
Billie Robinson, *Admin Sec*
EMP: 30
SQ FT: 4,800
SALES (est): 2.6MM **Privately Held**
WEB: www.bayfurnace.com
SIC: 1711 Warm air heating & air conditioning contractor

(G-19464)
BAY VILLAGE MONTESSORI INC
Also Called: MONTESSORI CHILDREN SCHOOL
28370 Bassett Rd (44145-3022)
PHONE..................440 871-8773
Barbara Kincade, *President*
EMP: 30
SQ FT: 1,092
SALES: 1MM **Privately Held**
SIC: 8351 Montessori child development center

(G-19465)
BELLA CAPELLI INC
Also Called: Bella Capelli Salon
24350 Center Ridge Rd (44145-4212)
PHONE..................440 899-1225
Fax: 440 899-1270
Sandra Borrelli, *President*
Serina Peck, *Vice Pres*
Michelle Mackenson, *Director*
Maggi Milia, *Director*
Nicole Gilsdorf, *Master*
EMP: 30 EST: 1997
SALES (est): 1.3MM **Privately Held**
WEB: www.bellacapelli.com
SIC: 7231 Hairdressers

(G-19466)
BORCHERS AMERICAS INC (HQ)
Also Called: Om Group
811 Sharon Dr (44145-1522)
PHONE..................440 899-2950
Fax: 440 808-7117
Joseph Scaminace, *CEO*
Alice Ramsey, *Office Mgr*
Wendy Kozel, *Manager*
Hugo Martin, *Manager*
EMP: 60
SQ FT: 30,000
SALES (est): 51MM
SALES (corp-wide): 791.7MM **Privately Held**
SIC: 8731 2819 2899 2992 Commercial physical research; industrial inorganic chemicals; chemical preparations; lubricating oils & greases; industrial organic chemicals
PA: The Jordan Company L P
399 Park Ave Fl 30
New York NY 10022
212 572-0800

(G-19467)
BROOKDALE SENIOR LIVING INC
28550 Westlake Village Dr (44145-7608)
PHONE..................440 892-4200
Jeanne Barnard, *Branch Mgr*
EMP: 35
SALES (corp-wide): 4.7B **Publicly Held**
SIC: 8059 Convalescent home
PA: Brookdale Senior Living
111 Westwood Pl Ste 400
Brentwood TN 37027
615 221-2250

(G-19468)
BUDGET DUMPSTER LLC (PA)
Also Called: Budget Dumpster Rental
830 Canterbury Rd (44145-1419)
PHONE..................866 284-6164
John Fenn,
Mark Campbell,
EMP: 25 EST: 2009
SALES (est): 3.8MM **Privately Held**
SIC: 7359 Equipment rental & leasing

(G-19469)
CAREER CNNCTIONS STAFFING SVCS
Also Called: Go 2 It Group
26260 Center Ridge Rd (44145-4016)
PHONE..................440 471-8210
Beverly Sandvick, *President*
EMP: 50
SQ FT: 1,500
SALES (est): 5.6MM **Privately Held**
WEB: www.go2itgroup.com
SIC: 7361 Employment agencies

(G-19470)
CARNEGIE MANAGEMENT & DEV CORP
27500 Detroit Rd Ste 300 (44145-5913)
PHONE..................440 892-6800
Fax: 440 892-6804
Rustom R Khouri, *CEO*
Steven M Edelman, *COO*
Clayton Lareux, *Vice Pres*
James McKinney, *Vice Pres*
Steve Rigo, *Personnel Exec*
EMP: 30
SQ FT: 17,000
SALES (est): 4.9MM **Privately Held**
SIC: 6512 6552 Commercial & industrial building operation; subdividers & developers

(G-19471)
CASTON HOLDINGS LLC (PA)
Also Called: Learning Express Toys
30061 Detroit Rd (44145-1944)
PHONE..................440 871-8697
Fax: 440 871-0407
Mark H Caston, *Mng Member*
EMP: 200
SALES (est): 40.2MM **Privately Held**
SIC: 6719 Personal holding companies, except banks

(G-19472)
CERES ENTERPRISES LLC
Also Called: Hilton
835 Sharon Dr Ste 400 (44145-7704)
PHONE..................440 617-9385
Lori Hansen, *Exec VP*
Kelli Peterson, *Purch Agent*
Diane Beach, *CFO*
David Crisafi, *Mng Member*
Frank Crisafi, *Mng Member*
EMP: 55
SALES (est): 1.2MM **Privately Held**
SIC: 7011 Hotels & motels

(G-19473)
CHARLES SCHWAB CORPORATION
2211 Crocker Rd Ste 100 (44145-7603)
PHONE..................440 617-2301
Karen Barrett, *Manager*
Roger Baranovic, *Manager*
Deborah Brock, *Manager*
EMP: 26
SALES (corp-wide): 8.6B **Publicly Held**
WEB: www.schwab.com
SIC: 6211 Brokers, security
PA: The Charles Schwab Corporation
211 Main St Fl 17
San Francisco CA 94105
415 667-7000

(G-19474)
CHILDRENS FOREVER HAVEN INC
Also Called: Center Ridge House
28700 Center Ridge Rd (44145-5213)
PHONE..................440 250-9182
Fax: 440 892-7768
Lynne Urbanski, *Director*
Denise Mendiola, *Admin Asst*
EMP: 45
SALES (corp-wide): 96.1K **Privately Held**
SIC: 8052 Home for the mentally retarded, with health care
PA: Childrens Forever Haven Inc
10983 Abboy Rd
North Royalton OH 44133
440 652-6749

(G-19475)
CITY OF WESTLAKE
Also Called: Meadowood Golf Course
29800 Center Ridge Rd (44145-5121)
PHONE..................440 835-6442
Fax: 440 835-6412
Bret Smith, *Manager*
EMP: 25 **Privately Held**
SIC: 7992 Public golf courses
PA: City Of Westlake
27700 Hilliard Blvd
Cleveland OH 44145
440 871-3300

Westlake - Cuyahoga County (G-19476)

(G-19476)
CLEVELAND AIRPORT HOSPITALITY
1100 Crocker Rd (44145-1033)
PHONE.................................440 871-6000
Fax: 216 252-3850
Steve Burroughs, *General Mgr*
Tom Hipman, *General Mgr*
Gloria Maciak, *Controller*
Preston Triggs, *Manager*
EMP: 96
SALES (est): 8.1MM **Publicly Held**
SIC: 7011 5813 5812 Hotels; drinking places; eating places
PA: Wyndham Worldwide Corporation
   22 Sylvan Way
   Parsippany NJ 07054

(G-19477)
CLEVELAND WESTLAKE
29690 Detroit Rd (44145-1934)
PHONE.................................440 892-0333
Gia Polo, *General Mgr*
Tyler Wulf, *Manager*
EMP: 25
SALES (est): 780K **Privately Held**
SIC: 7011 Hotels

(G-19478)
COMCAST SPOTLIGHT
Also Called: Adelphia
27887 Clemens Rd Ste 3 (44145-1181)
PHONE.................................440 617-2280
Fax: 440 617-2290
Michelle Radio, *Manager*
EMP: 50
SALES (corp-wide): 84.5B **Publicly Held**
WEB: www.cablecomcast.com
SIC: 4841 Cable television services
HQ: Comcast Spotlight
   55 W 46th St Fl 33
   New York NY 10036
   212 907-8641

(G-19479)
COMPREHENSIVE PEDIATRICS
2001 Crocker Rd Ste 600 (44145-6972)
PHONE.................................440 835-8270
Fax: 440 871-5610
Cynthia Strieter, *Partner*
Carolyn King, *Director*
Lori Setterman, *Nursing Dir*
Laura Kilbane, *Admin Sec*
Catherine D Arora, *Pediatrics*
EMP: 35
SALES (est): 3.5MM **Privately Held**
WEB: www.comprehensivepediatrics.com
SIC: 8011 Pediatrician

(G-19480)
CORPORATE UNITED INC
24651 Center Ridge Rd # 527 (44145-5674)
PHONE.................................440 895-0938
Fax: 440 895-0939
Gregg Mylett, *CEO*
Doug Blossey, *President*
Christopher Zirke, *President*
ARA Arslanian, *Vice Pres*
Mary Petzinger, *Vice Pres*
EMP: 27
SALES (est): 4.9MM **Privately Held**
WEB: www.corporateunited.com
SIC: 7389 Personal service agents, brokers & bureaus

(G-19481)
COURTYARD BY MARRIOTT
25050 Sperry Dr (44145-1535)
PHONE.................................440 871-3756
Fax: 440 871-4273
David Bragan, *General Mgr*
Al Schreiber, *Principal*
EMP: 31
SALES (est): 1MM **Privately Held**
SIC: 7011 Hotels & motels

(G-19482)
DCT TELECOM GROUP INC
27877 Clemens Rd (44145-1167)
PHONE.................................440 892-0300
Anthony S Romano, *CEO*
Anthony Rehak, *President*
Molly Fratalonie, *Project Mgr*
Michael Litten, *Opers Staff*
Theresa Videc, *Opers Staff*
EMP: 35 EST: 1993
SALES (est): 13MM **Privately Held**
WEB: www.4dct.com
SIC: 4813 ; local & long distance telephone communications; local telephone communications; long distance telephone communications

(G-19483)
FACTS MANAGEMENT COMPANY
Also Called: Private School Aid Service
909 Canterbury Rd Ste P (44145-7212)
P.O. Box 451160 (44145-0629)
PHONE.................................440 892-4272
Fax: 440 892-7727
David J Byrnes, *Branch Mgr*
EMP: 50
SALES (corp-wide): 1.2B **Publicly Held**
SIC: 7389 Financial services
HQ: Facts Management Company
   121 S 13th St Ste 201
   Lincoln NE 68508
   402 466-1063

(G-19484)
FAIRVIEW HOSPITAL
850 Columbia Rd Ste 100 (44145-7213)
PHONE.................................440 871-1063
Mary K Kelly, *Manager*
EMP: 100
SALES (corp-wide): 8B **Privately Held**
SIC: 8062 General medical & surgical hospitals
HQ: Fairview Hospital
   18101 Lorain Ave
   Cleveland OH 44111
   216 476-7000

(G-19485)
FASTENER CORP OF AMERICA INC
1133 Bassett Rd (44145-1193)
PHONE.................................440 835-5100
Fax: 440 835-9369
Rufus Lumbgao, *President*
Harvey Lumchek, *Principal*
Bob Douglas, *Sales Staff*
Sharon Eggert, *Office Admin*
EMP: 25
SQ FT: 12,000
SALES (est): 2.8MM **Privately Held**
WEB: www.fastenercorp.com
SIC: 5072 Miscellaneous fasteners

(G-19486)
GLOBAL TCHNICAL RECRUITERS INC (PA)
27887 Clemens Rd Ste 1 (44145-1181)
PHONE.................................216 251-9560
Robert J Murphy, *President*
Patrick T Murphy, *Principal*
Jackie Anderson, *Sales Associate*
Nick Calaway, *Consultant*
EMP: 33
SALES (est): 7.8MM **Privately Held**
SIC: 7361 Executive placement

(G-19487)
GROUND EFFECTS LLC
31000 Viking Pkwy (44145-1019)
PHONE.................................440 565-5925
Jim Scott, *President*
EMP: 50
SALES (corp-wide): 5.7B **Privately Held**
SIC: 4231 Trucking terminal facilities
HQ: Ground Effects Llc
   3302 Kent St
   Flint MI 48503
   810 250-5560

(G-19488)
HARBORSIDE CLVELAND LTD PARTNR
Also Called: West Bay Care Rhbilitation Ctr
27601 Westchester Pkwy (44145-1251)
PHONE.................................440 871-5900
Lillian Werntz, *Manager*
Bob Kuhn, *Info Tech Mgr*
Nadine Kodysz, *Director*
EMP: 85 **Publicly Held**
SIC: 8051 Skilled nursing care facilities
HQ: Harborside Of Cleveland Limited Partnership
   101 Sun Ave Ne
   Albuquerque NM

(G-19489)
HCR MANORCARE MED SVCS FLA LLC
Also Called: Arden Crts Manorcare Hlth Svcs
28400 Center Ridge Rd (44145-3805)
PHONE.................................440 808-9275
Fax: 440 808-9332
Allison Marrow, *Manager*
EMP: 50
SQ FT: 24,400
SALES (corp-wide): 3.6B **Publicly Held**
WEB: www.manorcare.com
SIC: 8051 Convalescent home with continuous nursing care
HQ: Hcr Manorcare Medical Services Of Florida, Llc
   333 N Summit St Ste 100
   Toledo OH 43604
   419 252-5500

(G-19490)
HEAD MERCANTILE CO INC
29065 Clemens Rd Ste 200 (44145-1179)
PHONE.................................440 847-2700
Fax: 440 333-4216
James Scharfeld, *President*
Steven Scharfeld, *Vice Pres*
EMP: 80 EST: 1975
SQ FT: 12,000
SALES (est): 722.3K **Privately Held**
SIC: 7322 Adjustment & collection services

(G-19491)
HMC GROUP INC
29065 Clemens Rd Ste 200 (44145-1179)
PHONE.................................440 847-2720
Fax: 440 892-3600
Leonard B Scharfeld, *President*
Lee Scharfeld, *Corp Secy*
James Scharfeld, *Exec VP*
Steven Scharfeld, *Exec VP*
Kim Sikora, *Manager*
EMP: 30
SQ FT: 4,100
SALES (est): 4.8MM **Privately Held**
WEB: www.hmcgrp.com
SIC: 7322 Collection agency, except real estate

(G-19492)
HOWLEY BREAD GROUP LTD (PA)
Also Called: Panera Bread
159 Crocker Park Blvd # 290 (44145-8131)
PHONE.................................440 808-1600
Lee Howley, *President*
Leslie Pakush, *Vice Pres*
Dennis Abbuhl, *CFO*
Carol Patsko, *Manager*
EMP: 84
SQ FT: 3,500
SALES (est): 26MM **Privately Held**
SIC: 5812 6794 Cafe; franchises, selling or licensing

(G-19493)
HS FINANCIAL GROUP LLC
25651 Detroit Rd Ste 203 (44145-2415)
P.O. Box 451193 (44145-0630)
PHONE.................................440 871-8484
Henny Cummings, *Office Mgr*
Timothy M Sullivan, *Mng Member*
Ken Wojtach, *Manager*
Krystina Dolamore, *Office Admin*
Sheilah Steiner, *Info Tech Mgr*
EMP: 50
SALES (est): 4.8MM **Privately Held**
SIC: 7322 Collection agency, except real estate

(G-19494)
HUB CITY TERMINALS INC
27476 Detroit Rd Ste 102 (44145-2394)
PHONE.................................440 779-2226
EMP: 51
SALES (corp-wide): 4B **Publicly Held**
SIC: 4731 Freight transportation arrangement
HQ: Hub City Terminals, Inc.
   2000 Clearwater Dr
   Oak Brook IL 60523
   630 271-3600

(G-19495)
HYLAND LLC (DH)
Also Called: Lexmark Enterprise Sftwr LLC
28500 Clemens Rd (44145-1145)
PHONE.................................440 788-5045
Bill Premier, *CEO*
Teresa Carter, *President*
Steve McQueen, *Business Mgr*
Howard Dratler, *Exec VP*
David Lintz, *Exec VP*
EMP: 320
SQ FT: 95,655
SALES (est): 158MM
SALES (corp-wide): 546.5MM **Privately Held**
WEB: www.imagenow.com
SIC: 7371 7372 Computer software development; prepackaged software

(G-19496)
HYLAND SOFTWARE INC (HQ)
28500 Clemens Rd (44145-1145)
PHONE.................................440 788-5000
Fax: 440 788-5100
Bill Priemer, *CEO*
Christopher J Hyland, *Ch of Bd*
Miguel A Zubizarreta, *Exec VP*
Noreen Kilbane, *Senior VP*
Brenda Kirk, *Senior VP*
EMP: 1800
SQ FT: 150,000
SALES (est): 437.7MM
SALES (corp-wide): 546.5MM **Privately Held**
WEB: www.onbase.com
SIC: 7372 Application computer software
PA: Thoma Cressey Bravo, Inc.
   300 N La Salle Dr # 4350
   Chicago IL 60654
   312 254-3300

(G-19497)
IEWC CORP
1991 Crocker Rd Ste 110 (44145-6970)
PHONE.................................440 835-5601
Michael Triplett, *Accounts Mgr*
Jim Wojan, *Systems Staff*
EMP: 25
SALES (corp-wide): 154.5MM **Privately Held**
WEB: www.iewc.com
SIC: 5063 Electronic wire & cable
PA: Iewc Corp.
   5001 S Towne Dr
   New Berlin WI 53151
   262 782-2255

(G-19498)
INFINITY HEALTH SERVICES INC (PA)
Also Called: American Home Health Services,
975 Crocker Rd A (44145-1030)
PHONE.................................440 614-0145
Fax: 216 521-0206
Norma Goodman, *President*
EMP: 68
SQ FT: 2,700
SALES (est): 2.6MM **Privately Held**
SIC: 8082 Home health care services

(G-19499)
IRISH ENVY LLC
Also Called: Massage Envy
30307 Detroit Rd (44145-1950)
PHONE.................................440 808-8000
Kevin Flynn, *Mng Member*
Brian Quinn,
EMP: 30
SQ FT: 2,500
SALES (est): 680.5K **Privately Held**
SIC: 7299 Massage parlor

(G-19500)
ITS TRAFFIC SYSTEMS INC
28915 Clemens Rd Ste 200 (44145-1177)
PHONE.................................440 892-4500
Randall Houlas, *President*
Robert Houlas, *Principal*
Lori Spencer, *Opers Staff*
Jennifer Kalassay, *Accounts Mgr*
Abbey Dewitt, *Director*

EMP: 57
SQ FT: 10,000
SALES (est): 10.9MM **Privately Held**
WEB: www.itstraffic.com
SIC: 8748 Traffic consultant

(G-19501)
J P FARLEY CORPORATION (PA)
29055 Clemens Rd (44145-1135)
P.O. Box 458022 (44145-8022)
PHONE.....................................440 250-4300
James P Farley, *President*
Patricia Hannigan, *Vice Pres*
Mike Farley, *CFO*
EMP: 50
SQ FT: 15,000
SALES (est): 30.7MM **Privately Held**
WEB: www.jpfarley.com
SIC: 6311 6321 6324 Life insurance; accident & health insurance; hospital & medical service plans

(G-19502)
JORDAN KYLI ENTERPRISES INC
Also Called: Jke
24650 Center Ridge Rd (44145-5637)
PHONE.....................................216 256-3773
EMP: 25
SALES (est): 560K **Privately Held**
SIC: 7349 Janitorial Services And Cleaning Chemical Distribution

(G-19503)
JTEKT AUTO TENN MORRISTOWN
29570 Clemens Rd (44145-1007)
PHONE.....................................440 835-1000
▲ EMP: 204
SALES (est): 128.3K
SALES (corp-wide): 11.6B **Privately Held**
SIC: 7538 General automotive repair shops
HQ: Jtekt Automotive Tennessee-Morristown, Inc.
5932 Commerce Blvd
Morristown TN 37814
423 585-2544

(G-19504)
KING JAMES GROUP IV LTD
Also Called: Westwat Management
24700 Center Ridge Rd G50 (44145-5636)
PHONE.....................................440 250-1851
Lewis Wallner Jr, *Owner*
Bob Lubick, *Partner*
Robert Miller, *Partner*
Lewis E Wallner Sr, *Partner*
EMP: 25
SALES (est): 1.7MM **Privately Held**
WEB: www.kingjameshomes.com
SIC: 6512 Commercial & industrial building operation

(G-19505)
KING JAMES PARK LTD
Also Called: King James Group
24700 Center Ridge Rd G50 (44145-5636)
PHONE.....................................440 835-1100
Fax: 440 835-1101
Robert J Lubick, *Partner*
EMP: 50 EST: 1975
SQ FT: 5,000
SALES (est): 3.1MM **Privately Held**
WEB: www.kingjamesgroup.com
SIC: 6512 Commercial & industrial building operation

(G-19506)
KNOXBI COMPANY LLC
27500 Detroit Rd (44145-5915)
PHONE.....................................440 892-6800
Robert Berryhill,
EMP: 55
SALES: 950K **Privately Held**
SIC: 6531 Real estate agent, commercial

(G-19507)
LAKE ERIE ELECTRIC INC (PA)
25730 1st St (44145-1432)
P.O. Box 450859 (44145-0619)
PHONE.....................................440 835-5565
Fax: 440 835-5688
Peter J Corogin, *President*
Eugene Ullrich, *Superintendent*
Linda L Bottegal, *Principal*
Kenneth R Beck, *Senior VP*
Armando Francisco, *Vice Pres*
EMP: 65 EST: 1952
SQ FT: 15,000
SALES (est): 137.9MM **Privately Held**
SIC: 1731 General electrical contractor

(G-19508)
LAKESIDE TITLE ESCROW AGCY INC
29550 Detroit Rd Ste 301 (44145-1994)
PHONE.....................................216 503-5600
Dennis L Obrien, *President*
Mark Fiala, *Vice Pres*
Alan Jaffa, *Vice Pres*
Diane Sapir, *Marketing Staff*
Amitha RAO, *Manager*
EMP: 45
SALES (est): 2.3MM **Privately Held**
SIC: 6541 Title & trust companies

(G-19509)
LE CHAPERON ROUGE COMPANY
27390 Center Ridge Rd (44145-3957)
PHONE.....................................440 899-9477
Fax: 440 835-2929
Stella Moga, *Owner*
EMP: 25
SALES (corp-wide): 1.2MM **Privately Held**
SIC: 8351 Child day care services
PA: Le Chaperon Rouge Company
30121 Lorain Rd
North Olmsted OH
440 779-5671

(G-19510)
LIFE CARE CENTERS AMERICA INC
Also Called: Life Care Center of Cleveland
26520 Center Ridge Rd (44145-4033)
PHONE.....................................440 871-3030
Laura Garsky, *Chf Purch Ofc*
Marie Ingmand, *Office Mgr*
Valerie Durica, *Manager*
Laura Quillin, *Manager*
June Ulin, *Nursing Dir*
EMP: 160
SALES (corp-wide): 101MM **Privately Held**
WEB: www.lcca.com
SIC: 8051 Convalescent home with continuous nursing care
PA: Life Care Centers Of America, Inc.
3570 Keith St Nw
Cleveland TN 37312
423 472-9585

(G-19511)
LORAD LLC
Also Called: Diversified Fall Protection
24400 Sperry Dr (44145-1565)
PHONE.....................................216 265-2862
John Powers, *Accountant*
Jeff Schneid, *Mng Member*
Carla R Burton,
▲ EMP: 30
SALES (est): 2.4MM **Privately Held**
SIC: 1799 Home/office interiors finishing, furnishing & remodeling

(G-19512)
MATRIX POINTE SOFTWARE LLC
30400 Detroit Rd Ste 400 (44145-1855)
PHONE.....................................216 333-1263
Joseph Whang,
EMP: 25
SQ FT: 10,000
SALES (est): 1.5MM **Privately Held**
SIC: 7371 Computer software development

(G-19513)
MEDICAL ADMINISTRATORS INC
28301 Ranney Pkwy (44145-1161)
PHONE.....................................440 899-2229
Fax: 440 899-2411
Tom Spooner, *President*
Margaret Carnish, *VP Opers*
Lisa Lachendro, *Exec Dir*
EMP: 30
SALES (est): 1.7MM **Privately Held**
WEB: www.medadmin.com
SIC: 7322 Adjustment & collection services

(G-19514)
MEDICAL DIAGNOSTIC LAB INC (PA)
Also Called: Premier Physican Centers
24651 Center Ridge Rd # 350 (44145-5635)
P.O. Box 74692, Cleveland (44194-0775)
PHONE.....................................440 333-1375
Kelly Mangan, *Human Resources*
Robert Harrison, *Corp Comm Staff*
Jeanette Monteleone, *Office Mgr*
M Sowden, *Manager*
Kim Cornelius, *Manager*
EMP: 85
SALES (est): 4.2MM **Privately Held**
SIC: 8011 8071 General & family practice, physician/surgeon; testing laboratories

(G-19515)
METROHEALTH SYSTEM
Also Called: Metrohealth Premier Health Ctr
25200 Center Ridge Rd (44145-4141)
PHONE.....................................216 957-3200
EMP: 26
SALES (corp-wide): 859.8MM **Privately Held**
SIC: 8062 General Hospital
PA: The Metrohealth System
2500 Metrohealth Dr
Cleveland OH 44109
216 398-6000

(G-19516)
MISA METALS INC
26926 Kenley Ct Ste 200 (44145-1457)
PHONE.....................................440 892-4944
James Banker, *President*
EMP: 250
SALES (corp-wide): 15.8B **Privately Held**
SIC: 5051 Steel
HQ: Misa Metals, Inc.
9050 Centre Pointe Dr
West Chester OH 45069
212 660-6000

(G-19517)
MONRO INC
Also Called: Monro Muffler Brake
29778 Detroit Rd (44145-1937)
PHONE.....................................440 835-2393
Fax: 440 835-2394
Jim Brewer, *Manager*
EMP: 98
SALES (corp-wide): 1B **Publicly Held**
SIC: 5531 7533 7538 Automotive tires; muffler shop, sale or repair & installation; general automotive repair shops
PA: Monro, Inc.
200 Holleder Pkwy
Rochester NY 14615
585 647-6400

(G-19518)
MORGAN STANLEY
159 Crocker Park Blvd # 460 (44145-8132)
PHONE.....................................440 835-6750
Tim Adkins, *Manager*
Kent Hageman, *Manager*
EMP: 50
SALES (corp-wide): 43.6B **Publicly Held**
SIC: 6211 Security brokers & dealers
PA: Morgan Stanley
1585 Broadway
New York NY 10036
212 761-4000

(G-19519)
NEFF GROUP DISTRIBUTORS INC
Also Called: Fluidtrols
909 Canterbury Rd Ste G (44145-7212)
PHONE.....................................440 835-7010
John J Neff, *CEO*
Larry Ostwinch, *Sales Mgr*
Rob Kirchner, *Manager*
Thomas Stabosz, *Manager*
EMP: 30
SALES (corp-wide): 57.8MM **Privately Held**
SIC: 5084 Instruments & control equipment
PA: Neff Group Distributors, Inc.
7114 Innovation Blvd
Fort Wayne IN 46818
260 489-6007

(G-19520)
NELSON STUD WELDING INC
821 Sharon Dr (44145-1522)
PHONE.....................................440 250-9242
Fax: 440 250-9246
Doug Philips, *Branch Mgr*
EMP: 40 **Privately Held**
SIC: 1799 Welding on site
HQ: Nelson Stud Welding, Inc.
7900 W Ridge Rd
Elyria OH 44035
440 329-0400

(G-19521)
NICK MAYER LINCOLN-MERCURY INC
24400 Center Ridge Rd (44145-4213)
PHONE.....................................440 835-3700
Fax: 440 835-3611
Patricia Mayer, *President*
Kevin Hoge, *General Mgr*
Chad Mayer, *General Mgr*
Mike Moran, *General Mgr*
Jack Gannon, *Vice Pres*
EMP: 40
SALES (est): 17.6MM **Privately Held**
SIC: 5511 7538 7515 Automobiles, new & used; general automotive repair shops; passenger car leasing

(G-19522)
NORTH BAY CONSTRUCTION INC
Also Called: Pe
25800 1st St Ste 1 (44145-1481)
PHONE.....................................440 835-1898
Fax: 440 835-0862
James J Manns, *CEO*
Michael S Kovatch, *Vice Pres*
Thomas Rice, *Project Mgr*
Marc Harcharik, *Purchasing*
Eugene Bittner, *Controller*
EMP: 25
SQ FT: 12,000
SALES (est): 5.7MM **Privately Held**
SIC: 8744 1799 7389 1796 Facilities support services; hydraulic equipment, installation & service; design, commercial & industrial; installing building equipment; plumbing, heating, air-conditioning contractors; water, sewer & utility lines

(G-19523)
NORTH EAST MECHANICAL INC
Also Called: Westland Heating & AC
26200 1st St (44145-1460)
PHONE.....................................440 871-7525
Fax: 440 937-9444
Zachary Mitchell, *President*
Tim Nelson, *Project Mgr*
Deborah Mitchell, *Treasurer*
Fran Banda, *Bookkeeper*
Andy France, *Sales Staff*
EMP: 50
SQ FT: 6,000
SALES (est): 6.6MM **Privately Held**
SIC: 1711 Refrigeration contractor; warm air heating & air conditioning contractor

(G-19524)
NORTH SHORE GSTRENTEROLOGY INC
Also Called: North Shore Gastroenterology &
850 Columbia Rd Ste 200 (44145-7215)
PHONE.....................................440 808-1212
Fax: 440 871-4640
Tabbaa Mousab MD, *President*
Marti Bauschka, *Manager*
Karl Dehaan, *Gastroenterlgy*
Mousab I Tabbaa, *Gastroenterlgy*
Mousab Tabbaa, *Gastroenterlgy*
EMP: 80
SALES (est): 11.1MM **Privately Held**
SIC: 8011 Gastronomist

Westlake - Cuyahoga County (G-19525)

(G-19525)
NORTHERN TIER HOSPITALITY LLC
Also Called: Best Western Grnd Victoria Inn
1100 Crocker Rd (44145-1033)
PHONE..............................570 888-7711
Satish Duggal,
EMP: 60
SALES (est): 3.1MM Privately Held
SIC: 7011 Hotels

(G-19526)
OBRIEN LAW FIRM COMPANY LPA
29550 Detroit Rd (44145-1994)
PHONE..............................216 685-7500
Dennis O'Brien, *President*
Pasquale Dimassa, *Managing Prtnr*
EMP: 32
SALES (est): 1.8MM Privately Held
SIC: 8111 Specialized law offices, attorneys

(G-19527)
OHIO CLINIC AESTHC PLSTC SRGY
2237 Crocker Rd Ste 140 (44145-7606)
PHONE..............................440 808-9315
Joan Stehlik, *General Mgr*
Jennifer Zwolinski, *COO*
EMP: 25
SALES (est): 1.9MM Privately Held
SIC: 8011 Plastic surgeon

(G-19528)
OHIO MEDICAL GROUP (PA)
29325 Health Campus Dr # 3 (44145-8201)
PHONE..............................440 414-9400
Fax: 440 899-4432
Othma Shemisa MD, *President*
EMP: 50
SALES (est): 4.3MM Privately Held
SIC: 8011 Cardiologist & cardio-vascular specialist

(G-19529)
OLMSTED MANOR RETIREMENT PRPTS
26612 Center Ridge Rd (44145-4035)
PHONE..............................440 250-4080
Timothy Coury,
EMP: 26
SALES: 1.2MM Privately Held
SIC: 8059 Rest home, with health care

(G-19530)
ORTHOPEDIC ASSOCIATES INC
24723 Detroit Rd (44145-2526)
PHONE..............................440 892-1440
Manuel Martinez, *Principal*
Robert Deswart, *Med Doctor*
Jeff Roberts, *Med Doctor*
Gail Crayne, *Manager*
Alan Fentner, *Manager*
EMP: 40
SALES (est): 891.4K Privately Held
SIC: 8011 Orthopedic physician

(G-19531)
OSBORN MARKETING RESEARCH CORP
1818 Century Oaks Dr (44145-3654)
PHONE..............................440 871-1047
Ronald Kornokovich, *President*
Frank Amelia, *Vice Pres*
EMP: 40
SQ FT: 5,000
SALES (est): 2.9MM Privately Held
SIC: 8732 Market analysis or research

(G-19532)
OUR HOUSE INC
27633 Bassett Rd (44145-3093)
PHONE..............................440 835-2110
Fax: 440 835-2115
Marguerite Vanderwyst, *President*
EMP: 47
SQ FT: 44,000
SALES (est): 3.7MM Privately Held
SIC: 6514 Dwelling operators, except apartments

(G-19533)
PHARMED CORPORATION
Also Called: Pharmed Institutional Pharmacy
24340 Sperry Dr (44145-1565)
PHONE..............................440 250-5400
Elias J Coury, *President*
Charles Freireich, *Principal*
Samuel Laderman, *Principal*
Nancy Thorne, *Principal*
Norman Fox, *Corp Secy*
EMP: 130 EST: 1971
SQ FT: 36,000
SALES (est): 54.4MM Privately Held
WEB: www.pharmedcorp.com
SIC: 5047 5122 Medical & hospital equipment; drugs & drug proprietaries; pharmaceuticals

(G-19534)
PINES MANUFACTURING INC (PA)
Also Called: Pines Technology
29100 Lakeland Blvd (44145)
PHONE..............................440 835-5553
Fax: 440 835-5556
Donald Rebar, *Ch of Bd*
Ian Williamson, *President*
Mickey McNamara, *Plant Mgr*
Dan Wilczynski, *Plant Mgr*
Darlene Wenzler, *Purchasing*
▲ **EMP:** 43
SQ FT: 48,000
SALES (est): 13.6MM Privately Held
WEB: www.pines-mfg.com
SIC: 5084 3542 3549 3547 Industrial machinery & equipment; bending machines; metalworking machinery; rolling mill machinery

(G-19535)
PREMIER PHYSICIANS CENTERS INC (PA)
24651 Center Ridge Rd # 350 (44145-5627)
PHONE..............................440 895-5085
Fax: 440 331-9531
Mark Wiedt, *CEO*
Antonios Paras, *President*
NI Dasari, *Vice Pres*
Jeff Dybiec, *CFO*
Isam Diab, *Treasurer*
EMP: 33
SQ FT: 7,000
SALES (est): 17.1MM Privately Held
SIC: 8011 Offices & clinics of medical doctors

(G-19536)
R AND J CORPORATION
Also Called: Haynes Manufacturing Company
24142 Detroit Rd (44145-1515)
PHONE..............................440 871-6009
Fax: 440 871-0855
Beth Kloos, *President*
Timothy Kloos, *Vice Pres*
Sheri Bohning, *Purchasing*
Ric Thornton, *Project Engr*
Matt Rogan, *Sales Engr*
EMP: 42
SQ FT: 23,000
SALES (est): 17.1MM Privately Held
WEB: www.haynesmfg.com
SIC: 3556 5084 7389 3053 Food products machinery; food industry machinery; design, commercial & industrial; gaskets, packing & sealing devices; lubricating oils & greases

(G-19537)
R E WARNER & ASSOCIATES INC
25777 Detroit Rd Ste 200 (44145-2484)
PHONE..............................440 835-9400
Fax: 440 835-9474
David W Sminchak, *President*
Ed Dziubek, *Project Mgr*
Terry McClain, *Project Mgr*
Vincent D Angelo, *Engineer*
Shane Kremser, *Engineer*
EMP: 68
SQ FT: 23,473
SALES (est): 10.2MM Privately Held
SIC: 8713 8712 8711 Surveying services; architectural engineering; mechanical engineering

(G-19538)
RADIOMETER AMERICA INC
810 Sharon Dr (44145-1598)
PHONE..............................440 925-2977
Fax: 440 835-8118
Ron Betts, *Vice Pres*
Robert Strenk, *Vice Pres*
Andy Siwierka, *QA Dir*
Jesper Isaksen, *VP Human Res*
Jenna Jackson, *Human Resources*
EMP: 100
SALES (corp-wide): 18.3B Publicly Held
SIC: 5047 Medical equipment & supplies
HQ: Radiometer America Inc.
250 S Kraemer Blvd Ms
Brea CA 92821
800 736-0600

(G-19539)
RAE-ANN HOLDINGS INC
Also Called: Rae Ann West Lake
28303 Detroit Rd (44145-2157)
PHONE..............................440 871-0500
Fax: 440 871-4668
Anne Hicks, *Office Mgr*
Sue Griffith, *Manager*
Kimberly Eiting, *Manager*
EMP: 80
SQ FT: 45,176
SALES (corp-wide): 36.6MM Privately Held
SIC: 8059 8052 8051 Nursing home, except skilled & intermediate care facility; intermediate care facilities; skilled nursing care facilities
PA: Rae-Ann Holdings, Inc.
27310 W Oviatt Rd
Bay Village OH 44140
440 835-3004

(G-19540)
RAE-ANN SUBURBAN INC
29505 Detroit Rd (44145-1932)
P.O. Box 40175, Bay Village (44140-0175)
PHONE..............................440 871-5181
Fax: 440 871-4692
John Griffiths, *President*
Michelle Salyan, *Admin Asst*
EMP: 125
SALES (est): 2.2MM Privately Held
SIC: 8051 Skilled nursing care facilities

(G-19541)
REGAL CINEMAS INC
Also Called: Regal Entertainment Group
30147 Detroit Rd (44145-1946)
PHONE..............................440 871-4546
Fax: 440 871-8778
Frank Scott, *General Mgr*
EMP: 30
SALES (corp-wide): 982.1MM Privately Held
WEB: www.regalcinemas.com
SIC: 7832 Motion picture theaters, except drive-in
HQ: Regal Cinemas, Inc.
101 E Blount Ave Ste 100
Knoxville TN 37920
865 922-1123

(G-19542)
RMS OF OHIO INC
Also Called: RMS Management
24651 Center Ridge Rd # 300 (44145-5635)
PHONE..............................440 617-6605
Terry Adams, *Manager*
Jim Cavins, *Manager*
Brandon Land, *Manager*
Laura Reese, *Manager*
Andrea Smith, *Manager*
EMP: 324
SALES (corp-wide): 11.8MM Privately Held
SIC: 8742 8741 Management consulting services; business management
PA: Rms Of Ohio, Inc
733 E Dublin Granville Rd # 100
Columbus OH 43229
614 844-6767

(G-19543)
ROMETRICS TOO HAIR NAIL GLLERY
26155 Detroit Rd (44145-2430)
PHONE..............................440 808-1391
Sherry Young, *Owner*
EMP: 25
SALES (est): 231.2K Privately Held
SIC: 7231 Beauty shops

(G-19544)
SCOTT FETZER COMPANY (DH)
Also Called: Kirby Vacuum Cleaner
28800 Clemens Rd (44145-1197)
PHONE..............................440 892-3000
Fax: 440 892-3060
Kenneth J Semelsberger, *Ch of Bd*
Bryan Telepak, *General Mgr*
Bob McBride, *Principal*
Vince Nardy, *COO*
Patricia Scanlon, *Vice Pres*
▲ **EMP:** 40
SQ FT: 80,000
SALES (est): 409.7MM
SALES (corp-wide): 242.1B Publicly Held
SIC: 7699 Industrial equipment services
HQ: Bhsf Inc.
1440 Kiewit Plz
Omaha NE 68131
402 346-1400

(G-19545)
SEA-LAND CHEMICAL CO (PA)
821 Westpoint Pkwy (44145-1545)
PHONE..............................440 871-7887
Fax: 440 871-7949
Joseph Clayton, *President*
Jennifer Altstadt, *President*
Rob Stubbs, *General Mgr*
Mark Christeon, *Exec VP*
Jack McKenna, *Vice Pres*
◆ **EMP:** 54
SQ FT: 8,000
SALES (est): 65.1MM Privately Held
SIC: 5169 Industrial chemicals

(G-19546)
SHAMROCK COMPANIES INC (PA)
Also Called: Shamrock Acquisition Company
24090 Detroit Rd (44145-1513)
P.O. Box 450980 (44145-0623)
PHONE..............................440 899-9510
Fax: 440 899-3288
Tim Connor, *CEO*
Robert E Troop, *Ch of Bd*
Tom Backus, *Business Mgr*
Dave Fechter, *COO*
Jim Spicuzza, *VP Sls/Mktg*
▲ **EMP:** 140
SQ FT: 42,500
SALES (est): 88.2MM Privately Held
WEB: www.shamrockcompanies.net
SIC: 5112 5199 7336 7389 Business forms; advertising specialties; art design services; brokers' services; commercial printing, gravure; pleating & stitching

(G-19547)
SIMPLIFIED LOGISTICS LLC
28915 Clemens Rd Ste 220 (44145-1177)
PHONE..............................440 250-8912
David Klugman, *CEO*
Rob Balawender, *President*
Doug Brownley, *President*
Robert H Maisch Jr, *President*
Sam Avampato, *COO*
EMP: 27
SALES (est): 9.9MM Privately Held
SIC: 7375 On-line data base information retrieval

(G-19548)
SPRING VALLEY GOLF & ATHC CLB
257 Crocker Park Blvd (44145-8142)
PHONE..............................440 365-1411
John Galligan, *President*
Wilfred Tremblay, *Treasurer*
Charles Bush, *Admin Sec*
EMP: 85
SQ FT: 5,000
SALES (est): 2.9MM Privately Held
SIC: 7997 Golf club, membership

(G-19549)
SPRINGCAR COMPANY LLC
27500 Detroit Rd Ste 300 (44145-5913)
PHONE..............................440 892-6800
Mary Cory,

GEOGRAPHIC SECTION

Wheelersburg - Scioto County (G-19572)

EMP: 28
SALES (est): 736K **Privately Held**
SIC: 6531 Real estate agents & managers

(G-19550)
ST JOHN MEDICAL CENTER
29000 Center Ridge Rd (44145-5219)
PHONE..................440 835-8000
Cliff Coker, *President*
Donald Sheldon, *President*
Eileen Hayes, *Vice Pres*
David Tolentino, *Vice Pres*
Ben Caplinger, *Manager*
EMP: 99
SALES: 157.8MM **Privately Held**
SIC: 8062 General medical & surgical hospitals

(G-19551)
STANDARD RETIREMENT SVCS INC
24610 Detroit Rd Ste 2000 (44145-2543)
PHONE..................440 808-2724
John J Griffith Jr, *President*
Don Daleffandro, *Manager*
EMP: 40
SALES (corp-wide): 34.1B **Privately Held**
SIC: 8741 6282 Administrative management; investment advisory service
HQ: Standard Retirement Services, Inc.
1100 Sw 6th Ave Ste 711
Portland OR 97204
412 249-3200

(G-19552)
SUNRISE SENIOR LIVING INC
Also Called: Brighton Gardens of Westlake
27819 Center Ridge Rd Ofc (44145-3920)
PHONE..................440 808-0074
Fax: 440 808-0564
Michael Beard, *Principal*
Mj J Giovanetti, *Telecom Exec*
EMP: 58
SALES (corp-wide): 4.3B **Publicly Held**
WEB: www.sunrise.com
SIC: 8051 Skilled nursing care facilities
HQ: Sunrise Senior Living, Llc
7902 Westpark Dr
Mc Lean VA 22102

(G-19553)
TA OPERATING LLC (HQ)
Also Called: Petro Stopping Center
24601 Center Ridge Rd # 200 (44145-5677)
PHONE..................440 808-9100
Fax: 440 808-3306
Thomas O Brien, *CEO*
Doug Parker, *General Mgr*
Terry Wilcox, *Superintendent*
ARA Bagdasarian, *Exec VP*
Andrew J Rebholz, *Exec VP*
EMP: 300
SQ FT: 60,000
SALES (est): 2.1B **Publicly Held**
SIC: 5541 7538 5812 5411 Filling stations, gasoline; truck stops; general truck repair; eating places; fast food restaurants & stands; convenience stores; franchises, selling or licensing

(G-19554)
TECHNOLOGY RECOVERY GROUP LTD (PA)
Also Called: Trg Repair
31390 Viking Pkwy (44145-1063)
PHONE..................440 250-9970
Sean Kennedy, *President*
Nick Young, *Vice Pres*
Dave Foyer, *VP Opera*
Ben Phlipot, *Project Dir*
Will McFadden, *Parts Mgr*
EMP: 69
SQ FT: 20,000
SALES (est): 33.4MM **Privately Held**
SIC: 7379 Computer related consulting services

(G-19555)
TRAVELCENTERS AMERICA INC (HQ)
24601 Center Ridge Rd # 200 (44145-5634)
PHONE..................440 808-9100
Timothy Doane, *Ch of Bd*
Edwin P Kuhn, *Chairman*
Michael J Lombardi, *Exec VP*
Andrew J Rebholz, *Exec VP*
Barry A Richards, *Exec VP*
EMP: 700
SQ FT: 60,000
SALES (est): 2.1B **Publicly Held**
WEB: www.tatravelcenters.com
SIC: 5541 7538 5812 5411 Filling stations, gasoline; truck stops; general truck repair; eating places; fast food restaurants & stands; convenience stores

(G-19556)
TRAVELCENTERS OF AMERICA LLC
Also Called: Quaker Steak and Lube
24601 Center Ridge Rd # 200 (44145-5634)
PHONE..................724 981-9464
Thomas M O'Brien, *Principal*
Tom Komos, *Human Resources*
EMP: 420 **Publicly Held**
SIC: 5812 6794 Chicken restaurant; franchises, selling or licensing
PA: Travelcenters Of America Llc
24601 Center Ridge Rd # 200
Westlake OH 44145

(G-19557)
TRAVELCENTERS OF AMERICA LLC (PA)
Also Called: Quaker Steak & Lube
24601 Center Ridge Rd # 200 (44145-5634)
P.O. Box 451100 (44145-0627)
PHONE..................440 808-9100
Thomas M O'Brien, *President*
Tim Hoekzema, *General Mgr*
Scott Rye, *General Mgr*
Jason Truitt, *General Mgr*
Margaret Ward, *General Mgr*
EMP: 600
SALES: 6B **Publicly Held**
WEB: www.iowa80group.com
SIC: 5541 5812 7538 Gasoline service stations; truck stops; American restaurant; coffee shop; general truck repair

(G-19558)
UBS FINANCIAL SERVICES INC
2055 Crocker Rd Ste 201 (44145-2197)
PHONE..................440 414-2740
Dale Alexander, *Senior VP*
John Bellow, *Branch Mgr*
Bradley T Boeckman, *Agent*
Brian Cahill, *Advisor*
EMP: 43
SALES (corp-wide): 28B **Privately Held**
SIC: 7389 6029 Financial services; commercial banks
HQ: Ubs Financial Services Inc.
1285 Ave Of The Americas
New York NY 10019
212 713-2000

(G-19559)
UHHS WESTLAKE MEDICAL CENTER
960 Clague Rd Ste 3201 (44145-1588)
PHONE..................440 250-2070
Anna Kessler, *Administration*
EMP: 200
SALES (est): 3.9MM **Privately Held**
SIC: 8099 Medical services organization

(G-19560)
UNIVERSITY HOSPITALS
960 Clague Rd Ste 2410 (44145-1587)
PHONE..................440 250-2001
Charles Nock, *Branch Mgr*
Robert Anderson, *Med Doctor*
Mary Greenberg, *Med Doctor*
Joan Tamburro, *Med Doctor*
Brian Victoroff, *Med Doctor*
EMP: 270
SALES (corp-wide): 2.3B **Privately Held**
SIC: 8062 8221 Hospital, medical school affiliation; university
PA: University Hospitals Health System, Inc.
3605 Warrensville Ctr Rd
Shaker Heights OH 44122
216 767-8900

(G-19561)
UNPACKING ETC
Also Called: Et Cetera Services
787 Bassett Rd (44145-1104)
PHONE..................440 871-0506
John Jones, *Partner*
EMP: 25
SALES (est): 760.5K **Privately Held**
SIC: 4214 4213 Furniture moving & storage, local; household goods transport

(G-19562)
VERIZON COMMUNICATIONS INC
30171 Detroit Rd (44145-1946)
PHONE..................440 892-4504
Fax: 440 892-4509
EMP: 107
SALES (corp-wide): 126B **Publicly Held**
SIC: 4813 4812 4841 Local & long distance telephone communications; local telephone communications; voice telephone communications; ; cellular telephone services; cable & other pay television services
PA: Verizon Communications Inc.
1095 Ave Of The Americas
New York NY 10036
212 395-1000

(G-19563)
VSM SEWING INC (DH)
31000 Viking Pkwy (44145-1019)
PHONE..................440 808-6550
Charlie Bayer, *CEO*
Stan Ingraham, *Senior VP*
Rick Drainville, *Vice Pres*
Don Zimmerman, *Controller*
▲ EMP: 150
SQ FT: 100,000
SALES (est): 104.7MM **Privately Held**
WEB: www.husqvarnaviking.com
SIC: 5064 Sewing machines, household; electric
HQ: Vsm Group Ab
Drottninggatan 1
Huskvarna 561 3
361 460-00

(G-19564)
WELLINGTON TECHNOLOGIES INC
802 Sharon Dr (44145-1521)
PHONE..................440 238-4377
Joseph Jasko, *President*
Jim Bizjak, *Vice Pres*
Ed Griglak, *Vice Pres*
Duane Harens, *Opers Mgr*
Brenda Miller, *Accounting Mgr*
EMP: 37
SQ FT: 13,000
SALES (est): 3.5MM **Privately Held**
WEB: www.wtimaintains.com
SIC: 7378 Computer maintenance & repair

(G-19565)
WELLS FARGO CLEARING SVCS LLC
Also Called: Wells Fargo Advisors
25 Main St Fl 2 (44145-6975)
PHONE..................440 835-9250
Susan Ross, *Pub Rel Dir*
Tim Atkins, *Systems Staff*
EMP: 30
SQ FT: 3,500
SALES (corp-wide): 97.7B **Publicly Held**
WEB: www.wachoviasec.com
SIC: 6211 Stock brokers & dealers
HQ: Wells Fargo Clearing Services, Llc
1 N Jefferson Ave
Saint Louis MO 63103
314 955-3000

(G-19566)
WEST-WAY MANAGEMENT COMPANY
24700 Center Ridge Rd G50 (44145-5636)
PHONE..................440 250-1851
Lewis E Wallner Jr, *President*
Lewis E Wallner Sr, *Vice Pres*
Robert J Lubick, *Treasurer*
EMP: 26
SQ FT: 2,000
SALES (est): 1.8MM **Privately Held**
SIC: 6531 Real estate managers

(G-19567)
WESTLAKE MARRIOTT
30100 Clemens Rd (44145-1013)
PHONE..................440 892-6887
Kristen Weaver, *Manager*
EMP: 30
SALES (est): 357.4K **Privately Held**
SIC: 7011 Motels

(G-19568)
WESTLAKE MNTSR SCHL & CHLD DV
Also Called: Creative Playrooms
26830 Detroit Rd (44145-2368)
PHONE..................440 835-5858
Fax: 440 349-0702
Joan Wenk, *President*
EMP: 31
SQ FT: 12,000
SALES (est): 565.3K **Privately Held**
SIC: 8351 Montessori child development center

(G-19569)
YOUNG MNS CHRSTN ASSN CLVELAND
Also Called: Westshore Ymca/Westlake Chrn
1575 Columbia Rd (44145-2404)
PHONE..................440 808-8150
Fax: 440 871-4154
Laurie Wise, *Branch Mgr*
EMP: 100
SALES (corp-wide): 29.2MM **Privately Held**
SIC: 8641 8661 8322 7991 Youth organizations; religious organizations; individual & family services; physical fitness facilities
PA: Young Men's Christian Association Of Cleveland
1801 Superior Ave E # 130
Cleveland OH 44114
216 781-1337

Wheelersburg
Scioto County

(G-19570)
BEST CARE NRSING RHBLTTION CTR
2159 Dogwood Ridge Rd (45694-9044)
PHONE..................740 574-2558
Fax: 740 574-5426
Wanda Meade, *Vice Pres*
Joe Donchantz, *Vice Pres*
Linda Collins, *Facilities Dir*
Kelly Daub, *Purchasing*
Kayla Culp, *Director*
EMP: 150
SQ FT: 40,000
SALES (est): 4.6MM
SALES (corp-wide): 574.7MM **Publicly Held**
SIC: 8051 8093 Skilled nursing care facilities; specialty outpatient clinics
HQ: Diversicare Management Services Co.
277 Mallory Station Rd # 130
Franklin TN 37067

(G-19571)
BROWN MEDICAL LLC
Also Called: Proactive Occpational Medicine
1661 State Route 522 # 3 (45694-8120)
P.O. Box 64 (45694-0064)
PHONE..................740 574-8728
Jeff Brown, *President*
Monica Clark, *Administration*
EMP: 40
SALES (est): 2MM **Privately Held**
SIC: 7361 Employment agencies

(G-19572)
CATSI INC
7991 Ohio River Rd (45694-1620)
P.O. Box 263 (45694-0263)
PHONE..................740 574-8417
Chris Rennion, *Principal*
EMP: 40
SALES (est): 1.6MM **Privately Held**
SIC: 7389 Inspection & testing services

Wheelersburg - Scioto County (G-19573)

(G-19573)
COLLINS & ASSOC TECHNICAL SVCS
7991 Ohio River Rd (45694-1620)
P.O. Box 263 (45694-0263)
PHONE..................................740 574-2320
James L Collins, *President*
EMP: 25
SQ FT: 8,000
SALES: 4.5MM **Privately Held**
WEB: www.catsi.com
SIC: 8741 Construction management

(G-19574)
COMMUNITY CHOICE HOME CARE
7318 Ohio River Rd (45694)
P.O. Box 148 (45694-0148)
PHONE..................................740 574-9900
Fax: 740 574-9064
L Cunningham, *Director*
EMP: 50 **EST:** 1996
SALES (est): 1.7MM **Privately Held**
SIC: 8082 Visiting nurse service

(G-19575)
CONCORD HLTH RHABILITATION CTR
1242 Crescent Dr (45694-9376)
PHONE..................................740 574-8441
Jennifer Chaffin, *Director*
EMP: 43 **EST:** 2010
SALES (est): 919.4K **Privately Held**
SIC: 8082 8059 8052 8051 Home health care services; nursing home, except skilled & intermediate care facility; personal care facility; skilled nursing care facilities

(G-19576)
DIVERSICARE LEASING CORP
2159 Dogwood Ridge Rd (45694-9044)
PHONE..................................615 771-7575
Brenda Wimsatt, *Director*
Lisa Tyler, *Admin Sec*
EMP: 99
SALES (est): 1.3MM **Privately Held**
SIC: 8051 Skilled nursing care facilities

(G-19577)
GIGGLES & WIGGLES INC (PA)
1207 Dogwood Ridge Rd (45694-9219)
PHONE..................................740 574-4536
Fax: 740 574-4536
Judie Hedrick, *President*
EMP: 32
SQ FT: 4,500
SALES (est): 894.4K **Privately Held**
SIC: 8351 Group day care center

(G-19578)
LOWES HOME CENTERS LLC
7915 Ohio River Rd (45694-1618)
PHONE..................................740 574-6200
Fax: 740 574-2104
Brian Clifford, *Manager*
John Swisher, *Executive*
EMP: 150
SALES (corp-wide): 68.6B **Publicly Held**
SIC: 5211 5031 5722 5064 Home centers; building materials, exterior; building materials, interior; household appliance stores; electrical appliances, television & radio
HQ: Lowe's Home Centers, Llc
1605 Curtis Bridge Rd
Wilkesboro NC 28697
336 658-4000

(G-19579)
NORFOLK SOUTHERN CORPORATION
914 Hayport Rd (45694-7504)
PHONE..................................740 574-8491
Fax: 740 574-8747
Charles Waggoner, *Branch Mgr*
Mullins Erbin, *Manager*
Josh Smith, *Executive*
EMP: 41
SALES (corp-wide): 10.5B **Publicly Held**
WEB: www.nscorp.com
SIC: 4111 Local & suburban transit
PA: Norfolk Southern Corporation
3 Commercial Pl Ste 1a
Norfolk VA 23510
757 629-2680

(G-19580)
PROACTIVE OCCPTNAL MDICINE INC
Also Called: Brown Medical Services
1661 State Route 522 # 2 (45694-8120)
PHONE..................................740 574-8728
Jeffrey A Brown, *President*
David Pack, *Business Mgr*
Melissa Sites, *Finance Mgr*
Todd Heitz, *Manager*
Wendi Collins, *Executive*
EMP: 45
SQ FT: 5,000
SALES: 3.5MM **Privately Held**
SIC: 8099 Health screening service; hearing testing service

(G-19581)
SELECTIVE NETWORKING INC
Also Called: Alternative Nursing & HM Care
8407 Hayport Rd (45694-1832)
P.O. Box 338 (45694-0338)
PHONE..................................740 574-2682
Fax: 740 574-1171
Tammy Hitower, *President*
EMP: 75
SALES (est): 1.7MM **Privately Held**
SIC: 8082 Visiting nurse service

(G-19582)
TRI-AMERICA CONTRACTORS INC (PA)
1664 State Route 522 (45694-7828)
PHONE..................................740 574-0148
Teresa Smith, *CEO*
Scott Taylor, *President*
John Mauk, *General Mgr*
Gregory Stanley, *General Mgr*
Paul Montgomery, *Superintendent*
EMP: 37
SQ FT: 34,000
SALES: 12MM **Privately Held**
WEB: www.triaminc.com
SIC: 3498 3441 1629 Fabricated pipe & fittings; fabricated structural metal; industrial plant construction

Whitehouse
Lucas County

(G-19583)
ANTHONY WAYNE LOCAL SCHOOLS
Also Called: Anthony Wayne Trnsp Dept
6320 Industrial Pkwy (43571-9792)
P.O. Box 2487 (43571-0487)
PHONE..................................419 877-0451
Fax: 419 877-5627
Randy Hardy, *Superintendent*
EMP: 100
SQ FT: 5,580
SALES (corp-wide): 46.8MM **Privately Held**
SIC: 4151 4111 School buses; local & suburban transit
PA: Anthony Wayne Local Schools
9565 Bucher Rd
Whitehouse OH 43571
419 877-0466

(G-19584)
BITTERSWEET INC (PA)
Also Called: BITTERSWEET FARMS
12660 Archbold Whthuse Rd (43571-9566)
PHONE..................................419 875-6986
Fax: 419 875-5593
Connie Olinger, *Vice Pres*
Jennifer Holloway, *Human Res Dir*
Vicki Obee-Hilty, *Exec Dir*
Charles Flowers, *Exec Dir*
Megan Daoust, *Director*
EMP: 51
SQ FT: 20,000
SALES: 6.8MM **Privately Held**
WEB: www.bittersweetfarms.org
SIC: 8361 2032 8052 Home for the mentally handicapped; canned specialties; intermediate care facilities

(G-19585)
DOTSON COMPANY
6848 Providence St (43571-9572)
P.O. Box 2429 (43571-0429)
PHONE..................................419 877-5176
Fax: 419 877-0736
Mark Dotson, *President*
Kurt Dotson, *Corp Secy*
Rodd Dotson, *Vice Pres*
Gary Dotson, *Safety Dir*
Colleen Dodson, *Manager*
EMP: 25
SQ FT: 2,700
SALES: 10.7MM **Privately Held**
WEB: www.dotsoncompany.com
SIC: 1541 1542 Industrial buildings, new construction; commercial & office building contractors

(G-19586)
FROG & TOAD INC
Also Called: Whitehouse Inn
10835 Waterville St (43571-9181)
P.O. Box 2506 (43571-0506)
PHONE..................................419 877-1180
Fax: 419 877-5105
John Fronk, *President*
Anthony Fronk, *Admin Sec*
EMP: 50
SALES (est): 1.3MM **Privately Held**
SIC: 7011 Inns

(G-19587)
KINDRED HEALTHCARE OPERATING
11239 Waterville St (43571-9813)
P.O. Box 2760 (43571-0760)
PHONE..................................419 877-5338
Linda Nijakowski, *General Mgr*
Deborah Townsend, *Manager*
Melissa Broadwater, *Nursing Dir*
Jodi Doran, *Administration*
EMP: 99
SALES (corp-wide): 6B **Publicly Held**
WEB: www.salemhaven.com
SIC: 8052 8051 Intermediate care facilities; skilled nursing care facilities
HQ: Kindred Healthcare Operating, Inc.
680 S 4th St
Louisville KY 40202
502 596-7300

(G-19588)
LEADERSHIP CIRCLE LLC
10918 Springbrook Ct (43571-9674)
PHONE..................................801 518-2980
William Adams, *CEO*
Betsy Leatherman, *President*
Nathan Delahunty, *CFO*
Robert J Anderson Jr,
EMP: 30
SALES: 7.5MM **Privately Held**
SIC: 7379

(G-19589)
PROGRESSIVE FISHING ASSN
8050 Schadel Rd (43571-9538)
PHONE..................................419 877-9909
Mike Adcok, *President*
EMP: 80
SQ FT: 3,282
SALES: 30.8K **Privately Held**
SIC: 7997 Country club, membership

(G-19590)
WHITEHOUSE OPERATOR LLC
Also Called: Whitehouse Country Manor
11239 Waterville St (43571-9813)
PHONE..................................419 877-5338
Fax: 419 877-1049
Amy Bates, *Vice Pres*
Luann Fortney, *Manager*
Jean Tenney, *Manager*
John Both, *Director*
Melvin Alexander, *Officer*
EMP: 99
SQ FT: 27,015
SALES (est): 5.6MM **Privately Held**
SIC: 8361 Geriatric residential care

Wickliffe
Lake County

(G-19591)
A AAA H JACKS PLUMBING HTG CO
29930 Lakeland Blvd (44092-1744)
PHONE..................................440 946-1166
John Langer, *Principal*
EMP: 40
SALES (est): 3.6MM **Privately Held**
SIC: 1711 Plumbing contractors

(G-19592)
A1 MR LIMO INC
29555 Lakeland Blvd (44092-2221)
PHONE..................................440 943-5466
Fax: 440 943-7866
Lawrence Chrystal, *President*
Judy Chrystal, *Vice Pres*
EMP: 35 **EST:** 1995
SALES: 1MM **Privately Held**
WEB: www.a1mrlimo.com
SIC: 4119 Limousine rental, with driver

(G-19593)
DINOS CATERING INC
30605 Ridge Rd (44092-1165)
PHONE..................................440 943-1010
Fax: 440 943-1337
Pat Tibaldi, *President*
Mark Tibaldi, *Vice Pres*
EMP: 50
SALES (est): 1.9MM **Privately Held**
WEB: www.dinoscatering.com
SIC: 7299 5812 Banquet hall facilities; eating places

(G-19594)
DMD MANAGEMENT INC
Also Called: Legacy Health Services
1919 Bishop Rd (44092-2518)
PHONE..................................440 944-9400
EMP: 236 **Privately Held**
SIC: 8741 Nursing & personal care facility management
PA: Dmd Management, Inc.
12380 Plaza Dr
Cleveland OH 44130

(G-19595)
EAST OHIO GAS COMPANY
Also Called: Dominion Energy Ohio
29555 Clayton Ave (44092-1924)
PHONE..................................216 736-6917
Mike Reed, *Manager*
Tom Kenny, *Supervisor*
EMP: 200
SALES (corp-wide): 12.5B **Publicly Held**
SIC: 4923 Gas transmission & distribution
HQ: The East Ohio Gas Company
19701 Libby Rd
Maple Heights OH 44137
800 362-7557

(G-19596)
FAIRWAYS
30630 Ridge Rd (44092-1166)
PHONE..................................440 943-2050
Fax: 440 943-0403
Erene Fairways, *Business Mgr*
Bill Gala, *Manager*
Michelle Gorman, *Exec Dir*
Joan Fair, *Administration*
Grace E Glasser, *Administration*
EMP: 56
SALES (est): 1.6MM **Privately Held**
WEB: www.fairwaysindoorgolf.com
SIC: 8361 Home for the aged

(G-19597)
FOTI CONSTRUCTION COMPANY LLP
1164 Lloyd Rd (44092-2314)
PHONE..................................440 347-0728
Fred Innamorato,
EMP: 50
SQ FT: 11,000

SALES (est): 2.4MM **Privately Held**
WEB: www.foticonstruction.com
SIC: 1741 1542 Masonry & other stonework; commercial & office building, new construction; commercial & office buildings, renovation & repair

(G-19598)
FOTI CONTRACTING LLC
1164 Lloyd Rd (44092-2314)
PHONE.................330 656-3454
Fred Innamorato,
Edward P Wojnaroski,
EMP: 250
SALES (est): 27MM **Privately Held**
SIC: 1542 Nonresidential construction

(G-19599)
GREAT LAKES CRUSHING LTD
30831 Euclid Ave (44092-1042)
PHONE.................440 944-5500
Fax: 440 953-8461
Mark M Belich, *General Ptnr*
Maxine Belich, *Manager*
EMP: 47 **EST:** 1996
SQ FT: 10,000
SALES (est): 23.9MM **Privately Held**
SIC: 1429 7359 1623 1629 Igneous rock, crushed & broken-quarrying; equipment rental & leasing; office machine rental, except computers; underground utilities contractor; land clearing contractor; grading

(G-19600)
GTM SERVICE INC (PA)
Also Called: Parts Pro Automotive Warehouse
1366 Rockefeller Rd (44092-1973)
PHONE.................440 944-5099
Michael McPhee, *President*
Sue Naght, *Sales Mgr*
Jean Sweigert, *Manager*
EMP: 40 **EST:** 1981
SQ FT: 12,000
SALES (est): 78.6MM **Privately Held**
WEB: www.partsproautomotive.com
SIC: 5013 Truck parts & accessories

(G-19601)
HI TECMETAL GROUP INC
Also Called: Brite Brazing
28910 Lakeland Blvd (44092-2321)
PHONE.................440 373-5101
Fax: 440 426-6837
Scott Featherston, *Engineer*
Duane Heinrich, *Manager*
EMP: 40
SALES (corp-wide): 22.9MM **Privately Held**
SIC: 3398 7692 Metal heat treating; welding repair
PA: Hi Tecmetal Group Inc
1101 E 55th St
Cleveland OH 44103
216 881-8100

(G-19602)
HORIZON PERSONNEL RESOURCES (PA)
1516 Lincoln Rd (44092-2411)
PHONE.................440 585-0031
Fax: 440 585-1011
Daniel L Schivitz, *President*
Stephen Majercik, *COO*
Walter Nelson, *Executive*
David Davies, *Administration*
EMP: 150
SQ FT: 2,200
SALES (est): 5.6MM **Privately Held**
WEB: www.hprjobs.com
SIC: 7363 7361 Temporary help service; employment agencies

(G-19603)
INN AT WICKLIFFE LLC
Also Called: Ramada Inn
28600 Ridgehills Dr (44092-2788)
PHONE.................440 585-0600
Ghanshyam Patel, *Mng Member*
Asmita Barot,
EMP: 34
SALES (est): 1.7MM **Privately Held**
SIC: 7011 Hotels & motels

(G-19604)
IWI INCORPORATED (PA)
1399 Rockefeller Rd (44092-1972)
PHONE.................440 585-5900
Fax: 440 585-2570
Robert J Iacco Sr, *Ch of Bd*
Jeffery Iacco, *President*
Mark Merickel, *Opers Mgr*
Sherrie Janz, *Accounts Mgr*
Marty Slunski, *Sales Engr*
EMP: 30 **EST:** 1972
SQ FT: 9,875
SALES (est): 22.7MM **Privately Held**
WEB: www.yalepart.com
SIC: 5084 Materials handling machinery

(G-19605)
LAKE DATA CENTER INC
800 Lloyd Rd (44092-2334)
PHONE.................440 944-2020
Fax: 440 944-3420
Tony Saranita, *President*
EMP: 70 **EST:** 1980
SQ FT: 3,500
SALES (est): 3.4MM **Privately Held**
WEB: www.lakedata.com
SIC: 7374 Data entry service

(G-19606)
LAZAR BROTHERS INC
Also Called: Stanley Steemer
30030 Lakeland Blvd (44092-1745)
PHONE.................440 585-9333
Fax: 440 585-0355
Terrance Lazar, *President*
Dennis E Lazar, *Corp Secy*
Donald Lazar, *Vice Pres*
EMP: 25
SQ FT: 8,100
SALES (est): 2.2MM **Privately Held**
SIC: 7217 Carpet & furniture cleaning on location; upholstery cleaning on customer premises

(G-19607)
MCSTEEN & ASSOCIATES INC
1415 E 286th St (44092-2506)
PHONE.................440 585-9800
Fax: 440 585-9801
Debbie Feller, *President*
Tim Feller, *Vice Pres*
Trellis Grubbs, *Marketing Staff*
Robert Dorner, *Manager*
Kathryn Kessler, *Manager*
EMP: 40
SQ FT: 4,000
SALES (est): 3.6MM **Privately Held**
SIC: 8713 Surveying services

(G-19608)
MULLINAX EAST LLC
Also Called: Autonation Ford East
28825 Euclid Ave (44092-2528)
PHONE.................440 296-3020
Fax: 440 585-0554
Charles E Mullinax, *President*
Rickey Limbers, *Manager*
EMP: 100
SQ FT: 34,000
SALES (est): 31.6MM
SALES (corp-wide): 21.5B **Publicly Held**
WEB: www.mullinaxfordeast.com
SIC: 5511 7538 7532 5521 Automobiles, new & used; general automotive repair shops; top & body repair & paint shops; used car dealers; automobiles & other motor vehicles
HQ: An Dealership Holding Corp.
200 Sw 1st Ave
Fort Lauderdale FL 33301
954 769-7000

(G-19609)
NORTHCOAST MOVING ENTERPRISING
Also Called: Two Men and A Truck/Cleveland
1420 Lloyd Rd (44092-2320)
PHONE.................440 943-3900
Fax: 440 943-3932
Lynn Meilander, *President*
Joseph Lora, *Manager*
EMP: 60
SQ FT: 27,000
SALES (est): 4.5MM **Privately Held**
SIC: 4212 Moving services

(G-19610)
OFEQ INSTITUTE INC
2620 Bishop Rd (44092-2642)
PHONE.................440 943-1497
Fax: 216 731-5567
Abraham Shoshana, *Director*
EMP: 26
SALES: 50.4K **Privately Held**
SIC: 8733 Noncommercial research organizations

(G-19611)
PERFECT CUT-OFF INC
29201 Anderson Rd (44092-2337)
PHONE.................440 943-0000
Fax: 440 943-0686
Michael V Picciano, *President*
Rudy Graham, *VP Opers*
Richard Kish, *QC Mgr*
Valerie Picciano, *Treasurer*
Jason Smith, *Controller*
EMP: 35 **EST:** 1973
SALES (est): 5.2MM **Privately Held**
WEB: www.perfectcutoff.com
SIC: 7389 Metal cutting services

(G-19612)
PROTERRA INC (PA)
29103 Euclid Ave (44092-2467)
PHONE.................216 383-8449
Michael Zychowski, *President*
Jonathan Varcelli, *Vice Pres*
EMP: 25
SQ FT: 8,000
SALES (est): 2.4MM **Privately Held**
SIC: 4214 5032 Local trucking with storage; stone, crushed or broken

(G-19613)
RIDGEHILLS HOTEL LTD PARTNR
Also Called: Holiday Inn
28600 Ridgehills Dr (44092-2788)
PHONE.................440 585-0600
Patti Martin, *Manager*
EMP: 60
SQ FT: 53,998
SALES (corp-wide): 1.7MM **Privately Held**
WEB: www.ridgehillshotel.com
SIC: 7011 5813 5812 Hotels & motels; drinking places; eating places
PA: Ridgehills Hotel Limited Partnership
1350 W 3rd St
Cleveland OH 44113
216 464-2860

(G-19614)
UNITED SKATES AMERICA INC
30325 Palisades Pkwy (44092-1567)
PHONE.................440 944-5300
Fax: 440 944-5310
Bruce Aster, *Manager*
EMP: 30
SALES (corp-wide): 8.8MM **Privately Held**
SIC: 7999 Roller skating rink operation
PA: United Skates Of America, Inc.
3362 Refugee Rd
Columbus OH 43232
614 802-2440

(G-19615)
WICKLIFFE ASSOCIATES PARTNR
Also Called: Wickliffe Lanes
30315 Euclid Ave (44092-1549)
PHONE.................440 585-3505
Gerald Appel, *Partner*
Frank King, *Partner*
Jeff Gierman, *Manager*
EMP: 40
SQ FT: 15,000
SALES (est): 2.1MM **Privately Held**
WEB: www.wickliffelanes.com
SIC: 6512 Commercial & industrial building operation

(G-19616)
WICKLIFFE COUNTRY PLACE LTD
1919 Bishop Rd (44092-2586)
PHONE.................440 944-9400
Fax: 440 944-0955
Sherri Liones, *Facilities Dir*
Roxann Stanescu, *Director*
Mark Yantek, *Administration*
Suzanne Carlton, *Administration*
EMP: 150
SALES (corp-wide): 11.3MM **Privately Held**
SIC: 8051 Convalescent home with continuous nursing care
PA: Wickliffe Country Place Ltd
12380 Plaza Dr
Parma OH 44130
216 898-8399

Willard
Huron County

(G-19617)
BUURMA FARMS INCORPORATED (PA)
3909 Kok Rd (44890-9700)
PHONE.................419 935-6411
Fax: 419 935-1918
Richard C Buurma, *President*
Steven Foster, *President*
Michael Murtha, *President*
Bruce Buurma, *Vice Pres*
Chadd Buurma, *Vice Pres*
EMP: 30 **EST:** 1896
SQ FT: 3,000
SALES: 19.3MM **Privately Held**
WEB: www.buurmafarms.com
SIC: 0161 Celery farm; rooted vegetable farms; lettuce farm

(G-19618)
CSX CORPORATION
2826 Liberty Rd (44890-9382)
PHONE.................419 933-5027
Bill Loar, *Manager*
EMP: 149
SALES (corp-wide): 11.4B **Publicly Held**
WEB: www.csx.com
SIC: 4011 Railroads, line-haul operating
PA: Csx Corporation
500 Water St Fl 15
Jacksonville FL 32202
904 359-3200

(G-19619)
FAMILY HEALTH PARTNERS INC
Also Called: Brown, Chris R & Vicki J
315 Crestwood Dr (44890-1652)
PHONE.................419 935-0196
Fax: 419 933-7616
Eric Prack, *President*
Marian Rohrbach, *Admin Sec*
EMP: 28
SALES (est): 2.7MM **Privately Held**
WEB: www.family-health-partners.com
SIC: 8011 Offices & clinics of medical doctors

(G-19620)
HOLTHOUSE FARMS OF OHIO INC (PA)
Also Called: Holthouse Farms of Michigan
4373 State Route 103 S (44890-9219)
PHONE.................419 935-1041
Fax: 419 933-2178
Stanton Holthouse, *Principal*
Carol Holthouse, *Principal*
Connie Holthouse, *Principal*
Jordon Holthouse, *Principal*
Kirk Holthouse, *Sales Executive*
EMP: 125
SQ FT: 20,000
SALES (est): 14.3MM **Privately Held**
SIC: 0161 0191 Vegetables & melons; general farms, primarily crop

(G-19621)
K & P TRUCKING LLC
3862 State Route 103 S (44890-9042)
P.O. Box 179 (44890-0179)
PHONE.................419 935-8646
William Koerner,
J Harold Cashman,
Kent Knaus,
EMP: 60
SALES (est): 3.3MM **Privately Held**
SIC: 4213 Trucking, except local

Willard - Huron County (G-19622)

(G-19622)
LIBERTY NURSING OF WILLARD
Also Called: Hillside Acres Nursing Home
370 E Howard St (44890-1656)
PHONE.................................419 935-0148
Fax: 419 933-6448
Linda Blackurek, *President*
Kathy Gumbert, *Office Mgr*
Mark Bigler, *Director*
EMP: 70
SQ FT: 58,000
SALES (est): 2.3MM **Privately Held**
WEB: www.lbkhealthcare.com
SIC: **8051** 8052 Skilled nursing care facilities; intermediate care facilities
PA: Lbk Health Care, Inc.
   4336 W Franklin St Ste A
   Bellbrook OH

(G-19623)
MERCY HEALTH
218 S Myrtle Ave (44890-1408)
PHONE.................................419 935-0187
EMP: 69
SALES (corp-wide): 4.2B **Privately Held**
SIC: **8011** Gynecologist
PA: Mercy Health
   1701 Mercy Health Pl
   Cincinnati OH 45237
   513 639-2800

(G-19624)
PAM TRANSPORTATION SVCS INC
2501 Miller Rd (44890-9555)
P.O. Box 383 (44890-0383)
PHONE.................................419 935-9501
Fred Blank, *Manager*
David R Grana, *Manager*
EMP: 60
SALES (corp-wide): 437.8MM **Publicly Held**
SIC: **4213** 4231 Trucking, except local; trucking terminal facilities
PA: P.A.M. Transportation Services, Inc.
   297 W Henri De Tonti Blvd
   Tontitown AR 72770
   479 361-9111

(G-19625)
PRISTINE SENIOR LIVING OF
Also Called: Pristine Senior Living and
370 E Howard St (44890-1656)
PHONE.................................419 935-0148
Brian Femia, *Mng Member*
EMP: 60
SALES (est): 645.4K **Privately Held**
SIC: **8059** Nursing & personal care

(G-19626)
SHARPNACK CHVRLET BICK CDILLAC
1330 S Conwell Ave (44890-9148)
PHONE.................................419 935-0194
Tom Sharpnack, *President*
Rhonda Holbrook, *Office Mgr*
EMP: 100
SALES: 10MM **Privately Held**
SIC: **5511** 7532 Automobiles, new & used; collision shops, automotive

(G-19627)
SISTERS OF MRCY OF WLLARD OHIO (DH)
Also Called: Mercy Hospital of Willard
1100 Neal Zick Rd (44890-9287)
PHONE.................................419 964-5000
Fax: 419 935-8966
Lynn Detterman, *President*
Ronald E Heinlen, *Principal*
Joan Kimmett, *QA Dir*
Deborah Donaldson, *Accountant*
Virgilio Tongson, *Med Doctor*
EMP: 175
SQ FT: 70,000
SALES: 24.7MM
SALES (corp-wide): 4.2B **Privately Held**
SIC: **8062** General medical & surgical hospitals
HQ: Mercy Health Cincinnati Llc
   1701 Mercy Health Pl
   Cincinnati OH 45237
   513 952-5000

(G-19628)
TRILOGY HEALTH SERVICES LLC
Also Called: Willows At Willard, The
1050 Neal Zick Rd (44890-9288)
PHONE.................................419 935-6511
Randall Bufford, *CEO*
Leigh Barney, *COO*
Danny Prosky, *Exec VP*
Mathieu Streiff, *Exec VP*
William Bryant, *Vice Pres*
EMP: 100
SQ FT: 28,442
SALES (corp-wide): 74.3MM **Privately Held**
SIC: **8051** 8361 Skilled nursing care facilities; residential care
HQ: Trilogy Health Services, Llc
   303 N Hurstbourne Pkwy # 200
   Louisville KY 40222

Williamsburg
Clermont County

(G-19629)
CECOS INTERNATIONAL INC
Also Called: Site K62
5092 Aber Rd (45176-9532)
PHONE.................................513 724-6114
Fax: 513 724-3234
Gary Saylor, *Engineer*
Connie Dall, *Controller*
EMP: 28
SALES (corp-wide): 10B **Publicly Held**
SIC: **4953** Refuse collection & disposal services
HQ: Cecos International, Inc.
   5600 Niagara Falls Blvd
   Niagara Falls NY 14304
   716 282-2676

(G-19630)
CLERCOM INC
Also Called: Diesel-Eagle
3710 State Route 133 (45176-9798)
PHONE.................................513 724-6101
Fax: 513 724-6103
Marlyon E Abrams, *President*
Les Willson, *General Mgr*
Jessie Abrams, *Corp Secy*
Jim Jones, *Accountant*
▲ EMP: 100 EST: 1968
SQ FT: 104,000
SALES (est): 10MM **Privately Held**
SIC: **5065** 5199 Communication equipment; citizens band radios; radio parts & accessories; general merchandise, nondurable

(G-19631)
CROSWELL OF WILLIAMSBURG LLC (PA)
Also Called: Croswell VIP Motor Couch Svc
975 W Main St (45176-1147)
PHONE.................................513 724-2206
Fax: 513 724-3261
John W Croswell, *President*
Marion Croswell, *Corp Secy*
Robert S Croswell III, *Vice Pres*
Robert Croswell, *Vice Pres*
Susan Mahan, *Vice Pres*
EMP: 25 EST: 1921
SQ FT: 21,000
SALES: 7MM **Privately Held**
WEB: www.croswell-bus.com
SIC: **4142** 4141 Bus charter service, except local; local bus charter service

(G-19632)
DUALITE SALES & SERVICE INC (PA)
1 Dualite Ln (45176-1121)
PHONE.................................513 724-7100
Fax: 513 724-9029
Gregory Schube, *CEO*
Kenneth Syberg, *Senior VP*
Greg Hoffer, *Vice Pres*
Marvin D Jett, *Vice Pres*
Paula Mueller, *Vice Pres*
◆ EMP: 250
SQ FT: 214,500
SALES: 32MM **Privately Held**
SIC: **5099** Signs, except electric

(G-19633)
LOCUST RIDGE NURSING HOME INC (PA)
12745 Elm Corner Rd (45176-9621)
PHONE.................................937 444-2920
Fax: 937 444-2182
Howard L Meeker, *President*
Ruth Osborn, *CFO*
Christopher Haas, *Director*
Maxine Snider, *Hlthcr Dir*
Steven L Meeker, *Admin Sec*
EMP: 125
SQ FT: 20,000
SALES (est): 4.7MM **Privately Held**
SIC: **8051** Convalescent home with continuous nursing care

(G-19634)
PINE RIDGE PINE VLLG RESDNTL H
146 N 3rd St (45176-1322)
PHONE.................................513 724-3460
Gladys Creighton, *Manager*
Tracy Watson, *Manager*
Verna Wiedenbein, *Administration*
EMP: 28
SALES (est): 893.4K **Privately Held**
SIC: **8361** Residential care for the handicapped

(G-19635)
RESCARE OHIO INC (DH)
Also Called: Willimsburg Rsdntial Altrntves
348 W Main St (45176-1352)
PHONE.................................513 724-1177
Fax: 513 724-3720
Dwight Finch, *Director*
Fred Duley, *Director*
Lynn Hibbard, *Director*
EMP: 50
SALES (est): 8.5MM
SALES (corp-wide): 24.5B **Privately Held**
SIC: **8361** 8052 Self-help group home; intermediate care facilities
HQ: Res-Care, Inc.
   9901 Linn Station Rd
   Louisville KY 40223
   502 394-2100

(G-19636)
RESIDENTIAL CONCEPTS INC
117 Kermit Ave (45176-1511)
PHONE.................................513 724-6067
Jim Sprags, *President*
EMP: 40
SALES (est): 699.3K **Privately Held**
SIC: **8052** Home for the mentally retarded, with health care

Williamsport
Pickaway County

(G-19637)
CONNECTIVITY SYSTEMS INC (PA)
Also Called: Csi International
8120 State Route 138 (43164-9767)
P.O. Box 417 (43164-0417)
PHONE.................................740 420-5400
Fax: 740 986-6022
John A Rankin, *Ch of Bd*
John Byrnes, *President*
EMP: 30
SQ FT: 4,000
SALES (est): 3MM **Privately Held**
WEB: www.e-vse.com
SIC: **7371** Computer software development

(G-19638)
INTERNATIONAL ASSN LIONS
Also Called: New Holland Lions Club
24920 Locust Grove Rd (43164-9780)
PHONE.................................740 986-6502
Fay Washburn, *President*
Marty Mace, *Treasurer*
Charlotte Riley, *Admin Sec*
EMP: 29
SALES (est): 278K **Privately Held**
SIC: **8641** Civic social & fraternal associations

Williston
Ottawa County

(G-19639)
LUTHER HOME OF MERCY
Also Called: Williston Luther Home of Mercy
5810 N Main St (43468)
P.O. Box 187 (43468-0187)
PHONE.................................419 836-3918
Fax: 419 836-9238
Dave Zyski, *Maint Spvr*
Mark Christophono, *CFO*
Renee Gibson, *Supervisor*
Mahalia Owens, *Supervisor*
Linda Tanner, *Supervisor*
EMP: 499
SQ FT: 150,000
SALES: 19.9MM **Privately Held**
SIC: **8052** Intermediate care facilities

Willoughby
Lake County

(G-19640)
A J GOULDER ELECTRIC CO
4307 Hamann Pkwy (44094-5625)
PHONE.................................440 942-4026
Fax: 440 354-2881
Keith Eldridge, *President*
Rich Cunningham, *President*
Connie Eldridge, *Corp Secy*
Amy Gallo, *Vice Pres*
Bret Thomas, *Vice Pres*
EMP: 44
SQ FT: 4,500
SALES (est): 3.2MM **Privately Held**
SIC: **1731** General electrical contractor

(G-19641)
AEROCON PHOTOGRAMMETRIC SVCS (PA)
4515 Glenbrook Rd (44094-8215)
PHONE.................................440 946-6277
Fax: 440 946-2646
Denny Sauers, *General Mgr*
James Liberty, *Principal*
Chad Bassett, *COO*
Bill Faunce, *Project Mgr*
Rose Brosius, *Human Res Dir*
EMP: 27
SQ FT: 10,000
SALES (est): 4.3MM **Privately Held**
WEB: www.aerocon.com
SIC: **7389** 7335 Photogrammatic mapping; aerial photography, except mapmaking

(G-19642)
ALL LIFT SERVICE COMPANY INC
Also Called: All Industrial Engine Service
4607 Hamann Pkwy (44094-5631)
PHONE.................................440 585-1542
John L Gelsimino, *President*
John P Gelsimino, *Owner*
Dave Gaydos, *Opers Mgr*
Sam Amato, *Accounts Mgr*
Chris Collins, *Accounts Mgr*
EMP: 47 EST: 1972
SQ FT: 38,000
SALES (est): 10.9MM **Privately Held**
WEB: www.alllift.com
SIC: **7699** 5013 7359 5084 Industrial truck repair; truck parts & accessories; industrial truck rental; trucks, industrial

(G-19643)
ALPHA IMAGING LLC (PA)
4455 Glenbrook Rd (44094-8215)
PHONE.................................440 953-3800
Fax: 440 953-1455
Albert D Perrico, *President*
Pete Davis, *President*
Jim Harrington, *Senior VP*
Scott Macgregor, *Vice Pres*
Michael Perrico, *Vice Pres*
EMP: 84
SQ FT: 7,500

SALES (est): 25.3MM **Privately Held**
WEB: www.alpha-imaging.com
SIC: **5047** 7699 X-ray machines & tubes; X-ray equipment repair

(G-19644)
ANDREWS APARTMENTS LTD
4420 Sherwin Rd (44094-7994)
PHONE..................440 946-3600
Douglas Price, *Principal*
EMP: 155 EST: 2008
SALES (est): 2.1MM
SALES (corp-wide): 26.2MM **Privately Held**
SIC: **6513** Apartment building operators
PA: The K&D Group Inc
4420 Sherwin Rd Ste 1
Willoughby OH 44094
440 946-3600

(G-19645)
ASCENDTECH INC
4772 E 355th St (44094-4632)
PHONE..................216 458-1101
Igor Lapinskiy, *President*
Gary Lapinskiy, *General Mgr*
Alexander Senik, *Sales Staff*
Jerry Latin, *Office Mgr*
EMP: 35
SALES (est): 8.3MM **Privately Held**
SIC: **5045** 7379 3571 7378 Computer peripheral equipment; computer related maintenance services; electronic computers; computer peripheral equipment repair & maintenance; electrical repair shops; scrap & waste materials

(G-19646)
AT&T CORP
34808 Euclid Ave (44094-4504)
PHONE..................440 951-5309
EMP: 69
SALES (corp-wide): 160.5B **Publicly Held**
SIC: **4813** Local & long distance telephone communications
HQ: At&T Corp.
1 At&T Way
Bedminster NJ 07921
800 403-3302

(G-19647)
BEVCORP LLC (PA)
4711 E 355th St (44094-4631)
PHONE..................440 954-3500
Fax: 440 954-3501
Cathy Connelly, *Safety Dir*
John Schein, *Plant Supt*
Chuck Sobecki, *Project Mgr*
Brian Warner, *Project Mgr*
John Mitchell, *Engineer*
▲ EMP: 65
SQ FT: 40,000
SALES (est): 42.1MM **Privately Held**
WEB: www.bevcorp.com
SIC: **5084** Industrial machinery & equipment

(G-19648)
CASCIA LLC
Also Called: Lake Cnty Captains Prof Basbal Classic Pk 35300 Vine St Classic Park (44095)
PHONE..................440 975-8085
Brad Seymour, *General Mgr*
Rob Demko, *Controller*
Kevin Brodzinski, *Manager*
Josh Porter, *Manager*
Jen Yorko, *Manager*
EMP: 45
SALES: 2MM **Privately Held**
SIC: **7997** 7941 Baseball club, except professional & semi-professional; baseball club, professional & semi-professional

(G-19649)
CITY OF WILLOUGHBY
Also Called: Willoughby City Garage
37400 N Industrial Pkwy (44094-6213)
PHONE..................440 942-0215
Neil Pinckney, *Superintendent*
George Trost, *Supervisor*
EMP: 35 **Privately Held**
WEB: www.willoughbyohio.com
SIC: **4173** Maintenance facilities for motor vehicle passenger transport

PA: City Of Willoughby
1 Public Sq
Willoughby OH 44094
440 953-4191

(G-19650)
CITY OF WILLOUGHBY
Road Department
1 Public Sq (44094-7827)
PHONE..................440 953-4111
Fax: 440 953-4382
Sam Trost, *Manager*
EMP: 75 **Privately Held**
WEB: www.willoughbyohio.com
SIC: **1611** Highway & street maintenance
PA: City Of Willoughby
1 Public Sq
Willoughby OH 44094
440 953-4191

(G-19651)
CITY OF WILLOUGHBY
Service Dept
1 Public Sq (44094-7827)
PHONE..................440 953-4111
David E Anderson, *Mayor*
EMP: 254 **Privately Held**
WEB: www.willoughbyohio.com
SIC: **6531** Cemetery management service
PA: City Of Willoughby
1 Public Sq
Willoughby OH 44094
440 953-4191

(G-19652)
CITY OF WILLOUGHBY
Also Called: Lost Nation Golf Course
38890 Hodgson Rd (44094-7572)
PHONE..................440 953-4280
Fax: 440 953-4136
Mitch Allan, *Manager*
Peter Brooks, *Manager*
EMP: 30 **Privately Held**
WEB: www.willoughbyohio.com
SIC: **7992** Public golf courses
PA: City Of Willoughby
1 Public Sq
Willoughby OH 44094
440 953-4191

(G-19653)
CLEVELAND COIN MCH EXCH INC (HQ)
3860 Ben Hur Ave Unit 2 (44094-6377)
PHONE..................847 842-6310
Herman Fox, *President*
Adrienne Gallender, *Publisher*
Sheldon M Gisser, *Exec VP*
Jeff Lonchor, *Controller*
EMP: 60 EST: 1947
SQ FT: 40,000
SALES (est): 16.6MM **Privately Held**
SIC: **5087** 5046 Vending machines & supplies; commercial equipment
PA: Family Entertainment Group Llc
1265 Hamilton Pkwy
Itasca IL 60143
847 842-6310

(G-19654)
CLEVELAND DAIRY QUEEN INC (PA)
4067 Erie St Ste 2 (44094-7873)
P.O. Box 109 (44096-0109)
PHONE..................440 946-3690
Jeff Baker, *President*
EMP: 111
SALES (est): 4.2MM **Privately Held**
SIC: **5012** 5451 8742 Ice cream stands or dairy bars; ice cream (packaged); franchising consultant

(G-19655)
COMMUNITY CHOICE FINANCIAL INC
34302 Euclid Ave Unit 7 (44094-3334)
PHONE..................440 602-9922
Jim Frauenberg, *President*
EMP: 100 **Privately Held**
WEB: www.buckeyecheckcashing.com
SIC: **6099** Check cashing agencies
HQ: Buckeye Check Cashing, Inc.
6785 Bobcat Way Ste 200
Dublin OH 43016
614 798-5900

(G-19656)
COUNTY OF LAKE
Also Called: Lake Cnty Deptmntl Retrdtn/Dvl
2100 Joseph Lloyd Pkwy (44094-8032)
PHONE..................440 269-2193
Fax: 440 269-2191
Wiegand Ken, *Plant Mgr*
Carol Krider, *Production*
Marcie Barbic, *Sls & Mktg Exec*
Michael Betz, *Sales Executive*
Gary Metelko, *Director*
EMP: 72 **Privately Held**
WEB: www.lakecountyohio.gov
SIC: **8322** 8331 3441 Individual & family services; job training & vocational rehabilitation services; fabricated structural metal
PA: County Of Lake
8 N State St Ste 215
Painesville OH 44077
440 350-2500

(G-19657)
CUSTOM CLEANING AND MAINT
38046 2nd St (44094-6105)
PHONE..................440 946-7028
Fax: 440 946-0862
Joe Lambardo, *President*
Sandra Sidley, *Vice Pres*
EMP: 30
SALES (est): 792.8K **Privately Held**
SIC: **7349** Janitorial service, contract basis

(G-19658)
DAWNCHEM INC
Also Called: Dawn Chemical
30510 Lakeland Blvd Frnt (44095-5239)
PHONE..................440 943-3332
Fax: 440 943-5644
Edward Rossi, *President*
Janine Thomas, *Opers Mgr*
Dave Vranic, *Purch Mgr*
Greg Grattino, *Accounts Mgr*
Robert Mercuri, *Regl Sales Mgr*
EMP: 40 EST: 1977
SQ FT: 40,000
SALES (est): 27.8MM **Privately Held**
WEB: www.dawnchem.com
SIC: **5169** 5087 5113 Specialty cleaning & sanitation preparations; cleaning & maintenance equipment & supplies; industrial & personal service paper

(G-19659)
DEPENDABLE CLEANING CONTRS
Also Called: Willo Maintenance
38230 Glenn Ave (44094-7808)
PHONE..................440 953-9191
Fax: 440 918-6626
Wayne A Trubiano, *President*
Steve Jenkins, *Vice Pres*
Sam Tagliarini, *Vice Pres*
Steve Allen, *Manager*
EMP: 70
SQ FT: 2,500
SALES (est): 2MM **Privately Held**
WEB: www.unimar.com
SIC: **7349** Janitorial service, contract basis

(G-19660)
EAST END RO BURTON INC
Also Called: Riders Inn
792 Mentor Ave (44094)
PHONE..................440 942-2742
Elaine R Crane, *President*
EMP: 25
SQ FT: 7,001
SALES (est): 910K **Privately Held**
SIC: **7011** Motels

(G-19661)
EMERITUS CORPORATION
Also Called: Brookdale Willoughby
35300 Kaiser Ct (44094-6633)
PHONE..................440 269-8600
Laurie Bonarrigo, *Exec Dir*
EMP: 39
SALES (corp-wide): 4.7B **Publicly Held**
SIC: **8361** Residential care
HQ: Emeritus Corporation
3131 Elliott Ave Ste 500
Milwaukee WI 53214

(G-19662)
ERIESIDE MEDICAL GROUP
38429 Lake Shore Blvd (44094-7009)
PHONE..................440 918-6270
Winston Ho, *Partner*
Harris Freedman, *Partner*
James Mandelick, *Partner*
EMP: 30
SALES (est): 2.8MM **Privately Held**
SIC: **8011** Internal medicine practitioners

(G-19663)
EXODUS INTEGRITY SERVICE
Also Called: Eis
37111 Euclid Ave Ste F (44094-5659)
PHONE..................440 918-0140
Jim Ciricola, *President*
Pete Mc Millan, *Vice Pres*
Ben Juengel, *Director*
EMP: 63
SQ FT: 2,200
SALES (est): 3.9MM **Privately Held**
WEB: www.exodusintegrity.com
SIC: **7371** 7361 Custom computer programming services; employment agencies

(G-19664)
FEDEX OFFICE & PRINT SVCS INC
34800 Euclid Ave (44094-4504)
PHONE..................440 946-6353
Fax: 440 946-6389
EMP: 34
SALES (corp-wide): 60.3B **Publicly Held**
WEB: www.fedex.com
SIC: **4513** Package delivery, private air
HQ: Fedex Office And Print Services, Inc.
7900 Legacy Dr
Plano TX 75024
214 550-7000

(G-19665)
FIVE STAR TRUCKING INC
4380 Glenbrook Rd (44094-8213)
PHONE..................440 953-9300
Fax: 440 953-1863
John J Gramc, *President*
Jeff Ratcliffe, *COO*
Ralph Godic, *Vice Pres*
Joseph J Gramc, *Vice Pres*
Bob Ratcliffe, *Opers Staff*
EMP: 32
SQ FT: 19,000
SALES: 7.1MM **Privately Held**
WEB: www.fivestartrucking.com
SIC: **4213** 4212 Contract haulers; local trucking, without storage

(G-19666)
GLENRIDGE MACHINE CO
4610 Beidler Rd (44094-4603)
PHONE..................440 975-1055
Fax: 440 975-3490
Mark Negrelli Jr, *Ch of Bd*
Jerry Negrelli, *President*
Mark Negrelli III, *Vice Pres*
Michael Genzen, *Engineer*
Phil Zendarski, *Senior Engr*
▲ EMP: 33
SQ FT: 66,000
SALES (est): 7.8MM **Privately Held**
WEB: www.glenridgemachine.com
SIC: **3599** 7692 Machine shop, jobbing & repair; welding repair

(G-19667)
GOLDEN LIVING LLC
Also Called: Beverly
9679 Chillicothe Rd (44094-8503)
PHONE..................440 256-8100
Robert Laird, *Sales Mgr*
Jim Homa, *Exec Dir*
EMP: 200
SALES (corp-wide): 7.4MM **Privately Held**
SIC: **8059** Convalescent home
PA: Golden Living Llc
5220 Tennyson Pkwy # 400
Plano TX 75024
972 372-6300

Willoughby - Lake County (G-19668)

(G-19668)
HHC OHIO INC
Also Called: Winds Laure Cente For Behav ME
35900 Euclid Ave (44094-4623)
PHONE.................................440 953-3000
Leonard Barley, *Principal*
Pam Connell, *Executive*
EMP: 29
SALES (est): 3.9MM **Privately Held**
SIC: 8093 Substance abuse clinics (outpatient)

(G-19669)
HI TECMETAL GROUP INC
HI Tech Aero
34800 Lakeland Blvd (44095-5224)
PHONE.................................440 946-2280
Fax: 440 946-2283
Scott St Claire, *Branch Mgr*
Scott Stclair, *Manager*
EMP: 27
SQ FT: 17,433
SALES (est): 5.3MM
SALES (corp-wide): 22.9MM **Privately Held**
SIC: 3398 7692 Metal heat treating; brazing (hardening) of metal; welding repair
PA: Hi Tecmetal Group Inc
  1101 E 55th St
  Cleveland OH 44103
  216 881-8100

(G-19670)
HOLDEN ARBORETUM
9500 Sperry Rd (44094-5172)
PHONE.................................440 946-4400
Fax: 440 256-1655
Clem Hamilton, *President*
Cait Anastis, *Editor*
Dave Lowery, *Vice Pres*
Al Picciano, *Facilities Mgr*
Sarah Kyker, *Research*
EMP: 62
SQ FT: 80,000
SALES (est): 7.2MM **Privately Held**
WEB: www.holdenarb.org
SIC: 8422 Arboretum

(G-19671)
HOWARD HANNA SMYTHE CRAMER
Also Called: Paul Paratto
34601 Ridge Rd Ste 3 (44094-3032)
PHONE.................................440 516-4444
Fax: 440 944-5371
Nancy Tracz, *Sales/Mktg Mgr*
Belinda Fulton, *Manager*
Janet Horvath, *Manager*
Angelo Petronzio, *Manager*
EMP: 27
SALES (corp-wide): 76.4MM **Privately Held**
WEB: www.smythecramer.com
SIC: 6531 Real estate agent, residential
HQ: Howard Hanna Smythe Cramer
  6000 Parkland Blvd
  Cleveland OH 44124
  216 447-4477

(G-19672)
K & D ENTERPRISES INC
4420 Sherwin Rd Ste 1 (44094-7995)
P.O. Box 219 (44096-0219)
PHONE.................................440 946-3600
Karen Harrison, *President*
Doug Price, *Admin Sec*
EMP: 50
SALES (est): 2.3MM **Privately Held**
SIC: 6513 Apartment building operators

(G-19673)
K&D GROUP INC (PA)
4420 Sherwin Rd Ste 1 (44094-7995)
P.O. Box 219 (44096-0219)
PHONE.................................440 946-3600
Douglas E Price III, *CEO*
Karen M Harrison, *President*
Mauri-Lynn Feemster, *Controller*
Karen Palmer, *Controller*
Ziga Peljko, *Portfolio Mgr*
EMP: 25
SQ FT: 33,000
SALES (est): 26.2MM **Privately Held**
SIC: 6513 Apartment building operators

(G-19674)
KAISER FOUNDATION HOSPITALS
Also Called: Willoughby Medical Offices
5105 S O M Center Rd (44094)
PHONE.................................216 524-7377
EMP: 454
SALES (corp-wide): 19.1B **Privately Held**
SIC: 6733 Trust Management
PA: Kaiser Foundation Hospitals Inc
  1 Kaiser Plz Ste 2600
  Oakland CA 94612
  510 271-5800

(G-19675)
KIRTLAND COUNTRY CLUB
39438 Kirtland Rd (44094-9201)
PHONE.................................440 942-4400
Roy Johnson, *Controller*
EMP: 50
SQ FT: 15,000
SALES: 5.2MM **Privately Held**
WEB: www.kirtlandcc.org
SIC: 7997 Country club, membership

(G-19676)
KIRTLAND COUNTRY CLUB COMPANY
39438 Kirtland Rd (44094-9201)
PHONE.................................440 942-4400
Fax: 440 942-5124
Brian Bollar, *President*
Mark T Petzinc, *General Mgr*
Olivia Maitland, *Manager*
EMP: 100
SALES: 6.2MM **Privately Held**
SIC: 7997 Country club, membership

(G-19677)
KOTTLER METAL PRODUCTS CO INC
1595 Lost Nation Rd (44094-7329)
PHONE.................................440 946-7473
Barry Feldman, *President*
Harold Feldman, *Vice Pres*
Pat Garrett, *Sales Mgr*
Barbara Boic, *Office Mgr*
Barbara Voic, *Office Admin*
▲ EMP: 25
SALES: 7.4MM **Privately Held**
WEB: www.kottlermetal.com
SIC: 3498 3441 7692 3547 Pipe sections fabricated from purchased pipe; tube fabricating (contract bending & shaping); fabricated structural metal; welding repair; rolling mill machinery

(G-19678)
KUCERA INTERNATIONAL INC (PA)
38133 Western Pkwy (44094-7589)
PHONE.................................440 975-4230
Fax: 440 975-4238
John W Antalovich Sr, *Ch of Bd*
John W Antalovich Jr, *President*
Antalovich John, *Vice Pres*
John Anta-Lovick, *Project Mgr*
Robert Weston, *Project Mgr*
EMP: 65 EST: 1948
SQ FT: 20,000
SALES: 7MM **Privately Held**
WEB: www.hendersonaerial.com
SIC: 7335 8713 7389 8711 Aerial photography, except mapmaking; surveying services; photogrammetric engineering; photogrammatic mapping; mining engineer

(G-19679)
LABORATORY CORPORATION AMERICA
38429 Lake Shore Blvd (44094-7009)
PHONE.................................440 951-6841
EMP: 25
SALES (corp-wide): 8.6B **Publicly Held**
SIC: 8071 Medical Laboratory
HQ: Laboratory Corporation Of America
  358 S Main St Ste 458
  Burlington NC 27215
  336 229-1127

(G-19680)
LAKE COUNTY YMCA
Also Called: West End Branch
37100 Euclid Ave (44094-5612)
PHONE.................................440 946-1160
Robert Hoffman, *Systems Staff*
Abby Begeman, *Director*
Sonja Cesen, *Director*
Jacob Daling, *Director*
Michele Kuester, *Director*
EMP: 150
SALES (corp-wide): 8.9MM **Privately Held**
SIC: 8641 7991 8351 7032 Youth organizations; physical fitness facilities; child day care services; youth camps; individual & family services
PA: Lake County Ymca
  933 Mentor Ave Fl 2
  Painesville OH 44077
  440 352-3303

(G-19681)
LAKE HOSPITAL SYSTEM INC
Also Called: Lake-West Hospital
36000 Euclid Ave (44094-4625)
PHONE.................................440 953-9600
Fax: 440 953-6081
Cynthia Moore Hardy, *Principal*
Cynthia Hardy, *Principal*
Harris Freedman, *Vice Pres*
Ted Nichols, *Vice Pres*
Jennifer Manka, *Manager*
EMP: 1000
SALES (corp-wide): 334.1MM **Privately Held**
WEB: www.lakehospitalsystem.com
SIC: 8062 General medical & surgical hospitals
PA: Lake Hospital System, Inc.
  7590 Auburn Rd
  Painesville OH 44077
  440 375-8100

(G-19682)
LAKE METROPARKS
8668 Kirtland Chardon Rd (44094-8608)
PHONE.................................440 256-1404
Ann Bugeda, *General Mgr*
Dan Burnett, *Manager*
Brad Geletka, *Manager*
Deb Berkebile, *Director*
EMP: 30
SALES (est): 437.8K **Privately Held**
WEB: www.lakemetroparks.com
SIC: 7999 Recreation services
PA: Lake Metroparks
  11211 Spear Rd
  Painesville OH 44077
  440 639-7275

(G-19683)
LAKELAND FOUNDATION
7700 Clocktower Dr C2089 (44094-5198)
PHONE.................................440 525-7094
Bob Cahen, *Exec Dir*
EMP: 48
SALES (est): 163.4K **Privately Held**
SIC: 8299 7371 Educational services; computer software development & applications

(G-19684)
LANHAN CONTRACTORS INC
2220 Lost Nation Rd (44094-7535)
PHONE.................................440 918-1099
William Lanhan, *Owner*
EMP: 30
SALES (est): 1MM **Privately Held**
SIC: 0781 Landscape architects

(G-19685)
LAURELWOOD HOSPITAL (PA)
Also Called: LAURELWOOD CENTER FOR BEHAVIOU
35900 Euclid Ave (44094-4648)
PHONE.................................440 953-3000
Fax: 440 602-3938
Richard Warden, *President*
Ruth S Martin, *Med Doctor*
EMP: 319
SQ FT: 160,000
SALES: 37.9MM **Privately Held**
WEB: www.laurelwoodhospital.com
SIC: 8063 8069 Psychiatric hospitals; substance abuse hospitals

(G-19686)
LEIKIN MOTOR COMPANIES INC
38750 Mentor Ave (44094-7929)
PHONE.................................440 946-6900
Fax: 440 269-2922
Ronald Leikin, *President*
Brian Rapoport, *Business Mgr*
Brian Flick, *Parts Mgr*
Dave Pecek, *Sales Staff*
Mike Bonitati, *Manager*
EMP: 62
SQ FT: 40,000
SALES (est): 25.2MM **Privately Held**
WEB: www.leikenvolvo.com
SIC: 5511 7532 7514 5531 Automobiles, new & used; top & body repair & paint shops; passenger car rental; automotive & home supply stores; used car dealers

(G-19687)
LOST NATION SPORTS PARK
38630 Jet Center Pl (44094-8174)
PHONE.................................440 602-4000
Mike Srsen, *Mng Member*
Dave Boyza, *Director*
Eddie Strauss, *Director*
Danny Bartulovic, *Program Dir*
EMP: 30
SALES (est): 2MM **Privately Held**
WEB: www.lnsportspark.com
SIC: 7996 Amusement parks

(G-19688)
LOWES HOME CENTERS LLC
36300 Euclid Ave (44094-4415)
PHONE.................................440 942-2759
Fax: 440 942-5336
Ken Mohrbach, *Office Mgr*
Richard Brown, *Branch Mgr*
EMP: 150
SALES (corp-wide): 68.6B **Publicly Held**
SIC: 5211 5031 5722 5064 Home centers; building materials, exterior; building materials, interior; household appliance stores; electrical appliances, television & radio
HQ: Lowe's Home Centers, Llc
  1605 Curtis Bridge Rd
  Wilkesboro NC 28697
  336 658-4000

(G-19689)
M J LANESE LANDSCAPING INC
37115 Code Ave (44094-6337)
PHONE.................................440 942-3444
Fax: 440 942-3549
Matt Lanese, *Owner*
EMP: 30
SALES (est): 1.4MM **Privately Held**
SIC: 0782 Landscape contractors

(G-19690)
MANOR CARE OF AMERICA INC
37603 Euclid Ave (44094-5923)
PHONE.................................440 951-5551
Fax: 440 951-1914
Erlinda Gonzalez, *Branch Mgr*
EMP: 110
SALES (corp-wide): 3.6B **Publicly Held**
WEB: www.trisunhealthcare.com
SIC: 8051 Convalescent home with continuous nursing care
HQ: Manor Care Of America, Inc.
  333 N Summit St Ste 103
  Toledo OH 43604
  419 252-5500

(G-19691)
MARKETING COMM RESOURCE INC
4800 E 345th St (44094-4607)
PHONE.................................440 484-3010
Dominic Tiunno, *CEO*
Frank Tiunno, *Exec VP*
EMP: 57
SALES (est): 6.9MM **Privately Held**
SIC: 4961 2759 Air conditioning supply services; laser printing

(G-19692)
MAROUS BROTHERS CNSTR INC
1702 Joseph Lloyd Pkwy (44094-8028)
PHONE.................................440 951-3904
Fax: 440 951-3781

Adelbert Marous, *President*
Doug Richardson, *General Mgr*
Douglas Richardson, *General Mgr*
Vince Coughlin, *Superintendent*
Brian Dudich, *Superintendent*
EMP: 300
SQ FT: 22,000
SALES (est): 124.3MM **Privately Held**
WEB: www.marousbrothers.com
SIC: 1521 1751 New construction, single-family houses; carpentry work

(G-19693)
MOODY NAT CY WILLOUGHBY MT LLC
Also Called: Courtyard By Marriott
35103 Maplegrove Rd (44094-9698)
PHONE.................................440 530-1100
Fax: 440 530-1100
Chris Cornett, *General Mgr*
Dena Heinlein, *Manager*
EMP: 50
SALES: 950K **Privately Held**
SIC: 7011 Hotels

(G-19694)
MORRIS SCHNEIDER WITTSTADT LLC
35110 Euclid Ave Ste 2 (44094-4523)
PHONE.................................440 942-5168
Dean Talaganis, *Branch Mgr*
EMP: 28
SALES (corp-wide): 12MM **Privately Held**
SIC: 8111 Legal services
PA: Morris Schneider Wittstadt Llc
      120 Interstate North Pkwy
      Atlanta GA 30339
      678 298-2100

(G-19695)
NATIONAL METAL TRADING LLC
3950 Ben Hur Ave (44094-6371)
PHONE.................................440 487-9771
Ron Vaughn,
Frank Demilta,
EMP: 35
SQ FT: 5,000
SALES (est): 5.2MM **Privately Held**
WEB: www.demiltairon.com
SIC: 5051 Iron or steel flat products

(G-19696)
NELSON & BOLD INC
Also Called: Bold, E Luke MD PH D
36060 Euclid Ave Ste 201 (44094-4661)
PHONE.................................440 975-1422
Fax: 440 942-4790
Scott Nelson, *President*
EMP: 30
SALES (est): 745.9K **Privately Held**
SIC: 8011 5999 Offices & clinics of medical doctors; hearing aids

(G-19697)
NEUNDORFER INC
Also Called: Neundorfer Engineering Service
4590 Hamann Pkwy (44094-5691)
PHONE.................................440 942-8990
Fax: 440 942-6824
Michael Neundorfer, *CEO*
Jean Ockuly, *Vice Pres*
Conne Tuttle, *Vice Pres*
Steve Ostanek, *Human Res Mgr*
Maggie Zeller, *Manager*
EMP: 42
SQ FT: 38,000
SALES (est): 8.4MM **Privately Held**
WEB: www.neundorfer.com
SIC: 8711 3564 Pollution control engineering; precipitators, electrostatic

(G-19698)
NORTHWEST COUNTRY PLACE INC
9223 Amber Wood Dr (44094-9350)
PHONE.................................440 488-2700
Thomas A Armagno, *Branch Mgr*
EMP: 52 **Privately Held**
SIC: 8742 Management consulting services
PA: Northwest Country Place Inc
      9223 Amber Wood Dr
      Willoughby OH 44094

(G-19699)
OHIO BROACH & MACHINE COMPANY
35264 Topps Indus Pkwy (44094-4684)
PHONE.................................440 946-1040
Fax: 440 946-6475
Charles P Van De Motter, *CEO*
Christopher C Van De Motter, *President*
Neil Van De Motter, *Vice Pres*
Richard Van De Motter, *Vice Pres*
Pat Doptis, *QC Mgr*
▼ **EMP:** 34 **EST:** 1956
SQ FT: 52,000
SALES (est): 6.2MM **Privately Held**
WEB: www.ohiobroach.com
SIC: 3541 7699 3545 3599 Broaching machines; knife, saw & tool sharpening & repair; machine tool accessories; machine shop, jobbing & repair

(G-19700)
OHIO LIVING
Also Called: Breckenridge Village
36855 Ridge Rd (44094-4128)
PHONE.................................440 942-4342
Fax: 440 942-4150
Carrie McGlaughlin, *Opers Staff*
Jeannie Zuydhoek, *Branch Mgr*
Elaine Kuhl, *Manager*
Michael Baranouskas, *Director*
EMP: 400 **Privately Held**
WEB: www.oprs.org
SIC: 8361 Home for the aged
PA: Ohio Living
      1001 Kingsmill Pkwy
      Columbus OH 43229

(G-19701)
OHIO PAVING & CNSTR CO INC
38220 Willoughby Pkwy (44094-7583)
PHONE.................................440 975-8929
Fax: 440 975-9019
John Delillo, *President*
Deborah Handy, *Bookkeeper*
EMP: 35
SQ FT: 10,000
SALES (est): 5.2MM **Privately Held**
WEB: www.ohiopaving.com
SIC: 1771 Blacktop (asphalt) work

(G-19702)
PALMER EXPRESS INCORPORATED
Also Called: Willo Transportation
34799 Curtis Blvd Ste A (44095-4025)
PHONE.................................440 942-3333
Robert Palmer, *President*
EMP: 47
SQ FT: 500
SALES (est): 2.5MM **Privately Held**
SIC: 4151 4215 School buses; package delivery, vehicular

(G-19703)
PAULO PRODUCTS COMPANY
Also Called: American Brzing Div Paulo Pdts
4428 Hamann Pkwy (44094-5628)
PHONE.................................440 942-0153
Fax: 440 946-3091
Bob Muto, *Branch Mgr*
Jim Loveland, *Manager*
EMP: 38
SALES (corp-wide): 92.8MM **Privately Held**
WEB: www.paulo.com
SIC: 7692 1799 Brazing; coating of concrete structures with plastic
PA: Paulo Products Company
      5711 W Park Ave
      Saint Louis MO 63110
      314 647-7500

(G-19704)
PLATINUM RE PROFESSIONALS LLC
10 Public Sq (44094-7843)
PHONE.................................440 942-2100
Monica Wilson, *Office Mgr*
Sara Breese, *Director*
Steven Sears,
Mark Zervos, *Asst Broker*
Eric Barbee, *Real Est Agnt*
EMP: 42

SALES: 827K **Privately Held**
WEB: MyPlatinumRealEstate.com
SIC: 6531 Real estate agent, residential

(G-19705)
POWER-PACK CONVEYOR COMPANY
38363 Airport Pkwy (44094-7562)
PHONE.................................440 975-9955
Fax: 440 975-0505
Kevin Ensinger, *President*
James L Ensinger, *President*
Donnell Ensinger, *Exec VP*
Harry Cook, *VP Mfg*
Eric Ensinger, *CFO*
EMP: 25 **EST:** 1929
SQ FT: 48,000
SALES: 5.6MM **Privately Held**
WEB: www.power-packconveyor.com
SIC: 3535 5084 3531 Conveyors & conveying equipment; unit handling conveying systems; belt conveyor systems, general industrial use; bucket type conveyor systems; industrial machinery & equipment; road construction & maintenance machinery

(G-19706)
PSYCHIATRIC SOLUTIONS INC
35900 Euclid Ave (44094-4623)
PHONE.................................440 953-3000
Cynthia Danko, *Branch Mgr*
EMP: 137
SALES (corp-wide): 10.4B **Publicly Held**
SIC: 8011 8049 Psychiatric clinic; clinical psychologist
HQ: Psychiatric Solutions, Inc.
      6640 Carothers Pkwy # 500
      Franklin TN 37067
      615 312-5700

(G-19707)
RED OAK CAMP
Also Called: Red Barn
9057 Kirtland Chardon Rd (44094-5156)
PHONE.................................440 256-0716
Fax: 440 256-0716
Leonard K Roskos, *Director*
EMP: 40
SALES: 464.4K **Privately Held**
SIC: 7032 Youth camps

(G-19708)
REGAL CINEMAS INC
Also Called: Willoughby Commons 16
36655 Euclid Ave (44094-4450)
PHONE.................................440 975-8820
EMP: 35
SALES (corp-wide): 982.1MM **Privately Held**
WEB: www.regalcinemas.com
SIC: 7832 Motion picture theaters, except drive-in
HQ: Regal Cinemas, Inc.
      101 E Blount Ave Ste 100
      Knoxville TN 37920
      865 922-1123

(G-19709)
REMAX HOMESOURCE
3500 Kaiser Ct Ste 300 (44095)
PHONE.................................440 951-2500
Fax: 440 951-2502
Michael Sivo, *Partner*
Alan Benjamin, *Partner*
Phil Mann, *Software Dev*
EMP: 40
SALES (est): 1.3MM **Privately Held**
SIC: 6531 Real estate agent, residential

(G-19710)
RENTECH SOLUTIONS INC
4934 Campbell Rd Ste C (44094-3332)
PHONE.................................216 398-1111
Daniel E Collins, *President*
Todd Lochan, *Opers Mgr*
Todd Cochan, *Manager*
Catherine Hernandez, *Manager*
Michelle Martinez, *Manager*
EMP: 89
SQ FT: 4,000
SALES (est): 9.2MM **Privately Held**
SIC: 7359 Audio-visual equipment & supply rental

(G-19711)
RYNO 24 INC
Also Called: Eagle Protective Services
4429 Hamann Pkwy Frnt (44094-5627)
PHONE.................................440 946-7700
Fax: 440 946-7771
Stephen Tryon, *President*
William Tryon, *Vice Pres*
EMP: 47
SALES (est): 1.2MM **Privately Held**
WEB: www.eagle-protective.com
SIC: 7381 Security guard service

(G-19712)
SENIOR INDEPENDENCE ADULT
36855 Ridge Rd (44094-4128)
PHONE.................................440 954-8372
Tina Witt, *Branch Mgr*
EMP: 35
SALES (corp-wide): 2.7MM **Privately Held**
SIC: 8322 Adult day care center
PA: Senior Independence Adult Day Services
      717 Neil Ave
      Columbus OH 43215
      614 224-5344

(G-19713)
SIGNATURE HEALTH INC
Also Called: North Coast Center
38882 Mentor Ave (44094-7875)
PHONE.................................440 953-9999
Ryan Wood, *CFO*
Dawn Brumfield, *Human Res Dir*
Elizabeth Whitworth, *Hum Res Coord*
Paul Brickman, *Mktg Dir*
Kirstin Esch, *Psychologist*
EMP: 312
SALES (est): 9MM **Privately Held**
SIC: 8093 Mental health clinic, outpatient

(G-19714)
SIMA MARINE SALES INC (PA)
200 Forest Dr (44095-1504)
PHONE.................................440 269-3200
John Sima, *President*
Barbara Remley, *Corp Secy*
James C Sima, *Vice Pres*
Eleanor Sima, *Asst Sec*
EMP: 30
SQ FT: 15,000
SALES (est): 5.2MM **Privately Held**
SIC: 5551 4493 Motor boat dealers; marinas

(G-19715)
SNPJ RECREATION FARM
10946 Heath Rd (44094-5183)
PHONE.................................440 256-3423
Joseph Blotneck, *Admin Sec*
EMP: 25
SALES (est): 457.9K **Privately Held**
WEB: www.snpj.org
SIC: 7299 Banquet hall facilities

(G-19716)
STEWART TITLE COMPANY
4212 State Route 306 (44094-9248)
PHONE.................................440 520-7130
Matt Morris, *Branch Mgr*
EMP: 25
SALES (corp-wide): 1.9B **Publicly Held**
SIC: 6361 Real estate title insurance
HQ: Stewart Title Company
      1980 Post Oak Blvd Ste 80
      Houston TX 77056
      713 625-8100

(G-19717)
TECHNICAL ASSURANCE INC
38112 2nd St (44094-6107)
PHONE.................................440 953-3147
Fax: 440 953-2621
William Roess, *President*
James Solether, *Vice Pres*
Gregory Taylor, *Vice Pres*
David Bebout, *Opers Staff*
Glenn Burkey, *Engineer*
EMP: 50
SQ FT: 6,500

Willoughby - Lake County (G-19718)

SALES (est): 4.1MM **Privately Held**
WEB: www.technicalassurance.com
SIC: **7389** 8711 8744 1541 Building inspection service; engineering services; facilities support services; industrial buildings & warehouses; architectural engineering; computer facilities management

(G-19718)
TRAMZ HOTELS LLC
Also Called: Fairfield Inn
35110 Maplegrove Rd (44094-9692)
PHONE.................................440 975-9922
Fax: 440 975-9922
Craig Roback, *Vice Pres*
Hudson Victoria, *Sales Executive*
EMP: 51
SQ FT: 2,400
SALES (corp-wide): 27.2MM **Privately Held**
SIC: **7011** Hotels & motels
PA: Tramz Hotels, Llc
   31 Mountain Blvd Bldg U
   Warren NJ 07059
   908 753-7400

(G-19719)
TWO M PRECISION CO INC
Also Called: United Hydraulics
1747 Joseph Lloyd Pkwy # 3 (44094-8067)
PHONE.................................440 946-2120
Fax: 440 946-2120
Mate Brkic, *President*
Nate Brkic, *Vice Pres*
Frank Bortnick, *Purchasing*
Doris Brkic, *Treasurer*
EMP: 45
SQ FT: 35,000
SALES (est): 7.2MM **Privately Held**
WEB: www.twomprecision.com
SIC: **3599** 3569 7692 Machine shop, jobbing & repair; grinding castings for the trade; filter elements, fluid, hydraulic line; welding repair

(G-19720)
UNIVERSITY PRMRY CARE PRCTICES (HQ)
Also Called: University Hosp Hlth Sys Shake
4212 State Route 306 # 304 (44094-9258)
PHONE.................................440 946-7391
Fax: 440 946-7594
Michael Nochomitz, *President*
Phyllis Hall, *CFO*
Mary Ella Rohwer, *Controller*
Jeff Tomaszewski, *Marketing Staff*
Terri Stalker, *Office Mgr*
EMP: 26
SALES (est): 6.6MM
SALES (corp-wide): 2.3B **Privately Held**
SIC: **8011** Pediatrician
PA: University Hospitals Health System, Inc.
   3605 Warrensville Ctr Rd
   Shaker Heights OH 44122
   216 767-8900

(G-19721)
US MOLDING MACHINERY CO INC
38294 Pelton Rd (44094-7765)
PHONE.................................440 918-1701
Fax: 440 918-1720
Zac Cohen, *President*
Jerry Harper, *Vice Pres*
Robert Luck, *Vice Pres*
Bill Sprowls, *Vice Pres*
Roger Anderson, *Plant Engr*
EMP: 28
SQ FT: 12,500
SALES (est): 5.2MM **Privately Held**
WEB: www.usmolding.com
SIC: **3089** 7699 Injection molding of plastics; industrial equipment services

(G-19722)
VECTOR TECHNICAL INC
38033 Euclid Ave Ste T9 (44094-6162)
PHONE.................................440 946-8800
Tim Bleich, *President*
EMP: 110
SALES: 5MM **Privately Held**
WEB: www.vectortechnicalinc.com
SIC: **7361** Executive placement

(G-19723)
WILLO SECURITY INC (PA)
38230 Glenn Ave (44094-7808)
PHONE.................................440 953-9191
Fax: 216 918-6626
Raymond D Disanto, *President*
EMP: 32
SQ FT: 1,200
SALES (est): 7.4MM **Privately Held**
SIC: **7381** Security guard service

(G-19724)
WILLOUGHBY LODGING LLC
Also Called: Courtyard By Marriott
35103 Maplegrove Rd Fl 3 (44094-9698)
PHONE.................................440 530-1100
Ken Hiller, *Manager*
EMP: 25
SALES (corp-wide): 1.1MM **Privately Held**
SIC: **7011** Hotels & motels
PA: Willoughby Lodging Llc
   5966 Heisley Rd
   Mentor OH 44060
   440 701-1000

(G-19725)
WILLOUGHBY MONTESSORI DAY SCHL
5543 Som Center Rd (44094-4281)
PHONE.................................440 942-5602
Fax: 440 942-4533
Kathy LI, *Director*
EMP: 30
SQ FT: 10,000
SALES (est): 890K **Privately Held**
SIC: **8351** Preschool center; group day care center; Montessori child development center

(G-19726)
WOODHILL SUPPLY INC (PA)
4665 Beidler Rd (44094-4645)
PHONE.................................440 269-1100
Fax: 440 269-1027
Arnold Kaufman, *President*
Scott Densmore, *Buyer*
Bruce Silverberg, *Purchasing*
Bruce Shaw, *Controller*
Ann Norris, *Credit Mgr*
EMP: 47 EST: 1958
SQ FT: 150,000
SALES: 13MM **Privately Held**
WEB: www.woodhillsupply.com
SIC: **5074** Plumbing fittings & supplies

(G-19727)
WRG SERVICES INC
38585 Apollo Pkwy (44094-7793)
P.O. Box 380 (44096-0380)
PHONE.................................440 942-8650
Michael J Stevenson, *CEO*
James Penza, *President*
Heather Napper, *Accounts Mgr*
Steve Farley, *Sales Executive*
Greg Randall, *Manager*
EMP: 52
SQ FT: 26,000
SALES (est): 2.8MM **Privately Held**
WEB: www.wrgservices.com
SIC: **7378** Computer maintenance & repair; computer & data processing equipment repair/maintenance; computer peripheral equipment repair & maintenance

Willoughby Hills
Lake County

(G-19728)
ANIMAL HOSPITAL INC
2735 Som Center Rd (44094-9121)
PHONE.................................440 946-2800
Fax: 440 946-9853
Deborah Dennis, *President*
Dr J S Murray, *President*
Kelli Kerwin, *Financial Exec*
Jennifer Johnston, *Associate*
EMP: 25
SALES (est): 3.2MM **Privately Held**
WEB: www.animalhospitalinc.com
SIC: **0742** Veterinarian, animal specialties

(G-19729)
CITY OF WILLOUGHBY HILLS
Also Called: Fire Department
35455 Chardon Rd (44094-9195)
PHONE.................................440 942-7207
Fax: 440 975-3534
Robert Disanto, *Chief*
EMP: 35 **Privately Held**
WEB: www.willoughbyhills.net
SIC: **9224** 8322 ; hotline
PA: City Of Willoughby Hills
   35405 Chardon Rd
   Willoughby Hills OH 44094
   440 942-9111

(G-19730)
GOLDBERG COMPANIES INC
Also Called: Pine Ridge Valley Apartments
2252 Par Ln (44094-2923)
PHONE.................................440 944-8656
Fax: 440 944-2369
Dennis M Bush, *Vice Pres*
Christine Dukowski, *Manager*
EMP: 28
SALES (corp-wide): 17.5MM **Privately Held**
WEB: www.goldbergcompanies.com
SIC: **6512** 6531 Commercial & industrial building operation; real estate agents & managers
PA: Goldberg Companies, Inc.
   25101 Chagrin Blvd # 300
   Beachwood OH 44122
   216 831-6100

(G-19731)
KAVAL-LEVINE MANAGEMENT CO
34500 Chardon Rd Ste 5 (44094-8239)
PHONE.................................440 944-5402
Fax: 216 781-6652
Marcie Levine, *President*
EMP: 25
SALES (est): 2.6MM **Privately Held**
SIC: **6531** Real estate managers

(G-19732)
MICRO PRODUCTS CO INC
26653 Curtiss Wright Pkwy (44092-2832)
PHONE.................................440 943-0258
Fax: 440 943-1599
Arthur Anton, *President*
Reese Armstrong, *Safety Mgr*
Scott Tracy, *Engineer*
Frank Roddy, *CFO*
Debbie Rubble, *Accountant*
EMP: 70 EST: 1981
SQ FT: 10,000
SALES (est): 3.7MM
SALES (corp-wide): 1.1B **Privately Held**
WEB: www.swagelok.com
SIC: **3471** 7389 Plating & polishing; grinding, precision: commercial or industrial
PA: Swagelok Company
   29500 Solon Rd
   Solon OH 44139
   440 248-4600

(G-19733)
PRIMEHALTH WNS HLTH SPECIALIST
35040 Chardon Rd Ste 205 (44094-9004)
PHONE.................................440 918-4630
Fax: 440 918-4632
Cynthia Moore-Heardy, *CEO*
EMP: 30
SALES (est): 1.7MM **Privately Held**
SIC: **8011** Obstetrician

(G-19734)
S & P SOLUTIONS INC
35000 Chardon Rd Ste 110 (44094-9018)
PHONE.................................440 918-9111
Fax: 440 918-1429
Gary Bates, *President*
Cathy Brankar, *Finance Dir*
Holly Corrao, *Office Mgr*
Donna Silvaroli, *Recruiter*
EMP: 130
SQ FT: 8,500

SALES (est): 11.4MM **Privately Held**
WEB: www.sps-solutions.com
SIC: **7379** 5734 8243 5045 Data processing consultant; computer software & accessories; operator training, computer; computers, peripherals & software

(G-19735)
SOUTH EAST CHEVROLET CO
2810 Bishop Rd (44092-2604)
PHONE.................................440 585-9300
Patt Obrien, *President*
EMP: 42
SQ FT: 48,000
SALES (est): 7.7MM **Privately Held**
SIC: **5511** 7515 7513 5012 Automobiles, new & used; passenger car leasing; truck rental & leasing, no drivers; automobiles & other motor vehicles

Willow Wood
Lawrence County

(G-19736)
MANNON PIPELINE LLC
9160 State Route 378 (45696-9014)
PHONE.................................740 643-1534
Darren Mannon,
EMP: 39 EST: 2010
SALES (est): 5.9MM **Privately Held**
SIC: **1623** Pipeline construction

Willowick
Lake County

(G-19737)
BAUR LEO CENTURY 21 REALTY
32801 Vine St Ste D (44095-3380)
PHONE.................................440 585-2300
Fax: 440 944-0046
Tim Baur, *Owner*
Eileen Baur, *Broker*
Joan Cameron, *Broker*
Christopher Scalese, *Broker*
Steve Baird, *Real Est Agnt*
EMP: 26
SALES: 1.4MM **Privately Held**
SIC: **6531** Real estate agent, residential

(G-19738)
CITY OF WILLOWICK
Also Called: Manary Pool
30100 Arnold Rd (44095-4961)
PHONE.................................440 944-1575
Martin Gusauskas, *Manager*
EMP: 70 **Privately Held**
WEB: www.cityofwillowick.com
SIC: **7999** Swimming pool, non-membership
PA: City Of Willowick
   30435 Lake Shore Blvd
   Willowick OH 44095
   440 585-1234

(G-19739)
EXCALIBUR AUTO BODY INC (PA)
Also Called: Excalibur Body & Frame
30520 Lakeland Blvd (44095-5202)
PHONE.................................440 942-5550
Fax: 440 942-8685
Mitchell Rudolph, *Principal*
EMP: 32
SQ FT: 14,000
SALES (est): 4.4MM **Privately Held**
SIC: **7532** Body shop, automotive; paint shop, automotive

Wilmington
Clinton County

(G-19740)
797 ELKS GOLF CLUB INC
2593 E Us Highway 22 3 (45177-8947)
P.O. Box 469 (45177-0469)
PHONE.................................937 382-2666
John Wynn, *Superintendent*

GEOGRAPHIC SECTION
Wilmington - Clinton County (G-19763)

Robert Holmes, *Treasurer*
David McCune, *Office Mgr*
EMP: 27
SQ FT: 1,152
SALES (est): 740.3K **Privately Held**
SIC: 7992 7997 7999 5941 Public golf courses; golf club, membership; golf driving range; golf goods & equipment

(G-19741)
ABX AIR INC (HQ)
145 Hunter Dr (45177-9550)
PHONE 937 382-5591
Fax: 937 382-0896
Joe Hete, *CEO*
John Starkovich, *President*
James E Bushman, *Principal*
James H Carey, *Principal*
Jeffrey A Dominick, *Principal*
EMP: 500
SQ FT: 37,000
SALES (est): 152.8MM **Publicly Held**
SIC: 4513 5088 4581 8299 Letter delivery, private air; package delivery, private air; parcel delivery, private air; aircraft & parts; aircraft servicing & repairing; flying instruction

(G-19742)
ABX AIR INC
Abx Equipment and Facility Svc
145 Hunter Dr (45177-9550)
PHONE 937 366-2282
Jim Osborne, *Branch Mgr*
EMP: 849 **Publicly Held**
SIC: 4513 Letter delivery, private air
HQ: Abx Air, Inc.
145 Hunter Dr
Wilmington OH 45177
937 382-5591

(G-19743)
AIR TRANSPORT SVCS GROUP INC (PA)
Also Called: ATSG
145 Hunter Dr (45177-9550)
P.O. Box 966 (45177-0966)
PHONE 937 382-5591
Fax: 937 382-3935
Randy D Rademacher, *Ch of Bd*
Joseph C Hete, *President*
Richard F Corrado, *COO*
W Joseph Payne, *Senior VP*
Steve Janasov, *Safety Dir*
EMP: 50
SQ FT: 310,000
SALES: 1B **Publicly Held**
SIC: 4513 Air courier services

(G-19744)
AIRBORNE MAINT ENGRG SVCS INC
1111 Airport Rd (45177-8904)
PHONE 937 366-2559
Brady Price, *Branch Mgr*
Christy Palmer, *Admin Asst*
EMP: 502 **Publicly Held**
SIC: 7699 5088 Aircraft & heavy equipment repair services; aircraft & parts
HQ: Airborne Maintenance And Engineering Services, Inc.
145 Hunter Dr
Wilmington OH 45177

(G-19745)
AIRBORNE MAINT ENGRG SVCS INC (HQ)
145 Hunter Dr (45177-9550)
PHONE 937 382-5591
Brady Templeton, *President*
Scott Glasser, *President*
Joseph Ryan, *COO*
Gary Stover, *Vice Pres*
Richard Ratliff, *Project Mgr*
EMP: 86
SALES (est): 91.1MM **Publicly Held**
SIC: 7699 5088 Aircraft & heavy equipment repair services; aircraft & parts

(G-19746)
AMES MATERIAL SERVICES INC
145 Hunter Dr (45177-9550)
P.O. Box 966 (45177-0966)
PHONE 937 382-5591
Joseph Hete, *President*

John Graver, *President*
Trisha Richards, *Controller*
Lynn Bare, *Accounts Mgr*
EMP: 800
SALES (est): 73MM **Publicly Held**
WEB: www.abxair.com
SIC: 4513 Air courier services
PA: Air Transport Services Group, Inc.
145 Hunter Dr
Wilmington OH 45177

(G-19747)
CHAMPONS IN MAKING DAYCARE LLC
160 Park Dr (45177-2041)
PHONE 937 728-4886
Tamara Rollins, *Director*
Hope Wilson-Belle,
EMP: 28 **EST:** 2006
SALES (est): 397.1K **Privately Held**
SIC: 8351 Group day care center

(G-19748)
CITY OF WILMINGTON
Also Called: Wilmington City Cab Service
260 Charles St (45177-2883)
PHONE 937 382-7961
Fax: 937 382-2301
Jeanie Foster, *Branch Mgr*
EMP: 45 **Privately Held**
WEB: www.ci.wilmington.oh.us
SIC: 4111 9111 Airport transportation; mayors' offices
PA: City Of Wilmington
69 N South St
Wilmington OH 45177
937 382-1880

(G-19749)
CLINTON COUNTY BOARD OF
Also Called: Clinton County Offices
4425 State Route 730 (45177-8661)
PHONE 937 382-7519
Fax: 937 382-6676
Kyle Lewis, *Superintendent*
EMP: 27
SALES (est): 1.4MM **Privately Held**
SIC: 8322 8093 Referral service for personal & social problems; specialty outpatient clinics

(G-19750)
CLINTON COUNTY COMMUNITY ACTN (PA)
789 N Nelson Ave (45177-8348)
P.O. Box 32 (45177-0032)
PHONE 937 382-8365
Ray Camp, *Comptroller*
Doug Tucker, *Manager*
Dean Knapp, *Director*
Stella Cramer, *Director*
Susan Stai, *Director*
EMP: 65
SQ FT: 11,782
SALES: 4.9MM **Privately Held**
SIC: 8399 Community action agency

(G-19751)
CLINTON COUNTY COMMUNITY ACTN
Also Called: Clinton County Head Start
789 N Nelson Ave (45177-8348)
P.O. Box 32 (45177-0032)
PHONE 937 382-5624
Fax: 937 383-0292
Carole Erdman, *Director*
EMP: 32
SALES (corp-wide): 4.9MM **Privately Held**
SIC: 8399 8351 Community action agency; head start center, except in conjunction with school
PA: Clinton County Community Action Program, Inc
789 N Nelson Ave
Wilmington OH 45177
937 382-8365

(G-19752)
CLINTON COUNTY DEPT JOBS/FMLY
Also Called: Job & Family Svcs Clinton Cnty
1025 S South St Ste 200 (45177-2788)
PHONE 937 382-0963
Fax: 937 382-7039

Mike Cooper, *Manager*
Bart Barber, *Director*
EMP: 60 **Privately Held**
SIC: 9441 6371 Administration of social & manpower programs; ; pension, health & welfare funds

(G-19753)
CLINTON MEMORIAL HOSPITAL (PA)
610 W Mn St (45177)
P.O. Box 600 (45177-0600)
PHONE 937 382-6611
Fax: 937 382-9254
Mark Dooley, *President*
Bradley Mabry, *COO*
Bob Curtis, *Maint Spvr*
Sheila Rose, *Buyer*
Bradley Boggus, *CFO*
EMP: 630 **EST:** 1951
SQ FT: 200,000
SALES (est): 66.1MM **Privately Held**
WEB: www.cmhregional.com
SIC: 8062 General medical & surgical hospitals

(G-19754)
CLINTON MEMORIAL HOSPITAL
Also Called: Clinton Memorial Fmly Hlth Ctr
825 W Locust St (45177-2118)
PHONE 937 383-3402
Fax: 937 383-0610
Greg Taulbee, *Principal*
David Hockman, *Manager*
Julie Wickline, *Manager*
EMP: 41
SALES (est): 2.2MM
SALES (corp-wide): 66.1MM **Privately Held**
WEB: www.cmhregional.com
SIC: 6733 8011 8093 Trusts; general & family practice, physician/surgeon; specialty outpatient clinics
PA: Clinton Memorial Hospital
610 W Mn St
Wilmington OH 45177
937 382-6611

(G-19755)
COMMUNITY ACTION PROGRAM INC
789 N Nelson Ave (45177-8348)
P.O. Box 32 (45177-0032)
PHONE 937 382-0225
Fax: 937 382-0390
Adam Morris, *Marketing Staff*
Sara Colegate, *Manager*
Madelyn Caplinger, *Exec Dir*
Alberta Jones, *Exec Dir*
Dean Knapp, *Administration*
EMP: 85
SALES (est): 1.6MM **Privately Held**
SIC: 8399 Community action agency

(G-19756)
COMMUNITY CARE HOSPICE
1669 Rombach Ave (45177-1965)
P.O. Box 123 (45177-0123)
PHONE 937 382-5400
Fax: 937 383-3898
Pam Skinner, *Office Admin*
Patricia Settlemyre, *Administration*
EMP: 43
SALES: 2.2MM **Privately Held**
SIC: 8069 Specialty hospitals, except psychiatric

(G-19757)
COMPTON METAL PRODUCTS INC
416 Steele Rd (45177-9332)
PHONE 937 382-2403
Fax: 937 382-2403
James Compton, *President*
Kandi Compton, *Admin Sec*
EMP: 82
SQ FT: 2,000
SALES (est): 2.4MM **Privately Held**
SIC: 7699 3599 7692 Engine repair & replacement, non-automotive; machine shop, jobbing & repair; welding repair

(G-19758)
COUNTY OF CLINTON
Also Called: Clinton County Childrens Svcs
1025 S South St Ste 300 (45177-2788)
PHONE 937 382-2449
Fax: 937 382-1165
John Hosler, *Director*
EMP: 40 **Privately Held**
WEB: www.clincohd.com
SIC: 8322 Child related social services
PA: County Of Clinton
46 S South St Rm 213
Wilmington OH 45177
937 382-2103

(G-19759)
COUNTY OF CLINTON
Also Called: Clinton County Highway Dept
1326 Fife Ave (45177-2462)
PHONE 937 382-2078
Fax: 937 382-5318
Jeffrey Linkous, *Principal*
Christian Dunlap, *Assistant*
EMP: 40 **Privately Held**
WEB: www.clincohd.com
SIC: 1611 Highway & street maintenance
PA: County Of Clinton
46 S South St Rm 213
Wilmington OH 45177
937 382-2103

(G-19760)
DASH LOGISTICS INC
259 Olinger Cir (45177-2484)
PHONE 937 382-9110
Tim Williams, *President*
Steve Barton, *Admin Sec*
EMP: 30
SALES (est): 2.8MM **Privately Held**
SIC: 7389 Courier or messenger service

(G-19761)
EQUIPMENT MGT SVC & REPR INC
Also Called: Emsar
270 Davids Dr (45177-2491)
PHONE 937 383-1052
Fax: 937 383-0022
Renee Lapine, *President*
Janet Fife, *Materials Dir*
Conor Boland, *Accounts Mgr*
Donna Burnett, *CTO*
Joseph Whalen, *Info Tech Mgr*
▲ **EMP:** 27
SQ FT: 10,000
SALES (est): 6.9MM **Privately Held**
WEB: www.emsar.com
SIC: 7699 Medical equipment repair, non-electric

(G-19762)
FERNO-WASHINGTON INC (PA)
70 Weil Way (45177-9300)
PHONE 877 733-0911
Fax: 937 382-6569
Elroy Bourgraf, *Ch of Bd*
Joseph Bourgraf, *President*
Becky Jenkins, *General Mgr*
Silvia Vancova, *Managing Dir*
Ron Beymer, *Exec VP*
◆ **EMP:** 151 **EST:** 1955
SQ FT: 212,000
SALES (est): 93.5MM **Privately Held**
SIC: 5047 Medical equipment & supplies

(G-19763)
G & J PEPSI-COLA BOTTLERS INC
3500 Progress Way (45177-8974)
PHONE 937 393-5744
Fax: 937 393-5745
Jim Malone, *Branch Mgr*
EMP: 25
SALES (corp-wide): 475.8MM **Privately Held**
WEB: www.gjpepsi.com
SIC: 4225 General warehousing
PA: G & J Pepsi-Cola Bottlers Inc
9435 Waterstone Blvd # 390
Cincinnati OH 45249
513 785-6060

Wilmington - Clinton County (G-19764)

(G-19764)
JET MINTENANCE CONSULTING CORP
1113 Airport Rd Ste Jmcc (45177-8904)
PHONE...................................937 205-2406
Joseph Merry, *President*
Stephen Huffman, *Manager*
EMP: 25
SALES: 500K **Privately Held**
SIC: 7363 8249 Pilot service, aviation; aviation school

(G-19765)
LABORATORY CORPORATION AMERICA
630 W Main St (45177-2170)
PHONE...................................937 383-6964
Brian Ondulick, *Branch Mgr*
EMP: 25 **Publicly Held**
SIC: 8071 Testing laboratories
HQ: Laboratory Corporation Of America
358 S Main St Ste 458
Burlington NC 27215
336 229-1127

(G-19766)
LGSTX SERVICES INC
145 Hunter Dr (45177-9550)
PHONE...................................866 931-2337
Gary Stover, *President*
Judy Anderson, *Managing Dir*
Kevin Yeary, *Regional Mgr*
Bladimir Chamorro, *Area Mgr*
Nicholas Reed, *Opers Spvr*
EMP: 68
SALES (est): 1.1MM **Publicly Held**
SIC: 4513 Air courier services
PA: Air Transport Services Group, Inc.
145 Hunter Dr
Wilmington OH 45177

(G-19767)
LIBERTY CAPITAL INC (PA)
3435 Airborne Rd Ste B (45177-8951)
PHONE...................................937 382-1000
James R Powell, *President*
Fiona M Carthy, *Vice Pres*
Isabelle Cochrane, *Vice Pres*
Jeanna Francis, *Vice Pres*
Deborah Lauer, *Vice Pres*
EMP: 71
SALES: 30.5MM **Privately Held**
SIC: 6035 Federal savings & loan associations

(G-19768)
LIBERTY SAVINGS BANK FSB (HQ)
2251 Rombach Ave (45177-1995)
P.O. Box 1000 (45177-1000)
PHONE...................................937 382-1000
Fax: 937 382-6255
James R Powell, *Ch of Bd*
John H Powell, *Vice Ch Bd*
Robert E Reed, *President*
Fred Blume, *Principal*
Beerling Darlene, *COO*
EMP: 113
SQ FT: 50,000
SALES: 28.1MM
SALES (corp-wide): 30.5MM **Privately Held**
WEB: www.liberty-direct.com
SIC: 6035 Federal savings banks
PA: Liberty Capital, Inc.
3435 Airborne Rd Ste B
Wilmington OH 45177
937 382-1000

(G-19769)
LOWES HOME CENTERS LLC
1175 Rombach Ave (45177-1940)
PHONE...................................937 383-7000
Fax: 937 383-4204
Sam Segrist, *Office Mgr*
Darryl Allen, *Branch Mgr*
EMP: 150
SALES (corp-wide): 68.6B **Publicly Held**
SIC: 5211 5031 5722 5064 Home centers; building materials, exterior; building materials, interior; household appliance stores; electrical appliances, television & radio
HQ: Lowe's Home Centers, Llc
1605 Curtis Bridge Rd
Wilkesboro NC 28697
336 658-4000

(G-19770)
LT LAND DEVELOPMENT LLC
94 N South St Ste A (45177-2097)
PHONE...................................937 382-0072
Ralph Larry Roberts, *Mng Member*
Terri Roberts,
EMP: 30 EST: 2008
SALES (est): 1.4MM **Privately Held**
SIC: 6552 6531 Subdividers & developers; real estate leasing & rentals

(G-19771)
M C TRUCKING COMPANY LLC
Also Called: Melvin Stone
228 Melvin Rd (45177-8750)
P.O. Box 158, Sabina (45169-0158)
PHONE...................................937 584-2486
Bob Lambers, *Manager*
Dennis Garrison,
EMP: 40 EST: 1951
SQ FT: 2,000
SALES (est): 3.5MM **Privately Held**
SIC: 4212 Local trucking, without storage

(G-19772)
MB FINANCIAL INC
2251 Rombach Ave (45177-1995)
PHONE...................................937 283-2027
EMP: 94 **Publicly Held**
SIC: 8742 6162 6029 Financial consultant; mortgage bankers & correspondents; commercial banks
PA: Mb Financial, Inc.
800 W Madison St
Chicago IL 60607

(G-19773)
MENTAL HEALTH & RECOVERY CTR (PA)
Also Called: Crisis Counseling Center
953 S South St (45177-2921)
PHONE...................................937 383-3031
Phyllis Mitchell, *Director*
EMP: 25
SQ FT: 5,200
SALES: 5.3K **Privately Held**
WEB: www.mhrccc.org
SIC: 8093 8322 8069 Alcohol clinic, outpatient; drug clinic, outpatient; general counseling services; drug addiction rehabilitation hospital

(G-19774)
NATIONAL WEATHER SERVICE
Also Called: Ohio River Forecast
1901 S State Route 134 (45177-9708)
PHONE...................................937 383-0031
Fax: 937 383-0033
Ken Haydu, *Manager*
EMP: 44 **Publicly Held**
SIC: 8999 9611 7389 Weather forecasting; administration of general economic programs; ; music & broadcasting services
HQ: National Weather Service
1325 E West Hwy
Silver Spring MD 20910

(G-19775)
PC CONNECTION INC
3336 Progress Way Bldg 11 (45177-8928)
PHONE...................................937 382-4800
Fax: 937 382-4040
Angie Hargett, *Controller*
Gretchen Myers, *Human Res Mgr*
Rob Debeau, *Sales Mgr*
Faith Dungan, *Office Mgr*
John Moran, *Manager*
EMP: 175
SALES (corp-wide): 2.9B **Publicly Held**
SIC: 4226 5045 Special warehousing & storage; computers, peripherals & software
PA: Pc Connection, Inc.
730 Milford Rd
Merrimack NH 03054
603 683-2000

(G-19776)
PC CONNECTION SALES CORP
2870 Old State 1 (45177)
PHONE...................................937 382-4800
John Moran, *Manager*
EMP: 125
SALES (corp-wide): 2.9B **Publicly Held**
SIC: 4225 5961 General warehousing & storage; computers & peripheral equipment, mail order
HQ: Pc Connection Sales Corp
730 Milford Rd
Merrimack NH 03054
603 423-2000

(G-19777)
PC CONNECTION SERVICES
Also Called: Distribution Center
2870 Old State Route 73 # 1 (45177-8997)
PHONE...................................937 382-4800
EMP: 148
SALES (est): 47.7MM **Privately Held**
SIC: 7379 Computer Related Services

(G-19778)
PEOPLES BANK
48 N South St (45177-2212)
PHONE...................................937 382-1441
John Limbert, *President*
EMP: 200
SALES (corp-wide): 182.1MM **Publicly Held**
SIC: 6021 National commercial banks
HQ: Peoples Bank
138 Putnam St
Marietta OH 45750
740 373-3155

(G-19779)
PREMIER FEEDS LLC
238 Melvin Rd (45177-8750)
PHONE...................................937 584-2411
Chris Meter, *Controller*
John Heinz, *Mktg Dir*
John Haynes, *Manager*
EMP: 25
SALES (corp-wide): 16.2MM **Privately Held**
SIC: 5191 Feed
HQ: Premier Feeds, Llc
292 N Howard St
Sabina OH 45169
937 584-2411

(G-19780)
R+L PRAMOUNT TRNSP SYSTEMS INC
Also Called: RI Global Services
600 Gilliam Rd (45177-9089)
P.O. Box 271 (45177-0271)
PHONE...................................937 382-1494
Michael Shroyer, *President*
Ralph L Roberts, *Vice Pres*
Robby L Roberts, *Vice Pres*
Tom Roberts, *Vice Pres*
Janielle Runyon, *Accountant*
EMP: 400
SALES (est): 27.7MM **Privately Held**
WEB: www.rlcarriers.com
SIC: 4213 Trucking, except local
PA: R & L Carriers, Inc.
600 Gilliam Rd
Wilmington OH 45177

(G-19781)
RCHP - WILMINGTON LLC (PA)
Also Called: Clinton Memorial Hospital
610 W Main St (45177-2125)
P.O. Box 600 (45177-0600)
PHONE...................................937 382-6611
Greg Nielsen, *CEO*
Marcy Hawley, *Chairman*
James Reynolds, *Chairman*
Mark Rembert, *Vice Chairman*
Eric Jost, *CFO*
EMP: 72
SALES: 78.4MM **Privately Held**
SIC: 8062 8361 General medical & surgical hospitals; rehabilitation center, residential: health care incidental

(G-19782)
RENAL LIFE LINK INC
Also Called: Willow Dialysis Cntr
1675 Alex Dr (45177-2446)
PHONE...................................937 383-3338
Fax: 937 383-3631
Angela Parkins, *Branch Mgr*
EMP: 25 **Publicly Held**
WEB: www.davita.com
SIC: 8092 Kidney dialysis centers
HQ: Renal Life Link, Inc.
2000 16th St
Denver CO 80202
253 280-9501

(G-19783)
RLR INVESTMENTS LLC
600 Gilliam Rd (45177-9089)
PHONE...................................937 382-1494
Dustin Owen, *Project Mgr*
James S Wachs,
EMP: 100
SALES (est): 17.3MM **Privately Held**
SIC: 4222 Warehousing, cold storage or refrigerated

(G-19784)
ROSE & DOBYNS AN OHIO PARTNR (PA)
97 N South St (45177-1644)
PHONE...................................937 382-2838
Fax: 937 382-7748
Gordon Rose, *Partner*
Michael Campbell, *Partner*
J Michael Dobyns, *Partner*
Richard Federle Jr, *Partner*
John Porter, *Partner*
EMP: 68
SALES (est): 4.9MM **Privately Held**
WEB: www.rosedobynslaw.com
SIC: 8111 General practice attorney, lawyer

(G-19785)
S & S MANAGEMENT INC
Also Called: Holiday Inn
155 Holiday Dr (45177-8763)
PHONE...................................937 382-5858
Fax: 937 382-0457
Bryan Powell, *General Mgr*
Tonya Fausnaugh, *General Mgr*
EMP: 25
SALES (est): 1.1MM
SALES (corp-wide): 8.6MM **Privately Held**
SIC: 7011 Hotels & motels
PA: S & S Management Inc
550 Folkerth Ave 100
Sidney OH 45365
937 498-9645

(G-19786)
SABER HEALTHCARE GROUP LLC
Also Called: Wilmington Nursing
75 Hale St (45177-2104)
PHONE...................................937 382-1621
Fax: 937 383-1215
Brian Hill, *Administration*
EMP: 36
SALES (corp-wide): 68.5MM **Privately Held**
SIC: 8051 Skilled nursing care facilities
PA: Saber Healthcare Group, L.L.C.
26691 Richmond Rd Frnt
Bedford OH 44146
216 292-5706

(G-19787)
SEWELL MOTOR EXPRESS CO (PA)
370 Davids Dr (45177-2424)
PHONE...................................937 382-3847
Fax: 937 382-7602
Janet Sewell, *CEO*
Jay Sewell, *President*
Leslie Williams, *Vice Pres*
EMP: 70 EST: 1921
SQ FT: 90,000
SALES (est): 9.9MM **Privately Held**
WEB: www.sewellmotorexpress.com
SIC: 4213 4212 Contract haulers; local trucking, without storage

(G-19788)
STOKES FRUIT FARM
3182 Center Rd (45177-9490)
PHONE...................................937 382-4004
Dale Stokes, *Owner*
EMP: 40

GEOGRAPHIC SECTION

Wintersville - Jefferson County (G-19809)

SALES (est): 1.6MM **Privately Held**
SIC: **0171** 0115 0111 Raspberry farm; corn; wheat

(G-19789)
SUNRISE COOPERATIVE INC
1425 Rombach Ave (45177-1946)
P.O. Box 512 (45177-0512)
PHONE.....................937 382-1633
Steve Haines, *Branch Mgr*
EMP: 28
SALES (corp-wide): 56.3MM **Privately Held**
SIC: **5191** Feed
PA: Sunrise Cooperative, Inc.
2025 W State St Ste A
Fremont OH 43420
419 332-6468

(G-19790)
TECHNICOLOR THOMSON GROUP
Also Called: Technicolor Entertainment Svcs
3418 Progress Way (45177-8952)
PHONE.....................937 383-6000
Fax: 937 383-6095
Cheryl Stone, *Human Res Dir*
Tony Butcher, *Business Anlyst*
Tim Burke, *Manager*
EMP: 250
SALES (corp-wide): 63.6MM **Privately Held**
WEB: www.technicolor.com
SIC: **7819** 7822 7829 5043 Video tape or disk reproduction; developing & printing of commercial motion picture film; motion picture & tape distribution; motion picture distribution services; photographic equipment & supplies
HQ: Technicolor Thomson Group, Inc
2233 N Ontario St Ste 300
Burbank CA 91504
818 260-3600

(G-19791)
UNITED PARCEL SERVICE INC OH
Also Called: UPS
2500 S Us Highway 68 (45177-8698)
PHONE.....................937 382-0658
Dan Fraley, *VP Sls/Mktg*
Tom Holback, *Sales/Mktg Dir*
Dave Bartko, *Manager*
Mark Moscinski, *Manager*
EMP: 158
SALES (corp-wide): 65.8B **Publicly Held**
WEB: www.martrac.com
SIC: **4215** Package delivery, vehicular
HQ: United Parcel Service, Inc. (Oh)
55 Glenlake Pkwy
Atlanta GA 30328
404 828-6000

(G-19792)
VERIZON NORTH INC
215 E Main St (45177-2312)
P.O. Box 769 (45177-0769)
PHONE.....................937 382-6961
Christina A Chamberlain, *Branch Mgr*
EMP: 58
SALES (corp-wide): 126B **Publicly Held**
SIC: **4813** Telephone communication, except radio
HQ: Verizon North Inc
140 West St
New York NY 10007
212 395-1000

(G-19793)
WILMINGTN NURSNG/REHAB RESDIDN
75 Hale St (45177-2104)
PHONE.....................937 382-1621
Tony Deaton, *Administration*
Jenny Mason, *Administration*
EMP: 100
SQ FT: 15,000
SALES (est): 3.6MM **Privately Held**
SIC: **8051** Skilled nursing care facilities

(G-19794)
WILMINGTON IRON AND MET CO INC
2149 S Us Highway 68 (45177-8629)
PHONE.....................937 382-3867
Fax: 937 382-3860
Robert Raizk, *President*
Dennis Hayes, *Vice Pres*
Penny Fouch, *Accountant*
EMP: 25
SQ FT: 2,500
SALES (est): 6.3MM **Privately Held**
SIC: **5093** Ferrous metal scrap & waste; nonferrous metals scrap

(G-19795)
WILMINGTON MEDICAL ASSOCIATES
1184 W Locust St (45177-2009)
PHONE.....................937 382-1616
Fax: 937 382-8781
Thomas Neville MD, *President*
Tracy Coomer, *Administration*
Mary A Merling, *Pediatrics*
EMP: 65
SQ FT: 10,000
SALES (est): 5.8MM **Privately Held**
SIC: **8011** General & family practice, physician/surgeon; pediatrician

(G-19796)
WRIGHT EXECUTIVE HT LTD PARTNR
123 Gano Rd (45177-8848)
PHONE.....................937 283-3200
Gray Campbell, *Manager*
EMP: 128 **Privately Held**
WEB: www.hwdaytonfairborn.com
SIC: **7011** Hotels & motels
PA: Wright Executive Hotel Limited Partnership
2800 Presidential Dr
Beavercreek OH 45324

Wilmot
Stark County

(G-19797)
AMISH DOOR INC (PA)
Also Called: Amish Door Restaurant
1210 Winesburg St (44689)
P.O. Box 215 (44689-0215)
PHONE.....................330 359-5464
Fax: 330 359-7159
Milo Miller, *President*
Eric Gerber, *Vice Pres*
Yvonne Torrence, *Treasurer*
Katherine Miller, *Shareholder*
EMP: 294
SQ FT: 7,500
SALES (est): 17.4MM **Privately Held**
WEB: www.amishdoor.com
SIC: **5947** 5812 7011 2051 Gift shop; restaurant, family: independent; hotels & motels; bread, cake & related products

Winchester
Adams County

(G-19798)
1ST STOP INC (PA)
Also Called: Cantrell's Motel
18856 State Route 136 (45697-9793)
P.O. Box 175 (45697-0175)
PHONE.....................937 695-0318
Fax: 937 695-1353
Robert Cantrell, *President*
Mike Gregory, *Info Tech Mgr*
Chad Moore, *Technology*
Skip Tilton, *Technology*
Linda Cantrell, *Admin Sec*
EMP: 30
SQ FT: 12,000
SALES (est): 39.3MM **Privately Held**
SIC: **5411** 7011 Convenience stores, independent; motels

(G-19799)
ADAMS & BROWN COUNTIES ECONOMI
Also Called: Adams Brown Wthrzation Program
19211 Main St (45697)
P.O. Box 188 (45697-0188)
PHONE.....................937 695-0316
Gary Tabor, *Admin Director*
EMP: 30
SALES (corp-wide): 10.4MM **Privately Held**
SIC: **8399** Community action agency
PA: Adams & Brown Counties Economic Opportunities, Inc.
406 W Plum St
Georgetown OH 45121
937 378-6041

(G-19800)
CANTRELL OIL COMPANY
Also Called: Winchester Wholesale
18856 State Route 136 (45697-9793)
P.O. Box 175 (45697-0175)
PHONE.....................937 695-8003
Robert Cantrell Jr, *President*
Tracy Derlmey, *Manager*
Melissa Oconnell, *Manager*
Linda Cantrell, *Admin Sec*
EMP: 46
SQ FT: 4,800
SALES (est): 29.7MM **Privately Held**
SIC: **5141** 5169 Food brokers; essential oils

(G-19801)
FIRST STATE BANK (PA)
19230 State Route 136 (45697-9571)
PHONE.....................937 695-0331
Fax: 937 695-0355
Michael Pell, *President*
Chris Baxla, *Chairman*
David Richey, *CFO*
David Roush, *CFO*
Jo Hanson, *Human Res Mgr*
EMP: 30 EST: 1884
SQ FT: 9,363
SALES (est): 19.8MM **Privately Held**
WEB: www.fsbadamscounty.com
SIC: **6022** State commercial banks

(G-19802)
HANSON AGGREGATES EAST LLC
13526 Overstake Rd (45697-9644)
PHONE.....................937 442-6009
Fax: 937 442-0219
Robert Roades, *Plant Mgr*
Bobby Roades, *Branch Mgr*
EMP: 30
SALES (corp-wide): 16B **Privately Held**
SIC: **5032** Aggregate
HQ: Hanson Aggregates East Llc
3131 Rdu Center Dr
Morrisville NC 27560
919 380-2500

Windham
Portage County

(G-19803)
RICK KUNTZ TRUCKING INC
9056 State Route 88 (44288-9726)
P.O. Box 775, Ravenna (44266-0775)
PHONE.....................330 296-9311
Fax: 330 527-2808
Rick Kuntz, *President*
Valarie Kuntz, *Corp Secy*
EMP: 35
SQ FT: 7,000
SALES (est): 4.9MM **Privately Held**
SIC: **4212** Local trucking, without storage

(G-19804)
TURNPIKE AND INFRASTRUCTURE CO
Also Called: Hiram Maintenance Bldg
9196 State Route 700 (44288-9744)
PHONE.....................330 527-2169
Fax: 330 527-2160
R Underwood, *Superintendent*
EMP: 80 **Privately Held**
WEB: www.ohioturnpike.net
SIC: **1611** 0782 9621 Highway & street maintenance; highway lawn & garden maintenance services; regulation, administration of transportation;
HQ: Ohio Turnpike And Infrastructure Commission
682 Prospect St
Berea OH 44017
440 234-2081

Windsor
Ashtabula County

(G-19805)
LYNNHAVEN V LLC
Also Called: Grand Valley Country Manor
5165 State Route 322 (44099-9623)
PHONE.....................440 272-5600
Fax: 440 272-1040
Dr Kenneth Hubbard, *CEO*
Stanley Huffman, *President*
EMP: 125
SALES (est): 3.5MM **Privately Held**
SIC: **8051** 8052 Skilled nursing care facilities; intermediate care facilities

Winesburg
Holmes County

(G-19806)
R W SAUDER INC
Also Called: Sauder's Quality Eggs
2648 Us Rt 62 (44690)
PHONE.....................330 359-5440
Wayne Troyer, *Manager*
EMP: 48
SALES (est): 5.3MM
SALES (corp-wide): 180MM **Privately Held**
WEB: www.sauderseggs.com
SIC: **5144** Eggs
PA: R. W. Sauder Inc.
570 Furnace Hills Pike
Lititz PA 17543
717 626-2074

Wintersville
Jefferson County

(G-19807)
ADDUS HOMECARE CORPORATION
Also Called: Addus Home Care
1406 Cadiz Rd (43953-9058)
PHONE.....................866 684-0385
EMP: 1118 **Publicly Held**
SIC: **8099** Blood related health services
PA: Addus Homecare Corporation
6801 Gaylord Pkwy Ste 110
Frisco TX 75034

(G-19808)
BATES BROS AMUSEMENT CO
1506 Fernwood Rd (43953-7640)
PHONE.....................740 266-2950
Eric Bates, *President*
Dolores Bates, *President*
EMP: 75
SALES (est): 4.1MM **Privately Held**
WEB: www.batesbros.com
SIC: **7999** Amusement ride

(G-19809)
COMMUNICARE HEALTH SVCS INC
Also Called: Salem West Healthcare Center
135 Reichart Ave (43953-4050)
PHONE.....................877 366-5306
Fax: 330 448-8080
Toni Fuzo, *Manager*
David Pertic, *Director*
EMP: 140
SQ FT: 33,805
SALES (corp-wide): 103.9MM **Privately Held**
WEB: www.atriumlivingcenters.com
SIC: **8051** Skilled nursing care facilities
PA: Communicare Health Services, Inc.
4700 Ashwood Dr Ste 200
Blue Ash OH 45241
513 530-1654

Wintersville - Jefferson County (G-19810)

(G-19810)
FAYETTE PARTS SERVICE INC
618 Canton Rd (43953-4118)
PHONE.................................724 880-3616
Carl Dellapenna, *Branch Mgr*
EMP: 103
SALES (corp-wide): 58MM **Privately Held**
SIC: 7549 Automotive maintenance services
PA: Fayette Parts Service, Inc.
325 E Main St
Uniontown PA
724 785-2506

(G-19811)
WALMART INC
843 State Route 43 (43952-7099)
PHONE.................................740 765-5700
Doug Corbolotti, *Branch Mgr*
EMP: 477
SALES (corp-wide): 500.3B **Publicly Held**
WEB: www.walmartstores.com
SIC: 4225 General warehousing & storage
PA: Walmart Inc.
702 Sw 8th St
Bentonville AR 72716
479 273-4000

Woodsfield
Monroe County

(G-19812)
BOARD MENTAL RETARDATION DVLPM
Also Called: Monroe Achievement Center
47011 State Route 26 (43793-9330)
P.O. Box 623 (43793-0623)
PHONE.................................740 472-1712
Fax: 740 472-0445
Helen Ring, *Superintendent*
Duane Burton, *Principal*
EMP: 32
SALES (est): 1MM **Privately Held**
SIC: 8322 Social services for the handicapped

(G-19813)
CITIZENS NATIONAL BANK (PA)
143 S Main St (43793-1022)
P.O. Box 230 (43793-0230)
PHONE.................................740 472-1696
Fax: 740 472-1979
Stanley Heft, *Ch of Bd*
Carey Bott, *President*
Bruce Climber, *Vice Pres*
EMP: 30
SQ FT: 3,500
SALES: 3.1MM **Privately Held**
SIC: 6021 National commercial banks

(G-19814)
COUNTY OF MONROE
Also Called: Monroe County Engineers Dept
47026 Moore Ridge Rd (43793-9050)
P.O. Box 555 (43793-0555)
PHONE.................................740 472-0760
Bruce Jones, *Superintendent*
Lonnie Tustin, *Principal*
EMP: 32 **Privately Held**
WEB: www.monroevets.net
SIC: 1611 Highway & street construction
PA: County Of Monroe
101 N Main St Rm 34
Woodsfield OH 43793
740 472-1341

(G-19815)
COUNTY OF MONROE
Also Called: Monroe County Care Center
47045 Moore Ridge Rd (43793-9484)
P.O. Box 352 (43793-0352)
PHONE.................................740 472-0144
Fax: 740 472-2504
Marilyn Stepp, *Manager*
Joan Michener, *Director*
Himalaya Patcha, *Director*
John Shreve, *Director*
Robin Groves, *Program Dir*
EMP: 78 **Privately Held**
WEB: www.monroevets.net
SIC: 8051 Skilled nursing care facilities

PA: County Of Monroe
101 N Main St Rm 34
Woodsfield OH 43793
740 472-1341

(G-19816)
MACO INC
Also Called: MONROE ADULT CRAFTS ORGANIZATI
47013 State Route 26 (43793-9330)
P.O. Box 564 (43793-0564)
PHONE.................................740 472-5445
Don Longwel, *Principal*
Daniel Lollathin, *Human Res Dir*
Misty Dierkes, *Admin Sec*
EMP: 50
SALES: 173.2K **Privately Held**
WEB: www.maco.com
SIC: 8322 Individual & family services

(G-19817)
MONROE COUNTY ASSOCIATION FOR
47011 State Route 26 (43793-9330)
P.O. Box 623 (43793-0623)
PHONE.................................740 472-1712
Helen Ring, *President*
Misty Douglas, *Admin Sec*
EMP: 32
SALES (est): 597.4K **Privately Held**
SIC: 8621 Professional membership organizations

(G-19818)
MONROE FAMILY HEALTH CENTER
Also Called: Ohio Hills Health Service
37984 Airport Rd (43793-9247)
P.O. Box 658 (43793-0658)
PHONE.................................740 472-0757
Fax: 740 472-0283
Donna Secrest, *Manager*
Jackie Vinson, *Manager*
Theodore Koler, *Exec Dir*
EMP: 25
SALES (est): 1.8MM **Privately Held**
SIC: 8011 8071 Clinic, operated by physicians; medical laboratories

(G-19819)
SAFE AUTO INSURANCE COMPANY
47060 Black Walnut Pkwy (43793-9521)
PHONE.................................740 472-1900
Jon P Diamond, *Branch Mgr*
EMP: 156
SALES (corp-wide): 678.8MM **Privately Held**
SIC: 6331 Automobile insurance
HQ: Safe Auto Insurance Company
4 Easton Oval
Columbus OH 43219

(G-19820)
WOODSFIELD OPCO LLC
Also Called: Arbors At Woodsfield
37930 Airport Rd (43793-9247)
PHONE.................................502 429-8062
Robert Norcross, *CEO*
Benjamin Sparks, *Clerk*
EMP: 99
SQ FT: 60,000
SALES (est): 1MM **Privately Held**
SIC: 8051 Skilled nursing care facilities

Woodstock
Champaign County

(G-19821)
SABER HEALTHCARE GROUP LLC
Also Called: Spring Meadows Care Center
1649 Park Rd (43084-9713)
PHONE.................................937 826-3351
Heather Mudgett, *Administration*
EMP: 36
SALES (corp-wide): 68.5MM **Privately Held**
SIC: 8051 Skilled nursing care facilities

PA: Saber Healthcare Group, L.L.C.
26691 Richmond Rd Frnt
Bedford OH 44146
216 292-5706

(G-19822)
WOODSTOCK CARE CENTER INC
Also Called: Spring Meadows Care Center
1649 Park Rd (43084-9713)
PHONE.................................937 826-3351
Fax: 937 826-6515
Ed Telle, *President*
William Soroka, *Vice Pres*
Ramalingam Selbarajah, *Director*
Peggy Dupler, *Admin Sec*
EMP: 50
SQ FT: 20,000
SALES (est): 3.3MM **Privately Held**
WEB: www.chicagowilderness.org
SIC: 8051 Skilled nursing care facilities

Woodville
Sandusky County

(G-19823)
PREDATOR TRUCKING COMPANY
1121 State Route 105 (43469-9754)
PHONE.................................419 849-2601
Fax: 419 849-3134
Steve Frasure, *General Mgr*
EMP: 25 **Privately Held**
SIC: 4213 Trucking, except local
PA: Predator Trucking Company
3181 Trumbull Ave
Mc Donald OH 44437

(G-19824)
ROUEN CHRYSLER PLYMOUTH DODGE
Also Called: Rouen Dodge
1091 Fremont Pike (43469-9606)
P.O. Box 1330, Maumee (43537-8330)
PHONE.................................419 837-6228
Fax: 419 837-6240
Michael J Rouen, *President*
EMP: 31 EST: 1948
SQ FT: 20,000
SALES (est): 12.3MM **Privately Held**
SIC: 5511 7515 7513 5521 Automobiles, new & used; passenger car leasing; truck rental & leasing, no drivers; used car dealers

Wooster
Wayne County

(G-19825)
ALAN MANUFACTURING INC
3927 E Lincoln Way (44691-8997)
P.O. Box 24875, Cleveland (44124-0875)
PHONE.................................330 262-1555
Richard Bluestone, *President*
Dean Weidner, *Manager*
▲ EMP: 36
SQ FT: 110,000
SALES (est): 3.9MM **Privately Held**
SIC: 3444 3822 1711 1761 Sheet metalwork; auto controls regulating residntl & coml environmt & appincs; plumbing, heating, air-conditioning contractors; roofing, siding & sheet metal work

(G-19826)
ALBRIGHT WELDING SUPPLY CO INC (PA)
3132 E Lincoln Way (44691-3757)
P.O. Box 35 (44691-0035)
PHONE.................................330 264-2021
Fax: 330 263-7484
James E Horst, *President*
Richard E Mang, *General Mgr*
Rebecca Horst, *Corp Secy*
Robert V Horst Jr, *Vice Pres*
Jeremey Frederick, *Store Mgr*
EMP: 35 EST: 1928
SQ FT: 14,500

SALES (est): 11.8MM **Privately Held**
WEB: www.albrightwelding.com
SIC: 5084 5085 5999 Welding machinery & equipment; welding supplies; welding supplies

(G-19827)
ALICE NOBLE ICE ARENA
851 Oldman Rd (44691-9072)
PHONE.................................330 345-8686
Fax: 330 345-5014
David Noble, *Principal*
Ryan Vogelsberger, *Opers Mgr*
Cathy Rohe, *Office Mgr*
EMP: 25
SQ FT: 1,296
SALES (est): 772.5K **Privately Held**
SIC: 7999 Ice skating rink operation

(G-19828)
ANAZAO COMMUNITY PARTNERS (PA)
2587 Back Orrville Rd (44691-9523)
PHONE.................................330 264-9597
Kevin Bowen, *Finance Dir*
Ken Ward, *Exec Dir*
EMP: 27
SQ FT: 4,000
SALES: 2.3MM **Privately Held**
SIC: 8322 8093 Substance abuse counseling; specialty outpatient clinics

(G-19829)
ASAP HOMECARE INC
133 Beall Ave (44691-3676)
PHONE.................................330 263-4733
Fax: 330 601-0309
EMP: 96
SALES (corp-wide): 6.9MM **Privately Held**
SIC: 8082 Home health care services
PA: Asap Homecare Inc
1 Park Centre Dr Ste 107
Wadsworth OH 44281
330 334-7027

(G-19830)
BAUER CORPORATION (PA)
Also Called: Bauer Ladder
2540 Progress Dr (44691-7970)
P.O. Box 165 (44691-0165)
PHONE.................................800 321-4760
Fax: 330 264-4888
Mark McConnell, *President*
Ward McConnel, *Chairman*
John Vasichko, *Vice Pres*
Beth Raff, *Accountant*
Rich Stoner, *Manager*
EMP: 50
SQ FT: 71,500
SALES (est): 15.5MM **Privately Held**
WEB: www.bauerladder.com
SIC: 5082 3499 3446 3441 Ladders; metal ladders; architectural metalwork; fabricated structural metal

(G-19831)
BEST WOOSTER INC
Also Called: Best Western Wooster Plaza
243 E Liberty St Ste 11 (44691-4366)
PHONE.................................330 264-7750
Fax: 330 262-5840
Stephen Sun, *President*
Elizabeth Feldman, *Office Mgr*
EMP: 40
SQ FT: 97,000
SALES (est): 2.7MM **Privately Held**
SIC: 7011 Hotels

(G-19832)
BLACK TIE AFFAIR INC
Also Called: Greenbriar CONference & Pty Ctr
50 Riffel Rd (44691-8596)
PHONE.................................330 345-8333
Fax: 330 345-9820
Betty Steine, *President*
Dorene Miller, *President*
Shanda Good, *Office Mgr*
Betty Stine, *Admin Sec*
EMP: 50
SQ FT: 40,000
SALES (est): 1.6MM **Privately Held**
SIC: 5812 7299 Caterers; facility rental & party planning services

GEOGRAPHIC SECTION — Wooster - Wayne County (G-19855)

(G-19833) BOGNER CONSTRUCTION COMPANY
305 Mulberry St (44691-4735)
P.O. Box 887 (44691-0887)
PHONE..................330 262-6730
Theodore R Bogner, *President*
Robert E Bogner, *Vice Pres*
Adam Bogner, *Project Mgr*
Michael Bogner, *Project Mgr*
Jaime Naujoks, *Marketing Staff*
EMP: 75 **EST:** 1979
SQ FT: 5,000
SALES (est): 23.8MM **Privately Held**
WEB: www.bognergroup.com
SIC: 1542 Commercial & office building, new construction

(G-19834) BROOKDALE PLACE WOOSTER LLC
1615 Cleveland Rd (44691-2335)
PHONE..................330 262-1615
Ann Worley, *Manager*
Jeff Vanek, *Food Svc Dir*
EMP: 48 **EST:** 2009
SALES (est): 429.9K
SALES (corp-wide): 4.7B **Publicly Held**
SIC: 8322 Rehabilitation services
PA: Brookdale Senior Living
111 Westwood Pl Ste 400
Brentwood TN 37027
615 221-2250

(G-19835) BROOKDALE SENIOR LIVING INC
1615 Cleveland Rd (44691-2335)
PHONE..................330 262-1615
Ann Worley, *Branch Mgr*
EMP: 36
SALES (corp-wide): 4.7B **Publicly Held**
SIC: 8082 Home health care services
PA: Brookdale Senior Living
111 Westwood Pl Ste 400
Brentwood TN 37027
615 221-2250

(G-19836) CAMPBELL CONSTRUCTION INC (PA)
1159 Blachleyville Rd (44691-9750)
PHONE..................330 262-5186
Fax: 330 262-7835
John Campbell, *President*
Nancy J Campbell, *Principal*
Robert B Campbell, *Principal*
Mary Louise Campbell, *Corp Secy*
Richard Hauenstein, *Exec VP*
EMP: 68
SQ FT: 12,000
SALES (est): 9.4MM **Privately Held**
SIC: 6512 Commercial & industrial building operation

(G-19837) CCJ ENTERPRISES INC
Also Called: Acres of Fun
3889 Friendsville Rd (44691-9601)
PHONE..................330 345-4386
Fax: 330 345-9868
Darlene Johns, *President*
Bob Johns, *Corp Secy*
EMP: 30
SQ FT: 15,750
SALES (est): 1.2MM **Privately Held**
SIC: 7999 Recreation center

(G-19838) CELLCO PARTNERSHIP
Also Called: Verizon
4164 Burbank Rd (44691-9077)
PHONE..................330 345-6465
Amy Schafer, *Manager*
EMP: 71
SALES (corp-wide): 126B **Publicly Held**
SIC: 4812 5999 Cellular telephone services; communication equipment
HQ: Cellco Partnership
1 Verizon Way
Basking Ridge NJ 07920

(G-19839) CERTIFIED ANGUS BEEF LLC (HQ)
206 Riffel Rd (44691-8588)
PHONE..................330 345-2333
Fax: 330 345-0808
John Stika, *President*
Brent Eichar, *Senior VP*
Mark A McCully, *Assistant VP*
Tracey Erickson, *Vice Pres*
Pam Cottrell, *Human Res Dir*
EMP: 90
SQ FT: 42,000
SALES (est): 15MM
SALES (corp-wide): 55.4MM **Privately Held**
SIC: 8611 Business associations
PA: American Angus Association Inc
3201 Frederick Ave
Saint Joseph MO 64506
816 383-5100

(G-19840) CERTIFIED ANGUS BEEF LLC
344 Riffel Rd (44691-8590)
PHONE..................330 345-2333
John Stika, *President*
EMP: 48
SALES (corp-wide): 55.4MM **Privately Held**
SIC: 8611 Business associations
HQ: Certified Angus Beef, Llc
206 Riffel Rd
Wooster OH 44691
330 345-2333

(G-19841) CHRISTIAN CHLD HM OHIO INC
2685 Armstrong Rd (44691-9041)
P.O. Box 765 (44691-0765)
PHONE..................330 345-7949
Steve Porter, *President*
Kevin R Hewitt, *Exec Dir*
Shawn Pedani, *Director*
John Smith, *Director*
Peggy Smith, *Director*
EMP: 100
SQ FT: 12,000
SALES (est): 8.2MM **Privately Held**
WEB: www.ccho.org
SIC: 8361 8093 8322 Children's home; substance abuse clinics (outpatient); individual & family services

(G-19842) CHRISTIAN WOOSTER SCHOOL
4599 Burbank Rd Ste B (44691-9099)
PHONE..................330 345-6436
Fax: 330 345-4330
Randy Claes, *Principal*
Deb Carpenter, *Librarian*
Karen Anderson, *Admin Sec*
Greg Brenneman, *Tech/Comp Coord*
Joyce Atkins, *Teacher*
EMP: 43
SALES (est): 1.2MM **Privately Held**
WEB: www.woosterchristianschool.com
SIC: 8211 8351 Private elementary & secondary schools; preschool center

(G-19843) CINEMARK USA INC
Also Called: Cinemark Movies 10
4108 Burbank Rd (44691-9077)
PHONE..................330 345-2610
Nancy Keller, *Manager*
Jeff Cernava, *Manager*
EMP: 27 **Publicly Held**
SIC: 7832 Motion picture theaters, except drive-in
HQ: Cinemark Usa, Inc.
3900 Dallas Pkwy Ste 500
Plano TX 75093
972 665-1000

(G-19844) CITY OF WOOSTER
1761 Beall Ave (44691-2342)
PHONE..................330 263-8636
Alex Davis, *Manager*
EMP: 25 **Privately Held**
WEB: www.woosteroh.com
SIC: 8082 Home health care services
PA: City Of Wooster
538 N Market St
Wooster OH 44691
330 263-5200

(G-19845) CITY OF WOOSTER
Also Called: Wooster Division Fire
510 N Market St (44691-3406)
PHONE..................330 263-5266
Fax: 330 263-5281
Robert Eyler, *Chief*
EMP: 40 **Privately Held**
WEB: www.woosteroh.com
SIC: 7389 9111 Fire protection service other than forestry or public; mayors' offices
PA: City Of Wooster
538 N Market St
Wooster OH 44691
330 263-5200

(G-19846) CITY OF WOOSTER
Also Called: Wooster Community Hospital
1761 Beall Ave (44691-2342)
PHONE..................330 263-8100
Fax: 330 262-8013
William Sheron, *CEO*
Judith Kestner, *Superintendent*
David Rice, *Superintendent*
Gary L Whittaker, *Superintendent*
Rhonda Warren, *QA Dir*
EMP: 854 **Privately Held**
WEB: www.woosteroh.com
SIC: 8062 5912 General medical & surgical hospitals; drug stores
PA: City Of Wooster
538 N Market St
Wooster OH 44691
330 263-5200

(G-19847) CLASSIC IMPORTS INC (PA)
Also Called: Funky People
2018 Great Trails Dr (44691-3740)
PHONE..................330 262-5277
Fax: 330 264-4528
Raj Arora, *President*
Ramesh Arora, *Vice Pres*
Sarvesh Arora, *Vice Pres*
Rachna Walia, *Vice Pres*
Pavan Kumar, *Administration*
▲ **EMP:** 37
SQ FT: 45,000
SALES (est): 10MM **Privately Held**
SIC: 5137 Women's & children's clothing

(G-19848) CLEVELAND CLINIC FOUNDATION
Also Called: Womans Health Center
1739 Cleveland Rd (44691-2203)
PHONE..................330 287-4930
Fax: 330 264-2085
Scott Steele, *Research*
Cathy Fischer, *Manager*
EMP: 30
SALES (corp-wide): 8B **Privately Held**
SIC: 8011 8062 Physicians' office, including specialists; general medical & surgical hospitals
PA: The Cleveland Clinic Foundation
9500 Euclid Ave
Cleveland OH 44195
216 636-8335

(G-19849) CLEVELAND CLINIC FOUNDATION
Also Called: Cleveland Clinic Wooster
1740 Cleveland Rd (44691-2204)
PHONE..................330 287-4500
Jennifer Lonzer, *Editor*
Tess Parry, *Editor*
Rose Jeric, *Project Mgr*
Juanita Phillips, *Purch Agent*
Duane Golden, *Engineer*
EMP: 85
SALES (corp-wide): 8B **Privately Held**
SIC: 6733 Trusts
PA: The Cleveland Clinic Foundation
9500 Euclid Ave
Cleveland OH 44195
216 636-8335

(G-19850) CLEVELND CLNC HLTH SYSTM EAST
Also Called: Cleveland Clinic Wooster
721 E Milltown Rd (44691-1331)
PHONE..................330 287-4830
Wendy Simmons, *Principal*
Greg Barton, *Med Doctor*
Richard Guttmajr, *Med Doctor*
EMP: 30
SALES (corp-wide): 8B **Privately Held**
SIC: 8062 8093 General medical & surgical hospitals; specialty outpatient clinics
HQ: Cleveland Clinic Health System-East Region
6803 Mayfield Rd Ste 500
Cleveland OH 44124
440 312-6010

(G-19851) COMMUNITY ACTION-WAYNE/MEDINA (PA)
905 Pittsburg Ave (44691-4296)
PHONE..................330 264-8677
Fax: 330 264-5170
Donald Ackerman, *CFO*
EMP: 80
SQ FT: 1,700
SALES (est): 7.5MM **Privately Held**
WEB: www.cawm.org
SIC: 8322 Social service center

(G-19852) COUNTRY ACRES OF WAYNE COUNTY
1240 Wildwood Dr (44691-1984)
PHONE..................330 698-2031
Leota Hutchinson, *President*
EMP: 26
SALES (est): 320.6K **Privately Held**
SIC: 8059 Nursing home, except skilled & intermediate care facility

(G-19853) COUNTRY POINTE SKILLED NURSING
3071 N Elyria Rd (44691-9379)
PHONE..................330 264-7881
Rachel Moore, *Consultant*
Rick Gebhard, *Administration*
Thomas S Lehner, *Gnrl Med Prac*
EMP: 35 **EST:** 1999
SALES (est): 1.6MM **Privately Held**
SIC: 8051 Extended care facility

(G-19854) COUNTY OF WAYNE
Also Called: Wayne County Care Center
876 S Geyers Chapel Rd (44691-3908)
PHONE..................330 262-1786
Fax: 330 262-0118
James Bay, *Director*
Jan Miller, *Nursing Dir*
Angela Young, *Nursing Dir*
Becky Sprinkle, *Records Dir*
Carol Van Pelt, *Administration*
EMP: 100 **Privately Held**
WEB: www.waynecsb.org
SIC: 8059 9111 Personal care home, with health care; county supervisors' & executives' offices
PA: County Of Wayne
428 W Liberty St
Wooster OH 44691
330 287-5400

(G-19855) COUNTY OF WAYNE
Also Called: Wayne Employment Training Ctr
356 W North St (44691-4822)
P.O. Box 76 (44691-0076)
PHONE..................330 264-5060
Fax: 330 287-5893
Becky Wagner, *Director*
EMP: 32 **Privately Held**
SIC: 7361 Employment agencies
PA: County Of Wayne
428 W Liberty St
Wooster OH 44691
330 287-5400

Wooster - Wayne County (G-19856)

(G-19856)
COUNTY OF WAYNE
Also Called: Wayne County Childrens Svcs
2534 Burbank Rd (44691-1675)
PHONE.................................330 345-5340
Fax: 330 345-7082
Pam Varnes, *MIS Staff*
Thomas Roelant, *Director*
EMP: 62 **Privately Held**
SIC: 8361 9111 Children's home; county supervisors' & executives' offices
PA: County Of Wayne
    428 W Liberty St
    Wooster OH 44691
    330 287-5400

(G-19857)
COUNTY OF WAYNE
Also Called: Wayne County Child Support
428 W Liberty St Ste 11 (44691-4851)
PHONE.................................330 287-5600
Fax: 330 287-5623
Marjorie Butler, *Director*
EMP: 32 **Privately Held**
WEB: www.waynecsb.org
SIC: 8322 Child related social services
PA: County Of Wayne
    428 W Liberty St
    Wooster OH 44691
    330 287-5400

(G-19858)
COUNTY OF WAYNE
Also Called: Wayne County Engineers Wooster
3151 W Old Lincoln Way (44691-3262)
PHONE.................................330 287-5500
Fax: 330 287-5520
Creed Parsons, *Asst Supt*
Darrell Collins, *Engineer*
Roger K Terrell, *Branch Mgr*
EMP: 52 **Privately Held**
WEB: www.waynecsb.org
SIC: 8711 Engineering services; heating & ventilation engineering
PA: County Of Wayne
    428 W Liberty St
    Wooster OH 44691
    330 287-5400

(G-19859)
CRITCHFELD CRTCHFIELD JOHNSTON (PA)
Also Called: Ccj
225 N Market St (44691-3511)
P.O. Box 599 (44691-0599)
PHONE.................................330 264-4444
Fax: 330 263-9278
Robert C Berry, *Partner*
J Douglas Drushal, *Partner*
Robert C Gorman, *Partner*
John C Johnston III, *Partner*
Daniel H Plumly, *Partner*
EMP: 88
SALES (est) 12MM **Privately Held**
SIC: 8111 General practice law office

(G-19860)
D C CURRY LUMBER COMPANY
331 W Henry St (44691-4719)
P.O. Box 197 (44691-0197)
PHONE.................................330 264-5223
Fax: 330 263-4599
David Nally, *President*
Wayne Hochstetler, *Corp Secy*
Tom Oller, *Marketing Staff*
Mose Yoder, *Representative*
EMP: 25
SQ FT: 19,600
SALES: 5.1MM **Privately Held**
SIC: 1522 5211 Residential construction; lumber & other building materials

(G-19861)
DANBURY WOODS OF WOOSTER
939 Portage Rd (44691-2039)
PHONE.................................330 264-0355
Wesley Hess, *Director*
EMP: 45
SALES (est) 697.9K **Privately Held**
SIC: 8322 Old age assistance

(G-19862)
ENGINEERING ASSOCIATES INC
1935 Eagle Pass (44691-5316)
PHONE.................................330 345-6556
Fax: 330 345-8077
Kent Baker, *President*
Frederick A Seling, *Vice Pres*
Gary Daugherty, *Treasurer*
Ronny Portz, *Admin Sec*
EMP: 25 **EST:** 1957
SQ FT: 9,000
SALES (est) 3.2MM **Privately Held**
WEB: www.eaohio.com
SIC: 8711 Civil engineering

(G-19863)
GLENDORA HEALTH CARE CENTER
1552 N Honeytown Rd (44691-9511)
PHONE.................................330 264-0912
Fax: 330 263-4321
Shaw Flank, *President*
Terry J Ferguson, *President*
Linda Ferguson, *Vice Pres*
Sherry Schartiger, *Pub Rel Dir*
Allen Lifer, *Office Mgr*
EMP: 56
SQ FT: 11,000
SALES (est) 2.8MM **Privately Held**
WEB: www.glendoracarecenter.com
SIC: 8051 Convalescent home with continuous nursing care

(G-19864)
GOLF COURSE MAINTENANCE
1599 Mechanicsburg Rd (44691-2766)
PHONE.................................330 262-9141
Joe Hatila, *President*
Larry Barnett, *President*
Scott McLain, *Principal*
EMP: 76
SQ FT: 1,200
SALES (est) 697.6K **Privately Held**
SIC: 7997 Country club, membership

(G-19865)
GOODWILL INDUSTRIES (PA)
1034 Nold Ave (44691-3642)
P.O. Box 1188 (44691-7083)
PHONE.................................330 264-1300
Judy Delaney, *President*
Sherri Clark, *Director*
EMP: 30
SQ FT: 21,000
SALES: 5.4MM **Privately Held**
WEB: www.woostergoodwill.org
SIC: 8331 5932 Sheltered workshop; used merchandise stores

(G-19866)
H & R BLOCK INC
2831 Cleveland Rd (44691-1737)
PHONE.................................330 345-1040
Fax: 330 345-5988
Sandy Easterday, *Manager*
EMP: 25
SALES (corp-wide): 3B **Publicly Held**
WEB: www.hrblock.com
SIC: 7291 Tax return preparation services
PA: H&R Block, Inc.
    1 H&R Block Way
    Kansas City MO 64105
    816 854-3000

(G-19867)
HERMAN BAIR ENTERPRISE
Also Called: Ej Therapy
210 E Milltown Rd A (44691-1246)
PHONE.................................330 262-4449
Eunice Herman, *President*
EMP: 27
SALES: 800K **Privately Held**
SIC: 8049 Nutrition specialist

(G-19868)
HOMETOWN URGENT CARE
4164 Burbank Rd (44691-9077)
PHONE.................................937 252-2000
EMP: 125
SALES (corp-wide): 73.2MM **Privately Held**
SIC: 8049 8011 7291 Occupational therapist; medical centers; tax return preparation services

PA: Hometown Urgent Care
    2400 Corp Exchange Dr # 102
    Columbus OH 43231
    614 505-7633

(G-19869)
HORIZONS TUSCARAWAS/CARROLL
527 N Market St (44691-3495)
PHONE.................................330 262-4183
Fax: 330 262-5291
Jack Robinson, *Manager*
EMP: 35
SALES (corp-wide): 6.8MM **Privately Held**
SIC: 8361 Home for the mentally handicapped
PA: Horizons Of Tuscarawas/Carroll
    220 W 4th St
    Dover OH 44622
    330 874-1060

(G-19870)
HORN NURSING AND REHAB CENTER (HQ)
Also Called: Horn Nursing Rehabilitation Ctr
230 N Market St (44691-3512)
PHONE.................................330 262-2951
Fax: 330 264-1254
Anthony L Sprenger, *President*
Donel L Sprenger, *Vice Pres*
Amy Jolloff, *Director*
EMP: 70 **EST:** 1960
SQ FT: 5,000
SALES (est) 8.6MM **Privately Held**
SIC: 8051 8052 Skilled nursing care facilities; intermediate care facilities

(G-19871)
HORN NURSING AND REHAB CENTER
Also Called: Smithville Western Commons
4110 E Smithville Wstn Rd (44691)
PHONE.................................330 345-9050
Fax: 330 345-9212
Sheila Kries, *Director*
Carrie Horst, *Administration*
EMP: 150 **Privately Held**
SIC: 8051 8052 Skilled nursing care facilities; intermediate care facilities
HQ: Horn Nursing And Rehab Center
    230 N Market St
    Wooster OH 44691
    330 262-2951

(G-19872)
HOWARD HANNA SMYTHE CRAMER
177 W Milltown Rd Unit A (44691-7289)
PHONE.................................330 345-2244
Fax: 330 345-2256
Howard Hannah, *Principal*
Cindy Householder, *Manager*
EMP: 30
SALES (corp-wide): 76.4MM **Privately Held**
SIC: 6531 Real estate brokers & agents
HQ: Howard Hanna Smythe Cramer
    6000 Parkland Blvd
    Cleveland OH 44124
    216 447-4477

(G-19873)
HUNTINGTON INSURANCE INC
121 N Market St Ste 600 (44691-4880)
PHONE.................................330 262-6611
Scott Schaffter, *President*
EMP: 37
SALES (corp-wide): 4.7B **Publicly Held**
WEB: www.skyinsure.com
SIC: 6411 Insurance agents, brokers & service
HQ: Huntington Insurance, Inc.
    519 Madison Ave
    Toledo OH 43604
    419 720-7900

(G-19874)
JPMORGAN CHASE BANK NAT ASSN
601 Portage Rd (44691-2029)
PHONE.................................330 287-5101
Fax: 330 287-5158
Glenda Farver, *Principal*
EMP: 26

SALES (corp-wide): 99.6B **Publicly Held**
SIC: 6021 National commercial banks
HQ: Jpmorgan Chase Bank, National Association
    1111 Polaris Pkwy
    Columbus OH 43240
    614 436-3055

(G-19875)
JPMORGAN CHASE BANK NAT ASSN
601 Portage Rd (44691-2029)
PHONE.................................330 287-5101
Rob Carter, *Manager*
EMP: 26
SALES (corp-wide): 99.6B **Publicly Held**
WEB: www.chase.com
SIC: 6021 National commercial banks
HQ: Jpmorgan Chase Bank, National Association
    1111 Polaris Pkwy
    Columbus OH 43240
    614 436-3055

(G-19876)
K S BANDAG INC
737 Industrial Blvd (44691-8999)
PHONE.................................330 264-9237
John Kauffman, *President*
Earl Shaw, *Corp Secy*
Mark Hershberger, *Vice Pres*
Carol Six, *Bookkeeper*
EMP: 25
SALES (est) 1.6MM **Privately Held**
SIC: 7534 Rebuilding & retreading tires

(G-19877)
KEIM CONCRETE LLC
4175 W Old Lincoln Way (44691-3241)
PHONE.................................330 264-5313
Jonas Keim,
EMP: 31 **EST:** 1974
SALES (est) 3.1MM **Privately Held**
SIC: 1771 Concrete work

(G-19878)
KEN MILLER SUPPLY INC
1537 Blachleyville Rd (44691-9752)
P.O. Box 1086 (44691-7081)
PHONE.................................330 264-9146
Fax: 330 263-7441
Kirk Miller, *CEO*
Lindy Chandler, *CEO*
Troy Poling, *Sales Mgr*
Dave Tracey, *Sales Mgr*
Cole Miller, *Sales Executive*
▲ **EMP:** 70 **EST:** 1959
SQ FT: 5,000
SALES (est) 105.8MM **Privately Held**
SIC: 5084 Oil field tool joints

(G-19879)
KENOIL INC
1537 Blachleyville Rd (44691-9752)
P.O. Box 1085 (44691-7081)
PHONE.................................330 262-1144
Steve Fleisher, *Vice Pres*
Martha Morris, *Office Mgr*
EMP: 50 **EST:** 1982
SALES (est) 2.7MM **Privately Held**
SIC: 1311 Crude petroleum & natural gas production

(G-19880)
KMB MANAGEMENT SERVICES CORP
Also Called: Wooster Inn, The
801 E Wayne Ave (44691-2388)
PHONE.................................330 263-2660
Fax: 330 263-2661
Ken Bogucki, *President*
Kenneth J Bogucki, *Vice Pres*
Kathy Kruse, *Manager*
EMP: 30
SALES (est) 2.1MM **Privately Held**
SIC: 7011 Hotels

(G-19881)
KOKOSING CONSTRUCTION INC
1516 Timken Rd (44691-9401)
PHONE.................................330 263-4168
Fax: 330 522-0989
Brian Burgett, *President*

Brian Wilson, *Controller*
▲ **EMP:** 2500
SQ FT: 20,000
SALES (est): 99.7MM **Privately Held**
SIC: 1611 Highway & street paving contractor

(G-19882)
LADDER MAN INC
1505 E Bowman St (44691)
PHONE..................614 784-1120
Jeff Monastra, *Vice Pres*
Tom Rosso, *Manager*
EMP: 25
SALES (est): 1.2MM **Privately Held**
SIC: 8748 Business consulting

(G-19883)
LIFECARE HOSPICE (PA)
Also Called: Lifecare Palliative Medicine
1900 Akron Rd (44691-2518)
PHONE..................330 264-4899
Kurt Holmes, *CEO*
Tim Pettorini, *Ch of Bd*
EMP: 30
SQ FT: 8,006
SALES: 10.5MM **Privately Held**
WEB: www.wchospice.org
SIC: 8322 Individual & family services

(G-19884)
LOWES HOME CENTERS LLC
3788 Burbank Rd (44691-9076)
PHONE..................330 287-2261
Fax: 330 287-2264
EMP: 150
SALES (corp-wide): 68.6B **Publicly Held**
SIC: 5211 5031 5722 5064 Home centers; building materials, exterior; building materials, interior; household appliance stores; electrical appliances, television & radio
HQ: Lowe's Home Centers, Llc
1605 Curtis Bridge Rd
Wilkesboro NC 28697
336 658-4000

(G-19885)
LUK TRANSMISSION SYSTEM LLC (PA)
3177 Old Airport Rd (44691-9520)
PHONE..................330 464-4184
David Marlar, *CFO*
◆ **EMP:** 36
SALES (est): 24.7MM **Privately Held**
SIC: 7537 Automotive transmission repair shops

(G-19886)
MCCLINTOCK ELECTRIC INC
402 E Henry St (44691-4393)
PHONE..................330 264-6380
Fax: 330 262-6232
Michael J McClintock, *President*
Steve Curtis, *Superintendent*
Ralph D McClintock, *Vice Pres*
Aaron Shields, *Project Mgr*
Misty Shields, *Warehouse Mgr*
EMP: 35 **EST:** 1963
SQ FT: 2,400
SALES (est): 6.8MM **Privately Held**
WEB: www.mcclintockelectric.com
SIC: 1731 General electrical contractor; fiber optic cable installation; voice, data & video wiring contractor; fire detection & burglar alarm systems specialization

(G-19887)
METALS USA CRBN FLAT RLLED INC (DH)
1070 W Liberty St (44691-3308)
P.O. Box 999 (44691-0999)
PHONE..................330 264-8416
Don Gingery, *President*
Tom Pacek, *Purch Mgr*
Jeffrey Aultz, *Sls & Mktg Exec*
James Zimmermann, *CFO*
Brian Schmidt, *Treasurer*
▲ **EMP:** 102
SQ FT: 140,000
SALES (est): 81MM
SALES (corp-wide): 9.7B **Publicly Held**
SIC: 3312 5051 Blast furnaces & steel mills; steel
HQ: Metals Usa, Inc.
4901 Nw 17th Way Ste 405
Fort Lauderdale FL 33309
954 202-4000

(G-19888)
MILITARY RESOURCES LLC
1036 Burbank Rd (44691)
PHONE..................330 263-1040
EMP: 50
SALES (corp-wide): 3MM **Privately Held**
SIC: 3559 7389 Mfg Misc Industry Machinery Business Services
PA: Military Resources, Llc
1834 Cleveland Rd Ste 301
Wooster OH 44691
330 309-9970

(G-19889)
MILITARY RESOURCES LLC (PA)
1834 Cleveland Rd Ste 301 (44691-2206)
PHONE..................330 309-9970
William D Johnson, *CEO*
Arthur Summerville,
Roger Williams,
▼ **EMP:** 59
SQ FT: 3,000
SALES: 3MM **Privately Held**
WEB: www.militaryresources.com
SIC: 3559 7389 Ammunition & explosives, loading machinery; design, commercial & industrial

(G-19890)
MILLER SUPPLY OF WVA INC (PA)
1537 Blachleyville Rd (44691-9752)
P.O. Box 1086 (44691-7081)
PHONE..................330 264-9146
Jack K Miller, *President*
Kenneth R Miller, *Corp Secy*
Max A Miller, *Vice Pres*
Joe Sanders, *CFO*
Max Miller, *Credit Mgr*
▲ **EMP:** 50
SALES (est): 30.7MM **Privately Held**
SIC: 5084 Oil well machinery, equipment & supplies

(G-19891)
MILLTOWN FAMILY PHYSICIANS
128 E Milltown Rd Ste 105 (44691-1276)
PHONE..................330 345-8016
Fax: 330 345-5983
John K Miller, *Principal*
EMP: 25
SALES (est): 2.7MM **Privately Held**
SIC: 8011 General & family practice, physician/surgeon

(G-19892)
NEW PITTSBURGH FIRE & RESCUE F
3311 N Elyria Rd (44691-7645)
PHONE..................330 264-1230
Ken Becker, *Chief*
EMP: 31
SALES (est): 386.3K **Privately Held**
SIC: 8641 Civic social & fraternal associations

(G-19893)
NICK AMSTER INC (PA)
1700b Old Mansfield Rd (44691-7212)
PHONE..................330 264-9667
Fax: 330 345-0996
Rich Patterson, *CEO*
Heather Wells, *Production*
David Spar, *Admin Sec*
Corie Enkemann, *Associate*
Karen Keplar, *Associate*
EMP: 120 **EST:** 1965
SQ FT: 18,000
SALES: 2.9MM **Privately Held**
WEB: www.nickamster.com
SIC: 8331 Sheltered workshop

(G-19894)
NICK AMSTER INC
326 N Hillcrest Dr Ste C (44691-3745)
PHONE..................330 264-9667
Rich Patterson, *General Mgr*
EMP: 74
SALES (est): 435.7K
SALES (corp-wide): 2.9MM **Privately Held**
WEB: www.nickamster.com
SIC: 8322 Social service center
PA: Nick Amster, Inc.
1700 Old Mansfield Rd
Wooster OH 44691
330 264-9667

(G-19895)
NOBLE TECHNOLOGIES CORP (PA)
Also Called: Nobletek
2020 Noble Dr (44691-5353)
PHONE..................330 287-1530
Uday Vaidya, *CEO*
Jan D Bruyckere, *Managing Dir*
Jan De Bruyckere, *Managing Dir*
Vinit Palshikar, *Business Mgr*
Abhay Jahirabadkar, *Vice Pres*
EMP: 40
SALES: 8.8MM **Privately Held**
WEB: www.tgstech.com
SIC: 7371 Computer software development

(G-19896)
OHIO LIGHT OPERA
1189 Beall Ave (44691-2393)
PHONE..................330 263-2345
Steven Daigle, *Director*
EMP: 100
SALES (est): 5.6MM **Privately Held**
SIC: 7832 7922 Motion picture theaters, except drive-in; theatrical producers & services

(G-19897)
OHIO POWER COMPANY
500 Maple St (44691-4293)
PHONE..................330 264-1616
Thomas Smith, *Manager*
EMP: 29
SALES (corp-wide): 15.4B **Publicly Held**
SIC: 4911 Distribution, electric power
HQ: Ohio Power Company
1 Riverside Plz
Columbus OH 43215
614 716-1000

(G-19898)
OHIO STATE UNIVERSITY
Also Called: O A R D C
1680 Madison Ave (44691-4114)
PHONE..................330 263-3700
Fax: 330 263-3695
Gail Vornholt, *Human Res Mgr*
Steven A Slack, *Director*
Thomas Payne, *Director*
EMP: 550
SALES (corp-wide): 5.5B **Privately Held**
WEB: www.ohio-state.edu
SIC: 8731 8221 Agricultural research; university
PA: The Ohio State University
Student Acade Servi Bldg
Columbus OH 43210
614 292-6446

(G-19899)
OHIO STATE UNIVERSITY
Also Called: Ohio Agriculture RES & Dev Ctr
1680 Madison Ave (44691-4114)
PHONE..................330 263-3701
Steven A Slack, *Director*
EMP: 400
SALES (corp-wide): 5.5B **Privately Held**
WEB: www.ohio-state.edu
SIC: 8733 8221 Physical research, non-commercial; university
PA: The Ohio State University
Student Acade Servi Bldg
Columbus OH 43210
614 292-6446

(G-19900)
ONEEIGHTY INC
Also Called: Steps At Liberty Center
104 Spink St (44691-3652)
PHONE..................330 263-6021
Fax: 330 262-6245
Thomas Fenzl, *Ch of Bd*
Laura Ginsburg, *Opers Staff*
Amy Davis, *Manager*
Bobbi Douglas, *Exec Dir*
Tammy Cruise, *Director*
EMP: 75
SQ FT: 25,000
SALES: 4.8MM **Privately Held**
WEB: www.everywomanshouse.org
SIC: 8322 Family counseling services

(G-19901)
OUTREACH CMNTY LIVING SVCS INC
337 W North St (44691-4821)
PHONE..................330 263-0862
Mary Lloyd, *Exec Dir*
EMP: 30
SQ FT: 4,500
SALES: 662.1K **Privately Held**
WEB: www.oclswooster.org
SIC: 8322 Social services for the handicapped

(G-19902)
PERFORMANCE PONTC-OLDMBL GM TR
Also Called: Performance Toyota Volkswagen
1363 W Old Lincoln Way (44691-3323)
PHONE..................330 264-1113
Ray Remark, *Manager*
EMP: 40
SALES (corp-wide): 8.9MM **Privately Held**
WEB: www.vwcars4u.com
SIC: 5511 5012 Automobiles, new & used; automobiles & other motor vehicles
PA: Performance Pontiac-Oldsmobile Gmc Truck Inc
1363 W Old Lincoln Way
Wooster OH 44691
330 264-1113

(G-19903)
PERSONAL TOUCH HM CARE IPA INC
543 Riffel Rd Ste F (44691-8591)
PHONE..................330 263-1112
Norene Scheck, *Branch Mgr*
Ann Plecha, *Manager*
EMP: 1509
SALES (corp-wide): 363MM **Privately Held**
SIC: 8082 Home health care services
PA: Personal Touch Home Care Ipa, Inc.
1985 Marcus Ave Ste 202
New Hyde Park NY 11042
718 468-4747

(G-19904)
PLAZ-WAY INC
Also Called: Wayne Lanes
1983 E Lincoln Way (44691-3813)
PHONE..................330 264-9025
Fax: 330 262-2825
Raymond Jeffries, *President*
Carol Jeffries, *Vice Pres*
EMP: 27 **EST:** 1956
SQ FT: 25,000
SALES (est): 1MM **Privately Held**
WEB: www.waynelanes.com
SIC: 7933 5812 5813 Ten pin center; snack bar; bars & lounges

(G-19905)
PSC METALS - WOOSTER LLC
972 Columbus Rd (44691-4600)
PHONE..................330 264-8956
David N Spector,
EMP: 90
SQ FT: 43,200
SALES (est): 9.9MM
SALES (corp-wide): 21.7B **Publicly Held**
WEB: www.pscmetals.com
SIC: 5093 Ferrous metal scrap & waste; nonferrous metals scrap
HQ: Psc Metals, Inc.
5875 Landerbrook Dr # 200
Mayfield Heights OH 44124
440 753-5400

(G-19906)
REALTY ONE INC
177 W Milltown Rd Unit A (44691-7289)
PHONE..................330 262-7200
Fax: 330 262-5097
Pamela Schrock, *Manager*
EMP: 31

Wooster - Wayne County (G-19907)

SALES (corp-wide): 67.8MM **Privately Held**
WEB: www.realty-1st.com
SIC: **6531** Real estate agents & managers
HQ: Realty One, Inc.
800 W Saint Clair Ave
Cleveland OH 44113
216 328-2500

(G-19907)
RK FAMILY INC
3541 E Lincoln Way (44691-3758)
PHONE.................................330 264-5475
Fax: 330 264-5432
Tom Waites, *Principal*
EMP: 301
SALES (corp-wide): 1.2B **Privately Held**
SIC: **5099** Firearms & ammunition, except sporting
PA: Rk Family, Inc.
4216 Dewitt Ave
Mattoon IL 61938
217 235-7102

(G-19908)
ROD LIGHTNING MUTUAL INSUR CO (PA)
1685 Cleveland Rd (44691-2335)
P.O. Box 36 (44691-0036)
PHONE.................................330 262-9060
F Emerson Logee, *Vice Ch Bd*
John P Murphy, *President*
Kevin Day, *Exec VP*
Jim Geopfert, *Assistant VP*
Greg Owen, *Vice Pres*
EMP: 265
SQ FT: 46,100
SALES: 77.1MM **Privately Held**
WEB: www.wrg-ins.com
SIC: **6331** Fire, marine & casualty insurance & carriers

(G-19909)
RXP WIRELESS LLC
Also Called: Verizon Wireless
3417 Cleveland Rd (44691-1213)
PHONE.................................330 264-1500
Jared Bogner, *Branch Mgr*
EMP: 25
SALES (corp-wide): 20MM **Privately Held**
SIC: **4813** Telephone communication, except radio
HQ: Rxp Wireless, Llc
262 S 3rd St
Columbus OH 43215
614 397-2844

(G-19910)
S C WOOSTER BUS GARAGE
1494 Old Mansfield Rd (44691-9050)
PHONE.................................330 264-4060
Dan Good, *Superintendent*
EMP: 40
SALES (est): 737.1K **Privately Held**
SIC: **4151** School buses

(G-19911)
SANTMYER OIL CO INC (PA)
3000 Old Airport Rd (44691-9520)
P.O. Box 146 (44691-0146)
PHONE.................................330 262-6501
Fax: 330 264-8023
Terry Santmyer, *Principal*
Robert Slauterbeck, *Vice Pres*
Mike Crossen, *Manager*
Don Hawke, *Manager*
EMP: 55
SQ FT: 1,000
SALES (est): 104.2MM **Privately Held**
WEB: www.santmyeroil.com
SIC: **5172** 5983 4212 5531 Fuel oil; gasoline; fuel oil dealers; petroleum haulage, local; automotive parts

(G-19912)
SCHMID MECHANICAL INC
207 N Hillcrest Dr (44691-3720)
PHONE.................................330 264-3633
Fax: 330 263-6553
Timothy Schmid, *President*
Tim Lucas, *Superintendent*
Dustin Fishburn, *Vice Pres*
Chalet Smith, *Project Mgr*
Dan Chojnacki, *Financial Exec*
EMP: 45

SQ FT: 2,400
SALES (est): 7.2MM **Privately Held**
WEB: www.schmid-net.com
SIC: **1711** Plumbing contractors; sprinkler contractors; warm air heating & air conditioning contractor

(G-19913)
SCHMIDS SERVICE NOW INC
Also Called: Snyder's Service Now
258 S Columbus Ave (44691-4826)
PHONE.................................330 264-2040
Fax: 330 263-7784
Lee Painter, *Branch Mgr*
EMP: 42 **Privately Held**
SIC: **1711** 5722 Warm air heating & air conditioning contractor; electric household appliances
PA: Schmid's Service Now, Inc
807 N Main St
Canton OH 44720

(G-19914)
SCOT INDUSTRIES INC
6578 Ashland Rd (44691-9233)
P.O. Box 1106 (44691-7081)
PHONE.................................330 262-7585
Fax: 330 263-4702
David Speigle, *Vice Pres*
Mike Bannert, *Plant Mgr*
Cody Wesson, *Prdtn Mgr*
Bob Gralinski, *Facilities Mgr*
Tammy Myers, *Human Resources*
EMP: 40
SQ FT: 2,018
SALES (corp-wide): 180.3MM **Privately Held**
WEB: www.scotindustries.com
SIC: **5051** 7389 3498 3471 Steel; pipe & tubing, steel; metal cutting services; fabricated pipe & fittings; plating & polishing
PA: Scot Industries, Inc.
3756 Fm 250 N
Lone Star TX 75668
903 639-2551

(G-19915)
SHEARER FARM INC (PA)
Also Called: John Deere Authorized Dealer
7762 Cleveland Rd (44691-7700)
PHONE.................................330 345-9023
Fax: 330 345-9348
Brian Giauque, *President*
Gerald Shearer, *Principal*
Dan Pycraft, *Materials Mgr*
James Croskey, *Manager*
EMP: 45 **EST**: 1937
SQ FT: 9,400
SALES (est): 59.5MM **Privately Held**
WEB: www.shearerequipment.com
SIC: **3523** 5082 Fertilizing machinery, farm; construction & mining machinery

(G-19916)
SHEER PROFESSIONALS INC
2912 Cleveland Rd (44691-1655)
PHONE.................................330 345-8666
Fax: 330 345-9686
Donna Beem, *Owner*
EMP: 32
SALES (est): 534.4K **Privately Held**
WEB: www.sheerprofessionals.com
SIC: **7231** Hairdressers

(G-19917)
SUNRISE SENIOR LIVING LLC
Also Called: Sunrise of Wooster
1615 Cleveland Rd (44691-2335)
PHONE.................................330 262-1615
Leslie Masters, *Sales Executive*
Ann Worley, *Manager*
James Schnabel, *Director*
EMP: 48
SALES (corp-wide): 4.3B **Publicly Held**
WEB: www.sunrise.com
SIC: **8051** 8361 Skilled nursing care facilities; residential care
HQ: Sunrise Senior Living, Llc
7902 Westpark Dr
Mc Lean VA 22102

(G-19918)
SURREAL ENTERTAINMENT LLC
2018 Great Trails Dr (44691-3740)
PHONE.................................330 262-5277
Sarvish Arora, *Mng Member*

▲ EMP: 27 **EST**: 2014
SALES: 100K **Privately Held**
SIC: **5162** Plastics products

(G-19919)
TRICOR INDUSTRIAL INC (PA)
Also Called: Tricor Metals
3225 W Old Lincoln Way (44691-3258)
P.O. Box 752 (44691-0752)
PHONE.................................330 264-3299
Fax: 330 262-7311
Nancy A Stitzlein, *CEO*
Michael D Stitzlein, *President*
◆ EMP: 77
SQ FT: 140,000
SALES: 50MM **Privately Held**
WEB: www.tricormetals.com
SIC: **5085** 5051 5169 3444 Industrial supplies; fasteners, industrial: nuts, bolts, screws, etc.; metals service centers & offices; chemicals & allied products; sheet metalwork

(G-19920)
TRICOR METALS
Also Called: Tricor Industrial
3225 W Old Lincoln Way (44691-3258)
P.O. Box 752 (44691-0752)
PHONE.................................330 264-3299
Mike Ftitzlein, *President*
Janelle Lentz, *Administration*
EMP: 100
SALES (est): 33.5MM **Privately Held**
SIC: **5085** Industrial supplies

(G-19921)
UNITED PARCEL SERVICE INC OH
Also Called: UPS
3250 Old Airport Rd (44691-9580)
PHONE.................................440 826-3320
EMP: 158
SALES (corp-wide): 65.8B **Publicly Held**
SIC: **4215** Parcel delivery, vehicular
HQ: United Parcel Service, Inc. (Oh)
55 Glenlake Pkwy
Atlanta GA 30328
404 828-6000

(G-19922)
VILLAGE NETWORK (PA)
2000 Noble Dr (44691-5353)
P.O. Box 518, Smithville (44677-0518)
PHONE.................................330 264-0650
James T Miller, *CEO*
Richard W Rodman, *Exec VP*
Bel Klockenga, *CFO*
Amy Saylor, *Admin Asst*
EMP: 216
SQ FT: 16,816
SALES: 38.8MM **Privately Held**
SIC: **8361** Boys' Towns

(G-19923)
WASTE MANAGEMENT OHIO INC
116 N Bauer Rd (44691-8624)
PHONE.................................800 910-2831
Ginger Kaladas, *Credit Staff*
Bill Sigler, *Manager*
Lee Hicks, *Contract Law*
EMP: 43
SALES (corp-wide): 14.4B **Publicly Held**
WEB: www.wm.com
SIC: **4953** Waste materials, disposal at sea
HQ: Waste Management Of Ohio, Inc.
1700 N Broad St
Fairborn OH 45324

(G-19924)
WAYNE MUTUAL INSURANCE CO
3873 Cleveland Rd (44691-1297)
PHONE.................................330 345-8100
Fax: 330 345-8775
Ralph Gresser, *Ch of Bd*
Alvin C Ramseyer, *Vice Ch Bd*
Tod Carmony, *President*
Edward Dark, *Counsel*
David Jarrett, *Counsel*
EMP: 38
SQ FT: 5,600

SALES: 15MM **Privately Held**
WEB: www.waynemutual.com
SIC: **6331** Fire, marine & casualty insurance

(G-19925)
WAYNE SAVINGS BANCSHARES INC (PA)
151 N Market St (44691-4809)
PHONE.................................330 264-5767
Peggy J Schmitz, *Ch of Bd*
James Rvansickle II, *President*
Joel Beckler, *Senior VP*
Jeff King, *Vice Pres*
Myron L Swartzentruber, *CFO*
EMP: 114
SALES: 17.5MM **Publicly Held**
SIC: **6035** Savings institutions, federally chartered

(G-19926)
WAYNE SAVINGS COMMUNITY BANK (HQ)
151 N Market St (44691-4809)
P.O. Box 858 (44691-0858)
PHONE.................................330 264-5767
Fax: 330 263-6490
James Rvansickle II, *President*
Jeneffer Gray, *Assistant VP*
EMP: 124
SQ FT: 12,500
SALES: 18.5MM **Publicly Held**
WEB: www.waynesavings.com
SIC: **6035** Savings institutions, federally chartered

(G-19927)
WEAVER CUSTOM HOMES INC
124 E Liberty St Ste A (44691-4421)
PHONE.................................330 264-5444
Fax: 330 263-4012
Ken Weaver, *CEO*
Ron Wenger, *Vice Pres*
Diann Miller, *Treasurer*
Mark Poulton, *Manager*
EMP: 40
SQ FT: 2,300
SALES (est): 7.8MM **Privately Held**
SIC: **1531** 1521 1542 Speculative builder, single-family houses; new construction, single-family houses; commercial & office building, new construction

(G-19928)
WEST VIEW MANOR INC
Also Called: West View Manor Retirement Ctr
1715 Mechanicsburg Rd (44691-2640)
PHONE.................................330 264-8640
Fax: 330 264-8396
Robert Wetter, *CFO*
Mike Jackson, *Director*
Theresa Ketler, *Director*
Mary Norris, *Director*
Linda Rogers, *Director*
EMP: 225
SQ FT: 126,000
SALES: 10.6MM **Privately Held**
WEB: www.westviewmanor.org
SIC: **8051** 8361 Convalescent home with continuous nursing care; geriatric residential care

(G-19929)
WESTERN RESERVE GROUP (PA)
1685 Cleveland Rd (44691-2335)
P.O. Box 36 (44691-0036)
PHONE.................................330 262-9060
Michael Reardon, *Ch of Bd*
F Emerson Logee, *Vice Ch Bd*
David Chandler, *President*
Kevin W Day, *President*
Dennis Manzella, *President*
EMP: 255 **EST**: 1937
SQ FT: 46,100
SALES (est): 333.5MM **Privately Held**
SIC: **6331** Fire, marine & casualty insurance: mutual

(G-19930)
WOLFF BROS SUPPLY INC
565 N Applecreek Rd (44691-9599)
PHONE.................................330 264-5900
Fax: 330 263-4410
Michael Huttinger, *Vice Pres*

Tina Sentelik, *Opers Mgr*
Andrew Bumgardner, *Sales Staff*
Joseph Ricci, *Sales Staff*
Doug Schnell, *Sales Staff*
EMP: 40
SQ FT: 1,632
SALES (corp-wide): 114.4MM **Privately Held**
WEB: www.wolffbros.com
SIC: 5074 5063 Plumbing fittings & supplies; electrical supplies
PA: Wolff Bros. Supply, Inc
6078 Wolff Rd
Medina OH 44256
330 725-3451

(G-19931)
WOOSTER CLINIC INC
1740 Cleveland Rd (44691-2296)
PHONE...........................330 264-1512
James Murphy MD, *President*
John Malgieri, *Treasurer*
Keith Wehr, *Administration*
EMP: 210 **EST:** 1939
SALES (est): 8.3MM **Privately Held**
SIC: 8011 Physicians' office, including specialists

(G-19932)
WOOSTER MOTOR WAYS INC (PA)
3501 W Old Lincoln Way (44691-3253)
P.O. Box 19 (44691-0019)
PHONE...........................330 264-9557
Fax: 330 264-8214
Paul M Williams, *President*
Jack Simmons, *Vice Pres*
Jack R Simmons, *Vice Pres*
Robin Engel, *Opers Mgr*
Jeff Schneider, *Opers Mgr*
EMP: 140
SQ FT: 40,000
SALES (est): 34.7MM **Privately Held**
WEB: www.woostermotorways.com
SIC: 4214 4226 4212 Local trucking with storage; special warehousing & storage; local trucking, without storage

(G-19933)
WOOSTER OPHTHALMOLOGISTS INC
Also Called: Eye Surgery Center of Wooster
3519 Friendsville Rd (44691-1241)
PHONE...........................330 345-7800
Fax: 330 345-8029
Harry A Zink, *President*
John W Thomas, *Vice Pres*
Thomas C Fenzl, *Treasurer*
Jeffrey Perkins, *Med Doctor*
Jeffrey W Perkins, *Admin Sec*
EMP: 45
SQ FT: 20,000
SALES (est): 5.2MM **Privately Held**
SIC: 8011 Ophthalmologist

(G-19934)
WOOSTER PRODUCTS INC
3503 Old Airport Rd (44691)
PHONE...........................330 264-2844
Poonam Harvey, *COO*
Rashmi Jeirath, *Controller*
EMP: 45
SALES (est): 2.3MM **Privately Held**
SIC: 7389

(G-19935)
WWST CORPORATION LLC
Also Called: Wqkt/Wkvx
186 S Hillcrest Dr (44691-3727)
PHONE...........................330 264-5122
Craig Walton, *General Mgr*
EMP: 1629 **EST:** 1996
SALES (est): 40.6MM
SALES (corp-wide): 573.2MM **Privately Held**
SIC: 4833 Television broadcasting stations
PA: Wooster Republican Printing Co
212 E Liberty St
Wooster OH
330 264-3511

(G-19936)
YOUNG MENS CHRISTIAN ASSOC
Also Called: YMCA OF THE USA
680 Woodland Ave (44691-2743)
PHONE...........................330 264-3131
Fax: 330 262-7227
Jeff Vincent, *Office Mgr*
W Robert Johnston, *Director*
Lori Colon, *Director*
William Seeden, *Director*
EMP: 60
SQ FT: 30,000
SALES: 2.2MM **Privately Held**
SIC: 7999 8641 7997 7991 Recreation center; youth organizations; membership sports & recreation clubs; physical fitness facilities

Worthington
Franklin County

(G-19937)
AAA OHIO AUTO CLUB
90 E Wilson Bridge Rd (43085-2325)
PHONE...........................614 431-7800
Ronald Carr, *President*
Dave Wood, *Vice Pres*
EMP: 60
SALES (est): 9.1MM **Privately Held**
SIC: 7549 Automotive maintenance services

(G-19938)
AJM WORTHINGTON INC
Also Called: Primrose School of Worthington
6902 N High St (43085-2510)
PHONE...........................614 888-5800
Dam Simonds, *President*
Dan Simonds, *President*
Tobie Simonds, *Vice Pres*
EMP: 30
SALES (est): 651.2K **Privately Held**
SIC: 8351 Preschool center

(G-19939)
ALLIEDBARTON SECURITY SVCS LLC
57 E Wilson Bridge Rd # 300 (43085-2368)
PHONE...........................614 225-9061
Gary Jones, *Principal*
Jim Soden, *Business Mgr*
Pam Armistead, *Recruiter*
EMP: 139
SALES (corp-wide): 2.6B **Privately Held**
SIC: 7381 Security guard service
HQ: Alliedbarton Security Services Llc
8 Tower Bridge 161 Wshgtn
Conshohocken PA 19428
610 239-1100

(G-19940)
AMERIPRISE FINANCIAL SVCS INC
250 W Old Wlsn Brg Rd # 150 (43085-2215)
PHONE...........................614 846-8723
Fax: 614 846-6529
Ray Jones, *Opers-Prdtn-Mfg*
Karen Cookston, *Advisor*
EMP: 67
SALES (corp-wide): 12B **Publicly Held**
WEB: www.amps.com
SIC: 6211 6411 6202 Mutual funds, selling by independent salesperson; insurance agents; investment advice
HQ: Ameriprise Financial Services Inc.
500 2nd St S Ste 101
La Crosse WI 54601
608 783-2639

(G-19941)
ANTHEM INSURANCE COMPANIES INC
Also Called: Blue Cross
6740 N High St (43085-7500)
P.O. Box 182361, Columbus (43218-2361)
PHONE...........................614 438-3542
Joe Bobey, *Branch Mgr*
EMP: 81
SALES (corp-wide): 90B **Publicly Held**
WEB: www.anthem-inc.com
SIC: 6324 Hospital & medical service plans
HQ: Anthem Insurance Companies, Inc.
120 Monument Cir Ste 200
Indianapolis IN 46204
317 488-6000

(G-19942)
ASSOCIATION OF PROSTHODONTICS
Also Called: Worthlington Dental Group
7227 N High St Ste 1 (43085-2575)
PHONE...........................614 885-2022
Fax: 614 888-0284
Bob Toottle, *Partner*
Richard P Cunningham, *Partner*
Melody Thomas, *Admin Asst*
Melissa Fast, *Dental Hygienist*
Christine Nobis, *Dental Hygienist*
EMP: 26
SALES (est): 1.7MM **Privately Held**
SIC: 8021 Prosthodontist

(G-19943)
BESTTRANSPORTCOM INC
400 W Wilson Bridge Rd (43085-2259)
PHONE...........................614 888-2378
Fax: 614 433-9748
Michael Dolan, *President*
Scott Cummans, *Vice Pres*
Pete Scolieri, *Sales Dir*
Patrick Ryan, *Sales Executive*
Nikki Brewer, *Manager*
EMP: 30
SQ FT: 11,000
SALES (est): 5.2MM **Privately Held**
WEB: www.besttransport.com
SIC: 7372 Prepackaged software

(G-19944)
CANNELL GRAPHICS LLC
5787 Linworth Rd (43085-3307)
PHONE...........................614 781-9760
Biz Phil Ferguson, *General Mgr*
Nicole Dobson, *Principal*
Pete Lauer, *Production*
Marcus McElas, *Manager*
EMP: 25
SALES (est): 3.8MM **Privately Held**
WEB: www.cannellgraphics.com
SIC: 7334 5199 Blueprinting service; art goods

(G-19945)
CAPITAL PARTNERS REALTY LLC
Keller Williams Commercial
100 E Wilson Bridge Rd # 100 (43085-2326)
PHONE...........................614 888-1000
Fax: 614 888-3880
Joann Rasmussen, *Sales Associate*
Tom Spangler, *Sales Associate*
Judy Ackerman, *Manager*
Ann Hunger, *Director*
Mellisa Thompson,
EMP: 39
SALES (est): 1MM
SALES (corp-wide): 1.2MM **Privately Held**
SIC: 6531 Real estate agent, residential
PA: Capital Partners Realty, Llc
100 E Wilson Bridge Rd # 100
Worthington OH 43085
614 888-1000

(G-19946)
CENTRAL OHIO PRIMARY CARE
760 Lakeview Plaza Blvd # 500 (43085-4734)
PHONE...........................614 540-7339
Fax: 614 540-7338
Carol Jenkins, *General Ptnr*
EMP: 50 **Privately Held**
SIC: 8011 Pediatrician
PA: Central Ohio Primary Care Physicians, Inc.
570 Polaris Pkwy Ste 250
Westerville OH 43082

(G-19947)
CHOICES FOR VCTIMS DOM VOLENCE
500 W Wilson Bridge Rd (43085-2238)
PHONE...........................614 224-6617
Larry Cowell, *CEO*
Larry Rinehart, *Treasurer*
Henry Kassab, *Accounting Mgr*
Stanley Gay, *Manager*
Gail Heller, *Director*
EMP: 29
SALES: 5.6MM **Privately Held**
SIC: 8399 8322 Advocacy group; emergency shelters

(G-19948)
COLUMBUS VTRINARY EMRGNCY SVCS
300 E Wilson Bridge Rd (43085-2300)
PHONE...........................614 846-5800
Fax: 614 846-5803
Paul Knapp, *Vice Pres*
Don White, *Treasurer*
Elizabeth Kellogg, *Admin Sec*
David Cook, *Administration*
EMP: 40
SQ FT: 20,000
SALES (est): 866.8K **Privately Held**
SIC: 0742 Veterinary services, specialties

(G-19949)
COMMERCIAL PAINTING INC
530 Lkview Plz Blvd Ste F (43085)
PHONE...........................614 298-9963
Fax: 614 298-9733
Greg Scott, *President*
Doug Lovelace, *Vice Pres*
Kevin Kobbeman, *VP Sales*
Pam Byerly, *Manager*
EMP: 25
SQ FT: 2,000
SALES (est): 2.1MM **Privately Held**
WEB: www.commercialpaintingohio.com
SIC: 1721 Residential painting

(G-19950)
COMPASSIONATE IN HOME CARE
7100 N High St Ste 200 (43085-2535)
PHONE...........................614 888-5683
Joe Govern, *President*
EMP: 40
SALES (est): 1.2MM **Privately Held**
WEB: www.compinhomecare.com
SIC: 8082 Home health care services

(G-19951)
COUGHLIN HOLDINGS LTD PARTNR
Also Called: Coughlin Realty
71 E Wilson Bridge Rd (43085-2358)
PHONE...........................614 847-1002
Al Coughlin Jr, *President*
Jean Flager, *CFO*
EMP: 50
SALES (est): 2MM **Privately Held**
SIC: 6512 Nonresidential building operators

(G-19952)
CSI INTERNATIONAL INC
690 Lkview Plz Blvd Ste C (43085)
PHONE...........................614 781-1571
J Espinosa, *President*
EMP: 779
SALES (corp-wide): 53MM **Privately Held**
SIC: 7349 Janitorial service, contract basis
PA: Csi International, Inc.
6700 N Andrews Ave # 400
Fort Lauderdale FL 33309
954 308-4300

(G-19953)
DATAFIELD INC
Also Called: A P T
25 W New England Ave (43085-3582)
PHONE...........................614 847-9600
Fax: 614 847-9599
Courtland Bishop, *CEO*
Michael F Mizesko, *Principal*
Britney Showalter, *CFO*
Brad Haarala, *Director*
EMP: 126
SQ FT: 8,000

Worthington - Franklin County (G-19954)

SALES (est): 12.8MM **Privately Held**
WEB: www.appliedperformance.com
SIC: 7379 Computer related consulting services

(G-19954)
DAYHUFF GROUP LLC (PA)
740 Lakeview Plaza Blvd # 300 (43085-6724)
PHONE.................614 854-9999
Corey Dayhuff, *President*
Lauren Maddern, *Business Mgr*
Edgar Alatorre, *Technology*
EMP: 32
SALES (est): 4.2MM **Privately Held**
WEB: www.dayhuffgroup.com
SIC: 7379

(G-19955)
ECS HOLDCO INC
705 Lkview Plz Blvd Ste A (43085)
PHONE.................614 433-0170
Dave Zappa, *Manager*
EMP: 33
SALES (corp-wide): 34MM **Privately Held**
SIC: 8748 Environmental consultant
PA: Ecs Holdco, Inc.

Agawam MA 01001

(G-19956)
ELITE EXPEDITING CORP (PA)
450 W Wilson Bridge Rd # 345 (43085-5226)
PHONE.................614 279-1181
Fax: 614 785-1186
D Jay Floyd, *President*
EMP: 75
SALES: 5.1MM **Privately Held**
WEB: www.eliteexp.com
SIC: 4215 Package delivery, vehicular

(G-19957)
EPIQURIAN INNS
Also Called: Worthington Inn, The
649 High St (43085-4105)
PHONE.................614 885-2600
Burke Showe, *Owner*
Hugh Showe II, *Manager*
EMP: 80
SQ FT: 28,000
SALES: 3MM **Privately Held**
SIC: 7011 5812 5813 Hotels; American restaurant; drinking places

(G-19958)
EVEREST TECHNOLOGIES INC
740 Lakeview Plaza Blvd # 250 (43085-4784)
PHONE.................614 436-3120
Fax: 614 436-3130
Vineet Arya, *President*
Puneet Arya, *Vice Pres*
Anil Bakhshi, *Vice Pres*
Bob Malik, *Treasurer*
Kapil Malik, *Treasurer*
EMP: 30
SALES (est): 5.3MM **Privately Held**
WEB: www.everesttech.com
SIC: 7379

(G-19959)
EXCEL ELECTRICAL CONTRACTOR
7484 Reliance St (43085-1703)
PHONE.................740 965-3795
Kenneth B White, *President*
Daniel R Howard, *Vice Pres*
EMP: 28
SQ FT: 2,700
SALES: 1.7MM **Privately Held**
SIC: 1731 Electrical work

(G-19960)
FARRIS ENTERPRISES INC (PA)
Also Called: Mammoth Restoration and Clg
7465 Worthington Galena (43085-6714)
PHONE.................614 367-9611
Matthew Farris, *President*
EMP: 36
SQ FT: 2,700
SALES: 4.6MM **Privately Held**
SIC: 1521 Repairing fire damage, single-family houses

(G-19961)
HE HARI INC
Also Called: Holiday Inn
7007 N High St (43085-2329)
PHONE.................614 436-0700
Vijay Phapha, *Branch Mgr*
Nitin Patel, *Admin Sec*
EMP: 89
SALES (est): 4.1MM
SALES (corp-wide): 1.8MM **Privately Held**
SIC: 7011 Hotels & motels
PA: He Hari Inc
600 Enterprise Dr
Lewis Center OH 43035
614 846-6600

(G-19962)
HECO OPERATIONS INC
Also Called: SERVPRO
7440 Pingue Dr (43085-1741)
PHONE.................614 888-5700
Fax: 614 888-0112
Patricia Heid, *Owner*
Robert Heid, *Owner*
Richard Cottrill, *Vice Pres*
Jean Dickey, *Manager*
EMP: 36
SQ FT: 19,150
SALES (est): 1.8MM **Privately Held**
WEB: www.spohio.com
SIC: 7349 Building maintenance services

(G-19963)
HER INC
Also Called: H E R Realtors
681 High St (43085-4105)
PHONE.................614 888-7400
Fax: 614 888-1126
Robert Case, *President*
Jessica McClurg, *Opers Mgr*
Karen Gorski, *Sales Associate*
Paul Bean, *Manager*
Maureen McCabe, *Manager*
EMP: 60
SALES (corp-wide): 14.3MM **Privately Held**
WEB: www.eassent.com
SIC: 6531 Real estate agent, residential
PA: Her, Inc
4261 Morse Rd
Columbus OH 43230
614 221-7400

(G-19964)
HOME HEALTH CONNECTION INC
6797 N High St Ste 113 (43085-2533)
PHONE.................614 839-4545
Fax: 614 540-1088
Shirine Mafi, *President*
Shawn Mafi, *Vice Pres*
Lynn Gray, *Director*
EMP: 30 **EST:** 2000
SALES (est): 2.1MM **Privately Held**
SIC: 8059 8011 Personal care home, with health care; offices & clinics of medical doctors

(G-19965)
HOMEREACH INC (HQ)
404 E Wilson Bridge Rd (43085-2369)
PHONE.................614 566-0850
Fax: 614 786-7070
Frances Baby, *President*
Mike Lazar, *CFO*
Elieen Kidner, *Accounts Mgr*
Mandy Sanford, *Mktg Dir*
Mary Shoemaker, *Office Mgr*
EMP: 125
SALES (est): 13.1MM
SALES (corp-wide): 3.7B **Privately Held**
WEB: www.homereach.net
SIC: 8082 Home health care services
PA: Ohiohealth Corporation
180 E Broad St
Columbus OH 43215
614 788-8860

(G-19966)
KINDERCARE LEARNING CTRS INC
Also Called: Kindercare Child Care Network
77 Caren Ave (43085-2513)
PHONE.................614 888-9696
Charles Freed, *Manager*
Laura Walker, *Director*
EMP: 25
SALES (corp-wide): 1.2B **Privately Held**
WEB: www.kindercare.com
SIC: 8351 Group day care center
HQ: Kindercare Learning Centers, Llc
650 Ne Holladay St # 1400
Portland OR 97232
503 872-1300

(G-19967)
KLINGBEIL CAPITAL MGT LLC (PA)
500 W Wilson Bridge Rd (43085-2238)
P.O. Box 1474, Centreville VA (20122-8474)
PHONE.................614 396-4919
James D Klingbeil Jr, *CEO*
Kasey Stevens, *Vice Pres*
Brett Bickley, *Controller*
Audra McIntosh, *Marketing Staff*
Lisa Aguirre, *Manager*
EMP: 55
SALES (est): 154.3MM **Privately Held**
SIC: 6799 8741 Real estate investors, except property operators; management services

(G-19968)
LAUREL HEALTH CARE COMPANY
Also Called: Laurels of Norworth
6830 N High St (43085-2510)
PHONE.................614 888-4553
Rylie Hacker, *Chf Purch Ofc*
Julie Falk, *Office Mgr*
Kelly Foster, *Info Tech Dir*
Jeff Allen, *Info Tech Mgr*
Don Appericio, *Director*
EMP: 115 **Privately Held**
WEB: www.laurelsofnorworth.com
SIC: 8741 8051 Nursing & personal care facility management; skilled nursing care facilities
HQ: Laurel Health Care Company
8181 Worthington Rd Uppr
Westerville OH 43082

(G-19969)
LAUREL HEALTH CARE COMPANY
Also Called: Worlds of Worthington
1030 High St (43085-4014)
PHONE.................614 885-0408
Chris Hudson, *Manager*
Leo Lawver, *Maintence Staff*
EMP: 200 **Privately Held**
WEB: www.laurelsofnorworth.com
SIC: 8741 8051 8059 Nursing & personal care facility management; hotel or motel management; skilled nursing care facilities; convalescent home
HQ: Laurel Health Care Company
8181 Worthington Rd Uppr
Westerville OH 43082

(G-19970)
LEADERS MOVING COMPANY
Also Called: Leaders Moving & Storage Co
7455 Alta View Blvd (43085-5891)
PHONE.................614 785-9595
Craig Crotinger, *Owner*
Steve Lambert, *COO*
Ericka Barr, *Opers Mgr*
Zachary Zieman, *Opers Mgr*
Jason Farley, *Opers Staff*
EMP: 50
SQ FT: 30,000
SALES (est): 8.1MM **Privately Held**
WEB: www.leadersmoving.com
SIC: 4212 4214 Moving services; furniture moving & storage, local

(G-19971)
LEI CBUS LLC
7492 Sancus Blvd (43085-4923)
PHONE.................614 302-8830
Matthew Jackson,
EMP: 50
SALES (est): 1.8MM **Privately Held**
SIC: 1521 Single-family housing construction

(G-19972)
LEVEL 3 TELECOM LLC
250 W Old Wilson Brg 13 (43085-2285)
PHONE.................614 255-2000
Mark Watson, *Accounts Exec*
Robert Miracle, *Manager*
EMP: 45
SALES (corp-wide): 17.6B **Publicly Held**
WEB: www.twtelecom.com
SIC: 4813
HQ: Level 3 Telecom, Llc
10475 Park Meadows Dr
Lone Tree CO 80124
303 566-1000

(G-19973)
LIBERTY CAPITAL SERVICES LLC
438 E Wilson Bridge Rd (43085-2382)
PHONE.................614 505-0620
Kenneth Wichman, *CEO*
EMP: 25 **EST:** 2011
SALES (est): 2.8MM **Privately Held**
SIC: 6162 Mortgage bankers

(G-19974)
LUTHERAN SCIAL SVCS CENTL OHIO (PA)
500 W Wilson Bridge Rd (43085-2238)
PHONE.................419 289-3523
Fax: 614 228-1471
Larry Crowell, *President*
Leah Schwalbe, *President*
Rose Craig, *Vice Pres*
Rick Davis, *Vice Pres*
Heather McCracken, *Vice Pres*
EMP: 40
SQ FT: 9,000
SALES: 49.2MM **Privately Held**
SIC: 8322 Outreach program

(G-19975)
LUTHERAN SOCIAL SERVICES OF
500 W Wilson Bridge Rd # 245 (43085-2283)
PHONE.................614 228-5200
Larry Crowell, *CEO*
Henry Kassab, *Accounting Mgr*
EMP: 25
SQ FT: 8,000
SALES (est): 247.3K **Privately Held**
SIC: 8082 Home health care services

(G-19976)
MEDVET ASSOCIATES INC (PA)
Also Called: Med Vet Associates
300 E Wilson Bridge Rd # 100 (43085-2300)
PHONE.................614 846-5800
Eric Schertel, *President*
John Gordon, *Treasurer*
Linda Lehmkuhl, *Chief Mktg Ofcr*
Troy Collins, *Director*
William Dehoff Dvm Ms, *Shareholder*
EMP: 696
SALES (est): 57.6MM **Privately Held**
WEB: www.medvetassociates.com
SIC: 0742 Veterinarian, animal specialties

(G-19977)
MIDWEST LIQUIDATORS INC
6827 N High St Ste 109 (43085-2517)
PHONE.................614 433-7355
Fax: 614 433-9020
Robert Cassel, *President*
Deborah R Cassel, *Vice Pres*
Julie Clement, *Manager*
EMP: 40
SQ FT: 2,400
SALES: 7.5MM **Privately Held**
WEB: www.casselauctions.com
SIC: 7389 6531 Merchandise liquidators; auctioneers, fee basis; real estate agents & managers

(G-19978)
MILE INC (PA)
Also Called: Lion's Den
110 E Wilson Bridge Rd # 100 (43085-2317)
PHONE.................614 794-2203
Michael R Moran, *President*
Eric Bomer, *Opers Mgr*
Patricia Dixon, *Executive*

GEOGRAPHIC SECTION
Worthington - Franklin County (G-20003)

EMP: 64
SALES (est): 12.8MM **Privately Held**
SIC: 7841 5942 Video tape rental; book stores

(G-19979)
NEW ENGLAND RMS INC
402 E Wilson Bridge Rd A (43085-2366)
PHONE.................................401 384-6759
Dixon Buehler, *CEO*
Joseph Cozzolino, *President*
EMP: 40
SQ FT: 8,000
SALES (est): 1.5MM **Privately Held**
SIC: 8361 Residential care for the handicapped

(G-19980)
OHIO AUTOMOBILE CLUB (PA)
Also Called: AAA
90 E Wilson Bridge Rd # 1 (43085-2387)
PHONE.................................614 431-7901
Fax: 614 431-7918
Mark Shaw, *President*
Tom Keyes, *COO*
Mark Grunden, *Director*
EMP: 200
SQ FT: 1,172
SALES (est): 55.9MM **Privately Held**
SIC: 8699 Automobile owners' association

(G-19981)
ORGANIZATIONAL HORIZONS INC
5721 N High St Ste L1a (43085-3978)
P.O. Box 14425, Columbus (43214-0425)
PHONE.................................614 268-6013
Fax: 614 841-0744
Sandra Shullman, *President*
EMP: 40
SQ FT: 2,600
SALES: 1.7MM **Privately Held**
SIC: 8742 Management consulting services

(G-19982)
PAYCHEX INC
600 Lkview Plz Blvd Ste G (43085)
PHONE.................................614 781-6143
Dale Warcewicz, *Branch Mgr*
EMP: 37
SALES (corp-wide): 3.1B **Publicly Held**
SIC: 8721 Payroll accounting service
PA: Paychex, Inc.
 911 Panorama Trl S
 Rochester NY 14625
 585 385-6666

(G-19983)
PAYCOR INC
250 E Wilson Bridge Rd # 110 (43085-2323)
PHONE.................................614 985-6140
Tammy Jamison, *Vice Pres*
Lorinda Binzer, *Sales Staff*
Brittany Brigadoi, *Sales Staff*
Becky Fusco, *Branch Mgr*
Brian Craft, *Manager*
EMP: 27
SALES (corp-wide): 105.2MM **Privately Held**
SIC: 8721 Payroll accounting service
PA: Paycor, Inc.
 4811 Montgomery Rd
 Cincinnati OH 45212
 513 381-0505

(G-19984)
PHIL GIESSLER
Also Called: Camtaylor Co Realtors
882 High St Ste A (43085-4159)
PHONE.................................614 888-0307
Phil Giessler, *Owner*
EMP: 30
SALES (est): 1.2MM **Privately Held**
WEB: www.cam-taylor.com
SIC: 6531 6512 Real estate brokers & agents; nonresidential building operators

(G-19985)
PREMIER CARE
500 W Wilson Bridge Rd # 235 (43085-2287)
PHONE.................................614 431-0599
Fax: 614 734-0519
Debbie Ittikraichereon, *Principal*

EMP: 55
SALES (est): 755K **Privately Held**
SIC: 8082 Home health care services

(G-19986)
PRIORITY MORTGAGE CORP
150 E Wilson Bridge Rd # 350 (43085-6302)
PHONE.................................614 431-1141
Fax: 614 431-0690
Samuel J Hill, *CEO*
Gary W Erler, *President*
Lisa Kendle, *Assistant VP*
Marianne Viola, *Assistant VP*
David McKee, *Vice Pres*
EMP: 28
SQ FT: 6,000
SALES (est): 5.4MM **Privately Held**
SIC: 6162 Mortgage bankers

(G-19987)
PSP OPERATIONS INC
7440 Pingue Dr (43085-1741)
PHONE.................................614 888-5700
Kenneth Parker, *Principal*
EMP: 27 EST: 2014
SALES (est): 660.5K **Privately Held**
SIC: 7349 Building maintenance services

(G-19988)
QUALITY AERO INC (PA)
Also Called: Acquisition Logistics Engrg
6797 N High St Ste 324 (43085-2598)
PHONE.................................614 436-1609
Fax: 614 436-1295
Renee Coogan, *President*
Steephen Brinson, *Vice Pres*
Joseph Coogan, *Vice Pres*
Lillian Coogan, *Director*
Delana Haldy, *Admin Sec*
EMP: 25
SQ FT: 5,000
SALES (est): 3.2MM **Privately Held**
WEB: www.ale.com
SIC: 8711 Consulting engineer

(G-19989)
R DORSEY & COMPANY INC
Also Called: R.dorsey & Company
400 W Wilson Bridge Rd # 105 (43085-2259)
P.O. Box 12328, Columbus (43212-0328)
PHONE.................................614 486-8900
Fax: 614 486-3698
Robert J Dorsey, *President*
EMP: 50
SQ FT: 2,000
SALES: 4MM **Privately Held**
WEB: www.dorseyplus.com
SIC: 7379 Computer related consulting services

(G-19990)
R P CUNNINGHAM DDS INC
7227 N High St Ste 1 (43085-2575)
PHONE.................................614 885-2022
R Cunningham DDS, *Principal*
Richard Cunningham DDS, *Principal*
Robert Tootle DDS, *Vice Pres*
EMP: 25 EST: 1975
SALES (est): 751K **Privately Held**
SIC: 8021 Offices & clinics of dentists

(G-19991)
RECYCLED SYSTEMS FURNITURE INC
Also Called: Rsfi Office Furniture
401 E Wilson Bridge Rd (43085-2320)
PHONE.................................614 880-9110
Fax: 614 880-9112
Ron Morris, *President*
Jim Ellison, *Vice Pres*
Joanne Simmons, *Office Admin*
EMP: 25
SQ FT: 100,000
SALES (est): 4.4MM **Privately Held**
WEB: www.rsfi.com
SIC: 7641 5712 2522 Office furniture repair & maintenance; furniture upholstery repair; office furniture; office furniture, except wood

(G-19992)
RESIDENTIAL MANAGEMENT SYSTEMS (PA)
402 E Wilson Bridge Rd (43085-2366)
PHONE.................................614 880-6014
Fax: 614 847-0601
Joseph Cozzolino, *President*
Anita Allen, *COO*
Dixon Buehler, *CFO*
Joe McCain, *Accountant*
Rose Childers, *Manager*
EMP: 41
SQ FT: 8,325
SALES: 4.5MM **Privately Held**
SIC: 8361 Home for the mentally handicapped

(G-19993)
RESOURCE ONE CMPT SYSTEMS INC
651 Lkview Plz Blvd Ste E (43085)
PHONE.................................614 485-4800
Stampp W Corbin, *President*
Mary Jobe, *Marketing Staff*
Lou Dellapina, *Manager*
EMP: 100
SALES (est): 12.6MM **Privately Held**
SIC: 5734 7378 Computer & software stores; computer maintenance & repair

(G-19994)
RICOH USA INC
300 W Wilson Bridge Rd # 110 (43085-2235)
PHONE.................................614 310-6500
Marsha Vanderstel, *Regional Mgr*
Christopher Gilligan, *Accounts Exec*
Heather Grace, *Accounts Exec*
Georg Shannon, *Manager*
Pat Brown, *Executive*
EMP: 70
SALES (corp-wide): 17.8B **Privately Held**
WEB: www.ikon.com
SIC: 5044 Photocopy machines
HQ: Ricoh Usa, Inc.
 70 Valley Stream Pkwy
 Malvern PA 19355
 610 296-8000

(G-19995)
SAFELITE GLASS CORP
Guardian Auto Glass
600 Lkview Plz Blvd Ste A (43085)
P.O. Box 29167, Columbus (43229-0167)
PHONE.................................614 431-4936
Fax: 614 891-5954
Reuben Lo, *Vice Pres*
Shannon Slade, *Plant Mgr*
Davanh Brown, *Store Mgr*
Tonie Jones, *Store Mgr*
Michael Kuehlthau, *Store Mgr*
EMP: 25
SALES (corp-wide): 3.1B **Privately Held**
SIC: 7536 Automotive glass replacement shops
HQ: Safelite Glass Corp.
 7400 Safelite Way
 Columbus OH 43235
 614 210-9000

(G-19996)
SECURE TRNSP CO OHIO LLC
777 Dearborn Park Ln S (43085-5716)
PHONE.................................800 856-9994
David Kurtz, *CFO*
Steve Dobbs,
Anne Marin,
EMP: 25
SALES (est): 534.7K **Privately Held**
SIC: 4789 Pipeline terminal facilities, independently operated

(G-19997)
SERVICES ON MARK INC
705 Lkview Plz Blvd Ste L (43085)
PHONE.................................614 846-5400
Fax: 614 901-3533
Mark Stuntz, *President*
EMP: 40
SALES (est): 1.5MM **Privately Held**
SIC: 8322 Child related social services

(G-19998)
SOUTHAST CMNTY MENTAL HLTH CTR
Also Called: Southeast Counseling
445 E Granville Rd (43085-3192)
PHONE.................................614 293-9613
Amy Price, *Branch Mgr*
EMP: 25
SALES (corp-wide): 12.5MM **Privately Held**
WEB: www.southeastinc.com
SIC: 8093 8322 Mental health clinic, outpatient; general counseling services
PA: Southeast Community Mental Health Center Inc
 16 W Long St
 Columbus OH 43215
 614 225-0980

(G-19999)
ST MORITZ SECURITY SVCS INC
705 Lkview Plz Blvd Ste G (43085)
PHONE.................................614 351-8798
Fax: 614 351-8874
Gary Harney, *Branch Mgr*
EMP: 45
SALES (corp-wide): 87.5MM **Privately Held**
WEB: www.smssi.com
SIC: 7381 Security guard service; detective services
PA: St. Moritz Security Services, Inc.
 4600 Clairton Blvd
 Pittsburgh PA 15236
 412 885-3144

(G-20000)
STAT EXPRESS DELIVERY LLC (PA)
705 Lkview Plz Blvd Ste M (43085)
PHONE.................................614 880-7828
Fax: 614 880-9240
Kathy Rittenhouse,
EMP: 47
SQ FT: 8,600
SALES (est): 2.1MM **Privately Held**
WEB: www.statexpress.com
SIC: 4215 Package delivery, vehicular

(G-20001)
SUNRISE SENIOR LIVING INC
Also Called: Sunrise Pl For Memory Impaired
6525 N High St (43085-4045)
PHONE.................................614 846-6500
Debra Guzman, *Principal*
EMP: 42
SALES (corp-wide): 4.3B **Publicly Held**
WEB: www.sunrise.com
SIC: 8361 8059 8051 Home for the aged; nursing home, except skilled & intermediate care facility; skilled nursing care facilities
HQ: Sunrise Senior Living, Llc
 7902 Westpark Dr
 Mc Lean VA 22102

(G-20002)
SWIM INCORPORATED
Also Called: WORTHINGTON SWIMMING POOL
400 W Dublin Granville Rd (43085-3590)
PHONE.................................614 885-1619
Fax: 614 885-4833
Tom Bubenik, *President*
Ron Lemerech, *President*
Phil Sobers, *General Mgr*
Dan McCarthy, *Asst Mgr*
Chris Hadden, *Director*
EMP: 50 EST: 1953
SALES: 1.1MM **Privately Held**
WEB: www.worthingtonswimclub.org
SIC: 7997 5812 7991 Swimming club, membership; concessionary; physical fitness facilities

(G-20003)
THOMAS GLASS COMPANY INC (PA)
400 E Wilson Bridge Rd A (43085-2363)
PHONE.................................614 268-8611
Andrew T Gum, *President*
Joe Bronson, *Business Mgr*
Charles Condit, *Vice Pres*
Lori Gum, *Engineer*
Madelyne Shepelak, *Human Res Mgr*

Worthington - Franklin County (G-20004)

EMP: 35
SQ FT: 4,000
SALES (est): 3.6MM **Privately Held**
WEB: www.thomasglass.com
SIC: **1793** Glass & glazing work

(G-20004)
UNITED METHODIST CHILDRENS (PA)
Also Called: United Methodist Childrens HM
1033 High St (43085-4026)
PHONE..................................614 885-5020
Fax: 614 885-4058
David Kurtz, *CFO*
Jamie Burks, *Human Res Dir*
Sean Reilly, *Exec Dir*
Bill Brownson, *Director*
Steven Putka, *Director*
EMP: 83
SQ FT: 7,000
SALES: 3.9MM **Privately Held**
WEB: www.umchohio.org
SIC: **8361** 8322 Home for the emotionally disturbed; group foster home; adoption services

(G-20005)
VERISK CRIME ANALYTICS INC
Also Called: Netmap Analytics
250 Old Wilson Brg (43085-2285)
PHONE..................................614 865-6000
Joseph Hirt, *Branch Mgr*
EMP: 33 **Publicly Held**
SIC: **7375** Information retrieval services
HQ: Verisk Crime Analytics, Inc.
  545 Washington Blvd
  Jersey City NJ 07310
  201 469-3000

(G-20006)
WARD & WERNER CO
6620 Plesenton Dr W (43085-2945)
P.O. Box 340497, Columbus (43234-0497)
PHONE..................................614 885-0741
Anthony Werner, *President*
Cheryl Werner, *Corp Secy*
Randy Ward, *Vice Pres*
EMP: 120
SALES (est): 2.4MM **Privately Held**
SIC: **7349** Building maintenance services

(G-20007)
WEST OHIO CONFERENCE OF (PA)
Also Called: United Methodist Camps
32 Wesley Blvd (43085-3585)
PHONE..................................614 844-6200
Fax: 614 781-2642
Gregory V Palmer, *Principal*
Barb Sholis, *Principal*
Bruce R Ouch, *Bishop*
Bill Brownson, *CFO*
Joy Monpanye, *Treasurer*
EMP: 39
SQ FT: 16,587
SALES (est): 5.6MM **Privately Held**
WEB: www.cliftonumc.com
SIC: **7032** 8661 Recreational camps; Methodist Church

(G-20008)
WHALEN AND COMPANY INC
Also Called: Whalen & Co CPA
250 W Old Wlsn Brg Rd # 300 (43085-2215)
PHONE..................................614 396-4200
Fax: 614 891-5504
Richard D Crabtree, *Partner*
Linda Hickey, *Partner*
Lisa G Shuneson, *Partner*
Laura B Wojciechowski, *Partner*
Dawn Malone, *CPA*
EMP: 32
SQ FT: 7,500
SALES (est): 3.2MM **Privately Held**
SIC: **8721** Certified public accountant

(G-20009)
WHITING-TURNER CONTRACTING CO
250 W Old Wilson Bridge R (43085-5227)
PHONE..................................614 459-6515
Tom Garske, *Regional Mgr*
EMP: 214
SALES (corp-wide): 5.5B **Privately Held**
SIC: **1542** Nonresidential construction
PA: The Whiting-Turner Contracting Company
  300 E Joppa Rd Ste 800
  Baltimore MD 21286
  410 821-1100

(G-20010)
WORTHINGTON PUBLIC LIBRARY
820 High St (43085-3182)
PHONE..................................614 807-2626
Fax: 614 807-2642
Margaret Doone, *Business Mgr*
John Mills, *Business Mgr*
Phyllis Winfield, *Human Res Mgr*
Kara Reuter, *Librarian*
Jessi Tisdale, *Manager*
EMP: 130
SALES: 54.9K **Privately Held**
WEB: www.worthingtonmemory.net
SIC: **8231** 8742 Public library; management consulting services

(G-20011)
WORTHINGTON UNITED METHDST CH
600 High St (43085-4116)
PHONE..................................614 885-5365
Andrew J Browning, *Manager*
Wendy Colbart, *Director*
EMP: 25
SALES (est): 710.1K **Privately Held**
WEB: www.worthingtonumc.com
SIC: **8351** Child day care services

Wright Patterson Afb
Greene County

(G-20012)
BOEING COMPANY
5200 Vincent Ave (45433-5127)
PHONE..................................937 431-3503
EMP: 275
SALES (corp-wide): 93.3B **Publicly Held**
SIC: **8711** Aviation &/or aeronautical engineering
PA: The Boeing Company
  100 N Riverside Plz
  Chicago IL 60606
  312 544-2000

Wshngtn CT Hs
Fayette County

(G-20013)
ADENA HEALTH SYSTEM
308 Highland Ave Unit C (43160-1993)
PHONE..................................740 779-7500
Adedoyin Adetoro, *Principal*
EMP: 213
SALES (corp-wide): 111.9MM **Privately Held**
SIC: **8062** General medical & surgical hospitals
PA: Adena Health System
  272 Hospital Rd
  Chillicothe OH 45601
  740 779-7360

(G-20014)
CARROLL HALLIDAY INC
1700 Columbus Ave (43160-1705)
PHONE..................................740 335-1670
Fax: 740 335-3713
David Ogan, *President*
Bill Picklesimer, *Manager*
EMP: 34
SALES: 12MM **Privately Held**
SIC: **7514** 5511 7539 Passenger car rental; new & used car dealers; machine shop, automotive

(G-20015)
CLARK ROYSTER INC
717 Robinson Rd Se (43160-8630)
PHONE..................................740 335-3810
Steve Emery, *President*
EMP: 30
SALES (est): 672.8K **Privately Held**
SIC: **0711** Soil chemical treatment services

(G-20016)
COMMU ACT COMM OF FAYETTE CNTY (PA)
1400 Us Highway 22 Nw (43160-8604)
PHONE..................................740 335-7282
Fax: 740 335-6802
Mekia Rhoades, *Manager*
Bill Davis, *Supervisor*
Lucinda Baughn, *Exec Dir*
Vicki Carrozza, *Director*
EMP: 95
SQ FT: 2,000
SALES: 7MM **Privately Held**
SIC: **8322** Social service center

(G-20017)
COUNTY OF FAYETTE
Also Called: County Engineer
1600 Robinson Rd Se (43160-9205)
PHONE..................................740 335-1541
Fax: 740 333-3573
Ron Longberry, *Superintendent*
Karla Morrison, *Admin Sec*
Julie Hidy, *Admin Asst*
Dana Foor, *Assistant*
EMP: 36 **Privately Held**
SIC: **8711** Engineering services
PA: County Of Fayette
  133 S Main St Rm 401
  Wshngtn Ct Hs OH 43160
  740 335-0720

(G-20018)
COX PAVING INC
2754 Us Highway 22 Nw (43160-9510)
PHONE..................................937 780-3075
Fax: 937 780-5201
Fred B Cox Jr, *President*
Fred B Cox III, *Vice Pres*
Gregory R Cox, *Vice Pres*
Misty Lawson, *Manager*
Jeff West, *Manager*
EMP: 93
SALES (est): 12.3MM **Privately Held**
WEB: www.coxpavinginc.com
SIC: **1794** 7631 1771 Excavation & grading, building construction; watch repair; driveway contractor

(G-20019)
CUSTOM LAWN CARE & LDSCPG LLC
2411 Us Highway 22 Sw (43160-8652)
PHONE..................................740 333-1669
Fax: 740 333-7381
Jaret L Bishop,
EMP: 25
SALES (est): 3.5MM **Privately Held**
SIC: **0781** Landscape services

(G-20020)
DOUG MARINE MOTORS INC
1120 Clinton Ave (43160-1215)
PHONE..................................740 335-3700
Fax: 740 333-3966
Doug Marine, *President*
Bill D Marine, *Admin Sec*
EMP: 31
SQ FT: 8,000
SALES (est): 9.8MM **Privately Held**
WEB: www.dougmarinemotors.com
SIC: **5511** 7538 5531 5012 Automobiles, new & used; general automotive repair shops; automotive & home supply stores; automobiles & other motor vehicles; motor vehicle parts & accessories

(G-20021)
FAYETTE COUNTY FAMILY YMCA
Also Called: Fayette County Family YMCA
100 Civic Dr (43160-9186)
P.O. Box 1021 (43160-8021)
PHONE..................................740 335-0477
Douglas Saunders, *CEO*
EMP: 85
SQ FT: 35,000
SALES: 1.5MM **Privately Held**
SIC: **8641** Youth organizations

(G-20022)
FAYETTE COUNTY MEMORIAL HOSP (PA)
1430 Columbus Ave (43160-1791)
P.O. Box 310 (43160-0310)
PHONE..................................740 335-1210
Fax: 740 333-2997
Beverly Hughes, *Vice Pres*
Mike Senter, *Vice Pres*
Tammie Wilson, *Vice Pres*
Kevin Anderson, *Plant Mgr*
Tammy Wilson, *QA Dir*
EMP: 224
SALES: 42MM **Privately Held**
SIC: **8062** General medical & surgical hospitals

(G-20023)
FAYETTE PROGRESSIVE INDUSTRIES
Also Called: Fayette County Mrdd
1330 Robinson Rd Se (43160-9201)
PHONE..................................740 335-7453
Fax: 740 335-2185
Steve Hilgeman, *Superintendent*
Mark Schwartz, *Director*
EMP: 40
SALES: 300.2K **Privately Held**
WEB: www.fayettemrdd.com
SIC: **8322** Individual & family services

(G-20024)
FOUR SEASONS WASHINGTON LLC
201 Courthouse Pkwy (43160-6001)
PHONE..................................740 895-6101
Tim A Ross, *Mng Member*
Tracy Ross,
EMP: 80 EST: 2014
SALES (est): 1.5MM **Privately Held**
SIC: **8051** Convalescent home with continuous nursing care

(G-20025)
HCF OF COURT HOUSE INC
Also Called: Court House Manor
555 N Glenn Ave (43160-2711)
PHONE..................................740 335-9290
Fax: 740 335-9337
Belinda Ross, *Sls & Mktg Exec*
Scott Hollaway, *Nursing Dir*
Tonya Duncan, *Executive*
Penny Henize, *Executive*
India Williamson, *Administration*
EMP: 256
SALES: 1,000K
SALES (corp-wide): 154.8MM **Privately Held**
SIC: **8051** Convalescent home with continuous nursing care
PA: Hcf Management, Inc.
  1100 Shawnee Rd
  Lima OH 45805
  419 999-2010

(G-20026)
HCF OF WASHINGTON INC
Also Called: St. Cthrnes Manor Wash Crt Hse
555 N Glenn Ave (43160-2711)
PHONE..................................419 999-2010
Barbara Masella, *Vice Pres*
Penny Henize, *Persnl Dir*
EMP: 35 **Privately Held**
SIC: **8059** Nursing home, except skilled & intermediate care facility
PA: Hcf Of Washington, Inc.
  250 Glenn Ave
  Wshngtn Ct Hs OH 43160

(G-20027)
HUNTINGTON NATIONAL BANK
Also Called: Advantage Bank
134 E Court St (43160-1358)
PHONE..................................740 335-3771
Ann Lenzer, *Branch Mgr*
EMP: 27
SALES (corp-wide): 4.7B **Publicly Held**
SIC: **6036** Savings & loan associations, not federally chartered
HQ: The Huntington National Bank
  17 S High St Fl 1
  Columbus OH 43215
  614 480-4293

Xenia — Greene County

(G-20028) KROGER CO
548 Clinton Ave (43160-1299)
PHONE 740 335-4030
Fax: 740 333-3827
William Drum, *Manager*
Tim Houseman, *Administration*
EMP: 110
SALES (corp-wide): 122.6B **Publicly Held**
WEB: www.kroger.com
SIC: **5411** 5122 2051 Supermarkets, chain; drugs, proprietaries & sundries; bread, cake & related products
PA: The Kroger Co
1014 Vine St Ste 1000
Cincinnati OH 45202
513 762-4000

(G-20029) LOWES HOME CENTERS LLC
1895 Lowes Blvd (43160-8611)
PHONE 740 636-2100
Fax: 740 636-0098
Tom Montgomery, *Branch Mgr*
EMP: 45
SALES (corp-wide): 68.6B **Publicly Held**
SIC: **4225** General warehousing & storage
HQ: Lowe's Home Centers, Llc
1605 Curtis Bridge Rd
Wilkesboro NC 28697
336 658-4000

(G-20030) MCKESSON CORPORATION
3000 Kenskill Ave (43160-8615)
PHONE 740 636-3500
Fax: 740 636-3526
Becky Pitakos, *Manager*
Karla Stokley, *Supervisor*
Robert Kearney, *Director*
EMP: 150
SALES (corp-wide): 198.5B **Publicly Held**
WEB: www.imckesson.com
SIC: **5122** Pharmaceuticals
PA: Mckesson Corporation
1 Post St Fl 18
San Francisco CA 94104
415 983-8300

(G-20031) MERRILL LYNCH PIERCE FENNER
209 E Court St (43160-1301)
PHONE 740 335-2930
John Bryan, *Branch Mgr*
George Smith, *Administration*
Andrew Cimis, *Advisor*
EMP: 55
SALES (corp-wide): 100.2B **Publicly Held**
SIC: **6282** Investment advisory service
HQ: Merrill Lynch, Pierce, Fenner & Smith Incorporated
111 8th Ave
New York NY 10011
800 637-7455

(G-20032) MID ATLANTIC STOR SYSTEMS INC
1551 Robinson Rd Se (43160-9201)
PHONE 740 335-2019
Fax: 740 335-0584
Jerry Morris, *President*
Jeanette Morris, *Corp Secy*
John Fox, *Vice Pres*
EMP: 75
SQ FT: 25,000
SALES (est): 23.9MM **Privately Held**
SIC: **1791** Storage tanks, metal: erection

(G-20033) RITEN INDUSTRIES
1110 Lakeview Ave (43160)
P.O. Box 340 (43160-0340)
PHONE 740 335-5353
J Andrew Lachat, *President*
Patricia Simon, *Manager*
EMP: 60
SALES (est): 11.7MM **Privately Held**
SIC: **5085** Industrial supplies

(G-20034) SCIOTO PNT VLY MENTAL HLTH CTR
Also Called: Scioto Pnt Vly Mental Hlth Ctr
1300 E Paint St (43160-1676)
PHONE 740 335-6935
Fax: 740 335-7423
Ed Sipe, *Manager*
EMP: 25
SALES (corp-wide): 14.2MM **Privately Held**
SIC: **8093** 8322 8069 Mental health clinic, outpatient; crisis intervention center; drug addiction rehabilitation hospital
PA: Scioto Paint Valley Mental Health Center
4449 State Route 159
Chillicothe OH 45601
740 775-1260

(G-20035) SEED CONSULTANTS INC (DH)
648 Miami Trace Rd Sw (43160-9661)
P.O. Box 370 (43160-0370)
PHONE 740 333-8644
Fax: 740 333-8544
Chris Jeffries, *General Mgr*
Dan Fox, *Vice Pres*
Bryan Smith, *Sales Mgr*
Connie Dement, *Accounts Mgr*
Brian George, *Regl Sales Mgr*
EMP: 50
SQ FT: 32,500
SALES (est): 11MM
SALES (corp-wide): 62.4B **Publicly Held**
WEB: www.seedconsultants.com
SIC: **5261** 5191 Nursery stock, seeds & bulbs; seeds: fruit, garden & flower
HQ: Pioneer Hi-Bred International, Inc.
7100 Nw 62nd Ave
Johnston IA 50131
515 535-3200

(G-20036) WALMART INC
1400 Old Chllicothe Rd Se (43160-9305)
PHONE 740 636-5400
Trenda Allen, *General Mgr*
Gary Brasseur, *General Mgr*
Matt Storrs, *General Mgr*
Michelle Spurling, *QA Dir*
Paul Herring, *Manager*
EMP: 850
SALES (corp-wide): 500.3B **Publicly Held**
WEB: www.walmartstores.com
SIC: **4225** General warehousing & storage
PA: Walmart Inc.
702 Sw 8th St
Bentonville AR 72716
479 273-4000

(G-20037) WASHINGTON COURT HSE HOLDG LLC
Also Called: G K Packaging
1850 Lowes Blvd (43160-8611)
PHONE 614 873-7733
Wyane Whitaker, *General Mgr*
EMP: 35
SALES (corp-wide): 24MM **Privately Held**
WEB: www.gkpackaging.com
SIC: **6719** Personal holding companies, except banks
PA: Gk Packaging, Inc.
7680 Commerce Pl
Plain City OH 43064
614 873-3900

(G-20038) WESTROCK CP LLC
1010 Mead St (43160-9310)
PHONE 770 448-2193
Larry Markham, *QC Dir*
Mark Badgley, *Branch Mgr*
EMP: 93
SALES (corp-wide): 14.8B **Publicly Held**
WEB: www.smurfit-stone.com
SIC: **2653** 5113 3412 Boxes, corrugated: made from purchased materials; corrugated & solid fiber boxes; metal barrels, drums & pails
HQ: Westrock Cp, Llc
504 Thrasher St
Norcross GA 30071

Xenia
Greene County

(G-20039) A-1 BAIL BONDS INC
20 S Detroit St (45385-3502)
P.O. Box 771 (45385-0771)
PHONE 937 372-2400
Judy Miller, *President*
Jeff Brown, *President*
EMP: 50
SALES (est): 1.3MM **Privately Held**
WEB: www.a-1bailbonds.net
SIC: **7389** Bail bonding

(G-20040) AK GROUP HOTELS INC
Also Called: Ramada Xenia
300 Xenia Towne Sq (45385-2949)
PHONE 937 372-9921
Rajesh Agrawala, *President*
Ketan Kadkia, *Vice Pres*
Sharon Hammond, *Sales Mgr*
EMP: 25
SQ FT: 40,000
SALES (est): 1.3MM **Privately Held**
SIC: **7011** 5812 Hotels; restaurant, family: independent

(G-20041) AMERICAN RED CROSS
Also Called: Green County Housing Program
1080 E Main St (45385-3310)
PHONE 937 376-3111
Tom Foder, *Branch Mgr*
EMP: 29
SALES (corp-wide): 2.5B **Privately Held**
SIC: **8322** Social service center
HQ: American Red Cross
370 W 1st St
Dayton OH 45402
937 222-0124

(G-20042) AT&T CORP
767 Industrial Blvd (45385-4031)
PHONE 937 372-9945
Fax: 937 372-8140
EMP: 107
SALES (corp-wide): 160.5B **Publicly Held**
SIC: **4813** Telephone communication, except radio
HQ: At&T Corp.
1 At&T Way
Bedminster NJ 07921
800 403-3302

(G-20043) ATHLETES IN ACTION SPORTS (HQ)
651 Taylor Dr (45385-7246)
PHONE 937 352-1000
Mark Householder, *President*
Kyle Wenig, *Pastor*
Jerry Dendinger, *Vice Pres*
Dave McDowell, *Vice Pres*
Sonny Mounts, *Maint Spvr*
EMP: 100
SQ FT: 5,227,200
SALES (est): 16.8MM
SALES (corp-wide): 234.2MM **Privately Held**
WEB: www.aia.com
SIC: **8699** Charitable organization
PA: Campus Crusade For Christ Inc
100 Lake Hart Dr
Orlando FL 32832
407 826-2000

(G-20044) BALANCED CARE CORPORATION
Also Called: Outlook Point At Xenia
60 Paceline Cir (45385-1281)
PHONE 937 372-7205
Fax: 937 372-1730
Ana Ellen, *Manager*
Felicia McCombs, *Manager*
EMP: 50 **Privately Held**
SIC: **8741** 8051 Nursing & personal care facility management; skilled nursing care facilities
PA: Balanced Care Corporation
5000 Ritter Rd Ste 202
Mechanicsburg PA 17055

(G-20045) CITY OF XENIA
Also Called: Xenia Waster Water
779 Ford Rd (45385-9538)
PHONE 937 376-7271
Chris Burger, *Principal*
EMP: 25 **Privately Held**
SIC: **4953**
PA: City Of Xenia
101 N Detroit St
Xenia OH 45385
937 376-7231

(G-20046) CITY OF XENIA
Sanitation Division
966 Towler Rd (45385-2412)
PHONE 937 376-7260
Fax: 937 376-7254
Kenneth Johnson, *Human Res Dir*
Paul Gultice, *Manager*
Jim Jones, *Director*
EMP: 40
SQ FT: 730 **Privately Held**
SIC: **8744** Base maintenance (providing personnel on continuing basis)
PA: City Of Xenia
101 N Detroit St
Xenia OH 45385
937 376-7231

(G-20047) COUNTRY CLUB OF NORTH
1 Club North Dr (45385-9399)
PHONE 937 374-5000
Fax: 937 374-5049
Michael A Mess, *President*
Steve Cash, *Asst Supt*
Jennifer Bouanani, *Sales Staff*
Lisa Renshaw, *Sales Executive*
Cheri Dalton, *Food Svc Dir*
EMP: 37
SALES (est): 2.3MM **Privately Held**
SIC: **7997** Country club, membership

(G-20048) CREATIVE DIVERSIFIED SERVICES
335 E Market St (45385-3114)
PHONE 937 376-7810
Fax: 937 376-9407
James Wickline, *President*
Matt Bottorff, *Manager*
EMP: 30
SALES: 446.5K **Privately Held**
SIC: **8322** Individual & family services

(G-20049) DAVITA INC
215 S Allison Ave Ste B (45385-3694)
PHONE 937 376-1453
Kim White, *Administration*
EMP: 26 **Publicly Held**
SIC: **8092** Kidney dialysis centers
PA: Davita Inc.
2000 16th St
Denver CO 80202

(G-20050) FILE SHARPENING COMPANY INC
Also Called: Save Edge USA
360 W Church St (45385-2900)
PHONE 937 376-8268
Fax: 937 376-8052
George Whyde, *President*
Randy Stout, *Manager*
▲ EMP: 25
SALES (est): 7.8MM **Privately Held**
SIC: **5085** 7699 3423 3315 Industrial tools; knife, saw & tool sharpening & repair; hand & edge tools; steel wire & related products

Xenia - Greene County (G-20051)

(G-20051) FOUR OAKS EARLY INTERVENTION
245 N Valley Rd (45385-9301)
PHONE..................937 562-6779
Fax: 937 562-7539
Mary Ann Campbell, *Principal*
EMP: 38
SALES (est): 696.3K **Privately Held**
SIC: 8351 Child day care services

(G-20052) GREENE CNTY CHLD SVC BRD FRBRN
601 Ledbetter Rd Ste A (45385-5363)
PHONE..................937 878-1415
Susan Alberter, *Program Dir*
Rhonda Reagh, *Administration*
Monica Schiffler, *Relations*
EMP: 75 EST: 2001
SALES (est): 1.2MM **Privately Held**
SIC: 8399 Social service information exchange

(G-20053) GREENE CNTY COMBINED HLTH DST
Also Called: Greene County Public Health
360 Wilson Dr (45385-1810)
PHONE..................937 374-5600
Fax: 937 376-3361
Melissa Branum, *CEO*
EMP: 69
SQ FT: 13,000
SALES: 4MM **Privately Held**
WEB: www.gcchd.org
SIC: 8322 Social service center

(G-20054) GREENE COUNTY
Also Called: Green County Engineer
615 Dayton Xenia Rd (45385-2605)
PHONE..................937 562-7500
Fax: 937 562-7510
Robert Geyer, *Branch Mgr*
Ken Hunley, *Supervisor*
EMP: 40 **Privately Held**
SIC: 8711 9221 Engineering services; state highway patrol
PA: Greene County
 35 Greene St
 Xenia OH 45385
 937 562-5006

(G-20055) GREENE COUNTY
Also Called: Human Services
541 Ledbetter Rd (45385-5334)
PHONE..................937 562-6000
Fax: 937 376-5377
Philip Mastn, *Director*
Beth Rubin, *Director*
Charlotte Rangi, *Asst Director*
EMP: 140 **Privately Held**
WEB: www.greeneworks.com
SIC: 8322 Public welfare center
PA: Greene County
 35 Greene St
 Xenia OH 45385
 937 562-5006

(G-20056) GREENE COUNTY
Also Called: Greene County Services
641 Dayton Xenia Rd (45385-2605)
PHONE..................937 562-7800
Fax: 937 562-7801
Kim Farmer, *Financial Exec*
Marvin Reid, *Commissioner*
Alan G Anderson, *Cnty Cmsnr*
Midge Fletcher, *Technology*
Robert Raglin, *Technology*
EMP: 32 **Privately Held**
WEB: www.greeneworks.com
SIC: 8744 Base maintenance (providing personnel on continuing basis)
PA: Greene County
 35 Greene St
 Xenia OH 45385
 937 562-5006

(G-20057) GREENE COUNTY CAREER CENTER
2960 W Enon Rd (45385-9545)
PHONE..................937 372-6941
Matt Lindley, *Principal*
Quinn Maureen, *Dept Chairman*
Kimberly Torrence, *Dept Chairman*
Ron Bolender, *Pub Rel Dir*
Cathy Mullen, *Inst Media Dir*
EMP: 40
SALES (est): 1.1MM **Privately Held**
SIC: 8399 Fund raising organization, non-fee basis

(G-20058) GREENE INC
Also Called: DOCUMENT SOLUTIONS
121 Fairground Rd (45385-9543)
PHONE..................937 562-4200
Fax: 937 376-8544
Mary Nissen, *Business Mgr*
Myra Jackson, *Financial Exec*
Dennis Rhodes, *Sales Mgr*
Robyn Marconet, *Manager*
Greg Geyer, *Info Tech Mgr*
EMP: 100
SQ FT: 2,086
SALES: 3.5MM **Privately Held**
WEB: www.greeneinc.org
SIC: 8331 Sheltered workshop

(G-20059) GREENE MEMORIAL HOSPITAL INC (DH)
1141 N Monroe Dr (45385-1600)
PHONE..................937 352-2000
Fax: 937 376-6983
Michael R Stephens, *CEO*
Jacqueline Weckesser, *Pastor*
Tracy Price, *Purch Agent*
Jim Pollard, *CFO*
Timothy Pollard, *CFO*
EMP: 600
SALES: 42.8MM
SALES (corp-wide): 1.7B **Privately Held**
WEB: www.greenememorialhospital.com
SIC: 8062 Hospital, affiliated with AMA residency
HQ: Greene Health Partners
 1141 N Monroe Dr
 Xenia OH 45385
 937 352-2000

(G-20060) GREENE OAKS
Also Called: MIDWEST HOME INFUSION
164 Office Park Dr (45385-1647)
PHONE..................937 352-2800
Fax: 937 376-8219
Frannita Porter, *Sls & Mktg Exec*
Dwayne Tracy, *Information Mgr*
John Flannigan, *Exec Dir*
Katie Dickens, *Hlthcr Dir*
EMP: 100
SQ FT: 18,000
SALES: 6.8MM
SALES (corp-wide): 1.7B **Privately Held**
SIC: 8051 Skilled nursing care facilities
HQ: Kettering Affiliated Health Services, Inc
 3535 Southern Blvd
 Dayton OH 45429
 937 298-4331

(G-20061) HOME RUN INC (PA)
1299 Lavelle Dr (45385-7402)
PHONE..................800 543-9198
Fax: 937 376-1379
Gary Harlow, *President*
Thomas Baker, *Vice Pres*
Dennis Harlow, *Vice Pres*
Chad Harlow, *VP Opers*
Donna Glispie, *Recruiter*
EMP: 35
SQ FT: 12,800
SALES: 31.4MM **Privately Held**
WEB: www.homeruninc.com
SIC: 4213 4212 Building materials transport; local trucking, without storage

(G-20062) HOMETOWN URGENT CARE
101 S Orange St (45385-3603)
PHONE..................937 372-6012
Ritu Singla, *Principal*
Brenda Lewis, *Director*
EMP: 126
SALES (corp-wide): 73.2MM **Privately Held**
SIC: 8031 8011 Offices & clinics of osteopathic physicians; clinic, operated by physicians
PA: Hometown Urgent Care
 2400 Corp Exchange Dr # 102
 Columbus OH 43231
 614 505-7633

(G-20063) HOSPICE OF MIAMI VALLEY LLC (PA)
46 N Detroit St Ste B (45385-2984)
PHONE..................937 458-6028
Carol L Brad, *CEO*
EMP: 28
SALES (est): 2.9MM **Privately Held**
SIC: 8052 Personal care facility

(G-20064) JAMES ADVANTAGE FUNDS
1349 Fairground Rd (45385-9514)
PHONE..................937 426-7640
Frank James, *Owner*
Barry James, *Vice Pres*
Diane M Rose, *Vice Pres*
Jeff Battles, *Sales Executive*
Michelle Sarmiento, *Marketing Staff*
EMP: 25
SALES (est): 2.1MM **Privately Held**
SIC: 6722 Management investment, open-end

(G-20065) KIL KARE INC
Also Called: Kil-Kare Speedway & Drag Strip
1166 Dayton Xenia Rd (45385-7107)
PHONE..................937 429-2961
Fax: 937 427-2001
David Cotereo, *President*
Noah Lemons, *Director*
Tommy Schloss, *Director*
EMP: 80
SQ FT: 2,000
SALES (est): 2.5MM **Privately Held**
WEB: www.kilkare.com
SIC: 7948 Automotive race track operation

(G-20066) KROGER CO
1700 W Park Sq (45385-2667)
PHONE..................937 376-7962
Fax: 937 376-3997
Amy Bohman, *Pharmacist*
Paul Fullencamb, *Manager*
EMP: 260
SALES (corp-wide): 122.6B **Publicly Held**
WEB: www.kroger.com
SIC: 5411 5141 Supermarkets, chain; supermarkets, 66,000-99,000 square feet; convenience stores, chain; groceries, general line
PA: The Kroger Co
 1014 Vine St Ste 1000
 Cincinnati OH 45202
 513 762-4000

(G-20067) LIBERTY NURSING HOME INC
Also Called: Heathergreene Nursing Homes
126 Wilson Dr (45385-1899)
PHONE..................937 376-2121
Fax: 937 376-1457
Linda Black-Kurek, *President*
Maryann La Vigne, *Vice Pres*
Mandy Sparkman, *Manager*
EMP: 75
SALES (est): 3.9MM **Privately Held**
SIC: 8051 Extended care facility

(G-20068) LOWES HOME CENTERS LLC
126 Hospitality Dr (45385-2777)
PHONE..................937 347-4000
Fax: 937 347-4003
Kimberly Leeper, *Store Mgr*
Jeremy Austin, *Manager*
EMP: 150
SALES (corp-wide): 68.6B **Publicly Held**
SIC: 5211 5031 5722 5064 Home centers; building materials, exterior; building materials, interior; household appliance stores; electrical appliances, television & radio
HQ: Lowe's Home Centers, Llc
 1605 Curtis Bridge Rd
 Wilkesboro NC 28697
 336 658-4000

(G-20069) MACAIR AVIATION LLC
140 N Valley Rd (45385-9301)
PHONE..................937 347-1302
Ross McNutt,
EMP: 32
SALES (est): 1.1MM **Privately Held**
SIC: 8299 7363 7997 4581 Airline training; pilot service, aviation; flying field, maintained by aviation clubs; airports & flying fields; confinement surveillance systems maintenance & monitoring

(G-20070) MIAMI VLY JVNILE RHBLTTION CTR
2100 Greene Way Blvd (45385-2677)
PHONE..................937 562-4000
Fax: 937 562-4170
Tawnya Henry, *Program Mgr*
Amanda Opicka, *Technology*
Gary Neidenthal, *Director*
EMP: 30
SALES (est): 559.2K **Privately Held**
SIC: 8322 Rehabilitation services

(G-20071) NATIONWIDE BIWEEKLY ADM INC
Also Called: Nba
855 Lower Bellbrook Rd (45385-7306)
PHONE..................937 376-5800
Daniel Lipsky, *President*
Sherry A Scott, *General Mgr*
Eric Clouse, *Business Mgr*
Mozelle Jackson, *CFO*
Bassam Rassi, *Sales Mgr*
EMP: 105
SQ FT: 25,000
SALES (est): 51.5MM **Privately Held**
WEB: www.nbabiweekly.com
SIC: 6099 Clearinghouse associations, bank or check

(G-20072) REDDY ELECTRIC CO
1145 Bellbrook Ave (45385-4061)
PHONE..................937 372-8205
Fax: 937 372-1556
Robert L La Freniere, *President*
Jeff Eldridge, *Vice Pres*
Steve Stanek, *Vice Pres*
Ted Nicholson, *Project Mgr*
Frank Carone, *Purch Agent*
EMP: 140
SQ FT: 7,000
SALES: 22MM **Privately Held**
WEB: www.reddyelectric.com
SIC: 1731 General electrical contractor

(G-20073) REPTILES BY MACK LLC
37 S Detroit St Ste 101 (45385-3581)
PHONE..................937 372-9570
John Mack, *Principal*
Amy Mack, *Vice Pres*
EMP: 50
SALES (est): 3.2MM **Privately Held**
SIC: 0752 Animal specialty services

(G-20074) ROGOSIN INSTITUTE INC
740 Birch Rd (45385-9606)
PHONE..................937 374-3116
Albert L Rubin, *President*
EMP: 25
SALES (corp-wide): 100MM **Privately Held**
WEB: www.thf.org
SIC: 8733 8731 Medical research; commercial physical research
PA: The Rogosin Institute Inc
 505 E 70th St Fl 2
 New York NY 10021
 212 746-1551

GEOGRAPHIC SECTION

(G-20075)
SENIOR CARE INC
Elmcroft Assisted Living
60 Paceline Cir (45385-1281)
PHONE..................937 372-1530
Diana Alan, *Branch Mgr*
Dan Shiplett, *Director*
EMP: 50 **Privately Held**
SIC: 8361 8051 Home for the aged; skilled nursing care facilities
PA: Senior Care, Inc.
700 N Hurstbourne Pkwy # 200
Louisville KY 40222

(G-20076)
SHOUPES CONSTUCTION
1410 Ludlow Rd (45385-7900)
PHONE..................937 352-6457
Roger L Shoupes, *Owner*
EMP: 25 **EST:** 1986
SALES: 850K **Privately Held**
SIC: 1521 Single-family housing construction

(G-20077)
TCN BEHAVIORAL HEALTH SVCS INC (PA)
Also Called: COMMUNITY NETWORK THE
452 W Market St (45385-2815)
PHONE..................937 376-8700
Fax: 937 376-0113
Lynn West, *CEO*
Sharon Brown, *HR Admin*
Franklin Halley, *Med Doctor*
Sena Harris, *Case Mgr*
Bobbie Fussichen, *Info Tech Dir*
EMP: 190
SALES: 13MM **Privately Held**
SIC: 8322 8093 Individual & family services; specialty outpatient clinics

(G-20078)
TEAM GREEN LAWN LLC
1070 Union Rd (45385-7216)
PHONE..................937 673-4315
Josh Anderson, *Mng Member*
EMP: 40 **EST:** 2009
SALES: 3.5MM **Privately Held**
SIC: 0782 Lawn care services

(G-20079)
TOWARD INDEPENDENCE INC (PA)
81 E Main St (45385-3201)
PHONE..................937 376-3996
Fax: 937 376-2046
Robert L Archer, *Exec Dir*
EMP: 25 **EST:** 1975
SQ FT: 2,000
SALES: 10.4MM **Privately Held**
WEB: www.ti-inc.org
SIC: 8361 Home for the mentally retarded; home for the mentally handicapped

(G-20080)
TRIAD GOVERNMENTAL SYSTEMS
358 S Monroe St (45385-3442)
PHONE..................937 376-5446
Tod A Rapp, *President*
EMP: 27
SALES (est): 2.6MM **Privately Held**
WEB: www.triadgsi.com
SIC: 7371 7372 Computer software development; prepackaged software

(G-20081)
TWIST INC
Also Called: ACC-U-Coil
1380 Lavelle Dr (45385-5676)
P.O. Box 356 (45385-0356)
PHONE..................937 675-9581
Fax: 937 376-4771
Jill Eright, *President*
Jim Chaney, *Plant Mgr*
Ron Pasco, *Draft/Design*
EMP: 35
SALES (corp-wide): 50.2MM **Privately Held**
SIC: 4225 General warehousing & storage
PA: Twist Inc.
47 S Limestone St
Jamestown OH 45335
937 675-9581

(G-20082)
US ONCOLOGY INC
Also Called: Ruth McMillan Cancer Center
1141 N Monroe Dr (45385-1619)
PHONE..................937 352-2140
Mark Collins, *Manager*
EMP: 36
SALES (corp-wide): 198.5B **Publicly Held**
WEB: www.mohpa.com
SIC: 8011 Oncologist
HQ: Us Oncology, Inc.
10101 Woodloch Forest Dr
The Woodlands TX 77380

(G-20083)
WICKLINE LANDSCAPING INC (PA)
Also Called: Wickline Floral & Garden Ctr
1625 N Detroit St (45385-1200)
PHONE..................937 372-0521
James Wickline, *President*
Helen B Wickline, *Vice Pres*
Mark Wickline, *Vice Pres*
Doug Wickline, *Admin Sec*
EMP: 32
SQ FT: 3,936
SALES (est): 1.8MM **Privately Held**
SIC: 5992 0782 5261 Flowers, fresh; landscape contractors; nursery stock, seeds & bulbs

(G-20084)
WOMENS RECOVERY CENTER
515 Martin Dr (45385-1615)
PHONE..................937 562-2400
Fax: 937 352-2930
Stephanie Harvey, *Psychologist*
Gretchen Hohnson, *Manager*
Michelle Cox, *Director*
Jim Barger, *Director*
EMP: 40
SALES: 2.2MM **Privately Held**
SIC: 8361 Halfway home for delinquents & offenders

(G-20085)
XENIA AREA CMNTY THEATER INC
Also Called: Xact
45 E 2nd St (45385-3415)
PHONE..................937 372-0516
Alan King, *President*
Allan King, *President*
EMP: 99
SALES: 58.9K **Privately Held**
EST: 1975
SIC: 7922 Community theater production

(G-20086)
XENIA EAST MANAGEMENT SYSTEMS
Also Called: Hospitality Home East
1301 N Monroe Dr (45385-1623)
PHONE..................937 372-4495
Fax: 937 372-8038
Grace Mc Cormick, *Social Dir*
John Flanagan, *Administration*
EMP: 95
SALES: 7.5MM **Privately Held**
SIC: 8051 Skilled nursing care facilities

(G-20087)
XENIA WEST MANAGEMENT SYSTEMS
Also Called: Hospitality Home West
1384 N Monroe Dr (45385-1653)
PHONE..................937 372-8081
Fax: 937 372-3224
Anthony Deaton, *Administration*
EMP: 100
SALES (est): 1.9MM **Privately Held**
SIC: 8051 Skilled nursing care facilities

Yellow Springs
Greene County

(G-20088)
ANTIOCH UNIVERSITY
1 Morgan Pl (45387-1683)
PHONE..................937 769-1366
Joan Straumanis, *Principal*
Jennifer Bennett, *Manager*
EMP: 100
SALES (corp-wide): 65.7MM **Privately Held**
WEB: www.antiochla.edu
SIC: 8731 8221 Commercial physical research; colleges universities & professional schools
PA: Antioch University
900 Dayton St
Yellow Springs OH 45387
937 769-1370

(G-20089)
FRIENDS HEALTH CARE ASSN (PA)
Also Called: FRIENDS CARE CENTER
150 E Herman St (45387-1601)
PHONE..................937 767-7363
Fax: 937 767-2333
Brenda McFann, *COO*
Pam Haislip, *Human Res Mgr*
Karl Zalar, *Director*
EMP: 140
SQ FT: 25,000
SALES: 5.5MM **Privately Held**
WEB: www.friendshealthcare.org
SIC: 8051 Skilled nursing care facilities

(G-20090)
LAYH & ASSOCIATES
416 Xenia Ave (45387-1836)
PHONE..................937 767-9171
Fax: 937 767-9175
John Layh, *Owner*
EMP: 30
SQ FT: 1,967
SALES (est): 783.8K **Privately Held**
SIC: 8049 8011 Psychologist, psychotherapist & hypnotist; offices & clinics of medical doctors

(G-20091)
YOUNGS JERSEY DAIRY INC
Also Called: Golden Jersey Inn
6880 Springfield Xenia Rd (45387-9610)
PHONE..................937 325-0629
Fax: 937 325-3226
C Daniel Young, *President*
C Robert Young, *President*
Brian Patterson, *General Mgr*
William H Young, *Vice Pres*
Debra Whittaker, *Treasurer*
EMP: 300 **EST:** 1964
SQ FT: 35,000
SALES (est): 12.1MM **Privately Held**
SIC: 5812 5451 5947 7999 Ice cream stands or dairy bars; family restaurants; dairy products stores; gift shop; golf driving range; miniature golf course operation; dairy farms; ice cream & frozen desserts

Yorkshire
Darke County

(G-20092)
ROBERT WINNER SONS INC (PA)
Also Called: Winner's Meat Service
8544 State Route 705 (45388-9784)
P.O. Box 39, Osgood (45351-0039)
PHONE..................419 582-4321
Fax: 419 582-2123
Brian K Winner, *President*
Alan Winner, *Senior VP*
Ted Winner, *Vice Pres*
Terrance Winner, *Vice Pres*
Steven Winner, *Treasurer*
EMP: 40 **EST:** 1928
SQ FT: 6,500
SALES: 33.9MM **Privately Held**
SIC: 0213 0751 5154 5147 Hog feedlot; slaughtering; custom livestock services; hogs; meats & meat products; sausages & other prepared meats; meat packing plants

Yorkville
Jefferson County

(G-20093)
ROSEWOOD MANOR
Also Called: Rosewood Manor Nursing Home
212 4th St (43971-1212)
PHONE..................740 859-7673
Fax: 740 859-2813
Renato De La Cruz, *Director*
Roger Davis Jr, *Administration*
EMP: 46
SALES (est): 2.8MM **Privately Held**
SIC: 8051 Skilled nursing care facilities

Youngstown
Mahoning County

(G-20094)
A A S AMELS SHEET METAL INC
222 Steel St (44509-2547)
P.O. Box 2407 (44509-0407)
PHONE..................330 793-9326
Fax: 330 793-0072
Andrew A Samuels Jr, *President*
George Timar, *Admin Sec*
EMP: 40
SQ FT: 12,000
SALES (est): 6.7MM **Privately Held**
SIC: 1711 3585 3564 3444 Ventilation & duct work contractor; warm air heating & air conditioning contractor; refrigeration & heating equipment; blowers & fans; sheet metalwork; fabricated plate work (boiler shop)

(G-20095)
A P OHORO COMPANY
3130 Belmont Ave (44505-1802)
P.O. Box 2228 (44504-0228)
PHONE..................330 759-9317
Fax: 330 759-8965
Daniel P O Horo, *President*
Daniel J O Horo, *Chairman*
Fred Leunis, *Corp Secy*
Thomas P Metzinger, *Vice Pres*
Duane C Thompson, *Vice Pres*
EMP: 90
SQ FT: 6,000
SALES: 52MM **Privately Held**
WEB: www.apohoro.com
SIC: 1629 1622 1623 1611 Waste water & sewage treatment plant construction; bridge construction; sewer line construction; highway & street construction

(G-20096)
ABM PARKING SERVICES INC
20 W Federal St Ste M9 (44503-1430)
PHONE..................330 747-7678
Dan Strong, *Principal*
Darnell Frazier, *Manager*
EMP: 26
SALES (corp-wide): 5.4B **Publicly Held**
SIC: 7521 Indoor parking services
HQ: Abm Parking Services, Inc.
1150 S Olive St Fl 19
Los Angeles CA 90015
213 284-7600

(G-20097)
ADO HEALTH SERVICES INC
Also Called: Anesthesiologists, D.O., Inc.
1011 Boardman Canfield Rd (44512-4226)
PHONE..................330 629-2888
Tracy Neuendorf, *President*
EMP: 70
SQ FT: 14,000
SALES (est): 1.4MM **Privately Held**
SIC: 8062 General medical & surgical hospitals

(G-20098)
ADVANCED UROLOGY INC (PA)
904 Sahara Trl Ste 1 (44514-3695)
PHONE..................330 758-9787
Fax: 330 758-9792
Richard D Nord MD, *President*
Harold Muir, *Manager*

Youngstown - Mahoning County (G-20099)   GEOGRAPHIC SECTION

Rosemary Hager, *Administration*
EMP: 27
SQ FT: 10,000
SALES (est): 3.2MM **Privately Held**
SIC: 8011 Urologist; surgeon

(G-20099)
AEY ELECTRIC INC
801 N Meridian Rd (44509-1008)
PHONE.................................330 792-5745
Fax: 330 792-3055
Robert Aey, *President*
Scott Byer, *Project Mgr*
Richard J Aey, *Admin Sec*
EMP: 25 **EST:** 1964
SQ FT: 10,000
SALES (est): 4MM **Privately Held**
WEB: www.aeyelectric.com
SIC: 1731 General electrical contractor

(G-20100)
ALLIANCE HOSPITALITY
Also Called: Fairfield Inn
801 N Canfield Niles Rd (44515-1106)
PHONE.................................330 505-2173
Fax: 330 505-3629
Naresh Patel, *President*
EMP: 30
SALES (est): 1.2MM **Privately Held**
WEB: www.alliancehospitalityinc.com
SIC: 7011 Hotels & motels

(G-20101)
ALLIED ERCT & DISMANTLING CO
2100 Poland Ave (44502-2775)
PHONE.................................330 744-0808
Fax: 330 744-3218
John R Ramun, *President*
Jay Collins, *Controller*
Dalene Lawless, *Accounts Mgr*
Louise Ramun, *Admin Sec*
▲ **EMP:** 200
SQ FT: 24,000
SALES (est): 27.8MM
SALES (corp-wide): 29MM **Privately Held**
SIC: 1796 1795 Installing building equipment; wrecking & demolition work
PA: Allied Consolidated Industries Inc
2100 Poland Ave
Youngstown OH 44502
330 744-0808

(G-20102)
ALTA CARE GROUP INC
711 Belmont Ave (44502-1039)
PHONE.................................330 793-2487
Frank Paden, *Vice Pres*
Meg Harris, *Opers Spvr*
Jamie Miller, *CFO*
Stacey Roberts, *Psychologist*
Barbara Forgac, *Manager*
EMP: 50
SQ FT: 7,428
SALES: 9.4MM **Privately Held**
WEB: www.dandecenter.com
SIC: 8093 Mental health clinic, outpatient

(G-20103)
AMERICAN BULK COMMODITIES INC (PA)
Also Called: R & J Trucking
8063 Southern Blvd (44512-6306)
P.O. Box 9454 (44513-0454)
PHONE.................................330 758-0841
Fax: 330 758-8170
Ronald Carrocce, *President*
Mark Carrocce, *Vice Pres*
Troy Carrocce, *Treasurer*
Stan Simons, *Human Res Dir*
Gary Carrocce, *Admin Sec*
EMP: 200
SQ FT: 50,000
SALES (est): 92.9MM **Privately Held**
SIC: 4212 7532 6531 7363 Local trucking, without storage; paint shop, automotive; real estate managers; truck driver services

(G-20104)
AMERICAN MAINTENANCE SVCS INC
20 W Federal St Fl 2b (44503-1432)
PHONE.................................330 744-3400
Fax: 330 746-6180
Rodney Turner, *CEO*
Shirley Casey, *Opers Mgr*
EMP: 30
SALES (est): 890K **Privately Held**
SIC: 7349 Janitorial service, contract basis

(G-20105)
ASHLEY PLACE HEALTH CARE INC
5291 Ashley Cir (44515-1160)
PHONE.................................330 793-3010
Fax: 330 799-8082
Patricia Andrews, *President*
Maryann Barnett, *Vice Pres*
EMP: 160
SALES (est): 8.8MM **Privately Held**
SIC: 8051 Skilled nursing care facilities

(G-20106)
AT&T MOBILITY LLC
Also Called: Dobson Cellular Call Center
8089 South Ave (44512-6154)
PHONE.................................330 565-5000
Lynn Gherrardi, *Manager*
EMP: 200
SALES (corp-wide): 160.5B **Publicly Held**
WEB: www.dobsoncellular.com
SIC: 4812 Cellular telephone services
HQ: At&T Mobility Llc
1025 Lenox Park Blvd Ne
Brookhaven GA 30319
800 331-0500

(G-20107)
AUSTIN WOODS NURSING CENTER
Also Called: Austin Wods Rehabilitation Ctr
4780 Kirk Rd (44515-5403)
PHONE.................................330 792-7681
Fax: 330 792-9282
Karapini Prasad MD, *President*
Kathy Prasad, *Exec Dir*
Andy Douglas, *Director*
Sally Beil, *Administration*
EMP: 250
SQ FT: 90,000
SALES (est): 14.1MM **Privately Held**
WEB: www.austinwoods.com
SIC: 8051 Convalescent home with continuous nursing care

(G-20108)
AUSTINTOWN DAIRY INC
780 Bev Rd (44512-6424)
P.O. Box 9484 (44513-0484)
PHONE.................................330 629-6170
Fax: 330 629-6180
Joseph Creighton, *President*
Thomas Creighton, *Vice Pres*
Brian Cooper, *Sales Mgr*
EMP: 40
SALES (est): 15.4MM **Privately Held**
WEB: www.austintowndairy.com
SIC: 5143 5451 Milk; ice cream & ices; ice cream (packaged)

(G-20109)
B & B CONTRS & DEVELOPERS INC
2781 Salt Springs Rd (44509-1035)
PHONE.................................330 270-5020
Philip M Beshara, *President*
Donald D'Andrea, *President*
Dominic Cappibianca, *Vice Pres*
Joseph Tahos, *Vice Pres*
Geno Leshnack, *Project Mgr*
EMP: 80
SQ FT: 12,000
SALES (est): 24.4MM **Privately Held**
SIC: 1542 1541 Commercial & office building, new construction; shopping center construction; hospital construction; institutional building construction; industrial buildings, new construction

(G-20110)
BALOG STEINES HENDRICKS & MANC
15 Central Sq Ste 300 (44503-1517)
PHONE.................................330 744-4401
Gary G Balog, *President*
Byron Manchester, *Vice Pres*
Jeffrey J Beadle, *Director*
Mary O Dennis, *Sr Associate*
Stephen Zerefos, *Assistant*
EMP: 27 **EST:** 1960
SQ FT: 2,500
SALES (est): 3.1MM **Privately Held**
SIC: 8712 Architectural engineering

(G-20111)
BECHTL BLDNG MNTNC CRPRTN OF
Also Called: B B M
3734 Logan Gate Rd (44505-2324)
PHONE.................................330 759-2797
Fax: 330 759-7419
John L Bechtel, *President*
EMP: 75
SQ FT: 2,000
SALES (est): 1.8MM **Privately Held**
SIC: 7349 7217 5085 5064 Janitorial service, contract basis; carpet & upholstery cleaning; industrial supplies; vacuum cleaners, household

(G-20112)
BEL-PARK ANESTHESIA
1044 Belmont Ave (44504-1006)
PHONE.................................330 480-3658
Steve Scharf, *Principal*
Tom Deascentis, *Manager*
Linda Berry, *Anesthesiology*
Luz Gotham, *Anesthesiology*
Stephen Kitzmiller, *Anesthesiology*
EMP: 29
SALES (est): 4.4MM **Privately Held**
SIC: 8011 Anesthesiologist

(G-20113)
BELMONT BHC PINES HOSPITAL INC
615 Churchill Hubbard Rd (44505-1332)
PHONE.................................330 759-2700
Fax: 330 759-2776
George Perry, *President*
Kathy Bolmer, *Exec VP*
Carol Smith, *Materials Mgr*
Sue Deangelo DDS, *Fmly & Gen Dent*
EMP: 175
SQ FT: 32,000
SALES (est): 16.7MM **Privately Held**
WEB: www.belmontpines.com
SIC: 8063 8011 8093 8062 Psychiatric hospitals; offices & clinics of medical doctors; mental health clinic, outpatient; general medical & surgical hospitals

(G-20114)
BELMONT EYE CLINIC INC (PA)
3020 Belmont Ave (44505-1860)
PHONE.................................330 759-7672
Fax: 330 759-7699
Asher Zeev Rabinovitz, *President*
EMP: 28
SQ FT: 2,000
SALES (est): 2.5MM **Privately Held**
WEB: www.belmonteyeclinic.com
SIC: 8011 Ophthalmologist

(G-20115)
BIG LOTS INC
7110 South Ave (44512-3635)
PHONE.................................330 726-0796
Lucille Antonucci, *Branch Mgr*
Brad Seehoffer, *Manager*
EMP: 30
SALES (corp-wide): 5.2B **Publicly Held**
SIC: 5021 Furniture
PA: Big Lots, Inc.
300 Phillipi Rd
Columbus OH 43228
614 278-6800

(G-20116)
BLAKEMANS VALLEY OFF EQP INC
8534 South Ave (44514-3620)
PHONE.................................330 729-1000
Fax: 330 726-2810
Steve A Blakeman, *President*
Kathy L Blakeman, *Vice Pres*
Gary Mariano, *Sales Mgr*
Joette Martuccio, *Marketing Staff*
Paula Davis, *Manager*
EMP: 37
SQ FT: 8,000
SALES (est): 5.1MM **Privately Held**
SIC: 5999 7629 5044 Business machines & equipment; facsimile equipment; business machine repair, electric; copying equipment; calcvlators, electronic; typewriters

(G-20117)
BLUE CROSS & BLUE SHIELD MICH
2405 Market St (44507-1432)
PHONE.................................330 783-3841
Fax: 330 783-3878
EMP: 620
SALES (corp-wide): 12.4B **Privately Held**
SIC: 6321 Health insurance carriers
PA: Blue Cross And Blue Shield Of Michigan
600 E Lafayette Blvd
Detroit MI 48226
313 225-9000

(G-20118)
BOAK & SONS INC
75 Victoria Rd (44515-2023)
PHONE.................................330 793-5646
Fax: 330 793-1999
Samuel G Boak, *President*
Pam Morgan, *Office Mgr*
EMP: 200 **EST:** 1974
SQ FT: 38,000
SALES (est): 18.9MM **Privately Held**
WEB: www.boakandsons.com
SIC: 1761 1742 1542 1541 Roofing contractor; insulation, buildings; nonresidential construction; industrial buildings & warehouses

(G-20119)
BOARD MAN FRST UNTD METHDST CH
Also Called: Boardman Methodist Daycare
6809 Market St (44512-4504)
PHONE.................................330 758-4527
Peg Welch, *Pastor*
Rev Peg Ash Welch, *Pastor*
EMP: 27
SALES (est): 392.5K **Privately Held**
SIC: 8661 8351 Methodist Church; child day care services

(G-20120)
BOARDMAN MOLDED INTL LLC
1110 Thalia Ave (44512-1825)
PHONE.................................330 788-2400
EMP: 120
SALES (est): 1.2MM
SALES (corp-wide): 25MM **Privately Held**
SIC: 7389
PA: Boardman Molded Products, Inc.
1110 Thalia Ave
Youngstown OH 44512
330 788-2400

(G-20121)
BOARDMAN SCHOOL BUS GARAGE
7410 Market St (44512-5612)
PHONE.................................330 726-3425
Ross McPherson, *Manager*
EMP: 59
SALES (est): 1.2MM **Privately Held**
SIC: 4151 School buses

(G-20122)
BOLT CONSTRUCTION INC
Also Called: BOLT CONSTRUCTION CO
10422 South Ave (44514-3459)
P.O. Box 5470 (44514-0470)
PHONE.................................330 549-0349
Fax: 330 549-0344
Bruno Miletta, *President*
John T Miller Jr, *Vice Pres*
Shirley Miletta, *Treasurer*
Deanna Maker, *Manager*
Melinda Miletta-Mill, *Admin Sec*
EMP: 90 **EST:** 1981
SQ FT: 15,000
SALES: 21.2MM **Privately Held**
SIC: 1623 Pipeline construction; oil & gas pipeline construction

GEOGRAPHIC SECTION
Youngstown - Mahoning County (G-20146)

(G-20123)
BOSTON RETAIL PRODUCTS INC
Boston Group
225 Hubbard Rd (44505-3120)
PHONE..................................330 744-8100
Fax: 330 744-8080
James Bellstrom, *Office Mgr*
Sandford Kessler, *Manager*
EMP: 60
SALES (est): 4.7MM
SALES (corp-wide): 21.3MM Privately Held
WEB: www.bostonretail.com
SIC: 5051 Metals service centers & offices
PA: Boston Retail Products, Inc.
400 Riverside Ave
Medford MA 02155
781 395-7417

(G-20124)
BRIAN BROCKER DR
1616 Covington St (44510-1244)
PHONE..................................330 747-9215
Dr Brian Brocker, *Owner*
Linda J Eisenbraun, *Manager*
EMP: 30
SALES (est): 944.8K Privately Held
SIC: 8011 Offices & clinics of medical doctors

(G-20125)
BRIARFIELD AT ASHLEY CIRCLE
5291 Ashley Cir (44515-1141)
PHONE..................................330 793-3010
Jack Depizzo, *Owner*
Joe Vince, *Controller*
EMP: 150 **EST:** 1998
SALES (est): 4.2MM Privately Held
SIC: 8051 8052 Convalescent home with continuous nursing care; intermediate care facilities

(G-20126)
BRINKS INCORPORATED
6971 Southern Blvd Ste F (44512-4652)
PHONE..................................330 758-7379
Cathy Pannunzio, *Manager*
EMP: 35
SALES (corp-wide): 3.3B Publicly Held
SIC: 7381 Armored car services
HQ: Brink's, Incorporated
1801 Bayberry Ct Ste 400
Richmond VA 23226
804 289-9600

(G-20127)
BROCK & ASSOCIATES BUILDERS
118 Heron Bay Dr (44514-4234)
PHONE..................................330 757-7150
Fax: 330 757-7174
Paul Brock, *President*
Jane Brock, *Corp Secy*
Brian Brock, *Vice Pres*
EMP: 30
SALES: 1.5MM Privately Held
SIC: 1521 1751 Single-family housing construction; carpentry work

(G-20128)
BROOKDALE SNIOR LVING CMMNTIES
Also Called: Sterling House of Youngstown
2300 Canfield Rd Ofc (44511-2981)
PHONE..................................330 793-0085
Fax: 330 793-8597
Doug Love, *Director*
EMP: 25
SALES (corp-wide): 4.7B Publicly Held
WEB: www.assisted.com
SIC: 8059 Rest home, with health care
HQ: Brookdale Senior Living Communities, Inc.
6737 W Wa St Ste 2300
Milwaukee WI 53214
414 918-5000

(G-20129)
BROWNING-FERRIS INDS OF OHIO (DH)
Also Called: Allied Wste Svcs Yngstown Coml
3870 Hendricks Rd (44515-1528)
PHONE..................................330 793-7676
James E Oconnor, *CEO*
Thomas Van Weelden, *President*
Charlene Alderman, *Controller*
EMP: 55
SQ FT: 5,300
SALES (est): 52.2MM
SALES (corp-wide): 10B Publicly Held
SIC: 4953 Garbage: collecting, destroying & processing; sanitary landfill operation

(G-20130)
BUCKEYE LEASING INC
8063 Southern Blvd (44512-6306)
PHONE..................................330 758-0841
Ronald Carrocce, *President*
Gary Carrocce, *Corp Secy*
Mark Carrocce, *Vice Pres*
EMP: 50
SQ FT: 50,000
SALES (est): 1.3MM Privately Held
SIC: 7363 Truck driver services
PA: American Bulk Commodities Inc
8063 Southern Blvd
Youngstown OH 44512

(G-20131)
BUTLER INSTITUTE OF AMERCN ART (PA)
524 Wick Ave (44502-1213)
PHONE..................................330 743-1711
Fax: 330 743-9567
Martha Menk, *Marketing Staff*
Louis A Zona, *Exec Dir*
Louis A Zon, *Exec Dir*
Jean Shreffler, *Director*
EMP: 28
SQ FT: 80,000
SALES (est): 2.2MM Privately Held
WEB: www.butlerart.com
SIC: 8412 Museum

(G-20132)
CALLOS RESOURCE LLC (PA)
Also Called: Callos Prof Employment II
755 Boardman Canfield Rd (44512-4300)
PHONE..................................330 788-3033
Fax: 330 788-6940
Thomas Walsh, *President*
John Callos, *Chairman*
Eric Sutton, *Senior VP*
Mary Beth Dipaolo, *Vice Pres*
Jeffrey McGraw, *Vice Pres*
EMP: 30
SQ FT: 8,200
SALES (est): 25.4MM Privately Held
SIC: 7363 Temporary help service

(G-20133)
CARDIOVASCULAR ASSOCIATES INC
Also Called: Ohio Heart Instit
1001 Belmont Ave (44504-1003)
PHONE..................................330 747-6446
Fax: 330 747-6843
Sadiq Husain MD, *President*
Shawki Habib MD, *Vice Pres*
Ates Labib MD, *Treasurer*
Paul Wright, *Admin Sec*
EMP: 27
SQ FT: 23,000
SALES (est): 2MM Privately Held
SIC: 8011 Cardiologist & cardio-vascular specialist

(G-20134)
CATHOLIC CHRTIES REGIONAL AGCY
319 W Rayen Ave (44502-1119)
PHONE..................................330 744-3320
John Edwards, *Principal*
Lisa Janci, *Manager*
Nancy Voitus, *Exec Dir*
EMP: 52
SALES (est): 2MM Privately Held
SIC: 8399 Community development groups

(G-20135)
CELTIC HEALTHCARE NE OHIO INC
299 Edwards St (44502-1504)
PHONE..................................724 742-4360
Arnold E Burchianti, *Principal*
EMP: 31
SALES (est): 356.4K
SALES (corp-wide): 2.5B Publicly Held
SIC: 8099 Health & allied services
HQ: Celtic Healthcare, Inc.
150 Scharberry Ln
Mars PA 16046
724 742-4360

(G-20136)
CERNI MOTOR SALES INC (PA)
5751 Cerni Pl (44515-1174)
P.O. Box 4176 (44515-0176)
PHONE..................................330 652-9917
John P Cerni, *President*
Jeanne Cerni Et Al, *Principal*
Charles Cerni, *Principal*
William Thompson, *Parts Mgr*
Joe Notarianni, *CFO*
EMP: 72 **EST:** 1961
SQ FT: 37,000
SALES (est): 22.9MM Privately Held
WEB: www.cernimotors.com
SIC: 5012 Trucks, commercial

(G-20137)
CHANDER M KOHLI MD FACS INC
540 Parmalee Ave Ste 310 (44510-1605)
PHONE..................................330 759-6978
Chander M Kohli MD, *President*
Karen Kohli, *Corp Secy*
EMP: 25
SALES (est): 1.8MM Privately Held
SIC: 8011 Neurosurgeon

(G-20138)
CHEMICAL BANK
476 Boardman Canfield Rd (44512-4790)
PHONE..................................330 965-5806
Fax: 330 747-1662
Trisha Minnie, *Branch Mgr*
EMP: 100
SALES (corp-wide): 776.1MM Publicly Held
SIC: 6099 Check clearing services
HQ: Chemical Bank
333 E Main St
Midland MI 48640
989 631-9200

(G-20139)
CHEMICAL BANK
3900 Market St (44512-1111)
PHONE..................................330 314-1380
Steven R Lewis, *Branch Mgr*
EMP: 80
SALES (corp-wide): 776.1MM Publicly Held
WEB: www.dlkbank.com
SIC: 6035 Federal savings & loan associations
HQ: Chemical Bank
333 E Main St
Midland MI 48640
989 631-9200

(G-20140)
CHILDRENS HOSP MED CTR AKRON
8423 Market St Ste 300 (44512-6778)
PHONE..................................330 629-6085
Patrick J Doherty, *Branch Mgr*
Stacia Erdos, *Director*
EMP: 40
SALES (corp-wide): 747.4MM Privately Held
SIC: 8069 Children's hospital
PA: Childrens Hospital Medical Center Of Akron
1 Perkins Sq
Akron OH 44308
330 543-1000

(G-20141)
CINEMARK USA INC
Also Called: Cinemark Tinseltown 7
7401 Market St Rear (44512-5624)
PHONE..................................330 965-2335
Greg Wigley, *Manager*
EMP: 25 Publicly Held
SIC: 7832 Motion picture theaters, except drive-in
HQ: Cinemark Usa, Inc.
3900 Dallas Pkwy Ste 500
Plano TX 75093
972 665-1000

(G-20142)
CITY MACHINE TECHNOLOGIES INC
Electric Machinery Division
825 Martin Luther King Jr (44502-1105)
P.O. Box 1466 (44501-1466)
PHONE..................................330 740-8186
Michael J Kovach, *President*
Mike Perello, *QC Mgr*
EMP: 40
SALES (corp-wide): 13.7MM Privately Held
WEB: www.cmtcompanies.com
SIC: 3599 7694 3621 3568 Machine shop, jobbing & repair; armature rewinding shops; motors & generators; power transmission equipment
PA: City Machine Technologies, Inc.
773 W Rayen Ave
Youngstown OH 44502
330 747-2639

(G-20143)
CITY OF YOUNGSTOWN (PA)
26 S Phelps St Bsmt (44503-1318)
PHONE..................................330 742-8700
Fax: 330 742-8999
Charles Sammaron, *Mayor*
Dave Vinion, *Foreman/Supr*
Jason Whitehead, *Manager*
Roger Linker, *Senior Mgr*
Dia Alessi, *Supervisor*
EMP: 300
SQ FT: 45,000
SALES (est): 76.2MM Privately Held
WEB: www.cityofyoungstown.com
SIC: 8741 Administrative management

(G-20144)
CITY OF YOUNGSTOWN
Also Called: Youngstown Water Dept
26 S Phelps St Fl 3a (44503-1318)
P.O. Box 6219 (44501-6219)
PHONE..................................330 742-8749
Fax: 330 742-8751
Joseph Dunlap, *Plant Mgr*
John Casciano, *Manager*
John Castiano, *Manager*
Charles Sammarone, *Manager*
EMP: 30
SALES (corp-wide): 76.2MM Privately Held
WEB: www.cityofyoungstown.com
SIC: 4941 9111 Water supply; mayors' offices
PA: City Of Youngstown
26 S Phelps St Bsmt
Youngstown OH 44503
330 742-8700

(G-20145)
COCCA DEVELOPMENT LTD
100 Debartolo Pl Ste 400 (44512-6099)
PHONE..................................330 729-1010
Fax: 330 729-1008
Anthony L Cocca, *CEO*
Marc Barca, *Vice Pres*
Jim Shipley, *Vice Pres*
Michael Hatfield, *Engineer*
Lynn E Davenport, *CFO*
EMP: 70
SQ FT: 20,000
SALES (est): 20.1MM Privately Held
SIC: 1542 Nonresidential construction

(G-20146)
COHEN & COMPANY LTD
Also Called: COHEN & COMPANY,LTD
201 E Commerce St Ste 400 (44503-1690)
PHONE..................................330 743-1040
Fax: 330 744-0111
Richard Schiraldi, *Partner*
Janet Meub, *Counsel*
Jack Savage, *Counsel*
John Zimmerman, *Vice Pres*
Gina Nocera, *Accountant*
EMP: 35
SALES (corp-wide): 36MM Privately Held
WEB: www.cohencpa.com
SIC: 8721 Certified public accountant
PA: Cohen & Company, Ltd.
1350 Euclid Ave Ste 800
Cleveland OH 44115
216 579-1040

Youngstown - Mahoning County (G-20147)

(G-20147)
COMMERCE TITLE AGCY YOUNGSTOWN
201 E Commerce St (44503-1659)
PHONE..................330 743-1171
Fax: 330 743-2185
Martha Bushey, *President*
Jeffrey Heintz, *Manager*
EMP: 30
SALES (est): 960.3K **Privately Held**
SIC: 6541 Title & trust companies

(G-20148)
COMMUNICARE HEALTH SVCS INC
Also Called: Greenbriar Healthcare Center
8064 South Ave (44512-6153)
PHONE..................330 726-3700
Fax: 330 726-2324
James Demidovich, *Director*
Tracy Wainwright, *Nursing Dir*
Melissa Shevetc, *Administration*
EMP: 99
SALES (corp-wide): 103.9MM **Privately Held**
SIC: 8051 Skilled nursing care facilities
PA: Communicare Health Services, Inc.
4700 Ashwood Dr Ste 200
Blue Ash OH 45241
513 530-1654

(G-20149)
COMMUNICARE HEALTH SVCS INC
Also Called: Austintown Healthcare Center
650 S Meridian Rd (44509-2932)
PHONE..................330 792-7799
Fax: 330 793-7433
Toni Fuzo, *Administration*
EMP: 80
SALES (corp-wide): 103.9MM **Privately Held**
WEB: www.atriumlivingcenters.com
SIC: 6531 8051 Real estate agents & managers; skilled nursing care facilities
PA: Communicare Health Services, Inc.
4700 Ashwood Dr Ste 200
Blue Ash OH 45241
513 530-1654

(G-20150)
COMMUNICARE HEALTH SVCS INC
Also Called: Canfield Healthcare Center
2958 Canfield Rd (44511-2805)
PHONE..................330 792-5511
Fax: 330 792-5511
Rick Cook, *Manager*
Prabhuda Lakhani, *Director*
EMP: 80
SALES (corp-wide): 103.9MM **Privately Held**
WEB: www.atriumlivingcenters.com
SIC: 6531 8051 Real estate agents & managers; skilled nursing care facilities
PA: Communicare Health Services, Inc.
4700 Ashwood Dr Ste 200
Blue Ash OH 45241
513 530-1654

(G-20151)
COMMUNITY CAREGIVERS
888 Boardman Canfield Rd D (44512-4276)
PHONE..................330 533-3427
Barbara E Scott, *Branch Mgr*
EMP: 71
SALES (corp-wide): 2.2MM **Privately Held**
SIC: 8322 Senior citizens' center or association
PA: Community Caregivers
66 S Miller Rd Ste 200
Fairlawn OH 44333
330 836-8585

(G-20152)
COMMUNITY CENTER
Also Called: Help Hotline Crisis Center
1344 5th Ave (44504-1703)
PHONE..................330 746-7721
Vince Brancaccio, *CEO*
Paul Guggenheim, *Manager*
EMP: 52 **EST:** 2010
SALES (est): 368.4K **Privately Held**
SIC: 8322 Crisis center

(G-20153)
COMPASS FAMILY AND CMNTY SVCS (PA)
Also Called: FAMILY SERVICE AGENCY
535 Marmion Ave (44502-2323)
PHONE..................330 743-9275
Fax: 330 782-1614
Joseph F Caruso, *CEO*
David Arnold, *COO*
Mark Wingert, *CFO*
Danielle M Lazor, *Human Res Dir*
Kim Barrett, *Info Tech Mgr*
EMP: 34
SQ FT: 9,600
SALES: 9.4MM **Privately Held**
WEB: www.familyserviceagency.com
SIC: 8322 Family (marriage) counseling; child guidance agency; emergency shelters

(G-20154)
COMPASS FAMILY AND CMNTY SVCS
284 Broadway Ave (44504-1752)
PHONE..................330 743-9275
Dean Wennerstrom, *Dean*
Melissa Toot, *Project Mgr*
Nancy L Flinn, *Human Res Dir*
Danielle M Lazor, *Human Res Dir*
Kathe Klem, *Human Resources*
EMP: 96
SALES (corp-wide): 9.4MM **Privately Held**
SIC: 8322 Family (marriage) counseling
PA: Compass Family And Community Services
535 Marmion Ave
Youngstown OH 44502
330 743-9275

(G-20155)
COMPCO LAND COMPANY (DH)
85 E Hylda Ave (44507-1762)
PHONE..................330 482-0200
Fax: 330 758-7621
Gregory B Smith Sr, *President*
Clarence R Smith Jr, *Chairman*
Douglas A Hagy, *CFO*
EMP: 88
SQ FT: 42,000
SALES (est): 2.5MM
SALES (corp-wide): 24.1MM **Privately Held**
SIC: 6512 Commercial & industrial building operation
HQ: Compco Industries, Incorporated
400 W Railroad St Ste 1
Columbiana OH 44408
330 482-6488

(G-20156)
COMPENSATION PROGRAMS OF OHIO
33 Fitch Blvd (44515-2202)
PHONE..................330 652-9821
Tim Myers, *Owner*
EMP: 25 **EST:** 2001
SALES (est): 1.3MM **Privately Held**
SIC: 8721 Billing & bookkeeping service

(G-20157)
COMPREHENSIVE BEHAVIORAL HLTH (PA)
104 Javit Ct Ste A (44515-2439)
P.O. Box 4174 (44515-0174)
PHONE..................330 797-4050
Fax: 330 797-4090
Kotes Wara Kaza, *Director*
Bob Roth, *Administration*
EMP: 32
SQ FT: 3,000
SALES (est): 3.2MM **Privately Held**
SIC: 8093 Mental health clinic, outpatient

(G-20158)
COMPREHENSIVE LOGISTICS CO INC
365 Victoria Rd (44512-2027)
PHONE..................330 793-0504
Tom Welsh, *Sales Executive*
Doug Caswell, *Branch Mgr*
Edward H Jones, *Manager*
Trey Lyda, *Director*
EMP: 50 **Privately Held**
SIC: 8742 4226 3714 3711 Transportation consultant; special warehousing & storage; motor vehicle parts & accessories; motor vehicles & car bodies
PA: Comprehensive Logistics Co., Inc.
4944 Belmont Ave Ste 202
Youngstown OH 44505

(G-20159)
COMPREHENSIVE LOGISTICS CO INC (PA)
4944 Belmont Ave Ste 202 (44505-1055)
P.O. Box 6127 (44501-6127)
PHONE..................800 734-0372
Fax: 330 793-2159
Don Constantini, *Ch of Bd*
Brian Hume, *General Mgr*
Andy Kromer, *Superintendent*
Brad Constantini, *Exec VP*
Rick Diefenderfer, *Vice Pres*
EMP: 28
SQ FT: 1,200
SALES: 104.2MM **Privately Held**
WEB: www.complog.com
SIC: 4225 4731 General warehousing; customs clearance of freight

(G-20160)
CONCORD HEALTH CARE INC (PA)
202 Churchill Hubbard Rd (44505-1325)
PHONE..................330 759-2357
Fax: 330 759-3365
Debra Ifft, *President*
EMP: 50
SALES (est): 5.2MM **Privately Held**
SIC: 8051 8052 Skilled nursing care facilities; intermediate care facilities

(G-20161)
CONSTELLATIONS ENTERPRISE LLC (PA)
1775 Logan Ave (44505-2622)
PHONE..................330 740-8208
Steve Witter,
Jan Doughty,
EMP: 199
SALES (est): 125.8MM **Privately Held**
SIC: 8741 Management services

(G-20162)
CORECIVIC INC
Also Called: Northeast Ohio Corrections
2240 Hubbard Rd (44505-3157)
P.O. Box 1857 (44501-1857)
PHONE..................330 746-3777
Fax: 330 746-3318
D Bryan Gardner, *Principal*
Vicki Caron, *Purchasing*
EMP: 450
SALES (corp-wide): 1.8B **Publicly Held**
WEB: www.correctionscorp.com
SIC: 8744 Correctional facility
PA: Corecivic, Inc.
10 Burton Hills Blvd
Nashville TN 37215
615 263-3000

(G-20163)
CUMULUS BROADCASTING LLC
Also Called: Wyfm Fm
4040 Simon Rd (44512-1362)
PHONE..................330 783-1000
Clyde Bass, *Manager*
EMP: 80
SALES (corp-wide): 1.1B **Publicly Held**
WEB: www.rockofsavannah.com
SIC: 4832 Radio broadcasting stations, music format
HQ: Cumulus Broadcasting, Llc
3280 Peachtree Rd Nw Ste
Atlanta GA 30305
404 949-0700

(G-20164)
CUSTOM MAINT
73 Country Green Dr (44515-2214)
PHONE..................330 793-2523
Dennis Gagne, *Owner*
EMP: 52
SALES (est): 564.4K **Privately Held**
SIC: 7349 Building maintenance services

(G-20165)
DANIEL A TERRERI & SONS INC
1091 N Meridian Rd (44509-1016)
PHONE..................330 538-2950
Fax: 330 538-2433
Daniel Terreri, *President*
Thomas Corroto, *Principal*
Karen Augustine, *Controller*
EMP: 40
SQ FT: 5,000
SALES (est): 2MM **Privately Held**
SIC: 1791 1795 1794 Storage tanks, metal: erection; demolition, buildings & other structures; asbestos removal & encapsulation

(G-20166)
DANRIDGE NURSING HOME INC
31 Maranatha Ct (44505-4970)
PHONE..................330 746-5157
Fax: 330 746-2508
Julius Blunt, *President*
Leigh Greene, *Vice Pres*
Joanne Blunt, *Administration*
EMP: 80
SQ FT: 29,000
SALES (est): 2.5MM **Privately Held**
SIC: 8051 Convalescent home with continuous nursing care

(G-20167)
DEMPSEY INC
Also Called: ServiceMaster
2803 South Ave (44502-2409)
PHONE..................330 758-2309
Fax: 330 758-3090
Donald F Dempsey Jr, *CEO*
Tony Dimpsey, *Owner*
EMP: 100
SALES (est): 2.4MM **Privately Held**
SIC: 7349 Building maintenance services

(G-20168)
DEYOR PERFORMING ARTS CENTER
260 W Federal St (44503-1206)
PHONE..................330 744-4269
Patricia Syak, *President*
EMP: 35
SALES (est): 442.2K **Privately Held**
SIC: 7299 7922 8412 Banquet hall facilities; performing arts center production; arts or science center

(G-20169)
DIRECT MAINTENANCE LLC
100 E Federal St Ste 600 (44503-1811)
PHONE..................330 744-5211
Daniel P Dascenzo, *Principal*
EMP: 35 **EST:** 2007
SALES (est): 3.5MM **Privately Held**
SIC: 6282 Investment advice

(G-20170)
DISTRICT BOARD HEALTH MAHONING
50 Westchester Dr (44515-3991)
PHONE..................330 270-2855
Patricia Sweeney, *General Mgr*
Matthew Stefanak, *Commander*
Kyle Gabrick, *Manager*
Matthew A Stefanak, *Commissioner*
Kathleen Affagato, *Info Tech Mgr*
EMP: 49
SALES (est): 1.6MM **Privately Held**
SIC: 8099 Health & allied services

(G-20171)
DIVER STEEL CITY AUTO CRUSHERS
590 Himrod Ave (44506-1414)
P.O. Box 1293 (44501-1293)
PHONE..................330 744-5083
Fax: 330 742-4805
John Diver, *President*
Alice Vestal, *Bookkeeper*
EMP: 31
SQ FT: 5,000
SALES (est): 4.6MM **Privately Held**
SIC: 5093 Automotive wrecking for scrap

Youngstown - Mahoning County

(G-20172)
DON WALTER KITCHEN DISTRS INC (PA)
260 Victoria Rd (44515-2024)
PHONE.................330 793-9338
Fax: 330 793-9406
Gary Walter, *President*
Randy Walter, *Vice Pres*
EMP: 30
SQ FT: 60,000
SALES (est): 17.8MM **Privately Held**
SIC: 5064 5031 Electrical appliances, major; kitchen cabinets

(G-20173)
DONALD P PIPINO COMPANY LTD
7600 Market St (44512-6078)
PHONE.................330 726-8177
Fax: 330 723-1891
Mary Pipino, *President*
Joseph Pipino, *Exec VP*
Anita E Chearno, *Vice Pres*
Kelly Cope, *Vice Pres*
Jack Kessler, *Vice Pres*
EMP: 75
SQ FT: 20,000
SALES (est): 21.8MM **Privately Held**
WEB: www.ajg.com
SIC: 6411 Insurance agents

(G-20174)
DUTCHESS DRY CLEANERS
Also Called: Dutchess Cleaner
2710 Belmont Ave Ste D (44505-1835)
PHONE.................330 759-9382
George Rondinelli, *President*
Jeno Pondinelli, *Owner*
EMP: 30
SALES (est): 304.2K **Privately Held**
SIC: 7216 Curtain cleaning & repair

(G-20175)
EAST OHIO GAS COMPANY
Also Called: Dominion Energy Ohio
1165 W Rayen Ave (44502-1394)
PHONE.................330 742-8121
Fax: 330 742-8189
EMP: 176
SQ FT: 224
SALES (corp-wide): 12.5B **Publicly Held**
SIC: 4924 Natural gas distribution
HQ: The East Ohio Gas Company
19701 Libby Rd
Maple Heights OH 44137
800 362-7557

(G-20176)
EASTER SEAL SOCIETY OF (PA)
Also Called: Easter Seals
299 Edwards St (44502-1599)
PHONE.................330 743-1168
Fax: 330 743-1616
Kenan Sklenar, *CEO*
Diane Hardenbrook, *CFO*
Beth Volosin, *CFO*
Jodi Harmon, *Associate*
EMP: 75
SQ FT: 26,265
SALES: 6.9MM **Privately Held**
SIC: 8322 8093 Individual & family services; rehabilitation center, outpatient treatment; speech defect clinic

(G-20177)
EDM MANAGEMENT INC
1419 Boardman Poland Rd # 500 (44514)
PHONE.................330 726-5790
Edward Reese, *CEO*
Diane Reese, *President*
Rob Rupeka, *CFO*
Constance E Pierce, *Admin Sec*
EMP: 50
SQ FT: 5,000
SALES (est): 5.5MM **Privately Held**
SIC: 8741 Business management

(G-20178)
EINSTRUCTION CORPORATION (HQ)
255 W Federal St (44503-1207)
PHONE.................330 746-3015
Rich Fennessy, *CEO*
Mike Logan, *Regional Mgr*
Michael Ottiano, *Engineer*
Tim Torno, *CFO*
Mike Torrenti, *Sales Dir*
EMP: 100
SQ FT: 8,000
SALES (est): 44.2MM
SALES (corp-wide): 98.4MM **Privately Held**
WEB: www.einstruction.com
SIC: 7371 7379 5045 7372 Computer software development; computer related consulting services; computers, peripherals & software; prepackaged software
PA: Turning Technologies, Llc
255 W Federal St
Youngstown OH 44503
330 746-3015

(G-20179)
ELIZABETH H FARBMAN
100 E Federal St (44503-1838)
PHONE.................330 744-5211
David Barbee, *Principal*
EMP: 31
SALES (est): 804.9K **Privately Held**
SIC: 8111 General practice attorney, lawyer

(G-20180)
ELLIOTT HELLER MAAS MORROW LPA
Also Called: Heller Mass Morrow and Migue
54 Westchester Dr Ste 10 (44515-3903)
PHONE.................330 792-6611
Robert Heller, *President*
Rush Elliott, *President*
EMP: 26
SALES (est): 1.6MM **Privately Held**
SIC: 8111 General practice attorney, lawyer

(G-20181)
ESEC CORPORATION (PA)
44 Victoria Rd (44515-2022)
PHONE.................330 799-1536
David Hutter, *President*
Robert Savich, *Vice Pres*
Mary C Hutter, *Treasurer*
Georgetta Darr, *Admin Sec*
EMP: 34
SALES (est): 7.6MM **Privately Held**
SIC: 5084 5012 Materials handling machinery; trucks, commercial

(G-20182)
EVENTS ON TOP
143 Boardman Canfield Rd (44512-4804)
PHONE.................330 757-3786
EMP: 45 **EST:** 2008
SALES (est): 597.6K **Privately Held**
SIC: 7922 Theatrical Producers/Services

(G-20183)
EYE CARE ASSOCIATES INC (PA)
10 Dutton Dr (44502-1899)
PHONE.................330 746-7691
Fax: 330 743-8322
H S Wang MD, *President*
Robert J Gerberry MD, *Vice Pres*
Sergul Erzurum MD, *Vice Pres*
Keith Wilson MD, *Vice Pres*
Diane Volosin, *Controller*
EMP: 55
SQ FT: 10,000
SALES (est): 8.1MM **Privately Held**
WEB: www.eyecareassociates.com
SIC: 8011 Ophthalmologist

(G-20184)
FAB LIMOUSINES INC
Also Called: Fab Tours & Travel
3681 Connecticut Ave (44515-3002)
PHONE.................330 792-6700
Fax: 330 792-4177
Mark Bagnoli, *CEO*
James Erickson, *Manager*
EMP: 47
SQ FT: 10,000
SALES (est): 2.3MM **Privately Held**
WEB: www.fablimo.com
SIC: 4119 Limousine rental, with driver

(G-20185)
FALCON TRANSPORT CO (PA)
4944 Belmont Ave Ste 201 (44505-1055)
P.O. Box 6147 (44501-6147)
PHONE.................330 793-1345
Barbara Takach, *President*
Brad Constantini, *Exec VP*
Steve Olender, *Vice Pres*
Lee Simmerman, *Vice Pres*
Tom Welsh, *Vice Pres*
EMP: 229
SQ FT: 10,000
SALES (est): 387.4MM **Privately Held**
WEB: www.falcontransport.com
SIC: 4213 Heavy hauling

(G-20186)
FALCON TRANSPORT CO
4944 Belmont Ave Ste 201 (44505-1055)
PHONE.................330 793-1345
John Serich, *Branch Mgr*
EMP: 80
SALES (corp-wide): 387.4MM **Privately Held**
WEB: www.falcontransport.com
SIC: 4212 7521 4213 Local trucking, without storage; outdoor parking services; trucking, except local
PA: Falcon Transport Co.
4944 Belmont Ave Ste 201
Youngstown OH 44505
330 793-1345

(G-20187)
FAMILY STATIONS INC
3930 Sunset Blvd (44512-1307)
PHONE.................330 783-9986
Harold Camping, *President*
EMP: 49
SALES (corp-wide): 7.4MM **Privately Held**
SIC: 4832 Radio broadcasting stations
PA: Family Stations, Inc.
1350 S Loop Rd
Alameda CA 94502
510 568-6200

(G-20188)
FIRST ACCEPTANCE CORPORATION
4774 Mahoning Ave Ste 5 (44515-1643)
PHONE.................330 792-7181
Annette Kelley, *Principal*
EMP: 31
SALES (corp-wide): 347.5MM **Publicly Held**
SIC: 6411 Insurance agents, brokers & service
PA: First Acceptance Corporation
3813 Green Hills Vlg Dr
Nashville TN 37215
615 844-2800

(G-20189)
FIRST NATIONAL BANK PA
1 W Federal St (44503-1438)
PHONE.................330 747-0292
Gary J Roberts, *Principal*
Walter Tomich, *Manager*
EMP: 25
SALES (corp-wide): 1.2B **Publicly Held**
SIC: 6021 6022 National commercial banks; state commercial banks
HQ: First National Bank Of Pennsylvania
166 Main St
Greenville PA 16125
724 588-6770

(G-20190)
FOR KIDS SAKE INC
1245 Boardman Canfield Rd (44512-4004)
PHONE.................330 726-6878
Cindy Alagretto, *President*
EMP: 30
SALES: 225K **Privately Held**
SIC: 8351 Preschool center

(G-20191)
FORGE INDUSTRIES INC (PA)
4450 Market St (44512-1512)
PHONE.................330 782-8301
Fax: 330 782-4064
William T James II, *Ch of Bd*
Carl G James, *President*
W Thomas James III, *Vice Pres*
Dan Maisonville, *CFO*
Robert Ruester, *Controller*
▲ **EMP:** 1250 **EST:** 1900
SQ FT: 1,500
SALES (est): 493.6MM **Privately Held**
WEB: www.forgeindustries.com
SIC: 5085 3566 3599 3531 Bearings; power transmission equipment & apparatus; gears, power transmission, except automotive; machine shop, jobbing & repair; road construction & maintenance machinery; insurance brokers; industrial equipment services

(G-20192)
FYDA FREIGHTLINER YOUNGSTOWN
Also Called: Fyda Truck & Equipment
5260 76 Dr (44515-1148)
PHONE.................330 797-0224
Fax: 330 797-0230
Walter R Fyda, *President*
Greg Kopp, *Parts Mgr*
Billie Baker, *Executive*
Elizabeth Fyda, *Admin Sec*
EMP: 70
SQ FT: 60,000
SALES (est): 18MM **Privately Held**
SIC: 5012 7538 Trucks, commercial; general truck repair

(G-20193)
GALAXIE INDUSTRIAL SVCS LLC
837 E Western Reserve Rd (44514-3360)
P.O. Box 11140 (44511-0140)
PHONE.................330 503-2334
Vince Pecchia, *Business Mgr*
Cortland Love, *Mng Member*
Donald Myler,
Timothy Potts,
EMP: 34
SQ FT: 20,000
SALES (est): 1.5MM **Privately Held**
SIC: 7349 Cleaning service, industrial or commercial

(G-20194)
GATEWAYS TO BETTER LIVING INC
945 W Rayen Ave (44502-1314)
PHONE.................330 480-9870
Gail Reiss, *Principal*
EMP: 40
SALES (corp-wide): 17.3MM **Privately Held**
SIC: 8051 Mental retardation hospital
PA: Gateways To Better Living Inc
6000 Mahoning Ave Ste 234
Youngstown OH 44515
330 792-2854

(G-20195)
GATEWAYS TO BETTER LIVING INC
230 Idaho Rd (44515-3702)
PHONE.................330 270-0952
Chris Ellis, *Branch Mgr*
Elaine Hamilton, *Manager*
EMP: 35
SALES (corp-wide): 17.3MM **Privately Held**
WEB: www.gatewaystbl.com
SIC: 8361 Home for the mentally retarded
PA: Gateways To Better Living Inc
6000 Mahoning Ave Ste 234
Youngstown OH 44515
330 792-2854

(G-20196)
GATEWAYS TO BETTER LIVING INC (PA)
6000 Mahoning Ave Ste 234 (44515-2225)
PHONE.................330 792-2854
Fax: 330 790-4395
James Linert, *CFO*
Mary O'Brien, *Human Res Dir*
Gail Riess, *Exec Dir*
EMP: 30
SQ FT: 3,000
SALES: 17.3MM **Privately Held**
WEB: www.gatewaystbl.com
SIC: 8361 Home for the mentally retarded

Youngstown - Mahoning County (G-20197)

GEOGRAPHIC SECTION

(G-20197)
GBS CORP
Also Called: Computer Solutions
1035 N Meridian Rd (44509-1016)
PHONE.................................330 797-2700
Fax: 330 797-2724
Michele Benson, *Vice Pres*
Eugene Calabria, *Vice Pres*
James Carey, *Vice Pres*
Bill Kinner, *Vice Pres*
John Lane, *Vice Pres*
EMP: 50
SQ FT: 1,100
SALES (corp-wide): 72.8MM Privately Held
SIC: 5045 Computer software
PA: Gbs Corp.
   7233 Freedom Ave Nw
   North Canton OH 44720
   330 494-5330

(G-20198)
GENEVA LIBERTY STEEL LTD (PA)
Also Called: GENMAK GENEVA LIBERTY
947 Martin Luther King Jr (44502-1106)
P.O. Box 6124 (44501-6124)
PHONE.................................330 740-0103
Fax: 330 740-0113
David T McLeroy, *President*
Enzo Dechellis, *CFO*
Barb McLeroy, *Human Res Mgr*
Dave Bauschard, *Regl Sales Mgr*
EMP: 47
SQ FT: 85,000
SALES: 37.5MM Privately Held
SIC: 3316 7389 Strip steel, flat bright, cold-rolled: purchased hot-rolled; scrap steel cutting

(G-20199)
GEORGE G ELLIS JR MD
910 Boardman Canfield Rd (44512-4218)
PHONE.................................330 965-0832
George G Ellis Jr, *Owner*
George Ellis Jr, *Internal Med*
EMP: 35 **EST:** 1999
SALES (est): 2.4MM Privately Held
SIC: 8011 Internal medicine, physician/surgeon

(G-20200)
GIFFIN MANAGEMENT GROUP INC
Also Called: Chelsea Court Apartments
6300 South Ave Apt 1200 (44512-3639)
PHONE.................................330 758-4695
Dale Giffin, *President*
EMP: 44
SALES (corp-wide): 4.8MM Privately Held
SIC: 6513 Apartment building operators
PA: Giffin Management Group Inc
   2725 Airview Blvd Ste 204
   Portage MI 49002
   269 743-4181

(G-20201)
GIRARD TECHNOLOGIES INC
1101 E Indianola Ave (44502-2643)
PHONE.................................330 783-2495
Alex C Bugno, *President*
Alex Bugno, *President*
EMP: 25
SQ FT: 4,500
SALES: 5.5MM Privately Held
SIC: 7379 Computer related consulting services

(G-20202)
GOLD CROSS AMBULANCE SVCS INC
1122 E Midlothian Blvd (44502-2839)
PHONE.................................330 744-4161
Daniel H Becker, *Principal*
Robert Evans, *Opers Mgr*
Ray Poynter, *Finance Mgr*
EMP: 200
SALES (est): 273.5K
SALES (corp-wide): 7.8B Publicly Held
SIC: 4119 Ambulance service; automobile rental, with driver

HQ: Rural/Metro Corporation
   8465 N Pima Rd
   Scottsdale AZ 85258
   480 606-3886

(G-20203)
GOLDEN STRING INC
16 S Phelps St (44503-1316)
PHONE.................................330 503-3894
Dini Isle, *Treasurer*
James F Sutman, *Exec Dir*
EMP: 25
SALES: 374.3K Privately Held
SIC: 8322 Individual & family services

(G-20204)
GRAYBAR ELECTRIC COMPANY INC
Also Called: Graybar Youngstown Nat Zone
1100 Ohio Works Dr (44510-1072)
PHONE.................................330 799-3220
Fax: 330 799-6646
Dennis Daloisio, *Branch Mgr*
EMP: 43
SALES (corp-wide): 6.6B Privately Held
WEB: www.graybar.com
SIC: 4225 General warehousing & storage
PA: Graybar Electric Company, Inc.
   34 N Meramec Ave
   Saint Louis MO 63105
   314 573-9200

(G-20205)
GREAT EXPECTATIONS D CA CENTER
755 Boardman Canfield Rd F8 (44512-4300)
PHONE.................................330 782-9500
Fax: 330 629-7640
Linda Beraduce, *President*
EMP: 25
SALES (est): 496.4K Privately Held
SIC: 8351 Child day care services

(G-20206)
GREAT LAKES CARTAGE COMPANY (PA)
555 N Meridian Rd Ste 1 (44509-1232)
PHONE.................................330 702-1930
Fax: 330 793-6505
James Cleary, *President*
David C Spagnola, *Vice Pres*
EMP: 68
SQ FT: 5,000
SALES (est): 6.7MM Privately Held
SIC: 4213 4212 Trucking, except local; local trucking, without storage

(G-20207)
GREAT LAKES TELCOM LTD
Also Called: Broadband Hospitality
590 E Western Reserve Rd (44514-3354)
PHONE.................................330 629-8848
Vincent Lucci Jr, *Partner*
Jeanne Mafodda, *Vice Pres*
Ed Santor, *VP Sales*
Larry Borders, *Manager*
Ed Joseph, *Technical Staff*
EMP: 30
SQ FT: 9,200
SALES (est): 8.7MM Privately Held
WEB: www.broadbandhospitality.com
SIC: 4813 3663 ; satellites, communications

(G-20208)
GREEN HAINES SGAMBATI LPA
100 E Federal St Ste 800 (44503-1871)
P.O. Box 849 (44501-0849)
PHONE.................................330 743-5101
Fax: 440 797-2969
Richard Abrams, *President*
EMP: 28
SALES (corp-wide): 6MM Privately Held
SIC: 8111 General practice law office
PA: Green, Haines Sgambati Lpa
   100 E Federal St Ste 800
   Youngstown OH 44503
   330 743-5101

(G-20209)
GREENWOOD CHEVROLET INC
4695 Mahoning Ave (44515-1687)
PHONE.................................330 270-1299
Fax: 330 792-2902

Gregory Greenwood, *President*
Dave Roberts, *General Mgr*
Wayne C Greenwood Jr, *Vice Pres*
Teri Simon, *Sls & Mktg Exec*
Angie Leemans, *Controller*
EMP: 146
SQ FT: 50,000
SALES (est): 67MM Privately Held
WEB: www.greenwoodchevy.com
SIC: 5511 7538 5521 Automobiles, new & used; general automotive repair shops; used car dealers

(G-20210)
GROUND TECH INC
240 Sinter Ct (44510-1076)
PHONE.................................330 270-0700
Mathew Frontino, *President*
Joseph Bianco, *Vice Pres*
Gregg Meece, *Manager*
EMP: 30
SQ FT: 40,000
SALES (est): 3.1MM Privately Held
WEB: www.groundtech-inc.com
SIC: 1794 Excavation work

(G-20211)
GUARDIAN PROTECTION SVCS INC
Also Called: Guardian Home Technology
5401 Ashley Cir Ste A (44515-1176)
PHONE.................................330 797-1570
Al Cochran, *Branch Mgr*
EMP: 30 Privately Held
WEB: www.guardianprotection.com
SIC: 1731 5999 7382 Safety & security specialization; fire detection & burglar alarm systems specialization; alarm signal systems; security systems services
HQ: Guardian Protection Services, Inc.
   174 Thorn Hill Rd
   Warrendale PA 15086
   412 788-2580

(G-20212)
HARDROCK EXCAVATING LLC
2761 Salt Springs Rd (44509-1035)
PHONE.................................330 792-9524
Ben Lupo, *Mng Member*
EMP: 68
SALES (est): 5.1MM Privately Held
SIC: 1794 Excavation work

(G-20213)
HARRINGTON HOPPE MITCHELL LTD
26 Market St Ste 1200 (44503-1769)
P.O. Box 6077 (44501-6077)
PHONE.................................330 744-1111
James L Blomstrom, *Partner*
Frederick S Coombs, *Partner*
Paul M Dutton, *Partner*
Robert A Lenga, *Partner*
Beth Bacon, *Corp Counsel*
EMP: 25
SALES (est): 2.4MM Privately Held
SIC: 8111 General practice attorney, lawyer

(G-20214)
HEART CENTER OF N EASTRN OHIO (PA)
Also Called: Heart Center Northeastern Ohio
250 Debartolo Pl Ste 2750 (44512-6026)
PHONE.................................330 758-7703
Paula Peterson, *Administration*
EMP: 47
SALES (est): 3.1MM Privately Held
SIC: 8011 Cardiologist & cardio-vascular specialist

(G-20215)
HELLER MAAS MORO & MAGILL
54 Westchester Dr Ste 10 (44515-3903)
PHONE.................................330 393-6602
Fax: 330 792-7486
Robert Heller, *Partner*
Richard L Magill, *Partner*
Joseph Moro, *Partner*
C Douglas Ames,
Rush E Elliott,
EMP: 26
SQ FT: 7,000

SALES (est): 3.2MM Privately Held
WEB: www.hmmmcolpa.com
SIC: 8111 General practice attorney, lawyer

(G-20216)
HELP HOTLINE CRISIS CENTER
Also Called: Help Network of Northeast Ohio
261 E Wood St (44503-1629)
P.O. Box 46 (44501-0046)
PHONE.................................330 747-5111
Fax: 330 747-4055
Dean Wennerstrom, *CFO*
Duane Piccirilli, *Director*
EMP: 34
SALES: 2.3MM Privately Held
SIC: 8322 Crisis center

(G-20217)
HILLTRUX TANK LINES INC
6331 Southern Blvd (44512-3313)
P.O. Box 696, North Jackson (44451-0696)
PHONE.................................330 965-1103
Fax: 330 965-1158
Brad G Hille, *President*
Bob Johnson, *Vice Pres*
EMP: 35
SQ FT: 1,600
SALES (est): 3.3MM Privately Held
WEB: www.hilltrux.com
SIC: 4212 Petroleum haulage, local

(G-20218)
HOME INSTEAD SENIOR CARE
5437 Mahoning Ave Ste 22 (44515-2421)
PHONE.................................330 729-1233
Fax: 330 729-0112
Carol Haus, *President*
EMP: 100 **EST:** 2001
SALES (est): 2.3MM Privately Held
WEB: www.homecarealternatives.com
SIC: 8082 Home health care services

(G-20219)
HOMETOWN URGENT CARE
1305 Boardman Poland Rd (44514-1935)
PHONE.................................330 629-2300
Tammy Russell, *Branch Mgr*
EMP: 175
SALES (corp-wide): 73.2MM Privately Held
SIC: 8049 8011 7291 Occupational therapist; medical centers; tax return preparation services
PA: Hometown Urgent Care
   2400 Corp Exchange Dr # 102
   Columbus OH 43231
   614 505-7633

(G-20220)
HOPES DRAMS CHILDCARE LRNG CTR
33 N Wickliffe Cir (44515-2926)
PHONE.................................330 793-8260
Fax: 330 799-1445
EMP: 29
SALES (est): 1.1MM
SALES (corp-wide): 811K Privately Held
SIC: 8351 Group day care center
PA: Hopes And Dreams Childcare & Learning Center
   4490 Norquest Blvd
   Austintown OH 44515
   330 793-3535

(G-20221)
HOSPICE OF THE VALLEY INC (PA)
5190 Market St (44512-2198)
PHONE.................................330 788-1992
Fax: 330 788-1998
Karen Sitzterald, *Business Mgr*
Terry Kilbury, *Director*
Kellie Durner, *Director*
Kelly Lyons, *Director*
Shannon McNally, *Director*
EMP: 75
SQ FT: 4,700
SALES: 21.7MM Privately Held
SIC: 8069 8322 Specialty hospitals, except psychiatric; individual & family services

GEOGRAPHIC SECTION

Youngstown - Mahoning County (G-20247)

(G-20222)
HUMILITY HOUSE
755 Ohltown Rd (44515-1075)
PHONE..............................330 505-0144
Donna Reedy, *Human Res Dir*
Marylou Clatterbuck, *Manager*
Roco Parrell, *Director*
Kris Mariotti, *Hlthcr Dir*
EMP: 100
SALES: 6.7MM **Privately Held**
SIC: 8051 8052 Skilled nursing care facilities; intermediate care facilities

(G-20223)
HUMILITY OF MARY INFO SYSTEMS
250 E Federal St Ste 200 (44503-1814)
PHONE..............................330 884-6600
Ed Rober, *Treasurer*
Charles Folkwein, *CIO*
Dennis Belter, *Prgrmr*
Maureen Kordupel, *Director*
EMP: 82
SQ FT: 14,000
SALES (est): 3.2MM
SALES (corp-wide): 4.2B **Privately Held**
SIC: 7299 Personal document & information services
PA: Mercy Health
1701 Mercy Health Pl
Cincinnati OH 45237
513 639-2800

(G-20224)
HUNTINGTON NATIONAL BANK
23 Federal Plaza Central (44503-1503)
PHONE..............................330 742-7013
Fax: 330 742-7418
Walter Tomich, *Manager*
EMP: 30
SALES (corp-wide): 4.7B **Publicly Held**
WEB: www.huntingtonnationalbank.com
SIC: 6029 6022 Commercial banks; state commercial banks
HQ: The Huntington National Bank
17 S High St Fl 1
Columbus OH 43215
614 480-4293

(G-20225)
HYDROCHEM LLC
Also Called: Inland Waters of Ohio
428 Thacher Ln (44515-1509)
PHONE..............................216 861-3949
Claude Kubrak, *Vice Pres*
EMP: 40
SQ FT: 30,000
SALES (est): 4.3MM **Privately Held**
WEB: www.inlandwaters.com
SIC: 4953 Hazardous waste collection & disposal; liquid waste, collection & disposal
HQ: Hydrochem Llc
900 Georgia Ave
Deer Park TX 77536
713 393-5600

(G-20226)
HYDROCHEM LLC
428 Thacher Ln (44515-1509)
PHONE..............................330 792-6569
Fax: 330 792-1474
Ronald Sundman, *Sales Staff*
Kevin Maloy, *Manager*
Terry Hall, *Manager*
Paul Sullivan, *Supervisor*
EMP: 34 **Privately Held**
WEB: www.hydrochem.com
SIC: 7349 Chemical cleaning services
HQ: Hydrochem Llc
900 Georgia Ave
Deer Park TX 77536
713 393-5600

(G-20227)
HYNES INDUSTRIES INC (PA)
Also Called: Roll Formed Products Co Div
3805 Hendricks Rd Ste A (44515-3046)
PHONE..............................330 799-3221
Fax: 330 799-9098
William W Bresnahan, *Ch of Bd*
William J Bresnahan, *President*
D R Golding, *President*
C A Covington Jr, *Principal*
Joseph S Donchess, *Principal*
▲ EMP: 124

SQ FT: 154,000
SALES (est): 75MM **Privately Held**
WEB: www.hynesind.com
SIC: 5051 3449 3316 3441 Steel; strip, metal; custom roll formed products; wire, flat, cold-rolled strip: not made in hot-rolled mills; fabricated structural metal

(G-20228)
ICE ZONE LTD
2445 Belmont Ave (44505-2405)
PHONE..............................330 965-1423
Fax: 330 965-9923
Thomas Hutch,
Bruce Zoldan,
EMP: 25
SALES (est): 906.2K **Privately Held**
WEB: www.icezone.com
SIC: 7999 Ice skating rink operation

(G-20229)
IDEXX LABORATORIES INC
945 Boardman Canfield Rd (44512-4239)
PHONE..............................330 629-6076
EMP: 100
SALES (corp-wide): 1.9B **Publicly Held**
SIC: 8734 Testing laboratories
PA: Idexx Laboratories, Inc.
1 Idexx Dr
Westbrook ME 04092
207 556-0300

(G-20230)
IHEARTCOMMUNICATIONS INC
7461 South Ave (44512-5789)
PHONE..............................330 965-0057
Bill Kelly, *General Mgr*
EMP: 80 **Publicly Held**
SIC: 4832 Radio broadcasting stations
HQ: Iheartcommunications, Inc.
20880 Stone Oak Pkwy
San Antonio TX 78258
210 822-2828

(G-20231)
INDEPENDENT RADIO TAXI INC
308 And One Half W (44503)
P.O. Box 1134 (44501-1134)
PHONE..............................330 746-8844
Fax: 330 746-5653
Carl Pasternack, *President*
Randall Park, *Manager*
EMP: 35
SALES (est): 1MM **Privately Held**
SIC: 4121 Taxicabs

(G-20232)
INDUSTRIAL MILL MAINTENANCE
1609 Wilson Ave Ste 2 (44506-1838)
P.O. Box 1465 (44501-1465)
PHONE..............................330 746-1155
Fax: 330 747-7017
Michael McCarthy Sr, *President*
Kathy McCarthy, *Vice Pres*
EMP: 50
SQ FT: 5,600
SALES: 4MM **Privately Held**
SIC: 3471 1721 3444 3441 Sand blasting of metal parts; industrial painting; sheet metalwork; fabricated structural metal

(G-20233)
INDUSTRIAL WASTE CONTROL INC
240 Sinter Ct (44510-1076)
PHONE..............................330 270-9900
Fax: 330 744-7910
Bobbi J Frontino, *President*
Joseph Bianco, *Principal*
Matt Frontino, *Principal*
John Bordell, *Purchasing*
Pasquerrella Joe, *Sales Executive*
EMP: 75
SQ FT: 40,000
SALES (est): 9.2MM **Privately Held**
WEB: www.iwc-inc.com
SIC: 1799 4953 Exterior cleaning, including sandblasting; refuse collection & disposal services

(G-20234)
INFOCISION MANAGEMENT CORP
6951 Southern Blvd Ste E (44512-4655)
PHONE..............................330 726-0872
Carl Albright, *Manager*
Mickey Grubbs, *Manager*
EMP: 272
SALES (corp-wide): 242.3MM **Privately Held**
WEB: www.infocision.com
SIC: 7389 Telemarketing services
PA: Infocision Management Corporation
325 Springside Dr
Akron OH 44333
330 668-1411

(G-20235)
INFOCISION MANAGEMENT CORP
5740 Interstate Blvd (44515-1170)
PHONE..............................330 544-1400
Fax: 330 544-1776
Diane Walker, *Manager*
EMP: 423
SALES (corp-wide): 242.3MM **Privately Held**
WEB: www.infocision.com
SIC: 7389 8732 Telemarketing services; commercial nonphysical research
PA: Infocision Management Corporation
325 Springside Dr
Akron OH 44333
330 668-1411

(G-20236)
INN AT CHRISTINE VALLEY
3150 S Schenley Ave (44511-2862)
PHONE..............................330 270-3347
Fax: 330 799-2499
Ed Reese, *Owner*
Melonie Torres, *Director*
EMP: 40
SALES (est): 945.9K **Privately Held**
WEB: www.theinnatchristinevalley.com
SIC: 8361 8322 Home for the aged; adult day care center

(G-20237)
INTERNTIONAL TOWERS I OHIO LTD
25 Market St (44503-1731)
PHONE..............................216 520-1250
Frank Sinito, *General Ptnr*
EMP: 99
SALES (est): 868K **Privately Held**
SIC: 6513 Apartment building operators

(G-20238)
IVAN LAW INC
2200 Hubbard Rd (44505-3191)
P.O. Box 14459 (44514-7459)
PHONE..............................330 533-5000
Fax: 330 746-1825
Daniel Garver, *President*
Carol Lynn Price, *Corp Secy*
Cynthia Garver, *Vice Pres*
George Seiders, *Treasurer*
EMP: 50
SQ FT: 9,000
SALES: 3MM **Privately Held**
WEB: www.ivanlaw.com
SIC: 1771 Concrete work

(G-20239)
JOHN BROWN TRUCKING INC
8063 Southern Blvd (44512-0306)
PHONE..............................330 758-0841
Anne Marie Naples, *Principal*
EMP: 50
SALES (est): 5.1MM **Privately Held**
SIC: 4212 Local trucking, without storage

(G-20240)
JOHN ZIDIAN CO INC (PA)
574 Mcclurg Rd (44512-6405)
PHONE..............................330 743-6050
Fax: 330 743-0739
Tom Zidian, *President*
Alice Loftus, *Purchasing*
John Angelilli, *CFO*
Aaron Stamp, *CFO*
Jim Zidian, *Treasurer*
◆ EMP: 64
SQ FT: 29,000

SALES (est): 15.6MM **Privately Held**
WEB: www.giarussa.com
SIC: 5141 Groceries, general line

(G-20241)
JOHNSON CONTROLS INC
1044 N Meridian Rd Ste A (44509-1070)
PHONE..............................330 270-4385
Fax: 330 794-4944
Edward Dunkerley, *Manager*
EMP: 40 **Privately Held**
SIC: 1711 Plumbing, heating, air-conditioning contractors
HQ: Johnson Controls, Inc.
5757 N Green Bay Ave
Milwaukee WI 53209
414 524-1200

(G-20242)
JPMORGAN CHASE BANK NAT ASSN
3999 Belmont Ave (44505-1409)
PHONE..............................330 759-1750
Jeanette Howell, *Manager*
EMP: 26
SQ FT: 5,185
SALES (corp-wide): 99.6B **Publicly Held**
WEB: www.chase.com
SIC: 6021 National commercial banks
HQ: Jpmorgan Chase Bank, National Association
1111 Polaris Pkwy
Columbus OH 43240
614 436-3055

(G-20243)
JVC SPORTS CORP
Also Called: Sportsworld
8249 South Ave (44512-6416)
PHONE..............................330 726-1757
Fax: 330 726-1757
Joe Corroto, *President*
Eugene Pirko, *Corp Secy*
Chuck Duke, *Vice Pres*
EMP: 40
SALES (est): 3MM **Privately Held**
SIC: 6512 Commercial & industrial building operation

(G-20244)
KIDNEY CENTER PARTNERSHIP
139 Javit Ct (44515-2410)
PHONE..............................330 799-1150
Fax: 330 799-9145
Guss Biscardi, *Partner*
Chester Amedia, *Partner*
Diane Crafton, *Partner*
Leon G Vassilaros, *Partner*
EMP: 75
SALES (est): 1.3MM **Privately Held**
SIC: 8092 Kidney dialysis centers

(G-20245)
KIDNEY GROUP INC
1340 Belmont Ave Ste 2300 (44504-1129)
PHONE..............................330 746-1488
Fax: 330 746-5611
Nathaniel DOE, *President*
Anup Bains, *Vice Pres*
Kathlyn Padgitt, *Vice Pres*
Ramish Soundararajan, *Vice Pres*
Leon G Vassilaros, *Treasurer*
EMP: 35
SALES (est): 4.7MM **Privately Held**
WEB: www.kidneygroup.com
SIC: 8011 8092 Nephrologist; kidney dialysis centers

(G-20246)
KIDSTOWN LLC
55 Stadium Dr (44512-5519)
PHONE..............................330 502-4484
Fax: 330 729-5437
Prisha Couche,
EMP: 25
SALES (est): 447.6K **Privately Held**
SIC: 8351 Preschool center

(G-20247)
KING COLLISION (PA)
8020 Market St (44512-6239)
PHONE..............................330 729-0525
Fax: 330 729-0085
Douglas J Fenstermaker, *Owner*
EMP: 25

Youngstown - Mahoning County (G-20248) — GEOGRAPHIC SECTION

SALES (est): 2.7MM Privately Held
SIC: 7532 Collision shops, automotive

(G-20248)
KOMAR PLUMBING CO
49 Roche Way (44512-6214)
PHONE.................................330 758-5073
Fax: 330 726-9976
James Grantz, *President*
EMP: 35
SQ FT: 5,000
SALES: 4.5MM Privately Held
SIC: 1711 Plumbing contractors; warm air heating & air conditioning contractor

(G-20249)
KREATIVE COMMUNICATION NETWORK
951 Cameron Ave (44502-2103)
PHONE.................................330 743-1612
David Marino Jr, *President*
EMP: 35
SALES (est): 1.3MM Privately Held
SIC: 4813

(G-20250)
KREPS RON DRYWALL & PLST CO
6042 Market St (44512-2918)
PHONE.................................330 726-8252
Sean Kreps, *President*
Ron Kreps, *President*
Karen Kreps, *Admin Sec*
EMP: 35
SALES: 1.5MM Privately Held
WEB: www.ronkreps.com
SIC: 1742 Drywall

(G-20251)
LA FRANCE SOUTH INC (PA)
Also Called: La France Crystal Dry Cleaners
2607 Glenwood Ave (44511-2401)
PHONE.................................330 782-1400
Fax: 330 782-9611
Steven Weiss, *President*
EMP: 30
SALES (est): 2MM Privately Held
SIC: 7216 Cleaning & dyeing, except rugs

(G-20252)
LAKESIDE REALTY LLC
1749 S Raccoon Rd (44515-4703)
PHONE.................................330 793-4200
George Berick, *Mng Member*
EMP: 50 EST: 2009
SALES (est): 1.5MM Privately Held
SIC: 6531 Real estate brokers & agents

(G-20253)
LANE LIFE CORP (PA)
Also Called: Lane Life Trans
5801 Mahoning Ave (44515-2222)
PHONE.................................330 799-1002
Joseph Lane, *President*
Dave Knarr, *Purch Agent*
Carol Ferko, *Human Res Dir*
EMP: 34
SALES (est): 7.4MM Privately Held
WEB: www.lanelifetrans.com
SIC: 4119 Ambulance service

(G-20254)
LENCYK MASONRY CO INC
7671 South Ave (44512-5724)
PHONE.................................330 729-9780
Lawrence Lencyk, *President*
Jacquelyn Lencyk, *Corp Secy*
Dave Detwiler, *Project Mgr*
EMP: 30
SALES (est): 3.5MM Privately Held
SIC: 1741 Tuckpointing or restoration

(G-20255)
LIBERTY MAINTENANCE INC
777 N Meridian Rd (44509-1006)
P.O. Box 631, Campbell (44405-0631)
PHONE.................................330 755-7711
Fax: 330 755-1847
Emanouel Frangos, *President*
Nikolaos Frangos, *Vice Pres*
John Frangos, *Treasurer*
Michele Lasko, *Admin Sec*
EMP: 70
SQ FT: 7,900
SALES (est): 10.1MM Privately Held
SIC: 1721 Bridge painting

(G-20256)
LOVING HANDS HOME CARE INC
4179 Nottingham Ave (44511-1017)
PHONE.................................330 792-7032
Kathy Stelluto, *President*
EMP: 30
SALES (est): 613.6K Privately Held
SIC: 8082 Home health care services

(G-20257)
LOWES HOME CENTERS LLC
1100 Doral Dr (44514-1904)
PHONE.................................330 965-4500
Fax: 330 965-4518
Bran Heckert, *Branch Mgr*
Brad Parker, *Executive*
EMP: 150
SALES (corp-wide): 68.6B Publicly Held
SIC: 5211 5031 5722 5064 Lumber & other building materials; building materials, exterior; building materials, interior; household appliance stores; electrical appliances, television & radio
HQ: Lowe's Home Centers, Llc
 1605 Curtis Bridge Rd
 Wilkesboro NC 28697
 336 658-4000

(G-20258)
LYDEN OIL COMPANY
3711 Leharps Dr Ste A (44515-1457)
PHONE.................................330 792-1100
Paul Lyden, *Branch Mgr*
Tony Pellegrene, *Manager*
Gary Richmond, *Manager*
EMP: 38
SALES (est): 11.7MM Privately Held
WEB: www.spartanoilcorp.com
SIC: 5172 Crude oil
PA: Lyden Oil Company
 30692 Tracy Rd
 Walbridge OH 43465

(G-20259)
MAHONING CLMBANA TRAINING ASSN
20 W Federal St Ste 604 (44503-1423)
PHONE.................................330 747-5639
Tonya Hawkin, *Manager*
Bert R Cene, *Director*
Gloria Mathews, *Assistant*
EMP: 40 EST: 2000
SALES (est): 2.2MM Privately Held
WEB: www.mctaworkforce.org
SIC: 8611 Business associations

(G-20260)
MAHONING COUNTY
Sanitary Engineering Dept
761 Industrial Rd (44509-2921)
PHONE.................................330 793-5514
Joseph Warinf, *Manager*
EMP: 35 Privately Held
WEB: www.mahoningcountygov.com
SIC: 9511 4953 Sanitary engineering agency, government; garbage: collecting, destroying & processing
PA: The Mahoning County
 21 W Boardman St Ste 200
 Youngstown OH 44503
 330 740-2130

(G-20261)
MAHONING COUNTY
Also Called: Mahoning County Engineers
940 Bears Den Rd (44511-1218)
PHONE.................................330 799-1581
Fax: 330 799-4600
Richard Marsico, *Principal*
Patrick Ginnetti, *Engineer*
EMP: 150 Privately Held
WEB: www.mahoningcountygov.com
SIC: 8711 4959 Engineering services; road, airport & parking lot maintenance services
PA: The Mahoning County
 21 W Boardman St Ste 200
 Youngstown OH 44503
 330 740-2130

(G-20262)
MAHONING COUNTY
Also Called: Transportatin Office
4795 Woodridge Dr (44515-5115)
PHONE.................................330 797-2837
Fax: 330 797-2929
Jeffrey Thompson, *Superintendent*
EMP: 70 Privately Held
WEB: www.mahoningcountygov.com
SIC: 4151 9111 8322 4119 School buses; county supervisors' & executives' offices; individual & family services; local passenger transportation
PA: The Mahoning County
 21 W Boardman St Ste 200
 Youngstown OH 44503
 330 740-2130

(G-20263)
MAHONING COUNTY CHILDRENS SVCS
222 N Federal St Fl 4 (44503-1206)
PHONE.................................330 941-8888
Denise Stewart, *Director*
EMP: 135
SALES (est): 2.5MM Privately Held
SIC: 8322 Adoption services

(G-20264)
MAHONING VALLEY DENTAL SERVICE (PA)
Also Called: Castilla, Dr David DDS
5100 Belmont Ave Ste 1 (44505-1043)
PHONE.................................330 759-1771
Fax: 330 759-1227
Robert Sabatini, *President*
David Castilla, *Fmly & Gen Dent*
EMP: 30
SALES (est): 3.4MM Privately Held
WEB: www.warrenfamilydental.com
SIC: 8021 Dentists' office

(G-20265)
MAHONING VLY HMTLGY ONCLGY ASO
Also Called: Cancer Care Center
500 Gypsy Ln (44504-1315)
P.O. Box 240 (44501-0240)
PHONE.................................330 318-1100
Fax: 330 740-6011
Trish Hrina, *Vice Pres*
Kathy Clark, *Manager*
EMP: 25
SALES (est): 780.7K Privately Held
SIC: 8011 8093 Hematologist; specialty outpatient clinics

(G-20266)
MAHONING VLY INFUSIONCARE INC (PA)
Also Called: Mvi Home Care
4891 Belmont Ave (44505-1015)
PHONE.................................330 759-9487
Kevin McGuire, *President*
Jim Linert, *CFO*
Sharyl Pancallo, *Manager*
Kevin McGwire, *CIO*
Diane Brookbank, *Executive*
EMP: 120
SQ FT: 16,200
SALES (est): 3.5MM Privately Held
WEB: www.mvihomecare.com
SIC: 8059 8082 Personal care home, with health care; home health care services

(G-20267)
MAHONING YOUNGSTOWN COMMUNITY
Also Called: Wic Womens Infants Program
737 N Garland Ave (44506-1018)
PHONE.................................330 747-5661
Fax: 330 743-2323
Anna Cappitti, *Branch Mgr*
EMP: 25
SALES (corp-wide): 2.8MM Privately Held
WEB: www.my-cap.org
SIC: 8732 8322 Economic research; individual & family services
PA: Mahoning Youngstown Community Action Partnership
 1325 5th Ave
 Youngstown OH 44504
 330 747-7921

(G-20268)
MAHONING YOUNGSTOWN COMMUNITY (PA)
Also Called: MYCAP
1325 5th Ave (44504-1702)
PHONE.................................330 747-7921
Fax: 330 747-5708
Anthony B Flask, *Principal*
Harry Meshel, *Principal*
J Ronald Pittman, *Principal*
Donna Morre, *Accountant*
Richard A Roller II, *Exec Dir*
EMP: 51
SALES (est): 2.8MM Privately Held
WEB: www.my-cap.org
SIC: 8732 8399 8322 Economic research; advocacy group; community center

(G-20269)
MALL PARK SOUTHERN
7401 Market St Rm 267 (44512-5650)
PHONE.................................330 758-4511
David Simon, *President*
John Sabino, *Manager*
EMP: 60
SALES (est): 3.1MM Privately Held
SIC: 6512 Shopping center, regional (300,000 - 1,000,000 sq ft)

(G-20270)
MAMMOVAN INC
61 Midgewood Dr (44512-5960)
PHONE.................................330 726-2064
EMP: 20
SALES (est): 1.4MM Privately Held
SIC: 8011 Medical Doctor's Office

(G-20271)
MANCHESTER BENNETT TOWERS & UL
201 E Commerce St Ste 200 (44503-1657)
PHONE.................................330 743-1171
Stephen Bolton, *President*
Timothy Acob, *Vice Pres*
Timothy J Jacob, *Vice Pres*
John F Zimmerman Jr, *Vice Pres*
Joseph Houser, *Bd of Directors*
EMP: 30
SALES (est): 4MM Privately Held
WEB: www.mbpu.com
SIC: 8111 General practice law office

(G-20272)
MARCUS THOMAS LLC
5212 Mahoning Ave Ste 311 (44515-1857)
PHONE.................................330 793-3000
Fax: 330 797-5522
James Nash, *Manager*
EMP: 60
SALES (est): 6.6MM
SALES (corp-wide): 20.7MM Privately Held
WEB: www.marcusthomasad.com
SIC: 7311 8743 Advertising consultant; public relations services
PA: Marcus Thomas, Llc.
 4781 Richmond Rd
 Cleveland OH 44128
 216 292-4700

(G-20273)
MARUCCI AND GAFFNEY EXCVTG CO (PA)
18 Hogue St (44502-1425)
PHONE.................................330 743-8170
William Gaffney Sr, *President*
Steve Shives, *Project Mgr*
William Thornton, *Project Mgr*
Scott Marucci, *Treasurer*
Linda Booth, *Office Mgr*
EMP: 50
SQ FT: 700
SALES (est): 8.9MM Privately Held
WEB: www.maruccigaffney.com
SIC: 1794 1795 1623 Excavation & grading, building construction; demolition, buildings & other structures; sewer line construction; water main construction

(G-20274)
MASCO INC
160 Marwood Cir (44512-6215)
PHONE.................................330 797-2904
John Beal, *Treasurer*
George Winsen, *Manager*

GEOGRAPHIC SECTION

Youngstown - Mahoning County (G-20297)

Sarah Zeisler, *Manager*
EMP: 25
SALES (est): 843.4K
SALES (corp-wide): 601.6K **Privately Held**
SIC: 8322 Individual & family services
PA: Masco Inc
   160 Marwood Cir
   Youngstown OH

(G-20275)
MEADOWBROOK MALL COMPANY (PA)
2445 Belmont Ave (44505-2405)
P.O. Box 2186 (44504-0186)
PHONE.................................330 747-2661
Anthony M Cafaro, *Partner*
EMP: 45 EST: 1980
SQ FT: 12,000
SALES (est): 1.9MM **Privately Held**
SIC: 6512 6531 Commercial & industrial building operation; real estate agents & managers

(G-20276)
MEANDER INN INC
Also Called: Best Western Meander Inn
870 N Canfield Niles Rd (44515-1105)
P.O. Box 6428, Delray Beach FL (33482-6428)
PHONE.................................330 544-2378
Fax: 330 544-7926
Bill Kovass, *President*
EMP: 35
SALES (est): 1.3MM **Privately Held**
SIC: 7011 Hotels

(G-20277)
MEANDER INN INCORPORATED
Also Called: Hampton Inn Youngstown West
880 N Canfield Niles Rd (44515-1105)
PHONE.................................330 544-0660
Sheree Moore, *Principal*
Janet Perry, *Manager*
EMP: 35
SALES: 950K **Privately Held**
SIC: 7011 Hotels

(G-20278)
MEANDER TIRE COMPANY INC
Also Called: Drywall Barn, The
408 N Meridian Rd (44509-1224)
PHONE.................................330 750-6155
Fax: 330 793-4000
Mark Markota, *CEO*
Vickie Shrader, *Manager*
Jack Sloan, *Manager*
EMP: 25
SALES (est): 14.3MM **Privately Held**
SIC: 5032 Drywall materials

(G-20279)
MEDICAL IMGING DIAGNOSTICS LLC
Also Called: Boardman Xray Mri
819 Mckay Ct Ste B103 (44512-5796)
PHONE.................................330 726-0322
Fax: 330 629-2766
Albert M Bleggi,
EMP: 45
SQ FT: 10,000
SALES (est): 2.7MM **Privately Held**
SIC: 8071 X-ray laboratory, including dental

(G-20280)
MERCY HEALTH
250 Debartolo Pl (44512-7004)
P.O. Box 1854 (44501-1854)
PHONE.................................330 729-1372
Molly Seals, *Senior VP*
EMP: 173
SALES (corp-wide): 4.2B **Privately Held**
SIC: 8062 General medical & surgical hospitals
PA: Mercy Health
   1701 Mercy Health Pl
   Cincinnati OH 45237
   513 639-2800

(G-20281)
MERCY HEALTH
6252 Mahoning Ave (44515-2003)
PHONE.................................330 792-7418
Fax: 330 792-9086
Jan Divelbiss, *Manager*
Gilbert Palmer, *Emerg Med Spec*
EMP: 42
SALES (corp-wide): 4.2B **Privately Held**
SIC: 8011 8062 Clinic, operated by physicians; general medical & surgical hospitals
PA: Mercy Health
   1701 Mercy Health Pl
   Cincinnati OH 45237
   513 639-2800

(G-20282)
MERCY HEALTH
Also Called: St. Elizabeth Youngstown Hosp
1044 Belmont Ave (44504-1006)
PHONE.................................330 746-7211
Fax: 330 480-7974
Barbara Stoos, *Dean*
Molly Seals, *Senior VP*
Shannon Hatfield, *Development*
Fran Vitullo, *Pub Rel Mgr*
Liz Baynes, *Manager*
EMP: 159
SALES (corp-wide): 4.2B **Privately Held**
SIC: 8099 Childbirth preparation clinic
PA: Mercy Health
   1701 Mercy Health Pl
   Cincinnati OH 45237
   513 639-2800

(G-20283)
MERCY HEALTH YOUNGSTOWN LLC
Also Called: St Elizabeth Boardman Hospital
8401 Market St (44512-6725)
PHONE.................................330 729-1420
Fax: 330 629-7504
Margaret Baker, *Manager*
Stephanie Muren, *Director*
EMP: 800
SALES (corp-wide): 4.2B **Privately Held**
SIC: 8011 8071 Freestanding emergency medical center; medical laboratories
HQ: Mercy Health Youngstown Llc
   1044 Belmont Ave
   Youngstown OH 44504

(G-20284)
MERCY HEALTH YOUNGSTOWN LLC (HQ)
Also Called: St Elizabeth Health Center
1044 Belmont Ave (44504-1006)
P.O. Box 1790 (44501-1790)
PHONE.................................330 746-7211
Fax: 330 480-2617
Robert Shroder, *President*
Genie Aubel, *President*
Sarah Quinn, *Principal*
James Davis, *VP*
Don Koenig, *COO*
EMP: 2500
SALES: 309.7MM
SALES (corp-wide): 4.2B **Privately Held**
SIC: 8062 8071 Hospital, affiliated with AMA residency; ultrasound laboratory
PA: Mercy Health
   1701 Mercy Health Pl
   Cincinnati OH 45237
   513 639-2800

(G-20285)
MERIDIAN HEALTHCARE (PA)
Also Called: McCdp
527 N Meridian Rd (44509-1227)
PHONE.................................330 797-0070
Lawrence J Moliterno, *CEO*
Darla Gallagher, *Business Mgr*
Darla S Gallagher, *COO*
Gary Holsopple, *COO*
Meghan Fortner, *Vice Pres*
EMP: 60
SALES: 10.6MM **Privately Held**
WEB: www.meridianservices.org
SIC: 8093 Substance abuse clinics (outpatient)

(G-20286)
MIDWEST MOTORS INC
Also Called: J D Byrider
7871 Market St (44512-5970)
PHONE.................................330 758-5800
Robert Palmer, *President*
EMP: 35
SALES (est): 5.6MM **Privately Held**
SIC: 5521 5012 Automobiles, used cars only; automobiles

(G-20287)
MILL CREEK METROPOLITAN PARK
Also Called: Mill Creek Golf Course
Boardman Canfield Rd (44502)
P.O. Box 596, Canfield (44406-0596)
PHONE.................................330 740-7112
Fax: 330 629-9459
Perry Toth, *Opers Staff*
Ray Novotny, *Manager*
Dennis Miller, *Director*
Brian Tolnar, *Director*
EMP: 60
SALES (corp-wide): 6.1MM **Privately Held**
WEB: www.millcreekmetroparks.com
SIC: 7992 Public golf courses
PA: Mill Creek Metropolitan Park
   7574 Clmbiana Canfield Rd
   Canfield OH 44406
   330 702-3000

(G-20288)
MODERN BUILDERS SUPPLY INC
500 Victoria Rd (44515-2030)
PHONE.................................330 726-7000
Jack Narstellar, *President*
EMP: 100
SALES (corp-wide): 437.3MM **Privately Held**
WEB: www.polaristechnologies.com
SIC: 5032 Brick, stone & related material
PA: Modern Builders Supply, Inc.
   302 Mcclurg Rd
   Youngstown OH 44512
   330 729-2690

(G-20289)
MODERN BUILDERS SUPPLY INC (PA)
Also Called: Polaris Technologies
302 Mcclurg Rd (44512-6401)
P.O. Box 9393 (44513-0393)
PHONE.................................330 729-2690
Fax: 330 729-2696
Kevin Leggett, *CEO*
Larry Leggett, *Ch of Bd*
Kevin Buchholtz, *General Mgr*
Eric Leggett, *Vice Pres*
Jack Marstellar, *Vice Pres*
EMP: 200
SQ FT: 40,000
SALES (corp-wide): 437.3MM **Privately Held**
WEB: www.polaristechnologies.com
SIC: 5032 3089 3446 3442 Brick, stone & related material; windows, plastic; doors, folding; plastic or plastic coated fabric; architectural metalwork; metal doors, sash & trim

(G-20290)
MROEKI INC
8571 Foxwood Ct Ste A (44514-4313)
PHONE.................................330 318-3926
Garry Mrozek, *CEO*
Robert Ekiert, *President*
Wanda Mrozek, *Manager*
EMP: 156
SALES (est): 152.3K **Privately Held**
SIC: 7389

(G-20291)
MS CONSULTANTS INC (PA)
333 E Federal St (44503-1821)
PHONE.................................330 744-5321
Fax: 330 744-5256
Thomas E Mosure, *President*
Michael D Kratofil, *COO*
Don Killmeyer, *Vice Pres*
Jason Longbrake, *Vice Pres*
John Pierko, *Vice Pres*
EMP: 105
SQ FT: 20,000
SALES (est): 39.8MM **Privately Held**
WEB: www.moshsolutions.com
SIC: 8711 8712 Consulting engineer; architectural services

(G-20292)
MURPHY CONTRACTING CO
285 Andrews Ave (44505-3059)
P.O. Box 1833 (44501-1833)
PHONE.................................330 743-8915
Fax: 330 743-4418
Donald Gubany, *President*
Len Summers, *Vice Pres*
Michael A Gentile, *Admin Sec*
EMP: 30
SQ FT: 7,000
SALES (est): 9.4MM **Privately Held**
SIC: 1542 1541 Commercial & office building, new construction; industrial buildings, new construction

(G-20293)
NANNICOLA WHOLESALE CO
Also Called: Bingo Division
2750 Salt Springs Rd (44509-4001)
PHONE.................................330 799-0888
Charles Nannicola, *Manager*
EMP: 70
SALES (est): 2.7MM
SALES (corp-wide): 7.9MM **Privately Held**
SIC: 5092 5199 Bingo games & supplies; gifts & novelties
PA: Nannicola Wholesale Co.
   2750 Salt Springs Rd
   Youngstown OH 44509
   330 799-0888

(G-20294)
NASCO ROOFING AND CNSTR INC
1900 Mccartney Rd (44505-5033)
PHONE.................................330 746-3566
Iraj Nasseri, *Principal*
EMP: 28
SALES (est): 1.8MM **Privately Held**
SIC: 1521 1761 Single-family housing construction; roofing contractor

(G-20295)
NATIO ASSOC FOR THE ADVAN OF
Also Called: N A A C P
1350 5th Ave (44504-1728)
P.O. Box 6103 (44501-6103)
PHONE.................................330 782-9777
Willie R Oliver, *President*
EMP: 28
SALES (corp-wide): 22.8MM **Privately Held**
WEB: www.detroitnaacp.org
SIC: 8641 Social associations
PA: National Association For The Advancement Of Colored People
   4805 Mount Hope Dr
   Baltimore MD 21215
   410 580-5777

(G-20296)
NATIONAL HEAT EXCH CLG CORP
8397 Southern Blvd (44512-6319)
PHONE.................................330 482-0893
Carroll Joseph, *President*
Brian Antal, *Vice Pres*
Natalie Joseph, *Safety Mgr*
Natalie Morton, *Safety Mgr*
Mark Mulcahy, *Purch Mgr*
EMP: 40
SQ FT: 52,000
SALES: 9.6MM
SALES (corp-wide): 3.2MM **Privately Held**
WEB: www.nationalheatexchange.com
SIC: 7699 Industrial equipment cleaning
PA: Gbhx Holding Corporation
   131 Varick St Rm 1034
   New York NY 10013
   212 929-0358

(G-20297)
NATIONAL HERITG ACADEMIES INC
Also Called: Stambaugh Charter Academy
2420 Donald Ave (44509-1306)
PHONE.................................330 792-4806
EMP: 59 **Privately Held**
SIC: 8741 Management services
PA: National Heritage Academies, Inc.
   3850 Broadmoor Ave Se # 201
   Grand Rapids MI 49512

Youngstown - Mahoning County (G-20298)   GEOGRAPHIC SECTION

(G-20298)
NATIONAL MENTOR HOLDINGS INC
100 Debartolo Pl Ste 330 (44512-7011)
PHONE..................................330 491-4331
Kristy Devan, *Program Dir*
EMP: 959
SALES (corp-wide): 741.5MM **Privately Held**
SIC: 8093 Mental health clinic, outpatient
PA: National Mentor Holdings, Inc.
    313 Congress St Fl 5
    Boston MA 02210
    617 790-4800

(G-20299)
NATIONAL MULTIPLE SCLEROSIS
4300 Belmont Ave (44505-1084)
PHONE..................................330 759-9066
Janet Kramer, *Director*
EMP: 40
SALES (est): 584.8K **Privately Held**
SIC: 8399 Fund raising organization, non-fee basis

(G-20300)
NICHALEX INC
Also Called: Wee Care Day Care Lrng Centre
801 Kentwood Dr (44512-5004)
PHONE..................................330 726-1422
Fax: 330 726-0516
Donna McGrath, *President*
Allison Carrocce, *Opers Staff*
Kimberly Smrek, *CFO*
Patti Scheetz, *Administration*
EMP: 27
SALES (est): 587.5K **Privately Held**
SIC: 8351 Preschool center

(G-20301)
NICHOLAS CARNEY-MC INC (PA)
Also Called: Carney McNicholas
100 Victoria Rd (44515-2037)
P.O. Box 4717 (44515-0717)
PHONE..................................330 792-5460
Fax: 330 792-1732
Thomas J Carney, *President*
Dennis Cleland, *General Mgr*
Brett Dibell, *Warehouse Mgr*
Pat Finn, *Controller*
Patrick Finn, *Controller*
EMP: 71
SQ FT: 35,000
SALES: 2.2MM **Privately Held**
WEB: www.cmcn.com
SIC: 4213 4214 4212 Trucking, except local; household goods transport; furniture moving & storage, local; household goods moving & storage, local; local trucking, without storage

(G-20302)
NORTH STAR PAINTING CO INC
3526 Mccartney Rd (44505-5006)
PHONE..................................330 743-2333
Fax: 330 743-3434
Irene Kalouris, *President*
Nick Kalouris, *Corp Secy*
Tom Poole, *Accountant*
Beth Beeson, *Manager*
EMP: 50
SALES (est): 6MM **Privately Held**
SIC: 1721 Bridge painting

(G-20303)
NORTH WOOD REALTY (PA)
1315 Boardman Poland Rd # 7 (44514-1935)
PHONE..................................330 423-0837
Richard Salata, *President*
Kathy Miller, *Broker*
Tom Tsarnas, *Sales Staff*
Robin Whitehair, *Manager*
EMP: 105
SALES (est): 5.5MM **Privately Held**
WEB: www.mikeshomecenter.com
SIC: 6531 Real estate agent, residential

(G-20304)
OHIO EDISON COMPANY
100 E Federal St Ste 100 (44503-1800)
PHONE..................................330 747-2071
Fax: 330 740-7695
Doug S Elliott, *Branch Mgr*
EMP: 150 **Publicly Held**
SIC: 4911 Distribution, electric power
HQ: Ohio Edison Company
    76 S Main St Bsmt
    Akron OH 44308
    800 736-3402

(G-20305)
OHIO EDISON COMPANY
730 South Ave (44502-2011)
PHONE..................................330 740-7754
Daniel Knupp, *Engineer*
Jeff Elser, *Branch Mgr*
EMP: 150 **Publicly Held**
SIC: 8742 Industry specialist consultants
HQ: Ohio Edison Company
    76 S Main St Bsmt
    Akron OH 44308
    800 736-3402

(G-20306)
OHIO HEART INSTITUTE INC (PA)
1001 Belmont Ave (44504-1088)
PHONE..................................330 747-6446
Wahoub Hout, *President*
Beth Lavender, *Office Mgr*
EMP: 32
SQ FT: 23,000
SALES (est): 1.6MM **Privately Held**
SIC: 8093 Specialty outpatient clinics

(G-20307)
OHIO NORTH E HLTH SYSTEMS INC
One Health Ohio
726 Wick Ave (44505-2827)
PHONE..................................330 747-9551
Dionna Slagle, *Branch Mgr*
Sameera Rahman, *Med Doctor*
EMP: 25
SALES (est): 1.4MM **Privately Held**
WEB: www.ychcinc.com
SIC: 8011 Offices & clinics of medical doctors
PA: Ohio North East Health Systems, Inc.
    726 Wick Ave
    Youngstown OH 44505

(G-20308)
OHIO NORTH E HLTH SYSTEMS INC (PA)
Also Called: Youngstown Community Hlth Ctr
726 Wick Ave (44505-2827)
PHONE..................................330 747-9551
Fax: 330 747-9552
Ronald Dwinnells, *CEO*
William Addington, *COO*
Beth Haddle, *COO*
Maxine Speer, *CFO*
EMP: 32
SALES: 9.1MM **Privately Held**
SIC: 8099 8082 Physical examination & testing services; home health care services

(G-20309)
OHIO PRESBT RETIREMENT SVCS
Also Called: Park Vista Retirement Cmnty
1216 5th Ave (44504-1605)
PHONE..................................330 746-2944
Fax: 330 746-3427
Mary L Cochran, *Branch Mgr*
Kim Laurie, *Med Doctor*
Vivian Starr, *Director*
Jacque Pernice, *Nursing Dir*
Brenda Brady, *Hlthcr Dir*
EMP: 300 **Privately Held**
WEB: www.nwo.oprs.org
SIC: 8051 8052 6513 Skilled nursing care facilities; intermediate care facilities; apartment building operators
PA: Ohio Living
    1001 Kingsmill Pkwy
    Columbus OH 43229

(G-20310)
OHIO UTILITIES PROTECTION SVC
4740 Belmont Ave (44505-1014)
P.O. Box 729, North Jackson (44451-0729)
PHONE..................................330 759-0050
Fax: 330 759-2745
Roger L Lipscomb Jr, *President*

Jami Novak, *Vice Pres*
Kelli Peck, *Opers Spvr*
Lee Richards, *Sales Staff*
Maureen Beardman, *Manager*
EMP: 51
SQ FT: 2,000
SALES: 6.2MM **Privately Held**
SIC: 8611 8748 1623 Public utility association; business consulting; underground utilities contractor

(G-20311)
OMNI MANOR INC
Also Called: Omni Nursing Home
3245 Vestal Rd (44509-1069)
PHONE..................................330 793-5648
Fax: 330 793-4304
Amy Croake, *QA Dir*
Paul Fabian, *Manager*
David Del Liquadri, *Director*
Carrie Cohal, *Executive*
EMP: 200
SALES (corp-wide): 57.8K **Privately Held**
SIC: 8051 Convalescent home with continuous nursing care
PA: Omni Manor, Inc
    101 W Liberty St
    Girard OH 44420
    330 545-1550

(G-20312)
P&S BAKERY INC
3279 E Western Reserve Rd (44514-2844)
PHONE..................................330 707-4141
Fax: 330 707-1892
David George, *President*
Bonnie George, *Treasurer*
Juan Diaz, *Office Mgr*
EMP: 50
SQ FT: 20,000
SALES: 3MM **Privately Held**
SIC: 5149 Bakery products

(G-20313)
P-AMERICAS LLC
Also Called: Pepsico
500 Pepsi Pl (44502-1432)
PHONE..................................330 746-7652
Richard Plant, *Manager*
Ransom Lane, *Manager*
EMP: 105
SALES (corp-wide): 63.5B **Publicly Held**
SIC: 2086 5149 4225 Carbonated soft drinks, bottled & canned; groceries & related products; general warehousing & storage
HQ: P-Americas Llc
    1 Pepsi Way
    Somers NY 10589
    336 896-5740

(G-20314)
PAISLEY HOUSE FOR AGED WOMEN
1408 Mahoning Ave (44509-2595)
PHONE..................................330 799-9431
Fax: 330 799-8810
Audene Patterson, *Director*
Charles Wilkins, *Director*
EMP: 26
SALES: 795.7K **Privately Held**
SIC: 8361 Home for the aged

(G-20315)
PANELMATIC INC
Also Called: Panelmatic Youngstown
1125 Meadowbrook Ave (44512-1884)
PHONE..................................330 782-8007
Fax: 330 782-0047
Rod Fellows, *General Mgr*
Gary M Urso, *Branch Mgr*
EMP: 29
SALES (corp-wide): 38MM **Privately Held**
WEB: www.panelmatic.com
SIC: 3613 8711 Control panels, electric; cubicles (electric switchboard equipment); designing; ship, boat, machine & product
PA: Panelmatic, Inc.
    258 Donald Dr
    Fairfield OH 45014
    513 829-3666

(G-20316)
PATELLAS FLOOR CENTER INC
Also Called: Patella Carpet & Tile
6620 Market St (44512-3401)
PHONE..................................330 758-4099
Fax: 330 758-5704
Anthony Patella, *President*
Thomas Patella, *Vice Pres*
Karen Patella, *Treasurer*
Maryann Patella, *Admin Sec*
EMP: 25
SQ FT: 3,500
SALES (est): 4.9MM **Privately Held**
SIC: 5713 1752 Carpets; floor tile; carpet laying; vinyl floor tile & sheet installation; ceramic floor tile installation

(G-20317)
PENNSYLVANIA TL SLS & SVC INC (PA)
Also Called: Penn Tool
625 Bev Rd (44512-6421)
P.O. Box 5557, Poland (44514-0557)
PHONE..................................330 758-0845
Fax: 330 758-6028
Robert Baxter, *President*
John Frank, *Finance Mgr*
▲ EMP: 93
SQ FT: 100,000
SALES (est): 110MM **Privately Held**
SIC: 7699 5085 5084 Tool repair services; industrial tools; hoists

(G-20318)
PETSMART INC
1101 Doral Dr (44514-1962)
PHONE..................................330 629-2479
Fax: 330 629-6067
David Beemf, *Manager*
EMP: 30
SALES (corp-wide): 12.7B **Privately Held**
WEB: www.petsmart.com
SIC: 5999 0752 Pet food; animal specialty services
HQ: Petsmart, Inc.
    19601 N 27th Ave
    Phoenix AZ 85027
    623 580-6100

(G-20319)
PHARMACY DATA MANAGEMENT INC (PA)
Also Called: Pharmacy Benefit Direct
1170 E Western Reserve Rd (44514-3245)
P.O. Box 5300, Poland (44514-0300)
PHONE..................................330 757-1500
Douglas Wittenauer, *President*
Dawn Engler, *Opers Staff*
Richard Pavelick, *Controller*
Karen Cessna, *Sales Dir*
Jocelyn Bolling, *Accounts Mgr*
EMP: 41
SQ FT: 14,000
SALES: 6MM **Privately Held**
WEB: www.pdmi.org
SIC: 6371 Pension, health & welfare funds

(G-20320)
PHOENIX SYSTEMS GROUP INC
Also Called: P S G
755 Brdmn Cnfeld Rd Ste G (44512)
PHONE..................................330 726-6500
Fax: 330 726-9587
Jeffrey White, *President*
Constance While, *Treasurer*
Chris Ohle, *Office Mgr*
Bill Mentzer, *Manager*
Paul Reese, *Manager*
EMP: 25
SQ FT: 2,900
SALES (est): 2.8MM **Privately Held**
WEB: www.phoenix-sys.com
SIC: 7379

(G-20321)
PIPINO MANAGEMENT COMPANY (PA)
1275 Boardman Poland Rd (44514-3911)
P.O. Box 9036 (44513-0036)
PHONE..................................330 629-2261
James D Pipino, *President*
Patricia Pipino, *Vice Pres*
Alan Setz, *CFO*
EMP: 44

SALES (est): 3.4MM **Privately Held**
SIC: 8741 Management services

(G-20322)
PLANNED PRENTHOOD GREATER OHIO
Also Called: Youngstown Health Center
77 E Midlothian Blvd (44507-2021)
PHONE..............................330 788-2487
Stephanie Kight, CEO
EMP: 35
SALES (corp-wide): 20.7MM **Privately Held**
SIC: 8093 Family planning clinic
PA: Planned Parenthood Of Greater Ohio
  206 E State St
  Columbus OH 43215
  614 224-2235

(G-20323)
PLANNED PRNTHOOD OF MHNING VLY
77 E Midlothian Blvd (44507-2021)
PHONE..............................330 788-6506
Fax: 330 788-7805
Roberta Antoniotti, Director
EMP: 28
SALES (est): 712K **Privately Held**
SIC: 8093 Birth control clinic

(G-20324)
PLEVNIAK CONSTRUCTION INC
1235 Townsend Ave (44505-1293)
PHONE..............................330 718-1600
Christopher Plevniak, CEO
EMP: 31
SALES (est): 1.2MM **Privately Held**
SIC: 1542 Commercial & office buildings, renovation & repair; shopping center construction; hospital construction; custom builders, non-residential

(G-20325)
PLY-TRIM ENTERPRISES INC
550 N Meridian Rd (44509-1226)
PHONE..............................330 799-7876
Harry Hoffman, Ch of Bd
Robin Kempf, President
Cheryl Dunn, Treasurer
EMP: 25
SALES (est): 1.4MM **Privately Held**
SIC: 8748 8742 Business consulting; manufacturing management consultant

(G-20326)
PLY-TRIM SOUTH INC
550 N Meridian Rd (44509-1226)
PHONE..............................330 799-7876
Robin D Kempf, President
Kathleen A Hoffman, Principal
Wayne Johnson, Vice Pres
Jeniffer Skrofft, Admin Sec
EMP: 25
SQ FT: 4,000
SALES (est): 3MM **Privately Held**
SIC: 5031 Building materials, exterior

(G-20327)
PNC BANK NATIONAL ASSOCIATION
100 E Federal St Ste 100 (44503-1800)
PHONE..............................330 742-4426
EMP: 149
SALES (corp-wide): 18B **Publicly Held**
SIC: 6029 6021 Commercial banks; national commercial banks
HQ: Pnc Bank, National Association
  222 Delaware Ave
  Wilmington DE 19801
  877 762-2000

(G-20328)
POSTAL MAIL SORT INC
1024 Mahoning Ave Ste 8 (44502-1449)
P.O. Box 6542 (44501-6542)
PHONE..............................330 747-1515
Fax: 330 747-3803
Jeff Hill, President
EMP: 35
SQ FT: 13,000
SALES: 3MM **Privately Held**
WEB: www.postalmailsort.com
SIC: 7331 Mailing service

(G-20329)
PROGRESSIVE MAX INSURANCE CO
Also Called: Progressive Insurance
120 Westchester Dr Ste 1 (44515-3989)
PHONE..............................330 533-8733
Fax: 330 533-8969
Rodney Brady, Branch Mgr
Jim Marx, Manager
Lou Deluca, Senior Mgr
EMP: 45
SALES (corp-wide): 26.8B **Publicly Held**
SIC: 6331 Fire, marine & casualty insurance
HQ: Progressive Max Insurance Company
  6300 Wilson Mills Rd
  Cleveland OH 44143
  440 461-5000

(G-20330)
PROGRESSIVE WOMENS CARE
6505 Market St Ste C112 (44512-3467)
PHONE..............................330 629-8466
Fax: 330 629-9559
Joni S Candi, President
Charles Demario, Co-Owner
Joanne Muranski, Office Mgr
EMP: 25
SALES (est): 1.3MM **Privately Held**
WEB: www.progressivewomenscare.com
SIC: 8011 Obstetrician

(G-20331)
PROUT BOILER HTG & WLDG INC
3124 Temple St (44510-1048)
PHONE..............................330 744-0293
Fax: 330 744-0717
Wes Prout, President
Richard Dalleske, Vice Pres
Linda Prout, Shareholder
Donald Raybuck, Admin Sec
EMP: 50 EST: 1945
SQ FT: 3,000
SALES (est): 10.1MM **Privately Held**
WEB: www.proutboiler.com
SIC: 1711 7692 3443 Boiler maintenance contractor; heating & air conditioning contractors; plumbing contractors; mechanical contractor; welding repair; fabricated plate work (boiler shop)

(G-20332)
PSYCARE INC (PA)
2980 Belmont Ave (44505-1834)
PHONE..............................330 759-2310
Douglas Darnall, CEO
Tasha Colvin, Psychologist
Ronald Yendrek, Psychologist
Kathy Dix, Admin Asst
EMP: 122
SALES (est): 4.7MM **Privately Held**
SIC: 8049 Clinical psychologist; hypnotist; psychiatric social worker

(G-20333)
PSYCHIATRIC SOLUTIONS INC
615 Churchill Hubbard Rd (44505-1332)
PHONE..............................330 759-2700
Krishna Devulapalli, Branch Mgr
EMP: 137
SALES (corp-wide): 10.4B **Publicly Held**
WEB: www.intermountainhospital.com
SIC: 8011 Psychiatric clinic
HQ: Psychiatric Solutions, Inc.
  6640 Carothers Pkwy # 500
  Franklin TN 37067
  615 312-5700

(G-20334)
QUADAX INC
17 Colonial Dr Ste 101 (44505-2163)
PHONE..............................330 759-4600
Fax: 330 759-3506
Sharon Lloyd, Branch Mgr
Nelson Laracuente, Manager
Benjamin Frayser, Representative
EMP: 50
SALES (corp-wide): 34.6MM **Privately Held**
WEB: www.quadax.net
SIC: 8721 7389 7363 Billing & bookkeeping service; automobile recovery service; medical help service

PA: Quadax, Inc.
  7500 Old Oak Blvd
  Middleburg Heights OH 44130
  440 777-6300

(G-20335)
R & J TRUCKING INC (HQ)
8063 Southern Blvd (44512-6306)
P.O. Box 9454 (44513-0454)
PHONE..............................800 262-9365
Fax: 330 758-0786
Ronald Carrocce, President
Ron Carrocce, President
Mark Carrocce, Vice Pres
Rob Reed, Vice Pres
Robert Reed, Vice Pres
EMP: 40 EST: 1981
SQ FT: 7,800
SALES (est): 47.1MM **Privately Held**
WEB: www.rjtrucking.com
SIC: 4212 Dump truck haulage

(G-20336)
R & L TRANSFER INC
5550 Dunlap Rd (44515-2042)
PHONE..............................330 743-3609
Jim Laronde, Manager
EMP: 78 **Privately Held**
SIC: 4213 Automobiles, transport & delivery
HQ: R & L Transfer, Inc.
  600 Gilliam Rd
  Wilmington OH 45177
  937 382-1494

(G-20337)
R & M FLUID POWER INC
7953 Southern Blvd (44512-6091)
PHONE..............................330 758-2766
Fax: 330 758-2095
Robert Gustafson Sr, Ch of Bd
Robert Gustafson II, Vice Pres
Jennifer Kenetz, Treasurer
Melissa Ricciardi, Admin Sec
EMP: 25
SQ FT: 40,000
SALES (est): 5.6MM **Privately Held**
WEB: www.rmfluidpower.com
SIC: 3593 5084 Fluid power cylinders, hydraulic or pneumatic; hydraulic systems equipment & supplies

(G-20338)
R & R INC (PA)
Also Called: R & R Cleveland Mack Sales
44 Victoria Rd (44515-2022)
PHONE..............................330 799-1536
Fax: 330 799-6854
Daniel Ralich, President
David Hutter, Corp Secy
Evelyn Savich, Vice Pres
Jeff Gregory, Parts Mgr
Nichole Rodriguez, Executive
EMP: 29
SQ FT: 24,000
SALES (est): 38.1MM **Privately Held**
SIC: 5511 5012 7538 5013 Trucks, tractors & trailers: new & used; trucks, commercial; general truck repair; truck parts & accessories

(G-20339)
R C ENTERPRISES INC
Also Called: Remco Security
5234 Southern Blvd Ste C (44512-2245)
P.O. Box 2633 (44507-0633)
PHONE..............................330 782-2111
Fax: 330 788-1950
Richard P Clautti, President
Gina Clautti, Vice Pres
EMP: 55
SQ FT: 1,200
SALES (est): 1.1MM **Privately Held**
SIC: 7381 Security guard service

(G-20340)
R W SIDLEY INCORPORATED
3424 Oregon Ave (44509-1075)
PHONE..............................330 793-7374
Fax: 330 793-5761
Dave Moore, Managing Dir
Gary Hawkins, Manager
Jeff Hochendoner, Manager
Janey Mental, Manager
EMP: 25

SALES (corp-wide): 136.8MM **Privately Held**
WEB: www.rwsidleyinc.com
SIC: 5032 3273 Brick, stone & related material; ready-mixed concrete
PA: R. W. Sidley Incorporated
  436 Casement Ave
  Painesville OH 44077
  440 352-9343

(G-20341)
RAPE INFORMATION & COUNSELING
Also Called: Family Service Agency
535 Marmion Ave (44502-2323)
PHONE..............................330 782-3936
Dave Arnold, CEO
Patricia Jones, Owner
Linda Diehl, Admin Dir
EMP: 50
SALES (est): 468.2K **Privately Held**
SIC: 8322 Crisis intervention center

(G-20342)
REGAL CINEMAS INC
Also Called: Regal Cinema South 10
7420 South Ave (44512-5719)
PHONE..............................330 758-0503
Fax: 330 758-3430
Stacy Allsop, Manager
EMP: 25
SALES (corp-wide): 982.1MM **Privately Held**
WEB: www.regalcinemas.com
SIC: 7832 Motion picture theaters, except drive-in
HQ: Regal Cinemas, Inc.
  101 E Blount Ave Ste 100
  Knoxville TN 37920
  865 922-1123

(G-20343)
REGIONAL IMAGING CONS CORP
Also Called: Boardman X-Ray & Mri
819 Mckay Ct Ste B103 (44512-5796)
PHONE..............................330 726-9006
Albert M Bleggi, President
Sue Dolofril, Manager
EMP: 30
SALES (est): 937.9K **Privately Held**
SIC: 8071 X-ray laboratory, including dental

(G-20344)
RENTOKIL NORTH AMERICA INC
Also Called: Rentokil Initial PLC
5560 W Webb Rd (44515-1137)
PHONE..............................330 797-9090
Dennis Kopelic, District Mgr
Michael Griffith, Branch Mgr
EMP: 26
SALES (corp-wide): 2.6B **Privately Held**
SIC: 7342 Pest control in structures
HQ: Rentokil North America, Inc.
  1125 Berkshire Blvd # 150
  Wyomissing PA 19610
  610 372-9700

(G-20345)
REPUBLIC SERVICES INC
450 Thacher Ln (44515-1509)
PHONE..............................330 793-7676
EMP: 34
SALES (corp-wide): 10B **Publicly Held**
SIC: 4953 Sanitary landfill operation
PA: Republic Services, Inc.
  18500 N Allied Way # 100
  Phoenix AZ 85054
  480 627-2700

(G-20346)
REPUBLIC SERVICES INC
3870 Hendricks Rd (44515-1528)
PHONE..............................330 793-7676
John Carlson, General Mgr
Robert E Dak, Branch Mgr
EMP: 34
SALES (corp-wide): 10B **Publicly Held**
SIC: 4953 Sanitary landfill operation
PA: Republic Services, Inc.
  18500 N Allied Way # 100
  Phoenix AZ 85054
  480 627-2700

Youngstown - Mahoning County (G-20347)

(G-20347)
REPUBLIC SERVICES INC
Also Called: Allied Waste Division
3870 Henricks Rd (44515)
PHONE..................330 793-7676
EMP: 34
SALES (corp-wide): 10B Publicly Held
SIC: 4953 Refuse collection & disposal services
PA: Republic Services, Inc.
18500 N Allied Way # 100
Phoenix AZ 85054
480 627-2700

(G-20348)
REPUBLIC/CONSTRUCTION
460 E Federal St (44503-1817)
P.O. Box 6564 (44501-6564)
PHONE..................330 747-1510
Richard Teodori, President
Scott Thompson, General Mgr
Ben Bertok, Manager
EMP: 30
SQ FT: 46,000
SALES (est): 1.5MM Privately Held
WEB: www.csdohio.com
SIC: 1742 Acoustical & ceiling work

(G-20349)
RESCUE MISSION OF MAHONING VAL (PA)
962 Martin L King Jr Blvd (44510-1686)
P.O. Box 298 (44501-0298)
PHONE..................330 744-5485
Fax: 330 788-8518
Naomi Sparks, Financial Exec
Rev David Sherrard, Exec Dir
Jim Echement, Exec Dir
Lynn Wyant, Director
Liz Ray, Exec Sec
EMP: 36
SQ FT: 22,000
SALES: 3.6MM Privately Held
SIC: 8322 Social service center

(G-20350)
RESCUE MISSION OF MAHONING VAL
2246 Glenwood Ave (44511-1574)
P.O. Box 298 (44501-0298)
PHONE..................330 744-5485
David Sherrard, Pastor
Naomi Sparks, Opers Staff
EMP: 30
SALES (est): 379.3K
SALES (corp-wide): 3.6MM Privately Held
SIC: 8322 Social service center
PA: Rescue Mission Of Mahoning Valley, The (Inc)
962 Martin L King Jr Blvd
Youngstown OH 44510
330 744-5485

(G-20351)
RGIS LLC
5423 Mahoning Ave Ste C (44515-2435)
PHONE..................330 799-1566
Fax: 330 799-5178
Carl Fisher, Manager
EMP: 100
SALES (corp-wide): 7.1B Publicly Held
WEB: www.rgisinv.com
SIC: 7389 Inventory computing service
HQ: Rgis, Llc
2000 Taylor Rd
Auburn Hills MI 48326
248 651-2511

(G-20352)
RNW HOLDINGS INC
200 Division Street Ext (44510-1000)
P.O. Box 478 (44501-0478)
PHONE..................330 792-0600
Fax: 330 792-1459
Major Hammond, Branch Mgr
Thomas Norris, Director
EMP: 40
SALES (corp-wide): 64.2MM Privately Held
SIC: 5093 1795 3341 Scrap & waste materials; wrecking & demolition work; secondary nonferrous metals

HQ: Rnw Holdings, Inc.
26949 Chagrin Blvd # 305
Cleveland OH 44122
216 831-0510

(G-20353)
ROBERT HALF INTERNATIONAL INC
Also Called: Account Temps
970 Windham Ct Ste 1a (44512-5082)
PHONE..................330 629-9494
Carrie Votino, Branch Mgr
EMP: 92
SALES (corp-wide): 5.2B Publicly Held
WEB: www.rhii.com
SIC: 7361 Executive placement
PA: Robert Half International Inc.
2884 Sand Hill Rd Ste 200
Menlo Park CA 94025
650 234-6000

(G-20354)
ROCKNSTARR HOLDINGS LLC
112 S Meridian Rd (44509-2640)
PHONE..................330 509-9086
Ray Starr,
EMP: 28
SQ FT: 52,000
SALES: 12MM Privately Held
SIC: 5013 3312 Wheels, motor vehicle; wheels

(G-20355)
ROGER KREPS DRYWALL & PLST INC
939 Augusta Dr (44512-7923)
PHONE..................330 726-6090
Fax: 330 726-6114
Roger R Kreps, President
Mary Ann Kreps, Corp Secy
Joan Molinar, Manager
Joni Molinari, Manager
Phil Fry, Supervisor
EMP: 76
SQ FT: 2,500
SALES (est): 7.8MM Privately Held
WEB: www.rogerkrepsdrywall.com
SIC: 1751 1742 Carpentry work; drywall; plastering, plain or ornamental; acoustical & ceiling work

(G-20356)
ROMAN CTHLIC DOCESE YOUNGSTOWN
Also Called: Calvary Cemetery
248 S Belle Vista Ave (44509-2252)
PHONE..................330 792-4721
Fax: 330 792-1885
Don Goncy, Superintendent
EMP: 25
SALES (corp-wide): 23.6MM Privately Held
WEB: www.stjosephmantua.com
SIC: 6553 Cemeteries, real estate operation
PA: Roman Catholic Diocese Of Youngstown
144 W Wood St
Youngstown OH 44503
330 744-8451

(G-20357)
RON CARROCCE TRUCKING COMPANY
8063 Southern Blvd (44512-6306)
P.O. Box 9454 (44513-0454)
PHONE..................330 758-0841
Ronald Carrocce, President
Mark Carrocce, Corp Secy
Gary Carrocce, Vice Pres
EMP: 110
SQ FT: 50,000
SALES (est): 6.5MM Privately Held
SIC: 4212 Local trucking, without storage; dump truck haulage
PA: American Bulk Commodities Inc
8063 Southern Blvd
Youngstown OH 44512

(G-20358)
RONDINELLI COMPANY INC (PA)
Also Called: Dutchess Cleaners
207 Boardman Canfield Rd (44512-4806)
PHONE..................330 726-7643
Gino Rondinelli, President

Malini Hyner, Manager
EMP: 75
SALES (est): 5.5MM Privately Held
SIC: 7216 7299 Cleaning & dyeing, except rugs; tuxedo rental

(G-20359)
RONDINELLIS TUXEDO
207 Boardman Canfield Rd (44512-4806)
PHONE..................330 726-7768
Gino Rondinelli, President
George Rondinelli, Vice Pres
EMP: 35
SQ FT: 6,000
SALES (est): 3.7MM
SALES (corp-wide): 5.5MM Privately Held
SIC: 5136 5699 7299 Men's & boys' clothing; formal wear; tuxedo rental
PA: The Rondinelli Company Inc
207 Boardman Canfield Rd
Youngstown OH 44512
330 726-7643

(G-20360)
ROTH BROS INC (DH)
3847 Crum Rd (44515-1414)
P.O. Box 4209 (44515-0209)
PHONE..................330 793-5571
Fax: 330 799-9005
Thomas E Froelich, Exec VP
Stephen P Koneval, Exec VP
Richard M Wardle, Exec VP
Michael A Wardle, Vice Pres
Troy Brandon, Vice Pres
EMP: 240
SQ FT: 120,000
SALES (est): 84.8MM
SALES (corp-wide): 139.1MM Privately Held
SIC: 1711 1761 Warm air heating & air conditioning contractor; roofing contractor; sheet metalwork
HQ: Sodexo, Inc.
9801 Washingtonian Blvd # 1
Gaithersburg MD 20878
301 987-4000

(G-20361)
RUKH BOARDMAN PROPERTIES LLC
Also Called: Holiday Inn
7410 South Ave (44512-5719)
PHONE..................330 726-5472
Fax: 330 726-0717
Brent Reynolds, General Mgr
Mike Moliterno, Facilities Mgr
Darolyn Boivin, Controller
Melissa Kellish, Sales Mgr
Len Lesko, Manager
EMP: 95
SALES: 1,000K Privately Held
WEB: www.hiboardman.com
SIC: 7011 Inns

(G-20362)
RURAL/METRO CORPORATION
1122 E Midlothian Blvd (44502-2839)
PHONE..................216 749-2211
Jackie Lavoie, Human Resources
Kurt Narron, Branch Mgr
Andy Kwon, Technology
EMP: 165
SALES (corp-wide): 7.8B Publicly Held
WEB: www.ruralmetro.com
SIC: 4119 Ambulance service
HQ: Rural/Metro Corporation
8465 N Pima Rd
Scottsdale AZ 85258
480 606-3886

(G-20363)
RURAL/METRO CORPORATION
Also Called: Gold Cross
1122 E Midlothian Blvd (44502-2839)
PHONE..................330 744-4161
Patrick Sullivan, Manager
EMP: 200
SALES (corp-wide): 7.8B Publicly Held
WEB: www.ruralmetro.com
SIC: 4119 Ambulance service
HQ: Rural/Metro Corporation
8465 N Pima Rd
Scottsdale AZ 85258
480 606-3886

(G-20364)
RYAN SHERIDAN
45 N Canfield Niles Rd (44515-2343)
PHONE..................330 270-2380
Ryan Sheridan, Owner
EMP: 29 EST: 2015
SALES (est): 363.1K Privately Held
SIC: 8093 8099 8322 Detoxification center, outpatient; health screening service; general counseling services

(G-20365)
SAMI S RAFIDI
Also Called: Sfr Group
2000 Canfield Rd (44511-2984)
PHONE..................330 799-9508
Fax: 330 799-9757
Sami S Rafidi, Owner
EMP: 175
SQ FT: 1,000
SALES (est): 4.2MM Privately Held
WEB: www.sfrgroup.com
SIC: 6531 6519 Real estate agents & managers; real property lessors

(G-20366)
SAMRON INC
Also Called: Stanley Steamer
674 Bev Rd (44512-6422)
PHONE..................330 782-6539
Fax: 330 726-3969
Ronald Zockle, President
Dominic Zockle, Corp Secy
Jeff Opencar, Financial Exec
EMP: 28 EST: 1974
SQ FT: 6,500
SALES (est): 1.6MM Privately Held
WEB: www.samron.net
SIC: 7217 5713 1752 Carpet & furniture cleaning on location; floor covering stores; floor laying & floor work

(G-20367)
SATERI HOME INC (PA)
7246 Ronjoy Pl (44512-4357)
PHONE..................330 758-8106
Fax: 330 726-2234
Felix S Savon, President
EMP: 100
SQ FT: 26,000
SALES (est): 39.1MM Privately Held
SIC: 6513 8051 5999 7352 Apartment building operators; skilled nursing care facilities; medical apparatus & supplies; medical equipment rental; individual & family services; intermediate care facilities

(G-20368)
SEARS ROEBUCK AND CO
Also Called: Sears Product Service 1474
7401 Market St Rm 7 (44512-5619)
PHONE..................330 629-7700
Fax: 330 758-0894
Marge Radecki, Branch Mgr
Jeff Curry, Manager
EMP: 41
SALES (corp-wide): 16.7B Publicly Held
SIC: 7699 5722 Household appliance repair services; household appliance stores
HQ: Sears, Roebuck And Co.
3333 Beverly Rd
Hoffman Estates IL 60179
847 286-2500

(G-20369)
SECOND PHASE INC
191 S Four Mile Run Rd (44515-3123)
PHONE..................330 797-9930
Fax: 330 797-9931
Candy Palmer, President
EMP: 49
SQ FT: 1,596
SALES (est): 1.8MM Privately Held
WEB: www.secondphase.net
SIC: 8361 Home for the mentally handicapped

(G-20370)
SENIOR INDEPENDENCE
1110 5th Ave (44504-1604)
PHONE..................330 744-5071
Karen Ambrose, Director
EMP: 35

GEOGRAPHIC SECTION

Youngstown - Mahoning County (G-20394)

SALES (est): 259K **Privately Held**
WEB: www.parkvista.oprs.org
SIC: 8082 Home health care services

(G-20371)
SEREX CORPORATION (PA)
55 Victoria Rd (44515-2023)
P.O. Box 9022 (44513-0022)
PHONE...................330 726-6062
Russel Hodge, *President*
Leonard Morris, *Vice Pres*
Gregory Pastore, *VP Sales*
EMP: 34
SQ FT: 14,900
SALES (est): 7.5MM **Privately Held**
SIC: 7699 Vending machine repair

(G-20372)
SHANCLIFF INVESTMENTS LTD
1358 Meadowood Cir (44514-3291)
PHONE...................330 883-5560
EMP: 35
SALES (est): 1.8MM **Privately Held**
SIC: 6799 Investors

(G-20373)
SHEPHERD OF THE VALLEY LUTHERA (PA)
5525 Silica Rd (44515-1002)
PHONE...................330 530-4038
Fax: 330 530-4039
Tj Eisenbraun, *Purch Mgr*
Victoria Brown, *CFO*
Deidre Watson, *Human Res Dir*
Cheryl Lloyd, *Marketing Staff*
Lynn Miller, *Marketing Staff*
EMP: 41
SALES (est): 31.6MM **Privately Held**
WEB: www.shepherdofthevalley.com
SIC: 8051 Skilled nursing care facilities

(G-20374)
SHEPHERD OF THE VALLEY LUTHERA
Also Called: Shepards Wood Nursing
7148 West Blvd (44512-4336)
PHONE...................330 726-9061
Fax: 330 726-0442
Richard Limongi, *Manager*
James F Brandis, *Manager*
Robyn Musgrove, *Manager*
Teresa Williams, *Food Svc Dir*
Jennifer Joseph, *Hlthcr Dir*
EMP: 170
SALES (est): 2.6MM
SALES (corp-wide): 31.6MM **Privately Held**
WEB: www.shepherdofthevalley.com
SIC: 8051 Skilled nursing care facilities
PA: Shepherd Of The Valley Lutheran Retirement Services, Inc.
5525 Silica Rd
Youngstown OH 44515
330 530-4038

(G-20375)
SIFFRIN RESIDENTIAL ASSN
Also Called: Bridge The
136 Westchester Dr Ste 1 (44515-3965)
PHONE...................330 799-8932
Fax: 330 799-8936
EMP: 165
SALES (corp-wide): 9.8MM **Privately Held**
SIC: 8322 8051 7361 5047 Social services for the handicapped; mental retardation hospital; placement agencies; technical aids for the handicapped
PA: Siffrin Inc.
3688 Dressler Rd Nw
Canton OH 44718
330 478-0263

(G-20376)
SIMON ROOFING AND SHTMTL CORP (PA)
70 Karago Ave (44512-5949)
P.O. Box 951109, Cleveland (44193-0005)
PHONE...................330 629-7392
Fax: 330 629-7399
Stephen Manser, *President*
Calvin Aschoff, *General Mgr*
Rocco Augustine, *Vice Pres*
Rick Cook, *Vice Pres*
Jami Erjavic, *Vice Pres*
EMP: 105
SQ FT: 30,000
SALES: 82MM **Privately Held**
WEB: www.simonroofing.com
SIC: 1761 2952 Roofing contractor; asphalt felts & coatings

(G-20377)
SOUTH MILL PET CARE CENTER
8105 South Ave (44512-6414)
PHONE...................330 758-6479
Fax: 330 758-7787
Robert Renolds, *President*
EMP: 25
SQ FT: 2,000
SALES (est): 1.1MM **Privately Held**
WEB: www.southmillpetcare.com
SIC: 0752 0742 Grooming services, pet & animal specialties; veterinarian, animal specialties

(G-20378)
SOUTHWOOD AUTO SALES
5334 South Ave (44512-2450)
PHONE...................330 788-8822
Joseph Mileto III, *Owner*
EMP: 34
SALES (est): 646.4K **Privately Held**
SIC: 7521 7549 Automobile parking; towing service, automotive

(G-20379)
SOUTHWOODS SURGICAL HOSPITAL
7630 Southern Blvd (44512-5633)
PHONE...................330 729-8000
Edward Muransky, *CEO*
Tony Biondillo, *Business Dir*
Cindy Hutchison, *Infect Cntl Dir*
Angela Kerns, *Administration*
EMP: 30
SALES (est): 4.7MM **Privately Held**
SIC: 8093 Specialty outpatient clinics

(G-20380)
SPRINGFIELD LITTLE TIGERS FOOT
49 Philrose Ln (44514-3242)
PHONE...................330 549-2359
David Billock, *President*
EMP: 85
SALES: 100K **Privately Held**
SIC: 8641 Youth organizations

(G-20381)
ST MORITZ SECURITY SVCS INC
Also Called: Saint Moritz Security Services
32 N Four Mile Run Rd (44515-3003)
PHONE...................330 270-5922
Fax: 330 270-5924
Joe Bonacci, *Branch Mgr*
EMP: 73
SQ FT: 741
SALES (corp-wide): 87.5MM **Privately Held**
SIC: 7381 Security guard service
PA: St. Moritz Security Services, Inc.
4600 Clairton Blvd
Pittsburgh PA 15236
412 885-3144

(G-20382)
STATE ALARM INC (PA)
Also Called: State Alarm Systems
5956 Market St (44512-2916)
PHONE...................330 726-8111
Fax: 330 726-8104
Donald P Shury, *President*
Brenda Dull, *Corp Secy*
Alan Flanegin, *Opers Mgr*
Jim Wiseman, *Sales Associate*
Al Carpanelli, *Manager*
EMP: 35 **EST:** 1953
SQ FT: 2,300
SALES (est): 17.7MM **Privately Held**
WEB: www.state-alarm.com
SIC: 5999 5063 7382 1731 Alarm signal systems; burglar alarm systems; fire alarm systems; burglar alarm maintenance & monitoring; fire alarm maintenance & monitoring; fire detection & burglar alarm systems specialization; closed circuit television services

(G-20383)
STEWARD NORTHSIDE MED CTR INC
500 Gypsy Ln (44504-1315)
PHONE...................330 884-1000
Ralph De La Torre, *Principal*
EMP: 31
SALES (est): 1MM
SALES (corp-wide): 2.3B **Privately Held**
SIC: 8062 General medical & surgical hospitals
PA: Steward Health Care System Llc
111 Huntington Ave # 1800
Boston MA 02199
617 419-4700

(G-20384)
STROLLO ARCHITECTS INC
201 W Federal St (44503-1203)
PHONE...................330 743-1177
Fax: 330 743-2834
Gregg Strollo, *President*
Robert Hanahan, *Principal*
Rodney Lamberson, *Exec VP*
Joseph Yank, *Vice Pres*
Robert Salata, *Project Mgr*
EMP: 30 **EST:** 1956
SALES (est): 4.7MM **Privately Held**
SIC: 8712 Architectural engineering

(G-20385)
SURGICAL HOSP AT SOUTHWOODS
7630 Southern Blvd (44512-5633)
PHONE...................330 729-8000
Steve Davenport, *Sls & Mktg Exec*
Amy Kurcon, *Office Mgr*
Coleen Cooper, *Manager*
Brian Oshaughnessy, *CIO*
Diane Benedict, *Pharmacy Dir*
EMP: 40
SALES: 65MM **Privately Held**
SIC: 8011 Surgeon

(G-20386)
SUTTON MOTOR COACH TOURS INC
Also Called: Southern Park Limo Service
7338 Southern Blvd (44512-5627)
P.O. Box 3335 (44513-3335)
PHONE...................330 726-2800
Fax: 330 726-3824
Lorraine Sutton Parnell, *President*
EMP: 30
SQ FT: 4,000
SALES (est): 1.3MM **Privately Held**
SIC: 4111 4142 Airport transportation services, regular route; bus charter service, except local

(G-20387)
TAYLOR - WINFIELD CORPORATION
Portage Transformer Co Div
3200 Innovation Pl (44509-4025)
PHONE...................330 797-0300
Fax: 330 797-7543
Kirk Harrell, *Vice Pres*
Blake Rhein, *Vice Pres*
Karen Sanders, *Vice Pres*
Chris Morrone, *Project Mgr*
Steve Zimmer, *Safety Mgr*
EMP: 90
SALES (est): 7.9MM
SALES (corp-wide): 20.3MM **Privately Held**
WEB: www.coil-joining.com
SIC: 5084 Welding machinery & equipment
PA: The Taylor - Winfield Corporation
3200 Innovation Pl
Hubbard OH 44425
330 259-8500

(G-20388)
TELE-SOLUTIONS INC (PA)
6001 Suthern Blvd Ste 102 (44512)
PHONE...................330 782-2888
Fax: 330 782-2898
Deane Wurst, *President*
Jason Wurst, *Vice Pres*
Michelle Henderson, *Sales Associate*
Linda Devine, *Manager*
Jeffrey Payne, *Info Tech Dir*
EMP: 27
SQ FT: 4,200
SALES (est): 5.4MM **Privately Held**
WEB: www.tele-solutions.net
SIC: 5065 1731 Telephone equipment; telephone & telephone equipment installation

(G-20389)
TIME WARNER CABLE INC
755 Wick Ave (44505-2826)
PHONE...................330 633-9203
Fax: 330 747-5003
James Manning, *Branch Mgr*
Daryl Morrison, *Manager*
EMP: 42
SALES (corp-wide): 41.5B **Publicly Held**
SIC: 4841 Cable television services; subscription television services
HQ: Spectrum Management Holding Company, Llc
400 Atlantic St
Stamford CT 06901
203 905-7801

(G-20390)
TRANSIT SERVICE COMPANY
1130 Prfmce Pl Unit A (44502)
PHONE...................330 782-3343
Fax: 330 781-9436
Frank Bochenek, *President*
Kenneth Bochenek, *Vice Pres*
Mike Pollifrone, *Manager*
EMP: 50
SALES (est): 3.1MM **Privately Held**
SIC: 4141 Local bus charter service

(G-20391)
TRAVELCENTERS OF AMERICA LLC
I 80 Rte 46 Exit 223 A Rt 46 (44515)
P.O. Box 4296 (44515-0296)
PHONE...................330 793-4426
Mary Ault, *Manager*
EMP: 100 **Publicly Held**
WEB: www.iowa80group.com
SIC: 5172 Petroleum products
PA: Travelcenters Of America Llc
24601 Center Ridge Rd # 200
Westlake OH 44145

(G-20392)
TRI AREA ELECTRIC CO INC
37 Wayne Ave (44502-1900)
PHONE...................330 744-0151
Fax: 330 744-5714
William T Leone, *President*
Andrea Leone, *Corp Secy*
Tammy Leone, *Office Mgr*
EMP: 50 **EST:** 1976
SQ FT: 8,000
SALES (est): 7.7MM **Privately Held**
SIC: 1731 General electrical contractor

(G-20393)
TRUMBULL INDUSTRIES INC
1040 N Meridian Rd (44509-1090)
PHONE...................330 799-3333
Fax: 330 797-3215
Kyle Elliott, *Opers Mgr*
Tim Saloff, *Opers Staff*
Carol London, *Buyer*
Chuck Bidinger, *Purchasing*
Duane Myers, *Design Engr*
EMP: 65
SALES (corp-wide): 136.6MM **Privately Held**
SIC: 5074 Plumbing fittings & supplies
PA: Trumbull Industries, Inc.
400 Dietz Rd Ne
Warren OH 44483
330 393-6624

(G-20394)
TURNING PT COUNSELING SVCS INC (PA)
611 Belmont Ave (44502-1037)
PHONE...................330 744-2991
J H Wanamaker Et Al, *Principal*
S M Berkowitz, *Principal*
B P Massman, *Principal*
Jannie Tagger, *Bookkeeper*
Rick Schukert, *MIS Dir*
EMP: 80
SALES: 5.1MM **Privately Held**
WEB: www.turningpointcs.com
SIC: 8322 Alcoholism counseling, nontreatment; general counseling services

Youngstown - Mahoning County (G-20395)

(G-20395)
TURNING TECHNOLOGIES LLC (PA)
255 W Federal St (44503-1207)
PHONE..................................330 746-3015
Fax: 330 259-7615
Mike Broderick, *CEO*
Dave Kauer, *President*
Ethan Cohen, *COO*
Sheila Hura, *Vice Pres*
Kevin Owens, *Vice Pres*
EMP: 125
SQ FT: 26,200
SALES (est): 98.4MM **Privately Held**
WEB: www.turningtechnologies.com
SIC: 7372 Business oriented computer software; educational computer software

(G-20396)
TVC HOME HEALTH CARE
70 W Mckinley Way Ste 8 (44514-1967)
PHONE..................................330 755-1110
Jerry Melillo, *Owner*
EMP: 27
SALES (est): 673.9K **Privately Held**
SIC: 8082 8099 Visiting nurse service; health & allied services

(G-20397)
UNITED COMMUNITY FINCL CORP (PA)
275 W Federal St (44503-1200)
PHONE..................................330 742-0500
Fax: 330 742-0532
Gary M Small, *President*
Richard J Schiraldi, *Principal*
Sandra Beckwith, *Assistant VP*
Terry Mann, *Vice Pres*
Jude J Nohra, *Vice Pres*
EMP: 200
SALES: 118.7MM **Publicly Held**
WEB: www.ucfcorp.com
SIC: 6036 State savings banks, not federally chartered; savings & loan associations, not federally chartered

(G-20398)
UNITED METHODIST COMMUNITY CTR
2401 Belmont Ave (44505-2405)
PHONE..................................330 743-5149
Fax: 330 747-5858
Robert L Faulkner, *President*
Rev Jerry Krueger, *Vice Pres*
Jerry Savo, *Treasurer*
Juanita Pasley, *Info Tech Mgr*
Amanda Crosby, *Director*
EMP: 40
SQ FT: 6,000
SALES: 700.7K **Privately Held**
SIC: 8661 8399 Methodist Church; advocacy group

(G-20399)
UNITED PARCEL SERVICE INC OH
Also Called: UPS
95 Karago Ave Ste 4 (44512-5951)
PHONE..................................800 742-5877
EMP: 158
SALES (corp-wide): 65.8B **Publicly Held**
WEB: www.upsscs.com
SIC: 4215 Package delivery, vehicular; parcel delivery, vehicular
HQ: United Parcel Service, Inc. (Oh)
  55 Glenlake Pkwy
  Atlanta GA 30328
  404 828-6000

(G-20400)
V AND V APPLIANCE PARTS INC (PA)
27 W Myrtle Ave (44507-1193)
PHONE..................................330 743-5144
Fax: 330 743-3221
Victor Lazar, *Ch of Bd*
Bruce Lazar, *President*
Albert E Brennan, *Principal*
Vincent Rypien, *Principal*
Judy Lazar, *Treasurer*
EMP: 40
SQ FT: 16,000
SALES: 210MM **Privately Held**
WEB: www.vvapplianceparts.com
SIC: 5064 Appliance parts, household

(G-20401)
VALLEY ACOUSTICS INC
1203 N Meridian Rd (44509-1020)
PHONE..................................330 799-1894
Fax: 330 799-1882
David Olsavsky, *President*
Tom Olsavsky, *Vice Pres*
EMP: 30 EST: 1960
SQ FT: 3,200
SALES (est): 3.1MM **Privately Held**
SIC: 1751 1742 Carpentry work; acoustical & ceiling work

(G-20402)
VALLEY INDUSTRIAL TRUCKS INC (PA)
1152 Meadowbrook Ave (44512-1887)
PHONE..................................330 788-4081
Fax: 330 788-5432
James E Hammond, *President*
Mark Evans, *VP Opers*
Mike Ladesic, *Warehouse Mgr*
Patricia Wilson, *Controller*
David Lipely, *Sales Mgr*
EMP: 32
SQ FT: 45,000
SALES (est): 10.7MM **Privately Held**
SIC: 7359 5084 Equipment rental & leasing; materials handling machinery

(G-20403)
VETERANS HEALTH ADMINISTRATION
Also Called: Youngstown V A Otptient Clinic
2031 Belmont Ave (44505-2401)
PHONE..................................330 740-9200
Mukesh Jain, *Branch Mgr*
Ganesan Shobana, *Med Doctor*
EMP: 30 **Publicly Held**
WEB: www.veterans-ru.org
SIC: 8011 9451 Clinic, operated by physicians; administration of veterans' affairs
HQ: Veterans Health Administration
  810 Vermont Ave Nw
  Washington DC 20420

(G-20404)
VIBRA HEALTHCARE LLC
8049 South Ave (44512-6154)
PHONE..................................330 726-5050
EMP: 28
SALES (corp-wide): 320.2MM **Privately Held**
SIC: 8051 Skilled nursing care facilities
PA: Vibra Healthcare, Llc
  4600 Lena Dr
  Mechanicsburg PA 17055
  717 591-5700

(G-20405)
VIBRA HOSP MAHONING VLY LLC
Also Called: MAHONING VALLEY HOSPITAL
8049 South Ave (44512-6154)
PHONE..................................330 726-5000
Fax: 330 758-6767
Karen McCullough, *Purch Dir*
Kirsten Cheeks, *Human Resources*
Mary Jane Larmon, *Mng Member*
Catherine Cardelein, *Manager*
Tony Terlecky, *CIO*
EMP: 96
SALES: 18.1MM
SALES (corp-wide): 320.2MM **Privately Held**
WEB: www.mahoningvalleyhospital.com
SIC: 8069 Specialty hospitals, except psychiatric
PA: Vibra Healthcare, Llc
  4600 Lena Dr
  Mechanicsburg PA 17055
  717 591-5700

(G-20406)
VINDICATOR PRINTING COMPANY
Also Called: Wfmj-Tv21
101 W Boardman St (44503-1305)
P.O. Box 689 (44501-0689)
PHONE..................................330 744-8611
John Grdic, *Manager*
EMP: 85
SALES (corp-wide): 50.5MM **Privately Held**
WEB: www.vindy.com
SIC: 4833 Television broadcasting stations
PA: The Vindicator Printing Company
  107 Vindicator Sq
  Youngstown OH 44503
  330 747-1471

(G-20407)
VLP INC
Also Called: Panache Hair Salon
7301 West Blvd Ste A3 (44512-5268)
PHONE..................................330 758-8811
Fax: 330 758-9708
Frank Lucurell, *President*
Nancy Vasu, *Vice Pres*
Francie Patoella, *Admin Sec*
EMP: 30
SALES (est): 810K **Privately Held**
SIC: 7231 Cosmetology & personal hygiene salons

(G-20408)
W H O T INC (PA)
4040 Simon Rd Ste 1 (44512-1362)
PHONE..................................330 783-1000
Fax: 440 783-0060
Brad Marshall, *President*
EMP: 80
SQ FT: 4,000
SALES (est): 2.8MM **Privately Held**
SIC: 4832 Radio broadcasting stations

(G-20409)
WALDON MANAGEMENT CORP (PA)
111 Westchester Dr (44515-3964)
PHONE..................................330 792-7688
Walter Terlecky, *President*
EMP: 30
SALES (est): 2.5MM **Privately Held**
WEB: www.waldonmanagement.com
SIC: 6531 6512 Cooperative apartment manager; commercial & industrial building operation

(G-20410)
WEDGEWOOD LANES INC
1741 S Raccoon Rd (44515-4785)
PHONE..................................330 792-1949
Ed Zitnick, *President*
EMP: 37
SQ FT: 46,000
SALES (est): 951.2K **Privately Held**
SIC: 7933 5813 Ten pin center; cocktail lounge

(G-20411)
WESTERN & SOUTHERN LF INSUR CO
320 S Canfield Niles Rd (44515-4019)
PHONE..................................330 792-6818
Tina Scarpaci, *Manager*
EMP: 25 **Privately Held**
SIC: 6411 Life insurance agents
HQ: The Western & Southern Life Insurance Company
  400 Broadway St
  Cincinnati OH 45202
  513 629-1800

(G-20412)
WESTERN RESERVE TRANSIT AUTH (PA)
604 Mahoning Ave (44502-1491)
PHONE..................................330 744-8431
Fax: 330 744-7611
Dean Soroka, *Human Res Dir*
Rich McFadden, *Human Resources*
Judy Saccomen, *Info Tech Mgr*
Jim Ferraro, *Director*
Matt Kotanchek, *Executive*
EMP: 82
SALES: 11.1MM **Privately Held**
WEB: www.wrtaonline.com
SIC: 4111 Bus line operations

(G-20413)
WESTVIEW APARTMENTS OHIO LLC
3111 Leo Ave (44509-1051)
PHONE..................................216 520-1250
Fax: 330 797-0382
Frank Sinito,
EMP: 385
SALES (est): 6.9MM **Privately Held**
SIC: 6513 Apartment building operators

(G-20414)
WESTVIEW-YOUNGSTOWN LTD
3111 Leo Ave (44509-1051)
PHONE..................................330 799-2787
Leeann Morein, *Partner*
Paul Phleger, *Partner*
EMP: 99
SALES (est): 3MM **Privately Held**
SIC: 6514 Dwelling operators, except apartments

(G-20415)
WFMJ TELEVISION INC
101 W Boardman St (44503-1305)
P.O. Box 689 (44501-0689)
PHONE..................................330 744-8611
Fax: 330 744-3402
Betty Brown, *President*
John Grdic, *General Mgr*
Jim Brent, *Controller*
Madonna Pinkard, *Director*
Mark Brown, *Admin Sec*
EMP: 105
SALES (est): 11.9MM **Privately Held**
WEB: www.wfmj.com
SIC: 4833 Television broadcasting stations

(G-20416)
WINDSOR HOUSE INC
Also Called: Liberty Health Care Center
1355 Churchill Hubbard Rd (44505-1346)
PHONE..................................330 759-7858
Fax: 330 759-7285
Paulette Trexler, *Nursing Dir*
Aleda Florek, *Hlthcr Dir*
Joseph Lambert, *Administration*
EMP: 150
SALES (corp-wide): 25.7MM **Privately Held**
SIC: 8059 8051 Nursing home, except skilled & intermediate care facility; skilled nursing care facilities
PA: Windsor House, Inc.
  101 W Liberty St
  Girard OH
  330 545-1550

(G-20417)
WINDSOR HOUSE INC
Also Called: Windsor Health Care
1735 Belmont Ave (44504-1111)
PHONE..................................330 743-1393
Fax: 330 744-8913
Laurie Forence, *Manager*
Jennifer Connolly, *Administration*
EMP: 100
SALES (corp-wide): 25.7MM **Privately Held**
SIC: 8051 Skilled nursing care facilities
PA: Windsor House, Inc.
  101 W Liberty St
  Girard OH
  330 545-1550

(G-20418)
WINKLE ELECTRIC COMPANY INC (PA)
1900 Hubbard Rd (44505-3128)
P.O. Box 6014 (44501-6014)
PHONE..................................330 744-5303
Fax: 330 744-1635
Tony Sahli, *Division Mgr*
Larry A Teaberry Jr, *Exec VP*
Robert J Conger, *Vice Pres*
Brian Vennetti, *Vice Pres*
Gary Connors, *Prdtn Mgr*
EMP: 35
SQ FT: 50,000
SALES: 40MM **Privately Held**
WEB: www.winkle.com
SIC: 5063 Motor controls, starters & relays: electric

(G-20419)
Y TOWN REALTY INC
1641 5th Ave (44504-1859)
P.O. Box 6482 (44501-6482)
PHONE..................................330 743-8844
Fax: 330 743-8991
Jerome Williams, *President*
EMP: 47

GEOGRAPHIC SECTION

Zanesville - Muskingum County (G-20442)

SALES (est): 2MM **Privately Held**
SIC: 6531 Real estate agent, residential

(G-20420)
YORK-MAHONING MECH CONTRS INC
724 Canfield Rd (44511-2399)
P.O. Box 3077 (44511-0077)
PHONE..............................330 788-7011
Fax: 330 788-7513
Michael Fagert, *President*
Ron Fagert, *Vice Pres*
Mary Jo Fagert, *Treasurer*
Jimmy Petrolla, *Manager*
Frank Julian, *Director*
EMP: 80
SQ FT: 22,000
SALES: 20MM **Privately Held**
WEB: www.yorkmahoning.com
SIC: 1761 1711 Sheet metalwork; mechanical contractor

(G-20421)
YOUNG MENS CHRISTIAN ASSN (PA)
Also Called: YMCA OF YOUNGSTOWN
17 N Champion St (44503-1602)
P.O. Box 1287 (44501-1287)
PHONE..............................330 744-8411
Fax: 330 744-8416
Kenneth Rudge, *CEO*
Tom Lodge, *President*
Richard Hahn, *Trustee*
Donald Harrison, *Trustee*
Elizabeth Scheller, *Vice Pres*
EMP: 160
SALES: 11.9MM **Privately Held**
SIC: 8641 8322 7997 Youth organizations; youth center; membership sports & recreation clubs

(G-20422)
YOUNG WOMENS CHRISTIAN ASSN
Also Called: YWCA
25 W Rayen Ave (44503-1000)
PHONE..............................330 746-6361
Fax: 330 746-6361
Leah Brooks, *Exec Dir*
Connie Schaffer, *Director*
EMP: 45
SALES: 1.3MM **Privately Held**
WEB: www.ywcaofyoungstown.org
SIC: 8641 7991 8351 7032 Youth organizations; physical fitness facilities; child day care services; youth camps; individual & family services

(G-20423)
YOUNGSTOWN ARC ENGRAVING CO
Also Called: Youngstown Lithographing Co
380 Victoria Rd (44515-2026)
PHONE..............................330 793-2471
E Craig Olsen, *President*
Tim Merrifield, *Exec VP*
George B Snyder, *Vice Pres*
Ken Baytosh, *Purchasing*
Terry Dunn, *Marketing Staff*
EMP: 26 EST: 1900
SQ FT: 30,000
SALES (est): 2.9MM **Privately Held**
WEB: www.youngstownwholesale.com
SIC: 2752 2796 7335 2791 Commercial printing, lithographic; commercial printing, offset; photoengraving plates, linecuts or halftones; commercial photography; typesetting; bookbinding & related work; commercial printing

(G-20424)
YOUNGSTOWN AREA (PA)
2747 Belmont Ave (44505-1819)
PHONE..............................330 759-7921
Fax: 330 759-0678
Toby Mirto, *Vice Pres*
Al Slabe, *Opers Staff*
Gina Angle, *Human Res Mgr*
Michael Mc Bride, *Director*
Anissa Knapik, *Director*
EMP: 180
SQ FT: 84,000

SALES: 5.9MM **Privately Held**
WEB: www.goodwillyoungstown.org
SIC: 8331 5932 Vocational rehabilitation agency; vocational training agency; clothing & shoes, secondhand

(G-20425)
YOUNGSTOWN AREA JWISH FDRATION (PA)
Also Called: Heritage Mnr Jwsh HM For Aged
505 Gypsy Ln (44504-1314)
PHONE..............................330 746-3251
William Benedikt, *President*
Sam Kooperman, *Exec VP*
Gerald Peskin, *Vice Pres*
David Stauffer, *CFO*
Amy Hendricks, *Treasurer*
EMP: 210
SQ FT: 100,000
SALES (est): 10.1MM **Privately Held**
SIC: 8322 Social service center

(G-20426)
YOUNGSTOWN AREA JWISH FDRATION
Also Called: Heritage Manor
517 Gypsy Ln (44504-1314)
PHONE..............................330 746-1076
Gary Weiss, *Director*
Bruce Willner, *Director*
Thomas Skook, *Administration*
EMP: 80
SALES (corp-wide): 10.1MM **Privately Held**
SIC: 8059 8322 8051 4119 Nursing home, except skilled & intermediate care facility; individual & family services; general counseling services; skilled nursing care facilities; local passenger transportation
PA: Youngstown Area Jewish Federation Inc
505 Gypsy Ln
Youngstown OH 44504
330 746-3251

(G-20427)
YOUNGSTOWN AUTOMATIC DOOR CO
1223 Gibson St (44502-2051)
PHONE..............................330 747-3135
EMP: 25
SALES (est): 779.7K **Privately Held**
SIC: 1751 Carpentry Contractor

(G-20428)
YOUNGSTOWN CLUB
201 E Commerce St Ste 400 (44503-1660)
PHONE..............................330 744-3111
Fax: 330 744-2170
Ted Thronton, *Corp Secy*
Carol Hixson, *Bookkeeper*
Stacy Renzel, *Manager*
Stephen Grant, *Executive*
EMP: 35
SALES (est): 1.8MM **Privately Held**
SIC: 8641 Social club, membership; bars & restaurants, members only

(G-20429)
YOUNGSTOWN COMMITTEE ON ALCHOL
Also Called: NEIL KENNEDY RECOVERY CLINIC
2151 Rush Blvd (44507-1535)
PHONE..............................330 744-1181
Fax: 330 740-2849
Jan Belleville, *Treasurer*
Joanne Vivo, *Manager*
Jerry Carter, *Exec Dir*
Neil Capretto, *Director*
EMP: 94
SALES: 5.3MM **Privately Held**
SIC: 8069 8322 Alcoholism rehabilitation hospital; individual & family services

(G-20430)
YOUNGSTOWN COUNTRY CLUB
1402 Country Club Dr (44505-2299)
PHONE..............................330 759-1040
Fax: 330 759-8954
Jim Dibacco, *President*
Karl Schroedel, *Treasurer*

SALES: 1.8MM **Privately Held**
WEB: www.youngstowncountryclub.com
SIC: 7997 5941 5812 Country club, membership; sporting goods & bicycle shops; eating places

(G-20431)
YOUNGSTOWN HEARING SPEECH CTR (PA)
299 Edwards St (44502-1504)
PHONE..............................330 726-8391
Jude Nohra, *Treasurer*
Alfred Pasini, *Director*
EMP: 48
SQ FT: 7,000
SALES: 1.2MM **Privately Held**
SIC: 8093 Speech defect clinic

(G-20432)
YOUNGSTOWN NEIGHBORHOOD DEV
Also Called: Yndc
820 Canfield Rd (44511-2345)
PHONE..............................330 480-0423
Germaine Bennett, *Vice Pres*
June Johnson, *Treasurer*
Brandi Takas, *Mktg Coord*
Michael Dulay, *Manager*
Ryan Emborsky, *Manager*
EMP: 30
SQ FT: 1,200
SALES: 2.1MM **Privately Held**
SIC: 8322 8699 Social service center; charitable organization

(G-20433)
YOUNGSTOWN OHIO OTPATIENT SVCS
6426 Market St (44512-3434)
PHONE..............................330 884-2020
David Fikse, *CEO*
EMP: 37
SALES (est): 580K **Privately Held**
SIC: 8049 Offices of health practitioner

(G-20434)
YOUNGSTOWN PLASTIC TOOLING (PA)
1209 Velma Ct (44512-1829)
PHONE..............................330 782-7222
Fax: 330 782-1854
Donald J Liga, *President*
Janet Liga, *Admin Sec*
EMP: 35
SQ FT: 20,000
SALES (est): 6.8MM **Privately Held**
WEB: www.yptm.com
SIC: 3559 8711 Plastics working machinery; machine tool design; mechanical engineering

(G-20435)
YOUNGSTOWN PROPANE INC (PA)
Also Called: Yp
810 N Meridian Rd (44509-4003)
P.O. Box 2447 (44509-0447)
PHONE..............................330 792-6571
Fax: 330 792-8114
Robert Jones, *President*
Albert E Brennan, *Principal*
Richard Jones, *Vice Pres*
Vernon Jones, *Vice Pres*
Bob Jones, *Finance Mgr*
EMP: 26
SQ FT: 4,000
SALES (est): 10.6MM **Privately Held**
WEB: www.youngstownpropane.com
SIC: 5984 5172 5719 Propane gas, bottled; gases, liquefied petroleum (propane); fireplace equipment & accessories

(G-20436)
YOUNGSTOWN-WARREN REG CHAMBER (PA)
11 Central Sq Ste 1600 (44503-1512)
PHONE..............................330 744-2131
Thomas Humphries, *President*
Anthony Cafaro Jr, *Vice Chairman*
Rachel Flickinger, *Vice Pres*
Kim Gonda, *Vice Pres*
Helen Paes, *Vice Pres*
EMP: 32 EST: 1905
SQ FT: 7,000

SALES: 2.7MM **Privately Held**
SIC: 8611 Chamber of Commerce

(G-20437)
YSD INDUSTRIES INC
3710 Henricks Rd (44515)
PHONE..............................330 792-6521
Fax: 330 792-2422
Jerome D Hines, *President*
Bruce Wylie, *Vice Pres*
Michael Feschak, *CFO*
Karen Flavell, *Human Resources*
Ralph Boland, *Director*
▲ EMP: 100
SQ FT: 30,000
SALES (est): 20.3MM **Privately Held**
SIC: 5088 3444 3441 Railroad equipment & supplies; sheet metalwork; fabricated structural metal

(G-20438)
ZINZ CNSTR & RESTORATION
6487 Mahoning Ave (44515-2039)
PHONE..............................330 332-7939
Fax: 330 332-9079
Bruce L Zinz, *President*
Barbie Leffler, *Opers Mgr*
Crystal Murphy, *Bookkeeper*
Marcella Zinz, *Marketing Staff*
Debbie Pringle, *Admin Asst*
EMP: 30
SALES (est): 4.6MM **Privately Held**
WEB: www.zinzconstruction.com
SIC: 1521 Single-family housing construction

(G-20439)
ZION CHRISTIAN SCHOOL
3300 Canfield Rd (44511-2701)
PHONE..............................330 792-4066
Rachel Gonatas, *Principal*
Dale Giffin, *Pastor*
Geniene Hankey, *Director*
Cathy Diemer, *Admin Asst*
EMP: 25
SALES (est): 399.8K **Privately Held**
SIC: 8351 8211 Preschool center; private elementary & secondary schools

---

Zanesville
Muskingum County

(G-20440)
ALLWELL BEHAVIORAL HEALTH SVCS (PA)
2845 Bell St (43701-1720)
PHONE..............................740 454-9766
Fax: 740 455-4134
James A McDonald, *President*
Robert R Santos, *COO*
Tim Llewellyn, *Senior VP*
Sue Ellen Foraker, *Controller*
Ray Bishoff, *Mktg Dir*
EMP: 190
SQ FT: 10,000
SALES: 11.5MM **Privately Held**
SIC: 8093 8322 Mental health clinic, outpatient; individual & family services

(G-20441)
AMERICAN NURSING CARE INC
1206 Brandywine Blvd A (43701-1755)
PHONE..............................614 847-0555
Fax: 614 847-7546
Diana Phelps, *Manager*
Pam Sabo, *Manager*
Deb Cronin, *Director*
EMP: 200 **Privately Held**
WEB: www.americannursingcare.com
SIC: 8051 8361 Skilled nursing care facilities; residential care
HQ: American Nursing Care, Inc.
1700 Edison Dr Ste 300
Milford OH 45150
513 576-0262

(G-20442)
AMERICAN NURSING CARE INC
1206 Brandywine Blvd A (43701-1755)
PHONE..............................740 452-0569
Fax: 740 452-3706
Heather Bonifild, *Office Mgr*
Diana Phelps, *Director*

Zanesville - Muskingum County (G-20443)

GEOGRAPHIC SECTION

EMP: 100
SALES (est): 1.7MM **Privately Held**
SIC: 8049 8082 Nurses, registered & practical; home health care services

(G-20443)
ASSISTED LIVING CONCEPTS INC
Also Called: Clay House
3784 Frazeysburg Rd Ofc (43701-7576)
PHONE.................................740 450-2744
Fax: 740 450-4270
Shawna Milatodich, *Manager*
Barbie Wilson, *Manager*
EMP: 25
SALES (corp-wide): 380.5MM **Privately Held**
WEB: www.assistedlivingconcepts.com
SIC: 8322 Individual & family services
HQ: Assisted Living Concepts, Llc
    330 N Wabash Ave Ste 3700
    Chicago IL 60611

(G-20444)
AT&T CORP
3575 Maple Ave Ste 502 (43701-7020)
PHONE.................................740 455-3042
EMP: 69
SALES (corp-wide): 160.5B **Publicly Held**
SIC: 4813 Local & long distance telephone communications
HQ: At&T Corp.
    1 At&T Way
    Bedminster NJ 07921
    800 403-3302

(G-20445)
AVI FOOD SYSTEMS INC
333 Richards Rd (43701-4643)
PHONE.................................740 452-9363
Fax: 740 452-9365
Donald Hormann, *Manager*
EMP: 50
SALES (corp-wide): 661.7MM **Privately Held**
WEB: www.avifoodsystems.com
SIC: 5962 5812 5046 Merchandising machine operators; eating places; commercial equipment
PA: Avi Food Systems, Inc.
    2590 Elm Rd Ne
    Warren OH 44483
    330 372-6000

(G-20446)
BALLAS EGG PRODUCTS CORP
40 N 2nd St (43701-3402)
P.O. Box 2217 (43702-2217)
PHONE.................................614 453-0386
Fax: 740 453-0491
Leonard Ballas, *President*
Joseph G Saliba, *Vice Pres*
Craig Ballas, *Admin Sec*
▼ EMP: 100 EST: 1961
SQ FT: 200,000
SALES (est): 14.5MM **Privately Held**
SIC: 2015 5144 Egg processing; eggs, processed: desiccated (dried); eggs, processed: frozen; eggs

(G-20447)
BETHESDA HOSPITAL ASSOCIATION
2951 Maple Ave (43701-1465)
PHONE.................................740 454-4000
Thomas Sieber, *President*
Charles Hunter, *COO*
Paul Masterson, *CFO*
Martha Nash, *Controller*
Larry Cook, *Director*
EMP: 1100
SQ FT: 400,000
SALES: 187.4K
SALES (corp-wide): 462MM **Privately Held**
SIC: 8062 8063 8082 General medical & surgical hospitals; psychiatric hospitals; home health care services
PA: Genesis Healthcare System
    2951 Maple Ave
    Zanesville OH 43701
    740 454-5000

(G-20448)
BLOOMBERG ROSS MD
2935 Maple Ave (43701-1487)
PHONE.................................740 454-1216
Ross Bloomberg, *Owner*
EMP: 30
SALES (est): 93.3K **Privately Held**
SIC: 8011 Offices & clinics of medical doctors; ophthalmologist

(G-20449)
BRENWOOD INC
Also Called: Hairitage, The
1709 Maple Ave (43701-2207)
PHONE.................................740 452-7533
Fax: 740 452-4749
Brenda Atwood, *President*
EMP: 35
SQ FT: 2,100
SALES (est): 629.4K **Privately Held**
SIC: 7231 Manicurist, pedicurist

(G-20450)
BUCKEYE COMPANIES (PA)
999 Zane St (43701-3863)
P.O. Box 1480 (43702-1480)
PHONE.................................740 452-3641
C E Straker, *President*
Stephen R Straker, *President*
M Dean Cole, *Corp Secy*
EMP: 31
SALES (est): 15.5MM **Privately Held**
SIC: 3533 5083 Drill rigs; agricultural machinery & equipment

(G-20451)
BUCKEYE SUPPLY COMPANY (HQ)
999 Zane St Ste A (43701-3863)
P.O. Box 1480 (43702-1480)
PHONE.................................740 452-3641
C E Straker, *CEO*
Stephen R Straker, *President*
George French, *Vice Pres*
Don Moore, *Safety Mgr*
Larry Messner, *CFO*
▼ EMP: 30
SQ FT: 50,000
SALES (est): 14.6MM
SALES (corp-wide): 15.5MM **Privately Held**
SIC: 5083 5084 Lawn & garden machinery & equipment; farm implements; pumps & pumping equipment; petroleum industry machinery; oil well machinery, equipment & supplies
PA: Buckeye Companies
    999 Zane St
    Zanesville OH 43701
    740 452-3641

(G-20452)
BUCKINGHAM COAL COMPANY LLC
11 N 4th St (43701-3409)
P.O. Box 340 (43702-0340)
PHONE.................................740 767-2907
Fax: 740 347-4003
Clay Graham, *CEO*
Mike Matusik, *Plant Mgr*
EMP: 80 EST: 1994
SALES (est): 15.1MM
SALES (corp-wide): 1.3B **Publicly Held**
SIC: 1241 Coal mining services
PA: Westmoreland Coal Company
    9540 Maroon Cir Unit 200
    Englewood CO 80112
    855 922-6463

(G-20453)
CALICO COURT
1101 Colony Dr (43701-6442)
PHONE.................................740 455-2541
Cynthia Stiverson, *Owner*
EMP: 30
SALES (est): 910K **Privately Held**
SIC: 7231 Beauty shops

(G-20454)
CAMBRIDGE COUNSELING CENTER
Also Called: Zanesville
326 Main St (43701-3426)
PHONE.................................740 450-7790
Susan Lynch, *Owner*

EMP: 150
SALES (corp-wide): 4MM **Privately Held**
SIC: 8322 Family counseling services
PA: Cambridge Counseling Center
    317 Highland Ave
    Cambridge OH 43725
    740 435-9766

(G-20455)
CARDINAL HEALTH 107 LLC
Also Called: Pharmaceutical Repackaging
3540 East Pike (43701-9526)
PHONE.................................740 455-2462
Robert Walter, *Ch of Bd*
Patrick Moore, *Maint Spvr*
Brian Dixon, *Opers Staff*
Jill Trumm, *Sales/Mktg Mgr*
Andrew Burke, *Finance*
EMP: 120
SQ FT: 90,000
SALES (est): 52MM
SALES (corp-wide): 129.9B **Publicly Held**
SIC: 5122 Pharmaceuticals
PA: Cardinal Health, Inc.
    7000 Cardinal Pl
    Dublin OH 43017
    614 757-5000

(G-20456)
CARDIOLOGY ASSOCIATES OF
Also Called: Caffaratti, John MD
751 Forest Ave Ste 301 (43701-2875)
PHONE.................................740 454-6831
John Vangilder, *President*
EMP: 36
SALES (est): 2.4MM **Privately Held**
SIC: 8011 Cardiologist & cardio-vascular specialist

(G-20457)
CARESERVE (HQ)
Also Called: Sunny View Nursing Home
2991 Maple Ave (43701-1499)
PHONE.................................740 454-4000
Fax: 740 454-4048
Thomas Sieber, *President*
Paul Masterson, *Treasurer*
Shelly Fuller, *Admin Sec*
EMP: 151
SQ FT: 25,000
SALES (est): 2.7MM
SALES (corp-wide): 462MM **Privately Held**
SIC: 8051 Skilled nursing care facilities
PA: Genesis Healthcare System
    2951 Maple Ave
    Zanesville OH 43701
    740 454-5000

(G-20458)
CELLCO PARTNERSHIP
Also Called: Verizon Wireless
3575 Maple Ave (43701-7019)
PHONE.................................740 588-0018
Fax: 740 588-0103
EMP: 76
SALES (corp-wide): 126B **Publicly Held**
SIC: 4812 Cellular telephone services
HQ: Cellco Partnership
    1 Verizon Way
    Basking Ridge NJ 07920

(G-20459)
CELLCO PARTNERSHIP
Also Called: Verizon Wireless
2359 Maple Ave (43701-2028)
PHONE.................................740 450-1525
Derric Matz, *Manager*
EMP: 25
SALES (corp-wide): 126B **Publicly Held**
SIC: 4813 4812 Telephone communication, except radio; cellular telephone services
HQ: Cellco Partnership
    1 Verizon Way
    Basking Ridge NJ 07920

(G-20460)
CENTRAL OHIO BANDAG LP
1600 S Point Dr (43701-7366)
PHONE.................................740 454-9728
Fax: 740 454-3701
Steven Dickerson, *Partner*
Wayne Anderson, *Partner*
Bob Sumerel, *Partner*

EMP: 30 EST: 1971
SQ FT: 19,000
SALES (est): 2.9MM **Privately Held**
SIC: 7534 5014 Tire recapping; truck tires & tubes

(G-20461)
CENTURY NATIONAL BANK (HQ)
14 S 5th St (43701-3526)
PHONE.................................740 454-2521
Tom Lyall, *CEO*
William A Phillips, *Ch of Bd*
Jim Blythe, *Senior VP*
Barbara Gibbs, *Senior VP*
Patrick Nash, *Senior VP*
EMP: 39
SQ FT: 25,000
SALES (est): 2.5MM
SALES (corp-wide): 367MM **Publicly Held**
WEB: www.centurynationalbank.com
SIC: 6035 Federal savings banks
PA: Park National Corporation
    50 N 3rd St
    Newark OH 43055
    740 349-8451

(G-20462)
CENTURY NATIONAL BANK
33 S 5th St (43701-3510)
P.O. Box 1515 (43702-1515)
PHONE.................................800 548-3557
Michael Whiteman, *Senior VP*
Jeffrey Jordan, *Vice Pres*
Connie Laplante, *Treasurer*
Janice Pavatt, *Finance Mgr*
Barbara Sesher, *Finance Mgr*
EMP: 50
SALES (corp-wide): 367MM **Publicly Held**
WEB: www.centurynationalbank.com
SIC: 6021 National commercial banks
HQ: Century National Bank
    14 S 5th St
    Zanesville OH 43701
    740 454-2521

(G-20463)
CENTURY NATIONAL BANK
505 Market St (43701-3610)
PHONE.................................740 455-7330
Jack W Imes, *Senior VP*
Jeffrey Jordan, *Vice Pres*
Jenny Snoud, *Branch Mgr*
EMP: 45
SALES (corp-wide): 367MM **Publicly Held**
WEB: www.centurynationalbank.com
SIC: 6035 Federal savings banks
HQ: Century National Bank
    14 S 5th St
    Zanesville OH 43701
    740 454-2521

(G-20464)
CHILD CARE RESOURCES INC (PA)
Also Called: MUSKINGUM COUNTY HEADSTART
1580 Adams Ln Lbby (43701-2606)
PHONE.................................740 454-6251
Fax: 740 454-7369
Steve Huffman, *Manager*
Jeri Johnson, *Director*
EMP: 80
SALES: 3.1MM **Privately Held**
WEB: www.ccri.org
SIC: 8351 Head start center, except in conjunction with school

(G-20465)
CITY OF ZANESVILLE
Also Called: Waste Water Treatment Plant
401 Market St Rm 1 (43701-3520)
PHONE.................................740 455-0641
Fax: 740 455-0750
Dan Smith, *Superintendent*
EMP: 30 **Privately Held**
SIC: 4952 Sewerage systems
PA: City Of Zanesville
    401 Market St Rm 1
    Zanesville OH 43701
    740 455-0601

GEOGRAPHIC SECTION
Zanesville - Muskingum County (G-20489)

(G-20466)
COMFORT INN
500 Monroe St (43701-3884)
P.O. Box 160 (43702-0160)
PHONE..................740 454-4144
Fax: 740 454-4144
Timothy Longstreth, *President*
Larry L Wade, *Vice Pres*
EMP: 25
SALES (est): 1.6MM **Privately Held**
SIC: 7011 8661 Hotel, franchised; religious organizations

(G-20467)
COMMUNITY AMBULANCE SERVICE
952 Linden Ave (43701-3062)
PHONE..................740 454-6800
Fax: 740 454-1299
Greg Beauchemin, *President*
Paul Masterson, *Treasurer*
Tom Edminson, *Director*
EMP: 88
SQ FT: 8,000
SALES: 8.6MM
SALES (corp-wide): 462MM **Privately Held**
SIC: 4119 8661 Ambulance service; religious organizations
PA: Genesis Healthcare System
2951 Maple Ave
Zanesville OH 43701
740 454-5000

(G-20468)
DOLGENCORP LLC
Also Called: Dollar General
2505 E Pointe Dr (43701-7761)
PHONE..................740 588-5700
Sandra Byers, *Human Res Mgr*
Ron Dennis, *Manager*
Kathy Abbott, *Clerk*
EMP: 600
SALES (corp-wide): 23.4B **Publicly Held**
SIC: 4225 General warehousing
HQ: Dolgencorp, Llc
100 Mission Rdg
Goodlettsville TN 37072
615 855-4000

(G-20469)
DOWNTHEROAD INC
3625 Maple Ave (43701-1193)
P.O. Box 8071 (43702-8071)
PHONE..................740 452-4579
Timothy J Hoffer, *President*
Jeff Drennen, *President*
Mike Geinther, *Sales Mgr*
EMP: 33
SALES (est): 7.2MM **Privately Held**
SIC: 5511 7538 Automobiles, new & used; general automotive repair shops

(G-20470)
DUTRO FORD LINCOLN-MERCURY INC (PA)
Also Called: Dutro Nissan
132 S 5th St (43701-3513)
P.O. Box 1265 (43702-1265)
PHONE..................740 452-6334
Fax: 740 455-4415
James F Graham, *President*
Kenneth D Williams, *Vice Pres*
Kent Cornett, *Manager*
Bryan Graham, *Admin Sec*
Lori Finan, *Clerk*
EMP: 91
SQ FT: 30,000
SALES (est): 34.8MM **Privately Held**
SIC: 5511 7538 5012 7532 Automobiles, new & used; pickups, new & used; vans, new & used; general automotive repair shops; automobiles & other motor vehicles; top & body repair & paint shops; automobile & truck equipment & parts

(G-20471)
DVA RENAL HEALTHCARE INC
Also Called: Zanesville Dialysis
3120 Newark Rd (43701-9659)
PHONE..................740 454-2911
Dave Davis, *Branch Mgr*
Kelly Grimes, *Exec Dir*
EMP: 36 **Publicly Held**
SIC: 8092 Kidney dialysis centers
HQ: Dva Renal Healthcare, Inc.
2000 16th St
Denver CO 80202
253 258-9501

(G-20472)
ECLIPSE RESOURCES - OHIO LLC
4900 Boggs Rd (43701-9491)
P.O. Box 910 (43702-0910)
PHONE..................740 452-4503
Tj Blizzard, *Engineer*
Benjamin W Hulburt, *Mng Member*
Bruce Carpenter, *Manager*
Christopher K Hulburt,
Thomas S Liberatore,
EMP: 42
SALES (est): 8.9MM
SALES (corp-wide): 383.6MM **Publicly Held**
SIC: 1381 Drilling oil & gas wells
HQ: Eclipse Resources I, Lp
2121 Old Gteburg Rd Ste 1
State College PA 16803
814 308-9754

(G-20473)
ECONOMY LINEN & TOWEL SVC INC
508 Howard St (43701-3637)
PHONE..................740 454-6888
Fax: 740 454-2155
George Dube, *Manager*
Doug Manfein, *Manager*
Ed Salba, *Manager*
EMP: 200
SALES (est): 5.4MM
SALES (corp-wide): 11.4MM **Privately Held**
SIC: 7213 7211 Uniform supply; power laundries, family & commercial
PA: Economy Linen & Towel Service, Inc.
80 Mead St
Dayton OH 45402
937 222-4625

(G-20474)
EMCO USA LLC
1000 Linden Ave (43701-3098)
PHONE..................740 588-1722
Teresa Reef, *Principal*
Kavin Niggemyer, *CFO*
EMP: 31
SALES (est): 3.7MM **Privately Held**
SIC: 7389

(G-20475)
ENGLEFIELD INC
Also Called: Zanesville Bulk
1400 Moxahala Ave (43701-5947)
PHONE..................740 452-2707
Fax: 740 452-2972
EMP: 56
SALES (corp-wide): 503.4MM **Privately Held**
SIC: 5171 Petroleum bulk stations
PA: Englefield, Inc.
447 James Pkwy
Heath OH 43056
740 928-8215

(G-20476)
ENVIRO-FLOW COMPANIES LTD
4830 Northpointe Dr (43701-7273)
PHONE..................740 453-7980
Jeff Tanner, *General Ptnr*
▲ **EMP:** 31
SQ FT: 30,000
SALES (est): 3.9MM **Privately Held**
WEB: www.enviro-flow.com
SIC: 1711 1623 Plumbing contractors; heating & air conditioning contractors; septic system construction; pipeline construction

(G-20477)
FEDEX FREIGHT CORPORATION
1705 Moxahala Ave (43701-5952)
PHONE..................800 354-9489
Fax: 740 450-7402
Brook Winegar, *Sales Executive*
Pat Lion, *Manager*
Pat Lyon, *Manager*
John Rumpf, *Manager*
EMP: 25
SALES (corp-wide): 60.3B **Publicly Held**
SIC: 4213 4212 Trucking, except local; local trucking, without storage
HQ: Fedex Freight Corporation
1715 Aaron Brenner Dr
Memphis TN 38120

(G-20478)
FLOW-LINER SYSTEMS LTD
4830 Northpointe Dr (43701-7273)
PHONE..................800 348-0020
Jeff Tanner, *CEO*
Rick Boles, *Superintendent*
Pam Davis, *Sales Staff*
Brent Musselman, *Manager*
▲ **EMP:** 28 **EST:** 2000
SQ FT: 30,000
SALES (est): 5.8MM **Privately Held**
WEB: www.flow-liner.com
SIC: 3589 1799 Sewage & water treatment equipment; epoxy application

(G-20479)
G & J PEPSI-COLA BOTTLERS INC
Also Called: Pepsico
335 N 6th St (43701-3636)
PHONE..................740 452-2721
Rick Stone, *Branch Mgr*
EMP: 85
SALES (corp-wide): 475.8MM **Privately Held**
WEB: www.gjpepsi.com
SIC: 2086 5149 Soft drinks: packaged in cans, bottles, etc.; groceries & related products
PA: G & J Pepsi-Cola Bottlers Inc
9435 Waterstone Blvd # 390
Cincinnati OH 45249
513 785-6060

(G-20480)
GENESIS CAREGIVERS
2800 Maple Ave (43701-1716)
PHONE..................740 454-1370
Jenny Laurie, *General Mgr*
William A Phillips, *Trustee*
Thomas H Diehl, *Trustee*
Theresa Feldkamp, *Trustee*
Robert D Kessler, *Trustee*
EMP: 140
SQ FT: 1,700
SALES (est): 2.4MM
SALES (corp-wide): 462MM **Privately Held**
SIC: 8082 Visiting nurse service
PA: Genesis Healthcare System
2951 Maple Ave
Zanesville OH 43701
740 454-5000

(G-20481)
GENESIS HEALTHCARE SYSTEM (PA)
Also Called: Bethesda Care
2951 Maple Ave (43701-1406)
PHONE..................740 454-5000
Fax: 740 454-4529
Matthew Perry, *President*
Brad Hollingsworth, *General Mgr*
Rick Chester, *Editor*
Carolyn Latteier, *Editor*
Patricia Alexander, *Area Mgr*
EMP: 1500
SALES: 462MM **Privately Held**
SIC: 8082 Home health care services

(G-20482)
GENESIS HEALTHCARE SYSTEM
Also Called: Kiddie Kollege & Academy
1238 Pfeifer Dr (43701-1354)
PHONE..................740 453-4959
Fax: 740 453-6506
Barbara Fisher, *Director*
EMP: 50
SALES (corp-wide): 462MM **Privately Held**
SIC: 8351 Child day care services
PA: Genesis Healthcare System
2951 Maple Ave
Zanesville OH 43701
740 454-5000

(G-20483)
GOSS SUPPLY COMPANY (PA)
620 Marietta St (43701-3633)
P.O. Box 2580 (43702-2580)
PHONE..................740 454-2571
Fax: 740 454-7344
Terry L Goss, *President*
Pasquale Gallina, *Principal*
Clarence A Goss, *Principal*
Don J Hollingsworth, *Principal*
Andy Goss, *Vice Pres*
EMP: 47 **EST:** 1954
SQ FT: 40,000
SALES (est): 30MM **Privately Held**
WEB: www.gosssupply.com
SIC: 5085 Industrial supplies; hose, belting & packing; tools; abrasives

(G-20484)
GOTTLIEB JOHNSON BEAM DAL P
320 Main St (43701-3426)
P.O. Box 190 (43702-0190)
PHONE..................740 452-7555
Toll Free:..................888 -
Fax: 740 452-2257
Cole Gerzner, *Managing Prtnr*
Jeff R Beam, *Partner*
Miles D Fries, *Partner*
James R Krischak, *Partner*
Don Dal Ponte, *Partner*
EMP: 26
SQ FT: 3,500
SALES (est): 2.5MM **Privately Held**
SIC: 8111 General practice attorney, lawyer; general practice law office

(G-20485)
HARTLAND PETROLEUM LLC
4560 West Pike (43701-7175)
PHONE..................740 452-3115
Jim Douglas, *General Mgr*
Jeff Snedegar, *Vice Pres*
William Snedegar,
EMP: 50
SALES (est): 12.8MM **Privately Held**
SIC: 5172 Fuel oil

(G-20486)
HEALTH CARE SPECIALISTS
945 Bethesda Dr Ste 300 (43701-1880)
PHONE..................740 454-4530
Myron Knell, *President*
Marcy Hunter, *VP Finance*
EMP: 32
SALES (est): 2MM **Privately Held**
SIC: 8011 Medical centers

(G-20487)
HELEN PURCELL HOME
1854 Norwood Blvd (43701-2337)
PHONE..................740 453-1745
Fax: 740 453-6674
Robert Moehrman Jr, *President*
Nancy Rutledge, *Mktg Dir*
Bradley Coleman, *Director*
Gina Dilly, *Director*
Sheri Pitcock, *Director*
EMP: 50
SQ FT: 55,000
SALES: 2.2MM **Privately Held**
SIC: 8059 Personal care home, with health care

(G-20488)
HOSPICE OF GENESIS HEALTH
Also Called: Genesis Hspces Pallitaive Care
713 Forest Ave (43701-2819)
PHONE..................740 454-5381
Fax: 740 455-7592
Renee Sparks, *Manager*
Sally Scheffler, *Director*
EMP: 43
SALES (est): 1MM **Privately Held**
SIC: 8062 8082 8051 General medical & surgical hospitals; home health care services; skilled nursing care facilities

(G-20489)
HUNTINGTON NATIONAL BANK
422 Main St (43701-3516)
P.O. Box 4658 (43702)
PHONE..................740 452-8444
Fax: 740 455-7082
Wayne Wycoff, *Office Mgr*
Mark Carpenter, *Manager*

Zanesville - Muskingum County (G-20490)

Tom Downs, *Manager*
EMP: 50
SALES (corp-wide): 4.7B **Publicly Held**
WEB: www.huntingtonnationalbank.com
SIC: 6029 6021 Commercial banks; national commercial banks
HQ: The Huntington National Bank
 17 S High St Fl 1
 Columbus OH 43215
 614 480-4293

(G-20490)
INTER HEALT CARE OF NORTH OH I
Also Called: Interim Healthcare
2806 Bell St (43701-1721)
PHONE.................................740 453-5130
Fax: 740 453-8889
Denise Brosie, *Accounts Mgr*
Deb Studer, *Manager*
EMP: 100
SALES (corp-wide): 24.4MM **Privately Held**
SIC: 7363 Temporary help service
HQ: Interim Health Care Of Northwestern Ohio, Inc
 3100 W Central Ave # 250
 Toledo OH 43606

(G-20491)
JD EQUIPMENT INC
Also Called: John Deere Authorized Dealer
4394 Northpointe Dr (43701-5968)
PHONE.................................740 450-7446
EMP: 60
SALES (corp-wide): 147.6MM **Privately Held**
SIC: 5999 5082 Farm equipment & supplies; construction & mining machinery
PA: Jd Equipment, Inc.
 5850 Zarley St
 New Albany OH 43054
 614 527-8800

(G-20492)
JOE MCCLELLAND INC (PA)
Also Called: O K Coal & Concrete
98 E La Salle St (43701-6281)
P.O. Box 1815 (43702-1815)
PHONE.................................740 452-3036
Fax: 740 455-8781
Joe Mc Clelland, *President*
Jack Mc Clelland, *Vice Pres*
Richard Mc Clelland, *Treasurer*
Joe Nesselroad, *Manager*
Gala Lemon, *Admin Sec*
EMP: 25 **EST:** 1934
SQ FT: 1,500
SALES (est): 6.7MM **Privately Held**
WEB: www.okcoalandconcrete.com
SIC: 3273 7992 1442 Ready-mixed concrete; public golf courses; construction sand & gravel

(G-20493)
JUVENILE COURT CNTY MUSKINGUM
1860 East Pike (43701-4619)
PHONE.................................740 453-0351
Fax: 740 453-1066
Joseph A Gormley, *Principal*
EMP: 25
SALES (est): 808.1K **Privately Held**
SIC: 8322 Child related social services

(G-20494)
KESSLER SIGN COMPANY (PA)
Also Called: Kessler Outdoor Advertising
2669 National Rd (43701-8257)
P.O. Box 785 (43702-0785)
PHONE.................................740 453-0668
Fax: 740 453-5301
Robert Kessler, *President*
Rodger Kessler, *Vice Pres*
Elaine Kessler-Kuntz, *Treasurer*
Mark Cox, *Accounts Exec*
Doug Gabriel, *Mktg Dir*
EMP: 50
SQ FT: 25,000
SALES (est): 7.4MM **Privately Held**
WEB: www.kesslersignco.com
SIC: 3993 7312 Signs, not made in custom sign painting shops; outdoor advertising services

(G-20495)
LEPI ENTERPRISES INC
630 Gw Morse St (43701-3304)
P.O. Box 457 (43702-0457)
PHONE.................................740 453-2980
Fax: 740 453-4691
James Lepi, *President*
Cathy L George, *Principal*
Kenneth M Mortimer, *Principal*
Jeff Lepi, *Corp Secy*
Michael Lepi, *Vice Pres*
EMP: 100
SQ FT: 20,000
SALES (est): 16.7MM **Privately Held**
WEB: www.lepienterprises.com
SIC: 1799 1541 Asbestos removal & encapsulation; lead burning; industrial buildings & warehouses

(G-20496)
LOVE N COMFORT HOME CARE
2814 Maple Ave (43701-1716)
PHONE.................................740 450-7658
Mick Buck, *Branch Mgr*
EMP: 50 **EST:** 2008
SALES (est): 542.4K **Privately Held**
SIC: 8059 Personal care home, with health care

(G-20497)
LOWES HOME CENTERS LLC
3755 Frazeysburg Rd (43701-1015)
PHONE.................................740 450-5500
Fax: 740 455-5518
Chapman Joe, *Manager*
EMP: 150
SALES (corp-wide): 68.6B **Publicly Held**
SIC: 5211 5031 5722 5064 Home centers; building materials, exterior; building materials, interior; household appliance stores; electrical appliances, television & radio
HQ: Lowe's Home Centers, Llc
 1605 Curtis Bridge Rd
 Wilkesboro NC 28697
 336 658-4000

(G-20498)
LUBURGH INC (PA)
4174 East Pike (43701-8425)
PHONE.................................740 452-3668
Fax: 740 454-7225
Otto Luburgh, *President*
Henry Luburgh, *Vice Pres*
Andrew Luburgh, *Admin Sec*
EMP: 30
SALES (est): 10.2MM **Privately Held**
SIC: 1794 Excavation work

(G-20499)
MAN-TANSKY INC
Also Called: Tansky Honda
3260 Maple Ave (43701-1313)
PHONE.................................740 454-2512
Fax: 740 454-5171
James Kobunski, *Vice Pres*
James J Kobunski, *Vice Pres*
Donna Gee, *Office Mgr*
EMP: 38
SQ FT: 20,000
SALES (est): 11.7MM **Privately Held**
WEB: www.tansky.com
SIC: 5511 7538 5531 Automobiles, new & used; general automotive repair shops; automotive parts

(G-20500)
MATTINGLY FOODS INC (PA)
302 State St (43701-3200)
P.O. Box 760 (43702-0760)
PHONE.................................740 454-0136
Rick Barnes, *CEO*
Barbara Callahan, *President*
Angie Schmidt, *Exec VP*
Andrew Hess, *Vice Pres*
Benjamin Hess, *Vice Pres*
EMP: 235
SQ FT: 225,000
SALES (est): 104.9MM **Privately Held**
WEB: www.mattinglyfoods.com
SIC: 5149 5142 5141 Canned goods: fruit, vegetables, seafood, meats, etc.; milk, canned or dried; fruit juices, frozen; vegetables, frozen; fish, frozen: packaged; meat, frozen: packaged; groceries, general line

(G-20501)
MERRILL LYNCH PIERCE FENNER
905 Zane St Ste 3 (43701-3840)
PHONE.................................740 452-3681
Fax: 740 455-4034
Merrill Lhancock, *Branch Mgr*
EMP: 27
SALES (corp-wide): 100.2B **Publicly Held**
SIC: 6211 Security brokers & dealers
HQ: Merrill Lynch, Pierce, Fenner & Smith Incorporated
 111 8th Ave
 New York NY 10011
 800 637-7455

(G-20502)
MIDWEST RETINA INC
2935 Maple Ave (43701-1487)
PHONE.................................614 233-9500
EMP: 27
SALES (corp-wide): 2.9MM **Privately Held**
SIC: 8011 General & family practice, physician/surgeon
PA: Midwest Retina, Inc.
 6655 Post Rd
 Dublin OH 43016
 614 339-8500

(G-20503)
MODERN GLASS PNT & TILE CO INC
933 Linden Ave (43701-3049)
PHONE.................................740 454-1253
Fax: 740 454-6069
John W Melsheimer, *President*
James D Spargrove, *Corp Secy*
Robert R Melsheimer, *Vice Pres*
EMP: 31 **EST:** 1951
SQ FT: 12,000
SALES (est): 9.1MM **Privately Held**
SIC: 1793 5713 5231 Glass & glazing work; floor covering stores; paint; wallcoverings

(G-20504)
MUSKINGUM CNTY CTR FOR SENIORS
160 Nth St (43701)
PHONE.................................740 454-9761
Tara Rock, *Supervisor*
Ann Combs, *Exec Dir*
Kurt Ufholz, *Officer*
Janice Funk, *Executive Asst*
EMP: 30
SQ FT: 36,000
SALES: 1.5MM **Privately Held**
SIC: 8322 Senior citizens' center or association

(G-20505)
MUSKINGUM COUNTY ADULT AND CHI
Also Called: Avondale Youth Center
4155 Roseville Rd (43701-8224)
PHONE.................................740 849-2344
Fax: 740 849-2640
Gary King, *Director*
EMP: 25
SALES (est): 901.3K **Privately Held**
SIC: 8322 Youth center

(G-20506)
MUSKINGUM COUNTY OHIO
Also Called: Senior Nutrition
160 N 4th St (43701-3518)
PHONE.................................740 452-0678
Carol Morgan, *Supervisor*
Jodi Paul, *Supervisor*
Ann Combs, *Exec Dir*
Terry Dunn, *Director*
Becky Bruce, *Director*
EMP: 60 **Privately Held**
SIC: 8322 4119 Senior citizens' center or association; meal delivery program; local passenger transportation
PA: Muskingum County, Ohio
 401 Main St
 Zanesville OH 43701
 740 455-7100

(G-20507)
MUSKINGUM COUNTY OHIO
Also Called: Muskingum County Home
401 Main St (43701-3519)
PHONE.................................740 454-1911
Fax: 740 454-6950
Rebecca Cooper, *Director*
EMP: 100 **Privately Held**
SIC: 8051 8052 Convalescent home with continuous nursing care; intermediate care facilities
PA: Muskingum County, Ohio
 401 Main St
 Zanesville OH 43701
 740 455-7100

(G-20508)
MUSKINGUM COUNTY OHIO
Also Called: Muskingum County Engineers Off
155 Rehl Rd (43701-2730)
PHONE.................................740 453-0381
Fax: 740 455-7180
Dug Davis, *Manager*
EMP: 40 **Privately Held**
SIC: 8711 Engineering services
PA: Muskingum County, Ohio
 401 Main St
 Zanesville OH 43701
 740 455-7100

(G-20509)
MUSKINGUM IRON & METAL CO
345 Arthur St (43701-5850)
P.O. Box 815 (43702-0815)
PHONE.................................740 452-9351
Fax: 740 452-3251
Jack Joseph, *President*
Brian Ferguson, *General Mgr*
Arthur L Joseph, *Principal*
Shirley L Joseph, *Principal*
Stanley I Joseph, *Principal*
EMP: 36 **EST:** 1929
SQ FT: 30,000
SALES (est): 20.4MM **Privately Held**
WEB: www.muskingumiron.com
SIC: 5093 Nonferrous metals scrap

(G-20510)
MUSKINGUM LIVESTOCK SALES INC
Also Called: Muskingum Livestock Auction
944 Malinda St (43701-3854)
P.O. Box 2003 (43702-2003)
PHONE.................................740 452-9984
Fax: 740 452-3010
David Dailey, *CEO*
Dennis Ruff, *President*
Eloise Barnett, *Corp Secy*
EMP: 35 **EST:** 1941
SQ FT: 20,000
SALES (est): 4.9MM **Privately Held**
WEB: www.muskingumlivestock.com
SIC: 5154 Auctioning livestock; hogs; sheep

(G-20511)
MUSKINGUM RESIDENTIALS INC
1900 Montgomery Ave (43701-2617)
P.O. Box 2415 (43702-2415)
PHONE.................................740 453-5350
Fax: 740 453-7045
Jerri Elson, *Director*
EMP: 25
SALES: 1.3MM **Privately Held**
SIC: 8361 8052 Home for the mentally handicapped; intermediate care facilities

(G-20512)
MUSKINGUM STARLIGHT INDUSTRIES (PA)
1304 Newark Rd (43701-2621)
PHONE.................................740 453-4622
Fax: 740 455-4179
John E Hill, *Superintendent*
Michele Seward, *Business Mgr*
Mary Thompson Sufferd, *Director*
Larry Wheeler, *Director*
Patrick Fisher, *Maintence Staff*
EMP: 75 **EST:** 1959
SQ FT: 11,500
SALES: 673.3K **Privately Held**
SIC: 8331 Sheltered workshop

Zanesville - Muskingum County (G-20536)

(G-20513)
MUSKINGUM STARLIGHT INDUSTRIES
Also Called: Starlight Special School
1330 Newark Rd (43701-2623)
PHONE.....................740 453-4622
Larry Wheeler, *General Mgr*
Nancy Goff, *Principal*
EMP: 70
SALES (est): 3.3MM
SALES (corp-wide): 673.3K **Privately Held**
SIC: 8731 8211 Commercial physical research; private special education school
PA: Muskingum Starlight Industries Inc
1304 Newark Rd
Zanesville OH 43701
740 453-4622

(G-20514)
NATIONAL GAS & OIL CORPORATION
1423 Lake Dr (43701-5922)
PHONE.....................740 454-7252
Fax: 740 454-7230
Dan Price, *Manager*
EMP: 31
SALES (corp-wide): 72.4MM **Privately Held**
WEB: www.theenergycoop.com
SIC: 4923 4924 4922 Gas transmission & distribution; natural gas distribution; natural gas transmission
HQ: The National Gas & Oil Corporation
1500 Granville Rd
Newark OH 43055
740 344-2102

(G-20515)
NEFF MACHINERY AND SUPPLIES
Also Called: Neff Parts
112 S Shawnee Ave (43701-6221)
P.O. Box 1822 (43702-1822)
PHONE.....................740 454-0128
Fax: 740 454-8433
Robert Neff, *President*
EMP: 30
SQ FT: 20,000
SALES (est): 3.8MM **Privately Held**
SIC: 3599 5084 5013 Machine & other job shop work; machine tools & accessories; motor vehicle supplies & new parts

(G-20516)
NEFF PAVING LTD (PA)
6575 West Pike (43701-8163)
PHONE.....................740 453-3063
Fax: 740 455-3959
Clint Berkfield, *President*
Krysta Berkfield, *Treasurer*
Neff P Berkfield, *Info Tech Mgr*
EMP: 25
SALES (est): 5.3MM **Privately Held**
SIC: 1611 Highway & street paving contractor

(G-20517)
NORTH HILLS MANAGEMENT COMPANY
Also Called: Inn At North Hills
1575 Bowers Ln Apt C13 (43701-7021)
PHONE.....................740 450-9999
Fax: 740 452-5541
Jerry McClain, *President*
Debbie Booth, *Vice Pres*
Joann Butcher, *Vice Pres*
Diane Katon, *Admin Sec*
EMP: 82
SQ FT: 55,000
SALES (est): 3.9MM **Privately Held**
SIC: 8361 8052 Residential care; intermediate care facilities

(G-20518)
NORTH VALLEY BANK (PA)
2775 Maysville Pike (43701-9772)
P.O. Box 1115 (43702-1115)
PHONE.....................740 452-7920
Fax: 740 450-2120
Carl Raines, *President*
Julie Paxton, *General Mgr*
Tom Selock, *Senior VP*
Jesse Rollins, *Assistant VP*
Brendan Underwood, *Assistant VP*
EMP: 25 EST: 1904
SQ FT: 6,000
SALES: 9.9MM **Privately Held**
WEB: www.nvboh.com
SIC: 6022 State commercial banks

(G-20519)
OHIO MACHINERY CO
Also Called: Caterpillar Authorized Dealer
3415 East Pike (43701-8419)
PHONE.....................740 453-0563
Fax: 740 452-3605
Rick Hensel, *Manager*
Rick Hinsle, *Manager*
EMP: 50
SQ FT: 18,000
SALES (corp-wide): 222.7MM **Privately Held**
WEB: www.enginesnow.com
SIC: 5082 7629 General construction machinery & equipment; electrical repair shops
PA: Ohio Machinery Co.
3993 E Royalton Rd
Broadview Heights OH 44147
440 526-6200

(G-20520)
OHIO TEXTILE SERVICE INC
2270 Fairview Rd (43701-8810)
P.O. Box 8048 (43702-8048)
PHONE.....................740 450-4900
Fax: 740 453-9267
David M Struminger, *President*
Donald L Struminger, *Chairman*
Nancy Alley, *Vice Pres*
EMP: 45
SALES (est): 2.9MM
SALES (corp-wide): 21.7MM **Privately Held**
WEB: www.mohenis.com
SIC: 7211 Power laundries, family & commercial
PA: Mohenis Services, Inc.
875 E Bank St
Petersburg VA 23803
800 879-3315

(G-20521)
ORIGINAL HARTSTONE POTTERY INC
1719 Dearborn St (43701-5299)
PHONE.....................740 452-9999
John McMillan, *President*
Wess Foltz, *Vice Pres*
Cathy Wilson, *Manager*
EMP: 30
SALES (est): 6MM **Privately Held**
WEB: www.hartstonepottery.com
SIC: 5023 Pottery

(G-20522)
ORTHOPEDIC ASSOC OF ZANESVILLE
2854 Bell St (43701-1721)
PHONE.....................740 454-3273
Fax: 740 454-3943
Karl C Saunders, *President*
Karl Saunders, *Med Doctor*
Debbie Apperson, *Manager*
EMP: 45
SALES (est): 6.2MM **Privately Held**
SIC: 8011 Orthopedic physician

(G-20523)
P & D TRANSPORTATION INC (PA)
Also Called: Putnam Truck Load Direct
1705 Moxahala Ave (43701-5952)
P.O. Box 2909 (43702-2909)
PHONE.....................740 454-1221
Fax: 740 454-0310
Patrick L Hennessey, *President*
Dan Hennessey, *Vice Pres*
Ronald J Kunkel, *Treasurer*
Ralph Hennessey, *Admin Sec*
EMP: 115
SALES (est): 21.3MM **Privately Held**
SIC: 4213 Contract haulers

(G-20524)
PEABODY COAL COMPANY
2810 East Pike Apt 3 (43701-9197)
PHONE.....................740 450-2420
J T Kneen, *Principal*
EMP: 312
SALES (corp-wide): 4.7B **Publicly Held**
SIC: 1241 Coal mining services
HQ: Peabody Coal Company
701 Market St
Saint Louis MO 63101
314 342-3400

(G-20525)
PHILO BAND BOOSTERS
1359 Wheeling Ave (43701-4538)
PHONE.....................740 221-3023
Chad Stemm, *Finance Dir*
EMP: 30
SALES (est): 96.3K **Privately Held**
SIC: 7929 Entertainers & entertainment groups

(G-20526)
PRIMECARE SUTHEASTERN OHIO INC
1210 Ashland Ave (43701-2883)
PHONE.....................740 454-8551
Daniel Sher, *Vice Pres*
Ronald Harvey, *Med Doctor*
EMP: 45 **Privately Held**
SIC: 8011 Group health association
PA: Primecare Of Southeastern Ohio, Inc.
860 Bethesda Dr Ste 3
Zanesville OH 43701

(G-20527)
PROFESSIONAL PLUMBING SERVICES
3570 Old Wheeling Rd (43701-9684)
PHONE.....................740 454-1066
Fax: 740 454-4815
Michael L Burkhart, *President*
Larry Wilson, *Opers Mgr*
Catherine Nash Burkhart, *Treasurer*
Sandra Findeiss, *Info Tech Mgr*
EMP: 28
SQ FT: 5,200
SALES: 2.7MM **Privately Held**
SIC: 1711 Plumbing contractors; warm air heating & air conditioning contractor

(G-20528)
RANKIN & RANKIN INC
806 Market St (43701-3718)
P.O. Box 2547 (43702-2547)
PHONE.....................740 452-7575
Fax: 740 452-7509
Robert S Glass, *President*
Lisa Curby, *Manager*
Tawna Lyons, *Manager*
Cindy Warne, *Manager*
EMP: 25
SALES (est): 4.6MM **Privately Held**
WEB: www.rankininsurance.com
SIC: 6411 Insurance agents

(G-20529)
RESIDENTIAL HOME FOR THE DEVLP
Also Called: Rhdd
3484 Old Wheeling Rd (43701-0904)
PHONE.....................740 452-5133
Fax: 740 452-5133
Lisa Reed, *Director*
Tricia Rasor, *Nursing Dir*
Sandy Pisch, *Assistant*
EMP: 30
SALES (corp-wide): 8.4MM **Privately Held**
WEB: www.reliabledist.com
SIC: 8361 Home for the mentally handicapped
PA: Residential Home For The Developmentally Disabled Incorporated
925 Chestnut St
Coshocton OH 43812
740 622-9778

(G-20530)
ROBERT NEFF & SON INC
132 S Shawnee Ave (43701-6221)
P.O. Box 1822 (43702-1822)
PHONE.....................740 454-0128
Robert G Neff, *President*
Bobbie Creeks, *Office Mgr*
EMP: 40 EST: 1939
SQ FT: 7,000
SALES: 2MM **Privately Held**
SIC: 4212 4213 Coal haulage, local; mail carriers, contract; trucking, except local

(G-20531)
SHELLY AND SANDS INC
3840 Durant Rd (43701-7857)
PHONE.....................740 453-6260
Fax: 740 453-6980
Richard H Mc Clelland, *Branch Mgr*
EMP: 25
SALES (corp-wide): 260.8MM **Privately Held**
SIC: 1611 Highway & street paving contractor
PA: Shelly And Sands, Inc.
3570 S River Rd
Zanesville OH 43701
740 453-0721

(G-20532)
SHELLY AND SANDS INC
3570 S River Rd (43701-9052)
PHONE.....................740 453-0721
Matt Kelley, *Vice Pres*
EMP: 35
SALES (corp-wide): 260.8MM **Privately Held**
WEB: www.shellyandsands.com
SIC: 1611 2951 1442 1771 Highway & street paving contractor; asphalt & asphaltic paving mixtures (not from refineries); construction sand & gravel; concrete work
PA: Shelly And Sands, Inc.
3570 S River Rd
Zanesville OH 43701
740 453-0721

(G-20533)
SIDWELL MATERIALS INC
4200 Maysville Pike (43701-9372)
P.O. Box 192, White Cottage (43791-0192)
PHONE.....................740 849-2394
Jeffrey R Sidwell, *President*
Stan Archer, *General Mgr*
Jackie Harlow, *Manager*
EMP: 130
SALES (est): 21.3MM **Privately Held**
SIC: 1795 4953 2951 1422 Demolition, buildings & other structures; rubbish collection & disposal; asphalt paving mixtures & blocks; crushed & broken limestone; brick, stone & related material

(G-20534)
SOUTHEAST AREA TRANSIT (PA)
Also Called: Z-Bus
375 Fairbanks St (43701-3043)
PHONE.....................740 454-8574
Fax: 740 454-7449
Mark McClanan, *General Mgr*
Rich Wood, *Maintenance Dir*
Arlene Johnson, *Supervisor*
Dianne Gill, *Pharmacy Dir*
Holly Grimes, *Admin Asst*
EMP: 26
SQ FT: 9,974
SALES (est): 3MM **Privately Held**
SIC: 4111 Local & suburban transit

(G-20535)
SOUTHEASTERN OHIO BRDCSTG SYS
Also Called: Whiz Am-FM
629 Downard Rd (43701-5108)
PHONE.....................740 452-5431
Norma Littick, *Ch of Bd*
Henry Littick, *President*
Barbara Saunders, *Corp Secy*
Erin France, *Accounts Exec*
Brian Wagner, *Program Dir*
EMP: 25
SQ FT: 10,000
SALES (est): 1.8MM **Privately Held**
SIC: 4832 Radio broadcasting stations, music format

(G-20536)
SOUTHEASTERN OHIO TV SYS (PA)
Also Called: Whiz-TV
629 Downard Rd (43701-5108)
PHONE.....................740 452-5431

Fax: 740 452-6553
Henry Littick, *Partner*
Barbara Saunders, *Partner*
Dan Slentz, *Engineer*
Scott Lauka, *Finance*
Jay Benson, *Sales Mgr*
EMP: 26 **EST:** 1953
SQ FT: 10,000
SALES (est): 10.4MM **Privately Held**
WEB: www.whizamfmtv.com
SIC: 4832 4833 Radio broadcasting stations, music format; television broadcasting stations

(G-20537)
SPECTRUM MGT HOLDG CO LLC
Also Called: Time Warner
737 Howard St (43701-3757)
PHONE................................740 455-9705
Terry Oconnell, *President*
EMP: 83
SALES (corp-wide): 41.5B **Publicly Held**
SIC: 4841 Cable television services
HQ: Spectrum Management Holding Company, Llc
    400 Atlantic St
    Stamford CT 06901
    203 905-7801

(G-20538)
THOMAS E ROJEWSKI MD INC
Also Called: Booth, Jack B MD
2945 Maple Ave (43701-1762)
PHONE................................740 454-0158
Thomas E Rojewski MD, *President*
Jack B Booth, *Med Doctor*
EMP: 28
SALES (est): 1MM **Privately Held**
SIC: 8011 Surgeon

(G-20539)
TOWN HOUSE MOTOR LODGE CORP
Also Called: Best Western
135 N 7th St (43701-3707)
P.O. Box 160 (43702-0160)
PHONE................................740 452-4511
Fax: 740 452-4511
Larry Wade, *President*
Timothy Longstreth, *Corp Secy*
EMP: 32
SQ FT: 40,000
SALES: 500K **Privately Held**
SIC: 7011 5812 5813 Hotels & motels; American restaurant; cocktail lounge

(G-20540)
TRILOGY REHAB SERVICES LLC
2991 Maple Ave (43701-1499)
PHONE................................740 452-3000
EMP: 1059
SALES (corp-wide): 151.1MM **Privately Held**
SIC: 8051 Skilled nursing care facilities
PA: Trilogy Rehab Services, Llc
    2701 Chestnut Station Ct
    Louisville KY 40299
    800 335-1060

(G-20541)
U S XPRESS INC
2705 E Pointe Dr (43701-7294)
PHONE................................740 452-4153
Fax: 740 453-7292
Duane Stare, *Manager*
EMP: 124 **Privately Held**
SIC: 4213 Contract haulers
HQ: U. S. Xpress, Inc.
    4080 Jenkins Rd
    Chattanooga TN 37421
    866 266-7270

(G-20542)
UNITED PARCEL SERVICE INC OH
Also Called: UPS
1507 Augusta St (43701-4155)
PHONE................................800 742-5877
EMP: 158
SALES (corp-wide): 65.8B **Publicly Held**
WEB: www.upsscs.com
SIC: 4215 Package delivery, vehicular; parcel delivery, vehicular

HQ: United Parcel Service, Inc. (Oh)
    55 Glenlake Pkwy
    Atlanta GA 30328
    404 828-6000

(G-20543)
VALLEY VIEW PLACE
3200 Shale Dr (43701)
PHONE................................740 454-7720
EMP: 200 **EST:** 2014
SQ FT: 40,524
SALES (est): 2MM **Privately Held**
SIC: 6531 Real Estate Agent/Manager

(G-20544)
VICTOR MCKENZIE DRILLING CO
3596 Maple Ave Ste A (43701-1686)
P.O. Box 3323 (43702-3323)
PHONE................................740 453-0834
Victor McKenzie, *President*
Sandy McKenzie, *Corp Secy*
EMP: 27
SALES (est): 1.5MM **Privately Held**
SIC: 1381 Drilling oil & gas wells

(G-20545)
WESTON GROUP INC
1575 Bowers Ln (43701-1000)
PHONE................................740 454-2741
Janet Hurd, *Manager*
EMP: 41 **Privately Held**
SIC: 8049 Physical therapist
PA: The Weston Group Inc
    2222 Sullivan Trl Easton
    Easton PA 18040

(G-20546)
ZANDEX INC (PA)
Also Called: Zandex Health Care
1122 Taylor St (43701-2658)
P.O. Box 730 (43702-0730)
PHONE................................740 454-1400
Fax: 740 454-7439
Douglas L Ramsay, *President*
Stoey Stout, *Vice Pres*
Lyle Clark, *CFO*
Peggy Morrison, *Accounting Mgr*
Donald Williamson, *MIS Dir*
EMP: 25
SQ FT: 1,500
SALES (est): 34MM **Privately Held**
SIC: 8052 8051 Intermediate care facilities; skilled nursing care facilities

(G-20547)
ZANDEX INC
Also Called: Apartments of Cedar Hill
1126 Adair Ave (43701-2804)
PHONE................................740 452-2087
Cindy Clark, *Manager*
Mable Clapper, *Director*
EMP: 30
SALES (corp-wide): 34MM **Privately Held**
SIC: 8361 Home for the aged
PA: Zandex, Inc.
    1122 Taylor St
    Zanesville OH 43701
    740 454-1400

(G-20548)
ZANDEX INC
Also Called: Adams Lane Care Center
1856 Adams Ln (43701-2612)
PHONE................................740 454-9769
Dave Wilson, *Branch Mgr*
Paul Mumma, *Director*
Heather Lamp, *Hlthcr Dir*
Colleen Besser, *Records Dir*
EMP: 180
SALES (corp-wide): 34MM **Privately Held**
SIC: 8052 8051 Intermediate care facilities; skilled nursing care facilities
PA: Zandex, Inc.
    1122 Taylor St
    Zanesville OH 43701
    740 454-1400

(G-20549)
ZANDEX INC
Also Called: Cedar Hill Care Center
1136 Adair Ave (43701-2804)
PHONE................................740 454-6823
Fax: 740 454-6167

Rich Stephens, *Branch Mgr*
Paul Mumma, *Director*
Lyle Clark, *Executive*
EMP: 90
SALES (corp-wide): 34MM **Privately Held**
SIC: 8052 8051 Personal care facility; skilled nursing care facilities
PA: Zandex, Inc.
    1122 Taylor St
    Zanesville OH 43701
    740 454-1400

(G-20550)
ZANDEX HEALTH CARE CORPORATION
Also Called: Ceder Hill
1136 Adair Ave (43701-2804)
PHONE................................740 452-4636
Linda Calindine, *President*
Dr Kurt Southam, *President*
Rich Stephens, *Manager*
Dew Williamson, *Info Tech Mgr*
EMP: 155
SALES (corp-wide): 34MM **Privately Held**
SIC: 8052 8051 Intermediate care facilities; skilled nursing care facilities
HQ: Zandex Health Care Corporation
    1122 Taylor St
    Zanesville OH 43701

(G-20551)
ZANDEX HEALTH CARE CORPORATION
Also Called: Adams Lane Care Center
1856 Adams Ln (43701-2612)
P.O. Box 638 (43702-0638)
PHONE................................740 454-9769
Fax: 740 454-4493
Sondra Caplinger, *Personnel Exec*
Cathy Kocher, *Administration*
EMP: 175
SQ FT: 20,000
SALES (corp-wide): 34MM **Privately Held**
SIC: 8052 8051 Intermediate care facilities; skilled nursing care facilities
HQ: Zandex Health Care Corporation
    1122 Taylor St
    Zanesville OH 43701

(G-20552)
ZANDEX HEALTH CARE CORPORATION (HQ)
Also Called: Cedar Hill Care Center
1122 Taylor St (43701-2658)
P.O. Box 730 (43702-0730)
PHONE................................740 454-1400
Douglas Ramsey, *President*
Stoey Stout, *Vice Pres*
Lyle Clark, *CFO*
Luis Gatti, *Manager*
Katheryn Simpson, *Technology*
EMP: 25
SQ FT: 1,000
SALES (est): 34MM **Privately Held**
SIC: 8052 8059 8051 Intermediate care facilities; rest home, with health care; skilled nursing care facilities; extended care facility
PA: Zandex, Inc.
    1122 Taylor St
    Zanesville OH 43701
    740 454-1400

(G-20553)
ZANDEX HEALTH CARE CORPORATION
Also Called: Willow Haven Nursing Home
1020 Taylor St (43701-2656)
P.O. Box 2038 (43702-2038)
PHONE................................740 454-9747
Fax: 740 454-4837
Erika Wickham, *Sls & Mktg Exec*
Sheri Tucker, *Personnel Exec*
Mary Anne Whickham, *Office Mgr*
Mark Richard, *Manager*
Joyce Ford, *Nursing Dir*
EMP: 120

SALES (corp-wide): 34MM **Privately Held**
SIC: 8051 8052 8059 Convalescent home with continuous nursing care; intermediate care facilities; rest home, with health care
HQ: Zandex Health Care Corporation
    1122 Taylor St
    Zanesville OH 43701

(G-20554)
ZANESVILLE CHEVROLET CADILLAC
3657 Maple Ave (43701-1193)
PHONE................................740 452-3611
Derek A Truss, *President*
Henry Walters, *Treasurer*
EMP: 27 **EST:** 1922
SQ FT: 50,000
SALES: 12MM **Privately Held**
SIC: 5511 7538 Automobiles, new & used; pickups, new & used; general automotive repair shops

(G-20555)
ZANESVILLE COUNTRY CLUB
1300 Country Club Dr (43701-1464)
P.O. Box 2490 (43702-2490)
PHONE................................740 452-2726
Fax: 740 452-1269
Michael Micheli, *President*
Michael Barron, *General Mgr*
Ken Corbin, *Vice Pres*
Tim Dunn, *Manager*
EMP: 35
SQ FT: 15,000
SALES: 2.6MM **Privately Held**
SIC: 7997 Country club, membership; swimming club, membership; tennis club, membership; golf club, membership

(G-20556)
ZANESVILLE METRO HSING AUTH (PA)
407 Pershing Rd (43701-6871)
PHONE................................740 454-9714
Fax: 740 454-8567
Trayce Osburn, *Manager*
Steven G Randles, *Exec Dir*
EMP: 59
SALES: 12.8MM **Privately Held**
WEB: www.zanesvillehousing.org
SIC: 6513 Apartment building operators

(G-20557)
ZANESVILLE NH LLC
Also Called: Zanesvlle Hlth Rhblitation Ctr
4200 Harrington Dr (43701-6022)
PHONE................................740 452-4351
Mordecai Rosenberg, *President*
Ronald Swartz, *CFO*
Lisa Schwartz, *Admin Sec*
EMP: 54 **EST:** 2015
SALES (est): 339.2K **Privately Held**
SIC: 8051 Skilled nursing care facilities

(G-20558)
ZANESVILLE SURGERY CENTER LLC
2907 Bell St (43701-1720)
PHONE................................740 453-5713
Fax: 740 454-7748
Jean Spring, *Office Mgr*
Myron H Powelson, *Med Doctor*
Jung Rhee, *Executive*
Glenda Rogers, *Administration*
Terry Ganton, *Administration*
EMP: 55
SALES (est): 3.9MM **Privately Held**
SIC: 8011 Ambulatory surgical center

(G-20559)
ZANESVILLE WELFARE ORGANIZATIO
3610 West Pike (43701-9335)
PHONE................................740 450-6060
Fax: 740 454-3242
Lou Cventic, *President*
Brad E Lynch, *Treasurer*
Connie Kimble, *Manager*
M D Young, *Director*
EMP: 285

SALES: 7.3MM **Privately Held**
SIC: 8699 8331 Charitable organization; job training & vocational rehabilitation services; vocational training agency

(G-20560)
ZANESVLLE WELFRE ORGNZTN/GOODW (PA)
Also Called: GOODWILL RETAIL STORE
3610 West Pike (43701-9335)
PHONE..................................740 450-6060
Louis Cvetnic, *CEO*
EMP: 60 **EST:** 1914
SQ FT: 40,000
SALES: 10.3MM **Privately Held**
SIC: 8331 5932 Sheltered workshop; used merchandise stores

(G-20561)
ZEMBA BROS INC
3401 East Pike (43701-8419)
P.O. Box 1270 (43702-1270)
PHONE..................................740 452-1880
Fax: 740 450-4209
Scott M Zemba, *President*
Susan Zemba, *Administration*
EMP: 47
SQ FT: 36,000
SALES (est): 11.2MM **Privately Held**
SIC: 1794 1711 1623 4212 Excavation & grading, building construction; septic system construction; sewer line construction; local trucking, without storage

SIC INDEX

Standard Industrial Classification Alphabetical Index

SIC NO	PRODUCT

A

6321 Accident & Health Insurance
8721 Accounting, Auditing & Bookkeeping Svcs
7322 Adjustment & Collection Svcs
7311 Advertising Agencies
7319 Advertising, NEC
4513 Air Courier Svcs
4522 Air Transportation, Nonscheduled
4512 Air Transportation, Scheduled
4581 Airports, Flying Fields & Terminal Svcs
7999 Amusement & Recreation Svcs, NEC
7996 Amusement Parks
0752 Animal Specialty Svcs, Exc Veterinary
1231 Anthracite Mining
8422 Arboreta, Botanical & Zoological Gardens
8712 Architectural Services
7694 Armature Rewinding Shops
7521 Automobile Parking Lots & Garages
5012 Automobiles & Other Motor Vehicles Wholesale
7533 Automotive Exhaust System Repair Shops
7536 Automotive Glass Replacement Shops
7539 Automotive Repair Shops, NEC
7549 Automotive Svcs, Except Repair & Car Washes
7537 Automotive Transmission Repair Shops

B

7929 Bands, Orchestras, Actors & Entertainers
7241 Barber Shops
7231 Beauty Shops
0211 Beef Cattle Feedlots
5181 Beer & Ale Wholesale
0171 Berry Crops
1221 Bituminous Coal & Lignite: Surface Mining
1222 Bituminous Coal: Underground Mining
5192 Books, Periodicals & Newspapers Wholesale
7933 Bowling Centers
5032 Brick, Stone & Related Construction Mtrls Wholesale
1622 Bridge, Tunnel & Elevated Hwy Construction
7349 Building Cleaning & Maintenance Svcs, NEC
4142 Bus Charter Service, Except Local
4173 Bus Terminal & Svc Facilities
8611 Business Associations
8748 Business Consulting Svcs, NEC
7389 Business Svcs, NEC

C

4841 Cable & Other Pay TV Svcs
7542 Car Washes
1751 Carpentry Work
7217 Carpet & Upholstery Cleaning
0119 Cash Grains, NEC
6553 Cemetery Subdividers & Developers
6019 Central Reserve Depository, NEC
1479 Chemical & Fertilizer Mining
5169 Chemicals & Allied Prdts, NEC Wholesale
0251 Chicken & Poultry Farms
0252 Chicken Egg Farms
8351 Child Day Care Svcs
8641 Civic, Social & Fraternal Associations
5052 Coal & Other Minerals & Ores Wholesale
1241 Coal Mining Svcs
7215 Coin Operated Laundries & Cleaning
7993 Coin-Operated Amusement Devices & Arcades
4939 Combination Utilities, NEC
7336 Commercial Art & Graphic Design
6029 Commercial Banks, NEC
8732 Commercial Economic, Sociological & Educational Research
5046 Commercial Eqpt, NEC Wholesale
7335 Commercial Photography
8731 Commercial Physical & Biological Research
6221 Commodity Contracts Brokers & Dealers
4899 Communication Svcs, NEC
7376 Computer Facilities Management Svcs
7373 Computer Integrated Systems Design
7378 Computer Maintenance & Repair
7379 Computer Related Svcs, NEC
7377 Computer Rental & Leasing
5045 Computers & Peripheral Eqpt & Software Wholesale
1771 Concrete Work
5145 Confectionery Wholesale
5082 Construction & Mining Mach & Eqpt Wholesale
5039 Construction Materials, NEC Wholesale
1442 Construction Sand & Gravel
1021 Copper Ores
0115 Corn
0724 Cotton Ginning
4215 Courier Svcs, Except Air
6159 Credit Institutions, Misc Business
6153 Credit Institutions, Short-Term Business
7323 Credit Reporting Svcs
0191 Crop Farming, Misc
0723 Crop Preparation, Except Cotton Ginning
1311 Crude Petroleum & Natural Gas
4612 Crude Petroleum Pipelines
1423 Crushed & Broken Granite
1422 Crushed & Broken Limestone
1429 Crushed & Broken Stone, NEC
7371 Custom Computer Programming Svcs

D

0241 Dairy Farms
5143 Dairy Prdts, Except Dried Or Canned Wholesale
7911 Dance Studios, Schools & Halls
7374 Data & Computer Processing & Preparation
0175 Deciduous Tree Fruits
4412 Deep Sea Foreign Transportation Of Freight
4481 Deep Sea Transportation Of Passengers
8072 Dental Laboratories
7381 Detective & Armored Car Svcs
1411 Dimension Stone
7331 Direct Mail Advertising Svcs
7342 Disinfecting & Pest Control Svcs
1381 Drilling Oil & Gas Wells
5122 Drugs, Drug Proprietaries & Sundries Wholesale
7216 Dry Cleaning Plants, Except Rug Cleaning
5099 Durable Goods: NEC Wholesale

E

6732 Education, Religious & Charitable Trusts
4931 Electric & Other Svcs Combined
4911 Electric Svcs
7629 Electrical & Elex Repair Shop, NEC
5064 Electrical Appliances, TV & Radios Wholesale
1731 Electrical Work
5063 Electrl Apparatus, Eqpt, Wiring Splys Wholesale
5065 Electronic Parts & Eqpt Wholesale
7361 Employment Agencies
8711 Engineering Services
7359 Equipment Rental & Leasing, NEC
1794 Excavating & Grading Work

F

8744 Facilities Support Mgmt Svcs
5083 Farm & Garden Mach & Eqpt Wholesale
0761 Farm Labor Contractors & Crew Leaders
4221 Farm Product Warehousing & Storage
5191 Farm Splys Wholesale
5159 Farm-Prdt Raw Mtrls, NEC Wholesale
6111 Federal Credit Agencies
6061 Federal Credit Unions
6011 Federal Reserve Banks
6035 Federal Savings Institutions
4482 Ferries
1061 Ferroalloy Ores, Except Vanadium
6331 Fire, Marine & Casualty Insurance
5146 Fish & Seafood Wholesale
4785 Fixed Facilities, Inspection, Weighing Svcs Transptn
1752 Floor Laying & Other Floor Work, NEC
5193 Flowers, Nursery Stock & Florists' Splys Wholesale
0182 Food Crops Grown Under Cover
5139 Footwear Wholesale
0851 Forestry Svcs
4731 Freight Forwarding & Arrangement
4432 Freight Transportation On The Great Lakes
5148 Fresh Fruits & Vegetables Wholesale
6099 Functions Related To Deposit Banking, NEC
7261 Funeral Svcs & Crematories
5021 Furniture Wholesale

G

7212 Garment Pressing & Cleaners' Agents
4932 Gas & Other Svcs Combined
4925 Gas Production &/Or Distribution
7538 General Automotive Repair Shop
1541 General Contractors, Indl Bldgs & Warehouses
1542 General Contractors, Nonresidential & Non-indl Bldgs
1522 General Contractors, Residential Other Than Single Family
1521 General Contractors, Single Family Houses
8062 General Medical & Surgical Hospitals
4225 General Warehousing & Storage
1793 Glass & Glazing Work
5153 Grain & Field Beans Wholesale
0172 Grapes
5149 Groceries & Related Prdts, NEC Wholesale
5141 Groceries, General Line Wholesale

H

5072 Hardware Wholesale
8099 Health & Allied Svcs, NEC
5075 Heating & Air Conditioning Eqpt & Splys Wholesale
7353 Heavy Construction Eqpt Rental & Leasing
1629 Heavy Construction, NEC
7363 Help Supply Svcs
1611 Highway & Street Construction
0213 Hogs
5023 Home Furnishings Wholesale
8082 Home Health Care Svcs
6324 Hospital & Medical Svc Plans Carriers
7011 Hotels, Motels & Tourist Courts
0971 Hunting & Trapping

I

8322 Individual & Family Social Svcs
5113 Indl & Personal Svc Paper Wholesale
7218 Industrial Launderers
5084 Industrial Mach & Eqpt Wholesale
1446 Industrial Sand
5085 Industrial Splys Wholesale
7375 Information Retrieval Svcs
1796 Installation Or Erection Of Bldg Eqpt & Machinery, NEC
6411 Insurance Agents, Brokers & Svc
6399 Insurance Carriers, NEC
4131 Intercity & Rural Bus Transportation
8052 Intermediate Care Facilities
6282 Investment Advice
6799 Investors, NEC
0134 Irish Potatoes
1011 Iron Ores
4971 Irrigation Systems

J

5094 Jewelry, Watches, Precious Stones Wholesale
8331 Job Training & Vocational Rehabilitation Svcs

K

8092 Kidney Dialysis Centers

L

8631 Labor Unions & Similar Organizations
6552 Land Subdividers & Developers
0781 Landscape Counseling & Planning
7219 Laundry & Garment Svcs, NEC
0782 Lawn & Garden Svcs
8111 Legal Svcs
6519 Lessors Of Real Estate, NEC
6311 Life Insurance Carriers
7213 Linen Sply
0751 Livestock Svcs, Except Veterinary
5154 Livestock Wholesale
6163 Loan Brokers
4111 Local & Suburban Transit
4141 Local Bus Charter Svc
4119 Local Passenger Transportation: NEC
4214 Local Trucking With Storage
4212 Local Trucking Without Storage
5031 Lumber, Plywood & Millwork Wholesale

M

8742 Management Consulting Services
6722 Management Investment Offices
8741 Management Services
4493 Marinas
4491 Marine Cargo Handling
1741 Masonry & Other Stonework
5147 Meats & Meat Prdts Wholesale
7352 Medical Eqpt Rental & Leasing
8071 Medical Laboratories
5047 Medical, Dental & Hospital Eqpt & Splys Wholesale
8699 Membership Organizations, NEC
7997 Membership Sports & Recreation Clubs

SIC INDEX

SIC NO	PRODUCT
7041	Membership-Basis Hotels
5136	Men's & Boys' Clothing & Furnishings Wholesale
1081	Metal Mining Svcs
5051	Metals Service Centers
1499	Miscellaneous Nonmetallic Mining
7299	Miscellaneous Personal Svcs, NEC
6162	Mortgage Bankers & Loan Correspondents
7822	Motion Picture & Video Tape Distribution
7812	Motion Picture & Video Tape Production
7832	Motion Picture Theaters, Except Drive-In
5015	Motor Vehicle Parts, Used Wholesale
5013	Motor Vehicle Splys & New Parts Wholesale
8412	Museums & Art Galleries

N

SIC NO	PRODUCT
6021	National Commercial Banks
4924	Natural Gas Distribution
1321	Natural Gas Liquids
4922	Natural Gas Transmission
4923	Natural Gas Transmission & Distribution
7383	News Syndicates
8733	Noncommercial Research Organizations
5199	Nondurable Goods, NEC Wholesale
1481	Nonmetallic Minerals Svcs, Except Fuels
8059	Nursing & Personal Care Facilities, NEC

O

SIC NO	PRODUCT
5044	Office Eqpt Wholesale
8041	Offices & Clinics Of Chiropractors
8021	Offices & Clinics Of Dentists
8011	Offices & Clinics Of Doctors Of Medicine
8031	Offices & Clinics Of Doctors Of Osteopathy
8049	Offices & Clinics Of Health Practitioners, NEC
8042	Offices & Clinics Of Optometrists
8043	Offices & Clinics Of Podiatrists
6712	Offices Of Bank Holding Co's
6719	Offices Of Holding Co's, NEC
1382	Oil & Gas Field Exploration Svcs
1389	Oil & Gas Field Svcs, NEC
1531	Operative Builders
6513	Operators Of Apartment Buildings
6514	Operators Of Dwellings, Except Apartments
6512	Operators Of Nonresidential Bldgs
6515	Operators of Residential Mobile Home Sites
5048	Ophthalmic Goods Wholesale
0181	Ornamental Floriculture & Nursery Prdts
0783	Ornamental Shrub & Tree Svc
7312	Outdoor Advertising Svcs

P

SIC NO	PRODUCT
5142	Packaged Frozen Foods Wholesale
4783	Packing & Crating Svcs
1721	Painting & Paper Hanging Contractors
5198	Paints, Varnishes & Splys Wholesale
7515	Passenger Car Leasing
7514	Passenger Car Rental
4729	Passenger Transportation Arrangement, NEC
6794	Patent Owners & Lessors
6371	Pension, Health & Welfare Funds
6141	Personal Credit Institutions
5172	Petroleum & Petroleum Prdts Wholesale
5171	Petroleum Bulk Stations & Terminals
7334	Photocopying & Duplicating Svcs
7384	Photofinishing Labs
5043	Photographic Eqpt & Splys Wholesale
7221	Photographic Studios, Portrait
7991	Physical Fitness Facilities
5131	Piece Goods, Notions & Dry Goods Wholesale
1742	Plastering, Drywall, Acoustical & Insulation Work
5162	Plastics Materials & Basic Shapes Wholesale
5074	Plumbing & Heating Splys Wholesale
1711	Plumbing, Heating & Air Conditioning Contractors
8651	Political Organizations
5144	Poultry & Poultry Prdts Wholesale
0254	Poultry Hatcheries
7211	Power Laundries, Family & Commercial
7372	Prepackaged Software
5111	Printing & Writing Paper Wholesale
5049	Professional Eqpt & Splys, NEC Wholesale
8621	Professional Membership Organizations
7941	Professional Sports Clubs & Promoters
8063	Psychiatric Hospitals
7992	Public Golf Courses
8743	Public Relations Svcs

R

SIC NO	PRODUCT
7948	Racing & Track Operations
7622	Radio & TV Repair Shops
4832	Radio Broadcasting Stations
7313	Radio, TV & Publishers Adv Reps
4812	Radiotelephone Communications
4741	Railroad Car Rental
6517	Railroad Property Lessors
4011	Railroads, Line-Hauling Operations
6531	Real Estate Agents & Managers
6798	Real Estate Investment Trusts
4613	Refined Petroleum Pipelines
4222	Refrigerated Warehousing & Storage
7623	Refrigeration & Air Conditioning Svc & Repair Shop
5078	Refrigeration Eqpt & Splys Wholesale
4953	Refuse Systems
7699	Repair Shop & Related Svcs, NEC
8361	Residential Care
7641	Reupholstery & Furniture Repair
5033	Roofing, Siding & Insulation Mtrls Wholesale
1761	Roofing, Siding & Sheet Metal Work
7021	Rooming & Boarding Houses

S

SIC NO	PRODUCT
4959	Sanitary Svcs, NEC
6036	Savings Institutions, Except Federal
4151	School Buses
5093	Scrap & Waste Materials Wholesale
7338	Secretarial & Court Reporting Svcs
6289	Security & Commodity Svcs, NEC
6211	Security Brokers & Dealers
7382	Security Systems Svcs
5087	Service Establishment Eqpt & Splys Wholesale
7829	Services Allied To Motion Picture Distribution
7819	Services Allied To Motion Picture Prdtn
8999	Services Not Elsewhere Classified
4952	Sewerage Systems
8051	Skilled Nursing Facilities
8399	Social Svcs, NEC
0711	Soil Preparation Svcs
0721	Soil Preparation, Planting & Cultivating Svc
0116	Soybeans
1799	Special Trade Contractors, NEC
4226	Special Warehousing & Storage, NEC
8069	Specialty Hospitals, Except Psychiatric
8093	Specialty Outpatient Facilities, NEC
7032	Sporting & Recreational Camps
5091	Sporting & Recreational Goods & Splys Wholesale
6022	State Commercial Banks
6062	State Credit Unions
5112	Stationery & Office Splys Wholesale
4961	Steam & Air Conditioning Sply
1791	Structural Steel Erection
6351	Surety Insurance Carriers
8713	Surveying Services
4013	Switching & Terminal Svcs

T

SIC NO	PRODUCT
7291	Tax Return Preparation Svcs
4121	Taxi Cabs
4822	Telegraph & Other Message Communications
4813	Telephone Communications, Except Radio
4833	Television Broadcasting Stations
4231	Terminal & Joint Terminal Maint Facilities
1743	Terrazzo, Tile, Marble & Mosaic Work
8734	Testing Laboratories
7922	Theatrical Producers & Misc Theatrical Svcs
0811	Timber Tracts
7534	Tire Retreading & Repair Shops
5014	Tires & Tubes Wholesale
6541	Title Abstract Offices
6361	Title Insurance
5194	Tobacco & Tobacco Prdts Wholesale
7532	Top, Body & Upholstery Repair & Paint Shops
4725	Tour Operators
4492	Towing & Tugboat Svcs
5092	Toys & Hobby Goods & Splys Wholesale
7033	Trailer Parks & Camp Sites
5088	Transportation Eqpt & Splys, Except Motor Vehicles Wholesale
4789	Transportation Svcs, NEC
4724	Travel Agencies
7513	Truck Rental & Leasing, Without Drivers
4213	Trucking, Except Local
6733	Trusts Except Educational, Religious & Charitable
0253	Turkey & Turkey Egg Farms

U

SIC NO	PRODUCT
6726	Unit Investment Trusts, Face-Amount Certificate Offices
1094	Uranium, Radium & Vanadium Ores
7519	Utility Trailers & Recreational Vehicle Rental

V

SIC NO	PRODUCT
0161	Vegetables & Melons
0742	Veterinary Animal Specialties
0741	Veterinary Livestock Svcs
7841	Video Tape Rental

W

SIC NO	PRODUCT
7631	Watch, Clock & Jewelry Repair
4941	Water Sply
4449	Water Transportation Of Freight, NEC
4499	Water Transportation Svcs, NEC
1781	Water Well Drilling
1623	Water, Sewer & Utility Line Construction
7692	Welding Repair
0111	Wheat
5182	Wine & Distilled Alcoholic Beverages Wholesale
5137	Women's, Children's & Infants Clothing Wholesale
1795	Wrecking & Demolition Work

SIC INDEX

Standard Industrial Classification Numerical Index

SIC NO	PRODUCT

01 AGRICULTURAL PRODUCTION-CROPS
0111 Wheat
0115 Corn
0116 Soybeans
0119 Cash Grains, NEC
0134 Irish Potatoes
0161 Vegetables & Melons
0171 Berry Crops
0172 Grapes
0175 Deciduous Tree Fruits
0181 Ornamental Floriculture & Nursery Prdts
0182 Food Crops Grown Under Cover
0191 Crop Farming, Misc

02 AGRICULTURAL PRODUCTION-LIVESTOCK AND ANIMAL SPECIALTIES
0211 Beef Cattle Feedlots
0213 Hogs
0241 Dairy Farms
0251 Chicken & Poultry Farms
0252 Chicken Egg Farms
0253 Turkey & Turkey Egg Farms
0254 Poultry Hatcheries

07 AGRICULTURAL SERVICES
0711 Soil Preparation Svcs
0721 Soil Preparation, Planting & Cultivating Svc
0723 Crop Preparation, Except Cotton Ginning
0724 Cotton Ginning
0741 Veterinary Livestock Svcs
0742 Veterinary Animal Specialties
0751 Livestock Svcs, Except Veterinary
0752 Animal Specialty Svcs, Exc Veterinary
0761 Farm Labor Contractors & Crew Leaders
0781 Landscape Counseling & Planning
0782 Lawn & Garden Svcs
0783 Ornamental Shrub & Tree Svc

08 FORESTRY
0811 Timber Tracts
0851 Forestry Svcs

09 FISHING, HUNTING, AND TRAPPING
0971 Hunting & Trapping

10 METAL MINING
1011 Iron Ores
1021 Copper Ores
1061 Ferroalloy Ores, Except Vanadium
1081 Metal Mining Svcs
1094 Uranium, Radium & Vanadium Ores

12 COAL MINING
1221 Bituminous Coal & Lignite: Surface Mining
1222 Bituminous Coal: Underground Mining
1231 Anthracite Mining
1241 Coal Mining Svcs

13 OIL AND GAS EXTRACTION
1311 Crude Petroleum & Natural Gas
1321 Natural Gas Liquids
1381 Drilling Oil & Gas Wells
1382 Oil & Gas Field Exploration Svcs
1389 Oil & Gas Field Svcs, NEC

14 MINING AND QUARRYING OF NONMETALLIC MINERALS, EXCEPT FUELS
1411 Dimension Stone
1422 Crushed & Broken Limestone
1423 Crushed & Broken Granite
1429 Crushed & Broken Stone, NEC
1442 Construction Sand & Gravel
1446 Industrial Sand
1479 Chemical & Fertilizer Mining
1481 Nonmetallic Minerals Svcs, Except Fuels
1499 Miscellaneous Nonmetallic Mining

15 BUILDING CONSTRUCTION-GENERAL CONTRACTORS AND OPERATIVE BUILDERS
1521 General Contractors, Single Family Houses
1522 General Contractors, Residential Other Than Single Family
1531 Operative Builders
1541 General Contractors, Indl Bldgs & Warehouses
1542 General Contractors, Nonresidential & Non-indl Bldgs

16 HEAVY CONSTRUCTION OTHER THAN BUILDING CONSTRUCTION-CONTRACTORS
1611 Highway & Street Construction
1622 Bridge, Tunnel & Elevated Hwy Construction
1623 Water, Sewer & Utility Line Construction
1629 Heavy Construction, NEC

17 CONSTRUCTION-SPECIAL TRADE CONTRACTORS
1711 Plumbing, Heating & Air Conditioning Contractors
1721 Painting & Paper Hanging Contractors
1731 Electrical Work
1741 Masonry & Other Stonework
1742 Plastering, Drywall, Acoustical & Insulation Work
1743 Terrazzo, Tile, Marble & Mosaic Work
1751 Carpentry Work
1752 Floor Laying & Other Floor Work, NEC
1761 Roofing, Siding & Sheet Metal Work
1771 Concrete Work
1781 Water Well Drilling
1791 Structural Steel Erection
1793 Glass & Glazing Work
1794 Excavating & Grading Work
1795 Wrecking & Demolition Work
1796 Installation Or Erection Of Bldg Eqpt & Machinery, NEC
1799 Special Trade Contractors, NEC

40 RAILROAD TRANSPORTATION
4011 Railroads, Line-Hauling Operations
4013 Switching & Terminal Svcs

41 LOCAL AND SUBURBAN TRANSIT AND INTERURBAN HIGHWAY PASSENGER TRANSPORTATION
4111 Local & Suburban Transit
4119 Local Passenger Transportation: NEC
4121 Taxi Cabs
4131 Intercity & Rural Bus Transportation
4141 Local Bus Charter Svc
4142 Bus Charter Service, Except Local
4151 School Buses
4173 Bus Terminal & Svc Facilities

42 MOTOR FREIGHT TRANSPORTATION AND WAREHOUSING
4212 Local Trucking Without Storage
4213 Trucking, Except Local
4214 Local Trucking With Storage
4215 Courier Svcs, Except Air
4221 Farm Product Warehousing & Storage
4222 Refrigerated Warehousing & Storage
4225 General Warehousing & Storage
4226 Special Warehousing & Storage, NEC
4231 Terminal & Joint Terminal Maint Facilities

44 WATER TRANSPORTATION
4412 Deep Sea Foreign Transportation Of Freight
4432 Freight Transportation On The Great Lakes
4449 Water Transportation Of Freight, NEC
4481 Deep Sea Transportation Of Passengers
4482 Ferries
4491 Marine Cargo Handling
4492 Towing & Tugboat Svcs
4493 Marinas
4499 Water Transportation Svcs, NEC

45 TRANSPORTATION BY AIR
4512 Air Transportation, Scheduled
4513 Air Courier Svcs
4522 Air Transportation, Nonscheduled
4581 Airports, Flying Fields & Terminal Svcs

46 PIPELINES, EXCEPT NATURAL GAS
4612 Crude Petroleum Pipelines
4613 Refined Petroleum Pipelines

47 TRANSPORTATION SERVICES
4724 Travel Agencies
4725 Tour Operators
4729 Passenger Transportation Arrangement, NEC
4731 Freight Forwarding & Arrangement
4741 Railroad Car Rental
4783 Packing & Crating Svcs
4785 Fixed Facilities, Inspection, Weighing Svcs Transptn
4789 Transportation Svcs, NEC

48 COMMUNICATIONS
4812 Radiotelephone Communications
4813 Telephone Communications, Except Radio
4822 Telegraph & Other Message Communications
4832 Radio Broadcasting Stations
4833 Television Broadcasting Stations
4841 Cable & Other Pay TV Svcs
4899 Communication Svcs, NEC

49 ELECTRIC, GAS, AND SANITARY SERVICES
4911 Electric Svcs
4922 Natural Gas Transmission
4923 Natural Gas Transmission & Distribution
4924 Natural Gas Distribution
4925 Gas Production &/Or Distribution
4931 Electric & Other Svcs Combined
4932 Gas & Other Svcs Combined
4939 Combination Utilities, NEC
4941 Water Sply
4952 Sewerage Systems
4953 Refuse Systems
4959 Sanitary Svcs, NEC
4961 Steam & Air Conditioning Sply
4971 Irrigation Systems

50 WHOLESALE TRADE¨DURABLE GOODS
5012 Automobiles & Other Motor Vehicles Wholesale
5013 Motor Vehicle Splys & New Parts Wholesale
5014 Tires & Tubes Wholesale
5015 Motor Vehicle Parts, Used Wholesale
5021 Furniture Wholesale
5023 Home Furnishings Wholesale
5031 Lumber, Plywood & Millwork Wholesale
5032 Brick, Stone & Related Construction Mtrls Wholesale
5033 Roofing, Siding & Insulation Mtrls Wholesale
5039 Construction Materials, NEC Wholesale
5043 Photographic Eqpt & Splys Wholesale
5044 Office Eqpt Wholesale
5045 Computers & Peripheral Eqpt & Software Wholesale
5046 Commercial Eqpt, NEC Wholesale
5047 Medical, Dental & Hospital Eqpt & Splys Wholesale
5048 Ophthalmic Goods Wholesale
5049 Professional Eqpt & Splys, NEC Wholesale
5051 Metals Service Centers
5052 Coal & Other Minerals & Ores Wholesale
5063 Electrl Apparatus, Eqpt, Wiring Splys Wholesale
5064 Electrical Appliances, TV & Radios Wholesale
5065 Electronic Parts & Eqpt Wholesale
5072 Hardware Wholesale
5074 Plumbing & Heating Splys Wholesale
5075 Heating & Air Conditioning Eqpt & Splys Wholesale
5078 Refrigeration Eqpt & Splys Wholesale
5082 Construction & Mining Mach & Eqpt Wholesale
5083 Farm & Garden Mach & Eqpt Wholesale
5084 Industrial Mach & Eqpt Wholesale
5085 Industrial Splys Wholesale
5087 Service Establishment Eqpt & Splys Wholesale
5088 Transportation Eqpt & Splys, Except Motor Vehicles Wholesale
5091 Sporting & Recreational Goods & Splys Wholesale
5092 Toys & Hobby Goods & Splys Wholesale
5093 Scrap & Waste Materials Wholesale
5094 Jewelry, Watches, Precious Stones Wholesale
5099 Durable Goods: NEC Wholesale

51 WHOLESALE TRADE¨NONDURABLE GOODS
5111 Printing & Writing Paper Wholesale
5112 Stationery & Office Splys Wholesale
5113 Indl & Personal Svc Paper Wholesale
5122 Drugs, Drug Proprietaries & Sundries Wholesale
5131 Piece Goods, Notions & Dry Goods Wholesale
5136 Men's & Boys' Clothing & Furnishings Wholesale
5137 Women's, Children's & Infants Clothing Wholesale
5139 Footwear Wholesale
5141 Groceries, General Line Wholesale
5142 Packaged Frozen Foods Wholesale
5143 Dairy Prdts, Except Dried Or Canned Wholesale
5144 Poultry & Poultry Prdts Wholesale
5145 Confectionery Wholesale
5146 Fish & Seafood Wholesale
5147 Meats & Meat Prdts Wholesale
5148 Fresh Fruits & Vegetables Wholesale

SIC INDEX

SIC NO	PRODUCT
5149	Groceries & Related Prdts, NEC Wholesale
5153	Grain & Field Beans Wholesale
5154	Livestock Wholesale
5159	Farm-Prdt Raw Mtrls, NEC Wholesale
5162	Plastics Materials & Basic Shapes Wholesale
5169	Chemicals & Allied Prdts, NEC Wholesale
5171	Petroleum Bulk Stations & Terminals
5172	Petroleum & Petroleum Prdts Wholesale
5181	Beer & Ale Wholesale
5182	Wine & Distilled Alcoholic Beverages Wholesale
5191	Farm Splys Wholesale
5192	Books, Periodicals & Newspapers Wholesale
5193	Flowers, Nursery Stock & Florists' Splys Wholesale
5194	Tobacco & Tobacco Prdts Wholesale
5198	Paints, Varnishes & Splys Wholesale
5199	Nondurable Goods, NEC Wholesale

60 DEPOSITORY INSTITUTIONS

SIC NO	PRODUCT
6011	Federal Reserve Banks
6019	Central Reserve Depository, NEC
6021	National Commercial Banks
6022	State Commercial Banks
6029	Commercial Banks, NEC
6035	Federal Savings Institutions
6036	Savings Institutions, Except Federal
6061	Federal Credit Unions
6062	State Credit Unions
6099	Functions Related To Deposit Banking, NEC

61 NONDEPOSITORY CREDIT INSTITUTIONS

SIC NO	PRODUCT
6111	Federal Credit Agencies
6141	Personal Credit Institutions
6153	Credit Institutions, Short-Term Business
6159	Credit Institutions, Misc Business
6162	Mortgage Bankers & Loan Correspondents
6163	Loan Brokers

62 SECURITY AND COMMODITY BROKERS, DEALERS, EXCHANGES, AND SERVICES

SIC NO	PRODUCT
6211	Security Brokers & Dealers
6221	Commodity Contracts Brokers & Dealers
6282	Investment Advice
6289	Security & Commodity Svcs, NEC

63 INSURANCE CARRIERS

SIC NO	PRODUCT
6311	Life Insurance Carriers
6321	Accident & Health Insurance
6324	Hospital & Medical Svc Plans Carriers
6331	Fire, Marine & Casualty Insurance
6351	Surety Insurance Carriers
6361	Title Insurance
6371	Pension, Health & Welfare Funds
6399	Insurance Carriers, NEC

64 INSURANCE AGENTS, BROKERS, AND SERVICE

SIC NO	PRODUCT
6411	Insurance Agents, Brokers & Svc

65 REAL ESTATE

SIC NO	PRODUCT
6512	Operators Of Nonresidential Bldgs
6513	Operators Of Apartment Buildings
6514	Operators Of Dwellings, Except Apartments
6515	Operators of Residential Mobile Home Sites
6517	Railroad Property Lessors
6519	Lessors Of Real Estate, NEC
6531	Real Estate Agents & Managers
6541	Title Abstract Offices
6552	Land Subdividers & Developers
6553	Cemetery Subdividers & Developers

67 HOLDING AND OTHER INVESTMENT OFFICES

SIC NO	PRODUCT
6712	Offices Of Bank Holding Co's
6719	Offices Of Holding Co's, NEC
6722	Management Investment Offices
6726	Unit Investment Trusts, Face-Amount Certificate Offices
6732	Education, Religious & Charitable Trusts
6733	Trusts Except Educational, Religious & Charitable
6794	Patent Owners & Lessors
6798	Real Estate Investment Trusts
6799	Investors, NEC

70 HOTELS, ROOMING HOUSES, CAMPS, AND OTHER LODGING PLACES

SIC NO	PRODUCT
7011	Hotels, Motels & Tourist Courts
7021	Rooming & Boarding Houses
7032	Sporting & Recreational Camps
7033	Trailer Parks & Camp Sites
7041	Membership-Basis Hotels

72 PERSONAL SERVICES

SIC NO	PRODUCT
7211	Power Laundries, Family & Commercial
7212	Garment Pressing & Cleaners' Agents
7213	Linen Sply
7215	Coin Operated Laundries & Cleaning
7216	Dry Cleaning Plants, Except Rug Cleaning
7217	Carpet & Upholstery Cleaning
7218	Industrial Launderers
7219	Laundry & Garment Svcs, NEC
7221	Photographic Studios, Portrait
7231	Beauty Shops
7241	Barber Shops
7261	Funeral Svcs & Crematories
7291	Tax Return Preparation Svcs
7299	Miscellaneous Personal Svcs, NEC

73 BUSINESS SERVICES

SIC NO	PRODUCT
7311	Advertising Agencies
7312	Outdoor Advertising Svcs
7313	Radio, TV & Publishers Adv Reps
7319	Advertising, NEC
7322	Adjustment & Collection Svcs
7323	Credit Reporting Svcs
7331	Direct Mail Advertising Svcs
7334	Photocopying & Duplicating Svcs
7335	Commercial Photography
7336	Commercial Art & Graphic Design
7338	Secretarial & Court Reporting Svcs
7342	Disinfecting & Pest Control Svcs
7349	Building Cleaning & Maintenance Svcs, NEC
7352	Medical Eqpt Rental & Leasing
7353	Heavy Construction Eqpt Rental & Leasing
7359	Equipment Rental & Leasing, NEC
7361	Employment Agencies
7363	Help Supply Svcs
7371	Custom Computer Programming Svcs
7372	Prepackaged Software
7373	Computer Integrated Systems Design
7374	Data & Computer Processing & Preparation
7375	Information Retrieval Svcs
7376	Computer Facilities Management Svcs
7377	Computer Rental & Leasing
7378	Computer Maintenance & Repair
7379	Computer Related Svcs, NEC
7381	Detective & Armored Car Svcs
7382	Security Systems Svcs
7383	News Syndicates
7384	Photofinishing Labs
7389	Business Svcs, NEC

75 AUTOMOTIVE REPAIR, SERVICES, AND PARKING

SIC NO	PRODUCT
7513	Truck Rental & Leasing, Without Drivers
7514	Passenger Car Rental
7515	Passenger Car Leasing
7519	Utility Trailers & Recreational Vehicle Rental
7521	Automobile Parking Lots & Garages
7532	Top, Body & Upholstery Repair & Paint Shops
7533	Automotive Exhaust System Repair Shops
7534	Tire Retreading & Repair Shops
7536	Automotive Glass Replacement Shops
7537	Automotive Transmission Repair Shops
7538	General Automotive Repair Shop
7539	Automotive Repair Shops, NEC
7542	Car Washes
7549	Automotive Svcs, Except Repair & Car Washes

76 MISCELLANEOUS REPAIR SERVICES

SIC NO	PRODUCT
7622	Radio & TV Repair Shops
7623	Refrigeration & Air Conditioning Svc & Repair Shop
7629	Electrical & Elex Repair Shop, NEC
7631	Watch, Clock & Jewelry Repair
7641	Reupholstery & Furniture Repair
7692	Welding Repair
7694	Armature Rewinding Shops
7699	Repair Shop & Related Svcs, NEC

78 MOTION PICTURES

SIC NO	PRODUCT
7812	Motion Picture & Video Tape Production
7819	Services Allied To Motion Picture Prdtn
7822	Motion Picture & Video Tape Distribution
7829	Services Allied To Motion Picture Distribution
7832	Motion Picture Theaters, Except Drive-In
7841	Video Tape Rental

79 AMUSEMENT AND RECREATION SERVICES

SIC NO	PRODUCT
7911	Dance Studios, Schools & Halls
7922	Theatrical Producers & Misc Theatrical Svcs
7929	Bands, Orchestras, Actors & Entertainers
7933	Bowling Centers
7941	Professional Sports Clubs & Promoters
7948	Racing & Track Operations
7991	Physical Fitness Facilities
7992	Public Golf Courses
7993	Coin-Operated Amusement Devices & Arcades
7996	Amusement Parks
7997	Membership Sports & Recreation Clubs
7999	Amusement & Recreation Svcs, NEC

80 HEALTH SERVICES

SIC NO	PRODUCT
8011	Offices & Clinics Of Doctors Of Medicine
8021	Offices & Clinics Of Dentists
8031	Offices & Clinics Of Doctors Of Osteopathy
8041	Offices & Clinics Of Chiropractors
8042	Offices & Clinics Of Optometrists
8043	Offices & Clinics Of Podiatrists
8049	Offices & Clinics Of Health Practitioners, NEC
8051	Skilled Nursing Facilities
8052	Intermediate Care Facilities
8059	Nursing & Personal Care Facilities, NEC
8062	General Medical & Surgical Hospitals
8063	Psychiatric Hospitals
8069	Specialty Hospitals, Except Psychiatric
8071	Medical Laboratories
8072	Dental Laboratories
8082	Home Health Care Svcs
8092	Kidney Dialysis Centers
8093	Specialty Outpatient Facilities, NEC
8099	Health & Allied Svcs, NEC

81 LEGAL SERVICES

SIC NO	PRODUCT
8111	Legal Svcs

83 SOCIAL SERVICES

SIC NO	PRODUCT
8322	Individual & Family Social Svcs
8331	Job Training & Vocational Rehabilitation Svcs
8351	Child Day Care Svcs
8361	Residential Care
8399	Social Services, NEC

84 MUSEUMS, ART GALLERIES, AND BOTANICAL AND ZOOLOGICAL GARDENS

SIC NO	PRODUCT
8412	Museums & Art Galleries
8422	Arboreta, Botanical & Zoological Gardens

86 MEMBERSHIP ORGANIZATIONS

SIC NO	PRODUCT
8611	Business Associations
8621	Professional Membership Organizations
8631	Labor Unions & Similar Organizations
8641	Civic, Social & Fraternal Associations
8651	Political Organizations
8699	Membership Organizations, NEC

87 ENGINEERING, ACCOUNTING, RESEARCH, MANAGEMENT, AND RELATED SERVICES

SIC NO	PRODUCT
8711	Engineering Services
8712	Architectural Services
8713	Surveying Services
8721	Accounting, Auditing & Bookkeeping Svcs
8731	Commercial Physical & Biological Research
8732	Commercial Economic, Sociological & Educational Research
8733	Noncommercial Research Organizations
8734	Testing Laboratories
8741	Management Services
8742	Management Consulting Services
8743	Public Relations Svcs
8744	Facilities Support Mgmt Svcs
8748	Business Consulting Svcs, NEC

89 SERVICES, NOT ELSEWHERE CLASSIFIED

SIC NO	PRODUCT
8999	Services Not Elsewhere Classified

SIC SECTION

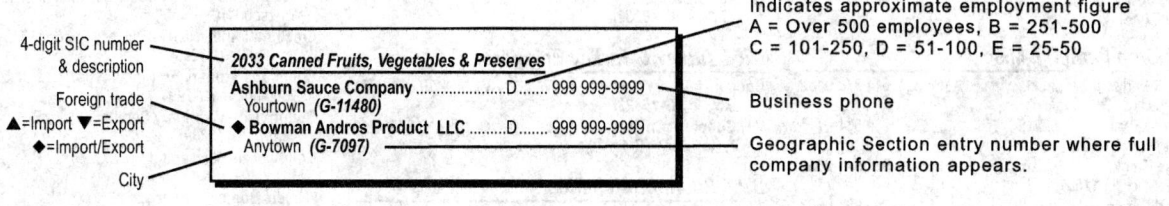

- See footnotes for symbols and codes identification.
- The SIC codes in this section are from the latest Standard Industrial Classification manual published by the U.S. Government's Office of Management and Budget. For more information regarding SICs, see the Explanatory Notes.
- Companies may be listed under multiple classifications.

01 AGRICULTURAL PRODUCTION-CROPS

0111 Wheat

Demmy Sand and Gravel LLC .... E 937 325-8840
  Springfield *(G-17189)*
Molyet Crop Production Inc .... E 419 992-4288
  Tiffin *(G-17688)*
Schlessman Seed Co .... E 419 499-2572
  Milan *(G-14499)*
Stokes Fruit Farm .... E 937 382-4004
  Wilmington *(G-19788)*

0115 Corn

Demmy Sand and Gravel LLC .... E 937 325-8840
  Springfield *(G-17189)*
George Darr .... E 740 498-5400
  Newcomerstown *(G-15269)*
Hartung Brothers Inc .... E 419 352-3000
  Bowling Green *(G-1780)*
Molyet Crop Production Inc .... E 419 992-4288
  Tiffin *(G-17688)*
Schlessman Seed Co .... E 419 499-2572
  Milan *(G-14499)*
Stokes Fruit Farm .... E 937 382-4004
  Wilmington *(G-19788)*
Tom Langhals .... E 419 659-5629
  Columbus Grove *(G-9031)*

0116 Soybeans

George Darr .... E 740 498-5400
  Newcomerstown *(G-15269)*
Molyet Crop Production Inc .... E 419 992-4288
  Tiffin *(G-17688)*
Schlessman Seed Co .... E 419 499-2572
  Milan *(G-14499)*

0119 Cash Grains, NEC

Ayers Farms Inc .... E 419 938-7707
  Perrysville *(G-16077)*
Demmy Sand and Gravel LLC .... E 937 325-8840
  Springfield *(G-17189)*
Douglas Walcher Farms .... D 419 744-2427
  North Fairfield *(G-15380)*
Hertzfeld Poultry Farms Inc .... D 419 832-2070
  Grand Rapids *(G-11450)*
McMaster Farms .... D 330 482-2913
  Columbiana *(G-6861)*
Movers and Shuckers LLC .... E 740 263-2164
  Mount Vernon *(G-14915)*

0134 Irish Potatoes

John F Stambaugh & Co .... E 419 687-6833
  Plymouth *(G-16217)*
McMaster Farms .... D 330 482-2913
  Columbiana *(G-6861)*

0161 Vegetables & Melons

Brenckle Farms Inc .... E 330 877-4426
  Hartville *(G-11815)*
Buurma Farms Incorporated .... E 419 935-6411
  Willard *(G-19617)*
Douglas Walcher Farms .... D 419 744-2427
  North Fairfield *(G-15380)*
George Darr .... E 740 498-5400
  Newcomerstown *(G-15269)*
George Knick .... E 937 548-2832
  Greenville *(G-11502)*
Hirzel Farms Inc .... E 419 837-2710
  Luckey *(G-13183)*
Holthouse Farms of Ohio Inc .... C 419 935-1041
  Willard *(G-19620)*
John F Stambaugh & Co .... E 419 687-6833
  Plymouth *(G-16217)*
McMaster Farms .... D 330 482-2913
  Columbiana *(G-6861)*
Molyet Crop Production Inc .... E 419 992-4288
  Tiffin *(G-17688)*
Rothert Farm Inc .... E 419 467-0095
  Elmore *(G-10589)*
Suter Produce Inc .... D 419 384-3665
  Pandora *(G-15894)*
White Pond Gardens Inc .... E 330 836-2727
  Akron *(G-509)*

0171 Berry Crops

James Recker .... E 419 837-5378
  Genoa *(G-11380)*
Stokes Fruit Farm .... E 937 382-4004
  Wilmington *(G-19788)*
Suter Produce Inc .... D 419 384-3665
  Pandora *(G-15894)*

0172 Grapes

Ferrante Wine Farm Inc .... E 440 466-8466
  Geneva *(G-11361)*
Mapleside Valley LLC .... C 330 225-5576
  Brunswick *(G-1987)*

0175 Deciduous Tree Fruits

Bauman Orchards Inc .... E 330 925-6861
  Rittman *(G-16551)*
George Darr .... E 740 498-5400
  Newcomerstown *(G-15269)*
Irons Fruit Farm .... E 513 932-2853
  Lebanon *(G-12614)*
Mac Queen Orchards Inc .... E 419 865-2916
  Holland *(G-12034)*
Mapleside Valley LLC .... C 330 225-5576
  Brunswick *(G-1987)*
Quality Plant Productions Inc .... E 440 526-8711
  Richfield *(G-16523)*
Scenic Ridge Fruit Farms .... E 419 368-3353
  Jeromesville *(G-12334)*
White House Fruit Farm Inc .... E 330 533-4161
  Canfield *(G-2215)*

0181 Ornamental Floriculture & Nursery Prdts

A Brown & Sons Nursery .... E 937 836-5826
  Brookville *(G-1958)*
▲ Acorn Farms Inc .... C 614 891-9348
  Galena *(G-11277)*
▲ Aris Horticulture Inc .... D 330 745-2143
  Barberton *(G-953)*
Barnes Nursery Inc .... E 800 421-8722
  Huron *(G-12161)*
Beroske Farms & Greenhouse Inc .... E 419 826-4547
  Delta *(G-10156)*
Cottage Gardens Inc .... D 440 259-2900
  Perry *(G-15960)*
▲ Cuthbert Greenhouse Inc .... E 614 836-3866
  Groveport *(G-11631)*
Davey Tree Expert Company .... C 330 673-9511
  Kent *(G-12363)*
Deckers Nursery Inc .... E 614 836-2130
  Groveport *(G-11632)*
▲ Dummen Na Inc .... D 614 850-9551
  Columbus *(G-7550)*
◆ Green Circle Growers Inc .... C 440 775-1411
  Oberlin *(G-15644)*
Green Circle Growers Inc .... B 440 775-1411
  Oberlin *(G-15645)*
Henderson Turf Farm Inc .... E 937 748-1559
  Franklin *(G-11158)*
Hirts Greenhouse Inc .... E 440 238-8200
  Strongsville *(G-17470)*
HJ Benken Flor & Greenhouses .... D 513 891-1040
  Cincinnati *(G-3772)*
Jeff Creque Farms Inc .... E 419 829-2941
  Sylvania *(G-15596)*
K W Zellers & Son Inc .... E 330 877-9371
  Hartville *(G-11825)*
Knollwood Florists Inc .... E 937 426-0861
  Beavercreek *(G-1183)*
▲ Lakewood Greenhouse Inc .... E 419 691-3541
  Northwood *(G-15535)*
Lowes Greenhouse & Gift Shop .... E 440 543-5123
  Chagrin Falls *(G-2722)*
Maria Gardens Inc .... E 440 238-7637
  Strongsville *(G-17489)*
Mike Ward Landscaping Inc .... E 513 683-6436
  Maineville *(G-13244)*
North Branch Nursery Inc .... E 419 287-4679
  Pemberville *(G-15942)*
Pennington Seed Inc .... D 513 642-8980
  Fairfield *(G-10894)*
Quality Plant Productions Inc .... E 440 526-8711
  Richfield *(G-16523)*
R & S Halley & Co Inc .... E 614 771-0388
  Hilliard *(G-11947)*
Ridge Manor Nuseries Inc .... C 440 466-5781
  Madison *(G-13235)*
Rosby Brothers Inc .... E 216 351-0850
  Cleveland *(G-6411)*
Scarffs Nursery Inc .... C 937 845-3130
  New Carlisle *(G-15031)*
▲ Schmidt Bros Inc .... E 419 826-3671
  Swanton *(G-17571)*
Schusters Greenhouse Ltd .... E 440 235-2440
  Cleveland *(G-6450)*
Studebaker Nurseries Inc .... D 800 845-0584
  New Carlisle *(G-15032)*
Sunny Border Ohio Inc .... D 440 858-9660
  Jefferson *(G-12332)*
▲ Thorsens Greenhouse LLC .... E 740 363-5069
  Delaware *(G-10129)*
Wade & Gatton Nurseries .... D 419 883-3191
  Bellville *(G-1427)*
White Pond Gardens Inc .... E 330 836-2727
  Akron *(G-509)*
Whiteford Greenhouse .... E 419 882-4110
  Toledo *(G-18308)*
▲ Willoway Nurseries Inc .... C 440 934-4435
  Avon *(G-920)*
▲ Willowbend Nurseries LLC .... C 440 259-3121
  Perry *(G-15968)*
Wilsons Hillview Farm Inc .... E 740 763-2873
  Newark *(G-15247)*

0182 Food Crops Grown Under Cover

Cover Crop Shop LLC .... D 937 417-3972
  Sidney *(G-16927)*
Nature Fresh Farms Usa Inc .... E 419 330-5080
  Delta *(G-10161)*

01 AGRICULTURAL PRODUCTION-CROPS

Sunny Border Ohio Inc .... D 440 858-9660
  Jefferson (G-12332)
White Pond Gardens Inc .... E 330 836-2727
  Akron (G-509)

0191 Crop Farming, Misc

Circle S Farms Inc .... E 614 878-9462
  Grove City (G-11546)
Deerfield Farms .... E 330 584-4715
  Deerfield (G-10018)
George Knick .... E 937 548-2832
  Greenville (G-11502)
Heimerl Farms Ltd .... E 740 967-0063
  Johnstown (G-12340)
Henderson Turf Farm Inc .... E 937 748-1559
  Franklin (G-11158)
Herb Thyme Farms Inc .... B 866 386-0854
  Perrysburg (G-16011)
Hertzfeld Poultry Farms Inc .... D 419 832-2070
  Grand Rapids (G-11450)
Holthouse Farms of Ohio Inc .... C 419 935-1041
  Willard (G-19620)
Jeff Creque Farms Inc .... E 419 829-2941
  Sylvania (G-17596)
Kunkle Farm Limited .... D 419 237-2748
  Alvordton (G-570)
Ringler Inc .... E 419 253-5300
  Marengo (G-13426)
Rk Family Inc .... C 419 443-1663
  Tiffin (G-17695)
Rohrs Farms .... E 419 757-0110
  Mc Guffey (G-14025)
Suter Produce Inc .... D 419 384-3665
  Pandora (G-15894)

02 AGRICULTURAL PRODUCTION-LIVESTOCK AND ANIMAL SPECIALTIES

0211 Beef Cattle Feedlots

Ayers Farms Inc .... E 419 938-7707
  Perrysville (G-16077)
Dairy Farmers America Inc .... E 330 670-7800
  Medina (G-14057)

0213 Hogs

Robert Winner Sons Inc .... E 419 582-4321
  Yorkshire (G-20092)

0241 Dairy Farms

Ayers Farms Inc .... E 419 938-7707
  Perrysville (G-16077)
Bridgewater Dairy LLC .... E 419 485-8157
  Montpelier (G-14738)
Calvary Christian Ch of Ohio .... E 740 828-9000
  Frazeysburg (G-11174)
Dovin Dairy Farms LLC .... E 440 653-7009
  Oberlin (G-15642)
Falling Star Farm Ltd .... E 419 945-2651
  Polk (G-16230)
▲ Miceli Dairy Products Co .... D 216 791-6222
  Cleveland (G-6045)
National All-Jersey Inc .... E 614 861-3636
  Reynoldsburg (G-16470)
Smithfoods Orrville Inc .... E 740 389-4643
  Marion (G-13580)
Springdale Ice Cream Beverage .... E 513 699-4984
  Cincinnati (G-4567)
Stoll Farms Inc .... E 330 682-5786
  Marshallville (G-13598)
Youngs Jersey Dairy Inc .... B 937 325-0629
  Yellow Springs (G-20091)

0251 Chicken & Poultry Farms

Chicn Fixins Inc .... E 614 929-8431
  Columbus (G-7257)

0252 Chicken Egg Farms

Cal-Maine Foods Inc .... E 937 337-9576
  Rossburg (G-16604)
Cal-Maine Foods Inc .... E 937 968-4874
  Union City (G-18500)
▲ Heartland Quality Egg Farm ...... E 937 355-5103
  West Mansfield (G-19266)
Ohio Fresh Eggs LLC .... E 937 354-2233
  Mount Victory (G-14929)

▲ Weaver Bros Inc .... D 937 526-3907
  Versailles (G-18731)
Weaver Bros Inc .... E 937 526-4777
  Versailles (G-18732)

0253 Turkey & Turkey Egg Farms

Cooper Hatchery Inc .... C 419 594-3325
  Oakwood (G-15623)
V H Cooper & Co Inc .... C 419 375-4116
  Fort Recovery (G-11120)

0254 Poultry Hatcheries

Cooper Hatchery Inc .... C 419 594-3325
  Oakwood (G-15623)
Cuddy Farms Inc .... E 740 599-7979
  Danville (G-9246)
Midwest Poultry Services Lp .... E 419 375-4417
  Fort Recovery (G-11119)
Select Genetics LLC .... E 740 599-7979
  Danville (G-9247)

07 AGRICULTURAL SERVICES

0711 Soil Preparation Svcs

Blanchard Tree and Lawn Inc .... D 419 865-7071
  Holland (G-12011)
Clark Royster Inc .... E 740 335-3810
  Wshngtn CT Hs (G-20015)
Henderson Turf Farm Inc .... E 937 748-1559
  Franklin (G-11158)
S & D Application LLC .... E 419 288-3660
  Wayne (G-18978)

0721 Soil Preparation, Planting & Cultivating Svc

Georgetown Vineyards Inc .... E 740 435-3222
  Cambridge (G-2115)

0723 Crop Preparation, Except Cotton Ginning

◆ Andersons Inc .... C 419 893-5050
  Maumee (G-13879)
Case Farms LLC .... C 330 832-0030
  Massillon (G-13793)
Custom Agri Systems Inc .... E 419 209-0940
  Upper Sandusky (G-18559)
Freshealth LLC .... E 614 231-3601
  Columbus (G-7704)
Great Lakes Packers Inc .... E 419 483-2956
  Bellevue (G-1411)
Movers and Shuckers LLC .... E 740 263-2164
  Mount Vernon (G-14915)
Ohigro Inc .... E 740 726-2429
  Waldo (G-18783)
Schlessman Seed Co .... E 419 499-2572
  Milan (G-14499)

0724 Cotton Ginning

▼ Compass Systems & Sales LLC ... D 330 733-2111
  Norton (G-15555)

0741 Veterinary Livestock Svcs

Howland Corners Twn & Ctry Vet .... E 330 856-1862
  Warren (G-18864)

0742 Veterinary Animal Specialties

Amherst Animal Hospital Inc .... E 440 282-5220
  Amherst (G-585)
Animal Care Unlimited Inc .... E 614 766-2317
  Columbus (G-7021)
Animal Hospital Inc .... E 440 946-2800
  Willoughby Hills (G-19728)
Animal Hospital Polaris LLC .... E 614 888-4050
  Lewis Center (G-12666)
Animal Protective League .... E 216 771-4616
  Cleveland (G-5039)
Annehurst Veterinary Hospital ...... E 614 818-4221
  Westerville (G-19363)
Avon Lake Animal Clinic Inc .... E 440 933-5297
  Avon Lake (G-922)
Beechmont Pet Hospital Inc .... E 513 232-0300
  Cincinnati (G-3090)
Beechwold Veterinary Hospital ..... E 614 268-8666
  Columbus (G-7097)
Beechwold Veterinary Hospital ..... E 614 766-1222
  Dublin (G-10260)

Bigger Road Veterinary Clinic .... E 937 435-3262
  Dayton (G-9357)
Cedar Creek Vterinary Svcs Inc .... E 740 467-2949
  Millersport (G-14630)
Cincinnati Anml Rfrrl .... D 513 530-0911
  Cincinnati (G-3280)
Columbus Vtrinary Emrgncy Svcs ... E 614 846-5800
  Worthington (G-19948)
Countryside Veterinary Service ..... E 330 847-7337
  Warren (G-18839)
County Animal Hospital .... E 513 398-8000
  Mason (G-13690)
Daniels Boarding Kennels .... E 440 238-7179
  Strongsville (G-17455)
Dayton Animal Hospital Assoc ...... E 937 890-4744
  Dayton (G-9456)
Detroit Dover Animals Hospital ..... E 440 871-5220
  Cleveland (G-5478)
Eastgate Animal Hospital Inc .... E 513 528-0700
  Cincinnati (G-3537)
Gahanna Animal Hospital Inc .... E 614 471-2201
  Gahanna (G-11243)
Grady Veterinary Hospital Inc .... E 513 931-8675
  Cincinnati (G-3691)
High Point Animal Hospital .... E 419 865-3611
  Maumee (G-13926)
Howland Corners Twn & Ctry Vet .... E 330 856-1862
  Warren (G-18864)
Kettering Animal Hospital Inc .... E 937 294-5211
  Dayton (G-9651)
Knapp Veterinary Hospital Inc ...... E 614 267-3124
  Columbus (G-8001)
Medvet Associates Inc .... B 937 293-2714
  Moraine (G-14804)
Medvet Associates Inc .... A 614 846-5800
  Worthington (G-19976)
Metropltan Vterinary Med Group ... E 330 253-2544
  Copley (G-9061)
Michael T Lee Dvm .... E 330 722-5076
  Medina (G-14105)
Midpark Animal Hospital .... E 216 362-6622
  Cleveland (G-6058)
National Veterinary Assoc Inc .... D 330 652-0055
  Niles (G-15298)
North Ridge Veterinary Hosp .... E 440 428-5166
  Madison (G-13234)
Ohio State University .... C 614 292-6661
  Columbus (G-8428)
Paws Inn Inc .... E 937 435-1500
  Dayton (G-9805)
Petsmart Inc .... D 614 418-9389
  Columbus (G-8540)
Riverside Drv Animal Care Ctr ..... E 614 414-2668
  Dublin (G-10441)
RMS Aquaculture Inc .... E 216 433-1340
  Cleveland (G-6401)
Shawnee Animal Clinic Inc .... E 740 353-5758
  Portsmouth (G-16309)
South Mill Pet Care Center .... E 330 758-6479
  Youngstown (G-20377)
Steven L Sawdai .... E 513 829-3830
  Fairfield (G-10911)
Stow-Kent Animal Hospital Inc ..... E 330 673-0049
  Kent (G-12396)
Stow-Kent Animal Hospital Inc ..... E 330 673-1002
  Kent (G-12397)
Suburban Veterinarian Clinic .... E 937 433-2160
  Dayton (G-9912)
Sylvania Veterinary Hospital .... E 419 885-4421
  Sylvania (G-17620)
Tipp City Veterinary Hosp Inc .... D 937 667-8489
  Tipp City (G-17728)
Tri Zob Inc .... E 216 252-4500
  Cleveland (G-6616)
VCA Animal Hospitals Inc .... E 419 423-7232
  Findlay (G-11098)
VCA Green Animal Medical Ctr .... E 330 896-4040
  Uniontown (G-18542)
Veterinary RFRrl&emer Ctr of .... E 330 665-4996
  Copley (G-9068)
Vma Inc .... E 614 475-7300
  Gahanna (G-11274)
Woodland Run Equin Vet Facilty ... E 614 871-4919
  Grove City (G-11619)

0751 Livestock Svcs, Except Veterinary

D H I Cooperative Inc .... D 614 545-0460
  Columbus (G-7479)
Hertzfeld Poultry Farms Inc .... D 419 832-2070
  Grand Rapids (G-11450)

SIC SECTION 07 AGRICULTURAL SERVICES

Landes Fresh Meats Inc ....E 937 836-3613
Clayton (G-4912)
Poultry Service Associates ....E 937 968-3339
Dayton (G-9248)
Robert Winner Sons Inc ....E 419 582-4321
Yorkshire (G-20092)
Rubin Erb ....E 330 852-4423
Sugarcreek (G-17547)

0752 Animal Specialty Svcs, Exc Veterinary

4 Paws Sake Inc ....E 419 304-7139
Grand Rapids (G-11447)
Anark Inc ....E 513 825-7387
Cincinnati (G-3021)
Animal Care Unlimited Inc ....E 614 766-2317
Columbus (G-7021)
Annehurst Veterinary Hospital ....E 614 818-4221
Westerville (G-19363)
Avon Lake Animal Clinic Inc ....E 440 933-5297
Avon Lake (G-922)
Barkley of Cleveland LLC ....E 440 248-2275
Chagrin Falls (G-2690)
Birchwood Genetics Inc ....E 937 678-9313
West Manchester (G-19265)
Cleveland All Breed Trning CLB ....D 216 398-1118
Cleveland (G-5290)
Coba/Select Sires Inc ....D 614 878-5333
Columbus (G-7312)
Csa Animal Nutrition LLC ....E 866 615-8084
Dayton (G-9447)
Dayton Animal Hospital Assoc ....E 937 890-4744
Dayton (G-9456)
Dayton Dog Training Club Inc ....E 937 293-5219
Moraine (G-14769)
Foxridge Farms Corp ....E 740 965-1369
Galena (G-11282)
Kettering Animal Hospital Inc ....E 937 294-5211
Dayton (G-9651)
Lake Erie Nature & Science Ctr ....E 440 871-2900
Bay Village (G-1040)
◆ Miraclecorp Products ....D 937 293-9994
Moraine (G-14808)
Orville Pet Spa & Resort ....E 330 683-3335
Orrville (G-15781)
Park Pet and Play LLC ....E 877 907-6222
Mentor (G-14227)
Paws Inn Inc ....E 937 435-1500
Dayton (G-9805)
Pet Central Lodge & Grooming ....E 440 282-1811
Amherst (G-601)
Petsmart Inc ....E 419 423-6869
Findlay (G-11075)
Petsmart Inc ....E 614 433-9361
Columbus (G-6900)
Petsmart Inc ....E 419 747-4544
Ontario (G-15711)
Petsmart Inc ....E 419 865-3941
Holland (G-12045)
Petsmart Inc ....E 513 336-0365
Mason (G-13746)
Petsmart Inc ....E 513 248-4954
Milford (G-14553)
Petsmart Inc ....E 513 752-8463
Cincinnati (G-2928)
Petsmart Inc ....E 937 236-1335
Huber Heights (G-12098)
Petsmart Inc ....D 614 418-9389
Columbus (G-8540)
Petsmart Inc ....E 330 922-4114
Cuyahoga Falls (G-9212)
Petsmart Inc ....E 330 629-2479
Youngstown (G-20318)
Petsmart Inc ....E 330 544-1499
Niles (G-15303)
Petsmart Inc ....E 614 497-3001
Groveport (G-11661)
Petsmart Inc ....E 440 974-1100
Mentor (G-14228)
Petsuites of America Inc ....E 513 554-4408
Cincinnati (G-4288)
Puppy Pals Rescue Inc ....E 937 426-2643
Beavercreek (G-1200)
Pups Paradise ....E 419 873-6115
Perrysburg (G-16047)
Red Dog Pet Resort & Spa ....E 513 733-3647
Cincinnati (G-4396)
Reptiles By Mack LLC ....E 937 372-9570
Xenia (G-20073)
Skyview Baptist Ranch Inc ....E 330 674-7511
Millersburg (G-14622)
South Mill Pet Care Center ....E 330 758-6479
Youngstown (G-20377)

0761 Farm Labor Contractors & Crew Leaders

Movers and Shuckers LLC ....E 740 263-2164
Mount Vernon (G-14915)

0781 Landscape Counseling & Planning

Aaron Landscape Inc ....E 440 838-8875
North Royalton (G-15479)
▲ Acro Tool & Die Company ....D 330 773-5173
Akron (G-17)
Bg Holding LLC ....A 513 489-1023
Blue Ash (G-1543)
Bladecutters Lawn Service Inc ....E 937 274-3861
Dayton (G-9360)
Blanchard Tree and Lawn Inc ....D 419 865-7071
Holland (G-12011)
Blendon Gardens Inc ....E 614 840-0500
Lewis Center (G-12670)
Brightview Landscape Svcs Inc ....E 614 801-1712
Columbus (G-7139)
Brightview Landscape Svcs Inc ....D 614 478-2085
Columbus (G-7140)
Brightview Landscape Svcs Inc ....D 740 369-4800
Columbus (G-7141)
Brightview Landscapes LLC ....E 937 235-9595
Dayton (G-9366)
Brightview Landscapes LLC ....D 513 874-6484
West Chester (G-19194)
Brightview Landscapes LLC ....E 216 398-1289
Oakwood Village (G-15626)
Brightview Landscapes LLC ....E 440 937-5126
Avon (G-882)
Brightview Landscapes LLC ....E 301 987-9200
Columbus (G-7142)
Brightview Landscapes LLC ....D 614 276-5500
Columbus (G-7143)
Brightview Landscapes LLC ....E 440 729-2302
Chesterland (G-2793)
Brightview Landscapes LLC ....D 614 741-8233
New Albany (G-14975)
▲ Buckeye Landscape Service Inc ....D 614 866-0088
Blacklick (G-1501)
Bzak Landscaping Inc ....E 513 831-0907
Milford (G-14508)
Civil & Environmental Cons Inc ....E 513 985-0226
Milford (G-14512)
Collaborative Inc ....E 419 242-7405
Toledo (G-17819)
Country Gardens ....E 740 522-8810
Granville (G-11463)
Custom Lawn Care & Ldscpg LLC ....E 740 333-1669
Wshngtn CT Hs (G-20019)
Dayton City Parks Golf Maint ....E 937 333-3378
Dayton (G-9466)
Detillion Landscaping Co Inc ....E 740 775-5305
Chillicothe (G-2835)
Eastside Landscaping Inc ....E 216 381-0070
Cleveland (G-5522)
Eastside Nursery Inc ....E 513 934-1661
Lebanon (G-12602)
Edwards Land Clearing Inc ....E 440 988-4477
Amherst (G-592)
Family Entertainment Services ....D 740 286-8587
Jackson (G-12311)
Five Seasons Landscape MGT Inc ....D 740 964-2915
Etna (G-10728)
Floralandscape Inc ....D 419 536-7640
Toledo (G-17897)
Garmann/Miller & Assoc Inc ....E 419 628-4240
Minster (G-14662)
Green Impressions LLC ....E 440 240-8508
Sheffield Village (G-16886)
Greenpro Services Inc ....E 937 748-1559
Franklin (G-11156)
Greenscapes Landscape Company ....D 614 837-1869
Columbus (G-7778)
H A M Landscaping Inc ....E 216 663-6666
Cleveland (G-5714)
Hemlock Landscapes Inc ....E 440 247-3631
Chagrin Falls (G-2719)
HWH Archtcts-Ngnrs-Plnners Inc ....D 216 875-4000
Cleveland (G-5794)
Impullitti Landscaping Inc ....E 440 834-1866
Burton (G-2063)
Joes Ldscpg Beavercreek Inc ....E 937 427-1133
Beavercreek Township (G-1272)
Kleingers Group Inc ....D 513 779-7851
West Chester (G-19103)
Knollwood Florists Inc ....E 937 426-0861
Beavercreek (G-1184)
Lanhan Contractors Inc ....E 440 918-1099
Willoughby (G-19684)
Lifestyle Landscaping Inc ....E 440 353-0333
North Ridgeville (G-15468)
Louderback Fmly Invstments Inc ....E 937 845-1762
New Carlisle (G-15026)
Madison Tree & Landscape Co ....E 614 207-5422
West Jefferson (G-19254)
Maslyk Landscaping Inc ....E 440 748-3635
Columbia Station (G-6849)
Mc Clurg & Creamer Inc ....E 419 866-7080
Holland (G-12036)
McGill Smith Punshon Inc ....E 513 759-0004
Cincinnati (G-4036)
Meyers Ldscp Svcs & Nurs Inc ....E 614 210-1194
Lewis Center (G-12695)
Mortons Lawn Service Inc ....E 440 236-3550
Columbia Station (G-6850)
Myers Industries Inc ....D 440 632-0230
Middlefield (G-14398)
Myers/Schmalenberger Inc ....E 614 621-2796
Columbus (G-8211)
Natorps Inc ....D 513 398-4769
Mason (G-13742)
Norvell Landscaping Inc ....E 513 423-9009
Middletown (G-14443)
▲ Oakland Nursery Inc ....E 614 268-3834
Columbus (G-8310)
Oasis Turf & Tree Inc ....E 513 697-9090
Loveland (G-13150)
Oberlanders Tree & Ldscp Ltd ....E 419 562-8733
Bucyrus (G-2045)
Ohio Valley Group Inc ....E 440 543-0500
Chagrin Falls (G-2727)
Pattie Group Inc ....D 440 338-1288
Novelty (G-15603)
Personal Lawn Care Inc ....E 440 934-5296
Avon (G-913)
Rentokil North America Inc ....E 614 837-0099
Groveport (G-11666)
Scarffs Nursery Inc ....C 937 845-3130
New Carlisle (G-15031)
Schill Landscaping and Lawn CA ....D 440 327-3030
North Ridgeville (G-15477)
Schoenbrunn Landscaping Inc ....E 330 364-3688
Dover (G-10211)
Seacrist Landscaping and Cnstr ....E 440 946-2731
Mentor (G-14240)
Southside Envmtl Group LLC ....E 330 299-0027
Niles (G-15306)
Spellacys Turf-Lawn Inc ....E 740 965-5508
Galena (G-11287)
Suncrest Gardens Inc ....C 330 650-4969
Peninsula (G-15951)
Thornton Landscape Inc ....E 513 683-8100
Maineville (G-13247)
Tim Mundy ....E 937 862-8686
Spring Valley (G-17111)
Todds Enviroscapes Inc ....E 330 875-0768
Louisville (G-13107)
Vance Property Management LLC ....D 419 467-9548
Toledo (G-18287)
Yardmaster of Columbus Inc ....E 614 863-4510
Blacklick (G-1513)

0782 Lawn & Garden Svcs

A Ressler Inc ....E 216 518-1804
Cleveland (G-4935)
Abbruzzese Brothers Inc ....E 614 873-1550
Plain City (G-16180)
Able Contracting Group Inc ....E 440 951-0880
Painesville (G-15832)
Ameriscape Inc ....E 614 863-5400
Blacklick (G-1499)
Barnes Nursery Inc ....E 800 421-8722
Huron (G-12161)
Bauer Lawn Maintenance Inc ....E 419 893-5296
Maumee (G-13886)
Benchmark Landscape Cnstr Inc ....E 614 873-8080
Plain City (G-16183)
Berns Grnhse & Grdn Ctr Inc ....E 513 423-5306
Middletown (G-14418)
Bladecutters Lawn Service Inc ....E 937 274-3861
Dayton (G-9360)
Blanchard Tree and Lawn Inc ....D 419 865-7071
Holland (G-12011)

S I C

07 AGRICULTURAL SERVICES

Brian-Kyles Construction Inc .... E 440 242-0298
  Lorain (G-13019)
Brightview Landscapes LLC .... E 440 729-2302
  Chesterland (G-2793)
Brightview Landscapes LLC .... D 614 741-8233
  New Albany (G-14975)
Buck and Sons Landscape Svc .... E 614 876-5359
  Hilliard (G-11885)
▲ Buckeye Landscape Service Inc .... D 614 866-0088
  Blacklick (G-1501)
Bzak Landscaping Inc .... E 513 831-0907
  Milford (G-14508)
C & B Buck Bros Asp Maint LLC .... E 419 536-7325
  Toledo (G-17789)
Camco Inc .... E 740 477-3682
  Circleville (G-4881)
Castle Care .... E 440 327-3700
  North Ridgeville (G-15457)
Chores Unlimited Inc .... D 440 439-5455
  Bedford Heights (G-1350)
Como Inc .... E 614 830-2666
  Pickerington (G-16092)
County of Gallia .... E 740 446-2665
  Gallipolis (G-11312)
County of Portage .... D 330 296-6411
  Ravenna (G-16379)
County of Warren .... E 513 695-1109
  Lebanon (G-12599)
Croys Mowing LLC .... E 419 523-5884
  Ottawa (G-15797)
Davey Tree Expert Company .... E 330 628-1499
  Mogadore (G-14674)
Davey Tree Expert Company .... E 330 928-4911
  Stow (G-17361)
Davey Tree Expert Company .... D 614 471-4144
  Columbus (G-7490)
Davey Tree Expert Company .... E 513 575-1733
  Milford (G-14515)
Davey Tree Expert Company .... E 440 439-4770
  Cleveland (G-5465)
Davey Tree Expert Company .... C 330 673-9511
  Kent (G-12363)
Dennis Top Soil & Landscaping .... E 419 865-5656
  Toledo (G-17849)
Detillion Landscaping Co Inc .... E 740 775-5305
  Chillicothe (G-2835)
Disanto Companies .... E 440 442-0600
  Cleveland (G-5487)
Dta Inc .... E 419 529-2920
  Ontario (G-15687)
Eastside Nursery Inc .... E 513 934-1661
  Lebanon (G-12602)
Eds Tree & Turf .... E 740 881-5800
  Delaware (G-10092)
Envircare Lawn Landscacape LLC .... E 419 874-6779
  Perrysburg (G-16002)
Environmental MGT Svcs Inc .... E 614 876-9988
  Plain City (G-16190)
Enviroscapes .... E 330 875-0768
  Louisville (G-13100)
Fackler Country Gardens Inc .... E 740 522-3128
  Granville (G-11465)
Fast Eddys Grounds Maint LLC .... E 740 599-2955
  Mount Vernon (G-14896)
Floralandscape Inc .... D 419 536-7640
  Toledo (G-17897)
Forevergreen Lawn Care .... E 440 327-8987
  North Ridgeville (G-15464)
Fredericks Landscaping Inc .... E 513 821-9407
  Cincinnati (G-3647)
Gears Garden Center Inc .... E 513 931-3800
  Cincinnati (G-3665)
Grandmas Gardens Inc .... E 937 885-2973
  Waynesville (G-18982)
Green King Company Inc .... E 614 861-4132
  Reynoldsburg (G-16457)
Greenleaf Landscapes Inc .... D 740 373-1639
  Marietta (G-13449)
Greenscapes Landscape Company .... D 614 837-1869
  Columbus (G-7778)
Greentech Corporation .... E 937 339-4758
  Troy (G-18355)
Grizzly Golf Center Inc .... B 513 398-5200
  Mason (G-13712)
Groundsystems Inc .... E 800 570-0213
  Blue Ash (G-1605)
Groundsystems Inc .... E 937 903-5325
  Moraine (G-14793)
H A M Landscaping Inc .... E 216 663-6666
  Cleveland (G-5714)
Hemlock Landscapes Inc .... E 440 247-3631
  Chagrin Falls (G-2719)
Henderson Turf Farm Inc .... E 937 748-1559
  Franklin (G-11158)
Hopewell Industries Inc .... C 740 622-3563
  Coshocton (G-9107)
Hyde Park Ldscp & Tree Svc Inc .... E 513 731-1334
  Cincinnati (G-3803)
Igh II Inc .... E 419 874-3575
  Mansfield (G-13310)
Impullitti Landscaping Inc .... E 440 834-1866
  Burton (G-2063)
J Gilmore Design Limited .... E 330 638-8224
  Cortland (G-9076)
Keller Group Limited .... E 614 866-9551
  Columbus (G-7971)
Kgk Gardening Design Corp .... E 330 656-1709
  Hudson (G-12127)
Knollwood Florists Inc .... E 937 426-0861
  Beavercreek (G-1184)
Land Art Inc .... E 419 666-5296
  Perrysburg (G-16026)
Lewis Landscaping Inc .... E 330 666-2655
  Copley (G-9058)
Lockes Garden Center Inc .... E 440 774-6981
  Oberlin (G-15648)
M J Lanese Landscaping Inc .... E 440 942-3444
  Willoughby (G-19689)
Mc Clurg & Creamer Inc .... E 419 866-7080
  Holland (G-12036)
McCallisters Landscaping & Sup .... E 440 259-3348
  Perry (G-15964)
McCoy Landscape Services Inc .... E 740 375-2730
  Marion (G-13566)
Miami Valley Memory Grdns Assn .... E 937 885-7779
  Dayton (G-9736)
Mike Ward Landscaping Inc .... E 513 683-6436
  Maineville (G-13244)
MJ Design Associates Inc .... E 614 873-7333
  Plain City (G-16200)
Mortons Lawn Service Inc .... E 440 236-3550
  Columbia Station (G-6850)
▲ Motz Group Inc .... E 513 533-6452
  Cincinnati (G-4123)
Natrop Inc .... D 513 242-1375
  Cincinnati (G-4146)
North Branch Nursery Inc .... E 419 287-4679
  Pemberville (G-15942)
Ohio Mulch Supply Inc .... D 614 445-4455
  Columbus (G-8361)
Ohio Tpk & Infrastructure Comm .... E 419 826-4831
  Swanton (G-17569)
Ohio Tpk & Infrastructure Comm .... C 440 234-2081
  Berea (G-1466)
Pace Sankar Landscaping Inc .... E 330 343-0858
  Dover (G-10205)
Paramount Lawn Service Inc .... E 513 984-5200
  Loveland (G-13152)
Peabody Landscape Cnstr Inc .... D 614 488-2877
  Columbus (G-8526)
Personal Lawn Care Inc .... E 440 934-5296
  Avon (G-913)
Peter A Wimberg Company Inc .... E 513 271-2332
  Cincinnati (G-4284)
Prusa Inc .... E 330 688-8500
  Stow (G-17387)
R & S Halley & Co Inc .... E 614 771-0388
  Hilliard (G-11947)
R B Stout Inc .... E 330 666-8811
  Akron (G-403)
Richland Newhope Industries .... C 419 774-4400
  Mansfield (G-13358)
Richter Landscaping .... E 513 539-0300
  Monroe (G-14710)
Riepenhoff Landscape Ltd .... E 614 876-4683
  Hilliard (G-11950)
River City Furniture LLC .... D 513 612-7303
  West Chester (G-19141)
Robiden Inc .... E 513 421-0000
  Fairfield Township (G-10935)
Rwc Inc .... E 614 890-0600
  Westerville (G-19351)
Scherzinger Corp .... D 513 531-7848
  Cincinnati (G-4480)
Schill Landscaping and Lawn CA .... D 440 327-3030
  North Ridgeville (G-15477)
Schoenbrunn Landscaping Inc .... E 330 364-3688
  Dover (G-10211)
◆ Scotts Company LLC .... A 937 644-3729
  Marysville (G-13650)
▲ Scotts Miracle-Gro Company .... B 937 644-0011
  Marysville (G-13651)
Seacrist Landscaping and Cnstr .... E 440 946-2731
  Mentor (G-14240)
Sharp Edge LLC .... E 440 255-5917
  Mentor (G-14241)
Siebenthaler Company .... D 937 427-4110
  Dayton (G-9882)
South Star Corp .... E 330 239-5466
  Medina (G-14128)
Spellacys Turf-Lawn Inc .... E 740 965-5508
  Galena (G-11287)
Spray A Tree Inc .... E 614 457-8257
  Columbus (G-8764)
Suncrest Gardens Inc .... C 330 650-4969
  Peninsula (G-15951)
Supers Landscaping Inc .... E 440 775-0027
  Oberlin (G-15661)
T L C Landscaping Inc .... E 440 248-4852
  Cleveland (G-6565)
Team Green Lawn LLC .... E 937 673-4315
  Xenia (G-20078)
Tersigni Cargill Entps LLC .... E 330 351-0942
  Stow (G-17396)
Thomsons Landscaping .... E 740 374-9353
  Marietta (G-13504)
Thornton Landscape Inc .... E 513 683-8100
  Maineville (G-13247)
Tim Mundy .... E 937 862-8686
  Spring Valley (G-17111)
Toledo Memorial Pk & Mausoleum .... E 419 882-7151
  Sylvania (G-17624)
Trugreen Limited Partnership .... D 614 527-7070
  Hilliard (G-11961)
Trugreen Limited Partnership .... E 937 557-0060
  Springboro (G-17140)
Trugreen Limited Partnership .... E 419 884-3636
  Mansfield (G-13377)
Trugreen Limited Partnership .... D 440 786-7200
  Bedford (G-1342)
Trugreen Limited Partnership .... E 513 223-3707
  Fairfield (G-10918)
Trugreen Limited Partnership .... E 440 290-3340
  Mentor (G-14250)
Trugreen Limited Partnership .... C 614 285-3721
  Lewis Center (G-12708)
Trugreen Limited Partnership .... D 440 540-4209
  Elyria (G-10685)
Trugreen Limited Partnership .... E 419 516-4200
  Lima (G-12908)
Trugreen Limited Partnership .... E 614 610-4142
  Groveport (G-11679)
Trugreen Limited Partnership .... E 740 598-4724
  Brilliant (G-1869)
Trugreen Limited Partnership .... E 330 409-2861
  Canton (G-2565)
Trugreen Limited Partnership .... E 937 866-8399
  Dayton (G-9939)
Trugreen Limited Partnership .... D 937 410-4055
  Vandalia (G-18702)
Trugreen-Chem Lawn .... D 330 533-2839
  Poland (G-16229)
Turfscape Inc .... C 330 405-0741
  Twinsburg (G-18479)
Turnpike and Infrastructure Co .... D 330 527-2169
  Windham (G-19804)
Tuttle Landscaping & Grdn Ctr .... E 419 756-7555
  Mansfield (G-13378)
University of Cincinnati .... A 513 556-6381
  Cincinnati (G-4761)
Vizmeg Landscape Inc .... E 330 686-0901
  Stow (G-17399)
Walden Turf Center .... E 330 995-0023
  Aurora (G-863)
Warstler Brothers Landscaping .... E 330 492-9500
  Canton (G-2582)
Weed Man Lawncare LLC .... E 513 683-6310
  Cincinnati (G-4827)
Wickline Landscaping Inc .... E 937 372-0521
  Xenia (G-20083)
Wilson Enterprises Inc .... E 614 444-8873
  Columbus (G-8999)
Winn-Scapes Inc .... D 614 866-9466
  Gahanna (G-11275)
Woody Tree Medics .... E 937 298-5316
  Dayton (G-10003)
Yardmaster Inc .... D 440 357-8400
  Painesville (G-15888)

SIC SECTION

0783 Ornamental Shrub & Tree Svc

Company	Code	Phone
Asplundh Tree Expert Co	B	740 435-4300
Cambridge *(G-2097)*		
Asplundh Tree Expert LLC	C	740 467-1028
Millersport *(G-14629)*		
Barberton Tree Service Inc	E	330 848-2344
Norton *(G-15554)*		
Blanchard Tree and Lawn Inc	D	419 865-7071
Holland *(G-12011)*		
Care of Trees Inc	E	800 445-8733
Kent *(G-12353)*		
Davey Resource Group Inc	E	330 673-9511
Kent *(G-12362)*		
Davey Tree Expert Company	E	330 908-0833
Macedonia *(G-13195)*		
Davey Tree Expert Company	C	330 673-9511
Kent *(G-12363)*		
Davey Tree Expert Company	E	330 928-4911
Stow *(G-17361)*		
Davey Tree Expert Company	D	614 471-4144
Columbus *(G-7490)*		
Davey Tree Expert Company	E	440 439-4770
Cleveland *(G-5465)*		
Dbi Services LLC	E	410 590-4181
South Point *(G-17082)*		
Fdc Enterprises Inc	E	614 774-9182
Springfield *(G-17197)*		
Forevergreen Lawn Care	E	440 327-8987
North Ridgeville *(G-15464)*		
Hyde Park Ldscp & Tree Svc Inc	E	513 731-1334
Cincinnati *(G-3803)*		
Land Art Inc	E	419 666-5296
Perrysburg *(G-16026)*		
Madison Tree Care & Ldscpg Inc	E	513 576-6391
Milford *(G-14536)*		
MBI Tree Service LLC	E	513 926-9857
Waynesville *(G-18985)*		
Merciers Incorporated	C	410 590-4181
South Point *(G-17094)*		
Metrohealth System	C	216 957-2100
Cleveland *(G-6043)*		
Nelson Tree Service Inc	E	937 294-1313
Dayton *(G-9772)*		
Oberlanders Tree & Ldscp Ltd	E	419 562-8733
Bucyrus *(G-2045)*		
Woody Tree Medics	E	937 298-5316
Dayton *(G-10003)*		

08 FORESTRY

0811 Timber Tracts

Company	Code	Phone
▲ Acro Tool & Die Company	D	330 773-5173
Akron *(G-17)*		
Davey Tree Expert Company	C	330 673-9511
Kent *(G-12363)*		

0851 Forestry Svcs

Company	Code	Phone
Belmont Cnty Fire & Squad Offi	E	740 312-5058
Bridgeport *(G-1859)*		
Cgh-Global Emerg Mngmt Strateg	E	800 376-0655
Cincinnati *(G-2905)*		
Middletown City Divison Fire	D	513 425-7996
Middletown *(G-14436)*		

09 FISHING, HUNTING, AND TRAPPING

0971 Hunting & Trapping

Company	Code	Phone
Miami Valley Gaming & Racg LLC	D	513 934-7070
Lebanon *(G-12628)*		

10 METAL MINING

1011 Iron Ores

Company	Code	Phone
◆ Cleveland-Cliffs Inc	D	216 694-5700
Cleveland *(G-5357)*		
Cliffs Minnesota Minerals Co	A	216 694-5700
Cleveland *(G-5361)*		
International Steel Group	C	330 841-2800
Warren *(G-18865)*		
The Cleveland-Cliffs Iron Co	C	216 694-5700
Cleveland *(G-6590)*		
Tilden Mining Company LC	A	216 694-5700
Cleveland *(G-6600)*		
Wabush Mines Cliffs Mining Co	A	216 694-5700
Cleveland *(G-6715)*		

1021 Copper Ores

Company	Code	Phone
◆ Warrenton Copper LLC	E	636 456-3488
Cleveland *(G-6723)*		

1061 Ferroalloy Ores, Except Vanadium

Company	Code	Phone
▲ Rhenium Alloys Inc	D	440 365-7388
North Ridgeville *(G-15475)*		

1081 Metal Mining Svcs

Company	Code	Phone
Alloy Metal Exchange LLC	E	216 478-0200
Bedford Heights *(G-1345)*		
Hahs Factory Outlet	E	330 405-4227
Twinsburg *(G-18426)*		
Hopedale Mining LLC	E	740 937-2225
Hopedale *(G-12079)*		

1094 Uranium, Radium & Vanadium Ores

Company	Code	Phone
Centrus Energy Corp	C	740 897-2457
Piketon *(G-16111)*		

12 COAL MINING

1221 Bituminous Coal & Lignite: Surface Mining

Company	Code	Phone
B&N Coal Inc	D	740 783-3575
Dexter City *(G-10170)*		
Coal Services Inc	D	740 795-5220
Powhatan Point *(G-16356)*		
Daron Coal Company LLC	C	614 643-0337
Cadiz *(G-2074)*		
J & D Mining Inc	E	330 339-4935
New Philadelphia *(G-15103)*		
Marietta Coal Co	E	740 695-2197
Saint Clairsville *(G-16643)*		
Murray American Energy Inc	A	740 338-3100
Saint Clairsville *(G-16645)*		
Nacco Industries Inc	E	440 229-5151
Cleveland *(G-6098)*		
Oxford Min Cmpany-Kentucky LLC	C	740 622-6302
Coshocton *(G-9114)*		
Oxford Mining Company Inc	E	740 342-7666
New Lexington *(G-15059)*		
Rosebud Mining Company	E	740 768-2097
Bergholz *(G-1476)*		
Rosebud Mining Company	E	740 922-9122
Uhrichsville *(G-18491)*		
Sands Hill Coal Hauling Co Inc	C	740 384-4211
Hamden *(G-11688)*		

1222 Bituminous Coal: Underground Mining

Company	Code	Phone
▲ American Energy Corporation	B	740 926-2430
Beallsville *(G-1139)*		
Coal Services Inc	D	740 795-5220
Powhatan Point *(G-16356)*		
Murray Kentucky Energy Inc	B	740 338-3100
Saint Clairsville *(G-16646)*		
Rosebud Mining Company	E	740 658-4217
Freeport *(G-11181)*		
Rosebud Mining Company	E	740 768-2097
Bergholz *(G-1476)*		
Rosebud Mining Company	E	740 922-9122
Uhrichsville *(G-18491)*		
Rosebud Mining Company	E	330 222-2334
Carrollton *(G-2627)*		
Western KY Coal Resources LLC	B	740 338-3100
Saint Clairsville *(G-16660)*		

1231 Anthracite Mining

Company	Code	Phone
Coal Services Inc	D	740 795-5220
Powhatan Point *(G-16356)*		

1241 Coal Mining Svcs

Company	Code	Phone
▲ American Energy Corporation	B	740 926-2430
Beallsville *(G-1139)*		
Buckingham Coal Company LLC	C	740 767-2907
Zanesville *(G-20452)*		
Coal Services Inc	D	740 795-5220
Powhatan Point *(G-16356)*		
Harrison County Coal Company	D	740 338-3100
Saint Clairsville *(G-16637)*		
Ohio Valley Coal Company	B	740 926-1351
Saint Clairsville *(G-16648)*		
Ohio Valley Resources Inc	E	740 795-5220
Saint Clairsville *(G-16649)*		
Ohio Valley Transloading Co	E	740 795-4967
Saint Clairsville *(G-16650)*		
Peabody Coal Company	B	740 450-2420
Zanesville *(G-20524)*		
Rosebud Mining Company	E	330 222-2334
Carrollton *(G-2627)*		
Suncoke Energy Nc	E	513 727-5571
Middletown *(G-14463)*		

13 OIL AND GAS EXTRACTION

1311 Crude Petroleum & Natural Gas

Company	Code	Phone
AB Resources LLC	E	440 922-1098
Brecksville *(G-1810)*		
Alliance Petroleum Corporation	D	330 493-0440
Canton *(G-2233)*		
Belden & Blake Corporation	E	330 602-5551
Dover *(G-10177)*		
Chevron Ae Resources LLC	E	330 654-4343
Deerfield *(G-10017)*		
City of Lancaster	E	740 687-6670
Lancaster *(G-12518)*		
Gulfport Energy Corporation	E	740 251-0407
Saint Clairsville *(G-16636)*		
Interstate Gas Supply Inc	C	614 659-5000
Dublin *(G-10378)*		
Kenoil Inc	E	330 262-1144
Wooster *(G-19879)*		
◆ Koch Knight LLC	D	330 488-1651
East Canton *(G-10504)*		
Resource America Inc	E	330 896-8510
Uniontown *(G-18536)*		
Resource Energy Inc	E	330 896-8510
Uniontown *(G-18537)*		
Williams Partners LP	C	330 966-3674
North Canton *(G-15379)*		
Xto Energy Inc	D	740 671-9901
Bellaire *(G-1369)*		

1321 Natural Gas Liquids

Company	Code	Phone
Husky Marketing and Supply Co	E	614 210-2300
Dublin *(G-10370)*		

1381 Drilling Oil & Gas Wells

Company	Code	Phone
Advent Drilling Inc	E	330 497-2533
Canton *(G-2227)*		
Decker Drilling Inc	D	740 749-3939
Vincent *(G-18743)*		
Eclipse Resources - Ohio LLC	E	740 452-4503
Zanesville *(G-20472)*		
J D Drilling Co	E	740 949-2512
Racine *(G-16371)*		
Kilbarger Construction Inc	C	740 385-5531
Logan *(G-12980)*		
Qes Pressure Control LLC	E	724 324-2391
Lore City *(G-13087)*		
Stratagraph Ne Inc	E	740 373-3091
Marietta *(G-13502)*		
Victor McKenzie Drilling Co	E	740 453-0834
Zanesville *(G-20544)*		
Warren Drilling Co Inc	C	740 783-2775
Dexter City *(G-10171)*		

1382 Oil & Gas Field Exploration Svcs

Company	Code	Phone
Alliance Petroleum Corporation	D	330 493-0440
Canton *(G-2233)*		
▲ American Envmtl Group Ltd	B	330 659-5930
Richfield *(G-16495)*		
Bakerwell Inc	D	614 898-7590
Westerville *(G-19286)*		
Belden & Blake Corporation	E	330 602-5551
Dover *(G-10177)*		
Chevron Ae Resources LLC	E	330 654-4343
Deerfield *(G-10017)*		
Dlz Ohio Inc	C	614 888-0040
Columbus *(G-7535)*		
Husky Marketing and Supply Co	E	614 210-2300
Dublin *(G-10370)*		
New World Energy Resources	B	740 344-4087
Newark *(G-15218)*		
Precision Geophysical Inc	E	330 674-2198
Millersburg *(G-14617)*		
Range Rsrces - Appalachia LLC	E	330 866-3301
Dover *(G-10207)*		
Resource America Inc	E	330 896-8510
Uniontown *(G-18536)*		
Resource Energy Inc	D	330 896-8510
Uniontown *(G-18537)*		
Triad Energy Corporation	E	740 374-2940
Marietta *(G-13505)*		

Employee Codes: A=Over 500 employees, B=251-500 C=101-250, D=51-100, E=25-50

13 OIL AND GAS EXTRACTION

True North Energy LLC .... E 440 442-0060
  Mayfield Heights *(G-14009)*

1389 Oil & Gas Field Svcs, NEC

Acuren Inspection Inc .... D 937 228-9729
  Dayton *(G-9306)*
Acuren Inspection Inc .... E 513 671-7073
  Cincinnati *(G-2971)*
▲ Bdi Inc .... B 216 642-9100
  Cleveland *(G-5104)*
Belden & Blake Corporation .... E 330 602-5551
  Dover *(G-10177)*
Cgh-Global Emerg Mngmt Strateg .... E 800 376-0655
  Cincinnati *(G-2905)*
Clearfield Ohio Holdings Inc .... D 740 947-5121
  Waverly *(G-18969)*
Express Energy Svcs Oper LP .... E 740 337-4530
  Toronto *(G-18337)*
Fishburn Tank Truck Service .... D 419 253-6031
  Marengo *(G-13424)*
Fts International Inc .... A 330 754-2375
  East Canton *(G-10503)*
Greer & Whitehead Cnstr Inc .... E 513 202-1757
  Harrison *(G-11799)*
Kelchner Inc .... C 937 704-9890
  Springboro *(G-17125)*
Siler Excavation Services .... E 513 400-8628
  Milford *(G-14563)*
▲ Stingray Pressure Pumping LLC .... E 405 648-4177
  Belmont *(G-1430)*
Stratagraph Ne Inc .... E 740 373-3091
  Marietta *(G-13502)*
Timothy Sinfield .... E 740 685-3684
  Pleasant City *(G-16213)*
Tk Gas Services Inc .... E 740 826-0303
  New Concord *(G-15038)*
Varco LP .... E 440 277-8696
  Lorain *(G-13084)*

14 MINING AND QUARRYING OF NONMETALLIC MINERALS, EXCEPT FUELS

1411 Dimension Stone

Heritage Marble of Ohio Inc .... E 614 436-1464
  Columbus *(G-7831)*
Irg Operating LLC .... E 440 963-4008
  Vermilion *(G-18711)*
National Lime and Stone Co .... D 419 562-0771
  Bucyrus *(G-2044)*
Stoneco Inc .... D 419 422-8454
  Findlay *(G-11086)*

1422 Crushed & Broken Limestone

Acme Company .... D 330 758-2313
  Poland *(G-16219)*
Allgeier & Son Inc .... E 513 574-3735
  Cincinnati *(G-2988)*
Chesterhill Stone Co .... E 740 849-2338
  East Fultonham *(G-10505)*
Conag Inc .... E 419 394-8870
  Saint Marys *(G-16673)*
Hanson Aggregates East LLC .... E 937 587-2671
  Peebles *(G-15939)*
Hanson Aggregates East LLC .... D 419 483-4390
  Castalia *(G-2630)*
Hanson Aggregates East LLC .... E 937 364-2311
  Hillsboro *(G-11976)*
▲ Lang Stone Company Inc .... D 614 235-4099
  Columbus *(G-8038)*
Martin Marietta Materials Inc .... D 513 353-1400
  North Bend *(G-15319)*
Martin Marietta Materials Inc .... E 513 701-1140
  West Chester *(G-19117)*
National Lime and Stone Co .... C 419 396-7671
  Carey *(G-2596)*
National Lime and Stone Co .... E 740 548-4206
  Delaware *(G-10117)*
National Lime and Stone Co .... E 419 423-3400
  Findlay *(G-11069)*
National Lime and Stone Co .... E 419 562-0771
  Bucyrus *(G-2044)*
◆ Omya Industries Inc .... D 513 387-4600
  Blue Ash *(G-1657)*
Piqua Materials Inc .... E 937 773-4824
  Piqua *(G-16158)*
Piqua Materials Inc .... E 513 771-0820
  Cincinnati *(G-4301)*

R W Sidley Incorporated .... E 440 352-9343
  Painesville *(G-15876)*
Shelly Materials Inc .... E 740 666-5841
  Ostrander *(G-15794)*
Shelly Materials Inc .... D 740 246-6315
  Thornville *(G-17668)*
Sidwell Materials Inc .... C 740 849-2394
  Zanesville *(G-20533)*
Stoneco Inc .... E 419 393-2555
  Oakwood *(G-15624)*
Wagner Quarries Company .... E 419 625-8141
  Sandusky *(G-16809)*
White Rock Quarry L P .... A 419 855-8388
  Clay Center *(G-4910)*

1423 Crushed & Broken Granite

Martin Marietta Materials Inc .... E 513 701-1140
  West Chester *(G-19117)*

1429 Crushed & Broken Stone, NEC

Great Lakes Crushing Ltd .... E 440 944-5500
  Wickliffe *(G-19599)*

1442 Construction Sand & Gravel

Barrett Paving Materials Inc .... C 513 271-6200
  Middletown *(G-14475)*
Carl E Oeder Sons Sand & Grav ...... E 513 494-1555
  Lebanon *(G-12594)*
Central Ready Mix LLC .... E 513 402-5001
  Cincinnati *(G-3216)*
Demmy Sand and Gravel LLC .... E 937 325-8840
  Springfield *(G-17189)*
Fleming Construction Co .... E 740 494-2177
  Prospect *(G-16365)*
FML Resin LLC .... E 440 214-3200
  Chesterland *(G-2796)*
FML Terminal Logistics LLC .... D 440 214-3200
  Chesterland *(G-2797)*
Hanson Aggregates East LLC .... E 740 773-2172
  Chillicothe *(G-2844)*
Hilltop Basic Resources Inc .... E 513 621-1500
  Cincinnati *(G-3768)*
J P Sand & Gravel Company .... E 614 497-0083
  Lockbourne *(G-12958)*
Joe McClelland Inc .... E 740 452-3036
  Zanesville *(G-20492)*
Kenmore Construction Co Inc .... E 330 832-8888
  Massillon *(G-13827)*
Lakeside Sand & Gravel Inc .... E 330 274-2569
  Mantua *(G-13390)*
Martin Marietta Materials Inc .... E 513 701-1140
  West Chester *(G-19117)*
Mecco Inc .... E 513 422-3651
  Middletown *(G-14434)*
Morrow Gravel Company Inc .... E 513 771-0820
  Cincinnati *(G-4120)*
National Lime and Stone Co .... E 614 497-0083
  Lockbourne *(G-12959)*
National Lime and Stone Co .... C 419 396-7671
  Carey *(G-2596)*
Oeder Carl E Sons Sand & Grav ...... E 513 494-1238
  Lebanon *(G-12632)*
▼ Osborne Materials Company .... E 440 357-7026
  Grand River *(G-11457)*
Phillips Ready Mix Co .... D 937 426-5151
  Beavercreek Township *(G-1281)*
Pioneer Sands LLC .... E 740 599-7773
  Howard *(G-12081)*
Rjw Trucking Company Ltd .... E 740 363-5343
  Delaware *(G-10124)*
Shelly and Sands Inc .... E 740 453-0721
  Zanesville *(G-20532)*
Shelly Materials Inc .... D 740 246-6315
  Thornville *(G-17668)*
Small Sand & Gravel Inc .... E 740 427-3130
  Gambier *(G-11349)*
Smith Concrete Co .... E 740 373-7441
  Dover *(G-10214)*
Stansley Mineral Resources Inc ...... E 419 843-2813
  Sylvania *(G-17617)*
Tri County Concrete Inc .... E 330 425-4464
  Twinsburg *(G-18477)*
Watson Gravel Inc .... D 513 863-0070
  Hamilton *(G-11784)*
Welch Holdings Inc .... E 513 353-3220
  Cincinnati *(G-4829)*

1446 Industrial Sand

Fairmount Minerals LLC .... C 269 926-9450
  Chesterland *(G-2795)*
Pioneer Sands LLC .... E 740 659-2241
  Glenford *(G-11433)*
Pioneer Sands LLC .... E 740 599-7773
  Howard *(G-12081)*
Standex International Corp .... E 513 871-3777
  Cincinnati *(G-4580)*

1479 Chemical & Fertilizer Mining

Cargill Incorporated .... C 216 651-7200
  Cleveland *(G-5184)*
◆ Everris NA Inc .... E 614 726-7100
  Dublin *(G-10340)*

1481 Nonmetallic Minerals Svcs, Except Fuels

Aluchem of Jackson Inc .... E 740 286-2455
  Jackson *(G-12306)*
Barr Engineering Incorporated .... E 614 714-0299
  Columbus *(G-7091)*
M G Q Inc .... E 419 992-4236
  Tiffin *(G-17683)*

1499 Miscellaneous Nonmetallic Mining

Graftech Holdings Inc .... C 216 676-2000
  Independence *(G-12214)*

15 BUILDING CONSTRUCTION- GENERAL CONTRACTORS AND OPERATIVE BUILDERS

1521 General Contractors, Single Family Houses

1522 Hess Street LLC .... E 614 291-6876
  Columbus *(G-6912)*
50 X 20 Holding Company Inc .... E 740 238-4262
  Belmont *(G-1428)*
50 X 20 Holding Company Inc .... D 330 478-4500
  Canton *(G-2220)*
50 X 20 Holding Company Inc .... E 330 865-4663
  Akron *(G-10)*
A & R Builders Ltd .... E 330 893-2111
  Millersburg *(G-14583)*
A-Sons Construction Inc .... D 614 846-2438
  Columbus *(G-6923)*
AAA Home Repair Services .... E 937 748-9988
  Springboro *(G-17112)*
AAA Standard Services Inc .... D 419 535-0274
  Toledo *(G-17737)*
Airko Inc .... E 440 333-0133
  Cleveland *(G-4978)*
Alexander and Bebout Inc .... D 419 238-9567
  Van Wert *(G-18626)*
Allan Hunter Construction LLC .... E 330 634-9882
  Akron *(G-67)*
Apco Industries Inc .... D 614 224-2345
  Columbus *(G-7027)*
Apex Restoration Contrs Ltd .... E 513 489-1795
  Cincinnati *(G-3035)*
Arnolds Home Improvement LLC ..... E 734 847-9600
  Toledo *(G-17759)*
Asplundh Construction Corp .... E 614 532-5224
  Columbus *(G-7052)*
Ayers Service Group LLC .... E 419 678-4811
  Coldwater *(G-6827)*
Belfor USA Group Inc .... E 330 916-6468
  Peninsula *(G-15947)*
Berlin Construction Ltd .... E 330 893-2003
  Millersburg *(G-14587)*
Bernard Busson Builder .... E 330 929-4926
  Akron *(G-99)*
Bob Schmitt Homes Inc .... D 440 327-9495
  North Ridgeville *(G-15455)*
Bob Webb Builders Inc .... E 740 548-5577
  Lewis Center *(G-12672)*
Brady Homes Inc .... E 440 937-6255
  Avon *(G-880)*
Brayman Construction Corp .... E 740 237-0000
  Ironton *(G-12282)*
Brian-Kyles Construction Inc .... E 440 242-0298
  Lorain *(G-13019)*
Brock & Associates Builders .... E 330 757-7150
  Youngstown *(G-20127)*

Buckeye Cmnty Hope Foundation C 614 942-2014 Columbus *(G-7158)*
Burge Building Co Inc E 440 245-6871 Lorain *(G-13021)*
Burkhart Trucking Inc E 740 896-2244 Lowell *(G-13168)*
Burkshire Construction Company E 440 885-9700 Cleveland *(G-5159)*
Bzak Landscaping Inc E 513 831-0907 Milford *(G-14508)*
C V Perry & Co E 614 221-4131 Columbus *(G-7176)*
Cardinal Builders Inc E 614 237-1000 Columbus *(G-7190)*
Cleveland Construction Inc E 440 255-8000 Mason *(G-13685)*
Columbus Drywall & Insulation D 614 257-0257 Columbus *(G-7347)*
Columbus Drywall Inc E 614 257-0257 Columbus *(G-7348)*
Combs Interior Specialties Inc D 937 879-2047 Fairborn *(G-10787)*
Community Improvement Corp E 440 466-4675 Geneva *(G-11360)*
Cooper Woda Companies Inc D 614 396-3200 Columbus *(G-7436)*
Cork Inc E 614 253-8400 Columbus *(G-7440)*
Craftsmen Restoration LLC E 877 442-3424 Akron *(G-174)*
Crapsey & Gillis Contractors E 513 891-6333 Loveland *(G-13117)*
Crock Construction Co E 740 732-2306 Caldwell *(G-2084)*
Cy Schwieterman Inc E 419 753-2566 Wapakoneta *(G-18794)*
Dan Marchetta Cnstr Co Inc E 330 668-4800 Akron *(G-186)*
Daugherty Construction Inc E 216 731-9444 Euclid *(G-10748)*
David W Milliken E 740 998-5023 Frankfort *(G-11145)*
Davis Paul Restoration Dayton E 937 436-3411 Moraine *(G-14766)*
Dayton Roof & Remodeling Co E 937 224-7667 Beavercreek *(G-1167)*
Deerfield Farms E 330 584-4715 Deerfield *(G-10018)*
Denny R King E 513 917-7968 Hamilton *(G-11721)*
Design Homes & Development Co E 937 438-3667 Dayton *(G-9499)*
Disaster Reconstruction Inc E 440 918-1523 Eastlake *(G-10545)*
Dixon Builders & Developers D 513 887-6400 West Chester *(G-19066)*
Dold Homes Inc E 419 874-2535 Perrysburg *(G-15999)*
Dominion Homes Inc D 614 356-5000 Dublin *(G-10323)*
Drees Company E 330 899-9554 Uniontown *(G-18518)*
Dry It Rite LLC E 614 295-8135 Columbus *(G-7546)*
Dublin Building Systems Co E 614 760-5831 Dublin *(G-10325)*
Duffy Homes Inc E 614 410-4100 Columbus *(G-7549)*
Dun Rite Home Improvement Inc E 330 650-5322 Macedonia *(G-13196)*
E A Zicka Co E 513 451-1440 Cincinnati *(G-3523)*
Edrich Supply Co E 440 238-9440 Strongsville *(G-17459)*
Elite Home Remodeling Inc E 614 785-6700 Columbus *(G-7589)*
Endeavor Construction Ltd E 513 469-1900 Pleasant Plain *(G-16214)*
Enterprise Construction Inc E 440 349-3443 Solon *(G-17003)*
Environmental Materials LLC E 330 558-9168 Hinckley *(G-11997)*
Equity Central LLC E 614 861-7777 Gahanna *(G-11240)*
Erie Construction Mid-West Inc E 937 898-4688 Dayton *(G-9530)*
Etech-Systems LLC D 216 221-6600 Lakewood *(G-12477)*
Farris Enterprises Inc E 614 367-9611 Worthington *(G-19960)*
Farrow Cleaners Co E 216 561-2355 Cleveland *(G-5574)*
Fetters Construction Inc C 419 542-0944 Hicksville *(G-11863)*
G Stephens Inc E 419 241-5188 Toledo *(G-17904)*
GCI Construction LLC E 216 831-6100 Beachwood *(G-1083)*
Goettle Co D 513 825-8100 Cincinnati *(G-3682)*
Gold Star Insulation L P E 614 221-3241 Columbus *(G-7757)*
Great Lakes Companies Inc C 513 554-0720 Cincinnati *(G-3702)*
Great Traditions Homes E 513 759-7444 West Chester *(G-19084)*
Greater Dayton Cnstr Ltd D 937 426-3577 Beavercreek *(G-1243)*
H&H Custom Homes LLC E 419 994-4070 Loudonville *(G-13090)*
Harrison Construction Inc E 740 373-7000 Marietta *(G-13450)*
Hays & Sons Construction Inc E 513 671-9110 Cincinnati *(G-3743)*
Hersh Construction Inc E 330 877-1515 Hartville *(G-11822)*
HMS Construction & Rental Co D 330 628-4811 Mogadore *(G-14679)*
Hochstedler Construction Ltd E 740 427-4880 Gambier *(G-11347)*
▲ Hoge Lumber Company E 419 753-2263 New Knoxville *(G-15052)*
Hometown Improvement Co E 614 846-1060 Columbus *(G-7853)*
Hoppes Construction LLC E 580 310-0090 Malvern *(G-13252)*
Icon Environmental Group LLC E 513 426-6767 Milford *(G-14526)*
Improve It Home Remodeling Inc E 614 297-5121 Columbus *(G-7886)*
Ingle-Barr Inc D 740 702-6117 Chillicothe *(G-2853)*
Investmerica limited D 216 618-3296 Chagrin Falls *(G-2701)*
Ivan Weaver Construction Co E 330 695-3461 Fredericksburg *(G-11177)*
J & D Home Improvement Inc D 740 927-0722 Reynoldsburg *(G-16459)*
J A A Interior & Coml Cnstr E 216 431-7633 Cleveland *(G-5839)*
J Russell Construction E 330 633-6462 Tallmadge *(G-17642)*
J W Enterprises Inc D 740 774-4500 Chillicothe *(G-2856)*
▲ Joshua Investment Company Inc E 614 428-5555 Columbus *(G-7951)*
K Hovnanian Summit Homes LLC E 330 454-4048 Canton *(G-2421)*
Kf Construction and Excvtg LLC E 419 547-7555 Clyde *(G-6817)*
Kokosing Construction Co Inc E 440 323-9346 Elyria *(G-10638)*
Lei Cbus LLC E 614 302-8830 Worthington *(G-19971)*
Lemmon & Lemmon Inc C 330 497-8686 North Canton *(G-15351)*
Luke Theis Enterprises Inc D 419 422-2040 Findlay *(G-11059)*
M M Construction E 513 553-0106 Bethel *(G-1483)*
Manufactured Housing Entps Inc C 419 636-4511 Bryan *(G-2011)*
Maronda Homes Inc Florida D 937 472-3907 Eaton *(G-10566)*
Marous Brothers Cnstr Inc B 440 951-3904 Willoughby *(G-19692)*
Menard Inc C 937 630-3550 Miamisburg *(G-14317)*
Menard Inc C 513 737-2204 Fairfield Township *(G-10934)*
Midwest Roofing & Furnace Co E 614 252-5241 Columbus *(G-8172)*
Miller Contracting Group Inc E 419 453-3825 Ottoville *(G-15808)*
Miller Homes of Kidron LLC E 330 857-0161 Kidron *(G-12444)*
Miracle Renovations E 513 371-0750 Cincinnati *(G-4103)*
Moyer Industries Inc E 937 832-7283 Clayton *(G-4915)*
MPW Construction Services E 440 647-6661 Wellington *(G-18995)*
Mural & Son Inc E 216 267-3322 Cleveland *(G-6090)*
Nasco Roofing and Cnstr Inc E 330 746-3566 Youngstown *(G-20294)*
Neals Construction Company E 513 489-7700 Cincinnati *(G-4149)*
New NV Co LLC C 330 896-7611 Uniontown *(G-18531)*
Nextt Corp E 513 813-6398 Cincinnati *(G-4165)*
Nhs - Totco Inc E 419 691-2900 Toledo *(G-18087)*
Nicholson Builders Inc E 614 846-8621 Columbus *(G-8278)*
Nitschke Sampson Dietz Inc E 614 464-1933 Columbus *(G-8281)*
North Branch Nursery Inc E 419 287-4679 Pemberville *(G-15942)*
Northern Style Cnstr LLC D 330 412-9594 Akron *(G-358)*
Nrp Contractors LLC E 216 475-8900 Cleveland *(G-6166)*
Nrp Group LLC D 216 475-8900 Cleveland *(G-6167)*
Nvr Inc E 440 933-7734 Avon *(G-910)*
Nvr Inc E 440 584-4200 Kent *(G-12389)*
Nvr Inc E 440 639-0525 Painesville *(G-15868)*
Nvr Inc E 513 494-0167 South Lebanon *(G-17079)*
Nvr Inc E 440 584-4250 Brecksville *(G-1838)*
Oberer Development Co E 937 910-0851 Miamisburg *(G-14328)*
Oberer Residential Cnstr C 937 278-0851 Miamisburg *(G-14329)*
Ohio Builders Resources LLC E 614 865-0306 Westerville *(G-19336)*
Olde Towne Windows Inc E 419 626-9613 Milan *(G-14496)*
▲ P T I Inc E 419 445-2800 Pettisville *(G-16082)*
Park Group Co of America Inc E 440 238-9440 Strongsville *(G-17499)*
Petros Homes Inc E 440 546-9000 Cleveland *(G-6272)*
Phil Wagler Construction Inc E 330 899-0316 Uniontown *(G-18532)*
Pirhl Contractors LLC E 216 378-9690 Cleveland *(G-6283)*
R A Hermes Inc E 513 251-5200 Cincinnati *(G-4377)*
Ram Restoration LLC E 937 347-7418 Dayton *(G-9841)*
RE Middleton Cnstr LLC E 513 398-9255 Mason *(G-13753)*
Registered Contractors Inc E 440 205-0873 Mentor *(G-14235)*
Residence Artists Inc E 440 286-8822 Chardon *(G-2764)*
Residntial Coml Rnovations Inc E 330 815-1476 Clinton *(G-6807)*
Robert C Verbon Inc E 419 867-6868 Toledo *(G-18160)*
Robert Lucke Homes Inc E 513 683-3300 Cincinnati *(G-4437)*
Rockford Homes Inc D 614 785-0015 Columbus *(G-6905)*
Romanelli & Hughes Building Co E 614 891-2042 Westerville *(G-19441)*
Rubber City Realty Inc D 330 745-9034 Akron *(G-421)*
Runyon & Sons Roofing Inc D 440 974-6810 Mentor *(G-14238)*
▲ Season Contractors Inc E 440 717-0188 Broadview Heights *(G-1891)*
Services On Deck Inc E 513 759-2854 Liberty Township *(G-12724)*
▲ Shade Tree Cool Living LLC E 614 844-5990 Columbus *(G-8719)*
Shoupes Constuction E 937 352-6457 Xenia *(G-20076)*
Simonson Construction Svcs Inc D 419 281-8299 Ashland *(G-699)*
Smb Construction Co Inc E 419 269-1473 Toledo *(G-18191)*

Employee Codes: A=Over 500 employees, B=251-500 C=101-250, D=51-100, E=25-50
2018 Harris Ohio Services Directory
895

Snavely Building Company E 440 585-9091
Chagrin Falls *(G-2705)*
Snavely Development Company E 440 585-9091
Chagrin Falls *(G-2706)*
Society Handicapped Citz Medin D 330 722-1710
Medina *(G-14127)*
Spartan Construction Co Inc E 419 389-1854
Toledo *(G-18194)*
Squires Construction Company E 216 252-0300
Rocky River *(G-16592)*
Steel Valley Construction Co E 330 392-8391
Warren *(G-18902)*
Sure Home Improvments LLC E 614 586-0610
Columbus *(G-8811)*
Swartz Enterprises Inc E 419 331-1024
Lima *(G-12895)*
Sws Environmental Services E 254 629-1718
Findlay *(G-11089)*
Toth Renovation LLC E 614 542-9683
Columbus *(G-8855)*
Towne Development Group Ltd E 513 381-8696
Cincinnati *(G-4667)*
Trimat Construction Inc E 740 388-9515
Bidwell *(G-1496)*
Trinity Home Builders Inc E 614 889-7830
Columbus *(G-8874)*
Tusing Builders Ltd E 419 465-3100
Monroeville *(G-14723)*
Two-X Engners Constructers LLC E 330 995-0592
Aurora *(G-857)*
US Home Center LLC E 614 737-9000
Columbus *(G-8924)*
Van Con Inc E 937 890-8400
Dayton *(G-9962)*
Vibo Construction Inc E 614 210-6780
Columbus *(G-8938)*
Weaver Custom Homes Inc E 330 264-5444
Wooster *(G-19927)*
Wh Midwest LLC C 330 896-7611
Uniontown *(G-18543)*
Wingler Construction Corp E 614 626-8546
Columbus *(G-9000)*
Woda Construction Inc E 614 396-3200
Columbus *(G-9002)*
Zinz Cnstr & Restoration E 330 332-7939
Youngstown *(G-20438)*

1522 General Contractors, Residential Other Than Single Family

Abco Contracting LLC E 419 973-4772
Toledo *(G-17739)*
Advocate Property Servic E 330 952-1313
Medina *(G-14032)*
Ahv Development LLC D 614 890-1440
Westerville *(G-19283)*
Akron Citicenter Hotel LLC D 330 253-8355
Akron *(G-31)*
Al Neyer LLC D 513 271-6400
Cincinnati *(G-2981)*
Amsdell Construction Inc C 216 458-0670
Cleveland *(G-5031)*
Asbuilt Construction Ltd E 937 550-4900
Franklin *(G-11149)*
Bernard Busson Builder E 330 929-4926
Akron *(G-99)*
Bob Schmitt Homes Inc D 440 327-9495
North Ridgeville *(G-15455)*
Cardinal Builders Inc E 614 237-1000
Columbus *(G-7190)*
Central Ohio Contractors Inc D 740 369-7700
Delaware *(G-10078)*
CFS Construction Inc E 513 559-4500
Cincinnati *(G-3222)*
Cooper Woda Companies Inc D 614 396-3200
Columbus *(G-7436)*
Cy Schwieterman Inc E 419 753-2566
Wapakoneta *(G-18794)*
D C Curry Lumber Company E 330 264-5223
Wooster *(G-19860)*
Danis Industrial Cnstr Co D 937 228-1225
Miamisburg *(G-14292)*
Dependble Bldrs Renovators LLC E 614 761-8250
Dublin *(G-10320)*
Dixon Builders & Developers D 513 887-6400
West Chester *(G-19066)*
Donald R Kenney & Company E 614 540-2404
Westerville *(G-19300)*
Douglas Company E 419 865-8600
Holland *(G-12021)*
Douglas Construction Company E 419 865-8600
Holland *(G-12022)*
Dr Michael J Hulit E 330 863-7173
Malvern *(G-13250)*
Dugan & Meyers Construction Co C 513 891-4300
Blue Ash *(G-1579)*
Dugan & Meyers Interests Inc E 513 891-4300
Blue Ash *(G-1580)*
Endeavor Construction Ltd E 513 469-1900
Pleasant Plain *(G-16214)*
Equity Central LLC E 614 861-7777
Gahanna *(G-11240)*
Etech-Systems LLC D 216 221-6600
Lakewood *(G-12477)*
Fairfield Homes Inc E 740 653-3583
Lancaster *(G-12534)*
Fairfield Homes Inc C 614 873-3533
Plain City *(G-16192)*
Forest City Residential Dev E 216 621-6060
Cleveland *(G-5621)*
G III Reitter Walls LLC E 614 545-4444
Columbus *(G-7718)*
G J Goudreau & Co E 216 351-5233
Cleveland *(G-5646)*
Garland Group Inc E 614 294-4411
Columbus *(G-7730)*
GCI Construction LLC E 216 831-6100
Beachwood *(G-1083)*
Greater Dayton Cnstr Ltd D 937 426-3577
Beavercreek *(G-1243)*
Habitat For Humanity Mid Ohio E 614 422-4828
Columbus *(G-7790)*
Hills Communities Inc C 513 984-0300
Blue Ash *(G-1611)*
Homewood Corporation C 614 898-7200
Columbus *(G-7857)*
I & M J Gross Company E 440 237-1681
Cleveland *(G-5798)*
Iacovetta Builders Inc E 614 272-6464
Columbus *(G-7880)*
Installed Building Pdts Inc C 614 221-3399
Columbus *(G-7908)*
Interstate Construction Inc E 614 539-1188
Grove City *(G-11572)*
K-Y Residential Coml Indus Dev D 330 448-4055
Brookfield *(G-1897)*
Klingbeil Management Group Co E 614 220-8900
Columbus *(G-7997)*
Lake Erie Home Repair E 419 871-0687
Norwalk *(G-15579)*
Lemmon & Lemmon Inc C 330 497-8686
North Canton *(G-15351)*
Lifestyle Communities Ltd D 614 918-2000
Columbus *(G-8065)*
Messer Construction Co D 513 242-1541
Cincinnati *(G-4083)*
Mv Residential Cnstr Inc A 513 588-1000
Cincinnati *(G-4133)*
National Housing Corporation E 614 481-8106
Columbus *(G-8220)*
Nitschke Sampson Dietz Inc E 614 464-1933
Columbus *(G-8281)*
Nrp Contractors LLC E 216 475-8900
Cleveland *(G-6166)*
Oberer Development Co E 937 910-0851
Miamisburg *(G-14328)*
Oberer Residential Cnstr C 937 278-0851
Miamisburg *(G-14329)*
Oliver House Rest Complex D 419 243-1302
Toledo *(G-18105)*
Optima 777 LLC E 216 771-7700
Cleveland *(G-6208)*
Otterbein Snior Lfstyle Chices B 513 933-5400
Lebanon *(G-12636)*
Patriot Roofing Company Inc E 513 469-7663
Blue Ash *(G-1662)*
◆ **Pivotek LLC** E 513 372-6205
West Chester *(G-19128)*
Property Estate Management LLC E 513 684-0418
Cincinnati *(G-4348)*
Pulte Homes Inc E 330 239-1587
Medina *(G-14116)*
Ram Restoration LLC E 937 347-7418
Dayton *(G-9841)*
Residntial Coml Rnovations Inc E 330 815-1476
Clinton *(G-6807)*
Rockford Homes Inc D 614 785-0015
Columbus *(G-6905)*
Rubber City Realty Inc D 330 745-9034
Akron *(G-421)*
Runyon & Sons Roofing Inc D 440 974-6810
Mentor *(G-14238)*
Safeguard Properties MGT LLC A 216 739-2900
Cleveland *(G-6434)*
Schnippel Construction Inc E 937 693-3831
Botkins *(G-1753)*
◆ **Schroeder Company** E 419 473-3139
Toledo *(G-18175)*
Showe Builders Inc E 614 481-8106
Columbus *(G-8729)*
Snavely Building Company E 440 585-9091
Chagrin Falls *(G-2705)*
Snavely Development Company E 440 585-9091
Chagrin Falls *(G-2706)*
Strawser Construction Inc E 614 276-5501
Columbus *(G-8796)*
Superior Kraft Homes LLC D 740 947-7710
New Boston *(G-15015)*
T O J Inc E 440 352-1900
Mentor *(G-14247)*
Topmind/Planex Construction E 248 719-0474
Middletown *(G-14469)*
Towne Building Group Inc D 513 381-8696
Cincinnati *(G-4666)*
Transcon Builders Inc E 440 439-3400
Cleveland *(G-6609)*
Turner Construction Company C 513 721-4224
Cincinnati *(G-4705)*
Upgrade Homes E 614 975-8532
Columbus *(G-8912)*
Wb Services Inc D 330 390-5722
Millersburg *(G-14628)*
Wirtzberger Enterprises Corp E 440 428-1901
Madison *(G-13238)*
Woda Construction Inc E 614 396-3200
Columbus *(G-9002)*

1531 Operative Builders

American Prservation Bldrs LLC D 216 236-2007
Cleveland *(G-5019)*
Bernard Busson Builder E 330 929-4926
Akron *(G-99)*
CV Perry Builders E 614 221-4131
Columbus *(G-7475)*
Dixon Builders & Developers D 513 887-6400
West Chester *(G-19066)*
Dold Homes Inc E 419 874-2535
Perrysburg *(G-15999)*
Douglas Construction Company E 419 865-8600
Holland *(G-12022)*
Duffy Homes Inc E 614 410-4100
Columbus *(G-7549)*
Epcon Cmmnties Franchising Inc D 614 761-1010
Dublin *(G-10337)*
Epcon Communities Inc D 614 761-1010
Dublin *(G-10338)*
Glencoe Restoration Group LLC E 330 752-1244
Akron *(G-237)*
M/I Homes Inc B 614 418-8000
Columbus *(G-8095)*
M/I Homes of Austin LLC E 614 418-8000
Columbus *(G-8096)*
Mainthia Technologies Inc D 216 433-2198
Cleveland *(G-5970)*
Multicon Construction Co E 614 351-2683
Columbus *(G-8208)*
Nrp Holdings LLC C 216 475-8900
Cleveland *(G-6168)*
Nvr Inc C 513 202-0323
Harrison *(G-11807)*
Nvr Inc C 937 529-7000
Dayton *(G-9777)*
▲ **P R Machine Works Inc** D 419 529-5748
Ontario *(G-15710)*
Phil Wagler Construction Inc E 330 899-0316
Uniontown *(G-18532)*
Plus Realty Cincinnati Inc E 513 575-4500
Milford *(G-14554)*
Weaver Custom Homes Inc E 330 264-5444
Wooster *(G-19927)*
Zicka Walker Builders Ltd E 513 247-3500
Cincinnati *(G-4871)*

1541 General Contractors, Indl Bldgs & Warehouses

AA Boos & Sons Inc D 419 691-2329
Oregon *(G-15721)*
Adena Corporation C 419 529-4456
Ontario *(G-15682)*

Adolph Johnson & Son Co ... E ... 330 544-8900
Mineral Ridge *(G-14635)*

Aecom Energy & Cnstr Inc ... B ... 216 622-2300
Cleveland *(G-4962)*

Agridry LLC ... E ... 419 459-4399
Edon *(G-10585)*

Akron Public Schools ... B ... 330 761-1660
Akron *(G-52)*

Al Neyer LLC ... D ... 513 271-6400
Cincinnati *(G-2981)*

Albert M Higley Company ... C ... 216 404-5783
Cleveland *(G-4982)*

Allen-Keith Construction Co ... D ... 330 266-2220
Canton *(G-2231)*

Amsdell Construction Inc ... C ... 216 458-0670
Cleveland *(G-5031)*

Austin Building and Design Inc ... C ... 440 544-2600
Cleveland *(G-5081)*

Ayrshire Inc ... E ... 440 286-9507
Chardon *(G-2740)*

B & B Contrs & Developers Inc ... D ... 330 270-5020
Youngstown *(G-20109)*

Beem Construction Inc ... E ... 937 693-3176
Botkins *(G-1751)*

Belfor USA Group Inc ... E ... 330 916-6468
Peninsula *(G-15947)*

Bell Hensley Inc ... E ... 937 498-1718
Sidney *(G-16915)*

Ben D Imhoff Inc ... E ... 330 683-4498
Orrville *(G-15766)*

Bilfinger Westcon Inc ... E ... 330 818-9734
Canton *(G-2263)*

Boak & Sons Inc ... C ... 330 793-5646
Youngstown *(G-20118)*

Butt Construction Company Inc ... E ... 937 426-1313
Dayton *(G-9259)*

C Tucker Cope & Assoc Inc ... E ... 330 482-4472
Columbiana *(G-6854)*

Central Ohio Building Co Inc ... E ... 614 475-6392
Columbus *(G-7229)*

Chapman Industrial Cnstr Inc ... D ... 330 343-1632
Louisville *(G-13095)*

Chemsteel Construction Company ... E ... 440 234-3930
Middleburg Heights *(G-14379)*

Cm-Gc LLC ... E ... 513 527-4141
Cincinnati *(G-3372)*

▲ **Compak Inc** ... E ... 419 207-8888
Ashland *(G-675)*

Continental RE Companies ... C ... 614 221-1800
Columbus *(G-7431)*

▲ **Corna Kokosing Construction Co** ... C ... 614 901-8844
Westerville *(G-19392)*

D & G Focht Construction Co ... E ... 419 732-2412
Port Clinton *(G-16243)*

D E Huddleston Inc ... E ... 740 773-2130
Chillicothe *(G-2832)*

DAG Construction Co Inc ... E ... 513 542-8597
Cincinnati *(G-3459)*

Danis Building Construction Co ... B ... 937 228-1225
Miamisburg *(G-14291)*

Dawn Incorporated ... E ... 330 652-7711
Warren *(G-18847)*

Deerfield Construction Co Inc ... E ... 513 984-4096
Loveland *(G-13122)*

Delventhal Company ... E ... 419 244-5570
Millbury *(G-14578)*

Desalvo Construction Company ... E ... 330 759-8145
Hubbard *(G-12085)*

DKM Construction Inc ... E ... 740 289-3006
Piketon *(G-16113)*

Dorsten Industries Inc ... E ... 419 628-2327
Minster *(G-14660)*

Dotson Company ... E ... 419 877-5176
Whitehouse *(G-19585)*

Dugan & Meyers Construction Co ... C ... 513 891-4300
Blue Ash *(G-1579)*

Dugan & Meyers Construction Co ... E ... 614 257-7430
Columbus *(G-6880)*

Dugan & Meyers Interests Inc ... E ... 513 891-4300
Blue Ash *(G-1580)*

Dunlop and Johnston Inc ... E ... 330 220-2700
Valley City *(G-18616)*

Dynamic Structures Inc ... E ... 330 892-0164
New Waterford *(G-15137)*

Elford Inc ... C ... 614 488-4000
Columbus *(G-7588)*

▲ **Enerfab Inc** ... B ... 513 641-0500
Cincinnati *(G-3557)*

Equity Inc ... E ... 614 802-2900
Hilliard *(G-11900)*

Exxcel Project Management LLC ... E ... 614 621-4500
Columbus *(G-7624)*

Farrow Cleaners Co ... E ... 216 561-2355
Cleveland *(G-5574)*

Ferguson Construction Company ... C ... 937 498-2381
Sidney *(G-16933)*

Ferguson Construction Company ... D ... 937 274-1173
Dayton *(G-9545)*

Ferrous Metal Transfer ... E ... 216 671-8500
Brooklyn *(G-1906)*

Fleming Construction Co ... E ... 740 494-2177
Prospect *(G-16365)*

Floyd P Bucher & Son Inc ... E ... 419 867-8792
Toledo *(G-17898)*

Fortney & Weygandt Inc ... E ... 440 716-4000
North Olmsted *(G-15422)*

Fryman-Kuck General Contrs Inc ... E ... 937 274-2892
Dayton *(G-9564)*

Geis Construction Inc ... D ... 330 528-3500
Streetsboro *(G-17413)*

Genco of Lebanon Inc ... A ... 330 837-0561
Massillon *(G-13813)*

Grunwell-Cashero Co ... E ... 419 476-2426
Toledo *(G-17927)*

Hammond Construction Inc ... D ... 330 455-7039
Canton *(G-2389)*

Head Inc ... E ... 614 338-8501
Columbus *(G-7808)*

Helm and Associates Inc ... E ... 419 893-1480
Maumee *(G-13924)*

Higgins Building Company Inc ... E ... 740 439-5553
Cambridge *(G-2120)*

Hume Supply Inc ... E ... 419 991-5751
Lima *(G-12800)*

Hummel Construction Company ... E ... 330 274-8584
Ravenna *(G-16388)*

Icon Environmental Group LLC ... E ... 513 426-6767
Milford *(G-14526)*

Ingle-Barr Inc ... D ... 740 702-6117
Chillicothe *(G-2853)*

J & F Construction and Dev Inc ... E ... 419 562-6662
Bucyrus *(G-2042)*

J & J General Maintenance Inc ... E ... 740 533-9729
Ironton *(G-12293)*

Jack Gibson Construction Co ... D ... 330 394-5280
Warren *(G-18867)*

Justice & Business Svcs LLC ... E ... 740 423-5005
Belpre *(G-1440)*

▲ **Kajima International Inc** ... C ... 440 544-2600
Cleveland *(G-5880)*

Kapp Construction Inc ... E ... 937 324-0134
Springfield *(G-17219)*

Knoch Corporation ... D ... 330 244-1440
Canton *(G-2428)*

▲ **Kokosing Construction Co Inc** ... C ... 614 228-1029
Columbus *(G-8007)*

Koroseal Interior Products LLC ... E ... 855 753-5474
Marietta *(G-13461)*

Kramer & Feldman Inc ... E ... 513 821-7444
Cincinnati *(G-3942)*

Lathrop Company Inc ... E ... 419 893-7000
Toledo *(G-18001)*

Lcs Inc ... E ... 419 678-8600
Saint Henry *(G-16666)*

Lepi Enterprises Inc ... D ... 740 453-2980
Zanesville *(G-20495)*

Liebel-Flarsheim Company LLC ... C ... 513 761-2700
Cincinnati *(G-3977)*

Lm Constrction Trry Lvrini Inc ... E ... 740 695-9604
Saint Clairsville *(G-16641)*

Luke Theis Enterprises Inc ... D ... 419 422-2040
Findlay *(G-11059)*

M & W Construction Entps LLC ... E ... 419 227-2000
Lima *(G-12835)*

Maco Construction Services ... E ... 330 482-4472
Columbiana *(G-6860)*

Maintenance Unlimited Inc ... E ... 440 238-1162
Strongsville *(G-17486)*

Matt Construction Services ... D ... 216 641-0030
Cleveland *(G-5994)*

Mc Meechan Construction Co ... E ... 216 581-9373
Cleveland *(G-5999)*

McDonalds Design & Build Inc ... E ... 419 782-4191
Defiance *(G-10047)*

McGraw/Kokosing Inc ... B ... 614 212-5700
Monroe *(G-14705)*

McNerney & Son Inc ... E ... 419 666-0200
Toledo *(G-18046)*

McTech Corp ... E ... 216 391-7700
Cleveland *(G-6009)*

Mel Lanzer Co ... E ... 419 592-2801
Napoleon *(G-14945)*

Messer Construction Co ... D ... 513 242-1541
Cincinnati *(G-4083)*

Mid-Continent Construction Co ... E ... 440 439-6100
Oakwood Village *(G-15631)*

Miencorp Inc ... E ... 330 978-8511
Niles *(G-15296)*

Mike Coates Cnstr Co Inc ... C ... 330 652-0190
Niles *(G-15297)*

Miles-Mcclellan Cnstr Co Inc ... E ... 614 487-7744
Columbus *(G-8173)*

Miller-Valentine Construction ... D ... 937 293-0900
Dayton *(G-9749)*

Monarch Construction Company ... C ... 513 351-6900
Cincinnati *(G-4114)*

Movers and Shuckers LLC ... E ... 740 263-2164
Mount Vernon *(G-14915)*

Mowry Construction & Engrg Inc ... E ... 419 289-2262
Ashland *(G-690)*

Mullett Company ... E ... 440 564-9000
Newbury *(G-15259)*

Mural & Son Inc ... E ... 216 267-3322
Cleveland *(G-6090)*

Murphy Contracting Co ... E ... 330 743-8915
Youngstown *(G-20292)*

Mv Commercial Construction LLC ... C ... 937 293-0900
Dayton *(G-9763)*

Nicolozakes Trckg & Cnstr Inc ... E ... 740 432-5648
Cambridge *(G-2124)*

Norris Brothers Co Inc ... C ... 216 771-2233
Cleveland *(G-6137)*

Nyman Construction Co ... E ... 216 475-7800
Cleveland *(G-6173)*

Ors Nasco Inc ... E ... 918 781-5300
West Chester *(G-19219)*

Oswald Company Inc ... E ... 513 745-4424
Cincinnati *(G-4241)*

Palmetto Construction Svcs LLC ... E ... 614 503-7150
Columbus *(G-8512)*

Pawnee Maintenance Inc ... D ... 740 373-6861
Marietta *(G-13483)*

Pepper Cnstr Co Ohio LLC ... E ... 614 793-4477
Dublin *(G-10425)*

QBS Inc ... E ... 330 821-8801
Alliance *(G-552)*

Quantum Construction Company ... E ... 513 351-6903
Cincinnati *(G-4361)*

R G Smith Company ... E ... 419 524-4778
Mansfield *(G-13352)*

Ram Construction Services of ... D ... 513 297-1857
West Chester *(G-19137)*

Ray Fogg Building Methods Inc ... E ... 216 351-7976
Cleveland *(G-6354)*

Refrigeration Systems Company ... D ... 614 263-0913
Columbus *(G-8603)*

Registered Contractors Inc ... E ... 440 205-0873
Mentor *(G-14235)*

Reinnovations Contracting Inc ... E ... 330 505-9035
Mineral Ridge *(G-14638)*

Resers Fine Foods Inc ... E ... 216 231-7112
Cleveland *(G-6382)*

Righter Construction Svcs Inc ... E ... 614 272-9700
Columbus *(G-8630)*

Robertson Cnstr Svcs Inc ... D ... 740 929-1000
Heath *(G-11842)*

Rudolph Libbe Inc ... B ... 419 241-5000
Walbridge *(G-18777)*

Rudolph/Libbe Companies Inc ... A ... 419 241-5000
Walbridge *(G-18778)*

Ruhlin Company ... C ... 330 239-2800
Sharon Center *(G-16877)*

Ruscilli Construction Co Inc ... D ... 614 876-9484
Columbus *(G-8658)*

Schirmer Construction Co ... E ... 440 716-4900
North Olmsted *(G-15443)*

Schnippel Construction Inc ... E ... 937 693-3831
Botkins *(G-1753)*

Simmons Brothers Corporation ... E ... 330 722-1415
Medina *(G-14125)*

Skanska USA Building Inc ... E ... 513 421-0082
Cincinnati *(G-4538)*

Spieker Company ... E ... 419 872-7000
Perrysburg *(G-16062)*

Stamm Contracting Co Inc ... E ... 330 274-8230
Mantua *(G-13395)*

Standard Contg & Engrg Inc ... D ... 440 243-1001
Brookpark *(G-1955)*

Stanley Miller Construction Co ... E ... 330 484-2229
East Sparta *(G-10541)*

Employee Codes: A=Over 500 employees, B=251-500
C=101-250, D=51-100, E=25-50
2018 Harris Ohio
Services Directory
897

15 BUILDING CONSTRUCTION-GENERAL CONTRACTORS AND OPERATIVE BUILDERS

Star Builders Inc .... E 440 986-5951
  Amherst (G-606)
Steel Warehouse Cleveland LLC 888 225-3760
  Cleveland (G-6534)
Stevens Engineers Constrs Inc .... E 440 277-6207
  Lorain (G-13079)
Structural Building Systems .... D 330 656-9353
  Hudson (G-12145)
Studer-Obringer Inc .... E 419 492-2121
  New Washington (G-15136)
Sunrush Construction Co Inc .... E 740 775-1300
  Chillicothe (G-2889)
Suresite Consulting Group LLC ...... E 216 593-0400
  Beachwood (G-1129)
Technical Assurance Inc .... E 440 953-3147
  Willoughby (G-19717)
Testa Enterprises Inc .... E 330 926-9060
  Cuyahoga Falls (G-9225)
Tradesmen Group Inc .... E 614 799-0889
  Plain City (G-16210)
Tri State Corporation .... E 513 763-0215
  Cincinnati (G-4683)
Trisco Systems Incorporated .... C 419 339-9912
  Lima (G-12906)
Troy Built Building LLC .... D 419 425-1093
  Findlay (G-11094)
Turner Construction Company ..... C 513 721-4224
  Cincinnati (G-4705)
TWC Concrete Services LLC .... E 513 771-8192
  Cincinnati (G-4709)
Union Industrial Contractors .... E 440 998-7871
  Ashtabula (G-765)
Universal Contracting Corp .... E 513 482-2700
  Cincinnati (G-4747)
▲ Universal Fabg Cnstr Svcs Inc ... D 614 274-1128
  Columbus (G-8905)
Van Tassel Construction Corp .... E 419 873-0188
  Perrysburg (G-16068)
Virginia Ohio-West Excvtg Co .... C 740 676-7464
  Shadyside (G-16852)
Wenco Inc .... C 937 849-6002
  New Carlisle (G-15033)
Whiting-Turner Contracting Co ..... D 440 449-9200
  Cleveland (G-6750)
Williams Bros Builders Inc .... E 440 365-3261
  Elyria (G-10692)

1542 General Contractors, Nonresidential & Non-indl Bldgs

A & A Wall Systems Inc .... E 513 489-0086
  Cincinnati (G-2950)
A P & P Dev & Cnstr Co .... D 330 833-8886
  Massillon (G-13782)
A2 Services LLC .... D 440 466-6611
  Geneva (G-11358)
AA Boos & Sons Inc .... D 419 691-2329
  Oregon (G-15721)
Abco Contracting LLC .... E 419 973-4772
  Toledo (G-17739)
Adena Corporation .... C 419 529-4456
  Ontario (G-15682)
Adolph Johnson & Son Co .... E 330 544-8900
  Mineral Ridge (G-14635)
Advanced Intgrted Slutions LLC ... E 313 724-8600
  Blue Ash (G-1524)
Aecom Energy & Cnstr Inc .... C 419 698-6277
  Oregon (G-15723)
Aecom Energy & Cnstr Inc .... B 216 622-2300
  Cleveland (G-4962)
Airko Inc .... E 440 333-0133
  Cleveland (G-4978)
Al Neyer LLC .... D 513 271-6400
  Cincinnati (G-2981)
Albert M Higley Company .... C 216 404-5783
  Cleveland (G-4982)
Alpine Structures LLC .... E 330 359-5708
  Dundee (G-10499)
Alvada Const Inc .... C 419 595-4224
  Alvada (G-568)
▼ Ams Inc .... E 513 244-8500
  Cincinnati (G-3020)
Amsdell Construction Inc .... E 216 458-0670
  Cleveland (G-5031)
Apex Restoration Contrs Ltd .... E 513 489-1795
  Cincinnati (G-3035)
Arbor Construction Co .... E 216 360-6989
  Cleveland (G-5059)
Arnolds Home Improvement LLC .. E 734 847-9600
  Toledo (G-17759)

Austin Building and Design Inc ..... C 440 544-2600
  Cleveland (G-5081)
B & B Contrs & Developers Inc .... D 330 270-5020
  Youngstown (G-20109)
Becker Construction Inc .... E 937 859-8308
  Dayton (G-9352)
Belfor USA Group Inc .... E 330 916-6468
  Peninsula (G-15947)
Ben D Imhoff Inc .... E 330 683-4498
  Orrville (G-15766)
Berlin Construction Ltd .... E 330 893-2003
  Millersburg (G-14587)
Boak & Sons Inc .... C 330 793-5646
  Youngstown (G-20118)
Bogner Construction Company ..... D 330 262-6730
  Wooster (G-19833)
Boyas Excavating Inc .... E 216 524-3620
  Cleveland (G-5131)
Brackett Builders Inc .... E 937 339-7505
  Troy (G-18350)
Brenmar Construction Inc .... D 740 286-2151
  Jackson (G-12307)
Brocon Construction Inc .... E 614 871-7300
  Grove City (G-11538)
▲ Brumbaugh Construction Inc ..... E 937 692-5107
  Arcanum (G-629)
▲ Bruns Building & Dev Corp Inc . D 419 925-4095
  Saint Henry (G-16665)
Burge Building Co Inc .... E 440 245-6871
  Lorain (G-13021)
Butt Construction Company Inc ... E 937 426-1313
  Dayton (G-9259)
C Tucker Cope & Assoc Inc .... E 330 482-4472
  Columbiana (G-6854)
Calvary Contracting Inc .... E 937 754-0300
  Tipp City (G-17711)
Camargo Construction Company .. E 513 248-1500
  Cincinnati (G-3168)
Canton Floors Inc .... E 330 492-1121
  Canton (G-2288)
Cattrell Companies Inc .... D 740 537-2481
  Toronto (G-18336)
Cedarwood Construction Company ... D ... 330 836-9971
  Akron (G-125)
Central Ohio Building Co Inc .... E 614 475-6392
  Columbus (G-7229)
CFS Construction Inc .... E 513 559-4500
  Cincinnati (G-3222)
Chaney Roofing Maintenance ...... E 419 639-2761
  Clyde (G-6811)
Cincinnati Coml Contg LLC .... E 513 561-6633
  Cincinnati (G-3294)
▲ Cleveland Construction Inc .... E 440 255-8000
  Mentor (G-14159)
Cleveland Construction Inc .... E 740 927-9000
  Columbus (G-7298)
Cleveland Construction Inc .... E 440 255-8000
  Mason (G-13685)
Cm-Gc LLC .... E 513 527-4141
  Cincinnati (G-3372)
Cocca Development Ltd .... D 330 729-1010
  Youngstown (G-20145)
Colaianni Construction Inc .... E 740 769-2362
  Dillonvale (G-10173)
Columbus City Trnsp Div .... C 614 645-3182
  Columbus (G-7338)
Combs Interior Specialties Inc ..... D 937 879-2047
  Fairborn (G-10787)
Conger Construction Group Inc ... E 513 932-1206
  Lebanon (G-12597)
Construction One Inc .... E 614 961-1140
  Columbus (G-7424)
Continental RE Companies .... C 614 221-1800
  Columbus (G-7431)
▲ Corna Kokosing Construction Co ... C ... 614 901-8844
  Westerville (G-19392)
Corporate Cleaning Inc .... E 614 203-6051
  Columbus (G-7441)
Crapsey & Gillis Contractors .... E 513 891-6333
  Loveland (G-13117)
Crock Construction Co .... E 740 732-2306
  Caldwell (G-2084)
D & G Focht Construction Co .... E 419 732-2412
  Port Clinton (G-16243)
D E Huddleston Inc .... E 740 773-2130
  Chillicothe (G-2832)
◆ Da Vinci Group Inc .... E 614 419-2393
  Reynoldsburg (G-16442)
DAG Construction Co Inc .... E 513 542-8597
  Cincinnati (G-3459)

Dan Marchetta Cnstr Co Inc .... E 330 668-4800
  Akron (G-186)
Danis Building Construction Co ... B 937 228-1225
  Miamisburg (G-14291)
Daugherty Construction Inc .... E 216 731-9444
  Euclid (G-10748)
Daytep Inc .... E 937 456-5860
  Eaton (G-10556)
Deerfield Construction Co Inc ...... E 513 984-4096
  Loveland (G-13122)
Delventhal Company .... E 419 244-5570
  Millbury (G-14578)
Desalvo Construction Company ... E 330 759-8145
  Hubbard (G-12085)
Design Homes & Development Co ... E ... 937 438-3667
  Dayton (G-9499)
Disaster Reconstruction Inc .... E 440 918-1523
  Eastlake (G-10545)
DKM Construction Inc .... E 740 289-3006
  Piketon (G-16113)
Donleys Inc .... C 216 524-6800
  Cleveland (G-5503)
Dorsten Industries Inc .... E 419 628-2327
  Minster (G-14660)
Dotson Company .... E 419 877-5176
  Whitehouse (G-19585)
Douglas Company .... E 419 865-8600
  Holland (G-12021)
Dugan & Meyers Construction Co ... C ... 513 891-4300
  Blue Ash (G-1579)
Dugan & Meyers Construction Co ... E ... 614 257-7430
  Columbus (G-6880)
Dugan & Meyers Interests Inc ..... E 513 891-4300
  Blue Ash (G-1580)
Dugan & Meyers LLC .... C 513 891-4300
  Blue Ash (G-1581)
Duncan Oil Co .... E 937 426-5945
  Dayton (G-9267)
Dunlop and Johnston Inc .... E 330 220-2700
  Valley City (G-18616)
Dynamic Structures Inc .... E 330 892-0164
  New Waterford (G-15137)
Early Construction Co .... E 740 894-5150
  South Point (G-17085)
Eckinger Construction Company .. E 330 453-2566
  Canton (G-2350)
Elford Inc .... C 614 488-4000
  Columbus (G-7588)
Enterprise Construction Inc .... E 440 349-3443
  Solon (G-17003)
Equity Inc .... E 614 802-2900
  Hilliard (G-11900)
Ernest Fritsch .... E 614 436-5995
  Columbus (G-7606)
Etech-Systems LLC .... D 216 221-6600
  Lakewood (G-12477)
Exxcel Project Management LLC .. E 614 621-4500
  Columbus (G-7624)
Fairfield Homes Inc .... C 614 873-3533
  Plain City (G-16192)
Fc 1346 LLC .... E 330 864-8170
  Akron (G-221)
Feick Contractors Inc .... E 419 625-3241
  Sandusky (G-16756)
Ferguson Construction Company .. C 937 498-2381
  Sidney (G-16933)
Ferguson Construction Company .. D 937 274-1173
  Dayton (G-9545)
Finneytown Contracting Corp ...... E 513 482-2700
  Cincinnati (G-3612)
Fiorilli Construction Co Inc .... E 216 696-5845
  Medina (G-14065)
Fleming Construction Co .... E 740 494-2177
  Prospect (G-16365)
Floyd P Bucher & Son Inc .... E 419 867-8792
  Toledo (G-17898)
Ford Development Corp .... D 513 772-1521
  Cincinnati (G-3637)
Forest City Residential Dev .... E 216 621-6060
  Cleveland (G-5621)
Fortney & Weygandt Inc .... E 440 716-4000
  North Olmsted (G-15422)
Foti Construction Company LLP ... E 440 347-0728
  Wickliffe (G-19597)
Foti Contracting LLC .... C 330 656-3454
  Wickliffe (G-19598)
▲ Fred Olivieri Construction Co .... C 330 494-1007
  North Canton (G-15338)
Fryman-Kuck General Contrs Inc . E 937 274-2892
  Dayton (G-9564)

G III Reitter Walls LLC ....E 614 545-4444
Columbus *(G-7718)*

G J Goudreau & Co ....E 216 351-5233
Cleveland *(G-5646)*

G Stephens Inc ....E 419 241-5188
Toledo *(G-17904)*

Gem Interiors Inc ....E 513 831-6535
Milford *(G-14521)*

Gilbane Building Company ....E 614 948-4000
Columbus *(G-7750)*

Gold Star Insulation L P ....E 614 221-3241
Columbus *(G-7757)*

Goliath Contracting Ltd ....E 614 568-7878
Reynoldsburg *(G-16455)*

Gowdy Partners LLC ....E 614 488-4424
Columbus *(G-7764)*

Grae-Con Construction Inc ....D 740 282-6830
Steubenville *(G-17321)*

Greater Dayton Cnstr Ltd ....D 937 426-3577
Beavercreek *(G-1243)*

Greystone Group-Avery Ltd ....E 216 464-3580
Cleveland *(G-5705)*

Gutknecht Construction Company ....E 614 532-5410
Columbus *(G-7787)*

Hal Homes Inc ....E 513 984-5360
Blue Ash *(G-1606)*

Hammond Construction Inc ....D 330 455-7039
Canton *(G-2389)*

Hanlin-Rainaldi Construction ....E 614 436-4204
Columbus *(G-7799)*

Head Inc ....E 614 338-8501
Columbus *(G-7808)*

Hi-Five Development Svcs Inc ....E 513 336-9280
Mason *(G-13716)*

Higgins Building Company Inc ....E 740 439-5553
Cambridge *(G-2120)*

▲ Homan Inc ....E 419 925-4349
Maria Stein *(G-13428)*

Hughes & Knollman Construction ....D 614 237-6167
Columbus *(G-7862)*

Icon Environmental Group LLC ....E 513 426-6767
Milford *(G-14526)*

Ideal Company Inc ....E 937 836-8683
Clayton *(G-4911)*

Ingle-Barr Inc ....D 740 702-6117
Chillicothe *(G-2853)*

Interstate Construction Inc ....E 614 539-1188
Grove City *(G-11572)*

Ivan Weaver Construction Co ....E 330 695-3461
Fredericksburg *(G-11177)*

J & F Construction and Dev Inc ....E 419 562-6662
Bucyrus *(G-2042)*

J & R Associates ....A 440 250-4080
Brookpark *(G-1947)*

J&H Rnfrcing Strl Erectors Inc ....C 740 355-0141
Portsmouth *(G-16292)*

Jack Gibson Construction Co ....D 330 394-5280
Warren *(G-18867)*

James Hunt Construction Co ....E 513 721-0559
Cincinnati *(G-3861)*

Jeffrey Carr Construction Inc ....E 330 879-5210
Massillon *(G-13826)*

Jhi Group Inc ....C 419 465-4611
Monroeville *(G-14721)*

JJO Construction Inc ....E 440 255-1515
Mentor *(G-14199)*

JKL Construction Inc ....E 513 553-3333
New Richmond *(G-15128)*

Jtf Construction Inc ....D 513 860-9835
Fairfield *(G-10866)*

Justice & Business Svcs LLC ....E 740 423-5005
Belpre *(G-1440)*

K-Y Residential Coml Indus Dev ....D 330 448-4055
Brookfield *(G-1897)*

▲ Kajima International Inc ....C 440 544-2600
Cleveland *(G-5880)*

Kapp Construction Inc ....E 937 324-0134
Springfield *(G-17219)*

Kbj-Summit LLC ....D 440 232-3334
Bedford *(G-1314)*

Kenny Obayashi Joint Venture V ....C 703 969-0611
Akron *(G-304)*

Kirila Contractors Inc ....D 330 448-4055
Brookfield *(G-1898)*

Knoch Corporation ....D 330 244-1440
Canton *(G-2428)*

▲ Kokosing Construction Co Inc ....C 614 228-1029
Columbus *(G-8007)*

Kramer & Feldman Inc ....E 513 821-7444
Cincinnati *(G-3942)*

Krumroy-Cozad Cnstr Corp ....E 330 376-4136
Akron *(G-309)*

▲ L Brands Store Dsign Cnstr Inc ....C 614 415-7000
Columbus *(G-8021)*

L Jack Ruscilli ....E 614 876-9484
Columbus *(G-8023)*

Lathrop Company Inc ....E 419 893-7000
Toledo *(G-18001)*

LEWaro-D&j-A Joint Venture Co ....E 937 443-0000
Dayton *(G-9678)*

Link Construction Group Inc ....E 937 292-7774
Bellefontaine *(G-1385)*

Lm Constrction Trry Lvrini Inc ....E 740 695-9604
Saint Clairsville *(G-16641)*

Ludy Greenhouse Mfg Corp ....D 800 255-5839
New Madison *(G-15072)*

Luke Theis Enterprises Inc ....D 419 422-2040
Findlay *(G-11059)*

M & W Construction Entps LLC ....E 419 227-2000
Lima *(G-12835)*

M-A Building and Maint Co ....E 216 391-5577
Independence *(G-12231)*

Marietta Silos LLC ....E 740 373-2822
Marietta *(G-13473)*

Mark-L Inc ....E 614 863-8832
Gahanna *(G-11256)*

Mattlin Construction Inc ....E 513 598-5402
Cleves *(G-6804)*

Mc Meechan Construction Co ....E 216 581-9373
Cleveland *(G-5999)*

McDonalds Design & Build Inc ....E 419 782-4191
Defiance *(G-10047)*

McNerney & Son Inc ....E 419 666-0200
Toledo *(G-18046)*

MCR Services Inc ....E 614 421-0860
Columbus *(G-8138)*

Mel Lanzer Co ....E 419 592-2801
Napoleon *(G-14945)*

Messer Construction Co ....E 513 672-5000
Cincinnati *(G-4082)*

Messer Construction Co ....D 513 242-1541
Cincinnati *(G-4083)*

Messer Construction Co ....D 937 291-1300
Dayton *(G-9721)*

Messer Construction Co ....D 614 275-0141
Columbus *(G-8152)*

MI - De - Con Inc ....D 740 532-2277
Ironton *(G-12299)*

Mid-Continent Construction Co ....E 440 439-6100
Oakwood Village *(G-15631)*

Midwest Church Cnstr Ltd ....E 419 874-0838
Perrysburg *(G-16033)*

Midwest Roofing & Furnace Co ....E 614 252-5241
Columbus *(G-8172)*

Mike Coates Cnstr Co Inc ....C 330 652-0190
Niles *(G-15297)*

Miles-Mcclellan Cnstr Co Inc ....E 614 487-7744
Columbus *(G-8173)*

Miller Contracting Group Inc ....E 419 453-3825
Ottoville *(G-15808)*

Miller-Valentine Construction ....D 937 293-0900
Dayton *(G-9749)*

Monarch Construction Company ....C 513 351-6900
Cincinnati *(G-4114)*

Mowry Construction & Engrg Inc ....E 419 289-2262
Ashland *(G-690)*

Mpower Inc ....E 614 783-0478
Gahanna *(G-11258)*

Muha Construction Inc ....E 937 435-0678
Dayton *(G-9760)*

Mullett Company ....E 440 564-9000
Newbury *(G-15259)*

Multicon Builders Inc ....E 614 241-2070
Columbus *(G-8206)*

Multicon Builders Inc ....E 614 463-1142
Columbus *(G-8207)*

Mural & Son Inc ....E 216 267-3322
Cleveland *(G-6090)*

Murphy Contracting Co ....E 330 743-8915
Youngstown *(G-20292)*

N Cook Inc ....E 513 275-9872
Cincinnati *(G-4135)*

National Housing Corporation ....E 614 481-8106
Columbus *(G-8220)*

Nitschke Sampson Dietz Inc ....E 614 464-1933
Columbus *(G-8281)*

Nordmann Roofing Co Inc ....E 419 691-5737
Toledo *(G-18089)*

Nyman Construction Co ....E 216 475-7800
Cleveland *(G-6173)*

Oberer Development Co ....E 937 910-0851
Miamisburg *(G-14328)*

Ohio Maint & Renovation Inc ....E 330 315-3101
Akron *(G-367)*

Ohio Technical Services Inc ....E 614 372-0829
Columbus *(G-8450)*

Oliver House Rest Complex ....D 419 243-1302
Toledo *(G-18105)*

Oswald Company Inc ....E 513 745-4424
Cincinnati *(G-4241)*

Ozanne Construction Co Inc ....E 216 696-2876
Cleveland *(G-6224)*

Palmetto Construction Svcs LLC ....E 614 503-7150
Columbus *(G-8512)*

Pepper Cnstr Co Ohio LLC ....E 614 793-4477
Dublin *(G-10425)*

Peterson Construction Company ....C 419 941-2233
Wapakoneta *(G-18806)*

◆ Pivotek LLC ....E 513 372-6205
West Chester *(G-19128)*

Plevniak Construction Inc ....E 330 718-1600
Youngstown *(G-20324)*

Prestige Interiors Inc ....E 330 425-1690
Twinsburg *(G-18456)*

Property Estate Management LLC ....E 513 684-0418
Cincinnati *(G-4348)*

QBS Inc ....E 330 821-8801
Alliance *(G-552)*

Quality Masonry Company Inc ....E 740 387-6720
Marion *(G-13573)*

Quandel Construction Group Inc ....E 717 657-0909
Westerville *(G-19439)*

Quantum Construction Company ....E 513 351-6903
Cincinnati *(G-4361)*

R A Hermes Inc ....E 513 251-5200
Cincinnati *(G-4377)*

R B Development Company Inc ....B 513 829-8100
Fairfield *(G-10897)*

R L Fortney Management Inc ....C 440 716-4000
North Olmsted *(G-15441)*

Ram Construction Services of ....D 513 297-1857
West Chester *(G-19137)*

Ray Fogg Building Methods Inc ....E 216 351-7976
Cleveland *(G-6354)*

Reece-Campbell Inc ....D 513 542-4600
Cincinnati *(G-4397)*

Registered Contractors Inc ....E 440 205-0873
Mentor *(G-14235)*

Renier Construction Corp ....E 614 866-4580
Columbus *(G-8613)*

Residence Artists Inc ....E 440 286-8822
Chardon *(G-2764)*

Residntial Coml Rnovations Inc ....E 330 815-1476
Clinton *(G-6807)*

Restaurant Specialties Inc ....E 614 885-9707
Sunbury *(G-17561)*

Retail Renovations Inc ....E 330 334-4501
Wadsworth *(G-18770)*

Righter Co Inc ....E 614 272-9700
Columbus *(G-8629)*

Righter Construction Svcs Inc ....E 614 272-9700
Columbus *(G-8630)*

Romanelli & Hughes Building Co ....E 614 891-2042
Westerville *(G-19441)*

◆ Rough Brothers Mfg Inc ....D 513 242-0310
Cincinnati *(G-4446)*

Rudolph Libbe Inc ....B 419 241-5000
Walbridge *(G-18777)*

Rudolph/Libbe Companies Inc ....A 419 241-5000
Walbridge *(G-18778)*

Ruhlin Company ....C 330 239-2800
Sharon Center *(G-16877)*

Runyon & Sons Roofing Inc ....D 440 974-6810
Mentor *(G-14238)*

Ruscilli Construction Co Inc ....D 614 876-9484
Columbus *(G-8658)*

Schirmer Construction Co ....E 440 716-4900
North Olmsted *(G-15443)*

Schnippel Construction Inc ....E 937 693-3831
Botkins *(G-1753)*

Scs Construction Services Inc ....E 513 929-0260
Cincinnati *(G-4487)*

▲ Season Contractors Inc ....E 440 717-0188
Broadview Heights *(G-1891)*

Shelly and Sands Inc ....D 740 859-2104
Rayland *(G-16418)*

Shelly and Sands Inc ....E 614 444-5100
Columbus *(G-8725)*

Simonson Construction Svcs Inc ....D 419 281-8299
Ashland *(G-699)*

S I C

Site Worx LLC D 513 229-0295
Lebanon *(G-12647)*
Skanska USA Building Inc E 513 421-0082
Cincinnati *(G-4538)*
Smb Construction Co Inc E 419 269-1473
Toledo *(G-18191)*
Smith Construction Group Inc E 937 426-0500
Beavercreek Township *(G-1284)*
Snavely Building Company E 440 585-9091
Chagrin Falls *(G-2705)*
Spieker Company E 419 872-7000
Perrysburg *(G-16062)*
Stamm Contracting Co Inc E 330 274-8230
Mantua *(G-13395)*
Stanley Miller Construction Co E 330 484-2229
East Sparta *(G-10541)*
Star Builders Inc E 440 986-5951
Amherst *(G-606)*
Stockmeister Enterprises Inc E 740 286-1619
Jackson *(G-12318)*
Studer-Obringer Inc E 419 492-2121
New Washington *(G-15136)*
Sunrush Construction Co Inc E 740 775-1300
Chillicothe *(G-2889)*
Swartz Enterprises Inc E 419 331-1024
Lima *(G-12895)*
T Allen Inc E 440 234-2366
Berea *(G-1472)*
T O J Inc E 440 352-1900
Mentor *(G-14247)*
Tab Construction Company Inc E 330 454-5228
Canton *(G-2557)*
Tri State Corporation E 513 763-0215
Cincinnati *(G-4683)*
Tri-Con Incorporated E 513 530-9844
Blue Ash *(G-1701)*
Trisco Systems Incorporated C 419 339-9912
Lima *(G-12906)*
Trubuilt Construction Svcs LLC E 614 279-4800
Columbus *(G-8875)*
Turner Construction Company E 216 522-1180
Cleveland *(G-6623)*
Turner Construction Company D 513 363-0883
Cincinnati *(G-4706)*
Turner Construction Company D 614 984-3000
Columbus *(G-8879)*
Turner Construction Company C 513 721-4224
Cincinnati *(G-4705)*
Tusing Builders Ltd E 419 465-3100
Monroeville *(G-14723)*
Twok General Co E 740 417-9195
Delaware *(G-10131)*
Union Industrial Contractors E 440 998-7871
Ashtabula *(G-765)*
Universal Contracting Corp E 513 482-2700
Cincinnati *(G-4747)*
Universal Development MGT Inc E 330 759-7017
Girard *(G-11428)*
Valley View Fire Dept E 216 524-7200
Cleveland *(G-6685)*
Van Con Inc E 937 890-8400
Dayton *(G-9962)*
Van Tassel Construction Corp E 419 873-0188
Perrysburg *(G-16068)*
Vig Property Development LLC E 888 384-5970
Cincinnati *(G-4814)*
VIP Restoration Inc D 216 426-9500
Cleveland *(G-6699)*
VIP Restoration Inc D 216 426-9500
Cuyahoga Falls *(G-9232)*
Watertown Steel Company LLC E 740 749-3512
Waterford *(G-18940)*
Weaver Custom Homes Inc E 330 264-5444
Wooster *(G-19927)*
Welty Building Company Ltd D 330 867-2400
Fairlawn *(G-10981)*
Wenco Inc C 937 849-6002
New Carlisle *(G-15033)*
Wenger Temperature Control E 614 586-4016
Columbus *(G-8978)*
▲ **West Roofing Systems Inc** E 800 356-5748
Lagrange *(G-12462)*
Whiting-Turner Contracting Co C 614 459-6515
Worthington *(G-20009)*
Whiting-Turner Contracting Co D 440 449-9200
Cleveland *(G-6750)*
Williams Bros Builders Inc E 440 365-3261
Elyria *(G-10692)*
Wingler Construction Corp E 614 626-8546
Columbus *(G-9000)*
Winsupply Inc D 937 294-5331
Moraine *(G-14836)*
Wise Services Inc E 937 854-0281
Dayton *(G-10001)*
Witmers Inc E 330 427-2147
Salem *(G-16719)*
Woodward Construction Inc E 513 247-9241
Blue Ash *(G-1721)*
Xtreme Contracting Ltd E 614 568-7030
Reynoldsburg *(G-16492)*

16 HEAVY CONSTRUCTION OTHER THAN BUILDING CONSTRUCTION-CONTRACTORS

1611 Highway & Street Construction

A & A Safety Inc E 513 943-6100
Amelia *(G-571)*
A P OHoro Company D 330 759-9317
Youngstown *(G-20095)*
Able Contracting Group Inc E 440 951-0880
Painesville *(G-15832)*
Aecom Energy & Cnstr Inc B 216 622-2300
Cleveland *(G-4962)*
Akil Incorporated E 419 625-0857
Sandusky *(G-16724)*
Alan Stone Company D 740 448-1100
Cutler *(G-9157)*
Allied Paving Inc E 419 666-3100
Holland *(G-12006)*
American Precast Refractories B 614 876-8416
Columbus *(G-7003)*
Anthony Allega Cement Contr E 216 447-0814
Cleveland *(G-5042)*
Armor Paving & Sealing E 614 751-6900
Reynoldsburg *(G-16429)*
Ashtabula County Commissioners E 440 576-2816
Jefferson *(G-12329)*
◆ **Baker Concrete Cnstr Inc** A 513 539-4000
Monroe *(G-14688)*
Barbicas Construction Co E 330 733-9101
Akron *(G-89)*
Barrett Paving Materials Inc C 513 271-6200
Middletown *(G-14475)*
Beaver Constructors Inc D 330 478-2151
Canton *(G-2261)*
Becdir Construction Company E 330 547-2134
Berlin Center *(G-1480)*
Belmont County of Ohio E 740 695-1580
Saint Clairsville *(G-16625)*
Brock & Sons Inc E 513 874-4555
Fairfield *(G-10824)*
Butler Asphalt Co LLC E 937 890-1141
Vandalia *(G-18666)*
C J & L Construction Inc E 513 769-3600
Cincinnati *(G-3160)*
C Tucker Cope & Assoc Inc E 330 482-4472
Columbiana *(G-6854)*
Camargo Construction Company E 513 248-1500
Cincinnati *(G-3168)*
Canton Public Works E 330 489-3030
Canton *(G-2295)*
Chemcote Inc C 614 792-2683
Dublin *(G-10290)*
Cincinnati Fill Inc E 513 242-7526
Cincinnati *(G-3304)*
City of Aurora D 330 562-8662
Aurora *(G-836)*
City of Avon E 440 937-5740
Avon *(G-889)*
City of Brecksville E 440 526-1384
Brecksville *(G-1818)*
City of Cuyahoga Falls E 330 971-8030
Cuyahoga Falls *(G-9176)*
City of Euclid E 216 289-2800
Cleveland *(G-5260)*
City of Kent D 330 678-8105
Kent *(G-12359)*
City of Lima E 419 221-5165
Lima *(G-12754)*
City of North Ridgeville E 440 327-8326
North Ridgeville *(G-15460)*
City of North Royalton E 440 582-3002
Cleveland *(G-5270)*
City of Norwalk E 419 663-6715
Norwalk *(G-15563)*
City of Portsmouth E 740 353-5419
Portsmouth *(G-16269)*
City of Streetsboro E 330 626-2856
Streetsboro *(G-17410)*
City of Westerville E 614 901-6500
Westerville *(G-19382)*
City of Willoughby D 440 953-4111
Willoughby *(G-19650)*
Colas Solutions Inc E 513 272-5348
Cincinnati *(G-3380)*
Columbus Asphalt Paving Inc E 614 759-9800
Gahanna *(G-11235)*
Cook Paving and Cnstr Co E 216 267-7705
Independence *(G-12201)*
County of Clinton E 937 382-2078
Wilmington *(G-19759)*
County of Delaware D 740 833-2400
Delaware *(G-10083)*
County of Holmes E 330 674-5076
Millersburg *(G-14598)*
County of Monroe E 740 472-0760
Woodsfield *(G-19814)*
County of Portage D 330 296-6411
Ravenna *(G-16379)*
County of Seneca E 419 447-3863
Tiffin *(G-17674)*
County of Shelby E 937 498-7244
Sidney *(G-16925)*
County of Summit C 330 643-2860
Akron *(G-171)*
County of Trumbull D 330 675-2640
Warren *(G-18840)*
Crp Contracting D 614 338-8501
Columbus *(G-7469)*
Cunningham Paving Company E 216 581-8600
Bedford *(G-1302)*
D B Bentley Inc E 440 352-8495
Painesville *(G-15849)*
D G M Inc D 740 226-1950
Beaver *(G-1141)*
D&M Carter LLC E 513 831-8843
Miamiville *(G-14375)*
Decorative Paving Company E 513 576-1222
Loveland *(G-13121)*
Dept of Public Works R B E 216 661-2800
Cleveland *(G-5477)*
Don S Cisle Contractor Inc D 513 867-1400
Hamilton *(G-11724)*
Double Z Construction Company D 614 274-9334
Columbus *(G-7542)*
E S Wagner Company D 419 691-8651
Oregon *(G-15733)*
Eaton Construction Co Inc D 740 474-3414
Circleville *(G-4887)*
Ebony Construction Co E 419 841-3455
Sylvania *(G-17585)*
Erie Blacktop Inc E 419 625-7374
Sandusky *(G-16751)*
Erie Construction Group Inc E 419 625-7374
Sandusky *(G-16752)*
Fabrizi Trucking & Pav Co Inc C 330 483-3291
Cleveland *(G-5564)*
Ferrous Metal Transfer E 216 671-8500
Brooklyn *(G-1906)*
Franklin Cnty Bd Commissioners C 614 462-3030
Columbus *(G-7682)*
Fred A Nemann Co E 513 467-9400
Cincinnati *(G-3645)*
Fryman-Kuck General Contrs Inc E 937 274-2892
Dayton *(G-9564)*
George Kuhn Enterprises Inc E 614 481-8838
Columbus *(G-7743)*
Great Lakes Crushing Ltd E 440 944-5500
Wickliffe *(G-19599)*
Hardin County Engineer E 419 673-2232
Kenton *(G-12415)*
Hi-Way Paving Inc D 614 876-1700
Hilliard *(G-11910)*
Hicon Inc D 513 242-3612
Cincinnati *(G-3760)*
Image Pavement Maintenance E 937 833-9200
Brookville *(G-1963)*
▲ **Independence Excavating Inc** E 216 524-1700
Independence *(G-12218)*
J A Donadee Corporation E 330 533-3305
Canfield *(G-2197)*
J K Enterprises Inc D 614 481-8838
Columbus *(G-7931)*
J K Meurer Corp E 513 831-7500
Loveland *(G-13135)*
J&B Steel Erectors Inc C 513 874-1722
West Chester *(G-19096)*

16 HEAVY CONSTRUCTION OTHER THAN BUILDING CONSTRUCTION-CONTRACTORS

K & M Construction Company ..... C 330 723-3681
  Medina (G-14089)
K West Group LLC ..... C 972 722-3874
  Perrysburg (G-16022)
Ken Heiberger Paving Inc ..... D 614 837-0290
  Canal Winchester (G-2162)
▲ Kenmore Construction Co Inc ..... C 330 762-8936
  Akron (G-303)
Kenmore Construction Co Inc ..... E 330 832-8888
  Massillon (G-13827)
Kirila Contractors Inc ..... D 330 448-4055
  Brookfield (G-1898)
▲ Kokosing Construction Inc ..... A 330 263-4168
  Wooster (G-19881)
▲ Kokosing Construction Co Inc ..... C 614 228-1029
  Columbus (G-8007)
Kokosing Construction Co Inc ..... E 614 228-1029
  Columbus (G-8008)
Kokosing Inc ..... D 614 212-5700
  Westerville (G-19417)
Lake Erie Construction Co ..... C 419 668-3302
  Norwalk (G-15578)
Lash Paving Inc ..... D 740 635-4335
  Bridgeport (G-1864)
LEWaro-D&j-A Joint Venture Co ..... E 937 443-0000
  Dayton (G-9678)
Lyndco Inc ..... E 740 671-9098
  Shadyside (G-16850)
M P Dory Co ..... D 614 444-2138
  Columbus (G-8093)
Maco Construction Services ..... E 330 482-4472
  Columbiana (G-6860)
Maintenance Systerms of N Ohio ..... E 440 323-1291
  Elyria (G-10648)
MBC Holdings Inc ..... A 419 445-1015
  Archbold (G-638)
McDaniels Cnstr Corp Inc ..... D 614 252-5852
  Columbus (G-8134)
Miller Bros Const Inc ..... E 419 445-1015
  Archbold (G-639)
Moyer Industries Inc ..... E 937 832-7283
  Clayton (G-4915)
Nas Ventures ..... D 614 338-8501
  Columbus (G-8213)
Neff Paving Ltd ..... E 740 453-3063
  Zanesville (G-20516)
Nerone & Sons Inc ..... E 216 662-2235
  Cleveland (G-6120)
Northstar Asphalt Inc ..... E 330 497-0936
  North Canton (G-15358)
Ohio Department Transportation ..... C 740 363-1251
  Delaware (G-10119)
Ohio Department Transportation ..... E 937 548-3015
  Greenville (G-11515)
Ohio Department Transportation ..... E 419 738-4214
  Wapakoneta (G-18805)
Ohio Department Transportation ..... E 330 533-4351
  Canfield (G-2205)
Ohio Tpk & Infrastructure Comm ..... E 419 826-4831
  Swanton (G-17569)
Ohio Tpk & Infrastructure Comm ..... C 440 234-2081
  Berea (G-1466)
Paul Peterson Company ..... E 614 486-4375
  Columbus (G-8522)
Pdk Construction Inc ..... E 740 992-6451
  Pomeroy (G-16234)
Perk Company Inc ..... E 216 391-1444
  Cleveland (G-6265)
Precision Paving Inc ..... E 419 499-7283
  Milan (G-14498)
Premier Asphalt Paving Co Inc ..... E 440 237-6600
  North Royalton (G-15498)
Prime Polymoro Inc ..... E 330 662-4200
  Medina (G-14113)
Queen City Blacktop Company ..... E 513 251-8400
  Cincinnati (G-4362)
R B Jergens Contractors Inc ..... D 937 669-9799
  Vandalia (G-18696)
R D Jergens Contractors Inc ..... D 937 669-9799
  Vandalia (G-18697)
R T Vernal Paving Inc ..... E 330 549-3189
  North Lima (G-15407)
Rack Seven Paving Co Inc ..... E 513 271-4863
  Cincinnati (G-4382)
Ray Bertolini Trucking Co ..... E 330 867-0666
  Akron (G-405)
Rick Eplion Paving ..... E 740 446-3000
  Gallipolis (G-11338)
Ruhlin Company ..... C 330 239-2800
  Sharon Center (G-16877)

S & K Asphalt & Concrete ..... E 330 848-6284
  Akron (G-422)
Samples Chuck-General Contr ..... E 419 586-1434
  Celina (G-2663)
Schweitzer Construction Co ..... E 513 761-4980
  Cincinnati (G-4485)
Scot Burton Contractors LLC ..... E 440 564-1011
  Newbury (G-15261)
Security Fence Group Inc ..... E 513 681-3700
  Cincinnati (G-4489)
Shelly and Sands Inc ..... E 740 453-6260
  Zanesville (G-20531)
Shelly and Sands Inc ..... E 614 444-5100
  Columbus (G-8725)
Shelly and Sands Inc ..... D 419 529-8455
  Ontario (G-15713)
Shelly and Sands Inc ..... E 740 453-0721
  Zanesville (G-20532)
Shelly Company ..... E 419 396-7641
  Carey (G-2598)
Shelly Company ..... E 740 441-1714
  Circleville (G-4904)
Shelly Company ..... D 419 422-8854
  Findlay (G-11080)
Shelly Company ..... E 330 425-7861
  Twinsburg (G-18469)
Shelly Materials Inc ..... E 740 666-5841
  Ostrander (G-15794)
Smalls Asphalt Paving Inc ..... E 740 427-4096
  Gambier (G-11350)
Spieker Company ..... E 419 872-7000
  Perrysburg (G-16062)
Springboro Service Center ..... E 937 748-0020
  Springboro (G-17138)
Stonegate Construction Inc ..... D 740 423-9170
  Belpre (G-1444)
Sunesis Construction Company ..... C 513 326-6000
  West Chester (G-19161)
Superior Paving & Materials ..... E 330 499-5849
  Canton (G-2556)
Tab Construction Company Inc ..... E 330 454-5228
  Canton (G-2557)
▲ Terminal Ready-Mix Inc ..... E 440 288-0181
  Lorain (G-13081)
Township of Copley ..... E 330 666-1853
  Copley (G-9067)
Trafftech Inc ..... E 216 361-8808
  Cleveland (G-6608)
Transportation Ohio Department ..... E 740 773-3191
  Chillicothe (G-2891)
Tri State Corporation ..... E 513 763-0215
  Cincinnati (G-4683)
Trucco Construction Co Inc ..... C 740 417-9010
  Delaware (G-10130)
Tucson Inc ..... E 330 339-4935
  New Philadelphia (G-15118)
Turnpike and Infrastructure Co ..... D 330 527-2169
  Windham (G-19804)
Unicustom Inc ..... E 513 874-9806
  Fairfield (G-10919)
Vandalia Blacktop Seal Coating ..... E 937 454-0571
  Dayton (G-9965)
Velotta Company ..... E 330 239-1211
  Sharon Center (G-16880)
Virginia Ohio-West Excvtg Co ..... C 740 676-7464
  Shadyside (G-16852)
W G Lockhart Construction Co ..... D 330 745-6520
  Akron (G-501)
Waltek Inc ..... E 614 469-0156
  Columbus (G-8965)
Westpatrick Corp ..... E 614 875-8200
  Columbus (G-8981)

1622 Bridge, Tunnel & Elevated Hwy Construction

A P OHoro Company ..... D 330 759-9317
  Youngstown (G-20095)
Aecom Energy & Cnstr Inc ..... B 216 622-2300
  Cleveland (G-4962)
Akil Incorporated ..... E 419 625-0857
  Sandusky (G-16724)
Armstrong Steel Erectors Inc ..... E 740 345-4503
  Newark (G-15144)
Becdir Construction Company ..... E 330 547-2134
  Berlin Center (G-1480)
▲ Brumbaugh Construction Inc ..... E 937 692-5107
  Arcanum (G-629)
Capitol Tunneling Inc ..... E 614 444-0255
  Columbus (G-7188)

CJ Mahan Construction Co LLC ..... D 614 277-4545
  Columbus (G-7288)
Clayton Railroad Cnstr LLC ..... E 937 549-2952
  West Union (G-19276)
Colas Solutions Inc ..... E 513 272-5348
  Cincinnati (G-3380)
Complete General Cnstr Co ..... C 614 258-9515
  Columbus (G-7414)
E S Wagner Company ..... E 419 691-8651
  Oregon (G-15733)
Eagle Bridge Co ..... D 937 492-5654
  Sidney (G-16930)
▲ Fenton Rigging & Contg Inc ..... E 513 631-5500
  Cincinnati (G-3602)
Foundation Steel LLC ..... D 419 402-4241
  Swanton (G-17564)
Fryman-Kuck General Contrs Inc ..... E 937 274-2892
  Dayton (G-9564)
J & J Schlaegel Inc ..... E 937 652-2045
  Urbana (G-18592)
K M & M ..... C 216 651-3333
  Cleveland (G-5879)
Kassouf Company ..... E 216 651-3333
  Avon (G-902)
▲ Kokosing Construction Co Inc ..... C 614 228-1029
  Columbus (G-8007)
Kokosing Construction Co Inc ..... E 614 228-1029
  Columbus (G-8008)
MBC Holdings Inc ..... A 419 445-1015
  Archbold (G-638)
National Engrg & Contg Co ..... A 440 238-3331
  Cleveland (G-6107)
▼ Ohio Bridge Corporation ..... C 740 432-6334
  Cambridge (G-2125)
Prus Construction Company ..... E 513 321-7774
  Cincinnati (G-4354)
Righter Co Inc ..... E 614 272-9700
  Columbus (G-8629)
Righter Construction Svcs Inc ..... E 614 272-9700
  Columbus (G-8630)
Ruhlin Company ..... C 330 239-2800
  Sharon Center (G-16877)
Rwb Properties and Cnstr LLC ..... D 513 541-0900
  Cincinnati (G-4459)
Sunesis Construction Company ..... C 513 326-6000
  West Chester (G-19161)
Tri State Corporation ..... E 513 763-0215
  Cincinnati (G-4683)
Velotta Company ..... E 330 239-1211
  Sharon Center (G-16880)
Westpatrick Corp ..... E 614 875-8200
  Columbus (G-8981)

1623 Water, Sewer & Utility Line Construction

A Crano Excavating Inc ..... E 330 630-1061
  Akron (G-11)
A P OHoro Company ..... D 330 759-9317
  Youngstown (G-20095)
AAA Flexible Pipe Cleaning ..... E 216 341-2900
  Cleveland (G-4941)
ABC Piping Co ..... E 216 398-4000
  Brooklyn Heights (G-1908)
Adams-Robinson Enterprises Inc ..... C 937 274-5318
  Dayton (G-9308)
Adleta Inc ..... E 513 554-1469
  Cincinnati (G-2973)
Aecom Energy & Cnstr Inc ..... B 216 622-2300
  Cleveland (G-4962)
Amboy Contractors LLc ..... D 419 644-2111
  Metamora (G-14264)
American Boring Inc ..... E 740 969-8000
  Carroll (G-2607)
Anderzack-Pitzen Cnstr Inc ..... E 419 553-7015
  Metamora (G-14265)
Bitzel Excavating Inc ..... E 330 477-9653
  Canton (G-2265)
Bluefoot Industrial LLC ..... E 740 314-5299
  Steubenville (G-17304)
Bolt Construction Inc ..... D 330 549-0349
  Youngstown (G-20122)
Boone Coleman Construction Inc ..... E 740 858-6661
  Portsmouth (G-16266)
Broadband Express LLC ..... D 419 536-9127
  Toledo (G-17783)
Brock & Sons Inc ..... E 513 874-4555
  Fairfield (G-10824)
Ch2m Hill Constructors Inc ..... E 937 228-4285
  Dayton (G-9395)

Charles H Hamilton Co....D....513 683-2442
Maineville *(G-13241)*
City of Dayton....E....937 333-3725
Dayton *(G-9410)*
City of Englewood....E....937 836-2434
Englewood *(G-10700)*
Cook Paving and Cnstr Co....E....216 267-7705
Independence *(G-12201)*
County of Clermont....E....513 732-7970
Batavia *(G-1007)*
County of Delaware....C....740 833-2240
Delaware *(G-10082)*
County of Union....D....937 645-4145
Marysville *(G-13614)*
Darby Creek Excavating Inc....D....740 477-8600
Circleville *(G-4886)*
Dave Sugar Excavating LLC....E....330 542-1100
Petersburg *(G-16081)*
Digioia/Suburban Excvtg LLC....D....440 237-1978
North Royalton *(G-15487)*
Don Wartko Construction Co....D....330 673-5252
Kent *(G-12366)*
Dynamic Construction Inc....D....740 927-8898
Pataskala *(G-15923)*
E S Wagner Company....D....419 691-8651
Oregon *(G-15733)*
▲ **Enviro-Flow Companies Ltd**....E....740 453-7980
Zanesville *(G-20476)*
Fabrizi Trucking & Pav Co Inc....C....330 483-3291
Cleveland *(G-5564)*
Finlaw Construction Inc....E....330 889-2074
Bristolville *(G-1871)*
Fishel Company....D....614 274-8100
Columbus *(G-7667)*
Fishel Company....C....614 850-9012
Columbus *(G-7668)*
Fishel Company....C....937 233-2268
Dayton *(G-9551)*
Fishel Company....D....614 850-4400
Columbus *(G-7669)*
Fleming Construction Co....E....740 494-2177
Prospect *(G-16365)*
Ford Development Corp....D....513 772-1521
Cincinnati *(G-3637)*
George J Igel & Co Inc....A....614 445-8421
Columbus *(G-7742)*
Geotex Construction Svcs Inc....E....614 444-5690
Columbus *(G-7745)*
Gleason Construction Co Inc....D....419 865-7480
Holland *(G-12024)*
Great Lakes Crushing Ltd....E....440 944-5500
Wickliffe *(G-19599)*
Gudenkauf Corporation....C....614 488-1776
Columbus *(G-7786)*
H & W Contractors Inc....E....330 833-0982
Massillon *(G-13816)*
H M Miller Construction Co....D....330 628-4811
Mogadore *(G-14677)*
Inliner American Inc....E....614 529-6440
Hilliard *(G-11914)*
J & J General Maintenance Inc....E....740 533-9729
Ironton *(G-12293)*
J B Express Inc....D....740 702-9830
Chillicothe *(G-2854)*
J Daniel & Company Inc....D....513 575-3100
Loveland *(G-13134)*
Jack Conie & Sons Corp....D....614 291-5931
Columbus *(G-7933)*
JS Bova Excavating LLC....E....234 254-4040
Struthers *(G-17532)*
Kenneth G Myers Cnstr Co Inc....D....419 639-2051
Green Springs *(G-11478)*
Kirk Bros Co Inc....D....419 595-4020
Alvada *(G-569)*
▲ **Kokosing Construction Co Inc**....C....614 228-1029
Columbus *(G-8007)*
Kokosing Industrial Inc....B....614 212-5700
Westerville *(G-19418)*
Larry Smith Contractors Inc....E....513 367-0218
Cleves *(G-6803)*
Main Lite Electric Co Inc....E....330 369-8333
Warren *(G-18877)*
Maintenance Unlimited Inc....E....440 238-1162
Strongsville *(G-17486)*
Majaac Inc....E....419 636-5678
Bryan *(G-2010)*
Mannon Pipeline LLC....E....740 643-1534
Willow Wood *(G-19736)*
Marucci and Gaffney Excvtg Co....E....330 743-8170
Youngstown *(G-20273)*
Microwave Leasing Services LLC....E....614 308-5433
Columbus *(G-8161)*
Mid-Ohio Contracting Inc....C....330 343-2925
Dover *(G-10199)*
Mid-Ohio Pipeline Company Inc....E....419 884-3772
Mansfield *(G-13346)*
Mike Enyart & Sons Inc....D....740 523-0235
South Point *(G-17095)*
Miller Pipeline LLC....B....937 506-8837
Tipp City *(G-17722)*
Miller Pipeline LLC....B....614 777-8377
Hilliard *(G-11936)*
Minnesota Limited LLC....C....330 343-4612
Dover *(G-10200)*
Miracle Plumbing & Heating Co....E....330 477-2402
Canton *(G-2464)*
Municpal Cntrs Saling Pdts Inc....E....513 482-3300
Cincinnati *(G-4131)*
National Engrg & Contg Co....A....440 238-3331
Cleveland *(G-6107)*
Nelson Stark Company....C....513 489-0866
Cincinnati *(G-4154)*
Nerone & Sons Inc....E....216 662-2235
Cleveland *(G-6120)*
North Bay Construction Inc....E....440 835-1898
Westlake *(G-19522)*
O C I Construction Co Inc....E....440 338-3166
Novelty *(G-15602)*
Ohio Utilities Protection Svc....D....330 759-0050
Youngstown *(G-20310)*
Ots-NJ LLC....D....732 833-0600
Butler *(G-2067)*
Parallel Technologies Inc....D....614 798-9700
Dublin *(G-10421)*
Precision Pipeline Svcs LLC....E....740 652-1679
Lancaster *(G-12565)*
Quality Lines Inc....C....740 815-1165
Findlay *(G-11078)*
R & R Pipeline Inc....D....740 345-3692
Newark *(G-15230)*
R D Jergens Contractors Inc....D....937 669-9799
Vandalia *(G-18697)*
Rla Investments Inc....E....513 554-1470
Cincinnati *(G-4430)*
Russell Hawk Enterprises Inc....E....330 343-4612
Dover *(G-10210)*
Schaffer Mark Excvtg & Trcking....D....419 668-5990
Norwalk *(G-15592)*
Schweitzer Construction Co....E....513 761-4980
Cincinnati *(G-4485)*
Six C Fabrication Inc....D....330 296-5594
Ravenna *(G-16412)*
Sky Climber Twr Solutions LLC....E....740 203-3900
Delaware *(G-10127)*
South Shore Cable Cnstr Inc....D....440 816-0033
Cleveland *(G-6498)*
Southtown Heating & Cooling....E....937 320-9900
Moraine *(G-14827)*
Steelial Wldg Met Fbrction Inc....E....740 669-5300
Vinton *(G-18744)*
Stg Communication Services Inc....E....330 482-0500
Columbiana *(G-6864)*
Sunesis Construction Company....C....513 326-6000
West Chester *(G-19161)*
Sunesis Environmental LLC....D....513 326-6000
Fairfield *(G-10912)*
Terrace Construction Co Inc....D....216 739-3170
Cleveland *(G-6585)*
Thayer Pwr Comm Line Cnstr LLC....E....814 474-1174
Reynoldsburg *(G-16483)*
Todd Alspaugh & Associates....E....419 476-8126
Toledo *(G-18224)*
▼ **Tri County Tower Service**....E....330 538-9874
North Jackson *(G-15389)*
Tribute Contracting & Cons LLC....E....740 451-1010
South Point *(G-17098)*
Trucco Construction Co Inc....C....740 417-9010
Delaware *(G-10130)*
Underground Utilities Inc....D....419 465-2587
Monroeville *(G-14724)*
Universal Recovery Systems....D....614 299-0184
Columbus *(G-8907)*
Usic Locating Services LLC....E....419 874-9988
North Baltimore *(G-15316)*
Usic Locating Services LLC....D....513 554-0456
Cincinnati *(G-4799)*
Utilicon Corporation....E....216 391-8500
Cleveland *(G-6680)*
Vallejo Company....E....216 741-3933
Cleveland *(G-6682)*
Wachter Inc....C....513 777-0701
West Chester *(G-19243)*
Wenger Excavating Inc....E....330 837-4767
Dalton *(G-9244)*
Woodward Excavating Co....E....614 866-4384
Reynoldsburg *(G-16491)*
Zemba Bros Inc....E....740 452-1880
Zanesville *(G-20561)*

1629 Heavy Construction, NEC

A P OHoro Company....D....330 759-9317
Youngstown *(G-20095)*
Aecom Energy & Cnstr Inc....B....216 622-2300
Cleveland *(G-4962)*
Amtrac of Ohio Inc....D....330 683-7206
Orrville *(G-15763)*
Apex Environmental LLC....D....740 543-4389
Amsterdam *(G-607)*
Aquarius Marine LLC....E....614 875-8200
Columbus *(G-7031)*
Babcock & Wilcox Cnstr Co Inc....D....330 860-6301
Barberton *(G-954)*
◆ **Babcock & Wilcox Company**....A....330 753-4511
Barberton *(G-955)*
Brunk Excavating Inc....E....513 360-0308
Monroe *(G-14691)*
▲ **Buckeye Landscape Service Inc**....D....614 866-0088
Blacklick *(G-1501)*
Byrnes-Conway Company....D....513 948-8882
Cincinnati *(G-3159)*
C & B Buck Bros Asp Maint LLC....E....419 536-7325
Toledo *(G-17789)*
CDM Constructors Inc....D....740 947-7500
Waverly *(G-18968)*
▲ **Delta Railroad Cnstr Inc**....D....440 992-2997
Ashtabula *(G-741)*
E S Wagner Company....D....419 691-8651
Oregon *(G-15733)*
▲ **Enerfab Inc**....B....513 641-0500
Cincinnati *(G-3557)*
Fritz-Rumer-Cooke Co Inc....E....614 444-8844
Columbus *(G-7710)*
Fryman-Kuck General Contrs Inc....E....937 274-2892
Dayton *(G-9564)*
▲ **Goettle Holding Company Inc**....C....513 825-8100
Cincinnati *(G-3683)*
Great Lakes Crushing Ltd....E....440 944-5500
Wickliffe *(G-19599)*
Image Pavement Maintenance....E....937 833-9200
Brookville *(G-1963)*
▲ **Independence Excavating Inc**....E....216 524-1700
Independence *(G-12218)*
ISI Systems Inc....E....740 942-0050
Cadiz *(G-2078)*
J Way Leasing Ltd....E....440 934-1020
Avon *(G-899)*
Jack Conie & Sons Corp....D....614 291-5931
Columbus *(G-7933)*
Jack Gibson Construction Co....D....330 394-5280
Warren *(G-18867)*
Jacobs Constructors Inc....D....419 226-1344
Lima *(G-12806)*
Jacobs Constructors Inc....E....513 595-7900
Cincinnati *(G-3854)*
Kirk Bros Co Inc....D....419 595-4020
Alvada *(G-569)*
Kokosing Construction Co Inc....E....440 323-9346
Elyria *(G-10638)*
▲ **Kokosing Construction Co Inc**....C....614 228-1029
Columbus *(G-8007)*
Kokosing Industrial Inc....B....614 212-5700
Westerville *(G-19418)*
Landscping Rclmtion Spcialists....E....330 339-4900
New Philadelphia *(G-15106)*
M T Golf Course Managment Inc....E....513 923-1188
Cincinnati *(G-4006)*
Maintenance Unlimited Inc....E....440 238-1162
Strongsville *(G-17486)*
McDermott International Inc....C....740 687-4292
Lancaster *(G-12554)*
Metropolitan Envmtl Svcs Inc....D....614 771-1881
Hilliard *(G-11930)*
Miller Logging Inc....E....330 279-4721
Holmesville *(G-12074)*
Mollett Seamless Gutter Co....E....513 825-0500
West Chester *(G-19123)*
Ohio Irrigation Lawn Sprinkler....E....937 432-9911
Dayton *(G-9786)*
Pae & Associates Inc....E....937 833-0013
Dayton *(G-9798)*

Parks Drilling Company E 614 761-7707
Dublin *(G-10422)*
Peterson Construction Company C 419 941-2233
Wapakoneta *(G-18806)*
Petro Environmental Tech E 513 489-6789
Cincinnati *(G-4287)*
Platinum Restoration Inc E 440 327-0699
Elyria *(G-10671)*
Railworks Corporation B 330 538-2261
North Jackson *(G-15387)*
Riepenhoff Landscape Ltd E 614 876-4683
Hilliard *(G-11950)*
Righter Construction Svcs Inc E 614 272-9700
Columbus *(G-8630)*
Scg Fields LLC E 440 546-1200
Brecksville *(G-1849)*
Scherzinger Drilling Inc E 513 738-2000
Harrison *(G-11808)*
Schweitzer Construction Co E 513 761-4980
Cincinnati *(G-4485)*
Siemens Energy Inc B 740 393-8897
Mount Vernon *(G-14923)*
Sports Surfaces Cnstr LLC E 440 546-1200
Brecksville *(G-1852)*
Sunesis Environmental LLC D 513 326-6000
Fairfield *(G-10912)*
Todd Alspaugh & Associates E 419 476-8126
Toledo *(G-18224)*
Toledo Refining Company LLC C 419 698-6600
Oregon *(G-15752)*
Tri-America Contractors Inc E 740 574-0148
Wheelersburg *(G-19582)*
Ulliman Schutte Cnstr LLC B 937 247-0375
Miamisburg *(G-14363)*
Uranium Disposition Svcs LLC C 740 289-3620
Piketon *(G-16130)*
W Pol Contracting Inc E 330 325-7177
Ravenna *(G-16415)*
Whiting-Turner Contracting Co D 440 449-9200
Cleveland *(G-6750)*
Zinni Golf Co Inc E 330 533-7155
Canfield *(G-2218)*

17 CONSTRUCTION-SPECIAL TRADE CONTRACTORS

1711 Plumbing, Heating & Air Conditioning Contractors

A A S Amels Sheet Meta L Inc E 330 793-9326
Youngstown *(G-20094)*
A A Astro Service Inc D 216 459-0363
Cleveland *(G-4928)*
A AAA H Jacks Plumbing Htg Co E 440 946-1166
Wickliffe *(G-19591)*
A J Stockmeister Inc E 740 286-2106
Jackson *(G-12305)*
A Team LLC E 216 271-7223
Cleveland *(G-4936)*
A To Zoff Co Inc E 330 733-7902
Akron *(G-12)*
A-1 Advanced Plumbing Inc E 614 873-0548
Plain City *(G-16178)*
AAA Pipe Cleaning Corporation C 216 341-2900
Cleveland *(G-4942)*
ABC Fire Inc E 440 237-6677
North Royalton *(G-15480)*
ABC Piping Co E 216 398-4000
Brooklyn Heights *(G-1908)*
Accurate Heating & Cooling E 740 775-5005
Chillicothe *(G-2807)*
Accurate Mechanical Inc E 740 664 5898
Lancaster *(G-12506)*
Adelmos Electric Sewer Clg Co E 216 641-2301
Brooklyn Heights *(G-1909)*
Advance Mechanical Plbg & Htg E 937 879-9405
Fairborn *(G-10782)*
▲ **Advanced Mechanical Svcs Inc** E 937 879-7426
Fairborn *(G-10783)*
Aetna Building Maintenance Inc B 614 476-1818
Columbus *(G-6953)*
Aggressive Mechanical Inc E 614 443-3280
Columbus *(G-6956)*
Air Comfort Systems Inc E 216 587-4125
Cleveland *(G-4971)*
Air Conditioning Entps Inc E 440 729-0900
Cleveland *(G-4973)*
Air-Temp Climate Control Inc E 216 579-1552
Cleveland *(G-4974)*
Aire-Tech Inc E 614 836-5670
Groveport *(G-11621)*
Airtron LP D 614 274-2345
Columbus *(G-6960)*
Airtron LP D 513 860-5959
Cincinnati *(G-2902)*
▲ **Alan Manufacturing Inc** E 330 262-1555
Wooster *(G-19825)*
All About Heating Cooling E 513 621-4620
Cincinnati *(G-2984)*
All Temp Refrigeration Inc E 419 692-5016
Delphos *(G-10137)*
Allied Restaurant Svc Ohio Inc E 419 589-4759
Mansfield *(G-13260)*
American Air Furnace Company D 614 876-1702
Grove City *(G-11528)*
American Residential Svcs LLC D 216 561-8880
Cleveland *(G-5020)*
Apollo Heating and AC Inc E 513 271-3600
Cincinnati *(G-3036)*
Apple Heating Inc E 440 997-1212
Barberton *(G-952)*
Applied Mechanical Systems Inc D 513 825-1800
Cincinnati *(G-3037)*
Arco Heating & AC Co E 216 663-3211
Solon *(G-16976)*
Area Energy & Electric Inc C 937 498-4784
Sidney *(G-16913)*
Arise Incorporated E 440 746-8860
Brecksville *(G-1814)*
ARS Rescue Rooter Inc E 440 842-8494
Cleveland *(G-5068)*
Ashland Comfort Control Inc E 419 281-0144
Ashland *(G-656)*
Atlas Capital Services Inc D 614 294-7373
Columbus *(G-7069)*
Ayers-Sterrett Inc E 419 238-5480
Van Wert *(G-18628)*
Ayrshire Inc D 440 992-0743
Ashtabula *(G-728)*
Aztec Plumbing Inc E 513 732-3320
Milford *(G-14506)*
◆ **Babcock & Wilcox Company** A 330 753-4511
Barberton *(G-955)*
Bachmans Inc E 513 943-5300
Batavia *(G-995)*
Bay Furnace Sheet Metal Co E 440 871-3777
Westlake *(G-19463)*
Bay Mechanical & Elec Corp D 440 282-6816
Lorain *(G-13017)*
Bayes Inc E 419 661-3933
Perrysburg *(G-15975)*
Bellman Plumbing Inc E 440 324-4477
Elyria *(G-10596)*
Best Plumbing Limited E 614 855-1919
New Albany *(G-14974)*
Blind & Son LLC D 330 753-7711
Barberton *(G-959)*
Blue Chip Plumbing Inc D 513 941-4010
Cincinnati *(G-3120)*
Brady Plumbing & Heating Inc E 440 324-4261
Elyria *(G-10599)*
Brennan & Associates Inc E 216 391-4822
Cleveland *(G-5135)*
Brewer-Garrett Co C 440 243-3535
Middleburg Heights *(G-14378)*
Bruner Corporation C 614 334-9000
Hilliard *(G-11884)*
Buck and Sons Landscape Svc E 614 876-5359
Hilliard *(G-11885)*
▲ **Buckeye Landscape Service Inc** D 614 866-0088
Blacklick *(G-1501)*
Buckeye Mechanical Contg Inc E 740 282-0089
Toronto *(G-18334)*
Budde Sheet Metal Works Inc E 937 224-0868
Dayton *(G-9372)*
Building Integrated Svcs LLC D 330 733-9191
Oakwood Village *(G-15627)*
Burrier Service Company Inc E 440 946-6019
Mentor *(G-14151)*
Cahill Corporation E 330 724-1224
Uniontown *(G-18510)*
Campbell Inc D 419 476-4444
Northwood *(G-15529)*
Castle Heating & Air Inc E 216 696-3940
Solon *(G-16989)*
Cattrell Companies Inc D 740 537-2481
Toronto *(G-18336)*
Century Mech Solutions Inc E 513 681-5700
Cincinnati *(G-3220)*
Chemed Corporation D 513 762-6690
Cincinnati *(G-3237)*
Chemsteel Construction Company E 440 234-3930
Middleburg Heights *(G-14379)*
◆ **Chick Master Incubator Company** C 330 722-5591
Medina *(G-14045)*
Cincinnati Air Conditioning Co D 513 721-5622
Cincinnati *(G-3279)*
Clearcreek Construction E 740 420-3568
Stoutsville *(G-17349)*
Coleman Spohn Corporation E 216 431-8070
Cleveland *(G-5370)*
Colonial Heating & Cooling Co E 614 837-6100
Pickerington *(G-16091)*
Columbs/Worthington Htg AC Inc E 614 771-5381
Columbus *(G-7325)*
Columbus Heating & Vent Co C 614 274-1177
Columbus *(G-7357)*
Comfort Systems USA Ohio Inc E 440 703-1600
Bedford *(G-1300)*
Commercial Comfort Systems Inc E 419 481-4444
Perrysburg *(G-15988)*
Commercial Hvac Inc E 513 396-6100
Cincinnati *(G-3399)*
Complete Mechanical Svcs LLC D 513 489-3080
Blue Ash *(G-1565)*
Corcoran and Harnist Htg & AC E 513 921-2227
Cincinnati *(G-3421)*
Crane Heating & AC Co E 513 641-4700
Cincinnati *(G-3438)*
Crawford Mechanical Svcs Inc D 614 478-9424
Columbus *(G-7455)*
Crown Heating & Cooling Inc D 330 499-4988
Uniontown *(G-18516)*
Custom AC & Htg Co D 614 552-4822
Gahanna *(G-11238)*
D C Minnick Contracting Ltd E 937 322-1012
Springfield *(G-17186)*
Dar Plumbing E 614 445-8243
Columbus *(G-7489)*
Dave Pinkerton E 740 477-8888
Chillicothe *(G-2834)*
David R White Services Inc E 740 594-8381
Athens *(G-782)*
Debra-Kuempel Inc D 513 271-6500
Cincinnati *(G-3476)*
Del Monde Inc E 859 371-7780
Miamisburg *(G-14296)*
Detmer & Sons Inc E 937 879-2373
Fairborn *(G-10793)*
Dickson Industrial Park Inc E 740 377-9162
South Point *(G-17083)*
Diewald & Pope Inc E 614 861-6160
Reynoldsburg *(G-16446)*
Dimech Services Inc E 419 727-0111
Toledo *(G-17853)*
Dival Inc D 216 831-4200
Warrensville Heights *(G-18932)*
Division Drnking Ground Waters D 614 644-2752
Columbus *(G-7530)*
Dooley Heating and AC LLC E 614 278-9944
Columbus *(G-7541)*
Dovetail Construction Co Inc E 740 592-1800
Cleveland *(G-5508)*
Drake State Air E 937 472-3740
Eaton *(G-10557)*
Drake State Air Systems Inc E 937 472-0640
Eaton *(G-10558)*
Dunbar Mechanical Inc D 734 856-6601
Toledo *(G-17859)*
Dynamic Mechanical Systems E 513 858-6722
Fairfield *(G-10843)*
Eaton Plumbing Inc E 614 891-7005
Westerville *(G-19396)*
Eckert Fire Protec E 513 948-1030
Cincinnati *(G-3541)*
Ecoplumbers Inc E 614 299-9903
Hilliard *(G-11899)*
Edwards Electrical & Mech E 614 485-2003
Columbus *(G-7584)*
Ellerbrock Heating & AC E 419 782-1834
Defiance *(G-10029)*
Emcor Fclities Svcs N Amer Inc D 614 430-5078
Columbus *(G-7591)*
▲ **Enerfab Inc** B 513 641-0500
Cincinnati *(G-3557)*
Energy MGT Specialists Inc E 216 676-9045
Cleveland *(G-5539)*
Enervise Incorporated C 513 761-6000
Blue Ash *(G-1586)*

Employee Codes: A=Over 500 employees, B=251-500
C=101-250, D=51-100, E=25-50
2018 Harris Ohio
Services Directory
903

17 CONSTRUCTION-SPECIAL TRADE CONTRACTORS

Enervise Incorporated .... E 614 885-9800
  Columbus *(G-7593)*
Engineering Excellence .... D 972 535-3756
  Blue Ash *(G-1587)*
Envirnmental Engrg Systems Inc ...... E 937 228-6492
  Dayton *(G-9527)*
▲ Enviro-Flow Companies Ltd .... E 740 453-7980
  Zanesville *(G-20476)*
Euclid Heat Treating Co .... D 216 481-8444
  Euclid *(G-10752)*
Excellence Alliance Group Inc .... E 513 619-4800
  Cincinnati *(G-3585)*
Falls Heating & Cooling Inc .... E 330 929-8777
  Cuyahoga Falls *(G-9183)*
Family Entertainment Services .... D 740 286-8587
  Jackson *(G-12311)*
▲ Farber Corporation .... E 614 294-1626
  Columbus *(G-7637)*
Favret Company .... D 614 488-5211
  Columbus *(G-7644)*
Feldkamp Enterprises Inc .... C 513 347-4500
  Cincinnati *(G-3600)*
Fire Guard LLC .... E 740 625-5181
  Sunbury *(G-17556)*
Fitzenrider Inc .... E 419 784-0828
  Defiance *(G-10032)*
Flickinger Piping Company Inc .... E 330 364-4224
  Dover *(G-10189)*
Fowler Electric Co .... E 440 735-2385
  Bedford *(G-1307)*
Franck and Fric Incorporated .... D 216 524-4451
  Cleveland *(G-5631)*
Freeland Contracting Co .... E 614 443-2718
  Columbus *(G-7702)*
G Mechanical Inc .... E 614 844-6750
  Columbus *(G-7719)*
Gardiner Service Company .... E 440 248-3400
  Solon *(G-17008)*
Geauga Mechanical Company .... D 440 285-2000
  Chardon *(G-2750)*
Gem Industrial Inc .... D 419 467-3287
  Walbridge *(G-18775)*
Gene Tolliver Corp .... D 440 324-7727
  Medina *(G-14068)*
General Temperature Ctrl Inc .... E 614 837-3888
  Canal Winchester *(G-2159)*
Genes Refrigeration Htg & AC .... E 330 723-4104
  Medina *(G-14069)*
Gilbert Heating & AC .... E 419 625-8875
  Sandusky *(G-16762)*
Glennco Systems Inc .... E 740 353-4328
  Portsmouth *(G-16280)*
Gorjanc Comfort Services Inc .... E 440 449-4411
  Cleveland *(G-5681)*
Grabill Plumbing & Heating .... E 330 756-2075
  Beach City *(G-1043)*
Greer & Whitehead Cnstr Inc .... E 513 202-1757
  Harrison *(G-11799)*
Gross Plumbing Incorporated .... E 440 324-9999
  Elyria *(G-10632)*
Guenther Mechanical Inc .... C 419 289-6900
  Ashland *(G-681)*
Gundlach Sheet Metal Works Inc .... D 419 626-4525
  Sandusky *(G-16766)*
Gundlach Sheet Metal Works Inc .... E 419 734-7351
  Port Clinton *(G-16246)*
H & M Plumbing Co .... E 614 491-4880
  Columbus *(G-7789)*
Haslett Heating & Cooling Inc .... E 614 299-2133
  Dublin *(G-10358)*
Hattenbach Company .... D 216 881-5200
  Cleveland *(G-5731)*
Havsco Inc .... E 440 439-8900
  Bedford *(G-1310)*
HEat Ttal Fclty Slutions Inc .... E 740 965-3005
  Galena *(G-11283)*
Helm and Associates Inc .... E 419 893-1480
  Maumee *(G-13924)*
Horizon Mechanical and Elec .... E 419 529-2738
  Mansfield *(G-13309)*
Houston Dick Plbg & Htg Inc .... E 740 763-3961
  Newark *(G-15176)*
Imperial Heating and Coolg Inc .... D 440 498-1788
  Solon *(G-17017)*
Industrial Power Systems Inc .... C 419 531-3121
  Rossford *(G-16608)*
Inloes Mechanical Inc .... E 513 896-9499
  Hamilton *(G-11744)*
J & D Home Improvement Inc .... D 740 927-0722
  Reynoldsburg *(G-16459)*

J & J General Maintenance Inc .... E 740 533-9729
  Ironton *(G-12293)*
J A Guy Inc .... E 937 642-3415
  Marysville *(G-13629)*
J F Bernard Inc .... E 330 785-3830
  Akron *(G-285)*
J Feldkamp Design Build Ltd .... E 513 870-0601
  Fairfield *(G-10864)*
J W Geopfert Co Inc .... E 330 762-2293
  Akron *(G-287)*
Jackson Comfort Systems Inc .... E 330 468-3111
  Northfield *(G-15518)*
Jacobs Mechanical Co .... C 513 681-6800
  Cincinnati *(G-3857)*
Jarvis Mechanical Constrs Inc .... E 513 831-0055
  Milford *(G-14528)*
Jeff Plumber Inc .... E 330 940-2600
  Akron *(G-292)*
Jennings Heating Company Inc ...... E 330 784-1286
  Akron *(G-293)*
John F Gallagher Plumbing Co .... E 440 946-4256
  Eastlake *(G-10547)*
Johnson Controls .... D 513 874-1227
  West Chester *(G-19098)*
Johnson Controls .... E 614 602-2000
  Dublin *(G-10381)*
Johnson Controls .... D 614 717-9079
  Dublin *(G-10382)*
Johnson Controls .... C 440 268-1160
  Strongsville *(G-17478)*
Johnson Controls Inc .... D 614 895-6600
  Westerville *(G-19412)*
Johnson Controls Inc .... E 330 270-4385
  Youngstown *(G-20241)*
Johnson Controls Inc .... D 513 489-0950
  Cincinnati *(G-3881)*
Jonle Co Inc .... E 513 662-2282
  Cincinnati *(G-3885)*
Julian Speer Co .... D 614 261-6331
  Columbus *(G-7958)*
K Company Incorporated .... C 330 773-5125
  Coventry Township *(G-9127)*
▼ KA Bergquist Inc .... E 419 865-4196
  Toledo *(G-17989)*
Ke Gutridge LLC .... C 614 252-0420
  Columbus *(G-7969)*
Ken Neyer Plumbing Inc .... C 513 353-3311
  Cleves *(G-6801)*
Kessler Heating & Cooling .... E 614 837-9961
  Canal Winchester *(G-2163)*
Kidron Electric Inc .... E 330 857-2871
  Kidron *(G-12443)*
Kirk Williams Company Inc .... D 614 875-9023
  Grove City *(G-11573)*
Komar Plumbing Co .... E 330 758-5073
  Youngstown *(G-20248)*
Kuempel Service Inc .... E 513 271-6500
  Cincinnati *(G-3948)*
Kusan Inc .... E 614 262-1818
  Columbus *(G-8018)*
Lakes Heating and AC .... E 330 644-7811
  Coventry Township *(G-9128)*
▲ Langdon Inc .... E 513 733-5955
  Cincinnati *(G-3960)*
Lawn Management Sprinkler Co ..... E 513 272-3808
  Cincinnati *(G-3964)*
Limbach Company LLC .... E 614 299-2175
  Columbus *(G-8066)*
Limbach Company LLC .... C 614 299-2175
  Columbus *(G-8067)*
Lippincott Plumbing-Heating AC ..... E 419 222-0856
  Lima *(G-12829)*
Litter Bob Fuel & Heating Co .... E 740 773-2196
  Chillicothe *(G-2860)*
Lochard Inc .... D 937 492-8811
  Sidney *(G-16940)*
Lucas Plumbing & Heating Inc .... E 440 282-4567
  Lorain *(G-13059)*
Luxury Heating Co .... E 440 366-0971
  Sheffield Village *(G-16890)*
M K Moore & Sons Inc .... E 937 236-1812
  Dayton *(G-9693)*
M&M Heating & Cooling Inc .... D 419 243-3005
  Toledo *(G-18024)*
Mac Mechanical Corporation .... E 216 531-0444
  Cleveland *(G-5962)*
Mack Industries .... C 419 353-7081
  Bowling Green *(G-1785)*
Mansfield Plumbing Pdts LLC .... E 330 496-2301
  Big Prairie *(G-1498)*

Marlin Mechanical LLC .... E 800 669-2645
  Cleveland *(G-5981)*
Marvin W Mielke Inc .... D 330 725-8845
  Medina *(G-14095)*
Mc Clurg & Creamer Inc .... E 419 866-7080
  Holland *(G-12036)*
Mc Phillips Plbg Htg & AC Co .... E 216 481-1400
  Cleveland *(G-6000)*
McAfee Heating & AC Co Inc .... E 937 438-1976
  Dayton *(G-9706)*
Mechancal/Industrial Contg Inc ...... E 513 489-8282
  Cincinnati *(G-4040)*
Mechanical Cnstr Managers LLC ... C 937 274-1987
  Dayton *(G-9709)*
Mechanical Construction Co .... E 740 353-5668
  Portsmouth *(G-16295)*
Mechanical Systems Dayton Inc ..... D 937 254-3235
  Dayton *(G-9277)*
Metal Masters Inc .... E 330 343-3515
  Dover *(G-10198)*
Metro Heating and AC Co .... E 614 777-1237
  Hilliard *(G-11929)*
Mid-Ohio Mechanical Inc .... E 740 587-3362
  Granville *(G-11470)*
Midwest Roofing & Furnace Co ...... E 614 252-5241
  Columbus *(G-8172)*
Midwestern Plumbing Service .... E 513 753-0050
  Cincinnati *(G-4094)*
Miracle Plumbing & Heating Co ..... E 330 477-2402
  Canton *(G-2464)*
Mj Baumann Co Inc .... D 614 759-7100
  Columbus *(G-8180)*
Monroe Mechanical Incorporated ... E 513 539-7555
  Monroe *(G-14706)*
Morrison Inc .... E 740 373-5869
  Marietta *(G-13478)*
Muetzel Plumbing & Heating Co ..... D 614 299-7700
  Columbus *(G-8205)*
Naragon Companies Inc .... E 330 745-7700
  Norton *(G-15556)*
Nbw Inc .... E 216 377-1700
  Cleveland *(G-6114)*
Nelson Stark Company .... C 513 489-0866
  Cincinnati *(G-4154)*
Neptune Plumbing & Heating Co .... D 216 475-9100
  Cleveland *(G-6119)*
Nieman Plumbing Inc .... D 513 851-5588
  Cincinnati *(G-4169)*
Noron Inc .... E 419 726-2677
  Toledo *(G-18092)*
North Bay Construction Inc .... E 440 835-1898
  Westlake *(G-19522)*
North East Mechanical Inc .... E 440 871-7525
  Westlake *(G-19523)*
Northern Ohio Plumbing Co .... E 440 951-3370
  Eastlake *(G-10550)*
Northern Plumbing Systems .... E 513 831-5111
  Goshen *(G-11437)*
Ogrinc Mechanical Corporation ...... E 216 765-8010
  Cleveland *(G-6183)*
Ohio Fabricators Inc .... E 216 391-2400
  Cleveland *(G-6190)*
Ohio Heating and Refrigeration ...... E 614 863-6666
  Columbus *(G-8351)*
Ohio Irrigation Lawn Sprinkler .... E 937 432-9911
  Dayton *(G-9786)*
Osterfeld Champion Service .... E 937 254-8437
  Dayton *(G-9795)*
Osterwisch Company Inc .... D 513 791-3282
  Cincinnati *(G-4240)*
Overcashier and Horst Htg & AC .... E 419 841-3333
  Sylvania *(G-17605)*
P K Wadsworth Heating & Coolg .... E 440 248-4821
  Solon *(G-17037)*
Paramount Plumbing Inc .... E 330 336-1096
  Norton *(G-15558)*
◆ Park Corporation .... B 216 267-4870
  Cleveland *(G-6234)*
Peck-Hannaford Briggs Svc Corp ... D 513 681-1200
  Cincinnati *(G-4271)*
Perfection Group Inc .... C 513 772-7545
  Cincinnati *(G-4279)*
Perfection Mechanical Svcs Inc ...... E 513 772-7545
  Cincinnati *(G-4280)*
Perfection Services Inc .... E 513 772-7545
  Cincinnati *(G-4281)*
Perry Kelly Plumbing Inc .... E 513 528-6554
  Cincinnati *(G-4282)*
Peterman Plumbing and Htg Inc ..... E 330 364-4497
  Dover *(G-10206)*

▲ **Pioneer Pipe Inc**...B....... 740 376-2400
Marietta *(G-13488)*
Piper Plumbing Inc...E....... 330 274-0160
Mantua *(G-13394)*
PNC Mortgage Company...C....... 412 762-2000
Miamisburg *(G-14337)*
Pre-Fore Inc...E....... 740 467-2206
Millersport *(G-14631)*
Premier Rstrtion Mech Svcs LLC...E....... 513 420-1600
Middletown *(G-14451)*
Process Construction Inc...D....... 513 251-2211
Cincinnati *(G-4339)*
Professional Plumbing Services...E....... 740 454-1066
Zanesville *(G-20527)*
Prout Boiler Htg & Wldg Inc...E....... 330 744-0293
Youngstown *(G-20331)*
Quality Electrical & Mech Inc...E....... 419 294-3591
Lima *(G-12865)*
Queen City Mechanicals Inc...E....... 513 353-1430
Cincinnati *(G-4366)*
R & R Hvac Systems...E....... 419 861-0266
Holland *(G-12048)*
R Kelly Inc...E....... 513 631-8488
Cincinnati *(G-4379)*
Rapid Plumbing Inc...D....... 513 575-1509
Loveland *(G-13154)*
Ray Esser & Sons Inc...E....... 440 324-2018
Elyria *(G-10673)*
▲ **Recker and Boerger Inc**...D....... 513 942-9663
West Chester *(G-19224)*
Regal Plumbing & Heating Co...E....... 937 492-2894
Sidney *(G-16949)*
Relmec Mechanical LLC...C....... 216 391-1030
Cleveland *(G-6372)*
Reupert Heating and AC Co Inc...E....... 513 922-5050
Cincinnati *(G-4410)*
Rexs Air Conditioning Company...E....... 330 499-8733
Canton *(G-2513)*
River Plumbing Inc...E....... 440 934-3720
Avon *(G-916)*
Rmf Nooter Inc...D....... 419 727-1970
Toledo *(G-18159)*
Robinson Htg Air-Conditioning...E....... 513 422-6812
Middletown *(G-14455)*
Roman Plumbing Company...D....... 330 455-5155
Canton *(G-2515)*
Ron Johnson Plumbing and Htg...E....... 419 433-5365
Norwalk *(G-15591)*
Roth Bros Inc...C....... 330 793-5571
Youngstown *(G-20360)*
Roto-Rooter Development Co...D....... 513 762-6690
Cincinnati *(G-4442)*
Roto-Rooter Services Company...D....... 513 762-6690
Cincinnati *(G-4444)*
Roto-Rooter Services Company...D....... 513 541-3840
Cincinnati *(G-4445)*
RPC Mechanical Services...C....... 513 733-1641
Cincinnati *(G-4449)*
S&D/Osterfeld Mech Contrs Inc...E....... 937 277-1700
Dayton *(G-9862)*
Sals Heating and Cooling Inc...E....... 216 676-4949
Cleveland *(G-6438)*
Sauer Group Inc...C....... 614 853-2500
Columbus *(G-8685)*
Sauer Incorporated...D....... 614 853-2500
Columbus *(G-8686)*
Schibi Heating & Cooling Corp...E....... 513 385-3344
Cincinnati *(G-4481)*
Schmid Mechanical Inc...E....... 330 264-3633
Wooster *(G-19912)*
Schmid Mechanical Co...E....... 614 261-6331
Columbus *(G-8696)*
Schmids Service Now Inc...E....... 330 264-2040
Wooster *(G-19913)*
Schneller Heating and AC Co...E....... 859 341-1200
Cincinnati *(G-2930)*
Schumm Richard A Plbg & Htg...E....... 419 238-4994
Van Wert *(G-18643)*
Schweizer Dipple Inc...D....... 440 786-8090
Cleveland *(G-6451)*
Scioto Services LLc...E....... 937 644-0888
Marysville *(G-13649)*
Service Experts Htg & AC LLC...E....... 937 426-3444
Springfield *(G-17274)*
Service Experts Htg & AC LLC...E....... 513 489-3361
Blue Ash *(G-1688)*
Service Experts Htg & AC LLC...E....... 614 859-6993
Columbus *(G-8715)*
Service Experts LLC...E....... 330 577-3918
Akron *(G-435)*

Sexton Industrial Inc...C....... 513 530-5555
West Chester *(G-19228)*
Sisler Heating & Cooling Inc...E....... 330 722-7101
Medina *(G-14126)*
Slagle Mechanical Contractors...E....... 937 492-4151
Sidney *(G-16956)*
Smith & Oby Company...D....... 440 735-5333
Walton Hills *(G-18791)*
Smith & Oby Service Co...E....... 440 735-5322
Bedford *(G-1337)*
Smylie One Heating & Cooling...E....... 440 449-4328
Bedford *(G-1338)*
Southtown Heating & Cooling...E....... 937 320-9900
Moraine *(G-14827)*
Speer Industries Incorporated...C....... 614 261-6331
Columbus *(G-8761)*
Spellacys Turf-Lawn Inc...E....... 740 965-5508
Galena *(G-11287)*
Standard Plumbing & Heating Co...D....... 330 453-5150
Canton *(G-2537)*
Steel Valley Construction Co...E....... 330 392-8391
Warren *(G-18902)*
Steingass Mechanical Contg...E....... 330 725-6090
Medina *(G-14129)*
Superior Mechanical Svcs Inc...E....... 937 259-0082
Dayton *(G-9284)*
Supply Network Inc...E....... 614 527-5800
Columbus *(G-8806)*
Tanner Heating & AC Inc...E....... 937 299-2500
Moraine *(G-14829)*
Tfh-Eb Inc...D....... 614 253-7246
Columbus *(G-8833)*
TH Martin Inc...D....... 216 741-2020
Cleveland *(G-6588)*
The Peck-Hannaford Briggs Co...D....... 513 681-4600
Cincinnati *(G-4645)*
Thomas J Dyer Company...C....... 513 321-8100
Cincinnati *(G-4653)*
Thompson Heating & Cooling...E....... 513 242-4450
Cincinnati *(G-4656)*
Thompson Heating Corporation...D....... 513 769-7696
Cincinnati *(G-4657)*
Timmerman John P Heating AC Co...E....... 419 229-4015
Lima *(G-12900)*
Trame Mechanical Inc...E....... 937 258-1000
Dayton *(G-9936)*
Trane Inc...E....... 440 946-7823
Mentor *(G-14248)*
Triton Services Inc...C....... 513 679-6800
Mason *(G-13774)*
U S A Plumbing Company...E....... 614 882-6402
Columbus *(G-8882)*
United Group Services Inc...C....... 800 633-9690
West Chester *(G-19238)*
Universal Enterprises Inc...C....... 419 529-3500
Ontario *(G-15718)*
V M Systems Inc...D....... 419 535-1044
Toledo *(G-18285)*
▲ **Vaughn Industries LLC**...B....... 419 396-3900
Carey *(G-2599)*
Vaughn Industries LLC...E....... 740 548-7100
Lewis Center *(G-12710)*
Volpone Enterprises Inc...E....... 440 969-1141
Ashtabula *(G-767)*
Vulcan Enterprises Inc...E....... 419 396-3535
Carey *(G-2600)*
Wadsworth Service Inc...E....... 419 861-8181
Middleburg Heights *(G-14391)*
Waibel Heating Company...E....... 614 837-7615
Canal Winchester *(G-2176)*
Warner Mechanical Corporation...E....... 419 332-7116
Fremont *(G-11229)*
Watkins Mechanical Inc...E....... 937 748-0220
Springboro *(G-17141)*
Wells Brother Electric Inc...D....... 937 394-7559
Anna *(G-618)*
Wenger Temperature Control...E....... 614 586-4016
Columbus *(G-8978)*
West Jefferson Plumbing Htg...E....... 614 879-9606
West Jefferson *(G-19256)*
Western Reserve Mechanical Inc...E....... 330 652-3888
Niles *(G-15311)*
Whisler Plumbing & Heating Inc...E....... 330 833-2875
Massillon *(G-13861)*
Whitt Inc...E....... 513 753-7707
Amelia *(G-584)*
Wilkes & Company Inc...E....... 419 433-2325
Huron *(G-12176)*
Willis One Hour Heating & AC...D....... 513 752-2512
Cincinnati *(G-2938)*

Wojos Heating & AC Inc...E....... 419 693-3220
Northwood *(G-15552)*
York-Mahoning Mech Contrs Inc...D....... 330 788-7011
Youngstown *(G-20420)*
Zemba Bros Inc...E....... 740 452-1880
Zanesville *(G-20561)*

1721 Painting & Paper Hanging Contractors

A & A Safety Inc...E....... 513 943-6100
Amelia *(G-571)*
A B Industrial Coatings...E....... 614 228-0383
Columbus *(G-6918)*
Aero-Mark Inc...E....... 330 995-0100
Streetsboro *(G-17405)*
Allstate Painting & Contg Co...D....... 330 220-5533
Brunswick *(G-1968)*
American Star Painting Co LLC...E....... 740 373-5634
Marietta *(G-13432)*
Apbn Inc...E....... 724 964-8252
Campbell *(G-2138)*
Apostolos Group Inc...D....... 330 670-9900
Copley *(G-9052)*
August Groh & Sons Inc...E....... 513 821-0090
Cincinnati *(G-3064)*
Barbara Gheens Painting Inc...E....... 740 949-0405
Long Bottom *(G-13009)*
Cipriano Painting...E....... 440 892-1827
Cleveland *(G-5241)*
Classic Papering & Painting...E....... 614 221-0505
Columbus *(G-7294)*
Cleveland Construction Inc...E....... 440 255-8000
Mason *(G-13685)*
Clubhouse Pub N Grub...E....... 440 884-2582
Cleveland *(G-5368)*
Commercial Painting Inc...E....... 614 298-9963
Worthington *(G-19949)*
Costello Pntg Bldg Restoration...E....... 513 321-3326
Cincinnati *(G-3425)*
Cummins Building Maint Inc...D....... 740 726-9800
Prospect *(G-16363)*
David W Steinbach Inc...E....... 330 497-5959
Canton *(G-2334)*
Dennis Todd Painting Inc...E....... 614 879-7952
West Jefferson *(G-19250)*
Dependable Painting Co...E....... 216 431-4470
Cleveland *(G-5476)*
Eagle Industrial Painting LLC...E....... 330 866-5965
Magnolia *(G-13239)*
Flamos Enterprises Inc...E....... 330 478-0009
Canton *(G-2369)*
Frank Novak & Sons Inc...D....... 216 475-2495
Cleveland *(G-5632)*
Gpc Contracting Company...E....... 740 264-6060
Steubenville *(G-17320)*
Industrial Mill Maintenance...E....... 330 746-1155
Youngstown *(G-20232)*
Ionno Properties s Corp...E....... 330 479-9267
Dennison *(G-10165)*
Johnson & Fischer Inc...E....... 614 276-8868
Columbus *(G-7943)*
Kendrick-Mollenauer Pntg Co...E....... 614 443-7037
Columbus *(G-7977)*
Kneisel Contracting Corp...E....... 513 615-8816
Cincinnati *(G-3935)*
Lehn Painting Inc...E....... 513 732-1515
Batavia *(G-1019)*
Liberty Maintenance Inc...D....... 330 755-7711
Youngstown *(G-20255)*
Liberty-Alpha III JV...E....... 330 755-7711
Campbell *(G-2139)*
Lou Ritenour Decorators Inc...D....... 330 425-3232
Twinsburg *(G-10443)*
Mark Dura Inc...E....... 330 995-0883
Aurora *(G-847)*
Masterpiece Painting Company...E....... 330 395-9900
Warren *(G-18878)*
Mike Morris...E....... 330 767-4122
Brewster *(G-1856)*
Mrap LLC...E....... 614 545-3190
Columbus *(G-8202)*
Muha Construction Inc...E....... 937 435-0678
Dayton *(G-9760)*
▲ **National Electro-Coatings Inc**...D....... 216 898-0080
Cleveland *(G-6106)*
North Star Painting Co Inc...E....... 330 743-2333
Youngstown *(G-20302)*
P & W Painting Contractors Inc...E....... 419 698-2209
Toledo *(G-18115)*
Painting Company...C....... 614 873-1334
Plain City *(G-16203)*

S
I
C

Employee Codes: A=Over 500 employees, B=251-500
C=101-250, D=51-100, E=25-50
2018 Harris Ohio
Services Directory
905

Performance Painting LLC ....E.... 440 735-3340
Oakwood Village (G-15632)
Perry Interiors Inc ....E.... 513 761-9333
Batavia (G-1021)
Preferred Acquisition Co LLC ....D.... 216 587-0957
Cleveland (G-6298)
Reilly Painting Co ....E.... 216 371-8160
Cleveland Heights (G-6796)
Residence Artists Inc ....E.... 440 286-8822
Chardon (G-2764)
Rl Painting and Mfg Inc ....E.... 937 968-5526
Union City (G-18503)
South Town Painting Inc ....E.... 937 847-1600
Miamisburg (G-14353)
Unique Construction Svcs Inc ....E.... 513 608-1363
Blue Ash (G-1711)
Vimas Painting Company Inc ....E.... 330 536-2222
Lowellville (G-13175)
W F Bolin Company Inc ....E.... 614 276-6397
Columbus (G-8958)
Yerman & Young Painting Inc ....E.... 330 861-0022
Barberton (G-986)

1731 Electrical Work

A J Goulder Electric Co ....E.... 440 942-4026
Willoughby (G-19640)
Abbott Electric ....D.... 330 452-6601
Canton (G-2222)
ABC Fire Inc ....E.... 440 237-6677
North Royalton (G-15480)
Accurate Electric Cnstr Inc ....C.... 614 863-1844
Reynoldsburg (G-16424)
Acpi Systems Inc ....E.... 513 738-3840
Cincinnati (G-2968)
Advanced Service Tech LLC ....E.... 937 435-4376
Miamisburg (G-14268)
AE Electric Inc ....E.... 419 392-8468
Grand Rapids (G-11448)
Aero Electrical Contractors ....E.... 614 834-8181
Canal Winchester (G-2152)
Aetna Building Maintenance Inc ....B.... 614 476-1818
Columbus (G-6953)
Aey Electric Inc ....E.... 330 792-5745
Youngstown (G-20099)
Akron Foundry Co ....E.... 330 745-3101
Barberton (G-950)
All Phase Power and Ltg Inc ....E.... 419 624-9640
Sandusky (G-16725)
Allcan Global Services Inc ....E.... 513 825-1655
Cincinnati (G-2987)
American Electric Power Co Inc ....E.... 740 829-4129
Conesville (G-9035)
American Electric Power Co Inc ....E.... 419 998-5106
Lima (G-12740)
American Electric Power Co Inc ....E.... 614 856-2750
Columbus (G-6987)
American Electric Power Co Inc ....E.... 740 295-3070
Coshocton (G-9087)
American Electric Power Co Inc ....E.... 614 716-1000
Columbus (G-6989)
AMS Construction Inc ....C.... 513 398-6689
Maineville (G-13240)
AMS Construction Inc ....E.... 513 794-0410
Loveland (G-13110)
Apollo Heating and AC Inc ....E.... 513 271-3600
Cincinnati (G-3036)
Archiable Electric Company ....D.... 513 621-1307
Cincinnati (G-3043)
Area Energy & Electric Inc ....E.... 937 642-0386
Marysville (G-13606)
Area Energy & Electric Inc ....C.... 937 498-4784
Sidney (G-16913)
Atkins & Stang Inc ....D.... 513 242-8300
Cincinnati (G-3057)
Atlas Electrical Construction ....E.... 440 323-5418
Elyria (G-10595)
Atlas Industrial Contrs LLC ....B.... 614 841-4500
Columbus (G-7072)
B & J Electrical Company Inc ....E.... 513 351-7100
Cincinnati (G-3072)
Bansal Construction Inc ....E.... 513 874-5410
Fairfield (G-10822)
Banta Electrical Contrs Inc ....D.... 513 353-4446
Cleves (G-6797)
Bay Mechanical & Elec Corp ....D.... 440 282-6816
Lorain (G-13017)
BCU Electric Inc ....E.... 419 281-8944
Ashland (G-663)
Beacon Electric Company ....D.... 513 851-0711
Cincinnati (G-3087)
Becdel Controls Incorporated ....E.... 330 652-1386
Niles (G-15284)
Benevento Enterprises Inc ....D.... 216 621-5890
Cleveland (G-5114)
Berwick Electric Company ....E.... 614 834-2301
Canal Winchester (G-2153)
Biz Com Electric Inc ....E.... 513 961-7200
Cincinnati (G-3110)
Bodie Electric Inc ....E.... 419 435-3672
Fostoria (G-11123)
Bp-Ls-Pt Co ....D.... 614 841-4500
Columbus (G-7128)
Brennan Electric LLC ....E.... 513 353-2229
Miamitown (G-14370)
Broadband Express Inc ....E.... 614 823-6464
Westerville (G-19288)
Broadband Express LLC ....E.... 513 834-8085
Cincinnati (G-3136)
Broadband Express LLC ....D.... 419 536-9127
Toledo (G-17783)
Brush Contractors Inc ....D.... 614 850-8500
Columbus (G-7154)
Bryan Electric Inc ....E.... 740 695-9834
Saint Clairsville (G-16630)
Buckeye Cable Systems Inc ....E.... 419 724-2539
Toledo (G-17787)
Busy Bee Electric Inc ....E.... 513 353-3553
Hooven (G-12076)
Butchko Electric Inc ....E.... 440 985-3180
Amherst (G-589)
Cable TV Services Inc ....E.... 440 816-0033
Cleveland (G-5170)
Capital City Electric LLC ....E.... 614 933-8700
New Albany (G-14978)
Carey Electric Co ....E.... 937 669-3399
Vandalia (G-18667)
Cattrell Companies Inc ....D.... 740 537-2481
Toronto (G-18336)
Chapel Electric Co LLC ....C.... 937 222-2290
Dayton (G-9397)
Chapel-Romanoff Tech LLC ....E.... 937 222-9840
Dayton (G-9398)
Cincinnati Voice and Data ....D.... 513 683-4127
Loveland (G-13115)
Claypool Electric Inc ....C.... 740 653-5683
Lancaster (G-12519)
Cls Facilities MGT Svcs Inc ....E.... 440 602-4600
Mentor (G-14160)
Cochran Electric Inc ....E.... 614 847-0035
Powell (G-16329)
Colgan-Davis Inc ....E.... 419 893-6116
Maumee (G-13895)
Commercial Electric Pdts Corp ....E.... 216 241-2886
Cleveland (G-5376)
Controls Inc ....E.... 330 239-4345
Medina (G-14051)
Converse Electric Inc ....D.... 614 808-4377
Grove City (G-11549)
Copp Systems Inc ....E.... 937 228-4188
Dayton (G-9427)
Corporate Electric Company LLC ....E.... 330 331-7517
Barberton (G-962)
Countryside Electric Inc ....E.... 614 478-7960
Columbus (G-7450)
▲ Craftsman Electric Inc ....D.... 513 891-4426
Cincinnati (G-3437)
CTS Construction Inc ....D.... 513 489-8290
Cincinnati (G-3445)
D B A Inc ....E.... 513 541-6600
Cincinnati (G-3454)
D C Minnick Contracting Ltd ....E.... 937 322-1012
Springfield (G-17186)
D E Williams Electric Inc ....E.... 440 543-1222
Chagrin Falls (G-2695)
▲ Darana Hybrid Inc ....D.... 513 785-7540
Hamilton (G-11720)
Davis H Elliot Cnstr Co Inc ....C.... 937 847-8025
Miamisburg (G-14293)
Davis Pickering & Company Inc ....D.... 740 373-5896
Marietta (G-13441)
Dayton/Cncinnati Tech Svcs LLC ....E.... 513 892-3940
Blue Ash (G-1575)
Delta Electrical Contrs Ltd ....E.... 513 421-7744
Cincinnati (G-3483)
Denier Electric Co Inc ....C.... 513 738-2641
Harrison (G-11796)
Denier Electric Co Inc ....E.... 614 338-4664
Grove City (G-11553)
DIA Electric Inc ....E.... 513 281-0783
Cincinnati (G-3488)
Diebold Incorporated ....C.... 330 588-3619
Canton (G-2340)
Diebold Nixdorf Incorporated ....D.... 513 870-1400
Hamilton (G-11722)
Dillard Electric Inc ....E.... 937 836-5381
Union (G-18498)
Dovetail Construction Co Inc ....E.... 740 592-1800
Cleveland (G-5508)
Dss Installations Ltd ....E.... 513 761-7000
Cincinnati (G-3505)
Dynalectric Company ....E.... 614 529-7500
Columbus (G-7555)
Dynamic Currents Corp ....E.... 419 861-2036
Holland (G-12023)
Dynamic Mechanical Systems ....E.... 513 858-6722
Fairfield (G-10843)
E S I Inc ....D.... 513 454-3741
West Chester (G-19195)
Eco Engineering Inc ....D.... 513 985-8300
Cincinnati (G-3543)
Efficient Electric Corp ....E.... 614 552-0200
Columbus (G-7587)
▲ Eighth Day Sound Systems Inc ....E.... 440 995-2647
Cleveland (G-5529)
Elect General Contractors Inc ....E.... 740 420-3437
Circleville (G-4888)
Electric Connection Inc ....D.... 614 436-1121
Westerville (G-19397)
Electrical Corp America Inc ....D.... 440 245-3007
Lorain (G-13038)
▲ Enertech Electrical Inc ....E.... 330 536-2131
Lowellville (G-13171)
Erb Electric Co ....C.... 740 633-5055
Bridgeport (G-1862)
Excel Electrical Contractor ....E.... 740 965-3795
Worthington (G-19959)
Fine- Line Communications Inc ....E.... 330 562-0731
Aurora (G-838)
Fishel Company ....D.... 614 274-8100
Columbus (G-7667)
Fishel Company ....D.... 614 850-4400
Columbus (G-7669)
Fowler Electric Co ....D.... 440 735-2385
Bedford (G-1307)
Frey Electric Inc ....D.... 513 385-0700
Cincinnati (G-3653)
Frontier Security LLC ....E.... 937 247-2824
Miamisburg (G-14303)
GA Business Purchaser LLC ....D.... 419 255-8400
Toledo (G-17905)
Garber Electrical Contrs Inc ....D.... 937 771-5202
Englewood (G-10704)
▲ Gatesair Inc ....E.... 513 459-3400
Mason (G-13704)
Gateway Electric Incorporated ....C.... 216 518-5500
Cleveland (G-5657)
Gem Electric ....E.... 440 286-6200
Chardon (G-2751)
Gem Industrial Inc ....D.... 419 467-3287
Walbridge (G-18775)
Gene Ptacek Son Fire Eqp Inc ....E.... 216 651-8300
Cleveland (G-5666)
General Electric Company ....D.... 330 256-5331
Cuyahoga Falls (G-9192)
General Electric Company ....E.... 614 527-1078
Hilliard (G-11902)
General Electric Company ....C.... 513 583-3500
Cincinnati (G-3669)
Gillmore Security Systems Inc ....E.... 440 232-1000
Cleveland (G-5672)
Goodin Electric Inc ....E.... 740 522-3113
Newark (G-15171)
Gorjanc Comfort Services Inc ....E.... 440 449-4411
Cleveland (G-5681)
Guardian Protection Svcs Inc ....E.... 330 797-1570
Youngstown (G-20211)
Harrington Electric Company ....D.... 216 361-5101
Cleveland (G-5727)
Hatzel & Buehler Inc ....E.... 740 420-3088
Circleville (G-4889)
Helm and Associates Inc ....E.... 419 893-1480
Maumee (G-13924)
Hilscher-Clarke Electric Co ....E.... 330 452-9806
Canton (G-2400)
Hilscher-Clarke Electric Co ....D.... 740 622-5557
Coshocton (G-9105)
Horizon Mechanical and Elec ....E.... 419 529-2738
Mansfield (G-13309)
Hoskins International LLC ....E.... 419 628-6015
Minster (G-14664)

SIC SECTION
17 CONSTRUCTION-SPECIAL TRADE CONTRACTORS

Ies Infrstrcture Solutions LLC .... E 330 830-3500
  Massillon *(G-13823)*
Indrolect Co .... E 513 821-4788
  Cincinnati *(G-3815)*
Industrial Comm & Sound Inc .... E 614 276-8123
  Cincinnati *(G-3816)*
Industrial Power Systems Inc .... C 419 531-3121
  Rossford *(G-16608)*
Insight Communications of Co .... E 614 236-1200
  Columbus *(G-7905)*
▲ Instrmntation Ctrl Systems Inc ...... E 513 662-2600
  Cincinnati *(G-3822)*
Intercnnect Cbling Netwrk Svcs ...... E 440 891-0465
  Berea *(G-1461)*
Interstate Fire & SEC Systems .... E 330 453-9495
  Canton *(G-2414)*
J & J General Maintenance Inc .... E 740 533-9729
  Ironton *(G-12293)*
J W Didado Electric Inc .... C 330 374-0070
  Akron *(G-286)*
Jess Howard Electric Company .... C 614 864-2167
  Blacklick *(G-1509)*
Jims Electric Inc .... E 440 327-8800
  North Ridgeville *(G-15465)*
Joe Dickey Electric Inc .... D 330 549-3976
  North Lima *(G-15403)*
John A Becker Co .... E 614 272-8800
  Columbus *(G-7942)*
John H Cooper Elec Contg Co .... E 513 271-5000
  Cincinnati *(G-3877)*
John P Novatny Electric Co .... E 330 630-8900
  Akron *(G-296)*
JZE Electric Inc .... C 440 243-7600
  Cleveland *(G-5878)*
K Ray Holding Co .... E 614 861-4738
  Brice *(G-1858)*
Kal Electric Inc .... E 740 593-8720
  Athens *(G-796)*
Kastle Electric Co LLC .... D 937 254-2681
  Moraine *(G-14794)*
Kastle Electric Company .... C 937 254-2681
  Moraine *(G-14795)*
Kastle Electric Company .... E 513 360-2901
  Monroe *(G-14701)*
Kastle Technologies Co LLC .... E 513 360-2901
  Monroe *(G-14702)*
Kastle Technologies Co LLC .... E 614 433-9860
  Columbus *(G-7968)*
Kathman Electric Co Inc .... E 513 353-3465
  Cleves *(G-6800)*
Kenmarc Inc .... E 513 541-2791
  Cincinnati *(G-3913)*
Kidron Electric Inc .... E 330 857-2871
  Kidron *(G-12443)*
Koorsen Fire & Security Inc .... E 937 324-9405
  Vandalia *(G-18687)*
Kraft Electrical Contg Inc .... E 513 467-0500
  Cincinnati *(G-3941)*
Kween Industries Inc .... E 513 932-2293
  Lebanon *(G-12617)*
Laibe Electric Co .... D 419 724-8200
  Toledo *(G-17999)*
Lake Erie Electric Inc .... D 440 835-5565
  Westlake *(G-19507)*
Lake Erie Electric Inc .... E 330 724-1241
  Akron *(G-312)*
Lake Erie Electric Inc .... E 419 529-4611
  Ontario *(G-15697)*
Lake Horry Electric .... D 440 808-8791
  Chagrin Falls *(G-2702)*
Lawn Management Sprinkler Co .... E 513 272-3808
  Cincinnati *(G-3964)*
Legrand North America LLC .... D 937 224-0639
  Moraine *(G-14798)*
Legrand North America LLC .... C 937 224-0639
  Dayton *(G-9676)*
Lighting Services Inc .... E 330 405-4879
  Twinsburg *(G-18442)*
Lin R Rogers Elec Contrs Inc .... B 614 876-9336
  Hilliard *(G-11922)*
Lippincott Plumbing-Heating AC ...... E 419 222-0856
  Lima *(G-12829)*
Live Technologies Holdings Inc .... D 614 278-7777
  Columbus *(G-8074)*
Lowry Controls Inc .... E 513 583-0182
  Loveland *(G-13142)*
M & L Electric Inc .... E 937 833-5154
  Lewisburg *(G-12712)*
Main Lite Electric Co Inc .... E 330 369-8333
  Warren *(G-18877)*

Mayers Electric Co Inc .... C 513 272-2900
  Cincinnati *(G-4032)*
Mc Phillips Plbg Htg & AC Co .... E 216 481-1400
  Cleveland *(G-6000)*
McClintock Electric Inc .... E 330 264-6380
  Wooster *(G-19886)*
McKeever & Niekamp Elc Inc .... E 937 431-9363
  Beavercreek *(G-1191)*
MDU Resources Group Inc .... E 937 424-2550
  Moraine *(G-14801)*
Megacity Fire Protection Inc .... E 937 335-0775
  Dayton *(G-9717)*
Miller Cable Company .... D 419 639-2091
  Green Springs *(G-11479)*
Mills Security Alarm Systems .... E 513 921-4600
  Cincinnati *(G-4101)*
Mitel (delaware) Inc .... E 513 733-8000
  West Chester *(G-19122)*
Mutual Electric Company .... E 937 254-6211
  Dayton *(G-9762)*
Nationwide Energy Partners LLC ...... E 614 918-2031
  Columbus *(G-8240)*
New River Electrical Corp .... E 614 891-1142
  Westerville *(G-19430)*
Newcome Corp .... E 614 848-5688
  Columbus *(G-6897)*
▼ Ngn Electric Corp .... E 330 923-2777
  Brecksville *(G-1837)*
North Electric Inc .... E 216 331-4141
  Cleveland *(G-6140)*
▼ Northeast Ohio Electric LLC .... B 216 587-9510
  Cleveland *(G-6155)*
▲ Northwest Electrical Contg Inc ..... E 419 865-4757
  Holland *(G-12041)*
Northwestern Ohio SEC Systems ..... E 419 227-1655
  Lima *(G-12845)*
O D Miller Electric Co Inc .... E 330 875-1651
  Louisville *(G-13103)*
Ohio Power Company .... E 888 216-3523
  Canton *(G-2483)*
Ohio Power Company .... E 419 443-4634
  Tiffin *(G-17691)*
Ohio Valley Elec Svcs LLC .... D 513 771-2410
  Blue Ash *(G-1655)*
Osterwisch Company Inc .... D 513 791-3282
  Cincinnati *(G-4240)*
Oyer Electric Inc .... D 740 773-2828
  Chillicothe *(G-2868)*
Paladin Protective Systems Inc .... E 216 441-6900
  Cleveland *(G-6229)*
Palazzo Brothers Electric Inc .... E 419 668-1100
  Norwalk *(G-15587)*
Penn-Ohio Electrical Company .... E 330 448-1234
  Masury *(G-13867)*
Perram Electric Inc .... E 330 239-2661
  Wadsworth *(G-18768)*
Pomeroy It Solutions Sls Inc .... E 440 717-1364
  Brecksville *(G-1842)*
Positive Electric Inc .... E 937 428-0606
  Dayton *(G-9816)*
Precision Broadbnd Installatns .... C 614 523-2917
  Westerville *(G-19343)*
Precision Electrical Services .... E 740 474-4490
  Circleville *(G-4901)*
Primetech Communications Inc .... D 513 942-6000
  West Chester *(G-19132)*
Professional Telecom Svcs .... E 513 232-7700
  Cincinnati *(G-4344)*
Proline Electric Inc .... E 740 687-4571
  Lancaster *(G-12567)*
Protech Security Inc .... E 330 499-3555
  Canton *(G-2496)*
Quebe Holdings Inc .... D 937 222-2290
  Dayton *(G-9838)*
Queen City Electric Inc .... E 513 591-2600
  Cincinnati *(G-4363)*
R & R Wiring Contractors Inc .... E 513 752-6304
  Batavia *(G-1022)*
R J Martin Elec Svcs Inc .... D 216 662-7100
  Bedford Heights *(G-1358)*
Rapier Electric Inc .... D 513 868-9087
  Hamilton *(G-11767)*
Reddy Electric Co .... C 937 372-8205
  Xenia *(G-20072)*
Regent Electric Inc .... D 419 476-8333
  Toledo *(G-18147)*
Rei Telecom Inc .... E 614 255-3100
  Canal Winchester *(G-2167)*
Reliable Contractors Inc .... D 937 433-0262
  Dayton *(G-9846)*

Research & Investigation Assoc ...... E 419 526-1299
  Mansfield *(G-13355)*
Reynolds Electric Company Inc .... D 419 228-5448
  Lima *(G-12868)*
RJ Runge Company Inc .... E 419 740-5781
  Port Clinton *(G-16253)*
Rmf Nooter Inc .... D 419 727-1970
  Toledo *(G-18159)*
Robinson Htg Air-Conditioning .... E 513 422-6812
  Middletown *(G-14455)*
Roehrenbeck Electric Inc .... E 614 443-9709
  Columbus *(G-8644)*
Romanoff Electric Inc .... C 614 755-4500
  Gahanna *(G-11266)*
Romanoff Electric Co LLC .... C 419 726-2627
  Toledo *(G-18164)*
Romanoff Electric Co LLC .... D 937 640-7925
  Toledo *(G-18165)*
Royal Electric Cnstr Corp .... E 614 253-6600
  Columbus *(G-8653)*
Ruhl Electric Co .... E 330 823-7230
  Alliance *(G-559)*
S & E Electric Inc .... E 330 425-7866
  Twinsburg *(G-18465)*
Sabroske Electric Inc .... E 419 332-6444
  Fremont *(G-11218)*
Safeway Electric Company Inc .... E 614 443-7672
  Columbus *(G-8674)*
Saturn Electric Inc .... E 937 278-2580
  Dayton *(G-9868)*
Schneder Elc Bldngs Amrcas Inc ...... D 513 398-9800
  Lebanon *(G-12644)*
Security Fence Group Inc .... E 513 681-3700
  Cincinnati *(G-4489)*
Servall Electric Company Inc .... E 513 771-5584
  Cincinnati *(G-4499)*
Settle Muter Electric Ltd .... C 614 866-7554
  Columbus *(G-8718)*
Shawntech Communications Inc ...... E 937 898-4900
  Miamisburg *(G-14350)*
Sidney Electric Company .... D 419 222-1109
  Sidney *(G-16954)*
Siemens Energy Inc .... B 740 393-8897
  Mount Vernon *(G-14923)*
Simplex Time Recorder LLC .... E 800 746-7539
  West Chester *(G-19154)*
Simplex Time Recorder LLC .... E 513 874-1227
  West Chester *(G-19229)*
Smink Electric Inc .... E 440 322-5518
  Elyria *(G-10680)*
South Shore Electric Inc .... E 440 366-6289
  Elyria *(G-10681)*
Southeast Security Corporation .... E 330 239-4600
  Sharon Center *(G-16879)*
Southtown Heating & Cooling .... E 937 320-9900
  Moraine *(G-14827)*
Speelman Electric Inc .... D 330 633-1410
  Tallmadge *(G-17650)*
Staley Inc .... E 614 552-2333
  Plain City *(G-16207)*
Star Dist & Manufacturring LLC .... D 513 860-3573
  West Chester *(G-19231)*
State Alarm Inc .... E 330 726-8111
  Youngstown *(G-20382)*
Studebaker Electric Company .... E 937 890-9510
  Dayton *(G-9911)*
Sunpro Inc .... D 330 966-0910
  North Canton *(G-15370)*
Superior Group .... C 614 488-8035
  Columbus *(G-8805)*
Supply Tech of Columbus LLC .... E 614 299-0184
  Columbus *(G-8807)*
T & B Electric Ltd .... E 740 881-5696
  Ostrander *(G-15795)*
T J Williams Electric Co .... E 513 738-5366
  Harrison *(G-11809)*
Taylor Telecommunications Inc .... D 330 628-5501
  Mogadore *(G-14685)*
Tele-Solutions Inc .... E 330 782-2888
  Youngstown *(G-20388)*
Telecom Expertise Inds Inc .... D 937 548-5254
  Greenville *(G-11521)*
Telephone & Cmpt Contrs Inc .... E 419 726-8142
  Toledo *(G-18215)*
Thompson Electric Inc .... C 330 686-2300
  Munroe Falls *(G-14933)*
Timmerman John P Heating AC Co .. E 419 229-4015
  Lima *(G-12900)*
Transtar Electric Inc .... D 419 385-7573
  Toledo *(G-18260)*

Employee Codes: A=Over 500 employees, B=251-500
C=101-250, D=51-100, E=25-50

Tri Area Electric Co Inc....E.... 330 744-0151
Youngstown *(G-20392)*
Triec Electrical Services Inc....E.... 937 323-3721
Springfield *(G-17290)*
Unicustom Inc....E.... 513 874-9806
Fairfield *(G-10919)*
United Electric Company Inc....E.... 502 459-5242
Cincinnati *(G-4732)*
Universal Recovery Systems....D.... 614 299-0184
Columbus *(G-8907)*
US Communications and Elc Inc....D.... 440 519-0880
Cleveland *(G-6676)*
Valley Electrical Cnsld Inc....C.... 330 539-4044
Girard *(G-11429)*
▲ Vaughn Industries LLC....B.... 419 396-3900
Carey *(G-2599)*
Vaughn Industries LLC....E.... 740 548-7100
Lewis Center *(G-12710)*
Vec Inc....E.... 330 539-4044
Girard *(G-11430)*
Vector Security Inc....E.... 440 466-7233
Geneva *(G-11372)*
Vector Security Inc....E.... 330 726-9841
Boardman *(G-1745)*
VIP Electric Company....E.... 440 255-0180
Mentor *(G-14256)*
W W Schaub Electric Co....E.... 330 494-3560
Canton *(G-2581)*
Wachter Inc....C.... 513 777-0701
West Chester *(G-19243)*
Wagner Industrial Electric Inc....E.... 937 298-7481
Moraine *(G-14833)*
Wells Brother Electric Inc....D.... 937 394-7559
Anna *(G-618)*
Westfield Electric Inc....E.... 419 862-0078
Gibsonburg *(G-11405)*
▲ Wireless Environment LLC....E.... 216 455-0192
Mayfield Village *(G-14014)*
Wood Electric Inc....D.... 330 339-7002
New Philadelphia *(G-15123)*
Woolace Electric Corp....E.... 419 428-3161
Stryker *(G-17539)*
X F Construction Svcs Inc....E.... 614 575-2700
Columbus *(G-9012)*
Yeck Brothers Company....E.... 937 294-4000
Moraine *(G-14837)*
Zender Electric....E.... 419 436-1538
Fostoria *(G-11143)*
Zenith Systems LLC....C.... 216 587-9510
Cleveland *(G-6783)*
Zenith Systems LLC....B.... 216 406-7916
Atwater *(G-823)*

1741 Masonry & Other Stonework

Able Company Ltd Partnership....D.... 614 444-7663
Columbus *(G-6926)*
Albert Freytag Inc....E.... 419 628-2018
Minster *(G-14659)*
Allen Refractories Company....C.... 740 927-8000
Pataskala *(G-15920)*
American International Cnstr....E.... 440 243-5535
Berea *(G-1445)*
Bama Masonry Inc....E.... 440 834-4175
Burton *(G-2060)*
Beaver Constructors Inc....D.... 330 478-2151
Canton *(G-2261)*
Benchmark Masonry Contractors....D.... 937 228-1225
Middletown *(G-14417)*
Buckner and Sons Masonry Inc....E.... 614 279-9777
Columbus *(G-7163)*
Casagrande Masonry Inc....E.... 740 964-0781
New Albany *(G-14980)*
Centennial Prsrvtion Group LLC....E.... 614 238-0730
Columbus *(G-7222)*
▲ Cleveland Marble Mosaic Co....C.... 216 749-2840
Cleveland *(G-5324)*
◆ Crowe Masonry....E.... 330 296-5539
Ravenna *(G-16382)*
Debello Masonry Inc....E.... 937 235-2096
Carlisle *(G-2603)*
Duer Construction Co Inc....D.... 330 848-9930
Akron *(G-202)*
Empire Masonry Company Inc....D.... 440 230-2800
North Royalton *(G-15488)*
F B and S Masonry Inc....E.... 330 608-3442
Silver Lake *(G-16962)*
Foti Construction Company LLP....E.... 440 347-0728
Wickliffe *(G-19597)*
Giambrone Masonry Inc....D.... 216 475-1200
Hudson *(G-12118)*
Harold K Phllips Rstration Inc....E.... 614 443-5699
Columbus *(G-7802)*
Hester Masonry Co Inc....E.... 937 890-2283
Vandalia *(G-18685)*
Hicon Inc....D.... 513 242-3612
Cincinnati *(G-3760)*
Hovest Construction....E.... 419 456-3426
Ottawa *(G-15798)*
Hummel Industries Incorporated....E.... 513 242-1321
Cincinnati *(G-3798)*
Industrial First Inc....C.... 216 991-8605
Bedford *(G-1313)*
International Masonry Inc....D.... 614 469-8338
Columbus *(G-7917)*
J & D Home Improvement Inc....D.... 740 927-0722
Reynoldsburg *(G-16459)*
J C Masonry Construction Inc....E.... 330 823-9795
Alliance *(G-542)*
Jess Hauer Masonry Inc....E.... 513 521-2178
Cincinnati *(G-3866)*
Kapton Caulking & Building....E.... 440 526-0670
Cleveland *(G-5883)*
Karst & Sons Inc....E.... 614 501-9530
Reynoldsburg *(G-16462)*
Kurzhals Inc....E.... 513 941-4624
Cincinnati *(G-3950)*
Lang Masonry Contractors Inc....D.... 740 749-3512
Waterford *(G-18939)*
Lencyk Masonry Co Inc....E.... 330 729-9780
Youngstown *(G-20254)*
Medhurst Mason Contractors Inc....C.... 440 543-8885
Chagrin Falls *(G-2725)*
Miter Masonry Contractors....E.... 513 821-3334
Arlington Heights *(G-648)*
Mural & Son Inc....E.... 216 267-3322
Cleveland *(G-6090)*
▲ OBrien Cut Stone Company....E.... 216 663-7800
Cleveland *(G-6178)*
Ohio State Home Services Inc....D.... 614 850-5600
Hilliard *(G-11940)*
▲ Onex Construction Inc....E.... 330 995-9015
Streetsboro *(G-17424)*
Pioneer Cldding Glzing Systems....E.... 216 816-4242
Cleveland *(G-6282)*
Platinum Restoration Inc....E.... 440 327-0699
Elyria *(G-10671)*
Ray St Clair Roofing Inc....E.... 513 874-1234
Fairfield *(G-10898)*
S A Storer and Sons Company....D.... 419 843-3133
Sylvania *(G-17614)*
▲ S P S & Associates Inc....E.... 330 283-4267
Silver Lake *(G-16963)*
Steven H Byerly Inc....E.... 614 882-0092
Columbus *(G-8788)*
Technical Construction Spc....E.... 330 929-1088
Cuyahoga Falls *(G-9224)*
Van Ness Stone Inc....E.... 440 564-1111
Newbury *(G-15263)*
VIP Restoration Inc....D.... 216 426-9500
Cuyahoga Falls *(G-9232)*
Warren Guillard Bricklayers....E.... 330 633-3855
Tallmadge *(G-17660)*
Wasiniak Construction Inc....D.... 419 668-8624
Norwalk *(G-15596)*
Whitaker Masonry Inc....E.... 330 225-7970
Brunswick *(G-1996)*
William Kerfoot Masonry Inc....E.... 330 772-6460
Burghill *(G-2056)*
Zavarella Brothers Cnstr Co....E.... 440 232-2243
Cleveland *(G-6782)*

1742 Plastering, Drywall, Acoustical & Insulation Work

All Construction Services Inc....E.... 330 225-1653
Brunswick *(G-1967)*
Anstine Drywall Inc....E.... 330 784-3867
Akron *(G-77)*
Apex Interiors Inc....E.... 330 327-2226
Avon *(G-875)*
Architectural Intr Restoration....E.... 216 241-2255
Cleveland *(G-5065)*
Blackstar Drywall Inc....E.... 614 242-4242
Sunbury *(G-17550)*
Boak & Sons Inc....C.... 330 793-5646
Youngstown *(G-20118)*
Buckholz Wall Systems LLC....E.... 614 870-1775
Hilliard *(G-11886)*
Builder Services Group Inc....D.... 614 263-9378
Columbus *(G-7166)*
Builder Services Group Inc....E.... 513 942-2204
Hamilton *(G-11695)*
Central Insulation Systems Inc....E.... 513 242-0600
Cincinnati *(G-3214)*
Century Contractors Inc....E.... 440 232-2626
Cleveland *(G-5215)*
Certanteed Gyps Ciling Mfg Inc....E.... 800 233-8990
Aurora *(G-835)*
Cincinnati Drywall Inc....E.... 513 321-7322
Cincinnati *(G-3299)*
▲ Cleveland Construction Inc....E.... 440 255-8000
Mentor *(G-14159)*
Cleveland Construction Inc....E.... 740 927-9000
Columbus *(G-7298)*
Cleveland Construction Inc....E.... 440 255-8000
Mason *(G-13685)*
Clubhouse Pub N Grub....E.... 440 884-2582
Cleveland *(G-5368)*
Columbus Drywall & Insulation....D.... 614 257-0257
Columbus *(G-7347)*
Columbus Drywall Inc....E.... 614 257-0257
Columbus *(G-7348)*
Community Action Comsn Belmont....E.... 740 695-0293
Saint Clairsville *(G-16632)*
Compass Construction Inc....D.... 614 761-7800
Dublin *(G-10305)*
Competitive Interiors Inc....C.... 330 297-1281
Ravenna *(G-16378)*
Construction Systems Inc....D.... 614 252-0708
Columbus *(G-7425)*
Dayton Walls & Ceilings Inc....D.... 937 277-0531
Dayton *(G-9494)*
Edwards Mooney & Moses....D.... 614 351-1439
Columbus *(G-7582)*
Fairfield Insul & Drywall Inc....E.... 740 654-8811
Lancaster *(G-12536)*
Frank Novak & Sons Inc....D.... 216 475-2495
Cleveland *(G-5632)*
Giorgi of Chesapeake Inc....E.... 740 256-1724
Crown City *(G-9155)*
Global Insulation Inc....E.... 330 479-3100
Canton *(G-2381)*
Halker Drywall Inc....E.... 419 646-3679
Columbus Grove *(G-9030)*
Hughes & Knollman Construction....D.... 614 237-6167
Columbus *(G-7862)*
Immaculate Interiors....E.... 440 324-9300
Elyria *(G-10635)*
Industrial Insul Coatings LLC....E.... 800 506-1399
Girard *(G-11414)*
Installed Building Pdts II LLC....D.... 626 812-6070
Columbus *(G-7907)*
Installed Building Pdts LLC....E.... 614 308-9900
Columbus *(G-7909)*
Installed Building Pdts LLC....E.... 330 798-9640
Akron *(G-280)*
Installed Building Pdts LLC....E.... 419 662-4524
Northwood *(G-15534)*
Insulating Sales Co Inc....E.... 513 742-2600
Cincinnati *(G-3823)*
Integrity Wall & Ceiling Inc....E.... 419 381-1855
Toledo *(G-17976)*
Knollman Construction LLC....C.... 614 841-0130
Columbus *(G-8004)*
Kramig Co....E.... 513 761-4010
Cincinnati *(G-3943)*
Kreps Ron Drywall & Plst Co....E.... 330 726-8252
Youngstown *(G-20250)*
Larry L Minges....E.... 513 738-4901
Hamilton *(G-11752)*
Liberty Insulation Co Inc....D.... 513 621-0108
Beavercreek *(G-1186)*
Lm Constrction Trry Lvrini Inc....E.... 740 695-9604
Saint Clairsville *(G-16641)*
Luke Collison....E.... 740 969-2283
Lancaster *(G-12552)*
M & S Drywall Inc....E.... 513 738-1510
Harrison *(G-11805)*
M K Moore & Sons Inc....E.... 937 236-1812
Dayton *(G-9693)*
Newark Drywall Inc....E.... 740 763-3572
Nashport *(G-14952)*
OCP Contractors Inc....E.... 419 865-7168
Holland *(G-12043)*
OK Interiors Corp....C.... 513 742-3278
Cincinnati *(G-4217)*
Omni Fireproofing Co LLC....D.... 513 870-9115
West Chester *(G-19126)*
Overhead Door Co- Cincinnati....C.... 513 346-4000
West Chester *(G-19127)*

17 CONSTRUCTION-SPECIAL TRADE CONTRACTORS

Pedersen Insulation Company .... E 614 471-3788
 Columbus (G-8529)
Porter Drywall Inc .... D 614 890-2111
 Westerville (G-19437)
Priority 1 Construction Svcs .... E 513 922-0203
 Cincinnati (G-4332)
R E Kramig & Co Inc .... C 513 761-4010
 Cincinnati (G-4378)
Rak Corrosion Control Inc .... E 440 985-2171
 Amherst (G-602)
Republic/Construction .... E 330 747-1510
 Youngstown (G-20348)
Robinson Insulation Co Inc .... E 937 323-9599
 Springfield (G-17264)
Roger Kreps Drywall & Plst Inc .... D 330 726-6090
 Youngstown (G-20355)
Roofing By Insulation Inc .... E 937 315-5024
 New Carlisle (G-15030)
Roricks Inc .... E 330 497-6888
 Canton (G-2516)
Sandel Corp .... E 614 475-5898
 Gahanna (G-11267)
Sports Facility Acoustics Inc .... E 440 323-1400
 Elyria (G-10682)
Synthetic Stucco Corporation .... E 513 897-9227
 Waynesville (G-18987)
T and D Interiors Incorporated .... E 419 331-4372
 Lima (G-12897)
Thermal Solutions Inc .... D 513 742-2836
 Fairfield (G-10914)
Thermal Solutions Inc .... D 740 886-2861
 Proctorville (G-16262)
Thermo-TEC Insulation Inc .... E 216 663-3842
 Euclid (G-10779)
Truteam LLC .... E 513 942-2204
 Hamilton (G-11779)
Unified Cnstr Systems Ltd .... E 330 773-2511
 Akron (G-483)
United Insulation Co Inc .... E 614 263-9378
 Columbus (G-8893)
Valley Acoustics Inc .... E 330 799-1894
 Youngstown (G-20401)
Valley Interior Systems Inc .... E 937 890-7319
 Dayton (G-9961)
Valley Interior Systems Inc .... B 513 961-0400
 Cincinnati (G-4801)
Valley Interior Systems Inc .... C 614 351-8440
 Columbus (G-8930)
Western Reserve Interiors Inc .... E 216 447-1081
 Cleveland (G-6745)

1743 Terrazzo, Tile, Marble & Mosaic Work

▲ Cleveland Marble Mosaic Co .... C 216 749-2840
 Cleveland (G-5324)
▼ Cutting Edge Countertops Inc ..... E 419 873-9500
 Perrysburg (G-15992)
Midwest Mosaic Inc .... E 419 377-3894
 Toledo (G-18062)
OCP Contractors Inc .... E 419 865-7168
 Holland (G-12043)
Rite Rug Co .... E 614 552-1190
 Reynoldsburg (G-16478)
Southwestern Tile and MBL Co ...... E 614 464-1257
 Columbus (G-8757)
▲ T H Winston Company .... E 513 271-2123
 Cincinnati (G-4613)
Virginia Tile Company .... E 216 741-8400
 Brooklyn Heights (G-1931)

1751 Carpentry Work

Advance Door Company .... E 216 883-2424
 Cleveland (G-4957)
Airko Inc .... E 440 333-0133
 Cleveland (G-4978)
Brock & Associates Builders .... E 330 757-7150
 Youngstown (G-20127)
Builders Firstsource Inc .... E 937 898-1358
 Vandalia (G-18665)
Burbank Inc .... E 419 698-3434
 Toledo (G-17788)
Casegoods Inc .... E 330 825-2461
 Barberton (G-960)
Castle Construction Co Inc .... E 419 289-1122
 Ashland (G-669)
Combs Interior Specialties Inc .... D 937 879-2047
 Fairborn (G-10787)
Command Roofing Co .... C 937 298-1155
 Moraine (G-14760)
Competitive Interiors Inc .... C 330 297-1281
 Ravenna (G-16378)

Contract Lumber Inc .... C 740 964-3147
 Pataskala (G-15921)
Countertop Alternatives Inc .... E 937 254-3334
 Dayton (G-9430)
Dayton Door Sales Inc .... E 937 253-9181
 Dayton (G-9471)
Dilly Door Co .... E 419 782-1181
 Defiance (G-10028)
Door Shop & Service Inc .... E 614 423-8043
 Westerville (G-19301)
Dortronic Service Inc .... E 216 739-3667
 Cleveland (G-5506)
Dynamic Structures Inc .... E 330 892-0164
 New Waterford (G-15137)
Erie Construction Mid-West Inc ...... E 419 472-4200
 Toledo (G-17869)
▲ Fortune Brands Windows Inc ...... B 614 532-3500
 Columbus (G-7681)
▲ Forum Manufacturing Inc .... E 937 349-8685
 Milford Center (G-14576)
Garage Door Systems LLC .... C 513 321-9600
 West Chester (G-19204)
Goliath Contracting Ltd .... E 614 568-7878
 Reynoldsburg (G-16455)
Graf and Sons Inc .... E 614 481-2020
 Columbus (G-7765)
Hgc Construction Co .... D 513 861-8866
 Cincinnati (G-3759)
J & B Equipment & Supply Inc .... D 419 884-1155
 Mansfield (G-13314)
Mammana Custom Woodworking Inc .... E 216 581-9059
 Maple Heights (G-13410)
Marous Brothers Cnstr Inc .... B 440 951-3904
 Willoughby (G-19692)
Metal Framing Enterprises LLC ...... E 216 433-7080
 Cleveland (G-6032)
Midwest Curtainwalls Inc .... D 216 641-7900
 Cleveland (G-6060)
Mjr-Construction Co .... E 216 523-8050
 Cincinnati (G-6071)
▼ Nofziger Door Sales Inc .... E 419 337-9900
 Wauseon (G-18960)
OCP Contractors Inc .... E 419 865-7168
 Holland (G-12043)
Ohio Builders Resources LLC .... E 614 865-0306
 Westerville (G-19336)
OK Interiors Corp .... C 513 742-3278
 Cincinnati (G-4217)
Overhead Door Co- Cincinnati .... C 513 346-4000
 West Chester (G-19127)
Overhead Inc .... E 419 476-7811
 Toledo (G-18113)
Premier Construction Company ...... E 513 874-2611
 Fairfield (G-10896)
Ray St Clair Roofing Inc .... E 513 874-1234
 Fairfield (G-10898)
Regency Windows Corporation ...... D 330 963-4077
 Twinsburg (G-18459)
Riverside Cnstr Svcs Inc .... E 513 723-0900
 Cincinnati (G-4427)
Roger Kreps Drywall & Plst Inc .... D 330 726-6090
 Youngstown (G-20355)
Ryans All-Glass Incorporated .... E 513 771-4440
 Cincinnati (G-4461)
Schlabach Wood Design Inc .... E 330 897-2600
 Baltic (G-947)
▲ Season Contractors Inc .... E 440 717-0188
 Broadview Heights (G-1891)
Thiels Replacement Systems Inc ... E 419 289-6139
 Ashland (G-701)
Traichal Construction Company ..... E 800 255-3667
 Niles (G-15307)
Valley Acoustics Inc .... E 330 799-1894
 Youngstown (G-20401)
Williams Bros Roofg Siding Co .... E 937 434-3838
 Dayton (G-9999)
Window Factory of America .... D 440 439-3050
 Bedford (G-1344)
Woodpeckers Inc .... E 440 238-1824
 Strongsville (G-17525)
Youngstown Automatic Door Co ..... E 330 747-3135
 Youngstown (G-20427)

1752 Floor Laying & Other Floor Work, NEC

American Star Painting Co LLC ...... E 740 373-5634
 Marietta (G-13432)
Andover Floor Covering .... E 440 293-5339
 Newbury (G-15254)
Bcf LLC .... E 937 746-0721
 Miamisburg (G-14274)

Centimark Corporation .... C 330 920-3560
 Stow (G-17356)
Cincinnati Floor Company Inc .... E 513 641-4500
 Cincinnati (G-3305)
Clays Heritage Carpet Inc .... E 330 497-1280
 Canton (G-2312)
▲ Cleveland Construction Inc .... E 440 255-8000
 Mentor (G-14159)
Cleveland Construction Inc .... E 740 927-9000
 Columbus (G-7298)
Command Carpet .... E 330 673-7404
 Kent (G-12361)
Company Inc .... E 216 431-2334
 Cleveland (G-5387)
◆ Continental Office Furn Corp .... E 614 262-5010
 Columbus (G-7428)
Corporate Floors Inc .... E 216 475-3232
 Cleveland (G-5409)
Dominguez Inc .... E 513 425-9955
 Middletown (G-14424)
▲ Done-Rite Bowling Service Co .... E 440 232-3280
 Bedford (G-1304)
Florline Group Inc .... E 330 830-3380
 Massillon (G-13808)
Frank Novak & Sons Inc .... D 216 475-2495
 Cleveland (G-5632)
Hoover & Wells Inc .... E 419 691-9220
 Toledo (G-17959)
JD Music Tile Co .... E 740 420-9611
 Circleville (G-4892)
K H F Inc .... E 330 928-0694
 Cuyahoga Falls (G-9200)
Legacy Commercial Flooring Ltd .... B 614 476-1043
 Columbus (G-8048)
▲ Marble Restoration Inc .... D 419 865-9000
 Maumee (G-13939)
OCP Contractors Inc .... E 419 865-7168
 Holland (G-12043)
OK Interiors Corp .... C 513 742-3278
 Cincinnati (G-4217)
Patellas Floor Center Inc .... E 330 758-4099
 Youngstown (G-20316)
Preferred Acquisition Co LLC .... D 216 587-0957
 Cleveland (G-6298)
Prime Polymers Inc .... E 330 662-4200
 Medina (G-14113)
Progressive Flooring Svcs Inc .... E 614 868-9005
 Etna (G-10738)
PTX Flooring Inc .... E 419 726-1775
 Toledo (G-18143)
Regal Carpet Center Inc .... E 216 475-1844
 Cleveland (G-6366)
Rite Rug Co .... E 614 882-4322
 Westerville (G-19350)
Rite Rug Co .... E 513 942-0010
 West Chester (G-19225)
Rite Rug Co .... E 937 318-9197
 Fairborn (G-10803)
River City Furniture LLC .... D 513 612-7303
 West Chester (G-19141)
Samron Inc .... E 330 782-6539
 Youngstown (G-20366)
Schoch Tile & Carpet Inc .... E 513 922-3466
 Cincinnati (G-4484)
Schumacher & Co Inc .... E 859 655-9000
 Milford (G-14560)
Stedman Floor Co Inc .... E 614 836-3190
 Groveport (G-11674)
T and D Interiors Incorporated .... E 419 331-4372
 Lima (G-12897)
◆ Tremco Incorporated .... B 216 292-5000
 Beachwood (G-1133)
W R Shepherd Inc .... E 614 889-2896
 Powell (G-16353)
Weiffenbach Marble & Tile Co .... E 937 832-7055
 Englewood (G-10724)

1761 Roofing, Siding & Sheet Metal Work

1st Choice Roofing Company .... E 216 227-7755
 Cleveland (G-4923)
Able Company Ltd Partnership ...... D 614 444-7663
 Columbus (G-6926)
Able Roofing LLC .... E 614 444-7663
 Columbus (G-6927)
Advanced Industrial Roofg Inc .... D 330 837-1999
 Massillon (G-13784)
AH Sturgill Roofing Inc .... E 937 254-2955
 Dayton (G-9250)
Airko Inc .... E 440 333-0133
 Cleveland (G-4978)

▲ Alan Manufacturing Inc ....E....... 330 262-1555
Wooster *(G-19825)*
All-Type Welding & Fabrication ....E....... 440 439-3990
Cleveland *(G-4991)*
Ameridian Specialty Services ....E....... 513 769-0150
Cincinnati *(G-3014)*
Anchor Metal Processing Inc ....E....... 216 362-1850
Cleveland *(G-5035)*
Apco Industries Inc ....D....... 614 224-2345
Columbus *(G-7027)*
Architectural Systems Inc ....D....... 614 873-2057
Plain City *(G-16182)*
Atlas Roofing Company ....E....... 330 467-7683
Cleveland *(G-5079)*
Avon Lake Sheet Metal Co ....E....... 440 933-3505
Avon Lake *(G-923)*
Aw Farrell Son Inc ....E....... 513 334-0715
Milford *(G-14505)*
B & B Roofing Inc ....E....... 740 772-4759
Chillicothe *(G-2815)*
Beck Company ....E....... 216 883-0909
Cleveland *(G-5110)*
Bh Group LLC ....D....... 513 671-3300
West Chester *(G-19028)*
Boak & Sons Inc ....C....... 330 793-5646
Youngstown *(G-20118)*
Budde Sheet Metal Works Inc ....E....... 937 224-0868
Dayton *(G-9372)*
Building Technicians Corp ....E....... 440 466-1651
Geneva *(G-11359)*
Burbank Inc ....E....... 419 698-3434
Toledo *(G-17788)*
Burns & Scalo Roofing Co Inc ....E....... 740 383-4639
Marion *(G-13527)*
Campeon Roofg & Waterproofing ....E....... 513 271-8972
Cincinnati *(G-3173)*
Cardinal Builders Inc ....E....... 614 237-1000
Columbus *(G-7190)*
Cardinal Maintenance & Svc Co ....C....... 330 252-0282
Akron *(G-122)*
Centimark Corporation ....E....... 614 536-1960
Reynoldsburg *(G-16435)*
Centimark Corporation ....E....... 937 704-9909
Franklin *(G-11152)*
Centimark Corporation ....C....... 330 920-3560
Stow *(G-17356)*
▲ Champion Opco LLC ....B....... 513 924-4858
Cincinnati *(G-3228)*
Chaney Roofing Maintenance ....E....... 419 639-2761
Clyde *(G-6811)*
Chemcote Roofing Company ....D....... 614 792-2683
Dublin *(G-10291)*
Christen & Sons Company ....E....... 419 243-4161
Toledo *(G-17805)*
Command Roofing Co ....C....... 937 298-1155
Moraine *(G-14760)*
Contract Lumber Inc ....C....... 740 964-3147
Pataskala *(G-15921)*
Cornelius Joel Roofing Inc ....E....... 513 367-4401
Harrison *(G-11795)*
D&T Installed Siding LLC ....E....... 614 444-8445
Columbus *(G-7482)*
Dahm Brothers Company Inc ....E....... 937 461-5627
Dayton *(G-9449)*
Dalton Roofing Co ....D....... 513 871-2800
Cincinnati *(G-3460)*
Damschroder Roofing Inc ....E....... 419 332-5000
Fremont *(G-11194)*
Daugherty Construction Inc ....E....... 216 731-9444
Euclid *(G-10748)*
Dayton Roof & Remodeling Co ....E....... 937 224-7667
Beavercreek *(G-1167)*
Deer Park Roofing Inc ....E....... 513 891-9151
Cincinnati *(G-3478)*
Detmer & Sons Inc ....E....... 937 879-2373
Fairborn *(G-10793)*
Diamond Roofing Systems LLP ....E....... 330 856-2500
Warren *(G-18849)*
Dimensional Metals Inc ....D....... 740 927-3633
Reynoldsburg *(G-16447)*
Division 7 Inc ....E....... 740 965-1970
Galena *(G-11281)*
Ducts Inc ....E....... 216 391-2400
Cleveland *(G-5511)*
Dun Rite Home Improvement Inc ....E....... 330 650-5322
Macedonia *(G-13196)*
▲ Durable Slate Co ....D....... 614 299-5522
Columbus *(G-7552)*
Durable Slate Co ....E....... 216 751-0151
Shaker Heights *(G-16859)*
Eastside Roofg Restoration Co ....E....... 513 471-0434
Cincinnati *(G-3539)*
Eckstein Roofing Company ....E....... 513 941-1511
Cincinnati *(G-3542)*
Erie Construction Mid-West Inc ....E....... 419 472-4200
Toledo *(G-17869)*
Erie Construction Mid-West Inc ....E....... 937 898-4688
Dayton *(G-9530)*
Facility Products & Svcs LLC ....E....... 330 533-8943
Canfield *(G-2189)*
Feazel Roofing Company ....E....... 614 898-7663
Westerville *(G-19306)*
Franck and Fric Incorporated ....D....... 216 524-4451
Cleveland *(G-5631)*
Fred Christen & Sons Company ....D....... 419 243-4161
Toledo *(G-17900)*
Frost Roofing Inc ....D....... 419 739-2701
Wapakoneta *(G-18796)*
Geauga Mechanical Company ....D....... 440 285-2000
Chardon *(G-2750)*
Giorgi of Chesapeake Inc ....E....... 740 256-1724
Crown City *(G-9155)*
Global Insulation Inc ....E....... 330 479-3100
Canton *(G-2381)*
Harold J Becker Company Inc ....E....... 614 279-1414
Beavercreek *(G-1245)*
Hart Roofing Inc ....E....... 330 452-4055
Canton *(G-2396)*
▲ Hickey Metal Fabrication Roofg ....E....... 330 337-9329
Salem *(G-16698)*
Hicks Roofing Inc ....E....... 330 364-7737
New Philadelphia *(G-15100)*
Hinckley Roofing Inc ....E....... 330 722-7663
Medina *(G-14076)*
Holland Roofing Inc ....E....... 330 963-0237
Twinsburg *(G-18430)*
Holland Roofing Inc ....E....... 614 430-3724
Columbus *(G-7847)*
Holmes Siding Contractors ....D....... 330 674-2867
Millersburg *(G-14605)*
Industrial Energy Systems Inc ....E....... 216 267-9590
Cleveland *(G-5816)*
Industrial First Inc ....C....... 216 991-8605
Bedford *(G-1313)*
J A Guy Inc ....E....... 937 642-3415
Marysville *(G-13629)*
K & W Roofing Inc ....E....... 740 927-3122
Etna *(G-10735)*
Kelley Brothers Roofing Inc ....D....... 513 829-7717
Fairfield *(G-10868)*
Kerkan Roofing Inc ....D....... 513 821-0556
Cincinnati *(G-3917)*
◆ Kirk & Blum Manufacturing Co ....C....... 513 458-2600
Cincinnati *(G-3929)*
Kirk & Blum Manufacturing Co ....E....... 419 782-9885
Defiance *(G-10043)*
Korman Construction Corp ....E....... 614 274-2170
Columbus *(G-8011)*
Leaffilter North LLC ....D....... 330 655-7950
Hudson *(G-12131)*
Meade Construction Inc ....E....... 740 694-5525
Lexington *(G-12715)*
Mechanical Cnstr Managers LLC ....C....... 937 274-1987
Dayton *(G-9709)*
Mechanical Construction Co ....E....... 740 353-5668
Portsmouth *(G-16295)*
Mid-America Gutters Inc ....E....... 513 671-4000
West Chester *(G-19215)*
Midwest Roofing & Furnace Co ....E....... 614 252-5241
Columbus *(G-8172)*
Moisture Guard Corporation ....E....... 330 928-7200
Stow *(G-17383)*
Mollett Seamless Gutter Co ....E....... 513 825-0500
West Chester *(G-19123)*
Molloy Roofing Company ....E....... 513 791-7400
Blue Ash *(G-1645)*
N F Mansuetto & Sons Inc ....E....... 740 633-7320
Martins Ferry *(G-13600)*
Nasco Roofing and Cnstr Inc ....E....... 330 746-3566
Youngstown *(G-20294)*
National Blanking LLC ....E....... 419 385-0636
Toledo *(G-18073)*
Nations Roof of Ohio LLC ....E....... 937 439-4160
Springboro *(G-17132)*
Nordmann Roofing Co Inc ....E....... 419 691-5737
Toledo *(G-18089)*
Northern Ohio Roofg Shtmtl Inc ....E....... 440 322-8262
Elyria *(G-10664)*
Ohio & Indiana Roofing ....E....... 937 339-8768
Troy *(G-18368)*
Ohio Fabricators Inc ....E....... 216 391-2400
Cleveland *(G-6190)*
Olde Towne Windows Inc ....E....... 419 626-9613
Milan *(G-14496)*
Ontario Mechanical LLC ....E....... 419 529-2578
Ontario *(G-15709)*
Overhead Door Co- Cincinnati ....C....... 513 346-4000
West Chester *(G-19127)*
◆ Owens Corning Sales LLC ....A....... 419 248-8000
Toledo *(G-18114)*
Patriot Roofing Company Inc ....E....... 513 469-7663
Blue Ash *(G-1662)*
Pcy Enterprises Inc ....E....... 513 241-5566
Cincinnati *(G-4270)*
▼ Phinney Industrial Roofing ....D....... 614 308-9000
Columbus *(G-8542)*
Preferred Roofing Ohio Inc ....E....... 216 587-0957
Cleveland *(G-6300)*
Preferred Roofing Services LLC ....E....... 216 587-0957
Cleveland *(G-6301)*
Promanco Inc ....E....... 740 374-2120
Marietta *(G-13491)*
Quality Electrical & Mech Inc ....E....... 419 294-3591
Lima *(G-12865)*
R & B Contractors LLC ....E....... 513 738-0954
Shandon *(G-16873)*
Ray St Clair Roofing Inc ....E....... 513 874-1234
Fairfield *(G-10898)*
Regency Roofing Companies Inc ....E....... 330 468-1021
Macedonia *(G-13208)*
Regency Windows Corporation ....D....... 330 963-4077
Twinsburg *(G-18459)*
Reilly Painting Co ....E....... 216 371-8160
Cleveland Heights *(G-6796)*
Residntial Coml Rnovations Inc ....E....... 330 815-1476
Clinton *(G-6807)*
Richland Co & Associates Inc ....E....... 419 782-0141
Defiance *(G-10054)*
Roofing By Insulation Inc ....E....... 937 315-5024
New Carlisle *(G-15030)*
Roth Bros Inc ....C....... 330 793-5571
Youngstown *(G-20360)*
Scs Construction Services Inc ....E....... 513 929-0260
Cincinnati *(G-4487)*
Simon Roofing and Shtmtl Corp ....C....... 330 629-7392
Youngstown *(G-20376)*
Slagle Mechanical Contractors ....E....... 937 492-4151
Sidney *(G-16956)*
Squires Construction Company ....E....... 216 252-0300
Rocky River *(G-16592)*
T & F Systems Inc ....D....... 216 881-3525
Cleveland *(G-6563)*
Tecta America Corp ....D....... 419 447-1716
Tiffin *(G-17703)*
Tecta America Zero Company LLC ....D....... 513 541-1848
Cincinnati *(G-4632)*
Tendon Manufacturing Inc ....E....... 216 663-3200
Cleveland *(G-6582)*
Terik Roofing Inc ....E....... 330 785-0060
Coventry Township *(G-9134)*
Thiels Replacement Systems Inc ....D....... 419 289-6139
Ashland *(G-701)*
◆ Tremco Incorporated ....B....... 216 292-5000
Beachwood *(G-1133)*
Tycor Roofing Inc ....E....... 330 452-8150
Canton *(G-2566)*
United GL & Panl Systems Inc ....E....... 330 244-9745
Canton *(G-2568)*
Valley Roofing LLC ....E....... 513 831-9444
Milford *(G-14572)*
Weatherproofing Tech Inc ....D....... 216 292-5000
Beachwood *(G-1136)*
Weatherproofing Tech Inc ....A....... 281 480-7900
Beachwood *(G-1137)*
▲ West Roofing Systems Inc ....E....... 800 356-5748
Lagrange *(G-12462)*
Williams Bros Roofg & Siding ....E....... 937 434-3838
Piqua *(G-16177)*
Williams Bros Roofg Siding Co ....E....... 937 434-3838
Dayton *(G-9999)*
Wm Kramer and Sons Inc ....D....... 513 353-1142
Cleves *(G-6806)*
Wolfes Roofing Inc ....E....... 419 666-6233
Walbridge *(G-18781)*
York-Mahoning Mech Contrs Inc ....D....... 330 788-7011
Youngstown *(G-20420)*

1771 Concrete Work

21st Century Con Cnstr Inc ....E....... 216 362-0900
Cleveland *(G-4925)*

17 CONSTRUCTION-SPECIAL TRADE CONTRACTORS

Company	Code	Phone
Adleta Inc — Cincinnati (G-2973)	E	513 554-1469
Aerodynamic Concrete & Cnstr — Akron (G-23)	E	330 906-7477
Akron Concrete Corp — Akron (G-35)	E	330 864-1188
Alan Stone Co Inc — Cutler (G-9156)	E	740 448-1100
Allied Paving Inc — Holland (G-12006)	E	419 666-3100
American Coatings Corporation — Plain City (G-16181)	E	614 335-1000
Architctural Con Solutions Inc — Columbus (G-7038)	E	614 940-5399
Arledge Construction Inc — Columbus (G-7041)	E	614 732-4258
Atlas Construction Company — Columbus (G-7070)	D	614 475-4705
B & D Concrete Footers Inc — Etna (G-10731)	E	740 964-2294
B G Trucking & Construction — Akron (G-88)	E	330 620-8734
◆ Baker Concrete Cnstr Inc — Monroe (G-14688)	A	513 539-4000
Barbicas Construction Co — Akron (G-89)	E	330 733-9101
Barrett Paving Materials Inc — Middletown (G-14475)	C	513 271-6200
Berlin Contractors — Berlin (G-1477)	E	330 893-2904
Bh Group LLC — West Chester (G-19027)	D	513 671-3300
Brown County Asphalt Inc — Georgetown (G-11387)	E	937 446-2481
Buckholz Wall Systems LLC — Hilliard (G-11886)	E	614 870-1775
Ceco Concrete Cnstr Del LLC — West Chester (G-19034)	E	734 455-3535
Ceco Concrete Cnstr Del LLC — West Chester (G-19033)	D	513 874-6953
Cem-Base Inc — Twinsburg (G-18399)	E	330 963-3101
Central Ohio Poured Walls Inc — Dublin (G-10285)	E	614 889-0505
Charles H Hamilton Co — Maineville (G-13241)	D	513 683-2442
Cioffi & Son Construction — Akron (G-137)	E	330 794-9448
Cleveland Concrete Cnstr Inc — Brooklyn Heights (G-1913)	D	216 741-3954
Concrete Coring Company Inc — Enon (G-10726)	E	937 864-7325
Cook Paving and Cnstr Co — Independence (G-12201)	E	216 267-7705
Cornerstone Concrete Cnstr Inc — Sardinia (G-16812)	E	937 442-2805
Cox Paving Inc — Wshngtn CT Hs (G-20018)	D	937 780-3075
Day Precision Wall Inc — Cleves (G-6798)	E	513 353-2999
Depuy Paving Inc — Columbus (G-7509)	E	614 272-0256
Donley Concrete Cutting — Pickerington (G-16094)	D	614 834-0300
DOT Diamond Core Drilling Inc — Elyria (G-10617)	E	440 322-6466
Dwyer Concrete Lifting Inc — Groveport (G-11635)	E	614 501-0998
E&I Construction LLC — Cincinnati (G-3525)	E	513 421-2045
Elastizell Systems Inc — Moraine (G-14779)	E	937 298-1313
Engineered Con Structures Corp — Cleveland (G-5540)	E	216 520-2000
Foor Concrete Co Inc — Delaware (G-10098)	D	740 513-4346
Formwork Services LLC — Monroe (G-14695)	E	513 539-4000
Freisthler Paving Inc — Sidney (G-16935)	E	937 498-4802
G Big Inc — Chesapeake (G-2784)	E	740 867-5758
Gardner Cement Contractors — Toledo (G-17909)	D	419 389-0768
Gateway Concrete Forming Svcs — Miamitown (G-14371)	E	513 353-2000
Geddis Paving & Excavating — Toledo (G-17910)	E	419 536-8501
George Kuhn Enterprises Inc — Columbus (G-7743)	E	614 481-8838
Gironda Vito & Bros Inc — Akron (G-236)	E	330 630-9399
▲ Goettle Holding Company Inc — Cincinnati (G-3683)	C	513 825-8100
H & M Precision Concrete LLC — Greenville (G-11508)	E	937 547-0012
H & R Concrete Inc — Dayton (G-9594)	E	937 885-2910
Halcomb Concrete Construction — Fairfield (G-10856)	E	513 829-3576
Hanson Concrete Products Ohio — Columbus (G-7800)	E	614 443-4846
Hayes Concrete Construction — Cincinnati (G-3742)	E	513 648-9400
Holland Enterprises Inc — Cleveland (G-5766)	E	216 671-9333
Hovest Construction — Ottawa (G-15798)	E	419 456-3426
Hoyer Poured Walls Inc — Marysville (G-13628)	E	937 642-6148
Image Pavement Maintenance — Brookville (G-1963)	E	937 833-9200
▲ Independence Excavating Inc — Independence (G-12218)	E	216 524-1700
Ivan Law Inc — Youngstown (G-20238)	E	330 533-5000
J & D Home Improvement Inc — Reynoldsburg (G-16459)	D	740 927-0722
J K Enterprises Inc — Columbus (G-7931)	D	614 481-8838
Jennite Co — Toledo (G-17984)	E	419 531-1791
Jostin Construction Inc — Cincinnati (G-3889)	E	513 559-9390
K & M Construction Company — Medina (G-14089)	C	330 723-3681
Keim Concrete LLC — Wooster (G-19877)	E	330 264-5313
L & I Custom Walls Inc — Loveland (G-13137)	E	513 683-2045
Lavy Concrete Construction — Covington (G-9137)	E	937 606-4754
Lithko Contracting LLC — Plain City (G-16196)	C	614 733-0300
Lithko Contracting LLC — West Chester (G-19110)	E	513 564-2000
Lithko Contracting LLC — Monroe (G-14703)	D	513 863-5100
Lithko Restoration Tech LLC — Monroe (G-14704)	E	513 863-5500
Lithko Restoration Tech LLC — Columbus (G-8072)	E	614 221-0711
Lockhart Concrete Co — Akron (G-325)	D	330 745-6520
Lucas County Asphalt Inc — Toledo (G-18016)	E	419 476-0705
Maintenance Systerms of N Ohio — Elyria (G-10648)	E	440 323-1291
Mattlin Construction Inc — Cleves (G-6804)	E	513 598-5402
Menke Bros Construction Co — Delphos (G-10147)	E	419 286-2086
Metcon Ltd — Bradford (G-1807)	E	937 447-9200
Milcon Concrete Inc — Troy (G-18366)	E	937 339-6274
Miller Yount Paving Inc — Cortland (G-9079)	E	330 372-4408
Modern Day Concrete Cnstr — Harrison (G-11806)	E	513 738-1026
Modern Poured Walls Inc — Wellington (G-18994)	D	440 647-6661
Morrow Gravel Company Inc — Cincinnati (G-4120)	C	513 771-0820
Newcomer Concrete Services Inc — Norwalk (G-15581)	D	419 668-2789
Norris Brothers Co Inc — Cleveland (G-6137)	C	216 771-2233
North Coast Concrete Inc — Cleveland (G-6139)	E	216 642-1114
Northeast Concrete & Cnstr — Westerville (G-19333)	E	614 898-5728
Northstar Asphalt Inc — North Canton (G-15358)	E	330 497-0936
Ohio Con Sawing & Drlg Inc — Sylvania (G-17603)	E	419 841-1330
Ohio Con Sawing & Drlg Inc — Columbus (G-8322)	E	614 252-1122
Ohio Paving & Cnstr Co Inc — Willoughby (G-19701)	E	440 975-8929
Ohio Paving Group LLC — Cleveland (G-6193)	E	216 475-1700
Pavement Protectors Inc — Grove City (G-11590)	E	614 875-9989
Perrin Asphalt Co Inc — Akron (G-386)	D	330 253-1020
Phillips Companies — Beavercreek Township (G-1280)	E	937 426-5461
Phillips Ready Mix Co — Beavercreek Township (G-1281)	D	937 426-5151
Platform Cement Inc — Mentor (G-14229)	E	440 602-9750
Premier Asphalt Paving Co Inc — North Royalton (G-15498)	E	440 237-6600
Prime Polymers Inc — Medina (G-14113)	E	330 662-4200
Prus Construction Company — Cincinnati (G-4354)	C	513 321-7774
Quality Cement Inc — Cleveland (G-6333)	E	216 676-8838
Queen City Blacktop Company — Cincinnati (G-4362)	E	513 251-8400
▲ R W Sidley Incorporated — Painesville (G-15875)	E	440 352-9343
Reitter Stucco Inc — Columbus (G-8609)	E	614 291-2212
Reitter Wall Systems Inc — Columbus (G-8610)	D	614 545-4444
S & K Asphalt & Concrete — Akron (G-422)	E	330 848-6284
Scioto-Darby Concrete Inc — Hilliard (G-11951)	E	614 876-3114
Sheedy Paving Inc — Columbus (G-8724)	E	614 252-2111
Shelly and Sands Inc — Columbus (G-8725)	E	614 444-5100
Shelly and Sands Inc — Zanesville (G-20532)	E	740 453-0721
Shepherd Excavating Inc — Dublin (G-10452)	D	614 889-1115
Signature Concrete Inc — Dayton (G-9884)	E	937 723-8435
Smalls Asphalt Paving Inc — Gambier (G-11350)	E	740 427-4096
Sowder Concrete Corporation — Dayton (G-9893)	E	937 890-1633
Spano Brothers Cnstr Co — Akron (G-445)	E	330 645-1544
Spaulding Construction Co Inc — Canton (G-2534)	D	330 494-1776
◆ Spillman Company — Columbus (G-8762)	E	614 444-2184
Staarmann Concrete Inc — Hamilton (G-11774)	E	513 756-9191
Stamm Contracting Co Inc — Mantua (G-13395)	E	330 274-8230
Standard Contg & Engrg Inc — Brookpark (G-1955)	D	440 243-1001
Suburban Maint & Cnstr Inc — North Royalton (G-15503)	E	440 237-7765
Tallmadge Asphalt & Pav Co Inc — Kent (G-12399)	D	330 677-0000
Technical Construction Spc — Cuyahoga Falls (G-9224)	E	330 929-1088
Thompson Concrete Ltd — Carroll (G-2609)	C	740 756-7256
Towne Construction Svcs LLC — Batavia (G-1028)	C	513 561-3700
Tri-Mor Corp — Twinsburg (G-18478)	C	330 963-3101
Triple Q Foundations Co Inc — Lebanon (G-12654)	E	513 932-3121
Trucco Construction Co Inc — Delaware (G-10130)	C	740 417-9010
Tscs Inc — Metamora (G-14266)	E	419 644-3921
U S A Concrete Specialists — Columbiana (G-6865)	E	330 482-9150
Vandra Bros Construction Inc — Cleveland (G-6687)	E	440 232-3030
Wasiniak Construction Inc — Norwalk (G-15596)	D	419 668-8624
Wenger Asphalt Inc — Dalton (G-9243)	E	330 837-4767
Williams Concrete Cnstr Co Inc — Norton (G-15560)	E	330 745-6388

1781 Water Well Drilling

Company	Code	Phone
Collector Wells Intl Inc — Columbus (G-7320)	E	614 888-6263

Moodys of Dayton Inc....E....614 443-3898
Miamisburg (G-14323)
Ohio Drilling Company....E....330 832-1521
Massillon (G-13842)
Patterson-Uti Drilling Co LLC....E....724 239-2812
Saint Clairsville (G-16652)

1791 Structural Steel Erection

Akron Erectors Inc....E....330 745-7100
Akron (G-39)
Black Swamp Steel Inc....E....419 867-8050
Holland (G-12010)
◆ Columbiana Boiler Company LLC....E....330 482-3373
Columbiana (G-6855)
Columbus Steel Erectors Inc....E....614 876-5050
Columbus (G-7388)
Daniel A Terreri & Sons Inc....E....330 538-2950
Youngstown (G-20165)
Dublin Building Systems Co....E....614 760-5831
Dublin (G-10325)
Evers Welding Co Inc....E....513 385-7352
Cincinnati (G-3582)
Forest City Erectors Inc....D....330 425-2345
Twinsburg (G-18417)
Foundation Steel LLC....D....419 402-4241
Swanton (G-17564)
Frameco Inc....E....216 433-7080
Cleveland (G-5629)
Frederick Steel Company LLC....D....513 821-6400
Cincinnati (G-3646)
FSRc Tanks Inc....E....234 221-2015
Bolivar (G-1747)
GL Nause Co Inc....E....513 722-9500
Loveland (G-13128)
Henry Gurtzweiler Inc....D....419 729-3955
Toledo (G-17953)
Hovest Construction....E....419 456-3426
Ottawa (G-15798)
Industrial First Inc....C....216 991-8605
Bedford (G-1313)
J&H Rnfrcing Strl Erectors Inc....C....740 355-0141
Portsmouth (G-16292)
Kelley Steel Erectors Inc....D....440 232-1573
Cleveland (G-5891)
Legacy Industrial Services LLC....E....606 584-8953
Ripley (G-16547)
Marysville Steel Inc....E....937 642-5971
Marysville (G-13636)
Mason Steel Erecting Inc....E....440 439-1040
Cleveland (G-5992)
Mid Atlantic Stor Systems Inc....D....740 335-2019
Wshngtn CT Hs (G-20032)
Midwest Reinforcing Contrs....E....937 390-8998
Springfield (G-17248)
Mohawk RE-Bar Services Inc....E....440 268-0780
Strongsville (G-17495)
Mound Technologies Inc....E....937 748-2937
Springboro (G-17131)
▲ Northbend Archtctural Pdts Inc....E....513 577-7988
Cincinnati (G-4179)
Ontario Mechanical LLC....E....419 529-2578
Ontario (G-15709)
Orbit Movers & Erectors Inc....E....937 277-8080
Dayton (G-9793)
R&F Erectors Inc....E....513 574-8273
Cincinnati (G-4381)
▼ Reading Rock Residential LLC....E....513 874-4770
West Chester (G-19223)
Rittman Inc....D....330 927-6855
Rittman (G-16556)
Sawyer Steel Erectors Inc....E....419 867-8050
Holland (G-12052)
Seneca Steel Erectors Inc....E....740 385-0517
Logan (G-12987)
Smith Brothers Erection Inc....E....740 373-3575
Marietta (G-13500)
Sofco Erectors Inc....C....513 771-1600
Cincinnati (G-4549)
Stein Inc....D....216 883-4277
Cleveland (G-6535)
Vmi Group Inc....D....330 405-4146
Macedonia (G-13216)

1793 Glass & Glazing Work

A E D Inc....E....419 661-9999
Northwood (G-15526)
▲ Advanced Auto Glass Inc....E....412 373-6675
Akron (G-21)
▲ AGC Automotive Americas....D....937 599-3131
Bellefontaine (G-1375)
Anderson Aluminum Corporation....D....614 476-4877
Columbus (G-7017)
E J Robinson Glass Co....E....513 242-9250
Cincinnati (G-3524)
J & B Equipment & Supply Inc....D....419 884-1155
Mansfield (G-13314)
Lakeland Glass Co....E....440 277-4527
Lorain (G-13047)
Lorain Glass Co Inc....D....440 277-6004
Lorain (G-13054)
▲ Medina Glass Block Inc....E....330 239-0239
Medina (G-14100)
Modern Glass Pnt & Tile Co Inc....E....740 454-1253
Zanesville (G-20503)
Pioneer Cldding Glzing Systems....E....216 816-4242
Cleveland (G-6282)
▲ Pioneer Cldding Glzing Systems....D....513 583-5925
Mason (G-13747)
R C Hemm Glass Shops Inc....E....937 773-5591
Piqua (G-16163)
Richardson Glass Service Inc....D....740 366-5090
Newark (G-15232)
Ryans All-Glass Incorporated....E....513 771-4440
Cincinnati (G-4461)
Thomas Glass Company Inc....E....614 268-8611
Worthington (G-20003)
Toledo Glass LLC....E....419 241-3151
Toledo (G-18237)
United GL & Panl Systems Inc....E....330 244-9745
Canton (G-2568)
Wiechart Enterprises Inc....E....419 227-0027
Lima (G-12921)

1794 Excavating & Grading Work

A Crano Excavating Inc....E....330 630-1061
Akron (G-11)
Allard Excavation LLC....D....740 778-2242
South Webster (G-17102)
Allgeier & Son Inc....E....513 574-3735
Cincinnati (G-2988)
Anderzack-Pitzen Cnstr Inc....E....419 553-7015
Metamora (G-14265)
B & B Wrecking & Excvtg Inc....E....216 429-1700
Cleveland (G-5089)
Bansal Construction Inc....E....513 874-5410
Fairfield (G-10822)
Bontrager Excavating Co Inc....E....330 499-8775
Uniontown (G-18508)
Boyas Excavating Inc....E....216 524-3620
Cleveland (G-5131)
Brunk Excavating Inc....E....513 360-0308
Monroe (G-14691)
Burkhart Excavating Inc....E....740 896-3312
Lowell (G-13167)
C & J Contractors Inc....E....216 391-5700
Cleveland (G-5167)
Camargo Construction Company....E....513 248-1500
Cincinnati (G-3168)
Charles F Jergens Cnstr Inc....E....937 233-1830
Dayton (G-9399)
Charles H Hamilton Co....D....513 683-2442
Maineville (G-13241)
Charles Jergens Contractor....E....937 233-1830
Dayton (G-9400)
Chieftain Trucking & Excav Inc....E....216 485-8034
Cleveland (G-5235)
Clemson Excavating Inc....E....440 286-4757
Chardon (G-2744)
Cox Paving Inc....D....937 780-3075
Wshngtn CT Hs (G-20018)
D B Bentley Inc....E....440 352-8495
Painesville (G-15849)
Darby Creek Excavating Inc....D....740 477-8600
Circleville (G-4886)
Dave Sugar Excavating LLC....E....330 542-1100
Petersburg (G-16081)
Demmy Construction Inc....E....937 325-9429
Springfield (G-17188)
Digioia/Suburban Excvtg LLC....D....440 237-1978
North Royalton (G-15487)
Don Wartko Construction Co....D....330 673-5252
Kent (G-12366)
E S Wagner Company....D....419 691-8651
Oregon (G-15733)
Elite Excavating Company Inc....E....419 683-4200
Mansfield (G-13297)
Eslich Wrecking Company....E....330 488-8300
Louisville (G-13101)
Facemyer Backhoe and Dozer Svc....E....740 965-1137
Sunbury (G-17555)
Fechko Excavating Inc....D....330 722-2890
Medina (G-14064)
Fishel Company....C....937 233-2268
Dayton (G-9551)
Fleming Construction Co....E....740 494-2177
Prospect (G-16365)
Ford Development Corp....D....513 772-1521
Cincinnati (G-3637)
Geddis Paving & Excavating....E....419 536-8501
Toledo (G-17910)
Geo Gradel Co....D....419 691-7123
Toledo (G-17912)
George J Igel & Co Inc....A....614 445-8421
Columbus (G-7742)
Geotex Construction Svcs Inc....E....614 444-5690
Columbus (G-7745)
GMC Excavation & Trucking....E....419 468-0121
Galion (G-11300)
▲ Goettle Holding Company Inc....C....513 825-8100
Cincinnati (G-3683)
Ground Tech Inc....E....330 270-0700
Youngstown (G-20210)
H & R Concrete Inc....E....937 885-2910
Dayton (G-9594)
Hardrock Excavating LLC....D....330 792-9524
Youngstown (G-20212)
Harris & Heavener Excavating....E....740 927-1423
Etna (G-10729)
▲ Independence Excavating Inc....E....216 524-1700
Independence (G-12218)
Indian Nation Inc....E....740 532-6143
North Canton (G-15345)
J & J General Maintenance Inc....E....740 533-9729
Ironton (G-12293)
J D Williamson Cnstr Co Inc....D....330 633-1258
Tallmadge (G-17641)
John Eramo & Sons Inc....D....614 777-0020
Hilliard (G-11916)
John F Gallagher Plumbing Co....E....440 946-4256
Eastlake (G-10547)
JS Bova Excavating LLC....E....234 254-4040
Struthers (G-17532)
JS Paris Excavating Inc....E....330 538-3048
North Jackson (G-15382)
Kelchner Inc....C....937 704-9890
Springboro (G-17125)
KMu Trucking & Excvtg Inc....E....440 934-1008
Avon (G-903)
Larry Lang Excavating Inc....E....740 984-4750
Beverly (G-1491)
Law Excavating Inc....E....740 745-3420
Saint Louisville (G-16669)
Layton Inc....E....740 349-7101
Newark (G-15182)
Layton Trucking Inc....E....740 366-1447
Newark (G-15183)
Loveland Excavating Inc....E....513 965-6600
Fairfield (G-10873)
Luburgh Inc....E....740 452-3668
Zanesville (G-20498)
Maintenance Unlimited Inc....E....440 238-1162
Strongsville (G-17486)
Martin Greg Excavating Inc....E....513 727-9300
Middletown (G-14433)
Marucci and Gaffney Excvtg Co....E....330 743-8170
Youngstown (G-20273)
McConnell Excavating Ltd....E....440 774-4578
Oberlin (G-15649)
Menke Bros Construction Co....E....419 286-2086
Delphos (G-10147)
Metropolitan Envmtl Svcs Inc....D....614 771-1881
Hilliard (G-11930)
Mike Enyart & Sons Inc....D....740 523-0235
South Point (G-17095)
Mike George Excavating....E....419 855-4147
Genoa (G-11382)
Mike Pusateri Excavating Inc....E....330 385-5221
East Liverpool (G-10525)
Miller Yount Paving Inc....E....330 372-4408
Cortland (G-9079)
Modern Poured Walls Inc....D....440 647-6661
Wellington (G-18994)
Movers and Shuckers LLC....E....740 263-2164
Mount Vernon (G-14915)
Mr Excavator Inc....D....440 256-2008
Kirtland (G-12458)
Nelson Stark Company....C....513 489-0866
Cincinnati (G-4154)
Newcomer Concrete Services Inc....D....419 668-2789
Norwalk (G-15581)

Nicolozakes Trckg & Cnstr Inc ....E 740 432-5648
Cambridge *(G-2124)*
Northast Ohio Trnching Svc Inc ....E 216 663-6006
Cleveland *(G-6149)*
Nuway Incorporated ....E 740 587-2452
Heath *(G-11841)*
Ohio Heavy Equipment Lsg LLC ....E 513 965-6600
Fairfield *(G-10888)*
Ohio State Home Services Inc ....D 614 850-5600
Hilliard *(G-11940)*
Osborne Co ....D 440 942-7000
Mentor *(G-14226)*
Otto Falkenberg Excavating ....E 330 626-4215
Mantua *(G-13393)*
Phillips Ready Mix Co ....D 937 426-5151
Beavercreek Township *(G-1281)*
R D Jones Excavating Inc ....E 419 648-5870
Harrod *(G-11813)*
R T Vernal Paving Inc ....E 330 549-3189
North Lima *(G-15407)*
Rack & Ballauer Excvtg Co Inc ....E 513 738-7000
Hamilton *(G-11766)*
Ray Bertolini Trucking Co ....E 330 867-0666
Akron *(G-405)*
Rbm Environmental and Cnstr ....E 419 693-5840
Oregon *(G-15748)*
Ricketts Excavating Inc ....E 740 687-0338
Lancaster *(G-12569)*
Rudzik Excavating Inc ....E 330 755-1540
Struthers *(G-17534)*
S E T Inc ....E 330 536-6724
Lowellville *(G-13174)*
Schaffer Mark Excvtg & Trcking ....D 419 668-5990
Norwalk *(G-15592)*
Schumm Richard A Plbg & Htg ....E 419 238-4994
Van Wert *(G-18643)*
Seals Construction Inc ....E 614 836-7200
Canal Winchester *(G-2170)*
Sehlhorst Equipment Svcs Inc ....E 513 353-9300
Hooven *(G-12077)*
Siler Excavation Services ....E 513 400-8628
Milford *(G-14563)*
Sisler Heating & Cooling Inc ....E 330 722-7101
Medina *(G-14126)*
Smith & Associates Excavating ....E 740 362-3355
Columbus *(G-8745)*
Spano Brothers Cnstr Co ....E 330 645-1544
Akron *(G-445)*
Stahlheber & Sons Inc ....E 513 726-4446
Hamilton *(G-11775)*
Standard Contg & Engrg Inc ....D 440 243-1001
Brookpark *(G-1955)*
Star-Ex Inc ....E 937 473-2397
Covington *(G-9139)*
Steingass Mechanical Contg ....E 330 725-6090
Medina *(G-14129)*
Stonegate Construction Inc ....D 740 423-9170
Belpre *(G-1444)*
Stover Excavating Inc ....E 614 873-5865
Plain City *(G-16208)*
Sws Environmental Services ....E 254 629-1718
Findlay *(G-11089)*
Taylor Construction Company ....E 330 628-9310
Mogadore *(G-14684)*
Todd Alspaugh & Associates ....E 419 476-8126
Toledo *(G-18224)*
Trafzer Excavating Inc ....E 740 383-2616
Marion *(G-13586)*
Triad Engineering & Contg Co ....E 440 786-1000
Cleveland *(G-6617)*
Trimat Construction Inc ....E 740 388-9515
Bidwell *(G-1496)*
Trucco Construction Co Inc ....C 740 417-9010
Delaware *(G-10130)*
Utter Construction Inc ....C 513 876-2246
Bethel *(G-1484)*
Vandalia Blacktop Seal Coating ....E 937 454-0571
Dayton *(G-9965)*
Wenger Excavating Inc ....E 330 837-4767
Dalton *(G-9244)*
Zemba Bros Inc ....E 740 452-1880
Zanesville *(G-20561)*

1795 Wrecking & Demolition Work

Allgeier & Son Inc ....E 513 574-3735
Cincinnati *(G-2988)*
▲ Allied Erct & Dismantling Co ....C 330 744-0808
Youngstown *(G-20101)*
Aztec Services Group Inc ....D 513 541-2002
Cincinnati *(G-3071)*
B & B Wrecking & Excvtg Inc ....E 216 429-1700
Cleveland *(G-5089)*
Bladecutters Lawn Service Inc ....E 937 274-3861
Dayton *(G-9360)*
Boyas Excavating Inc ....E 216 524-3620
Cleveland *(G-5131)*
Brunk Excavating Inc ....E 513 360-0308
Monroe *(G-14691)*
C & J Contractors Inc ....E 216 391-5700
Cleveland *(G-5167)*
Charles F Jergens Cnstr Inc ....E 937 233-1830
Dayton *(G-9399)*
Cook Paving and Cnstr Co ....E 216 267-7705
Independence *(G-12201)*
Daniel A Terreri & Sons Inc ....E 330 538-2950
Youngstown *(G-20165)*
Dave Sugar Excavating LLC ....E 330 542-1100
Petersburg *(G-16081)*
Eslich Wrecking Company ....E 330 488-8300
Louisville *(G-13101)*
Fluor-Bwxt Portsmouth LLC ....A 866 706-6992
Piketon *(G-16115)*
▲ Independence Excavating Inc ....E 216 524-1700
Independence *(G-12218)*
JS Paris Excavating Inc ....E 330 538-3048
North Jackson *(G-15382)*
Marucci and Gaffney Excvtg Co ....E 330 743-8170
Youngstown *(G-20273)*
Miller Brothers Cnstr Dem LLC ....E 513 257-1082
Oxford *(G-15824)*
Mosier Industrial Services ....E 419 683-4000
Crestline *(G-9148)*
ORourke Wrecking Company ....D 513 871-1400
Cincinnati *(G-4235)*
Ray Bertolini Trucking Co ....E 330 867-0666
Akron *(G-405)*
Rnw Holdings Inc ....E 330 792-0600
Youngstown *(G-20352)*
S G Loewendick and Sons Inc ....E 614 539-2582
Grove City *(G-11594)*
Schaffer Mark Excvtg & Trcking ....D 419 668-5990
Norwalk *(G-15592)*
Sidwell Materials Inc ....C 740 849-2394
Zanesville *(G-20533)*
Sunesis Environmental LLC ....D 513 326-6000
Fairfield *(G-10912)*

1796 Installation Or Erection Of Bldg Eqpt & Machinery, NEC

A and A Millwright Rigging Svcs ....E 513 396-6212
Cincinnati *(G-2951)*
Advanced Tool & Supply Inc ....E 937 278-7337
Dayton *(G-9310)*
▲ Allied Erct & Dismantling Co ....C 330 744-0808
Youngstown *(G-20101)*
Atlas Industrial Contrs LLC ....B 614 841-4500
Columbus *(G-7072)*
▲ Canton Erectors Inc ....E 330 453-7363
Canton *(G-2287)*
▲ Clopay Corporation ....C 800 282-2260
Mason *(G-13686)*
CTS Construction Inc ....D 513 489-8290
Cincinnati *(G-3445)*
▲ Fenton Rigging & Contg Inc ....C 513 631-5500
Cincinnati *(G-3602)*
Gardner Contracting Company ....E 216 881-3800
Cleveland *(G-5654)*
Gem Industrial Inc ....D 419 467-3287
Walbridge *(G-18775)*
Glt Inc ....E 937 395-0508
Moraine *(G-14791)*
Grubb Construction Inc ....F 419 293-2316
Mc Comb *(G-14021)*
Hensley Industries Inc ....E 513 769-6666
Cincinnati *(G-3757)*
Hgc Construction Co ....D 513 861-8866
Cincinnati *(G-3759)*
▲ Hy-Tek Material Handling Inc ....D 614 497-2500
Columbus *(G-7873)*
Industrial Power Systems Inc ....C 419 531-3121
Rossford *(G-16608)*
◆ Intertec Corporation ....B 419 537-9711
Toledo *(G-17977)*
J R Mead Industrial Contrs ....E 614 891-4466
Galena *(G-11284)*
K F T Inc ....D 513 241-5910
Cincinnati *(G-3897)*
◆ McGill Airclean LLC ....D 614 829-1200
Columbus *(G-8136)*
Myers Machinery Movers Inc ....E 614 871-5052
Grove City *(G-11582)*
Nbw Inc ....E 216 377-1700
Cleveland *(G-6114)*
Norris Brothers Co Inc ....C 216 771-2233
Cleveland *(G-6137)*
North Bay Construction Inc ....E 440 835-1898
Westlake *(G-19522)*
Orbit Movers & Erectors Inc ....E 937 277-8080
Dayton *(G-9793)*
Otis Elevator Company ....D 513 531-7888
Cincinnati *(G-4242)*
Otis Elevator Company ....D 216 573-2333
Cleveland *(G-6218)*
Piqua Steel Co ....D 937 773-3632
Piqua *(G-16159)*
Schindler Elevator Corporation ....C 419 867-5100
Holland *(G-12053)*
Schindler Elevator Corporation ....D 216 370-9524
Cleveland *(G-6447)*
Schindler Elevator Corporation ....E 614 573-2777
Columbus *(G-8694)*
▲ Sk Rigging Co Inc ....E 513 771-7766
Cincinnati *(G-4536)*
▲ Spallinger Millwright Svc Co ....D 419 225-5830
Lima *(G-12879)*
Standard Contg & Engrg Inc ....D 440 243-1001
Brookpark *(G-1955)*
Tesar Industrial Contrs Inc ....E 216 741-8008
Cleveland *(G-6587)*
Thyssenkrupp Elevator Corp ....E 513 241-6000
Cincinnati *(G-4659)*
Thyssenkrupp Elevator Corp ....E 614 895-8930
Westerville *(G-19445)*

1799 Special Trade Contractors, NEC

AAA American Abatement Asb Corp ....D 216 281-9400
Cleveland *(G-4940)*
Adelmos Electric Sewer Clg Co ....E 216 641-2301
Brooklyn Heights *(G-1909)*
Advanced Industrial Svcs LLC ....D 419 661-8522
Toledo *(G-17743)*
Aerco Sandblasting Company ....E 419 224-2464
Lima *(G-12732)*
▲ AGC Automotive Americas ....D 937 599-3131
Bellefontaine *(G-1375)*
Aic Contracting Inc ....E 513 881-5900
Cincinnati *(G-2978)*
Allied Builders Inc ....E 937 226-0311
Dayton *(G-9316)*
Allied Environmental Svcs Inc ....E 419 227-4004
Lima *(G-12739)*
Alloyd Insulation Co Inc ....E 937 890-7900
Dayton *(G-9319)*
Allstate Painting & Contg Co ....D 330 220-5533
Brunswick *(G-1968)*
▲ AM Industrial Group LLC ....E 216 433-7171
Brookpark *(G-1935)*
American International Cnstr ....E 440 243-5535
Berea *(G-1445)*
American Star Painting Co LLC ....E 740 373-5634
Marietta *(G-13432)*
Angelos Caulking & Sealants Co ....E 614 236-1350
Columbus *(G-7020)*
Apco Aluminum Awning Co ....E 614 334-2726
Columbus *(G-7026)*
Aquarian Pools Inc ....E 513 576-9771
Loveland *(G-13111)*
Archer Corporation ....E 330 455-9995
Canton *(G-2244)*
Architectural Metal Erectors ....E 513 242-5106
Cincinnati *(G-3044)*
Barr Engineering Incorporated ....E 614 714-0299
Columbus *(G-7091)*
Basement Systems Ohio Inc ....C 330 423-4430
Twinsburg *(G-18396)*
◆ BASF Construction Chem LLC ....E 216 831-5500
Cleveland *(G-5098)*
Bathroom Alternatives Inc ....E 937 434-1984
Dayton *(G-9349)*
Belfor USA Group Inc ....E 513 860-3111
West Chester *(G-19192)*
Bogie Industries Inc Ltd ....E 330 745-3105
Akron *(G-106)*
Boyas Excavating Inc ....E 216 524-3620
Cleveland *(G-5131)*
Brilliant Electric Sign Co Ltd ....D 216 741-3800
Brooklyn Heights *(G-1911)*
Brown Contracting & Dev LLC ....E 419 341-3939
Port Clinton *(G-16238)*

SIC

Employee Codes: A=Over 500 employees, B=251-500
C=101-250, D=51-100, E=25-50
2018 Harris Ohio
Services Directory
913

17 CONSTRUCTION-SPECIAL TRADE CONTRACTORS

Company		Phone
Buckeye Cable Systems Inc — Toledo (G-17787)	E	419 724-2539
Buckeye Pool Inc — Dayton (G-9370)	E	937 434-7916
Burbank Inc — Toledo (G-17788)	E	419 698-3434
Burdens Machine & Welding — Newark (G-15153)	E	740 345-9246
Burnett Pools Inc — Cortland (G-9074)	E	330 372-1725
Bwxt Nclear Oprtions Group Inc — Cleveland (G-5166)	E	216 912-3000
C M S Enterprises Inc — Lancaster (G-12512)	E	740 653-1940
Camco Inc — Circleville (G-4881)	E	740 477-3682
Capital Fire Protection Co — Columbus (G-7183)	E	614 279-9448
Cardinal Builders Inc — Columbus (G-7190)	E	614 237-1000
Cardinal Environmental Svc Inc — Akron (G-121)	E	330 252-0220
Carpe Diem Industries LLC — Columbus Grove (G-9029)	D	419 659-5639
Carpe Diem Industries LLC — Bluffton (G-1729)	E	419 358-0129
Ceco Concrete Cnstr Del LLC — West Chester (G-19033)	D	513 874-6953
Ceco Concrete Cnstr Del LLC — West Chester (G-19034)	E	734 455-3535
Central Fire Protection Co Inc — Springfield (G-17158)	E	937 322-0713
Central Insulation Systems Inc — Cincinnati (G-3214)	E	513 242-0600
Central Ohio Custom Contg LLC — Mount Vernon (G-14882)	E	614 579-4971
Chemsteel Construction Company — Middleburg Heights (G-14379)	E	440 234-3930
Clarke Contractors Corp — West Chester (G-19045)	E	513 285-7844
Complete Services Inc — Mason (G-13688)	E	513 770-5575
Coon Caulking & Sealants Inc — Louisville (G-13098)	D	330 875-2100
Corporate Environments of Ohio — Columbus (G-7442)	E	614 358-3375
Countertop Alternatives Inc — Dayton (G-9430)	E	937 254-3334
Curtiss-Wright Flow Control — Batavia (G-1008)	D	513 735-2538
Curtiss-Wright Flow Control — Cincinnati (G-2909)	D	513 528-7900
Daniel A Terreri & Sons Inc — Youngstown (G-20165)	E	330 538-2950
Daniels Basement Waterproofing — Berlin Heights (G-1481)	E	440 965-4332
Danite Holdings Ltd — Columbus (G-7488)	E	614 444-3333
Decoating Inc — Shelby (G-16899)	E	419 347-9191
Deerfield Farms — Deerfield (G-10018)	E	330 584-4715
Design Rstrtion Reconstruction — North Canton (G-15332)	E	330 563-0010
Disaster Reconstruction Inc — Eastlake (G-10545)	E	440 918-1523
Early Construction Co — South Point (G-17085)	E	740 894-5150
Empaco Equipment Corporation — Richfield (G-16505)	E	330 659-9393
Erie Construction Mid-West Inc — Dayton (G-9530)	E	937 898-4688
Euclid Indus Maint Clg Contrs — Cleveland (G-5553)	C	216 361-0288
Extreme Detail Clg Cnstr Svcs — Toledo (G-17874)	E	419 392-3243
Feecorp Corporation — Canal Winchester (G-2158)	E	614 837-3010
Flamos Enterprises Inc — Canton (G-2369)	E	330 478-0009
▲ Flow-Liner Systems Ltd — Zanesville (G-20478)	E	800 348-0020
Gem City Waterproofing — Dayton (G-9569)	E	937 220-6800
▲ Goettle Holding Company Inc — Cincinnati (G-3683)	C	513 825-8100
Ground Penetrating Radar Sys — Toledo (G-17926)	E	419 843-9804
Gus Holthaus Signs Inc — Cincinnati (G-3720)	E	513 861-0060
Harold J Becker Company Inc — Beavercreek (G-1245)	E	614 279-1414
▲ High-Tech Pools Inc — North Olmsted (G-15425)	E	440 979-5070
Hughes Kitchens and Bath LLC — Canton (G-2407)	E	330 455-5269
Hummel Industries Incorporated — Cincinnati (G-3798)	E	513 242-1321
Identitek Systems Inc — Massillon (G-13826)	D	330 832-9844
Image Pavement Maintenance — Brookville (G-1963)	E	937 833-9200
Industrial Fiberglass Spc Inc — Dayton (G-9630)	E	937 222-9000
Industrial Waste Control Inc — Youngstown (G-20233)	D	330 270-9900
Ionno Properties s Corp — Dennison (G-10165)	E	330 479-9267
J & D Home Improvement Inc — Reynoldsburg (G-16459)	D	740 927-0722
J R Mead Industrial Contrs — Galena (G-11284)	E	614 891-4466
Jaco Waterproofing LLC — Fairfield (G-10865)	E	513 738-0084
Janson Industries — Canton (G-2417)	D	330 455-7029
Jtc Contracting Inc — Cleveland (G-5875)	E	216 635-0745
Kapton Caulking & Building — Cleveland (G-5883)	E	440 526-0670
Keen & Cross Envmtl Svcs Inc — Cincinnati (G-3905)	E	513 674-1700
Kens Beverage Inc — Fairfield (G-10869)	E	513 874-8200
Korman Construction Corp — Columbus (G-8011)	E	614 274-2170
Kramig Co — Cincinnati (G-3943)	E	513 761-4010
L B Foster Company — Mineral Ridge (G-14637)	E	330 652-1461
Lawn Management Sprinkler Co — Cincinnati (G-3964)	E	513 272-3808
▲ Lefeld Welding & Stl Sups Inc — Coldwater (G-6832)	E	419 678-2397
Lepi Enterprises Inc — Zanesville (G-20495)	D	740 453-2980
Lighting Maint Harmon Sign — Toledo (G-18006)	D	419 841-6658
Lincoln Moving & Storage Co — Cleveland (G-5943)	D	216 741-5500
▲ Lorad LLC — Westlake (G-19511)	E	216 265-2862
M K Moore & Sons Inc — Dayton (G-9693)	E	937 236-1812
M T Golf Course Managment Inc — Cincinnati (G-4006)	E	513 923-1188
Marsam Metalfab Inc — Twinsburg (G-18444)	E	330 405-1520
Maxwell Lightning Protection — Dayton (G-9703)	E	937 228-7250
Mc Fadden Construction Inc — Norwalk (G-15580)	E	419 668-4165
Metropolitan Pool Service Co — Parma (G-15910)	E	216 741-9451
Midwest Contracting Inc — Holland (G-12037)	E	419 866-4560
Midwest Industrial Supply Inc — Toledo (G-18061)	E	800 321-0699
Mike Morris — Brewster (G-1856)	E	330 767-4122
▲ Mills Fence Co Inc — Cincinnati (G-4100)	E	513 631-0333
▲ Modlich Stoneworks Inc — Columbus (G-8181)	E	614 276-2848
Modular Systems Technicians — Cleveland (G-6072)	E	216 459-2630
▲ Motz Group Inc — Cincinnati (G-4123)	E	513 533-6452
MPS Group Inc — Carlisle (G-2604)	D	937 746-2117
Mrap LLC — Columbus (G-8202)	E	614 545-3190
MRM Construction Inc — Gallipolis (G-11329)	E	740 388-0079
Multi Cntry SEC Slutions Group — Cleveland (G-6089)	E	216 973-0291
Mural & Son Inc — Cleveland (G-6090)	E	216 267-3322
Nelson Stud Welding Inc — Westlake (G-19520)	E	440 250-9242
North Bay Construction Inc — Westlake (G-19522)	E	440 835-1898
Northpointe Property MGT LLC — Columbus (G-8294)	C	614 579-9712
Northwest Firestop Inc — Toledo (G-18093)	E	419 517-4777
OCP Contractors Inc — Holland (G-12043)	E	419 865-7168
Ohio Concrete Resurfacing Inc — Bedford (G-1221)	E	440 786-9100
▲ Ohio Pools & Spas Inc — Canton (G-2482)	E	330 494-7755
Ohio State Home Services Inc — Macedonia (G-13207)	C	330 467-1055
Ohio State Home Services Inc — Hilliard (G-11940)	E	614 850-5600
Omni Fireproofing Co LLC — West Chester (G-19126)	D	513 870-9115
P-N-D Communications Inc — Crestline (G-9149)	E	419 683-1922
Palazzo Brothers Electric Inc — Norwalk (G-15587)	E	419 668-1100
Paul Peterson Company — Columbus (G-8522)	E	614 486-4375
Paulo Products Company — Willoughby (G-19703)	E	440 942-0153
Pedersen Insulation Company — Columbus (G-8529)	E	614 471-3788
Perrysburg Rsdntial Seal Cting — Perrysburg (G-16043)	E	419 872-7325
Precision Environmental Co — Independence (G-12244)	B	216 642-6040
Prime Polymers Inc — Medina (G-14113)	E	330 662-4200
Priority 1 Construction Svcs — Cincinnati (G-4332)	E	513 922-0203
Priority III Contracting Inc — Cincinnati (G-4333)	E	513 922-0203
▲ Ptmj Enterprises — Solon (G-17042)	E	440 543-8000
Purple Marlin Inc — Elyria (G-10672)	E	440 323-1291
Quality Fabricated Metals Inc — Salem (G-16707)	E	330 332-7008
R E Kramig & Co Inc — Cincinnati (G-4378)	C	513 761-4010
Rak Corrosion Control Inc — Amherst (G-602)	E	440 985-2171
Ram Construction Services — Broadview Heights (G-1890)	E	440 740-0100
Ram Construction Services of — West Chester (G-19137)	D	513 297-1857
Ram Restoration LLC — Dayton (G-9841)	E	937 347-7418
Regency Roofing Companies Inc — Macedonia (G-13208)	E	330 468-1021
Resource International Inc — Columbus (G-8622)	C	614 823-4949
Riverfront Diversified Inc — West Chester (G-19142)	D	513 874-7200
Rudzik Excavating Inc — Struthers (G-17534)	E	330 755-1540
Rusk Industries Inc — Toledo (G-18168)	D	419 841-6055
Safety Grooving & Grinding LP — Napoleon (G-14950)	E	419 592-8666
Sayles Company LLC — Columbus (G-8689)	E	614 801-0432
Security Fence Group Inc — Cincinnati (G-4489)	E	513 681-3700
Signature Control Systems LLC — Columbus (G-8731)	E	614 864-2222
Six C Fabrication Inc — Ravenna (G-16412)	D	330 296-5594
Southway Fence Company — Canton (G-2533)	E	330 477-5251
Stachler Concrete Inc — Saint Henry (G-16667)	E	419 678-3867
Stanley Stemer of Akron Canton — Coventry Township (G-9133)	E	330 785-5005
Style-Line Incorporated — Columbus (G-8798)	E	614 291-0600
Suburban Maint & Cnstr Inc — North Royalton (G-15503)	E	440 237-7765
◆ Sws Equipment Services Inc — Akron (G-470)	E	330 806-2767
Systems Jay LLC Nanogate — Mansfield (G-13369)	A	419 524-3778
Terrafirm Construction LLC — Columbus (G-8832)	E	913 433-2998

41 LOCAL AND SUBURBAN TRANSIT AND INTERURBAN HIGHWAY PASSENGER TRANSPORTATION

Thermal Solutions Inc ....D...... 740 886-2861
 Proctorville (G-16362)
Thiels Replacement Systems Inc ....D...... 419 289-6139
 Ashland (G-701)
TNT Mobile Powerwash Inc ....E...... 614 402-7474
 Canal Winchester (G-2172)
Toledo Area Insulator Wkrs Jac .....D...... 419 531-5911
 Toledo (G-18226)
Trak-1 Technology Inc ....E...... 513 204-5530
 Mason (G-13772)
Trinity Contracting Inc ....D...... 614 905-4410
 Columbus (G-8871)
U S A Waterproofing Inc ....E...... 330 425-2440
 Twinsburg (G-18481)
Unified Cnstr Systems Ltd ....E...... 330 773-2511
 Akron (G-483)
United-Maier Signs Inc ....D...... 513 681-6600
 Cincinnati (G-4743)
▲ Universal Fabg Cnstr Svcs Inc ......D...... 614 274-1128
 Columbus (G-8905)
Vwc Liquidation Company LLC ......C...... 330 372-6776
 Warren (G-18922)
Wegman Construction Company .....E...... 513 381-1111
 Cincinnati (G-4828)
X F Construction Svcs Inc ....E...... 614 575-2700
 Columbus (G-9012)

40 RAILROAD TRANSPORTATION

4011 Railroads, Line-Hauling Operations

Ann Arbor Railroad Inc ....E...... 419 726-4181
 Toledo (G-17752)
Ashland Railway Inc ....E...... 419 525-2822
 Mansfield (G-13262)
Cleveland Harbor Belt RR LLC ....E...... 440 746-0801
 Solon (G-16993)
Cleveland Works Railway Co ....D...... 216 429-7267
 Cleveland (G-5355)
Cliffs Resources Inc ....C...... 216 694-5700
 Cleveland (G-5362)
Columbus & Ohio River RR Co ......D...... 740 622-8092
 Coshocton (G-9092)
CSX Corporation ....C...... 419 225-4121
 Lima (G-12769)
CSX Corporation ....C...... 419 933-5027
 Willard (G-19618)
CSX Transportation Inc ....E...... 440 992-0871
 Ashtabula (G-740)
CSX Transportation Inc ....E...... 513 369-5514
 Cincinnati (G-3444)
CSX Transportation Inc ....E...... 614 898-3651
 Westerville (G-19295)
CSX Transportation Inc ....E...... 937 642-2221
 Marysville (G-13615)
CSX Transportation Inc ....E...... 419 257-1225
 North Baltimore (G-15312)
CSX Transportation Inc ....E...... 513 422-2031
 Middletown (G-14423)
CSX Transportation Inc ....D...... 419 697-2323
 Oregon (G-15729)
Illinois & Midland RR Inc ....D...... 217 670-1242
 Columbus (G-7884)
Illinois Central Railroad Co ....E...... 419 726-6028
 Toledo (G-17970)
Indiana & Ohio Central RR ....C...... 740 385-3127
 Logan (G-12978)
Indiana & Ohio Rail Corp ....E...... 513 860-1000
 Cincinnati (G-3813)
Indiana & Ohio Rail Corp ....E...... 419 229-1010
 Lima (G-12804)
Indiana & Ohio Railway Company ..D...... 513 860-1000
 Cincinnati (G-3814)
Nimishillen & Tuscarawas LLC ......E...... 330 438-5821
 Canton (G-2473)
Norfolk Southern Corporation ....D...... 419 436-2408
 Fostoria (G-11136)
Norfolk Southern Corporation ....D...... 614 251-2684
 Columbus (G-8284)
Norfolk Southern Corporation ....E...... 419 381-5505
 Toledo (G-18090)
Norfolk Southern Corporation ....E...... 419 254-1562
 Toledo (G-18091)
Norfolk Southern Corporation ....E...... 440 992-2274
 Ashtabula (G-757)
Norfolk Southern Corporation ....D...... 440 992-2215
 Ashtabula (G-758)
Norfolk Southern Corporation ....E...... 513 271-0972
 Cincinnati (G-4173)
Norfolk Southern Corporation ....E...... 216 362-6087
 Cleveland (G-6134)
Norfolk Southern Corporation ....E...... 419 529-4574
 Ontario (G-15706)
Norfolk Southern Corporation ....C...... 419 483-1423
 Bellevue (G-1414)
Norfolk Southern Corporation ....E...... 419 485-3510
 Montpelier (G-14747)
Norfolk Southern Corporation ....E...... 216 362-6087
 Cleveland (G-6135)
Norfolk Southern Corporation ....E...... 419 626-4323
 Sandusky (G-16781)
Norfolk Southern Corporation ....D...... 740 353-4529
 Portsmouth (G-16296)
Norfolk Southern Corporation ....E...... 937 297-5420
 Moraine (G-14813)
Norfolk Southern Corporation ....D...... 513 977-3246
 Cincinnati (G-4174)
Norfolk Southern Railway Co ....D...... 440 439-1827
 Bedford (G-1323)
Republic N&T Railroad Inc ....C...... 330 438-5826
 Canton (G-2508)
Trans-Continental Systems Inc ......E...... 513 769-4774
 Canton (G-4678)
Wheeling & Lake Erie Rlwy Co ......B...... 330 767-3401
 Brewster (G-1857)

4013 Switching & Terminal Svcs

Ashland Railway Inc ....E...... 419 525-2822
 Mansfield (G-13262)
National Railroad Pass Corp ....E...... 419 246-0159
 Toledo (G-18078)
Norfolk Southern Corporation ....D...... 740 535-4102
 Mingo Junction (G-14656)
Rail Logistics Inc ....D...... 440 933-6500
 Avon Lake (G-938)

41 LOCAL AND SUBURBAN TRANSIT AND INTERURBAN HIGHWAY PASSENGER TRANSPORTATION

4111 Local & Suburban Transit

Allen Cnty Regional Trnst Auth ......E...... 419 222-2782
 Lima (G-12733)
Anthony Wayne Local Schools ......D...... 419 877-0451
 Whitehouse (G-19583)
Central Ohio Transit Authority ....C...... 614 275-5800
 Columbus (G-7241)
Central Ohio Transit Authority ....A...... 614 275-5800
 Columbus (G-7242)
Charter Vans Inc ....E...... 937 898-4043
 Vandalia (G-18669)
City of North Olmsted ....E...... 440 777-8000
 North Olmsted (G-15415)
City of Wilmington ....E...... 937 382-7961
 Wilmington (G-19748)
City Taxicab & Transfer Co ....E...... 440 992-2156
 Ashtabula (G-734)
Columbus Public School Dst ....C...... 614 365-6542
 Columbus (G-7380)
First Group Investment Partnr ....D...... 513 241-2200
 Cincinnati (G-3618)
First Transit Inc ....D...... 937 652-4175
 Urbana (G-18587)
Firstgroup America Inc ....D...... 513 241-2200
 Cincinnati (G-3626)
Firstgroup America Inc ....C...... 513 241-2200
 Cincinnati (G-3628)
Firstgroup Usa Inc ....B...... 513 241-2200
 Cincinnati (G-3629)
Greater Cleveland ....A...... 216 566-5107
 Cleveland (G-5094)
Greater Cleveland Regional ....D...... 216 575-3932
 Cleveland (G-5699)
Greater Dyton Rgnal Trnst Auth ....D...... 937 425-8310
 Dayton (G-9590)
Hopkins Airport Limousine Svc .....C...... 216 267-8810
 Cleveland (G-5771)
Intercoastal Trnsp Systems ....D...... 513 829-1287
 Fairfield (G-10862)
Ironton and Lawrence County ....B...... 740 532-3534
 Ironton (G-12291)
Ironton and Lawrence County ....E...... 740 532-7855
 Ironton (G-12292)
Laketran ....E...... 440 350-1000
 Painesville (G-15862)
Led Transportation ....E...... 330 484-2772
 Canton (G-2431)
Lifecare Ambulance Inc ....E...... 440 323-6111
 Elyria (G-10642)
Metro Regional Transit Auth ....B...... 330 762-0341
 Akron (G-341)
Mv Transportation Inc ....D...... 419 627-0740
 Sandusky (G-16780)
Mv Transportation Inc ....D...... 740 681-5086
 Cincinnati (G-4134)
Norfolk Southern Corporation ....E...... 740 574-8491
 Wheelersburg (G-19579)
Park-N-Go Inc ....E...... 937 890-7275
 Vandalia (G-18692)
Pickaway County Community Acti .D...... 740 477-1655
 Circleville (G-4894)
Southeast Area Transit ....E...... 740 454-8574
 Zanesville (G-20534)
Southwest OH Trans Auth ....A...... 513 621-4455
 Cincinnati (G-4553)
Southwest OH Trans Auth ....A...... 513 632-7511
 Cincinnati (G-4554)
Stark Area Regional Trnst Auth .....C...... 330 477-2782
 Canton (G-2539)
Sutton Motor Coach Tours Inc ....E...... 330 726-2800
 Youngstown (G-20386)
Toledo Area Rgional Trnst Auth .....D...... 419 243-7433
 Toledo (G-18227)
United Scoto Senior Activities ....E...... 740 354-6672
 Portsmouth (G-16316)
Universal Transportation Syste ......C...... 513 829-1287
 Fairfield (G-10920)
Universal Transportation Syste ......E...... 513 539-9491
 Monroe (G-14716)
Universal Work and Power LLC ....E...... 513 981-1111
 Blue Ash (G-1714)
Western Reserve Transit Auth ....D...... 330 744-8431
 Youngstown (G-20412)

4119 Local Passenger Transportation: NEC

1st Advanced Ems LLC ....D...... 614 348-9991
 Gahanna (G-11232)
A1 Mr Limo Inc ....E...... 440 943-5466
 Wickliffe (G-19592)
Above & Beyond Caregivers LLC ..E...... 614 478-1700
 Columbus (G-6928)
Aladdins Enterprises Inc ....E...... 614 891-3440
 Westerville (G-19361)
American Livery Service Inc ....E...... 216 221-9330
 Cleveland (G-5011)
American Med ....C...... 216 251-5319
 Cleveland (G-5013)
American Med ....B...... 330 762-8999
 Akron (G-71)
Americas Urgent Care ....E...... 614 929-2721
 Upper Arlington (G-18546)
Anna Rescue Squad ....E...... 937 394-7377
 Anna (G-617)
Asv Services LLC ....E...... 216 797-1701
 Euclid (G-10743)
Athens County Emrgncy Med Svcs .D...... 740 797-9560
 The Plains (G-17664)
Bellevue Four Cnty Ems N Centl ...C...... 419 483-3322
 Milan (G-14492)
Bkp Ambulance District ....E...... 419 674-4574
 Kenton (G-12408)
Brookside Ambulance Services .....E...... 419 476-7442
 Toledo (G-17784)
Buckeye Ambulance LLC ....D...... 937 435-1584
 Kettering (G-12428)
C C & S Ambulance Service Inc ....E...... 330 868-4114
 Minerva (G-14642)
Capital Transportation Inc ....C...... 614 258-0400
 Columbus (G-7184)
Carlson Amblnce Trnspt Svc Inc ...E...... 330 225-2400
 Brunswick (G-1971)
Catholic Charities of SW Ohio ....D...... 513 241-7745
 Cincinnati (G-3194)
City of Cleveland ....B...... 216 664-2555
 Cleveland (G-5249)
City of Cleveland ....B...... 216 664-2555
 Cleveland (G-5250)
City of Lakewood ....E...... 216 521-1288
 Cleveland (G-5269)
City of Westlake ....E...... 440 871-3441
 Cleveland (G-5278)
Clark County Board of Developm ..D...... 937 328-5240
 Springfield (G-17162)
Clemente-Mc Kay Ambulance Inc .E...... 330 755-1401
 Struthers (G-17528)
Cleveland Auto Livery Inc ....E...... 216 421-1101
 Cleveland (G-5291)

41 LOCAL AND SUBURBAN TRANSIT AND INTERURBAN HIGHWAY PASSENGER TRANSPORTATION

Cloverleaf Transport Co .... E 419 599-5015
  Napoleon *(G-14935)*
Community Ambulance Service .... D 740 454-6800
  Zanesville *(G-20467)*
Community Care Amblance Netwrk ... D 440 992-1401
  Ashtabula *(G-735)*
Contract Transport Services .... E 216 524-8435
  Cleveland *(G-5403)*
Coshocton Cnty Emrgncy Med Svc .... E 740 622-4294
  Coshocton *(G-9094)*
County of Hardin .... E 419 634-7729
  Ada *(G-5)*
County of Lorain .... E 440 647-5803
  Wellington *(G-18989)*
County of Meigs .... E 740 992-6617
  Pomeroy *(G-16231)*
County of Ottawa .... E 419 898-7433
  Oak Harbor *(G-15606)*
County of Seneca .... E 419 937-2340
  Bascom *(G-993)*
Courtesy Ambulance Inc .... E 740 522-8588
  Newark *(G-15163)*
Cremation Service Inc .... E 216 861-2334
  Cleveland *(G-5435)*
Critical Care Transport Inc .... D 614 775-0564
  Columbus *(G-7463)*
Critical Life Inc .... E 419 525-0502
  Mansfield *(G-13285)*
Cusa LI Inc .... C 216 267-8810
  Brookpark *(G-1942)*
Direct Expediting LLC .... E 513 459-0100
  Mason *(G-13696)*
Donty Horton HM Care Dhhc LLC ..... E 513 463-3442
  Cincinnati *(G-3499)*
Eastern Horizon Inc .... E 614 253-7000
  Columbus *(G-7564)*
Eaton Rescue Squad .... E 937 456-5361
  Eaton *(G-10560)*
Elite Ambulance Service LLC .... E 888 222-1356
  Loveland *(G-13124)*
Emergency Medical Transport .... D 330 484-4000
  North Canton *(G-15334)*
Eric Boeppler Fmly Ltd Partnr .... D 513 336-8108
  Fairfield *(G-10848)*
Fab Limousines Inc .... E 330 792-6700
  Youngstown *(G-20184)*
Firelands Ambulance Service .... E 419 929-1487
  New London *(G-15067)*
First Class Limos Inc .... E 440 248-1114
  Cleveland *(G-5594)*
Firstgroup America Inc .... D 513 241-2200
  Cincinnati *(G-3626)*
Firstgroup America Inc .... D 513 241-2200
  Cincinnati *(G-3628)*
Franklin Township Fire and Ems ...... E 513 876-2996
  Felicity *(G-10985)*
Georgetown Life Squad .... E 937 378-3082
  Georgetown *(G-11394)*
Gold Cross Ambulance Svcs Inc .... C 330 744-4161
  Youngstown *(G-20202)*
Gold Cross Limousine Service .... E 330 757-3053
  Struthers *(G-17531)*
Greater Cleveland Regional .... C 216 781-1110
  Cleveland *(G-5700)*
Greenville Township Rescue .... E 937 548-9339
  Greenville *(G-11507)*
Guernsey Health Enterprises .... A 740 439-3561
  Cambridge *(G-2118)*
Guernsey Health Systems Inc .... A 740 439-3561
  Cambridge *(G-2119)*
Hanco Ambulance Inc .... E 419 423-2912
  Findlay *(G-11040)*
Harter Ventures Inc .... D 419 224-4075
  Lima *(G-12790)*
Henderson Road Rest Systems .... E 614 442-3310
  Columbus *(G-7825)*
Hillcrest Ambulance Svc Inc .... C 216 797-4000
  Euclid *(G-10760)*
Hopkin Arprt Lmsine Shttle Svc .... E 216 267-8282
  Brookpark *(G-1946)*
Hustead Emergency Medical Svc ..... E 937 324-3031
  Springfield *(G-17209)*
Intercoastal Trnsp Systems .... D 513 829-1287
  Fairfield *(G-10862)*
J & C Ambulance Services Inc .... C 330 899-0022
  North Canton *(G-15346)*
Jls Enterprises Inc .... E 513 769-1888
  West Chester *(G-19097)*
Kare Medical Trnspt Svcs LLP .... E 937 578-0263
  Marysville *(G-13630)*

Lacp St Ritas Medical Ctr LLC .... D 419 324-4075
  Lima *(G-12814)*
Lakefront Lines Inc .... C 216 267-8810
  Brookpark *(G-1949)*
Lakefront Lines Inc .... E 419 537-0677
  Toledo *(G-18000)*
Lakefront Lines Inc .... E 614 476-1113
  Columbus *(G-8031)*
Lakefront Lines Inc .... D 513 829-8290
  Fairfield *(G-10872)*
Lane Life Corp .... E 330 799-1002
  Youngstown *(G-20253)*
Liberty Ems Services LLC .... E 216 630-6626
  Cleveland *(G-5938)*
Lifecare Ambulance Inc .... D 440 323-2527
  Elyria *(G-10641)*
Lifecare Ambulance Inc .... E 440 323-6111
  Elyria *(G-10642)*
Lifecare Medical Services .... E 614 258-2545
  Columbus *(G-8064)*
Lifestar Ambulance Inc .... E 419 245-6210
  Toledo *(G-18005)*
Lifeteam Ems Inc .... E 330 386-9284
  East Liverpool *(G-10523)*
Lorain Life Care Ambulance Svc ...... D 440 244-6467
  Lorain *(G-13055)*
Mahoning County .... D 330 797-2837
  Youngstown *(G-20262)*
Mansfield Ambulance Inc .... E 419 525-3311
  Mansfield *(G-13329)*
Martens Donald & Sons .... D 216 265-4211
  Cleveland *(G-5988)*
Med Ride Ems .... D 614 747-9744
  Columbus *(G-8142)*
Med Star Emgncy Mdcl Srv .... E 330 394-6611
  Warren *(G-18879)*
Med-Trans Inc .... E 937 325-4926
  Springfield *(G-17231)*
Med-Trans Inc .... E 937 293-9771
  Moraine *(G-14802)*
Medcorp Inc .... C 419 425-9700
  Findlay *(G-11065)*
Medcorp Inc .... D 419 727-7000
  Toledo *(G-18047)*
Medic Response Service Inc .... E 419 522-1998
  Mansfield *(G-13342)*
Medical Transport Systems Inc .... D 330 837-9818
  North Canton *(G-15352)*
Medpro LLC .... D 937 336-5586
  Eaton *(G-10567)*
Mercy Health .... E 440 775-1211
  Oberlin *(G-15651)*
Metrohealth System .... E 216 778-3867
  Cleveland *(G-6042)*
Metrohealth System .... E 216 957-4000
  Cleveland *(G-6039)*
Mid County Ems .... E 419 898-9366
  Oak Harbor *(G-15612)*
Morgan County Public Transit .... E 740 962-1322
  McConnelsville *(G-14029)*
Morrow Cnty Fire Fighter .... D 419 946-7976
  Mount Gilead *(G-14856)*
Mt Orab Fire Department Inc .... E 937 444-3945
  Mount Orab *(G-14870)*
Muskingum County Ohio .... D 740 452-0678
  Zanesville *(G-20506)*
Mycity Transporatation Co .... E 216 591-1900
  Shaker Heights *(G-16864)*
National Express Transit Corp .... D 513 322-6214
  Cincinnati *(G-4137)*
Non Emergency Ambulance Svc .... E 330 296-4541
  Ravenna *(G-16394)*
North Star Critical Care LLC .... D 330 386-9110
  East Liverpool *(G-10528)*
Northwest Fire Ambulance .... E 937 437-8354
  New Paris *(G-15079)*
Northwest Limousine Inc .... E 440 322-5804
  Elyria *(G-10665)*
Norwalk Area Health Services .... E 419 499-2515
  Milan *(G-14495)*
Norwalk Area Health Services .... C 419 668-8101
  Norwalk *(G-15583)*
Ohio Medical Trnsp Inc .... E 614 791-4400
  Columbus *(G-8360)*
Patriot Emergency Med Svcs Inc ..... E 740 532-2222
  Ironton *(G-12301)*
Physicians Ambulance Svc Inc .... E 216 332-1667
  Cleveland *(G-6279)*
Pickaway County Community Acti ... D 740 477-1655
  Circleville *(G-4894)*

Pickaway Plains Ambulance Svc ...... C 740 474-4180
  Circleville *(G-4900)*
Portage Path Behavorial Health .... D 330 762-6110
  Akron *(G-398)*
Portsmouth Ambulance .... C 740 289-2932
  Portsmouth *(G-16298)*
Portsmuth Emrgncy Amblance Svc ... B 740 354-3122
  Portsmouth *(G-16302)*
Precious Cargo Transportation .... E 440 564-8039
  Newbury *(G-15260)*
Professional Transportation .... C 419 661-0576
  Walbridge *(G-18776)*
Pymatuning Ambulance Service ...... E 440 293-7991
  Andover *(G-613)*
Quad Ambulance District .... D 330 866-9847
  Waynesburg *(G-18981)*
Rittman City of Inc .... E 330 925-2065
  Rittman *(G-16555)*
Rural/Metro Corporation .... C 216 749-2211
  Youngstown *(G-20362)*
Rural/Metro Corporation .... C 330 744-4161
  Youngstown *(G-20363)*
Rural/Metro Corporation .... C 440 543-3313
  Chagrin Falls *(G-2732)*
Sardinia Life Squad .... E 937 446-2178
  Sardinia *(G-16814)*
Seneca-Crawford Area Trnsp .... E 419 937-2428
  Tiffin *(G-17702)*
Senior Outreach Services .... E 216 421-6900
  Cleveland *(G-6470)*
Shima Limousine Services Inc .... E 440 918-6400
  Mentor *(G-14242)*
Smith Ambulance Service Inc .... E 330 825-0205
  Dover *(G-10212)*
Smith Ambulance Service Inc .... E 330 602-0050
  Dover *(G-10213)*
Spirit Medical Transport LLC .... D 937 548-2800
  Greenville *(G-11520)*
Sterling Joint Ambulance Dst .... E 740 869-3006
  Mount Sterling *(G-14875)*
Stofcheck Ambulance Inc .... C 740 383-2787
  Marion *(G-13581)*
Stofcheck Ambulance Svc Inc .... E 740 499-2200
  La Rue *(G-12459)*
Toronto Emergency Medical Svc ...... E 740 537-3891
  Toronto *(G-18339)*
Tri Village Rescue Service .... E 937 996-3155
  New Madison *(G-15073)*
Tri-State Amblnce Pramedic Svc ..... C 304 233-2331
  North Canton *(G-15375)*
Tricounty Ambulance Service .... D 440 951-4600
  Mentor *(G-14249)*
United Amblnce Svc of Cmbridge .... E 740 439-7787
  Cambridge *(G-2132)*
United Ambulance Service .... E 740 732-5653
  Caldwell *(G-2091)*
United Scoto Senior Activities .... E 740 354-6672
  Portsmouth *(G-16316)*
Universal Work and Power LLC .... E 513 981-1111
  Blue Ash *(G-1714)*
Village of Antwerp .... E 419 258-6631
  Antwerp *(G-622)*
Youngstown Area Jwish Fdration .... D 330 746-1076
  Youngstown *(G-20426)*

4121 Taxi Cabs

Americab Inc .... E 216 429-1134
  Cleveland *(G-5002)*
City Taxicab & Transfer Co .... E 440 992-2156
  Ashtabula *(G-734)*
City Yellow Cab Company .... E 330 253-3141
  Akron *(G-144)*
Columbus Green Cabs Inc .... E 614 444-4444
  Columbus *(G-7355)*
Independent Radio Taxi Inc .... E 330 746-8844
  Youngstown *(G-20231)*
Knox Area Transit .... E 740 392-7433
  Mount Vernon *(G-14902)*
Pickaway County Community Acti ... D 740 477-1655
  Circleville *(G-4894)*
Shamrock Taxi Ltd .... E 614 263-8294
  Columbus *(G-8723)*
United Garage & Service Corp .... D 216 623-1550
  Cleveland *(G-6639)*
Westlake Cab Service .... D 440 331-5000
  Cleveland *(G-6746)*
Yellow Cab Co of Cleveland .... D 216 623-1500
  Cleveland *(G-6769)*

42 MOTOR FREIGHT TRANSPORTATION AND WAREHOUSING

4131 Intercity & Rural Bus Transportation

Company	Code	Phone
Atlantic Greyhound Lines	E	513 721-4450
Cincinnati (G-3059)		
First Transit Inc	D	513 732-1206
Batavia (G-1013)		
Firstgroup America Inc	D	513 241-2200
Cincinnati (G-3626)		
Greater Dayton Rta	A	937 425-8400
Dayton (G-9588)		
Greyhound Lines Inc	E	513 421-7442
Cincinnati (G-3713)		
Greyhound Lines Inc	E	614 221-0577
Columbus (G-7779)		
Laidlaw Transit Services Inc	D	513 241-2200
Cincinnati (G-3959)		
Muskingum Coach Company	E	740 622-2545
Coshocton (G-9112)		
Precious Cargo Transportation	E	440 564-8039
Newbury (G-15260)		
Stark Area Regional Trnst Auth	C	330 477-2782
Canton (G-2539)		

4141 Local Bus Charter Svc

Company	Code	Phone
A T V Inc	C	614 252-5060
Columbus (G-6920)		
Charter Vans Inc	E	937 898-4043
Vandalia (G-18669)		
Croswell of Williamsburg LLC	E	513 724-2206
Williamsburg (G-19631)		
Cusa LI Inc	C	216 267-8810
Brookpark (G-1942)		
Cuyahoga Marketing Service	E	440 526-5350
Cleveland (G-5457)		
Firstgroup America Inc	D	513 241-2200
Cincinnati (G-3626)		
Lakefront Lines Inc	D	513 829-8290
Fairfield (G-10872)		
Lakefront Lines Inc	C	216 267-8810
Brookpark (G-1949)		
Marfre Inc	C	513 321-3477
Cincinnati (G-4021)		
Precious Cargo Transportation	E	440 564-8039
Newbury (G-15260)		
Queen City Transportation LLC	B	513 941-8700
Cincinnati (G-4372)		
S B S Transit Inc	B	440 288-2222
Lorain (G-13075)		
Transit Service Company	E	330 782-3343
Youngstown (G-20390)		

4142 Bus Charter Service, Except Local

Company	Code	Phone
Buckeye Charter Service Inc	E	419 222-2455
Lima (G-12750)		
Buckeye Charter Service Inc	E	937 879-3000
Dayton (G-9368)		
Croswell of Williamsburg LLC	E	513 724-2206
Williamsburg (G-19631)		
Cusa LI Inc	C	216 267-8810
Brookpark (G-1942)		
Cuyahoga Marketing Service	E	440 526-5350
Cleveland (G-5457)		
Garfield Hts Coach Line Inc	D	440 232-4550
Chagrin Falls (G-2697)		
Greyhound Lines Inc	E	614 221-0577
Columbus (G-7779)		
Hat White Management LLC	E	800 525-7967
Akron (G-257)		
Lakefront Lines Inc	C	216 267-8810
Brookpark (G-1949)		
Lakefront Lines Inc	E	419 537-0677
Toledo (G-18000)		
Lakefront Lines Inc	E	614 476-1113
Columbus (G-8031)		
Pioneer Trails Inc	E	330 674-1234
Millersburg (G-14616)		
Put In Bay Transportation	E	419 285-4855
Put In Bay (G-16370)		
Queen City Transportation LLC	B	513 941-8700
Cincinnati (G-4372)		
S B S Transit Inc	B	440 288-2222
Lorain (G-13075)		
Starforce National Corporation	C	513 979-3600
Cincinnati (G-4586)		
Sutton Motor Coach Tours Inc	E	330 726-2800
Youngstown (G-20386)		
Tesco-Transportion Eqp Sls	E	419 836-2835
Oregon (G-15751)		

4151 School Buses

Company	Code	Phone
Akron School Trnsp Svcs	D	330 761-1390
Akron (G-55)		
Anthony Wayne Local Schools	D	419 877-0451
Whitehouse (G-19583)		
Beachwood City Schools	E	216 464-6609
Cleveland (G-5106)		
Benton-Carroll-Salem	E	419 898-6214
Oak Harbor (G-15605)		
Berea B O E Trnsp Dept	E	216 898-8300
Berea (G-1447)		
Boardman School Bus Garage	D	330 726-3425
Youngstown (G-20121)		
Canton City School District	D	330 456-6710
Canton (G-2285)		
Chillicothe City School Dst	E	740 775-2936
Chillicothe (G-2818)		
Clark Shawnee Schl Trnsprtn	E	937 328-5382
Springfield (G-17165)		
Cleveland Municipal School Dst	B	216 634-7005
Cleveland (G-5332)		
Cleveland Municipal School Dst	B	216 432-4600
Cleveland (G-5333)		
Dublin City Schools	C	614 764-5926
Dublin (G-10326)		
First Group Investment Partnr	D	513 241-2200
Cincinnati (G-3618)		
First Student Inc	D	513 531-6888
Cincinnati (G-3620)		
First Student Inc	E	937 645-0201
Marysville (G-13617)		
First Student Inc	D	513 761-6100
Cincinnati (G-3621)		
First Student Inc	B	513 761-5136
Cincinnati (G-3622)		
First Student Inc	E	419 382-9915
Toledo (G-17894)		
First Student Inc	E	513 241-2200
Cincinnati (G-3623)		
Firstgroup America Inc	D	513 241-2200
Cincinnati (G-3626)		
Firstgroup America Inc	B	513 419-8611
Cincinnati (G-3627)		
Firstgroup America Inc	D	513 241-2200
Cincinnati (G-3628)		
Firstgroup Usa Inc	D	513 241-2200
Cincinnati (G-3629)		
Gahanna-Jefferson Pub Schl Dst	D	614 751-7581
Columbus (G-7724)		
Geneva Area City School Dst	E	440 466-2684
Geneva (G-11362)		
Lakota Local School District	C	513 777-2150
Liberty Township (G-12722)		
Lima City School District	E	419 996-3450
Lima (G-12817)		
Mahoning County	D	330 797-2837
Youngstown (G-20262)		
Marfre Inc	C	513 321-3477
Cincinnati (G-4021)		
Massillon City School Bus Gar	E	330 830-1849
Massillon (G-13834)		
Mentor Exempted Vlg Schl Dst	C	440 974-5260
Mentor (G-14212)		
Miamisburg City School Dst	D	937 866-1283
Miamisburg (G-14321)		
Middletown School Vhcl Svc Ctr	E	513 420-4568
Middletown (G-14437)		
New Albany Plain Loc SC Transp	E	614 855-2033
New Albany (G-15000)		
North Canton City School Dst	D	330 497-5615
Canton (G-2475)		
Northmont Service Center	D	937 832-5050
Englewood (G-10713)		
Ontario Local School District	E	419 529-3814
Ontario (G-15708)		
Palmer Express Incorporated	E	440 942-3333
Willoughby (G-19702)		
Pauls Bus Service Inc	E	513 851-5089
Cincinnati (G-4265)		
Perry Transportation Dept	E	440 259-3005
Perry (G-15966)		
Perrysburg Board of Education	E	419 874-3127
Perrysburg (G-16041)		
Peterman	E	513 722-2229
Goshen (G-11438)		
Peterman	E	513 539-0324
Monroe (G-14709)		
Petermann Ltd	D	330 653-3323
Hudson (G-12140)		
Petermann Northeast LLC	A	513 351-7383
Cincinnati (G-4286)		
Queen City Transportation LLC	B	513 941-8700
Cincinnati (G-4372)		
S B S Transit Inc	B	440 288-2222
Lorain (G-13075)		
S C Wooster Bus Garage	E	330 264-4060
Wooster (G-19910)		
SC Madison Bus Garage	E	419 589-3373
Mansfield (G-13362)		
Streetsboro Board Education	E	330 626-4909
Streetsboro (G-17432)		
Suburban Transportation Co Inc	E	440 846-9291
Brunswick (G-1990)		
Vermilion Board of Education	E	440 204-1700
Vermilion (G-18718)		
Washington Local Schools	D	419 473-8356
Toledo (G-18299)		

4173 Bus Terminal & Svc Facilities

Company	Code	Phone
City of Willoughby	E	440 942-0215
Willoughby (G-19649)		
Hans Truck and Trlr Repr Inc	E	216 581-0046
Cleveland (G-5724)		
Lakota Local School District	C	513 777-2150
Liberty Township (G-12722)		
Meigs Local School District	E	740 742-2990
Middleport (G-14408)		
Ottawa County Transit Board	E	419 898-7433
Oak Harbor (G-15615)		
Reynoldsburg City Schools	E	614 501-1041
Reynoldsburg (G-16475)		
Washington Local Schools	D	419 473-8356
Toledo (G-18299)		

42 MOTOR FREIGHT TRANSPORTATION AND WAREHOUSING

4212 Local Trucking Without Storage

Company	Code	Phone
1st Carrier Corp	D	740 477-2587
Circleville (G-4875)		
44444 LLC	E	330 502-2023
Austintown (G-867)		
A L Smith Trucking Inc	E	937 526-3651
Versailles (G-18722)		
Accelerated Moving & Stor Inc	E	614 836-1007
Columbus (G-6932)		
Aci Const Co Inc	E	419 595-4284
Alvada (G-567)		
Advantage Tank Lines Inc	C	330 427-1010
Leetonia (G-12661)		
AG Trucking Inc	E	937 497-7770
Sidney (G-16911)		
Aim Integrated Logistics Inc	B	330 759-0438
Girard (G-11406)		
Aim Leasing Company	D	330 759-0438
Girard (G-11407)		
Alan Woods Trucking Inc	E	513 738-3314
Hamilton (G-11690)		
Allan Hunter Construction LLC	E	330 634-9882
Akron (G-67)		
American Bulk Commodities Inc	C	330 758-0841
Youngstown (G-20103)		
American Waste MGT Svcs Inc	E	330 856-8800
Warren (G-18816)		
Arrowhead Transport Co	E	330 638-2900
Cortland (G-9072)		
Atlantic Coastal Trucking	C	201 438-6500
Delaware (G-10072)		
Autumn Industries Inc	E	330 372-5002
Warren (G-18821)		
B & H Industries Inc	E	419 485-8373
Montpelier (G-14736)		
B & L Transport Inc	E	866 848-2888
Millersburg (G-14586)		
B D Transportation Inc	E	937 773-9280
Piqua (G-16135)		
Back In Black Co	E	419 425-5555
Findlay (G-10992)		
Bell Moving and Storage Inc	E	513 942-7500
Fairfield (G-10823)		
Berner Trucking	E	419 476-0207
Toledo (G-17770)		
Berner Trucking Inc	E	330 343-5812
Dover (G-10178)		
Besl Transfer Co	E	513 242-3456
Cincinnati (G-3100)		

Employee Codes: A=Over 500 employees, B=251-500
C=101-250, D=51-100, E=25-50

42 MOTOR FREIGHT TRANSPORTATION AND WAREHOUSING

BFI Waste Services LLC ....E 800 437-1123
  Salem *(G-16689)*
Big Blue Trucking Inc ....E 330 372-1421
  Warren *(G-18830)*
Blatt Trucking Co Inc ....E 419 898-0002
  Rocky Ridge *(G-16566)*
Blb Transport Inc ....E 740 474-1341
  Circleville *(G-4879)*
Blood Courier Inc ....E 216 251-3050
  Cleveland *(G-5123)*
Bob Miller Rigging Inc ....E 419 422-7477
  Findlay *(G-11005)*
Bobs Moraine Trucking Inc ....E 937 746-8420
  Franklin *(G-11150)*
Bowling Transportation Inc ....D 419 436-9590
  Fostoria *(G-11124)*
Brookside Holdings LLC ....E 419 224-7019
  Lima *(G-12749)*
Brookside Holdings LLC ....E 419 925-4457
  Maria Stein *(G-13427)*
Browning-Ferris Industries LLC .....D 330 393-0385
  Warren *(G-18832)*
Bryan Truck Line Inc ....D 419 485-8373
  Montpelier *(G-14739)*
Building Systems Trnsp Co ....C 740 852-9700
  London *(G-12994)*
Burch Hydro Inc ....E 740 694-9146
  Fredericktown *(G-11178)*
Burch Hydro Trucking Inc ....E 740 694-9146
  Fredericktown *(G-11179)*
Burkhart Trucking Inc ....E 740 896-2244
  Lowell *(G-13168)*
C & G Transportation Inc ....E 419 288-2653
  Wayne *(G-18977)*
C-Z Trucking Co ....D 330 758-2313
  Poland *(G-16221)*
Capitol Express Entps Inc ....D 614 279-2819
  Columbus *(G-7187)*
Carl E Oeder Sons Sand & Grav ...E 513 494-1555
  Lebanon *(G-12594)*
Carrier Industries Inc ....B 614 851-6363
  Columbus *(G-7203)*
Century Lines Inc ....E 216 271-0700
  Cleveland *(G-5219)*
Certified Oil Inc ....D 614 421-7500
  Columbus *(G-7244)*
Chambers Leasing Systems Corp ..E 419 726-9747
  Toledo *(G-17801)*
Chapin Logistics Inc ....E 440 327-1360
  North Ridgeville *(G-15459)*
Charles D McIntosh Trckg Inc ....E 937 378-3803
  Georgetown *(G-11389)*
Cheeseman LLC ....B 419 375-4132
  Fort Recovery *(G-11114)*
Circle S Transport Inc ....E 614 207-2184
  Columbus *(G-7276)*
City Dash Inc ....C 513 562-2000
  Cincinnati *(G-3357)*
City of Marion ....D 740 382-1479
  Marion *(G-13531)*
Clary Trucking Inc ....E 740 702-4242
  Chillicothe *(G-2827)*
Clayton Weaver Trucking Inc ....E 513 896-6932
  Fairfield *(G-10837)*
Clp Towne Inc ....E 440 234-3324
  Brookpark *(G-1940)*
Competitive Transportation ....E 419 529-5300
  Bellville *(G-1422)*
Containerport Group Inc ....E 216 692-3124
  Euclid *(G-10747)*
Containerport Group Inc ....E 440 333-1330
  Columbus *(G-7426)*
Continental Express Inc ....B 937 497-2100
  Sidney *(G-16922)*
Continental Office Furn Corp ....E 614 781-0080
  Columbus *(G-7429)*
Continental Transport Inc ....E 513 360-2960
  Monroe *(G-14692)*
Corrigan Moving Systems-Ann AR ..E 419 874-2900
  Perrysburg *(G-15989)*
Coshocton Trucking South Inc .....C 740 622-1311
  Coshocton *(G-9097)*
Cotter Moving & Storage Co ....E 330 535-5115
  Akron *(G-167)*
Cousins Waste Control LLC ....D 419 726-1500
  Toledo *(G-17839)*
Cowen Truck Line Inc ....D 419 938-3401
  Perrysville *(G-16078)*
Custom Movers Services Inc ....E 330 564-0507
  Stow *(G-17358)*

D & V Trucking Inc ....E 330 482-9440
  Columbiana *(G-6857)*
D&D Trucking and Services Inc .....E 419 692-3205
  Delphos *(G-10140)*
Dale Ross Trucking Inc ....E 937 981-2168
  Greenfield *(G-11484)*
Daves Sand & Stone Inc ....E 419 445-9256
  Wauseon *(G-18950)*
Davidson Trucking Inc ....E 419 288-2318
  Bradner *(G-1809)*
DD&b Inc ....E 614 577-0550
  Columbus *(G-7496)*
Dedicated Logistics Inc ....D 513 275-1135
  West Chester *(G-19060)*
Dedicated Transport LLC ....C 216 641-2500
  Brooklyn Heights *(G-1914)*
Dill-Elam Inc ....E 513 575-0017
  Loveland *(G-13123)*
Dingledine Trucking Company ......E 937 652-3454
  Urbana *(G-18585)*
Disttech LLC ....E 800 321-3143
  Cleveland *(G-5490)*
DOT Smith LLC ....E 740 245-5105
  Thurman *(G-17670)*
Drasc Enterprises Inc ....E 330 852-3254
  Sugarcreek *(G-17544)*
Dyno Nobel Transportation ....E 740 439-5050
  Cambridge *(G-2111)*
E & V Ventures Inc ....E 330 794-6683
  Akron *(G-203)*
Early Express Services Inc ....E 937 223-5801
  Dayton *(G-9511)*
Ed Wilson & Son Trucking Inc ......E 330 549-9287
  New Springfield *(G-15129)*
Edw C Levy Co ....E 419 822-8286
  Delta *(G-10157)*
Emory Rothenbuhler & Sons ....E 740 458-1432
  Beallsville *(G-1140)*
Falcon Transport Co ....D 330 793-1345
  Youngstown *(G-20186)*
Federal Express Corporation ....C 800 463-3339
  Bedford *(G-1306)*
Fedex Freight Inc ....D 330 645-0879
  Akron *(G-223)*
Fedex Freight Corporation ....E 800 354-9489
  Zanesville *(G-20477)*
Fedex Ground Package Sys Inc ....C 412 859-2653
  Steubenville *(G-17317)*
Fedex Ground Package Sys Inc ....B 800 463-3339
  Toledo *(G-17884)*
Fedex Ground Package Sys Inc ....E 513 942-4330
  West Chester *(G-19200)*
Fedex Ground Package Sys Inc ....B 800 463-3339
  Grove City *(G-11560)*
Ferrous Metal Transfer ....E 216 671-8500
  Brooklyn *(G-1906)*
Findlay Truck Line Inc ....D 419 422-1945
  Findlay *(G-11029)*
First Group Investment Partnr ......D 513 241-2200
  Cincinnati *(G-3618)*
Firstgroup Usa Inc ....B 513 241-2200
  Cincinnati *(G-3629)*
Five Star Trucking Inc ....E 440 953-9300
  Willoughby *(G-19665)*
Forrest Trucking Company ....E 614 879-8642
  West Jefferson *(G-19252)*
Fraley & Schilling Inc ....C 740 598-4118
  Brilliant *(G-1868)*
Fultz & Son Inc ....E 419 547-9365
  Clyde *(G-6813)*
G & S Transfer Inc ....E 330 673-3899
  Kent *(G-12370)*
Garber Ag Freight Inc ....E 937 548-8400
  Greenville *(G-11501)*
Garner Trucking Inc ....E 419 422-5742
  Findlay *(G-11035)*
Glm Transport Inc ....E 419 363-2041
  Rockford *(G-16562)*
GMC Excavation & Trucking ....E 419 468-0121
  Galion *(G-11300)*
Golden Hawk Inc ....D 419 683-3304
  Crestline *(G-9145)*
Great Lakes Cartage Company .....D 330 702-1930
  Youngstown *(G-20206)*
Greater Dayton Mvg & Stor Co .....E 937 235-0011
  Dayton *(G-9586)*
H & W Holdings LLC ....E 800 826-3560
  South Point *(G-17087)*
H L C Trucking Inc ....D 740 676-6181
  Shadyside *(G-16849)*

H T I Express ....E 419 423-9555
  Findlay *(G-11039)*
Hc Transport Inc ....E 513 574-1800
  Cincinnati *(G-3744)*
Heartland Express Inc ....C 614 870-8628
  Columbus *(G-7817)*
Henderson Trucking Inc ....E 740 369-6100
  Delaware *(G-10105)*
Henderson Turf Farm Inc ....E 937 748-1559
  Franklin *(G-11158)*
Hilltrux Tank Lines Inc ....E 330 965-1103
  Youngstown *(G-20217)*
Hirzel Transfer Co ....E 419 287-3288
  Pemberville *(G-15941)*
Home Run Inc ....E 800 543-9198
  Xenia *(G-20061)*
Hyway Trucking Company ....D 419 423-7145
  Findlay *(G-11049)*
Iddings Trucking Inc ....C 740 568-1780
  Marietta *(G-13453)*
Imperial Express Inc ....E 937 399-9400
  Springfield *(G-17210)*
Innovative Logistics Svcs Inc ....D 330 468-6422
  Northfield *(G-15517)*
Integrity Ex Logistics LLC ....E 888 374-5138
  Cincinnati *(G-3828)*
International Truck & Eng Corp ....A 937 390-4045
  Springfield *(G-17214)*
J M T Cartage Inc ....E 330 478-2430
  Canton *(G-2416)*
J M Towning Inc ....E 614 876-7335
  Hilliard *(G-11915)*
J P Jenks Inc ....E 440 428-4500
  Madison *(G-13226)*
J P Transportation Company ....E 513 424-6978
  Middletown *(G-14430)*
J T Express Inc ....E 513 727-8185
  Monroe *(G-14699)*
J-Trac Inc ....E 419 524-3456
  Mansfield *(G-13315)*
James Air Cargo Inc ....E 440 243-9095
  Cleveland *(G-5849)*
James H Alvis Trucking Inc ....E 513 623-8121
  Harrison *(G-11803)*
Jet Express Inc ....D 937 274-7033
  Dayton *(G-9640)*
John Brown Trucking Inc ....E 330 758-0841
  Youngstown *(G-20239)*
K R Drenth Trucking Inc ....D 708 983-6340
  Cincinnati *(G-3898)*
Kace Logistics LLC ....D 419 273-3388
  Toledo *(G-17990)*
Kenan Advantage Group Inc ....C 877 999-2524
  North Canton *(G-15349)*
KF Express LLC ....E 614 258-8858
  Powell *(G-16342)*
Klingshirn & Sons Trucking ....E 937 338-5000
  Burkettsville *(G-2058)*
KMu Trucking & Excvtg Inc ....E 440 934-1008
  Avon *(G-903)*
Knight Transportation Inc ....D 614 308-4900
  Columbus *(G-8002)*
Ktib Inc ....E 330 722-7935
  Medina *(G-14093)*
Kuhnle Brothers Inc ....C 440 564-7168
  Newbury *(G-15258)*
Kuntzman Trucking Inc ....E 330 821-9160
  Alliance *(G-543)*
L V Trucking Inc ....E 614 275-4994
  Columbus *(G-8024)*
Lairson Trucking LLC ....E 513 894-0452
  Hamilton *(G-11751)*
Leaders Moving Company ....E 614 785-9595
  Worthington *(G-19970)*
Lesaint Logistics Inc ....C 513 874-3900
  West Chester *(G-19105)*
Lewis & Michael Mvg & Stor Co ...E 614 275-2997
  Columbus *(G-8054)*
Locker Moving & Storage Inc ....E 330 784-0477
  Canton *(G-2439)*
LT Harnett Trucking Inc ....E 440 997-5528
  Ashtabula *(G-753)*
M C Trucking Company LLC ....E 937 584-2486
  Wilmington *(G-19771)*
Mail Contractors America Inc ......C 513 769-5967
  Cincinnati *(G-4014)*
Martin Trnsp Systems Inc ....D 419 726-1348
  Toledo *(G-18045)*
Masur Trucking Inc ....E 513 860-9600
  Cincinnati *(G-4029)*

SIC SECTION

42 MOTOR FREIGHT TRANSPORTATION AND WAREHOUSING

Mid America Trucking Company ....E 216 447-0814
  Cleveland (G-6051)
Midway Delivery Service ....E 216 391-0700
  Cleveland (G-6059)
Midwest Logistics Systems ....B 419 584-1414
  Celina (G-2658)
Mikes Trucking Ltd ....E 614 879-8808
  Galloway (G-11346)
Moeller Trucking Inc ....D 419 925-4799
  Maria Stein (G-13429)
Monesi Trucking & Eqp Repr Inc ....E 614 921-9183
  Columbus (G-8184)
Montgomery Trucking Company ....E 740 384-2138
  Wellston (G-19004)
Murray Leasing Inc ....C 330 386-4757
  East Liverpool (G-10526)
Myers Machinery Movers Inc ....E 614 871-5052
  Grove City (G-11582)
National Highway Equipment Co ....D 614 459-4900
  Columbus (G-8219)
National Trnsp Solutions Inc ....D 330 405-2660
  Twinsburg (G-18450)
Nb Trucking Inc ....E 740 335-9331
  Washington Court Hou (G-18937)
Neighborhood Logistics Co Inc ....E 440 466-0020
  Geneva (G-11366)
Nest Tenders Limited ....D 614 901-1570
  Columbus (G-8257)
Nicholas Carney-Mc Inc ....E 330 792-5460
  Youngstown (G-20301)
Nicolozakes Trckg & Cnstr Inc ....E 740 432-5648
  Cambridge (G-2124)
Northcoast Moving Enterprising ....D 440 943-3900
  Wickliffe (G-19609)
Northcutt Trucking Inc ....E 440 458-5139
  Elyria (G-10663)
Ohio Oil Gathering Corporation ....E 740 828-2892
  Nashport (G-14953)
Ohio Transport Corporation ....D 513 539-0576
  Middletown (G-14446)
One Way Express Incorporated ....E 440 439-9182
  Cleveland (G-6206)
Otis Wright & Sons Inc ....E 419 227-4400
  Lima (G-12852)
P & D Transportation Inc ....E 614 577-1130
  Columbus (G-8500)
P I & I Motor Express Inc ....C 330 448-4035
  Masury (G-13866)
Panther II Transportation Inc ....C 800 685-0657
  Medina (G-14111)
Panther Premium Logistics Inc ....B 800 685-0657
  Medina (G-14112)
Peak Transportation Inc ....D 419 874-5201
  Perrysburg (G-16038)
Peoples Services Inc ....E 330 453-3709
  Canton (G-2490)
PGT Trucking Inc ....E 419 943-3437
  Leipsic (G-12664)
Pierceton Trucking Co Inc ....E 740 446-0114
  Gallipolis (G-11335)
Pitt-Ohio Express LLC ....D 419 729-8173
  Toledo (G-18127)
Pitt-Ohio Express LLC ....D 513 860-3424
  West Chester (G-19221)
Pitt-Ohio Express LLC ....B 216 433-9000
  Cleveland (G-6284)
Powers Equipment ....E 740 746-8220
  Sugar Grove (G-17542)
Prestige Delivery Systems LLC ....E 614 836-8980
  Groveport (G-11663)
Pride Transportation Inc ....E 419 424-2145
  Findlay (G-11077)
Priority Dispatch Inc ....E 513 791-3900
  Blue Ash (G-1665)
Priority Dispatch Inc ....E 216 332-9852
  Solon (G-17041)
Proline Xpress Inc ....E 440 777-8120
  North Olmsted (G-15440)
Quick Delivery Service Inc ....E 330 453-3709
  Canton (G-2500)
R & J Trucking Inc ....E 800 262-9365
  Youngstown (G-20335)
R & J Trucking Inc ....D 330 758-0841
  Shelby (G-16903)
R & J Trucking Inc ....D 740 374-3050
  Marietta (G-13492)
R & J Trucking Inc ....D 440 960-1508
  Lorain (G-13072)
R & J Trucking Inc ....E 419 837-9937
  Perrysburg (G-16049)

R & L Transfer Inc ....C 216 531-3324
  Norwalk (G-15589)
R & L Transfer Inc ....C 330 482-5800
  Columbiana (G-6862)
R & M Delivery ....E 740 574-2113
  Franklin Furnace (G-11173)
R & R Sanitation Inc ....E 330 325-2311
  Mogadore (G-14683)
R E Watson Inc ....E 513 863-0070
  Hamilton (G-11765)
Ramos Trucking Corporation ....E 216 781-0770
  Cleveland (G-6351)
Rands Trucking Inc ....E 740 397-1144
  Mount Vernon (G-14918)
Rapid Delivery Service Co Inc ....E 513 733-0500
  Cincinnati (G-4385)
Ray Bertolini Trucking Co ....E 330 867-0666
  Akron (G-405)
Ray Hamilton Companies ....E 513 641-5400
  Blue Ash (G-1676)
Reis Trucking Inc ....E 513 353-1960
  Cleves (G-6805)
Reliable Appl Installation Inc ....E 614 246-6840
  Columbus (G-8612)
Reliable Appl Installation Inc ....D 330 784-7474
  Akron (G-409)
Republic Services Inc ....E 513 771-4200
  Cincinnati (G-4408)
Rick Kuntz Trucking Inc ....E 330 296-9311
  Windham (G-19803)
Ricketts Excavating Inc ....E 740 687-0338
  Lancaster (G-12569)
Rising Sun Express LLC ....E 937 596-6167
  Jackson Center (G-12324)
River City Furniture LLC ....D 513 612-7303
  West Chester (G-19141)
Rjw Trucking Company Ltd ....E 740 363-5343
  Delaware (G-10124)
Rmx Freight Systems Inc ....E 740 849-2374
  Roseville (G-16602)
Robert M Neff Inc ....D 614 444-1562
  Columbus (G-8642)
Robert Neff & Son Inc ....E 740 454-0128
  Zanesville (G-20530)
Ron Carrocce Trucking Company ....C 330 758-0841
  Youngstown (G-20357)
Rood Trucking Company Inc ....C 330 652-3519
  Mineral Ridge (G-14639)
Ross Consolidated Corp ....D 440 748-5800
  Grafton (G-11444)
Rt80 Express Inc ....E 330 706-0900
  Barberton (G-978)
Rumpke Waste Inc ....D 937 378-4126
  Georgetown (G-11397)
Rumpke Waste Inc ....D 513 242-4401
  Cincinnati (G-4456)
Rumpke Waste Inc ....C 937 548-1939
  Greenville (G-11517)
Rush Package Delivery Inc ....E 937 297-6182
  Dayton (G-9859)
S B Morabito Trucking Inc ....D 216 441-3070
  Cleveland (G-6426)
Sanfrey Freight Services Inc ....E 330 372-1883
  Warren (G-18896)
Santmyer Oil Co Inc ....D 330 262-6501
  Wooster (G-19911)
Schindewolf Express Inc ....D 937 585-5919
  De Graff (G-10016)
Schroeder Associates Inc ....E 419 258-5075
  Antwerp (G-620)
SDS Earth Moving Inc ....E 330 358-2132
  Diamond (G-10172)
Sebastiani Trucking Inc ....D 330 286-0059
  Canfield (G-2210)
Sewell Motor Express Co ....D 937 382-3847
  Wilmington (G-19787)
Shoreline Transportation Inc ....D 440 878-2000
  Strongsville (G-17508)
Sidle Transit Service Inc ....E 330 683-2807
  Orrville (G-15787)
Slay Transportation Co Inc ....E 740 865-2910
  Sardis (G-16815)
Spears Transf & Expediting Inc ....E 937 275-2443
  Dayton (G-9895)
Spring Grove Rsrce Rcovery Inc ....D 513 681-6242
  Cincinnati (G-4565)
Stack Container Service Inc ....E 216 531-7555
  Euclid (G-10777)
State-Wide Express Inc ....D 216 676-4600
  Cleveland (G-6532)

Store & Haul Inc ....E 419 238-4284
  Van Wert (G-18644)
Strawser Equipment & Lsg Inc ....D 614 444-2521
  Columbus (G-8797)
Style Crest Transport Inc ....E 419 332-7369
  Fremont (G-11225)
Su-Jon Enterprises ....E 330 372-1100
  Warren (G-18905)
Sylvester Materials Co ....C 419 841-3874
  Sylvania (G-17621)
T R L Inc ....C 330 448-4071
  Brookfield (G-1901)
T&T Enterprises of Ohio Inc ....E 513 942-1141
  West Chester (G-19236)
Ted Ruck Co Inc ....E 419 738-2613
  Wapakoneta (G-18808)
Tesar Industrial Contrs Inc ....E 216 741-8008
  Cleveland (G-6587)
Tfh-Eb Inc ....D 614 253-7246
  Columbus (G-8833)
Thomas Transport Delivery Inc ....E 330 908-3100
  Macedonia (G-13212)
Todd A Ruck Inc ....E 614 527-9927
  Hilliard (G-11959)
Top Dawg Group LLC ....E 216 398-1066
  Brooklyn Heights (G-1928)
Total Package Express Inc ....E 513 741-5500
  Cincinnati (G-4662)
Trans Vac Inc ....E 419 229-8192
  Lima (G-12903)
Trans-States Express Inc ....D 513 679-7100
  Cincinnati (G-4679)
Transmerica Svcs Technical Sup ....E 740 282-3695
  Steubenville (G-17338)
Transportation Unlimited Inc ....A 216 426-0088
  Cleveland (G-6613)
Tricont Trucking Company ....C 614 527-7398
  Columbus (G-8869)
Trio Trucking Inc ....E 513 679-7100
  Cincinnati (G-4701)
Triple Ladys Agency Inc ....E 330 274-1100
  Mantua (G-13396)
Tsm Logistics LLC ....E 419 234-6074
  Rockford (G-16565)
TV Minority Company Inc ....E 937 226-1559
  Dayton (G-9941)
Two Men & Truck Inc ....E 419 882-1002
  Toledo (G-18265)
U-Haul Neighborhood Dealer -Ce ....E 419 929-3724
  New London (G-15071)
Universal Disposal Inc ....E 440 286-3153
  Chardon (G-2773)
UPS Ground Freight Inc ....C 330 659-6693
  Richfield (G-16531)
UPS Ground Freight Inc ....E 937 236-4700
  Dayton (G-9957)
USF Holland Inc ....D 740 441-1200
  Gallipolis (G-11340)
USF Holland LLC ....C 937 233-7600
  Dayton (G-9959)
USF Holland LLC ....C 513 874-8960
  West Chester (G-19241)
USF Holland LLC ....C 614 529-9300
  Columbus (G-8926)
USF Holland LLC ....C 216 941-4340
  Cleveland (G-6678)
Vallejo Company ....E 216 741-3933
  Cleveland (G-6682)
Van Howards Lines Inc ....E 937 235-0007
  Dayton (G-9963)
Van Mills Lines Inc ....C 440 846-0200
  Strongsville (G 17521)
Varney Dispatch Inc ....E 513 682-4200
  Cincinnati (G-4804)
▲ Vexor Technology Inc ....E 330 721-9773
  Medina (G-14137)
Veyance Industrial Svcs Inc ....C 307 682-7855
  Fairlawn (G-10980)
Vin Devers ....C 888 847-9535
  Sylvania (G-17626)
Vision Express Inc ....E 740 922-8848
  Uhrichsville (G-18496)
Vitran Express Inc ....E 614 870-2255
  Columbus (G-8947)
W L Logan Trucking Company ....C 330 478-1404
  Canton (G-2580)
Wannemacher Enterprises Inc ....E 419 225-9060
  Lima (G-12912)
Waste Management Ohio Inc ....D 440 201-1235
  Solon (G-17066)

Employee Codes: A=Over 500 employees, B=251-500
C=101-250, D=51-100, E=25-50

2018 Harris Ohio
Services Directory

Waste Management Ohio Inc ....D....... 800 343-6047
Fairborn ***(G-10811)***
Waste Management Ohio Inc ....E....... 440 286-7116
Chardon ***(G-2777)***
Waste Management Ohio Inc ....C....... 800 343-6047
Fairborn ***(G-10812)***
Wendel Poultry Service Inc ....E....... 419 375-2439
Fort Recovery ***(G-11121)***
Werlor Inc ....E....... 419 784-4285
Defiance ***(G-10063)***
Westhafer Trucking Inc ....E....... 330 698-3030
Apple Creek ***(G-628)***
William Hafer Drayage Inc ....E....... 513 771-5000
Cincinnati ***(G-4849)***
Wnb Group LLC ....E....... 513 641-5400
Cincinnati ***(G-4855)***
Wooster Motor Ways Inc ....C....... 330 264-9557
Wooster ***(G-19932)***
Wright Brothers Aero Inc ....E....... 937 454-8475
Dayton ***(G-10004)***
Xpo Logistics Freight Inc ....E....... 937 898-9808
Dayton ***(G-10005)***
Xpo Logistics Freight Inc ....E....... 937 364-2361
Hillsboro ***(G-11993)***
Xpo Logistics Freight Inc ....E....... 740 922-5614
Uhrichsville ***(G-18497)***
Xpo Logistics Freight Inc ....C....... 513 870-0044
West Chester ***(G-19244)***
Xpo Logistics Freight Inc ....C....... 216 433-1000
Parma ***(G-15919)***
Xpo Logistics Freight Inc ....C....... 614 876-7100
Columbus ***(G-9014)***
Xpo Logistics Freight Inc ....D....... 330 896-7300
Uniontown ***(G-18544)***
Yrc Inc ....D....... 330 659-4151
Richfield ***(G-16534)***
Yrc Inc ....B....... 419 729-0631
Toledo ***(G-18327)***
Zeiter Trucking Inc ....E....... 419 668-2229
Norwalk ***(G-15597)***
Zemba Bros Inc ....E....... 740 452-1880
Zanesville ***(G-20561)***
Zone Transportation Co ....D....... 440 324-3544
Elyria ***(G-10695)***

4213 Trucking, Except Local

1st Carrier Corp ....D....... 740 477-2587
Circleville ***(G-4875)***
A C Leasing Company ....E....... 513 771-3676
Cincinnati ***(G-2953)***
A L Smith Trucking Inc ....E....... 937 526-3651
Versailles ***(G-18722)***
A&R Logistics Inc ....D....... 614 444-4111
Columbus ***(G-6921)***
ABF Freight System Inc ....D....... 440 843-4600
Cleveland ***(G-4947)***
ABF Freight System Inc ....E....... 614 294-3537
Columbus ***(G-6925)***
ABF Freight System Inc ....E....... 937 236-2210
Dayton ***(G-9301)***
ABF Freight System Inc ....E....... 513 779-7888
West Chester ***(G-19011)***
ABF Freight System Inc ....E....... 330 549-3800
North Lima ***(G-15395)***
Accelerated Moving & Stor Inc ....E....... 614 836-1007
Columbus ***(G-6932)***
Advantage Tank Lines Inc ....E....... 330 491-0474
North Canton ***(G-15321)***
Advantage Tank Lines Inc ....C....... 330 427-1010
Leetonia ***(G-12661)***
AG Trucking Inc ....E....... 937 497-7770
Sidney ***(G-16911)***
Akron Centl Engrv Mold Mch Inc ....E....... 330 794-8704
Akron ***(G-30)***
All Industrial Group Inc ....E....... 216 441-2000
Newburgh Heights ***(G-15250)***
All Pro Freight Systems Inc ....D....... 440 934-2222
Avon ***(G-874)***
Alpha Freight Systems Inc ....D....... 800 394-9001
Hudson ***(G-12104)***
Ameri-Line Inc ....E....... 440 316-4500
Columbia Station ***(G-6840)***
American Power LLC ....E....... 937 235-0418
Dayton ***(G-9331)***
American Way Van and Stor Inc ....E....... 937 898-7294
Vandalia ***(G-18658)***
Arctic Express Inc ....C....... 614 876-4008
Hilliard ***(G-11879)***
Arms Trucking Co Inc ....E....... 800 362-1343
Huntsburg ***(G-12156)***
As Logistics Inc ....D....... 513 863-4627
Hamilton ***(G-11693)***
Autumn Industries Inc ....E....... 330 372-5002
Warren ***(G-18821)***
Awl Transport Inc ....E....... 330 899-3444
Mantua ***(G-13384)***
Awrs LLC ....E....... 888 611-2292
Cincinnati ***(G-3068)***
B & H Industries Inc ....E....... 419 485-8373
Montpelier ***(G-14736)***
B & T Express Inc ....D....... 330 549-0000
North Lima ***(G-15399)***
B D Transportation Inc ....E....... 937 773-9280
Piqua ***(G-16135)***
Bantam Leasing Inc ....E....... 513 734-6696
Amelia ***(G-578)***
Barnets Inc ....E....... 937 452-3275
Camden ***(G-2136)***
Bell Moving and Storage Inc ....E....... 513 942-7500
Fairfield ***(G-10823)***
Berlin Transportaion LLC ....E....... 330 674-3395
Millersburg ***(G-14588)***
Besl Transfer Co ....E....... 513 242-3456
Cincinnati ***(G-3100)***
Bestway Transport Co ....E....... 419 687-2000
Plymouth ***(G-16216)***
Black Horse Carriers Inc ....C....... 330 225-2250
Hinckley ***(G-11995)***
Blatt Trucking Co Inc ....E....... 419 898-0002
Rocky Ridge ***(G-16566)***
Blb Transport Inc ....E....... 740 474-1341
Circleville ***(G-4879)***
Bowling Transportation Inc ....D....... 419 436-9590
Fostoria ***(G-11124)***
Brendamour Moving & Stor Inc ....D....... 800 354-9715
Cincinnati ***(G-3129)***
Brent Burris Trucking LLC ....E....... 419 759-2020
Ada ***(G-3)***
Brookside Holdings LLC ....E....... 419 925-4457
Maria Stein ***(G-13427)***
Bryan Truck Line Inc ....D....... 419 485-8373
Montpelier ***(G-14739)***
Buckeye Waste Industries Inc ....E....... 330 645-9900
Coventry Township ***(G-9123)***
Building Systems Trnsp Co ....C....... 740 852-9700
London ***(G-12994)***
Bulk Transit Corporation ....E....... 614 873-4632
Plain City ***(G-16185)***
Bulk Transit Corporation ....E....... 937 497-9573
Sidney ***(G-16917)***
Bulkmatic Transport Company ....E....... 614 497-2372
Columbus ***(G-7168)***
Burd Brothers Inc ....D....... 800 538-2873
Batavia ***(G-996)***
BWC Trucking Company Inc ....E....... 740 532-5188
Ironton ***(G-12284)***
By-Line Transit Inc ....E....... 937 642-2500
Marysville ***(G-13608)***
C&K Trucking LLC ....E....... 440 657-5249
Elyria ***(G-10600)***
Carrier Industries Inc ....B....... 614 851-6363
Columbus ***(G-7203)***
Carry Transport Inc ....E....... 937 236-0026
Dayton ***(G-9386)***
Cassens Transport Company ....C....... 937 644-8886
Marysville ***(G-13610)***
Cassens Transport Company ....C....... 419 727-0520
Toledo ***(G-17794)***
Cavins Trucking & Garage LLC ....E....... 419 661-9947
Perrysburg ***(G-15985)***
Century Lines Inc ....E....... 216 271-0700
Cleveland ***(G-5219)***
Ceva Logistics US Inc ....E....... 937 578-1160
East Liberty ***(G-10507)***
Chambers Leasing Systems ....E....... 937 547-9777
Greenville ***(G-11492)***
Cimarron Express Inc ....D....... 419 855-7713
Genoa ***(G-11375)***
Circle S Transport Inc ....E....... 614 207-2184
Columbus ***(G-7276)***
City Dash Inc ....C....... 513 562-2000
Cincinnati ***(G-3357)***
Clark Trucking Inc ....C....... 937 642-0335
East Liberty ***(G-10508)***
Classic Carriers Inc ....E....... 937 604-8118
Versailles ***(G-18724)***
Clayton Weaver Trucking Inc ....E....... 513 896-6932
Fairfield ***(G-10837)***
Cle Transportation Company ....D....... 567 805-4008
Norwalk ***(G-15565)***
Cleveland Express Trckg Co Inc ....D....... 216 348-0922
Cleveland ***(G-5313)***
Clopay Transportation Company ....D....... 513 381-4800
Cincinnati ***(G-3368)***
Clp Towne Inc ....E....... 440 234-3324
Brookpark ***(G-1940)***
Competitive Transportation ....E....... 419 529-5300
Bellville ***(G-1422)***
Concept Freight Service Inc ....E....... 330 784-1134
New Franklin ***(G-15043)***
Containerport Group Inc ....E....... 440 333-1330
Columbus ***(G-7426)***
Containerport Group Inc ....E....... 216 341-4800
Cleveland ***(G-5401)***
Continental Express Inc ....B....... 937 497-2100
Sidney ***(G-16922)***
Contract Freighters Inc ....A....... 614 577-0447
Reynoldsburg ***(G-16441)***
Cooper Brothers Trucking LLC ....E....... 330 784-1717
Akron ***(G-164)***
Corrigan Moving Systems-Ann AR ....E....... 419 874-2900
Perrysburg ***(G-15989)***
Cotter Moving & Storage Co ....E....... 330 535-5115
Akron ***(G-167)***
Cowan Systems LLC ....C....... 513 769-4774
Cincinnati ***(G-3436)***
Cowan Systems LLC ....C....... 513 721-6444
West Chester ***(G-19056)***
Cowan Systems LLC ....E....... 330 963-8483
Twinsburg ***(G-18405)***
Cowen Truck Line Inc ....D....... 419 938-3401
Perrysville ***(G-16078)***
Coy Brothers Inc ....E....... 330 533-6864
Canfield ***(G-2187)***
Craig Transportation Co ....E....... 419 874-7981
Maumee ***(G-13901)***
Crescent Park Corporation ....C....... 513 759-7000
West Chester ***(G-19059)***
Crete Carrier Corporation ....C....... 614 853-4500
Columbus ***(G-7461)***
CRST International Inc ....D....... 740 599-0008
Danville ***(G-9245)***
Crw Inc ....D....... 330 264-3785
Shreve ***(G-16907)***
D L Belknap Trucking Inc ....D....... 330 868-7766
Paris ***(G-15895)***
Dart Trucking Company Inc ....E....... 330 549-0994
North Lima ***(G-15401)***
Daves Sand & Stone Inc ....E....... 419 445-9256
Wauseon ***(G-18950)***
Davidson Trucking Inc ....E....... 419 288-2318
Bradner ***(G-1809)***
Dayton Freight Lines Inc ....E....... 419 661-8600
Perrysburg ***(G-15993)***
Dayton Freight Lines Inc ....E....... 614 860-1080
Columbus ***(G-7493)***
Dayton Freight Lines Inc ....D....... 937 236-4880
Dayton ***(G-9475)***
Dayton Freight Lines Inc ....E....... 330 346-0750
Kent ***(G-12364)***
Dearman Moving & Storage Co ....E....... 419 524-3456
Mansfield ***(G-13291)***
Dedicated Logistics Inc ....D....... 513 275-1135
West Chester ***(G-19060)***
Dedicated Transport LLC ....C....... 216 641-2500
Brooklyn Heights ***(G-1914)***
Dhl Supply Chain (usa) ....E....... 614 492-6614
Lockbourne ***(G-12950)***
Dhl Supply Chain (usa) ....E....... 513 942-1575
Cincinnati ***(G-3487)***
Diamond Heavy Haul Inc ....E....... 330 677-8061
Kent ***(G-12365)***
Dick Lavy Trucking Inc ....C....... 937 448-2104
Bradford ***(G-1806)***
Dill-Elam Inc ....E....... 513 575-0017
Loveland ***(G-13123)***
Dingledine Trucking Company ....E....... 937 652-3454
Urbana ***(G-18585)***
Direct Express Delivery Svc ....E....... 513 541-0600
Cincinnati ***(G-3492)***
Dist-Trans Inc ....C....... 614 497-1660
Columbus ***(G-7526)***
Distribution and Trnsp Svc Inc ....E....... 937 295-3343
Fort Loramie ***(G-11110)***
Disttech LLC ....D....... 800 321-3143
Cleveland ***(G-5490)***
Dlc Transport Inc ....E....... 740 282-1763
Steubenville ***(G-17315)***
Drasc Enterprises Inc ....E....... 330 852-3254
Sugarcreek ***(G-17544)***

SIC SECTION
42 MOTOR FREIGHT TRANSPORTATION AND WAREHOUSING

Drew Ag-Transport Inc D 937 548-3200
Greenville *(G-11499)*
Durbin Trucking Inc E 419 334-2422
Oak Harbor *(G-15609)*
Dworkin Inc E 216 271-5318
Cleveland *(G-5515)*
Elmco Trucking Inc E 419 983-2010
Bloomville *(G-1519)*
Erie Trucking Inc E 419 625-7374
Sandusky *(G-16755)*
Estes Express Lines Inc D 440 327-3884
North Ridgeville *(G-15463)*
Estes Express Lines Inc C 614 275-6000
Columbus *(G-7614)*
Estes Express Lines Inc E 419 531-1500
Toledo *(G-17871)*
Estes Express Lines Inc D 937 237-7536
Huber Heights *(G-12095)*
Estes Express Lines Inc D 419 522-2641
Mansfield *(G-13298)*
Estes Express Lines Inc D 513 779-9581
West Chester *(G-19070)*
Estes Express Lines Inc E 740 401-0410
Belpre *(G-1437)*
Excel Trucking LLC E 614 826-1988
Columbus *(G-7617)*
Exel Holdings (usa) Inc C 614 865-8500
Westerville *(G-19303)*
Exel Inc B 614 865-8500
Westerville *(G-19305)*
Express Twing Recovery Svc Inc E 513 881-1900
West Chester *(G-19199)*
F S T Express Inc D 614 529-7900
Columbus *(G-7626)*
Falcon Transport Co C 330 793-1345
Youngstown *(G-20185)*
Falcon Transport Co D 330 793-1345
Youngstown *(G-20186)*
FANTON Logistics Inc D 216 341-2400
Cleveland *(G-5572)*
Federal Express Corporation B 614 492-6106
Columbus *(G-7646)*
Fedex Custom Critical Inc B 234 310-4090
Uniontown *(G-18519)*
Fedex Freight Inc D 330 645-0879
Akron *(G-223)*
Fedex Freight Inc C 937 233-4826
Dayton *(G-9543)*
Fedex Freight Corporation E 877 661-8956
Mentor *(G-14175)*
Fedex Freight Corporation E 419 729-1755
Toledo *(G-17883)*
Fedex Freight Corporation E 800 390-0159
Mansfield *(G-13301)*
Fedex Freight Corporation E 800 521-3505
Lima *(G-12781)*
Fedex Freight Corporation D 800 344-6448
West Jefferson *(G-19251)*
Fedex Freight Corporation C 800 728-8190
Northwood *(G-15532)*
Fedex Freight Corporation E 800 354-9489
Zanesville *(G-20477)*
Fedex Ground Package Sys Inc C 614 863-8000
Columbus *(G-7649)*
Fedex Ground Package Sys Inc D 513 942-4330
West Chester *(G-19200)*
Fedex Ground Package Sys Inc B 800 463-3339
Grove City *(G-11560)*
Ferrous Metal Transfer E 216 671-8500
Brooklyn *(G-1906)*
Fetter and Son LLC E 740 465-2961
Morral *(G-14840)*
Fetter Son Farms Ltd Lblty Co E 740 465-2961
Morral *(G-14841)*
First Group Investment Partnr D 513 241-2200
Cincinnati *(G-3618)*
Firstenterprises Inc B 740 369-5100
Delaware *(G-10096)*
Firstgroup Usa Inc B 513 241-2200
Cincinnati *(G-3629)*
Five Star Trucking Inc E 440 953-9300
Willoughby *(G-19665)*
Foodliner Inc E 563 451-1047
Dayton *(G-9555)*
Foster Sales & Delivery Inc D 740 245-0200
Bidwell *(G-1495)*
Fraley & Schilling Inc C 740 598-4118
Brilliant *(G-1868)*
Franklin Specialty Trnspt Inc D 614 529-7900
Columbus *(G-7699)*

G & S Transfer Inc E 330 673-3899
Kent *(G-12370)*
Garber Ag Freight Inc E 937 548-8400
Greenville *(G-11501)*
Gardner Contracting Company E 216 881-3800
Cleveland *(G-5654)*
Garner Trucking Inc C 419 422-5742
Findlay *(G-11035)*
General Transport Incorporated E 330 786-3400
Akron *(G-234)*
Glm Transport Inc E 419 363-2041
Rockford *(G-16562)*
Global Workplace Solutions LLC D 513 759-6000
West Chester *(G-19082)*
Globe Trucking Inc D 419 727-8307
Toledo *(G-17917)*
GMC Excavation & Trucking E 419 468-0121
Galion *(G-11300)*
Golden Hawk Transportation Co D 419 683-3304
Crestline *(G-9146)*
Great Lakes Cartage Company D 330 702-1930
Youngstown *(G-20206)*
Greater Dayton Mvg & Stor Co E 937 235-0011
Dayton *(G-9586)*
Green Lines Transportation Inc E 330 863-2111
Malvern *(G-13251)*
Guenther & Sons Inc E 513 738-1448
Ross *(G-16603)*
H O C J Inc E 614 539-4601
Grove City *(G-11569)*
Harbor Freight Tools Usa Inc D 513 598-4897
Cincinnati *(G-3736)*
Harris Distributing Co E 513 541-4222
Cincinnati *(G-3737)*
Harte-Hanks Trnsp Svcs D 513 458-7600
Cincinnati *(G-3739)*
Hillandale Farms Trnsp D 740 893-2232
Johnstown *(G-12341)*
Hillsboro Transportation Co E 513 772-9223
Cincinnati *(G-3766)*
Hilltrux Tank Lines Inc E 330 538-3700
North Jackson *(G-15381)*
Homan Transportation Inc D 419 465-2626
Monroeville *(G-14720)*
Home Moving & Storage Co Inc E 614 445-6377
Columbus *(G-7851)*
Home Run Inc E 800 543-9198
Xenia *(G-20061)*
Hoosier Express Inc E 419 436-9590
Fostoria *(G-11132)*
Horizon Freight System Inc E 216 341-3322
Cleveland *(G-5773)*
Horizon Freight System Inc E 216 341-7410
Cleveland *(G-5774)*
Hs Express LLC D 419 729-2400
Toledo *(G-17963)*
HTI - Hall Trucking Inc E 419 423-9555
Findlay *(G-11047)*
Hyway Trucking Company D 419 423-7145
Findlay *(G-11049)*
Iddings Trucking Inc C 740 568-1780
Marietta *(G-13453)*
Integres Global Logistics Inc D 866 347-2101
Medina *(G-14081)*
J & B Leasing Inc of Ohio E 419 269-1440
Toledo *(G-17979)*
J & J Carriers LLC E 614 447-2615
Columbus *(G-7929)*
J B Hunt Transport Inc C 440 786-8436
Bedford Heights *(G-1354)*
J B Hunt Transport Inc C 419 547-2777
Clyde *(G-6816)*
J M T Cartage Inc E 330 478-2430
Canton *(G-2416)*
J P Jenks Inc E 440 428-4500
Madison *(G-13226)*
J P Transportation Company E 513 424-6978
Middletown *(G-14430)*
J T Express Inc E 513 727-8185
Monroe *(G-14699)*
J-Trac Inc E 419 524-3456
Mansfield *(G-13315)*
Jack Cooper Transport Co Inc C 440 949-2044
Sheffield Village *(G-16888)*
Jaro Transportation Svcs Inc D 330 393-5659
Warren *(G-18868)*
Jarrells Moving & Transport Co D 330 764-4333
Seville *(G-16841)*
JB Hunt Transport Svcs Inc A 614 335-6681
Columbus *(G-7937)*

Jet Express Inc D 937 274-7033
Dayton *(G-9640)*
K & L Trucking Inc E 419 822-3836
Delta *(G-10160)*
K & P Trucking LLC D 419 935-8646
Willard *(G-19621)*
K-Limited Carrier Ltd C 419 269-0002
Toledo *(G-17988)*
Kaplan Trucking Company D 216 341-3322
Cleveland *(G-5882)*
Kenan Advantage Group Inc C 877 999-2524
North Canton *(G-15349)*
Keystone Freight Corp E 614 542-0320
Columbus *(G-7984)*
KF Express LLC E 614 258-8858
Powell *(G-16342)*
Klingshirn & Sons Trucking E 937 338-5000
Burkettsville *(G-2058)*
Kllee Trucking Inc D 740 867-6454
Chesapeake *(G-2785)*
Kmj Leasing Ltd E 614 871-3883
Orient *(G-15761)*
Knight Transportation Inc D 614 308-4900
Columbus *(G-8002)*
Knight-Swift Trnsp Hldings Inc D 614 274-5204
Columbus *(G-8003)*
Kuhnle Brothers Inc C 440 564-7168
Newbury *(G-15258)*
Kuntzman Trucking Inc E 330 821-9160
Alliance *(G-543)*
L A King Trucking Inc E 419 727-9398
Toledo *(G-17998)*
L J Navy Trucking Company E 614 754-8929
Columbus *(G-8022)*
L O G Transportation Inc E 440 891-0850
Berea *(G-1462)*
L V Trucking Inc E 614 275-4994
Columbus *(G-8024)*
La King Trucking Inc E 419 225-9039
Lima *(G-12813)*
Lewis & Michael Inc E 937 252-6683
Dayton *(G-9679)*
Lincoln Moving & Storage Co D 216 741-5500
Cleveland *(G-5943)*
Liquid Transport Corp E 513 769-4777
Cincinnati *(G-3989)*
Locker Moving & Storage Inc E 330 784-0477
Canton *(G-2439)*
LT Harnett Trucking Inc E 440 997-5528
Ashtabula *(G-753)*
Lt Trucking Inc E 440 997-5528
Ashtabula *(G-754)*
Lyden Company E 419 868-6800
Toledo *(G-18022)*
Lykins Companies Inc C 513 831-8820
Milford *(G-14533)*
Lykins Transportation Inc D 513 831-8820
Milford *(G-14535)*
M & B Trucking Express Corp E 440 236-8820
Columbia Station *(G-6848)*
Maines Collision Repr & Bdy Sp D 937 322-4618
Springfield *(G-17228)*
Mansfield Whsng & Dist Inc C 419 522-3510
Ontario *(G-15699)*
Martin Trnsp Systems Inc D 419 726-1348
Toledo *(G-18045)*
Mast Trucking Inc D 330 674-8913
Millersburg *(G-14611)*
Material Suppliers Inc E 419 298-2440
Edgerton *(G-10583)*
McMullen Transportation LLC E 937 981-4455
Greenfield *(G-11488)*
Merchants 5 Star Ltd D 740 373-0313
Marietta *(G-13475)*
Miami Valley Bekins Inc E 937 278-4296
Dayton *(G-9726)*
Miarer Transportation Inc E 419 665-2334
Gibsonburg *(G-11403)*
Mid State Systems Inc D 740 928-1115
Hebron *(G-11853)*
Midfitz Inc E 216 663-8816
Cleveland *(G-6055)*
Midwest Logistics Systems B 419 584-1414
Celina *(G-2658)*
Miller Transfer and Rigging Co E 330 325-2521
Rootstown *(G-16598)*
Millis Transfer Inc E 513 863-0222
Hamilton *(G-11760)*
Mitchell & Sons Moving & Stor E 419 289-3311
Ashland *(G-689)*

S I C

Employee Codes: A=Over 500 employees, B=251-500
C=101-250, D=51-100, E=25-50
2018 Harris Ohio
Services Directory
921

42 MOTOR FREIGHT TRANSPORTATION AND WAREHOUSING

Company		Phone
Mizar Motors Inc	D	419 729-2400
Toledo (G-18065)		
Moeller Trucking Inc	D	419 925-4799
Maria Stein (G-13429)		
Montgomery Trucking Company	E	740 384-2138
Wellston (G-19004)		
Motor Carrier Service Inc	C	419 693-6207
Northwood (G-15537)		
Murray Leasing Inc	C	330 386-4757
East Liverpool (G-10526)		
◆ Mxd Group Inc	D	866 711-3129
New Albany (G-14995)		
Myers Machinery Movers Inc	E	614 871-5052
Grove City (G-11582)		
National Highway Equipment Co	D	614 459-4900
Columbus (G-8219)		
National Trnsp Solutions Inc	D	330 405-2660
Twinsburg (G-18450)		
Nationwide Truck Brokers Inc	E	937 335-9229
Troy (G-18367)		
Neighborhood Logistics Co Inc	E	440 466-0020
Geneva (G-11366)		
New England Motor Freight Inc	D	513 782-0017
Cincinnati (G-4155)		
New World Van Lines Ohio Inc	E	614 836-5720
Groveport (G-11658)		
Nicholas Carney-Mc Inc	D	330 792-5460
Youngstown (G-20301)		
Nicholas Carney-Mc Inc	E	440 243-8560
Sheffield Village (G-16894)		
Nick Strimbu Inc	D	330 448-4046
Brookfield (G-1900)		
Nick Strimbu Inc	D	330 448-4046
Dover (G-10203)		
Nicolozakes Trckg & Cnstr Inc	E	740 432-5648
Cambridge (G-2124)		
Noramco Transport Corp	E	513 245-9050
Cincinnati (G-4172)		
Oeder Carl E Sons Sand & Grav	E	513 494-1238
Lebanon (G-12632)		
Ohio Auto Delivery Inc	E	614 277-1445
Grove City (G-11587)		
Ohio Carriers Corp	D	330 878-5311
Dover (G-10204)		
Ohio Oil Gathering Corporation	E	740 828-2892
Nashport (G-14953)		
Old Dominion Freight Line Inc	D	330 545-8628
Girard (G-11422)		
Old Dominion Freight Line Inc	E	937 235-1596
Dayton (G-9790)		
Old Dominion Freight Line Inc	E	513 771-1486
West Chester (G-19125)		
Old Dominion Freight Line Inc	E	419 726-4032
Toledo (G-18104)		
Old Dominion Freight Line Inc	B	614 491-3903
Columbus (G-8463)		
Old Dominion Freight Line Inc	E	216 641-5566
Cleveland (G-6198)		
OMI Transportation Inc	E	419 241-8711
Toledo (G-18106)		
One Way Express Incorporated	E	440 439-9182
Cleveland (G-6206)		
Osborne Trucking Company	D	513 874-2090
Fairfield (G-10890)		
Otis Wright & Sons Inc	E	419 227-4400
Lima (G-12852)		
P & D Transportation Inc	E	614 577-1130
Columbus (G-8500)		
P & D Transportation Inc	C	740 454-1221
Zanesville (G-20523)		
P C C Refrigerated Ex Inc	E	614 754-8929
Columbus (G-8501)		
P I & I Motor Express Inc	C	330 448-4035
Masury (G-13866)		
PAm Transportation Svcs Inc	D	419 935-9501
Willard (G-19624)		
Panther II Transportation Inc	C	800 685-0657
Medina (G-14111)		
Panther Premium Logistics Inc	B	800 685-0657
Medina (G-14112)		
Partnership LLC	E	440 471-8310
Cleveland (G-6248)		
Peak Transportation Inc	D	419 874-5201
Perrysburg (G-16038)		
Penske Logistics LLC	D	216 765-5475
Beachwood (G-1114)		
Penske Logistics LLC	D	330 626-7623
Streetsboro (G-17425)		
Peoples Services Inc	E	330 453-3709
Canton (G-2490)		
PGT Trucking Inc	E	419 943-3437
Leipsic (G-12664)		
Piqua Transfer & Storage Co	D	937 773-3743
Piqua (G-16160)		
Pitt-Ohio Express LLC	C	614 801-1064
Grove City (G-11592)		
Pitt-Ohio Express LLC	E	419 726-6523
Toledo (G-18126)		
Pitt-Ohio Express LLC	D	513 860-3424
West Chester (G-19221)		
Pitt-Ohio Express LLC	B	216 433-9000
Cleveland (G-6284)		
Planes Moving & Storage Inc	C	513 759-6000
West Chester (G-19129)		
Planes Mvg & Stor Co Columbus	E	614 777-9090
Columbus (G-8548)		
Platinum Express Inc	D	937 235-9540
Dayton (G-9812)		
Predator Trucking Company	E	419 849-2601
Woodville (G-19823)		
Premium Trnsp Logistics LLC	E	419 861-3430
Toledo (G-18133)		
Pride Transportation Inc	E	419 424-2145
Findlay (G-11077)		
Pros Freight Corporation	E	440 543-7555
Chagrin Falls (G-2730)		
Quality Carriers Inc	E	419 222-6800
Lima (G-12864)		
R & J Trucking Inc	D	740 374-3050
Marietta (G-13492)		
R & L Carriers Inc	E	419 874-5976
Perrysburg (G-16050)		
R & L Transfer Inc	E	216 531-3324
Norwalk (G-15589)		
R & L Transfer Inc	D	330 743-3609
Youngstown (G-20336)		
R & L Transfer Inc	C	330 482-5800
Columbiana (G-6862)		
R & S Lines Inc	E	419 682-7807
Stryker (G-17538)		
R E Watson Inc	E	513 863-0070
Hamilton (G-11765)		
R K Campf Corp	E	330 332-7089
Salem (G-16709)		
R+I Pramount Trnsp Systems Inc	B	937 382-1494
Wilmington (G-19780)		
Ray Bertolini Trucking Co	D	330 867-0666
Akron (G-405)		
Richard Wolfe Trucking Inc	E	740 392-2445
Mount Vernon (G-14920)		
Rising Sun Express LLC	D	937 596-6167
Jackson Center (G-12324)		
Rjw Inc	E	216 398-6090
Independence (G-12250)		
RL Trucking Inc	C	419 732-4177
Port Clinton (G-16254)		
Robert G Owen Trucking Inc	E	330 756-1013
Navarre (G-14956)		
Robert M Neff Inc	D	614 444-1562
Columbus (G-8642)		
Robert Neff & Son Inc	E	740 454-0128
Zanesville (G-20530)		
Roeder Cartage Company Inc	D	419 221-1600
Lima (G-12870)		
Rollins Moving and Storage Inc	E	937 525-4013
Springfield (G-17267)		
Ron Burge Trucking Inc	E	330 624-5373
Burbank (G-2055)		
Rood Trucking Company Inc	C	330 652-3519
Mineral Ridge (G-14639)		
Rose Transport Inc	E	614 864-4004
Reynoldsburg (G-16480)		
Roseville Motor Express Inc	E	614 921-2121
Columbus (G-8650)		
Ross Transportation Svcs Inc	D	440 748-5900
Grafton (G-11446)		
Rrr Express LLC	C	800 723-3424
West Chester (G-19143)		
Rt80 Express Inc	E	330 706-0900
Barberton (G-978)		
S & T Truck and Auto Svc Inc	E	614 272-8163
Columbus (G-8667)		
Saia Motor Freight Line LLC	E	419 726-9761
Toledo (G-18170)		
Saia Motor Freight Line LLC	E	330 659-4277
Richfield (G-16528)		
Saia Motor Freight Line LLC	D	614 870-8778
Columbus (G-8676)		
Sanfrey Freight Services Inc	E	330 372-1883
Warren (G-18896)		
Saro Truck Dispatch Inc	E	419 873-1358
Perrysburg (G-16056)		
Scheiderer Transport Inc	D	614 873-5103
Plain City (G-16204)		
Schindewolf Express Inc	D	937 585-5919
De Graff (G-10016)		
Schneider Nat Carriers Inc	E	740 362-6910
Delaware (G-10126)		
Schneider National Inc	B	419 673-0254
Kenton (G-12423)		
Schroeder Associates Inc	E	419 258-5075
Antwerp (G-620)		
Security Storage Co Inc	D	513 961-2700
Cincinnati (G-4490)		
Sewell Motor Express Co	E	937 382-3847
Wilmington (G-19787)		
Shetler Moving & Stor of Ohio	E	513 755-0700
West Chester (G-19151)		
Shippers Consolidated Dist	E	216 579-9303
Cleveland (G-6478)		
Shoreline Transportation Inc	C	440 878-2000
Strongsville (G-17508)		
Short Freight Lines Inc	E	419 729-1691
Toledo (G-18185)		
Slay Transportation Co Inc	C	740 865-2910
Sardis (G-16815)		
Smith Trucking Inc	E	419 841-8676
Sylvania (G-17616)		
SMS Transport LLC	E	937 813-8897
Dayton (G-9886)		
Spader Freight Carriers Inc	D	419 547-1117
Clyde (G-6823)		
Spader Freight Services Inc	E	419 547-1117
Clyde (G-6824)		
State-Wide Express Inc	D	216 676-4600
Cleveland (G-6532)		
STC Transporation Inc	E	216 441-6217
Cleveland (G-6533)		
Style Crest Transport Inc	D	419 332-7369
Fremont (G-11225)		
Superior Bulk Logistics Inc	E	513 874-3440
West Chester (G-19233)		
Swx Enterprises Inc	E	216 676-4600
Brookpark (G-1956)		
T & L Transport Inc	E	330 674-0655
Millersburg (G-14623)		
▲ Tersher Corporation	D	440 439-8383
Strongsville (G-17516)		
Tesar Industrial Contrs Inc	E	216 741-8008
Cleveland (G-6587)		
Tfi Transportation Inc	E	330 332-4655
Salem (G-16717)		
Thoman Weil Moving & Stor Co	E	513 251-5000
Cincinnati (G-4651)		
Thomas E Keller Trucking Inc	C	419 784-4805
Defiance (G-10061)		
Thomas Trucking Inc	E	513 731-8411
Cincinnati (G-4654)		
Three-D Transport Inc	E	419 924-5368
West Unity (G-19281)		
Thyssenkrupp Logistics Inc	D	419 662-1800
Northwood (G-15545)		
Titan Transfer Inc	D	513 458-4233
West Chester (G-19163)		
Tkx Logistics	E	419 662-1800
Northwood (G-15546)		
Total Package Express Inc	E	513 741-5500
Cincinnati (G-4675)		
Tpg Noramco LLC	E	513 245-9050
Cincinnati (G-4676)		
Trans-States Express Inc	D	513 679-7100
Cincinnati (G-4679)		
Transport Corp America Inc	E	330 538-3328
North Jackson (G-15388)		
Transportation Unlimited Inc	A	216 426-0088
Cleveland (G-6613)		
Triad Transport Inc	E	614 491-9497
Columbus (G-8868)		
Trio Trucking Inc	E	513 679-7100
Cincinnati (G-4701)		
Triple Ladys Agency Inc	E	330 274-1100
Mantua (G-13396)		
U S Xpress Inc	E	937 328-4100
Springfield (G-17291)		
U S Xpress Inc	E	740 363-0700
Delaware (G-10132)		
U S Xpress Inc	C	740 452-4153
Zanesville (G-20541)		
United Road Services Inc	D	419 837-2703
Toledo (G-18272)		

SIC SECTION 42 MOTOR FREIGHT TRANSPORTATION AND WAREHOUSING

Unpacking Etc .... E 440 871-0506
Westlake *(G-19561)*
UPS Ground Freight Inc .... C 330 659-6693
Richfield *(G-16531)*
UPS Ground Freight Inc .... E 937 236-4700
Dayton *(G-9957)*
UPS Ground Freight Inc .... E 330 448-0440
Masury *(G-13869)*
US Expediting Logistics LLC .... E 937 235-1014
Vandalia *(G-18704)*
USF Holland Inc .... D 740 441-1200
Gallipolis *(G-11340)*
USF Holland LLC .... C 513 874-8960
West Chester *(G-19241)*
USF Holland LLC .... D 419 354-6633
Bowling Green *(G-1796)*
USF Holland LLC .... C 614 529-9300
Columbus *(G-8926)*
USF Holland LLC .... C 330 549-2917
North Lima *(G-15408)*
USF Holland LLC .... C 937 233-7600
Dayton *(G-9959)*
USF Holland LLC .... C 216 941-4340
Cleveland *(G-6678)*
Valley Transportation Inc .... C 419 289-6200
Ashland *(G-704)*
Van Howards Lines Inc .... E 937 235-0007
Dayton *(G-9963)*
Van Mayberrys & Storage Inc .... E 937 298-8800
Moraine *(G-14832)*
Van Mills Lines Inc .... C 440 846-0200
Strongsville *(G-17521)*
Van Stevens Lines Inc .... E 419 729-8871
Toledo *(G-18286)*
Vance Road Enterprises Inc .... E 937 268-6953
Dayton *(G-9964)*
Venezia Transport Service Inc .... E 330 542-9735
New Middletown *(G-15074)*
Vision Express Inc .... E 740 922-8848
Uhrichsville *(G-18496)*
Vitran Express Inc .... D 216 426-8584
Cleveland *(G-6707)*
Vitran Express Inc .... E 513 771-4894
West Chester *(G-19182)*
W L Logan Trucking Company .... C 330 478-1404
Canton *(G-2580)*
Wannemacher Enterprises Inc .... D 419 225-9060
Lima *(G-12912)*
Ward Trucking LLC .... E 330 659-6658
Richfield *(G-16532)*
Ward Trucking LLC .... E 614 275-3800
Columbus *(G-8966)*
Werner Enterprises Inc .... D 937 325-5403
Springfield *(G-17297)*
William R Morse .... E 440 352-2600
Painesville *(G-15887)*
World Shipping Inc .... E 440 356-7676
Cleveland *(G-6759)*
Xpo Cnw Inc .... C 440 716-8971
North Olmsted *(G-15451)*
Xpo Logistics Freight Inc .... C 513 870-0044
West Chester *(G-19244)*
Xpo Logistics Freight Inc .... E 419 499-8888
Milan *(G-14500)*
Xpo Logistics Freight Inc .... C 216 433-1000
Parma *(G-15919)*
Xpo Logistics Freight Inc .... E 740 894-3859
South Point *(G-17099)*
Xpo Logistics Freight Inc .... C 330 824-2242
Warren *(G-18930)*
Xpo Logistics Freight Inc .... E 419 294-5728
Upper Sandusky *(G-18572)*
Xpo Logistics Freight Inc .... D 419 666-3022
Perrysburg *(G-16075)*
Xpo Logistics Freight Inc .... D 330 896-7300
Uniontown *(G-18544)*
Xpo Logistics Freight Inc .... E 937 492-3899
Sidney *(G-16961)*
Xpo Logistics Freight Inc .... C 614 876-7100
Columbus *(G-9014)*
Yowell Transportation Svc Inc .... D 937 294-5933
Moraine *(G-14838)*
Yrc Inc .... C 513 874-9320
West Chester *(G-19245)*
Yrc Inc .... D 330 659-4151
Richfield *(G-16534)*
Yrc Inc .... B 419 729-0631
Toledo *(G-18327)*
Yrc Inc .... C 330 665-0274
Copley *(G-9070)*
Yrc Inc .... D 614 878-9281
Columbus *(G-9023)*
Zipline Logistics LLC .... D 888 469-4754
Columbus *(G-9027)*
Zone Transportation Co .... D 440 324-3544
Elyria *(G-10695)*

4214 Local Trucking With Storage

A C Leasing Company .... E 513 771-3676
Cincinnati *(G-2953)*
A Plus Expediting & Logistics .... E 937 424-0220
Dayton *(G-9298)*
Abco Contracting LLC .... E 419 973-4772
Toledo *(G-17739)*
Accelerated Moving & Stor Inc .... E 614 836-1007
Columbus *(G-6932)*
All My Sons Moving & Storge of .... E 614 405-7202
Hilliard *(G-11877)*
All Pro Freight Systems Inc .... D 440 934-2222
Avon *(G-874)*
Arms Trucking Co Inc .... E 800 362-1343
Huntsburg *(G-12156)*
Atlas Home Moving & Storage .... E 614 445-8831
Columbus *(G-7071)*
Bell Moving and Storage Inc .... E 513 942-7500
Fairfield *(G-10823)*
Brendamour Moving & Stor Inc .... D 800 354-9715
Cincinnati *(G-3129)*
Bridge Logistics Inc .... E 513 874-7444
West Chester *(G-19193)*
Circle T Logistics Inc .... E 740 262-5096
Marion *(G-13530)*
Clark Trucking Inc .... C 937 642-0335
East Liberty *(G-10508)*
Cleveland Express Trckg Co Inc .... D 216 348-0922
Cleveland *(G-5313)*
Containerport Group Inc .... E 216 341-4800
Cleveland *(G-5401)*
Corrigan Moving Systems-Ann AR .... E 419 874-2900
Perrysburg *(G-15989)*
County of Hancock .... E 419 422-7433
Findlay *(G-11018)*
Dhl Supply Chain (usa) .... E 419 727-4318
Toledo *(G-17852)*
Distribution and Trnsp Svc Inc .... E 937 295-3343
Fort Loramie *(G-11110)*
Essential Freight Systems Inc .... D 330 468-5898
Northfield *(G-15514)*
Getgo Transportation Co LLC .... E 419 666-6850
Millbury *(G-14579)*
Greater Dayton Mvg & Stor Co .... E 937 235-0011
Dayton *(G-9586)*
Henderson Trucking Inc .... E 740 369-6100
Delaware *(G-10105)*
J-Trac Inc .... E 419 524-3456
Mansfield *(G-13315)*
King Tut Logistics LLC .... E 614 538-0509
Columbus *(G-7994)*
Leaders Moving Company .... E 614 785-9595
Worthington *(G-19970)*
Lewis & Michael Inc .... E 937 252-6683
Dayton *(G-9679)*
Lincoln Moving & Storage Co .... D 216 741-5500
Cleveland *(G-5943)*
Locker Moving & Storage Inc .... E 330 784-0477
Canton *(G-2439)*
M G Q Inc .... E 419 992-4236
Tiffin *(G-17683)*
Mano Logistics LLC .... E 330 454-1307
Canton *(G-2444)*
Marietta Industrial Entps Inc .... D 740 373-2252
Marietta *(G-13470)*
Miami Valley Bekins Inc .... E 937 278-4296
Dayton *(G-9726)*
Midfitz Inc .... E 216 663-8816
Cleveland *(G-6055)*
Mitchell & Sons Moving & Stor .... E 419 289-3311
Ashland *(G-689)*
Moving Solutions Inc .... D 440 946-9300
Mentor *(G-14223)*
◆ **Mxd Group Inc** .... D 866 711-3129
New Albany *(G-14995)*
Neighborhood Logistics Co Inc .... E 440 466-0020
Geneva *(G-11366)*
Nicholas Carney-Mc Inc .... D 330 792-5460
Youngstown *(G-20301)*
Picklesimer Trucking Inc .... E 937 642-1091
Marysville *(G-13644)*
Piqua Transfer & Storage Co .... D 937 773-3743
Piqua *(G-16160)*
Planes Moving & Storage Inc .... C 513 759-6000
West Chester *(G-19129)*
Planes Mvg & Stor Co Columbus .... D 614 777-9090
Columbus *(G-8548)*
Proterra Inc .... E 216 383-8449
Wickliffe *(G-19612)*
R K Campf Corp .... E 330 332-7089
Salem *(G-16709)*
Ray Hamilton Companies .... E 513 641-5400
Blue Ash *(G-1676)*
River City Furniture LLC .... D 513 612-7303
West Chester *(G-19141)*
Rmb Enterprises Inc .... D 513 539-3431
Middletown *(G-14454)*
Rollins Moving and Storage Inc .... E 937 525-4013
Springfield *(G-17267)*
Security Storage Co Inc .... D 513 961-2700
Cincinnati *(G-4490)*
Shetler Moving & Stor of Ohio .... E 513 755-0700
West Chester *(G-19151)*
Shippers Consolidated Dist .... E 216 579-9303
Cleveland *(G-6478)*
Shoreline Express Inc .... E 440 878-3750
Strongsville *(G-17507)*
Smithfoods Trucking Inc .... E 330 684-6502
Orrville *(G-15788)*
Spartan Whse & Dist Co Inc .... D 614 497-1777
Columbus *(G-8758)*
Spears Transf & Expediting Inc .... E 937 275-2443
Dayton *(G-9895)*
State-Wide Express Inc .... D 216 676-4600
Cleveland *(G-6532)*
Taylor Distributing Company .... D 513 771-1850
Cincinnati *(G-4626)*
▲ **Tersher Corporation** .... D 440 439-8383
Strongsville *(G-17516)*
Thoman Weil Moving & Stor Co .... E 513 251-5000
Cincinnati *(G-4651)*
Tri Modal Service Inc .... E 614 876-6325
Columbus *(G-8867)*
University Moving & Storage Co .... E 248 615-7000
West Chester *(G-19174)*
Unpacking Etc .... E 440 871-0506
Westlake *(G-19561)*
Van Howards Lines Inc .... E 937 235-0007
Dayton *(G-9963)*
Van Mayberrys & Storage Inc .... E 937 298-8800
Moraine *(G-14832)*
Van Mills Lines Inc .... C 440 846-0200
Strongsville *(G-17521)*
Van Stevens Lines Inc .... E 419 729-8871
Toledo *(G-18286)*
Vance Property Management LLC .... D 419 467-9548
Toledo *(G-18287)*
William R Morse .... E 440 352-2600
Painesville *(G-15887)*
Willis Day Management Inc .... E 419 476-8000
Toledo *(G-18311)*
Wnb Group LLC .... E 513 641-5400
Cincinnati *(G-4855)*
Wooster Motor Ways Inc .... C 330 264-9557
Wooster *(G-19932)*
Yowell Transportation Svc Inc .... D 937 294-5933
Moraine *(G-14838)*

4215 Courier Svcs, Except Air

Centaur Mail Inc .... E 419 887-5857
Maumee *(G-13893)*
City Dash Inc .... C 513 562-2000
Cincinnati *(G-3357)*
City Taxicab & Transfer Co .... E 440 992-2156
Ashtabula *(G-731)*
Clockwork Logistics Inc .... E 216 587-5371
Garfield Heights *(G-11351)*
Clp Towne Inc .... E 440 234-3324
Brookpark *(G-1940)*
Elite Expediting Corp .... D 614 279-1181
Worthington *(G-19956)*
Fed Ex Rob Carpenter .... E 419 260-1889
Maumee *(G-13915)*
Federal Express Corporation .... D 800 463-3339
Miamisburg *(G-14301)*
Federal Express Corporation .... D 937 898-3474
Vandalia *(G-18680)*
Federal Express Corporation .... B 614 492-6106
Columbus *(G-7646)*
Fedex Freight Corporation .... E 800 521-3505
Lima *(G-12781)*
Fedex Ground Package Sys Inc .... E 330 244-1534
Canton *(G-2366)*

S I C

Employee Codes: A=Over 500 employees, B=251-500
C=101-250, D=51-100, E=25-50

2018 Harris Ohio
Services Directory

923

Fedex Ground Package Sys Inc ....C....... 800 463-3339
Richfield *(G-16509)*
Fedex Ground Package Sys Inc ....B....... 800 463-3339
Toledo *(G-17884)*
Fedex Smartpost Inc ....D....... 800 463-3339
Grove City *(G-11561)*
Firelands Security Services ....E....... 419 627-0562
Sandusky *(G-16759)*
Keller Logistics Group Inc ....D....... 419 784-4805
Defiance *(G-10039)*
Palmer Express Incorporated ....E....... 440 942-3333
Willoughby *(G-19702)*
Prestige Delivery Systems LLC ....D....... 216 332-8000
Cleveland *(G-6304)*
Prime Time Enterprises Inc ....E....... 440 891-8855
Cleveland *(G-6306)*
Priority Dispatch Inc ....E....... 216 332-9852
Solon *(G-17041)*
Robert M Neff Inc ....D....... 614 444-1562
Columbus *(G-8642)*
Rush Package Delivery Inc ....C....... 937 224-7874
Dayton *(G-9858)*
SMS Transport LLC ....E....... 937 813-8897
Dayton *(G-9886)*
Stat Express Delivery LLC ....E....... 614 880-7828
Worthington *(G-20000)*
United Parcel Service Inc ....B....... 440 826-2591
Cleveland *(G-6643)*
United Parcel Service Inc ....D....... 937 859-2314
West Carrollton *(G-19010)*
United Parcel Service Inc ....E....... 800 742-5877
Chillicothe *(G-2892)*
United Parcel Service Inc ....E....... 614 431-0600
Columbus *(G-8896)*
United Parcel Service Inc ....E....... 440 846-6000
Strongsville *(G-17519)*
United Parcel Service Inc OH ....C....... 419 747-3080
Mansfield *(G-13380)*
United Parcel Service Inc OH ....C....... 513 852-6135
Cincinnati *(G-4736)*
United Parcel Service Inc OH ....C....... 800 742-5877
Cleveland *(G-6644)*
United Parcel Service Inc OH ....C....... 740 373-0772
Marietta *(G-13511)*
United Parcel Service Inc OH ....D....... 419 222-7399
Lima *(G-12909)*
United Parcel Service Inc OH ....C....... 440 826-3320
Wooster *(G-19921)*
United Parcel Service Inc OH ....A....... 419 891-6776
Maumee *(G-13990)*
United Parcel Service Inc OH ....C....... 419 424-9494
Findlay *(G-11095)*
United Parcel Service Inc OH ....C....... 330 545-0177
Girard *(G-11427)*
United Parcel Service Inc OH ....D....... 440 275-3301
Austinburg *(G-866)*
United Parcel Service Inc OH ....C....... 330 339-6281
New Philadelphia *(G-15120)*
United Parcel Service Inc OH ....C....... 740 598-4293
Brilliant *(G-1870)*
United Parcel Service Inc OH ....E....... 740 592-4570
Athens *(G-818)*
United Parcel Service Inc OH ....E....... 740 968-3508
Saint Clairsville *(G-16658)*
United Parcel Service Inc OH ....C....... 614 841-7159
Columbus *(G-8897)*
United Parcel Service Inc OH ....C....... 800 742-5877
Zanesville *(G-20542)*
United Parcel Service Inc OH ....D....... 419 891-6841
Toledo *(G-18271)*
United Parcel Service Inc OH ....C....... 330 478-1007
Canton *(G-2570)*
United Parcel Service Inc OH ....C....... 419 586-8556
Celina *(G-2665)*
United Parcel Service Inc OH ....C....... 513 241-5289
Cincinnati *(G-4737)*
United Parcel Service Inc OH ....C....... 614 383-4580
Marion *(G-13593)*
United Parcel Service Inc OH ....C....... 513 782-4000
Cincinnati *(G-4738)*
United Parcel Service Inc OH ....D....... 513 241-5316
Cincinnati *(G-4739)*
United Parcel Service Inc OH ....C....... 419 872-0211
Perrysburg *(G-16066)*
United Parcel Service Inc OH ....C....... 614 272-8500
Obetz *(G-15672)*
United Parcel Service Inc OH ....D....... 513 863-1681
Hamilton *(G-11781)*
United Parcel Service Inc OH ....C....... 937 773-4762
Piqua *(G-16170)*
United Parcel Service Inc OH ....D....... 419 782-3552
Defiance *(G-10062)*
United Parcel Service Inc OH ....C....... 937 382-0658
Wilmington *(G-19791)*
United Parcel Service Inc OH ....C....... 800 742-5877
Youngstown *(G-20399)*
United Parcel Service Inc OH ....B....... 740 363-0636
Delaware *(G-10133)*
United States Cargo & Courier ....E....... 216 325-0483
Cleveland *(G-6646)*
United States Cargo & Courier ....E....... 614 449-2854
Columbus *(G-8900)*

4221 Farm Product Warehousing & Storage

Consolidated Grain & Barge Co ....E....... 513 941-4805
Cincinnati *(G-3411)*
Consolidated Grain & Barge Co ....D....... 419 785-1941
Defiance *(G-10023)*
Deerfield Farms Service Inc ....D....... 330 584-4715
Deerfield *(G-10019)*
Mercer Landmark Inc ....E....... 419 586-7443
Celina *(G-2655)*

4222 Refrigerated Warehousing & Storage

Americold Logistics LLC ....D....... 330 834-1742
Massillon *(G-13785)*
Cloverleaf Cold Storage Co ....E....... 330 833-9870
Massillon *(G-13797)*
Cloverleaf Cold Storage Co ....C....... 419 599-5015
Napoleon *(G-14934)*
Crescent Park Corporation ....C....... 513 759-7000
West Chester *(G-19059)*
D & D Investment Co ....E....... 614 272-6567
Columbus *(G-7476)*
Exel N Amercn Logistics Inc ....C....... 937 854-7900
Dayton *(G-9535)*
Fresh Mark Inc ....B....... 330 833-9870
Massillon *(G-13811)*
Gorbett Enterprises of Solon ....E....... 440 248-3950
Solon *(G-17011)*
Interstate Warehousing VA LLC ....D....... 513 874-6500
Fairfield *(G-10863)*
RLR Investments LLC ....D....... 937 382-1494
Wilmington *(G-19783)*
Woodruff Enterprises Inc ....E....... 937 399-9300
Springfield *(G-17301)*

4225 General Warehousing & Storage

A Duie Pyle Inc ....D....... 330 342-7750
Streetsboro *(G-17404)*
A1 Quality Labor Svc ....E....... 513 353-0173
Cincinnati *(G-2957)*
Aero Fulfillment Services Corp ....D....... 800 225-7145
Mason *(G-13658)*
Aero Fulfillment Services Corp ....D....... 513 874-4112
West Chester *(G-19014)*
Akron Porcelain & Plastics Co ....E....... 330 745-2159
Barberton *(G-951)*
Al-Mar Lanes ....E....... 419 352-4637
Bowling Green *(G-1757)*
Albring Vending Company ....E....... 419 726-8059
Toledo *(G-17746)*
Aldi Inc ....D....... 330 273-7351
Hinckley *(G-11994)*
All Pro Freight Systems Inc ....D....... 440 934-2222
Avon *(G-874)*
AM Industrial Group LLC ....E....... 216 267-6783
Cleveland *(G-5000)*
Andersen Distribution Inc ....C....... 937 898-7844
Dayton *(G-9336)*
Andersons Inc ....C....... 419 891-6479
Maumee *(G-13877)*
Andersons Inc ....C....... 419 893-5050
Maumee *(G-13880)*
Arett Sales Corp ....D....... 937 552-2005
Troy *(G-18348)*
Asw Global LLC ....D....... 330 733-6291
Mogadore *(G-14670)*
Asw Global LLC ....D....... 330 899-1003
Canton *(G-2247)*
Asw Global LLC ....D....... 330 798-5184
Mogadore *(G-14671)*
Atotech USA Inc ....D....... 216 398-0550
Cleveland *(G-5080)*
Bartram & Sons Groceries ....E....... 740 532-5216
Ironton *(G-12281)*
Basista Furniture Inc ....E....... 216 398-5900
Cleveland *(G-5099)*
BDS Inc ....E....... 513 921-8441
Cincinnati *(G-3086)*
Big Sandy Distribution Inc ....C....... 740 574-2113
Franklin Furnace *(G-11168)*
Big Sandy Furniture Inc ....D....... 740 574-2113
Franklin Furnace *(G-11169)*
Big Sandy Furniture Inc ....E....... 740 354-3193
Portsmouth *(G-16265)*
Big Sandy Furniture Inc ....E....... 740 775-4244
Chillicothe *(G-2816)*
Big Sandy Furniture Inc ....E....... 740 894-4242
Chesapeake *(G-2781)*
Briar-Gate Realty Inc ....E....... 614 299-2121
Columbus *(G-7133)*
Building Systems Trnsp Co ....C....... 740 852-9700
London *(G-12994)*
Burd Brothers Inc ....D....... 800 538-2873
Batavia *(G-996)*
Calypso Logistics LLC ....C....... 614 262-8911
Columbus *(G-7179)*
Caterpillar Inc ....D....... 614 834-2400
Canal Winchester *(G-2155)*
Central Equity Investments Inc ....E....... 937 454-1270
Vandalia *(G-18668)*
Childrens Hospital Medical Ctr ....A....... 513 636-4200
Cincinnati *(G-3253)*
Cloverleaf Cold Storage Co ....C....... 419 599-5015
Napoleon *(G-14934)*
Compass Self Storage LLC ....E....... 216 458-0670
Cleveland *(G-5388)*
Comprehensive Logistics Co Inc ....E....... 330 233-0805
Parma *(G-15902)*
Comprehensive Logistics Co Inc ....E....... 440 934-0870
Lorain *(G-13032)*
Comprehensive Logistics Co Inc ....E....... 800 734-0372
Youngstown *(G-20159)*
Containerport Group Inc ....E....... 216 341-4800
Cleveland *(G-5401)*
Cotter Mdse Stor of Ohio ....E....... 330 773-9177
Akron *(G-166)*
Cotter Moving & Storage Co ....E....... 330 535-5115
Akron *(G-167)*
Crescent Park Corporation ....C....... 513 759-7000
West Chester *(G-19059)*
D M I Distribution Inc ....E....... 765 584-3234
Columbus *(G-7481)*
Daikin Applied Americas Inc ....E....... 763 553-5009
Dayton *(G-9450)*
Daniel Logistics Inc ....D....... 614 367-9442
Columbus *(G-7487)*
Dayton Heidelberg Distrg Co ....C....... 419 666-9783
Perrysburg *(G-15994)*
Dedicated Logistics Inc ....D....... 513 275-1135
West Chester *(G-19060)*
Dhl Supply Chain (usa) ....E....... 419 727-4318
Toledo *(G-17852)*
Dhl Supply Chain (usa) ....D....... 513 482-6015
Cincinnati *(G-3486)*
Dhl Supply Chain (usa) ....D....... 614 895-1959
Westerville *(G-19299)*
Dhl Supply Chain (usa) ....D....... 740 929-2113
Hebron *(G-11848)*
Dhl Supply Chain (usa) ....B....... 614 662-9247
Groveport *(G-11634)*
Dhl Supply Chain (usa) ....E....... 513 942-1575
Cincinnati *(G-3487)*
Dhl Supply Chain (usa) ....E....... 513 745-7445
Blue Ash *(G-1578)*
Dolgencorp LLC ....A....... 740 588-5700
Zanesville *(G-20468)*
Doylestown Telephone Company ....E....... 330 658-6666
Doylestown *(G-10229)*
DSC Logistics Inc ....D....... 847 390-6800
Toledo *(G-17857)*
E and P Warehouse Services Ltd ....E....... 330 898-4800
Warren *(G-18852)*
Efco Corp ....E....... 614 876-1226
Columbus *(G-7586)*
Enterprise Vending Inc ....E....... 513 772-1373
Cincinnati *(G-3560)*
Essilor of America Inc ....C....... 614 492-0888
Groveport *(G-11637)*
Exel Inc ....D....... 419 996-7703
Lima *(G-12774)*
Exel Inc ....D....... 419 226-5500
Lima *(G-12775)*
Exel Inc ....E....... 614 865-8294
Westerville *(G-19304)*
Exel Inc ....D....... 740 927-1762
Etna *(G-10734)*
Exel Inc ....E....... 614 670-6473
Lockbourne *(G-12952)*

42 MOTOR FREIGHT TRANSPORTATION AND WAREHOUSING

Exel Inc .... B 614 865-8500
  Westerville *(G-19305)*
Faro Services Inc .... B 614 497-1700
  Groveport *(G-11639)*
Federal Express Corporation .... B 614 492-6106
  Columbus *(G-7646)*
Fedex Sup Chain Dist Sys Inc .... C 614 277-3970
  Groveport *(G-11640)*
Fedex Supply Chain .... B 412 820-3700
  Lockbourne *(G-12954)*
First Group Investment Partnr .... D 513 241-2200
  Cincinnati *(G-3618)*
Firstgroup Usa Inc .... B 513 241-2200
  Cincinnati *(G-3629)*
Fremont Logistics LLC .... D 419 333-0669
  Fremont *(G-11202)*
Frito-Lay North America Inc .... E 330 786-6000
  Akron *(G-231)*
Fuchs Lubricants Co .... E 330 963-0400
  Twinsburg *(G-18419)*
Fulfillment Technologies LLC .... C 513 346-3100
  West Chester *(G-19203)*
Fusion Ceramics Inc .... E 330 627-5821
  Carrollton *(G-2620)*
G & J Pepsi-Cola Bottlers Inc .... D 740 593-3366
  Athens *(G-788)*
G & J Pepsi-Cola Bottlers Inc .... E 937 393-5744
  Wilmington *(G-19763)*
G & S Metal Products Co Inc .... C 216 831-2388
  Cleveland *(G-5644)*
General Motors LLC .... C 513 874-0535
  West Chester *(G-19080)*
Getgo Transportation Co LLC .... E 419 666-6850
  Millbury *(G-14579)*
GMI Holdings Inc .... D 330 794-0846
  Akron *(G-239)*
Goodwill Ester Seals Miami Vly .... B 937 461-4800
  Dayton *(G-9580)*
Graham Investment Co .... D 740 382-0902
  Marion *(G-13541)*
Graybar Electric Company Inc .... E 330 799-3220
  Youngstown *(G-20204)*
Great Value Storage .... E 614 848-8420
  Columbus *(G-7772)*
H & O Distribution Inc .... E 513 874-2090
  Fairfield *(G-10855)*
Handl-It Inc .... C 330 468-0734
  Macedonia *(G-13201)*
Home Depot USA Inc .... D 513 360-1100
  Monroe *(G-14698)*
Hyperlogistics Group Inc .... E 614 497-0800
  Columbus *(G-7876)*
Ieh Auto Parts LLC .... E 216 351-2560
  Cleveland *(G-5802)*
Ingersoll-Rand Company .... E 419 633-6800
  Bryan *(G-2008)*
Inter Distr Svcs of Cleve .... E 330 468-4949
  Macedonia *(G-13203)*
J B Express Inc .... D 740 702-9830
  Chillicothe *(G-2854)*
J-Trac Inc .... E 419 524-3456
  Mansfield *(G-13315)*
Jacobson Warehouse Company Inc ... E 614 409-0003
  Groveport *(G-11650)*
Jacobson Warehouse Company Inc ... D 614 497-6300
  Groveport *(G-11651)*
Keller Warehousing & Dist LLC .... C 419 784-4805
  Defiance *(G-10041)*
Kenco Group Inc .... E 614 409-8754
  Groveport *(G-11653)*
King Tut Logistics LLC .... E 614 538-0509
  Columbus *(G-7994)*
Kmart Corporation .... B 614 836-5000
  Groveport *(G-11654)*
Kmart Corporation .... A 330 372-6688
  Warren *(G-18871)*
Kuehne + Nagel Inc .... E 419 635-4051
  Port Clinton *(G-16249)*
Kyocera SGS Precision Tools .... E 330 922-1953
  Cuyahoga Falls *(G-9204)*
Lakota Local School District .... C 513 777-2150
  Liberty Township *(G-12722)*
Lesaint Logistics Inc .... C 513 874-3900
  West Chester *(G-19105)*
Lesaint Logistics LLC .... C 513 874-3900
  West Chester *(G-19106)*
Lesaint Logistics LLC .... D 513 988-0101
  Trenton *(G-18341)*
Lewis & Michael Inc .... E 937 252-6683
  Dayton *(G-9679)*

Liberty Insulation Co Inc .... E 513 621-0108
  Milford *(G-14530)*
Locker Moving & Storage Inc .... E 330 784-0477
  Canton *(G-2439)*
Lowes Home Centers LLC .... C 419 429-5700
  Findlay *(G-11058)*
Lowes Home Centers LLC .... E 740 636-2100
  Wshngtn CT Hs *(G-20029)*
M A Folkes Company Inc .... E 513 785-4200
  Hamilton *(G-11756)*
Malleys Candies Inc .... E 216 529-6262
  Cleveland *(G-5974)*
Mansfield Whsng & Dist Inc .... C 419 522-3510
  Ontario *(G-15699)*
Marc Glassman Inc .... E 216 265-7700
  Cleveland *(G-5977)*
McM Electronics Inc .... D 937 434-0031
  Dayton *(G-9708)*
Menlo Logistics Inc .... E 740 963-1154
  Etna *(G-10736)*
Micro Electronics Inc .... D 614 334-1430
  Columbus *(G-8160)*
Mid-Ohio Development Corp .... E 614 836-0606
  Groveport *(G-11657)*
Mid-Ohio Mechanical Inc .... E 740 587-3362
  Granville *(G-11470)*
Midwest Trmnals Tledo Intl Inc .... E 419 698-8171
  Toledo *(G-18064)*
Mxd Group Inc .... E 614 801-0621
  Columbus *(G-8210)*
Nifco America Corporation .... C 614 836-8733
  Groveport *(G-11659)*
North Coast Logistics Inc .... E 216 362-7159
  Brookpark *(G-1952)*
Oatey Supply Chain Svcs Inc .... E 216 267-7100
  Cleveland *(G-6177)*
Odw Logistics Inc .... B 614 549-5000
  Columbus *(G-8313)*
Ohio Desk Co .... E 216 623-0600
  Brooklyn Heights *(G-1922)*
Osborne Trucking Company .... D 513 874-2090
  Fairfield *(G-10890)*
P-Americas LLC .... C 330 746-7652
  Youngstown *(G-20313)*
Parker-Hannifin Corporation .... D 419 878-7000
  Waterville *(G-18943)*
Parker-Hannifin Corporation .... A 216 531-3000
  Cleveland *(G-6241)*
PC Connection Sales Corp .... C 937 382-4800
  Wilmington *(G-19776)*
Peoples Cartage Inc .... E 330 833-8571
  Massillon *(G-13843)*
Peoples Services Inc .... E 330 453-3709
  Canton *(G-2490)*
Pepsi-Cola Metro Btlg Co Inc .... E 330 336-3553
  Wadsworth *(G-18767)*
Pepsi-Cola Metro Btlg Co Inc .... E 440 323-5524
  Elyria *(G-10669)*
Piqua Steel Co .... E 937 773-3632
  Piqua *(G-16159)*
Prime Time Enterprises Inc .... E 440 891-8855
  Cleveland *(G-6306)*
Public Storage .... E 216 220-7978
  Bedford Heights *(G-1357)*
Restaurant Depot LLC .... E 216 525-0101
  Cleveland *(G-6386)*
Restaurant Equippers Inc .... E 614 358-6622
  Columbus *(G-8624)*
Roppe Holding Company .... E 419 435-9335
  Fostoria *(G-11139)*
RR Donnelley & Sons Company .... E 614 539-5527
  Grove City *(G-11593)*
Safelite Fulfillment Inc .... E 614 781-5449
  Columbus *(G-8670)*
Safelite Fulfillment Inc .... E 216 475-7781
  Cleveland *(G-6435)*
Sally Beauty Supply LLC .... C 937 548-7684
  Greenville *(G-11518)*
Sally Beauty Supply LLC .... C 614 278-1691
  Columbus *(G-8678)*
SH Bell Company .... E 412 963-9910
  East Liverpool *(G-10534)*
South E Harley Davidson Sls Co ...... E 440 439-3013
  Cleveland *(G-6437)*
Springs Window Fashions LLC .... D 614 492-6770
  Groveport *(G-11673)*
Surface Combustion Inc .... E 419 878-8444
  Waterville *(G-18946)*
Sygma Network Inc .... B 614 734-2500
  Dublin *(G-10469)*

Synnex Corporation .... E 614 539-6995
  Grove City *(G-11603)*
Taylor Warehouse Corporation .... E 513 771-2956
  Cincinnati *(G-4627)*
Terminal Warehouse Inc .... E 330 453-3709
  Canton *(G-2559)*
Terminal Warehouse Inc .... D 330 773-2056
  Akron *(G-475)*
The C-Z Company .... E 740 432-6334
  Cambridge *(G-2131)*
The Maple City Ice Company .... E 419 747-4777
  Mansfield *(G-13373)*
Tmarzetti Company .... C 614 277-3577
  Grove City *(G-11605)*
Top Dawg Group LLC .... E 216 398-1066
  Brooklyn Heights *(G-1928)*
Total Warehousing Services .... D 419 562-2878
  Bucyrus *(G-2048)*
Triple Ladys Agency Inc .... E 330 274-1100
  Mantua *(G-13396)*
TRT Management Corporation .... E 419 661-1233
  Perrysburg *(G-16065)*
Twist Inc .... E 937 675-9581
  Xenia *(G-20081)*
Utility Trailer Mfg Co .... E 513 436-2600
  Batavia *(G-1031)*
Verst Group Logistics Inc .... C 513 782-1725
  Cincinnati *(G-4809)*
Verst Group Logistics Inc .... E 513 772-2494
  Cincinnati *(G-4810)*
Victory White Metal Company .... E 216 271-7200
  Cleveland *(G-6695)*
W W Williams Company LLC .... E 614 228-5000
  Columbus *(G-8960)*
Walmart Inc .... B 937 843-3681
  Belle Center *(G-1373)*
Walmart Inc .... A 740 636-5400
  Wshngtn CT Hs *(G-20036)*
Walmart Inc .... A 614 871-7094
  Grove City *(G-11611)*
Walmart Inc .... B 740 765-5700
  Wintersville *(G-19811)*
Walmart Inc .... B 614 409-5500
  Lockbourne *(G-12962)*
Warehouse Services Group Llc .... E 419 868-6400
  Holland *(G-12068)*
Westway Trml Cincinnati LLC .... E 513 921-8441
  Cincinnati *(G-4846)*
Whirlpool Corporation .... C 419 547-2610
  Clyde *(G-6825)*
Willis Day Management Inc .... E 419 476-8000
  Toledo *(G-18311)*
Willis Day Storage Co .... E 419 470-6255
  Toledo *(G-18312)*
Wright Distribution Centers .... E 419 227-7621
  Lima *(G-12922)*

4226 Special Warehousing & Storage, NEC

Andreas Furniture Company .... E 330 852-2494
  Sugarcreek *(G-17543)*
Atrium Apparel Corporation .... D 612 889-0959
  Johnstown *(G-12335)*
Auto Warehousing Co Inc .... E 419 727-1534
  Toledo *(G-17761)*
Ballreich Bros Inc .... C 419 447-1814
  Tiffin *(G-17672)*
BDS Inc .... E 513 921-8441
  Cincinnati *(G-3086)*
Briar-Gate Realty Inc .... E 614 299-2122
  Grove City *(G-11536)*
Briar-Gate Realty Inc .... D 614 299-2121
  Grove City *(G-11537)*
Comprehensive Logistics Co Inc ..... E 330 793-0504
  Youngstown *(G-20158)*
Distribution and Trnsp Svc Inc .... E 937 295-3343
  Fort Loramie *(G-11110)*
Eddie Bauer LLC .... E 614 278-9281
  Columbus *(G-7576)*
Exel Holdings (usa) Inc .... C 614 865-8500
  Westerville *(G-19303)*
General Motors LLC .... C 513 603-6600
  West Chester *(G-19081)*
Great Value Storage .... E 614 848-8420
  Columbus *(G-7772)*
High Line Corporation .... E 330 848-8800
  Akron *(G-264)*
Honda Logistics North Amer Inc ..... A 937 642-0335
  East Liberty *(G-10509)*
Infostore LLC .... E 216 749-4636
  Cleveland *(G-5820)*

Employee Codes: A=Over 500 employees, B=251-500
C=101-250, D=51-100, E=25-50

42 MOTOR FREIGHT TRANSPORTATION AND WAREHOUSING

Interstate Warehousing VA LLC .... D 513 874-6500
  Fairfield *(G-10863)*
Iron Mountain Incorporated .... D 513 874-3535
  West Chester *(G-19094)*
Iron Mountain Incorporated .... D 614 801-0151
  Urbancrest *(G-18605)*
Iron Mountain Info MGT LLC .... E 513 297-3268
  Cincinnati *(G-3844)*
Iron Mountain Info MGT LLC .... E 513 942-7300
  Hamilton *(G-11747)*
Iron Mountain Info MGT LLC .... E 513 297-1906
  West Chester *(G-19095)*
Iron Mountain Info MGT LLC .... E 614 840-9321
  Columbus *(G-7922)*
Iron Mountain Info MGT LLC .... C 440 248-0999
  Solon *(G-17019)*
Iron Mountain Info MGT LLC .... E 513 247-2183
  Blue Ash *(G-1617)*
Jacobson Warehouse Company Inc ..... C 614 314-1091
  Obetz *(G-15668)*
Kitchen Collection LLC .... E 740 773-9150
  Chillicothe *(G-2858)*
Kuhlman Corporation .... C 419 897-6000
  Maumee *(G-13934)*
Lefco Worthington LLC .... E 216 432-4422
  Cleveland *(G-5931)*
Locker Moving & Storage Inc .... E 330 784-0477
  Canton *(G-2439)*
Midwest Express Inc .... A 937 642-0335
  East Liberty *(G-10510)*
Nex Transport Inc .... C 937 645-3761
  East Liberty *(G-10512)*
Odw Logistics Inc .... B 614 549-5000
  Columbus *(G-8313)*
PC Connection Inc .... C 937 382-4800
  Wilmington *(G-19775)*
Radial South LP .... C 678 584-4047
  Groveport *(G-11665)*
Ray Hamilton Companies .... E 513 641-5400
  Blue Ash *(G-1676)*
SH Bell Company .... E 412 963-9910
  East Liverpool *(G-10534)*
Ship Shape Marine Inc .... E 419 734-1554
  Port Clinton *(G-16255)*
Target Corporation .... C 513 671-8603
  Cincinnati *(G-4625)*
Target Corporation .... B 614 801-6700
  West Jefferson *(G-19255)*
Vista Industrial Packaging LLC .... D 800 454-6117
  Columbus *(G-8945)*
Warren City Board Education .... E 330 841-2265
  Warren *(G-18923)*
Wooster Motor Ways Inc .... C 330 264-9557
  Wooster *(G-19932)*

4231 Terminal & Joint Terminal Maint Facilities

Chieftain Trucking & Excav Inc .... E 216 485-8034
  Cleveland *(G-5235)*
Dayton Freight Lines Inc .... D 937 236-4880
  Dayton *(G-9475)*
Disttech LLC .... D 800 321-3143
  Cleveland *(G-5490)*
Eab Truck Service .... D 216 525-0020
  Cleveland *(G-5517)*
Fedex Freight Corporation .... E 877 661-8956
  Mentor *(G-14175)*
Ground Effects LLC .... E 440 565-5925
  Westlake *(G-19487)*
PAm Transportation Svcs Inc .... D 419 935-9501
  Willard *(G-19624)*
Pitt-Ohio Express LLC .... B 216 433-9000
  Cleveland *(G-6284)*
Short Freight Lines Inc .... E 419 729-1691
  Toledo *(G-18185)*
Slay Transportation Co Inc .... C 740 865-2910
  Sardis *(G-16815)*
Stover Transportation Inc .... E 614 777-4184
  Hilliard *(G-11955)*
STS Logistics Inc .... E 419 294-1498
  Upper Sandusky *(G-18567)*
Xpo Logistics Freight Inc .... C 614 876-7100
  Columbus *(G-9014)*
Xpo Logistics Freight Inc .... D 330 896-7300
  Uniontown *(G-18544)*
Yrc Inc .... D 614 878-9281
  Columbus *(G-9023)*

44 WATER TRANSPORTATION

4412 Deep Sea Foreign Transportation Of Freight

APL Logistics Ltd .... C 440 930-2822
  Avon Lake *(G-921)*
Toula Industries Ltd LLC .... C 937 689-1818
  Dayton *(G-9934)*

4432 Freight Transportation On The Great Lakes

The Interlake Steamship Co .... E 440 260-6900
  Middleburg Heights *(G-14388)*

4449 Water Transportation Of Freight, NEC

Consolidated Grain & Barge Co .... E 513 941-4805
  Cincinnati *(G-3411)*

4481 Deep Sea Transportation Of Passengers

AAA Allied Group Inc .... D 513 228-0866
  Lebanon *(G-12586)*

4482 Ferries

Kelleys Isle Ferry Boat Lines .... E 419 798-9763
  Marblehead *(G-13421)*
▲ Miller Boat Line Inc .... D 419 285-2421
  Put In Bay *(G-16369)*

4491 Marine Cargo Handling

A-1 Quality Labor Services LLC .... E 513 678-0724
  Cincinnati *(G-2956)*
Bellaire Harbor Service LLC .... E 740 676-4305
  Bellaire *(G-1361)*
Cincinnati Bulk Terminals LLC .... E 513 621-4800
  Cincinnati *(G-3290)*
Consolidated Grain & Barge Co .... E 513 941-4805
  Cincinnati *(G-3411)*
Cooper/T Smith Corporation .... E 419 626-0801
  Sandusky *(G-16747)*
Kinder Mrgan Lqds Trminals LLC .... E 513 841-0500
  Cincinnati *(G-3924)*
Marietta Industrial Entps Inc .... D 740 373-2252
  Marietta *(G-13470)*
McGinnis Inc .... C 740 377-4391
  South Point *(G-17092)*
McGinnis Inc .... E 513 941-8070
  Cincinnati *(G-4037)*
McNational Inc .... E 740 377-4391
  South Point *(G-17093)*
◆ Pinney Dock & Transport LLC .... E 440 964-7186
  Ashtabula *(G-760)*
Reserve Ftl LLC .... E 440 519-1768
  Twinsburg *(G-18460)*
Toledo-Lucas County Port Auth .... E 419 243-8251
  Toledo *(G-18255)*
Toledo-Lucas County Port Auth .... E 419 865-2351
  Swanton *(G-17573)*

4492 Towing & Tugboat Svcs

A M & O Towing Inc .... E 330 385-0639
  Negley *(G-14958)*
Great Lakes Group .... C 216 621-4854
  Cleveland *(G-5689)*
Shelly Materials Inc .... D 740 246-6315
  Thornville *(G-17668)*

4493 Marinas

Catawba-Cleveland Dev Corp .... D 419 797-4424
  Port Clinton *(G-16239)*
Containerport Group Inc .... E 513 771-0275
  West Chester *(G-19049)*
Erie Island Resort and Marina .... E 419 734-9117
  Warren *(G-18856)*
Island Service Company .... C 419 285-3695
  Put In Bay *(G-16368)*
S B S Transit Inc .... B 440 288-2222
  Lorain *(G-13075)*
Sandusky Harbor Marina Inc .... E 419 627-1201
  Sandusky *(G-16791)*
Saw Mill Creek Ltd .... C 419 433-3800
  Huron *(G-12170)*
Sima Marine Sales Inc .... E 440 269-3200
  Willoughby *(G-19714)*
Tack-Anew Inc .... E 419 734-4212
  Port Clinton *(G-16257)*
Tappan Lake Marina Inc .... E 740 269-2031
  Scio *(G-16817)*
Vermilion Boat Club Inc .... E 440 967-6634
  Vermilion *(G-18719)*

4499 Water Transportation Svcs, NEC

MPW Industrial Water Svcs Inc .... C 800 827-8790
  Hebron *(G-11856)*
Ship Shape Marine Inc .... E 419 734-1554
  Port Clinton *(G-16255)*
South Shore Marine Services .... E 419 433-5798
  Huron *(G-12174)*

45 TRANSPORTATION BY AIR

4512 Air Transportation, Scheduled

American Airlines Inc .... E 937 890-6668
  Vandalia *(G-18657)*
American Airlines Inc .... E 216 898-1347
  Cleveland *(G-5004)*
Champlain Enterprises LLC .... A 440 779-4588
  North Olmsted *(G-15413)*
City of Dayton .... C 937 454-8200
  Vandalia *(G-18672)*
Delta Air Lines Inc .... D 614 239-4440
  Columbus *(G-7506)*
Distribution and Trnsp Svc Inc .... E 937 295-3343
  Fort Loramie *(G-11110)*
Envoy Air Inc .... D 614 231-4391
  Columbus *(G-7601)*
Executive Jet Management Inc .... B 513 979-6600
  Cincinnati *(G-3586)*
Federal Express Corporation .... E 614 492-6106
  Columbus *(G-7646)*
Flight Express Inc .... D 305 379-8686
  Columbus *(G-7675)*
Lane Aviation Corporation .... C 614 237-3747
  Columbus *(G-8037)*
Menzies Aviation (texas) Inc .... E 216 362-6565
  Cleveland *(G-6026)*
Psa Airlines Inc .... D 937 454-9338
  Vandalia *(G-18694)*
Psa Airlines Inc .... C 937 454-1116
  Vandalia *(G-18695)*
United Airlines Inc .... E 937 454-2009
  Vandalia *(G-18703)*
United Airlines Inc .... C 216 501-4700
  Cleveland *(G-6633)*
United Parcel Service Inc OH .... B 740 363-0636
  Delaware *(G-10133)*

4513 Air Courier Svcs

Abx Air Inc .... B 937 382-5591
  Wilmington *(G-19741)*
Abx Air Inc .... A 937 366-2282
  Wilmington *(G-19742)*
Air Transport Svcs Group Inc .... E 937 382-5591
  Wilmington *(G-19743)*
Ames Material Services Inc .... A 937 382-5591
  Wilmington *(G-19746)*
Clp Towne Inc .... E 440 234-3324
  Brookpark *(G-1940)*
Dhl Express (usa) Inc .... E 614 865-8325
  Westerville *(G-19297)*
Dhl Express (usa) Inc .... E 800 225-5345
  Lockbourne *(G-12949)*
Dhl Express (usa) Inc .... E 440 239-0670
  Cleveland *(G-5480)*
Federal Express Corporation .... D 800 463-3339
  Miamisburg *(G-14301)*
Federal Express Corporation .... E 800 463-3339
  Mansfield *(G-13300)*
Federal Express Corporation .... B 614 492-6106
  Columbus *(G-7646)*
Federal Express Corporation .... E 800 463-3339
  Lima *(G-12780)*
Federal Express Corporation .... C 800 463-3339
  Northwood *(G-15531)*
Federal Express Corporation .... C 800 463-3339
  Columbus *(G-7647)*
Federal Express Corporation .... C 800 463-3339
  Columbus *(G-7648)*
Federal Express Corporation .... D 800 463-3339
  Vandalia *(G-18679)*
Federal Express Corporation .... E 800 463-3339
  Canton *(G-2365)*
Federal Express Corporation .... D 937 898-3474
  Vandalia *(G-18680)*

Fedex Corporation E 440 234-0315
Cleveland *(G-5584)*

Fedex Corporation E 614 801-0953
Grove City *(G-11559)*

Fedex Freight Corporation E 800 979-9232
Chillicothe *(G-2837)*

Fedex Ground Package Sys Inc E 800 463-3339
Chillicothe *(G-2838)*

Fedex Ground Package Sys Inc E 800 463-3339
Richfield *(G-16508)*

Fedex Office & Print Svcs Inc E 440 946-6353
Willoughby *(G-19664)*

Garda CL Technical Svcs Inc E 937 294-4099
Moraine *(G-14788)*

Lgstx Services Inc D 866 931-2337
Wilmington *(G-19766)*

Prestige Delivery Systems LLC D 216 332-8000
Cleveland *(G-6304)*

Prime Time Enterprises Inc E 440 891-8855
Cleveland *(G-6306)*

United Parcel Service Inc D 614 385-9100
Columbus *(G-8895)*

United Parcel Service Inc OH D 419 222-7399
Lima *(G-12909)*

United Parcel Service Inc OH C 330 339-6281
New Philadelphia *(G-15120)*

United Parcel Service Inc OH D 419 782-3552
Defiance *(G-10062)*

United States Cargo & Courier E 216 325-0483
Cleveland *(G-6646)*

4522 Air Transportation, Nonscheduled

Aerodynmics Inc Ardynamics Inc E 404 596-8751
Beachwood *(G-1048)*

Airnet Systems Inc C 614 409-4900
Columbus *(G-6958)*

Business Aircraft Group Inc D 216 348-1415
Cleveland *(G-5162)*

Executive Jet Management Inc B 513 979-6600
Cincinnati *(G-3586)*

Federal Express Corporation B 614 492-6106
Columbus *(G-7646)*

Jetselect LLC D 614 338-4380
Columbus *(G-7939)*

◆ **Jilco Industries Inc** E 330 698-0280
Kidron *(G-12441)*

Lane Aviation Corporation C 614 237-3747
Columbus *(G-8037)*

McKinley Air Transport Inc E 330 497-6956
Canton *(G-2453)*

Netjets Inc E 614 239-5500
Columbus *(G-8261)*

Netjets International Inc A 614 239-5500
Columbus *(G-8262)*

Netjets Sales Inc C 614 239-5500
Columbus *(G-8264)*

Ohio Medical Trnsp Inc E 937 747-3540
Marysville *(G-13643)*

Ohio Medical Trnsp Inc D 740 962-2055
McConnelsville *(G-14030)*

Ohio Medical Trnsp Inc C 614 791-4400
Columbus *(G-8360)*

One Sky Flight LLC A 877 703-2348
Cleveland *(G-6204)*

Options Flight Support Inc C 216 261-3500
Cleveland *(G-6209)*

Panther II Transportation Inc C 800 685-0657
Medina *(G-14111)*

4581 Airports, Flying Fields & Terminal Svcs

Abx Air Inc B 937 382-5591
Wilmington *(G-19741)*

Aitheras Aviation Group LLC E 216 298-9060
Cleveland *(G-4979)*

Akron-Canton Regional Airport E 330 499-4059
North Canton *(G-15322)*

American Airlines Inc E 216 706-0702
Cleveland *(G-5003)*

American Airlines Inc D 937 454-7472
Vandalia *(G-18656)*

American Airlines Inc E 216 898-1347
Cleveland *(G-5004)*

ATI Aviation Services LLC E 216 268-4888
Cleveland *(G-5077)*

Aviation Manufacturing Co Inc D 419 435-7448
Fostoria *(G-11122)*

Boeing Company A 740 788-4000
Newark *(G-15147)*

Cessna Aircraft Company D 419 866-6761
Swanton *(G-17562)*

City of Dayton C 937 454-8200
Vandalia *(G-18672)*

City of Dayton E 937 454-8231
Vandalia *(G-18673)*

Columbus Regional Airport Auth E 614 239-4000
Columbus *(G-7381)*

Columbus Regional Airport Auth B 614 239-4015
Columbus *(G-7382)*

Constant Aviation LLC C 800 440-9004
Cleveland *(G-5396)*

Corporate Wngs - Cleveland LLC E 216 261-9000
Cleveland *(G-5411)*

Duncan Aviation Inc D 513 873-7523
Cincinnati *(G-3513)*

Executive Jet Management Inc B 513 979-6600
Cincinnati *(G-3586)*

Exel Inc B 614 865-8500
Westerville *(G-19305)*

Flight Options Inc B 216 261-3880
Richmond Heights *(G-16537)*

Flight Options Intl Inc E 216 261-3500
Richmond Heights *(G-16538)*

GE Aviation Systems LLC B 513 786-4555
West Chester *(G-19079)*

General Electric Company A 513 552-2000
Cincinnati *(G-3668)*

Huntleigh USA Corporation B 216 265-3707
Cleveland *(G-5793)*

James Air Cargo Inc E 440 243-9095
Cleveland *(G-5849)*

Lane Aviation Corporation C 614 237-3747
Columbus *(G-8037)*

Legndary Cleaners LLC E 216 374-1205
Cleveland *(G-5935)*

Macair Aviation LLC E 937 347-1302
Xenia *(G-20069)*

McKinley Air Transport Inc E 330 497-6956
Canton *(G-2453)*

National Flight Services Inc D 419 865-2311
Swanton *(G-17568)*

Netjets Large Aircraft Inc D 614 239-4853
Columbus *(G-8263)*

Park-N-Go Inc E 937 890-7275
Vandalia *(G-18692)*

Plane Detail LLC E 614 734-1201
Mount Gilead *(G-14862)*

Servisair LLC C 216 267-9910
Cleveland *(G-6472)*

Stevens Aviation Inc D 937 890-0189
Vandalia *(G-18699)*

Ultimate Jetcharters LLC D 330 497-3344
North Canton *(G-15377)*

Unison Industries LLC B 937 426-0621
Dayton *(G-9285)*

Unison Industries LLC B 937 427-0550
Beavercreek *(G-1215)*

Winner Aviation Corporation D 330 856-5000
Vienna *(G-18742)*

Wright Brothers Aero Inc D 937 890-8900
Vandalia *(G-18707)*

46 PIPELINES, EXCEPT NATURAL GAS

4612 Crude Petroleum Pipelines

Bluefoot Industrial LLC E 740 314-5299
Steubenville *(G-17304)*

▲ **Marathon Pipe Line LLC** C 419 422-2121
Findlay *(G-11062)*

Ohio Oil Gathering Corporation E 740 828-2802
Nashport *(G-14953)*

4613 Refined Petroleum Pipelines

Buckeye Pipe Line Services Co E 419 698-8770
Oregon *(G-15726)*

Integrity Kokosing Pipeline Sv C 740 694-6315
Fredericktown *(G-11180)*

▲ **Marathon Pipe Line LLC** C 419 422-2121
Findlay *(G-11062)*

Three Rivers Energy LLC E 740 623-3035
Coshocton *(G-9119)*

47 TRANSPORTATION SERVICES

4724 Travel Agencies

AAA Allied Group Inc E 419 228-1022
Lima *(G-12730)*

AAA Allied Group Inc B 513 762-3100
Cincinnati *(G-2958)*

AAA Miami Valley D 937 224-2896
Dayton *(G-9300)*

AAA Shelby County Motor Club E 937 492-3167
Sidney *(G-16910)*

Allstars Travel Group Inc C 614 901-4100
New Albany *(G-14973)*

Avalon Holdings Corporation D 330 856-8800
Warren *(G-18823)*

Central Travel & Ticket Inc E 419 897-2070
Toledo *(G-17799)*

Chima Travel Bureau Inc E 330 867-4770
Fairlawn *(G-10942)*

Croswell of Williamsburg LLC D 800 782-8747
Dayton *(G-9446)*

Independence Travel E 216 447-9950
Cleveland *(G-5813)*

Khm Consulting Inc E 330 460-5635
Brunswick *(G-1985)*

Kollander World Travel Inc E 216 692-1000
Cleveland *(G-5909)*

Maritz Travel Company B 660 626-1501
Maumee *(G-13940)*

Muskingum Coach Company E 740 622-2545
Coshocton *(G-9112)*

Pier n Port Travel Inc E 513 841-9900
Cincinnati *(G-4298)*

Professional Travel Inc D 440 734-8800
North Olmsted *(G-15439)*

Provident Travel Corporation D 513 247-1100
Cincinnati *(G-4351)*

Travel Authority E 513 272-2887
Cincinnati *(G-4681)*

4725 Tour Operators

Keeptryan Inc D 330 319-1866
Akron *(G-302)*

Newport Walking Tours LLC E 859 951-8560
Cincinnati *(G-4161)*

Tours of Black Heritage Inc D 440 247-2737
Cleveland *(G-6606)*

Trolley Tours of Cleveland E 216 771-4484
Cleveland *(G-6619)*

4729 Passenger Transportation Arrangement, NEC

Daugwood Inc E 937 429-9465
Beavercreek *(G-1165)*

Delta Air Lines Inc E 216 265-2400
Cleveland *(G-5475)*

Rush Expediting Inc E 937 885-0894
Dayton *(G-9857)*

4731 Freight Forwarding & Arrangement

ABF Freight System Inc C 419 525-0118
Mansfield *(G-13258)*

Ace Doran Hauling & Rigging Co E 513 681-7900
Cincinnati *(G-2966)*

Action Engneered Logistics LLC D 513 681-7900
Cincinnati *(G-2970)*

Advance Trnsp Systems Inc E 513 818-4311
Cincinnati *(G-2975)*

Airnet Systems Inc C 614 409-4900
Columbus *(G-6958)*

Alpha Freight Systems Inc D 800 394-9001
Hudson *(G-12104)*

Ameri-Line Inc E 440 316-4500
Columbia Station *(G-6840)*

American Marine Express Inc E 216 268-3005
Cleveland *(G-5012)*

Ardmore Power Logistics LLC E 216 502-0640
Westlake *(G-19461)*

Bleckmann USA LLC E 740 809-2645
Johnstown *(G-12337)*

Blood Courier Inc E 216 251-3050
Cleveland *(G-5123)*

Bnsf Logistics LLC E 937 526-3141
Versailles *(G-18723)*

Bolt Express LLC C 419 729-6698
Toledo *(G-17777)*

Burd Brothers Inc E 513 708-7787
Dayton *(G-9373)*

C & M Express Logistics Inc E 440 350-0802
Painesville *(G-15838)*

Ceva Freight LLC D 614 482-5100
Groveport *(G-11627)*

Ceva Freight LLC E 216 898-6765
Cleveland *(G-5221)*

S I C

47 TRANSPORTATION SERVICES

Company		Phone
Ceva Logistics LLC Groveport (G-11628)	B	614 482-5000
Ceva Logistics US Inc Columbus (G-7245)	E	614 482-5107
CH Robinson Company Inc Columbus (G-7248)	E	614 933-5100
CH Robinson Freight Svcs Ltd Cleveland (G-5223)	E	440 234-7811
Colonial Courier Service Inc Maumee (G-13896)	E	419 891-0922
Colonial Courier Service Inc Maumee (G-13897)	E	419 891-0922
Commercial Traffic Company Cleveland (G-5377)	C	216 267-2000
Commercial Traffic Company Cleveland (G-5378)	D	216 267-2000
Complete Qlty Trnsp Sltons LLC Cincinnati (G-3404)	E	513 914-4882
Comprehensive Logistics Co Inc Youngstown (G-20159)		800 734-0372
Containerport Group Inc Cleveland (G-5400)		440 333-1330
Containerport Group Inc Euclid (G-10747)	D	216 692-3124
Contech Trckg & Logistics LLC West Chester (G-19050)	D	513 645-7000
Cos Express Inc Columbus (G-7446)	D	614 276-9000
County of Medina Medina (G-14055)	E	330 723-9670
Covenant Transport Inc Columbus (G-7453)	D	423 821-1212
Craig Transportation Co Maumee (G-13901)	E	419 874-7981
Dayton Freight Lines Inc Dayton (G-9475)	D	937 236-4880
Dhl Supply Chain (usa) Groveport (G-11633)	D	614 836-1265
Dhl Supply Chain (usa) Lockbourne (G-12951)	D	614 662-9200
Dick Lavy Trucking Inc Bradford (G-1806)	C	937 448-2104
Distribution Data Incorporated Brookpark (G-1943)		216 362-3009
Elite Transportation Svcs LLC Seville (G-16839)	E	330 769-5830
Esj Carrier Corporation Fairfield (G-10849)		513 728-7388
Estes Express Lines Inc Richfield (G-16506)	E	330 659-9750
Exel Freight Connect Inc Columbus (G-7619)	D	855 393-5378
Exel Global Logistics Inc Cleveland (G-5561)	D	440 243-5900
Exel Global Logistics Inc Columbus (G-7620)	E	614 409-4500
Exel N Amercn Logistics Inc Westerville (G-19398)	C	800 272-1052
Expeditors Intl Wash Inc Cleveland (G-5562)	D	440 243-9900
Expeditors Intl Wash Inc Lockbourne (G-12953)	E	614 492-9840
Faf Inc Groveport (G-11638)	A	800 496-4696
Faro Services Inc Groveport (G-11639)	B	614 497-1700
FCA US LLC Toledo (G-17882)	D	419 729-5959
Fedex Freight Corporation Lima (G-12781)	E	800 521-3505
Fedex Freight Corporation Northwood (G-15552)	C	800 728-8190
Fedex Supply Chain Lockbourne (G-12955)		614 491-1518
Fedex Truckload Brokerage Inc Uniontown (G-18520)	C	234 310-4090
Freedom Enterprises Inc Kenton (G-12411)	E	419 675-1192
Freshway Foods Inc Sidney (G-16937)		937 498-4664
Garner Trucking Inc Findlay (G-11035)	C	419 422-5742
Garys Pharmacy Inc Eaton (G-10561)	E	937 456-5777
Gateway Distribution Inc Cincinnati (G-3664)	E	513 891-4477
GKN Freight Services Inc Van Wert (G-18633)	E	419 232-5623
Global Transportation Services Reynoldsburg (G-16454)	E	614 409-0770
Globaltranz Enterprises Inc Blue Ash (G-1603)	C	513 745-0138
Haid Acquisitions LLC Cincinnati (G-3728)	D	513 941-8700
Horizon South Inc Cleveland (G-5775)	D	800 480-6829
Hub City Terminals Inc Westlake (G-19494)	D	440 779-2226
Hub City Terminals Inc Toledo (G-17964)	E	419 217-5200
Innovative Logistics Group Inc Englewood (G-10710)	E	937 832-9350
Innovel Solutions Inc Columbus (G-7901)	D	614 878-2092
Innovel Solutions Inc Columbus (G-7902)	A	614 492-5304
Integrity Ex Logistics LLC Cincinnati (G-3828)	C	888 374-5138
J B Express Inc Chillicothe (G-2854)	D	740 702-9830
J Rayl Transport Inc Euclid (G-10765)	E	330 940-1668
Jarrett Logistics Systems Inc Orrville (G-15775)	C	330 682-0099
JB Hunt Transport Svcs Inc Columbus (G-7937)	A	614 335-6681
Keller Logistics Group Inc Defiance (G-10040)	E	866 276-9486
Kgbo Holdings Inc West Chester (G-19101)		800 580-3101
Kgbo Holdings Inc Cincinnati (G-2922)	E	513 831-2600
Krakowski Trucking Inc Medina (G-14092)		330 722-7935
Lesaint Logistics LLC Trenton (G-18341)	D	513 988-0101
Logikor LLC Cincinnati (G-3993)	D	513 762-7678
Martin Logistics Inc Canton (G-2450)	D	330 456-8000
Mid Ohio Vly Bulk Trnspt Inc Marietta (G-13476)	E	740 373-2481
◆ Millwood Inc Vienna (G-18740)		330 393-4400
Millwood Natural LLC Vienna (G-18741)	C	330 393-4400
Moving Solutions Inc Mentor (G-14223)	D	440 946-9300
Nationwide Transport Llc Cincinnati (G-4144)	E	513 554-0203
Newark Parcel Service Company Columbus (G-8274)		614 253-3777
Nippon Express USA Inc Grove City (G-11585)	D	614 801-5695
Nissin Intl Trnspt USA Inc Marysville (G-13642)		937 644-2644
Noramco Transport Corp Cincinnati (G-4172)	E	513 245-9050
Norfolk Southern Corporation Mingo Junction (G-14656)	D	740 535-4102
Norfolk Southern Corporation Maple Heights (G-13411)	E	216 518-8407
Nutrition Trnsp Svcs LLC Lewisburg (G-12713)	C	937 962-2661
Ohio Transport Inc Cleveland (G-6196)	E	216 741-8000
Omni Interglobal Inc Cleveland (G-6202)	E	216 239-3833
Overland Xpress LLC Cincinnati (G-4245)	E	513 528-1158
Packship Usa Inc Orrville (G-15782)	D	330 682-7225
Ploger Transportation LLC Bellevue (G-1415)	E	419 465-2100
Pride Transportation Inc Findlay (G-11077)	E	419 424-2145
Ray Hamilton Companies Blue Ash (G-1676)	E	513 641-5400
RDF Trucking Corporation Lorain (G-13073)	D	440 282-9060
Rehrig Penn Logistics Inc Canal Winchester (G-2166)	E	614 833-2564
Reliable Trnsp Solutions LLC Georgetown (G-11396)	E	937 378-2700
Ringler Feedlots LLC Marengo (G-13425)	E	419 253-5300
Rk Express International LLC Cincinnati (G-4429)	D	513 574-2400
Roadrunner Trnsp Systems Inc Peninsula (G-15950)	E	330 920-4101
Roe Transport Inc Sidney (G-16951)	E	937 497-7161
Rondy Fleet Services Inc Barberton (G-977)	C	330 745-9016
Ryan Logistics Inc Marysville (G-13648)	D	937 642-4158
Schneider Nat Carriers Inc Delaware (G-10126)	E	740 362-6910
Shoreline Transportation Inc Strongsville (G-17508)	C	440 878-2000
SMS Transport LLC Dayton (G-9886)	E	937 813-8897
Stack Container Service Inc Euclid (G-10777)	D	216 531-7555
Tazmanian Freight Fwdg Inc Middleburg Heights (G-14387)	E	216 265-7881
▲ Tersher Corporation Strongsville (G-17516)	D	440 439-8383
Tier One Distribution LLC Springfield (G-17288)	D	937 323-6325
Total Package Express Inc Cincinnati (G-4662)	E	513 741-5500
Total Quality Logistics LLC Milford (G-14568)	E	513 831-2600
Total Quality Logistics LLC Cincinnati (G-4663)	E	513 831-2600
Total Quality Logistics LLC Milford (G-14569)	C	513 831-2600
Total Quality Logistics LLC Cincinnati (G-2936)	E	513 831-2600
Tpg Noramco LLC Cincinnati (G-4676)	E	513 245-9050
Transfreight Inc Troy (G-18381)	E	937 332-0366
Triple T Transport Inc Lewis Center (G-12707)	D	740 657-3244
Trx Great Plains Inc Cleveland (G-6620)	D	855 259-9259
TV Minority Company Inc Englewood (G-10722)	E	937 832-9350
United Parcel Service Inc OH Delaware (G-10133)	B	740 363-0636
USF Holland LLC Cleveland (G-6678)	C	216 941-4340
Verst Group Logistics Inc Cincinnati (G-4810)	E	513 772-2494
William R Morse Painesville (G-15887)		440 352-2600
Wnb Group LLC Cincinnati (G-4855)	E	513 641-5400
World Shipping Inc Cleveland (G-6759)	E	440 356-7676
Wright Distribution Centers Lima (G-12922)	E	419 227-7621
Xpo Intermodal Inc Dublin (G-10494)	D	614 923-1400
Xpo Intermodal Solutions Inc Dublin (G-10495)	A	614 923-1400
Xpo Stacktrain LLC Dublin (G-10496)	E	614 923-1400
Yrc Inc Copley (G-9071)	E	913 344-5174

4741 Railroad Car Rental

Company		Phone
◆ Andersons Inc Maumee (G-13879)	C	419 893-5050
▼ Djj Holding Corporation Cincinnati (G-3496)	C	513 621-8770

4783 Packing & Crating Svcs

Company		Phone
▲ Amerisource Health Svcs LLC Columbus (G-7012)	D	614 492-8177
Bates Metal Products Inc Port Washington (G-16260)	D	740 498-8371
Calypso Logistics LLC Columbus (G-7179)	C	614 262-8911
Containerport Group Inc Columbus (G-7426)	E	440 333-1330
Crescent Park Corporation West Chester (G-19059)	C	513 759-7000
Deufol Worldwide Packaging LLC Bedford (G-1303)	D	440 232-1100
Deufol Worldwide Packaging LLC Fairfield (G-10840)	D	414 967-8000
Flick Lumber Co Inc Galion (G-11296)	E	419 468-6278
Genpak LLC Columbus (G-7739)	E	614 276-5156
Hcg Inc Monroe (G-14697)	E	513 539-9269

Inquiry Systems Inc..........E....... 614 464-3800
Columbus *(G-7904)*
Kenco Group Inc..........E....... 614 409-8754
Groveport *(G-11653)*
Lefco Worthington LLC..........E....... 216 432-4422
Cleveland *(G-5931)*
◆ **McNerney & Associates LLC**..........E....... 513 241-9951
Cincinnati *(G-4039)*
Morral Companies LLC..........E....... 740 465-3251
Morral *(G-14842)*
Packship Usa Inc..........D....... 330 682-7225
Orrville *(G-15782)*
Reynolds Industries Inc..........E....... 330 889-9466
West Farmington *(G-19246)*
Southeast Diversified Inds..........D....... 740 432-4241
Cambridge *(G-2128)*
Star Packaging Inc..........E....... 614 564-9936
Columbus *(G-8777)*
Sugar Creek Packing Co..........E....... 513 551-5255
Blue Ash *(G-1691)*
Vista Industrial Packaging LLC..........D....... 800 454-6117
Columbus *(G-8945)*

4785 Fixed Facilities, Inspection, Weighing Svcs Transptn

Argus International Inc..........E....... 513 852-1010
Cincinnati *(G-3046)*
Johnson Mirmiran Thompson Inc..........D....... 614 714-0270
Columbus *(G-7944)*
Magnum Management Corporation..........A....... 419 627-2334
Sandusky *(G-16778)*
Ohio Tpk & Infrastructure Comm..........C....... 440 234-2081
Berea *(G-1465)*
Pti Qlity Cntnment Sltions LLC..........D....... 313 304-8677
Toledo *(G-18142)*
Pti Qlity Cntnment Sltions LLC..........E....... 330 306-0125
Warren *(G-18892)*

4789 Transportation Svcs, NEC

Access Home Care LLC..........E....... 937 224-9991
Dayton *(G-9304)*
Age Line Inc..........E....... 216 941-9990
Cleveland *(G-4968)*
Ahoy Transport LLC..........E....... 740 596-0536
Creola *(G-9141)*
All American Trnsp Svcs LLC..........E....... 419 589-7433
Ontario *(G-15684)*
Alstom Signaling Operation LLC..........B....... 513 552-6485
Cincinnati *(G-2996)*
American Linehaul Corporation..........E....... 614 409-8568
Columbus *(G-7000)*
Ameripro Logistics LLC..........E....... 410 375-3469
Dayton *(G-9333)*
Andersons Inc..........E....... 419 891-6634
Maumee *(G-13878)*
◆ **Andersons Inc**..........C....... 419 893-5050
Maumee *(G-13879)*
Ashtabula Chemical Corp..........E....... 440 998-0100
Ashtabula *(G-714)*
Brothers Auto Transport LLC..........E....... 330 824-0082
Warren *(G-18831)*
Coldliner Express Inc..........E....... 614 570-0836
Columbus *(G-7316)*
Commercial Warehouse & Cartage..........D....... 614 409-3901
Groveport *(G-11629)*
CSX Corporation..........A....... 614 242-3932
Columbus *(G-7472)*
CT Logistics Inc..........C....... 216 267-1636
Cleveland *(G-5446)*
Dayton Freight Lines Inc..........C....... 419 589-0350
Mansfield *(G-13290)*
DSV Solutions LLC..........D....... 740 989-1200
Little Hocking *(G-12943)*
Euclid SC Transportation..........D....... 216 797-7600
Cleveland *(G-5554)*
Fidelitone Inc..........D....... 440 260-6523
Middleburg Heights *(G-14381)*
Genox Transportation Inc..........E....... 419 837-2023
Perrysburg *(G-16006)*
Great Lakes Cold Logistics..........E....... 216 520-0930
Independence *(G-12215)*
Hoc Transport Company..........E....... 330 630-0100
Akron *(G-267)*
Hogan Services Inc..........E....... 614 491-8402
Columbus *(G-7844)*
Hometech Healthcare Svcs LLC..........E....... 216 295-9120
Cleveland *(G-5769)*
Jarrells Moving & Transport Co..........E....... 330 952-1240
Medina *(G-14086)*
▼ **Jk-Co LLC**..........E....... 419 422-5240
Findlay *(G-11051)*
Jti Transportation Inc..........E....... 419 661-9360
Stony Ridge *(G-17347)*
Kettering City School District..........D....... 937 499-1770
Dayton *(G-9653)*
Lake Local Board of Education..........B....... 330 877-9383
Hartville *(G-11826)*
Marietta Transfer Company..........E....... 740 896-3565
Lowell *(G-13169)*
Meda-Care Transportation Inc..........E....... 513 521-4799
Cincinnati *(G-4041)*
Midwest Trmnals Tledo Intl Inc..........E....... 419 698-8171
Toledo *(G-18064)*
Mikesell Transportation Broker..........E....... 937 996-5731
Arcanum *(G-630)*
Mkm Distribution Services Inc..........D....... 330 549-9670
North Lima *(G-15405)*
Moore Trnspt Tulsa Ltd Lblty..........D....... 419 726-4499
Toledo *(G-18069)*
Movers and Shuckers LLC..........E....... 740 263-2164
Mount Vernon *(G-14915)*
Multi Flow Transport Inc..........E....... 216 641-0200
Brooklyn Heights *(G-1920)*
Mwd Logistics Inc..........D....... 419 522-3510
Ontario *(G-15705)*
Niese Transport Inc..........E....... 419 523-4400
Ottawa *(G-15800)*
Nye F A & Sons Enterprises..........E....... 419 986-5400
Tiffin *(G-17689)*
OH St Trans Dist 02 Outpost..........E....... 419 693-8870
Northwood *(G-15542)*
Ohio State University..........E....... 614 292-6122
Columbus *(G-8426)*
PAm Transportation Svcs Inc..........A....... 330 270-7900
North Jackson *(G-15385)*
Parsec Inc..........E....... 513 621-6111
Cincinnati *(G-4256)*
Precision Vhcl Solutions LLC..........E....... 513 651-9444
Cincinnati *(G-4320)*
R W Godbey Railroad Services..........E....... 513 651-3800
Cincinnati *(G-4380)*
Schenker Inc..........E....... 614 662-7217
Groveport *(G-11670)*
Schroeder Associates Inc..........E....... 419 258-5075
Antwerp *(G-620)*
Secure Trnsp Co Ohio LLC..........E....... 800 856-9994
Worthington *(G-19996)*
Specialty Logistics Inc..........E....... 513 421-2041
Cincinnati *(G-4558)*
Tmt Inc..........C....... 419 592-1041
Perrysburg *(G-16064)*
Total Transportation Trckg Inc..........E....... 216 398-6090
Cleveland *(G-6604)*
Universal Transportation Syste..........E....... 513 539-9491
Monroe *(G-14716)*
Water Transport LLC..........E....... 740 937-2199
Hopedale *(G-12080)*
Wmk Inc..........E....... 630 782-1900
Richfield *(G-16533)*
Woodruff Enterprises Inc..........E....... 937 399-9300
Springfield *(G-17301)*
World Trck Towing Recovery Inc..........E....... 330 723-1116
Seville *(G-16848)*

48 COMMUNICATIONS

4812 Radiotelephone Communications

Aka Wireless Inc..........E....... 216 213-8040
Hartville *(G-11814)*
Alltel Communications Corp..........D....... 740 349-8551
Newark *(G-15141)*
Answering Service Inc..........E....... 440 473-1200
Cleveland *(G-5041)*
AT&T Corp..........D....... 614 798-3898
Dublin *(G-10257)*
AT&T Corp..........D....... 614 539-0165
Grove City *(G-11532)*
AT&T Corp..........D....... 614 575-3044
Columbus *(G-7063)*
AT&T Corp..........D....... 614 851-2400
Columbus *(G-7064)*
AT&T Corp..........E....... 330 505-4200
Niles *(G-15282)*
AT&T Corp..........A....... 513 629-5000
Cincinnati *(G-3054)*
AT&T Inc..........E....... 937 320-9648
Beavercreek *(G-1227)*
AT&T Mobility LLC..........E....... 614 291-2500
Columbus *(G-7066)*
AT&T Mobility LLC..........C....... 330 565-5000
Youngstown *(G-20106)*
AT&T Mobility LLC..........E....... 440 846-3232
Strongsville *(G-17445)*
AT&T Mobility LLC..........E....... 216 382-0825
Cleveland *(G-5076)*
AT&T Mobility LLC..........E....... 419 516-0602
Lima *(G-12743)*
AT&T Mobility LLC..........E....... 513 381-6800
Cincinnati *(G-3055)*
AT&T Mobility LLC..........E....... 937 439-4900
Centerville *(G-2674)*
AT&T Services Inc..........C....... 937 456-2330
Eaton *(G-10553)*
Cellco Partnership..........B....... 614 560-2000
Dublin *(G-10281)*
Cellco Partnership..........D....... 330 486-1005
Twinsburg *(G-18398)*
Cellco Partnership..........D....... 614 560-8552
Lewis Center *(G-12673)*
Cellco Partnership..........D....... 513 923-2700
Cincinnati *(G-3202)*
Cellco Partnership..........D....... 614 476-9786
Columbus *(G-7220)*
Cellco Partnership..........D....... 330 764-7380
Medina *(G-14044)*
Cellco Partnership..........D....... 330 823-7758
Alliance *(G-531)*
Cellco Partnership..........D....... 419 333-1009
Fremont *(G-11187)*
Cellco Partnership..........D....... 440 886-5461
Parma *(G-15901)*
Cellco Partnership..........D....... 330 928-4382
Cuyahoga Falls *(G-9170)*
Cellco Partnership..........D....... 419 353-0904
Bowling Green *(G-1771)*
Cellco Partnership..........D....... 740 652-9540
Lancaster *(G-12515)*
Cellco Partnership..........D....... 740 695-3600
Saint Clairsville *(G-16631)*
Cellco Partnership..........D....... 419 784-3800
Defiance *(G-10021)*
Cellco Partnership..........D....... 740 432-7785
Cambridge *(G-2103)*
Cellco Partnership..........D....... 330 376-8275
Akron *(G-126)*
Cellco Partnership..........D....... 513 755-1666
West Chester *(G-19035)*
Cellco Partnership..........D....... 513 697-1190
Cincinnati *(G-3203)*
Cellco Partnership..........D....... 440 934-0576
Avon *(G-885)*
Cellco Partnership..........D....... 419 381-1726
Toledo *(G-17795)*
Cellco Partnership..........C....... 216 765-1444
Beachwood *(G-1061)*
Cellco Partnership..........D....... 440 998-3111
Ashtabula *(G-731)*
Cellco Partnership..........D....... 513 422-3437
Middletown *(G-14477)*
Cellco Partnership..........D....... 740 588-0018
Zanesville *(G-20458)*
Cellco Partnership..........E....... 513 688-1300
Cincinnati *(G-3204)*
Cellco Partnership..........E....... 419 424-2351
Findlay *(G-11011)*
Cellco Partnership..........E....... 419 331-4644
Lima *(G-12752)*
Cellco Partnership..........D....... 419 897-9133
Maumee *(G-13892)*
Cellco Partnership..........E....... 614 759-4400
Reynoldsburg *(G-16434)*
Cellco Partnership..........D....... 419 625-7900
Sandusky *(G-16736)*
Cellco Partnership..........E....... 440 953-1155
Mentor *(G-14155)*
Cellco Partnership..........E....... 440 646-9625
Cleveland *(G-5203)*
Cellco Partnership..........E....... 440 846-8881
Strongsville *(G-17448)*
Cellco Partnership..........E....... 740 397-6609
Mount Vernon *(G-14881)*
Cellco Partnership..........E....... 614 459-7200
Columbus *(G-7221)*
Cellco Partnership..........E....... 937 429-4000
Beavercreek *(G-1158)*
Cellco Partnership..........E....... 513 671-2200
Cincinnati *(G-3205)*
Cellco Partnership..........E....... 513 697-0222
Cincinnati *(G-3206)*

S I C

Cellco Partnership ... E ... 330 665-5220
Fairlawn *(G-10941)*

Cellco Partnership ... E ... 419 843-2995
Toledo *(G-17796)*

Cellco Partnership ... E ... 330 493-7979
Canton *(G-2302)*

Cellco Partnership ... E ... 216 573-5880
Independence *(G-12195)*

Cellco Partnership ... D ... 937 578-0022
Marysville *(G-13611)*

Cellco Partnership ... D ... 440 542-9631
Solon *(G-16990)*

Cellco Partnership ... D ... 330 626-0524
Streetsboro *(G-17408)*

Cellco Partnership ... D ... 740 362-2408
Delaware *(G-10077)*

Cellco Partnership ... E ... 440 324-9479
Elyria *(G-10601)*

Cellco Partnership ... E ... 614 793-8989
Dublin *(G-10283)*

Cellco Partnership ... D ... 614 277-2900
Grove City *(G-11544)*

Cellco Partnership ... E ... 740 522-6446
Newark *(G-15155)*

Cellco Partnership ... D ... 330 345-6465
Wooster *(G-19838)*

Cellco Partnership ... E ... 330 722-6622
Medina *(G-14043)*

Cellco Partnership ... E ... 440 984-5200
Amherst *(G-590)*

Cellco Partnership ... E ... 740 450-1525
Zanesville *(G-20459)*

Century Tel of Odon Inc ... C ... 440 244-8544
Lorain *(G-13022)*

Horizon Pcs Inc ... C ... 740 772-8200
Chillicothe *(G-2850)*

Maximum Communications Inc ... E ... 513 489-3414
Cincinnati *(G-4031)*

Nextel Communications Inc ... D ... 513 891-9200
Cincinnati *(G-4163)*

Nextel Communications Inc ... D ... 614 801-9267
Grove City *(G-11584)*

Nextel Partners Operating Corp ... E ... 330 305-1365
North Canton *(G-15357)*

Nextel Partners Operating Corp ... E ... 419 380-2000
Toledo *(G-18086)*

Prime Communications LP ... E ... 281 240-7800
Canton *(G-2494)*

Round Room LLC ... E ... 440 888-0322
North Royalton *(G-15500)*

Sprint Spectrum LP ... E ... 614 575-5500
Columbus *(G-8765)*

Sprint Spectrum LP ... E ... 614 428-2300
Columbus *(G-8767)*

Supermedia LLC ... D ... 740 369-2391
Marion *(G-13583)*

TSC Communications Inc ... E ... 419 739-2200
Wapakoneta *(G-18810)*

Twin Comm Inc ... E ... 740 774-4701
Marietta *(G-13508)*

Verizon Communications Inc ... D ... 419 281-1714
Ashland *(G-705)*

Verizon Communications Inc ... C ... 330 334-1268
Wadsworth *(G-18772)*

Verizon Communications Inc ... C ... 440 892-4504
Westlake *(G-19562)*

Verizon New York Inc ... E ... 330 364-0508
Dover *(G-10222)*

Verizon Wireless Inc ... D ... 937 434-2355
Dayton *(G-9969)*

Wireless Center Inc ... B ... 216 503-3777
Cleveland *(G-6755)*

4813 Telephone Communications, Except Radio

1 Community ... E ... 216 923-2272
Cleveland *(G-4917)*

▲ 4mybenefits Inc ... E ... 513 891-6648
Blue Ash *(G-1521)*

Advanced Cmpt Connections LLC ... E ... 419 668-4080
Norwalk *(G-15561)*

Alltel Communications Corp ... D ... 740 349-8551
Newark *(G-15141)*

Alltel Communications Corp ... E ... 330 656-8000
Chardon *(G-2739)*

Armstrong Utilities Inc ... E ... 740 894-3886
South Point *(G-17080)*

At T Broadband & Intern ... E ... 614 839-4271
Columbus *(G-7060)*

AT&T Corp ... D ... 937 320-9648
Beavercreek *(G-1226)*

AT&T Corp ... D ... 330 337-3505
Salem *(G-16687)*

AT&T Corp ... D ... 614 223-5318
Westerville *(G-19367)*

AT&T Corp ... C ... 614 271-8911
Powell *(G-16325)*

AT&T Corp ... D ... 614 223-6513
Columbus *(G-7061)*

AT&T Corp ... D ... 740 455-3042
Zanesville *(G-20444)*

AT&T Corp ... D ... 740 549-4546
Lewis Center *(G-12667)*

AT&T Corp ... D ... 330 665-3100
Akron *(G-82)*

AT&T Corp ... D ... 440 951-5309
Willoughby *(G-19646)*

AT&T Corp ... C ... 937 372-9945
Xenia *(G-20042)*

AT&T Corp ... C ... 330 752-7776
Akron *(G-83)*

AT&T Corp ... D ... 513 741-1700
Cincinnati *(G-3053)*

AT&T Corp ... C ... 216 672-0809
Cleveland *(G-5075)*

AT&T Corp ... A ... 513 629-5000
Cincinnati *(G-3054)*

AT&T Corp ... D ... 330 723-1717
Medina *(G-14037)*

AT&T Corp ... D ... 614 337-3902
Columbus *(G-7065)*

AT&T Corp ... A ... 614 223-8236
Columbus *(G-7062)*

AT&T Datacomm LLC ... E ... 614 223-5799
Westerville *(G-19368)*

AT&T Mobility LLC ... E ... 614 291-2500
Columbus *(G-7066)*

AT&T Services Inc ... C ... 937 456-2330
Eaton *(G-10553)*

AVI-Spl Employee ... E ... 937 836-4787
Englewood *(G-10697)*

Bluespring Software Inc ... E ... 513 794-1764
Blue Ash *(G-1547)*

Broadvox LLC ... E ... 216 373-4600
Cleveland *(G-5142)*

Buckeye Telesystem Inc ... D ... 419 724-9898
Northwood *(G-15528)*

C T Wireless ... D ... 937 653-2208
Urbana *(G-18574)*

Cass Information Systems Inc ... E ... 614 839-4503
Columbus *(G-7206)*

Cellco Partnership ... E ... 440 984-5200
Amherst *(G-590)*

Cellco Partnership ... C ... 937 498-2371
Sidney *(G-16918)*

Cellco Partnership ... E ... 330 922-5997
Stow *(G-17355)*

Cellco Partnership ... E ... 740 450-1525
Zanesville *(G-20459)*

Champaign Telephone Company ... E ... 937 653-4000
Urbana *(G-18579)*

Chillicothe Telephone Company ... C ... 740 772-8200
Chillicothe *(G-2825)*

Chillicothe Telephone Company ... D ... 740 772-8361
Chillicothe *(G-2826)*

▲ Cincinnati Bell Inc ... D ... 513 397-9900
Cincinnati *(G-3285)*

Cincinnati Bell Tele Co LLC ... C ... 513 565-9402
Cincinnati *(G-3288)*

Cinciti Bl Etd Trts LLC ... D ... 513 397-0963
Cincinnati *(G-3340)*

Com Net Inc ... D ... 419 739-3100
Wapakoneta *(G-18792)*

Communication Options Inc ... E ... 614 901-7095
New Albany *(G-14982)*

Community Isp Inc ... E ... 419 867-6060
Toledo *(G-17824)*

Conneaut Telephone Company ... E ... 440 593-7140
Conneaut *(G-9041)*

Connect Call Global LLC ... E ... 513 348-1800
Mason *(G-13689)*

Connectlink Inc ... E ... 740 867-5095
Chesapeake *(G-2783)*

Construction Biddingcom LLC ... E ... 440 716-4087
North Olmsted *(G-15418)*

Cox Ohio Telcom LLC ... D ... 216 535-3500
Parma *(G-15904)*

Cypress Communications Inc ... C ... 404 965-7248
Cleveland *(G-5459)*

Datzap LLC ... E ... 330 785-2100
Akron *(G-187)*

Dct Telecom Group Inc ... E ... 440 892-0300
Westlake *(G-19482)*

Deliass Assets Corp ... D ... 614 891-0101
Westerville *(G-19393)*

Doylestown Telephone Company ... E ... 330 658-2121
Doylestown *(G-10228)*

Doylestown Telephone Company ... E ... 330 658-6666
Doylestown *(G-10229)*

Echo 24 Inc ... E ... 740 964-7081
Reynoldsburg *(G-16450)*

Ecommerce Inc ... D ... 800 861-9394
Columbus *(G-7573)*

▲ F+w Media Inc ... B ... 513 531-2690
Blue Ash *(G-1591)*

First Communications LLC ... E ... 330 835-2323
Fairlawn *(G-10953)*

▲ First Communications LLC ... B ... 330 835-2323
Fairlawn *(G-10954)*

Fte Networks Inc ... D ... 502 657-3500
Cincinnati *(G-3657)*

Great Lakes Telcom Ltd ... E ... 330 629-8848
Youngstown *(G-20207)*

Horizon Telcom Inc ... B ... 740 772-8200
Chillicothe *(G-2851)*

Infotelecom Holdings LLC ... B ... 216 373-4811
Cleveland *(G-5821)*

Intellinet Corporation ... E ... 216 289-4100
Cleveland *(G-5827)*

Intellinex LLC ... B ... 216 685-6000
Independence *(G-12220)*

Intgrted Bridge Communications ... E ... 513 381-1380
Cincinnati *(G-3839)*

J E Davis Corporation ... E ... 440 377-4700
Sheffield Village *(G-16887)*

Jumplinecom Inc ... E ... 614 859-1170
Columbus *(G-7959)*

Kraft Electrical Contg Inc ... E ... 614 836-9300
Groveport *(G-11655)*

Kraftmaid Trucking Inc ... D ... 440 632-2531
Middlefield *(G-14396)*

Kreative Communication Network ... E ... 330 743-1612
Youngstown *(G-20249)*

Level 3 Communications Inc ... E ... 330 256-8999
Akron *(G-315)*

Level 3 Telecom LLC ... E ... 614 255-2000
Worthington *(G-19972)*

Level 3 Telecom LLC ... E ... 234 542-6279
Akron *(G-316)*

Level 3 Telecom LLC ... E ... 513 841-0000
Cincinnati *(G-3970)*

Level 3 Telecom LLC ... E ... 513 841-0000
Cincinnati *(G-3971)*

Level 3 Telecom LLC ... E ... 513 682-7806
West Chester *(G-19107)*

Level 3 Telecom LLC ... E ... 513 682-7806
West Chester *(G-19108)*

Level 3 Telecom LLC ... E ... 513 682-7806
West Chester *(G-19109)*

Level 3 Telecom LLC ... E ... 513 841-0000
Cincinnati *(G-3972)*

Link Iq LLC ... E ... 859 983-6080
Dayton *(G-9684)*

Making Evrlasting Memories LLC ... E ... 513 864-0100
Cincinnati *(G-4016)*

Marietta College ... E ... 740 376-4790
Marietta *(G-13467)*

Massillon Cable TV Inc ... D ... 330 833-4134
Massillon *(G-13833)*

MCI Communications Svcs Inc ... B ... 216 265-9953
Cleveland *(G-6005)*

MCI Communications Svcs Inc ... B ... 440 635-0418
Chardon *(G-2757)*

Mitel (delaware) Inc ... E ... 513 733-8000
West Chester *(G-19122)*

Morelia Group LLC ... E ... 513 469-1500
Cincinnati *(G-4117)*

Mvd Communications LLC ... D ... 513 683-4711
Mason *(G-13741)*

Ohio Bell Telephone Company ... A ... 216 822-3439
Cleveland *(G-6185)*

Ohio State University ... E ... 614 292-6291
Columbus *(G-8416)*

Orwell Communications Inc ... E ... 937 855-6511
Germantown *(G-11400)*

Oxcyon Inc ... E ... 440 239-3345
Cleveland *(G-6223)*

Pearl Interactive Network Inc ... B ... 614 258-2943
Columbus *(G-8527)*

Png Telecommunications Inc ....D 513 942-7900
Cincinnati *(G-4311)*

Premier System Integrators Inc ....D 513 217-7294
Middletown *(G-14452)*

Primax Marketing Group ....E 513 443-2797
Cincinnati *(G-4329)*

Professional Telecom Svcs ....E 513 232-7700
Cincinnati *(G-4344)*

Profit Recovery of Ohio ....C 440 243-1743
Cleveland *(G-6310)*

Quality One Technologies Inc ....E 937 855-6511
Germantown *(G-11401)*

Quanexus Inc ....E 937 885-7272
Dayton *(G-9837)*

Qwest Corporation ....D 614 793-9258
Dublin *(G-10435)*

Raco Wireless LLC ....D 513 870-6480
Blue Ash *(G-1673)*

Revolution Group Inc ....D 614 212-1111
Westerville *(G-19349)*

Round Room LLC ....E 330 880-0660
Massillon *(G-13851)*

Round Room LLC ....E 937 429-2230
Beavercreek *(G-1206)*

Roundtable Online Learning LLC ....E 440 220-5252
Chagrin Falls *(G-2731)*

Rxp Ohio LLC ....D 614 937-2844
Columbus *(G-8663)*

Rxp Wireless LLC ....E 330 264-1500
Wooster *(G-19909)*

▼ Skycasters LLC ....E 330 785-2100
Akron *(G-440)*

Spectrum Networks Inc ....E 513 697-2000
Cincinnati *(G-4560)*

Sprint Communications Co LP ....E 419 725-2444
Toledo *(G-18197)*

Sprint Spectrum LP ....E 440 686-2600
North Olmsted *(G-15445)*

Sprint Spectrum LP ....E 614 575-5500
Columbus *(G-8765)*

Sprint Spectrum LP ....E 614 793-2500
Columbus *(G-8766)*

Sprint Spectrum LP ....E 614 428-2300
Columbus *(G-8767)*

Suite 224 Internet ....E 440 593-7113
Conneaut *(G-9047)*

Swn Communications Inc ....E 877 698-3262
Dayton *(G-9917)*

Telemaxx Communications LLC ....E 216 371-8800
Cleveland *(G-6578)*

Time Warner Cable Inc ....E 330 800-3874
Akron *(G-477)*

Tpusa Inc ....A 614 621-5512
Columbus *(G-8860)*

Tremor LLC ....E 513 983-1100
Blue Ash *(G-1700)*

TSC Communications Inc ....E 419 739-2200
Wapakoneta *(G-18810)*

TSC Television Inc ....D 419 941-6001
Wapakoneta *(G-18811)*

TW Telecom Inc ....E 234 542-6279
Akron *(G-482)*

United Telephone Company Ohio ....B 419 227-1660
Lima *(G-12910)*

Verizon Bus Netwrk Svcs Inc ....E 513 897-1501
Waynesville *(G-18988)*

Verizon Business Global LLC ....E 440 457-4049
North Royalton *(G-15505)*

Verizon Business Global LLC ....E 330 505-2368
Niles *(G-15308)*

Verizon Business Global LLC ....E 614 219-2317
Hilliard *(G-11963)*

Verizon Communications Inc ....C 330 334-1268
Wadsworth *(G-18772)*

Verizon Communications Inc ....C 440 892-4504
Westlake *(G-19562)*

Verizon Communications Inc ....C 740 383-0527
Marion *(G-13594)*

Verizon New York Inc ....C 740 383-0411
Marion *(G-13595)*

Verizon North Inc ....E 740 942-2566
Cadiz *(G-2081)*

Verizon North Inc ....D 937 382-6961
Wilmington *(G-19792)*

Verizon North Inc ....E 419 734-5000
Port Clinton *(G-16258)*

Verizon North Inc ....E 330 339-7733
New Philadelphia *(G-15121)*

Verizon South Inc ....D 740 354-0544
Portsmouth *(G-16321)*

Verizon Wireless ....E 330 963-1300
Twinsburg *(G-18484)*

Vox Mobile ....E 800 536-9030
Independence *(G-12274)*

West Central Ohio Internet ....E 419 229-2645
Lima *(G-12916)*

Windstream Ohio LLC ....C 440 329-4000
Elyria *(G-10693)*

Windstream Ohio LLC ....D 330 650-8436
Hudson *(G-12152)*

Windstream Western Reserve LLC ....C 330 650-8000
Hudson *(G-12153)*

Xo Communications LLC ....E 216 619-3200
Cleveland *(G-6768)*

4822 Telegraph & Other Message Communications

AT&T Corp ....A 513 629-5000
Cincinnati *(G-3054)*

Cosmic Concepts Ltd ....C 614 228-1104
Columbus *(G-7447)*

Maximum Communications Inc ....E 513 489-3414
Cincinnati *(G-4031)*

▲ Stratacache Inc ....C 937 224-0485
Dayton *(G-9910)*

Verizon Business Global LLC ....E 614 219-2317
Hilliard *(G-11963)*

Verizon Select Services Inc ....E 908 559-2054
North Royalton *(G-15506)*

4832 Radio Broadcasting Stations

Alpha Media LLC ....E 937 294-5858
Dayton *(G-9322)*

Ashtabula Broadcasting Station ....E 440 993-2126
Ashtabula *(G-713)*

Bonneville International Corp ....D 513 699-5102
Cincinnati *(G-3126)*

Bowling Green State University ....D 419 372-8657
Bowling Green *(G-1767)*

CBS Corporation ....C 513 749-1035
Cincinnati *(G-3197)*

CBS Radio Inc ....D 513 699-5105
Cincinnati *(G-3198)*

CBS Radio Inc ....E 216 861-0100
Cleveland *(G-5199)*

Cd1025 ....E 614 221-9923
Columbus *(G-7217)*

Cincinnati Public Radio Inc ....E 513 241-8282
Cincinnati *(G-3323)*

City Casters ....E 937 224-1137
Dayton *(G-9408)*

Cumulus Broadcasting LLC ....E 850 243-7676
Cincinnati *(G-3447)*

Cumulus Broadcasting LLC ....D 330 783-1000
Youngstown *(G-20163)*

Cumulus Media Inc ....D 419 725-5700
Toledo *(G-17842)*

Cumulus Media Inc ....D 513 241-9898
Cincinnati *(G-3448)*

Cumulus Media Inc ....D 419 240-1000
Toledo *(G-17843)*

D A Peterson Inc ....E 330 821-1111
Alliance *(G-537)*

Dayton Public School District ....D 937 542-3000
Dayton *(G-9489)*

Educational and Community Rdo ....E 513 724-3939
Batavia *(G-1011)*

Elyria-Lorain Broadcasting Co ....E 440 322-3761
Elyria *(G-10623)*

Fairborn Sftball Offcials Assn ....E 937 902-9920
Dayton *(G-9538)*

Family Stations Inc ....E 330 783-9986
Youngstown *(G-20187)*

Findlay Publishing Company ....E 419 422-4545
Findlay *(G-11028)*

Franklin Communications Inc ....D 614 451-2191
Columbus *(G-7691)*

Franklin Communications Inc ....D 614 459-9769
Columbus *(G-7692)*

Gap Radio Broadcasting LLC ....E 440 992-9700
Ashtabula *(G-744)*

Hubbard Radio Cincinnati LLC ....D 513 699-5102
Cincinnati *(G-3794)*

Iheartcommunications Inc ....E 419 625-1010
Sandusky *(G-16770)*

Iheartcommunications Inc ....E 937 224-1137
Dayton *(G-9626)*

Iheartcommunications Inc ....D 614 486-6101
Columbus *(G-7882)*

Iheartcommunications Inc ....C 937 224-1137
Dayton *(G-9627)*

Iheartcommunications Inc ....C 216 520-2600
Cleveland *(G-5803)*

Iheartcommunications Inc ....E 419 289-2605
Ashland *(G-683)*

Iheartcommunications Inc ....E 419 529-2211
Mansfield *(G-13311)*

Iheartcommunications Inc ....D 330 965-0057
Youngstown *(G-20230)*

Iheartcommunications Inc ....E 216 409-9673
Cleveland *(G-5804)*

Iheartcommunications Inc ....D 419 782-9336
Defiance *(G-10037)*

Iheartcommunications Inc ....D 419 223-2060
Lima *(G-12803)*

Ingleside Investments Inc ....E 614 221-1025
Columbus *(G-7898)*

Johnny Appleseed Broadcasting ....E 419 529-5900
Ontario *(G-15695)*

Kent State University ....E 330 672-3114
Kent *(G-12380)*

Marietta College ....E 740 376-4790
Marietta *(G-13467)*

Maverick Media ....E 419 331-1600
Lima *(G-12838)*

Media-Com Inc ....E 330 673-2323
Kent *(G-12386)*

North American Broadcasting ....D 614 481-7800
Columbus *(G-8286)*

Ohio State University ....C 614 292-4510
Columbus *(G-8406)*

Ohio University ....E 740 593-1771
Athens *(G-806)*

Ohio University ....E 740 593-1771
Athens *(G-805)*

Pillar of Fire ....E 513 542-1212
Cincinnati *(G-4300)*

Public Broadcasting Found NW ....D 419 380-4600
Toledo *(G-18144)*

Radio Promotions ....C 513 381-5000
Cincinnati *(G-4383)*

Radio Seaway Inc ....E 216 916-6100
Cleveland *(G-6343)*

Radiohio Incorporated ....D 614 460-3850
Columbus *(G-8584)*

Rubber City Radio Group ....D 330 869-9800
Akron *(G-420)*

Saga Communications Neng Inc ....D 614 451-2191
Columbus *(G-8675)*

Salem Media Group Inc ....D 216 901-0921
Cleveland *(G-6437)*

Sandusky Newspapers Inc ....C 419 625-5500
Sandusky *(G-16792)*

Southeastern Ohio Brdcstg Sys ....E 740 452-5431
Zanesville *(G-20535)*

Southeastern Ohio TV Sys ....E 740 452-5431
Zanesville *(G-20536)*

Sunrise Television Corp ....E 419 244-2197
Toledo *(G-18209)*

Urban One Inc ....D 216 579-1111
Cleveland *(G-6673)*

Urban One Inc ....E 513 749-1009
Cincinnati *(G-4788)*

Urban One Inc ....E 614 487-1444
Columbus *(G-8918)*

Urban One Inc ....D 216 861-0100
Cleveland *(G-6674)*

Urban One Inc ....E 513 679-6000
Cincinnati *(G-4789)*

W H O T Inc ....D 330 783-1000
Youngstown *(G-20408)*

W K H R Radio ....E 440 708-0915
Bainbridge *(G-943)*

W M V O 1300 AM ....E 740 397-1000
Mount Vernon *(G-14924)*

Weol ....E 440 236-9283
Elyria *(G-10688)*

Wqio 93q Request ....E 740 392-9370
Mount Vernon *(G-14926)*

Wqmx Love Fund ....D 330 869-9800
Akron *(G-512)*

Wrwk 1065 ....E 419 725-5700
Toledo *(G-18315)*

Wzrx ....E 419 223-2060
Lima *(G-12924)*

Xavier University ....E 513 745-3335
Cincinnati *(G-4863)*

Employee Codes: A=Over 500 employees, B=251-500
C=101-250, D=51-100, E=25-50
2018 Harris Ohio
Services Directory
931

48 COMMUNICATIONS

4833 Television Broadcasting Stations

Barrington Toledo LLC .... E 419 535-0024
  Toledo (G-17763)
Bowling Green State University .... E 419 372-2700
  Bowling Green (G-1769)
Dispatch Printing Company .... A 614 461-5000
  Columbus (G-7524)
Dispatch Printing Company .... C 740 548-5331
  Lewis Center (G-12684)
Fox Television Stations Inc .... C 216 432-4278
  Cleveland (G-5627)
Gray Television Group Inc .... D 419 531-1313
  Toledo (G-17920)
Greater Cincinnati TV Educ Fnd .... D 513 381-4033
  Cincinnati (G-3711)
Greater Dayton Public TV .... D 937 220-1600
  Dayton (G-9587)
▲ Ideastream .... C 216 916-6100
  Cleveland (G-5801)
Iheartcommunications Inc .... E 513 763-5500
  Cincinnati (G-3807)
Iheartcommunications Inc .... C 216 520-2600
  Cleveland (G-5803)
Johnny Appleseed Broadcasting .... E 419 529-5900
  Ontario (G-15695)
Lima Communications Corp .... D 419 228-8835
  Lima (G-12819)
Miami Valley Broadcasting Corp ...... C 937 259-2111
  Dayton (G-9727)
New Wrld Cmmunications of Ohio ... D 216 432-4041
  Cleveland (G-6125)
Nexstar Broadcasting Inc .... C 614 263-4444
  Columbus (G-8275)
Nexstar Broadcasting Inc .... D 937 293-2101
  Moraine (G-14811)
Northastern Eductl TV Ohio Inc .... E 330 677-4549
  Kent (G-12388)
Ohio News Network .... D 216 367-7493
  Cleveland (G-6192)
Ohio State University .... C 614 292-4510
  Columbus (G-8406)
Ohio University .... E 740 593-1771
  Athens (G-805)
Ohio University .... E 740 593-1771
  Athens (G-806)
Ohio/Oklahoma Hearst TV Inc .... C 513 412-5000
  Cincinnati (G-4215)
Ohio/Oklahoma Hearst TV Inc .... C 513 412-5000
  Cincinnati (G-4216)
Public Broadcasting Found NW .... D 419 380-4600
  Toledo (G-18144)
Raycom Media Inc .... C 216 367-7300
  Cleveland (G-6355)
Raycom Media Inc .... B 513 421-1919
  Cincinnati (G-4387)
Sinclair Broadcast Group Inc .... C 513 641-4400
  Cincinnati (G-4530)
Sinclair Broadcast Group Inc .... D 513 641-4400
  Cincinnati (G-4531)
Sinclair Media II Inc .... C 614 481-6666
  Columbus (G-8738)
Sinclair Media II Inc .... C 614 481-6666
  Columbus (G-8739)
Sinclair Media II Inc .... D 614 481-6666
  Columbus (G-8740)
Southeastern Ohio TV Sys .... E 740 452-5431
  Zanesville (G-20536)
Sunrise Television Corp .... C 937 293-2101
  Moraine (G-14828)
Sunrise Television Corp .... D 740 282-9999
  Mingo Junction (G-14658)
Sunrise Television Corp .... E 419 244-2197
  Toledo (G-18209)
Thinktv Network .... E 937 220-1600
  Dayton (G-9927)
Toledo Television Investors LP .... D 419 535-0024
  Toledo (G-18252)
Vindicator Printing Company .... D 330 744-8611
  Youngstown (G-20406)
W B N X T V 55 .... E 330 922-5500
  Cuyahoga Falls (G-9234)
W L W T T V 5 .... C 513 412-5000
  Cincinnati (G-4820)
Wbns Tv Inc .... C 614 460-3700
  Columbus (G-8973)
Wfmj Television Inc .... C 330 744-8611
  Youngstown (G-20415)
Wfts .... C 216 431-5555
  Cleveland (G-6749)
Wfts .... C 513 721-9900
  Cincinnati (G-4847)
Winston Brdcstg Netwrk Inc .... E 330 928-5711
  Cuyahoga Falls (G-9236)
Wkyc-Tv Inc .... C 216 344-3300
  Cleveland (G-6756)
Wupw LLC .... E 419 244-3600
  Toledo (G-18316)
Wwst Corporation LLC .... A 330 264-5122
  Wooster (G-19935)

4841 Cable & Other Pay TV Svcs

Armstrong Utilities Inc .... E 330 758-6411
  North Lima (G-15396)
ASC of Cincinnati Inc .... E 513 886-7100
  Lebanon (G-12590)
C T Wireless .... D 937 653-2208
  Urbana (G-18574)
Chillicothe Telephone Company ...... C 740 772-8200
  Chillicothe (G-2825)
Coaxial Communications of Sout .... D 513 797-4400
  Columbus (G-7311)
Comcast Cble Cmmunications LLC . C 503 372-9144
  Steubenville (G-17312)
Comcast Corporation .... D 740 633-3437
  Bridgeport (G-1861)
Comcast Corporation .... D 419 586-1458
  Celina (G-2640)
Comcast Spotlight .... E 440 617-2280
  Westlake (G-19478)
Comcast Spotlight Inc .... B 216 575-8016
  Cleveland (G-5373)
Conneaut Telephone Company .... E 440 593-7140
  Conneaut (G-9041)
Cox Cable Cleveland Area Inc .... C 216 676-8300
  Cleveland (G-5431)
Cox Communications Inc .... D 216 712-4500
  Parma (G-15903)
Cox Communications Inc .... D 937 222-5700
  Dayton (G-9442)
Dish Network Corporation .... D 614 534-2001
  Hilliard (G-11896)
Doylestown Communications .... E 330 658-7000
  Doylestown (G-10226)
▲ DSI Systems Inc .... E 614 871-1456
  Grove City (G-11557)
Erie County Cablevision Inc .... E 419 627-0800
  Sandusky (G-16753)
Fulfillment Technologies LLC .... C 513 346-3100
  West Chester (G-19203)
Insight Communications of Co .... C 614 236-1200
  Columbus (G-7905)
Massillon Cable TV Inc .... D 330 833-4134
  Massillon (G-13833)
Ohio News Network .... D 614 460-3700
  Columbus (G-8362)
Satcom Service LLC .... D 614 863-6470
  Reynoldsburg (G-16481)
Spectrum MGT Holdg Co LLC .... C 614 481-5408
  Columbus (G-8759)
Spectrum MGT Holdg Co LLC .... D 740 455-9705
  Zanesville (G-20537)
Spectrum MGT Holdg Co LLC .... D 330 856-2343
  Warren (G-18901)
Spectrum MGT Holdg Co LLC .... C 419 386-0040
  Port Clinton (G-16256)
Spectrum MGT Holdg Co LLC .... D 740 762-0291
  Chillicothe (G-2888)
Spectrum MGT Holdg Co LLC .... D 513 469-1112
  Cincinnati (G-4559)
Spectrum MGT Holdg Co LLC .... E 614 344-4159
  Columbus (G-8760)
Spectrum MGT Holdg Co LLC .... D 937 552-5760
  Springfield (G-17276)
Spectrum MGT Holdg Co LLC .... D 740 200-3385
  Athens (G-812)
Spectrum MGT Holdg Co LLC .... D 614 503-4153
  Hilliard (G-11952)
Spectrum MGT Holdg Co LLC .... D 440 319-3271
  Ashtabula (G-764)
Spectrum MGT Holdg Co LLC .... D 419 775-9292
  Mansfield (G-13366)
Spectrum MGT Holdg Co LLC .... E 330 208-9028
  Akron (G-446)
Spectrum MGT Holdg Co LLC .... D 937 684-8891
  Dayton (G-9896)
Spectrum MGT Holdg Co LLC .... E 740 772-7809
  Lancaster (G-12576)
Spectrum MGT Holdg Co LLC .... D 937 294-6800
  Dayton (G-9897)
Spectrum MGT Holdg Co LLC .... D 937 306-6082
  Piqua (G-16166)
State Alarm Inc .... E 330 726-8111
  Youngstown (G-20382)
Time Warner Cable Entps LLC .... A 614 255-6289
  Columbus (G-8845)
Time Warner Cable Entps LLC .... C 513 489-5000
  Blue Ash (G-1695)
Time Warner Cable Entps LLC .... E 614 481-5072
  Columbus (G-8846)
Time Warner Cable Inc .... C 614 236-1200
  Columbus (G-8847)
Time Warner Cable Inc .... D 440 366-0416
  Elyria (G-10684)
Time Warner Cable Inc .... D 419 331-1111
  Lima (G-12899)
Time Warner Cable Inc .... D 614 481-5050
  Columbus (G-8848)
Time Warner Cable Inc .... E 330 800-3874
  Akron (G-477)
Time Warner Cable Inc .... A 614 481-5000
  Columbus (G-8849)
Time Warner Cable Inc .... D 330 494-9200
  Canton (G-2562)
Time Warner Cable Inc .... E 330 633-9203
  Youngstown (G-20389)
Time Warner Cable Inc .... D 513 489-5000
  Blue Ash (G-1697)
Time Warner Cable Inc .... D 937 471-1572
  Eaton (G-10577)
Time Warner Cable Inc .... D 513 523-6333
  Oxford (G-15831)
Time Warner Cable Inc .... E 937 483-5152
  Troy (G-18379)
Time Warner Cable Inc .... D 740 345-4329
  Newark (G-15240)
Time Warner Cable Inc .... D 937 667-8302
  Tipp City (G-17727)
Time Warner Cable Inc .... D 937 492-4145
  Sidney (G-16957)
TSC Television Inc .... D 419 941-6001
  Wapakoneta (G-18811)
USI Cable Corp .... E 937 606-2636
  Piqua (G-16173)
Verizon Communications Inc .... C 440 892-4504
  Westlake (G-19562)

4899 Communication Svcs, NEC

A M Communications Ltd .... D 419 528-3051
  Vandalia (G-18655)
Armstrong Utilities Inc .... E 740 894-3886
  South Point (G-17080)
Brand Technologies Inc .... E 419 873-6600
  Perrysburg (G-15980)
◆ Calvert Wire & Cable Corp .... E 216 433-7600
  Cleveland (G-5173)
Cellco Partnership .... D 330 308-0549
  New Philadelphia (G-15084)
Cellco Partnership .... D 614 793-8989
  Dublin (G-10282)
Cincinnati Voice and Data .... D 513 683-4127
  Loveland (G-13115)
Communication Svc For Deaf Inc .... C 937 299-0917
  Moraine (G-14762)
Inet Interactive LLC .... E 513 322-5600
  West Chester (G-19093)
Jay Blue Communications .... E 216 661-2828
  Cleveland (G-5853)
Oovoo LLC .... D 917 515-2074
  Kettering (G-12434)
Springdot Inc .... D 513 542-4000
  Cincinnati (G-4568)
Telcom Construction Svcs Inc .... D 330 239-6900
  Medina (G-14134)
Time Warner Cable Inc .... E 513 354-1100
  Blue Ash (G-1696)
Velocity Grtest Phone Ever Inc .... C 419 868-9983
  Holland (G-12066)
Verizon Communications Inc .... C 419 874-3933
  Perrysburg (G-16069)
Vox Mobile .... E 800 536-9030
  Independence (G-12274)

49 ELECTRIC, GAS, AND SANITARY SERVICES

4911 Electric Svcs

Adams Rural Electric Coop Inc .... E 937 544-2305
  West Union (G-19274)

49 ELECTRIC, GAS, AND SANITARY SERVICES

AEP Energy Partners Inc...............E...... 614 716-1000
  Columbus (G-6949)
AEP Generating Company..............A...... 614 223-1000
  Columbus (G-6951)
AEP Power Marketing Inc................A...... 614 716-1000
  Columbus (G-6952)
American Electric Power Co Inc........E...... 419 420-3011
  Findlay (G-10990)
American Electric Power Co Inc........E...... 740 594-1988
  Athens (G-771)
American Electric Power Co Inc........C...... 330 438-7024
  Canton (G-2237)
American Electric Power Co Inc........E...... 740 779-5261
  Chillicothe (G-2814)
American Electric Power Co Inc........D...... 614 351-3715
  Columbus (G-6988)
American Electric Power Co Inc........E...... 740 384-7981
  Wellston (G-18997)
American Electric Power Co Inc........E...... 330 580-5085
  Canton (G-2238)
American Electric Power Co Inc........E...... 740 598-4164
  Brilliant (G-1865)
▲ American Electric Pwr Svc Corp.....B...... 614 716-1000
  Columbus (G-6990)
American Electric Pwr Svc Corp........E...... 614 582-1742
  Columbus (G-6991)
◆ American Municipal Power Inc......C...... 614 540-1111
  Columbus (G-7002)
▲ Appalachian Power Company........C...... 614 716-1000
  Columbus (G-7029)
Appalachian Power Company............D...... 330 438-7102
  Canton (G-2243)
Buckeye Power Inc..............................B...... 740 598-6534
  Brilliant (G-1866)
Buckeye Power Inc..............................E...... 614 781-0573
  Columbus (G-7160)
Buckeye Rural Elc Coop Inc................E...... 740 379-2025
  Patriot (G-15926)
Butler Rural Electric Coop..................E...... 513 867-4400
  Oxford (G-15812)
Butterfly Inc......................................E...... 440 892-7777
  Independence (G-12191)
Cardinal Operating Company............C...... 740 598-4164
  Brilliant (G-1867)
Carroll Electric Coop Inc....................E...... 330 627-2116
  Carrollton (G-2611)
▲ Cinergy Corp.................................A...... 513 421-9500
  Cincinnati (G-3346)
Cinergy Pwr Gneration Svcs LLC.......A...... 513 421-9500
  Cincinnati (G-3347)
City of Cuyahoga Falls.......................E...... 330 971-8000
  Cuyahoga Falls (G-9173)
City of Dublin....................................E...... 614 410-4750
  Dublin (G-10294)
City of Hamilton.................................D...... 513 785-7450
  Hamilton (G-11711)
City of Hudson Village.......................D...... 330 650-1052
  Hudson (G-12112)
City of Painesville.............................E...... 440 392-5954
  Painesville (G-15840)
City of Toledo...................................D...... 419 245-1800
  Toledo (G-17807)
City of Westerville.............................E...... 614 901-6700
  Westerville (G-19383)
Cleveland Elc Illuminating Co.............D...... 800 589-3101
  Akron (G-147)
Cleveland Elc Illuminating Co.............D...... 440 953-7650
  Painesville (G-15843)
Columbus Southern Power Co...........E...... 614 716-1000
  Columbus (G-7385)
Columbus Southern Power Co...........D...... 740 829-2378
  Conesville (G-9036)
Consolidated Electric Coop................E...... 740 363-2041
  Delaware (G-10081)
Consolidated Electric Coop Inc..........D...... 419 947-3055
  Mount Gilead (G-14852)
Dayton Power and Light Company......C...... 937 224-6000
  Dayton (G-9264)
Dayton Power and Light Company......B...... 937 549-2641
  Aberdeen (G-2)
Dayton Power and Light Company......E...... 937 331-3032
  Miamisburg (G-14294)
Dayton Power and Light Company......D...... 937 549-2641
  Manchester (G-13255)
Dayton Power and Light Company......D...... 937 331-4123
  Moraine (G-14774)
Deepwell Energy Services LLC..........C...... 740 685-2253
  Senecaville (G-16823)
DPL Inc..E...... 937 331-4063
  Dayton (G-9266)
Duke Energy Beckjord LLC................A...... 513 287-2561
  Cincinnati (G-3506)
▲ Duke Energy Ohio Inc...................D...... 704 382-3853
  Cincinnati (G-3508)
Duke Energy Ohio Inc.......................C...... 800 544-6900
  Cincinnati (G-3509)
Duke Energy Ohio Inc.......................E...... 513 287-1120
  Cincinnati (G-3510)
Duke Energy Ohio Inc.......................C...... 513 467-5000
  New Richmond (G-15127)
Duquesne Light Company..................C...... 330 385-6103
  East Liverpool (G-10519)
Dynegy Inc......................................C...... 513 467-4900
  North Bend (G-15318)
Dynegy Washington II LLC................E...... 713 507-6400
  Beverly (G-1490)
▲ Echogen Power Systems Del Inc....E...... 234 542-4379
  Akron (G-206)
Firstenergy Corp...............................A...... 800 736-3402
  Akron (G-225)
Firstenergy Nuclear Oper Co..............A...... 800 646-0400
  Akron (G-226)
Frontier Power Company....................E...... 740 622-6755
  Coshocton (G-9103)
Gavin AEP Plant................................E...... 740 925-3166
  Cheshire (G-2791)
Granger Elc Hancock Cnty LLC.........E...... 517 371-9765
  Findlay (G-11038)
Great Lakes Energy...........................E...... 440 582-4662
  Broadview Heights (G-1880)
Guernsy-Muskingum Elc Coop Inc.....E...... 740 826-7661
  New Concord (G-15034)
Hancock-Wood Electric Coop Inc......E...... 419 257-3241
  North Baltimore (G-15313)
Hearthstone Utilities Inc...................D...... 440 974-3770
  Cleveland (G-5744)
Holmes-Wayne Electric Coop.............E...... 330 674-1055
  Millersburg (G-14606)
Igs Solar LLC..................................E...... 844 447-7652
  Dublin (G-10373)
Indiana Michigan Power Company.....C...... 614 716-1000
  Columbus (G-7889)
▲ Jersey Central Pwr & Light Co.......C...... 800 736-3402
  Akron (G-294)
Jersey Central Pwr & Light Co...........D...... 440 994-8271
  Ashtabula (G-751)
Jersey Central Pwr & Light Co...........D...... 419 366-2915
  Sandusky (G-16771)
Jersey Central Pwr & Light Co...........E...... 330 315-6713
  Fairlawn (G-10960)
Jersey Central Pwr & Light Co...........D...... 937 327-1218
  Springfield (G-17216)
Jersey Central Pwr & Light Co...........C...... 740 537-6308
  Stratton (G-17403)
Jersey Central Pwr & Light Co...........D...... 440 326-3222
  Elyria (G-10637)
Jersey Central Pwr & Light Co...........D...... 216 432-6330
  Cleveland (G-5860)
Jersey Central Pwr & Light Co...........A...... 440 546-8609
  Brecksville (G-1829)
Jersey Central Pwr & Light Co...........D...... 330 336-9884
  Wadsworth (G-18758)
Jersey Central Pwr & Light Co...........D...... 216 479-1132
  Cleveland (G-5861)
Jersey Central Pwr & Light Co...........D...... 440 953-7651
  Painesville (G-15858)
Licking Rural Electrification...............D...... 740 892-2071
  Utica (G-18612)
Metropolitan Edison Company............C...... 800 736-3402
  Newark (G-342)
Mid-Ohio Energy Cooperative.............E...... 419 568-5321
  Kenton (G-12421)
National Gas & Oil Corporation..........D...... 740 344-2102
  Newark (G-15216)
Nisource Inc....................................E...... 614 460-4878
  Columbus (G-8280)
North Central Elc Coop Inc...............E...... 800 426-3072
  Attica (G-822)
NRG Power Midwest LP....................D...... 440 930-6401
  Avon Lake (G-936)
NRG Power Midwest LP....................D...... 330 505-4327
  Niles (G-15301)
Ohio Edison Company......................C...... 800 736-3402
  Akron (G-365)
Ohio Edison Company......................C...... 330 747-2071
  Youngstown (G-20304)
Ohio Edison Company......................C...... 740 671-2900
  Shadyside (G-16851)
Ohio Edison Company......................C...... 330 336-9880
  Wadsworth (G-18766)
Ohio Power Company........................C...... 614 716-1000
  Columbus (G-8366)
Ohio Power Company........................E...... 330 264-1616
  Wooster (G-19897)
Ohio Power Company........................D...... 614 836-2570
  Groveport (G-11660)
Ohio Power Company........................E...... 614 836-2570
  Gahanna (G-11262)
Ohio Power Company........................E...... 614 836-2570
  Columbus (G-8367)
Ohio Power Company........................E...... 740 695-7800
  Saint Clairsville (G-16647)
Ohio Valley Electric Corp..................D...... 740 289-7200
  Piketon (G-16121)
Ohio Valley Electric Corp..................D...... 740 289-7225
  Piketon (G-16122)
Paulding-Putnam Electric Coop.........E...... 419 399-5015
  Paulding (G-15935)
Pennsylvania Electric Company..........C...... 800 545-7741
  Akron (G-382)
Pennsylvania Power Company............C...... 800 720-3600
  Akron (G-383)
Pioneer Rural Electric Coop...............D...... 800 762-0997
  Piqua (G-16155)
Public Service Company Okla............C...... 614 716-1000
  Columbus (G-8578)
South Central Power Company..........E...... 740 474-6045
  Circleville (G-4905)
▲ South Central Power Company......C...... 740 653-4422
  Lancaster (G-12575)
South Central Power Company..........E...... 614 837-4351
  Canal Winchester (G-2171)
South Central Power Company..........E...... 740 425-4018
  Barnesville (G-991)
Southwestern Electric Power Co........C...... 614 716-1000
  Columbus (G-8756)
Toledo Edison Company....................C...... 800 447-3333
  Akron (G-478)
Toledo Edison Company....................E...... 419 321-8488
  Oak Harbor (G-15617)
Toledo Edison Company....................D...... 419 249-5364
  Holland (G-12062)
Union Rural Electric Coop Inc............E...... 937 642-1826
  Marysville (G-13657)

4922 Natural Gas Transmission

Belden & Blake Corporation...............E...... 330 602-5551
  Dover (G-10177)
Columbia Gas of Ohio Inc..................E...... 740 264-5577
  Steubenville (G-17311)
Columbia Gas Transmission LLC........E...... 614 460-6000
  Columbus (G-7323)
Columbia Gas Transmission LLC........E...... 740 397-8242
  Mount Vernon (G-14884)
Columbia Gas Transmission LLC........E...... 614 460-4704
  Columbus (G-7324)
Columbia Gas Transmission LLC........E...... 740 892-2552
  Homer (G-12075)
Consumers Gas Cooperative..............E...... 330 682-4144
  Orrville (G-15768)
Dominion Energy Transm Inc.............E...... 513 932-5793
  Lebanon (G-12601)
▲ Duke Energy Ohio Inc...................D...... 704 382-3853
  Cincinnati (G-3508)
Eureka Midstream LLC.....................E...... 740 868-1325
  Marietta (G-13444)
◆ Koch Knight LLC...........................D...... 330 488-1651
  East Canton (G-10504)
National Gas & Oil Corporation..........D...... 740 344-2102
  Newark (G-15216)
National Gas & Oil Corporation..........F...... 740 454-7252
  Zanesville (G-20514)
Ohio Gas Company...........................E...... 419 636-3642
  Bryan (G-2014)
Texas Eastern Transmission LP.........E...... 513 932-1816
  Lebanon (G-12653)
Utica East Ohio Midstream LLC.........A...... 740 431-4168
  Dennison (G-10168)

4923 Natural Gas Transmission & Distribution

ARC Gas & Supply LLC....................E...... 216 341-5882
  Cleveland (G-5063)
Aspire Energy of Ohio LLC................E...... 330 682-7726
  Orrville (G-15764)
Columbia Gas Transmission LLC........E...... 740 432-1612
  Cambridge (G-2105)
Columbia Gulf Transmission LLC.......E...... 740 746-9105
  Sugar Grove (G-17540)

49 ELECTRIC, GAS, AND SANITARY SERVICES

Dayton Power and Light Company ....D....... 937 331-4123
  Moraine (G-14774)
East Ohio Gas Company ....A....... 800 362-7557
  Maple Heights (G-13406)
East Ohio Gas Company ....B....... 330 266-2169
  New Franklin (G-15044)
East Ohio Gas Company ....C....... 330 477-9411
  Canton (G-2345)
East Ohio Gas Company ....D....... 330 499-2501
  Canton (G-2346)
East Ohio Gas Company ....C....... 216 736-6917
  Wickliffe (G-19595)
East Ohio Gas Company ....C....... 330 478-1700
  Canton (G-2347)
National Gas & Oil Corporation ....E....... 740 454-7252
  Zanesville (G-20514)

4924 Natural Gas Distribution

AEP Energy Services Inc ....B....... 614 583-2900
  Columbus (G-6950)
Bay State Gas Company ....B....... 614 460-4292
  Columbus (G-7094)
▲ Cinergy Corp ....A....... 513 421-9500
  Cincinnati (G-3346)
City of Lancaster ....E....... 740 687-6670
  Lancaster (G-12518)
City of Toledo ....D....... 419 245-1800
  Toledo (G-17807)
Columbia Gas of Ohio Inc ....B....... 614 460-6000
  Columbus (G-7321)
Columbia Gas of Ohio Inc ....D....... 440 891-2458
  Cleveland (G-5372)
Columbia Gas of Ohio Inc ....E....... 419 435-7725
  Findlay (G-11015)
Columbia Gas of Ohio Inc ....C....... 614 481-1000
  Columbus (G-7322)
Columbia Gas Transmission LLC ....E....... 937 327-7108
  Springfield (G-17168)
Delta Energy LLC ....E....... 614 761-3603
  Dublin (G-10318)
▲ Duke Energy Ohio Inc ....D....... 704 382-3853
  Cincinnati (G-3508)
East Ohio Gas Company ....C....... 330 742-8121
  Youngstown (G-20175)
East Ohio Gas Company ....E....... 216 736-6959
  Cleveland (G-5520)
East Ohio Gas Company ....E....... 216 736-6120
  Ashtabula (G-743)
East Ohio Gas Company ....C....... 330 478-1700
  Canton (G-2347)
Hearthstone Utilities Inc ....D....... 440 974-3770
  Cleveland (G-5744)
National Gas & Oil Corporation ....D....... 740 344-2102
  Newark (G-15216)
National Gas & Oil Corporation ....E....... 740 454-7252
  Zanesville (G-20514)
National Gas Oil Corp ....E....... 740 348-1243
  Hebron (G-11857)
Ohio Gas Company ....E....... 419 636-1117
  Bryan (G-2013)
Stand Energy Corporation ....E....... 513 621-1113
  Cincinnati (G-4578)
Volunteer Energy Services Inc ....E....... 614 856-3128
  Pickerington (G-16107)

4925 Gas Production &/Or Distribution

Heritage Cooperative Inc ....D....... 419 294-2371
  West Mansfield (G-19267)
True North Energy LLC ....E....... 614 222-0198
  Columbus (G-8876)
Usher Transport Inc ....E....... 614 875-0528
  Grove City (G-11607)

4931 Electric & Other Svcs Combined

AEP Dresden Plant ....E....... 740 450-1964
  Dresden (G-10230)
City of Columbus ....C....... 614 645-7627
  Columbus (G-7278)
Cliffs Minnesota Minerals Co ....A....... 216 694-5700
  Cleveland (G-5361)
Dayton Power and Light Company ....D....... 937 549-2641
  Manchester (G-13255)
Dayton Power and Light Company ....D....... 937 331-4123
  Moraine (G-14774)
Dayton Power and Light Company ....C....... 937 224-6000
  Dayton (G-9264)
Dayton Power and Light Company ....E....... 937 331-3032
  Miamisburg (G-14294)
Duke Energy Kentucky Inc ....C....... 704 594-6200
  Cincinnati (G-3507)

▲ Duke Energy Ohio Inc ....D....... 704 382-3853
  Cincinnati (G-3508)
Medical Center Co (inc) ....E....... 216 368-4256
  Cleveland (G-6014)
Stockport Mill Country Inn Inc ....E....... 740 559-2822
  Stockport (G-17346)

4932 Gas & Other Svcs Combined

Columbia Gas of Ohio Inc ....D....... 419 539-6046
  Toledo (G-17820)
Dayton Power and Light Company ....D....... 937 549-2641
  Manchester (G-13255)
Dayton Power and Light Company ....E....... 937 331-3032
  Miamisburg (G-14294)
Dayton Power and Light Company ....D....... 937 331-4123
  Moraine (G-14774)
Duke Energy Kentucky Inc ....C....... 704 594-6200
  Cincinnati (G-3507)
G & O Resources Ltd ....D....... 330 253-2525
  Akron (G-232)
Heritage Cooperative Inc ....D....... 419 294-2371
  West Mansfield (G-19267)
National Gas & Oil Corporation ....D....... 740 344-2102
  Newark (G-15216)

4939 Combination Utilities, NEC

City of Lorain ....C....... 440 204-2500
  Lorain (G-13024)
City of Painesville ....B....... 440 392-5795
  Painesville (G-15841)
Jersey Central Pwr & Light Co ....E....... 330 315-6713
  Fairlawn (G-10960)
Ohio Edison Company ....C....... 740 671-2900
  Shadyside (G-16851)
Universal Green Energy Solutio ....E....... 844 723-7768
  Reynoldsburg (G-16487)
University of Cincinnati ....D....... 513 558-1799
  Cincinnati (G-4772)

4941 Water Sply

Aqua Ohio Inc ....E....... 330 832-5764
  Massillon (G-13787)
Aqua Pennsylvania Inc ....E....... 614 882-6586
  Westerville (G-19364)
Belmont County of Ohio ....E....... 740 695-3144
  Saint Clairsville (G-16622)
City Alliance Water Sewer Dst ....E....... 330 823-5216
  Alliance (G-533)
City of Akron ....E....... 330 678-0077
  Kent (G-12358)
City of Akron ....C....... 330 375-2420
  Akron (G-139)
City of Avon Lake ....E....... 440 933-6226
  Avon Lake (G-925)
City of Celina ....E....... 419 586-2451
  Celina (G-2639)
City of Cleveland ....E....... 216 664-3121
  Cleveland (G-5251)
City of Cleveland Heights ....E....... 216 291-5995
  Cleveland Heights (G-6788)
City of Columbus ....E....... 614 645-7490
  Columbus (G-7279)
City of Columbus ....E....... 614 645-8297
  Columbus (G-7285)
City of Columbus ....D....... 614 645-8270
  Columbus (G-7283)
City of Cuyahoga Falls ....E....... 330 971-8130
  Cuyahoga Falls (G-9175)
City of Dayton ....C....... 937 333-6070
  Dayton (G-9412)
City of Dayton ....E....... 937 333-3725
  Dayton (G-9410)
City of Huron ....D....... 419 433-5000
  Huron (G-12163)
City of Lorain ....E....... 440 288-0281
  Lorain (G-13023)
City of Lorain ....C....... 440 204-2500
  Lorain (G-13024)
City of Massillon ....E....... 330 833-3304
  Massillon (G-13796)
City of Toledo ....D....... 419 245-1800
  Toledo (G-17807)
City of Troy ....E....... 937 335-1914
  Troy (G-18351)
City of Westerville ....E....... 614 901-6500
  Westerville (G-19382)
City of Youngstown ....E....... 330 742-8749
  Youngstown (G-20144)
Clearwater Services Inc ....D....... 330 836-4946
  Akron (G-146)

Cleveland Water Department ....A....... 216 664-3168
  Cleveland (G-5354)
County of Licking ....E....... 740 967-5951
  Johnstown (G-12339)
County of Warren ....D....... 513 925-1377
  Lebanon (G-12600)
Del-Co Water Company Inc ....C....... 740 548-7746
  Delaware (G-10086)
East Liverpool Water Dept ....E....... 330 385-8812
  East Liverpool (G-10520)
Employment Relations Board ....E....... 513 863-0828
  Hamilton (G-11726)
Highland County Water Co Inc ....E....... 937 393-4281
  Hillsboro (G-11980)
Medical Center Co (inc) ....E....... 216 368-4256
  Cleveland (G-6014)
New Lexington City of ....E....... 740 342-1633
  New Lexington (G-15057)
Northern Ohio Rural Water ....E....... 419 668-7213
  Norwalk (G-15582)
Northwestern Water & Sewer Dst ....E....... 419 354-9090
  Bowling Green (G-1787)
Ohio-American Water Co Inc ....E....... 740 382-3993
  Marion (G-13570)
Ross County Water Company Inc ....E....... 419 774-4117
  Chillicothe (G-2881)
Rural Lorain County Water Auth ....D....... 440 355-5121
  Lagrange (G-12461)
Scioto County Region Wtr Dst 1 ....E....... 740 259-2301
  Lucasville (G-13182)
Syracuse Water Dept ....E....... 740 992-7777
  Pomeroy (G-16235)
Toledo Cy Pub Utlty Wtr Distr ....C....... 419 936-2506
  Toledo (G-18235)
Victory White Metal Company ....E....... 216 271-7200
  Cleveland (G-6695)

4952 Sewerage Systems

Belmont County of Ohio ....E....... 740 695-3144
  Saint Clairsville (G-16622)
City of Akron ....E....... 330 375-2666
  Akron (G-140)
City of Avon Lake ....E....... 440 933-6226
  Avon Lake (G-925)
City of Columbus ....D....... 614 645-3248
  Lockbourne (G-12947)
City of Dayton ....D....... 937 333-1837
  Dayton (G-9411)
City of Findlay ....E....... 419 424-7179
  Findlay (G-11014)
City of Hamilton ....E....... 513 785-7551
  Hamilton (G-11709)
City of Hamilton ....E....... 513 868-5971
  Hamilton (G-11710)
City of Kent ....D....... 330 678-8105
  Kent (G-12359)
City of Lima ....E....... 419 221-5175
  Lima (G-12756)
City of Lorain ....C....... 440 204-2500
  Lorain (G-13024)
City of Sandusky ....E....... 419 627-5906
  Sandusky (G-16737)
City of Sandusky ....E....... 419 627-5907
  Sandusky (G-16739)
City of Toledo ....E....... 419 936-2924
  Toledo (G-17810)
City of Toledo ....D....... 419 245-1800
  Toledo (G-17807)
City of Westerville ....E....... 614 901-6500
  Westerville (G-19382)
City of Zanesville ....E....... 740 455-0641
  Zanesville (G-20465)
Clermont Cnty Wtr Rsrces Dept ....D....... 513 732-7970
  Batavia (G-999)
County of Lorain ....D....... 440 329-5584
  Elyria (G-10609)
County of Stark ....A....... 330 451-2303
  Canton (G-2323)
County of Warren ....E....... 513 925-1377
  Lebanon (G-12600)
New Lexington City of ....E....... 740 342-1633
  New Lexington (G-15057)
Northeast Ohio Rgonal Sewer Dst ....C....... 216 641-6000
  Cleveland (G-6147)
Northeast Ohio Rgonal Sewer Dst ....D....... 216 531-4892
  Cleveland (G-6148)
Northeast Ohio Rgonal Sewer Dst ....C....... 216 641-3200
  Cleveland (G-6145)
Northwestern Water & Sewer Dst ....E....... 419 354-9090
  Bowling Green (G-1787)

4953 Refuse Systems

Company	Code	Phone
Allied Waste Industries LLC, Oberlin (G-15639)	E	440 774-3100
Allied Waste Systems Inc, Dayton (G-9318)	E	937 268-8110
Allied Waste Systems Inc, Celina (G-2633)	E	419 925-4592
Allied Waste Systems Inc, Bellefontaine (G-1376)	D	937 593-3566
Allied Waste Systems Inc, Bryan (G-2001)	E	419 636-2242
American Landfill Inc, Waynesburg (G-18980)	E	330 866-3265
Appliance Recycl Ctrs Amer Inc, Hilliard (G-11878)	D	614 876-8771
Athens-Hcking Cnty Recycl Ctrs, Athens (G-777)	E	740 797-4208
Avalon Holdings Corporation, Warren (G-18823)	D	330 856-8800
B & B Plastics Recyclers Inc, Columbus (G-7081)	C	614 409-2880
BFI Waste Services LLC, Salem (G-16689)	E	800 437-1123
Big O Refuse Inc, Granville (G-11458)	E	740 344-7544
Boral Resources LLC, Coshocton (G-9088)	D	740 622-8042
Browning-Ferris Inds of Ohio, Youngstown (G-20129)	D	330 793-7676
Browning-Ferris Inds of Ohio, Lowellville (G-13170)	D	330 536-8013
Browning-Ferris Industries Inc, Morrow (G-14844)	E	513 899-2942
Browning-Ferris Industries LLC, Solon (G-16986)	E	440 786-9390
Browning-Ferris Industries LLC, Warren (G-18832)	D	330 393-0385
Builders Trash Service, Columbus (G-7167)	E	614 444-7060
Caraustar Industries Inc, Moraine (G-14758)	E	937 298-9969
Cecos International Inc, Williamsburg (G-19629)	E	513 724-6114
Central Ohio Contractors Inc, Grove City (G-11545)	D	614 539-2579
Central Ohio Contractors Inc, Delaware (G-10078)	D	740 369-7700
Chemtron Corporation, Avon (G-888)	E	440 937-6348
City of Canton, Canton (G-2311)	E	330 489-3080
City of Cleveland Heights, Cleveland (G-5259)	E	216 691-7300
City of Elyria, Elyria (G-10604)	D	440 366-2211
City of Lakewood, Cleveland (G-5265)	E	216 252-4322
City of Perrysburg, Perrysburg (G-15987)	E	419 872-8020
City of Xenia, Xenia (G-20045)	E	937 376-7271
Clean Harbors Envmtl Svcs Inc, Cleveland (G-5283)	E	216 429-2402
Clean Harbors Envmtl Svcs Inc, Cleveland (G-5284)	D	216 429-2401
Clean Harbors Envmtl Svcs Inc, Cincinnati (G-3361)	E	513 681-6242
Clean Harbors Envmtl Svcs Inc, Hebron (G-11846)	E	740 929-3532
Clm Pallet Recycling Inc, Columbus (G-7306)	D	614 272-5761
County of Erie, Milan (G-14493)	D	419 433-0617
County of Montgomery, Moraine (G-14764)	E	937 781-3046
County of Portage, Ravenna (G-16380)	E	330 297-3670
Eco Global Corp, Rockford (G-16561)	E	419 363-2681
Envirite of Ohio Inc, Canton (G-2356)	E	330 456-6238
Environmental Enterprises Inc, Cincinnati (G-3561)	D	513 541-1823
Envirosafe Services of Ohio, Oregon (G-15735)	E	419 698-3500
Envision Waste Services LLC, Cleveland (G-5547)	D	216 831-1818
▲ Fpt Cleveland LLC, Cleveland (G-5628)	C	216 441-3800
Fultz & Son Inc, Clyde (G-6813)	E	419 547-9365
▲ Garden Street Iron & Metal, Cincinnati (G-3662)	E	513 853-3700
Gateway Products Recycling Inc, Cleveland (G-5659)	E	216 341-8777
General Environmental MGT LLC, Chagrin Falls (G-2717)	D	216 621-3694
Global Scrap Management Inc, Batavia (G-1015)	E	513 576-6600
▼ Grasan Equipment Company Inc, Mansfield (G-13306)	D	419 526-4440
Greenstar Mid-America LLC, Akron (G-248)	E	330 784-1167
Hpj Industries Inc, North Baltimore (G-15314)	D	419 278-1000
Hydrochem LLC, Youngstown (G-20225)	E	216 861-3949
▲ Imco Recycling of Ohio LLC, Uhrichsville (G-18490)	C	740 922-2373
In-Plas Recycling Inc, Cincinnati (G-3811)	E	513 541-9800
Industrial Waste Control Inc, Youngstown (G-20233)	D	330 270-9900
▲ Interstate Shredding LLC, Girard (G-11415)	E	330 545-5477
Kimble Companies Inc, Twinsburg (G-18437)	D	330 963-5493
Kimble Companies Inc, Dover (G-10194)	C	330 343-5665
Lafarge North America Inc, Warren (G-18872)	E	330 393-5656
Liberty Tire Recycling LLC, Grove City (G-11576)	E	614 871-8097
Mahoning County, Youngstown (G-20260)	E	330 793-5514
Metalico Akron Inc, Akron (G-340)	E	330 376-1400
Micro Construction LLC, Baltimore (G-948)	E	740 862-0751
Milliron Recycling Inc, Mansfield (G-13347)	D	419 747-6522
Mondo Polymer Technologies Inc, Reno (G-16422)	E	740 376-9396
Novotec Recycling LLC, Columbus (G-8300)	E	614 231-8326
Nucor Corporation, Cincinnati (G-4189)	E	407 855-2990
OK Industries Inc, Fostoria (G-11137)	E	419 435-2361
Perma-Fix of Dayton Inc, Dayton (G-9807)	E	937 268-6501
Pinnacle Recycling LLC, Akron (G-390)	E	330 745-3700
Plastic Recycling Tech Inc, Piqua (G-16161)	E	937 615-9286
Plastic Recycling Tech Inc, Van Wert (G-18641)	E	419 238-9395
Polychem Corporation, Clyde (G-6820)	D	419 547-1400
R & R Sanitation Inc, Mogadore (G-14683)	E	330 325-2311
Recycling Services Inc, Maumee (G-13968)	E	419 381-7762
Republic Services Inc, Bellefontaine (G-1392)	E	937 593-3566
Republic Services Inc, Lowellville (G-13173)	E	330 536-8013
Republic Services Inc, Celina (G-2662)	E	419 925-4592
Republic Services Inc, Sandusky (G-16788)	E	419 626-2454
Republic Services Inc, Cleveland (G-6379)	E	216 741-4013
Republic Services Inc, Cleveland (G-6380)	D	216 741-4013
Republic Services Inc, Elyria (G-10676)	E	440 458-5191
Republic Services Inc, Massillon (G-13847)	E	330 830-9050
Republic Services Inc, Youngstown (G-20345)	E	330 793-7676
Republic Services Inc, Youngstown (G-20346)	E	330 793-7676
Republic Services Inc, Youngstown (G-20347)	E	330 793-7676
Republic Services Inc, Bryan (G-2020)	E	419 636-5109
Republic Services Inc, Oberlin (G-15659)	E	440 774-4060
Republic Services Inc, Cincinnati (G-4407)	E	513 554-0237
Republic Services Inc, Dayton (G-9849)	E	937 268-8110
Republic Services Inc, Cincinnati (G-4408)	D	513 771-4200
Republic Services Inc, Columbus (G-8614)	E	614 308-3000
Republic Services Inc, Columbus (G-8615)	D	740 969-4487
Republic Services Inc, Massillon (G-13848)	E	800 247-3644
Republic Services Inc, Akron (G-412)	E	330 434-9183
Republic Services Inc, Gallipolis (G-11336)	E	800 331-0988
Republic Services Inc, Carey (G-2597)	E	419 396-3581
Republic Services Inc, Port Clinton (G-16252)	E	419 635-2367
Republic Services Inc, Toledo (G-18152)	E	419 726-9465
Republic Services Inc, Sidney (G-16950)	E	937 492-3470
Rls Disposal Company Inc, Chillicothe (G-2875)	E	740 773-1440
Ross Consolidated Corp, Grafton (G-11444)	D	440 748-5800
▼ Ross Incineration Services Inc, Grafton (G-11445)	C	440 366-2000
Royal Paper Stock Company Inc, West Chester (G-19226)	E	513 870-5780
Rpg Inc, Ashland (G-695)	D	419 289-2757
Rumpke Cnsld Companies Inc, Hamilton (G-11771)	C	513 738-0800
Rumpke Sanitary Landfill Inc, Cincinnati (G-4453)	E	513 851-0122
Rumpke Transportation Co LLC, Dayton (G-9856)	E	937 461-0004
Rumpke Transportation Co LLC, Cincinnati (G-4454)	C	513 242-4600
Rumpke Waste Inc, Cincinnati (G-4455)	D	513 851-0122
Rumpke Waste Inc, Greenville (G-11517)	C	937 548-1939
Rumpke Waste Inc, Georgetown (G-11397)	D	937 378-4126
Rumpke Waste Inc, Cincinnati (G-4456)	D	513 242-4401
Rumpke Waste Inc, Circleville (G-4902)	D	740 474-9790
Safety-Kleen Systems Inc, Hebron (G-11860)	D	740 929-3532
Shredded Bedding Corporation, Centerburg (G-2668)	E	740 893-3567
Sidwell Materials Inc, Zanesville (G-20533)	C	740 849-2394
Solid Waste Auth Centl Ohio, Grove City (G-11598)	C	614 871-5100
Spring Grove Rsrce Rcovery Inc, Cincinnati (G-4565)	D	513 681-6242
Stericycle Inc, Warren (G-18903)	D	330 393-0370
Stericycle Inc, Middletown (G-14461)	E	513 539-6213
Stericycle Inc, Toledo (G-18202)	E	419 729-1934
T C Rumpke Waste Collection, Cincinnati (G-4612)	E	513 385-7627
Triad Transport Inc, Columbus (G-8868)	E	614 491-9497
Veolia Es Tchncal Slutions LLC, Miamisburg (G-14365)	D	937 859-6101
▲ Vexor Technology Inc, Medina (G-14137)	E	330 721-9773
Waste Management Ohio Inc, Solon (G-17066)	D	440 201-1235
Waste Management Ohio Inc, Chillicothe (G-2896)	D	800 356-5235
Waste Management Ohio Inc, Wooster (G-19923)	E	800 910-2831
Waste Management Ohio Inc, Canton (G-2583)	E	330 452-9000
Waste Management Ohio Inc, Vickery (G-18734)	E	419 547-7791
Waste Management Ohio Inc, North Jackson (G-15390)	E	866 797-9018
Waste Management Ohio Inc, Northwood (G-15550)	D	866 409-4671

Employee Codes: A=Over 500 employees, B=251-500
C=101-250, D=51-100, E=25-50

49 ELECTRIC, GAS, AND SANITARY SERVICES

Waste Management Ohio Inc .... E 440 286-7116
  Chardon (G-2777)
Waste Management Ohio Inc .... D 740 345-1212
  Newark (G-15245)
Waste Management Ohio Inc .... D 419 221-3644
  Lima (G-12913)
Waste Management Ohio Inc .... D 614 833-5290
  Canal Winchester (G-2178)
Waste Management Ohio Inc .... C 800 343-6047
  Fairborn (G-10812)
Waste Management Ohio Inc .... E 440 285-6767
  Geneva (G-11373)
Waste Management Ohio Inc .... E 419 221-2029
  Lima (G-12914)
Waste Parchment Inc .... E 330 674-6868
  Millersburg (G-14627)
▼ Wws Associates Inc .... C 513 761-5333
  Blue Ash (G-1723)

4959 Sanitary Svcs, NEC

AST Environmental Inc .... E 937 743-0002
  Springboro (G-17115)
Bauer Lawn Maintenance Inc .... E 419 893-5296
  Maumee (G-13886)
Bladecutters Lawn Service Inc .... E 937 274-3861
  Dayton (G-9360)
Board Amercn Township Trustees .... E 419 331-8651
  Elida (G-10586)
Brunk Excavating Inc .... E 513 360-0308
  Monroe (G-14691)
C & B Buck Bros Asp Maint LLC .... E 419 536-7325
  Toledo (G-17789)
C & K Industrial Services Inc .... D 216 642-0055
  Independence (G-12192)
C & K Industrial Services Inc .... E 513 829-5353
  Fairfield (G-10827)
Chemtron Corporation .... E 440 937-6348
  Avon (G-888)
City of Lima .... B 419 221-5294
  Lima (G-12755)
City of Toledo .... C 419 936-2924
  Toledo (G-17810)
Contract Sweepers & Eqp Co .... E 614 221-7441
  Columbus (G-7435)
Cousins Waste Control LLC .... E 419 726-1500
  Toledo (G-17839)
Cuyahoga County Sani Engrg Svc .... C 216 443-8211
  Cleveland (G-5456)
Digestive Disease Consultants .... E 330 225-6468
  Brunswick (G-1975)
▼ Diproinduca (usa) Limited LLC .... D 330 722-4442
  Medina (G-14058)
Dun Rite Home Improvement Inc .... E 330 650-5322
  Macedonia (G-13196)
Environment Control of Greater .... D 614 868-9788
  Columbus (G-7599)
Green Impressions LLC .... E 440 240-8508
  Sheffield Village (G-16886)
Greenscapes Landscape Company ..... D 614 837-1869
  Columbus (G-7778)
H A M Landscaping Inc .... E 216 663-6666
  Cleveland (G-5714)
Image Pavement Maintenance .... E 937 833-9200
  Brookville (G-1963)
Interdyne Corporation .... E 419 229-8192
  Lima (G-12805)
Los Alamos Technical Assoc Inc .... E 614 508-1200
  Westerville (G-19420)
Mahoning County .... C 330 799-1581
  Youngstown (G-20261)
Mc Clurg & Creamer Inc .... E 419 866-7080
  Holland (G-12036)
Northeast Ohio Rgonal Sewer Dst .... C 216 881-6600
  Cleveland (G-6144)
Northeast Ohio Rgonal Sewer Dst .... C 216 641-3200
  Cleveland (G-6145)
Ohio Irrigation Lawn Sprinkler .... E 937 432-9911
  Dayton (G-9786)
Ohio State University .... E 614 293-8732
  Columbus (G-8421)
Paramount Lawn Service Inc .... E 513 984-5200
  Loveland (G-13152)
Petro Environmental Tech .... E 513 489-6789
  Cincinnati (G-4287)
Progrssive Sweeping Contrs Inc .... E 419 464-0130
  Toledo (G-18138)
Reilly Sweeping Inc .... E 440 786-8400
  Cleveland (G-6369)
▲ Samsel Rope & Marine Supply Co ... E 216 241-0333
  Cleveland (G-6442)

Schill Landscaping and Lawn CA .... D 440 327-3030
  North Ridgeville (G-15477)
Spellacys Turf-Lawn Inc .... E 740 965-5508
  Galena (G-11287)
Superior Envmtl Solutions LLC .... B 513 874-8355
  West Chester (G-19235)
Supers Landscaping Inc .... E 440 775-0027
  Oberlin (G-15661)
T J D Industrial Clg & Maint .... E 419 425-5025
  Findlay (G-11090)
T L C Landscaping Inc .... E 440 248-4852
  Cleveland (G-6565)
T O J Inc .... E 440 352-1900
  Mentor (G-14247)
Warstler Brothers Landscaping .... E 330 492-9500
  Canton (G-2582)
Wastren Advantage Inc .... E 970 254-1277
  Piketon (G-16132)
Yardmaster of Columbus Inc .... E 614 863-4510
  Blacklick (G-1513)
Z Snow Removal Inc .... E 513 683-7719
  Maineville (G-13248)

4961 Steam & Air Conditioning Sply

Akron Energy Systems LLC .... D 330 374-0600
  Akron (G-38)
Brewer-Garrett Co .... C 440 243-3535
  Middleburg Heights (G-14378)
Cleveland Thermal LLC .... E 216 241-3636
  Cleveland (G-5352)
Honeywell International Inc .... D 216 459-6053
  Cleveland (G-5770)
Marketing Comm Resource Inc .... E 440 484-3010
  Willoughby (G-19691)
Medical Center Co (inc) .... E 216 368-4256
  Cleveland (G-6014)

4971 Irrigation Systems

City of Dayton .... D 937 333-7138
  Dayton (G-9413)
City of Westerville .... E 614 901-6500
  Westerville (G-19382)
♦ Pentair Rsdntial Fltration LLC .... E 440 286-4116
  Chardon (G-2762)

50 WHOLESALE TRADE¨DURABLE GOODS

5012 Automobiles & Other Motor Vehicles Wholesale

1106 West Main Inc .... E 330 673-2122
  Kent (G-12350)
ABC Detroit/Toledo Auto Auctn .... E 419 872-0872
  Perrysburg (G-15971)
Abers Garage Inc .... E 419 281-5500
  Ashland (G-649)
Ace Truck Body Inc .... E 614 871-3100
  Grove City (G-11527)
Adesa Corporation LLC .... C 937 746-5361
  Franklin (G-11148)
Adesa-Ohio Llc .... C 330 467-8280
  Northfield (G-15508)
Akron Auto Auction Inc .... C 330 724-7708
  Coventry Township (G-9122)
▼ Albert Mike Leasing Inc .... C 513 563-1400
  Cincinnati (G-2982)
Auction Broadcasting Co LLC .... C 419 872-0872
  Perrysburg (G-15972)
Baker Vehicle Systems Inc .... E 330 467-2250
  Macedonia (G-13189)
Beechmont Motors Inc .... E 513 388-3883
  Cincinnati (G-3089)
Beechmont Toyota Inc .... D 513 388-3800
  Cincinnati (G-3092)
Bob Sumerel Tire Co Inc .... E 513 792-6600
  Cincinnati (G-3125)
Bobb Automotive Inc .... E 614 853-3000
  Columbus (G-7123)
Brown Industrial Inc .... E 937 693-3838
  Botkins (G-1752)
Buckeye Truck Equipment Inc .... E 614 299-1136
  Columbus (G-7162)
Bulk Carrier Trnsp Eqp Co .... E 330 339-3333
  New Philadelphia (G-15083)
Bulldawg Holdings LLC .... E 419 423-3131
  Findlay (G-11010)
Central Hummr East .... E 216 514-2700
  Cleveland (G-5212)

Cerni Motor Sales Inc .... D 330 652-9917
  Youngstown (G-20136)
Chuck Nicholson Pntc-GMC Trcks ..... E 330 343-7781
  Dover (G-10180)
Columbus Fair Auto Auction Inc .... A 614 497-2000
  Obetz (G-15666)
Community Emrgcy Med Svcs Ohio .. C 614 751-6651
  Columbus (G-7404)
Copart Inc .... E 614 497-1590
  Columbus (G-7437)
Coughlin Chevrolet Inc .... D 740 964-9191
  Pataskala (G-15922)
Cox Automotive Inc .... C 513 874-9310
  West Chester (G-19057)
Cox Automotive Inc .... B 614 871-2771
  Grove City (G-11550)
Dave Knapp Ford Lincoln Inc .... E 937 547-3000
  Greenville (G-11496)
Donley Ford-Lincoln Inc .... E 419 281-3673
  Ashland (G-679)
Dons Automotive Group LLC .... E 419 337-3010
  Wauseon (G-18951)
Dons Brooklyn Chevrolet Inc .... E 216 741-1500
  Cleveland (G-5504)
Doug Bigelow Chevrolet Inc .... D 330 644-7500
  Akron (G-198)
Doug Marine Motors Inc .... E 740 335-3700
  Wshngtn CT Hs (G-20020)
Downtown Ford Lincoln Inc .... D 330 456-2781
  Canton (G-2344)
Dutro Ford Lincoln-Mercury Inc .... D 740 452-6334
  Zanesville (G-20470)
Ed Schmidt Auto Inc .... E 419 874-4331
  Perrysburg (G-16001)
Ed Tomko Chryslr Jep Dge Inc .... E 440 835-5900
  Avon Lake (G-929)
Esec Corporation .... E 330 799-1536
  Youngstown (G-20181)
Esec Corporation .... E 614 875-3732
  Grove City (G-11558)
Freightliner Trcks of Cncinnati .... E 513 772-7171
  Cincinnati (G-3651)
Fyda Freightliner Youngstown .... D 330 797-0224
  Youngstown (G-20192)
Gallipolis Auto Auction Inc .... E 740 446-1576
  Gallipolis (G-11317)
Gene Stevens Auto & Truck Ctr .... E 419 429-2000
  Findlay (G-11036)
George P Ballas Buick GMC Trck .... D 419 535-1000
  Toledo (G-17913)
Graham Chevrolet-Cadillac Co .... E 419 989-4012
  Ontario (G-15690)
Great Dane Columbus Inc .... E 614 876-0666
  Hilliard (G-11904)
Great Dane LLC .... E 614 876-0666
  Hilliard (G-11905)
Greater Cleveland Auto Auction .... D 216 433-7777
  Cleveland (G-5695)
Haydocy Automotive Inc .... E 614 279-8880
  Columbus (G-7804)
Helton Enterprises Inc .... E 419 423-4180
  Findlay (G-11046)
Hidy Motors Inc .... D 937 426-9564
  Dayton (G-9272)
▼ Honda North America Inc .... E 937 642-5000
  Marysville (G-13625)
Interstate Truckway Inc .... E 614 771-1220
  Columbus (G-7919)
Interstate Truckway Inc .... D 513 542-5500
  Cincinnati (G-3838)
Kempthorn Automall .... C 330 456-8287
  Canton (G-2423)
Kenworth of Cincinnati Inc .... E 513 771-5831
  Cincinnati (G-3916)
Klaben Lincoln Ford Inc .... D 330 673-3139
  Kent (G-12383)
▲ Ktm North America Inc .... D 855 215-6360
  Amherst (G-598)
Laria Chevrolet-Buick Inc .... E 330 925-2015
  Rittman (G-16553)
Liberty Ford Southwest Inc .... D 440 888-2600
  Cleveland (G-5939)
Life Star Rescue Inc .... E 419 238-2507
  Van Wert (G-18637)
Lower Great Lakes Kenworth Inc .... E 419 874-3511
  Perrysburg (G-16029)
M H EBY Inc .... E 614 879-6901
  West Jefferson (G-19253)
▲ Mac Manufacturing Inc .... A 330 823-9900
  Alliance (G-546)

Mac Manufacturing Inc ....C....... 330 829-1680
Salem *(G-16704)*

▲ **Mac Trailer Manufacturing Inc** ....C....... 330 823-9900
Alliance *(G-547)*

Mansfield Truck Sales & Svc ....E....... 419 522-9811
Mansfield *(G-13335)*

McCluskey Chevrolet Inc ....C....... 513 761-1111
Cincinnati *(G-4035)*

Medina Management Company LLC ....D....... 330 723-3291
Medina *(G-14102)*

Midwest Motors Inc ....E....... 330 758-5800
Youngstown *(G-20286)*

Montpelier Auto Auction Ohio ....C....... 419 485-1691
Montpelier *(G-14744)*

Mullinax East LLC ....D....... 440 296-3020
Wickliffe *(G-19608)*

▼ **National Car Mart III Inc** ....E....... 216 398-2228
Cleveland *(G-6102)*

Nollenberger Truck Center ....E....... 419 837-5996
Stony Ridge *(G-17348)*

Performance Autoplex LLC ....D....... 513 870-5033
Fairfield *(G-10895)*

Performance Pontc-Oldmbl GM Tr ....E....... 330 264-1113
Wooster *(G-19902)*

Peterbilt of Cincinnati ....E....... 513 772-1740
Cincinnati *(G-4285)*

Peterbilt of Northwest Ohio ....E....... 419 423-3441
Findlay *(G-11073)*

R & R Inc ....E....... 330 799-1536
Youngstown *(G-20338)*

R & R Truck Sales Inc ....E....... 330 784-5881
Akron *(G-402)*

Rush Truck Centers Ohio Inc ....D....... 513 733-8500
Cincinnati *(G-4458)*

Rush Truck Centers Ohio Inc ....E....... 419 224-6045
Lima *(G-12872)*

Rush Truck Leasing Inc ....E....... 614 876-3500
Columbus *(G-8660)*

Schodorf Truck Body & Eqp Co ....E....... 614 228-6793
Columbus *(G-8698)*

Sharpnack Chevrolet Co ....E....... 440 967-3144
Vermilion *(G-18716)*

Sharron Group Inc ....E....... 614 873-5856
Plain City *(G-16206)*

Sims Buick-G M C Truck Inc ....D....... 330 372-3500
Warren *(G-18900)*

Slimans Sales & Service Inc ....E....... 440 988-4484
Amherst *(G-604)*

South East Chevrolet Co ....E....... 440 585-9300
Willoughby Hills *(G-19735)*

State Park Motors Inc ....E....... 740 264-3113
Steubenville *(G-17334)*

Stoops Frghtlnr-Qlity Trlr Inc ....E....... 937 236-4092
Dayton *(G-9909)*

Stoops of Lima Inc ....C....... 419 228-4334
Lima *(G-12894)*

Stratton Chevrolet Co ....E....... 330 537-3151
Beloit *(G-1432)*

Stykemain Pntiac-Buick-Gmc Ltd ....D....... 419 784-5252
Defiance *(G-10059)*

Tesco-Transportion Eqp Sls ....E....... 419 836-2835
Oregon *(G-15751)*

Tri-State Trailer Sales Inc ....E....... 412 747-7777
West Chester *(G-19237)*

Truck Country Indiana Inc ....C....... 419 228-4334
Lima *(G-12907)*

◆ **Valley Ford Truck Inc** ....D....... 216 524-2400
Cleveland *(G-6683)*

Value Auto Auction LLC ....D....... 740 982-3030
Crooksville *(G-9153)*

▲ **Venco Venturo Industries LLC** ....E....... 513 772-8448
Cincinnati *(G-4806)*

Village Motors Inc ....D....... 330 074-2055
Millersburg *(G-14626)*

Voss Auto Network Inc ....E....... 937 428-2447
Dayton *(G-9976)*

Voss Chevrolet Inc ....C....... 937 428-2500
Dayton *(G-9978)*

Voss Dodge ....E....... 937 435-7800
Dayton *(G-9979)*

Voss Toyota Inc ....E....... 937 427-3700
Beavercreek *(G-1218)*

Walt Sweeney Fleet Sales ....E....... 513 932-2717
Lebanon *(G-12657)*

Warner Buick-Nissan Inc ....E....... 419 423-7161
Findlay *(G-11099)*

White Family Companies Inc ....C....... 937 222-3701
Dayton *(G-9996)*

Whites Service Center Inc ....E....... 937 653-5279
Urbana *(G-18602)*

▼ **Wholecycle Inc** ....E....... 330 929-8123
Peninsula *(G-15953)*

Worldwide Equipment Inc ....D....... 513 563-6363
Cincinnati *(G-4860)*

Youngstown-Kenworth Inc ....E....... 330 534-9761
Hubbard *(G-12093)*

5013 Motor Vehicle Splys & New Parts Wholesale

▲ **Accel Performance Group LLC** ....C....... 216 658-6413
Independence *(G-12177)*

Ace Truck Body Inc ....E....... 614 871-3100
Grove City *(G-11527)*

◆ **Adelmans Truck Parts Corp** ....E....... 330 456-0206
Canton *(G-2225)*

Admiral Truck Parts Inc ....E....... 330 659-6311
Bath *(G-1033)*

Advance Auto Parts Inc ....E....... 440 226-3150
Chardon *(G-2738)*

Advance Stores Company Inc ....C....... 740 369-4491
Delaware *(G-10067)*

▲ **Aftermarket Parts Company LLC** ....D....... 888 333-6224
Delaware *(G-10068)*

Alex Products Inc ....C....... 419 399-4500
Paulding *(G-15927)*

All Lift Service Company Inc ....E....... 440 585-1542
Willoughby *(G-19642)*

Allied Truck Parts Co ....E....... 330 477-8127
Canton *(G-2234)*

Atlas Industries Inc ....B....... 419 637-2117
Tiffin *(G-17671)*

▲ **Auto Aftermarket Concepts** ....E....... 513 942-2535
Cincinnati *(G-3065)*

Automotive Distributors Co Inc ....D....... 614 476-1315
Columbus *(G-7077)*

Automotive Distributors Co Inc ....E....... 330 785-7290
Akron *(G-85)*

Automotive Distributors Co Inc ....E....... 216 398-2014
Cleveland *(G-5083)*

Beechmont Ford Inc ....C....... 513 752-6611
Cincinnati *(G-2904)*

Beechmont Motors Inc ....E....... 513 388-3883
Cincinnati *(G-3089)*

Beechmont Toyota Inc ....D....... 513 388-3800
Cincinnati *(G-3092)*

◆ **Bendix Coml Vhcl Systems LLC** ....B....... 440 329-9000
Elyria *(G-10597)*

◆ **Better Brake Parts Inc** ....E....... 419 227-0685
Lima *(G-12747)*

Bills Battery Company Inc ....E....... 513 922-0100
Cincinnati *(G-3108)*

Bridgeport Auto Parts Inc ....E....... 740 635-0441
Bridgeport *(G-1860)*

Brookville Roadster Inc ....E....... 937 833-4605
Brookville *(G-1961)*

▲ **Building 8 Inc** ....E....... 513 771-8000
Cincinnati *(G-3148)*

▲ **Buyers Products Company** ....C....... 440 974-8888
Mentor *(G-14152)*

▲ **Cadna Rubber Company Inc** ....E....... 901 566-9090
Fairlawn *(G-10940)*

Car Parts Warehouse Inc ....E....... 440 259-2991
Perry *(G-15959)*

▲ **Car Parts Warehouse Inc** ....E....... 216 281-4500
Brookpark *(G-1937)*

Columbus Diesel Supply Co Inc ....E....... 614 445-8391
Reynoldsburg *(G-16439)*

Columbus Public School Dst ....C....... 614 365-5263
Columbus *(G-7376)*

Commercial Truck & Trailer ....E....... 330 545-9717
Girard *(G-11411)*

Contitech North America Inc ....E....... 440 225-5363
Akron *(G-162)*

Cornwell Quality Tools Company ....E....... 330 335-2933
Wadsworth *(G-18751)*

Cross Truck Equipment Co Inc ....E....... 330 477-8151
Canton *(G-2329)*

Crown Dielectric Inds Inc ....C....... 614 224-5161
Columbus *(G-7467)*

D-G Custom Chrome LLC ....D....... 513 531-1881
Cincinnati *(G-3457)*

Dana Heavy Vehicle Systems ....D....... 419 866-3900
Holland *(G-12018)*

Denso International Amer Inc ....B....... 937 393-6800
Hillsboro *(G-11972)*

◆ **Durable Corporation** ....D....... 800 537-1603
Norwalk *(G-15571)*

▼ **East Manufacturing Corporation** ....B....... 330 325-9921
Randolph *(G-16372)*

▲ **Faurecia Exhaust Systems LLC** ....C....... 419 727-5000
Toledo *(G-17880)*

Fayette Parts Service Inc ....C....... 740 282-4547
Steubenville *(G-17316)*

Finishmaster Inc ....D....... 614 228-4328
Columbus *(G-7657)*

◆ **Four Wheel Drive Hardware LLC** ....C....... 330 482-4733
Columbiana *(G-6859)*

Freudenberg-Nok General Partnr ....B....... 419 499-2502
Milan *(G-14494)*

Frontier Tank Center Inc ....E....... 330 659-3888
Richfield *(G-16510)*

Fuyao Glass America Inc ....C....... 937 496-5777
Dayton *(G-9566)*

G & C Finishes From The Future ....E....... 937 890-3002
Dayton *(G-9567)*

▲ **G S Wiring Systems Inc** ....B....... 419 423-7111
Findlay *(G-11034)*

▼ **G-Cor Automotive Corp** ....E....... 614 443-6735
Columbus *(G-7721)*

General Motors LLC ....C....... 513 874-0535
West Chester *(G-19080)*

General Motors LLC ....C....... 513 603-6600
West Chester *(G-19081)*

General Parts Inc ....D....... 330 220-6500
Brunswick *(G-1980)*

General Parts Inc ....E....... 614 267-5197
Columbus *(G-7734)*

Genuine Parts Company ....B....... 614 766-6865
Columbus *(G-7740)*

GKN Driveline North Amer Inc ....D....... 419 354-3955
Bowling Green *(G-1777)*

◆ **Goodyear Tire & Rubber Company** ....A....... 330 796-2121
Akron *(G-243)*

Greenleaf Auto Recyclers LLC ....E....... 330 832-6001
Massillon *(G-13814)*

GTM Service Inc ....E....... 440 944-5099
Wickliffe *(G-19600)*

H & H Auto Parts Inc ....D....... 330 456-4778
Canton *(G-2386)*

H & H Auto Parts Inc ....E....... 330 494-2975
Canton *(G-2387)*

Hahn Automotive Warehouse Inc ....E....... 937 223-1068
Dayton *(G-9597)*

Hamilton Automotive Warehouse ....D....... 513 896-4000
Hamilton *(G-11738)*

Hamilton Automotive Warehouse ....D....... 513 896-4100
Hamilton *(G-11739)*

Hankook Tire America Corp ....E....... 330 896-6199
Uniontown *(G-18523)*

▲ **Harris Battery Company Inc** ....E....... 330 874-0205
Bolivar *(G-1748)*

Hebco Products Inc ....A....... 419 562-7987
Bucyrus *(G-2039)*

Herbert E Orr Company ....C....... 419 399-4866
Paulding *(G-15931)*

Hite Parts Exchange Inc ....E....... 614 272-5115
Columbus *(G-7842)*

Honda Trading America Corp ....C....... 937 644-8004
Marysville *(G-13627)*

▲ **Hy-Tek Material Handling Inc** ....D....... 614 497-2500
Columbus *(G-7873)*

Ieh Auto Parts LLC ....E....... 740 373-8327
Marietta *(G-13454)*

Ieh Auto Parts LLC ....E....... 740 732-2395
Caldwell *(G-2086)*

Ieh Auto Parts LLC ....E....... 740 373-8151
Marietta *(G-13455)*

▲ **Interstate Diesel Service Inc** ....C....... 216 881-0015
Cleveland *(G-5834)*

▲ **Jegs Automotive Inc** ....C....... 614 294-5050
Delaware *(G-10110)*

Jim Hayden Inc ....D....... 513 563-8828
Cincinnati *(G-3873)*

Joseph Russo ....E....... 440 748-2690
Grafton *(G-11441)*

Jr Engineering Inc ....C....... 330 848-0960
Barberton *(G-968)*

K - O - I Warehouse Inc ....E....... 937 323-5585
Springfield *(G-17218)*

▲ **K - O - I Warehouse Inc** ....E....... 513 357-2400
Cincinnati *(G-3896)*

◆ **Kaffenbarger Truck Eqp Co** ....C....... 937 845-3804
New Carlisle *(G-15025)*

Kar Products ....A....... 216 416-7200
Cleveland *(G-5884)*

◆ **Keihin Thermal Tech Amer Inc** ....B....... 740 869-3000
Mount Sterling *(G-14873)*

Kenton Auto and Truck Wrecking ....E....... 419 673-8234
Kenton *(G-12420)*

S I C

Employee Codes: A=Over 500 employees, B=251-500
C=101-250, D=51-100, E=25-50

2018 Harris Ohio
Services Directory

937

50 WHOLESALE TRADE¨DURABLE GOODS

Kenworth of Cincinnati Inc ....D....... 513 771-5831
  Cincinnati (G-3916)
Keystone Automotive Inds Inc ....D....... 513 961-5500
  Cincinnati (G-3920)
Keystone Automotive Inds Inc ....E....... 330 759-8019
  Girard (G-11419)
Klase Enterprises Inc ....E....... 330 452-6300
  Canton (G-2427)
▲ KOI Enterprises Inc ....D....... 513 357-2400
  Cincinnati (G-3939)
Lower Great Lakes Kenworth Inc ....E....... 419 874-3511
  Perrysburg (G-16029)
◆ Luk-Aftermarket Service Inc ....D....... 330 273-4383
  Valley City (G-18620)
▲ Mac Trailer Manufacturing Inc ....C....... 330 823-9900
  Alliance (G-547)
▲ Matco Tools Corporation ....B....... 330 929-4949
  Stow (G-17382)
▲ McBee Supply Corporation ....E....... 216 881-0015
  Cleveland (G-6001)
◆ MJ Auto Parts Inc ....E....... 440 205-6272
  Mentor (G-14221)
◆ Myers Industries Inc ....E....... 330 253-5592
  Akron (G-348)
National Marketshare Group ....E....... 513 921-0800
  Cincinnati (G-4140)
Neff Machinery and Supplies ....E....... 740 454-0128
  Zanesville (G-20515)
Nk Parts Industries Inc ....E....... 937 493-4651
  Sidney (G-16943)
Nu-Di Products Co Inc ....D....... 216 251-9070
  Cleveland (G-6170)
▲ Ohashi Technica USA Inc ....E....... 740 965-5115
  Sunbury (G-17560)
Ohio Auto Supply Company ....E....... 330 454-5105
  Canton (G-2478)
Ohio Automotive Supply Co ....E....... 419 422-1655
  Findlay (G-11072)
OReilly Automotive Inc ....D....... 330 494-0042
  North Canton (G-15360)
OReilly Automotive Inc ....E....... 419 630-0811
  Bryan (G-2015)
OReilly Automotive Inc ....D....... 330 318-3136
  Boardman (G-1742)
P & M Exhaust Systems Whse ....E....... 513 825-2660
  Cincinnati (G-4247)
▼ Par International Inc ....E....... 614 529-1300
  Obetz (G-15669)
Pat Young Service Co Inc ....E....... 440 891-1550
  Avon (G-912)
▲ Pat Young Service Co Inc ....E....... 216 447-8550
  Cleveland (G-6250)
Perkins Motor Service Ltd ....E....... 440 277-1256
  Lorain (G-13071)
Peterbilt of Cincinnati ....E....... 513 772-1740
  Cincinnati (G-4285)
Pgw Auto Glass LLC ....E....... 419 993-2421
  Lima (G-12859)
▲ Pioneer Automotive Tech Inc ....C....... 937 746-2293
  Springboro (G-17136)
▲ Power Train Components Inc ....D....... 419 636-4430
  Bryan (G-2018)
Premier Truck Parts Inc ....E....... 216 642-5000
  Cleveland (G-6302)
R & R Inc ....E....... 330 799-1536
  Youngstown (G-20338)
▲ R L Morrissey & Assoc Inc ....E....... 440 498-3730
  Solon (G-17044)
Rocknstarr Holdings LLC ....E....... 330 509-9086
  Youngstown (G-20354)
Rubini Enterprises Inc ....E....... 419 729-7010
  Toledo (G-18166)
Shiloh Manufacturing LLC ....E....... 330 558-2693
  Valley City (G-18624)
▲ Shrader Tire & Oil Inc ....E....... 419 472-2128
  Toledo (G-18186)
Smyth Automotive Inc ....D....... 513 528-2800
  Cincinnati (G-4543)
Smyth Automotive Inc ....E....... 513 528-0061
  Cincinnati (G-4544)
Smyth Automotive Inc ....E....... 513 777-6400
  West Chester (G-19157)
▲ Snyders Antique Auto Parts Inc ....E....... 330 549-5313
  New Springfield (G-15131)
▲ Stellar Srkg Acquisition LLC ....E....... 330 769-8484
  Seville (G-16847)
▲ Stoddard Imported Cars Inc ....D....... 440 951-1040
  Mentor (G-14245)
Thyssenkrupp Bilstein Amer Inc ....E....... 513 881-7600
  West Chester (G-19162)

◆ Thyssenkrupp Bilstein Amer Inc ....C....... 513 881-7600
  Hamilton (G-11778)
Tk Holdings Inc ....E....... 937 778-9713
  Piqua (G-16168)
Transport Services Inc ....E....... 440 582-4900
  Cleveland (G-6612)
Truckomat Corporation ....E....... 740 467-2818
  Hebron (G-11861)
Turbo Parts LLC ....E....... 740 223-1695
  Marion (G-13587)
▼ Valley Ford Truck Inc ....E....... 216 524-2400
  Cleveland (G-6683)
▲ Ventra Salem LLC ....A....... 330 337-8002
  Salem (G-16718)
W W Williams Company LLC ....E....... 419 837-5067
  Perrysburg (G-16071)
W W Williams Company LLC ....E....... 419 837-5067
  Perrysburg (G-16070)
◆ Western Tradewinds Inc ....E....... 937 859-4300
  Miamisburg (G-14368)
Whites Service Center Inc ....E....... 937 653-5279
  Urbana (G-18602)
▲ Winston Products LLC ....D....... 440 478-1418
  Cleveland (G-6754)
World Auto Parts Inc ....E....... 216 781-8418
  Cleveland (G-6758)
◆ Wz Management Inc ....E....... 330 628-4881
  Akron (G-514)
Young Truck Sales Inc ....E....... 330 477-6271
  Canton (G-2592)
Youngstown-Kenworth Inc ....E....... 330 534-9761
  Hubbard (G-12093)

5014 Tires & Tubes Wholesale

▲ American Kenda Rbr Indus Ltd ....E....... 866 536-3287
  Reynoldsburg (G-16428)
Belle Tire Distributors Inc ....E....... 419 473-1393
  Toledo (G-17768)
▲ Best One Tire & Svc Lima Inc ....E....... 419 229-2380
  Lima (G-12746)
Bob Sumerel Tire Co Inc ....E....... 513 792-6600
  Cincinnati (G-3125)
Bob Sumerel Tire Co Inc ....E....... 614 527-9700
  Columbus (G-7122)
▲ Capital Tire Inc ....E....... 419 241-5111
  Toledo (G-17790)
Capital Tire Inc ....E....... 419 865-7151
  Toledo (G-17791)
Central Ohio Bandag LP ....E....... 740 454-9728
  Zanesville (G-20460)
Conrads Tire Service Inc ....E....... 216 941-3333
  Cleveland (G-5392)
Dayton Marshall Tire Sales Co ....E....... 937 293-8330
  Moraine (G-14782)
◆ Dealer Tire LLC ....B....... 216 432-0088
  Cleveland (G-5472)
▲ Grismer Tire Company ....E....... 937 643-2526
  Centerville (G-2678)
Hankook Tire America Corp ....E....... 330 896-6199
  Uniontown (G-18523)
Joseph Russo ....E....... 440 748-2690
  Grafton (G-11441)
▲ K & M Tire Inc ....E....... 419 695-1061
  Delphos (G-10145)
K & M Tire Inc ....E....... 419 695-1060
  Delphos (G-10146)
▲ Malone Warehouse Tire Inc ....E....... 740 592-2893
  Athens (G-800)
▲ Millersburg Tire Service Inc ....E....... 330 674-1085
  Millersburg (G-14612)
◆ Myers Industries Inc ....E....... 330 253-5592
  Akron (G-348)
North Gateway Tire Co Inc ....E....... 330 725-8473
  Medina (G-14108)
Reville Tire Co ....D....... 330 468-1900
  Northfield (G-15523)
Rush Truck Centers Ohio Inc ....D....... 513 733-8500
  Cincinnati (G-4458)
Rush Truck Centers Ohio Inc ....E....... 419 224-6045
  Lima (G-12872)
Rush Truck Leasing Inc ....E....... 614 876-3500
  Columbus (G-8660)
▲ Shrader Tire & Oil Inc ....E....... 419 472-2128
  Toledo (G-18186)
▲ Speck Sales Incorporated ....E....... 419 353-8312
  Bowling Green (G-1794)
▲ Stoney Hollow Tire Inc ....D....... 740 635-5200
  Martins Ferry (G-13601)
◆ Technical Rubber Company Inc ....B....... 740 967-9015
  Johnstown (G-12343)

Tire Waste Transport Inc ....B....... 419 363-2681
  Rockford (G-16564)
▲ W D Tire Warehouse Inc ....E....... 614 461-8944
  Columbus (G-8957)
Ziegler Tire and Supply Co ....E....... 330 353-1499
  Massillon (G-13865)

5015 Motor Vehicle Parts, Used Wholesale

Advance Auto Parts Inc ....E....... 440 226-3150
  Chardon (G-2738)
Beheydts Auto Wrecking ....E....... 330 658-6109
  Doylestown (G-10223)
Bob Sumerel Tire Co Inc ....E....... 614 527-9700
  Columbus (G-7122)
▼ Dales Truck Parts Inc ....E....... 937 766-2551
  Cedarville (G-2632)
▼ G-Cor Automotive Corp ....E....... 614 443-6735
  Columbus (G-7721)
General Motors LLC ....C....... 513 603-6600
  West Chester (G-19081)
Greenleaf Ohio LLC ....E....... 330 832-6001
  Massillon (G-13815)
Lkq Triplettasap Inc ....C....... 330 733-6333
  Akron (G-323)
▲ Mac Trailer Manufacturing Inc ....C....... 330 823-9900
  Alliance (G-547)
Myers Bus Parts and Sups Co ....E....... 330 533-2275
  Canfield (G-2202)
Nk Parts Industries Inc ....E....... 937 493-4651
  Sidney (G-16943)
Speedie Auto Salvage Ltd ....E....... 330 878-9961
  Dover (G-10215)
▼ Stricker Bros Inc ....E....... 513 732-1152
  Batavia (G-1026)

5021 Furniture Wholesale

Apg Office Furnishings Inc ....E....... 216 621-4590
  Cleveland (G-5048)
Big Lots Inc ....E....... 330 726-0796
  Youngstown (G-20115)
▲ Big Lots Stores Inc ....B....... 614 278-6800
  Columbus (G-7107)
Business Furniture LLC ....E....... 937 293-1010
  Dayton (G-9375)
Cbf Industries Inc ....E....... 216 229-9300
  Bedford (G-1298)
Central Business Equipment Co ....E....... 513 891-4430
  Cincinnati (G-3210)
Collaborative Inc ....E....... 419 242-7405
  Toledo (G-17819)
◆ Continental Office Furn Corp ....C....... 614 262-5010
  Columbus (G-7428)
◆ Cornerstone Brands Inc ....A....... 513 603-1000
  West Chester (G-19052)
EBO Inc ....E....... 216 229-9300
  Bedford (G-1305)
Everybodys Inc ....E....... 937 293-1010
  Moraine (G-14782)
Federated Logistics ....E....... 937 294-3074
  Moraine (G-14784)
Friends Service Co Inc ....D....... 419 427-1704
  Findlay (G-11033)
Indepndence Office Bus Sup Inc ....D....... 216 398-8880
  Cleveland (G-5815)
Jones Group Interiors Inc ....E....... 330 253-9180
  Akron (G-297)
King Business Interiors Inc ....E....... 614 430-0020
  Columbus (G-7992)
La-Z-Boy Incorporated ....C....... 614 478-0898
  Columbus (G-8026)
Loth Inc ....D....... 614 487-4000
  Columbus (G-8077)
Loth Inc ....D....... 614 225-1933
  Columbus (G-8078)
▲ Mantua Manufacturing Co ....C....... 800 333-8333
  Bedford (G-1320)
Mat Innovative Solutions LLC ....E....... 216 398-8010
  Independence (G-12232)
McNerney & Son Inc ....E....... 419 666-0200
  Toledo (G-18046)
▲ Mill Distributors Inc ....D....... 330 995-9200
  Aurora (G-848)
Office Furniture Resources Inc ....E....... 216 781-8200
  Cleveland (G-6180)
Patterson Pope Inc ....D....... 513 891-4430
  Cincinnati (G-4263)
Pottery Barn Inc ....E....... 216 378-1211
  Cleveland (G-6293)
▲ Progressive Furniture Inc ....E....... 419 446-4500
  Archbold (G-641)

SIC SECTION 50 WHOLESALE TRADE¨DURABLE GOODS

▲ Regency Seating Inc .... E 330 848-3700
Akron *(G-408)*

S P Richards Company .... E 614 497-2270
Obetz *(G-15670)*

◆ Sauder Woodworking Co .... A 419 446-3828
Archbold *(G-645)*

Seagate Office Products Inc .... E 419 861-6161
Holland *(G-12055)*

Signal Office Supply Inc .... E 513 821-2280
Cincinnati *(G-4528)*

Springfield Business Eqp Co .... E 937 322-3828
Springfield *(G-17279)*

Staples Inc .... E 614 472-2014
Columbus *(G-8775)*

Thomas W Ruff and Company .... B 800 828-0234
Columbus *(G-8838)*

Value City Furniture Inc .... E 330 929-2111
Cuyahoga Falls *(G-9231)*

W B Mason Co Inc .... D 216 267-5000
Cleveland *(G-6713)*

◆ Wasserstrom Company .... B 614 228-6525
Columbus *(G-8970)*

Workshops of David T Smith .... E 513 932-2472
Morrow *(G-14848)*

5023 Home Furnishings Wholesale

Accent Drapery Co Inc .... E 614 488-0741
Columbus *(G-6933)*

▲ American Frame Corporation .... E 419 893-5595
Maumee *(G-13874)*

▲ Americas Floor Source LLC .... D 614 808-3915
Columbus *(G-7011)*

Bcf LLC .... E 937 746-0721
Miamisburg *(G-14274)*

▲ Bostwick-Braun Company .... D 419 259-3600
Toledo *(G-17778)*

Business Furniture LLC .... E 937 293-1010
Dayton *(G-9375)*

Century Glass Co .... E 216 361-7700
Cleveland *(G-5218)*

◆ Cinmar LLC .... C 513 603-1000
West Chester *(G-19040)*

Creative Products Inc .... E 419 866-5501
Holland *(G-12017)*

▲ Culver Art & Frame Co .... E 740 548-6868
Lewis Center *(G-12679)*

D & S Crtive Cmmunications Inc .... E 419 524-4312
Mansfield *(G-13289)*

▲ Dealers Supply North Inc .... E 614 274-6285
Lockbourne *(G-12948)*

Dwa Mrkting Prmtional Pdts LLC .... E 216 476-0635
Strongsville *(G-17457)*

Everfast Inc .... B 216 360-9176
Cleveland *(G-5557)*

Everybodys Inc .... E 937 293-1010
Moraine *(G-14782)*

Famous Distribution Inc .... D 330 762-9621
Akron *(G-215)*

▲ G G Marck & Associates Inc .... E 419 478-0900
Toledo *(G-17903)*

Ghp II LLC .... B 740 681-6825
Lancaster *(G-12544)*

▲ Hayward Distributing Co .... E 614 272-5953
Columbus *(G-7805)*

Hobby Lobby Stores Inc .... E 330 686-1508
Stow *(G-17371)*

◆ Interdesign Inc .... B 440 248-0136
Solon *(G-17018)*

JP Flooring Systems Inc .... E 513 346-4300
West Chester *(G-19099)*

Lumenomics Inc .... E 614 798-3500
Lewis Center *(G-12693)*

Luminex Home Decor .... A 513 563-1113
Blue Ash *(G-1632)*

◆ Marketing Results Ltd .... E 614 575-9300
Columbus *(G-8111)*

▲ Mill Distributors Inc .... D 330 995-9200
Aurora *(G-848)*

National Marketshare Group .... E 513 921-0800
Cincinnati *(G-4140)*

Newell Brands Inc .... C 419 662-2225
Bowling Green *(G-1786)*

▲ Norwood Hardware & Supply Co .... E 513 733-1175
Cincinnati *(G-4185)*

▲ Ohio Valley Flooring Inc .... D 513 271-3434
Cincinnati *(G-4212)*

Old Time Pottery Inc .... D 513 825-5211
Cincinnati *(G-4219)*

Old Time Pottery Inc .... D 440 842-1244
Cleveland *(G-6199)*

Old Time Pottery Inc .... D 614 337-1258
Columbus *(G-8464)*

Original Hartstone Pottery Inc .... E 740 452-9999
Zanesville *(G-20521)*

Pfpc Enterprises Inc .... B 513 941-6200
Cincinnati *(G-4290)*

Pottery Barn Inc .... E 614 478-3154
Columbus *(G-8553)*

PTX Flooring Inc .... E 419 726-1775
Toledo *(G-18143)*

Regal Carpet Center Inc .... E 216 475-1844
Cleveland *(G-6366)*

Rite Rug Co .... E 440 945-4100
Strongsville *(G-17502)*

◆ State Crest Carpet & Flooring .... E 440 232-3980
Bedford *(G-1340)*

Style-Line Incorporated .... E 614 291-0600
Columbus *(G-8798)*

Ten Thousand Villages Cleveland .... E 216 575-1058
Cleveland *(G-6580)*

Walter F Stephens Jr Inc .... E 937 746-0521
Franklin *(G-11167)*

Wholesale Decor LLC .... E 330 587-7100
Hartville *(G-11833)*

Workshops of David T Smith .... E 513 932-2472
Morrow *(G-14848)*

▲ World Tableware Inc .... D 419 325-2608
Toledo *(G-18314)*

5031 Lumber, Plywood & Millwork Wholesale

Acord Rk Lumber Company .... E 740 289-3761
Piketon *(G-16108)*

Advance Door Company .... E 216 883-2424
Cleveland *(G-4957)*

Allied Building Products Corp .... E 513 784-9090
Cincinnati *(G-2989)*

American Warming and Vent .... D 419 288-2703
Bradner *(G-1808)*

Andersen Distribution Inc .... C 937 898-7844
Dayton *(G-9336)*

Apco Industries Inc .... D 614 224-2345
Columbus *(G-7027)*

Appalachia Wood Inc .... E 740 596-2551
Mc Arthur *(G-14015)*

▲ Appalachian Hardwood Lumber Co .... E 440 232-6767
Cleveland *(G-5049)*

▲ Associated Materials LLC .... B 330 929-1811
Cuyahoga Falls *(G-9161)*

Associated Materials Group Inc .... E 330 929-1811
Cuyahoga Falls *(G-9162)*

Associated Mtls Holdings LLC .... A 330 929-1811
Cuyahoga Falls *(G-9163)*

Baillie Lumber Co LP .... E 419 462-2000
Galion *(G-11292)*

▼ Bennett Supply of Ohio LLC .... E 800 292-5577
Macedonia *(G-13190)*

Bluelinx Corporation .... E 330 794-1141
Akron *(G-105)*

Boise Cascade Company .... E 740 382-6766
Marion *(G-13525)*

▼ Brenneman Lumber Co .... E 740 397-0573
Mount Vernon *(G-14879)*

Brower Products Inc .... D 937 563-1111
Cincinnati *(G-3142)*

Buckeye Components LLC .... E 330 482-5163
Columbiana *(G-6853)*

Builders Firstsource Inc .... E 937 898-1358
Vandalia *(G-18665)*

Builders Firstsource Inc .... E 513 874-9950
Cincinnati *(G-3147)*

Carter-Jones Companies Inc .... E 330 673-6100
Kent *(G-12354)*

Carter-Jones Lumber Company .... C 330 674-9060
Millersburg *(G-14591)*

▲ Carter-Jones Lumber Company .... C 330 673-6100
Kent *(G-12355)*

Carter-Jones Lumber Company .... D 330 784-5441
Akron *(G-123)*

Carter-Jones Lumber Company .... A 330 673-6000
Kent *(G-12356)*

Clark Son Actn Liquidation Inc .... E 330 837-9710
Canal Fulton *(G-2142)*

▲ Clem Lumber and Distrg Co .... D 330 821-2130
Alliance *(G-534)*

Daniels Lumber Co Inc .... D 330 533-2211
Canfield *(G-2188)*

Dayton Door Sales Inc .... E 937 253-9181
Dayton *(G-9472)*

Dayton Door Sales Inc .... E 937 253-9181
Dayton *(G-9471)*

▲ Direct Import Home Decor Inc .... E 216 898-9758
Cleveland *(G-5485)*

Don Walter Kitchen Distrs Inc .... E 330 793-9338
Youngstown *(G-20172)*

Dortronic Service Inc .... E 216 739-3667
Cleveland *(G-5506)*

Dublin Millwork Co Inc .... E 614 889-7776
Dublin *(G-10331)*

▼ Eagle Hardwoods Inc .... E 330 339-8838
Newcomerstown *(G-15267)*

Edrich Supply Co .... E 440 238-9440
Strongsville *(G-17459)*

▲ Enclosure Suppliers LLC .... E 513 782-3900
Cincinnati *(G-3555)*

Famous Enterprises Inc .... E 330 762-9621
Akron *(G-217)*

Fifth Avenue Lumber Co .... D 614 294-0068
Columbus *(G-7654)*

Francis-Schulze Co .... E 937 295-3941
Russia *(G-16614)*

Garick LLC .... E 937 462-8350
South Charleston *(G-17076)*

Gorell Enterprises Inc .... B 724 465-1800
Streetsboro *(G-17414)*

Graf and Sons Inc .... E 614 481-2020
Columbus *(G-7765)*

Gross Lumber Inc .... E 330 683-2055
Apple Creek *(G-625)*

Gunton Corporation .... C 216 831-2420
Cleveland *(G-5710)*

▲ Hamilton-Parker Company .... D 614 358-7800
Columbus *(G-7797)*

▼ Hartzell Hardwoods Inc .... D 937 773-7054
Piqua *(G-16146)*

Hd Supply Inc .... E 614 771-4849
Groveport *(G-11643)*

Holmes Lumber & Bldg Ctr Inc .... C 330 674-9060
Millersburg *(G-14604)*

Hrh Door Corp .... E 330 893-3233
Dundee *(G-10500)*

Huttig Building Products Inc .... E 614 492-8248
Obetz *(G-15667)*

J McCoy Lumber Co Ltd .... E 937 587-3423
Peebles *(G-15940)*

Kansas City Hardwood Corp .... E 913 621-1975
Lakewood *(G-12484)*

Keidel Supply Company Inc .... E 513 351-1600
Cincinnati *(G-3906)*

Keim Lumber Company .... E 330 893-2251
Baltic *(G-946)*

Khempco Bldg Sup Co Ltd Partnr .... D 740 549-0465
Delaware *(G-10113)*

Koch Aluminum Mfg Inc .... E 419 625-5956
Sandusky *(G-16774)*

La Force Inc .... E 513 772-0783
Cincinnati *(G-3954)*

◆ Litco International Inc .... E 330 539-5433
Vienna *(G-18739)*

Lowes Home Centers LLC .... C 216 351-4723
Cleveland *(G-5953)*

Lowes Home Centers LLC .... C 419 739-1300
Wapakoneta *(G-18803)*

Lowes Home Centers LLC .... C 937 235-2920
Dayton *(G-9688)*

Lowes Home Centers LLC .... C 740 574-6200
Wheelersburg *(G-19578)*

Lowes Home Centers LLC .... C 330 665-9356
Akron *(G-328)*

Lowes Home Centers LLC .... C 330 829-2700
Alliance *(G-545)*

Lowes Home Centers LLC .... C 937 599-4000
Bellefontaine *(G-1300)*

Lowes Home Centers LLC .... C 419 420-7531
Findlay *(G-11057)*

Lowes Home Centers LLC .... C 330 832-1901
Massillon *(G-13829)*

Lowes Home Centers LLC .... C 513 741-0585
Cincinnati *(G-3996)*

Lowes Home Centers LLC .... C 614 433-9957
Columbus *(G-6892)*

Lowes Home Centers LLC .... C 740 389-9737
Marion *(G-13549)*

Lowes Home Centers LLC .... C 740 450-5500
Zanesville *(G-20497)*

Lowes Home Centers LLC .... C 513 598-7050
Cincinnati *(G-3997)*

Lowes Home Centers LLC .... C 614 769-9940
Reynoldsburg *(G-16466)*

Lowes Home Centers LLC .... C 614 853-6200
Columbus *(G-8079)*

SIC

Employee Codes: A=Over 500 employees, B=251-500
C=101-250, D=51-100, E=25-50

2018 Harris Ohio
Services Directory

939

50 WHOLESALE TRADE¨DURABLE GOODS

Lowes Home Centers LLC ....C....... 440 937-3500
  Avon (G-906)
Lowes Home Centers LLC ....C....... 513 445-1000
  South Lebanon (G-17078)
Lowes Home Centers LLC ....B....... 216 831-2860
  Bedford (G-1318)
Lowes Home Centers LLC ....C....... 937 327-6000
  Springfield (G-17226)
Lowes Home Centers LLC ....C....... 419 331-3598
  Lima (G-12832)
Lowes Home Centers LLC ....C....... 740 681-3464
  Lancaster (G-12551)
Lowes Home Centers LLC ....C....... 614 659-0530
  Dublin (G-10392)
Lowes Home Centers LLC ....C....... 614 238-2601
  Columbus (G-8080)
Lowes Home Centers LLC ....C....... 740 522-0003
  Newark (G-15199)
Lowes Home Centers LLC ....C....... 740 773-7777
  Chillicothe (G-2862)
Lowes Home Centers LLC ....C....... 440 998-6555
  Ashtabula (G-752)
Lowes Home Centers LLC ....B....... 513 753-5094
  Cincinnati (G-2924)
Lowes Home Centers LLC ....C....... 614 497-6170
  Columbus (G-8081)
Lowes Home Centers LLC ....C....... 513 731-6127
  Cincinnati (G-3998)
Lowes Home Centers LLC ....C....... 330 287-2261
  Wooster (G-19884)
Lowes Home Centers LLC ....C....... 937 339-2544
  Troy (G-18362)
Lowes Home Centers LLC ....C....... 440 392-0027
  Mentor (G-14210)
Lowes Home Centers LLC ....C....... 440 942-2759
  Willoughby (G-19688)
Lowes Home Centers LLC ....C....... 740 374-2151
  Marietta (G-13462)
Lowes Home Centers LLC ....C....... 419 874-6758
  Perrysburg (G-16030)
Lowes Home Centers LLC ....C....... 330 626-2980
  Streetsboro (G-17419)
Lowes Home Centers LLC ....C....... 419 389-9464
  Toledo (G-18013)
Lowes Home Centers LLC ....C....... 419 843-9758
  Toledo (G-18014)
Lowes Home Centers LLC ....C....... 614 447-2851
  Columbus (G-8082)
Lowes Home Centers LLC ....C....... 330 245-4300
  Akron (G-329)
Lowes Home Centers LLC ....C....... 513 965-3280
  Milford (G-14532)
Lowes Home Centers LLC ....C....... 330 908-2750
  Northfield (G-15519)
Lowes Home Centers LLC ....C....... 419 470-2491
  Toledo (G-18015)
Lowes Home Centers LLC ....C....... 513 336-9741
  Mason (G-13733)
Lowes Home Centers LLC ....C....... 937 498-8400
  Sidney (G-16941)
Lowes Home Centers LLC ....C....... 740 699-3000
  Saint Clairsville (G-16642)
Lowes Home Centers LLC ....C....... 330 920-9280
  Stow (G-17381)
Lowes Home Centers LLC ....C....... 740 589-3750
  Athens (G-799)
Lowes Home Centers LLC ....C....... 740 393-5350
  Mount Vernon (G-14910)
Lowes Home Centers LLC ....C....... 937 547-2400
  Greenville (G-11513)
Lowes Home Centers LLC ....C....... 330 335-1900
  Wadsworth (G-18763)
Lowes Home Centers LLC ....C....... 937 347-4000
  Xenia (G-20068)
Lowes Home Centers LLC ....C....... 440 239-2630
  Strongsville (G-17485)
Lowes Home Centers LLC ....C....... 513 755-4300
  West Chester (G-19113)
Lowes Home Centers LLC ....C....... 513 671-2093
  Cincinnati (G-3999)
Lowes Home Centers LLC ....C....... 440 331-1027
  Rocky River (G-16585)
Lowes Home Centers LLC ....C....... 330 677-3040
  Kent (G-12384)
Lowes Home Centers LLC ....C....... 419 747-1920
  Ontario (G-15698)
Lowes Home Centers LLC ....C....... 330 339-1936
  New Philadelphia (G-15107)
Lowes Home Centers LLC ....C....... 440 985-5700
  Lorain (G-13058)

Lowes Home Centers LLC ....C....... 419 447-4101
  Tiffin (G-17682)
Lowes Home Centers LLC ....C....... 937 578-4440
  Marysville (G-13632)
Lowes Home Centers LLC ....C....... 440 324-5004
  Elyria (G-10647)
Lowes Home Centers LLC ....C....... 937 438-4900
  Dayton (G-9689)
Lowes Home Centers LLC ....C....... 937 427-1110
  Beavercreek (G-1189)
Lowes Home Centers LLC ....C....... 937 848-5600
  Dayton (G-9690)
Lowes Home Centers LLC ....C....... 614 529-5900
  Hilliard (G-11923)
Lowes Home Centers LLC ....C....... 513 737-3700
  Hamilton (G-11755)
Lowes Home Centers LLC ....C....... 740 894-7120
  South Point (G-17091)
Lowes Home Centers LLC ....C....... 513 727-3900
  Middletown (G-14431)
Lowes Home Centers LLC ....C....... 419 355-0221
  Fremont (G-11210)
Lowes Home Centers LLC ....C....... 419 624-6000
  Sandusky (G-16777)
Lowes Home Centers LLC ....C....... 419 782-9000
  Defiance (G-10045)
Lowes Home Centers LLC ....C....... 330 609-8000
  Warren (G-18876)
Lowes Home Centers LLC ....C....... 330 965-4500
  Youngstown (G-20257)
Lowes Home Centers LLC ....C....... 937 383-7000
  Wilmington (G-19769)
Lowes Home Centers LLC ....C....... 937 854-8200
  Dayton (G-9691)
Lowes Home Centers LLC ....C....... 330 497-2720
  Canton (G-2440)
Lowes Home Centers LLC ....C....... 740 266-3500
  Steubenville (G-17327)
Lowes Home Centers LLC ....C....... 614 476-7100
  Columbus (G-8083)
Lumberjacks Inc ....E....... 330 762-2401
  Akron (G-330)
Lute Supply Inc ....E....... 740 353-1447
  Portsmouth (G-16294)
Mae Holding Company ....E....... 513 751-2424
  Cincinnati (G-4011)
Marsh Building Products Inc ....E....... 937 222-3321
  Dayton (G-9700)
Mason Structural Steel Inc ....D....... 440 439-1040
  Walton Hills (G-18790)
Mentor Lumber and Supply Co ....C....... 440 255-8814
  Mentor (G-14214)
▲ Meyer Decorative Surfaces USA .....E....... 800 776-3900
  Hudson (G-12133)
Milestone Ventures LLC ....E....... 317 908-2093
  Newark (G-15208)
Milliken Millwork Inc ....D....... 513 874-6771
  West Chester (G-19217)
Millwood Inc ....C....... 440 914-0540
  Solon (G-17028)
Modern Builders Supply Inc ....E....... 513 531-1000
  Cincinnati (G-4113)
▼ Muth Lumber Company Inc ....E....... 740 533-0800
  Ironton (G-12300)
Nilco LLC ....E....... 888 248-5151
  Hartville (G-11827)
Nilco LLC ....E....... 330 538-3386
  North Jackson (G-15384)
Norandex Bldg Mtls Dist Inc ....A....... 330 656-8924
  Hudson (G-12136)
North Shore Door Co Inc ....E....... 800 783-6112
  Elyria (G-10662)
Northwest Building Resources ....E....... 419 286-5400
  Fort Jennings (G-11109)
▲ Norwood Hardware & Supply Co ....E....... 513 733-1175
  Cincinnati (G-4185)
OK Interiors Corp ....C....... 513 742-3278
  Cincinnati (G-4217)
Olde Towne Windows Inc ....E....... 419 626-9613
  Milan (G-14496)
Orrville Trucking & Grading Co ....E....... 330 682-4010
  Orrville (G-15780)
Pallet Distributors Inc ....C....... 888 805-9670
  Lakewood (G-12494)
Palmer-Donavin Mfg Co ....D....... 614 277-2777
  Urbancrest (G-18607)
Paxton Hardwoods LLC ....E....... 513 984-8200
  Cincinnati (G-4266)
Pella Corporation ....D....... 513 948-8480
  Cincinnati (G-4275)

Ply-Trim South Inc ....E....... 330 799-7876
  Youngstown (G-20326)
Premier Construction Company ....E....... 513 874-2611
  Fairfield (G-10896)
▼ Price Woods Products Inc ....E....... 513 722-1200
  Loveland (G-13153)
▲ Professional Laminate Mllwk Inc ....E....... 513 891-7858
  Milford (G-14556)
Provia Holdings Inc ....C....... 330 852-4711
  Sugarcreek (G-17546)
S R Door Inc ....D....... 740 927-3558
  Hebron (G-11859)
Schneider Home Equipment Co ....E....... 513 522-1200
  Cincinnati (G-4483)
▲ Sims-Lohman Inc ....E....... 513 651-3510
  Cincinnati (G-4529)
Southern Ohio Door Contrls Inc ....E....... 513 353-4793
  Miamitown (G-14373)
▲ Stephen M Trudick ....E....... 440 834-1891
  Burton (G-2065)
◆ Style Crest Inc ....B....... 419 332-7369
  Fremont (G-11223)
◆ T J Ellis Enterprises Inc ....E....... 419 999-5026
  Lima (G-12898)
Toledo Molding & Die Inc ....D....... 419 354-6050
  Bowling Green (G-1795)
Toledo Molding & Die Inc ....D....... 419 692-6022
  Delphos (G-10152)
Traichal Construction Company ....E....... 800 255-3667
  Niles (G-15307)
Tri-County Pallet Recycl Inc ....E....... 330 848-0313
  Akron (G-481)
▲ Tri-State Forest Products Inc ....E....... 937 323-6325
  Springfield (G-17289)
◆ Usavinyl LLC ....E....... 614 771-4805
  Groveport (G-11682)
Vwc Liquidation Company LLC ....C....... 330 372-6776
  Warren (G-18922)
Wappoo Wood Products Inc ....E....... 937 492-1166
  Sidney (G-16960)
Window Factory of America ....D....... 440 439-3050
  Bedford (G-1344)

5032 Brick, Stone & Related Construction Mtrls Wholesale

▲ Accco Inc ....E....... 740 697-2005
  Roseville (G-16600)
Acme Company ....D....... 330 758-2313
  Poland (G-16219)
Allega Recycled Mtls & Sup Co ....E....... 216 447-0814
  Cleveland (G-4992)
Arrowhead Transport Co ....E....... 330 638-2900
  Cortland (G-9072)
Barrett Paving Materials Inc ....C....... 513 271-6200
  Middletown (G-14475)
Boral Resources LLC ....D....... 740 622-8042
  Coshocton (G-9088)
▼ Bruder Inc ....E....... 216 791-9800
  Maple Heights (G-13402)
C & B Buck Bros Asp Maint LLC ....E....... 419 536-7325
  Toledo (G-17789)
CCI Supply Inc ....C....... 440 953-0045
  Mentor (G-14154)
▲ Clay Burley Products Co ....E....... 740 452-3633
  Roseville (G-16601)
Columbus Coal & Lime Co ....E....... 614 224-9241
  Columbus (G-7340)
Digeronimo Aggregates LLC ....E....... 216 524-2950
  Independence (G-12204)
▲ Direct Import Home Decor Inc ....E....... 216 898-9758
  Cleveland (G-5485)
Gms Inc ....E....... 937 222-4444
  Dayton (G-9575)
▲ Hamilton-Parker Company ....D....... 614 358-7800
  Columbus (G-7797)
Hanson Aggregates East LLC ....E....... 937 442-6009
  Winchester (G-19802)
Hull Builders Supply Inc ....E....... 440 967-3159
  Vermilion (G-18710)
Huron Cement Products Company ....E....... 419 433-4161
  Huron (G-12166)
Hwz Distribution Group LLC ....E....... 513 618-0300
  West Chester (G-19209)
Hwz Distribution Group LLC ....E....... 513 723-1150
  Cincinnati (G-3800)
Hy-Grade Corporation ....E....... 216 341-7711
  Cleveland (G-5795)
▲ Indus Trade & Technology LLC ......E....... 614 527-0257
  Columbus (G-7892)

SIC SECTION
50 WHOLESALE TRADE¨DURABLE GOODS

J & B Equipment & Supply Inc .... D 419 884-1155
  Mansfield *(G-13314)*
▲ Jainco International Inc .... C 440 519-0100
  Solon *(G-17020)*
▲ Justice & Co Inc .... E 330 225-6000
  Medina *(G-14088)*
▲ Kenmore Construction Co Inc .... C 330 762-8936
  Akron *(G-303)*
Koltcz Concrete Block Co .... E 440 232-3630
  Bedford *(G-1315)*
Kuhlman Corporation .... C 419 897-6000
  Maumee *(G-13934)*
L & W Supply Corporation .... E 614 276-6391
  Columbus *(G-8019)*
Lafarge North America Inc .... D 419 798-4486
  Marblehead *(G-13422)*
▲ Lang Stone Company Inc .... D 614 235-4099
  Columbus *(G-8038)*
Martin Marietta Materials Inc. .... E 513 829-6446
  Fairfield *(G-10875)*
Martin Marietta Materials Inc. .... E 614 871-6708
  Grove City *(G-11579)*
▲ Maza Inc .... E 614 760-0003
  Plain City *(G-16198)*
Meander Tire Company Inc .... E 330 750-6155
  Youngstown *(G-20278)*
▲ Mees Distributors Inc .... E 513 541-2311
  Cincinnati *(G-4051)*
Micro Construction LLC .... E 740 862-0751
  Baltimore *(G-948)*
Mid-Ohio Valley Lime Inc .... E 740 373-1006
  Marietta *(G-13477)*
Modern Builders Supply Inc .... D 330 726-7000
  Youngstown *(G-20288)*
Modern Builders Supply Inc .... C 330 729-2690
  Youngstown *(G-20289)*
Modern Builders Supply Inc .... E 419 241-3961
  Toledo *(G-18068)*
Nexgen Enterprises Inc .... C 513 618-0300
  Cincinnati *(G-4162)*
◆ Pinney Dock & Transport LLC .... E 440 964-7186
  Ashtabula *(G-760)*
Proterra Inc .... E 216 383-8449
  Wickliffe *(G-19612)*
Quality Block & Supply Inc .... E 330 364-4411
  Mount Eaton *(G-14850)*
R W Sidley Incorporated .... E 330 793-7374
  Youngstown *(G-20340)*
Robinson Insulation Co Inc .... E 937 323-9599
  Springfield *(G-17264)*
Sewer Rodding Equipment Co .... E 419 991-2065
  Lima *(G-12876)*
Sidwell Materials Inc .... C 740 849-2394
  Zanesville *(G-20533)*
▲ Snyder Concrete Products Inc ..... E 937 885-5176
  Moraine *(G-14825)*
Stamm Contracting Co Inc .... E 330 274-8230
  Mantua *(G-13395)*
Stone Coffman Company LLC .... E 614 861-4668
  Gahanna *(G-11270)*
Sylvester Materials Co .... C 419 841-3874
  Sylvania *(G-17621)*
Westfall Aggregate & Mtls Inc .... D 740 420-9090
  Circleville *(G-4907)*

5033 Roofing, Siding & Insulation Mtrls Wholesale

Allied Building Products Corp .... E 216 362-1764
  Cleveland *(G-4993)*
Allied Building Products Corp .... E 513 784-9090
  Cincinnati *(G-2989)*
Allied Building Products Corp .... E 614 488-0717
  Columbus *(G-6969)*
Alpine Insulation I LLC .... A 614 221-3399
  Columbus *(G-6977)*
Apco Industries Inc .... D 614 224-2345
  Columbus *(G-7027)*
Associated Materials LLC .... E 614 985-4611
  Columbus *(G-7055)*
▲ Associated Materials LLC .... B 330 929-1811
  Cuyahoga Falls *(G-9161)*
Associated Materials Group Inc ...... E 330 929-1811
  Cuyahoga Falls *(G-9162)*
Associated Mtls Holdings LLC .... A 330 929-1811
  Cuyahoga Falls *(G-9163)*
Beacon Sales Acquisition Inc .... C 330 425-3359
  Twinsburg *(G-18397)*
CCI Supply Inc .... D 440 953-0045
  Mentor *(G-14154)*

◆ Great Lakes Textiles Inc .... E 440 439-1300
  Solon *(G-17012)*
Hd Supply Inc .... E 614 771-4849
  Groveport *(G-11643)*
Installed Building Pdts Inc .... C 614 221-3399
  Columbus *(G-7908)*
Johns Manville Corporation .... D 419 784-7000
  Defiance *(G-10038)*
Lindsey Cnstr & Design Inc .... E 330 785-9931
  Akron *(G-321)*
Modern Builders Supply Inc .... E 937 222-2627
  Dayton *(G-9753)*
Modern Builders Supply Inc .... E 513 531-1000
  Cincinnati *(G-4113)*
Norandex Bldg Mtls Dist Inc .... A 330 656-8924
  Hudson *(G-12136)*
▲ Palmer-Donavin Mfg Co .... C 614 486-0975
  Columbus *(G-8511)*
R E Kramig & Co Inc .... C 513 761-4010
  Cincinnati *(G-4378)*
Vinyl Design Corporation .... E 419 283-4009
  Holland *(G-12067)*
Willoughby Supply Company .... E 440 942-7939
  Mentor *(G-14258)*

5039 Construction Materials, NEC Wholesale

▲ Agratronix LLC .... E 330 562-2222
  Streetsboro *(G-17406)*
American Warming and Vent .... D 419 288-2703
  Bradner *(G-1808)*
Anderson Glass Co Inc .... E 614 476-4877
  Columbus *(G-7018)*
Apco Industries Inc .... D 614 224-2345
  Columbus *(G-7027)*
Century Glass Co .... E 216 361-7700
  Cleveland *(G-5218)*
▼ Cleveland Glass Block Inc .... E 216 531-6363
  Cleveland *(G-5316)*
Cleveland Glass Block Inc .... E 614 252-5888
  Cleveland *(G-7299)*
D & S Crtive Cmmunications Inc .... E 419 524-4312
  Mansfield *(G-13289)*
Efficient Services Ohio Inc .... E 330 627-4440
  Carrollton *(G-2619)*
Eger Products Inc .... D 513 753-4200
  Amelia *(G-580)*
▲ Glenny Glass Company .... E 513 489-2233
  Milford *(G-14522)*
Harmon Inc .... E 513 645-1550
  West Chester *(G-19089)*
Marysville Steel Inc .... E 937 642-5971
  Marysville *(G-13636)*
▲ Medina Glass Block Inc .... E 330 239-0239
  Medina *(G-14100)*
▲ Mills Fence Co Inc .... E 513 631-0333
  Cincinnati *(G-4100)*
Morton Buildings Inc .... D 419 675-2311
  Kenton *(G-12422)*
Olde Towne Windows Inc .... E 419 626-9613
  Milan *(G-14496)*
Palmer-Donavin Mfg Co .... E 419 692-5000
  Delphos *(G-10148)*
Real America Inc .... B 216 261-1177
  Cleveland *(G-6357)*
▲ Richards Whl Fence Co Inc .... E 330 773-0423
  Akron *(G-415)*
Schneider Home Equipment Co .... E 513 522-1200
  Cincinnati *(G-4483)*
Security Fence Group Inc .... E 513 681-3700
  Cincinnati *(G-4489)*
Six C Fabrication Inc .... D 330 296-5594
  Ravenna *(G-16412)*
▼ Valicor Environmental Svcs LLC D 513 733-4666
  Monroe *(G-14717)*
▲ Will-Burt Company .... E 330 682-7015
  Orrville *(G-15789)*
Will-Burt Company .... E 330 682-7015
  Orrville *(G-15790)*

5043 Photographic Eqpt & Splys Wholesale

Collins KAO Inc .... E 513 948-9000
  Cincinnati *(G-3388)*
▲ KAO Collins Inc .... D 513 948-9000
  Cincinnati *(G-3901)*
Technicolor Thomson Group .... C 937 383-6000
  Wilmington *(G-19790)*

5044 Office Eqpt Wholesale

American Copy Equipment Inc .... C 330 922-9555
  Cleveland *(G-5008)*

Andrew Belmont Sargent .... E 513 769-7800
  Cincinnati *(G-3027)*
Apg Office Furnishings Inc .... E 216 621-4590
  Cleveland *(G-5048)*
▲ Big Lots Stores Inc .... B 614 278-6800
  Columbus *(G-7107)*
Blakemans Valley Off Eqp Inc .... E 330 729-1000
  Youngstown *(G-20116)*
Blue Technologies Inc .... E 216 271-4800
  Cleveland *(G-5126)*
Blue Technologies Inc .... E 330 499-9300
  Canton *(G-2266)*
Business Alternatives Inc .... E 724 325-2777
  Uniontown *(G-18509)*
Business Data Systems Inc .... E 330 633-1221
  Tallmadge *(G-17633)*
Canon Solutions America Inc .... D 937 260-4495
  Miamisburg *(G-14278)*
Collaborative Inc .... E 419 242-7405
  Toledo *(G-17819)*
Comdoc Inc .... E 330 539-4822
  Girard *(G-11410)*
Comdoc Inc .... C 330 896-2346
  Uniontown *(G-18514)*
David Francis Corporation .... C 216 524-0900
  Cleveland *(G-5466)*
Document Imging Spcialists LLC .. E 614 868-9008
  Columbus *(G-7538)*
Document Solutions Ohio LLC ..... E 614 846-2400
  Columbus *(G-7539)*
Donnellon Mc Carthy Inc .... E 937 299-3564
  Moraine *(G-14775)*
Donnellon Mc Carthy Inc .... E 513 681-3200
  Cincinnati *(G-3498)*
Essendant Co .... C 330 425-4001
  Twinsburg *(G-18412)*
Essendant Co .... D 614 876-7774
  Columbus *(G-7610)*
Franklin Imaging Llc .... E 614 885-6894
  Columbus *(G-7697)*
Friends Service Co Inc .... D 419 427-1704
  Findlay *(G-11033)*
Giesecke & Devrient Amer Inc ..... C 330 425-1515
  Twinsburg *(G-18423)*
Goodremonts .... E 419 476-1492
  Toledo *(G-17918)*
Gordon Flesch Company Inc .... E 419 884-2031
  Mansfield *(G-13305)*
▲ Graphic Enterprises Inc .... D 800 553-6616
  North Canton *(G-15340)*
Graphic Entps Off Slutions Inc ..... D 800 553-6616
  North Canton *(G-15341)*
Konica Minolta Business Soluti ... E 910 990-5837
  Cleveland *(G-5911)*
Lorain Cnty Sty Off Eqp Co Inc ... D 440 960-7070
  Amherst *(G-599)*
M T Business Technologies .... E 440 933-7682
  Avon Lake *(G-935)*
Meritech Inc .... D 216 459-8333
  Cleveland *(G-6028)*
Modern Office Methods Inc .... D 513 791-0909
  Blue Ash *(G-1644)*
Mt Business Technologies Inc .... C 419 529-6100
  Mansfield *(G-13348)*
Northcoast Duplicating Inc .... C 216 573-6681
  Cleveland *(G-6150)*
Office Depot Inc .... E 800 463-3768
  Cleveland *(G-6179)*
Office Products Inc/Cleveland .... E 919 754-3700
  Cleveland *(G-6181)*
Office Products Toledo Inc .... E 419 865-7001
  Holland *(G-12044)*
Office World Inc .... E 419 991-4694
  Lima *(G-12928)*
Ohio Business Machines LLC .... E 216 485-2000
  Cleveland *(G-6187)*
P-N-D Communications Inc .... E 419 683-1922
  Crestline *(G-9149)*
Perry Pro Tech Inc .... E 419 475-9030
  Perrysburg *(G-16040)*
Perry Pro Tech Inc .... D 419 228-1360
  Lima *(G-12857)*
Ricoh Usa Inc .... D 513 984-9898
  Blue Ash *(G-1683)*
Ricoh Usa Inc .... D 614 310-6500
  Worthington *(G-19994)*
Ricoh Usa Inc .... E 330 523-3900
  Richfield *(G-16527)*
Schenker Inc .... D 614 257-8365
  Lockbourne *(G-12960)*

Employee Codes: A=Over 500 employees, B=251-500
C=101-250, D=51-100, E=25-50

50 WHOLESALE TRADE¨DURABLE GOODS SIC SECTION

Springfield Business Eqp Co....E....937 322-3828
Springfield *(G-17279)*
Symatic Inc....E....330 225-1510
Brunswick *(G-1991)*
Viking Office Products Inc....B....513 881-7200
West Chester *(G-19181)*
Visual Edge Technology Inc....C....330 494-9694
Canton *(G-2579)*
W B Mason Co Inc....D....216 267-5000
Cleveland *(G-6713)*
Xerox Corporation....D....216 642-7806
Cleveland *(G-6767)*
Xerox Corporation....B....513 554-3200
Blue Ash *(G-1724)*

5045 Computers & Peripheral Eqpt & Software Wholesale

3sg Corporation....C....614 309-3600
Dublin *(G-10232)*
Advanced Cmpt Connections LLC....E....419 668-4080
Norwalk *(G-15561)*
Advantech Corporation....D....513 742-8895
Blue Ash *(G-1528)*
Agilysys Inc....E....440 519-6262
Solon *(G-16971)*
Arrow Globl Asset Dspstion Inc....D....614 328-4100
Gahanna *(G-11233)*
Ascendtech Inc....E....216 458-1101
Willoughby *(G-19645)*
Avid Technologies Inc....E....330 487-0770
Twinsburg *(G-18395)*
Blue Tech Smart Solutions LLC....E....216 271-4800
Cleveland *(G-5125)*
Blue Technologies Inc....E....330 499-9300
Canton *(G-2266)*
Bsl - Applied Laser Tech LLC....E....216 663-8181
Cleveland *(G-5154)*
Business Data Systems Inc....E....330 633-1221
Tallmadge *(G-17633)*
Canon Solutions America Inc....D....937 260-4495
Miamisburg *(G-14278)*
Cincinnati Bell Techno....D....513 841-6700
Cincinnati *(G-3286)*
Cisco Systems Inc....D....614 764-4987
Dublin *(G-10293)*
Commercial Time Sharing Inc....E....330 644-3059
Akron *(G-152)*
Computer Helper Publishing....E....614 939-9094
Columbus *(G-7417)*
Cranel Incorporated....D....614 431-8000
Columbus *(G-6879)*
Datavantage Corporation....B....440 498-4414
Cleveland *(G-5464)*
▲ Decision One....E....614 883-0215
Grove City *(G-11552)*
Digital Controls Corporation....D....513 746-8118
Miamisburg *(G-14297)*
DMC Technology Group....E....419 535-2900
Toledo *(G-17855)*
Dolbey Systems Inc....E....440 392-9900
Painesville *(G-15852)*
Einstruction Corporation....D....330 746-3015
Youngstown *(G-20178)*
Enhanced Software Inc....E....877 805-8388
Columbus *(G-7596)*
Environmental Systems Research....D....614 933-8698
Columbus *(G-7600)*
Evanhoe & Associates Inc....E....937 235-2995
Dayton *(G-9269)*
Exact Software North Amer LLC....C....978 539-6186
Dublin *(G-10341)*
▲ GBS Corp....C....330 494-5330
North Canton *(G-15339)*
GBS Corp....E....330 797-2700
Youngstown *(G-20197)*
Global Gvrnment Edcatn Sltions....D....937 368-2308
Dayton *(G-9574)*
Global Mall Unlimited....E....740 533-7203
Delaware *(G-10101)*
Gordon Flesch Company Inc....E....419 884-2031
Mansfield *(G-13305)*
Government Acquisitions Inc....E....513 721-8700
Cincinnati *(G-3689)*
Horizon Payroll Services Inc....B....937 434-8244
Dayton *(G-9621)*
HP Inc....E....513 983-2817
Cincinnati *(G-3791)*
Indico LLC....D....440 775-7777
Oberlin *(G-15646)*
Insight Direct Usa Inc....D....614 456-0423
Columbus *(G-7906)*
Isqft Inc....C....513 645-8004
Cincinnati *(G-3845)*
▲ King Memory LLC....E....614 418-6044
Columbus *(G-7993)*
Kiwiplan Inc....E....513 554-1500
Cincinnati *(G-3931)*
Legrand North America LLC....B....937 224-0639
Moraine *(G-14798)*
Manatron Inc....E....937 431-4000
Beavercreek *(G-1252)*
Manatron Sabre Systems and Svc....D....937 431-4000
Beavercreek *(G-1253)*
Mapsys Inc....E....614 255-7258
Columbus *(G-8104)*
McPc Inc....C....440 238-0102
Brookpark *(G-1951)*
Mediquant Inc....D....440 746-2300
Brecksville *(G-1833)*
▼ Meyer Hill Lynch Corporation....E....419 897-9797
Maumee *(G-13947)*
Micro Center Inc....B....614 850-3000
Hilliard *(G-11931)*
Micro Center Online Inc....C....614 326-8500
Columbus *(G-8159)*
Micro Electronics Inc....D....614 334-1430
Columbus *(G-8160)*
▲ Micro Electronics Inc....B....614 850-3000
Hilliard *(G-11932)*
Micro Electronics Inc....D....614 850-3500
Hilliard *(G-11933)*
Micro Electronics Inc....C....440 449-7000
Cleveland *(G-6049)*
Micro Electronics Inc....C....513 782-8500
Cincinnati *(G-4090)*
Microplex Inc....E....330 498-0600
North Canton *(G-15353)*
Mitel (delaware) Inc....E....513 733-8000
West Chester *(G-19122)*
Mtm Technologies (texas) Inc....E....513 786-6600
Blue Ash *(G-1648)*
Netsmart Technologies Inc....D....614 764-0143
Dublin *(G-10407)*
Netwave Corporation....E....614 850-6300
Dublin *(G-10408)*
Office Depot Inc....E....800 463-3768
Cleveland *(G-6179)*
Office World Inc....E....419 991-4694
Lima *(G-12928)*
Oracle Systems Corporation....D....216 328-9100
Beachwood *(G-1112)*
Park Place International LLC....D....877 991-1991
Chagrin Falls *(G-2728)*
PC Connection Inc....C....937 382-4800
Wilmington *(G-19775)*
Pcm Sales Inc....E....501 342-1000
Cleveland *(G-6255)*
Pcm Sales Inc....C....513 842-3500
Blue Ash *(G-1663)*
Pcm Sales Inc....E....740 548-2222
Lewis Center *(G-12702)*
Pomeroy It Solutions Sls Inc....E....440 717-1364
Brecksville *(G-1842)*
Positive Bus Solutions Inc....D....513 772-2255
Cincinnati *(G-4317)*
▼ Provantage LLC....D....330 494-3781
North Canton *(G-15362)*
Quilalea Corporation....E....330 487-0777
Richfield *(G-16524)*
Raco Industries LLC....D....513 984-2101
Blue Ash *(G-1672)*
Radial South LP....C....678 584-4047
Groveport *(G-11665)*
S & P Solutions Inc....C....440 918-9111
Willoughby Hills *(G-19734)*
Sadler-Necamp Financial Svcs....E....513 489-5477
Cincinnati *(G-4466)*
Software Info Systems LLC....E....513 791-7777
Cincinnati *(G-4550)*
Software Solutions Inc....E....513 932-6667
Lebanon *(G-12648)*
Sophisticated Systems Inc....D....614 418-4600
Columbus *(G-8750)*
▲ Systemax Manufacturing Inc....C....937 368-2300
Dayton *(G-9919)*
Total Loop Inc....D....888 614-5667
Uniontown *(G-18541)*
Transcriptiongear Inc....E....888 834-2392
Painesville *(G-15882)*
▲ Vecmar Corporation....E....440 953-1119
Mentor *(G-14254)*
Xerox Corporation....D....216 642-7806
Cleveland *(G-6767)*

5046 Commercial Eqpt, NEC Wholesale

Access Catalog Company LLC....E....440 572-5377
Strongsville *(G-17438)*
Acorn Distributors Inc....E....614 294-6444
Columbus *(G-6940)*
AVI Food Systems Inc....E....740 452-9363
Zanesville *(G-20445)*
Bakemark USA LLC....D....513 870-0880
West Chester *(G-19023)*
Brechbuhler Scales Inc....E....330 458-3060
Canton *(G-2269)*
▼ Burkett and Sons Inc....E....419 242-7377
Perrysburg *(G-15982)*
Burns Industrial Equipment Inc....E....330 425-2476
Macedonia *(G-13191)*
Business Data Systems Inc....E....330 633-1221
Tallmadge *(G-17633)*
▲ Carroll Manufacturing & Sales....E....440 937-3900
Avon *(G-884)*
Cbf Industries Inc....E....216 229-9300
Bedford *(G-1298)*
▼ Century Marketing Corporation....C....419 354-2591
Bowling Green *(G-1772)*
Cleveland Coin Mch Exch Inc....D....847 842-6310
Willoughby *(G-19653)*
Cmbb LLC....C....937 652-2151
Urbana *(G-18581)*
▲ CMC Daymark Corporation....C....419 354-2591
Bowling Green *(G-1773)*
▲ Door Fabrication Services Inc....E....937 454-9207
Vandalia *(G-18677)*
Dtv Inc....E....216 226-5465
Mayfield Heights *(G-14001)*
EBO Inc....E....216 229-9300
Bedford *(G-1305)*
Filing Scale Company Inc....E....330 425-3092
Twinsburg *(G-18415)*
▲ General Data Company Inc....C....513 752-7978
Cincinnati *(G-2916)*
▲ Globe Food Equipment Company....E....937 299-5493
Moraine *(G-14790)*
▲ Harry C Lobalzo & Sons Inc....E....330 666-6758
Akron *(G-253)*
◆ Hubert Company LLC....B....513 367-8600
Harrison *(G-11802)*
◆ ITW Food Equipment Group LLC....A....937 332-2396
Troy *(G-18359)*
John H Kappus Co....E....216 367-6677
Cleveland *(G-5867)*
Koenig Equipment Inc....D....937 877-1920
Tipp City *(G-17721)*
◆ N Wasserstrom & Sons Inc....C....614 228-5550
Columbus *(G-8212)*
Nemco Inc....D....419 542-7751
Hicksville *(G-11866)*
OK Interiors Corp....C....513 742-3278
Cincinnati *(G-4217)*
Productivity Qulty Systems Inc....E....937 885-2255
Dayton *(G-9833)*
Quality Supply Co....E....937 890-6114
Cincinnati *(G-4360)*
Restaurant Equippers Inc....E....614 358-6622
Columbus *(G-8624)*
◆ Russell T Bundy Associates Inc....D....937 652-2151
Urbana *(G-18600)*
S S Kemp & Company....C....216 271-7062
Cleveland *(G-6428)*
Service Solutions Group LLC....E....513 772-6600
Cincinnati *(G-4501)*
Shearer Farm Inc....E....419 465-4622
Monroeville *(G-14722)*
Sign America Incorporated....E....740 765-5555
Richmond *(G-16535)*
▲ Specialty Equipment Sales Co....E....216 351-2559
Brooklyn Heights *(G-1927)*
Sprayworks Equipment Group LLC....E....330 587-4141
Canton *(G-2536)*
▲ Takkt America Holding Inc....C....513 367-8600
Harrison *(G-11810)*
The Cottingham Paper Co....E....614 294-6444
Columbus *(G-8834)*
Trimark Usa LLC....D....216 271-7700
Cleveland *(G-6618)*
Vulcan Feg....D....937 332-2763
Troy *(G-18387)*

50 WHOLESALE TRADE¨DURABLE GOODS

◆ Wasserstrom Company ....B 614 228-6525
  Columbus (G-8970)
▲ Zink Foodservice Group.................E 800 492-7400
  Westerville (G-19359)

5047 Medical, Dental & Hospital Eqpt & Splys Wholesale

Advanced Medical Equipment Inc........E 937 534-1080
  Kettering (G-12426)
Advantage Appliance Services...........C 330 498-8101
  Canton (G-2226)
Alliance Medical Inc..........................E 800 890-3092
  Dublin (G-10242)
Alpha Imaging LLC............................D 440 953-3800
  Willoughby (G-19643)
American Home Health Care Inc........E 614 237-1133
  Columbus (G-6996)
Americas Best Medical Eqp Co.........E 330 928-0884
  Akron (G-73)
Amerimed Inc...................................E 513 942-3670
  West Chester (G-19019)
Apria Healthcare LLC........................D 419 471-1919
  Maumee (G-13883)
Ardus Medical Inc.............................D 855 592-7387
  Blue Ash (G-1535)
Assuramed Inc..................................E 330 963-6998
  Twinsburg (G-18393)
Benco Dental Supply Co....................D 513 874-2990
  Cincinnati (G-3098)
Benco Dental Supply Co....................D 614 761-1053
  Dublin (G-10261)
Biorx LLC..D 866 442-4679
  Cincinnati (G-3109)
◆ Biotech Medical Inc......................A 330 494-5504
  Canton (G-2264)
▲ Blatchford Inc...............................D 937 291-3636
  Miamisburg (G-14276)
▲ Bound Tree Medical LLC..............D 614 760-5000
  Dublin (G-10266)
Braden Med Services Inc..................E 740 732-2356
  Caldwell (G-2082)
◆ Butler Animal Health Sup LLC......C 614 761-9095
  Dublin (G-10273)
▼ Butler Animal Hlth Holdg LLC.......E 614 761-9095
  Dublin (G-10274)
Cando Pharmaceutical.......................E 513 354-2694
  Loveland (G-13112)
◆ Cardinal Health Inc......................A 614 757-5000
  Dublin (G-10275)
Cardinal Health Inc...........................D 614 497-9552
  Obetz (G-15665)
Cardinal Health 100 Inc....................B 614 757-5000
  Dublin (G-10276)
Cardinal Health 200 LLC..................E 440 349-1247
  Cleveland (G-5180)
Cardinal Health 200 LLC..................C 614 491-0050
  Columbus (G-7194)
▲ Cardinal Health 301 LLC.............A 614 757-5000
  Dublin (G-10277)
Cardio Partners Inc..........................D 614 760-5038
  Dublin (G-10278)
Centura Inc......................................E 216 593-0226
  Cleveland (G-5213)
Cintas Corporation No 2....................D 513 459-1200
  Mason (G-13681)
Clinical Specialties Inc.....................C 614 659-6580
  Columbus (G-7302)
Clinical Technology Inc.....................E 440 526-0160
  Brecksville (G-1821)
Columbus Prescr Phrms Inc..............C 614 294-1600
  Westerville (G-19389)
Community Srgl Sply Toms Rvr........C 614 307 2075
  Columbus (G-7411)
Community Srgl Sply Toms Rvr........C 216 475-8440
  Cleveland (G-5386)
◆ Compass Health Brands Corp......C 800 947-1728
  Middleburg Heights (G-14380)
Concordnce Hlthcare Sltons LLC.......D 419 455-2153
  Tiffin (G-17673)
Cornerstone Med Svcs Midwest.......C 513 554-0222
  Blue Ash (G-1566)
Cornerstone Medical Associates.......E 330 374-0229
  Akron (G-165)
Cornerstone Medical Services...........E 513 554-0222
  Blue Ash (G-1567)
CT Medical Electronics Co................E 440 526-3551
  Broadview Heights (G-1876)
▲ Demarius Corporation..................E 760 957-5500
  Dublin (G-10319)

Dentronix Inc....................................E 330 916-7300
  Cuyahoga Falls (G-9179)
▲ Dermamed Coatings Company LLC.E 330 634-9449
  Tallmadge (G-17637)
Eastern Medical Equipment Co.........E 330 394-5555
  Warren (G-18853)
▲ Edwards Gem Inc........................D 330 342-8300
  Hudson (G-12115)
Espt Liquidation Inc..........................D 330 698-4711
  Apple Creek (G-624)
◆ Ferno-Washington Inc.................C 877 733-0911
  Wilmington (G-19762)
Frantz Medical Group.........................E 440 974-8522
  Mentor (G-14176)
Fresenius Usa Inc.............................E 419 691-2475
  Oregon (G-15736)
Garys Pharmacy Inc..........................E 937 456-5777
  Eaton (G-10561)
Gulf South Medical Supply Inc..........E 614 501-9080
  Gahanna (G-11245)
Haag-Streit USA Inc..........................E 513 336-7255
  Mason (G-13713)
Haag-Streit USA Inc..........................C 513 336-7255
  Mason (G-13714)
Henry Schein Inc..............................E 440 349-0891
  Cleveland (G-5750)
▲ Hitachi Hlthcare Americas Corp...B 330 425-1313
  Twinsburg (G-18429)
Homereach Inc..................................E 614 566-0850
  Lewis Center (G-12688)
Institutional Care Pharmacy..............C 419 447-6216
  Tiffin (G-17681)
Jones Metal Products Company........E 740 545-6341
  West Lafayette (G-19257)
▲ Julius Zorn Inc.............................D 330 923-4999
  Cuyahoga Falls (G-9199)
Keysource Acquisition LLC................E 513 469-7881
  Cincinnati (G-3919)
Kunkel Pharmaceuticals Inc.............E 513 231-1943
  Cincinnati (G-3949)
Lake Erie Med Surgical Sup Inc........E 734 847-3847
  Holland (G-12032)
Lima Medical Supplies Inc................E 419 226-9581
  Lima (G-12823)
M & R Fredericktown Ltd Inc............E 440 801-1563
  Akron (G-331)
Marquis Mobility Inc.........................D 330 497-5373
  Canton (G-2448)
McKesson Medical-Surgical Inc........C 614 539-2600
  Urbancrest (G-18606)
McKesson Medical-Surgical Top........E 513 985-0525
  Cincinnati (G-4038)
▲ Medline Diamed LLC..................E 330 484-1450
  Canton (G-2457)
Medpace Inc.....................................A 513 579-9911
  Cincinnati (G-4049)
▲ Mill Rose Laboratories Inc..........E 440 974-6730
  Mentor (G-14219)
Modern Medical Inc...........................C 800 547-3330
  Westerville (G-19329)
Neighborcare Inc...............................A 513 719-2600
  Cincinnati (G-4151)
Nightngl-Alan Med Eqp Svcs LLC.....E 513 247-8200
  Blue Ash (G-1653)
Noor Home Health Care....................D 216 320-0803
  Cleveland Heights (G-6794)
▲ O E Meyer Co..............................D 419 625-1256
  Sandusky (G-16784)
Ohio State University........................E 614 293-8588
  Columbus (G-8422)
Omnicare Inc.....................................C 513 719-2600
  Cincinnati (G-4220)
Partssource Inc.................................C 330 562-9900
  Aurora (G-849)
▲ Pdi Communication Systems Inc.D 937 743-6010
  Springboro (G-17133)
Pel LLC..E 216 267-5775
  Cleveland (G-6261)
◆ Perio Inc......................................E 614 791-1207
  Dublin (G-10426)
Pharmed Corporation........................C 440 250-5400
  Westlake (G-19533)
◆ Philips Medical Systems Clevel...B 440 247-2652
  Cleveland (G-6273)
Phoenix Resource Network LLC........E 800 990-4948
  Cincinnati (G-4294)
▲ PMI Supply Inc............................D 760 598-1128
  Dublin (G-10425)
Precision Products Group Inc...........D 330 698-4711
  Apple Creek (G-626)

Professional Sales Associates..........E 330 299-7343
  Seville (G-16842)
Radebaugh-Fetzer Company.............E 440 878-4700
  Strongsville (G-17501)
Radiometer America Inc...................D 440 925-2977
  Westlake (G-19538)
Riverain Technologies LLC...............E 937 425-6811
  Miamisburg (G-14345)
▲ Safety Today Inc.........................E 614 409-7200
  Grove City (G-11595)
Sarnova Inc.......................................D 614 760-5000
  Dublin (G-10448)
Seeley Medical Oxygen Co................E 440 255-7163
  Andover (G-615)
▲ Seneca Medical LLC...................C 419 447-0236
  Tiffin (G-17701)
Siffrin Residential Assn....................C 330 799-8932
  Youngstown (G-20375)
Sourceone Healthcare Tech Inc........C 440 701-1200
  Mentor (G-14244)
Therapy Support Inc..........................D 513 469-6999
  Blue Ash (G-1694)
Thermo Fisher Scientific Inc............C 800 871-8909
  Oakwood Village (G-15635)
▲ Tosoh America Inc......................B 614 539-8622
  Grove City (G-11606)
▲ Tri-Anim Health Services Inc......E 614 760-5000
  Dublin (G-10477)
United Seating & Mobility LLC..........E 567 302-4000
  Maumee (G-13991)
▲ Viewray Incorporated..................D 440 703-3210
  Oakwood Village (G-15636)
▲ Wbc Group LLC...........................D 866 528-2144
  Hudson (G-12150)
Ziks Family Pharmacy 100................E 937 225-9350
  Dayton (G-10015)

5048 Ophthalmic Goods Wholesale

Haag-Streit USA Inc..........................C 513 336-7255
  Mason (G-13714)
▲ Interstate Optical Co...................D 419 529-6800
  Ontario (G-15694)
Sight Resource Corporation..............D 513 942-4423
  West Chester (G-19153)
Toledo Optical Laboratory Inc...........D 419 248-3384
  Toledo (G-18246)
Walman Optical Company..................B 419 248-3384
  Toledo (G-18298)
Walmart Inc......................................B 740 286-8203
  Jackson (G-12321)

5049 Professional Eqpt & Splys, NEC Wholesale

Champion Optical Network................E 216 831-1800
  Beachwood (G-1062)
Diebold Incorporated.........................C 330 588-3619
  Canton (G-2340)
Diebold Nixdorf Incorporated............D 513 870-1400
  Hamilton (G-11722)
Essilor Laboratories Amer Inc..........E 614 274-0840
  Columbus (G-7613)
Euclid City Schools............................D 216 261-2900
  Euclid (G-10751)
Franklin Imaging Llc.........................E 614 885-6894
  Columbus (G-7697)
Hamilton Safe Products Co Inc.........E 614 268-5530
  Hilliard (G-11906)
▼ ICM Distributing Company Inc....E 234 212-3030
  Twinsburg (G-18431)
▲ Key Blue Prints Inc.....................D 614 228-3285
  Columbus (G-7983)
▲ Lorenz Corporation.....................D 937 228-6118
  Dayton (G-9687)
▲ Monarch Steel Company Inc.......E 216 587-8000
  Cleveland (G-6074)
▲ Panini North America Inc............E 937 291-2195
  Dayton (G-9800)
Perkinelmer Hlth Sciences Inc.........E 330 825-4525
  Akron (G-385)
Pts Prfssnal Technical Svc Inc.........D 513 642-0111
  West Chester (G-19134)
Queen City Reprographics..................C 513 326-2300
  Cincinnati (G-4371)
▲ S&V Industries Inc.....................E 330 666-1986
  Medina (G-14121)
Shawnee Optical Inc.........................D 440 997-2020
  Ashtabula (G-763)
Teledyne Instruments Inc.................E 513 229-7000
  Mason (G-13767)

50 WHOLESALE TRADE¨DURABLE GOODS SIC SECTION

Teledyne Tekmar Company ....E 513 229-7000
Mason (G-13768)
Testamerica Laboratories Inc ....D 937 294-6856
Moraine (G-14830)
US Tsubaki Power Transm LLC ....C 419 626-4560
Sandusky (G-16807)
▲ Zaner-Bloser Inc ....D 614 486-0221
Columbus (G-9025)

5051 Metals Service Centers

▲ A J Oster Foils LLC ....D 330 823-1700
Alliance (G-521)
A M Castle & Co ....D 330 425-7000
Bedford (G-1292)
Advanced Graphite Machining US ....E 216 658-6521
Parma (G-15898)
Albco Sales Inc ....E 330 424-9446
Lisbon (G-12931)
◆ All Foils Inc ....D 440 572-3645
Strongsville (G-17441)
▲ All Metal Sales Inc ....E 440 617-1234
Westlake (G-19456)
Alro Steel Corporation ....E 330 929-4660
Cuyahoga Falls (G-9160)
Alro Steel Corporation ....E 419 720-5300
Toledo (G-17747)
Alro Steel Corporation ....E 937 253-6121
Dayton (G-9323)
▲ Aluminum Line Products Company ....D 440 835-8880
Westlake (G-19459)
◆ American Consolidated Inds Inc ....E 216 587-8000
Cleveland (G-5007)
American Posts LLC ....E 419 720-0652
Toledo (G-17751)
▲ American Tank & Fabricating Co ....D 216 252-1500
Cleveland (G-5023)
Anchor Bronze and Metals Inc ....E 440 549-5653
Cleveland (G-5033)
Associated Steel Company Inc ....E 216 475-8000
Cleveland (G-5073)
▲ Atlas Bolt & Screw Company LLC ....C 419 289-6171
Ashland (G-660)
Atlas Recycling Inc ....E 800 837-1520
Warren (G-18818)
◆ Atlas Steel Products Co ....D 330 425-1600
Twinsburg (G-18394)
Avalon Precision Cast Co LLC ....C 216 362-4100
Brookpark (G-1936)
◆ Beck Aluminum Intl LLC ....D 440 684-4848
Cleveland (G-5108)
Benjamin Steel Company Inc ....E 937 233-1212
Springfield (G-17150)
Benjamin Steel Company Inc ....E 419 229-8045
Lima (G-12745)
Benjamin Steel Company Inc ....E 419 522-5500
Mansfield (G-13265)
▲ Bico Akron Inc ....D 330 794-1716
Mogadore (G-14672)
Blackburns Fabrication Inc ....E 614 875-0784
Columbus (G-7117)
Boston Retail Products Inc ....D 330 744-8100
Youngstown (G-20123)
Canfield Metal Coating Corp ....D 330 702-3876
Canfield (G-2184)
Central Steel and Wire Company ....C 513 242-2233
Cincinnati (G-3217)
Chapel Steel Corp ....E 800 570-7674
Bedford Heights (G-1349)
Chatham Steel Corporation ....E 740 377-9310
South Point (G-17081)
Cincinnati Steel Products Co ....E 513 871-4444
Cincinnati (G-3330)
▲ Clifton Steel Company ....D 216 662-6111
Maple Heights (G-13403)
▲ Clinton Aluminum Dist Inc ....C 330 882-6743
New Franklin (G-15042)
▲ Cme Acquisitions LLC ....E 216 464-4480
Twinsburg (G-18403)
Coilplus Inc ....D 614 866-1338
Columbus (G-7315)
Coilplus Inc ....E 937 322-4455
Springfield (G-17167)
Coilplus Inc ....D 937 778-8884
Piqua (G-16139)
▲ Contractors Materials Company ....E 513 733-3000
Cincinnati (G-3413)
Contractors Steel Company ....E 330 425-3050
Twinsburg (G-18404)
Earle M Jorgensen Company ....E 513 771-3223
Cincinnati (G-3530)
Earle M Jorgensen Company ....D 330 425-1500
Twinsburg (G-18407)
Efco Corp ....E 614 876-1226
Columbus (G-7586)
▲ F I L US Inc ....E 440 248-9500
Solon (G-17005)
▲ Fay Industries Inc ....D 440 572-5030
Strongsville (G-17464)
▲ Ferralloy Inc ....E 440 250-1900
Cleveland (G-5585)
▲ Flack Steel LLC ....E 216 456-0700
Cleveland (G-5603)
▲ Fpt Cleveland LLC ....C 216 441-3800
Cleveland (G-5628)
Freedom Steel Inc ....E 440 266-6800
Mentor (G-14177)
Graber Metal Works Inc ....E 440 237-8422
North Royalton (G-15490)
▲ H & D Steel Service Inc ....E 440 237-3390
North Royalton (G-15491)
▲ Haverhill Coke Company LLC ....D 740 355-9819
Franklin Furnace (G-11172)
Heidtman Steel Products ....A 419 691-4646
Toledo (G-17952)
Holub Iron & Steel Company ....E 330 252-5655
Akron (G-270)
◆ Howmet Corporation ....E 800 242-9898
Newburgh Heights (G-15251)
▲ Hynes Industries Inc ....C 330 799-3221
Youngstown (G-20227)
▲ Independent Steel Company LLC ....E 330 225-7741
Valley City (G-18618)
▲ Industrial Tube and Steel Corp ....D 330 474-5530
Kent (G-12374)
Infra-Metals Co ....E 740 353-1350
Portsmouth (G-16290)
▲ Is Acquisition Inc ....E 440 287-0150
Streetsboro (G-17417)
▲ Jade-Sterling Steel Co Inc ....E 330 425-3141
Twinsburg (G-18434)
Joseph T Ryerson & Son Inc ....D 513 542-5800
Columbus (G-7950)
Joseph T Ryerson & Son Inc ....E 513 896-4600
Hamilton (G-11748)
Kloeckner Metals Corporation ....D 513 769-4000
Cincinnati (G-3932)
L B Industries Inc ....E 330 750-1002
Struthers (G-17533)
Lapham-Hickey Steel Corp ....E 614 443-4881
Columbus (G-8039)
◆ Latrobe Spcialty Mtls Dist Inc ....D 330 609-5137
Vienna (G-18738)
◆ Liberty Steel Products Inc ....E 330 538-2236
North Jackson (G-15383)
Liberty Steel Products Inc ....C 330 534-7998
Hubbard (G-12089)
Louis Arthur Steel Company ....D 440 997-5545
Geneva (G-11365)
▼ Loveman Steel Corporation ....D 440 232-6200
Bedford (G-1317)
▲ Majestic Steel Usa Inc ....C 440 786-2666
Cleveland (G-5973)
Major Metals Company ....E 419 886-4600
Mansfield (G-13327)
Master-Halco Inc ....E 513 869-7600
Fairfield (G-10876)
Matandy Steel & Metal Pdts LLC ....D 513 844-2277
Hamilton (G-11757)
Mazzella Holding Company Inc ....D 513 772-4466
Cleveland (G-5997)
McWane Inc ....B 740 622-6651
Coshocton (G-9111)
▲ Mes Inc ....D 740 201-8112
Lewis Center (G-12694)
▲ Metal Conversions Ltd ....E 419 525-0011
Mansfield (G-13343)
Metals USA Crbn Flat Rlled Inc ....D 937 882-6354
Springfield (G-17245)
▲ Metals USA Crbn Flat Rlled Inc ....C 330 264-8416
Wooster (G-19887)
▼ Miami Valley Steel Service Inc ....C 937 773-7127
Piqua (G-16153)
Mid-America Steel Corp ....E 800 282-3466
Cleveland (G-6052)
Mid-West Materials Inc ....E 440 259-5200
Perry (G-15965)
Miller Consolidated Industries ....C 937 294-2681
Moraine (G-14806)
▲ Misa Metals Inc ....D 212 660-6000
West Chester (G-19120)
Misa Metals Inc ....C 440 892-4944
Westlake (G-19516)
Modern Welding Co Ohio Inc ....E 740 344-9425
Newark (G-15209)
▲ Monarch Steel Company Inc ....E 216 587-8000
Cleveland (G-6074)
▲ National Bronze Mtls Ohio Inc ....E 440 277-1226
Lorain (G-13063)
National Metal Trading LLC ....E 440 487-9771
Willoughby (G-19695)
New Technology Steel LLC ....D 419 385-0636
Toledo (G-18084)
▲ New Technology Steel LLC ....E 419 385-0636
Toledo (G-18085)
Northstar Alloys & Machine Co ....E 440 234-3069
Berea (G-1464)
Ohio Metal Processing Inc ....E 740 286-6457
Jackson (G-12316)
Ohio Steel Sheet & Plate Inc ....E 800 827-2401
Hubbard (G-12090)
▲ Olympic Steel Inc ....D 216 292-3800
Cleveland (G-6200)
Olympic Steel Inc ....D 216 292-3800
Cleveland (G-6201)
Olympic Steel Inc ....E 440 287-0150
Streetsboro (G-17423)
Olympic Steel Inc ....C 216 292-3800
Bedford (G-1327)
◆ Panacea Products Corporation ....E 614 850-7000
Columbus (G-8513)
▲ Parker Steel International Inc ....E 419 473-2481
Maumee (G-13957)
Phoenix Corporation ....E 513 727-4763
Middletown (G-14449)
Phoenix Steel Service Inc ....E 216 332-0600
Cleveland (G-6276)
Precesion Finning Bending Inc ....E 330 382-9351
East Liverpool (G-10533)
Precision Steel Services Inc ....D 419 476-5702
Toledo (G-18132)
Quality Steels Corp ....E 937 294-4133
Moraine (G-14818)
▲ R L Morrissey & Assoc Inc ....E 440 498-3730
Solon (G-17044)
Radix Wire Co ....D 216 731-9191
Cleveland (G-6345)
▲ Riverfront Steel Inc ....D 513 769-9999
Cincinnati (G-4424)
▲ Samsel Rope & Marine Supply Co ....E 216 241-0333
Cleveland (G-6442)
Samuel Son & Co Inc ....D 419 470-7070
Toledo (G-18171)
Samuel Steel Pickling Company ....D 330 963-3777
Twinsburg (G-18467)
Scot Industries Inc ....E 330 262-7585
Wooster (G-19914)
Select Steel Inc ....E 330 652-1756
Niles (G-15305)
▲ Shadco Inc ....E 310 217-8777
Toronto (G-18338)
Shells Inc ....D 330 808-5558
Copley (G-9063)
SL Wellspring LLC ....D 513 948-2339
Cincinnati (G-4540)
Specialty Steel Co Inc ....E 800 321-8500
Cleveland (G-6516)
◆ St Lawrence Steel Corporation ....E 330 562-9000
Streetsboro (G-17431)
Stark Metal Sales Inc ....E 330 823-7383
Alliance (G-562)
Steel Plate LLC ....E 888 894-8818
Twinsburg (G-18473)
Steelsummit Holdings Inc ....E 513 825-8550
Cincinnati (G-4588)
Swagelok Company ....D 440 349-5934
Solon (G-17059)
Symcox Grinding & Steele Co ....E 330 678-1080
Kent (G-12398)
Thompson Steel Company Inc ....E 937 236-6940
Dayton (G-9928)
▲ Three D Metals Inc ....D 330 220-0451
Valley City (G-18625)
Thyssenkrupp Materials NA Inc ....D 216 883-8100
Independence (G-12267)
Thyssenkrupp Materials NA Inc ....C 440 234-7500
Cleveland (G-6599)
◆ Timken Corporation ....E 330 471-3378
North Canton (G-15374)
Tomson Steel Company ....E 513 420-8600
Middletown (G-14468)

SIC SECTION — 50 WHOLESALE TRADE¨DURABLE GOODS

Tri-State Aluminium Inc .... E 419 666-0100
Toledo *(G-18261)*
◆ **Tricor Industrial Inc** .... D 330 264-3299
Wooster *(G-19919)*
◆ **Tylinter Inc** .... D 800 321-6188
Mentor *(G-14251)*
◆ **United Performance Metals Inc** .... C 513 860-6500
Hamilton *(G-11782)*
▲ **United Steel Service LLC** .... C 330 448-4057
Brookfield *(G-1902)*
▲ **Universal Steel Company** .... D 216 883-4972
Cleveland *(G-6650)*
Van Pelt Corporation .... E 513 242-6000
Cincinnati *(G-4803)*
◆ **Voestlpine Precision Strip LLC** .... D 330 220-7800
Brunswick *(G-1994)*
▲ **Waelzholz North America LLC** .... E 216 267-5500
Cleveland *(G-6717)*
◆ **Watteredge LLC** .... D 440 933-6110
Avon Lake *(G-940)*
Westfield Steel Inc .... D 937 322-2414
Springfield *(G-17299)*
William Wood .... E 740 543-4052
Bloomingdale *(G-1518)*
Witt Glvnzing - Cincinnati Inc .... E 513 871-5700
Cincinnati *(G-4854)*
Worthington Industries Inc .... C 513 539-9291
Monroe *(G-14718)*
Worthngton Stelpac Systems LLC .... C 614 438-3205
Columbus *(G-9009)*

5052 Coal & Other Minerals & Ores Wholesale

Graphel Corporation .... C 513 779-6166
West Chester *(G-19083)*
▲ **Tosoh America Inc** .... B 614 539-8622
Grove City *(G-11606)*

5063 Electrl Apparatus, Eqpt, Wiring Splys Wholesale

ABB Inc .... C 614 818-6300
Westerville *(G-19282)*
ABB Inc .... E 440 585-7804
Beachwood *(G-1045)*
Accurate Mechanical Inc .... E 740 654-5898
Lancaster *(G-12506)*
Afc Cable Systems Inc .... D 740 435-3340
Cambridge *(G-2092)*
Akron Electric Inc .... D 330 745-8891
Akron *(G-37)*
Akron Foundry Co .... C 330 745-3101
Akron *(G-40)*
Ametek Tchnical Indus Pdts Inc .... D 330 677-3754
Kent *(G-12352)*
▲ **Applied Indus Tech - CA LLC** .... B 216 426-4000
Cleveland *(G-5053)*
Associated Mtls Holdings LLC .... A 330 929-1811
Cuyahoga Falls *(G-9163)*
▲ **Bearing & Drive Systems Inc** .... D 440 846-9700
Strongsville *(G-17446)*
Belting Company of Cincinnati .... E 937 498-2104
Sidney *(G-16916)*
▲ **Belting Company of Cincinnati** .... C 513 621-9050
Cincinnati *(G-3097)*
◆ **Best Lighting Products Inc** .... D 740 964-0063
Etna *(G-10732)*
▲ **Bostwick-Braun Company** .... D 419 259-3600
Toledo *(G-17778)*
Buckeye Power Sales Co Inc .... D 513 755-2323
Blacklick *(G-1502)*
Buckeye Power Sales Co Inc .... E 937 340-8322
Moraine *(G-14756)*
◆ **Calvert Wire & Cable Corp** .... E 216 433-7600
Cleveland *(G-5173)*
▲ **Capital Lighting Inc** .... D 614 841-1200
Columbus *(G-6871)*
Cls Facilities MGT Svcs Inc .... E 440 602-4600
Mentor *(G-14160)*
Communications Supply Corp .... E 330 208-1900
Cleveland *(G-5381)*
Consolidated Elec Distrs Inc .... E 614 445-8871
Columbus *(G-7423)*
Dickman Supply Inc .... C 937 492-6166
Sidney *(G-16928)*
Dickman Supply Inc .... E 937 492-6166
Sidney *(G-16929)*
Dickman Supply Inc .... E 937 492-6166
Greenville *(G-11498)*
Dxp Enterprises Inc .... E 513 242-2227
Cincinnati *(G-3517)*
Edison Equipment .... E 614 883-5710
Columbus *(G-7577)*
Electric Motor Tech LLC .... E 513 821-9999
Cincinnati *(G-3546)*
Fenton Bros Electric Co .... E 330 343-0093
New Philadelphia *(G-15094)*
Furbay Electric Supply Co .... D 330 454-3033
Canton *(G-2373)*
GA Business Purchaser LLC .... D 419 255-8400
Toledo *(G-17905)*
◆ **GE Lighting Solutions LLC** .... E 216 266-4800
Cleveland *(G-5663)*
Gene Ptacek Son Fire Eqp Inc .... E 216 651-8300
Cleveland *(G-5666)*
Graybar Electric Company Inc .... E 216 573-6144
Cleveland *(G-5688)*
Graybar Electric Company Inc .... D 513 719-7400
Cincinnati *(G-3695)*
Graybar Electric Company Inc .... E 614 486-4391
Columbus *(G-7770)*
Gross Electric Inc .... E 419 537-1818
Toledo *(G-17925)*
H Leff Electric Company .... C 216 325-0941
Cleveland *(G-5715)*
Handl-It Inc .... D 440 439-9400
Bedford *(G-1309)*
Horner Industrial Services Inc .... E 937 390-6667
Springfield *(G-17208)*
Hughes Corporation .... E 440 238-2550
Strongsville *(G-17473)*
Iewc Corp .... E 440 835-5601
Westlake *(G-19497)*
Illinois Tool Works Inc .... E 216 292-7161
Bedford *(G-1312)*
Interstate Fire & SEC Systems .... E 330 453-9495
Canton *(G-2414)*
John A Becker Co .... D 937 226-1341
Dayton *(G-9643)*
John A Becker Co .... D 513 771-2550
Cincinnati *(G-3876)*
John A Becker Co .... E 614 272-8800
Columbus *(G-7942)*
Johnson Cntrls SEC Sltions LLC .... D 440 262-1084
Brecksville *(G-1830)*
Johnson Electric Supply Co .... E 513 421-3700
Cincinnati *(G-3882)*
▲ **Kirk Key Interlock Company LLC** .... E 330 833-8223
North Canton *(G-15350)*
Laughlin Music & Vending Svc .... E 740 593-7778
Athens *(G-798)*
Legrand North America LLC .... B 937 224-0639
Moraine *(G-14798)*
▲ **Loeb Electric Company** .... D 614 294-6351
Columbus *(G-8075)*
LSI Industries Inc .... C 913 281-1100
Blue Ash *(G-1631)*
M & R Electric Motor Svc Inc .... E 937 222-6282
Dayton *(G-9692)*
▲ **Major Electronix Corp** .... E 440 942-0054
Eastlake *(G-10548)*
Manufactured Assemblies Corp .... D 937 898-2060
Vandalia *(G-18688)*
Mars Electric Company .... D 440 946-2250
Cleveland *(G-5984)*
Matlock Electric Co Inc .... E 513 731-9600
Cincinnati *(G-4030)*
▲ **McNaughton-Mckay Elc Ohio Inc** .... D 614 476-2800
Columbus *(G-8137)*
McNaughton-Mckay Elc Ohio Inc .... E 419 422-2984
Findlay *(G-11064)*
McNaughton-Mckay Elc Ohio Inc .... E 419 891-0262
Maumee *(G-13946)*
Mid-Ohio Electric Co .... E 614 274-8000
Columbus *(G-8165)*
◆ **Monarch Electric Service Co** .... D 216 433-7800
Cleveland *(G-6073)*
▲ **Multilink Inc** .... C 440 366-6966
Elyria *(G-10656)*
New Haven Estates Inc .... E 419 933-2181
New Haven *(G-15051)*
Newark Electronics Corporation .... C 330 523-4912
Richfield *(G-16518)*
▲ **Noco Company** .... B 216 464-8131
Solon *(G-17035)*
◆ **Noland Company** .... C 937 396-7980
Moraine *(G-14812)*
Ohio Alarm Inc .... E 216 692-1204
Independence *(G-12241)*
Ohio Rural Electric Coops Inc .... E 614 846-5757
Columbus *(G-8371)*
Powell Electrical Systems Inc .... D 330 966-1750
Canton *(G-2491)*
Professional Electric Pdts Co .... E 419 269-3790
Toledo *(G-18137)*
Research & Investigation Assoc .... E 419 526-1299
Mansfield *(G-13355)*
Rexel Usa Inc .... E 216 778-6400
Cleveland *(G-6388)*
Rexel Usa Inc .... D 440 248-3800
Solon *(G-17047)*
Rexel Usa Inc .... E 419 625-6761
Sandusky *(G-16789)*
Rexel Usa Inc .... E 614 771-7373
Hilliard *(G-11949)*
▲ **Richards Electric Sup Co Inc** .... C 513 242-8800
Cincinnati *(G-4416)*
▲ **Riverside Drives Inc** .... E 216 362-1211
Cleveland *(G-6399)*
Sabroske Electric Inc .... E 419 332-6444
Fremont *(G-11218)*
Schneider Electric Usa Inc .... E 440 526-9070
Richfield *(G-16529)*
Schneider Electric Usa Inc .... D 513 755-5000
West Chester *(G-19145)*
Scott Fetzer Company .... C 216 267-9000
Cleveland *(G-6452)*
▲ **Shoemaker Electric Company** .... E 614 294-5626
Columbus *(G-8728)*
Siemens Industry Inc .... D 513 742-5590
Cincinnati *(G-4526)*
Sievers Security Systems Inc .... E 216 383-1234
Cleveland *(G-6481)*
Signature Control Systems LLC .... E 614 864-2222
Columbus *(G-8731)*
Simplex Time Recorder LLC .... E 513 874-1227
West Chester *(G-19229)*
State Alarm Inc .... E 330 726-8111
Youngstown *(G-20382)*
Stock Fairfield Corporation .... C 440 543-6000
Chagrin Falls *(G-2735)*
Sumitomo Elc Wirg Systems Inc .... E 937 642-7579
Marysville *(G-13653)*
▲ **Technical Consumer Pdts Inc** .... B 800 324-1496
Aurora *(G-856)*
▲ **Thomas Door Controls Inc** .... E 614 263-1756
Columbus *(G-8837)*
▲ **TPC Wire & Cable Corp** .... D 800 521-7935
Macedonia *(G-13213)*
Tri-City Industrial Power Inc .... E 937 866-4099
Miamisburg *(G-14361)*
Vincent Ltg Systems Co Inc .... E 216 475-7600
Solon *(G-17065)*
W W Grainger Inc .... C 330 425-8387
Macedonia *(G-13217)*
W W Williams Company LLC .... E 419 837-5067
Perrysburg *(G-16070)*
Wesco Distribution Inc .... E 216 741-0441
Cleveland *(G-6734)*
Wesco Distribution Inc .... E 937 228-9668
Dayton *(G-9991)*
Western Branch Diesel Inc .... E 330 454-8800
Canton *(G-2585)*
Westfield Electric Inc .... E 419 862-0078
Gibsonburg *(G-11405)*
Winkle Electric Company Inc .... E 330 744-5303
Youngstown *(G-20418)*
▲ **Winkle Industries Inc** .... D 330 823-9730
Alliance *(G-565)*
Wolff Bros Supply Inc .... E 330 400-5990
Sandusky *(G-16810)*
Wolff Bros Supply Inc .... E 419 425-8511
Findlay *(G-11101)*
Wolff Bros Supply Inc .... E 330 786-4140
Akron *(G-511)*
Wolff Bros Supply Inc .... E 330 264-5900
Wooster *(G-19930)*
Wright State University .... A 937 775-3333
Beavercreek *(G-1222)*
WW Grainger Inc .... E 614 276-5231
Columbus *(G-9010)*
WW Grainger Inc .... E 513 563-7100
Blue Ash *(G-1722)*

5064 Electrical Appliances, TV & Radios Wholesale

Bechtl Bldng Mntnc Crprtn of .... D 330 759-2797
Youngstown *(G-20111)*

SIC

Employee Codes: A=Over 500 employees, B=251-500
C=101-250, D=51-100, E=25-50

50 WHOLESALE TRADE¨DURABLE GOODS

C C Mitchell Supply Company ....E 440 526-2040
  Cleveland *(G-5168)*
Colonial Sales Inc ....E 740 397-4970
  Mount Vernon *(G-14883)*
▲ Danby Products Inc ....E 519 425-8627
  Findlay *(G-11020)*
Dayton Appliance Parts Co ....E 937 224-0487
  Dayton *(G-9458)*
Don Walter Kitchen Distrs Inc ....E 330 793-9338
  Youngstown *(G-20172)*
Lowes Home Centers LLC ....C 216 351-4723
  Cleveland *(G-5953)*
Lowes Home Centers LLC ....C 419 739-1300
  Wapakoneta *(G-18803)*
Lowes Home Centers LLC ....C 937 235-2920
  Dayton *(G-9688)*
Lowes Home Centers LLC ....C 740 574-6200
  Wheelersburg *(G-19578)*
Lowes Home Centers LLC ....C 330 665-9356
  Akron *(G-328)*
Lowes Home Centers LLC ....C 330 829-2700
  Alliance *(G-545)*
Lowes Home Centers LLC ....C 937 599-4000
  Bellefontaine *(G-1388)*
Lowes Home Centers LLC ....C 419 420-7531
  Findlay *(G-11057)*
Lowes Home Centers LLC ....C 330 832-1901
  Massillon *(G-13829)*
Lowes Home Centers LLC ....C 513 741-0585
  Cincinnati *(G-3996)*
Lowes Home Centers LLC ....C 614 433-9957
  Columbus *(G-6892)*
Lowes Home Centers LLC ....C 740 389-9737
  Marion *(G-13549)*
Lowes Home Centers LLC ....C 740 450-5500
  Zanesville *(G-20497)*
Lowes Home Centers LLC ....C 513 598-7050
  Cincinnati *(G-3997)*
Lowes Home Centers LLC ....C 614 769-9940
  Reynoldsburg *(G-16466)*
Lowes Home Centers LLC ....C 614 853-6200
  Columbus *(G-8079)*
Lowes Home Centers LLC ....C 440 937-3500
  Avon *(G-906)*
Lowes Home Centers LLC ....C 513 445-1000
  South Lebanon *(G-17078)*
Lowes Home Centers LLC ....B 216 831-2860
  Bedford *(G-1318)*
Lowes Home Centers LLC ....C 937 327-6000
  Springfield *(G-17226)*
Lowes Home Centers LLC ....C 419 331-3598
  Lima *(G-12832)*
Lowes Home Centers LLC ....C 740 681-3464
  Lancaster *(G-12551)*
Lowes Home Centers LLC ....C 614 659-0530
  Dublin *(G-10392)*
Lowes Home Centers LLC ....C 614 238-2601
  Columbus *(G-8080)*
Lowes Home Centers LLC ....C 740 522-0003
  Newark *(G-15199)*
Lowes Home Centers LLC ....C 740 773-7777
  Chillicothe *(G-2862)*
Lowes Home Centers LLC ....C 440 998-6555
  Ashtabula *(G-752)*
Lowes Home Centers LLC ....B 513 753-5094
  Cincinnati *(G-2924)*
Lowes Home Centers LLC ....C 614 497-6170
  Columbus *(G-8081)*
Lowes Home Centers LLC ....C 513 731-6127
  Cincinnati *(G-3998)*
Lowes Home Centers LLC ....C 330 287-2261
  Wooster *(G-19884)*
Lowes Home Centers LLC ....C 937 339-2544
  Troy *(G-18362)*
Lowes Home Centers LLC ....C 440 392-0027
  Mentor *(G-14210)*
Lowes Home Centers LLC ....C 440 942-2759
  Willoughby *(G-19688)*
Lowes Home Centers LLC ....C 740 374-2151
  Marietta *(G-13462)*
Lowes Home Centers LLC ....C 419 874-6758
  Perrysburg *(G-16030)*
Lowes Home Centers LLC ....C 330 626-2980
  Streetsboro *(G-17419)*
Lowes Home Centers LLC ....C 419 389-9464
  Toledo *(G-18013)*
Lowes Home Centers LLC ....C 419 843-9758
  Toledo *(G-18014)*
Lowes Home Centers LLC ....C 614 447-2851
  Columbus *(G-8082)*

Lowes Home Centers LLC ....C 330 245-4300
  Akron *(G-329)*
Lowes Home Centers LLC ....C 513 965-3280
  Milford *(G-14532)*
Lowes Home Centers LLC ....C 330 908-2750
  Northfield *(G-15519)*
Lowes Home Centers LLC ....C 419 470-2491
  Toledo *(G-18015)*
Lowes Home Centers LLC ....C 513 336-9741
  Mason *(G-13733)*
Lowes Home Centers LLC ....C 937 498-8400
  Sidney *(G-16941)*
Lowes Home Centers LLC ....C 740 699-3000
  Saint Clairsville *(G-16642)*
Lowes Home Centers LLC ....C 330 920-9280
  Stow *(G-17381)*
Lowes Home Centers LLC ....C 740 589-3750
  Athens *(G-799)*
Lowes Home Centers LLC ....C 740 393-5350
  Mount Vernon *(G-14910)*
Lowes Home Centers LLC ....C 937 547-2400
  Greenville *(G-11513)*
Lowes Home Centers LLC ....C 330 335-1900
  Wadsworth *(G-18763)*
Lowes Home Centers LLC ....C 937 347-4000
  Xenia *(G-20068)*
Lowes Home Centers LLC ....C 440 239-2630
  Strongsville *(G-17485)*
Lowes Home Centers LLC ....C 513 755-4300
  West Chester *(G-19113)*
Lowes Home Centers LLC ....C 513 671-2093
  Cincinnati *(G-3999)*
Lowes Home Centers LLC ....C 440 331-1027
  Rocky River *(G-16585)*
Lowes Home Centers LLC ....C 330 677-3040
  Kent *(G-12384)*
Lowes Home Centers LLC ....C 419 747-1920
  Ontario *(G-15698)*
Lowes Home Centers LLC ....C 330 339-1936
  New Philadelphia *(G-15107)*
Lowes Home Centers LLC ....C 440 985-5700
  Lorain *(G-13058)*
Lowes Home Centers LLC ....C 419 447-4101
  Tiffin *(G-17682)*
Lowes Home Centers LLC ....C 937 578-4440
  Marysville *(G-13632)*
Lowes Home Centers LLC ....C 937 438-4900
  Dayton *(G-9689)*
Lowes Home Centers LLC ....C 937 427-1110
  Beavercreek *(G-1189)*
Lowes Home Centers LLC ....C 937 848-5600
  Dayton *(G-9690)*
Lowes Home Centers LLC ....C 614 529-5900
  Hilliard *(G-11923)*
Lowes Home Centers LLC ....C 513 737-3700
  Hamilton *(G-11755)*
Lowes Home Centers LLC ....C 740 894-7120
  South Point *(G-17091)*
Lowes Home Centers LLC ....C 513 727-3900
  Middletown *(G-14431)*
Lowes Home Centers LLC ....C 419 355-0221
  Fremont *(G-11210)*
Lowes Home Centers LLC ....C 419 624-6000
  Sandusky *(G-16777)*
Lowes Home Centers LLC ....C 419 782-9000
  Defiance *(G-10045)*
Lowes Home Centers LLC ....C 330 609-8000
  Warren *(G-18876)*
Lowes Home Centers LLC ....C 330 965-4500
  Youngstown *(G-20257)*
Lowes Home Centers LLC ....C 937 383-7000
  Wilmington *(G-19769)*
Lowes Home Centers LLC ....C 937 854-8200
  Dayton *(G-9691)*
Lowes Home Centers LLC ....C 330 497-2720
  Canton *(G-2440)*
Lowes Home Centers LLC ....C 740 266-3500
  Steubenville *(G-17327)*
Lowes Home Centers LLC ....C 740 476-7100
  Columbus *(G-8083)*
◆ Mas Inc ....E 330 659-3333
  Richfield *(G-16514)*
▲ Merc Acquisitions Inc ....E 216 925-5918
  Twinsburg *(G-18448)*
Mobilcomm Inc ....D 513 742-5555
  Cincinnati *(G-4110)*
Panasonic Corp North America ....D 513 770-9294
  Mason *(G-13745)*
Panasonic Corp North America ....E 201 392-6872
  Troy *(G-18371)*

▲ Pdi Communication Systems Inc ......D 937 743-6010
  Springboro *(G-17133)*
Rieman Arszman Cstm Distrs Inc ....E 513 874-5444
  Fairfield *(G-10899)*
◆ Royal Appliance Mfg Co ....C 440 996-2000
  Cleveland *(G-6415)*
RPC Electronics Inc ....E 877 522-7927
  Cleveland *(G-6420)*
Super Laundry Inc ....E 614 258-5147
  Columbus *(G-8804)*
V and V Appliance Parts Inc ....E 330 743-5144
  Youngstown *(G-20400)*
▲ Vsm Sewing Inc ....C 440 808-6550
  Westlake *(G-19563)*
W W W M ....E 419 240-1055
  Toledo *(G-18296)*
Whirlpool Corporation ....D 419 423-6097
  Findlay *(G-11100)*
Whirlpool Corporation ....C 740 383-7122
  Marion *(G-13596)*

5065 Electronic Parts & Eqpt Wholesale

ABC Appliance Inc ....E 419 693-4414
  Oregon *(G-15722)*
Acadia Solutions Inc ....E 614 505-6135
  Dublin *(G-10233)*
Access Catalog Company LLC ....E 440 572-5377
  Strongsville *(G-17438)*
Acuative Corporation ....D 440 202-4500
  Strongsville *(G-17439)*
Agilysys Inc ....E 440 519-6262
  Solon *(G-16971)*
Airborn Electronics Inc ....E 330 245-2630
  Akron *(G-25)*
▲ Allied Enterprises Inc ....E 440 808-8760
  Westlake *(G-19457)*
Arrow Electronics Inc ....D 440 498-3617
  Solon *(G-16977)*
AT&T Corp ....E 330 505-4200
  Niles *(G-15282)*
▲ Audio-Technica US Inc ....D 330 686-2600
  Stow *(G-17353)*
Avnet Inc ....E 440 479-3607
  Eastlake *(G-10544)*
Avnet Inc ....E 614 865-1400
  Columbus *(G-7078)*
Avnet Inc ....E 440 349-7600
  Beachwood *(G-1054)*
C A E C Inc ....E 614 337-1091
  Columbus *(G-7173)*
Cellco Partnership ....E 330 722-6622
  Medina *(G-14043)*
Cellco Partnership ....E 440 779-1313
  North Olmsted *(G-15412)*
Cincinnati Voice and Data ....D 513 683-4127
  Loveland *(G-13115)*
▲ Clercom Inc ....D 513 724-6101
  Williamsburg *(G-19630)*
Commercial Electronics Inc ....E 740 281-0180
  Newark *(G-15157)*
Communications III Inc ....E 614 901-7720
  Westerville *(G-19390)*
Comproducts Inc ....E 614 276-5552
  Columbus *(G-7416)*
Consolidated Communications ....E 330 896-3905
  Canton *(G-2321)*
Convergint Technologies LLC ....C 513 771-1717
  Cincinnati *(G-3416)*
Copp Systems Inc ....E 937 228-4188
  Dayton *(G-9427)*
Donnellon Mc Carthy Inc ....E 937 299-0200
  Moraine *(G-14776)*
E-Cycle LLC ....D 614 832-7032
  Hilliard *(G-11897)*
Electra Sound Inc ....D 216 433-9600
  Parma *(G-15906)*
Enviro It LLC ....E 614 453-0709
  Columbus *(G-7598)*
Exonic Systems LLC ....E 330 315-3100
  Akron *(G-212)*
Famous Industries Inc ....E 330 535-1811
  Akron *(G-219)*
▼ Fox International Limited Inc ....E 216 454-1001
  Beachwood *(G-1080)*
▲ Funai Service Corporation ....E 614 409-2600
  Groveport *(G-11641)*
General Electric Company ....E 614 899-8923
  Westerville *(G-19403)*
Gordon Flesch Company Inc ....E 419 884-2031
  Mansfield *(G-13305)*

SIC SECTION

50 WHOLESALE TRADE¨DURABLE GOODS

Graybar Electric Company Inc .... E 216 573-6144
  Cleveland *(G-5688)*
▲ Harris Battery Company Inc .... E 330 874-0205
  Bolivar *(G-1748)*
Honeywell International Inc .... E 614 717-2270
  Columbus *(G-7858)*
Hubbell Power Systems Inc .... D 330 335-2361
  Wadsworth *(G-18757)*
Hughes Corporation .... E 440 238-2550
  Strongsville *(G-17474)*
Keithley Instruments Intl Corp .... B 440 248-0400
  Cleveland *(G-5889)*
▲ Koehlke Components Inc .... E 937 435-5435
  Franklin *(G-11160)*
Konica Minolta Business Soluti .... D 440 546-5795
  Broadview Heights *(G-1882)*
▲ Ladd Distribution LLC .... D 937 438-2646
  Kettering *(G-12432)*
◆ Mace Personal Def & SEC Inc .... E 440 424-5321
  Cleveland *(G-5964)*
▲ Major Electronix Corp .... E 440 942-0054
  Eastlake *(G-10548)*
◆ Mark Feldstein & Assoc Inc .... E 419 867-9500
  Sylvania *(G-17600)*
McM Electronics Inc .... D 937 434-0031
  Dayton *(G-9708)*
Mega Techway Inc .... C 440 605-0700
  Cleveland *(G-6019)*
Mendelson Electronics Co Inc .... E 937 461-3525
  Dayton *(G-9718)*
Midwest Communications Inc .... D 800 229-4756
  North Canton *(G-15354)*
Midwest Digital Inc .... D 330 966-4744
  North Canton *(G-15355)*
Mitel (delaware) Inc .... E 513 733-8000
  West Chester *(G-19122)*
Mobilcomm Inc .... D 513 742-5555
  Cincinnati *(G-4110)*
Neteam Systems LLC .... E 330 523-5100
  Cleveland *(G-6121)*
Newark Corporation .... B 330 523-4457
  Richfield *(G-16517)*
Newark Electronics Corporation .... C 330 523-4912
  Richfield *(G-16518)*
P & R Communications Svc Inc .... E 937 222-0861
  Dayton *(G-9796)*
Pager Plus One Inc .... C 513 748-3788
  Milford *(G-14548)*
▲ Pepperl + Fuchs Inc .... C 330 425-3555
  Twinsburg *(G-18452)*
Polycom Inc .... E 937 245-1853
  Englewood *(G-10716)*
▲ Pro Oncall Technologies LLC .... D 513 489-7660
  Cincinnati *(G-4337)*
Quasonix Inc .... E 513 942-1287
  West Chester *(G-19135)*
REM Electronics Supply Co Inc .... E 330 373-1300
  Warren *(G-18893)*
Ricoh Usa Inc .... D 513 984-9898
  Blue Ash *(G-1683)*
Schuster Electronics Inc .... E 330 425-8134
  Twinsburg *(G-18468)*
Shawntech Communications Inc .... E 937 898-4900
  Miamisburg *(G-14350)*
Sound Com Corporation .... D 440 234-2604
  Berea *(G-1469)*
Tele-Solutions Inc .... E 330 782-2888
  Youngstown *(G-20388)*
Teletronic Services Inc .... E 216 778-6500
  Strongsville *(G-17515)*
Visual Edge Technology Inc .... C 330 494-9694
  Canton *(G-2579)*
Warwick Communications Inc .... E 216 787-0300
  Broadview Heights *(G-1895)*
◆ Western Tradewinds Inc .... E 937 859-4300
  Miamisburg *(G-14368)*
◆ Wholesale House Inc .... D 419 542-1315
  Hicksville *(G-11867)*
◆ Winncom Technologies Corp .... E 440 498-9510
  Solon *(G-17068)*
◆ Wurtec Incorporated .... D 419 726-1066
  Toledo *(G-18317)*

5072 Hardware Wholesale

◆ A M Leonard Inc .... D 937 773-2694
  Piqua *(G-16133)*
Ace Hardware Corporation .... C 440 333-4223
  Rocky River *(G-16568)*
Akron Hardware Consultants Inc ...... D 330 644-7167
  Akron *(G-47)*

▲ Atlas Bolt & Screw Company LLC .... C 419 289-6171
  Ashland *(G-660)*
Barnes Group Inc .... E 419 891-9292
  Maumee *(G-13885)*
▲ Bostwick-Braun Company .... D 419 259-3600
  Toledo *(G-17778)*
Brighton-Best Intl Inc .... E 440 238-1350
  Strongsville *(G-17447)*
▲ Country Saw and Knife Inc .... E 330 332-1611
  Salem *(G-16692)*
Do Cut Sales & Service Inc .... E 330 533-9878
  Warren *(G-18851)*
Do It Best Corp .... C 330 725-3859
  Medina *(G-14061)*
Elliott Tool Technologies Ltd .... D 937 253-6133
  Dayton *(G-9524)*
◆ F & M Mafco Inc .... C 513 367-2151
  Harrison *(G-11797)*
◆ Facil North America Inc .... C 330 487-2500
  Twinsburg *(G-18414)*
Fastener Corp of America Inc .... E 440 835-5100
  Westlake *(G-19485)*
GMI Holdings Inc .... D 330 794-0846
  Akron *(G-239)*
Hd Supply Facilities Maint Ltd .... E 440 542-9188
  Solon *(G-17014)*
Hillman Companies Inc .... D 513 851-4900
  Cincinnati *(G-3762)*
Hillman Companies Inc .... B 513 851-4900
  Cincinnati *(G-3763)*
◆ Hillman Companies Inc .... B 513 851-4900
  Cincinnati *(G-3764)*
◆ Hillman Group Inc .... C 513 851-4900
  Cincinnati *(G-3765)*
Hman Group Holdings Inc .... A 513 851-4900
  Cincinnati *(G-3773)*
▲ Hodell-Natco Industries Inc .... E 773 472-2305
  Cleveland *(G-5765)*
Kar Products .... A 216 416-7200
  Cleveland *(G-5884)*
Khempco Bldg Sup Co Ltd Partnr .... D 740 549-0465
  Delaware *(G-10113)*
La Force Inc .... E 614 875-2545
  Grove City *(G-11574)*
▲ LE Smith Company .... D 419 636-4555
  Bryan *(G-2009)*
Mae Holding Company .... E 513 751-2424
  Cincinnati *(G-4011)*
▲ Matco Tools Corporation .... B 330 929-4949
  Stow *(G-17382)*
Mazzella Holding Company Inc .... D 513 772-4466
  Cleveland *(G-5997)*
Menards Contractor Sales .... E 419 726-4029
  Toledo *(G-18050)*
▲ Mid-State Bolt and Nut Co Inc .... E 614 253-8631
  Columbus *(G-8166)*
Midland Hardware Company .... E 216 228-7721
  Cleveland *(G-6056)*
▲ Noco Company .... B 216 464-8131
  Solon *(G-17035)*
▲ Norwood Hardware & Supply Co .... E 513 733-1175
  Cincinnati *(G-4185)*
▲ Ohashi Technica USA Inc .... E 740 965-5115
  Sunbury *(G-17560)*
▲ Omni Fasteners Inc .... E 440 838-1800
  Broadview Heights *(G-1888)*
Reitter Stucco Inc .... E 614 291-2212
  Columbus *(G-8609)*
▲ Saw Service and Supply Company .. E 216 252-5600
  Cleveland *(G-6444)*
◆ Serv-A-Lite Products Inc .... E 309 762-7741
  Cincinnati *(G-4498)*
▼ State Industrial Products Corp ...... B 877 747-6986
  Cleveland *(G-6530)*
▼ The Mau-Sherwood Supply Co ..... E 330 405-1200
  Twinsburg *(G-18475)*
▲ TTI Floor Care North Amer Inc ...... B 440 996-2000
  Solon *(G-17061)*
▲ Waxman Consumer Pdts Group Inc .. D 440 439-1830
  Cleveland *(G-6725)*
Waxman Consumer Pdts Group Inc .. D 614 491-0500
  Groveport *(G-11686)*
▲ Waxman Industries Inc .... C 440 439-1830
  Cleveland *(G-6726)*
WW Grainger Inc .... E 614 276-5231
  Columbus *(G-9010)*
Ziegler Bolt & Parts Co .... D 330 478-2542
  Canton *(G-2595)*

5074 Plumbing & Heating Splys Wholesale

Accurate Mechanical Inc .... E 740 654-5898
  Lancaster *(G-12506)*
▲ Chandler Systems Incorporated .... D 888 363-9434
  Ashland *(G-673)*
▲ Corrosion Fluid Products Corp ...... E 248 478-0100
  Columbus *(G-7445)*
Eastway Supplies Inc .... E 614 252-3650
  Columbus *(G-7569)*
Edelman Plumbing Supply Inc .... E 216 591-0150
  Bedford Heights *(G-1351)*
▲ Empire Brass Co .... E 216 431-6565
  Cleveland *(G-5537)*
▲ Enting Water Conditioning Inc .... E 937 294-5100
  Moraine *(G-14781)*
Famous Distribution Inc .... D 330 762-9621
  Akron *(G-215)*
Famous Distribution Inc .... E 330 434-5194
  Akron *(G-216)*
Famous Enterprises Inc .... E 330 938-6350
  Sebring *(G-16822)*
Famous Enterprises Inc .... E 330 762-9621
  Akron *(G-217)*
Famous II Inc .... D 330 762-9621
  Akron *(G-218)*
Famous Industries Inc .... E 330 535-1811
  Akron *(G-219)*
Famous Industries Inc .... E 330 535-1811
  Akron *(G-220)*
Ferguson Enterprises Inc .... E 513 771-6566
  West Chester *(G-19073)*
Ferguson Enterprises Inc .... E 614 876-8555
  Hilliard *(G-11901)*
Gordon Brothers Inc .... E 800 331-7611
  Salem *(G-16697)*
Habegger Corporation .... E 330 499-4328
  North Canton *(G-15342)*
Habegger Corporation .... D 513 612-4700
  Cincinnati *(G-3725)*
Hague Water Conditioning Inc .... E 614 482-8121
  Groveport *(G-11642)*
Hajoca Corporation .... E 216 447-0050
  Cleveland *(G-5721)*
Industrial Controls Distrs LLC .... E 513 733-5200
  West Chester *(G-19092)*
Keidel Supply Company Inc .... E 513 351-1600
  Cincinnati *(G-3906)*
L B Brunk & Sons Inc .... E 330 332-0359
  Salem *(G-16702)*
Lakeside Supply Co .... E 216 941-6800
  Cleveland *(G-5920)*
Lute Supply Inc .... E 740 353-1447
  Portsmouth *(G-16294)*
Macomb Group Inc .... E 419 666-6899
  Northwood *(G-15536)*
◆ Mansfield Plumbing Pdts LLC .... A 419 938-5211
  Perrysville *(G-16079)*
Mason Structural Steel Inc .... D 440 439-1040
  Walton Hills *(G-18790)*
Maumee Plumbing & Htg Sup Inc .... E 419 874-7991
  Perrysburg *(G-16031)*
Morrow Control and Supply Inc .... E 330 452-9791
  Canton *(G-2465)*
▲ Nelsen Corporation .... E 330 745-6000
  Norton *(G-15557)*
New Haven Estates Inc .... E 419 933-2181
  New Haven *(G-15051)*
◆ Noland Company .... C 937 396-7980
  Moraine *(G-14812)*
▲ Oatey Supply Chain Svcs Inc .... C 216 267-7100
  Cleveland *(G-6176)*
Palmer-Donavin Mfg Co .... E 419 692-5000
  Delphos *(G-10148)*
Parker-Hannifin Corporation .... B 937 456-5571
  Eaton *(G-10572)*
Parker-Hannifin Corporation .... E 614 279-7070
  Columbus *(G-8516)*
Pickrel Brothers Inc .... E 937 461-5960
  Dayton *(G-9808)*
▼ Reading Rock Residential LLC .... E 513 874-4770
  West Chester *(G-19223)*
Rexel Usa Inc .... E 419 625-6761
  Sandusky *(G-16789)*
Robertson Heating Sup Co Ohio ...... E 800 433-9532
  Alliance *(G-553)*
▲ Robertson Htg Sup Aliance Ohio .... C 330 821-9180
  Alliance *(G-554)*
Robertson Htg Sup Canton Ohio ...... E 330 821-9180
  Alliance *(G-555)*

50 WHOLESALE TRADE¨DURABLE GOODS SIC SECTION

Robertson Htg Sup Clumbus Ohio........C....... 330 821-9180
Alliance (G-556)
Ssi Fabricated Inc........E....... 513 217-3535
Middletown (G-14459)
The Famous Manufacturing Co........E....... 330 762-9621
Akron (G-476)
Trumbull Industries Inc........E....... 330 393-6624
Warren (G-18913)
Trumbull Industries Inc........D....... 330 799-3333
Youngstown (G-20393)
▲ Trumbull Manufacturing Inc........D....... 330 393-6624
Warren (G-18914)
United Atmtc Htng Spply of Clv........E....... 216 621-5571
Cleveland (G-6634)
Waxman Consumer Pdts Group Inc......D....... 614 491-0500
Groveport (G-11686)
▲ Waxman Consumer Pdts Group Inc.D....... 440 439-1830
Cleveland (G-6725)
▲ Waxman Industries Inc........C....... 440 439-1830
Cleveland (G-6726)
▲ Wayne/Scott Fetzer Company........C....... 800 237-0987
Harrison (G-11812)
Winsupply Inc........E....... 937 865-0796
Miamisburg (G-14369)
Winsupply Inc........D....... 937 294-5331
Moraine (G-14836)
Wolff Bros Supply Inc........E....... 419 425-8511
Findlay (G-11101)
Wolff Bros Supply Inc........E....... 330 264-5900
Wooster (G-19930)
Wolff Bros Supply Inc........E....... 330 786-4140
Akron (G-511)
Woodhill Supply Inc........E....... 440 269-1100
Willoughby (G-19726)
Worly Plumbing Supply Inc........D....... 614 445-1000
Columbus (G-9008)
Zekelman Industries Inc........C....... 740 432-2146
Cambridge (G-2135)

5075 Heating & Air Conditioning Eqpt & Splys Wholesale

Air Systems of Ohio Inc........E....... 216 741-1700
Brooklyn Heights (G-1910)
Airtron LP........D....... 614 274-2345
Columbus (G-6960)
Allied Supply Company Inc........E....... 937 224-9833
Dayton (G-9317)
American Hood Systems Inc........E....... 440 365-4567
Elyria (G-10593)
Best Aire Compressor Service........D....... 419 726-0055
Millbury (G-14577)
Buckeye Heating and AC Sup Inc........E....... 216 831-0066
Bedford Heights (G-1348)
Controls Center Inc........D....... 513 772-2665
Cincinnati (G-3415)
▲ Copeland Access + Inc........E....... 937 498-3802
Sidney (G-16923)
Daikin Applied Americas Inc........E....... 763 553-5009
Dayton (G-9450)
Diversified Air Systems Inc........E....... 330 784-3366
Akron (G-194)
Famous Distribution Inc........E....... 330 434-5194
Akron (G-216)
Famous Distribution Inc........D....... 330 762-9621
Akron (G-215)
Famous Enterprises Inc........E....... 330 762-9621
Akron (G-217)
Famous Enterprises Inc........E....... 216 529-1010
Cleveland (G-5571)
Famous Enterprises Inc........E....... 419 478-0343
Toledo (G-17879)
Famous II Inc........D....... 330 762-9621
Akron (G-218)
Gardiner Service Company........C....... 440 248-3400
Solon (G-17008)
▲ Habegger Corporation........E....... 513 853-6644
Cincinnati (G-3724)
Habegger Corporation........D....... 513 612-4700
Cincinnati (G-3725)
▲ Hamilton-Parker Company........D....... 614 358-7800
Columbus (G-7797)
Honeywell International Inc........D....... 216 459-6053
Cleveland (G-5770)
Honeywell International Inc........E....... 614 717-2270
Columbus (G-7858)
Industrial Controls Distrs LLC........E....... 513 733-5200
West Chester (G-19092)
Lakeside Supply Co........E....... 216 941-6800
Cleveland (G-5920)
Lennox Industries Inc........E....... 614 871-3017
Grove City (G-11575)
Lute Supply Inc........E....... 740 353-1447
Portsmouth (G-16294)
Luxury Heating Co........D....... 440 366-0971
Sheffield Village (G-16890)
Monroe Mechanical Incorporated........E....... 513 539-7555
Monroe (G-14706)
◆ Noland Company........C....... 937 396-7980
Moraine (G-14812)
OEM Parts Outlet........E....... 419 472-2237
Toledo (G-18102)
Robertson Heating Sup Co Ohio........E....... 800 433-9532
Alliance (G-553)
Siemens Industry Inc........D....... 216 365-7030
Cleveland (G-6480)
Slawson Equipment Co Inc........E....... 216 391-7263
Cleveland (G-6489)
Style Crest Inc........C....... 419 332-7369
Fremont (G-11222)
◆ Style Crest Inc........B....... 419 332-7369
Fremont (G-11223)
Style Crest Enterprises Inc........D....... 419 355-8586
Fremont (G-11224)
Swift Filters Inc........E....... 440 735-0995
Oakwood Village (G-15634)
The Famous Manufacturing Co........E....... 330 762-9621
Akron (G-476)
Thompson Heating Corporation........D....... 513 769-7696
Cincinnati (G-4657)
United Atmtc Htng Spply of Clv........E....... 216 621-5571
Cleveland (G-6634)
▼ Verantis Corporation........E....... 440 243-0700
Middleburg Heights (G-14390)
Wadsworth-Slawson Inc........E....... 216 391-7263
Perrysburg (G-16072)
Wolff Bros Supply Inc........E....... 419 425-8511
Findlay (G-11101)
Wolff Bros Supply Inc........E....... 330 786-4140
Akron (G-511)
WW Grainger Inc........E....... 614 276-5231
Columbus (G-9010)
Yanfeng US Automotive........D....... 419 662-4905
Northwood (G-15553)

5078 Refrigeration Eqpt & Splys Wholesale

Allied Supply Company Inc........E....... 937 224-9833
Dayton (G-9317)
Buckeye Heating and AC Sup Inc........E....... 216 831-0066
Bedford Heights (G-1348)
Controls Center Inc........D....... 513 772-2665
Cincinnati (G-3415)
D & D Investment Co........E....... 614 272-6567
Columbus (G-7476)
Gordon Brothers Inc........E....... 800 331-7611
Salem (G-16697)
Hattenbach Company........D....... 216 881-5200
Cleveland (G-5731)
Scotts Towing Co........E....... 419 729-7888
Toledo (G-18176)
Slush Puppie........D....... 513 771-0940
West Chester (G-19230)
WW Grainger Inc........E....... 614 276-5231
Columbus (G-9010)

5082 Construction & Mining Mach & Eqpt Wholesale

Advanced Industrial Svcs LLC........D....... 800 846-9094
Toledo (G-17742)
▼ Advanced Specialty Products........D....... 419 882-6528
Bowling Green (G-1756)
American Crane Inc........E....... 614 496-2268
Reynoldsburg (G-16426)
▲ American Producers Sup Co Inc........D....... 740 373-5050
Marietta (G-13431)
Baker & Sons Equipment Co........E....... 740 567-3317
Lewisville (G-12714)
Bauer Corporation........E....... 800 321-4760
Wooster (G-19830)
Belden & Blake Corporation........E....... 330 602-5551
Dover (G-10177)
▲ Bobcat Enterprises Inc........C....... 513 874-8945
West Chester (G-19030)
Carmichael Equipment Inc........E....... 740 446-2412
Bidwell (G-1494)
Cecil I Walker Machinery Co........E....... 740 286-7566
Jackson (G-12308)
▼ Columbus Equipment Company........E....... 614 437-0352
Columbus (G-7352)
Columbus Equipment Company........E....... 513 771-3922
Cincinnati (G-3389)
Columbus Equipment Company........E....... 330 659-6681
Richfield (G-16502)
Columbus Equipment Company........E....... 614 443-6541
Columbus (G-7353)
Cope Farm Equipment Inc........E....... 330 821-5867
Alliance (G-536)
Dover Investments Inc........E....... 440 235-5511
Olmsted Falls (G-15673)
E T B Ltd........E....... 740 373-6686
Marietta (G-13443)
Ebony Construction Co........E....... 419 841-3455
Sylvania (G-17585)
Equipment Maintenance Inc........E....... 513 353-3518
Cleves (G-6799)
EZ Grout Corporation Inc........E....... 740 962-2024
Malta (G-13249)
◆ F & M Mafco Inc........C....... 513 367-2151
Harrison (G-11797)
Fabco Inc........D....... 419 427-0872
Findlay (G-11022)
Findlay Implement Co........E....... 419 424-0471
Findlay (G-11026)
▲ Hartville Hardware Inc........C....... 330 877-4690
Hartville (G-11820)
JD Equipment Inc........D....... 740 450-7446
Zanesville (G-20491)
K & M Contracting Ohio Inc........E....... 330 759-1090
Girard (G-11418)
Koenig Equipment Inc........D....... 937 877-1920
Tipp City (G-17721)
Kuester Implement Company Inc........E....... 740 944-1502
Bloomingdale (G-1517)
▲ Lefeld Implement Inc........E....... 419 678-2375
Coldwater (G-6831)
Leppo Inc........C....... 330 633-3999
Tallmadge (G-17643)
◆ Mesa Industries Inc........D....... 513 321-2950
Cincinnati (G-4081)
Murphy Tractor & Eqp Co Inc........E....... 513 772-3232
Cincinnati (G-4132)
◆ Npk Construction Equipment Inc......D....... 440 232-7900
Bedford (G-1324)
Ohio Machinery Co........C....... 419 874-7975
Perrysburg (G-16036)
Ohio Machinery Co........E....... 740 942-4626
Cadiz (G-2080)
Ohio Machinery Co........E....... 330 478-6525
Canton (G-2481)
Ohio Machinery Co........E....... 740 453-0563
Zanesville (G-20519)
Ohio Machinery Co........C....... 513 771-0515
Cincinnati (G-4209)
Ohio Machinery Co........B....... 614 878-2287
Columbus (G-8359)
Ohio Machinery Co........D....... 440 526-0520
Broadview Heights (G-1887)
Ohio Machinery Co........D....... 937 335-7660
Troy (G-18370)
Ohio Machinery Co........E....... 330 530-9010
Girard (G-11421)
Ohio Machinery Co........E....... 330 874-1003
Bolivar (G-1750)
◆ Ohio Machinery Co........C....... 440 526-6200
Broadview Heights (G-1886)
▲ Reco Equipment Inc........E....... 740 619-8071
Belmont (G-1429)
◆ Richard Goettle Inc........D....... 513 825-8100
Cincinnati (G-4415)
Safway Services LLC........E....... 513 860-2626
West Chester (G-19144)
Shearer Farm Inc........E....... 330 345-9023
Wooster (G-19915)
Shearer Farm Inc........E....... 419 465-4622
Monroeville (G-14722)
Shetlers Sales & Service Inc........E....... 330 760-3358
Copley (G-9064)
Simpson Strong-Tie Company Inc........C....... 614 876-8060
Columbus (G-8737)
Southeastern Equipment Co Inc........C....... 614 889-1073
Dublin (G-10458)
Stallion Oilfield Cnstr LLC........E....... 330 868-2083
Paris (G-15896)
▼ Stone Products Inc........E....... 800 235-6088
Canton (G-2552)
Terry Asphalt Materials Inc........E....... 513 874-6192
Hamilton (G-11777)
TNT Equipment Company........E....... 614 882-1549
Columbus (G-8852)

Vermeer Sales & Service Inc ..... E 330 723-8383
Medina (G-14136)
▲ Wrench Ltd Company ..... D 740 654-5304
Carroll (G-2610)
Yoder Drilling and Geothermal ..... E 330 852-4342
Sugarcreek (G-17548)

5083 Farm & Garden Mach & Eqpt Wholesale

▲ Agrinomix LLC ..... E 440 774-2981
Oberlin (G-15637)
Apple Farm Service Inc ..... E 937 526-4851
Covington (G-9135)
Baker & Sons Equipment Co ..... E 740 567-3317
Lewisville (G-12714)
▲ Bostwick-Braun Company ..... D 419 259-3600
Toledo (G-17778)
Buckeye Companies ..... E 740 452-3641
Zanesville (G-20450)
▼ Buckeye Supply Company ..... E 740 452-3641
Zanesville (G-20451)
Bzak Landscaping Inc ..... E 513 831-0907
Milford (G-14508)
Cahall Bros Inc ..... E 937 378-4439
Georgetown (G-11388)
Century Equipment Inc ..... E 419 865-7400
Toledo (G-17800)
Century Equipment Inc ..... E 513 285-1800
Hamilton (G-11707)
Century Equipment Inc ..... E 216 292-6911
Cleveland (G-5216)
Coughlin Chevrolet Inc ..... E 740 852-1122
London (G-12995)
Crouse Implement ..... E 740 892-2086
Utica (G-18611)
Deerfield Farms Service Inc ..... D 330 584-4715
Deerfield (G-10019)
Dta Inc ..... E 419 529-2920
Ontario (G-15687)
Evolution Ag LLC ..... E 740 363-1341
Plain City (G-16191)
Fackler Country Gardens Inc ..... E 740 522-3128
Granville (G-11465)
Farmers Equipment Inc ..... E 419 339-7000
Lima (G-12778)
Farmers Equipment Inc ..... E 419 339-7000
Urbana (G-18586)
◆ Fort Recovery Equipment Inc ..... E 419 375-1006
Fort Recovery (G-11116)
Gardner-Connell LLC ..... E 614 456-4000
Columbus (G-7729)
▲ Hayward Distributing Co ..... E 614 272-5953
Columbus (G-7805)
Homier & Sons Inc ..... E 419 596-3965
Continental (G-9049)
Hull Bros Inc ..... E 419 375-2827
Fort Recovery (G-11118)
▼ JD Equipment Inc ..... D 614 527-8800
New Albany (G-14989)
Kenmar Lawn & Grdn Care Co LLC ..... E 330 239-2924
Medina (G-14091)
Krystowski Tractor Sales Inc ..... E 440 647-2015
Wellington (G-18993)
▼ Lesco Inc ..... C 216 706-9250
Cleveland (G-5936)
Liechty Inc ..... E 419 445-1565
Archbold (G-637)
▼ Myers Equipment Corporation ..... E 330 533-5556
Canfield (G-2203)
Ohio Irrigation Lawn Sprinkler ..... E 937 432-9911
Dayton (G-9786)
Pax Steel Products Inc ..... E 419 678-1481
Coldwater (G-6834)
Rk Family Inc ..... C 513 737-0436
Hamilton (G-11770)
Roger Shawn Houck ..... E 513 933-0563
Oregonia (G-15758)
Schmidt Machine Company ..... E 419 294-3814
Upper Sandusky (G-18566)
Shearer Farm Inc ..... E 419 529-6160
Ontario (G-15712)
Shearer Farm Inc ..... E 440 237-4806
North Royalton (G-15502)
▲ Speck Sales Incorporated ..... E 419 353-8312
Bowling Green (G-1794)
Streacker Tractor Sales Inc ..... E 419 422-6973
Findlay (G-11087)
◆ Western Tradewinds Inc ..... E 937 859-4300
Miamisburg (G-14368)
Wyandot Tractor & Implement Co ..... E 419 294-2349
Upper Sandusky (G-18571)

5084 Industrial Mach & Eqpt Wholesale

A & A Safety Inc ..... E 513 943-6100
Amelia (G-571)
A P O Holdings Inc ..... D 330 650-1330
Hudson (G-12100)
ABB Inc ..... C 440 585-8500
Cleveland (G-4944)
ABB Inc ..... E 440 585-7804
Beachwood (G-1045)
▲ Absolute Machine Tools Inc ..... D 440 839-9696
Lorain (G-13010)
▲ Addisonmckee Inc ..... C 513 228-7000
Lebanon (G-12587)
Advanced Tool & Supply Inc ..... E 937 278-7337
Dayton (G-9310)
Aerocontrolex Group Inc ..... D 440 352-6182
Painesville (G-15833)
▲ Agrinomix LLC ..... E 440 774-2981
Oberlin (G-15637)
Air Systems of Ohio Inc ..... E 216 741-1700
Brooklyn Heights (G-1910)
Airgas Usa LLC ..... E 513 563-8070
Cincinnati (G-2979)
Airgas Usa LLC ..... B 216 642-6600
Independence (G-12183)
Alba Manufacturing Inc ..... D 513 874-0551
Fairfield (G-10818)
Albright Welding Supply Co Inc ..... E 330 264-2021
Wooster (G-19826)
Aldrich Chemical ..... D 937 859-1808
Miamisburg (G-14269)
▲ Alfons Haar Inc ..... E 937 560-2031
Springboro (G-17114)
▲ Alkon Corporation ..... D 419 355-9111
Fremont (G-11184)
Alkon Corporation ..... E 614 799-6650
Dublin (G-10241)
All Lift Service Company Inc ..... E 440 585-1542
Willoughby (G-19642)
▲ AM Industrial Group LLC ..... E 216 433-7171
Brookpark (G-1935)
Andersen & Associates Inc ..... E 330 425-8500
Twinsburg (G-18391)
Anderson & Vreeland Inc ..... D 419 636-5002
Bryan (G-2002)
Area Wide Protective Inc ..... E 614 272-7840
Columbus (G-7040)
▲ Argo-Hytos Inc ..... A 419 353-6070
Bowling Green (G-1758)
Atlas Machine and Supply Inc ..... E 502 584-7262
West Chester (G-19190)
▲ Ats Systems Oregon Inc ..... B 541 738-0932
Lewis Center (G-12668)
▲ Becker Pumps Corporation ..... E 330 928-9966
Cuyahoga Falls (G-9165)
▲ Best & Donovan N A Inc ..... E 513 791-9180
Blue Ash (G-1542)
▲ Bettcher Industries Inc ..... C 440 965-4422
Wakeman (G-18774)
▲ Bevcorp LLC ..... D 440 954-3500
Willoughby (G-19647)
Bionix Safety Technologies ..... E 419 727-0552
Toledo (G-17773)
◆ Blastmaster Holdings Usa LLC ..... D 877 725-2781
Columbus (G-7118)
Bobcat of Dayton Inc ..... E 937 293-3176
Moraine (G-14755)
Bohl Crane Inc ..... D 419 476-7525
Toledo (G-17774)
▲ Bohl Equipment Company ..... D 419 476-7525
Toledo (G-17775)
Boler Company ..... C 330 445-6728
Canton (G-2267)
Bollin & Sons Inc ..... E 419 693-6573
Toledo (G-17776)
Bosch Rexroth Corporation ..... E 614 527-7400
Grove City (G-11535)
▲ Bostwick-Braun Company ..... D 419 259-3600
Toledo (G-17778)
Breathing Air Systems Inc ..... E 614 864-1235
Reynoldsburg (G-16431)
Brennan Industrial Truck Co ..... E 419 867-6000
Holland (G-12012)
Brown Industrial Inc ..... E 937 693-3838
Botkins (G-1752)
▼ Buckeye Supply Company ..... E 740 452-3641
Zanesville (G-20451)
C H Bradshaw Co ..... E 614 871-2087
Grove City (G-11543)
Cecil I Walker Machinery Co ..... E 740 286-7566
Jackson (G-12308)
Cinc ..... E 419 663-6644
Collins (G-6839)
◆ Cintas Corporation ..... A 513 459-1200
Cincinnati (G-3349)
Cintas Corporation ..... D 513 631-5750
Cincinnati (G-3350)
Cintas Corporation No 2 ..... A 513 459-1200
Mason (G-13679)
▲ Cintas Corporation No 2 ..... A 513 459-1200
Mason (G-13680)
▲ Clarke Power Services Inc ..... D 513 771-2200
Cincinnati (G-3360)
Clarke Power Services Inc ..... E 937 684-4402
Huber Heights (G-12094)
Cleveland Tank & Supply Inc ..... E 216 771-8265
Cleveland (G-5350)
Columbus Equipment Company ..... E 513 771-3922
Cincinnati (G-3389)
Contract Sweepers & Eqp Co ..... E 614 221-7441
Columbus (G-7435)
▲ Corrosion Fluid Products Corp ..... E 248 478-0100
Columbus (G-7445)
▲ CPI - Cnstr Polymers Inc ..... E 330 861-5200
North Canton (G-15329)
Cross Truck Equipment Co Inc ..... E 330 477-8151
Canton (G-2329)
◆ Crown Equipment Corporation ..... A 419 629-2311
New Bremen (G-15018)
Crown Equipment Corporation ..... D 419 629-2311
New Bremen (G-15019)
Ctm Integration Incorporated ..... E 330 332-1800
Salem (G-16693)
Cummins Bridgeway Columbus LLC ..... D 614 771-1000
Hilliard (G-11893)
Cummins Inc ..... E 614 771-1000
Hilliard (G-11894)
D M I Distribution Inc ..... E 765 584-3234
Columbus (G-7481)
▲ Daifuku America Corporation ..... C 614 863-1888
Reynoldsburg (G-16443)
▲ Daihen Inc ..... E 937 667-0800
Tipp City (G-17715)
▼ Decker Equipment Company Inc ..... E 866 252-4395
Cleveland (G-5473)
Detroit Diesel Corporation ..... B 330 430-4300
Canton (G-2339)
▼ Devirsified Material Handling ..... E 419 865-8025
Holland (G-12019)
Dickman Supply Inc ..... C 937 492-6166
Sidney (G-16928)
Dickman Supply Inc ..... E 937 492-6166
Greenville (G-11498)
▲ Double A Trailer Sales Inc ..... E 419 692-7626
Delphos (G-10142)
Dreier & Maller Inc ..... E 614 575-0065
Reynoldsburg (G-16448)
Dxp Enterprises Inc ..... E 513 242-2227
Cincinnati (G-3517)
E F Bavis & Associates Inc ..... E 513 677-0500
Maineville (G-13243)
Eaton Corporation ..... B 216 523-5000
Beachwood (G-1075)
Eaton Corporation ..... B 216 920-2000
Cleveland (G-5524)
Ellison Technologies Inc ..... E 440 546-1920
Brecksville (G-1823)
▲ EMI Corp ..... D 937 596-5511
Jackson Center (G-12322)
Equipment Depot Ohio Inc ..... E 513 934-2121
Lebanon (G-12603)
▲ Equipment Depot Ohio Inc ..... E 513 891-0600
Blue Ash (G-1590)
Equipment Depot Ohio Inc ..... E 513 539-8464
Monroe (G-14694)
Equipment Depot Ohio Inc ..... E 513 934-2121
Lebanon (G-12604)
▲ Equipment Manufacturers Intl ..... E 216 651-6700
Cleveland (G-5548)
Esec Corporation ..... E 330 799-1536
Youngstown (G-20181)
Esec Corporation ..... E 614 875-3732
Grove City (G-11558)
▲ Esko-Graphics Inc ..... D 937 454-1721
Miamisburg (G-14299)
Estabrook Corporation ..... E 440 234-8566
Berea (G-1457)
▲ Eurolink Inc ..... E 740 392-1549
Mount Vernon (G-14895)

S I C

50 WHOLESALE TRADE¨DURABLE GOODS

Fairborn Equipment Company Inc ....D........ 419 209-0760
Upper Sandusky *(G-18560)*

▲ Fallsway Equipment Co Inc ....C........ 330 633-6000
Akron *(G-214)*

Fastener Industries Inc ....E........ 440 891-2031
Berea *(G-1459)*

▲ Fcx Performance Inc ....E........ 614 324-6050
Columbus *(G-7645)*

◆ Federal Machinery & Eqp Co ....E........ 800 652-2466
Cleveland *(G-5582)*

▲ Feintool Equipment Corporation ....E........ 513 791-1118
Blue Ash *(G-1593)*

▲ Fischer Pump & Valve Company .....E........ 513 583-4800
Loveland *(G-13125)*

Fluid Mechanics LLC ....E........ 216 362-7800
Avon Lake *(G-930)*

Forte Indus Eqp Systems Inc ....E........ 513 398-2800
Mason *(G-13703)*

Freeman Manufacturing & Sup Co ......E........ 440 934-1902
Avon *(G-893)*

Gardner Inc ....C........ 614 456-4000
Columbus *(G-7728)*

Gateway Products Recycling Inc ....E........ 216 341-8777
Cleveland *(G-5659)*

Ged Holdings Inc ....C........ 330 963-5401
Twinsburg *(G-18421)*

▲ General Data Company Inc ....C........ 513 752-7978
Cincinnati *(G-2916)*

General Electric Company ....E........ 513 530-7107
Blue Ash *(G-1599)*

General Electric Intl Inc ....E........ 330 963-2066
Twinsburg *(G-18422)*

▲ Giant Industries Inc ....E........ 419 531-4600
Toledo *(G-17915)*

Glavin Industries Inc ....E........ 440 349-0049
Solon *(G-17009)*

◆ Goettsch Int Inc ....E........ 513 563-6500
Blue Ash *(G-1604)*

◆ Gosiger Inc ....C........ 937 228-5174
Dayton *(G-9581)*

Gosiger Inc ....C........ 937 228-5174
Dayton *(G-9582)*

Graco Ohio Inc ....D........ 330 494-1313
Canton *(G-2385)*

▲ Great Lakes Power Products Inc .....D........ 440 951-5111
Mentor *(G-14185)*

Great Lakes Water Treatment ....E........ 216 464-8292
Cleveland *(G-5692)*

▲ Hagglunds Drives Inc ....E........ 614 527-7400
Columbus *(G-7793)*

Hannon Company ....D........ 330 456-4728
Canton *(G-2393)*

Heidelberg USA Inc ....E........ 937 492-1281
Sidney *(G-16938)*

Hendrickson International Corp ....D........ 740 929-5600
Hebron *(G-11849)*

Henry P Thompson Company ....E........ 513 248-3200
Milford *(G-11925)*

▲ Heritage Equipment Company ....E........ 614 873-3941
Plain City *(G-16193)*

▼ Hgr Industrial Surplus Inc ....E........ 216 486-4567
Euclid *(G-10759)*

◆ Hiab USA Inc ....D........ 419 482-6000
Perrysburg *(G-16012)*

Hirsch International Holdings ....D........ 513 733-4111
Cincinnati *(G-3769)*

Howden American Fan Company ....E........ 513 874-2400
Fairfield *(G-10860)*

▲ Howden North America Inc ....C........ 513 874-2400
Fairfield *(G-10861)*

▲ Hy-Tek Material Handling Inc ....D........ 614 497-2500
Columbus *(G-7873)*

Hydraulic Parts Store Inc ....E........ 330 364-6667
New Philadelphia *(G-15102)*

I L T Diversified Mtl Hdlg ....E........ 419 865-8025
Holland *(G-12029)*

Imco Carbide Tool Inc ....E........ 419 661-6313
Perrysburg *(G-16015)*

▲ Impact Products LLC ....C........ 419 841-2891
Toledo *(G-17971)*

◆ IMS Company ....D........ 440 543-1615
Chagrin Falls *(G-2720)*

Industrial Air Centers Inc ....E........ 614 274-9171
Columbus *(G-7893)*

Industrial Maint Svcs Inc ....E........ 440 729-2068
Chagrin Falls *(G-2721)*

◆ Industrial Parts & Service Co ....E........ 330 966-5025
Canton *(G-2411)*

Innovative Enrgy Solutions LLC ....E........ 937 228-3044
Hamilton *(G-11745)*

▲ Intelligrated Systems Inc ....A........ 866 936-7300
Mason *(G-13720)*

Intelligrated Systems LLC ....A........ 513 701-7300
Mason *(G-13721)*

◆ Intelligrated Systems Ohio LLC ......A........ 513 701-7300
Mason *(G-13722)*

Interstate Lift Trucks Inc ....E........ 216 328-0970
Cleveland *(G-5835)*

Isaacs Company ....E........ 513 336-8500
Mason *(G-13724)*

Iwi Incorporated ....E........ 440 585-5900
Wickliffe *(G-19604)*

J and S Tool Incorporated ....E........ 216 676-8330
Cleveland *(G-5840)*

Jed Industries Inc ....E........ 440 639-9973
Grand River *(G-11456)*

▲ Jergens Inc ....B........ 216 486-5540
Cleveland *(G-5859)*

▲ Joseph Industries Inc ....D........ 330 528-0091
Streetsboro *(G-17418)*

Jr Engineering Inc ....C........ 330 848-0960
Barberton *(G-968)*

▲ JWF Technologies Llc ....E........ 513 769-9611
Fairfield *(G-10867)*

▼ KA Bergquist Inc ....E........ 419 865-4196
Toledo *(G-17989)*

Kar Products ....A........ 216 416-7200
Cleveland *(G-5884)*

▲ Ken Miller Supply Inc ....D........ 330 264-9146
Wooster *(G-19878)*

Kennametal Inc ....D........ 216 898-6120
Cleveland *(G-5894)*

Kmh Systems Inc ....E........ 513 469-9400
Cincinnati *(G-3934)*

▲ Kolbus America Inc ....E........ 216 931-5100
Cleveland *(G-5908)*

Kyocera SGS Precision Tools ....D........ 330 686-4151
Cuyahoga Falls *(G-9203)*

▲ Kyocera SGS Precision Tools ....E........ 330 688-6667
Munroe Falls *(G-14931)*

◆ Lawrence Industries Inc ....E........ 216 518-7000
Cleveland *(G-5929)*

▲ Lefeld Welding & Stl Sups Inc ....E........ 419 678-2397
Coldwater *(G-6832)*

Linden Industries Inc ....E........ 330 928-4064
Cuyahoga Falls *(G-9205)*

▲ Lns America Inc ....D........ 513 528-5674
Cincinnati *(G-2923)*

M Conley Company ....D........ 330 456-8243
Canton *(G-2442)*

Maag Automatik Inc ....E........ 330 677-2225
Kent *(G-12385)*

Maple Mountain Industries Inc ....C........ 330 948-2510
Lodi *(G-12965)*

Marcy Industries Company LLC ....E........ 740 943-2343
Marion *(G-13552)*

Matheson Tri-Gas Inc ....E........ 614 771-1311
Hilliard *(G-11925)*

McCormick Equipment Co Inc ....E........ 513 677-8888
Loveland *(G-13145)*

Mh Equipment Company ....E........ 937 890-6800
Dayton *(G-9725)*

Mh Equipment Company ....E........ 614 871-1571
Grove City *(G-11580)*

Mh Equipment Company ....D........ 513 681-2200
Cincinnati *(G-4085)*

MH Logistics Corp ....E........ 330 425-2476
Hudson *(G-12134)*

Miami Industrial Trucks Inc ....D........ 937 293-4194
Moraine *(G-14805)*

Mid-Ohio Forklifts Inc ....E........ 330 633-1230
Akron *(G-344)*

▲ Midlands Millroom Supply Inc ....E........ 330 453-9100
Canton *(G-2462)*

▲ Miller Supply of WvA Inc ....E........ 330 264-9146
Wooster *(G-19890)*

Mine Equipment Services LLC ....E........ 740 936-5427
Sunbury *(G-17558)*

Minerva Welding and Fabg Inc ....E........ 330 868-7731
Minerva *(G-14649)*

Modal Shop Inc ....D........ 513 351-9919
Cincinnati *(G-4111)*

Monode Marking Products Inc ....E........ 440 975-8802
Mentor *(G-14222)*

▲ Multi Products Company ....E........ 330 674-5981
Millersburg *(G-14613)*

Neff Group Distributors Inc ....E........ 440 835-7010
Westlake *(G-19519)*

Neff Machinery and Supplies ....E........ 740 454-0128
Zanesville *(G-20515)*

Neopost USA Inc ....E........ 440 526-3196
Brecksville *(G-1836)*

▲ Newtown Nine Inc ....D........ 440 781-0623
Macedonia *(G-13206)*

Newtown Nine Inc ....E........ 330 376-7741
Akron *(G-351)*

Nfm/Welding Engineers Inc ....E........ 330 837-3868
Massillon *(G-13841)*

▲ O E Meyer Co ....D........ 419 625-1256
Sandusky *(G-16784)*

Ohio Hydraulics Inc ....E........ 513 771-2590
Cincinnati *(G-4207)*

Ohio Tool Systems Inc ....D........ 330 659-4181
Richfield *(G-16521)*

◆ Ohio Transmission Corporation ......C........ 614 342-6247
Columbus *(G-8451)*

Ohio Transmission Corporation ....E........ 419 468-7866
Galion *(G-11304)*

Ohio Transmission Corporation ....E........ 513 539-8411
Middletown *(G-14445)*

Otis Elevator Company ....E........ 614 777-6500
Columbus *(G-8498)*

◆ Park Corporation ....B........ 216 267-4870
Cleveland *(G-6234)*

Parker-Hannifin Corporation ....E........ 216 896-3000
Cleveland *(G-6240)*

Paul Peterson Company ....E........ 614 486-4375
Columbus *(G-8522)*

▲ Pennsylvania TI Sls & Svc Inc ....D........ 330 758-0845
Youngstown *(G-20317)*

Pfpc Enterprises Inc ....B........ 513 941-6200
Cincinnati *(G-4290)*

▲ Pines Manufacturing Inc ....E........ 440 835-5553
Westlake *(G-19534)*

▲ Power Distributors LLC ....D........ 614 876-3533
Columbus *(G-8554)*

Power-Pack Conveyor Company ....E........ 440 975-9955
Willoughby *(G-19705)*

Praxair Distribution Inc ....D........ 330 376-2242
Akron *(G-400)*

Precision Supply Company Inc ....D........ 330 225-5530
Brunswick *(G-1988)*

Primetals Technologies USA LLC ......E........ 419 929-1554
New London *(G-15070)*

Process Pump & Seal Inc ....E........ 513 988-7000
Trenton *(G-18343)*

▲ Prospect Mold & Die Company ......D........ 330 929-3311
Cuyahoga Falls *(G-9214)*

Quality Trailers of Oh Inc ....E........ 330 332-9630
Salem *(G-16708)*

▼ Questar Solutions LLC ....E........ 330 966-2070
North Canton *(G-15363)*

R & M Fluid Power Inc ....E........ 330 758-2766
Youngstown *(G-20337)*

R and J Corporation ....E........ 440 871-6009
Westlake *(G-19536)*

▼ R&M Materials Handling Inc ....E........ 937 328-5100
Springfield *(G-17262)*

▲ Raymond Storage Concepts Inc ....E........ 513 891-7290
Blue Ash *(G-1677)*

Rde System Corp ....E........ 513 933-8000
Lebanon *(G-12640)*

Reid Asset Management Company .....E........ 216 642-3223
Cleveland *(G-6368)*

Remtec Engineering ....E........ 513 860-4299
Mason *(G-13756)*

Rilco Industrial Controls Inc ....E........ 513 530-0055
Cincinnati *(G-4420)*

▲ Robeck Fluid Power Co ....D........ 330 562-1140
Aurora *(G-852)*

▲ Rodem Inc ....E........ 513 922-6140
Cincinnati *(G-4439)*

▼ RSR Partners LLC ....B........ 440 519-1768
Twinsburg *(G-18463)*

▲ Rubber City Machinery Corp ....E........ 330 434-3500
Akron *(G-419)*

▲ Rumpke/Kenworth Contract ....D........ 740 774-5111
Chillicothe *(G-2883)*

S & S Inc ....E........ 216 383-1880
Cleveland *(G-6425)*

Safety Solutions Inc ....D........ 614 799-9900
Dublin *(G-10446)*

▲ Safety Today Inc ....E........ 614 409-7200
Grove City *(G-11595)*

▲ Salvagnini America Inc ....E........ 513 874-8284
Hamilton *(G-11772)*

Samuel Strapping Systems Inc ....D........ 740 522-2500
Heath *(G-11843)*

Schindler Elevator Corporation ....E........ 614 573-2777
Columbus *(G-8694)*

SIC SECTION 50 WHOLESALE TRADE¨DURABLE GOODS

Scott Industrial Systems Inc.................D....... 937 233-8146
Dayton (G-9869)
Select Industries Corp............................E....... 937 233-9191
Dayton (G-9874)
Sentinel Fluid Controls LLC..................E....... 419 478-9086
Toledo (G-18179)
▲ Sgl Carbon Technic LLC ....E....... 440 572-3600
Strongsville (G-17506)
Shawcor Pipe Protection LLC................E....... 513 683-7800
Loveland (G-13159)
Shearer Farm Inc...................................E....... 440 237-4806
North Royalton (G-15502)
Siemens Industry Inc.............................E....... 440 526-2770
Brecksville (G-1850)
Simco Supply Co ....E....... 614 253-1999
Columbus (G-8733)
South Shore Controls Inc.......................E....... 440 259-2500
Perry (G-15967)
◆ Spillman Company ....E....... 614 444-2184
Columbus (G-8762)
Staufs Coffee Roasters II Inc ....E....... 614 487-6050
Columbus (G-8785)
Stolle Machinery Company LLC............E....... 330 493-0444
Canton (G-2550)
Stolle Machinery Company LLC............D....... 330 453-2015
North Canton (G-15369)
STS Operating Inc..................................E....... 513 941-6200
Cincinnati (G-4596)
Sumitomo Demag Plstc Machinery.......E....... 440 876-8960
Strongsville (G-17514)
Super Systems Inc..................................E....... 513 772-0060
Cincinnati (G-4602)
▲ System Seals Inc.................................D....... 440 735-0200
Cleveland (G-6562)
Tank Leasing Corp..................................E....... 330 339-3333
New Philadelphia (G-15117)
▲ Tape Products Company ....D....... 513 489-8840
Cincinnati (G-4624)
Taylor - Winfield Corporation.................D....... 330 797-0300
Youngstown (G-20387)
Tech Products Corporation.....................E....... 937 438-1100
Miamisburg (G-14355)
Thyssenkrupp Elevator Corp..................E....... 440 717-0080
Broadview Heights (G-1893)
Thyssenkrupp Elevator Corp..................E....... 614 895-8930
Westerville (G-19445)
Tiffin Loader Crane Company.................D....... 419 448-8156
Tiffin (G-17705)
Tkf Conveyor Systems LLC ....C....... 513 621-5260
Cincinnati (G-4660)
Tom Langhals..E....... 419 659-5629
Columbus Grove (G-9031)
▲ Tomita USA Inc....................................E....... 614 873-6509
Plain City (G-16209)
▲ Total Fleet Solutions LLC ....E....... 419 868-8853
Holland (G-12063)
▲ Towlift Inc ....C....... 216 749-6800
Brooklyn Heights (G-1929)
Towlift Inc ....E....... 419 666-1333
Northwood (G-15548)
Towlift Inc ....D....... 614 851-1001
Columbus (G-8856)
Towlift Inc ....E....... 419 531-6110
Toledo (G-18258)
Toyota Industrial Eqp Dlr ....E....... 419 865-8025
Holland (G-12064)
Toyota Industries N Amer Inc ....E....... 513 779-7500
West Chester (G-19164)
Toyota Industries N Amer Inc ....E....... 937 237-0976
Dayton (G-9935)
Toyota Material Hdlg Ohio Inc ....D....... 216 328-0970
Independence (G-12268)
Triad Technologies LLC ....E....... 937 832-2861
Vandalia (G-18701)
▲ Tripack LLC ....E....... 859 282-7914
Milford (G-14570)
Union Supply Group Inc.........................E....... 614 409-1444
Groveport (G-11680)
▲ United Grinding North Amer Inc.......D....... 937 859-1975
Miamisburg (G-14364)
US Safetygear Inc ....E....... 330 898-1344
Warren (G-18919)
Valley Industrial Trucks Inc....................E....... 330 788-4081
Youngstown (G-20402)
Vargo Integrated Systems Inc................E....... 614 876-1163
Hilliard (G-11962)
▲ Venco Venturo Industries LLC...........E....... 513 772-8448
Cincinnati (G-4806)
Venturo Manufacturing Inc.....................E....... 513 772-8448
Cincinnati (G-4807)
Veritiv Operating Company....................D....... 216 901-5700
Cleveland (G-6689)
W W Williams Company LLC ....E....... 330 534-1161
Hubbard (G-12092)
W W Williams Company LLC ....D....... 800 336-6651
West Chester (G-19242)
W W Williams Company LLC ....E....... 330 225-7751
Brunswick (G-1995)
W W Williams Company LLC ....E....... 419 837-5067
Perrysburg (G-16070)
Weiler Welding Company Inc.................D....... 937 222-8312
Moraine (G-14835)
Weld Plus Inc..E....... 513 941-4411
Cincinnati (G-4830)
Western Branch Diesel Inc.....................E....... 330 454-8800
Canton (G-2585)
◆ Western Tradewinds Inc ....E....... 937 859-4300
Miamisburg (G-14368)
Wilkris Company.....................................E....... 513 271-9344
Terrace Park (G-17663)
Williams Super Service Inc ....E....... 330 733-7750
East Sparta (G-10542)
Willis Day Management Inc...................E....... 419 476-8000
Toledo (G-18311)
Winelco Inc..E....... 513 755-8050
West Chester (G-19187)
Wolf Machine Company ....C....... 513 791-5194
Blue Ash (G-1719)
Woodworkers Outlet................................E....... 440 286-3942
Chardon (G-2779)
◆ Wurtec Incorporated ....D....... 419 726-1066
Toledo (G-18317)
WW Grainger Inc.....................................E....... 513 563-7100
Blue Ash (G-1722)
WW Grainger Inc.....................................E....... 614 276-5231
Columbus (G-9010)
Yoder Machinery Sales Company ....E....... 419 865-5555
Holland (G-12069)

5085 Industrial Splys Wholesale

3b Holdings Inc ....D....... 800 791-7124
Cleveland (G-4926)
▲ A-T Controls Inc ....E....... 513 530-5175
West Chester (G-19188)
▲ Advanced Elastomer Systems LP ....C....... 800 352-7866
Akron (G-22)
Advanced Tool & Supply Inc..................E....... 937 278-7337
Dayton (G-9310)
▲ Afc Industries Inc................................E....... 513 874-7456
Fairfield (G-10816)
Albright Welding Supply Co Inc ....E....... 330 264-2021
Wooster (G-19826)
▲ Alkon Corporation...............................D 419 355-9111
Fremont (G-11184)
Alkon Corporation ....E....... 614 799-6650
Dublin (G-10241)
▲ All Ohio Threaded Rod Co Inc ....E....... 216 426-1800
Cleveland (G-4990)
Allen Refractories Company...................C....... 740 927-8000
Pataskala (G-15920)
◆ Alliance Knife Inc................................E....... 513 367-9000
Harrison (G-11789)
Allied Supply Company Inc....................E....... 937 224-9833
Dayton (G-9317)
Alro Steel Corporation.............................E....... 419 720-5300
Toledo (G-17747)
▲ American Producers Sup Co Inc ......D....... 740 373-5050
Marietta (G-13431)
Andre Corporation ....E....... 574 293-0207
Mason (G-13662)
Apex Gear..E....... 614 539-3002
Grove City (G-11531)
▲ Applied Industrial Tech Inc ....B....... 216 426-4000
Cleveland (G-5055)
Applied Mint Sups Slutions LLC ....E....... 216 456-3600
Strongsville (G-17443)
▲ ARC Abrasives Inc ....D....... 800 888-4885
Troy (G-18347)
▲ Atlas Bolt & Screw Company LLC....C....... 419 289-6171
Ashland (G-660)
B W Grinding Co ....E....... 419 923-1376
Lyons (G-13185)
▲ Bearing & Drive Systems Inc ....D....... 440 846-9700
Strongsville (G-17446)
◆ Bearing Distributors Inc ....C....... 216 642-9100
Cleveland (G-5107)
▲ Bearing Technologies Ltd ....D....... 440 937-4770
Avon (G-879)
Bechtl Bldng Mntnc Crprtn of................D....... 330 759-2797
Youngstown (G-20111)
▲ Belting Company of Cincinnati.........C....... 513 621-9050
Cincinnati (G-3097)
Binkelman Corporation ....E....... 419 537-9333
Toledo (G-17771)
Brand Energy & Infrastructure ....E....... 419 324-1305
Toledo (G-17781)
▲ Brennan Industries Inc......................E....... 440 248-1880
Cleveland (G-5136)
Brennan Industries Inc...........................E....... 440 248-7088
Solon (G-16985)
▲ Buckeye Rubber & Packing Co ....E....... 216 464-8900
Beachwood (G-1058)
Buffalo Abrasives Inc ....E....... 614 891-6450
Westerville (G-19374)
▲ CB Manufacturing & Sls Co Inc........D....... 937 866-5986
Miamisburg (G-14279)
Chandler Products LLC..........................E....... 216 481-4400
Cleveland (G-5226)
Chardon Tool & Supply Co Inc ....E....... 440 286-6440
Chardon (G-2743)
Ci Disposition Co....................................E....... 216 587-5200
Brooklyn Heights (G-1912)
Cincinnati Gearing Systems Inc............D....... 513 527-8600
Cincinnati (G-3306)
◆ Clippard Instrument Lab Inc..............C....... 513 521-4261
Cincinnati (G-3367)
Commercial Electric Pdts Corp ....E....... 216 241-2886
Cleveland (G-5376)
Cornwell Quality Tools Company..........D....... 330 628-2627
Mogadore (G-14673)
Cornwell Quality Tools Company..........E....... 330 335-2933
Wadsworth (G-18751)
Crane Pumps & Systems Inc ....B....... 937 773-2442
Piqua (G-16142)
◆ Datwyler Sling Sltions USA Inc.........D....... 937 387-2800
Vandalia (G-18676)
Dayton Industrial Drum Inc....................E....... 937 253-8933
Dayton (G-9263)
Dayton Windustrial Co ....E....... 937 461-2603
Dayton (G-9495)
Delille Oxygen Company........................E....... 614 444-1177
Columbus (G-7504)
Dolin Supply Co ....E....... 304 529-4171
South Point (G-17084)
Dynatech Systems Inc...........................E....... 440 365-1774
Elyria (G-10618)
Eagle Equipment Corporation ....E....... 937 746-0510
Franklin (G-11154)
◆ Eagle Industrial Truck Mfg LLC.........E....... 734 442-1000
Swanton (G-17563)
▲ Earnest Machine Products Co ....E....... 440 895-8400
Rocky River (G-16577)
Edward W Daniel LLC.............................E....... 440 647-1960
Wellington (G-18990)
Ellison Technologies Inc........................E....... 310 323-2121
Hamilton (G-11725)
◆ F & M Mafco Inc..................................C....... 513 367-2151
Harrison (G-11797)
F B Wright Co Cincinnati........................E....... 513 874-9100
West Chester (G-19071)
◆ Facil North America Inc ....C....... 330 487-2500
Twinsburg (G-18414)
Famous Distribution Inc.........................D....... 330 762-9621
Akron (G-215)
▲ Faster Inc...E....... 419 868-8197
Maumee (G-13914)
▲ Fcx Performance Inc...........................E....... 614 324-6050
Columbus (G-7645)
Federal-Mogul LLC.................................C....... 740 432-2393
Cambridge (G-2113)
▲ File Sharpening Company Inc ....E....... 937 376-8268
Xenia (G-20050)
First Francis Company Inc.....................E....... 440 352-8927
Painesville (G-15857)
▲ Fischer Pump & Valve Company ......E....... 513 583-4800
Loveland (G-13125)
Flodraulic Group Incorporated...............E....... 614 276-8141
Columbus (G-7676)
▲ Forge Industries Inc............................A....... 330 782-8301
Youngstown (G-20191)
General Factory Sups Co Inc.................E....... 513 864-6007
Cincinnati (G-3674)
▲ Ges Graphite Inc ....E....... 205 838-0820
Parma (G-15908)
◆ Gorilla Glue Company........................E....... 513 271-3300
Cincinnati (G-3688)
Goss Supply Company...........................E....... 740 454-2571
Zanesville (G-20483)
▲ Great Lakes Fasteners Inc ....E....... 330 425-4488
Twinsburg (G-18425)

S I C

50 WHOLESALE TRADE¨DURABLE GOODS

▲ Great Lakes Power Products Inc ...... D 440 951-5111
   Mentor *(G-14185)*
◆ Great Lakes Textiles Inc .... E 440 439-1300
   Solon *(G-17012)*
▲ H & D Steel Service Inc .... E 440 237-3390
   North Royalton *(G-15491)*
▲ Hart Industries Inc .... E 513 541-4278
   Middletown *(G-14427)*
Hd Supply Facilities Maint Ltd .... E 440 542-9188
   Solon *(G-17014)*
Ishikawa Gasket America Inc .... C 419 353-7300
   Bowling Green *(G-1783)*
J & J Entps Westerville Inc .... E 614 898-5997
   Sunbury *(G-17557)*
Jet Rubber Company .... E 330 325-1821
   Rootstown *(G-16597)*
Kaman Corporation .... E 330 468-1811
   Macedonia *(G-13205)*
▲ Kaufman Container Company .... C 216 898-2000
   Cleveland *(G-5887)*
Koi Siferd Hossellman .... E 419 228-1221
   Lima *(G-12812)*
L & J Fasteners Inc .... E 614 876-7313
   Hilliard *(G-11919)*
Lakeside Supply Co .... E 216 941-6800
   Cleveland *(G-5920)*
◆ Lancaster Commercial Pdts LLC .... E 740 286-5081
   Columbus *(G-8032)*
◆ Lawrence Industries Inc .... E 216 518-7000
   Cleveland *(G-5929)*
Liberty Casting Company LLC .... E 740 363-1941
   Delaware *(G-10116)*
▲ Logan Clutch Corporation .... E 440 808-4258
   Cleveland *(G-5950)*
Luke Collison .... E 740 969-2283
   Lancaster *(G-12552)*
Lute Supply Inc .... E 740 353-1447
   Portsmouth *(G-16294)*
◆ Main Line Supply Co Inc .... E 937 254-6910
   Dayton *(G-9695)*
Mauser Usa LLC .... E 740 397-1762
   Mount Vernon *(G-14912)*
Mazzella Holding Company Inc .... D 513 772-4466
   Cleveland *(G-5997)*
Mc Neal Industries Inc .... E 440 721-0400
   Painesville *(G-15865)*
▲ McNeil Industries Inc .... E 440 951-7756
   Painesville *(G-15866)*
McWane Inc .... B 740 622-6651
   Coshocton *(G-9111)*
Megacity Fire Protection Inc .... E 937 335-0775
   Dayton *(G-9717)*
◆ Merchandise Inc .... D 513 353-2200
   Miamitown *(G-14372)*
◆ Mesa Industries Inc .... E 513 321-2950
   Cincinnati *(G-4081)*
▲ Mid-State Bolt and Nut Co Inc .... E 614 253-8631
   Columbus *(G-8166)*
▲ Mill-Rose Company .... C 440 255-9171
   Mentor *(G-14220)*
▲ Mirka USA Inc .... D 330 963-6421
   Twinsburg *(G-18449)*
MRC Global (us) Inc .... E 419 324-0039
   Toledo *(G-18071)*
MRC Global (us) Inc .... E 513 489-6922
   Cincinnati *(G-4126)*
▲ Mullins International Sls Corp ...... D 937 233-4213
   Dayton *(G-9761)*
New Haven Estates Inc .... E 419 933-2181
   New Haven *(G-15051)*
▲ Newman International Inc .... D 513 932-7379
   Lebanon *(G-12630)*
◆ Noland Company .... E 937 396-7980
   Moraine *(G-14812)*
▲ North Coast Bearings LLC .... E 440 930-7600
   Avon *(G-908)*
◆ Ohio Transmission Corporation .... D 614 342-6247
   Columbus *(G-8451)*
Ohio Transmission Corporation .... E 419 468-7866
   Galion *(G-11304)*
Ors Nasco Inc .... E 918 781-5300
   West Chester *(G-19219)*
Pallet Distributors Inc .... C 888 805-9670
   Lakewood *(G-12494)*
▲ Pennsylvania TI Sls & Svc Inc .... D 330 758-0845
   Youngstown *(G-20317)*
Precision Supply Company Inc .... D 330 225-5530
   Brunswick *(G-1988)*
Process Pump & Seal Inc .... E 513 988-7000
   Trenton *(G-18343)*

R L Morrissey & Assoc Inc .... E 440 498-3730
   Solon *(G-17044)*
Riten Industries .... D 740 335-5353
   Wshngtn CT Hs *(G-20033)*
Roger Zatkoff Company .... E 248 478-2400
   Twinsburg *(G-18462)*
Ruthman Pump and Engineering .... E 937 783-2411
   Blanchester *(G-1516)*
▲ Sabco Industries Inc .... E 419 531-5347
   Toledo *(G-18169)*
▲ Samsel Rope & Marine Supply Co ...... E 216 241-0333
   Cleveland *(G-6442)*
Samuel Strapping Systems Inc .... D 740 522-2500
   Heath *(G-11843)*
Scioto Services Llc .... E 937 644-0888
   Marysville *(G-13649)*
Selinsky Force LLC .... C 330 477-4527
   Canton *(G-2525)*
Sign Source USA Inc .... D 419 224-1130
   Lima *(G-12878)*
▲ SSP Fittings Corp .... D 330 425-4250
   Twinsburg *(G-18472)*
▲ Stafast Products Inc .... E 440 357-5546
   Painesville *(G-15880)*
▼ Stark Industrial LLC .... E 330 493-9773
   North Canton *(G-15368)*
State Industrial Products Corp .... C 216 861-6363
   Cleveland *(G-6531)*
▲ Summers Acquisition Corp .... E 216 941-7700
   Cleveland *(G-6546)*
Superior Products LLC .... D 216 651-9400
   Cleveland *(G-6555)*
◆ Superior Products Llc .... D 216 651-9400
   Cleveland *(G-6554)*
▲ Supply Technologies LLC .... C 440 947-2100
   Cleveland *(G-6556)*
▼ The Mau-Sherwood Supply Co .... D 330 405-1200
   Twinsburg *(G-18475)*
Timco Rubber Products Inc .... E 216 267-6242
   Berea *(G-1473)*
▼ Timken Corporation .... D 330 471-3378
   North Canton *(G-15374)*
▲ Tolco Corporation .... D 419 241-1113
   Toledo *(G-18225)*
◆ Tricor Industrial Inc .... D 330 264-3299
   Wooster *(G-19919)*
Tricor Metals .... D 330 264-3299
   Wooster *(G-19920)*
Vallen Distribution Inc .... D 513 942-9100
   West Chester *(G-19177)*
▲ Victory White Metal Company .... D 216 271-1400
   Cleveland *(G-6694)*
W W Grainger Inc .... C 330 425-8387
   Macedonia *(G-13217)*
◆ Watteredge LLC .... D 440 933-6110
   Avon Lake *(G-940)*
Wesco Distribution Inc .... E 419 666-1670
   Northwood *(G-15551)*
Wesco Distribution Inc .... E 216 741-0441
   Cleveland *(G-6734)*
Wesco Distribution Inc .... E 937 228-9668
   Dayton *(G-9991)*
Winsupply Inc .... E 937 294-5331
   Moraine *(G-14836)*
▲ Wulco Inc .... D 513 679-2600
   Cincinnati *(G-4862)*
WW Grainger Inc .... E 614 276-5231
   Columbus *(G-9010)*
Ziegler Bolt & Parts Co .... D 330 478-2542
   Canton *(G-2595)*

5087 Service Establishment Eqpt & Splys Wholesale

A-1 Sprinkler Company Inc .... D 937 859-6198
   Miamisburg *(G-14267)*
Acorn Distributors Inc .... E 614 294-6444
   Columbus *(G-6940)*
▲ Action Coupling & Eqp Inc .... D 330 279-4242
   Holmesville *(G-12070)*
Airgas Usa LLC .... B 216 642-6600
   Independence *(G-12183)*
▲ Alco-Chem Inc .... E 330 253-3535
   Akron *(G-64)*
Alco-Chem Inc .... E 330 833-8551
   Canton *(G-2230)*
American Sales Inc .... E 937 253-9520
   Dayton *(G-9254)*
Anixter Inc .... E 513 881-4600
   West Chester *(G-19021)*

Baxter Burial Vault Service .... E 513 641-1010
   Cincinnati *(G-3082)*
Brakefire Incorporated .... E 330 535-4343
   Akron *(G-107)*
Century Equipment Inc .... E 513 285-1800
   Hamilton *(G-11707)*
Clean Innovations .... E 614 299-1187
   Columbus *(G-7295)*
Cleveland Coin Mch Exch Inc .... D 847 842-6310
   Willoughby *(G-19653)*
Commercial Parts & Ser .... E 614 221-0057
   Columbus *(G-7400)*
Dawnchem Inc .... E 440 943-3332
   Willoughby *(G-19658)*
Envirochemical Inc .... E 440 287-2200
   Solon *(G-17004)*
Finley Fire Equipment Co .... D 740 962-4328
   McConnelsville *(G-14027)*
▼ Fox International Limited Inc .... E 216 454-1001
   Beachwood *(G-1080)*
▲ Fredrics Corporation .... E 513 874-2226
   West Chester *(G-19076)*
Friends Service Co Inc .... D 419 427-1704
   Findlay *(G-11033)*
H & H Green LLC .... E 419 674-4152
   Kenton *(G-12412)*
H P Products Corporation .... D 513 683-8553
   Cincinnati *(G-3723)*
Hd Supply Facilities Maint Ltd .... E 440 542-9188
   Solon *(G-17014)*
Hillside Maint Sup Co Inc .... E 513 751-4100
   Cincinnati *(G-3767)*
I Supply Co .... C 937 878-5240
   Fairborn *(G-10798)*
▲ Impact Products LLC .... C 419 841-2891
   Toledo *(G-17971)*
Laughlin Music & Vending Svc .... E 740 593-7778
   Athens *(G-798)*
Lute Supply Inc .... E 740 353-1447
   Portsmouth *(G-16294)*
M Conley Company .... D 330 456-8243
   Canton *(G-2442)*
▲ Majestic Manufacturing Inc .... E 330 457-2447
   New Waterford *(G-15138)*
Mansfield City Building Maint .... E 419 755-9698
   Mansfield *(G-13330)*
Mapp Building Service LLC .... E 513 253-3990
   Blue Ash *(G-1633)*
Mark Humrichouser .... E 614 324-5231
   Westerville *(G-19327)*
Martin-Brower Company LLC .... B 513 773-2301
   West Chester *(G-19118)*
Mougianis Industries Inc .... D 740 264-6372
   Steubenville *(G-17331)*
MSA Group Inc .... B 614 334-0400
   Columbus *(G-8204)*
National Marketshare Group .... E 513 921-0800
   Cincinnati *(G-4140)*
▲ Norm Sharlotte Inc .... E 336 788-7705
   New Albany *(G-15002)*
North Central Sales Inc .... E 216 481-2418
   Cleveland *(G-6138)*
◆ Perio Inc .... E 614 791-1207
   Dublin *(G-10426)*
▲ Phillips Supply Company .... D 513 579-1762
   Cincinnati *(G-4292)*
Powell Company Ltd .... D 419 228-3552
   Lima *(G-12861)*
Pro-Touch Inc .... C 614 586-0303
   Columbus *(G-8563)*
Rde System Corp .... C 513 933-8000
   Lebanon *(G-12640)*
Rdp Foodservice Ltd .... D 614 261-5661
   Columbus *(G-8593)*
Rhiel Supply Co Inc .... E 330 799-7777
   Austintown *(G-873)*
Rose Products and Services Inc .... E 614 443-7647
   Columbus *(G-8649)*
Sally Beauty Supply LLC .... E 937 548-7684
   Greenville *(G-11518)*
Sally Beauty Supply LLC .... C 614 278-1691
   Columbus *(G-8678)*
Salon Success Intl LLC .... E 330 468-0476
   Macedonia *(G-13209)*
Salon Ware Inc .... E 330 665-2244
   Copley *(G-9062)*
Seaway Sponge & Chamois Co .... E 419 691-4694
   Toledo *(G-18177)*
ServiceMaster of Defiance Inc .... D 419 784-5570
   Defiance *(G-10057)*

SIC SECTION 50 WHOLESALE TRADE¨DURABLE GOODS

▲ Shaffer Distributing Company ....D....... 614 421-6800
Columbus (G-8721)
◆ Sutphen Corporation ....C....... 800 726-7030
Dublin (G-10468)
The Cottingham Paper Co..........E....... 614 294-6444
Columbus (G-8834)
◆ Wasserstrom Company ....B....... 614 228-6525
Columbus (G-8970)

5088 Transportation Eqpt & Splys, Except Motor Vehicles Wholesale

A & K Railroad Materials Inc ....E....... 419 537-9470
Toledo (G-17733)
Abx Air Inc ....B....... 937 382-5591
Wilmington (G-19741)
◆ Aim Mro Holdings Inc..........D....... 513 831-2938
Miamiville (G-14374)
Airborne Maint Engrg Svcs Inc..........A....... 937 366-2559
Wilmington (G-19744)
Airborne Maint Engrg Svcs Inc..........D....... 937 382-5591
Wilmington (G-19745)
Amsted Industries Incorporated..........C....... 614 836-2323
Groveport (G-11622)
▲ Buck Equipment Inc ....E....... 614 539-3039
Grove City (G-11540)
Century Equipment Inc..........E....... 419 865-7400
Toledo (G-17800)
Century Equipment Inc..........E....... 216 292-6911
Cleveland (G-5216)
Cleveland Wheels ....D....... 440 937-6211
Avon (G-890)
▼ Djj Holding Corporation ....C....... 513 621-8770
Cincinnati (G-3496)
▲ Eleet Cryogenics Inc..........E....... 330 874-4009
Bolivar (G-1746)
GE Engine Services LLC..........B....... 513 243-9404
Hamilton (G-11731)
▲ Greenfield Products Inc ....D....... 937 981-2696
Greenfield (G-11486)
Grimes Aerospace Company..........B....... 937 484-2001
Urbana (G-18590)
◆ Jilco Industries Inc..........E....... 330 698-0280
Kidron (G-12441)
Keeptryan Inc ....D....... 330 319-1866
Akron (G-302)
Mazzella Holding Company Inc ....D....... 513 772-4466
Cleveland (G-5997)
Netjets Inc..........E....... 614 239-5500
Columbus (G-8261)
Netjets Sales Inc ....C....... 614 239-5500
Columbus (G-8264)
NJ Executive Services Inc..........E....... 614 239-2996
Columbus (G-8282)
Norman-Spencer Agency Inc ....E....... 937 432-1600
Dayton (G-9775)
Roe Transport Inc ....E....... 937 497-7161
Sidney (G-16951)
Schuster Electronics Inc ....E....... 330 425-8134
Twinsburg (G-18468)
▲ Sportsmans Market Inc ....C....... 513 735-9100
Batavia (G-1025)
▲ Star Dynamics Corporation ....D....... 614 334-4510
Hilliard (G-11954)
Transdigm Group Incorporated..........C....... 216 706-2960
Cleveland (G-6611)
▲ Ysd Industries Inc..........D....... 330 792-6521
Youngstown (G-20437)

5091 Sporting & Recreational Goods & Splys Wholesale

21st Century Health Spa Inc ....E....... 419 476-5585
Toledo (G-17732)
4th and Goal Distribution LLC ....E....... 440 212-0769
Burbank (G-2054)
A K Athletic Equipment Inc..........E....... 614 920-3069
Canal Winchester (G-2151)
AB Marketing LLC..........E....... 513 385-6158
Fairfield (G-10814)
Acusport Corporation..........C....... 937 593-7010
Bellefontaine (G-1374)
Air Venturi Ltd ....D....... 216 292-2570
Solon (G-16973)
◆ Ball Bounce and Sport Inc..........B....... 419 289-9310
Ashland (G-661)
Beaver-Vu Bowl..........E....... 937 426-6771
Beavercreek (G-1150)
Brennan-Eberly Team Sports Inc ....E....... 419 865-8326
Holland (G-12013)
Cherry Valley Lodge ....E....... 740 788-1200
Newark (G-15156)
Coachs Sports Corner Inc..........E....... 419 609-3737
Sandusky (G-16742)
Competitor Swim Products Inc..........D....... 800 888-7946
Columbus (G-7413)
▲ Done-Rite Bowling Service Co ....E....... 440 232-3280
Bedford (G-1304)
Dtv Inc..........E....... 216 226-5465
Mayfield Heights (G-14001)
Durga Llc ....D....... 513 771-2080
Cincinnati (G-3515)
Dwa Mrkting Prmtional Pdts LLC ....E....... 216 476-0635
Strongsville (G-17457)
◆ Emsco..........E....... 440 238-2100
Strongsville (G-17460)
▲ Golf Galaxy Golfworks Inc ....C....... 740 328-4193
Newark (G-15170)
▲ Kohlmyer Sporting Goods Inc..........E....... 440 277-8296
Lorain (G-13045)
Lmn Development LLC..........D....... 419 433-7200
Sandusky (G-16775)
Mc Alarney Pool Spas and Billd ....E....... 740 373-6698
Marietta (G-13474)
Mc Gregor Family Enterprises..........E....... 513 583-0040
Cincinnati (G-4034)
Metropolitan Pool Service Co..........E....... 216 741-9451
Parma (G-15910)
▲ Miami Corporation ....E....... 513 451-6700
Cincinnati (G-4086)
▲ Micnan Inc ....E....... 330 920-6200
Cuyahoga Falls (G-9209)
R & A Sports Inc..........E....... 216 289-2254
Euclid (G-10773)
Riddell Inc..........E....... 440 366-8225
North Ridgeville (G-15476)
▲ Schneider Saddlery LLC ....E....... 440 543-2700
Chagrin Falls (G-2733)
Suarez Corporation Industries ....D....... 330 494-4282
Canton (G-2554)
▲ Weston Brands LLC..........E....... 216 901-6801
Independence (G-12276)
Willow and Cane LLC ....E....... 609 280-1150
Springboro (G-17142)
▲ Zebec of North America Inc ....E....... 513 829-5533
Fairfield (G-10923)
Zide Sport Shop of Ohio Inc ....D....... 740 373-6446
Marietta (G-13521)

5092 Toys & Hobby Goods & Splys Wholesale

Anderson Press Incorporated ....E....... 615 370-9922
Ashland (G-650)
▲ AW Faber-Castell Usa Inc..........D....... 216 643-4660
Cleveland (G-5086)
Ball Bounce and Sport Inc ....E....... 419 759-3838
Dunkirk (G-10501)
Ball Bounce and Sport Inc ....E....... 614 662-5381
Columbus (G-7087)
◆ Ball Bounce and Sport Inc..........B....... 419 289-9310
Ashland (G-661)
Ball Bounce and Sport Inc ....E....... 419 289-9310
Ashland (G-662)
▲ Bendon Inc ....D....... 419 207-3600
Ashland (G-664)
▲ Closeout Distribution Inc ....A....... 614 278-6800
Columbus (G-7307)
▼ Craft Wholesalers Inc ....C....... 740 964-6210
Groveport (G-11630)
Dwa Mrkting Prmtional Pdts LLC ....E....... 216 476-0635
Strongsville (G-17457)
Flower Factory Inc..........D....... 614 275-6220
Columbus (G-7677)
▲ Galaxy Balloons Incorporated..........C....... 216 476-3360
Cleveland (G-5651)
▼ ICM Distributing Company Inc..........E....... 234 212-3030
Twinsburg (G-18431)
◆ K & K Interiors Inc ....D....... 419 627-0039
Sandusky (G-16772)
▲ K & M International Inc..........D....... 330 425-2550
Twinsburg (G-18435)
Lamrite West Inc ....E....... 440 268-0634
Strongsville (G-17484)
▲ Lamrite West Inc ....C....... 440 238-7318
Strongsville (G-17482)
▲ Lancaster Bingo Company Inc ....D....... 740 681-4759
Lancaster (G-12548)
◆ Mas Inc ....E....... 330 659-3333
Richfield (G-16514)
▲ Miller Fireworks Company Inc ....E....... 419 865-7329
Holland (G-12039)
Nannicola Wholesale Co ....D....... 330 799-0888
Youngstown (G-20293)
National Marketshare Group..........E....... 513 921-0800
Cincinnati (G-4140)
◆ Neil Kravitz Group Sales Inc ....E....... 513 961-8697
Cincinnati (G-4153)
▲ Pyramyd Air Ltd ....E....... 216 896-0893
Solon (G-17043)
R and G Enterprises of Ohio..........E....... 440 845-6870
Cleveland (G-6337)

5093 Scrap & Waste Materials Wholesale

◆ Aci Industries Ltd ....E....... 740 368-4160
Delaware (G-10065)
▲ Agmet LLC..........E....... 440 439-7400
Cleveland (G-4969)
Agmet LLC..........E....... 216 662-6939
Maple Heights (G-13399)
Allen County Recyclers Inc..........E....... 419 223-5010
Lima (G-12735)
Ascendtech Inc ....E....... 216 458-1101
Willoughby (G-19645)
Associated Paper Stock Inc..........E....... 330 549-5311
North Lima (G-15397)
Byer Steel Recycling Inc ....E....... 513 948-0300
Cincinnati (G-3158)
City Scrap & Salvage Co ....E....... 330 753-5051
Akron (G-143)
Cohen Electronics Inc ....D....... 513 425-6911
Middletown (G-14421)
Crispin Iron & Metal Co LLC ....E....... 740 616-6213
Granville (G-11464)
▼ Diproinduca (usa) Limited LLC..........D....... 330 722-4442
Medina (G-14058)
Diver Steel City Auto Crushers..........E....... 330 744-5083
Youngstown (G-20171)
▼ Djj Holding Corporation ....C....... 513 621-8770
Cincinnati (G-3496)
▲ Fpt Cleveland LLC ....C....... 216 441-3800
Cleveland (G-5628)
Frankes Wood Products LLC..........E....... 937 642-0706
Marysville (G-13620)
▲ Franklin Iron & Metal Corp..........C....... 937 253-8184
Dayton (G-9561)
▼ G-Cor Automotive Corp..........E....... 614 443-6735
Columbus (G-7721)
Hamilton Scrap Processors..........E....... 513 863-3474
Hamilton (G-11741)
Harry Rock & Company..........E....... 330 644-3748
Cleveland (G-5728)
Heritage Envmtl Svcs LLC ....E....... 419 729-1321
Toledo (G-17954)
Holub Iron & Steel Company ....E....... 330 252-5655
Akron (G-270)
I H Schlezinger Inc..........E....... 614 252-1188
Columbus (G-7877)
◆ I-Tran Inc ....E....... 330 659-0801
Richfield (G-16512)
Imperial Alum - Minerva LLC ....D....... 330 868-7765
Minerva (G-14646)
▼ Intex Supply Company ....E....... 216 535-4300
Richmond Heights (G-16539)
▼ Jasar Recycling Inc ....D....... 864 233-5421
East Palestine (G-10538)
Kenton Auto and Truck Wrecking ....E....... 419 673-8234
Kenton (G-12420)
▲ Legend Smelting and Recycl Inc......D....... 740 928-0139
Hebron (G-11851)
Lkq Corporation ....E....... 614 575-8200
Groveport (G-11656)
Lkq Corporation ....E....... 330 733-6333
Akron (G-322)
M & M Metals International Inc ....E....... 513 221-4411
Cincinnati (G-4005)
Mauser Usa LLC..........E....... 740 397-1762
Mount Vernon (G-14911)
Metal Management Ohio Inc ....E....... 419 782-7791
Defiance (G-10049)
Metalico Akron Inc ....E....... 330 376-1400
Akron (G-340)
Midwest Iron and Metal Co..........D....... 937 222-5992
Dayton (G-9745)
Miles Alloy Inc..........E....... 216 245-8893
Cleveland (G-6062)
Montgomery Iron & Paper Co Inc..........D....... 937 222-4059
Dayton (G-9755)
Moskowitz Bros Inc ....E....... 513 242-2100
Cincinnati (G-4121)

SIC

50 WHOLESALE TRADE¨DURABLE GOODS

Muskingum Iron & Metal Co .... E 740 452-9351
  Zanesville (G-20509)
Niles Iron & Metal Company LLC .... E 330 652-2262
  Niles (G-15300)
Omnisource LLC .... D 419 537-1631
  Toledo (G-18107)
Omnisource LLC .... E 419 227-3411
  Lima (G-12849)
Omnisource LLC .... E 419 394-3351
  Saint Marys (G-16681)
Omnisource LLC .... C 419 537-9400
  Toledo (G-18108)
PSC Metals Inc .... E 330 455-0212
  Canton (G-2497)
PSC Metals Inc .... E 614 299-4175
  Columbus (G-8576)
PSC Metals Inc .... D 234 208-2331
  Barberton (G-974)
PSC Metals Inc .... E 330 794-8300
  Barberton (G-975)
PSC Metals Inc .... E 330 745-4437
  Barberton (G-976)
PSC Metals Inc .... E 330 484-7610
  Canton (G-2498)
PSC Metals Inc .... E 216 341-3400
  Cleveland (G-6329)
PSC Metals - Wooster LLC .... D 330 264-8956
  Wooster (G-19905)
◆ Quantum Metals Inc .... E 513 573-0144
  Lebanon (G-12638)
R L S Corporation .... E 740 773-1440
  Chillicothe (G-2872)
Reserve Ftl LLC .... E 773 721-8740
  Canton (G-2512)
▼ River Recycling Entps Ltd .... E 216 459-2100
  Cleveland (G-6398)
Rnw Holdings Inc .... E 330 792-0600
  Youngstown (G-20352)
Royal Paper Stock Company Inc .... D 614 851-4714
  Columbus (G-8655)
Scrap Yard LLC .... E 216 271-5823
  Cleveland (G-6454)
Shredded Bedding Corporation .... E 740 893-3567
  Centerburg (G-2668)
Slesnick Iron & Metal Co .... E 330 453-8475
  Canton (G-2532)
Tms International LLC .... E 419 747-5500
  Mansfield (G-13375)
◆ Unico Alloys & Metals Inc .... D 614 299-0545
  Columbus (G-8887)
W R G Inc .... E 216 351-8494
  Cleveland (G-6714)
Wall St Recycling LLC .... E 330 296-8657
  Ravenna (G-16416)
Wilmington Iron and Met Co Inc .... E 937 382-3867
  Wilmington (G-19794)

5094 Jewelry, Watches, Precious Stones Wholesale

Anderson Press Incorporated .... E 615 370-9922
  Ashland (G-650)
▲ Cas-Ker Company Inc .... E 513 674-7700
  Cincinnati (G-3190)
Equity Diamond Brokers Inc .... E 513 793-4760
  Cincinnati (G-3570)
J L Swaney Inc .... E 740 884-4450
  Chillicothe (G-2855)
Marfo Company .... D 614 276-3352
  Columbus (G-8109)
Toledo Jewelers Supply Co .... E 419 241-4181
  Toledo (G-18240)
United States Commemrtv Art GA .... E 330 494-5504
  Canton (G-2571)

5099 Durable Goods: NEC Wholesale

3s Incorporated .... E 513 202-5070
  Harrison (G-11788)
77 Coach Supply Ltd .... E 330 674-1454
  Millersburg (G-14582)
ABC Fire Inc .... E 440 237-6677
  North Royalton (G-15480)
Abco Fire LLC .... E 800 875-7200
  Cincinnati (G-2960)
▼ Abco Holdings LLC .... D 216 433-7200
  Cleveland (G-4946)
Bladecutters Lawn Service Inc .... E 937 274-3861
  Dayton (G-9360)
▲ Chester West Holdings Inc .... C 800 647-1900
  Cincinnati (G-3241)

◆ Dualite Sales & Service Inc .... C 513 724-7100
  Williamsburg (G-19632)
Earth n Wood Products Inc .... E 330 644-1858
  Akron (G-204)
Gene Ptacek Son Fire Eqp Inc .... E 216 651-8300
  Cleveland (G-5666)
Gia USA Inc .... E 216 831-8678
  Cleveland (G-5670)
Gross Lumber Inc .... E 330 683-2055
  Apple Creek (G-625)
▲ Grover Musical Products Inc .... E 216 391-1188
  Cleveland (G-5708)
Keidel Supply Company Inc .... E 513 351-1600
  Cincinnati (G-3906)
Koorsen Fire & Security Inc .... E 614 878-2228
  Columbus (G-8009)
Koorsen Fire & Security Inc .... E 614 878-2228
  Columbus (G-8010)
Live Technologies Holdings Inc .... D 614 278-7777
  Columbus (G-8074)
◆ Merchandise Inc .... D 513 353-2200
  Miamitown (G-14372)
▲ Midwest Tape LLC .... B 419 868-9370
  Holland (G-12038)
◆ Pipeline Packaging Corporation .... E 440 349-3200
  Solon (G-17040)
◆ Premium Beverage Supply Ltd .... E 614 777-1007
  Hilliard (G-11944)
▲ Recaro Child Safety LLC .... E 248 904-1570
  Cincinnati (G-4392)
Rk Family Inc .... C 740 389-2674
  Marion (G-13577)
Rk Family Inc .... C 419 355-8230
  Fremont (G-11216)
Rk Family Inc .... B 330 264-5475
  Wooster (G-19907)
Rk Family Inc .... C 513 934-0015
  Lebanon (G-12643)
RLM Fabricating Inc .... E 419 729-6130
  Toledo (G-18158)
Roofing Supply Group LLC .... E 614 239-1111
  Columbus (G-8647)
▲ Safety Today Inc .... E 614 409-7200
  Grove City (G-11595)
Southern Ohio Gun Distrs Inc .... E 513 932-8148
  Lebanon (G-12649)
Superr-Spdie Portable Svcs Inc .... E 330 733-9000
  Akron (G-469)
Telarc International Corp .... E 216 464-2313
  Beachwood (G-1130)
TS Tech Americas Inc .... E 740 593-5958
  Athens (G-817)
▲ TS Tech Americas Inc .... B 614 575-4100
  Reynoldsburg (G-16486)
U-Haul Neighborhood Dealer -Ce .... E 419 929-3724
  New London (G-15071)
Union Tank Car Company .... C 419 864-7216
  Marion (G-13589)
Vinifera Imports Ltd .... E 440 942-9463
  Mentor (G-14255)
▲ Wcm Holdings Inc .... C 513 705-2100
  Cincinnati (G-4826)
Windy Hill Ltd Inc .... D 216 391-4800
  Cleveland (G-6753)
Woodcraft Supply LLC .... D 513 407-8371
  Cincinnati (G-4859)

51 WHOLESALE TRADE¨NONDURABLE GOODS

5111 Printing & Writing Paper Wholesale

Catalyst Paper (usa) Inc .... E 937 528-3800
  Dayton (G-9389)
Commerce Paper Company .... E 419 241-9101
  Toledo (G-17821)
▲ Millcraft Group LLC .... D 216 441-5500
  Cleveland (G-6063)
▲ Millcraft Paper Company .... C 216 441-5505
  Cleveland (G-6064)
Millcraft Paper Company .... E 740 924-9470
  Columbus (G-8174)
Millcraft Paper Company .... E 937 222-7829
  Dayton (G-9748)
Millcraft Paper Company .... E 614 675-4800
  Columbus (G-8175)
Millcraft Paper Company .... E 216 441-5500
  Cleveland (G-6065)
Mohawk Fine Papers Inc .... C 440 969-2049
  Ashtabula (G-755)

OfficeMax Contract Inc .... D 216 898-2400
  Cleveland (G-6182)
Ohio & Michigan Paper Company .... E 419 666-1500
  Perrysburg (G-16035)
▲ Sterling Paper Co .... E 614 443-0303
  Columbus (G-8786)
The Cincinnati Cordage Ppr Co .... E 513 242-3600
  Cincinnati (G-4640)
Veritiv Operating Company .... E 419 243-6100
  Toledo (G-18289)
◆ Veritiv Pubg & Print MGT Inc .... E 330 650-5522
  Hudson (G-12149)

5112 Stationery & Office Splys Wholesale

▲ AW Faber-Castell Usa Inc .... D 216 643-4660
  Cleveland (G-5086)
Business Stationery LLC .... D 216 514-1192
  Cleveland (G-5164)
Canon Solutions America Inc .... E 216 750-2980
  Independence (G-12194)
▲ Dexxxon Digital Storage Inc .... E 740 548-7179
  Lewis Center (G-12681)
Electronic Printing Pdts Inc .... E 330 689-3930
  Stow (G-17362)
EMI Enterprises Inc .... E 419 666-0012
  Northwood (G-15530)
Envelope Mart of North E Ohio .... E 440 322-8862
  Elyria (G-10627)
Envelope Mart of Ohio Inc .... E 440 365-8177
  Elyria (G-10628)
Essendant Co .... D 330 650-9361
  Hudson (G-12116)
Essendant Co .... C 330 425-4001
  Twinsburg (G-18412)
Essendant Co .... D 513 942-1354
  West Chester (G-19197)
Essendant Co .... D 614 876-7774
  Columbus (G-7610)
Essendant Inc .... D 330 425-4001
  Twinsburg (G-18413)
Friends Service Co Inc .... D 419 427-1704
  Findlay (G-11033)
▲ GBS Corp .... C 330 494-5330
  North Canton (G-15339)
Indepndence Office Bus Sup Inc .... D 216 398-8880
  Cleveland (G-5815)
Med-Pass Incorporated .... E 937 438-8884
  Dayton (G-9711)
OfficeMax North America Inc .... E 330 666-4550
  Akron (G-362)
Ohio & Michigan Paper Company .... E 419 666-1500
  Perrysburg (G-16035)
Optimum System Products Inc .... E 614 885-4464
  Westerville (G-19433)
Pac Worldwide Corporation .... D 800 610-9367
  Middletown (G-14448)
Pfg Ventures LP .... D 216 520-8400
  Independence (G-12243)
Powell Company Ltd .... D 419 228-3552
  Lima (G-12861)
▼ Quick Tab II Inc .... D 419 448-6622
  Tiffin (G-17694)
Ricoh Usa Inc .... D 513 984-9898
  Blue Ash (G-1683)
S P Richards Company .... E 614 497-2270
  Obetz (G-15670)
Seagate Office Products Inc .... E 419 861-6161
  Holland (G-12055)
▲ Shamrock Companies Inc .... C 440 899-9510
  Westlake (G-19546)
Signal Office Supply Inc .... E 513 821-2280
  Cincinnati (G-4528)
Staples Inc .... E 740 845-5600
  London (G-13007)
W B Mason Co Inc .... D 216 267-5000
  Cleveland (G-6713)
◆ Wasserstrom Company .... B 614 228-6525
  Columbus (G-8970)
Western States Envelope Co .... D 419 666-7480
  Walbridge (G-18780)

5113 Indl & Personal Svc Paper Wholesale

◆ Aci Industries Converting Ltd .... E 740 368-4160
  Delaware (G-10066)
Acorn Distributors Inc .... E 614 294-6444
  Columbus (G-6940)
Alco-Chem Inc .... E 330 833-8551
  Canton (G-2230)
▲ Atlapac Corp .... D 614 252-2121
  Columbus (G-7067)

SIC SECTION 51 WHOLESALE TRADE¨NONDURABLE GOODS

Avalon Foodservice Inc ..... C 330 854-4551
Canal Fulton *(G-2140)*
▲ Berk Enterprises Inc ..... D 330 369-1192
Warren *(G-18829)*
Buckeye Boxes Inc ..... E 614 274-8484
Columbus *(G-7156)*
▼ Buckeye Paper Co Inc ..... E 330 477-5925
Canton *(G-2272)*
▲ Cannon Group Inc ..... E 614 890-0343
Westerville *(G-19375)*
Cardinal Container Corporation ..... E 614 497-3033
Columbus *(G-7191)*
▲ Compass Packaging LLC ..... E 330 274-2001
Mantua *(G-13386)*
Dawnchem Inc ..... E 440 943-3332
Willoughby *(G-19658)*
Dayton Industrial Drum Inc ..... E 937 253-8933
Dayton *(G-9263)*
Deufol Worldwide Packaging LLC ..... D 440 232-1100
Bedford *(G-1303)*
Deufol Worldwide Packaging LLC ..... D 414 967-8000
Fairfield *(G-10840)*
Espt Liquidation Inc ..... D 330 698-4711
Apple Creek *(G-624)*
Food Distributors Inc ..... E 740 439-2764
Cambridge *(G-2114)*
▲ G R B Inc ..... D 800 628-9195
West Chester *(G-19078)*
I Supply Co ..... C 937 878-5240
Fairborn *(G-10798)*
Impressive Packaging Inc ..... E 419 368-6808
Hayesville *(G-11834)*
J V Hansel Inc ..... E 330 716-0806
Warren *(G-18866)*
Jit Packaging Aurora Inc ..... E 330 562-8080
Aurora *(G-843)*
◆ Joshen Paper & Packaging Co ..... C 216 441-5600
Cleveland *(G-5872)*
Keystone Foods LLC ..... C 419 843-3009
Toledo *(G-17993)*
M Conley Company ..... D 330 456-8243
Canton *(G-2442)*
▲ Mailender Inc ..... D 513 942-5453
West Chester *(G-19115)*
Maines Paper & Food Svc Inc ..... E 216 643-7500
Bedford *(G-1319)*
▲ Mast Logistics Services Inc ..... C 614 415-7500
Columbus *(G-8125)*
▲ Millcraft Group LLC ..... D 216 441-5500
Cleveland *(G-6063)*
▲ Millcraft Paper Company ..... C 216 441-5505
Cleveland *(G-6064)*
Millcraft Paper Company ..... E 937 222-7829
Dayton *(G-9748)*
Millcraft Paper Company ..... E 614 675-4800
Columbus *(G-8175)*
Millcraft Paper Company ..... E 216 441-5500
Cleveland *(G-6065)*
Millers Textile Services Inc ..... D 419 738-3552
Wapakoneta *(G-18804)*
North American Plas Chem Inc ..... E 330 627-2210
Carrollton *(G-2624)*
Ohio & Michigan Paper Company ..... E 419 666-1500
Perrysburg *(G-16035)*
▲ Peck Distributors Inc ..... E 216 587-6814
Maple Heights *(G-13413)*
Pollak Distributing Co Inc ..... E 216 851-9911
Euclid *(G-10772)*
▲ Polymer Packaging Inc ..... D 330 832-2000
Massillon *(G-13844)*
Precision Products Group Inc ..... D 330 698-4711
Apple Creek *(G-626)*
Procter & Gamble Distrg LLC ..... D 513 626-2500
Blue Ash *(G-1667)*
Ricking Paper and Specialty Co ..... E 513 825-3551
Cincinnati *(G-4418)*
Sonoco Products Company ..... D 937 429-0040
Beavercreek Township *(G-1285)*
Sysco Cincinnati LLC ..... B 513 563-6300
Cincinnati *(G-4609)*
Systems Pack Inc ..... E 330 467-5729
Macedonia *(G-13211)*
▲ Tape Products Company ..... D 513 489-8840
Cincinnati *(G-4624)*
The Cincinnati Cordage Ppr Co ..... E 513 242-3600
Cincinnati *(G-4640)*
The Cottingham Paper Co ..... E 614 294-6444
Columbus *(G-8834)*
Tiffin Paper Company ..... E 419 447-2121
Tiffin *(G-17706)*

Veritiv Operating Company ..... E 614 251-7100
Columbus *(G-8935)*
Veritiv Operating Company ..... E 216 573-7400
Independence *(G-12273)*
Veritiv Operating Company ..... C 513 285-0999
Fairfield *(G-10922)*
Welch Packaging LLC ..... E 937 223-3958
Dayton *(G-9989)*
Westrock CP LLC ..... D 770 448-2193
Wshngtn CT Hs *(G-20038)*

5122 Drugs, Drug Proprietaries & Sundries Wholesale

ACS Acqco Corp ..... C 513 719-2600
Cincinnati *(G-2969)*
▲ American Cutting Edge Inc ..... C 937 438-2390
Centerville *(G-2673)*
Amerisourcebergen Corporation ..... C 610 727-7000
Columbus *(G-7013)*
Amerisourcebergen Corporation ..... D 614 497-3665
Lockbourne *(G-12944)*
Amerisourcebergen Drug Corp ..... D 614 409-0741
Lockbourne *(G-12945)*
Asd Specialty Healthcare LLC ..... D 513 682-3600
West Chester *(G-19022)*
Basic Drugs Inc ..... E 937 898-4010
Vandalia *(G-18662)*
Beiersdorf Inc ..... C 513 682-7300
West Chester *(G-19191)*
Biolife Plasma Services LP ..... D 419 425-8680
Findlay *(G-10994)*
Biorx LLC ..... D 866 442-4679
Cincinnati *(G-3109)*
▲ Boehringer Ingelheim USA Corp ..... E 440 232-3320
Bedford *(G-1297)*
Braden Med Services Inc ..... E 740 732-2356
Caldwell *(G-2082)*
◆ Brothers Trading Co Inc ..... C 937 746-1010
Springboro *(G-17117)*
Buderer Drug Company Inc ..... E 419 627-2800
Sandusky *(G-16730)*
◆ Butler Animal Health Sup LLC ..... C 614 761-9095
Dublin *(G-10273)*
Butler Animal Health Sup LLC ..... E 614 718-2000
Columbus *(G-7171)*
▼ Butler Animal Hlth Holdg LLC ..... E 614 761-9095
Dublin *(G-10274)*
Capital Wholesale Drug Company ..... D 614 297-8225
Columbus *(G-7185)*
◆ Cardinal Health Inc ..... A 614 757-5000
Dublin *(G-10275)*
Cardinal Health Inc ..... D 614 497-9552
Obetz *(G-15665)*
Cardinal Health Inc ..... D 614 757-7690
Columbus *(G-7193)*
Cardinal Health 100 Inc ..... B 614 757-5000
Dublin *(G-10276)*
Cardinal Health 107 LLC ..... C 740 455-2462
Zanesville *(G-20455)*
Cardinal Health 414 LLC ..... E 419 867-1077
Holland *(G-12014)*
Cardinal Health 414 LLC ..... E 937 438-1888
Moraine *(G-14759)*
Catamaran Home Dlvry Ohio Inc ..... D 440 930-5520
Avon Lake *(G-924)*
Columbus Serum Company ..... C 614 444-5211
Columbus *(G-7384)*
▲ Cosmax USA Inc Cosmax USA Corp ..... E 440 600-5738
Solon *(G-16996)*
▲ Discount Drug Mart Inc ..... C 330 725-2340
Medina *(G-14059)*
EBY-Brown Company LLC ..... C 937 324-1036
Springfield *(G-17192)*
▲ Edwards Gem Inc ..... D 330 342-8300
Hudson *(G-12115)*
Evergreen Pharmaceutical LLC ..... B 513 719-2600
Cincinnati *(G-3580)*
Evergreen Phrm Cal Inc ..... E 513 719-2600
Cincinnati *(G-3581)*
F Dohmen Co ..... C 614 757-5000
Dublin *(G-10344)*
▲ Fredrics Corporation ..... C 513 874-2226
West Chester *(G-19076)*
G E G Enterprises Inc ..... E 330 477-3133
Canton *(G-2375)*
Greenfield Hts Oper Group LLC ..... E 312 877-1153
Lima *(G-12787)*
Heartland Healthcare Svcs LLC ..... C 419 535-8435
Toledo *(G-17947)*

Home Care Pharmacy LLC ..... C 513 874-0009
West Chester *(G-19208)*
▼ ICM Distributing Company Inc ..... E 234 212-3030
Twinsburg *(G-18431)*
Imagepace LLC ..... B 513 579-9911
Cincinnati *(G-3809)*
Institutional Care Pharmacy ..... C 419 447-6216
Tiffin *(G-17681)*
Keysource Acquisition LLC ..... E 513 469-7881
Cincinnati *(G-3919)*
Kroger Co ..... C 740 335-4030
Wshngtn CT Hs *(G-20028)*
Kroger Co ..... B 614 898-3200
Westerville *(G-19419)*
Masters Drug Company Inc ..... D 800 982-7922
Lebanon *(G-12625)*
▲ Masters Pharmaceutical Inc ..... C 513 354-2690
Lebanon *(G-12626)*
Masters Pharmaceutical Inc ..... D 800 982-7922
Lebanon *(G-12627)*
McKesson Corporation ..... C 740 636-3500
Wshngtn CT Hs *(G-20030)*
Medpace Inc ..... A 513 579-9911
Cincinnati *(G-4049)*
◆ Merchandise Inc ..... D 513 353-2200
Miamitown *(G-14372)*
Miami-Luken Inc ..... D 937 743-7775
Springboro *(G-17128)*
Mimrx Co Inc ..... B 614 850-6672
Columbus *(G-8176)*
MSA Group Inc ..... B 614 334-0400
Columbus *(G-8204)*
Ncs Healthcare of Ohio LLC ..... E 330 364-5011
Dover *(G-10201)*
Ncs Healthcare of Ohio LLC ..... D 513 719-2600
Cincinnati *(G-4148)*
Ncs Healthcare of Ohio LLC ..... E 614 534-0400
Columbus *(G-8254)*
▲ Nehemiah Manufacturing Co LLC ..... E 513 351-5700
Cincinnati *(G-4150)*
Neighborcare Inc ..... A 513 719-2600
Cincinnati *(G-4151)*
Omnicare Inc ..... C 513 719-2600
Cincinnati *(G-4220)*
Omnicare Distribution Ctr LLC ..... D 419 720-8200
Cincinnati *(G-4221)*
Omnicare Phrm of Midwest LLC ..... D 513 719-2600
Cincinnati *(G-4223)*
Orchard Phrm Svcs LLC ..... C 330 491-4200
North Canton *(G-15359)*
Pca-Corrections LLC ..... E 614 297-8244
Columbus *(G-8525)*
Pharmed Corporation ..... C 440 250-5400
Westlake *(G-19533)*
Physicians Weight Ls Ctr Amer ..... E 330 666-7952
Akron *(G-389)*
▲ Prasco LLC ..... D 513 204-1100
Mason *(G-13748)*
Prescription Supply Inc ..... D 419 661-6600
Northwood *(G-15543)*
Procter & Gamble Distrg LLC ..... B 513 626-2500
Blue Ash *(G-1667)*
Raisin Rack Inc ..... E 614 882-5886
Westerville *(G-19440)*
Remedi Seniorcare of Ohio LLC ..... E 800 232-4239
Troy *(G-18377)*
Riser Foods Company ..... D 216 292-7000
Bedford Heights *(G-1359)*
River City Pharma ..... D 513 870-1680
Fairfield *(G-10900)*
▲ Robert J Matthews Company ..... D 330 834-3000
Massillon *(G-13849)*
Samuels Products Inc ..... E 513 891-4456
Blue Ash *(G-1686)*
Shaklee Corporation ..... C 614 409-2953
Groveport *(G-11671)*
Skilled Care Pharmacy Inc ..... C 513 459-7626
Mason *(G-13762)*
Specialized Pharmacy Svcs LLC ..... E 513 719-2600
Cincinnati *(G-4557)*
Suarez Corporation Industries ..... D 330 494-4282
Canton *(G-2554)*
Superior Care Pharmacy Inc ..... C 513 719-2600
Cincinnati *(G-4603)*
Teva Womens Health Inc ..... C 513 731-9900
Cincinnati *(G-4639)*
Trickeration Inc ..... E 216 360-9966
Warrensville Heights *(G-18935)*
▲ Triplefin LLC ..... D 855 877-5346
Blue Ash *(G-1703)*

S I C

Employee Codes: A=Over 500 employees, B=251-500
C=101-250, D=51-100, E=25-50

2018 Harris Ohio Services Directory 955

51 WHOLESALE TRADE¨NONDURABLE GOODS SIC SECTION

Vitamin Shoppe Inc....E.... 440 238-5987
Strongsville (G-17522)
Walter F Stephens Jr Inc....E.... 937 746-0521
Franklin (G-11167)
▲ Wbc Group LLC....D.... 866 528-2144
Hudson (G-12150)
Westhaven Services Co LLC....B.... 419 661-2200
Perrysburg (G-16073)

5131 Piece Goods, Notions & Dry Goods Wholesale

▲ Checker Notions Company Inc....D.... 419 893-3636
Maumee (G-13894)
Collotype Labels Usa Inc....D.... 513 381-1480
Batavia (G-1005)
Custom Products Corporation....D.... 440 528-7100
Solon (G-16999)
Electronic Printing Pdts Inc....E.... 330 689-3930
Stow (G-17362)
◆ Great Lakes Textiles Inc....E.... 440 439-1300
Solon (G-17012)
▲ Miami Corporation....E.... 513 451-6700
Cincinnati (G-4086)
R S Sewing Inc....E.... 330 478-3360
Canton (G-2502)
Style-Line Incorporated....E.... 614 291-0600
Columbus (G-8798)
Welspun Usa Inc....E.... 614 945-5100
Grove City (G-11613)

5136 Men's & Boys' Clothing & Furnishings Wholesale

▼ Abercrombie & Fitch Trading Co....E.... 614 283-6500
New Albany (G-14970)
Barbs Graffiti Inc....D.... 216 881-5550
Cleveland (G-5093)
▲ Barbs Graffiti Inc....E.... 216 881-5550
Cleveland (G-5094)
Brennan-Eberly Team Sports Inc....E.... 419 865-8326
Holland (G-12013)
▲ Chester West Holdings Inc....C.... 800 647-1900
Cincinnati (G-3241)
Cintas Corporation No 1....A.... 513 459-1200
Mason (G-13678)
Cintas Sales Corporation....B.... 513 459-1200
Cincinnati (G-3353)
◆ For Women Like Me Inc....E.... 407 848-7339
Chagrin Falls (G-2696)
Gymnastic World Inc....E.... 440 526-2970
Cleveland (G-5712)
Heritage Sportswear Inc....D.... 740 928-7771
Hebron (G-11850)
▲ J Peterman Company LLC....E.... 888 647-2555
Blue Ash (G-1619)
▲ K Amalia Enterprises Inc....D.... 614 733-3800
Plain City (G-16195)
▼ Lion-Vallen Ltd Partnership....B.... 937 898-1949
Dayton (G-9686)
▲ Mast Industries Inc....C.... 614 415-7000
Columbus (G-8124)
Mast Industries Inc....D.... 614 856-6000
Reynoldsburg (G-16468)
▲ McCc Sportswear Inc....E.... 513 583-9210
West Chester (G-19214)
▲ MGF Sourcing Us LLC....A.... 614 904-3300
Columbus (G-8156)
R & A Sports Inc....E.... 216 289-2254
Euclid (G-10773)
Rassak LLC....E.... 513 791-9453
Cincinnati (G-4386)
▲ RG Barry Corporation....D.... 614 864-6400
Pickerington (G-16105)
Rondinellis Tuxedo....E.... 330 726-7768
Youngstown (G-20359)
Safety Solutions Inc....D.... 614 799-9900
Dublin (G-10446)
◆ Standard Textile Co Inc....B.... 513 761-9255
Cincinnati (G-4579)
Walter F Stephens Jr Inc....E.... 937 746-0521
Franklin (G-11167)

5137 Women's, Children's & Infants Clothing Wholesale

▼ Abercrombie & Fitch Trading Co....E.... 614 283-6500
New Albany (G-14970)
▲ Atrium Buying Corporation....D.... 740 966-8200
Blacklick (G-1500)
Barbs Graffiti Inc....D.... 216 881-5550
Cleveland (G-5093)
▲ Barbs Graffiti Inc....E.... 216 881-5550
Cleveland (G-5094)
Brennan-Eberly Team Sports Inc....E.... 419 865-8326
Holland (G-12013)
Cheek-O Inc....E.... 513 942-4880
Cincinnati (G-3236)
▲ Chester West Holdings Inc....C.... 800 647-1900
Cincinnati (G-3241)
Cintas Corporation No 1....A.... 513 459-1200
Mason (G-13678)
Cintas Corporation No 2....D.... 937 401-0098
Vandalia (G-18670)
Cintas Sales Corporation....B.... 513 459-1200
Cincinnati (G-3353)
▲ Classic Imports Inc....E.... 330 262-5277
Wooster (G-19847)
◆ For Women Like Me Inc....E.... 407 848-7339
Chagrin Falls (G-2696)
Gymnastic World Inc....E.... 440 526-2970
Cleveland (G-5712)
Heritage Sportswear Inc....D.... 740 928-7771
Hebron (G-11850)
▲ J Peterman Company LLC....E.... 888 647-2555
Blue Ash (G-1619)
▼ Lion-Vallen Ltd Partnership....B.... 937 898-1949
Dayton (G-9686)
▲ Mast Industries Inc....C.... 614 415-7000
Columbus (G-8124)
Mast Industries Inc....D.... 614 856-6000
Reynoldsburg (G-16468)
▲ McCc Sportswear Inc....E.... 513 583-9210
West Chester (G-19214)
▲ MGF Sourcing Us LLC....A.... 614 904-3300
Columbus (G-8156)
◆ Philips Medical Systems Clevel....B.... 440 247-2652
Cleveland (G-6273)
Procter & Gamble Distrg LLC....B.... 513 626-2500
Blue Ash (G-1667)
R & A Sports Inc....E.... 216 289-2254
Euclid (G-10773)
Rassak LLC....E.... 513 791-9453
Cincinnati (G-4386)
▲ RG Barry Corporation....D.... 614 864-6400
Pickerington (G-16105)
Toys r Us Inc....E.... 614 759-7744
Reynoldsburg (G-16485)
▲ TSC Apparel LLC....D.... 513 771-1138
Cincinnati (G-4703)

5139 Footwear Wholesale

Brennan-Eberly Team Sports Inc....E.... 419 865-8326
Holland (G-12013)
▲ Drew Ventures Inc....E.... 740 653-4271
Lancaster (G-12528)
Georgia Boot LLC....D.... 740 753-1951
Nelsonville (G-14964)
◆ Lehigh Outfitters LLC....C.... 740 753-1951
Nelsonville (G-14965)
M & R Fredericktown Ltd Inc....E.... 440 801-1563
Akron (G-331)
▲ RG Barry Corporation....D.... 614 864-6400
Pickerington (G-16105)
Safety Solutions Inc....D.... 614 799-9900
Dublin (G-10446)

5141 Groceries, General Line Wholesale

Acosta Inc....D.... 440 498-7370
Solon (G-16970)
Advantage Sales & Mktg LLC....D.... 513 841-0500
Blue Ash (G-1527)
Advantage Waypoint LLC....E.... 248 919-3144
Twinsburg (G-18389)
Albert Guarnieri & Co....D.... 330 794-9834
Akron (G-63)
Anderson and Dubose Inc....D.... 440 248-8800
Warren (G-18817)
Atlantic Fish & Distrg Co....E.... 330 454-1307
Canton (G-2248)
◆ Brothers Trading Co Inc....C.... 937 746-1010
Springboro (G-17117)
Cantrell Oil Company....E.... 937 695-8003
Winchester (G-19800)
Chas G Buchy Packing Company....E.... 800 762-1060
Cincinnati (G-3232)
Circle S Farms Inc....E.... 614 878-9462
Grove City (G-11546)
Dwa Mrkting Prmtional Pdts LLC....E.... 216 476-0635
Strongsville (G-17457)
EBY-Brown Company LLC....C.... 937 324-1036
Springfield (G-17192)
Euclid Fish Company....D.... 440 951-6448
Mentor (G-14172)
Food Sample Express LLc....D.... 330 225-3550
Brunswick (G-1978)
Forths Foods Inc....E.... 740 886-9769
Proctorville (G-16358)
General Mills Inc....D.... 513 770-0558
Mason (G-13706)
Giant Eagle Inc....E.... 216 292-7000
Bedford Heights (G-1352)
Greeneview Foods LLC....E.... 937 675-4161
Jamestown (G-12326)
Gummer Wholesale Inc....D.... 740 928-0415
Heath (G-11838)
Hillandale Farms Corporation....E.... 330 724-3199
Akron (G-265)
Impact Sales Inc....D.... 937 274-1905
Dayton (G-9628)
J V Hansel Inc....E.... 330 716-0806
Warren (G-18866)
Jetro Cash and Carry Entps LLC....D.... 216 525-0101
Cleveland (G-5862)
◆ John Zidian Co Inc....D.... 330 743-6050
Youngstown (G-20240)
Kcbs LLC....E.... 513 421-9422
Cincinnati (G-3903)
Keystone Foods LLC....C.... 419 843-3009
Toledo (G-17993)
Kroger Co....D.... 740 363-4398
Delaware (G-10114)
Kroger Co....C.... 614 759-2745
Columbus (G-8015)
Kroger Co....B.... 937 376-7962
Xenia (G-20066)
Kroger Co....D.... 937 848-5990
Dayton (G-9667)
Larosas Inc....A.... 513 347-5660
Cincinnati (G-3962)
Mattingly Foods Inc....C.... 740 454-0136
Zanesville (G-20500)
Meadowbrook Meat Company Inc....C.... 614 771-9660
Columbus (G-8140)
◆ Mountain Foods Inc....E.... 440 286-7177
Chardon (G-2758)
Mpf Sales and Mktg Group LLC....C.... 513 793-6241
Blue Ash (G-1647)
Nestle Usa Inc....E.... 513 576-4930
Loveland (G-13148)
Novelart Manufacturing Company....C.... 513 351-7700
Cincinnati (G-4187)
Ovations Food Services LP....D.... 513 419-7254
Cincinnati (G-4244)
Physicians Weight Ls Ctr Amer....E.... 330 666-7952
Akron (G-389)
Pollak Distributing Co Inc....E.... 216 851-9911
Euclid (G-10772)
Queensgate Food Group LLC....D.... 513 721-5503
Cincinnati (G-4374)
R G Sellers Company....E.... 937 299-1545
Moraine (G-14819)
Restaurant Depot LLC....E.... 216 525-0101
Cleveland (G-6386)
Ricking Paper and Specialty Co....E.... 513 825-3551
Cincinnati (G-4418)
Riser Foods Company....D.... 216 292-7000
Bedford Heights (G-1359)
Sandridge Food Corporation....C.... 330 725-8883
Medina (G-14123)
Shaker Valley Foods Inc....E.... 216 961-8600
Cleveland (G-6476)
Sherwood Food Distributors LLC....B.... 216 662-6794
Maple Heights (G-13418)
Sommers Market LLC....D.... 330 352-7470
Hartville (G-11831)
Spartannash Company....A.... 937 599-1110
Bellefontaine (G-1397)
Spartannash Company....B.... 419 228-3141
Lima (G-12880)
Spartannash Company....D.... 419 998-2562
Lima (G-12881)
Spartannash Company....D.... 937 599-1110
Bellefontaine (G-1398)
Spartannash Company....D.... 513 793-6300
Cincinnati (G-4556)
Sygma Network Inc....C.... 614 771-3801
Columbus (G-8814)
Sysco Central Ohio Inc....B.... 614 272-0658
Columbus (G-8816)
Tasty Pure Food Company....E.... 330 434-8141
Akron (G-471)

SIC SECTION
51 WHOLESALE TRADE¨NONDURABLE GOODS

Total Wholesale Inc....E....216 361-5757
Cleveland *(G-6605)*
▼ Tusco Grocers Inc....D....740 922-8721
Dennison *(G-10167)*
US Foods Inc....C....330 963-6789
Twinsburg *(G-18483)*
US Foods Inc....A....614 539-7993
West Chester *(G-19240)*
Valley Wholesale Foods Inc....E....740 354-5216
Portsmouth *(G-16320)*
Vendors Supply Inc....E....513 755-2111
West Chester *(G-19179)*
Wrightway Fd Svc Rest Sup Inc....E....419 222-7911
Lima *(G-12923)*

5142 Packaged Frozen Foods Wholesale

A To Z Portion Ctrl Meats Inc....E....419 358-2926
Bluffton *(G-1726)*
Anderson and Dubose Inc....D....440 248-8800
Warren *(G-18817)*
Avalon Foodservice Inc....C....330 854-4551
Canal Fulton *(G-2140)*
Best Express Foods Inc....D....513 531-2378
Cincinnati *(G-3101)*
Blue Ribbon Meats Inc....D....216 631-8850
Cleveland *(G-5124)*
Euclid Fish Company....D....440 951-6448
Mentor *(G-14172)*
Food Distributors Inc....E....740 439-2764
Cambridge *(G-2114)*
Gordon Food Service Inc....E....419 747-1212
Ontario *(G-15689)*
Gordon Food Service Inc....E....419 225-8983
Lima *(G-12786)*
Gordon Food Service Inc....E....216 573-4900
Cleveland *(G-5680)*
Hillcrest Egg & Cheese Co....D....216 361-4625
Cleveland *(G-5757)*
Instantwhip Foods Inc....E....330 688-8825
Stow *(G-17375)*
Jetro Cash and Carry Entps LLC....D....216 525-0101
Cleveland *(G-5862)*
King Kold Inc....E....937 836-2731
Englewood *(G-10711)*
Koch Meat Co Inc....B....513 874-3500
Fairfield *(G-10871)*
Lori Holding Co....E....740 342-3230
New Lexington *(G-15055)*
Maines Paper & Food Svc Inc....E....216 643-7500
Bedford *(G-1319)*
Mattingly Foods Inc....C....740 454-0136
Zanesville *(G-20500)*
Northern Frozen Foods Inc....C....440 439-0600
Cleveland *(G-6158)*
▲ Peck Distributors Inc....E....216 587-6814
Maple Heights *(G-13413)*
Pinata Foods Inc....E....216 281-8811
Cleveland *(G-6280)*
Powell Company Ltd....D....419 228-3552
Lima *(G-12861)*
Produce One Inc....D....931 253-4749
Dayton *(G-9831)*
Ritchies Food Distributors Inc....E....740 443-6303
Piketon *(G-16127)*
Sherwood Food Distributors LLC....B....216 662-6794
Maple Heights *(G-13418)*
Smithfoods Orrville Inc....E....740 389-4643
Marion *(G-13580)*
Spartannash Company....D....513 793-6300
Cincinnati *(G-4556)*
Swd Corporation....E....419 227-2436
Lima *(G-12896)*
Sysco Central Ohio Inc....B....614 272-0658
Columbus *(G-8816)*
Tasty Pure Food Company....E....330 434-8141
Akron *(G-471)*
US Foods Inc....A....614 539-7993
West Chester *(G-19240)*
▲ White Castle System Inc....B....614 228-5781
Columbus *(G-8986)*
Z Produce Co Inc....E....614 224-4373
Columbus *(G-9024)*

5143 Dairy Prdts, Except Dried Or Canned Wholesale

Auburn Dairy Products Inc....E....614 488-2536
Columbus *(G-7073)*
Austintown Dairy Inc....E....330 629-6170
Youngstown *(G-20108)*
Barkett Fruit Co Inc....E....330 364-6645
Dover *(G-10176)*
Borden Dairy Co Cincinnati LLC....C....513 948-8811
Cincinnati *(G-3127)*
Coblentz Distributing Inc....C....330 852-2888
Walnut Creek *(G-18784)*
Euclid Fish Company....D....440 951-6448
Mentor *(G-14172)*
Giant Eagle Inc....E....216 292-7000
Bedford Heights *(G-1352)*
◆ Great Lakes Cheese Co Inc....B....440 834-2500
Hiram *(G-12002)*
Handels Homemade Ice Cream....E....330 922-4589
Cuyahoga Falls *(G-9193)*
▲ Hans Rothenbuhler & Son Inc....E....440 632-6000
Middlefield *(G-14395)*
Hillandale Farms Corporation....E....330 724-3199
Akron *(G-265)*
Hillcrest Egg & Cheese Co....D....216 361-4625
Cleveland *(G-5757)*
Instantwhip Foods Inc....E....330 688-8825
Stow *(G-17375)*
Instantwhip-Akron Inc....E....614 488-2536
Stow *(G-17376)*
Instantwhip-Columbus Inc....E....614 871-9447
Grove City *(G-11571)*
Lori Holding Co....E....740 342-3230
New Lexington *(G-15055)*
Louis Trauth Dairy LLC....B....859 431-7553
West Chester *(G-19213)*
Mds Foods Inc....E....330 879-9780
Navarre *(G-14955)*
S and S Gilardi Inc....D....740 397-2751
Mount Vernon *(G-14921)*
Siemer Distributing Company....E....740 342-3230
New Lexington *(G-15063)*
Sysco Cincinnati LLC....B....513 563-6300
Cincinnati *(G-4609)*
Troyer Cheese Inc....E....330 893-2479
Millersburg *(G-14625)*
United Dairy Farmers Inc....C....513 396-8700
Cincinnati *(G-4731)*
US Foods Inc....A....614 539-7993
West Chester *(G-19240)*
▲ Weaver Bros Inc....D....937 526-3907
Versailles *(G-18731)*

5144 Poultry & Poultry Prdts Wholesale

▼ Ballas Egg Products Corp....D....614 453-0386
Zanesville *(G-20446)*
Barkett Fruit Co Inc....E....330 364-6645
Dover *(G-10176)*
Borden Dairy Co Cincinnati LLC....C....513 948-8811
Cincinnati *(G-3127)*
C W Egg Products LLC....E....419 375-5800
Fort Recovery *(G-11113)*
Cooper Frms Spring Madow Farms....E....419 375-4119
Rossburg *(G-16605)*
Di Feo & Sons Poultry Inc....E....330 564-8172
Akron *(G-191)*
Euclid Fish Company....D....440 951-6448
Mentor *(G-14172)*
Hillandale Farms Inc....E....740 968-3597
Flushing *(G-11104)*
Hillandale Farms Corporation....E....330 724-3199
Akron *(G-265)*
Hillcrest Egg & Cheese Co....D....216 361-4625
Cleveland *(G-5757)*
Koch Meat Co Inc....B....513 874-3500
Fairfield *(G-10871)*
▲ Ohio Fresh Eggs LLC....C....740 893-7200
Croton *(G-9154)*
Ohio Fresh Eggs LLC....E....937 354-2233
Mount Victory *(G-14929)*
R W Sauder Inc....E....330 359-5440
Winesburg *(G-19806)*
Sfd Company LLC....D....216 662-8000
Maple Heights *(G-13417)*
Sysco Cincinnati LLC....B....513 563-6300
Cincinnati *(G-4609)*

5145 Confectionery Wholesale

Albert Guarnieri & Co....D....330 794-9834
Akron *(G-63)*
EBY-Brown Company LLC....C....937 324-1036
Springfield *(G-17192)*
Frito-Lay North America Inc....D....513 874-0112
West Chester *(G-19202)*
Frito-Lay North America Inc....C....216 491-4000
Cleveland *(G-5642)*
Frito-Lay North America Inc....E....937 224-8716
Dayton *(G-9563)*
Frito-Lay North America Inc....C....614 508-3004
Columbus *(G-7709)*
Gorant Chocolatier LLC....C....330 726-8821
Boardman *(G-1740)*
Grippo Foods Inc....E....513 923-1900
Cincinnati *(G-3714)*
Gummer Wholesale Inc....D....740 928-0415
Heath *(G-11838)*
JE Carsten Company....E....330 794-4440
Akron *(G-291)*
Jones Potato Chip Co....E....419 529-9424
Mansfield *(G-13317)*
Lobby Shoppes Inc....C....937 324-0002
Springfield *(G-17223)*
Mike-Sells Potato Chip Co....E....937 228-9400
Dayton *(G-9747)*
Multi-Flow Dispensers Ohio Inc....D....216 641-0200
Brooklyn Heights *(G-1921)*
Novelart Manufacturing Company....C....513 351-7700
Cincinnati *(G-4187)*
Ohio Hickory Harvest Brand Pro....E....330 644-6266
Coventry Township *(G-9130)*
Poppees Popcorn Inc....E....440 327-0775
North Ridgeville *(G-15474)*
Robert E McGrath Inc....E....440 572-7747
Strongsville *(G-17503)*
S-L Distribution Company Inc....D....740 676-6932
Bellaire *(G-1367)*
◆ Shearers Foods LLC....A....330 834-4030
Massillon *(G-13855)*
Tarrier Foods Corp....E....614 876-8594
Columbus *(G-8823)*
The Anter Brothers Company....E....216 252-4555
Cleveland *(G-6589)*
Tiffin Paper Company....E....419 447-2121
Tiffin *(G-17706)*

5146 Fish & Seafood Wholesale

101 River Inc....E....440 352-6343
Grand River *(G-11455)*
Farm House Food Distrs Inc....E....216 791-6948
Cleveland *(G-5573)*
Midwest Seafood Inc....D....937 746-8856
Springboro *(G-17129)*
Ocean Wide Seafood Company....E....937 610-5740
Cincinnati *(G-4197)*
◆ Omega Sea LLC....E....440 639-2372
Painesville *(G-15870)*
Omegasea Ltd Liability Co....E....440 639-2372
Painesville *(G-15871)*
Riser Foods Company....D....216 292-7000
Bedford Heights *(G-1359)*
Ritchies Food Distributors Inc....E....740 443-6303
Piketon *(G-16127)*
Sfd Company LLC....D....216 662-8000
Maple Heights *(G-13417)*
Sherwood Food Distributors LLC....B....216 662-6794
Maple Heights *(G-13418)*

5147 Meats & Meat Prdts Wholesale

A To Z Portion Ctrl Meats Inc....E....419 358-2926
Bluffton *(G-1726)*
Blue Ribbon Meats Inc....D....216 631-8850
Cleveland *(G-5124)*
Boars Head Provisions Co Inc....B....614 662-5300
Groveport *(G-11625)*
Carfagnas Incorporated....E....614 846-6340
Columbus *(G-7199)*
Carles Bratwurst Inc....E....419 562-7741
Bucyrus *(G-2028)*
Dutch Creek Foods Inc....E....330 852-2631
Sugarcreek *(G-17545)*
Empire Packing Company LP....D....513 942-5400
West Chester *(G-19196)*
Fresh Mark Inc....B....330 832-7491
Massillon *(G-13812)*
◆ Fresh Mark Inc....B....330 834-3669
Massillon *(G-13810)*
Giant Eagle Inc....E....216 292-7000
Bedford Heights *(G-1352)*
Hillandale Farms Corporation....E....330 724-3199
Akron *(G-265)*
Hillcrest Egg & Cheese Co....D....216 361-4625
Cleveland *(G-5757)*
Jetro Cash and Carry Entps LLC....D....216 525-0101
Cleveland *(G-5862)*
Kenosha Beef International Ltd....C....614 771-1330
Columbus *(G-7979)*

S I C

Employee Codes: A=Over 500 employees, B=251-500
C=101-250, D=51-100, E=25-50
2018 Harris Ohio
Services Directory
957

51 WHOLESALE TRADE¨NONDURABLE GOODS SIC SECTION

Landes Fresh Meats Inc ....E 937 836-3613
Clayton *(G-4912)*

Lori Holding Co ....E 740 342-3230
New Lexington *(G-15055)*

Marshallville Packing Co Inc ....E 330 855-2871
Marshallville *(G-13597)*

Meadowbrook Meat Company Inc ....C 614 771-9660
Columbus *(G-8140)*

Northern Frozen Foods Inc ....C 440 439-0600
Cleveland *(G-6158)*

Pioneer Packing Co ....D 419 352-5283
Bowling Green *(G-1790)*

Produce One Inc ....D 931 253-4749
Dayton *(G-9831)*

Ritchies Food Distributors Inc ....E 740 443-6303
Piketon *(G-16127)*

Robert Winner Sons Inc ....E 419 582-4321
Yorkshire *(G-20092)*

S and S Gilardi Inc ....D 740 397-2751
Mount Vernon *(G-14921)*

Sfd Company LLC ....D 216 662-8000
Maple Heights *(G-13417)*

Sherwood Food Distributors LLC ....B 216 662-6794
Maple Heights *(G-13418)*

Siemer Distributing Company ....E 740 342-3230
New Lexington *(G-15063)*

Smithfield Packaged Meats Corp ....B 513 782-3805
Cincinnati *(G-4542)*

Spartannash Company ....D 513 793-6300
Cincinnati *(G-4556)*

Steaks & Such Inc ....E 330 837-9296
Massillon *(G-13858)*

Storer Meat Co Inc ....E 216 621-7538
Cleveland *(G-6543)*

Tasty Pure Food Company ....E 330 434-8141
Akron *(G-471)*

Tri-State Beef Co Inc ....E 513 579-1722
Cincinnati *(G-4685)*

Troyer Cheese Inc ....E 330 893-2479
Millersburg *(G-14625)*

Tsg-Cincinnati LLC ....D 513 793-6241
Blue Ash *(G-1707)*

Weilands Fine Meats Inc ....E 614 267-9910
Columbus *(G-8975)*

5148 Fresh Fruits & Vegetables Wholesale

Al Peake & Sons Inc ....E 419 243-9284
Toledo *(G-17745)*

Anselmo Rssis Premier Prod Ltd ....E 800 229-5517
Cleveland *(G-5040)*

Barkett Fruit Co Inc ....E 330 364-6645
Dover *(G-10176)*

Bowman Organic Farms Ltd ....E 740 246-3936
Thornville *(G-17666)*

Cabbage Inc ....E 440 899-9171
Sheffield Village *(G-16885)*

▲ Caruso Inc ....C 513 860-9200
Cincinnati *(G-3188)*

Chariott Foods Inc ....E 419 243-1101
Toledo *(G-17802)*

Chefs Garden Inc ....C 419 433-4947
Huron *(G-12162)*

Circle S Farms Inc ....E 614 878-9462
Grove City *(G-11546)*

Del Monte Fresh Produce NA Inc ....E 614 527-7398
Columbus *(G-7503)*

Dno Inc ....D 614 231-3601
Columbus *(G-7536)*

Dole Fresh Vegetables Inc ....C 937 525-4300
Springfield *(G-17190)*

Farris Produce Inc ....E 330 837-4607
Massillon *(G-13807)*

Freshway Foods Inc ....C 937 498-4664
Sidney *(G-16936)*

Giant Eagle Inc ....E 216 292-7000
Bedford Heights *(G-1352)*

Greenline Foods Inc ....D 419 354-1149
Bowling Green *(G-1778)*

Hillcrest Egg & Cheese Co ....D 216 361-4625
Cleveland *(G-5757)*

Joe Lasita & Sons Inc ....E 513 241-5288
Cincinnati *(G-3875)*

Midwest Fresh Foods Inc ....E 614 469-1492
Columbus *(G-8169)*

Miles Farmers Market Inc ....C 440 248-5222
Solon *(G-17027)*

Mrs Dennis Potato Farm Inc ....E 419 335-2778
Wauseon *(G-18959)*

Pics Produce Inc ....E 513 381-1239
Cincinnati *(G-4297)*

Powell Company Ltd ....D 419 228-3552
Lima *(G-12861)*

Produce One Inc ....D 931 253-4749
Dayton *(G-9831)*

Reinhart Foodservice LLC ....C 513 421-9184
Cincinnati *(G-4400)*

Sirna & Sons Inc ....C 330 298-2222
Ravenna *(G-16411)*

Spartannash Company ....D 513 793-6300
Cincinnati *(G-4556)*

US Foods Inc ....A 614 539-7993
West Chester *(G-19240)*

Vermilion Farm Market ....E 440 967-9666
Vermilion *(G-18721)*

Z Produce Co Inc ....E 614 224-4373
Columbus *(G-9024)*

5149 Groceries & Related Prdts, NEC Wholesale

▲ Akron Coca-Cola Bottling Co ....A 330 784-2653
Akron *(G-34)*

Aladdins Baking Company Inc ....E 216 861-0317
Cleveland *(G-4981)*

Alfred Nickles Bakery Inc ....E 419 332-6418
Fremont *(G-11183)*

Alfred Nickles Bakery Inc ....D 330 628-9964
Mogadore *(G-14669)*

American Bottling Company ....D 614 237-4201
Columbus *(G-6985)*

▲ Antonio Sofo Son Importing Co ....C 419 476-4211
Toledo *(G-17754)*

▲ Atlantic Foods Corp ....D 513 772-3535
Cincinnati *(G-3058)*

Avalon Foodservice Inc ....C 330 854-4551
Canal Fulton *(G-2140)*

Bagel Place Inc ....E 419 885-1000
Toledo *(G-17762)*

Bakemark USA LLC ....D 513 870-0880
West Chester *(G-19023)*

▲ Bellas Co ....E 740 598-4171
Mingo Junction *(G-14653)*

Berardis Fresh Roast Inc ....E 440 582-4303
North Royalton *(G-15482)*

Bimbo Bakeries Usa Inc ....E 614 868-7565
Columbus *(G-7110)*

Bimbo Bakeries Usa Inc ....E 740 446-4552
Gallipolis *(G-11309)*

◆ Brothers Trading Co Inc ....C 937 746-1010
Springboro *(G-17117)*

▲ Buckeye Distributing Inc ....C 440 526-6668
Broadview Heights *(G-1873)*

Busken Bakery Inc ....D 513 871-2114
Cincinnati *(G-3157)*

▼ Butler Animal Hlth Holdg LLC ....E 614 761-9095
Dublin *(G-10274)*

Cassanos Inc ....E 937 294-8400
Dayton *(G-9388)*

Central Coca-Cola Btlg Co Inc ....C 419 476-6622
Toledo *(G-17798)*

Classic Delight Inc ....E 419 394-7955
Saint Marys *(G-16671)*

Cleveland Sysco Inc ....A 216 201-3000
Cleveland *(G-5349)*

Clintonville Community Mkt ....E 614 261-3663
Columbus *(G-7304)*

Coca-Cola Bottling Co Cnsld ....D 937 878-5000
Dayton *(G-9414)*

Coffee Break Corporation ....E 513 841-1100
Cincinnati *(G-3377)*

◆ Crowning Food Company ....D 937 323-4699
Springfield *(G-17185)*

Dayton Heidelberg Distrg Co ....C 937 220-6450
Moraine *(G-14772)*

Distillata Company ....D 216 771-2900
Cleveland *(G-5489)*

Dutchman Hospitality Group Inc ....C 614 873-3414
Plain City *(G-16189)*

EBY-Brown Company LLC ....C 937 324-1036
Springfield *(G-17192)*

▲ Esber Beverage Company ....E 330 456-4361
Canton *(G-2360)*

▲ Euro Usa Inc ....D 216 714-0500
Cleveland *(G-5555)*

Flavorfresh Dispensers Inc ....E 216 641-0200
Brooklyn Heights *(G-1916)*

Food Distributors Inc ....E 740 439-2764
Cambridge *(G-2114)*

Frito-Lay North America Inc ....C 216 491-4000
Cleveland *(G-5642)*

Frito-Lay North America Inc ....D 419 893-8171
Maumee *(G-13919)*

G & J Pepsi-Cola Bottlers Inc ....E 740 774-2148
Chillicothe *(G-2841)*

G & J Pepsi-Cola Bottlers Inc ....B 740 354-9191
Franklin Furnace *(G-11171)*

G & J Pepsi-Cola Bottlers Inc ....D 740 593-3366
Athens *(G-788)*

G & J Pepsi-Cola Bottlers Inc ....D 740 452-2721
Zanesville *(G-20479)*

Generations Coffee Company LLC ....E 440 546-0901
Brecksville *(G-1824)*

Gordon Food Service Inc ....E 419 747-1212
Ontario *(G-15689)*

Gordon Food Service Inc ....E 419 225-8983
Lima *(G-12786)*

Gordon Food Service Inc ....E 440 953-1785
Mentor *(G-14181)*

Gordon Food Service Inc ....E 216 573-4900
Cleveland *(G-5680)*

▲ Gust Gallucci Co ....E 216 881-0045
Cleveland *(G-5711)*

Hanson-Faso Sales & Marketing ....E 216 642-4500
Cleveland *(G-5725)*

Hiland Group Incorporated ....D 330 499-8404
Canton *(G-2399)*

▲ Hill Distributing Company ....D 614 276-6533
Dublin *(G-10361)*

Hillcrest Egg & Cheese Co ....D 216 361-4625
Cleveland *(G-5757)*

Interbake Foods LLC ....C 614 294-4931
Columbus *(G-7913)*

Interbake Foods LLC ....A 614 294-4931
Columbus *(G-7914)*

▲ Interntional Molasses Corp Ltd ....E 937 276-7980
Dayton *(G-9635)*

Klosterman Baking Co ....D 513 242-1004
Cincinnati *(G-3933)*

▲ Knall Beverage Inc ....D 216 252-2500
Cleveland *(G-5905)*

▲ Leo A Dick & Sons Co ....E 330 452-5010
Canton *(G-2432)*

Louis Trauth Dairy LLC ....B 859 431-7553
West Chester *(G-19213)*

Luxfer Magtech Inc ....E 513 772-3066
Cincinnati *(G-4003)*

M & M Wine Cellar Inc ....E 330 536-6450
Lowellville *(G-13172)*

Made From Scratch Inc ....E 614 873-3344
Plain City *(G-16197)*

Magnetic Springs Water Company ....D 614 421-1780
Columbus *(G-8098)*

Maines Paper & Food Svc Inc ....E 216 643-7500
Bedford *(G-1319)*

Mattingly Foods Inc ....C 740 454-0136
Zanesville *(G-20500)*

Michaels Bakery Inc ....E 216 351-7530
Cleveland *(G-6048)*

Michaels Gourmet Catering ....E 419 698-2988
Toledo *(G-18060)*

Mondelez Global LLC ....D 330 626-6500
Streetsboro *(G-17422)*

Morton Salt Inc ....C 330 925-3015
Rittman *(G-16554)*

National Marketshare Group ....E 513 921-0800
Cincinnati *(G-4140)*

▼ Natural Foods Inc ....E 419 537-1713
Toledo *(G-18079)*

Norcia Bakery ....E 330 454-1077
Canton *(G-2474)*

Northern Frozen Foods Inc ....C 440 439-0600
Cleveland *(G-6158)*

Ohio Citrus Juices Inc ....E 614 539-0030
Grove City *(G-11589)*

Ohio Hickory Harvest Brand Pro ....E 330 644-6266
Coventry Township *(G-9130)*

Ohio Pizza Products Inc ....D 937 294-6969
Monroe *(G-14707)*

Osf International Inc ....E 513 942-6620
Fairfield *(G-10891)*

P&S Bakery Inc ....E 330 707-4141
Youngstown *(G-20312)*

P-Americas LLC ....E 419 227-3541
Lima *(G-12853)*

P-Americas LLC ....D 216 252-7377
Cleveland *(G-6227)*

P-Americas LLC ....C 330 746-7652
Youngstown *(G-20313)*

▲ Peck Distributors Inc ....E 216 587-6814
Maple Heights *(G-13413)*

SIC SECTION
51 WHOLESALE TRADE¨NONDURABLE GOODS

Pepsi-Cola Metro Btlg Co Inc ... E ... 330 336-3553
Wadsworth *(G-18767)*
Pepsi-Cola Metro Btlg Co Inc ... B ... 937 461-4664
Dayton *(G-9806)*
Pepsi-Cola Metro Btlg Co Inc ... E ... 440 323-5524
Elyria *(G-10669)*
Pepsi-Cola Metro Btlg Co Inc ... B ... 330 963-0426
Twinsburg *(G-18453)*
Powell Company Ltd ... D ... 419 228-3552
Lima *(G-12861)*
Procter & Gamble Distrg LLC ... B ... 513 626-2500
Blue Ash *(G-1667)*
Produce One Inc ... D ... 931 253-4749
Dayton *(G-9831)*
R L Lipton Distributing LLC ... D ... 800 321-6553
Austintown *(G-872)*
▲ R L Lipton Distributing Co ... D ... 216 475-4150
Maple Heights *(G-13414)*
Rdp Foodservice Ltd ... D ... 614 261-5661
Columbus *(G-8593)*
Ritchies Food Distributors Inc ... E ... 740 443-6303
Piketon *(G-16127)*
Schwebel Baking Company ... C ... 440 248-1500
Solon *(G-17049)*
Servatii Inc ... D ... 513 271-5040
Cincinnati *(G-4500)*
Sherwood Food Distributors LLC ... B ... 216 662-6794
Maple Heights *(G-13418)*
Skallys Old World Bakery Inc ... E ... 513 931-1411
Cincinnati *(G-4537)*
▲ Skidmore Sales & Distrg Co Inc ... E ... 513 755-4200
West Chester *(G-19156)*
▲ Skyline Chili Inc ... C ... 513 874-1188
Fairfield *(G-10910)*
Spectrum Supportive Services ... C ... 216 761-2388
Cleveland *(G-6518)*
Staufs Coffee Roasters II Inc ... E ... 614 487-6050
Columbus *(G-8785)*
Superior Beverage Group Ltd ... D ... 614 294-3555
Lewis Center *(G-12706)*
▲ Superior Beverage Group Ltd ... C ... 440 703-4580
Solon *(G-17058)*
Swan Sales ... E ... 513 422-3100
Middletown *(G-14465)*
Swh Mimis Cafe LLC ... D ... 614 433-0441
Columbus *(G-6908)*
▲ Sygma Network Inc ... C ... 614 734-2500
Dublin *(G-10470)*
Sysco Cincinnati LLC ... B ... 513 563-6300
Cincinnati *(G-4609)*
Tarrier Foods Corp ... E ... 614 876-8594
Columbus *(G-8823)*
Thurns Bakery & Deli ... E ... 614 221-9246
Columbus *(G-8844)*
Tiffin Paper Company ... E ... 419 447-2121
Tiffin *(G-17706)*
Tony Packos Toledo LLC ... D ... 419 691-6054
Toledo *(G-18257)*
Troyer Cheese Inc ... E ... 330 893-2479
Millersburg *(G-14625)*
Troyers Home Pantry ... E ... 330 698-4182
Apple Creek *(G-627)*
US Foods Inc ... C ... 330 963-6789
Twinsburg *(G-18483)*
US Foods Inc ... A ... 614 539-7993
West Chester *(G-19240)*
Walnut Creek Chocolate Company ... E ... 330 893-2995
Walnut Creek *(G-18785)*
Wasserstrom Company ... E ... 614 228-6525
Columbus *(G-8971)*
▲ Wine-Art of Ohio Inc ... E ... 330 678-7733
Kent *(G-12406)*
Z Produce Co Inc ... E ... 614 224-4373
Columbus *(G-9024)*

5153 Grain & Field Beans Wholesale

◆ Andersons Inc ... C ... 419 893-5050
Maumee *(G-13879)*
Archbold Elevator Inc ... E ... 419 445-2451
Archbold *(G-632)*
Ardent Mills LLC ... E ... 614 274-2545
Columbus *(G-7039)*
Barnets Inc ... E ... 937 452-3275
Camden *(G-2136)*
Champaign Landmark Inc ... E ... 937 652-2135
Urbana *(G-18577)*
Consolidated Grain & Barge Co ... D ... 419 785-1941
Defiance *(G-10023)*
Consolidated Grain & Barge Co ... E ... 513 941-4805
Cincinnati *(G-3411)*
Cooper Hatchery Inc ... C ... 419 594-3325
Oakwood *(G-15623)*
Deerfield Farms Service Inc ... D ... 330 584-4715
Deerfield *(G-10019)*
Fort Recovery Equity Inc ... C ... 419 375-4119
Fort Recovery *(G-11117)*
Hanby Farms Inc ... E ... 740 763-3554
Nashport *(G-14951)*
Hansen-Mueller Co ... E ... 419 729-5535
Toledo *(G-17931)*
Heritage Cooperative Inc ... D ... 419 294-2371
West Mansfield *(G-19267)*
Pioneer Hi-Bred Intl Inc ... E ... 419 748-8051
Grand Rapids *(G-11452)*
Sunrise Cooperative Inc ... B ... 937 575-6780
Piqua *(G-16167)*
Trupointe Cooperative Inc ... B ... 937 575-6780
Piqua *(G-16169)*

5154 Livestock Wholesale

Barnesville Livestock Sales Co ... E ... 740 425-3611
Barnesville *(G-989)*
Hord Livestock Company Inc ... E ... 419 562-0277
Bucyrus *(G-2041)*
Kalmbach Pork Finishing LLC ... D ... 419 294-3838
Upper Sandusky *(G-18563)*
Kidron Auction Inc ... E ... 330 857-2641
Kidron *(G-12442)*
Mt Hope Auction Inc ... E ... 330 674-6188
Mount Hope *(G-14866)*
Muskingum Livestock Sales Inc ... E ... 740 452-9984
Zanesville *(G-20510)*
Robert Winner Sons Inc ... E ... 419 582-4321
Yorkshire *(G-20092)*
United Producers Inc ... E ... 937 456-4161
Eaton *(G-10579)*
United Producers Inc ... C ... 614 433-2150
Columbus *(G-8899)*

5159 Farm-Prdt Raw Mtrls, NEC Wholesale

Altria Group Distribution Co ... C ... 804 274-2000
Mason *(G-13660)*
Hills Supply Inc ... E ... 740 477-8994
Circleville *(G-4890)*
Inland Products Inc ... E ... 614 443-3425
Columbus *(G-7899)*

5162 Plastics Materials & Basic Shapes Wholesale

▲ Advanced Elastomer Systems LP ... C ... 800 352-7866
Akron *(G-22)*
Alro Steel Corporation ... E ... 419 720-5300
Toledo *(G-17747)*
Ampacet Corporation ... E ... 513 247-5400
Cincinnati *(G-3018)*
Bprex Plastic Packaging Inc ... C ... 419 423-3271
Findlay *(G-11007)*
▲ Cannon Group Inc ... E ... 614 890-0343
Westerville *(G-19375)*
▲ Checker Notions Company Inc ... D ... 419 893-3636
Maumee *(G-13894)*
F B Wright Co Cincinnati ... E ... 513 874-9100
West Chester *(G-19071)*
Florline Group Inc ... E ... 330 830-3380
Massillon *(G-13808)*
Hexpol Compounding LLC ... C ... 440 834-4644
Burton *(G-2062)*
HP Manufacturing Company Inc ... D ... 216 361-6500
Cleveland *(G-5788)*
Ilpea Industries Inc ... C ... 330 562-2916
Aurora *(G-842)*
▲ Inno-Pak LLC ... E ... 740 363-0090
Delaware *(G-10109)*
◆ Multi-Plastics Inc ... D ... 740 548-4894
Lewis Center *(G-12696)*
▲ Polymer Packaging Inc ... D ... 330 832-2000
Massillon *(G-13844)*
Polymershapes LLC ... E ... 937 877-1903
Tipp City *(G-17724)*
◆ Polyone Corporation ... D ... 440 930-1000
Avon Lake *(G-937)*
Queen City Polymers Inc ... E ... 513 779-0990
West Chester *(G-19136)*
▲ Surreal Entertainment LLC ... E ... 330 262-5277
Wooster *(G-19918)*
Tahoma Enterprises Inc ... D ... 330 745-9016
Barberton *(G-982)*
▼ Tahoma Rubber & Plastics Inc ... D ... 330 745-9016
Barberton *(G-983)*
Thyssenkrupp Materials NA Inc ... E ... 937 898-7400
Miamisburg *(G-14360)*
Wilbert Inc ... D ... 419 483-2300
Bellevue *(G-1419)*

5169 Chemicals & Allied Prdts, NEC Wholesale

Accurate Lubr & Met Wkg Fluids ... E ... 937 461-9906
Dayton *(G-9305)*
Airgas Inc ... B ... 866 935-3370
Cleveland *(G-4975)*
Airgas Inc ... B ... 440 632-1758
Middlefield *(G-14393)*
▲ Airgas Merchant Gases LLC ... B ... 800 242-0105
Cleveland *(G-4976)*
Airgas Safety Inc ... E ... 513 942-1465
Hamilton *(G-11689)*
Airgas Usa LLC ... B ... 216 642-6600
Independence *(G-12183)*
Airgas Usa LLC ... D ... 440 786-2864
Oakwood Village *(G-15625)*
Airgas Usa LLC ... E ... 513 563-8070
Cincinnati *(G-2979)*
Akrochem Corporation ... E ... 330 535-2108
Barberton *(G-949)*
Americas Best Medical Eqp Co ... E ... 330 928-0884
Akron *(G-73)*
Anatrace Products LLC ... E ... 419 740-6600
Maumee *(G-13876)*
▲ Applied Indus Tech - Dixie Inc ... C ... 216 426-4000
Cleveland *(G-5054)*
▲ Applied Industrial Tech Inc ... B ... 216 426-4000
Cleveland *(G-5055)*
Ashland LLC ... D ... 614 232-8510
Columbus *(G-7049)*
Ashland LLC ... E ... 614 276-6144
Columbus *(G-7050)*
Ashland LLC ... D ... 216 961-4690
Cleveland *(G-5070)*
Ashland LLC ... E ... 216 883-8200
Cleveland *(G-5071)*
Ashland LLC ... D ... 419 289-9588
Ashland *(G-658)*
Ashland LLC ... C ... 614 790-3333
Dublin *(G-10256)*
Avalon Foodservice Inc ... C ... 330 854-4551
Canal Fulton *(G-2140)*
Bleachtech LLC ... E ... 216 921-1980
Seville *(G-16838)*
▲ Bonded Chemicals Inc ... E ... 614 777-9240
Columbus *(G-7124)*
Braden Med Services Inc ... E ... 740 732-2356
Caldwell *(G-2082)*
◆ Budenheim Usa Inc ... E ... 614 345-2400
Columbus *(G-7164)*
▲ Calvary Industries Inc ... D ... 513 874-1113
Fairfield *(G-10828)*
Cantrell Oil Company ... E ... 937 695-8003
Winchester *(G-19800)*
Cargill Incorporated ... D ... 440 716-4664
North Olmsted *(G-15411)*
Chemical Services Inc ... E ... 937 898-5566
Dayton *(G-9401)*
▲ Chemical Solvents Inc ... E ... 216 741-9310
Cleveland *(G-5232)*
Chemical Solvents Inc ... D ... 216 741-9310
Cleveland *(G-5233)*
▲ Cimcool Industrial Pdts LLC ... D ... 888 246-2665
Cincinnati *(G-3275)*
▲ CL Zimmerman Delaware LLC ... E ... 513 860-9300
West Chester *(G-19042)*
Cr Brands Inc ... D ... 513 860-5039
West Chester *(G-19058)*
Custom Chemical Solutions ... E ... 800 291-1057
Loveland *(G-13119)*
D & D Investment Co ... E ... 614 272-6567
Columbus *(G-7476)*
D W Dickey and Son Inc ... E ... 330 424-1441
Lisbon *(G-12935)*
Dawnchem Inc ... E ... 440 943-3332
Willoughby *(G-19658)*
Dupont Inc ... D ... 937 268-3411
Dayton *(G-9509)*
▲ Electro Prime Group LLC ... D ... 419 476-0100
Toledo *(G-17863)*
▲ Eliokem Inc ... D ... 330 734-1100
Fairlawn *(G-10947)*
Flex Technologies Inc ... E ... 330 897-6311
Baltic *(G-945)*

S I C

51 WHOLESALE TRADE¨NONDURABLE GOODS SIC SECTION

Galaxy Associates Inc ..... E 513 731-6350
Cincinnati *(G-3660)*
◆ Gorilla Glue Company ..... E 513 271-3300
Cincinnati *(G-3688)*
◆ Harwick Standard Dist Corp ..... D 330 798-9300
Akron *(G-255)*
Hillside Maint Sup Co Inc ..... E 513 751-4100
Cincinnati *(G-3767)*
▲ Imcd Us LLC ..... E 216 228-8900
Lakewood *(G-12483)*
▲ Industrial Chemical Corp ..... E 330 725-0800
Medina *(G-14079)*
◆ Joshen Paper & Packaging Co ..... C 216 441-5600
Cleveland *(G-5872)*
◆ Koch Knight LLC ..... D 330 488-1651
East Canton *(G-10504)*
Kraton Polymers US LLC ..... B 740 423-7571
Belpre *(G-1441)*
Lanxess Corporation ..... C 440 279-2367
Chardon *(G-2755)*
Maines Paper & Food Svc Inc ..... E 216 643-7500
Bedford *(G-1319)*
Mantaline Corporation ..... D 330 274-2264
Mantua *(G-13392)*
Matheson Tri-Gas Inc ..... E 614 771-1311
Hilliard *(G-11925)*
Medi Home Health Agency Inc ..... E 740 266-3977
Steubenville *(G-17329)*
Midwest Industrial Supply Inc ..... E 800 321-0699
Toledo *(G-18061)*
▲ Mitsubshi Intl Fd Ingrdnts Inc ..... E 614 652-1111
Dublin *(G-10399)*
▲ National Colloid Company ..... E 740 282-1171
Steubenville *(G-17332)*
Nexeo Solutions LLC ..... E 330 405-0461
Twinsburg *(G-18451)*
▲ Palmer Holland Inc ..... D 440 686-2300
North Olmsted *(G-15438)*
▲ Phoenix Technologies Intl LLC ..... E 419 353-7738
Bowling Green *(G-1789)*
Polyone Corporation ..... D 440 930-1000
North Baltimore *(G-15315)*
Procter & Gamble Distrg LLC ..... B 513 945-7960
Cincinnati *(G-4341)*
Procter & Gamble Distrg LLC ..... C 937 387-5189
Union *(G-18499)*
Procter & Gamble Distrg LLC ..... B 513 626-2500
Blue Ash *(G-1667)*
Rde System Corp ..... C 513 933-8000
Lebanon *(G-12640)*
Rhiel Supply Co Inc ..... E 330 799-7777
Austintown *(G-873)*
Rudolph Brothers & Co ..... E 614 833-0707
Canal Winchester *(G-2169)*
Rwc Inc ..... E 614 890-0600
Westerville *(G-19351)*
Schaaf Drugs LLC ..... E 419 879-4327
Lima *(G-12873)*
◆ Sea-Land Chemical Co ..... D 440 871-7887
Westlake *(G-19545)*
Sika Corporation ..... D 740 387-9224
Marion *(G-13579)*
▲ Skidmore Sales & Distrg Co Inc ..... E 513 755-4200
West Chester *(G-19156)*
▲ Sunsource Inc ..... E 513 941-6200
Cincinnati *(G-4601)*
T&L Global Management LLC ..... D 614 586-0303
Columbus *(G-8818)*
▲ Tembec Btlsr Inc ..... E 419 244-5856
Toledo *(G-18216)*
Texo International Inc ..... D 513 731-6350
Norwood *(G-15600)*
▼ The Mau-Sherwood Supply Co ..... E 330 405-1200
Twinsburg *(G-18475)*
▲ Tosoh America Inc ..... B 614 539-8622
Grove City *(G-11606)*
◆ Tricor Industrial Inc ..... D 330 264-3299
Wooster *(G-19919)*
▲ United McGill Corporation ..... E 614 829-1200
Groveport *(G-11681)*
Univar USA Inc ..... C 513 714-5264
West Chester *(G-19239)*
Univar USA Inc ..... E 419 666-7880
Walbridge *(G-18779)*
Univar USA Inc ..... E 330 425-4330
Twinsburg *(G-18482)*
Univar USA Inc ..... E 513 870-4050
Hamilton *(G-11783)*
Univar USA Inc ..... D 440 238-8550
Strongsville *(G-17520)*
Viking Explosives LLC ..... E 218 263-8845
Cleveland *(G-6696)*
VWR Chemicals LLC ..... E 330 425-2522
Aurora *(G-860)*
Wampum Hardware Co ..... E 740 685-2585
Salesville *(G-16721)*
Wampum Hardware Co ..... E 419 273-2542
Forest *(G-11107)*
▼ Washing Systems LLC ..... C 800 272-1974
Loveland *(G-13163)*
Weiler Welding Company Inc ..... D 937 222-8312
Moraine *(G-14835)*
Young Chemical Co LLC ..... E 330 486-4210
Twinsburg *(G-18486)*
Zep Inc ..... E 440 239-1580
Cleveland *(G-6784)*

5171 Petroleum Bulk Stations & Terminals

Campbell Oil Company ..... D 330 833-8555
Massillon *(G-13792)*
Cincinnati - Vulcan Company ..... D 513 242-5300
Cincinnati *(G-3278)*
Englefield Inc ..... D 740 452-2707
Zanesville *(G-20475)*
New Vulco Mfg & Sales Co LLC ..... D 513 242-2672
Cincinnati *(G-4158)*
Ney Oil Company Inc ..... D 419 485-4009
Montpelier *(G-14746)*
Universal Oil Inc ..... E 216 771-4300
Cleveland *(G-6649)*

5172 Petroleum & Petroleum Prdts Wholesale

Accurate Lubr & Met Wkg Fluids ..... E 937 461-9906
Dayton *(G-9305)*
Afm East Archwood Oil Inc ..... E 330 786-1000
Akron *(G-24)*
▲ Applied Indus Tech - Dixie Inc ..... C 216 426-4000
Cleveland *(G-5054)*
Bazell Oil Co Inc ..... E 740 385-5420
Logan *(G-12968)*
Bd Oil Gathering Corp ..... E 740 374-9355
Marietta *(G-13435)*
Blue Star Lubrication Tech LLC ..... E 847 285-1888
Cincinnati *(G-3122)*
Centerra Co-Op ..... E 800 362-9598
Jefferson *(G-12331)*
Centerra Co-Op ..... E 419 281-2153
Ashland *(G-672)*
Champaign Landmark Inc ..... E 937 652-2135
Urbana *(G-18577)*
Circleville Oil Co ..... D 740 474-7568
Circleville *(G-4882)*
Clay Distributing Co ..... E 419 426-3051
Attica *(G-821)*
▲ Coolants Plus Inc ..... E 513 892-4000
Hamilton *(G-11718)*
Cuyahoga Landmark Inc ..... E 440 238-3900
Strongsville *(G-17454)*
D W Dickey and Son Inc ..... E 330 424-1441
Lisbon *(G-12935)*
Duncan Oil Co ..... E 937 426-5945
Dayton *(G-9267)*
Earhart Petroleum Inc ..... E 937 335-2928
Troy *(G-18353)*
Free Enterprises Incorporated ..... D 330 722-2031
Medina *(G-14067)*
Hartland Petroleum LLC ..... E 740 452-3115
Zanesville *(G-20485)*
Hearthstone Utilities Inc ..... D 440 974-3770
Cleveland *(G-5744)*
Heartland Petroleum LLC ..... E 614 441-4001
Columbus *(G-7820)*
Hightowers Petroleum Company ..... E 513 423-4272
Middletown *(G-14480)*
Holland Oil Company ..... D 330 835-1815
Akron *(G-269)*
Knisely Inc ..... D 330 343-5812
Dover *(G-10195)*
◆ Koch Knight LLC ..... D 330 488-1651
East Canton *(G-10504)*
Krebs Steve BP Oil Co ..... E 513 641-0150
Cincinnati *(G-3944)*
Lyden Oil Company ..... E 330 792-1100
Youngstown *(G-20258)*
Lykins Companies Inc ..... C 513 831-8820
Milford *(G-14533)*
Lykins Oil Company ..... E 513 831-8820
Milford *(G-14534)*
Marathon Petroleum Company LP ..... B 330 479-5688
Canton *(G-2446)*
Marathon Petroleum Company LP ..... E 614 274-1125
Columbus *(G-8105)*
Marathon Petroleum Company LP ..... E 513 932-6007
Lebanon *(G-12624)*
▲ Marathon Petroleum Corporation ..... B 419 422-2121
Findlay *(G-11061)*
McKinley Air Transport Inc ..... E 330 497-6956
Canton *(G-2453)*
Mplx Terminals LLC ..... E 440 526-4653
Cleveland *(G-6082)*
Mplx Terminals LLC ..... B 330 479-5539
Canton *(G-2466)*
Mplx Terminals LLC ..... E 504 252-8064
Heath *(G-11840)*
Mplx Terminals LLC ..... E 513 451-0485
Cincinnati *(G-4125)*
Northeast Lubricants Ltd ..... C 216 478-0507
Cleveland *(G-6151)*
Nzr Retail of Toledo Inc ..... D 419 724-0005
Toledo *(G-18100)*
Santmyer Oil Co Inc ..... D 330 262-6501
Wooster *(G-19911)*
▲ Shrader Tire & Oil Inc ..... E 419 472-2128
Toledo *(G-18186)*
Sines Inc ..... E 440 352-6572
Painesville *(G-15879)*
Specialty Lubricants Corp ..... E 330 425-2567
Macedonia *(G-13210)*
The Columbia Oil Co ..... D 513 868-8700
Liberty Twp *(G-12728)*
Travelcenters of America LLC ..... D 330 793-4426
Youngstown *(G-20391)*
Triumph Energy Corporation ..... E 513 367-9900
Harrison *(G-11811)*
Troutwine Auto Sales Inc ..... E 937 692-8373
Arcanum *(G-631)*
True North Energy LLC ..... E 877 245-9336
Brecksville *(G-1853)*
Ull Inc ..... E 440 543-5195
Chagrin Falls *(G-2737)*
Vesco Oil Corporation ..... E 614 367-1412
Blacklick *(G-1512)*
Winner Aviation Corporation ..... D 330 856-5000
Vienna *(G-18742)*
X F Construction Svcs Inc ..... E 614 575-2700
Columbus *(G-9012)*
Youngstown Propane Inc ..... E 330 792-6571
Youngstown *(G-20435)*

5181 Beer & Ale Wholesale

Anheuser-Busch LLC ..... C 513 381-3927
Cincinnati *(G-3031)*
▲ Bellas Co ..... E 740 598-4171
Mingo Junction *(G-14653)*
▲ Beverage Distributors Inc ..... C 216 431-1600
Cleveland *(G-5121)*
▲ Bonbright Distributors Inc ..... C 937 222-1001
Dayton *(G-9363)*
▲ Brown Distributing Inc ..... D 740 349-7999
Newark *(G-15151)*
▲ Cavalier Distributing Company ..... D 513 247-9222
Blue Ash *(G-1552)*
Cbo LLC ..... E 740 598-4121
Mingo Junction *(G-14654)*
Cdc Management Co ..... C 614 781-0216
Columbus *(G-7218)*
▲ Central Beverage Group Ltd ..... C 614 294-3555
Lewis Center *(G-12674)*
▲ City Beverage Company ..... E 419 782-7065
Defiance *(G-10022)*
▲ Columbus Distributing Company ..... B 614 846-1000
Columbus *(G-7346)*
Columbus Distributing Company ..... E 740 726-2211
Waldo *(G-18782)*
▲ Dayton Heidelberg Distrg Co ..... C 937 222-8692
Moraine *(G-14770)*
Dayton Heidelberg Distrg Co ..... C 937 220-6450
Moraine *(G-14772)*
Dayton Heidelberg Distrg Co ..... D 513 421-5000
Cincinnati *(G-3468)*
Dayton Heidelberg Distrg Co ..... C 614 308-0400
Columbus *(G-7494)*
Dayton Heidelberg Distrg Co ..... C 419 666-9783
Perrysburg *(G-15994)*
▲ Dickerson Distributing Company ..... D 513 539-8483
Monroe *(G-14693)*
▲ Donzells Flower & Grdn Ctr Inc ..... E 330 724-0550
Akron *(G-197)*

51 WHOLESALE TRADE¨NONDURABLE GOODS

▲ Esber Beverage Company ....E..... 330 456-4361
  Canton *(G-2360)*
Glazers Distributors Ohio Inc ....E..... 440 542-7000
  Solon *(G-17010)*
▲ Goodman Beverage Co Inc ....D..... 440 787-2255
  Lorain *(G-13040)*
Hanson Distributing Co Inc ....D..... 419 435-3214
  Fostoria *(G-11130)*
▲ Heritage Beverage Company LLC ...D..... 440 255-5550
  Mentor *(G-14190)*
▲ Hill Distributing Company ....D..... 614 276-6533
  Dublin *(G-10361)*
House of La Rose Cleveland ....C..... 440 746-7500
  Brecksville *(G-1827)*
Jetro Cash and Carry Entps LLC ....D..... 216 525-0101
  Cleveland *(G-5862)*
K M C Corporation ....E..... 740 598-4171
  Mingo Junction *(G-14655)*
▲ Knall Beverage Inc ....E..... 216 252-2500
  Cleveland *(G-5905)*
Litter Distributing Co Inc ....D..... 740 774-2831
  Chillicothe *(G-2861)*
M & A Distributing Co Inc ....D..... 440 703-4580
  Solon *(G-17024)*
▲ Matesich Distributing Co ....D..... 740 349-8686
  Newark *(G-15201)*
Nwo Beverage Inc ....E..... 419 725-2162
  Northwood *(G-15541)*
▲ Ohio Valley Wine Company ....D..... 513 771-9370
  Cincinnati *(G-4213)*
▲ R L Lipton Distributing Co ....E..... 216 475-4150
  Maple Heights *(G-13414)*
▲ Rhinegeist LLC ....D..... 513 381-1367
  Cincinnati *(G-4414)*
Southern Glazers Wine and Sp ....D..... 330 422-9463
  Streetsboro *(G-17430)*
▲ Southern Glzers Dstrs Ohio LLC .....D..... 614 552-7900
  Columbus *(G-8754)*
Superior Beverage Company Inc ....D..... 440 703-4580
  Solon *(G-17057)*
The Maple City Ice Company ....E..... 419 668-2531
  Norwalk *(G-15594)*
Treu House of Munch Inc ....D..... 419 666-7770
  Northwood *(G-15549)*
▲ Warsteiner Importers Agency ....E..... 513 942-9872
  West Chester *(G-19183)*

5182 Wine & Distilled Alcoholic Beverages Wholesale

August Food & Wine LLC ....E..... 513 421-2020
  Cincinnati *(G-3063)*
▲ Bellas Co ....E..... 740 598-4171
  Mingo Junction *(G-14653)*
Dayton Heidelberg Distrg Co ....C..... 216 520-2626
  Cleveland *(G-5471)*
Dayton Heidelberg Distrg Co ....D..... 419 666-9783
  Perrysburg *(G-15995)*
Dayton Heidelberg Distrg Co ....D..... 614 308-0400
  Columbus *(G-7494)*
Dayton Heidelberg Distrg Co ....C..... 419 666-9783
  Perrysburg *(G-15994)*
Dayton Heidelberg Distrg Co ....C..... 937 220-6450
  Moraine *(G-14772)*
E & J Gallo Winery ....E..... 513 381-4050
  Cincinnati *(G-3520)*
▲ Esber Beverage Company ....E..... 330 456-4361
  Canton *(G-2360)*
Fredericks Wine & Dine ....E..... 216 581-5299
  Cleveland *(G-5635)*
Glazers Distributors Ohio Inc ....E..... 440 542-7000
  Solon *(G-17010)*
▲ Goodman Beverage Co Inc ....D..... 440 787-2255
  Lorain *(G-13040)*
▲ H Dennert Distributing Corp ....C..... 513 871-7272
  Cincinnati *(G-3722)*
K M C Corporation ....E..... 740 598-4171
  Mingo Junction *(G-14655)*
M & A Distributing Co Inc ....E..... 440 703-4580
  Solon *(G-17024)*
M & A Distributing Co Inc ....D..... 614 294-3555
  Columbus *(G-8091)*
M & M Wine Cellar Inc ....E..... 330 536-6450
  Lowellville *(G-13172)*
▲ Mid-Ohio Wines Inc ....E..... 440 989-1011
  Lorain *(G-13061)*
▲ Ohio Valley Wine Company ....D..... 513 771-9370
  Cincinnati *(G-4213)*
▲ R L Lipton Distributing Co ....D..... 216 475-4150
  Maple Heights *(G-13414)*

Southern Glazers Wine and Sp ....D..... 330 422-9463
  Streetsboro *(G-17430)*
▲ Southern Glzers Dstrs Ohio LLC ....D..... 614 552-7900
  Columbus *(G-8754)*
Superior Beverage Company Inc ......D..... 440 703-4580
  Solon *(G-17057)*
▲ Vanguard Wines LLC ....D..... 614 291-3493
  Columbus *(G-8934)*
Vervasi Vineyard & Itln Bistro ....E..... 330 497-1000
  Canton *(G-2576)*
Vintage Wine Distributor Inc ....E..... 614 876-2580
  Columbus *(G-8942)*
▲ Wine Trends Inc ....E..... 216 520-2626
  Independence *(G-12277)*

5191 Farm Splys Wholesale

◆ A M Leonard Inc ....D..... 937 773-2694
  Piqua *(G-16133)*
Alabama Farmers Coop Inc ....E..... 419 655-2289
  Cygnet *(G-9238)*
◆ Andersons Inc ....C..... 419 893-5050
  Maumee *(G-13879)*
◆ Andersons Agriculture Group LP ....E..... 419 893-5050
  Maumee *(G-13881)*
Archbold Elevator Inc ....E..... 419 445-2451
  Archbold *(G-632)*
Berns Grnhse & Grdn Ctr Inc ....E..... 513 423-5306
  Middletown *(G-14418)*
▲ Bfg Supply Co Llc ....E..... 440 834-1883
  Burton *(G-2061)*
Centerra Co-Op ....E..... 800 362-9598
  Jefferson *(G-12331)*
Champaign Landmark Inc ....E..... 937 652-2135
  Urbana *(G-18577)*
Cooper Farms Inc ....D..... 419 375-4116
  Fort Recovery *(G-11115)*
Deerfield Farms Service Inc ....D..... 330 584-4715
  Deerfield *(G-10019)*
Do Cut Sales & Service Inc ....E..... 330 533-9878
  Warren *(G-18851)*
▲ Express Seed Company ....E..... 440 774-2259
  Oberlin *(G-15643)*
Gardenlife Inc ....E..... 440 352-6195
  Concord Twp *(G-9033)*
Gardner-Connell LLC ....E..... 614 456-4000
  Columbus *(G-7729)*
Gerber Feed Service Inc ....E..... 330 857-4421
  Dalton *(G-9241)*
Hanby Farms Inc ....E..... 740 763-3554
  Nashport *(G-14951)*
◆ Jiffy Products America Inc ....E..... 440 282-2818
  Lorain *(G-13043)*
K M B Inc ....E..... 330 889-3451
  Bristolville *(G-1872)*
Keynes Bros Inc ....E..... 740 385-6824
  Logan *(G-12979)*
Land OLakes Inc ....E..... 330 879-2158
  Massillon *(G-13828)*
▼ Lesco Inc ....C..... 216 706-9250
  Cleveland *(G-5936)*
▲ Mac Kenzie Nursery Supply Inc ....E..... 440 259-3517
  Perry *(G-15963)*
Morral Companies LLC ....E..... 740 465-3251
  Morral *(G-14842)*
Noxious Vegetation Control Inc ....D..... 614 486-8994
  Ashville *(G-770)*
Ohigro Inc ....E..... 740 726-2429
  Waldo *(G-18783)*
Phillips Ready Mix Co ....D..... 937 426-5151
  Beavercreek Township *(G-1281)*
Pioneer Hi-Bred Intl Inc ....E..... 740 657-6120
  Delaware *(G-10120)*
Pioneer Hi-Bred Intl Inc ....E..... 419 748-8051
  Grand Rapids *(G-11452)*
Premier Feeds LLC ....E..... 937 584-2411
  Wilmington *(G-19779)*
◆ Provimi North America Inc ....B..... 937 770-2400
  Brookville *(G-1965)*
Purina Animal Nutrition LLC ....E..... 419 224-2015
  Lima *(G-12863)*
Purina Animal Nutrition LLC ....E..... 330 682-1951
  Orrville *(G-15784)*
Purina Animal Nutrition LLC ....E..... 330 879-2158
  Massillon *(G-13846)*
S & D Application LLC ....E..... 419 288-3660
  Wayne *(G-18978)*
Schlessman Seed Co ....E..... 419 499-2572
  Milan *(G-14499)*
Seed Consultants Inc ....E..... 740 333-8644
  Wshngtn CT Hs *(G-20035)*

Sunrise Cooperative Inc ....E..... 937 462-8341
  South Charleston *(G-17077)*
Sunrise Cooperative Inc ....E..... 937 382-1633
  Wilmington *(G-19789)*
Sunrise Cooperative Inc ....E..... 937 323-7536
  Springfield *(G-17284)*
Sunrise Cooperative Inc ....B..... 937 575-6780
  Piqua *(G-16167)*
Trupointe Cooperative Inc ....E..... 937 575-6780
  Piqua *(G-16169)*
United States Dept Agriculture ....D..... 419 626-8439
  Sandusky *(G-16806)*
Univar Inc ....E..... 440 510-1259
  Eastlake *(G-10551)*
Waterworks America Inc ....C..... 440 526-4815
  Cleveland *(G-6724)*

5192 Books, Periodicals & Newspapers Wholesale

Afit Ls Usaf ....E..... 937 255-3636
  Dayton *(G-9249)*
Alliance Medical Inc ....E..... 800 890-3092
  Dublin *(G-10242)*
Anderson Press Incorporated ....E..... 615 370-9922
  Ashland *(G-650)*
◆ Barbour Publishing Inc ....E..... 740 922-1321
  Uhrichsville *(G-18487)*
Bookmasters Inc ....C..... 419 281-1802
  Ashland *(G-665)*
CSS Publishing Co Inc ....E..... 419 227-1818
  Lima *(G-12768)*
Ed Map Inc ....D..... 740 753-3439
  Nelsonville *(G-14962)*
▲ Findaway World LLC ....D..... 440 893-0808
  Solon *(G-17007)*
Friends of The Lib Cyahoga FLS ......C..... 330 928-2117
  Cuyahoga Falls *(G-9190)*
▲ H & M Patch Company ....D..... 614 339-8950
  Columbus *(G-7788)*
Hecks Direct Mail & Prtg Svc ....E..... 419 661-6028
  Toledo *(G-17951)*
Hubbard Company ....E..... 419 784-4455
  Defiance *(G-10034)*
Indico LLC ....D..... 440 775-7777
  Oberlin *(G-15646)*
McGraw-Hill School Education H ......B..... 419 207-7400
  Ashland *(G-687)*
Media Source Inc ....D..... 614 873-7635
  Plain City *(G-16199)*
Scholastic Book Fairs Inc ....D..... 513 714-1000
  West Chester *(G-19146)*
Scholastic Book Fairs Inc ....D..... 440 572-4880
  Strongsville *(G-17504)*
Windy Hill Ltd Inc ....D..... 216 391-4800
  Cleveland *(G-6753)*
▲ Zaner-Bloser Inc ....D..... 614 486-0221
  Columbus *(G-9025)*

5193 Flowers, Nursery Stock & Florists' Splys Wholesale

▲ August Corso Sons Inc ....C..... 419 626-0765
  Sandusky *(G-16727)*
Beroske Farms & Greenhouse Inc ....E..... 419 826-4547
  Delta *(G-10156)*
C M Brown Nurseries Inc ....E..... 440 259-5403
  Perry *(G-15958)*
Claprood Roman J Co ....E..... 614 221-5515
  Columbus *(G-7290)*
Cottage Gardens Inc ....D..... 440 259-2900
  Perry *(G-15960)*
◆ Darice Inc ....C..... 440 238-9150
  Strongsville *(G-17456)*
Davis Tree Farm & Nursery Inc ....E..... 330 483-3324
  Valley City *(G-18615)*
Dennis Top Soil & Landscaping ....E..... 419 865-5656
  Toledo *(G-17849)*
Denver Wholesale Florists Co ....E..... 419 241-7241
  Toledo *(G-17850)*
▲ Express Seed Company ....E..... 440 774-2259
  Oberlin *(G-15643)*
Flower Factory Inc ....D..... 614 275-6220
  Columbus *(G-7677)*
▲ Flowerland Garden Centers ....E..... 440 439-8636
  Oakwood Village *(G-15629)*
Giant Eagle Inc ....D..... 330 364-5301
  Dover *(G-10190)*
Gs Ohio Inc ....D..... 614 885-5350
  Powell *(G-16337)*

Employee Codes: A=Over 500 employees, B=251-500
C=101-250, D=51-100, E=25-50

Kens Flower Shop Inc ....E ....419 841-9590 Perrysburg *(G-16023)*
Lcn Holdings Inc ....E ....440 259-5571 Madison *(G-13229)*
▲ Mac Kenzie Nursery Supply Inc ....E ....440 259-3517 Perry *(G-15963)*
Maria Gardens Inc ....E ....440 238-7637 Strongsville *(G-17489)*
◆ New Diamond Line Cont Corp ....E ....330 644-9993 Coventry Township *(G-9129)*
North Branch Nursery Inc ....E ....419 287-4679 Pemberville *(G-15942)*
North Coast Perennials Inc ....E ....440 428-1277 Madison *(G-13233)*
▲ Oberers Flowers Inc ....E ....937 223-1253 Dayton *(G-9781)*
Petitti Enterprises Inc ....E ....440 236-5055 Columbia Station *(G-6851)*
Plantscaping Inc ....D ....216 367-1200 Cleveland *(G-6285)*
Rentokil North America Inc ....E ....216 739-0200 Brooklyn Heights *(G-1925)*
Rentokil North America Inc ....E ....614 837-0099 Groveport *(G-11666)*
Rusty Oak Nursery Ltd ....E ....330 225-7704 Valley City *(G-18623)*
Scarffs Nursery Inc ....C ....937 845-3130 New Carlisle *(G-15031)*
▲ Schmidt Bros Inc ....E ....419 826-3671 Swanton *(G-17571)*
Siebenthaler Company ....D ....937 427-4110 Dayton *(G-9882)*
▲ Straders Garden Centers Inc ....C ....614 889-1314 Columbus *(G-8792)*
▲ Thorsens Greenhouse LLC ....E ....740 363-5069 Delaware *(G-10129)*
Warner Nurseries Inc ....E ....440 946-0880 Madison *(G-13237)*

5194 Tobacco & Tobacco Prdts Wholesale

Albert Guarnieri & Co ....D ....330 794-9834 Akron *(G-63)*
Core-Mark Ohio ....C ....650 589-9445 Solon *(G-16994)*
Dittman-Adams Company ....E ....513 870-7530 West Chester *(G-19065)*
EBY-Brown Company LLC ....C ....937 324-1036 Springfield *(G-17192)*
Gummer Wholesale Inc ....D ....740 928-0415 Heath *(G-11838)*
JE Carsten Company ....E ....330 794-4440 Akron *(G-291)*
Jetro Cash and Carry Entps LLC ....D ....216 525-0101 Cleveland *(G-5862)*
K M C Corporation ....E ....740 598-4171 Mingo Junction *(G-14655)*
McKirnan Bros Inc ....E ....419 586-2428 Celina *(G-2651)*
Novelart Manufacturing Company ....C ....513 351-7700 Cincinnati *(G-4187)*
Swd Corporation ....E ....419 227-2436 Lima *(G-12896)*
The Anter Brothers Company ....E ....216 252-4555 Cleveland *(G-6589)*

5198 Paints, Varnishes & Splys Wholesale

Carlisle Fluid Tech Inc ....E ....419 825-5186 Toledo *(G-17792)*
◆ Comex North America Inc ....D ....303 307-2100 Cleveland *(G-5374)*
Continental Products Company ....E ....216 531-0710 Cleveland *(G-5402)*
Fashion Wallcoverings Inc ....D ....216 432-1600 Cleveland *(G-5575)*
Finishmaster Inc ....D ....614 228-4328 Columbus *(G-7657)*
Matrix Sys Auto Finishes LLC ....D ....248 668-8135 Massillon *(G-13837)*
Miller Bros Wallpaper Company ....E ....513 231-4470 Cincinnati *(G-4095)*
Systems Jay LLC Nanogate ....E ....419 747-6639 Mansfield *(G-13371)*
▲ Teknol Inc ....D ....937 264-0190 Dayton *(G-9922)*

5199 Nondurable Goods, NEC Wholesale

▲ A-Roo Company LLC ....D ....440 238-8850 Strongsville *(G-17437)*
▲ Albrecht Inc ....E ....513 576-9900 Milford *(G-14501)*
▲ Ameri Interntl Trade Grp Inc ....E ....419 586-6433 Celina *(G-2634)*
▼ Armaly LLC ....E ....740 852-3621 London *(G-12992)*
Aunties Attic ....E ....740 548-5059 Lewis Center *(G-12669)*
◆ Aurora Wholesalers LLC ....D ....440 248-5200 Solon *(G-16980)*
Avery Dennison Corporation ....C ....440 534-6000 Mentor *(G-14145)*
◆ B D G Wrap-Tite Inc ....D ....440 349-5400 Solon *(G-16981)*
Berlin Packaging LLC ....E ....614 777-6282 Grove City *(G-11533)*
Boost Technologies LLC ....D ....800 223-2203 Dayton *(G-9364)*
Buy Below Retail Inc ....E ....216 292-7805 Cleveland *(G-5165)*
Cambridge Packaging Inc ....E ....740 432-3351 Cambridge *(G-2101)*
Cannell Graphics LLC ....E ....614 781-9760 Worthington *(G-19944)*
▼ Century Marketing Corporation ....C ....419 354-2591 Bowling Green *(G-1772)*
▲ Checker Notions Company Inc ....D ....419 893-3636 Maumee *(G-13894)*
▲ Clercom Inc ....D ....513 724-6101 Williamsburg *(G-19630)*
Columbus Serum Company ....C ....614 444-5211 Columbus *(G-7384)*
▲ Corporate Imageworks LLC ....E ....216 292-8800 Streetsboro *(G-17411)*
Custom Products Corporation ....D ....440 528-7100 Solon *(G-16999)*
▲ Dayton Bag & Burlap Co ....C ....937 258-8000 Dayton *(G-9461)*
Dayton Heidelberg Distrg Co ....D ....937 220-6450 Moraine *(G-14771)*
Distribution Data Incorporated ....E ....216 362-3009 Brookpark *(G-1943)*
Diversified Products & Svcs ....C ....740 393-6202 Mount Vernon *(G-14893)*
Dollar Paradise ....E ....216 432-0421 Cleveland *(G-5498)*
Don Drumm Studios & Gallery ....E ....330 253-6840 Akron *(G-196)*
Dwa Mrkting Prmtional Pdts LLC ....E ....216 476-0635 Strongsville *(G-17457)*
Earthbound Holding LLC ....E ....972 248-0228 Strongsville *(G-17458)*
▲ Esc and Company Inc ....E ....614 794-0568 Columbus *(G-7608)*
Evolution Crtive Solutions LLC ....E ....513 681-4450 Cincinnati *(G-3584)*
▲ First 2 Market Products LLC ....E ....419 874-5444 Perrysburg *(G-16003)*
Flower Factory Inc ....D ....614 275-6220 Columbus *(G-7677)*
▲ Galaxy Balloons Incorporated ....C ....216 476-3360 Cleveland *(G-5651)*
Glen Surplus Sales Inc ....E ....419 347-1212 Shelby *(G-16900)*
▲ Global-Pak Inc ....E ....330 482-1993 Lisbon *(G-12938)*
◆ Glow Industries Inc ....D ....419 872-4772 Perrysburg *(G-16007)*
Gordon Bernard Company LLC ....E ....513 248-7600 Milford *(G-14523)*
Gpax Ltd ....E ....614 501-7622 Reynoldsburg *(G-16456)*
Graham Packaging Holdings Co ....E ....419 628-1070 Minster *(G-14663)*
Graham Packg Plastic Pdts Inc ....C ....419 423-3271 Findlay *(G-11037)*
Gummer Wholesale Inc ....D ....740 928-0415 Heath *(G-11838)*
Hammacher Schlemmer & Co Inc ....C ....513 860-4570 West Chester *(G-19088)*
Harold Tatman & Sons Entps Inc ....E ....740 655-2880 Kingston *(G-12450)*
Hays Enterprises Inc ....E ....330 299-8639 Warren *(G-18861)*
▲ Hi-Way Distributing Corp Amer ....D ....330 645-6633 Coventry Township *(G-9125)*
Home City Ice Company ....E ....614 836-2877 Groveport *(G-11644)*
▼ ICM Distributing Company Inc ....E ....234 212-3030 Twinsburg *(G-18431)*
Impressive Packaging Inc ....E ....419 368-6808 Hayesville *(G-11834)*
▲ Johnson Bros Rubber Co Inc ....D ....419 853-4122 West Salem *(G-19270)*
Johnson Bros Rubber Co Inc ....E ....419 752-4814 Greenwich *(G-11526)*
▲ K & M International Inc ....D ....330 425-2550 Twinsburg *(G-18435)*
Kapstone Container Corporation ....C ....330 562-6111 Aurora *(G-844)*
L M Berry and Company ....D ....513 768-7700 Cincinnati *(G-3953)*
Labelle News Agency Inc ....E ....740 282-9731 Steubenville *(G-17324)*
Lamrite West Inc ....E ....440 572-9946 Strongsville *(G-17483)*
▲ Lamrite West Inc ....C ....440 238-7318 Strongsville *(G-17482)*
▲ Leader Promotions Inc ....D ....614 416-6565 Columbus *(G-8047)*
▲ Leather Gallery Inc ....E ....513 312-1722 Lebanon *(G-12619)*
Lori Holding Co ....E ....740 342-3230 New Lexington *(G-15055)*
M & M Wintergreens Inc ....D ....216 398-1288 Cleveland *(G-5961)*
Marathon Mfg & Sup Co ....D ....330 343-2656 New Philadelphia *(G-15108)*
◆ Mark Feldstein & Assoc Inc ....E ....419 867-9500 Sylvania *(G-17600)*
◆ Merchandise Inc ....D ....513 353-2200 Miamitown *(G-14372)*
▲ Millennium Leather LLC ....E ....201 541-7121 Mason *(G-13740)*
Nannicola Wholesale Co ....D ....330 799-0888 Youngstown *(G-20293)*
◆ Novelty Advertising Co Inc ....E ....740 622-3113 Coshocton *(G-9113)*
▼ Nutis Press Inc ....C ....614 237-8626 Columbus *(G-8307)*
▼ Pacific MGT Holdings LLC ....E ....440 324-3339 Elyria *(G-10667)*
Packaging & Pads R Us LLC ....E ....419 499-2905 Milan *(G-14497)*
▼ Pakmark LLC ....E ....513 285-1040 Fairfield *(G-10892)*
▼ Par International Inc ....E ....614 529-1300 Obetz *(G-15669)*
▲ Peter Graham Dunn Inc ....E ....330 816-0035 Dalton *(G-9242)*
Petland Inc ....D ....740 775-2464 Chillicothe *(G-2870)*
▲ Potter Inc ....E ....419 636-5624 Bryan *(G-2017)*
▼ Questar Solutions LLC ....E ....330 966-2070 North Canton *(G-15363)*
Raco Industries LLC ....D ....513 984-2101 Blue Ash *(G-1672)*
Red Apple Packaging LLC ....E ....513 228-5522 Lebanon *(G-12642)*
▲ Relay Gear Ltd ....E ....888 735-2943 Columbus *(G-8611)*
Riser Foods Company ....D ....216 292-7000 Bedford Heights *(G-1359)*
Rrp Packaging ....E ....419 666-6119 Perrysburg *(G-16053)*
S & S Inc ....E ....216 383-1880 Cleveland *(G-6425)*
Samuel Strapping Systems Inc ....D ....740 522-2500 Heath *(G-11843)*
Scholastic Book Fairs Inc ....D ....513 714-1000 West Chester *(G-19146)*
Screen Works Inc ....E ....937 264-9111 Dayton *(G-9870)*
▲ Shamrock Companies Inc ....C ....440 899-9510 Westlake *(G-19546)*
▲ Ship-Paq Inc ....E ....513 860-0700 Fairfield *(G-10905)*
▲ Shumsky Enterprises Inc ....D ....937 223-2203 Dayton *(G-9880)*
Siemer Distributing Company ....E ....740 342-3230 New Lexington *(G-15063)*
SJS Packaging Group Inc ....E ....513 841-1351 Cincinnati *(G-4535)*
Skybox Packaging LLC ....D ....419 525-7209 Mansfield *(G-13364)*
Star Packaging Inc ....E ....614 564-9936 Columbus *(G-8777)*
▲ Sterling Paper Co ....E ....614 443-0303 Columbus *(G-8786)*
▲ Storopack Inc ....E ....513 874-0314 West Chester *(G-19232)*

Superior Packaging Toledo LLC .... E 419 380-3335
  Toledo (G-18211)
Systems Pack Inc .... E 330 467-5729
  Macedonia (G-13211)
Tahoma Enterprises Inc .... D 330 745-9016
  Barberton (G-982)
▼ Tahoma Rubber & Plastics Inc .... D 330 745-9016
  Barberton (G-983)
Third Dimension Inc .... E 877 926-3223
  Geneva (G-11370)
▲ Trademark Global LLC .... D 440 960-6226
  Lorain (G-13082)
Traichal Construction Company .... E 800 255-3667
  Niles (G-15307)
Two Happy Frogs Incorporated .... E 330 633-1666
  Tallmadge (G-17658)
US Safetygear Inc .... E 330 898-1344
  Warren (G-18919)
▲ Waterbeds n Stuff Inc .... E 614 871-1171
  Grove City (G-11612)
White Barn Candle Co .... A 614 856-6000
  Reynoldsburg (G-16490)
Wolverton Inc .... E 330 220-3320
  Brunswick (G-1999)
◆ X-S Merchandise Inc .... E 216 524-5620
  Independence (G-12278)

60 DEPOSITORY INSTITUTIONS

6011 Federal Reserve Banks
Federal Rsrve Bnk of Cleveland .... A 216 579-2000
  Cleveland (G-5583)
Federal Rsrve Bnk of Cleveland .... C 513 721-4787
  Cincinnati (G-3599)

6019 Central Reserve Depository, NEC
Federal Home Ln Bnk Cincinnati .... A 513 852-7500
  Cincinnati (G-3596)

6021 National Commercial Banks
Century National Bank .... E 800 548-3557
  Zanesville (G-20462)
Champaign National Bank Urbana .... E 614 798-1321
  Dublin (G-10287)
Chase Equipment Finance Inc .... C 800 678-2601
  Columbus (G-6876)
Citizens Bank National Assn .... D 330 580-1913
  Canton (G-2310)
Citizens Nat Bnk of Bluffton .... E 419 358-8040
  Bluffton (G-1730)
Citizens Nat Bnk of Bluffton .... E 419 224-0400
  Lima (G-12753)
Citizens Nat Bnk Urbana Ohio .... E 937 653-1200
  Urbana (G-18580)
Citizens National Bank .... E 740 472-1696
  Woodsfield (G-19813)
Civista Bank .... E 419 744-3100
  Norwalk (G-15564)
Colonial Banc Corp .... E 937 456-5544
  Eaton (G-10554)
Consumers National Bank .... E 330 868-7701
  Minerva (G-14644)
Credit First NA .... C 216 362-5000
  Brookpark (G-1941)
Croghan Bancshares Inc .... D 419 794-9399
  Maumee (G-13902)
Eastern Ohio P-16 .... E 330 675-7623
  Warren (G-18854)
Fairfield National Bank .... E 740 653-7242
  Lancaster (G-12538)
Farmers Nat Bnk of Canfield .... C 330 533-3341
  Canfield (G-2190)
Farmers National Bank .... D 330 544-7447
  Niles (G-15293)
Farmers National Bank .... C 330 682-1010
  Orrville (G-15771)
Farmers National Bank .... D 330 385-9200
  East Liverpool (G-10521)
Farmers National Bank .... D 330 682-1030
  Orrville (G-15772)
Fifth Third Bank .... C 513 574-4457
  Cincinnati (G-3606)
Fifth Third Bank .... C 440 984-2402
  Amherst (G-594)
Fifth Third Bank of NW Ohio .... B 419 259-7820
  Toledo (G-17887)
First Capital Bancshares Inc .... D 740 775-6777
  Chillicothe (G-2839)

First Citizens Nat Bnk Inc .... E 419 294-2351
  Upper Sandusky (G-18561)
First Financial Bancorp .... C 513 551-5640
  Cincinnati (G-3615)
First Financial Bank .... E 513 979-5800
  Cincinnati (G-3616)
First Nat Bnk of Nelsonville .... E 740 753-1941
  Nelsonville (G-14963)
First National Bank Bellevue .... E 419 483-7340
  Bellevue (G-1410)
First National Bank of Pandora .... E 419 384-3221
  Pandora (G-15890)
First National Bank of Waverly .... E 740 947-2136
  Waverly (G-18971)
First National Bank of Waverly .... E 740 493-3372
  Piketon (G-16114)
First National Bank PA .... E 330 747-0292
  Youngstown (G-20189)
First National Bnk of Dennison .... E 740 922-2532
  Dennison (G-10163)
First-Knox National Bank .... C 740 399-5500
  Mount Vernon (G-14897)
FNB Corporation .... E 440 439-2200
  Cleveland (G-5610)
FNB Corporation .... D 330 425-1818
  Twinsburg (G-18416)
Futura Banc Corp .... D 937 653-1167
  Urbana (G-18588)
Greenville National Bank .... E 937 548-1114
  Greenville (G-11506)
Huntington Bancshares Inc .... C 614 480-8300
  Columbus (G-7865)
Huntington National Bank .... A 330 996-6300
  Akron (G-273)
Huntington National Bank .... A 330 384-7201
  Akron (G-274)
Huntington National Bank .... E 330 384-7092
  Akron (G-275)
Huntington National Bank .... E 216 621-1717
  Cleveland (G-5791)
Huntington National Bank .... D 614 480-8300
  Columbus (G-7871)
Huntington National Bank .... E 330 343-6611
  Dover (G-10193)
Huntington National Bank .... E 740 452-8444
  Zanesville (G-20489)
Huntington National Bank .... E 216 515-6401
  Cleveland (G-5792)
Huntington National Bank .... C 513 762-1860
  Cincinnati (G-3799)
Huntington National Bank .... E 740 773-2681
  Chillicothe (G-2852)
Huntington National Bank .... E 419 226-8200
  Lima (G-12801)
Huntington Technology Finance .... B 614 480-5169
  Columbus (G-7872)
Icx Corporation .... E 330 656-3611
  Cleveland (G-5800)
Jpmorgan Chase Bank Nat Assn .... E 614 876-7650
  Hilliard (G-11917)
Jpmorgan Chase Bank Nat Assn .... E 614 248-2410
  Reynoldsburg (G-16461)
Jpmorgan Chase Bank Nat Assn .... E 614 794-7398
  Westerville (G-19413)
Jpmorgan Chase Bank Nat Assn .... E 614 476-1910
  Columbus (G-7952)
Jpmorgan Chase Bank Nat Assn .... E 513 221-1040
  Cincinnati (G-3890)
Jpmorgan Chase Bank Nat Assn .... E 513 826-2317
  Blue Ash (G-1621)
Jpmorgan Chase Bank Nat Assn .... E 419 358-4055
  Bluffton (G-1733)
Jpmorgan Chase Bank Nat Assn .... E 216 781-2127
  Columbus (G-7953)
Jpmorgan Chase Bank Nat Assn .... E 614 248-5391
  Columbus (G-7954)
Jpmorgan Chase Bank Nat Assn .... E 513 985-5120
  Cincinnati (G-3891)
Jpmorgan Chase Bank Nat Assn .... E 513 784-0770
  Cincinnati (G-3892)
Jpmorgan Chase Bank Nat Assn .... A 740 363-8032
  Delaware (G-10112)
Jpmorgan Chase Bank Nat Assn .... E 330 364-7242
  New Philadelphia (G-15104)
Jpmorgan Chase Bank Nat Assn .... E 419 394-2358
  Saint Marys (G-16678)
Jpmorgan Chase Bank Nat Assn .... E 419 294-4944
  Upper Sandusky (G-18562)
Jpmorgan Chase Bank Nat Assn .... E 740 676-2671
  Bellaire (G-1366)

Jpmorgan Chase Bank Nat Assn .... E 330 972-1905
  Cuyahoga Falls (G-9198)
Jpmorgan Chase Bank Nat Assn .... E 513 985-5350
  Milford (G-14529)
Jpmorgan Chase Bank Nat Assn .... E 513 595-6450
  Cincinnati (G-3893)
Jpmorgan Chase Bank Nat Assn .... E 440 442-7800
  Cleveland (G-5873)
Jpmorgan Chase Bank Nat Assn .... E 330 972-1735
  New Franklin (G-15045)
Jpmorgan Chase Bank Nat Assn .... E 330 287-5101
  Wooster (G-19874)
Jpmorgan Chase Bank Nat Assn .... E 330 650-0476
  Hudson (G-12126)
Jpmorgan Chase Bank Nat Assn .... E 440 352-5491
  Perry (G-15961)
Jpmorgan Chase Bank Nat Assn .... E 419 424-7570
  Findlay (G-11052)
Jpmorgan Chase Bank Nat Assn .... A 937 534-8218
  Dayton (G-9646)
Jpmorgan Chase Bank Nat Assn .... E 330 225-1330
  Brunswick (G-1984)
Jpmorgan Chase Bank Nat Assn .... E 330 325-7855
  Randolph (G-16373)
Jpmorgan Chase Bank Nat Assn .... E 330 287-5101
  Wooster (G-19875)
Jpmorgan Chase Bank Nat Assn .... E 419 946-3015
  Mount Gilead (G-14854)
Jpmorgan Chase Bank Nat Assn .... E 419 586-6668
  Celina (G-2648)
Jpmorgan Chase Bank Nat Assn .... B 440 352-5969
  Painesville (G-15859)
Jpmorgan Chase Bank Nat Assn .... E 330 545-2551
  Girard (G-11416)
Jpmorgan Chase Bank Nat Assn .... E 440 286-6111
  Chardon (G-2753)
Jpmorgan Chase Bank Nat Assn .... E 330 972-1915
  Akron (G-298)
Jpmorgan Chase Bank Nat Assn .... E 330 759-1750
  Youngstown (G-20242)
Jpmorgan Chase Bank Nat Assn .... E 419 424-7512
  Findlay (G-11053)
Jpmorgan Chase Bank Nat Assn .... D 614 248-5800
  Westerville (G-19414)
Jpmorgan Chase Bank Nat Assn .... E 614 920-4182
  Canal Winchester (G-2161)
Jpmorgan Chase Bank Nat Assn .... E 614 834-3120
  Pickerington (G-16098)
Jpmorgan Chase Bank Nat Assn .... E 614 853-2999
  Galloway (G-11344)
Jpmorgan Chase Bank Nat Assn .... E 614 248-3315
  Powell (G-16340)
Jpmorgan Chase Bank Nat Assn .... E 740 657-8906
  Lewis Center (G-12690)
Jpmorgan Chase Bank Nat Assn .... E 216 524-0600
  Seven Hills (G-16831)
Jpmorgan Chase Bank Nat Assn .... E 740 374-2263
  Marietta (G-13459)
Jpmorgan Chase Bank Nat Assn .... E 614 248-7505
  Westerville (G-19415)
Jpmorgan Chase Bank Nat Assn .... C 614 248-5800
  Westerville (G-19416)
Jpmorgan Chase Bank Nat Assn .... E 419 739-3600
  Wapakoneta (G-18800)
Jpmorgan Chase Bank Nat Assn .... E 330 722-6626
  Medina (G-14087)
Jpmorgan Chase Bank Nat Assn .... E 614 248-2083
  Columbus (G-7956)
Jpmorgan Chase Bank Nat Assn .... E 216 781-4437
  Cleveland (G-5874)
Jpmorgan Chase Bank Nat Assn .... E 614 759-8955
  Reynoldsburg (C-16400)
Keybanc Capital Markets Inc .... B 800 553-2240
  Cleveland (G-5898)
Keybank National Association .... B 800 539-2968
  Cleveland (G-5899)
Kingston National Bank Inc .... E 740 642-2191
  Kingston (G-12451)
Lcnb National Bank .... D 513 932-1414
  Lebanon (G-12618)
Lcnb National Bank .... E 740 775-6777
  Chillicothe (G-2859)
Lcnb National Bank .... D 937 456-5544
  Eaton (G-10565)
Lorain National Bank .... C 440 244-6000
  Lorain (G-13056)
Merchants National Bank .... E 937 393-1134
  Hillsboro (G-11987)
Merrill Lynch Business .... E 513 791-5700
  Blue Ash (G-1642)

60 DEPOSITORY INSTITUTIONS SIC SECTION

National City Mortgage ......E 614 401-5030
Dublin *(G-10404)*
Northwest Bank ......B 330 342-4018
Hudson *(G-12137)*
Pandora Bancshares Inc ......E 419 384-3221
Pandora *(G-15893)*
Park National Bank ......C 740 349-8451
Newark *(G-15225)*
Park National Bank ......E 614 228-0063
Columbus *(G-8515)*
Peoples Bancorp Inc ......E 740 373-3155
Marietta *(G-13484)*
Peoples Bank ......E 937 748-0067
Springboro *(G-17134)*
Peoples Bank ......E 740 286-6773
Wellston *(G-19005)*
Peoples Bank ......C 937 382-1441
Wilmington *(G-19778)*
Peoples Bank National Assn ......E 937 746-5733
Franklin *(G-11163)*
Peoples Nat Bnk of New Lxngton ......E 740 342-5111
New Lexington *(G-15060)*
PNC Banc Corp Ohio ......E 513 651-8738
Cincinnati *(G-4307)*
PNC Bank National Association ......C 330 375-8342
Akron *(G-394)*
PNC Bank National Association ......E 740 349-8431
Newark *(G-15228)*
PNC Bank National Association ......B 513 721-2500
Cincinnati *(G-4308)*
PNC Bank National Association ......E 513 455-9522
Cincinnati *(G-4309)*
PNC Bank National Association ......E 419 621-2930
Sandusky *(G-16785)*
PNC Bank National Association ......B 419 259-5466
Toledo *(G-18129)*
PNC Bank National Association ......C 330 742-4426
Youngstown *(G-20327)*
PNC Bank National Association ......C 330 562-9700
Aurora *(G-850)*
Riverhills Bank ......E 513 553-6700
Milford *(G-14557)*
Second National Bank ......E 937 548-2122
Greenville *(G-11519)*
Security National Bank & Tr Co ......C 740 426-6384
Newark *(G-15233)*
Security National Bank & Tr Co ......C 937 324-6800
Springfield *(G-17272)*
Standing Stone National Bank ......E 740 653-5115
Lancaster *(G-12577)*
State Bank and Trust Company ......E 419 485-5521
Montpelier *(G-14748)*
The First Central National Bnk ......E 937 663-4186
Saint Paris *(G-16686)*
The Liberty Nat Bankof Ada ......E 419 673-1217
Kenton *(G-12424)*
United Bank National Assn ......E 419 562-3040
Bucyrus *(G-2049)*
US Bank National Association ......A 513 632-4234
Cincinnati *(G-4792)*
US Bank National Association ......E 740 353-4151
Portsmouth *(G-16318)*
US Bank National Association ......A 513 979-1000
Cincinnati *(G-4793)*
US Bank National Association ......E 513 458-2844
Cincinnati *(G-4794)*
US Bank National Association ......D 937 873-7845
Fairborn *(G-10807)*
US Bank National Association ......E 937 335-8351
Troy *(G-18384)*
US Bank National Association ......E 937 498-1131
Sidney *(G-16958)*
Wells Fargo Bank National Assn ......D 513 424-6640
Middletown *(G-14470)*

6022 State Commercial Banks

Andover Bancorp Inc ......E 440 293-7605
Andover *(G-609)*
Apple Creek Banking Co (inc) ......E 330 698-2631
Apple Creek *(G-623)*
Buckeye Community Bank ......E 440 233-8800
Lorain *(G-13020)*
Citizens Bank Company ......E 740 984-2381
Beverly *(G-1488)*
Citizens Bank of Ashville Ohio ......E 740 983-2511
Ashville *(G-769)*
Citizens Bnk of Logan Ohio Inc ......E 740 380-2561
Logan *(G-12970)*
Civista Bank ......D 419 625-4121
Sandusky *(G-16740)*
Civista Bank ......E 419 744-3100
Norwalk *(G-15564)*
CNB Bank ......D 419 562-7040
Bucyrus *(G-2030)*
Commercial Svgs Bank Millersbu ......E 330 674-9015
Millersburg *(G-14595)*
Consumers Bancorp Inc ......C 330 868-7701
Minerva *(G-14643)*
Crogan Colonial Bank ......E 419 483-2541
Bellevue *(G-1407)*
Croghan Colonial Bank ......E 419 332-7301
Fremont *(G-11193)*
CSB Bancorp Inc ......E 330 674-9015
Millersburg *(G-14602)*
Farmers & Merchants State Bank ......C 419 446-2501
Archbold *(G-636)*
Farmers Bank & Savings Co Inc ......E 740 992-0088
Pomeroy *(G-16232)*
Farmers Citizens Bank ......E 419 562-7040
Bucyrus *(G-2037)*
Farmers National Bank ......D 330 544-7447
Niles *(G-15293)*
Federal Home Ln Bnk Cincinnati ......D 513 852-5719
Cincinnati *(G-3597)*
Fifth Third Bancorp ......D 800 972-3030
Cincinnati *(G-3605)*
Fifth Third Bank ......A 513 579-5203
Cincinnati *(G-3607)*
Fifth Third Bank ......E 419 259-7820
Toledo *(G-17886)*
Fifth Third Bank ......D 330 686-0511
Cuyahoga Falls *(G-9188)*
Fifth Third Bank of Sthrn OH ......E 937 840-5353
Hillsboro *(G-11974)*
Fifth Third Bnk of Columbus OH ......A 614 744-7553
Columbus *(G-7655)*
First Commonwealth Bank ......E 740 548-3340
Delaware *(G-10094)*
First Commonwealth Bank ......E 740 369-0048
Delaware *(G-10095)*
First Commonwealth Bank ......E 614 336-2280
Powell *(G-16335)*
First Commonwealth Bank ......C 740 657-7000
Lewis Center *(G-12685)*
First Federal Bank of Midwest ......E 419 695-1055
Delphos *(G-10143)*
First Financial Bank ......C 877 322-9530
Cincinnati *(G-3617)*
First National Bank PA ......E 330 747-0292
Youngstown *(G-20189)*
First State Bank ......E 937 695-0331
Winchester *(G-19801)*
Fort Jennings State Bank ......E 419 286-2527
Fort Jennings *(G-11108)*
Genoa Banking Company ......E 419 855-8381
Genoa *(G-11378)*
Heartland Bank ......E 614 337-4600
Gahanna *(G-11247)*
Henry County Bank ......E 419 599-1065
Napoleon *(G-14942)*
Hicksville Bank Inc ......E 419 542-7726
Hicksville *(G-11865)*
Hocking Vly Bnk of Athens Co ......E 740 592-4441
Athens *(G-792)*
Huntington National Bank ......E 330 742-7013
Youngstown *(G-20224)*
Huntington National Bank ......E 740 695-3323
Saint Clairsville *(G-16638)*
Huntington National Bank ......E 419 782-5050
Defiance *(G-10035)*
Independence Bank ......E 216 447-1444
Cleveland *(G-5809)*
◆ **Jpmorgan Chase Bank Nat Assn** ......A 614 436-3055
Columbus *(G-6888)*
Jpmorgan Chase Bank Nat Assn ......E 614 759-8955
Reynoldsburg *(G-16460)*
Keybank National Association ......B 800 539-2968
Cleveland *(G-5899)*
Killbuck Savings Bank Co Inc ......E 330 276-4881
Killbuck *(G-12445)*
Minster Bank ......E 419 628-2351
Minster *(G-14666)*
North Side Bank and Trust Co ......D 513 542-7800
Cincinnati *(G-4177)*
North Side Bank and Trust Co ......D 513 533-8000
Cincinnati *(G-4178)*
North Valley Bank ......E 740 452-7920
Zanesville *(G-20518)*
Northwest Ohio Chapter Cfma ......E 419 891-1040
Maumee *(G-13950)*
Ohio Valley Bank Company ......D 740 446-2168
Gallipolis *(G-11330)*
Ohio Valley Bank Company ......C 740 446-2631
Gallipolis *(G-11331)*
Ohio Valley Bank Company ......E 740 446-1646
Gallipolis *(G-11332)*
Ohio Valley Bank Company ......E 740 446-2631
Gallipolis *(G-11333)*
Old Fort Banking Company ......D 419 447-4790
Tiffin *(G-17692)*
Osgood State Bank (inc) ......E 419 582-2681
Osgood *(G-15792)*
Park National Bank ......C 740 349-8451
Newark *(G-15226)*
Park National Bank ......E 937 324-6800
Springfield *(G-17258)*
Peoples Banking and Trust Co ......C 740 373-3155
Marietta *(G-13486)*
Peoples Banking and Trust Co ......E 740 439-2767
Cambridge *(G-2126)*
Portage Community Bank Inc ......D 330 296-8090
Ravenna *(G-16397)*
Richland Trust Company ......D 419 525-8700
Mansfield *(G-13361)*
Richwood Banking Co ......E 740 943-2317
Richwood *(G-16544)*
Savings Bank ......E 740 474-3191
Circleville *(G-4903)*
Sb Financial Group Inc ......C 419 783-8950
Defiance *(G-10056)*
◆ **State Bank and Trust Company** ......E 419 783-8950
Defiance *(G-10058)*
State Bank and Trust Company ......E 419 485-5521
Montpelier *(G-14748)*
The Cortland Sav & Bnkg Co ......D 330 637-8040
Cortland *(G-9083)*
The Liberty Nat Bankof Ada ......E 419 673-1217
Kenton *(G-12424)*
The Middlefield Banking Co ......E 440 632-1666
Middlefield *(G-14403)*
The Peoples Bank Co Inc ......E 419 678-2385
Coldwater *(G-6835)*
The Peoples Bank Co Inc ......E 419 678-2385
Coldwater *(G-6836)*
Unified Bank ......E 740 633-0445
Martins Ferry *(G-13602)*
Union Bank Company ......E 740 387-2265
Marion *(G-13588)*
Vinton County Nat Bnk McArthur ......E 740 596-2525
Mc Arthur *(G-14019)*
Wesbanco Inc ......E 740 532-0263
Ironton *(G-12304)*
Wesbanco Bank Inc ......D 740 425-1927
Barnesville *(G-992)*

6029 Commercial Banks, NEC

Croghan Bancshares Inc ......D 419 794-9399
Maumee *(G-13902)*
Farm Credit Mid-America ......E 740 441-9312
Albany *(G-519)*
First Merchants Bank ......E 614 486-9000
Columbus *(G-7666)*
FNB Corporation ......D 330 425-1818
Twinsburg *(G-18416)*
Huntington Insurance Inc ......E 419 429-4627
Findlay *(G-11048)*
Huntington National Bank ......C 513 762-1860
Cincinnati *(G-3799)*
Huntington National Bank ......E 330 742-7013
Youngstown *(G-20224)*
Huntington National Bank ......E 330 343-6611
Dover *(G-10193)*
Huntington National Bank ......E 740 773-2681
Chillicothe *(G-2852)*
Huntington National Bank ......E 614 480-4293
Columbus *(G-7869)*
Huntington National Bank ......E 740 452-8444
Zanesville *(G-20489)*
Huntington National Bank ......B 614 480-4293
Columbus *(G-7870)*
Huntington National Bank ......E 740 695-3323
Saint Clairsville *(G-16638)*
Huntington National Bank ......E 419 226-8200
Lima *(G-12801)*
Huntington National Bank ......E 216 515-6401
Cleveland *(G-5792)*
Huntington National Bank ......E 419 782-5050
Defiance *(G-10035)*
Jpmorgan Chase Bank Nat Assn ......E 614 759-8955
Reynoldsburg *(G-16460)*

Jpmorgan Chase Bank Nat Assn .... E 740 382-7362
Marion *(G-13544)*

Jpmorgan Chase Bank Nat Assn .... E 440 277-1038
Lorain *(G-13044)*

MB Financial Inc .... D 937 283-2027
Wilmington *(G-19772)*

PNC Bank National Association .... C 330 742-4426
Youngstown *(G-20327)*

PNC Bank National Association .... C 330 562-9700
Aurora *(G-850)*

PNC Bank National Association .... C 330 854-0974
Canal Fulton *(G-2145)*

Raymond James Fincl Svcs Inc .... E 419 586-5121
Celina *(G-2661)*

Republic Bank .... B 513 793-7666
Blue Ash *(G-1680)*

UBS Financial Services Inc .... E 440 414-2740
Westlake *(G-19558)*

Wesbanco Inc .... E 614 208-7298
Columbus *(G-8979)*

Westfield Bank Fsb .... E 800 368-8930
Westfield Center *(G-19453)*

6035 Federal Savings Institutions

American Savings Bank .... E 740 354-3177
Portsmouth *(G-16264)*

Belmont Federal Sav & Ln Assn .... E 740 676-1165
Bellaire *(G-1363)*

Century National Bank .... E 740 454-2521
Zanesville *(G-20461)*

Century National Bank .... E 740 455-7330
Zanesville *(G-20463)*

Chemical Bank .... E 440 779-0807
North Olmsted *(G-15414)*

Chemical Bank .... E 513 232-0800
Cincinnati *(G-3238)*

Chemical Bank .... E 440 926-2191
Grafton *(G-11440)*

Chemical Bank .... E 330 314-1395
Poland *(G-16222)*

Chemical Bank .... E 440 323-7451
Elyria *(G-10603)*

Chemical Bank .... D 330 298-0510
Ravenna *(G-16376)*

Chemical Bank .... D 330 314-1380
Youngstown *(G-20139)*

Cheviot Mutual Holding Company .... D 513 661-0457
Cincinnati *(G-3242)*

Cincinnati Federal .... E 513 574-3025
Cincinnati *(G-3302)*

Cincinnatus Savings & Loan .... E 513 661-6903
Cincinnati *(G-3338)*

Citizens Federal Sav & Ln Assn .... E 937 593-0015
Bellefontaine *(G-1379)*

Congressional Bank .... E 614 441-9230
Columbus *(G-7420)*

Eagle Financial Bancorp Inc .... E 513 574-0700
Cincinnati *(G-3527)*

Fairfield Federal Sav Ln Assn .... E 740 653-3863
Lancaster *(G-12533)*

First Defiance Financial Corp .... E 419 353-8611
Bowling Green *(G-1776)*

First Fdral Sav Ln Assn Galion .... D 419 468-1518
Galion *(G-11294)*

First Fdral Sav Ln Assn Lkwood .... C 216 221-7300
Lakewood *(G-12478)*

First Fdral Sav Ln Assn Lorain .... D 440 282-6188
Lorain *(G-13039)*

First Fdral Sav Ln Assn Newark .... E 740 345-3494
Newark *(G-15166)*

First Fdral Sving Ln Assn Dlta .... E 419 822-3131
Delta *(G-10158)*

First Federal Bank of Midwest .... E 419 782-5015
Defiance *(G-10031)*

First Federal Bank of Midwest .... E 419 695-1055
Delphos *(G-10143)*

First Federal Bank of Midwest .... D 419 855-8326
Genoa *(G-11376)*

First Federal Bank of Ohio .... D 419 468-1518
Galion *(G-11295)*

First Federal Cmnty Bnk Assn .... D 330 364-7777
Dover *(G-10188)*

First Financial Bancorp .... C 513 551-5640
Cincinnati *(G-3615)*

Greenville Federal .... E 937 548-4158
Greenville *(G-11504)*

Guardian Savings Bank .... E 513 942-3535
West Chester *(G-19086)*

Guardian Savings Bank .... E 513 528-8787
Cincinnati *(G-3717)*

Harrison Building and Ln Assn .... E 513 367-2015
Harrison *(G-11801)*

Home City Federal Savings Bank .... E 937 390-0470
Springfield *(G-17205)*

Liberty Capital Inc .... D 937 382-1000
Wilmington *(G-19767)*

Liberty Savings Bank FSB .... C 937 382-1000
Wilmington *(G-19768)*

New York Community Bank .... E 440 734-7040
North Olmsted *(G-15434)*

New York Community Bank .... E 216 741-7333
Cleveland *(G-6126)*

Peoples Bank .... D 740 373-3155
Marietta *(G-13485)*

Peoples Federal Sav & Ln Assn .... E 937 492-6129
Sidney *(G-16947)*

Talmer Bank and Trust .... E 330 726-3396
Canfield *(G-2211)*

Third Federal Savings .... B 800 844-7333
Cleveland *(G-6592)*

Third Federal Savings .... E 440 885-4900
Cleveland *(G-6593)*

Third Federal Savings .... E 440 716-1865
North Olmsted *(G-15448)*

Third Federal Savings .... E 440 843-6300
Cleveland *(G-6594)*

Union Savings Bank .... D 937 434-1254
Dayton *(G-9944)*

Unity National Bank .... E 937 773-0752
Piqua *(G-16171)*

Wayne Savings Bancshares Inc .... C 330 264-5767
Wooster *(G-19925)*

Wayne Savings Community Bank .... C 330 264-5767
Wooster *(G-19926)*

Wesbanco Inc .... E 740 532-0263
Ironton *(G-12304)*

6036 Savings Institutions, Except Federal

Belmont Savings Bank .... E 740 695-0140
Saint Clairsville *(G-16627)*

Farmers Savings Bank .... E 330 648-2441
Spencer *(G-17106)*

Fort Jennings State Bank .... E 419 286-2527
Fort Jennings *(G-11108)*

Geauga Savings Bank .... E 440 564-9441
Newbury *(G-15257)*

Harrison Building and Ln Assn .... E 513 367-2015
Harrison *(G-11801)*

Home Savings Bank .... D 330 499-1900
North Canton *(G-15344)*

Hometown Bank .... E 330 673-9827
Kent *(G-12373)*

Huntington National Bank .... E 740 335-3771
Wshngtn CT Hs *(G-20027)*

Mechanics Bank .... E 419 524-0831
Mansfield *(G-13337)*

Resolute Bank .... D 419 868-1750
Maumee *(G-13970)*

The Peoples Savings and Ln Co .... E 937 653-1600
Urbana *(G-18601)*

Union Savings Bank .... D 937 434-1254
Dayton *(G-9944)*

United Community Fincl Corp .... C 330 742-0500
Youngstown *(G-20397)*

Wesbanco Bank Inc .... E 513 741-5766
Cincinnati *(G-4833)*

6061 Federal Credit Unions

Aur Group Financial Credit Un .... E 513 737-0508
Hamilton *(G-11694)*

Aurgroup Financial Credit Un .... D 513 942-4422
Fairfield *(G-10821)*

B F G Federal Credit Union .... D 330 374-2990
Akron *(G-87)*

Bayer Heritage Federal Cr Un .... C 740 929-2015
Hebron *(G-11845)*

Best Reward Credit Union .... E 216 367-8000
Cleveland *(G-5119)*

Bmi Federal Credit Union .... D 614 707-4000
Dublin *(G-10264)*

Bmi Federal Credit Union .... D 614 298-8527
Columbus *(G-7120)*

Canton School Employees Fed Cr .... E 330 452-9801
Canton *(G-2298)*

Century Federal Credit Union .... E 216 535-3600
Cleveland *(G-5217)*

Cincinnati Central Cr Un Inc .... D 513 241-2050
Cincinnati *(G-3291)*

Cinco Credit Union .... E 513 281-9988
Cincinnati *(G-3341)*

Cinfed Federal Credit Union .... D 513 333-3800
Cincinnati *(G-3348)*

Clyde-Findlay Area Cr Un Inc .... E 419 547-7781
Clyde *(G-6812)*

Columbus Municipal Employees .... E 614 224-8890
Columbus *(G-7371)*

Corporate One Federal Cr Un .... D 614 825-9314
Columbus *(G-6878)*

Desco Federal Credit Union .... D 740 354-7791
Portsmouth *(G-16275)*

Dover Phila Federal Credit Un .... D 330 364-8874
Dover *(G-10187)*

Education First Credit Un Inc .... E 614 221-9376
Columbus *(G-7580)*

Fairview Hlth Sys Fderal Cr Un .... A 216 476-7000
Cleveland *(G-5567)*

Firelands Federal Credit Union .... E 419 483-4180
Bellevue *(G-1409)*

First Day Fincl Federal Cr Un .... E 937 222-4546
Dayton *(G-9548)*

First Miami Student Credit Un .... E 513 529-1251
Oxford *(G-15815)*

Fremont Federal Credit Union .... C 419 334-4434
Fremont *(G-11201)*

Glass City Federal Credit Un .... E 419 887-1000
Maumee *(G-13922)*

Honda Federal Credit Union .... E 937 642-6000
Marysville *(G-13624)*

Lima Superior Federal Cr Un .... C 419 223-9746
Lima *(G-12828)*

Miami University .... E 513 529-1251
Oxford *(G-15822)*

Midwest Cmnty Federal Cr Un .... E 419 782-9856
Defiance *(G-10050)*

Ohio Catholic Federal Cr Un .... E 216 663-6800
Cleveland *(G-6188)*

Ohio Healthcare Federal Cr Un .... E 614 737-6034
Dublin *(G-10413)*

River Valley Credit Union Inc .... D 937 859-1970
Miamisburg *(G-14344)*

Saint Francis De Sales Church .... E 440 884-2319
Cleveland *(G-6436)*

School Employees Lorain County .... E 440 324-3400
Elyria *(G-10678)*

Sun Federal Credit Union .... E 800 786-0945
Maumee *(G-13981)*

Sun Federal Credit Union .... D 419 537-0200
Toledo *(G-18207)*

True Core Federal Credit Union .... E 740 345-6608
Newark *(G-15241)*

Vacationland Federal Credit Un .... E 440 967-5155
Sandusky *(G-16808)*

6062 State Credit Unions

Advantage Credit Union Inc .... E 419 529-5603
Ontario *(G-15683)*

Atomic Credit Union Inc .... E 740 289-5060
Piketon *(G-16109)*

Aur Group Financial Credit Un .... E 513 737-0508
Hamilton *(G-11694)*

Buckeye State Credit Union .... D 330 253-9197
Akron *(G-117)*

C E S Credit Union Inc .... E 561 203-5443
Loudonville *(G-13088)*

C E S Credit Union Inc .... E 740 397-1136
Mount Vernon *(G-14880)*

C E S Credit Union Inc .... E 740 892-3323
Utica *(G-18610)*

Chaco Credit Union Inc .... E 513 785-3500
Hamilton *(G-11708)*

Credit Union of Ohio Inc .... E 614 487-6650
Hilliard *(G-11892)*

Cuso Corporation .... D 513 984-2876
Cincinnati *(G-3450)*

Day Air Credit Union Inc .... E 937 643-2160
Dayton *(G-9454)*

Day-Met Credit Union Inc .... E 937 236-2562
Moraine *(G-14767)*

Directions Credit Union Inc .... D 419 720-4769
Sylvania *(G-17583)*

Directions Credit Union Inc .... E 419 524-7113
Mansfield *(G-13292)*

Education First Credit Un Inc .... E 614 221-9376
Columbus *(G-7580)*

Erie Shores Credit Union Inc .... E 419 897-8110
Maumee *(G-13912)*

Firefighters Cmnty Cr Un Inc .... E 216 621-4644
Cleveland *(G-5587)*

General Electric Credit Union .... D 513 243-4328
Cincinnati *(G-3671)*

Employee Codes: A=Over 500 employees, B=251-500
C=101-250, D=51-100, E=25-50

2018 Harris Ohio
Services Directory

965

60 DEPOSITORY INSTITUTIONS

Greater Cincinnati Credit Un .... E 513 559-1234
  Mason *(G-13711)*
Hancock Federal Credit Union .... E 419 420-0338
  Findlay *(G-11041)*
Homeland Credit Union Inc .... D 740 775-3024
  Chillicothe *(G-2847)*
Homeland Credit Union Inc .... E 740 775-3331
  Chillicothe *(G-2848)*
Kemba Credit Union Inc .... C 513 762-5070
  West Chester *(G-19100)*
Kemba Financial Credit Un Inc .... C 614 853-9774
  Columbus *(G-7974)*
Kemba Financial Credit Union .... D 614 235-2395
  Columbus *(G-7975)*
Lima Superior Federal Cr Un .... E 419 738-4512
  Wapakoneta *(G-18802)*
Midusa Credit Union .... E 513 420-8640
  Middletown *(G-14440)*
Midusa Credit Union .... E 513 420-8640
  Middletown *(G-14482)*
Ohio Educational Credit Union .... E 216 621-6296
  Seven Hills *(G-16833)*
Pse Credit Union Inc .... E 440 843-8300
  Cleveland *(G-6330)*
Seven Seventeen Credit Un Inc .... C 330 372-8100
  Warren *(G-18897)*
Seven Seventeen Credit Un Inc .... E 330 372-8100
  Warren *(G-18898)*
Sun Federal Credit Union .... D 419 537-0200
  Toledo *(G-18207)*
Taleris Credit Union Inc .... E 216 739-2300
  Cleveland *(G-6568)*
Telhio Credit Union Inc .... E 614 221-3233
  Columbus *(G-8829)*
Telhio Credit Union Inc .... E 614 221-3233
  Columbus *(G-8830)*
Universal 1 Credit Union Inc .... D 800 762-9555
  Dayton *(G-9950)*
Wright-Patt Credit Union Inc .... E 937 912-7000
  Beavercreek *(G-1223)*

6099 Functions Related To Deposit Banking, NEC

Allied Cash Holdings LLC .... D 305 371-3141
  Cincinnati *(G-2991)*
Buckeye Check Cashing Inc .... C 614 798-5900
  Dublin *(G-10271)*
Cashland Financial Svcs Inc .... E 937 253-7842
  Dayton *(G-9387)*
Check N Go of Iowa Inc .... E 563 359-7800
  Cincinnati *(G-3235)*
Checksmart Financial Company .... E 614 798-5900
  Dublin *(G-10289)*
Chemical Bank .... D 330 965-5806
  Youngstown *(G-20138)*
CNG Financial Corporation .... B 513 336-7735
  Cincinnati *(G-3375)*
Community Choice Financial Inc .... D 440 602-9922
  Willoughby *(G-19655)*
First Data Gvrnment Sltions LP .... D 513 489-9599
  Blue Ash *(G-1594)*
Huntington National Bank .... D 614 480-0067
  Columbus *(G-7868)*
Huntington National Bank .... D 614 336-4620
  Dublin *(G-10369)*
Jpmorgan Chase Bank Nat Assn .... E 740 423-4111
  Belpre *(G-1439)*
◆ Jpmorgan Chase Bank Nat Assn ...... A 614 436-3055
  Columbus *(G-6888)*
Klarna Inc .... E 614 615-4705
  Columbus *(G-7995)*
Mary C Enterprises Inc .... D 937 253-6169
  Dayton *(G-9701)*
National Consumer Coop Bnk .... E 937 393-4246
  Hillsboro *(G-11988)*
Nationwide Biweekly ADM Inc .... C 937 376-5800
  Xenia *(G-20071)*
Ohio Check Cashers Inc .... E 513 559-0220
  Cincinnati *(G-4203)*
PNC Bank-Atm .... E 937 865-6800
  Miamisburg *(G-14336)*
Ptc Holdings Inc .... B 216 771-6960
  Cleveland *(G-6331)*
Sack n Save Inc .... E 740 382-2464
  Marion *(G-13578)*
Southwestern PCF Spclty Fin Inc .... E 513 336-7735
  Cincinnati *(G-4555)*

61 NONDEPOSITORY CREDIT INSTITUTIONS

6111 Federal Credit Agencies

Columbus Metro Federal Cr Un .... E 614 239-0210
  Columbus *(G-7368)*
Columbus Metro Federal Cr Un .... E 614 239-0210
  Columbus *(G-7369)*
Hanna Holdings Inc .... E 440 971-5600
  North Royalton *(G-15492)*
National Cooperative Bank NA .... D 937 393-4246
  Hillsboro *(G-11989)*

6141 Personal Credit Institutions

722 Redemption Funding Inc .... E 513 679-8302
  Cincinnati *(G-2948)*
Affordable Cars & Finance Inc .... E 440 777-2424
  North Olmsted *(G-15410)*
Caliber Home Loans Inc .... E 937 435-5363
  Dayton *(G-9376)*
Central Credit Corp .... D 614 856-5840
  Reynoldsburg *(G-16436)*
Citizens Capital Markets Inc .... E 216 589-0900
  Cleveland *(G-5244)*
Dfs Corporate Services LLC .... E 614 283-2499
  New Albany *(G-14983)*
Education Loan Servicing Corp .... D 216 706-8130
  Cleveland *(G-5527)*
Farm Credit Mid-America .... E 740 441-9312
  Albany *(G-519)*
General Electric Company .... A 330 433-5163
  Canton *(G-2378)*
General Revenue Corporation .... B 513 469-1472
  Mason *(G-13707)*
Homeland Credit Union Inc .... E 740 775-3331
  Chillicothe *(G-2848)*
Howard Hanna Smythe Cramer .... D 330 725-4137
  Medina *(G-14078)*
Macys Cr & Customer Svcs Inc .... A 513 398-5221
  Mason *(G-13734)*
▼ Mtd Holdings Inc .... B 330 225-2600
  Valley City *(G-18622)*
PNC Bank National Association .... D 440 546-6760
  Brecksville *(G-1841)*
Security Nat Auto Accptnce LLC .... C 513 459-8118
  Mason *(G-13758)*
Security National Bank & Tr Co .... C 937 324-6800
  Springfield *(G-17272)*
Stark Federal Credit Union .... E 330 493-8325
  Canton *(G-2547)*
Student Loan Strategies LLC .... E 513 645-5400
  Cincinnati *(G-4597)*
Tebo Financial Services Inc .... E 234 207-2500
  Canton *(G-2558)*
Toyota Motor Credit Corp .... D 513 984-7100
  Blue Ash *(G-1698)*
United Consumer Fincl Svcs Co .... C 440 835-3230
  Cleveland *(G-6637)*

6153 Credit Institutions, Short-Term Business

Ally Financial Inc .... E 330 533-7300
  Canfield *(G-2182)*
Business Backer LLC .... E 513 792-6866
  Cincinnati *(G-3155)*
General Electric Company .... C 440 255-0930
  Mentor *(G-14179)*
General Electric Company .... E 937 534-2000
  Dayton *(G-9571)*
General Electric Company .... A 937 534-6920
  Dayton *(G-9570)*
Lakewood Acceptance Corp .... E 216 658-1234
  Cleveland *(G-5921)*
Morgan Stanley .... E 330 670-4600
  Akron *(G-347)*
Preferred Capital Lending Inc .... E 216 472-1391
  Cleveland *(G-6299)*
Relentless Recovery Inc .... D 216 621-8333
  Cleveland *(G-6301)*
Scott Fetzer Financial Group .... E 440 892-3000
  Cleveland *(G-6453)*
Sherman Financial Group LLC .... E 513 707-3000
  Cincinnati *(G-4516)*
Unifund Ccr LLC .... D 513 489-8877
  Blue Ash *(G-1709)*
Unifund Corporation .... E 513 489-8877
  Blue Ash *(G-1710)*

6159 Credit Institutions, Misc Business

BMW Financial Services Na LLC .... E 614 718-6900
  Hilliard *(G-11882)*
BMW Financial Services Na LLC .... C 614 718-6900
  Dublin *(G-10265)*
Dana Credit Corporation .... D 419 887-3000
  Maumee *(G-13903)*
Ford Motor Company .... E 513 573-1101
  Mason *(G-13702)*
Kempthorn Motors Inc .... D 330 452-6511
  Canton *(G-2424)*
Keybank National Association .... B 800 539-2968
  Cleveland *(G-5899)*
Kings Cove Automotive LLC .... D 513 677-0177
  Fairfield *(G-10870)*
Klaben Leasing and Sales Inc .... D 330 673-9971
  Kent *(G-12382)*
Lancaster Pollard Mrtg Co LLC .... D 614 224-8800
  Columbus *(G-8034)*
Mtd Acceptance Corp Inc .... B 330 225-2600
  Valley City *(G-18621)*
N C B International Department .... D 216 488-7990
  Cleveland *(G-6097)*
◆ Ohio Machinery Co .... C 440 526-6200
  Broadview Heights *(G-1886)*
PNC Equipment Finance LLC .... D 513 421-9191
  Cincinnati *(G-4310)*
Producers Credit Corporation .... E 614 433-2150
  Columbus *(G-8565)*
Reynolds and Reynolds Company .... A 937 485-2000
  Kettering *(G-12435)*
Ricoh Usa Inc .... D 513 984-9898
  Blue Ash *(G-1683)*
Security Nat Auto Accptnce LLC .... C 513 459-8118
  Mason *(G-13758)*
Summit Funding Group Inc .... D 513 489-1222
  Mason *(G-13765)*

6162 Mortgage Bankers & Loan Correspondents

American Equity Mortgage Inc .... D 800 236-2600
  Dublin *(G-10247)*
American Midwest Mortgage Corp .... E 440 882-5210
  Cleveland *(G-5014)*
Amerifirst Financial Corp .... D 216 452-5120
  Lakewood *(G-12470)*
Broadview Mortgage Company .... E 614 854-7000
  Powell *(G-16327)*
Chase Manhattan Mortgage Corp .... C 614 422-7982
  Columbus *(G-7253)*
Chase Manhattan Mortgage Corp .... A 614 422-6900
  Columbus *(G-7254)*
Fairway Independent Mrtg Corp .... E 513 367-6344
  Harrison *(G-11798)*
Fairway Independent Mrtg Corp .... E 614 930-6552
  Columbus *(G-7632)*
Farm Credit Mid-America .... E 740 441-9312
  Albany *(G-519)*
Fifth Third Bank .... D 513 579-5203
  Cincinnati *(G-3608)*
Fifth Third Bank of Sthrn OH .... E 937 840-5353
  Hillsboro *(G-11974)*
First Day Fincl Federal Cr Un .... E 937 222-4546
  Dayton *(G-9548)*
First Federal Bank of Midwest .... E 419 695-1055
  Delphos *(G-10143)*
First Ohio Banc & Lending Inc .... B 216 642-8900
  Cleveland *(G-5599)*
First Ohio Home Finance Inc .... E 937 322-3396
  Springfield *(G-17199)*
First Union Banc Corp .... E 330 896-1222
  Uniontown *(G-18521)*
Firstmerit Mortgage Corp .... D 330 478-3400
  Canton *(G-2368)*
FNB Corporation .... D 330 721-7484
  Medina *(G-14066)*
FNB Corporation .... D 330 425-1818
  Twinsburg *(G-18416)*
G & G Investment LLC .... E 513 984-0300
  Blue Ash *(G-1598)*
Hallmark Home Mortgage LLC .... E 614 568-1960
  Columbus *(G-7795)*
Home Loan Financial Corp .... E 740 622-0444
  Coshocton *(G-9106)*
Huntington National Bank .... C 513 762-1860
  Cincinnati *(G-3799)*
Huntington National Bank .... E 740 773-2681
  Chillicothe *(G-2852)*
Huntington National Bank .... E 419 226-8200
  Lima *(G-12801)*

62 SECURITY AND COMMODITY BROKERS, DEALERS, EXCHANGES, AND SERVICES

◆ Jpmorgan Chase Bank Nat Assn ......A 614 436-3055
   Columbus *(G-6888)*
Lancaster Pollard Mrtg Co LLC ....D 614 224-8800
   Columbus *(G-8034)*
Liberty Capital Services LLC ....E 614 505-0620
   Worthington *(G-19973)*
Liberty Mortgage Company Inc ....E 614 224-4000
   Columbus *(G-8057)*
M/I Financial LLC ....D 614 418-8650
   Columbus *(G-8094)*
M/I Homes Inc ....B 614 418-8000
   Columbus *(G-8095)*
MB Financial Inc ....D 937 283-2027
   Wilmington *(G-19772)*
Mortgage Now Inc ....E 800 245-1050
   Cleveland *(G-6079)*
National City Mortgage Inc ....A 937 910-1200
   Miamisburg *(G-14325)*
Nations Lending Corporation ....D 440 842-4817
   Independence *(G-12238)*
Nationstar Mortgage LLC ....D 614 985-9500
   Columbus *(G-8228)*
Northern Ohio Investment Co ....D 419 885-8300
   Sylvania *(G-17601)*
Old Rpblic Ttle Nthrn Ohio LLC ....A 216 524-5700
   Independence *(G-12242)*
Pgim Inc ....E 419 331-6604
   Lima *(G-12858)*
Precision Funding Corp ....E 330 405-1313
   Twinsburg *(G-18455)*
Primero Home Loans LLC ....D 877 959-2921
   Dublin *(G-10431)*
Priority Mortgage Corp ....E 614 431-1141
   Worthington *(G-19986)*
Quicken Loans Inc ....E 216 586-8900
   Cleveland *(G-6336)*
Rapid Mortgage Company ....E 937 748-8888
   Dayton *(G-9842)*
Realty Corporation of America ....E 216 522-0020
   Cleveland Heights *(G-6795)*
Red Mortgage Capital LLC ....E 614 857-1400
   Columbus *(G-8599)*
Residential Finance Corp ....B 614 324-4700
   Columbus *(G-8619)*
Security Savings Mortgage Corp ....D 330 455-2833
   Canton *(G-2524)*
Sibcy Cline Inc ....D 513 777-8100
   West Chester *(G-19152)*
Sirva Mortgage Inc ....D 800 531-3837
   Independence *(G-12258)*
Sunrise Mortgage Services Inc ....E 614 989-5412
   Gahanna *(G-11271)*
Union Home Mortgage Corp ....E 440 234-4300
   Strongsville *(G-17517)*
Vinton County Nat Bnk McArthur ....E 740 596-2525
   Mc Arthur *(G-14019)*
Wells Fargo Home Mortgage Inc ....E 614 781-8847
   Dublin *(G-10490)*

6163 Loan Brokers

All State Home Mortgage Inc ....D 216 261-7700
   Euclid *(G-10742)*
American Eagle Mortgage Co LLC ....E 440 988-2900
   Lorain *(G-13011)*
Best Reward Credit Union ....E 216 367-8000
   Cleveland *(G-5119)*
Board of Dir of Wittenbe ....E 937 327-6310
   Springfield *(G-17152)*
Caliber Home Loans Inc ....E 937 435-5363
   Dayton *(G-9376)*
Clyde-Findlay Area Cr Un Inc ....E 419 547-7781
   Clyde *(G-6812)*
Columbus Metro Federal Cr Un ....E 614 239-0210
   Columbus *(G-7369)*
Commonwealth Financial Svcs ....E 440 449-7709
   Cleveland *(G-5379)*
Directions Credit Union Inc ....E 419 524-7113
   Mansfield *(G-13292)*
Equitable Mortgage Corporation ....E 614 764-1232
   Columbus *(G-7602)*
Equity Consultants LLC ....D 330 659-7600
   Seven Hills *(G-16829)*
Firefighters Cmnty Cr Un Inc ....E 216 621-4644
   Cleveland *(G-5587)*
Firelands Federal Credit Union ....E 419 483-4180
   Bellevue *(G-1409)*
First Merchants Bank ....E 614 486-9000
   Columbus *(G-7666)*
Forest City Residential Dev ....E 216 621-6060
   Cleveland *(G-5621)*

Fremont Federal Credit Union ....C 419 334-4434
   Fremont *(G-11201)*
George W Mc Cloy ....D 614 457-6233
   Columbus *(G-7744)*
Guardian Savings Bank ....E 513 942-3535
   West Chester *(G-19086)*
Guardian Savings Bank ....E 513 528-8787
   Cincinnati *(G-3717)*
Henry County Bank ....E 419 599-1065
   Napoleon *(G-14942)*
Manhattan Mortgage Group Ltd ....E 614 933-8955
   Blacklick *(G-1510)*
Nations Lending Corporation ....D 440 842-4817
   Independence *(G-12238)*
Nationstar Mortgage LLC ....D 614 985-9500
   Columbus *(G-8228)*
Osgood State Bank (inc) ....E 419 582-2681
   Osgood *(G-15792)*
Precision Funding Corp ....E 330 405-1313
   Twinsburg *(G-18455)*
Premiere Service Mortgage Corp ....E 513 546-9895
   West Chester *(G-19130)*
Randall Mortgage Services ....E 614 336-7948
   Dublin *(G-10437)*
Real Estate Mortgage Corp ....D 440 356-5373
   Chagrin Falls *(G-2704)*
Second National Bank ....E 937 548-2122
   Greenville *(G-11519)*
Seven Seventeen Credit Un Inc ....C 330 372-8100
   Warren *(G-18897)*
Seven Seventeen Credit Un Inc ....E 330 372-8100
   Warren *(G-18898)*
Sibcy Cline Mortgage Services ....E 513 984-6776
   Cincinnati *(G-4524)*
◆ State Bank and Trust Company ....E 419 783-8950
   Defiance *(G-10058)*
The Peoples Savings and Ln Co ....E 937 653-1600
   Urbana *(G-18601)*
Union Mortgage Services Inc ....E 614 457-4815
   Columbus *(G-8889)*
Welles Bowen Realty Inc ....D 419 535-0011
   Toledo *(G-18300)*
William D Taylor Sr Inc ....D 614 653-6683
   Etna *(G-10740)*

62 SECURITY AND COMMODITY BROKERS, DEALERS, EXCHANGES, AND SERVICES

6211 Security Brokers & Dealers

Ameriprise Financial Svcs Inc ....D 614 846-8723
   Worthington *(G-19940)*
Axa Advisors LLC ....C 614 985-3015
   Columbus *(G-7079)*
Bowers Insurance Agency Inc ....E 330 638-6146
   Cortland *(G-9073)*
Brown Gibbons Lang & Co LLC ....E 216 241-2800
   Cleveland *(G-5150)*
Cadle Company II Inc ....C 330 872-0918
   Newton Falls *(G-15273)*
Charles Schwab & Co Inc ....E 330 908-4478
   Richfield *(G-16500)*
Charles Schwab Corporation ....E 440 617-2301
   Westlake *(G-19473)*
Charles Schwab Corporation ....E 216 291-9333
   Cleveland *(G-5229)*
Cincinnati Financial Corp ....A 513 870-2000
   Fairfield *(G-10833)*
Citigroup Global Markets Inc ....D 860 291-4181
   Beavercreek *(G-1233)*
Citigroup Global Markets Inc ....D 513 579-8300
   Cincinnati *(G-3355)*
Citigroup Global Markets Inc ....E 419 842-5383
   Toledo *(G-17806)*
Citigroup Global Markets Inc ....E 440 617-2000
   Cleveland *(G-5243)*
Columbus Metro Federal Cr Un ....E 614 239-0210
   Columbus *(G-7368)*
Corporate Fin Assoc of Clumbus ....E 614 457-9219
   Columbus *(G-7444)*
Cowen and Company LLC ....E 440 331-3531
   Rocky River *(G-16575)*
Deutsche Bank Securities Inc ....E 440 237-0188
   Broadview Heights *(G-1878)*
Diamond Hill Capital MGT Inc ....E 614 255-3333
   Columbus *(G-7516)*
Equity Resources Inc ....E 513 518-6318
   Cincinnati *(G-3571)*

First Command Fincl Plg Inc ....E 937 429-4490
   Beavercreek *(G-1241)*
Haven Financial Enterprise ....E 800 265-2401
   Cleveland *(G-5732)*
Hbi Payments Ltd ....D 614 944-5788
   Columbus *(G-7806)*
Huntington Insurance Inc ....E 614 480-3800
   Columbus *(G-7866)*
Ifs Financial Services Inc ....E 513 362-8000
   Westerville *(G-19410)*
Independence Capital Corp ....E 440 888-7000
   Cleveland *(G-5810)*
Jdel Inc ....E 614 436-2418
   Columbus *(G-7938)*
◆ Jpmorgan Chase Bank Nat Assn ....A 614 436-3055
   Columbus *(G-6888)*
Keybanc Capital Markets Inc ....B 800 553-2240
   Cleveland *(G-5898)*
Kgbo Holdings Inc ....E 800 580-3101
   Centerville *(G-2682)*
Kidney & Hypertension Con ....E 330 649-9400
   Canton *(G-2425)*
Lancaster Pollard & Co LLC ....E 614 224-8800
   Columbus *(G-8033)*
Linsalata Capital Partners Fun ....C 440 684-1400
   Cleveland *(G-5945)*
MAI Capital Management LLC ....E 216 920-4913
   Cleveland *(G-5968)*
Mc Cloy Financial Services ....D 614 457-6233
   Columbus *(G-8133)*
McM Capital Partners ....B 216 514-1840
   Beachwood *(G-1098)*
Merrill Lynch Pierce Fenner ....E 419 891-2091
   Perrysburg *(G-16032)*
Merrill Lynch Pierce Fenner ....E 614 475-2798
   Columbus *(G-8150)*
Merrill Lynch Pierce Fenner ....E 740 452-3681
   Zanesville *(G-20501)*
Merrill Lynch Pierce Fenner ....E 614 225-3197
   Springfield *(G-17243)*
Merrill Lynch Pierce Fenner ....E 937 847-4000
   Miamisburg *(G-14319)*
Merrill Lynch Pierce Fenner ....E 614 225-3000
   Columbus *(G-8151)*
Merrill Lynch Pierce Fenner ....E 330 670-2400
   Akron *(G-338)*
Merrill Lynch Pierce Fenner ....C 216 363-6500
   Cleveland *(G-6030)*
Merrill Lynch Pierce Fenner ....D 330 670-2400
   Akron *(G-339)*
Merrill Lynch Pierce Fenner ....E 614 825-0350
   Columbus *(G-6895)*
Merrill Lynch Pierce Fenner ....E 216 292-8000
   Cleveland *(G-6031)*
Merrill Lynch Pierce Fenner ....E 513 562-2100
   Cincinnati *(G-4080)*
Merrill Lynch Pierce Fenner ....E 614 798-4354
   Dublin *(G-10395)*
Merrill Lynch Pierce Fenner ....E 330 497-6600
   Canton *(G-2460)*
Merrill Lynch Pierce Fenner ....E 330 702-7300
   Canfield *(G-2200)*
Merrill Lynch Pierce Fenner ....E 330 702-0535
   Canfield *(G-2201)*
Merrill Lynch Pierce Fenner ....E 330 655-2312
   Hudson *(G-12132)*
Merrill Lynch Pierce Fenner ....E 330 670-2400
   Bath *(G-1034)*
Morgan Stanley ....E 513 721-2000
   Cincinnati *(G-4118)*
Morgan Stanley ....E 440 835-6750
   Westlake *(G-19518)*
Morgan Stanley ....E 216 523-3000
   Cleveland *(G-6076)*
Morgan Stanley ....D 614 473-2086
   Columbus *(G-8188)*
Morgan Stanley & Co LLC ....E 614 798-3100
   Dublin *(G-10400)*
Morgan Stanley & Co LLC ....E 614 228-0600
   Columbus *(G-8189)*
Morgan Stnley Smith Barney LLC ....E 216 360-4900
   Cleveland *(G-6077)*
Nationwide Fin Inst Dis Agency ....D 614 249-6825
   Columbus *(G-8241)*
Nationwide Inv Svcs Corp ....D 614 249-7111
   Columbus *(G-8244)*
◆ Nationwide Life Insur Co Amer ....A 800 688-5175
   Columbus *(G-8245)*
O N Equity Sales Company ....A 513 794-6794
   Montgomery *(G-14728)*

Ohio Department of Commerce ..... E 614 644-7381
Columbus *(G-8325)*

Old Rpblic Ttle Nthrn Ohio LLC ..... A 216 524-5700
Independence *(G-12242)*

R B C Apollo Equity Partners ..... E 216 875-2626
Cleveland *(G-6338)*

Raymond James Fincl Svcs Inc ..... E 513 287-6777
Cincinnati *(G-4388)*

Raymond James Fincl Svcs Inc ..... E 419 586-5121
Celina *(G-2661)*

Red Capital Markets LLC ..... C 614 857-1400
Columbus *(G-8597)*

Riverside Partners LLC ..... E 216 344-1040
Cleveland *(G-6400)*

Robert W Baird & Co Inc ..... E 216 737-7330
Cleveland *(G-6404)*

Ross Sinclaire & Assoc LLC ..... E 513 381-3939
Cincinnati *(G-4441)*

Shane Security Services Inc ..... D 330 757-4001
Poland *(G-16226)*

Sirak Financial Services Inc ..... D 330 493-0642
Canton *(G-2530)*

Southwest Financial Svcs Ltd ..... C 513 621-6699
Cincinnati *(G-4552)*

Stateco Financial Services ..... C 614 464-5000
Columbus *(G-8784)*

Stonehenge Fincl Holdings Inc ..... E 614 246-2500
Columbus *(G-8791)*

The Cadle Company ..... C 330 872-0918
Newton Falls *(G-15278)*

The Huntington Investment Co ..... E 614 480-3600
Columbus *(G-8836)*

The Huntington Investment Co ..... E 513 351-2555
Cincinnati *(G-4643)*

UBS Financial Services Inc ..... D 513 576-5000
Cincinnati *(G-4715)*

UBS Financial Services Inc ..... D 419 318-5525
Sylvania *(G-17625)*

UBS Financial Services Inc ..... E 937 428-1300
Dayton *(G-9942)*

UBS Financial Services Inc ..... E 513 792-2146
Cincinnati *(G-4716)*

UBS Financial Services Inc ..... E 216 831-3400
Cleveland *(G-6628)*

UBS Financial Services Inc ..... E 614 460-6559
Columbus *(G-8883)*

UBS Financial Services Inc ..... E 614 442-6240
Columbus *(G-8884)*

UBS Financial Services Inc ..... E 937 223-3141
Miamisburg *(G-14362)*

UBS Financial Services Inc ..... E 513 792-2100
Cincinnati *(G-4717)*

Ultimus Fund Solutions LLC ..... E 513 587-3400
Cincinnati *(G-4725)*

Valmark Insurance Agency LLC ..... D 330 576-1234
Akron *(G-492)*

Valmark Securities Inc ..... E 330 576-1234
Akron *(G-493)*

Van Dyk Mortgage Corporation ..... E 513 429-2122
Mason *(G-13777)*

Wells Fargo Clearing Svcs LLC ..... E 614 764-2040
Dublin *(G-10489)*

Wells Fargo Clearing Svcs LLC ..... E 216 378-2722
Cleveland *(G-6730)*

Wells Fargo Clearing Svcs LLC ..... E 614 221-8371
Columbus *(G-8976)*

Wells Fargo Clearing Svcs LLC ..... E 419 356-3272
Toledo *(G-18302)*

Wells Fargo Clearing Svcs LLC ..... E 440 835-9250
Westlake *(G-19565)*

Wells Fargo Clearing Svcs LLC ..... E 419 720-9700
Toledo *(G-18303)*

Wells Fargo Clearing Svcs LLC ..... E 513 241-9900
Cincinnati *(G-4831)*

Wells Fargo Clearing Svcs LLC ..... D 216 574-7300
Cleveland *(G-6731)*

Western & Southern Lf Insur Co ..... A 513 629-1800
Cincinnati *(G-4839)*

Western Southern Mutl Holdg Co ..... A 866 832-7719
Cincinnati *(G-4844)*

Western Sthern Fincl Group Inc ..... A 866 832-7719
Cincinnati *(G-4845)*

Westmnster Fncl Securities Inc ..... E 937 898-5010
Dayton *(G-9995)*

Wunderlich Securities Inc ..... E 440 646-1400
Cleveland *(G-6763)*

6221 Commodity Contracts Brokers & Dealers

Merrill Lynch Pierce Fenner ..... E 937 847-4000
Miamisburg *(G-14319)*

Merrill Lynch Pierce Fenner ..... D 330 670-2400
Akron *(G-339)*

Wells Fargo Clearing Svcs LLC ..... D 216 574-7300
Cleveland *(G-6731)*

6282 Investment Advice

American Money Management Corp ..... E 513 579-2592
Cincinnati *(G-3008)*

Ameriprise Financial Svcs Inc ..... E 330 494-9300
Akron *(G-74)*

Ameriprise Financial Svcs Inc ..... E 614 934-4057
Dublin *(G-10253)*

Ameriprise Financial Svcs Inc ..... D 614 846-8723
Worthington *(G-19940)*

Bartlett & Co LLC ..... D 513 621-4612
Cincinnati *(G-3081)*

Brookdale Senior Living Inc ..... D 855 308-2438
Cincinnati *(G-3138)*

Brown WD General Agency Inc ..... D 216 241-5840
Cleveland *(G-5152)*

C H Dean Inc ..... D 937 222-9531
Beavercreek *(G-1156)*

Carnegie Capital Asset MGT LLC ..... E 216 595-1349
Cleveland *(G-5185)*

Centaurus Financial Inc ..... D 419 756-9747
Mansfield *(G-13273)*

Cleveland Research Company LLC ..... E 216 649-7250
Cleveland *(G-5343)*

CNG Financial Corp ..... A 513 336-7735
Cincinnati *(G-3374)*

Crestview Partners II Gp LP ..... B 216 898-2400
Brooklyn *(G-1905)*

Cw Financial LLC ..... B 941 907-9490
Beachwood *(G-1070)*

Diamond Hill Funds ..... E 614 255-3333
Columbus *(G-7517)*

Direct Maintenance LLC ..... E 330 744-5211
Youngstown *(G-20169)*

Eubel Brady Suttman Asset Mgt ..... E 937 291-1223
Miamisburg *(G-14300)*

Financial Engines Inc ..... E 330 726-3100
Boardman *(G-1739)*

Financial Network Group Ltd ..... E 513 469-7500
Cincinnati *(G-3610)*

Financial Plnners of Cleveland ..... E 440 473-1115
Cleveland *(G-5586)*

Fort Wash Inv Advisors Inc ..... D 513 361-7600
Cincinnati *(G-3639)*

Fund Evaluation Group LLC ..... E 513 977-4400
Cincinnati *(G-3658)*

Ifs Financial Services Inc ..... E 513 362-8000
Westerville *(G-19410)*

Johnson Trust Co ..... C 513 598-8859
Cincinnati *(G-3884)*

Jpmorgan Inv Advisors Inc ..... A 614 248-5800
Columbus *(G-6890)*

Kemba Financial Credit Un Inc ..... D 614 235-2395
Columbus *(G-7973)*

Lancaster Pollard Mrtg Co LLC ..... D 614 224-8800
Columbus *(G-8034)*

Lang Financial Group Inc ..... E 513 699-2966
Blue Ash *(G-1626)*

Lassiter Corporation ..... E 216 391-4800
Cleveland *(G-5927)*

Lincoln Fincl Advisors Corp ..... E 216 765-7400
Beachwood *(G-1096)*

Longbow Research LLC ..... D 216 986-0700
Independence *(G-12230)*

MAI Capital Management LLC ..... D 216 920-4800
Cleveland *(G-5967)*

Mc Cormack Advisors Intl ..... E 216 522-1200
Cleveland *(G-5998)*

Meeder Asset Management Inc ..... D 614 760-2112
Dublin *(G-10394)*

Merrill Lynch Pierce Fenner ..... D 614 225-3152
Columbus *(G-8149)*

Merrill Lynch Pierce Fenner ..... D 740 335-2930
Wshngtn CT Hs *(G-20031)*

Merrill Lynch Pierce Fenner ..... C 216 363-6500
Cleveland *(G-6030)*

Merrill Lynch Pierce Fenner ..... E 937 847-4000
Miamisburg *(G-14319)*

Merrill Lynch Pierce Fenner ..... D 614 225-3000
Columbus *(G-8151)*

Merrill Lynch Pierce Fenner ..... D 330 670-2400
Akron *(G-339)*

Morgan Stanley ..... D 614 473-2086
Columbus *(G-8188)*

Morgan Stanley ..... E 513 721-2000
Cincinnati *(G-4118)*

Mt Washington Care Center Inc ..... C 513 231-4561
Cincinnati *(G-4130)*

Mutual Shareholder Svcs LLC ..... E 440 922-0067
Broadview Heights *(G-1884)*

Oak Associates Ltd ..... E 330 666-5263
Akron *(G-360)*

Parkwood Corporation ..... E 216 875-6500
Cleveland *(G-6244)*

Red Capital Partners LLC ..... D 614 857-1400
Columbus *(G-8598)*

S&P Global Inc ..... C 614 835-2444
Groveport *(G-11669)*

S&P Global Inc ..... C 330 482-9544
Leetonia *(G-12662)*

Sena Weller Rohs Williams ..... E 513 241-6443
Cincinnati *(G-4495)*

Standard Retirement Svcs Inc ..... E 440 808-2724
Westlake *(G-19551)*

Stepstone Group Real Estate LP ..... E 216 522-0330
Cleveland *(G-6538)*

Sterling Ltd Co ..... E 216 464-8850
Cleveland *(G-6539)*

Stonehenge Capital Company LLC ..... E 614 246-2456
Columbus *(G-8790)*

Stratos Wealth Partners Ltd ..... D 440 519-2500
Beachwood *(G-1127)*

Summit Financial Strategies ..... E 614 885-1115
Columbus *(G-8801)*

The Cadle Company ..... C 330 872-0918
Newton Falls *(G-15278)*

Victory Capital Management Inc ..... C 216 898-2400
Brooklyn *(G-1907)*

Westminster Financial Company ..... E 937 898-5010
Dayton *(G-9994)*

William D Taylor Sr Inc ..... D 614 653-6683
Etna *(G-10740)*

6289 Security & Commodity Svcs, NEC

Flex Fund Inc ..... E 614 766-7000
Dublin *(G-10348)*

63 INSURANCE CARRIERS

6311 Life Insurance Carriers

21st Century Financial Inc ..... E 330 668-9065
Akron *(G-9)*

Allstate Insurance Company ..... E 330 650-2917
Hudson *(G-12102)*

American Financial Group Inc ..... C 513 579-2121
Cincinnati *(G-3006)*

American Income Life Insur Co ..... D 440 582-0040
Cleveland *(G-5010)*

American Mutual Life Assn ..... E 216 531-1900
Cleveland *(G-5016)*

Ameritas Life Insurance Corp ..... E 513 595-2334
Cincinnati *(G-3015)*

Bankers Life & Casualty Co ..... E 614 987-0590
Columbus *(G-6870)*

Cincinnati Financial Corp ..... A 513 870-2000
Fairfield *(G-10833)*

Cincinnati Life Insurance Co ..... A 513 870-2000
Fairfield *(G-10836)*

Columbus Financial Gr ..... E 614 785-5100
Columbus *(G-6877)*

Columbus Life Insurance Co ..... D 513 361-6700
Cincinnati *(G-3390)*

Employers Mutual Casualty Co ..... D 513 221-6010
Blue Ash *(G-1585)*

Farmers Group Inc ..... C 614 406-2424
Columbus *(G-7638)*

Grange Indemnity Insurance Co ..... D 614 445-2900
Columbus *(G-7767)*

Grange Life Insurance Company ..... E 800 445-3030
Columbus *(G-7768)*

Great American Life Insur Co ..... E 513 357-3300
Cincinnati *(G-3699)*

Guardian Life Insur Co of Amer ..... E 513 579-1114
Cincinnati *(G-3716)*

Home Loan Financial Corp ..... E 740 622-0444
Coshocton *(G-9106)*

Howard Hanna Smythe Cramer ..... D 330 725-4137
Medina *(G-14078)*

Hylant Administrative Services ..... E 419 255-1020
Toledo *(G-17967)*

Irongate Inc ..... C 937 433-3300
Centerville *(G-2680)*

SIC SECTION — 63 INSURANCE CARRIERS

J P Farley Corporation .... E 440 250-4300
  Westlake *(G-19501)*
Kelley Companies .... D 330 668-6100
  Copley *(G-9057)*
Lafayette Life Insurance Co .... C 800 443-8793
  Cincinnati *(G-3958)*
Loyal American Life Insur Co .... C 800 633-6752
  Cincinnati *(G-4000)*
Massachusetts Mutl Lf Insur Co .... E 513 579-8555
  Cincinnati *(G-4028)*
Massachusetts Mutl Lf Insur Co .... E 216 592-7359
  Cleveland *(G-5993)*
Midland-Guardian Co .... A 513 943-7100
  Amelia *(G-582)*
Motorists Life Insurance Co .... E 614 225-8211
  Columbus *(G-8192)*
Nationwide Financial Svcs Inc ...... C 614 249-7111
  Columbus *(G-8242)*
Nationwide General Insur Co .... D 614 249-7111
  Columbus *(G-8243)*
Nationwide Mutual Insurance Co .. E 614 430-3047
  Lewis Center *(G-12697)*
Nationwide Mutual Insurance Co .. E 614 249-7111
  Columbus *(G-8247)*
New York Life Insurance Co .... D 216 221-1100
  Lakewood *(G-12492)*
Northwestern Mutl Lf Insur Co ...... E 614 221-5287
  Columbus *(G-8299)*
Ohio Casualty Insurance Co .... A 800 843-6446
  Fairfield *(G-10887)*
Ohio Nat Mutl Holdings Inc .... A 513 794-6100
  Montgomery *(G-14729)*
Ohio National Fincl Svcs Inc .... A 513 794-6100
  Montgomery *(G-14730)*
Ohio Pia Service Corporation .... E 614 552-8000
  Gahanna *(G-11261)*
Penn Mutual Life Insurance Co ..... E 330 668-9065
  Akron *(G-381)*
Progressive Bayside Insur Co .... B 440 395-4460
  Cleveland *(G-6312)*
Sirak Financial Services .... D 330 493-3211
  Canton *(G-2529)*
State Farm Mutl Auto Insur Co ...... A 614 775-2001
  New Albany *(G-15008)*
Summa Insurance Company Inc ... B 800 996-8411
  Akron *(G-462)*
Transamerica Premier Lf Insur ...... E 614 488-5983
  Columbus *(G-8864)*
Ulysses Caremark Holding Corp ... C 440 542-4214
  Solon *(G-17063)*
Union Central Life Insur Co .... A 866 696-7478
  Cincinnati *(G-4726)*
United American Insurance Co ..... E 440 265-9200
  Strongsville *(G-17518)*
United Omaha Life Insurance Co .. E 216 573-6900
  Cleveland *(G-6642)*
Voya Financial Inc .... E 614 431-5000
  Columbus *(G-8953)*
Western & Southern Lf Insur Co ... E 614 277-4800
  Grove City *(G-11615)*
Western & Southern Lf Insur Co ... E 419 524-1800
  Ontario *(G-15720)*
Western & Southern Lf Insur Co ... A 513 629-1800
  Cincinnati *(G-4839)*
Western & Southern Lf Insur Co ... E 234 380-4525
  Hudson *(G-12151)*

6321 Accident & Health Insurance

1-888 Ohio Comp LLC .... D 216 426-0646
  Cleveland *(G-4918)*
American Financial Group Inc .... C 513 579-2121
  Cincinnati *(G-3006)*
American Modern Home Svc Co .. E 513 943-7100
  Amelia *(G-575)*
American Modrn Insur Group Inc .. C 800 543-2644
  Amelia *(G-576)*
Aultcare Insurance Company .... B 330 363-6360
  Canton *(G-2250)*
Blue Cross & Blue Shield Mich ..... A 330 783-3841
  Youngstown *(G-20117)*
Caresource Management Group Co ... A 937 224-3300
  Dayton *(G-9381)*
Caresource Management Group Co ... E 614 221-3370
  Hilliard *(G-11888)*
Caresource Management Group Co ... E 937 224-3300
  Dayton *(G-9382)*
▲ Cincinnati Equitable Insur Co .... E 513 621-1826
  Cincinnati *(G-3301)*
Dawson Companies .... D 440 333-9000
  Richfield *(G-16503)*
Employers Mutual Casualty Co ..... D 513 221-6010
  Blue Ash *(G-1585)*
Farmers New World Lf Insur Co ... C 614 764-9975
  Columbus *(G-7642)*
Hometown Hospital Health Plan ... C 330 834-2200
  Massillon *(G-13820)*
J P Farley Corporation .... E 440 250-4300
  Westlake *(G-19501)*
James B Oswald Company .... E 330 723-3637
  Medina *(G-14085)*
Liberty Mutual Insurance Co .... E 614 855-6193
  Westerville *(G-19325)*
Medical Benefits Mutl Lf Insur ...... C 740 522-8425
  Newark *(G-15204)*
Medical Bnfits Admnstrtors Inc ..... D 740 522-8425
  Newark *(G-15205)*
Medical Mutual of Ohio .... B 216 292-0400
  Beachwood *(G-1099)*
Nationwide Corporation .... E 614 249-7111
  Columbus *(G-8238)*
Nationwide Mutual Insurance Co .. A 614 249-7111
  Columbus *(G-8247)*
Noor Home Health Care .... D 216 320-0803
  Cleveland Heights *(G-6794)*
Paramount Care Inc .... B 419 887-2500
  Maumee *(G-13955)*
Progressive Casualty Insur Co ..... D 440 603-4033
  Cleveland *(G-6314)*
Progressive Casualty Insur Co ..... A 440 461-5000
  Mayfield Village *(G-14012)*
Royal Health Services LLC .... E 614 826-1316
  Columbus *(G-8654)*
Signature Healthcare LLC .... C 440 232-1800
  Bedford *(G-1336)*
State Farm Mutl Auto Insur Co ...... A 614 775-2001
  New Albany *(G-15008)*
Summa Insurance Company Inc ... B 800 996-8411
  Akron *(G-462)*
Superior Dental Care Inc .... E 937 438-0283
  Dayton *(G-9916)*
Transamerica Premier Lf Insur ...... E 614 488-5983
  Columbus *(G-8864)*
Union Central Life Insur Co .... A 866 696-7478
  Cincinnati *(G-4726)*

6324 Hospital & Medical Svc Plans Carriers

1-888 Ohio Comp LLC .... D 216 426-0646
  Cleveland *(G-4918)*
Aetna Health California Inc .... E 614 933-6000
  New Albany *(G-14972)*
Aetna Life Insurance Company ..... E 330 659-8000
  Richfield *(G-16493)*
Amerigroup Ohio Inc .... E 513 733-2300
  Blue Ash *(G-1532)*
Anthem Insurance Companies Inc .... D 614 438-3542
  Worthington *(G-19941)*
Anthem Insurance Companies Inc .... E 330 492-2151
  Canton *(G-2242)*
Anthem Insurance Companies Inc .... C 330 783-9800
  Seven Hills *(G-16826)*
Aultcare Corp .... B 330 363-6360
  Canton *(G-2249)*
Aultman Hospital .... A 330 363-6262
  Canton *(G-2255)*
Benefit Services Inc .... D 330 666-0337
  Copley *(G-9053)*
Cigna Corporation .... C 216 642-1700
  Independence *(G-12197)*
Clinical Research Center .... D 513 636-4412
  Cincinnati *(G-3366)*
Close To Home Health Care Ctr ... E 614 932-9013
  Dublin *(G-10296)*
Community Insurance Company ... E 859 282-7888
  Cincinnati *(G-3401)*
Custom Design Benefits Inc .... E 513 598-2929
  Cincinnati *(G-3451)*
Dcp Holding Company .... D 513 554-1100
  Sharonville *(G-16881)*
Deaconess Associations Inc .... B 513 559-2100
  Cincinnati *(G-3471)*
Ebso Inc .... E 419 423-3823
  Findlay *(G-11021)*
Ebso Inc .... E 440 262-1133
  Cleveland *(G-5525)*
Family Health Plan Inc .... E 419 241-6501
  Toledo *(G-17877)*
Firelands Regional Health Sys ..... C 419 626-7400
  Sandusky *(G-16758)*
Healthspan Integrated Care .... E 440 937-2350
  Avon *(G-897)*
Healthspan Integrated Care .... E 216 621-5600
  Cleveland *(G-5740)*
Healthspan Integrated Care .... E 216 524-7377
  Cleveland *(G-5741)*
Healthspan Integrated Care .... E 440 572-1000
  Cleveland *(G-5743)*
Healthspan Integrated Care .... E 330 767-3436
  Brewster *(G-1855)*
Healthspan Integrated Care .... E 330 486-2800
  Twinsburg *(G-18428)*
Healthspan Integrated Care .... E 330 877-4018
  Hartville *(G-11821)*
Healthspan Integrated Care .... E 330 334-1549
  Wadsworth *(G-18754)*
Healthspan Integrated Care .... E 330 633-8400
  Akron *(G-261)*
Healthspan Integrated Care .... E 216 362-2277
  Lakewood *(G-12481)*
Humana Health Plan Ohio Inc ...... D 513 784-5200
  Cincinnati *(G-3796)*
Humana Inc .... E 330 877-5464
  Hartville *(G-11824)*
Humana Inc .... E 216 328-2047
  Independence *(G-12217)*
Humana Inc .... E 614 210-1038
  Dublin *(G-10368)*
J P Farley Corporation .... E 440 250-4300
  Westlake *(G-19501)*
Kelley Companies .... D 330 668-6100
  Copley *(G-9057)*
Massillon Cmnty Hosp Hlth Plan ... C 330 837-6880
  Massillon *(G-13835)*
Medical Mutual of Ohio .... A 216 687-7000
  Cleveland *(G-6015)*
Medical Mutual of Ohio .... B 419 473-7100
  Toledo *(G-18049)*
Metrohealth System .... E 216 778-3867
  Cleveland *(G-6042)*
Miami Valley Hospitalist Group ..... D 937 208-8394
  Dayton *(G-9734)*
Molina Healthcare Inc .... A 800 642-4168
  Columbus *(G-8183)*
Ohio Health Choice Inc .... D 800 554-0027
  Cleveland *(G-6191)*
Oxford Blazer Company Inc .... E 614 792-2220
  Dublin *(G-10419)*
Promedica Health Systems Inc .... A 567 585-7454
  Toledo *(G-18141)*
Uc Health Llc .... B 513 585-7600
  Cincinnati *(G-4719)*
United Healthcare Ohio Inc .... D 216 694-4080
  Cleveland *(G-6640)*
United Healthcare Ohio Inc .... B 614 410-7000
  Columbus *(G-8891)*
United Healthcare Ohio Inc .... C 513 603-6200
  Blue Ash *(G-1713)*
Unitedhealth Group Inc .... B 513 603-6200
  Cincinnati *(G-4744)*
Vitamin Shoppe Inc .... E 440 238-5987
  Strongsville *(G-17522)*

6331 Fire, Marine & Casualty Insurance

Affiliated FM Insurance Co .... E 216 362-4820
  North Olmsted *(G-15409)*
American Commerce Insurance Co ... C 614 272-6951
  Columbus *(G-6986)*
American Emprie Srpls Lines In ... D 513 369-3000
  Cincinnati *(G-3003)*
American Financial Group Inc .... C 513 579-2121
  Cincinnati *(G-3006)*
American Modern Home Insur Co .... D 513 943-7100
  Amelia *(G-574)*
American Select Insurance Co ..... A 330 887-0101
  Westfield Center *(G-19451)*
American Western Home Insur Co ... B 513 943-7100
  Amelia *(G-577)*
Amica Mutual Insurance Company ... E 866 942-6422
  West Chester *(G-19020)*
Amtrust North America Inc .... C 216 328-6100
  Cleveland *(G-5032)*
Broadspire Services Inc .... E 614 436-8990
  Columbus *(G-7148)*
Buckeye State Mutual Insur Co .... D 937 778-5000
  Piqua *(G-16138)*
Carrara Companies Inc .... D 330 659-2800
  Richfield *(G-16499)*
Celina Mutual Insurance Co .... C 419 586-5181
  Celina *(G-2638)*
Central Mutual Insurance Co .... B 419 238-1010
  Van Wert *(G-18629)*

63 INSURANCE CARRIERS

Century Surety Company ....E 614 895-2000
  Westerville (G-19293)
Cincinnati Casualty Company ....D 513 870-2000
  Fairfield (G-10832)
▲ Cincinnati Equitable Insur Co ....E 513 621-1826
  Cincinnati (G-3301)
Cincinnati Financial Corp ....A 513 870-2000
  Fairfield (G-10833)
Cincinnati Indemnity Co ....A 513 870-2000
  Fairfield (G-10835)
Erie Insurance Exchange ....D 330 568-1802
  Hubbard (G-12086)
Erie Insurance Exchange ....D 330 479-1010
  Canton (G-2358)
Erie Insurance Exchange ....C 614 436-0224
  Columbus (G-7605)
Erie Insurance Exchange ....D 330 433-1925
  Canton (G-2359)
Factory Mutual Insurance Co ....C 440 779-0651
  North Olmsted (G-15421)
Farmers Group Inc ....C 614 406-2424
  Columbus (G-7638)
Foremost Insurance Company ....D 216 674-7000
  Independence (G-12212)
Geico General Insurance Co ....B 513 794-3426
  Cincinnati (G-3666)
Grange Mutual Casualty Company ....A 614 445-2900
  Columbus (G-7769)
Grange Mutual Casualty Company ....E 513 671-3722
  Cincinnati (G-3692)
Great American Insurance Co ....A 513 369-5000
  Cincinnati (G-3697)
Great American Insurance Co ....D 513 603-2570
  Fairfield (G-10853)
Great American Insurance Co ....D 513 763-7035
  Cincinnati (G-3698)
Home and Farm Insurance Co ....D 937 778-5000
  Piqua (G-16149)
James B Oswald Company ....E 330 723-3637
  Medina (G-14085)
L Calvin Jones & Company ....E 330 533-1195
  Canfield (G-2198)
Lancer Insurance Company ....E 440 473-1634
  Cleveland (G-5925)
Liberty Mutual Insurance Co ....D 614 864-4100
  Gahanna (G-11253)
Liberty Mutual Insurance Co ....E 614 855-6193
  Westerville (G-19325)
Liberty Mutual Insurance Co ....D 513 984-0550
  Blue Ash (G-1628)
Midland-Guardian Co ....A 513 943-7100
  Amelia (G-582)
Motorists Coml Mutl Insur Co ....E 614 225-8211
  Columbus (G-8191)
Motorists Mutual Insurance Co ....A 614 225-8211
  Columbus (G-8193)
Motorists Mutual Insurance Co ....E 440 779-8900
  North Olmsted (G-15433)
Motorists Mutual Insurance Co ....E 330 896-9311
  Uniontown (G-18529)
Motorists Mutual Insurance Co ....E 937 435-5540
  Dayton (G-9759)
Munich Reinsurance America Inc ....E 614 221-7123
  Columbus (G-8209)
National Interstate Corp ....D 330 659-8900
  Richfield (G-16515)
National Interstate Insur Co ....C 330 659-8900
  Richfield (G-16516)
Nationwide General Insur Co ....D 614 249-7111
  Columbus (G-8243)
Nationwide Mutual Insurance Co ....A 614 249-7111
  Columbus (G-8247)
Northwestrn Natl Insur Company ....E 513 425-5899
  Middletown (G-14442)
Occupational Health Link ....E 614 885-0039
  Columbus (G-8312)
Ohic Insurance Company ....D 614 221-7777
  Columbus (G-8315)
Ohio Casualty Insurance Co ....A 800 843-6446
  Fairfield (G-10887)
Ohio Casualty Insurance Co ....C 513 867-3000
  Hamilton (G-11761)
Ohio Fair Plan Undwrt Assn ....E 614 839-6446
  Columbus (G-8344)
Ohio Farmers Insurance Company ....A 800 243-0210
  Westfield Center (G-19452)
Ohio Indemnity Company ....E 614 228-1601
  Columbus (G-8355)
Ohio Mutual Insurance Company ....C 419 562-3011
  Bucyrus (G-2046)

Ohio National Life Insur Co ....D 513 794-6100
  Montgomery (G-14732)
Permanent Gen Asrn Corp Ohio ....E 216 986-3000
  Cleveland (G-6266)
Personal Service Insurance Co ....B 800 282-9416
  Columbus (G-8538)
Platinum Restoration Contrs ....E 440 327-0699
  Elyria (G-10670)
Progressive Agency Inc ....C 440 461-5000
  Cleveland (G-6311)
Progressive Casualty Insur Co ....A 440 461-5000
  Mayfield Village (G-14012)
Progressive Casualty Insur Co ....E 440 683-8164
  Cleveland (G-6313)
Progressive Casualty Insur Co ....D 440 603-4033
  Cleveland (G-6314)
Progressive Choice Insur Co ....A 440 461-5000
  Cleveland (G-6315)
Progressive Corporation ....B 440 461-5000
  Cleveland (G-6317)
Progressive Max Insurance Co ....E 330 533-8733
  Youngstown (G-20329)
Progressive Northwestern Insur ....E 440 461-5000
  Cleveland (G-6319)
Progressive Select Insur Co ....A 440 461-5000
  Cleveland (G-6322)
Rod Lightning Mutual Insur Co ....B 330 262-9060
  Wooster (G-19908)
Rtw Inc ....E 614 594-9217
  Columbus (G-8657)
Safe Auto Insurance Company ....C 740 472-1900
  Woodsfield (G-19819)
Safe Auto Insurance Group Inc ....D 614 231-0200
  Columbus (G-8669)
Seven Hills Fireman Assn ....E 216 524-3321
  Seven Hills (G-16836)
State Auto Financial Corp ....E 614 464-5000
  Columbus (G-8780)
State Auto Prperty Cslty Insur ....E 440 842-6200
  Strongsville (G-17511)
State Automobile Mutl Insur Co ....A 833 724-3577
  Columbus (G-8781)
Utica National Insurance Group ....E 614 823-5300
  Columbus (G-8928)
Verti Insurance Company ....D 844 448-3784
  Columbus (G-8936)
Wayne Mutual Insurance Co ....E 330 345-8100
  Wooster (G-19924)
Western Reserve Group ....B 330 262-9060
  Wooster (G-19929)
Workers Compensation Ohio Bur ....A 614 644-6292
  Columbus (G-9007)

6351 Surety Insurance Carriers

American Commerce Insurance Co ....C 614 272-6951
  Columbus (G-6986)
Progressive Casualty Insur Co ....A 440 461-5000
  Mayfield Village (G-14012)
Progressive Corporation ....B 440 461-5000
  Cleveland (G-6317)
State Automobile Mutl Insur Co ....A 833 724-3577
  Columbus (G-8781)

6361 Title Insurance

A R E A Title Agency Inc ....E 419 242-5485
  Toledo (G-17735)
Accurate Group Holdings Inc ....D 216 520-1740
  Independence (G-12178)
Barristers of Ohio LLC ....E 330 898-5600
  Warren (G-18828)
Chicago Title Insurance Co ....D 330 873-9393
  Akron (G-132)
Entitle Direct Group Inc ....C 216 236-7800
  Independence (G-12209)
Fidelity National Fincl Inc ....E 614 865-1562
  Westerville (G-19401)
First American Equity Ln Svcs ....C 800 221-8683
  Cleveland (G-5588)
First American Title Insur Co ....E 216 241-1278
  Cleveland (G-5589)
First American Title Insur Co ....E 419 625-8505
  Sandusky (G-16760)
First American Title Insur Co ....C 740 450-0006
  South Zanesville (G-17103)
First Amrcn Cash Advnce SC LLC ....D 330 644-9144
  Akron (G-224)
Howard Hanna Smythe Cramer ....D 330 725-4137
  Medina (G-14078)
Landsel Title Agency Inc ....E 614 337-1928
  Gahanna (G-11252)

Lawyers Title Cincinnati Inc ....D 513 421-1313
  Cincinnati (G-3965)
Lawyers Title Company ....E 330 376-0000
  Akron (G-314)
Midland Title Security Inc ....D 216 241-6045
  Cleveland (G-6057)
Mortgage Information Services ....D 216 514-7480
  Cleveland (G-6078)
Northwest Hts Title Agcy LLC ....E 614 451-6313
  Columbus (G-8296)
Northwest Ttl Agy of OH MI In ....D 419 241-8195
  Toledo (G-18096)
Ohio Real Title Agency LLC ....E 216 373-9900
  Cleveland (G-6194)
Omega Title Agency LLC ....D 330 436-0600
  Stow (G-17384)
Port Lawrence Title and Tr Co ....E 419 244-4605
  Toledo (G-18130)
Resource Title Agency Inc ....D 216 520-0050
  Cleveland (G-6385)
Resource Title Nat Agcy Inc ....D 216 520-0050
  Independence (G-12248)
Search 2 Close Columbus Ltd ....E 614 389-5353
  Powell (G-16351)
Service Center Title Agency ....E 937 312-3080
  Dayton (G-9877)
Southern Title of Ohio Ltd ....E 419 525-4600
  Mansfield (G-13365)
Sterling Land Title Agency ....E 937 438-2000
  Dayton (G-9906)
Sterling Land Title Agency ....E 513 755-3700
  West Chester (G-19160)
Stewart Advnced Land Title Ltd ....E 513 753-2800
  Cincinnati (G-2933)
Stewart Title Company ....E 440 520-7130
  Willoughby (G-19716)
Title First Agency Inc ....E 614 224-9207
  Columbus (G-8850)
U S Title Agency Inc ....E 216 621-1424
  Cleveland (G-6627)
Valmer Land Title Agency ....E 614 860-0005
  Reynoldsburg (G-16488)
Valmer Land Title Agency ....E 614 875-7001
  Grove City (G-11608)

6371 Pension, Health & Welfare Funds

Ashtabula County Commissioners ....D 440 994-1206
  Ashtabula (G-717)
Clinton County Dept Jobs/Fmly ....D 937 382-0963
  Wilmington (G-19752)
County of Gallia ....D 740 446-3222
  Gallipolis (G-11311)
County of Seneca ....D 419 447-5011
  Tiffin (G-17675)
Great Amrcn Fncl Resources Inc ....C 513 333-5300
  Cincinnati (G-3700)
Great Amrcn Plan Admin Inc ....D 513 412-2316
  Cincinnati (G-3701)
Nationwide Rtirement Solutions ....C 614 854-8300
  Dublin (G-10405)
Ohio Pub Employees Rtrement Sys ....B 614 228-8471
  Columbus (G-8370)
Pharmacy Data Management Inc ....E 330 757-1500
  Youngstown (G-20319)
School Employees Retirement ....C 614 222-5853
  Columbus (G-8701)
State Tchers Rtrement Sys Ohio ....C 614 227-4090
  Columbus (G-8783)

6399 Insurance Carriers, NEC

American Contrs Indemnity Co ....E 513 688-0800
  Cincinnati (G-3001)
American Mutl Share Insur Corp ....E 614 764-1900
  Dublin (G-10251)
Dimension Service Corporation ....C 614 226-7455
  Dublin (G-10321)
Excess Share Insurance Corp ....E 614 764-1900
  Dublin (G-10343)
Hartville Group Inc ....E 330 484-8166
  Akron (G-254)
Heritage Wrranty Insur Rrg Inc ....D 800 753-5236
  Dublin (G-10360)
Ohio Farmers Insurance Company ....C 330 484-5660
  Canton (G-2479)

64 INSURANCE AGENTS, BROKERS, AND SERVICE

6411 Insurance Agents, Brokers & Svc

A A Hammersmith Insurance Inc ....E 330 832-7411
  Massillon (G-13781)
A-1 General Insurance Agency ....D 216 986-3000
  Cleveland (G-4939)
AAA Cincinnati Insurance Svc ....E 513 345-5600
  Cincinnati (G-2959)
AAA Club Alliance Inc ....C 937 427-5884
  Beavercreek (G-1144)
Aba Insurance Services Inc ....D 800 274-5222
  Mayfield Heights (G-13998)
Ability Network Inc ....E 513 943-8888
  Cincinnati (G-2901)
Accurate Group Holdings Inc ....D 216 520-1740
  Independence (G-12178)
Advanced Group Corp ....E 216 431-8800
  Cleveland (G-4959)
AFLAC Incorporated ....C 614 410-1696
  Columbus (G-6954)
Alex N Sill Company ....E 216 524-9999
  Seven Hills (G-16825)
All America Insurance Company ....B 419 238-1010
  Van Wert (G-18627)
Allan Miller Insurance Agency ....E 513 863-2629
  Hamilton (G-11691)
Allan Peace & Associates Inc ....E 513 579-1700
  Cincinnati (G-2986)
Allen Gardiner Deroberts ....E 614 221-1500
  Columbus (G-6966)
Allstate Insurance Company ....E 330 650-2917
  Hudson (G-12102)
Allstate Insurance Company ....D 330 656-6000
  Hudson (G-12103)
Alpha Group Agency Inc ....E 216 520-0440
  Cleveland (G-4996)
Alpha Investment Partnership ....D 513 621-1826
  Cincinnati (G-2994)
Alternative Care Mgt Systems ....E 614 761-0035
  Dublin (G-10243)
Althans Insurance Agency Inc ....E 440 247-6422
  Chagrin Falls (G-2689)
American Empire Surplus Lines ....E 513 369-3000
  Cincinnati (G-3002)
American Family Home Insur Co ....D 513 943-7100
  Amelia (G-573)
American Fidelity Assurance Co ....A 800 437-1011
  Columbus (G-6992)
American Gen Lf Insur Co Del ....E 513 762-7807
  Cincinnati (G-3007)
American Highways Insur Agcy ....C 330 659-8900
  Richfield (G-16496)
American Income Life Insur Co ....D 440 582-0040
  Cleveland (G-5010)
American Insur Administrators ....E 614 486-5388
  Dublin (G-10248)
American Modrn Insur Group Inc ....C 800 543-2644
  Amelia (G-576)
American Risk Services LLC ....E 513 772-3712
  Cincinnati (G-3013)
American Security Insurance Co ....E 937 327-7700
  Springfield (G-17147)
American Title of Ohio LLC ....E 303 868-2250
  Cleveland (G-5024)
Ameriprise Financial Svcs Inc ....D 614 846-8723
  Worthington (G-19940)
Amtrust North America Inc ....C 216 328-6100
  Cleveland (G-5032)
Anthem Midwest Inc ....A 614 433-8350
  Mason (G-13663)
AON Consulting Inc ....E 614 436-8100
  Columbus (G-7023)
AON Consulting Inc ....D 614 847-4670
  Columbus (G-7024)
AON Consulting Inc ....E 216 621-8100
  Cleveland (G-5046)
AON Risk Svcs Northeast Inc ....A 216 621-8100
  Cleveland (G-5047)
Archer-Meek-Weiler Agency Inc ....E 614 212-1009
  Westerville (G-19285)
Art Hauser Insurance Inc ....D 513 745-9200
  Cincinnati (G-3050)
Arthur J Gallagher & Co ....E 513 977-3100
  Cincinnati (G-3051)
Auto-Owners Insurance Company ....D 937 432-6740
  Miamisburg (G-14273)

Auto-Owners Life Insurance Co ....D 419 227-1452
  Lima (G-12744)
Axa Advisors LLC ....E 513 762-7705
  Cincinnati (G-3069)
Axa Advisors LLC ....D 216 621-7715
  Cleveland (G-5087)
Benefit ADM Agcy LLC ....E 614 791-1143
  Dublin (G-10262)
Bowers Insurance Agency Inc ....E 330 638-6146
  Cortland (G-9073)
Brands Insurance Agency Inc ....E 513 777-7775
  West Chester (G-19031)
Britton-Gallagher & Assoc Inc ....D 216 658-7100
  Cleveland (G-5141)
Brooks & Stafford Co ....E 216 696-3000
  Cleveland (G-5147)
Brown & Brown of Ohio LLC ....C 419 874-1974
  Perrysburg (G-15981)
Brown WD General Agency Inc ....D 216 241-5840
  Cleveland (G-5152)
Bruce Klinger ....E 419 473-2270
  Toledo (G-17786)
Brunswick Companies ....E 330 864-8800
  Fairlawn (G-10939)
Buren Insurance Group Inc ....E 419 281-8060
  Ashland (G-668)
Business Admnstrators Cons Inc ....E 614 863-8780
  Reynoldsburg (G-16433)
Cai/Insurance Agency Inc ....E 513 221-1140
  Cincinnati (G-3165)
Careworks of Ohio Inc ....B 614 792-1085
  Dublin (G-10280)
Carriage Town Chrysler Plymouth ......D 740 369-9611
  Delaware (G-10076)
Cbiz Inc ....D 330 644-2044
  Uniontown (G-18512)
Central Bnfits Admnstrtors Inc ....E 614 797-5200
  Westerville (G-19377)
Chapman & Chapman Inc ....E 440 934-4102
  Avon (G-887)
Cincinnati Equitable Insur Co ....E 440 349-2210
  Solon (G-16991)
Cincinnati Financial Corp ....A 513 870-2000
  Fairfield (G-10833)
Clark Theders Insurance Agency ....E 513 779-2800
  West Chester (G-19043)
Cobos Insurance Centre LLC ....E 440 324-3732
  Elyria (G-10606)
Colonial Lf Accident Insur Co ....B 614 793-8622
  Dublin (G-10299)
Columbus Life Insurance Co ....E 513 361-6700
  Cincinnati (G-3390)
Combined Insurance Co Amer ....D 614 210-6209
  Columbus (G-7396)
Compmanagement Inc ....E 614 376-5300
  Dublin (G-10306)
Cornerstone Broker Ins Svcs AG ....E 513 241-7675
  Cincinnati (G-3423)
Corporate Health Benefits ....E 740 348-1401
  Newark (G-15161)
Corporate Plans Inc ....E 440 542-7800
  Solon (G-16995)
Crawford & Company ....E 440 243-8710
  Cleveland (G-5432)
CSC Insurance Agency Inc ....D 614 895-2000
  Westerville (G-19294)
Defense Info Systems Agcy ....C 614 692-4433
  Columbus (G-7502)
Donald P Pipino Company Ltd ....D 330 726-8177
  Youngstown (G-20173)
Ebso Inc ....E 419 423-3823
  Findlay (G-11021)
Employee Benefit Management ....E 614 766-5800
  Dublin (G-10336)
Employers Mutual Casualty Co ....D 513 221-6010
  Blue Ash (G-1585)
Employers Select Plan Agcy Inc ....E 216 642-4200
  Independence (G-12208)
Envision Phrm Svcs LLC ....B 330 405-8080
  Twinsburg (G-18411)
Erie Indemnity Company ....D 330 433-6300
  Canton (G-2357)
Erie Insurance Exchange ....D 330 430-8530
  Columbus (G-7604)
Executive Insurance Agency ....E 330 576-1234
  Akron (G-210)
Explorer Rv Insurance Agcy Inc ....C 330 659-8900
  Richfield (G-16507)
F W Arnold Agency Co Inc ....E 330 832-1556
  Massillon (G-13805)

Factory Mutual Insurance Co ....D 513 742-9516
  Cincinnati (G-3588)
Family Heritg Lf Insur Co Amer ....E 440 922-5200
  Broadview Heights (G-1879)
Farmers Financial Services ....E 937 424-0643
  Beavercreek (G-1240)
Farmers Group Inc ....E 330 467-6575
  Northfield (G-15515)
Farmers Group Inc ....E 614 766-6005
  Columbus (G-7639)
Farmers Group Inc ....E 614 799-3200
  Columbus (G-7640)
Farmers Group Inc ....E 216 750-4010
  Independence (G-12211)
Farmers Insurance of Columbus ....B 614 799-3200
  Columbus (G-7641)
Farmers New World Lf Insur Co ....C 614 764-9975
  Columbus (G-7642)
Fedeli Group Inc ....D 216 328-8080
  Cleveland (G-5580)
Federal Insurance Company ....E 216 687-1700
  Cleveland (G-5581)
Federal Insurance Company ....D 513 721-0601
  Cincinnati (G-3598)
Financial Design Group Inc ....E 419 843-4737
  Toledo (G-17889)
Financial Plnners of Cleveland ....E 440 473-1115
  Cleveland (G-5586)
First Acceptance Corporation ....E 614 237-9700
  Columbus (G-7659)
First Acceptance Corporation ....E 937 778-8888
  Piqua (G-16144)
First Acceptance Corporation ....E 513 741-0811
  Cincinnati (G-3613)
First Acceptance Corporation ....E 614 492-1446
  Columbus (G-7660)
First Acceptance Corporation ....E 330 792-7181
  Youngstown (G-20188)
First Acceptance Corporation ....E 614 853-3344
  Columbus (G-7661)
First Defiance Financial Corp ....E 419 353-8611
  Bowling Green (G-1776)
▲ Forge Industries Inc ....A 330 782-8301
  Youngstown (G-20191)
▲ Freedom Specialty Insurance Co .....C 614 249-1545
  Columbus (G-7701)
Gallagher Bassett Services ....E 614 764-7616
  Dublin (G-10352)
Gallagher Benefit Services Inc ....E 216 623-2600
  Cleveland (G-5652)
Galt Enterprises Inc ....E 216 464-6744
  Moreland Hills (G-14839)
George W Mc Cloy ....D 614 457-6233
  Columbus (G-7744)
German Mutual Insurance Co ....E 419 599-3993
  Napoleon (G-14940)
Grange Mutual Casualty Company ....E 614 337-4400
  Cleveland (G-5686)
Great American Advisors Inc ....E 513 357-3300
  Cincinnati (G-3696)
Guardian Business Services ....E 614 416-6090
  Columbus (G-7781)
Hanover Insurance Company ....D 614 408-9000
  Dublin (G-10356)
Hanover Insurance Company ....D 513 829-4555
  Fairfield (G-10857)
Harrington Health Services Inc ....C 614 212-7000
  Westerville (G-19406)
Hartford Fire Insurance Co ....C 216 447-1000
  Cleveland (G-5729)
Health Design Plus Inc ....D 330 656-1072
  Hudson (C-12120)
Home and Farm Insurance Co ....E 937 778-5000
  Piqua (G-16149)
Hummel Group Inc ....E 330 683-1050
  Orrville (G-15774)
Huntington Insurance Inc ....C 419 720-7900
  Toledo (G-17966)
Huntington Insurance Inc ....E 614 480-3800
  Columbus (G-7866)
Huntington Insurance Inc ....E 216 206-1787
  Cleveland (G-5790)
Huntington Insurance Inc ....E 330 262-6611
  Wooster (G-19873)
Huntington Insurance Inc ....D 614 899-8500
  Columbus (G-7867)
Huntington Insurance Inc ....E 330 337-9933
  Salem (G-16700)
Huntington Insurance Inc ....E 330 430-1300
  Canton (G-2409)

Employee Codes: A=Over 500 employees, B=251-500
C=101-250, D=51-100, E=25-50

64 INSURANCE AGENTS, BROKERS, AND SERVICE

Huntington Insurance Inc .... E 330 674-2931
  Millersburg (G-14608)
Hyatt Legal Plans Inc .... D 216 241-0022
  Cleveland (G-5796)
Hylant Group Inc .... E 513 985-2400
  Cincinnati (G-3805)
Hylant Group Inc .... E 614 932-1200
  Dublin (G-10371)
Hylant Group Inc .... C 419 255-1020
  Toledo (G-17968)
Hylant Group Inc .... D 216 447-1050
  Cleveland (G-5797)
Hylant-Maclean Inc .... E 614 932-1200
  Dublin (G-10372)
Infoquest Information Services .... E 614 761-3003
  Columbus (G-7895)
Insurance Intermediaries Inc .... D 614 846-1111
  Columbus (G-7911)
International Healthcare Corp .... D 513 731-3338
  Cincinnati (G-3836)
James B Oswald Company .... E 330 723-3637
  Medina (G-14085)
Jpmorgan Chase Bank Nat Assn ...... B 843 679-3653
  Columbus (G-7955)
Kellison & Co .... D 216 464-5160
  Cleveland (G-5892)
Keybank National Association .... C 216 813-0000
  Cleveland (G-5901)
Knight Crockett Miller Ins .... E 419 254-2400
  Toledo (G-17996)
Lang Financial Group Inc .... E 513 699-2966
  Blue Ash (G-1626)
Leonard Insur Svcs Agcy Inc .... E 330 266-1904
  Canton (G-2433)
Licking Memorial Hlth Systems .... A 220 564-4000
  Newark (G-15191)
Life Insurance Mktg Co Inc .... E 330 867-1707
  Akron (G-318)
Lighthouse Insurance Group LLC ..... D 216 503-2439
  Independence (G-12228)
Lincoln Fincl Advisors Corp .... D 614 888-6516
  Columbus (G-8069)
Louiveille Title Agncy For Nrt .... D 419 248-4611
  Toledo (G-18010)
Louisvlle Title Agcy For NW OH .... D 419 248-4611
  Toledo (G-18011)
Luce Smith & Scott Inc .... E 440 746-1700
  Brecksville (G-1832)
Marsh & McLennan Agency LLC ..... E 513 248-4888
  Loveland (G-13143)
Marsh & McLennan Agency LLC ..... C 937 228-4135
  Dayton (G-9699)
Marsh USA Inc .... B 216 937-1700
  Cleveland (G-5985)
Marsh USA Inc .... D 513 287-1600
  Cincinnati (G-4027)
Marsh USA Inc .... D 614 227-6200
  Columbus (G-8119)
Marsh USA Inc .... D 216 830-8000
  Cleveland (G-5986)
Masters Agency Inc .... E 330 805-5985
  Wadsworth (G-18764)
Mc Cloy Financial Services .... D 614 457-6233
  Columbus (G-8133)
McGohan/Brabender Agency Inc ..... D 937 293-1600
  Moraine (G-14800)
McGowan & Company Inc .... D 800 545-1538
  Cleveland (G-6003)
Medical Mutual of Ohio .... D 440 878-4800
  Strongsville (G-17491)
Medical Mutual of Ohio .... B 216 292-0400
  Beachwood (G-1099)
MetLife Auto HM Insur Agcy Inc .... A 815 266-5301
  Dayton (G-9722)
Metropolitan Life Insur Co .... E 440 746-8699
  Broadview Heights (G-1883)
Metropolitan Life Insur Co .... D 614 792-1463
  Dublin (G-10396)
Motorists Mutual Insurance Co .... E 440 779-8900
  North Olmsted (G-15433)
Motorists Mutual Insurance Co .... E 937 435-5540
  Dayton (G-9759)
National Auto Care Corporation .... D 800 548-1875
  Westerville (G-19330)
National General Insurance .... B 212 380-9462
  Cleveland (G-6108)
National Interstate Corp .... D 330 659-8900
  Richfield (G-16515)
Nations Title Agency of Ohio .... E 614 839-3848
  Columbus (G-8227)

Nationwide Corporation .... E 614 249-7111
  Columbus (G-8238)
Nationwide Corporation .... D 614 249-4302
  Columbus (G-8239)
Nationwide Corporation .... A 330 452-8705
  Canton (G-2471)
Nationwide Corporation .... B 614 277-5103
  Grove City (G-11583)
Nationwide Financial Svcs Inc .... C 614 249-7111
  Columbus (G-8242)
♦ Nationwide Life Insur Co Amer ..... A 800 688-5177
  Columbus (G-8245)
Nationwide Mutl Fire Insur Co .... E 614 249-7111
  Columbus (G-8246)
Nationwide Mutual Insurance Co ..... A 330 489-5000
  Canton (G-2472)
Nationwide Mutual Insurance Co ..... E 614 948-4153
  Westerville (G-19332)
Nationwide Rtirement Solutions .... E 614 854-8300
  Dublin (G-10405)
Nb and T Insurance Agency Inc .... E 937 393-1985
  Hillsboro (G-11990)
Neace Assoc Insur Agcy of Ohio ..... E 614 224-0772
  Columbus (G-8255)
New England Life Insurance Co .... E 614 457-6233
  Columbus (G-8272)
New York Life Insurance Co .... C 216 520-1345
  Independence (G-12239)
New York Life Insurance Co .... D 513 621-9999
  Cincinnati (G-4159)
NI of Ky Inc .... E 740 689-9876
  Lancaster (G-12562)
NI of Ky Inc .... E 216 643-7100
  Rocky River (G-16587)
NI of Ky Inc .... E 614 224-0772
  Columbus (G-8283)
Noble-Davis Consulting Inc .... E 440 519-0850
  Solon (G-17034)
Northwestern Mutl Lf Insur Co .... D 513 366-3600
  Cincinnati (G-4183)
Northwestern Ohio Admnistrators .... E 419 248-2401
  Holland (G-12042)
Ohic Insurance Company .... D 614 221-7777
  Columbus (G-8315)
Ohio Farmers Insurance Company ... A 800 243-0210
  Westfield Center (G-19452)
Ohio Farmers Insurance Company ... C 330 484-5660
  Canton (G-2479)
Ohio Farmers Insurance Company ... D 614 848-6174
  Columbus (G-6898)
Ohio Indemnity Company .... E 614 228-1601
  Columbus (G-8355)
Ohio Mutual Insurance Company ..... C 419 562-3011
  Bucyrus (G-2046)
Ohio National Life Assurance .... A 513 794-6100
  Montgomery (G-14731)
Old Rpblic Ttle Nthrn Ohio LLC .... A 216 524-5700
  Independence (G-12242)
Optumrx Inc .... A 614 794-3300
  Westerville (G-19338)
Pasco Inc .... B 330 650-0613
  Hudson (G-12138)
Paul Moss LLC .... E 216 765-1580
  Solon (G-17038)
Phelan Insurance Agency Inc .... E 800 843-3069
  Versailles (G-18727)
Postema Insurance & Investment ... E 419 782-2500
  Defiance (G-10052)
Producer Group LLC .... E 440 871-7700
  Rocky River (G-16589)
Progressive Casualty Insur Co .... E 440 683-8164
  Cleveland (G-6313)
Progressive Casualty Insur Co .... A 440 461-5000
  Mayfield Village (G-14012)
Progressive Corporation .... A 800 925-2886
  Cleveland (G-6316)
Progressive Hawaii Insurance C ...... A 440 461-5000
  Cleveland (G-6318)
Progressive Premier Insurance .... A 440 461-5000
  Cleveland (G-6321)
Prudential Insur Co of Amer .... E 513 612-6400
  Cincinnati (G-4353)
Prudential Insur Co of Amer .... E 330 896-7200
  Uniontown (G-18533)
Prudential Insur Co of Amer .... E 440 684-4409
  Cleveland (G-6327)
Prudential Insur Co of Amer .... E 419 893-6227
  Maumee (G-13962)
Qualchoice Inc .... B 330 656-1231
  Beachwood (G-1117)

R L King Insurance Agency .... E 419 255-9947
  Holland (G-12049)
Rankin & Rankin Inc .... E 740 452-7575
  Zanesville (G-20528)
Richfield Financial Group Inc .... E 440 546-4288
  Brecksville (G-1847)
Rick Allman .... E 330 699-1660
  Canton (G-2514)
Rick Blazing Insurance Agency .... E 513 677-8300
  Cincinnati (G-4417)
Royalton Financial Group .... E 440 582-3020
  Cleveland (G-6419)
S & S Halthcare Strategies Ltd .... C 513 772-8866
  Cincinnati (G-4464)
Safe Auto Insurance Company .... B 614 231-0200
  Columbus (G-8668)
Safe Auto Insurance Group Inc .... D 614 231-0200
  Columbus (G-8669)
▲ Safelite Group Inc .... A 614 210-9000
  Columbus (G-8672)
Savage and Associates Inc .... D 419 475-8665
  Toledo (G-18174)
Sbm Business Services Inc .... E 330 396-7000
  Akron (G-429)
Schauer Group Incorporated .... E 330 453-7721
  Canton (G-2523)
Schiff John J & Thomas R & Co ..... E 513 870-2580
  Fairfield (G-10903)
Schwendeman Agency Inc .... E 740 373-6793
  Marietta (G-13496)
Seibert-Keck Insurance Agency ...... E 330 867-3140
  Fairlawn (G-10974)
Self-Funded Plans Inc .... E 216 566-1455
  Cleveland (G-6468)
Selman & Company .... D 440 646-9336
  Cleveland (G-6469)
Seymour & Associates .... E 419 517-7079
  Maumee (G-13975)
Sirak Financial Services Inc .... D 330 493-0642
  Canton (G-2530)
Sirak-Moore Insurance Agcy Inc ...... E 330 493-3211
  Canton (G-2531)
♦ Smart .... C 216 228-9400
  North Olmsted (G-15444)
State Auto Prperty Cslty Insur .... E 440 842-6200
  Strongsville (G-17511)
State Automobile Mutl Insur Co .... A 833 724-3577
  Columbus (G-8781)
State Farm General Insur Co .... D 740 364-5000
  Newark (G-15235)
State Farm Life Insurance Co .... E 937 276-1900
  Dayton (G-9905)
State Farm Mutl Auto Insur Co .... D 419 873-0100
  Perrysburg (G-16063)
State Farm Mutl Auto Insur Co .... D 216 621-3723
  Cleveland (G-6528)
State Farm Mutl Auto Insur Co .... A 614 775-2001
  New Albany (G-15008)
State Farm Mutl Auto Insur Co .... A 740 364-5000
  Newark (G-15236)
State Farm Mutl Auto Insur Co .... A 216 321-1422
  Cleveland (G-6529)
Steele W W Jr Agency Inc .... E 330 453-7721
  Canton (G-2549)
Stephens-Matthews Mktg Inc .... E 740 984-8011
  Beverly (G-1493)
Stolly Insurance Agency Inc .... E 419 227-2570
  Lima (G-12893)
Strategic Research Group Inc .... E 614 220-8860
  Columbus (G-8795)
Summit Claim Services LLC .... D 330 706-9898
  New Franklin (G-15050)
Support Insur Systems Agcy Inc ..... E 937 434-5700
  Centerville (G-2687)
Supreme Court of Ohio .... E 614 387-9800
  Columbus (G-8809)
The Sheakley Group Inc .... E 513 771-2277
  Cincinnati (G-4646)
Thomas Gentz .... E 513 247-7300
  Cincinnati (G-4652)
Todd Associates Inc .... D 440 461-1101
  Beachwood (G-1132)
Transamerica Premier Lf Insur .... E 216 524-1436
  Independence (G-12269)
Travelers Property Cslty Corp .... E 513 639-5300
  Cincinnati (G-4682)
Travelers Property Cslty Corp .... C 216 643-2100
  Cleveland (G-6615)
Uct Property Inc .... E 614 228-3276
  Columbus (G-8885)

Ues Metals Group ... E ... 937 255-9340 Beavercreek *(G-1214)*
Union Security Insurance Co ... E ... 513 621-1924 Cincinnati *(G-4727)*
United Agencies Inc ... E ... 216 696-8044 Cleveland *(G-6632)*
United American Insurance Co ... E ... 440 265-9200 Strongsville *(G-17518)*
United Insurance Company Amer ... E ... 513 771-6771 Cincinnati *(G-4733)*
United Insurance Company Amer ... E ... 419 531-4289 Toledo *(G-18270)*
United Insurance Company Amer ... E ... 216 514-1904 Beachwood *(G-1134)*
United Ohio Insurance Company ... C ... 419 562-3011 Bucyrus *(G-2050)*
UNUM Life Insurance Co Amer ... E ... 614 807-2500 Columbus *(G-8911)*
Usi Inc ... D ... 419 243-1191 Toledo *(G-18284)*
USI Insurance Services Nat ... E ... 614 228-5565 Columbus *(G-8927)*
USI Midwest LLC ... C ... 513 852-6300 Cincinnati *(G-4798)*
Valmark Insurance Agency LLC ... D ... 330 576-1234 Akron *(G-492)*
Vision Service Plan ... C ... 614 471-7511 Columbus *(G-8944)*
Voya Financial Inc ... E ... 614 431-5000 Columbus *(G-8953)*
W P Dolle LLC ... E ... 513 421-6515 Cincinnati *(G-4821)*
Wabe Maquaw Holdings Inc ... D ... 419 243-1191 Toledo *(G-18297)*
Wallace & Turner Insurance Inc ... E ... 937 324-8492 Springfield *(G-17294)*
Wellington F Roemer Insurance ... E ... 419 473-0258 Toledo *(G-18301)*
Western & Southern Lf Insur Co ... E ... 234 380-4525 Hudson *(G-12151)*
Western & Southern Lf Insur Co ... E ... 440 324-2626 Elyria *(G-10691)*
Western & Southern Lf Insur Co ... E ... 330 792-6818 Youngstown *(G-20411)*
Western & Southern Lf Insur Co ... E ... 330 825-9935 Barberton *(G-985)*
Western & Southern Lf Insur Co ... E ... 937 435-1964 Dayton *(G-9993)*
Western & Southern Lf Insur Co ... E ... 740 653-3210 Lancaster *(G-12583)*
Western & Southern Lf Insur Co ... E ... 513 891-0777 Loveland *(G-13165)*
Western & Southern Lf Insur Co ... E ... 614 898-1066 Columbus *(G-6910)*
Western & Southern Lf Insur Co ... E ... 937 773-5303 Piqua *(G-16176)*
Western & Southern Lf Insur Co ... E ... 937 399-7696 Springfield *(G-17298)*
Western & Southern Lf Insur Co ... E ... 740 354-2848 Portsmouth *(G-16322)*
Western & Southern Lf Insur Co ... E ... 937 393-1969 Hillsboro *(G-11992)*
Westfield Services Inc ... E ... 614 796-7700 Columbus *(G-6911)*
William D Taylor Sr Inc ... D ... 614 653-6683 Etna *(G-10740)*
Willis of Ohio Inc ... E ... 614 457-7000 Columbus *(G-8997)*
Wilmared Inc ... E ... 513 891-6615 Loveland *(G-13166)*
Workers Compensation Ohio Bur ... A ... 800 644-6292 Columbus *(G-9006)*
York Risk Services Group Inc ... C ... 866 391-9675 Dublin *(C-10497)*
York Risk Services Group Inc ... E ... 440 863-2500 Cleveland *(G-6771)*
Zurich American Insurance Co ... E ... 216 328-9400 Independence *(G-12279)*

65 REAL ESTATE

6512 Operators Of Nonresidential Bldgs

127 PS Fee Owner LLC ... D ... 216 520-1250 Cleveland *(G-4920)*
Ad Investments LLC ... E ... 614 857-2340 Columbus *(G-6943)*
American Maritime Officers ... E ... 419 255-3940 Toledo *(G-17749)*
Americas Best Value Inn ... E ... 419 626-9890 Sandusky *(G-16726)*
Anderson Jeffery R RE Inc ... E ... 513 241-5800 Cincinnati *(G-3024)*
Ashtabula Chemical Corp ... E ... 440 998-0100 Ashtabula *(G-714)*
Assembly Center ... E ... 800 582-1099 Monroe *(G-14687)*
Barcus Company Inc ... E ... 614 451-9000 Columbus *(G-7089)*
Best Western Columbus N Hotel ... E ... 614 888-8230 Columbus *(G-7103)*
C M Limited ... E ... 614 888-4567 Columbus *(G-7174)*
Campbell Construction Inc ... D ... 330 262-5186 Wooster *(G-19836)*
Canal Road Partners ... E ... 216 447-0814 Cleveland *(G-5176)*
Cararo Co Inc ... E ... 330 652-6980 Niles *(G-15287)*
Carew Realty Inc ... E ... 513 241-3888 Cincinnati *(G-3184)*
Carnegie Management & Dev Corp ... E ... 440 892-6800 Westlake *(G-19470)*
Casto Communities Cnstr Ltd ... B ... 614 228-8545 Columbus *(G-7209)*
Catholic Diocese of Cleveland ... E ... 419 289-7224 Ashland *(G-671)*
Cavaliers Holdings LLC ... C ... 216 420-2000 Cleveland *(G-5193)*
Cbl & Associates Prpts Inc ... E ... 513 424-8517 Middletown *(G-14476)*
Central Ohio Associates Ltd ... E ... 419 342-2045 Shelby *(G-16897)*
Centro Properties Group LLC ... E ... 440 324-6610 Elyria *(G-10602)*
Ch Relty Iv/Clmbus Partners LP ... D ... 614 885-3334 Columbus *(G-7247)*
Chapel Hill Management Inc ... D ... 330 633-7100 Akron *(G-129)*
Cincinnati Sports Mall Inc ... D ... 513 527-4000 Cincinnati *(G-3329)*
Cincinnatian Hotel ... C ... 513 381-3000 Cincinnati *(G-3336)*
City of Cleveland ... E ... 216 621-4231 Cleveland *(G-5253)*
Coldwell Bnkr Hritg Rltors LLC ... E ... 937 434-7600 Dayton *(G-9416)*
Columbian Corporation Mantua ... E ... 330 274-2576 Mantua *(G-13385)*
Columbus Association For The P ... A ... 614 469-1045 Columbus *(G-7331)*
Compco Land Company ... D ... 330 482-0200 Youngstown *(G-20155)*
Continental Properties ... B ... 614 221-1800 Columbus *(G-7430)*
Cornerstone Managed Prpts LLC ... E ... 440 263-7708 Lorain *(G-13033)*
Coughlin Holdings Ltd Partnr ... E ... 614 847-1002 Worthington *(G-19951)*
Court Stret Center Associates ... E ... 513 241-0415 Cincinnati *(G-3435)*
Daniel Maury Construction Co ... E ... 513 984-4096 Loveland *(G-13120)*
Dayton Hara Arena Conf Exhibtn ... E ... 937 278-4776 Dayton *(G-9476)*
Dayton Hcri Place Denver ... E ... 419 247-2800 Toledo *(G-17845)*
Duke Realty Corporation ... D ... 614 932-6000 Dublin *(G-10333)*
Easton Town Center II LLC ... D ... 614 416-7000 Columbus *(G-7567)*
Easton Town Center LLC ... C ... 614 337-2560 Columbus *(G-7568)*
Emmett Dan House Ltd Partnr ... E ... 740 392-6886 Mount Vernon *(G-14894)*
Equity Residential Properties ... E ... 216 861-2700 Cleveland *(G-5549)*
F H Bonn ... E ... 937 323-7024 Springfield *(G-17195)*
Fairfield Homes Inc ... C ... 614 873-3533 Plain City *(G-16192)*
Fairlawn Associates Ltd ... C ... 330 867-5000 Fairlawn *(G-10949)*
Findlay Inn & Conference Ctr ... D ... 419 422-5682 Findlay *(G-11027)*
First Interstate Properties ... E ... 216 381-2900 Cleveland *(G-5598)*
Forest City Enterprises LP ... B ... 216 621-6060 Cleveland *(G-5614)*
Forest City Enterprises LP ... E ... 216 416-3756 Cleveland *(G-5615)*
Forest City Enterprises LP ... E ... 440 888-8664 Cleveland *(G-5616)*
Forest City Enterprises LP ... E ... 216 416-3780 Cleveland *(G-5617)*
Forest City Enterprises LP ... D ... 216 416-3766 Cleveland *(G-5618)*
Forest City Properties LLC ... C ... 216 621-6060 Cleveland *(G-5619)*
Friedman Management Company ... D ... 614 224-2424 Columbus *(G-7705)*
Gardner Inc ... C ... 614 456-4000 Columbus *(G-7728)*
Garland/Dbs Inc ... C ... 216 641-7500 Cleveland *(G-5655)*
Glemsure Realty Trust ... E ... 740 522-6620 Heath *(G-11837)*
Glen Arbors Ltd Partnership ... D ... 937 293-0900 Moraine *(G-14789)*
Gms Management Co Inc Iowa ... E ... 216 766-6000 Cleveland *(G-5676)*
Goldberg Companies Inc ... E ... 440 944-8656 Willoughby Hills *(G-19730)*
Goldberg Companies Inc ... E ... 216 475-2600 Cleveland *(G-5677)*
Goodall Properties Ltd ... E ... 513 621-5522 Cincinnati *(G-3686)*
Goodman Properties Inc ... E ... 740 264-7781 Steubenville *(G-17318)*
Graham Investment Co ... D ... 740 382-0902 Marion *(G-13541)*
Greater Clumbus Convention Ctr ... C ... 614 827-2500 Columbus *(G-7773)*
Hadler-Zimmerman Inc ... E ... 614 457-6650 Columbus *(G-7792)*
Hall Nazareth Inc ... D ... 419 832-2900 Grand Rapids *(G-11449)*
Highland Village Ltd Partnr ... D ... 614 863-4640 New Albany *(G-14988)*
Hills Property Management Inc ... D ... 513 984-0300 Blue Ash *(G-1613)*
Hit Portfolio I Misc Trs LLC ... C ... 614 228-1234 Columbus *(G-7840)*
Holland Management Inc ... B ... 330 239-4474 Sharon Center *(G-16874)*
Hoty Enterprises Inc ... E ... 419 609-7000 Sandusky *(G-16769)*
I-X Center Corporation ... C ... 216 265-2675 Cleveland *(G-5799)*
Islander Company ... E ... 440 243-0593 Cleveland *(G-5837)*
Jacobs Real Estate Services ... E ... 216 514-9830 Beachwood *(G-1090)*
Jade Investments ... E ... 330 425-3141 Twinsburg *(G-18433)*
Judy Mills Company Inc ... E ... 513 271-4241 Cincinnati *(G-3895)*
Jvc Sports Corp ... E ... 330 726-1757 Youngstown *(G-20243)*
Keybank National Association ... E ... 216 689-8481 Cleveland *(G-5900)*
King Group Inc ... E ... 216 831-9330 Beachwood *(G-1095)*
King James Group IV Ltd ... E ... 440 250-1851 Westlake *(G-19504)*
King James Park Ltd ... E ... 440 835-1100 Westlake *(G-19505)*
Kingsmason Properties Ltd ... E ... 513 932-6010 Lebanon *(G-12616)*
Kohr Royer Griffith Dev Co LLC ... E ... 614 228-2471 Columbus *(G-8006)*
L and M Investment Co ... E ... 740 653-3583 Lancaster *(G-12517)*
L Brands Service Company LLC ... D ... 614 415-7000 Columbus *(G-8020)*
Ladera Healthcare Company ... E ... 614 459-1313 Columbus *(G-8030)*
Laudan Properties LLC ... E ... 234 212-3225 Twinsburg *(G-18439)*
Lewis Price Realty Co ... E ... 330 856-1911 Warren *(G-18875)*
Lima Mall Inc ... E ... 419 331-6255 Lima *(G-12822)*
Lmt Enterprises Maumee Inc ... E ... 419 891-7325 Maumee *(G-13936)*
Lofinos Inc ... D ... 937 431-1662 Beavercreek *(G-1250)*
M & L Leasing Co ... E ... 330 343-8910 Mineral City *(G-14633)*
Majestic Steel Properties Inc ... D ... 440 786-2666 Cleveland *(G-5972)*

Employee Codes: A=Over 500 employees, B=251-500 C=101-250, D=51-100, E=25-50
2018 Harris Ohio Services Directory
973

Makoy Center Inc E 614 777-1211 Hilliard *(G-11924)*
Mall Park Southern D 330 758-4511 Youngstown *(G-20269)*
Manleys Manor Nursing Home Inc C 419 424-0402 Findlay *(G-11060)*
Marion Road Enterprises C 614 228-6525 Columbus *(G-8110)*
Matco Properties Inc D 440 366-5501 Elyria *(G-10649)*
McM General Properties Ltd E 216 851-8000 Cleveland *(G-6008)*
Meadowbrook Mall Company E 330 747-2661 Youngstown *(G-20275)*
MEI Hotels Incorporated C 216 589-0441 Cleveland *(G-6021)*
Mendelson Realty Ltd E 937 461-3525 Dayton *(G-9719)*
Mid-Ohio Development Corp D 614 836-0606 Groveport *(G-11657)*
Miller-Valentine Partners C 937 293-0900 Moraine *(G-14807)*
Mills Corporation E 513 671-2882 Cincinnati *(G-4099)*
▲ Musical Arts Association C 216 231-7300 Cleveland *(G-6093)*
Oak Health Care Investor E 614 794-8800 Westerville *(G-19334)*
Ohio State University A 614 688-3939 Columbus *(G-8389)*
Olentangy Village Associates E 614 515-4680 Columbus *(G-8465)*
Oliver House Rest Complex D 419 243-1302 Toledo *(G-18105)*
Park Cincinnati Board D 513 421-4086 Cincinnati *(G-4252)*
◆ Park Corporation B 216 267-4870 Cleveland *(G-6234)*
Phil Giessler E 614 888-0307 Worthington *(G-19984)*
PNC Banc Corp Ohio E 513 651-8738 Cincinnati *(G-4307)*
Polaris Towne Center LLC E 614 456-0123 Columbus *(G-6901)*
Power Management Inc E 937 222-2909 Dayton *(G-9817)*
Primo Properties LLC E 330 606-6746 Austintown *(G-871)*
◆ Pubco Corporation D 216 881-5300 Cleveland *(G-6332)*
Quincy Mall Inc E 614 228-5331 Columbus *(G-8582)*
Raf Celina LLC E 216 464-6626 Celina *(G-2660)*
Reed Hartman Corporate Center E 513 984-3030 Blue Ash *(G-1678)*
Ricco Enterprises Incorporated E 216 883-7775 Cleveland *(G-6389)*
Richard E Jacobs Group LLC E 440 871-4800 Cleveland *(G-6390)*
Robinson Investments Ltd E 937 593-1849 Bellefontaine *(G-1393)*
Rockside Center Ltd E 216 447-0070 Cleveland *(G-6408)*
Roemer Land Investment Co E 419 475-5151 Toledo *(G-18163)*
Rootstown Township E 330 296-8240 Ravenna *(G-16409)*
Rose Properties Inc E 216 881-6000 Cleveland *(G-6413)*
Sanico Inc D 440 439-5686 Cleveland *(G-6443)*
Saw Mill Creek Ltd C 419 433-3800 Huron *(G-12170)*
Schottenstein Realty LLC E 614 445-8461 Columbus *(G-8704)*
Simon Property Group E 614 717-9300 Dublin *(G-10454)*
Smg Holdings Inc C 614 827-2500 Columbus *(G-8744)*
Southwest Associates C 440 243-7888 Cleveland *(G-6499)*
Stranahan Theatre Trust D 419 381-8851 Toledo *(G-18204)*
Ted Graham E 740 223-3509 Marion *(G-13584)*
The C-Z Company E 740 432-6334 Cambridge *(G-2131)*
Thompson Hall & Jordan Fnrl HM E 513 761-8881 Cincinnati *(G-4655)*
Three M Associates D 330 674-9646 Millersburg *(G-14624)*
Traders World Inc E 513 424-2052 Monroe *(G-14715)*
U S Development Corp E 330 673-6900 Kent *(G-12401)*
United Fd Coml Wkrs Local 880 E 216 241-5930 Cleveland *(G-6638)*
United Management Inc D 614 228-5331 Columbus *(G-8894)*
Universal Veneer Mill Corp C 740 522-1147 Newark *(G-15243)*
Valley Title & Escro Agency E 330 392-6171 Warren *(G-18920)*
Visconsi Management Inc E 216 464-5550 Cleveland *(G-6701)*
Waldon Management Corp E 330 792-7688 Youngstown *(G-20409)*
Washington PRI C 614 621-9000 Columbus *(G-8967)*
Washington Prime Group Inc D 614 621-9000 Columbus *(G-8969)*
Waterfront & Associates Inc B 859 581-1414 Cincinnati *(G-4824)*
Wernli Realty Inc D 937 258-7878 Beavercreek *(G-1262)*
Weston Inc E 440 349-9000 Cleveland *(G-6748)*
White & Chambers Partnership E 740 594-8381 Athens *(G-820)*
Whitford Woods Co Inc E 440 693-4344 Middlefield *(G-14405)*
Wickliffe Associates Partnr E 440 585-3505 Wickliffe *(G-19615)*
Willis Day Management Inc E 419 476-8000 Toledo *(G-18311)*
Willis Day Storage Co E 419 470-6255 Toledo *(G-18312)*
Zaremba LLC D 216 221-6600 Cleveland *(G-6780)*
Zucker Building Company D 216 861-7114 Cleveland *(G-6785)*
Zvn Properties Inc D 330 854-5890 Canal Fulton *(G-2149)*

6513 Operators Of Apartment Buildings

12000 Edgewater Drive LLC D 216 520-1250 Lakewood *(G-12469)*
A P & P Dev & Cnstr Co D 330 833-8886 Massillon *(G-13782)*
Akron Metropolitan Hsing Auth C 330 920-1652 Stow *(G-17350)*
Alcohol Drug Addiction D 330 564-4075 Akron *(G-65)*
Allen Metropolitan Hsing Auth E 419 228-6065 Lima *(G-12737)*
Alliance Towers LLC A 330 823-1063 Alliance *(G-526)*
Alpha PHI Alpha Homes Inc D 330 376-2115 Akron *(G-70)*
Andrews Apartments Ltd C 440 946-3600 Willoughby *(G-19644)*
Arbor Park Phase Two Assoc E 561 998-0700 Cleveland *(G-5060)*
Arbor Pk Phase Three Assoc LP E 561 998-0700 Cleveland *(G-5061)*
Aspen Management Usa LLC E 419 281-3367 Ashland *(G-659)*
Atria Senior Living Group Inc E 513 923-3711 Cincinnati *(G-3062)*
Aurora Hotel Partners LLC E 330 562-0767 Aurora *(G-826)*
Azalea Alabama Investment LLC D 216 520-1250 Cleveland *(G-5088)*
Baptist Home and Center C 513 662-5880 Cincinnati *(G-3076)*
Barcus Company Inc E 614 451-9000 Columbus *(G-7089)*
Belmont Metro Hsing Auth E 740 633-5085 Martins Ferry *(G-13599)*
Biltmore Apartments Ltd D 937 461-9695 Dayton *(G-9359)*
Brethren Care Inc C 419 289-0803 Ashland *(G-666)*
Brodhead Village Ltd D 614 863-4640 New Albany *(G-14976)*
Brookdale Lving Cmmunities Inc E 330 666-4545 Akron *(G-113)*
Brookdale Senior Living Inc D 937 203-8596 Beavercreek Township *(G-1287)*
Brookdale Senior Living Inc E 216 321-6331 Cleveland *(G-5145)*
Brookdale Senior Living Inc D 330 723-5825 Medina *(G-14041)*
Buckeye Cmnty Eighty One LP E 614 942-2020 Columbus *(G-7157)*
Buckeye Cmnty Thirty Five LP D 614 942-2020 Akron *(G-116)*
Burton Carol Management E 216 464-5130 Cleveland *(G-5160)*
Cardinal Retirement Village E 330 928-7888 Cuyahoga Falls *(G-9168)*
Cassady Vlg Aprtments Ohio LLC D 216 520-1250 Columbus *(G-7208)*
Chelmsford Apartments Ltd E 419 389-0800 Toledo *(G-17803)*
Cincinnati Metro Hsing Auth E 513 421-2642 Cincinnati *(G-3315)*
Cincinnati Metro Hsing Auth E 513 333-0670 Cincinnati *(G-3317)*
Claremont Retirement Village D 614 761-2011 Columbus *(G-7291)*
Commons of Providence D 419 624-1171 Sandusky *(G-16744)*
Community Mercy Foundation C 937 390-9000 Springfield *(G-17172)*
Community Prpts Ohio III LLC D 614 253-0984 Columbus *(G-7407)*
Community Prpts Ohio MGT Svcs D 614 253-0984 Columbus *(G-7408)*
Copeland Oaks B 330 938-1050 Sebring *(G-16820)*
Creative Living Inc E 614 421-1131 Columbus *(G-7456)*
Creative Living Housing Corp E 614 421-1226 Columbus *(G-7457)*
Crestview Manor Nursing Home C 740 654-2634 Lancaster *(G-12524)*
Cwb Property Managment Inc E 614 793-2244 Dublin *(G-10315)*
D & S Properties E 614 224-6663 Columbus *(G-7478)*
E A Zicka Co E 513 451-1440 Cincinnati *(G-3523)*
Ea Vica Co E 513 481-3500 Cincinnati *(G-3526)*
Eaglewood Care Center C 937 399-7195 Springfield *(G-17191)*
Ebenezer Road Corp C 513 941-0099 Cincinnati *(G-3540)*
Eci Inc B 419 986-5566 Burgoon *(G-2057)*
Edward Rose Associates Inc E 513 752-2727 Batavia *(G-1012)*
Emerald Dev Ecnomic Netwrk Inc D 216 961-9690 Cleveland *(G-5533)*
Englewood Square Ltd D 937 836-4117 Englewood *(G-10703)*
Episcopal Retirement Homes D 513 271-9610 Cincinnati *(G-3566)*
Equity Residential Properties E 216 861-2700 Cleveland *(G-5549)*
Fairfield Homes Inc E 740 653-3583 Lancaster *(G-12535)*
Fairfield Homes Inc C 614 873-3533 Plain City *(G-16192)*
Fay Limited Partnership E 513 542-8333 Cincinnati *(G-3594)*
Fay Limited Partnership E 513 241-1911 Cincinnati *(G-3595)*
Fieldstone Limited Partnership C 937 293-0900 Moraine *(G-14786)*
Fish Creek Plaza Ltd D 330 688-0450 Stow *(G-17366)*
Forest City Enterprises LP B 216 621-6060 Cleveland *(G-5614)*
Forest City Properties LLC C 216 621-6060 Cleveland *(G-5619)*
Fort Austin Ltd Partnership C 440 892-4200 Cleveland *(G-5624)*
FTM Associates LLC D 614 846-1834 Columbus *(G-7712)*
G J Goudreau Operating Co E 216 741-7524 Cleveland *(G-5647)*
Galion East Ohio I LP D 216 520-1250 Galion *(G-11299)*
Garland Group Inc E 614 294-4411 Columbus *(G-7730)*
Gemini Properties E 419 531-9211 Toledo *(G-17911)*

SIC SECTION — 65 REAL ESTATE

Company	Code	Phone
Gemini Properties — Dublin (G-10353)	E	614 764-2800
Giffin Management Group Inc — Youngstown (G-20200)	E	330 758-4695
Glen Wesley Inc — Columbus (G-7755)	D	614 888-7492
Gms Management Co Inc Iowa — Cleveland (G-5676)	E	216 766-6000
Goldberg Companies Inc — Cleveland (G-5677)	E	216 475-2600
Harvest Facility Holdings LP — Toledo (G-17937)	E	419 472-7115
Harvest Facility Holdings LP — Cleveland (G-5730)	E	440 268-9555
Hcf Management Inc — Lima (G-12791)	D	419 999-2010
Hcf of Bowling Green Inc — Bowling Green (G-1782)	C	419 352-4694
Highland Village Ltd Partnr — New Albany (G-14988)	D	614 863-4640
Hills Property Management Inc — Blue Ash (G-1613)	D	513 984-0300
Hilltop Village — Cleveland (G-5758)	E	216 261-8383
Holland Management Inc — Sharon Center (G-16874)	B	330 239-4474
Horizon House Apartments LLC — Portsmouth (G-16288)	D	740 354-6393
Huber Investment Corporation — Dayton (G-9624)	E	937 233-1122
Iacovetta Builders Inc — Columbus (G-7880)	E	614 272-6464
Indian Hills Senior Community — Euclid (G-10763)	E	216 486-7700
Interntional Towers I Ohio Ltd — Youngstown (G-20237)	D	216 520-1250
Intown Suites Management Inc — Dayton (G-9636)	E	937 433-9038
Islander Company — Cleveland (G-5837)	E	440 243-0593
Judson — Cleveland (G-5876)	D	216 791-2004
K & D Enterprises Inc — Willoughby (G-19672)	E	440 946-3600
K&D Group Inc — Willoughby (G-19673)	E	440 946-3600
Kensington Place Inc — Columbus (G-7980)	E	614 252-5276
Kettering Medical Center — Miamisburg (G-14311)	D	937 866-2984
Kingsbury Tower I Ltd — Cleveland (G-5904)	D	216 795-3950
Klingbeil Multifamily Fund IV — Columbus (G-7998)	D	415 398-0106
Kopf Construction Corporation — Avon Lake (G-933)	D	440 933-0250
L S C Service Corp — Lakewood (G-12485)	E	216 521-7260
Lakewoods II Ltd — Dayton (G-9671)	D	937 254-6141
Links — Marysville (G-13631)	E	937 644-9988
Little Bark View Limited — Cleveland (G-5946)	E	216 520-1250
Marsol Apartments — Cleveland (G-5987)	E	440 449-5800
Menorah Park Center For Senio — Beachwood (G-1100)	E	216 831-6515
Menorah Park Center For Senio — Cleveland (G-6024)	A	216 831-6500
Mercy Health West Park — Cincinnati (G-4076)	C	513 451-8900
Miami Cnty Cmnty Action Cuncil — Troy (G-18363)	E	937 335-7921
Millennia Housing MGT Ltd — Cleveland (G-6066)	E	216 520-1250
Mrn Limited Partnership — Cleveland (G-6084)	E	216 589-5631
Mulberry Garden A L S — Munroe Falls (G-14932)	E	330 630-3980
Murray Guttman — Blue Ash (G-1649)	D	513 984-0300
National Church Residences — Columbus (G-8215)	C	614 451-2151
National Housing Corporation — Columbus (G-8220)	E	614 481-8106
Neighborhood Properties Inc — Toledo (G-18082)	E	419 473-2604
Network Restorations II — Columbus (G-8266)	D	614 253-0984
Network Restorations III LLC — Columbus (G-8267)	D	614 253-0984
New Birch Manor I Assoc LLC — Medina (G-14106)	D	330 723-3404
Northeast Cincinnati Hotel LLC — Mason (G-13743)	C	513 459-9800
Northwesterly Ltd — Cleveland (G-6162)	E	216 228-2266
Notre Dame Academy Apartments — Cleveland (G-6164)	E	216 707-1590
Npa Associates — Beachwood (G-1109)	D	614 258-4053
Oak Brook Gardens — North Royalton (G-15497)	D	440 237-3613
Oakleaf Toledo Ltd Partnership — Toledo (G-18101)	E	419 885-3934
Oakwood Management Company — Chillicothe (G-2865)	E	740 774-3570
Oberer Development Co — Miamisburg (G-14328)	E	937 910-0851
Ohio Eastern Star Home — Mount Vernon (G-14917)	C	740 397-1706
Ohio Living — Columbus (G-8357)	B	614 224-1651
Ohio Presbt Retirement Svcs — Youngstown (G-20309)	B	330 746-2944
Olentangy Village Associates — Columbus (G-8465)	E	614 515-4680
Oliver House Rest Complex — Toledo (G-18105)	D	419 243-1302
Olmsted Mnor Rtrment Cmnty Ltd — North Olmsted (G-15437)	E	440 779-8886
One Lincoln Park — Dayton (G-9791)	D	937 298-0594
Original Partners Ltd Partnr — Cincinnati (G-4234)	C	513 381-8696
Orrvilla Inc — Orrville (G-15776)	E	330 683-4455
Otterbein Portage Valley Inc — Pemberville (G-15943)	C	888 749-4950
Overbrook Park Ltd — Chillicothe (G-2867)	D	740 773-1159
Owners Management Company — Bedford (G-1328)	E	440 439-3800
Parklane Manor of Akron Inc — Akron (G-377)	E	330 724-2315
Paul Dennis — Brecksville (G-1839)	E	440 746-8600
Phoenix Residential Centers — Cleveland (G-6275)	D	440 887-6097
Pickaway County Community Acti — Circleville (G-4894)	D	740 477-1655
Pinewood Place Apartments — Toledo (G-18125)	A	419 243-1413
Plaza Properties Inc — Columbus (G-8552)	E	614 237-3726
Pleasant Lake Apartments Ltd — Cleveland (G-6288)	E	440 845-2694
Power Management Inc — Dayton (G-9817)	E	937 222-2909
Province Kent OH LLC — Kent (G-12392)	E	330 673-3808
Rahf IV Kent LLC — Kent (G-12393)	E	216 621-6060
Real Estate Investors Mgt Inc — Columbus (G-8594)	E	614 777-2444
Riverside Commons Ltd Partnr — Reynoldsburg (G-16479)	D	614 863-4640
Saint Edward Housing Corp — Fairlawn (G-10971)	E	330 668-2828
Sateri Home Inc — Youngstown (G-20367)	D	330 758-8106
Senior Lifestyle Corporation — West Chester (G-19150)	D	513 777-4457
Senior Lifestyle Evergreen Ltd — Cincinnati (G-4496)	C	513 948-2308
Sh-91 Limited Partnership — Akron (G-436)	E	330 535-1581
Shaker House — Cleveland (G-6475)	D	216 991-6000
Shepherd of The Valley Luthera — Poland (G-16227)	E	330 726-7110
Sherman Thompson Oh Tc LP — Ironton (G-12302)	D	216 520-1250
SKW Management LLC — Lynchburg (G-13184)	E	937 382-7938
Slaters Inc — Lancaster (G-12574)	E	740 654-2204
Smb Construction Co Inc — Toledo (G-18191)	E	419 269-1473
Smith Tandy Company — Columbus (G-8746)	E	614 224-9255
South Franklin Circle — Chagrin Falls (G-2734)	C	440 247-1300
Spruce Bough Homes LLC — Columbus (G-8768)	D	614 253-0984
St Regis Investment LLC — Cleveland (G-6522)	D	216 520-1250
Stautberg Family LLC — Cincinnati (G-4587)	E	513 941-5070
Summerfield Homes LLC — Columbus (G-8800)	D	614 253-0984
Summit Management Services Inc — Medina (G-14131)	E	330 723-0864
Sunpoint Senior Living Hamlet — Chagrin Falls (G-2708)	E	440 247-4200
Sunset Rtrment Communities Inc — Ottawa Hills (G-15807)	D	419 724-1200
Superior Apartments — Cleveland (G-6553)	E	216 861-6405
Tm Wallick Rsdntl Prpts I Ltd — Reynoldsburg (G-16484)	D	614 863-4640
Towne Properties Asset MGT — Cincinnati (G-4669)	A	513 381-8696
Towne Properties Assoc Inc — Cincinnati (G-4672)	E	513 874-3737
Townhomes Management Inc — Columbus (G-8858)	E	614 228-3578
Transcon Builders Inc — Cleveland (G-6609)	E	440 439-3400
Twin Towers — Cincinnati (G-4710)	B	513 853-2000
Tyrone Townhouses PA Inv LLC — Cleveland (G-6624)	D	216 520-1250
Unite Churc Resid of Oxfor Mis — Marion (G-13590)	E	740 382-4885
United Church Homes — Marion (G-13591)	D	740 382-4885
United Church Res of Kenton — Kenton (G-12425)	D	740 382-4885
United Church Residences of — Canal Winchester (G-2174)	D	614 837-2008
Universal Development MGT Inc — Girard (G-11428)	E	330 759-7017
Urbancrest Affrdbl Hsing LLC — Columbus (G-8919)	E	614 228-3578
Vancrest Apts — Delphos (G-10154)	E	419 695-7335
Victory Sq Aprtmnts Ltd Partnr — Canton (G-2578)	D	330 455-8035
Wallace F Ackley Co — Columbus (G-8963)	E	614 231-3661
Wallick Construction Co — Springfield (G-17295)	E	937 399-7009
Walnut Hills Preservation LP — Cincinnati (G-4822)	D	513 281-1288
Washington Square Apartments — Newark (G-15244)	E	740 349-8353
Westgate Limited Partnership — Toledo (G-18307)	C	419 535-7070
Westlake Village Inc — Cleveland (G-6747)	C	440 892-4200
Westview Apartments Ohio LLC — Youngstown (G-20413)	B	216 520-1250
Whitehurst Company — Maumee (G-13994)	E	419 865-0799
Windsorwood Place Inc — Coshocton (G-9121)	E	740 623-4600
Zanesville Metro Hsing Auth — Zanesville (G-20556)	D	740 454-9714
Zepf Housing Corp One Inc — Toledo (G-18333)	C	419 531-0019

6514 Operators Of Dwellings, Except Apartments

Company	Code	Phone
Birchaven Village — Findlay (G-10996)	D	419 424-3000
Cincinnati Metro Hsing Auth — Cincinnati (G-3316)	E	513 421-8190
Cincinnati Metro Hsing Auth — Cincinnati (G-3317)	E	513 333-0670
Cwb Property Managment Inc — Dublin (G-10315)	E	614 793-2244
Huber Investment Corporation — Dayton (G-9624)	E	937 233-1122
J & R Associates — Brookpark (G-1947)	A	440 250-4080
Kent Place Housing — Columbus (G-7981)	D	614 942-2020

Employee Codes: A=Over 500 employees, B=251-500, C=101-250, D=51-100, E=25-50

L and M Investment Co..........E....... 740 653-3583
Lancaster *(G-12547)*
North Park Care Center LLC..........D....... 440 250-4080
Brookpark *(G-1953)*
Norwalk Golf Properties Inc..........E....... 419 668-8535
Norwalk *(G-15586)*
Original Partners Ltd Partnr..........C....... 513 381-8696
Cincinnati *(G-4234)*
Our House Inc..........E....... 440 835-2110
Westlake *(G-19532)*
Rv Properties LLC..........E....... 330 928-7888
Cuyahoga Falls *(G-9218)*
Towne Properties Assoc Inc..........E....... 513 874-3737
Cincinnati *(G-4672)*
Westview-Youngstown Ltd..........D....... 330 799-2787
Youngstown *(G-20414)*

6515 Operators of Residential Mobile Home Sites

Mercelina Mobile Home Park..........D....... 419 586-5407
Celina *(G-2652)*
Park Management Specialist..........D....... 419 893-4879
Maumee *(G-13956)*

6517 Railroad Property Lessors

Feridean Group Inc..........E....... 614 898-7488
Westerville *(G-19308)*

6519 Lessors Of Real Estate, NEC

Baker Bnngson Rlty Auctioneers..........E....... 419 547-7777
Clyde *(G-6810)*
Bessemer and Lake Erie RR Co..........C....... 440 593-1102
Conneaut *(G-9039)*
Catawba-Cleveland Dev Corp..........D....... 419 797-4424
Port Clinton *(G-16239)*
Cutler Real Estate Inc..........E....... 614 339-4664
Dublin *(G-10314)*
Darfus..........E....... 740 380-1710
Logan *(G-12971)*
Employers Mutual Casualty Co..........D....... 513 221-6010
Blue Ash *(G-1585)*
Etb University Properties LLC..........C....... 440 826-2212
Berea *(G-1458)*
Fairlawn Associates Ltd..........C....... 330 867-5000
Fairlawn *(G-10949)*
Hertz Clvland 600 Superior LLC..........E....... 310 584-8108
Cleveland *(G-5754)*
J & E LLC..........E....... 513 241-0429
Cincinnati *(G-3850)*
James Lafontaine..........E....... 740 474-5052
Circleville *(G-4891)*
Mapleview Farms Inc..........E....... 419 826-3671
Swanton *(G-17567)*
Midway Realty Company..........E....... 440 324-2404
Elyria *(G-10654)*
Mwa Enterprises Ltd..........E....... 419 599-3835
Napoleon *(G-14946)*
Ohio Living..........A....... 330 638-2420
Cortland *(G-9081)*
Real Living Inc..........D....... 614 560-9942
Powell *(G-16347)*
Realty One Inc..........E....... 440 333-8700
Rocky River *(G-16590)*
Royalton 6001 Ltd..........E....... 216 447-0070
Independence *(G-12256)*
Sami S Rafidi..........C....... 330 799-9508
Youngstown *(G-20365)*
Schottenstein Realty LLC..........E....... 614 445-8461
Columbus *(G-8704)*
Select Hotels Group LLC..........E....... 513 754-0003
Mason *(G-13759)*
Stranahan Theatre Trust..........D....... 419 381-8851
Toledo *(G-18204)*

6531 Real Estate Agents & Managers

0714 Inc..........E....... 440 327-2123
North Ridgeville *(G-15452)*
1440 Corporation Inc..........E....... 513 424-2421
Middletown *(G-14410)*
2780 Airport Drive LLC..........E....... 513 563-7555
Cincinnati *(G-2944)*
36 E Seventh LLC..........E....... 513 699-2279
Cincinnati *(G-2945)*
AA Green Realty Inc..........E....... 419 352-5331
Bowling Green *(G-1755)*
Abco Contracting LLC..........E....... 419 973-4772
Toledo *(G-17739)*
Adena Commercial LLC..........E....... 614 436-9800
Columbus *(G-6868)*
Al Neyer LLC..........D....... 513 271-6400
Cincinnati *(G-2980)*
Al-Mar Lanes..........E....... 419 352-4637
Bowling Green *(G-1757)*
Allen Est Mangement Ltd..........E....... 419 526-6505
Mansfield *(G-13259)*
Allen Metro Hsing MGT Dev Corp..........E....... 419 228-6065
Lima *(G-12736)*
Altobelli Realestate..........E....... 330 652-0200
Niles *(G-15280)*
American Bulk Commodities Inc..........C....... 330 758-0841
Youngstown *(G-20103)*
American Title Services Inc..........E....... 330 652-1609
Niles *(G-15281)*
Amsdell Construction Inc..........C....... 216 458-0670
Cleveland *(G-5031)*
Appraisal Research Corporation..........C....... 419 423-3582
Findlay *(G-10991)*
Arena Management Holdings LLC..........A....... 513 421-4111
Cincinnati *(G-3045)*
Baker Bnngson Rlty Auctioneers..........E....... 419 547-7777
Clyde *(G-6810)*
Baur Leo Century 21 Realty..........E....... 440 585-2300
Willowick *(G-19737)*
Bellwether Entp RE Capitl LLC..........E....... 216 820-4500
Cleveland *(G-5112)*
Best Realty Inc..........E....... 513 932-3948
Lebanon *(G-12591)*
Beyond 2000 Realty Inc..........E....... 440 842-7200
Cleveland *(G-5122)*
Big Hill Realty Corp..........D....... 937 426-4420
Beavercreek *(G-1229)*
Big Hill Realty Corp..........C....... 937 435-1177
Dayton *(G-9356)*
Big Hill Realty Corp..........E....... 937 429-2200
Beavercreek *(G-1230)*
Blossom Hill Elderly Housing L..........D....... 330 385-4310
East Liverpool *(G-10516)*
Blue Ash Distribution Ctr LLC..........E....... 513 699-2279
Cincinnati *(G-3117)*
Boyd Property Group LLC..........E....... 614 725-5228
Columbus *(G-7126)*
Bre Ddr Parker Pavilions LLC..........E....... 216 755-6451
Beachwood *(G-1056)*
Brg Realty Group LLC..........C....... 513 936-5960
Cincinnati *(G-3130)*
Brookdale Senior Living Inc..........D....... 614 277-1200
Grove City *(G-11539)*
Brookwood Management Company..........E....... 330 497-6565
Canton *(G-2271)*
Buckeye Cmnty Twenty Six LP..........E....... 614 942-2020
Columbus *(G-7159)*
Butler County of Ohio..........D....... 513 887-3154
Hamilton *(G-11696)*
C V Perry & Co..........E....... 614 221-4131
Columbus *(G-7176)*
Calabresem Racek & Markos Inc..........E....... 216 696-5442
Cleveland *(G-5171)*
Capital Partners Realty LLC..........E....... 614 888-1000
Worthington *(G-19945)*
Capital Properties MGT Ltd..........E....... 216 991-3057
Cleveland *(G-5178)*
Capital Senior Living..........E....... 440 356-5444
Rocky River *(G-16572)*
Carleton Realty Inc..........E....... 740 653-5200
Lancaster *(G-12513)*
Carnegie Companies Inc..........E....... 440 232-2300
Solon *(G-16987)*
Cassidy Trley Coml RE Svcs Inc..........E....... 513 771-2580
Cincinnati *(G-3192)*
Cbre Inc..........D....... 513 369-1300
Cincinnati *(G-3196)*
Cbre Inc..........E....... 216 687-1800
Cleveland *(G-5198)*
Cbre Inc..........E....... 614 419-7429
Blacklick *(G-1503)*
Cbre Inc..........D....... 614 438-5488
Columbus *(G-7216)*
Century 21 Elite Performance..........E....... 937 438-8221
Spring Valley *(G-17109)*
Century 21 Trammell Odonnell..........D....... 440 888-6800
Cleveland *(G-5214)*
Century 21-Joe Walker & Assoc..........E....... 614 899-1400
Columbus *(G-6873)*
Chartwell Group LLC..........E....... 216 360-0009
Cleveland *(G-5230)*
Cincinnati Coml Contg LLC..........E....... 513 561-6633
Cincinnati *(G-3294)*
City of Willoughby..........B....... 440 953-4111
Willoughby *(G-19651)*
Classic Real Estate Co..........E....... 937 393-3416
Hillsboro *(G-11968)*
Cleveland Real Estate Partners..........E....... 216 623-1600
Cleveland *(G-5342)*
Coffman Family Partnership..........E....... 614 864-5400
Columbus *(G-7314)*
Coldwell Banker..........E....... 513 321-9944
Cincinnati *(G-3382)*
Coldwell Banker First Place RE..........D....... 330 726-8161
Poland *(G-16223)*
Coldwell Banker King Thompson..........D....... 614 759-0808
Pickerington *(G-16090)*
Coldwell Banker West Shell..........E....... 513 829-4000
West Chester *(G-19046)*
Coldwell Banker West Shell..........D....... 513 922-9400
Cincinnati *(G-3383)*
Coldwell Banker West Shell..........D....... 513 385-9300
Cincinnati *(G-3384)*
Coldwell Banker West Shell..........D....... 513 777-7900
West Chester *(G-19047)*
Coldwell Banker West Shell..........E....... 513 271-7200
Cincinnati *(G-3385)*
Coldwell Bnkr Hritg Rltors LLC..........E....... 937 304-8500
Dayton *(G-9415)*
Coldwell Bnkr Hritg Rltors LLC..........E....... 937 748-5500
Springboro *(G-17119)*
Coldwell Bnkr Hritg Rltors LLC..........E....... 937 434-7600
Dayton *(G-9416)*
Coldwell Bnkr Hritg Rltors LLC..........E....... 937 426-6060
Beavercreek Township *(G-1266)*
Coldwell Bnkr Hritg Rltors LLC..........E....... 937 439-4500
Dayton *(G-9417)*
Coldwell Bnkr Hritg Rltors LLC..........E....... 937 890-2200
Vandalia *(G-18675)*
Comey & Shepherd LLC..........E....... 513 489-2100
Cincinnati *(G-3391)*
Comey & Shepherd LLC..........C....... 513 561-5800
Cincinnati *(G-3392)*
Comey & Shepherd LLC..........E....... 513 321-4343
Cincinnati *(G-3393)*
Comey & Shepherd LLC..........E....... 513 231-2800
Cincinnati *(G-3394)*
Comey & Shepherd LLC..........E....... 513 891-4444
Cincinnati *(G-3395)*
Communicare Health Svcs Inc..........D....... 419 485-8307
Montpelier *(G-14740)*
Communicare Health Svcs Inc..........D....... 330 792-7799
Youngstown *(G-20149)*
Communicare Health Svcs Inc..........D....... 419 394-7611
Saint Marys *(G-16672)*
Communicare Health Svcs Inc..........E....... 330 454-6508
Canton *(G-2317)*
Communicare Health Svcs Inc..........D....... 330 792-5511
Youngstown *(G-20150)*
Communicare Health Svcs Inc..........C....... 330 454-2152
Canton *(G-2318)*
Communicare Health Svcs Inc..........D....... 330 630-9780
Tallmadge *(G-17635)*
Connor Group A RE Inv Firm LLC..........B....... 937 434-3095
Miamisburg *(G-14286)*
Continental Realty Ltd..........E....... 614 221-6260
Columbus *(G-7432)*
County of Allen..........E....... 419 228-6065
Lima *(G-12762)*
Crawford Hoying Ltd..........C....... 614 335-2020
Dublin *(G-10312)*
Croxton Realty Company..........E....... 330 492-1697
Canton *(G-2330)*
Cushman & Wakefield Inc..........E....... 513 631-1121
Norwood *(G-15598)*
Cushman & Wakefield Inc..........E....... 937 222-7884
Moraine *(G-14765)*
Cutler and Associates Inc..........D....... 330 896-1680
Akron *(G-182)*
Cutler and Associates Inc..........E....... 330 688-2100
Stow *(G-17359)*
Cutler and Associates Inc..........E....... 330 493-9323
Canton *(G-2331)*
Cutler Real Estate..........D....... 330 499-9922
North Canton *(G-15331)*
Cutler Real Estate..........C....... 330 836-9141
Fairlawn *(G-10943)*
Cutler Real Estate..........E....... 330 688-2100
Stow *(G-17360)*
Cutler Real Estate..........E....... 330 644-0644
Akron *(G-183)*
Cutler Real Estate..........D....... 330 733-7575
Ravenna *(G-16383)*
Cutler Real Estate..........D....... 330 492-7230
Canton *(G-2332)*

SIC SECTION 65 REAL ESTATE

Cutler Real Estate Inc ... E ... 614 339-4664
Dublin (G-10314)
Cwb Property Managment Inc ... E ... 614 793-2244
Dublin (G-10315)
Danberry Co ... D ... 419 866-8888
Maumee (G-13904)
Darfus ... E ... 740 380-1710
Logan (G-12971)
Dari Pizza Enterprises II Inc ... C ... 419 534-3000
Maumee (G-13905)
David Campbell ... E ... 937 266-7064
Dayton (G-9451)
Ddr Corp ... E ... 216 755-5547
Canton (G-2337)
Deed Realty Co ... E ... 330 225-5220
Brunswick (G-1974)
Design Homes & Development Co ... E ... 937 438-3667
Dayton (G-9499)
Di Salle Real Estate Co ... E ... 419 885-4475
Sylvania (G-17582)
Ducru Spe LLC ... E ... 937 228-2224
Dayton (G-9507)
Duke Realty Corporation ... D ... 513 651-3900
Mason (G-13698)
E A Zicka Co ... E ... 513 451-1440
Cincinnati (G-3523)
E M Columbus LLC ... E ... 614 861-3232
Columbus (G-7559)
Eagle Realty Group LLC ... E ... 513 361-7700
Cincinnati (G-3528)
Eastgate Professional Off Pk V ... E ... 513 943-0050
Cincinnati (G-2914)
Eaton Group GMAC Real Estate ... E ... 330 726-9999
Warren (G-18855)
Echoing Hills Village Inc ... A ... 740 327-2311
Warsaw (G-18936)
Elden Properties Ltd Partnr ... E ... 440 967-0521
Vermilion (G-18709)
Ellis Richard CB Reichle Klein ... E ... 419 861-1100
Toledo (G-17864)
Equity Central LLC ... E ... 614 861-7777
Gahanna (G-11240)
Erhal Inc ... E ... 513 272-5555
Cincinnati (G-3572)
Essex Healthcare Corporation ... E ... 614 416-0600
Columbus (G-7612)
Executive Properties Inc ... E ... 330 376-4037
Akron (G-211)
Fairfield Homes Inc ... E ... 740 653-3583
Lancaster (G-12534)
Fairfield Homes Inc ... C ... 614 873-3533
Plain City (G-16192)
Fay Limited Partnership ... E ... 513 241-1911
Cincinnati (G-3595)
Fc Continental Landlord LLC ... A ... 216 621-6060
Cleveland (G-5579)
First Realty Property MGT Ltd ... E ... 440 720-0100
Mayfield Village (G-14011)
Five & Company Realty Inc ... E ... 419 423-8004
Findlay (G-11032)
Fleetwood Management Inc ... E ... 614 538-1277
Columbus (G-7674)
Flex Realty ... E ... 419 841-6208
Toledo (G-17896)
Forest City Commercial MGT Inc ... C ... 216 621-6060
Cleveland (G-5612)
Forest Cy Residential MGT Inc ... C ... 216 621-6060
Cleveland (G-5623)
Fujiyama International Inc ... E ... 614 891-2224
Columbus (G-7713)
G H A Inc ... E ... 440 729-2130
Chesterland (G-2798)
G J Goudreau & Co ... E ... 216 351-5233
Cleveland (G-5646)
Garland Group Inc ... E ... 614 294-4411
Columbus (G-7730)
Geneva Chervenic Realty Inc ... D ... 330 686-8400
Stow (G-17370)
Giammarco Properties LLC ... E ... 419 885-4844
Toledo (G-17914)
Gideon ... D ... 800 395-6014
Cleveland (G-5671)
Goldberg Companies Inc ... E ... 440 944-8656
Willoughby Hills (G-19730)
Green Springs Residential Ltd ... C ... 419 639-2581
Green Springs (G-11477)
Greentown Center LLC ... D ... 937 490-4990
Beavercreek (G-1244)
Greystone Group-Avery Ltd ... E ... 216 464-3580
Cleveland (G-5705)

Hadler Realty Company ... E ... 614 457-6650
Columbus (G-7791)
Hallmark Management Associates ... E ... 216 681-0080
Cleveland (G-5722)
Hanna Holdings Inc ... E ... 440 971-5600
North Royalton (G-15492)
Hanna Holdings Inc ... E ... 440 933-6195
Avon (G-896)
Hanna Holdings Inc ... D ... 330 707-1000
Poland (G-16225)
Henkle-Schueler & Associates ... E ... 513 932-6070
Lebanon (G-12611)
Her Inc ... E ... 614 240-7400
Columbus (G-7826)
Her Inc ... E ... 614 221-7400
Columbus (G-7827)
Her Inc ... D ... 614 888-7400
Worthington (G-19963)
Her Inc ... E ... 614 239-7400
Columbus (G-7828)
Her Inc ... E ... 614 878-4734
Columbus (G-7829)
Her Inc ... D ... 614 864-7400
Pickerington (G-16095)
Her Inc ... C ... 614 889-7400
Dublin (G-10359)
Her Inc ... E ... 614 771-7400
Hilliard (G-11907)
Her Inc ... C ... 614 890-7400
Westerville (G-19313)
Hidden Lake Condominiums ... D ... 614 488-1131
Columbus (G-7832)
Hmshost Corporation ... C ... 419 547-8667
Clyde (G-6814)
Hoeting Inc ... D ... 513 451-4800
Cincinnati (G-3775)
Home Town Realtors LLC ... D ... 937 890-9111
Dayton (G-9617)
Homelife Companies Inc ... E ... 740 369-1297
Delaware (G-10106)
Howard Hanna Smythe Cramer ... E ... 440 237-8888
North Royalton (G-15495)
Howard Hanna Smythe Cramer ... E ... 330 345-2244
Wooster (G-19872)
Howard Hanna Smythe Cramer ... E ... 440 248-3000
Solon (G-17015)
Howard Hanna Smythe Cramer ... E ... 800 656-7356
Canfield (G-2195)
Howard Hanna Smythe Cramer ... E ... 216 831-0210
Beachwood (G-1086)
Howard Hanna Smythe Cramer ... C ... 216 447-4477
Cleveland (G-5782)
Howard Hanna Smythe Cramer ... E ... 440 333-6500
Rocky River (G-16581)
Howard Hanna Smythe Cramer ... D ... 216 447-4477
Akron (G-272)
Howard Hanna Smythe Cramer ... E ... 330 468-6833
Macedonia (G-13202)
Howard Hanna Smythe Cramer ... D ... 330 725-4137
Medina (G-14078)
Howard Hanna Smythe Cramer ... E ... 440 835-2800
Cleveland (G-5783)
Howard Hanna Smythe Cramer ... E ... 440 282-8002
Amherst (G-597)
Howard Hanna Smythe Cramer ... E ... 330 686-1166
Stow (G-17374)
Howard Hanna Smythe Cramer ... E ... 440 516-4444
Willoughby (G-19671)
Howard Hanna Smythe Cramer ... E ... 440 248-3380
Cleveland (G-5784)
Howard Hanna Smythe Cramer ... E ... 216 751-8550
Beachwood (G-1087)
Howard Hanna Smythe Cramer ... D ... 216 831-9310
Pepper Pike (G-15956)
Howard Hanna Smythe Cramer ... D ... 330 562-6188
Aurora (G-841)
Howard Hanna Smythe Cramer ... E ... 440 428-1818
Madison (G-13225)
Howard Hanna Smythe Cramer ... E ... 330 493-6555
Canton (G-2406)
Howard Hanna Smythe Cramer ... E ... 330 896-3333
Uniontown (G-18524)
Howard Hanna Smythe Cramer ... E ... 440 526-1800
Cleveland (G-5785)
Hunt Club LLC ... E ... 419 885-4647
Sylvania (G-17594)
Hunter Realty Inc ... E ... 216 831-2911
Cleveland (G-5789)
Hunter Realty Inc ... E ... 440 466-9177
Geneva (G-11364)

I H S Services Inc ... E ... 419 224-8811
Lima (G-12802)
Inc/Ballew A Head Joint Ventr ... D ... 614 338-5801
Columbus (G-7888)
Integra Cncinnati/Columbus Inc ... E ... 614 764-8040
Dublin (G-10377)
Investek Realty LLC ... E ... 419 873-1236
Perrysburg (G-16019)
Irg Realty Advisors LLC ... E ... 330 659-4060
Richfield (G-16513)
Irongate Inc ... C ... 937 433-3300
Centerville (G-2680)
Irongate Inc ... E ... 937 298-6000
Dayton (G-9637)
Irongate Inc ... D ... 937 432-3432
Dayton (G-9638)
J S N Holdings ... E ... 216 447-0070
Cleveland (G-5843)
J W Enterprises Inc ... D ... 740 774-4500
Chillicothe (G-2856)
Jacobs Real Estate Services ... E ... 216 514-9830
Beachwood (G-1090)
Jobar Enterprise Inc ... E ... 216 561-5184
Cleveland (G-5866)
John Dellagnese & Assoc Inc ... E ... 330 668-4000
Akron (G-295)
Jones Lang Lsalle Americas Inc ... E ... 216 447-5276
Brecksville (G-1831)
Jordan Realtors Inc ... E ... 513 791-0281
Cincinnati (G-3886)
Joseph Schmidt Realty Inc ... E ... 330 225-6688
Brunswick (G-1983)
Joseph Walker Inc ... E ... 614 895-3840
Columbus (G-6887)
Karam & Simon Realty Inc ... E ... 330 929-0707
Cuyahoga Falls (G-9201)
Kaval-Levine Management Co ... E ... 440 944-5402
Willoughby Hills (G-19731)
Keller Williams Advisors LLC ... E ... 513 766-9200
Cincinnati (G-3907)
Keller Williams Advisory Rlty ... E ... 513 372-6500
Cincinnati (G-3908)
Keller Williams Classic Pro ... D ... 614 451-8500
Columbus (G-7972)
Keller Williams Rlty M Walker ... E ... 330 571-2020
Stow (G-17378)
Kencor Properties Inc ... E ... 513 984-3870
Cincinnati (G-3911)
Kettering Medical Center ... D ... 937 866-2984
Miamisburg (G-14311)
Key Realty Ltd ... C ... 419 270-7445
Holland (G-12031)
Klingbeil Management Group Co ... E ... 614 220-8900
Columbus (G-7997)
Knoxbi Company LLC ... D ... 440 892-6800
Westlake (G-19506)
Kramer & Kramer Inc ... E ... 937 456-1101
Eaton (G-10563)
Kwik Parking ... E ... 419 246-0454
Toledo (G-17997)
L J F Management Inc ... E ... 513 688-0104
Blue Ash (G-1623)
L O M Inc ... E ... 216 363-6009
Cleveland (G-5914)
Lakeside Realty LLC ... E ... 330 793-4200
Youngstown (G-20252)
Lee & Associates Inc ... E ... 614 923-3300
Dublin (G-10386)
Lenz Inc ... E ... 937 277-9364
Dayton (G-9677)
Lewis Price Realty Co ... E ... 330 856-1911
Warren (G-18875)
Linn Street Holdings LLC ... E ... 513 699-8825
Cincinnati (G-3988)
Longwood Phase One Assoc LP ... E ... 561 998-0700
Cleveland (G-5951)
Lt Land Development LLC ... E ... 937 382-0072
Wilmington (G-19770)
Lucien Realty ... D ... 440 331-8500
Cleveland (G-5958)
Mall Realty Inc ... E ... 937 866-3700
Dayton (G-9696)
Manatron Sabre Systems and Svc ... D ... 937 431-4000
Beavercreek (G-1253)
Marcus Mllchap RE Inv Svcs Inc ... E ... 614 360-9800
Columbus (G-8107)
Marion Plaza Inc ... D ... 330 747-2661
Niles (G-15295)
Martin + WD Apprisal Group Ltd ... E ... 419 241-4998
Toledo (G-18044)

S I C

Employee Codes: A=Over 500 employees, B=251-500
C=101-250, D=51-100, E=25-50
2018 Harris Ohio
Services Directory
977

65 REAL ESTATE — SIC SECTION

Company	Code	Phone
Maryann McEowen, Cortland (G-9078)	D	330 638-6385
Mc Mahon Realestate Co, Newark (G-15203)	E	740 344-2250
Meadowbrook Mall Company, Youngstown (G-20275)	E	330 747-2661
Mendelson Realty Ltd, Dayton (G-9719)	E	937 461-3525
Midland Atlantic Prpts LLC, Cincinnati (G-4091)	E	513 792-5000
Midwest Liquidators Inc, Worthington (G-19977)	E	614 433-7355
Mike Sikora Realty Inc, Mentor (G-14218)	E	440 255-7777
Miller-Valentine Partners Ltd, Cincinnati (G-4097)	E	513 588-1000
Miller-Vlentine Operations Inc, Dayton (G-9750)	E	937 293-0900
Miller-Vlentine Operations Inc, Dayton (G-9751)	A	513 771-0900
Miller-Vlntine Partners Ltd Lc, Cincinnati (G-4098)	E	513 588-1000
Model Group Inc, Cincinnati (G-4112)	E	513 559-0048
Morelia Consultants LLC, Cincinnati (G-4116)	E	513 469-1500
Mortgage Information Services, Cleveland (G-6078)	D	216 514-7480
Mrap LLC, Columbus (G-8202)	E	614 545-3190
Mri Software LLC, Solon (G-17030)	C	800 327-8770
Multi Builders Inc, Cleveland (G-6088)	E	216 831-1400
Murwood Real Estate Group LLC, Beachwood (G-1106)	E	216 839-5500
Mv Land Development Company, Dayton (G-9764)	B	937 293-0900
National Church Residences, Columbus (G-8215)	C	614 451-2151
National Realty Services Inc, Columbus (G-8222)	E	614 798-0971
Nationwide Mutual Insurance Co, Columbus (G-8247)	A	614 249-7111
Neighborhood Properties Inc, Toledo (G-18082)	E	419 473-2604
Newmark & Company RE Inc, Cleveland (G-6127)	E	216 453-3000
Neyer Real Estate MGT LLC, Cincinnati (G-4167)	E	513 618-6000
Nisbet Corporation, Cincinnati (G-4170)	C	513 563-1111
Noakes Rooney Rlty & Assoc Co, Findlay (G-11070)	E	419 423-4861
Noneman Real Estate Company, Toledo (G-18088)	E	419 531-4020
NOR Corp, Elyria (G-10659)	E	440 366-0099
Normandy Office Associates, Cincinnati (G-4175)	D	513 381-8696
North American Properties Inc, Cincinnati (G-4176)	E	513 721-2744
North Star Realty Incorporated, Fairfield (G-10884)	E	513 737-1700
North Wood Realty, Youngstown (G-20303)	C	330 423-0837
North Wood Realty, Warren (G-18886)	E	330 856-3915
Northpointe Plaza, Columbus (G-8293)	D	614 744-2229
Nrt Commercial Utah LLC, Columbus (G-8301)	D	614 239-0808
Nrt Commercial Utah LLC, Dublin (G-10411)	E	614 889-0808
Nwd Arena District II LLC, Columbus (G-8308)	E	614 857-2330
Oak Brook Gardens, North Royalton (G-15497)	D	440 237-3613
Oakwood Management Company, Reynoldsburg (G-16471)	E	614 866-8702
Oberer Residential Cnstr, Miamisburg (G-14329)	C	937 278-0851
Ohio Equities LLC, Columbus (G-8341)	E	614 469-0058
Olmsted Residence Corporation, Olmsted Twp (G-15680)	C	440 235-7100
One Lincoln Park, Dayton (G-9791)	E	937 298-0594
Owners Management Company, Bedford (G-1328)	E	440 439-3800
Pache Management Company Inc, Columbus (G-8504)	E	614 451-9236
Paran Management Company Ltd, Cleveland (G-6233)	E	216 921-5663
Petros Homes Inc, Cleveland (G-6272)	E	440 546-9000
Pfh Partners LLC, Cincinnati (G-4289)	E	513 241-5800
Phil Giessler, Worthington (G-19984)	E	614 888-0307
Phillips Edison & Company LLC, Cincinnati (G-4291)	E	513 554-1110
Pizzuti Inc, Columbus (G-8547)	E	614 280-4000
Platinum RE Professionals LLC, Willoughby (G-19704)	E	440 942-2100
Plaza Properties Inc, Columbus (G-8552)	E	614 237-3726
Plus Realty Cincinnati Inc, Milford (G-14554)	E	513 575-4500
Port Lawrence Title and Tr Co, Toledo (G-18130)	E	419 244-4605
Preferred RE Investments LLC, Westerville (G-19344)	E	614 901-2400
Premier Prpts Centl Ohio Inc, Columbus (G-8556)	E	614 755-4275
Prudential Calhoon Co Realtors, Hilliard (G-11945)	E	614 777-1000
Prudential Lucien Realty, Lakewood (G-12495)	E	216 226-4673
Prudential Select Properties, Mentor (G-14230)	D	440 255-1111
Prudential Welsh Realty, Mentor (G-14231)	E	440 974-3100
R A Hermes Inc, Cincinnati (G-4377)	E	513 251-5200
Randolph and Associates RE, Columbus (G-8588)	E	614 269-8418
Re/Max, Beavercreek (G-1257)	E	937 477-4997
Re/Max Consultant Group, New Albany (G-15004)	D	614 855-2822
RE/Max Experts Realty, Dover (G-10208)	E	330 364-7355
RE/Max Real Estate Experts, Mentor (G-14233)	E	440 255-6505
Real Estate Capital Fund LLC, Cleveland (G-6358)	E	216 491-3990
Real Estate II Inc, Springfield (G-17263)	E	937 390-3119
Real Estate Showcase, Marion (G-13574)	E	740 389-2000
Real Living Inc, Powell (G-16347)	D	614 560-9942
Real Living Title Agency Ltd, Painesville (G-15877)	E	440 974-7810
Real Living Title Agency Ltd, Columbus (G-8595)	D	614 459-7400
Real Property Management Inc, Dublin (G-10439)	E	614 766-6500
Realty One Inc, Stow (G-17389)	E	330 686-1166
Realty One Inc, Mentor (G-14234)	C	440 951-2123
Realty One Inc, Lakewood (G-12497)	E	216 221-6585
Realty One Inc, Brecksville (G-1846)	D	440 526-2900
Realty One Inc, North Royalton (G-15499)	D	440 888-8600
Realty One Inc, Uniontown (G-18535)	E	330 896-5225
Realty One Inc, Cleveland (G-6359)	D	440 238-1400
Realty One Inc, Elyria (G-10674)	E	440 365-8392
Realty One Inc, Rocky River (G-16590)	E	440 333-8700
Realty One Inc, Aurora (G-851)	E	330 562-2277
Realty One Inc, Wooster (G-19906)	E	330 262-7200
Realty One Inc, Amherst (G-603)	D	440 282-8002
Realty One Inc, Bay Village (G-1041)	D	440 835-6500
Red Brick Property MGT LLC, Oxford (G-15830)	E	513 524-9340
Remax Homesource, Willoughby (G-19709)	E	440 951-2500
REO Network Inc, Marietta (G-13494)	E	740 374-8900
Residential Hm Assn of Marion, Marion (G-13575)	C	740 387-9999
Residential One Realty Inc, Columbus (G-8620)	E	614 436-9830
Resource Title Agency Inc, Cleveland (G-6385)	D	216 520-0050
Resource Title Nat Agcy Inc, Independence (G-12248)	D	216 520-0050
Reuben Co, Toledo (G-18155)	E	419 241-3400
Richard H Freyhof, Urbana (G-18599)	E	937 653-5837
Richland Mall Shopping Ctr, Mansfield (G-13357)	E	419 529-4003
Rlj Management Co Inc, Columbus (G-8639)	C	614 942-2020
Robert F Lindsay Co, Toledo (G-18161)	D	419 476-6221
Roediger Realty Inc, Springfield (G-17266)	E	937 322-0352
Rolls Realty, Powell (G-16348)	E	614 792-5662
Ron Neff Real Estate, Chillicothe (G-2876)	E	740 773-4670
Rose Community Management LLC, Independence (G-12254)	C	917 542-3600
RPM Midwest LLC, Cincinnati (G-4451)	E	513 762-9000
Rubber City Realty Inc, Akron (G-421)	D	330 745-9034
Rybac Inc, Columbus (G-8664)	E	614 228-3578
S & S Real Estate Managers LLC, Dayton (G-9283)	D	937 256-7000
Sami S Rafidi, Youngstown (G-20365)	C	330 799-9508
Sawmill Road Management Co LLC, Springfield (G-17270)	E	937 342-9071
Sawyer Realtors, Middletown (G-14456)	E	513 423-6521
Saxton Real Estate Co, Grove City (G-11596)	D	614 875-2327
Schottenstein RE Group LLC, Columbus (G-8703)	E	614 418-8900
◆ Schroeder Company, Toledo (G-18175)	E	419 473-3139
Sibcy Cline Inc, Dayton (G-9881)	E	937 610-3404
Sibcy Cline Inc, Cincinnati (G-2931)	E	513 752-4000
Sibcy Cline Inc, Cincinnati (G-4520)	D	513 793-2121
Sibcy Cline Inc, Fairfield (G-10908)	E	513 385-3330
Sibcy Cline Inc, Cincinnati (G-4521)	E	513 984-4100
Sibcy Cline Inc, Fairfield (G-10909)	D	513 829-0044
Sibcy Cline Inc, West Chester (G-19152)	D	513 777-8100
Sibcy Cline Inc, Cincinnati (G-4522)	D	513 793-2700
Sibcy Cline Inc, Cincinnati (G-4523)	E	513 931-7700
Sibcy Cline Inc, Mason (G-13761)	D	513 677-1830
Sibcy Cline Inc, Beavercreek (G-1208)	E	937 429-2101
Sibcy Cline Inc, Lebanon (G-12646)	D	513 932-6334
Siena Springs II, Dayton (G-9883)	E	513 639-2800
Signature Associates Inc, Toledo (G-18188)	E	419 244-7505
Skye Development Company LLC, Cleveland (G-6485)	E	216 223-0160
Springcar Company LLC, Westlake (G-19549)	E	440 892-6800
Star One Holdings Inc, Cincinnati (G-4584)	E	513 474-9100
Star One Holdings Inc, West Chester (G-19159)	E	513 779-9500
Star One Holdings Inc, Cincinnati (G-4585)	E	513 300-6663
Sterling Heights Gsa Prpts Ltd, Sandusky (G-16801)	E	419 609-7000
Steve Brown, Dayton (G-9907)	D	937 436-2700

SIC SECTION — 65 REAL ESTATE

Company	Code	Phone
Stickelman Schneider Assoc LLC Fairborn (G-10804)	E	513 475-6000
Stouffer Realty Inc Fairlawn (G-10978)	E	330 835-4900
STS Restaurant Management Inc Toledo (G-18205)	D	419 246-0730
Sue Smedley Springfield (G-17282)	E	937 399-5155
Sweda Sweda Associates Inc Avon (G-917)	E	419 433-4841
Sweeney Team Inc Lebanon (G-12651)	E	513 934-0700
Sweeney Team Inc Cincinnati (G-4606)	E	513 241-3400
T & R Properties Dublin (G-10472)	E	614 923-4000
Tiger 2010 LLC North Canton (G-15373)	E	330 236-5100
Tolson Enterprises Inc Toledo (G-18256)	E	419 843-6465
Tom Baier & Assoc Inc Canton (G-2563)	E	330 497-3115
Tom Properties LLC Columbus (G-8853)	D	614 781-0055
Towne Properties Assoc Inc Cincinnati (G-4671)	E	513 489-4059
Towne Properties Assoc Inc Cincinnati (G-4672)	E	513 874-3737
Townhomes Management Inc Columbus (G-8858)	E	614 228-3578
Triad PII Marietta (G-13507)	E	740 374-2940
Triangle Office Park LLC Cincinnati (G-4686)	E	513 563-7555
TSS Real Estate Ltd Cincinnati (G-4704)	C	513 772-7000
U S Associates Realty Inc Cleveland (G-6625)	E	216 663-3400
U S Title Agency Inc Cleveland (G-6627)	E	216 621-1424
Ufcw 75 Real Estate Corp Dayton (G-9943)	D	937 677-0075
United Management Inc Cincinnati (G-4735)	E	513 936-8568
University Circle Incorporated Cleveland (G-6653)	E	216 791-3900
Valley View Place Zanesville (G-20543)	C	740 454-7720
Village Communities LLC Westerville (G-19357)	C	614 540-2400
Visconsi Companies Ltd Cleveland (G-6700)	E	216 464-5550
Waldon Management Corp Youngstown (G-20409)	E	330 792-7688
Wallick Properties Midwest LLC Grove City (G-11610)	C	614 539-9041
Wallick Properties Midwest LLC New Albany (G-15010)	A	614 863-4640
Ward Realestate Inc Ashland (G-707)	E	419 281-2000
Washington Square Apartments Newark (G-15244)	E	740 349-8353
Welles Bowen Realty Inc Toledo (G-18300)	D	419 535-0011
West Shell Commercial Inc Cincinnati (G-4837)	D	513 721-4200
West Shell Gale Schnetzer Loveland (G-13164)	E	513 683-3833
West-Way Management Company Westlake (G-19566)	E	440 250-1851
Western Reserve Realty LLC Chagrin Falls (G-2710)	E	440 247-3707
Whitehurst Company Maumee (G-13994)	E	419 865-0799
Wilbur Realty Inc Kent (G-12405)	E	330 673-5883
William Zamarelli Realtors Warren (G-18927)	E	330 856-2299
Williams Homes LLC Toledo (G-18310)	E	419 472-1005
Y Town Realty Inc Youngstown (G-20419)	E	330 743-8844
Yocum Realty Company Lima (G-12925)	E	419 222-3040
Zaremba Group Incorporated Cleveland (G-6779)	E	216 221-6600
Zaremba Group LLC Lakewood (G-12504)	C	216 221-6600
Zaremba LLC Cleveland (G-6780)	E	216 221-6600
Zaremba Zanesville LLC Lakewood (G-12505)	E	216 221-6600

6541 Title Abstract Offices

Company	Code	Phone
A R E A Title Agency Inc Toledo (G-17735)	E	419 242-5485
American Title Services Inc Niles (G-15281)	E	330 652-1609
Chicago Title Insurance Co Cleveland (G-5234)	E	216 241-6045
Commerce Title Agcy Youngstown Youngstown (G-20147)	E	330 743-1171
County of Delaware Lewis Center (G-12678)	D	740 657-3945
First Fincl Title Agcy of Ohio Cleveland (G-5597)	E	216 664-1920
Intitle Agency Inc Cincinnati (G-3840)	D	513 241-8780
Lakeside Title Escrow Agcy Inc Westlake (G-19508)	E	216 503-5600
Landsel Title Agency Inc Gahanna (G-11252)	E	614 337-1928
Lawyers Title Company Akron (G-314)	E	330 376-0000
Real Living Title Agency Ltd Columbus (G-8595)	D	614 459-7400
Security Title Guarantee Agcy Cincinnati (G-4491)	C	513 651-3393
Talon Title Agency LLC Westerville (G-19355)	E	614 818-0500
Valley Title & Escrow Agency Middlefield (G-14404)	E	440 632-9833
Weston Inc Cleveland (G-6748)	E	440 349-9000

6552 Land Subdividers & Developers

Company	Code	Phone
Al Neyer LLC Cincinnati (G-2981)	D	513 271-6400
Bob Schmitt Homes Inc North Ridgeville (G-15455)	D	440 327-9495
Breezy Point Ltd Partnership Solon (G-16984)	C	440 247-3363
C V Perry & Co Columbus (G-7176)	E	614 221-4131
Cardida Corporation Kimbolton (G-12446)	E	740 439-4359
Carnegie Management & Dev Corp Westlake (G-19470)	E	440 892-6800
Carter-Jones Companies Inc Kent (G-12354)	E	330 673-6100
Columbus Housing Partnr Inc Columbus (G-7360)	D	614 221-8889
Coral Company Cleveland (G-5408)	E	216 932-8822
Creekside II LLC Columbus (G-7459)	E	614 280-4000
Duke Realty Corporation Mason (G-13698)	D	513 651-3900
Eagle Realty Group LLC Cincinnati (G-3528)	E	513 361-7700
Edwards Land Company Columbus (G-7585)	E	614 241-2070
Equity Inc Hilliard (G-11900)	E	614 802-2900
Forest City Enterprises LP Cleveland (G-5614)	B	216 621-6060
Forest City Washington LLC Cleveland (G-5622)	E	202 496-6600
Forest Cy Residential MGT Inc Cleveland (G-5623)	C	216 621-6060
Forrer Development Ltd Dayton (G-9557)	E	937 431-6489
George J Igel & Co Inc Columbus (G-7742)	A	614 445-8421
Goodman Properties Inc Steubenville (G-17318)	E	740 264-7781
Greystone Group-Avery Ltd Cleveland (G-5705)	E	216 464-3580
Henkle-Schueler & Associates Lebanon (G-12611)	E	513 932-6070
Highland Som Development Streetsboro (G-17416)	E	330 528-3500
Laurel Development Corporation Westerville (G-19321)	E	614 794-8800
Lha Developments Akron (G-317)	E	330 785-3219
Lt Land Development LLC Wilmington (G-19770)	E	937 382-0072
Magnum Management Corporation Sandusky (G-16778)	A	419 627-2334
Mid-Ohio Development Corp Groveport (G-11657)	D	614 836-0606
Midwestern Plumbing Service Cincinnati (G-4094)	E	513 753-0050
Miller-Vlentine Operations Inc Dayton (G-9750)	E	937 293-0900
Miller-Vlentine Operations Inc Dayton (G-9751)	A	513 771-0900
Multicon Builders Inc Columbus (G-8206)	E	614 241-2070
Multicon Builders Inc Columbus (G-8207)	E	614 463-1142
Mv Residential Development LLC Moraine (G-14810)	E	937 293-0900
Nationwide Rlty Investors Ltd Columbus (G-8248)	E	614 857-2330
Newcomerstown Development Inc Newcomerstown (G-15270)	C	740 498-5165
North American Properties Inc Cincinnati (G-4176)	E	513 721-2744
Oberer Development Co Miamisburg (G-14328)	E	937 910-0851
Ostendorf-Morris Properties Cleveland (G-6217)	D	216 861-7200
Phillips Edison & Company LLC Cincinnati (G-4291)	E	513 554-1110
Piatt Park Ltd Partnership Cincinnati (G-4296)	D	513 381-8696
Pizzuti Builders LLC Columbus (G-8546)	E	614 280-4000
Pizzuti Inc Columbus (G-8547)	E	614 280-4000
Rama Tika Developers LLC Mansfield (G-13353)	E	419 806-6446
Req/Jqh Holdings Inc Blue Ash (G-1681)	D	513 891-1066
Richland Mall Shopping Ctr Mansfield (G-13357)	E	419 529-4003
Robert C Verbon Inc Toledo (G-18160)	E	419 867-6868
Robert L Stark Enterprises Inc Cleveland (G-6403)	E	216 292-0242
Rockford Homes Inc Columbus (G-6905)	D	614 785-0015
Sawyer Realtors Middletown (G-14456)	E	513 423-6521
Seg of Ohio Inc Columbus (G-8711)	E	614 414-7300
Signature Associates Inc Toledo (G-18188)	E	419 244-7505
Slavic Village Development Cleveland (G-6488)	E	216 429-1182
Soho Development Company Johnstown (G-12342)	D	614 207-3261
Sommerset Development Ltd Chardon (G-2768)	C	440 286-6194
Southgate Corp Newark (G-15234)	E	740 522-2151
Sunrise Land Co Cleveland (G-6550)	E	216 621-6060
T O J Inc Mentor (G-14247)	E	440 352-1900
The Daimler Group Inc Columbus (G-8835)	E	614 488-4424
Towne Development Group Ltd Cincinnati (G-4667)	E	513 381-8696
TP Mechanical Contractors Inc Cincinnati (G-4675)	A	513 851-8881
TP Mechanical Contractors Inc Columbus (G-8859)	C	614 253-8556
Urban Retail Properties LLC Cincinnati (G-4790)	E	513 346-4482
Visconsi Companies Ltd Cleveland (G-6700)	E	216 464-5550
Wallick Enterprises Inc New Albany (G-15009)	D	614 863-4640
Warren Housing Development Warren (G-18925)	D	330 369-1533
Windsor Companies Lancaster (G-12584)	E	740 653-8822
Wryneck Development LLC Bowling Green (G-1805)	E	419 354-2535
Zaremba Group Incorporated Cleveland (G-6779)	E	216 221-6600
Zaremba Group LLC Lakewood (G-12504)	C	216 221-6600

6553 Cemetery Subdividers & Developers

Company	Code	Phone
Arlington Memorial Grdns Assn Cincinnati (G-3047)	E	513 521-7003

Employee Codes: A=Over 500 employees, B=251-500
C=101-250, D=51-100, E=25-50

65 REAL ESTATE

Catholic Cemeteries .... E 614 491-2751
  Lockbourne (G-12946)
Catholic Diocese of Cleveland .... E 216 267-2850
  Cleveland (G-5192)
City of Cleveland .... E 216 348-7210
  Cleveland (G-5256)
Green Haven Memorial Gardens .... E 330 533-6811
  Canfield (G-2192)
Green Lawn Cemetery Assn .... E 614 444-1123
  Columbus (G-7777)
Miami Valley Memory Grdns Assn .... E 937 885-7779
  Dayton (G-9736)
Ottawa Hills Memorial Park .... E 419 539-0218
  Ottawa Hills (G-15806)
Roman Cthlic Docese Youngstown .... E 330 792-4721
  Youngstown (G-20356)
Spring Grove Cmtry & Arboretum .... D 513 681-7526
  Cincinnati (G-4563)
Stonemor Partners LP .... E 330 491-8001
  Canton (G-2553)
Stonemor Partners LP .... E 937 866-4135
  Dayton (G-9908)
Stonemor Partners LP .... E 330 425-8128
  Twinsburg (G-18474)
Sunset Hills Cemetery Corp .... E 330 494-2051
  Canton (G-2555)
Sunset Memorial Park Assn .... E 440 777-0450
  North Olmsted (G-15447)
Toledo Memorial Pk & Mausoleum .... E 419 882-7151
  Sylvania (G-17624)

67 HOLDING AND OTHER INVESTMENT OFFICES

6712 Offices Of Bank Holding Co's

Community Invstors Bancorp Inc .... E 419 562-7055
  Bucyrus (G-2032)
Comunibanc Corp .... D 419 599-1065
  Napoleon (G-14936)
First Capital Bancshares Inc .... D 740 775-6777
  Chillicothe (G-2839)
Genbanc .... E 419 855-8381
  Genoa (G-11377)
Greenville National Bancorp .... E 937 548-1114
  Greenville (G-11505)
Portage Bancshares Inc .... D 330 296-8090
  Ravenna (G-16396)

6719 Offices Of Holding Co's, NEC

A and S Ventures Inc .... E 419 376-3934
  Toledo (G-17734)
◆ Ampac Holdings LLC .... A 513 671-1777
  Cincinnati (G-3017)
Amrstrong Distributors Inc .... E 419 483-4840
  Bellevue (G-1402)
Aprecia Pharmaceuticals Co .... C 513 864-4107
  Blue Ash (G-1534)
Betco Corporation .... C 419 241-2156
  Bowling Green (G-1763)
Bleux Holdings LLC .... E 859 414-5060
  Cincinnati (G-3114)
Caston Holdings LLC .... C 440 871-8697
  Westlake (G-19471)
Che International Group LLC .... E 513 444-2072
  Cincinnati (G-3233)
CV Perry Builders .... E 614 221-4131
  Columbus (G-7475)
Drt Holdings Inc .... D 937 298-7391
  Dayton (G-9505)
Elyria Foundry Holdings LLC .... B 440 322-4657
  Elyria (G-10622)
Entelco Corporation .... D 419 872-4620
  Maumee (G-13910)
Global Cnsld Holdings Inc .... D 513 703-0965
  Mason (G-13709)
Global Graphene Group Inc .... E 937 331-9884
  Dayton (G-9573)
Going Home Medical Holding Co .... E 305 340-1034
  Strongsville (G-17466)
Hman Group Holdings Inc .... A 513 851-4900
  Cincinnati (G-3773)
Jbo Holding Company .... C 216 367-8787
  Cleveland (G-5855)
Lion Group Inc .... D 937 898-1949
  Dayton (G-9685)
Liqui-Box International Inc .... D 614 888-9280
  Columbus (G-8071)
Live Technologies Holdings Inc .... D 614 278-7777
  Columbus (G-8074)

M J S Holding .... E 614 410-2512
  Columbus (G-8092)
Mssl Consolidated Inc .... B 330 766-5510
  Warren (G-18883)
◆ Nationwide Life Insur Co Amer .... A 800 688-5177
  Columbus (G-8245)
Nri Global Inc .... E 905 790-2828
  Delta (G-10162)
Ocr Services Corporation .... C 513 719-2600
  Cincinnati (G-4199)
Pet Food Holdings Inc .... D 419 394-3374
  Saint Marys (G-16683)
Pf Holdings LLC .... D 740 549-3558
  Lewis Center (G-12703)
Premix Holding Company .... B 330 666-3751
  Fairlawn (G-10968)
Qsr Parent Co .... A 330 425-8472
  Twinsburg (G-18458)
Savare Corporation .... D 770 517-3749
  Columbus (G-8687)
◆ Select-Arc Inc .... C 937 295-5215
  Fort Loramie (G-11111)
Towne Investment Company LP .... D 513 381-8696
  Cincinnati (G-4668)
Vala Holdings Ltd .... C 216 398-2980
  Parma (G-15918)
Washington Court Hse Holdg LLC .... E 614 873-7733
  Wshngtn CT Hs (G-20037)
Wasserstrom Holdings Inc .... C 614 228-6525
  Columbus (G-8972)

6722 Management Investment Offices

James Advantage Funds .... E 937 426-7640
  Xenia (G-20064)
Jpmorgan High Yield Fund .... E 614 248-7017
  Columbus (G-6889)

6726 Unit Investment Trusts, Face-Amount Certificate Offices

National Housing Tr Ltd Partnr .... E 614 451-9929
  Columbus (G-8221)
Rockbridge Capital LLC .... E 614 246-2400
  Columbus (G-8643)
Rockwood Equity Partners LLC .... E 216 378-9326
  Cleveland (G-6409)

6732 Education, Religious & Charitable Trusts

Altruism Society Inc .... D 877 283-4001
  Beachwood (G-1049)
Cleveland Foundation .... D 216 861-3810
  Cleveland (G-5315)
Golden Endings Golden Ret Resc .... E 614 486-0773
  Columbus (G-7758)
Miami Valley Community Action .... D 937 222-1009
  Dayton (G-9728)
Shawnee Weekday Early Lrng Ctr .... E 419 991-4806
  Lima (G-12930)

6733 Trusts Except Educational, Religious & Charitable

Charles V Francis Trust .... E 513 528-5600
  Cincinnati (G-3230)
Cleveland Clinic Foundation .... D 330 505-2280
  Niles (G-15288)
Cleveland Clinic Foundation .... D 614 451-0489
  Columbus (G-7297)
Cleveland Clinic Foundation .... D 216 444-2820
  Cleveland (G-5297)
Cleveland Clinic Foundation .... E 216 445-8585
  Cleveland (G-5298)
Cleveland Clinic Foundation .... B 216 444-5000
  Cleveland (G-5299)
Cleveland Clinic Foundation .... D 330 287-4500
  Wooster (G-19849)
Cleveland Clinic Foundation .... D 216 444-2200
  Cleveland (G-5303)
Cleveland Clinic Foundation .... D 440 930-6800
  Avon Lake (G-926)
Cleveland Clinic Foundation .... D 440 366-9444
  Elyria (G-10605)
Cleveland Clinic Foundation .... D 440 204-7800
  Lorain (G-13027)
Cleveland Clinic Foundation .... D 216 986-4000
  Independence (G-12200)
Cleveland Clinic Foundation .... D 216 445-6439
  Cleveland (G-5304)

Clinton Memorial Hospital .... E 937 383-3402
  Wilmington (G-19754)
Community Mercy Foundation .... B 937 652-3645
  Urbana (G-18582)
County of Preble .... E 937 839-5845
  West Alexandria (G-19007)
Huntington Auto Trust 2015-1 .... C 302 636-5401
  Columbus (G-7863)
Huntington Auto Trust 2016-1 .... C 302 636-5401
  Columbus (G-7864)
Kaiser Foundation Hospitals .... B 216 524-7377
  Willoughby (G-19674)
Raymond James Fincl Svcs Inc .... E 419 586-5121
  Celina (G-2661)
Sky Financial Capital Tr III .... C 614 480-3278
  Columbus (G-8742)

6794 Patent Owners & Lessors

Cassanos Inc .... E 937 294-8400
  Dayton (G-9388)
Clark Brands LLC .... A 330 723-9886
  Medina (G-14048)
Cleveland Rest Oper Ltd Partnr .... C 216 328-1121
  Cleveland (G-5344)
Convenient Food Mart Inc .... E 800 860-4844
  Mentor (G-14163)
Covelli Family Ltd Partnership .... B 330 856-3176
  Warren (G-18842)
Diet Center Worldwide Inc .... E 330 665-5861
  Akron (G-192)
East of Chicago Pizza Inc .... E 419 225-7116
  Lima (G-12771)
Epcon Cmmnties Franchising Inc .... D 614 761-1010
  Dublin (G-10337)
Escape Enterprises Inc .... E 614 224-0300
  Columbus (G-7609)
Giant Eagle Inc .... E 216 292-7000
  Bedford Heights (G-1352)
Gold Star Chili Inc .... E 513 231-4541
  Cincinnati (G-3684)
Gosh Enterprises Inc .... E 614 923-4700
  Columbus (G-7762)
Hobby Lobby Stores Inc .... D 419 861-1862
  Holland (G-12027)
Howley Bread Group Ltd .... D 440 808-1600
  Westlake (G-19492)
Larosas Inc .... A 513 347-5660
  Cincinnati (G-3962)
Marcos Inc .... C 419 885-4844
  Toledo (G-18042)
McDonalds Corporation .... E 614 682-1128
  Columbus (G-8135)
Moto Franchise Corporation .... E 937 291-1900
  Dayton (G-9758)
Ohio Valley Acquisition Inc .... B 513 553-0768
  Cincinnati (G-4211)
Ohio/Oklahoma Hearst TV Inc .... C 513 412-5000
  Cincinnati (G-4216)
Petland Inc .... D 740 775-2464
  Chillicothe (G-2870)
Physicians Weight Ls Ctr Amer .... E 330 666-7952
  Akron (G-389)
Premier Broadcasting Co Inc .... E 614 866-0700
  Columbus (G-8555)
Red Robin Gourmet Burgers Inc .... D 330 305-1080
  Canton (G-2505)
ServiceMaster of Defiance Inc .... D 419 784-5570
  Defiance (G-10057)
▲ Skyline Chili Inc .... C 513 874-1188
  Fairfield (G-10910)
Stanley Steemer Intl Inc .... C 614 764-2007
  Dublin (G-10461)
Ta Operating LLC .... B 440 808-9100
  Westlake (G-19553)
Travelcenters of America LLC .... B 724 981-9464
  Westlake (G-19556)
Tuffy Associates Corp .... E 419 865-6900
  Toledo (G-18264)
United Mercantile Corporation .... E 513 831-1300
  Milford (G-14571)
◆ Wendys Company .... B 614 764-3100
  Dublin (G-10491)
Wendys Restaurants LLC .... C 614 764-3100
  Dublin (G-10492)

6798 Real Estate Investment Trusts

845 Yard Street LLC .... D 614 857-2330
  Columbus (G-6917)
Ddr Corp .... E 614 785-6445
  Columbus (G-7497)

Ddr Corp ......C....... 216 755-5500 Beachwood *(G-1071)*
Ddr Tucson Spectrum I LLC ......E....... 216 755-5500 Beachwood *(G-1072)*
Forest City Realty Trust Inc ......E....... 216 621-6060 Cleveland *(G-5620)*
Investmerica limited ......D....... 216 618-3296 Chagrin Falls *(G-2701)*
Morelia Consultants LLC ......D....... 513 469-1500 Cincinnati *(G-4116)*
Moskowitz Family Ltd ......C....... 513 729-2300 Cincinnati *(G-4122)*
Washington Prime Group LP ......A....... 614 621-9000 Columbus *(G-8968)*
Washington Prime Group Inc ......D....... 614 621-9000 Columbus *(G-8969)*
▲ Welltower Inc ......D....... 419 247-2800 Toledo *(G-18304)*

6799 Investors, NEC

Arthur Middleton Capital Holdn ......C....... 330 966-3033 Canton *(G-2245)*
Blackbird Capital Group LLC ......C....... 513 762-7890 Cincinnati *(G-3113)*
Capital Investment Group Inc ......E....... 513 241-5090 Cincinnati *(G-3174)*
Community Choice Financial Inc ......D....... 614 798-5900 Dublin *(G-10304)*
Ctd Investments LLC ......E....... 614 570-9949 Columbus *(G-7473)*
First Business Fincl Svcs Inc ......E....... 216 573-3792 Cleveland *(G-5591)*
◆ Jpmorgan Chase Bank Nat Assn ......A....... 614 436-3055 Columbus *(G-6888)*
K M Clemens DDS Inc ......E....... 419 228-4036 Lima *(G-12807)*
Klingbeil Capital MGT LLC ......D....... 614 396-4919 Worthington *(G-19967)*
Lti Inc ......D....... 614 278-7777 Columbus *(G-8085)*
M-E Companies Inc ......D....... 614 818-4900 Westerville *(G-19423)*
Natl City Coml Capitol LLC ......E....... 513 455-9746 Cincinnati *(G-4145)*
Newmark & Company RE Inc ......E....... 216 453-3000 Cleveland *(G-6127)*
Rev1 Ventures ......E....... 614 487-3700 Columbus *(G-8627)*
Rightway Investments LLC ......E....... 216 854-7697 Twinsburg *(G-18461)*
Roulston Research Corp ......E....... 216 431-3000 Cleveland *(G-6414)*
Shancliff Investments Ltd ......E....... 330 883-5560 Youngstown *(G-20372)*
Shields Capital Corporation ......D....... 216 767-1340 Beachwood *(G-1123)*
Superior Street Partners LLC ......D....... 216 862-0058 Shaker Heights *(G-16868)*
The Huntington Investment Co ......E....... 513 351-2555 Cincinnati *(G-4643)*
Weinberg Capital Group Inc ......D....... 216 503-8307 Cleveland *(G-6728)*
Wings Investors Company Ltd ......E....... 513 241-5800 Cincinnati *(G-4853)*

70 HOTELS, ROOMING HOUSES, CAMPS, AND OTHER LODGING PLACES

7011 Hotels, Motels & Tourist Courts

1100 Carnegie LP ......D....... 216 658-6400 Cleveland *(G-4919)*
1460 Ninth St Assoc Ltd Partnr ......E....... 216 241-6600 Cleveland *(G-4921)*
16644 Snow Rd LLC ......E....... 216 676-5200 Brookpark *(G-1934)*
1st Stop Inc ......E....... 937 695-0318 Winchester *(G-19798)*
21c Cincinnati LLC ......D....... 513 578-6600 Cincinnati *(G-2942)*
5 Star Hotel Management IV LP ......D....... 614 431-1819 Columbus *(G-6913)*
50 S Front LLC ......D....... 614 224-4600 Columbus *(G-6914)*
506 Phelps Holdings LLC ......E....... 513 651-1234 Cincinnati *(G-2946)*
5901 Pfffer Rd Htels Sites LLC ......D....... 513 793-4500 Blue Ash *(G-1522)*
6300 Sharonville Assoc LLC ......C....... 513 489-3636 Cincinnati *(G-2947)*
631 South Main Street Dev LLC ......D....... 419 423-0631 Findlay *(G-10987)*
75 East State LLC ......E....... 614 365-4500 Columbus *(G-6916)*
A C Management Inc ......E....... 440 461-9200 Cleveland *(G-4931)*
AIR Management Group LLC ......D....... 330 856-1900 Warren *(G-18814)*
Airport Core Hotel LLC ......C....... 614 536-0500 Columbus *(G-6959)*
AK Group Hotels Inc ......E....... 937 372-9921 Xenia *(G-20040)*
Akron Inn Limited Partnership ......E....... 330 336-7692 Wadsworth *(G-18745)*
Alexander House Inc ......E....... 513 523-4569 Oxford *(G-15810)*
Alliance Hospitality ......E....... 330 505-2173 Youngstown *(G-20100)*
Alliance Hospitality Inc ......E....... 440 951-7333 Mentor *(G-14141)*
Alsan Corporation ......D....... 330 385-3636 East Liverpool *(G-10514)*
American Prprty-Mnagement Corp ......D....... 330 454-5000 Canton *(G-2239)*
Americas Best Value Inn ......E....... 419 626-9890 Sandusky *(G-16726)*
Amish Door Inc ......B....... 330 359-5464 Wilmot *(G-19797)*
Amitel Beachwood Ltd Partnr ......E....... 216 831-3030 Cleveland *(G-5027)*
Amitel Limited Partnership ......E....... 440 234-6688 Cleveland *(G-5028)*
Amitel Mentor Ltd Partnership ......E....... 440 392-0800 Mentor *(G-14143)*
Amitel Rockside Ltd Partnr ......E....... 216 520-1450 Cleveland *(G-5029)*
Ap/Aim Dublin Suites Trs LLC ......D....... 614 790-9000 Dublin *(G-10254)*
Ap/Aim Indpndnce Sites Trs LLC ......D....... 216 986-9900 Independence *(G-12186)*
Apple Gate Operating Co Inc ......E....... 330 405-4488 Twinsburg *(G-18392)*
Army & Air Force Exchange Svc ......C....... 937 257-2928 Dayton *(G-9255)*
Arvind Sagar Inc ......E....... 614 428-8800 Columbus *(G-7047)*
Ashford Trs Lessee LLC ......E....... 937 436-2400 Miamisburg *(G-14272)*
At Hospitality LLC ......D....... 513 527-9962 Cincinnati *(G-3052)*
Athens OH 1013 LLC ......E....... 740 589-5839 Athens *(G-776)*
Aurora Hotel Partners LLC ......E....... 330 562-0767 Aurora *(G-826)*
Avalon Inn Services Inc ......C....... 330 856-1900 Warren *(G-18824)*
Avalon Resort and Spa LLC ......D....... 330 856-1900 Warren *(G-18826)*
Awe Hospitality Group LLC ......C....... 330 888-8836 Macedonia *(G-13188)*
B & I Hotel Management LLC ......C....... 330 995-0200 Aurora *(G-828)*
Bass Lake Tavern Inc ......D....... 440 285-3100 Chardon *(G-2741)*
Bellville Hotel Company ......E....... 419 886-7000 Bellville *(G-1421)*
Bennett Enterprises Inc ......B....... 419 874-3111 Perrysburg *(G-15978)*
Bennett Enterprises Inc ......E....... 419 893-1004 Maumee *(G-13887)*
Best Western Columbus N Hotel ......E....... 614 888-8230 Columbus *(G-7103)*
Best Western Executive Inn ......E....... 330 794-1050 Akron *(G-101)*
Best Wooster Inc ......E....... 330 264-7750 Wooster *(G-19831)*
Beverly Hills Inn La Llc ......E....... 859 494-9151 Aberdeen *(G-1)*
Bindu Associates LLC ......E....... 440 324-0099 Elyria *(G-10598)*
Bird Enterprises LLC ......E....... 330 674-1457 Millersburg *(G-14589)*
Black Sapphire C Columbus Univ ......D....... 614 297-9912 Columbus *(G-7116)*
Blue-Kenwood LLC ......E....... 513 469-6900 Blue Ash *(G-1546)*
Bob Mor Inc ......C....... 419 485-5555 Montpelier *(G-14737)*
Boulevard Motel Corp ......E....... 440 234-3131 Cleveland *(G-5130)*
Brice Hotel Inc ......D....... 614 864-1280 Reynoldsburg *(G-16432)*
Broad Street Hotel Assoc LP ......D....... 614 861-0321 Columbus *(G-7147)*
Brookdale Senior Living Inc ......D....... 937 738-7342 Marysville *(G-13607)*
Brothers Properties Corp ......C....... 513 381-3000 Cincinnati *(G-3141)*
Buffalo-Gtb Associates LLC ......E....... 216 831-3735 Beachwood *(G-1059)*
Buxton Inn Inc ......E....... 740 587-0001 Granville *(G-11459)*
Ca-Mj Hotel Associates Ltd ......D....... 330 494-6494 Canton *(G-2278)*
Cabin Restaurant ......E....... 330 562-9171 Aurora *(G-832)*
Cafaro Peachcreek Co Ltd ......D....... 419 625-6280 Sandusky *(G-16731)*
Cambria Green Management LLC ......E....... 330 899-1263 Uniontown *(G-18511)*
Cambridge Associates Ltd ......E....... 740 432-7313 Cambridge *(G-2098)*
Cambridge Property Investors ......E....... 740 432-7313 Cambridge *(G-2102)*
Canter Inn Inc ......E....... 740 354-7711 Portsmouth *(G-16267)*
Canton Hotel Holdings Inc ......E....... 330 492-1331 Canton *(G-2289)*
Canus Hospitality LLC ......E....... 937 323-8631 Springfield *(G-17155)*
Cardida Corporation ......E....... 740 439-4359 Kimbolton *(G-12446)*
Carlisle Hotels Inc ......E....... 614 851-5599 Columbus *(G-7201)*
Carlson Hotels Ltd Partnership ......D....... 740 386-5451 Marion *(G-13528)*
Carol Burton Management LLC ......E....... 419 666-5120 Toledo *(G-17793)*
Carroll Properties ......E....... 513 398-8075 Mason *(G-13671)*
Cedar Point Park LLC ......D....... 419 627-2500 Sandusky *(G-16735)*
CER Hotels LLC ......E....... 330 422-1855 Streetsboro *(G-17409)*
Ceres Enterprises LLC ......D....... 440 617-9385 Westlake *(G-19472)*
Cerruti LLC ......E....... 330 562-0120 Aurora *(G-834)*
Ch Relty Iv/Clmbus Partners LP ......D....... 614 885-3334 Columbus *(G-7247)*
Charter Hotel Group Ltd Partnr ......E....... 216 772-4538 Mentor *(G-14156)*
Cherry Valley Lodge ......E....... 740 788-1200 Newark *(G-15156)*
Chillicothe Motel LLC ......E....... 740 773-3903 Chillicothe *(G-2822)*
Chimneys Inn ......E....... 937 567-7850 Dayton *(G-9404)*
Choice Hotels Intl Inc ......D....... 330 656-1252 Hudson *(G-12111)*
Chu Airport Inn Inc ......E....... 216 267-5100 Brookpark *(G-1939)*
Cincinnati Netherland Ht LLC ......B....... 513 421-9100 Cincinnati *(G-3320)*
Claire De Leigh Corp ......E....... 614 459-6575 Columbus *(G-7289)*
Clermont Hills Co LLC ......D....... 513 752-4400 Cincinnati *(G-2908)*
Cleveland Airport Hospitality ......D....... 440 871-6000 Westlake *(G-19476)*
Cleveland Bchwood Hsptlity LLC ......D....... 216 464-5950 Beachwood *(G-1063)*
Cleveland Crowne Plaza Airport ......E....... 440 243-4040 Cleveland *(G-5311)*
Cleveland East Hotel LLC ......D....... 216 378-9191 Cleveland *(G-5312)*
Cleveland S Hospitality LLC ......E....... 216 447-1300 Cleveland *(G-5345)*
Cleveland Westlake ......E....... 440 892-0333 Westlake *(G-19477)*
Clinic Care Inc ......D....... 216 707-4200 Cleveland *(G-5364)*
Clp Gw Sandusky Tenant LP ......B....... 419 609-6000 Sandusky *(G-16741)*
Cmp I Blue Ash Owner LLC ......E....... 513 733-4334 Blue Ash *(G-1561)*
Cmp I Columbus I Owner LLC ......E....... 614 764-9393 Dublin *(G-10297)*

Employee Codes: A=Over 500 employees, B=251-500
C=101-250, D=51-100, E=25-50
2018 Harris Ohio
Services Directory
981

70 HOTELS, ROOMING HOUSES, CAMPS, AND OTHER LODGING PLACES SIC SECTION

Cmp I Columbus II Owner LLC..............E....... 614 436-7070
Columbus *(G-7309)*
Columbia Properties Lima LLC............D....... 419 222-0004
Lima *(G-12757)*
Columbus Airport Ltd Partnr................C....... 614 475-7551
Columbus *(G-7326)*
Columbus Concord Ltd Partnr..............D....... 614 228-3200
Columbus *(G-7342)*
Columbus Easton Hotel LLC.................E....... 614 414-1000
Columbus *(G-7349)*
Columbus Easton Hotel LLC.................D....... 614 414-5000
Columbus *(G-7350)*
Columbus Easton Hotel LLC.................E....... 614 383-2005
Columbus *(G-7351)*
Columbus Hospitality..............................E....... 614 461-2648
Columbus *(G-7358)*
Columbus Hotel Partners........................E....... 513 891-1066
Blue Ash *(G-1563)*
Columbus Hotel Partnership LLC.........D....... 614 890-8600
Columbus *(G-7359)*
Columbus Leasing LLC..........................D....... 614 885-1885
Columbus *(G-7363)*
Columbus Oh-16 Airport Gahanna........E....... 614 501-4770
Gahanna *(G-11236)*
Columbus Worthington Hospitali..........D....... 614 885-3334
Columbus *(G-7394)*
Comfort Inn..E....... 740 454-4144
Zanesville *(G-20466)*
Comfort Inn Northeast...........................E....... 513 683-9700
Cincinnati *(G-3396)*
Comfort Inns..E....... 614 885-4084
Columbus *(G-7398)*
Commodore Prry Inns Suites LLC........D....... 419 732-2645
Port Clinton *(G-16240)*
Commodore Resorts Inc........................E....... 419 285-3101
Port Clinton *(G-16241)*
Commonwealth Hotels LLC..................D....... 216 524-5814
Cleveland *(G-5380)*
Commonwealth Hotels LLC..................C....... 614 790-9000
Dublin *(G-10303)*
Concord Dayton Hotel II LLC...............D....... 937 223-1000
Dayton *(G-9422)*
Concord Hamiltonian Rvrfrnt Ho...........D....... 513 896-6200
Hamilton *(G-11717)*
Concord Testa Hotel Assoc LLC...........D....... 330 252-9228
Akron *(G-160)*
▲ **Continental GL Sls & Inv Group**.......B....... 614 679-1201
Powell *(G-16332)*
Continental/Olentangy Ht LLC..............D....... 614 297-9912
Columbus *(G-7433)*
Cork Enterprises Inc.............................E....... 740 654-1842
Lancaster *(G-12523)*
Corporate Exchange Hotel Assoc.........C....... 614 890-8600
Columbus *(G-7443)*
Coshocton Village Inn Suites................E....... 740 622-9455
Coshocton *(G-9098)*
Courtyard By Marriott............................E....... 216 765-1900
Cleveland *(G-5429)*
Courtyard By Marriott............................E....... 513 341-4140
West Chester *(G-19055)*
Courtyard By Marriott............................E....... 440 871-3756
Westlake *(G-19481)*
Courtyard By Marriott............................D....... 937 433-3131
Miamisburg *(G-14288)*
Courtyard By Marriott Dayton...............E....... 937 220-9060
Dayton *(G-9441)*
Courtyard By Marriott Rossford............E....... 419 872-5636
Rossford *(G-16607)*
Courtyard Management Corp................E....... 614 475-8530
Columbus *(G-7451)*
Courtyard Management Corp................E....... 216 901-9988
Cleveland *(G-5430)*
CPX Canton Airport LLC.......................C....... 330 305-0500
North Canton *(G-15330)*
CPX Carrollton Es LLC..........................E....... 330 627-1200
Carrollton *(G-2617)*
Crefiii Waramaug...................................D....... 937 322-3600
Springfield *(G-17184)*
Crowne Plaza Toledo.............................D....... 419 241-1411
Toledo *(G-17841)*
Cs Hotels Limited Partnership..............D....... 614 771-8999
Columbus *(G-7470)*
Cumberland Gap LLC............................E....... 513 681-9300
Cincinnati *(G-3446)*
Cwb Property Managment Inc...............E....... 614 793-2244
Dublin *(G-10315)*
Das Dutch Village Inn............................D....... 330 482-5050
Columbiana *(G-6858)*
Days Inn..E....... 740 695-0100
Saint Clairsville *(G-16635)*
Dayton Choa...E....... 937 278-4871
Dayton *(G-9465)*
Dayton Hotels LLC..................................E....... 937 832-2222
Englewood *(G-10702)*
DB&p Logistics Inc..................................E....... 614 491-4035
Columbus *(G-7495)*
Dbp Enterprises LLC...............................E....... 740 513-2399
Sunbury *(G-17554)*
Detroit Westfield LLC..............................D....... 330 666-4131
Akron *(G-190)*
Dino Persichetti..E....... 330 821-9600
Alliance *(G-538)*
Donlen Inc...D....... 216 961-6767
Cleveland *(G-5502)*
Doubletree Guest Suites Dayton...........D....... 937 436-2400
Miamisburg *(G-14298)*
Drury Hotels Company LLC...................E....... 614 798-8802
Dublin *(G-10324)*
Drury Hotels Company LLC...................E....... 614 221-7008
Columbus *(G-7545)*
Drury Hotels Company LLC...................E....... 937 454-5200
Dayton *(G-9506)*
Drury Hotels Company LLC...................E....... 513 771-5601
Cincinnati *(G-3503)*
Drury Hotels Company LLC...................E....... 614 798-8802
Grove City *(G-11556)*
Dure Investments LLC............................E....... 419 697-7800
Oregon *(G-15732)*
Durga Llc..D....... 513 771-2080
Cincinnati *(G-3515)*
East End Ro Burton Inc..........................E....... 440 942-2742
Willoughby *(G-19660)*
Eastlake Lodging LLC.............................E....... 440 953-8000
Eastlake *(G-10546)*
Econo Lodge...D....... 419 627-8000
Sandusky *(G-16750)*
Edmond Hotel Investors LLC..................D....... 614 891-2900
Columbus *(G-7579)*
Elbe Properties...A....... 513 489-1955
Cincinnati *(G-3545)*
Elden Motels LP..D....... 440 967-8770
Vermilion *(G-18708)*
Emmett Dan House Ltd Partnr...............E....... 740 392-6886
Mount Vernon *(G-14894)*
Epiqurian Inns..D....... 614 885-2600
Worthington *(G-19957)*
Fairfeld Inn Stes Clmbus Arprt..............E....... 614 237-2100
Columbus *(G-7630)*
Fairfield Inn..D....... 614 267-1111
Columbus *(G-7631)*
Fairlawn Associates Ltd..........................C....... 330 867-5000
Fairlawn *(G-10949)*
Falcon Plaza LLC.....................................E....... 419 352-4671
Bowling Green *(G-1775)*
Fh TCH...E....... 614 781-1645
Powell *(G-16334)*
Findlay Inn & Conference Ctr................D....... 419 422-5682
Findlay *(G-11027)*
First Hospitality Company LLC..............E....... 614 864-4555
Reynoldsburg *(G-16452)*
First Hotel Associates LP........................D....... 614 228-3800
Columbus *(G-7665)*
First Hotel Management LLC.................E....... 614 864-1280
Reynoldsburg *(G-16453)*
Fmw Rri Opco LLC...................................E....... 614 744-2659
Columbus *(G-7678)*
Frog & Toad Inc..E....... 419 877-1180
Whitehouse *(G-19586)*
Gallipolis Hospitality Inc..........................E....... 740 446-0090
Gallipolis *(G-11319)*
Gateway Hospitality Group Inc..............C....... 330 405-9800
Twinsburg *(G-18420)*
Geeta Hospitality Inc...............................E....... 937 642-3777
Marysville *(G-13622)*
Glenlaurel Inc...E....... 740 385-4070
Rockbridge *(G-16560)*
Glidden House Associates Ltd...............E....... 216 231-8900
Cleveland *(G-5674)*
Golden Lamb..C....... 513 932-5065
Lebanon *(G-12608)*
Goodnight Inn Inc....................................E....... 419 334-9551
Fremont *(G-11203)*
Grand Heritage Hotel Portland...............E....... 440 734-4477
North Olmsted *(G-15424)*
Grand View Inn Inc...................................D....... 740 377-4388
South Point *(G-17086)*
Grandview Ht Ltd Partnr Ohio................D....... 937 766-5519
Springfield *(G-17203)*
Granville Hospitality Llc...........................D....... 740 587-3333
Granville *(G-11466)*
Great Bear Lodge Sandusky LLC...........B....... 419 609-6000
Sandusky *(G-16765)*
Green Township Hospitality LLC............B....... 513 574-6000
Cincinnati *(G-3712)*
Hampton Inn & Suite Inc.........................E....... 440 234-0206
Middleburg Heights *(G-14382)*
Hampton Inns LLC...................................E....... 330 492-0151
Canton *(G-2391)*
Hampton Inns LLC...................................E....... 330 422-0500
Streetsboro *(G-17415)*
Hardage Hotels I LLC...............................E....... 614 766-7762
Dublin *(G-10357)*
Haribol Haribol Inc...................................E....... 330 339-7731
New Philadelphia *(G-15099)*
Hauck Hospitality LLC..............................D....... 513 563-8330
Cincinnati *(G-3741)*
Hdi Ltd..C....... 937 224-0800
Dayton *(G-9602)*
He Hari Inc..D....... 614 436-0700
Worthington *(G-19961)*
He Hari Inc..D....... 614 846-6600
Lewis Center *(G-12687)*
Hide-A-Way Hills Club..............................E....... 740 746-9589
Sugar Grove *(G-17541)*
Hilton Garden Inn.....................................D....... 614 263-7200
Columbus *(G-7837)*
Hilton Garden Inn Akron..........................E....... 330 966-4907
Canton *(G-2401)*
Hilton Garden Inn Beavercreek...............D....... 937 458-2650
Dayton *(G-9273)*
Hilton Grdn Inn Clmbus Polaris..............E....... 614 846-8884
Columbus *(G-6883)*
Hilton Grdn Inn Columbus Arprt.............D....... 614 231-2869
Columbus *(G-7838)*
Hilton Polaris...D....... 614 885-1600
Columbus *(G-6884)*
Hit Portfolio I Hil Trs LLC........................E....... 614 235-0717
Dublin *(G-10362)*
Hit Portfolio I Misc Trs LLC......................C....... 216 575-1234
Cleveland *(G-5760)*
Hit Portfolio I Misc Trs LLC......................E....... 614 846-4355
Columbus *(G-7839)*
Hit Portfolio I Misc Trs LLC......................C....... 513 241-3575
Cincinnati *(G-3770)*
Hit Portfolio I Misc Trs LLC......................C....... 614 228-1234
Columbus *(G-7840)*
Hit Swn Trs LLC.......................................E....... 614 228-3200
Columbus *(G-7841)*
Hmshost Corporation..............................C....... 419 547-8667
Clyde *(G-6814)*
Holiday Inn..E....... 419 691-8800
Oregon *(G-15739)*
Holiday Inn Express.................................E....... 419 332-7700
Fremont *(G-11206)*
Holiday Inn Express.................................E....... 937 424-5757
Dayton *(G-9612)*
Holiday Inn Express.................................E....... 614 447-1212
Columbus *(G-7845)*
Holiday Inn of Englewood.........................D....... 937 832-1234
Englewood *(G-10708)*
Hollywood Casino Toledo.........................D....... 419 661-5200
Toledo *(G-17956)*
Home2 By Hilton......................................E....... 513 422-3454
West Chester *(G-19091)*
Honey Run Retreats LLC..........................E....... 330 674-0011
Millersburg *(G-14607)*
Hopkins Partners.....................................C....... 216 267-1500
Cleveland *(G-5772)*
Horseshoe Cleveland MGT LLC...............E....... 216 297-4777
Cleveland *(G-5776)*
Host Cincinnati Hotel LLC........................C....... 513 621-7700
Cincinnati *(G-3788)*
Hoster Hotels LLC....................................E....... 419 931-8900
Perrysburg *(G-16014)*
Hotel 2345 LLC..E....... 614 766-7762
Dublin *(G-10365)*
Hotel 50 S Front Opco LP.........................D....... 614 228-4600
Columbus *(G-7860)*
Hotel Stow LP...E....... 330 945-9722
Stow *(G-17373)*
Howard Johnson.......................................D....... 513 825-3129
Cincinnati *(G-3790)*
Hst Lessee Cincinnati LLC........................C....... 513 852-2702
Cincinnati *(G-3793)*
Hyatt Corporation....................................B....... 614 463-1234
Columbus *(G-7874)*
Hyatt Regency Columbus.........................B....... 614 463-1234
Columbus *(G-7875)*
IA Urban Htels Bchwood Trs LLC...........D....... 216 765-8066
Beachwood *(G-1088)*

SIC SECTION

70 HOTELS, ROOMING HOUSES, CAMPS, AND OTHER LODGING PLACES

Ihg Management (maryland) LLC ....C 614 461-4100
  Columbus *(G-7883)*
Independent Hotel Partners LLC ....D 216 524-0700
  Cleveland *(G-5814)*
Indus Airport Hotel II LLC ....D 614 235-0717
  Columbus *(G-7890)*
Indus Airport Hotels I LLC ....D 614 231-2869
  Columbus *(G-7891)*
Indus Hilliard Hotel LLC ....E 614 334-1800
  Hilliard *(G-11913)*
Inn At Marietta Ltd ....D 740 373-9600
  Marietta *(G-13456)*
Inn At Wickliffe LLC ....E 440 585-0600
  Wickliffe *(G-19603)*
Integrated CC LLC ....E 216 707-4132
  Cleveland *(G-5825)*
Integrity Hotel Group ....C 937 224-0800
  Dayton *(G-9633)*
Intercntnntal Ht Group Rsurces ....D 216 707-4300
  Cleveland *(G-5828)*
Intercontinental Hotels Group ....E 216 707-4100
  Cleveland *(G-5829)*
Island Hospitality MGT LLC ....E 614 864-8844
  Columbus *(G-7927)*
Island House Inc ....E 419 734-0100
  Port Clinton *(G-16248)*
Jackson I-94 Ltd Partnership ....E 614 793-2244
  Dublin *(G-10379)*
Jagi Clveland Independence LLC ....C 216 524-8050
  Cleveland *(G-5848)*
Jagi Juno LLC ....E 513 489-1955
  Cincinnati *(G-3858)*
Jagi Springhill LLC ....E 216 264-4190
  Independence *(G-12221)*
Janus Hotels and Resorts Inc ....E 513 631-8500
  Lewisburg *(G-12711)*
Johnson Howard International ....E 513 825-3129
  Cincinnati *(G-3883)*
Kenyon College ....E 740 427-2202
  Gambier *(G-11348)*
Kmb Management Services Corp ....D 330 263-2660
  Wooster *(G-19880)*
Kribha LLC ....E 740 788-8991
  Newark *(G-15180)*
Lancaster Host LLC ....E 740 654-4445
  Lancaster *(G-12550)*
Lawnfield Properties LLC ....E 440 974-3572
  Mentor *(G-14208)*
Legacy Village Hospitality LLC ....D 216 382-3350
  Cleveland *(G-5932)*
Levis Commons Hotel LLC ....D 419 873-3573
  Perrysburg *(G-16027)*
Liberty Ashtabula Holdings ....E 330 872-6000
  Newton Falls *(G-15277)*
Liberty Ctr Lodging Assoc LLC ....E 608 833-4100
  Liberty Township *(G-12723)*
Lieben Wooster LP ....E 330 390-5722
  Millersburg *(G-14610)*
Lmn Development LLC ....D 419 433-7200
  Sandusky *(G-16775)*
Lodging Industry Inc ....E 440 323-7488
  Sandusky *(G-16776)*
Lodging Industry Inc ....E 419 732-2929
  Port Clinton *(G-16250)*
Lodging Industry Inc ....E 440 324-3911
  Elyria *(G-10645)*
Longaberger Company ....D 740 349-8411
  Newark *(G-15197)*
Lq Management LLC ....E 614 866-6456
  Reynoldsburg *(G-16467)*
Lq Management LLC ....D 513 771-0300
  Cincinnati *(G-4002)*
Lq Management LLC ....E 216 447-1133
  Cleveland *(G-5954)*
Lq Management LLC ....E 216 251-8500
  Cleveland *(G-5955)*
M&C Hotel Interests Inc ....E 937 778-8100
  Piqua *(G-16151)*
Mansfield Hotel Partnership ....E 419 529-2100
  Mansfield *(G-13331)*
Mansfield Hotel Partnership ....D 419 529-1000
  Mansfield *(G-13332)*
March Investors Ltd ....E 740 373-5353
  Marietta *(G-13463)*
Marcus Hotels Inc ....E 614 228-3800
  Columbus *(G-8106)*
Marios International Spa & Ht ....C 330 562-5141
  Aurora *(G-846)*
Marriott ....E 440 542-2375
  Solon *(G-17026)*

Marriott Hotel Services Inc ....C 216 252-5333
  Cleveland *(G-5982)*
Marriott International Inc ....C 614 861-1400
  Columbus *(G-8112)*
Marriott International Inc ....E 330 484-0300
  Canton *(G-2449)*
Marriott International Inc ....C 513 487-3800
  Cincinnati *(G-4025)*
Marriott International Inc ....B 216 696-9200
  Cleveland *(G-5983)*
Marriott International Inc ....B 614 228-5050
  Columbus *(G-8113)*
Marriott International Inc ....E 614 436-7070
  Columbus *(G-8114)*
Marriott International Inc ....C 614 475-8530
  Columbus *(G-8115)*
Marriott International Inc ....C 614 864-8844
  Columbus *(G-8116)*
Marriott International Inc ....C 614 222-2610
  Columbus *(G-8117)*
Marriott International Inc ....E 614 885-0799
  Columbus *(G-8118)*
Marriott International Inc ....E 330 666-4811
  Copley *(G-9060)*
Marriott International Inc ....C 419 866-1001
  Holland *(G-12035)*
Marriott International Inc ....E 440 716-9977
  North Olmsted *(G-15431)*
Marriott International Inc ....C 513 530-5060
  Blue Ash *(G-1636)*
Mason Family Resorts LLC ....B 513 339-0141
  Mason *(G-13736)*
Maumee Lodging Enterprises ....D 419 865-1380
  Maumee *(G-13944)*
McPaul Corp ....E 419 447-6313
  Tiffin *(G-17684)*
Meander Hospitality Group Inc ....E 330 702-0226
  Canfield *(G-2199)*
Meander Hsptality Group II LLC ....E 330 422-0500
  Streetsboro *(G-17420)*
Meander Inn Inc ....E 330 544-2378
  Youngstown *(G-20276)*
Meander Inn Incorporated ....E 330 544-0660
  Youngstown *(G-20277)*
Middletown Innkeepers Inc ....E 513 942-3440
  Fairfield *(G-10882)*
Moody Nat Cy Dt Clumbus Mt LLC ....D 614 228-3200
  Columbus *(G-8186)*
Moody Nat Cy Willoughby Mt LLC ....E 440 530-1100
  Willoughby *(G-19693)*
Motel 6 Operating LP ....E 614 431-2525
  Columbus *(G-8190)*
Motel Investments Marietta Inc ....E 740 374-8190
  Marietta *(G-13479)*
Motel Partners LLC ....E 740 594-3000
  Athens *(G-802)*
Moti Corporation ....E 440 734-4500
  Cleveland *(G-6080)*
Mrn-Newgar Hotel Ltd ....E 216 443-1000
  Cleveland *(G-6085)*
Msk Hospitality Inc ....E 513 771-0370
  Cincinnati *(G-4127)*
N P Motel System Inc ....E 330 339-7731
  New Philadelphia *(G-15110)*
Natural Resources Ohio Dept ....D 419 938-5411
  Perrysville *(G-16080)*
Newark Management Partners LLC ....D 740 322-6455
  Newark *(G-15220)*
Nf II Cleveland Op Co LLC ....E 216 443-9043
  Cleveland *(G-6130)*
Norstar Aluminum Molds Inc ....D 440 632-0853
  Middlefield *(G-14399)*
Northeast Cincinnati Hotel LLC ....C 513 459-9800
  Mason *(G-13743)*
Northern Tier Hospitality LLC ....D 570 888-7711
  Westlake *(G-19525)*
Northland Hotel Inc ....E 614 885-1601
  Columbus *(G-8292)*
Northtown Square Ltd Partnr ....E 419 691-8911
  Oregon *(G-15742)*
Ntk Hotel Group II LLC ....D 614 559-2000
  Columbus *(G-8302)*
Oakwood Hospitality Corp ....E 440 786-1998
  Bedford *(G-1325)*
Oberlin College ....D 440 935-1475
  Oberlin *(G-15656)*
Oh-16 Clvlnd Arprt S Prprty Su ....E 440 243-8785
  Middleburg Heights *(G-14383)*
Ohio Inns Inc ....E 937 440-9303
  Troy *(G-18369)*

Ohio State Parks Inc ....D 513 664-3504
  College Corner *(G-6838)*
Ohio State University ....E 614 247-4000
  Columbus *(G-8404)*
Ohio State University ....B 614 292-3238
  Columbus *(G-8427)*
Olshan Hotel Management Inc ....E 614 414-1000
  Columbus *(G-8467)*
Olshan Hotel Management Inc ....E 614 416-8000
  Columbus *(G-8468)*
Oxford Hospitality Group Inc ....E 513 524-0114
  Oxford *(G-15828)*
Pacific Heritg Inn Polaris LLC ....E 614 880-9080
  Columbus *(G-6899)*
Paradise Hospitality Inc ....C 419 255-6190
  Toledo *(G-18116)*
Park Hotels & Resorts Inc ....C 216 447-0020
  Cleveland *(G-6236)*
Park Hotels & Resorts Inc ....B 216 464-5950
  Cleveland *(G-6237)*
Park Hotels & Resorts Inc ....E 937 436-2400
  Miamisburg *(G-14331)*
Park Inn ....E 419 241-3000
  Toledo *(G-18117)*
Parkins Incorporated ....E 614 334-1800
  Hilliard *(G-11942)*
Peitro Properties Ltd Partnr ....E 216 328-7777
  Cleveland *(G-6260)*
PH Fairborn Ht Owner 2800 LLC ....E 937 426-7800
  Beavercreek *(G-1197)*
Pinecraft Land Holdings LLC ....E 330 390-5722
  Millersburg *(G-14615)*
Plaza Inn Foods Inc ....E 937 354-2181
  Mount Victory *(G-14930)*
Polaris Innkeepers Inc ....E 614 568-0770
  Westerville *(G-19341)*
Primary Dayton Innkeepers LLC ....E 937 938-9550
  Dayton *(G-9827)*
Qh Management Company LLC ....D 440 497-1100
  Concord Twp *(G-9034)*
Quail Hollow Management Inc ....D 440 639-4000
  Painesville *(G-15874)*
R & H Service Inc ....E 330 626-2888
  Streetsboro *(G-17427)*
R & K Gorby LLC ....E 419 222-0004
  Lima *(G-12866)*
R & Y Holding ....E 419 353-3464
  Bowling Green *(G-1792)*
R P L Corporation ....C 937 335-0021
  Troy *(G-18373)*
Radisson Hotel Cleve ....E 440 734-5060
  North Olmsted *(G-15442)*
Radisson Hotel Cleveland Gtwy ....D 216 377-9000
  Cleveland *(G-6344)*
Radius Hospitality MGT LLC ....D 330 735-2211
  Sherrodsville *(G-16906)*
Rama Inc ....E 614 473-9888
  Columbus *(G-8587)*
Red Roof Inns Inc ....A 614 744-2600
  Columbus *(G-8600)*
Red Roof Inns Inc ....E 614 224-6539
  Columbus *(G-8601)*
Red Roof Inns Inc ....E 440 892-7920
  Cleveland *(G-6363)*
Red Roof Inns Inc ....E 740 695-4057
  Saint Clairsville *(G-16654)*
Red Roof Inns Inc ....E 440 243-5166
  Cleveland *(G-6364)*
Renaissance Corporation ....E 937 526-3672
  Versailles *(G-18729)*
Renaissance Hotel Operating Co ....A 216 696-5600
  Cleveland *(G-6374)*
Renthotel Dayton LLC ....D 937 461-4700
  Dayton *(G-9847)*
Req/Jqh Holdings Inc ....D 937 432-0000
  Miamisburg *(G-14341)*
Residence Inn ....E 614 222-2610
  Columbus *(G-8618)*
Residence Inn By Marriott Beav ....E 937 427-3914
  Beavercreek *(G-1204)*
Richfield Banquet & Confer ....E 330 659-6151
  Richfield *(G-16526)*
Riders 1812 Inn ....E 440 354-0922
  Painesville *(G-15878)*
Ridgehills Hotel Ltd Partnr ....D 440 585-0600
  Wickliffe *(G-19613)*
River Road Hotel Corp ....E 614 267-7461
  Columbus *(G-8634)*
Riverside Cmnty Urban Redev ....C 330 929-3000
  Cuyahoga Falls *(G-9215)*

Employee Codes: A=Over 500 employees, B=251-500
C=101-250, D=51-100, E=25-50

Riverview Hotel LLC E 614 268-8700
Columbus *(G-8637)*
Rlj III - Em Clmbus Lessee LLC D 614 890-8600
Columbus *(G-8638)*
Roce Group LLC E 330 969-2627
Stow *(G-17390)*
Rockside Hospitality LLC D 216 524-0700
Independence *(G-12251)*
Roschmans Restaurant ADM E 419 225-8300
Lima *(G-12871)*
Rose Gracias E 614 785-0001
Columbus *(G-8648)*
Rossford Hospitality Group Inc E 419 874-2345
Rossford *(G-16611)*
Rukh Boardman Properties LLC D 330 726-5472
Youngstown *(G-20361)*
Rukh-Jagi Holdings LLC D 330 494-2770
Canton *(G-2518)*
S & S Management Inc E 937 382-5858
Wilmington *(G-19785)*
S & S Management Inc E 937 235-2000
Dayton *(G-9861)*
S & S Management Inc E 567 356-4151
Wapakoneta *(G-18807)*
S P S Inc E 937 339-7801
Troy *(G-18378)*
Sadguru Krupa LLC E 330 644-2111
Akron *(G-425)*
Sage Hospitality Resources LLC D 513 771-2080
Cincinnati *(G-4469)*
Salt Fork Resort Club Inc A 740 498-8116
Kimbolton *(G-12447)*
Sar Biren E 419 865-0407
Maumee *(G-13974)*
Sauder Haritage Inn E 419 445-6408
Archbold *(G-643)*
Saw Mill Creek Ltd C 419 433-3800
Huron *(G-12170)*
Sawmill Creek Resort Ltd C 419 433-3800
Huron *(G-12172)*
Sb Hotel LLC E 614 793-2244
Dublin *(G-10449)*
SDC Unvrsity Cir Developer LLC D 216 791-5333
Cleveland *(G-6456)*
Seagate Hospitality Group LLC E 216 252-7700
Cleveland *(G-6457)*
Seal Mayfield LLC E 440 684-4100
Mayfield Heights *(G-14007)*
Select Hotels Group LLC E 513 754-0003
Mason *(G-13759)*
Select Hotels Group LLC E 216 328-1060
Cleveland *(G-6466)*
Select Hotels Group LLC E 614 799-1913
Dublin *(G-10451)*
Shaker House D 216 991-6000
Cleveland *(G-6475)*
Shiv Hotels LLC E 740 374-8190
Marietta *(G-13499)*
Signature Boutique Hotel LP E 216 595-0900
Beachwood *(G-1125)*
Six Continents Hotels Inc C 513 563-8330
Cincinnati *(G-4533)*
Skyline Clvland Rnaissance LLC D 216 696-5600
Cleveland *(G-6487)*
SM Double Tree Hotel Lake E 216 241-5100
Cleveland *(G-6491)*
Sojourn Lodging Inc E 330 422-1855
Streetsboro *(G-17429)*
Solon Lodging Associates LLC E 440 248-9600
Solon *(G-17053)*
Somnus Corporation E 740 695-3961
Saint Clairsville *(G-16656)*
Son-Rise Hotels Inc E 330 769-4949
Seville *(G-16846)*
Sonesta Intl Hotels Corp C 614 791-8554
Dublin *(G-10457)*
Sortino Management & Dev Co E 419 626-6761
Sandusky *(G-16796)*
South Beach Resort E 419 798-4900
Lakeside Marblehead *(G-12466)*
Spread Eagle Tavern Inc E 330 223-1583
Hanoverton *(G-11787)*
Sree Hotels LLC E 513 354-2430
Cincinnati *(G-4570)*
Star Group Ltd E 614 428-8678
Gahanna *(G-11269)*
Starwood Hotels & Resorts C 614 345-9291
Columbus *(G-8778)*
Starwood Hotels & Resorts C 614 888-8230
Columbus *(G-8779)*
Sterling Lodging LLC E 419 879-4000
Lima *(G-12892)*
Stockport Mill Country Inn Inc E 740 559-2822
Stockport *(G-17346)*
Stoney Lodge Inc D 419 837-6409
Millbury *(G-14581)*
Stoney Ridge Inn South Ltd D 513 539-9247
Monroe *(G-14713)*
Strang Corporation E 216 961-6767
Cleveland *(G-6545)*
Strongsville Lodging Assoc 1 C 440 238-8800
Strongsville *(G-17512)*
Summit Associates Inc D 216 831-3300
Cleveland *(G-6547)*
Summit Hotel Trs 144 LLC E 216 443-9043
Cleveland *(G-6548)*
Summithotel D 513 527-9900
Cincinnati *(G-4598)*
Sycamore Lake Inc C 440 729-9775
Chesterland *(G-2804)*
Synergy Hotels LLC E 614 492-9000
Obetz *(G-15671)*
Tharaldson Hospitality MGT E 513 947-9402
Cincinnati *(G-2935)*
Toledo Inns Inc E 440 243-4040
Cleveland *(G-6601)*
Town House Motor Lodge Corp E 740 452-4511
Zanesville *(G-20539)*
Town Inn Co LLC D 614 221-3281
Columbus *(G-8857)*
TownePlace Suites By Marriott E 419 425-9545
Findlay *(G-11093)*
TownePlace Suites By Marriott E 513 774-0610
Cincinnati *(G-4673)*
Tramz Hotels LLC D 440 975-9922
Willoughby *(G-19718)*
Travelcenters of America LLC D 330 769-2053
Lodi *(G-12966)*
TW Recreational Services Inc E 440 564-9144
Newbury *(G-15262)*
Union Centre Hotel LLC C 513 874-7335
West Chester *(G-19173)*
United Hsptality Solutions LLC A 800 238-0487
Buffalo *(G-2053)*
Uph Holdings LLC D 614 447-9777
Columbus *(G-8913)*
Valley Hospitality Inc E 740 374-9660
Marietta *(G-13513)*
Valleyview Management Co Inc E 419 886-4000
Bellville *(G-1426)*
Visicon Inc D 937 879-2696
Fairborn *(G-10809)*
Vjp Hospitality Ltd E 614 475-8383
Columbus *(G-8948)*
W & H Realty Inc E 513 891-1066
Blue Ash *(G-1717)*
W2005/Fargo Hotels (pool C) E 937 890-6112
Dayton *(G-9980)*
W2005/Fargo Hotels (pool C) D 614 791-8675
Dublin *(G-10486)*
W2005/Fargo Hotels (pool C) E 937 322-2200
Springfield *(G-17293)*
W2005/Fargo Hotels (pool C) E 937 429-5505
Fairborn *(G-10810)*
West Montrose Properties D 330 867-4013
Fairlawn *(G-10982)*
Westgate Limited Partnership C 419 535-7070
Toledo *(G-18307)*
Westlake Marriott E 440 892-6887
Westlake *(G-19567)*
Westpost Columbus LLC D 614 885-1885
Columbus *(G-8982)*
Willoughby Lodging LLC E 440 530-1100
Willoughby *(G-19724)*
Winegardner & Hammons Inc C 614 791-1000
Dublin *(G-10493)*
Wm Columbus Hotel LLC C 614 228-3800
Columbus *(G-9001)*
Wph Cincinnati LLC C 513 771-2080
Cincinnati *(G-4861)*
Wright Executive Ht Ltd Partnr C 937 283-3200
Wilmington *(G-19796)*
Wright Executive Ht Ltd Partnr C 937 426-7800
Beavercreek *(G-1219)*
Wright Executive Ht Ltd Partnr C 937 429-0600
Beavercreek *(G-1220)*
Wyndham International Inc E 330 666-9300
Copley *(G-9069)*
Wyndham International Inc C 216 615-7500
Cleveland *(G-6764)*
Xanterra Parks & Resorts Inc C 740 439-2751
Cambridge *(G-2134)*
Xanterra Parks & Resorts Inc C 419 836-1466
Oregon *(G-15755)*
Xanterra Parks & Resorts Inc C 740 869-2020
Mount Sterling *(G-14876)*
Xanterra Parks & Resorts Inc D 440 564-9144
Newbury *(G-15265)*
Zincks Inn E 330 893-6600
Berlin *(G-1479)*

7021 Rooming & Boarding Houses

A M Management Inc E 937 426-6500
Beavercreek *(G-1143)*
Lodging First LLC E 614 792-2770
Dublin *(G-10390)*

7032 Sporting & Recreational Camps

Archdiocese of Cincinnati D 513 729-1725
Cincinnati *(G-3041)*
Camp Patmos Inc E 419 746-2214
Kelleys Island *(G-12348)*
Camp Pinecliff Inc D 614 236-5698
Columbus *(G-7181)*
Classroom Antics Inc E 800 595-3776
North Royalton *(G-15484)*
Columbus Frkln Cnty Pk E 614 891-0700
Westerville *(G-19388)*
Community Services Inc D 937 667-8631
Tipp City *(G-17714)*
Echoing Hills Village Inc D 740 594-3541
Athens *(G-785)*
Echoing Hills Village Inc A 740 327-2311
Warsaw *(G-18936)*
Echoing Hills Village Inc D 937 854-5151
Dayton *(G-9518)*
Echoing Hills Village Inc E 937 237-7881
Dayton *(G-9519)*
Echoing Hills Village Inc D 440 989-1400
Lorain *(G-13037)*
Echoing Hills Village Inc D 440 986-3085
South Amherst *(G-17073)*
Family YMCA of LANcstr&fairfld D 740 277-7373
Lancaster *(G-12541)*
Findlay Y M C A Child Dev E 419 422-3174
Findlay *(G-11031)*
First Community Church E 740 385-3827
Logan *(G-12972)*
Friars Club Inc D 513 488-8777
Cincinnati *(G-3654)*
Galion Community Center YMCA E 419 468-7754
Galion *(G-11297)*
Great Miami Valley YMCA D 513 887-0001
Hamilton *(G-11733)*
Great Miami Valley YMCA C 513 892-9622
Fairfield Township *(G-10930)*
Great Miami Valley YMCA D 513 887-0014
Hamilton *(G-11735)*
Great Miami Valley YMCA D 513 868-9622
Hamilton *(G-11736)*
Great Miami Valley YMCA D 513 829-3091
Fairfield *(G-10854)*
Hardin County Family YMCA E 419 673-6131
Kenton *(G-12416)*
Highland County Family YMCA E 937 840-9622
Hillsboro *(G-11978)*
Huber Heights YMCA D 937 236-9622
Dayton *(G-9623)*
Lake County YMCA A 440 352-3303
Painesville *(G-15860)*
Lake County YMCA C 440 946-1160
Willoughby *(G-19680)*
Lake County YMCA E 440 259-2724
Perry *(G-15962)*
Lake County YMCA D 440 428-5125
Madison *(G-13227)*
Mideast Baptist Conference E 440 834-8984
Burton *(G-2064)*
Midwest Gymnstics Cheerleading E 614 764-0775
Dublin *(G-10398)*
Ohio Camp Cherith Inc E 330 725-4202
Medina *(G-14110)*
Ohio F F A Camps Inc E 330 627-2208
Carrollton *(G-2625)*
Pike County YMCA E 740 947-8862
Waverly *(G-18974)*
Procamps Inc E 513 745-5855
Blue Ash *(G-1666)*
Red Oak Camp E 440 256-0716
Willoughby *(G-19707)*

72 PERSONAL SERVICES

Rockwell Springs Trout Club .... E 419 684-7971
  Clyde *(G-6821)*
Salvation Army .... D 330 735-2671
  Carrollton *(G-2629)*
Scribes & Scrbblr Chld Dev Ctr .... E 440 884-5437
  Cleveland *(G-6455)*
Sheldon Harry E Calvary Camp .... D 440 593-4381
  Conneaut *(G-9046)*
Skyview Baptist Ranch Inc .... E 330 674-7511
  Millersburg *(G-14622)*
Springfield Family Y M C A .... D 937 323-3781
  Springfield *(G-17281)*
Sycamore Board of Education .... D 513 489-3937
  Cincinnati *(G-4608)*
Ucc Childrens Center .... E 513 217-5501
  Middletown *(G-14488)*
West Ohio Conference of .... E 614 844-6200
  Worthington *(G-20007)*
Y M C A Central Stark County .... E 330 305-5437
  Canton *(G-2590)*
Y M C A Central Stark County .... E 330 875-1611
  Louisville *(G-13108)*
Y M C A Central Stark County .... E 330 877-8933
  Uniontown *(G-18545)*
Y M C A Central Stark County .... E 330 830-6275
  Massillon *(G-13862)*
Y M C A Central Stark County .... E 330 498-4082
  Canton *(G-2591)*
Y M C A of Ashland Ohio Inc .... D 419 289-0626
  Ashland *(G-709)*
YMCA .... E 330 823-1930
  Alliance *(G-566)*
YMCA Inc .... D 330 385-6400
  East Liverpool *(G-10536)*
YMCA of Clermont County Inc .... E 513 724-9622
  Batavia *(G-1032)*
YMCA of Massillon .... E 330 879-0800
  Navarre *(G-14957)*
Young Mens Christian .... B 513 932-1424
  Lebanon *(G-12660)*
Young Mens Christian Assn .... E 419 238-0443
  Van Wert *(G-18653)*
Young Mens Christian Assoc .... D 513 932-3756
  Oregonia *(G-15759)*
Young Mens Christian Assoc .... C 614 885-4252
  Columbus *(G-9017)*
Young Mens Christian Assoc .... C 614 871-9622
  Grove City *(G-11620)*
Young Mens Christian Assoc .... A 937 223-5201
  Dayton *(G-10009)*
Young Mens Christian Assoc .... D 330 923-5223
  Cuyahoga Falls *(G-9237)*
Young Mens Christian Assoc .... E 330 467-8366
  Macedonia *(G-13219)*
Young Mens Christian Assoc .... E 330 784-0408
  Akron *(G-515)*
Young Mens Christian Assoc .... C 614 416-9622
  Gahanna *(G-11276)*
Young Mens Christian Assoc .... C 740 881-1058
  Powell *(G-16355)*
Young Mens Christian Assoc .... C 614 334-9622
  Hilliard *(G-11967)*
Young Mens Christian Assoc .... E 937 312-1810
  Dayton *(G-10010)*
Young Mens Christian Assoc .... E 614 539-1770
  Urbancrest *(G-18609)*
Young Mens Christian Assoc .... D 614 252-3166
  Columbus *(G-9019)*
Young Mens Christian Assoc .... E 937 593-9001
  Bellefontaine *(G-1401)*
Young Mens Christian Associat .... E 419 729-8135
  Toledo *(G-18320)*
Young Mens Christian Associat .... D 513 241-9622
  Cincinnati *(G-4868)*
Young Mens Christian Associat .... D 513 923-4466
  Cincinnati *(G-4869)*
Young Mens Christian Associat .... E 419 474-3995
  Toledo *(G-18322)*
Young Mens Christian Associat .... D 419 866-9622
  Maumee *(G-13997)*
Young Mens Christian Associat .... C 419 475-3496
  Toledo *(G-18323)*
Young Mens Christian Associat .... D 419 691-3523
  Oregon *(G-15756)*
Young Mens Christian Mt Vernon .... E 740 392-9622
  Mount Vernon *(G-14927)*
Young MNS Chrstn Assn Clveland .... E 216 521-8400
  Lakewood *(G-12502)*
Young MNS Chrstn Assn Clveland .... D 440 842-5200
  North Royalton *(G-15507)*
Young MNS Chrstn Assn Clveland .... E 216 731-7454
  Cleveland *(G-6774)*
Young MNS Chrstn Assn Clveland .... D 440 285-7543
  Chardon *(G-2780)*
Young MNS Chrstn Assn Grter NY .... D 740 392-9622
  Mount Vernon *(G-14928)*
Young Womens Christian .... D 419 241-3235
  Toledo *(G-18325)*
Young Womens Christian 937 461-5550
  Dayton *(G-10013)*
Young Womens Christian .... E 419 238-6639
  Van Wert *(G-18654)*
Young Womens Christian Assn 614 224-9121
  Columbus *(G-9021)*
Young Womens Christian Assn 330 746-6361
  Youngstown *(G-20422)*
Young Womens Christian Associ 216 881-6878
  Cleveland *(G-6776)*
Young Womns Chrstn Assc Canton .... D 330 453-0789
  Canton *(G-2594)*
YWCA of Greater Cincinnati .... D 513 241-7090
  Cincinnati *(G-4870)*
YWCA Shelter & Housing Network .... E 937 222-6333
  Dayton *(G-10014)*

7033 Trailer Parks & Camp Sites

Big Broth and Big Siste of Cen .... E 614 839-2447
  Columbus *(G-7106)*
Clare-Mar Camp Inc .... E 440 647-3318
  New London *(G-15066)*
Dayton Tall Timbers Resort .... E 937 833-3888
  Brookville *(G-1962)*
Elbe Properties .... A 513 489-1955
  Cincinnati *(G-3545)*
Great Miami Valley YMCA .... E 513 867-0600
  Hamilton *(G-11734)*
Muskingum Wtrshed Cnsrvncy Dst .... E 330 343-6780
  Mineral City *(G-14634)*
Natural Resources Ohio Dept .... E 419 394-3611
  Saint Marys *(G-16680)*
Parks Recreation Athens .... E 740 592-0046
  Athens *(G-810)*
Real America Inc .... B 216 261-1177
  Cleveland *(G-6357)*

7041 Membership-Basis Hotels

Air Force US Dept of 937 257-6068
  Dayton *(G-9252)*
Alpha CHI Omega .... E 614 291-3871
  Columbus *(G-6974)*
Alpha Epsilon PHI .... E 614 294-5243
  Columbus *(G-6975)*
CHI Omega Sorority .... E 937 325-9323
  Springfield *(G-17159)*
Cincinnati Fifth Street Ht LLC .... D 513 579-1234
  Cincinnati *(G-3303)*
Ohio State University .... E 614 294-2635
  Columbus *(G-8430)*
Rockwell Springs Trout Club 419 684-7971
  Clyde *(G-6821)*
Sigma CHI Frat .... E 614 297-8783
  Columbus *(G-8730)*

72 PERSONAL SERVICES

7211 Power Laundries, Family & Commercial

Buckeye Launderer and Clrs LLC .... D 419 592-2941
  Sylvania *(G-17577)*
Dee Jay Cleaners Inc .... E 216 731-7060
  Euclid *(G-10750)*
Economy Linen & Towel Svc Inc .... C 740 454-6888
  Zanesville *(G-20473)*
Evergreen Cooperative Ldry Inc .... E 216 268-3548
  Cleveland *(G-5558)*
George Gardner .... D 419 636-4277
  Bryan *(G-2006)*
Heights Laundry & Dry Cleaning .... E 216 932-9666
  Cleveland Heights *(G-6789)*
Midwest Laundry Inc .... D 513 563-5560
  Cincinnati *(G-4092)*
Ohio Textile Service Inc .... E 740 450-4900
  Zanesville *(G-20520)*

7212 Garment Pressing & Cleaners' Agents

Apc2 Inc .... D 513 231-5540
  Cincinnati *(G-3033)*
C&C Clean Team Enterprises LLC .... C 513 321-5100
  Cincinnati *(G-3163)*
R & E Joint Venture Inc .... E 614 891-9404
  Westerville *(G-19348)*

7213 Linen Sply

Aramark Unf & Career AP LLC .... D 937 223-6667
  Dayton *(G-9340)*
Aramark Unf & Career AP LLC .... C 614 445-8341
  Columbus *(G-7032)*
Aramark Unf & Career AP LLC .... C 216 341-7400
  Cleveland *(G-5058)*
Barberton Laundry & Cleaning .... E 330 825-6911
  Barberton *(G-958)*
Buckeye Linen Service Inc .... D 740 345-4046
  Newark *(G-15152)*
Cintas Corporation No 1 .... A 513 459-1200
  Mason *(G-13678)*
Cintas Corporation No 2 .... C 419 661-8714
  Perrysburg *(G-15986)*
Cintas Corporation No 2 .... D 440 238-5565
  Strongsville *(G-17449)*
Cintas Corporation No 2 .... D 614 878-7313
  Columbus *(G-7274)*
Cintas Corporation No 2 .... D 440 352-4003
  Painesville *(G-15839)*
Cintas Corporation No 2 .... E 740 687-6230
  Lancaster *(G-12517)*
Cintas Corporation No 2 .... 614 860-9152
  Blacklick *(G-1504)*
Cintas Corporation No 2 .... D 937 401-0098
  Vandalia *(G-18670)*
Cintas Corporation No 2 .... C 513 965-0800
  Milford *(G-14511)*
Economy Linen & Towel Svc Inc .... C 740 454-6888
  Zanesville *(G-20473)*
Kimmel Cleaners Inc .... D 419 294-1959
  Upper Sandusky *(G-18564)*
Kramer Enterprises Inc .... D 419 422-7924
  Findlay *(G-11055)*
Midwest Laundry Inc .... D 513 563-5560
  Cincinnati *(G-4092)*
Millers Textile Services Inc .... D 419 738-3552
  Wapakoneta *(G-18804)*
Millers Textile Services Inc .... E 614 262-1206
  Springfield *(G-17249)*
Morgan Services Inc .... E 419 243-2214
  Toledo *(G-18070)*
Morgan Services Inc .... C 216 241-3107
  Cleveland *(G-6075)*
Morgan Services Inc .... D 937 223-5241
  Dayton *(G-9757)*
Paris Cleaners Inc .... C 330 296-3300
  Ravenna *(G-16395)*
Springfeld Unfrm-Linen Sup Inc 937 323-5544
  Springfield *(G-17278)*
Superior Linen & AP Svcs Inc .... D 513 751-1345
  Cincinnati *(G-4604)*
Synergy Health North Amer Inc .... D 513 398-6406
  Mason *(G-13766)*
Unifirst Corporation .... E 614 575-9999
  Blacklick *(G-1511)*
Unifirst Corporation .... D 937 746-0531
  Franklin *(G-11166)*
Van Dyne-Crotty Co .... E 614 684-0048
  Columbus *(G-8932)*
Van Dyne-Crotty Co .... C 614 491-3903
  Columbus *(G-8933)*
Van Dyne-Crotty Co 440 248-6935
  Solon *(G-17064)*

7215 Coin Operated Laundries & Cleaning

American Sales Inc .... E 937 253-9520
  Dayton *(G-9254)*
Fox Cleaners Inc .... D 937 276-4171
  Dayton *(G-9559)*
Joseph S Mischell .... E 513 542-9800
  Cincinnati *(G-3888)*

7216 Dry Cleaning Plants, Except Rug Cleaning

A One Fine Dry Cleaners Inc .... D 513 351-2663
  Cincinnati *(G-2955)*
Apc2 Inc .... D 513 231-5540
  Cincinnati *(G-3033)*
Aramark Unf & Career AP LLC .... D 937 223-6667
  Dayton *(G-9340)*
Caskey Cleaning Co .... D 614 443-7448
  Columbus *(G-7204)*
Cintas Corporation No 2 .... 440 238-5565
  Strongsville *(G-17449)*

Coit Services of Ohio Inc D 216 626-0040
Cleveland *(G-5369)*
Dee Jay Cleaners Inc E 216 731-7060
Euclid *(G-10750)*
Dublin Cleaners Inc D 614 764-9934
Columbus *(G-7548)*
Dutchess Dry Cleaners E 330 759-9382
Youngstown *(G-20174)*
Edco Cleaners Inc E 330 477-3357
Canton *(G-2351)*
Farrow Cleaners Co E 216 561-2355
Cleveland *(G-5574)*
Fox Cleaners Inc D 937 276-4171
Dayton *(G-9559)*
George Gardner D 419 636-4277
Bryan *(G-2006)*
Heider Cleaners Inc E 937 298-6631
Dayton *(G-9609)*
Heights Laundry & Dry Cleaning E 216 932-9666
Cleveland Heights *(G-6789)*
Kimmel Cleaners Inc D 419 294-1959
Upper Sandusky *(G-18564)*
Kramer Enterprises Inc D 419 422-7924
Findlay *(G-11055)*
La France South Inc E 330 782-1400
Youngstown *(G-20251)*
Midwest Laundry Inc D 513 563-5560
Cincinnati *(G-4092)*
Pierce Cleaners Inc E 614 888-4225
Columbus *(G-8543)*
Quality Cleaners of Ohio Inc E 330 688-5616
Stow *(G-17388)*
Rentz Corp E 937 434-2774
Dayton *(G-9848)*
Rockwood Dry Cleaners Corp E 614 471-3700
Gahanna *(G-11265)*
Rondinelli Company Inc D 330 726-7643
Youngstown *(G-20358)*
Sunset Carpet Cleaning E 937 836-5531
Englewood *(G-10721)*
Velco Inc E 513 772-4226
Cincinnati *(G-4805)*
Widmers LLC C 513 321-5100
Cincinnati *(G-4848)*

7217 Carpet & Upholstery Cleaning

Allen-Keith Construction Co D 330 266-2220
Canton *(G-2231)*
Americas Floor Source LLC E 216 342-4929
Bedford Heights *(G-1346)*
Arslanian Bros Crpt Rug Clg Co E 216 271-6888
Warrensville Heights *(G-18931)*
Bechtl Bldng Mntnc Crprtn of D 330 759-2797
Youngstown *(G-20111)*
C M S Enterprises Inc E 740 653-1940
Lancaster *(G-12512)*
C&C Clean Team Enterprises LLC C 513 321-5100
Cincinnati *(G-3163)*
Carpet Services Plus Inc E 330 458-2409
Canton *(G-2301)*
Coit Services of Ohio Inc D 216 626-0040
Cleveland *(G-5369)*
D & J Master Clean Inc D 614 847-1181
Columbus *(G-7477)*
Farrow Cleaners Co E 216 561-2355
Cleveland *(G-5574)*
Icon Environmental Group LLC E 513 426-6767
Milford *(G-14526)*
Image By J & K LLC B 888 667-6929
Maumee *(G-13927)*
Lazar Brothers Inc E 440 585-9333
Wickliffe *(G-19606)*
Marks Cleaning Service Inc E 330 725-5702
Medina *(G-14094)*
Martin Carpet Cleaning Company E 614 443-4655
Columbus *(G-8121)*
Merlene Enterprises Inc E 440 593-6771
Conneaut *(G-9044)*
New Albany Cleaning Services E 614 855-9990
New Albany *(G-14997)*
Ohio Building Service Inc E 513 761-0268
Cincinnati *(G-4202)*
Samron Inc E 330 782-6539
Youngstown *(G-20366)*
Springfeld Unfrm-Linen Sup Inc D 937 323-5544
Springfield *(G-17278)*
Stanley Steemer Intl Inc C 614 764-2007
Dublin *(G-10461)*
Stanley Steemer Intl Inc E 419 227-1212
Lima *(G-12891)*
Stanley Steemer Intl Inc E 513 771-0213
Cincinnati *(G-4582)*
Stanley Steemer Intl Inc E 614 652-2241
Dublin *(G-10462)*
Stanley Steemer Intl Inc E 937 431-3205
Beavercreek Township *(G-1286)*
Stanley Stemer of Akron Canton E 330 785-5005
Coventry Township *(G-9133)*
Sunset Carpet Cleaning E 937 836-5531
Englewood *(G-10721)*
Teasdale Fenton Carpet Cleanin D 513 797-0900
Cincinnati *(G-4628)*
Velco Inc E 513 772-4226
Cincinnati *(G-4805)*
Widmers LLC C 513 321-5100
Cincinnati *(G-4848)*
Wiggins Clg & Crpt Svc Inc D 937 279-9080
Dayton *(G-9998)*

7218 Industrial Launderers

Aramark Unf & Career AP LLC D 513 533-1000
Cincinnati *(G-3039)*
Aramark Unf & Career AP LLC D 937 223-6667
Dayton *(G-9340)*
Aramark Unf & Career AP LLC C 614 445-8341
Columbus *(G-7032)*
Aramark Unf & Career AP LLC C 216 341-7400
Cleveland *(G-5058)*
Brent Industries Inc E 419 382-8693
Toledo *(G-17782)*
◆ **Cintas Corporation** A 513 459-1200
Cincinnati *(G-3349)*
Cintas Corporation D 330 821-2220
Alliance *(G-532)*
Cintas Corporation D 513 671-7717
Cincinnati *(G-3351)*
Cintas Corporation D 513 631-5750
Cincinnati *(G-3350)*
Cintas Corporation No 2 D 440 746-7777
Girard *(G-11409)*
Cintas Corporation No 2 D 440 746-7777
Brecksville *(G-1817)*
Cintas Corporation No 2 C 513 965-0800
Milford *(G-14511)*
Cintas Corporation No 2 D 330 966-7800
Canton *(G-2309)*
Cintas Corporation No 2 D 440 238-5565
Strongsville *(G-17449)*
Cintas Corporation No 2 D 614 878-7313
Columbus *(G-7274)*
Cintas Corporation No 2 C 614 860-9152
Blacklick *(G-1504)*
Cintas R US Inc A 513 459-1200
Cincinnati *(G-3352)*
Cintas Sales Corporation B 513 459-1200
Cincinnati *(G-3353)*
Cintas-Rus LP E 513 459-1200
Mason *(G-13683)*
Duckworth Enterprises LLC E 614 575-2900
Reynoldsburg *(G-16449)*
G&K Services Inc D 937 873-4500
Fairborn *(G-10797)*
Kimmel Cleaners Inc D 419 294-1959
Upper Sandusky *(G-18564)*
Midwest Laundry Inc D 513 563-5560
Cincinnati *(G-4092)*
Morgan Services Inc E 419 243-2214
Toledo *(G-18070)*
Morgan Services Inc C 216 241-3107
Cleveland *(G-6075)*
Rentwear Inc D 330 535-2301
Canton *(G-2506)*
Runt Ware & Sanitary Service E 330 494-5776
Canton *(G-2519)*
Springfeld Unfrm-Linen Sup Inc D 937 323-5544
Springfield *(G-17278)*
Unifirst Corporation E 614 575-9999
Blacklick *(G-1511)*
Unifirst Corporation D 937 746-0531
Franklin *(G-11166)*
Van Dyne-Crotty Co E 614 684-0048
Columbus *(G-8932)*
Van Dyne-Crotty Co C 614 491-3903
Columbus *(G-8933)*
Van Dyne-Crotty Co E 440 248-6935
Solon *(G-17064)*

7219 Laundry & Garment Svcs, NEC

Central Ohio Medical Textiles C 614 453-9274
Columbus *(G-7231)*
Clean Living Laundry LLC E 513 569-0439
Cincinnati *(G-3362)*
Hyo OK Inc E 614 876-7644
Hilliard *(G-11912)*
Pins & Needles Inc E 440 243-6400
Cleveland *(G-6281)*
Quality Cleaners of Ohio Inc E 330 688-5616
Stow *(G-17388)*
Springfeld Unfrm-Linen Sup Inc D 937 323-5544
Springfield *(G-17278)*
Van Dyne-Crotty Co E 614 684-0048
Columbus *(G-8932)*

7221 Photographic Studios, Portrait

Childers Photography E 937 256-0501
Dayton *(G-9261)*
Lifetouch Inc E 419 435-2646
Fostoria *(G-11134)*
Lifetouch Inc E 937 298-6275
Dayton *(G-9682)*
Lifetouch Nat Schl Studios Inc E 419 483-8200
Bellevue *(G-1412)*
Lifetouch Nat Schl Studios Inc E 330 497-1291
Canton *(G-2438)*
Lifetouch Nat Schl Studios Inc E 513 772-2110
Cincinnati *(G-3979)*
Pam Johnsonident D 419 946-4551
Mount Gilead *(G-14861)*
Peters Main Street Photography E 740 852-2731
London *(G-13005)*
Rapid Mortgage Company E 937 748-8888
Dayton *(G-9842)*
Ripcho Studio E 216 631-0664
Cleveland *(G-6397)*
Royal Color Inc B 440 234-1337
Bellevue *(G-1417)*
Universal Technology Corp D 937 426-2808
Beavercreek *(G-1216)*
Usam Inc D 330 244-8782
Canton *(G-2575)*
Woodard Photographic Inc E 419 483-3364
Bellevue *(G-1420)*

7231 Beauty Shops

Alsan Corporation D 330 385-3636
East Liverpool *(G-10514)*
Anthony David Salon & Spa E 440 233-8570
Lorain *(G-13013)*
Anthony Roccos Hair Design E 440 646-1925
Cleveland *(G-5044)*
Attitudes New Inc E 330 856-1143
Warren *(G-18819)*
Attractions E 740 592-5600
Athens *(G-778)*
Bajon Salon Montgomery E 513 984-8880
Cincinnati *(G-3073)*
Beauty Bar LLC E 419 537-5400
Toledo *(G-17766)*
Bella Capelli Inc E 440 899-1225
Westlake *(G-19465)*
Bellazio Salon & Day Spa E 937 432-6722
Dayton *(G-9354)*
Best Cuts Inc E 440 884-6300
Cleveland *(G-5118)*
Beverly Hills Inn La Llc E 859 494-9151
Aberdeen *(G-1)*
Brenwood Inc E 740 452-7533
Zanesville *(G-20449)*
Calico Court E 740 455-2541
Zanesville *(G-20453)*
Casals Hair Salon Inc E 330 533-6766
Canfield *(G-2185)*
Castilian & Co E 937 836-9671
Englewood *(G-10699)*
Changes Hair Designers Inc E 614 846-6666
Columbus *(G-6875)*
Collins Salon Inc E 513 683-1700
Loveland *(G-13116)*
Cookie Cutters Haircutters E 614 522-0220
Pickerington *(G-16093)*
Creative Images College of B E 937 478-7922
Dayton *(G-9443)*
Dana Lauren Salon & Spa E 440 262-1092
Broadview Heights *(G-1877)*
David Scott Salon E 440 734-7595
North Olmsted *(G-15419)*
Definitions of Design Inc E 419 891-0188
Maumee *(G-13906)*
Diane Babiuch E 419 867-8837
Holland *(G-12020)*

SIC SECTION

72 PERSONAL SERVICES

Ecotage ....E 513 782-2229
  Cincinnati *(G-3544)*
Edge Hair Design & Spa ....E 330 477-2300
  Canton *(G-2352)*
Englefield Inc ....D 740 323-2077
  Thornville *(G-17667)*
Esbi International Salon ....E 330 220-3724
  Brunswick *(G-1977)*
Flux A Salon By Hazelton ....E 419 841-5100
  Perrysburg *(G-16004)*
Frank Santo LLC ....E 216 831-9374
  Pepper Pike *(G-15955)*
G E G Enterprises Inc ....E 330 494-9160
  Canton *(G-2374)*
G E G Enterprises Inc ....E 330 477-3133
  Canton *(G-2375)*
Hair Forum ....E 513 245-0800
  Cincinnati *(G-3729)*
Hair Shoppe Inc ....D 330 497-1651
  Canton *(G-2388)*
Hairy Cactus Salon Inc ....E 513 771-9335
  West Chester *(G-19087)*
Head Quarters Inc ....E 440 233-8508
  Lorain *(G-13041)*
Image Engineering Inc ....E 513 541-8544
  Cincinnati *(G-3808)*
Intl Europa Salon & Spa ....E 216 292-6969
  Cleveland *(G-5836)*
Intrigue Salon & Day Spa ....E 330 493-7003
  Canton *(G-2415)*
Jbentley Studio & Spa LLC ....D 614 790-8828
  Powell *(G-16339)*
Jbj Enterprises Inc ....E 440 992-6051
  Ashtabula *(G-750)*
JC Penney Corporation Inc ....B 330 633-7700
  Akron *(G-290)*
John Rbrts Hair Studio Spa Inc ......D 216 839-1430
  Cleveland *(G-5868)*
Kenneths Hair Salons & Day Sp ....B 614 457-7712
  Columbus *(G-7978)*
Kerr House Inc ....E 419 832-1733
  Grand Rapids *(G-11451)*
Kristie Warner ....E 330 650-4450
  Hudson *(G-12129)*
L A Hair Force ....E 419 756-3101
  Mansfield *(G-13321)*
Laser Hair Removal Center ....D 937 433-7536
  Dayton *(G-9674)*
Le Nails ....E 440 846-1866
  Cleveland *(G-5930)*
Legrand Services Inc ....E 740 682-6046
  Oak Hill *(G-15619)*
Linda Cpers Idntity Hair Dsign ....D 513 791-2555
  Cincinnati *(G-3985)*
M C Hair Consultants Inc ....E 234 678-3987
  Cuyahoga Falls *(G-9206)*
Marios International Spa & Ht ....C 330 562-5141
  Aurora *(G-846)*
Marios International Spa & Ht ....E 440 845-7373
  Cleveland *(G-5979)*
Mark Luikart Inc ....E 330 339-9141
  New Philadelphia *(G-15109)*
Mato Inc ....E 440 729-9008
  Chesterland *(G-2799)*
Merle-Holden Enterprises Inc ....E 216 661-6887
  Cleveland *(G-6029)*
Mfh Inc ....E 937 435-4701
  Dayton *(G-9723)*
Mfh Inc ....D 937 435-4701
  Dayton *(G-9724)*
Michael A Garcia Salon ....E 614 235-1605
  Columbus *(G-8157)*
Michael Christopher Salon Inc ....E 440 449-0999
  Cleveland *(G-6047)*
Mitchells Salon & Day Spa ....B 513 793-0900
  Cincinnati *(G-4104)*
Mitchells Salon & Day Spa ....E 513 772-3200
  Cincinnati *(G-4105)*
Mitchells Salon & Day Spa ....D 513 731-0600
  Cincinnati *(G-4106)*
Mzf Inc ....E 216 464-3910
  Cleveland *(G-6096)*
Noggins Hair Design Inc ....E 513 474-4405
  Cincinnati *(G-4171)*
Nurtur Holdings LLC ....E 614 487-3033
  Loveland *(G-13149)*
P JS Hair Styling Shoppe ....E 440 333-1244
  Cleveland *(G-6226)*
Paragon Salons Inc ....E 513 651-4600
  Cincinnati *(G-4250)*

Paragon Salons Inc ....E 513 683-6700
  Cincinnati *(G-4251)*
Philip Icuss Jr ....E 740 264-4647
  Steubenville *(G-17333)*
Phyllis At Madison ....E 513 321-1300
  Cincinnati *(G-4295)*
PS Lifestyle LLC ....A 440 600-1595
  Cleveland *(G-6328)*
Pure Concept Salon Inc ....E 513 770-2120
  Mason *(G-13751)*
R L O Inc ....E 937 620-9998
  Dayton *(G-9839)*
Raphaels Schl Buty Culture Inc .....E 330 782-3395
  Boardman *(G-1743)*
Reflections Hair Studio Inc ....E 330 725-5782
  Medina *(G-14119)*
Reves Salon & Spa ....E 419 885-1140
  Sylvania *(G-17611)*
Rometrics Too Hair Nail Gllery ......E 440 808-1391
  Westlake *(G-19543)*
Salon Alexandre Inc ....E 513 207-8406
  West Chester *(G-19227)*
Salon Communication Services ....E 614 233-8500
  Columbus *(G-8680)*
Salon Hazelton ....E 419 874-9404
  Perrysburg *(G-16055)*
Salon La ....E 513 784-1700
  Cincinnati *(G-4473)*
Salon Ware Inc ....E 330 665-2244
  Copley *(G-9062)*
Shamas Ltd ....E 419 872-9908
  Perrysburg *(G-16058)*
Sheer Professionals Inc ....E 330 345-8666
  Wooster *(G-19916)*
Soto Salon & Spa ....E 419 872-5555
  Perrysburg *(G-16060)*
Star Beauty Plus LLC ....E 216 662-9750
  Maple Heights *(G-13419)*
Tanos Salon ....E 216 831-7880
  Cleveland *(G-6569)*
Tanyas Image LLC ....E 513 386-9981
  Cincinnati *(G-4623)*
Tara Flaherty ....E 419 565-1334
  Mansfield *(G-13372)*
Ulta Beauty Inc ....C 440 248-5618
  Solon *(G-17062)*
Uptown Hair Studio Inc ....E 937 832-2111
  Englewood *(G-10723)*
Urban Oasis Inc ....E 614 766-9946
  Dublin *(G-10480)*
Vlp Inc ....E 330 758-8811
  Youngstown *(G-20407)*
Walmart Inc ....C 937 399-0370
  Springfield *(G-17296)*
Yearwood Corporation ....E 937 223-3572
  Dayton *(G-10006)*
Z A F Inc ....E 216 291-1234
  Cleveland *(G-6778)*

7241 Barber Shops

Attractions ....E 740 592-5600
  Athens *(G-778)*
Head Quarters Inc ....E 440 233-8508
  Lorain *(G-13041)*
Lucas Metropolitan Hsing Auth .....D 419 259-9457
  Toledo *(G-18018)*
Mfh Inc ....E 937 435-4701
  Dayton *(G-9723)*
Ricks Hair Center ....E 330 545-5120
  Girard *(G-11425)*
Ulta Beauty Inc ....D 513 752-1472
  Cincinnati *(G-2937)*
Ulta Beauty Inc ....D 419 621-1345
  Sandusky *(G-16804)*

7261 Funeral Svcs & Crematories

Busch Development Corporation ..E 440 842-7800
  Cleveland *(G-5161)*
Cole Selby Funeral Inc ....E 330 856-4695
  Vienna *(G-18736)*
Cremation Service Inc ....E 216 861-2334
  Cleveland *(G-5435)*
Cremation Service Inc ....E 216 621-6222
  Cleveland *(G-5436)*
Cummings and Davis Fnrl HM Inc .E 216 541-1111
  Cleveland *(G-5448)*
Davidson Becker Inc ....E 330 755-2111
  Struthers *(G-17530)*
Domajaparo Inc ....E 513 742-3600
  Cincinnati *(G-3497)*

E F Boyd & Son Inc ....E 216 791-0770
  Cleveland *(G-5516)*
Ferfolia Funeral Homes Inc ....E 216 663-4222
  Northfield *(G-15516)*
Keller Ochs Koch Inc ....E 419 332-8288
  Fremont *(G-11208)*
Martin Altmeyer Funeral Home .....E 330 385-3650
  East Liverpool *(G-10524)*
Newcomer Funeral Svc Group Inc .B 513 521-1971
  Cincinnati *(G-4160)*
Paul R Young Funeral Homes ....E 513 521-9303
  Cincinnati *(G-4264)*
Rutherford Funeral Home Inc ....E 614 451-0593
  Columbus *(G-8662)*
Spring Grove Funeral Homes Inc ..E 513 681-7526
  Cincinnati *(G-4564)*

7291 Tax Return Preparation Svcs

Barnes Wendling Cpas Inc ....E 216 566-9000
  Cleveland *(G-5095)*
Colonial Banc Corp ....E 937 456-5544
  Eaton *(G-10554)*
Damon Tax Service ....E 513 574-9087
  Cincinnati *(G-3461)*
Delaneys Tax Accunting Svc Ltd ...E 513 248-2829
  Milford *(G-14516)*
Deloitte & Touche LLP ....B 513 784-7100
  Cincinnati *(G-3482)*
Dw Together LLC ....E 330 225-8200
  Brunswick *(G-1976)*
E T Financial Service Inc ....E 937 716-1726
  Trotwood *(G-18346)*
H & R Block ....E 419 352-9467
  Bowling Green *(G-1779)*
H & R Block Inc ....E 330 345-1040
  Wooster *(G-19866)*
H & R Block Inc ....E 216 271-7108
  Cleveland *(G-5713)*
H & R Block Inc ....E 513 868-1818
  Hamilton *(G-11737)*
H&R Block Inc ....E 330 773-0412
  Akron *(G-250)*
H&R Block Inc ....E 440 282-4288
  Amherst *(G-596)*
H&R Block Inc ....E 216 861-1185
  Cleveland *(G-5717)*
Hometown Urgent Care ....C 330 629-2300
  Youngstown *(G-20219)*
Hometown Urgent Care ....D 740 363-3133
  Delaware *(G-10107)*
Hometown Urgent Care ....E 937 252-2000
  Wooster *(G-19868)*
Jennings & Associates ....E 740 369-4426
  Delaware *(G-10111)*
Liberty Tax Inc ....E 614 853-1090
  Galloway *(G-11345)*
Phillip Mc Guire ....E 740 482-2701
  Nevada *(G-14969)*
Skoda Minotti Holdings LLC ....E 440 449-6800
  Cleveland *(G-6484)*
Village of Coldwater ....D 419 678-2685
  Coldwater *(G-6837)*

7299 Miscellaneous Personal Svcs, NEC

A Tara Tiffanys Property ....E 330 448-0778
  Brookfield *(G-1896)*
Action For Children Inc ....E 614 224-0222
  Columbus *(G-6941)*
Administrative Svcs Ohio Dept .....D 614 466-5090
  Columbus *(G-6944)*
Akron Metropolitan Hsing Auth .....C 330 920-1652
  Stow *(C-17350)*
Alpha PHI Alpha Homes Inc ....D 330 376-2115
  Akron *(G-70)*
American Commodore Tu ....D 216 291-4601
  Cleveland *(G-5006)*
Assembly Center 800 582-1099
  Monroe *(G-14687)*
Attractions ....E 740 592-5600
  Athens *(G-778)*
Banquets Unlimited 859 689-4000
  Cincinnati *(G-3075)*
Barberton Laundry & Cleaning ......E 330 825-6911
  Barberton *(G-958)*
Best Upon Request Corp Inc ....D 513 605-7800
  Cincinnati *(G-3102)*
Black Tie Affair Inc ....E 330 345-8333
  Wooster *(G-19832)*
Blue Chip Mailing Services Inc .....E 513 541-4800
  Blue Ash *(G-1545)*

72 PERSONAL SERVICES

Brown Derby Roadhouse ..... E 330 528-3227
  Hudson *(G-12105)*
Buffalo Jacks ..... E 937 473-2524
  Covington *(G-9136)*
Buns of Delaware Inc ..... E 740 363-2867
  Delaware *(G-10075)*
Cabin Restaurant ..... E 330 562-9171
  Aurora *(G-832)*
Camargo Rental Center Inc ..... E 513 271-6510
  Cincinnati *(G-3170)*
Carol Scudere ..... E 614 839-4357
  New Albany *(G-14979)*
Carrie Cerino Restaurants Inc ..... C 440 237-3434
  Cleveland *(G-5186)*
Cec Entertainment Inc ..... D 937 439-1108
  Miamisburg *(G-14280)*
Cheers Chalet ..... E 740 654-9036
  Lancaster *(G-12516)*
Child & Elder Care Insights ..... E 440 356-2900
  Rocky River *(G-16573)*
Cintas Document Management LLC ..... E 800 914-1960
  Mason *(G-13682)*
City Life Inc ..... E 216 523-5899
  Cleveland *(G-5246)*
City of Beavercreek ..... D 937 320-0742
  Beavercreek *(G-1161)*
City of Centerville ..... D 937 438-3585
  Dayton *(G-9409)*
City of Vandalia ..... E 937 890-1300
  Vandalia *(G-18674)*
Cleveland Metroparks ..... C 216 661-6500
  Cleveland *(G-5326)*
Connor Concepts Inc ..... D 937 291-1661
  Dayton *(G-9423)*
Consumer Credit Coun ..... E 614 552-2222
  Gahanna *(G-11237)*
Continntal Mssage Solution Inc ..... D 614 224-4534
  Columbus *(G-7434)*
Coshocton Village Inn Suites ..... E 740 622-9455
  Coshocton *(G-9098)*
Costume Specialists Inc ..... E 614 464-2115
  Columbus *(G-7448)*
Cuyahoga County ..... D 216 443-8920
  Cleveland *(G-5454)*
D H Packaging Co ..... A 513 791-2022
  Cincinnati *(G-3455)*
Davis Catering Inc ..... D 513 241-3464
  Cincinnati *(G-3464)*
De Lucas Place In Park ..... D 440 233-7272
  Lorain *(G-13035)*
Delaware Golf Club Inc ..... E 740 362-2582
  Delaware *(G-10089)*
Deyor Performing Arts Center ..... E 330 744-4269
  Youngstown *(G-20168)*
Diane Babiuch ..... E 419 867-8837
  Holland *(G-12020)*
Diet Center Worldwide Inc ..... E 330 665-5861
  Akron *(G-192)*
Dinos Catering Inc ..... E 440 943-1010
  Wickliffe *(G-19593)*
Eagle Industries Ohio Inc ..... E 513 247-2900
  Fairfield *(G-10844)*
Emmys Bridal Inc ..... E 419 628-7555
  Minster *(G-14661)*
Engle Management Group ..... D 513 232-9729
  Cincinnati *(G-3558)*
Eventions Ltd ..... E 216 952-9898
  Cleveland *(G-5556)*
Excel Decorators Inc ..... E 614 522-0056
  Columbus *(G-7616)*
Farm Inc ..... E 513 922-7020
  Cincinnati *(G-3592)*
Findlay Inn & Conference Ctr ..... E 419 422-5682
  Findlay *(G-11027)*
Formu3 International Inc ..... E 330 668-1461
  Akron *(G-228)*
Fun Day Events LLC ..... E 740 549-9000
  Gahanna *(G-11242)*
G E G Enterprises Inc ..... E 330 477-3133
  Canton *(G-2375)*
German Family Society Inc ..... E 330 678-8229
  Kent *(G-12371)*
Goldfish Swim School ..... E 216 364-9090
  Chagrin Falls *(G-2718)*
Grandview Ht Ltd Partnr Ohio ..... D 937 766-5519
  Springfield *(G-17203)*
Great Southern Video Inc ..... E 216 642-8855
  Cleveland *(G-5693)*
Guys Party Center ..... E 330 724-6373
  Akron *(G-249)*
Hall Nazareth Inc ..... D 419 832-2900
  Grand Rapids *(G-11449)*
Handy Hubby ..... E 419 754-1150
  Toledo *(G-17930)*
Haribol Haribol Inc ..... E 330 339-7731
  New Philadelphia *(G-15099)*
Heatherwoode Golf Course ..... C 937 748-3222
  Springboro *(G-17122)*
Humility of Mary Info Systems ..... D 330 884-6600
  Youngstown *(G-20223)*
Iacominis Papa Joes Inc ..... D 330 923-7999
  Akron *(G-276)*
Intelisol Inc ..... D 614 409-0052
  Lockbourne *(G-12956)*
Irish Envy LLC ..... E 440 808-8000
  Westlake *(G-19499)*
Jack & Jill Babysitting Svc ..... E 513 731-5261
  Cincinnati *(G-3853)*
Kiddie Party Company LLC ..... E 440 273-7680
  Mayfield Heights *(G-14003)*
Kinane Inc ..... D 513 459-0177
  Mason *(G-13727)*
Kitchen Katering Inc ..... E 216 481-8080
  Euclid *(G-10766)*
Kohler Foods Inc ..... E 937 291-3600
  Dayton *(G-9665)*
La Villa Cnference Banquet Ctr ..... E 216 265-9305
  Cleveland *(G-5915)*
Lazer Kraze ..... E 513 339-1030
  Galena *(G-11286)*
Lees Roby Inc ..... E 330 872-0983
  Newton Falls *(G-15276)*
Leos La Piazza Inc ..... E 937 339-5553
  Troy *(G-18361)*
Life Time Fitness Inc ..... C 614 428-6000
  Columbus *(G-8062)*
Little Miami River Catering Co ..... E 937 848-2464
  Bellbrook *(G-1372)*
Longworth Enterprises Inc ..... B 513 738-4663
  West Chester *(G-19112)*
Lorain Party Center ..... E 440 282-5599
  Lorain *(G-13057)*
Mackil Inc ..... E 937 833-3310
  Brookville *(G-1964)*
Makoy Center Inc ..... E 614 777-1211
  Hilliard *(G-11924)*
Mandalay Inc ..... E 937 294-6600
  Moraine *(G-14799)*
Mark Luikart Inc ..... E 330 339-9141
  New Philadelphia *(G-15109)*
Mason Family Resorts LLC ..... B 513 339-0141
  Mason *(G-13736)*
Massage Envy ..... E 440 878-0500
  Strongsville *(G-17490)*
Menard Inc ..... B 614 501-1654
  Columbus *(G-8146)*
Mercy Health ..... D 419 407-3990
  Toledo *(G-18053)*
Michaels Inc ..... D 440 357-0384
  Mentor *(G-14217)*
Mitchells Salon & Day Spa ..... C 513 793-0900
  West Chester *(G-19121)*
Mocha House Inc ..... E 330 392-3020
  Warren *(G-18882)*
Monaco Palace Inc ..... E 614 475-4817
  Newark *(G-15210)*
Mustard Seed Health Fd Mkt Inc ..... E 440 519-3663
  Solon *(G-17031)*
Nelson Financial Group ..... E 513 686-7800
  Dayton *(G-9278)*
New Jersey Aquarium LLC ..... D 614 414-7300
  Columbus *(G-8273)*
Noggins Hair Design Inc ..... E 513 474-4405
  Cincinnati *(G-4171)*
Occasions Party Centre ..... E 330 882-5113
  New Franklin *(G-15046)*
Old Barn Out Back Inc ..... D 419 999-3989
  Lima *(G-12848)*
Parking Solutions Inc ..... A 614 469-7000
  Columbus *(G-8517)*
Pccw Teleservices (us) Inc ..... A 614 652-6300
  Dublin *(G-10424)*
Pines Golf Club ..... E 330 684-1414
  Orrville *(G-15783)*
Public Safety Ohio Department ..... A 614 752-7600
  Columbus *(G-8577)*
Pure Romance LLC ..... D 513 248-8656
  Cincinnati *(G-4356)*
Raymond Recepton House ..... E 614 276-6127
  Columbus *(G-8589)*
Refectory Restaurant Inc ..... E 614 451-9774
  Columbus *(G-8602)*
Research Associates Inc ..... D 440 892-1000
  Cleveland *(G-6381)*
Riverside Cmnty Urban Redev ..... C 330 929-3000
  Cuyahoga Falls *(G-9215)*
Rondinelli Company Inc ..... E 330 726-7643
  Youngstown *(G-20358)*
Rondinellis Tuxedo ..... E 330 726-7768
  Youngstown *(G-20359)*
Roscoe Village Foundation ..... D 740 622-2222
  Coshocton *(G-9116)*
Sam BS Restaurant ..... E 419 353-2277
  Bowling Green *(G-1793)*
Sauder Village ..... B 419 446-2541
  Archbold *(G-644)*
Snpj Recreation Farm ..... E 440 256-3423
  Willoughby *(G-19715)*
Spagnas ..... E 740 376-9245
  Marietta *(G-13501)*
Sr Improvements Services LLC ..... E 567 207-6488
  Vickery *(G-18733)*
Super Tan ..... E 330 722-2799
  Medina *(G-14132)*
Teasdale Fenton Carpet Cleanin ..... D 513 797-0900
  Cincinnati *(G-4628)*
The Oaks Lodge ..... E 330 769-2601
  Chippewa Lake *(G-2899)*
Toris Station ..... E 513 829-7815
  Fairfield *(G-10915)*
Twin Haven Reception Hall ..... E 330 425-1616
  Twinsburg *(G-18480)*
Ussa Inc ..... E 740 354-6672
  Portsmouth *(G-16319)*
Valley Hospitality Inc ..... E 740 374-9660
  Marietta *(G-13513)*
Villa Milano Inc ..... E 614 882-2058
  Columbus *(G-8941)*
Vulcan Machinery Corporation ..... E 330 376-6025
  Akron *(G-500)*
William Royce Inc ..... D 513 771-3361
  Cincinnati *(G-4850)*
Winking Lizard Inc ..... D 330 467-1002
  Peninsula *(G-15954)*
Winking Lizard Inc ..... D 330 220-9944
  Brunswick *(G-1998)*

73 BUSINESS SERVICES

7311 Advertising Agencies

▲ Airmate Company ..... D 419 636-3184
  Bryan *(G-2000)*
AMG Marketing Resources Inc ..... E 216 621-1835
  Solon *(G-16975)*
AMP Advertising Inc ..... E 513 333-4100
  Cincinnati *(G-3016)*
Arras Group Inc ..... E 216 621-1601
  Cleveland *(G-5067)*
Barefoot LLC ..... E 513 861-3668
  Cincinnati *(G-3078)*
BBDO Worldwide Inc ..... E 513 861-3668
  Cincinnati *(G-3084)*
Bbs & Associates Inc ..... E 330 665-5227
  Akron *(G-92)*
Brand Build Inc ..... E 513 579-1950
  Blue Ash *(G-1548)*
Brokaw Inc ..... E 216 241-8003
  Cleveland *(G-5143)*
Charles W Powers & Assoc Inc ..... E 513 721-5353
  Cincinnati *(G-3231)*
Chisano Mktg Cmmunications Inc ..... E 937 847-0607
  Miamisburg *(G-14282)*
Commerce Holdings Inc ..... E 513 579-1950
  Cincinnati *(G-3398)*
Cooper-Smith Advertising LLC ..... E 419 470-5900
  Toledo *(G-17832)*
Curiosity LLC ..... D 513 744-6000
  Cincinnati *(G-3449)*
D & D Advertising Enterprises ..... E 513 921-6827
  Cincinnati *(G-3453)*
D & S Crtive Cmmunications Inc ..... D 419 524-6699
  Mansfield *(G-13288)*
David Group ..... E 216 685-4400
  Cleveland *(G-5467)*
Deanhouston Creative Group Inc ..... E 513 421-6622
  Cincinnati *(G-3475)*
Detroit Royalty Incorporated ..... D 216 771-5700
  Cleveland *(G-5479)*
Dix & Eaton Incorporated ..... E 216 241-0405
  Cleveland *(G-5493)*

73 BUSINESS SERVICES

Epipheo Incorporated ....E 888 687-7620
  Cincinnati *(G-3565)*
Eric Mower and Associates Inc ....E 513 381-8855
  Cincinnati *(G-3573)*
Fahlgren Inc ....E 614 383-1500
  Columbus *(G-7628)*
Fahlgren Inc ....D 614 383-1500
  Columbus *(G-7629)*
Guardian Enterprise Group Inc ....E 614 416-6080
  Columbus *(G-7784)*
Gypc Inc ....C 309 677-0405
  Dayton *(G-9593)*
Hart Associates Inc ....D 419 893-9600
  Toledo *(G-17936)*
Hitchcock Fleming & Assoc Inc ....D 330 376-2111
  Akron *(G-266)*
Hsr Marketing Communications ....D 513 671-3811
  Cincinnati *(G-3792)*
Inquiry Systems Inc ....E 614 464-3800
  Columbus *(G-7904)*
Kreber Graphics Inc ....D 614 529-5701
  Columbus *(G-8013)*
Kuno Creative Group LLC ....E 440 225-4144
  Avon *(G-904)*
L M Berry and Company ....A 937 296-2121
  Moraine *(G-14797)*
Madison Avenue Mktg Group Inc ....E 419 473-9000
  Toledo *(G-18026)*
Marcus Thomas Llc ....D 216 292-4700
  Cleveland *(G-5978)*
Marcus Thomas Llc ....D 330 793-3000
  Youngstown *(G-20272)*
Marketing Support Services Inc ....D 513 752-1200
  Cincinnati *(G-4024)*
Matrix Media Services Inc ....E 614 228-2200
  Columbus *(G-8129)*
Melamed Riley Advertising LLC ....E 216 241-2141
  Cleveland *(G-6022)*
Monster Worldwide Inc ....D 513 719-3331
  Cincinnati *(G-4115)*
Nas Rcrtment Cmmunications LLC ....D 216 478-0300
  Cleveland *(G-6100)*
People To My Site LLC ....E 614 452-8179
  Columbus *(G-8532)*
Quad/Graphics Inc ....C 614 276-4800
  Columbus *(G-8579)*
Real Art Design Group Inc ....E 937 223-9955
  Dayton *(G-9844)*
Rockfish Interactive Corp ....D 513 381-1583
  Cincinnati *(G-4438)*
Roman/Peshoff Inc ....E 419 241-2221
  Holland *(G-12051)*
Ron Foth Retail Inc ....D 614 888-7771
  Columbus *(G-8646)*
SBC Advertising Ltd ....C 614 891-7070
  Columbus *(G-8692)*
Sgk LLC ....D 513 569-9900
  Cincinnati *(G-4506)*
Stern Advertising Inc ....E 216 464-4850
  Cleveland *(G-6540)*
Thread Information Design Inc ....E 419 887-6801
  Toledo *(G-18218)*
Touchstone Mdse Group LLC ....D 513 741-0400
  Mason *(G-13771)*
Universal Advertising Assoc ....E 513 522-5000
  Cincinnati *(G-4746)*
Vivial Media LLC ....D 937 610-4100
  Dayton *(G-9973)*
Wern-Rausch Locke Advertising ....E 330 493-8866
  Canton *(G-2584)*
Whitespace Design Group Inc ....E 330 762-9320
  Akron *(G-510)*
Wyse Advertising Inc ....D 216 696-2424
  Cleveland *(G-6765)*

7312 Outdoor Advertising Svcs

Clear Channel Outdoor Inc ....E 614 276-9781
  Columbus *(G-7296)*
Kessler Sign Company ....E 740 453-0668
  Zanesville *(G-20494)*
Lamar Advertising Company ....E 216 676-4321
  Cleveland *(G-5924)*
Lamar Advertising Company ....E 740 699-0000
  Saint Clairsville *(G-16639)*
Matrix Media Services Inc ....E 614 228-2200
  Columbus *(G-8129)*
Orange Barrel Media LLC ....E 614 294-4898
  Columbus *(G-8477)*

7313 Radio, TV & Publishers Adv Reps

Agri Communicators Inc ....E 614 273-0465
  Columbus *(G-6957)*
American City Bus Journals Inc ....E 937 528-4400
  Dayton *(G-9328)*
B G News ....E 419 372-2601
  Bowling Green *(G-1759)*
Copley Ohio Newspapers Inc ....C 330 364-5577
  New Philadelphia *(G-15087)*
Creative Crafts Group LLC ....D 303 215-5600
  Blue Ash *(G-1570)*
Ctv Media Inc ....E 614 848-5800
  Powell *(G-16333)*
Iheartcommunications Inc ....E 937 224-1137
  Dayton *(G-9627)*
Killer Spotscom Inc ....D 513 201-1380
  Cincinnati *(G-3923)*
Madison Avenue Mktg Group Inc ....E 419 473-9000
  Toledo *(G-18026)*
Manta Media Inc ....E 888 875-5833
  Columbus *(G-6893)*
Maverick Media ....E 419 331-1600
  Lima *(G-12838)*
Sandusky Register ....E 419 625-5500
  Sandusky *(G-16793)*
Segmint Inc ....E 330 594-5379
  Akron *(G-431)*
Thinktv Network ....E 937 220-1600
  Dayton *(G-9927)*

7319 Advertising, NEC

Berry Network LLC ....C 800 366-1264
  Moraine *(G-14753)*
Catalina Marketing Corporation ....E 513 564-8200
  Cincinnati *(G-3193)*
Ctv Media Inc ....E 614 848-5800
  Powell *(G-16333)*
Digital Color Intl LLC ....E 330 762-6959
  Akron *(G-193)*
Dismas Distribution Services ....E 614 861-2525
  Blacklick *(G-1506)*
Dispatch Consumer Services ....D 740 687-1893
  Lancaster *(G-12527)*
Dispatch Consumer Services ....E 740 548-5555
  Columbus *(G-7523)*
Elyria-Lorain Broadcasting Co ....E 440 322-3761
  Elyria *(G-10624)*
Empower Mediamarketing Inc ....C 513 871-7779
  Cincinnati *(G-3554)*
Groupcle LLC ....E 216 251-9641
  Cleveland *(G-5707)*
Harmon Media Group ....E 330 478-5325
  Canton *(G-2395)*
Hillman Group Inc ....E 513 874-5905
  West Chester *(G-19207)*
Innomark Communications LLC ....E 937 425-6152
  Sharonville *(G-16882)*
Ohs LLC ....E 513 252-2249
  Blue Ash *(G-1656)*
Paul Werth Associates Inc ....E 614 224-8114
  Columbus *(G-8524)*
Signum LLC ....D 440 248-2233
  Solon *(G-17051)*
Team Management Inc ....C 614 486-0864
  Columbus *(G-8827)*

7322 Adjustment & Collection Svcs

Allied Interstate LLC ....D 715 386-1810
  Columbus *(G-6971)*
Apelles LLC ....E 614 899-7322
  Columbus *(G-7028)*
Axcess Rcvery Cr Solutions Inc ....E 513 229-6700
  Cincinnati *(G-3070)*
C & S Associates Inc ....E 440 461-9661
  Highland Heights *(G-11868)*
Celco Ltd ....E 330 655-7000
  Hudson *(G-12107)*
Choice Recovery Inc ....D 614 358-9900
  Columbus *(G-7266)*
Controlled Credit Corporation ....E 513 921-2600
  Cincinnati *(G-3414)*
Credit Adjustments Inc ....D 419 782-3709
  Defiance *(G-10024)*
Credit Bur Collectn Svcs Inc ....E 614 223-0688
  Columbus *(G-7458)*
Credit Bur Collectn Svcs Inc ....E 937 496-2577
  Dayton *(G-9444)*
Dfs Corporate Services LLC ....B 614 777-7020
  Hilliard *(G-11895)*
Estate Information Svcs LLC ....D 614 729-1700
  Gahanna *(G-11241)*
Fidelity Properties Inc ....E 330 821-9700
  Alliance *(G-539)*
Finance System of Toledo Inc ....E 419 578-4300
  Toledo *(G-17888)*
First Federal Credit Control ....E 216 360-2000
  Cleveland *(G-5596)*
General Audit Corp ....E 419 993-2900
  Lima *(G-12782)*
General Revenue Corporation ....B 513 469-1472
  Mason *(G-13707)*
Guardian Water & Power Inc ....D 614 291-3141
  Columbus *(G-7785)*
Head Mercantile Co Inc ....D 440 847-2700
  Westlake *(G-19490)*
HMC Group Inc ....E 440 847-2720
  Westlake *(G-19491)*
Hs Financial Group LLC ....E 440 871-8484
  Westlake *(G-19493)*
Innovtive Cllectn Concepts Inc ....E 513 489-5500
  Blue Ash *(G-1615)*
Jared Galleria of Jewelery ....D 614 476-6532
  Columbus *(G-7935)*
JP Recovery Services Inc ....E 440 356-5048
  Rocky River *(G-16583)*
Macys Cr & Customer Svcs Inc ....A 513 398-5221
  Mason *(G-13734)*
McCarthy Burgess & Wolff Inc ....C 440 735-5100
  Bedford *(G-1321)*
Media Collections Inc ....D 216 831-5626
  Twinsburg *(G-18447)*
Medical Administrators Inc ....E 440 899-2229
  Westlake *(G-19513)*
Medical Care PSC Inc ....E 513 281-4400
  Cincinnati *(G-4042)*
National Entp Systems Inc ....B 440 542-1360
  Solon *(G-17032)*
Ncs Incorporated ....D 440 684-9455
  Cleveland *(G-6115)*
PRC Medical LLC ....D 330 493-9004
  Cuyahoga Falls *(G-9213)*
Receivable MGT Svcs Corp ....D 330 659-1000
  Richfield *(G-16525)*
Recovery One LLC ....D 614 336-4207
  Columbus *(G-8596)*
Reliant Capital Solutions LLC ....C 614 452-6100
  Gahanna *(G-11264)*
Revenue Assistance Corporation ....C 216 763-2100
  Cleveland *(G-6387)*
Roddy Group Inc ....E 216 763-0088
  Beachwood *(G-1121)*
Rossman ....E 614 523-4150
  New Albany *(G-15006)*
Security Check LLC ....C 614 944-5788
  Columbus *(G-8710)*
Tek-Collect Incorporated ....E 614 299-2766
  Columbus *(G-8828)*
United Collection Bureau Inc ....C 419 866-6227
  Toledo *(G-18269)*
United Collection Bureau Inc ....E 419 866-6227
  Maumee *(G-13989)*

7323 Credit Reporting Svcs

Cbc Companies Inc ....E 614 222-4343
  Columbus *(G-7213)*
Cbc Companies Inc ....D 614 538-6100
  Columbus *(G-7214)*
Cbcinnovis International Inc ....E 614 222-4343
  Columbus *(G-7215)*
Corps Security Agency Inc ....D 513 631-3200
  Blue Ash *(G-1568)*
Credit Infonet Inc ....E 937 235-2546
  Dayton *(G-9445)*
Innovis Data Solutions Inc ....E 614 222-4343
  Columbus *(G-7903)*
Kreller Bus Info Group Inc ....E 513 723-8900
  Cincinnati *(G-3945)*
Open Online LLC ....E 614 481-6999
  Columbus *(G-8470)*
Pasco Inc ....B 330 650-0613
  Hudson *(G-12138)*

7331 Direct Mail Advertising Svcs

A W S Inc ....C 440 333-1791
  Rocky River *(G-16567)*
A W S Inc ....B 216 749-0356
  Cleveland *(G-4937)*
Aero Fulfillment Services Corp ....D 800 225-7145
  Mason *(G-13658)*

73 BUSINESS SERVICES

Amerimark Holdings LLC .... B 440 325-2000
  Cleveland *(G-5025)*
Angstrom Graphics Inc Midwest .... E 330 225-8950
  Cleveland *(G-5038)*
Angstrom Graphics Inc Midwest .... B 216 271-5300
  Cleveland *(G-5037)*
Atco Inc .... C 740 592-6659
  Athens *(G-773)*
Bindery & Spc Pressworks Inc .... D 614 873-4623
  Plain City *(G-16184)*
Blue Chip Mailing Services Inc .... E 513 541-4800
  Blue Ash *(G-1545)*
Bpm Realty Inc .... E 614 221-6811
  Columbus *(G-7129)*
Brothers Publishing Co LLC .... E 937 548-3330
  Greenville *(G-11491)*
Case Western Reserve Univ .... E 216 368-2560
  Cleveland *(G-5187)*
Centurion of Akron Inc .... D 330 645-6699
  Copley *(G-9054)*
Clipper Magazine LLC .... D 513 794-4100
  Blue Ash *(G-1559)*
▲ Consolidated Graphics Group Inc .... C 216 881-9191
  Cleveland *(G-5393)*
Ctrac Inc .... E 440 572-1000
  Cleveland *(G-5447)*
Dayton Mailing Services Inc .... E 937 222-5056
  Dayton *(G-9480)*
Ddm-Digital Imaging Data .... D 740 928-1110
  Hebron *(G-11847)*
Deepwood Industries Inc .... E 440 350-5231
  Mentor *(G-14168)*
Digital Color Intl LLC .... E 330 762-6959
  Akron *(G-193)*
Directconnectgroup Ltd .... A 216 281-2866
  Cleveland *(G-5486)*
Early Express Services Inc .... E 937 223-5801
  Dayton *(G-9511)*
▲ Fine Line Graphics Corp .... C 614 486-0276
  Columbus *(G-7656)*
▲ Haines & Company Inc .... C 330 494-9111
  North Canton *(G-15343)*
Hecks Direct Mail & Prtg Svc .... E 419 697-3505
  Toledo *(G-17950)*
Hecks Direct Mail & Prtg Svc .... E 419 661-6028
  Toledo *(G-17951)*
Hkm Drect Mkt Cmmnications Inc .... E 216 651-9500
  Cleveland *(G-5762)*
J C Direct Mail Inc .... C 614 836-4848
  Groveport *(G-11649)*
Literature Fulfillment Svcs .... E 513 774-8600
  Blue Ash *(G-1629)*
Macke Brothers Inc .... D 513 771-7500
  Cincinnati *(G-4008)*
Macys Cr & Customer Svcs Inc .... D 513 881-9950
  West Chester *(G-19114)*
Mail It Corp .... E 419 249-4848
  Toledo *(G-18027)*
New Pros Communications Inc .... D 740 201-0410
  Powell *(G-16345)*
Patented Acquisition Corp .... D 937 353-2299
  Miamisburg *(G-14332)*
Pickaway Diversfied Industries .... D 740 474-1522
  Circleville *(G-4897)*
Popper & Associates Msrp LLC .... E 614 798-8991
  Dublin *(G-10428)*
Postal Mail Sort Inc .... E 330 747-1515
  Youngstown *(G-20328)*
Power Management Inc .... E 937 222-2909
  Dayton *(G-9817)*
Presort America Ltd .... D 614 836-5120
  Groveport *(G-11662)*
Resource Interactive .... E 614 621-2888
  Columbus *(G-8621)*
Sourcelink Ohio LLC .... C 937 885-8000
  Miamisburg *(G-14352)*
TMR Inc .... C 330 220-8564
  Brunswick *(G-1992)*
Traxium LLC .... E 330 572-8200
  Stow *(G-17397)*
United Mail LLC .... D 513 482-7429
  Cincinnati *(G-4734)*
W C National Mailing Corp .... B 614 836-5703
  Groveport *(G-11685)*
Weekleys Mailing Service Inc .... D 440 234-4325
  Berea *(G-1475)*
Yeck Brothers Company .... E 937 294-4000
  Moraine *(G-14837)*

7334 Photocopying & Duplicating Svcs

A-A Blueprint Co Inc .... E 330 794-8803
  Akron *(G-13)*
American Reprographics Co LLC .... E 614 224-5149
  Columbus *(G-7005)*
ARC Document Solutions Inc .... D 216 281-1234
  Cleveland *(G-5062)*
ARC Document Solutions Inc .... E 513 326-2300
  Cincinnati *(G-3040)*
ARC Document Solutions Inc .... E 937 277-7930
  Dayton *(G-9341)*
Cannell Graphics LLC .... E 614 781-9760
  Worthington *(G-19944)*
Fedex Office & Print Svcs Inc .... E 937 436-0677
  Dayton *(G-9544)*
Fedex Office & Print Svcs Inc .... E 614 621-1100
  Columbus *(G-7650)*
Fedex Office & Print Svcs Inc .... E 614 538-1429
  Columbus *(G-7651)*
Fedex Office & Print Svcs Inc .... E 614 898-0000
  Westerville *(G-19400)*
Fedex Office & Print Svcs Inc .... E 216 292-2679
  Beachwood *(G-1079)*
Franklin Imaging Llc .... E 614 885-6894
  Columbus *(G-7697)*
▲ Key Blue Prints Inc .... D 614 228-3285
  Columbus *(G-7983)*
Mike Rennie .... E 513 830-0020
  Dayton *(G-9746)*
Oscar Rbrtsn Doc Mgmt Svcs .... E 800 991-4611
  Blue Ash *(G-1661)*
Profile Digital Printing LLC .... E 937 866-4241
  Dayton *(G-9835)*
Queen City Reprographics .... C 513 326-2300
  Cincinnati *(G-4371)*
Ricoh Usa Inc .... D 216 574-9111
  Cleveland *(G-6394)*
Ricoh Usa Inc .... E 330 384-9111
  Akron *(G-416)*
Ricoh Usa Inc .... D 513 984-9898
  Blue Ash *(G-1683)*
TMR Inc .... C 330 220-8564
  Brunswick *(G-1992)*

7335 Commercial Photography

Aerocon Photogrammetric Svcs .... E 440 946-6277
  Willoughby *(G-19641)*
AG Interactive Inc .... C 216 889-5000
  Cleveland *(G-4967)*
Childers Photography .... E 937 256-0501
  Dayton *(G-9261)*
Eclipsecorp LLC .... E 614 626-8536
  Columbus *(G-7572)*
Ideal Image Inc .... D 937 832-1660
  Englewood *(G-10709)*
Interphase Phtgrphy Cmmnctions .... E 254 289-6270
  Amelia *(G-581)*
Kucera International Inc .... D 440 975-4230
  Willoughby *(G-19678)*
Marsh Inc .... E 513 421-1234
  Cincinnati *(G-4026)*
Phantom Photography LLC .... E 419 215-8060
  Toledo *(G-18123)*
Queen City Reprographics .... C 513 326-2300
  Cincinnati *(G-4371)*
Rapid Mortgage Company .... E 937 748-8888
  Dayton *(G-9842)*
Tj Metzgers Inc .... D 419 861-8611
  Toledo *(G-18219)*
Woodard Photographic Inc .... E 419 483-3364
  Bellevue *(G-1420)*
Youngstown ARC Engraving Co .... E 330 793-2471
  Youngstown *(G-20423)*

7336 Commercial Art & Graphic Design

Academy Graphic Comm Inc .... E 216 661-2550
  Cleveland *(G-4952)*
Adcom Group Inc .... E 216 574-9100
  Cleveland *(G-4955)*
Art-American Printing Plates .... E 216 241-4420
  Cleveland *(G-5069)*
Austin Foam Plastics Inc .... E 614 921-0824
  Columbus *(G-7075)*
Container Graphics Corp .... D 419 531-5133
  Toledo *(G-17831)*
Coyne Graphic Finishing Inc .... E 740 397-6232
  Mount Vernon *(G-14889)*
Digital Color Intl LLC .... E 330 762-6959
  Akron *(G-193)*

SIC SECTION

Diversipak Inc .... C 513 321-7884
  Cincinnati *(G-3495)*
Don Drumm Studios & Gallery .... E 330 253-6840
  Akron *(G-196)*
Edward Howard & Co .... E 216 781-2400
  Cleveland *(G-5528)*
Evolution Crtive Solutions LLC .... E 513 681-4450
  Cincinnati *(G-3584)*
Exhibitpro Inc .... E 614 885-9541
  New Albany *(G-14985)*
Fisher Design Inc .... E 513 417-8235
  Cincinnati *(G-3630)*
Fitch Inc .... D 614 885-3453
  Columbus *(G-7670)*
Fx Digital Media Inc .... E 216 241-4040
  Cleveland *(G-5643)*
▲ Galaxy Balloons Incorporated .... C 216 476-3360
  Cleveland *(G-5651)*
General Theming Contrs LLC .... E 614 252-6342
  Columbus *(G-7736)*
Graffiti Inc .... D 216 881-5550
  Cleveland *(G-5685)*
▲ Graphic Publications Inc .... E 330 674-2300
  Millersburg *(G-14603)*
Haney Inc .... E 513 561-1441
  Cincinnati *(G-3735)*
Innovtive Crtive Solutions LLC .... E 614 491-9638
  Groveport *(G-11647)*
Interbrand Hulefeld Inc .... D 513 421-2210
  Cincinnati *(G-3835)*
Libby Prszyk Kthman Hldngs Inc .... C 513 241-6330
  Cincinnati *(G-3974)*
Marsh Inc .... E 513 421-1234
  Cincinnati *(G-4026)*
▲ Mc Sign Company .... C 440 209-6200
  Mentor *(G-14211)*
Mitosis LLC .... E 937 557-3440
  Dayton *(G-9752)*
Mueller Art Cover & Binding Co .... E 440 238-3303
  Strongsville *(G-17496)*
Northeast Scene Inc .... E 216 241-7550
  Cleveland *(G-6157)*
Northern Ohio Printing Inc .... E 216 398-0000
  Cleveland *(G-6160)*
Nottingham-Spirk Des .... E 216 800-5782
  Cleveland *(G-6165)*
ONeil & Associates Inc .... C 937 865-0800
  Miamisburg *(G-14330)*
Real Art Design Group Inc .... E 937 223-9955
  Dayton *(G-9844)*
RGI Inc .... E 513 221-2121
  Cincinnati *(G-4411)*
Screen Works Inc .... E 937 264-9111
  Dayton *(G-9870)*
Sfc Graphics Inc .... E 419 255-1283
  Toledo *(G-18181)*
▲ Shamrock Companies Inc .... C 440 899-9510
  Westlake *(G-19546)*
Suntwist Corp .... D 800 935-3534
  Maple Heights *(G-13420)*
Taylor Made Graphics .... E 440 882-6318
  Cleveland *(G-6571)*
Third Dimension Inc .... E 877 926-3223
  Geneva *(G-11370)*
Univenture Inc .... D 937 645-4600
  Dublin *(G-10478)*
Visual Art Graphic Services .... E 330 274-2775
  Mantua *(G-13397)*
Whitespace Design Group Inc .... E 330 762-9320
  Akron *(G-510)*
Woodrow Manufacturing Co .... E 937 399-9333
  Springfield *(G-17300)*
Young & Rubicam Inc .... C 513 419-2300
  Cincinnati *(G-4864)*
Young Mens Christian .... E 513 791-5000
  Blue Ash *(G-1725)*

7338 Secretarial & Court Reporting Svcs

Academy Court Reporting Inc .... E 216 861-3222
  Cleveland *(G-4951)*
Ace-Merit LLC .... E 513 241-3200
  Cincinnati *(G-2967)*
Chase Transcriptions Inc .... E 330 650-0539
  Hudson *(G-12110)*
Mehler and Hagestrom Inc .... E 216 621-4984
  Cleveland *(G-6020)*
National Service Information .... E 740 387-6806
  Marion *(G-13567)*
Robert Erney .... E 312 788-9005
  Brookpark *(G-1954)*

7342 Disinfecting & Pest Control Svcs

All Gone Termite & Pest Ctrl.................E....... 513 874-7500
West Chester *(G-19016)*
Central Exterminating Company...........E....... 216 771-0555
Cleveland *(G-5210)*
Corporate Cleaning Inc.........................E....... 614 203-6051
Columbus *(G-7441)*
DCS Sanitation Management Inc...........D....... 513 891-4980
Cincinnati *(G-3469)*
General Pest Control Company.............E....... 216 252-7140
Cleveland *(G-5668)*
Image By J & K LLC...............................B....... 888 667-6929
Maumee *(G-13927)*
Living Matters LLC.................................E....... 866 587-8074
Cleveland *(G-5948)*
Ohio Exterminating Co Inc......................E....... 614 294-6311
Columbus *(G-8343)*
Orkin LLC..E....... 614 888-5811
Columbus *(G-8481)*
Rentokil North America Inc...................E....... 330 797-9090
Youngstown *(G-20344)*
Rentokil North America Inc...................E....... 216 328-0700
Brooklyn Heights *(G-1924)*
Scherzinger Corp....................................D....... 513 531-7848
Cincinnati *(G-4480)*
▲ **Scotts Miracle-Gro Company**............B....... 937 644-0011
Marysville *(G-13651)*
Steve Shaffer..E....... 614 276-6355
Columbus *(G-8787)*
Terminix Intl Co Ltd Partnr....................E....... 513 942-6670
Fairfield *(G-10913)*
Terminix Intl Co Ltd Partnr....................E....... 216 518-1091
Cleveland *(G-6584)*
Terminix Intl Co Ltd Partnr....................E....... 419 868-8290
Maumee *(G-13986)*
Terminix Intl Co Ltd Partnr....................E....... 513 539-7846
Middletown *(G-14466)*
Terminix Intl Co Ltd Partnr....................E....... 978 744-2402
Canton *(G-2560)*
Terminix Intl Coml Xenia.......................E....... 513 539-7846
Middletown *(G-14467)*

7349 Building Cleaning & Maintenance Svcs, NEC

A 1 Janitorial Cleaning Svc....................E....... 513 932-8003
Lebanon *(G-12585)*
A B M Inc...E....... 419 421-2292
Findlay *(G-10988)*
A Bee C Service Inc.................................E....... 440 735-1505
Cleveland *(G-4930)*
AAA Standard Services Inc.....................D....... 419 535-0274
Toledo *(G-17737)*
ABM Facility Services Inc.......................E....... 859 767-4393
Cincinnati *(G-2961)*
ABM Janitorial Services Inc...................C....... 216 861-1199
Cleveland *(G-4948)*
ABM Janitorial Services Inc...................C....... 513 731-1418
Cincinnati *(G-2962)*
Absolute Cleaning Services....................D....... 440 542-1742
Solon *(G-16968)*
Academic Support Services LLC...........E....... 740 274-6138
Columbus *(G-6930)*
Access Cleaning Service Inc..................E....... 937 276-2605
Dayton *(G-9303)*
Accomodaire Total Cleaning LLC..........E....... 614 367-1347
Columbus *(G-6935)*
Ace Building Maintenance LLC..............E....... 614 471-2223
Columbus *(G-6937)*
Advanced Facilities Maint Corp.............E....... 614 389-3495
Columbus *(G-6946)*
Aetna Building Maintenance Inc............B....... 614 476-1818
Columbus *(G-6953)*
Aetna Building Maintenance Inc............D....... 937 324-5711
Springfield *(G-17146)*
Aetna Building Maintenance Inc............C....... 866 238-6201
Dayton *(G-9312)*
Ajax Cleaning Contractors Co...............D....... 216 881-8484
Cleveland *(G-4980)*
Ajax Commercial Cleaning Inc...............D....... 330 928-4543
Cuyahoga Falls *(G-9158)*
Akron Area Commercial Cleaning..........E....... 330 434-0767
Akron *(G-26)*
Akron Public School Maint Svcs............D....... 330 761-2640
Akron *(G-51)*
All Pro Cleaning Services Inc................D....... 440 519-0055
Solon *(G-16974)*
Allen-Keith Construction Co...................D....... 330 266-2220
Canton *(G-2231)*
Alpha & Omega Bldg Svcs Inc...............E....... 513 429-5082
Blue Ash *(G-1529)*
Alpha & Omega Bldg Svcs Inc...............D....... 937 229-3536
Dayton *(G-9320)*
Alpha & Omega Bldg Svcs Inc...............B....... 937 298-2125
Dayton *(G-9321)*
American Maintenance Svcs Inc............E....... 330 744-3400
Youngstown *(G-20104)*
AMF Facility Services Inc.......................E....... 800 991-2273
Dayton *(G-9334)*
Anchor Cleaning Contractors..................E....... 216 961-7343
Cleveland *(G-5034)*
Any Domest Work Inc..............................D....... 440 845-9911
Cleveland *(G-5045)*
Apex Environmental Svcs LLC...............D....... 513 772-2739
Cincinnati *(G-3034)*
Aramark Facility Services LLC...............E....... 216 687-5000
Cleveland *(G-5057)*
Ashland Cleaning LLC............................E....... 419 281-1747
Ashland *(G-653)*
Atlantis Co Inc...D....... 888 807-3272
Cleveland *(G-5078)*
Ats Group LLC..C....... 216 744-5757
Solon *(G-16979)*
August Groh & Sons Inc..........................E....... 513 821-0090
Cincinnati *(G-3064)*
Basol Maintenance Service Inc..............D....... 419 422-0946
Findlay *(G-10993)*
Bebley Enterprises Inc............................E....... 419 389-9424
Toledo *(G-17767)*
Bechtl Bldng Mntnc Crprtn of.................D....... 330 759-2797
Youngstown *(G-20111)*
Belfor USA Group Inc..............................E....... 513 860-3111
West Chester *(G-19192)*
Beneficial Building Services...................D....... 330 848-2556
Akron *(G-97)*
Bkg Services Inc......................................E....... 614 476-1800
Columbus *(G-7114)*
Blanchard Valley Health System............A....... 419 423-4500
Findlay *(G-10997)*
Bleachtech LLC..E....... 216 921-1980
Seville *(G-16838)*
Blue Chip 2000 Coml Clg Inc..................B....... 513 561-2999
Cincinnati *(G-3119)*
Buckeye Commercial Cleaning...............E....... 614 866-4700
Pickerington *(G-16087)*
Butchko Electric Inc................................E....... 440 985-3180
Amherst *(G-589)*
Butterfield Co Inc.....................................D....... 330 832-1282
Massillon *(G-13790)*
C & K Industrial Services Inc..................D....... 216 642-0055
Independence *(G-12192)*
C M S Enterprises Inc..............................E....... 740 653-1940
Lancaster *(G-12512)*
Camco Inc..E....... 740 477-3682
Circleville *(G-4881)*
Cardinal Maintenance & Svc Co.............C....... 330 252-0282
Akron *(G-122)*
Carol Scudere...E....... 614 839-4357
New Albany *(G-14979)*
Carrara Companies Inc............................D....... 330 659-2800
Richfield *(G-16499)*
Caveney Inc...D....... 330 497-4600
North Canton *(G-15328)*
Champion Clg Specialists Inc.................E....... 513 871-2333
Cincinnati *(G-3227)*
▲ **Chemical Solvents Inc**........................E....... 216 741-9310
Cleveland *(G-5232)*
Circle Building Services Inc....................D....... 614 228-6090
Columbus *(G-7275)*
Clean All Services Inc.............................C....... 937 498-4146
Sidney *(G-16921)*
Clean Break Inc..E....... 330 638-5648
Warren *(G-18834)*
Clean Care Inc...C....... 419 725-2100
Toledo *(G-17815)*
Cleaner Carpet & Jantr Inc......................E....... 513 469-2070
Mason *(G-13684)*
Clearview Cleaning Contractors............E....... 216 621-6688
Cleveland *(G-5285)*
Clinton-Carvell Inc...................................E....... 614 351-8858
Columbus *(G-7303)*
CMS Business Services LLC..................D....... 740 687-0577
Lancaster *(G-12520)*
Coleman Professional Svcs Inc..............B....... 330 673-1347
Kent *(G-12360)*
Columbus Public School Dst...................B....... 614 365-5043
Columbus *(G-7378)*
Commercial Cleaning Solutions..............E....... 937 981-4870
Greenfield *(G-11483)*
Complete Building Maint LLC.................E....... 513 235-7511
Cincinnati *(G-3403)*
Control Cleaning Solutions.....................E....... 330 220-3333
Brunswick *(G-1973)*
Corporate Cleaning Inc............................E....... 614 203-6051
Columbus *(G-7441)*
County of Cuyahoga.................................A....... 216 443-6954
Cleveland *(G-5423)*
Crystal Clear Bldg Svcs Inc....................D....... 440 439-2288
Oakwood Village *(G-15628)*
Csi International Inc................................A....... 614 781-1571
Worthington *(G-19952)*
Cummins Building Maint Inc....................D....... 740 726-9800
Prospect *(G-16363)*
Cummins Facility Services LLC..............B....... 740 726-9800
Prospect *(G-16364)*
Custom Cleaning and Maint....................E....... 440 946-7028
Willoughby *(G-19657)*
Custom Cleaning Service LLC................E....... 440 774-1222
Oberlin *(G-15641)*
Custom Maid Cleaning Services.............E....... 513 351-6571
Cincinnati *(G-3452)*
Custom Maint..D....... 330 793-2523
Youngstown *(G-20164)*
D & J Master Clean Inc............................D....... 614 847-1181
Columbus *(G-7477)*
Dave & Barb Enterprises Inc....................D....... 513 553-0050
New Richmond *(G-15125)*
DCS Sanitation Management Inc...........D....... 513 891-4980
Cincinnati *(G-3469)*
Dempsey Inc..D....... 330 758-2309
Youngstown *(G-20167)*
Dependable Cleaning Contrs..................D....... 440 953-9191
Willoughby *(G-19659)*
Dove Building Services Inc.....................D....... 614 299-4700
Columbus *(G-7543)*
Dublin Coml Property Svcs Inc...............E....... 419 732-6732
Port Clinton *(G-16244)*
E Wynn Inc...E....... 614 444-5288
Columbus *(G-7562)*
Environment Control of Greater..............D....... 614 868-9788
Columbus *(G-7599)*
Environment Ctrl Beachwood Inc..........D....... 330 405-6201
Twinsburg *(G-18408)*
Environment Ctrl of Miami Cnty.............D....... 937 669-9900
Tipp City *(G-17716)*
Ermc II LP..E....... 513 424-8517
Middletown *(G-14478)*
Essentialprofile1corp...............................D....... 614 805-4794
Columbus *(G-7611)*
Euclid Indus Maint Clg Contrs................C....... 216 361-0288
Cleveland *(G-5553)*
Executive Management Services...........C....... 419 529-8800
Ontario *(G-15688)*
Extreme Detail Clg Cnstr Svcs...............E....... 419 392-3243
Toledo *(G-17874)*
Family Entertainment Services...............D....... 740 286-8587
Jackson *(G-12311)*
Feecorp Industrial Services....................C....... 740 533-1445
Ironton *(G-12288)*
Four Corners Cleaning Inc......................E....... 330 644-0834
Barberton *(G-963)*
G J Goudreau & Co...................................E....... 216 351-5233
Cleveland *(G-5646)*
Galaxie Industrial Svcs LLC....................E....... 330 503-2334
Youngstown *(G-20193)*
Gca Services Group Inc...........................D....... 800 422-8760
Cleveland *(G-5661)*
General Building Maintenance................D....... 330 682-2238
Orrville *(G-15773)*
General Services Cleaning Co................E....... 614 840-0562
Columbus *(G-7735)*
George Gardner..D....... 419 636-4277
Bryan *(G-2000)*
Green Impressions LLC...........................E....... 440 240-8508
Sheffield Village *(G-16886)*
Gsf North American Jantr Svc................C....... 513 733-1451
West Chester *(G-19205)*
Guardian Care Services...........................E....... 614 436-8500
Columbus *(G-7782)*
H & B Window Cleaning Inc.....................E....... 440 934-6158
Avon Lake *(G-931)*
Harrison Industries Inc............................D....... 740 942-2988
Cadiz *(G-2077)*
Heco Operations Inc.................................E....... 614 888-5700
Worthington *(G-19962)*
Heits Building Svcs Cnkd LLC................D....... 855 464-3487
Cincinnati *(G-3756)*
High Power Inc..E....... 937 667-1772
Tipp City *(G-17717)*
High-TEC Industrial Services..................C....... 937 667-1772
Tipp City *(G-17718)*

S I C

Employee Codes: A=Over 500 employees, B=251-500
C=101-250, D=51-100, E=25-50
2018 Harris Ohio
Services Directory
991

73 BUSINESS SERVICES

Company	Location	Class	Phone
Hopewell Industries Inc	Coshocton (G-9107)	C	740 622-3563
House Calls LLC	Cincinnati (G-3789)	E	513 841-9800
Hydrochem LLC	Youngstown (G-20226)	E	330 792-6569
Image By J & K LLC	Maumee (G-13927)	B	888 667-6929
Industrial Air Control Inc	Hubbard (G-12088)	D	330 772-6422
Inner-Space Cleaning Corp	Cleveland (G-5823)	C	440 646-0701
Inovative Facility Svcs LLC	Maumee (G-13928)	B	419 861-1710
Ivory Services Inc	Cleveland (G-5838)	E	216 344-3094
J B M Cleaning & Supply Co	Massillon (G-13825)	E	330 837-8805
J Rutledge Enterprises Inc	Cincinnati (G-3852)	E	502 241-4100
J V Janitorial Services Inc	Cleveland (G-5845)	E	216 749-1150
Jancoa Janitorial Services Inc	Cincinnati (G-3862)	B	513 351-7200
Jani-Source Inc	Marietta (G-13458)	E	740 374-6298
Janitorial Services Inc	Cleveland (G-5851)	B	216 341-8601
Jantech Building Services Inc	Brooklyn Heights (G-1917)	C	216 661-6102
Jenkins Enterprises LLC	Cincinnati (G-2920)	E	513 752-7896
John O Bostock Jr	Dayton (G-9644)	E	937 263-8540
Jordan Kyli Enterprises Inc	Westlake (G-19502)	E	216 256-3773
Justin L Paulk	Middletown (G-14481)	D	513 422-7060
K & L Floormasters LLC	Canton (G-2420)	E	330 493-0869
K & M Kleening Service Inc	Groveport (G-11652)	E	614 737-3750
Kellermyer Bergensons Svcs LLC	Maumee (G-13932)	E	419 867-4300
Kelli Woods Management Inc	Toledo (G-17992)	C	419 478-1200
Kettering City School District	Dayton (G-9652)	D	937 297-1990
Key Center Properties LP	Cleveland (G-5897)	E	216 687-0500
Kleman Services LLC	Lima (G-12811)	E	419 339-0871
Ktm Enterprises Inc	Greenville (G-11512)	E	937 548-8357
Lake Side Building Maintenance	Cleveland (G-5919)	E	216 589-9900
Larue Enterprises Inc	Beavercreek (G-1248)	E	937 438-5711
Leadec Corp	Blue Ash (G-1627)	E	513 731-3590
Licking-Knox Goodwill Inds Inc	Columbus (G-8058)	D	614 235-7675
Lima Sheet Metal Machine & Mfg	Lima (G-12827)	E	419 229-1161
Living Matters LLC	Cleveland (G-5948)	E	866 587-8074
Logan-Hocking School District	Logan (G-12985)	E	740 385-7844
Louderback Fmly Invstments Inc	New Carlisle (G-15026)	E	937 845-1762
Lucas Building Mainenance LLC	Ironton (G-12297)	A	740 479-1800
Mapp Building Service LLC	Blue Ash (G-1633)	E	513 253-3990
Marks Cleaning Service Inc	Medina (G-14094)	E	330 725-5702
Mathews Josiah	Lima (G-12837)	E	567 204-8818
Metropolitan Envmtl Svcs Inc	Hilliard (G-11930)	D	614 771-1881
Mid-American Clg Contrs Inc	Findlay (G-11067)	C	419 429-6222
Mid-American Clg Contrs Inc	Lima (G-12840)	D	419 229-3899
Mid-American Clg Contrs Inc	Columbus (G-8163)	C	614 291-7170
Milford Coml Clg Svcs Inc	Milford (G-14542)	E	513 575-5678
Molly Maid of Lorain County	Elyria (G-10655)	E	440 327-0000
Mougianis Industries Inc	Steubenville (G-17331)	D	740 264-6372
MPW Industrial Services Inc	Canton (G-2467)	D	330 454-1898
MPW Industrial Services Inc	Hebron (G-11854)	A	800 827-8790
MPW Industrial Services Inc	Chillicothe (G-2864)	D	740 774-5251
MPW Industrial Services Inc	East Liberty (G-10511)	D	937 644-0200
MPW Industrial Services Inc	Lorain (G-13062)	E	440 277-9072
MPW Industrial Svcs Group Inc	Hebron (G-11855)	D	740 927-8790
Mrap LLC	Columbus (G-8202)	E	614 545-3190
N Services Inc	Blue Ash (G-1651)	D	513 793-2000
New Albany Cleaning Services	New Albany (G-14997)	E	614 855-9990
Nicholas D Starr Inc	Lima (G-12843)	C	419 229-3192
North Coast Sales	Middlefield (G-14400)	E	440 632-0793
Northpointe Property MGT LLC	Columbus (G-8294)	C	614 579-9712
Nortone Service Inc	Buckeye Lake (G-2022)	E	740 527-2057
Ohio Building Service Inc	Cincinnati (G-4202)	E	513 761-0268
Ohio Custodial Maintenance	Columbus (G-8323)	C	614 443-1232
Ohio State University	Columbus (G-8445)	A	614 292-6158
Ohio Window Cleaning Inc	Tipp City (G-17723)	D	937 877-0832
Perry Contract Services Inc	Columbus (G-8537)	D	614 274-4350
Pinnacle Building Services Inc	Chillicothe (G-2871)	C	614 871-6190
Priority Building Services Inc	Beavercreek Township (G-1282)	D	937 233-7030
Pro Care Janitor Supply	Piqua (G-16162)	E	937 778-2275
Pro-Touch Inc	Columbus (G-8563)	C	614 586-0303
Professional Hse Clg Svcs Inc	Chesterland (G-2801)	E	440 729-7866
Professional Maint Dayton	Dayton (G-9834)	D	937 461-5259
Professional Maint of Columbus	Columbus (G-8567)	C	614 443-6528
Professional Maint of Columbus	Cincinnati (G-4343)	B	513 579-1762
Professional Restoration Svc	Medina (G-14114)	E	330 825-1803
Professnal Mint Cincinnati Inc	Cincinnati (G-4345)	A	513 579-1161
Promanco Inc	Marietta (G-13491)	E	740 374-2120
Psp Operations Inc	Worthington (G-19987)	E	614 888-5700
Putman Janitorial Service Inc	West Chester (G-19222)	E	513 942-1900
Quality Assured Cleaning Inc	Columbus (G-8580)	A	614 798-1505
Quality Cleaning Systems LLC	Shreve (G-16908)	E	330 567-2050
Quality Clg Svc of NW Ohio	Wauseon (G-18961)	D	419 335-9105
R K Hydro-Vac Inc	Piqua (G-16164)	E	937 773-8600
R T Industries Inc	Troy (G-18374)	C	937 335-5784
Rcs Enterprises Inc	Columbus (G-8591)	D	614 337-8520
Rde System Corp	Lebanon (G-12640)	C	513 933-8000
Rde System Corporation	Dayton (G-9843)	D	513 933-8000
Red Carpet Janitorial Service	Cincinnati (G-4395)	B	513 242-7575
Restoration Resources Inc	Hudson (G-12141)	E	330 650-4486
Richland Newhope Industries	Mansfield (G-13358)	C	419 774-4400
Romaster Corp	Norton (G-15559)	D	330 825-1945
Rwk Services Inc	Cleveland (G-6423)	E	440 526-2144
Saftek Industrial Service Inc	Tipp City (G-17726)	E	937 667-1772
Scarlet & Gray Cleaning Svc	Cincinnati (G-4479)	C	513 661-4483
Schenker Inc	Swanton (G-17570)	E	419 491-1055
Scioto Services LLc	Marysville (G-13649)	E	937 644-0888
Seaway Sponge & Chamois Co	Toledo (G-18177)	E	419 691-4694
ServiceMaster By Sidwell Inc	Lancaster (G-12573)	E	740 687-1077
ServiceMaster By Steinbach	Canton (G-2526)	E	330 497-5959
ServiceMaster Clean	Bedford (G-1335)	E	440 349-0979
ServiceMaster of Defiance Inc	Defiance (G-10057)	D	419 784-5570
Shining Company	Columbus (G-8727)	E	614 588-4115
Southtown Heating & Cooling	Moraine (G-14827)	E	937 320-9900
Sr Improvements Services LLC	Vickery (G-18733)	E	567 207-6488
Stanley Stemer of Akron Canton	Coventry Township (G-9133)	E	330 785-5005
Star Inc	Portsmouth (G-16314)	C	740 354-1517
Starlight Enterprises Inc	New Philadelphia (G-15116)	C	330 339-2020
Stb Enterprises	Canton (G-2548)	E	330 478-0044
Stout Lori Cleaning & Such	Gibsonburg (G-11404)	E	419 637-7644
Suburban Maint Contrs Inc	North Royalton (G-15504)	E	440 237-7765
Super Shine Inc	Middletown (G-14464)	E	513 423-8999
Sylvania Lighting Svcs Corp	Solon (G-17060)	E	440 742-8208
T & L Enterprises Inc	Berea (G-1471)	E	440 234-5900
T N C Construction Inc	Grove City (G-11604)	E	614 554-5330
T&L Global Management LLC	Columbus (G-8818)	D	614 586-0303
The Maids	Bedford Heights (G-1360)	D	440 735-6243
TNT Power Wash Inc	Groveport (G-11676)	E	614 662-3110
TNT Power Wash Inc	Groveport (G-11677)	E	614 662-3110
Toledo Building Services Co	Toledo (G-18228)	A	419 241-3101
Toledo Public Schools	Toledo (G-18247)	D	419 243-6422
Trg Maintenance LLC	Westerville (G-19356)	A	614 891-4850
Tri Tech Service Systems Inc	Somerville (G-17071)	C	937 787-4664
Turn Around Group Inc	Warren (G-18917)	D	330 372-0064
Twin Cedars Services Inc	Lebanon (G-12655)	D	513 932-0399
Two Men & A Vacuum LLC	Columbus (G-8881)	D	614 300-7970
Ultimate Building Maintenance	Warren (G-18918)	D	330 369-9771
United Scoto Senior Activities	Portsmouth (G-16316)	E	740 354-6672
University of Cincinnati	Cincinnati (G-4761)	A	513 556-6381
Vadakin Inc	Marietta (G-13512)	E	740 373-7518
Veolia Es Industrial Svcs Inc	Dayton (G-9968)	C	937 425-0512
W David Maupin Inc	Toledo (G-18294)	E	419 389-0458
Ward & Werner Co	Worthington (G-20006)	E	614 885-0741
Wells & Sons Janitorial Svc	Fairborn (G-10813)	E	937 878-4375
Wheeler Cleaning LLC	Westerville (G-19450)	E	614 818-0981
White Glove Executive Services	Grove City (G-11617)	E	614 226-2553
Wiggins Clg & Crpt Svc Inc	Dayton (G-9998)	D	937 279-9080
Wj Service Co Inc	Warren (G-18928)	E	330 372-5040

York Building Maintenance Inc ....C 216 398-8100
Cleveland *(G-6770)*

Youngstown Window Cleaning Co ....C 330 743-3880
Girard *(G-11431)*

7352 Medical Eqpt Rental & Leasing

American Home Health Care Inc ....E 614 237-1133
Columbus *(G-6996)*

Americas Best Medical Eqp Co ....E 330 928-0884
Akron *(G-73)*

Ancillary Medical Investments ....E 937 456-5520
Eaton *(G-10552)*

Apria Healthcare LLC ....E 614 351-5920
Columbus *(G-7030)*

Apria Healthcare LLC ....E 216 485-1180
Cleveland *(G-5056)*

Apria Healthcare LLC ....D 419 471-1919
Maumee *(G-13883)*

▲ Boardman Medical Supply Co ....C 330 545-6700
Girard *(G-11408)*

Braden Med Services Inc ....E 740 732-2356
Caldwell *(G-2082)*

Cornerstone Medical Associates ....E 330 374-0229
Akron *(G-165)*

Fairfield Medical Center ....A 740 687-8000
Lancaster *(G-12537)*

Fortec Medical Inc ....E 330 463-1265
Hudson *(G-12117)*

Fortec Medical Inc ....E 513 742-9100
Cincinnati *(G-3640)*

Medic Home Health Care LLC ....E 440 449-7727
Cleveland *(G-6012)*

Medical Service Company ....D 440 232-3000
Bedford *(G-1322)*

Medical Specialties Distrs LLC ....E 440 232-0320
Oakwood Village *(G-15630)*

Millers Rental and Sls Co Inc ....D 330 753-8600
Akron *(G-345)*

North Ohio Heart Center ....D 440 204-4000
Lorain *(G-13069)*

Pharmerica Long-Term Care Inc ....E 330 425-4450
Twinsburg *(G-18454)*

Sateri Home Inc ....D 330 758-8106
Youngstown *(G-20367)*

Seeley Enterprises Company ....E 440 293-6600
Andover *(G-614)*

Seeley Medical Oxygen Co ....E 440 255-7163
Andover *(G-615)*

St Ritas Medical Center ....A 419 227-3361
Lima *(G-12885)*

Toledo Medical Equipment Co ....E 419 866-7120
Maumee *(G-13987)*

7353 Heavy Construction Eqpt Rental & Leasing

1st Choice LLC ....D 877 564-6658
Cleveland *(G-4922)*

A and A Millwright Rigging Svcs ....E 513 396-6212
Cincinnati *(G-2951)*

Ahern Rentals Inc ....E 440 498-0869
Solon *(G-16972)*

All Aerials LLC ....E 330 659-9600
Richfield *(G-16494)*

All Crane Rental Corp ....D 614 261-1800
Columbus *(G-6964)*

All Erection & Crane Rental ....C 216 524-6550
Cleveland *(G-4986)*

All Erection & Crane Rental ....D 216 524-6550
Cleveland *(G-4987)*

American Crane Inc ....E 614 496-2268
Reynoldsburg *(G-16426)*

AVI Food Systems Inc ....E 440 255-3468
Mentor *(G-14146)*

Bluefoot Industrial LLC ....E 740 314-5299
Steubenville *(G-17304)*

▲ Bobcat Enterprises Inc ....C 513 874-8945
West Chester *(G-19030)*

▲ Canton Erectors Inc ....E 330 453-7363
Canton *(G-2287)*

Cecil I Walker Machinery Co ....E 740 286-7566
Jackson *(G-12308)*

Charles Jergens Contractor ....E 937 233-1830
Dayton *(G-9400)*

▼ Columbus Equipment Company ....E 614 437-0352
Columbus *(G-7352)*

Columbus Equipment Company ....E 614 443-6541
Columbus *(G-7353)*

Dolin Supply Co ....E 304 529-4171
South Point *(G-17084)*

Eastland Crane Service Inc ....E 614 868-9750
Columbus *(G-7565)*

Efco Corp ....E 614 876-1226
Columbus *(G-7586)*

▲ Eleet Cryogenics Inc ....E 330 874-4009
Bolivar *(G-1746)*

◆ F & M Mafco Inc ....C 513 367-2151
Harrison *(G-11797)*

General Crane Rental LLC ....E 330 908-0001
Macedonia *(G-13198)*

Grady Rentals LLC ....E 330 627-2022
Carrollton *(G-2621)*

H M Miller Construction Co ....D 330 628-4811
Mogadore *(G-14677)*

Holt Rental Services ....E 513 771-0515
Cincinnati *(G-3776)*

Indian Nation Inc ....E 740 532-6143
North Canton *(G-15345)*

Interstate Lift Trucks Inc ....E 216 328-0970
Cleveland *(G-5835)*

JBK Group Inc ....E 216 901-0000
Cleveland *(G-5854)*

Jeffers Crane Service Inc ....D 419 693-0421
Oregon *(G-15740)*

Kelley Steel Erectors Inc ....D 440 232-1573
Cleveland *(G-5891)*

▲ Lefeld Welding & Stl Sups Inc ....E 419 678-2397
Coldwater *(G-6832)*

Leppo Inc ....E 330 456-2930
Canton *(G-2434)*

Leppo Inc ....C 330 633-3999
Tallmadge *(G-17643)*

Malavite Excavating Inc ....E 330 484-1274
East Sparta *(G-10540)*

Miami Industrial Trucks Inc ....E 419 424-0042
Findlay *(G-11066)*

Midwest Equipment Co ....E 216 441-1400
Cleveland *(G-6061)*

Ohio Machinery Co ....E 330 530-9010
Girard *(G-11421)*

◆ Ohio Machinery Co ....C 440 526-6200
Broadview Heights *(G-1886)*

Phillips Ready Mix Co ....D 937 426-5151
Beavercreek Township *(G-1281)*

Piqua Steel Co ....D 937 773-3632
Piqua *(G-16159)*

Pollock Research & Design Inc ....E 330 332-3300
Salem *(G-16706)*

RELAM Inc ....E 440 232-3354
Solon *(G-17046)*

Sommerset Development Ltd ....C 440 286-6194
Chardon *(G-2768)*

Sunbelt Rentals Inc ....E 216 362-0300
Cleveland *(G-6549)*

TNT Equipment Company ....E 614 882-1549
Columbus *(G-8852)*

Towlift Inc ....E 419 666-1333
Northwood *(G-15548)*

▲ Trimble Engineering & Cnstr ....E 937 233-8921
Dayton *(G-9938)*

United Rentals North Amer Inc ....E 800 877-3687
Perrysburg *(G-16067)*

7359 Equipment Rental & Leasing, NEC

A & A Safety Inc ....E 513 943-6100
Amelia *(G-571)*

A B C Rental Center East Inc ....E 216 475-8240
Cleveland *(G-4929)*

Aarons Inc ....E 330 823-1879
Alliance *(G-522)*

Aarons Inc ....E 216 251-4500
Cleveland *(G-4943)*

Aarons Inc ....E 330 385-7201
East Liverpool *(G-10513)*

Aarons Inc ....E 937 778-3577
Piqua *(G-16134)*

Aarons Inc ....E 216 587-2745
Maple Heights *(G-13398)*

Ace Rental Place ....D 937 642-2891
Marysville *(G-13605)*

Advance Vending Corp ....E 216 587-9500
Cleveland *(G-4958)*

Advanced Tenting Solutions ....E 216 291-3300
Newbury *(G-15253)*

All Erection & Crane Rental ....C 216 524-6550
Cleveland *(G-4986)*

All Erection & Crane Rental ....D 216 524-6550
Cleveland *(G-4987)*

All Lift Service Company Inc ....E 440 585-1542
Willoughby *(G-19642)*

All Occasions Event Rental ....E 513 563-0600
Cincinnati *(G-2985)*

All Temp Refrigeration Inc ....E 419 692-5016
Delphos *(G-10137)*

American Roadway Logistics Inc ....E 330 659-2003
Richfield *(G-16497)*

Ayrshire Inc ....D 440 992-0743
Ashtabula *(G-728)*

Baker Bnngson Rlty Auctioneers ....E 419 547-7777
Clyde *(G-6810)*

Baker Equipment and Mtls Ltd ....E 513 422-6697
Monroe *(G-14689)*

Baker Vehicle Systems Inc ....E 330 467-2250
Macedonia *(G-13189)*

Beacon Company ....E 330 733-8322
Akron *(G-95)*

Bkg Holdings LLC ....E 614 252-7455
Columbus *(G-7113)*

Black Swamp Equipment LLC ....E 419 445-0030
Archbold *(G-633)*

Bluefoot Industrial LLC ....E 740 314-5299
Steubenville *(G-17304)*

Bnd Rentals Inc ....E 937 898-5061
Vandalia *(G-18663)*

Bobcat of Dayton Inc ....E 937 293-3176
Moraine *(G-14755)*

Brennan Industrial Truck Co ....E 419 867-6000
Holland *(G-12012)*

Budco Group Inc ....E 513 621-6111
Cincinnati *(G-3146)*

Budget Dumpster LLC ....E 866 284-6164
Westlake *(G-19468)*

Camargo Rental Center Inc ....E 513 271-6510
Cincinnati *(G-3170)*

Chase Phipps ....E 330 754-0467
Canton *(G-2303)*

Cleveland Corporate Svcs Inc ....C 216 397-1492
Cleveland *(G-5310)*

Colortone Audio Visual ....E 216 928-1530
Cleveland *(G-5371)*

Columbus AAA Corp ....E 614 889-2840
Dublin *(G-10300)*

Comdoc Inc ....C 330 896-2346
Uniontown *(G-18514)*

Cort Business Services Corp ....D 513 759-8181
West Chester *(G-19054)*

Countryside Rentals Inc ....E 740 634-2666
Bainbridge *(G-941)*

Csr Colortone Staging Rentals ....E 440 914-9500
Cleveland *(G-5444)*

Cuyahoga Vending Co Inc ....D 216 663-1457
Maple Heights *(G-13404)*

David Francis Corporation ....C 216 524-0900
Cleveland *(G-5466)*

◆ De Nora Tech LLC ....E 440 710-5300
Painesville *(G-15850)*

Diane Sauer Chevrolet Inc ....D 330 373-1600
Warren *(G-18850)*

E T B Ltd ....E 740 373-6686
Marietta *(G-13443)*

Easton Sales and Rental LLC ....E 440 708-0099
Chagrin Falls *(G-2714)*

Elliott Tool Technologies Ltd ....D 937 253-6133
Dayton *(G-9524)*

Equipment Depot Ohio Inc ....E 513 934-2121
Lebanon *(G-12604)*

▲ Fallsway Equipment Co Inc ....C 330 633-6000
Akron *(G-214)*

Fern Exposition Services LLC ....E 513 621-6111
Cincinnati *(G-3603)*

Fifth Third Equipment Fin Co ....E 800 972-3030
Cincinnati *(G-3609)*

Filing Scale Company Inc ....E 330 425-3092
Twinsburg *(G-18415)*

Flight Options LLC ....C 216 261-3500
Cleveland *(G-5608)*

Garda CL Great Lakes Inc ....B 561 939-7000
Columbus *(G-7727)*

Gordon Brothers Inc ....E 800 331-7611
Salem *(G-16697)*

Gordon Flesch Company Inc ....E 419 884-2031
Mansfield *(G-13305)*

Great Lakes Crushing Ltd ....E 440 944-5500
Wickliffe *(G-19599)*

HEat Ttal Fclty Slutions Inc ....E 740 965-3005
Galena *(G-11283)*

Home Depot USA Inc ....C 614 523-0600
Columbus *(G-7848)*

Home Depot USA Inc ....C 330 965-4790
Boardman *(G-1741)*

SIC

73 BUSINESS SERVICES

Company	Col	Phone
Home Depot USA Inc	C	330 497-1810
Canton *(G-2402)*		
Home Depot USA Inc	C	513 688-1654
Cincinnati *(G-3778)*		
Home Depot USA Inc	C	330 922-3448
Cuyahoga Falls *(G-9194)*		
Home Depot USA Inc	C	937 312-9053
Dayton *(G-9614)*		
Home Depot USA Inc	C	937 312-9076
Dayton *(G-9615)*		
Home Depot USA Inc	C	216 692-2780
Euclid *(G-10762)*		
Home Depot USA Inc	C	216 676-9969
Cleveland *(G-5767)*		
Home Depot USA Inc	C	216 581-6611
Maple Heights *(G-13408)*		
Home Depot USA Inc	D	937 431-7346
Beavercreek *(G-1177)*		
Home Depot USA Inc	C	330 245-0280
Akron *(G-271)*		
Home Depot USA Inc	D	937 837-1551
Dayton *(G-9616)*		
Home Depot USA Inc	C	216 297-1303
Cleveland Heights *(G-6790)*		
Home Depot USA Inc	C	513 661-2413
Cincinnati *(G-3779)*		
Home Depot USA Inc	C	513 887-1450
Fairfield Township *(G-10931)*		
Home Depot USA Inc	C	419 476-4573
Toledo *(G-17957)*		
Home Depot USA Inc	C	440 357-0428
Mentor *(G-14191)*		
Home Depot USA Inc	C	513 631-1705
Cincinnati *(G-3780)*		
Home Depot USA Inc	C	440 684-1343
Highland Heights *(G-11869)*		
Home Depot USA Inc	C	419 537-1920
Toledo *(G-17958)*		
Home Depot USA Inc	C	614 878-9150
Columbus *(G-7849)*		
Home Depot USA Inc	C	440 826-9092
Strongsville *(G-17471)*		
Home Depot USA Inc	C	614 939-5036
Columbus *(G-7850)*		
Home Depot USA Inc	D	440 937-2240
Avon *(G-898)*		
Home Depot USA Inc	C	614 577-1601
Reynoldsburg *(G-16458)*		
Home Depot USA Inc	C	330 220-2654
Brunswick *(G-1981)*		
Home Depot USA Inc	C	419 626-6493
Sandusky *(G-16768)*		
Home Depot USA Inc	C	614 876-5558
Hilliard *(G-11911)*		
Home Depot USA Inc	C	440 324-7222
Elyria *(G-10633)*		
Home Depot USA Inc	C	419 529-0015
Ontario *(G-15691)*		
Home Depot USA Inc	C	216 251-3091
Cleveland *(G-5768)*		
I L T Diversified Mtl Hdlg	E	419 865-8025
Holland *(G-12029)*		
Independence Equipment Lsg Co		216 642-3408
Cleveland *(G-5811)*		
J Way Leasing Ltd		440 934-1020
Avon *(G-899)*		
Jbjs Acquisitions LLC	E	513 769-0393
Cincinnati *(G-3864)*		
JBK Group Inc		216 901-0000
Cleveland *(G-5854)*		
Lasting Impressions Event	D	614 252-5400
Columbus *(G-8042)*		
Live Technologies Holdings Inc	D	614 278-7777
Columbus *(G-8074)*		
M & L Leasing Co	E	330 343-8910
Mineral City *(G-14633)*		
Made From Scratch Inc		614 873-3344
Plain City *(G-16197)*		
Maloney & Associates Inc	E	330 479-7084
Canton *(G-2443)*		
Mapleview Farms Inc	E	419 826-3671
Swanton *(G-17567)*		
MH Logistics Corp	E	330 425-2476
Hudson *(G-12134)*		
Miami Industrial Trucks Inc	D	937 293-4194
Moraine *(G-14805)*		
Miller & Co Portable Toil Svcs	D	330 453-9472
Canton *(G-2463)*		
Millers Rental and Sls Co Inc	E	216 642-1447
Cleveland *(G-6067)*		
Mitel (delaware) Inc	E	513 733-8000
West Chester *(G-19122)*		
Mobilcomm Inc	D	513 742-5555
Cincinnati *(G-4110)*		
Modal Shop Inc	D	513 351-9919
Cincinnati *(G-4111)*		
Modern Office Methods Inc	D	513 791-0909
Blue Ash *(G-1644)*		
Multi-Flow Dispensers Ohio Inc	D	216 641-0200
Brooklyn Heights *(G-1921)*		
Netjets Inc	E	614 239-5500
Columbus *(G-8261)*		
Northeast Projections Inc	E	330 375-9444
Cleveland *(G-6156)*		
Office Products Toledo Inc	E	419 865-7001
Holland *(G-12044)*		
Ohio Machinery Co	C	419 874-7975
Perrysburg *(G-16036)*		
ONeil Awning and Tent Inc	D	614 837-6352
Canal Winchester *(G-2165)*		
Oscar Rbrtsn Doc Mgmt Svcs	E	800 991-4611
Blue Ash *(G-1661)*		
Paul Peterson Company	E	614 486-4375
Columbus *(G-8522)*		
Paul Peterson Safety Div Inc	E	614 486-4375
Columbus *(G-8523)*		
Piqua Steel Co	D	937 773-3632
Piqua *(G-16159)*		
Pitney Bowes Inc		203 426-7025
Brecksville *(G-1840)*		
Pitney Bowes Inc	D	740 374-5535
Marietta *(G-13489)*		
Prestige Audio Visual Inc	D	513 641-1600
Cincinnati *(G-4326)*		
Prime Time Party Rental Inc	E	937 296-9262
Moraine *(G-14815)*		
Pro-Kleen Industrial Svcs Inc	E	740 689-1886
Lancaster *(G-12566)*		
Quality Supply & Rental Inc	E	740 286-7517
Jackson *(G-12317)*		
Rent-A-Center Inc	D	330 337-1107
Salem *(G-16710)*		
Rent-A-Center Inc	D	419 382-8585
Toledo *(G-18151)*		
Rent-N-Roll	D	513 528-6929
Cincinnati *(G-4406)*		
Rentech Solutions Inc	D	216 398-1111
Willoughby *(G-19710)*		
Ricoh Usa Inc	D	513 984-9898
Blue Ash *(G-1683)*		
Rumpke Transportation Co LLC	E	937 461-0004
Dayton *(G-9856)*		
Rumpke Waste Inc	C	937 548-1939
Greenville *(G-11517)*		
S and R Leasing		330 276-3061
Millersburg *(G-14620)*		
Safety-Kleen Systems Inc	E	440 992-8665
Ashtabula *(G-761)*		
Setiawan Associates LLC	E	614 285-5815
Columbus *(G-8717)*		
Springfield Cartage LLC	D	937 222-2120
Dayton *(G-9898)*		
Stout Lori Cleaning & Such	E	419 637-7644
Gibsonburg *(G-11404)*		
Sunbelt Rentals Inc	E	216 362-0300
Cleveland *(G-6549)*		
Superr-Spdie Portable Svcs Inc	E	330 733-9000
Akron *(G-469)*		
▲ Thomas Do-It Center Inc	E	740 446-2002
Gallipolis *(G-11339)*		
▲ Towlift Inc	C	216 749-6800
Brooklyn Heights *(G-1929)*		
Two Men & A Vacuum LLC	D	614 300-7970
Columbus *(G-8881)*		
U Haul Co of Northwestern Ohio	E	419 478-1101
Toledo *(G-18266)*		
United Rentals North Amer Inc	E	800 877-3687
Perrysburg *(G-16067)*		
Valley Industrial Trucks Inc	C	330 788-4081
Youngstown *(G-20402)*		
Vincent Ltg Systems Co Inc	E	216 475-7600
Solon *(G-17065)*		
Waids Rainbow Rental Inc	E	216 524-3736
Akron *(G-502)*		
Warwick Communications Inc	E	216 787-0300
Broadview Heights *(G-1895)*		
Waste Management Ohio Inc	D	800 343-6047
Fairborn *(G-10811)*		
Winner Aviation Corporation	D	330 856-5000
Vienna *(G-18742)*		
Yockey Group Inc	E	513 899-2188
Morrow *(G-14849)*		

7361 Employment Agencies

Company	Col	Phone
56 Plus Management LLC	E	937 323-4114
Springfield *(G-17145)*		
A-1 Nursing Care Inc	C	614 268-3800
Columbus *(G-6922)*		
Abacus Corporation	B	614 367-7000
Reynoldsburg *(G-16423)*		
Abilities First Foundation	C	513 423-9496
Middletown *(G-14411)*		
Accentcare Home Health Cal Inc	C	740 387-4568
Marion *(G-13522)*		
Accountants To You LLC	E	513 651-2855
Cincinnati *(G-2965)*		
Adecco Usa Inc	E	419 720-0111
Toledo *(G-17741)*		
Advantage Resourcing Amer Inc	E	781 472-8900
Cincinnati *(G-2976)*		
Advantage Rn LLC	D	866 301-4045
West Chester *(G-19012)*		
Alexander Mann Solutions Corp	B	216 336-6756
Cleveland *(G-4984)*		
Allcan Global Services Inc	E	513 825-1655
Cincinnati *(G-2987)*		
Alliance Legal Solutions LLC	E	216 525-0100
Independence *(G-12184)*		
Alliance Solutions Group LLC	E	216 525-0100
Independence *(G-12185)*		
Alternate Solutions First LLC	C	937 298-1111
Dayton *(G-9325)*		
American Bus Personnel Svcs	E	513 770-3300
Mason *(G-13661)*		
Aspen Community Living	C	614 880-6000
Columbus *(G-7051)*		
Assured Health Care Inc		937 294-2803
Dayton *(G-9346)*		
Atrium Apparel Corporation	D	612 889-0959
Johnstown *(G-12335)*		
Backtrack Inc	D	440 205-8280
Mentor *(G-14147)*		
Belflex Staffing Network LLC	C	513 488-8588
Cincinnati *(G-3096)*		
Berns Oneill SEC & Safety LLC	E	330 374-9133
Akron *(G-100)*		
Blanchard Valley Health System	D	419 424-3000
Findlay *(G-10998)*		
Blanchard Valley Industries	D	419 422-6386
Findlay *(G-11000)*		
Bmch Inc	D	216 642-1300
Independence *(G-12189)*		
Brown Medical LLC	E	740 574-8728
Wheelersburg *(G-19571)*		
Cardinalcommerce Corporation	D	877 352-8444
Mentor *(G-14153)*		
Career Cnnctions Staffing Svcs	E	440 471-8210
Westlake *(G-19469)*		
Carestar Inc	C	513 618-8300
Cincinnati *(G-3183)*		
Careworks of Ohio Inc	B	614 792-1085
Dublin *(G-10280)*		
Chad Downing	E	614 532-5127
Columbus *(G-7250)*		
Childrens Home Care Dayton	D	937 641-4663
Dayton *(G-9402)*		
Cleveland Job Corps Center	C	216 541-2500
Cleveland *(G-5323)*		
Cnsld Humacare- Employee MGT	E	513 605-3522
Cincinnati *(G-3376)*		
Collier Nursing Service Inc	C	513 791-4357
Montgomery *(G-14725)*		
Community Hlth Prfssionals Inc		419 238-9223
Van Wert *(G-18630)*		
Community Hlth Prfssionals Inc	D	419 586-6266
Celina *(G-2642)*		
Community Home Care	E	330 971-7011
Cuyahoga Falls *(G-9177)*		
Comprehensive Health Care Svcs	C	513 245-0100
Cincinnati *(G-3406)*		
Construction Labor Contrs LLC	D	614 932-9937
Dublin *(G-10309)*		
Corporate Ladder Search	E	330 776-4390
Uniontown *(G-18515)*		
County of Guernsey	D	740 432-2381
Cambridge *(G-2108)*		
County of Holmes	E	330 674-5035
Millersburg *(G-14597)*		
County of Huron	D	419 668-8126
Norwalk *(G-15568)*		

County of Wayne....E.... 330 264-5060
Wooster (G-19855)
Csu/Career Services Center....E.... 216 687-2233
Cleveland (G-5445)
Ctpartners Exec Search Inc....D.... 216 464-8710
Beachwood (G-1069)
Custom Halthcare Proffessional....E.... 216 381-1010
Cleveland (G-5449)
Custom Staffing Inc....E.... 419 221-3097
Lima (G-12770)
Daily Services LLC....C.... 614 431-5100
Columbus (G-7483)
Damascus Staffing LLC....D.... 513 954-8941
Maineville (G-13242)
Dawson Resources....E.... 614 255-1400
Columbus (G-7491)
Dawson Resources....B.... 614 274-8900
Columbus (G-7492)
Dedicated Nursing Assoc Inc....D.... 937 886-4559
Miamisburg (G-14295)
Dedicated Nursing Assoc Inc....E.... 866 450-5550
Cincinnati (G-3477)
Dedicated Nursing Assoc Inc....E.... 877 411-8350
Galloway (G-11343)
Dedicated Nursing Assoc Inc....E.... 877 547-9144
Parma (G-15905)
Dedicated Nursing Assoc Inc....C.... 888 465-6929
Beavercreek (G-1237)
Dedicated Technologies Inc....D.... 614 460-3200
Columbus (G-7499)
Discover Training Inc....D.... 614 871-0010
Grove City (G-11554)
Diversity Search Group LLC....B.... 614 352-2988
Columbus (G-7528)
E & L Premier Corporation....C.... 330 836-9901
Fairlawn (G-10946)
Employment Network....E.... 440 324-5244
Elyria (G-10626)
Endevis LLc....E.... 419 482-4848
Toledo (G-17867)
Epilogue Inc....D.... 440 582-5555
North Royalton (G-15489)
Everstaff LLC....E.... 877 392-6151
Cleveland (G-5559)
Exodus Integrity Service....D.... 440 918-0140
Willoughby (G-19663)
Experis Us Inc....E.... 614 223-2300
Columbus (G-7622)
Fast Switch Ltd....B.... 614 336-1122
Dublin (G-10347)
First Choice Med Staff of Ohio....D.... 419 521-2700
Mansfield (G-13303)
First Choice Medical Staffing....D.... 419 861-2722
Toledo (G-17892)
First Choice Medical Staffing....B.... 216 521-2222
Cleveland (G-5593)
First Diversity Staffing Group....B.... 937 323-4114
Springfield (G-17198)
Firstat Nursing Services....D.... 216 295-1500
Cleveland (G-5600)
Future Unlimited Inc....E.... 330 273-6677
Brunswick (G-1979)
Gallery Holdings LLC....D.... 773 693-6220
Independence (G-12213)
Global Exec Slutions Group LLC....E.... 330 666-3354
Akron (G-238)
Global Tchnical Recruiters Inc....E.... 216 251-9560
Westlake (G-19486)
Global Tchnical Recruiters Inc....E.... 440 365-1670
Elyria (G-10630)
Goodwill Industries Inc....E.... 330 724-6995
Akron (G-241)
Gus Perdikakis Associates....D.... 513 583-0900
Cincinnati (G-3721)
Health & HM Care Concepts Inc....E.... 740 383-4968
Marion (G-13542)
Health Care Plus....E.... 614 340-7587
Columbus (G-6882)
Heitmeyer Group LLC....B.... 614 573-5571
Westerville (G-19312)
HJ Ford Associates Inc....C.... 937 429-9711
Beavercreek (G-1176)
Home Care Network Inc....D.... 937 435-1142
Dayton (G-9613)
Horizon Personnel Resources....C.... 440 585-0031
Wickliffe (G-19602)
Horizons Employment Svcs LLC....B.... 419 254-9644
Toledo (G-17960)
Hospice of Darke County Inc....E.... 419 678-4808
Coldwater (G-6830)

Hr Services Inc....E.... 419 224-2462
Lima (G-12799)
Human Resources Services....E.... 740 587-3484
Westerville (G-19314)
I-Force LLC....C.... 614 431-5100
Columbus (G-7879)
Integrity Enterprizes....E.... 216 289-8801
Euclid (G-10764)
Interim Halthcare Columbus Inc....E.... 330 836-5571
Fairlawn (G-10958)
Its Technologies Inc....D.... 419 842-2100
Holland (G-12030)
Jacor LLC....A.... 330 441-4182
Medina (G-14084)
Job 1 USA....D.... 419 255-5005
Toledo (G-17985)
Key Career Place....D.... 216 987-3029
Cleveland (G-5896)
Kforce Inc....E.... 614 436-4027
Columbus (G-7985)
Kforce Inc....E.... 216 643-8141
Independence (G-12222)
Kilgore Group Inc....E.... 513 684-3721
Cincinnati (G-3922)
Lane Wood Industries....B.... 419 352-5059
Bowling Green (G-1784)
Licking-Knox Goodwill Inds Inc....D.... 740 397-0051
Mount Vernon (G-14909)
Management Recruiters Intl Inc....E.... 614 252-6200
Columbus (G-8102)
Mancan Inc....A.... 440 884-9675
Strongsville (G-17487)
Marvel Consultants....E.... 216 292-2855
Cleveland (G-5989)
Medi Home Health Agency Inc....E.... 740 266-3977
Steubenville (G-17329)
Medical Solutions LLC....D.... 513 936-3468
Blue Ash (G-1638)
Mid Ohio Employment Services....E.... 419 747-5466
Ontario (G-15703)
Midwest Emergency Services LLC....E.... 586 294-2700
Fairlawn (G-10965)
Mj-6 LLC....E.... 419 517-7725
Toledo (G-18066)
Murtech Consulting LLC....D.... 216 328-8580
Cleveland (G-6091)
National Staffing Group Ltd....E.... 440 546-0800
Brecksville (G-1835)
Nurses Care Inc....E.... 513 791-0233
Cincinnati (G-4193)
Nurses Heart Med Staffing LLC....E.... 614 648-5111
Columbus (G-8306)
Ohio Dept of Job & Fmly Svcs....D.... 330 484-5402
Akron (G-364)
Ohio State University....A.... 614 293-2494
Columbus (G-8412)
On Search Partners LLC....E.... 440 318-1006
Solon (G-17036)
Onestaff Inc....E.... 859 815-1345
Cincinnati (G-4227)
P E Miller & Assoc....D.... 614 231-4743
Columbus (G-8502)
Pathway Inc....E.... 419 242-7304
Toledo (G-18122)
Pearl Interactive Network Inc....B.... 614 258-2943
Columbus (G-8527)
Per Diem Nurse Staffing LLT....E.... 419 878-8880
Waterville (G-18944)
Personal Touch HM Care IPA Inc....E.... 937 456-4447
Eaton (G-10573)
Pps Holding LLC....D.... 513 985-6400
Cincinnati (G-4319)
Private Practice Nurses Inc....E.... 216 481-1305
Cleveland (G-6307)
Prn Health Services Inc....D.... 513 792-2217
Cincinnati (G-4336)
Prn Nurse Inc....B.... 614 864-9292
Columbus (G-8562)
Professional Contract Systems....C.... 513 469-8800
Cincinnati (G-4342)
Professional Data Resources Inc....C.... 513 792-5100
Blue Ash (G-1668)
Promedica Physcn Cntinuum Svcs....C.... 419 824-7200
Sylvania (G-17608)
PSI Associates Inc....B.... 330 425-8474
Twinsburg (G-18457)
Psychpros Inc....E.... 513 651-9500
Cincinnati (G-4355)
R E Richards Inc....E.... 330 499-1001
Canton (G-2501)

Randstad Technologies LLC....D.... 614 436-0961
Columbus (G-6903)
Randstad Technologies LLC....D.... 216 520-0206
Independence (G-12246)
Randstad Technologies LP....E.... 614 552-3280
Hilliard (G-11948)
Reserves Network Inc....E.... 440 779-1400
Cleveland (G-6383)
Rightthing LLC....B.... 419 420-1830
Findlay (G-11079)
Rkpl Inc....D.... 419 224-2121
Lima (G-12869)
Robert Half International Inc....D.... 937 224-7376
Dayton (G-9854)
Robert Half International Inc....D.... 330 629-9494
Youngstown (G-20353)
Robert Half International Inc....D.... 513 563-0770
Blue Ash (G-1684)
Robert Half International Inc....D.... 614 221-8326
Columbus (G-8640)
Robert Half International Inc....D.... 614 602-0505
Dublin (G-10442)
Robert Half International Inc....D.... 513 621-8367
Cincinnati (G-4436)
Robert Half International Inc....D.... 614 221-1544
Columbus (G-8641)
Rumpf Corporation....E.... 419 255-5005
Toledo (G-18167)
Rvet Operating LLC....E.... 513 683-5020
Loveland (G-13157)
S & H Risner Inc....D.... 937 778-8563
Piqua (G-16165)
Safegard Bckgrund Screning LLC....C.... 216 370-7345
Cleveland (G-6432)
Seifert & Group Inc....D.... 330 833-2700
Massillon (G-13852)
Siffrin Residential Assn....C.... 330 799-8932
Youngstown (G-20375)
St Ritas Medical Center....C.... 419 538-7025
Lima (G-12887)
Staffmark Holdings Inc....D.... 513 651-1111
Cincinnati (G-4573)
Staffmark Investment LLC....C.... 513 651-3600
Cincinnati (G-4574)
Stearns Companies LLC....E.... 419 422-0241
Findlay (G-11085)
Tailored Management Services....D.... 614 859-1500
Columbus (G-8820)
Talemed LLC....B.... 513 774-7300
Loveland (G-13162)
Taylor Strategy Partners LLC....E.... 614 436-6650
Columbus (G-8825)
Taylors Staffing....D.... 740 446-3305
Pomeroy (G-16236)
Tech Center Inc....E.... 330 762-6212
Akron (G-472)
Telamon Corporation....E.... 937 254-2004
Dayton (G-9923)
Telecmmnctons Stffing Slutions....E.... 614 799-9300
Dublin (G-10475)
Thinkpath Engineering Svcs LLC....D.... 937 291-8374
Miamisburg (G-14358)
Tradesmen International LLC....E.... 440 349-3432
Macedonia (G-13214)
Tradesmen Services LLC....D.... 440 349-3432
Macedonia (G-13215)
Tradesource Inc....C.... 216 801-4944
Parma (G-15916)
Tradesource Inc....C.... 614 824-3883
Columbus (G-8862)
Trak Staffing Services Inc....E.... 513 333-4199
Cincinnati (G-4677)
Ulrich Professional Group....E.... 330 673-9501
Kent (G-12402)
United Steelworkers....E.... 440 244-1358
Lorain (G-13083)
Vector Technical Inc....C.... 440 946-8800
Willoughby (G-19722)
Vishnia & Associates Inc....D.... 330 929-5512
Cuyahoga Falls (G-9233)
Willory LLC....E.... 330 576-5486
Bath (G-1037)
Wise Medical Staffing Inc....D.... 740 775-4108
Chillicothe (G-2898)
Wjcb LLC....E.... 513 631-3200
Blue Ash (G-1718)
Wood County Ohio....E.... 419 352-5059
Bowling Green (G-1804)
Work Solutions Group LLC....E.... 440 205-8297
Mentor (G-14259)

SIC

Wtw Delaware Holdings LLC ....C....... 216 937-4000
Cleveland *(G-6762)*

Youth Opportunities Unlimited ....E....... 216 566-5445
Cleveland *(G-6777)*

7363 Help Supply Svcs

A B S Temps Inc ....E....... 937 252-9888
Dayton *(G-9297)*

A Jacobs Inc ....E....... 614 774-6757
Hilliard *(G-11874)*

Acloche LLC ....E....... 888 608-0889
Columbus *(G-6938)*

Act I Temporaries Findlay Inc ....B....... 419 423-0713
Findlay *(G-10989)*

Ado Staffing Inc ....E....... 419 222-8395
Lima *(G-12731)*

Aerotek Inc ....E....... 330 517-7330
Uniontown *(G-18506)*

Aerotek Inc ....E....... 216 573-5520
Independence *(G-12181)*

Aldo Peraza ....D....... 614 804-0403
Columbus *(G-6963)*

Alliance Solutions Group LLC ....E....... 216 525-0100
Independence *(G-12185)*

Alternate Solutions Healthcare ....D....... 937 299-1111
Dayton *(G-9326)*

American Bulk Commodities Inc ....C....... 330 758-0841
Youngstown *(G-20103)*

Amerimed Inc ....E....... 513 942-3670
West Chester *(G-19019)*

Arcadia Services Inc ....D....... 330 869-9520
Akron *(G-79)*

Arcadia Services Inc ....D....... 937 912-5800
Beavercreek *(G-1147)*

Area Temps Inc ....A....... 216 227-8200
Lakewood *(G-12471)*

Area Temps Inc ....E....... 216 781-5350
Independence *(G-12187)*

Area Temps Inc ....A....... 216 518-2000
Maple Heights *(G-13400)*

Ashtabula Stevedore Company ....E....... 440 964-7186
Ashtabula *(G-727)*

Aspen Community Living ....C....... 614 880-6000
Columbus *(G-7051)*

Atrium Apparel Corporation ....D....... 612 889-0959
Johnstown *(G-12335)*

Belcan LLC ....A....... 513 645-1509
West Chester *(G-19026)*

Belcan LLC ....A....... 513 891-0972
Blue Ash *(G-1538)*

Belcan LLC ....A....... 513 217-4562
Middletown *(G-14416)*

Belcan LLC ....A....... 740 393-8888
Mount Vernon *(G-14878)*

Belcan Corporation ....A....... 513 985-7777
Blue Ash *(G-1539)*

Belcan Corporation ....D....... 513 891-0972
Solon *(G-16983)*

Belcan Corporation ....A....... 614 224-6080
Columbus *(G-7099)*

Belcan Svcs Group Ltd Partnr ....C....... 937 586-5053
Dayton *(G-9353)*

Belcan Svcs Group Ltd Partnr ....C....... 513 891-0972
Blue Ash *(G-1541)*

Belcan Svcs Group Ltd Partnr ....D....... 937 859-8880
Miamisburg *(G-14275)*

Belflex Staffing Network LLC ....C....... 513 488-8588
Cincinnati *(G-3096)*

Buckeye Leasing Inc ....E....... 330 758-0841
Youngstown *(G-20130)*

Callos Resource LLC ....E....... 330 788-3033
Youngstown *(G-20132)*

Carol Scudere ....E....... 614 839-4357
New Albany *(G-14979)*

Cbiz Inc ....C....... 216 447-9000
Cleveland *(G-5196)*

Central Ohio Hospitalists ....E....... 614 255-6900
Columbus *(G-7230)*

CHI Health At Home ....E....... 513 576-0262
Milford *(G-14510)*

▲ Cima Inc ....E....... 513 682-5900
Fairfield *(G-10831)*

Columbiana Service Company LLC ....D....... 330 482-5511
Columbiana *(G-6856)*

Constant Aviation LLC ....C....... 800 440-9004
Cleveland *(G-5396)*

CPC Logistics Inc ....D....... 513 874-5787
Fairfield *(G-10838)*

Custom Staffing Inc ....E....... 419 221-3097
Lima *(G-12770)*

D C Transportation Service ....C....... 440 237-0900
North Royalton *(G-15485)*

Dawson Resources ....E....... 614 255-1400
Columbus *(G-7491)*

Dedicated Nursing Assoc Inc ....E....... 866 450-5550
Cincinnati *(G-3477)*

Dedicated Nursing Assoc Inc ....E....... 877 411-8350
Galloway *(G-11343)*

Dedicated Nursing Assoc Inc ....E....... 877 547-9144
Parma *(G-15905)*

Dedicated Nursing Assoc Inc ....C....... 888 465-6929
Beavercreek *(G-1237)*

Dedicated Tech Services Inc ....D....... 614 309-0059
Dublin *(G-10317)*

Diversfied Emplyee Sltions Inc ....B....... 330 764-4125
Medina *(G-14060)*

Diversified Labor Support LLC ....B....... 440 234-3090
Cleveland *(G-5492)*

Doepker Group Inc ....E....... 419 355-1409
Fremont *(G-11195)*

E & L Premier Corporation ....C....... 330 836-9901
Fairlawn *(G-10946)*

Edge Plastics Inc ....E....... 419 522-6696
Mansfield *(G-13296)*

Emily Management Inc ....D....... 440 354-6713
Painesville *(G-15854)*

Emp Holdings Ltd ....A....... 330 493-4443
Canton *(G-2354)*

Everstaff LLC ....E....... 440 992-0238
Mentor *(G-14173)*

Firstat Nursing Services ....D....... 216 295-1500
Cleveland *(G-5600)*

Flex Temp Employment Services ....C....... 419 355-9675
Fremont *(G-11199)*

Focus Solutions Inc ....C....... 513 376-8349
Cincinnati *(G-3635)*

Franklin Cnty Crt Common Pleas ....E....... 614 525-5775
Columbus *(G-7690)*

Frontline National LLC ....D....... 513 528-7823
Milford *(G-14519)*

Future Unlimited Inc ....E....... 330 273-6677
Brunswick *(G-1979)*

Health Carousel LLC ....C....... 866 665-4544
Cincinnati *(G-3752)*

Heartland Employment Svcs LLC ....A....... 419 252-5500
Toledo *(G-17945)*

Heiser Staffing Services LLC ....E....... 614 800-4188
Columbus *(G-7823)*

Hogan Truck Leasing Inc ....E....... 513 454-3500
Fairfield *(G-10859)*

Horizon Personnel Resources ....C....... 440 585-0031
Wickliffe *(G-19602)*

Hr Services Inc ....E....... 419 224-2462
Lima *(G-12799)*

▲ Industrial Repair & Mfg Inc ....E....... 419 822-4232
Delta *(G-10159)*

Innovtive Sltons Unlimited LLC ....E....... 740 289-3282
Piketon *(G-16118)*

Innovtive Sltons Unlimited LLC ....D....... 740 289-3282
Piketon *(G-16119)*

Integrated Marketing Tech Inc ....D....... 330 225-3550
Brunswick *(G-1982)*

Inter Healt Care of North OH I ....D....... 740 453-5130
Zanesville *(G-20490)*

Inter Healt Care of North OH I ....E....... 419 422-5328
Findlay *(G-11050)*

Interim Halthcare Columbus Inc ....A....... 740 349-8700
Newark *(G-15177)*

Interim Halthcare Columbus Inc ....E....... 330 836-5571
Fairlawn *(G-10958)*

Interim Healthcare of Dayton ....B....... 937 291-5330
Dayton *(G-9634)*

Its Technologies Inc ....D....... 419 842-2100
Holland *(G-12030)*

JB Management Inc ....D....... 419 841-2596
Toledo *(G-17983)*

Jet Mintenance Consulting Corp ....E....... 937 205-2406
Wilmington *(G-19764)*

Job 1 USA ....D....... 419 255-5005
Toledo *(G-17985)*

Kilgore Group Inc ....E....... 513 684-3721
Cincinnati *(G-3922)*

Larue Enterprises Inc ....E....... 937 438-5711
Beavercreek *(G-1248)*

Lee Personnel Inc ....E....... 513 744-6780
Cincinnati *(G-3967)*

Locum Medical Group LLC ....D....... 216 464-2125
Independence *(G-12229)*

Macair Aviation LLC ....E....... 937 347-1302
Xenia *(G-20069)*

Maids Home Service of Cincy ....E....... 513 396-6900
Cincinnati *(G-4013)*

Medlink of Ohio Inc ....B....... 330 773-9434
Akron *(G-337)*

Medport Inc ....D....... 216 244-6832
Cleveland *(G-6017)*

Medsearch Staffing Service ....E....... 440 243-6363
Cleveland *(G-6018)*

Minute Men Inc ....D....... 216 426-2225
Cleveland *(G-6069)*

MPW Industrial Services Inc ....D....... 937 644-0200
East Liberty *(G-10511)*

Msstaff LLC ....C....... 419 868-8536
Toledo *(G-18072)*

Neo-Pet LLC ....E....... 440 893-9949
Cleveland *(G-6118)*

Netjets Assn Shred Arcft Plots ....D....... 614 863-2008
Columbus *(G-8260)*

Nursing Resources Corp ....C....... 419 333-3000
Maumee *(G-13951)*

Ohio Dept of Job & Fmly Svcs ....E....... 419 334-3891
Fremont *(G-11215)*

P E Miller & Associates Inc ....D....... 614 231-4743
Columbus *(G-8503)*

Paradigm Industrial LLC ....E....... 937 224-4415
Dayton *(G-9801)*

Patrick Staffing Inc ....E....... 937 743-5585
Franklin *(G-11162)*

Physician Staffing Inc ....B....... 440 542-1950
Solon *(G-17039)*

Poison Information Center ....E....... 513 636-5111
Cincinnati *(G-4313)*

Pontoon Solutions Inc ....D....... 855 881-1533
Maumee *(G-13959)*

Preferred Temporary Services ....E....... 330 494-5502
Canton *(G-2492)*

Prestige Technical Svcs Inc ....E....... 513 779-6800
West Chester *(G-19131)*

Prn Nurse Inc ....B....... 614 864-9292
Columbus *(G-8562)*

Production Design Services Inc ....D....... 937 866-3377
Dayton *(G-9832)*

Professional Drivers GA Inc ....E....... 614 529-8282
Columbus *(G-8566)*

Professional Transportation ....C....... 419 661-0576
Walbridge *(G-18776)*

Prueter Enterprises Ltd ....C....... 419 872-5343
Perrysburg *(G-16046)*

Quadax Inc ....E....... 330 759-4600
Youngstown *(G-20334)*

Ran Temps Inc ....E....... 216 991-5500
Cleveland *(G-6352)*

Randstad Professionals Us LLC ....E....... 419 893-2400
Maumee *(G-13966)*

Randstad Professionals Us LLC ....E....... 513 792-6658
Blue Ash *(G-1674)*

Randstad Professionals Us LP ....E....... 513 791-8600
Blue Ash *(G-1675)*

Renhill Stffing Srvces-America ....E....... 419 254-2800
Perrysburg *(G-16051)*

Reserves Network Inc ....E....... 440 779-1400
Cleveland *(G-6383)*

Rkpl Inc ....D....... 419 224-2121
Lima *(G-12869)*

Robert Half International Inc ....E....... 216 621-4253
Cleveland *(G-6402)*

Rumpf Corporation ....E....... 419 255-5005
Toledo *(G-18167)*

S & B Trucking Inc ....E....... 614 554-4090
Hubbard *(G-12091)*

Salo Inc ....A....... 740 623-2331
Coshocton *(G-9117)*

Select Staffing ....D....... 513 247-9772
West Chester *(G-19149)*

Sequent Inc ....D....... 614 436-5880
Columbus *(G-6907)*

Sfn Group Inc ....E....... 419 727-4104
Toledo *(G-18182)*

Spherion of Lima Inc ....A....... 419 224-8367
Lima *(G-12882)*

Staffmark Holdings Inc ....D....... 513 651-1111
Cincinnati *(G-4573)*

Stage Works ....E....... 513 522-3118
Cincinnati *(G-4575)*

Super Shine Inc ....E....... 513 423-8999
Middletown *(G-14464)*

Taylors Staffing ....D....... 740 446-3305
Pomeroy *(G-16236)*

Top Echelon Contracting Inc ....B....... 330 454-3508
Canton *(G-2564)*

Township of Chester E 440 729-9951
Chesterland *(G-2805)*

Tradesmen International LLC D 513 771-1115
Blue Ash *(G-1699)*

Transportation Unlimited Inc A 216 426-0088
Cleveland *(G-6613)*

Trueblue Inc E 740 282-1079
Steubenville *(G-17345)*

Tsl Ltd A 419 843-3200
Toledo *(G-18262)*

Verified Person Inc E 901 767-6121
Independence *(G-12272)*

Volt Management Corp D 513 791-2600
Cincinnati *(G-4818)*

Wayne Industries Inc E 937 548-6025
Greenville *(G-11525)*

Waypoint Aviation LLC E 800 769-4765
Cincinnati *(G-4825)*

Yrs Inc D 330 665-3906
Akron *(G-518)*

7371 Custom Computer Programming Svcs

1 Edi Source Inc C 440 519-7800
Solon *(G-16967)*

22nd Century Technologies Inc D 866 537-9191
Beavercreek *(G-1142)*

Acadia Solutions Inc E 614 505-6135
Dublin *(G-10233)*

Aclara Technologies LLC C 440 528-7200
Solon *(G-16969)*

Advanced Prgrm Resources Inc E 614 761-9994
Dublin *(G-10234)*

Advantage Technology Group E 513 563-3560
West Chester *(G-19013)*

Aktion Associates Incorporated E 419 893-7001
Maumee *(G-13873)*

Alien Technology LLC C 408 782-3900
Miamisburg *(G-14270)*

American Systems Cnsulting Inc D 614 282-7180
Dublin *(G-10252)*

Assured Information SEC Inc D 937 427-9720
Beavercreek *(G-1148)*

Astute Inc E 614 508-6100
Columbus *(G-7058)*

Auto Des Sys Inc E 614 488-7984
Upper Arlington *(G-18548)*

◆ **B-Tek Scales LLC** E 330 471-8900
Canton *(G-2259)*

Batch Labs Inc D 216 901-9366
Cleveland *(G-5100)*

Big Red Rooster D 614 255-0200
Columbus *(G-7108)*

Billback Systems LLC E 937 433-1844
Dayton *(G-9358)*

Bluespring Software Inc E 513 794-1764
Blue Ash *(G-1547)*

Boundless Flight Inc E 440 610-3683
Rocky River *(G-16571)*

Briteskies LLC E 216 369-3600
Cleveland *(G-5140)*

Btas Inc C 937 431-9431
Beavercreek *(G-1155)*

Business Equipment Co Inc E 513 948-1500
Cincinnati *(G-3156)*

Camgen Ltd D 330 204-8636
Cleveland *(G-5174)*

Camgen Ltd E 330 204-8636
Canal Winchester *(G-2154)*

Campuseai Inc C 216 589-9626
Cleveland *(G-5175)*

Care Information Systems LLC D 614 496-4338
Dublin *(G-10279)*

Cdo Technologies Inc D 937 258-0022
Dayton *(G-9260)*

Cengage Learning Inc B 513 229-1000
Mason *(G-13674)*

Certified SEC Solutions Inc E 216 785-2986
Independence *(G-12196)*

Checkfree Services Corporation A 614 564-3000
Dublin *(G-10288)*

Cimx LLC E 513 248-7700
Cincinnati *(G-3276)*

Cincom Intrnational Operations B 513 612-2300
Cincinnati *(G-3342)*

Cintech LLC D 513 731-6000
Cincinnati *(G-3354)*

Click4care Inc D 614 431-3700
Powell *(G-16328)*

Cloudroute LLC E 216 373-4601
Cleveland *(G-5365)*

Clubessential LLC E 800 448-1475
Blue Ash *(G-1560)*

Cochin Technologies LLC E 440 941-4856
Avon *(G-891)*

Coleman Professional Svcs Inc B 330 673-1347
Kent *(G-12360)*

Command Alkon Incorporated D 614 799-0600
Dublin *(G-10302)*

Commercial Time Sharing Inc E 330 644-3059
Akron *(G-152)*

Commsys Inc E 937 220-4990
Moraine *(G-14761)*

Computer Helper Publishing E 614 939-9094
Columbus *(G-7417)*

Comtech Global Inc D 614 796-1148
Columbus *(G-7419)*

Connectivity Systems Inc E 740 420-5400
Williamsport *(G-19637)*

Cott Systems Inc D 614 847-4405
Columbus *(G-7449)*

County of Montgomery B 937 496-3103
Dayton *(G-9439)*

Critical Business Analysis Inc E 419 874-0800
Perrysburg *(G-15991)*

Crosschx Inc D 800 501-3161
Columbus *(G-7465)*

CT Logistics Inc C 216 267-1636
Cleveland *(G-5446)*

Dassault Systemes Simulia Corp E 513 275-1430
Mason *(G-13694)*

Datavantage Corporation B 440 498-4414
Cleveland *(G-5464)*

Dedicated Tech Services Inc D 614 309-0059
Dublin *(G-10317)*

Deemsys Inc D 614 322-9928
Gahanna *(G-11239)*

Devcare Solutions Ltd E 614 221-2277
Columbus *(G-7511)*

▲ **Dexxxon Digital Storage Inc** E 740 548-7179
Lewis Center *(G-12681)*

Digiknow Inc E 888 482-4455
Cleveland *(G-5483)*

Digitek Software Inc E 614 764-8875
Lewis Center *(G-12683)*

Diskcopy Duplication Services E 440 460-0800
Cleveland *(G-5488)*

Distribution Data Incorporated E 216 362-3009
Brookpark *(G-1943)*

Diversified Systems Inc E 614 476-9939
Westerville *(G-19394)*

Dizer Corp E 440 368-0200
Painesville *(G-15851)*

DMC Technology Group E 419 535-2900
Toledo *(G-17855)*

Domin-8 Entp Solutions Inc D 513 492-5800
Mason *(G-13697)*

Dotloop LLC C 513 257-0550
Cincinnati *(G-3500)*

Drb Systems LLC D 330 645-3299
Akron *(G-200)*

Drs Signal Technologies Inc E 937 429-7470
Beavercreek *(G-1169)*

Dynamite Technologies LLC D 614 538-0095
Columbus *(G-7556)*

Eclipse Blind Systems Inc C 330 296-0112
Ravenna *(G-16384)*

Edaptive Computing Inc D 937 433-0477
Dayton *(G-9520)*

Einstruction Corporation D 330 746-3015
Youngstown *(G-20178)*

Electronic Registry Systems E 513 771-7330
Cincinnati *(G-3549)*

Eliassen Group LLC E 781 205-8100
Blue Ash *(G-1583)*

Erp Analysts Inc B 614 718-9222
Dublin *(G-10339)*

Evanhoe & Associates Inc E 937 235-2995
Dayton *(G-9269)*

Exact Software North Amer LLC C 978 539-6186
Dublin *(G-10341)*

Exceptional Innovation Inc D 614 901-8899
Westerville *(G-19302)*

Exodus Integrity Service D 440 918-0140
Willoughby *(G-19663)*

Expert Technical Consultants E 614 430-9113
Piqua *(G-16143)*

Fascor Inc E 513 421-1777
Cincinnati *(G-3593)*

Fastems LLC E 513 779-4614
West Chester *(G-19072)*

First Data Gvrnmnt Solutns Inc C 513 489-9599
Blue Ash *(G-1595)*

Flairsoft Ltd E 614 888-0700
Columbus *(G-7673)*

Foresight Corporation E 614 791-1600
Dublin *(G-10349)*

Formsoft Group Ltd E 937 885-5015
Dayton *(G-9556)*

Foundation Software Inc D 330 220-8383
Strongsville *(G-17465)*

Frontier Technology Inc E 937 429-3302
Beavercreek Township *(G-1269)*

Fund Evaluation Group LLC E 513 977-4400
Cincinnati *(G-3658)*

Gannett Media Tech Intl E 513 665-3777
Cincinnati *(G-3661)*

▲ **Gatesair Inc** E 513 459-3400
Mason *(G-13704)*

Gb Liquidating Company Inc E 513 248-7600
Milford *(G-14520)*

Genomoncology LLC E 216 496-4216
Cleveland *(G-5669)*

Gensuite LLC D 513 774-1000
Mason *(G-13708)*

Gracie Plum Investments Inc E 740 355-9029
Portsmouth *(G-16282)*

Harley-Dvidson Dlr Systems Inc D 216 573-1393
Cleveland *(G-5726)*

Health Care Dataworks Inc D 614 255-5400
Columbus *(G-7809)*

Henry Call Inc C 216 433-5609
Cleveland *(G-5749)*

Holo Pundits Inc E 614 707-5225
Dublin *(G-10364)*

Horizon Payroll Services Inc B 937 434-8244
Dayton *(G-9621)*

Hyland LLC B 440 788-5045
Westlake *(G-19495)*

Icr Inc D 513 900-7007
Mason *(G-13718)*

Ils Technology LLC E 800 695-8650
Cleveland *(G-5805)*

Imflux Inc E 513 488-1017
Hamilton *(G-11743)*

Incubit LLC D 740 362-1401
Delaware *(G-10108)*

Indecon Solutions LLC E 614 799-1850
Dublin *(G-10374)*

Indigo Group E 513 557-8794
Liberty Twp *(G-12726)*

Inet Interactive LLC E 513 322-5600
West Chester *(G-19093)*

Infor (us) Inc B 678 319-8000
Columbus *(G-7896)*

Infovision 21 Inc E 614 761-8844
Dublin *(G-10376)*

Inreality LLC E 513 218-9603
Cincinnati *(G-3820)*

Integrated Telehealth Inc E 216 373-2221
Hudson *(G-12124)*

▲ **Intelligrated Systems Inc** A 866 936-7300
Mason *(G-13720)*

Intelligrated Systems LLC A 513 701-7300
Mason *(G-13721)*

International Technegroup Inc D 513 576-3900
Milford *(G-14527)*

Iq Innovations LLC E 614 222-0882
Columbus *(G-7921)*

Irth Solutions Inc E 614 459-2328
Columbus *(G-7923)*

Isqft Inc C 513 645-8004
Cincinnati *(G-3845)*

Itcube LLC D 513 891-7300
Blue Ash *(G-1618)*

▲ **Jenne Inc** C 440 835-0040
Avon *(G-900)*

Jjr Solutions LLC E 937 912-0288
Beavercreek *(G-1180)*

Jyg Innovations LLC E 937 630-3858
Dayton *(G-9647)*

▲ **Keithley Instruments LLC** C 440 248-0400
Solon *(G-17021)*

Keystone Technology Cons E 330 666-6200
Akron *(G-306)*

Kiwiplan Inc E 513 554-1500
Cincinnati *(G-3931)*

Kmi Inc E 614 326-6304
Columbus *(G-8000)*

Knowledge MGT Interactive Inc E 614 224-0664
Columbus *(G-8005)*

Employee Codes: A=Over 500 employees, B=251-500
C=101-250, D=51-100, E=25-50

Lakeland Foundation....E.... 440 525-7094
Willoughby *(G-19683)*
Lap Technology LLC....E.... 937 415-5794
Dayton *(G-9673)*
Leader Technologies Inc....E.... 614 890-1986
Lewis Center *(G-12692)*
Liberty Comm Sftwr Sltions Inc....E.... 614 318-5000
Columbus *(G-8056)*
Lifecycle Solutions Jv LLC....D.... 937 938-1321
Beavercreek *(G-1187)*
Lisnr Inc....E.... 513 322-8400
Cincinnati *(G-3990)*
Logic Soft Inc....D.... 614 884-5544
Dublin *(G-10391)*
London Computer Systems Inc....D.... 513 583-0840
Loveland *(G-13140)*
Main Sequence Technology Inc....E.... 440 946-5214
Mentor On The Lake *(G-14261)*
Managed Technology Svcs LLC....D.... 937 247-8915
Miamisburg *(G-14315)*
Manhattan Associates Inc....D.... 440 878-0771
Strongsville *(G-17488)*
Manifest Solutions Corp....D.... 614 930-2800
Upper Arlington *(G-18555)*
Mapsys Inc....E.... 614 255-7258
Columbus *(G-8104)*
Marshall Information Svcs LLC....E.... 614 430-0355
Columbus *(G-8120)*
Marxent Labs LLC....D.... 937 999-5005
Kettering *(G-12433)*
Matrix Pointe Software LLC....E.... 216 333-1263
Westlake *(G-19512)*
Maximation LLC....D.... 614 526-2260
Columbus *(G-8131)*
Mede America of Ohio LLC....A.... 330 425-3241
Twinsburg *(G-18446)*
Metacarta Incorporated....E.... 937 458-0345
Springfield *(G-17244)*
Mirifex Systems LLC....C.... 440 891-1210
Sharon Center *(G-16876)*
Mitosis LLC....E.... 937 557-3440
Dayton *(G-9752)*
Morphick Inc....E.... 844 506-6774
Blue Ash *(G-1646)*
Mri Software LLC....C.... 800 327-8770
Solon *(G-17030)*
MSI International LLC....E.... 330 869-6459
Cleveland *(G-6087)*
Netrada North America LLC....E.... 866 345-5835
West Chester *(G-19218)*
Netsmart Technologies Inc....D.... 614 764-0143
Dublin *(G-10407)*
New Innovations Inc....E.... 330 899-9954
Uniontown *(G-18530)*
Noble Technologies Corp....E.... 330 287-1530
Wooster *(G-19895)*
Northwods Cnslting Prtners Inc....C.... 614 781-7800
Dublin *(G-10410)*
Nsb Retail Systems Inc....D.... 614 840-1421
Lewis Center *(G-12698)*
Ntt Data Inc....D.... 513 794-1400
Cincinnati *(G-4188)*
Odyssey Consulting Services....C.... 614 523-4248
Columbus *(G-8314)*
Oeconnection LLC....C.... 888 776-5792
Richfield *(G-16519)*
Office World Inc....E.... 419 991-4694
Lima *(G-12928)*
Ohio University....D.... 740 593-1000
Athens *(G-804)*
Online Mega Sellers Corp....D.... 888 384-6468
Toledo *(G-18109)*
Parker-Hannifin Corporation....D.... 513 831-2340
Milford *(G-14550)*
Patterson Pope Inc....D.... 513 891-4430
Cincinnati *(G-4263)*
Paychex Inc....D.... 800 939-2462
Lima *(G-12855)*
Pcms Datafit Inc....D.... 513 587-3100
Cincinnati *(G-4269)*
Pegasus Technical Services Inc....E.... 513 793-0094
Cincinnati *(G-4274)*
Persistent Systems Inc....E.... 727 786-0379
Marion *(G-13572)*
Pillar Technology Group LLC....D.... 614 535-7868
Columbus *(G-8544)*
Plumbline Solutions Inc....E.... 419 581-2963
Findlay *(G-11076)*
Positive Bus Solutions Inc....D.... 513 772-2255
Cincinnati *(G-4317)*
Primatech Inc....E.... 614 841-9800
Columbus *(G-8560)*
Primax Marketing Group....E.... 513 443-2797
Cincinnati *(G-4329)*
Productivity Qulty Systems Inc....E.... 937 885-2255
Dayton *(G-9833)*
Quest Software Inc....D.... 614 336-9223
Dublin *(G-10434)*
Qvidian Corporation....E.... 513 631-1155
Blue Ash *(G-1669)*
Raco Wireless LLC....D.... 513 870-6480
Blue Ash *(G-1673)*
Rainbow Data Systems Inc....E.... 937 431-8000
Beavercreek *(G-1202)*
Resource International Inc....C.... 614 823-4949
Columbus *(G-8622)*
Retalix Usa Inc....C.... 937 384-2277
Miamisburg *(G-14343)*
Rippe & Kingston Systems Inc....D.... 513 241-1375
Cincinnati *(G-4421)*
Roadtrippers Inc....E.... 917 688-9887
Cincinnati *(G-4432)*
Sadler-Necamp Financial Svcs....E.... 513 489-5477
Cincinnati *(G-4466)*
Saec/Kinetic Vision Inc....C.... 513 793-4959
Cincinnati *(G-4467)*
Sanctuary Software Studio Inc....E.... 330 666-9690
Fairlawn *(G-10972)*
Sap America Inc....E.... 513 762-7630
Cincinnati *(G-4478)*
Sawdey Solution Services Inc....E.... 937 490-4060
Beavercreek *(G-1259)*
Scientific Forming Tech Corp....E.... 614 451-8330
Columbus *(G-8705)*
Seapine Software Inc....E.... 513 754-1655
Mason *(G-13757)*
Seifert & Group Inc....D.... 330 833-2700
Massillon *(G-13852)*
Service Pronet Inc....E.... 614 874-4300
Columbus *(G-8716)*
Shoptech Industrial Sftwr....D.... 513 985-9900
Cincinnati *(G-4517)*
Siemens Product Life Mgmt Sftw....D.... 513 576-2400
Milford *(G-14562)*
Solutions Through Innovative T....D.... 937 320-9994
Beavercreek *(G-1209)*
Sordyl & Associates Inc....E.... 419 866-6811
Maumee *(G-13979)*
Srinsoft Inc....E.... 614 893-6535
Dublin *(G-10459)*
Staid Logic LLC....E.... 309 807-0575
Columbus *(G-8772)*
Strategic Data Systems Inc....E.... 513 772-7374
Cincinnati *(G-4595)*
Strategic Insurance Sftwr Inc....E.... 614 915-9769
Columbus *(G-8794)*
Sumaria Systems Inc....D.... 937 429-6070
Beavercreek *(G-1210)*
Sumtotal Systems LLC....C.... 352 264-2800
Columbus *(G-8802)*
Sunstorm Games LLC....E.... 216 403-4820
Beachwood *(G-1128)*
Synoran....E.... 614 236-4014
Columbus *(G-8815)*
Systems Alternatives Intl....E.... 419 891-1100
Maumee *(G-13985)*
Systems Evolution Inc....D.... 513 459-1992
Cincinnati *(G-4611)*
Tata America Intl Corp....B.... 513 677-6500
Milford *(G-14565)*
Tech Mahindra (americas) Inc....D.... 216 912-2002
Cleveland *(G-6577)*
Teradata Corporation....B.... 866 548-8348
Miamisburg *(G-14356)*
Thinkware Incorporated....E.... 513 598-3300
Cincinnati *(G-4650)*
Timeware Inc....E.... 330 963-2700
Twinsburg *(G-18476)*
TOA Technologies Inc....D.... 216 360-8106
Beachwood *(G-1131)*
Triad Governmental Systems....E.... 937 376-5446
Xenia *(G-20080)*
Tridec Technologies LLC....E.... 937 938-8160
Huber Heights *(G-12099)*
Triplett & Adams Entps Inc....D.... 816 221-1024
New Concord *(G-15039)*
Tyco International MGT Co LLC....E.... 888 787-8324
Cincinnati *(G-4712)*
Unicon International Inc....C.... 614 861-7070
Columbus *(G-8888)*
Vediscovery LLC....E.... 216 241-3443
Cleveland *(G-6688)*
Ventech Solutions Inc....D.... 614 757-1167
Columbus *(G-6909)*
Virtual Hold Technology LLC....D.... 330 666-1181
Akron *(G-498)*
Widepint Intgrted Sltions Corp....E.... 614 410-1587
Columbus *(G-8992)*
Wtw Delaware Holdings LLC....C.... 216 937-4000
Cleveland *(G-6762)*
Yashco Systems Inc....E.... 614 467-4600
Hilliard *(G-11966)*

7372 Prepackaged Software

Advanced Prgrm Resources Inc....E.... 614 761-9994
Dublin *(G-10234)*
Advant-E Corporation....D.... 937 429-4288
Beavercreek *(G-1145)*
Agile Global Solutions Inc....E.... 916 655-7745
Independence *(G-12182)*
Air Force US Dept of....B.... 937 656-2354
Dayton *(G-9251)*
Auto Des Sys Inc....E.... 614 488-7984
Upper Arlington *(G-18548)*
Besttransportcom Inc....E.... 614 888-2378
Worthington *(G-19943)*
Cimx LLC....E.... 513 248-7700
Cincinnati *(G-3276)*
Cincom Systems Inc....C.... 513 459-1470
Mason *(G-13677)*
Citynet Ohio LLC....E.... 614 364-7881
Columbus *(G-7287)*
Clinicl Otcms Mngmnt Syst LLC....D.... 330 650-9900
Broadview Heights *(G-1875)*
Creative Microsystems Inc....D.... 937 836-4499
Englewood *(G-10701)*
Dakota Software Corporation....D.... 216 765-7100
Cleveland *(G-5461)*
Datatrak International Inc....E.... 440 443-0082
Mayfield Heights *(G-14000)*
Delta Media Group Inc....E.... 330 493-0350
Canton *(G-2338)*
Digital Controls Corporation....D.... 513 746-8118
Miamisburg *(G-14297)*
Drb Systems LLC....D.... 330 645-3299
Akron *(G-200)*
Edict Systems Inc....E.... 937 429-4288
Beavercreek *(G-1172)*
Einstruction Corporation....D.... 330 746-3015
Youngstown *(G-20178)*
EMC Corporation....D.... 513 794-9624
Blue Ash *(G-1584)*
EMC Corporation....E.... 216 606-2000
Independence *(G-12206)*
▲ **Esko-Graphics Inc**....D.... 937 454-1721
Miamisburg *(G-14299)*
Estreamz Inc....E.... 513 278-7836
Cincinnati *(G-3577)*
Exact Software North Amer LLC....C.... 978 539-6186
Dublin *(G-10341)*
Explorys Inc....D.... 216 767-4700
Cleveland *(G-5563)*
Exponentia US Inc....E.... 614 944-5103
Columbus *(G-7623)*
Finastra USA Corporation....E.... 937 435-2335
Miamisburg *(G-14302)*
Flexnova Inc....E.... 216 288-6961
Cleveland *(G-5607)*
Flypaper Studio Inc....E.... 602 801-2208
Cincinnati *(G-3634)*
Foundation Software Inc....D.... 330 220-8383
Strongsville *(G-17465)*
Gracie Plum Investments Inc....E.... 740 355-9029
Portsmouth *(G-16282)*
Honeywell International Inc....D.... 513 745-7200
Cincinnati *(G-3782)*
Hyland LLC....B.... 440 788-5045
Westlake *(G-19495)*
Hyland Software Inc....A.... 440 788-5000
Westlake *(G-19496)*
Infoaccessnet LLC....E.... 216 328-0100
Cleveland *(G-5819)*
Juniper Networks Inc....D.... 614 932-1432
Dublin *(G-10383)*
Mapsys Inc....E.... 614 255-7258
Columbus *(G-8104)*
Matrix Management Solutions....C.... 330 470-3700
Canton *(G-2451)*
Microsoft Corporation....E.... 614 719-5900
Columbus *(G-6896)*

SIC SECTION

73 BUSINESS SERVICES

Microsoft Corporation ....E 216 986-1440
Cleveland (G-6050)
Microsoft Corporation ....D 513 339-2800
Mason (G-13739)
Mim Software Inc ....E 216 896-9798
Beachwood (G-1103)
Netsmart Technologies Inc ....E 440 942-4040
Solon (G-17033)
Nextmed Systems Inc ....E 216 674-0511
Cincinnati (G-4164)
Nsa Technologies LLC ....C 330 576-4600
Akron (G-359)
Ohio Cllbrtive Lrng Sltons Inc ....E 216 595-5289
Beachwood (G-1110)
Onx USA LLC ....D 440 569-2300
Cleveland (G-6207)
Open Text Inc ....E 614 658-3588
Hilliard (G-11941)
Oracle Corporation ....C 513 826-5632
Beavercreek (G-1195)
Oracle Systems Corporation ....E 513 826-6000
Blue Ash (G-1658)
Parallel Technologies Inc ....D 614 798-9700
Dublin (G-10421)
Patrick J Burke & Co ....E 513 455-8200
Cincinnati (G-4262)
Peco II Inc ....D 614 431-0694
Columbus (G-8528)
Preemptive Solutions LLC ....E 440 443-7200
Cleveland (G-6297)
Retalix Inc ....C 937 384-2277
Miamisburg (G-14342)
Revolution Group Inc ....D 614 212-1111
Westerville (G-19349)
Rivals Sports Grille LLC ....E 216 267-0005
Middleburg Heights (G-14386)
Sanctuary Software Studio Inc ....C 330 666-9690
Fairlawn (G-10972)
Seapine Software Inc ....E 513 754-1655
Mason (G-13757)
Sigmatek Systems LLC ....E 513 674-0005
Cincinnati (G-4527)
Skillsoft Corporation ....D 216 524-5200
Independence (G-12260)
Software Management Group ....E 513 618-2165
Cincinnati (G-4551)
Software Solutions Inc ....E 513 932-6667
Lebanon (G-12648)
Starwin Industries Inc ....E 937 293-8568
Dayton (G-9904)
Symantec Corporation ....D 216 643-6700
Independence (G-12264)
Tata America Intl Corp ....B 513 677-6500
Milford (G-14565)
Teradata Corporation ....B 866 548-8348
Miamisburg (G-14356)
Thinkware Incorporated ....E 513 598-3300
Cincinnati (G-4650)
Tmw Systems Inc ....C 216 831-6606
Mayfield Heights (G-14008)
To Scale Software LLC ....E 513 253-0053
Mason (G-13769)
Triad Governmental Systems ....E 937 376-5446
Xenia (G-20080)
Triplett & Adams Entps Inc ....D 816 221-1024
New Concord (G-15039)
Turning Technologies LLC ....C 330 746-3015
Youngstown (G-20395)
Virtual Hold Technology LLC ....D 330 666-1181
Akron (G-498)
Workspeed Management LLC ....E 917 369-9025
Solon (G-17069)
Zipscene LLC ....D 513 201-5174
Cincinnati (G-4872)

7373 Computer Integrated Systems Design

Acadia Solutions Inc ....E 614 505-6135
Dublin (G-10233)
Aclara Technologies LLC ....C 440 528-7200
Solon (G-16969)
Advanced Prgrm Resources Inc ....E 614 761-9994
Dublin (G-10234)
Advanced Service Tech LLC ....E 937 435-4376
Miamisburg (G-14268)
Afidence Inc ....E 513 234-5822
Mason (G-13659)
Aisling Enterprises LLC ....E 937 203-1757
Centerville (G-2670)
Assured Information SEC Inc ....D 937 427-9720
Beavercreek (G-1148)

Attevo Inc ....D 216 928-2800
Beachwood (G-1053)
Axia Consulting Inc ....D 614 675-4050
Columbus (G-7080)
Baxter Hodell Donnelly Preston ....C 513 271-1634
Cincinnati (G-3083)
Bpi Infrmtion Systems Ohio Inc ....E 440 717-4112
Brecksville (G-1815)
Brandmuscle Inc ....C 216 464-4342
Cleveland (G-5133)
Cameo Solutions Inc ....E 513 645-4220
West Chester (G-19032)
Cdo Technologies Inc ....D 937 258-0022
Dayton (G-9260)
Cdw Technologies LLC ....E 513 677-4100
Cincinnati (G-3199)
▲ Cincinnati Bell Inc ....D 513 397-9900
Cincinnati (G-3285)
Cincom Intrnational Operations ....B 513 612-2300
Cincinnati (G-3342)
Cincom Systems Inc ....B 513 612-2300
Cincinnati (G-3343)
Cisco Systems Inc ....C 330 523-2000
Richfield (G-16501)
Commercial Time Sharing Inc ....E 330 644-3059
Akron (G-152)
Commsys Inc ....E 937 220-4990
Moraine (G-14761)
Computers Universal Inc ....C 614 543-0473
Beavercreek (G-1162)
Convergys Corporation ....A 513 723-7000
Cincinnati (G-3417)
Cott Systems Inc ....D 614 847-4405
Columbus (G-7449)
Courtview Justice Solutions ....E 330 497-0033
Canton (G-2326)
Creative Microsystems Inc ....D 937 836-4499
Englewood (G-10701)
Datascan Field Services LLC ....E 440 914-7300
Solon (G-17000)
Dayton/Cncinnati Tech Svcs LLC ......E 513 892-3940
Blue Ash (G-1575)
Dedicated Tech Services Inc ....D 614 309-0059
Dublin (G-10317)
Deemsys Inc ....D 614 322-9928
Gahanna (G-11239)
Definitive Solutions Co Inc ....D 513 719-9100
Cincinnati (G-3479)
Devcare Solutions Ltd ....E 614 221-2277
Columbus (G-7511)
Document Tech Systems Ltd ....E 330 928-5311
Cuyahoga Falls (G-9181)
Drb Systems LLC ....D 330 645-3299
Akron (G-200)
Dyncorp ....C 513 942-6500
West Chester (G-19067)
Dyncorp ....D 513 569-7415
Cincinnati (G-3518)
E&I Solutions LLC ....E 937 912-0288
Beavercreek (G-1171)
Easy2 Technologies Inc ....E 216 479-0482
Cleveland (G-5523)
Evanhoe & Associates Inc ....E 937 235-2995
Dayton (G-9269)
Exact Software North Amer LLC ....C 614 410-2600
Dublin (G-10342)
Expert System Applications ....E 440 248-0110
Beachwood (G-1077)
Honeywell International Inc ....D 513 745-7200
Cincinnati (G-3782)
HP Inc ....E 440 234-7022
Cleveland (G-5787)
ID Networks Inc ....E 440 992-0062
Ashtabula (G-749)
Infor (us) Inc ....B 678 319-8000
Columbus (G-7896)
Infor (us) Inc ....D 614 781-2325
Columbus (G-6886)
Infotelecom Holdings LLC ....B 216 373-4811
Cleveland (G-5821)
Integrted Prcision Systems Inc ....D 330 963-0064
Twinsburg (G-18432)
Jaekle Group Inc ....E 330 405-9353
Macedonia (G-13204)
Juniper Networks Inc ....D 614 932-1432
Dublin (G-10383)
Knotice LLC ....D 800 801-4194
Akron (G-308)
Leidos Inc ....B 858 826-6000
Columbus (G-8051)

Manatron Inc ....E 937 431-4000
Beavercreek (G-1252)
Manifest Solutions Corp ....D 614 930-2800
Upper Arlington (G-18555)
Matrix Management Solutions ....C 330 470-3700
Canton (G-2451)
Matrix Technologies Inc ....D 419 897-7200
Maumee (G-13942)
Microman Inc ....E 614 923-8000
Dublin (G-10397)
Mid-Amrica Cnsulting Group Inc ....D 216 432-6925
Cleveland (G-6053)
Millenium Control Systems LLC ....E 440 510-0050
Eastlake (G-10549)
Natural Resources Ohio Dept ....E 614 265-6852
Columbus (G-8250)
Netsmart Technologies Inc ....D 614 764-0143
Dublin (G-10407)
Northern Datacomm Corp ....E 330 665-0344
Akron (G-357)
Northrop Grumman Systems Corp .....E 937 429-6450
Beavercreek (G-1255)
Northrop Grumman Technical ....C 937 320-3100
Beavercreek Township (G-1276)
Ohio State University ....E 614 728-8100
Columbus (G-8432)
Online Mega Sellers Corp ....D 888 384-6468
Toledo (G-18109)
Pcms Datafit Inc ....D 513 587-3100
Cincinnati (G-4269)
Peerless Technologies Corp ....D 937 490-5000
Beavercreek Township (G-1279)
Pegasus Technical Services Inc ....E 513 793-0094
Cincinnati (G-4274)
Pomeroy It Solutions Sls Inc ....E 440 717-1364
Brecksville (G-1842)
Presidio Infrastructure ....D 419 241-8303
Toledo (G-18134)
Presidio Infrastructure ....E 614 381-1400
Dublin (G-10429)
Rainbow Data Systems Inc ....E 937 431-8000
Beavercreek (G-1202)
Ranac Computer Corporation ....E 317 844-0141
Moraine (G-14820)
Reynolds and Reynolds Company .....A 937 485-2000
Kettering (G-12435)
Robots and Pencils LP ....D 587 350-4095
Beachwood (G-1120)
Rockwell Automation Ohio Inc ....D 513 576-6151
Milford (G-14558)
Rolta Advizex Technologies LLC ....E 216 901-1818
Independence (G-12253)
Rovisys Building Tech LLC ....E 330 954-7600
Aurora (G-853)
Security Investments LLC ....D 614 441-4601
Westerville (G-19443)
Sgi Matrix LLC ....D 937 438-9033
Miamisburg (G-14349)
Siemens PLM Software ....E 513 576-2400
Milford (G-14561)
Soaring Eagle Inc ....E 330 385-5579
East Liverpool (G-10535)
Software Solutions Inc ....E 513 932-6667
Lebanon (G-12648)
Sogeti USA LLC ....E 614 847-4477
Westerville (G-19353)
Sterling Buying Group LLC ....E 513 564-9000
Cincinnati (G-4589)
Suite 224 Internet ....E 440 593-7113
Conneaut (G-9047)
Sumaria Systems Inc ....D 937 429-6070
Beavercreek (G-1210)
▲ Systemax Manufacturing Inc ....C 937 368-2300
Dayton (G-9919)
Sytronics Inc ....E 937 431-6100
Beavercreek (G-1211)
Talx Corporation ....E 614 527-9404
Hilliard (G-11956)
Tata America Intl Corp ....B 513 677-6500
Milford (G-14565)
Teknobility LLC ....E 216 255-9433
Medina (G-14133)
Telligen Tech Inc ....E 614 934-1554
Columbus (G-8831)
Thinkpath Engineering Svcs LLC ......E 937 291-8374
Miamisburg (G-14358)
Tour De Force Crm Inc ....E 419 425-4800
Findlay (G-11092)
Tsi Inc ....E 419 468-1855
Galion (G-11307)

73 BUSINESS SERVICES

Twism Enterprises LLC ....E 513 800-1098
  Cincinnati (G-4711)
Tyco International MGT Co LLC ....E 888 787-8324
  Cincinnati (G-4712)
United Technical Support Svcs ....D 330 562-3330
  Aurora (G-858)
Velocity Grtest Phone Ever Inc ....E 419 868-9983
  Holland (G-12066)
Ventech Solutions Inc ....D 614 757-1167
  Columbus (G-6909)
Warnock Tanner & Assoc Inc ....E 419 897-6999
  Maumee (G-13993)
Wescom Solutions Inc ....E 513 831-1207
  Milford (G-14574)

7374 Data & Computer Processing & Preparation

1st All File Recovery Usa ....E 800 399-7150
  Shaker Heights (G-16855)
Aero Fulfillment Services Corp ....D 800 225-7145
  Mason (G-13658)
Alliance Data Systems Corp ....B 614 729-4000
  Columbus (G-6968)
Aurora Imaging Company ....E 614 761-1390
  Dublin (G-10258)
Automatic Data Processing Inc ....C 216 447-1980
  Cleveland (G-5082)
Automatic Data Processing Inc ....E 614 212-4831
  Westerville (G-19370)
Btas Inc ....C 937 431-9431
  Beavercreek (G-1155)
Cache Next Generation LLC ....D 614 850-9444
  Hilliard (G-11887)
Cbc Companies Inc ....E 614 538-6100
  Columbus (G-7214)
Central Command Inc ....E 330 723-2062
  Columbia Station (G-6842)
Change Healthcare Holdings Inc ....E 330 405-0001
  Hudson (G-12108)
Change Healthcare Holdings Inc ....E 216 589-5878
  Cleveland (G-5227)
▲ Cincinnati Bell Inc............................D 513 397-9900
  Cincinnati (G-3285)
City of Cleveland..................................D 216 664-2430
  Cleveland (G-5254)
Cleveland State University ....E 216 687-3786
  Cleveland (G-5348)
Clubessential LLC ....E 800 448-1475
  Blue Ash (G-1560)
Coleman Professional Svcs Inc ....C 330 628-2275
  Akron (G-151)
Coleman Professional Svcs Inc ....B 330 673-1347
  Kent (G-12360)
Convergys Corporation ....A 513 723-7000
  Cincinnati (G-3417)
Convergys Gvrnment Sltions LLC ......D 513 723-7006
  Cincinnati (G-3419)
County of Cuyahoga ....C 216 443-8011
  Cleveland (G-5421)
Csi Complete Inc ....E 800 343-0461
  Plain City (G-16186)
Ctrac Inc...E 440 572-1000
  Cleveland (G-5447)
Data Direction Inc ....E 216 362-5900
  Cleveland (G-5463)
Datatrak International Inc...................E 440 443-0082
  Mayfield Heights (G-14000)
Decisionone Corporation ....E 614 883-0228
  Urbancrest (G-18604)
Definitive Solutions Co Inc ....D 513 719-9100
  Cincinnati (G-3479)
Early Express Services Inc ....E 937 223-5801
  Dayton (G-9511)
Eliassen Group LLC ....E 781 205-8100
  Blue Ash (G-1583)
Enterprise Data Management Inc ......E 513 791-7272
  Blue Ash (G-1588)
Enterprise Services LLC ....D 740 423-9501
  Belpre (G-1436)
Expedata LLC ....E 937 439-6767
  Dayton (G-9536)
Gracie Plum Investments Inc............E 740 355-9029
  Portsmouth (G-16282)
Great Lakes Publishing Company.......D 216 771-2833
  Cleveland (G-5691)
Hyperquake LLC ....E 513 563-6555
  Cincinnati (G-3806)
Illumination Works LLC ....D 937 938-1321
  Beavercreek (G-1178)

Infovision 21 Inc ....E 614 761-8844
  Dublin (G-10376)
Integrated Data Services Inc ....D 937 656-5496
  Dayton (G-9631)
Integrated Marketing Tech Inc ....D 330 225-3550
  Brunswick (G-1982)
Interact One Inc ....E 513 469-7042
  Blue Ash (G-1616)
International Data MGT Inc ....E 330 869-8500
  Fairlawn (G-10959)
Karcher Group Inc ....E 330 493-6141
  North Canton (G-15348)
Kuno Creative Group LLC ....E 440 225-4144
  Avon (G-904)
Lake Data Center Inc ....D 440 944-2020
  Wickliffe (G-19605)
Lockheed Martin ....A 330 796-2800
  Akron (G-326)
Lou-Ray Associates Inc ....E 330 220-1999
  Brunswick (G-1986)
Mast Technology Services Inc ....A 614 415-7000
  Columbus (G-8126)
Medical Mutual Services LLC ....C 440 878-4800
  Strongsville (G-17492)
Merchant Data Service Inc ....E 937 847-6585
  Miamisburg (G-14318)
▲ Midwest Tape LLC ....B 419 868-9370
  Holland (G-12038)
Mri Software LLC ....E 800 327-8770
  Solon (G-17030)
New Pros Communications Inc ....D 740 201-0410
  Powell (G-16345)
Northwest Ohio Computer Assn ....D 419 267-5565
  Archbold (G-640)
Office World Inc ....E 419 991-4694
  Lima (G-12928)
Personalized Data Corporation ....E 216 289-2200
  Cleveland (G-6268)
Quadax Inc ....E 614 882-1200
  Westerville (G-19438)
Racksquared LLC ....E 614 737-8812
  Columbus (G-8583)
Record Express LLC ....E 513 685-7329
  Batavia (G-1023)
Rgis LLC ....D 248 651-2511
  Reynoldsburg (G-16477)
Rurbanc Data Services Inc................E 419 782-2530
  Defiance (G-10055)
Sedlak Management Cons Inc ....E 216 206-4700
  Cleveland (G-6464)
Service Pronet Inc ....E 614 874-4300
  Columbus (G-8716)
Sourcelink Ohio LLC ....C 937 885-8000
  Miamisburg (G-14352)
Speedeon Data LLC ....E 440 264-2100
  Cleveland (G-6519)
Sumaria Systems Inc ....D 937 429-6070
  Beavercreek (G-1210)
Thinkware Incorporated ....E 513 598-3300
  Cincinnati (G-4650)
Universal Enterprises Inc ....C 419 529-3500
  Ontario (G-15718)
Vantiv LLC ....B 877 713-5964
  Symmes Twp (G-17630)
Vediscovery LLC ....E 216 241-3443
  Cleveland (G-6688)

7375 Information Retrieval Svcs

Acxiom Corporation ....C 216 520-3181
  Independence (G-12179)
Advant-E Corporation ....D 937 429-4288
  Beavercreek (G-1145)
AGS Custom Graphics Inc ....D 330 963-7770
  Macedonia (G-13186)
Amaxx Inc ....E 614 486-3481
  Dublin (G-10244)
Bluespring Software Inc ....E 513 794-1764
  Blue Ash (G-1547)
Cobalt Group Inc ....D 614 876-4013
  Hilliard (G-11891)
Com Net Inc ....D 419 739-3100
  Wapakoneta (G-18792)
Community Isp Inc ....E 419 867-6060
  Toledo (G-17824)
Cyxtera Data Centers Inc ....B 216 986-2742
  Cleveland (G-5460)
Doylestown Communications ....E 330 658-7000
  Doylestown (G-10226)
Ecommerce LLC ....D 800 861-9394
  Columbus (G-7574)

Hkm Drect Mkt Cmmnications Inc .....C 216 651-9500
  Cleveland (G-5762)
Innovative Technologies Corp ....D 937 252-2145
  Dayton (G-9275)
Intellicorp Records Inc ....D 216 450-5200
  Beachwood (G-1089)
▲ Lexisnexis Group..............................C 937 865-6800
  Miamisburg (G-14314)
Medical Mutual Services LLC ....C 440 878-4800
  Strongsville (G-17492)
Mirifex Systems LLC ....C 440 891-1210
  Sharon Center (G-16876)
Oclc Inc ....A 614 764-6000
  Dublin (G-10412)
One Source Technology LLC ....E 216 420-1700
  Cleveland (G-6205)
Peoplefacts LLC ....E 800 849-1071
  Maumee (G-13958)
Png Telecommunications Inc ....D 513 942-7900
  Cincinnati (G-4311)
Relx Inc ....C 937 865-6800
  Miamisburg (G-14339)
▲ Repro Acquisition Company LLC ...E 216 738-3800
  Cleveland (G-6378)
Salvagedata Recovery LLC ....E 914 600-2434
  Cleveland (G-6439)
Security Hut Inc ....C 216 226-0461
  Lakewood (G-12500)
Seifert & Group Inc ....D 330 833-2700
  Massillon (G-13852)
Simplified Logistics LLC ....E 440 250-8912
  Westlake (G-19547)
Title First Agency Inc ....E 614 224-9207
  Columbus (G-8850)
TSC Communications Inc ....E 419 739-2200
  Wapakoneta (G-18810)
Verisk Crime Analytics Inc ....E 614 865-6000
  Worthington (G-20005)
Verizon Business Global LLC ....E 614 219-2317
  Hilliard (G-11963)
Webmd Health Corp ....E 330 425-3241
  Twinsburg (G-18485)

7376 Computer Facilities Management Svcs

Ability Network Inc ....E 513 943-8888
  Cincinnati (G-2901)
City of Cleveland ....E 216 664-2941
  Cleveland (G-5252)
Computer Sciences Corporation ....E 937 904-5113
  Dayton (G-9262)
Computer Sciences Corporation ....C 614 801-2343
  Grove City (G-11548)
CSRA LLC ....B 937 429-9774
  Beavercreek (G-1164)
Dedicated Tech Services Inc ....D 614 309-0059
  Dublin (G-10317)
Dyn Marine Services Inc ....E 937 427-2663
  Beavercreek (G-1170)
E&I Solutions LLC ....E 937 912-0288
  Beavercreek (G-1171)
Evanhoe & Associates Inc ....E 937 235-2995
  Dayton (G-9269)
General Electric Company ....C 513 583-3500
  Cincinnati (G-3669)
Jjr Solutions LLC ....E 937 912-0288
  Beavercreek (G-1180)
Jyg Innovations LLC ....E 937 630-3858
  Dayton (G-9647)
Med3000 Group Inc ....E 937 291-7850
  Miamisburg (G-14316)
Selecttech Services Corp ....C 937 438-9905
  Centerville (G-2685)
Technical Assurance Inc ....E 440 953-3147
  Willoughby (G-19717)

7377 Computer Rental & Leasing

Information Builders Inc ....E 513 891-2338
  Montgomery (G-14726)
Pomeroy It Solutions Sls Inc ....E 440 717-1364
  Brecksville (G-1842)

7378 Computer Maintenance & Repair

Ascendtech Inc ....E 216 458-1101
  Willoughby (G-19645)
Bpi Infrmtion Systems Ohio Inc ....E 440 717-4112
  Brecksville (G-1815)
Bsl - Applied Laser Tech LLC ....E 216 663-8181
  Cleveland (G-5154)
Butler County of Ohio ....E 513 887-3418
  Hamilton (G-11705)

Cincinnati Copiers Inc ....C 513 769-0606
Blue Ash (G-1556)
Cincinnati Voice and Data ....D 513 683-4127
Loveland (G-13115)
County of Montgomery ....B 937 496-3103
Dayton (G-9439)
CTS Construction Inc ....D 513 489-8290
Cincinnati (G-3445)
Decisionone Corporation ....E 614 883-0228
Urbancrest (G-18604)
Diebold Nixdorf Incorporated ....D 513 870-1400
Hamilton (G-11722)
DMC Technology Group ....E 419 535-2900
Toledo (G-17855)
Efix Computer Repair & Svc LLC ....E 937 985-4447
Kettering (G-12429)
Enterprise Data Management Inc ....E 513 791-7272
Blue Ash (G-1588)
Evanhoe & Associates Inc ....E 937 235-2995
Dayton (G-9269)
Government Acquisitions Inc ....E 513 721-8700
Cincinnati (G-3689)
Great Lakes Computer Corp ....D 440 937-1100
Avon (G-895)
HP Inc ....E 513 983-2817
Cincinnati (G-3791)
Intelligent Information Inc ....E 513 860-4233
West Chester (G-19210)
Mt Business Technologies Inc ....C 419 529-6100
Mansfield (G-13348)
Northcoast Duplicating Inc ....C 216 573-6681
Cleveland (G-6150)
Park Place Technologies LLC ....B 610 544-0571
Mayfield Heights (G-14005)
Park Place Technologies LLC ....C 877 778-8707
Mayfield Heights (G-14006)
Perry Pro Tech Inc ....D 419 228-1360
Lima (G-12857)
Pomeroy It Solutions Sls Inc ....E 440 717-1364
Brecksville (G-1842)
Positive Bus Solutions Inc ....D 513 772-2255
Cincinnati (G-4317)
Realm Technologies LLC ....E 513 297-3095
Lebanon (G-12641)
Resource One Cmpt Systems Inc ....D 614 485-4800
Worthington (G-19993)
Sjn Data Center LLC ....E 513 386-7871
Cincinnati (G-4534)
Systems Alternatives Intl ....E 419 891-1100
Maumee (G-13985)
Uptime Corporation ....E 216 661-1655
Brooklyn Heights (G-1930)
Wellington Technologies Inc ....E 440 238-4377
Westlake (G-19564)
Wrg Services Inc ....D 440 942-8650
Willoughby (G-19727)
Xerox Corporation ....D 216 642-7806
Cleveland (G-6767)

7379 Computer Related Svcs, NEC

1 Edi Source Inc ....C 440 519-7800
Solon (G-16967)
3sg Corporation ....E 614 761-8394
Dublin (G-10231)
Advanced Prgrm Resources Inc ....E 614 761-9994
Dublin (G-10234)
Advantage Technology Group ....E 513 563-3560
West Chester (G-19013)
American Bus Solutions Inc ....D 614 888-2227
Lewis Center (G-12665)
American Systems Cnsulting Inc ....D 614 282-7180
Dublin (G-10252)
Arrow Electronics Inc ....D 440 498-6400
Solon (G-16978)
Arszman & Lyons LLC ....E 513 527-4900
Blue Ash (G-1536)
Ascendtech Inc ....E 216 458-1101
Willoughby (G-19645)
Atos It Solutions and Svcs Inc ....B 513 336-1000
Mason (G-13665)
Attevo Inc ....D 216 928-2800
Beachwood (G-1053)
Baseline Consulting LLC ....D 440 336-5382
Cleveland (G-5096)
Bcg Systems That Work Inc ....E 330 864-4816
Akron (G-93)
Blue Chip Consulting Group LLC ....E 216 503-6001
Seven Hills (G-16827)
Cache Next Generation LLC ....D 614 850-9444
Hilliard (G-11887)
Cadre Computer Resources Co ....E 513 762-7350
Cincinnati (G-3164)
Cardinal Solutions Group Inc ....D 513 984-6700
Cincinnati (G-3179)
Cgi Technologies Solutions Inc ....C 216 687-1480
Cleveland (G-5222)
Cgi Technologies Solutions Inc ....D 614 228-2245
Columbus (G-7246)
Cgi Technologies Solutions Inc ....D 614 880-2200
Columbus (G-6874)
▲ Cincinnati Bell Inc ....D 513 397-9900
Cincinnati (G-3285)
Cincinnati Bell Techno ....D 513 841-6700
Cincinnati (G-3286)
▼ Cincinnati Bell Techno ....B 513 841-2287
Cincinnati (G-3287)
Cincom Systems Inc ....E 513 389-2344
Cincinnati (G-3344)
Cisco Systems Inc ....A 937 427-4264
Beavercreek (G-1160)
Comptech Computer Tech Inc ....E 937 228-2667
Dayton (G-9420)
Comresource Inc ....E 614 221-6348
Columbus (G-7418)
Creek Technologies Company ....C 937 272-4581
Beavercreek (G-1163)
Datacomm Tech ....E 614 755-5100
Reynoldsburg (G-16444)
Datafield Inc ....C 614 847-9600
Worthington (G-19953)
Datalysys LLC ....E 614 495-0260
Dublin (G-10316)
Dayhuff Group LLC ....E 614 854-9999
Worthington (G-19954)
Dedicated Tech Services Inc ....D 614 309-0059
Dublin (G-10317)
Definitive Solutions Co Inc ....D 513 719-9100
Cincinnati (G-3479)
Digital Controls Corporation ....D 513 746-8118
Miamisburg (G-14297)
Digital Management Inc ....D 240 223-4800
Mason (G-13695)
Diversified Systems Inc ....E 614 476-9939
Westerville (G-19394)
DMC Technology Group ....E 419 535-2900
Toledo (G-17855)
E&I Solutions LLC ....E 937 912-0288
Beavercreek (G-1171)
E-Mek Technologies LLC ....D 937 424-3163
Dayton (G-9510)
E2b Teknologies Inc ....E 440 352-4700
Chardon (G-2748)
Echo-Tape LLC ....E 614 892-3246
Columbus (G-7571)
Einstruction Corporation ....D 330 746-3015
Youngstown (G-20178)
Enterprise Data Management Inc ....E 513 791-7272
Blue Ash (G-1588)
Enterprise Systems Sftwr LLC ....D 419 841-3179
Toledo (G-17868)
Entrust Solutions LLC ....E 614 504-4900
Columbus (G-7597)
Entrypoint Consulting LLC ....D 216 674-9070
Cleveland (G-5544)
Enviro It LLC ....E 614 453-0709
Columbus (G-7598)
Estreamz Inc ....E 513 278-7836
Cincinnati (G-3577)
Evanhoe & Associates Inc ....E 937 235-2995
Dayton (G-9269)
Everest Technologies Inc ....E 614 436-3120
Worthington (G-19958)
Fhc Enterprises LLC ....E 614 271-3513
Columbus (G-7653)
Fit Technologies LLC ....E 216 583-0733
Cleveland (G-5601)
Forsythe Solutions Group Inc ....D 513 697-5100
Cincinnati (G-3638)
Franklin Cmpt Svcs Group Inc ....E 614 431-3327
New Albany (G-14986)
Genesis Corp ....D 330 597-4100
Akron (G-235)
Genesis Corp ....E 614 934-1211
Columbus (G-7738)
Girard Technologies Inc ....E 330 783-2495
Youngstown (G-20201)
GP Strategies Corporation ....E 513 583-8810
Mason (G-13710)
Great Nthrn Cnsulting Svcs Inc ....E 614 890-9999
Columbus (G-7771)
Greentree Group Inc ....D 937 490-5500
Dayton (G-9591)
Illumination Works LLC ....D 937 938-1321
Beavercreek (G-1178)
Indecon Solutions LLC ....E 614 799-1850
Dublin (G-10374)
Indus Valley Consultants Inc ....C 937 660-4748
Dayton (G-9629)
Information Control Corp ....B 614 523-3070
Columbus (G-7897)
Infovision 21 Inc ....E 614 761-8844
Dublin (G-10376)
Integrated Solutions and ....E 513 826-1932
Dayton (G-9632)
Integrity Information Tech Inc ....E 937 846-1769
New Carlisle (G-15024)
Interactive Bus Systems Inc ....E 513 984-2205
Cincinnati (G-3832)
International Association of ....E 330 628-3012
Canton (G-2413)
International Bus Mchs Corp ....B 917 406-7400
Beavercreek (G-1179)
Intralot Inc ....E 440 268-2900
Strongsville (G-17477)
Itelligence Inc ....D 513 956-2000
Cincinnati (G-3847)
Itelligence Outsourcing Inc ....D 513 956-2000
Cincinnati (G-3848)
Jjr Solutions LLC ....E 937 912-0288
Beavercreek (G-1180)
Jyg Innovations LLC ....E 937 630-3858
Dayton (G-9647)
Kristi Britton ....E 614 868-7612
Reynoldsburg (G-16464)
Laketec Communications Inc ....E 440 892-2001
North Olmsted (G-15429)
Lan Solutions Inc ....E 513 469-6500
Blue Ash (G-1624)
Lanco Global Systems Inc ....D 937 660-8090
Dayton (G-9672)
Leadership Circle LLC ....E 801 518-2980
Whitehouse (G-19588)
Liebert Field Services Inc ....E 614 841-5763
Westerville (G-19326)
Lightwell Inc ....E 614 310-2700
Dublin (G-10389)
Link Iq LLC ....E 859 983-6080
Dayton (G-9684)
London Computer Systems Inc ....D 513 583-0840
Loveland (G-13140)
Main Sail LLC ....D 216 472-5100
Cleveland (G-5969)
Maxim Technologies Inc ....E 614 457-6325
Hilliard (G-11926)
Mt Business Technologies Inc ....C 419 529-6100
Mansfield (G-13348)
Myca Mltmdia Trning Sltons LLC ....E 513 544-2379
Blue Ash (G-1650)
Natural Resources Ohio Dept ....E 614 265-6852
Columbus (G-8250)
Navigtor MGT Prtners Ltd Lblty ....E 614 796-0090
Columbus (G-8251)
Netsmart Technologies Inc ....E 440 942-4040
Solon (G-17033)
Netwave Corporation ....E 614 850-6300
Dublin (G-10408)
Nova Technology Solutions LLC ....E 937 426-2596
Beavercreek (G-1194)
Oasis Systems Inc ....E 937 426-1295
Beavercreek Township (G-1277)
Ohio State University ....C 614 292-4843
Columbus (G-8407)
Onx USA LLC ....D 440 569-2300
Cleveland (G-6207)
Optimum Technology Inc ....E 614 785-1110
Columbus (G-8474)
PC Connection Services ....C 937 382-4800
Wilmington (G-19777)
Pcm Sales Inc ....D 937 885-6444
Miamisburg (G-14333)
Perceptis LLC ....C 216 458-4122
Cleveland (G-6264)
Phoenix Systems Group Inc ....E 330 726-6500
Youngstown (G-20320)
Platinum Technologies ....E 216 926-1080
Akron (G-392)
Plus One Communications LLC ....B 330 255-4500
Akron (G-393)
Prime Prodata Inc ....E 330 497-2578
North Canton (G-15361)

S I C

Employee Codes: A=Over 500 employees, B=251-500
C=101-250, D=51-100, E=25-50

2018 Harris Ohio
Services Directory

1001

73 BUSINESS SERVICES

Company	Location	Code	Phone
Professional Data Resources Inc	Blue Ash (G-1668)	C	513 792-5100
Qbase LLC	Beavercreek (G-1201)	E	888 458-0345
Quanexus Inc	Dayton (G-9837)	E	937 885-7272
R Dorsey & Company Inc	Worthington (G-19989)	E	614 486-8900
Rainbow Data Systems Inc	Beavercreek (G-1202)	E	937 431-8000
Recker Consulting LLC	Cincinnati (G-4393)	D	513 924-5500
Regent Systems Inc	Dayton (G-9845)	D	937 640-8010
Revolution Group Inc	Westerville (G-19349)		614 212-1111
Rippe & Kingston Systems Inc	Cincinnati (G-4421)	D	513 241-1375
Rockwell Automation Ohio Inc	Milford (G-14558)	D	513 576-6151
Roundtower Technologies LLC	Cincinnati (G-4447)		513 247-7900
S & P Solutions Inc	Willoughby Hills (G-19734)	C	440 918-9111
Sjn Data Center LLC	Cincinnati (G-4534)	E	513 386-7871
Snapblox Hosted Solutions LLC	Cincinnati (G-4545)	E	866 524-7707
Sogeti USA LLC	Westerville (G-19353)		614 847-4477
Sogeti USA LLC	Dayton (G-9887)	D	937 433-3334
Sogeti USA LLC	Miamisburg (G-14351)		937 291-8100
Sogeti USA LLC	Cleveland (G-6493)	E	216 654-2230
Sogeti USA LLC	Blue Ash (G-1689)	E	513 824-3000
Sonit Systems LLC	Archbold (G-646)		419 446-2151
Sophisticated Systems Inc	Columbus (G-8750)	D	614 418-4600
Speedeon Data LLC	Cleveland (G-6519)		440 264-2100
Staid Logic LLC	Columbus (G-8772)	E	309 807-0575
Strategic Systems Inc	Dublin (G-10464)	C	614 717-4774
Technology Recovery Group Ltd	Westlake (G-19554)	D	440 250-9970
Techsoft Systems Inc	Cincinnati (G-4630)	E	513 772-5010
Teksystems Inc	Independence (G-12265)	E	216 606-3600
Teksystems Inc	Cincinnati (G-4633)	E	513 719-3950
Telligen Tech Inc	Columbus (G-8831)		614 934-1554
Teradata Operations Inc	Miamisburg (G-14357)	D	937 242-4030
Top Gun Sales Performance Inc	Mason (G-13770)		513 770-0870
Unicon International Inc	Columbus (G-8888)	C	614 861-7070
Vana Solutions LLC	Beavercreek (G-1217)	E	937 242-6399
Ventech Solutions Inc	Columbus (G-6909)	D	614 757-1167
Vertical Knowledge LLC	Chagrin Falls (G-2709)	D	216 920-7790
Vital Resources Inc	Huron (G-12175)	E	440 614-5150
Vitalyst	Cleveland (G-6705)	D	216 201-9070
Warnock Tanner & Assoc Inc	Maumee (G-13993)	E	419 897-6999
Web Yoga Inc	Dayton (G-9987)	E	937 428-0000
Wolcott Group	Medina (G-14139)		330 666-5900
Wolters Kluwer Clinical Drug	Hudson (G-12154)	D	330 650-6506
Zin Technologies Inc	Middleburg Heights (G-14392)		440 625-2200

7381 Detective & Armored Car Svcs

Company	Location	Code	Phone
1st Advnce SEC Invstgtions Inc	Dayton (G-9292)	E	937 317-4433
1st Choice Security Inc	Cincinnati (G-2940)	C	513 381-6789
Acrux Investigation Agency	Lakeview (G-12467)	B	937 842-5780
All Secured Security Svcs LLC	Columbus (G-6965)	E	614 861-0482
Allied Security LLC	Cincinnati (G-2992)	B	513 771-3776
Alliedbarton Security Svcs LLC	Worthington (G-19939)	C	614 225-9061
Alliedbarton Security Svcs LLC	Rossford (G-16606)	E	419 874-9005
Alpha Security LLC	Poland (G-16220)		330 406-2181
American Svcs & Protection LLC	Columbus (G-7009)	D	614 884-0177
Anderson Security Inc	Moraine (G-14749)	D	937 294-1478
Andy Frain Services Inc	Maumee (G-13882)	B	419 897-7909
Area Wide Protective Inc	Fairfield (G-10820)		513 321-9889
Aset Corporation	Vandalia (G-18659)	E	937 890-8881
Atlantis Co Inc	Cleveland (G-5078)	D	888 807-3272
Awp Inc	North Canton (G-15327)	A	330 677-7401
Bdtk Private Security	Dayton (G-9350)	E	937 520-1784
Belayusa Corporation	Columbus (G-7098)	E	614 878-8200
Brinks Incorporated	Columbus (G-7144)	E	614 291-1268
Brinks Incorporated	Columbus (G-7145)	E	614 291-0624
Brinks Incorporated	Cleveland (G-5139)	D	216 621-7493
Brinks Incorporated	Akron (G-112)		330 633-5351
Brinks Incorporated	Cincinnati (G-3135)	D	513 621-9310
Brinks Incorporated	Dayton (G-9258)		937 253-9777
Brinks Incorporated	Massillon (G-13789)		330 832-6130
Brinks Incorporated	Dublin (G-10268)	E	614 761-1205
Brinks Incorporated	Youngstown (G-20126)	E	330 758-7379
Buckeye Protective Service	Canton (G-2274)	B	330 456-2671
Cal Crim Inc	Trenton (G-18340)	C	513 563-5500
Cefaratti Investigation & Prcs	Cleveland (G-5201)	E	216 696-1161
Celebrity Security Inc	Cleveland (G-5202)	E	216 671-6425
Community Crime Patrol	Columbus (G-7402)	E	614 247-1765
Cooperate Screening Services	Cleveland (G-5407)	E	440 816-0500
Corporate Screening Svcs Inc	Cleveland (G-5410)	D	440 816-0500
Corps Security Agency Inc	Blue Ash (G-1568)	D	513 631-3200
D B A Inc	Cincinnati (G-3454)	E	513 541-6600
Danson Inc	Cincinnati (G-3462)	C	513 948-0066
Darke County Sheriffs Patrol	Greenville (G-11495)	D	937 548-3399
Deacon 10	Euclid (G-10749)	D	216 731-4000
Donty Horton HM Care Dhhc LLC	Cincinnati (G-3499)	E	513 463-3442
Dunbar Armored Inc	Cincinnati (G-3512)	E	513 381-8000
Dunbar Armored Inc	Columbus (G-7551)	E	614 475-1969
Dunbar Armored Inc	Cleveland (G-5512)	E	216 642-5700
Dusk To Dawn Protective Svcs	Massillon (G-13802)	E	330 837-9992
Elite Isg	Dayton (G-9521)	E	937 668-6858
Firelands Security Services	Sandusky (G-16759)	E	419 627-0562
G4s Secure Solutions (usa)	Cincinnati (G-3659)	C	513 874-0941
Garda CL Great Lakes Inc	Columbus (G-7726)		614 863-4044
Garda CL Great Lakes Inc	Toledo (G-17907)	E	419 385-2411
Garda CL Great Lakes Inc	Columbus (G-7727)	B	561 939-7000
Garda CL Technical Svcs Inc	Moraine (G-14788)	E	937 294-4099
Guardsmark LLC	Cincinnati (G-3718)		513 851-5523
Guardsmark LLC	Lima (G-12789)	E	419 229-9300
Highway Patrol	Lucasville (G-13181)		740 354-2888
Infinite SEC Solutions LLC	Toledo (G-17973)	E	419 720-5678
Info Trak Incorporated	Mansfield (G-13312)	E	419 747-9296
Jefferson Invstgtors Scurities	Steubenville (G-17323)	D	740 283-3681
Job 1 USA	Toledo (G-17985)	D	419 255-5005
Key II Security Inc	Troy (G-18360)		937 339-8530
Kreller Bus Info Group Inc	Cincinnati (G-3945)		513 723-8900
Marshall & Associates Inc	Loveland (G-13144)		513 683-6396
McKeen Security Inc	Saint Clairsville (G-16644)	D	740 699-1301
Merchants Scrty Srvc of Dayton	Dayton (G-9720)	B	937 256-9373
Metro Safety and Security LLC	Columbus (G-8154)	D	614 792-2770
Metropolitan Security Svcs Inc	Cleveland (G-6044)	A	216 298-4076
Metropolitan Security Svcs Inc	Akron (G-343)	B	330 253-6459
Moonlight Security Inc	Moraine (G-14809)	D	937 252-1600
NASA-Trmi Group Inc	Dayton (G-9767)	D	937 387-6517
National Alliance SEC Agcy Inc	Dayton (G-9768)		937 387-6517
Official Investigations Inc	Cincinnati (G-4200)	D	844 263-3424
Ohio Entertainment Security	South Vienna (G-17100)	D	937 325-7216
Ohio Support Services Corp	Columbus (G-8448)	C	614 443-0291
Patrol Urban Services LLC	Westerville (G-19436)	E	614 620-4672
Pennington International Inc	Cincinnati (G-4276)	E	513 631-2130
Pls Protective Services	Cincinnati (G-4306)	E	513 521-3581
Public Safety Ohio Department	Mount Gilead (G-14863)	E	419 768-3955
R C Enterprises Inc	Youngstown (G-20339)	D	330 782-2111
R-Cap Security LLC	Cleveland (G-6341)	C	216 761-6355
Rmi International Inc	Marysville (G-13647)	D	937 642-5032
Rumpf Corporation	Toledo (G-18167)	E	419 255-5005
Ryno 24 Inc	Willoughby (G-19711)	E	440 946-7700
Safeguard Properties LLC	Cleveland (G-6433)	A	216 739-2900
Sam-Tom Inc	Cleveland (G-6441)	C	216 426-7752
Securitas SEC Svcs USA Inc	Cleveland (G-6461)	C	216 431-3139
Securitas SEC Svcs USA Inc	Cincinnati (G-4488)	D	513 639-7615
Securitas SEC Svcs USA Inc	Grove City (G-11597)	C	614 871-6051
Securitas SEC Svcs USA Inc	Cleveland (G-6462)	A	440 887-6800
Securitas SEC Svcs USA Inc	Cleveland (G-6463)	C	216 503-2021
Security Hut Inc	Lakewood (G-12500)	C	216 226-0461
Seven Secured Inc	Strongsville (G-17505)	E	281 362-2887
Shane Security Services Inc	Poland (G-16226)	D	330 757-4001
Shield Security Service	Hudson (G-12144)		330 650-2001
St Moritz Security Svcs Inc	Youngstown (G-20381)	D	330 270-5922

St Moritz Security Svcs Inc ....E 614 351-8798
Worthington *(G-19999)*

Start-Black Servicesjv LLC ....D 740 598-4891
Mingo Junction *(G-14657)*

Sterling Infosystems Inc ....E 216 685-7600
Independence *(G-12262)*

Tenable Protective Svcs Inc ....A 216 361-0002
Cleveland *(G-6581)*

Tenable Protective Svcs Inc ....A 513 741-3560
Cincinnati *(G-4634)*

US Protection Service LLC ....D 513 422-7910
Cincinnati *(G-4796)*

US Security Associates Inc ....C 513 381-7033
Cincinnati *(G-4797)*

US Security Associates Inc ....C 937 454-9035
Vandalia *(G-18705)*

US Security Holdings Inc ....D 614 488-6110
Columbus *(G-8925)*

Veteran Security Patrol Co ....E 937 222-7333
Dayton *(G-9971)*

Veteran Security Patrol Co ....C 513 381-4482
Cincinnati *(G-4811)*

Whittguard Security Services ....C 440 288-7233
Avon *(G-918)*

Willo Security Inc ....C 614 481-9456
Columbus *(G-8998)*

Willo Security Inc ....E 440 953-9191
Willoughby *(G-19723)*

7382 Security Systems Svcs

ABC Fire Inc ....E 440 237-6677
North Royalton *(G-15480)*

ADT Security ....D 440 397-5751
Strongsville *(G-17440)*

American Svcs & Protection LLC ....D 614 884-0177
Columbus *(G-7009)*

Anderson Security Inc ....D 937 294-1478
Moraine *(G-14749)*

Area Wide Protective Inc ....E 513 321-9889
Fairfield *(G-10820)*

Bass Security Services Inc ....D 216 755-1200
Bedford Heights *(G-1347)*

Brawnstone Security LLC ....D 330 800-9006
Canton *(G-2268)*

Brentley Institute Inc ....E 216 225-0087
Cleveland *(G-5137)*

Bureau Workers Compensation ....E 614 466-5109
Pickerington *(G-16088)*

D B A Inc ....E 513 541-6600
Cincinnati *(G-3454)*

Electra Sound Inc ....C 216 433-1050
Cleveland *(G-5531)*

G4s Secure Solutions (usa) ....C 614 322-5100
Columbus *(G-7722)*

GA Business Purchaser LLC ....D 419 255-8400
Toledo *(G-17905)*

Gene Ptacek Son Fire Eqp Inc ....E 216 651-8300
Cleveland *(G-5666)*

Gillmore Security Systems Inc ....E 440 232-1000
Cleveland *(G-5672)*

Guardian Protection Svcs Inc ....D 513 422-5319
West Chester *(G-19085)*

Guardian Protection Svcs Inc ....E 330 797-1570
Youngstown *(G-20211)*

Habitec Security Inc ....D 419 537-6768
Holland *(G-12025)*

Henley & Assoc SEC Group LLC ....E 614 378-3727
Blacklick *(G-1507)*

Honeywell International Inc ....E 614 717-2270
Columbus *(G-7858)*

Integrated Protection Svcs Inc ....D 513 631-5505
Cincinnati *(G-3827)*

▲ **Jenne Inc** ....C 440 835-0040
Avon *(G-900)*

Johnson Cntrls SEC Sltions LLC ....C 330 497-0850
Canton *(G-2419)*

Johnson Cntrls SEC Sltions LLC ....D 440 262-1084
Brecksville *(G-1830)*

Johnson Cntrls SEC Sltions LLC ....C 561 988-3600
Dublin *(G-10380)*

Johnson Cntrls SEC Sltions LLC ....E 513 277-4966
Cincinnati *(G-3880)*

Johnson Cntrls SEC Sltions LLC ....E 419 243-8400
Maumee *(G-13931)*

Koorsen Fire & Security Inc ....E 937 324-9405
Vandalia *(G-18687)*

Kst Security Inc ....E 614 878-2228
Columbus *(G-8017)*

Macair Aviation LLC ....E 937 347-1302
Xenia *(G-20069)*

Metro Safety and Security LLC ....D 614 792-2770
Columbus *(G-8154)*

Mills Security Alarm Systems ....E 513 921-4600
Cincinnati *(G-4101)*

Northwestern Ohio SEC Systems ....E 419 227-1655
Lima *(G-12845)*

OGara Group Inc ....D 513 338-0660
Cincinnati *(G-4201)*

Ohio Valley Integration Svcs ....E 937 492-0008
Sidney *(G-16946)*

Protech Security Inc ....E 330 499-3555
Canton *(G-2496)*

Research & Investigation Assoc ....E 419 526-1299
Mansfield *(G-13355)*

Safe-N-Sound Security Inc ....D 330 491-1148
Millersburg *(G-14621)*

Safeguard Properties LLC ....A 216 739-2900
Cleveland *(G-6433)*

Securestate LLC ....E 216 927-0115
Cleveland *(G-6460)*

Securitas Electronic SEC Inc ....D 855 331-0359
Uniontown *(G-18539)*

Securitas SEC Svcs USA Inc ....C 937 224-7432
Dayton *(G-9873)*

Security Investments LLC ....D 614 441-4601
Westerville *(G-19443)*

Shiver Security Systems Inc ....E 513 719-4000
Mason *(G-13760)*

State Alarm Inc ....E 330 726-8111
Youngstown *(G-20382)*

Surmount Solutions Group LLC ....E 937 842-5780
Lakeview *(G-12468)*

United States Protective ....E 216 475-8550
Independence *(G-12271)*

Universal Green Energy Solutio ....E 844 723-7768
Reynoldsburg *(G-16487)*

Vector Security Inc ....E 440 466-7233
Geneva *(G-11372)*

Vector Security Inc ....E 330 726-9841
Boardman *(G-1745)*

Vigilant Defense ....E 513 309-0672
West Chester *(G-19180)*

Whitestone Group Inc ....B 614 501-7007
Columbus *(G-8990)*

Wj Service Co Inc ....E 330 372-5040
Warren *(G-18928)*

Xentry Systems Integration LLC ....E 614 452-7300
Columbus *(G-9013)*

7383 News Syndicates

Associated Press ....E 614 885-3444
Columbus *(G-7056)*

Ohio News Network ....D 614 460-3700
Columbus *(G-8362)*

7384 Photofinishing Labs

Buckeye Prof Imaging Inc ....E 800 433-1292
Canton *(G-2273)*

Buehler Food Markets Inc ....C 330 364-3079
Dover *(G-10179)*

Click Camera & Video ....E 937 435-3072
Miamisburg *(G-14285)*

Digico Imaging Inc ....D 614 239-5200
Columbus *(G-7519)*

Discount Drug Mart Inc ....E 330 343-7700
Dover *(G-10183)*

Fred W Albrecht Grocery Co ....C 330 645-6222
Coventry Township *(G-9124)*

Fred W Albrecht Grocery Co ....C 330 666-6781
Akron *(G-230)*

Kroger Co ....C 937 294-7210
Dayton *(G-9666)*

Marc Glassman Inc ....C 330 995-9246
Aurora *(G-845)*

Marco Photo Service Inc ....D 419 529-9010
Ontario *(G-15700)*

Solar Imaging LLC ....E 614 626-8536
Gahanna *(G-11268)*

Target Stores Inc ....C 614 279-4224
Columbus *(G-8822)*

Vista Color Imaging Inc ....E 216 651-2830
Brooklyn Heights *(G-1932)*

Walgreen Co ....E 937 433-5314
Dayton *(G-9981)*

Walgreen Co ....E 614 236-8622
Columbus *(G-8961)*

Walgreen Co ....E 330 677-5650
Kent *(G-12404)*

Walgreen Co ....E 330 745-2674
Barberton *(G-984)*

Walgreen Co ....E 937 396-1358
Kettering *(G-12438)*

Walgreen Co ....E 937 781-9561
Dayton *(G-9982)*

Walgreen Co ....E 330 733-4237
Akron *(G-503)*

Walgreen Co ....E 937 277-6022
Dayton *(G-9983)*

Walgreen Co ....E 740 368-9380
Delaware *(G-10134)*

Walgreen Co ....E 614 336-0431
Dublin *(G-10487)*

Walgreen Co ....E 937 859-3879
Miamisburg *(G-14366)*

Walgreen Co ....E 330 928-5444
Cuyahoga Falls *(G-9235)*

7389 Business Svcs, NEC

1 Financial Corporation ....E 513 936-1400
Blue Ash *(G-1520)*

3-D Technical Services Company ....E 937 746-2901
Franklin *(G-11147)*

6200 Rockside LLC ....D 216 642-8004
Cleveland *(G-4927)*

A-1 Bail Bonds Inc ....E 937 372-2400
Xenia *(G-20039)*

A2z Field Services LLC ....C 614 873-0211
Plain City *(G-16179)*

AA Fire Protection LLC ....E 440 327-0060
Elyria *(G-10590)*

Abco Fire LLC ....D 216 433-7200
Cleveland *(G-4945)*

Abco Fire LLC ....E 800 875-7200
Cincinnati *(G-2960)*

▼ **Abco Holdings LLC** ....D 216 433-7200
Cleveland *(G-4946)*

Ability Works Inc ....C 419 626-1048
Sandusky *(G-16723)*

Abraham Ford LLC ....E 440 233-7402
Elyria *(G-10592)*

Academy Answering Service Inc ....E 440 442-8500
Cleveland *(G-4950)*

Accel Inc ....C 614 656-1100
New Albany *(G-14971)*

Accurate Inventory and C ....B 800 777-9414
Columbus *(G-6936)*

Ace Assembly Packaging Inc ....E 330 866-9117
Waynesburg *(G-18979)*

Acuren Inspection Inc ....E 937 228-9729
Dayton *(G-9307)*

Acxiom Info SEC Svcs Inc ....B 216 685-7600
Independence *(G-12180)*

▼ **Advanced Specialty Products** ....D 419 882-6528
Bowling Green *(G-1756)*

Advanced Translation/Cnsltng ....E 440 716-0820
Westlake *(G-19455)*

Adventure Cmbat Operations LLC ....E 330 818-1029
Canton *(G-2228)*

Aecom Energy & Cnstr Inc ....A 216 523-5600
Cleveland *(G-4963)*

Aecom Energy & Cnstr Inc ....A 216 523-5600
Cleveland *(G-4964)*

Aerocon Photogrammetric Svcs ....E 440 946-6277
Willoughby *(G-19641)*

Affinity Disp Expositions Inc ....C 513 771-2339
Cincinnati *(G-2977)*

◆ **Affinity Specialty Apparel Inc** ....D 866 548-8434
Fairborn *(G-10784)*

Akron-Summit Convention ....E 330 374-7560
Akron *(G-62)*

Al-Mar Lanes ....E 419 352-4637
Bowling Green *(G-1757)*

Alliance Data Systems Corp ....B 614 729-5000
Westerville *(G-19362)*

Alliance Data Systems Corp ....C 614 729-5800
Reynoldsburg *(G-16425)*

Allied Infotech Corporation ....D 330 745-8529
Akron *(G-68)*

Allstate Insurance Company ....E 330 650-2917
Hudson *(G-12102)*

Almost Family Inc ....E 513 662-3400
Cincinnati *(G-2993)*

Alorica Customer Care Inc ....A 216 525-3311
Cleveland *(G-4995)*

Alternative Services Inc ....E 419 861-2121
Holland *(G-12007)*

American Crane Inc ....E 614 496-2268
Reynoldsburg *(G-16426)*

American Publishers LLC ....D 419 626-0623
Huron *(G-12160)*

Employee Codes: A=Over 500 employees, B=251-500
C=101-250, D=51-100, E=25-50
2018 Harris Ohio
Services Directory
1003

American Signature Inc........C....... 614 449-6107
Columbus (G-7007)
Ameridial Inc........B....... 800 445-7128
Canton (G-2240)
Ameridial Inc........D....... 330 479-8044
North Canton (G-15324)
Ameridial Inc........B....... 330 497-4888
North Canton (G-15325)
Ameridial Inc........D....... 330 339-7222
New Philadelphia (G-15082)
Ameridial Inc........D....... 330 868-2000
Minerva (G-14641)
▲ Amos Media Company........B....... 937 498-2111
Sidney (G-16912)
Ampersand Group LLC........E....... 330 379-0044
Akron (G-75)
Another Chance Inc........E....... 614 868-3541
Pickerington (G-16084)
Answering Service Inc........E....... 440 473-1200
Cleveland (G-5041)
Argus International Inc........E....... 513 852-1010
Cincinnati (G-3046)
ARS Ohio LLC........E....... 513 327-7645
Cincinnati (G-3049)
▲ Asm International........D....... 440 338-5151
Novelty (G-15601)
Auction Services Inc........A....... 614 497-2000
Obetz (G-15663)
Avery Dennison Corporation........C....... 440 534-6000
Mentor (G-14145)
Baker Bnngson Rlty Auctioneers........E....... 419 547-7777
Clyde (G-6810)
Banc Certified Merch Svcs LLC........E....... 614 850-2740
Hilliard (G-11880)
Banc One Services Corporation........A....... 614 248-5800
Columbus (G-6869)
▲ Baumfolder Corporation........D....... 937 492-1281
Sidney (G-16914)
Bay Mechanical & Elec Corp........D....... 440 282-6816
Lorain (G-13017)
Bbs & Associates Inc........E....... 330 665-5227
Akron (G-92)
Bdo Usa LLP........E....... 513 592-2400
Cincinnati (G-3085)
BDS Packaging Inc........D....... 937 643-0530
Moraine (G-14752)
Beheydts Auto Wrecking........E....... 330 658-6109
Doylestown (G-10223)
Benchmark Craftsman Inc........E....... 330 975-4214
Seville (G-16837)
Benchmark National Corporation........E....... 419 660-1100
Bellevue (G-1406)
Bermex Inc........B....... 330 945-7500
Akron (G-98)
Board of Dir of Wittenbe........D....... 937 327-6231
Springfield (G-17151)
Boardman Molded Intl LLC........C....... 330 788-2400
Youngstown (G-20120)
Bollin & Sons Inc........E....... 419 693-6573
Toledo (G-17776)
Bookmasters Inc........C....... 419 281-1802
Ashland (G-665)
Bowling Green State Univ Fdn........E....... 419 372-2551
Bowling Green (G-1766)
Boyd Property Group LLC........E....... 614 725-5228
Columbus (G-7126)
Bpf Enterprises Ltd........D....... 419 855-2545
Maumee (G-13888)
▲ Bron-Shoe Company........E....... 614 252-0967
Columbus (G-7150)
Bst & G Joint Fire District........E....... 740 965-3841
Sunbury (G-17551)
Buckeye Pool Inc........E....... 937 434-7916
Dayton (G-9370)
Burgess & Niple / Heapy Engine........D....... 614 459-2050
Columbus (G-7170)
Business Backer LLC........E....... 513 792-6866
Cincinnati (G-3155)
Calvin Lanier........E....... 937 952-4221
Dayton (G-9377)
Camargo Rental Center Inc........E....... 513 271-6510
Cincinnati (G-3170)
Canon Solutions America Inc........D....... 216 446-3830
Independence (G-12193)
Canton Inventory Service........E....... 330 453-1633
Canton (G-2290)
Canton S-Group Ltd........B....... 419 625-7003
Sandusky (G-16732)
Cardio Partners Inc........D....... 614 760-5038
Dublin (G-10278)
Carol Reese........E....... 513 347-0252
Cincinnati (G-3187)
Cass Information Systems Inc........C....... 614 766-2277
Columbus (G-7207)
Catsi Inc........E....... 740 574-8417
Wheelersburg (G-19572)
Cbiz Inc........C....... 216 447-9000
Cleveland (G-5196)
Cdc Technologies Inc........D....... 937 886-9713
Dayton (G-9392)
Cdd LLC........B....... 905 829-2794
Mason (G-13673)
Cec Combustion Safety LLC........E....... 216 749-2992
Brookpark (G-1938)
Ceiba Enterprises Incorporated........C....... 614 818-3220
Westerville (G-19376)
Cgh-Global Security LLC........E....... 800 376-0655
Cincinnati (G-3224)
Chapel Hl Chrstn Schl Endwment........D....... 330 929-1901
Cuyahoga Falls (G-9171)
Chardon Laboratories Inc........E....... 614 860-1000
Reynoldsburg (G-16438)
Christ Hospital........C....... 513 564-1340
Cincinnati (G-3263)
Chute Gerdeman Inc........D....... 614 469-1001
Columbus (G-7271)
Cincilingua Inc........E....... 513 721-8782
Cincinnati (G-3277)
Cincinnati Financial Corp........A....... 513 870-2000
Fairfield (G-10833)
Cincinnati Indus Actoneers Inc........E....... 513 241-9701
Cincinnati (G-3311)
Cintas Corporation No 2........D....... 440 838-8611
Cleveland (G-5240)
CIP International Inc........D....... 513 874-9925
West Chester (G-19041)
Citicorp Credit Services Inc........B....... 212 559-1000
Columbus (G-7277)
Citigroup Inc........B....... 740 548-0594
Delaware (G-10080)
Citizens Financial Svcs Inc........D....... 513 385-3200
Cincinnati (G-3356)
City of Cleveland........E....... 216 664-2620
Cleveland (G-5255)
City of Cleveland........E....... 216 664-3922
Cleveland (G-5258)
City of North Olmsted........E....... 440 777-0678
North Olmsted (G-15417)
City of Solon........E....... 440 248-6939
Solon (G-16992)
City of Wooster........E....... 330 263-5266
Wooster (G-19845)
Clearwater Services Inc........D....... 330 836-4946
Akron (G-146)
Cleveland Clinic Foundation........B....... 216 444-5000
Cleveland (G-5299)
Clgt Solutions LLC........E....... 740 920-4795
Granville (G-11462)
Clovernook Center For The Bli........C....... 513 522-3860
Cincinnati (G-3370)
Clovvr LLC........E....... 740 653-2224
Columbus (G-7308)
Coast To Coast Studios LLC........E....... 614 861-9800
Blacklick (G-1505)
Colerain Volunteer Fire Co........E....... 740 738-0735
Dillonvale (G-10174)
Collaborative Inc........E....... 419 242-7405
Toledo (G-17819)
Collections Acquisition Co LLC........C....... 614 944-5788
Columbus (G-7319)
Columbus Bride........D....... 614 888-4567
Columbus (G-7334)
Comenity Servicing LLC........C....... 614 729-4000
Columbus (G-7397)
Compliant Healthcare Tech LLC........E....... 216 255-9607
Cleveland (G-5389)
Continental Business Services........E....... 614 224-4534
Columbus (G-7427)
Controls Inc........E....... 330 239-4345
Medina (G-14051)
Convention & Vistors Bureau of........E....... 216 875-6603
Cleveland (G-5405)
Convergys Cstmer MGT Group Inc........B....... 513 723-6104
Cincinnati (G-3418)
Conversa Language Center Inc........E....... 513 651-5679
Cincinnati (G-3420)
▲ Conversion Tech Intl Inc........E....... 419 924-5566
West Unity (G-19280)
Convivo Network LLC........E....... 216 631-9000
Cleveland (G-5406)
Corporate Fin Assoc of Clumbus........D....... 614 457-9219
Columbus (G-7444)
Corporate Support Inc........E....... 419 221-3838
Lima (G-12761)
Corporate United Inc........E....... 440 895-0938
Westlake (G-19480)
Covelli Enterprises Inc........D....... 614 889-7802
Dublin (G-10311)
Crain Communications Inc........D....... 330 836-9180
Akron (G-175)
Crane 1 Services Inc........E....... 937 704-9900
Miamisburg (G-14289)
Credit First National Assn........B....... 216 362-5300
Cleveland (G-5434)
Crescent Park Corporation........C....... 513 759-7000
West Chester (G-19059)
Cronins Inc........E....... 513 851-5900
Cincinnati (G-3440)
Custom Pkg & Inspecting Inc........E....... 330 399-8961
Warren (G-18845)
Custom Products Corporation........D....... 440 528-7100
Solon (G-16999)
Custom-Pak Inc........D....... 330 725-0800
Medina (G-14056)
Cwm Envronmental Cleveland LLC........E....... 216 663-0808
Cleveland (G-5458)
D H Packaging Co........A....... 513 791-2022
Cincinnati (G-3455)
Dash Logistics Inc........E....... 937 382-9110
Wilmington (G-19760)
Dayton Cvb........E....... 937 226-8211
Dayton (G-9468)
Dayton Digital Media Inc........E....... 937 223-8335
Dayton (G-9469)
Definitive Solutions Co Inc........D....... 513 719-9100
Cincinnati (G-3479)
Dennis & Carol Liederbach........E....... 256 582-6200
Northfield (G-15513)
Design Central Inc........E....... 614 890-0202
Columbus (G-7510)
Dfs Corporate Services LLC........B....... 614 777-7020
Hilliard (G-11895)
Dialamerica Marketing Inc........C....... 330 836-5293
Fairlawn (G-10945)
Dialamerica Marketing Inc........C....... 440 234-4410
Cleveland (G-5481)
Division 7 Inc........E....... 740 965-1970
Galena (G-11281)
Dlr Group Inc........D....... 216 522-1350
Cleveland (G-5495)
DMR Management Inc........E....... 513 771-1700
Avon Lake (G-928)
Document Concepts Inc........E....... 330 575-5685
North Canton (G-15333)
Domino Foods Inc........D....... 216 432-3222
Cleveland (G-5499)
Douglas R Denny........E....... 216 236-2400
Independence (G-12205)
Douglas Webb & Associates........D....... 614 873-9830
Plain City (G-16188)
Dreier & Maller Inc........E....... 614 575-0065
Reynoldsburg (G-16448)
Dwellworks LLC........D....... 216 682-4200
Cleveland (G-5513)
E & A Pedco Services Inc........D....... 513 782-4920
Cincinnati (G-3519)
E T Financial Service Inc........E....... 937 716-1726
Trotwood (G-18346)
Ebsco Industries Inc........B....... 330 478-0281
Canton (G-2349)
▲ Elder-Beerman Stores Corp........A....... 937 296-2700
Moraine (G-14780)
Electrovations Inc........E....... 330 274-3558
Aurora (G-837)
Elevar Design Group Inc........E....... 513 721-0600
Cincinnati (G-3550)
Elite Enclosure Company LLC........E....... 937 492-3548
Sidney (G-16931)
Emco Usa LLC........E....... 740 588-1722
Zanesville (G-20474)
Emersion Design LLC........E....... 513 841-9100
Cincinnati (G-3553)
Empire One LLC........E....... 330 628-9310
Mogadore (G-14676)
Employeescreeniq Inc........D....... 216 514-2800
Independence (G-12207)
Essilor of America Inc........C....... 614 492-0888
Groveport (G-11637)
Evanston Bulldogs Youth Footba........E....... 513 254-9500
Cincinnati (G-3579)

Eventions Ltd E 216 952-9898
Cleveland *(G-5556)*
Evolution Crtive Solutions LLC E 513 681-4450
Cincinnati *(G-3584)*
Exhibitpro Inc E 614 885-9541
New Albany *(G-14985)*
Express Packaging Ohio Inc A 740 498-4700
Newcomerstown *(G-15268)*
Facts Management Company E 440 892-4272
Westlake *(G-19483)*
Ferguson Hills Inc D 513 539-4497
Dayton *(G-9546)*
Filterfresh Coffee Service Inc E 513 681-8911
West Chester *(G-19201)*
Finastra USA Corporation E 937 435-2335
Miamisburg *(G-14302)*
▲ **First Choice Packaging Inc** C 419 333-4100
Fremont *(G-11198)*
Flamos Enterprises Inc E 330 478-0009
Canton *(G-2369)*
Flight Services & Systems Inc C 216 328-0090
Cleveland *(G-5609)*
Fnb Inc E 740 922-2532
Dennison *(G-10164)*
FNB Corporation D 330 425-1818
Twinsburg *(G-18416)*
▼ **Fox International Limited Inc** E 216 454-1001
Beachwood *(G-1080)*
Frankes Unlimited Inc E 937 642-0706
Marysville *(G-13619)*
Freudenberg-Nok General Partnr B 419 499-2502
Milan *(G-14494)*
Future Poly Tech Inc E 614 942-1209
Columbus *(G-7716)*
G Herschman Architects Inc D 216 223-3200
Cleveland *(G-5645)*
G Robert Toney & Assoc Inc E 954 791-9601
Cleveland *(G-5648)*
Gabriel Partners LLC E 216 771-1250
Cleveland *(G-5650)*
Garda CL Great Lakes Inc B 561 939-7000
Columbus *(G-7727)*
Gateway Distribution Inc E 513 891-4477
Cincinnati *(G-3664)*
General Electric Company A 937 534-6920
Dayton *(G-9570)*
General Theming Contrs LLC C 614 252-6342
Columbus *(G-7736)*
Genesis Respiratory Svcs Inc E 740 456-4363
Athens *(G-789)*
Geneva Liberty Steel Ltd E 330 740-0103
Youngstown *(G-20198)*
Gerdau Macsteel Atmosphere Ann D 330 478-0314
Canton *(G-2379)*
Global Spectrum D 513 419-7300
Cincinnati *(G-3680)*
Greenspace Enterprise Tech Inc E 888 309-8517
Franklin *(G-11157)*
Greentown Vlntr Fire Dept Inc E 330 494-3002
Uniontown *(G-18522)*
Guardian Water & Power Inc D 614 291-3141
Columbus *(G-7785)*
Hague Water Conditioning Inc E 614 482-8121
Groveport *(G-11642)*
Hamilton Cnty Auditor Office C 513 946-4000
Cincinnati *(G-3730)*
Hanco International D 330 456-9407
Canton *(G-2392)*
Hastings Water Works Inc E 440 832-7700
Brecksville *(G-1826)*
Haven Financial Enterprise E 800 265-2401
Cleveland *(G-5732)*
Heartland Payment Systems LLC D 513 518-6125
Loveland *(G-13130)*
High Line Corporation E 330 848-8800
Akron *(G-264)*
Hochstedler Construction Ltd E 740 427-4880
Gambier *(G-11347)*
Horter Investment MGT LLC E 513 984-9933
Cincinnati *(G-3784)*
▲ **Hrm Enterprises Inc** C 330 877-9353
Hartville *(G-11823)*
Huffy Corporation D 937 743-5011
Springboro *(G-17124)*
Human Resource Profile Inc E 513 388-4300
Cincinnati *(G-3795)*
Hunt Products Inc E 440 667-2457
Newburgh Heights *(G-15252)*
I-X Center Corporation C 216 265-2675
Cleveland *(G-5799)*
Ies Systems Inc E 330 533-6683
Canfield *(G-2196)*
Improvedge LLC E 614 793-1738
Powell *(G-16338)*
In Terminal Services Corp E 216 518-8407
Maple Heights *(G-13409)*
Incept Corporation C 330 649-8000
Canton *(G-2410)*
▲ **Independent Steel Company LLC** E 330 225-7741
Valley City *(G-18618)*
▲ **Industrial Chemical Corp** E 330 725-0800
Medina *(G-14079)*
Industrial Insul Coatings LLC E 800 506-1399
Girard *(G-11414)*
Infocision Management Corp B 330 668-1411
Akron *(G-278)*
Infocision Management Corp B 330 726-0872
Youngstown *(G-20234)*
Infocision Management Corp D 419 529-8685
Mansfield *(G-13313)*
Infocision Management Corp C 330 668-6615
Akron *(G-279)*
Infocision Management Corp B 330 544-1400
Youngstown *(G-20235)*
Infoverity LLC E 614 327-5173
Dublin *(G-10375)*
Innovairre Communications LLC D 330 869-8500
Fairlawn *(G-10957)*
Inquiry Systems Inc E 614 464-3800
Columbus *(G-7904)*
Inspection Group Incorporated E 614 891-3606
Westerville *(G-19316)*
Interbrand Design Forum Inc C 937 439-4400
Cincinnati *(G-3834)*
Interior Supply Cincinnati LLC E 614 424-6611
Columbus *(G-7915)*
◆ **Interscope Manufacturing Inc** E 513 423-8866
Middletown *(G-14429)*
J & B Systems Company Inc C 513 732-2000
Batavia *(G-1017)*
J Cherie LLC E 216 453-1051
Shaker Heights *(G-16862)*
J Schoen Enterprises Inc E 419 536-0970
Toledo *(G-17981)*
Jacqueline Kumi-Sakyi D 740 282-5955
Steubenville *(G-17322)*
James Ray Lozier E 419 884-2656
Mansfield *(G-13316)*
Jason Wilson E 937 604-8209
Tipp City *(G-17720)*
Jbjs Acquisitions LLC E 513 769-0393
Cincinnati *(G-3864)*
Jean R Wagner D 614 430-0065
Westerville *(G-19317)*
JLW Marketing LLC D 513 260-8418
Cincinnati *(G-3874)*
John Stewart Company D 513 703-5412
Cincinnati *(G-3878)*
Jones Group Interiors Inc E 330 253-9180
Akron *(G-297)*
◆ **Jpmorgan Chase Bank Nat Assn** A 614 436-3055
Columbus *(G-6888)*
Jrb Industries LLC E 567 825-7022
Greenville *(G-11511)*
Juice Technologies Inc E 800 518-5576
Columbus *(G-7957)*
K & R Distributors Inc E 937 864-5495
Fairborn *(G-10799)*
Karlsberger Companies C 614 461-9500
Columbus *(G-7966)*
Keller Logistics Group Inc E 866 276-9486
Defiance *(G-10040)*
▼ **Kent Adhesive Products Co** D 330 678-1626
Kent *(G-12376)*
King Tut Logistics LLC E 614 538-0509
Columbus *(G-7994)*
Knisely Inc D 330 343-5812
Dover *(G-10195)*
Koorsen Fire & Security Inc E 937 324-9405
Vandalia *(G-18687)*
Kramer & Kramer Inc E 937 456-1101
Eaton *(G-10563)*
Kucera International Inc D 440 975-4230
Willoughby *(G-19678)*
Landmark America Inc E 330 372-6800
Warren *(G-18873)*
Laser Craft Inc E 440 327-4300
North Ridgeville *(G-15467)*
Laserflex Corporation D 614 850-9600
Hilliard *(G-11920)*
Lawnview Industries Inc C 937 653-5217
Urbana *(G-18593)*
Legacy Industrial Services LLC E 606 584-8953
Ripley *(G-16547)*
Legend Equities Corporation D 216 741-3113
Independence *(G-12223)*
Liberty Healthshare Inc E 855 585-4237
Canton *(G-2436)*
Lighthouse Youth Services Inc D 513 861-1111
Cincinnati *(G-3981)*
Limitless Solutions Inc E 614 577-1550
Columbus *(G-8068)*
Lindsey Cnstr & Design Inc E 330 785-9931
Akron *(G-321)*
Lions Gate SEC Solutions Inc E 440 539-8382
Euclid *(G-10767)*
Logistics Inc E 419 478-1514
Toledo *(G-18007)*
Loth Inc C 513 554-4900
Cincinnati *(G-3995)*
M A Folkes Company Inc E 513 785-4200
Hamilton *(G-11756)*
M P & A Fibers Inc E 440 926-1074
Grafton *(G-11442)*
Macys Cr & Customer Svcs Inc D 513 881-9950
West Chester *(G-19114)*
Macys Cr & Customer Svcs Inc A 513 398-5221
Mason *(G-13734)*
Madison Cnty Lndon Cy Hlth Dst E 740 852-3065
London *(G-12999)*
Marcums Don Pool Care Inc E 513 561-7050
Cincinnati *(G-4020)*
Matvest Inc E 614 487-8720
Columbus *(G-8130)*
Maximum Communications Inc E 513 489-3414
Cincinnati *(G-4031)*
McConnell Excavating Ltd E 440 774-4578
Oberlin *(G-15649)*
McDonalds 3490 E 330 762-7747
Akron *(G-333)*
Medigistics Inc D 614 430-5700
Columbus *(G-8144)*
Megacity Fire Protection Inc E 937 335-0775
Dayton *(G-9717)*
Merchant Data Service Inc C 937 847-6585
Miamisburg *(G-14318)*
Metal Shredders Inc E 937 866-0777
Miamisburg *(G-14320)*
Metropolitan Pool Service Co E 216 741-9451
Parma *(G-15910)*
Metzenbaum Sheltered Inds C 440 729-1919
Chesterland *(G-2800)*
Miami University D 513 529-1230
Oxford *(G-15823)*
Miami University D 513 529-6911
Oxford *(G-15821)*
Michael Schuster Associates E 513 241-5666
Cincinnati *(G-4089)*
Micro Products Co Inc D 440 943-0258
Willoughby Hills *(G-19732)*
Microanalysis Society Inc B 614 256-8063
Hilliard *(G-11934)*
Midwest Liquidators Inc E 614 433-7355
Worthington *(G-19977)*
▲ **Midwest Tape LLC** B 419 868-9370
Holland *(G-12038)*
Miencorp Inc E 330 978-8511
Niles *(G-15296)*
Military Resources LLC E 330 263-1040
Wooster *(G-19888)*
▼ **Military Resources LLC** D 330 309-9970
Wooster *(G-19889)*
Millennium Cpitl Recovery Corp E 330 528-1450
Hudson *(G-12135)*
Miller Products Inc E 330 238-4200
Alliance *(G-549)*
Mission Essntial Personnel LLC C 614 416-2345
New Albany *(G-14992)*
Mistras Group Inc E 419 227-4100
Lima *(G-12841)*
Mount Auburn Community Hdo D 513 659-4514
Cincinnati *(G-4124)*
Mroeki Inc C 330 318-3926
Youngstown *(G-20290)*
Mt Hope Auction Inc E 330 674-6188
Mount Hope *(G-14866)*
Mt Washington Care Center Inc C 513 231-4561
Cincinnati *(G-4130)*
N Safe Sound Security Inc E 888 317-7233
Millersburg *(G-14614)*

S I C

Employee Codes: A=Over 500 employees, B=251-500
C=101-250, D=51-100, E=25-50
2018 Harris Ohio
Services Directory
1005

73 BUSINESS SERVICES

SIC SECTION

Company	Code	Phone
National Board of Boiler	D	614 888-8320
Columbus (G-8214)		
National Weather Service	E	937 383-0031
Wilmington (G-19774)		
Nationwide General Insur Co	D	614 249-7111
Columbus (G-8243)		
Neighborcare Inc	A	513 719-2600
Cincinnati (G-4151)		
Nelson Packaging Company Inc	D	419 229-3471
Lima (G-12842)		
Netrada North America LLC	E	866 345-5835
West Chester (G-19218)		
▲ New Path International LLC	E	614 410-3974
Powell (G-16344)		
Nexxtshow Exposition Svcs LLC		877 836-3131
Cincinnati (G-4166)		
Ngm Inc	E	513 821-7363
Cincinnati (G-4168)		
North Bay Construction Inc	E	440 835-1898
Westlake (G-19522)		
Notoweega Nation Inc	D	740 777-1480
Logan (G-12986)		
Npc Group Inc	A	312 627-6000
Symmes Twp (G-17629)		
Nucentury Textile Services LLC	D	419 241-2267
Toledo (G-18097)		
Official Investigations Inc	D	844 263-3424
Cincinnati (G-4200)		
Ohio Design Centre	D	216 831-1245
Beachwood (G-1111)		
Ohio Fabricators Inc	E	216 391-2400
Cleveland (G-6190)		
▲ Ohio Gasket and Shim Co Inc	E	330 630-0626
Akron (G-366)		
Ohio Laminating & Binding Inc	E	614 771-4868
Hilliard (G-11939)		
Ohio Metal Processing Inc	E	740 286-6457
Jackson (G-12316)		
Ohio Presbyterian Rtr Svcs	E	614 888-7800
Columbus (G-8369)		
Ohio Steel Slitters Inc	E	330 477-6741
Canton (G-2486)		
Ohio-Kentucky Steel Corp	E	937 743-4600
Franklin (G-11161)		
Orbit Industries Inc	D	440 243-3311
Cleveland (G-6211)		
OReilly Automotive Inc	D	216 642-7591
Seven Hills (G-16835)		
OReilly Automotive Inc	D	213 332-0427
Maple Heights (G-13412)		
OReilly Automotive Inc	D	330 238-1416
Alliance (G-551)		
Oriana House Inc	A	330 374-9610
Akron (G-372)		
P C Workshop Inc		419 399-4805
Paulding (G-15932)		
P3 Infrastructure Inc	A	330 686-1129
Stow (G-17385)		
Packship Usa Inc	D	330 682-7225
Orrville (G-15782)		
Pactiv LLC	C	614 777-4019
Columbus (G-8506)		
Pactiv LLC	C	614 771-5400
Columbus (G-8505)		
Pak Lab	B	513 735-4777
Batavia (G-1020)		
Pandora Manufacturing Llc	D	419 384-3241
Ottawa (G-15802)		
Patented Acquisition Corp	D	937 353-2299
Miamisburg (G-14332)		
Pathway House LLC	E	872 223-9797
Cleveland (G-6251)		
Pccw Teleservices (us) Inc	A	614 652-6300
Dublin (G-10424)		
Penske Logistics LLC	E	419 547-2615
Clyde (G-6819)		
Perceptionist Inc	E	614 384-7500
Columbus (G-8535)		
Perfect Cut-Off Inc	E	440 943-0000
Wickliffe (G-19611)		
Piqua Industrial Cut & Sew	E	937 773-7397
Piqua (G-16157)		
Pitney Bowes Presort Svcs Inc	E	513 860-3607
West Chester (G-19220)		
Platinum Prestige Property	E	614 705-2251
Columbus (G-8550)		
Pmwi LLC	E	614 975-5004
Hilliard (G-11943)		
Polaris Automation Inc	D	614 431-0170
Lewis Center (G-12704)		
Pollock Research & Design Inc	E	330 332-3300
Salem (G-16706)		
Popper & Associates Msrp LLC	E	614 798-8991
Dublin (G-10428)		
Precision Strip Inc	D	937 667-6255
Tipp City (G-17725)		
Precision Strip Inc	C	419 628-2343
Minster (G-14668)		
Precision Strip Inc	D	419 661-1100
Perrysburg (G-16044)		
Precision Strip Inc	D	513 423-4166
Middletown (G-14450)		
Predictive Service LLC	D	866 772-6770
Cleveland (G-6296)		
Printing Services	E	440 708-1999
Chagrin Falls (G-2729)		
Printpack Inc	C	513 891-7886
Cincinnati (G-4331)		
Priority Designs Inc	D	614 337-9979
Columbus (G-8561)		
Producers Credit Corporation	E	614 433-2150
Columbus (G-8565)		
Progressive Quality Care Inc	E	216 661-6800
Parma (G-15914)		
Project Packaging Inc	E	216 451-7878
Cleveland (G-6323)		
Promohouse Inc	E	614 324-9200
Columbus (G-8571)		
Pxp Ohio	E	614 575-4242
Reynoldsburg (G-16473)		
Quadax Inc	E	330 759-4600
Youngstown (G-20334)		
Quality Control Inspection	D	440 359-1900
Cleveland (G-6334)		
Quality Lines Inc	C	740 815-1165
Findlay (G-11078)		
Quintus Technologies LLC	E	614 891-2732
Lewis Center (G-12705)		
Quotient Technology Inc	E	513 229-8659
Mason (G-13752)		
R and J Corporation	E	440 871-6009
Westlake (G-19536)		
R D D Inc	C	216 781-5858
Cleveland (G-6339)		
R P Marketing Public Relations	E	419 241-2221
Holland (G-12050)		
R Square Inc	E	216 328-2077
Cleveland (G-6340)		
Raco Industries LLC	D	513 984-2101
Blue Ash (G-1672)		
Rainbow Flea Market Inc	E	614 291-3133
Columbus (G-8585)		
Rapid Mortgage Company	E	937 748-8888
Dayton (G-9842)		
Ray Meyer Sign Company Inc	E	513 984-5446
Loveland (G-13155)		
Rdi Corporation	D	513 524-3320
Oxford (G-15829)		
Rdl Architects Inc	E	216 752-4300
Cleveland (G-6356)		
Recording Workshop	E	740 663-1000
Chillicothe (G-2873)		
Reid Asset Management Company	E	216 642-3223
Cleveland (G-6368)		
▲ Relay Gear Ltd		888 735-2943
Columbus (G-8611)		
Reliable Polymer Services LP	E	800 321-0954
Wadsworth (G-18769)		
Reliable Rnners Curier Svc Inc	E	440 578-1011
Mentor (G-14236)		
Reliance Financial Services NA	E	419 783-8007
Defiance (G-10053)		
Relx Inc	E	937 865-6800
Miamisburg (G-14340)		
Renaissance Hotel Operating Co	A	216 696-5600
Toledo (G-18192)		
Rentokil North America Inc	E	614 837-0099
Canal Winchester (G-2168)		
Republic Telcom Worldwide LLC	D	330 244-8285
North Canton (G-15364)		
Republic Telcom Worldwide LLC	C	330 966-4586
Canton (G-2509)		
Resilience Capitl Partners LLC	A	216 292-0200
Cleveland (G-6384)		
Resource Interactive	E	614 621-2888
Columbus (G-8621)		
Return Polymers Inc	D	419 289-1998
Ashland (G-694)		
Rgis LLC	D	216 447-1744
Independence (G-12249)		
Rgis LLC	D	330 799-1566
Youngstown (G-20351)		
Rgis LLC	D	248 651-2511
Reynoldsburg (G-16477)		
Rgis LLC	D	330 896-9802
Akron (G-414)		
Rgis LLC	C	513 772-5990
Cincinnati (G-4412)		
▲ Richardson Printing Corp	D	740 373-5362
Marietta (G-13495)		
Richland Newhope Industries	E	419 774-4400
Mansfield (G-13358)		
Rite Rug Co	E	614 478-3365
Columbus (G-8632)		
River City Furniture LLC	E	513 612-7303
West Chester (G-19141)		
Riverside Medical Inc	E	513 936-5360
Cincinnati (G-4428)		
Rolling Hocevar & Associa	E	614 760-8320
Dublin (G-10443)		
Roy J Miller	E	330 674-2405
Millersburg (G-14619)		
Rush Package Delivery Inc	E	513 771-7874
Cincinnati (G-4457)		
Rush Package Delivery Inc	D	937 297-6182
Dayton (G-9859)		
Rvet Operating LLC	E	513 683-5020
Loveland (G-13157)		
S&P Data Ohio LLC	B	216 965-0018
Cleveland (G-6429)		
Safety-Kleen Systems Inc	D	740 929-3532
Hebron (G-11860)		
Samuel Steel Pickling Company	E	330 963-3777
Twinsburg (G-18467)		
Sander Woody Ford	D	513 541-5586
Cincinnati (G-4476)		
Sanese Services Inc	B	614 436-1234
Warren (G-18895)		
Sb Capital Group LLC	E	516 829-2400
Columbus (G-8691)		
Scot Industries Inc	E	330 262-7585
Wooster (G-19914)		
Screen Works Inc	E	937 264-9111
Dayton (G-9870)		
Security Check LLC	C	614 944-5788
Columbus (G-8710)		
Seifert Technologies Inc	E	330 833-2700
Massillon (G-13853)		
Service Pronet Inc	E	614 874-4300
Columbus (G-8716)		
Servicelink Field Services LLC	A	440 424-0058
Solon (G-17050)		
▲ Shamrock Companies Inc	C	440 899-9510
Westlake (G-19546)		
Shotstop Ballistics LLC	E	330 686-0020
Stow (G-17392)		
Shred-It USA LLC	E	800 697-4733
Fairfield (G-10907)		
Shredded Bedding Corporation	E	740 893-3567
Centerburg (G-2668)		
Side Effects Inc	E	937 704-9696
Franklin (G-11165)		
Sirva Inc	E	216 606-4000
Independence (G-12257)		
Sirva Relocation LLC	E	216 606-4000
Independence (G-12259)		
Skipco Financial Adjusters	D	330 854-4800
Canal Fulton (G-2146)		
Skylight Financial Group LLC	E	216 621-5680
Cleveland (G-6486)		
Snapblox Hosted Solutions LLC	E	866 524-7707
Cincinnati (G-4545)		
Snl Designs Ltd	E	440 247-2344
Chagrin Falls (G-2707)		
Solomon Lei & Associates Inc	E	419 246-6931
Toledo (G-18192)		
Solupay Consulting Inc	D	216 535-9016
Twinsburg (G-18471)		
Sonoco Products Company	E	513 381-2088
Blue Ash (G-1690)		
Sonoco Prtective Solutions Inc	E	937 890-7628
Dayton (G-9888)		
Soundtrack Printing	C	330 606-7117
Cuyahoga Falls (G-9219)		
Southern Graphic Systems Inc	B	419 662-9873
Perrysburg (G-16061)		
Sparkbase Inc	E	216 867-0877
Cleveland (G-6514)		
Specialty Lubricants Corp	E	330 425-2567
Macedonia (G-13210)		

Spectrum Networks Inc ....E 513 697-2000
Cincinnati *(G-4560)*
Startek Inc ....C 419 528-7801
Ontario *(G-15717)*
Steriltek Inc ....E 615 627-0241
Painesville *(G-15881)*
Sterling Buying Group LLC ....E 513 564-9000
Cincinnati *(G-4589)*
Sterling Infosystems Inc ....E 216 685-7600
Independence *(G-12262)*
Streamline Technical Svcs LLC ....D 614 441-7448
Lockbourne *(G-12961)*
Summit Advantage LLC ....D 330 835-2453
Fairlawn *(G-10979)*
Summit Claim Services LLC ....D 330 706-9898
New Franklin *(G-15050)*
Systems Pack Inc ....E 330 467-5729
Macedonia *(G-13211)*
T W I International Inc ....C 440 439-1830
Cleveland *(G-6566)*
Tbn Acquisition LLC ....D 740 653-2091
Lancaster *(G-12580)*
TDS Document Management Ltd ....E 614 367-9633
Columbus *(G-8826)*
Team Sports LLC ....E 419 865-8326
Holland *(G-12059)*
Technical Assurance Inc ....E 440 953-3147
Willoughby *(G-19717)*
Tekni-Plex Inc ....E 419 491-2407
Holland *(G-12060)*
Telarc International Corp ....E 216 464-2313
Beachwood *(G-1130)*
Telemessaging Services Inc ....E 440 845-5400
Cleveland *(G-6579)*
Telinx Solutions LLC ....E 330 819-0657
Medina *(G-14135)*
Terminix Intl Co Ltd Partnr ....E 513 539-7846
Middletown *(G-14466)*
Teva Womens Health Inc ....C 513 731-9900
Cincinnati *(G-4639)*
Things Remembered Inc ....C 440 473-2000
Highland Heights *(G-11872)*
Third Dimension Inc ....E 877 926-3223
Geneva *(G-11370)*
Tim Mundy ....E 937 862-8686
Spring Valley *(G-17111)*
Tipp Machine & Tool Inc ....C 937 890-8428
Dayton *(G-9931)*
Toledo Shredding LLC ....E 419 698-1153
Toledo *(G-18249)*
Toledo Sign Company Inc ....E 419 244-4444
Toledo *(G-18250)*
Tommy Bahama Group Inc ....C 614 750-9668
Columbus *(G-8854)*
Toms Installation Co Inc ....E 419 584-1218
Celina *(G-2664)*
Top Tier Soccer LLC ....E 937 903-6114
Dayton *(G-9932)*
Tpusa Inc ....B 330 374-1232
Akron *(G-479)*
Traders World Inc ....E 513 424-2052
Monroe *(G-14715)*
Traffic Ctrl Safety Svcs LLC ....E 330 904-2732
Alliance *(G-564)*
▼ Tri County Tower Service ....E 330 538-9874
North Jackson *(G-15389)*
Tri Green Interstate Equipment ....E 614 879-7731
London *(G-13008)*
Tricor Emplyment Screening Ltd ....E 800 818-5116
Berea *(G-1474)*
Triplefin LLC ....E 513 794-9870
Bluo Ash *(G 1704)*
Truechoicepack Corp ....E 937 630-3832
Mason *(G-13775)*
Trumbull Special Courier Inc ....E 330 841-0074
Warren *(G-18916)*
Twin Comm Inc ....E 740 774-4701
Marietta *(G-13508)*
Tyler Technologies Inc ....C 937 276-5261
Moraine *(G-14831)*
UBS Financial Services Inc ....E 330 655-8319
Hudson *(G-12147)*
UBS Financial Services Inc ....E 440 414-2740
Westlake *(G-19558)*
UBS Financial Services Inc ....E 419 624-6800
Sandusky *(G-16803)*
UBS Financial Services Inc ....E 740 336-7823
Marietta *(G-13509)*
▲ Ultra Tech Machinery Inc ....E 330 929-5544
Cuyahoga Falls *(G-9228)*
Unirush LLC ....D 866 766-2229
Blue Ash *(G-1712)*
United Art and Education Inc ....E 800 322-3247
Dayton *(G-9945)*
United Parcel Service Inc ....E 440 243-3344
Middleburg Heights *(G-14389)*
United Parcel Service Inc OH ....B 216 676-4560
Cleveland *(G-6645)*
United Parcel Service Inc OH ....B 740 363-0636
Delaware *(G-10133)*
United Parcel Service Inc OH ....B 614 277-3300
Urbancrest *(G-18608)*
United Parcel Service Inc OH ....B 614 870-4111
Columbus *(G-8898)*
United Parcel Service Inc OH ....B 740 962-7971
Portsmouth *(G-16315)*
Univenture Inc ....D 937 645-4600
Dublin *(G-10478)*
Univenture Inc ....E 937 645-4600
Dublin *(G-10479)*
Universal Grinding Corporation ....E 216 631-9410
Cleveland *(G-6648)*
Universal Packg Systems Inc ....B 513 732-2000
Batavia *(G-1029)*
Universal Packg Systems Inc ....E 513 735-4777
Batavia *(G-1030)*
Universal Packg Systems Inc ....B 513 674-9400
Cincinnati *(G-4748)*
US Bronco Services Inc ....E 513 829-9880
Fairfield *(G-10921)*
US Protection Service LLC ....D 513 422-7910
Cincinnati *(G-4796)*
Venture Plastics Inc ....E 330 872-6262
Newton Falls *(G-15279)*
◆ Veritiv Pubg & Print MGT Inc ....E 330 650-5522
Hudson *(G-12149)*
Verizon New York Inc ....C 614 301-2498
Hilliard *(G-11964)*
Vigilant Global Trade Svcs LLC ....E 260 417-1825
Shaker Heights *(G-16871)*
Vista Industrial Packaging LLC ....D 800 454-6117
Columbus *(G-8945)*
Vocalink Inc ....B 937 223-1415
Dayton *(G-9974)*
Vocon Design Inc ....D 216 588-0800
Cleveland *(G-6710)*
Walter Alexander Entps Inc ....E 513 841-1100
Cincinnati *(G-4823)*
Weaver Industries Inc ....C 330 379-3606
Akron *(G-505)*
Weaver Industries Inc ....E 330 379-3660
Akron *(G-506)*
Weaver Industries Inc ....C 330 666-5114
Akron *(G-507)*
Weaver Industries Inc ....C 330 733-2431
Tallmadge *(G-17661)*
Weaver Industries Inc ....C 330 745-2400
Akron *(G-508)*
Wegman Construction Company ....E 513 381-1111
Cincinnati *(G-4828)*
West Corporation ....B 330 574-0510
Niles *(G-15310)*
White Oak Investments Inc ....D 614 491-1000
Columbus *(G-8987)*
Wiegands Lake Park Inc ....E 440 338-5795
Novelty *(G-15604)*
Wooster Products Inc ....E 330 264-2844
Wooster *(G-19934)*
Worldpay Inc ....C 513 900-5250
Symmes Twp *(G-17631)*
Wtb Inc ....E 216 298-1895
Cleveland *(G-6761)*

75 AUTOMOTIVE REPAIR, SERVICES, AND PARKING

7513 Truck Rental & Leasing, Without Drivers

Aim Integrated Logistics Inc ....B 330 759-0438
Girard *(G-11406)*
Aim Leasing Company ....D 330 759-0438
Girard *(G-11407)*
▼ Albert Mike Leasing Inc ....C 513 563-1400
Cincinnati *(G-2982)*
Benedict Enterprises Inc ....E 513 539-9216
Monroe *(G-14690)*
Diane Sauer Chevrolet Inc ....D 330 373-1600
Warren *(G-18850)*
E H Schmidt Executive ....D 419 874-4331
Perrysburg *(G-16000)*
First Group Investment Partnr ....D 513 241-2200
Cincinnati *(G-3618)*
Firstgroup Usa Inc ....B 513 241-2200
Cincinnati *(G-3629)*
Fountain City Leasing Inc ....D 419 785-3100
Defiance *(G-10033)*
Geo Byers Sons Holding Inc ....E 614 239-1084
Columbus *(G-7741)*
Graham Chevrolet-Cadillac Co ....D 419 989-4012
Ontario *(G-15690)*
▼ Grogans Towne Chrysler Inc ....C 419 476-0761
Toledo *(G-17924)*
Helton Enterprises Inc ....E 419 423-4180
Findlay *(G-11046)*
Hogan Truck Leasing Inc ....E 513 454-3500
Fairfield *(G-10859)*
▲ Hy-Tek Material Handling Inc ....D 614 497-2500
Columbus *(G-7873)*
Interstate Truckway Inc ....D 513 542-5500
Cincinnati *(G-3838)*
Kempthorn Automall ....C 330 456-8287
Canton *(G-2423)*
Kempthorn Automall ....D 800 451-3877
Canton *(G-2422)*
Kenworth of Cincinnati Inc ....D 513 771-5831
Cincinnati *(G-3916)*
Kirk NationaLease Co ....E 937 498-1151
Sidney *(G-16939)*
Knisely Inc ....D 330 343-5812
Dover *(G-10195)*
▲ Krieger Ford Inc ....C 614 888-3320
Columbus *(G-8014)*
Lanes Transfer Inc ....E 419 222-8692
Lima *(G-12815)*
McCluskey Chevrolet Inc ....C 513 761-1111
Cincinnati *(G-4035)*
Miami Valley Intl Trcks Inc ....D 513 733-8500
Cincinnati *(G-4087)*
Montrose Ford Inc ....D 330 666-0711
Fairlawn *(G-10966)*
Murray Leasing Inc ....C 330 386-4757
East Liverpool *(G-10526)*
Northern Management & Leasing ....D 216 676-4600
Cleveland *(G-6159)*
◆ Ohio Machinery Co ....C 440 526-6200
Broadview Heights *(G-1886)*
Os Hill Leasing Inc ....E 330 386-6440
East Liverpool *(G-10531)*
Paccar Leasing Corporation ....E 937 235-2589
Dayton *(G-9797)*
Penske Logistics LLC ....D 440 232-5811
Cleveland *(G-6262)*
Penske Truck Leasing Co LP ....E 419 873-8611
Perrysburg *(G-16039)*
Penske Truck Leasing Co LP ....E 614 658-0000
Columbus *(G-8531)*
Penske Truck Leasing Co LP ....E 513 771-7701
Cincinnati *(G-4278)*
Penske Truck Leasing Co LP ....E 330 645-3100
Akron *(G-384)*
Penske Truck Leasing Co LP ....E 440 232-5811
Bedford *(G-1330)*
Predator Trucking Company ....E 330 530-0712
Mc Donald *(G-14024)*
Premier Truck Parts Inc ....E 216 642-5000
Cleveland *(G-6302)*
▼ Premier Truck Sls & Rentl Inc ....E 216 642-5000
Cleveland *(G-6303)*
Rjw Inc ....E 216 398-6090
Independence *(G-12250)*
Roger Bettis Trucking Inc ....C 330 863-2111
Malvern *(G-13254)*
Rouen Chrysler Plymouth Dodge ....E 419 837-6228
Woodville *(G-19824)*
Roush Equipment Inc ....C 614 882-1535
Westerville *(G-19442)*
Rush Truck Centers Ohio Inc ....D 513 733-8500
Cincinnati *(G-4458)*
Rush Truck Centers Ohio Inc ....E 419 224-6045
Lima *(G-12872)*
Rush Truck Leasing Inc ....E 614 876-3500
Columbus *(G-8660)*
Ryder Truck Rental Inc ....E 614 409-6550
Groveport *(G-11668)*
Ryder Truck Rental Inc ....E 614 846-6780
Columbus *(G-8665)*
Ryder Truck Rental Inc ....E 513 241-7736
Cincinnati *(G-4462)*
Ryder Truck Rental Inc ....E 419 666-9833
Perrysburg *(G-16054)*

75 AUTOMOTIVE REPAIR, SERVICES, AND PARKING

Ryder Truck Rental Inc .... E 614 876-0405
  Columbus (G-8666)
Ryder Truck Rental Inc .... E 937 236-1650
  Dayton (G-9860)
Ryder Truck Rental Inc .... E 513 772-0223
  Cincinnati (G-4463)
Ryder Truck Rental Inc .... C 216 433-4700
  Cleveland (G-6424)
Schoner Chevrolet Inc .... E 330 877-6731
  Hartville (G-11830)
South East Chevrolet Co .... E 440 585-9300
  Willoughby Hills (G-19735)
Star Leasing Co .... D 614 278-9999
  Columbus (G-8776)
▼ Truck Sales Leasing Inc .... E 330 343-5581
  Midvale (G-14491)
U Haul Co of Northwestern Ohio .... E 419 478-1101
  Toledo (G-18266)
U-Haul Neighborhood Dealer -Ce ..... E 419 929-3724
  New London (G-15071)
Vin Devers .... C 888 847-9535
  Sylvania (G-17626)
Voss Auto Network Inc .... E 937 428-2447
  Dayton (G-9976)
White Family Companies Inc .... C 937 222-3701
  Dayton (G-9996)

7514 Passenger Car Rental

Afford-A-Car Inc .... E 937 235-2700
  Tipp City (G-17710)
Avis Administration .... D 937 898-2581
  Vandalia (G-18660)
Budget Rent A Car System Inc .... D 216 267-2080
  Cleveland (G-5157)
Budget Rent A Car System Inc .... E 937 898-1396
  Vandalia (G-18664)
Carroll Halliday Inc .... E 740 335-1670
  Wshngtn CT Hs (G-20014)
Cartemp USA Inc .... C 440 715-1000
  Solon (G-16988)
Clerac LLC .... E 440 345-3999
  Strongsville (G-17450)
Crawford Group Inc .... D 419 873-7360
  Perrysburg (G-15990)
Crawford Group Inc .... D 330 665-5432
  Akron (G-176)
Dealers Group Limited .... E 440 352-4970
  Beachwood (G-1073)
Edison Local School District .... E 740 543-4011
  Amsterdam (G-608)
Enterprise Holdings Inc .... D 614 866-1480
  Reynoldsburg (G-16451)
Enterprise Holdings Inc .... E 937 879-0023
  Cincinnati (G-3559)
Falls Motor City Inc .... E 330 929-3066
  Cuyahoga Falls (G-9184)
Family Ford Lincoln Inc .... D 740 373-9127
  Marietta (G-13445)
Geo Byers Sons Holding Inc .... E 614 239-1084
  Columbus (G-7741)
George P Ballas Buick GMC Trck .... D 419 535-1000
  Toledo (G-17913)
Hertz Corporation .... D 216 267-8900
  Cleveland (G-5755)
Hertz Corporation .... E 513 533-3161
  Cincinnati (G-3758)
Hertz Corporation .... E 937 890-2721
  Vandalia (G-18683)
Hertz Corporation .... D 937 898-5806
  Vandalia (G-18684)
Leikin Motor Companies Inc .... D 440 946-6900
  Willoughby (G-19686)
Lincoln Mrcury Kings Auto Mall .... C 513 683-3800
  Cincinnati (G-3984)
National Rental (us) Inc .... E 937 890-0100
  Vandalia (G-18690)
National Rental (us) Inc .... E 614 239-3270
  Columbus (G-8223)
Precision Coatings Systems .... E 937 642-4727
  Marysville (G-13645)
Rental Concepts Inc .... E 216 525-3870
  Cleveland (G-6377)
Schmidt Daily Rental Inc .... D 419 874-4331
  Perrysburg (G-16057)
Schoner Chevrolet Inc .... E 330 877-6731
  Hartville (G-11830)
Spitzer Chevrolet Company .... E 330 966-9524
  Canton (G-2535)
Sweeny Walt Pntc GMC Trck Sles ... E 513 621-4888
  Cincinnati (G-4607)

Taylor Chevrolet Inc .... C 740 653-2091
  Lancaster (G-12579)
Thrifty Rent-A-Car System Inc .... E 440 842-1660
  Cleveland (G-6598)
U Save Auto Rental .... E 330 925-2015
  Rittman (G-16557)

7515 Passenger Car Leasing

1106 West Main Inc .... E 330 673-2122
  Kent (G-12350)
▼ Albert Mike Leasing Inc .... C 513 563-1400
  Cincinnati (G-2982)
Auto Center USA Inc .... E 513 683-4900
  Cincinnati (G-3066)
Beechmont Ford Inc .... C 513 752-6611
  Cincinnati (G-2904)
Bob Pulte Chevrolet Inc .... E 513 932-0303
  Lebanon (G-12593)
Bobb Automotive Inc .... E 614 853-3000
  Columbus (G-7123)
Brondes All Makes Auto Leasing .... D 419 887-1511
  Maumee (G-13891)
Brown Motor Sales Co .... E 419 531-0151
  Toledo (G-17785)
Budget Rent A Car System Inc .... E 937 898-1396
  Vandalia (G-18664)
▼ Carcorp Inc .... C 877 857-2801
  Columbus (G-7189)
Chesrown Oldsmobile GMC Inc ...... E 614 846-3040
  Columbus (G-7255)
Chuck Nicholson Inc .... E 330 674-4015
  Millersburg (G-14594)
City Yellow Cab Company .... E 330 253-3141
  Akron (G-144)
Classic Buick Olds Cadillac .... D 440 639-4500
  Painesville (G-15842)
Clerac LLC .... E 440 345-3999
  Strongsville (G-17450)
Columbus SAI Motors LLC .... E 614 851-3273
  Columbus (G-7383)
Dave White Chevrolet Inc .... C 419 885-4444
  Sylvania (G-17581)
Dunning Motor Sales Inc .... E 740 439-4465
  Logan (G-2110)
E H Schmidt Executive .... D 419 874-4331
  Perrysburg (G-16000)
Ed Schmidt Chevrolet Inc .... D 419 897-8600
  Maumee (G-13908)
Ed Tomko Chryslr Jep Dge Inc .... E 440 835-5900
  Avon Lake (G-929)
Enterprise Holdings Inc .... E 937 879-0023
  Cincinnati (G-3559)
Germain On Scarborough LLC .... C 614 868-0300
  Columbus (G-7748)
Graham Chevrolet-Cadillac Co .... D 419 989-4012
  Ontario (G-15690)
Greenwoods Hubbard Chevy-Olds .. E 330 568-4335
  Hubbard (G-12087)
▼ Grogans Towne Chrysler Inc .... C 419 476-0761
  Toledo (G-17924)
Hidy Motors Inc .... D 937 426-9564
  Dayton (G-9921)
Jake Sweeney Automotive Inc .... C 513 782-2800
  Cincinnati (G-3859)
Jim Brown Chevrolet Inc .... C 440 255-5511
  Mentor (G-14197)
Joe Dodge Kidd Inc .... E 513 752-1804
  Cincinnati (G-2921)
Kempthorn Automall .... C 330 456-8287
  Canton (G-2423)
Kempthorn Automall .... D 800 451-3877
  Canton (G-2422)
Kent Automotive Inc .... E 330 678-5520
  Kent (G-12377)
Kerns Chevrolet-Buick-Gmc Inc ...... E 419 586-5131
  Celina (G-2649)
Kerry Ford Inc .... D 513 671-6400
  Cincinnati (G-3918)
Kings Toyota Inc .... E 513 583-4333
  Cincinnati (G-3928)
Klaben Family Dodge Inc .... E 330 673-9971
  Kent (G-12381)
Klaben Lincoln Ford Inc .... D 330 673-3139
  Kent (G-12383)
▲ Krieger Ford Inc .... C 614 888-3320
  Columbus (G-8014)
Lakewood Chrysler-Plymouth .... E 216 521-1000
  Brookpark (G-1950)
Lang Chevrolet Co .... D 937 426-2313
  Beavercreek Township (G-1274)

Lariche Subaru Inc .... D 419 422-1855
  Findlay (G-11056)
Lavery Chevrolet-Buick Inc .... E 330 823-1100
  Alliance (G-544)
Lebanon Chrysler - Plymouth Inc .... E 513 932-2717
  Lebanon (G-12620)
Lima Auto Mall Inc .... D 419 993-6000
  Lima (G-12816)
Lincoln Mrcury Kings Auto Mall .... C 513 683-3800
  Cincinnati (G-3984)
Mathews Dodge Chrysler Jeep .... E 740 389-2341
  Marion (G-13563)
Mathews Kennedy Ford L-M Inc ..... D 740 387-3673
  Marion (G-13564)
Mc Daniel Motor Co (Inc) .... E 740 389-2355
  Marion (G-13565)
McCluskey Chevrolet Inc .... C 513 761-1111
  Cincinnati (G-4035)
Medina World Cars Inc .... E 330 725-4901
  Strongsville (G-17493)
Merrick Chevrolet Co .... D 440 878-6700
  Strongsville (G-17494)
Montrose Ford Inc .... D 330 666-0711
  Fairlawn (G-10966)
Mullinax Ford North Canton Inc .... C 330 238-3206
  Canton (G-2468)
Nick Mayer Lincoln-Mercury Inc ...... E 440 835-3700
  Westlake (G-19521)
Northgate Chrysler Jeep Inc .... E 513 385-3900
  Cincinnati (G-4180)
Oregon Ford Inc .... C 419 698-4444
  Oregon (G-15746)
Partners Auto Group Bdford Inc ...... E 440 439-2323
  Bedford (G-1329)
Ron Marhofer Automall Inc .... E 330 923-5059
  Cuyahoga Falls (G-9217)
Rouen Chrysler Plymouth Dodge .... E 419 837-6228
  Woodville (G-19824)
Roush Equipment Inc .... C 614 882-1535
  Westerville (G-19442)
Saturn of Toledo Inc .... E 419 841-9070
  Toledo (G-18173)
Schoner Chevrolet Inc .... E 330 877-6731
  Hartville (G-11830)
Sharpnack Chevrolet Co .... E 440 967-3144
  Vermilion (G-18716)
Sonic Automotive .... E 614 870-8200
  Columbus (G-8748)
Sonic Automotive-1495 Automall ..... E 614 317-4326
  Columbus (G-8749)
Sorbir Inc .... E 440 449-1000
  Cleveland (G-6495)
South East Chevrolet Co .... E 440 585-9300
  Willoughby Hills (G-19735)
Spitzer Auto World Amherst .... E 440 988-4444
  Amherst (G-605)
Sunnyside Toyota Inc .... D 440 777-9911
  North Olmsted (G-15446)
Tansky Motors Inc .... E 650 322-7069
  Logan (G-12989)
Team Rahal of Dayton Inc .... E 937 438-3800
  Dayton (G-9921)
Tom Ahl Chryslr-Plymouth-Dodge ... C 419 227-0202
  Lima (G-12901)
Toyota of Bedford .... D 440 439-8600
  Bedford (G-1341)
Van Devere Inc .... D 330 253-6137
  Akron (G-494)
Vin Devers .... C 888 847-9535
  Sylvania (G-17626)
Yark Automotive Group Inc .... C 419 841-7771
  Toledo (G-18319)

7519 Utility Trailers & Recreational Vehicle Rental

A Duie Pyle Inc .... D 330 342-7750
  Streetsboro (G-17404)
Ample Trailer Leasing & Sales .... E 513 563-2550
  Cincinnati (G-3019)
Benedict Enterprises Inc .... E 513 539-9216
  Monroe (G-14690)
Brown Gibbons Lang Ltd Ptrship ..... E 216 241-2800
  Cleveland (G-5151)
D & D Rv and Auto LLC .... E 937 839-4555
  West Alexandria (G-19008)
E & J Trailer Leasing Inc .... E 513 563-7366
  Cincinnati (G-3521)
E & J Trailer Sales & Service .... E 513 563-2550
  Cincinnati (G-3522)

▲ Eleet Cryogenics Inc........E....... 330 874-4009
Bolivar (G-1746)
Ryder Truck Rental Inc........E....... 614 846-6780
Columbus (G-8665)
Ryder Truck Rental Inc........E....... 513 772-0223
Cincinnati (G-4463)
Transport Services Inc........E....... 440 582-4900
Cleveland (G-6612)
U Haul Co of Northwestern Ohio........E....... 419 478-1101
Toledo (G-18266)
U-Haul Neighborhood Dealer -Ce........E....... 419 929-3724
New London (G-15071)

7521 Automobile Parking Lots & Garages

ABM Parking Services Inc........E....... 937 461-2113
Dayton (G-9302)
ABM Parking Services Inc........E....... 330 747-7678
Youngstown (G-20096)
ABM Parking Services Inc........E....... 216 621-6600
Cleveland (G-4949)
Allpro Parking Ohio LLC........E....... 614 221-9696
Columbus (G-6972)
Amherst Exempted Vlg Schools........E....... 440 988-2633
Amherst (G-586)
Asv Services LLC........E....... 216 797-1701
Euclid (G-10743)
Central Parking System Inc........E....... 513 381-2621
Cincinnati (G-3215)
Chillicothe City School Dst........E....... 740 775-2936
Chillicothe (G-2818)
City of Garfield Heights........E....... 216 475-1107
Cleveland (G-5261)
City of Lakewood........D....... 216 941-1116
Cleveland (G-5268)
City of New Philadelphia........E....... 330 339-2121
New Philadelphia (G-15086)
City of Parma........D....... 440 885-8983
Cleveland (G-5271)
City of Portsmouth........E....... 740 353-3459
Portsmouth (G-16270)
County of Holmes........E....... 330 674-5916
Millersburg (G-14599)
Falcon Transport Co........D....... 330 793-1345
Youngstown (G-20186)
Kwik Parking........E....... 419 246-0454
Toledo (G-17997)
Ohio Department Transportation........E....... 330 637-5951
Cortland (G-9080)
Park n Fly Inc........E....... 404 264-1000
Cleveland (G-6238)
Park Place Management Inc........E....... 216 362-1080
Cleveland (G-6239)
Park-N-Go Inc........E....... 937 890-7275
Vandalia (G-18692)
Parking Company America Inc........B....... 513 241-0415
Cincinnati (G-4254)
Parking Company America Inc........E....... 216 265-0500
Cleveland (G-6243)
Parking Company America Inc........E....... 513 381-2179
Cincinnati (G-4255)
Prestige Valet Inc........D....... 513 871-4220
Cincinnati (G-4327)
Republic Parking System Inc........E....... 937 415-0016
Vandalia (G-18698)
Shaias Parking Inc........E....... 216 621-0328
Cleveland (G-6474)
Sharps Valet Parking........E....... 513 863-1777
Fairfield (G-10904)
Southwood Auto Sales........E....... 330 788-8822
Youngstown (G-20378)
Sp Plus Corporation........D....... 216 444-2255
Cleveland (G-6508)
Sp Plus Corporation........E....... 216 687-0141
Cleveland (G-6509)
Sp Plus Corporation........D....... 216 267-7275
Cleveland (G-6510)
Sp Plus Corporation........D....... 216 267-5030
Cleveland (G-6511)
United Parcel Service Inc OH........C....... 419 424-9494
Findlay (G-11095)
USA Parking Systems Inc........D....... 216 621-9255
Cleveland (G-6677)

7532 Top, Body & Upholstery Repair & Paint Shops

Advantage Ford Lincoln Mercury........E....... 419 334-9751
Fremont (G-11182)
American Bulk Commodities Inc........C....... 330 758-0841
Youngstown (G-20103)
American Nat Fleet Svc Inc........D....... 216 447-6060
Cleveland (G-5017)
Arch Abraham Susuki Ltd........E....... 440 934-6001
Elyria (G-10594)
Auto Additions Inc........E....... 614 899-9100
Westerville (G-19369)
Auto Body North Inc........E....... 614 436-3700
Columbus (G-7076)
Bakers Cllsion Repr Specialist........E....... 419 524-1350
Mansfield (G-13263)
Bauman Chrysler Jeep Dodge........E....... 419 332-8291
Fremont (G-11185)
Bobbart Industries Inc........E....... 419 350-5477
Sylvania (G-17576)
Brown Motor Sales Co........E....... 419 531-0151
Toledo (G-17785)
Buddies Inc........E....... 216 642-3362
Cleveland (G-5156)
Burtons Collision........E....... 513 984-3396
Cincinnati (G-3154)
Busam Fairfield LLC........E....... 513 771-8100
Fairfield (G-10825)
Carls Body Shop Inc........E....... 937 253-5166
Dayton (G-9383)
Chesrown Oldsmobile GMC Inc........E....... 614 846-3040
Columbus (G-7255)
Cincinnati Collision Center........E....... 513 984-4445
Blue Ash (G-1555)
Coughlin Chevrolet Inc........E....... 740 852-1122
London (G-12995)
Coughlin Chevrolet Inc........D....... 740 964-9191
Pataskala (G-15922)
Coughlin Chevrolet Toyota Inc........D....... 740 366-1381
Newark (G-15162)
Dan Tobin Pontiac Buick GMC........D....... 614 889-6300
Columbus (G-7484)
Dave Dnnis Chrysler Jeep Dodge........D....... 937 429-5566
Beavercreek Township (G-1267)
Dave White Chevrolet Inc........C....... 419 885-4444
Sylvania (G-17581)
Decorative Paint Incorporated........D....... 419 485-0632
Montpelier (G-14743)
Dent Magic........E....... 614 864-3368
Columbus (G-7507)
Don Tester Ford Lincoln Inc........E....... 419 668-8233
Norwalk (G-15570)
Donnell Ford-Lincoln........E....... 330 332-0031
Salem (G-16694)
Doug Bigelow Chevrolet Inc........D....... 330 644-7500
Akron (G-198)
Downtown Ford Lincoln Inc........D....... 330 456-2781
Canton (G-2344)
Dutro Ford Lincoln-Mercury Inc........D....... 740 452-6334
Zanesville (G-20470)
Eastside Body Shop........E....... 513 624-1145
Cincinnati (G-3538)
Ed Mullinax Ford LLC........C....... 440 984-2431
Amherst (G-591)
Ed Schmidt Auto Inc........C....... 419 874-4331
Perrysburg (G-16001)
Excalibur Auto Body Inc........E....... 440 942-5550
Willowick (G-19739)
Family Ford Lincoln Inc........D....... 740 373-9127
Marietta (G-13445)
George P Ballas Buick GMC Trck........D....... 419 535-1000
Toledo (G-17913)
▼ Grogans Towne Chrysler Inc........C....... 419 476-0761
Toledo (G-17924)
Haydocy Automotive Inc........D....... 614 279-8880
Columbus (G-7804)
Jake Sweeney Automotive Inc........C....... 513 782-2800
Cincinnati (G-3859)
Jake Sweeney Body Shop........E....... 513 782-1100
Cincinnati (G-3860)
Jeff Wyler Chevrolet Inc........B....... 513 752-3447
Batavia (G-1018)
Jeff Wyler Ft Thomas Inc........D....... 513 752-7450
Cincinnati (G-2919)
Jim Brown Chevrolet Inc........E....... 440 255-5511
Mentor (G-14198)
Joe Dodge Kidd Inc........E....... 513 752-1804
Cincinnati (G-2921)
Joseph Chevrolet Oldsmobile Co........C....... 513 741-6700
Cincinnati (G-3887)
Joyce Buick Inc........E....... 419 529-3211
Ontario (G-15696)
Kallas Enterprises Inc........E....... 330 253-6893
Akron (G-300)
Kerry Ford Inc........D....... 513 671-6400
Cincinnati (G-3918)
King Collision........E....... 330 729-0525
Youngstown (G-20247)
King Collision Inc........E....... 330 372-3242
Warren (G-18870)
Kumler Collision Inc........E....... 740 653-4301
Lancaster (G-12546)
Lang Chevrolet Co........D....... 937 426-2313
Beavercreek Township (G-1274)
Lavery Chevrolet-Buick Inc........E....... 330 823-1100
Alliance (G-544)
Leikin Motor Companies Inc........D....... 440 946-6900
Willoughby (G-19686)
Lennys Auto Sales Inc........E....... 330 848-2993
Barberton (G-970)
Lima Auto Mall Inc........D....... 419 993-6000
Lima (G-12816)
Magic Industries Inc........E....... 614 759-8422
Columbus (G-8097)
Maines Collision Repr & Bdy Sp........D....... 937 322-4618
Springfield (G-17228)
Mark Thomas Ford Inc........E....... 330 638-1010
Cortland (G-9077)
Mathews Kennedy Ford L-M Inc........D....... 740 387-3673
Marion (G-13564)
Matia Motors Inc........E....... 440 365-7311
Elyria (G-10650)
Medina World Cars Inc........E....... 330 725-4901
Strongsville (G-17493)
Merrick Body Shop........E....... 440 243-6700
Berea (G-1463)
Mike Castrucci Ford........C....... 513 831-7010
Milford (G-14541)
Montrose Ford Inc........D....... 330 666-0711
Fairlawn (G-10966)
Mowerys Collision Inc........E....... 614 274-6072
Columbus (G-8201)
Mullinax East LLC........D....... 440 296-3020
Wickliffe (G-19608)
Oregon Ford Inc........C....... 419 698-4444
Oregon (G-15746)
Palmer Trucks Inc........E....... 937 235-3318
Dayton (G-9799)
Paul Hrnchar Ford-Mercury Inc........E....... 330 533-3673
Canfield (G-2207)
Pierson Automotive Inc........E....... 513 424-1881
Middletown (G-14485)
Precision Coatings Systems........E....... 937 642-4727
Marysville (G-13645)
▼ QT Equipment Company........E....... 330 724-3055
Akron (G-401)
Ron Marhofer Automall Inc........B....... 330 835-6707
Cuyahoga Falls (G-9216)
Ron Marhofer Automall Inc........E....... 330 923-5059
Cuyahoga Falls (G-9217)
Ron Marhofer Collision Center........E....... 330 686-2262
Stow (G-17391)
Roush Equipment Inc........C....... 614 882-1535
Westerville (G-19442)
Sharonville Car Wash........E....... 513 769-4219
Cincinnati (G-4509)
Sharpnack Chevrolet Co........E....... 440 967-3144
Vermilion (G-18716)
Sharpnack Chvrlet Bick Cdillac........D....... 419 935-0194
Willard (G-19626)
Skinner Diesel Services Inc........E....... 614 491-8785
Columbus (G-8741)
Sonic Automotive-1495 Automall........E....... 614 317-4326
Columbus (G-8749)
St Clair Auto Body........E....... 216 531-7300
Cleveland (G-6521)
Suburban Collision Centers........E....... 440 243-5533
Berea (G-1470)
Sunnyside Toyota Inc........D....... 440 777-9911
North Olmsted (G-15446)
Surfside Motors Inc........E....... 419 462-1746
Galion (G-11306)
Tallmadge Collision Center........E....... 330 630-2188
Tallmadge (G-17657)
Tansky Motors Inc........E....... 650 322-7069
Logan (G-12989)
Target Auto Body Inc........E....... 216 391-1942
Cleveland (G-6570)
Three C Body Shop Inc........D....... 614 274-9700
Columbus (G-8842)
Three C Body Shop Inc........E....... 614 885-0900
Columbus (G-8843)
▲ Transitworks LLC........D....... 330 861-1118
Akron (G-480)
True2form Collision Repair Ctr........E....... 330 399-6659
Warren (G-18907)

SIC

Employee Codes: A=Over 500 employees, B=251-500
C=101-250, D=51-100, E=25-50
2018 Harris Ohio
Services Directory
1009

Voss Auto Network Inc ....B.... 937 433-1444
Dayton (G-9977)
Walker Auto Group Inc ....D.... 937 433-4950
Miamisburg (G-14367)
Warner Buick-Nissan Inc ....E.... 419 423-7161
Findlay (G-11099)
White Family Collision Center ....E.... 419 885-8885
Sylvania (G-17628)

7533 Automotive Exhaust System Repair Shops

Dayton-Dixie Mufflers Inc ....E.... 419 243-7281
Toledo (G-17846)
Monro Inc ....D.... 440 835-2393
Westlake (G-19517)
Tuffy Associates Corp ....E.... 419 865-6900
Toledo (G-18264)

7534 Tire Retreading & Repair Shops

Belle Tire ....E.... 440 735-0800
Bedford (G-1296)
▲ Best One Tire & Svc Lima Inc ....E.... 419 229-2380
Lima (G-12746)
Bob Sumerel Tire Co Inc ....E.... 937 235-0062
Dayton (G-9361)
Bob Sumerel Tire Co Inc ....E.... 614 527-9700
Columbus (G-7122)
Bridgestone Ret Operations LLC ....E.... 513 367-7888
Harrison (G-11792)
Bridgestone Ret Operations LLC ....E.... 513 522-2525
Cincinnati (G-3132)
Bridgestone Ret Operations LLC ....E.... 513 741-9701
Cincinnati (G-3133)
Bridgestone Ret Operations LLC ....E.... 419 691-7111
Northwood (G-15527)
Bridgestone Ret Operations LLC ....E.... 513 271-7100
Cincinnati (G-3134)
Bridgestone Ret Operations LLC ....E.... 419 586-1600
Celina (G-2636)
Central Ohio Bandag LP ....E.... 740 454-9728
Zanesville (G-20460)
Goodyear Tire & Rubber Company ....E.... 440 735-9910
Walton Hills (G-18789)
Goodyear Tire & Rubber Company ....E.... 614 871-1881
Grove City (G-11565)
◆ Goodyear Tire & Rubber Company ....A.... 330 796-2121
Akron (G-243)
▲ Grismer Tire Company ....E.... 937 643-2526
Centerville (G-2678)
H & H Retreading Inc ....D.... 740 682-7721
Oak Hill (G-15618)
K S Bandag Inc ....E.... 330 264-9237
Wooster (G-19876)
Tire Centers LLC ....E.... 419 287-3227
Pemberville (G-15945)

7536 Automotive Glass Replacement Shops

▲ Advanced Auto Glass Inc ....E.... 412 373-6675
Akron (G-21)
▲ Belletech Corp ....D.... 937 599-3774
Bellefontaine (G-1378)
▲ C-Auto Glass Inc ....E.... 216 351-2193
Cleveland (G-5169)
Mels Auto Glass Inc ....E.... 513 563-7771
Cincinnati (G-4054)
Pgw Auto Glass LLC ....E.... 419 993-2421
Lima (G-12859)
Ryans All-Glass Incorporated ....E.... 513 771-4440
Cincinnati (G-4461)
Safelite Fulfillment Inc ....E.... 614 781-5449
Columbus (G-8670)
Safelite Fulfillment Inc ....E.... 216 475-7781
Cleveland (G-6435)
Safelite Glass Corp ....E.... 614 431-4936
Worthington (G-19995)
▲ Safelite Group Inc ....A.... 614 210-9000
Columbus (G-8672)
Techna Glass Inc ....E.... 513 685-3800
Milford (G-14566)
Wiechart Enterprises Inc ....E.... 419 227-0027
Lima (G-12921)

7537 Automotive Transmission Repair Shops

◆ Luk Transmission System LLC ....E.... 330 464-4184
Wooster (G-19885)
Ohio Transmission Corporation ....E.... 614 342-6247
Columbus (G-8452)
W W Williams Company LLC ....D.... 614 228-5000
Columbus (G-8959)
W W Williams Company LLC ....E.... 330 225-7751
Brunswick (G-1995)

7538 General Automotive Repair Shop

1st Gear Auto Inc ....E.... 216 458-0791
Bedford (G-1291)
Abers Garage Inc ....E.... 419 281-5500
Ashland (G-649)
Abraham Ford LLC ....E.... 440 233-7402
Elyria (G-10592)
Advantage Ford Lincoln Mercury ....E.... 419 334-9751
Fremont (G-11182)
Aim Leasing Company ....D.... 330 759-0438
Girard (G-11407)
Allied Truck Parts Co ....E.... 330 477-8127
Canton (G-2234)
Allstate Trk Sls of Estrn OH ....E.... 330 339-5555
New Philadelphia (G-15080)
American Nat Fleet Svc Inc ....D.... 216 447-6060
Cleveland (G-5017)
Ashtabula Area City School Dst ....E.... 440 992-1221
Ashtabula (G-712)
Auto Center USA Inc ....E.... 513 683-4900
Cincinnati (G-3066)
Beaverdam Fleet Services Inc ....E.... 419 643-8880
Beaverdam (G-1288)
Beechmont Ford Inc ....C.... 513 752-6611
Cincinnati (G-2904)
Benedict Enterprises Inc ....E.... 513 539-9216
Monroe (G-14690)
Bill Delord Autocenter Inc ....D.... 513 932-3000
Lebanon (G-12592)
Bob-Boyd Ford Inc ....D.... 614 860-0606
Lancaster (G-12510)
Bowling Green Lncln-Mrcury Inc ....E.... 419 352-2553
Bowling Green (G-1765)
▲ Brentlinger Enterprises ....C.... 614 889-2571
Dublin (G-10267)
Brown Motor Sales Co ....E.... 419 531-0151
Toledo (G-17785)
Burtons Collision ....E.... 513 984-3396
Cincinnati (G-3154)
Cain Motors Inc ....E.... 330 494-5588
Canton (G-2280)
Carl E Oeder Sons Sand & Grav ....E.... 513 494-1555
Lebanon (G-12594)
Cascade Group Inc ....E.... 330 929-1861
Cuyahoga Falls (G-9169)
Central Cadillac Limited ....D.... 216 861-5800
Cleveland (G-5209)
Chillicothe City School Dst ....E.... 740 775-2936
Chillicothe (G-2818)
City of Berea ....E.... 440 826-5853
Berea (G-1451)
City of Toledo ....D.... 419 936-2507
Toledo (G-17812)
Classic International Inc ....D.... 440 975-1222
Mentor (G-14158)
Cole-Valley Motor Co ....D.... 330 372-1665
Warren (G-18835)
Columbus Col-Weld Corporation ....E.... 614 276-5303
Columbus (G-7341)
Columbus Diesel Supply Co Inc ....E.... 614 445-8391
Reynoldsburg (G-16439)
Columbus SAI Motors LLC ....E.... 614 851-3273
Columbus (G-7383)
Commercial Truck & Trailer ....E.... 330 545-9717
Girard (G-11411)
Conrads Tire Service Inc ....E.... 216 941-3333
Cleveland (G-5392)
Contitech North America Inc ....E.... 440 225-5363
Akron (G-162)
Coughlin Chevrolet Inc ....D.... 740 964-9191
Pataskala (G-15922)
County Engineering Office ....E.... 419 334-9731
Fremont (G-11189)
County Engineers Office ....E.... 740 702-3130
Chillicothe (G-2829)
County of Lorain ....D.... 440 326-5880
Elyria (G-10615)
Crestmont Cadillac Corporation ....E.... 216 831-5300
Cleveland (G-5437)
Cummins Inc ....E.... 614 771-1000
Hilliard (G-11894)
Dan Tobin Pontiac Buick GMC ....D.... 614 889-6300
Columbus (G-7484)
Dave Dnnis Chrysler Jeep Dodge ....D.... 937 429-5566
Beavercreek Township (G-1267)
Dave White Chevrolet Inc ....C.... 419 885-4444
Sylvania (G-17581)
Dcr Systems LLC ....E.... 440 205-9900
Mentor (G-14167)
Decosky Motor Holdings Inc ....E.... 740 397-9122
Mount Vernon (G-14892)
Delaware City School District ....E.... 740 363-5901
Delaware (G-10087)
Dickinson Fleet Services LLC ....E.... 513 772-3629
Cincinnati (G-3490)
Don Wood Bck Oldsmble Pntiac C ....D.... 740 593-6641
Athens (G-783)
Don Wood Inc ....D.... 740 593-6641
Athens (G-784)
Donnell Ford-Lincoln ....E.... 330 332-0031
Salem (G-16694)
Doug Bigelow Chevrolet Inc ....D.... 330 644-7500
Akron (G-198)
Doug Marine Motors Inc ....E.... 740 335-3700
Wshngtn CT Hs (G-20020)
Downtheroad Inc ....E.... 740 452-4579
Zanesville (G-20469)
Downtown Ford Lincoln Inc ....D.... 330 456-2781
Canton (G-2344)
Dunning Motor Sales Inc ....E.... 740 439-4465
Cambridge (G-2110)
Dutro Ford Lincoln-Mercury Inc ....D.... 740 452-6334
Zanesville (G-20470)
Ed Mullinax Ford LLC ....C.... 440 984-2431
Amherst (G-591)
Ed Schmidt Auto Inc ....C.... 419 874-4331
Perrysburg (G-16001)
Ed Tomko Chryslr Jep Dge Inc ....E.... 440 835-5900
Avon Lake (G-929)
Family Ford Lincoln Inc ....D.... 740 373-9127
Marietta (G-13445)
FCA US LLC ....E.... 419 727-2800
Toledo (G-17881)
Flagship Services of Ohio Inc ....D.... 740 533-1657
Ironton (G-12289)
Fyda Freightliner Youngstown ....D.... 330 797-0224
Youngstown (G-20192)
Germain On Scarborough LLC ....C.... 614 868-0300
Columbus (G-7748)
Giles Marathon Inc ....E.... 440 974-8815
Mentor (G-14180)
Glenway Automotive Service ....E.... 513 921-2117
Cincinnati (G-3679)
◆ Goodyear Tire & Rubber Company ....A.... 330 796-2121
Akron (G-243)
Greenwood Chevrolet Inc ....C.... 330 270-1299
Youngstown (G-20209)
Greenwoods Hubbard Chevy-Olds ....E.... 330 568-4335
Hubbard (G-12087)
Greg Ford Sweet Inc ....E.... 440 593-7714
North Kingsville (G-15391)
▲ Grismer Tire Company ....E.... 937 643-2526
Centerville (G-2678)
▼ Grogans Towne Chrysler Inc ....C.... 419 476-0761
Toledo (G-17924)
Guess Motors Inc ....E.... 866 890-0522
Carrollton (G-2622)
Hartwig Transit Inc ....E.... 513 563-1765
Cincinnati (G-3740)
Haydocy Automotive Inc ....D.... 614 279-8880
Columbus (G-7804)
▼ Hill Intl Trcks NA LLC ....D.... 330 386-6440
East Liverpool (G-10522)
Hoss Value Cars & Trucks Inc ....E.... 937 428-2400
Dayton (G-9622)
▲ Hy-Tek Material Handling Inc ....D.... 614 497-2500
Columbus (G-7873)
Irace Inc ....E.... 330 836-7247
Akron (G-283)
J D S Leasing Inc ....E.... 440 236-6575
Columbia Station (G-6847)
Jake Sweeney Automotive Inc ....C.... 513 782-2800
Cincinnati (G-3859)
Jeff Wyler Chevrolet Inc ....B.... 513 752-3447
Batavia (G-1018)
Jerry Haag Motors Inc ....E.... 937 402-2090
Hillsboro (G-11984)
Jim Brown Chevrolet Inc ....E.... 440 255-5511
Mentor (G-14198)
Jim Keim Ford ....D.... 614 888-3333
Columbus (G-7941)
Joe Dodge Kidd Inc ....E.... 513 752-1804
Cincinnati (G-2921)
Joseph Chevrolet Oldsmobile Co ....C.... 513 741-6700
Cincinnati (G-3887)
Joseph Russo ....E.... 440 748-2690
Grafton (G-11441)

75 AUTOMOTIVE REPAIR, SERVICES, AND PARKING

▲ Jtekt Auto Tenn Morristown .... C 440 835-1000
  Westlake (G-19503)
▲ K & M Tire Inc .... C 419 695-1061
  Delphos (G-10145)
Kaffenbarger Truck Eqp Co .... E 513 772-6800
  Cincinnati (G-3900)
Kempthorn Automall .... C 330 456-8287
  Canton (G-2423)
Kempthorn Automall .... D 800 451-3877
  Canton (G-2422)
Kennedy Mint Inc .... D 440 572-3222
  Cleveland (G-5895)
Kent Automotive Inc .... E 330 678-5520
  Kent (G-12377)
Kenworth of Cincinnati Inc .... D 513 771-5831
  Cincinnati (G-3916)
Kerry Ford Inc .... D 513 671-6400
  Cincinnati (G-3918)
Kings Toyota Inc .... D 513 583-4333
  Cincinnati (G-3928)
Kirk NationaLease Co .... E 937 498-1151
  Sidney (G-16939)
Klaben Family Dodge Inc .... E 330 673-9971
  Kent (G-12381)
▲ Krieger Ford Inc .... C 614 888-3320
  Columbus (G-8014)
Lakewood Chrysler-Plymouth .... E 216 521-1000
  Brookpark (G-1950)
Lakota Bus Garage .... E 419 986-5558
  Kansas (G-12347)
Lane Chevrolet .... D 937 426-2313
  Beavercreek Township (G-1273)
Lang Chevrolet Co .... D 937 426-2313
  Beavercreek Township (G-1274)
Lariche Subaru Inc .... D 419 422-1855
  Findlay (G-11056)
Lavery Chevrolet-Buick Inc .... E 330 823-1100
  Alliance (G-544)
Lebanon Chrysler - Plymouth Inc ..... E 513 932-2717
  Lebanon (G-12620)
Lebanon Ford Inc .... D 513 932-1010
  Lebanon (G-12621)
Lima Auto Mall Inc .... D 419 993-6000
  Lima (G-12816)
Lima City School District .... E 419 996-3450
  Lima (G-12817)
Lincoln Mrcury Kings Auto Mall .... C 513 683-3800
  Cincinnati (G-3984)
Lindsey Accura Inc .... E 800 980-8199
  Columbus (G-8070)
Loves Travel Stops .... E 419 643-8482
  Beaverdam (G-1290)
Lower Great Lakes Kenworth Inc .... E 419 874-3511
  Perrysburg (G-16029)
Madison Motor Service Inc .... E 419 332-0727
  Fremont (G-11211)
Maines Collision Repr & Bdy Sp ...... D 937 322-4618
  Springfield (G-17228)
Man-Tansky Inc .... E 740 454-2512
  Zanesville (G-20499)
Mansfield Truck Sales & Svc .... E 419 522-9811
  Mansfield (G-13335)
Mark Thomas Ford Inc .... E 330 638-1010
  Cortland (G-9077)
Martin Chevrolet Inc .... E 937 849-1381
  New Carlisle (G-15027)
Mathews Dodge Chrysler Jeep .... E 740 389-2341
  Marion (G-13563)
Mathews Ford Inc .... D 740 522-2181
  Newark (G-15202)
Mathews Kennedy Ford L-M Inc ...... D 740 387-3673
  Marion (G-13564)
Matia Motors Inc .... E 440 365-7311
  Elyria (G-10650)
May Jim Auto Sales LLC .... E 419 422-9797
  Findlay (G-11063)
Medina World Cars Inc .... E 330 725-4901
  Strongsville (G-17493)
Midway Garage Inc .... E 740 345-0699
  Newark (G-15207)
Midwest Trailer Sales & Svc .... E 513 772-2818
  West Chester (G-19119)
Mike Castrucci Ford .... C 513 831-7010
  Milford (G-14541)
Mizar Motors Inc .... D 419 729-2400
  Toledo (G-18065)
Monro Inc .... D 440 835-2393
  Westlake (G-19517)
Montrose Ford Inc .... D 330 666-0711
  Fairlawn (G-10966)

Morris Cadillac Buick GMC .... D 440 327-4181
  North Olmsted (G-15432)
Mullinax East LLC .... D 440 296-3020
  Wickliffe (G-19608)
Nassief Automotive Inc .... E 440 997-5151
  Austinburg (G-865)
National Auto Experts LLC .... E 440 274-5114
  Strongsville (G-17497)
Navistar Intl Trnsp Corp .... C 937 390-4242
  Springfield (G-17250)
Newtown Nine Inc .... E 330 376-7741
  Akron (G-351)
Nick Mayer Lincoln-Mercury Inc ...... E 440 835-3700
  Westlake (G-19521)
Northern Automotive Inc .... E 614 436-2001
  Columbus (G-8290)
Northgate Chrysler Jeep Inc .... D 513 385-3900
  Cincinnati (G-4180)
Ohio Automobile Club .... E 614 559-0000
  Columbus (G-8320)
Oregon Ford Inc .... C 419 698-4444
  Oregon (G-15746)
OReilly Automotive Inc .... E 937 660-3040
  Germantown (G-11399)
OReilly Automotive Inc .... E 419 324-2077
  Toledo (G-18112)
OReilly Automotive Inc .... E 740 845-1016
  London (G-13004)
OReilly Automotive Inc .... E 614 444-5352
  Columbus (G-8480)
OReilly Automotive Inc .... E 513 731-7700
  Cincinnati (G-4233)
OReilly Automotive Inc .... E 330 267-4383
  Hartville (G-11828)
Palmer Trucks Inc .... E 937 235-3318
  Dayton (G-9799)
Parrish Tire Company of Akron .... E 330 628-6800
  Mogadore (G-14682)
Pep Boys - Manny Moe & Jack .... E 614 864-2092
  Columbus (G-8534)
Peterbilt of Cincinnati .... E 513 772-1740
  Cincinnati (G-4285)
PGT Trucking Inc .... E 419 943-3437
  Leipsic (G-12664)
Pierson Automotive Inc .... E 513 424-1881
  Middletown (G-14485)
Progrssive Oldsmobile Cadillac ...... E 330 833-8585
  Massillon (G-13845)
R & R Inc .... E 330 799-1536
  Youngstown (G-20338)
Rebman Truck Service Inc .... E 419 589-8161
  Mansfield (G-13354)
▲ Ricart Ford Inc .... B 614 836-5321
  Groveport (G-11667)
Ron Marhofer Automall Inc .... E 330 923-5059
  Cuyahoga Falls (G-9217)
Rondy Fleet Services Inc .... C 330 745-9016
  Barberton (G-977)
Roush Equipment Inc .... C 614 882-1535
  Westerville (G-19442)
Rubini Enterprises Inc .... E 419 729-7010
  Toledo (G-18166)
Rush Motor Sales Inc .... E 614 471-9980
  Columbus (G-8659)
Rush Truck Centers Ohio Inc .... D 513 733-8500
  Cincinnati (G-4458)
Rush Truck Centers Ohio Inc .... E 419 224-6045
  Lima (G-12872)
Rush Truck Leasing Inc .... E 614 876-3500
  Columbus (G-8660)
Schoner Chevrolet Inc .... E 330 877-6731
  Hartville (G-11830)
Scotts Towing Co .... E 419 729-7888
  Toledo (G-18176)
Sharpnack Chevrolet Co .... E 440 967-3144
  Vermilion (G-18716)
Skinner Diesel Services Inc .... E 614 491-8785
  Columbus (G-8741)
Sonic Automotive .... D 614 870-8200
  Columbus (G-8748)
Specialized Services Inc .... E 330 448-4035
  Masury (G-13868)
Spires Motors Inc .... E 614 771-2345
  Hilliard (G-11953)
Spitzer Chevrolet Inc .... D 330 467-4141
  Northfield (G-15524)
Spitzer Motor City Inc .... E 567 307-7119
  Ontario (G-15716)
Spurlock Truck Service .... E 937 268-6100
  Dayton (G-9900)

Steubenville Truck Center Inc .... E 740 282-2711
  Steubenville (G-17337)
Stoops Frghtlnr-Qlity Trlr Inc .... E 937 236-4092
  Dayton (G-9909)
Stratton Chevrolet Co .... E 330 537-3151
  Beloit (G-1432)
Sunnyside Toyota Inc .... D 440 777-9911
  North Olmsted (G-15446)
Surfside Motors Inc .... E 419 462-1746
  Galion (G-11306)
Ta Operating LLC .... B 440 808-9100
  Westlake (G-19553)
Tallmadge Board of Education .... E 330 633-2215
  Tallmadge (G-17656)
Tansky Motors Inc .... E 650 322-7069
  Logan (G-12989)
Taylor Chevrolet Inc .... C 740 653-2091
  Lancaster (G-12579)
Ted Ruck Co Inc .... E 419 738-2613
  Wapakoneta (G-18808)
Trader Buds Westside Dodge .... D 614 272-0000
  Columbus (G-8861)
Travelcenters America Inc .... A 440 808-9100
  Westlake (G-19555)
Travelcenters of America LLC .... A 440 808-9100
  Westlake (G-19557)
Travelcenters of America LLC .... E 330 769-2053
  Lodi (G-12966)
Trepanier Daniels & Trepanier .... D 740 286-1288
  Jackson (G-12319)
United Parcel Service Inc OH .... C 419 872-0211
  Perrysburg (G-16066)
Valentine Buick Gmc Inc .... D 937 878-7371
  Fairborn (G-10808)
Vin Devers .... C 888 847-9535
  Sylvania (G-17626)
Volvo BMW Dyton Evans Volkswag ... E 937 890-6200
  Dayton (G-9975)
Voss Auto Network Inc .... E 937 428-2447
  Dayton (G-9976)
Voss Toyota Inc .... E 937 427-3700
  Beavercreek (G-1218)
W W Williams Company LLC .... E 419 837-5067
  Perrysburg (G-16070)
W W Williams Company LLC .... D 614 228-5000
  Columbus (G-8959)
W W Williams Company LLC .... E 614 527-9400
  Hilliard (G-11965)
W W Williams Company LLC .... E 330 225-7751
  Brunswick (G-1995)
Wagner Lincoln-Mercury Inc .... E 419 435-8131
  Carey (G-2601)
Walker Auto Group Inc .... D 937 433-4950
  Miamisburg (G-14367)
Warner Buick-Nissan Inc .... E 419 423-7161
  Findlay (G-11099)
Workforce Services Inc .... E 330 484-2566
  Canton (G-2589)
Young Truck Sales Inc .... E 330 477-6271
  Canton (G-2592)
Youngstown-Kenworth Inc .... E 330 534-9761
  Hubbard (G-12093)
Zanesville Chevrolet Cadillac .... E 740 452-3611
  Zanesville (G-20554)
Zender Electric .... E 419 436-1538
  Fostoria (G-11143)
Ziegler Tire and Supply Co .... E 513 539-7574
  Monroe (G-14719)

7539 Automotive Repair Shops, NEC

Bbt Fleet Services LLC .... E 419 462-7722
  Mansfield (G-13264)
Beechmont Motors Inc .... E 513 388-3883
  Cincinnati (G-3089)
Beechmont Toyota Inc .... D 513 388-3800
  Cincinnati (G-3092)
Bridgestone Ret Operations LLC .... E 330 929-3391
  Cuyahoga Falls (G-9167)
Broad & James Inc .... E 614 231-8697
  Columbus (G-7146)
Burtons Collision .... E 513 984-3396
  Cincinnati (G-3154)
Capitol City Trailers Inc .... D 614 491-2616
  Obetz (G-15664)
Carroll Halliday Inc .... E 740 335-1670
  Wshngtn CT Hs (G-20014)
Coates Car Care Inc .... E 330 652-4180
  Niles (G-15289)
▲ Double A Trailer Sales Inc .... E 419 692-7626
  Delphos (G-10142)

Employee Codes: A=Over 500 employees, B=251-500
C=101-250, D=51-100, E=25-50

75 AUTOMOTIVE REPAIR, SERVICES, AND PARKING

East Manufacturing Corporation......B...... 330 325-9921
　Randolph (G-16372)
First Services Inc...........................A...... 513 241-2200
　Cincinnati (G-3619)
First Transit Inc............................B...... 513 241-2200
　Cincinnati (G-3624)
Fleetpride West Inc........................E...... 419 243-3161
　Toledo (G-17895)
Fred Martin Nissan LLC..................E...... 330 644-8888
　Akron (G-229)
Germain Ford LLC..........................C...... 614 889-7777
　Columbus (G-7747)
◆ Goodyear Tire & Rubber Company....A...... 330 796-2121
　Akron (G-243)
Haasz Automall LLC........................E...... 330 296-2866
　Ravenna (G-16387)
Hans Truck and Trlr Repr Inc............E...... 216 581-0046
　Cleveland (G-5724)
Heritage Truck Equipment Inc.........E...... 330 699-4491
　Akron (G-262)
Irace Inc..E...... 330 836-7247
　Akron (G-283)
Jeff Wyler Chevrolet Inc..................B...... 513 752-3447
　Batavia (G-1018)
Jones Truck & Spring Repr Inc.........D...... 614 443-4619
　Columbus (G-7949)
Kings Cove Automotive LLC............D...... 513 677-0177
　Fairfield (G-10870)
▲ Mac Trailer Manufacturing Inc........C...... 330 823-9900
　Alliance (G-547)
Mac Trailer Service Inc..................E...... 330 823-9190
　Alliance (G-548)
Marmon Highway Tech LLC..............E...... 330 878-5595
　Dover (G-10197)
Monro Inc......................................D...... 614 360-3883
　Columbus (G-8185)
Monro Muffler Brake Inc..................D...... 937 999-3202
　Springboro (G-17130)
Montrose Sheffield LLC..................E...... 440 934-6699
　Sheffield Village (G-16892)
▼ Nelson Manufacturing Company......D...... 419 523-5321
　Ottawa (G-15799)
Paul Hrnchar Ford-Mercury Inc........E...... 330 533-3673
　Canfield (G-2207)
Perkins Motor Service Ltd................E...... 440 277-1256
　Lorain (G-13071)
Reliability First Corporation............E...... 216 503-0600
　Cleveland (G-6371)
◆ RL Best Company..........................E...... 330 758-8601
　Boardman (G-1744)
Rubini Enterprises Inc....................E...... 419 729-7010
　Toledo (G-18166)
S&S Car Care Inc............................E...... 330 494-9535
　Canton (G-2521)
Sanoh America Inc.........................C...... 740 392-9200
　Mount Vernon (G-14922)
▲ Speck Sales Incorporated..............E...... 419 353-8312
　Bowling Green (G-1794)
Spitzer Chevrolet Inc......................D...... 330 467-4141
　Northfield (G-15524)
Star Leasing Co..............................D...... 614 278-9999
　Columbus (G-8776)
Stoops Frghtlnr-Qlity Trlr Inc............E...... 937 236-4092
　Dayton (G-9909)
Three C Body Shop Inc...................D...... 614 274-9700
　Columbus (G-8842)
Transport Services Inc...................E...... 440 582-4900
　Cleveland (G-6612)
Tuffy Associates Corp.....................E...... 419 865-6900
　Toledo (G-18264)
United Garage & Service Corp.........D...... 216 623-1550
　Cleveland (G-6639)

7542 Car Washes

3 B Ventures LLC.............................E...... 419 236-9461
　Lima (G-12729)
Allied Car Wash Inc........................E...... 513 559-1733
　Cincinnati (G-2990)
Beheydts Auto Wrecking..................E...... 330 658-6109
　Doylestown (G-10223)
Blue Beacon of Hubbard Inc............E...... 330 534-4419
　Hubbard (G-12082)
Blue Beacon USA LP II....................E...... 330 534-4419
　Hubbard (G-12083)
Blue Beacon USA LP II....................E...... 419 643-8146
　Beaverdam (G-1289)
Blue Beacon USA LP II....................E...... 937 437-5533
　New Paris (G-15075)
Bp..E...... 216 731-3826
　Euclid (G-10745)
Car Wash..E...... 216 662-6289
　Cleveland (G-5179)
Car Wash Plus Ltd..........................E...... 513 683-4228
　Cincinnati (G-3175)
Coates Car Care Inc........................E...... 330 652-4180
　Niles (G-15289)
Consumer Foods..............................E...... 440 284-5972
　Elyria (G-10608)
Covington Car Wash Inc..................E...... 513 831-6164
　Milford (G-14514)
Elliott Auto Bath Inc........................E...... 513 422-3700
　Middletown (G-14425)
Expresso Car Wash Systems Inc......D...... 419 536-7540
　Toledo (G-17872)
Expresso Car Wash Systems Inc......E...... 419 866-7099
　Toledo (G-17873)
Falls Supersonic Car Wash Inc........E...... 330 928-1657
　Cuyahoga Falls (G-9186)
Four Season Car Wash....................E...... 330 372-4163
　Warren (G-18858)
Henderson Road Rest Systems........E...... 614 442-3310
　Columbus (G-7825)
J & T Washes Inc............................E...... 614 486-9093
　Columbus (G-7930)
JKL Development Company..............E...... 937 390-0358
　Springfield (G-17217)
John Atwood Inc..............................E...... 440 777-4147
　North Olmsted (G-15428)
Johnnys Carwash............................D...... 513 474-6603
　Cincinnati (G-3879)
Klean A Kar Inc..............................E...... 614 221-3145
　Columbus (G-7996)
Lawnview Industries Inc..................C...... 937 653-5217
　Urbana (G-18593)
Mikes Carwash Inc........................C...... 513 677-4700
　Loveland (G-13146)
Moo Moo North Hamilton LLC...........E...... 614 751-9274
　Etna (G-10730)
Mr Magic Carnegie Inc....................E...... 440 461-7572
　Beachwood (G-1105)
Napoleon Wash-N-Fill Inc................C...... 419 422-7216
　Findlay (G-11068)
Napoleon Wash-N-Fill Inc................D...... 419 592-0851
　Napoleon (G-14947)
North Lima Dairy Queen Inc.............E...... 330 549-3220
　North Lima (G-15406)
Red Carpet Car Wash Inc................E...... 330 477-5772
　Canton (G-2504)
Robert Stough Ventures Corp..........E...... 419 882-4073
　Toledo (G-18162)
Royal Car Wash Inc........................E...... 513 385-2777
　Cincinnati (G-4448)
Royal Sheen Service Center............E...... 330 966-7200
　Canton (G-2517)
Sax 5th Ave Car Wash Inc...............E...... 614 486-9093
　Columbus (G-8688)
Sharonville Car Wash......................E...... 513 769-4219
　Cincinnati (G-4509)
Susan A Smith Crystal Care............E...... 419 747-2666
　Butler (G-2068)
Truckomat Corporation....................E...... 740 467-2818
　Hebron (G-11861)
Waterway Gas & Wash Company......E...... 330 995-2900
　Aurora (G-864)
Yund Inc..E...... 330 837-9358
　Massillon (G-13864)

7549 Automotive Svcs, Except Repair & Car Washes

AAA Ohio Auto Club.........................D...... 614 431-7800
　Worthington (G-19937)
Abers Garage Inc............................E...... 419 281-5500
　Ashland (G-649)
▲ AGC Automotive Americas..............D...... 937 599-3131
　Bellefontaine (G-1375)
Air Compliance Testing Inc..............E...... 216 525-0900
　Cleveland (G-4972)
Arlington Towing Inc........................E...... 614 488-2006
　Columbus (G-7043)
Atlas Towing Service........................E...... 513 451-1854
　Cincinnati (G-3060)
Auto Concepts Cincinnatti LLC........E...... 513 769-4540
　Cincinnati (G-3067)
Auto Warehousing Co Inc................E...... 330 824-5149
　Warren (G-18820)
B & D Auto & Towing Inc..................E...... 440 237-3737
　North Royalton (G-15481)
Beaverdam Fleet Services Inc........E...... 419 643-8880
　Beaverdam (G-1288)
Broad & James Inc........................E...... 614 231-8697
　Columbus (G-7146)
Buddies Inc....................................E...... 216 642-3362
　Cleveland (G-5156)
Charlie Towing Service Inc..............E...... 440 234-5300
　Berea (G-1450)
Chesrown Oldsmobile Cadillac........E...... 740 366-7373
　Granville (G-11461)
Cintas Corporation No 1..................A...... 513 459-1200
　Mason (G-13678)
Cleveland Pick-A-Part Inc..............E...... 440 236-5031
　Columbia Station (G-6843)
Coates Car Care Inc........................E...... 330 652-4180
　Niles (G-15289)
Cresttek LLC..................................E...... 248 602-2083
　Dublin (G-10313)
Dave Marshall Inc...........................D...... 937 878-9135
　Fairborn (G-10790)
Dealer Supply and Eqp Ltd..............E...... 419 724-8473
　Toledo (G-17847)
Delphi Automotive Systems LLC.....E...... 248 724-5953
　Warren (G-18848)
Dutys Towing..................................E...... 614 252-3336
　Columbus (G-7553)
Eastland Crane Service Inc.............E...... 614 868-9750
　Columbus (G-7565)
Eaton Corporation...........................B...... 440 523-5000
　Beachwood (G-1074)
Eitel Towing Service Inc.................E...... 614 877-4139
　Orient (G-15760)
Envirotest Systems Corp.................E...... 330 963-4464
　Twinsburg (G-18409)
Envirotest Systems Corp.................E...... 330 963-4464
　Berea (G-1456)
Envirotest Systems Corp.................E...... 330 963-4464
　Cleveland (G-5545)
Envirotest Systems Corp.................E...... 330 963-4464
　Kent (G-12368)
Envirotest Systems Corp.................E...... 330 963-4464
　Elyria (G-10629)
Envirotest Systems Corp.................E...... 330 963-4464
　Cleveland (G-5546)
Envirotest Systems Corp.................E...... 330 963-4464
　Chagrin Falls (G-2716)
Envirotest Systems Corp.................E...... 330 963-4464
　Painesville (G-15855)
Envirotest Systems Corp.................E...... 330 963-4464
　Medina (G-14063)
Envirotest Systems Corp.................E...... 330 963-4464
　Chardon (G-2749)
Envirotest Systems Corp.................E...... 330 963-4464
　Amherst (G-593)
Envirotest Systems Corp.................E...... 330 963-4464
　Spencer (G-17105)
Envirotest Systems Corp.................E...... 330 963-4464
　Twinsburg (G-18410)
Fayette Parts Service Inc...............C...... 724 880-3616
　Wintersville (G-19810)
First Vehicle Services Inc..............C...... 513 241-2200
　Cincinnati (G-3625)
G&M Towing and Recovery LLC......E...... 216 271-0581
　Cleveland (G-5649)
Genicon Inc....................................E...... 419 491-4478
　Swanton (G-17565)
Herrnstein Chrysler Inc..................D...... 740 773-2203
　Chillicothe (G-2846)
Industrial Sorting Svcs Inc..............E...... 513 772-6501
　Cincinnati (G-3817)
Jo Lynn Inc....................................D...... 419 994-3204
　Loudonville (G-13092)
Madison Motor Service Inc..............E...... 419 332-0727
　Fremont (G-11211)
Maines Collision Repr & Bdy Sp......D...... 937 322-4618
　Springfield (G-17228)
Pete Baur Buick Gmc Inc...............E...... 440 238-5600
　Cleveland (G-6270)
Precision Coatings Systems............E...... 937 642-4727
　Marysville (G-13645)
Pro-Tow Inc....................................E...... 614 444-8697
　Columbus (G-8564)
Quest Quality Services LLC............D...... 419 704-7407
　Maumee (G-13965)
Reladyne LLC..................................E...... 513 489-6000
　Cincinnati (G-4402)
Richs Towing & Service Inc............E...... 440 234-3435
　Middleburg Heights (G-14385)
Rustys Towing Service Inc..............D...... 614 491-6288
　Columbus (G-8661)
Sandys Auto & Truck Svc Inc..........D...... 937 461-4980
　Moraine (G-14823)

Sandys Towing .... E 937 461-4980
Moraine (G-14824)
Scotts Towing Co .... E 419 729-7888
Toledo (G-18176)
Sears Roebuck and Co .... C 614 797-2095
Columbus (G-6906)
Sears Roebuck and Co .... E 937 427-8528
Beavercreek (G-1207)
Sears Roebuck and Co .... D 419 226-4172
Lima (G-12874)
Sears Roebuck and Co .... D 614 760-7195
Dublin (G-10450)
Sears Roebuck and Co .... C 330 652-5128
Niles (G-15304)
Sears Roebuck and Co .... C 440 846-3595
Cleveland (G-6459)
SGS North America Inc .... E 513 674-7048
Cincinnati (G-4507)
Shamrock Towing Inc .... E 614 882-3555
Westerville (G-19352)
Southwood Auto Sales .... E 330 788-8822
Youngstown (G-20378)
Sprandel Enterprises Inc .... E 513 777-6622
West Chester (G-19158)
Spurlock Truck Service .... E 937 268-6100
Dayton (G-9900)
Star Leasing Co .... D 614 278-9999
Columbus (G-8776)
Steve Austin Auto Group .... E 937 592-3015
Bellefontaine (G-1399)
Steve S Towing and Recovery .... E 513 422-0254
Middletown (G-14462)
Valvoline Instant Oil Change .... C 937 548-0123
Greenville (G-11522)
Valvoline LLC .... D 513 557-3100
Cincinnati (G-4802)
Van Wert County Engineers .... E 419 238-0210
Van Wert (G-18648)
World Trck Towing Recovery Inc .... E 330 723-1116
Seville (G-16848)
Yund Inc .... E 330 837-9358
Massillon (G-13864)

76 MISCELLANEOUS REPAIR SERVICES

7622 Radio & TV Repair Shops

Central USA Wireless LLC .... E 513 469-1500
Cincinnati (G-3218)
Comproducts Inc .... E 614 276-5552
Columbus (G-7416)
Consolidated Communications .... E 330 896-3905
Canton (G-2321)
Dss Installations Ltd .... E 513 761-7000
Cincinnati (G-3505)
Electra Sound Inc .... C 216 433-1050
Cleveland (G-5531)
Electra Sound Inc .... D 216 433-9600
Parma (G-15906)
Household Centralized Svc Inc .... E 419 474-5754
Toledo (G-17962)
K M T Service .... E 614 777-7770
Hilliard (G-11918)
Mobilcomm Inc .... D 513 742-5555
Cincinnati (G-4110)
Office World Inc .... E 419 991-4694
Lima (G-12928)
P & R Communications Svc Inc .... E 937 222-0861
Dayton (G-9796)
Professional Telecom Svcs .... E 513 232-7700
Cincinnati (G-4344)
Staley Technologies Inc .... E 330 339-2898
New Philadelphia (G-15115)
Sunrise Television Corp .... D 740 282-9999
Mingo Junction (G-14658)

7623 Refrigeration & Air Conditioning Svc & Repair Shop

Columbs/Worthington Htg AC Inc .... E 614 771-5381
Columbus (G-7325)
Cov-Ro Inc .... E 330 856-3176
Warren (G-18841)
Dickson Industrial Park Inc .... E 740 377-9162
South Point (G-17083)
Electrical Appl Repr Svc Inc .... E 216 459-8700
Brooklyn Heights (G-1915)
Gardiner Service Company .... C 440 248-3400
Solon (G-17008)
Honeywell International Inc .... D 216 459-6053
Cleveland (G-5770)
Mid-Ohio Air Conditioning .... E 614 291-4664
Columbus (G-8164)
Osterfeld Champion Service .... E 937 254-8437
Dayton (G-9795)
Refrigeration Systems Company .... D 614 263-0913
Columbus (G-8603)
Roto-Rooter Services Company .... D 513 541-3840
Cincinnati (G-4445)
Smith & Oby Service Co .... E 440 735-5322
Bedford (G-1337)
▲ Transport Specialists Inc .... E 513 771-2220
Cincinnati (G-4680)

7629 Electrical & Elex Repair Shop, NEC

Alco-Chem Inc .... E 330 833-8551
Canton (G-2230)
▲ Amko Service Company .... E 330 364-8857
Midvale (G-14489)
Ascendtech Inc .... E 216 458-1101
Willoughby (G-19645)
AT&T Corp .... A 614 223-8236
Columbus (G-7062)
▲ Automation & Control Tech Ltd .... E 419 661-6400
Perrysburg (G-15973)
Blakemans Valley Off Eqp Inc .... E 330 729-1000
Youngstown (G-20116)
Blue Technologies Inc .... E 330 499-9300
Canton (G-2266)
Boeing Company .... E 740 788-4000
Newark (G-15148)
Casey Equipment Corporation .... E 330 750-1005
Struthers (G-17527)
Cellco Partnership .... E 440 779-1313
North Olmsted (G-15412)
Central Repair Service Inc .... E 513 943-0500
Point Pleasant (G-16218)
Centurylink Inc .... A 614 215-4223
Dublin (G-10286)
City of Wadsworth .... E 330 334-1581
Wadsworth (G-18749)
DTE Inc .... E 419 522-3428
Mansfield (G-13295)
Electric Motor Tech LLC .... E 513 821-9999
Cincinnati (G-3546)
Electric Service Co Inc .... E 513 271-6387
Cincinnati (G-3547)
Electrical Appl Repr Svc Inc .... E 216 459-8700
Brooklyn Heights (G-1915)
▲ Enprotech Industrial Tech LLC .... C 216 883-3220
Cleveland (G-5542)
Fak Group Inc .... E 440 498-8465
Solon (G-17006)
▲ Fosbel Inc .... C 216 362-3900
Brookpark (G-1945)
General Electric Company .... D 216 883-1000
Cleveland (G-5667)
General Electric Company .... B 513 977-1500
Cincinnati (G-3667)
High Line Corporation .... E 330 848-8800
Akron (G-264)
Honeywell International Inc .... D 440 243-8877
Strongsville (G-17472)
Household Centralized Svc Inc .... E 419 474-5754
Toledo (G-17962)
▲ Instrmntation Ctrl Systems Inc .... E 513 662-2600
Cincinnati (G-3822)
Internash Global Svc Group LLC .... D 513 772-0430
West Chester (G-19211)
▲ J-C-R Tech Inc .... E 937 783-2296
Blanchester (G-1515)
Jersey Central Pwr & Light Co .... E 419 321-7207
Oak Harbor (G-15611)
Kiemle-Hankins Company .... E 419 661-2430
Perrysburg (G-16024)
Leppo Inc .... C 330 633-3999
Tallmadge (G-17643)
Liebert Corporation .... D 614 841-6104
Columbus (G-8060)
◆ Liebert Corporation .... A 614 888-0246
Columbus (G-8059)
▲ Magnetech Industrial Svcs Inc .... D 330 830-3500
Massillon (G-13830)
Mid-Ohio Electric Co .... E 614 274-8000
Columbus (G-8165)
Mmi-Cpr LLC .... E 216 674-0645
Independence (G-12234)
Modern Office Methods Inc .... D 513 791-0909
Blue Ash (G-1644)
Modern Office Methods Inc .... E 614 891-3693
Westerville (G-19426)
Narrow Way Custom Technology .... E 937 743-1611
Carlisle (G-2605)
Ohio Business Machines LLC .... E 216 485-2000
Cleveland (G-6187)
Ohio Machinery Co .... E 740 453-0563
Zanesville (G-20519)
Ohio State University .... A 614 292-6158
Columbus (G-8445)
Professional Telecom Svcs .... E 513 232-7700
Cincinnati (G-4344)
▲ Rubber City Machinery Corp .... E 330 434-3500
Akron (G-419)
S D Myers Inc .... C 330 630-7000
Tallmadge (G-17648)
Service Solutions Group LLC .... E 513 772-6600
Cincinnati (G-4501)
Star Dist & Manufacturring LLC .... D 513 860-3573
West Chester (G-19231)
▲ Steel Eqp Specialists Inc .... D 330 823-8260
Alliance (G-563)
Tegam Inc .... E 440 466-6100
Geneva (G-11369)
Terex Utilities Inc .... D 513 539-9770
Monroe (G-14714)
Toshiba Amer Bus Solutions Inc .... E 216 642-7555
Cleveland (G-6603)
◆ Vertiv Energy Systems Inc .... A 440 288-1122
Lorain (G-13085)
▲ Wauseon Machine & Mfg Inc .... D 419 337-0940
Wauseon (G-18964)

7631 Watch, Clock & Jewelry Repair

Cox Paving Inc .... D 937 780-3075
Wshngtn CT Hs (G-20018)
Sdr Services LLC .... E 513 625-0695
Goshen (G-11439)

7641 Reupholstery & Furniture Repair

Business Furniture LLC .... E 937 293-1010
Dayton (G-9375)
▲ Casco Mfg Solutions Inc .... D 513 681-0003
Cincinnati (G-3191)
Everybodys Inc .... E 937 293-1010
Moraine (G-14782)
OfficeMax North America Inc .... E 614 899-6186
Westerville (G-19431)
Recycled Systems Furniture Inc .... E 614 880-9110
Worthington (G-19991)
Soft Touch Wood LLC .... E 330 545-4204
Girard (G-11426)

7692 Welding Repair

A & C Welding Inc .... E 330 762-4777
Peninsula (G-15946)
▲ A & G Manufacturing Co Inc .... E 419 468-7433
Galion (G-11288)
Abbott Tool Inc .... E 419 476-6742
Toledo (G-17738)
All-Type Welding & Fabrication .... E 440 439-3990
Cleveland (G-4991)
Allied Fabricating & Wldg Co .... E 614 751-6664
Columbus (G-6970)
Arctech Fabricating Inc .... E 937 525-9353
Springfield (G-17149)
Athens Mold and Machine Inc .... D 740 593-6613
Akron (G-84)
Bayloff Stmped Pdts Knsman Inc .... D 330 876-4511
Kinsman (G-12452)
Blevins Metal Fabrication Inc .... E 419 522-6082
Mansfield (G-13267)
Breitinger Company .... C 419 526-4255
Mansfield (G-13269)
Brown Industrial Inc .... E 937 693-3838
Botkins (G-1752)
C & R Inc .... E 614 497-1130
Groveport (G-11626)
C-N-D Industries Inc .... E 330 478-8811
Massillon (G-13791)
Carter Manufacturing Co Inc .... E 513 398-7303
Mason (G-13672)
Chipmatic Tool & Machine Inc .... D 419 862-2737
Elmore (G-10587)
Compton Metal Products Inc .... D 937 382-2403
Wilmington (G-19757)
Creative Mold and Machine Inc .... E 440 338-5146
Newbury (G-15255)
Crest Bending Inc .... E 419 492-2108
New Washington (G-15134)

S
I
C

Custom Machine Inc .... E 419 986-5122
Tiffin *(G-17676)*

Dynamic Weld Corporation .... E 419 582-2900
Osgood *(G-15791)*

▲ East End Welding Company .... C 330 677-6000
Kent *(G-12367)*

Falls Stamping & Welding Co .... C 330 928-1191
Cuyahoga Falls *(G-9185)*

▲ Fosbel Inc .... C 216 362-3900
Brookpark *(G-1945)*

Fosbel Holding Inc .... E 216 362-3900
Cleveland *(G-5625)*

Gaspar Inc .... D 330 477-2222
Canton *(G-2376)*

▲ General Tool Company .... C 513 733-5500
Cincinnati *(G-3675)*

George Steel Fabricating Inc .... E 513 932-2887
Lebanon *(G-12606)*

▲ Glenridge Machine Co .... E 440 975-1055
Willoughby *(G-19666)*

Habco Tool and Dev Co Inc .... E 440 946-5546
Mentor *(G-14187)*

HI Tecmetal Group Inc .... E 440 373-5101
Wickliffe *(G-19601)*

HI Tecmetal Group Inc .... E 440 946-2280
Willoughby *(G-19669)*

▲ Hi-Tek Manufacturing Inc .... C 513 459-1094
Mason *(G-13717)*

Hobart Bros Stick Electrode .... C 937 332-5375
Troy *(G-18357)*

▲ Industry Products Co .... B 937 778-0585
Piqua *(G-16150)*

J & S Industrial Mch Pdts Inc .... D 419 691-1380
Toledo *(G-17980)*

Jerl Machine Inc .... D 419 873-0270
Perrysburg *(G-16020)*

JMw Welding and Mfg .... E 330 484-2428
Canton *(G-2418)*

K-M-S Industries Inc .... E 440 243-6680
Brookpark *(G-1948)*

Kings Welding and Fabg Inc .... E 330 738-3592
Mechanicstown *(G-14031)*

▲ Kottler Metal Products Co Inc .... E 440 946-7473
Willoughby *(G-19677)*

L B Industries Inc .... E 330 750-1002
Struthers *(G-17533)*

Laserflex Corporation .... D 614 850-9600
Hilliard *(G-11920)*

Liberty Casting Company LLC .... E 740 363-1941
Delaware *(G-10116)*

Lima Sheet Metal Machine & Mfg .... E 419 229-1161
Lima *(G-12827)*

▲ Long-Stanton Mfg Company .... E 513 874-8020
West Chester *(G-19111)*

Majestic Tool and Machine Inc .... E 440 248-5058
Solon *(G-17025)*

Marsam Metalfab Inc .... E 330 405-1520
Twinsburg *(G-18444)*

Meta Manufacturing Corporation .... E 513 793-6382
Blue Ash *(G-1643)*

Norman Noble Inc .... C 216 761-2133
Cleveland *(G-6136)*

Northwind Industries Inc .... E 216 433-0666
Cleveland *(G-6163)*

Ohio Hydraulics Inc .... E 513 771-2590
Cincinnati *(G-4207)*

Ohio State University .... E 614 292-4139
Columbus *(G-8399)*

Paulo Products Company .... E 440 942-0153
Willoughby *(G-19703)*

◆ Pentaflex Inc .... C 937 325-5551
Springfield *(G-17260)*

Perkins Motor Service Ltd .... E 440 277-1256
Lorain *(G-13071)*

Phillips Mfg and Tower Co .... D 419 347-1720
Shelby *(G-16902)*

Precision Mtal Fabrication Inc .... D 937 235-9261
Dayton *(G-9818)*

Precision Welding Corporation .... E 216 524-6110
Cleveland *(G-6295)*

Prout Boiler Htg & Wldg Inc .... E 330 744-0293
Youngstown *(G-20331)*

Quality Welding Inc .... E 419 483-6067
Bellevue *(G-1416)*

▲ R K Industries Inc .... D 419 523-5001
Ottawa *(G-15804)*

Rbm Environmental and Cnstr .... E 419 693-5840
Oregon *(G-15748)*

▲ Rose City Manufacturing Inc .... D 937 325-5561
Springfield *(G-17268)*

Schmidt Machine Company .... E 419 294-3814
Upper Sandusky *(G-18566)*

Steubenville Truck Center Inc .... E 740 282-2711
Steubenville *(G-17337)*

Systems Jay LLC Nanogate .... B 419 747-4161
Mansfield *(G-13370)*

Tendon Manufacturing Inc .... E 216 663-3200
Cleveland *(G-6582)*

Triangle Precision Industries .... D 937 299-6776
Dayton *(G-9937)*

Turn-Key Industrial Svcs LLC .... D 614 274-1128
Columbus *(G-8878)*

Two M Precision Co Inc .... E 440 946-2120
Willoughby *(G-19719)*

Valley Machine Tool Co Inc .... E 513 899-2737
Morrow *(G-14847)*

Viking Fabricators Inc .... E 740 374-5246
Marietta *(G-13515)*

Wayne Trail Technologies Inc .... D 937 295-2120
Fort Loramie *(G-11112)*

7694 Armature Rewinding Shops

▲ 3-D Service Ltd .... C 330 830-3500
Massillon *(G-13780)*

City Machine Technologies Inc .... E 330 740-8186
Youngstown *(G-20142)*

Dolin Supply Co .... E 304 529-4171
South Point *(G-17084)*

Fenton Bros Electric Co .... E 330 343-0093
New Philadelphia *(G-15094)*

Horner Industrial Services Inc .... E 937 390-6667
Springfield *(G-17208)*

Integrated Power Services LLC .... E 216 433-7808
Cleveland *(G-5826)*

Integrated Power Services LLC .... E 513 863-8816
Hamilton *(G-11746)*

Kiemle-Hankins Company .... E 419 661-2430
Perrysburg *(G-16024)*

M & R Electric Motor Svc Inc .... E 937 222-6282
Dayton *(G-9692)*

Magnetech Industrial Svcs Inc .... C 330 830-3500
Massillon *(G-13831)*

Matlock Electric Co Inc .... E 513 731-9600
Cincinnati *(G-4030)*

Mid-Ohio Electric Co .... E 614 274-8000
Columbus *(G-8165)*

◆ National Electric Coil Inc .... B 614 488-1151
Columbus *(G-8217)*

▲ Setco Sales Company .... D 513 941-5110
Cincinnati *(G-4502)*

▲ Shoemaker Electric Company .... E 614 294-5626
Columbus *(G-8728)*

Whelco Industrial Ltd .... E 419 873-6134
Perrysburg *(G-16074)*

7699 Repair Shop & Related Svcs, NEC

1157 Design Concepts LLC .... E 937 497-1157
Sidney *(G-16909)*

▲ 3-D Service Ltd .... C 330 830-3500
Massillon *(G-13780)*

A and A Millwright Rigging Svcs .... E 513 396-6212
Cincinnati *(G-2951)*

A P O Holdings Inc .... D 330 650-1330
Hudson *(G-12100)*

AAA Pipe Cleaning Corporation .... C 216 341-2900
Cleveland *(G-4942)*

Acpx2 .... E 513 829-2100
Fairfield *(G-10815)*

AD Farrow LLC .... E 614 228-6353
Columbus *(G-6942)*

Adelmos Electric Sewer Clg Co .... E 216 641-2301
Brooklyn Heights *(G-1909)*

Advance Door Company .... E 216 883-2424
Cleveland *(G-4957)*

Adventure Harley Davidson .... E 330 343-2295
Dover *(G-10175)*

Airborne Maint Engrg Svcs Inc .... A 937 366-2559
Wilmington *(G-19744)*

Airborne Maint Engrg Svcs Inc .... D 937 382-5591
Wilmington *(G-19745)*

◆ Ajax Tocco Magnethermic Corp .... C 330 372-8511
Warren *(G-18815)*

Akil Incorporated .... E 419 625-0857
Sandusky *(G-16724)*

▲ All American Sports Corp .... A 440 366-8225
North Ridgeville *(G-15453)*

All Lift Service Company Inc .... E 440 585-1542
Willoughby *(G-19642)*

Alpha Imaging LLC .... D 440 953-3800
Willoughby *(G-19643)*

Altaquip LLC .... E 513 674-6464
Harrison *(G-11790)*

▲ American Frame Corporation .... E 419 893-5595
Maumee *(G-13874)*

American Residential Svcs LLC .... E 888 762-7752
Columbus *(G-7006)*

▲ Amko Service Company .... E 330 364-8857
Midvale *(G-14489)*

Andrew Belmont Sargent .... E 513 769-7800
Cincinnati *(G-3027)*

Apple Farm Service Inc .... E 937 526-4851
Covington *(G-9135)*

▲ Applied Industrial Tech Inc .... B 216 426-4000
Cleveland *(G-5055)*

Ashland Cleaning LLC .... E 419 281-1747
Ashland *(G-654)*

Atm Solutions Inc .... D 513 742-4900
Cincinnati *(G-3061)*

◆ Babcock & Wilcox Company .... A 330 753-4511
Barberton *(G-955)*

Bedford Heights City Waste .... E 440 439-5343
Bedford *(G-1295)*

Benchmark Technologies Corp .... E 419 843-6691
Toledo *(G-17769)*

Best Aire Compressor Service .... D 419 726-0055
Millbury *(G-14577)*

Boc Water Hydraulics Inc .... E 330 332-4444
Salem *(G-16691)*

Brechbuhler Scales Inc .... E 330 458-3060
Canton *(G-2269)*

Burch Hydro Inc .... E 740 694-9146
Fredericktown *(G-11178)*

C & W Tank Cleaning Company .... D 419 691-1995
Oregon *(G-15727)*

C H Bradshaw Co .... E 614 871-2087
Grove City *(G-11543)*

Calvin Klein Inc .... E 330 562-2746
Aurora *(G-833)*

Capitol Varsity Sports Inc .... E 513 523-4126
Oxford *(G-15813)*

Cbord Group Inc .... C 330 498-2702
Uniontown *(G-18513)*

Cecil I Walker Machinery Co .... E 740 286-7566
Jackson *(G-12308)*

Chemed Corporation .... D 513 762-6690
Cincinnati *(G-3237)*

Cincinnati Hydraulic Svc Inc .... E 513 874-0540
West Chester *(G-19039)*

Cleveland Electric Labs Co .... E 800 447-2207
Twinsburg *(G-18401)*

Cleveland Pump Repr & Svcs LLC .... E 330 963-3100
Twinsburg *(G-18402)*

Cmbb LLC .... C 937 652-2151
Urbana *(G-18581)*

Columbs/Worthington Htg AC Inc .... E 614 771-5381
Columbus *(G-7325)*

Comdoc Inc .... C 330 896-2346
Uniontown *(G-18514)*

Commercial Electric Pdts Corp .... E 216 241-2886
Cleveland *(G-5376)*

▲ Compak Inc .... E 419 207-8888
Ashland *(G-675)*

Compton Metal Products Inc .... D 937 382-2403
Wilmington *(G-19757)*

Consolidated Rail Corporation .... D 440 786-3014
Macedonia *(G-13194)*

Constant Aviation LLC .... E 216 261-7119
Cleveland *(G-5395)*

Convergint Technologies LLC .... C 513 771-1717
Cincinnati *(G-3416)*

Cope Farm Equipment Inc .... E 330 821-5867
Alliance *(G-536)*

Corporate Cleaning Inc .... E 614 203-6051
Columbus *(G-7441)*

Corrotec Inc .... E 937 325-3585
Springfield *(G-17177)*

▲ Country Saw and Knife Inc .... E 330 332-1611
Salem *(G-16692)*

County of Stark .... E 330 477-3609
Massillon *(G-13799)*

Cov-Ro Inc .... E 330 856-3176
Warren *(G-18841)*

Damarc Inc .... E 330 454-6171
Canton *(G-2333)*

Dayton Door Sales Inc .... E 937 253-9181
Dayton *(G-9471)*

Dayton Door Sales Inc .... E 937 253-9181
Dayton *(G-9472)*

Dayton Industrial Drum Inc .... E 937 253-8933
Dayton *(G-9263)*

SIC SECTION

76 MISCELLANEOUS REPAIR SERVICES

Diversified Air Systems Inc ....E 330 784-3366
Akron *(G-194)*
Document Imging Spcialists LLC ....E 614 868-9008
Columbus *(G-7538)*
Dortronic Service Inc ....E 216 739-3667
Cleveland *(G-5506)*
▲ Dover Hydraulics Inc ....D 330 364-1617
Dover *(G-10185)*
Dreier & Maller Inc ....E 614 575-0065
Reynoldsburg *(G-16448)*
Dtv Inc ....E 216 226-5465
Mayfield Heights *(G-14001)*
▲ Eagleburgmann Ke Inc ....E 859 746-0091
Cincinnati *(G-3529)*
Eastern Medical Equipment Co ....E 330 394-5555
Warren *(G-18853)*
Elmco Engineering Oh Inc ....E 419 238-1100
Van Wert *(G-18632)*
▲ Emsco Inc ....E 330 830-7125
Massillon *(G-13803)*
Emsco Inc ....E 330 833-5600
Massillon *(G-13804)*
Enterprise Vending Inc ....E 513 772-1373
Cincinnati *(G-3560)*
Equipment Maintenance Inc ....E 513 353-3518
Cleves *(G-6799)*
▲ Equipment MGT Svc & Repr Inc ....E 937 383-1052
Wilmington *(G-19761)*
Estabrook Corporation ....E 440 234-8566
Berea *(G-1457)*
▲ Fallsway Equipment Co Inc ....C 330 633-6000
Akron *(G-214)*
Famous Enterprises Inc ....E 330 762-9621
Akron *(G-217)*
Fdc Machine Repair Inc ....E 216 362-1082
Parma *(G-15907)*
▲ File Sharpening Company Inc ....E 937 376-8268
Xenia *(G-20050)*
Filing Scale Company Inc ....E 330 425-3092
Twinsburg *(G-18415)*
Fire Foe Corp ....E 330 759-9834
Girard *(G-11413)*
▲ Forge Industries Inc ....A 330 782-8301
Youngstown *(G-20191)*
Freedom Harley-Davidson Inc ....E 330 494-2453
Canton *(G-2371)*
French Company LLC ....D 330 963-4344
Twinsburg *(G-18418)*
Frontier Tank Center Inc ....E 330 659-3888
Richfield *(G-16510)*
▲ Fusion Interior Services Ltd ....E 513 759-4100
West Chester *(G-19077)*
General Plastex Inc ....E 330 745-7775
Barberton *(G-964)*
GL Nause Co Inc ....E 513 722-9500
Loveland *(G-13128)*
Graphic Systems Services Inc ....E 937 746-0708
Springboro *(G-17120)*
Grimes Aerospace Company ....B 937 484-2001
Urbana *(G-18590)*
◆ Grob Systems Inc ....C 419 358-9015
Bluffton *(G-1731)*
▲ Hall Contracting Services Inc ....D 440 930-0050
Avon Lake *(G-932)*
Hans Truck and Trlr Repr Inc ....E 216 581-0046
Cleveland *(G-5724)*
▲ Harry C Lobalzo & Sons Inc ....E 330 666-6758
Akron *(G-253)*
Hays Enterprises Inc ....E 330 299-8639
Warren *(G-18861)*
Henry P Thompson Company ....E 513 248-3200
Milford *(G-14524)*
◆ Hillman Companies Inc ....B 513 851-4900
Cincinnati *(G-3764)*
Hman Group Holdings Inc ....A 513 851-4900
Cincinnati *(G-3773)*
Honeywell International Inc ....D 216 459-6053
Cleveland *(G-5770)*
Huffy Corporation ....D 937 743-5011
Springboro *(G-17124)*
Hydraulic Specialists Inc ....E 740 922-3343
Midvale *(G-14490)*
I L T Diversified Mtl Hdlg ....E 419 865-8025
Holland *(G-12029)*
Industrial Air Control Inc ....D 330 772-6422
Hubbard *(G-12088)*
Industrial Maint Svcs Inc ....E 440 729-2068
Chagrin Falls *(G-2721)*
◆ Industrial Parts & Service Co ....E 330 966-5025
Canton *(G-2411)*
▲ Industrial Repair & Mfg Inc ....E 419 822-4232
Delta *(G-10159)*
Inertial Airline Services Inc ....E 440 995-6555
Cleveland *(G-5818)*
Integrity Processing LLC ....E 330 285-6937
Barberton *(G-966)*
Interstate Lift Trucks Inc ....E 216 328-0970
Cleveland *(G-5835)*
J and J Environmental Inc ....E 513 398-4521
Mason *(G-13725)*
J&J Precision Machine Ltd ....E 330 923-5783
Cuyahoga Falls *(G-9197)*
Keaney Investment Group LLC ....E 937 263-6429
Dayton *(G-9648)*
Kens Beverage Inc ....E 513 874-8200
Fairfield *(G-10869)*
Kone Inc ....E 330 762-8886
Cleveland *(G-5910)*
Kone Inc ....E 614 866-1751
Gahanna *(G-11251)*
Konecranes Inc ....E 513 755-2800
West Chester *(G-19104)*
Lance A1 Cleaning Services LLC ....D 614 370-0550
Columbus *(G-8035)*
Laserflex Corporation ....D 614 850-9600
Hilliard *(G-11920)*
◆ Lawrence Industries Inc ....C 216 518-7000
Cleveland *(G-5929)*
Leppo Inc ....E 330 456-2930
Canton *(G-2434)*
Liberty Casting Company LLC ....E 740 363-1941
Delaware *(G-10116)*
▲ Lucas Precision LLC ....E 216 451-5588
Cleveland *(G-5957)*
Magnetech Industrial Svcs Inc ....C 330 830-3500
Massillon *(G-13831)*
Maintenance & Repair Tech Inc ....E 513 422-1198
Middletown *(G-14432)*
Marsh Building Products Inc ....E 937 222-3321
Dayton *(G-9700)*
McNational Inc ....E 740 377-4391
South Point *(G-17093)*
Med Clean ....C 614 207-3317
Columbus *(G-8141)*
Miami Industrial Trucks Inc ....D 937 293-4194
Moraine *(G-14805)*
Mid-American Clg Contrs Inc ....C 937 859-6222
Dayton *(G-9743)*
Mid-Ohio Harley-Davidson Inc ....E 937 322-3590
Springfield *(G-17247)*
Mine Equipment Services LLC ....E 740 936-5427
Sunbury *(G-17558)*
Mispace Inc ....E 614 626-2602
Columbus *(G-8179)*
Mmic Inc ....D 513 697-0445
Loveland *(G-13147)*
Mobile Instr Svc & Repr Inc ....C 937 592-5025
Bellefontaine *(G-1391)*
◆ Monarch Electric Service Co ....D 216 433-7800
Cleveland *(G-6073)*
MPW Container Management Corp ....D 216 362-8400
Cleveland *(G-6083)*
▲ Mr Rooter Plumbing Corporation ....E 419 625-4444
Independence *(G-12236)*
Mt Texas LLC ....E 513 853-4400
Cincinnati *(G-4129)*
National Compressor Svcs LLC ....E 419 868-4980
Holland *(G-12040)*
National Heat Exch Clg Corp ....E 330 482-0893
Youngstown *(G-20296)*
Nbw Inc ....E 216 377-1700
Cleveland *(G-6114)*
No Cages Harley-Davidson ....E 614 764-2453
Plain City *(G-16202)*
Norris Brothers Co Inc ....C 216 771-2233
Cleveland *(G-6137)*
Nurotoco Massachusetts Inc ....C 513 762-6690
Cincinnati *(G-4192)*
Obr Cooling Towers Inc ....E 419 243-3443
Rossford *(G-16610)*
▼ Ohio Broach & Machine Company ....E 440 946-1040
Willoughby *(G-19699)*
Ohio Hydraulics Inc ....E 513 771-2590
Cincinnati *(G-4207)*
Ohio Machinery Co ....E 330 530-9010
Girard *(G-11421)*
Ohio Machinery Co ....E 330 874-1003
Bolivar *(G-1750)*
◆ Ohio Machinery Co ....C 440 526-6200
Broadview Heights *(G-1886)*
◆ OKL Can Line Inc ....E 513 825-1655
Cincinnati *(G-4218)*
Omni Cart Services Inc ....E 440 205-8363
Mentor *(G-14225)*
Oregon Clean Energy Center ....E 419 566-9466
Oregon *(G-15745)*
Osterfeld Champion Service ....E 937 254-8437
Dayton *(G-9795)*
Otis Elevator Company ....D 216 573-2333
Cleveland *(G-6218)*
Otis Elevator Company ....D 513 531-7888
Cincinnati *(G-4242)*
Otis Elevator Company ....E 614 777-6500
Columbus *(G-8498)*
Paradigm Industrial LLC ....E 937 224-4415
Dayton *(G-9801)*
Pas Technologies Inc ....D 937 840-1000
Hillsboro *(G-11991)*
Patriot Indus Contg Svcs LLC ....E 513 248-8222
Milford *(G-14552)*
▲ Pennsylvania Tl Sls & Svc Inc ....D 330 758-0845
Youngstown *(G-20317)*
Perkins Motor Service Ltd ....E 440 277-1256
Lorain *(G-13071)*
Petro-Com Corp ....E 440 327-6900
North Ridgeville *(G-15473)*
Precision Endoscopy Amer Inc ....E 410 527-9598
Stow *(G-17386)*
Premier Cleaning Services Inc ....E 513 831-2492
Milford *(G-14555)*
Primetals Technologies USA LLC ....E 419 929-1554
New London *(G-15070)*
Pro-Kleen Industrial Svcs Inc ....E 740 689-1886
Lancaster *(G-12566)*
Providian Med Field Svc LLC ....E 440 833-0460
Highland Heights *(G-11871)*
Quintus Technologies LLC ....E 614 891-2732
Lewis Center *(G-12705)*
Randy L Fork Inc ....E 419 891-1230
Maumee *(G-13967)*
▲ Raymond Storage Concepts Inc ....E 513 891-7290
Blue Ash *(G-1677)*
Rbm Environmental and Cnstr ....E 419 693-5840
Oregon *(G-15748)*
Reladyne LLC ....E 513 489-6000
Cincinnati *(G-4402)*
Riverside Marine Inds Inc ....D 419 729-1621
Toledo *(G-18157)*
Rmf Nooter Inc ....D 419 727-1970
Toledo *(G-18159)*
Roto-Rooter Development Co ....D 513 762-6690
Cincinnati *(G-4442)*
Roto-Rooter Group Inc ....C 513 762-6690
Cincinnati *(G-4443)*
Roto-Rooter Services Company ....E 614 238-8006
Columbus *(G-8652)*
Roto-Rooter Services Company ....D 513 762-6690
Cincinnati *(G-4444)*
Roto-Rooter Services Company ....D 513 541-3840
Cincinnati *(G-4445)*
Roto-Rooter Services Company ....E 216 429-1928
Solon *(G-17048)*
◆ Russell T Bundy Associates Inc ....D 937 652-2151
Urbana *(G-18600)*
S & S Inc ....E 216 383-1880
Cleveland *(G-6425)*
▲ Sabco Industries Inc ....E 419 531-5347
Toledo *(G-18169)*
▲ Saw Service and Supply Company ....E 216 252-5600
Cleveland *(G-6444)*
Schindler Elevator Corporation ....D 216 391-8600
Cleveland *(G-6446)*
Schindler Elevator Corporation ....E 614 573-2777
Columbus *(G-8694)*
Schindler Elevator Corporation ....E 419 861-5900
Holland *(G-12054)*
▲ Scott Fetzer Company ....E 440 892-3000
Westlake *(G-19544)*
Sears Roebuck and Co ....E 330 629-7700
Youngstown *(G-20368)*
Seilkop Industries Inc ....E 513 761-1035
Cincinnati *(G-4492)*
Serex Corporation ....E 330 726-6062
Youngstown *(G-20371)*
Sharron Group Inc ....E 614 873-5856
Plain City *(G-16206)*
Sirpilla Recrtl Vhcl Ctr Inc ....D 330 494-2525
Akron *(G-439)*
Smith & Oby Service Co ....E 440 735-5322
Bedford *(G-1337)*

SIC

Employee Codes: A=Over 500 employees, B=251-500
C=101-250, D=51-100, E=25-50

2018 Harris Ohio
Services Directory

1015

76 MISCELLANEOUS REPAIR SERVICES SIC SECTION

SMS Technical Services LLC ....E....... 330 426-4126
East Palestine *(G-10539)*
Southern Ohio Door Contrls Inc ....E....... 513 353-4793
Miamitown *(G-14373)*
Spartan Supply Co Inc ....E....... 513 932-6954
Lebanon *(G-12650)*
Ssi Fabricated Inc ....E....... 513 217-3535
Middletown *(G-14459)*
St Marys City Board Education ....E....... 419 394-1116
Saint Marys *(G-16684)*
Standrdaero Component Svcs Inc ....A....... 513 618-9588
Cincinnati *(G-4581)*
▲ **Steel Eqp Specialists Inc** ....D....... 330 823-8260
Alliance *(G-563)*
Steven H Byerly Inc ....E....... 614 882-0092
Columbus *(G-8788)*
Straders Nrthwst Schwinn ....E....... 614 889-2453
Columbus *(G-8793)*
Superior Marine Ways Inc ....C....... 740 894-6224
Proctorville *(G-16361)*
Supers Landscaping Inc ....E....... 440 775-0027
Oberlin *(G-15661)*
Team Industrial Services Inc ....E....... 440 498-9494
Cleveland *(G-6575)*
▲ **Tech Pro Inc** ....E....... 330 923-3546
Akron *(G-473)*
Terex Utilities Inc ....E....... 614 444-7373
Etna *(G-10739)*
Terex Utilities Inc ....C....... 937 293-6526
Springfield *(G-17287)*
Tfh-Eb Inc ....D....... 614 253-7246
Columbus *(G-8833)*
▲ **Thomas Door Controls Inc** ....E....... 614 263-1756
Columbus *(G-8837)*
Thyssenkrupp Elevator Corp ....E....... 440 717-0080
Broadview Heights *(G-1893)*
Thyssenkrupp Elevator Corp ....E....... 513 241-6000
Cincinnati *(G-4659)*
Thyssenkrupp Elevator Corp ....E....... 614 895-8930
Westerville *(G-19445)*
TNT Equipment Company ....E....... 614 882-1549
Columbus *(G-8852)*
▲ **Towlift Inc** ....C....... 216 749-6800
Brooklyn Heights *(G-1929)*
Towlift Inc ....D....... 614 851-1001
Columbus *(G-8856)*
Towlift Inc ....E....... 419 666-1333
Northwood *(G-15548)*
Toyota Industries N Amer Inc ....E....... 937 237-0976
Dayton *(G-9935)*
Tracy Refrigeration Inc ....E....... 419 223-4786
Lima *(G-12902)*
Transco Railway Products Inc ....E....... 419 726-3383
Toledo *(G-18259)*
Transforce Inc ....E....... 513 860-4402
West Chester *(G-19165)*
Tri-City Industrial Power Inc ....E....... 937 866-4099
Miamisburg *(G-14361)*
United Technical Support Svcs ....E....... 330 562-3330
Aurora *(G-859)*
US Molding Machinery Co Inc ....E....... 440 918-1701
Willoughby *(G-19721)*
Valley Harley Davidson Co ....E....... 740 695-9591
Belmont *(G-1431)*
Vermeer Sales & Service Inc ....E....... 330 723-8383
Medina *(G-14136)*
Victory Machine and Fab ....E....... 937 693-3171
Sidney *(G-16959)*
◆ **Walker National Inc** ....E....... 614 492-1614
Columbus *(G-8962)*
Williams Super Service Inc ....E....... 330 733-7750
East Sparta *(G-10542)*
Winelco Inc ....E....... 513 755-8050
West Chester *(G-19187)*
▲ **Winkle Industries Inc** ....D....... 330 823-9730
Alliance *(G-565)*
Witmers Inc ....E....... 330 427-2147
Salem *(G-16719)*
◆ **Wood Graphics Inc** ....E....... 513 771-6300
Cincinnati *(G-4858)*
Woodhull LLC ....E....... 937 294-5311
Springboro *(G-17143)*
Xerox Corporation ....E....... 419 418-6500
Toledo *(G-18318)*
Xerox Corporation ....D....... 216 642-7806
Cleveland *(G-6767)*

78 MOTION PICTURES

7812 Motion Picture & Video Tape Production

Bkg Holdings LLC ....E....... 614 252-7455
Columbus *(G-7113)*
Estreamz Inc ....E....... 513 278-7836
Cincinnati *(G-3577)*
Fastball Spt Productions LLC ....E....... 440 746-8000
Cleveland *(G-5576)*
For Women Like Me Inc ....E....... 407 848-7339
Cleveland *(G-5611)*
◆ **For Women Like Me Inc** ....E....... 407 848-7339
Chagrin Falls *(G-2696)*
Fox Television Stations Inc ....C....... 216 432-4278
Cleveland *(G-5627)*
Greater Cincinnati TV Educ Fnd ....D....... 513 381-4033
Cincinnati *(G-3711)*
Intgrted Bridge Communications ....E....... 513 381-1380
Cincinnati *(G-3839)*
Madison Avenue Mktg Group Inc ....E....... 419 473-9000
Toledo *(G-18026)*
Mills/James Inc ....C....... 614 777-9933
Hilliard *(G-11937)*
Mitosis LLC ....E....... 937 557-3440
Dayton *(G-9752)*
Pagetech Ltd ....D....... 614 238-0518
Columbus *(G-8507)*
Province of St John The Baptis ....D....... 513 241-5615
Cincinnati *(G-4352)*
Ron Foth Retail Inc ....D....... 614 888-7771
Columbus *(G-8646)*
Shadoart Productions Inc ....D....... 614 227-6125
Columbus *(G-8720)*
Shalom Ministries Intl Inc ....E....... 614 504-6052
Plain City *(G-16205)*
Universal Technology Corp ....D....... 937 426-2808
Beavercreek *(G-1216)*
▲ **Video Duplication Services Inc** ....E....... 614 871-3827
Columbus *(G-8940)*
Video Works ....D....... 419 865-6800
Toledo *(G-18291)*
World Harvest Church Inc ....B....... 614 837-1990
Canal Winchester *(G-2180)*

7819 Services Allied To Motion Picture Prdtn

Click Camera & Video ....E....... 937 435-3072
Miamisburg *(G-14285)*
Litigation Support Svcs Inc ....E....... 513 241-5605
Cincinnati *(G-3992)*
Live Technologies Holdings Inc ....D....... 614 278-7777
Columbus *(G-8074)*
Mills/James Inc ....C....... 614 777-9933
Hilliard *(G-11937)*
Signal Productions Inc ....E....... 323 382-0000
Cleveland *(G-6482)*
Technicolor Thomson Group ....C....... 937 383-6000
Wilmington *(G-19790)*

7822 Motion Picture & Video Tape Distribution

▲ **Midwest Tape LLC** ....B....... 419 868-9370
Holland *(G-12038)*
Technicolor Thomson Group ....C....... 937 383-6000
Wilmington *(G-19790)*
Zebo Productions ....D....... 937 339-0397
Troy *(G-18388)*

7829 Services Allied To Motion Picture Distribution

Technicolor Thomson Group ....C....... 937 383-6000
Wilmington *(G-19790)*

7832 Motion Picture Theaters, Except Drive-In

AMC Entertainment Inc ....E....... 614 846-6575
Columbus *(G-6982)*
AMC Entertainment Inc ....E....... 614 428-5716
Columbus *(G-6983)*
AMC Entertainment Inc ....E....... 614 429-0100
Columbus *(G-6984)*
AMC Entertainment Inc ....E....... 216 749-0260
Brooklyn *(G-1904)*
American Multi-Cinema Inc ....D....... 614 801-9130
Grove City *(G-11530)*
American Multi-Cinema Inc ....E....... 614 889-0580
Dublin *(G-10250)*
American Multi-Cinema Inc ....E....... 216 749-0260
Cleveland *(G-5015)*
American Multi-Cinema Inc ....E....... 440 331-2826
Rocky River *(G-16569)*
B and D Investment Partnership ....E....... 937 233-6698
Dayton *(G-9348)*
Carmike Cinemas Inc ....E....... 740 264-1680
Steubenville *(G-17306)*
Cincinnati Museum Center ....B....... 513 287-7000
Cincinnati *(G-3319)*
Cinemark Usa Inc ....E....... 330 965-2335
Youngstown *(G-20141)*
Cinemark Usa Inc ....C....... 216 447-8820
Cleveland *(G-5239)*
Cinemark Usa Inc ....E....... 330 908-1005
Macedonia *(G-13193)*
Cinemark Usa Inc ....E....... 419 589-7300
Ontario *(G-15685)*
Cinemark Usa Inc ....E....... 614 538-0403
Columbus *(G-7272)*
Cinemark Usa Inc ....E....... 330 497-9118
Canton *(G-2308)*
Cinemark Usa Inc ....E....... 614 527-3773
Hilliard *(G-11890)*
Cinemark Usa Inc ....E....... 614 471-7620
Gahanna *(G-11234)*
Cinemark Usa Inc ....E....... 330 345-2610
Wooster *(G-19843)*
Cinemark Usa Inc ....E....... 614 529-8547
Columbus *(G-7273)*
Danbarry Linemas Inc ....E....... 740 779-6115
Chillicothe *(G-2833)*
Drc Holdings Inc ....E....... 419 230-0188
Pandora *(G-15889)*
Great Eastern Theatre Company ....D....... 419 691-9668
Oregon *(G-15737)*
M E Theaters Inc ....E....... 937 596-6424
Jackson Center *(G-12323)*
Marcus Theatres Corporation ....E....... 614 759-6500
Pickerington *(G-16101)*
Marcus Theatres Corporation ....D....... 614 436-9818
Columbus *(G-8108)*
National Amusements Inc ....E....... 513 699-1500
Milford *(G-14544)*
National Amusements Inc ....E....... 513 699-1500
Cincinnati *(G-4136)*
National Amusements Inc ....D....... 419 215-3095
Maumee *(G-13949)*
Ohio Light Opera ....D....... 330 263-2345
Wooster *(G-19896)*
Quincy Amusements Inc ....E....... 419 874-2154
Perrysburg *(G-16048)*
Regal Cinemas Inc ....E....... 614 853-0850
Columbus *(G-8604)*
Regal Cinemas Inc ....E....... 330 723-4416
Medina *(G-14120)*
Regal Cinemas Inc ....E....... 440 975-8820
Willoughby *(G-19708)*
Regal Cinemas Inc ....E....... 937 431-9418
Beavercreek *(G-1203)*
Regal Cinemas Inc ....E....... 440 934-3356
Elyria *(G-10675)*
Regal Cinemas Inc ....E....... 330 666-9373
Akron *(G-406)*
Regal Cinemas Inc ....E....... 440 871-4546
Westlake *(G-19541)*
Regal Cinemas Inc ....E....... 330 758-0503
Youngstown *(G-20342)*
Regal Cinemas Inc ....E....... 330 633-7668
Akron *(G-407)*
Regal Cinemas Corporation ....E....... 513 770-0713
Mason *(G-13754)*
Regal Cinemas Corporation ....E....... 440 720-0500
Richmond Heights *(G-16541)*
Regal Cinemas Inc ....E....... 440 891-9845
Cleveland *(G-6367)*
Seminole Theater Co LLC ....E....... 440 934-6998
Avon Lake *(G-939)*

7841 Video Tape Rental

Emerge Ministries Inc ....E....... 330 865-8351
Akron *(G-208)*
Family Video Movie Club Inc ....E....... 937 846-1021
New Carlisle *(G-15023)*
Mile Inc ....D....... 614 794-2203
Worthington *(G-19978)*

79 AMUSEMENT AND RECREATION SERVICES

7911 Dance Studios, Schools & Halls

Applause Talent Presentation .... E 513 844-6788
  Hamilton *(G-11692)*
Artistic Dance Enterprises .... E 614 761-2882
  Columbus *(G-7046)*
Ballet Metropolitan Inc .... C 614 229-4860
  Columbus *(G-7088)*
Cincinnati Ballet Company Inc .... E 513 621-5219
  Cincinnati *(G-3283)*
Cleveland Mus Schl Settlement .... C 216 421-5806
  Cleveland *(G-5339)*
Eldora Enterprises Inc .... E 937 338-3815
  New Weston *(G-15140)*
Ohio Chamber Ballet .... E 330 972-7900
  Akron *(G-363)*
Piqua Country Club Holding Co .... E 937 773-7744
  Piqua *(G-16156)*
Truenorth Cultural Arts .... E 440 949-5200
  Sheffield Village *(G-16895)*

7922 Theatrical Producers & Misc Theatrical Svcs

Ballet Metropolitan Inc .... C 614 229-4860
  Columbus *(G-7088)*
Beck Center For Arts .... C 216 521-2540
  Cleveland *(G-5109)*
Cincinnati Opera Association .... E 513 768-5500
  Cincinnati *(G-3321)*
Cincinnati Shakespeare Company .... E 513 381-2273
  Cincinnati *(G-3327)*
City of Cleveland .... D 216 664-6800
  Cleveland *(G-5257)*
Columbus Association For The P .... D 614 469-0939
  Columbus *(G-7332)*
Deyor Performing Arts Center .... E 330 744-4269
  Youngstown *(G-20168)*
Events On Top .... E 330 757-3786
  Youngstown *(G-20182)*
Funny Bone Comedy Club & Cafe .... E 614 471-5653
  Columbus *(G-7714)*
Hanson Productions Inc .... E 419 327-6100
  Maumee *(G-13923)*
◆ International Management Group .... B 216 522-1200
  Cleveland *(G-5830)*
Interntnal Aliance Thea Stage .... E 440 734-4883
  North Olmsted *(G-15427)*
Licking County Players Inc .... E 740 349-2287
  Newark *(G-15189)*
Little Theater Off Broadway .... E 614 875-3919
  Grove City *(G-11578)*
Ohio Chamber Ballet .... E 330 972-7900
  Akron *(G-363)*
Ohio Light Opera .... D 330 263-2345
  Wooster *(G-19896)*
Ovations .... E 216 687-9292
  Cleveland *(G-6220)*
Playhouse Square Foundation .... B 216 771-4444
  Cleveland *(G-6286)*
Playhouse Square Holdg Co LLC .... C 216 771-4444
  Cleveland *(G-6287)*
Rock and Roll of Fame and Muse .... D 216 781-7625
  Cleveland *(G-6406)*
Stranahan Theatre Trust .... D 419 381-8851
  Toledo *(G-18204)*
The In Cincinnati Playhouse .... D 513 421-3888
  Cincinnati *(G-4644)*
Theatre Management Corporation .... E 513 723-1180
  Cincinnati *(G-4647)*
University of Findlay .... C 419 434-4531
  Findlay *(G-11097)*
Venture Productions Inc .... D 937 544-2823
  West Union *(G-19279)*
Xenia Area Cmnty Theater Inc .... D 937 372-0516
  Xenia *(G-20085)*

7929 Bands, Orchestras, Actors & Entertainers

A To Z Golf Managment Co .... E 937 434-4911
  Dayton *(G-9299)*
Adventure Cmbat Operations LLC ...... E 330 818-1029
  Canton *(G-2228)*
Bird Enterprises LLC .... E 330 674-1457
  Millersburg *(G-14589)*
Blue Water Chamber Orchestra .... E 440 781-6215
  Cleveland *(G-5127)*
Catholic Diocese of Columbus .... D 614 276-5263
  Columbus *(G-7210)*
Cincinnati Circus Company LLC .... D 513 921-5454
  Cincinnati *(G-3292)*
Cincinnati Symphony Orchestra .... C 513 621-1919
  Cincinnati *(G-3332)*
Cleveland Phlhrmonic Orchestra .... D 216 556-1800
  Rocky River *(G-16574)*
Club Life Entertainment LLC .... E 216 831-1134
  Beachwood *(G-1066)*
Columbus Association For The P .... D 614 469-0939
  Columbus *(G-7332)*
Columbus Symphony Orchestra .... D 614 228-9600
  Columbus *(G-7389)*
Dayton Metro Chapter .... E 937 294-0192
  Dayton *(G-9482)*
Dayton Performing Arts Aliance .... D 937 224-3521
  Dayton *(G-9485)*
Etc Gameco LLC .... E 614 428-7529
  Columbus *(G-7615)*
Food Concepts Intl Inc .... D 513 336-7449
  Mason *(G-13701)*
Fountain Square MGT Group LLC ..... E 513 621-4400
  Cincinnati *(G-3642)*
Greater Akron Musical Assn .... D 330 535-8131
  Akron *(G-246)*
Henrys King Touring Company .... E 330 628-1886
  Mogadore *(G-14678)*
Ingram Entrmt Holdings Inc .... E 419 662-3132
  Perrysburg *(G-16017)*
J S P A Inc .... E 407 957-6664
  Columbus *(G-7932)*
▲ Musical Arts Association .... C 216 231-7300
  Cleveland *(G-6093)*
Muskingum Vly Symphonic Winds ..... E 740 826-8095
  New Concord *(G-15035)*
Northeast Ohio Dukes .... E 330 360-0968
  Warren *(G-18889)*
Nulife Music Group .... E 216 870-3720
  Cleveland *(G-6171)*
Philo Band Boosters .... E 740 221-3023
  Zanesville *(G-20525)*
Radio Seaway Inc .... E 216 916-6100
  Cleveland *(G-6343)*
Rcwc Col Inc .... D 614 564-9344
  Columbus *(G-8592)*
▲ Rock House Entrmt Group Inc .... C 440 232-7625
  Oakwood Village *(G-15633)*
Run Jump-N-Play .... E 513 701-7529
  Blue Ash *(G-1685)*
Southeastern Ohio Symphony Orc ...... E 740 826-8197
  New Concord *(G-15037)*
Toledo Swiss Singers .... E 419 693-4110
  Oregon *(G-15753)*
▲ Zink Calls .... E 419 732-6171
  Port Clinton *(G-16259)*

7933 Bowling Centers

Al-Mar Lanes .... E 419 352-4637
  Bowling Green *(G-1757)*
AMF Bowling Centers Inc .... E 330 725-4548
  Medina *(G-14036)*
AMF Bowling Centers Inc .... E 614 889-0880
  Columbus *(G-7015)*
Beaver-Vu Bowl .... E 937 426-6771
  Beavercreek *(G-1150)*
Big Western Operating Co Inc .... E 614 274-1169
  Columbus *(G-7109)*
Bigelow Corporation .... E 937 339-3315
  Troy *(G-18349)*
Bowlmor AMF Corp .... E 440 327-1190
  North Ridgeville *(G-15456)*
Brookpark Freeway Lanes LLC .... E 216 267-2150
  Cleveland *(G-5146)*
Capri Bowling Lanes Inc .... E 937 832-4000
  Dayton *(G-9379)*
Cherry Grove Sports Center .... E 513 232-7199
  Cincinnati *(G-3239)*
Chillicothe Bowling Lanes Inc .... E 740 773-3300
  Chillicothe *(G-2817)*
Cloverleaf Bowling Center Inc .... E 216 524-4833
  Cleveland *(G-5366)*
Columbus Square Bowling Palace .... E 614 895-1122
  Columbus *(G-7387)*
Coshocton Bowling Center .... E 740 622-6332
  Coshocton *(G-9093)*
Crossgate Lanes Inc .... E 513 891-0310
  Blue Ash *(G-1572)*
East Mentor Recreation Inc .... E 440 354-2000
  Mentor *(G-14170)*
Eastbury Bowling Center .... E 330 452-3700
  Canton *(G-2348)*
Eastland Lanes Inc .... E 614 868-9866
  Columbus *(G-7566)*
Freeway Lanes Bowl Group LLC .... E 440 946-5131
  Mentor *(G-14178)*
Holiday Lanes Inc .... E 614 861-1600
  Columbus *(G-7846)*
Interstate Lanes of Ohio Ltd .... E 419 666-2695
  Rossford *(G-16609)*
Madison Bowl Inc .... E 513 271-2700
  Cincinnati *(G-4010)*
Mahalls 20 Lanes .... E 216 521-3280
  Cleveland *(G-5966)*
Midway Bowling Lanes Inc .... E 330 762-7477
  Cuyahoga Falls *(G-9210)*
Northland Lanes Inc .... E 419 224-1961
  Lima *(G-12844)*
Olmsted Lanes Inc .... E 440 777-6363
  North Olmsted *(G-15435)*
Park Centre Lanes Inc .... E 330 499-0555
  Canton *(G-2488)*
Plaz-Way Inc .... E 330 264-9025
  Wooster *(G-19904)*
Poelking Bowling Centers .... E 937 435-3855
  Dayton *(G-9813)*
Poelking Lanes Inc .... D 937 299-5573
  Dayton *(G-9814)*
Rainbow Lanes Inc .... E 614 491-7155
  Columbus *(G-8586)*
Rebman Recreation Inc .... E 440 282-6761
  Lorain *(G-13074)*
Roseland Lanes Inc .... D 440 439-0097
  Bedford *(G-1332)*
Sequoia Pro Bowl .... E 614 885-7043
  Columbus *(G-8713)*
Skylane LLC .... E 330 527-9999
  Garrettsville *(G-11352)*
Sortino Management & Dev Co .... E 419 626-6761
  Sandusky *(G-16796)*
Stonehedge Enterprises Inc .... E 330 928-2161
  Akron *(G-451)*
Suburban Gala Lanes Inc .... E 419 468-7488
  Bucyrus *(G-2047)*
Thompson Capri Lanes Inc .... E 614 888-3159
  Columbus *(G-8839)*
Tiki Bowling Lanes Inc .... E 740 654-4513
  Lancaster *(G-12581)*
Toledo Sports Center Inc .... E 419 693-0687
  Toledo *(G-18251)*
Victory Lanes Inc .... E 937 323-8684
  Springfield *(G-17292)*
Wedgewood Lanes Inc .... E 330 792-1949
  Youngstown *(G-20410)*
Westgate Lanes Incorporated .... E 419 229-3845
  Lima *(G-12920)*

7941 Professional Sports Clubs & Promoters

Alliance Hot Stove Baseball L .... E 330 823-7034
  Alliance *(G-525)*
Ap23 Sports Complex LLC .... E 614 452-0760
  Columbus *(G-7025)*
Arena Management Holdings LLC ..... A 513 421-4111
  Cincinnati *(G-3045)*
Brixx Ice Company .... E 937 222-2257
  Dayton *(G-9367)*
Cascia LLC .... E 440 975-8085
  Willoughby *(G-19648)*
Cavaliers Holdings LLC .... C 216 420-2000
  Cleveland *(G-5193)*
Cavaliers Operating Co LLC .... A 216 420-2000
  Cleveland *(G-5194)*
Cincinnati Bengals Inc .... E 513 621-3550
  Cincinnati *(G-3289)*
▼ Cincinnati Reds LLC .... C 513 765-7000
  Cincinnati *(G-3324)*
Cincinnati Reds LLC .... E 513 765-7923
  Cincinnati *(G-3325)*
Cleveland Browns Football LLC .... C 440 891-5000
  Berea *(G-1452)*
Cleveland Indians Baseball Com .... E 216 420-4487
  Cleveland *(G-5321)*
▲ Colhoc Limited Partnership .... C 614 246-4625
  Columbus *(G-7318)*
▲ Columbus Team Soccer LLC .... E 614 447-1301
  Columbus *(G-7390)*
Crew Soccer Stadium LLC .... E 614 447-2739
  Columbus *(G-7462)*
Dayton Prof Basbal CLB LLC .... E 937 228-2287
  Dayton *(G-9488)*

79 AMUSEMENT AND RECREATION SERVICES SIC SECTION

Five Seasons Spt Cntry CLB Inc ....D 937 848-9200
Dayton *(G-9553)*
◆ International Management Group ....B 216 522-1200
Cleveland *(G-5830)*
International Mdsg Corp ....B 216 522-1200
Cleveland *(G-5831)*
National Football Museum Inc ....E 330 456-8207
Canton *(G-2470)*
Ohio High School Football Coac ....E 419 673-1286
Etna *(G-10737)*
Ohio State University ....E 614 292-2624
Columbus *(G-8400)*
Palisdes Bsbal A Cal Ltd Prtnr ....C 330 505-0000
Niles *(G-15302)*
Phoenix ....D 513 721-8901
Cincinnati *(G-4293)*
Toledo Mud Hens Basbal CLB Inc ....D 419 725-4367
Toledo *(G-18243)*
Towne Properties Assoc Inc ....E 513 489-9700
Cincinnati *(G-4670)*
Wall2wall Soccer LLC ....E 513 573-9898
Mason *(G-13779)*
Windwood Swim & Tennis Club ....E 513 777-2552
West Chester *(G-19186)*

7948 Racing & Track Operations

Brush Creek Motorsports ....E 937 515-1353
West Union *(G-19275)*
Columbus Motor Speedway Inc ....D 614 491-1047
Grove City *(G-11547)*
Eldora Enterprises Inc ....E 937 338-3815
New Weston *(G-15140)*
Fast Traxx Promotions LLC ....E 740 767-3740
Millfield *(G-14632)*
Kil Kare Inc ....D 937 429-2961
Xenia *(G-20065)*
National Hot Rod Association ....C 740 928-5706
Hebron *(G-11858)*
Park Raceway Inc ....C 419 476-7751
Dayton *(G-9802)*
Pnk (ohio) LLC ....A 513 232-8000
Cincinnati *(G-4312)*
Portsmouth Raceway Park Inc ....E 740 354-3278
Portsmouth *(G-16301)*
Raceway Foods Inc ....E 513 932-2457
Lebanon *(G-12639)*
River Downs Turf Club Inc ....E 513 232-8000
Cincinnati *(G-4423)*
Scioto Downs Inc ....A 614 295-4700
Columbus *(G-8706)*
Stonehedge Enterprises Inc ....E 330 928-2161
Akron *(G-451)*
◆ Team Rahal Inc ....D 614 529-7000
Hilliard *(G-11957)*
Thistledown Inc ....C 216 662-8600
Cleveland *(G-6595)*

7991 Physical Fitness Facilities

Akron General Medical Center ....C 330 665-8000
Akron *(G-46)*
Alsan Corporation ....D 330 385-3636
East Liverpool *(G-10514)*
Amitel Limited Partnership ....E 440 234-6688
Cleveland *(G-5028)*
Aussiefit I LLC ....E 614 755-4400
Columbus *(G-7074)*
Avalon Holdings Corporation ....D 330 856-8800
Warren *(G-18823)*
B & I Hotel Management LLC ....C 330 995-0200
Aurora *(G-828)*
Beechmont Racquet Club Inc ....E 513 528-5700
Cincinnati *(G-3091)*
Bennett Enterprises Inc ....B 419 874-3111
Perrysburg *(G-15978)*
Best Western Columbus N Hotel ....E 614 888-8230
Columbus *(G-7103)*
Breezy Point Ltd Partnership ....E 330 995-0600
Aurora *(G-831)*
Broad Street Hotel Assoc LP ....D 614 861-0321
Columbus *(G-7147)*
Canter Inn Inc ....E 740 354-7711
Portsmouth *(G-16267)*
Carroll Properties ....E 513 398-8075
Mason *(G-13671)*
Centerville Fitness Inc ....E 937 291-7990
Centerville *(G-2675)*
Chagrin Valley Athletic Club ....D 440 543-5141
Chagrin Falls *(G-2712)*
Chalk Box Get Fit LLC ....E 440 992-9619
Ashtabula *(G-732)*
Champions Gym ....E 937 294-8202
Dayton *(G-9396)*
Changes Hair Designers Inc ....E 614 846-6666
Columbus *(G-6875)*
Chillicothe Motel LLC ....E 740 773-3903
Chillicothe *(G-2822)*
Chillicothe Racquet Club ....E 740 773-4928
Chillicothe *(G-2824)*
Cincinnati Sports Mall Inc ....D 513 527-4000
Cincinnati *(G-3329)*
City of Brecksville ....D 440 526-4109
Brecksville *(G-1819)*
Columbus Country Club ....D 614 861-1332
Columbus *(G-7343)*
Compel Fitness LLC ....C 216 965-5694
Cincinnati *(G-3402)*
Coshocton Village Inn Suites ....E 740 622-9455
Coshocton *(G-9098)*
Emh Regional Medical Center ....D 440 988-6800
Avon *(G-892)*
Family YMCA of LANcstr&fairfld ....C 740 654-0616
Lancaster *(G-12542)*
Family YMCA of LANcstr&fairfld ....D 740 277-7373
Lancaster *(G-12541)*
Findlay Country Club ....E 419 422-9263
Findlay *(G-11025)*
Findlay Y M C A Child Dev ....E 419 422-3174
Findlay *(G-11031)*
Fitness International LLC ....E 513 298-0134
West Chester *(G-19074)*
Fitness International LLC ....E 937 427-0700
Beavercreek *(G-1173)*
Fitness International LLC ....E 419 482-7740
Maumee *(G-13917)*
Fitworks Holding LLC ....E 330 688-2329
Stow *(G-17367)*
Fitworks Holding LLC ....E 440 333-4141
Rocky River *(G-16578)*
Fitworks Holding LLC ....E 513 531-1500
Cincinnati *(G-3632)*
Flexeco Incorporated ....E 216 812-3304
Cleveland *(G-5606)*
Frans Child Care-Mansfield ....C 419 775-2500
Mansfield *(G-13304)*
Friars Club Inc ....D 513 488-8777
Cincinnati *(G-3654)*
Galion Community Center YMCA ....E 419 468-7754
Galion *(G-11297)*
Geeta Hospitality Inc ....E 937 642-3777
Marysville *(G-13622)*
General Electric Company ....E 513 243-9404
Cincinnati *(G-3670)*
Grandview Ht Ltd Partnr Ohio ....D 937 766-5519
Springfield *(G-17203)*
Great Miami Valley YMCA ....D 513 887-0001
Hamilton *(G-11733)*
Great Miami Valley YMCA ....C 513 892-9622
Fairfield Township *(G-10930)*
Great Miami Valley YMCA ....D 513 887-0014
Hamilton *(G-11735)*
Great Miami Valley YMCA ....D 513 868-9622
Hamilton *(G-11736)*
Great Miami Valley YMCA ....D 513 829-3091
Fairfield *(G-10854)*
Grooveryde Cle ....E 323 595-1701
Cleveland *(G-5706)*
Hardin County Family YMCA ....E 419 673-6131
Kenton *(G-12416)*
Highland County Family YMCA ....E 937 840-9622
Hillsboro *(G-11978)*
Holzer Clinic LLC ....E 740 446-5412
Gallipolis *(G-11323)*
Huber Heights YMCA ....D 937 236-9622
Dayton *(G-9623)*
Island Hospitality MGT LLC ....E 614 864-8844
Columbus *(G-7927)*
Jbentley Studio & Spa LLC ....D 614 790-8828
Powell *(G-16339)*
Jto Club Corp ....D 440 352-1900
Mentor *(G-14200)*
Kerr House Inc ....E 419 832-1733
Grand Rapids *(G-11451)*
Kettering Recreation Center ....E 937 296-2587
Dayton *(G-9657)*
Kinsale Golf & Fitnes CLB LLC ....C 740 881-6500
Powell *(G-16343)*
Kristie Warner ....E 330 650-4450
Hudson *(G-12129)*
L A Fitness Intl LLC ....E 937 439-2795
Washington Township *(G-18938)*
Lake County YMCA ....A 440 352-3303
Painesville *(G-15860)*
Lake County YMCA ....C 440 946-1160
Willoughby *(G-19680)*
Lake County YMCA ....E 440 259-2724
Perry *(G-15962)*
Lake County YMCA ....D 440 428-5125
Madison *(G-13227)*
Life Time Fitness Inc ....C 513 234-0660
Mason *(G-13732)*
Life Time Fitness Inc ....C 952 229-7158
Dublin *(G-10388)*
Life Time Fitness Inc ....C 614 428-6000
Columbus *(G-8062)*
Lima Family YMCA ....E 419 223-6045
Lima *(G-12821)*
Mansfield Hotel Partnership ....D 419 529-1000
Mansfield *(G-13332)*
Marios International Spa & Ht ....C 330 562-5141
Aurora *(G-846)*
Meadowbrook Country Club ....D 937 836-5186
Clayton *(G-4913)*
Medallion Club ....C 614 794-6999
Westerville *(G-19328)*
Mitchells Salon & Day Spa ....B 513 793-0900
Cincinnati *(G-4104)*
Mitchells Salon & Day Spa ....D 513 731-0600
Cincinnati *(G-4106)*
N C R Employee Benefit Assn ....C 937 299-3571
Dayton *(G-9766)*
New Carlisle Spt & Fitnes Ctr ....E 937 846-1000
New Carlisle *(G-15029)*
Ohio State University ....E 614 293-2800
Columbus *(G-8391)*
Ohio State University ....B 614 292-3238
Columbus *(G-8427)*
Oid Associates ....E 330 666-3161
Akron *(G-370)*
Paragon Salons Inc ....E 513 574-7610
Cincinnati *(G-4249)*
Pike County YMCA ....E 740 947-8862
Waverly *(G-18974)*
Queen City Racquet Club LLC ....D 513 771-2835
Cincinnati *(G-4370)*
Redefine Enterprises LLC ....E 330 952-2024
Medina *(G-14118)*
Ross County YMCA ....D 740 772-4340
Chillicothe *(G-2882)*
S P S Inc ....E 937 339-7801
Troy *(G-18378)*
Scioto Reserve Inc ....D 740 881-9082
Powell *(G-16349)*
Select Hotels Group LLC ....E 614 799-1913
Dublin *(G-10451)*
Shadow Valley Tennis & Fitness ....E 419 861-3986
Toledo *(G-18183)*
Shady Hollow Cntry CLB Co Inc ....D 330 832-1581
Massillon *(G-13854)*
Southwest General Health Ctr ....D 440 816-4202
Cleveland *(G-6502)*
Spa Fitness Centers Inc ....E 419 476-6018
Toledo *(G-18193)*
Springfield Family Y M C A ....D 937 323-3781
Springfield *(G-17281)*
Swim Incorporated ....E 614 885-1619
Worthington *(G-20002)*
Sycamore Board of Education ....D 513 489-3937
Cincinnati *(G-4608)*
Synergy Hotels LLC ....E 614 492-9000
Obetz *(G-15671)*
T O J Inc ....E 440 352-1900
Mentor *(G-14247)*
Tippecanoe Country Club Inc ....E 330 758-7518
Canfield *(G-2213)*
TLC Health Wellness & Fitness ....E 330 527-4852
Garrettsville *(G-11354)*
Tuscany Spa Salon ....E 513 489-8872
Cincinnati *(G-4708)*
Ucc Childrens Center ....E 513 217-5501
Middletown *(G-14488)*
Uptown Hair Studio Inc ....E 937 832-2111
Englewood *(G-10723)*
Vermilion Family YMCA ....E 440 967-4208
Vermilion *(G-18720)*
▼ Victory Ftnes Ctrs of Columbus ....E 614 351-1688
Columbus *(G-8939)*
W T Sports Inc ....E 740 654-0035
Dublin *(G-10485)*
Washington Twnship Mntgomery ....C 937 433-0130
Dayton *(G-9986)*

SIC SECTION — 79 AMUSEMENT AND RECREATION SERVICES

Wyandotte Athletic Club .... E 614 861-6303
  Columbus *(G-9011)*
Y M C A Central Stark County .... E 330 305-5437
  Canton *(G-2590)*
Y M C A Central Stark County .... E 330 875-1611
  Louisville *(G-13108)*
Y M C A Central Stark County .... E 330 877-8933
  Uniontown *(G-18545)*
Y M C A Central Stark County .... E 330 830-6275
  Massillon *(G-13862)*
Y M C A Central Stark County .... E 330 498-4082
  Canton *(G-2591)*
Y M C A of Ashland Ohio Inc .... D 419 289-0626
  Ashland *(G-709)*
YMCA .... E 330 823-1930
  Alliance *(G-566)*
YMCA .... D 937 653-9622
  Urbana *(G-18603)*
YMCA Inc .... D 330 385-6400
  East Liverpool *(G-10536)*
YMCA of Clermont County Inc .... E 513 724-9622
  Batavia *(G-1032)*
YMCA of Massillon .... E 330 879-0800
  Navarre *(G-14957)*
Young Mens Christian .... B 513 932-1424
  Lebanon *(G-12660)*
Young Mens Christian Assn .... E 419 238-0443
  Van Wert *(G-18653)*
Young Mens Christian Assoc .... C 614 871-9622
  Grove City *(G-11620)*
Young Mens Christian Assoc .... A 937 223-5201
  Dayton *(G-10009)*
Young Mens Christian Assoc .... D 330 923-5223
  Cuyahoga Falls *(G-9237)*
Young Mens Christian Assoc .... E 330 467-8366
  Macedonia *(G-13219)*
Young Mens Christian Assoc .... E 330 784-0408
  Akron *(G-515)*
Young Mens Christian Assoc .... C 614 416-9622
  Gahanna *(G-11276)*
Young Mens Christian Assoc .... C 740 881-1058
  Powell *(G-16355)*
Young Mens Christian Assoc .... C 614 334-9622
  Hilliard *(G-11967)*
Young Mens Christian Assoc .... E 937 312-1810
  Dayton *(G-10010)*
Young Mens Christian Assoc .... E 614 539-1770
  Urbancrest *(G-18609)*
Young Mens Christian Assoc .... D 614 252-3166
  Columbus *(G-9019)*
Young Mens Christian Assoc .... E 937 593-9001
  Bellefontaine *(G-1401)*
Young Mens Christian Assoc .... D 740 477-1661
  Circleville *(G-4909)*
Young Mens Christian Assoc .... D 330 264-3131
  Wooster *(G-19936)*
Young Mens Christian Assoc .... E 937 228-9622
  Dayton *(G-10012)*
Young Mens Christian Assoc .... C 937 223-5201
  Springboro *(G-17144)*
Young Mens Christian Assoc .... C 614 834-9622
  Canal Winchester *(G-2181)*
Young Mens Christian Associat .... E 419 729-8135
  Toledo *(G-18320)*
Young Mens Christian Associat .... D 513 241-9622
  Cincinnati *(G-4868)*
Young Mens Christian Associat .... D 513 923-4466
  Cincinnati *(G-4869)*
Young Mens Christian Associat .... E 419 474-3995
  Toledo *(G-18322)*
Young Mens Christian Associat .... D 419 866-9622
  Maumee *(G-13997)*
Young Mens Christian Associat .... C 419 475-3496
  Toledo *(G-18323)*
Young Mens Christian Associat .... D 419 691-3523
  Oregon *(G-15756)*
Young Mens Christian Associat .... E 513 731-0115
  Cincinnati *(G-4866)*
Young Mens Christian Associat .... C 513 474-1400
  Cincinnati *(G-4867)*
Young Mens Christian Mt Vernon ..... D 740 392-9622
  Mount Vernon *(G-14927)*
Young Mens Christian Assn Shelby .... D 419 347-1312
  Shelby *(G-16904)*
Young MNS Christn Assn Findlay ..... D 419 422-4424
  Findlay *(G-11102)*
Young MNS Chrstn Assn Clveland .... E 216 521-8400
  Lakewood *(G-12502)*
Young MNS Chrstn Assn Clveland .... D 440 842-5200
  North Royalton *(G-15507)*

Young MNS Chrstn Assn Clveland .... E 216 731-7454
  Cleveland *(G-6774)*
Young MNS Chrstn Assn Clveland .... D 440 285-7543
  Chardon *(G-2780)*
Young MNS Chrstn Assn Clveland .... D 216 382-4300
  Cleveland *(G-6775)*
Young MNS Chrstn Assn Clveland .... D 440 808-8150
  Westlake *(G-19569)*
Young MNS Chrstn Assn Grter NY .... D 740 392-9622
  Mount Vernon *(G-14928)*
Young Womens Christian .... D 937 461-5550
  Dayton *(G-10013)*
Young Womens Christian .... E 419 238-6639
  Van Wert *(G-18654)*
Young Womens Christian Assn .... E 614 224-9121
  Columbus *(G-9021)*
Young Womens Christian Assn .... E 330 746-6361
  Youngstown *(G-20422)*
Young Womens Christian Associ ...... E 216 881-6878
  Cleveland *(G-6776)*
Young Womns Chrstn Assc Canton .... D 330 453-0789
  Canton *(G-2594)*
YWCA of Greater Cincinnati .... E 513 241-7090
  Cincinnati *(G-4870)*
YWCA Shelter & Housing Network ... E 937 222-6333
  Dayton *(G-10014)*

7992 Public Golf Courses

797 Elks Golf Club Inc .... E 937 382-2666
  Wilmington *(G-19740)*
A To Z Golf Managment Co .... E 937 434-4911
  Dayton *(G-9299)*
▲ Aboutgolf Limited .... D 419 482-9095
  Maumee *(G-13871)*
American Golf Corporation .... E 740 965-5122
  Galena *(G-11278)*
Amix Inc .... E 513 539-7220
  Middletown *(G-14413)*
Aston Oaks Golf Club .... E 513 467-0070
  North Bend *(G-15317)*
Avalon Golf & Country Club .... D 330 539-5008
  Vienna *(G-18735)*
Avalon Lakes Golf Inc .... E 330 856-8898
  Warren *(G-18825)*
Avon Properties Inc .... E 440 934-6217
  Avon *(G-877)*
Avondale Golf Club .... E 440 934-4398
  Avon *(G-878)*
Bayview Retirees Golf Course .... E 419 726-8081
  Toledo *(G-17764)*
Beckett Ridge Country Club .... D 513 874-2710
  West Chester *(G-19024)*
Black Diamond Golf Course .... E 330 674-6110
  Millersburg *(G-14590)*
Blackbrook Country Club Inc .... E 440 951-0010
  Mentor *(G-14150)*
Blue Heron Golf Course Inc .... E 330 722-0227
  Medina *(G-14039)*
Bramarjac Inc .... E 419 884-3434
  Mansfield *(G-13268)*
Brandywine Country Club Inc .... E 330 657-2525
  Peninsula *(G-15948)*
Brentwood Golf Club Inc .... E 440 322-9254
  Sheffield Village *(G-16884)*
Bw Enterprises Inc .... E 937 568-9660
  South Charleston *(G-17075)*
Cambridge Country Club Company .. E 740 439-2744
  Byesville *(G-2070)*
Championship Management Co ...... D 740 524-4653
  Sunbury *(G-17552)*
Chardon Lakes Golf Course Inc ...... E 440 285-4653
  Chardon *(G-2742)*
Chgc Inc .... D 330 225-6122
  Valley City *(G-18614)*
Chippewa Golf Corp .... E 330 658-2566
  Doylestown *(G-10224)*
Circling Hills Golf Course .... E 513 367-5858
  Harrison *(G-11794)*
City of Akron .... E 330 864-0020
  Akron *(G-138)*
City of Beavercreek .... D 937 320-0742
  Beavercreek *(G-1161)*
City of Blue Ash .... E 513 745-8577
  Blue Ash *(G-1558)*
City of Cuyahoga Falls .... E 330 971-8416
  Cuyahoga Falls *(G-9174)*
City of Miamisburg .... E 937 866-4653
  Miamisburg *(G-14284)*
City of Parma .... E 440 885-8876
  Cleveland *(G-5272)*

City of Pickerington .... E 614 645-8474
  Pickerington *(G-16089)*
City of Vandalia .... E 937 890-1300
  Vandalia *(G-18674)*
City of Westlake .... E 440 835-6442
  Westlake *(G-19475)*
City of Willoughby .... E 440 953-4280
  Willoughby *(G-19652)*
Cleveland Metroparks .... D 440 526-4285
  Brecksville *(G-1820)*
Cleveland Metroparks .... D 440 232-7184
  Cleveland *(G-5330)*
Cleveland Metroparks .... E 440 331-1070
  Cleveland *(G-5331)*
Columbus Frkln Cnty Pk .... E 614 861-3193
  Reynoldsburg *(G-16440)*
Columbus Zoological Park Assn ..... C 614 645-3400
  Powell *(G-16330)*
Creekside Golf Ltd .... E 513 785-2999
  Fairfield Township *(G-10928)*
Creekside Ltd LLC .... D 513 583-4977
  Loveland *(G-13118)*
Crooked Tree Golf Course .... E 513 398-3933
  Cincinnati *(G-3441)*
Darby Creek Golf Course Inc .... E 937 349-7491
  Marysville *(G-13616)*
Dorlon Golf Club .... E 440 236-8234
  Columbia Station *(G-6845)*
E J Links Co The Inc .... E 440 235-0501
  Olmsted Twp *(G-15675)*
Emerald Woods Golf Course .... E 440 236-8940
  Columbia Station *(G-6846)*
Fox Den Fairways Inc .... E 330 678-6792
  Stow *(G-17368)*
Ganzfair Investment Inc .... E 614 792-6630
  Delaware *(G-10100)*
Gc At Stonelick Hills .... E 513 735-4653
  Batavia *(G-1014)*
Golf Club of Dublin LLC .... E 614 889-5469
  Dublin *(G-10354)*
Grizzly Golf Center Inc .... B 513 398-5200
  Mason *(G-13712)*
Hawkins Markets Inc .... E 330 435-4611
  Creston *(G-9150)*
Heatherwoode Golf Course .... C 937 748-3222
  Springboro *(G-17122)*
Heritage Golf Club Ltd Partnr .... D 614 777-1690
  Hilliard *(G-11908)*
Hickory Woods Golf Course Inc .... E 513 575-3900
  Loveland *(G-13131)*
Homestead Golf Course Inc .... E 937 698-4876
  Tipp City *(G-17719)*
Indian Ridge Golf Club L L C .... E 513 524-4653
  Oxford *(G-15816)*
Joe McClelland Inc .... E 740 452-3036
  Zanesville *(G-20492)*
Kinsale Golf & Fitnes CLB LLC ..... C 740 881-6500
  Powell *(G-16343)*
Lake Metroparks .... E 440 428-3164
  Madison *(G-13228)*
Link & Reneissance Inc .... E 440 235-0501
  Olmsted Twp *(G-15678)*
Links At Windy Knoll LLC .... D 937 631-3744
  Springfield *(G-17222)*
Locust Hills Golf Inc .... E 937 265-5152
  Springfield *(G-17224)*
Loyal Oak Golf Course Inc .... E 330 825-2904
  Barberton *(G-971)*
Madison Route 20 LLC .... E 440 358-7888
  Painesville *(G-15864)*
Mahoning Country Club Inc .... E 330 545-2517
  Girard *(G-11420)*
Mayfair Country Club Inc .... D 330 699-2209
  Uniontown *(G-18528)*
Meadowlake Corporation .... E 330 492-2010
  Canton *(G-2456)*
Mill Creek Golf Course Corp .... E 740 666-7711
  Ostrander *(G-15793)*
Mill Creek Metropolitan Park ...... D 330 740-7112
  Youngstown *(G-20287)*
Mohican Hills Golf Club Inc .... E 419 368-4700
  Jeromesville *(G-12333)*
Moundbuilders Country Club Co .. D 740 344-4500
  Newark *(G-15213)*
Norwalk Golf Properties Inc .... E 419 668-8535
  Norwalk *(G-15586)*
Ohio State Parks Inc .... D 513 664-3504
  College Corner *(G-6838)*
Park Arrowhead Golf Club Inc ..... E 419 628-2444
  Minster *(G-14667)*

Phoenix Golf Links ... E ... 614 539-3636
Grove City *(G-11591)*
Pine Brook Golf Club Inc ... E ... 440 748-2939
Grafton *(G-11443)*
Pine Hills Golf Club Inc ... E ... 330 225-4477
Hinckley *(G-11999)*
Pines Golf Club ... E ... 330 684-1414
Orrville *(G-15783)*
Quail Hollow Management Inc ... D ... 440 639-4000
Painesville *(G-15874)*
River Greens Golf Course Inc ... E ... 740 545-7817
West Lafayette *(G-19259)*
Sable Creek Golf Course Inc ... E ... 330 877-9606
Hartville *(G-11829)*
Scioto Reserve Inc ... D ... 740 881-9082
Powell *(G-16349)*
Scioto Reserve Inc ... D ... 740 881-6500
Powell *(G-16350)*
Shady Hollow Cntry CLB Co Inc ... D ... 330 832-1581
Massillon *(G-13854)*
Shaker Run Golf Club ... D ... 513 727-0007
Lebanon *(G-12645)*
Silver Lake Country Club ... D ... 330 688-6066
Silver Lake *(G-16964)*
Split Rock Golf Club Inc ... E ... 614 877-9755
Orient *(G-15762)*
Spring Hills Golf Club ... E ... 330 825-2439
New Franklin *(G-15047)*
Sugarbush Golf Inc ... E ... 330 527-4202
Garrettsville *(G-11353)*
Tamaron Golf LLC ... D ... 419 474-5067
Toledo *(G-18213)*
TW Recreational Services ... E ... 419 836-1466
Oregon *(G-15754)*
Valley View Golf Club Inc ... E ... 330 928-9034
Cuyahoga Falls *(G-9230)*
Vieira Inc ... E ... 937 599-3221
Bellefontaine *(G-1400)*
Wicked Woods Gulf Club Inc ... E ... 440 564-7960
Newbury *(G-15264)*
Win Tamer Corporation ... E ... 330 637-2881
Cortland *(G-9085)*
Wmvh LLC ... D ... 513 425-7886
Middletown *(G-14471)*
Yankee Run Golf Course ... D ... 330 448-8096
Brookfield *(G-1903)*

7993 Coin-Operated Amusement Devices & Arcades

16 Bit Bar ... E ... 513 381-1616
Cincinnati *(G-2939)*
Bell Music Company ... E ... 330 376-6337
Akron *(G-96)*
Entertrainment Inc ... E ... 513 898-8000
West Chester *(G-19069)*
Jack Thistledown Racino LLC ... E ... 216 662-8600
Cleveland *(G-5846)*
Magic Castle Inc ... E ... 937 434-4911
Dayton *(G-9694)*
Pnk (ohio) LLC ... A ... 513 232-8000
Cincinnati *(G-4312)*
S & B Enterprises LLC ... E ... 740 753-2646
Nelsonville *(G-14967)*
Stonehedge Enterprises Inc ... E ... 330 928-2161
Akron *(G-451)*
Strike Zone Inc ... D ... 440 235-4420
Olmsted Twp *(G-15681)*

7996 Amusement Parks

▲ Cedar Fair LP ... A ... 419 626-0830
Sandusky *(G-16734)*
Cedar Point Park LLC ... D ... 419 627-2500
Sandusky *(G-16735)*
Columbus Frkln Cnty Pk ... E ... 614 895-6219
Westerville *(G-19386)*
Columbus Frkln Cnty Pk ... E ... 614 891-0700
Galloway *(G-11342)*
Columbus Frkln Cnty Pk ... E ... 614 846-9962
Lewis Center *(G-12676)*
▲ Fun n Stuff Amusements Inc ... D ... 330 467-0821
Macedonia *(G-13197)*
Funtime Parks Inc ... C ... 330 562-7131
Aurora *(G-839)*
▲ Kings Island Company ... C ... 513 754-5700
Kings Mills *(G-12448)*
Kings Island Park LLC ... C ... 513 754-5901
Kings Mills *(G-12449)*
Linwood Park Company ... E ... 440 963-0481
Vermilion *(G-18713)*
Little Squirt Sports Park ... E ... 419 227-6200
Lima *(G-12830)*
Lmn Development LLC ... D ... 419 433-7200
Sandusky *(G-16775)*
Lodge Stone Wood ... E ... 513 769-4325
Blue Ash *(G-1630)*
Lost Nation Sports Park ... E ... 440 602-4000
Willoughby *(G-19687)*
Magnum Management Corporation ... A ... 419 627-2334
Sandusky *(G-16778)*
Muskingum Wtrshed Cnsrvncy Dst ... E ... 740 685-6013
Senecaville *(G-16824)*
Muskingum Wtrshed Cnsrvncy Dst ... E ... 330 343-6780
Mineral City *(G-14634)*
Rumpke Amusements Inc ... E ... 513 738-2646
Cincinnati *(G-4452)*
Seaworld Entertainment Inc ... E ... 330 562-8101
Aurora *(G-855)*
Strongville Recreation Complex ... C ... 440 580-3230
Strongsville *(G-17513)*

7997 Membership Sports & Recreation Clubs

797 Elks Golf Club Inc ... E ... 937 382-2666
Wilmington *(G-19740)*
Akron Management Corp ... B ... 330 644-8441
Akron *(G-48)*
Alano Club Inc ... D ... 419 335-6211
Wauseon *(G-18948)*
Alexander J Abernethy ... E ... 740 432-2107
Byesville *(G-2069)*
American Golf Corporation ... D ... 440 286-9544
Chesterland *(G-2792)*
American Golf Corporation ... E ... 740 965-5122
Galena *(G-11278)*
American Golf Corporation ... E ... 310 664-4278
Grove City *(G-11529)*
American Italian Golf ... D ... 614 889-2551
Dublin *(G-10249)*
Armco Association Park ... E ... 513 695-3980
Lebanon *(G-12589)*
Ashland Golf Club ... E ... 419 289-2917
Ashland *(G-657)*
Athens Golf & Country Club ... E ... 740 592-1655
Athens *(G-774)*
Atwood Yacht Club Inc ... E ... 330 735-2135
Sherrodsville *(G-16905)*
Avalon Golf & Country Club ... D ... 330 539-5008
Vienna *(G-18735)*
Avalon Golf and Cntry CLB Inc ... D ... 330 856-8898
Warren *(G-18822)*
Avon Oaks Country Club ... D ... 440 892-0660
Avon *(G-876)*
Avondale Golf Club ... E ... 440 934-4398
Avon *(G-878)*
Barrington Golf Club Inc ... D ... 330 995-0600
Aurora *(G-829)*
Barrington Golf Club Inc ... D ... 330 995-0821
Aurora *(G-830)*
Beechmont Inc ... D ... 216 831-9100
Cleveland *(G-5111)*
Beechmont Racquet Club Inc ... E ... 513 528-5700
Cincinnati *(G-3091)*
Bel-Wood Country Club Inc ... D ... 513 899-3361
Morrow *(G-14843)*
Belmont Country Club ... D ... 419 666-1472
Perrysburg *(G-15977)*
Belmont Hills Country Club ... D ... 740 695-2181
Saint Clairsville *(G-16626)*
Big Red LP ... D ... 740 548-7799
Galena *(G-11280)*
Blennerhassett Yacht Club Inc ... E ... 740 423-9062
Belpre *(G-1434)*
Brass Ring Golf Club Ltd ... E ... 740 385-8966
Logan *(G-12969)*
Breezy Point Ltd Partnership ... E ... 330 995-0600
Aurora *(G-831)*
Breezy Point Ltd Partnership ... C ... 440 247-3363
Solon *(G-16984)*
Brook Plum Country Club ... D ... 419 625-5394
Sandusky *(G-16729)*
Brookside Country Club Inc ... D ... 330 477-6505
Canton *(G-2270)*
Brookside Golf & Cntry CLB Co ... C ... 614 889-2581
Columbus *(G-7153)*
Browns Run Country Club ... D ... 513 423-6291
Middletown *(G-14419)*
Buckeye Golf Club Co Inc ... E ... 419 636-6984
Bryan *(G-2003)*
Buckeye Lake Yacht Club Inc ... E ... 740 929-4466
Buckeye Lake *(G-2021)*
Camargo Club ... C ... 513 561-9292
Cincinnati *(G-3167)*
Cambridge Country Club Company ... E ... 740 439-2744
Byesville *(G-2070)*
Canterbury Golf Club Inc ... D ... 216 561-1914
Cleveland *(G-5177)*
Caravon Golf Company Ltd ... D ... 440 937-6018
Avon *(G-883)*
Cascia LLC ... E ... 440 975-8085
Willoughby *(G-19648)*
Catawba-Cleveland Dev Corp ... D ... 419 797-4424
Port Clinton *(G-16239)*
Chagrin Valley Country Club Co ... D ... 440 248-4310
Chagrin Falls *(G-2692)*
Chagrin Valley Hunt Club ... E ... 440 423-4414
Gates Mills *(G-11356)*
Chillicothe Country Club Co ... E ... 740 775-0150
Chillicothe *(G-2819)*
Chillicothe Racquet Club ... E ... 740 773-4928
Chillicothe *(G-2824)*
Cincinnati Country Club ... C ... 513 533-5200
Cincinnati *(G-3295)*
Cincinnati Sports Mall Inc ... D ... 513 527-4000
Cincinnati *(G-3329)*
City of Parma ... E ... 440 885-8876
Cleveland *(G-5272)*
City of Sylvania ... E ... 419 885-1167
Sylvania *(G-17579)*
Cleveland Hts Tigers Youth Spo ... E ... 216 906-4168
Cleveland *(G-5319)*
Cleveland Racquet Club Inc ... D ... 216 831-2155
Cleveland *(G-5341)*
Cleveland Skating Club ... C ... 216 791-2800
Cleveland *(G-5346)*
Cleveland Yachting Club Inc ... D ... 440 333-1155
Cleveland *(G-5356)*
Clovernook Country Club ... D ... 513 521-0333
Cincinnati *(G-3371)*
Club At Hillbrook Inc ... E ... 440 247-4940
Chagrin Falls *(G-2694)*
Clubcorp Usa Inc ... E ... 216 851-2582
Cleveland *(G-5367)*
Coldstream Country Club ... E ... 513 231-3900
Cincinnati *(G-3381)*
Columbia Hills Country CLB Inc ... E ... 440 236-5051
Columbia Station *(G-6844)*
Columbia Recreation Assn ... E ... 740 849-2466
East Fultonham *(G-10506)*
Columbus Country Club ... D ... 614 861-1332
Columbus *(G-7343)*
Columbus Sail and Pwr Squadron ... C ... 614 384-0245
Lewis Center *(G-12677)*
Congress Lake Club Company ... E ... 330 877-9318
Hartville *(G-11816)*
Country Club Inc ... C ... 216 831-9200
Cleveland *(G-5417)*
Country Club At Muirfield Vlg ... E ... 614 764-1714
Dublin *(G-10310)*
Country Club of Hudson ... E ... 330 650-1188
Hudson *(G-12113)*
Country Club of North ... E ... 937 374-5000
Xenia *(G-20047)*
County of Perry ... E ... 740 342-0416
New Lexington *(G-15053)*
Cumberland Trail Golf CLB Crse ... E ... 740 964-9336
Etna *(G-10733)*
Dayton Country Club Company ... D ... 937 294-3352
Dayton *(G-9467)*
Dayton Toro Motorcycle Club ... D ... 937 723-9133
Dayton *(G-9492)*
Dornoch Golf Club Inc ... E ... 740 369-0863
Delaware *(G-10091)*
Dry Run Limited Partnership ... E ... 513 561-9119
Cincinnati *(G-3504)*
Dunsiane Swim Club ... E ... 937 433-7946
Dayton *(G-9508)*
Elm Valley Fishing Club ... D ... 937 845-0584
New Carlisle *(G-15022)*
Elms Country Club Inc ... E ... 330 833-2668
North Lawrence *(G-15392)*
Elms of Massillon Inc ... E ... 330 833-2668
North Lawrence *(G-15393)*
Elyria Country Club Company ... C ... 440 322-6391
Elyria *(G-10621)*
Fairfield Tempo Club ... E ... 513 863-2081
Fairfield *(G-10850)*
Fairlawn Country Club Company ... D ... 330 836-5541
Akron *(G-213)*
Family YMCA of LANcstr&fairfld ... C ... 740 654-0616
Lancaster *(G-12542)*

Field & Stream Bowhunters D 419 423-9861
Findlay *(G-11024)*
Findlay Country Club E 419 422-9263
Findlay *(G-11025)*
Fitworks Holding LLC E 440 333-4141
Rocky River *(G-16578)*
Five Seasons Spt Cntry CLB Inc D 513 842-1188
Cincinnati *(G-3633)*
Five Seasons Spt Cntry CLB Inc D 937 848-9200
Dayton *(G-9553)*
Five Seasons Spt Cntry CLB Inc D 440 899-4555
Cleveland *(G-5602)*
Four Bridges Country Club Ltd D 513 759-4620
Liberty Township *(G-12720)*
Frontier Bassmasters Inc E 740 423-9293
Belpre *(G-1438)*
Ganzfair Investment Inc E 614 792-6630
Delaware *(G-10100)*
Gardens Hockey Inc E 513 351-3999
Cincinnati *(G-3663)*
General Electric Employees E 513 243-2129
Cincinnati *(G-3672)*
Geneva Area Recreational E 440 466-1002
Geneva *(G-11363)*
German Family Society Inc E 330 678-8229
Kent *(G-12371)*
Glenmoor Country Club Inc C 330 966-3600
Canton *(G-2380)*
Golf Club Co E 614 855-7326
New Albany *(G-14987)*
Golf Course Maintenance D 330 262-9141
Wooster *(G-19864)*
Grove City Community Club E 614 875-6074
Grove City *(G-11567)*
Grove Walnut Country Club Inc E 937 253-3109
Dayton *(G-9270)*
Hawthorne Valley Country Club D 440 232-1400
Bedford *(G-1311)*
Heritage Club D 513 459-7711
Mason *(G-13715)*
Heritage Golf Club Ltd Partnr D 614 777-1690
Hilliard *(G-11908)*
Hyde Park Golf & Country Club D 513 321-3721
Cincinnati *(G-3801)*
Inverness Club D 419 578-9000
Toledo *(G-17978)*
Island Service Company C 419 285-3695
Put In Bay *(G-16368)*
Jefferson Golf & Country Club E 614 759-7500
Blacklick *(G-1508)*
Kenwood Country Club Inc C 513 527-3590
Cincinnati *(G-3914)*
Kettenring Country Club Inc E 419 782-2101
Defiance *(G-10042)*
Kettering Tennis Center E 937 434-6602
Dayton *(G-9658)*
Kirtland Country Club E 440 942-4400
Willoughby *(G-19675)*
Kirtland Country Club Company D 440 942-4400
Willoughby *(G-19676)*
Lake Front II Inc E 330 337-8033
Salem *(G-16703)*
Lake Wynoka Prprty Owners Assn E 937 446-3774
Lake Waynoka *(G-12463)*
Lakes Country Club Inc C 614 882-4167
Galena *(G-11285)*
Lakes Golf & Country Club Inc E 614 882-2582
Westerville *(G-19320)*
Lakewood Country Club Company D 440 871-0400
Cleveland *(G-5922)*
Lancaster Country Club D 740 654-3535
Lancaster *(G-12549)*
Legend Lake Golf Club Inc E 440 285-3110
Chardon *(G-2756)*
Leisure Sports Inc E 419 829-2891
Sylvania *(G-17599)*
Lenau Park E 440 235-2646
Olmsted Twp *(G-15677)*
Lions Club International Inc E 330 424-3490
Lisbon *(G-12939)*
Losantiville Country Club D 513 631-4133
Cincinnati *(G-3994)*
Lost Creek Country Club Inc E 419 229-2026
Lima *(G-12831)*
M&C Hotel Interests Inc E 440 543-1331
Chagrin Falls *(G-2723)*
Macair Aviation LLC E 937 347-1302
Xenia *(G-20069)*
Madison Route 20 LLC E 440 358-7888
Painesville *(G-15864)*

Maketewah Country Club Company D 513 242-9333
Cincinnati *(G-4015)*
Marietta Bantam Baseball Leag E 740 350-9844
Marietta *(G-13465)*
Marietta Country Club Inc E 740 373-7722
Marietta *(G-13468)*
Marion Country Club Company E 740 387-0974
Marion *(G-13555)*
Mayfield Sand Ridge Club D 216 381-0826
Cleveland *(G-5995)*
Meadowbrook Country Club D 937 836-5186
Clayton *(G-4914)*
Meadowbrook Country Club D 937 836-5186
Clayton *(G-4913)*
Medallion Club C 614 794-6999
Westerville *(G-19328)*
Mentor Lagoons Yacht Club Inc D 440 205-3625
Mentor *(G-14213)*
Miami Rifle Pistol Club D 513 732-9943
Milford *(G-14539)*
Miami Valley Golf Club D 937 278-7381
Dayton *(G-9730)*
Michael Brothers Inc E 419 332-5716
Fremont *(G-11213)*
Midwest Gymnstics Cheerleading E 614 764-0775
Dublin *(G-10398)*
Mill Creek Golf Course Corp E 740 666-7711
Ostrander *(G-15793)*
Mohawk Golf Club E 419 447-5876
Tiffin *(G-17687)*
Montgomery Swim & Tennis Club E 513 793-6433
Montgomery *(G-14727)*
Moraine Country Club E 937 294-6200
Dayton *(G-9756)*
Moundbuilders Country Club Co D 740 344-4500
Newark *(G-15213)*
Muirfield Village Golf Club E 614 889-6700
Dublin *(G-10402)*
N C R Employee Benefit Assn C 937 299-3571
Dayton *(G-9766)*
National Exchange Club E 419 535-3232
Toledo *(G-18074)*
New Albany Athc Booster CLB E 614 413-8325
New Albany *(G-14996)*
New Albany Country Club Comm A C 614 939-8500
New Albany *(G-14998)*
New Albany Links Dev Co Ltd D 614 939-5914
New Albany *(G-14999)*
New Wembley LLC E 440 543-8171
Chagrin Falls *(G-2726)*
Newlex Classic Riders Inc D 740 342-3885
New Lexington *(G-15058)*
Northwest Swim Club Inc E 614 442-8716
Columbus *(G-8298)*
Oak Hills Swim & Racquet E 513 922-1827
Cincinnati *(G-4195)*
Oakwood Club Inc D 216 381-7755
Cleveland *(G-6174)*
OBannon Creek Golf Club E 513 683-5657
Loveland *(G-13151)*
Oberlin College C 440 775-8519
Oberlin *(G-15654)*
Ohio Automobile Club E 614 277-1310
Grove City *(G-11588)*
Ohio Automobile Club E 513 870-0951
West Chester *(G-19124)*
Orchard Hill Swim Club D 513 385-0211
Cincinnati *(G-4232)*
Oxford Country Club Inc E 513 524-0801
Oxford *(G-15827)*
Pepper Pike Club Company Inc D 216 831-9400
Cleveland *(G-6263)*
Pike Run Golf Club Inc E 419 538-7000
Ottawa *(G-15803)*
Piqua Country Club Holding Co E 937 773-7744
Piqua *(G-16156)*
Portage Country Club Company D 330 836-8565
Akron *(G-396)*
Progressive Fishing Assn D 419 877-9909
Whitehouse *(G-19589)*
Quail Hollow Management Inc D 440 639-4000
Painesville *(G-15874)*
Radius Hospitality MGT LLC D 330 735-2211
Sherrodsville *(G-16906)*
Raintree Country Club Inc E 330 699-3232
Uniontown *(G-18534)*
Rawiga Country Club Inc D 330 336-2220
Seville *(G-16843)*
Reynoldsburg Swim Club Inc E 614 866-3211
Reynoldsburg *(G-16476)*

Salt Fork Resort Club Inc A 740 498-8116
Kimbolton *(G-12447)*
Sand Ridge Golf Club D 440 285-8088
Chardon *(G-2767)*
Sandusky Rotary Club Charitabl E 419 625-1707
Huron *(G-12169)*
Sandusky Yacht Club Inc D 419 625-6567
Sandusky *(G-16794)*
Sawmill Creek Golf Racquet CLB D 419 433-4945
Huron *(G-12171)*
Sawmill Greek Golf Racquet CLB D 419 433-3789
Huron *(G-12173)*
Scarbrough E Tennis Fitnes Ctr E 614 751-2597
Columbus *(G-8693)*
Scioto Reserve Inc D 740 881-9082
Powell *(G-16349)*
Shadow Valley Tennis Club E 419 865-1141
Maumee *(G-13976)*
Shady Hollow Cntry CLB Co Inc D 330 832-1581
Massillon *(G-13854)*
Shaker Heights Country Club Co C 216 991-3324
Shaker Heights *(G-16865)*
Shawnee Country Club D 419 227-7177
Lima *(G-12877)*
Silver Lake Country Club D 330 688-6066
Silver Lake *(G-16964)*
Silver Lake Management Corp C 330 688-6066
Silver Lake *(G-16965)*
Snow Hill Country Club Inc E 937 987-2491
New Vienna *(G-15132)*
Soccer Centre Inc E 419 893-5419
Maumee *(G-13977)*
Sportsman Gun & Reel Club Inc C 440 233-8287
Lorain *(G-13077)*
Spring Valley Golf & Athc CLB D 440 365-1411
Westlake *(G-19548)*
Springfield Country Club Co E 937 399-4215
Springfield *(G-17280)*
Steubenville Country Club Inc D 740 264-0521
Steubenville *(G-17336)*
Stone Oak Country Club D 419 867-0969
Holland *(G-12058)*
Swim Incorporated E 614 885-1619
Worthington *(G-20002)*
Sycamore Creek Country Club C 937 748-0791
Springboro *(G-17139)*
Sylvania Country Club D 419 392-0530
Sylvania *(G-17619)*
Tartan Fields Golf Club Ltd D 614 792-0900
Dublin *(G-10473)*
Tennis Unlimited Inc E 330 928-8763
Akron *(G-474)*
Terrace Park Country Club Inc D 513 965-4061
Milford *(G-14567)*
Tiffin Cmnty YMCA Rcration Ctr D 419 447-8711
Tiffin *(G-17704)*
Tippecanoe Country Club Inc E 330 758-7518
Canfield *(G-2213)*
Toledo Club D 419 243-2200
Toledo *(G-18234)*
Tri County Nite Hunter Assn Ci E 740 385-7341
Logan *(G-12990)*
Troy Country Club Inc E 937 335-5691
Troy *(G-18383)*
Turpin Hills Swim Racquet CLB E 513 231-3242
Cincinnati *(G-4707)*
Turtle Golf Management Ltd E 614 882-5920
Westerville *(G-19446)*
Union Country Club E 330 343-5544
Dover *(G-10218)*
US Swimming Lake Erie Swimming E 330 423-0485
Bay Village *(G-1042)*
Valleaire Golf Club Inc E 440 237-9191
Hinckley *(G-12000)*
Valleywood Golf Club Inc E 419 826-3991
Swanton *(G-17574)*
Vermilion Boat Club Inc E 440 967-6634
Vermilion *(G-18719)*
Vermilion Family YMCA E 440 967-4208
Vermilion *(G-18720)*
Walden Club D 330 995-7162
Aurora *(G-861)*
Walden Company Ltd C 330 562-7145
Aurora *(G-862)*
Wedgewood Golf & Country Club C 614 793-9600
Powell *(G-16354)*
West Denison Baseball League E 216 251-5790
Cleveland *(G-6735)*
Western Hills Country Club D 513 922-0011
Cincinnati *(G-4842)*

S I C

Employee Codes: A=Over 500 employees, B=251-500
C=101-250, D=51-100, E=25-50
2018 Harris Ohio
Services Directory
1021

Western Hills Sportsplex Inc D 513 451-4900
Cincinnati *(G-4843)*

Western Reserve Racquet Club E 330 653-3103
Streetsboro *(G-17436)*

Westwood Country Club Company D 440 331-3016
Rocky River *(G-16595)*

Wetherngton Golf Cntry CLB Inc D 513 755-2582
West Chester *(G-19185)*

Weymouth Valley Inc E 440 498-8888
Solon *(G-17067)*

Wickertree Tnnis Ftnes CLB LLC E 614 882-5724
Columbus *(G-8991)*

Wildwood Yacht Club Inc D 216 531-9052
Cleveland *(G-6752)*

YMCA of Ashtabula County Inc D 440 997-5321
Ashtabula *(G-768)*

York Temple Country Club Inc E 614 885-5459
Columbus *(G-9015)*

Young Mens Christian C 513 791-5000
Blue Ash *(G-1725)*

Young Mens Christian Assn E 419 332-9622
Fremont *(G-11231)*

Young Mens Christian Assn C 330 744-8411
Youngstown *(G-20421)*

Young Mens Christian Assoc D 740 477-1661
Circleville *(G-4909)*

Young Mens Christian Assoc D 937 426-9622
Dayton *(G-10011)*

Young Mens Christian Assoc E 614 878-7269
Columbus *(G-9020)*

Young Mens Christian Assoc D 330 264-3131
Wooster *(G-19936)*

Young Mens Christian Assoc D 937 836-9622
Englewood *(G-10725)*

Young Mens Christian Assoc E 937 228-9622
Dayton *(G-10012)*

Young Mens Christian Assoc C 937 223-5201
Springboro *(G-17144)*

Young Mens Christian Assoc C 614 834-9622
Canal Winchester *(G-2181)*

Young Mens Christian Associat C 419 251-9622
Perrysburg *(G-16076)*

Young Mens Christian Associat D 513 521-7112
Cincinnati *(G-4865)*

Young Mens Christian Associat E 513 731-0115
Cincinnati *(G-4866)*

Young Mens Christian Associat C 513 474-1400
Cincinnati *(G-4867)*

Young Mens Christn Assn Shelby D 419 347-1312
Shelby *(G-16904)*

Young MNS Christn Assn Findlay D 419 422-4424
Findlay *(G-11102)*

Young MNS Chrstn Assn Clveland D 216 382-4300
Cleveland *(G-6775)*

Young MNS Chrstn Assn Clveland E 216 941-4654
Cleveland *(G-6773)*

Youngstown Country Club D 330 759-1040
Youngstown *(G-20430)*

Zanesville Country Club E 740 452-2726
Zanesville *(G-20555)*

7999 Amusement & Recreation Svcs, NEC

797 Elks Golf Club Inc E 937 382-2666
Wilmington *(G-19740)*

Alice Noble Ice Arena E 330 345-8686
Wooster *(G-19827)*

Alliance Hospitality Inc E 440 951-7333
Mentor *(G-14141)*

Amusements of America Inc C 614 297-8863
Columbus *(G-7016)*

Army & Air Force Exchange Svc A 937 257-7736
Dayton *(G-9256)*

▲ **Asm International** D 440 338-5151
Novelty *(G-15601)*

Avalon Holdings Corporation D 330 856-8800
Warren *(G-18823)*

Baldwin Wallace University E 440 826-2285
Berea *(G-1446)*

Bates Bros Amusement Co D 740 266-2950
Wintersville *(G-19808)*

Beaver-Vu Bowl E 937 426-6771
Beavercreek *(G-1150)*

Bramarjac Inc E 419 884-3434
Mansfield *(G-13268)*

CCJ Enterprises Inc E 330 345-4386
Wooster *(G-19837)*

Centennial Terrace & Quarry E 419 885-7106
Sylvania *(G-17578)*

Central Ohio Ice Rinks Inc E 614 475-7575
Dublin *(G-10284)*

Chiller LLC D 614 764-1000
Dublin *(G-10292)*

Chiller LLC E 740 549-0009
Lewis Center *(G-12675)*

Chiller LLC E 614 475-7575
Columbus *(G-7265)*

Christian Twigs Gymnastics CLB E 937 866-8356
Dayton *(G-9406)*

Cincinnati Gymnastics Academy E 513 860-3082
Fairfield *(G-10834)*

Cincinnati Pool Management Inc A 513 777-1444
Cincinnati *(G-3322)*

Cincinnati Tae Kwon Do Inc E 513 271-6900
Cincinnati *(G-3333)*

Circle S Farms Inc E 614 878-9462
Grove City *(G-11546)*

City of Brook Park E 216 433-1545
Cleveland *(G-5248)*

City of Gallipolis E 740 441-6003
Gallipolis *(G-11310)*

City of Independence E 216 524-3262
Cleveland *(G-5263)*

City of Miamisburg E 937 866-4532
Miamisburg *(G-14283)*

City of North Olmsted D 440 734-8200
North Olmsted *(G-15416)*

City of Rocky River E 440 356-5656
Cleveland *(G-5274)*

City of Seven Hills C 216 524-6262
Seven Hills *(G-16828)*

City of South Euclid E 216 291-3902
Cleveland *(G-5276)*

City of Sylvania E 419 885-1167
Sylvania *(G-17579)*

City of Willowick D 440 944-1575
Willowick *(G-19738)*

Cleveland Metroparks D 440 331-5530
Cleveland *(G-5327)*

Cleveland Metroparks B 216 635-3200
Cleveland *(G-5328)*

Cleveland Metroparks B 216 739-6040
Strongsville *(G-17451)*

Cleveland Metroparks E 440 572-9990
Strongsville *(G-17452)*

Cloverleaf Bowling Center Inc E 216 524-4833
Cleveland *(G-5366)*

Clubcorp Usa Inc E 330 724-4444
Akron *(G-149)*

Columbus Frkln Cnty Pk E 614 891-0700
Westerville *(G-19387)*

Community Action Columbiana CT E 330 385-7251
East Liverpool *(G-10518)*

▲ **Coney Island Inc** E 513 232-8230
Cincinnati *(G-3410)*

County of Hancock E 419 425-7275
Findlay *(G-11019)*

Creekside Golf Dome E 330 545-5000
Girard *(G-11412)*

Cuyahoga County AG Soc E 440 243-0090
Berea *(G-1454)*

Darby Creek Golf Course Inc E 937 349-7491
Marysville *(G-13616)*

David Barber Civic Center E 740 498-4383
Newcomerstown *(G-15266)*

Dayton History C 937 293-2841
Dayton *(G-9478)*

Delaware Golf Club Inc E 740 362-2582
Delaware *(G-10089)*

Deshler Amusements Inc E 330 532-2922
Wellsville *(G-19006)*

Dicks Sporting Goods Inc E 740 522-5555
Heath *(G-11836)*

Dicks Sporting Goods Inc E 614 472-4250
Columbus *(G-7518)*

Dutch Heritage Farms Inc E 330 893-3232
Berlin *(G-1478)*

Edgewood Skate Arena E 419 331-0647
Lima *(G-12772)*

Fat Jacks Pizza II Inc E 419 227-1813
Lima *(G-12779)*

Flash Seats LLC E 216 420-2000
Cleveland *(G-5604)*

Flytz Gymnastics Inc E 330 926-2900
Cuyahoga Falls *(G-9189)*

Foxridge Farms Corp E 740 965-1369
Galena *(G-11282)*

Goldfish Swim School E 216 364-9090
Chagrin Falls *(G-2718)*

Goodrich Gnnett Nghborhood Ctr E 216 432-1717
Cleveland *(G-5678)*

Goofy Golf II Inc D 419 732-6671
Port Clinton *(G-16245)*

Goofy Golf Inc E 419 625-1308
Sandusky *(G-16764)*

Gymnastic World Inc E 440 526-2970
Cleveland *(G-5712)*

Hamilton County Parks District E 513 825-3701
Cincinnati *(G-3732)*

Heaven Bound Ascensions E 330 633-3288
Tallmadge *(G-17640)*

Huntington Hlls Recreation CLB E 614 837-0293
Pickerington *(G-16097)*

Ice Land USA Lakewood E 216 529-1200
Lakewood *(G-12482)*

Ice Land USA Ltd D 440 268-2800
Strongsville *(G-17475)*

Ice Zone Ltd E 330 965-1423
Youngstown *(G-20228)*

▲ **Integrity Global Marketing LLC** E 330 492-9989
Canton *(G-2412)*

Integrity Gymnstics Chrleading E 614 733-0818
Plain City *(G-16194)*

◆ **International Management Group** B 216 522-1200
Cleveland *(G-5830)*

International Mdsg Corp B 216 522-1200
Cleveland *(G-5831)*

Island Bike Rental Inc E 419 285-2016
Put In Bay *(G-16367)*

Iticketscom E 614 410-4140
Columbus *(G-7928)*

J&B Sprafka Enterprises Inc E 330 733-4212
Akron *(G-288)*

Kettering Recreation Center E 937 296-2587
Dayton *(G-9657)*

Kissel Bros Shows Inc E 513 741-1080
Cincinnati *(G-3930)*

Know Theatre of Cincinnati E 513 300-5669
Cincinnati *(G-3936)*

Lake Metroparks D 440 256-2122
Kirtland *(G-12457)*

Lake Metroparks E 440 256-1404
Willoughby *(G-19682)*

Lakewood City School District E 216 529-4400
Lakewood *(G-12487)*

Leaders Family Farms E 419 599-1570
Napoleon *(G-14944)*

M & R Amusement Services Inc E 937 525-0404
Springfield *(G-17227)*

Magic Castle Inc E 937 434-4911
Dayton *(G-9694)*

Makoy Center Inc E 614 777-1211
Hilliard *(G-11924)*

Man Golf Ohio LLC E 440 635-5178
Huntsburg *(G-12158)*

Marietta Aquatic Center E 740 373-2445
Marietta *(G-13464)*

Max Dixons Expressway Park E 513 831-2273
Milford *(G-14537)*

Meadowbrook Country Club D 937 836-5186
Clayton *(G-4913)*

Metropolitan Pool Service Co E 216 741-9451
Parma *(G-15910)*

Miami Valley Gaming & Racg LLC D 513 934-7070
Lebanon *(G-12628)*

Midwest Gymnstics Cheerleading E 614 764-0775
Dublin *(G-10398)*

National Concession Company E 216 881-9911
Cleveland *(G-6104)*

Oberlin College C 440 775-8519
Oberlin *(G-15654)*

Ohio Dept Natural Resources E 740 869-3124
Mount Sterling *(G-14874)*

Ohio Exposition Center D 614 644-4000
Columbus *(G-8342)*

Ohio Skate Inc E 419 476-2808
Toledo *(G-18103)*

Our Lady Prptul Hlp Cnmty Bngo E 513 742-3200
Cincinnati *(G-4243)*

◆ **Park Corporation** B 216 267-4870
Cleveland *(G-6234)*

Paul A Ertel D 216 696-8888
Cleveland *(G-6252)*

Recreational Golf Inc E 513 677-0347
Loveland *(G-13156)*

Relx Inc E 937 865-6800
Miamisburg *(G-14340)*

Roto Group LLC D 614 760-8690
Dublin *(G-10444)*

S & S Management Inc E 567 356-4151
Wapakoneta *(G-18807)*

SIC SECTION

80 HEALTH SERVICES

Skate Town U S A	E	513 874-9855

West Chester *(G-19155)*

Skateworld Inc .... E 937 294-4032
  Dayton *(G-9885)*
Sky Zone Indoor Trampoline Pk .... D 614 302-6093
  Cincinnati *(G-4539)*
Snows Lakeside Tavern .... E 513 954-5626
  Cincinnati *(G-4546)*
Soccer Centre Owners Ltd .... E 419 893-5425
  Maumee *(G-13978)*
Society of The Transfiguration .... E 513 771-7462
  Cincinnati *(G-4548)*
South E Harley Davidson Sls Co ...... E 440 439-5300
  Cleveland *(G-6496)*
Spring Hills Golf Club .... E 740 543-3270
  East Springfield *(G-10543)*
Stark County Park District .... D 330 477-3552
  Canton *(G-2545)*
Stockport Mill Country Inn Inc .... E 740 559-2822
  Stockport *(G-17346)*
Stonehedge Enterprises Inc .... E 330 928-2161
  Akron *(G-451)*
Strike Zone Inc .... D 440 235-4420
  Olmsted Twp *(G-15681)*
Therapeutic Riding Center Inc .... E 440 708-0013
  Chagrin Falls *(G-2736)*
Three D Golf LLC .... E 513 732-0295
  Batavia *(G-1027)*
United Skates America Inc .... E 440 944-5300
  Wickliffe *(G-19614)*
Valley Riding .... E 216 267-2525
  Cleveland *(G-6684)*
Washington Township Park Dst ...... E 937 433-5155
  Dayton *(G-9985)*
Washington Twnship Mntgomery ..... C 937 433-0130
  Dayton *(G-9986)*
Western Hills Sportsplex Inc .... D 513 451-4900
  Cincinnati *(G-4843)*
Wiegands Lake Park Inc .... E 440 338-5795
  Novelty *(G-15604)*
Wonderworker Inc .... D 234 249-3030
  Hudson *(G-12155)*
Wyandot County AG Soc .... E 419 294-4320
  Upper Sandusky *(G-18569)*
YMCA .... D 937 653-9622
  Urbana *(G-18603)*
Young Mens Christian Assoc .... D 330 264-3131
  Wooster *(G-19936)*
Young Mens Christian Assoc .... D 614 276-8224
  Columbus *(G-9018)*
Young Mens Christian Assoc .... D 740 477-1661
  Circleville *(G-4909)*
Young Mens Christian Assoc .... C 614 885-4252
  Columbus *(G-9017)*
Young Mens Christian Assoc .... E 937 228-9622
  Dayton *(G-10012)*
Youngs Jersey Dairy Inc .... B 937 325-0629
  Yellow Springs *(G-20091)*
YWCA of Hamilton .... E 513 856-9800
  Hamilton *(G-11785)*

80 HEALTH SERVICES

8011 Offices & Clinics Of Doctors Of Medicine

3rd Street Community Clinic .... D 419 522-6191
  Mansfield *(G-13257)*
A Thomas Dalagiannis MD .... E 419 887-7000
  Maumee *(G-13870)*
Adena Pckwy-Ross Fmly Physcans .. E 740 779-4500
  Chillicothe *(G-2813)*
Adrian M Schnall MD .... D 216 291-4300
  Cleveland *(G-4956)*
Advanced Urology Inc .... E 330 758-9787
  Youngstown *(G-20098)*
Advocate Radiology Bil .... C 614 210-1885
  Powell *(G-16323)*
Affiliates In Oral & Maxlofcl .... E 513 829-8080
  West Chester *(G-19015)*
Akron General Health System .... E 330 665-8200
  Akron *(G-42)*
Akron Neonatology Inc .... E 330 379-9473
  Akron *(G-49)*
Akron Plastic Surgeons Inc .... E 330 253-9161
  Akron *(G-50)*
Akron Radiology Inc .... E 330 375-3043
  Akron *(G-53)*
Allergy & Asthma Inc .... E 740 654-8623
  Lancaster *(G-12507)*

Allergy & Asthma Centre Dayton ..... E 937 435-8999
  Centerville *(G-2672)*
Alliance For Womens Health .... E 419 228-1000
  Lima *(G-12738)*
Alta Partners LLC .... E 440 808-3654
  Westlake *(G-19458)*
Ambulatory Medical Care Inc .... C 513 831-8555
  Milford *(G-14502)*
American Health Network Inc .... E 614 794-4500
  Columbus *(G-6993)*
American Health Network Inc .... E 740 363-5437
  Delaware *(G-10071)*
American Hlth Netwrk Ohio LLC ...... D 614 794-4500
  Columbus *(G-6995)*
American Hlth Ntwrk & Fmly PRC .... E 419 524-2212
  Mansfield *(G-13261)*
American Para Prof Systems Inc ..... E 513 531-2900
  Cincinnati *(G-3011)*
Ameripath Cincinnati Inc .... E 513 745-8330
  Blue Ash *(G-1533)*
Amherst Hospital Association .... C 440 988-6000
  Amherst *(G-587)*
Anderson Hills Pediatrics Inc .... E 513 232-8100
  Cincinnati *(G-3023)*
Anesthesia Associates Inc .... E 440 350-0832
  Painesville *(G-15834)*
Anesthesiology Assoc of Akron .... E 330 344-6401
  Akron *(G-76)*
Anesthesiology Consultant Inc .... E 614 566-9983
  Columbus *(G-7019)*
Anesthesiology Services Netwrk ..... E 937 208-6173
  Dayton *(G-9337)*
Anesthsia Assoc Cincinnati Inc .... D 513 585-0577
  Cincinnati *(G-3028)*
AP Cchmc .... E 513 636-4200
  Cincinnati *(G-3032)*
▲ Arlington Contact Lens Svc Inc .... E 614 921-9894
  Columbus *(G-7042)*
Ashtabula Clinic Inc .... D 440 997-6980
  Ashtabula *(G-715)*
Ashtabula County Medical Ctr .... C 440 997-6960
  Ashtabula *(G-723)*
Associated Specialists .... E 937 208-7272
  Dayton *(G-9345)*
Associates In Dermatology Inc .... E 440 249-0274
  Westlake *(G-19462)*
Asscoted Ctract Laser Surgeons ..... E 419 693-4444
  Oregon *(G-15724)*
Aultman Health Foundation .... C 330 305-6999
  Canton *(G-2251)*
Aultman Health Foundation .... E 330 452-9911
  Canton *(G-2252)*
Aultman North Canton Med Group ... B 330 433-1200
  Canton *(G-2257)*
Aultman North Inc .... C 330 305-6999
  Canton *(G-2258)*
Avita Health System .... C 419 468-4841
  Galion *(G-11291)*
Axesspointe Cmnty Hlth Ctr Inc ...... E 330 724-5471
  Akron *(G-86)*
Barb Linden .... E 440 233-1068
  Lorain *(G-13016)*
Barberton Area Family Practice .... E 330 615-3205
  Barberton *(G-956)*
Bel-Park Anesthesia .... E 330 480-3658
  Youngstown *(G-20112)*
Belmont Bhc Pines Hospital Inc .... C 330 759-2700
  Youngstown *(G-20113)*
Belmont Eye Clinic Inc .... E 330 759-7672
  Youngstown *(G-20114)*
Bernstein Allergy Group Inc .... E 513 931-0775
  Cincinnati *(G-3099)*
Bethesda Hospital Inc .... E 513 563-1505
  Cincinnati *(G-3107)*
Big Run Urgent Care Center .... E 614 871-7130
  Grove City *(G-11534)*
Bio-Mdical Applications RI Inc .... E 740 389-4111
  Marion *(G-13524)*
Blanchard Valley Hospital .... E 419 423-4335
  Findlay *(G-10999)*
Blanchard Valley Medical Assoc ...... D 419 424-0380
  Findlay *(G-11001)*
Blanchard Vly Rgional Hlth Ctr .... C 419 427-0809
  Findlay *(G-11003)*
Blanchard Vly Rgional Hlth Ctr .... E 419 358-9010
  Bluffton *(G-1727)*
Bloomberg Ross MD .... E 740 454-1216
  Zanesville *(G-20448)*
Brian Brocker Dr .... E 330 747-9215
  Youngstown *(G-20124)*

Bruce R Bracken .... E 513 558-3700
  Cincinnati *(G-3144)*
Buckeye Drmtlogy Drmthphthlogy ... E 614 389-6331
  Dublin *(G-10272)*
Buckeye Drmtlogy Drmthphthlogy ... E 614 317-9630
  Grove City *(G-11541)*
Bucyrus Community Physicians ...... D 419 492-2200
  New Washington *(G-15133)*
Butler Cnty Cmnty Hlth Cnsrtm .... D 513 454-1460
  Hamilton *(G-11699)*
Campolo Michael MD .... E 740 522-7600
  Newark *(G-15154)*
Canal Physician Group .... E 330 344-4000
  Akron *(G-120)*
Canton Altman Emrgncy Physcans .. E 330 456-2695
  Canton *(G-2281)*
Canton Ophthalmology Assoc .... E 330 994-1286
  Canton *(G-2294)*
Canyon Medical Center Inc .... E 614 864-6010
  Columbus *(G-7182)*
Capitol City Cardiology Inc .... E 614 464-0884
  Columbus *(G-7186)*
Cardiac Vsclar Thrcic Surgeons ...... E 513 421-3494
  Cincinnati *(G-3177)*
Cardinal Orthopaedic Group Inc ...... E 614 759-1186
  Columbus *(G-7196)*
Cardio Thoracic Surgery .... E 614 293-4509
  Columbus *(G-7197)*
Cardiologist .... D 440 882-0075
  Cleveland *(G-5181)*
Cardiologist Clark & Champaign ...... E 937 653-8897
  Urbana *(G-18575)*
Cardiologist of Clark & Champ .... E 937 323-1404
  Springfield *(G-17156)*
Cardiology Associates of .... E 740 454-6831
  Zanesville *(G-20456)*
Cardiology Consultants Inc .... D 330 454-8076
  Canton *(G-2299)*
Cardiology Ctr of Cincinnati .... E 513 745-9800
  Cincinnati *(G-3180)*
Cardiology Specialists Inc .... E 330 297-6110
  Ravenna *(G-16375)*
Cardiovascular Associates Inc .... E 330 747-6446
  Youngstown *(G-20133)*
Cardiovascular Clinic Inc .... D 440 882-0075
  Cleveland *(G-5182)*
Cardiovascular Consultants Inc .... D 330 454-8076
  Canton *(G-2300)*
Cardiovascular Medicine Assoc .... E 440 816-2708
  Cleveland *(G-5183)*
Cei Physicians Inc .... B 513 984-5133
  Blue Ash *(G-1553)*
Cei Physicians PSC Inc .... C 513 984-5133
  Blue Ash *(G-1554)*
Cei Physicians PSC Inc .... E 513 233-2700
  Cincinnati *(G-3200)*
Cei Physicians PSC Inc .... E 513 531-2020
  Cincinnati *(G-3201)*
Center For Dagnstc Imaging Inc ...... C 614 841-0800
  Columbus *(G-6872)*
Center For Dlysis Cre of Cnfld .... E 330 702-3040
  Canfield *(G-2186)*
Center For Srgcal Drmtlogy Inc .... D 614 847-4100
  Westerville *(G-19289)*
Center For Urologic Health LLC .... E 330 375-0924
  Akron *(G-128)*
Centers For Dialysis Care Inc .... E 216 295-7000
  Shaker Heights *(G-16858)*
Central Ohio Geriatrics LLC .... E 614 530-4077
  Granville *(G-11460)*
Central Ohio Nrlgical Surgeons .... D 614 268-9561
  Westerville *(G-19378)*
Central Ohio Primary Care .... E 614 459-3687
  Columbus *(G-7234)*
Central Ohio Primary Care .... E 614 451-1551
  Columbus *(G-7235)*
Central Ohio Primary Care .... E 614 473-1300
  Columbus *(G-7237)*
Central Ohio Primary Care .... D 614 508-0110
  Westerville *(G-19380)*
Central Ohio Primary Care .... E 614 891-9505
  Westerville *(G-19290)*
Central Ohio Primary Care .... E 614 882-0708
  Westerville *(G-19381)*
Central Ohio Primary Care .... C 614 268-8164
  Columbus *(G-7238)*
Central Ohio Primary Care .... E 614 834-8042
  Canal Winchester *(G-2156)*
Central Ohio Primary Care .... E 614 540-7339
  Worthington *(G-19946)*

Employee Codes: A=Over 500 employees, B=251-500
C=101-250, D=51-100, E=25-50

Central Ohio Primary Care D 614 326-2672
Westerville (G-19291)
Central Ohio Primary Care D 614 818-9550
Westerville (G-19379)
Central Ohio Primary Care E 614 442-7550
Columbus (G-7239)
Central Ohio Surgical Assoc E 614 222-8000
Columbus (G-7240)
Chander M Kohli MD Facs Inc E 330 759-6978
Youngstown (G-20137)
Charles L Maccallum MD Inc E 330 655-2161
Hudson (G-12109)
Chester West Dentistry E 330 753-7734
Akron (G-131)
Child & Adolescent Speciality E 937 667-7711
Tipp City (G-17713)
Children Medical Group Inc E 330 762-9033
Akron (G-133)
Childrens Hosp Med Ctr Akron E 330 543-8004
Akron (G-136)
Childrens Hospital Medical Ctr A 513 636-4200
Cincinnati (G-3247)
Childrens Hospital Medical Ctr A 513 636-4366
Cincinnati (G-3250)
Childrens Hospital Medical Ctr A 513 636-8778
Cincinnati (G-3254)
Childrens Hospital Medical Ctr A 513 803-9600
Liberty Township (G-12719)
Childrens Hospital Medical Ctr A 513 636-4200
Cincinnati (G-3252)
Childrens Hospital Medical Ctr E 513 636-6800
Mason (G-13676)
Childrens Physician Inc E 330 494-5600
Canton (G-2306)
Childrens Surgery Center Inc D 614 722-2920
Columbus (G-7264)
Chillicothe Family Physicians E 740 779-4100
Chillicothe (G-2820)
Chirst Hospital Surgery Center E 513 272-3448
Cincinnati (G-3257)
Christ Hospital D 513 721-8272
Cincinnati (G-3259)
Christ Hospital D 513 585-0050
Cincinnati (G-3265)
Christ Hospital C 513 755-4700
West Chester (G-19038)
Christ Hospital D 513 631-3300
Cincinnati (G-3267)
Christ Hospital C 513 351-0800
Cincinnati (G-3268)
Christ Hospital E 513 564-4000
Cincinnati (G-3260)
Christ Hospital C 513 561-7809
Cincinnati (G-3261)
Christ Hospital Corporation C 513 347-2300
Cincinnati (G-3269)
▲ Christian Community Hlth Svcs E 513 381-2247
Cincinnati (G-3272)
Christian Healthcare E 330 848-1511
Barberton (G-961)
Christopher C Kaeding E 614 293-3600
Columbus (G-7270)
Cincinnati Hand Surgery Cons E 513 961-4263
Cincinnati (G-3307)
Cincinnati Head and Neck Inc E 513 232-3277
Cincinnati (G-3308)
City of Columbus E 614 645-1600
Columbus (G-7280)
City of Whitehall E 614 237-5478
Columbus (G-7286)
Clevelan Clinic Hlth Sys W Reg E 216 476-7606
Cleveland (G-5288)
Clevelan Clinic Hlth Sys W Reg D 216 476-7007
Cleveland (G-5289)
Cleveland Anesthesia Group E 216 901-5706
Independence (G-12198)
Cleveland Clinic Cole Eye Inst E 216 444-4508
Cleveland (G-5295)
Cleveland Clinic Community Onc E 216 447-9747
Independence (G-12199)
Cleveland Clinic Foundation E 330 287-4930
Wooster (G-19848)
Cleveland Clinic Foundation B 216 448-4325
Cleveland (G-5302)
▲ Cleveland Clinic Foundation A 216 636-8335
Cleveland (G-5296)
Cleveland Ear Nose Throat Ctr E 440 550-4179
Mayfield Heights (G-13999)
Cleveland Preterm E 216 991-4577
Cleveland (G-5340)

Clinton Memorial Hospital E 937 383-3402
Wilmington (G-19754)
Clyo Internal Medicine Inc D 937 435-5857
Centerville (G-2676)
Coleman Professional Svcs Inc B 330 673-1347
Kent (G-12360)
Columbus Cardiology Cons Inc C 614 224-2281
Columbus (G-7335)
Columbus Cardiology Cons Inc C 614 224-2281
Columbus (G-7336)
Columbus Gstrntrlogy Group Inc D 614 457-1213
Columbus (G-7356)
Columbus Medical Rheumatology E 614 486-5200
Columbus (G-7367)
Columbus Neighborhood Health C C 614 445-0685
Columbus (G-7373)
Columbus Obsttrcans Gynclgists E 614 434-2400
Columbus (G-7374)
▲ Columbus Oncology Associates D 614 442-3130
Columbus (G-7375)
Columbus Surgical Center LLP E 614 932-9503
Dublin (G-10301)
Community Action Comm Pike CNT E 740 947-7726
Waverly (G-18970)
Community Health Partners Regi E 440 960-4000
Lorain (G-13029)
Community Mental Health Svc D 740 695-9344
Saint Clairsville (G-16633)
Community Mercy Foundation B 937 652-3645
Urbana (G-18582)
Compass Community Health E 740 355-7102
Portsmouth (G-16273)
Comprehensive Health Care Inc E 419 238-7777
Van Wert (G-18631)
Comprehensive Pediatrics E 440 835-8270
Westlake (G-19479)
Comprhensive Cardiologist Cons E 513 936-9191
Cincinnati (G-3408)
Comprhnsive Care Orthpdics Inc E 419 473-9500
Toledo (G-17827)
Concorde Therapy Group Inc E 330 493-4210
Alliance (G-535)
Consolidated Care Inc E 937 465-8065
West Liberty (G-19262)
Consultnts In Gastroenterology E 440 386-2250
Painesville (G-15846)
Corporate Health Dimensions E 740 775-6119
Chillicothe (G-2828)
County of Delaware D 740 203-2040
Delaware (G-10084)
County of Lucas C 419 213-4018
Toledo (G-17836)
County of Montgomery E 937 225-4156
Dayton (G-9440)
Covenant Care Ohio Inc D 937 526-5570
Versailles (G-18726)
Cranley Surgical Associates E 513 961-4335
Cincinnati (G-3439)
Crossroads Lake County Adole D 440 255-1700
Mentor (G-14165)
Crystal Arthritis Center Inc E 330 668-4045
Akron (G-177)
Crystal Clinic Surgery Ctr Inc A 330 668-4040
Akron (G-178)
David Lee Grossman MD E 419 843-8150
Toledo (G-17844)
David M Schneider MD Inc E 513 752-5700
Cincinnati (G-2912)
Davis Eye Center E 330 923-5676
Cuyahoga Falls (G-9178)
Davita Inc E 615 341-6311
Georgetown (G-11393)
Davue Ob-Gyn Associates Inc D 937 277-8988
Dayton (G-9453)
Dayton Cardiology Consultants E 937 223-3053
Dayton (G-9462)
Dayton Childrens Hospital E 937 641-3376
Dayton (G-9463)
Dayton Ear Nose Throat Srgeons E 937 434-0555
Dayton (G-9473)
Dayton Eye Surgery Center E 937 431-9531
Beavercreek (G-1236)
Dayton Heart Center Inc D 937 277-4274
Dayton (G-9477)
Dayton Medical Imaging D 937 439-0390
Dayton (G-9481)
Dayton Ob Gyn E 937 439-7550
Centerville (G-2677)
Dayton Physicians LLC D 937 280-8400
Dayton (G-9486)

Dayton Physicians LLC C 937 547-0563
Greenville (G-11497)
Dayton Primary & Urgent Care E 937 461-0800
Dayton (G-9487)
Dayton Regional Dialysis Inc E 937 898-5526
Dayton (G-9490)
Defiance Family Physicians E 419 785-3281
Defiance (G-10026)
Dennis C McCluskey MD & Assoc E 330 628-2686
Mogadore (G-14675)
Dermatlgists of Southwest Ohio E 937 435-2094
Dayton (G-9498)
Digestive Care Inc D 937 320-5050
Beavercreek (G-1238)
▲ Digestive Specialists Inc E 937 534-7330
Dayton (G-9501)
Dignity Health C 330 493-4443
Canton (G-2341)
Doctors Hosp Physcn Svcs LLC E 330 834-4725
Massillon (G-13801)
Doctors Ohiohealth Corporation A 614 544-5424
Columbus (G-7537)
Doctors Urgent Care E 419 586-1611
Celina (G-2646)
Drs Hill & Thomas Co E 440 944-8887
Cleveland (G-5509)
Drs Paul Boyles & Kennedy E 614 734-3347
Columbus (G-7544)
Drs Ravin Birndorf Ravin Inc E 877 852-8463
Toledo (G-17856)
Dublin Family Care Inc E 614 761-2244
Dublin (G-10327)
Dublin Surgical Center LLC E 614 932-9548
Dublin (G-10332)
Dunlap Family Physicians Inc E 330 684-2015
Orrville (G-15769)
E N T Toledo Inc E 419 578-7555
Toledo (G-17860)
Eastern Hill Internal Medicine E 513 232-3500
Cincinnati (G-3535)
Eastern Hills Pediatric Assoc E 513 231-3345
Cincinnati (G-3536)
Elizabeth Place Holdings LLC E 323 300-3700
Dayton (G-9522)
Emerald Pediatrics E 614 932-5050
Dublin (G-10335)
Emergency Medical Group Inc E 419 866-6009
Toledo (G-17865)
Emergency Medicine Specialists D 937 438-8910
Dayton (G-9526)
Emergency Services Inc E 614 224-6420
Columbus (G-7592)
Emp Management Group Ltd D 330 493-4443
Canton (G-2355)
Endo-Surgical Center Fla LLC B 440 708-0582
Chagrin Falls (G-2715)
Endoscopy Center E 419 843-7993
Sylvania (G-17586)
Endoscopy Center of Dayton E 937 320-5050
Beavercreek (G-1239)
▲ ENt and Allergy Health Svcs E 440 779-1112
North Olmsted (G-15420)
Envision Healthcare Corp A 937 534-7330
Dayton (G-9528)
Equitas Health Inc C 614 299-2437
Columbus (G-7603)
Eric Hasemeier Do E 740 594-7979
Athens (G-787)
Erieside Medical Group E 440 918-6270
Willoughby (G-19662)
Evokes LLC E 513 947-8433
Mason (G-13700)
Eye Care Associates Inc D 330 746-7691
Youngstown (G-20183)
Eye Center E 614 228-3937
Columbus (G-7625)
Eye Centers of Ohio Inc E 330 966-1111
North Canton (G-15336)
Eye Centers of Ohio Inc E 330 966-1111
Canton (G-2362)
Eye Inst of Northwestern OH In E 419 865-3866
Toledo (G-17875)
Fairview Eye Center Inc E 440 333-3060
Cleveland (G-5566)
Fairview Hospital E 216 476-7000
Cleveland (G-5568)
Fallen Timbers Fmly Physicians D 419 893-3321
Maumee (G-13913)
Falls Family Practice Inc E 330 923-9585
Cuyahoga Falls (G-9182)

Family Health Care Center Inc ....E 614 274-4171
Columbus *(G-7635)*
Family Health Partners Inc ....E 419 935-0196
Willard *(G-19619)*
Family Health Plan Inc ....C 419 241-6501
Toledo *(G-17877)*
Family Hlth Svcs Drke Cnty Inc ....C 937 548-3806
Greenville *(G-11500)*
Family Medical Group ....E 513 389-1400
Cincinnati *(G-3589)*
Family Medicine Center Minerva ....E 330 868-4184
Minerva *(G-14645)*
Family Medicine Stark County ....E 330 499-5600
Canton *(G-2363)*
Family Physician Associates ....E 614 901-2273
Westerville *(G-19399)*
Family Physicians Associates ....E 440 442-3866
Cleveland *(G-5570)*
Family Physicians Inc ....E 330 494-7099
Canton *(G-2364)*
Family Physicians of Coshocton ....E 740 622-0332
Coshocton *(G-9102)*
Family Physicians of Gahanna ....E 614 471-9654
Columbus *(G-7636)*
Family Practice & Associates ....E 937 399-6650
Springfield *(G-17196)*
Family Practice Ctr Salem Inc ....E 330 332-9961
Salem *(G-16695)*
Far Oaks Orthopedists Inc ....E 937 433-5309
Dayton *(G-9539)*
Far Oaks Orthopedists Inc ....E 937 298-0452
Vandalia *(G-18678)*
Far Oaks Orthopedists Inc ....E 937 433-5309
Dayton *(G-9540)*
Fauster-Cameron Inc ....B 419 784-1414
Defiance *(G-10030)*
Findlay Womens Care LLC ....E 419 420-0904
Findlay *(G-11030)*
First Med Urgent & Fmly Ctr ....E 740 756-9238
Lancaster *(G-12543)*
First Settlement Orthopaedics ....E 740 373-8756
Marietta *(G-13446)*
Five Rivers Health Centers ....E 937 734-6841
Dayton *(G-9552)*
Flowers Family Practice Inc ....E 614 277-9631
Grove City *(G-11562)*
Foot & Ankle Care Center ....E 937 492-1211
Sidney *(G-16934)*
Fortunefavorsthe Bold LLC ....E 216 469-2845
Lakewood *(G-12479)*
Foundations Hlth Solutions Inc ....D 440 793-0200
North Olmsted *(G-15423)*
Franklin & Seidelmann Inc ....E 216 255-5700
Beachwood *(G-1081)*
Frederick C Smith Clinic Inc ....B 740 383-7000
Marion *(G-13540)*
Frederick C Smith Clinic Inc ....E 740 363-9021
Delaware *(G-10099)*
Fresenius Med Care Hldings Inc ....E 216 267-1451
Cleveland *(G-5637)*
Gastrntrlogy Assoc Clvland Inc ....E 216 593-7700
Cleveland *(G-5656)*
Gastroenterology Associates ....E 330 493-1480
Canton *(G-2377)*
Gem City Urologist Inc ....E 937 832-8400
Englewood *(G-10705)*
Generations Family Medicine ....E 614 337-1282
Gahanna *(G-11244)*
Geoff Answini ....E 513 792-7800
Cincinnati *(G-3677)*
George G Ellis Jr MD ....E 330 965-0832
Youngstown *(G-20199)*
George P Pettit MD Inc ....E 740 354-1434
Portsmouth *(G-16279)*
Good Samaritan Hosp Cincinnati ....E 513 569-6251
Cincinnati *(G-3685)*
Good Samaritan Hospital ....C 937 276-6784
Englewood *(G-10706)*
Goudy Internal Medicine Inc ....D 419 468-8323
Galion *(G-11301)*
Grandview Family Practice ....E 740 258-9267
Columbus *(G-7766)*
Greater Cin Cardi Consults In ....E 513 751-4222
Cincinnati *(G-3706)*
Greater Cincinnati Gastro Assc ....D 513 336-8636
Cincinnati *(G-3709)*
Greater Cincinnati Ob/Gyn Inc ....D 513 245-3103
Cincinnati *(G-3710)*
GTE Internet ....D 614 508-6000
Columbus *(G-7780)*

Gw Sutherland MD ....E 419 578-7200
Toledo *(G-17928)*
H M T Dermatology Inc ....E 330 725-0569
Medina *(G-14073)*
Hand Ctr At Orthopaedic Inst ....D 937 298-4417
Dayton *(G-9598)*
Hand Rehabilitation Associates ....E 330 668-4055
Akron *(G-251)*
Hans Zwart MD & Associates ....E 937 433-4183
Dayton *(G-9599)*
Health Care Specialists ....E 740 454-4530
Zanesville *(G-20486)*
Health Collaborative ....D 513 618-3600
Cincinnati *(G-3753)*
Health Works Mso Inc ....E 740 368-5366
Delaware *(G-10103)*
Healthsource of Ohio Inc ....E 937 392-4381
Georgetown *(G-11395)*
Healthsource of Ohio Inc ....E 937 981-7707
Greenfield *(G-11487)*
Healthspan Integrated Care ....C 216 621-5600
Cleveland *(G-5742)*
Heart Care ....D 614 533-5000
Gahanna *(G-11246)*
Heart Center of N Eastrn Ohio ....E 330 758-7703
Youngstown *(G-20214)*
Heart Ohio Family Health Ctrs ....E 614 235-5555
Columbus *(G-7814)*
Heart Specialists of Ohio ....E 614 538-0527
Columbus *(G-7815)*
Hector A Buch Jr MD ....E 419 227-7399
Lima *(G-12797)*
Helen M Torok MD ....E 330 722-5477
Medina *(G-14075)*
Hernando Zegarra ....E 216 831-5700
Cleveland *(G-5753)*
Herzig-Krall Medical Group ....E 513 896-9595
Fairfield *(G-10858)*
Hickman Cancer Center ....D 419 824-1952
Sylvania *(G-17593)*
Hillsboro Health Center Inc ....E 937 393-5781
Hillsboro *(G-11982)*
Holzer Clinic LLC ....C 304 746-3701
Gallipolis *(G-11320)*
Holzer Clinic LLC ....A 740 446-5411
Gallipolis *(G-11321)*
Holzer Clinic LLC ....C 304 744-2300
Gallipolis *(G-11322)*
Holzer Clinic LLC ....E 740 886-9403
Proctorville *(G-16359)*
Holzer Clinic LLC ....C 740 589-3100
Athens *(G-793)*
Holzer Clinic LLC ....E 740 446-5412
Gallipolis *(G-11323)*
Home Health Connection Inc ....E 614 839-4545
Worthington *(G-19964)*
Hometown Urgent Care ....C 614 263-4400
Columbus *(G-7854)*
Hometown Urgent Care ....C 330 505-9400
Warren *(G-18862)*
Hometown Urgent Care ....C 614 472-2880
Columbus *(G-7855)*
Hometown Urgent Care ....C 614 272-1100
Columbus *(G-7856)*
Hometown Urgent Care ....C 937 236-8630
Dayton *(G-9619)*
Hometown Urgent Care ....C 937 322-6222
Springfield *(G-17207)*
Hometown Urgent Care ....C 614 835-0400
Groveport *(G-11645)*
Hometown Urgent Care ....C 937 372-6012
Xenia *(G-20062)*
Hometown Urgent Care ....C 330 629-2300
Youngstown *(G-20219)*
Hometown Urgent Care ....D 740 363-3133
Delaware *(G-10107)*
Hometown Urgent Care ....C 937 252-2000
Wooster *(G-19868)*
Hometown Urgent Care ....C 513 831-5900
Milford *(G-14525)*
Hometown Urgent Care ....C 937 342-9520
Springfield *(G-17206)*
Hope Ctr For Cncer Care Warren ....D 330 856-8600
Warren *(G-18863)*
Hopewell Health Centers Inc ....E 740 596-5249
Mc Arthur *(G-14016)*
HRP Capital Inc ....E 419 865-3111
Holland *(G-12028)*
Immediate Health Associates ....E 614 794-0481
Westerville *(G-19411)*

Immediate Medical Service Inc ....E 330 823-0400
Alliance *(G-540)*
Independence Oncology ....E 216 524-7979
Cleveland *(G-5812)*
Institute/Reproductive Health ....E 513 585-2355
Cincinnati *(G-3821)*
Internal Mdcine Cons of Clmbus ....E 614 878-6413
Columbus *(G-7916)*
Internal Medical Physicians ....E 330 868-3711
Minerva *(G-14647)*
Internal Medicine of Akron ....E 330 376-2728
Akron *(G-281)*
Ironton and Lawrence County ....B 740 532-3534
Ironton *(G-12291)*
Johnson Adams & Protrouski ....E 419 238-6251
Van Wert *(G-18636)*
Joint Implant Surgeons Inc ....E 614 221-6331
New Albany *(G-14990)*
Joint Township Dst Mem Hosp ....D 419 394-9959
Saint Marys *(G-16675)*
Jon R Dvorak MD ....E 419 872-7700
Perrysburg *(G-16021)*
Joseph A Girgis MD Inc ....E 440 930-6095
Sheffield Village *(G-16889)*
Joslin Diabetes Center Inc ....E 937 401-7575
Dayton *(G-9645)*
Jyg Innovations LLC ....E 937 630-3858
Dayton *(G-9647)*
Kaiser Foundation Hospitals ....A 440 350-3614
Concord Township *(G-9032)*
Kaiser Foundation Hospitals ....A 330 633-8400
Akron *(G-299)*
Kaiser Foundation Hospitals ....A 216 524-7377
Avon *(G-901)*
Kaiser Foundation Hospitals ....A 800 524-7377
Cleveland Heights *(G-6792)*
Kaiser Foundation Hospitals ....A 216 524-7377
Brooklyn Heights *(G-1918)*
Kaiser Foundation Hospitals ....A 800 524-7377
North Canton *(G-15347)*
Kaiser Foundation Hospitals ....A 800 524-7377
Medina *(G-14090)*
Kaiser Foundation Hospitals ....A 800 524-7377
Fairlawn *(G-10961)*
Kaiser Foundation Hospitals ....A 800 524-7377
Mentor *(G-14201)*
Kaiser Foundation Hospitals ....A 800 524-7377
Kent *(G-12375)*
Kaiser Foundation Hospitals ....A 216 524-7377
Rocky River *(G-16584)*
Kaiser Foundation Hospitals ....A 800 524-7377
Brooklyn Heights *(G-1919)*
Kaiser Foundation Hospitals ....A 216 524-7377
Strongsville *(G-17479)*
Kaiser Foundation Hospitals ....A 330 486-2800
Twinsburg *(G-18436)*
Kathleen K Karol MD ....D 419 878-7992
Toledo *(G-17991)*
Kentucky Heart Institute Inc ....E 740 353-8100
Portsmouth *(G-16293)*
Kettering Adventist Healthcare ....D 937 298-3399
Kettering *(G-12430)*
Kettering Anesthesia Assoc Inc ....D 937 298-4331
Dayton *(G-9650)*
Kevin C McDonnell MD ....D 330 344-6401
Akron *(G-305)*
Kiddie West Pediatric Center ....E 614 276-7733
Columbus *(G-7986)*
Kidney & Hypertension Center ....E 513 861-0800
Cincinnati *(G-3921)*
Kidney Group Inc ....E 330 746-1488
Youngstown *(G-20245)*
Kindred Healthcare Inc ....D 937 222-5963
Dayton *(G-9660)*
Kolczun & Kolczun Orthopedics ....E 440 985-3113
Lorain *(G-13046)*
Kunesh Eye Center Inc ....E 937 298-1703
Oakwood *(G-15621)*
Labcare ....E 330 753-3649
Barberton *(G-969)*
Lake County Family Practice ....E 440 352-4880
Mentor *(G-14204)*
Lake Hospital System Inc ....A 440 632-3024
Middlefield *(G-14397)*
Lake Urgent & Family Med Ctr ....E 440 255-6400
Mentor *(G-14206)*
Lakewood Clveland Fmly Med Ctr ....E 216 227-2162
Lakewood *(G-12488)*
Lakewood Hospital Association ....E 216 228-5437
Cleveland *(G-5923)*

S I C

Employee Codes: A=Over 500 employees, B=251-500
C=101-250, D=51-100, E=25-50
2018 Harris Ohio
Services Directory
1025

Laser Hair Removal Center D 937 433-7536
Dayton *(G-9674)*
Lasik Plus Vision Center D 513 794-9964
Cincinnati *(G-3963)*
Lawrence A Cervino MD E 330 668-4065
Akron *(G-313)*
Layh & Associates E 937 767-9171
Yellow Springs *(G-20090)*
Lca-Vision Inc C 513 792-9292
Cincinnati *(G-3966)*
Life Line Screening D 216 581-6556
Independence *(G-12226)*
Lifecare Fmly Hlth & Dntl Ctr E 330 454-2000
Canton *(G-2437)*
Lifestges Smrtan Ctr For Women E 937 277-8988
Dayton *(G-9681)*
Lu-Jean Feng Clinic LLC E 216 831-7007
Cleveland *(G-5956)*
Luis F Soto MD E 330 649-9400
Canton *(G-2441)*
Luke Immediate Care Center E 419 227-2245
Lima *(G-12833)*
Lutheran Medical Center B 216 696-4300
Solon *(G-17023)*
Magnum Medical Overseas JV LLC D 979 848-8169
Cincinnati *(G-4012)*
Mahoning Vly Hmtlgy Onclgy Aso E 330 318-1100
Youngstown *(G-20265)*
Mammovan Inc E 330 726-2064
Youngstown *(G-20270)*
Margaret B Shipley Child Hlth E 330 478-6333
Canton *(G-2447)*
Marietta Gynecologic Assoc D 740 374-3622
Marietta *(G-13469)*
Markowitz Rosenberg Assoc Drs E 440 646-2200
Cleveland *(G-5980)*
Marysvlle Obsttrics Gynecology E 937 644-1244
Marysville *(G-13637)*
Marysvlle Ohio Srgical Ctr LLC A 937 578-4200
Marysville *(G-13639)*
Matern Ohio Management Inc D 614 457-7660
Columbus *(G-8127)*
Maumee Ob Gyn Assoc E 419 891-6201
Maumee *(G-13945)*
Mayfield Clinic Inc D 513 221-1100
Cincinnati *(G-4033)*
MBC Cardiologist Inc D 937 223-4461
Dayton *(G-9704)*
Med -Center/Med Partners E 440 349-6400
Cleveland *(G-6011)*
Med Center One Streetsboro E 330 626-3455
Streetsboro *(G-17421)*
Medcentral Health System E 419 526-8900
Ontario *(G-15701)*
Medical Arts Physician Center D 216 431-1500
Cleveland *(G-6013)*
Medical Assoc Cambridge Inc E 740 439-3515
Cambridge *(G-2123)*
Medical Associates of Mid-Ohio E 419 289-1331
Ashland *(G-688)*
Medical College of Ohio E 419 383-7100
Toledo *(G-18048)*
Medical Diagnostic Lab Inc D 440 333-1375
Westlake *(G-19514)*
Medical Group Associates Inc E 740 283-4773
Steubenville *(G-17330)*
Medical Mutual of Ohio E 614 621-4585
Columbus *(G-8143)*
Medical Onclgy-Hematology Assn E 937 223-2183
Dayton *(G-9714)*
Medicine Midwest LLC E 513 533-1199
Cincinnati *(G-4045)*
Medicine Midwest LLC E 937 435-8786
Dayton *(G-9715)*
Mercer Cnty Joint Townshp Hosp E 419 586-1611
Celina *(G-2654)*
Mercy Health D 419 935-0187
Willard *(G-19623)*
Mercy Health E 330 792-7418
Youngstown *(G-20281)*
Mercy Health E 513 829-1700
Fairfield *(G-10879)*
Mercy Health E 513 686-5392
Cincinnati *(G-4059)*
Mercy Health E 419 492-1300
New Washington *(G-15135)*
Mercy Health E 440 355-4206
Lagrange *(G-12460)*
Mercy Health D 937 390-1700
Springfield *(G-17236)*
Mercy Health E 513 248-0100
Milford *(G-14538)*
Mercy Health D 513 232-7100
Cincinnati *(G-4063)*
Mercy Health E 513 686-8100
Blue Ash *(G-1640)*
Mercy Health E 440 937-4600
Avon *(G-907)*
Mercy Health E 440 336-2239
Elyria *(G-10651)*
Mercy Health E 440 327-7372
North Ridgeville *(G-15469)*
Mercy Health E 440 775-1881
Oberlin *(G-15650)*
Mercy Health E 440 934-8344
Sheffield Village *(G-16891)*
Mercy Health E 440 967-8713
Vermilion *(G-18714)*
Mercy Health D 513 233-6736
Cincinnati *(G-4065)*
Mercy Health C 419 251-2659
Toledo *(G-18052)*
Mercy Health E 440 366-5577
North Ridgeville *(G-15470)*
Mercy Health D 513 585-9600
Cincinnati *(G-4066)*
Mercy Health D 419 475-4666
Toledo *(G-18054)*
Mercy Health E 419 476-2124
Toledo *(G-18055)*
Mercy Health D 419 264-5800
Holgate *(G-12003)*
Mercy Health Youngstown LLC A 330 729-1420
Youngstown *(G-20283)*
Mercy Hlth St Vincent Med LLC A 419 251-0580
Toledo *(G-18058)*
Mercy Hospital Tiffin Ohio B 419 455-8101
Tiffin *(G-17685)*
Mercy Medical Associates E 513 686-4840
Cincinnati *(G-4077)*
Mercy Medical Center Inc D 330 649-4380
Canton *(G-2458)*
Mercy Medical Center Inc E 330 627-7641
Carrollton *(G-2623)*
Mercy Professional Care E 330 832-2280
Massillon *(G-13839)*
Metro Health System D 330 669-2249
Smithville *(G-16966)*
Metrohealth System D 216 778-8446
Cleveland *(G-6040)*
Metropolitan Family Care Inc E 614 237-1067
Reynoldsburg *(G-16469)*
Miamisburg Family Practice E 937 866-2494
Miamisburg *(G-14322)*
Mid-Ohio Heart Clinic Inc E 419 524-8151
Mansfield *(G-13345)*
Mid-Ohio Pdiatrics Adolescents E 614 899-0000
Westerville *(G-19425)*
Middltown Crdvscular Assoc Inc E 513 217-6400
Middletown *(G-14439)*
Midohio Crdiolgy Vascular Cons C 614 262-6772
Columbus *(G-8167)*
Midwest Allergy Associates E 614 846-5944
Columbus *(G-8168)*
Midwest Cmnty Hlth Assoc Inc C 419 633-4034
Bryan *(G-2012)*
Midwest Physcans Ansthsia Svcs D 614 884-0641
Columbus *(G-8171)*
Midwest Retina Inc E 614 233-9500
Zanesville *(G-20502)*
Mill Pond Family Physicians E 330 928-3111
Cuyahoga Falls *(G-9211)*
Miller-Valentine Construction D 937 293-0900
Dayton *(G-9749)*
Milltown Family Physicians E 330 345-8016
Wooster *(G-19891)*
Mobile Cardiac Imaging LLC E 419 251-3711
Toledo *(G-18067)*
Monroe Family Health Center E 740 472-0757
Woodsfield *(G-19818)*
Moyal and Petroff MD E 440 461-6477
Cleveland *(G-6081)*
Mrp Inc E 513 965-9700
Milford *(G-14543)*
Mvhe Inc E 937 499-8211
Dayton *(G-9765)*
National Guard Ohio D 614 492-3166
Columbus *(G-8218)*
National Rgstry Emrgncy Mdcl E 614 888-4484
Columbus *(G-8224)*
Neighborhood Health Care Inc E 216 281-8945
Cleveland *(G-6116)*
Nelson & Bold Inc E 440 975-1422
Willoughby *(G-19696)*
Neurological Associates Inc D 614 544-4455
Columbus *(G-8268)*
Neurology Nroscience Assoc Inc E 330 572-1011
Akron *(G-350)*
Neurosurgical Network Inc E 419 251-1155
Toledo *(G-18083)*
New Beginnings Pediatrics Inc E 419 483-4122
Bellevue *(G-1413)*
New Horizons Surgery Center E 740 375-5854
Marion *(G-13568)*
North Coast Prof Co LLC C 419 557-5541
Sandusky *(G-16782)*
North Ohio Heart Center Inc E 440 414-9500
Cleveland *(G-6141)*
North Ohio Heart Center Inc E 440 366-3600
Elyria *(G-10660)*
North Ohio Heart Center Inc E 440 204-4000
Avon *(G-909)*
North Ohio Heart Center Inc E 440 204-4000
Lorain *(G-13070)*
North Ohio Heart Center Inc E 440 326-4120
Elyria *(G-10661)*
North Shore Gstrenterology Inc D 440 808-1212
Westlake *(G-19524)*
Northast Ohio Eye Surgeons Inc E 330 678-0201
Kent *(G-12387)*
Northast Ohio Eye Surgeons Inc E 330 836-8545
Akron *(G-353)*
Northast Ohio Orthpedics Assoc E 330 344-1980
Akron *(G-354)*
Northast Srgical Assoc of Ohio E 216 643-2780
Independence *(G-12240)*
Northeast Family Health Care E 330 630-2332
Tallmadge *(G-17645)*
Northeast OH Neighborhood Heal C 216 231-2323
Cleveland *(G-6152)*
Northeast Ohio Cardiology Svcs E 330 253-8195
Akron *(G-356)*
Northern Ohio Med Spclists LLC E 419 625-2841
Sandusky *(G-16783)*
Northwest Columbus Urology E 937 342-9260
Springfield *(G-17253)*
Northwest Eye Surgeons Inc E 614 451-7550
Columbus *(G-8295)*
Northwest Ohio Cardiology Cons D 419 842-3000
Toledo *(G-18094)*
Northwest Ohio Orthopedics E 419 885-2553
Sylvania *(G-17602)*
Northwest Ohio Urgent Care Inc E 419 720-7363
Toledo *(G-18095)*
Norwalk Clinic Inc E 419 668-4851
Norwalk *(G-15585)*
Norwood Endoscopy Center E 513 731-5600
Cincinnati *(G-4184)*
Nuerocare Center Inc D 330 494-2917
Canton *(G-2477)*
Nuerological & Sleep Disorders E 513 721-7533
Cincinnati *(G-4190)*
Nueterra Holdings LLC E 614 451-0500
Columbus *(G-8304)*
Nuray Radiologists Inc E 513 965-8059
Cincinnati *(G-4191)*
Nwo Gastroenterology Assoc Inc E 419 471-1317
Toledo *(G-18099)*
Oakhill Medical Associates E 937 599-1411
West Liberty *(G-19263)*
Ob Gyn Associates of Lancaster E 740 653-5088
Lancaster *(G-12563)*
Ob-Gyn Specialists Lima Inc E 419 227-0610
Lima *(G-12846)*
Oberlin Clinic Inc C 440 774-7337
Oberlin *(G-15653)*
Obstetrics & Gynecology Assoc D 513 221-3800
Fairfield *(G-10886)*
Obstetrics & Gynecology S Inc E 937 296-0167
Dayton *(G-9782)*
Obstetrics Gynclogy of Reserve E 330 666-1166
Akron *(G-361)*
Occupational Health Services E 937 492-7296
Sidney *(G-16944)*
Ohio Cancer Specialists E 419 756-2122
Mansfield *(G-13351)*
Ohio Clinic Aesthc Plstc Srgy E 440 808-9315
Westlake *(G-19527)*
Ohio Eye Alliance E 330 823-1680
Alliance *(G-550)*

80 HEALTH SERVICES

Ohio Eyecare Specialists Inc ....E 937 222-3937
  Oakwood *(G-15622)*
Ohio Gstroenterology Group Inc ....E 614 221-8355
  Columbus *(G-8346)*
Ohio Gstroenterology Group Inc ....E 614 754-5500
  Columbus *(G-8347)*
Ohio Gstroenterology Group Inc ....D 614 754-5500
  Columbus *(G-8348)*
Ohio Head & Neck Surgeons Inc ....E 330 492-2844
  Canton *(G-2480)*
Ohio Health Group LLC ....E 614 566-0010
  Columbus *(G-8350)*
Ohio Heart ....E 513 206-1320
  Cincinnati *(G-4204)*
Ohio Heart and Vascular ....E 513 206-1800
  Cincinnati *(G-4205)*
Ohio Heart Health Center Inc ....C 513 351-9900
  Cincinnati *(G-4206)*
Ohio Institute of Cardiac Care ....E 937 322-1700
  Springfield *(G-17255)*
Ohio Medical Group ....E 440 414-9400
  Westlake *(G-19528)*
Ohio North E Hlth Systems Inc ....E 330 747-9551
  Youngstown *(G-20307)*
Ohio Orthpd Surgery Inst LLC ....E 614 827-8777
  Columbus *(G-8364)*
Ohio Pediatrics Inc ....E 937 299-2339
  Dayton *(G-9787)*
Ohio Pediatrics Inc ....E 937 299-2743
  Dayton *(G-9788)*
Ohio Retina Associates Inc ....E 330 966-9800
  Canton *(G-2484)*
Ohio State Univ Managed Health ....E 614 292-8405
  Columbus *(G-8380)*
Ohio State Univ Wexner Med Ctr ....C 614 293-2663
  Columbus *(G-8382)*
Ohio State Univ Wexner Med Ctr ....A 614 227-0562
  Columbus *(G-8383)*
Ohio State Univ Wexner Med Ctr ....A 614 293-6255
  Columbus *(G-8387)*
Ohio State Univ Wexner Med Ctr ....A 614 293-7521
  Columbus *(G-8385)*
Ohio State University ....A 614 366-3692
  Columbus *(G-8388)*
Ohio State University ....A 614 293-8045
  Columbus *(G-8390)*
Ohio State University ....A 614 293-7417
  Columbus *(G-8394)*
Ohio State University ....A 614 293-8116
  Columbus *(G-8396)*
Ohio State University ....A 614 293-3860
  Columbus *(G-8403)*
Ohio State University ....E 614 293-4997
  Columbus *(G-8411)*
Ohio State University ....E 614 293-8732
  Columbus *(G-8415)*
Ohio State University ....D 614 293-2222
  Columbus *(G-8433)*
Ohio State University ....B 614 293-8133
  Columbus *(G-8434)*
Ohio State University ....A 614 293-5066
  Columbus *(G-8436)*
Ohio State University ....A 614 293-4967
  Columbus *(G-8444)*
Ohio State University ....A 614 257-3000
  Columbus *(G-8393)*
Ohio Surgery Center Ltd ....D 614 451-0500
  Columbus *(G-8449)*
Ohio University ....D 740 593-2195
  Athens *(G-807)*
Ohio University ....E 740 593-1660
  Athens *(G-808)*
Ohio Valley Medical Center LLC ....D 937 521-3900
  Springfield *(G-17257)*
Ohio Vally Ambulatory Surgery ....E 740 423-4684
  Belpre *(G-1443)*
Ohiocare Ambulatory Surgery ....E 419 897-5501
  Maumee *(G-13952)*
Oncolgy/Hmatology Care Inc PSC ....D 513 751-2145
  Cincinnati *(G-4226)*
Ophthalmology Associates of ....E 419 865-3866
  Maumee *(G-13953)*
Ophthlmic Srgeons Cons of Ohio ....E 614 221-7464
  Columbus *(G-8472)*
Optivue Inc ....C 419 891-1391
  Oregon *(G-15743)*
Oral & Maxillofacial Surgeons ....E 419 471-0300
  Toledo *(G-18111)*
Orthoneuro ....E 614 890-6555
  Westerville *(G-19434)*

Orthoneuro ....D 614 890-6555
  Columbus *(G-8482)*
Orthoneuro ....D 614 890-6555
  Columbus *(G-8483)*
Orthopaedic & Spine Center At ....E 614 468-0300
  Dublin *(G-10417)*
Orthopaedic Institute Ohio Inc ....D 419 222-6622
  Lima *(G-12851)*
Orthopaedic Offices Inc ....E 513 221-5500
  Blue Ash *(G-1659)*
Orthopdic Spt Mdicine Cons Inc ....E 513 777-7714
  Middletown *(G-14447)*
Orthopedic Assoc of Zanesville ....E 740 454-3273
  Zanesville *(G-20522)*
Orthopedic Associates ....E 937 415-9100
  Centerville *(G-2683)*
Orthopedic Associates Dayton ....E 937 280-4988
  Dayton *(G-9794)*
Orthopedic Associates Inc ....E 440 892-1440
  Westlake *(G-19530)*
▲ Orthopedic Cons Cincinnati ....C 513 733-8894
  Blue Ash *(G-1660)*
Orthopedic Cons Cincinnati ....E 513 753-7488
  Cincinnati *(G-2926)*
Orthopedic Cons Cincinnati ....E 513 232-6677
  Cincinnati *(G-4236)*
Orthopedic Cons Cincinnati ....E 513 245-2500
  Cincinnati *(G-4237)*
Orthopedic Cons Cincinnati ....E 513 347-9999
  Cincinnati *(G-4238)*
Orthopedic Diagnstc Trtmnt Ctr ....E 513 791-6611
  Montgomery *(G-14733)*
Orthopedic Diagnstc Trtmnt Ctr ....E 513 221-4848
  Cincinnati *(G-4239)*
Orthopedic One Inc ....D 614 827-8700
  Columbus *(G-8484)*
Orthorpdics Mltspcialty Netwrk ....E 330 493-1630
  Canton *(G-2487)*
Osu Emergency Medicine LLC ....D 614 947-3700
  Columbus *(G-8486)*
Osu Physical Medicine LLC ....E 614 366-6398
  Columbus *(G-8491)*
Osu Psychiatry LLC ....E 614 794-1818
  Columbus *(G-8492)*
Osu Radiology LLC ....E 614 293-8315
  Columbus *(G-8493)*
OSu Spt Mdcine Physicians Inc ....E 614 293-3600
  Columbus *(G-8494)*
Osu Surgery LLC ....E 614 293-8116
  Columbus *(G-8495)*
Osu Surgery LLC ....C 614 261-1141
  Columbus *(G-8496)*
Osup Community Outreach LLC ....E 614 685-1542
  Columbus *(G-8497)*
P C Vpa ....E 937 293-2133
  Moraine *(G-14814)*
Pain Control Consultants Inc ....E 614 430-5727
  Columbus *(G-8508)*
Pain Net Inc ....D 614 481-5960
  Columbus *(G-8509)*
Pajka Eye Center Inc ....E 419 228-7432
  Lima *(G-12854)*
Parkway Surgery Center Inc ....D 419 531-7860
  Toledo *(G-18120)*
Patricia A Dickerson MD ....E 937 436-1117
  Dayton *(G-9804)*
Pediatric Assoc Cincinnati ....E 513 791-1222
  Cincinnati *(G-4272)*
Pediatric Assoc of Fairfield ....E 513 874-9460
  Fairfield *(G-10893)*
Pediatric Assoc of Springfield ....D 937 328-2320
  Springfield *(G-17259)*
Pediatric Associatoc Inc ....E 614 501-7337
  Columbus *(G-8530)*
Pediatric Associates of Dayton ....E 937 832-7337
  Englewood *(G-10715)*
Pediatric Care Inc ....E 513 931-6357
  Cincinnati *(G-4273)*
Pediatric Services Inc ....E 440 845-1500
  Cleveland *(G-6259)*
Pediatrics Assoc of Mt Carmel ....E 513 752-3650
  Cincinnati *(G-2927)*
Pediatrics of Akron Inc ....E 330 253-7753
  Akron *(G-380)*
Pediatrics of Lima Inc ....E 419 222-4045
  Lima *(G-12856)*
Perrysburg Pediatrics ....E 419 872-7700
  Perrysburg *(G-16042)*
Physicians Care of Marietta ....D 740 373-2519
  Marietta *(G-13487)*

Physicians In Family Practice ....E 440 775-1881
  Oberlin *(G-15658)*
Physicians Surgeons For Women ....E 937 323-7340
  Springfield *(G-17261)*
Pioneer Physicians Networking ....E 330 633-6601
  Tallmadge *(G-17647)*
Plastic Surgery Group Inc ....E 513 791-4440
  Cincinnati *(G-4303)*
Portage Family Medicine ....E 330 626-5566
  Streetsboro *(G-17426)*
Portage Pediatrics ....E 330 297-8824
  Ravenna *(G-16401)*
Preble County General Hlth Dst ....E 937 472-0087
  Eaton *(G-10575)*
Premier Health Group LLC ....E 937 535-4100
  Dayton *(G-9819)*
Premier Health Partners ....D 937 526-3235
  Versailles *(G-18728)*
Premier Health Specialists Inc ....E 937 223-4518
  Dayton *(G-9821)*
Premier Heart Associates Inc ....E 937 832-2425
  Dayton *(G-9822)*
Premier Heart Inc ....E 937 832-2425
  Englewood *(G-10717)*
Premier Integrated Med Assoc ....D 937 291-6813
  Centerville *(G-2684)*
Premier Physicians Centers Inc ....E 440 895-5085
  Westlake *(G-19535)*
Premier Radiology Group Inc ....E 937 431-9729
  Beavercreek *(G-1198)*
Primary Care Nursing Services ....D 614 764-0960
  Dublin *(G-10430)*
Primary Care Physicians Assn ....E 330 499-9944
  Canton *(G-2493)*
Primary Cr Ntwrk Prmr Hlth Prt ....E 513 492-5940
  Mason *(G-13749)*
Primary Cr Ntwrk Prmr Hlth Prt ....E 937 890-6644
  Vandalia *(G-18693)*
Primary Cr Ntwrk Prmr Hlth Prt ....E 937 278-5854
  Dayton *(G-9823)*
Primary Cr Ntwrk Prmr Hlth Prt ....D 937 208-9090
  Dayton *(G-9824)*
Primary Cr Ntwrk Prmr Hlth Prt ....E 937 743-5965
  Franklin *(G-11164)*
Primary Cr Ntwrk Prmr Hlth Prt ....E 513 420-5233
  Middletown *(G-14486)*
Primary Cr Ntwrk Prmr Hlth Prt ....E 937 226-7085
  Dayton *(G-9825)*
Primary Cr Ntwrk Prmr Hlth Prt ....D 937 424-9800
  Dayton *(G-9826)*
Primary Eyecare Associates ....E 937 492-2351
  Sidney *(G-16948)*
Primecare Sutheastern Ohio Inc ....E 740 454-8551
  Zanesville *(G-20526)*
Primed ....E 937 435-9013
  Dayton *(G-9828)*
Primed Physicians ....E 937 298-8058
  Dayton *(G-9829)*
Primed Premier Integrated Med ....C 937 291-6893
  Dayton *(G-9830)*
Primehalth Wns Hlth Specialist ....E 440 918-4630
  Willoughby Hills *(G-19733)*
Professionals For Womens Hlth ....E 614 268-8800
  Columbus *(G-8569)*
Progressive Womens Care ....E 330 629-8466
  Youngstown *(G-20330)*
Promedica ....D 419 291-3450
  Maumee *(G-13960)*
Promedica GI Physicians LLC ....E 419 843-7996
  Toledo *(G-18139)*
Promedica Gnt-Urinary Surgeons ....E 419 531-8558
  Toledo *(G-18140)*
Promedica Health Systems Inc ....E 419 891-6201
  Maumee *(G-13961)*
Provider Physicians Inc ....D 614 755-3000
  Columbus *(G-8574)*
Psy-Care Inc ....E 330 856-6663
  Warren *(G-18891)*
Psychiatric Solutions Inc ....C 440 953-3000
  Willoughby *(G-19706)*
Psychiatric Solutions Inc ....C 330 759-2700
  Youngstown *(G-20333)*
Psychiatric Solutions Inc ....C 419 891-9333
  Maumee *(G-13963)*
Psychiatric Solutions Inc ....C 740 695-2131
  Saint Clairsville *(G-16653)*
Public Safety Ohio Department ....E 937 335-6209
  Troy *(G-18372)*
Pulmonary & Medicine Dayton ....E 937 439-3600
  Miamisburg *(G-14338)*

80 HEALTH SERVICES

Name	Code	Phone
Pulmonary Crtcal Care Spcalist	E	419 843-7800
Maumee *(G-13964)*		
Queen City General & Vascular	E	513 232-8181
Cincinnati *(G-4364)*		
Queen City Medical Group	E	513 528-5600
Cincinnati *(G-4367)*		
Queen City Physicians	D	513 872-2061
Cincinnati *(G-4368)*		
Queen City Physicians Ltd	E	513 791-6992
Cincinnati *(G-4369)*		
Queen Cy Spt Mdcine Rhbltation	E	513 561-1111
Cincinnati *(G-4373)*		
R I D Inc	E	419 251-4790
Toledo *(G-18145)*		
Radiology & Imaging Services	E	330 864-0832
Akron *(G-404)*		
Radiology Physicians Inc	E	614 717-9840
Delaware *(G-10121)*		
Rakesh Ranjan MD & Assoc Inc	E	216 375-9897
Cleveland *(G-6350)*		
Reading Family Practice	E	513 563-6934
Cincinnati *(G-4391)*		
Reconstructive Orthopedics	D	513 793-3933
Cincinnati *(G-4394)*		
Regency Park Eye Associates	E	419 882-0588
Toledo *(G-18146)*		
Rehab Continuum Inc	E	513 984-8070
Blue Ash *(G-1679)*		
Reid Physician Associates Inc	B	937 456-4400
Eaton *(G-10576)*		
Reproductive Gynecology Inc	E	330 375-7722
Akron *(G-411)*		
Reproductive Gynecology Inc	E	330 452-6010
Canton *(G-2507)*		
Reserve	E	330 666-1166
Akron *(G-413)*		
Retina Associate of Cleveland	E	216 831-5700
Beachwood *(G-1119)*		
Retina Associate of Cleveland	E	216 221-2878
Lakewood *(G-12498)*		
Retina Group Inc	E	614 464-3937
Columbus *(G-8626)*		
Retina Vitreous Associates	E	419 517-6599
Toledo *(G-18154)*		
Richard J Nelson MD	E	419 578-7555
Maumee *(G-13971)*		
Richard L Liston MD	D	937 320-2020
Beavercreek *(G-1258)*		
Richard Tomm MD	D	216 297-3060
Cleveland *(G-6393)*		
Richmond Medical Center	B	440 585-6500
Richmond Heights *(G-16542)*		
River Road Family Physicians	E	419 872-7745
Perrysburg *(G-16052)*		
River Vly Orthpdics Spt Mdcine	E	740 687-3346
Lancaster *(G-12570)*		
Riverhills Healthcare Inc	E	513 241-2370
Cincinnati *(G-4425)*		
Riverhills Healthcare Inc	E	513 791-6400
Cincinnati *(G-4426)*		
Riverside Nephrology Assoc Inc	E	614 538-2250
Columbus *(G-8635)*		
Riverside Radiology and	C	614 340-7747
Columbus *(G-8636)*		
Riverview Health Institute	E	937 222-5390
Dayton *(G-9852)*		
Riverview Surgery Center	E	740 681-2700
Lancaster *(G-12571)*		
Robert E Kose	E	419 843-7800
Maumee *(G-13973)*		
Robert E Lubow MD	E	513 961-8861
Cincinnati *(G-4434)*		
Robert Ellis	E	513 821-0275
Cincinnati *(G-4435)*		
Robert F Arrom Md Inc	E	513 893-4107
Fairfield *(G-10901)*		
Robert Wiley MD Inc	E	216 621-3211
Cleveland *(G-6405)*		
Robinson Health System Inc	A	330 297-0811
Ravenna *(G-16407)*		
Robinson Memorial Hospital	E	330 626-3455
Streetsboro *(G-17428)*		
Rocking Horse Chld Hlth Ctr	E	937 328-7266
Springfield *(G-17265)*		
Roger S Palutsis MD	E	330 821-0201
Alliance *(G-557)*		
Russell D Ens Do	E	330 499-5700
Canton *(G-2520)*		
Russell Weisman Jr MD	C	216 844-3127
Cleveland *(G-6422)*		
Sabry Hospital	E	216 476-7052
Cleveland *(G-6431)*		
Sagar Satyavolu MD	E	937 323-1404
Springfield *(G-17269)*		
Salem Internal Medicine Assoc	E	330 332-5232
Salem *(G-16716)*		
Samaritan Professional Corp	E	419 289-0491
Ashland *(G-696)*		
Saras Garden	D	419 335-7272
Wauseon *(G-18962)*		
Schoenbrunn Healthcare	E	330 339-3595
New Philadelphia *(G-15114)*		
Schuster Cardiology	E	937 866-0637
Miamisburg *(G-14346)*		
Senior Lifestyle Corporation	D	513 777-4457
West Chester *(G-19150)*		
Seven Hills Obgyn Associates	E	513 922-6666
Cincinnati *(G-4503)*		
Seven Hills Womens Health Ctrs	C	513 721-3200
Cincinnati *(G-4504)*		
Shapiro Shapiro & Shapiro	E	216 927-2030
Cleveland *(G-6477)*		
Shawneespring Hlth Cre Cntr RI	B	513 943-4000
Loveland *(G-13160)*		
Signature Healthcare LLC	C	440 232-1800
Bedford *(G-1336)*		
Signature Optical Inc	E	216 831-6299
Beachwood *(G-1126)*		
Sister of Mercy of Clerm Count	D	513 732-8200
Batavia *(G-1024)*		
Somc Foundation Inc	D	740 356-5000
Portsmouth *(G-16310)*		
South Dayton Acute Care Cons	E	937 433-8990
Dayton *(G-9890)*		
South Dyton Urlgcal Asscations	E	937 294-1489
Dayton *(G-9891)*		
Southast Cmnty Mental Hlth Ctr	C	614 225-0980
Columbus *(G-8751)*		
Southern Ohio Eye Assoc LLC	E	740 773-6347
Chillicothe *(G-2886)*		
Southern Ohio Wns Cancer Prj	D	740 775-7332
Chillicothe *(G-2887)*		
Southwest Family Physicians	E	440 816-2750
Cleveland *(G-6501)*		
Southwest General Health Ctr	C	440 816-4900
Strongsville *(G-17510)*		
Southwest Internal Medicine	E	440 816-2777
Cleveland *(G-6506)*		
Southwest Ohio Amblatry Srgery	E	513 425-0930
Middletown *(G-14458)*		
Southwest Ohio Ent Spclsts Inc	E	937 496-2600
Dayton *(G-9892)*		
Southwest Urology LLC	E	440 845-0900
Cleveland *(G-6507)*		
Southwestern Obstetricians & G	E	614 875-0444
Grove City *(G-11600)*		
Spectrum Eye Care Inc	E	419 423-8665
Findlay *(G-11083)*		
Spectrum Orthpedics Inc Canton	E	330 455-5367
North Canton *(G-15367)*		
Sports Care Rehabilitation	E	419 578-7530
Toledo *(G-18196)*		
Springdale Family Medicine PC	E	513 771-7213
Cincinnati *(G-4566)*		
St Ritas Medical Center	D	419 227-3361
Lima *(G-12888)*		
St Ritas Medical Center	E	419 996-5895
Lima *(G-12889)*		
Stark Cnty Emrgncy Physicians	E	330 492-7950
Canton *(G-2541)*		
Stark County Neurologists Inc	D	330 494-2097
Canton *(G-2544)*		
Stark County Womens Clinic Inc	D	330 493-0313
Canton *(G-2546)*		
Stark Medical Specialties Inc	E	330 837-1111
Massillon *(G-13857)*		
Stephen A Rudolph Inc	E	216 381-1367
Cleveland *(G-6537)*		
Summa Health	A	330 873-1518
Akron *(G-452)*		
Summa Health System	C	330 252-0095
Akron *(G-455)*		
Summa Health System	E	330 630-9726
Tallmadge *(G-17651)*		
Summa Health System	C	330 375-3315
Akron *(G-459)*		
Summa Health System	B	330 864-8060
Akron *(G-461)*		
Summa Health System	D	330 375-3584
Akron *(G-457)*		
Summa Health System	E	330 375-3000
Akron *(G-460)*		
Summa Health System	C	330 375-3315
Akron *(G-458)*		
Summit Cnty Internists & Assoc	E	330 375-3690
Akron *(G-466)*		
Summit Hand Center Inc	E	330 668-4055
Akron *(G-467)*		
Summit Opthomology Optical	E	330 864-8060
Akron *(G-468)*		
Sunforest Ob Gyn Associates	E	419 473-6622
Toledo *(G-18208)*		
Superior Med Inc	E	740 439-8839
Cambridge *(G-2130)*		
Superior Medical Care Inc	E	440 282-7420
Lorain *(G-13080)*		
Surgery Center Cincinnati LLC	D	513 947-1130
Cincinnati *(G-2934)*		
Surgery Center Howland Ltd	E	330 609-7874
Warren *(G-18906)*		
Surgery Ctr An Ohio Ltd Partnr	D	440 826-3240
Cleveland *(G-6559)*		
Surgical Hosp At Southwoods	E	330 729-8000
Youngstown *(G-20385)*		
Surgicenter Ltd	E	740 522-3937
Newark *(G-15237)*		
System Optics Csmt Srgcal Arts	E	330 630-9699
Tallmadge *(G-17653)*		
System Optics Laser Vision Ctr	E	330 630-2451
Tallmadge *(G-17654)*		
Talmage N Porter MD	E	937 435-9013
Dayton *(G-9920)*		
Taylor Stn Surgical Ctr Ltd	D	614 751-4466
Columbus *(G-8824)*		
Teater Orthopedic Surgeons	E	330 343-3335
Dover *(G-10216)*		
Terence Isakov MD	D	440 449-1014
Cleveland *(G-6583)*		
The Healthcare Connection Inc	E	513 588-3623
Cincinnati *(G-4642)*		
Thomas E Rojewski MD Inc	E	740 454-0158
Zanesville *(G-20538)*		
Thomas L Stover Inc	E	330 665-8060
Mogadore *(G-14686)*		
TLC Eyecare	E	419 882-2020
Toledo *(G-18222)*		
Toledo Cardiology Cons Inc	D	419 251-6183
Toledo *(G-18229)*		
Toledo Cardiology Inc	E	419 479-5690
Toledo *(G-18230)*		
▲ Toledo Clinic Inc	B	419 473-3561
Toledo *(G-18232)*		
Toledo Family Health Center	D	419 241-1554
Toledo *(G-18236)*		
Toledo Hospital	A	419 291-4000
Toledo *(G-18238)*		
Total Renal Care Inc	E	937 294-6711
Kettering *(G-12436)*		
Township of Colerain	C	513 741-7551
Cincinnati *(G-4674)*		
Tri County Family Physicians	E	614 837-6363
Canal Winchester *(G-2173)*		
Tri County Mental Health Svcs	C	740 592-3091
Athens *(G-815)*		
Tri State Urlogic Svcs PSC Inc	D	513 841-7400
Cincinnati *(G-4684)*		
Trihealth Inc	E	513 891-1627
Blue Ash *(G-1702)*		
Trihealth G LLC	D	513 732-0700
Cincinnati *(G-4693)*		
Trihealth G LLC	D	513 624-5535
Cincinnati *(G-4695)*		
Trihealth G LLC	E	513 346-5000
Cincinnati *(G-4694)*		
Trihealth G LLC	D	513 922-1200
Cincinnati *(G-4696)*		
Trihealth Inc	C	513 985-0900
Montgomery *(G-14734)*		
Trihealth Oncology Inst LLC	E	513 451-4033
Cincinnati *(G-4697)*		
Trinity Health System	B	740 283-7000
Steubenville *(G-17342)*		
Trinity Hospital Twin City	B	740 922-2800
Dennison *(G-10166)*		
Trumbull Mem Hosp Foundation	A	330 841-9376
Warren *(G-18915)*		
Trumbull-Mahoning Med Group	D	330 372-8800
Cortland *(G-9084)*		
Uc Health Llc	B	513 584-6999
Mason *(G-13776)*		

Name	Code	Phone
Uc Health Llc	A	513 475-7458
West Chester (G-19167)		
Uc Health Llc	A	513 475-7880
Cincinnati (G-4718)		
Uc Health Llc	A	513 475-8881
West Chester (G-19169)		
Uc Health Llc	C	513 475-7777
West Chester (G-19171)		
Uc Health Llc	A	513 648-9077
Cincinnati (G-4720)		
Uc Health Llc	A	513 475-7500
West Chester (G-19172)		
Uhmg Department of Urologist	E	216 844-3009
Cleveland (G-6629)		
Union Hospital Association	D	330 343-3311
Dover (G-10219)		
United Health Network Ltd	E	330 492-2102
Canton (G-2569)		
United Srgcal Prtners Intl Inc	E	330 702-1489
Canfield (G-2214)		
Unity Health Network LLC	E	330 678-7782
Kent (G-12403)		
Unity Health Network LLC	E	330 626-0549
Streetsboro (G-17435)		
Univ Dermatology	D	513 475-7630
Cincinnati (G-4745)		
University Anesthesiologists	E	216 844-3777
Cleveland (G-6652)		
University Dermatology Cons	E	513 584-4775
Cincinnati (G-4750)		
University Dermatology Cons	E	513 475-7630
Cincinnati (G-4751)		
University Eye Surgeons	C	614 293-5635
Columbus (G-8908)		
University Family Physicians	E	513 929-0104
Cincinnati (G-4752)		
University Family Physicians	D	513 475-7505
Cincinnati (G-4753)		
University GYN&ob Cnsltnts Inc	E	614 293-8697
Columbus (G-8909)		
University Hospitals	E	216 767-8500
Cleveland (G-6658)		
▲ University Hospitals	A	216 767-8900
Shaker Heights (G-16869)		
University Hospitals	A	440 743-3000
Parma (G-15917)		
University Hospitals	D	216 844-8797
Cleveland (G-6657)		
University Hospitals Cleveland	E	440 205-5755
Mentor (G-14252)		
University Hospitals Cleveland	D	216 721-8457
Beachwood (G-1135)		
University Medical Assoc Inc	C	740 593-0753
Athens (G-819)		
University Mednet	C	440 255-0800
Mentor (G-14253)		
University Mednet	E	440 285-9079
Bedford (G-1343)		
University Neurology Inc	D	513 475-8730
Cincinnati (G-4754)		
University of Cincinnati	E	513 558-4194
Cincinnati (G-4755)		
University of Cincinnati	D	513 558-4516
Cincinnati (G-4757)		
University of Cincinnati	D	513 558-7700
Cincinnati (G-4758)		
University of Cincinnati	E	513 475-8771
Cincinnati (G-4759)		
University of Cincinnati	B	513 558-1200
Cincinnati (G-4760)		
University of Cincinnati	E	513 558-5471
Cincinnati (G-4774)		
University of Cincinnati	D	513 475-8524
Cincinnati (G-4775)		
University of Cincinnati	E	513 558-4831
Cincinnati (G-4777)		
University of Cincinnati Phys	E	513 475-8000
West Chester (G-19175)		
University of Cincinnati Phys	C	513 475-7934
Cincinnati (G-4781)		
University of Cncnnati Srgeons	E	513 245-3300
Cincinnati (G-4782)		
University of Toledo	D	419 534-3770
Toledo (G-18277)		
University of Toledo	E	419 383-3556
Toledo (G-18278)		
University of Toledo	E	419 383-5322
Toledo (G-18280)		
University Ophthalmology Assoc	E	216 382-8022
Cleveland (G-6666)		
University Orthopaedic Cnsltnt	E	513 475-8690
Cincinnati (G-4783)		
University Orthpedic Assoc Inc	E	216 844-1000
Cleveland (G-6667)		
University Otolaryngologists	E	614 273-2241
Columbus (G-8910)		
University Prmry Care Prctices	E	440 946-7391
Willoughby (G-19720)		
University Radiology Assoc	D	513 475-8760
Cincinnati (G-4784)		
University Rdlgsts of Clveland	D	216 844-1700
Cleveland (G-6668)		
University Suburban Health Ctr	E	216 382-8920
Cleveland (G-6670)		
University Surgeons Inc	E	216 844-3021
Cleveland (G-6671)		
Universty of Cincinnti Medcl C	A	513 475-8000
Cincinnati (G-4786)		
Universty of Cincinnti Medcl C	A	513 475-8300
West Chester (G-19176)		
Upper Valley Family Care	E	937 339-5355
Piqua (G-16172)		
Urological Associates Inc	E	614 221-5189
Columbus (G-8920)		
US Dept of the Air Force	D	937 257-0837
Dayton (G-9287)		
US Oncology Inc	E	937 352-2140
Xenia (G-20082)		
Ushc Physicians Inc	E	216 382-2036
Cleveland (G-6679)		
Valley Regional Surgery Center	E	877 858-5029
Piqua (G-16174)		
Van Wert County Hospital Assn	C	419 232-2077
Van Wert (G-18650)		
Vanguard Imaging Partners	E	937 236-4780
Dayton (G-9966)		
Veterans Affairs US Dept	A	937 268-6511
Dayton (G-9972)		
Veterans Health Administration	B	740 568-0412
Marietta (G-13514)		
Veterans Health Administration	A	202 461-4800
Chillicothe (G-2895)		
Veterans Health Administration	A	513 861-3100
Cincinnati (G-4812)		
Veterans Health Administration	B	513 943-3680
Cincinnati (G-4813)		
Veterans Health Administration	A	216 791-3800
Cleveland (G-6691)		
Veterans Health Administration	C	614 257-5524
Columbus (G-8937)		
Veterans Health Administration	B	866 463-0912
Ashtabula (G-766)		
Veterans Health Administration	B	740 695-9321
Saint Clairsville (G-16659)		
Veterans Health Administration	D	419 259-2000
Toledo (G-18290)		
Veterans Health Administration	E	330 740-9200
Youngstown (G-20403)		
Veterans Health Administration	B	216 939-0699
Cleveland (G-6692)		
Veterans Health Administration	D	330 489-4600
Canton (G-2577)		
Veterinary RFRrl&emer Ctr of	E	330 665-4996
Copley (G-9068)		
Vision Associates Inc	D	419 578-7598
Toledo (G-18292)		
▲ Volk Optical Inc	D	440 942-6161
Mentor (G-14257)		
Warren Drmatology Allergies PC	E	330 856-6365
Warren (G-18924)		
West Central Ohio Group Ltd	D	419 224-7586
Lima (G-12915)		
West Central Ohio Surgery & En	E	419 226-8700
Lima (G-12917)		
West Park Family Physician	E	419 472-1124
Toledo (G-18305)		
West Side Cardiology Assoc	E	440 333-8600
Cleveland (G-6737)		
West Side Cardiology Assoc	E	440 333-8600
Cleveland (G-6738)		
West Side Pediatrics Inc	E	513 922-8200
Cincinnati (G-4838)		
Western Family Physicians	E	513 853-4900
Cincinnati (G-4840)		
Westerville Dermatology Inc	E	614 895-0400
Westerville (G-19448)		
Westshore Prmry Care Assoc Inc	D	440 934-0276
Sheffield Village (G-16896)		
Westside Family Practice Inc	E	614 878-4541
Columbus (G-8983)		
Wheeling Hospital Inc	D	740 695-2090
Saint Clairsville (G-16661)		
Wheeling Hospital Inc	D	740 633-4765
Martins Ferry (G-13604)		
Whole Health Management Inc	E	216 921-8601
Cleveland (G-6751)		
Wilmington Medical Associates	D	937 382-1616
Wilmington (G-19795)		
Women Health Partners	E	740 363-9021
Delaware (G-10136)		
Women Physicans of Ob/Gyn Inc	E	614 734-3340
Columbus (G-9003)		
Womens Care Inc	D	419 756-6000
Mansfield (G-13383)		
Wooster Clinic Inc	C	330 264-1512
Wooster (G-19931)		
Wooster Ophthalmologists Inc	E	330 345-7800
Wooster (G-19933)		
Wright State Physcans Drmtlogy	E	937 224-7546
Beavercreek (G-1221)		
Yeater Alene K MD	E	740 348-4694
Newark (G-15249)		
Youngstown Orthopaedic Assoc	E	330 726-1466
Canfield (G-2217)		
Zanesville Surgery Center LLC	D	740 453-5713
Zanesville (G-20558)		
Zepf Center	E	419 255-4050
Toledo (G-18331)		

8021 Offices & Clinics Of Dentists

Name	Code	Phone
Advance Implant Dentistry Inc	E	513 271-0821
Cincinnati (G-2974)		
Affiliates In Oral & Maxlofcl	E	513 829-8080
West Chester (G-19015)		
▲ Ashtabula Dental Associates	E	440 992-3146
Ashtabula (G-724)		
Association of Prosthodontics	E	614 885-2022
Worthington (G-19942)		
C Ted Forsberg	E	440 992-3145
Ashtabula (G-730)		
Charles C Smith DDS Inc	E	937 667-2417
Tipp City (G-17712)		
Chester West Dental Group Inc	E	513 942-8181
West Chester (G-19036)		
Chester West Dentistry	E	330 753-7734
Akron (G-131)		
Cincinnati Dental Services	E	513 753-6446
Cincinnati (G-2907)		
Cincinnati Dental Services	E	513 741-7779
Cincinnati (G-3297)		
Cincinnati Dental Services	D	513 721-8888
Cincinnati (G-3298)		
Cincinnati Dental Services	E	513 774-8800
Loveland (G-13114)		
Concorde Therapy Group Inc	C	330 493-4210
Canton (G-2319)		
Dental Facility	E	614 292-1472
Columbus (G-7508)		
Dental Health Group PA	E	330 630-9222
Akron (G-189)		
▲ Dental Health Services	E	330 864-9090
Fairlawn (G-10944)		
Dental One Inc	E	216 584-1000
Independence (G-12203)		
Dental Servics of Ohio Daniel	D	614 863-2222
Reynoldsburg (G-16445)		
Denture Center	E	440 964-0542
Ashtabula (G-742)		
Donald Bowen and Assoc DDS	E	614 274-0454
Columbus (G-7540)		
Dr Michael J Hulit	E	330 863-7173
Malvern (G-13250)		
Equitas Health Inc	C	614 299-2437
Columbus (G-7603)		
Family Dental Team Inc	E	330 733-7911
Fairlawn (G-10951)		
Family Dentistry Inc	E	513 932-6991
Lebanon (G-12605)		
Fixari Family Dental Inc	E	614 866-7445
Columbus (G-7672)		
Health Smile Center	E	440 992-2700
Ashtabula (G-747)		
Hopewell Dental Care	E	740 522-5000
Newark (G-15174)		
Hudec Dental Associates Inc	D	216 485-5788
Brecksville (G-1828)		
Lawrence M Shell DDS	E	614 235-3444
Columbus (G-8045)		
Lima Dental Assoc Risolvato Lt	E	419 228-4036
Lima (G-12820)		

Employee Codes: A=Over 500 employees, B=251-500
C=101-250, D=51-100, E=25-50

80 HEALTH SERVICES

Locust Dental Center ....E........ 330 535-7876
  Akron (G-327)
▲ Lucas & Clark Family Dentistry ....E........ 937 393-3494
  Hillsboro (G-11986)
Mahoning Valley Dental Service ....E........ 330 759-1771
  Youngstown (G-20264)
Martin Ls DDS Ms ....E........ 513 829-8999
  Fairfield (G-10874)
Metro Health Dental Associates ....E........ 216 778-4982
  Cleveland (G-6034)
Metrohealth Dept of Dentistry ....E........ 216 778-4739
  Cleveland (G-6035)
Metrohealth System ....E........ 216 957-1500
  Cleveland (G-6041)
Ohio State University ....D........ 614 292-5578
  Columbus (G-8392)
Ohio State University ....E........ 614 292-5144
  Columbus (G-8420)
Ohio State University ....D........ 614 292-1472
  Columbus (G-8439)
Ohio State University ....D........ 614 292-2751
  Columbus (G-8443)
Oral & Maxillofacial Surgeons ....E........ 419 385-5743
  Toledo (G-18110)
Orthodontic Associates LLC ....E........ 419 229-8771
  Lima (G-12850)
Osu Orthodontic Clinic ....E........ 614 292-1058
  Columbus (G-8488)
Painesville Dental Group Inc ....E........ 440 354-2183
  Painesville (G-15872)
R P Cunningham DDS Inc ....E........ 614 885-2022
  Worthington (G-19990)
Rahn Dental Group Inc ....E........ 937 435-0324
  Dayton (G-9840)
Raymond A Greiner DDS Inc ....E........ 440 951-6688
  Mentor (G-14232)
Smile Brands Inc ....E........ 419 627-1255
  Sandusky (G-16795)
Smile Development Inc ....E........ 419 882-7187
  Sylvania (G-17615)
State Valley Dental Center ....E........ 330 920-8060
  Cuyahoga Falls (G-9220)
Stow Dental Group Inc ....E........ 330 688-6456
  Stow (G-17393)
Thomas and Associates ....E........ 330 494-2111
  Canton (G-2561)
Thomas E Anderson DDS Inc ....E........ 330 467-6446
  Northfield (G-15525)
US Dental Care/M D Gelender ....E........ 614 252-3181
  Columbus (G-8923)
Van Buren Dental Associates ....E........ 937 253-9115
  Kettering (G-12437)

8031 Offices & Clinics Of Doctors Of Osteopathy

Adena Health System ....E........ 740 779-7201
  Chillicothe (G-2808)
Christ Hospital ....C........ 513 561-7809
  Cincinnati (G-3261)
Davis Eye Center ....E........ 330 923-5676
  Cuyahoga Falls (G-9178)
Doctors Hospital Health Center ....E........ 614 544-0101
  Grove City (G-11555)
Eric Hasemeier Do ....E........ 740 594-7979
  Athens (G-787)
Family Practice Center Inc ....E........ 330 682-3075
  Orrville (G-15770)
Grandview Family Practice ....E........ 740 258-9267
  Columbus (G-7766)
Hometown Urgent Care ....C........ 937 372-6012
  Xenia (G-20062)
Internal Mdcine Cons of Clmbus ....E........ 614 878-6413
  Columbus (G-7916)
Medical Surgical Associates ....E........ 740 522-7600
  Newark (G-15206)
Mercy Health ....D........ 419 264-5800
  Holgate (G-12003)
Metro Health System ....D........ 330 669-2249
  Smithville (G-16966)
Michael G Lawley ....E........ 513 793-3933
  Cincinnati (G-4088)
Mount Carmel Health ....E........ 614 855-4878
  New Albany (G-14993)
Physicians In Family Practice ....E........ 440 775-1881
  Oberlin (G-15658)
R I D Inc ....E........ 419 251-4790
  Toledo (G-18145)
Sports Medicine Grant Inc ....D........ 614 461-8174
  Columbus (G-8763)

Ulrich Professional Group ....E........ 330 673-9501
  Kent (G-12402)

8041 Offices & Clinics Of Chiropractors

Active Chiropractic 440 893-8800
  Chagrin Falls (G-2688)
Lbi Starbucks DC 3 ....C........ 614 415-6363
  Columbus (G-8046)

8042 Offices & Clinics Of Optometrists

James D Egbert Optometrist ....E........ 937 236-1770
  Huber Heights (G-12096)
Ohio Eye Specialists Inc ....E........ 800 948-3937
  Chillicothe (G-2866)
Optivue Inc ....C........ 419 891-1391
  Oregon (G-15743)
Ottivue ....D........ 419 693-4444
  Oregon (G-15747)
Primary Eyecare Associates ....E........ 937 492-2351
  Sidney (G-16948)
Rinkov Eyecare Center ....E........ 614 224-2414
  Columbus (G-8631)
Shawnee Optical Inc ....D........ 440 997-2020
  Ashtabula (G-763)
Sight Resource Corporation ....D........ 513 942-4423
  West Chester (G-19153)
Systems Temoptics Coop Opt Un ....E........ 330 633-4321
  Tallmadge (G-17655)
Thomas R Truitt Od ....E........ 937 644-8637
  Marysville (G-13655)

8043 Offices & Clinics Of Podiatrists

Ankle and Foot Care Center ....E........ 330 385-2413
  East Liverpool (G-10515)
Center For Foot & Ankle Care ....E........ 513 533-1199
  Cincinnati (G-3208)
Toledo Clinic Inc ....C........ 419 381-9977
  Toledo (G-18233)
Unity Health Network LLC ....E........ 330 626-0549
  Streetsboro (G-17435)

8049 Offices & Clinics Of Health Practitioners, NEC

A+ Solutions LLC ....E........ 216 896-0111
  Beachwood (G-1044)
Abilities First Foundation ....C........ 513 423-9496
  Middletown (G-14411)
Accurate Nurse Staffing ....E........ 419 475-2424
  Toledo (G-17740)
Amedisys Inc ....E........ 740 373-8549
  Marietta (G-13430)
American Nursing Care Inc ....D........ 740 452-0569
  Zanesville (G-20442)
Appleseed Cmnty Mntal Hlth Ctr ....E........ 419 281-3716
  Ashland (G-651)
Around Clock Home Care ....D........ 440 350-2547
  Painesville (G-15835)
Atrium Medical Center ....E........ 513 420-5013
  Middletown (G-14414)
Aultman Health Foundation ....B........ 330 875-6050
  Louisville (G-13094)
Bellefontaine Physical Therapy ....E........ 937 592-1625
  Bellefontaine (G-1377)
Blue Ash Fire Department ....E........ 513 745-8534
  Blue Ash (G-1544)
Carington Health Systems ....C........ 513 961-8881
  Cincinnati (G-3185)
Center For Cognitive and Beh ....E........ 614 459-4490
  Columbus (G-7223)
Central Ohio Nutrition Center ....E........ 614 864-7225
  Columbus (G-7232)
Central Ohio Primary Care ....D........ 614 818-9550
  Westerville (G-19379)
Central Ohio Primary Care ....E........ 614 268-6555
  Columbus (G-7236)
Central Ohio Primary Care ....E........ 614 442-7550
  Columbus (G-7239)
Central Ohio Sleep Medicine ....E........ 614 475-6700
  Westerville (G-19292)
Cgh-Glbal Operations Logistics ....E........ 800 376-0655
  Cincinnati (G-3223)
Chcc Home Health Care ....E........ 330 759-4069
  Austintown (G-869)
Childrens Aid Society ....E........ 216 521-6911
  Cleveland (G-5237)
Christ Hospital ....B........ 513 688-1111
  Cincinnati (G-3262)
Cincinnati Occupational Therap ....E........ 513 791-5688
  Blue Ash (G-1557)

Coleman Professional Svcs Inc ....D........ 330 296-8313
  Ravenna (G-16377)
Colerain Volunteer Fire Co ....E........ 740 738-0735
  Dillonvale (G-10174)
Comprehensive Services Inc ....E........ 614 442-0664
  Columbus (G-7415)
Concorde Therapy Group Inc ....E........ 330 493-4210
  Canton (G-2319)
Concorde Therapy Group Inc ....E........ 330 478-1752
  Canton (G-2320)
Concorde Therapy Group Inc ....E........ 330 493-4210
  Louisville (G-13097)
Concorde Therapy Group Inc ....E........ 330 493-4210
  Alliance (G-535)
Consolidated Care Inc ....E........ 937 465-8065
  West Liberty (G-19262)
County of Cuyahoga ....D........ 216 721-5610
  Cleveland (G-5420)
County of Hamilton ....E........ 513 221-4524
  Cincinnati (G-3432)
Crisis Intervention & Rcvy Ctr ....D........ 330 455-9407
  Canton (G-2327)
Dietary Solutions Inc ....E........ 614 985-6567
  Lewis Center (G-12682)
Emerge Counseling Service ....E........ 330 865-8351
  Akron (G-207)
Equitas Health Inc ....C........ 614 299-2437
  Columbus (G-7603)
First Settlement Orthopaedics ....E........ 740 373-8756
  Marietta (G-13446)
George W Arensberg Phrm Inc ....E........ 740 344-2195
  Newark (G-15169)
Health Services Inc ....E........ 330 837-7678
  Massillon (G-13818)
Healthsource Inc ....C........ 330 278-2781
  Hinckley (G-11998)
Herman Bair Enterprise ....E........ 330 262-4449
  Wooster (G-19867)
Hilty Memorial Home Inc ....E........ 419 384-3218
  Pandora (G-15892)
Holzer Clinic LLC ....E........ 740 886-9403
  Proctorville (G-16359)
Hometown Urgent Care ....C........ 330 629-2300
  Youngstown (G-20219)
Hometown Urgent Care ....D........ 740 363-3133
  Delaware (G-10107)
Hometown Urgent Care ....C........ 937 252-2000
  Wooster (G-19868)
Hometown Urgent Care ....C........ 513 831-5900
  Milford (G-14525)
Hometown Urgent Care ....C........ 937 342-9520
  Springfield (G-17206)
Inter Healt Care of Cambr Zane ....E........ 513 984-1110
  Cincinnati (G-3830)
Jewish Home of Cincinnati ....B........ 513 754-3100
  Mason (G-13726)
Just In Time Care Inc ....E........ 614 985-3555
  Columbus (G-7961)
Kindred Healthcare Inc ....C........ 440 232-1800
  Bedford Heights (G-1355)
Kindred Healthcare Oper Inc ....C........ 740 387-7537
  Marion (G-13545)
Layh & Associates ....E........ 937 767-9171
  Yellow Springs (G-20090)
Licking Rhabilitation Svcs Inc ....E........ 740 345-2837
  Newark (G-15194)
Lifeteam Ems Inc ....E........ 330 386-9284
  East Liverpool (G-10523)
Maxim Healthcare Services Inc ....D........ 740 772-4100
  Chillicothe (G-2863)
Medcentral Health System ....C........ 419 342-5015
  Shelby (G-16901)
Medcentral Health System ....C........ 419 683-1040
  Crestline (G-9147)
Medlink of Ohio Inc ....B........ 216 751-5900
  Cleveland (G-6016)
Medlink of Ohio Inc ....B........ 330 773-9434
  Akron (G-337)
Medwork LLC ....D........ 937 449-0800
  Dayton (G-9716)
Mercy Health ....E........ 937 390-5515
  Springfield (G-17238)
Mercy Health ....D........ 937 328-8700
  Springfield (G-17239)
Mercy Health ....E........ 937 390-5075
  Springfield (G-17240)
Mercy Health ....C........ 440 774-6800
  Oberlin (G-15652)
Midwest Behavioral Care Ltd ....E........ 937 454-0092
  Dayton (G-9744)

80 HEALTH SERVICES

Company	Code	Phone
Msstaff LLC	C	419 868-8536
Toledo (G-18072)		
Netcare Corporation	D	614 274-9500
Columbus (G-8258)		
Netcare Corporation	E	614 274-9500
Columbus (G-8259)		
Newcomerstown Progress Corp	C	740 498-5165
Newcomerstown (G-15271)		
Nexstep Healthcare LLC	C	216 797-4040
Cleveland (G-6128)		
Occupational Health Services	E	937 492-7296
Sidney (G-16944)		
Ohio Hi Point Career Center	E	937 599-3010
Urbana (G-18598)		
Ohio Presbt Retirement Svcs	C	614 228-8888
Columbus (G-8368)		
Ohio State University	D	614 292-6741
Columbus (G-8419)		
Ohio State University	A	614 366-3692
Columbus (G-8388)		
Ohio State University	A	614 257-3000
Columbus (G-8393)		
Ohiohealth Corporation	A	614 788-8860
Columbus (G-8457)		
Orthoneuro	D	614 890-6555
Columbus (G-8482)		
Pastoral Counseling Svc Summit	C	330 996-4600
Akron (G-378)		
Primary Cr Ntwrk Prmr Hlth Prt	E	937 208-7000
Beavercreek (G-1199)		
Prohealth Partners Inc	E	419 491-7150
Perrysburg (G-16045)		
PSI Associates Inc	B	330 425-8474
Twinsburg (G-18457)		
Psycare Inc	C	330 759-2310
Youngstown (G-20332)		
Psychiatric Solutions Inc	C	440 953-3000
Willoughby (G-19706)		
Quality Care Nursing Svc Inc	B	740 377-9095
South Point (G-17096)		
R & F Inc	E	419 868-2909
Holland (G-12047)		
Rehab Center	E	330 297-2770
Ravenna (G-16405)		
Rehab Continuum Inc	E	513 984-8070
Blue Ash (G-1679)		
Rehabilitation Aquatics	E	419 843-2500
Toledo (G-18148)		
Reverse Center Clinic	E	419 885-8800
Sylvania (G-17610)		
Samaritan Regional Health Sys	E	419 281-1330
Ashland (G-697)		
Sandy Creek Joint Fire Dst	E	330 868-5193
Minerva (G-14650)		
Selby General Hospital	C	740 568-2037
Marietta (G-13497)		
Sisters of Mercy Amer Reg Comm	D	419 696-7203
Oregon (G-15750)		
Society For Rehabilitation	E	440 209-0135
Mentor (G-14243)		
Sports Therapy Inc	E	513 671-5841
Cincinnati (G-4561)		
Sports Therapy Inc	E	513 531-1698
Cincinnati (G-4562)		
Stephen R Saddemi MD	E	419 578-7200
Toledo (G-18201)		
Steward Trumbull Mem Hosp Inc	A	330 841-9011
Warren (G-18904)		
Summa Health	B	330 926-0384
Cuyahoga Falls (G-9221)		
Summa Rehab Hospital LLC	E	330 572-7300
Akron (G-463)		
Therapy In Motion LLC	C	216 459-2846
Independence (G-12266)		
Tky Associates LLC	D	419 535-7777
Toledo (G-18221)		
Toledo District Nurses Assn	C	419 255-0983
Sylvania (G-17622)		
Total Rhabilitation Specialist	E	440 236-8527
Columbia Station (G-6852)		
Trihealth G LLC	D	513 922-1200
Cincinnati (G-4696)		
United Rehabilitation Services	D	937 233-1420
Dayton (G-9947)		
Walnut Hills Physical Therapy	E	614 234-8000
Columbus (G-8964)		
Weinstein Donald Jay PHD	E	216 831-1040
Painesville (G-15886)		
Weston Group Inc	E	740 454-2741
Zanesville (G-20545)		
Wsb Rehabilitation Svcs Inc	D	330 533-1338
Canfield (G-2216)		
Youngstown Ohio Otpatient Svcs	E	330 884-2020
Youngstown (G-20433)		

8051 Skilled Nursing Facilities

Company	Code	Phone
10 Wilmington Place	D	937 253-1010
Dayton (G-9291)		
204 W Main Street Oper Co LLC	D	419 929-1563
New London (G-15065)		
3g Operating Company LLC	B	440 944-9400
Parma (G-15897)		
5440 Charlesgate Rd Oper LLC	D	937 236-6707
Dayton (G-9293)		
A L K Inc	D	740 369-8741
Delaware (G-10064)		
A Provide Care Inc	C	330 828-2278
Dalton (G-9239)		
Adams County Manor	D	937 544-2205
West Union (G-19272)		
Adena NH LLC	E	740 546-3620
Adena (G-7)		
Advance Care Inc	C	513 932-1121
Lebanon (G-12588)		
Ahf Ohio Inc	D	330 725-4123
Medina (G-14033)		
Ahf Ohio Inc	D	740 532-6188
Ironton (G-12280)		
Ahf Ohio Inc	D	614 760-8870
Dublin (G-10237)		
Ahf Ohio Inc	D	937 256-4663
Dayton (G-9313)		
Ahf/Central States Inc	E	615 383-3570
Dublin (G-10238)		
Alexson Services Inc	B	513 874-0423
Fairfield (G-10819)		
▲ Allen Medical Center	C	440 986-4000
Oberlin (G-15638)		
Alpha Nursing Homes Inc	D	740 345-9197
Newark (G-15142)		
Altenheim Foundation Inc	E	440 238-3361
Strongsville (G-17442)		
Altercare Inc	C	330 335-2555
Wadsworth (G-18746)		
Altercare Inc	E	440 327-5285
North Ridgeville (G-15454)		
Altercare Nobles Pond Inc	D	330 834-4800
Canton (G-2235)		
Altercare of Bucyrus Inc	C	419 562-7644
Bucyrus (G-2023)		
Altercare of Louisville Center	D	330 875-4224
Louisville (G-13093)		
Altercare of Mentor Center	C	440 953-4421
Mentor (G-14142)		
Altercare of Millersburg	D	330 674-4444
Millersburg (G-14584)		
Amberwood Manor	D	330 339-2151
New Philadelphia (G-15081)		
Amedisys Inc	E	740 373-8549
Marietta (G-13430)		
American Eagle Hlth Care Svcs	C	440 428-5103
Madison (G-13220)		
American Nursing Care Inc	E	513 731-4600
Cincinnati (G-3009)		
American Nursing Care Inc	D	513 245-1500
Cincinnati (G-3010)		
American Nursing Care Inc	D	513 576-0262
Milford (G-14503)		
American Nursing Care Inc	D	937 438-3844
Dayton (G-9330)		
American Nursing Care Inc	C	614 847-0555
Zanesville (G-20441)		
American Nursing Caro Inc	D	419 228-0888
Lima (G-12741)		
Anchor Lodge Nursing Home Inc	C	440 244-2019
Lorain (G-13012)		
Anderson Healthcare Ltd	D	513 474-6200
Cincinnati (G-3022)		
Andover Vlg Retirement Cmnty	C	440 293-5416
Andover (G-610)		
Anna Maria of Aurora Inc	C	330 562-6171
Aurora (G-824)		
Anna Maria of Aurora Inc	D	330 562-3120
Aurora (G-825)		
Apostolic Christian Home Inc	D	330 927-1010
Rittman (G-16550)		
Appalachian Respite Care Ltd	D	740 984-4262
Beverly (G-1487)		
April Enterprises Inc	B	937 293-7703
Moraine (G-14751)		
Arbors East LLC	D	614 575-9003
Columbus (G-7033)		
Arbors West LLC	D	614 879-7661
West Jefferson (G-19247)		
Aristocrat W Nursing Hm Corp	C	216 252-7730
Cleveland (G-5066)		
Arlington Care Ctr	C	740 344-0303
Newark (G-15143)		
Arlington Court Nursing	C	614 545-5502
Upper Arlington (G-18547)		
Ashley Enterprises LLC	D	330 726-5790
Boardman (G-1737)		
Ashley Place Health Care Inc	C	330 793-3010
Youngstown (G-20105)		
Assisted Living Concepts Inc	E	419 586-2484
Celina (G-2635)		
Assumption Village	C	330 549-2434
North Lima (G-15398)		
Astoria Place Columbus LLC	D	614 228-5900
Columbus (G-7057)		
Astoria Place of Clyde LLC	D	419 547-9595
Clyde (G-6809)		
Audrich Inc	C	419 483-6225
Bellevue (G-1403)		
Aurora Manor Special Care	E	440 424-4000
Aurora (G-827)		
Austin Woods Nursing Center	C	330 792-7681
Youngstown (G-20107)		
Autumn Aegis Inc	D	440 282-6768
Lorain (G-13015)		
Autumn Hills Care Center Inc	C	330 652-2053
Niles (G-15283)		
Balanced Care Corporation	E	330 908-1166
Northfield (G-15509)		
Balanced Care Corporation	E	937 372-7205
Xenia (G-20044)		
Baptist Home and Center	C	513 662-5880
Cincinnati (G-3076)		
Barnesville Healthcare Rehab	D	740 425-3648
Barnesville (G-987)		
Bath Manor Limited Partnership	E	330 836-1006
Akron (G-90)		
Beacon of Light Ltd	E	419 531-9060
Toledo (G-17765)		
Beechwood Home	E	513 321-9294
Cincinnati (G-3093)		
Beechwood Terrace Care Ctr Inc	E	513 578-6200
Cincinnati (G-3094)		
Bel Air Care Center	D	330 821-3939
Alliance (G-527)		
Bellbrook Rhbltttion Healthcare	D	937 848-8421
Bellbrook (G-1370)		
Belmont County Home	D	740 695-4925
Saint Clairsville (G-16620)		
Belmore Leasing Co LLC	C	216 268-3600
Cleveland (G-5113)		
Bentley Leasing Co LLC	A	330 337-9503
Salem (G-16688)		
Best Care Nrsing Rhbltttion Ctr	C	740 574-2558
Wheelersburg (G-19570)		
Bethany Nursing Home Inc	E	330 492-7171
Canton (G-2262)		
Bethesda Foundation Inc	E	513 569-6575
Cincinnati (G-3104)		
Biorx LLC	D	866 442-4679
Cincinnati (G-3109)		
Birchaven Village	D	419 424-3000
Findlay (G-10996)		
Blanchard Vly Residential Ctr	D	419 422-6503
Findlay (G-11002)		
Blossom Hills Nursing Home	D	440 635-5567
Huntsburg (G-12157)		
Blossom Nursing & Rehab Center	C	330 337-3033
Salem (G-16690)		
Blue Ash Healthcare Group Inc	E	513 793-3362
Cincinnati (G-3118)		
Bmnh Inc	C	937 845-3561
New Carlisle (G-15020)		
Bradley Road Nursing Home	C	440 871-3474
Bay Village (G-1039)		
Braeview Manor Inc	C	216 486-9300
Cleveland (G-5132)		
Brecksville Leasing Co LLC	C	330 659-6166
Richfield (G-16498)		
Brenn Field Nursing Center	C	330 683-4075
Orrville (G-15767)		
Brentwood Life Care Company	C	330 468-2273
Northfield (G-15511)		
Brethren Care Inc	C	419 289-0803
Ashland (G-666)		

Employee Codes: A=Over 500 employees, B=251-500
C=101-250, D=51-100, E=25-50

Brewster Parke Inc..........D....... 330 767-4179
Brewster *(G-1854)*
Briar Hl Hlth Care Rsdence Inc..........D....... 440 632-5241
Middlefield *(G-14394)*
Briarfield At Ashley Circle..........C....... 330 793-3010
Youngstown *(G-20125)*
Briarwood Ltd..........D....... 330 688-1828
Stow *(G-17354)*
Bridges To Independence Inc..........E....... 740 375-5533
Marion *(G-13526)*
Broadview NH LLC..........D....... 614 337-1066
Columbus *(G-7149)*
Broadview Nursing Home Inc..........C....... 216 661-5084
Parma *(G-15900)*
Brook Willow Chrstn Cmmunities..........D....... 614 885-3300
Columbus *(G-7151)*
Brookdale Senior Living Inc..........C....... 937 294-1772
Oakwood *(G-15620)*
Brookdale Snior Lving Cmmnties..........E....... 330 249-1071
Austintown *(G-868)*
Brookview Healthcare Ctr..........D....... 419 784-1014
Defiance *(G-10020)*
Brookville Enterprises Inc..........B....... 937 833-2133
Brookville *(G-1960)*
Bryant Eliza Village..........B....... 216 361-6141
Cleveland *(G-5153)*
Bryant Health Center Inc..........C....... 740 532-6188
Ironton *(G-12283)*
Bryden Place Inc..........C....... 614 258-6623
Beachwood *(G-1057)*
Burlington House Inc..........D....... 513 851-7888
Cincinnati *(G-3153)*
Butler County of Ohio..........C....... 513 887-3728
Fairfield Township *(G-10926)*
Camargo Manor Inc..........D....... 513 605-3000
Cincinnati *(G-3169)*
Cambridge Home Healthcare..........E....... 740 432-6191
Cambridge *(G-2099)*
Cambridge NH LLC..........D....... 740 432-7717
Cambridge *(G-2100)*
Camillus Villa Inc..........D....... 440 236-5091
Columbia Station *(G-6841)*
Canterbury Villa of Alliance..........D....... 330 821-1391
Alliance *(G-529)*
Canton Assisted Living..........C....... 330 492-7131
Canton *(G-2282)*
Capital Health Services Inc..........E....... 937 278-0404
Dayton *(G-9378)*
Caprice Health Care Inc..........C....... 330 965-9200
North Lima *(G-15400)*
Care One LLC..........C....... 937 236-6707
Dayton *(G-9380)*
Careserve..........C....... 740 454-4000
Zanesville *(G-20457)*
Careserve Inc..........C....... 740 962-3761
McConnelsville *(G-14026)*
Carington Health Systems..........B....... 513 732-6500
Batavia *(G-997)*
Carington Health Systems..........C....... 513 961-8881
Cincinnati *(G-3185)*
Carington Health Systems..........C....... 937 743-2754
Franklin *(G-11151)*
Carington Health Systems..........E....... 513 682-2700
Hamilton *(G-11706)*
Caritas Inc..........E....... 419 332-2589
Fremont *(G-11186)*
Carlisle Health Care Inc..........E....... 937 746-2662
Carlisle *(G-2602)*
Carriage Court Company Inc..........E....... 740 654-4422
Lancaster *(G-12514)*
Carriage House Assisted Living..........E....... 740 264-7667
Steubenville *(G-17307)*
Carriage Inn of Cadiz Inc..........E....... 740 942-8084
Cadiz *(G-2073)*
Carriage Inn of Steubenville..........C....... 740 264-7161
Steubenville *(G-17308)*
Carriage Inn of Trotwood Inc..........C....... 937 854-1180
Trotwood *(G-18345)*
Carriage Inn of Trotwood Inc..........D....... 937 277-0505
Dayton *(G-9384)*
Carriage Inn Retirement Cmnty..........C....... 937 278-0404
Dayton *(G-9385)*
Carroll Health Care Center..........C....... 330 627-5501
Carrollton *(G-2613)*
Castle Nursing Homes Inc..........C....... 330 674-0015
Millersburg *(G-14592)*
Casto Health Care..........D....... 419 884-6400
Mansfield *(G-13272)*
Catherines Care Center Inc..........D....... 740 282-3605
Steubenville *(G-17309)*

Center Ridge Nursing Home Inc..........C....... 440 327-1295
North Ridgeville *(G-15458)*
Centerburg Two LLC..........D....... 740 625-5774
Centerburg *(G-2666)*
Childs Investment Co..........E....... 330 837-2100
Massillon *(G-13794)*
Chillicothe Long Term Care..........C....... 740 773-6161
Chillicothe *(G-2821)*
Chillicothe Long Term Care..........D....... 513 793-8804
Cincinnati *(G-3256)*
Chillicothe Opco LLC..........D....... 740 772-5900
Chillicothe *(G-2823)*
Christian Worthington Vlg Inc..........E....... 614 846-6076
Columbus *(G-7269)*
CHS Miami Valley Inc..........E....... 330 204-1040
Sidney *(G-16920)*
CHS Norwood Inc..........D....... 513 242-1360
Cincinnati *(G-3273)*
CHS of Bowerston Oper Co Inc..........D....... 937 277-0505
Dayton *(G-9407)*
CHS-Lake Erie Inc..........C....... 440 964-8446
Ashtabula *(G-733)*
Chs-Norwood Inc..........C....... 513 351-7007
Cincinnati *(G-3274)*
Church of God Retirement Cmnty..........C....... 513 422-5600
Middletown *(G-14420)*
Cincinnati Senior Care LLC..........E....... 513 272-0600
Cincinnati *(G-3326)*
City View Nursing & Rehab LLC..........C....... 216 361-1414
Cleveland *(G-5279)*
Clermont Care Inc..........C....... 513 831-1770
Milford *(G-14513)*
Clifton Care Center Inc..........C....... 513 530-1600
Cincinnati *(G-3365)*
Clime Leasing Co LLC..........D....... 614 276-4400
Columbus *(G-7300)*
Clovernook Inc..........C....... 513 605-4000
Cincinnati *(G-3369)*
Coal Grove Long Term Care Inc..........D....... 740 532-0449
Ironton *(G-12287)*
Colonial Manor Health Care Ctr..........C....... 419 994-4191
Loudonville *(G-13089)*
Columbus Alzheimers Care Ctr..........C....... 614 459-7050
Columbus *(G-7327)*
Columbus Area..........D....... 614 251-6561
Columbus *(G-7328)*
Columbus Clny For Elderly Care..........C....... 614 891-5055
Westerville *(G-19385)*
Columbus W Hlth Care Co Partnr..........C....... 614 274-4222
Columbus *(G-7393)*
Communi Care Inc..........E....... 419 382-2200
Toledo *(G-17822)*
Communicare Health Svcs Inc..........D....... 440 234-0454
Berea *(G-1453)*
Communicare Health Svcs Inc..........D....... 330 726-3700
Youngstown *(G-20148)*
Communicare Health Svcs Inc..........C....... 937 399-9217
Springfield *(G-17170)*
Communicare Health Svcs Inc..........C....... 877 366-5306
Wintersville *(G-19809)*
Communicare Health Svcs Inc..........D....... 330 792-7799
Youngstown *(G-20149)*
Communicare Health Svcs Inc..........D....... 330 792-5511
Youngstown *(G-20150)*
Communicare Health Svcs Inc..........C....... 330 454-2152
Canton *(G-2318)*
Communicare Health Svcs Inc..........D....... 330 630-9780
Tallmadge *(G-17635)*
Communicare Health Svcs Inc..........D....... 419 394-7611
Saint Marys *(G-16672)*
Community Hlth Prfssionals Inc..........E....... 419 634-7443
Ada *(G-4)*
Community Hospital Springfield..........A....... 937 325-0531
Springfield *(G-17171)*
Community Mercy Foundation..........C....... 937 278-8211
Dayton *(G-9418)*
Community Mercy Hlth Partners..........C....... 937 653-5432
Urbana *(G-18583)*
Community Skilled Health Care..........C....... 330 373-1160
Warren *(G-18837)*
Concord Health Care Inc..........E....... 330 759-2357
Youngstown *(G-20160)*
Concord Hlth Rhabilitation Ctr..........E....... 740 574-8441
Wheelersburg *(G-19575)*
Congregate Living of America..........D....... 513 899-2801
Morrow *(G-14845)*
Congregate Living of America..........E....... 937 393-6700
Hillsboro *(G-11969)*
Consulate Healthcare Inc..........E....... 419 865-1248
Maumee *(G-13899)*

Consulate Management Co LLC..........D....... 330 837-1001
Massillon *(G-13798)*
Consulate Management Co LLC..........D....... 419 886-3922
Bellville *(G-1423)*
Consulate Management Co LLC..........D....... 440 237-7966
Cleveland *(G-5398)*
Consulate Management Co LLC..........C....... 419 683-3255
Crestline *(G-9143)*
Consulate Management Co LLC..........D....... 419 867-7926
Maumee *(G-13900)*
Consulate Management Co LLC..........D....... 740 259-2351
Lucasville *(G-13176)*
Continent Hlth Co Cortland LLC..........E....... 330 637-7906
Cortland *(G-9075)*
Copley Health Center Inc..........C....... 330 666-0980
Copley *(G-9055)*
Coshocton Opco LLC..........D....... 740 622-1220
Coshocton *(G-9096)*
Cottingham Retirement Cmnty..........C....... 513 563-3600
Cincinnati *(G-3426)*
Country Club Center Homes Inc..........D....... 330 343-6351
Dover *(G-10182)*
Country Club Center II Ltd..........C....... 740 397-2350
Mount Vernon *(G-14886)*
Country Club Retirement Center..........C....... 740 671-9330
Bellaire *(G-1365)*
Country Court Ltd..........C....... 740 397-4125
Mount Vernon *(G-14887)*
Country Mdow Fclty Oprtons LLC..........D....... 419 886-3922
Bellville *(G-1424)*
Country Pointe Skilled Nursing..........E....... 330 264-7881
Wooster *(G-19853)*
Countryview of Sunbury..........D....... 740 965-3984
Sunbury *(G-17553)*
County of Allen..........C....... 419 221-1103
Lima *(G-12763)*
County of Erie..........C....... 419 627-8733
Huron *(G-12164)*
County of Logan..........C....... 937 592-2901
Bellefontaine *(G-1382)*
County of Lucas..........D....... 419 385-6021
Toledo *(G-17838)*
County of Marion..........D....... 740 389-4624
Marion *(G-13533)*
County of Monroe..........D....... 740 472-0144
Woodsfield *(G-19815)*
County of Montgomery..........B....... 937 264-0460
Dayton *(G-9434)*
County of Ottawa..........C....... 419 898-6459
Oak Harbor *(G-15607)*
County of Perry..........E....... 740 342-0416
New Lexington *(G-15053)*
County of Sandusky..........D....... 419 334-2602
Fremont *(G-11191)*
County of Sandusky..........C....... 419 334-2602
Fremont *(G-11192)*
County of Shelby..........C....... 937 492-6900
Sidney *(G-16926)*
County of Van Wert..........E....... 419 968-2141
Middle Point *(G-14376)*
County of Williams..........C....... 419 636-4508
Bryan *(G-2005)*
Covenant Care Ohio Inc..........D....... 419 898-5506
Port Clinton *(G-16242)*
Covenant Care Ohio Inc..........D....... 419 531-4201
Toledo *(G-17840)*
Covenant Care Ohio Inc..........D....... 937 378-0188
Georgetown *(G-11392)*
Covenant Care Ohio Inc..........D....... 937 399-5551
Springfield *(G-17183)*
Covenant Care Ohio Inc..........D....... 937 526-5570
Versailles *(G-18726)*
Covenant Care Ohio Inc..........D....... 937 878-7046
Fairborn *(G-10788)*
Covington Snf Inc..........E....... 330 426-2920
East Palestine *(G-10537)*
Creative Foundations Inc..........E....... 614 832-2121
Mount Vernon *(G-14890)*
Crestline Nursing Home Inc..........E....... 419 683-3255
Crestline *(G-9144)*
Crestmont Nursing Home N Corp..........C....... 216 228-9550
Lakewood *(G-12475)*
Crestmont Nursing Home N Corp..........D....... 216 228-9550
Lakewood *(G-12476)*
Crestview Health Care Center..........D....... 740 695-2500
Saint Clairsville *(G-16634)*
Crestview Manor Nursing Home..........C....... 740 654-2634
Lancaster *(G-12524)*
Crestview Manor Nursing Home..........C....... 740 654-2634
Lancaster *(G-12525)*

80 HEALTH SERVICES

Company	Code	Phone
Crestview Ridge Nursing, Hillsboro (G-11971)	E	937 393-6700
Cridersville Health Care Ctr, Cridersville (G-9151)	E	419 645-4468
Crotinger Nursing Home Inc, Union City (G-18502)	D	937 968-5284
Crystal Care Centers Inc, Ashland (G-677)	E	419 281-9595
Crystal Care Centers Inc, Mansfield (G-13286)	E	419 747-2666
Crystal Care Centers Inc, Mansfield (G-13287)	D	419 747-2666
Crystal Care Ctr of Portsmouth, Portsmouth (G-16274)	E	740 354-6619
D James Incorporated, Cincinnati (G-3456)	C	513 574-4550
Danridge Nursing Home Inc, Youngstown (G-20166)	D	330 746-5157
Day Spring Health Care Corp, Beverly (G-1489)	D	740 984-4262
Dayspring Health Care Center, Fairborn (G-10792)	C	937 864-5800
Dayton Dmh Inc, Dayton (G-9470)	C	937 436-2273
Dayton Nwborn Care Spclsts Inc, Dayton (G-9483)	A	937 641-3329
Deaconess Long Term Care of MI, Cincinnati (G-3474)	A	513 487-3600
Dearth Management Company, Marengo (G-13423)	C	419 253-0144
Dearth Management Company, Marion (G-13537)	E	740 389-1214
Dearth Management Company, New Philadelphia (G-15092)	C	330 339-3595
Dedicated Nursing Assoc Inc, Beavercreek (G-1237)	C	888 465-6929
Dedicated Nursing Assoc Inc, Cincinnati (G-3477)	E	866 450-5550
Dedicated Nursing Assoc Inc, Galloway (G-11343)	E	877 411-8350
Dedicated Nursing Assoc Inc, Parma (G-15905)	E	877 547-9144
Delaware Opco LLC, Delaware (G-10090)	D	502 429-8062
Diverscare Healthcare Svcs Inc, Dayton (G-9502)	E	937 278-8211
Diverscare Healthcare Svcs Inc, Cincinnati (G-3494)	E	513 271-7010
Diversicare Leasing Corp, Wheelersburg (G-19576)	D	615 771-7575
Diversicare of Avon LLC, Cleveland (G-5491)	C	440 937-6201
Diversicare of Mansfield LLC, Ontario (G-15686)	D	419 529-6447
DMD Management Inc, Twinsburg (G-18406)	E	330 405-6040
DMD Management Inc, Cleveland (G-5497)	A	216 371-3600
Doctors Hospital Cleveland Inc, Nelsonville (G-14961)	C	740 753-7300
Dover Nursing Center, Dover (G-10186)	D	330 364-4436
Doylestown Health Care Center, Doylestown (G-10227)	C	330 658-1533
Drake Center LLC, Cincinnati (G-3501)	A	513 418-2500
Dublin Geriatric Care Co LP, Dublin (G-10328)	E	614 761-1188
Eagle Creek Nursing Center, West Union (G-19278)	E	937 544-5531
Eaglewood Care Center, Springfield (G-17191)	C	937 399-7195
East Carroll Nursing Home, Carrollton (G-2618)	D	330 627-6900
East Galbraith Nursing Home, Cincinnati (G-3532)	C	513 984-5220
East Water Leasing Co LLC, Deshler (G-10169)	D	419 278-6921
Eastern Star Hm of Cyhoga Cnty, Cleveland (G-5521)	D	216 761-0170
Eastgate Health Care Center, Cincinnati (G-2913)	C	513 752-3710
Eastside Multi Care Inc, Maple Heights (G-13407)	C	216 662-3343
Eaton Gardens Rehabilitation A, Eaton (G-10559)	D	937 456-5537
Ebenezer Road Corp, Cincinnati (G-3540)	C	513 941-0099
Echoing Hills Village Inc, Warsaw (G-18936)	A	740 327-2311
Echoing Hills Village Inc, Dayton (G-9518)	D	937 854-5151
Echoing Hills Village Inc, Lorain (G-10756)	D	440 989-1400
Edgewood Manor of Lucasville, Lucasville (G-13178)	C	740 259-5536
Elms Retirement Village Inc, Wellington (G-18991)	D	440 647-2414
Embassy Autumnwood MGT LLC, Rittman (G-16552)	D	330 927-2060
Embassy Healthcare Inc, Fairfield (G-10847)	D	513 868-6500
Emery Leasing Co LLC, Cleveland (G-5536)	B	216 475-8880
Encore Healthcare LLC, Seville (G-16840)	C	330 769-2015
Episcopal Retirement Homes Inc, Cincinnati (G-3567)	E	513 271-9610
Es3 Management Inc, Conneaut (G-9042)	D	440 593-6266
Euclid Health Care Inc, Cincinnati (G-3578)	C	513 561-4105
Evangelical Lutheran, Arlington (G-647)	D	419 365-5115
Ezra Health Care Inc, Beachwood (G-1078)	C	440 498-3000
Fairchild MD Leasing Co LLC, Kent (G-12369)	C	330 678-4912
Fairhope Hospice and Palliativ, Lancaster (G-12540)	D	740 654-7077
Fairlawn Opco LLC, Fairlawn (G-10950)	D	502 429-8062
Fairmont Nursing Home Inc, Newbury (G-15256)	D	440 338-8220
Fairport Enterprises Inc, Massillon (G-13806)	C	330 830-9988
Falling Leasing Co LLC, Strongsville (G-17463)	C	440 238-1100
Falls Village Retirement Cmnty, Cuyahoga Falls (G-9187)	D	330 945-9797
Feridean Commons LLC, Westerville (G-19307)	E	614 898-7488
First Community Village, Columbus (G-7664)	B	614 324-4455
First Louisville Arden LLC, Toledo (G-17893)	E	419 252-5500
First Richmond Corp, Blanchester (G-1514)	D	937 783-4949
Five Star Senior Living Inc, Columbus (G-7671)	D	614 451-6793
Flower Hospital, Sylvania (G-17587)	B	419 824-1000
Fountainhead Nursing Home Inc, Franklin Furnace (G-11170)	E	740 354-9113
Four Seasons Washington LLC, Wshngtn CT Hs (G-20024)	D	740 895-6101
Franciscan Care Ctr Sylvania, Toledo (G-17899)	C	419 882-2087
Franciscan Sisters of Chicago, Cleveland (G-5630)	C	440 843-7800
Franklin Boulevard Nursing Hm, Cleveland (G-5633)	C	216 651-1600
Franklin Shcp Inc, Columbus (G-7698)	D	440 614-0160
Friendly Nursing Home Inc, Franklin (G-11155)	E	937 855-2363
Friends Health Care Assn, Yellow Springs (G-20089)	C	937 767-7363
Friendship Vlg of Clumbus Ohio, Columbus (G-7707)	D	614 890-8287
Friendship Vlg of Clumbus Ohio, Columbus (G-7708)	C	614 890-8282
Friendship Vlg of Dublin Ohio, Dublin (G-10351)	E	614 764-1600
Front Leasing Co LLC, Berea (G-1460)	C	440 243-4000
Fulton County Health Center, Wauseon (G-18953)	E	419 335-2017
Gables At Green Pastures, Marysville (G-13621)	C	937 642-3893
Gables Care Center Inc, Hopedale (G-12078)	C	740 937-2900
Gahanna Health Care Center, Columbus (G-7723)	E	614 475-7222
Galion Community Hospital, Galion (G-11298)	B	419 468-4841
Gallipolis Care LLC, Gallipolis (G-11318)	C	740 446-7112
Garden Manor Extended Care Cen, Middletown (G-14426)	C	513 420-5972
Gardens At Wapakoneta, Wapakoneta (G-18797)	E	419 738-0725
Gateway Family House, Euclid (G-10756)	E	216 531-5400
Gateway Health Care Center, Cleveland (G-5658)	C	216 486-4949
Gateways To Better Living Inc, Youngstown (G-20194)	E	330 480-9870
Gaymont Nursing Homes Inc, Norwalk (G-15576)	D	419 668-8258
Generation Health & Rehab Cntr, Newark (G-15168)	D	740 344-9465
Generation Health Corp, Columbus (G-7737)	C	614 337-1066
GFS Leasing Inc, Kent (G-12372)	D	330 296-6415
GFS Leasing Inc, Hartville (G-11818)	D	330 877-2666
Gibsonburg Health Llc, Gibsonburg (G-11402)	C	419 637-2104
Gillette Nursing Home Inc, Warren (G-18860)	D	330 372-1960
Glen Wesley Inc, Columbus (G-7755)	D	614 888-7492
Glendale Place Care Center LLC, Cincinnati (G-3678)	E	513 771-1779
Glendora Health Care Center, Wooster (G-19863)	D	330 264-0912
Glenn View Manor Inc, Mineral Ridge (G-14636)	C	330 652-9901
Glenward Inc, Fairfield Township (G-10929)	C	513 863-3100
Golden Living LLC, Napoleon (G-14941)	E	419 599-4070
Golden Living LLC, Akron (G-240)	C	330 762-6486
Golden Living LLC, Medina (G-14071)	D	330 725-3393
Golden Living LLC, Lima (G-12784)	D	419 227-2154
Golden Living LLC, Saint Marys (G-16674)	D	419 394-3308
Golden Living LLC, Columbus (G-7759)	C	614 861-6666
Golden Living LLC, Ravenna (G-16386)	C	330 297-5781
Golden Living LLC, Wadsworth (G-18753)	D	330 335-1558
Golden Years Nursing Home Inc, Hamilton (G-11732)	E	513 893-0471
Good Shepard Village LLC, Springfield (G-17202)	D	937 322-1911
Good Shepherd Home, Fostoria (G-11129)	C	419 937-1801
Good Shepherd Home For Aged, Ashland (G-680)	C	614 228-5200
Governors Village LLC, Cleveland (G-5682)	E	440 449-8788
Grace Brethren Village Inc, Englewood (G-10707)	E	937 836-4011
Graceworks Lutheran Services, Dayton (G-9584)	A	937 433-2140
Greenbrier Senior Living Cmnty, Cleveland (G-5702)	C	440 888-5900
Greenbrier Senior Living Cmnty, Cleveland (G-5703)	D	440 888-0400
Greene Oaks, Xenia (G-20060)	D	937 352-2800
Greens of Lyndhurst The Inc, Cleveland (G-5704)	C	440 460-1000
Guardian Elder Care LLC, North Lima (G-15402)	C	330 549-0898
Hamlet Village In Chagrin FLS, Chagrin Falls (G-2700)	D	216 263-6033
Hampton Woods Nursing Ctr Inc, Poland (G-16224)	E	330 707-1400
Hanover House Inc, Massillon (G-13817)	C	330 837-1741
Harborside Clveland Ltd Partnr, Westlake (G-19488)	D	440 871-5900
Harborside Clveland Ltd Partnr, Broadview Heights (G-1881)	C	440 526-4770
Harborside Healthcare Corp, Swanton (G-17566)	C	419 825-1111
Harborside Healthcare NW Ohio, Bryan (G-2007)	C	419 636-5071
Harborside Pointe Place LLC, Toledo (G-17935)	C	419 727-7870
Harborside Sylvania LLC, Sylvania (G-17592)	D	419 882-1875

Employee Codes: A=Over 500 employees, B=251-500
C=101-250, D=51-100, E=25-50

80 HEALTH SERVICES

Harborside Troy LLC ....D...... 937 335-7161 Troy *(G-18356)*	Health Care Rtrement Corp Amer......D...... 740 773-5000 Chillicothe *(G-2845)*	Hospice of North Central Ohio ....E...... 419 281-7107 Ashland *(G-682)*
Havar Inc ....E...... 740 373-7175 Marietta *(G-13451)*	Health Care Rtrement Corp Amer......C...... 740 354-4505 Portsmouth *(G-16284)*	Hospice of The Western Reserve ......D...... 440 951-8692 Mentor *(G-14192)*
Hcf Management Inc ....C...... 740 289-2394 Piketon *(G-16117)*	Health Care Rtrement Corp Amer......D...... 614 882-3782 Westerville *(G-19408)*	Hospice of The Western Reserve ......E...... 440 787-2080 Lorain *(G-13042)*
Hcf Management Inc ....D...... 419 999-2010 Lima *(G-12791)*	Health Care Rtrement Corp Amer......C...... 937 599-5123 Bellefontaine *(G-1384)*	Hosser Assisted Living ....E...... 740 286-8785 Jackson *(G-12314)*
Hcf Management Inc ....C...... 419 999-2055 Lima *(G-12792)*	Health Care Rtrement Corp Amer......D...... 614 464-2273 Columbus *(G-7811)*	House of Loreto ....D...... 330 453-8137 Canton *(G-2405)*
Hcf of Bowl Green Care Ctr Inc ......D...... 419 352-7558 Bowling Green *(G-1781)*	Health Care Rtrement Corp Amer......D...... 937 390-0005 Springfield *(G-17204)*	Huffman Health Care Inc ....C...... 937 476-1000 Dayton *(G-9625)*
Hcf of Briarwood Inc ....B...... 419 678-2311 Coldwater *(G-6829)*	Health Care Rtrement Corp Amer......D...... 740 894-3287 South Point *(G-17088)*	Humility House ....D...... 330 505-0144 Youngstown *(G-20222)*
Hcf of Court House Inc ....B...... 740 335-9290 Wshngtn CT Hs *(G-20025)*	Health Care Rtrement Corp Amer......C...... 937 393-5766 Hillsboro *(G-11977)*	Huron Health Care Center Inc ....C...... 419 433-4990 Huron *(G-12167)*
Hcf of Crestview Inc ....D...... 937 426-5033 Beavercreek *(G-1246)*	Health Care Rtrement Corp Amer......C...... 440 946-1912 Mentor *(G-14188)*	Huston Nursing Home ....D...... 740 384-3485 Hamden *(G-11687)*
Hcf of Fox Run Inc ....D...... 419 424-0832 Findlay *(G-11045)*	Health Care Rtrement Corp Amer......D...... 740 635-4600 Bridgeport *(G-1863)*	I Vrable Inc ....C...... 614 545-5500 Columbus *(G-7878)*
Hcf of Lima Inc ....D...... 419 999-2010 Lima *(G-12793)*	Health Care Rtrement Corp Amer......D...... 937 773-9346 Piqua *(G-16148)*	Independence Care Community ......D...... 419 435-8505 Fostoria *(G-11133)*
Hcf of Perrysburg Inc ....D...... 419 874-0306 Perrysburg *(G-16008)*	Health Care Rtrement Corp Amer......C...... 419 874-3578 Perrysburg *(G-16009)*	Ioof Home of Ohio Inc ....E...... 937 399-8631 Springfield *(G-17215)*
Hcf of Piqua Inc ....D...... 937 773-0040 Piqua *(G-16147)*	Health Care Rtrement Corp Amer......C...... 937 866-8885 Miamisburg *(G-14306)*	Isabelle Ridgway Care Ctr Inc ....C...... 614 252-4931 Columbus *(G-7926)*
Hcf of Roselawn Inc ....C...... 419 647-4115 Spencerville *(G-17108)*	Health Care Rtrement Corp Amer......C...... 937 548-3141 Greenville *(G-11509)*	Ivy Health Care Inc ....C...... 513 251-2557 Cincinnati *(G-3849)*
Hcf of Shawnee Inc ....C...... 419 999-2055 Lima *(G-12794)*	Health Care Rtrement Corp Amer......E...... 419 337-3050 Wauseon *(G-18958)*	J W J Investments Inc ....C...... 419 643-3161 Bluffton *(G-1732)*
Hcf of Van Wert Inc ....D...... 419 999-2010 Van Wert *(G-18634)*	Health Care Rtrement Corp Amer......C...... 419 878-8523 Waterville *(G-19042)*	Jackson County Hlth Facilities ....D...... 740 384-0722 Wellston *(G-19002)*
Hcf of Wapakoneta Inc ....D...... 419 738-3711 Wapakoneta *(G-18798)*	Health Care Rtrement Corp Amer......C...... 513 751-0880 Cincinnati *(G-3751)*	Jacobs Dwelling Nursing Home ......E...... 740 824-3635 Coshocton *(G-9109)*
Hcr Manor Care Svc Fla III Inc ....E...... 419 252-5500 Toledo *(G-17938)*	Healthcare Facility MGT LLC ....D...... 419 382-2200 Toledo *(G-17944)*	Jada Inc ....E...... 419 512-1713 Mount Vernon *(G-14901)*
Hcr Manorcare Med Svcs Fla LLC ...E...... 513 745-9600 Cincinnati *(G-3746)*	Healthcare Facility MGT LLC ....C...... 330 836-7953 Akron *(G-260)*	Jennings Eliza Home Inc ....C...... 216 226-0282 Cleveland *(G-5857)*
Hcr Manorcare Med Svcs Fla LLC ...D...... 513 233-0831 Cincinnati *(G-3747)*	Heartland Fort Myers Fl LLC ....E...... 419 252-5500 Toledo *(G-17946)*	Jennings Eliza Senior Care ....A...... 216 226-5000 Olmsted Twp *(G-15676)*
Hcr Manorcare Med Svcs Fla LLC ...C...... 419 252-5500 Portsmouth *(G-16283)*	Heartlnd-Riverview S Pt OH LLC .....C...... 740 894-3287 South Point *(G-17089)*	Jennings Ctr For Older Adults ....B...... 216 581-2900 Cleveland *(G-5858)*
Hcr Manorcare Med Svcs Fla LLC ...C...... 419 531-2127 Toledo *(G-17939)*	Heath Nursing Care Center ....C...... 740 522-1171 Newark *(G-15173)*	Jewish Fdrtion of Grter Dayton ....D...... 937 837-2651 Dayton *(G-9641)*
Hcr Manorcare Med Svcs Fla LLC ...C...... 330 753-5005 Barberton *(G-965)*	Heather Knoll Retirement Vlg ....C...... 330 688-8600 Tallmadge *(G-17639)*	Jewish Home of Cincinnati ....B...... 513 754-3100 Mason *(G-13726)*
Hcr Manorcare Med Svcs Fla LLC ...C...... 513 561-4111 Cincinnati *(G-3748)*	Heatherhill Care Communities ....E...... 440 285-4040 Chardon *(G-2752)*	Jma Healthcare LLC ....C...... 440 439-7976 Cleveland *(G-5865)*
Hcr Manorcare Med Svcs Fla LLC ...C...... 614 882-1511 Westerville *(G-19407)*	Hempstead Manor ....C...... 740 354-8150 Portsmouth *(G-16286)*	Jo Lin Health Center Inc ....C...... 740 532-0860 Ironton *(G-12295)*
Hcr Manorcare Med Svcs Fla LLC ...D...... 330 668-6889 Akron *(G-259)*	Hennis Nursing Home ....C...... 330 364-8849 Dover *(G-10191)*	Joint Township Dst Mem Hosp ....B...... 419 394-3335 Saint Marys *(G-16676)*
Hcr Manorcare Med Svcs Fla LLC ...C...... 419 252-5500 Toledo *(G-17940)*	Heritage Park Rehabilita ....E...... 937 437-2311 New Paris *(G-15078)*	Judson Care Center Inc ....E...... 216 292-5706 Cincinnati *(G-3894)*
Hcr Manorcare Med Svcs Fla LLC ...C...... 216 251-3300 Cleveland *(G-5735)*	Hermenia Inc ....D...... 216 795-5710 Cleveland *(G-5752)*	Karl Hc LLC ....B...... 614 846-5420 Columbus *(G-7965)*
Hcr Manorcare Med Svcs Fla LLC ...D...... 440 473-0090 Cleveland *(G-5736)*	Hgcc of Allentown Inc ....D...... 419 252-5500 Toledo *(G-17955)*	Kendal At Oberlin ....C...... 440 775-0094 Oberlin *(G-15647)*
Hcr Manorcare Med Svcs Fla LLC ...C...... 216 486-2300 Cleveland *(G-5737)*	Hickory Creek Healthcare ....D...... 419 542-7795 Hicksville *(G-11864)*	Kenwood Ter Hlth Care Ctr Inc ....C...... 513 793-2255 Cincinnati *(G-3915)*
Hcr Manorcare Med Svcs Fla LLC ...C...... 937 436-9700 Centerville *(G-2679)*	Highbanks Care Center LLC ....D...... 614 888-2021 Columbus *(G-7833)*	Kimes Convalescent Center ....E...... 740 593-3391 Athens *(G-797)*
Hcr Manorcare Med Svcs Fla LLC ...C...... 419 691-3088 Oregon *(G-15738)*	Hill Side Plaza ....D...... 216 486-6300 Cleveland *(G-5756)*	Kindred Healthcare Inc ....D...... 937 222-5963 Dayton *(G-9660)*
Hcr Manorcare Med Svcs Fla LLC ...E...... 440 808-9275 Westlake *(G-19489)*	Hill View Retirement Center ....C...... 740 354-3135 Portsmouth *(G-16287)*	Kindred Healthcare Oper Inc ....D...... 740 545-6355 West Lafayette *(G-19258)*
Hcr Manorcare Med Svcs Fla LLC ...C...... 513 591-0400 Cincinnati *(G-3749)*	Hillandale Healthcare Inc ....D...... 513 777-1400 West Chester *(G-19090)*	Kindred Healthcare Oper Inc ....D...... 614 882-2490 Columbus *(G-7990)*
Hcr Manorcare Med Svcs Fla LLC ...D...... 440 887-1442 North Royalton *(G-15494)*	Hillspring Health Care Center ....E...... 937 748-1100 Springboro *(G-17123)*	Kindred Healthcare Oper Inc ....C...... 740 387-7537 Marion *(G-13545)*
Health Care Opportunities Inc ....E...... 513 932-4861 Lebanon *(G-12610)*	Hilty Memorial Home Inc ....C...... 419 384-3218 Pandora *(G-15892)*	Kindred Healthcare Oper Inc ....C...... 740 439-4437 Cambridge *(G-2122)*
Health Care Retirement Corp ....B...... 419 252-5500 Toledo *(G-17941)*	Home Echo Club Inc ....C...... 614 864-1718 Pickerington *(G-16096)*	Kindred Healthcare Operating ....D...... 330 762-0901 Akron *(G-307)*
Health Care Rtrement Corp Amer......C...... 419 252-5500 Toledo *(G-17942)*	Home The Friends Inc ....C...... 513 897-6050 Waynesville *(G-18983)*	Kindred Healthcare Operating ....D...... 419 877-5338 Whitehouse *(G-19587)*
Health Care Rtrement Corp Amer......D...... 419 474-6021 Toledo *(G-17943)*	Hooberry Associates Inc ....D...... 330 872-1991 Newton Falls *(G-15274)*	Kindred Nursing Centers E LLC ......C...... 513 932-0105 Lebanon *(G-12615)*
Health Care Rtrement Corp Amer......D...... 740 286-5026 Jackson *(G-12312)*	Horizon Health Management LLC ....D...... 513 793-5220 Cincinnati *(G-3783)*	Kindred Nursing Centers E LLC ......C...... 614 276-8222 Columbus *(G-7991)*
Health Care Rtrement Corp Amer......D...... 419 562-9907 Bucyrus *(G-2038)*	Horn Nursing and Rehab Center .....D...... 330 262-2951 Wooster *(G-19870)*	Kindred Nursing Centers E LLC ......C...... 614 837-9666 Canal Winchester *(G-2164)*
Health Care Rtrement Corp Amer......D...... 937 298-8084 Dayton *(G-9604)*	Horn Nursing and Rehab Center .....C...... 330 345-9050 Wooster *(G-19871)*	Kindred Nursing Centers E LLC ......C...... 314 631-3000 Pickerington *(G-16099)*
Health Care Rtrement Corp Amer......D...... 740 373-8920 Marietta *(G-13452)*	Hospice Cincinnati Inc ....E...... 513 862-1100 Cincinnati *(G-3785)*	Kindred Nursing Centers E LLC ......C...... 740 344-0357 Newark *(G-15179)*
Health Care Rtrement Corp Amer......D...... 937 429-1106 Dayton *(G-9271)*	Hospice Cincinnati Inc ....D...... 513 891-7700 Cincinnati *(G-3786)*	Kindred Nursing Centers E LLC ......C...... 502 596-7300 Logan *(G-12981)*
Health Care Rtrement Corp Amer......D...... 937 456-5537 Eaton *(G-10562)*	Hospice of Genesis Health ....E...... 740 454-5381 Zanesville *(G-20488)*	King Tree Leasing Co LLC ....D...... 937 278-0723 Dayton *(G-9663)*

80 HEALTH SERVICES

Company	Code	Phone
Kingston Healthcare Company	C	937 866-9089
Miamisburg (G-14312)		
Kingston Healthcare Company	C	440 967-1800
Vermilion (G-18712)		
Kingston Healthcare Company	C	419 289-3859
Ashland (G-684)		
Kingston Rsdnce Perrysburg LLC	D	419 872-6200
Perrysburg (G-16025)		
Lakewood Health Care Center	C	216 226-3103
Lakewood (G-12490)		
Lancia Nursing Home Inc	E	740 695-4404
Saint Clairsville (G-16640)		
Larchwood Health Group LLC	E	216 941-6100
Cleveland (G-5926)		
Laurel Health Care Company	C	614 888-4553
Worthington (G-19968)		
Laurel Health Care Company	C	614 885-0408
Worthington (G-19969)		
Laurel Healthcare	C	419 782-7879
Defiance (G-10044)		
Laurel Hlth Care Battle Creek	E	614 794-8800
Westerville (G-19323)		
Laurel Hlth Care of Mt Plasant	D	614 794-8800
Westerville (G-19324)		
Laurel Lk Retirement Cmnty Inc	B	330 650-0681
Hudson (G-12130)		
Laurels of Hillsboro	D	937 393-1925
Hillsboro (G-11985)		
Leader Nuring & Rehabilitation	C	419 252-5718
Toledo (G-18002)		
Lebanon Nursing & Rehab Ctr	D	513 932-1121
Lebanon (G-12622)		
Levering Management Inc	C	419 756-4747
Mansfield (G-13323)		
Levering Management Inc	D	740 387-9545
Marion (G-13548)		
Levering Management Inc	D	740 369-6400
Delaware (G-10115)		
Lexington Court Care Center	D	419 884-2000
Mansfield (G-13324)		
Liberty Nrsing Ctr of Jmestown	D	937 675-3311
Jamestown (G-12327)		
Liberty Nrsing Ctr Rvrside LLC	D	513 557-3621
Cincinnati (G-3975)		
Liberty Nursing Center	E	937 836-5143
Englewood (G-10712)		
Liberty Nursing Home Inc	D	937 376-2121
Xenia (G-20067)		
Liberty Nursing of Willard	D	419 935-0148
Willard (G-19622)		
Life Care Centers America Inc	C	440 365-5200
Elyria (G-10640)		
Life Care Centers America Inc	C	440 871-3030
Westlake (G-19510)		
Life Care Centers America Inc	D	614 889-6320
Columbus (G-8061)		
Life Care Centers America Inc	C	330 483-3131
Valley City (G-18619)		
Lima Cnvlscent HM Fndation Inc	D	419 227-5450
Lima (G-12818)		
Lincoln Crawford Nrsg/Rehab CT	E	513 861-2044
Cincinnati (G-3983)		
Lincoln Park Associates II LP	C	937 297-4300
Dayton (G-9683)		
Livin Care Alter of Kirke Inc	E	740 927-3209
Kirkersville (G-12455)		
Living Care Alternatives	E	740 927-3209
Kirkersville (G-12456)		
Locust Ridge Nursing Home Inc	C	937 444-2920
Williamsburg (G-19633)		
Lodge Care Center Inc	C	513 683-9966
Loveland (G-13139)		
Logan Health Care Center	C	740 385-2155
Logan (G-12983)		
Logan Healthcare Leasing LLC	D	216 367-1214
Logan (G-12984)		
Longterm Lodging Inc	C	614 224-0614
Columbus (G-8076)		
Lorantffy Care Center Inc	D	330 666-2631
Copley (G-9059)		
Loveland Health Care Ctr LLC	C	513 605-6000
Loveland (G-13141)		
Loving Care Hospice Inc	E	740 852-7755
London (G-12998)		
Lutheran Home	B	440 871-0090
Cleveland (G-5959)		
Lutheran Scial Svcs Centl Ohio	C	419 289-3523
Ashland (G-686)		
Lutheran Senior City Inc	B	614 228-5200
Columbus (G-8089)		
Lutheran Village At Wolf Creek	C	419 861-2233
Holland (G-12033)		
Lynnhaven V LLC	C	440 272-5600
Windsor (G-19805)		
Lynnhaven Xii LLC	C	419 756-7111
Mansfield (G-13325)		
Madeira Health Care Center	C	513 561-4105
Cincinnati (G-4009)		
Madison Care Inc	D	440 428-1492
Madison (G-13230)		
Main Street Terrace Care Ctr	D	740 653-8767
Lancaster (G-12553)		
Mallard Cove Senior Dev LLC	C	513 772-6655
Cincinnati (G-4018)		
Manleys Manor Nursing Home Inc	C	419 424-0402
Findlay (G-11060)		
Manor Care Inc	D	419 252-5500
Toledo (G-18028)		
Manor Care Nursing Center	E	419 252-5500
Toledo (G-18029)		
Manor Care of America Inc	D	440 543-6766
Chagrin Falls (G-2724)		
Manor Care of America Inc	C	330 867-8530
Akron (G-332)		
Manor Care of America Inc	C	330 492-7835
Canton (G-2445)		
Manor Care of America Inc	C	440 779-6900
North Olmsted (G-15430)		
Manor Care of America Inc	C	440 951-5551
Willoughby (G-19690)		
Manor Care of America Inc	C	440 345-9300
North Royalton (G-15496)		
Manor Care of Boynton Beach	C	419 252-5500
Toledo (G-18030)		
Manor Care of Kansas Inc	D	419 252-5500
Toledo (G-18031)		
Manor Care of North Olmsted	B	419 252-5500
Toledo (G-18032)		
Manor Care of Plantation Inc	C	419 252-5500
Toledo (G-18033)		
Manor Care of York North Inc	C	419 252-5500
Toledo (G-18034)		
Manor Care Wilmington Inc	E	419 252-5500
Toledo (G-18035)		
Manor Care York (south) Inc	C	419 252-5500
Toledo (G-18036)		
Manor Cr-Mprial Rchmond VA LLC	D	419 252-5000
Toledo (G-18037)		
Manorcare Health Services LLC	E	419 252-5500
Toledo (G-18038)		
Manorcare Health Svcs VA Inc	D	419 252-5500
Toledo (G-18039)		
Manorcare of Kingston Court	C	419 252-5500
Toledo (G-18040)		
Manorcare of Willoughby Inc	C	419 252-5500
Toledo (G-18041)		
Mansfield Memorial Homes LLC	C	419 774-5100
Mansfield (G-13333)		
Mansfield Opco LLC	D	502 429-8062
Mansfield (G-13334)		
Maple Knoll Communities Inc	E	513 524-7990
Oxford (G-15817)		
Maple Knoll Communities Inc	B	513 782-2400
Cincinnati (G-4019)		
Maplewood Nursing Center Inc	E	740 383-2126
Marion (G-13550)		
Marietta Center For Health &	C	740 373-1867
Marietta (G-13466)		
Marion Manor	D	740 387-9545
Marion (G-13562)		
▲ Marymount Hospital Inc	B	216 581-0500
Cleveland (G-5991)		
Mason Health Care Center	D	513 398-2881
Mason (G-13737)		
Masonic Healthcare Inc	B	937 525-3001
Springfield (G-17229)		
Mayfair Nursing Care Centers	D	614 889-6320
Columbus (G-8132)		
Mayflower Nursing Home Inc	C	330 492-7131
Canton (G-2452)		
Mc Auley Center	C	937 653-5432
Urbana (G-18594)		
McClellan Management Inc	C	419 855-7755
Genoa (G-11381)		
McGregor Senior Ind Hsing	D	216 851-8200
Cleveland (G-6004)		
McKinley Hall Inc	E	937 328-5300
Springfield (G-17230)		
McKinley Life Care Center LLC	D	330 456-1014
Canton (G-2455)		
McV Health Care Facilities	C	513 398-1486
Mason (G-13738)		
Meadow Wind Hlth Care Ctr Inc	C	330 833-2026
Massillon (G-13838)		
Meadowbrook Manor of Hartford	D	330 772-5253
Fowler (G-11144)		
Medina Meadows	D	330 725-1550
Medina (G-14103)		
Medina Medical Investors Ltd	C	330 483-3131
Medina (G-14104)		
Megco Management Inc	C	330 874-9999
Bolivar (G-1749)		
Meigs Center Ltd	C	740 992-6472
Middleport (G-14407)		
Mennonite Memorial Home Inc	C	419 358-1015
Bluffton (G-1734)		
Menorah Park Center For Senio	A	216 831-6500
Cleveland (G-6024)		
Mental Rtrdtion Preble Cnty Bd	D	937 456-5891
Eaton (G-10568)		
Mentor Way Nursing & Rehab Cen	C	440 255-9309
Mentor (G-14216)		
Mercy Health West Park	C	513 451-8900
Cincinnati (G-4076)		
Mercy St Theresa Center Inc	C	513 271-7010
Cincinnati (G-4078)		
Merit House LLC	C	419 478-5131
Toledo (G-18059)		
Merit Leasing Co LLC	C	216 261-9592
Cleveland (G-6027)		
Mff Somerset LLc	E	216 752-5600
Shaker Heights (G-16863)		
Mill Creek Nursing	E	419 468-4046
Galion (G-11302)		
Mill Manor Nursing Home Inc	E	440 967-6614
Vermilion (G-18715)		
Mill Run Care Center LLC	D	614 527-3000
Hilliard (G-11935)		
Minerva Elder Care Inc	E	330 868-4147
Minerva (G-14648)		
Mkjb Inc	C	513 851-8400
Cincinnati (G-4108)		
Montefiore Home	B	216 360-9080
Beachwood (G-1104)		
Mount Vernon NH LLC	E	740 392-1099
Mount Vernon (G-14914)		
Mt Washington Care Center Inc	C	513 231-4561
Cincinnati (G-4130)		
Multi-Care Inc	D	440 352-0788
Painesville (G-15867)		
Multicare Management Group	C	513 868-6500
Fairfield (G-10883)		
Muskingum County Ohio	D	740 454-1911
Zanesville (G-20507)		
Myocare Nursing Home Inc	C	216 252-7555
Cleveland (G-6095)		
National Church Residences	C	614 451-2151
Columbus (G-8215)		
Ncop LLC	D	419 599-4070
Napoleon (G-14948)		
Nentwick Convalescent Home	C	330 385-5001
East Liverpool (G-10527)		
New Albany Care Center LLC	C	614 855-8866
Columbus (G-8270)		
New Dawn Health Care Inc	C	330 343-5521
Dover (G-10202)		
New Life Hospice Inc	E	440 934-1458
Lorain (G-13064)		
New Life Hospice Inc	D	440 934-1458
Sheffield Village (G-16893)		
Newark Care Center LLC	D	740 366-2321
Newark (G-15219)		
Newark NH LLC	D	740 345-9197
Newark (G-15221)		
Newcomerstown Progress Corp	C	740 498-5165
Newcomerstown (G-15271)		
Nightingale Holdings LLC	B	330 645-0200
Akron (G-352)		
Normandy Manor of Rocky River	C	440 333-5401
Rocky River (G-16588)		
Northpoint Senior Services LLC	D	740 369-9614
Delaware (G-10118)		
Northpoint Senior Services LLC	C	740 373-3597
Marietta (G-13480)		
Northpoint Senior Services LLC	D	513 248-1655
Milford (G-14545)		
Norwalk Area Hlth Systems Inc	A	419 668-8101
Norwalk (G-15584)		
Norwood Health Care Center LLC	D	513 351-0153
Cincinnati (G-4186)		

Employee Codes: A=Over 500 employees, B=251-500
C=101-250, D=51-100, E=25-50

80 HEALTH SERVICES

Company	Location	Code	Phone
Nursing Care MGT Amer Inc	Pataskala (G-15924)	D	740 927-9888
Nursing Care MGT Amer Inc	Cincinnati (G-4194)	D	513 793-5092
Nursing Home Management Inc	Geneva (G-11367)	D	440 466-1181
Oak Creek Terrace Inc	Dayton (G-9778)	C	937 439-1454
Oak Grove Manor Inc	Mansfield (G-13350)	C	419 589-6222
Oak Health Care Investors	Mount Vernon (G-14916)	D	740 397-3200
Oak Health Care Investors	Westerville (G-19335)	E	614 794-8800
Oaktree LLC	Cincinnati (G-4196)	D	513 598-8000
October Enterprises Inc	Eaton (G-10571)	C	937 456-9535
Ohio Department Veterans Svcs	Columbus (G-8331)	A	614 644-0898
Ohio Eastern Star Home	Mount Vernon (G-14917)	C	740 397-1706
Ohio Living	Columbus (G-8357)	B	614 224-1651
Ohio Living	Cincinnati (G-4208)	C	513 681-4230
Ohio Presbt Retirement Svcs	Youngstown (G-20309)	B	330 746-2944
Ohio Presbt Retirement Svcs	Akron (G-368)	C	330 867-2150
Ohio Presbt Retirement Svcs	Sidney (G-16945)	B	937 498-2391
Ohio Presbt Retirement Svcs	Monroe (G-14708)	C	513 539-7391
Ohio Valley Manor Inc	Ripley (G-16548)	C	937 392-4318
Ohioguidestone	Berea (G-1467)		440 234-2006
Ohiohealth Corporation	Columbus (G-8457)	A	614 788-8860
Olmsted Health and Svc Corp	Olmsted Twp (G-15679)	B	440 235-7100
Olmsted Manor Nursing Home	North Olmsted (G-15436)	C	440 250-4080
Olmsted Mnor Rtrment Cmnty Ltd	North Olmsted (G-15437)	E	440 779-8886
Omni Manor Inc	Girard (G-11423)	C	330 545-1550
Omni Manor Inc	Youngstown (G-20311)	C	330 793-5648
Orchard Villa Inc	Oregon (G-15744)	C	419 697-4100
Orion Care Services LLC	Cleveland (G-6215)	C	216 752-3600
Otterbein Portage Valley Inc	Pemberville (G-15943)		888 749-4950
Otterbein Snior Lfstyle Chices	Lebanon (G-12636)	B	513 933-5400
Otterbein Snior Lfstyle Chices	Cridersville (G-9152)	C	419 645-5114
Otterbein Snior Lfstyle Chices	Middletown (G-14483)	C	513 260-7690
Otterbein Snior Lfstyle Chices	Saint Marys (G-16682)	C	419 394-2366
Ovm Investment Group LLC	Ripley (G-16549)	C	937 392-0145
Parkcliffe Development	Toledo (G-18118)	D	419 381-9447
Parkview Manor Inc	Toledo (G-18119)	C	419 243-5191
Parkview Manor Inc	Englewood (G-10714)	D	937 296-1550
Parma Care Center Inc	Cleveland (G-6245)	C	216 661-6800
Pebble Creek Cnvlscnt Ctr	Akron (G-379)	C	330 645-0200
Phyllis Wheatley Assn Dev	Cleveland (G-6278)	E	216 391-4443
Pickaway Manor Inc	Circleville (G-4899)	C	740 474-5400
Piketon Nursing Center Inc	Piketon (G-16125)	D	740 289-4074
Pine Hills Continuing Care Ctr	Nelsonville (G-14966)	E	740 753-1931
Pleasant Hill Leasing LLC	Piketon (G-16126)	C	740 289-2394
Pleasant Lake Nursing Home	Cleveland (G-6289)	B	440 842-2273
Pleasant Ridge Care Center Inc	Cincinnati (G-4305)	C	513 631-1310
Pleasant View Nursing Home	Barberton (G-972)	D	330 745-6028
Premier Estates 521 LLC	Cincinnati (G-4322)	D	765 288-2488
Premier Health Care MGT Inc	Blue Ash (G-1664)	E	248 644-5522
Progressive Green Meadows LLC	Louisville (G-13105)	C	330 875-1456
Progressive Park LLC	Cleveland (G-6320)	C	330 434-4514
Quaker Heights Nursing HM Inc	Waynesville (G-18986)	D	513 897-6050
Quality Care Nursing Svc Inc	South Point (G-17096)	B	740 377-9095
R & F Inc	Holland (G-12047)	E	419 868-2909
R & J Investment Co Inc	Avon (G-915)	C	440 934-5204
Rae-Ann Holdings Inc	Cleveland (G-6347)	D	440 871-5181
Rae-Ann Holdings Inc	Westlake (G-19539)	D	440 871-0500
Rae-Ann Suburban Inc	Westlake (G-19540)	C	440 871-5181
Raeann Inc	Cleveland (G-6348)	E	440 871-5181
Raeann Inc	Geneva (G-11368)	D	440 466-5733
Rapids Nursing Homes Inc	Grand Rapids (G-11453)	E	216 292-5706
Rcr East Inc	Cincinnati (G-4389)	C	513 793-2090
Rcr East Inc	Cincinnati (G-4390)	C	513 231-8292
Red Carpet Health Care Center	Cambridge (G-2127)	C	740 439-4401
Regency Leasing Co LLC	Columbus (G-8606)	B	614 542-3100
Rescare Ohio Inc	Centerburg (G-2667)	E	740 625-6873
Rest Haven Nursing Home Inc	Greenville (G-11516)	C	937 548-1138
Ridge Murray Prod Ctr Oberlin	Oberlin (G-15660)	E	440 774-7400
Ridge Pleasant Valley Inc	Cleveland (G-6395)	C	440 845-0200
Rivers Bend Health Care LLC	South Point (G-17097)	D	740 894-3476
Riverside Care Center LLC	Mc Connelsville (G-14022)	D	740 962-5303
Rocky River Leasing Co LLC	Berea (G-1468)	C	440 243-5688
Rolling Hlls Rhab Wellness Ctr	Brunswick (G-1989)	C	330 225-9121
Roman Cthlic Docese Youngstown	Louisville (G-13106)	C	330 875-5562
Rosary Care Center	Sylvania (G-17613)	D	419 824-3600
Rose Ln Hlth Rhabilitation Inc	Massillon (G-13850)	C	330 833-3174
Rosewood Manor	Yorkville (G-20093)	E	740 859-7673
Rossford Grtric Care Ltd Prtnr	Columbus (G-8651)	C	614 459-0445
Royal Manor Health Care Inc	Cleveland (G-6416)	E	216 752-3600
Royal Oak Nrsing Rhblttion Ctr	Cleveland (G-6417)	D	440 884-9191
Royce Leasing Co LLC	Portsmouth (G-16305)	D	740 354-1240
Ruffing Care Inc	Tiffin (G-17696)	D	419 447-4662
Rwdop LLC	Fairlawn (G-10970)	C	330 666-3776
Saber Healthcare Group LLC	Warren (G-18894)	E	330 369-4672
Saber Healthcare Group LLC	Ravenna (G-16410)	E	330 297-4564
Saber Healthcare Group LLC	Wilmington (G-19786)	E	937 382-1621
Saber Healthcare Group LLC	Brecksville (G-1848)	E	440 546-0643
Saber Healthcare Group LLC	Cincinnati (G-4465)	E	513 631-6800
Saber Healthcare Group LLC	Euclid (G-10775)	E	216 486-5736
Saber Healthcare Group LLC	Cleveland (G-6430)	E	216 795-5710
Saber Healthcare Group LLC	Maple Heights (G-13416)	E	216 662-3343
Saber Healthcare Group LLC	Woodstock (G-19821)	E	937 826-3351
Saber Healthcare Group LLC	Bellevue (G-1418)	E	419 483-6225
Saber Healthcare Group LLC	Cortland (G-9082)	E	330 638-4015
Saber Healthcare Group LLC	Grand Rapids (G-11454)	E	419 484-1111
Saber Healthcare Group LLC	Bedford (G-1333)	E	216 292-5706
Saber Healthcare Group LLC	Akron (G-423)	E	216 292-5706
Saber Healthcare Group LLC	Hudson (G-12142)	E	330 650-0436
Salem Community Hospital	Salem (G-16713)	A	330 332-1551
Salutary Providers Inc	Ashtabula (G-762)	C	440 964-8446
Samaritan Care Center & Villa	Medina (G-14122)	D	330 725-4123
Sanctuary At Tuttle Crossing	Dublin (G-10447)	D	614 408-0182
Sanctuary At Wilmington Place	Dayton (G-9867)	D	937 256-4663
Sarah Jane Living Center Ltd	Delphos (G-10150)	E	419 692-6618
Sateri Home Inc	Youngstown (G-20367)	D	330 758-8106
Schoenbrunn Healthcare	New Philadelphia (G-15114)	D	330 339-3595
Schroer Properties Inc	Lancaster (G-12572)	D	740 687-5100
Schroer Properties Inc	North Canton (G-15365)	D	330 498-8200
Schroer Properties Inc	Mentor (G-14239)	C	440 357-7900
Select Spclty Hsptal-Akron LLC	Akron (G-433)	D	330 761-7500
Semma Enterprises Inc	Middletown (G-14457)	C	513 863-7775
Senior Care Inc	Xenia (G-20075)	E	937 372-1530
Senior Care Inc	Miamisburg (G-14347)	E	937 291-3211
Sensi Care 3	Elyria (G-10679)	E	440 323-6310
Shelby County Mem Hosp Assn	Sidney (G-16953)	D	937 492-9591
Shepherd of The Valley Luthera	Youngstown (G-20373)	E	330 530-4038
Shepherd of The Valley Luthera	Youngstown (G-20374)		330 726-9061
Shg Whitehall Holdings LLC	Columbus (G-8726)	C	216 292-5706
Sienna Hills Nursing & Rehab	Adena (G-8)	E	740 546-3013
Siffrin Residential Assn	Youngstown (G-20375)	C	330 799-8932
Singleton Health Care Center	Cleveland (G-6483)	E	216 231-0076
Sisters Od Saint Joseph of SAI	Euclid (G-10776)	B	216 531-7426
Sisters of Charity of Cinc	Mount Saint Joseph (G-14871)	D	513 347-5200
Sisters of Charity of Cinc	Mount Saint Joseph (G-14872)		513 347-5436
Sisters of Little	Warrensville Heights (G-18934)	C	216 464-1222
Sisters of Little	Oregon (G-15749)		419 698-4331
Slovene Home For The Aged	Cleveland (G-6490)	C	216 486-0268
Snf Wadsworth LLC	Solon (G-17052)	D	330 336-3472
Solon Pnte At Emrald Ridge LLC	Solon (G-17054)	E	440 498-3000
Somerset NH LLC	Somerset (G-17070)	D	740 743-2924
Southbrook Health Care Ctr Inc	Springfield (G-17275)	C	937 322-3436
Sprenger Entrprises Inc	Lorain (G-13078)	D	440 244-2019
Spring Meadow Extended Care Ce	Holland (G-12057)	D	419 866-6124
Springhills LLC	Dayton (G-9899)	C	937 274-1400
Springhills LLC	Middletown (G-14487)	D	513 424-9999
Springview Manor Nursing Home	Lima (G-12883)	E	419 227-3661

80 HEALTH SERVICES

St Augustine Corporation ....B 216 939-7600
  Lakewood (G-12501)
St Catherines Care Centers O ....C 419 435-8112
  Fostoria (G-11141)
St Catherines Care Ctr Findlay ....C 419 422-3978
  Findlay (G-11084)
St Edward Home ....C 330 668-2828
  Fairlawn (G-10977)
Stone Crossing Assisted Living ....C 330 492-7131
  Canton (G-2551)
Stow Opco LLC ....D 502 429-8062
  Stow (G-17394)
Streetsboro Opco LLC ....D 502 429-8062
  Streetsboro (G-17433)
Summit Facility Operations LLC ......C 330 633-0555
  Tallmadge (G-17652)
Summitt Ohio Leasing Co LLC ....C 937 436-2273
  Dayton (G-9914)
Sumner Home For The Aged Inc .....C 330 666-2952
  Copley (G-9065)
Sun Healthcare Group Inc ....C 419 784-1450
  Defiance (G-10060)
Sunbrdge Marion Hlth Care Corp .....D 740 389-6306
  Marion (G-13582)
Sunbridge Care Enterprises Inc ....D 740 653-8630
  Lancaster (G-12578)
Sunbridge Circleville ....E 740 477-1695
  Circleville (G-4906)
Sunbridge Healthcare LLC ....C 740 342-5161
  New Lexington (G-15064)
Sunrise Connecticut Avenue Ass ....E 614 451-6766
  Columbus (G-8803)
Sunrise Senior Living Inc ....D 937 438-0054
  Dayton (G-9915)
Sunrise Senior Living Inc ....E 614 418-9775
  Gahanna (G-11272)
Sunrise Senior Living Inc ....D 440 895-2383
  Rocky River (G-16593)
Sunrise Senior Living Inc ....D 440 808-0074
  Westlake (G-19552)
Sunrise Senior Living Inc ....D 216 751-0930
  Cleveland (G-6551)
Sunrise Senior Living Inc ....D 614 457-3500
  Upper Arlington (G-18556)
Sunrise Senior Living Inc ....E 614 846-6500
  Worthington (G-20001)
Sunrise Senior Living LLC ....E 330 262-1615
  Wooster (G-19917)
Sunrise Senior Living LLC ....E 419 425-3440
  Findlay (G-11088)
Sunrise Senior Living LLC ....E 513 729-5233
  Cincinnati (G-4600)
Sunrise Senior Living LLC ....D 330 929-8500
  Cuyahoga Falls (G-9223)
Sunrise Senior Living LLC ....E 216 447-8909
  Cleveland (G-6552)
Sunrise Senior Living LLC ....E 513 893-9000
  Hamilton (G-11776)
Swa Inc ....C 440 243-7888
  Cleveland (G-6560)
Swan Pnte Fclty Operations LLC .....D 419 867-7926
  Maumee (G-13983)
Swanton Hlth Care Rtrement Ctr ......D 419 825-1145
  Swanton (G-17572)
Tender Nursing Care ....E 614 856-3508
  Reynoldsburg (G-16482)
The Maria-Joseph Center ....B 937 278-2692
  Dayton (G-9926)
Thornville NH LLC ....D 740 246-5253
  Thornville (G-17669)
Tlevay Inc ....C 419 385-3958
  Toledo (G-18223)
Toledo Opco LLC ....D 502 429-8062
  Toledo (G-18245)
Traditions At Bath Rd Inc ....C 330 929-6272
  Cuyahoga Falls (G-9226)
Tri County Extended Care Ctr ....C 513 829-3555
  Fairfield (G-10917)
Trilogy Health Services LLC ....D 419 935-6511
  Willard (G-19628)
Trilogy Healthcare Allen LLC ....D 419 643-3161
  Bluffton (G-1736)
Trilogy Healthcare Putnam LLC ......C 419 532-2961
  Kalida (G-12346)
Trilogy Rehab Services LLC ....A 740 452-3000
  Zanesville (G-20540)
Trinity Health Corporation ....B 614 846-5420
  Columbus (G-8872)
Trinity Healthcare Corporation ....C 513 489-2444
  Cincinnati (G-4700)

Triumph Hospital Mansfield ....E 419 526-0777
  Mansfield (G-13376)
Twilight Gardens Healthcare ....E 419 668-2086
  Norwalk (G-15595)
Twin Maples Nursing Home ....E 740 596-5955
  Mc Arthur (G-14018)
Twin Oaks Care Center Inc ....E 419 524-1205
  Mansfield (G-13379)
U C M Residential Services ....D 937 643-3757
  Union City (G-18504)
Uhrichsville Health Care Ctr ....D 740 922-2208
  Uhrichsville (G-18494)
Union Christel Manor Inc ....D 937 968-6265
  Union City (G-18505)
United Church Homes Inc ....C 513 922-1440
  Cincinnati (G-4730)
United Church Homes Inc ....C 330 854-4177
  Canal Fulton (G-2148)
United Church Homes Inc ....C 937 426-8481
  Beavercreek (G-1261)
United Church Homes Inc ....D 740 382-4885
  Marion (G-13592)
United Church Homes Inc ....C 419 621-1900
  Sandusky (G-16805)
United Church Homes Inc ....C 937 878-0262
  Fairborn (G-10806)
United Church Homes Inc ....D 740 376-5600
  Marietta (G-13510)
United Church Homes Inc ....D 740 286-7551
  Jackson (G-12320)
University Hospitals Health ....A 440 285-4040
  Chardon (G-2775)
University Manor Hlth Care Ctr ....C 216 721-1400
  Cleveland (G-6665)
Uvmc Management Corporation .....D 937 440-4000
  Troy (G-18385)
Uvmc Nursing Care Inc ....D 937 440-7663
  Troy (G-18386)
Uvmc Nursing Care Inc ....C 937 667-7500
  Tipp City (G-17731)
Uvmc Nursing Care Inc ....C 937 473-2075
  Covington (G-9140)
V Clew LLC ....E 740 687-2273
  Lancaster (G-12582)
V Vrable Inc ....C 614 545-5500
  Columbus (G-8929)
Valley Hospice Inc ....D 740 859-5041
  Rayland (G-16419)
Valley View Alzhimers Care Ctr ....D 740 998-2948
  Frankfort (G-11146)
Van Rue Incorporated ....C 419 238-0715
  Van Wert (G-18646)
Vancare Inc ....C 937 898-4202
  Vandalia (G-18706)
Vancrest Ltd ....C 419 695-2871
  Delphos (G-10153)
Vancrest Ltd ....C 419 749-2194
  Convoy (G-9050)
Vancrest Ltd ....C 937 456-3010
  Eaton (G-10580)
Vibra Healthcare LLC ....E 330 726-5050
  Youngstown (G-20404)
Vienna Enterprises Inc ....E 937 568-4524
  South Vienna (G-17101)
Village Green Healthcare Ctr ....D 937 548-1993
  Greenville (G-11523)
Vista Centre ....D 330 424-5852
  Lisbon (G-12942)
Volunters Amer Care Facilities ....C 419 447-7151
  Tiffin (G-17708)
Volunters Amer Care Facilities ....C 419 225-9040
  Lima (G-12911)
Volunters Amer Care Facilities ....C 419 334-9521
  Fremont (G-11226)
Vrable Healthcare Inc ....E 614 545-5500
  Columbus (G-8954)
Vrable II Inc ....D 614 545-5502
  Columbus (G-8955)
Vrable IV Inc ....D 614 545-5502
  Columbus (G-8956)
Walnut Hills Inc ....C 330 852-2457
  Walnut Creek (G-18786)
Walton Manor Health Care Ctr ....C 440 439-4433
  Cleveland (G-6721)
Washington Manor Inc ....E 937 433-3441
  Dayton (G-9984)
Water Leasing Co LLC ....C 440 285-9400
  Chardon (G-2778)
Waterville Care LLC ....D 419 878-3901
  Waterville (G-18947)

Waverly Care Center Inc ....E 740 947-2113
  Waverly (G-18976)
Wayside Farms Inc ....D 330 666-7716
  Peninsula (G-15952)
Weber Health Care Center Inc ....C 440 647-2088
  Wellington (G-18996)
Wessell Generations Inc ....C 440 775-1491
  Oberlin (G-15662)
West Liberty Care Center Inc ....C 937 465-5065
  West Liberty (G-19264)
West Park Retirement Community ...C 513 451-8900
  Cincinnati (G-4836)
West Side Dtscher Fruen Verein .....E 440 238-3361
  Strongsville (G-17524)
West View Manor Inc ....C 330 264-8640
  Wooster (G-19928)
Western Hills Care Center ....C 513 941-0099
  Cincinnati (G-4841)
Western Rsrve Msonic Cmnty Inc ...C 330 721-3000
  Medina (G-14138)
Wexner Heritage Village ....B 614 231-4900
  Columbus (G-8984)
Whetstone Care Center LLC ....C 614 875-7700
  Grove City (G-11616)
Whetstone Care Center LLC ....C 614 457-1100
  Columbus (G-8985)
Whetstone Care Center LLC ....C 740 474-6036
  Circleville (G-4908)
Wickliffe Country Place Ltd ....C 440 944-9400
  Wickliffe (G-19616)
Widows Home of Dayton Ohio ....D 937 252-1661
  Dayton (G-9997)
Willow Brook Chrstn Cmmunities ....D 740 369-0048
  Delaware (G-10135)
Willowood Care Center ....C 330 225-3156
  Brunswick (G-1997)
Wilmingtn Nursng/Rehab Resdidn ..D 937 382-1621
  Wilmington (G-19793)
Winchester Place Leasing LLC ....D 614 834-2273
  Canal Winchester (G-2179)
Windsor House Inc ....D 330 743-1393
  Youngstown (G-20417)
Windsor House Inc ....D 330 482-1375
  Columbiana (G-6866)
Windsor House Inc ....C 330 549-9259
  Columbiana (G-6867)
Windsor House Inc ....C 330 759-7858
  Youngstown (G-20416)
Windsor House Inc ....E 440 834-0544
  Burton (G-2066)
Windsor Medical Center Inc ....D 330 499-8300
  Canton (G-2587)
Womens Welsh Clubs of America ...D 440 331-0420
  Rocky River (G-16596)
Wood County Ohio ....C 419 353-8411
  Bowling Green (G-1802)
Woodland Assisted Living Resi ....E 614 755-7591
  Columbus (G-9004)
Woodland Country Manor Inc ....E 513 523-4449
  Somerville (G-17072)
Woodsfield Opco LLC ....D 502 429-8062
  Woodsfield (G-19820)
Woodside Village Care Center ....D 419 947-2015
  Mount Gilead (G-14865)
Woodstock Care Center Inc ....E 937 826-3351
  Woodstock (G-19822)
Wyant Leasing Co LLC ....B 330 836-7953
  Akron (G-513)
Xenia East Management Systems ...D 937 372-4495
  Xenia (G-20086)
Xenia West Management Systems ..D 937 372-8081
  Xenia (G-20087)
Youngstown Area Jwish Fdration ....D 330 746-1076
  Youngstown (G-20426)
Zandex Inc ....C 740 676-8381
  Shadyside (G-16854)
Zandex Inc ....E 740 454-1400
  Zanesville (G-20546)
Zandex Inc ....C 740 454-9769
  Zanesville (G-20548)
Zandex Inc ....C 740 695-7233
  Saint Clairsville (G-16663)
Zandex Inc ....D 740 967-1111
  Johnstown (G-12344)
Zandex Inc ....D 740 454-6823
  Zanesville (G-20549)
Zandex Inc ....C 740 872-0809
  New Concord (G-15040)
Zandex Health Care Corporation ....C 740 454-9747
  Zanesville (G-20553)

Zandex Health Care Corporation.......C....... 740 452-4636
Zanesville *(G-20550)*
Zandex Health Care Corporation.......C....... 740 454-9769
Zanesville *(G-20551)*
Zandex Health Care Corporation.......C....... 740 695-7233
Saint Clairsville *(G-16664)*
Zandex Health Care Corporation.......C....... 740 454-1400
New Concord *(G-15041)*
Zandex Health Care Corporation.......E....... 740 454-1400
Zanesville *(G-20552)*
Zanesville NH LLC.......D....... 740 452-4351
Zanesville *(G-20557)*

8052 Intermediate Care Facilities

10 Wilmington Place.......D....... 937 253-1010
Dayton *(G-9291)*
599 W Main Corporation.......E....... 440 466-5901
Geneva *(G-11357)*
A M Mc Gregor Home.......B....... 216 851-8200
Cleveland *(G-4933)*
A Provide Care Inc.......C....... 330 828-2278
Dalton *(G-9239)*
Adams County Manor.......D....... 937 544-2205
West Union *(G-19272)*
Advance Care Inc.......D....... 513 932-1121
Lebanon *(G-12588)*
Alexson Services Inc.......B....... 513 874-0423
Fairfield *(G-10819)*
Algart Health Care Inc.......D....... 216 631-1550
Cleveland *(G-4985)*
Alpha Nursing Homes Inc.......D....... 740 345-9197
Newark *(G-15142)*
Alpha Nursing Homes Inc.......D....... 740 622-2074
Coshocton *(G-9086)*
Altercare Inc.......C....... 330 335-2555
Wadsworth *(G-18746)*
Altercare Nobles Pond Inc.......D....... 330 834-4800
Canton *(G-2235)*
Alternative Residences Two.......C....... 740 526-0514
Saint Clairsville *(G-16616)*
Alternative Residences Two.......E....... 330 453-0200
Canton *(G-2236)*
American Retirement Corp.......D....... 216 291-6140
Cleveland *(G-5021)*
Amherst Manor Nursing Home.......D....... 440 988-4415
Amherst *(G-588)*
Anchor Lodge Nursing Home Inc.......C....... 440 244-2019
Lorain *(G-13012)*
Angels 4 Life LLC.......E....... 513 474-5683
Cincinnati *(G-3029)*
Anne Grady Corporation.......C....... 419 380-8985
Holland *(G-12009)*
Apostolic Christian Home Inc.......D....... 330 927-1010
Rittman *(G-16550)*
Arbors East LLC.......D....... 614 575-9003
Columbus *(G-7033)*
Arlington Care Ctr.......C....... 740 344-0303
Newark *(G-15143)*
Arlington Court Nursing.......C....... 614 545-5502
Upper Arlington *(G-18547)*
Audrich Inc.......C....... 419 483-6225
Bellevue *(G-1403)*
Baptist Home and Center.......C....... 513 662-5880
Cincinnati *(G-3076)*
Beeghly Oaks Operating LLC.......C....... 330 884-2300
Boardman *(G-1738)*
Bel Air Care Center.......D....... 330 821-3939
Alliance *(G-527)*
Bittersweet Inc.......D....... 419 875-6986
Whitehouse *(G-19584)*
Blossom Hills Nursing Home.......D....... 440 635-5567
Huntsburg *(G-12157)*
Boyds Kinsman Home Inc.......E....... 330 876-5581
Kinsman *(G-12453)*
Braeview Manor Inc.......C....... 216 486-9300
Cleveland *(G-5132)*
Brethren Care Inc.......C....... 419 289-0803
Ashland *(G-666)*
Brewster Parke Inc.......D....... 330 767-4179
Brewster *(G-1854)*
Briarfield At Ashley Circle.......C....... 330 793-3010
Youngstown *(G-20125)*
Brook Willow Chrstn Cmmunities.......D....... 614 885-3300
Columbus *(G-7151)*
Brookville Enterprises Inc.......B....... 937 833-2133
Brookville *(G-1960)*
Brown Memorial Home Inc.......D....... 740 474-6238
Circleville *(G-4880)*
Butler County of Ohio.......C....... 513 887-3728
Fairfield Township *(G-10926)*
Butler County Board of Develop.......E....... 513 867-5913
Fairfield *(G-10826)*
C R G Health Care Systems.......E....... 330 498-8107
Niles *(G-15285)*
Camargo Manor Inc.......D....... 513 605-3000
Cincinnati *(G-3169)*
Canton Assisted Living.......C....... 330 492-7131
Canton *(G-2282)*
Capital Senior Living Corp.......B....... 513 829-6200
Fairfield *(G-10829)*
Caprice Health Care Inc.......C....... 330 965-9200
North Lima *(G-15400)*
Cardinal Retirement Village.......E....... 330 928-7888
Cuyahoga Falls *(G-9168)*
Carington Health Systems.......C....... 937 743-2754
Franklin *(G-11151)*
Carriage Crt Mrysvlle Ltd Prtn.......E....... 937 642-2202
Marysville *(G-13609)*
Carriage Inn of Bowerston Inc.......D....... 740 269-8001
Bowerston *(G-1754)*
Carroll Golden Age Retreat.......E....... 330 627-4665
Carrollton *(G-2612)*
Carroll Health Care Center.......C....... 330 627-5501
Carrollton *(G-2613)*
Center For Eating Disorders.......E....... 614 896-8222
Columbus *(G-7225)*
Center Ridge Nursing Home Inc.......C....... 440 327-1295
North Ridgeville *(G-15458)*
Chelmsford Apartments Ltd.......E....... 419 389-0800
Toledo *(G-17803)*
Childrens Forever Haven Inc.......E....... 440 652-6749
North Royalton *(G-15483)*
Childrens Forever Haven Inc.......E....... 440 250-9182
Westlake *(G-19474)*
Childs Investment Co.......E....... 330 837-2100
Massillon *(G-13794)*
Choices In Community Living.......C....... 937 898-3655
Dayton *(G-9405)*
Church of God Retirement Cmnty.......C....... 513 422-5600
Middletown *(G-14420)*
Co Open Options Inc.......E....... 513 932-0724
Lebanon *(G-12595)*
Columbus Area Integrated Healt.......D....... 614 252-0711
Columbus *(G-7330)*
Commons of Providence.......D....... 419 624-1171
Sandusky *(G-16744)*
Communicare Health Svcs Inc.......D....... 419 394-7611
Saint Marys *(G-16672)*
Community Assisted Living Inc.......E....... 740 653-2575
Lancaster *(G-12522)*
Concord Health Care Inc.......E....... 419 626-5373
Sandusky *(G-16746)*
Concord Health Care Inc.......E....... 330 759-2357
Youngstown *(G-20160)*
Concord Hlth Rhabilitation Ctr.......E....... 740 574-8441
Wheelersburg *(G-19575)*
Congregate Living of America.......E....... 937 393-6700
Hillsboro *(G-11969)*
Congregate Living of America.......D....... 513 899-2801
Morrow *(G-14845)*
Consulate Healthcare Inc.......E....... 419 865-1248
Maumee *(G-13899)*
Consulate Management Co LLC.......D....... 440 237-7966
Cleveland *(G-5398)*
Country Club Center Homes Inc.......D....... 330 343-6351
Dover *(G-10182)*
Country Club Center II Ltd.......C....... 740 397-2350
Mount Vernon *(G-14886)*
Country Club Retirement Center.......C....... 740 671-9330
Bellaire *(G-1365)*
County of Lorain.......E....... 440 282-3074
Lorain *(G-13034)*
County of Montgomery.......B....... 937 264-0460
Dayton *(G-9434)*
County of Shelby.......C....... 937 492-6900
Sidney *(G-16926)*
County of Wood.......B....... 419 686-6951
Portage *(G-16261)*
Covenant Care Ohio Inc.......D....... 937 878-7046
Fairborn *(G-10788)*
Cred-Kap Inc.......D....... 330 755-1466
Struthers *(G-17529)*
Cridersville Health Care Ctr.......E....... 419 645-4468
Cridersville *(G-9151)*
Crystal Care Centers Inc.......E....... 419 747-2666
Mansfield *(G-13286)*
Crystalwood Inc.......D....... 513 605-1000
Cincinnati *(G-3443)*
Cypress Hospice LLC.......E....... 440 973-0250
Berea *(G-1455)*
Dayspring Health Care Center.......C....... 937 864-5800
Fairborn *(G-10792)*
Deaconess Long Term Care of MI.......A....... 513 487-3600
Cincinnati *(G-3474)*
Dearth Management Company.......E....... 740 389-1214
Marion *(G-13537)*
Dearth Management Company.......C....... 614 847-1070
Columbus *(G-7498)*
Dearth Management Company.......C....... 330 339-3595
New Philadelphia *(G-15092)*
Dearth Management Company.......C....... 419 253-0144
Marengo *(G-13423)*
Develpmntal Dsblties Ohio Dept.......A....... 740 446-1642
Gallipolis *(G-11314)*
Develpmntal Dsblties Ohio Dept.......B....... 614 272-0509
Columbus *(G-7513)*
Dover Nursing Center.......D....... 330 364-4436
Dover *(G-10186)*
Doylestown Health Care Center.......C....... 330 658-1533
Doylestown *(G-10227)*
Eagle Creek Nursing Center.......E....... 937 544-5531
West Union *(G-19278)*
Earley & Ross Ltd.......D....... 740 634-3301
Sabina *(G-16615)*
East Galbraith Nursing Home.......C....... 513 984-5220
Cincinnati *(G-3532)*
Eastern Star Hm of Cyhoga Cnty.......D....... 216 761-0170
Cleveland *(G-5521)*
Ebenezer Road Corp.......C....... 513 941-0099
Cincinnati *(G-3540)*
Echoing Hills Village Inc.......D....... 440 989-1400
Lorain *(G-13037)*
Edgewood Manor of Wellston.......E....... 740 384-5611
Wellston *(G-18999)*
Elms Retirement Village Inc.......D....... 440 647-2414
Wellington *(G-18991)*
Elmwood Center Inc.......D....... 419 639-2581
Green Springs *(G-11474)*
Elmwood Center Inc.......D....... 419 447-6885
Tiffin *(G-17677)*
Elmwood Center Inc.......D....... 419 639-2626
Green Springs *(G-11475)*
Emeritus Corporation.......E....... 330 342-0934
Stow *(G-17363)*
Emeritus Corporation.......E....... 614 836-5990
Groveport *(G-11636)*
Fairmont Nursing Home Inc.......D....... 440 338-8220
Newbury *(G-15256)*
Falls Village Retirement Cmnty.......D....... 330 945-9797
Cuyahoga Falls *(G-9187)*
Filling Memorial Home of Mercy.......B....... 419 592-6451
Napoleon *(G-14938)*
Fisher-Titus Medical Center.......E....... 419 668-4228
Norwalk *(G-15574)*
▲ **Fisher-Titus Medical Center**.......A....... 419 668-8101
Norwalk *(G-15575)*
Flower Hospital.......B....... 419 824-1000
Sylvania *(G-17587)*
Fort Austin Ltd Partnership.......C....... 440 892-4200
Cleveland *(G-5624)*
Foundations.......D....... 937 437-2311
New Paris *(G-15077)*
Foundations Hlth Solutions Inc.......D....... 440 793-0200
North Olmsted *(G-15423)*
Franciscan At St Leonard.......B....... 937 433-0480
Dayton *(G-9560)*
Friends of Good Shepherd Manor.......D....... 740 289-2861
Lucasville *(G-13179)*
Furney Group Home.......E....... 419 389-0152
Toledo *(G-17902)*
Garbry Ridge Assisted Living.......E....... 937 778-9385
Piqua *(G-16145)*
Gaslite Villa Convalescent Ctr.......D....... 330 494-4500
Canal Fulton *(G-2143)*
Gateway Health Care Center.......C....... 216 486-4949
Cleveland *(G-5658)*
Gaymont Nursing Homes Inc.......D....... 419 668-8258
Norwalk *(G-15576)*
Generation Health & Rehab Cntr.......D....... 740 344-9465
Newark *(G-15168)*
Gillette Nursing Home Inc.......D....... 330 372-1960
Warren *(G-18860)*
Golden Living LLC.......D....... 419 227-2154
Lima *(G-12784)*
Golden Living LLC.......D....... 419 394-3308
Saint Marys *(G-16674)*
Golden Living LLC.......C....... 614 861-6666
Columbus *(G-7759)*
Golden Living LLC.......C....... 330 297-5781
Ravenna *(G-16386)*

80 HEALTH SERVICES

Company	Code	Phone
Golden Living LLC, Wadsworth (G-18753)	D	330 335-1558
Good Shepherd Home, Fostoria (G-11129)	C	419 937-1801
Grace Hospice LLC, Cincinnati (G-3690)	C	513 458-5545
Grace Hospice LLC, Moraine (G-14792)	C	937 293-1381
Grace Hospice LLC, Mentor (G-14183)	C	216 288-7413
Greens of Lyndhurst The Inc, Cleveland (G-5704)	C	440 460-1000
Guardian Elde, Lima (G-12788)	D	419 225-9040
Guernsey Health Systems Inc, Cambridge (G-2119)	A	740 439-3561
Harbor, Toledo (G-17934)	E	800 444-3353
Harborside Sylvania LLC, Sylvania (G-17592)	D	419 882-1875
Hattie Larlham Center For, Mantua (G-13387)	C	330 274-2272
Healthcare Facility MGT LLC, Akron (G-260)	C	330 836-7953
Healthcare Management Cons, Rockford (G-16563)	E	419 363-2193
Heinzerling Foundation, Columbus (G-7821)	C	614 272-8888
Hempstead Manor, Portsmouth (G-16286)	C	740 354-8150
Hennis Nursing Home, Dover (G-10191)	C	330 364-8849
Heritage Park Rehabilita, New Paris (G-15078)	E	937 437-2311
Heritage Professional Services, New Boston (G-15011)	E	740 456-8245
Hill Side Plaza, Cleveland (G-5756)	D	216 486-6300
Home Echo Club Inc, Pickerington (G-16096)	C	614 864-1718
Horn Nursing and Rehab Center, Wooster (G-19870)	D	330 262-2951
Horn Nursing and Rehab Center, Wooster (G-19871)	C	330 345-9050
Hospice of Hope Inc, Mount Orab (G-14869)	D	937 444-4900
Hospice of Miami Valley LLC, Xenia (G-20063)	E	937 458-6028
Hospice Southwest Ohio Inc, Cincinnati (G-3787)	C	513 770-0820
Humility House, Youngstown (G-20222)	D	330 505-0144
Independence of Portage County, Ravenna (G-16390)	C	330 296-2851
Inn At Lakeview, Groveport (G-11646)	D	614 836-2866
Inn At Marietta Ltd, Marietta (G-13456)	D	740 373-9600
Inn At Univ Vlg MGT Co LLC, Massillon (G-13824)	E	330 837-3000
Inner City Nursing Home, Cleveland (G-5822)	C	216 795-1363
Isabelle Ridgway Care Ctr Inc, Columbus (G-7926)	C	614 252-4931
Jennings Eliza Home Inc, Cleveland (G-5857)	C	216 226-0282
Jennings Ctr For Older Adults, Cleveland (G-5858)	B	216 581-2900
Judson, Cleveland (G-5876)	D	216 791-2004
Judson Care Center Inc, Cincinnati (G-3894)	E	216 292-5706
Kendal At Oberlin, Oberlin (G-15647)	C	440 775-0094
Kindred Healthcare Oper Inc, West Lafayette (G-19258)	D	740 545-6355
Kindred Healthcare Operating, Whitehouse (G-19587)	D	419 877-5338
Kindred Nursing Centers E LLC, Chillicothe (G-2857)	C	740 772-5900
Kingston Healthcare Company, Sylvania (G-17598)	D	419 824-4200
Lakeside Manor Inc, North Lima (G-15404)	E	330 549-2545
Laurels of Hillsboro, Hillsboro (G-11985)	D	937 393-1925
Leeda Services Inc, Warren (G-18874)	E	330 392-6006
Levering Management Inc, Delaware (G-10115)	D	740 369-6400
Lexington Court Care Center, Mansfield (G-13324)	D	419 884-2000
Liberty Nursing Center, Englewood (G-10712)	E	937 836-5143
Liberty Nursing Center of Thre, Cincinnati (G-3976)	C	513 941-0787
Liberty Nursing of Willard, Willard (G-19622)	D	419 935-0148
Liberty Residence II, Wadsworth (G-18760)	E	330 334-3262
Life Care Centers America Inc, Valley City (G-18619)	C	330 483-3131
Lifeservices Development Corp, Mentor (G-14209)	E	440 257-3866
Light of Hearts Villa, Cleveland (G-5941)	D	440 232-1991
Lincoln Park Associates II LP, Dayton (G-9683)	C	937 297-4300
Living Care Altrntves of Utica, Utica (G-18613)	E	740 892-3414
Longmeadow Care Center Inc, Ravenna (G-16392)	C	330 297-5781
Lucas County Board of Developm, Toledo (G-18017)	D	419 380-4000
Luther Home of Mercy, Williston (G-19639)	B	419 836-3918
Lutheran Home, Cleveland (G-5959)		440 871-0090
Lutheran Memorial Home Inc, Toledo (G-18021)	D	419 502-5700
Lutheran Village At Wolf Creek, Holland (G-12033)	C	419 861-2233
Lynnhaven V LLC, Windsor (G-19805)	C	440 272-5600
Main Street Terrace Care Ctr, Lancaster (G-12553)	D	740 653-8767
Manorcare of Willoughby Inc, Toledo (G-18041)	C	419 252-5500
Mansfield Memorial Homes LLC, Mansfield (G-13333)	C	419 774-5100
Maple Knoll Communities Inc, Cincinnati (G-4019)	B	513 782-2400
Mary Scott Nursing Home Inc, Dayton (G-9702)	D	937 278-0761
McClellan Management Inc, Genoa (G-11381)	C	419 855-7755
McV Health Care Facilities, Mason (G-13738)	C	513 398-1486
Meigs Center Ltd, Middleport (G-14407)	C	740 992-6472
Mennonite Memorial Home Inc, Bluffton (G-1734)	C	419 358-1015
Mental Health Service, Springfield (G-17232)	E	937 399-9500
Mercer Residential Svcs Inc, Celina (G-2657)	D	419 586-4709
Mercy Health, Springfield (G-17237)	C	937 390-9665
Miami Valley Hsing Assn I Inc, Dayton (G-9735)	E	937 263-4449
Mill Manor Nursing Home Inc, Vermilion (G-18715)	E	440 967-6614
Mill Run Care Center LLC, Hilliard (G-11935)	D	614 527-3000
Mount Aloysius Corp, New Lexington (G-15056)	C	740 342-3343
Muskingum County Ohio, Zanesville (G-20507)	D	740 454-1911
Muskingum Residentials Inc, Zanesville (G-20511)	E	740 453-5350
New Dawn Health Care Inc, Dover (G-10202)	C	330 343-5521
New Hope & Horizons, Cincinnati (G-4156)	E	513 761-7999
North Hills Management Company, Zanesville (G-20517)	D	740 450-9999
North Point Eductl Svc Ctr, Huron (G-12168)	E	440 967-0904
North Shore Retirement Cmnty, Lakeside (G-12465)	E	419 798-8203
Northpoint Senior Services LLC, Marietta (G-13480)	C	740 373-3597
Northpoint Senior Services LLC, Milford (G-14545)	D	513 248-1655
Norwood Health Care Center LLC, Cincinnati (G-4186)	C	513 351-0153
Oak Health Care Investors, Mount Vernon (G-14916)	D	740 397-3200
October Enterprises Inc, Eaton (G-10571)	C	937 456-9535
Ohio Eastern Star Home, Mount Vernon (G-14917)	C	740 397-1706
Ohio Living, Cincinnati (G-4208)	C	513 681-4230
Ohio Living, Columbus (G-8357)	B	614 224-1651
Ohio Presbt Retirement Svcs, Youngstown (G-20309)	B	330 746-2944
Ohio Presbt Retirement Svcs, Monroe (G-14708)	C	513 539-7391
Ohio Presbt Retirement Svcs, Sidney (G-16945)	B	937 498-2391
Ohio Valley Manor Inc, Ripley (G-16548)	C	937 392-4318
Olmsted Manor Nursing Home, North Olmsted (G-15436)	C	440 250-4080
On-Call Nursing Inc, Lakewood (G-12493)	D	216 577-8890
Orchard Villa Inc, Oregon (G-15744)	C	419 697-4100
Orion Care Services LLC, Cleveland (G-6215)	C	216 752-3600
Otterbein Portage Valley Inc, Pemberville (G-15943)	C	888 749-4950
Otterbein Snior Lfstyle Chices, Lebanon (G-12636)	B	513 933-5400
Palm Crest East Inc, Elyria (G-10668)	E	440 322-0726
Park Creek Rtirement Cmnty Inc, Cleveland (G-6235)	E	440 842-5100
Parkview Manor Inc, Englewood (G-10714)	D	937 296-1550
Parma Care Center Inc, Cleveland (G-6245)	C	216 661-6800
◆ Perio Inc, Dublin (G-10426)	E	614 791-1207
Personacare of Ohio Inc, Painesville (G-15873)	C	440 357-1311
Pickaway Manor Inc, Circleville (G-4899)	C	740 474-5400
Places Inc, Dayton (G-9810)	D	937 461-4300
Pleasant Lake Nursing Home, Cleveland (G-6289)	B	440 842-2273
Pleasant View Nursing Home, Barberton (G-973)	E	330 848-5028
Protem Homecare LLC, Cleveland (G-6324)	E	216 663-8188
Queen City Hospice LLC, Cincinnati (G-4365)	E	513 510-4406
Rae-Ann Holdings Inc, Westlake (G-19539)	D	440 871-0500
Raeann Inc, Geneva (G-11368)	D	440 466-5733
Renaissance House Inc, Sandusky (G-16787)	D	419 626-1110
RES-Care Inc, Saint Clairsville (G-16655)	E	740 526-0285
RES-Care Inc, West Chester (G-19139)	E	513 858-4550
RES-Care Inc, Flushing (G-11106)	E	740 968-0181
RES-Care Inc, Carrollton (G-2626)	E	330 627-7552
RES-Care Inc, Waverly (G-18975)	E	740 941-1178
RES-Care Inc, Fostoria (G-11138)	E	419 435-6620
RES-Care Inc, Gallipolis (G-11337)	D	740 446-7549
RES-Care Inc, Canton (G-2510)	E	330 453-4144
Rescare, Chesapeake (G-2787)	E	740 867-3051
Rescare Ohio Inc, Williamsburg (G-19635)	E	513 724-1177
Residence of Chardon, Chardon (G-2765)	D	440 286-2277
Residential Concepts Inc, Williamsburg (G-19636)	E	513 724-6067
Rest Haven Nursing Home Inc, Greenville (G-11516)	C	937 548-1138
Ridge Pleasant Valley Inc, Cleveland (G-6395)	C	440 845-0200
Ridgewood At Friendship Vlg, Columbus (G-8628)	E	614 890-8285
Rivers Bend Health Care LLC, South Point (G-17097)	D	740 894-3476
Roman Cthlic Docese Youngstown, Louisville (G-13106)	C	330 875-5562

Employee Codes: A=Over 500 employees, B=251-500
C=101-250, D=51-100, E=25-50

80 HEALTH SERVICES

Rose Mary Johanna Grassell .... C 216 481-4823
  Cleveland (G-6412)
Royal Manor Health Care Inc .... E 216 752-3600
  Cleveland (G-6416)
Saint Johns Villa .... C 330 627-4662
  Carrollton (G-2628)
Salutary Providers Inc .... C 440 964-8446
  Ashtabula (G-762)
Samaritan Care Center & Villa .... D 330 725-4123
  Medina (G-14122)
Sarah Moore Hlth Care Ctr Inc .... D 740 362-9641
  Delaware (G-10125)
Sateri Home Inc .... D 330 758-8106
  Youngstown (G-20367)
Senior Care Inc .... C 330 721-2000
  Medina (G-14124)
Senior Care Inc .... C 419 516-4788
  Lima (G-12875)
Sensi Care 3 .... E 440 323-6310
  Elyria (G-10679)
Singleton Health Care Center .... E 216 231-0076
  Cleveland (G-6483)
Sisters of Little .... C 216 464-1222
  Warrensville Heights (G-18934)
Sisters of Little .... C 513 281-8001
  Cincinnati (G-4532)
Society Handicapped Citz Medin .... E 330 722-1900
  Seville (G-16844)
Sociey For Handicapped Citizen .... C 330 725-7041
  Seville (G-16845)
Spring Meadow Extended Care Ce ..... D 419 866-6124
  Holland (G-12057)
Spring Meadow Extended Care Ce ..... D 419 866-6124
  Mansfield (G-13367)
St Augustine Corporation .... B 216 939-7600
  Lakewood (G-12501)
St Joseph Infant Maternity Hm .... C 513 563-2520
  Cincinnati (G-4572)
St Luke Lutheran Community .... D 330 644-3914
  New Franklin (G-15048)
St Luke Lutheran Community .... D 330 644-3914
  New Franklin (G-15049)
Stein Hospice Services Inc .... D 419 663-3222
  Norwalk (G-15593)
Stratford Commons Inc .... C 440 914-0900
  Solon (G-17056)
Summit Acres Inc .... E 740 732-2364
  Caldwell (G-2089)
Summit Facility Operations LLC .... D 330 633-0555
  Tallmadge (G-17652)
Sunbridge Healthcare LLC .... C 740 342-5161
  New Lexington (G-15064)
Sunrise Manor Convalescent Ctr .... D 513 797-5144
  Amelia (G-583)
Sunset House Inc .... C 419 536-4645
  Toledo (G-18210)
Sunshine Communities .... B 419 865-0251
  Maumee (G-13982)
Supportcare Inc .... C 216 446-2650
  Independence (G-12263)
Swanton Hlth Care Rtrement Ctr .... D 419 825-1145
  Swanton (G-17572)
The Maria-Joseph Center .... B 937 278-2692
  Dayton (G-9926)
The Villa At Lake MGT Co .... D 440 599-1999
  Conneaut (G-9048)
Triad Residential .... E 419 482-0711
  Maumee (G-13988)
Twilight Gardens Healthcare .... E 419 668-2086
  Norwalk (G-15595)
Twin Maples Nursing Home .... E 740 596-5955
  Mc Arthur (G-14018)
Twin Pines Retreat Care Center .... E 330 688-5553
  Stow (G-17398)
Twin Towers .... B 513 853-2000
  Cincinnati (G-4710)
United Cerebral Palsy .... C 216 381-9993
  Cleveland (G-6636)
United Church Homes Inc .... C 937 878-0262
  Fairborn (G-18806)
United Church Homes Inc .... D 740 286-7551
  Jackson (G-12320)
United Church Homes Inc .... C 513 922-1440
  Cincinnati (G-4730)
United Church Homes Inc .... C 937 426-8481
  Beavercreek (G-1261)
United Church Homes Inc .... C 419 294-4973
  Upper Sandusky (G-18568)
University Hospitals Health .... A 440 285-4040
  Chardon (G-2775)

University Manor Hlth Care Ctr .... C 216 721-1400
  Cleveland (G-6665)
Vancare Inc .... C 937 898-4202
  Vandalia (G-18706)
Vienna Enterprises Inc .... E 937 568-4524
  South Vienna (G-17101)
Vista Centre .... D 330 424-5852
  Lisbon (G-12942)
Voca of Ohio .... E 419 435-5836
  Fostoria (G-11142)
Voiers Enterprises Inc .... E 740 259-2838
  Mc Dermott (G-14023)
Volunters Amer Care Facilities .... C 419 225-9040
  Lima (G-12911)
Walnut Hills Inc .... C 330 852-2457
  Walnut Creek (G-18786)
Warren County Board Devlpmntal ..... E 513 925-1813
  Lebanon (G-12658)
Washington Manor Inc .... C 937 433-3441
  Dayton (G-9984)
Weber Health Care Center Inc .... C 440 647-2088
  Wellington (G-18996)
Wedgewood Estates .... E 419 756-7400
  Westerville (G-19358)
Wellington Place LLC .... D 440 734-9933
  North Olmsted (G-15450)
Wesley Ridge Inc .... C 614 759-0023
  Reynoldsburg (G-16489)
West Liberty Care Center Inc .... C 937 465-5065
  West Liberty (G-19264)
West Park Retirement Community ..... C 513 451-8900
  Cincinnati (G-4836)
Western Rsrve Msonic Cmnty Inc ..... C 330 721-3000
  Medina (G-14138)
Wexner Heritage Village .... B 614 231-4900
  Columbus (G-8984)
Willglo Services Inc .... E 614 443-3020
  Columbus (G-8994)
Willow Brook Chrstn Cmmunities ...... D 740 369-0048
  Delaware (G-10135)
Windsor House Inc .... C 330 549-9259
  Columbiana (G-6867)
Windsor Medical Center Inc .... D 330 499-8300
  Canton (G-2587)
Woodside Village Care Center .... D 419 947-2015
  Mount Gilead (G-14865)
Zandex Inc .... E 740 695-3281
  Saint Clairsville (G-16662)
Zandex Inc .... E 740 454-1400
  Zanesville (G-20546)
Zandex Inc .... C 740 454-9769
  Zanesville (G-20548)
Zandex Inc .... C 740 695-7233
  Saint Clairsville (G-16663)
Zandex Inc .... D 740 967-1111
  Johnstown (G-12344)
Zandex Inc .... D 740 454-6823
  Zanesville (G-20549)
Zandex Inc .... C 740 872-0809
  New Concord (G-15040)
Zandex Health Care Corporation .... C 740 452-4636
  Zanesville (G-20550)
Zandex Health Care Corporation .... C 740 454-9769
  Zanesville (G-20551)
Zandex Health Care Corporation .... C 740 695-7233
  Saint Clairsville (G-16664)
Zandex Health Care Corporation .... E 740 454-1400
  Zanesville (G-20552)
Zandex Health Care Corporation .... D 740 454-1400
  Johnstown (G-12345)
Zandex Health Care Corporation .... C 740 454-1400
  New Concord (G-15041)
Zandex Health Care Corporation .... C 740 454-9747
  Zanesville (G-20553)
Zusman Community Hospice .... E 614 559-0350
  Columbus (G-9028)

8059 Nursing & Personal Care Facilities, NEC

Ability Matters LLC .... E 614 214-9652
  Hilliard (G-11875)
Access Home Care LLC .... E 937 224-9991
  Dayton (G-9304)
Accurate Healthcare Inc .... E 513 208-6988
  West Chester (G-19189)
Age Line Inc .... E 216 941-9990
  Cleveland (G-4968)
Alpha Nursing Homes Inc .... D 740 622-2074
  Coshocton (G-9086)
American Retirement Corp .... D 216 291-6140
  Cleveland (G-5021)

Americas Dream Homes LLC .... E 614 252-7834
  Columbus (G-7010)
Angel Hearts Home Health Inc .... C 937 263-6194
  Moraine (G-14750)
Antioch Cnnction Canton MI LLC ...... E 614 531-9285
  Pickerington (G-16085)
Antioch Salem Fields Frederick .... E 614 531-9285
  Pickerington (G-16086)
Apostolic Christian Home Inc .... D 330 927-1010
  Rittman (G-16550)
Arbors West LLC .... D 614 879-7661
  West Jefferson (G-19247)
ASAP Homecare Inc .... D 330 674-3306
  Millersburg (G-14585)
ASAP Homecare Inc .... D 330 491-0700
  Canton (G-2246)
Bel Air Care Center .... D 330 821-3939
  Alliance (G-527)
Berea Lk Twers Rtirement Cmnty ..... E 440 243-9050
  Berea (G-1449)
Birchaven Village .... C 419 424-3000
  Findlay (G-10995)
Blue Ash Healthcare Group Inc .... E 513 793-3362
  Cincinnati (G-3118)
Bmnh Inc .... C 937 845-3561
  New Carlisle (G-15020)
Boyds Kinsman Home Inc .... E 330 876-5581
  Kinsman (G-12453)
Brethren Care Village LLC .... C 419 289-1585
  Ashland (G-667)
Brewster Parke Inc .... D 330 767-4179
  Brewster (G-1854)
Briarwood Ltd. .... D 330 688-1828
  Stow (G-17354)
Bristol Village Homes .... E 740 947-2118
  Waverly (G-18966)
Broken Arrow Inc .... E 419 562-3480
  Bucyrus (G-2024)
Brookdale Deer Park .... E 513 745-7600
  Cincinnati (G-3137)
Brookdale Lving Cmmunities Inc ...... D 614 734-1000
  Columbus (G-7152)
Brookdale Lving Cmmunities Inc ...... E 937 399-1216
  Springfield (G-17153)
Brookdale Senior Living Commun ..... E 330 829-0180
  Alliance (G-528)
Brookdale Senior Living Commun ..... E 937 203-8443
  Beavercreek (G-1231)
Brookdale Senior Living Commun ..... E 937 548-6800
  Greenville (G-11490)
Brookdale Senior Living Inc .... E 419 756-5599
  Mansfield (G-13270)
Brookdale Senior Living Inc .... D 330 666-7011
  Akron (G-114)
Brookdale Senior Living Inc .... E 440 892-4200
  Westlake (G-19467)
Brookdale Snior Lving Cmmnties ..... E 740 366-0005
  Newark (G-15149)
Brookdale Snior Lving Cmmnties ..... E 937 832-8500
  Englewood (G-10698)
Brookdale Snior Lving Cmmnties ..... E 419 354-5300
  Bowling Green (G-1770)
Brookdale Snior Lving Cmmnties ..... E 740 681-9903
  Lancaster (G-12511)
Brookdale Snior Lving Cmmnties ..... E 419 423-4440
  Findlay (G-11009)
Brookdale Snior Lving Cmmnties ..... E 330 249-1071
  Austintown (G-868)
Brookdale Snior Lving Cmmnties ..... E 419 756-5599
  Mansfield (G-13271)
Brookdale Snior Lving Cmmnties ..... E 937 773-0500
  Piqua (G-16137)
Brookdale Snior Lving Cmmnties ..... E 330 793-0085
  Youngstown (G-20128)
Brookside Extended Care Center ..... C 513 398-1020
  Mason (G-13669)
Brookview Healthcare Ctr .... D 419 784-1014
  Defiance (G-10020)
Bryant Health Center Inc .... C 740 532-6188
  Ironton (G-12283)
Buckeye Community Services Inc .... C 740 941-1639
  Waverly (G-18967)
Buckeye Home Health Care .... E 937 291-3780
  Dayton (G-9369)
Burchwood Care Center .... E 513 868-3300
  Fairfield Township (G-10925)
Capital Health Services Inc .... E 937 278-0404
  Dayton (G-9378)
Capital Senior Living .... E 440 356-5444
  Rocky River (G-16572)

Careworks of Ohio Inc ....B.... 614 792-1085
Dublin ***(G-10280)***

Carriage Court Company Inc ....E.... 740 654-4422
Lancaster ***(G-12514)***

Carroll Golden Age Retreat ....E.... 330 627-4665
Carrollton ***(G-2612)***

Center Ridge Nursing Home Inc ....C.... 440 327-1295
North Ridgeville ***(G-15458)***

Center Street Cmnty Clinic Inc ....E.... 740 751-6380
Marion ***(G-13529)***

Chcc Home Health Care ....E.... 330 759-4069
Austintown ***(G-869)***

Columbus Alzheimers Care Ctr ....C.... 614 459-7050
Columbus ***(G-7327)***

Columbus Ctr For Humn Svcs Inc ....C.... 614 641-2904
Columbus ***(G-7344)***

Columbus Ctr For Humn Svcs Inc ....E.... 614 245-8180
New Albany ***(G-14981)***

Communicare Health Svcs Inc ....D.... 740 264-1155
Steubenville ***(G-17313)***

Community Concepts Inc ....C.... 513 398-8181
Mason ***(G-13687)***

Community Mercy Foundation ....C.... 937 390-9000
Springfield ***(G-17172)***

Concord Care Center of Toledo ....D.... 419 385-6616
Toledo ***(G-17829)***

Concord Hlth Rhabilitation Ctr ....E.... 740 574-8441
Wheelersburg ***(G-19575)***

Consulate Management Co LLC ....D.... 740 259-2351
Lucasville ***(G-13176)***

Consumer Support Services Inc ....B.... 740 788-8257
Newark ***(G-15158)***

Consumer Support Services Inc ....D.... 330 764-4785
Medina ***(G-14050)***

Country Acres of Wayne County ....E.... 330 698-2031
Wooster ***(G-19852)***

Country Club Center Homes Inc ....D.... 330 343-6351
Dover ***(G-10182)***

Country Club Retirement Center ....D.... 440 992-0022
Ashtabula ***(G-738)***

Country Club Retirement Center ....C.... 740 671-9330
Bellaire ***(G-1365)***

Country Meadow Care Center LLC ....E.... 419 886-3922
Bellville ***(G-1425)***

Countryview Assistant Living ....E.... 740 489-5351
Lore City ***(G-13086)***

County of Auglaize ....C.... 419 738-3816
Wapakoneta ***(G-18793)***

County of Henry ....E.... 419 592-8075
Napoleon ***(G-14937)***

County of Richland ....B.... 419 774-4200
Mansfield ***(G-13284)***

County of Shelby ....C.... 937 492-6900
Sidney ***(G-16926)***

County of Wayne ....D.... 330 262-1786
Wooster ***(G-19854)***

County of Wood ....B.... 419 686-6951
Portage ***(G-16261)***

County of Wyandot ....D.... 419 294-1714
Upper Sandusky ***(G-18558)***

Crystal Care Centers Inc ....D.... 419 747-2666
Mansfield ***(G-13287)***

Crystalwood Inc ....D.... 513 605-1000
Cincinnati ***(G-3443)***

Csi Managed Care Inc ....D.... 440 717-1700
Brecksville ***(G-1822)***

Deaconess Long Term Care of MI ....A.... 513 487-3600
Cincinnati ***(G-3474)***

Dobbins Nursing Home Inc ....C.... 513 553-4139
New Richmond ***(G-15126)***

Dublin Geriatric Care Co LP ....E.... 614 761-1188
Dublin ***(G-10328)***

East Carroll Nursing Home ....D.... 330 627-6900
Carrollton ***(G-2618)***

East Galbraith Health Care Ctr ....B.... 513 984-5220
Cincinnati ***(G-3531)***

Echoing Hills Village Inc ....E.... 937 237-7881
Dayton ***(G-9519)***

Echoing Hills Village Inc ....D.... 440 986-3085
South Amherst ***(G-17073)***

Elizabeth Scott Inc ....C.... 419 865-3002
Maumee ***(G-13909)***

Elms Retirement Village Inc ....D.... 440 647-2414
Wellington ***(G-18991)***

Encore Healthcare LLC ....C.... 330 769-2015
Seville ***(G-16840)***

Evangelical Lutheran ....D.... 419 365-5115
Arlington ***(G-647)***

Faithful Companions Inc ....E.... 440 255-4357
Mentor ***(G-14174)***

First Choice Medical Staffing ....C.... 216 521-2222
Cleveland ***(G-5592)***

First Community Village ....B.... 614 324-4455
Columbus ***(G-7664)***

Franciscan At St Leonard ....B.... 937 433-0480
Dayton ***(G-9560)***

Friendship Vlg of Dublin Ohio ....C.... 614 764-1600
Dublin ***(G-10351)***

Gardens Western Reserve Inc ....D.... 330 342-9100
Streetsboro ***(G-17412)***

Gaslite Villa Convalescent Ctr ....D.... 330 494-4500
Canal Fulton ***(G-2143)***

Gem City Home Care LLC ....E.... 614 588-0228
Columbus ***(G-7733)***

Gentiva Health Services Inc ....D.... 419 887-6700
Maumee ***(G-13920)***

Gillette Associates LP ....D.... 330 372-1960
Warren ***(G-18859)***

Golden Living LLC ....D.... 419 599-4070
Napoleon ***(G-14941)***

Golden Living LLC ....D.... 419 227-2154
Lima ***(G-12784)***

Golden Living LLC ....D.... 419 394-3308
Saint Marys ***(G-16674)***

Golden Living LLC ....C.... 440 247-4200
Chagrin Falls ***(G-2698)***

Golden Living LLC ....C.... 614 861-6666
Columbus ***(G-7759)***

Golden Living LLC ....C.... 440 256-8100
Willoughby ***(G-19667)***

Golden Living LLC ....C.... 330 297-5781
Ravenna ***(G-16386)***

Golden Living LLC ....C.... 330 762-6486
Akron ***(G-240)***

Golden Living LLC ....D.... 330 335-1558
Wadsworth ***(G-18753)***

Golden Living LLC ....D.... 330 725-3393
Medina ***(G-14071)***

Governors Pointe LLC ....E.... 440 205-1570
Mentor ***(G-14182)***

Guardian Elder Care Columbus ....D.... 614 868-9306
Columbus ***(G-7783)***

Guernsey Health Enterprises ....A.... 740 439-3561
Cambridge ***(G-2118)***

H C F Inc ....C.... 740 289-2528
Piketon ***(G-16116)***

H C R Corp ....D.... 419 472-0076
Toledo ***(G-17929)***

Hamlet Village In Chagrin FLS ....D.... 440 247-4200
Chagrin Falls ***(G-2699)***

Hampton Woods Nursing Ctr Inc ....E.... 330 707-1400
Poland ***(G-16224)***

Harborside Healthcare NW Ohio ....C.... 419 636-5071
Bryan ***(G-2007)***

Hardin County Home ....D.... 419 673-0961
Kenton ***(G-12417)***

Harrison Pavilion ....E.... 513 662-5800
Cincinnati ***(G-3738)***

Hcf Management Inc ....D.... 419 435-8112
Fostoria ***(G-11131)***

Hcf of Findlay Inc ....D.... 419 999-2010
Findlay ***(G-11044)***

Hcf of Fox Run Inc ....D.... 419 424-0832
Findlay ***(G-11045)***

Hcf of Washington Inc ....E.... 419 999-2010
Wshngtn CT Hs ***(G-20026)***

Health Care Opportunities Inc ....E.... 513 932-0300
Lebanon ***(G-12609)***

Heartland Home Care LLC ....D.... 419 252-5500
Toledo ***(G-17948)***

Heath Nursing Care Center ....C.... 740 522-1171
Newark ***(G-15173)***

Heinzerling Foundation ....C.... 614 272-8888
Columbus ***(G-7821)***

Heinzerling Foundation ....A.... 614 272-2000
Columbus ***(G-7822)***

Helen Purcell Home ....E.... 740 453-1745
Zanesville ***(G-20487)***

Hickory Health Care Inc ....D.... 330 762-6486
Akron ***(G-263)***

Home Health Connection Inc ....E.... 614 839-4545
Worthington ***(G-19964)***

Hospice of Darke County Inc ....E.... 937 548-2999
Greenville ***(G-11510)***

Hospice of North Central Ohio ....E.... 419 281-7107
Ashland ***(G-682)***

Hospice of The Western Reserve ....D.... 440 357-5833
Mentor ***(G-14193)***

Hospice of The Western Reserve ....C.... 216 383-2222
Cleveland ***(G-5779)***

Hospice of The Western Reserve ....C.... 216 227-9048
Cleveland ***(G-5781)***

Hospice Tuscarawas County Inc ....D.... 330 343-7605
New Philadelphia ***(G-15101)***

Inn At Hillenvale Ltd ....D.... 740 392-8245
Mount Vernon ***(G-14900)***

J E F Inc ....D.... 513 921-4130
Cincinnati ***(G-3851)***

J W J Investments Inc ....C.... 419 643-3161
Bluffton ***(G-1732)***

Jacobs Dwelling Nursing Home ....E.... 740 824-3635
Coshocton ***(G-9109)***

Jennings Ctr For Older Adults ....B.... 216 581-2900
Cleveland ***(G-5858)***

Judson ....D.... 216 791-2004
Cleveland ***(G-5876)***

Judson Palmer Home Corp ....E.... 419 422-9656
Findlay ***(G-11054)***

Just In Time Care Inc ....E.... 614 985-3555
Columbus ***(G-7961)***

Karrington Operating Co Inc ....D.... 614 324-5951
Columbus ***(G-7967)***

Kingston Healthcare Company ....E.... 419 247-2880
Toledo ***(G-17995)***

Kingston Healthcare Company ....C.... 440 967-1800
Vermilion ***(G-18712)***

Koinonia Homes Inc ....D.... 216 351-5361
Cleveland ***(G-5907)***

Lancia Nursing Home Inc ....E.... 740 264-7101
Steubenville ***(G-17325)***

Laurel Health Care Company ....D.... 740 264-5042
Steubenville ***(G-17326)***

Laurel Health Care Company ....C.... 614 885-0408
Worthington ***(G-19969)***

Lcd Home Health Agency LLC ....E.... 513 497-0441
Hamilton ***(G-11753)***

Levering Management Inc ....D.... 740 369-6400
Delaware ***(G-10115)***

Levering Management Inc ....E.... 419 768-2401
Chesterville ***(G-2806)***

Liberty Vlg Senior Communities ....E.... 614 889-5002
Dublin ***(G-10387)***

Lima Cnvlscent HM Fndation Inc ....D.... 419 227-5450
Lima ***(G-12818)***

Lincoln Park Associates II LP ....C.... 937 297-4300
Dayton ***(G-9683)***

Love N Comfort Home Care ....E.... 740 450-7658
Zanesville ***(G-20496)***

Lutheran Memorial Home Inc ....D.... 419 502-5700
Toledo ***(G-18021)***

Lutheran Village At Wolf Creek ....C.... 419 861-2233
Holland ***(G-12033)***

Mahoning Vly Infusioncare Inc ....C.... 330 759-9487
Youngstown ***(G-20266)***

Maplewood At Bath Creek LLC ....D.... 234 208-9872
Cuyahoga Falls ***(G-9207)***

Marion Manor ....D.... 740 387-9545
Marion ***(G-13562)***

Marymount Health Care Systems ....E.... 216 332-1100
Cleveland ***(G-5990)***

Mayflower Nursing Home Inc ....C.... 330 492-7131
Canton ***(G-2452)***

McV Health Care Facilities ....C.... 513 398-1486
Mason ***(G-13738)***

Medina Medical Investors Ltd ....C.... 330 483-3131
Medina ***(G-14104)***

Mennonite Memorial Home Inc ....E.... 419 358-7654
Bluffton ***(G-1735)***

Mennonite Memorial Home Inc ....C.... 419 358-1015
Bluffton ***(G-1734)***

Mercer Residential Services ....E.... 419 586-4709
Celina ***(G-2656)***

Mercy Health West Park ....C.... 513 451-8900
Cincinnati ***(G-4076)***

Miami Valley Urgent Care ....E.... 937 252-2000
Dayton ***(G-9739)***

Mikouis Enterprise Inc ....D.... 330 424-1418
Lisbon ***(G-12940)***

Mill Run Care Center LLC ....D.... 614 527-3000
Hilliard ***(G-11935)***

Minamyer Residential Mr/Dd Svc ....E.... 614 802-0190
Columbus ***(G-8177)***

Minford Retirement Center LLC ....E.... 740 820-2821
Minford ***(G-14652)***

Mkjb Inc ....C.... 513 851-8400
Cincinnati ***(G-4108)***

Mohun Health Care Center ....E.... 614 416-6132
Columbus ***(G-8182)***

Msab Park Creek LLC ....E.... 440 842-5100
Rocky River ***(G-16586)***

Employee Codes: A=Over 500 employees, B=251-500
C=101-250, D=51-100, E=25-50
2018 Harris Ohio
Services Directory
1041

Mt Healthy Christian Home Inc ....C 513 931-5000
Cincinnati *(G-4128)*
National Church Residences ....C 614 451-2151
Columbus *(G-8215)*
Nentwick Convalescent Home ....C 330 385-5001
East Liverpool *(G-10527)*
New Concord Health Center ....C 740 826-4135
New Concord *(G-15036)*
North Park Retirement Cmnty ....E 216 267-0555
Cleveland *(G-6142)*
Norwood Health Care Center LLC ....D 513 351-0153
Cincinnati *(G-4186)*
Nursing Care MGT Amer Inc ....D 740 927-9888
Pataskala *(G-15924)*
Nursing Care MGT Amer Inc ....D 513 793-5092
Cincinnati *(G-4194)*
Nursing Resources Corp ....C 419 333-3000
Maumee *(G-13951)*
Oakhill Manor Care Center ....C 330 875-5060
Louisville *(G-13104)*
Oakwood Health Care Svcs Inc ....D 440 439-7976
Cleveland *(G-6175)*
Ohio Hills Health Services ....D 740 425-5165
Barnesville *(G-990)*
Ohio Presbt Retirement Svcs ....B 937 498-2391
Sidney *(G-16945)*
Ohio Presbt Retirement Svcs ....C 937 415-5666
Dayton *(G-9789)*
Ohio Valley Manor Inc ....C 937 392-4318
Ripley *(G-16548)*
Olmsted Manor Retirement Prpts ....E 440 250-4080
Westlake *(G-19529)*
On-Call Nursing Inc ....D 216 577-8890
Lakewood *(G-12493)*
Orchard Villa Inc ....C 419 697-4100
Oregon *(G-15744)*
Otterbein Lebanon ....E 513 933-5465
Lebanon *(G-12635)*
Otterbein Snior Lfstyle Chices ....C 513 260-7690
Middletown *(G-14483)*
Overlook House ....E 216 795-3550
Cleveland *(G-6221)*
Park Haven Inc ....E 440 992-9441
Ashtabula *(G-759)*
Partners of City View LLC ....C 216 361-1414
Cleveland *(G-6247)*
Prime Home Care LLC ....E 419 535-1414
Toledo *(G-18136)*
Pristine Senior Living of ....D 419 935-0148
Willard *(G-19625)*
Provider Services Inc ....D 614 888-2021
Columbus *(G-8575)*
Rae-Ann Enterprises Inc ....D 440 249-5092
Cleveland *(G-6346)*
Rae-Ann Holdings Inc ....D 440 871-0500
Westlake *(G-19539)*
Rae-Ann Holdings Inc ....D 440 871-5181
Cleveland *(G-6347)*
Red Carpet Health Care Center ....C 740 439-4401
Cambridge *(G-2127)*
Regency Park ....D 330 682-2273
Orrville *(G-15785)*
Regency Park Nursing & Rehab ....D 330 682-2273
Orrville *(G-15786)*
Residence At Kensington Place ....C 513 863-4218
Hamilton *(G-11769)*
Rest Haven Nursing Home Inc ....C 937 548-1138
Greenville *(G-11516)*
Rittenhouse ....E 513 423-2322
Middletown *(G-14453)*
RMS of Ohio Inc ....E 513 841-0990
Cincinnati *(G-4431)*
Roselawn Health Services Corp ....E 330 823-0618
Alliance *(G-558)*
Royalton Senior Living Inc ....E 440 582-4111
North Royalton *(G-15501)*
Salutary Providers Inc ....C 440 964-8446
Ashtabula *(G-762)*
Samaritan Care Center & Villa ....D 330 725-4123
Medina *(G-14122)*
Sarah Moore Hlth Care Ctr Inc ....D 740 362-9641
Delaware *(G-10125)*
Schoenbrunn Healthcare ....D 330 339-3595
New Philadelphia *(G-15114)*
Senior Care Inc ....E 937 291-3211
Miamisburg *(G-14347)*
Senior Lifestyle Corporation ....D 513 777-4457
West Chester *(G-19150)*
Serenity Center Inc ....C 614 891-1111
Columbus *(G-8714)*
Shiloh Group ....C 937 833-2219
Brookville *(G-1966)*
Society of The Transfiguration ....E 513 771-7462
Cincinnati *(G-4548)*
Steubenville Country CLB Manor ....D 740 266-6118
Steubenville *(G-17335)*
Stewart Lodge Inc ....D 440 417-1898
Madison *(G-13236)*
Stratford Commons Inc ....C 440 914-0900
Solon *(G-17056)*
Summit At Park Hills LLC ....E 317 462-8048
Fairborn *(G-10805)*
Sumner On Ridgewood ....E 330 664-1360
Copley *(G-9066)*
Sunrise Senior Living Inc ....D 614 457-3500
Upper Arlington *(G-18556)*
Sunrise Senior Living Inc ....E 614 846-6500
Worthington *(G-20001)*
Susan A Smith Crystal Care ....E 419 747-2666
Butler *(G-2068)*
The Villa At Lake MGT Co ....D 440 599-1999
Conneaut *(G-9048)*
Traditions At Mill Run ....D 614 771-0100
Hilliard *(G-11960)*
Traditions of Chillicothe ....E 740 773-8107
Chillicothe *(G-2890)*
United Cerebral Palsy ....D 216 381-9993
Cleveland *(G-6636)*
United Church Homes Inc ....C 419 294-4973
Upper Sandusky *(G-18568)*
United Rest Homes Inc ....E 440 354-2131
Painesville *(G-15884)*
University Hospitals Health ....A 440 285-4040
Chardon *(G-2775)*
Uvmc Nursing Care Inc ....C 937 473-2075
Covington *(G-9140)*
Valley View Alzhimers Care Ctr ....D 740 998-2948
Frankfort *(G-11146)*
Viaquest Home Health LLC ....E 800 645-3267
Dublin *(G-10483)*
Victorian Oaks LLC ....E 740 432-2262
Cambridge *(G-2133)*
Vienna Enterprises Inc ....E 937 568-4524
South Vienna *(G-17101)*
Wedgewood Estates ....E 419 756-7400
Westerville *(G-19358)*
Wesley Ridge Inc ....C 614 759-0023
Reynoldsburg *(G-16489)*
Western Rsrve Msonic Cmnty Inc ....C 330 721-3000
Medina *(G-14138)*
Whetstone Care Center LLC ....C 614 457-1100
Columbus *(G-8985)*
Whetstone Care Center LLC ....C 740 474-6036
Circleville *(G-4908)*
Whispering Hills Care Center ....E 740 392-3982
Mount Vernon *(G-14925)*
Williamsburg of Cincinnati Mgt ....C 513 948-2308
Cincinnati *(G-4852)*
Windsor House Inc ....C 330 759-7858
Youngstown *(G-20416)*
Windsor Medical Center Inc ....D 330 499-8300
Canton *(G-2587)*
Windsorwood Place Inc ....E 740 623-4600
Coshocton *(G-9121)*
Yorkland Health Care Inc ....D 614 751-2525
Columbus *(G-9016)*
Youngstown Area Jwish Fdration ....D 330 746-1076
Youngstown *(G-20426)*
Zandex Health Care Corporation ....E 740 454-1400
Zanesville *(G-20552)*
Zandex Health Care Corporation ....D 740 454-1400
Johnstown *(G-12345)*
Zandex Health Care Corporation ....C 740 695-7233
Saint Clairsville *(G-16664)*
Zandex Health Care Corporation ....C 740 454-9747
Zanesville *(G-20553)*

8062 General Medical & Surgical Hospitals

Acute Care Specialty Hospital ....A 330 363-4860
Canton *(G-2224)*
Adams County Regional Med Ctr ....C 937 386-3001
Seaman *(G-16818)*
Adams County Regional Med Ctr ....D 937 386-3400
Seaman *(G-16819)*
Adena Health System ....E 740 779-7201
Chillicothe *(G-2808)*
Adena Health System ....A 740 779-7360
Chillicothe *(G-2809)*
Adena Health System ....C 740 779-7500
Wshngtn CT Hs *(G-20013)*
Adena Health System ....C 740 420-3000
Circleville *(G-4877)*
Adena Health System ....C 937 981-9444
Greenfield *(G-11482)*
Adena Health System ....C 740 779-8995
Chillicothe *(G-2810)*
Adena Health System ....E 740 779-4801
Chillicothe *(G-2811)*
Ado Health Services Inc ....D 330 629-2888
Youngstown *(G-20097)*
Affiliates In Oral & Maxlofcl ....E 513 829-8080
Fairfield *(G-10817)*
Akron City Hospital Inc ....A 330 253-5046
Akron *(G-32)*
Akron General Medical Center ....C 330 344-1980
Akron *(G-44)*
Akron General Medical Center ....C 330 344-1444
Akron *(G-45)*
Akron General Medical Center ....C 330 665-8000
Akron *(G-46)*
▲ **Allen Medical Center** ....C 440 986-4000
Oberlin *(G-15638)*
Allianalce Hospitalist Group ....E 330 823-5626
Alliance *(G-523)*
Alliance Citizens Health Assn ....A 330 596-6000
Alliance *(G-524)*
Ashtabula County Medical Ctr ....A 440 997-2262
Ashtabula *(G-722)*
Ashtabula County Medical Ctr ....C 440 997-6960
Ashtabula *(G-723)*
Atrium Medical Center ....E 513 420-5013
Middletown *(G-14414)*
Aultman Hospital ....A 330 452-9911
Canton *(G-2253)*
Aultman Hospital ....B 330 452-9911
Canton *(G-2254)*
Aultman Hospital ....A 330 363-6262
Canton *(G-2255)*
Aultman Hospital ....E 330 452-2273
Canton *(G-2256)*
Aultman North Inc ....E 330 305-6999
Canton *(G-2258)*
Auxiliary Bd Fairview Gen Hosp ....A 216 476-7000
Cleveland *(G-5084)*
Barnesville Hospital Assn Inc ....B 740 425-3941
Barnesville *(G-988)*
Bay Park Community Hospital ....D 419 690-7900
Oregon *(G-15725)*
Beavercreek Medical Center ....D 937 558-3000
Beavercreek *(G-1152)*
Beavercreek Medical Center ....D 937 558-3000
Beavercreek *(G-1153)*
Beckett Springs LLC ....E 513 942-9500
West Chester *(G-19025)*
Bellevue Hospital ....B 419 483-4040
Bellevue *(G-1404)*
Bellevue Hospital ....B 419 547-0074
Bellevue *(G-1405)*
Belmont Bhc Pines Hospital Inc ....C 330 759-2700
Youngstown *(G-20113)*
Belmont Community Hospital ....B 740 671-1200
Bellaire *(G-1362)*
Bethesda Hospital Inc ....E 513 894-8888
Fairfield Township *(G-10924)*
Bethesda Hospital Inc ....A 513 569-6100
Cincinnati *(G-3105)*
Bethesda Hospital Inc ....A 513 745-1111
Cincinnati *(G-3106)*
Bethesda Hospital Inc ....E 513 563-1505
Cincinnati *(G-3107)*
Bethesda Hospital Association ....A 740 454-4000
Zanesville *(G-20447)*
▲ **Blanchard Vly Rgional Hlth Ctr** ....A 419 423-4500
Findlay *(G-11004)*
Blue Chp Srgcl Ctr Ptns LLC ....D 513 561-8900
Cincinnati *(G-3121)*
Bon Secours Health System ....E 740 966-3116
Johnstown *(G-12338)*
Bridgeshome Health Care ....E 330 764-1000
Medina *(G-14040)*
Brown Memorial Hospital ....B 440 593-1131
Conneaut *(G-9040)*
Bucyrus Community Hospital Inc ....C 419 562-4677
Bucyrus *(G-2026)*
Bucyrus Community Hospital LLC ....D 419 562-4677
Bucyrus *(G-2027)*
Caep-Dunlap LLC ....E 330 456-2695
Canton *(G-2279)*
Center For Health Affairs ....D 800 362-2628
Cleveland *(G-5208)*

SIC SECTION — 80 HEALTH SERVICES

Center For Spinal Disorders ..... E 419 383-4878
  Toledo (G-17797)
Change Healthcare Tech Enabled ..... D 614 566-5861
  Columbus (G-7252)
Charles Mercy Hlth-St Hospita ..... D 419 696-7200
  Oregon (G-15728)
Chester West Medical Center ..... A 513 298-3000
  West Chester (G-19037)
Childrens Hosp Med Ctr Akron ..... A 330 308-5432
  New Philadelphia (G-15085)
Childrens Hospital Medical Ctr ..... A 513 803-9600
  Liberty Township (G-12719)
Childrens Hospital Medical Ctr ..... A 513 636-8778
  Cincinnati (G-3255)
Christ Hospital ..... E 513 564-4000
  Cincinnati (G-3260)
Christ Hospital ..... C 513 561-7809
  Cincinnati (G-3261)
Christ Hospital ..... B 513 688-1111
  Cincinnati (G-3262)
Christ Hospital ..... B 513 272-3448
  Cincinnati (G-3264)
Christ Hospital ..... A 513 585-2000
  Cincinnati (G-3266)
Christ Hospital Spine Surgery ..... E 513 619-5899
  Cincinnati (G-3270)
City Hospital Association ..... A 330 385-7200
  East Liverpool (G-10517)
City of Wooster ..... A 330 263-8100
  Wooster (G-19846)
▲ Cleveland Clinic Foundation ..... A 216 636-8335
  Cleveland (G-5296)
Cleveland Clinic Foundation ..... A 440 282-6669
  Lorain (G-13025)
Cleveland Clinic Foundation ..... A 800 223-2273
  Cleveland (G-5300)
Cleveland Clinic Foundation ..... A 216 444-5755
  Cleveland (G-5301)
Cleveland Clinic Foundation ..... A 440 327-1050
  North Ridgeville (G-15461)
Cleveland Clinic Foundation ..... A 216 448-0116
  Beachwood (G-1065)
Cleveland Clinic Foundation ..... A 440 986-4000
  Broadview Heights (G-1874)
Cleveland Clinic Foundation ..... D 216 444-5757
  Cleveland (G-5305)
Cleveland Clinic Foundation ..... A 216 444-2200
  Cleveland (G-5306)
Cleveland Clinic Foundation ..... E 330 287-4930
  Wooster (G-19848)
Cleveland Clinic Foundation ..... D 216 444-2820
  Cleveland (G-5297)
Cleveland Clinic Foundation ..... D 440 988-5651
  Lorain (G-13026)
Cleveland Clinic Health System ..... E 440 449-4500
  Cleveland (G-5307)
Cleveland Clinic Health System ..... E 216 692-7555
  Cleveland (G-5308)
Cleveland Clinic Lerner Colleg ..... D 216 445-3853
  Cleveland (G-5309)
Clevelnd Clnc Hlth Systm East ..... E 330 287-4830
  Wooster (G-19850)
Clevelnd Clnc Hlth Systm East ..... D 330 468-0190
  Northfield (G-15512)
Clevelnd Clnc Hlth Systm East ..... E 216 761-3300
  Cleveland (G-5358)
Clinical Research Center ..... D 513 636-4412
  Cincinnati (G-3366)
Clinton Memorial Hospital ..... A 937 382-6611
  Wilmington (G-19753)
Columbia-Csa/Hs Greater Canton ..... A 330 489-1000
  Canton (G-2315)
Community Health Ptnrs Reg Fou ..... A 440 960-4000
  Lorain (G-13030)
Community Hlth Ptnr Reg Hlth S ..... A 440 960-4000
  Lorain (G-13031)
Community Hospital of Bedford ..... B 440 735-3900
  Bedford (G-1301)
Community Hospital Springfield ..... A 937 325-0531
  Springfield (G-17171)
Community Hsptals Wllness Ctrs ..... D 419 485-3154
  Montpelier (G-14741)
Community Hsptals Wllness Ctrs ..... D 419 445-2015
  Archbold (G-635)
Community Hsptals Wllness Ctrs ..... C 419 636-1131
  Bryan (G-2004)
Community Memorial Hospital ..... C 419 542-6692
  Hicksville (G-11485)
Community Mercy Hlth Partners ..... E 937 523-6670
  Springfield (G-17175)

Copc Hospitals ..... E 614 268-8164
  Columbus (G-7438)
County of Holmes ..... C 330 674-1015
  Millersburg (G-14600)
Dayton Osteopathic Hospital ..... A 937 762-1629
  Dayton (G-9484)
Deaconess Hospital of Cincinna ..... D 513 559-2100
  Cincinnati (G-3472)
Defiance Hospital Inc ..... B 419 782-6955
  Defiance (G-10027)
Delphos Ambulatory Care Center ..... E 419 692-2662
  Delphos (G-10141)
▲ Dhsc LLC ..... D 330 832-8761
  Massillon (G-13800)
Doctors Hospital Cleveland Inc ..... C 740 753-7300
  Nelsonville (G-14961)
Doctors Ohiohealth Corporation ..... A 614 544-5424
  Columbus (G-7537)
Elmwood of Green Springs Ltd ..... D 419 639-2626
  Green Springs (G-11476)
Emh Regional Medical Center ..... D 440 988-6800
  Avon (G-892)
Encompass Health Corporation ..... E 205 970-4869
  Springfield (G-17194)
Euclid Hospital ..... D 216 531-9000
  Euclid (G-10753)
Fairfield Medical Center ..... A 740 687-8000
  Lancaster (G-12537)
Fairview Hospital ..... E 216 476-7000
  Cleveland (G-5568)
Fairview Hospital ..... D 440 871-1063
  Westlake (G-19484)
Fayette County Memorial Hosp ..... C 740 335-1210
  Wshngtn CT Hs (G-20022)
Firelands Regional Health Sys ..... A 419 557-7400
  Sandusky (G-16757)
Firelands Regional Health Sys ..... E 419 332-5524
  Fremont (G-11197)
▲ Fisher-Titus Medical Center ..... A 419 668-8101
  Norwalk (G-15575)
Flower Hospital ..... A 419 824-1444
  Sylvania (G-17588)
Fort Hamilton Hospital ..... D 513 867-2000
  Hamilton (G-11728)
Fostoria Hospital Association ..... B 419 435-7734
  Fostoria (G-11126)
Fulton County Health Center ..... C 419 335-2017
  Wauseon (G-18953)
Fulton County Health Center ..... A 419 335-2015
  Wauseon (G-18955)
G M A Surgery Inc ..... E 937 429-7350
  Beavercreek (G-1174)
Galion Community Hospital ..... B 419 468-4841
  Galion (G-11298)
Garden II Leasing Co LLC ..... D 419 381-0037
  Toledo (G-17908)
Glenmont ..... E 614 876-0084
  Hilliard (G-11903)
Good Samaritan Hosp Cincinnati ..... E 513 569-6251
  Cincinnati (G-3685)
Good Samaritan Hospital ..... E 937 224-4646
  Dayton (G-9576)
Good Samaritan Hospital ..... A 937 278-2612
  Dayton (G-9577)
Good Samaritan Hospital ..... C 937 276-6784
  Englewood (G-10706)
Good Samaritan Hospital ..... E 937 734-2612
  Dayton (G-9578)
Grace Hospital ..... D 216 476-2704
  Cleveland (G-5684)
Grace Hospital ..... D 216 687-1500
  Bedford (G-1308)
Grace Hospital ..... D 216 687-1500
  Warrensville Heights (G-18933)
Grace Hospital ..... D 216 687-4013
  Amherst (G-595)
Grady Memorial Hospital ..... E 740 615-1000
  Delaware (G-10102)
Greater Dayton Surgery Ctr LLC ..... E 937 535-2200
  Dayton (G-9589)
Greene Memorial Hosp Svcs Inc ..... D 937 352-2000
  Miamisburg (G-14304)
Greene Memorial Hospital Inc ..... A 937 352-2000
  Xenia (G-20059)
Greene Memorial Hospital Inc ..... E 937 458-4500
  Beavercreek (G-1175)
Greenfield Area Medical Ctr ..... D 937 981-9400
  Greenfield (G-11485)
Guernsey Health Systems Inc ..... A 740 439-3561
  Cambridge (G-2119)

Hardin Memorial Hospital ..... E 419 673-0761
  Kenton (G-12418)
Harrison Community Hosp Inc ..... C 740 942-4631
  Cadiz (G-2076)
Hcl of Dayton Inc ..... C 937 384-8300
  Miamisburg (G-14305)
Healthspan Integrated Care ..... D 216 362-2000
  Cleveland (G-5739)
Heart Hospital of Dto LLC ..... B 937 734-8000
  Dayton (G-9606)
Henry County Hospital Inc ..... E 419 592-4015
  Napoleon (G-14943)
Highland County Joint ..... B 937 393-6100
  Hillsboro (G-11979)
Hocking Valley Community Ho ..... C 740 380-8336
  Logan (G-12974)
Holzer Health System ..... E 740 446-5060
  Gallipolis (G-11324)
Holzer Hospital Foundation ..... A 740 446-5000
  Gallipolis (G-11325)
Holzer Hospital Foundation ..... B 740 446-5000
  Gallipolis (G-11326)
Holzer Medical Ctr - Jackson ..... B 740 288-4625
  Jackson (G-12313)
Hometown Hospital Health Plan ..... C 330 834-2200
  Massillon (G-13820)
Hometown Urgent Care ..... C 937 342-9520
  Springfield (G-17206)
Hospice of Genesis Health ..... E 740 454-5381
  Zanesville (G-20488)
Humana Inc ..... A 330 498-0537
  Canton (G-2408)
▲ Jewish Hospital LLC ..... E 513 686-3000
  Cincinnati (G-3871)
▲ Jewish Hospital Cincinnati Inc ..... A 513 686-3303
  Cincinnati (G-3872)
Joel Pomerene Memorial Hosp ..... B 330 674-1015
  Millersburg (G-14609)
Joint Township Dst Mem Hosp ..... B 419 394-3335
  Saint Marys (G-16676)
Kettering Adventist Healthcare ..... E 937 534-4651
  Moraine (G-14796)
Kettering Adventist Healthcare ..... D 937 878-8644
  Fairborn (G-10800)
Kettering Medical Center ..... D 937 702-4000
  Beavercreek (G-1181)
Kettering Medical Center ..... E 937 298-4331
  Kettering (G-12431)
Kettering Medical Center ..... B 937 866-0551
  Miamisburg (G-14310)
Kettering Medical Center ..... E 937 384-8750
  Dayton (G-9656)
Kindred Healthcare Inc ..... D 937 222-5963
  Dayton (G-9660)
Kindred Healthcare Inc ..... D 937 222-5963
  Dayton (G-9662)
Kindred Hospital Central Ohio ..... E 419 526-0777
  Lima (G-12810)
Knox Community Hospital ..... A 740 393-9000
  Mount Vernon (G-14904)
Lake Hospital System Inc ..... A 440 953-9600
  Willoughby (G-19681)
Lake Hospital System Inc ..... A 440 632-3024
  Middlefield (G-14397)
Lake Hospital System Inc ..... A 440 375-8100
  Painesville (G-15861)
Lakewood Hospital Association ..... A 216 529-7160
  Lakewood (G-12491)
Lakewood Hospital Association ..... E 216 228-5437
  Cleveland (G-5923)
Licking Memorial Hospital ..... A 740 348-4137
  Newark (G-15192)
Life Line Screening ..... D 216 581-6556
  Independence (G-12226)
Lima Memorial Hospital ..... D 419 228-3335
  Lima (G-12824)
Lima Memorial Hospital La ..... B 419 738-5151
  Wapakoneta (G-18801)
Lima Memorial Joint Oper Co ..... A 419 228-5165
  Lima (G-12825)
Lodi Community Hospital ..... C 330 948-1222
  Lodi (G-12964)
Ltac Investors LLC ..... C 740 346-2600
  Steubenville (G-17328)
Lutheran Medical Center ..... B 216 696-4300
  Solon (G-17023)
Madison Family Health Corp ..... C 740 845-7000
  London (G-13000)
Madison Medical Campus ..... E 440 428-6800
  Madison (G-13232)

Employee Codes: A=Over 500 employees, B=251-500
C=101-250, D=51-100, E=25-50

2018 Harris Ohio
Services Directory

80 HEALTH SERVICES

Name	Code	Phone
Manor Care Inc — Toledo (G-18028)	D	419 252-5500
Marietta Memorial Hospital — Belpre (G-1442)	B	740 401-0362
Marietta Memorial Hospital — Marietta (G-13471)	A	740 374-1400
Marietta Memorial Hospital — Marietta (G-13472)	E	740 373-8549
Marion Gen Social Work Dept — Marion (G-13557)	E	740 383-8788
Marion General Hospital Inc — Marion (G-13559)	D	740 383-8400
Mary Rutan Hospital — Bellefontaine (G-1390)	A	937 592-4015
▲ Marymount Hospital Inc — Cleveland (G-5991)	B	216 581-0500
Marysvlle Ohio Srgical Ctr LLC — Marysville (G-13638)	D	937 642-6622
Massillon Health System LLC — Massillon (G-13836)	A	330 837-7200
McCullough-Hyde Mem Hosp Inc — Oxford (G-15818)	E	513 523-2111
McCullough-Hyde Mem Hosp Inc — Hamilton (G-11758)	B	513 863-2215
Med America Hlth Systems Corp — Dayton (G-9710)	A	937 223-6192
Medcath Intermediate Holdings — Dayton (G-9712)	B	937 221-8016
Medcentral Health System — Ontario (G-15701)	E	419 526-8900
Medcentral Health System — Mansfield (G-13338)	E	419 526-8442
Medcentral Health System — Mansfield (G-13339)	D	419 526-8000
Medcentral Health System — Mansfield (G-13340)	D	419 526-8970
Medcentral Health System — Crestline (G-9147)	C	419 683-1040
Medcentral Health System — Shelby (G-16901)	C	419 342-5015
Medcentral Health System — Mansfield (G-13341)	E	419 526-8043
Medical Center At Elizabeth Pl — Dayton (G-9713)	C	937 223-6237
Medina Hospital — Medina (G-14101)	E	330 723-3117
Medone Hospital Physicians — Columbus (G-8145)	E	314 255-6900
Memorial Hospital — Fremont (G-11212)	A	419 334-6657
Memorial Hospital — Clyde (G-6818)	E	419 547-6419
Memorial Hospital Union County — Marysville (G-13640)	C	937 644-1001
Memorial Hospital Union County — Marysville (G-13641)	A	937 644-6115
Mental Health and Addi Serv — Columbus (G-8148)	C	614 752-0333
Mentor Surgery Center Ltd — Mentor (G-14215)	E	440 205-5725
Mercer Cnty Joint Townshp Hosp — Coldwater (G-6833)	D	419 678-2341
Mercer Cnty Joint Townshp Hosp — Celina (G-2654)	E	419 586-1611
Mercy Franciscan Hosp Mt Airy — Cincinnati (G-4057)	A	513 853-5101
Mercy Frncscan Hosp Wstn Hills — Cincinnati (G-4058)	A	513 389-5000
Mercy Hamilton Hospital — Fairfield (G-10878)	E	513 603-8600
Mercy Health — Youngstown (G-20280)	C	330 729-1372
Mercy Health — Cincinnati (G-4060)	D	513 639-0250
Mercy Health — Cincinnati (G-4062)	C	513 639-2800
Mercy Health — Cincinnati (G-4064)	E	513 639-2800
Mercy Health — Youngstown (G-20281)	E	330 792-7418
Mercy Health — Lorain (G-13060)	A	440 233-1000
Mercy Health - St — Oregon (G-15741)	E	419 696-7465
Mercy Health Anderson Hospital — Cincinnati (G-4067)	A	513 624-4500
Mercy Health Anderson Hospital — Cincinnati (G-4068)	E	513 624-1950
Mercy Health Anderson Hospital — Cincinnati (G-4069)	E	513 624-4025
Mercy Health Cincinnati LLC — Cincinnati (G-4070)	D	513 952-5000
Mercy Health Partners — Cincinnati (G-4071)	D	513 233-2444
Mercy Health Partners — Cincinnati (G-4072)	D	513 389-5000
Mercy Health Partners — Cincinnati (G-4073)	C	513 853-5101
Mercy Health Partners — Blue Ash (G-1641)	D	513 981-5056
Mercy Health Partners — Cincinnati (G-4075)	D	513 686-4800
Mercy Health Sys - Nthrn Reg — Toledo (G-18056)	B	419 251-1359
Mercy Health Youngstown LLC — Youngstown (G-20284)	A	330 746-7211
Mercy Health Youngstown LLC — Warren (G-18881)	A	330 841-4000
Mercy Hlth St Vincent Med LLC — Toledo (G-18057)	A	419 251-3232
Mercy Hospital of Defiance — Defiance (G-10048)	C	419 782-8444
Mercy Hospital Tiffin Ohio — Tiffin (G-17686)	B	419 455-7000
Mercy Medical Center — Springfield (G-17242)	A	937 390-5000
Mercy Medical Center Inc — Canton (G-2459)	E	330 489-1000
Mercy Mem Hosp Urbana Ohio — Urbana (G-18596)	B	937 653-5231
Metrohealth Medical Center — Cleveland (G-6036)	A	216 778-7800
Metrohealth System — Cleveland (G-6038)	A	216 398-6000
Metrohealth System — Cleveland (G-6039)	C	216 957-4000
Metrohealth System — Cleveland (G-6041)	E	216 957-1500
Metrohealth System — Beachwood (G-1101)	E	216 765-0733
Metrohealth System — Westlake (G-19515)	E	216 957-3200
Metrohealth System — Beachwood (G-1102)	E	216 591-0523
Miami Valley Hospital — Dayton (G-9731)	C	937 436-5200
Miami Valley Hospital — Vandalia (G-18689)	A	937 208-7065
Miami Valley Hospital — Dayton (G-9732)	A	937 208-8000
Morrow County Hospital — Mount Gilead (G-14859)	B	419 949-3085
Morrow County Hospital — Mount Gilead (G-14860)	B	419 947-9127
Mount Carmel East Hospital — Columbus (G-8195)	A	614 234-6000
Mount Carmel Health — Columbus (G-8196)	A	614 234-5000
Mount Carmel Health System — Columbus (G-8198)	A	614 234-6000
Mount Carmel Health System — New Albany (G-14994)	E	614 775-6600
Neuroscience Center Inc — Columbus (G-8269)	D	614 293-8930
New Albany Surgery Center LLC — New Albany (G-15001)	C	614 775-1616
New Lfcare Hspitals Dayton LLC — Miamisburg (G-14326)	B	937 384-8300
Niagara Health Corporation — Columbus (G-8277)	C	614 898-4000
Norwalk Area Hlth Systems Inc — Norwalk (G-15584)	A	419 668-8101
Ohio Osteopathic Hospital Assn — Columbus (G-8365)	E	614 299-2107
Ohio State Univ Wexner Med Ctr — Columbus (G-8384)	A	614 293-8000
Ohio State Univ Wexner Med Ctr — Columbus (G-8386)	A	614 366-3687
Ohio State University — Columbus (G-8393)	A	614 257-3000
Ohio State University — Columbus (G-8395)	C	614 293-8750
Ohio State University — Columbus (G-8417)	E	614 293-8158
Ohio State University — Columbus (G-8431)	C	614 292-6251
Ohio State University — Columbus (G-8437)	E	614 293-8419
Ohio State University — Columbus (G-8440)	E	614 293-8196
Ohio State University — Columbus (G-8441)	E	614 293-8333
Ohio State University — Columbus (G-8442)	A	614 293-8000
Ohiohealth Corporation — Columbus (G-8454)	C	614 566-5456
Ohiohealth Corporation — Dublin (G-10416)	B	614 544-8000
Ohiohealth Corporation — Columbus (G-8455)	C	614 566-2124
Ohiohealth Corporation — Columbus (G-8458)	D	614 566-5977
Ohiohealth Corporation — Columbus (G-8459)	C	614 566-4800
Ohiohealth Corporation — Columbus (G-8460)	E	614 566-5414
Ohiohealth Corporation — Columbus (G-8457)	A	614 788-8860
Ohiohlth Rverside Methdst Hosp — Columbus (G-8462)	A	614 566-5000
Orrville Hospital Foundation — Orrville (G-15779)	C	330 684-4700
Osu Nephrology Medical Ctr — Columbus (G-8487)	E	614 293-8300
Parma Community General Hosp — Parma (G-15912)	A	440 743-3000
Paulding County Hospital — Paulding (G-15933)	C	419 399-4080
Promedica Health Systems Inc — Toledo (G-18141)	A	567 585-7454
Providence Care Center — Sandusky (G-16786)	C	419 627-2273
Providence Hospital — Cincinnati (G-4350)	A	513 853-5000
Rchp - Wilmington LLC — Wilmington (G-19781)	D	937 382-6611
Regency Hospital Toledo LLC — Sylvania (G-17609)	E	419 318-5700
Research Institute At Nation — Columbus (G-8617)	C	614 722-2700
Richmond Medical Center — Richmond Heights (G-16542)	B	440 585-6500
Robinson Health System Inc — Ravenna (G-16406)	E	330 678-4100
Robinson Health System Inc — Ravenna (G-16407)	A	330 297-0811
Robinson Health System Inc — Kent (G-12394)	A	330 297-0811
Robinson Memorial Hospital — Streetsboro (G-17428)	E	330 626-3455
Salem Community Hospital — Salem (G-16713)	A	330 332-1551
Samaritan Health Partners — Dayton (G-9865)	A	937 208-8400
Samaritan N Surgery Ctr Ltd — Englewood (G-10719)	E	937 567-6100
Samaritan Regional Health Sys — Ashland (G-697)	E	419 281-1330
Samaritan Regional Health Sys — Ashland (G-698)	B	419 289-0491
Selby General Hospital — Marietta (G-13498)	C	740 568-2000
Select Medical Corporation — Cleveland (G-6467)	C	216 983-8030
Select Medical Corporation — Akron (G-432)	D	330 761-7500
Select Specialty Hosp Columbus — Columbus (G-8712)	D	614 291-8467
Select Specialty Hospital — Cincinnati (G-4493)	D	513 862-4700
Shelby County Mem Hosp Assn — Sidney (G-16952)	A	937 498-2311
Shelby County Mem Hosp Assn — Sidney (G-16953)	D	937 492-9591
Sheltering Arms Hospital Found — Athens (G-811)	B	740 592-9300
Sister of Mercy of Clerm Count — Batavia (G-1024)	D	513 732-8200
Sisters of Mrcy of Wllard Ohio — Willard (G-19627)	C	419 964-5000
Skilled Nurse Ctr of — Barberton (G-979)	E	330 615-3717
▲ Southern Ohio Medical Center — Portsmouth (G-16311)	A	740 354-5000
Southstern Ohio Rgonal Med Ctr — Cambridge (G-2129)	E	740 439-3561
Southwest Cmnty Hlth Systems — Cleveland (G-6500)	A	440 816-8000
Southwest General Health Ctr — Cleveland (G-6502)	D	440 816-4202

Southwest General Health Ctr ... C ... 440 816-4900
Strongsville *(G-17510)*

Southwest General Health Ctr ... D ... 440 816-8200
Cleveland *(G-6503)*

Southwest General Health Ctr ... A ... 440 816-8000
Cleveland *(G-6504)*

Southwest General Health Ctr ... E ... 440 816-8005
Cleveland *(G-6505)*

Southwest Healthcare of Brown ... D ... 937 378-7800
Georgetown *(G-11398)*

Specialty Hosp Cleveland Inc ... B ... 216 592-2830
Cleveland *(G-6515)*

St Anne Mercy Hospital ... E ... 419 407-2663
Toledo *(G-18199)*

St John Medical Center ... D ... 440 835-8000
Westlake *(G-19550)*

St Lukes Hospital ... A ... 419 893-5911
Maumee *(G-13980)*

St Ritas Medical Center ... A ... 419 227-3361
Lima *(G-12885)*

St Ritas Medical Center ... E ... 419 538-6288
Glandorf *(G-11432)*

St Vincent Charity Med Ctr ... A ... 216 861-6200
Cleveland *(G-6523)*

Steward Northside Med Ctr Inc ... E ... 330 884-1000
Youngstown *(G-20383)*

Steward Trumbull Mem Hosp Inc ... A ... 330 841-9011
Warren *(G-18904)*

Summa Health ... D ... 330 753-3649
Barberton *(G-980)*

Summa Health ... E ... 330 688-4531
Stow *(G-17395)*

Summa Health ... A ... 330 615-3000
Barberton *(G-981)*

Summa Health System ... D ... 330 535-7319
Akron *(G-453)*

Summa Health System ... E ... 330 375-3000
Akron *(G-456)*

Summa Health System ... A ... 330 334-1504
Wadsworth *(G-18771)*

Summa Health System ... D ... 330 375-3584
Akron *(G-457)*

Summa Health System ... C ... 330 375-3315
Akron *(G-458)*

Summa Health System ... E ... 330 375-3000
Akron *(G-460)*

Surgery and Gynecology Inc ... E ... 614 294-1603
Columbus *(G-8812)*

Sylvania Franciscan Health ... E ... 419 882-8373
Maumee *(G-13984)*

Toledo Hospital ... D ... 419 291-8701
Toledo *(G-18239)*

Toledo Hospital ... A ... 419 291-4000
Toledo *(G-18238)*

Trihealth Evendale Hospital ... C ... 513 454-2222
Cincinnati *(G-4692)*

Trinity Health System ... B ... 740 283-7000
Steubenville *(G-17342)*

Trinity Health System ... A ... 740 264-8000
Steubenville *(G-17340)*

Trinity Health System ... E ... 740 264-8101
Steubenville *(G-17341)*

Trinity Hospital Holding Co ... A ... 740 264-8000
Steubenville *(G-17343)*

Trinity Hospital Twin City ... B ... 740 922-2800
Dennison *(G-10166)*

Trinity West ... A ... 740 264-8000
Steubenville *(G-17344)*

Tripoint Medical Center ... A ... 440 375-8100
Painesville *(G-15883)*

Uc Health Llc ... E ... 513 584-8600
Cincinnati *(G-4721)*

Uhhs-Memorial Hosp of Geneva ... C ... 440 466-1141
Geneva *(G-11371)*

Union Hospital Association ... D ... 330 343-3311
Dover *(G-10219)*

University Hospitals ... B ... 440 250-2001
Westlake *(G-19560)*

University Hospitals ... B ... 216 593-5500
Cleveland *(G-6654)*

University Hospitals ... E ... 216 536-3020
Cleveland *(G-6655)*

University Hospitals ... A ... 440 285-6000
Chardon *(G-2774)*

▲ **University Hospitals** ... A ... 216 767-8900
Shaker Heights *(G-16869)*

University Hospitals ... A ... 440 743-3000
Parma *(G-15917)*

University Hospitals ... E ... 216 844-6400
Cleveland *(G-6656)*

University Hospitals Cleveland ... A ... 216 844-1000
Cleveland *(G-6659)*

University Hospitals Cleveland ... E ... 440 205-5755
Mentor *(G-14252)*

▲ **University Hospitals Cleveland** ... A ... 216 844-1000
Cleveland *(G-6660)*

University Hospitals Cleveland ... D ... 216 844-4663
Cleveland *(G-6661)*

University Hospitals Cleveland ... A ... 216 844-3323
Shaker Heights *(G-16870)*

University Hospitals Cleveland ... D ... 216 721-8457
Beachwood *(G-1135)*

University Hospitals Cleveland ... E ... 216 844-3528
Cleveland *(G-6662)*

University Hospitals Health Sy ... E ... 216 844-4663
Cleveland *(G-6664)*

University of Cincinnati ... E ... 513 584-7522
Cincinnati *(G-4756)*

University of Cincinnati ... E ... 513 584-4396
Cincinnati *(G-4763)*

University of Cincinnati ... E ... 513 584-1000
Cincinnati *(G-4776)*

University of Cincinnati ... E ... 513 584-1000
Cincinnati *(G-4778)*

University of Toledo ... A ... 419 383-4000
Toledo *(G-18279)*

University of Toledo ... A ... 419 383-3759
Toledo *(G-18281)*

University of Toledo ... B ... 419 383-4229
Toledo *(G-18282)*

▲ **Universty of Cincinnti Medcl C** ... E ... 513 584-1000
Cincinnati *(G-4785)*

Uvmc Management Corporation ... D ... 937 440-4000
Troy *(G-18385)*

VA Medical Center Automated RE ... E ... 740 772-7118
Chillicothe *(G-2894)*

Van Wert County Hospital Assn ... D ... 419 238-2390
Van Wert *(G-18649)*

Van Wert Medical Services Ltd ... B ... 419 238-7727
Van Wert *(G-18651)*

Vibra Healthcare LLC ... D ... 330 675-5555
Warren *(G-18921)*

Wayne Healthcare ... B ... 937 548-1141
Greenville *(G-11524)*

Wood County Hospital Assoc ... A ... 419 354-8900
Bowling Green *(G-1800)*

Wright Center ... E ... 216 382-1868
Cleveland *(G-6760)*

Wyandot Memorial Hospital ... C ... 419 294-4991
Upper Sandusky *(G-18570)*

8063 Psychiatric Hospitals

Adriel School Inc ... D ... 937 465-0010
West Liberty *(G-19260)*

Belmont Bhc Pines Hospital Inc ... C ... 330 759-2700
Youngstown *(G-20113)*

Bethesda Hospital Association ... A ... 740 454-4000
Zanesville *(G-20447)*

Bhc Fox Run Hospital Inc ... C ... 740 695-2131
Saint Clairsville *(G-16628)*

Center For Chemical Addictions ... D ... 513 381-6672
Cincinnati *(G-3207)*

Central Commnty Hlth Brd of Ha ... C ... 513 559-2000
Cincinnati *(G-3211)*

Central Community ... D ... 513 559-2000
Cincinnati *(G-3213)*

Community Mental Healthcare ... E ... 330 343-1811
Dover *(G-10181)*

County of Paulding ... E ... 419 399-3636
Paulding *(G-15930)*

Develpmntal Dsblties Ohio Dept ... A ... 740 446-1642
Gallipolis *(G-11314)*

Develpmntal Dsblties Ohio Dept ... B ... 614 272-0509
Columbus *(G-7513)*

Eastway Corporation ... C ... 937 496-2000
Dayton *(G-9516)*

Eastway Corporation ... C ... 937 531-7000
Dayton *(G-9517)*

Focus Healthcare of Ohio LLC ... E ... 419 891-9333
Maumee *(G-13918)*

Heartland Bhavioral Healthcare ... B ... 330 833-3135
Massillon *(G-13819)*

Laurelwood Hospital ... B ... 440 953-3000
Willoughby *(G-19685)*

▲ **Marymount Hospital Inc** ... B ... 216 581-0500
Cleveland *(G-5991)*

Mental Health and Addi Serv ... C ... 419 381-1881
Toledo *(G-18051)*

Mental Health and Addi Serv ... B ... 513 948-3600
Cincinnati *(G-4055)*

Mental Health and Addi Serv ... D ... 614 752-0333
Columbus *(G-8147)*

Mental Health and Addi Serv ... B ... 330 467-7131
Northfield *(G-15520)*

Mental Hlth Serv For CL & Mad ... E ... 937 390-7980
Springfield *(G-17233)*

Mental Hlth Serv For CL & Mad ... C ... 937 399-9500
Springfield *(G-17234)*

Mental Hlth Serv For CL & Mad ... E ... 740 852-6256
London *(G-13003)*

Mercy Health ... A ... 440 233-1000
Lorain *(G-13060)*

Oglethorpe Middlepoint LLC ... E ... 419 968-2950
Middle Point *(G-14377)*

Ohio Hospital For Psychiatry ... E ... 877 762-9026
Columbus *(G-8354)*

Rehab Continuum Inc ... E ... 513 984-8070
Blue Ash *(G-1679)*

Rescue Incorporated ... C ... 419 255-9585
Toledo *(G-18153)*

Southast Cmnty Mental Hlth Ctr ... E ... 614 444-0800
Columbus *(G-8752)*

St Ritas Medical Center ... E ... 419 226-9067
Lima *(G-12884)*

8069 Specialty Hospitals, Except Psychiatric

Affiliates In Oral & Maxlofcl ... E ... 513 829-8080
Fairfield *(G-10817)*

Affiliates In Oral & Maxlofcl ... E ... 513 829-8080
West Chester *(G-19015)*

Akron Gen Edwin Shaw Rhbltion ... C ... 330 375-1300
Cuyahoga Falls *(G-9159)*

Alcohol Drug Addction & Mental ... E ... 937 443-0416
Dayton *(G-9314)*

Anderson Healthcare Ltd ... D ... 513 474-6200
Cincinnati *(G-3022)*

Arthur G James Cancer ... A ... 614 293-4878
Columbus *(G-7044)*

Arthur G James Cancer Hospital ... E ... 614 293-3300
Columbus *(G-7045)*

Aultman Hospital ... A ... 330 452-9911
Canton *(G-2253)*

Aultman Hospital ... B ... 330 452-9911
Canton *(G-2254)*

Behavral Cnnctions WD Cnty Inc ... E ... 419 352-5387
Bowling Green *(G-1761)*

Center For Chemical Addictions ... D ... 513 381-6672
Cincinnati *(G-3207)*

Charity Hospice Inc ... E ... 740 264-2280
Steubenville *(G-17310)*

Childrens Hosp Med Ctr Akron ... A ... 330 425-3344
Twinsburg *(G-18400)*

Childrens Hosp Med Ctr Akron ... A ... 330 308-5432
New Philadelphia *(G-15085)*

Childrens Hosp Med Ctr Akron ... E ... 330 629-6085
Youngstown *(G-20140)*

Childrens Hosp Med Ctr Akron ... A ... 330 543-1000
Akron *(G-135)*

Childrens Hosp Med Ctr Akron ... E ... 330 543-8004
Akron *(G-136)*

Childrens Hosp Med Ctr Akron ... E ... 330 676-1020
Kent *(G-12357)*

Childrens Hospital ... E ... 513 636-4051
Cincinnati *(G-3245)*

Childrens Hospital Medical Ctr ... A ... 513 636-4200
Cincinnati *(G-3249)*

Childrens Hospital Medical Ctr ... A ... 513 636-6036
Cincinnati *(G-2906)*

Childrens Hospital Medical Ctr ... A ... 513 636-4200
Cincinnati *(G-3252)*

Childrens Hospital Medical Ctr ... E ... 513 636-6800
Mason *(G-13676)*

Childrens Medical Ctr Toledo ... A ... 937 641-3000
Dayton *(G-9403)*

Community Care Hospice ... E ... 937 382-5400
Wilmington *(G-19756)*

Community Counseling Services ... E ... 419 468-8211
Bucyrus *(G-2031)*

Compass Corp For Recovery Svcs ... D ... 419 241-8827
Toledo *(G-17825)*

Cornell Companies Inc ... C ... 419 747-3322
Shelby *(G-16898)*

County of Clark ... D ... 937 390-5615
Springfield *(G-17180)*

County of Stark ... E ... 330 455-6644
Canton *(G-2325)*

Covenant Care Ohio Inc ... D ... 937 878-7046
Fairborn *(G-10788)*

Crossroads Center ... C ... 513 475-5300
Cincinnati *(G-3442)*

SIC

80 HEALTH SERVICES

Crystal Clnic Orthpdic Ctr LLC ....D 330 668-4040
  Akron (G-179)
Crystal Clnic Orthpdic Ctr LLC ....D 330 535-3396
  Akron (G-180)
▲ Dayton Childrens Hospital ....A 937 641-3000
  Dayton (G-9464)
Encompass Health Corporation ....C 513 418-5600
  Cincinnati (G-3556)
Firelands Regional Health Sys ....E 419 332-5524
  Fremont (G-11197)
Frs Counseling Inc ....E 937 393-0585
  Hillsboro (G-11975)
Glenbeigh Health Sources Inc ....C 440 951-7000
  Rock Creek (G-16558)
Glenbeigh Hospital ....E 440 563-3400
  Rock Creek (G-16559)
Greenbrier Senior Living Cmnty ....C 440 888-5900
  Cleveland (G-5702)
Hcr Manorcare Med Svcs Fla LLC ....C 614 882-1511
  Westerville (G-19407)
Health Recovery Services Inc ....C 740 592-6720
  Athens (G-791)
HealthSouth ....C 937 424-8200
  Dayton (G-9605)
Heart Hospital of Dto LLC ....B 937 734-8000
  Dayton (G-9606)
Hospice of Central Ohio ....C 740 344-0311
  Newark (G-15175)
Hospice of Middletown ....E 513 424-2273
  Middletown (G-14428)
Hospice of Northwest Ohio ....D 419 661-4001
  Toledo (G-17961)
Hospice of The Valley Inc ....D 330 788-1992
  Youngstown (G-20221)
Hospice of The Western Reserve ....D 330 800-2240
  Medina (G-14077)
Laurelwood Hospital ....B 440 953-3000
  Willoughby (G-19685)
Liberty Nrsing Ctr Rvrside LLC ....D 513 557-3621
  Cincinnati (G-3975)
Lorain County Alcohol and Drug ....E 440 989-4900
  Lorain (G-13051)
Lutheran Medical Center ....B 216 696-4300
  Solon (G-17023)
Marietta Memorial Hospital ....A 740 374-1400
  Marietta (G-13471)
Maryhaven Inc ....C 614 449-1530
  Columbus (G-8123)
Maryhaven Inc ....E 937 644-9192
  Marysville (G-13634)
McKinley Hall Inc ....E 937 328-5300
  Springfield (G-17230)
Medcath Intermediate Holdings ....B 937 221-8016
  Dayton (G-9712)
Mental Health & Recovery Ctr ....E 937 383-3031
  Wilmington (G-19773)
Mercy Health ....E 419 226-9064
  Lima (G-12839)
Mercy Health - Springfield C ....E 937 323-5001
  Springfield (G-17241)
Mercy Health Anderson Hospital ....E 513 624-4025
  Cincinnati (G-4069)
Metrohealth System ....C 216 957-2100
  Cleveland (G-6043)
Metrohealth System ....E 216 778-3867
  Cleveland (G-6042)
Morrow County Council On Drugs ....E 419 947-4055
  Mount Gilead (G-14858)
Nationwide Childrens Hospital ....C 614 722-2700
  Columbus (G-8229)
Nationwide Childrens Hospital ....B 614 722-5750
  Columbus (G-8230)
◆ Nationwide Childrens Hospital ....A 614 722-2000
  Columbus (G-8231)
Nationwide Childrens Hospital ....B 513 636-6000
  Cincinnati (G-2925)
Nationwide Childrens Hospital ....E 330 253-5200
  Akron (G-349)
Nationwide Childrens Hospital ....A 614 722-2000
  Columbus (G-8232)
Nationwide Childrens Hospital ....E 614 355-8300
  Westerville (G-19331)
Nationwide Childrens Hospital ....A 614 722-8200
  Columbus (G-8233)
Nationwide Childrens Hospital ....A 614 864-9216
  Pickerington (G-16102)
Nationwide Childrens Hospital ....A 614 355-0802
  Columbus (G-8234)
Nationwide Childrens Hospital ....B 614 355-8100
  Columbus (G-8235)
Nationwide Childrens Hospital ....B 614 355-9200
  Columbus (G-8236)
Nationwide Childrens Hospital ....B 614 355-8000
  Columbus (G-8237)
Newark Sleep Diagnostic Center ....E 740 522-9499
  Newark (G-15223)
Nord Center Associates Inc ....E 440 233-7232
  Lorain (G-13068)
Northwest Ohio Orthopedic & Sp ....C 419 427-1984
  Findlay (G-11071)
Ohio Department Youth Services ....E 740 881-3337
  Columbus (G-8332)
Ohio State University ....E 614 293-4925
  Columbus (G-8446)
Oriana House Inc ....C 216 361-9655
  Cleveland (G-6214)
Oriana House Inc ....D 330 996-7730
  Akron (G-374)
Orthopedic One Inc ....E 614 545-7900
  Columbus (G-8485)
Parkside Behavioral Healthcare ....E 614 471-2552
  Gahanna (G-11263)
Parma Clinic Cancer Center ....E 440 743-4747
  Cleveland (G-6246)
Pike Cnty Recovery Council Inc ....E 740 835-8437
  Waverly (G-18973)
Recovery Works Healing Ctr LLC ....E 937 384-0580
  West Carrollton (G-19009)
Salvation Army ....C 330 773-3331
  Akron (G-428)
Scioto Pnt Vly Mental Hlth Ctr ....E 740 335-6935
  Wshngtn CT Hs (G-20034)
Select Spclty Hsptal-Akron LLC ....D 330 761-7500
  Akron (G-433)
Shriners Hspitals For Children ....B 513 872-6000
  Cincinnati (G-4519)
Southast Cmnty Mental Hlth Ctr ....E 614 444-0800
  Columbus (G-8752)
Southwest General Health Ctr ....D 440 816-8200
  Cleveland (G-6503)
Stein Hospice Services Inc ....D 419 447-0475
  Sandusky (G-16798)
Stein Hospice Services Inc ....D 419 502-0019
  Sandusky (G-16799)
▲ Stein Hospice Services Inc ....B 800 625-5269
  Sandusky (G-16800)
Stein Hospice Services Inc ....D 419 663-3222
  Norwalk (G-15593)
Stella Maris Inc ....E 216 781-0550
  Cleveland (G-6536)
Syntero Inc ....E 614 889-5722
  Dublin (G-10471)
Talbert House ....C 513 751-7747
  Cincinnati (G-4618)
Talbert House ....D 513 684-7968
  Cincinnati (G-4621)
Toledo Childrens Hosp Fdn ....E 419 824-9072
  Toledo (G-18231)
Transitional Living Inc ....D 513 863-6383
  Fairfield Township (G-10936)
Trihealth Os LLC ....D 513 791-6611
  Montgomery (G-14735)
Trinity Health Corporation ....B 614 846-5420
  Columbus (G-8872)
Twin Oaks Care Center Inc ....E 419 524-1205
  Mansfield (G-13379)
▲ University Hospitals Cleveland ....A 216 844-1000
  Cleveland (G-6660)
University Hospitals Health ....A 440 285-4040
  Chardon (G-2775)
University Mednet ....B 216 383-0100
  Euclid (G-10780)
Uvmc Nursing Care Inc ....C 937 473-2075
  Covington (G-9140)
Vibra Hosp Mahoning Vly LLC ....D 330 726-5000
  Youngstown (G-20405)
Whetstone Care Center LLC ....C 614 875-7700
  Grove City (G-11616)
Youngstown Committee On Alchol ....D 330 744-1181
  Youngstown (G-20429)

8071 Medical Laboratories

Alliance Imaging Inc ....C 330 493-5100
  Canton (G-2232)
Amerathon LLC ....B 513 752-7300
  Cincinnati (G-2903)
Arbor View Family Medicine Inc ....E 740 687-3386
  Lancaster (G-12509)
Associated Imaging Corporation ....E 419 517-0500
  Toledo (G-17760)
Bayless Pathmark Inc ....E 440 274-2494
  Cleveland (G-5103)
Berkebile Russell & Associates ....E 440 989-4480
  Lorain (G-13018)
Blossom Nursing & Rehab Center ....C 330 337-3033
  Salem (G-16690)
Brook Haven Home Health Care ....E 937 833-6945
  Brookville (G-1959)
Cadx Systems Inc ....D 937 431-1464
  Beavercreek (G-1157)
Cellular Technology Limited ....E 216 791-5084
  Shaker Heights (G-16857)
Childrens Hospital Medical Ctr ....E 513 636-6400
  Fairfield (G-10830)
▼ Cleveland Heartlab Inc ....D 866 358-9828
  Cleveland (G-5317)
Cols Health & Wellness Testing ....E 614 839-2781
  Westerville (G-19384)
Compunet Clinical Labs LLC ....D 937 427-2655
  Beavercreek (G-1234)
Compunet Clinical Labs LLC ....D 937 342-0015
  Springfield (G-17176)
Compunet Clinical Labs LLC ....E 937 296-0844
  Moraine (G-14763)
Compunet Clinical Labs LLC ....B 937 208-3555
  Dayton (G-9421)
Connie Parks ....E 330 759-8334
  Hubbard (G-12084)
Consultants Laboratory Medici ....E 419 535-9629
  Toledo (G-17830)
Dayton Medical Imaging ....D 937 439-0390
  Dayton (G-9481)
Drew Medical Inc ....E 407 363-6700
  Hudson (G-12114)
Drs Hill & Thomas Co ....E 440 944-8887
  Cleveland (G-5509)
Ecg Scanning & Medical Svcs ....E 888 346-5837
  Moraine (G-14778)
Gloria Gadmack Do ....C 216 363-2353
  Cleveland (G-5675)
Heart To Heart Home Health ....E 330 335-9999
  Wadsworth (G-18755)
Labcare ....E 330 753-3649
  Barberton (G-969)
Labone Inc ....A 513 585-9000
  Cincinnati (G-3955)
Laboratory Corporation America ....E 614 475-7852
  Columbus (G-8027)
Laboratory Corporation America ....E 937 383-6964
  Wilmington (G-19765)
Laboratory Corporation America ....E 330 865-3624
  Akron (G-311)
Laboratory Corporation America ....E 440 951-6841
  Willoughby (G-19679)
Laboratory Corporation America ....E 614 882-6278
  Columbus (G-8028)
Laboratory Corporation America ....E 513 242-6800
  Cincinnati (G-3956)
Laboratory Corporation America ....E 419 281-7100
  Ashland (G-685)
Laboratory Corporation America ....E 937 866-8188
  Miamisburg (G-14313)
Laboratory Corporation America ....A 614 336-3993
  Dublin (G-10385)
Laboratory Corporation America ....E 440 328-3275
  Mansfield (G-13322)
Laboratory Corporation America ....E 440 884-1591
  Cleveland (G-5917)
Laboratory Corporation America ....E 740 522-2034
  Newark (G-15181)
Laboratory Corporation America ....E 330 686-0194
  Stow (G-17379)
Laboratory Corporation America ....E 440 838-0404
  Cleveland (G-5918)
Laboratory of Dermatopathology ....E 937 434-2351
  Dayton (G-9669)
Lexamed ....E 419 693-5307
  Toledo (G-18004)
Lima Pathology Associates Labs ....E 419 226-9595
  Lima (G-12826)
Maternohio Clinical Assoicates ....E 614 457-7660
  Columbus (G-8128)
Medcentral Workable ....E 419 526-8444
  Ontario (G-15702)
Medical Diagnostic Lab Inc ....D 440 333-1375
  Westlake (G-19514)
Medical Imging Diagnostics LLC ....E 330 726-0322
  Youngstown (G-20279)
Medpace Inc ....A 513 366-3220
  Cincinnati (G-4048)

80 HEALTH SERVICES

Medpace Bioanalytical Labs LLC .... E 513 366-3260
  Cincinnati *(G-4050)*
Mercy Health Youngstown LLC .... A 330 729-1420
  Youngstown *(G-20283)*
Mercy Health Youngstown LLC .... A 330 746-7211
  Youngstown *(G-20284)*
Midwest Ultrasound Inc .... E 513 936-0444
  Cincinnati *(G-4093)*
Midwest Ultrasound Inc .... D 513 248-8885
  Milford *(G-14540)*
Monroe Family Health Center .... E 740 472-0757
  Woodsfield *(G-19818)*
Mount Carmel Imaging & Therapy ..... E 614 234-8080
  Columbus *(G-8199)*
Mp Biomedicals LLC .... C 440 337-1200
  Solon *(G-17029)*
Nationwide Childrens Hospital .... C 614 722-2700
  Columbus *(G-8229)*
Northeast OH Neighborhood Heal ..... C 216 231-2323
  Cleveland *(G-6152)*
Oncodiagnostic Laboratory Inc .... E 216 861-5846
  Cleveland *(G-6203)*
Osu Pathology Services LLC .... D 614 293-5905
  Columbus *(G-8489)*
Osu Pathology Services LLC .... B 614 247-6461
  Columbus *(G-8490)*
Pathology Laboratories Inc .... C 419 255-4600
  Toledo *(G-18121)*
Proscan Imaging LLC .... D 513 281-3400
  Cincinnati *(G-4349)*
Proscan Imaging LLC .... E 513 759-7350
  West Chester *(G-19133)*
Regional Imaging Cons Corp .... E 330 726-9006
  Youngstown *(G-20343)*
Ridgepark Medical Associates .... E 216 749-8256
  Cleveland *(G-6396)*
Shared PET Imaging Llc .... C 330 491-0480
  Canton *(G-2527)*
St Ritas Medical Center .... D 419 226-9229
  Lima *(G-12886)*
▲ Standards Testing Labs Inc .... E 330 833-8548
  Massillon *(G-13856)*
Stembanc Inc .... E 440 332-4279
  Chardon *(G-2770)*
Stork Studios Inc .... E 419 841-7766
  Toledo *(G-18203)*
Suburban Medical Laboratory .... C 330 929-7992
  Euclid *(G-10778)*
Summa Health .... D 330 753-3649
  Barberton *(G-980)*
Summa Health .... E 330 688-4531
  Stow *(G-17395)*
Superior Medical Care Inc .... E 440 282-7420
  Lorain *(G-13080)*
Triad Group Inc .... D 419 228-8800
  Lima *(G-12904)*
Trident USA Health Svcs LLC .... E 614 888-2226
  Columbus *(G-8870)*
University of Cincinnati .... E 513 558-4444
  Cincinnati *(G-4762)*
University of Cincinnati .... C 513 558-5439
  Cincinnati *(G-4766)*
University of Cincinnati .... D 513 584-5331
  Cincinnati *(G-4769)*
Vet Path Services Inc .... E 513 469-0777
  Mason *(G-13778)*
Womens Centers-Dayton .... E 937 228-2222
  Dayton *(G-10002)*
X-Ray Industries Inc .... E 216 642-0100
  Cleveland *(G-6766)*
Zak Enterprises Ltd .... D 216 261-9700
  Euclid *(G-10781)*

8072 Dental Laboratories

Classic Dental Labs Inc .... E 614 443-0328
  Columbus *(G-7293)*
Dental Ceramics Inc .... E 330 523-5240
  Richfield *(G-16504)*
Doling & Associates Dental Lab .... E 937 254-0075
  Dayton *(G-9503)*
Dresch Tolson Dental Labs .... D 419 842-6730
  Sylvania *(G-17584)*
Greater Cincinnati Dental Labs .... E 513 385-4222
  Cincinnati *(G-3708)*
Health Smile Center .... E 440 992-2700
  Ashtabula *(G-747)*
National Dentex LLC .... E 216 671-0577
  Cleveland *(G-6105)*
Roe Dental Laboratory Inc .... D 216 663-2233
  Independence *(G-12252)*

Sentage Corporation .... E 937 865-5900
  Miamisburg *(G-14348)*
State Valley Dental Center .... E 330 920-8060
  Cuyahoga Falls *(G-9220)*
United Dental Laboratories .... E 330 253-1810
  Akron *(G-484)*

8082 Home Health Care Svcs

A Touch of Grace Inc .... D 740 397-7971
  Mount Vernon *(G-14877)*
A-1 Nursing Care Inc .... C 614 268-3800
  Columbus *(G-6922)*
Ability Matters LLC .... E 614 214-9652
  Hilliard *(G-11875)*
Above & Beyond Caregivers LLC .... E 614 478-1700
  Columbus *(G-6928)*
Accentcare Home Health Cal Inc .... C 740 387-4568
  Marion *(G-13522)*
Accentcare Home Health Cal Inc .... C 740 474-7826
  Circleville *(G-4876)*
Acute Care Homenursing Service ...... E 216 271-9100
  Warren *(G-18813)*
Advance Home Care LLC .... D 614 436-3611
  Columbus *(G-6945)*
Advance Home Care LLC .... D 937 723-6335
  Dayton *(G-9309)*
Advantage Home Health Care .... D 800 636-2330
  Portsmouth *(G-16263)*
Advantage Home Health Svcs Inc ..... E 330 491-8161
  North Canton *(G-15320)*
All About Home Care Svcs LLC .... E 937 222-2980
  Dayton *(G-9315)*
All Heart Home Care LLC .... E 419 298-0034
  Edgerton *(G-10581)*
All Hearts Home Health Care .... E 440 342-2026
  Cleveland *(G-4988)*
Almost Family Inc .... E 614 457-1900
  Columbus *(G-6973)*
Almost Family Inc .... E 330 724-7545
  Akron *(G-69)*
Almost Family Inc .... E 216 464-0443
  Cleveland *(G-4994)*
Alpine Nursing Care .... E 216 650-6295
  Cleveland *(G-4998)*
Alternacare Home Health Inc .... E 740 689-1589
  Lancaster *(G-12508)*
Alternate Sltions Private Duty .... D 937 298-1111
  Dayton *(G-9324)*
Alternate Solutions First LLC .... C 937 298-1111
  Dayton *(G-9325)*
Alternative Home Care & Stffng .... E 513 794-0571
  Cincinnati *(G-2997)*
Alternative Home Health Care .... E 513 794-0555
  Cincinnati *(G-2998)*
Altimate Care LLC .... E 614 794-9600
  Columbus *(G-6978)*
Amandacare Inc .... C 614 884-8880
  Columbus *(G-6980)*
Amber Home Care LLC .... E 614 523-0668
  Columbus *(G-6981)*
Amedisys Inc .... E 740 373-8549
  Marietta *(G-13430)*
Amenity Home Health Care LLC .... E 513 931-3689
  Cincinnati *(G-3000)*
American Nursing Care Inc .... E 513 731-4600
  Cincinnati *(G-3009)*
American Nursing Care Inc .... E 937 438-3844
  Dayton *(G-9330)*
American Nursing Care Inc .... D 419 228-0888
  Lima *(G-12741)*
American Nursing Care Inc .... D 740 452-0569
  Zanesville *(G-20442)*
Angel Above Byond Hm Hlth Svcs .... E 513 553-9955
  New Richmond *(G-15124)*
Angels 4 Life LLC .... E 513 474-5683
  Cincinnati *(G-3029)*
Angels Home Care LLC .... E 419 947-9373
  Mount Gilead *(G-14851)*
Angels In Waiting Home Care .... E 440 946-0349
  Mentor *(G-14144)*
Angels Touch Nursing Care .... E 513 661-4111
  Cincinnati *(G-3030)*
Angels Visiting .... D 419 298-0034
  Edgerton *(G-10582)*
Angmar Medical Holdings Inc .... D 330 835-9663
  Fairlawn *(G-10937)*
Answercare LLC .... D 855 213-1511
  Canton *(G-2241)*
Appalachian Community Visi .... D 740 594-8226
  Athens *(G-772)*

Apria Healthcare LLC .... E 937 291-2842
  Miamisburg *(G-14271)*
Arcadia Services Inc .... D 330 869-9520
  Akron *(G-79)*
Arcadia Services Inc .... D 937 912-5800
  Beavercreek *(G-1147)*
Area Agency On Aging Planni .... C 800 258-7277
  Dayton *(G-9343)*
Area Office On Aging of Nwstrn .... D 419 382-0624
  Toledo *(G-17758)*
Arlingworth Home Health Inc .... E 614 659-0961
  Dublin *(G-10255)*
Around Clock Home Care .... D 440 350-2547
  Painesville *(G-15835)*
ASAP Homecare Inc .... E 330 334-7027
  Wadsworth *(G-18748)*
ASAP Homecare Inc .... D 330 263-4733
  Wooster *(G-19829)*
Ashtabula Rgional Hm Hlth Svcs .... E 440 992-4663
  Ashtabula *(G-726)*
Assured Health Care Inc .... E 937 294-2803
  Dayton *(G-9346)*
Atrium Health System .... A 937 499-5606
  Middletown *(G-14473)*
B & L Agency LLC .... E 740 373-8272
  Marietta *(G-13434)*
B H C Services Inc .... A 216 289-5300
  Euclid *(G-10744)*
Benjamin Rose Institute .... D 216 791-8000
  Cleveland *(G-5117)*
Bethesda Hospital Association .... A 740 454-4000
  Zanesville *(G-20447)*
Beyond The Horizons Home Healt ..... E 608 630-0617
  Columbus *(G-7105)*
Black Stone Cincinnati LLC .... D 937 424-1370
  Moraine *(G-14754)*
Black Stone Cincinnati LLC .... E 513 924-1370
  Cincinnati *(G-3112)*
Blanchard Valley Health System .... D 419 424-3000
  Findlay *(G-10998)*
Bracor Inc .... E 216 289-5300
  Euclid *(G-10746)*
Braden Med Services Inc .... E 740 732-2356
  Caldwell *(G-2082)*
Bradley Bay Assisted Living .... E 440 871-4509
  Bay Village *(G-1038)*
Bridgeshome Health Care .... E 330 764-1000
  Medina *(G-14040)*
Brightstar Healthcare .... E 513 321-4688
  Blue Ash *(G-1549)*
Brook Haven Home Health Care .... E 937 833-6945
  Brookville *(G-1959)*
Brookdale Senior Living Commun ..... E 937 548-6800
  Greenville *(G-11490)*
Brookdale Senior Living Inc .... E 614 336-3677
  Dublin *(G-10269)*
Brookdale Senior Living Inc .... E 513 745-9292
  Cincinnati *(G-3139)*
Brookdale Senior Living Inc .... E 330 262-1615
  Wooster *(G-19835)*
Buckeye Hills-Hck Vly Reg Dev .... E 740 373-6400
  Reno *(G-16421)*
Buckeye Home Health Care .... C 513 791-6446
  Blue Ash *(G-1550)*
Buckeye Home Healthcare Inc .... E 614 776-3372
  Westerville *(G-19373)*
Buckeye Rsdntial Solutions LLC .... D 330 235-9183
  Ravenna *(G-16374)*
C K of Cincinnati Inc .... E 513 752-5533
  Cincinnati *(G-3161)*
C R G Health Care Systems .... E 330 498-8107
  Niles *(G-15285)*
Capital Health Homecare .... E 740 264-8815
  Steubenville *(G-17305)*
Capital Senior Living Corp .... C 330 748-4204
  Macedonia *(G-13192)*
Caprice Health Care Inc .... C 330 965-9200
  North Lima *(G-15400)*
Care Connection of Cincinnati .... D 513 842-1101
  Cincinnati *(G-3181)*
Caregivers Health Network Inc .... D 513 662-3400
  Cincinnati *(G-3182)*
Carestar Inc .... C 513 618-8300
  Cincinnati *(G-3183)*
Caring Hands Inc .... C 330 821-6310
  Alliance *(G-530)*
Caring Hands Home Health Care .... E 740 532-9020
  Ironton *(G-12285)*
Caring Hearts Home Health Care .... B 513 339-1237
  Mason *(G-13670)*

Carl Mills D 740 282-2382 Toronto *(G-18335)*
Central Star C 419 756-9449 Mansfield *(G-13275)*
Chcc Home Health Care E 330 759-4069 Austintown *(G-869)*
Chemed Corporation D 513 762-6690 Cincinnati *(G-3237)*
Chestnut Hill Management Co D 614 855-3700 Columbus *(G-7256)*
CHI Health At Home D 513 576-0262 Milford *(G-14509)*
Childrens Home Care Dayton D 937 641-4663 Dayton *(G-9402)*
Childrens Home Care Group B 330 543-5000 Akron *(G-134)*
Childrens Homecare Services C 614 355-1100 Columbus *(G-7261)*
Choice Healthcare Limited D 937 254-6220 Beavercreek *(G-1159)*
Circle J Home Health Care D 330 482-0877 Salineville *(G-16722)*
City of Wooster E 330 263-8636 Wooster *(G-19844)*
Clearpath HM Hlth Hospice LLC D 330 784-2162 Akron *(G-145)*
Colt Enterprises Inc E 567 336-6062 Maumee *(G-13898)*
Columbus W Hlth Care Co Partnr E 614 274-4005 Columbus *(G-7392)*
Comfort Healthcare E 216 281-9999 Cleveland *(G-5375)*
Comfort Keepers E 419 229-1031 Lima *(G-12758)*
Comfort Keepers E 440 721-0100 Painesville *(G-15844)*
Comfort Keepers Inc E 937 322-6288 Springfield *(G-17169)*
Committed To Care Inc E 513 245-1190 Cincinnati *(G-3400)*
Community Caregivers E 330 725-9800 Wadsworth *(G-18750)*
Community Choice Home Care E 740 574-9900 Wheelersburg *(G-19574)*
Community Concepts Inc C 513 398-8181 Mason *(G-13687)*
Community Health Systems Inc D 330 841-9011 Warren *(G-18836)*
Community Hlth Prfssionals Inc E 419 634-7443 Ada *(G-4)*
Community Hlth Prfssionals Inc E 419 445-5128 Archbold *(G-634)*
Community Hlth Prfssionals Inc C 419 238-9223 Van Wert *(G-18630)*
Community Hlth Prfssionals Inc E 419 399-4708 Paulding *(G-15928)*
Community Hlth Prfssionals Inc E 419 991-1822 Lima *(G-12926)*
Community Hlth Prfssionals Inc E 419 586-1999 Celina *(G-2641)*
Community Hlth Prfssionals Inc D 419 586-6266 Celina *(G-2642)*
Community Hlth Prfssionals Inc E 419 695-8101 Delphos *(G-10139)*
Community Home Care E 330 971-7011 Cuyahoga Falls *(G-9177)*
Companions of Ashland LLC E 419 281-2273 Ashland *(G-676)*
Compassionate In Home Care E 614 888-5683 Worthington *(G-19950)*
Comprehensive Health Care Svcs C 513 245-0100 Cincinnati *(G-3406)*
Concord Hlth Rhabilitation Ctr E 740 574-8441 Wheelersburg *(G-19575)*
Constance Care Home Hlth Care D 740 477-6360 Circleville *(G-4884)*
Consumer Support Services Inc C 330 652-8800 Niles *(G-15290)*
Consumer Support Services Inc B 740 788-8257 Newark *(G-15158)*
Continued Care Inc E 419 222-2273 Lima *(G-12759)*
Continuum Home Care Inc E 440 964-3332 Ashtabula *(G-737)*
Cori Care Inc D 614 848-4357 Columbus *(G-7439)*
Cottages of Clayton E 937 280-0300 Dayton *(G-9429)*
County of Knox E 740 392-2200 Mount Vernon *(G-14888)*
County of Washington E 740 373-2028 Marietta *(G-13439)*
County of Williams E 419 485-3141 Montpelier *(G-14742)*
Covington Square Senior APT E 740 623-4603 Coshocton *(G-9101)*
Crawford Cnty Shared Hlth Svcs E 419 468-7985 Galion *(G-11293)*
Dacas Nursing Systems Inc C 330 884-2530 Warren *(G-18846)*
Daugwood Inc E 937 429-9465 Beavercreek *(G-1165)*
Daynas Homecare LLC E 216 323-0323 Maple Heights *(G-13405)*
Dayton Hospice Incorporated B 937 256-4490 Dayton *(G-9479)*
Dayton Hospice Incorporated C 513 422-0300 Franklin *(G-11153)*
Decahealth Inc D 866 908-3514 Toledo *(G-17848)*
Diamonds Pearls Hlth Svcs LLC D 216 752-8500 Cleveland *(G-5482)*
Diane Vishnia Rn and Assoc D 330 929-1113 Cuyahoga Falls *(G-9180)*
Dillon Holdings LLC C 513 942-5600 West Chester *(G-19062)*
▲ **Discount Drug Mart Inc** C 330 725-2340 Medina *(G-14059)*
Diversified Health Management E 614 338-8888 Columbus *(G-7527)*
EJq Home Health Care Inc D 440 323-7004 Elyria *(G-10620)*
Eldercare Services Inst LLC D 216 791-8000 Cleveland *(G-5530)*
Ember Complete Care C 740 922-6888 Uhrichsville *(G-18488)*
Ember Home Care B 740 922-6968 Uhrichsville *(G-18489)*
Emh Regional Homecare Agency E 440 329-7519 Elyria *(G-10625)*
Enhanced Home Health Care LLC D 614 433-7266 Columbus *(G-7595)*
Enhanced Homecare Medina Inc E 330 952-2331 Medina *(G-14062)*
Every Child Succeeds C 513 636-2830 Cincinnati *(G-3583)*
Everyday Homecare E 937 444-1672 Mount Orab *(G-14868)*
Excel Health Services LLC D 614 794-0006 Delaware *(G-10093)*
Exclusive Homecare Services D 937 236-6750 Dayton *(G-9534)*
Fairfield Community Health Ctr E 740 277-6043 Lancaster *(G-12530)*
Fairhope Hospice and Palliativ D 740 654-7077 Lancaster *(G-12540)*
Family Nursing Services Inc E 740 775-5463 Chillicothe *(G-2836)*
Family Senior Care Inc E 740 441-1428 Gallipolis *(G-11315)*
Family Service of NW Ohio D 419 321-6455 Toledo *(G-17878)*
Fidelity Health Care B 937 208-6400 Moraine *(G-14785)*
First Community Hlth Svcs LLC E 937 247-0400 Dayton *(G-9547)*
First Community Village B 614 324-4455 Columbus *(G-7664)*
Frencor Inc D 330 332-1203 Salem *(G-16696)*
Gardens Western Reserve Inc D 330 928-4500 Cuyahoga Falls *(G-9191)*
Genesis Caregivers C 740 454-1370 Zanesville *(G-20480)*
Genesis Healthcare System A 740 454-5000 Zanesville *(G-20481)*
Good Samaritan Hosp Cincinnati E 513 569-6251 Cincinnati *(G-3685)*
Graceworks Lutheran Services B 937 436-6850 Dayton *(G-9583)*
Great Lakes Home Hlth Svcs Inc E 888 260-9835 Toledo *(G-17921)*
Great Lakes Home Hlth Svcs Inc E 888 260-9835 Akron *(G-245)*
Great Lakes Home Hlth Svcs Inc E 888 260-9835 Mentor *(G-14184)*
Guardian Angls Home Hlth Svcs D 419 517-7797 Sylvania *(G-17590)*
Hamilton Homecare Inc E 614 221-0022 Columbus *(G-7796)*
Hanson Services Inc C 216 226-5425 Lakewood *(G-12480)*
Hastings Home Health Ctr Inc E 216 898-3300 Medina *(G-14074)*
Hattie Larlham Community Svcs E 330 274-2272 Mantua *(G-13389)*
Hcr Manorcare Med Svcs Fla LLC D 513 233-0831 Cincinnati *(G-3747)*
Healing Hands Home Health Ltd E 740 385-0710 Logan *(G-12973)*
Health Care Depo of Ohio LLC D 614 776-3333 Columbus *(G-7810)*
Health Care Facility MGT LLC D 513 489-7100 Blue Ash *(G-1608)*
Health Care Plus E 614 340-7587 Columbus *(G-6882)*
Health Services Coshocton Cnty E 740 622-7311 Coshocton *(G-9104)*
Healthcare Circle Inc D 440 331-7347 Strongsville *(G-17468)*
Healthcare Holdings Inc D 513 530-1600 Blue Ash *(G-1609)*
Healthlinx Inc E 513 402-2018 Cincinnati *(G-3754)*
Healthsource of Ohio Inc E 937 981-7707 Greenfield *(G-11487)*
Heart To Heart Home Health E 330 335-9999 Wadsworth *(G-18755)*
Heartland Home Care LLC E 614 433-0423 Columbus *(G-7818)*
Heartland Hospice Services LLC D 614 433-0423 Columbus *(G-7819)*
Heartland Hospice Services LLC D 740 351-0575 Portsmouth *(G-16285)*
Heartland Hospice Services LLC D 740 259-0281 Lucasville *(G-13180)*
Heartland Hospice Services LLC D 419 531-0440 Perrysburg *(G-16010)*
Heartland Hospice Services LLC D 216 901-1464 Independence *(G-12216)*
Heartland Hospice Services LLC E 937 299-6980 Dayton *(G-9607)*
Heavenly Home Health E 740 859-4735 Rayland *(G-16417)*
Helping Hands Health Care Inc C 513 755-4181 West Chester *(G-19206)*
Heritage Day Health Centers E 614 451-2151 Columbus *(G-7830)*
Heritage Health Care Services D 419 222-2404 Lima *(G-12798)*
Heritage Health Care Services C 419 867-2002 Maumee *(G-13925)*
Heritage Home Health Care E 440 333-1925 Rocky River *(G-16580)*
Hillebrand Home Health Inc E 513 598-6648 Cincinnati *(G-3761)*
Holy Family Hospice D 440 888-7722 Parma *(G-15909)*
Home Care Advantage D 330 337-4663 Salem *(G-16699)*
Home Care Network Inc D 937 435-1142 Dayton *(G-9613)*
Home Care Relief Inc D 216 692-2270 Euclid *(G-10761)*
Home Helpers D 937 393-8600 Hillsboro *(G-11983)*
Home Helpers In Home Care D 330 455-5440 Canton *(G-2403)*
Home Instead Senior Care D 330 334-4664 Wadsworth *(G-18756)*
Home Instead Senior Care E 740 393-2500 Mount Vernon *(G-14898)*
Home Instead Senior Care D 330 729-1233 Youngstown *(G-20218)*
Home Instead Senior Care D 614 432-8524 Upper Arlington *(G-18551)*
Homecare Mtters HM Hlth Hspice D 419 562-2001 Bucyrus *(G-2040)*
Homereach Inc C 614 566-0850 Worthington *(G-19965)*
Hometech Healthcare Svcs LLC E 216 295-9120 Cleveland *(G-5769)*
Hope Homes Inc E 330 688-4935 Stow *(G-17372)*
Horizon HM Hlth Care Agcy LLC E 614 279-2933 Columbus *(G-7859)*
Hospice Care Ohio E 330 665-1455 Fairlawn *(G-10956)*
Hospice Caring Way D 419 238-9223 Van Wert *(G-18635)*

80 HEALTH SERVICES

Hospice Cincinnati Inc .... E 513 862-1100
Cincinnati (G-3785)
Hospice Cincinnati Inc .... D 513 891-7700
Cincinnati (G-3786)
Hospice of Genesis Health .... E 740 454-5381
Zanesville (G-20488)
Hospice of Knox County .... E 740 397-5188
Mount Vernon (G-14899)
Hospice of Memorial Hospita L .... E 419 334-6626
Clyde (G-6815)
Hospice of Miami County Inc .... E 937 335-5191
Troy (G-18358)
Hospice of North Central Ohio .... E 419 524-9200
Ontario (G-15692)
Hospice of North Central Ohio .... E 419 281-7107
Ashland (G-682)
Hospice of Ohio LLC .... D 440 286-2500
Cleveland (G-5777)
Hospice of The Western Reserve .... D 330 800-2240
Medina (G-14077)
Hospice of The Western Reserve .... D 800 707-8921
Cleveland (G-5778)
Hospice of The Western Reserve .... D 440 997-6619
Ashtabula (G-748)
Hospice of The Western Reserve .... D 800 707-8922
Cleveland (G-5780)
Huntsey Corporation .... E 614 568-5030
Westerville (G-19315)
In Home Health LLC .... E 419 531-0440
Toledo (G-17972)
In Home Health LLC .... E 513 831-5800
Cincinnati (G-3810)
In Home Health LLC .... E 419 355-9209
Fremont (G-11207)
Independent Living of Ohio .... E 937 323-8400
Springfield (G-17211)
Infinity Health Services Inc .... D 440 614-0145
Westlake (G-19498)
▲ Infusion Partners Inc .... E 513 396-6060
Cincinnati (G-3818)
Inter Healt Care of Cambr Zane .... E 614 436-9404
Columbus (G-7912)
Inter Healt Care of Cambr Zane .... E 513 984-1110
Cincinnati (G-3830)
Interim Halthcare Columbus Inc .... E 614 888-3130
Gahanna (G-11249)
Interim Halthcare Columbus Inc .... E 330 836-5571
Fairlawn (G-10958)
Interim Healthcare .... D 740 354-5550
Portsmouth (G-16291)
Interim Healthcare SE Ohio Inc .... D 740 373-3800
Marietta (G-13457)
International Healthcare Corp .... D 513 731-3338
Cincinnati (G-3836)
Intervention For Peace Inc .... E 330 725-1298
Medina (G-14083)
Jag Healthcare Inc .... A 440 385-4370
Rocky River (G-16582)
Kaiser-Wells Inc .... E 419 668-7651
Norwalk (G-15577)
Karopa Incorporate .... E 513 860-1616
Hamilton (G-11749)
Kindred Healthcare Inc .... C 440 232-1800
Bedford Heights (G-1355)
Kindred Healthcare Inc .... A 937 433-2400
Dayton (G-9661)
Labelle Hmhealth Care Svcs LLC .... D 440 842-3005
Cleveland (G-5916)
Labelle Hmhealth Care Svcs LLC .... D 740 392-1405
Mount Vernon (G-14908)
Laurie Ann Home Health Care .... E 330 872-7512
Newton Falls (G-15275)
Lbs International Inc .... D 614 866-3688
Pickerington (G-16100)
Liberty Health Care Center Inc .... E 937 296-1550
Bellbrook (G-1371)
Lifecare Alliance .... C 614 278-3130
Columbus (G-8063)
Lighthouse Medical Staffing .... D 614 937-6259
Hilliard (G-11921)
Little Miami Home Care Inc .... E 513 248-8988
Milford (G-14531)
Living Assistance Services .... D 330 733-1532
Tallmadge (G-17644)
Loft Services LLC .... E 614 855-2452
New Albany (G-14991)
Loving Family Home Care Inc .... D 888 469-2178
Toledo (G-18012)
Loving Hands Home Care Inc .... E 330 792-7032
Youngstown (G-20256)

Lutheran Social Services of .... E 614 228-5200
Worthington (G-19975)
Mahoning Vly Infusioncare Inc .... C 330 759-9487
Youngstown (G-20266)
Main Street Fmly Medicine LLC .... E 614 253-8537
Columbus (G-8100)
Majastan Group LLC .... D 216 231-6400
Cleveland (G-5971)
Manor Care Inc .... D 419 252-5500
Toledo (G-18028)
Maple Knoll Communities Inc .... B 513 782-2400
Cincinnati (G-4019)
Maplecrst Asistd Lvg Intl Ordr .... E 419 562-4988
Bucyrus (G-2043)
Marietta Memorial Hospital .... E 740 373-8549
Marietta (G-13472)
Marion General Hosp HM Hlth .... E 740 383-8770
Marion (G-13558)
▲ Marymount Hospital Inc .... B 216 581-0500
Cleveland (G-5991)
Mch Services Inc .... C 260 432-9699
Dayton (G-9707)
Med America Hlth Systems Corp .... A 937 223-6192
Dayton (G-9710)
Medcentral Health System .... E 419 526-8442
Mansfield (G-13338)
Medcorp Inc .... D 419 727-7000
Toledo (G-18047)
Medcorp Inc .... C 419 425-9700
Findlay (G-11065)
Medi Home Health Agency Inc .... E 740 266-3977
Steubenville (G-17329)
Medi Home Health Agency Inc .... E 740 441-1779
Gallipolis (G-11328)
Medlink of Ohio Inc .... B 216 751-5900
Cleveland (G-6016)
Memorial Hospital .... E 419 547-6419
Clyde (G-6818)
Menorah Park Center For Senio .... D 330 867-2143
Cuyahoga Falls (G-9208)
Mercer Cnty Joint Townshp Hosp .... E 419 584-0143
Celina (G-2653)
Mid Ohio Home Health Ltd .... E 419 529-3883
Ontario (G-15704)
Mircale Health Care .... C 614 237-7702
Columbus (G-8178)
Mount Carmel Health .... D 614 234-0100
Westerville (G-19427)
Mount Crmel Hospice Evrgrn Ctr .... D 614 234-0200
Columbus (G-8200)
Multicare Home Health Services .... D 216 731-8900
Euclid (G-10768)
National Church Residences .... E 614 451-2151
Columbus (G-8216)
National Mentor Holdings Inc .... A 419 443-0867
Fostoria (G-11135)
National Mentor Holdings Inc .... A 330 835-1468
Fairlawn (G-10967)
National Mentor Holdings Inc .... A 234 806-5361
Warren (G-18884)
Nationwide Childrens Hospital .... E 614 355-8300
Westerville (G-19331)
Nationwide Health MGT LLC .... D 440 888-8888
Parma (G-15911)
NC Hha Inc .... D 216 593-7750
Elyria (G-10658)
NCR At Home Health & Wellness .... E 614 451-2151
Columbus (G-8253)
New Life Hospice Inc .... E 440 934-1458
Lorain (G-13064)
New Life Hospice Inc .... D 440 934-1458
Sheffield Village (G-16893)
Nightingale Home Care .... E 614 457-6006
Columbus (G-8279)
Nightingale Home Healthcare .... E 614 408-0104
Dublin (G-10409)
Northeast Professional Hm Care .... E 330 966-2311
Canton (G-2476)
Nurse Medicinal Healthcare Svcs .... D 614 801-1300
Grove City (G-11586)
Nurses Care Inc .... D 513 424-1141
Miamisburg (G-14327)
Nurses Care Inc .... E 513 424-1141
Fairfield (G-10885)
Nursing Resources Corp .... E 419 333-3000
Maumee (G-13951)
Odyssey Healthcare Inc .... C 614 414-0500
Gahanna (G-11260)
Ohio Home Health Care Inc .... E 937 853-0271
Dayton (G-9785)

Ohio North E Hlth Systems Inc .... E 330 747-9551
Youngstown (G-20308)
Ohio Senior Home Hlth Care LLC .... D 614 470-6070
Columbus (G-8375)
Ohio Valley Home Care LLC .... E 330 385-2333
East Liverpool (G-10529)
Ohio Valley Home Health Inc .... E 740 249-4219
Athens (G-809)
Ohio Valley Home Health Inc .... E 740 441-1393
Gallipolis (G-11334)
Ohio Valley Home Hlth Svcs Inc .... E 330 385-2333
East Liverpool (G-10530)
Ohioans Home Health Care Inc .... D 419 843-4422
Perrysburg (G-16037)
Ohiohealth Corporation .... A 614 788-8860
Columbus (G-8457)
Omni Park Health Care LLC .... C 216 289-8963
Euclid (G-10770)
Omnicare Inc .... C 513 719-2600
Cincinnati (G-4220)
On-Call Nursing Inc .... D 216 577-8890
Lakewood (G-12493)
Open Arms Health Systems LLC .... E 614 385-8354
Columbus (G-8469)
Option Care Enterprises Inc .... C 513 576-8400
Milford (G-14546)
Option Care Infusion Svcs Inc .... E 614 431-6453
Columbus (G-8475)
Option Care Infusion Svcs Inc .... D 513 576-8400
Milford (G-14547)
P E Miller & Assoc .... D 614 231-4743
Columbus (G-8502)
P E Miller & Associates Inc .... E 614 231-4743
Columbus (G-8503)
Palladium Healthcare LLC .... C 216 644-4383
Cleveland (G-6230)
Paramount Support Service .... D 740 526-0540
Saint Clairsville (G-16651)
Parkside Care Corporation .... D 440 286-2273
Chardon (G-2761)
Passion To Heal Healthcare .... E 216 849-0180
Cleveland (G-6249)
Paula Jo Moore .... E 330 894-2910
Kensington (G-12349)
Personal Touch HM Care IPA Inc .... C 216 986-0885
Cleveland (G-6267)
Personal Touch HM Care IPA Inc .... E 937 456-4447
Eaton (G-10573)
Personal Touch HM Care IPA Inc .... C 513 868-2272
Hamilton (G-11763)
Personal Touch HM Care IPA Inc .... E 513 984-9600
Cincinnati (G-4283)
Personal Touch HM Care IPA Inc .... D 614 227-6952
Columbus (G-8539)
Personal Touch HM Care IPA Inc .... A 330 263-1112
Wooster (G-19903)
Phoenix Homes Inc .... E 419 692-2421
Delphos (G-10149)
Physicians Choice Inc .... E 513 844-1608
Liberty Twp (G-12727)
Preferred Medical Group Inc .... C 404 403-8310
Beachwood (G-1115)
Premier Care .... D 614 431-0599
Worthington (G-19985)
Premier Health Partners .... A 937 499-9596
Dayton (G-9820)
Premierfirst Home Health Care .... E 614 443-3110
Columbus (G-8557)
Pressley Ridge Foundation .... E 513 737-0400
Hamilton (G-11764)
Primary Care Nursing Services .... D 614 764-0960
Dublin (C 10430)
Prime Home Care LLC .... E 513 340-4183
Maineville (G-13245)
Prime Home Care LLC .... E 419 535-1414
Toledo (G-18136)
Private Duty Services Inc .... C 419 238-3714
Van Wert (G-18642)
Private HM Care Foundation Inc .... D 513 662-8999
Cincinnati (G-4335)
Pro Health Care Services Ltd .... E 614 856-9111
Groveport (G-11664)
Prome Conti Care Serv Corpo .... A 419 885-1715
Sylvania (G-17657)
Quality Care Nursing Svc Inc .... B 740 377-9095
South Point (G-17096)
Quality Life Providers LLC .... E 614 527-9999
Hilliard (G-11946)
Quantum Health Inc .... D 614 846-4318
Columbus (G-8581)

Employee Codes: A=Over 500 employees, B=251-500
C=101-250, D=51-100, E=25-50

2018 Harris Ohio Services Directory

80 HEALTH SERVICES

Name	Code	Phone
R & F Inc	E	419 868-2909
Holland (G-12047)		
Reflektions Ltd	E	614 560-6994
Delaware (G-10123)		
REM Corp	E	740 828-2601
Frazeysburg (G-11176)		
RES-Care Inc	E	740 782-1476
Bethesda (G-1486)		
RES-Care Inc	E	440 729-2432
Chesterland (G-2802)		
Rescare Ohio Inc	E	740 867-4568
Chesapeake (G-2788)		
Right At Home	D	937 291-2244
Springboro (G-17137)		
Right At Home LLC	E	614 734-1110
Columbus (G-6904)		
RMS of Ohio Inc	D	937 291-3622
Dayton (G-9853)		
Robinson Visitn Nrs Asoc/Hospc	E	330 297-8899
Ravenna (G-16408)		
Ross County Health District	C	740 775-1114
Chillicothe (G-2880)		
RWS Enterprises LLC	D	513 598-6770
Cincinnati (G-4460)		
Salem Area Vsiting Nurse Assoc	E	330 332-9986
Salem (G-16711)		
Salo Inc	D	614 436-9404
Columbus (G-8679)		
Sand Run Supports LLC	E	330 256-2127
Fairlawn (G-10973)		
Sar Enterprises LLC	D	419 472-8181
Toledo (G-18172)		
Sdx Home Care Operations LLC	D	877 692-0345
Springfield (G-17271)		
Selective Networking Inc	D	740 574-2682
Wheelersburg (G-19581)		
Senior Care Management Inc	E	419 578-7000
Toledo (G-18178)		
Senior Independence	E	330 744-5071
Youngstown (G-20370)		
Senior Independence	D	330 873-3468
Fairlawn (G-10975)		
Senior Independence Adult	E	513 539-2697
Monroe (G-14712)		
Senior Select Home Health Care	E	330 665-4663
Fairlawn (G-10976)		
Signature Health Services LLC	E	740 522-6017
Heath (G-11844)		
Simone Health Management Inc	E	614 224-1347
Columbus (G-8735)		
Source Diagnostics LLC	D	440 542-9481
Solon (G-17055)		
Southern Care Inc	E	419 774-0555
Ontario (G-15715)		
Special Touch Homecare LLC	E	937 549-1843
Manchester (G-13256)		
Ssth LLC	D	614 884-0793
Columbus (G-8769)		
St Augustine Towers	E	216 634-7444
Cleveland (G-6520)		
St Ritas Medical Center	C	419 538-7025
Lima (G-12887)		
Summa Health Center Lk Medina	E	330 952-0014
Medina (G-14130)		
Summit Acres Inc	C	740 732-2364
Caldwell (G-2089)		
Sunshine Homecare	E	419 207-9900
Ashland (G-700)		
Supportcare Inc	E	614 889-5837
Dublin (G-10467)		
Supreme Touch Home Health Svcs	D	614 783-1115
Columbus (G-8810)		
Svh Holdings LLC	D	844 560-7775
Columbus (G-8813)		
Synergy Homecare South Dayton	E	937 610-0555
Dayton (G-9918)		
Think-Ability LLC	E	419 589-2238
Mansfield (G-13374)		
Tk Homecare Llc	C	419 517-7000
Toledo (G-18220)		
Tky Associates LLC	D	419 535-7777
Toledo (G-18221)		
TLC Home Health Care Inc	E	740 732-5211
Caldwell (G-2090)		
Toledo District Nurses Assn	C	419 255-0983
Sylvania (G-17622)		
Toledo Hospital	C	419 291-2273
Sylvania (G-17623)		
Traditions At Stygler Road	E	614 475-8778
Columbus (G-8863)		
Tri County Visitng Nrs Prvt	E	419 738-7430
Wapakoneta (G-18809)		
Trusted Homecare Solutions	E	937 506-7063
Dayton (G-9940)		
Tsk Assisted Living Services	E	330 297-2000
Ravenna (G-16414)		
TVC Home Health Care	E	330 755-1110
Youngstown (G-20396)		
Twin Maples Home Health Care	E	740 596-1022
Mc Arthur (G-14017)		
Uahs Heather Hill Home Health	E	440 285-5098
Chardon (G-2772)		
Union Hospital Home Hlth Care	E	330 343-6909
Dover (G-10221)		
United Home Health Services	D	614 880-8686
Columbus (G-8892)		
Universal Health Care Svcs Inc	C	614 547-0282
Columbus (G-8906)		
Universal Nursing Services	E	330 434-7318
Akron (G-487)		
University Hospitals Cleveland	D	216 844-4663
Cleveland (G-6661)		
University Hospitals He	B	216 844-4663
Cleveland (G-6663)		
University Mednet		216 383-0100
Euclid (G-10780)		
Ussa Inc	E	740 354-6672
Portsmouth (G-16319)		
Vancrest Health Care Center	D	419 264-0700
Holgate (G-12004)		
VIP Homecare Inc	D	330 929-2838
Akron (G-497)		
Vishnia & Associates Inc	D	330 929-5512
Cuyahoga Falls (G-9233)		
Visions Matter LLC	D	513 934-1934
Lebanon (G-12656)		
Visiting Nrse Assn of Clveland	B	419 281-2480
Ashland (G-706)		
Visiting Nrse Assn of Clveland	E	419 522-4969
Mansfield (G-13381)		
Visiting Nrse Assn of Clveland	B	216 931-1400
Cleveland (G-6702)		
Visiting Nrse Assn of Mid-Ohio	E	216 931-1300
Cleveland (G-6703)		
Visiting Nurse Associat	C	513 345-8000
Cincinnati (G-4815)		
Visiting Nurse Service Inc	B	330 745-1601
Akron (G-499)		
Visiting Nurse Service Inc	E	440 286-9461
Chardon (G-2776)		
Vistacare USA Inc	E	614 975-3230
Columbus (G-8946)		
Vitas Healthcare Corporation	D	513 742-6310
Cincinnati (G-4816)		
Vitas Healthcare Corporation	E	216 706-2100
Cleveland (G-6706)		
Vrable III Inc	D	740 446-7150
Bidwell (G-1497)		
Western Reserve Area Agency	C	216 621-0303
Cleveland (G-6742)		
Ziks Family Pharmacy 100	E	937 225-9350
Dayton (G-10015)		

8092 Kidney Dialysis Centers

Name	Code	Phone
Alomie Dialysis LLC	E	740 941-1688
Waverly (G-18965)		
Amelia Davita Dialysis Center	E	513 797-0713
Amelia (G-572)		
Barrington Dialysis LLC	E	740 346-2740
Steubenville (G-17303)		
Basin Dialysis LLC	E	937 643-2337
Kettering (G-12427)		
Beck Dialysis LLC	E	513 422-6879
Middletown (G-14415)		
Bio-Mdcal Applcations Ohio Inc	E	937 279-3120
Trotwood (G-18344)		
Bio-Mdcal Applcations Ohio Inc	E	419 874-3447
Perrysburg (G-15979)		
Bio-Mdcal Applcations Ohio Inc	E	330 928-4511
Cuyahoga Falls (G-9166)		
Bio-Mdcal Applcations Ohio Inc	E	330 376-4905
Akron (G-102)		
Bio-Mdcal Applcations Ohio Inc	E	419 774-0180
Mansfield (G-13266)		
Bio-Mdcal Applcations Ohio Inc	E	330 896-6311
Uniontown (G-18507)		
Bio-Mdcal Applcations Ohio Inc	E	614 338-8202
Columbus (G-7112)		
Bio-Mdical Applications RI Inc	E	740 389-4111
Marion (G-13524)		
Cdc of Shaker Heights	E	216 295-7000
Cleveland (G-5200)		
Centers For Dialysis Care Inc	E	216 295-7000
Shaker Heights (G-16858)		
Columbus-Rna-Davita LLC	E	614 985-1732
Columbus (G-7395)		
Comm Ltd Care Dialysis Center	E	513 784-1800
Cincinnati (G-3397)		
Community Dialysis Center	C	216 229-6170
Cleveland (G-5384)		
Community Dialysis Ctr Mentor	E	440 255-5999
Mentor (G-14161)		
Court Dialysis LLC	E	740 773-3733
Chillicothe (G-2831)		
Crestview Health Care Center	D	740 695-2500
Saint Clairsville (G-16634)		
Davita Healthcare Partners Inc	E	216 961-6498
Cleveland (G-5469)		
Davita Healthcare Partners Inc	E	440 353-0114
North Ridgeville (G-15462)		
Davita Inc	E	513 939-1110
Fairfield (G-10839)		
Davita Inc	E	216 712-4700
Rocky River (G-16576)		
Davita Inc	E	440 891-5645
Cleveland (G-5470)		
Davita Inc	E	740 376-2622
Marietta (G-13442)		
Davita Inc	E	937 456-1174
Eaton (G-10555)		
Davita Inc	E	330 494-2091
Canton (G-2335)		
Davita Inc	E	216 525-0990
Independence (G-12202)		
Davita Inc	E	937 879-0433
Fairborn (G-10791)		
Davita Inc	E	937 426-6475
Beavercreek (G-1166)		
Davita Inc	E	937 435-4030
Dayton (G-9452)		
Davita Inc	E	937 376-1453
Xenia (G-20049)		
Davita Inc	E	513 784-1800
Cincinnati (G-3465)		
Davita Inc	E	740 401-0607
Belpre (G-1435)		
Davita Inc	E	330 335-2300
Wadsworth (G-18752)		
Davita Inc	E	440 251-6237
Madison (G-13222)		
Davita Inc	E	330 733-1861
Akron (G-188)		
Davita Inc	E	419 697-2191
Oregon (G-15730)		
Davita Inc	E	513 624-0400
Cincinnati (G-3466)		
Dayton Regional Dialysis Inc	E	937 898-5526
Dayton (G-9490)		
Desoto Dialysis LLC	E	419 691-1514
Oregon (G-15731)		
Dialysis Center of Dayton East	E	937 252-1867
Dayton (G-9500)		
Dialysis Clinic Inc	D	513 281-0091
Cincinnati (G-3489)		
Dialysis Clinic Inc	E	740 351-0596
Portsmouth (G-16276)		
Dialysis Clinic Inc	E	513 777-0855
West Chester (G-19061)		
Dialysis Clinic Inc	E	740 264-6687
Steubenville (G-17314)		
Dialysis Specialists Fairfield	E	513 863-6331
Fairfield (G-10841)		
Dome Dialysis LLC	E	614 882-1734
Westerville (G-19395)		
DSI East	E	330 733-1861
Akron (G-201)		
Dva Healthcare - South	E	513 347-0444
Cincinnati (G-3516)		
Dva Renal Healthcare Inc	E	740 454-2911
Zanesville (G-20471)		
Fort Dialysis LLC	E	330 837-7730
Massillon (G-13809)		
Fresenius Med Care Butler Cty	E	513 737-1415
Hamilton (G-11730)		
Fresenius Med Care Hldings Inc	E	800 881-5101
Columbus (G-7703)		
Fresenius Medical Care Vro LLC	E	614 875-2349
Grove City (G-11564)		
Goza Dialysis LLC	E	513 738-0276
Fairfield (G-10852)		

Greater Columbus Regional ....D 614 228-9114
  Columbus (G-7775)
Greenfield Health Systems Corp ....E 419 389-9681
  Toledo (G-17923)
Hemodialysis Services Inc ....E 216 378-2691
  Beachwood (G-1085)
Heyburn Dialysis LLC ....E 614 876-3610
  Hilliard (G-11909)
Innovative Dialysis of Toledo ....E 419 473-9900
  Toledo (G-17975)
Isd Renal Inc ....D 330 375-6848
  Akron (G-284)
Kidney Center of Bexley LLC ....C 614 231-2200
  Columbus (G-7987)
Kidney Center Partnership ....D 330 799-1150
  Youngstown (G-20244)
Kidney Group Inc ....E 330 746-1488
  Youngstown (G-20245)
Kidney Services W Centl Ohio ....E 419 227-0918
  Lima (G-12808)
Kinswa Dialysis LLC ....E 419 332-0310
  Fremont (G-11209)
Lakeshore Dialysis LLC ....E 937 278-0516
  Dayton (G-9670)
Lory Dialysis LLC ....E 740 522-2955
  Newark (G-15198)
Mahoney Dialysis LLC ....E 937 642-0676
  Marysville (G-13633)
Manzano Dialysis LLC ....E 937 879-0433
  Fairborn (G-10802)
Mesilla Dialysis LLC ....E 937 484-4600
  Urbana (G-18597)
Morro Dialysis LLC ....E 937 865-0633
  Miamisburg (G-14324)
Mount Carmel E Dialysis Clnc ....E 614 322-0433
  Columbus (G-8194)
Ohio Renal Care Group LLC ....D 440 974-3459
  Mentor (G-14224)
Pendster Dialysis LLC ....E 937 237-0769
  Huber Heights (G-12097)
Renal Life Link Inc ....E 937 383-3338
  Wilmington (G-19782)
Seneca Dialysis LLC ....E 419 443-1051
  Tiffin (G-17700)
Steele Dialysis LLC ....E 419 462-1028
  Galion (G-11305)
Tonka Bay Dialysis LLC ....E 740 375-0849
  Marion (G-13585)
Total Renal Care Inc ....E 937 294-6711
  Kettering (G-12436)
Total Renal Care Inc ....E 937 252-1867
  Dayton (G-9933)
Trinity Health Corporation ....B 614 846-5420
  Columbus (G-8872)
Vogel Dialysis LLC ....E 614 834-3564
  Canal Winchester (G-2175)
Wakoni Dialysis LLC ....E 937 294-7188
  Moraine (G-14834)
Wallowa Dialysis LLC ....E 419 747-4039
  Ontario (G-15719)
Wauseon Dialysis LLC ....E 419 335-0695
  Wauseon (G-18963)

8093 Specialty Outpatient Facilities, NEC

A W S Inc ....D 216 941-8800
  Cleveland (G-4938)
A+ Solutions LLC ....E 216 896-0111
  Beachwood (G-1044)
Accelerated Health Systems LLC ....D 614 334-5135
  Hilliard (G-11876)
Akron General Medical Center ....C 330 665-8000
  Akron (G-46)
Alcohol Drug Addiction & Mental ....E 937 443-0416
  Dayton (G-9314)
Allwell Behavioral Health Svcs ....C 740 454-9766
  Zanesville (G-20440)
Allwell Behavioral Health Svcs ....E 740 439-4428
  Cambridge (G-2094)
Alta Care Group Inc ....E 330 793-2487
  Youngstown (G-20102)
Alternative Paths Inc ....E 330 725-9195
  Medina (G-14035)
American Kidney Stone MGT Ltd 800 637-5188
  Columbus (G-6999)
Amethyst Inc ....D 614 242-1284
  Columbus (G-7014)
Anazao Community Partners ....E 330 264-9597
  Wooster (G-19828)
Appleseed Cmnty Mntal Hlth Ctr ....E 419 281-3716
  Ashland (G-651)

Audrich Inc ....C 419 483-6225
  Bellevue (G-1403)
Aurora Manor Special Care ....E 440 424-4000
  Aurora (G-827)
Bayshore Counseling Service ....E 419 626-9156
  Sandusky (G-16728)
Beacon Health ....C 440 354-9924
  Mentor (G-14148)
Behavorial Healthcare ....E 740 522-8477
  Newark (G-15146)
Behavral Cnnctions WD Cnty Inc ....C 419 352-5387
  Bowling Green (G-1760)
Behavral Cnnctions WD Cnty Inc ....E 419 872-2419
  Perrysburg (G-15976)
Behavral Cnnctions WD Cnty Inc ....E 419 352-5387
  Bowling Green (G-1761)
Behavral Cnnctions WD Cnty Inc ....E 419 352-5387
  Bowling Green (G-1762)
Belmont Bhc Pines Hospital Inc ....C 330 759-2700
  Youngstown (G-20113)
Best Care Nrsing Rhbltition Ctr ....C 740 574-2558
  Wheelersburg (G-19570)
Bhc Fox Run Hospital Inc ....E 740 695-2131
  Saint Clairsville (G-16628)
Blick Clinic Inc ....C 330 762-5425
  Akron (G-103)
Blick Clinic Inc ....E 330 762-5425
  Akron (G-104)
Brecksville Hlthcare Group Inc ....D 440 546-0643
  Brecksville (G-1816)
Bridgeway Inc ....B 216 688-4114
  Cleveland (G-5138)
Butler Bhavioral Hlth Svcs Inc ....E 513 896-7887
  Hamilton (G-11698)
Cancer Ntwk of W Cent ....E 419 226-9085
  Lima (G-12751)
Caprice Health Care Inc ....C 330 965-9200
  North Lima (G-15400)
Center 5 ....D 330 379-5900
  Akron (G-127)
Center For Chemical Addictions ....D 513 381-6672
  Cincinnati (G-3207)
Center For Families & Children ....E 216 252-5800
  Cleveland (G-5207)
Center For Individual and Fmly ....C 419 522-4357
  Mansfield (G-13274)
Central Commnty Hlth Brd of Ha ....E 513 559-2981
  Cincinnati (G-3212)
Central Commnty Hlth Brd of Ha ....E 513 559-2000
  Cincinnati (G-3211)
Central Ohio Mental Health Ctr ....C 740 368-7831
  Delaware (G-10079)
Century Health Inc ....D 419 425-5050
  Findlay (G-11012)
CHI Health At Home ....E 513 576-0262
  Milford (G-14510)
Child Focus Inc ....D 513 752-1555
  Cincinnati (G-3243)
Childrens Hospital Medical Ctr ....E 513 636-6100
  Cincinnati (G-3251)
Childrens Hospital Medical Ctr ....E 513 636-6800
  Mason (G-13676)
Childrens Rehabilitation Ctr ....E 330 856-2107
  Warren (G-18833)
Choices Behavioral Healthcare ....E 216 881-4060
  Cleveland (G-5238)
Christ Hospital Spine Surgery ....E 513 619-5899
  Cincinnati (G-3270)
Christian Chld HM Ohio Inc ....D 330 345-7949
  Wooster (G-19841)
Cincinnati Speech Hearing Ctr ....E 513 221-0527
  Cincinnati (G-3328)
Clermont Recovery Center Inc ....E 513 735-8100
  Batavia (G-1003)
Cleveland Clinic Foundation ....D 440 988-5651
  Lorain (G-13026)
Cleveland Preterm ....E 216 991-4577
  Cleveland (G-5340)
Clevelnd Clnc Hlth Systm East ....E 330 287-4830
  Wooster (G-19850)
Clevelnd Clnc Hlth Systm East ....E 330 468-0190
  Northfield (G-15512)
Clinton County Board of ....E 937 382-7519
  Wilmington (G-19749)
Clinton Memorial Hospital ....E 937 383-3402
  Wilmington (G-19754)
Coleman Professional Svcs Inc ....B 330 673-1347
  Kent (G-12360)
Coleman Professional Svcs Inc ....D 330 296-8313
  Ravenna (G-16377)

Columbus Area ....D 614 251-6561
  Columbus (G-7328)
Columbus Area Inc ....E 614 252-0711
  Columbus (G-7329)
Columbus Area Integrated Healt ....D 614 252-0711
  Columbus (G-7330)
Community Action Against Addic ....E 216 881-0765
  Cleveland (G-5382)
Community Assesment and Treatm .....D 216 441-0200
  Cleveland (G-5383)
Community Behavioral Hlth Inc ....C 513 887-8500
  Hamilton (G-11716)
Community Counseling Services ....E 419 468-8211
  Bucyrus (G-2031)
Community Counsing Ctr Ashtabu ....D 440 998-4210
  Ashtabula (G-736)
Community Drug Board Inc ....D 330 315-5590
  Akron (G-153)
Community Health Centers Ohio ....D 216 831-1494
  Beachwood (G-1067)
Community Mental Health Svc ....D 740 695-9344
  Saint Clairsville (G-16633)
Community Solutions Assn ....E 330 394-9090
  Warren (G-18838)
Community Support Services Inc ....C 330 253-9388
  Akron (G-157)
Community Support Services Inc ....E 330 253-9675
  Akron (G-158)
Community Support Services Inc ....E 330 733-6203
  Akron (G-159)
Communty Mntl Hlth Ctr ....D 513 228-7800
  Lebanon (G-12596)
Compass Community Health ....E 740 355-7102
  Portsmouth (G-16273)
Comprehensive Addiction Svc Sy ....D 419 241-8827
  Toledo (G-17826)
Comprehensive Behavioral Hlth ....E 330 797-4050
  Youngstown (G-20157)
Comprehensive Counseling Svc ....E 513 424-0921
  Middletown (G-14422)
Concept Rehab Inc ....D 419 843-6002
  Toledo (G-17828)
Consolidated Care Inc ....E 937 465-8065
  West Liberty (G-19262)
Consumer Advocacy Model ....E 937 222-2400
  Dayton (G-9424)
▲ Cora Health Services Inc ....E 419 221-3004
  Lima (G-12760)
Cornerstone Support Services ....D 330 339-7850
  New Philadelphia (G-15088)
Counseling Center Huron County ....E 419 663-3737
  Norwalk (G-15567)
Counseling Source Inc ....E 513 984-9838
  Blue Ash (G-1569)
Country Meadow Care Center LLC ......E 419 886-3922
  Bellville (G-1425)
County of Allen ....E 419 221-1226
  Lima (G-12766)
County of Carroll ....E 330 627-7651
  Carrollton (G-2616)
County of Cuyahoga ....E 216 443-7035
  Cleveland (G-5418)
County of Geauga ....C 440 286-6264
  Chardon (G-2745)
County of Hamilton ....B 513 598-2965
  Cincinnati (G-3431)
County of Lorain ....E 440 989-4900
  Elyria (G-10614)
Craig and Frances Lindner Cent ....C 513 536-4673
  Mason (G-13691)
Crossroads Center ....C 513 475-5300
  Cincinnati (G-3442)
Crossroads Lake County Adole ....E 440 255-1700
  Mentor (G-14165)
Darke Cnty Mental Hlth Clinic ....E 937 548-1635
  Greenville (G-11494)
Day-Mont Bhvoral Hlth Care Inc ....D 937 222-8111
  Moraine (G-14768)
East Way Behavioral Hlth Care ....C 937 222-4900
  Dayton (G-9515)
Easter Seal Society of ....D 330 743-1168
  Youngstown (G-20176)
Eastway Corporation ....C 937 531-7000
  Dayton (G-9517)
Education Alternatives ....D 216 332-9360
  Brookpark (G-1944)
Emerge Counseling Service ....E 330 865-8351
  Akron (G-207)
Empowered For Excellence ....E 567 316-7253
  Toledo (G-17866)

Equitas Health Inc..........C....... 614 299-2437
Columbus *(G-7603)*
F R S Connections..........E....... 937 393-9662
Hillsboro *(G-11973)*
Fairfld Ctr For Disablts & CER..........E....... 740 653-1186
Lancaster *(G-12539)*
Family Planning Center..........E....... 740 439-3340
Cambridge *(G-2112)*
Family Plnning Assoc of Ne..........E....... 440 352-0608
Painesville *(G-15856)*
Family Recovery Center Inc..........E....... 330 424-1468
Lisbon *(G-12937)*
Family Rsource Ctr NW Ohio Inc..........E....... 419 222-1168
Lima *(G-12777)*
Family Rsource Ctr NW Ohio Inc..........E....... 419 422-8616
Findlay *(G-11023)*
Firelands Regional Health Sys..........E....... 419 332-5524
Fremont *(G-11197)*
Firelands Regional Health Sys..........E....... 419 663-3737
Norwalk *(G-15573)*
First Call For Help Inc..........E....... 419 599-1660
Napoleon *(G-14939)*
Formu3 International Inc..........E....... 330 668-1461
Akron *(G-228)*
Foundtion Behavioral Hlth Svcs..........E....... 419 584-1000
Celina *(G-2647)*
Frs Counseling Inc..........E....... 937 393-0585
Hillsboro *(G-11975)*
Fulton County Health Center..........E....... 419 337-8661
Wauseon *(G-18954)*
Fulton County Health Dept..........E....... 419 337-6979
Wauseon *(G-18956)*
Genesis Respiratory Svcs Inc..........E....... 740 354-4363
Portsmouth *(G-16278)*
Giving Tree Inc..........E....... 419 898-0077
Oak Harbor *(G-15610)*
Harbor..........D....... 419 479-3233
Toledo *(G-17932)*
Harbor..........D....... 419 241-6191
Toledo *(G-17933)*
Harbor..........E....... 800 444-3353
Toledo *(G-17934)*
HCA Holdings Inc..........D....... 440 826-3240
Cleveland *(G-5734)*
Hcf of Roselawn Inc..........C....... 419 647-4115
Spencerville *(G-17108)*
▲ **Health Partners Health Clinic**..........E....... 937 645-8488
Marysville *(G-13623)*
Healthsource of Ohio Inc..........E....... 513 707-1997
Batavia *(G-1016)*
Healthsource of Ohio Inc..........E....... 937 981-7707
Greenfield *(G-11487)*
Heartland Rhblitation Svcs Inc..........D....... 419 537-0764
Toledo *(G-17949)*
Heartlnd-Riverview S Pt OH LLC..........C....... 740 894-3287
South Point *(G-17089)*
HHC Ohio Inc..........E....... 440 953-3000
Willoughby *(G-19668)*
Hill Manor 1 Inc..........E....... 740 972-3227
Columbus *(G-7836)*
Hitchcock Center For Women Inc..........E....... 216 421-0662
Cleveland *(G-5761)*
Hope Ctr For Cncer Care Warren..........D....... 330 856-8600
Warren *(G-18863)*
Hopewell Health Centers Inc..........E....... 740 385-6594
Logan *(G-12977)*
Hospice of Darke County Inc..........E....... 419 678-4808
Coldwater *(G-6830)*
Integrated Youth Services Inc..........E....... 937 427-3837
Springfield *(G-17213)*
Ironton and Lawrence County..........B....... 740 532-3534
Ironton *(G-12291)*
Jac-Lin Manor..........D....... 419 994-5700
Loudonville *(G-13091)*
Kindred Healthcare Oper Inc..........D....... 740 545-6355
West Lafayette *(G-19258)*
Kindred Healthcare Oper Inc..........C....... 740 387-7537
Marion *(G-13545)*
Kindred Nursing Centers E LLC..........C....... 502 596-7300
Logan *(G-12981)*
Legacy Freedom Treatment Ctr..........E....... 614 741-2100
Columbus *(G-8049)*
Lorain County Alcohol and Drug..........D....... 440 246-0109
Lorain *(G-13050)*
Lorain County Alcohol and Drug..........E....... 440 989-4900
Lorain *(G-13051)*
Lorain County Board..........E....... 440 329-3734
Elyria *(G-10646)*
Lutheran Social..........E....... 419 229-2222
Lima *(G-12834)*
Mahoning Vly Hmtlgy Onclgy Aso..........E....... 330 318-1100
Youngstown *(G-20265)*
Main Place Inc..........E....... 740 345-6246
Newark *(G-15200)*
Manor Care of Kansas Inc..........D....... 419 252-5500
Toledo *(G-18031)*
Marca Terrace Widows..........D....... 937 252-1661
Dayton *(G-9698)*
Marietta Center For Health &..........C....... 740 373-1867
Marietta *(G-13466)*
Marion Area Counseling Ctr..........C....... 740 387-5210
Marion *(G-13553)*
Maryhaven Inc..........E....... 419 946-6734
Mount Gilead *(G-14855)*
Maumee Valley Guidance Center..........E....... 419 782-8856
Defiance *(G-10046)*
McKinley Hall Inc..........E....... 937 328-5300
Springfield *(G-17230)*
Medcentral Health System..........C....... 419 683-1040
Crestline *(G-9147)*
Medcentral Health System..........E....... 419 526-8442
Mansfield *(G-13338)*
Meigs Center Ltd..........C....... 740 992-6472
Middleport *(G-14407)*
Mental Health & Recovery Ctr..........E....... 937 383-3031
Wilmington *(G-19773)*
Mental Health and Addi Serv..........E....... 740 594-5000
Athens *(G-801)*
Mental Health and Addi Serv..........C....... 614 752-0333
Columbus *(G-8148)*
Mental Hlth Serv For CL & Mad..........E....... 740 852-6256
London *(G-13003)*
Mercy Healthplexm LLC..........E....... 513 870-7101
Fairfield *(G-10881)*
Mercy Medical Center Inc..........E....... 330 627-7641
Carrollton *(G-2623)*
Meridian Healthcare..........D....... 330 797-0070
Youngstown *(G-20285)*
Met Group..........E....... 330 864-1916
Fairlawn *(G-10964)*
Metrohealth System..........E....... 216 957-5000
Cleveland *(G-6037)*
Metrohealth System..........D....... 216 778-8446
Cleveland *(G-6040)*
Mid-Ohio Psychlogical Svcs Inc..........E....... 740 687-0042
Lancaster *(G-12558)*
Midwest Behavioral Care Ltd..........E....... 937 454-0092
Dayton *(G-9744)*
Midwest Rehab Inc..........D....... 419 238-3405
Ada *(G-6)*
Moundbuilders Guidance Ctr Inc..........E....... 740 397-0442
Mount Vernon *(G-14913)*
National Mentor Holdings Inc..........A....... 330 491-4331
Youngstown *(G-20298)*
Nationwide Childrens Hospital..........B....... 614 355-8000
Columbus *(G-8237)*
Neighborhood Health Asso..........D....... 419 720-7883
Toledo *(G-18080)*
Neighborhood House..........D....... 614 252-4941
Columbus *(G-8256)*
Noble Cnty Nble Cnty Cmmsoners..........E....... 740 732-4958
Caldwell *(G-2088)*
Norcare Enterprises Inc..........B....... 440 233-7232
Lorain *(G-13065)*
Nord Center..........E....... 440 233-7232
Lorain *(G-13066)*
▲ **Nord Center Associates Inc**..........C....... 440 233-7232
Lorain *(G-13067)*
North Cntl Mntal Hlth Svcs Inc..........D....... 614 227-6865
Columbus *(G-8288)*
North Community Counseling Ctr..........D....... 614 846-2588
Columbus *(G-8289)*
North East Ohio Health Svcs..........D....... 216 831-6466
Beachwood *(G-1107)*
Northpoint Senior Services LLC..........D....... 740 369-9614
Delaware *(G-10118)*
Northwest Mental Health Svcs..........E....... 614 457-7876
Columbus *(G-8297)*
Odyssey Healthcare Inc..........E....... 937 298-2800
Dayton *(G-9783)*
Ohio Heart Institute Inc..........E....... 330 747-6446
Youngstown *(G-20306)*
Ohio State University..........A....... 614 257-3000
Columbus *(G-8393)*
Opportunities For Ohioans..........E....... 513 852-3260
Cincinnati *(G-4229)*
Oral & Maxillofacial Surgeons..........E....... 419 385-5743
Toledo *(G-18110)*
Orca House..........E....... 216 231-3772
Cleveland *(G-6212)*
Pain Management Associates Inc..........E....... 937 252-2000
Dayton *(G-9281)*
Peak Performance Center Inc..........E....... 440 838-5600
Broadview Heights *(G-1889)*
Philio Inc..........E....... 419 531-5544
Toledo *(G-18124)*
Planned Parenthood Association..........E....... 937 226-0780
Dayton *(G-9811)*
Planned Parenthood NW Ohio Inc..........E....... 419 255-1115
Toledo *(G-18128)*
Planned Parenthood of SW OH..........E....... 513 721-7635
Cincinnati *(G-4302)*
Planned Prenthood Greater Ohio..........E....... 614 224-2235
Columbus *(G-8549)*
Planned Prenthood Greater Ohio..........E....... 330 535-2671
Akron *(G-391)*
Planned Prenthood Greater Ohio..........E....... 216 961-8804
Bedford Heights *(G-1356)*
Planned Prenthood Greater Ohio..........E....... 330 788-2487
Youngstown *(G-20322)*
Planned Prnthood of Mhning Vly..........E....... 330 788-6506
Youngstown *(G-20323)*
Plastic Surgery Group Inc..........E....... 513 791-4440
Cincinnati *(G-4303)*
Portage Path Behavorial Health..........D....... 330 253-3100
Akron *(G-397)*
Portage Path Behavorial Health..........D....... 330 762-6110
Akron *(G-398)*
Portage Physical Therapists..........D....... 330 297-9020
Ravenna *(G-16402)*
Positive Education Program..........E....... 440 471-8200
Cleveland *(G-6292)*
Pregnancy Care of Cincinnati..........E....... 513 487-7777
Cincinnati *(G-4321)*
Pressley Ridge Foundation..........A....... 513 752-4548
Cincinnati *(G-2929)*
Project C U R E Inc..........E....... 937 262-3500
Dayton *(G-9836)*
Psy-Care Inc..........E....... 330 856-6663
Warren *(G-18891)*
Psychlgcal Behavioral Cons LLC..........E....... 216 456-8123
Beachwood *(G-1116)*
Ravenwood Mental Health Center..........E....... 440 632-5355
Middlefield *(G-14401)*
Ravenwood Mental Hlth Ctr Inc..........E....... 440 285-3568
Chardon *(G-2763)*
Recovery Center..........E....... 740 687-4500
Lancaster *(G-12568)*
Recovery Prv RES of Del & Mor..........E....... 740 369-6811
Delaware *(G-10122)*
Recovery Resources..........E....... 216 431-4131
Cleveland *(G-6361)*
Recovery Resources..........D....... 216 431-4131
Cleveland *(G-6362)*
Rehab Center..........E....... 330 297-2770
Ravenna *(G-16405)*
Rehab Medical Inc..........C....... 513 381-3740
Cincinnati *(G-4398)*
Rehabcare Group MGT Svcs Inc..........E....... 740 779-6732
Chillicothe *(G-2874)*
Rehabcare Group MGT Svcs Inc..........D....... 740 356-6160
Portsmouth *(G-16303)*
Rehabltion Ctr At Mrietta Mem..........D....... 740 374-1407
Marietta *(G-13493)*
Rescue Incorporated..........C....... 419 255-9585
Toledo *(G-18153)*
Reynolds Road Surgical Ctr LLC..........D....... 419 578-7500
Toledo *(G-18156)*
Robinson Health System Inc..........E....... 330 678-4100
Ravenna *(G-16406)*
Ryan Sheridan..........E....... 330 270-2380
Youngstown *(G-20364)*
Samaritan Behavioral Health..........E....... 937 276-8333
Dayton *(G-9864)*
Scioto Pnt Vly Mental Hlth Ctr..........E....... 740 335-6935
Wshngtn CT Hs *(G-20034)*
Scioto Pnt Vly Mental Hlth Ctr..........C....... 740 775-1260
Chillicothe *(G-2884)*
Shr Management Resources Corp..........E....... 937 274-1546
Dayton *(G-9879)*
Signature Health Inc..........B....... 440 953-9999
Willoughby *(G-19713)*
Sleep Care Inc..........E....... 614 901-8989
Columbus *(G-8743)*
Society For Rehabilitation..........E....... 440 209-0135
Mentor *(G-14243)*
South Community Inc..........C....... 937 293-8300
Moraine *(G-14826)*
South Community Inc..........E....... 937 252-0100
Dayton *(G-9889)*

Southast Cmnty Mental Hlth Ctr............C...... 614 225-0980
Columbus (G-8751)
Southast Cmnty Mental Hlth Ctr............E...... 614 445-6832
Columbus (G-8753)
Southast Cmnty Mental Hlth Ctr............E...... 614 293-9613
Worthington (G-19998)
Southast Cmnty Mental Hlth Ctr............E...... 614 444-0800
Columbus (G-8752)
Southern Ohio Bhvoral Hlth LLC..........E...... 740 533-0055
Ironton (G-12303)
Southwoods Surgical Hospital..............E...... 330 729-8000
Youngstown (G-20379)
Springfeld Rgnal Otpatient Ctr ....E...... 937 390-8310
Springfield (G-17277)
St Aloysius Services Inc ....E...... 513 482-1745
Cincinnati (G-4571)
St Ritas Medical Center..........................E...... 419 226-9067
Lima (G-12884)
St Ritas Medical Center..........................E...... 419 228-1535
Lima (G-12890)
St Vincent Family Centers......................C...... 614 252-0731
Columbus (G-8771)
Stark County Board of Developm..........A...... 330 477-5200
Canton (G-2543)
Summa Health System ....C...... 330 375-3315
Akron (G-458)
Summit Acres Inc...................................C...... 740 732-2364
Caldwell (G-2089)
Sunbrdge Marion Hlth Care Corp..........D...... 740 389-6306
Marion (G-13582)
Surgicenter of Mansfield........................E...... 419 774-9410
Mansfield (G-13368)
Syntero Inc ....E...... 614 889-5722
Dublin (G-10471)
Taylor Murtis Human Svcs Sys.............D...... 216 283-4400
Cleveland (G-6573)
Taylor Murtis Human Svcs Sys.............D...... 216 281-7192
Cleveland (G-6574)
Tcn Behavioral Health Svcs Inc............C...... 937 376-8700
Xenia (G-20077)
Therapeutic Riding Center Inc..............E...... 440 708-0013
Chagrin Falls (G-2736)
Theratrust ....E...... 740 345-7688
Newark (G-15239)
Thompkins Child Adlescent Svcs ....D...... 740 622-4470
Coshocton (G-9118)
Tri County Mental Health Svcs ....C...... 740 592-3091
Athens (G-815)
Tri County Mental Health Svcs ....D...... 740 594-5045
Athens (G-816)
Trihealth Inc...E...... 513 569-6777
Cincinnati (G-4689)
Trihealth G LLC......................................E...... 513 346-5000
Cincinnati (G-4694)
Ultimate Rehab Ltd ....D...... 513 563-8777
Blue Ash (G-1708)
Unison Behavioral Health Group...........D...... 419 242-9577
Toledo (G-18267)
Unison Behavioral Health Group...........C...... 419 693-0631
Toledo (G-18268)
United Disability Services Inc...............C...... 330 374-1169
Akron (G-485)
United Rehabilitation Services ....D...... 937 233-1230
Dayton (G-9947)
Univ Dermatology ....D...... 513 475-7630
Cincinnati (G-4745)
University Mednet...................................C...... 440 255-0800
Mentor (G-14253)
University of Cincinnati..........................C...... 513 584-3200
Cincinnati (G-4773)
University Radiology Assoc ....D...... 513 475-8760
Cincinnati (G-4784)
Upper Arlington Surgery Center............E...... 614 442-6515
Columbus (G-8916)
Wendt-Bristol Health Services...............E...... 614 403-9966
Columbus (G-8977)
West End Health Center Inc ....E...... 513 621-2726
Cincinnati (G-4835)
Westwood Behavioral Health Ctr ....E...... 419 238-3434
Van Wert (G-18652)
Wood County Chld Svcs Assn...............D...... 419 352-7588
Bowling Green (G-1798)
Woodland Centers Inc............................D...... 740 446-5500
Gallipolis (G-11341)
Wsb Rehabilitation Svcs Inc..................A...... 330 847-7819
Warren (G-18929)
Youngstown Hearing Speech Ctr ....E...... 330 726-8391
Youngstown (G-20431)
Zepf Center..E...... 419 255-4050
Toledo (G-18328)
Zepf Center..D...... 419 841-7701
Toledo (G-18329)
Zepf Center..E...... 419 213-5627
Toledo (G-18330)
Zepf Center..E...... 419 255-4050
Toledo (G-18331)
Zepf Center..E...... 419 213-5627
Toledo (G-18332)

8099 Health & Allied Svcs, NEC

24 - Seven Home Hlth Care LLC ....E...... 614 794-0325
Hilliard (G-11873)
Abbott Laboratories................................A...... 614 624-3191
Columbus (G-6924)
Addus Homecare Corporation...............A...... 866 684-0385
Wintersville (G-19807)
Advantage Imaging LLC.......................E...... 216 292-9998
Beachwood (G-1047)
Aksm/Genesis Medical Svcs Inc ....E...... 614 447-0281
Columbus (G-6961)
Alveo Health LLC ....E...... 513 557-3502
Cincinnati (G-2999)
Athens Medical Associates LLC...........D...... 740 594-8819
Athens (G-775)
Atrium Medical Center............................A...... 937 499-9596
Middletown (G-14474)
Baltic Health Care Corp.........................D...... 330 897-4311
Baltic (G-944)
Beall Inc ....E...... 440 974-8719
Mentor (G-14149)
Bio-Blood Components Inc...................E...... 614 294-3183
Columbus (G-7111)
Biolife Plasma Services LP ....E...... 419 224-0117
Lima (G-12748)
Biolife Plasma Services LP ....D...... 419 425-8680
Findlay (G-10994)
Black Stone Cincinnati LLC ....E...... 937 773-8573
Piqua (G-16136)
Blood Services Centl Ohio Reg ....C...... 614 253-7981
Columbus (G-7119)
Brecksvlle Halthcare Group Inc.............D...... 440 546-0643
Brecksville (G-1816)
Broadspire Services Inc.........................E...... 614 436-8990
Columbus (G-7148)
Cardinal Health Inc ....C...... 614 473-0786
Columbus (G-7192)
Cardinal Healthcare ....E...... 954 202-1883
Columbus (G-7195)
Carespring Health Care MGT LLC........E...... 513 943-4000
Loveland (G-13113)
Celtic Healthcare Ne Ohio Inc...............E...... 724 742-4360
Youngstown (G-20135)
Central Ohio Poison Center ....E...... 800 222-1222
Columbus (G-7233)
Central Ohio Primary Care ....D...... 614 552-2300
Reynoldsburg (G-16437)
Cincinnati Speech Hearing Ctr ....E...... 513 221-0527
Cincinnati (G-3328)
Clevelnd Clnc Chagrn Flls Fmly ....E...... 440 893-9393
Chagrin Falls (G-2693)
Clinic5..E...... 614 598-9960
Columbus (G-7301)
Cols Health & Wellness Testing ....E...... 614 839-2781
Westerville (G-19384)
Community & Rural Health Svcs ....E...... 419 334-8943
Fremont (G-11188)
Consulate Management Co LLC............D...... 740 259-5536
Lucasville (G-13177)
County of Carroll.....................................E...... 330 627-4866
Carrollton (G-2615)
County of Clark ....D...... 937 390-5600
Springfield (G-17178)
Covenant Home Health Care LLC.........E...... 614 465-2017
Columbus (G-7452)
Csl Plasma Inc..D...... 937 331-9186
Dayton (G-9448)
Csl Plasma Inc..D...... 614 267-4982
Columbus (G-7471)
Csl Plasma Inc..D...... 330 535-4338
Akron (G-181)
Csl Plasma Inc..D...... 216 398-0440
Cleveland (G-5443)
District Board Health Mahoning ....E...... 330 270-2855
Youngstown (G-20170)
Diverscare Healthcare Svcs Inc.............E...... 513 867-4100
Hamilton (G-11723)
Divine Healthcare Services LLC ....E...... 614 899-6767
Columbus (G-7529)
Engaged Health Care Bus Svcs.............E...... 614 457-8180
Columbus (G-7594)
Excelas LLC..E...... 440 442-7310
Cleveland (G-5560)
F R S Connections ....E...... 937 393-9662
Hillsboro (G-11973)
Fairfield Diagnstc Imaging LLC ....E...... 740 654-7559
Lancaster (G-12532)
Family Birth Center Lima Mem ....E...... 419 998-4570
Lima (G-12776)
First Choice Med Staff of Ohio ....E...... 330 867-1409
Fairlawn (G-10952)
First Choice Medical Staffing.................D...... 513 631-5656
Cincinnati (G-3614)
Foundation For Communit.....................C...... 937 461-3450
Dayton (G-9558)
Franklin County Adamh Board ....E...... 614 224-1057
Columbus (G-7694)
G and H Management ....E...... 614 268-2273
Columbus (G-7717)
Good Night Medical Ohio LLC...............E...... 614 384-7433
Westerville (G-19404)
Gratis Ems..E...... 937 787-4285
Gratis (G-11473)
Greater Clvland Halthcare Assn ....D...... 216 696-6900
Cleveland (G-5701)
H B Magruder Memorial Hospital ....B...... 419 734-4539
Port Clinton (G-16247)
Hanger Inc ....E...... 419 841-9852
Sylvania (G-17591)
Harter Ventures Inc................................D...... 419 224-4075
Lima (G-12790)
Healing Touch Healthcare ....E...... 937 610-5555
Dayton (G-9603)
Health Data MGT Solutions Inc.............D...... 216 595-1232
Beachwood (G-1084)
Health Partners Western Ohio ....E...... 419 679-5994
Kenton (G-12419)
Heartspring Home Hlth Care LLC..........D...... 937 531-6920
Dayton (G-9608)
Highpoint Home Healthcare Agcy ....E...... 330 491-1805
Canton (G-2398)
Hopewell Health Centers Inc................E...... 740 596-5249
Mc Arthur (G-14016)
Hopewell Health Centers Inc................E...... 740 773-1006
Chillicothe (G-2849)
Horizon Home Health Care.....................E...... 937 264-3155
Vandalia (G-18686)
Hospice of Northwest Ohio....................B...... 419 661-4001
Perrysburg (G-16013)
Hyde Park Health Center ....E...... 513 272-0600
Cincinnati (G-3802)
Ironton and Lawrence County ....E...... 740 532-7855
Ironton (G-12292)
Ironton and Lawrence County ....B...... 740 532-3534
Ironton (G-12291)
Joint Emergency Med Svc Inc ....E...... 937 746-3471
Franklin (G-11159)
Kettering Adventist Healthcare ....E...... 937 401-6306
Centerville (G-2681)
Kettering Medical Center........................E...... 937 298-4331
Dayton (G-9654)
Kettering Medical Center........................E...... 937 299-0099
Dayton (G-9655)
Kindred Healthcare Inc..........................E...... 513 336-0178
Mason (G-13728)
Kindred Healthcare Inc..........................D...... 419 224-1888
Lima (G-12809)
Kindred Healthcare Inc..........................A...... 937 433-2400
Dayton (G-9661)
Larlham Care Hattie Group ....D...... 330 274-2272
Mantua (G-13391)
Leroy Twp Fire Dept...............................E...... 440 254-4124
Painesville (G-15803)
Life Connection of Ohio ....E...... 419 893-4891
Maumee (G-13935)
Life Connection of Ohio Inc...................E...... 937 223-8223
Dayton (G-9680)
Life Line Screening Amer Ltd ....C...... 216 581-6556
Independence (G-12227)
Lifebanc..D...... 216 752-5433
Cleveland (G-5940)
Lifecenter Organ Donor Network ....E...... 513 558-5555
Cincinnati (G-3978)
Lifeshare Cmnty Blood Svcs Inc...........E...... 440 322-6159
Elyria (G-10643)
Lifeshare Community Blood Svcs.........E...... 440 322-6573
Elyria (G-10644)
Lifestges Smrtan Ctr For Women..........E...... 937 277-8988
Dayton (G-9681)
Maxim Healthcare Services Inc ....D...... 740 522-6094
Hebron (G-11852)

Employee Codes: A=Over 500 employees, B=251-500
C=101-250, D=51-100, E=25-50
2018 Harris Ohio
Services Directory
1053

80 HEALTH SERVICES

Maxim Healthcare Services Inc ....D..... 740 772-4100
  Chillicothe (G-2863)
Maxim Healthcare Services Inc ....D..... 216 606-3000
  Independence (G-12233)
Maxim Healthcare Services Inc ....D..... 614 986-3001
  Gahanna (G-11257)
Medical Arts Physician Center ....D..... 216 431-1500
  Cleveland (G-6013)
Medical Specialties Distrs LLC ....E..... 614 888-7939
  Columbus (G-6894)
Mercy Health ....E..... 937 323-4585
  Springfield (G-17235)
Mercy Health ....C..... 513 981-5750
  Cincinnati (G-4061)
Mercy Health ....E..... 440 988-1009
  Amherst (G-600)
Mercy Health ....D..... 937 653-3445
  Urbana (G-18595)
Mercy Health ....E..... 440 324-0400
  Elyria (G-10652)
Mercy Health ....C..... 330 746-7211
  Youngstown (G-20282)
Metro Health System ....D..... 330 669-2249
  Smithville (G-16966)
Metrohealth System ....E..... 216 957-5000
  Cleveland (G-6037)
Molina Healthcare Inc ....B..... 216 606-1400
  Independence (G-12235)
Mount Crmel Hospice Evrgrn Ctr ....D..... 614 234-0200
  Columbus (G-8200)
Mutual Health Services Company ......D..... 216 687-7000
  Cleveland (G-6094)
Mvhe Inc ....E..... 937 499-8211
  Dayton (G-9765)
New Carlisle Spt & Fitnes Ctr ....E..... 937 846-1000
  New Carlisle (G-15029)
Northast Ohio Med Rserve Corps ......E..... 216 789-6653
  Broadview Heights (G-1885)
Northeast OH Neighborhood Heal .....C..... 216 231-2323
  Cleveland (G-6152)
Northeast Ohio Orthopedics ....E..... 330 856-1070
  Warren (G-18890)
Novus Clinic ....D..... 330 630-9699
  Tallmadge (G-17646)
Ohio Kepro Inc ....E..... 216 447-9604
  Seven Hills (G-16834)
Ohio North E Hlth Systems Inc ....D..... 330 747-9551
  Youngstown (G-20308)
Ohio State University ....E..... 614 292-5504
  Columbus (G-8397)
Ohio State University ....D..... 614 257-5200
  Columbus (G-8409)
Ohio State University ....D..... 614 292-0110
  Columbus (G-8418)
Ohio State University ....D..... 614 293-8074
  Columbus (G-8447)
P C Vpa ....E..... 440 826-0500
  Cleveland (G-6225)
P N P Inc ....D..... 330 386-1231
  East Liverpool (G-10532)
Palestine Chld Relief Fund ....E..... 330 678-2645
  Kent (G-12390)
Peregrine Health Services Inc ....D..... 419 586-4135
  Celina (G-2659)
Peregrine Health Services Inc ....D..... 419 298-2321
  Edgerton (G-10584)
◆ Philips Healthcare Cleveland ....D..... 440 483-3235
  Highland Heights (G-11870)
Primary Cr Ntwrk Prmr Hlth Prt ....E..... 513 204-5785
  Mason (G-13750)
Proactive Occptnal Mdicine Inc ....E..... 740 574-8728
  Wheelersburg (G-19580)
Prosperity Care Service ....E..... 614 430-8626
  Columbus (G-8572)
Regensis Stna Training Program ....E..... 614 849-0115
  Columbus (G-8607)
Renaissance Home Health Care ....D..... 216 662-8702
  Bedford (G-1331)
Ryan Sheridan ....E..... 330 270-2380
  Youngstown (G-20364)
Salo Incorporated ....A..... 740 964-2904
  Pataskala (G-15925)
Seneca County Ems ....C..... 419 447-0266
  Tiffin (G-17698)
Serenity HM Halthcare Svcs LLC ....D..... 937 222-0002
  Dayton (G-9876)
Signature Healthcare LLC ....C..... 330 372-1977
  Warren (G-18899)
Sports Medicine Grant Inc ....E..... 614 461-8199
  Pickerington (G-16106)

Spryance Inc ....E..... 678 808-0600
  Toledo (G-18198)
Sterling Medical Associates ....D..... 513 984-1800
  Cincinnati (G-4590)
Summa Health System ....A..... 330 836-9023
  Akron (G-454)
Summacare Inc ....B..... 330 996-8410
  Akron (G-464)
Taylor Murtis Human Svcs Sys ....C..... 216 283-4400
  Cleveland (G-6572)
Toledo Clinic Inc ....C..... 419 865-3111
  Holland (G-12061)
Trihealth Hf LLC ....E..... 513 398-3445
  Mason (G-13773)
TVC Home Health Care ....E..... 330 755-1110
  Youngstown (G-20396)
Uhhs Westlake Medical Center ....C..... 440 250-2070
  Westlake (G-19559)
Unity Health Network LLC ....E..... 330 655-3820
  Hudson (G-12148)
Unity Health Network LLC ....D..... 330 923-5899
  Cuyahoga Falls (G-9229)
Unity Health Network LLC ....E..... 330 633-7782
  Tallmadge (G-17659)
Unity I Home Healthcare LLC ....E..... 740 351-0500
  Portsmouth (G-16317)
University Womens Healthcare ....E..... 937 208-2948
  Dayton (G-9956)
Wheeling Hospital Inc ....D..... 740 671-0850
  Shadyside (G-16853)
Wheeling Hospital Inc ....D..... 740 676-4623
  Bellaire (G-1368)
Wright Nutrition Inc ....E..... 614 873-0418
  Plain City (G-16212)
Young Mens Christian Associat ....C..... 419 794-7304
  Maumee (G-13996)

81 LEGAL SERVICES

8111 Legal Svcs

Advoctes For Bsic Lgal Eqality ....E..... 419 255-0814
  Toledo (G-17744)
Agee Clymer Mitchell & Laret ....E..... 614 221-3318
  Columbus (G-6955)
Allen Khnle Stovall Neuman LLP ....E..... 614 221-8500
  Columbus (G-6967)
Altick & Corwin Co Lpa ....E..... 937 223-1201
  Dayton (G-9327)
American Financial Corporation ....D..... 513 579-2121
  Cincinnati (G-3005)
American Title Services Inc ....E..... 330 652-1609
  Niles (G-15281)
Amin Turocy & Watson LLP ....E..... 216 696-8730
  Cleveland (G-5026)
Anspach Meeks Ellenberger LLP ....E..... 614 745-8350
  Columbus (G-7022)
Anspach Meeks Ellenberger LLP ....E..... 419 447-6181
  Toledo (G-17753)
Anthony Omalley Atty ....E..... 216 479-6100
  Cleveland (G-5043)
Arthur Middleton Capital Holdn ....E..... 330 966-9000
  North Canton (G-15326)
Auman Mahan & Furry A Legal ....E..... 937 223-6003
  Dayton (G-9347)
Bailey Cavalieri LLC ....E..... 614 221-3258
  Columbus (G-7085)
Baker & Hostetler LLP ....B..... 216 861-7587
  Cleveland (G-5091)
Baker & Hostetler LLP ....B..... 216 621-0200
  Cleveland (G-5092)
Baker & Hostetler LLP ....C..... 614 228-1541
  Columbus (G-7086)
Baker & Hostetler LLP ....E..... 513 929-3400
  Cincinnati (G-3074)
Baker Dblkar Beck Wley Mathews .....E..... 330 499-6000
  Canton (G-2260)
Barkan & Neff Co Lpa ....E..... 614 221-4221
  Columbus (G-7090)
Bavan & Associates ....E..... 330 650-0088
  Northfield (G-15510)
Benesch Friedlander Coplan & ....E..... 614 223-9300
  Columbus (G-7100)
Bhatti Enterprises Inc ....E..... 513 886-6000
  West Chester (G-19029)
Bieser Greer & Landis LLP ....E..... 937 223-3277
  Dayton (G-9355)
Bigmar Inc ....E..... 740 966-5800
  Johnstown (G-12336)
Bolotin Law Offices ....E..... 419 424-9800
  Findlay (G-11006)

SIC SECTION

Bonezzi Swtzer Mrphy Plito Lpa ....E..... 216 875-2767
  Cleveland (G-5128)
Bordas & Bordas Pllc ....E..... 740 695-8141
  Saint Clairsville (G-16629)
Brennan Manna & Diamond LLC ......E..... 330 253-5060
  Akron (G-109)
Bricker & Eckler LLP ....B..... 614 227-2300
  Columbus (G-7134)
Bricker & Eckler LLP ....C..... 513 870-6700
  Cincinnati (G-3131)
Brouse McDowell Lpa ....E..... 216 830-6830
  Cleveland (G-5148)
Brown and Margolius Co Lpa ....E..... 216 621-2034
  Cleveland (G-5149)
Bruce M Allman ....D..... 513 352-6712
  Cincinnati (G-3143)
Buckingham Dlttle Brroughs LLC ......C..... 330 376-5300
  Akron (G-118)
Buckingham Dlttle Brroughs LLC ......E..... 888 811-2825
  Canton (G-2275)
Buckingham Dlttle Brroughs LLC ......D..... 330 492-8717
  Canton (G-2276)
Buckingham Dlttle Brroughs LLC ......E..... 330 492-8717
  Canton (G-2277)
Buckingham Dlttle Brroughs LLC ......E..... 216 621-5300
  Cleveland (G-5155)
Burke Manley Lpa ....E..... 513 721-5525
  Cincinnati (G-3152)
Butler Cincione and Dicuccio ....E..... 614 221-3151
  Columbus (G-7172)
Butler County Clerk of Courts ....D..... 513 887-3282
  Hamilton (G-11701)
Butler County of Ohio ....E..... 513 887-3090
  Hamilton (G-11704)
C T Corporation System ....E..... 614 473-9749
  Columbus (G-7175)
Calfee Halter & Griswold LLP ....B..... 216 831-2732
  Cleveland (G-5172)
Calfee Halter & Griswold LLP ....E..... 513 693-4880
  Cincinnati (G-3166)
Calfee Halter & Griswold LLP ....E..... 614 621-1500
  Columbus (G-7177)
Calfee Halgerr Griswold LLC ....E..... 614 621-7003
  Columbus (G-7178)
Carlile Patchen & Murphy LLP ....D..... 614 228-6135
  Columbus (G-7200)
Carlisle McNellie Rini Kram ....E..... 216 360-7200
  Beachwood (G-1060)
Carpenter Lipps & Leland LLP ....E..... 614 365-4100
  Columbus (G-7202)
Cavitch Familo & Durkin Co Lpa ....E..... 216 621-7860
  Cleveland (G-5195)
Chamberlain Hr ....C..... 216 589-9280
  Avon (G-886)
City of Columbus ....E..... 614 645-6624
  Columbus (G-7284)
City of Lakewood ....E..... 216 529-6170
  Cleveland (G-5267)
City of Marion ....D..... 740 382-1479
  Marion (G-13531)
Cleveland Metro Bar Assn ....E..... 216 696-3525
  Cleveland (G-5325)
Cleveland Teachers Union Inc ....E..... 216 861-7676
  Cleveland (G-5351)
Climaco Lefkwtz Peca Wlcox & ....D..... 216 621-8484
  Cleveland (G-5363)
Cohen Todd Kite Stanford LLC ....E..... 513 205-7286
  Cincinnati (G-3378)
Community Legal Aid Services ....E..... 330 725-1231
  Medina (G-14049)
Community Legal Aid Services ....D..... 330 535-4191
  Akron (G-156)
Connor Evans Hafenstein LLP ....E..... 614 464-2025
  Columbus (G-7422)
Coolidge Law ....D..... 937 223-8177
  Dayton (G-9425)
Coolidge Wall Co LPA ....E..... 937 223-8177
  Dayton (G-9426)
Cors & Bassett LLC ....D..... 513 852-8200
  Cincinnati (G-3424)
County of Lucas ....C..... 419 213-4700
  Toledo (G-17834)
County of Montgomery ....E..... 937 225-5623
  Dayton (G-9437)
County of Ottawa ....C..... 419 898-6459
  Oak Harbor (G-15607)
County of Ottawa ....E..... 419 898-2089
  Oak Harbor (G-15608)
County of Portage ....E..... 330 297-3850
  Ravenna (G-16381)

81 LEGAL SERVICES

Firm	Location	Code	Phone
Crabbe Brown & James LLP	Columbus (G-7454)	E	614 229-4587
Critchfeld Crtchfield Johnston	Wooster (G-19859)	D	330 264-4444
Dacia R Crum	Cincinnati (G-3458)	D	513 698-5000
Dagger Johnston Miller	Lancaster (G-12526)	E	740 653-6464
Dana & Pariser Attys	Columbus (G-7485)	E	614 253-1010
David L Barth Lwyr	Cincinnati (G-3463)	D	513 852-8228
Davis Young A Legal Prof Assn	Cleveland (G-5468)	E	216 348-1700
Day Ketterer Ltd	Canton (G-2336)	D	330 455-0173
Dinn Hochman and Potter LLC	Cleveland (G-5484)	E	440 446-1100
Dinsmore & Shohl LLP	Cincinnati (G-3491)	B	513 977-8200
Douglass & Associates Co Lpa	Cleveland (G-5507)	E	216 362-7777
Duane Morris LLP	Cleveland (G-5510)	E	202 577-3075
Duane Morris LLP	Columbus (G-7547)	E	937 424-7086
Dworken & Bernstein Co Lpa	Cleveland (G-5514)	E	216 861-4211
Dworken & Bernstein Co Lpa	Painesville (G-15853)	E	440 352-3391
E S Gallon & Associates	Moraine (G-14777)	E	937 586-3100
Eastman & Smith Ltd	Toledo (G-17862)	C	419 241-6000
Elizabeth H Farbman	Youngstown (G-20179)	E	330 744-5211
Elk & Elk Co Lpa	Mayfield Heights (G-14002)	D	800 355-6446
Elliott Heller Maas Morrow Lpa	Youngstown (G-20180)	E	330 792-6611
Ernest V Thomas Jr	Cincinnati (G-3574)	E	513 961-5311
Executives Agencies	Columbus (G-7618)	E	614 466-2980
Fairfield Federal Sav Ln Assn	Lancaster (G-12533)	E	740 653-3863
Faruki Ireland & Cox Pllc	Dayton (G-9541)	E	937 227-3700
Faulkner Grmhsen Keister Shenk	Sidney (G-16932)	E	937 492-1271
Fay Sharpe LLP	Cleveland (G-5578)	D	216 363-9000
Firm Hahn Law	Columbus (G-7658)	E	614 221-0240
Flanagan Lberman Hoffman Swaim	Dayton (G-9554)	E	937 223-5200
Franklin Cnty Bd Commissioners	Columbus (G-7688)	C	614 462-3194
Frantz Ward LLP	Cleveland (G-5634)	C	216 515-1660
Freeze/Arnold A Freund Legal	Dayton (G-9562)	D	937 222-2424
Freking Betz	Cincinnati (G-3652)	E	513 721-1975
Friedberg Meyers Roman	Cleveland (G-5638)	E	216 831-0042
Friedman Domiano Smith Co Lpa	Cleveland (G-5639)	E	216 621-0070
Frost Brown Todd LLC	Cincinnati (G-3656)	B	513 651-6800
Frost Brown Todd LLC	Columbus (G-7711)	E	614 464-1211
Fuller & Henry Ltd	Toledo (G-17901)	E	419 247-2500
Gallagher Gams Pryor Tallan	Columbus (G-7725)	E	614 228-5151
Gallagher Sharp	Cleveland (G-5653)	C	216 241-5310
Gallon Takacs Boissoneault & S	Toledo (G-17906)	D	419 843-2001
Garretson Firm Resolution	Loveland (G-13126)	C	513 794-0400
General Audit Corp	Lima (G-12782)	E	419 993-2900
Gottlieb Johnson Beam Dal P	Zanesville (G-20484)	E	740 452-7555
Green Haines Sgambati Lpa	Youngstown (G-20208)	E	330 743-5101
Hahmooeser & Parks	Cleveland (G-5719)	E	330 864-5550
Hahn Loeser & Parks LLP	Cleveland (G-5720)	C	216 621-0150
Hammond Law Group LLC	Cincinnati (G-3734)	E	513 381-2011
Hanna Cambell & Powell	Akron (G-252)	E	330 670-7300
Harrington Hoppe Mitchell Ltd	Youngstown (G-20213)	E	330 744-1111
Harris & Burgin	Blue Ash (G-1607)	E	513 891-3270
Hawkins & Co Lpa Ltd	Cleveland (G-5733)	E	216 861-1365
Heller Maas Moro & Magill	Youngstown (G-20215)	E	330 393-6602
Hermann Cahn & Schneider LLP	Cleveland (G-5751)	E	216 781-5515
Heyman Ralph E Attorney At Law	Dayton (G-9610)	D	937 449-2820
Hoglund Chwlkowski Mrozik Pllc	Akron (G-268)	C	330 252-8009
Horenstein Nicho & Blume A L	Dayton (G-9620)	E	937 224-7200
Ice Miller LLP	Columbus (G-7881)	E	614 462-2700
International Paper Compa	Loveland (G-13133)	D	513 248-6000
Isaac Brant Ledman Teetor LLP	Columbus (G-7924)	E	614 221-2121
Isaac Wiles Burkholder & Teeto	Columbus (G-7925)	D	614 221-5216
Jackson Kelly Pllc	Akron (G-289)	D	330 252-9060
Jackson Kohrman & Pll Krantz	Cleveland (G-5847)	D	216 696-8700
James C Sass Atty	Toledo (G-17982)	E	419 843-3545
James L Jacobson	Dayton (G-9639)	E	937 223-1130
Janik LLP	Cleveland (G-5850)	D	440 838-7600
Javitch Block LLC	Cincinnati (G-3863)	E	513 381-3051
Javitch Block LLC	Cleveland (G-5852)	C	216 623-0000
Javitch Block LLC	Columbus (G-7936)	D	216 623-0000
Jefferson Medical Co	Cleveland (G-5856)	E	216 443-9000
Jeffrey W Smith	Ironton (G-12294)	E	740 532-9000
Jones Day Limited Partnership	Columbus (G-7947)	C	614 469-3939
Jones Day Limited Partnership	Cleveland (G-5871)	A	216 586-3939
Jones Law Group LLC	Columbus (G-7948)	E	614 545-9998
Joseph R Harrison Company Lpa	Barberton (G-967)	E	330 666-6900
Jurus Stanley R Atty At Law	Columbus (G-7960)	E	614 486-0297
Kademenos Wisehart Hines	Mansfield (G-13318)	E	419 524-6011
Katz Teller Brant Hild Co Lpa	Cincinnati (G-3902)	D	513 721-4532
Keating Muething & Klekamp Pll	Cincinnati (G-3907)	B	513 579-6400
Kegler Brown Hl Ritter Co Lpa	Columbus (G-7970)	C	614 462-5400
Kegler Brown Hl Ritter Co Lpa	Cleveland (G-5888)	D	216 586-6650
Kelley & Ferraro LLP	Cleveland (G-5890)	D	216 575-0777
Kelly Farrish Lpa	Cincinnati (G-3909)	E	513 621-8700
Kendis & Associates Co Lpa	Cleveland (G-5893)	E	216 579-1818
Kenneth Zerrusen	Fairlawn (G-10962)	D	330 869-9007
Kimberly Williford Attorney	Toledo (G-17994)	E	419 241-1220
Kohnen & Patton	Cincinnati (G-3938)	E	513 381-0656
Krugliak Wilkins Grifiyhd &	New Philadelphia (G-15105)	E	330 364-3472
Krugliak Wilkins Grifiyhd &	Canton (G-2430)	D	330 497-0700
Lane Alton & Horst LLC	Columbus (G-8036)	E	614 228-6885
Larrimer & Larrimer LLC	Columbus (G-8040)	E	419 222-6266
Larrimer & Larrimer LLC	Columbus (G-8041)	E	614 221-7548
Larrimer & Larrimer LLC	Granville (G-11469)	E	740 366-0184
Laurito & Laurito LLC	Dayton (G-9675)	E	937 743-4878
Law Offces Rbert A Schrger Lpa	Columbus (G-8043)	E	614 824-5731
Law Offices of John D Clunk C	Stow (G-17380)	D	330 436-0300
Lawrence Cnty Hstorical Museum	Ironton (G-12296)	E	740 532-1222
Legal Aid Society Cincinnati	Cincinnati (G-3968)	D	513 241-9400
Legal Aid Society of Cleveland	Cleveland (G-5934)	E	216 861-5500
Legal Aid Society of Columbus	Columbus (G-8050)	D	614 737-0139
Legal Aid Western Ohio Inc	Toledo (G-18003)	D	419 724-0030
Lerner Sampson & Rothfuss	Cincinnati (G-3969)	B	513 241-3100
Levine Arnold S Law Offices	Cincinnati (G-3973)	E	513 241-6748
Levy & Associates LLC	Columbus (G-8053)	E	614 898-5200
Lewis Adkins W Jr	Cleveland (G-5937)	D	216 623-0501
Lewis P C Jackson	Independence (G-12225)	E	216 750-0404
Lewis P C Jackson	Beavercreek (G-1249)	E	937 306-6304
Lindhorst & Dreidame Co Lpa	Cincinnati (G-3986)	E	513 421-6630
Litigation Management Inc	Mayfield Heights (G-14004)	B	440 484-2000
Litigation Support Svcs Inc	Cincinnati (G-3992)	E	513 241-5605
Littler Mendelson PC	Cleveland (G-5947)	D	216 696-7600
LLP Ziegler Metzger	Cleveland (G-5949)	E	216 781-5470
London City Admin Offices	London (G-12997)	D	740 852-3243
Loveland & Brosius LLC	Upper Arlington (G-18554)	E	614 488-4092
Luper Neidental & Logan A Leg	Columbus (G-8087)	E	614 221-7663
Lyons Doughty & Veldhuis PC	Columbus (G-8090)	E	614 229-3888
Macmillan Sobanski & Todd LLC	Toledo (G-18025)	E	419 255-5900
Magolius Margolius & Assoc Lpa	Cleveland (G-5965)	D	216 621-2034
Maguire & Schneider LLP	Columbus (G-8099)	E	614 224-1222
Manchester Bennett Towers & Ul	Youngstown (G-20271)	E	330 743-1171
Manley Deas & Kochalski LLC	Columbus (G-8103)	E	614 220-5611
Mannion & Gray Co LpA	Cleveland (G-5976)	E	216 344-9422
Marshall & Associates Inc	Loveland (G-13144)	E	513 683-6396
Marshall & Melhorn LLC	Toledo (G-18043)	D	419 249-7100
Mazanec Raskin & Ryder Co Lpa	Cleveland (G-5996)	D	440 248-7906
MCDONALD HOPKINS LLC	Cleveland (G-6002)	C	216 348-5400
Micha Ltd	Lancaster (G-12557)	E	740 653-6464
Miller Cnfeld Pddock Stone PLC	Cincinnati (G-4096)	D	513 394-5252
Millikin and Fitton Law Firm	Hamilton (G-11759)	E	513 829-6700
Morris Schneider Wittstadt LLC	Willoughby (G-19694)	E	440 942-5168
Murray & Murray Co Lpa	Sandusky (G-16779)	E	419 624-3000
Nadler Nadler & Burdman Co Lpa	Canfield (G-2204)	E	330 533-6195
National Labor Relations Board	Cleveland (G-6053)	E	216 522-3716
National Service Information	Marion (G-13567)	E	740 387-6806
Nicholas E Davis	Dayton (G-9773)	E	937 228-2838
Nicola Gudbranson & Cooper LLC	Cleveland (G-6131)	E	216 621-7227

Employee Codes: A=Over 500 employees, B=251-500
C=101-250, D=51-100, E=25-50

2018 Harris Ohio Services Directory

Northwest Ttl Agy of OH MI In D 419 241-8195
Toledo *(G-18096)*
Nurenberg Plevin Heller D 440 423-0750
Cleveland *(G-6172)*
OBrien Law Firm Company Lpa E 216 685-7500
Westlake *(G-19526)*
OConnor Acciani & Levy LLC E 513 241-7111
Cincinnati *(G-4198)*
Ohio Disability Rights Law Pol E 614 466-7264
Columbus *(G-8337)*
Ohio Northern University C 419 227-0061
Lima *(G-12847)*
Ohio State Bar Association E 614 487-2050
Columbus *(G-8377)*
Opers Legal Dept E 614 227-0550
Columbus *(G-8471)*
Palmer Volkema Thomas Inc E 614 221-4400
Columbus *(G-8510)*
Pappas Leah E 614 621-7007
Columbus *(G-8514)*
Pearne & Gordon LLP E 216 579-1700
Cleveland *(G-6257)*
Peter M Kostoff D 330 849-6681
Akron *(G-387)*
Peterj Brodhead E 216 696-3232
Cleveland *(G-6271)*
Pickrel Schaeffer Ebeling Lpa D 937 223-1130
Dayton *(G-9809)*
Porter Wrght Morris Arthur LLP E 513 381-4700
Cincinnati *(G-4316)*
Porter Wrght Morris Arthur LLP D 216 443-2506
Cleveland *(G-6290)*
Porter Wrght Morris Arthur LLP E 937 449-6810
Dayton *(G-9815)*
Rathbone Group LLC D 800 870-5521
Cleveland *(G-6353)*
Recovery One LLC D 614 336-4207
Columbus *(G-8596)*
Reese Pyle Drake & Meyer E 740 345-3431
Newark *(G-15231)*
Reimer Law Co C 440 600-5500
Solon *(G-17045)*
Reisenfeld & Assoc Lpa LLC C 513 322-7000
Cincinnati *(G-4401)*
Reminger Co LPA C 216 687-1311
Cleveland *(G-6373)*
Reminger Co LPA D 419 254-1311
Toledo *(G-18150)*
Reminger Co LPA E 513 721-1311
Cincinnati *(G-4403)*
Rendigs Fry Kiely & Dennis LLP D 513 381-9200
Cincinnati *(G-4404)*
Renner Kenner Grieve Bobak E 330 376-1242
Akron *(G-410)*
Renner Otto Boiselle & Sklar E 216 621-1113
Cleveland *(G-6375)*
Rennie & Jonson Montgomery E 513 241-4722
Cincinnati *(G-4405)*
Rich Crites & Dittmer LLC E 614 228-5822
Dublin *(G-10440)*
Richard A Broock E 937 449-2840
Dayton *(G-9851)*
Rickerier and Eckler E 513 870-6565
West Chester *(G-19140)*
Ritter & Randolph LLC E 513 381-5700
Cincinnati *(G-4422)*
Robbins Kelly Patterson Tucker E 513 721-3330
Cincinnati *(G-4433)*
Roderick Linton Belfance LLP E 330 434-3000
Akron *(G-417)*
Roetzel and Andress A Legal P C 330 376-2700
Akron *(G-418)*
Roetzel and Andress A Legal P E 614 463-9489
Columbus *(G-8645)*
Roetzel and Andress A Legal P E 216 623-0150
Cleveland *(G-6410)*
Rose & Dobyns An Ohio Partnr D 937 382-2838
Wilmington *(G-19784)*
Ross Brittain Schonberg Lpa E 216 447-1551
Independence *(G-12255)*
Schimpf Ginocchio Mullins Lpa E 513 977-5570
Cincinnati *(G-4482)*
Scott D Phillips E 513 870-8200
West Chester *(G-19148)*
Scott Scriven & Wahoff LLP E 614 222-8686
Columbus *(G-8708)*
Sebaly Shillito & Dyer Lpa E 937 222-2500
Dayton *(G-9871)*
Seeley Svdge Ebert Gourash Lpa E 216 566-8200
Cleveland *(G-6465)*
Shared Services LLC D 513 821-4278
Cincinnati *(G-4508)*
Shindler Neff Holmes Schlag E 419 243-6281
Toledo *(G-18184)*
Shumaker Loop & Kendrick LLP C 419 241-9000
Toledo *(G-18187)*
Siegel Siegel J & Jennings Co E 216 763-1004
Beachwood *(G-1124)*
Smith Peter Kalail Co Lpa E 216 503-5055
Independence *(G-12261)*
Smith Rolfes & Skazdahl Lpa E 513 579-0080
Cincinnati *(G-4541)*
Spangenberg Shibley Liber LLP E 216 215-7445
Cleveland *(G-6512)*
Spengler Nathanson PLL D 419 241-2201
Toledo *(G-18195)*
Squire Patton Boggs (us) LLP E 513 361-1200
Cincinnati *(G-4569)*
Stagnaro Saba Patterson Co Lpa E 513 533-2700
Cincinnati *(G-4576)*
Stagnaro Saba Patterson Co Lpa E 513 533-2700
Cincinnati *(G-4577)*
Standley Law Group LLP E 614 792-5555
Dublin *(G-10460)*
Stark Knoll E 330 376-3300
Akron *(G-450)*
Supreme Court of Ohio E 937 898-3996
Vandalia *(G-18700)*
Sweeney Robert E Co Lpa E 216 696-0606
Cleveland *(G-6561)*
Tafaro John D 513 381-0656
Cincinnati *(G-4614)*
Taft Stettinius Hollister LLP B 513 381-2838
Cincinnati *(G-4616)*
Taft Stettinius Hollister LLP D 614 221-4000
Columbus *(G-8819)*
Taft Stettinius Hollister LLP D 216 241-3141
Cleveland *(G-6567)*
Thompson Hine LLP C 614 469-3200
Columbus *(G-8840)*
Thompson Hine LLP C 614 469-3200
Columbus *(G-8841)*
Thompson Hine LLP C 937 443-6859
Miamisburg *(G-14359)*
Thompson Hine LLP B 216 566-5500
Cleveland *(G-6596)*
Thos A Lupica D 419 252-6298
Toledo *(G-18217)*
Thrasher Dinsmore & Dolan E 440 285-2242
Chardon *(G-2771)*
Toledo Legal Aid Society E 419 720-3048
Toledo *(G-18241)*
Tucker Ellis LLP D 720 897-4400
Cleveland *(G-6621)*
Tucker Ellis LLP C 216 592-5000
Cleveland *(G-6622)*
Tucker Ellis LLP D 614 358-9717
Columbus *(G-8877)*
Ulmer & Berne LLP B 216 583-7000
Cleveland *(G-6630)*
Ulmer & Berne LLP D 513 698-5000
Cincinnati *(G-4723)*
Ulmer & Berne LLP C 513 698-5058
Cincinnati *(G-4724)*
Ulmer & Berne LLP E 614 229-0000
Columbus *(G-8886)*
United Scoto Senior Activities E 740 354-6672
Portsmouth *(G-16316)*
Value Recovery Group Inc E 614 324-5959
Columbus *(G-8931)*
Village of Strasburg E 330 878-7115
Strasburg *(G-17402)*
Vorys Sater Seymour Pease LLP E 216 479-6100
Cleveland *(G-6712)*
Vorys Sater Seymour Pease LLP C 513 723-4000
Cincinnati *(G-4819)*
Walter Haverfield LLP D 216 781-1212
Cleveland *(G-6719)*
Warner Dennehey Marshall D 216 912-3787
Cleveland *(G-6722)*
Wegman Hessler Vanderburg D 216 642-3342
Cleveland *(G-6727)*
Weiner Keith D Co L P A Inc E 216 771-6500
Cleveland *(G-6729)*
Weltman Weinberg & Reis Co Lpa C 216 739-5100
Brooklyn Heights *(G-1933)*
Weltman Weinberg & Reis Co Lpa A 216 685-1000
Cleveland *(G-6732)*
Weltman Weinberg & Reis Co Lpa C 614 801-2600
Grove City *(G-11614)*
Weltman Weinberg & Reis Co Lpa C 513 723-2200
Cincinnati *(G-4832)*
Weltman Weinberg & Reis Co Lpa C 216 459-8633
Cleveland *(G-6733)*
Wickens Hrzer Pnza Cook Btista D 440 695-8000
Avon *(G-919)*
Wiles Boyle Burkholder & D 614 221-5216
Columbus *(G-8993)*
Wilmer Cutler Pick Hale Dorr B 937 395-2100
Dayton *(G-10000)*
Wong Margaret W Assoc Co Lpa E 313 527-9989
Cleveland *(G-6757)*
Wood Herron & Evans LLP D 513 241-2324
Cincinnati *(G-4856)*
Wood & Lamping LLP D 513 852-6000
Cincinnati *(G-4857)*
Young & Alexander Co Lpa D 937 224-9291
Dayton *(G-10008)*
Zaremba Group Incorporated E 216 221-6600
Cleveland *(G-6779)*
Zaremba Group LLC C 216 221-6600
Lakewood *(G-12504)*
Zashin & Rich Co LPA E 216 696-4441
Cleveland *(G-6781)*
Zeiger Tigges & Little LLP E 614 365-9900
Columbus *(G-9026)*

83 SOCIAL SERVICES

8322 Individual & Family Social Svcs

2100 Lakeside Shelter For Men E 216 566-0047
Cleveland *(G-4924)*
6th Circuit Court E 614 719-3100
Columbus *(G-6915)*
6th Circuit Court E 614 719-3100
Dayton *(G-9294)*
A Better Choice Child Care LLC E 614 268-8503
Columbus *(G-6919)*
A Renewed Mind D 419 214-0606
Perrysburg *(G-15970)*
A Team LLC E 216 271-7223
Cleveland *(G-4936)*
A W S Inc E 216 486-0600
Euclid *(G-10741)*
Ability Works Inc C 419 626-1048
Sandusky *(G-16723)*
Absolute Care Management Llc E 614 846-8053
Columbus *(G-6929)*
Access Counseling Services LLC C 513 649-8008
Middletown *(G-14472)*
Achievement Ctrs For Children D 216 292-9700
Cleveland *(G-4954)*
Achievement Ctrs For Children E 440 250-2520
Westlake *(G-19454)*
Action For Children Inc E 614 224-0222
Columbus *(G-6941)*
Adams County Senior Citizens E 937 544-7459
West Union *(G-19273)*
Addiction Services Council E 513 281-7880
Cincinnati *(G-2972)*
Adena Health System E 740 779-4888
Chillicothe *(G-2812)*
Adena NH LLC E 740 546-3620
Adena *(G-7)*
Aids Tskfrce Grter Clvland Inc D 216 357-3131
Cleveland *(G-4970)*
Akron General Foundation E 330 344-6888
Akron *(G-41)*
Akron General Medical Center D 330 344-6000
Akron *(G-43)*
Alexson Services Inc E 614 889-5837
Dublin *(G-10240)*
All Star Training Club E 330 352-5602
Akron *(G-66)*
Allwell Behavioral Health Svcs C 740 454-9766
Zanesville *(G-20440)*
Allwell Behavioral Health Svcs E 740 439-4428
Cambridge *(G-2094)*
Alternative Paths Inc E 330 725-9195
Medina *(G-14035)*
American Cancer Society East E 800 227-2345
Cleveland *(G-5005)*
American National Red Cross D 216 303-5476
Parma *(G-15899)*
American National Red Cross C 419 382-2707
Toledo *(G-17750)*
American National Red Cross E 330 535-6131
Akron *(G-72)*
American Red Cross D 513 579-3000
Cincinnati *(G-3012)*

83 SOCIAL SERVICES

Name	Code	Phone
American Red Cross — Dayton (G-9332)	E	937 222-0124
American Red Cross — Xenia (G-20041)	E	937 376-3111
Amethyst Inc — Columbus (G-7014)	D	614 242-1284
Anazao Community Partners — Wooster (G-19828)	E	330 264-9597
Ansonia Area Emergency Service — Ansonia (G-619)	E	937 337-2651
Applewood Centers Inc — Cleveland (G-5050)	B	216 696-6815
Applewood Centers Inc — Cleveland (G-5051)	D	216 521-6511
Applewood Centers Inc — Lorain (G-13014)	E	440 324-1300
Applewood Centers Inc — Cleveland (G-5052)	C	216 741-2241
Arbor Rehabilitation & Healtcr — Gates Mills (G-11355)	B	440 423-0206
ARC Industries Incorporated O — Groveport (G-11623)	B	614 836-0700
Archdiocese of Cincinnati — Springfield (G-17148)	E	937 323-6507
Area Agency On Aging Planni — Dayton (G-9343)	C	800 258-7277
Area Agency On Aging Dst 7 Inc — Rio Grande (G-16546)	C	800 582-7277
Area Agency On Aging Dst 7 Inc — Gallipolis (G-11308)	E	740 446-7000
Area Agency On Aging Reg 9 Inc — Cambridge (G-2096)	D	740 439-4478
Area Office On Aging of Nwstrn — Toledo (G-17758)	D	419 382-0624
Artis Senior Living — Mason (G-13664)	E	513 229-7450
Ashland Cnty Council On Aging — Ashland (G-655)	E	419 281-1477
Ashtabula Community Counseling — Ashtabula (G-716)	D	440 998-6032
Ashtabula County Commnty Actn — Conneaut (G-9037)	D	440 593-6441
Ashtabula County Commnty Actn — Jefferson (G-12330)	D	440 576-6911
Ashtabula County Community — Ashtabula (G-721)	C	440 997-1721
Ashtabula Job and Family Svcs — Ashtabula (G-725)	C	440 994-2020
Assisted Living Concepts Inc — Zanesville (G-20443)	E	740 450-2744
Assoc Dvlpmtly Disabled — Westerville (G-19365)	E	614 486-4361
Aultman Hospital — Canton (G-2255)	A	330 363-6262
Avalon Foodservice Inc — Canal Fulton (G-2140)	C	330 854-4551
Avita Health System — Galion (G-11290)	C	419 468-7059
Battered Womens Shelter — Medina (G-14038)	E	330 723-3900
Battered Womens Shelter — Akron (G-91)	D	330 374-0740
Battle Bullying Hotline Inc — Cleveland (G-5101)	D	216 731-1976
Beatitude House — Ashtabula (G-729)	E	440 992-0265
Beavercreek YMCA — Dayton (G-9351)	D	937 426-9622
Beech Acres Parenting Center — Cincinnati (G-3088)	C	513 231-6630
Beeghly Oaks Operating LLC — Boardman (G-1738)	C	330 884-2300
Behavioral Treatments — Hilliard (G-11881)	E	614 558-1968
Behavral Cnnctions WD Cnty Inc — Perrysburg (G-15976)	E	419 872-2419
Bellefaire Jewish Chld Bur — Shaker Heights (G-16856)	B	216 932-2800
Belmont County of Ohio — Saint Clairsville (G-16623)	E	740 695-3813
Belmont County of Ohio — Saint Clairsville (G-16624)	D	740 695-0460
Ben El Child Development Ctr — Urbana (G-18573)	E	937 465-0010
Benjamin Rose Institute — Cleveland (G-5117)	D	216 791-8000
Benjamin Rose Institute — Cleveland (G-5116)	D	216 791-3580
Beth-El Agape Christian Center — Columbus (G-7104)	E	614 445-0674
Big Broth and Big Siste of Cen — Columbus (G-7106)	E	614 839-2447
Biomat Usa Inc — Toledo (G-17772)	E	419 531-3332
Blick Clinic Inc — Akron (G-103)	C	330 762-5425
Bluebird Retirement Community — London (G-12993)	E	740 845-1880
Board Mental Retardation Dvlpm — Woodsfield (G-19812)	E	740 472-1712
Board of Delaware County — Lewis Center (G-12671)	D	740 201-3600
Bobby Tripodi Foundation Inc — Independence (G-12190)	E	216 524-3787
Box 21 Rescue Squad Inc — Dayton (G-9365)	E	937 223-2821
Brenn Field Nursing Center — Orrville (G-15767)	C	330 683-4075
Bridges To Independence Inc — Delaware (G-10074)	C	740 362-1996
Bridgeway Inc — Cleveland (G-5138)	B	216 688-4114
Broken Arrow Inc — Bucyrus (G-2024)	E	419 562-3480
Brook Beech — Cleveland (G-5144)	C	216 831-2255
Brookdale Place Wooster LLC — Wooster (G-19834)	C	330 262-1615
Brookdale Senior Living Inc — Fairborn (G-10786)	E	937 864-1500
Brown Cnty Snior Ctzen Council — Georgetown (G-11385)	E	937 378-6603
Bryant Eliza Village — Cleveland (G-5153)	B	216 361-6141
Butler County of Ohio — Fairfield Township (G-10926)	C	513 887-3728
CA Group — Celina (G-2637)	E	419 586-2137
Cambridge Counseling Center — Zanesville (G-20454)	C	740 450-7790
Canton Christian Home Inc — Canton (G-2283)	C	330 456-0004
Canton Jewish Community Center — Canton (G-2291)	D	330 452-6444
Caracole Inc — Cincinnati (G-3176)	E	513 761-1480
Care & Share of Erie Count — Sandusky (G-16733)	D	419 624-1411
Carriage Inn of Cadiz Inc — Cadiz (G-2073)	E	740 942-8084
Carvaka Inc — Cincinnati (G-3189)	E	513 381-1531
Casleo Corporation — Columbus (G-7205)	E	614 252-6508
Casto Health Care — Mansfield (G-13272)	D	419 884-6400
Catholic Charities Corporation — Medina (G-14042)	B	330 723-9615
Catholic Charities Corporation — Cleveland (G-5189)	E	216 939-3713
Catholic Charities Corporation — Cleveland (G-5190)	E	216 268-4006
Catholic Charities Corporation — Ashland (G-670)	E	419 289-1903
Catholic Charities of Southwst — Springfield (G-17157)	D	937 325-8715
Catholic Charities of SW Ohio — Cincinnati (G-3194)	C	513 241-7745
Catholic Diocese of Columbus — Columbus (G-7211)	E	614 221-5891
Catholic Residential Service — Cincinnati (G-3195)	E	513 784-0400
Catholic Social Services Inc — Columbus (G-7212)	D	614 221-5891
Catholic Social Svc Miami Vly — Dayton (G-9390)	E	937 223-7217
Center For Cognitv Behav Psych — Columbus (G-7224)	E	614 459-4490
Center For Families & Children — Cleveland (G-5205)	E	440 888-0300
Center For Families & Children — Cleveland (G-5206)	D	216 432-7200
Center For Families & Children — Cleveland Heights (G-6786)	E	216 932-9497
Center For Families & Children — Cleveland (G-5207)	E	216 252-5800
Center For Individual and Fmly — Mansfield (G-13274)	C	419 522-4357
Central Cmnty Hse of Columbus — Columbus (G-7227)	E	614 253-7267
Central OH Area Agency On Agng — Columbus (G-7228)	C	614 645-7250
Central Ohio Youth For Christ — Columbus (G-7243)	E	614 732-5260
Cgh-Global Emerg Mngmt Strateg — Cincinnati (G-2905)	E	800 376-0655
Chagrin Valley Dispatch — Bedford (G-1299)	E	440 247-7321
Champaign Cnty Board of Dd — Urbana (G-18576)	C	937 653-5217
Champaign Residential Services — Columbus (G-7251)	E	614 481-5550
Child Adlscent Behavioral Hlth — Canton (G-2304)	E	330 454-7917
Child Adlscent Behavioral Hlth — Canton (G-2305)	D	330 433-6075
Child Focus Inc — Batavia (G-998)	E	513 732-8800
Child Focus Inc — Cincinnati (G-3243)	E	513 752-1555
Child Focus Inc — Mount Orab (G-14867)	D	937 444-1613
Childrens Advocacy Center — Cambridge (G-2104)	E	740 432-6581
Childrens Cmprhensive Svcs Inc — Mansfield (G-13276)	D	419 589-5511
Childrens HM of Cncinnati Ohio — Cincinnati (G-3244)	C	513 272-2800
Childrens Homecare Services — Columbus (G-7261)	C	614 355-1100
Childrens Hosp Med Ctr Akron — Tallmadge (G-17634)	E	330 633-2055
Childrens Hospital Medical Ctr — Cincinnati (G-3246)	A	513 541-4500
Childrens Hunger Alliance — Columbus (G-7263)	D	614 341-7700
CHN Inc - Adult Day Care — Greenville (G-11493)	E	937 548-0506
Choices For Vctims Dom Volence — Columbus (G-7267)	D	614 258-6080
Choices For Vctims Dom Volence — Worthington (G-19947)	E	614 224-6617
Christian Aid Ministries — Millersburg (G-14593)	E	330 893-2428
Christian Chld HM Ohio Inc — Wooster (G-19841)	D	330 345-7949
Cincinnati Area Senior Svcs — Cincinnati (G-3281)	C	513 721-4330
Cincinnati Assn For The Blind — Cincinnati (G-3282)	C	513 221-8558
Cincinnati Ctr/Psychoanalysis — Cincinnati (G-3296)	E	513 961-8484
Cincinnati Youth Collaborative — Cincinnati (G-3335)	E	513 475-4165
Cincysmiles Foundation Inc — Cincinnati (G-3345)	E	513 621-0248
Circle Health Services — Cleveland (G-5242)	E	216 721-4010
City Gospel Mission — Cincinnati (G-3358)	E	513 241-5525
City Mission — Cleveland (G-5247)	E	216 431-3510
City of Brecksville — Brecksville (G-1819)	D	440 526-4109
City of Bucyrus — Bucyrus (G-2029)	E	419 562-3050
City of Canal Winchester — Canal Winchester (G-2157)	E	614 837-8276
City of Highland Heights — Cleveland (G-5262)	D	440 461-2441
City of Independence — Cleveland (G-5264)	E	216 524-7373
City of Lakewood — Lakewood (G-12473)	E	216 521-1515
City of Parma — Cleveland (G-5273)	E	440 888-4514
City of Willoughby Hills — Willoughby Hills (G-19729)	E	440 942-7207
Clark County Board of Developm — Springfield (G-17161)	E	937 328-2675
Cleaners Extraordinaire Inc — Springfield (G-17166)	D	937 324-8488
Clermont Counseling Center — Cincinnati (G-3363)	E	513 345-8555
Clermont Counseling Center — Amelia (G-579)	E	513 947-7000
Clermont County Community Svcs — Batavia (G-1000)	E	513 732-2277
Clermont Senior Services Inc — Batavia (G-1004)	E	513 724-1255

Employee Codes: A=Over 500 employees, B=251-500, C=101-250, D=51-100, E=25-50

83 SOCIAL SERVICES

Name		Phone
Cleveland Center For Etng Dsor .... E		216 765-2535
Beachwood (G-1064)		
Cleveland Christian Home Inc C		216 671-0977
Cleveland (G-5294)		
Cleveland Municipal School Dst .... D		216 521-6511
Cleveland (G-5337)		
Cleveland Soc For The Blind C		216 791-8118
Cleveland (G-5347)		
Clinton County Board of .... E		937 382-7519
Wilmington (G-19749)		
Clossman Catering Incorporated .... E		513 942-7744
Hamilton (G-11712)		
Clovernook Center For The Bli C		513 522-3860
Cincinnati (G-3370)		
Columbus Foundation .... E		614 251-4000
Columbus (G-7354)		
Columbus Spech Hearing Ctr Cpd .... D		614 263-5151
Columbus (G-7386)		
Comforcare Senior Services Inc .... E		513 777-4860
West Chester (G-19048)		
Commquest Services Inc C		330 455-0374
Canton (G-2316)		
Commu Act Comm of Fayette Cnty .... D		740 335-7282
Wshngtn CT Hs (G-20016)		
Community Action .... E		740 354-7541
Portsmouth (G-16271)		
Community Action Comm Pike CNT C		740 289-2371
Piketon (G-16112)		
Community Action Comm Pike CNT .... E		740 961-4011
Portsmouth (G-16272)		
Community Action Comm Pike CNT .... E		740 286-2826
Jackson (G-12310)		
Community Action Commission .... D		419 626-6540
Sandusky (G-16745)		
Community Action Comsn Belmont .... E		740 695-0293
Saint Clairsville (G-16632)		
Community Action Program Comm .... D		740 653-1711
Lancaster (G-12521)		
Community Action Program Corp .... E		740 373-6016
Marietta (G-13437)		
Community Action-Wayne/Medina .... D		330 264-8677
Wooster (G-19851)		
Community Caregivers .... D		330 533-3427
Youngstown (G-20151)		
Community Center .... D		330 746-7721
Youngstown (G-20152)		
Community Counseling Services .... E		419 468-8211
Bucyrus (G-2031)		
Community Drug Board Inc .... D		330 996-5114
Akron (G-154)		
Community Drug Board Inc .... D		330 315-5590
Akron (G-153)		
Community Refugee & Immigation .... D		614 235-5747
Columbus (G-7409)		
Community Services Inc .... D		937 667-8631
Tipp City (G-17714)		
Community Solutions Assn .... E		330 394-9090
Warren (G-18838)		
Compass Family and Cmnty Svcs .... D		330 743-9275
Youngstown (G-20153)		
Compass Family and Cmnty Svcs .... D		330 743-9275
Youngstown (G-20154)		
Compdrug .... D		614 224-4506
Columbus (G-7412)		
Comprehensive Cmnty Child Care .... E		513 221-0033
Cincinnati (G-3405)		
Concord .... E		614 882-9338
Westerville (G-19391)		
Concordia Care .... D		216 791-3580
Cleveland (G-5391)		
Consolidated Care Inc .... E		937 465-8065
West Liberty (G-19261)		
Consolidated Care Inc .... E		937 465-8065
West Liberty (G-19262)		
Consumer Support Services Inc .... D		740 522-5464
Newark (G-15159)		
Consumer Support Services Inc .... D		740 344-3600
Newark (G-15160)		
Consumer Support Services Inc .... B		740 788-8257
Newark (G-15158)		
Consumer Support Services Inc .... D		330 764-4785
Medina (G-14050)		
Corporation for OH Appalachian .... E		740 594-8499
Athens (G-779)		
Council For Economic Opport .... D		216 696-9077
Cleveland (G-5414)		
Council On Aging of Southweste C		513 721-1025
Cincinnati (G-3427)		
Council On Rur Svc Prgrams Inc .... E		937 773-0773
Piqua (G-16141)		
Counseling Center Huron County .... E		419 663-3737
Norwalk (G-15567)		
County of Adams .... E		937 544-5067
West Union (G-19277)		
County of Allen C		419 228-2120
Lima (G-12764)		
County of Allen .... E		419 227-8590
Lima (G-12765)		
County of Allen .... E		419 996-7050
Lima (G-12767)		
County of Ashtabula .... D		440 998-1811
Ashtabula (G-739)		
County of Brown .... E		937 378-6104
Georgetown (G-11391)		
County of Clark C		937 327-1700
Springfield (G-17179)		
County of Clark .... B		937 327-1700
Springfield (G-17181)		
County of Clark .... B		937 327-1700
Springfield (G-17182)		
County of Clinton .... E		937 382-2449
Wilmington (G-19758)		
County of Columbiana C		330 424-1386
Lisbon (G-12934)		
County of Coshocton .... D		740 622-1020
Coshocton (G-9100)		
County of Cuyahoga .... A		419 399-8260
Paulding (G-15929)		
County of Cuyahoga .... A		216 432-2621
Cleveland (G-5427)		
County of Cuyahoga .... E		216 443-5100
Cleveland (G-5422)		
County of Cuyahoga .... D		216 681-4433
Cleveland (G-5425)		
County of Darke .... E		937 526-4488
Versailles (G-18725)		
County of Erie C		419 626-6781
Sandusky (G-16748)		
County of Geauga .... D		440 285-9141
Chardon (G-2747)		
County of Geauga .... D		440 564-2246
Chardon (G-2746)		
County of Guernsey .... E		740 439-6681
Cambridge (G-2109)		
County of Guernsey .... D		740 432-2381
Cambridge (G-2108)		
County of Hamilton .... E		513 821-6946
Cincinnati (G-3433)		
County of Hamilton .... B		513 742-1576
Cincinnati (G-3428)		
County of Highland .... E		937 393-4278
Hillsboro (G-11970)		
County of Holmes .... E		330 674-1111
Millersburg (G-14601)		
County of Holmes .... E		330 674-1926
Millersburg (G-14596)		
County of Huron .... D		419 668-8126
Norwalk (G-15568)		
County of Huron .... D		419 663-5437
Norwalk (G-15569)		
County of Lake .... D		440 350-4000
Painesville (G-15847)		
County of Lake .... D		440 269-2193
Willoughby (G-19656)		
County of Logan .... E		937 599-7290
Bellefontaine (G-1383)		
County of Lorain .... E		440 329-3734
Elyria (G-10610)		
County of Lorain .... E		440 326-4700
Elyria (G-10611)		
County of Lorain .... D		440 284-1830
Elyria (G-10613)		
County of Lorain .... E		440 329-5340
Elyria (G-10616)		
County of Lucas C		419 213-3000
Toledo (G-17833)		
County of Lucas .... B		419 213-8999
Toledo (G-17835)		
County of Marion .... E		740 387-6688
Marion (G-13532)		
County of Marion .... E		740 389-2317
Marion (G-13534)		
County of Meigs .... E		740 992-2117
Middleport (G-14406)		
County of Mercer .... D		419 586-2369
Celina (G-2643)		
County of Mercer .... E		419 586-5106
Celina (G-2644)		
County of Mercer .... E		419 678-8071
Coldwater (G-6828)		
County of Montgomery .... B		937 224-5437
Dayton (G-9432)		
County of Montgomery .... D		937 224-5437
Dayton (G-9438)		
County of Montgomery .... B		937 225-4804
Dayton (G-9436)		
County of Ottawa .... E		419 898-2089
Oak Harbor (G-15608)		
County of Paulding .... E		419 399-3636
Paulding (G-15930)		
County of Pickaway .... D		740 474-7588
Circleville (G-4885)		
County of Richland .... E		419 774-5894
Mansfield (G-13279)		
County of Richland C		419 774-5400
Mansfield (G-13281)		
County of Richland C		419 774-4100
Mansfield (G-13280)		
County of Summit .... D		330 643-2300
Akron (G-168)		
County of Summit .... B		330 643-7217
Akron (G-172)		
County of Summit .... A		330 634-8193
Tallmadge (G-17636)		
County of Tuscarawas .... E		330 343-0099
New Philadelphia (G-15090)		
County of Tuscarawas .... D		330 339-7791
New Philadelphia (G-15091)		
County of Union .... D		937 645-6733
Marysville (G-13613)		
County of Warren .... E		513 695-1420
Lebanon (G-12598)		
County of Washington .... D		740 373-5513
Marietta (G-13440)		
County of Wayne .... E		330 287-5600
Wooster (G-19852)		
Couple To Couple Leag Intl Inc .... E		513 471-2000
Cincinnati (G-3434)		
Crawford County Children Svcs .... E		419 562-1200
Bucyrus (G-2035)		
Crawford County Council On Agi .... E		419 562-3050
Bucyrus (G-2036)		
Creative Diversified Services .... E		937 376-7810
Xenia (G-20048)		
Creative Foundations Inc .... D		740 362-5102
Delaware (G-10085)		
Crisis Intervention & Rcvy Ctr .... D		330 455-9407
Canton (G-2327)		
Crisis Intvntn Ctr Stark Cnty .... D		330 452-9812
Canton (G-2328)		
Crittenton Family Services .... E		614 251-0103
Columbus (G-7464)		
Crossroads Lake County Adole .... D		440 255-1700
Mentor (G-14165)		
Cuyahoga County .... A		216 431-4500
Cleveland (G-5452)		
Cuyahoga County .... D		216 420-6750
Cleveland (G-5450)		
Cyo & Community Services Inc .... E		330 762-2961
Akron (G-184)		
Danbury Woods of Wooster .... E		330 264-0355
Wooster (G-19861)		
Davita Inc .... E		440 293-6028
Andover (G-611)		
Day Share Ltd .... E		513 451-1100
Cincinnati (G-3467)		
Dayton Urban League .... E		937 226-1513
Dayton (G-9493)		
Deepwood Industries Inc C		440 350-5231
Mentor (G-14168)		
Defiance Cnty Bd Commissioners .... E		419 782-3233
Defiance (G-10025)		
Delhi Township .... D		513 922-0060
Cincinnati (G-3481)		
Developmental Disabilities C		513 732-7000
Batavia (G-1009)		
Developmental Disabilities .... D		513 732-7015
Owensville (G-15809)		
Develpmntal Dsblties Ohio Dept C		937 233-8108
Columbus (G-7514)		
Develpmntal Dsblties Ohio Dept C		513 732-9200
Batavia (G-1010)		
Direction Home Akron Canton AR C		330 896-9172
Uniontown (G-18517)		
Directions For Youth Families .... E		614 258-8043
Columbus (G-7520)		
Directions For Youth Families .... E		614 694-0203
Columbus (G-7521)		
Directions For Youth Families .... E		614 294-2661
Columbus (G-7522)		

83 SOCIAL SERVICES

Name	Code	Phone
Diverscare Healthcare Svcs Inc, Dayton (G-9502)	E	937 278-8211
DMD Management Inc, Cleveland (G-5497)	A	216 371-3600
Domestic Violence Project Inc, Canton (G-2343)	E	330 445-2000
Don Bosco Community Center Inc, Cleveland (G-5500)	D	816 421-3160
Don Bosco Community Center Inc, Cleveland (G-5501)	D	816 421-3160
East End Community Svcs Corp, Dayton (G-9514)	E	937 259-1898
East End Neighborhood Hse Assn, Cleveland (G-5519)	E	216 791-9378
East Toledo Family Center, Toledo (G-17861)	D	419 691-1429
Easter Seal Society of, Youngstown (G-20176)	D	330 743-1168
Easter Seals Center, Hilliard (G-11898)	D	614 228-5523
Easter Seals Tristate, Blue Ash (G-1582)	C	513 985-0515
Easter Seals Tristate LLC, Cincinnati (G-3534)	C	513 475-6791
Eastway Corporation, Dayton (G-9516)	C	937 496-2000
Echoing Hills Village Inc, Warsaw (G-18936)	A	740 327-2311
Economic & Cmnty Dev Inst Inc, Columbus (G-7575)	E	614 559-0104
Elderly United of Springfield, Springfield (G-17193)	D	937 323-4948
Emerge Counseling Service, Akron (G-207)	E	330 865-8351
Emerge Ministries Inc, Akron (G-208)	E	330 865-8351
Episcopal Retirement Homes Inc, Cincinnati (G-3567)	E	513 271-9610
Equitas Health Inc, Columbus (G-7603)	C	614 299-2437
Equitas Health Inc, Dayton (G-9529)	E	937 461-2437
F R S Connections, Hillsboro (G-11973)	E	937 393-9662
Fairborn Fish, Fairborn (G-10794)	E	937 879-1313
Fairborn YMCA, Fairborn (G-10796)	E	937 754-9622
Faith Mission Inc, Columbus (G-7633)	E	614 224-6617
Faith Mission Inc, Columbus (G-7634)	E	614 224-6617
Family & Child Abuse, Toledo (G-17876)	E	419 244-3053
Family Cmnty Svcs Portage Cnty, Ravenna (G-16385)	C	330 297-0078
Family Life Counseling, Mansfield (G-13299)	E	419 774-9969
Family Senior Care Inc, Gallipolis (G-11315)	E	740 441-1428
Family Service, Cincinnati (G-3591)	E	513 381-6300
Family Service Association, Moraine (G-14783)	E	937 222-9481
Family Service of NW Ohio, Toledo (G-17878)	D	419 321-6455
Family YMCA of LANcstr&fairfld, Lancaster (G-12541)	D	740 277-7373
Fayette Progressive Industries, Wshngtn CT Hs (G-20023)	E	740 335-7453
Feed Lucas County Children Inc, Toledo (G-17885)	D	419 260-1556
Findlay Y M C A Child Dev, Findlay (G-11031)	E	419 422-3174
Firelands Regional Health Sys, Norwalk (G-15573)	E	419 663-3737
First Community Village, Columbus (G-7664)	B	614 324-4455
Focus On Youth Inc, West Chester (G-19075)	E	513 644-1030
For Specialized Alternatives, Delphos (G-10144)	E	419 695-8010
Foundations Hlth Solutions Inc, North Olmsted (G-15423)	D	440 793-0200
Four County Family Center, Wauseon (G-18952)	E	800 693-6000
Franklin Cnty Bd Commissioners, Columbus (G-7683)	C	614 275-2571
Franklin Cnty Bd Commissioners, Columbus (G-7685)	B	614 462-3275
Franklin Cnty Bd Commissioners, Columbus (G-7687)	B	614 229-7100
Frans Child Care-Mansfield, Mansfield (G-13304)	C	419 775-2500
Free Store/Food Bank Inc, Cincinnati (G-3648)	E	513 482-4526
Free Store/Food Bank Inc, Cincinnati (G-3649)	E	513 241-1064
Freestore/Foodbank, Cincinnati (G-3650)	E	513 482-4500
Friend To Friend Program, Cleveland (G-5640)	E	216 861-1838
Friendly Inn Settlement House, Cleveland (G-5641)	E	216 431-7656
Frs Counseling Inc, Hillsboro (G-11975)	E	937 393-0585
Fulton County Senior Center, Wauseon (G-18957)	E	419 337-9299
Furniture Bank Central Ohio, Columbus (G-7715)	E	614 272-9544
G M N Tri Cnty Community Action, Caldwell (G-2085)	C	740 732-2388
Galion Community Center YMCA, Galion (G-11297)	E	419 468-7754
Gallia-Meigs Community Action, Cheshire (G-2790)	E	740 367-7341
Ganzhorn Suites Inc, Powell (G-16336)	E	614 356-9810
Gardens Western Reserve Inc, Streetsboro (G-17412)	D	330 342-9100
Gerlach John J Center For Sen, Columbus (G-7746)	E	614 566-5858
Girl Scuts Appleseed Ridge Inc, Lima (G-12783)	E	419 225-4085
Gladden Community House, Columbus (G-7753)	E	614 221-7801
Godman Guild, Columbus (G-7756)	E	614 294-5476
Golden String Inc, Youngstown (G-20203)	E	330 503-3894
Good Smaritan Netwrk Ross Cnty, Chillicothe (G-2842)	E	740 774-6303
Goodrich Gnnett Nghborhood Ctr, Cleveland (G-5678)	E	216 432-1717
Goodwill Inds of S Centl Ohio, Chillicothe (G-2843)	D	740 702-4000
Goodwill Inds Rhbilitation Ctr, Steubenville (G-17319)	C	740 264-6000
Goodwill Inds Rhbilitation Ctr, Canton (G-2384)	B	330 454-9461
Goodwill Industries Inc, Akron (G-241)	E	330 724-6995
Goodwill Industries of Erie, Fremont (G-11204)	D	419 355-1579
Goodwill Industries of Erie, Sandusky (G-16763)	E	419 625-4744
Goodwill Industries of Erie, Fremont (G-11205)	D	419 334-7566
Grace Resurrection Association, Greenville (G-11503)	E	937 548-2595
Graceworks Lutheran Services, Dayton (G-9585)	C	937 433-2110
Great Miami Valley YMCA, Hamilton (G-11733)	E	513 887-0001
Great Miami Valley YMCA, Fairfield Township (G-10930)	C	513 892-9622
Great Miami Valley YMCA, Hamilton (G-11735)	E	513 887-0014
Great Miami Valley YMCA, Hamilton (G-11736)	D	513 868-9622
Great Miami Valley YMCA, Fairfield (G-10854)	E	513 829-3091
Greater Cincinnati Behavioral, Walnut Hills (G-18787)	B	513 354-7000
Greater Cincinnati Behavioral, Walnut Hills (G-18788)	D	513 755-2203
Greater Cleveland Food Bnk Inc, Cleveland (G-5696)	C	216 738-2265
Greene Cnty Combined Hlth Dst, Xenia (G-20053)	D	937 374-5600
Greene County, Xenia (G-20055)	E	937 562-6000
Greenleaf Family Center, Akron (G-247)	E	330 376-9494
Grove Cy Chrstn Child Care Ctr, Grove City (G-11568)	D	614 875-2551
Hancock Job & Family Services, Findlay (G-11043)	D	419 424-7022
Handson Central Ohio Inc, Columbus (G-7798)	E	614 221-2255
Happy Hearts School, Ashtabula (G-746)	C	440 224-2157
Harbor House Inc, New Philadelphia (G-15096)	E	740 498-7213
Harcatus Tri-County Community, New Philadelphia (G-15097)	E	740 922-0933
Hardin Cnty Cncil On Aging Inc, Kenton (G-12414)	E	419 673-1102
Hardin County Family YMCA, Kenton (G-12416)	E	419 673-6131
Harrison Pavilion, Cincinnati (G-3738)	E	513 662-5800
Hattie Larlham Center For, Mantua (G-13387)	C	330 274-2272
Hattie Larlham Community Svcs, Twinsburg (G-18427)	C	330 274-2272
Havar Inc, Athens (G-790)	D	740 594-3533
Haven Bhavioral Healthcare Inc, Dayton (G-9601)	B	937 234-0100
Haven Rest Ministries Inc, Akron (G-258)	D	330 535-1563
Hcf Management Inc, Piketon (G-16117)	C	740 289-2394
Hcf of Roselawn Inc, Spencerville (G-17108)	C	419 647-4115
Hcr Manorcare Med Svcs Fla LLC, North Royalton (G-15494)	D	440 887-1442
Healing Hrts Cunseling Ctr Inc, Mansfield (G-13307)	E	419 528-5993
Heap Home Energy Assistance, Sandusky (G-16767)	E	419 626-6540
Hearing Spch Deaf Ctr Grtr Cnc, Cincinnati (G-3755)	E	513 221-0527
Heartbeat International Inc, Columbus (G-7816)	E	614 885-7577
Help Hotline Crisis Center, Youngstown (G-20216)	E	330 747-5111
Help Line of Dlware Mrrow Cnty, Delaware (G-10104)	E	740 369-3316
Help ME Grow, Wapakoneta (G-18799)	E	419 738-4773
Highland County Family YMCA, Hillsboro (G-11978)	E	937 840-9622
HighInd Cnty Commnty Action or, Hillsboro (G-11981)	E	937 393-3060
Hilty Memorial Home Inc, Pandora (G-15892)	C	419 384-3218
Hispanc Urbn Mnrty Alchlsm DRG, Cleveland (G-5759)	E	216 398-2333
Hocking College Addc, Glouster (G-11434)	E	740 541-2221
Hockingthensperry Cmnty Action, Logan (G-12976)	E	740 385-6813
Hockingthensperry Cmnty Action, Glouster (G-11435)	E	740 767-4500
Home Instead Senior Care, Wadsworth (G-18756)	D	330 334-4664
Homefull, Dayton (G-9618)	E	937 293-1945
Homeless Families Foundation, Columbus (G-7852)	E	614 461-9427
Homes For Kids of Ohio Inc, Niles (G-15294)	E	330 544-8005
Horizon Education Centers, Elyria (G-10634)	E	440 458-5115
Hospice of Knox County, Mount Vernon (G-14899)	E	740 397-5188
Hospice of The Valley Inc, Youngstown (G-20221)	D	330 788-1992
Hospice of The Western Reserve, Ashtabula (G-748)	D	440 997-6619
House of New Hope, Saint Louisville (G-16668)	E	740 345-5437
Huber Heights YMCA, Dayton (G-9623)	D	937 236-9622
Huckleberry House, Columbus (G-7861)	D	614 294-5553
Hudson City Engineering Dept, Hudson (G-12121)	E	330 342-1770
Impact Community Action, Columbus (G-7885)	D	614 252-2799
Info Line Inc, Akron (G-247)	E	330 252-8064
Inn At Christine Valley, Youngstown (G-20236)	E	330 270-3347
Inn At Medina Limited LLC, Medina (G-14080)	D	330 723-0110
Inside Out, Springfield (G-17212)	D	937 525-7880

Integrated Services of Appala ....D....... 740 594-6807
Athens *(G-794)*
Interfaith Hosptlty Ntwrk of W ....D....... 513 934-5250
Lebanon *(G-12613)*
Jackson County Board On Aging..........E....... 740 286-2909
Jackson *(G-12315)*
James Powers..........E....... 614 566-9397
Columbus *(G-7934)*
Jewish Cmnty Ctr of Toledo..........D....... 419 885-4485
Sylvania *(G-17597)*
Jewish Community Ctr Cleveland.........C....... 216 831-0700
Beachwood *(G-1091)*
Jewish Family Service of The C ....E....... 513 469-1188
Cincinnati *(G-3869)*
Jewish Family Services..........D....... 614 231-1890
Columbus *(G-7940)*
Jewish Family Services Associa ....E....... 216 292-3999
Cleveland *(G-5863)*
Jewish Family Services Associa ....E....... 216 292-3999
Cleveland *(G-5864)*
Jewish Fderation of Cincinnati..........E....... 513 985-1500
Cincinnati *(G-3870)*
Jewish Fdrtion of Grter Dayton ....D....... 937 837-2651
Dayton *(G-9641)*
Joint Township Dst Mem Hosp..........D....... 419 394-9992
Saint Marys *(G-16677)*
Juvenile Court Cnty Muskingum..........E....... 740 453-0351
Zanesville *(G-20493)*
KElly Youth Services Inc..........E....... 513 761-0700
Cincinnati *(G-3910)*
Kettering Recreation Center ....E....... 937 296-2587
Dayton *(G-9657)*
Kindred Healthcare Inc..........D....... 216 593-2200
Beachwood *(G-1094)*
Kingston Rsdnce Perrysburg LLC ....D....... 419 872-6200
Perrysburg *(G-16025)*
Kno-Ho-Co- Ashland Community A ......C....... 740 622-9801
Coshocton *(G-9110)*
Lake County Council On Aging..........E....... 440 205-8111
Mentor *(G-14203)*
Lake County YMCA..........A....... 440 352-3303
Painesville *(G-15860)*
Lake County YMCA..........C....... 440 946-1160
Willoughby *(G-19680)*
Lake County YMCA..........E....... 440 259-2724
Perry *(G-15962)*
Lake County YMCA..........D....... 440 428-5125
Madison *(G-13227)*
Lawrence Cnty Bd Dev Dsblities ....E....... 740 377-2356
South Point *(G-17090)*
Leads Inc..........E....... 740 349-8606
Newark *(G-15184)*
Liberty Nursing Center of Thre..........C....... 513 941-0787
Cincinnati *(G-3976)*
Licco Inc..........C....... 740 522-8345
Newark *(G-15185)*
Licking Cnty Alcoholism Prvntn..........E....... 740 281-3639
Newark *(G-15186)*
Licking County Aging Program..........D....... 740 345-0821
Newark *(G-15187)*
Licking County Board of Mrdd ....C....... 740 349-6588
Newark *(G-15188)*
Life Center Adult Day Care ....E....... 614 866-7212
Reynoldsburg *(G-16465)*
Lifecare Hospice..........E....... 330 264-4899
Wooster *(G-19883)*
Lifecare Hospice..........D....... 330 336-6595
Wadsworth *(G-18761)*
Lifespan Incorporated ....D....... 513 868-3210
Hamilton *(G-11754)*
Light of Hearts Villa ....D....... 440 232-1991
Cleveland *(G-5941)*
Lighthouse Youth Services Inc..........D....... 513 221-1017
Cincinnati *(G-3980)*
Lighthouse Youth Services Inc..........D....... 513 221-3350
Cincinnati *(G-3982)*
Lighthouse Youth Services Inc..........D....... 740 634-3094
Bainbridge *(G-942)*
Lima Family YMCA..........E....... 419 223-6045
Lima *(G-12821)*
Living In Family Environment..........D....... 614 475-5305
Gahanna *(G-11255)*
Lorain Cnty Bys Girls CLB Inc..........E....... 440 775-2582
Lorain *(G-13048)*
Lutheran Scial Svcs Centl Ohio..........E....... 419 289-3523
Worthington *(G-19974)*
Lyman W Liggins Urban Affairs..........D....... 419 385-2532
Toledo *(G-18023)*
Maco Inc..........E....... 740 472-5445
Woodsfield *(G-19816)*
Mahoning County..........D....... 330 797-2837
Youngstown *(G-20262)*
Mahoning County Childrens Svcs.........C....... 330 941-8888
Youngstown *(G-20263)*
Mahoning Youngstown Community ......E....... 330 747-5661
Youngstown *(G-20267)*
Mahoning Youngstown Community......D....... 330 747-7921
Youngstown *(G-20268)*
Marion Area Counseling Ctr ....C....... 740 387-5210
Marion *(G-13553)*
Marion Family YMCA ....D....... 740 725-9622
Marion *(G-13556)*
Marsh Foundation..........E....... 419 238-1695
Van Wert *(G-18639)*
Masco Inc..........E....... 330 797-2904
Youngstown *(G-20274)*
Matco Industries Inc ....E....... 740 852-7054
London *(G-13002)*
Meals On Wheels-Older Adult Al ....E....... 740 681-5050
Lancaster *(G-12555)*
Medina Creative Accessibility ....D....... 330 220-2112
Medina *(G-14099)*
Meigs County Council On Aging ....E....... 740 992-2161
Pomeroy *(G-16233)*
Menorah Park Center For Senio ....A....... 216 831-6500
Cleveland *(G-6024)*
Mental Health & Recovery Ctr..........E....... 937 383-3031
Wilmington *(G-19773)*
Mental Health Services..........E....... 216 623-6555
Cleveland *(G-6025)*
Mental Hlth Serv For CL & Mad ....E....... 937 390-7980
Springfield *(G-17233)*
Mercy Health..........A....... 440 233-1000
Lorain *(G-13060)*
Mercy Health..........E....... 440 324-0400
Elyria *(G-10652)*
Mercy Health - St..........E....... 419 696-7465
Oregon *(G-15741)*
Mercy Health Partners..........B....... 513 451-8900
Cincinnati *(G-4074)*
Miami County Childrens Svcs Bd..........E....... 937 335-4103
Troy *(G-18364)*
Miami Valley Community Action..........E....... 937 456-2800
Eaton *(G-10569)*
Miami Valley Community Action..........D....... 937 548-8143
Greenville *(G-11514)*
Miami Valley Community Action..........D....... 937 222-1009
Dayton *(G-9728)*
Miami Vly Jvnile Rhblttion Ctr ....E....... 937 562-4000
Xenia *(G-20070)*
Mid-Ohio Foodbank ....C....... 614 317-9400
Grove City *(G-11581)*
Mid-Ohio Psychlogical Svcs Inc..........E....... 740 687-0042
Lancaster *(G-12558)*
Middltown Area Senior Citizens ....D....... 513 423-1734
Middletown *(G-14438)*
Midwest Behavioral Care Ltd..........E....... 937 454-0092
Dayton *(G-9744)*
Miracle Spirtl Retrst Orgnsizn ....E....... 216 324-4287
Cleveland *(G-6070)*
Mobile Meals of Salem Inc ....E....... 330 332-2160
Salem *(G-16705)*
Mound Builders Guidance Center..........D....... 740 522-2828
Newark *(G-15212)*
Mount Carmel Health..........C....... 614 234-8170
Columbus *(G-8197)*
Mt Washington Care Center Inc..........C....... 513 231-4561
Cincinnati *(G-4130)*
Murray Ridge Production Center..........B....... 440 329-3734
Elyria *(G-10657)*
Muskingum Cnty Ctr For Seniors..........E....... 740 454-9761
Zanesville *(G-20504)*
Muskingum County Adult and CHI..........E....... 740 849-2344
Zanesville *(G-20505)*
Muskingum County Ohio ....D....... 740 452-0678
Zanesville *(G-20506)*
Muskingum Vly Nrsing Rhblttion ....D....... 740 984-4262
Beverly *(G-1492)*
Nami of Preble County Ohio ....E....... 937 456-4947
Eaton *(G-10570)*
National Exchange Club Foundat..........E....... 419 535-3232
Toledo *(G-18075)*
National Mentor Holdings Inc ....A....... 513 221-0175
Cincinnati *(G-4141)*
National Youth Advocate Progra ....E....... 740 349-7511
Newark *(G-15217)*
National Youth Advocate Progra ....E....... 614 487-8758
Columbus *(G-8225)*
National Youth Advocate Progra ....D....... 614 252-6927
Columbus *(G-8226)*
Neighborhood House ....D....... 614 252-4941
Columbus *(G-8256)*
New Horizon Youth Center Co ....E....... 740 782-0092
Bethesda *(G-1485)*
New Horizon Youth Family Ctr..........E....... 740 687-0835
Lancaster *(G-12560)*
Nick Amster Inc..........D....... 330 264-9667
Wooster *(G-19894)*
North East Ohio Health Svcs ....D....... 216 831-6466
Beachwood *(G-1107)*
Northeast Ohio Adoption Svcs..........E....... 330 856-5582
Warren *(G-18887)*
Northeast Ohio Chapter Natnl ....E....... 216 696-8220
Cleveland *(G-6154)*
Northern Ohio Recovery Assn..........E....... 216 391-6672
Cleveland *(G-6161)*
Northgate Pk Retirement Cmnty..........D....... 513 923-3711
Cincinnati *(G-4181)*
Northland Brdg Franklin Cnty..........E....... 614 846-2588
Columbus *(G-8291)*
Northwest Mental Health Svcs..........E....... 614 457-7876
Columbus *(G-8297)*
Northwestrn OH Communty Action.......C....... 419 784-2150
Defiance *(G-10051)*
Oaks of West Kettering Inc ....C....... 937 293-1152
Dayton *(G-9780)*
Ohio Department of Health ....B....... 330 792-2397
Austintown *(G-870)*
Ohio Department of Health ....B....... 614 645-3621
Columbus *(G-8327)*
Ohio Department of Health ....A....... 614 438-1255
Columbus *(G-8329)*
Ohio Department of Health ....D....... 937 285-6250
Dayton *(G-9784)*
Ohio Dept of Job & Fmly Svcs..........C....... 614 466-1213
Columbus *(G-8335)*
Ohio Dept Rhbilitation Corectn ....B....... 614 274-9000
Columbus *(G-8336)*
Ohio District 5 Area ....C....... 419 522-5612
Ontario *(G-15707)*
Ohio Hrtland Cmnty Action Comm..........E....... 419 468-5121
Galion *(G-11303)*
Ohio State University..........A....... 614 366-3692
Columbus *(G-8388)*
Ohio Yuth Advocate Program Inc..........D....... 614 252-6927
Columbus *(G-8453)*
Ohioguidestone..........E....... 440 234-2006
Berea *(G-1467)*
Ohioguidestone..........C....... 440 260-8900
Cleveland *(G-6197)*
Older Wiser Life Services LLC..........E....... 330 659-2111
Richfield *(G-16522)*
Olmsted Residence Corporation..........C....... 440 235-7100
Olmsted Twp *(G-15680)*
Oneeighty Inc..........D....... 330 263-6021
Wooster *(G-19900)*
ONeill Senior Center Inc..........E....... 740 373-3914
Marietta *(G-13482)*
Operation Thank You..........E....... 513 899-3134
Morrow *(G-14846)*
Opportunities For Ohioans ....E....... 614 438-1200
Columbus *(G-8473)*
Option Line..........E....... 614 586-1380
Columbus *(G-8476)*
Options For Family & Youth..........E....... 216 267-7070
Strongsville *(G-17498)*
Oriana House Inc ....A....... 330 535-8116
Akron *(G-373)*
Oriana House Inc ....D....... 330 996-7730
Akron *(G-374)*
Oriana House Inc ....E....... 216 881-5440
Cleveland *(G-6213)*
Oriana House Inc ....C....... 330 643-2171
Akron *(G-375)*
Otterbein Snior Lfstyle Chices ....C....... 419 394-2366
Saint Marys *(G-16682)*
Outreach Cmnty Living Svcs Inc..........E....... 330 263-0862
Wooster *(G-19901)*
Pastoral Care Management Svcs ....E....... 513 205-1398
Cincinnati *(G-4257)*
Pastoral Counseling Svc Summit..........C....... 330 996-4600
Akron *(G-378)*
Pathway Inc..........E....... 419 242-7304
Toledo *(G-18122)*
Pathway 2 Hope Inc ....E....... 866 491-3040
Cincinnati *(G-4258)*
Pathways of Central Ohio ....E....... 740 345-6166
Newark *(G-15227)*
Personal & Fmly Counseling Svc..........E....... 330 343-8171
New Philadelphia *(G-15111)*

Phillis Wheat Association Inc..........E....... 216 391-4443
Cleveland *(G-6274)*
Pickaway County Community Acti........D....... 740 477-1655
Circleville *(G-4894)*
Pickaway County Community Acti........E....... 740 474-7411
Circleville *(G-4895)*
Pickaway County Community Acti........E....... 740 477-1655
Circleville *(G-4896)*
Pickaway Diversified..........E....... 740 474-1522
Circleville *(G-4898)*
Pike County YMCA..........E....... 740 947-8862
Waverly *(G-18974)*
Planned Parenthood Association..........E....... 937 226-0780
Dayton *(G-9811)*
Portage County Board..........D....... 330 678-2400
Ravenna *(G-16398)*
Portsmouth Metro Hsing Auth..........E....... 740 354-4547
Portsmouth *(G-16300)*
Positive Education Program..........E....... 216 227-2730
Cleveland *(G-6291)*
Preble County Council On Aging..........E....... 937 456-4947
Eaton *(G-10574)*
Pregnancy Care of Cincinnati..........E....... 513 487-7777
Cincinnati *(G-4321)*
Pressley Ridge Pryde..........E....... 513 559-1402
Cincinnati *(G-4325)*
Private Duty Services Inc..........C....... 419 238-3714
Van Wert *(G-18642)*
Pro Seniors Inc..........E....... 513 345-4160
Cincinnati *(G-4338)*
Prokids Inc..........E....... 513 281-2000
Cincinnati *(G-4347)*
Providence House Inc..........E....... 216 651-5982
Cleveland *(G-6326)*
Pump House Ministries..........E....... 419 207-3900
Ashland *(G-692)*
Quest Recovery Prevention Svcs..........C....... 330 453-8252
Canton *(G-2499)*
Rape Information & Counseling..........E....... 330 782-3936
Youngstown *(G-20341)*
Rehab Resources..........E....... 513 474-4123
Cincinnati *(G-4399)*
Rehabltation Corectn Ohio Dept..........D....... 614 752-0800
Columbus *(G-8608)*
Rescue Mission of Mahoning Val..........E....... 330 744-5485
Youngstown *(G-20349)*
Rescue Mission of Mahoning Val..........E....... 330 744-5485
Youngstown *(G-20350)*
Richland County Child Support..........E....... 419 774-5700
Mansfield *(G-13356)*
River Rock Rehabilitation..........E....... 740 382-4035
Marion *(G-13576)*
Rocking Horse Chld Hlth Ctr..........E....... 937 328-7266
Springfield *(G-17265)*
Ross Cnty Cmmittee For Elderly..........E....... 740 773-3544
Chillicothe *(G-2877)*
Ross County Children Svcs Ctr..........D....... 740 773-2651
Chillicothe *(G-2878)*
Ross County Community..........E....... 740 702-7222
Chillicothe *(G-2879)*
Ross County YMCA..........D....... 740 772-4340
Chillicothe *(G-2882)*
Ryan Sheridan..........E....... 330 270-2380
Youngstown *(G-20364)*
Safely Home Inc..........E....... 440 232-9310
Bedford *(G-1334)*
Salem Community Center Inc..........D....... 330 332-5885
Salem *(G-16712)*
Saline Township..........E....... 330 532-2195
Hammondsville *(G-11786)*
Salvation Army..........D....... 614 252-7171
Columbus *(G-8681)*
Salvation Army..........E....... 937 528-5100
Dayton *(G-9863)*
Salvation Army..........D....... 859 255-5791
Cincinnati *(G-4474)*
Salvation Army..........D....... 800 728-7825
Columbus *(G-8682)*
Salvation Army..........D....... 513 762-5600
Cincinnati *(G-4475)*
Salvation Army..........D....... 216 861-8185
Cleveland *(G-6440)*
Santa Maria Community Svcs Inc..........E....... 513 557-2720
Cincinnati *(G-4477)*
Santantonio Diana and Assoc..........E....... 440 323-5121
Elyria *(G-10677)*
Sateri Home Inc..........D....... 330 758-8106
Youngstown *(G-20367)*
Scioto County Counseling Ctr..........D....... 740 354-6685
Portsmouth *(G-16307)*
Scioto County Ohio..........E....... 740 456-4164
New Boston *(G-15013)*
Scioto Pnt Vly Mental Hlth Ctr..........C....... 740 775-1260
Chillicothe *(G-2884)*
Scioto Pnt Vly Mental Hlth Ctr..........E....... 740 335-6935
Wshngtn CT Hs *(G-20034)*
Seamans Services..........E....... 216 621-4107
Cleveland *(G-6458)*
Sechkar Company..........E....... 740 385-8900
Nelsonville *(G-14968)*
Self Reliance Inc..........E....... 937 525-0809
Springfield *(G-17273)*
Senior Independence Adult..........E....... 440 954-8372
Willoughby *(G-19712)*
Senior Independence Adult..........E....... 513 681-8174
Monroe *(G-14711)*
Senior Independence Adult..........E....... 513 539-2697
Monroe *(G-14712)*
Senior Outreach Services..........E....... 216 421-6900
Cleveland *(G-6470)*
Senior Resource Connection..........C....... 937 223-8246
Dayton *(G-9875)*
Senior Star Management Company..........B....... 513 271-1747
Cincinnati *(G-4497)*
Services On Mark Inc..........E....... 614 846-5400
Worthington *(G-19997)*
Seven Hlls Neighborhood Houses..........D....... 513 407-5362
Cincinnati *(G-4505)*
Shaw Jewish Community Center..........C....... 330 867-7850
Akron *(G-437)*
Sheakley Cente..........E....... 513 487-7106
Cincinnati *(G-4511)*
Shelter House Volunteer Group..........E....... 513 721-0643
Cincinnati *(G-4515)*
Sickle Cell Awaremess Grp..........E....... 513 281-4450
Cincinnati *(G-4525)*
Sidney-Shelby County YMCA..........E....... 937 492-9134
Sidney *(G-16955)*
Siffrin Residential Assn..........C....... 330 799-8932
Youngstown *(G-20375)*
Simply Youth LLC..........D....... 330 284-2537
Canton *(G-2528)*
Sioto Paintsville Mental Hlth..........E....... 740 775-1260
Chillicothe *(G-2885)*
Skyview Baptist Ranch Inc..........E....... 330 674-7511
Millersburg *(G-14622)*
Society For Handicapped Citzns..........E....... 937 746-4201
Carlisle *(G-2606)*
Society of St Vincent De Paul..........E....... 513 421-2273
Cincinnati *(G-4547)*
Society St Vincent De Paul Cle..........D....... 216 696-6525
Cleveland *(G-6492)*
Sojourner Recovery Services..........D....... 513 868-7654
Hamilton *(G-11773)*
Sourcepoint..........D....... 740 363-6677
Delaware *(G-10128)*
Southast Cmnty Mental Hlth Ctr..........E....... 614 444-0800
Columbus *(G-8752)*
Southast Cmnty Mental Hlth Ctr..........E....... 614 445-6832
Columbus *(G-8753)*
Southast Cmnty Mental Hlth Ctr..........E....... 614 293-9613
Worthington *(G-19998)*
Southeast Diversified Inds..........D....... 740 432-4241
Cambridge *(G-2128)*
Southeastern Rehabilitation..........E....... 740 679-2111
Salesville *(G-16720)*
Southern Ohio Medical Center..........A....... 740 354-5000
Portsmouth *(G-16313)*
Southstern Ohio Rgional Fd Ctr..........E....... 740 385-6813
Logan *(G-12988)*
Spanish American Committee..........E....... 216 961-2100
Cleveland *(G-6513)*
Specialized Alternatives For F..........C....... 216 295-7239
Shaker Heights *(G-16867)*
Specialized Alternatives For F..........A....... 419 695-8010
Delphos *(G-10151)*
Spectrum Supportive Services..........E....... 216 875-0460
Cleveland *(G-6517)*
Springfield Family Y M C A..........D....... 937 323-3781
Springfield *(G-17281)*
St Joseph Infant Maternity Hm..........C....... 513 563-2520
Cincinnati *(G-4572)*
St Pauls Community Center..........D....... 419 255-5520
Toledo *(G-18200)*
St Stephens Community House..........D....... 614 294-6347
Columbus *(G-8770)*
St Vincent De Paul Scl Svs..........D....... 937 222-7349
Dayton *(G-9902)*
St Vincent Family Centers..........C....... 614 252-0731
Columbus *(G-8771)*
Stark Cnty Dept Job Fmly Svcs..........B....... 330 451-8400
Canton *(G-2540)*
Substance Abuse Services Inc..........E....... 419 243-7274
Toledo *(G-18206)*
Summit Cnty Dept Job Fmly Svcs..........D....... 330 643-8200
Akron *(G-465)*
Sunshine Communities..........B....... 419 865-0251
Maumee *(G-13982)*
Support To At Risk Teens..........E....... 216 696-5507
Cleveland *(G-6557)*
Supreme Court United States..........E....... 419 213-5800
Toledo *(G-18212)*
Supreme Court United States..........D....... 614 719-3107
Columbus *(G-8808)*
Supreme Court United States..........E....... 513 564-7575
Cincinnati *(G-4605)*
Supreme Court United States..........E....... 216 357-7300
Cleveland *(G-6558)*
Sycamore Board of Education..........D....... 513 489-3937
Cincinnati *(G-4608)*
Sycamore Senior Center..........D....... 513 984-1234
Blue Ash *(G-1692)*
Sylvania Community Svcs Ctr..........E....... 419 885-2451
Sylvania *(G-17618)*
Syntero Inc..........E....... 614 889-5722
Dublin *(G-10471)*
Talbert House..........E....... 513 541-0127
Cincinnati *(G-4617)*
Talbert House..........E....... 513 541-1184
Cincinnati *(G-4619)*
Talbert House..........D....... 513 872-5863
Cincinnati *(G-4620)*
Talbert House..........D....... 513 933-9304
Lebanon *(G-12652)*
Talbert House Health..........E....... 513 541-7577
Cincinnati *(G-4622)*
Tasc of Northwest Ohio Inc..........E....... 419 242-9955
Toledo *(G-18214)*
Tasc of Southeast Ohio..........E....... 740 594-2276
Athens *(G-814)*
Taylor Corporation..........E....... 419 420-0790
Findlay *(G-11091)*
Taylor Murtis Human Svcs Sys..........D....... 216 281-7192
Cleveland *(G-6574)*
Taylor Murtis Human Svcs Sys..........D....... 216 283-4400
Cleveland *(G-6573)*
Tcn Behavioral Health Svcs Inc..........C....... 937 376-8700
Xenia *(G-20077)*
Tender Mercies Inc..........E....... 513 721-8666
Cincinnati *(G-4635)*
The Foodbank Inc..........E....... 937 461-0265
Dayton *(G-9924)*
Tom Paige Catering Company..........E....... 216 431-4236
Cleveland *(G-6602)*
Townhall 2..........E....... 330 678-3006
Kent *(G-12400)*
Transformation Network..........E....... 419 207-1188
Ashland *(G-702)*
Tri County Help Center Inc..........E....... 740 695-5441
Saint Clairsville *(G-16657)*
Tri-County Community Act..........E....... 740 385-6812
Logan *(G-12991)*
Trihealth Rehabilitation Hosp..........C....... 513 601-0600
Cincinnati *(G-4698)*
Trillium Family Solutions Inc..........D....... 330 454-7066
Cuyahoga Falls *(G-9227)*
Trinity Action Partnership..........E....... 937 456-2800
Eaton *(G-10578)*
Trumball Cnty Fire Chiefs Assn..........D....... 330 675-6602
Warren *(G-18908)*
Trumbull County One Stop..........D....... 330 675-2000
Warren *(G-18911)*
Turning Pt Counseling Svcs Inc..........D....... 330 744-2991
Youngstown *(G-20394)*
Tuscarawas County Commitee..........D....... 330 364-6611
Dover *(G-10217)*
Tuscarawas County Help ME Grow..........E....... 330 339-3493
New Philadelphia *(G-15119)*
Twelve Inc..........E....... 330 837-3555
Massillon *(G-13859)*
Ucc Childrens Center..........E....... 513 217-5501
Middletown *(G-14488)*
United Disability Services Inc..........C....... 330 374-1169
Akron *(G-485)*
United Methodist Childrens..........D....... 614 885-5020
Worthington *(G-20004)*
United Rehabilitation Services..........D....... 937 233-1230
Dayton *(G-9947)*
United Scoto Senior Activities..........E....... 740 354-6672
Portsmouth *(G-16316)*

S I C

Employee Codes: A=Over 500 employees, B=251-500
C=101-250, D=51-100, E=25-50
2018 Harris Ohio
Services Directory
1061

83 SOCIAL SERVICES

United Way Greater Cincinnati ....D....... 513 762-7100
  Cincinnati *(G-4742)*
United Way of Greater Toledo ....D....... 419 254-4742
  Toledo *(G-18274)*
United Way of The Greater Dayt ....E....... 937 225-3060
  Dayton *(G-9949)*
University of Cincinnati ....D....... 513 556-3803
  Cincinnati *(G-4779)*
Upreach LLC ....B....... 614 442-7702
  Columbus *(G-8917)*
Ussa Inc 740 354-6672
  Portsmouth *(G-16319)*
Vantage Aging ....A....... 440 324-3588
  Elyria *(G-10686)*
Vantage Aging 330 253-4597
  Akron *(G-495)*
Vasconcellos Inc ....E....... 513 576-1250
  Milford *(G-14573)*
Vermilion Family YMCA ....E....... 440 967-4208
  Vermilion *(G-18720)*
Village of Groveport ....E....... 614 830-2060
  Groveport *(G-11684)*
Volunteers of America NW Ohio ....E....... 419 248-3733
  Toledo *(G-18293)*
Volunters of Amer Greater Ohio ....E....... 614 861-8551
  Columbus *(G-8949)*
Volunters of Amer Greater Ohio ....D....... 216 541-9000
  Cleveland *(G-6711)*
Volunters of Amer Greater Ohio ....C....... 614 372-3120
  Columbus *(G-8950)*
Volunters of Amer Greater Ohio ....C....... 614 253-6100
  Columbus *(G-8951)*
Volunters of Amer Greater Ohio ....E....... 419 524-5013
  Mansfield *(G-13382)*
Volunters of Amer Greater Ohio ....E....... 614 263-9134
  Columbus *(G-8952)*
Volunters of America Cntl Ohio ....D....... 614 801-1655
  Grove City *(G-11609)*
W S O S Community A ....E....... 419 333-6068
  Fremont *(G-11227)*
West Ohio Cmnty Action Partnr ....C....... 419 227-2586
  Lima *(G-12918)*
West Ohio Cmnty Action Partnr ....C....... 419 227-2586
  Lima *(G-12919)*
West Side Community House ....E....... 216 771-7297
  Cleveland *(G-6739)*
West Side Ecumenical Ministry ....C....... 216 325-9369
  Cleveland *(G-6740)*
Westark Family Services Inc ....E....... 330 832-5043
  Massillon *(G-13860)*
Western Reserve Area Agency ....C....... 216 621-0303
  Cleveland *(G-6742)*
Western Reserve Area Agency ....E....... 216 621-0303
  Cleveland *(G-6743)*
Whetstone Industries Inc ....E....... 419 947-9222
  Mount Gilead *(G-14864)*
Wood County Chld Svcs Assn ....D....... 419 352-7588
  Bowling Green *(G-1798)*
Wood County Committee On Aging ...E....... 419 353-5661
  Bowling Green *(G-1799)*
Wood County Ohio ....C....... 419 354-9201
  Bowling Green *(G-1801)*
WoodInds Srving Centl Ohio Inc ....E....... 740 349-7051
  Newark *(G-15248)*
Y M C A Central Stark County ....E....... 330 305-5437
  Canton *(G-2590)*
Y M C A Central Stark County ....E....... 330 875-1611
  Louisville *(G-13108)*
Y M C A Central Stark County ....E....... 330 877-8933
  Uniontown *(G-18545)*
Y M C A Central Stark County ....E....... 330 830-6275
  Massillon *(G-13862)*
Y M C A Central Stark County ....E....... 330 498-4082
  Canton *(G-2591)*
Y M C A of Ashland Ohio Inc ....D....... 419 289-0626
  Ashland *(G-709)*
YMCA ....D....... 937 653-9622
  Urbana *(G-18603)*
YMCA 330 823-1930
  Alliance *(G-566)*
YMCA Inc ....D....... 330 385-6400
  East Liverpool *(G-10536)*
YMCA of Clermont County Inc ....E....... 513 724-9622
  Batavia *(G-1032)*
YMCA of Massillon ....E....... 330 879-0800
  Navarre *(G-14957)*
Young Mens Christian ....B....... 513 932-1424
  Lebanon *(G-12660)*
Young Mens Christian Assn ....E....... 419 332-9622
  Fremont *(G-11231)*
Young Mens Christian Assn ....C....... 330 744-8411
  Youngstown *(G-20421)*
Young Mens Christian Assn ....E....... 419 238-0443
  Van Wert *(G-18653)*
Young Mens Christian Assoc ....C....... 614 885-4252
  Columbus *(G-9017)*
Young Mens Christian Assoc ....D....... 614 276-8224
  Columbus *(G-9018)*
Young Mens Christian Assoc ....C....... 614 834-9622
  Canal Winchester *(G-2181)*
Young Mens Christian Assoc 614 871-9622
  Grove City *(G-11620)*
Young Mens Christian Assoc ....A....... 937 223-5201
  Dayton *(G-10009)*
Young Mens Christian Assoc ....D....... 330 923-5223
  Cuyahoga Falls *(G-9237)*
Young Mens Christian Assoc ....E....... 330 467-8366
  Macedonia *(G-13219)*
Young Mens Christian Assoc ....E....... 330 784-0408
  Akron *(G-515)*
Young Mens Christian Assoc 614 416-9622
  Gahanna *(G-11276)*
Young Mens Christian Assoc ....C....... 740 881-1058
  Powell *(G-16355)*
Young Mens Christian Assoc 614 334-9622
  Hilliard *(G-11967)*
Young Mens Christian Assoc ....E....... 937 312-1810
  Dayton *(G-10010)*
Young Mens Christian Assoc ....E....... 614 539-1770
  Urbancrest *(G-18609)*
Young Mens Christian Assoc ....D....... 614 252-3166
  Columbus *(G-9019)*
Young Mens Christian Assoc ....C....... 937 223-5201
  Springboro *(G-17144)*
Young Mens Christian Assoc ....E....... 937 593-9001
  Bellefontaine *(G-1401)*
Young Mens Christian Associat ....E....... 419 729-8135
  Toledo *(G-18320)*
Young Mens Christian Associat 513 241-9622
  Cincinnati *(G-4868)*
Young Mens Christian Associat ....D....... 513 923-4466
  Cincinnati *(G-4869)*
Young Mens Christian Associat ....E....... 419 474-3995
  Toledo *(G-18322)*
Young Mens Christian Associat ....D....... 419 866-9622
  Maumee *(G-13997)*
Young Mens Christian Associat 419 475-3496
  Toledo *(G-18323)*
Young Mens Christian Associat ....D....... 419 691-3523
  Oregon *(G-15756)*
Young Mens Christian Mt Vernon 740 392-9622
  Mount Vernon *(G-14927)*
Young MNS Chrstn Assn Cleveland ....E....... 216 941-4654
  Cleveland *(G-6773)*
Young MNS Chrstn Assn Cleveland ....D....... 440 808-8150
  Westlake *(G-19569)*
Young MNS Chrstn Assn Cleveland ....E....... 216 521-8400
  Lakewood *(G-12502)*
Young MNS Chrstn Assn Cleveland ....D....... 440 842-5200
  North Royalton *(G-15507)*
Young MNS Chrstn Assn Cleveland ....E....... 216 731-7454
  Cleveland *(G-6774)*
Young MNS Chrstn Assn Cleveland ....D....... 440 285-7543
  Chardon *(G-2780)*
Young MNS Chrstn Assn Grter NY 740 392-9622
  Mount Vernon *(G-14928)*
Young Womens Christian ....D....... 419 241-3235
  Toledo *(G-18325)*
Young Womens Christian 937 461-5550
  Dayton *(G-10013)*
Young Womens Christian ....E....... 419 238-6639
  Van Wert *(G-18654)*
Young Womens Christian Assn ....D....... 614 224-9121
  Columbus *(G-9021)*
Young Womens Christian Assn ....E....... 330 746-6361
  Youngstown *(G-20422)*
Young Womens Christian Associ ....E....... 216 881-6878
  Cleveland *(G-6776)*
Young Womns Chrstn Assc Canton .....D....... 330 453-7644
  Canton *(G-2593)*
Young Womns Chrstn Assc Canton .....D....... 330 453-0789
  Canton *(G-2594)*
Youngstown Area Jwish Fdration ....C....... 330 746-3251
  Youngstown *(G-20425)*
Youngstown Area Jwish Fdration ....D....... 330 746-1076
  Youngstown *(G-20426)*
Youngstown Committee On Alchol 330 744-1181
  Youngstown *(G-20429)*
Youngstown Neighborhood Dev ....E....... 330 480-0423
  Youngstown *(G-20432)*

SIC SECTION

Youth Advocate Services ....E....... 614 258-9927
  Columbus *(G-9022)*
Youth Mntrng & At Rsk Intrvntn ....E....... 216 324-2451
  Richmond Heights *(G-16543)*
Youth Services Ohio Department ....C....... 419 875-6965
  Liberty Center *(G-12716)*
YWCA of Greater Cincinnati ....D....... 513 241-7090
  Cincinnati *(G-4870)*
YWCA Shelter & Housing Network .....E....... 937 222-6333
  Dayton *(G-10014)*

8331 Job Training & Vocational Rehabilitation Svcs

A W S Inc ....C....... 440 333-1791
  Rocky River *(G-16567)*
A W S Inc ....B....... 216 749-0356
  Cleveland *(G-4937)*
A W S Inc ....E....... 216 486-0600
  Euclid *(G-10741)*
A W S Inc 216 941-8800
  Cleveland *(G-4938)*
Abilities First Foundation ....C....... 513 423-9496
  Middletown *(G-14411)*
Ability Works Inc ....C....... 419 626-1048
  Sandusky *(G-16723)*
Akron Blind Center & Workshop ....D....... 330 253-2555
  Akron *(G-29)*
Alpha Group of Delaware Inc ....D....... 614 222-1855
  Columbus *(G-6976)*
Alpha Group of Delaware Inc ....D....... 740 368-5810
  Delaware *(G-10069)*
Alpha Group of Delaware Inc ....E....... 740 368-5820
  Delaware *(G-10070)*
American Line Builders Apprent ....D....... 937 849-4177
  Medway *(G-14140)*
Angeline Industries Inc ....D....... 419 294-4488
  Upper Sandusky *(G-18557)*
Anne Grady Corporation ....E....... 419 867-7501
  Holland *(G-12008)*
ARC Industries Incorporated O ....C....... 614 479-2500
  Columbus *(G-7034)*
ARC Industries Incorporated O ....B....... 614 436-4800
  Columbus *(G-7035)*
ARC Industries Incorporated O ....B....... 614 864-2406
  Columbus *(G-7036)*
ARC Industries Incorporated O ....D....... 614 267-1207
  Columbus *(G-7037)*
ARC Industries Incorporated O ....B....... 614 836-0700
  Groveport *(G-11623)*
Ash Craft Industries Inc ....C....... 440 224-2177
  Ashtabula *(G-711)*
Atco Inc ....C....... 740 592-6659
  Athens *(G-773)*
Belco Works Inc ....B....... 740 695-0500
  Saint Clairsville *(G-16617)*
Brookhill Center Industries ....C....... 419 876-3932
  Ottawa *(G-15796)*
Brown Cnty Bd Mntal Rtardation ....E....... 937 378-4891
  Georgetown *(G-11384)*
Butler County of Ohio ....E....... 513 785-6500
  Hamilton *(G-11697)*
Butler County Bd of Mental RE ....C....... 513 785-2870
  Fairfield Township *(G-10927)*
Capabilities Inc ....E....... 419 394-0003
  Saint Marys *(G-16670)*
Capano & Associates LLC ....E....... 513 403-6000
  Liberty Township *(G-12717)*
Carroll Hills Industries Inc ....D....... 330 627-5524
  Carrollton *(G-2614)*
Center of Voctnl Altrntvs Mntl ....D....... 614 294-7117
  Columbus *(G-7226)*
Cincinnati Assn For The Blind ....C....... 513 221-8558
  Cincinnati *(G-3282)*
Cleveland Christian Home Inc ....E....... 216 671-0977
  Cleveland *(G-5294)*
CLI Incorporated ....C....... 419 668-8840
  Norwalk *(G-15566)*
Collins Career Center ....D....... 740 867-6641
  Chesapeake *(G-2782)*
Community Action ....E....... 740 354-7541
  Portsmouth *(G-16271)*
Community Support Services Inc ....C....... 330 253-9388
  Akron *(G-157)*
Cornucopia Inc ....E....... 216 521-4600
  Lakewood *(G-12474)*
County of Crawford ....D....... 419 562-0015
  Bucyrus *(G-2033)*
County of Cuyahoga ....D....... 216 475-7066
  Cleveland *(G-5419)*

SIC SECTION

83 SOCIAL SERVICES

Company	Code	Phone
County of Geauga	D	440 564-2246
Chardon (G-2746)		
County of Hamilton	B	513 742-1576
Cincinnati (G-3428)		
County of Hancock	E	419 422-6387
Findlay (G-11016)		
County of Hardin	E	419 674-4158
Kenton (G-12410)		
County of Holmes	E	330 674-1111
Millersburg (G-14601)		
County of Lake	A	440 350-5100
Mentor (G-14164)		
County of Lake	D	440 269-2193
Willoughby (G-19656)		
County of Marion	D	740 387-1035
Marion (G-13535)		
County of Mercer	D	419 586-2369
Celina (G-2643)		
County of Montgomery	B	937 225-4804
Dayton (G-9436)		
County of Sandusky	D	419 637-2243
Fremont (G-11190)		
County of Seneca	D	419 435-0729
Fostoria (G-11125)		
County of Stark	D	330 484-4814
Canton (G-2322)		
Creative Learning Workshop	E	330 393-5929
Warren (G-18844)		
Creative Learning Workshop	E	937 437-0146
New Paris (G-15076)		
Cuyahoga County		216 265-3030
Cleveland (G-5451)		
D-R Training Center & Workshop	C	419 289-0470
Ashland (G-678)		
Dayton Urban League	E	937 226-1513
Dayton (G-9493)		
Deepwood Industries Inc	C	440 350-5231
Mentor (G-14168)		
Don Bosco Community Center Inc	D	816 421-3160
Cleveland (G-5500)		
Easter Seals Tristate	C	513 985-0515
Blue Ash (G-1582)		
Easter Seals Tristate LLC	D	513 281-2316
Cincinnati (G-3533)		
Employment Development Inc	C	330 424-7711
Lisbon (G-12936)		
Esc of Cuyahoga County	D	216 524-3000
Independence (G-12210)		
Fairfield Industries Inc	C	740 652-7230
Carroll (G-2608)		
Fairhaven Sheltered Workshop	C	330 652-1116
Niles (G-15291)		
Fairhaven Sheltered Workshop	C	330 847-7275
Warren (G-18857)		
Fairhaven Sheltered Workshop	C	330 505-3644
Niles (G-15292)		
▲ Findaway World LLC	D	440 893-0808
Solon (G-17007)		
First Capital Enterprises Inc	D	740 773-2166
Chillicothe (G-2840)		
Food For Good Thought Inc	E	614 447-0424
Columbus (G-7679)		
Gallco Inc	D	740 446-3775
Gallipolis (G-11316)		
Goodwill Ester Seals Miami Vly	C	937 461-4800
Dayton (G-9579)		
Goodwill Idstrs Grtr Clvlnd L	E	440 783-1168
Strongsville (G-17467)		
Goodwill Idstrs Grtr Clvlnd L	E	330 877-7921
Hartville (G-11819)		
Goodwill Idstrs Grtr Clvlnd L	E	216 581-6320
Cleveland (G-5679)		
Goodwill Idstrs Grtr Clvlnd L	D	330 454-9401
Canton (G-2383)		
Goodwill Inds Centl Ohio Inc	B	614 294-5181
Columbus (G-7760)		
Goodwill Inds Centl Ohio Inc	D	740 373-1304
Marietta (G-13448)		
Goodwill Inds Centl Ohio Inc	E	614 274-5296
Columbus (G-7761)		
Goodwill Inds Centl Ohio Inc	E	740 439-7000
Cambridge (G-2116)		
Goodwill Inds Lorain Cnty Inc	E	440 242-2124
Elyria (G-10631)		
Goodwill Inds NW Ohio Inc	D	419 255-0070
Toledo (G-17919)		
Goodwill Inds of Ashtabula	C	440 964-3565
Ashtabula (G-745)		
Goodwill Inds of S Centl Ohio	D	740 702-4000
Chillicothe (G-2843)		
Goodwill Inds Rhbilitation Ctr	B	330 454-9461
Canton (G-2384)		
Goodwill Industries	E	330 264-1300
Wooster (G-19865)		
Goodwill Industries Inc	E	330 724-6995
Akron (G-241)		
Goodwill Industries of Akron	C	330 724-6995
Akron (G-242)		
Goodwill Industries of Lima	D	419 228-4821
Lima (G-12785)		
GP Strategies Corporation	E	513 583-8810
Mason (G-13710)		
Great Oaks Inst Tech Creer Dev	E	513 771-8840
Cincinnati (G-3703)		
Great Oaks Inst Tech Creer Dev	E	513 771-8840
Cincinnati (G-3704)		
Greene Inc	D	937 562-4200
Xenia (G-20058)		
Gw Business Solutions LLC	C	740 645-9861
Newark (G-15172)		
Handson Central Ohio Inc	E	614 221-2255
Columbus (G-7798)		
Harco Industries Inc	E	419 674-4159
Kenton (G-12413)		
Harrison Industries Inc	D	740 942-2988
Cadiz (G-2077)		
Hocking Valley Industries Inc	E	740 385-2118
Logan (G-12975)		
Hockingthensperry Cmnty Action	E	740 767-4500
Glouster (G-11435)		
Holmes County Board of Dd	D	330 674-8045
Holmesville (G-12072)		
Hopewell Industries Inc	C	740 622-3563
Coshocton (G-9107)		
▲ Hunter Defense Tech Inc	E	216 438-6111
Solon (G-17016)		
Integrated Services of Appala	D	740 594-6807
Athens (G-794)		
Ironton and Lawrence County	B	740 532-3534
Ironton (G-12291)		
J-Vac Industries Inc	D	740 384-2155
Wellston (G-19000)		
Jewish Family Services	D	614 231-1890
Columbus (G-7940)		
Joe and Jill Lewis Inc	E	937 718-8829
Dayton (G-9642)		
Ken Harper	C	740 439-4452
Byesville (G-2071)		
Knox New Hope Industries Inc	E	740 397-4601
Mount Vernon (G-14907)		
L & M Products Inc	C	937 456-7141
Eaton (G-10564)		
Licco Inc	C	740 522-8345
Newark (G-15185)		
Licking-Knox Goodwill Inds Inc	D	740 345-9861
Newark (G-15196)		
Linking Employment Abilities	E	216 696-2716
Cleveland (G-5944)		
Lorain County Board	E	440 329-3734
Elyria (G-10646)		
Lott Industries Incorporated	B	419 476-2516
Toledo (G-18008)		
Lott Industries Incorporated	B	419 891-5215
Maumee (G-13937)		
Lott Industries Incorporated	B	419 534-4980
Toledo (G-18009)		
Lynn Hope Industries Inc	D	330 674-8045
Holmesville (G-12073)		
Marca Industries Inc	E	740 387-1035
Marion (G-13551)		
Marimor Industries Inc	C	419 221-1226
Lima (G-12836)		
Marion Cnty Bd Dev Dsabilities	D	740 387-1035
Marion (G-13554)		
Marion Goodwill Industries	E	740 387-7023
Marion (G-13560)		
Mary Hmmond Adult Actvties Ctr	D	740 962-4200
McConnelsville (G-14028)		
Matco Industries Inc	E	740 852-7054
London (G-13002)		
Medina County Sheltered Inds	B	330 334-4491
Wadsworth (G-18765)		
Meigs Industries Inc	E	740 992-6681
Syracuse (G-17632)		
Metzenbaum Sheltered Inds	E	440 729-1919
Chesterland (G-2800)		
Miami University	B	513 727-3200
Middletown (G-14435)		
Mickis Creative Options Inc	E	419 526-4254
Mansfield (G-13344)		
Monco Enterprises Inc	A	937 461-0034
Dayton (G-9754)		
Murray Ridge Production Center	B	440 329-3734
Elyria (G-10657)		
Muskingum Starlight Industries	D	740 453-4622
Zanesville (G-20512)		
Nick Amster Inc	C	330 264-9667
Wooster (G-19893)		
Ohio Dept of Job & Fmly Svcs	E	614 752-9494
Columbus (G-8334)		
Ohio Rehabilitation Svcs Comm	E	330 643-3080
Akron (G-369)		
Ohio State University	D	614 685-3192
Columbus (G-8401)		
Ohio State University	D	614 292-7788
Columbus (G-8413)		
Ohio State University	D	614 292-4353
Columbus (G-8410)		
Perco Inc	D	740 342-5156
New Lexington (G-15061)		
Pickaway Diversfied Industries	D	740 474-1522
Circleville (G-4897)		
Portage Industries Inc	C	330 296-2839
Ravenna (G-16400)		
Portage Private Industry	D	330 297-7795
Ravenna (G-16403)		
Production Services Unlimited	D	513 695-1658
Lebanon (G-12637)		
Project Rebuild Inc	E	330 639-1559
Canton (G-2495)		
Quadco Rehabilitation Center	B	419 682-1011
Stryker (G-17537)		
Quadco Rehabilitation Center	E	419 445-1950
Archbold (G-642)		
R T Industries Inc	C	937 339-8313
Troy (G-18375)		
R T Industries Inc	C	937 335-5784
Troy (G-18374)		
Richcreek Bailey Rehabilitatio	E	440 527-8610
Mentor (G-14237)		
Richland Newhope Industries	D	419 774-4200
Mansfield (G-13359)		
Richland Newhope Industries	D	419 774-4496
Mansfield (G-13360)		
Richland Newhope Industries	E	419 774-4400
Mansfield (G-13358)		
Ridge Murray Prod Ctr Oberlin	E	440 774-7400
Oberlin (G-15660)		
Riverview Industries Inc	E	419 898-5250
Oak Harbor (G-15616)		
Ross Training Center Inc	D	937 592-0025
Bellefontaine (G-1394)		
RTC Industries Inc	E	937 592-0534
Bellefontaine (G-1395)		
Sandco Industries	C	419 334-9090
Clyde (G-6822)		
Southeast Diversified Inds	D	740 432-4241
Cambridge (G-2128)		
Spanish American Committee	E	216 961-2100
Cleveland (G-6513)		
Spectrum Supportive Services	E	216 875-0460
Cleveland (G-6517)		
Spectrum Supportive Services	C	216 761-2388
Cleveland (G-6518)		
Star Inc	C	740 354-1517
Portsmouth (G-16314)		
Stark County Board of Developm	A	330 477-5200
Canton (G-2543)		
Starlight Enterprises Inc	C	330 339-2020
New Philadelphia (G-15116)		
Step By Step Emplyment Trining	E	440 967-9042
Vermilion (G-10717)		
TAC Industries Inc	B	937 328-5200
Springfield (G-17285)		
TAC Industries Inc	C	937 328-5200
Springfield (G-17286)		
Tri-State Industries Inc	E	740 532-0406
Coal Grove (G-6826)		
Trumbull Cmnty Action Program	E	330 393-2507
Warren (G-18909)		
U-Co Industries Inc	D	937 644-3021
Marysville (G-13656)		
United Cerebral Palsy	C	216 791-8363
Cleveland (G-6635)		
United Disability Services Inc	C	330 374-1169
Akron (G-485)		
Vgs Inc	C	216 431-7800
Cleveland (G-6693)		
Vision & Vocational Services	E	614 294-5571
Columbus (G-8943)		

Employee Codes: A=Over 500 employees, B=251-500
C=101-250, D=51-100, E=25-50

83 SOCIAL SERVICES

Voc Works Ltd .... D 614 760-3515
   Dublin *(G-10484)*
Vocational Guidance Services .... A 216 431-7800
   Cleveland *(G-6708)*
Vocational Guidance Services .... E 440 322-1123
   Elyria *(G-10687)*
Vocational Services Inc .... C 216 431-8085
   Cleveland *(G-6709)*
W S O S Community A .... E 419 639-2802
   Green Springs *(G-11480)*
W S O S Community A .... D 419 334-8511
   Fremont *(G-11228)*
W S O S Community A .... D 419 333-6068
   Fremont *(G-11227)*
Wasco Inc .... E 740 373-3418
   Marietta *(G-13518)*
Waycraft Inc .... D 419 563-0550
   Bucyrus *(G-2051)*
Waycraft Inc .... D 419 562-3321
   Bucyrus *(G-2052)*
Weaver Industries Inc .... E 330 379-3660
   Akron *(G-506)*
Weaver Industries Inc .... C 330 666-5114
   Akron *(G-507)*
Weaver Industries Inc .... C 330 733-2431
   Tallmadge *(G-17661)*
Wood County Ohio .... E 419 352-5059
   Bowling Green *(G-1804)*
Workforce Initiative Assn .... E 330 433-9675
   Canton *(G-2588)*
Youngstown Area .... C 330 759-7921
   Youngstown *(G-20424)*
Zanesville Welfare Organizatio .... B 740 450-6060
   Zanesville *(G-20559)*
Zanesville Welfre Orgnztn/Goodw .. D 740 450-6060
   Zanesville *(G-20560)*
Zepf Center .... E 419 213-5627
   Toledo *(G-18330)*

8351 Child Day Care Svcs

1 Amazing Place Co .... E 419 420-0424
   Findlay *(G-10986)*
A & D Daycare and Learning Ctr .... E 937 263-4447
   Dayton *(G-9296)*
A Better Child Care Corp .... E 513 353-5437
   Cincinnati *(G-2952)*
A CCS Day Care Centers Inc .... E 513 841-2227
   Cincinnati *(G-2954)*
A Childs Place Nursery School .... D 330 493-1333
   Canton *(G-2221)*
A New Beginning Preschool .... D 216 531-7465
   Cleveland *(G-4934)*
Abacus Child Care Centers Inc .... E 330 773-4200
   Akron *(G-14)*
ABC Child Care & Learning Ctr .... E 440 964-8799
   Ashtabula *(G-710)*
Abilities First Foundation .... C 513 423-9496
   Middletown *(G-14411)*
Academy Kids Learning Ctr Inc .... E 614 258-5437
   Columbus *(G-6931)*
Action For Children Inc .... E 614 224-0222
   Columbus *(G-6941)*
Adams Cnty /Ohio Vly Schl Dst .... D 937 544-2951
   West Union *(G-19271)*
Agj Kidz LLC .... E 937 350-1001
   Centerville *(G-2669)*
Ajm Worthington Inc .... E 614 888-5800
   Worthington *(G-19938)*
Akron Summit Cmnty Action Agcy .. E 330 733-2290
   Akron *(G-57)*
All About Kids .... E 937 885-7480
   Centerville *(G-2671)*
All About Kids Daycare N .... E 330 494-8700
   North Canton *(G-15323)*
All Around Children Montessori .... E 330 928-1444
   Stow *(G-17351)*
All For Kids Inc .... E 740 435-8050
   Cambridge *(G-2093)*
All My Sons Business Dev Corp ...... E 469 461-5000
   Cleveland *(G-4989)*
Allen County Eductl Svc Ctr .... D 419 222-1836
   Lima *(G-12734)*
Anderson Little .... E 513 474-7800
   Cincinnati *(G-3025)*
Angel Care Inc .... E 440 736-7267
   Brecksville *(G-1812)*
Angels On Earth Child Care Co ...... E 216 476-8100
   Cleveland *(G-5036)*
Apple Tree Nursery School Inc .... E 419 530-1070
   Toledo *(G-17755)*

Arlitt Child Development Ctr .... D 513 556-3802
   Cincinnati *(G-3048)*
Ashland City School District .... E 419 289-7967
   Ashland *(G-652)*
Assoc Dvlpmtly Disabled .... E 614 447-0606
   Columbus *(G-7054)*
Aultman Hospital .... E 330 452-2273
   Canton *(G-2256)*
Bailey & Long Inc .... E 614 937-9435
   Columbus *(G-7083)*
Balsara Enterprise Ltd .... E 330 497-7000
   Solon *(G-16982)*
Bay Village City School Dst .... E 440 617-7330
   Cleveland *(G-5102)*
Bay Village Montessori Inc .... E 440 871-8773
   Westlake *(G-19464)*
Beavercreek Church of Nazarene ... E 937 426-0079
   Beavercreek *(G-1151)*
Beavercreek YMCA .... D 937 426-9622
   Dayton *(G-9351)*
Bedford Church of Nazarene .... E 440 232-7440
   Bedford *(G-1294)*
Bethlehem Lutheran Ch Parma .... E 440 845-2230
   Cleveland *(G-5120)*
Board Man Frst Untd Methdst Ch .... E 330 758-4527
   Youngstown *(G-20119)*
Bombeck Family Learning Center ... E 937 229-2158
   Dayton *(G-9362)*
Bowling Green Coop Nurs Schl .... E 419 352-8675
   Bowling Green *(G-1764)*
Bright Beginnings .... E 937 748-2612
   Springboro *(G-17116)*
Bright Horizons Chld Ctrs LLC .... E 614 754-7023
   Columbus *(G-7135)*
Bright Horizons Chld Ctrs LLC .... E 614 566-9322
   Columbus *(G-7136)*
Bright Horizons Chld Ctrs LLC .... E 614 566-4847
   Columbus *(G-7138)*
Bright Horizons Chld Ctrs LLC .... E 330 375-7633
   Akron *(G-111)*
Brookdale Senior Living Inc .... D 513 745-7600
   Cincinnati *(G-3140)*
Brooksedge Day Care Center .... E 614 529-0077
   Hilliard *(G-11883)*
Brownstone Private Child Care .... E 216 221-1470
   Lakewood *(G-12472)*
Brunswick City Schools .... A 330 225-7731
   Brunswick *(G-1969)*
Butler County Bd of Mental RE .... E 513 785-2815
   Hamilton *(G-11700)*
Butler County Eductl Svc Ctr .... E 513 737-2817
   Hamilton *(G-11702)*
Campbell Family Childcare Inc .... E 614 855-4780
   New Albany *(G-10308)*
Canton City School District .... E 330 456-3167
   Canton *(G-2284)*
Canton Country Day School .... E 330 453-8279
   Canton *(G-2286)*
Canton Montessori Association .... E 330 452-0148
   Canton *(G-2293)*
Cardinal Pacelli School .... B 513 321-1048
   Cincinnati *(G-3178)*
Carol Scudere .... E 614 839-4357
   New Albany *(G-14979)*
Catholic Social Svc Miami Vly .... E 937 223-7217
   Dayton *(G-9390)*
Centerville Child Development .... E 937 434-5949
   Dayton *(G-9393)*
Chal-Ron LLC .... E 216 383-9050
   Cleveland *(G-5225)*
Champons In Making Daycare LLC . E 937 728-4886
   Wilmington *(G-19747)*
Cherished Childrens Early .... E 330 424-4402
   Negley *(G-14959)*
Child Care Resource Center .... E 216 575-0061
   Cleveland *(G-5236)*
Child Care Resources Inc .... D 740 454-6251
   Zanesville *(G-20464)*
Child Dev Ctr Jackson Cnty .... E 740 286-3995
   Jackson *(G-12309)*
Child Dvlpmnt Cncl of Frnkln .... D 614 221-1709
   Columbus *(G-7258)*
Child Dvlpmnt Cncl of Frnkln .... E 614 416-5178
   Columbus *(G-7259)*
Child Focus Inc .... D 937 444-1613
   Mount Orab *(G-14867)*
Child Focus Inc .... D 513 752-1555
   Cincinnati *(G-3243)*
Children First Inc .... E 614 466-0945
   Columbus *(G-7260)*

Childrens Discovery Center .... E 419 861-1060
   Holland *(G-12015)*
Childrens Rehabilitation Ctr .... E 330 856-2107
   Warren *(G-18833)*
Childtime Childcare Inc .... E 330 723-8697
   Medina *(G-14046)*
Childvine Inc .... E 937 748-1260
   Springboro *(G-17118)*
Chippewa School District .... E 330 658-4868
   Doylestown *(G-10225)*
Christian Missionary Alliance .... E 614 457-4085
   Columbus *(G-7268)*
Christian Perry Pre School .... E 330 477-7262
   Canton *(G-2307)*
Christian Rivertree School .... E 330 494-1860
   Massillon *(G-13795)*
Christian Schools Inc .... D 330 857-7311
   Kidron *(G-12440)*
Christian Wooster School .... E 330 345-6436
   Wooster *(G-19842)*
Cincinnati Early Learning Ctr .... E 513 961-2690
   Cincinnati *(G-3300)*
Cincinnati Early Learning Ctr .... E 513 367-2129
   Harrison *(G-11793)*
City of Lakewood .... E 216 226-0080
   Cleveland *(G-5266)*
Cleveland Child Care Inc .... E 216 631-3211
   Cleveland *(G-5293)*
Cleveland Mus Schl Settlement ...... C 216 421-5806
   Cleveland *(G-5339)*
Clinton County Community Actn ..... E 937 382-5624
   Wilmington *(G-19751)*
Coleeta Daycare Llc .... E 614 310-6465
   Columbus *(G-7317)*
Colerain Dry Rdge Chldcare Ltd ..... E 513 923-4300
   Cincinnati *(G-3387)*
Colonial Senior Services Inc .... C 513 867-4006
   Hamilton *(G-11714)*
Colonial Senior Services Inc .... C 513 856-8600
   Hamilton *(G-11713)*
Columbus Christian Center Inc .... E 614 416-9673
   Columbus *(G-7337)*
Columbus Day Care Center .... E 614 269-8980
   Columbus *(G-7345)*
Columbus Montessori Education .... E 614 231-3790
   Columbus *(G-7370)*
Columbus Public School Dst .... E 614 365-5456
   Columbus *(G-7377)*
Community Action Comsn Belmont . D 740 676-0800
   Bellaire *(G-1364)*
Community Action Comsn Belmont . E 740 695-0293
   Saint Clairsville *(G-16632)*
Consolidated Learning Ctrs Inc .... C 614 791-0050
   Dublin *(G-10308)*
Corporation For OH Appalachian .... E 330 364-8882
   New Philadelphia *(G-15089)*
Coshocton County Head Start .... E 740 622-3667
   Coshocton *(G-9095)*
Council For Economic Opport .... D 216 696-9077
   Cleveland *(G-5414)*
Council of Ecnmc Opprtnts of G ..... E 216 651-5154
   Cleveland *(G-5416)*
Council On Rur Svc Prgrams Inc .... D 937 452-1090
   Camden *(G-2137)*
Council On Rur Svc Prgrams Inc .... E 937 492-8787
   Sidney *(G-16924)*
Council On Rur Svc Prgrams Inc .... E 937 773-0773
   Piqua *(G-16141)*
County of Athens .... D 740 592-3061
   Athens *(G-781)*
County of Guernsey .... E 740 439-5555
   Cambridge *(G-2106)*
County of Mercer .... D 419 586-2369
   Celina *(G-2643)*
Creative Center For Children .... E 513 867-1118
   Hamilton *(G-11719)*
Creative Childrens World LLC .... E 513 336-7799
   Mason *(G-13692)*
Creative Learning Child Care .... E 440 729-9001
   Chesterland *(G-2794)*
Creative Playroom .... D 216 475-6464
   Cleveland *(G-5433)*
Creative Playroom .... E 440 248-3100
   Solon *(G-16997)*
Creative Playrooms Inc .... E 440 572-9365
   Strongsville *(G-17453)*
Creative Playrooms Inc .... E 440 349-9111
   Solon *(G-16998)*
Creme De La Creme Colorado Inc . E 513 459-4300
   Mason *(G-13693)*

83 SOCIAL SERVICES

Company	Code	Phone
Crossroads Lake County Adole	E	440 358-7370
Painesville (G-15848)		
Dakota Girls LLC	E	614 801-2558
Grove City (G-11551)		
Days of Discovery	E	937 862-4465
Spring Valley (G-17110)		
Delth Corporation	E	440 255-7655
Mentor (G-14169)		
Diocese of Toledo	E	419 243-7255
Toledo (G-17854)		
Discovery School	E	419 756-8880
Mansfield (G-13294)		
Dover City Schools	D	330 343-8880
Dover (G-10184)		
Dublin Latchkey Inc	D	614 793-0871
Dublin (G-10329)		
Dublin Learning Academy	E	614 761-1800
Dublin (G-10330)		
Early Childhood Enrichment Ctr	E	216 991-9761
Cleveland (G-5518)		
Early Childhood Learning Commu	D	614 451-6418
Columbus (G-7563)		
Early Learning Tree Chld Ctr	D	937 276-3221
Dayton (G-9512)		
Early Learning Tree Chld Ctr	D	937 293-7907
Dayton (G-9513)		
East Dayton Christian School	E	937 252-5400
Dayton (G-9268)		
East End Neighborhood Hse Assn	E	216 791-9378
Cleveland (G-5519)		
Edwards Creative Learning Ctr	E	614 492-8977
Columbus (G-7583)		
Elderly Day Care Center	E	419 228-2688
Lima (G-12773)		
Enrichment Center of Wishing W	D	440 237-5000
Cleveland (G-5543)		
Epworth Preschool and Daycare	E	740 387-1062
Marion (G-13538)		
Epworth United Methodist Ch	D	740 387-1062
Marion (G-13539)		
Erie Huron Cac Headstart Inc	E	419 663-2623
Norwalk (G-15572)		
Ernst Corporation	E	513 697-6970
Cincinnati (G-3576)		
Fairborn St Luke Untd Mthdst	E	937 878-5042
Fairborn (G-10795)		
Fairmount Montessori Assn	E	216 321-7571
Cleveland (G-5565)		
Family Lrng Ctr At Sentinel	E	419 448-5079
Tiffin (G-17678)		
Family YMCA of LANcstr&fairfld	D	740 277-7373
Lancaster (G-12541)		
Findlay Y M C A Child Dev	E	419 422-3174
Findlay (G-11031)		
First Apostolic Church	E	419 885-4888
Toledo (G-17891)		
First Assembly Child Care	E	419 529-6501
Mansfield (G-13302)		
First Baptist Day Care Center	E	216 371-9394
Cleveland (G-5590)		
First Christian Church	E	330 445-2700
Canton (G-2367)		
First Community Church	E	614 488-0681
Columbus (G-7662)		
First Community Church	E	614 488-0681
Columbus (G-7663)		
First Fruits Child Dev Ctr I	E	216 862-4715
Euclid (G-10755)		
First School Corp	E	937 433-3455
Dayton (G-9550)		
Flying Colors Public Preschool	E	740 349-1629
Newark (G-15167)		
For Kids Sake Inc	E	330 726-6878
Youngstown (G-20190)		
Four Oaks Early Intervention	E	937 562-6779
Xenia (G-20051)		
Frans Child Care-Mansfield	C	419 775-2500
Mansfield (G-13304)		
Friend-Ship Child Care Ctr LLC	E	330 484-2051
Canton (G-2372)		
Future Advantage Inc	E	330 686-7707
Stow (G-17369)		
Galion Community Center YMCA	E	419 468-7754
Galion (G-11297)		
Gearity Early Child Care Ctr	E	216 371-7356
Cleveland (G-5665)		
Geary Family YMCA Fostria	E	419 435-6608
Fostoria (G-11128)		
Genesis Healthcare System	E	740 453-4959
Zanesville (G-20482)		
Gethsemane Lutheran Church	E	614 885-4319
Columbus (G-7749)		
Giggles & Wiggles Inc	E	740 574-4536
Wheelersburg (G-19577)		
Gingerbread Inc	E	513 793-4122
Blue Ash (G-1601)		
Goddard School	E	513 697-9663
Loveland (G-13129)		
Goddard School	E	614 920-9810
Canal Winchester (G-2160)		
Goddard School	E	513 271-6311
Cincinnati (G-3681)		
Goddard School of Avon	E	440 934-3300
Avon (G-894)		
Goddard School of Twinsburg	E	330 487-0394
Twinsburg (G-18424)		
Golden Key Ctr For Excptnl Chl	E	330 493-4400
Canton (G-2382)		
Grace Baptist Church	E	937 652-1133
Urbana (G-18589)		
Grace Brthren Ch Columbus Ohio	E	614 888-7733
Westerville (G-19310)		
Great Expectations D CA Center	E	330 782-9500
Youngstown (G-20205)		
Great Miami Valley YMCA	D	513 887-0001
Hamilton (G-11733)		
Great Miami Valley YMCA	E	513 892-9622
Fairfield Township (G-10930)		
Great Miami Valley YMCA	D	513 887-0014
Hamilton (G-11735)		
Great Miami Valley YMCA	D	513 868-9622
Hamilton (G-11736)		
Great Miami Valley YMCA	E	513 829-3091
Fairfield (G-10854)		
Hamilton County Eductl Svc Ctr	D	513 674-4200
Cincinnati (G-3731)		
Hanna Perkins School	E	216 991-4472
Shaker Heights (G-16861)		
Harcatus Tri-County Community	D	330 602-5442
New Philadelphia (G-15098)		
Hardin County Family YMCA	E	419 673-6131
Kenton (G-12416)		
Harrison Ave Assembly of God	E	513 367-6100
Harrison (G-11800)		
Hcesc Early Learning Program	C	513 589-3021
Cincinnati (G-3745)		
Health Care Plus	E	614 340-7587
Columbus (G-6882)		
Hewlettco Inc	E	440 238-4600
Strongsville (G-17469)		
Highland County Family YMCA	E	937 840-9622
Hillsboro (G-11978)		
Hilty Child Care Center	E	419 384-3220
Pandora (G-15891)		
Hopes Drams Childcare Lrng Ctr	E	330 793-8260
Youngstown (G-20220)		
Horizon Education Centers	C	440 779-1930
North Olmsted (G-15426)		
Huber Heights YMCA	D	937 236-9622
Dayton (G-9623)		
Hudson Montessori Association	E	330 650-0424
Hudson (G-12122)		
Hyde Park Play School	E	513 631-2095
Cincinnati (G-3804)		
Independence Local Schools	E	216 642-5865
Independence (G-12219)		
Ironton and Lawrence County	B	740 532-3534
Ironton (G-12291)		
Israel Adath	E	513 793-1800
Cincinnati (G-3846)		
J Nan Enterprises LLC	E	330 653-3766
Hudson (G-12125)		
J&B Sprafka Enterprises Inc	E	330 733-4212
Akron (G-288)		
Jewish Day Schl Assoc Grtr Clv	D	216 763-1400
Pepper Pike (G-15957)		
Jolly Tots Too Inc	E	614 471-0688
Columbus (G-7946)		
Joseph and Florence Mandel	D	216 464-4055
Beachwood (G-1092)		
Just 4 Kidz Childcare	E	440 285-2221
Chardon (G-2754)		
Kandy Kane Childrens Lrng Ctr	E	330 864-6642
Akron (G-301)		
Kangaroo Pouch Daycare Inc	E	440 473-4725
Cleveland (G-5881)		
Kare A Lot	E	614 298-8933
Columbus (G-7963)		
Kare A Lot Infnt Tddlr Dev Ctr	E	614 481-7532
Columbus (G-7964)		
Kiddie Kollege Inc	E	440 327-5435
North Ridgeville (G-15466)		
Kiddle Korral	E	419 626-9082
Sandusky (G-16773)		
Kids Ahead Inc	E	330 628-7404
Mogadore (G-14680)		
Kids Country	E	330 899-0909
Uniontown (G-18525)		
Kids First Learning Centers	D	440 235-2500
Olmsted Falls (G-15674)		
Kids Kastle Day Care	E	419 586-0903
Celina (G-2650)		
Kids R Kids 2 Ohio	E	513 860-3197
West Chester (G-19102)		
Kids R Kids Schools Qulty Lrng	E	937 748-1260
Springboro (G-17126)		
Kids World	E	614 473-9229
Columbus (G-7988)		
Kids-Play Inc	E	330 896-2400
Uniontown (G-18526)		
Kids-Play Inc	E	330 896-2400
Canton (G-2426)		
Kidstown LLC	E	330 502-4484
Youngstown (G-20246)		
Kidz By Riverside Inc	E	330 392-0700
Warren (G-18869)		
Kinder Garden School	E	513 791-4300
Blue Ash (G-1622)		
Kinder Kare Day Nursery	E	740 886-6905
Proctorville (G-16360)		
Kindercare Education LLC	E	513 896-4769
Fairfield Township (G-10933)		
Kindercare Education LLC	E	330 405-5556
Twinsburg (G-18438)		
Kindercare Education LLC	E	614 337-2035
Gahanna (G-11250)		
Kindercare Education LLC	E	440 442-4360
Cleveland (G-5902)		
Kindercare Learning Ctrs Inc	E	937 435-2353
Dayton (G-9659)		
Kindercare Learning Ctrs Inc	E	614 888-9696
Worthington (G-19966)		
Kindercare Learning Ctrs LLC	E	440 248-5437
Solon (G-17022)		
Kindercare Learning Ctrs LLC	E	513 771-8787
Cincinnati (G-3925)		
Kindercare Learning Ctrs LLC	E	740 549-0264
Lewis Center (G-12691)		
Kindercare Learning Ctrs LLC	E	440 442-8067
Cleveland (G-5903)		
Kindercare Learning Ctrs LLC	E	614 866-4446
Reynoldsburg (G-16463)		
Kindercare Learning Ctrs LLC	E	513 961-3164
Cincinnati (G-3926)		
Kindercare Learning Ctrs LLC	E	614 759-6622
Columbus (G-7989)		
Kindercare Learning Ctrs LLC	E	513 791-4712
Cincinnati (G-3927)		
Kindertown Educational Centers	E	859 344-8802
Cleves (G-6802)		
Kingdom Kids Inc	E	513 851-6400
Hamilton (G-11750)		
Knox County Head Start Inc	E	740 397-1344
Mount Vernon (G-14906)		
Kozmic Korner	E	330 494-4148
Canton (G-2429)		
Krieger Enterprises Inc	E	513 573-9132
Mason (G-13729)		
Ladan Learning Center	E	614 426-4306
Columbus (G-8029)		
Lake County YMCA	A	440 352-3303
Painesville (G-15860)		
Lake County YMCA	C	440 946-1160
Willoughby (G-19680)		
Lake County YMCA	E	440 259-2724
Perry (G-15962)		
Lake County YMCA	D	440 428-5125
Madison (G-13227)		
Lakewood Catholic Academy	E	216 521-4352
Lakewood (G-12486)		
Lakewood Community Care Center	E	216 226-0080
Lakewood (G-12489)		
Laurel School	C	216 464-1441
Cleveland (G-5928)		
Lawrence Cnty Bd Dev Dsblities	E	740 377-2356
South Point (G-17090)		
Le Chaperon Rouge	E	440 934-0296
Avon (G-905)		
Le Chaperon Rouge Company	E	440 899-9477
Westlake (G-19509)		

Employee Codes: A=Over 500 employees, B=251-500
C=101-250, D=51-100, E=25-50

83 SOCIAL SERVICES

Name	Code	Phone
Learning Tree Childcare Ctr	E	419 229-5484
Lima (G-12927)		
Lebanon Presbyterian Church	E	513 932-0369
Lebanon (G-12623)		
Liberty Bible Academy Assn	E	513 754-1234
Mason (G-13731)		
Life Center Adult Day Care	E	614 866-7212
Reynoldsburg (G-16465)		
Lillian and Betty Ratner Schl	E	216 464-0033
Cleveland (G-5942)		
Lima Family YMCA	E	419 223-6045
Lima (G-12821)		
Little Dreamers Big Believers	E	614 294-2922
Columbus (G-8073)		
Little Lambs Childrens Center	E	614 471-9269
Gahanna (G-11254)		
Logan Housing Corp Inc	D	937 592-2009
Bellefontaine (G-1387)		
Lorain County Community Action	E	440 246-0480
Lorain (G-13053)		
Louis Stokes Head Start	E	216 295-0854
Cleveland (G-5952)		
Louisville Child Care Center	E	330 875-4303
Uniontown (G-18527)		
M J J B Ltd	E	937 748-4414
Springboro (G-17127)		
Madison Local School District	E	440 428-5111
Madison (G-13231)		
Madison Local School District	B	419 589-2600
Mansfield (G-13326)		
Marion Head Start Center	E	740 382-6858
Marion (G-13561)		
McKinley Early Childhood Ctr	E	330 454-4800
Canton (G-2454)		
McKinley Early Childhood Ctr	E	330 252-2552
Akron (G-334)		
Medcentral Health System	E	419 526-8043
Mansfield (G-13341)		
Medina Advantage Inc	E	330 723-8697
Medina (G-14096)		
Merry Moppets Early Learning	E	614 529-1730
Hilliard (G-11928)		
Miami Valley Family Care Ctr	E	937 268-0336
Dayton (G-9729)		
Miami Valley Hospital	E	937 224-3916
Dayton (G-9733)		
Miami Valley School	E	937 434-4444
Dayton (G-9738)		
Miami Vly Child Dev Ctrs Inc	D	937 226-5664
Dayton (G-9740)		
Miami Vly Child Dev Ctrs Inc	C	937 325-2559
Springfield (G-17246)		
Miami Vly Child Dev Ctrs Inc	E	937 228-1644
Dayton (G-9741)		
Migrant Head Start	E	937 846-0699
New Carlisle (G-15028)		
Mini University Inc	D	513 275-5184
Oxford (G-15825)		
Mini University Inc	C	937 426-1414
Beavercreek (G-1254)		
Ministerial Day Care-Headstart	E	216 541-7400
Cleveland (G-6068)		
Mk Childcare Warsaw Ave LLC	E	513 922-6279
Cincinnati (G-4107)		
Mlm Childcare LLC	E	513 623-8243
Cincinnati (G-4109)		
Montessori Community School	E	740 344-9411
Newark (G-15211)		
Morrow County Child Care Ctr	D	419 946-5007
Mount Gilead (G-14857)		
My Place Child Care	E	740 349-3505
Newark (G-15215)		
N & C Active Learning LLC	E	937 545-1342
Beavercreek (G-1193)		
Nanaeles Day Care Inc	E	216 991-6139
Cleveland (G-6099)		
National Benevolent Associatio	D	216 476-0333
Cleveland (G-6101)		
Nbdc II LLC	E	513 681-5439
Cincinnati (G-4147)		
Neighborhood House	D	614 252-4941
Columbus (G-8256)		
New Bgnnngs Assembly of God Ch	E	614 497-2658
Columbus (G-8271)		
New Dawn Health Care Inc	C	330 343-5521
Dover (G-10202)		
New Hope Christian Academy	E	740 477-6427
Circleville (G-4893)		
New Life Christian Center	E	740 687-1572
Lancaster (G-12561)		
New School Inc	E	513 281-7999
Cincinnati (G-4157)		
Nichalex Inc	E	330 726-1422
Youngstown (G-20300)		
Nicoles Child Care Center	D	216 751-6668
Cleveland (G-6132)		
Nightingale Montessori Inc	E	937 324-0336
Springfield (G-17252)		
Noahs Ark Child Care Inc	E	330 325-7236
Rootstown (G-16599)		
Noahs Ark Child Dev Ctr	E	513 988-0921
Trenton (G-18342)		
Noahs Ark Creative Care	E	740 323-3664
Newark (G-15224)		
Noahs Ark Learning Center	E	740 965-1668
Sunbury (G-17559)		
Nobel Learning Center	E	740 732-4722
Caldwell (G-2087)		
North Broadway Childrens Ctr	E	614 262-6222
Columbus (G-8287)		
Northfield Presbt Ch Day Care	E	330 467-4411
Northfield (G-15521)		
Northfield Presbt Day Care Ctr	E	330 467-4411
Northfield (G-15522)		
Northside Baptst Child Dev Ctr	E	513 932-5642
Lebanon (G-12631)		
Northwest Child Development An	E	937 559-9565
Dayton (G-9776)		
Northwest Local School Dst	D	513 923-1000
Cincinnati (G-4182)		
Notre Dame College of Ohio	E	440 279-1127
Chardon (G-2760)		
Nurtury		330 723-1800
Medina (G-14109)		
Oak Creek United Church	E	937 434-3941
Dayton (G-9779)		
Oberlin Early Childhood Center	E	440 774-8193
Oberlin (G-15657)		
Ohio Dept of Job & Fmly Svcs	C	614 466-1213
Columbus (G-8335)		
Ohio State University	D	614 292-4453
Columbus (G-8405)		
Ohioguidestone		440 234-2006
Berea (G-1467)		
Old Trail School	D	330 666-1118
Bath (G-1035)		
Open Door Christian School	D	440 322-6386
Elyria (G-10666)		
Our Lady of Bethlehem Schools	E	614 459-8285
Columbus (G-8499)		
Ourday At Messiah Preschool	E	614 882-4416
Westerville (G-19435)		
Oxford Blazer Company Inc	E	614 792-2220
Dublin (G-10419)		
P J & R J Connection Inc	E	513 398-2777
Mason (G-13744)		
Paulding Exempted Vlg Schl Dst	C	419 594-3309
Paulding (G-15934)		
Pickaway County Community Acti	E	740 474-7411
Circleville (G-4895)		
Pike County Head Start Inc	E	740 289-2371
Piketon (G-16124)		
Pike County YMCA	E	740 947-8862
Waverly (G-18974)		
Pilgrim United Church Christ	E	513 574-4208
Cincinnati (G-4299)		
Play Time Day Nursery Inc	E	513 385-8281
Cincinnati (G-4304)		
Playtime Preschool LLC	E	614 975-1005
Columbus (G-8551)		
Portage Private Industry	D	330 297-7795
Ravenna (G-16403)		
Powell Enterprises Inc	E	614 882-0111
Westerville (G-19342)		
Precious Angels Lrng Ctr Inc	E	440 886-1919
Cleveland (G-6294)		
Presbyterian Child Center	E	740 852-3190
London (G-13006)		
Pride -N- Joy Preschool Inc	E	740 522-3338
Newark (G-15229)		
Primrose School At Golf Vlg	E	740 881-3500
Powell (G-16346)		
Primrose School At Polaris	E	614 899-2588
Westerville (G-19345)		
Primrose School of Symmes	E	513 697-6970
Cincinnati (G-4330)		
Professional Maint of Columbus	B	513 579-1762
Cincinnati (G-4343)		
Promedica Health Systems Inc	A	567 585-7454
Toledo (G-18141)		
Pulaski Head Start	E	419 636-8862
Bryan (G-2019)		
R & J Investment Co Inc	C	440 934-5204
Avon (G-915)		
R L B Inc	E	513 793-3758
Blue Ash (G-1670)		
Rainbow Station Day Care Inc	E	614 759-8667
Pickerington (G-16104)		
Ravenna Assembly of God Inc	E	330 297-1493
Ravenna (G-16404)		
Ready Set Grow	E	614 855-5100
New Albany (G-15005)		
Robert A Kaufmann Inc	E	216 663-1150
Maple Heights (G-13415)		
Rockport United Methodist Ch	E	440 331-9434
Cleveland (G-6407)		
Ross County YMCA	D	740 772-4340
Chillicothe (G-2087)		
Royal Redeemer Lutheran Church	E	440 237-7958
Cleveland (G-6418)		
Ruffing Montessori School	E	440 333-2250
Rocky River (G-16591)		
Saint Cecilia Church	E	614 878-5353
Columbus (G-8677)		
Saint James Day Care Center	E	513 662-2287
Cincinnati (G-4470)		
Saint Johns Villa	C	330 627-4662
Carrollton (G-2628)		
Salem Church of God Inc	E	937 836-6500
Clayton (G-4916)		
Samkel Inc	E	614 491-3270
Columbus (G-8683)		
Sandusky Area YMCA Foundation	E	419 621-9622
Sandusky (G-16790)		
Santas Hide Away Hollow Inc	E	440 632-5000
Middlefield (G-14402)		
Scioto County C A O Headstart	E	740 354-3333
Portsmouth (G-16306)		
Scribes & Scrbblr Chld Dev Ctr	E	440 884-5437
Cleveland (G-6455)		
Seton Catholic School Hudson	E	330 342-4200
Hudson (G-12143)		
Sharonville Mthdist Wkdays Nrs	E	513 563-8278
Cincinnati (G-4510)		
Sisters of Notre D	E	419 471-0170
Toledo (G-18189)		
Smoky Row Childrens Center	E	614 766-2122
Powell (G-16352)		
Something Special Lrng Ctr Inc	E	419 422-1400
Findlay (G-11082)		
Something Special Lrng Ctr Inc	E	419 878-4190
Waterville (G-18945)		
South- Western City School Dst	D	614 801-8438
Grove City (G-11599)		
Southside Learning & Dev Ctr	E	614 444-1529
Columbus (G-8755)		
Spanish American Committee	E	216 961-2100
Cleveland (G-6513)		
Springfield Family Y M C A	D	937 323-3781
Springfield (G-17281)		
St Marys City Board Education	E	419 394-2616
Saint Marys (G-16685)		
St Pauls Catholic Church	E	330 724-1263
Akron (G-448)		
St Stephen United Church Chrst	E	419 624-1814
Sandusky (G-16797)		
St Stephens Community House	D	614 294-6347
Columbus (G-8770)		
St Thomas Episcopal Church	E	513 831-6908
Terrace Park (G-17662)		
Stark County Cmnty Action Agcy	E	330 821-5977
Alliance (G-561)		
Success Kidz 24-Hr Enrchmt Ctr	E	614 419-2276
Columbus (G-8799)		
Sunny Day Academy LLC	E	614 718-1717
Dublin (G-10465)		
Sycamore Board of Education	D	513 489-3937
Cincinnati (G-4608)		
Sylvania Community Svcs Ctr	E	419 885-2451
Sylvania (G-17618)		
T L C Child Development Center	E	330 655-2797
Hudson (G-12146)		
T M C Systems LLC	E	440 740-1234
Broadview Heights (G-1892)		
Tiny Tots Day Nursery	E	330 755-6473
Struthers (G-17535)		
Tri County Assembly of God	E	513 874-8575
Fairfield (G-10916)		
Trinity Luth Child Care	E	419 289-2126
Ashland (G-703)		

83 SOCIAL SERVICES

Trinity United Methodist Ch .... E 419 224-2909
  Lima *(G-12905)*
Troy Christian School .... D 937 339-5692
  Troy *(G-18382)*
Twinbrook Hills Baptist Church ..... E 513 863-3107
  Hamilton *(G-11780)*
U C Child Care Center Inc .... E 513 961-2825
  Cincinnati *(G-4713)*
Ucc Childrens Center .... E 513 217-5501
  Middletown *(G-14488)*
United Rehabilitation Services ...... D 937 233-1230
  Dayton *(G-9947)*
United States Enrichment Corp ..... A 740 897-2457
  Piketon *(G-16129)*
University of Akron .... E 330 972-8210
  Akron *(G-489)*
Upper Arlington City Schl Dst .... E 614 487-5133
  Columbus *(G-8914)*
Upper Arlington Lutheran Ch .... E 614 451-3736
  Columbus *(G-8915)*
Valentour Education Inc .... E 937 434-5949
  Dayton *(G-9960)*
Van Wert County Day Care Inc ..... E 419 238-9918
  Van Wert *(G-18647)*
Vermilion Family YMCA .... E 440 967-4208
  Vermilion *(G-18720)*
W S O S Community A .... E 419 729-8035
  Toledo *(G-18295)*
W S O S Community A .... D 419 333-6068
  Fremont *(G-11227)*
W S O S Community A .... D 419 334-8511
  Fremont *(G-11228)*
Wee Care Daycare .... E 330 856-1313
  Warren *(G-18926)*
Wee Care Learning Center .... E 937 454-9363
  Dayton *(G-9988)*
Wenzler Daycare Learning Ctr ...... E 937 435-8200
  Dayton *(G-9990)*
Wesley Educ Cntr For Chldrn .... E 513 569-1840
  Cincinnati *(G-4834)*
West Chester Chrstn Chld .... E 513 777-6300
  West Chester *(G-19184)*
West Liberty Care Center Inc .... C 937 465-5065
  West Liberty *(G-19264)*
West Ohio Cmnty Action Partnr .... C 419 227-2586
  Lima *(G-12919)*
West Ohio Conference of .... E 937 773-5313
  Piqua *(G-16175)*
West Shore Child Care Center ..... E 440 333-2040
  Cleveland *(G-6736)*
West Side Montessori .... D 419 866-1931
  Toledo *(G-18306)*
Westerville-Worthington Learni .... E 614 891-4105
  Westerville *(G-19449)*
Westlake Mntsr Schl & Chld Dv .... E 440 835-5858
  Westlake *(G-19568)*
Whitehall City Schools .... E 614 417-5680
  Columbus *(G-8988)*
Willoughby Montessori Day Schl .. E 440 942-5602
  Willoughby *(G-19725)*
Wise Choices In Learning Ltd ...... E 440 324-6056
  Elyria *(G-10694)*
Worthington United Methdst Ch ... E 614 885-5365
  Worthington *(G-20011)*
Wright State University .... E 937 775-4070
  Dayton *(G-9290)*
Wsos Child Development Program E 419 334-8511
  Fremont *(G-11230)*
Y M C A Central Stark County ...... E 330 305-5437
  Canton *(G-2590)*
Y M C A Central Stark County ...... E 330 875-1611
  Louisville *(G-13108)*
Y M C A Central Stark County ...... E 330 877-8933
  Uniontown *(G-18545)*
Y M C A Central Stark County ...... E 330 830-6275
  Massillon *(G-13862)*
Y M C A Central Stark County ...... E 330 498-4082
  Canton *(G-2591)*
Y M C A of Ashland Ohio Inc .... D 419 289-0626
  Ashland *(G-709)*
YMCA .... E 330 823-1930
  Alliance *(G-566)*
YMCA Inc .... D 330 385-6400
  East Liverpool *(G-10536)*
YMCA of Clermont County Inc ..... E 513 724-9622
  Batavia *(G-1032)*
YMCA of Massillon .... E 330 879-0800
  Navarre *(G-14957)*
Young Mens Christian .... C 513 791-5000
  Blue Ash *(G-1725)*

Young Mens Christian .... B 513 932-1424
  Lebanon *(G-12660)*
Young Mens Christian Assn .... D 740 373-2250
  Marietta *(G-13520)*
Young Mens Christian Assn .... E 419 238-0443
  Van Wert *(G-18653)*
Young Mens Christian Assoc .... E 330 724-1255
  Akron *(G-516)*
Young Mens Christian Assoc .... A 330 376-1335
  Akron *(G-517)*
Young Mens Christian Assoc .... D 419 523-5233
  Ottawa *(G-15805)*
Young Mens Christian Assoc .... E 937 228-9622
  Dayton *(G-10012)*
Young Mens Christian Assoc .... C 937 223-5201
  Springboro *(G-17144)*
Young Mens Christian Assoc .... C 614 871-9622
  Grove City *(G-11620)*
Young Mens Christian Assoc .... A 937 223-5201
  Dayton *(G-10009)*
Young Mens Christian Assoc .... D 330 923-5223
  Cuyahoga Falls *(G-9237)*
Young Mens Christian Assoc .... E 330 467-8366
  Macedonia *(G-13219)*
Young Mens Christian Assoc .... E 330 784-0408
  Akron *(G-515)*
Young Mens Christian Assoc .... C 614 416-9622
  Gahanna *(G-11276)*
Young Mens Christian Assoc .... C 740 881-1058
  Powell *(G-16355)*
Young Mens Christian Assoc .... C 614 334-9622
  Hilliard *(G-11967)*
Young Mens Christian Assoc .... E 937 312-1810
  Dayton *(G-10010)*
Young Mens Christian Assoc .... E 614 539-1770
  Urbancrest *(G-18609)*
Young Mens Christian Assoc .... D 614 252-3166
  Columbus *(G-9019)*
Young Mens Christian Assoc .... E 937 593-9001
  Bellefontaine *(G-1401)*
Young Mens Christian Associat .... E 513 731-0115
  Cincinnati *(G-4866)*
Young Mens Christian Associat .... C 513 474-1400
  Cincinnati *(G-4867)*
Young Mens Christian Associat .... E 419 729-8135
  Toledo *(G-18320)*
Young Mens Christian Associat .... D 513 241-9622
  Cincinnati *(G-4868)*
Young Mens Christian Associat .... D 513 923-4466
  Cincinnati *(G-4869)*
Young Mens Christian Associat .... E 419 474-3995
  Toledo *(G-18322)*
Young Mens Christian Associat .... D 419 866-9622
  Maumee *(G-13997)*
Young Mens Christian Associat .... E 419 475-3496
  Toledo *(G-18323)*
Young Mens Christian Associat .... D 419 691-3523
  Oregon *(G-15756)*
Young Mens Christian Mt Vernon . D 740 392-9622
  Mount Vernon *(G-14927)*
Young MNS Chrstn Assn Clveland E 216 521-8400
  Lakewood *(G-12502)*
Young MNS Chrstn Assn Clveland D 440 842-5200
  North Royalton *(G-15507)*
Young MNS Chrstn Assn Clveland E 216 731-7454
  Cleveland *(G-6774)*
Young MNS Chrstn Assn Clveland D 440 285-7543
  Chardon *(G-2780)*
Young MNS Chrstn Assn Grter NY D 740 392-9622
  Mount Vernon *(G-14928)*
Young Services Inc .... E 419 704-2009
  Toledo *(G-18324)*
Young Womens Christian .... D 419 241-3235
  Toledo *(G-18325)*
Young Womens Christian .... D 937 461-5550
  Dayton *(G-10013)*
Young Womens Christian .... E 419 238-6639
  Van Wert *(G-18654)*
Young Womens Christian Assn ..... D 614 224-9121
  Columbus *(G-9021)*
Young Womens Christian Assn ..... D 330 746-6361
  Youngstown *(G-20422)*
Young Womens Christian Associ .. E 216 881-6878
  Cleveland *(G-6776)*
Young Womns Chrstn Assc Canton D 330 453-0789
  Canton *(G-2594)*
YWCA of Greater Cincinnati .... D 513 241-7090
  Cincinnati *(G-4870)*
YWCA Shelter & Housing Network E 937 222-6333
  Dayton *(G-10014)*

Zion Christian School .... E 330 792-4066
  Youngstown *(G-20439)*

8361 Residential Care

A&L Home Care & Training Ctr ... C 740 886-7623
  Proctorville *(G-16357)*
Abbewood Limited Partnership .... E 440 366-8980
  Elyria *(G-10591)*
Abilities First Foundation .... C 513 423-9496
  Middletown *(G-14411)*
Ability Ctr of Greater Toledo .... E 419 517-7123
  Sylvania *(G-17575)*
Adriel School Inc .... D 937 465-0010
  West Liberty *(G-19260)*
Advanced Geriatric Education & .. E 888 393-9799
  Loveland *(G-13109)*
Ahf Ohio Inc .... D 330 725-4123
  Medina *(G-14033)*
Ahf Ohio Inc .... D 614 760-8870
  Dublin *(G-10237)*
Ahf Ohio Inc .... D 937 256-4663
  Dayton *(G-9313)*
Akron Summit Cmnty Action Agcy C 330 572-8532
  Akron *(G-56)*
Aleph Home & Senior Care Inc .... D 216 382-7689
  Cleveland *(G-4983)*
Alexson Services Inc .... B 513 874-0423
  Fairfield *(G-10819)*
Alternative Residences Two .... C 740 526-0514
  Saint Clairsville *(G-16616)*
Alternative Residences Two .... E 330 453-0200
  Canton *(G-2236)*
Alvis Inc .... C 614 252-1788
  Columbus *(G-6979)*
Amedisys Inc .... E 740 373-8549
  Marietta *(G-13430)*
American Nursing Care Inc .... C 614 847-0555
  Zanesville *(G-20441)*
American Retirement Corp .... D 216 321-6331
  Cleveland *(G-5022)*
Anne Grady Corporation .... C 419 380-8985
  Holland *(G-12009)*
Arbors At Clide Asssted Living .... E 419 547-7746
  Clyde *(G-6808)*
Archdiocese of Cincinnati .... E 513 231-5010
  Cincinnati *(G-3042)*
Ardmore Inc .... C 330 535-2601
  Akron *(G-81)*
Ashtabula County Residential I .... E 440 593-6404
  Conneaut *(G-9038)*
Aspen Woodside Village .... D 440 439-8666
  Cleveland *(G-5072)*
Assisted Living Concepts LLC ..... E 419 224-6327
  Lima *(G-12742)*
Assoc Dvlpmtly Disabled .... E 614 486-4361
  Westerville *(G-19365)*
Assoc Dvlpmtly Disabled .... E 614 447-0606
  Columbus *(G-7054)*
Autumn Health Care Inc .... E 740 366-2321
  Newark *(G-15145)*
Bastin Home Inc .... E 513 734-2662
  Bethel *(G-1482)*
Bellefaire Jewish Chld Bur .... B 216 932-2800
  Shaker Heights *(G-16856)*
Bellmont County .... E 740 695-9750
  Saint Clairsville *(G-16618)*
Benjamin Rose Institute .... D 216 791-3580
  Cleveland *(G-5116)*
Berea Lake Towers Inc .... E 440 243-9050
  Berea *(G-1448)*
Bittersweet Inc .... D 419 875-6986
  Whitehouse *(G-19584)*
Bradley Bay Assisted Living .... E 440 871-4509
  Bay Village *(G-1038)*
Brighter Horizons Residential ...... E 440 417-1751
  Madison *(G-13221)*
Broadway Care Ctr Mple Hts LLC E 216 662-0551
  Maple Heights *(G-13401)*
Brookdale Senior Living Inc .... D 513 229-3155
  Mason *(G-13668)*
Brookdale Senior Living Inc .... C 614 794-2499
  Westerville *(G-19372)*
Brookdale Senior Living Inc .... D 419 422-8657
  Findlay *(G-11008)*
Browning Mesonic Community .... E 419 878-4055
  Waterville *(G-18941)*
Buckeye Ranch Inc .... D 614 384-7700
  Columbus *(G-7161)*
Buckeye Ranch Inc .... B 614 875-2371
  Grove City *(G-11542)*

83 SOCIAL SERVICES

Butler County Bd of Mental RE .... E 513 785-2815
  Hamilton (G-11700)
Butler County Bd of Mental RE .... C 513 785-2870
  Fairfield Township (G-10927)
Butler County Board of Develop .... E 513 867-5913
  Fairfield (G-10826)
C Micah Rand Inc .... C 513 605-2000
  Cincinnati (G-3162)
Capital Senior Living Corp .... C 419 874-2564
  Perrysburg (G-15983)
Capital Senior Living Corp .... C 216 289-9800
  Richmond Heights (G-16536)
Caracole Inc .... E 513 761-1480
  Cincinnati (G-3176)
Cardinal Retirement Village .... E 330 928-7888
  Cuyahoga Falls (G-9168)
Caritas Inc .... E 419 332-2589
  Fremont (G-11186)
Carriage Court Company Inc .... E 740 654-4422
  Lancaster (G-12514)
Carriage Crt Mrysvlle Ltd Prtn .... E 937 642-2202
  Marysville (G-13609)
Champaign Residential Svcs Inc .... A 937 653-1320
  Urbana (G-18578)
Cherry St Mission Ministries .... E 419 242-5141
  Toledo (G-17804)
Childrens Cmprhensive Svcs Inc .... D 419 589-5511
  Mansfield (G-13276)
Choices For Vctims Dom Volence .... D 614 258-6080
  Columbus (G-7267)
Choices In Community Living .... C 937 898-3655
  Dayton (G-9405)
Christian Chld HM Ohio Inc .... D 330 345-7949
  Wooster (G-19841)
Church of God Retirement Cmnty .... C 513 422-5600
  Middletown (G-14420)
Cincinnatis Optimum RES Envir .... C 513 771-2673
  Cincinnati (G-3337)
City Mission .... E 216 431-3510
  Cleveland (G-5247)
Clark County Board of Developm .... C 937 328-5200
  Springfield (G-17163)
Clark Memorial Home Assn .... E 937 399-4262
  Springfield (G-17164)
Cleveland Christian Home Inc .... C 216 671-0977
  Cleveland (G-5294)
Cleveland Municipal School Dst .... C 216 459-9818
  Cleveland (G-5338)
Close To Home III .... E 740 534-1100
  Ironton (G-12286)
College Park Inc .... E 740 623-4607
  Coshocton (G-9091)
Commons of Providence .... D 419 624-1171
  Sandusky (G-16744)
Community Hbilitation Svcs Inc .... E 234 334-4288
  Akron (G-155)
Community Hsing Netwrk Dev Co .... C 614 487-6700
  Columbus (G-7405)
Community Living Experiences .... E 614 588-0320
  Columbus (G-7406)
Community Support Services Inc .... C 330 253-9388
  Akron (G-157)
Compdrug .... D 614 224-4506
  Columbus (G-7412)
Comprehensive Addiction Svc Sy .... D 419 241-8827
  Toledo (G-17826)
Concepts In Community Living .... E 740 393-0055
  Mount Vernon (G-14885)
Copeland Oaks .... B 330 938-6126
  Sebring (G-16821)
Cornell Companies Inc .... C 419 747-3322
  Shelby (G-16898)
County of Allen .... C 419 221-1103
  Lima (G-12763)
County of Auglaize .... D 419 629-2419
  New Bremen (G-15017)
County of Cuyahoga .... C 216 241-8230
  Cleveland (G-5424)
County of Hamilton .... C 513 552-1200
  Cincinnati (G-3429)
County of Hancock .... E 419 422-6387
  Findlay (G-11016)
County of Hancock .... D 419 424-7050
  Findlay (G-11017)
County of Holmes .... E 330 279-2801
  Holmesville (G-12071)
County of Logan .... C 937 592-2901
  Bellefontaine (G-1382)
County of Lorain .... E 440 282-3074
  Lorain (G-13034)
County of Lorain .... E 440 329-3734
  Elyria (G-10610)
County of Lorain .... C 440 329-5340
  Elyria (G-10616)
County of Medina .... E 330 723-9553
  Medina (G-14053)
County of Richland .... D 419 774-4300
  Mansfield (G-13277)
County of Richland .... C 419 774-4100
  Mansfield (G-13280)
County of Richland .... D 419 774-5578
  Mansfield (G-13282)
County of Ross .... E 740 773-4169
  Chillicothe (G-2830)
County of Summit .... C 330 643-2943
  Akron (G-169)
County of Wayne .... D 330 345-5340
  Wooster (G-19856)
Crestview Health Care Center .... D 740 695-2500
  Saint Clairsville (G-16634)
Crossroads Center .... C 513 475-5300
  Cincinnati (G-3442)
Crystalwood Inc .... D 513 605-1000
  Cincinnati (G-3443)
D-R Training Center & Workshop .... C 419 289-0470
  Ashland (G-678)
Deaconess Long Term Care of MI .... A 513 487-3600
  Cincinnati (G-3474)
Develpmntal Dsblties Ohio Dept .... B 419 385-0231
  Toledo (G-17851)
Develpmntal Dsblties Ohio Dept .... C 330 544-2231
  Columbus (G-7512)
Domestic Violence Project Inc .... E 330 445-2000
  Canton (G-2343)
Donty Horton HM Care Dhhc LLC .... E 513 463-3442
  Cincinnati (G-3499)
Drake Development Inc .... D 513 418-4370
  Cincinnati (G-3502)
Eastgate Village .... E 513 753-4400
  Cincinnati (G-2915)
Eastwood Residential Living .... E 440 417-0608
  Madison (G-13223)
Eastwood Residential Living .... E 440 428-1588
  Madison (G-13224)
ECHO Residential Support .... E 614 210-0944
  Columbus (G-7570)
Echoing Hills Village Inc .... D 740 594-3541
  Athens (G-785)
Echoing Hills Village Inc .... A 740 327-2311
  Warsaw (G-18936)
Eci Inc .... B 419 986-5566
  Burgoon (G-2057)
Embracing Autism Inc .... E 614 559-0077
  Columbus (G-7590)
Emeritus Corporation .... D 440 201-9200
  Cleveland (G-5535)
Emeritus Corporation .... E 440 269-8600
  Willoughby (G-19661)
Episcopal Retirement Homes Inc .... E 513 271-9610
  Cincinnati (G-3567)
Episcopal Retirement Homes Inc .... E 513 561-6363
  Cincinnati (G-3568)
Episcopal Retirement Homes Inc .... C 513 871-2090
  Cincinnati (G-3569)
Erie Residential Living Inc .... E 419 625-0060
  Sandusky (G-16754)
Evangelical Retirement .... C 937 837-5581
  Dayton (G-9532)
Evant .... E 330 920-1517
  Stow (G-17365)
Extended Family Concepts Inc .... E 330 966-2555
  Canton (G-2361)
Fairways .... D 440 943-2050
  Wickliffe (G-19596)
Firelands Regional Health Sys .... E 419 448-9440
  Tiffin (G-17679)
First Community Village .... B 614 324-4455
  Columbus (G-7664)
First Mental Retardation Corp .... E 937 262-3077
  Dayton (G-9549)
Five County Joint Juvenile Det .... E 937 642-1015
  Marysville (G-13618)
Flat Rock Care Center .... C 419 483-7330
  Flat Rock (G-11103)
Foundations Hlth Solutions Inc .... D 440 793-0200
  North Olmsted (G-15423)
Franklin Cnty Bd Commissioners .... E 614 462-3429
  Columbus (G-7686)
Franklin County Residential S .... B 614 844-5847
  Columbus (G-7696)
Friars Club Inc .... D 513 488-8777
  Cincinnati (G-3654)
Friedman Vlg Retirement Cmnty .... E 419 443-1540
  Tiffin (G-17680)
Friends of Good Shepherd Manor .... D 740 289-2861
  Lucasville (G-13179)
Friendship Vlg of Clumbus Ohio .... C 614 890-8282
  Columbus (G-7708)
Furney Group Home .... E 419 389-0152
  Toledo (G-17902)
G & D Alternative Living Inc .... E 937 446-2803
  Sardinia (G-16813)
Garden Manor Extended Care Cen .... C 513 420-5972
  Middletown (G-14426)
Gateways To Better Living Inc .... E 330 270-0952
  Youngstown (G-20195)
Gateways To Better Living Inc .... E 330 797-1764
  Canfield (G-2191)
Gateways To Better Living Inc .... E 330 792-2854
  Youngstown (G-20196)
Gentlebrook Inc .... C 330 877-3694
  Hartville (G-11817)
Gerspacher Companies .... E 330 725-1596
  Medina (G-14070)
Glen Wesley Inc .... D 614 888-7492
  Columbus (G-7755)
Glenwood Community Inc .... E 740 376-9555
  Marietta (G-13447)
Grace Hospice LLC .... C 440 826-0350
  Cleveland (G-5683)
Greenbrier Senior Living Cmnty .... D 440 888-0400
  Cleveland (G-5703)
Hackensack Meridian Health Inc .... D 513 792-9697
  Cincinnati (G-3727)
Harbor .... D 419 241-6191
  Toledo (G-17933)
Harmony Home Care Inc .... E 440 243-1332
  North Royalton (G-15493)
Harrison Co County Home .... E 740 942-3573
  Cadiz (G-2075)
Hattie Larlham Center For .... C 330 274-2272
  Mantua (G-13387)
Hattie Larlham Center For .... D 330 274-2272
  Mantua (G-13388)
Havar Inc .... D 740 594-3533
  Athens (G-790)
Hcf Management Inc .... C 419 999-2055
  Lima (G-12792)
Health Recovery Services Inc .... C 740 592-6720
  Athens (G-791)
Healthy Life HM Healthcare LLC .... E 614 865-3368
  Columbus (G-7813)
Heinzerling Foundation .... A 614 272-2000
  Columbus (G-7822)
Help Foundation Inc .... E 216 486-5258
  Cleveland (G-5748)
Hill Manor 1 Inc .... E 740 972-3227
  Columbus (G-7836)
Hitchcock Center For Women Inc .... E 216 421-0662
  Cleveland (G-5761)
Hopewell .... E 440 693-4074
  Mesopotamia (G-14263)
Horizons Tuscarawas/Carroll .... E 330 262-4183
  Wooster (G-19869)
I A R Inc .... E 740 432-3371
  Cambridge (G-2121)
Independence of Portage County .... C 330 296-2851
  Ravenna (G-16390)
Inn At Christine Valley .... E 330 270-3347
  Youngstown (G-20236)
Interval Brotherhood Homes .... D 330 644-4095
  Coventry Township (G-9126)
J & R Associates .... A 440 250-4080
  Brookpark (G-1947)
Jo Lin Health Center Inc .... C 740 532-0860
  Ironton (G-12295)
Josina Lott Foundation .... E 419 866-9013
  Toledo (G-17987)
Judson .... D 216 791-2555
  Cleveland (G-5877)
Kendal At Granville .... C 740 321-0400
  Granville (G-11467)
Kent Ridge At Golden Pond Ltd .... D 330 677-4040
  Kent (G-12378)
Kingston Healthcare Company .... D 419 824-4200
  Sylvania (G-17598)
Kingston Healthcare Company .... D 740 389-2311
  Marion (G-13546)
Lakeside Manor Inc .... E 330 549-2545
  North Lima (G-15404)

83 SOCIAL SERVICES

Larchwood Health Group LLC .... E 216 941-6100
  Cleveland *(G-5926)*
Laurel Lk Retirement Cmnty Inc .... B 330 650-0681
  Hudson *(G-12130)*
Lighthouse Youth Services Inc .... D 740 634-3094
  Bainbridge *(G-942)*
Lindley Inn .... E 740 797-9701
  The Plains *(G-17665)*
Lutheran Home .... D 419 724-1414
  Toledo *(G-18019)*
Lutheran Village At Wolf Creek .... C 419 861-2233
  Holland *(G-12033)*
Madison House Inc .... E 740 845-0145
  London *(G-13001)*
Manfield Living Center Ltd .... E 419 512-1711
  Mansfield *(G-13328)*
Maple Knoll Communities Inc .... E 513 524-7990
  Oxford *(G-15817)*
Mason Health Care Center .... D 513 398-2881
  Mason *(G-13737)*
McElvain Group Home .... E 419 589-6697
  Mansfield *(G-13336)*
Medina Cnty Jvnile Dtntion Ctr .... E 330 764-8408
  Medina *(G-14097)*
Mended Reeds Home .... E 740 533-1883
  Ironton *(G-12298)*
Miami Vly Hsing Oprtunties Inc .... E 937 263-4449
  Dayton *(G-9742)*
Mid-Western Childrens Home .... E 513 877-2141
  Pleasant Plain *(G-16215)*
Midwest Health Services Inc .... C 330 828-0779
  Massillon *(G-13840)*
Mount Aloysius Corp .... C 740 342-3343
  New Lexington *(G-15056)*
Mulberry Garden A L S .... E 330 630-3980
  Munroe Falls *(G-14932)*
Multi County Juvenile Det Ctr .... E 740 652-1525
  Lancaster *(G-12559)*
Multi-Cnty Jvnile Attntion Sys .... D 330 484-6471
  Canton *(G-2469)*
Muskingum Residentials Inc .... E 740 453-5350
  Zanesville *(G-20511)*
National Benevolent Associatio .... D 216 476-0333
  Cleveland *(G-6101)*
National Mentor Inc .... E 216 525-1885
  Cleveland *(G-6111)*
National Mentor Holdings Inc .... A 419 443-0867
  Fostoria *(G-11135)*
Necco Center .... D 740 534-1386
  Pedro *(G-15937)*
Network Housing 2005 Inc .... D 614 487-6700
  Columbus *(G-8265)*
New Avenues To Independence .... E 216 481-1907
  Cleveland *(G-6122)*
New Avenues To Independence .... E 216 671-8224
  Cleveland *(G-6123)*
New Avenues To Independence .... E 888 853-8905
  Ashtabula *(G-756)*
New Dawn Health Care Inc .... C 330 343-5521
  Dover *(G-10202)*
New Directions Inc .... D 216 591-0324
  Cleveland *(G-6124)*
New England Rms Inc .... E 401 384-6759
  Worthington *(G-19979)*
New Nghbors Rsdential Svcs Inc .... E 937 717-5731
  Springfield *(G-17251)*
Newark Resident Homes Inc .... D 740 345-7231
  Newark *(G-15222)*
Nickolas Rsidential Trtmnt Ctr .... E 937 496-7100
  Dayton *(G-9774)*
North Cntl Mntal Hlth Svcs Inc .... D 614 227-6865
  Columbus *(G-8288)*
North Hills Managemont Company .... D 740 450-9999
  Zanesville *(G-20517)*
Oakleaf Toledo Ltd Partnership .... E 419 885-3934
  Toledo *(G-18101)*
Oakleaf Village Ltd .... D 614 431-1739
  Columbus *(G-8311)*
Oasis Thrptic Fster Care Ntwrk .... E 740 698-0340
  Albany *(G-520)*
Oesterlen-Services For Youth .... C 937 399-6101
  Springfield *(G-17254)*
Ohio Department of Aging .... D 614 466-5500
  Columbus *(G-8324)*
Ohio Department of Health .... B 614 447-1450
  Tiffin *(G-17690)*
Ohio Living .... C 513 681-4230
  Cincinnati *(G-4208)*
Ohio Living .... B 440 942-4342
  Willoughby *(G-19700)*

Ohio Living .... E 614 888-7800
  Columbus *(G-8358)*
Ohio Presbt Retirement Svcs .... C 513 539-7391
  Monroe *(G-14708)*
Ohioguidestone .... E 440 234-2006
  Berea *(G-1467)*
One Way Farm of Fairfield Inc .... E 513 829-3276
  Fairfield *(G-10889)*
Opportunity Homes Inc .... E 330 424-1411
  Lisbon *(G-12941)*
Orrvilla Retirement Community .... E 330 683-4455
  Orrville *(G-15777)*
Otterbein Homes .... E 513 933-5439
  Lebanon *(G-12634)*
Otterbein Snior Lfstyle Chices .... C 513 260-7690
  Middletown *(G-14483)*
Otterbein Snior Lfstyle Chices .... B 513 933-5400
  Lebanon *(G-12636)*
Otterbein Snior Lfstyle Chices .... C 419 645-5114
  Cridersville *(G-9152)*
Otterbein Snior Lfstyle Chices .... E 419 943-4376
  Leipsic *(G-12663)*
Otterbein Snior Lfstyle Chices .... C 419 394-2366
  Saint Marys *(G-16682)*
Our Lady of Wayside Inc .... B 440 934-6152
  Avon *(G-911)*
Paisley House For Aged Women .... E 330 799-9431
  Youngstown *(G-20314)*
Parkcliffe Development .... D 419 381-9447
  Toledo *(G-18118)*
Pathway Caring For Children .... D 330 493-0083
  Canton *(G-2489)*
Paul Dennis .... E 440 746-8600
  Brecksville *(G-1839)*
Pine Ridge Pine Vllg Resdntl H .... E 513 724-3460
  Williamsburg *(G-19634)*
Portage County Board .... E 330 297-6209
  Ravenna *(G-16399)*
Premier Estates 525 LLC .... D 513 631-6800
  Cincinnati *(G-4323)*
Premier Estates 526 LLC .... D 513 922-1440
  Cincinnati *(G-4324)*
Primrose Rtrment Cmmnities LLC .... E 419 224-1200
  Lima *(G-12862)*
Pristine Senior Living .... D 513 471-8667
  Cincinnati *(G-4334)*
Pristine Snior Lving Englewood .... C 937 836-5143
  Englewood *(G-10718)*
Providence House Inc .... E 216 651-5982
  Cleveland *(G-6326)*
R T Industries Inc .... C 937 335-5784
  Troy *(G-18374)*
Rchp - Wilmington LLC .... D 937 382-6611
  Wilmington *(G-19781)*
Rehabltition Ctr At Mrietta Mem .... D 740 374-1407
  Marietta *(G-13493)*
REM-Ohio Inc .... E 937 335-8267
  Troy *(G-18376)*
REM-Ohio Inc .... D 330 644-9730
  Coventry Township *(G-9131)*
REM-Ohio Inc .... D 614 367-1370
  Reynoldsburg *(G-16474)*
Renaissance House Inc .... E 419 663-1316
  Norwalk *(G-15590)*
Rescare .... E 740 867-3051
  Chesapeake *(G-2787)*
Rescare Ohio Inc .... D 330 479-9841
  Canton *(G-2511)*
Rescare Ohio Inc .... E 513 724-1177
  Williamsburg *(G-19635)*
Rescare Ohio Inc .... D 513 829-8992
  Hamilton *(G-11768)*
Rescue Incorporated .... C 419 255-9585
  Toledo *(G-18153)*
Residential Hm Assn of Marion .... E 740 387-9999
  Marion *(G-13575)*
Residential Home For The Devlp .... C 740 622-9778
  Coshocton *(G-9115)*
Residential Home For The Devlp .... E 740 452-5133
  Zanesville *(G-20529)*
Residential Inc .... E 740 342-4158
  New Lexington *(G-15062)*
Residential Management Systems .... E 419 222-8806
  Lima *(G-12867)*
Residential Management Systems .... E 614 880-6014
  Worthington *(G-19992)*
Residential Management Systems .... D 419 255-6060
  Maumee *(G-13969)*
Rhc Inc .... E 513 389-7501
  Cincinnati *(G-4413)*

Roman Cthlic Docese Youngstown .... C 330 875-5562
  Louisville *(G-13106)*
Rose Mary Johanna Grassell .... C 216 481-4823
  Cleveland *(G-6412)*
Saint Johns Villa .... C 330 627-4662
  Carrollton *(G-2628)*
Saint Joseph Orphanage .... D 513 231-5010
  Cincinnati *(G-4471)*
Saint Joseph Orphanage .... D 513 741-3100
  Cincinnati *(G-4472)*
Saint Joseph Orphanage .... D 937 643-0398
  Moraine *(G-14822)*
Sattlerpearson Inc .... E 419 698-3822
  Northwood *(G-15544)*
Second Mental Retardation .... E 937 262-3077
  Dayton *(G-9872)*
Second Phase Inc .... E 330 797-9930
  Youngstown *(G-20369)*
Select Spclty Hsptal-Akron LLC .... D 330 761-7500
  Akron *(G-433)*
SEM Villa Inc .... E 513 831-3262
  Loveland *(G-13158)*
Senior Care Inc .... E 937 372-1530
  Xenia *(G-20075)*
Senior Care Inc .... E 937 291-3211
  Miamisburg *(G-14347)*
Senior Lifestyle Corporation .... D 513 777-4457
  West Chester *(G-19150)*
Shalom House Inc .... E 614 239-1999
  Columbus *(G-8722)*
Shurmer Place At Altenheim .... E 440 238-9001
  Strongsville *(G-17509)*
Sisters of Little .... E 513 281-8001
  Cincinnati *(G-4532)*
Sisters of Mercy .... E 419 332-8208
  Fremont *(G-11221)*
Society For Handicapped Citzns .... E 937 746-4201
  Carlisle *(G-2606)*
Society Handicapped Citz Medin .... E 330 722-1900
  Seville *(G-16844)*
Sociey For Handicapped Citizen .... C 330 725-7041
  Seville *(G-16845)*
Southeast Cmnty Mental Hlth Ctr .... C 614 225-0980
  Columbus *(G-8751)*
St Edward Home .... C 330 668-2828
  Fairlawn *(G-10977)*
St Luke Lutheran Community .... E 330 868-5600
  Minerva *(G-14651)*
St Vincent Family Centers .... C 614 252-0731
  Columbus *(G-8771)*
Stone Gardens .... D 216 292-0070
  Cleveland *(G-6541)*
Stonewood Residential Inc .... E 216 267-9777
  Cleveland *(G-6542)*
◆ Style Crest Inc .... B 419 332-7369
  Fremont *(G-11223)*
Summerville Senior Living Inc .... D 440 354-5499
  Mentor *(G-14246)*
Sunrise Senior Living Inc .... E 614 846-6500
  Worthington *(G-20001)*
Sunrise Senior Living Inc .... E 614 418-9775
  Gahanna *(G-11272)*
Sunrise Senior Living Inc .... D 440 895-2383
  Rocky River *(G-16593)*
Sunrise Senior Living LLC .... E 937 836-9617
  Englewood *(G-10720)*
Sunrise Senior Living LLC .... E 330 707-1313
  Poland *(G-16228)*
Sunrise Senior Living LLC .... E 614 718-2062
  Dublin *(G-10466)*
Sunrise Senior Living LLC .... E 330 262-1615
  Wooster *(G-19017)*
Sunrise Senior Living LLC .... E 419 425-3440
  Findlay *(G-11088)*
Sunrise Senior Living LLC .... E 216 447-8909
  Cleveland *(G-6552)*
Sunset House Inc .... C 419 536-4645
  Toledo *(G-18210)*
Sunset Rtrment Communities Inc .... D 419 724-1200
  Ottawa Hills *(G-15807)*
Sunshine Communities .... B 419 865-0251
  Maumee *(G-13982)*
Terre Forme Enterprises Inc .... E 330 847-6800
  Mineral Ridge *(G-14640)*
Toledo Hospital .... C 419 291-2273
  Sylvania *(G-17623)*
Toward Independence Inc .... E 937 376-3996
  Xenia *(G-20079)*
Traditions At Bath Rd Inc .... C 330 929-6272
  Cuyahoga Falls *(G-9226)*

83 SOCIAL SERVICES

Name	Code	Phone
Tri County Mental Health Svcs	C	740 592-3091
Athens (G-815)		
Trilogy Health Services LLC	D	419 935-6511
Willard (G-19628)		
Twelve Inc	E	330 837-3555
Massillon (G-13859)		
United Cerebral Palsy	C	216 791-8363
Cleveland (G-6635)		
United Cerebral Palsy	D	216 381-9993
Cleveland (G-6636)		
United Cerebral Palsy Gr Cinc	E	513 221-4606
Cincinnati (G-4729)		
United Church Homes Inc	D	740 376-5600
Marietta (G-13510)		
United Church Homes Inc	E	513 922-1440
Cincinnati (G-4730)		
United Church Homes Inc	C	937 426-8481
Beavercreek (G-1261)		
United Methodist Childrens	D	614 885-5020
Worthington (G-20004)		
Ursuline Convent Sacred Heart	E	419 531-8990
Toledo (G-18283)		
Uvmc Nursing Care Inc	C	937 667-7500
Tipp City (G-17731)		
Village Network	C	330 264-0650
Wooster (G-19922)		
Volunters of Amer Greater Ohio	C	614 253-6100
Columbus (G-8951)		
Wallick Construction Co	D	937 399-7009
Springfield (G-17295)		
Washington Manor Inc	E	937 433-3441
Dayton (G-9984)		
Wesleyan Senior Living	D	440 284-9000
Elyria (G-10689)		
Wesleyan Village	B	440 284-9000
Elyria (G-10690)		
West View Manor Inc	C	330 264-8640
Wooster (G-19928)		
Whitehouse Operator LLC	D	419 877-5338
Whitehouse (G-19590)		
Widows Home of Dayton Ohio	D	937 252-1661
Dayton (G-9997)		
Wiley Homes Inc	D	419 535-3988
Toledo (G-18309)		
Womens Recovery Center	E	937 562-2400
Xenia (G-20084)		
Womens Welsh Clubs of America	D	440 331-0420
Rocky River (G-16596)		
Wood County Chld Svcs Assn	D	419 352-7588
Bowling Green (G-1798)		
Wynn-Reeth Inc	E	419 639-2094
Green Springs (G-11481)		
Zandex Inc	E	740 452-2087
Zanesville (G-20547)		
Zandex Health Care Corporation	C	740 454-1400
New Concord (G-15041)		

8399 Social Services, NEC

Name	Code	Phone
Abcd Inc	E	330 455-6385
Canton (G-2223)		
Adams & Brown Counties Economi	E	937 695-0316
Winchester (G-19799)		
Adams & Brown Counties Economi	C	937 378-6041
Georgetown (G-11383)		
Adams County Senior Citizens	E	937 544-7459
West Union (G-19273)		
Air Frce Museum Foundation Inc	E	937 258-1218
Dayton (G-9253)		
Akron Cmnty Svc Ctr Urban Leag	E	234 542-4141
Akron (G-33)		
Akron Summit Cmnty Action Agcy	C	330 572-8532
Akron (G-56)		
Akron Summit Cmnty Action Agcy	D	330 733-2290
Akron (G-57)		
Akron Summit Cmnty Action Agcy	B	330 376-7730
Akron (G-58)		
American Red Cross of Grtr Col	E	614 253-7981
Columbus (G-7004)		
ARC Industries Incorporated O	E	614 836-6050
Groveport (G-11624)		
Ashtabula County Commnty Actn	C	440 997-1721
Ashtabula (G-718)		
Ashtabula County Commnty Actn	D	440 593-6441
Conneaut (G-9037)		
Ashtabula County Commnty Actn	D	440 576-6911
Jefferson (G-12330)		
Ashtabula County Commnty Actn	D	440 993-7716
Ashtabula (G-719)		
Ashtabula County Commnty Actn	D	440 997-5957
Ashtabula (G-720)		
Catholic Charities Corporation	E	216 939-3713
Cleveland (G-5189)		
Catholic Charities Corporation	E	216 268-4006
Cleveland (G-5190)		
Catholic Charities Corporation	E	419 289-1903
Ashland (G-670)		
Catholic Charities Corporation	E	216 334-2900
Cleveland (G-5191)		
Catholic Chrties Regional Agcy	D	330 744-3320
Youngstown (G-20134)		
Center For Community Solutions	E	216 781-2944
Cleveland (G-5204)		
Childrens Hospital Foundation	E	614 355-0888
Columbus (G-7262)		
Childrens Hunger Alliance	D	614 341-7700
Columbus (G-7263)		
Choices For Vctims Dom Volence	E	614 224-6617
Worthington (G-19947)		
Cincinnati Institute Fine Arts	E	513 871-2787
Cincinnati (G-3312)		
City of Columbus	D	614 645-3072
Columbus (G-7281)		
City of Columbus	D	614 645-7417
Columbus (G-7282)		
City of Portsmouth	E	740 353-5153
Portsmouth (G-16268)		
City of Warrensville Heights	E	216 587-1230
Cleveland (G-5277)		
Cleveland Jewish Federation	C	216 593-2900
Cleveland (G-5322)		
Cleveland Municipal School Dst	B	216 838-0000
Cleveland (G-5335)		
Cleveland Municipal School Dst	E	216 838-8700
Cleveland (G-5336)		
Clinton County Community Actn	D	937 382-8365
Wilmington (G-19750)		
Clinton County Community Actn	E	937 382-5624
Wilmington (G-19751)		
Colonial Senior Services Inc	C	513 856-8600
Hamilton (G-11713)		
Columbus Jewish Federation	E	614 237-7686
Columbus (G-7361)		
Columbus Landmarks Foundation	E	614 221-0227
Columbus (G-7362)		
Columbus Surgical Center LLP	E	614 932-9503
Dublin (G-10301)		
Columbus Urban League Inc	E	614 257-6300
Columbus (G-7391)		
Community Action Columbiana CT	D	330 424-7221
Lisbon (G-12932)		
Community Action Program Corp	D	740 373-3745
Marietta (G-13436)		
Community Action Program Corp	E	740 373-6016
Marietta (G-13437)		
Community Action Program Inc	D	937 382-0225
Wilmington (G-19755)		
Community Imprv Corp Nble Cnty	D	740 509-0248
Caldwell (G-2083)		
Community Re-Entry Inc	E	216 696-2717
Cleveland (G-5385)		
Concord	E	614 882-9338
Westerville (G-19391)		
Council For Economic Opport	D	216 541-7878
Cleveland (G-5412)		
Council For Economic Opport	D	216 696-9077
Cleveland (G-5414)		
Council For Economic Opport	E	216 692-4010
Cleveland (G-5415)		
Council On Aging of Southweste	C	513 721-1025
Cincinnati (G-3427)		
Council On Rur Svc Prgrams Inc	E	937 492-8787
Sidney (G-16924)		
Council On Rur Svc Prgrams Inc	E	937 778-5220
Piqua (G-16140)		
Council On Rur Svc Prgrams Inc	E	937 773-0773
Piqua (G-16141)		
County of Medina	D	330 995-5243
Medina (G-14054)		
County of Montgomery	E	937 225-4192
Dayton (G-9431)		
Daybreak Inc	E	937 395-4600
Dayton (G-9455)		
East End Community Svcs Corp	E	937 259-1898
Dayton (G-9514)		
Easter Seals Metro Chicago Inc	E	419 332-3016
Fremont (G-11196)		
Emeritus Corporation	E	330 477-5727
Canton (G-2353)		
Epilepsy Cntr of Nrthwstrn OH	D	419 867-5950
Maumee (G-13911)		
Fairfield Cnty Job & Fmly Svcs	D	800 450-8845
Lancaster (G-12529)		
Fairfield County	D	740 653-4060
Lancaster (G-12531)		
Famicos Foundation	E	216 791-6476
Cleveland (G-5569)		
Fort Hamilton Hosp Foundation	B	513 867-5492
Hamilton (G-11727)		
Gc Neighborhood Ctrs Assoc Inc	C	216 298-4440
Cleveland (G-5660)		
GE Reuter Stokes	E	216 749-6332
Cleveland (G-5664)		
Greater Cleveland Food Bnk Inc	C	216 738-2265
Cleveland (G-5696)		
Greene Cnty Chld Svc Brd Frbrn	E	937 878-1415
Xenia (G-20052)		
Greene County Career Center	E	937 372-6941
Xenia (G-20057)		
Guernsey County Cmnty Dev Corp	E	740 439-0020
Cambridge (G-2117)		
Habitat For Humanity	E	216 429-1299
Cleveland (G-5718)		
Habitat For Humanity Intl	E	513 721-4483
Cincinnati (G-3726)		
Hancock Hardin Wyandot Putnam	C	419 423-3755
Findlay (G-11042)		
Health Partners Western Ohio	D	419 221-3072
Lima (G-12795)		
Hockingthensperry Cmnty Action	E	740 767-4500
Glouster (G-11435)		
Integrated Services of Appala	D	740 594-6807
Athens (G-794)		
Interact For Health	E	513 458-6600
Cincinnati (G-3831)		
Jackson Co Bd of Dd	D	740 384-7938
Wellston (G-19001)		
Jackson-Vinton Cmnty Action	E	740 384-3722
Wellston (G-19003)		
Jewish Edcatn Ctr of Cleveland	D	216 371-0446
Cleveland Heights (G-6791)		
Karamu House Inc	E	216 795-7070
Cleveland (G-5885)		
Leads Inc	E	740 349-8606
Newark (G-15184)		
Licking County Aging Program	D	740 345-0821
Newark (G-15187)		
Life Enriching Communities	E	513 719-3510
Loveland (G-13138)		
Lifeline Systems Company	E	330 762-5627
Akron (G-319)		
Lifeservices Development Corp	E	440 257-3866
Mentor (G-14209)		
Lincare Inc	E	330 928-0884
Akron (G-320)		
Lorain County Community Action	E	440 245-2009
Lorain (G-13052)		
Lutheran Metropolitan Ministry	C	216 658-4638
Cleveland (G-5960)		
Mahoning Youngstown Community	D	330 747-7921
Youngstown (G-20268)		
Med Assist Prgram of Info Line	E	330 762-0609
Akron (G-335)		
Medill Elemntary Sch of Volntr	E	740 687-7352
Lancaster (G-12556)		
Miami Cnty Cmnty Action Cuncil	E	937 335-7921
Troy (G-18363)		
Miami Valley Community Action	D	937 222-1009
Dayton (G-9728)		
Miami Vly Fandom For Literacy	E	513 933-0452
Lebanon (G-12629)		
Mobile Meals Inc	D	330 376-7717
Akron (G-346)		
Montpelier Senior Center	E	419 485-3218
Montpelier (G-14745)		
National Multiple Sclerosis	E	330 759-9066
Youngstown (G-20299)		
Nationwide Childrens Hospital	B	614 722-8200
Columbus (G-8233)		
Nationwide Childrens Hospital	E	614 722-2700
Columbus (G-8229)		
Neighborhood Development Svcs	E	330 296-2003
Ravenna (G-16393)		
Neighborhood Health Care Inc	E	513 221-4949
Cincinnati (G-4152)		
Neighborhood Hsg Servs Toledo	E	419 691-2900
Toledo (G-18081)		
Neighborhood Progress Inc	E	216 830-2770
Cleveland (G-6117)		
Northwestrn OH Community Action	C	419 784-2150
Defiance (G-10051)		

SIC SECTION

86 MEMBERSHIP ORGANIZATIONS

Occupational Health Link .... E 614 885-0039
  Columbus *(G-8312)*
Ohio Citizen Action .... E 216 861-5200
  Cleveland *(G-6189)*
Ohio Hrtland Cmnty Action Comm ..... E 740 387-1039
  Marion *(G-13569)*
Ohio Hrtland Cmnty Action Comm ..... E 419 468-5121
  Galion *(G-11303)*
Ohio Legal Rights Service .... E 614 466-7264
  Columbus *(G-8356)*
Orphan Foundation of America .... E 571 203-0270
  Beachwood *(G-1113)*
Phyllis Wheatley Assn Dev .... E 216 391-4443
  Cleveland *(G-6278)*
Pike Cnty Adult Activities Ctr .... E 740 947-7503
  Waverly *(G-18972)*
Pilot Dogs Incorporated .... E 614 221-6367
  Columbus *(G-8545)*
Playhouse Square Holdg Co LLC ...... E 216 771-4444
  Cleveland *(G-6287)*
Prevent Blindness - Ohio .... E 614 464-2020
  Columbus *(G-8558)*
Provider Services Inc .... E 614 888-2021
  Columbus *(G-8575)*
Randall R Leab .... E 330 689-6263
  Ashland *(G-693)*
REM-Ohio Inc .... E 440 986-3337
  South Amherst *(G-17074)*
Rosemary Center .... E 216 481-4823
  Euclid *(G-10774)*
Salvation Army .... E 330 762-8481
  Akron *(G-427)*
Salvation Army .... D 513 762-5600
  Cincinnati *(G-4475)*
Salvation Army .... D 614 252-7171
  Columbus *(G-8681)*
Salvation Army .... D 800 728-7825
  Columbus *(G-8682)*
Scioto Residential Services .... E 740 353-0288
  Portsmouth *(G-16308)*
Senior Independence .... D 330 873-3468
  Fairlawn *(G-10975)*
Shafer Confession .... E 419 399-4662
  Paulding *(G-15936)*
Sharon Twnship Frfighters Assn .... E 330 239-4992
  Sharon Center *(G-16878)*
Solidarity Health Network Inc .... E 216 831-1220
  Cleveland *(G-6494)*
St Jude Social Concern Hot .... D 440 365-7971
  Elyria *(G-10683)*
Tipp-Monroe Community Svcs Inc .... E 937 667-8631
  Tipp City *(G-17729)*
Tri-County Community Act .... E 740 385-6812
  Logan *(G-12991)*
United Labor Agency Inc .... C 216 664-3446
  Cleveland *(G-6641)*
United Methodist Community Ctr ...... E 330 743-5149
  Youngstown *(G-20398)*
United Rehabilitation Services .... D 937 233-1230
  Dayton *(G-9947)*
United Way Central Ohio Inc .... D 614 227-2700
  Columbus *(G-8904)*
United Way Greater Cleveland .... C 216 436-2100
  Cleveland *(G-6647)*
United Way Greater Stark Cnty .... E 330 491-0445
  Canton *(G-2573)*
United Way of Summit County .... E 330 762-7601
  Akron *(G-486)*
United Way of The Greater Dayt .... E 937 225-3060
  Dayton *(G-9949)*
University of Tledo Foundation .... E 419 530-7730
  Toledo *(G-18276)*
University Settlement Inc .... E 216 641-8948
  Cleveland *(G-6669)*
Urban League of Greater Southw ...... D 513 281-9955
  Cincinnati *(G-4787)*
W T C S A Headstart Niles Ctr .... E 330 652-0338
  Niles *(G-15309)*
Warren County Community Svcs ...... C 513 695-2100
  Lebanon *(G-12659)*
West Ohio Cmnty Action Partnr .... C 419 227-2586
  Lima *(G-12919)*
Wood County Ohio .... D 419 353-6914
  Bowling Green *(G-1803)*

84 MUSEUMS, ART GALLERIES, AND BOTANICAL AND ZOOLOGICAL GARDENS

8412 Museums & Art Galleries

Akron Art Museum .... D 330 376-9185
  Akron *(G-27)*
Anderson Twnship Hstorical Soc .... E 513 231-2114
  Cincinnati *(G-3026)*
Ark Foundation of Dayton .... E 937 256-2759
  Dayton *(G-9344)*
Arts and Exhibitions Intl LLC .... D 330 995-9300
  Streetsboro *(G-17407)*
Belpre Historical Society .... E 740 423-7588
  Belpre *(G-1433)*
Butler Institute of Amercn Art .... E 330 743-1711
  Youngstown *(G-20131)*
Chagrin Falls Historical Soc .... E 440 247-4695
  Chagrin Falls *(G-2691)*
Cincinnati Institute Fine Arts .... E 513 241-0343
  Cincinnati *(G-3313)*
▲ Cincinnati Museum Association ..... C 513 721-5204
  Cincinnati *(G-3318)*
Cincinnati Museum Center .... B 513 287-7000
  Cincinnati *(G-3319)*
Cleveland Hungarian Heritg Soc .... E 216 523-3900
  Cleveland *(G-5320)*
▲ Clevelnd Museum of Natural His .... A 216 231-4600
  Cleveland *(G-5359)*
▲ Columbus Museum of Art .... D 614 221-6801
  Columbus *(G-7372)*
Contemporary Arts Center .... E 513 721-0390
  Cincinnati *(G-3412)*
▲ Dayton Art Institute .... D 937 223-5277
  Dayton *(G-9460)*
Dayton History .... C 937 293-2841
  Dayton *(G-9478)*
▲ Dayton Society Natural History ...... D 937 275-7431
  Dayton *(G-9491)*
Dayton Society Natural History .... E 513 932-4421
  Oregonia *(G-15757)*
Delaware County Historical Soc .... D 740 369-3831
  Delaware *(G-10088)*
Deyor Performing Arts Center .... E 330 744-4269
  Youngstown *(G-20168)*
Dumouchelle Art Galleries .... E 419 255-7606
  Toledo *(G-17858)*
◆ Franklin County Historical Soc .... C 614 228-2674
  Columbus *(G-7695)*
▲ Great Lakes Mseum of Scnce Env ... C 216 694-2000
  Cleveland *(G-5690)*
Greater Andrson Premotes Peace ..... E 513 588-8391
  Cincinnati *(G-3705)*
Kingwood Center .... E 419 522-0211
  Mansfield *(G-13320)*
Lake Erie Nature & Science Ctr .... D 440 871-2900
  Bay Village *(G-1040)*
Lawrence Cnty Hstorical Museum ..... E 740 532-1222
  Ironton *(G-12296)*
Miami University .... C 513 529-2232
  Oxford *(G-15819)*
Miami University .... C 513 529-8380
  Oxford *(G-15820)*
▲ Museum Cntmprary Art Cleveland .. E 216 421-8671
  Cleveland *(G-6092)*
National Underground Railroad .... D 513 333-7500
  Cincinnati *(G-4142)*
New London Area Historical Soc .... D 419 929-3674
  New London *(G-15068)*
Norhteast Ohio Museum .... E 330 336-7657
  Medina *(G-14107)*
Ohio Historical Society .... C 614 297-2300
  Columbus *(G-8352)*
Rock and Roll of Fame and Muse ..... D 216 781-7625
  Cleveland *(G-6406)*
Rthrford B Hayes Prsdntial Ctr .... E 419 332-2081
  Fremont *(G-11217)*
Salem Historical Soc Museum .... E 330 337-6733
  Salem *(G-16715)*
Sauder Village .... B 419 446-2541
  Archbold *(G-644)*
Stan Hywet Hall and Grdns Inc .... D 330 836-5533
  Akron *(G-449)*
Stark Cnty Historical Soc Inc .... D 330 455-7043
  Canton *(G-2542)*
Taft Museum of Art .... E 513 241-0343
  Cincinnati *(G-4615)*
▲ Toledo Museum of Art .... E 419 255-8000
  Toledo *(G-18244)*

Toledo Science Center .... E 419 244-2674
  Toledo *(G-18248)*
Western Reserve Historical Soc .... D 330 666-3711
  Bath *(G-1036)*
Western Reserve Historical Soc .... D 216 721-5722
  Cleveland *(G-6744)*

8422 Arboreta, Botanical & Zoological Gardens

Akron Zoological Park .... E 330 375-2550
  Akron *(G-60)*
Animal Mgt Svcs Ohio Inc .... E 248 398-6533
  Port Clinton *(G-16237)*
Cleveland Metroparks .... C 216 661-6500
  Cleveland *(G-5326)*
Cleveland Metroparks .... C 216 661-6500
  Cleveland *(G-5329)*
Columbus Zoological Park Assn .... C 614 645-3400
  Powell *(G-16330)*
Dawes Arboretum .... E 740 323-2355
  Newark *(G-15164)*
Holden Arboretum .... D 440 946-4400
  Willoughby *(G-19670)*
Park Cincinnati Board .... E 513 421-4086
  Cincinnati *(G-4252)*
Stan Hywet Hall and Grdns Inc .... D 330 836-5533
  Akron *(G-449)*
Toledo Zoo .... E 419 385-5721
  Toledo *(G-18253)*
Toledo Zoological Society .... B 419 385-4040
  Toledo *(G-18254)*
▲ Zoological Society Cincinnati .... B 513 281-4700
  Cincinnati *(G-4874)*

86 MEMBERSHIP ORGANIZATIONS

8611 Business Associations

A Fox Construction .... E 614 506-1685
  Canal Winchester *(G-2150)*
American Jersey Cattle Assn .... E 614 861-3636
  Reynoldsburg *(G-16427)*
American Legion Post .... E 330 872-5475
  Newton Falls *(G-15272)*
Barberton Jaycees .... E 330 745-3733
  Barberton *(G-957)*
Blue Ash Business Association .... D 513 253-1006
  Cincinnati *(G-3116)*
Bnai Brith Hillel Fdn At Osu .... E 614 294-4797
  Columbus *(G-7121)*
Buckeye Power Inc .... E 614 781-0573
  Columbus *(G-7160)*
Builders Exchange Inc .... E 216 393-6300
  Cleveland *(G-5158)*
Canton Reg Cham of Comm Fdn ...... E 330 456-7253
  Canton *(G-2296)*
Canton Rgnal Chmber of Cmmerce ... E 330 456-7253
  Canton *(G-2297)*
Certified Angus Beef LLC .... D 330 345-2333
  Wooster *(G-19839)*
Certified Angus Beef LLC .... E 330 345-2333
  Wooster *(G-19840)*
Chamber Commerce New Carlisle .... E 937 845-3911
  New Carlisle *(G-15021)*
Cincinnati USA Rgional Chamber ..... D 513 579-3100
  Cincinnati *(G-3334)*
City of Circleville .... E 740 477-8255
  Circleville *(G-4883)*
City of Kenton .... E 419 674-4850
  Kenton *(G-12409)*
City of Louisville .... D 330 875-3321
  Louisville *(G-13006)*
City of Oberlin .... E 440 775-1531
  Oberlin *(G-15640)*
City of Toledo .... A 419 245-1001
  Toledo *(G-17808)*
City of Toledo .... D 419 245-1400
  Toledo *(G-17811)*
Consolidated Electric Coop Inc .... D 419 947-3055
  Mount Gilead *(G-14852)*
County of Montgomery .... E 937 225-4010
  Dayton *(G-9435)*
Dayton Area Chamber Commerce .... E 937 226-1444
  Dayton *(G-9459)*
Enon Firemans Association .... E 937 864-7429
  Enon *(G-10727)*
Greater Cleveland Partnership .... D 216 621-3300
  Cleveland *(G-5698)*
Greater Clvland Halthcare Assn .... D 216 696-6900
  Cleveland *(G-5701)*

Greater Columbus Chmbr Commrce ....E....... 614 221-1321
Columbus *(G-7774)*
Gs1 Us Inc ....D....... 609 620-0200
Dayton *(G-9592)*
Hecla Water Association ....E....... 740 533-0526
Ironton *(G-12290)*
▲ **Hirzel Canning Company** ....D....... 419 693-0531
Northwood *(G-15533)*
Home Bldrs Assn Grter Cncnnati ....D....... 513 851-6300
Cincinnati *(G-3777)*
In His Prsence Ministries Intl ....E....... 614 516-1812
Columbus *(G-7887)*
Interstate Contractors LLC ....E....... 513 372-5393
Mason *(G-13723)*
Longaberger Company ....D....... 740 349-8411
Newark *(G-15197)*
Mahoning Clmbana Training Assn ....E....... 330 747-5639
Youngstown *(G-20259)*
National Hot Rod Association ....C....... 740 928-5706
Hebron *(G-11858)*
New Waterford Fireman ....E....... 330 457-2363
New Waterford *(G-15139)*
Oak Harbor Lions Club ....E....... 419 898-3828
Oak Harbor *(G-15613)*
Odd Fellows Hall ....E....... 440 599-7973
Conneaut *(G-9045)*
Ohio Assn Pub Treasurers ....C....... 937 415-2237
Vandalia *(G-18691)*
Ohio Association Realtors Inc ....E....... 614 228-6675
Columbus *(G-8319)*
Ohio Biliffs Crt Officers Assn ....D....... 419 354-9302
Bowling Green *(G-1788)*
Ohio Chamber of Commerce Inc ....E....... 614 228-4201
Columbus *(G-8321)*
Ohio Civil Service Employees A ....D....... 614 865-4700
Westerville *(G-19337)*
Ohio Department of Commerce ....C....... 614 728-8400
Columbus *(G-8326)*
Ohio Farm Bur Federation Inc ....D....... 614 249-2400
Columbus *(G-8345)*
Ohio Rural Electric Coops Inc ....E....... 614 846-5757
Columbus *(G-8371)*
Ohio Utilities Protection Svc ....D....... 330 759-0050
Youngstown *(G-20310)*
Precision Metalforming Assn ....E....... 216 241-1482
Independence *(G-12245)*
Ross County YMCA ....D....... 740 772-4340
Chillicothe *(G-2882)*
Saint Mary Parish ....D....... 440 285-7051
Chardon *(G-2766)*
Service Corps Retired Execs ....E....... 216 522-4194
Cleveland *(G-6471)*
Service Corps Retired Execs ....E....... 419 259-7598
Toledo *(G-18180)*
Southeast Area Law Enforcement ....E....... 216 475-1234
Bedford *(G-1339)*
◆ **Superior Clay Corp** ....D....... 740 922-4122
Uhrichsville *(G-18492)*
Toledo Elec Jint Apprnticeship ....E....... 419 666-8088
Rossford *(G-16612)*
Town of Canal Fulton ....E....... 330 854-9448
Canal Fulton *(G-2147)*
Union Rural Electric Coop Inc ....E....... 937 642-1826
Marysville *(G-13657)*
United States Trotting Assn ....D....... 614 224-2291
Westerville *(G-19447)*
Universal Advertising Assoc ....E....... 513 522-5000
Cincinnati *(G-4746)*
Vigilant Global Trade Svcs LLC ....E....... 260 417-1825
Shaker Heights *(G-16871)*
Village of Antwerp ....E....... 419 258-7422
Antwerp *(G-621)*
Village of Versailles ....E....... 937 526-4191
Versailles *(G-18730)*
Waste Management Ohio Inc ....D....... 614 382-6342
Canal Winchester *(G-2177)*
Westfield Belden Village ....E....... 330 494-5490
Canton *(G-2586)*
Youngstown-Warren Reg Chamber ....E....... 330 744-2131
Youngstown *(G-20436)*

8621 Professional Membership Organizations

Aauw Action Fund Inc ....E....... 330 833-0520
Massillon *(G-13783)*
Akron Council of Engineering ....E....... 330 535-8835
Akron *(G-36)*
Alzheimers Disease and ....E....... 216 721-8457
Beachwood *(G-1050)*
American Ceramic Society ....E....... 614 890-4700
Westerville *(G-19284)*
American Cllege Crdlgy Fndtion ....E....... 614 442-5950
Dublin *(G-10246)*
American Heart Association Inc ....E....... 614 848-6676
Columbus *(G-6994)*
American Society For Nondstctv ....E....... 614 274-6003
Columbus *(G-7008)*
Association For Middle Lvl Edu ....E....... 614 895-4730
Westerville *(G-19366)*
Balanced Care Corporation ....E....... 330 908-1166
Northfield *(G-15509)*
Breathing Association ....E....... 614 457-4570
Columbus *(G-7132)*
Buckeye Assn Schl Admnstrators ....E....... 614 846-4080
Columbus *(G-7155)*
Center School Association ....D....... 440 995-7400
Mayfield Village *(G-14010)*
Central Hospital Services Inc ....D....... 216 696-6900
Cleveland *(G-5211)*
Chesapeake Research Review LLC ....E....... 410 884-2900
Cincinnati *(G-3240)*
Cincinnati Bar Association ....E....... 513 381-8213
Cincinnati *(G-3284)*
Columbus Bar Association ....E....... 614 221-4112
Columbus *(G-7333)*
Columbus Med Assn Foundation ....E....... 614 240-7420
Columbus *(G-7365)*
Columbus Medical Association ....E....... 614 240-7410
Columbus *(G-7366)*
Community Shelter Board ....E....... 614 221-9195
Columbus *(G-7410)*
Consortium For Hlthy & Immunzd ....D....... 216 201-2001
Cleveland *(G-5394)*
Dayton Anthem ....D....... 937 428-8000
Dayton *(G-9457)*
Deaconis Assocation Inc ....D....... 419 874-9008
Perrysburg *(G-15997)*
Detox Health Care Corp Ohio ....B....... 513 742-6310
Cincinnati *(G-3485)*
Dignity Health ....C....... 330 493-4443
Canton *(G-2341)*
Dnv GL Healthcare Usa Inc ....E....... 281 396-1610
Milford *(G-14517)*
Emergency Medical Transport ....D....... 330 484-4000
North Canton *(G-15334)*
Greater Cleveland Hosp Assn ....D....... 216 696-6900
Cleveland *(G-5697)*
Greiner Dental Association ....E....... 440 255-2600
Mentor *(G-14186)*
Health Collaborative ....D....... 513 618-3600
Cincinnati *(G-3753)*
Lakeside Association ....E....... 419 798-4461
Lakeside *(G-12464)*
Monroe County Association For ....E....... 740 472-1712
Woodsfield *(G-19817)*
Mount Carmel Health System ....E....... 614 898-4000
Westerville *(G-19428)*
National Ground Water Assn Inc ....E....... 614 898-7791
Westerville *(G-19429)*
Ohio Association of Foodbanks ....E....... 614 221-4336
Columbus *(G-8318)*
Ohio Department of Health ....C....... 614 466-1521
Columbus *(G-8328)*
Ohio Health Council ....D....... 614 221-7614
Columbus *(G-8349)*
Ohio Hospital Association ....D....... 614 221-7614
Columbus *(G-8353)*
Ohio School Psychologists Assn ....E....... 614 414-5980
Columbus *(G-8374)*
Ohio Soc of Crtif Pub Accntnts ....D....... 614 764-2727
Columbus *(G-8376)*
Ohio State Bar Association ....D....... 614 487-2050
Columbus *(G-8378)*
Ohio State Medical Association ....D....... 614 527-6762
Dublin *(G-10415)*
Orthodontic Association ....E....... 419 523-4014
Ottawa *(G-15801)*
Pain Net Inc ....D....... 614 481-5960
Columbus *(G-8509)*
Physician Hospital Alliance ....E....... 937 558-3456
Miamisburg *(G-14335)*
Resident Home Association ....D....... 937 278-0791
Dayton *(G-9850)*
Schulman Assocs Instl Review ....C....... 513 761-4100
Blue Ash *(G-1687)*
Society Plastics Engineers Inc ....C....... 419 287-4898
Pemberville *(G-15944)*
State of Ohio ....E....... 614 466-3834
Grove City *(G-11602)*
Union Hospital Association ....A....... 330 602-0719
Dover *(G-10220)*
Visiting Nurse Association ....E....... 216 931-1300
Cleveland *(G-6704)*
Warren Twnship Vlntr Fire Dept ....E....... 740 373-2424
Marietta *(G-13517)*
William I Notz ....E....... 614 292-3154
Columbus *(G-8995)*
Wingspan Care Group ....E....... 216 932-2800
Shaker Heights *(G-16872)*

8631 Labor Unions & Similar Organizations

Amalgamated Transit Union ....E....... 216 861-3350
Cleveland *(G-5001)*
American Federation of Gov ....E....... 513 861-6047
Cincinnati *(G-3004)*
American Federation of State ....E....... 937 461-9983
Dayton *(G-9329)*
Brotherhood of Locomotive Engi ....E....... 740 345-0978
Newark *(G-15150)*
C W A Local 4326 ....E....... 937 322-2227
Springfield *(G-17154)*
Cleveland Teachers Union Inc ....E....... 216 861-7676
Cleveland *(G-5351)*
Healthcare and Social ....E....... 614 461-1199
Columbus *(G-7812)*
Humaserve Hr LLC ....E....... 513 605-3522
Cincinnati *(G-3797)*
International Chem Wkrs Cr Un ....E....... 330 926-1444
Akron *(G-282)*
International Union United Au ....E....... 216 447-6080
Cleveland *(G-5832)*
International Union United Au ....D....... 513 897-4939
Waynesville *(G-18984)*
International Union United Au ....D....... 513 563-1252
Cincinnati *(G-3837)*
International Union United Au ....E....... 419 893-4677
Maumee *(G-13929)*
Internatl Un Oper Eng 18 ....E....... 216 432-3131
Cleveland *(G-5833)*
Interntional Assn Firefighters ....E....... 330 823-5222
Alliance *(G-541)*
Lake County Local Hazmat ....E....... 440 350-5499
Mentor *(G-14205)*
Licking Knox Labor Council ....D....... 740 345-1765
Newark *(G-15190)*
Local 911 United Mine Workers ....E....... 740 256-6083
Gallipolis *(G-11327)*
Local Union 856 Uaw Bldg Corp ....E....... 330 733-6231
Akron *(G-324)*
National Assn Ltr Carriers ....E....... 419 289-8359
Ashland *(G-691)*
National Assn Ltr Carriers ....D....... 419 693-8392
Northwood *(G-15538)*
Ohio Assn Pub Schl Employees ....E....... 614 890-4770
Columbus *(G-8317)*
Ohio Assn Pub Schl Employees ....D....... 937 253-5100
Dayton *(G-9279)*
Ohio Assn Pub Schl Employees ....D....... 330 659-7335
Richfield *(G-16520)*
Ohio Civil Service Employees A ....D....... 614 865-4700
Westerville *(G-19337)*
Ohio Education Association ....D....... 614 485-6000
Columbus *(G-8338)*
Ohio Education Association ....D....... 614 228-4526
Columbus *(G-8339)*
Ohio Lbrers Frnge Bneft Prgram ....E....... 614 898-9006
Westerville *(G-19432)*
Ohio Operating Engineers Apprn ....E....... 614 487-6531
Columbus *(G-8363)*
Pace International Union ....E....... 419 929-1335
New London *(G-15069)*
Pace International Union ....E....... 740 772-2038
Chillicothe *(G-2869)*
Pace International Union ....E....... 740 289-2368
Piketon *(G-16123)*
Painters District Council 6 ....E....... 440 239-4575
Cleveland *(G-6228)*
Painters Local Union 555 ....D....... 740 353-1431
Portsmouth *(G-16297)*
◆ **Smart** ....C....... 216 228-9400
North Olmsted *(G-15444)*
U S Dept of Labor Occupational ....E....... 216 447-4194
Independence *(G-12270)*
Union Cnstr Wkrs Hlth Plan ....E....... 419 248-2401
Holland *(G-12065)*
United Fd & Coml Wkrs Intl Un ....E....... 216 241-2828
Broadview Heights *(G-1894)*
United Fd Coml Wkrs Local 880 ....E....... 216 241-5930
Cleveland *(G-6638)*

United Food & Commercial Wkr............E....... 330 452-4850
Canton *(G-2567)*
United Food and Coml Wkrs..................D....... 937 665-0075
Dayton *(G-9946)*
United Food Comml Wrkrs Un...............E....... 614 235-3635
Columbus *(G-8890)*
United Steelworkers...............................E....... 740 772-5988
Chillicothe *(G-2893)*
United Steelworkers...............................C....... 740 928-0157
Newark *(G-15242)*
United Steelworkers...............................E....... 440 979-1050
North Olmsted *(G-15449)*
United Steelworkers...............................E....... 419 238-7980
Van Wert *(G-18645)*
United Steelworkers...............................E....... 740 633-0899
Martins Ferry *(G-13603)*
United Steelworkers...............................E....... 440 244-1358
Lorain *(G-13083)*
United Steelworkers...............................E....... 440 354-2328
Painesville *(G-15885)*
United Steelworkers...............................E....... 614 272-8609
Columbus *(G-8902)*
United Steelworkers...............................E....... 740 622-8860
Coshocton *(G-9120)*
United Steelworkers...............................E....... 513 793-0272
Cincinnati *(G-4740)*
United Steelworkers of America............C....... 330 493-7721
Canton *(G-2572)*

8641 Civic, Social & Fraternal Associations

2444 Mdson Rd Cndo Owners Assn......E....... 513 871-0100
Cincinnati *(G-2943)*
Aerie Frtnrl Order Egles 2875................E....... 419 433-4611
Huron *(G-12159)*
Akron Womans City Club Inc.................E....... 330 762-6261
Akron *(G-59)*
American Legion...................................D....... 330 488-0119
East Canton *(G-10502)*
American Legion...................................E....... 440 834-8621
Burton *(G-2059)*
American Legion Post...........................D....... 330 393-9858
Southington *(G-17104)*
Amvets Post No 6 Inc............................E....... 330 833-5935
Massillon *(G-13786)*
Belmont & Monroe Lodge 6 of...............E....... 740 695-2121
Saint Clairsville *(G-16619)*
Benevolent/Protectv Order Elks............E....... 440 357-6943
Painesville *(G-15836)*
Beta RHO House Assoc Kappa..............D....... 513 221-1280
Cincinnati *(G-3103)*
Beta Theta PI Fraternity.........................E....... 513 523-7591
Oxford *(G-15811)*
Bluffton Family Recreation....................E....... 419 358-6978
Bluffton *(G-1728)*
Bowling Green State University............D....... 419 372-2186
Bowling Green *(G-1768)*
Boy Scouts of America..........................E....... 513 961-2336
Cincinnati *(G-3128)*
Boys & Girls Club of Columbus.............E....... 614 221-8830
Columbus *(G-7127)*
Boys & Girls Club of Toledo..................E....... 419 241-4258
Toledo *(G-17780)*
Bpo Elks of USA...................................E....... 740 622-0794
Coshocton *(G-9089)*
Brandywine Master Assn.......................D....... 419 866-0135
Maumee *(G-13889)*
Buckeye Trils Girl Scout Cncil...............E....... 937 275-7601
Dayton *(G-9371)*
Burkhardt Springfield Neighbor.............E....... 937 252-7076
Dayton *(G-9374)*
Cafaro Co..E....... 330 652-6980
Niles *(G-15286)*
Catholic Association of The Di..............C....... 216 641-7575
Cleveland *(G-5188)*
Central Ohio Youth For Christ...............E....... 614 732-5260
Columbus *(G-7243)*
Change Healthcare Tech Enabled.........D....... 614 566-5861
Columbus *(G-7252)*
Chester West YMCA..............................E....... 513 779-3917
Liberty Township *(G-12718)*
Clearmount Elementary School.............E....... 330 497-5640
Canton *(G-2313)*
Cleveland Botanical Garden..................E....... 216 721-1600
Cleveland *(G-5292)*
Cleveland Heights Highschool...............E....... 216 691-5452
Cleveland *(G-5318)*
Cleveland Municipal School Dst............D....... 216 459-4200
Cleveland *(G-5334)*
Columbus Club Co................................E....... 614 224-4131
Columbus *(G-7339)*

Columbus Maennerchor..........................E....... 614 444-3531
Columbus *(G-7364)*
Commodore Denig Post No 83..............E....... 419 625-3274
Sandusky *(G-16743)*
Communities In Schools........................D....... 614 268-2472
Columbus *(G-7401)*
Community Action Columbiana CT........E....... 330 385-7251
East Liverpool *(G-10518)*
Community Mercy Foundation...............D....... 937 328-7000
Springfield *(G-17174)*
County of Cuyahoga..............................D....... 216 443-7265
Cleveland *(G-5428)*
County of Darke....................................E....... 937 526-4488
Versailles *(G-18725)*
Cuyahoga County AG Soc......................E....... 440 243-0090
Berea *(G-1454)*
Delta Gamma Fraternity.........................E....... 614 481-8169
Upper Arlington *(G-18549)*
Delta Gamma Fraternity.........................E....... 614 487-5599
Upper Arlington *(G-18550)*
Delta Kappa Gamma Society..................E....... 419 586-6016
Celina *(G-2645)*
Disabled American Veterans..................E....... 330 875-5795
Louisville *(G-13099)*
Disabled American Veterans..................B....... 419 526-0203
Mansfield *(G-13293)*
Disabled American Veterans..................B....... 330 364-1204
New Philadelphia *(G-15093)*
Disabled American Veterans..................B....... 740 367-7973
Cheshire *(G-2789)*
Division Drnking Ground Waters...........D....... 614 644-2752
Columbus *(G-7530)*
Easter Seals Nothern Ohio Inc...............C....... 440 324-6600
Lorain *(G-13036)*
EMs Rams Youth Dev Group Inc...........E....... 216 282-4688
Cleveland *(G-5538)*
Enon Firemans Association...................E....... 937 864-7429
Enon *(G-10727)*
Fairborn YMCA.....................................E....... 937 754-9622
Fairborn *(G-10796)*
Family Motor Coach Assn Inc................E....... 513 474-3622
Cincinnati *(G-3590)*
Family YMCA of LANcstr&fairfld...........D....... 740 277-7373
Lancaster *(G-12541)*
Farmersville Fire Assn Inc.....................E....... 937 696-2863
Farmersville *(G-10983)*
Fayette County Family YMCA................D....... 740 335-0477
Wshngtn CT Hs *(G-20021)*
Feldys..D....... 513 474-2212
Cincinnati *(G-3601)*
Findlay Y M C A Child Dev.....................E....... 419 422-3174
Findlay *(G-11031)*
Frans Child Care-Mansfield...................C....... 419 775-2500
Mansfield *(G-13304)*
Fraternal Order Eagles Inc....................E....... 330 477-8059
Canton *(G-2370)*
Fraternal Order Eagles Inc....................E....... 419 738-2582
Wapakoneta *(G-18795)*
Fraternal Order Eagles Inc....................E....... 419 332-3961
Fremont *(G-11200)*
Fraternal Order Eagles Inc....................E....... 440 293-5997
Andover *(G-612)*
Fraternal Order Eagles Inc....................E....... 614 883-2200
Grove City *(G-11563)*
Fraternal Order of Eagles......................E....... 937 323-0671
Springfield *(G-17200)*
Fraternal Order of Police of O...............D....... 614 224-5700
Columbus *(G-7700)*
Friends of Art For Cultural....................E....... 614 888-9929
Columbus *(G-7706)*
Galion Community Center YMCA...........E....... 419 468-7754
Galion *(G-11297)*
Gamma PHI Beta Sorority Alpha...........D....... 937 324-3436
Springfield *(G-17201)*
Geary Family YMCA Fostria..................E....... 419 435-6608
Fostoria *(G-11128)*
Genoa Legion Post 324..........................E....... 419 855-7049
Genoa *(G-11379)*
Girl Scouts Lake Erie Council................E....... 330 864-9933
Macedonia *(G-13199)*
Girl Scouts North East Ohio..................D....... 216 481-1313
Cleveland *(G-5673)*
Girl Scouts North East Ohio..................D....... 330 864-9933
Macedonia *(G-13200)*
Girl Scouts of The US Amer...................C....... 614 487-8101
Columbus *(G-7751)*
Girl Scouts of Western Ohio..................E....... 513 489-1025
Blue Ash *(G-1602)*
Girl Scuts Appleseed Ridge Inc.............E....... 419 225-4085
Lima *(G-12783)*

Girl Scuts Ohios Heartland Inc..............D....... 614 340-8820
Columbus *(G-7752)*
Girl Scuts Wstn Ohio Tledo Div..............E....... 419 243-8216
Toledo *(G-17916)*
Goldwood Primary School Pta...............E....... 440 356-6720
Rocky River *(G-16579)*
Goodwill Service Guild..........................E....... 513 771-4800
Cincinnati *(G-3687)*
Grand Aerie of The Fraternal.................E....... 614 883-2200
Grove City *(G-11566)*
Great Miami Valley YMCA......................D....... 513 217-5501
Middletown *(G-14479)*
Great Miami Valley YMCA......................D....... 513 887-0001
Hamilton *(G-11733)*
Great Miami Valley YMCA......................C....... 513 892-9622
Fairfield Township *(G-10930)*
Great Miami Valley YMCA......................E....... 513 867-0600
Hamilton *(G-11734)*
Great Miami Valley YMCA......................D....... 513 887-0014
Hamilton *(G-11735)*
Great Miami Valley YMCA......................D....... 513 868-9622
Hamilton *(G-11736)*
Great Miami Valley YMCA......................D....... 513 829-3091
Fairfield *(G-10854)*
Greater Cincinnati Cnvntn/Vstr..............E....... 513 621-2142
Cincinnati *(G-3707)*
Grove City Community Club..................E....... 614 875-6074
Grove City *(G-11567)*
Hamilton Lodge 93 Benevolant P..........E....... 513 887-4384
Liberty Twp *(G-12725)*
Hardin County Family YMCA..................E....... 419 673-6131
Kenton *(G-12416)*
Heart of OH Cncl Bsa............................E....... 419 522-8300
Mansfield *(G-13308)*
Help Foundation Inc..............................E....... 216 289-7710
Euclid *(G-10757)*
Hide-A-Way Hills Club...........................E....... 740 746-9589
Sugar Grove *(G-17541)*
Highland County Family YMCA..............E....... 937 840-9622
Hillsboro *(G-11978)*
Highland Relief Organization.................E....... 614 843-5152
Columbus *(G-7834)*
Huber Heights YMCA.............................D....... 937 236-9622
Dayton *(G-9623)*
Independence Foundation Inc...............C....... 330 296-2851
Ravenna *(G-16389)*
Independent Order Odd Fellows............E....... 740 548-5038
Lewis Center *(G-12689)*
Intercity Amateur Rdo CLB Inc..............E....... 419 989-3429
Ontario *(G-15693)*
International Assn Lions.......................E....... 740 986-6502
Williamsport *(G-19638)*
International Frat of Del........................E....... 330 922-5959
Cuyahoga Falls *(G-9196)*
International Ordr of Rnbow Fo..............E....... 419 862-3009
Elmore *(G-10588)*
International Un Elev Constrs...............C....... 614 291-5859
Columbus *(G-7918)*
Jewish Community Center Inc...............D....... 513 761-7500
Cincinnati *(G-3868)*
Joey Boyle..E....... 216 273-8317
Athens *(G-795)*
Junior Achvment Mhning Vly Inc...........E....... 330 539-5268
Girard *(G-11417)*
Kappa Kappa Gamma Foundation..........E....... 614 228-6515
Columbus *(G-7962)*
Kiwanis International Inc......................E....... 740 385-5887
Logan *(G-12982)*
Knights of Columbus.............................E....... 937 890-2971
Dayton *(G-9664)*
Knights of Columbus.............................E....... 419 628-2089
Minster *(G-14665)*
Knights of Columbus.............................D....... 740 382-3671
Marion *(G-13547)*
Lake County YMCA................................A....... 440 352-3303
Painesville *(G-15860)*
Lake County YMCA................................C....... 440 946-1160
Willoughby *(G-19680)*
Lake County YMCA................................E....... 440 259-2724
Perry *(G-15962)*
Lake County YMCA................................D....... 440 428-5125
Madison *(G-13227)*
Lake Mhawk Prperty Owners Assn........E....... 330 863-0000
Malvern *(G-13253)*
Lenau Park...E....... 440 235-2646
Olmsted Twp *(G-15677)*
Leo Yannenoff Jewish Community........C....... 614 231-2731
Columbus *(G-8052)*
Lima Family YMCA................................E....... 419 223-6045
Lima *(G-12821)*

S I C

Employee Codes: A=Over 500 employees, B=251-500
C=101-250, D=51-100, E=25-50
2018 Harris Ohio
Services Directory
1073

86 MEMBERSHIP ORGANIZATIONS

Lithuanian World Community .... E 513 542-0076
  Cincinnati *(G-3991)*
Louisville Frternal Order of E .... E 330 875-2113
  Louisville *(G-13102)*
Marion Family YMCA .... D 740 725-9622
  Marion *(G-13556)*
Maumee Lodge No 1850 Bnvlt .... E 419 893-7272
  Maumee *(G-13943)*
Mercy Health .... E 513 870-7008
  Fairfield *(G-10880)*
Miami Co YMCA Child Care .... E 937 778-5241
  Piqua *(G-16152)*
Miami County Park District .... E 937 335-6273
  Troy *(G-18365)*
Mills Creek Association .... E 440 327-5336
  North Ridgeville *(G-15471)*
Minature Society Cincinnati .... D 513 931-9708
  Cincinnati *(G-4102)*
Moose International Inc .... E 513 422-6776
  Middletown *(G-14441)*
Muirfield Association Inc .... E 614 889-0922
  Dublin *(G-10401)*
Natio Assoc For The Advan of .... E 330 782-9777
  Youngstown *(G-20295)*
Neighborhood Development Svcs .... E 330 296-2003
  Ravenna *(G-16393)*
New Boston Aerie 2271 FOE .... E 740 456-0171
  New Boston *(G-15012)*
New Pittsburgh Fire & Rescue F ...... E 330 264-1230
  Wooster *(G-19892)*
Norwich Elementary Pto .... E 614 921-6000
  Hilliard *(G-11938)*
O S U Faculty Club .... E 614 292-2262
  Columbus *(G-8309)*
Ohio Dept Amvet Svc Foundation .... D 614 431-6990
  Columbus *(G-8333)*
Ohio Masonic Retirement Vlg .... D 937 525-1743
  Springfield *(G-17256)*
Ohio Rver Vly Wtr Snttion Comm ..... E 513 231-7719
  Cincinnati *(G-4210)*
Ohio State Univ Alumni Assn .... D 614 292-2200
  Columbus *(G-8379)*
Ohio State University .... E 614 688-5721
  Columbus *(G-8423)*
Optimist International .... D 419 238-5086
  Van Wert *(G-18640)*
Order of Symposiarchs America ...... E 740 387-9713
  Marion *(G-13571)*
Order of Unite Commercial Tra .... D 614 487-9680
  Columbus *(G-8479)*
Orrville Boys and Girls Club .... E 330 683-4888
  Orrville *(G-15778)*
Owners Management .... E 440 439-3800
  Cleveland *(G-6222)*
Parks Recreation Division .... E 937 496-7135
  Dayton *(G-9803)*
Pike County YMCA .... E 740 947-8862
  Waverly *(G-18974)*
Polish American Citizens Club .... E 330 253-0496
  Akron *(G-395)*
Port Clnton Bpo Elks Ldge 1718 .... E 419 734-1900
  Port Clinton *(G-16251)*
Portsmouth Lodge 154 B P O E .... E 740 353-1013
  Portsmouth *(G-16299)*
Ross County YMCA .... D 740 772-4340
  Chillicothe *(G-2882)*
S R Restaurant Corp .... E 216 781-6784
  Cleveland *(G-6427)*
Salvation Army .... D 216 861-8185
  Cleveland *(G-6440)*
Salvation Army .... D 419 447-2252
  Tiffin *(G-17697)*
Sandusky Area YMCA Foundation ... E 419 621-9622
  Sandusky *(G-16790)*
Saxon House Condo .... D 440 333-8675
  Cleveland *(G-6445)*
Schlee Malt House Condo Assn ...... E 614 463-1999
  Columbus *(G-8695)*
Seneca County Firemens Assn .... D 419 447-7909
  Tiffin *(G-17699)*
Seven Hills Fireman Assn .... E 216 524-3321
  Seven Hills *(G-16836)*
Sidney-Shelby County YMCA .... E 937 492-9134
  Sidney *(G-16955)*
Sigma CHI Frat .... E 614 297-8783
  Columbus *(G-8730)*
Simon Knton Cncil Byscuts Amer .... E 614 436-7200
  Columbus *(G-8734)*
Springfield Family Y M C A .... D 937 323-3781
  Springfield *(G-17281)*

Springfield Little Tigers Foot .... D 330 549-2359
  Youngstown *(G-20380)*
Sycamore Board of Education .... D 513 489-3937
  Cincinnati *(G-4608)*
The For Cincinnati Association .... D 513 744-3344
  Cincinnati *(G-4641)*
The For National Association .... E 937 470-1059
  Dayton *(G-9925)*
The Nature Conservancy .... E 614 717-2770
  Dublin *(G-10476)*
Three Village Condominium .... E 440 461-1483
  Cleveland *(G-6597)*
Tiffin Cmnty YMCA Rcration Ctr .... D 419 447-8711
  Tiffin *(G-17704)*
Toledo Club .... D 419 243-2200
  Toledo *(G-18234)*
Towards Employment Inc .... E 216 696-5750
  Cleveland *(G-6607)*
Tusco Imaa Chapter No 602 .... E 330 878-7369
  Strasburg *(G-17401)*
Ucc Childrens Center .... E 513 217-5501
  Middletown *(G-14488)*
Union Club Company .... D 216 621-4230
  Cleveland *(G-6631)*
University Club Inc .... E 513 721-2600
  Cincinnati *(G-4749)*
University of Findlay .... C 419 434-4516
  Findlay *(G-11096)*
Urban Leagu of Greater Clevlnd ...... E 216 622-0999
  Cleveland *(G-6672)*
Vermilion Family YMCA .... E 440 967-4208
  Vermilion *(G-18720)*
Veterans Fgn Wars Post 2850 .... D 216 631-2585
  Cleveland *(G-6690)*
Vietnam Veterans America Inc .... E 330 877-6017
  Hartville *(G-11832)*
Village of Cuyahoga Heights .... C 216 641-7020
  Cleveland *(G-6697)*
Wapakoneta YMCA .... D 419 739-9622
  Wapakoneta *(G-18812)*
Wesley Community Center Inc .... E 937 263-3556
  Dayton *(G-9992)*
Western Rsrve Girl Scout Cncil .... E 330 864-9933
  Macedonia *(G-13218)*
Western Rsrve Land Conservancy .. E 440 729-9621
  Chagrin Falls *(G-2711)*
Whitehall Frmens Bnvlence Fund .... E 614 237-5478
  Columbus *(G-8989)*
Wolves Club Inc .... E 419 476-4418
  Toledo *(G-18313)*
Y M C A Central Stark County .... E 330 305-5437
  Canton *(G-2590)*
Y M C A Central Stark County .... E 330 875-1611
  Louisville *(G-13108)*
Y M C A Central Stark County .... E 330 877-8933
  Uniontown *(G-18545)*
Y M C A Central Stark County .... E 330 830-6275
  Massillon *(G-13862)*
Y M C A Central Stark County .... E 330 498-4082
  Canton *(G-2591)*
Y M C A of Ashland Ohio Inc .... E 419 289-0626
  Ashland *(G-709)*
YMCA .... E 330 823-1930
  Alliance *(G-566)*
YMCA Inc .... D 330 385-6400
  East Liverpool *(G-10536)*
YMCA of Ashtabula County Inc .... D 440 997-5321
  Ashtabula *(G-768)*
YMCA of Clermont County Inc .... E 513 724-9622
  Batavia *(G-1032)*
YMCA of Massillon .... E 330 837-5116
  Massillon *(G-13863)*
YMCA of Massillon .... E 330 879-0800
  Navarre *(G-14957)*
YMCA of Sandusky Ohio Inc .... E 419 621-9622
  Sandusky *(G-16811)*
York Rite .... E 216 751-1417
  Cleveland *(G-6772)*
Young Mens Christian .... E 513 791-5000
  Blue Ash *(G-1725)*
Young Mens Christian .... B 513 932-1424
  Lebanon *(G-12660)*
Young Mens Christian Assn .... E 419 332-9622
  Fremont *(G-11231)*
Young Mens Christian Assn .... C 330 744-8411
  Youngstown *(G-20421)*
Young Mens Christian Assn .... D 740 373-2250
  Marietta *(G-13520)*
Young Mens Christian Assn .... E 419 238-0443
  Van Wert *(G-18653)*

Young Mens Christian Assoc .... C 614 491-0980
  Lockbourne *(G-12963)*
Young Mens Christian Assoc .... C 614 871-9622
  Grove City *(G-11620)*
Young Mens Christian Assoc .... A 937 223-5201
  Dayton *(G-10009)*
Young Mens Christian Assoc .... D 330 923-5223
  Cuyahoga Falls *(G-9237)*
Young Mens Christian Assoc .... E 330 467-8366
  Macedonia *(G-13219)*
Young Mens Christian Assoc .... E 330 784-0408
  Akron *(G-515)*
Young Mens Christian Assoc .... D 740 477-1661
  Circleville *(G-4909)*
Young Mens Christian Assoc .... C 614 885-4252
  Columbus *(G-9017)*
Young Mens Christian Assoc .... E 330 724-1255
  Akron *(G-516)*
Young Mens Christian Assoc .... A 330 376-1335
  Akron *(G-517)*
Young Mens Christian Assoc .... C 614 416-9622
  Gahanna *(G-11276)*
Young Mens Christian Assoc .... C 740 881-1058
  Powell *(G-16355)*
Young Mens Christian Assoc .... C 614 334-9622
  Hilliard *(G-11967)*
Young Mens Christian Assoc .... E 937 312-1810
  Dayton *(G-10010)*
Young Mens Christian Assoc .... E 614 539-1770
  Urbancrest *(G-18609)*
Young Mens Christian Assoc .... D 614 276-8224
  Columbus *(G-9018)*
Young Mens Christian Assoc .... D 513 932-3756
  Oregonia *(G-15759)*
Young Mens Christian Assoc .... D 614 252-3166
  Columbus *(G-9019)*
Young Mens Christian Assoc .... D 937 426-9622
  Dayton *(G-10011)*
Young Mens Christian Assoc .... D 937 836-9622
  Englewood *(G-10725)*
Young Mens Christian Assoc .... D 419 523-5233
  Ottawa *(G-15805)*
Young Mens Christian Assoc .... E 937 228-9622
  Dayton *(G-10012)*
Young Mens Christian Assoc .... C 937 223-5201
  Springboro *(G-17144)*
Young Mens Christian Assoc .... E 614 878-7269
  Columbus *(G-9020)*
Young Mens Christian Assoc .... E 937 593-9001
  Bellefontaine *(G-1401)*
Young Mens Christian Assoc .... C 614 834-9622
  Canal Winchester *(G-2181)*
Young Mens Christian Assoc .... D 330 264-3131
  Wooster *(G-19936)*
Young Mens Christian Associat .... E 419 729-8135
  Toledo *(G-18320)*
Young Mens Christian Associat .... B 419 475-3496
  Toledo *(G-18321)*
Young Mens Christian Associat .... D 513 521-7112
  Cincinnati *(G-4865)*
Young Mens Christian Associat .... E 513 731-0115
  Cincinnati *(G-4866)*
Young Mens Christian Associat .... C 513 474-1400
  Cincinnati *(G-4867)*
Young Mens Christian Associat .... D 513 241-9622
  Cincinnati *(G-4868)*
Young Mens Christian Associat .... D 513 923-4466
  Cincinnati *(G-4869)*
Young Mens Christian Associat .... E 419 474-3995
  Toledo *(G-18322)*
Young Mens Christian Associat .... D 419 866-9622
  Maumee *(G-13997)*
Young Mens Christian Associat .... C 419 475-3496
  Toledo *(G-18323)*
Young Mens Christian Associat .... E 419 691-3523
  Oregon *(G-15756)*
Young Mens Christian Mt Vernon .... D 740 392-9622
  Mount Vernon *(G-14927)*
Young Mens Christian Assn Shelby .E 419 347-1312
  Shelby *(G-16904)*
Young MNS Christn Assn Findlay ... D 419 422-4424
  Findlay *(G-11102)*
Young MNS Chrstn Assn Clveland .. E 216 521-8400
  Lakewood *(G-12502)*
Young MNS Chrstn Assn Clveland .. E 216 941-4654
  Cleveland *(G-6773)*
Young MNS Chrstn Assn Clveland .. D 440 842-5200
  North Royalton *(G-15507)*
Young MNS Chrstn Assn Clveland .. E 216 731-7454
  Cleveland *(G-6774)*

87 ENGINEERING, ACCOUNTING, RESEARCH, MANAGEMENT, AND RELATED SERVICES

Young MNS Chrstn Assn Clveland ....D...... 216 382-4300
  Cleveland *(G-6775)*
Young MNS Chrstn Assn Clveland ....D...... 440 285-7543
  Chardon *(G-2780)*
Young MNS Chrstn Assn Clveland ....D...... 440 808-8150
  Westlake *(G-19569)*
Young MNS Chrstn Assn Grter NY ....D...... 740 392-9622
  Mount Vernon *(G-14928)*
Young Womens Christian ....D...... 937 461-5550
  Dayton *(G-10013)*
Young Womens Christian ....E...... 419 238-6639
  Van Wert *(G-18654)*
Young Womens Christian Assn ....D...... 614 224-9121
  Columbus *(G-9021)*
Young Womens Christian Assn ....E...... 330 746-6361
  Youngstown *(G-20422)*
Young Womens Christian Associ ....E...... 216 881-6878
  Cleveland *(G-6776)*
Young Womns Chrstn Assc Canton ....E...... 330 453-0789
  Canton *(G-2594)*
Young Womns Chrstn Assc Lima ....E...... 419 241-3230
  Toledo *(G-18326)*
Youngstown Club ....E...... 330 744-3111
  Youngstown *(G-20428)*
YWCA of Greater Cincinnati ....D...... 513 241-7090
  Cincinnati *(G-4870)*
YWCA of Hamilton ....E...... 513 856-9800
  Hamilton *(G-11785)*
YWCA Shelter & Housing Network ....E...... 937 222-6333
  Dayton *(G-10014)*

8651 Political Organizations

County of Richland ....E...... 419 774-5676
  Mansfield *(G-13278)*
Republican Headquarters ....E...... 330 343-6131
  Dover *(G-10209)*
Republican State Central Execu ....E...... 614 228-2481
  Columbus *(G-8616)*

8699 Membership Organizations, NEC

AAA Allied Group Inc ....B...... 513 762-3100
  Cincinnati *(G-2958)*
AAA Club Alliance Inc ....D...... 419 843-1200
  Toledo *(G-17736)*
AAA Miami Valley ....E...... 937 224-2896
  Dayton *(G-9300)*
AAA South Central Ohio Inc ....E...... 740 354-5614
  Portsmouth *(G-16262)*
Access Inc ....E...... 330 535-2999
  Akron *(G-16)*
Affinion Group LLC ....A...... 614 895-1803
  Westerville *(G-19360)*
Akron Automobile Association ....D...... 330 762-0631
  Akron *(G-28)*
Akron-Canton Regional Foodbank ....B...... 330 535-6900
  Akron *(G-61)*
American Motorcycle Assn ....D...... 614 856-1900
  Pickerington *(G-16083)*
Animal Protective League ....E...... 216 771-4616
  Cleveland *(G-5039)*
Ardmore Inc ....C...... 330 535-2601
  Akron *(G-81)*
Athletes In Action Sports ....D...... 937 352-1000
  Xenia *(G-20043)*
Auxiliary St Lukes Hospital ....E...... 419 893-5911
  Maumee *(G-13884)*
Beachwood Prof Fire Fighters C ....E...... 216 292-1968
  Beachwood *(G-1055)*
Belmont County of Ohio ....E...... 740 695-4708
  Saint Clairsville *(G-16621)*
Broken Arrow Inc ....E...... 419 562-3480
  Bucyrus *(G-2024)*
Brunswick Food Pantry Inc ....E...... 330 225-0395
  Brunswick *(G-1970)*
Buckeye Drag Racing Assn LLC ....E...... 419 562-0869
  Bucyrus *(G-2025)*
Carmen Steering Committee ....E...... 330 756-2066
  Navarre *(G-14954)*
Carol A & Ralp V H US B Fdn Tr ....E...... 513 632-4426
  Cincinnati *(G-3186)*
Center For Health Affairs ....D...... 800 362-2628
  Cleveland *(G-5208)*
Cincinnati Health Network Inc ....E...... 513 961-0600
  Cincinnati *(G-3309)*
Cincinnati Humn Relations Comm ....E...... 513 352-3237
  Cincinnati *(G-3310)*
City of Brunswick ....C...... 330 225-9144
  Brunswick *(G-1972)*
City of Compassion ....D...... 419 422-7800
  Findlay *(G-11013)*

Cliffs Cleveland Foundation ....E...... 216 694-5700
  Cleveland *(G-5360)*
Columbus Landmarks Foundation ....E...... 614 221-0227
  Columbus *(G-7362)*
Community Dev For All People ....E...... 614 445-7342
  Columbus *(G-7403)*
Conserv For Cyhg Vlly Nat Prk ....D...... 330 657-2909
  Peninsula *(G-15949)*
Council For Economic Opport ....D...... 216 476-3201
  Cleveland *(G-5413)*
County of Summit Board of Mntl ....A...... 330 634-8100
  Akron *(G-173)*
Dayton Society Natural History ....E...... 513 932-4421
  Oregonia *(G-15757)*
Downtown Akron Partnership Inc ....E...... 330 374-7676
  Akron *(G-199)*
East Akron Neighborhood Dev ....E...... 330 773-6838
  Akron *(G-205)*
Eastern Mumee Bay Arts Council ....E...... 419 690-5718
  Oregon *(G-15734)*
Elizabeths New Life Center Inc ....D...... 937 226-7414
  Dayton *(G-9523)*
Ethnic Voice of America ....E...... 440 845-0922
  Cleveland *(G-5552)*
First Capital Enterprises Inc ....D...... 740 773-2166
  Chillicothe *(G-2840)*
Franklin Cnty Bd Commissioners ....E...... 614 462-4360
  Columbus *(G-7689)*
Frazeysburg Lions Club Inc ....E...... 740 828-2313
  Frazeysburg *(G-11175)*
Gideons International ....E...... 513 932-2857
  Lebanon *(G-12607)*
Goodwill Inds Centl Ohio Inc ....E...... 740 439-7000
  Cambridge *(G-2116)*
Granger Township ....E...... 330 239-2111
  Medina *(G-14072)*
Greatr Columbus Conventn & Vis ....E...... 614 221-6623
  Columbus *(G-7776)*
Hadassah Dayton Chapter ....E...... 937 275-0227
  Dayton *(G-9595)*
Hamilton County Society ....E...... 513 541-6100
  Cincinnati *(G-3733)*
Heartbeats To City Inc ....E...... 330 452-4524
  Canton *(G-2397)*
Heights Emergency Food Center ....D...... 216 381-0707
  Cleveland *(G-5747)*
Knox Community Hosp Foundation ....E...... 740 393-9814
  Mount Vernon *(G-14903)*
Koinonia Homes Inc ....B...... 216 588-8777
  Cleveland *(G-5906)*
Kroger Co Foundation ....E...... 513 762-4000
  Cincinnati *(G-3947)*
Leo Yannenoff Jewish Community ....C...... 614 231-2731
  Columbus *(G-8052)*
Licking Valley Lions Club ....C...... 740 763-3733
  Newark *(G-15195)*
Loves Travel Stops ....D...... 419 837-0071
  Perrysburg *(G-16028)*
Loves Travel Stops ....E...... 937 325-2961
  Springfield *(G-17225)*
Marysville Food Pantry ....E...... 937 644-3248
  Marysville *(G-13635)*
Massillon Automobile Club ....E...... 330 833-1084
  Massillon *(G-13832)*
Nami of Preble County Ohio ....E...... 937 456-4947
  Eaton *(G-10570)*
Niles Historical Society ....D...... 330 544-2143
  Niles *(G-15299)*
Northast Ohio Sstnble Cmmnties ....D...... 216 410-7698
  Akron *(G-355)*
Oberlin College ....E...... 440 775-8500
  Oberlin *(G-15655)*
Ohio Academy of Science ....E...... 614 488-2228
  Columbus *(G-8316)*
Ohio Automobile Club ....C...... 614 431-7901
  Worthington *(G-19980)*
Ohio Federation of Soil and WA ....E...... 614 784-1900
  Reynoldsburg *(G-16472)*
Ohio School Boards Association ....E...... 614 540-4000
  Columbus *(G-8372)*
Ohio School Boards Association ....E...... 614 540-4000
  Columbus *(G-8373)*
Ottawa County Board M R D D ....E...... 419 734-6650
  Oak Harbor *(G-15614)*
Parma Community General Hosp ....B...... 440 743-4280
  Parma *(G-15913)*
Pepper Pike Club Company Inc ....D...... 216 831-9400
  Cleveland *(G-6263)*
Professnl Glfers Assn of Amer ....E...... 419 882-3197
  Sylvania *(G-17606)*

Recovery Center ....E...... 740 687-4500
  Lancaster *(G-12568)*
Ridgeville Community Choir ....E...... 419 267-3820
  Ridgeville Corners *(G-16545)*
Ronald McDonald Hse Grtr Cinci ....E...... 513 636-5591
  Cincinnati *(G-4440)*
Royal Arch Masons of Ohio ....E...... 419 762-5565
  Napoleon *(G-14949)*
Ruritan ....E...... 330 542-2308
  New Springfield *(G-15130)*
School Choice Ohio Inc ....E...... 614 223-1555
  Columbus *(G-8700)*
Seneca RE ADS Ind Fostoria Div ....C...... 419 435-0729
  Fostoria *(G-11140)*
Shoreby Club Inc ....D...... 216 851-2587
  Cleveland *(G-6479)*
Sons of Un Vtrans of Civil War ....D...... 740 992-6144
  Middleport *(G-14409)*
Sporty Events ....E...... 440 342-5046
  Chesterland *(G-2803)*
Team NEO ....E...... 216 363-5400
  Cleveland *(G-6576)*
United Sttes Bowl Congress Inc ....D...... 740 922-3120
  Uhrichsville *(G-18495)*
United Sttes Bowl Congress Inc ....D...... 513 761-3338
  Cincinnati *(G-4741)*
United Sttes Bowl Congress Inc ....D...... 419 531-4058
  Toledo *(G-18273)*
United Sttes Bowl Congress Inc ....D...... 440 327-0102
  North Ridgeville *(G-15478)*
United Sttes Bowl Congress Inc ....D...... 614 237-3716
  Columbus *(G-8903)*
University of Cincinnati ....C...... 513 556-4603
  Cincinnati *(G-4771)*
Volunteers of America NW Ohio ....E...... 419 248-3733
  Toledo *(G-18293)*
Womens Civic Club Grove City ....E...... 614 871-0145
  Grove City *(G-11618)*
Youngstown Neighborhood Dev ....E...... 330 480-0423
  Youngstown *(G-20432)*
Zanesville Welfare Organizatio ....E...... 740 450-6060
  Zanesville *(G-20559)*
Zoo Cincinnati ....D...... 513 961-0041
  Cincinnati *(G-4873)*

87 ENGINEERING, ACCOUNTING, RESEARCH, MANAGEMENT, AND RELATED SERVICES

8711 Engineering Services

7nt Enterprises LLC ....E...... 937 435-3200
  Dayton *(G-9295)*
ABB Inc ....E...... 440 585-7804
  Beachwood *(G-1045)*
ACC Automation Co Inc ....E...... 330 928-3821
  Akron *(G-15)*
Accelerant Technologies LLC ....D...... 419 236-8768
  Genoa *(G-11374)*
Acpi Systems Inc ....E...... 513 738-3840
  Cincinnati *(G-2968)*
Adaptive Corporation ....E...... 440 257-7460
  Hudson *(G-12101)*
▲ Advanced Design Industries Inc ....E...... 440 277-4141
  Sheffield Village *(G-16883)*
Advanced Engrg Solutions Inc ....D...... 937 743-6900
  Springboro *(G-17113)*
Advantage Aerotech Inc ....E...... 614 759-8329
  Columbus *(G-6947)*
Aecom ....D...... 330 253-9741
  Cleveland *(G-4961)*
Aecom Energy & Cnstr Inc ....D...... 216 523-5600
  Cleveland *(G-4965)*
Aecom Global II LLC ....E...... 937 233-1230
  Dayton *(G-9311)*
Aecom Global II LLC ....E...... 216 523-5600
  Cleveland *(G-4966)*
Aecom Technical Services Inc ....E...... 937 233-1898
  Batavia *(G-994)*
Airgas Usa LLC ....C...... 440 232-1590
  Cleveland *(G-4977)*
Alexander & Associates Co ....C...... 513 731-7800
  Cincinnati *(G-2983)*
▲ Alfons Haar Inc ....E...... 937 560-2031
  Springboro *(G-17114)*
Alphaport Inc ....E...... 216 619-2400
  Cleveland *(G-4997)*
Alstom Grid LLC ....D...... 330 688-4061
  Stow *(G-17352)*

Employee Codes: A=Over 500 employees, B=251-500
C=101-250, D=51-100, E=25-50

87 ENGINEERING, ACCOUNTING, RESEARCH, MANAGEMENT, AND RELATED SERVICES

Company		Phone
Alt & Witzig Engineering Inc West Chester *(G-19018)*	E	513 777-9890
Amec Fstr Whlr Envrnmnt Infrst Blue Ash *(G-1531)*	E	513 489-6611
▲ American Electric Pwr Svc Corp Columbus *(G-6990)*	B	614 716-1000
American Rock Mechanics Inc Twinsburg *(G-18390)*	E	330 963-0550
Amg Inc Dayton *(G-9335)*	E	937 260-4646
Ann Corbett Design Inc Cambridge *(G-2095)*	E	740 432-2969
Aptim Corp Cincinnati *(G-3038)*	E	513 782-4700
Arcadis US Inc Akron *(G-80)*	D	330 434-1995
Atc Group Services LLC Cincinnati *(G-3056)*	D	513 771-2112
Austin Building and Design Inc Cleveland *(G-5081)*	C	440 544-2600
Avid Technologies Inc Twinsburg *(G-18395)*	E	330 487-0770
Azimuth Corporation Beavercreek Township *(G-1265)*	E	937 256-8571
B&N Coal Inc Dexter City *(G-10170)*	E	740 783-3575
Barr Engineering Incorporated Columbus *(G-7091)*	E	614 714-0299
Bayer & Becker Inc Mason *(G-13667)*	E	513 492-7401
BBC&m Engineering Inc Dublin *(G-10259)*	D	614 793-2226
Bbs Professional Corporation Columbus *(G-7095)*	E	614 888-3100
Belcan LLC Blue Ash *(G-1538)*	A	513 891-0972
Belcan Corporation Cincinnati *(G-3095)*	C	513 277-3100
Belcan Engineering Group LLC Blue Ash *(G-1540)*	A	513 891-0972
◆ Bendix Coml Vhcl Systems LLC Elyria *(G-10597)*	B	440 329-9000
Bertec Corporation Columbus *(G-7102)*	E	614 543-0962
BHF Incorporated Scio *(G-16816)*	E	740 945-6410
Black & Veatch Corporation Columbus *(G-7115)*	E	614 473-0921
Boeing Company Wright Patterson Afb *(G-20012)*	B	937 431-3503
Booz Allen Hamilton Inc Beavercreek *(G-1154)*	E	937 429-5580
Boral Resources LLC Coshocton *(G-9088)*	D	740 622-8042
Bowen Engineering Corporation Columbus *(G-7125)*	C	614 536-0273
Bramhall Engrg & Surveying Co Avon *(G-881)*	E	440 934-7878
Brewer-Garrett Co Middleburg Heights *(G-14378)*	C	440 243-3535
Brilligent Solutions Inc Fairborn *(G-10785)*	E	937 879-4148
Brown and Caldwell Dublin *(G-10270)*	E	614 410-6144
Brumbaugh Engrg Surveying LLC West Milton *(G-19268)*	E	937 698-3000
BSI Engineering LLC Cincinnati *(G-3145)*	C	513 201-3100
Burgess & Niple Inc Columbus *(G-7169)*	B	502 254-2344
Burgess & Niple Inc Painesville *(G-15837)*	D	440 354-9700
Burgess & Niple Inc Cincinnati *(G-3149)*	C	513 579-0042
Burgess & Niple / Heapy Engine Holland *(G-7170)*	D	614 459-2050
Butler County of Ohio Hamilton *(G-11703)*	D	513 867-5744
Camgen Ltd Canal Winchester *(G-2154)*	E	330 204-8636
Capano & Associates LLC Liberty Township *(G-12717)*	E	513 403-6000
Cbc Engineers & Associates Ltd Dayton *(G-9391)*	E	937 428-6150
CDM Smith Inc Piketon *(G-16110)*	E	740 897-2937
Cec Combustion Safety LLC Brookpark *(G-1938)*	E	216 749-2992
Ceso Inc Miamisburg *(G-14281)*	D	937 435-8584
Cetek Ltd Cleveland *(G-5220)*	E	216 362-3900
Cgh-Global Emerg Mngmt Strateg Cincinnati *(G-2905)*	E	800 376-0655
Ch2m Hill Inc Cincinnati *(G-3226)*	D	513 243-5070
Ch2m Hill Inc Columbus *(G-7249)*	E	614 888-3100
Ch2m Hill Constructors Inc Dayton *(G-9395)*	E	937 228-4285
Cha Consulting Inc Cleveland *(G-5224)*	C	216 443-1700
Chemstress Consultant Company Akron *(G-130)*	C	330 535-5591
Chipmatic Tool & Machine Inc Elmore *(G-10587)*	D	419 862-2737
Choice One Engineering Corp Sidney *(G-16919)*	E	937 497-0200
Circle Prime Manufacturing Cuyahoga Falls *(G-9172)*	E	330 923-0019
Circuits & Cables Inc Vandalia *(G-18671)*	E	937 415-2070
City of Akron Akron *(G-142)*	D	330 375-2355
City of Delphos Delphos *(G-10138)*	E	419 695-4010
City of Sandusky Sandusky *(G-16738)*	D	419 627-5829
City of Toledo Toledo *(G-17813)*	D	419 936-2275
Civil & Environmental Cons Inc Milford *(G-14512)*	E	513 985-0226
Clarkdietrich Engineering Serv West Chester *(G-19044)*	D	513 870-1100
Clear Vision Engineering LLC Toledo *(G-17816)*	E	419 478-7151
Cmta Inc Cincinnati *(G-3373)*	C	502 326-3085
Coal Services Inc Powhatan Point *(G-16356)*	D	740 795-5220
Control Concepts & Design Inc West Chester *(G-19051)*	D	513 771-7271
▼ Corrpro Companies Inc Medina *(G-14052)*	E	330 723-5082
County Engineering Office Fremont *(G-11189)*	E	419 334-9731
County Engineers Office Chillicothe *(G-2829)*	E	740 702-3130
County of Athens Athens *(G-780)*	E	740 593-5514
County of Brown Georgetown *(G-11390)*	E	937 378-6456
County of Champaign Urbana *(G-18584)*	E	937 653-4848
County of Coshocton Coshocton *(G-9099)*	E	740 622-2135
County of Crawford Bucyrus *(G-2034)*	E	419 562-7731
County of Delaware Delaware *(G-10083)*	D	740 833-2400
County of Erie Sandusky *(G-16749)*	E	419 627-7710
County of Fayette Wshngtn CT Hs *(G-20017)*	E	740 335-1541
County of Fulton Wauseon *(G-18949)*	E	419 335-3816
County of Gallia Gallipolis *(G-11313)*	E	740 446-4009
County of Hamilton Cincinnati *(G-3430)*	D	513 946-4250
County of Hancock Findlay *(G-11018)*	E	419 422-7433
County of Lorain Elyria *(G-10612)*	E	440 326-5884
County of Lucas Holland *(G-12016)*	D	419 213-2892
County of Madison London *(G-12996)*	E	740 852-9404
County of Montgomery Dayton *(G-9433)*	E	937 854-4576
County of Perry New Lexington *(G-15054)*	E	740 342-2191
County of Portage Ravenna *(G-16379)*	D	330 296-6411
County of Richland Mansfield *(G-13283)*	E	419 774-5591
County of Stark Canton *(G-2324)*	C	330 477-6781
County of Summit Akron *(G-170)*	C	330 643-2850
County of Union Marysville *(G-13612)*	E	937 645-3018
County of Washington Marietta *(G-13438)*	E	740 376-7430
County of Wayne Wooster *(G-19858)*	D	330 287-5500
Crowne Group LLC Cleveland *(G-5440)*	D	216 589-0198
CT Consultants Inc Blue Ash *(G-1573)*	E	513 791-1700
CT Consultants Inc Mentor *(G-14166)*	C	440 951-9000
Ctl Engineering Inc Columbus *(G-7474)*	C	614 276-8123
Curtiss-Wright Controls Fairborn *(G-10789)*	E	937 252-5601
Custom Materials Inc Chagrin Falls *(G-2713)*	D	440 543-8284
Cuyahoga County Cleveland *(G-5453)*	A	216 348-3800
Denmark Consultants Inc Blue Ash *(G-1576)*	E	513 530-9984
Design Homes & Development Co Dayton *(G-9499)*	E	937 438-3667
Design Knowledge Company Beavercreek *(G-1168)*	E	937 320-9244
Deskey Associates Inc Cincinnati *(G-3484)*	D	513 721-6800
Dillin Engineered Systems Corp Perrysburg *(G-15998)*	E	419 666-6789
Dizer Corp Painesville *(G-15851)*	E	440 368-0200
Dj Neff Enterpeises Inc Cleveland *(G-5494)*	E	440 884-3100
Dkmp Consulting Inc Plain City *(G-16187)*	C	614 733-0979
Dlhbowles Inc Canton *(G-2342)*	B	330 478-2503
Dlr Group Inc Cleveland *(G-5495)*	D	216 522-1350
Dlz American Drilling Inc Columbus *(G-7532)*	E	614 888-0040
Dlz Construction Services Inc Columbus *(G-7533)*	E	614 888-0040
Dlz National Inc Columbus *(G-7534)*	E	614 888-0040
Dlz Ohio Inc Columbus *(G-7535)*	C	614 888-0040
Dlz Ohio Inc Akron *(G-195)*	E	330 923-0401
Donald E Didion II Bellevue *(G-1408)*	E	419 483-2226
Dynamix Engineering Ltd Columbus *(G-7557)*	D	614 443-1178
Dynotec Inc Columbus *(G-7558)*	E	614 880-7320
E & A Pedco Services Inc Cincinnati *(G-3519)*	E	513 782-4920
E P Ferris & Associates Inc Columbus *(G-7560)*	E	614 299-2999
Earl Twinam Portsmouth *(G-16277)*	E	740 820-2654
Early Construction Co South Point *(G-17085)*	E	740 894-5150
Eaton-Aeroquip Llc Maumee *(G-13907)*	D	419 891-7775
Electrol Systems Inc Cincinnati *(G-3548)*	E	513 942-7777
Electrovations Inc Aurora *(G-837)*	E	330 274-3558
Emersion Design LLC Cincinnati *(G-3553)*	E	513 841-9100
Emerson Process MGT Lllp Columbus *(G-6881)*	E	877 468-6384
◆ Emh Inc Valley City *(G-18617)*	E	330 220-8600
Engineering Associates Inc Wooster *(G-19862)*	E	330 345-6556
Engineering Design and Testing Cleveland *(G-5541)*	D	440 239-0362
Engisystems Inc Mason *(G-13699)*	D	513 229-8860
▲ Enprotech Industrial Tech LLC Cleveland *(G-5542)*	C	216 883-3220
Environmental Quality MGT Cincinnati *(G-3562)*	D	513 825-7500
Essig Research Inc West Chester *(G-19198)*	E	513 942-7100
Euthenics Inc Strongsville *(G-17462)*	E	440 260-1555

SIC SECTION — 87 ENGINEERING, ACCOUNTING, RESEARCH, MANAGEMENT, AND RELATED SERVICES

- Evans Mechwart Ham .... B 614 775-4500
  New Albany (G-14984)
- Fed/Matrix A Joint Venture LLC .... E 863 665-6363
  Dayton (G-9542)
- Feller Finch & Associates Inc .... E 419 893-3680
  Maumee (G-13916)
- Fishbeck Thmpson Carr Hber Inc .... E 513 469-2370
  Blue Ash (G-1596)
- Fishel Company .... D 614 850-4400
  Columbus (G-7669)
- Fishel Company .... D 614 274-8100
  Columbus (G-7667)
- Forte Indus Eqp Systems Inc .... E 513 398-2800
  Mason (G-13703)
- Fosdick & Hilmer Inc .... D 513 241-5640
  Cincinnati (G-3641)
- Frontier Technology Inc .... E 937 429-3302
  Beavercreek Township (G-1269)
- Futura Design Service Inc .... E 937 890-5252
  Dayton (G-9565)
- G Herschman Architects Inc .... D 216 223-3200
  Cleveland (G-5645)
- Gannett Fleming Inc .... E 614 794-9424
  Westerville (G-19402)
- Garmann/Miller & Assoc Inc .... E 419 628-4240
  Minster (G-14662)
- Gbc Design Inc .... E 330 283-6870
  Akron (G-233)
- GE Aviation Systems LLC .... D 937 474-9397
  Dayton (G-9568)
- GE Aviation Systems LLC .... B 937 898-5881
  Vandalia (G-18681)
- General Electric Intl Inc .... C 617 443-0000
  Cincinnati (G-3673)
- Global Military Expert Co .... E 800 738-9795
  Beavercreek (G-1242)
- Global Risk Consultants Corp .... E 440 746-8861
  Brecksville (G-1825)
- Glowe-Smith Industrial Inc .... C 330 638-5088
  Vienna (G-18737)
- Greene County .... E 937 562-7500
  Xenia (G-20054)
- Gus Perdikakis Associates .... D 513 583-0900
  Cincinnati (G-3721)
- ▲ Hamilton Manufacturing Corp .... E 419 867-4858
  Holland (G-12026)
- Hammontree & Associates Ltd .... E 330 499-8817
  Canton (G-2390)
- Hardy Diagnostics .... D 937 550-2768
  Springboro (G-17121)
- Hawa Incorporated .... E 614 451-1711
  Columbus (G-7803)
- HDR Engineering Inc .... E 614 839-5770
  Columbus (G-7807)
- Heery International Inc .... E 216 781-1313
  Cleveland (G-5746)
- Henningson Drham Richardson PC .... D 513 984-7500
  Blue Ash (G-1610)
- High Voltage Maintenance Corp .... E 937 278-0811
  Dayton (G-9611)
- HJ Ford Associates Inc .... C 937 429-9711
  Beavercreek (G-1176)
- Hlg Engineering & Survey Inc .... E 614 760-8320
  Dublin (G-10363)
- Hntb Corporation .... E 216 522-1140
  Cleveland (G-5763)
- Hockaden & Associates Inc .... E 614 252-0993
  Columbus (G-7843)
- Hokuto USA Inc .... E 614 782-6200
  Grove City (G-11570)
- Honeywell International Inc .... D 937 484-2261
  Urbana (G-18591)
- Horn Electric Company .... E 330 364-7784
  Dover (G-10192)
- HP Inc .... E 513 983-2817
  Cincinnati (G-3791)
- Hull & Associates Inc .... E 614 793-8777
  Dublin (G-10367)
- Hull & Associates Inc .... E 419 385-2018
  Toledo (G-17965)
- ▲ Hunter Defense Tech Inc .... E 216 438-6111
  Solon (G-17016)
- HWH Archtcts-Ngnrs-Plnners Inc .... D 216 875-4000
  Cleveland (G-5794)
- ▲ Hydro-Dyne Inc .... E 330 832-5076
  Massillon (G-13821)
- I T E LLC .... D 513 576-6200
  Loveland (G-13132)
- Icr Inc .... D 513 900-7007
  Mason (G-13718)
- Iet Inc .... E 419 385-1233
  Toledo (G-17969)
- Ijus LLC .... D 614 470-9882
  Gahanna (G-11248)
- Industrial Origami Inc .... E 440 260-0000
  Cleveland (G-5817)
- Infoscitex Corporation .... E 937 429-9008
  Beavercreek Township (G-1270)
- Innovative Controls Corp .... D 419 691-6684
  Toledo (G-17974)
- Innovtive Sltons Unlimited LLC .... E 740 289-3282
  Piketon (G-16118)
- Innovtive Sltons Unlimited LLC .... D 740 289-3282
  Piketon (G-16119)
- Intren Inc .... E 815 482-0651
  Cincinnati (G-3841)
- Invotec Engineering Inc .... D 937 886-3232
  Miamisburg (G-14307)
- J R Johnson Engineering Inc .... E 440 234-9972
  Cleveland (G-5842)
- Jack A Hamilton & Assoc Inc .... E 740 968-4947
  Flushing (G-11105)
- Jacobs Constructors Inc .... E 419 226-1344
  Lima (G-12806)
- Jacobs Engineering Group Inc .... E 513 595-7500
  Cincinnati (G-3855)
- Jacobs Engineering Group Inc .... D 513 595-7500
  Cincinnati (G-3856)
- Jacobs Technology Inc .... E 937 429-5056
  Beavercreek Township (G-1271)
- Jdi Group Inc .... D 419 725-7161
  Maumee (G-13930)
- Jdrm Engineering Inc .... E 419 824-2400
  Sylvania (G-17595)
- Jedson Engineering Inc .... D 513 965-5999
  Cincinnati (G-3865)
- Jetson Engineering .... E 513 965-5999
  Cincinnati (G-3867)
- Jjr Solutions LLC .... E 937 912-0288
  Beavercreek (G-1180)
- Jobes Henderson & Assoc Inc .... E 740 344-5451
  Newark (G-15178)
- Johnson Mirmiran Thompson Inc .... D 614 714-0270
  Columbus (G-7944)
- Johnson Mirmiran Thompson Inc .... E 614 714-0270
  Blue Ash (G-1620)
- Johnson Mirmiran Thompson Inc .... E 614 714-0270
  Columbus (G-7945)
- Johnson Mirmiran Thompson Inc .... E 614 714-0270
  Cleveland (G-5869)
- Jones & Henry Engineers Ltd .... D 419 473-9611
  Toledo (G-17986)
- Juice Technologies Inc .... E 800 518-5576
  Columbus (G-7957)
- K&K Technical Group Inc .... C 513 202-1300
  Harrison (G-11804)
- Karpinski Engineering Inc .... E 614 430-9820
  Columbus (G-6891)
- Karpinski Engineering Inc .... D 216 391-3700
  Cleveland (G-5886)
- Kemron Environmental Svcs Inc .... D 740 373-4071
  Marietta (G-13460)
- ▲ Kendall Holdings Ltd .... E 614 486-4750
  Columbus (G-7976)
- ◆ Keuchel & Associates Inc .... E 330 945-9455
  Cuyahoga Falls (G-9202)
- Kevin Kennedy Associates Inc .... E 317 536-7000
  Columbus (G-7982)
- Keyw Corporation .... E 937 702-9512
  Beavercreek (G-1182)
- Kleingers Group Inc .... D 614 882-4311
  Westerville (G-19319)
- Kleingers Group Inc .... D 513 779-7851
  West Chester (G-19103)
- Knox County Engineer .... E 740 397-1590
  Mount Vernon (G-14905)
- KS Associates Inc .... D 440 365-4730
  Elyria (G-10639)
- Kucera International Inc .... D 440 975-4230
  Willoughby (G-19678)
- KZF Bwsc Joint Venture .... E 513 621-6211
  Cincinnati (G-3951)
- KZF Design Inc .... D 513 621-6211
  Cincinnati (G-3952)
- L R G Inc .... E 937 890-0510
  Dayton (G-9668)
- L&T Technology Services Ltd .... E 732 688-4402
  Dublin (G-9678)
- L-3 Cmmncations Nova Engrg Inc .... C 877 282-1168
  Mason (G-13730)
- L3 Aviation Products Inc .... D 614 825-2001
  Columbus (G-8025)
- Land Design Consultants .... E 440 255-8463
  Mentor (G-14207)
- Leidos Engineering LLC .... D 330 405-9810
  Twinsburg (G-18441)
- LEWaro-D&j-A Joint Venture Co .... E 937 443-0000
  Dayton (G-9678)
- Lockheed Martin Corporation .... C 937 429-0100
  Beavercreek (G-1188)
- Logan County Engineering Off .... E 937 592-2791
  Bellefontaine (G-1386)
- Los Alamos Technical Assoc Inc .... E 614 508-1200
  Westerville (G-19420)
- Louis Perry & Associates Inc .... C 330 334-1585
  Wadsworth (G-18762)
- LSI Adl Techonology LLC .... E 614 345-9040
  Columbus (G-8084)
- M Consultants LLC .... D 614 839-4639
  Westerville (G-19421)
- M Retail Engineering Inc .... E 614 818-2323
  Westerville (G-19422)
- M-E Companies Inc .... D 614 818-4900
  Westerville (G-19423)
- M-E Companies Inc .... E 513 942-3141
  Cincinnati (G-4007)
- Macaulay-Brown Inc .... B 937 426-3421
  Beavercreek (G-1251)
- Macdonald Mott LLC .... E 216 535-3640
  Cleveland (G-5963)
- Mahoning County .... C 330 799-1581
  Youngstown (G-20261)
- Majidzadeh Enterprises Inc .... E 614 823-4949
  Columbus (G-8101)
- Mannik & Smith Group Inc .... C 419 891-2222
  Maumee (G-13938)
- Mannik & Smith Group Inc .... E 740 942-4222
  Cadiz (G-2079)
- Manufacturing Services Intl .... E 937 299-9922
  Dayton (G-9697)
- Matrix Research Inc .... E 937 427-8433
  Beavercreek (G-1190)
- ▲ Maval Industries LLC .... C 330 405-1600
  Twinsburg (G-18445)
- McGill Smith Punshon Inc .... E 513 759-0004
  Cincinnati (G-4036)
- Mechanical Support Svcs Inc .... E 614 777-8808
  Hilliard (G-11927)
- Medina County Sanitary .... E 330 273-3610
  Medina (G-14098)
- Metamateria Partners LLC .... E 614 340-1690
  Columbus (G-8153)
- Metcalf & Eddy Inc .... E 216 910-2000
  Cleveland (G-6033)
- Michael Baker Intl Inc .... D 330 453-3110
  Canton (G-2461)
- Michael Baker Intl Inc .... E 412 269-6300
  Cleveland (G-6046)
- Michael Baker Intl Inc .... E 614 418-1773
  Columbus (G-8158)
- Michael Benza and Assoc Inc .... E 440 526-4206
  Brecksville (G-1834)
- ▲ Micro Industries Corporation .... D 740 548-7878
  Westerville (G-19424)
- Mid-Ohio Electric Co .... E 614 274-8000
  Columbus (G-8165)
- Middough Inc .... B 216 367-6000
  Cleveland (G-6054)
- Mistras Group Inc .... D 419 836-5904
  Millbury (G-14580)
- Mistras Group Inc .... D 330 244-1541
  North Canton (G-15356)
- Modal Shop Inc .... D 513 351-9919
  Cincinnati (G-4111)
- Modern Tech Solutions Inc .... D 937 426-9025
  Beavercreek Township (G-1275)
- Moody-Nolan Inc .... E 614 461-4664
  Columbus (G-8187)
- Morris Technologies Inc .... C 513 733-1611
  Cincinnati (G-4119)
- Ms Consultants Inc .... C 330 744-5321
  Youngstown (G-20291)
- Ms Consultants Inc .... C 614 898-7100
  Columbus (G-8203)
- Ms Consultants Inc .... E 216 522-1926
  Cleveland (G-6086)
- Muskingum County Ohio .... E 740 453-0381
  Zanesville (G-20508)
- Natural Resources Ohio Dept .... E 614 265-6948
  Columbus (G-8249)

Employee Codes: A=Over 500 employees, B=251-500
C=101-250, D=51-100, E=25-50

87 ENGINEERING, ACCOUNTING, RESEARCH, MANAGEMENT, AND RELATED SERVICES

Neteam Systems LLC ....E 330 523-5100
  Cleveland (G-6121)
Neundorfer Inc ....E 440 942-8990
  Willoughby (G-19697)
▲ New Path International LLC ....E 614 410-3974
  Powell (G-16344)
Nexus Engineering Group LLC ....D 216 404-7867
  Cleveland (G-6129)
Northast Ohio Rgonal Sewer Dst ....D 216 961-2187
  Cleveland (G-6146)
Northrop Grumman Technical ....C 937 320-3100
  Beavercreek Township (G-1276)
Nottingham-Spirk Des ....E 216 800-5782
  Cleveland (G-6165)
Nu Waves Ltd ....D 513 360-0800
  Middletown (G-14444)
Ohio Blow Pipe Company ....E 216 681-7379
  Cleveland (G-6186)
Ohio Structures Inc ....E 330 533-0084
  Canfield (G-2206)
On-Power Inc ....E 513 228-2100
  Lebanon (G-12633)
Optimetrics Inc ....E 937 306-7180
  Beavercreek Township (G-1278)
Optis Solutions ....E 513 948-2070
  Cincinnati (G-4230)
Osborn Engineering Company ....D 216 861-2020
  Cleveland (G-6216)
P E Systems Inc ....D 937 258-0141
  Dayton (G-9280)
Pakteem Technical Services ....D 513 772-1515
  Cincinnati (G-4248)
Panelmatic Inc ....E 330 782-8007
  Youngstown (G-20315)
Peco II Inc ....D 614 431-0694
  Columbus (G-8528)
Pegasus Technical Services Inc ....E 513 793-0094
  Cincinnati (G-4274)
Peterman Associates Inc ....E 419 722-9566
  Findlay (G-11074)
Peters Tschantz & Assoc Inc ....E 330 666-3702
  Akron (G-388)
Phantom Technical Services Inc ....E 614 868-9920
  Columbus (G-8541)
Phoenix Group Holding Co ....C 937 704-9850
  Springboro (G-17135)
Pioneer Solutions LLC ....E 216 383-3400
  Euclid (G-10771)
PMC Systems Limited ....E 330 538-2268
  North Jackson (G-15386)
Pmwi LLC ....D 614 975-5004
  Hilliard (G-11943)
Poggemeyer Design Group Inc ....C 419 244-8074
  Bowling Green (G-1791)
Poggemeyer Design Group Inc ....E 419 748-7438
  Mc Clure (G-14020)
Polaris Automation Inc ....D 614 431-0170
  Lewis Center (G-12704)
Pollock Research & Design Inc ....E 330 332-3300
  Salem (G-16706)
Power Engineers Incorporated ....E 513 326-1500
  Cincinnati (G-4318)
Power Engineers Incorporated ....E 234 678-9875
  Akron (G-399)
Power System Engineering Inc ....E 740 568-9220
  Marietta (G-13490)
Premier Integration ....E 330 545-8690
  Girard (G-11424)
Primatech Inc ....E 614 841-9800
  Columbus (G-8560)
Prime Ae Group Inc ....D 614 839-0250
  Columbus (G-6902)
Process Plus LLC ....E 513 742-7590
  Cincinnati (G-4340)
Production Design Services Inc ....D 937 866-3377
  Dayton (G-9832)
Professional Service Inds Inc ....E 614 876-8000
  Columbus (G-8568)
Professional Service Inds Inc ....D 216 447-1335
  Cleveland (G-6309)
Providence Rees Inc ....E 614 833-6231
  Columbus (G-8573)
Pyramid Control Systems Inc ....E 513 679-7400
  Cincinnati (G-4357)
Quality Aero Inc ....E 614 436-1609
  Worthington (G-19988)
Quest Global Services-Na Inc ....D 513 648-4900
  Cincinnati (G-4376)
Quilalea Corporation ....E 330 487-0777
  Richfield (G-16524)

R E Warner & Associates Inc ....D 440 835-9400
  Westlake (G-19537)
R W Earhart Company ....E 937 753-1191
  Covington (G-9138)
Ra Consultants LLC ....E 513 469-6600
  Blue Ash (G-1671)
Racaza International LLC ....E 614 973-9266
  Dublin (G-10436)
RAD-Con Inc ....E 440 871-5720
  Lakewood (G-12496)
RCT Engineering Inc ....E 561 684-7534
  Beachwood (G-1118)
Reed Westlake Leskosky Ltd ....D 216 522-0449
  Cleveland (G-6365)
Reps Resource LLC ....E 513 874-0500
  West Chester (G-19138)
Resource International ....D 513 769-6998
  Blue Ash (G-1682)
Resource International Inc ....C 614 823-4949
  Columbus (G-8622)
Richard L Bowen & Assoc Inc ....E 216 491-9300
  Cleveland (G-6391)
River Consulting LLC ....E 614 797-2480
  Columbus (G-8633)
Rovisys Company ....C 330 562-8600
  Aurora (G-854)
S&Me Inc ....D 614 793-2226
  Dublin (G-10445)
Saec/Kinetic Vision Inc ....C 513 793-4959
  Cincinnati (G-4467)
Safran Humn Rsrces Support Inc ......D 513 552-3230
  Cincinnati (G-4468)
Safran Power Usa LLC ....C 330 487-2000
  Twinsburg (G-18466)
Sands Decker Cps Llc ....E 614 459-6992
  Columbus (G-8684)
Sandusky County Engr & Hwy Gar ....E 419 334-9731
  Fremont (G-11219)
Scheeser Buckley Mayfield LLC ....E 330 896-4664
  Uniontown (G-18538)
Schneider Elc Systems USA Inc ....E 440 234-3900
  Cleveland (G-6448)
Schomer Glaus Pyle ....E 614 210-0751
  Columbus (G-8699)
Schomer Glaus Pyle ....E 216 518-5544
  Cleveland (G-6449)
Schomer Glaus Pyle ....B 330 572-2100
  Akron (G-430)
Schomer Glaus Pyle ....D 330 645-2131
  Coventry Township (G-9132)
Schooley Caldwell Associates ....D 614 628-0300
  Columbus (G-8702)
Sea Ltd ....D 614 888-4160
  Columbus (G-8709)
Sebesta Inc ....E 216 351-7621
  Parma (G-15915)
Seifert & Group Inc ....D 330 833-2700
  Massillon (G-13852)
Sgi Matrix LLC ....D 937 438-9033
  Miamisburg (G-14349)
Sgt Inc ....B 216 433-3982
  Cleveland (G-6473)
Shaffer Pomeroy Ltd ....E 419 756-7302
  Mansfield (G-13363)
Shotstop Ballistics LLC ....E 330 686-0020
  Stow (G-17392)
Sierra Lobo Inc ....E 419 332-7101
  Fremont (G-11220)
Sigma Technologies Ltd ....E 419 874-9262
  Perrysburg (G-16059)
Slick Automated Solutions Inc ....E 567 247-1080
  Ontario (G-15714)
Society Plastics Engineers Inc ....C 419 287-4898
  Pemberville (G-15944)
Sponseller Group Inc ....E 419 861-3000
  Holland (G-12056)
Ssoe Inc ....E 330 821-7198
  Alliance (G-560)
Stantec Arch & Engrg PC ....E 216 454-2150
  Cleveland (G-6524)
Stantec Arch & Engrg PC ....E 614 486-4383
  Columbus (G-8773)
Stantec Architecture Inc ....E 216 454-2150
  Cleveland (G-6525)
Stantec Consulting Svcs Inc ....E 614 210-2000
  Dublin (G-10463)
Stantec Consulting Svcs Inc ....E 216 621-2407
  Cleveland (G-6527)
Stantec Consulting Svcs Inc ....E 216 454-2150
  Cleveland (G-6526)

Stantec Consulting Svcs Inc ....D 513 842-8200
  Cincinnati (G-4583)
Stantec Consulting Svcs Inc ....C 614 486-4383
  Columbus (G-8774)
Steven Schaefer Associates Inc ....D 513 542-3300
  Cincinnati (G-4593)
Stilson & Associates Inc ....E 614 847-0300
  Columbus (G-8789)
Stock Fairfield Corporation ....C 440 543-6000
  Chagrin Falls (G-2735)
Straight 72 Inc ....D 740 943-5730
  Marysville (G-13652)
Strand Associates Inc ....E 513 861-5600
  Cincinnati (G-4594)
Strand Associates Inc ....E 614 835-0460
  Groveport (G-11675)
Stress Engineering Svcs Inc ....D 513 336-6701
  Mason (G-13764)
Sumaria Systems Inc ....E 937 429-6070
  Beavercreek (G-1210)
Sumitomo Elc Wirg Systems Inc ....E 937 642-7579
  Marysville (G-13654)
Sunpower Inc ....D 740 594-2221
  Athens (G-813)
Superior Mechanical Svcs Inc ....E 937 259-0082
  Dayton (G-9284)
T J Neff Holdings Inc ....E 440 884-3100
  Cleveland (G-6564)
Technical Assurance Inc ....D 440 953-3147
  Willoughby (G-19717)
Technical Construction Spc ....E 330 929-1088
  Cuyahoga Falls (G-9224)
Technical Consultants Inc ....E 513 521-2696
  Cincinnati (G-4629)
Technology House Ltd ....E 440 248-3025
  Streetsboro (G-17434)
Techsolve Inc ....D 513 948-2000
  Cincinnati (G-4631)
Telecom Expertise Inds Inc ....D 937 548-5254
  Greenville (G-11521)
Terracon Consultants Inc ....C 513 321-5816
  Cincinnati (G-4636)
Terracon Consultants Inc ....E 614 863-3113
  Gahanna (G-11273)
Thelen Associates Inc ....E 513 825-4350
  Cincinnati (G-4648)
Thermal Treatment Center Inc ....E 216 881-8100
  Cleveland (G-6591)
Thermaltech Engineering Inc ....E 513 561-2271
  Cincinnati (G-4649)
Thinkpath Engineering Svcs LLC ......D 937 291-8374
  Miamisburg (G-14358)
Thomas L Miller ....D 740 374-3041
  Marietta (G-13503)
Thorson Baker & Assoc Inc ....C 330 659-6688
  Richfield (G-16530)
Thp Limited Inc ....D 513 241-3222
  Cincinnati (G-4658)
TL Industries Inc ....C 419 666-8144
  Northwood (G-15547)
Transcore Its LLC ....E 440 243-2222
  Cleveland (G-6610)
Transystems Corporation ....E 614 433-7800
  Columbus (G-8866)
Transystems Corporation ....E 216 861-1780
  Cleveland (G-6614)
Trumbull County Engineering ....D 330 675-2640
  Warren (G-18910)
Tsi Inc ....E 419 468-1855
  Galion (G-11307)
▲ TSS Technologies Inc ....B 513 772-7000
  West Chester (G-19166)
Ttl Associates Inc ....C 419 241-4556
  Toledo (G-18263)
Turnkey Network Solutions LLC ....E 614 876-9944
  Columbus (G-8880)
Twism Enterprises LLC ....E 513 800-1098
  Cincinnati (G-4711)
U S Army Corps of Engineers ....D 740 269-2681
  Uhrichsville (G-18493)
U S Army Corps of Engineers ....D 740 767-3527
  Glouster (G-11436)
U S Army Corps of Engineers ....D 513 684-3048
  Cincinnati (G-4714)
Universal Technology Corp ....D 937 426-2808
  Beavercreek (G-1216)
University of Akron ....D 330 972-6008
  Akron (G-488)
University of Cincinnati ....E 513 556-3732
  Cincinnati (G-4770)

SIC SECTION 87 ENGINEERING, ACCOUNTING, RESEARCH, MANAGEMENT, AND RELATED SERVICES

URS Group Inc ....D .... 216 622-2300 Cleveland ***(G-6675)***
URS Group Inc ....C .... 614 464-4500 Columbus ***(G-8921)***
URS Group Inc ....D .... 513 651-3440 Cincinnati ***(G-4791)***
URS Group Inc ....D .... 330 836-9111 Akron ***(G-490)***
URS-Smith Group VA Idiq Joint ....E .... 614 464-4500 Columbus ***(G-8922)***
US Tech Arospc Engrg Corp ....D .... 330 455-1181 Canton ***(G-2574)***
Usaf Sctt ....E .... 937 257-0228 Dayton ***(G-9289)***
Utility Technologies Intl Corp ....E .... 614 879-7624 Groveport ***(G-11683)***
Vantage Partners LLC ....E .... 216 925-1302 Brookpark ***(G-1957)***
Varo Engineers Inc ....D .... 513 729-9313 West Chester ***(G-19178)***
Varo Engineers Inc ....E .... 740 587-2228 Granville ***(G-11472)***
W E Quicksall and Assoc Inc ....E .... 330 339-6676 New Philadelphia ***(G-15122)***
Wade Trim ....E .... 216 363-0300 Cleveland ***(G-6716)***
Wastren Advantage Inc ....E .... 970 254-1277 Piketon ***(G-16132)***
Wheaton & Sprague Engineering ....E .... 330 923-5560 Stow ***(G-17400)***
Wilkris Company ....E .... 513 271-9344 Terrace Park ***(G-17663)***
Woolpert Inc ....E .... 614 476-6000 Columbus ***(G-9005)***
Youngstown Plastic Tooling ....E .... 330 782-7222 Youngstown ***(G-20434)***
Zin Technologies Inc ....C .... 440 625-2200 Middleburg Heights ***(G-14392)***

8712 Architectural Services

A D A Architects Inc ....E .... 216 521-5134 Cleveland ***(G-4932)***
Acock Assoc Architects LLC ....E .... 614 228-1586 Columbus ***(G-6939)***
Aecom Global II LLC ....B .... 614 726-3500 Dublin ***(G-10235)***
Aecom Global II LLC ....D .... 216 523-5600 Cleveland ***(G-4966)***
Arcadis US Inc ....E .... 216 781-6177 Cleveland ***(G-5064)***
ASC Group Inc ....E .... 614 268-2514 Columbus ***(G-7048)***
Austin Building and Design Inc ....C .... 440 544-2600 Cleveland ***(G-5081)***
Balog Steines Hendricks & Manc ....E .... 330 744-4401 Youngstown ***(G-20110)***
Baxter Hodell Donnelly Preston ....C .... 513 271-1634 Cincinnati ***(G-3083)***
Berardi + Partners ....E .... 614 221-1110 Columbus ***(G-7101)***
Big Red Rooster ....D .... 614 255-0200 Columbus ***(G-7108)***
Bostwick Design Partnr Inc ....E .... 216 621-7900 Cleveland ***(G-5129)***
Braun & Steidl Architects Inc ....E .... 330 864-7755 Akron ***(G-108)***
Burgess & Niple Inc ....C .... 513 579-0042 Cincinnati ***(G-3149)***
Burgess & Niple Inc ....B .... 502 254-2344 Columbus ***(G-7169)***
Burgess & Niple Inc ....D .... 440 354-9700 Painesville ***(G-15837)***
Burgess & Niple / Heapy Engine ....D .... 614 459-2050 Columbus ***(G-7170)***
Ceso Inc ....D .... 937 435-8584 Miamisburg ***(G-14281)***
Cha Consulting Inc ....C .... 216 443-1700 Cleveland ***(G-5224)***
Champlin Haupt Architects Inc ....D .... 513 241-4474 Cincinnati ***(G-3229)***
Chemstress Consultant Company ....C .... 330 535-5591 Akron ***(G-130)***
Chute Gerdeman Inc ....D .... 614 469-1001 Columbus ***(G-7271)***
City Architecture Inc ....E .... 216 881-2444 Cleveland ***(G-5245)***
Cole + Russell Architects Inc ....E .... 513 721-8080 Cincinnati ***(G-3386)***
Collaborative Inc ....E .... 419 242-7405 Toledo ***(G-17819)***
Cornelia C Hodgson - Architec ....E .... 216 593-0057 Beachwood ***(G-1068)***
CT Consultants Inc ....E .... 513 791-1700 Blue Ash ***(G-1573)***
CT Consultants Inc ....C .... 440 951-9000 Mentor ***(G-14166)***
Dei Incorporated ....D .... 513 825-5800 Cincinnati ***(G-3480)***
Delphi Automotive Systems LLC ....E .... 248 724-5953 Warren ***(G-18848)***
Design Center ....E .... 513 618-3133 Blue Ash ***(G-1577)***
Dlr Group Inc ....D .... 216 522-1350 Cleveland ***(G-5495)***
Dlz Ohio Inc ....C .... 614 888-0040 Columbus ***(G-7535)***
Domokur Architects Inc ....E .... 330 666-7878 Copley ***(G-9056)***
Dorsky Hodgson + Partners Inc ....D .... 216 464-8600 Cleveland ***(G-5505)***
E & A Pedco Services Inc ....D .... 513 782-4920 Cincinnati ***(G-3519)***
Elevar Design Group Inc ....E .... 513 721-0600 Cincinnati ***(G-3550)***
Emersion Design LLC ....E .... 513 841-9100 Cincinnati ***(G-3553)***
Fanning/Howey Associates Inc ....D .... 614 764-4661 Dublin ***(G-10345)***
Fanning/Howey Associates Inc ....D .... 919 831-1831 Dublin ***(G-10346)***
Fed/Matrix A Joint Venture LLC ....E .... 863 665-6363 Dayton ***(G-9542)***
Feinknopf Macioce Schappa ARC ....E .... 614 297-1020 Columbus ***(G-7652)***
Frch Design Worldwide - Cincin ....B .... 513 241-3000 Cincinnati ***(G-3644)***
G Herschman Architects Inc ....D .... 216 223-3200 Cleveland ***(G-5645)***
Garland/Dbs Inc ....C .... 216 641-7500 Cleveland ***(G-5655)***
Garmann/Miller & Assoc Inc ....E .... 419 628-4240 Minster ***(G-14662)***
Gbc Design Inc ....E .... 330 283-6870 Akron ***(G-233)***
Glavan & Accociates Architects ....E .... 614 205-4060 Columbus ***(G-7754)***
Gpd Services Company Inc ....D .... 330 572-2100 Akron ***(G-244)***
Hardlines Design Company ....E .... 614 784-8733 Columbus ***(G-7801)***
Hasenstab Architects Inc ....E .... 330 434-4464 Akron ***(G-256)***
Heery International Inc ....E .... 216 510-4701 Cleveland ***(G-5745)***
Heery International Inc ....E .... 216 781-1313 Cleveland ***(G-5746)***
Hixson Incorporated ....C .... 513 241-1230 Cincinnati ***(G-3771)***
Holland Professional Group ....D .... 330 239-4474 Sharon Center ***(G-16875)***
HWH Archtcts-Ngnrs-Plnners Inc ....D .... 216 875-4000 Cleveland ***(G-5794)***
Jdi Group Inc ....D .... 419 725-7161 Maumee ***(G-13930)***
Johnson Mirmiran Thompson Inc ....D .... 614 714-0270 Columbus ***(G-7944)***
K4 Architecture LLC ....D .... 513 455-5005 Cincinnati ***(G-3899)***
Ka Inc ....C .... 216 781-9144 Seven Hills ***(G-16832)***
Karlsberger Companies ....C .... 614 461-9500 Columbus ***(G-7966)***
KZF Bwsc Joint Venture ....E .... 513 621-6211 Cincinnati ***(G-3951)***
KZF Design Inc ....D .... 513 621-6211 Cincinnati ***(G-3952)***
Lacaisse Inc ....D .... 513 621-6211 Cincinnati ***(G-3957)***
Loth Inc ....C .... 513 554-4900 Cincinnati ***(G-3995)***
Louis Perry & Associates Inc ....C .... 330 334-1585 Wadsworth ***(G-18762)***
Lusk & Harkin Ltd ....E .... 614 221-3707 Columbus ***(G-8088)***
McGill Smith Punshon Inc ....E .... 513 759-0004 Cincinnati ***(G-4036)***
Meacham & Apel Architects Inc ....D .... 614 764-0407 Columbus ***(G-8139)***
Meyers + Associates Arch LLC ....E .... 614 221-9433 Columbus ***(G-8155)***
Michael Schuster Associates ....E .... 513 241-5666 Cincinnati ***(G-4089)***
Middough Inc ....B .... 216 367-6000 Cleveland ***(G-6054)***
Moody-Nolan Inc ....C .... 614 461-4664 Columbus ***(G-8187)***
Ms Consultants Inc ....C .... 330 744-5321 Youngstown ***(G-20291)***
NBBJ LLC ....C .... 206 223-5026 Columbus ***(G-8252)***
Nitschke Sampson Dietz Inc ....E .... 614 464-1933 Columbus ***(G-8281)***
Orchard Hiltz & McCliment Inc ....D .... 614 418-0600 Columbus ***(G-8478)***
Osborn Engineering Company ....D .... 216 861-2020 Cleveland ***(G-6216)***
Perkfect Design Solutions ....E .... 614 778-3560 Columbus ***(G-8536)***
Perspectus Architecture LLC ....E .... 216 752-1800 Cleveland ***(G-6269)***
Poggemeyer Design Group Inc ....C .... 419 244-8074 Bowling Green ***(G-1791)***
Pond-Woolpert LLC ....D .... 937 461-5660 Beavercreek ***(G-1256)***
Prime Ae Group Inc ....D .... 614 839-0250 Columbus ***(G-6902)***
R E Warner & Associates Inc ....D .... 440 835-9400 Westlake ***(G-19537)***
Rdl Architects Inc ....E .... 216 752-4300 Cleveland ***(G-6356)***
Reed Westlake Leskosky Ltd ....D .... 216 522-0449 Cleveland ***(G-6365)***
Richard L Bowen & Assoc Inc ....D .... 216 491-9300 Cleveland ***(G-6391)***
Richard R Jencen & Associates ....E .... 216 781-0131 Cleveland ***(G-6392)***
Schomer Glaus Pyle ....D .... 614 210-0751 Columbus ***(G-8699)***
Schomer Glaus Pyle ....E .... 216 518-5544 Cleveland ***(G-6449)***
Schomer Glaus Pyle ....B .... 330 572-2100 Akron ***(G-430)***
Schooley Caldwell Associates ....D .... 614 628-0300 Columbus ***(G-8702)***
Sfa Architects Inc ....E .... 937 281-0600 Dayton ***(G-9878)***
Shp Leading Design ....D .... 513 381-2112 Cincinnati ***(G-4518)***
Shremshock Architects Inc ....D .... 614 545-4550 New Albany ***(G-15007)***
Simonson Construction Svcs Inc ....D .... 419 281-8299 Ashland ***(G-699)***
Ssoe Inc ....E .... 330 821-7198 Alliance ***(G-560)***
Stantec Arch & Engrg PC ....E .... 216 454-2150 Cleveland ***(G-6524)***
Stantec Arch & Engrg PC ....E .... 614 486-4383 Columbus ***(G-8773)***
Stantec Architecture Inc ....E .... 216 454-2150 Cleveland ***(G-6525)***
Stantec Consulting Svcs Inc ....E .... 216 454-2150 Cleveland ***(G-6526)***
Stantec Consulting Svcs Inc ....D .... 513 842-8200 Cincinnati ***(G-4583)***
Stantec Consulting Svcs Inc ....C .... 614 486-4383 Columbus ***(G-8774)***
Stilson & Associates Inc ....E .... 614 847-0300 Columbus ***(G-8789)***
Strollo Architects Inc ....E .... 330 743-1177 Youngstown ***(G-20384)***
Technical Assurance Inc ....E .... 440 953-3147 Willoughby ***(G-19717)***
Trinity Health Group Ltd ....E .... 614 899-4830 Columbus ***(G-8873)***
Twism Enterprises LLC ....E .... 513 800-1098 Cincinnati ***(G-4711)***
United Architectural Mtls Inc ....E .... 330 433-9220 North Canton ***(G-15378)***
URS Group Inc ....D .... 330 836-9111 Akron ***(G-490)***
URS Group Inc ....C .... 614 464-4500 Columbus ***(G-8921)***
WD Partners Inc ....E .... 614 634-7000 Dublin ***(G-10488)***
Woolprt-Mrrick Joint Ventr LLP ....E .... 937 461-5660 Beavercreek ***(G-1263)***

8713 Surveying Services

7nt Enterprises LLC ....E .... 937 435-3200 Dayton ***(G-9295)***

S I C

Employee Codes: A=Over 500 employees, B=251-500 C=101-250, D=51-100, E=25-50

2018 Harris Ohio Services Directory

1079

▲ **American Electric Pwr Svc Corp** ......B 614 716-1000
Columbus *(G-6990)*
ASC Group Inc ......E 614 268-2514
Columbus *(G-7048)*
Barr Engineering Incorporated ......E 614 714-0299
Columbus *(G-7091)*
Bayer & Becker Inc ......E 513 492-7297
Mason *(G-13666)*
Bayer & Becker Inc ......E 513 492-7401
Mason *(G-13667)*
Bramhall Engrg & Surveying Co ......E 440 934-7878
Avon *(G-881)*
Choice One Engineering Corp ......E 937 497-0200
Sidney *(G-16919)*
CT Consultants Inc ......C 440 951-9000
Mentor *(G-14166)*
CT Consultants Inc ......E 513 791-1700
Blue Ash *(G-1573)*
Ctl Engineering Inc ......C 614 276-8123
Columbus *(G-7474)*
Dj Neff Enterpeises Inc ......E 440 884-3100
Cleveland *(G-5494)*
Dlz Ohio Inc ......C 614 888-0040
Columbus *(G-7535)*
E P Ferris & Associates Inc ......E 614 299-2999
Columbus *(G-7560)*
Evans Mechwart Ham ......B 614 775-4500
New Albany *(G-14984)*
Feller Finch & Associates Inc ......E 419 893-3680
Maumee *(G-13916)*
Ground Penetrating Radar Sys ......E 419 843-9804
Toledo *(G-17926)*
Hammontree & Associates Ltd ......E 330 499-8817
Canton *(G-2390)*
Jack A Hamilton & Assoc Inc ......E 740 968-4947
Flushing *(G-11105)*
Jobes Henderson & Assoc Inc ......E 740 344-5451
Newark *(G-15178)*
Kleingers Group Inc ......D 513 779-7851
West Chester *(G-19103)*
KS Associates Inc ......D 440 365-4730
Elyria *(G-10639)*
Kucera International Inc ......D 440 975-4230
Willoughby *(G-19678)*
Land Design Consultants ......E 440 255-8463
Mentor *(G-14207)*
McGill Smith Punshon Inc ......E 513 759-0004
Cincinnati *(G-4036)*
McSteen & Associates Inc ......E 440 585-9800
Wickliffe *(G-19607)*
Peterman Associates Inc ......E 419 722-9566
Findlay *(G-11074)*
Poggemeyer Design Group Inc ......E 419 748-7438
Mc Clure *(G-14020)*
Poggemeyer Design Group Inc ......C 419 244-8074
Bowling Green *(G-1791)*
R E Warner & Associates Inc ......D 440 835-9400
Westlake *(G-19537)*
Resource International Inc ......C 614 823-4949
Columbus *(G-8622)*
Sands Decker Cps Llc ......E 614 459-6992
Columbus *(G-8684)*
T J Neff Holdings Inc ......E 440 884-3100
Cleveland *(G-6564)*
Usic Locating Services LLC ......C 330 733-9393
Akron *(G-491)*
Wade Trim ......E 216 363-0300
Cleveland *(G-6716)*

8721 Accounting, Auditing & Bookkeeping Svcs

415 Group Inc ......E 330 492-0094
Canton *(G-2219)*
Advance Payroll Funding Ltd ......C 216 831-8900
Beachwood *(G-1046)*
Ahola Corporation ......D 440 717-7620
Brecksville *(G-1811)*
Akron-Canton Regional Airport ......E 330 499-4059
North Canton *(G-15322)*
▲ **American Electric Pwr Svc Corp** ......B 614 716-1000
Columbus *(G-6990)*
▲ **Apple Growth Partners Inc** ......D 330 867-7350
Akron *(G-78)*
APS Medical Billing ......D 419 866-1804
Toledo *(G-17756)*
Archways Brookville Inc ......D 513 367-2649
Harrison *(G-11791)*
Arthur Middleton Capital Holdn ......E 330 966-9000
North Canton *(G-15326)*
Barnes Dennig & Co Ltd ......D 513 241-8313
Cincinnati *(G-3079)*
Barnes Wendling Cpas Inc ......E 216 566-9000
Cleveland *(G-5095)*
Bdo Usa LLP ......E 614 488-3126
Columbus *(G-7096)*
Bdo Usa LLP ......E 513 592-2400
Cincinnati *(G-3085)*
Bdo Usa LLP ......D 216 325-1700
Cleveland *(G-5105)*
Bdo Usa LLP ......D 330 668-9696
Akron *(G-94)*
Bhm CPA Group Inc ......D 740 474-5210
Circleville *(G-4878)*
Billing Connection Inc ......E 740 964-0043
Reynoldsburg *(G-16430)*
Bkd LLP ......D 513 621-8300
Cincinnati *(G-3111)*
Blue & Co LLC ......C 513 241-4507
Cincinnati *(G-3115)*
Bober Markey Fedorovich ......D 330 762-9785
Fairlawn *(G-10938)*
Bodine Perry LLC ......E 330 702-8100
Canfield *(G-2183)*
Brady Ware & Schoenfeld Inc ......D 614 885-7407
Columbus *(G-7130)*
Brady Ware & Schoenfeld Inc ......D 937 223-5247
Miamisburg *(G-14277)*
Brady Ware & Schoenfeld Inc ......D 614 825-6277
Columbus *(G-7131)*
Brott Mardis & Co ......E 330 762-5022
Akron *(G-115)*
Burke & Schindler Pllc ......E 859 344-8887
Cincinnati *(G-3151)*
C H Dean Inc ......D 937 222-9531
Beavercreek *(G-1156)*
Cassady Schiller & Associates ......E 513 483-6699
Blue Ash *(G-1551)*
Cbiz Accounting Tax ......D 330 668-6500
Akron *(G-124)*
Cbiz Med MGT Professionals Inc ......E 614 771-2222
Hilliard *(G-11889)*
Cbiz Mhm LLC ......C 216 447-9000
Cleveland *(G-5197)*
Central Accounting Systems ......E 513 605-2700
Cincinnati *(G-3209)*
Chard Snyder & Associates Inc ......C 513 459-9997
Mason *(G-13675)*
Cincinnati Medical Billing Svc ......E 513 965-8041
Cincinnati *(G-3314)*
City of Wellston ......D 740 384-2428
Wellston *(G-18998)*
Ciulla Smith & Dale LLP ......E 440 884-2036
Cleveland *(G-5280)*
Ciuni & Panichi Inc ......D 216 831-7171
Cleveland *(G-5281)*
Clark Schaefer Hackett & Co ......E 937 399-2000
Springfield *(G-17160)*
Clark Schaefer Hackett & Co ......E 513 241-3111
Cincinnati *(G-3359)*
Clark Schaefer Hackett & Co ......E 216 672-5252
Cleveland *(G-5282)*
Clark Schaefer Hackett & Co ......D 419 243-0218
Toledo *(G-17814)*
Clark Schaefer Hackett & Co ......D 614 885-2208
Columbus *(G-7292)*
Cliftonlarsonallen LLP ......D 330 497-2000
Canton *(G-2314)*
Cliftonlarsonallen LLP ......E 419 244-3711
Toledo *(G-17817)*
Cliftonlarsonallen LLP ......E 330 376-0100
Akron *(G-148)*
Cohen & Company Ltd ......E 330 743-1040
Youngstown *(G-20146)*
Cohen & Company Ltd ......D 330 374-1040
Akron *(G-150)*
Compensation Programs of Ohio ......E 330 652-9821
Youngstown *(G-20156)*
Comprehensive Med Data MGT LLC ......D 614 717-9840
Powell *(G-16331)*
County of Lucas ......E 419 213-4500
Toledo *(G-17837)*
Crowe Horwath LLP ......C 614 469-0001
Columbus *(G-7466)*
Crowe Horwath LLP ......E 216 623-7500
Cleveland *(G-5439)*
Csh Group ......E 937 226-0070
Miamisburg *(G-14290)*
Defense Fin & Accounting Svc ......E 410 436-9740
Columbus *(G-7500)*
Defense Fin & Accounting Svc ......A 614 693-6700
Columbus *(G-7501)*
Deloitte & Touche LLP ......D 937 223-8821
Dayton *(G-9496)*
Deloitte & Touche LLP ......B 513 784-7100
Cincinnati *(G-3482)*
Deloitte & Touche LLP ......C 614 221-1000
Columbus *(G-7505)*
Deloitte & Touche LLP ......C 216 589-1300
Cleveland *(G-5474)*
Doctors Consulting Service ......E 614 793-1980
Dublin *(G-10322)*
E T Financial Service Inc ......E 937 716-1726
Trotwood *(G-18346)*
Elliott Davis LLC ......E 513 579-1717
Cincinnati *(G-3551)*
Emergency Medical Svcs Billing ......E 216 664-2598
Cleveland *(G-5534)*
Ernst & Young LLP ......D 216 861-5000
Cleveland *(G-5550)*
Ernst & Young LLP ......C 216 583-1823
Cleveland *(G-5551)*
Ernst & Young LLP ......C 614 224-5678
Columbus *(G-7607)*
Ernst & Young LLP ......C 513 612-1400
Cincinnati *(G-3575)*
Ernst & Young LLP ......C 419 244-8000
Toledo *(G-17870)*
Essex and Associates Inc ......E 937 432-1040
Dayton *(G-9531)*
Euclid Hospital ......C 216 445-6440
Euclid *(G-10754)*
Experis Finance Us LLC ......D 614 223-2300
Columbus *(G-7621)*
Experis Finance Us LLC ......E 216 621-0200
Seven Hills *(G-16830)*
Fehr Services LLC ......E 513 829-9333
Fairfield *(G-10851)*
First-Knox National Bank ......C 740 399-5500
Mount Vernon *(G-14897)*
Flagel Huber Flagel & Co ......E 937 299-3400
Moraine *(G-14787)*
Flex Fund Inc ......E 614 766-7000
Dublin *(G-10348)*
Foundations Hlth Solutions Inc ......D 440 793-0200
North Olmsted *(G-15423)*
Foxx & Company ......E 513 241-1616
Cincinnati *(G-3643)*
Fruth & Co ......E 419 435-8541
Fostoria *(G-11127)*
Gbq Holdings LLC ......D 614 221-1120
Columbus *(G-7732)*
Gilmore Jasion Mahler Ltd ......E 419 794-2000
Maumee *(G-13921)*
Grant Thornton LLP ......C 216 771-1400
Cleveland *(G-5687)*
Grant Thornton LLP ......D 513 762-5000
Cincinnati *(G-3693)*
Healthpro Medical Billing Inc ......D 419 223-2717
Lima *(G-12796)*
Hill Barth & King LLC ......E 330 758-8613
Canfield *(G-2193)*
Hill Barth & King LLC ......D 614 228-4000
Columbus *(G-7835)*
Hill Barth & King LLC ......E 330 747-1903
Canfield *(G-2194)*
Hobe Lcas Crtif Pub Accntants ......E 216 524-7167
Cleveland *(G-5764)*
Holbrook & Manter ......E 740 387-8620
Marion *(G-13543)*
Howard Wershbale & Co ......D 216 831-1200
Cleveland *(G-5786)*
Hr Butler LLC ......E 614 923-2900
Dublin *(G-10366)*
Humaserve Hr LLC ......E 513 605-3522
Cincinnati *(G-3797)*
Jennings & Associates ......E 740 369-4426
Delaware *(G-10111)*
Jones Cochenour & Co Inc ......E 740 653-9581
Lancaster *(G-12545)*
Julian & Grube Inc ......E 614 846-1899
Westerville *(G-19318)*
Kaiser Consulting LLC ......E 614 378-5361
Powell *(G-16341)*
Kennedy Group Enterprises Inc ......E 440 879-0078
Strongsville *(G-17481)*
Kent State University ......D 330 672-2607
Kent *(G-12379)*
Klingbeil Management Group Co ......E 614 220-8900
Columbus *(G-7997)*

Kpmg LLP....C....513 421-6430
Cincinnati *(G-3940)*
Kpmg LLP....C....614 249-2300
Columbus *(G-8012)*
Kpmg LLP....C....216 696-9100
Cleveland *(G-5912)*
Lassiter Corporation....E....216 391-4800
Cleveland *(G-5927)*
Maloney + Novotny LLC....D....216 363-0100
Cleveland *(G-5975)*
MBI Solutions Inc....C....937 619-4000
Dayton *(G-9705)*
McCrate Delaet & Co....E....937 492-3161
Sidney *(G-16942)*
MD Business Solutions Inc....E....513 872-4500
Blue Ash *(G-1637)*
Meaden & Moore LLP....D....216 241-3272
Cleveland *(G-6010)*
Med3000 Group Inc....E....937 291-7850
Miamisburg *(G-14316)*
Medic Management Group LLC....D....330 670-5316
Akron *(G-336)*
Medical Account Services Inc....E....937 297-6072
Moraine *(G-14803)*
Medical Care PSC Inc....E....513 281-4400
Cincinnati *(G-4042)*
Medical Care Reimbursement....E....513 281-4400
Cincinnati *(G-4043)*
Medigistics Inc....D....614 430-5700
Columbus *(G-8144)*
Mellott & Mellott Pll....E....513 241-2940
Cincinnati *(G-4053)*
Midwest Emergency Services LLC....E....586 294-2700
Fairlawn *(G-10965)*
Mosley Pfundt & Glick Inc....E....419 861-1120
Maumee *(G-13948)*
Murray Wlls Wndeln Rbnson Cpas....E....937 773-6373
Piqua *(G-16154)*
Mutual Shareholder Svcs LLC....E....440 922-0067
Broadview Heights *(G-1884)*
Nationwide Childrens Hospital....E....330 253-5200
Akron *(G-349)*
Nms Inc Certif Pub Accountants....E....440 286-5222
Chardon *(G-2759)*
Norman Jones Enlow & Co....E....614 228-4000
Columbus *(G-8285)*
Northcoast Healthcare MGT Inc....C....216 591-2000
Beachwood *(G-1108)*
Ohio Bell Telephone Company....A....216 822-3439
Cleveland *(G-6185)*
Ohio State University....E....614 292-6831
Columbus *(G-8408)*
Patrick J Burke & Co....E....513 455-8200
Cincinnati *(G-4262)*
Paychex Inc....E....614 781-6143
Worthington *(G-19982)*
Paychex Inc....C....330 342-0530
Hudson *(G-12139)*
Paychex Inc....E....513 727-9182
Middletown *(G-14484)*
Paychex Inc....D....614 210-0400
Dublin *(G-10423)*
Paycom Software Inc....A....888 678-0796
Cincinnati *(G-4267)*
Paycor Inc....E....614 985-6140
Worthington *(G-19983)*
Paycor Inc....E....216 447-7913
Cleveland *(G-6253)*
Paycor Inc....C....513 381-0505
Cincinnati *(G-4268)*
Payne Nickles & Co CPA....E....419 668-2552
Norwalk *(G-15588)*
Payroll Services Unlimited....E....740 653-9581
Lancaster *(G-12564)*
Pease & Associates LLC....E....216 348-9600
Cleveland *(G-6258)*
Pioneer Physicians Networking....E....330 633-6601
Tallmadge *(G-17647)*
Pricewaterhousecoopers LLP....B....216 875-3000
Cleveland *(G-6305)*
Pricewaterhousecoopers LLP....E....419 254-2500
Toledo *(G-18135)*
Pricewaterhousecoopers LLP....D....513 723-4700
Cincinnati *(G-4328)*
Pricewaterhousecoopers LLP....C....614 225-8700
Columbus *(G-8559)*
Promedica Physcn Cntinuum Svcs....C....419 824-7200
Sylvania *(G-17608)*
Protiviti Inc....E....216 696-6010
Cleveland *(G-6325)*
Quadax Inc....E....330 759-4600
Youngstown *(G-20334)*
Quadax Inc....C....440 777-6300
Middleburg Heights *(G-14384)*
Quadax Inc....E....614 882-1200
Westerville *(G-19438)*
Radiology Assoc Canton Inc....E....330 363-2842
Canton *(G-2503)*
REA & Associates Inc....E....330 722-8222
Medina *(G-14117)*
REA & Associates Inc....D....330 339-6651
New Philadelphia *(G-15112)*
REA & Associates Inc....E....419 331-1040
Lima *(G-12929)*
REA & Associates Inc....E....330 674-6055
Millersburg *(G-14618)*
REA & Associates Inc....D....440 266-0077
New Philadelphia *(G-15113)*
REA & Associates Inc....E....614 889-8725
Dublin *(G-10438)*
Real Property Management Inc....E....614 766-6500
Dublin *(G-10439)*
Rehmann LLC....D....419 865-8118
Toledo *(G-18149)*
REM-Ohio Inc....D....330 644-9730
Coventry Township *(G-9131)*
Reynolds & Co Inc....E....740 353-1040
Portsmouth *(G-16304)*
Richland Trust Company....D....419 525-8700
Mansfield *(G-13361)*
Rlj Management Co Inc....C....614 942-2020
Columbus *(G-8639)*
RSM US LLP....C....937 298-0201
Moraine *(G-14821)*
RSM US LLP....E....614 224-7722
Columbus *(G-8656)*
RSM US LLP....C....216 523-1900
Cleveland *(G-6421)*
Safelite Fulfillment Inc....E....614 210-9050
Columbus *(G-8671)*
Schneider Downs & Co Inc....D....614 621-4060
Columbus *(G-8697)*
Schroedel Scullin & Bestic LLC....E....330 533-1131
Canfield *(G-2209)*
Sheakley Med MGT Resources LLC....D....513 891-1006
Cincinnati *(G-4512)*
Sheakley-Uniservice Inc....C....513 771-2277
Cincinnati *(G-4514)*
Skoda Mntti Crtif Pub Accntnts....D....440 449-6800
Mayfield Village *(G-14013)*
Smithpearlman & Co....E....513 248-9210
Milford *(G-14564)*
Specialty Medical Services....E....440 245-8010
Lorain *(G-13076)*
Superior Med Inc....E....740 439-8839
Cambridge *(G-2130)*
Terry J Reppa & Associates....E....440 888-8533
Cleveland *(G-6586)*
The Peoples Bank Co Inc....E....419 678-2385
Coldwater *(G-6835)*
The Sheakley Group Inc....E....513 771-2277
Cincinnati *(G-4646)*
Thomas Packer & Co....E....330 533-9777
Canfield *(G-2212)*
Thomas Rosser....C....614 890-2900
Westerville *(G-19444)*
Top Echelon Contracting Inc....B....330 454-3508
Canton *(G-2564)*
Verizon Business Global LLC....E....614 219-2317
Hilliard *(G-11963)*
Vernon F Glaser & Associates....E....937 298-5536
Dayton *(G-9970)*
Village of Byesville....E....740 685-5901
Byesville *(G-2072)*
Vivial Media LLC....E....513 768-7800
Cincinnati *(G-4817)*
Walthall LLP....E....216 573-2330
Cleveland *(G-6720)*
Warren Bros & Sons Inc....E....740 373-1430
Marietta *(G-13516)*
Weber Obrien Ltd....E....419 885-8338
Sylvania *(G-17627)*
Whalen and Company Inc....E....614 396-4200
Worthington *(G-20008)*
Whitcomb & Hess Inc....E....419 289-7007
Ashland *(G-708)*
Whited Seigneur Sams & Rahe....E....740 702-2600
Chillicothe *(G-2897)*
William Vaughan Company....D....419 891-1040
Maumee *(G-13995)*
Wilson Shannon & Snow Inc....E....740 345-6611
Newark *(G-15246)*
Zinner & Co....E....216 831-0733
Beachwood *(G-1138)*

8731 Commercial Physical & Biological Research

Akron Rubber Dev Lab Inc....D....330 794-6600
Akron *(G-54)*
Aktion Associates Incorporated....E....419 893-7001
Maumee *(G-13873)*
Alcatel-Lucent USA Inc....B....614 860-2000
Dublin *(G-10239)*
Alliance Imaging Inc....C....330 493-5100
Canton *(G-2232)*
American Showa Inc....E....740 965-4040
Sunbury *(G-17549)*
Antioch University....D....937 769-1366
Yellow Springs *(G-20088)*
Applied Medical Technology Inc....E....440 717-4000
Brecksville *(G-1813)*
Applied Research Assoc Inc....E....937 435-1016
Dayton *(G-9338)*
Applied Research Assoc Inc....E....937 873-8166
Dayton *(G-9339)*
Applied Sciences Inc....E....937 766-2020
Cedarville *(G-2631)*
Arthur G James Cancer....A....614 293-4878
Columbus *(G-7044)*
ASC Group Inc....E....614 268-2514
Columbus *(G-7048)*
Asymmetric Technologies LLC....E....614 725-5310
Columbus *(G-7059)*
Atk Space Systems Inc....E....937 490-4121
Beavercreek *(G-1228)*
Azimuth Corporation....E....937 256-8571
Beavercreek Township *(G-1265)*
BASF Catalysts LLC....D....216 360-5005
Cleveland *(G-5097)*
▲ **Battelle Memorial Institute**....A....614 424-6424
Columbus *(G-7092)*
Battelle Memorial Institute....E....937 254-0880
Dayton *(G-9257)*
Battelle Memorial Institute....B....614 424-5435
West Jefferson *(G-19248)*
Battelle Memorial Institute....C....614 424-5435
West Jefferson *(G-19249)*
Battelleed....D....614 859-6433
Columbus *(G-7093)*
Biosortia Pharmaceuticals Inc....E....614 636-4850
Dublin *(G-10263)*
Borchers Americas Inc....D....440 899-2950
Westlake *(G-19466)*
Bridgestone Research LLC....A....330 379-7570
Akron *(G-110)*
Brilligent Solutions Inc....E....937 879-4148
Fairborn *(G-10785)*
Cast Metals Technology Inc....E....937 968-5460
Union City *(G-18501)*
Center For Eating Disorders....E....614 896-8222
Columbus *(G-7225)*
Champaign Premium Grn Growers....E....937 826-3003
Milford Center *(G-14575)*
Charles River Laboratories Inc....C....419 647-4196
Spencerville *(G-17107)*
Charles Rver Labs Clveland Inc....D....216 332-1665
Cleveland *(G-5228)*
Chemimage Filter Tech LLC....E....330 686-2829
Stow *(G-17357)*
Childrens Hospital Medical Ctr....A....513 636-4200
Cincinnati *(G-3252)*
Circle Prime Manufacturing....E....330 923-0019
Cuyahoga Falls *(G-9172)*
Cleveland F E S Center....D....216 231-3257
Cleveland *(G-5314)*
Clinical Research MGT Inc....B....330 278-2343
Hinckley *(G-11996)*
Concord Biosciences LLC....D....440 357-3200
Painesville *(G-15845)*
Conwed Plas Acquisition V LLC....D....440 926-2607
Akron *(G-163)*
Ctl Engineering Inc....C....614 276-8123
Columbus *(G-7474)*
Curtiss-Wright Controls....E....937 252-5601
Fairborn *(G-10789)*
Defense Research Assoc Inc....E....937 431-1644
Dayton *(G-9265)*
Edison Biotechnology Institute....E....740 593-4713
Athens *(G-786)*

S I C

87 ENGINEERING, ACCOUNTING, RESEARCH, MANAGEMENT, AND RELATED SERVICES SIC SECTION

Edison Welding Institute Inc....C.... 614 688-5000
Columbus *(G-7578)*
EMD Millipore Corporation....C.... 513 631-0445
Norwood *(G-15599)*
Ensafe Inc....E.... 513 621-7233
West Chester *(G-19068)*
First Energy Nuclear Oper Co....D.... 440 604-9836
Cleveland *(G-5595)*
▼ Flexsys America LP....D.... 330 666-4111
Akron *(G-227)*
Fram Group Operations LLC....D.... 419 661-6700
Perrysburg *(G-16005)*
Ftech R&D North America Inc....D.... 937 339-2777
Troy *(G-18354)*
◆ Guild Associates Inc....D.... 614 798-8215
Dublin *(G-10355)*
▲ Heraeus Precious Metals North....E.... 937 264-1000
Vandalia *(G-18682)*
Hydrogeologic Inc....E.... 330 463-3303
Hudson *(G-12123)*
Illumination Research Inc....E.... 513 774-9531
Mason *(G-13719)*
Inc Research LLC....C.... 513 381-5550
Cincinnati *(G-3812)*
Keeptryan Inc....D.... 330 319-1866
Akron *(G-302)*
Kemron Environmental Svcs Inc....D.... 740 373-4071
Marietta *(G-13460)*
Kenmore Research Company....D.... 330 297-1407
Ravenna *(G-16391)*
Laboratory Corporation America....A.... 614 336-3993
Dublin *(G-10385)*
Leidos Inc....E.... 330 405-9810
Twinsburg *(G-18440)*
Leidos Inc....B.... 937 431-2220
Beavercreek *(G-1185)*
Leidos Technical Services Inc....D.... 513 672-8400
West Chester *(G-19212)*
Lg Fuel Cell Systems Inc....E.... 330 491-4800
Canton *(G-2435)*
Lindner Clinical Trial Center....E.... 513 585-1777
Cincinnati *(G-3987)*
Lubrizol Advanced Mtls Inc....E.... 440 933-0400
Avon Lake *(G-934)*
Lyondell Chemical Company....D.... 513 530-4000
Cincinnati *(G-4004)*
Medpace Inc....A.... 513 579-9911
Cincinnati *(G-4049)*
Midwest Optoelectronics LLC....C.... 419 724-0565
Toledo *(G-18063)*
Modern Tech Solutions Inc....D.... 937 426-9025
Beavercreek Township *(G-1275)*
Morris Technologies Inc....C.... 513 733-1611
Cincinnati *(G-4119)*
Mp Biomedicals LLC....C.... 440 337-1200
Solon *(G-17029)*
Muskingum Starlight Industries....D.... 740 453-4622
Zanesville *(G-20513)*
Nationwide Childrens Hospital....C.... 614 722-2700
Columbus *(G-8229)*
Natural Resources Ohio Dept....E.... 614 265-6852
Columbus *(G-8250)*
North Amercn Science Assoc Inc....C.... 419 666-9455
Northwood *(G-15539)*
North Amercn Science Assoc Inc....C.... 419 666-9455
Northwood *(G-15540)*
Nsa Technologies LLC....C.... 330 576-4600
Akron *(G-359)*
Ohio State University....A.... 330 263-3700
Wooster *(G-19898)*
Ohio State University....C.... 614 688-8220
Columbus *(G-8425)*
Ohio State University....E.... 330 263-3725
Canton *(G-2485)*
Olon Ricerca Bioscience LLC....D.... 440 357-3300
Painesville *(G-15869)*
Omnova Solutions Inc....D.... 330 794-6300
Akron *(G-371)*
Owens Corning Sales LLC....B.... 740 587-3562
Granville *(G-11471)*
Pen Brands LLC....E.... 216 447-1199
Brooklyn Heights *(G-1923)*
Phycal Inc....E.... 440 460-2477
Cleveland *(G-6277)*
Plastic Technologies Inc....D.... 419 867-5400
Holland *(G-12046)*
Potter Technologies LLC....D.... 419 380-8404
Toledo *(G-18131)*
PPG Architectural Finishes Inc....B.... 440 826-5100
Strongsville *(G-17500)*
Promerus LLC....E.... 440 922-0300
Brecksville *(G-1843)*
Q Labs LLC....C.... 513 471-1300
Cincinnati *(G-4359)*
Quest Global Services-Na Inc....D.... 513 563-8855
Cincinnati *(G-4375)*
Quest Global Services-Na Inc....D.... 513 648-4900
Cincinnati *(G-4376)*
R & D Nestle Center Inc....C.... 937 642-7015
Marysville *(G-13646)*
Rambus Inc....E.... 440 397-2549
Brecksville *(G-1845)*
Renovo Neural Inc....E.... 216 445-4252
Cleveland *(G-6376)*
Rogosin Institute Inc....E.... 937 374-3116
Xenia *(G-20074)*
Schneller LLC....D.... 330 673-1299
Kent *(G-12395)*
Sensation Research....E.... 513 602-1611
Maineville *(G-13246)*
Steiner Eoptics Inc....D.... 937 426-2341
Miamisburg *(G-14354)*
Stembanc Inc....E.... 440 332-4279
Chardon *(G-2770)*
Sunpower Inc....D.... 740 594-2221
Athens *(G-813)*
Sytronics Inc....E.... 937 431-6100
Beavercreek *(G-1211)*
Taitech Inc....E.... 937 431-1007
Beavercreek *(G-1260)*
Terracon Consultants Inc....E.... 614 863-3113
Gahanna *(G-11273)*
U S Laboratories Inc....E.... 440 248-1223
Cleveland *(G-6626)*
Ues Inc....C.... 937 426-6900
Beavercreek *(G-1213)*
Velocys Inc....D.... 614 733-3300
Plain City *(G-16211)*
Work Connections Intl LLC....E.... 419 448-4655
Tiffin *(G-17709)*
Wyle Laboratories Inc....C.... 937 320-2712
Beavercreek *(G-1264)*
Zin Technologies Inc....C.... 440 625-2200
Middleburg Heights *(G-14392)*

8732 Commercial Economic, Sociological & Educational Research

8451 LLC....C.... 513 632-1020
Cincinnati *(G-2949)*
AK Steel Corporation....C.... 513 425-6541
Middletown *(G-14412)*
Alphamicron Inc....E.... 330 676-0648
Kent *(G-12351)*
Applied Research Assoc Inc....E.... 937 873-8166
Dayton *(G-9339)*
Assistnce In Mktg Columbus Inc....E.... 614 583-2100
Columbus *(G-7053)*
Azg Inc....D.... 419 724-3000
Perrysburg *(G-15974)*
Bionetics Corporation....E.... 757 873-0900
Heath *(G-11835)*
Burke Inc....D.... 513 576-5700
Milford *(G-14507)*
Burke Inc....C.... 513 241-5663
Cincinnati *(G-3150)*
Business Research Services....E.... 216 831-5200
Cleveland *(G-5163)*
Canton Med Educatn Foundation....E.... 330 363-6783
Canton *(G-2292)*
Clinical Research MGT Inc....B.... 330 278-2343
Hinckley *(G-11996)*
Convergys Cstmer MGT Group Inc....B.... 513 723-6104
Cincinnati *(G-3418)*
Creative Marketing Enterprises....D.... 419 867-4444
Sylvania *(G-17580)*
Curator Video LLC....E.... 513 842-6605
Blue Ash *(G-1574)*
Deskey Associates Inc....D.... 513 721-6800
Cincinnati *(G-3484)*
Directions Research Inc....C.... 513 651-2990
Cincinnati *(G-3493)*
Division of Geological Survey....E.... 614 265-6576
Columbus *(G-7531)*
Douglas Webb & Associates....D.... 614 873-9830
Plain City *(G-16188)*
Dwight Spencer & Associates....E.... 614 488-3123
Columbus *(G-7554)*
Fields Marketing Research Inc....D.... 513 821-6266
Cincinnati *(G-3604)*
Freedonia Publishing LLC....D.... 440 684-9600
Cleveland *(G-5636)*
Friedman-Swift Associates Inc....D.... 513 772-9200
Cincinnati *(G-3655)*
Gfk Custom Research LLC....C.... 513 562-1507
Blue Ash *(G-1600)*
Great Lakes Mktg Assoc Inc....E.... 419 534-4700
Toledo *(G-17922)*
Honda R&D Americas Inc....E.... 937 644-0439
Raymond *(G-16420)*
I T E LLC....D.... 513 576-6200
Loveland *(G-13132)*
Illumination Research Inc....E.... 513 774-9531
Mason *(G-13719)*
Infocision Management Corp....B.... 330 544-1400
Youngstown *(G-20235)*
Integer Holdings Corporation....E.... 216 937-2800
Cleveland *(G-5824)*
Intelliq Health....D.... 513 489-8838
Cincinnati *(G-3829)*
Ipsos-Asi LLC....D.... 513 872-4300
Cincinnati *(G-3842)*
Ipsos-Insight LLC....C.... 513 552-1100
Cincinnati *(G-3843)*
Klein Associates Inc....E.... 937 873-8166
Fairborn *(G-10801)*
Leidos Inc....B.... 937 431-2220
Beavercreek *(G-1185)*
Lindner Clinical Trial Center....E.... 513 585-1777
Cincinnati *(G-3987)*
Mahoning Youngstown Community....E.... 330 747-5661
Youngstown *(G-20267)*
Mahoning Youngstown Community....D.... 330 747-7921
Youngstown *(G-20268)*
Maritzcx Research LLC....B.... 419 725-4000
Maumee *(G-13941)*
Market Inquiry Llc....E.... 513 794-1088
Blue Ash *(G-1634)*
Marketing Research Svcs Inc....D.... 513 772-7580
Cincinnati *(G-4022)*
Marketing Research Svcs Inc....D.... 513 579-1555
Cincinnati *(G-4023)*
Marketvision Research Inc....E.... 513 603-6340
West Chester *(G-19116)*
Marketvision Research Inc....D.... 513 791-3100
Blue Ash *(G-1635)*
National Rgstry Emrgncy Mdcl....E.... 614 888-4484
Columbus *(G-8224)*
Nielsen Consumer Insights Inc....D.... 513 489-9000
Blue Ash *(G-1652)*
Northrop Grumman Technical....C.... 937 320-3100
Beavercreek Township *(G-1276)*
Ohio State University....D.... 740 376-7431
Marietta *(G-13481)*
Ohio State University....D.... 740 593-2657
Athens *(G-803)*
Ohio State University....D.... 614 292-4353
Columbus *(G-8410)*
Ohio State University....D.... 614 442-7300
Columbus *(G-8414)*
Ohio State University....E.... 614 292-9404
Columbus *(G-8435)*
Ohio State University....D.... 614 292-0476
Columbus *(G-8438)*
Ohio State University....D.... 614 292-5491
Columbus *(G-8398)*
Opinions Ltd....E.... 440 893-0300
Chagrin Falls *(G-2703)*
Orc International Inc....E.... 419 893-0029
Maumee *(G-13954)*
Orc International Inc....D.... 513 579-1555
Cincinnati *(G-4231)*
Osborn Marketing Research Corp....E.... 440 871-1047
Westlake *(G-19531)*
Power Management Inc....E.... 937 222-2909
Dayton *(G-9817)*
Q Fact Marketing Research Inc....C.... 513 891-2271
Cincinnati *(G-4358)*
Quality Solutions Inc....E.... 440 933-9946
Cleveland *(G-6335)*
Rebiz LLC....E.... 844 467-3249
Cleveland *(G-6360)*
Ritter & Associates Inc....E.... 419 535-5757
Maumee *(G-13972)*
Scanner Applications LLC....E.... 513 248-5588
Milford *(G-14559)*
SSS Consulting Inc....E.... 937 259-1200
Dayton *(G-9901)*
Strategic Consumer Research....E.... 216 261-0308
Mentor On The Lake *(G-14262)*

SIC SECTION 87 ENGINEERING, ACCOUNTING, RESEARCH, MANAGEMENT, AND RELATED SERVICES

Sytronics Inc E 937 431-6100 Beavercreek *(G-1211)*
Tns North America Inc D 513 621-7887 Cincinnati *(G-4661)*
University of Cincinnati E 513 556-4054 Cincinnati *(G-4765)*
Various Views Research Inc D 513 489-9000 Blue Ash *(G-1715)*
Wolf Sensory Inc E 513 891-9100 Blue Ash *(G-1720)*

8733 Noncommercial Research Organizations

Advantage Aerotech Inc E 614 759-8329 Columbus *(G-6947)*
American Cancer Society East B 888 227-6446 Dublin *(G-10245)*
American Heart Assn Ohio Vly E 216 791-7500 Cleveland *(G-5009)*
American Institute Research B 614 221-8717 Columbus *(G-6997)*
American Institute Research B 614 310-8982 Columbus *(G-6998)*
Applied Optimization Inc C 937 431-5100 Beavercreek *(G-1146)*
Applied Research Solutions Inc D 937 912-6100 Beavercreek *(G-1225)*
Arthur G James Cancer A 614 293-4878 Columbus *(G-7044)*
ASC Group Inc E 614 268-2514 Columbus *(G-7048)*
Assured Information SEC Inc D 937 427-9720 Beavercreek *(G-1148)*
Barrett Center For Cancer Prev D 513 558-3200 Cincinnati *(G-3080)*
Benjamin Rose Institute D 216 791-8000 Cleveland *(G-5115)*
Charles River Labs Ashland LLC C 419 282-8700 Ashland *(G-674)*
Childrens Hosp Med Ctr Akron E 330 633-2055 Tallmadge *(G-17634)*
Childrens Hospital Medical Ctr A 513 803-1751 Cincinnati *(G-3248)*
Childrens Hospital Medical Ctr E 513 636-6100 Cincinnati *(G-3251)*
Childrens Hospital Medical Ctr A 513 636-4200 Cincinnati *(G-3252)*
Childrens Hospital Medical Ctr E 513 636-6400 Fairfield *(G-10830)*
Childrens Hospital Medical Ctr E 513 636-6800 Mason *(G-13676)*
Cincinnti Educ & RES For Vetrn E 513 861-3100 Cincinnati *(G-3339)*
Cleveland VA Medical Research E 216 791-2300 Cleveland *(G-5353)*
Cornerstone Research Group Inc C 937 320-1877 Miamisburg *(G-14287)*
Dayton Foundation Inc E 937 222-0410 Dayton *(G-9474)*
Jjr Solutions LLC E 937 912-0288 Beavercreek *(G-1180)*
Kendle International Inc E 513 763-1414 Cincinnati *(G-3912)*
Macaulay-Brown Inc B 937 426-3421 Beavercreek *(G-1251)*
Mp Biomedicals LLC C 440 337-1200 Solon *(G-17029)*
Nationwide Childrens Hospital A 614 722-2000 Columbus *(G-8232)*
Ofeq Institute Inc E 440 943-1497 Wickliffe *(G-19610)*
Ohio Aerospace Institute D 440 962-3000 Cleveland *(G 6184)*
Ohio Seed Improvement Assn D 614 889-1136 Dublin *(G-10414)*
Ohio State University D 614 292-1681 Columbus *(G-8402)*
Ohio State University B 330 263-3701 Wooster *(G-19899)*
Ohio State University C 614 292-5990 Columbus *(G-8429)*
Ohio Technical College Inc C 216 881-1700 Cleveland *(G-6195)*
Ohiohealth Research Institute E 614 566-4297 Columbus *(G-8461)*
Prologue Research Intl Inc D 614 324-1500 Columbus *(G-8570)*
Research Institute At Nation C 614 722-2700 Columbus *(G-8617)*
Riverside Research Institute D 937 431-3810 Beavercreek *(G-1205)*
Rogosin Institute Inc E 937 374-3116 Xenia *(G-20074)*
Roholt Vision Institute Inc E 330 702-8755 Canfield *(G-2208)*
Sunpower Inc D 740 594-2221 Athens *(G-813)*
Truenorth Cultural Arts E 440 949-5200 Sheffield Village *(G-16895)*
United States Dept of Navy E 937 938-3926 Dayton *(G-9286)*
Universities Space Res Assn E 216 368-0750 Cleveland *(G-6651)*
University Hospitals D 216 844-8797 Cleveland *(G-6657)*
University of Dayton C 937 229-2113 Dayton *(G-9953)*
University of Dayton B 937 229-3822 Dayton *(G-9954)*
University of Dayton A 937 229-2919 Dayton *(G-9952)*
US Dept of the Air Force B 937 255-5150 Dayton *(G-9288)*
Wright State University E 937 298-4331 Kettering *(G-12439)*

8734 Testing Laboratories

Advanced Testing Lab Inc C 513 489-8447 Blue Ash *(G-1525)*
Advanced Testing MGT Group Inc C 513 489-8447 Blue Ash *(G-1526)*
Agrana Fruit Us Inc C 937 693-3821 Anna *(G-616)*
Akzo Nobel Coatings Inc C 614 294-3361 Columbus *(G-6962)*
Als Group Usa Corp E 513 733-5336 Blue Ash *(G-1530)*
Als Services Usa Corp D 513 582-8277 West Chester *(G-19017)*
Als Services Usa Corp E 604 998-5311 Cleveland *(G-4999)*
Analytical Pace Services LLC E 937 832-8242 Englewood *(G-10696)*
Antech Diagnostics Inc E 330 665-4996 Copley *(G-9051)*
Aqua Tech Envmtl Labs Inc E 740 389-5991 Marion *(G-13523)*
Atc Group Services LLC D 513 771-2112 Cincinnati *(G-3056)*
Balancing Company Inc E 937 898-9111 Vandalia *(G-18661)*
Barr Engineering Incorporated E 614 714-0299 Columbus *(G-7091)*
Bayless Pathmark Inc E 440 274-2494 Cleveland *(G-5103)*
Bionetics Corporation E 757 873-0900 Heath *(G-11835)*
Bowser-Morner Inc E 419 691-4800 Toledo *(G-17779)*
Brookside Laboratories Inc E 419 977-2766 New Bremen *(G-15016)*
Bwi North America Inc E 937 212-2892 Moraine *(G-14757)*
Chemsultants International Inc E 440 974-3080 Mentor *(G-14157)*
Cincinnati Sub-Zero Pdts LLC C 800 989-7373 Cincinnati *(G-3331)*
Cliff North Consultants Inc E 513 251-4930 Cincinnati *(G-3364)*
Clinton-Carvell Inc E 614 351-8858 Columbus *(G-7303)*
Csa America Inc C 216 524-4990 Cleveland *(G-5441)*
Csa America Inc D 216 524-4990 Cleveland *(G-5442)*
Ctl Engineering Inc C 614 276-8123 Columbus *(G-7474)*
Curtiss-Wright Flow Control D 513 528-7900 Cincinnati *(G-2910)*
Curtiss-Wright Flow Ctrl Corp D 513 528-7900 Cincinnati *(G-2911)*
Daymark Food Safety Systems C 419 353-2458 Bowling Green *(G-1774)*
Dna Diagnostics Center Inc C 513 881-7800 Fairfield *(G-10842)*
Electro-Analytical Inc E 440 951-3514 Mentor *(G-14171)*
Element Cincinnati E 513 984-4112 Fairfield *(G-10845)*
Element Mtls Tech Cncnnati Inc E 513 771-2536 Fairfield *(G-10846)*
Element Mtrls Tchnlgy Hntngtn E 216 643-1208 Cleveland *(G-5532)*
Emlab P&K LLC D 330 497-9396 North Canton *(G-15335)*
Envirite of Ohio Inc E 330 456-6238 Canton *(G-2356)*
Enviroscience Inc D 330 688-0111 Stow *(G-17364)*
First Energy Nuclear Oper Co D 440 604-9836 Cleveland *(G-5595)*
Food Safety Net Services Ltd E 614 274-2070 Columbus *(G-7680)*
Fram Group Operations LLC D 419 661-6700 Perrysburg *(G-16005)*
General Electric Company C 937 587-2631 Peebles *(G-15938)*
Glowe-Smith Industrial Inc C 330 638-5088 Vienna *(G-18737)*
▲ Godfrey & Wing Inc E 330 562-1440 Aurora *(G-840)*
Grace Consulting Inc E 440 647-6672 Wellington *(G-18992)*
Grl Engineers Inc E 216 831-6131 Solon *(G-17013)*
High Voltage Maintenance Corp E 937 278-0811 Dayton *(G-9611)*
Idexx Laboratories Inc D 330 629-6076 Youngstown *(G-20229)*
Intertek Testing Svcs NA Inc E 614 279-8090 Columbus *(G-7920)*
Isomedix Operations Inc E 614 836-5757 Groveport *(G-11648)*
Isomedix Operations Inc C 440 354-2600 Mentor *(G-14196)*
J T Adams Co Inc E 216 641-3290 Cleveland *(G-5844)*
Juice Technologies Inc E 800 518-5576 Columbus *(G-7957)*
Kemron Environmental Svcs Inc D 740 373-4071 Marietta *(G-13460)*
Kenmore Research Company D 330 297-1407 Ravenna *(G-16391)*
Laboratory Corporation America E 440 205-8299 Mentor *(G-14202)*
Landing Gear Test Facility E 937 255-5740 Dayton *(G-9276)*
McCloy Engineering LLC E 513 984-4112 Fairfield *(G-10877)*
Mercy Health E 330 841-4406 Warren *(G-18880)*
Metcut Research Associates Inc D 513 271-5100 Cincinnati *(G-4084)*
Mistras Group Inc E 740 788-9188 Heath *(G-11839)*
Mobile Analytical Services E 614 873-1710 Plain City *(G-16201)*
MPW Industrial Services Inc E 740 345-2431 Newark *(G-15214)*
National Testing Laboratories E 440 449-2525 Cleveland *(G-6112)*
Nestle Usa Inc D 614 526-5300 Dublin *(G-10406)*
North Amercn Science Assoc Inc C 419 666-9455 Northwood *(G-15539)*
Northast Ohio Rgonal Sewer Dst C 216 641-6000 Cleveland *(G-6147)*
Nsl Analytical Services Inc D 216 438-5200 Cleveland *(G-6169)*
Nucon International Inc E 614 846-5710 Columbus *(G-8303)*
Ohio Department Transportation D 614 275-1324 Columbus *(G-8330)*
Ohio Rver Vly Wtr Snttion Comm E 513 231-7719 Cincinnati *(G-4210)*
Omega Laboratories Inc D 330 628-5748 Mogadore *(G-14681)*
Pace Analytical Services Inc E 614 486-5421 Dublin *(G-10420)*
Plastic Technologies Inc D 419 867-5400 Holland *(G-12046)*
Professional Service Inds Inc E 614 876-8000 Columbus *(G-8568)*
Q Labs LLC C 513 471-1300 Cincinnati *(G-4359)*
Raitz Inc E 513 769-1200 Cincinnati *(G-4384)*
Reid Asset Management Company E 216 642-3223 Cleveland *(G-6368)*

SIC

Employee Codes: A=Over 500 employees, B=251-500 C=101-250, D=51-100, E=25-50
2018 Harris Ohio Services Directory
1083

Resource International Inc C 614 823-4949
Columbus *(G-8622)*
Rev1 Ventures E 614 487-3700
Columbus *(G-8627)*
S D Myers Inc C 330 630-7000
Tallmadge *(G-17648)*
Sample Machining Inc E 937 258-3338
Dayton *(G-9866)*
SD Myers LLC D 330 630-7000
Tallmadge *(G-17649)*
Sensation Research E 513 602-1611
Maineville *(G-13246)*
Shaw Group Inc A 937 593-2022
Bellefontaine *(G-1396)*
Silliker Laboratories Ohio Inc E 614 486-0150
Columbus *(G-8732)*
Smithers Quality Assessments E 330 762-4231
Akron *(G-442)*
Smithers Rapra Inc E 330 297-1495
Ravenna *(G-16413)*
Smithers Rapra Inc D 330 762-7441
Akron *(G-443)*
Smithers Tire & Auto Testng TX E 330 762-7441
Akron *(G-444)*
Standard Laboratories Inc E 513 422-1088
Middletown *(G-14460)*
▲ **Standards Testing Labs Inc** E 330 833-8548
Massillon *(G-13856)*
Summit Environmental Tech Inc E 330 253-8211
Cuyahoga Falls *(G-9222)*
Testamerica Laboratories Inc C 800 456-9396
North Canton *(G-15372)*
Testamerica Laboratories Inc E 513 733-5700
Cincinnati *(G-4637)*
Tool Testing Lab Inc E 937 898-5696
Tipp City *(G-17730)*
Transportation Ohio Department E 614 275-1300
Columbus *(G-8865)*
US Inspection Services Inc E 937 660-9879
Dayton *(G-9958)*
US Inspection Services Inc E 513 671-7073
Cincinnati *(G-4795)*
US Tubular Products Inc D 330 832-1734
North Lawrence *(G-15394)*
Wallover Enterprises Inc E 440 238-9250
Strongsville *(G-17523)*
Wyle Laboratories Inc E 937 912-3470
Beavercreek *(G-1224)*
X-Ray Industries Inc E 216 642-0100
Cleveland *(G-6766)*
Yoder Industries Inc C 937 278-5769
Dayton *(G-10007)*

8741 Management Services

3c Technologies Inc D 419 868-8999
Holland *(G-12005)*
A-Sons Construction Inc D 614 846-2438
Columbus *(G-6923)*
Acuity Healthcare LP D 740 283-7499
Steubenville *(G-17302)*
Advocare Inc D 216 514-1451
Cleveland *(G-4960)*
Aecom Global II LLC D 216 523-5600
Cleveland *(G-4966)*
Aim Integrated Logistics Inc B 330 759-0438
Girard *(G-11406)*
Allcan Global Services Inc E 513 825-1655
Cincinnati *(G-2987)*
Alternative Home Health Care E 513 794-0555
Cincinnati *(G-2998)*
American Hospitality Group Inc B 330 336-6684
Wadsworth *(G-18747)*
American Mechanical Group Inc E 614 575-3720
Columbus *(G-7001)*
American Med B 330 762-8999
Akron *(G-71)*
Ameridian Specialty Services E 513 769-0150
Cincinnati *(G-3014)*
Andersen Distribution Inc C 937 898-7844
Dayton *(G-9336)*
Apollo Property Management LLC E 216 468-0050
Beachwood *(G-1051)*
Arthur Middleton Capital Holdn E 330 966-9000
North Canton *(G-15326)*
Astro Aluminum Enterprises Inc E 330 755-1414
Struthers *(G-17526)*
Atlantic Hospitality & MGT LLC E 216 454-5450
Beachwood *(G-1052)*
Aultcomp Inc E 330 830-4919
Massillon *(G-13788)*
Authentic Food LLC E 740 369-0377
Delaware *(G-10073)*
◆ **Babcock & Wilcox Company** A 330 753-4511
Barberton *(G-955)*
Bailey Associates C 614 760-7752
Columbus *(G-7084)*
Balanced Care Corporation E 330 908-1166
Northfield *(G-15509)*
Balanced Care Corporation E 937 372-7205
Xenia *(G-20044)*
Baxter Hodell Donnelly Preston C 513 271-1634
Cincinnati *(G-3083)*
Benchmark Technologies Corp E 419 843-6691
Toledo *(G-17769)*
Benjamin Rose Institute D 216 791-3580
Cleveland *(G-5116)*
Bernard Busson Builder E 330 929-4926
Akron *(G-99)*
Bistro Off Broadway E 937 316-5000
Greenville *(G-11489)*
Blanchard Valley Health System A 419 423-4500
Findlay *(G-10997)*
Blanchard Valley Health System D 419 424-3000
Findlay *(G-10998)*
Bon Appetit Management Co E 614 823-1880
Westerville *(G-19371)*
Bravo Wellness LLC E 216 658-9500
Cleveland *(G-5134)*
Bridgepoint Risk MGT LLC E 419 794-1075
Maumee *(G-13890)*
Brown Co Ed Service Center D 937 378-6118
Georgetown *(G-11386)*
C M M Inc E 330 656-3820
Hudson *(G-12106)*
Camden Management Inc E 513 383-1635
Cincinnati *(G-3171)*
Cameron Mitchell Rest LLC E 614 621-3663
Columbus *(G-7180)*
◆ **Cardinal Health Inc** A 614 757-5000
Dublin *(G-10275)*
Cardinal Health Inc D 614 497-9552
Obetz *(G-15665)*
Carespring Health Care MGT LLC E 513 943-4000
Loveland *(G-13113)*
Careworks of Ohio Inc B 614 792-1085
Dublin *(G-10280)*
Cargotec Services USA Inc D 419 482-6866
Perrysburg *(G-15984)*
Carington Health Systems E 513 682-2700
Hamilton *(G-11706)*
Cdc Management Co C 614 781-0216
Columbus *(G-7218)*
Cedarwood Construction Company D 330 836-9971
Akron *(G-125)*
CFM Religion Pubg Group LLC E 513 931-4050
Cincinnati *(G-3221)*
Chemstress Consultant Company C 330 535-5591
Akron *(G-130)*
Christian Benevolent Assocn C 513 931-5000
Cincinnati *(G-3271)*
Chu Management Co Inc E 330 725-4571
Medina *(G-14047)*
Cincinnati Health Network Inc E 513 961-0600
Cincinnati *(G-3309)*
City of Youngstown B 330 742-8700
Youngstown *(G-20143)*
Clermont North East School Dst E 513 625-8283
Batavia *(G-1002)*
Clevelan Clinic Hlth Sys W Reg B 216 518-3444
Cleveland *(G-5286)*
Clevelan Clinic Hlth Sys W Reg A 216 476-7000
Cleveland *(G-5287)*
Clevelan Clinic Hlth Sys W Reg E 216 476-7606
Cleveland *(G-5288)*
Clevelan Clinic Hlth Sys W Reg D 216 476-7007
Cleveland *(G-5289)*
▲ **Cleveland Clinic Foundation** A 216 636-8335
Cleveland *(G-5296)*
Clk Multi-Family MGT LLC C 614 891-0011
Columbus *(G-7305)*
Cmp I Owner-T LLC E 614 764-9393
Dublin *(G-10298)*
Cmp I Owner-T LLC E 614 436-7070
Columbus *(G-7310)*
Cmp I Owner-T LLC E 513 733-4334
Blue Ash *(G-1562)*
CMS & Co Management Svcs Inc E 440 989-5200
Lorain *(G-13028)*
Coal Services Inc D 740 795-5220
Powhatan Point *(G-16356)*
Collins & Assoc Technical Svcs E 740 574-2320
Wheelersburg *(G-19573)*
Colonial Senior Services Inc C 513 856-8600
Hamilton *(G-11713)*
Colonial Senior Services Inc C 513 867-4006
Hamilton *(G-11714)*
Colonial Senior Services Inc C 513 844-8004
Hamilton *(G-11715)*
Communicare Health Svcs Inc E 513 530-1654
Blue Ash *(G-1564)*
Community Mercy Foundation D 937 274-1569
Dayton *(G-9419)*
Community Mercy Foundation D 937 328-8134
Springfield *(G-17173)*
Community Mercy Hlth Partners C 937 653-5432
Urbana *(G-18583)*
Comprehensive Health Care A 440 329-7500
Elyria *(G-10607)*
Comprehensive Managed Care Sys E 513 533-0021
Cincinnati *(G-3407)*
Constellations Enterprise LLC C 330 740-8208
Youngstown *(G-20161)*
Consulate Management Co LLC A 419 683-3436
Crestline *(G-9142)*
Contech-Gdcg E 937 426-3577
Beavercreek *(G-1235)*
Continntal Mssage Solution Inc D 614 224-4534
Columbus *(G-7434)*
Cook Paving and Cnstr Co E 216 267-7705
Independence *(G-12201)*
Core Resources Inc D 513 731-1771
Cincinnati *(G-3422)*
Corporate Health Dimensions E 740 775-6119
Chillicothe *(G-2828)*
County of Cuyahoga B 216 443-7181
Cleveland *(G-5426)*
County of Morrow E 419 946-2618
Mount Gilead *(G-14853)*
Crawford & Company E 330 652-3296
Warren *(G-18843)*
Crescent Park Corporation C 513 759-7000
West Chester *(G-19059)*
Crestline Hotels & Resorts LLC E 614 846-4355
Columbus *(G-7460)*
Crestline Hotels & Resorts LLC E 513 489-3666
Blue Ash *(G-1571)*
Crestwood Mgmt LLC D 440 484-2400
Cleveland *(G-5438)*
Critical Business Analysis Inc E 419 874-0800
Perrysburg *(G-15991)*
Cypress Communications Inc C 404 965-7248
Cleveland *(G-5459)*
Cypress Companies Inc E 330 849-6500
Akron *(G-185)*
D J- Seve Group Inc E 614 888-6600
Lewis Center *(G-12680)*
Das Dutch Kitchen Inc D 330 683-0530
Dalton *(G-9240)*
Dave Commercial Ground MGT E 440 237-5394
North Royalton *(G-15486)*
Dayton Foundation Inc E 937 222-0410
Dayton *(G-9474)*
◆ **Dco LLC** B 419 931-9086
Perrysburg *(G-15996)*
DE Foxx & Associates Inc B 513 621-5522
Cincinnati *(G-3470)*
Deaconess Long Term Care Inc D 513 861-0400
Cincinnati *(G-3473)*
Dearth Management Company C 614 847-1070
Columbus *(G-7498)*
Dhl Supply Chain (usa) D 229 888-0699
Westerville *(G-19298)*
Dhl Supply Chain (usa) E 419 727-4318
Toledo *(G-17852)*
Dimensionmark Ltd E 513 305-3525
West Chester *(G-19063)*
Distribution Data Incorporated E 216 362-3009
Brookpark *(G-1943)*
DMD Management Inc C 440 944-9400
Wickliffe *(G-19594)*
DMD Management Inc E 216 898-8399
Cleveland *(G-5496)*
Early Learning Tree Chld Ctr D 937 293-7907
Dayton *(G-9513)*
Eclipse Co LLC E 440 552-9400
Cleveland *(G-5526)*
EDM Management Inc E 330 726-5790
Youngstown *(G-20177)*
Education Innovations Intl LLC C 614 339-3676
Dublin *(G-10334)*

87 ENGINEERING, ACCOUNTING, RESEARCH, MANAGEMENT, AND RELATED SERVICES

Company	Code	Phone
Educatonal Svc Ctr Lorain Cnty Elyria (G-10619)	E	440 244-1659
▲ Eleet Cryogenics Inc Bolivar (G-1746)	E	330 874-4009
Elford Inc Columbus (G-7588)	C	614 488-4000
Emp Management Group Ltd Canton (G-2355)	D	330 493-4443
Erie Indemnity Company Canton (G-2357)	D	330 433-6300
Excellence In Motivation Inc Dayton (G-9533)	C	763 445-3000
Executive Jet Management Inc Cincinnati (G-3586)	B	513 979-6600
Facilities Kahn Management Dayton (G-9537)	E	313 202-7607
FC Schwendler LLC Akron (G-222)	E	330 733-8715
First Services Inc Cincinnati (G-3619)	A	513 241-2200
First Transit Inc Cincinnati (G-3624)	B	513 241-2200
Fisher Foods Marketing Inc North Canton (G-15337)	C	330 497-3000
Flat Rock Care Center Flat Rock (G-11103)	C	419 483-7330
Focus Solutions Inc Cincinnati (G-3635)	C	513 376-8349
Folkers Management Corporation Cincinnati (G-3636)	E	513 421-0230
Fort Hmltn-Hghes Hlthcare Corp Hamilton (G-11729)	A	513 867-2000
Foseco Management Inc Cleveland (G-5626)	B	440 826-4548
Franklin & Seidelmann LLC Beachwood (G-1082)	D	216 255-5700
French Company LLC Twinsburg (G-18418)	D	330 963-4344
Frito-Lay North America Inc Maumee (G-13919)	D	419 893-8171
G Stephens Inc Columbus (G-7720)	E	614 227-0304
Gcha Cleveland (G-5662)	D	216 696-6900
Genesis Technology Partners Cincinnati (G-3676)	E	513 585-5800
Gentlebrook Inc Hartville (G-11817)	C	330 877-3694
Gilbane Building Company Columbus (G-7750)	E	614 948-4000
Grote Enterprises LLC Cincinnati (G-3715)	D	513 731-5700
Haiku Columbus (G-7794)	E	614 294-8168
Hammond Construction Inc Canton (G-2389)	D	330 455-7039
Hanger Prosthetics & Tallmadge (G-17638)	E	330 633-9807
Harborside Healthcare Corp Dayton (G-9600)	D	937 436-6155
Hat White Management LLC Akron (G-257)	E	800 525-7967
Hcesc Early Learning Program Cincinnati (G-3745)	C	513 589-3021
Healthcare Management Cons Rockford (G-16563)	E	419 363-2193
Healthscope Benefits Inc Westerville (G-19409)	E	614 797-5200
Heery International Inc Cleveland (G-5746)	E	216 781-1313
Helmsman Management Svcs LLC Columbus (G-7824)	D	614 478-8282
Help Foundation Inc Euclid (G-10758)	C	216 432 4810
Henkel Corporation Mentor (G-14189)	E	440 255-8900
Hernandez Cnstr Svcs Inc Fairlawn (G-10955)	E	330 796-0500
Hill Barth & King LLC Canfield (G-2193)	E	330 758-8613
Hills Developers Inc Blue Ash (G-1612)	C	513 984-0300
Hmshost Corporation Clyde (G-6814)	C	419 547-8667
Holzer Clinic LLC Gallipolis (G-11321)	A	740 446-5411
Hospice of Hamilton Hamilton (G-11742)	E	513 895-1270
Hospice of Southern Ohio Portsmouth (G-16289)	D	740 356-2567
Hospitalists MGT Group LLC Canton (G-2404)	A	866 464-7497
HRP Capital Inc Holland (G-12028)	E	419 865-3111
Ideal Setech LLC Defiance (G-10036)	E	419 782-5522
Illinois Tool Works Inc Blue Ash (G-1614)	E	513 891-7474
Illumetek Corp Cuyahoga Falls (G-9195)	E	330 342-7582
Imflux Inc Hamilton (G-11743)	E	513 488-1017
Infinite Shares LLC Mentor (G-14195)	E	216 317-1601
Infocision Management Corp Dayton (G-9274)	C	937 259-2400
Innovative Architectural Columbus (G-7900)	E	614 416-0614
Instantwhip-Columbus Inc Grove City (G-11571)	E	614 871-9447
Integra Ohio Inc Cincinnati (G-3825)	B	513 378-5214
Intergrated Consulting Bedford Heights (G-1353)	E	216 214-7547
Investek Management Svcs F/C Perrysburg (G-16018)	E	419 873-1236
Island Service Company Put In Bay (G-16368)	C	419 285-3695
J A G Black Gold Management Co Lockbourne (G-12957)	D	614 565-3246
Jack Gibson Construction Co Warren (G-18867)	D	330 394-5280
Jake Sweeney Automotive Inc Cincinnati (G-3859)	C	513 782-2800
Jeff Wyler Automotive Fmly Inc Cincinnati (G-2918)	E	513 752-7450
Jtd Health Systems Inc Saint Marys (G-16679)	A	419 394-3335
Juice Technologies Inc Columbus (G-7957)	E	800 518-5576
Kaiser Logistics LLC Monroe (G-14700)	D	937 534-0213
Kappa House Corp of Delta Upper Arlington (G-18552)	E	614 487-9461
Kerrington Health Systems Inc Fairfield Township (G-10932)	C	513 863-0360
Kettcor Inc Miamisburg (G-14308)	B	937 458-4949
Kettering Adventist Healthcare Dayton (G-9649)	E	937 298-4331
Kettering Adventist Healthcare Miamisburg (G-14309)	E	937 395-8816
Kingston Healthcare Company Toledo (G-17995)	E	419 247-2880
Klingbeil Capital MGT LLC Worthington (G-19967)	D	614 396-4919
Kmon Inc Maumee (G-13933)	E	419 873-0029
Kroger Co Cincinnati (G-3946)	C	513 782-3300
Kross Acquisition Company LLC Loveland (G-13136)	E	513 554-0555
Kurtz Bros Compost Services Akron (G-310)	E	330 864-2621
Lathrop Company Inc Toledo (G-18001)	E	419 893-7000
Laurel Health Care Company Westerville (G-19322)	C	614 794-8800
Laurel Health Care Company Worthington (G-19968)	C	614 888-4553
Laurel Health Care Company Worthington (G-19969)	C	614 885-0408
Leadec Corp Blue Ash (G-1627)	E	513 731-3590
Leatherman Nursing Ctrs Corp Wadsworth (G-18759)	A	330 336-6684
Legacy Village Management Off Cleveland (G-5933)	E	216 382-3871
Levering Management Inc Chesterville (G-2806)	E	419 768-2401
Levering Management Inc Marion (G-13548)	E	740 387-9545
LEWaro-D&j-A Joint Venture Co Dayton (G-9678)	E	937 443-0000
Licking Memorial Hlth Systems Newark (G-15191)	A	220 564-4000
Licking-Knox Goodwill Inds Inc Newark (G-15196)	D	740 345-9861
Lincolnview Local Schools Van Wert (G-18638)	E	419 968-2226
Lineage Logistics LLC Springfield (G-17221)	E	937 328-3349
Lutheran Housing Services Inc Toledo (G-18020)	E	419 861-4990
M A Folkes Company Inc Hamilton (G-11756)	E	513 785-4200
M&C Hotel Interests Inc Chagrin Falls (G-2723)	E	440 543-1331
Marsh Berry & Company Inc Beachwood (G-1097)	E	440 354-3230
Mary Rtan Hlth Assn Logan Cnty Bellefontaine (G-1389)	E	937 592-4015
Marymount Health Care Systems Cleveland (G-5990)	E	216 332-1100
McDaniels Cnstr Corp Inc Columbus (G-8134)	D	614 252-5852
McR LLC Beavercreek (G-1192)	D	937 879-5055
MD Business Solutions Inc Blue Ash (G-1637)	E	513 872-4500
Med America Hlth Systems Corp Dayton (G-9710)	A	937 223-6192
Medicount Management Inc Cincinnati (G-4046)	E	513 772-4465
Megen Construction Company Inc Cincinnati (G-4052)	E	513 742-9191
MEI Hotels Incorporated Cleveland (G-6021)	C	216 589-0441
Mercy Franciscan Hosp Mt Airy Cincinnati (G-4057)	E	513 853-5101
Michael Baker Intl Inc Canton (G-2461)	C	330 453-3110
Michael Baker Intl Inc Cleveland (G-6046)	E	412 269-6300
▲ Midwest Tape LLC Holland (G-12038)	B	419 868-9370
Ministerial Day Care-Headstart Cleveland (G-6068)	E	216 541-7400
National Heritg Academies Inc Dayton (G-9769)	D	937 223-2889
National Heritg Academies Inc Cincinnati (G-4138)	D	513 251-6000
National Heritg Academies Inc Toledo (G-18076)	D	419 269-2247
National Heritg Academies Inc Cincinnati (G-4139)	D	513 751-5555
National Heritg Academies Inc Toledo (G-18077)	D	419 531-3285
National Heritg Academies Inc Dayton (G-9770)	D	937 235-5498
National Heritg Academies Inc Dayton (G-9771)	D	937 278-6671
National Heritg Academies Inc Euclid (G-10769)	D	216 731-0127
National Heritg Academies Inc Cleveland (G-6109)	D	216 451-1725
National Heritg Academies Inc Youngstown (G-20297)	D	330 792-4806
Nationwide General Insur Co Columbus (G-8243)	D	614 249-7111
Netjets Aviation Inc Gahanna (G-11259)	E	614 239-5501
Nexstep Healthcare LLC Cleveland (G-6128)	E	216 797-4040
Niagara Health Corporation Columbus (G-8277)	C	614 898-4000
Niederst Management Ltd Cleveland (G-6133)	D	440 331-8800
North Randall Village Cleveland (G-6143)	D	216 663-1112
Northcoast Healthcare MGT Inc Beachwood (G-1108)	C	216 591-2000
Northwest Local School Dst Canal Fulton (G-2144)	D	330 854-2291
Nursing Care MGT Amer Inc Pataskala (G-15924)	D	740 927-9888
Nursing Care MGT Amer Inc Cincinnati (G-4194)	D	513 793-5092
Nursing Care MGT Amer Inc Toledo (G-18098)	C	419 385-3958
Ohio Cllbrtive Lrng Sltons Inc Beachwood (G-1110)	E	216 595-5289
Ohio Department of Education Piketon (G-16120)	E	740 289-2908
Ohio State Univ Res Foundation Columbus (G-8381)	D	614 292-3815
Omnicare Inc Cincinnati (G-4220)	E	513 719-2600
Omnicare Management Company Cincinnati (G-4222)	A	513 719-1535

Employee Codes: A=Over 500 employees, B=251-500
C=101-250, D=51-100, E=25-50

87 ENGINEERING, ACCOUNTING, RESEARCH, MANAGEMENT, AND RELATED SERVICES SIC SECTION

Omnicare Purch Ltd Partner Inc............C....... 800 990-6664
Cincinnati *(G-4224)*
Osu Internal Medicine LLC....................D....... 614 293-0080
Dublin *(G-10418)*
Outreach Professional Svcs Inc............D....... 216 472-4094
Cleveland *(G-6219)*
P I & I Motor Express Inc.......................C....... 330 448-4035
Masury *(G-13866)*
Parker-Hannifin Intl Corp.......................B....... 216 896-3000
Cleveland *(G-6242)*
Parkops Columbus LLC..........................B....... 877 499-9155
Columbus *(G-8518)*
Pazco Inc..E....... 216 447-9581
Cleveland *(G-6254)*
Perduco Group Inc...................................E....... 937 401-0271
Beavercreek *(G-1196)*
Permedion Inc...D....... 614 895-9900
Westerville *(G-19340)*
Pipino Management Company..............E....... 330 629-2261
Youngstown *(G-20321)*
Pk Management LLC................................C....... 216 472-1870
Richmond Heights *(G-16540)*
Plus Management Services Inc.............C....... 419 225-9018
Lima *(G-12860)*
Premier Management Co Inc..................E....... 740 867-2144
Chesapeake *(G-2786)*
Promedica Health Systems Inc.............A....... 567 585-7454
Toledo *(G-18141)*
Promedica Physcn Cntinuum Svcs.......C....... 419 824-7200
Sylvania *(G-17608)*
Providence Health Partners LLC..........E....... 937 297-8999
Moraine *(G-14816)*
Providence Medical Group Inc..............D....... 937 297-8999
Moraine *(G-14817)*
Quality Control Inspection......................D....... 440 359-1900
Cleveland *(G-6334)*
Quality Supply Chain Co-Op Inc............E....... 614 764-3124
Dublin *(G-10433)*
Quandel Construction Group Inc...........E....... 717 657-0909
Westerville *(G-19439)*
Rama Tika Developers LLC....................E....... 419 806-6446
Mansfield *(G-13353)*
Rbp Atlanta LLC.......................................D....... 614 246-2522
Columbus *(G-8590)*
Regal Hospitality LLC..............................E....... 614 436-0004
Columbus *(G-8605)*
Renaissance House Inc...........................D....... 419 626-1110
Sandusky *(G-16787)*
Renier Construction Corp........................E....... 614 866-4580
Columbus *(G-8613)*
Req/Jqh Holdings Inc..............................D....... 513 891-1066
Blue Ash *(G-1681)*
Resource International Inc....................C....... 614 823-4949
Columbus *(G-8622)*
Rev1 Ventures...E....... 614 487-3700
Columbus *(G-8627)*
Revolution Group Inc...............................D....... 614 212-1111
Westerville *(G-19349)*
Ricco Enterprises Incorporated.............E....... 216 883-7775
Cleveland *(G-6389)*
Richard L Bowen & Assoc Inc................D....... 216 491-9300
Cleveland *(G-6391)*
Richland Mall Shopping Ctr....................E....... 419 529-4003
Mansfield *(G-13357)*
RJ Runge Company Inc...........................E....... 419 740-5781
Port Clinton *(G-16253)*
Rjw Inc...E....... 216 398-6090
Independence *(G-12250)*
RMS of Ohio Inc...B....... 440 617-6605
Westlake *(G-19542)*
Ross Consolidated Corp..........................D....... 440 748-5800
Grafton *(G-11444)*
Roundstone Management Ltd...............E....... 440 617-0333
Lakewood *(G-12499)*
Ruscilli Construction Co Inc...................D....... 614 876-9484
Columbus *(G-8658)*
Saber Healthcare Group LLC..................E....... 216 292-5706
Bedford *(G-1333)*
Safeguard Properties LLC.......................A....... 216 739-2900
Cleveland *(G-6433)*
Safran Power Usa LLC............................C....... 330 487-2000
Twinsburg *(G-18466)*
Salem Healthcare MGT LLC....................E....... 330 332-1588
Salem *(G-16714)*
Salvation Army...D....... 419 447-2252
Tiffin *(G-17697)*
Salvation Army...C....... 330 773-3331
Akron *(G-428)*
Select Hotels Group LLC.........................E....... 513 754-0003
Mason *(G-13759)*
Shred-It USA LLC.....................................D....... 847 288-0377
Fairfield *(G-10906)*
Signature Inc..C....... 614 734-0010
Dublin *(G-10453)*
Simonson Construction Svcs Inc..........D....... 419 281-8299
Ashland *(G-699)*
Skanska USA Building Inc.......................E....... 513 421-0082
Cincinnati *(G-4538)*
Sleep Network Inc....................................E....... 419 535-9282
Toledo *(G-18190)*
Smg Holdings Inc.....................................C....... 614 827-2500
Columbus *(G-8744)*
Sperian Protection Usa Inc....................D....... 614 539-5056
Grove City *(G-11601)*
Ssoe Inc...E....... 330 821-7198
Alliance *(G-560)*
St Augustine Corporation........................B....... 216 939-7600
Lakewood *(G-12501)*
St George & Co Inc...................................E....... 330 733-7528
Akron *(G-447)*
Standard Retirement Svcs Inc...............E....... 440 808-2724
Westlake *(G-19551)*
Stat Integrated Tech Inc..........................E....... 440 286-7663
Chardon *(G-2769)*
Sterling Medical Corporation..................D....... 513 984-1800
Cincinnati *(G-4591)*
Sterling Medical Corporation..................C....... 513 984-1800
Cincinnati *(G-4592)*
Summit Advantage LLC............................D....... 330 835-2453
Fairlawn *(G-10979)*
Sylvania Franciscan Health....................E....... 419 882-8373
Maumee *(G-13984)*
T K Edwards LLC.......................................E....... 614 406-8064
Columbus *(G-8817)*
TAC Industries Inc....................................B....... 937 328-5200
Springfield *(G-17285)*
Technical Consultants Inc.......................E....... 513 521-2696
Cincinnati *(G-4629)*
The Sheakley Group Inc..........................E....... 513 771-2277
Cincinnati *(G-4646)*
Thomas Rosser..C....... 614 890-2900
Westerville *(G-19444)*
Tjm Clmbus LLC Tjm Clumbus LLC......D....... 614 885-1885
Columbus *(G-8851)*
Tradesmen International LLC................C....... 419 502-9140
Sandusky *(G-16802)*
Trihealth Inc...E....... 513 929-0020
Cincinnati *(G-4687)*
Trihealth Inc...E....... 513 865-1111
Cincinnati *(G-4688)*
Trihealth Inc...E....... 513 569-6777
Cincinnati *(G-4689)*
Trihealth Inc...E....... 513 891-1627
Blue Ash *(G-1702)*
Trihealth Inc...E....... 513 569-6111
Cincinnati *(G-4690)*
Trihealth Inc...E....... 513 871-2340
Cincinnati *(G-4691)*
Trihealth Inc...C....... 513 985-0900
Montgomery *(G-14734)*
Trinity Health System...............................C....... 740 283-7848
Steubenville *(G-17339)*
Trinity Health System...............................A....... 740 264-8000
Steubenville *(G-17340)*
Trinity Health System...............................E....... 740 264-8101
Steubenville *(G-17341)*
Trinity Hospital Holding Co.....................A....... 740 264-8000
Steubenville *(G-17343)*
Triversity Construction Co LLC..............E....... 513 733-0046
Cincinnati *(G-4702)*
Trustaff Management Inc........................A....... 513 272-3999
Blue Ash *(G-1706)*
Ttl Associates Inc......................................C....... 419 241-4556
Toledo *(G-18263)*
Uc Health Llc..C....... 513 298-3000
West Chester *(G-19170)*
Uc Health Llc..E....... 513 584-8600
Cincinnati *(G-4721)*
Uc Health Llc..A....... 513 585-6000
Cincinnati *(G-4722)*
United Telemanagement Corp...............E....... 937 454-1888
Dayton *(G-9948)*
▲ **University Hospitals**...............................A....... 216 767-8900
Shaker Heights *(G-16869)*
University Hospitals...................................A....... 440 743-3000
Parma *(G-15917)*
University Hospitals...................................D....... 216 844-8797
Cleveland *(G-6657)*
University Hospitals Cleveland..............E....... 216 844-3528
Cleveland *(G-6662)*
University of Cincinnati...........................E....... 513 556-4200
Cincinnati *(G-4767)*
University of Cincinnati...........................C....... 513 558-4231
Cincinnati *(G-4768)*
V Westaar Inc..E....... 740 803-2803
Lewis Center *(G-12709)*
Vance Property Management LLC........D....... 419 887-1878
Toledo *(G-18288)*
Verst Group Logistics Inc.......................E....... 513 772-2494
Cincinnati *(G-4810)*
Viaquest Inc...E....... 614 889-5837
Dublin *(G-10481)*
Viaquest Behavioral Health LLC............E....... 614 339-0868
Dublin *(G-10482)*
Village of Valley View................................C....... 216 524-6511
Cleveland *(G-6698)*
Voc Works Ltd..D....... 614 760-3515
Dublin *(G-10484)*
Vora Ventures LLC.....................................C....... 513 792-5100
Blue Ash *(G-1716)*
Wadsworth Galaxy Rest Inc...................D....... 330 334-3663
Wadsworth *(G-18773)*
Walnut Ridge Management.....................D....... 234 678-3900
Akron *(G-504)*
Wayne Street Development LLC...........E....... 740 373-5455
Marietta *(G-13519)*
Western Management Inc.......................E....... 216 941-3333
Cleveland *(G-6741)*
Westminster Management Company....C....... 614 274-5154
Columbus *(G-8980)*
William Royce Inc.......................................D....... 513 771-3361
Cincinnati *(G-4850)*
Windsor House Inc....................................E....... 440 834-0544
Burton *(G-2066)*
Wings Investors Company Ltd...............E....... 513 241-5800
Cincinnati *(G-4853)*
Zarcal Zanesville LLC...............................D....... 216 226-2132
Lakewood *(G-12503)*

8742 Management Consulting Services

0714 Inc..E....... 440 327-2123
North Ridgeville *(G-15452)*
1st Advnce SEC Invstgtions Inc.............E....... 937 317-4433
Dayton *(G-9292)*
2060 Digital LLC..E....... 513 699-5012
Cincinnati *(G-2941)*
5me LLC..E....... 513 719-1600
Cincinnati *(G-2900)*
Accelerant Technologies LLC.................D....... 419 236-8768
Genoa *(G-11374)*
Accenture LLP...C....... 216 685-1435
Cleveland *(G-4953)*
Accenture LLP...C....... 614 629-2000
Columbus *(G-6934)*
Accenture LLP...D....... 513 455-1000
Cincinnati *(G-2963)*
Accenture LLP...D....... 513 651-2444
Cincinnati *(G-2964)*
Accurate Inventory and C........................B....... 800 777-9414
Columbus *(G-6936)*
Acloche LLC...E....... 888 608-0889
Columbus *(G-6938)*
Acuity Healthcare LP................................D....... 740 283-7499
Steubenville *(G-17302)*
Advanced Computer Graphics...............E....... 513 936-5060
Blue Ash *(G-1523)*
Advanced Prgrm Resources Inc............E....... 614 761-9994
Dublin *(G-10234)*
Advocate Solutions LLC..........................E....... 614 444-5144
Columbus *(G-6948)*
Aeea LLC...E....... 330 497-5304
Canton *(G-2229)*
Affiliated Resource Group Inc................D....... 614 889-6555
Dublin *(G-10236)*
Ake Marketing..E....... 440 232-1661
Bedford *(G-1293)*
Akron Centl Engrv Mold Mch Inc...........E....... 330 794-8704
Akron *(G-30)*
Alps Services Inc.......................................E....... 513 671-6300
Cincinnati *(G-2995)*
Alternative Care Mgt Systems...............E....... 614 761-0035
Dublin *(G-10243)*
American Health Group Inc....................D....... 419 891-1212
Maumee *(G-13875)*
Ameriprise Financial Svcs Inc................E....... 614 934-4057
Dublin *(G-10253)*
Amotec Inc..E....... 440 250-4600
Cleveland *(G-5030)*
Antero Resources Corporation..............D....... 740 760-1000
Marietta *(G-13433)*

1086 2018 Harris Ohio Services Directory

87 ENGINEERING, ACCOUNTING, RESEARCH, MANAGEMENT, AND RELATED SERVICES

▲ Applied Marketing Services .... E 440 716-9962
  Westlake *(G-19460)*
Archway Marketing Services Inc .... C 440 572-0725
  Strongsville *(G-17444)*
Ardmore Power Logistics LLC .... E 216 502-0640
  Westlake *(G-19461)*
Armada Ltd .... D 614 505-7256
  Powell *(G-16324)*
Arras Group Inc .... E 216 621-1601
  Cleveland *(G-5067)*
Arysen Inc .... D 440 230-4400
  Independence *(G-12188)*
AT&T Government Solutions Inc .... D 937 306-3030
  Beavercreek *(G-1149)*
Atlas Advisors LLC .... E 888 282-0873
  Columbus *(G-7068)*
Attevo Inc .... D 216 928-2800
  Beachwood *(G-1053)*
Aultman Health Foundation .... A 330 682-3010
  Orrville *(G-15765)*
Austin Building and Design Inc .... C 440 544-2600
  Cleveland *(G-5081)*
Automotive Events Inc .... E 440 356-1383
  Rocky River *(G-16570)*
Avatar Management Services .... E 330 963-3900
  Macedonia *(G-13187)*
AVI Food Systems Inc .... C 330 372-6000
  Warren *(G-18827)*
Azimuth Corporation .... E 937 256-8571
  Beavercreek Township *(G-1265)*
B&F Capital Markets Inc .... E 216 472-2700
  Cleveland *(G-5090)*
Backoffice Associates LLC .... D 419 660-4600
  Norwalk *(G-15562)*
Banc Amer Prctice Slutions Inc .... C 614 794-8247
  Westerville *(G-19287)*
Barrett & Associates Inc .... E 330 928-2323
  Cuyahoga Falls *(G-9164)*
Baxter Hodell Donnelly Preston .... C 513 271-1634
  Cincinnati *(G-3083)*
Beacon of Light Ltd .... E 419 531-9060
  Toledo *(G-17765)*
Benchmark National Corporation .... E 419 660-1100
  Bellevue *(G-1406)*
Benchmark Technologies Corp .... E 419 843-6691
  Toledo *(G-17769)*
Bionetics Corporation .... E 757 873-0900
  Heath *(G-11835)*
Bodine Perry LLC .... E 330 702-8100
  Canfield *(G-2183)*
Boenning & Scattergood Inc .... E 614 336-8851
  Powell *(G-16326)*
Brandmuscle Inc .... C 216 464-4342
  Cleveland *(G-5133)*
Brentley Institute Inc .... E 216 225-0087
  Cleveland *(G-5137)*
Btas Inc .... C 937 431-9431
  Beavercreek *(G-1155)*
Budros Ruhlin & Roe Inc .... E 614 481-6900
  Columbus *(G-7165)*
Burke Inc .... C 513 241-5663
  Cincinnati *(G-3150)*
C H Dean Inc .... D 937 222-9531
  Beavercreek *(G-1156)*
Career Partners Intl LLC .... A 919 401-4260
  Columbus *(G-7198)*
Carol Scudere .... E 614 839-4357
  New Albany *(G-14979)*
Cbiz Inc .... C 216 447-9000
  Cleveland *(G-5196)*
Center For Health Affairs .... D 800 362-2628
  Cleveland *(G-5208)*
Chapman & Chapman Inc .... E 440 934-4102
  Avon *(G-887)*
Chartwell Group LLC .... E 216 360-0009
  Cleveland *(G-5230)*
Chattree and Associates Inc .... D 216 831-1494
  Cleveland *(G-5231)*
Chemsultants International Inc .... E 440 974-3080
  Mentor *(G-14157)*
Classic Real Estate Co .... E 937 393-3416
  Hillsboro *(G-11968)*
Clear Vision Engineering LLC .... E 419 478-7151
  Toledo *(G-17816)*
Clemans Nelson & Assoc Inc .... E 614 923-7700
  Dublin *(G-10295)*
Cleveland Dairy Queen Inc .... C 440 946-3690
  Willoughby *(G-19654)*
Clgt Solutions LLC .... E 740 920-4795
  Granville *(G-11462)*

Club Life Entertainment LLC .... E 216 831-1134
  Beachwood *(G-1066)*
Coho Creative LLC .... E 513 751-7500
  Cincinnati *(G-3379)*
Columbus Public School Dst .... E 614 365-5000
  Columbus *(G-7379)*
◆ Comex North America Inc .... D 303 307-2100
  Cleveland *(G-5374)*
Commercial Debt Cunseling Corp .... D 614 848-9800
  Columbus *(G-7399)*
Commquest Services Inc .... C 330 455-0374
  Canton *(G-2316)*
Communica Inc .... E 419 244-7766
  Toledo *(G-17823)*
Comprehensive Logistics Co Inc .... E 330 793-0504
  Youngstown *(G-20158)*
Comprehensive Logistics Co Inc .... E 330 233-2627
  Avon Lake *(G-927)*
Concordia Properties LLC .... E 513 671-0120
  Cincinnati *(G-3409)*
Consumer Credit Counseling .... E 800 254-4100
  Cleveland *(G-5399)*
Contract Marketing Inc .... D 440 639-9100
  Mentor *(G-14162)*
Corbus LLC .... D 937 226-7724
  Dayton *(G-9428)*
▼ Cornerstone Brands Group Inc .... A 513 603-1000
  West Chester *(G-19053)*
Corporate Fin Assoc of Clumbus .... D 614 457-9219
  Columbus *(G-7444)*
Corporate Plans Inc .... E 440 542-7800
  Solon *(G-16995)*
County of Marion .... E 740 382-0624
  Marion *(G-13536)*
CPC Logistics Inc .... D 513 874-5787
  Fairfield *(G-10838)*
Critical Business Analysis Inc .... E 419 874-0800
  Perrysburg *(G-15991)*
Crown Westfalen LLC .... C 614 488-1169
  Columbus *(G-7468)*
D L A Training Center .... D 614 692-5986
  Columbus *(G-7480)*
D L Ryan Companies LLC .... E 614 436-6558
  Westerville *(G-19296)*
Dari Pizza Enterprises II Inc .... E 419 534-3000
  Maumee *(G-13905)*
Davis 5 Star Holdings LLC .... E 954 470-8456
  Springfield *(G-17187)*
Dayton Aerospace Inc .... E 937 426-4300
  Beavercreek Township *(G-1268)*
Dayton Digital Media Inc .... E 937 223-8335
  Dayton *(G-9469)*
Dayton Foundation Inc .... E 937 222-0410
  Dayton *(G-9474)*
DE Foxx & Associates Inc .... B 513 621-5522
  Cincinnati *(G-3470)*
Dealers Group Limited .... E 440 352-4970
  Beachwood *(G-1073)*
Dedicated Tech Services Inc .... D 614 309-0059
  Dublin *(G-10317)*
Dedicated Technologies Inc .... D 614 460-3200
  Columbus *(G-7499)*
Deloitte & Touche LLP .... D 937 223-8821
  Dayton *(G-9496)*
Deloitte & Touche LLP .... C 216 589-1300
  Cleveland *(G-5474)*
Deloitte & Touche LLP .... B 513 784-7100
  Cincinnati *(G-3482)*
Deloitte Consulting LLP .... C 937 223-8821
  Dayton *(G-9497)*
Delta Energy LLC .... E 614 761-3603
  Dublin *(G 10318)*
Dental One Inc .... E 216 584-1000
  Independence *(G-12203)*
Devry University Inc .... C 614 251-6969
  Columbus *(G-7515)*
Digital Controls Corporation .... D 513 746-8118
  Miamisburg *(G-14297)*
Direct Options Inc .... E 513 779-4416
  West Chester *(G-19064)*
Distribution Data Incorporated .... E 216 362-3009
  Brookpark *(G-1943)*
Diversified Systems Inc .... E 614 476-9939
  Westerville *(G-19394)*
Duke Energy Ohio Inc .... C 513 421-9500
  Cincinnati *(G-3511)*
Duncan Falls Assoc .... D 740 674-7105
  Duncan Falls *(G-10498)*
Dunnhumby Inc .... E 513 579-3400
  Cincinnati *(G-3514)*

Dwight Spencer & Associates .... E 614 488-3123
  Columbus *(G-7554)*
East Way Behavioral Hlth Care .... C 937 222-4900
  Dayton *(G-9515)*
Efficient Collaborative Retail .... D 440 498-0500
  Solon *(G-17001)*
Emerald Health Network Inc .... D 216 479-2030
  Fairlawn *(G-10948)*
Enabling Partners LLC .... E 440 878-9418
  Strongsville *(G-17461)*
Engaged Health Care Bus Svcs .... E 614 457-8180
  Columbus *(G-7594)*
Enterprise Data Management Inc .... E 513 791-7272
  Blue Ash *(G-1588)*
Epiphany Management Group LLC .... E 330 706-4056
  Akron *(G-209)*
Epipheo Incorporated .... E 888 687-7620
  Cincinnati *(G-3565)*
Equity Resources Inc .... E 513 518-6318
  Cincinnati *(G-3571)*
Ernst & Young LLP .... C 614 224-5678
  Columbus *(G-7607)*
Ernst & Young LLP .... C 513 612-1400
  Cincinnati *(G-3575)*
Excellence Alliance Group Inc .... E 513 619-4800
  Cincinnati *(G-3585)*
Facilities MGT Solutions LLC .... E 513 639-2230
  Cincinnati *(G-3587)*
Fahlgren Inc .... E 614 383-1500
  Columbus *(G-7629)*
Fathom Seo LLC .... E 614 291-8456
  Columbus *(G-7643)*
Fathom Seo LLC .... D 216 525-0510
  Cleveland *(G-5577)*
Financial Design Group Inc .... E 419 843-4737
  Toledo *(G-17889)*
Financial Network Group Ltd .... E 513 469-7500
  Cincinnati *(G-3610)*
Findley Davies Inc .... D 419 255-1360
  Toledo *(G-17890)*
Finit Group LLC .... D 513 793-4648
  Cincinnati *(G-3611)*
First Choice Medical Staffing .... E 419 626-9740
  Sandusky *(G-16761)*
First Data Gvrnment Sltions LP .... D 513 489-9599
  Blue Ash *(G-1594)*
First Transit Inc .... B 513 241-2200
  Cincinnati *(G-3624)*
Fitworks Holding LLC .... B 513 923-9931
  Cincinnati *(G-3631)*
Focus Solutions Inc .... C 513 376-8349
  Cincinnati *(G-3635)*
Forest City Enterprises Inc .... D 216 621-6060
  Cleveland *(G-5613)*
Four Seasons Environmental Inc .... B 513 539-2978
  Monroe *(G-14696)*
Frank Gates Service Company .... B 614 793-8000
  Dublin *(G-10350)*
Frankes Wood Products LLC .... E 937 642-0706
  Marysville *(G-13620)*
Fusion Alliance LLC .... E 614 852-8000
  Westerville *(G-19309)*
Fusion Alliance LLC .... E 513 563-8444
  Blue Ash *(G-1597)*
G Stephens Inc .... E 419 241-5188
  Toledo *(G-17904)*
Garretyson Frm Resolution Grp .... C 513 794-0400
  Loveland *(G-13127)*
Gbq Consulting LLC .... D 614 221-1120
  Columbus *(G-7731)*
General Fncl Tax Cnsulting LLC .... E 888 496-2679
  Cincinnati *(G-2917)*
Genesis Corp .... E 614 934-1211
  Columbus *(G-7738)*
Germain & Co Inc .... E 937 885-5827
  Dayton *(G-9572)*
Global Cnsld Holdings Inc .... D 513 703-0965
  Mason *(G-13709)*
Global Military Expert Co .... E 800 738-9795
  Beavercreek *(G-1242)*
Goodwill Inds of Southern Ohio .... E 740 353-4394
  Portsmouth *(G-16281)*
GP Strategies Corporation .... E 513 583-8810
  Mason *(G-13710)*
Gray & Pape Inc .... E 513 287-7700
  Cincinnati *(G-3694)*
Greentree Group Inc .... E 937 490-5500
  Dayton *(G-9591)*
Group Management Services Inc .... E 330 659-0100
  Richfield *(G-16511)*

87 ENGINEERING, ACCOUNTING, RESEARCH, MANAGEMENT, AND RELATED SERVICES

Group Transportation Svcs Inc .... E 800 689-6255
  Hudson *(G-12119)*
Gund Sports Marketing Llc .... E 216 420-2000
  Cleveland *(G-5709)*
H T V Industries Inc .... D 216 514-0060
  Cleveland *(G-5716)*
Hafenbrack Mktg Cmmnctions Inc .... E 937 424-8950
  Dayton *(G-9596)*
Halley Consulting Group LLC .... E 614 899-7325
  Westerville *(G-19405)*
Hamilton Parks Conservancy .... E 513 785-7055
  Hamilton *(G-11740)*
Hanna Commercial LLC .... D 216 861-7200
  Cleveland *(G-5723)*
Harbor Freight Tools Usa Inc .... D 330 479-9852
  Canton *(G-2394)*
Harris Mackessy & Brennan .... C 614 221-6831
  Westerville *(G-19311)*
Hctec Partners LLC .... D 513 985-6400
  Cincinnati *(G-3750)*
HDR Engineering Inc .... E 614 839-5770
  Columbus *(G-7807)*
Healthcomp Inc .... D 216 696-6900
  Cleveland *(G-5738)*
Henry Call Inc .... C 216 433-5609
  Cleveland *(G-5749)*
HJ Ford Associates Inc .... C 937 429-9711
  Beavercreek *(G-1176)*
Homelife Companies Inc .... E 740 369-1297
  Delaware *(G-10106)*
Honda of America Mfg Inc .... C 937 644-0724
  Marysville *(G-13626)*
Hr Butler LLC .... E 614 923-2900
  Dublin *(G-10366)*
I T E LLC .... D 513 576-6200
  Loveland *(G-13132)*
Ilead LLC .... E 440 846-2346
  Strongsville *(G-17476)*
Impact Ceramics LLC .... E 440 554-3624
  Cleveland *(G-5807)*
Incentisoft Solutions LLC .... D 877 562-4461
  Cleveland *(G-5808)*
Incubit LLC .... D 740 362-1401
  Delaware *(G-10108)*
Independent Evaluators Inc .... D 419 872-5650
  Perrysburg *(G-16016)*
Industry Insights Inc .... E 614 389-2100
  Columbus *(G-7894)*
Infor (us) Inc .... D 614 781-2325
  Columbus *(G-6886)*
Ingleside Investments Inc .... E 614 221-1025
  Columbus *(G-7898)*
Innerworkings Inc .... E 513 984-9500
  Cincinnati *(G-3819)*
Innovative Technologies Corp .... D 937 252-2145
  Dayton *(G-9275)*
Inquiry Systems Inc .... E 614 464-3800
  Columbus *(G-7904)*
Institute For Human Services .... E 614 251-6000
  Columbus *(G-7910)*
Integra Group Inc .... E 513 326-5600
  Cincinnati *(G-3824)*
Integra Realty Resources - Cin .... B 513 561-2305
  Cincinnati *(G-3826)*
Integrated Prj Resources LLC .... E 330 272-0998
  Salem *(G-16701)*
Interbrand Design Forum Inc .... C 937 439-4400
  Cincinnati *(G-3834)*
Interchez Lgistics Systems Inc .... E 330 923-5080
  Stow *(G-17377)*
Ipsos-Asi LLC .... D 513 872-4300
  Cincinnati *(G-3842)*
Iron Mountain Info MGT LLC .... C 440 248-0999
  Solon *(G-17019)*
Island Hospitality MGT LLC .... E 614 864-8844
  Columbus *(G-7927)*
ITM Marketing Inc .... C 740 295-3575
  Coshocton *(G-9108)*
Its Financial LLC .... D 937 425-6889
  Beavercreek *(G-1247)*
J G Martin Inc .... D 216 491-1584
  Cleveland *(G-5841)*
Jarrett Logistics Systems Inc .... C 330 682-0099
  Orrville *(G-15775)*
Jersey Central Pwr & Light Co .... E 330 315-6713
  Fairlawn *(G-10960)*
Jjr Solutions LLC .... E 937 912-0288
  Beavercreek *(G-1180)*
Johnson Mirmiran Thompson Inc .... D 614 714-0270
  Columbus *(G-7944)*

Jonathon R Johnson & Assoc .... E 216 932-6529
  Cleveland *(G-5870)*
Jyg Innovations LLC .... E 937 630-3858
  Dayton *(G-9647)*
Kaiser Consulting LLC .... E 614 378-5361
  Powell *(G-16341)*
Kalypso LP .... D 216 378-4290
  Beachwood *(G-1093)*
Karlsberger Companies .... C 614 461-9500
  Columbus *(G-7966)*
Kelley Companies .... D 330 668-6100
  Copley *(G-9057)*
Kennedy Group Enterprises Inc .... E 440 879-0078
  Strongsville *(G-17481)*
Kettering Adventist Healthcare .... E 513 867-3166
  Liberty Township *(G-12721)*
Kings Medical Company .... C 330 653-3968
  Hudson *(G-12128)*
Klingbeil Management Group Co .... E 614 220-8900
  Columbus *(G-7997)*
Km2 Solutions LLC .... B 610 213-1408
  Columbus *(G-7999)*
Knowledgeworks Foundation .... D 513 241-1422
  Cincinnati *(G-3937)*
Kroger Refill Center .... E 614 333-5017
  Columbus *(G-8016)*
L and C Soft Serve Inc .... E 330 364-3823
  Dover *(G-10196)*
Landrum & Brown Incorporated .... D 513 530-5333
  Blue Ash *(G-1625)*
Lang Financial Group Inc .... E 513 699-2966
  Blue Ash *(G-1626)*
Language Logic .... E 513 241-9112
  Cincinnati *(G-3961)*
Lesaint Logistics LLC .... D 513 988-0101
  Trenton *(G-18341)*
Level Seven .... E 216 524-9055
  Independence *(G-12224)*
LEWaro-D&j-A Joint Venture Co .... E 937 443-0000
  Dayton *(G-9678)*
Lpl Financial Holdings Inc .... B 513 772-2592
  Cincinnati *(G-4001)*
Madison Avenue Mktg Group Inc .... E 419 473-9000
  Toledo *(G-18026)*
Malik Punam .... D 513 636-1333
  Cincinnati *(G-4017)*
Managed Technology Svcs LLC .... D 937 247-8915
  Miamisburg *(G-14315)*
Mancan Inc .... A 440 884-9675
  Strongsville *(G-17487)*
Marketing Indus Solutions Corp .... E 513 703-0965
  Mason *(G-13735)*
Marsh Berry & Company Inc .... E 440 354-3230
  Beachwood *(G-1097)*
MB Financial Inc .... D 937 283-2027
  Wilmington *(G-19772)*
Mc Cloy Financial Services .... D 614 457-6233
  Columbus *(G-8133)*
McKinsey & Company Inc .... E 216 274-4000
  Cleveland *(G-6006)*
McKinsey & Company Inc .... D 216 274-4000
  Cleveland *(G-6007)*
Med-Pass Incorporated .... E 937 438-8884
  Dayton *(G-9711)*
Med3000 Group Inc .... E 937 291-7850
  Miamisburg *(G-14316)*
Medco Health Solutions Inc .... A 614 822-2000
  Dublin *(G-10393)*
Medical Account Services Inc .... E 937 297-6072
  Moraine *(G-14803)*
Medical Recovery Systems Inc .... D 513 872-7000
  Cincinnati *(G-4044)*
Medisync Midwest Ltd Lblty Co .... D 513 533-1199
  Cincinnati *(G-4047)*
Melo International Inc .... B 440 519-0526
  Cleveland *(G-6023)*
Mercer (us) Inc .... E 513 632-2600
  Cincinnati *(G-4056)*
Merchandising Services Co .... D 866 479-8246
  Blue Ash *(G-1639)*
Merrill Lynch Pierce Fenner .... C 513 579-3600
  Cincinnati *(G-4079)*
Merrill Lynch Pierce Fenner .... E 937 847-4000
  Miamisburg *(G-14319)*
Merrill Lynch Pierce Fenner .... D 614 225-3000
  Columbus *(G-8151)*
Merrill Lynch Pierce Fenner .... D 330 670-2400
  Akron *(G-339)*
Merrill Lynch Pierce Fenner .... E 330 655-2312
  Hudson *(G-12132)*

▲ Mes Inc .... D 740 201-8112
  Lewis Center *(G-12694)*
Miami University .... B 513 727-3200
  Middletown *(G-14435)*
Mid-Amrica Cnsulting Group Inc .... D 216 432-6925
  Cleveland *(G-6053)*
Midwest Mfg Solutions LLC .... E 513 381-7200
  West Chester *(G-19216)*
▲ Midwest Motor Supply Co .... C 800 233-1294
  Columbus *(G-8170)*
Mission Pride Inc .... E 216 759-7404
  Cleveland Heights *(G-6793)*
Motion Controls Robotics Inc .... E 419 334-5886
  Fremont *(G-11214)*
Murtech Consulting LLC .... D 216 328-8580
  Cleveland *(G-6091)*
Mxd Group Inc .... E 614 801-0621
  Columbus *(G-8210)*
National Administative Svc LLC .... E 614 358-3607
  Dublin *(G-10403)*
National City Cmnty Dev Corp .... E 216 575-2000
  Cleveland *(G-6103)*
National Yllow Pages Media LLC .... E 216 447-9400
  Independence *(G-12237)*
Nationwide Financial Svcs Inc .... C 614 249-7111
  Columbus *(G-8242)*
Nationwide Rtirement Solutions .... C 614 854-8300
  Dublin *(G-10405)*
Navigtor MGT Prtners Ltd Lblty .... E 614 796-0090
  Columbus *(G-8251)*
Neighborhood Development Svcs .... E 330 296-2003
  Ravenna *(G-16393)*
Netsmart Technologies Inc .... D 614 764-0143
  Dublin *(G-10407)*
Normandy Group LLC .... E 513 745-0990
  Blue Ash *(G-1654)*
Northwest Country Place Inc .... D 440 488-2700
  Willoughby *(G-19698)*
Nsa Technologies LLC .... E 330 576-4600
  Akron *(G-359)*
Ohic Insurance Company .... D 614 221-7777
  Columbus *(G-8315)*
Ohio Custodial Maintenance .... E 614 443-1232
  Columbus *(G-8323)*
Ohio Edison Company .... C 330 740-7754
  Youngstown *(G-20305)*
Ohio Equities LLC .... E 614 207-1805
  Columbus *(G-8340)*
Ohio State University .... E 614 728-8100
  Columbus *(G-8432)*
Ohio-Kentucky-Indiana Regional .... E 513 621-6300
  Cincinnati *(G-4214)*
Ohiohealth Corporation .... D 614 566-3500
  Columbus *(G-8456)*
Ologie LLC .... D 614 221-1107
  Columbus *(G-8466)*
Oncall LLC .... E 513 381-4320
  Cincinnati *(G-4225)*
One10 LLC .... D 763 445-3000
  Dayton *(G-9792)*
Oppenheimer & Co Inc .... E 513 723-9200
  Cincinnati *(G-4228)*
Optimal Life Intgrtve Mdcne PA .... E 419 474-3657
  Sylvania *(G-17604)*
OR Colan Associates LLC .... E 440 827-6116
  Cleveland *(G-6210)*
Orbit Systems Inc .... E 614 504-8011
  Lewis Center *(G-12700)*
Organizational Horizons Inc .... E 614 268-6013
  Worthington *(G-19981)*
Paragon Consulting Inc .... E 440 684-3101
  Cleveland *(G-6231)*
Paragon Tec Inc .... D 216 361-5555
  Cleveland *(G-6232)*
Park International Theme Svcs .... E 513 381-6131
  Cincinnati *(G-4253)*
Parker Marketing Research LLC .... E 513 248-8100
  Milford *(G-14549)*
Parman Group Inc .... E 513 673-0077
  Columbus *(G-8519)*
Pat Henry Group LLC .... E 216 447-0831
  Milford *(G-14551)*
Patient Account MGT Svcs LLC .... E 614 575-0044
  Columbus *(G-8520)*
Patientpint Hosp Solutions LLC .... C 513 936-6800
  Cincinnati *(G-4259)*
Patientpint Ntwrk Slutions LLC .... D 513 936-6800
  Cincinnati *(G-4260)*
Patientpoint LLC .... E 513 936-6800
  Cincinnati *(G-4261)*

Patrick Mahoney E 614 292-5766
Columbus *(G-8521)*
Pcs Cost E 216 771-1090
Cleveland *(G-6256)*
Pension Corporation America E 513 281-3366
Cincinnati *(G-4277)*
Peoplefacts LLC E 800 849-1071
Maumee *(G-13958)*
Peopletomysitecom LLC E 800 295-4519
Columbus *(G-8533)*
Peopleworks Dev of Hr LLC E 419 636-4637
Bryan *(G-2016)*
Perduco Group Inc E 937 401-0271
Beavercreek *(G-1196)*
Phoenix Cosmopolitan Group LLC E 814 746-4863
Avon *(G-914)*
Phoenix Resource Network LLC E 800 990-4948
Cincinnati *(G-4294)*
Piasans Mill Inc E 419 448-0100
Tiffin *(G-17693)*
Pitmark Services Inc E 330 876-2217
Kinsman *(G-12454)*
Plus Management Services Inc C 419 225-9018
Lima *(G-12860)*
Ply-Trim Enterprises Inc E 330 799-7876
Youngstown *(G-20325)*
Pope & Associates Inc E 513 671-1277
Cincinnati *(G-4314)*
Portage Area Rgonal Trnsp Auth D 330 678-1287
Kent *(G-12391)*
Power Management Inc E 937 222-2909
Dayton *(G-9817)*
Producer Group LLC E 440 871-7700
Rocky River *(G-16589)*
Productivity Qulty Systems Inc E 937 885-2255
Dayton *(G-9833)*
Professnal Mint Cincinnati Inc A 513 579-1161
Cincinnati *(G-4345)*
Progressive Entps Holdings Inc A 614 794-3300
Westerville *(G-19346)*
Projetech Inc E 513 481-4900
Cincinnati *(G-4346)*
Protiviti Inc E 216 696-6010
Cleveland *(G-6325)*
Provenitfinance LLC E 888 958-1060
Pickerington *(G-16103)*
PSI Supply Chain Solutions LLC E 614 389-4717
Dublin *(G-10432)*
Quality Solutions Inc E 440 933-9946
Cleveland *(G-6335)*
Quick Solutions Inc C 614 825-8000
Westerville *(G-19347)*
Quotient Technology Inc E 513 229-8659
Mason *(G-13752)*
R D D Inc C 216 781-5858
Cleveland *(G-6339)*
R P Marketing Public Relations E 419 241-2221
Holland *(G-12050)*
Racksquared LLC E 614 737-8812
Columbus *(G-8583)*
Rahim Inc E 216 621-8977
Cleveland *(G-6349)*
Real Estate Capital Fund LLC E 216 491-3990
Cleveland *(G-6358)*
Redwood Living Inc C 216 360-9441
Independence *(G-12247)*
Regent Systems Inc D 937 640-8010
Dayton *(G-9845)*
Remtec Automation LLC E 877 759-8151
Mason *(G-13755)*
Residential Hm Assn of Marion C 740 387-9999
Marion *(G-13575)*
Resource Ventures Ltd D 614 621-2888
Columbus *(G-8623)*
Retail Forward Inc E 614 355-4000
Columbus *(G-8625)*
Revlocal Inc D 740 392-9246
Mount Vernon *(G-14919)*
Ride Share Information E 513 621-6300
Cincinnati *(G-4419)*
Risk International Svcs Inc E 216 255-3400
Fairlawn *(G-10969)*
RMS of Ohio Inc B 440 617-6605
Westlake *(G-19542)*
Root Inc D 419 874-0077
Sylvania *(G-17612)*
Royalton Financial Group E 440 582-3020
Cleveland *(G-6419)*
Rpf Consulting LLC E 678 494-8030
Cincinnati *(G-4450)*
Rse Group Inc D 937 596-6167
Jackson Center *(G-12325)*
Ruralogic Inc D 419 630-0500
Beachwood *(G-1122)*
Rx Options LLC D 330 405-8080
Twinsburg *(G-18464)*
Sacs Cnslting Training Ctr Inc E 330 255-1101
Akron *(G-424)*
Safelite Solutions LLC A 614 210-9000
Columbus *(G-8673)*
Safety Resources Company Ohio E 330 477-1100
Canton *(G-2522)*
Savage and Associates Inc D 419 731-4441
Upper Sandusky *(G-18565)*
Sb Capital Acquisitions LLC A 614 443-4080
Columbus *(G-8690)*
SBC Advertising Ltd C 614 891-7070
Columbus *(G-8692)*
Schrudder Prfmce Group LLC E 513 652-7675
West Chester *(G-19147)*
SCI Direct LLC A 330 494-5504
North Canton *(G-15366)*
Scrogginsgrear Inc C 513 672-4281
Cincinnati *(G-4486)*
Sedlak Management Cons Inc E 216 206-4700
Cleveland *(G-6464)*
Selection MGT Systems Inc D 513 522-8764
Cincinnati *(G-4494)*
Sheakley Unicomp Inc C 513 771-2277
Cincinnati *(G-4513)*
Sheakley-Uniservice Inc C 513 771-2277
Cincinnati *(G-4514)*
Shermco Industries Inc D 614 836-8556
Groveport *(G-11672)*
Shotstop Ballistics LLC E 330 686-0020
Stow *(G-17392)*
Shp Leading Design D 513 381-2112
Cincinnati *(G-4518)*
Signature Associates Inc E 419 244-7505
Toledo *(G-18188)*
Signet Management Co Ltd C 330 762-9102
Akron *(G-438)*
Smith & English II Inc E 513 697-9300
Loveland *(G-13161)*
Smithers Group Inc D 330 762-7441
Akron *(G-441)*
Smithers Quality Assessments E 330 762-4231
Akron *(G-442)*
Smithers Rapra Inc D 330 762-7441
Akron *(G-443)*
Smoot Construction Co Ohio E 614 257-0032
Columbus *(G-8747)*
Socius1 LLC D 614 280-9880
Dublin *(G-10455)*
Sodexo Inc E 330 425-0709
Twinsburg *(G-18470)*
Software Answers Inc E 440 526-0095
Brecksville *(G-1851)*
Solenis LLC E 614 336-1101
Dublin *(G-10456)*
Southern Ohio Medical Center E 740 356-5000
Portsmouth *(G-16312)*
Spirit Women Health Netwrk LLC E 561 544-2004
Cincinnati *(G-2932)*
SSS Consulting Inc E 937 259-1200
Dayton *(G-9901)*
Stagnaro Saba Patterson Co Lpa E 513 533-2700
Cincinnati *(G-4576)*
Standard Register Inc A 937 221-1000
Dayton *(G-9903)*
State of Ohio C 614 466-3455
Columbus *(G-8782)*
Stepstone Group Real Estate LP E 216 522-0330
Cleveland *(G-6538)*
Stohen Group LLC E 513 448-6288
Mason *(G-13763)*
Sumner Solutions Inc E 513 531-6382
Cincinnati *(G-4599)*
Sun Valley Infosys LLC D 937 267-6435
Springfield *(G-17283)*
Support Fincl Resources Inc E 800 444-5465
Centerville *(G-2686)*
Surgere Inc E 330 526-7971
North Canton *(G-15371)*
Synergy Consulting Group Inc E 330 899-9301
Uniontown *(G-18540)*
Tacg LLC D 937 203-8201
Beavercreek *(G-1212)*
Taylor Strategy Partners LLC E 614 436-6650
Columbus *(G-8825)*
Techncal Sltons Spcialists Inc E 513 792-8930
Blue Ash *(G-1693)*
Techsolve Inc D 513 948-2000
Cincinnati *(G-4631)*
Tek Systems D 614 789-6200
Dublin *(G-10474)*
Terry J Reppa & Associates E 440 888-8533
Cleveland *(G-6586)*
The Sheakley Group Inc E 513 771-2277
Cincinnati *(G-4646)*
Thomas and King Inc C 614 527-0571
Hilliard *(G-11958)*
Toni & Marie Bader E 937 339-3621
Troy *(G-18380)*
Top Echelon Contracting Inc B 330 454-3508
Canton *(G-2564)*
Total Marketing Resources LLC E 330 220-1275
Brunswick *(G-1993)*
Touchstone Group Assoc LLC E 513 791-1717
Cincinnati *(G-4664)*
Towers Watson Pennsylvania Inc E 513 345-4200
Cincinnati *(G-4665)*
Triad Oil & Gas Engineering D 740 374-2940
Marietta *(G-13506)*
Trilogy Fulfillment LLC E 614 491-0553
Groveport *(G-11678)*
Trinity Credit Counseling Inc E 513 769-0621
Cincinnati *(G-4699)*
Trinity Health Corporation E 419 448-3124
Tiffin *(G-17707)*
Truepoint Inc E 513 792-6648
Blue Ash *(G-1705)*
Tsg Resources Inc A 330 498-8200
North Canton *(G-15376)*
Turtle Golf Management Ltd E 614 882-5920
Westerville *(G-19446)*
TV Minority Company Inc E 937 832-9350
Englewood *(G-10722)*
United Audit Systems Inc C 513 723-1122
Cincinnati *(G-4728)*
United States Enrichment Corp A 740 897-2331
Piketon *(G-16128)*
United States Enrichment Corp A 740 897-2457
Piketon *(G-16129)*
Universal Marketing Group LLC D 419 720-9696
Toledo *(G-18275)*
Universal Transportation Syste C 513 829-1287
Fairfield *(G-10920)*
University of Cincinnati Phys E 513 475-8521
Cincinnati *(G-4780)*
University of Dayton C 937 255-3141
Dayton *(G-9951)*
University of Dayton C 937 229-3913
Dayton *(G-9955)*
Vand Corp E 216 481-3788
Cleveland *(G-6686)*
Vartek Services Inc E 937 438-3550
Dayton *(G-9967)*
Vediscovery LLC E 216 241-3443
Cleveland *(G-6688)*
Venator Holdings LLC D 248 792-9209
Maumee *(G-13992)*
Vernon F Glaser & Associates E 937 298-5536
Dayton *(G-9970)*
Versatex LLC E 513 639-3119
Cincinnati *(G-4808)*
Viaquest Behavioral Health LLC E 614 339-0868
Dublin *(G-10482)*
Walgreen Co E 216 595-1407
Cleveland *(G-6718)*
Weber Obrien Ltd E 419 885-8338
Sylvania *(G-17027)*
Weber Partners Ltd E 614 222-6806
Columbus *(G-8974)*
Wellington Group LLC E 216 525-2200
Independence *(G-12275)*
William Thomas Group Inc D 800 582-3107
Cincinnati *(G-4851)*
Willowood Care Center C 330 225-3156
Brunswick *(G-1997)*
Workplace Media Inc E 440 392-2171
Mentor *(G-14260)*
Worthington Public Library C 614 807-2626
Worthington *(G-20010)*
Wtw Delaware Holdings LLC C 216 937-4000
Cleveland *(G-6762)*
Xzamcorp E 330 629-2218
Perry *(G-15969)*
Young and Associates Inc E 330 678-0524
Kent *(G-12407)*

Employee Codes: A=Over 500 employees, B=251-500
C=101-250, D=51-100, E=25-50

8743 Public Relations Svcs

Automotive Events Inc E 440 356-1383
Rocky River *(G-16570)*
Babbage-Simmel & Assoc Inc E 614 481-6555
Columbus *(G-7082)*
Campbell Sales Company E 513 697-2900
Cincinnati *(G-3172)*
City of Cleveland Heights E 216 291-2323
Cleveland Heights *(G-6787)*
Code One Communications Inc E 614 338-0321
Columbus *(G-7313)*
County of Guernsey D 800 307-8422
Cambridge *(G-2107)*
County of Logan E 937 599-7252
Bellefontaine *(G-1380)*
D L Ryan Companies LLC E 614 436-6558
Westerville *(G-19296)*
Dix & Eaton Incorporated E 216 241-0405
Cleveland *(G-5493)*
Domestic Relations E 937 225-4063
Dayton *(G-9504)*
Edward Howard & Co E 216 781-2400
Cleveland *(G-5528)*
Fahlgren Inc D 614 383-1500
Columbus *(G-7629)*
Fast Traxx Promotions LLC E 740 767-3740
Millfield *(G-14632)*
Forwith Logistics LLC E 513 386-8310
Milford *(G-14518)*
Krajewski Corp E 740 522-2000
Granville *(G-11468)*
L Brands Service Company LLC D 614 415-7000
Columbus *(G-8020)*
Marcus Thomas Llc D 330 793-3000
Youngstown *(G-20272)*
Marsh Inc E 513 421-1234
Cincinnati *(G-4026)*
Midway Mall Merchants Assoc E 440 244-1245
Elyria *(G-10653)*
Nugrowth Solutions LLC E 800 747-9273
Columbus *(G-8305)*
Ohio State University E 614 293-3737
Columbus *(G-8424)*
Paul Werth Associates Inc E 614 224-8114
Columbus *(G-8524)*
Quotient Technology Inc E 513 229-8659
Mason *(G-13752)*
RA Staff Company Inc E 440 891-9900
Cleveland *(G-6342)*
Roman/Peshoff Inc E 419 241-2221
Holland *(G-12051)*
SBC Advertising Ltd C 614 891-7070
Columbus *(G-8692)*
United States Trotting Assn D 614 224-2291
Columbus *(G-8901)*
Ver-A-Fast Corp E 440 331-0250
Rocky River *(G-16594)*
Whitespace Design Group Inc E 330 762-9320
Akron *(G-510)*

8744 Facilities Support Mgmt Svcs

Alco Inc E 740 527-2991
Logan *(G-12967)*
Aramark Facility Services LLC E 216 687-5000
Cleveland *(G-5057)*
Aztec Services Group Inc D 513 541-2002
Cincinnati *(G-3071)*
City of Xenia E 937 376-7260
Xenia *(G-20046)*
Community Education Ctrs Inc B 330 424-4065
Lisbon *(G-12933)*
Corecivic Inc B 330 746-3777
Youngstown *(G-20162)*
Correction Commission NW Ohio C 419 428-3800
Stryker *(G-17536)*
Correctons Comm Sthastern Ohio D 740 753-4060
Nelsonville *(G-14960)*
County of Miami E 937 335-1314
Troy *(G-18352)*
Cuyahoga County Convention Fac D 216 928-1600
Cleveland *(G-5455)*
Emcor Facilities Services Inc D 888 846-9462
Cincinnati *(G-3552)*
Environmental Specialists Inc E 740 788-8134
Newark *(G-15165)*
Facilitysource LLC B 614 318-1700
Columbus *(G-7627)*
Firstgroup America Inc D 513 241-2200
Cincinnati *(G-3626)*
Four Seasons Environmental Inc B 513 539-2978
Monroe *(G-14696)*
Franklin Cnty Bd Commissioners C 614 462-3800
Columbus *(G-7684)*
Franklin Community Base Correc D 614 525-4600
Columbus *(G-7693)*
Greene County E 937 562-7800
Xenia *(G-20056)*
Henry Call Inc C 216 433-5609
Cleveland *(G-5749)*
Independence of Portage County C 330 296-2851
Ravenna *(G-16390)*
L B & B Associates Inc E 216 451-2672
Cleveland *(G-5913)*
Licking Muskingum Cmnty Correc E 740 349-6980
Newark *(G-15193)*
Management & Training Corp C 801 693-2600
Conneaut *(G-9043)*
Midwest Environmental Inc E 419 382-9200
Perrysburg *(G-16034)*
MPW Industrial Svcs Group Inc D 740 927-8790
Hebron *(G-11855)*
Neocap/Cbcf E 330 675-2669
Warren *(G-18885)*
North Bay Construction Inc E 440 835-1898
Westlake *(G-19522)*
Selecttech Services Corp C 937 438-9905
Centerville *(G-2685)*
Southside Envmtl Group LLC E 330 299-0027
Niles *(G-15306)*
Space Management Inc E 937 254-6622
Dayton *(G-9894)*
Sunpro Inc D 330 966-0910
North Canton *(G-15370)*
Technical Assurance Inc E 440 953-3147
Willoughby *(G-19717)*
Wastren - Energx Mission C 740 897-3724
Piketon *(G-16131)*
Wastren Advantage Inc E 970 254-1277
Piketon *(G-16132)*

8748 Business Consulting Svcs, NEC

A M Communications Ltd D 419 528-3051
Galion *(G-11289)*
ABC Fire Inc E 440 237-6677
North Royalton *(G-15480)*
Acadia Solutions Inc E 614 505-6135
Dublin *(G-10233)*
Accenture LLP C 216 685-1435
Cleveland *(G-4953)*
Accenture LLP C 614 629-2000
Columbus *(G-6934)*
Accessrn Inc D 419 698-1988
Maumee *(G-13872)*
Acrt Inc E 800 622-2562
Akron *(G-18)*
Acrt Services Inc A 330 945-7500
Akron *(G-19)*
Actionlink LLC A 888 737-8757
Akron *(G-20)*
Aecom Global II LLC D 419 774-9862
Delta *(G-10155)*
Alice Training Institute LLC D 330 661-0106
Medina *(G-14034)*
Allied Environmental Svcs Inc E 419 227-4004
Lima *(G-12739)*
Als Group Usa Corp E 513 733-5336
Blue Ash *(G-1530)*
American Broadband Telecom Co E 419 824-5800
Toledo *(G-17748)*
American Health Group Inc D 419 891-1212
Maumee *(G-13875)*
Andy Mark Inc C 513 248-8000
Milford *(G-14504)*
▲ **Apple Growth Partners Inc** D 330 867-7350
Akron *(G-78)*
Arcadis US Inc D 419 473-1121
Toledo *(G-17757)*
Ardent Technologies Inc C 937 312-1345
Dayton *(G-9342)*
Ashtabula Cnty Eductl Svc Ctr D 440 576-4085
Jefferson *(G-12328)*
AT&T Corp A 216 298-1513
Cleveland *(G-5074)*
Avantia Inc E 216 901-9366
Cleveland *(G-5085)*
Axiom Product Development LLC E 513 791-2425
Blue Ash *(G-1537)*
B2b Power Partners E 614 309-6964
Galena *(G-11279)*
Barbara S Desalvo Inc E 513 729-2111
Cincinnati *(G-3077)*
Bbs & Associates Inc E 330 665-5227
Akron *(G-92)*
Benchmark National Corporation E 419 660-1100
Bellevue *(G-1406)*
Benchmark Technologies Corp E 419 843-6691
Toledo *(G-17769)*
Big Red Rooster D 614 255-0200
Columbus *(G-7108)*
Biorx LLC D 866 442-4679
Cincinnati *(G-3109)*
Bjaam Environmental Inc E 330 854-5300
Canal Fulton *(G-2141)*
Bkd LLP D 513 621-8300
Cincinnati *(G-3111)*
Bravo Wellness LLC E 216 658-9500
Cleveland *(G-5134)*
Bright Horizons Chld Ctrs LLC E 614 227-0550
Columbus *(G-7137)*
Bureau Veritas North Amer Inc E 330 252-5100
Akron *(G-119)*
Calabresem Racek & Markos Inc E 216 696-5442
Cleveland *(G-5171)*
Capital City Indus Systems LLC E 614 519-5047
Put In Bay *(G-16366)*
Cardinal Maintenance & Svc Co C 330 252-0282
Akron *(G-122)*
Cash Flow Solutions Inc D 513 524-2320
Oxford *(G-15814)*
Cbiz Inc D 330 644-2044
Uniontown *(G-18512)*
CDM SMITH INC E 614 847-8340
Columbus *(G-7219)*
Celebrity Security Inc E 216 671-6425
Cleveland *(G-5202)*
Centric Consulting LLC D 888 781-7567
Dayton *(G-9394)*
Cgh-Global Technologies LLC E 800 376-0655
Cincinnati *(G-3225)*
Check It Out 4 Me LLC E 513 568-4269
Cincinnati *(G-3234)*
Cincinnati Cnslting Consortium E 513 233-0011
Cincinnati *(G-3293)*
City of Akron E 330 375-2851
Akron *(G-141)*
City of Coshocton D 740 622-1763
Coshocton *(G-9090)*
Clermont County Gen Hlth Dst E 513 732-7499
Batavia *(G-1001)*
Clgt Solutions LLC E 740 920-4795
Granville *(G-11462)*
Cliff North Consultants Inc E 513 251-4930
Cincinnati *(G-3364)*
Clinton-Carvell Inc E 614 351-8858
Columbus *(G-7303)*
Coact Associates Ltd E 866 646-4400
Toledo *(G-17818)*
Communications III Inc E 614 901-7720
Westerville *(G-19390)*
Compmanagement Health Systems D 614 766-5223
Dublin *(G-10307)*
Composite Tech Amer Inc E 330 562-5201
Cleveland *(G-5390)*
Connaissance Consulting LLC C 614 289-5200
Columbus *(G-7421)*
Construction Resources Inc E 440 248-9800
Cleveland *(G-5397)*
Consultants Collections E 330 666-6900
Akron *(G-161)*
Controlsoft Inc E 440 443-3900
Cleveland *(G-5404)*
Corporate Ladder Search E 330 776-4390
Uniontown *(G-18515)*
CTS Construction Inc D 513 489-8290
Cincinnati *(G-3445)*
Dan-Ray Construction LLC E 216 518-8484
Cleveland *(G-5462)*
Dancor Inc E 614 340-2155
Columbus *(G-7486)*
Datavantage Corporation B 440 498-4414
Cleveland *(G-5464)*
Dedicated Technologies Inc D 614 460-3200
Columbus *(G-7499)*
Deemsys Inc D 614 322-9928
Gahanna *(G-11239)*
Deloitte & Touche LLP B 513 784-7100
Cincinnati *(G-3482)*
Deloitte Consulting LLP C 937 223-8821
Dayton *(G-9497)*

87 ENGINEERING, ACCOUNTING, RESEARCH, MANAGEMENT, AND RELATED SERVICES

Company	Code	Phone
Devcare Solutions Ltd — Columbus (G-7511)	E	614 221-2277
E Retailing Associates LLC — Columbus (G-7561)	D	614 300-5785
Ecs Holdco Inc — Worthington (G-19955)	E	614 433-0170
Educational Solutions Co — Columbus (G-7581)	D	614 989-4588
Ellipse Solutions LLC — Dayton (G-9525)	E	937 312-1547
Emergency Response & Trnng — Solon (G-17002)	E	440 349-2700
Emersion Design LLC — Cincinnati (G-3553)	E	513 841-9100
Employee Benefit Management — Dublin (G-10336)	E	614 766-5800
Envirnmental Resources MGT Inc — Beachwood (G-1076)	E	216 593-5200
Envirnmental Resources MGT Inc — Blue Ash (G-1589)	E	513 830-9030
Environmental Solutions — Cincinnati (G-3563)	E	513 451-1777
Enviroscience Inc — Stow (G-17364)	D	330 688-0111
Envision Corporation — Cincinnati (G-3564)	D	513 772-5437
Equity Engineering Group Inc — Shaker Heights (G-16860)	D	216 283-9519
Excellence In Motivation Inc — Dayton (G-9533)	C	763 445-3000
Feg Consulting LLC — Blue Ash (G-1592)	E	412 224-2263
Flavik Village Development — Cleveland (G-5605)	E	216 429-1182
Floyd Browne Group Inc — Delaware (G-10097)	E	740 363-6792
General Electric Company — Mason (G-13705)	C	513 583-3626
Gleaming Systems LLC — Lewis Center (G-12686)	E	614 348-7475
Governan LLC — Columbus (G-7763)	E	614 761-2400
Grace Consulting Inc — Wellington (G-18992)	E	440 647-6672
Gunning & Associates Mktg Inc — Cincinnati (G-3719)	E	513 688-1370
Halley Consulting Group LLC — Westerville (G-19405)	E	614 899-7325
Hobsons Inc — Cincinnati (G-3774)	C	513 891-5444
Homeland Defense Solutions — Cincinnati (G-3781)	E	513 333-7800
Hoskins International LLC — Minster (G-14664)	E	419 628-6015
Hull & Associates Inc — Dublin (G-10367)	E	614 793-8777
Humantics Innovative Solutions — Huron (G-12165)	E	567 265-5200
Hzw Environmental Cons LLC — Mentor (G-14194)	E	800 804-8484
Icon Environmental Group LLC — Milford (G-14526)	E	513 426-6767
Image Consulting Services Inc — Cleveland (G-5806)	E	440 951-9919
Impact Medical Mgt Group — Elyria (G-10636)	E	440 365-7014
Improvedge LLC — Powell (G-16338)	E	614 793-1738
Incentisoft Solutions LLC — Cleveland (G-5808)	D	877 562-4461
Indecon Solutions LLC — Dublin (G-10374)	E	614 799-1850
Industrial Vibrations Cons — Lebanon (G 12612)	D	513 932-4678
Infoverity LLC — Dublin (G-10375)	E	614 327-5173
Integrated Solutions and — Dayton (G-9632)	E	513 826-1932
Interactive Engineering Corp — Medina (G-14082)	E	330 239-6888
Interactive Solutions Intl LLC — Cincinnati (G-3833)	E	513 619-5100
Interdyne Corporation — Lima (G-12805)	E	419 229-8192
Its Traffic Systems Inc — Westlake (G-19500)	D	440 892-4500
Jennings & Associates — Delaware (G-10111)	E	740 369-4426
Jones Group Interiors Inc — Akron (G-297)	E	330 253-9180
Juice Technologies Inc — Columbus (G-7957)	E	800 518-5576
Jyg Innovations LLC — Dayton (G-9647)	E	937 630-3858
Kemper Company — Strongsville (G-17480)	D	440 846-1100
Kemron Environmental Svcs Inc — Marietta (G-13460)	D	740 373-4071
Kenexis Consulting Corporation — Upper Arlington (G-18553)	E	614 451-7031
Kennedy Group Enterprises Inc — Strongsville (G-17481)	E	440 879-0078
Key Office Services — Mansfield (G-13319)	E	419 747-9749
Keyw Corporation — Beavercreek (G-1182)	E	937 702-9512
Kirila Fire Trning Fclties Inc — Brookfield (G-1899)	E	724 854-5207
Klais and Company Inc — Fairlawn (G-10963)	E	330 867-8443
Ladder Man Inc — Wooster (G-19882)	E	614 784-1120
Landrum & Brown Incorporated — Blue Ash (G-1625)	D	513 530-5333
Lateef Elmin Mhammad Inv Group — Springfield (G-17220)	D	937 450-3388
Lawhon and Associates Inc — Columbus (G-8044)	E	614 481-8600
Legacy Consultant Pharmacy — Bedford (G-1316)	E	336 760-1670
Lextant Corporation — Columbus (G-8055)	E	614 228-9711
Lorain Cnty Elderly Hsing Corp — Lorain (G-13049)	D	440 288-1600
Lumenance LLC — Columbus (G-8086)	E	319 541-6811
Mannik & Smith Group Inc — Maumee (G-13938)	C	419 891-2222
Mary Kelleys Inc — Columbus (G-8122)	D	614 760-7041
Massillon Cable TV Inc — Massillon (G-13833)	D	330 833-4134
Mediadvertiser Company — Fayetteville (G-10984)	E	513 651-0265
Miami Valley Regional Plg Comm — Dayton (G-9737)	E	937 223-6323
Mission Essntial Personnel LLC — New Albany (G-14992)	C	614 416-2345
Nas Rcrtment Cmmunications LLC — Cleveland (G-6100)	E	216 478-0300
Nationwide Energy Partners LLC — Columbus (G-8240)	E	614 918-2031
Nationwide Rtirement Solutions — Dublin (G-10405)	C	614 854-8300
Neutral Telecom Corporation — North Ridgeville (G-15472)	E	440 377-4700
Nexus Communications Inc — Columbus (G-8276)	E	740 549-1092
Northeast Ohio Areawide — Cleveland (G-6153)	E	216 621-3055
Northeast Ohio Communic — Warren (G-18888)	D	330 399-2700
Nugrowth Solutions LLC — Columbus (G-8305)	E	800 747-9273
Occupational Health Services — Sidney (G-16944)	E	937 492-7296
Ohio Utilities Protection Svc — Youngstown (G-20310)	D	330 759-0050
On Site Instruments LLC — Lewis Center (G-12699)	E	614 846-1900
Oracle Systems Corporation — Beachwood (G-1112)	D	216 328-9100
Orin Group LLC — Akron (G-376)	E	330 630-3937
▼ Orton Edward Jr Crmic Fndation — Westerville (G-19339)	E	614 895-2663
Peak 10 Inc — Hamilton (G-11762)	D	513 645-2900
Peq Services + Solutions Inc — Miamisburg (G-14334)	D	937 610-4800
Ply-Trim Enterprises Inc — Youngstown (G-20325)	E	330 799-7876
Poggemeyer Design Group Inc — Bowling Green (G-1791)	C	419 244-8074
Port Grter Cincinnati Dev Auth — Cincinnati (G-4315)	E	513 621-3000
Primatech Inc — Columbus (G-8560)	E	614 841-9800
Pro Ed Communications Inc — Cleveland (G-6308)	E	216 595-7919
Qwaide Enterprises LLC — New Albany (G-15003)	E	614 209-0551
Resolvit Resources LLC — Cincinnati (G-4409)	E	513 619-5900
RJ Runge Company Inc — Port Clinton (G-16253)	E	419 740-5781
Romitech Inc — Dayton (G-9855)	E	937 297-9529
Root Inc — Sylvania (G-17612)	D	419 874-0077
Sadler-Necamp Financial Svcs — Cincinnati (G-4466)	E	513 489-5477
Safety-Kleen Systems Inc — Fairfield (G-10902)	E	513 563-0931
Saloma Intl Co Since 1978 — Akron (G-426)	E	440 941-1527
Sawdey Solution Services Inc — Beavercreek (G-1259)	E	937 490-4060
Schooley Caldwell Associates — Columbus (G-8702)	D	614 628-0300
Scioto Packaging Inc — Columbus (G-8707)	E	614 491-1500
Seifert & Group Inc — Massillon (G-13852)	D	330 833-2700
Sequent Inc — Columbus (G-6907)	D	614 436-5880
Service Corps Retired Execs — Akron (G-434)	E	330 379-3163
Sheakley Med MGT Resources LLC — Cincinnati (G-4512)	D	513 891-1006
Shotstop Ballistics LLC — Stow (G-17392)	E	330 686-0020
Simplifi Eso LLC — Columbus (G-8736)	E	615 635-8679
Six Disciplines LLC — Findlay (G-11081)	E	419 424-6647
Sjn Data Center LLC — Cincinnati (G-4534)	E	513 386-7871
Smith & English II Inc — Loveland (G-13161)	E	513 697-9300
Smithers Quality Assessments — Akron (G-442)	E	330 762-4231
Software Support Group Inc — Shaker Heights (G-16866)	D	216 566-0555
Solar Testing Laboratories Inc — Brooklyn Heights (G-1926)	E	216 741-7007
Sordyl & Associates Inc — Maumee (G-13979)	E	419 866-6811
South Central Ohio Eductl Ctr — New Boston (G-15014)	C	740 456-0517
SSS Consulting Inc — Dayton (G-9901)	E	937 259-1200
Star County Home Consortium — Canton (G-2538)	E	330 451-7395
Status Solutions LLC — Westerville (G-19354)	E	866 846-7272
Stout Risius Ross LLC — Cleveland (G-6544)	E	216 685-5000
Summit Solutions Inc — Dayton (G-9913)	E	937 291-4333
Sunpro Inc — North Canton (G-15370)	D	330 966-0910
Systems Evolution Inc — Cincinnati (G-4610)	D	513 459-1992
Tangoe Inc — Columbus (G-8821)	D	614 842-9918
Team NEO — Cleveland (G-6576)	E	216 363-5400
Techsolve Inc — Cincinnati (G-4631)	D	513 948-2000
Tetra Tech Inc — Cincinnati (G-4638)	E	513 251-2730
Th Services — Newark (G-15238)	E	740 258-9054
Tipharah Group Corp — Dayton (G-9929)	C	937 430-6266
Tipharah Group Corp — Dayton (G-9930)	C	937 430-6266
Toledo Metro Area Cncl Gvrnmnt — Toledo (G-18242)	E	419 241-9155
Towe & Associates Inc — West Milton (G-19269)	E	937 275-0900
Tribute Contracting & Cons LLC — South Point (G-17098)	E	740 451-1010
Truechoicepack Corp — Mason (G-13775)	E	937 630-3832
Trumbull Housing Dev Corp — Warren (G-18912)	D	330 369-1533
Ttl Associates Inc — Toledo (G-18263)	C	419 241-4556

Employee Codes: A=Over 500 employees, B=251-500
C=101-250, D=51-100, E=25-50

87 ENGINEERING, ACCOUNTING, RESEARCH, MANAGEMENT, AND RELATED SERVICES

Turnkey Network Solutions LLC .... E 614 876-9944
  Columbus *(G-8880)*
Twism Enterprises LLC .... E 513 800-1098
  Cincinnati *(G-4711)*
Uc Health Llc .... A 513 475-7630
  West Chester *(G-19168)*
US Home Center LLC .... E 614 737-9000
  Columbus *(G-8924)*
Uts Inc .... E 513 332-9000
  Cincinnati *(G-4800)*
Vahalla Company Inc .... E 216 326-2245
  Cleveland *(G-6681)*
Vans Express Inc .... E 216 224-5388
  Hinckley *(G-12001)*
Weber Obrien Ltd .... E 419 885-8338
  Sylvania *(G-17627)*
William Sydney Druen .... E 614 444-7655
  Columbus *(G-8996)*
Wtb Inc .... E 216 298-1895
  Cleveland *(G-6761)*
Yashco Systems Inc .... E 614 467-4600
  Hilliard *(G-11966)*

89 SERVICES, NOT ELSEWHERE CLASSIFIED

8999 Services Not Elsewhere Classified

Accelerant Technologies LLC .... D 419 236-8768
  Genoa *(G-11374)*
American National Red Cross .... D 216 431-3152
  Cleveland *(G-5018)*
ASC Group Inc .... E 614 268-2514
  Columbus *(G-7048)*
Bob Sumerel Tire Co Inc .... E 513 528-1900
  Cincinnati *(G-3123)*
Bob Sumerel Tire Co Inc .... E 513 598-2300
  Cincinnati *(G-3124)*
Central Ohio Primary Care .... E 614 882-0708
  Westerville *(G-19381)*

Centre Communications Corp .... E 440 454-3262
  Beavercreek *(G-1232)*
Centric Consulting LLC .... E 513 791-3061
  Cincinnati *(G-3219)*
Chp AP Shared Services .... E 513 981-6704
  Cincinnati *(G-3258)*
City of Rocky River .... E 440 356-5630
  Cleveland *(G-5275)*
City of Toledo .... E 419 936-2875
  Toledo *(G-17809)*
Coleman Professional Svcs Inc .... B 330 673-1347
  Kent *(G-12360)*
County of Clermont .... E 513 732-7661
  Batavia *(G-1006)*
County of Logan .... E 937 599-4221
  Bellefontaine *(G-1381)*
Daily Services LLC .... C 740 326-6130
  Mount Vernon *(G-14891)*
▼ Diproinduca (usa) Limited LLC .... D 330 722-4442
  Medina *(G-14058)*
Dispatch Productions Inc .... D 614 460-3700
  Columbus *(G-7525)*
Don Drumm Studios & Gallery .... E 330 253-6840
  Akron *(G-196)*
Goodwill Idstrs Grtr Clvlnd L .... E 330 339-5746
  New Philadelphia *(G-15095)*
Grenada Stamping Assembly Inc .... E 419 842-3600
  Sylvania *(G-17589)*
Htp Inc .... E 614 885-1272
  Columbus *(G-6885)*
Lighthouse Youth Services Inc .... D 513 861-1111
  Cincinnati *(G-3981)*
Linemaster Services LLC .... E 614 507-9945
  Grove City *(G-11577)*
Madison Avenue Mktg Group Inc .... E 419 473-9000
  Toledo *(G-18026)*
Miami County Park District .... E 937 335-6273
  Troy *(G-18365)*
Mid Ohio Emergency Svcs LLC .... E 614 566-5070
  Columbus *(G-8162)*

Moon Co-Op Services .... D 513 523-3990
  Oxford *(G-15826)*
National Service Information .... E 740 387-6806
  Marion *(G-13567)*
National Valuation Consultants .... E 513 929-4100
  Cincinnati *(G-4143)*
National Weather Service .... E 937 383-0031
  Wilmington *(G-19774)*
National Weather Service .... E 216 265-2370
  Cleveland *(G-6113)*
National Weather Service .... E 419 522-1375
  Mansfield *(G-13349)*
ONeil & Associates Inc .... C 937 865-0800
  Miamisburg *(G-14330)*
P & D Removal Service .... E 513 226-7687
  Cincinnati *(G-4246)*
Pcm Inc .... E 614 854-1399
  Lewis Center *(G-12701)*
Provato LLC .... E 440 546-0768
  Brecksville *(G-1844)*
Psychology Consultants Inc .... E 330 764-7916
  Medina *(G-14115)*
Quantech Services Inc .... C 937 490-8461
  Beavercreek Township *(G-1283)*
Richland Township Fire Dept .... E 740 536-7313
  Rushville *(G-16613)*
Rxoc Information Operations .... E 937 255-1151
  Dayton *(G-9282)*
Stg Communication Services Inc .... E 330 482-0500
  Columbiana *(G-6863)*
Superior Envmtl Sltons SES Inc .... B 513 874-6910
  West Chester *(G-19234)*
Thinkpath Engineering Svcs LLC .... D 937 291-8374
  Miamisburg *(G-14358)*
University of Cincinnati .... A 513 556-5087
  Cincinnati *(G-4764)*
Vantage Aging .... A 330 785-9770
  Akron *(G-496)*
Wireless Source Entps LLC .... E 419 266-5556
  Bowling Green *(G-1797)*

89 SERVICES, NOT ELSEWHERE CLASSIFIED

Wtw Delaware Holdings LLC ....C....... 216 937-4000

Cleveland *(G-6762)*

ALPHABETIC SECTION

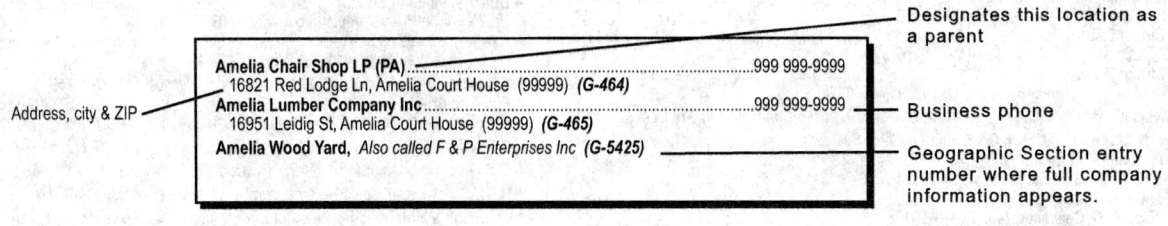

See footnotes for symbols and codes identification.
* Companies listed alphabetically.
* Complete physical or mailing address.

0714 Inc 440 327-2123
  32648 Center Ridge Rd North Ridgeville (44039) *(G-15452)*
1 Amazing Place Co 419 420-0424
  207 E Foulke Ave Findlay (45840) *(G-10986)*
1 Community 216 923-2272
  1375 Euclid Ave Cleveland (44115) *(G-4917)*
1 Edi Source Inc 440 519-7800
  31875 Solon Rd Solon (44139) *(G-16967)*
1 Financial Corporation 513 936-1400
  10123 Alliance Rd Ste 110 Blue Ash (45242) *(G-1520)*
1-888 Ohio Comp LLC 216 426-0646
  2900 Carnegie Ave Cleveland (44115) *(G-4918)*
10 Wilmington Place 937 253-1010
  10 Wilmington Ave Dayton (45420) *(G-9291)*
101 River Inc 440 352-6343
  101 River St Grand River (44045) *(G-11455)*
1100 Carnegie LP 216 658-6400
  1100 Carnegie Ave Cleveland (44115) *(G-4919)*
1106 West Main Inc 330 673-2122
  1106 W Main St Kent (44240) *(G-12350)*
1157 Design Concepts LLC 937 497-1157
  171 S Lester Ave Sidney (45365) *(G-16909)*
12000 Edgewater Drive LLC 216 520-1250
  12000 Edgewater Dr Lakewood (44107) *(G-12469)*
127 PS Fee Owner LLC 216 520-1250
  1300 Key Tower 127 Pub Sq Cleveland (44114) *(G-4920)*
1440 Corporation Inc 513 424-2421
  1440 S Breiel Blvd Middletown (45044) *(G-14410)*
1460 Ninth St Assoc Ltd Partnr 216 241-6600
  1460 E 9th St Cleveland (44114) *(G-4921)*
1522 Hess Street LLC 614 291-6876
  1522 Hess St Columbus (43212) *(G-6912)*
16 Bit Bar 513 381-1616
  1331 Walnut St Cincinnati (45202) *(G-2939)*
16644 Snow Rd LLC 216 676-5200
  16644 Snow Rd Brookpark (44142) *(G-1934)*
1st Advanced Ems LLC 614 348-9991
  735 Taylor Rd Ste 210 Gahanna (43230) *(G-11232)*
1st Advnce SEC Invstgtions Inc 937 317-4433
  111 W 1st St Ste 101 Dayton (45402) *(G-9292)*
1st All File Recovery Usa 800 399-7150
  3570 Warrensville Ctr Rd Shaker Heights (44122) *(G-16855)*
1st Carrier Corp 740 477-2587
  177 Neville St Circleville (43113) *(G-4875)*
1st Choice LLC 877 564-6658
  600 Superior Ave E # 1300 Cleveland (44114) *(G-4922)*
1st Choice Roofing Company 216 227-7755
  10311 Berea Rd Cleveland (44102) *(G-4923)*
1st Choice Security Inc 513 381-6789
  2245 Gilbert Ave Ste 400 Cincinnati (45206) *(G-2940)*
1st Gear Auto Inc 216 458-0791
  333 Broadway Ave Bedford (44146) *(G-1291)*
1st Stop Inc (PA) 937 695-0318
  18856 State Route 136 Winchester (45097) *(G-19798)*
204 W Main Street Oper Co LLC 419 929-1563
  204 W Main St New London (44851) *(G-15065)*
2060 Digital LLC 513 699-5012
  2060 Reading Rd Cincinnati (45202) *(G-2941)*
2100 Lakeside Shelter For Men 216 566-0047
  2100 Lakeside Ave E Cleveland (44114) *(G-4924)*
21c Cincinnati LLC 513 578-6600
  609 Walnut St Ste 2 Cincinnati (45202) *(G-2942)*
21c Museum Hotel Cincinnati, Cincinnati Also called 21c Cincinnati LLC *(G-2942)*
21st Century Con Cnstr Inc 216 362-0900
  13925 Enterprise Ave Cleveland (44135) *(G-4925)*
21st Century Financial Inc 330 668-9065
  130 Springside Dr Ste 100 Akron (44333) *(G-9)*
21st Century Health Spa Inc (PA) 419 476-5585
  343 New Towne Square Dr Toledo (43612) *(G-17732)*
22nd Century Technologies Inc 866 537-9191
  2601 Commons Blvd Ste 130 Beavercreek (45431) *(G-1142)*

24 - Seven Home Hlth Care LLC 614 794-0325
  5064 Edgeley Dr Hilliard (43026) *(G-11873)*
2444 Mdson Rd Cndo Owners Assn 513 871-0100
  2444 Madison Rd Ste 101 Cincinnati (45208) *(G-2943)*
2780 Airport Drive LLC 513 563-7555
  2135 Dana Ave Ste 200 Cincinnati (45207) *(G-2944)*
2trg, Blue Ash Also called Wws Associates Inc *(G-1723)*
3 B Ventures LLC 419 236-9461
  980 N Eastown Rd Lima (45807) *(G-12729)*
3-D Service Ltd (PA) 330 830-3500
  800 Nave Rd Se Massillon (44646) *(G-13780)*
3-D Technical Services Company 937 746-2901
  255 Industrial Dr Franklin (45005) *(G-11147)*
3-Dmed, Franklin Also called 3-D Technical Services Company *(G-11147)*
36 E Seventh LLC 513 699-2279
  2135 Dana Ave Ste 200 Cincinnati (45207) *(G-2945)*
3b Holdings Inc (PA) 800 791-7124
  11470 Euclid Ave Ste 407 Cleveland (44106) *(G-4926)*
3b Supply, Cleveland Also called 3b Holdings Inc *(G-4926)*
3c Technologies Inc 419 868-8999
  6834 Spring Valley Dr # 202 Holland (43528) *(G-12005)*
3g Operating Company LLC 440 944-9400
  12380 Plaza Dr Parma (44130) *(G-15897)*
3rd Street Community Clinic 419 522-6191
  600 W 3rd St Mansfield (44906) *(G-13257)*
3rd Street Family Health Svcs, Mansfield Also called 3rd Street Community Clinic *(G-13257)*
3s Incorporated (HQ) 513 202-5070
  8686 Southwest Pkwy Harrison (45030) *(G-11788)*
3sg Corporation (PA) 614 761-8394
  344 Cramer Creek Ct Dublin (43017) *(G-10231)*
3sg Corporation 614 309-3600
  344 Cramer Creek Ct Dublin (43017) *(G-10232)*
4 Paws Sake Inc 419 304-7139
  13244 Neowash Rd Grand Rapids (43522) *(G-11447)*
4 Seasons Car Wash, Lima Also called 3 B Ventures LLC *(G-12729)*
415 Group Inc (PA) 330 492-0094
  4100 Holiday St Nw # 100 Canton (44718) *(G-2219)*
44444 LLC 330 502-2023
  5783 Norquest Blvd Austintown (44515) *(G-867)*
4C FOR CHILDREN, Cincinnati Also called Comprehensive Cmnty Child Care *(G-3405)*
4mybenefits Inc 513 891-6648
  4665 Cornell Rd Ste 331 Blue Ash (45241) *(G-1521)*
4th and Goal Distribution LLC 440 212-0769
  9911 Avon Lake Rd Burbank (44214) *(G-2054)*
4wd, Columbiana Also called Four Wheel Drive Hardware LLC *(G-6859)*
5 Star Hotel Management IV LP 614 431-1819
  6191 Quarter Horse Dr Columbus (43229) *(G-6913)*
50 S Front LLC 614 224-4600
  50 S Front St Columbus (43215) *(G-6914)*
50 X 20 Holding Company Inc 740 238-4262
  41201 Bond Dr Belmont (43718) *(G-1428)*
50 X 20 Holding Company Inc (PA) 330 478-4500
  2715 Wise Ave Nw Canton (44708) *(G-2220)*
50 X 20 Holding Company Inc 330 865-4663
  779 White Pond Dr Akron (44320) *(G-10)*
506 Phelps Holdings LLC 513 651-1234
  506 E 4th St Cincinnati (45202) *(G-2946)*
5440 Charlesgate Rd Oper LLC 937 236-6707
  5440 Charlesgate Rd Dayton (45424) *(G-9293)*
55 Degrees, Streetsboro Also called Southern Glazers Wine and Sp *(G-17430)*
56 Plus Management LLC 937 323-4114
  560 E High St Springfield (45505) *(G-17145)*
5901 Pfffer Rd Htels Sites LLC 513 793-4500
  5901 Pfeiffer Rd Blue Ash (45242) *(G-1522)*
599 W Main Corporation 440 466-5901
  599 W Main St Geneva (44041) *(G-11357)*
5me LLC 513 719-1600
  4270 Ivy Pointe Blvd # 100 Cincinnati (45245) *(G-2900)*
6200 Rockside LLC 216 642-8004
  6200 Rockside Rd Ste 100 Cleveland (44131) *(G-4927)*

(PA)=Parent Co (HQ)=Headquarters (DH)=Div Headquarters

2018 Harris Ohio
Services Directory

ALPHABETIC

1095

6300 Sharonville Assoc LLC.....513 489-3636
6300 E Kemper Rd Cincinnati (45241) ***(G-2947)***
631 South Main Street Dev LLC.....419 423-0631
631 S Main St Findlay (45840) ***(G-10987)***
6th Circuit Court.....614 719-3100
200 W 2nd St Ste 702 Dayton (45402) ***(G-9294)***
6th Circuit Court.....614 719-3100
85 Marconi Blvd Rm 546 Columbus (43215) ***(G-6915)***
7 Physcian Fmly Practice Group, Mentor *Also called Lake County Family Practice* ***(G-14204)***
7 Up / R C/Canada Dry Btlg Co, Columbus *Also called American Bottling Company* ***(G-6985)***
722 Redemption Funding Inc.....513 679-8302
169 Northland Blvd Ste 2 Cincinnati (45246) ***(G-2948)***
75 East State LLC.....614 365-4500
75 E State St Columbus (43215) ***(G-6916)***
77 Coach Supply Ltd.....330 674-1454
7426 County Road 77 Millersburg (44654) ***(G-14582)***
797 Elks Golf Club Inc.....937 382-2666
2593 E Us Highway 22 3 Wilmington (45177) ***(G-19740)***
7nt Enterprises LLC (PA).....937 435-3200
531 E 3rd St Dayton (45402) ***(G-9295)***
8094, Groveport *Also called Shermco Industries Inc* ***(G-11672)***
845 Yard Street LLC (PA).....614 857-2330
375 N Front St Ste 200 Columbus (43215) ***(G-6917)***
8451 LLC (HQ).....513 632-1020
100 W 5th St Cincinnati (45202) ***(G-2949)***
94 5 Xkr Rdo Stn Bus & Sls Off, Toledo *Also called Wrwk 1065* ***(G-18315)***
A A S Amels Sheet Meta L Inc.....330 793-9326
222 Steel St Youngstown (44509) ***(G-20094)***
A & A Safety Inc (PA).....513 943-6100
1126 Ferris Rd Bldg A Amelia (45102) ***(G-571)***
A & A Truck Stop, Jackson *Also called Trepanier Daniels & Trepanier* ***(G-12319)***
A & A Wall Systems Inc.....513 489-0086
11589 Deerfield Rd Cincinnati (45242) ***(G-2950)***
A & C Welding Inc.....330 762-4777
80 Cuyhoga Fls Indus Pkwy Peninsula (44264) ***(G-15946)***
A & D Daycare and Learning Ctr.....937 263-4447
1049 Infirmary Rd Dayton (45417) ***(G-9296)***
A & G Manufacturing Co Inc (PA).....419 468-7433
280 Gelsanliter Rd Galion (44833) ***(G-11288)***
A & J Asphalt, Columbus *Also called J K Enterprises Inc* ***(G-7931)***
A & K Railroad Materials Inc.....419 537-9470
2750 Hill Ave Toledo (43607) ***(G-17733)***
A & R Builders Ltd.....330 893-2111
6914 County Road 672 Millersburg (44654) ***(G-14583)***
A 1 Janitorial Cleaning Svc.....513 932-8003
939 Old 122 Rd Lebanon (45036) ***(G-12585)***
A A Angelone, Cleveland *Also called Cleveland Auto Livery Inc* ***(G-5291)***
A A Astro Service Inc.....216 459-0363
5283 Pearl Rd Cleveland (44129) ***(G-4928)***
A A Hammersmith Insurance Inc (PA).....330 832-7411
210 Erie St N Massillon (44646) ***(G-13781)***
A AAA H Jacks Plumbing Htg Co.....440 946-1166
29930 Lakeland Blvd Wickliffe (44092) ***(G-19591)***
A and A Millwright Rigging Svcs.....513 396-6212
2205 Langdon Farm Rd Cincinnati (45237) ***(G-2951)***
A and S Ventures Inc.....419 376-3934
4311 Garden Estates Dr Toledo (43623) ***(G-17734)***
A B C D, Canton *Also called Abcd Inc* ***(G-2223)***
A B C Rental Center East Inc.....216 475-8240
5204 Warrensville Ctr Rd Cleveland (44137) ***(G-4929)***
A B Industrial Coatings.....614 228-0383
212 N Grant Ave Columbus (43215) ***(G-6918)***
A B M Inc.....419 421-2292
119 E Sandusky St Findlay (45840) ***(G-10988)***
A B S Temps Inc.....937 252-9888
2770 Wilmington Pike Dayton (45419) ***(G-9297)***
A Bee C Service Inc (PA).....440 735-1505
7589 First Pl Ste 1 Cleveland (44146) ***(G-4930)***
A Better Child Care Corp.....513 353-5437
6945 Harrison Ave Cincinnati (45247) ***(G-2952)***
A Better Choice Child Care LLC.....614 268-8503
2572 Cleveland Ave Columbus (43211) ***(G-6919)***
A Brown & Sons Nursery (PA).....937 836-5826
11506 Dyton Grnville Pike Brookville (45309) ***(G-1958)***
A C Homenursing, Warren *Also called Acute Care Homenursing Service* ***(G-18813)***
A C Leasing Company.....513 771-3676
3023 E Kemper Rd Bldg 9 Cincinnati (45241) ***(G-2953)***
A C Management Inc.....440 461-9200
780 Beta Dr Cleveland (44143) ***(G-4931)***
A C Supply, Strongsville *Also called Lamrite West Inc* ***(G-17483)***
A C Trucking, Cincinnati *Also called A C Leasing Company* ***(G-2953)***
A CCS Day Care Centers Inc.....513 841-2227
1705 Section Rd Cincinnati (45237) ***(G-2954)***
A Childs Place Nursery School.....330 493-1333
4770 Higbee Ave Nw Canton (44718) ***(G-2221)***
A Clean Sweep, Toledo *Also called Bebley Enterprises Inc* ***(G-17767)***
A Coach USA Company, Brookpark *Also called Cusa Ll Inc* ***(G-1942)***
A Crano Excavating Inc.....330 630-1061
1505 Industrial Pkwy Akron (44310) ***(G-11)***
A D A Architects Inc.....216 521-5134
17710 Detroit Ave Cleveland (44107) ***(G-4932)***
A D D, Westerville *Also called Assoc Dvlpmtly Disabled* ***(G-19365)***
A D M Crisis Center, Akron *Also called Oriana House Inc* ***(G-374)***
A Duie Pyle Inc.....330 342-7750
10225 Philipp Pkwy Streetsboro (44241) ***(G-17404)***
A E D Inc.....419 661-9999
2845 Crane Way Northwood (43619) ***(G-15526)***
A F P Ohio, Columbus *Also called Austin Foam Plastics Inc* ***(G-7075)***
A Fox Construction.....614 506-1685
6478 Winchester Blvd # 156 Canal Winchester (43110) ***(G-2150)***
A G Mercury, Galion *Also called A & G Manufacturing Co Inc* ***(G-11288)***
A G S Ohio, Macedonia *Also called AGS Custom Graphics Inc* ***(G-13186)***
A H G, Wadsworth *Also called American Hospitality Group Inc* ***(G-18747)***
A J Asphalt Maintenance & Pav, Columbus *Also called George Kuhn Enterprises Inc* ***(G-7743)***
A J Goulder Electric Co.....440 942-4026
4307 Hamann Pkwy Willoughby (44094) ***(G-19640)***
A J Oster Foils LLC.....330 823-1700
2081 Mccrea St Alliance (44601) ***(G-521)***
A J Stockmeister Inc (PA).....740 286-2106
702 E Main St Jackson (45640) ***(G-12305)***
A J'S Body Shop, Cleveland *Also called Buddies Inc* ***(G-5156)***
A Jacobs Inc.....614 774-6757
4410 Hansen Dr Hilliard (43026) ***(G-11874)***
A K Athletic Equipment Inc.....614 920-3069
8015 Howe Industrial Pkwy Canal Winchester (43110) ***(G-2151)***
A L K Inc.....740 369-8741
462 W Central Ave Delaware (43015) ***(G-10064)***
A L Smith Trucking Inc.....937 526-3651
8984 Murphy Rd Versailles (45380) ***(G-18722)***
A L T, Cleveland *Also called Bsl - Applied Laser Tech LLC* ***(G-5154)***
A M & O Towing Inc.....330 385-0639
11341 State Route 170 Negley (44441) ***(G-14958)***
A M Castle & Co.....330 425-7000
26800 Miles Rd Bedford (44146) ***(G-1292)***
A M Communications Ltd.....419 528-3051
4431 Old Springfield Rd Vandalia (45377) ***(G-18655)***
A M Communications Ltd (PA).....419 528-3051
5707 State Route 309 Galion (44833) ***(G-11289)***
A M Leonard Inc.....937 773-2694
241 Fox Dr Piqua (45356) ***(G-16133)***
A M Management Inc.....937 426-6500
2000 Zink Rd Beavercreek (45324) ***(G-1143)***
A M Mc Gregor Home.....216 851-8200
14900 Private Dr Ofc Cleveland (44112) ***(G-4933)***
A Miracle Home Care, Blue Ash *Also called N Services Inc* ***(G-1651)***
A New Beginning Preschool.....216 531-7465
18403 Euclid Ave Cleveland (44112) ***(G-4934)***
A O N, Cleveland *Also called AON Risk Svcs Northeast Inc* ***(G-5047)***
A One Fine Dry Cleaners Inc (PA).....513 351-2663
6223 Montgomery Rd Cincinnati (45213) ***(G-2955)***
A P & P Dev & Cnstr Co (PA).....330 833-8886
2851 Lincoln Way E Massillon (44646) ***(G-13782)***
A P O Holdings Inc (PA).....330 650-1330
6607 Chittenden Rd Hudson (44236) ***(G-12100)***
A P O Pumps and Compressors, Hudson *Also called A P O Holdings Inc* ***(G-12100)***
A P OHoro Company.....330 759-9317
3130 Belmont Ave Youngstown (44505) ***(G-20095)***
A P P S, Cincinnati *Also called American Para Prof Systems Inc* ***(G-3011)***
A P S Medical Billing, Toledo *Also called APS Medical Billing* ***(G-17756)***
A P T, Worthington *Also called Datafield Inc* ***(G-19953)***
A Plus Expediting & Logistics.....937 424-0220
2947 Boulder Ave Dayton (45414) ***(G-9298)***
A Provide Care Inc.....330 828-2278
15028 Old Lincoln Way Dalton (44618) ***(G-9239)***
A R C, Troy *Also called ARC Abrasives Inc* ***(G-18347)***
A R C, Cleveland *Also called ARC Document Solutions Inc* ***(G-5062)***
A R E A Title Agency Inc (PA).....419 242-5485
5450 Monroe St Ste 2 Toledo (43623) ***(G-17735)***
A Renewed Mind.....419 214-0606
885 Commerce Dr Ste C Perrysburg (43551) ***(G-15970)***
A Ressler Inc.....216 518-1804
12750 Broadway Ave Cleveland (44125) ***(G-4935)***
A S I, Dayton *Also called American Sales Inc* ***(G-9254)***
A S I, Plain City *Also called Architectural Systems Inc* ***(G-16182)***
A Savannah Nite Limousine Svcs, Fairfield *Also called Eric Boeppler Fmly Ltd Partnr* ***(G-10848)***
A T & F Co, Cleveland *Also called American Tank & Fabricating Co* ***(G-5023)***
A T V Inc.....614 252-5060
2047 Leonard Ave Columbus (43219) ***(G-6920)***
A Tara Tiffanys Property.....330 448-0778
601 Bedford Rd Se Brookfield (44403) ***(G-1896)***
A Team LLC.....216 271-7223
5280 W 161st St Frnt Ste Cleveland (44142) ***(G-4936)***
A Thomas Dalagiannis MD.....419 887-7000
1360 Arrowhead Dr Maumee (43537) ***(G-13870)***
A To Z Golf Managment Co.....937 434-4911
4990 Wilmington Pike Dayton (45440) ***(G-9299)***
A To Z Portion Ctrl Meats Inc.....419 358-2926
201 N Main St Bluffton (45817) ***(G-1726)***

ALPHABETIC SECTION

A To Zoff Co Inc 330 733-7902
  1105 Canton Rd Akron (44312) *(G-12)*
A Touch of Grace Inc (PA) 740 397-7971
  809 Coshocton Ave Ste B Mount Vernon (43050) *(G-14877)*
A W S Inc 440 333-1791
  20120 Detroit Rd Rocky River (44116) *(G-16567)*
A W S Inc 216 749-0356
  4720 Hinckley Indus Pkwy Cleveland (44109) *(G-4937)*
A W S Inc 216 486-0600
  1490 E 191st St Euclid (44117) *(G-10741)*
A W S Inc 216 941-8800
  10991 Memphis Ave Cleveland (44144) *(G-4938)*
A&L Home Care & Training Ctr 740 886-7623
  6101 County Road 107 Proctorville (45669) *(G-16357)*
A&L Imaging, Blue Ash Also called Arszman & Lyons   LLC *(G-1536)*
A&R Logistics Inc 614 444-4111
  1230 Harmon Ave Columbus (43223) *(G-6921)*
A+ Solutions LLC 216 896-0111
  3659 Green Rd Ste 112 Beachwood (44122) *(G-1044)*
A-1 Advanced Plumbing Inc 614 873-0548
  8299 Memorial Dr Plain City (43064) *(G-16178)*
A-1 Bail Bonds Inc 937 372-2400
  20 S Detroit St Xenia (45385) *(G-20039)*
A-1 Best Locksmith, Cincinnati Also called Serv-A-Lite Products Inc *(G-4498)*
A-1 General Insurance Agency (HQ) 216 986-3000
  9700 Rockside Rd Ste 250 Cleveland (44125) *(G-4939)*
A-1 Nursing Care Inc 614 268-3800
  2500 Corp Exchange Dr # 220 Columbus (43231) *(G-6922)*
A-1 Quality Labor Services LLC 513 678-0724
  Robertson Ave Ste 3021 Cincinnati (45209) *(G-2956)*
A-1 Sprinkler Company Inc 937 859-6198
  2383 Northpointe Dr Miamisburg (45342) *(G-14267)*
A-A Blueprint Co Inc 330 794-8803
  2757 Gilchrist Rd Akron (44305) *(G-13)*
A-Advnced Mvg Stor Systms-Self, Akron Also called Cotter Moving & Storage Co *(G-167)*
A-Roo Company LLC (HQ) 440 238-8850
  22360 Royalton Rd Strongsville (44149) *(G-17437)*
A-Sons Construction Inc 614 846-2438
  6427 Busch Blvd Columbus (43229) *(G-6923)*
A-T Controls Inc (PA) 513 530-5175
  9955 International Blvd West Chester (45246) *(G-19188)*
A1 Drywall Supply, Nashport Also called Newark Drywall Inc *(G-14952)*
A1 Mr Limo Inc 440 943-5466
  29555 Lakeland Blvd Wickliffe (44092) *(G-19592)*
A1 Quality Labor Svc 513 353-0173
  3055 Blue Rock Rd Cincinnati (45239) *(G-2957)*
A2 Services LLC 440 466-6611
  4749 N Ridge Rd E Geneva (44041) *(G-11358)*
A2z Field Services LLC 614 873-0211
  7450 Industrial Pkwy # 105 Plain City (43064) *(G-16179)*
AA Boos & Sons Inc 419 691-2329
  2015 Pickle Rd Oregon (43616) *(G-15721)*
AA Fire Protection LLC 440 327-0060
  620 Sugar Ln Elyria (44035) *(G-10590)*
AA Green Realty Inc 419 352-5331
  1045 N Main St Ste 2 Bowling Green (43402) *(G-1755)*
AAA, Worthington Also called Ohio Automobile Club *(G-19980)*
AAA Allied Group Inc 513 228-0866
  603 E Main St Lebanon (45036) *(G-12586)*
AAA Allied Group Inc 419 228-1022
  2115 Allentown Rd Lima (45805) *(G-12730)*
AAA Allied Group Inc (PA) 513 762-3100
  15 W Central Pkwy Cincinnati (45202) *(G-2958)*
AAA Amrican Abatement Asb Corp 216 281-9400
  15401 Chatfield Ave Cleveland (44111) *(G-4940)*
AAA Auto Wash, Cincinnati Also called Allied Car Wash Inc *(G-2990)*
AAA Car Care Plus, Columbus Also called Ohio Automobile Club *(G-8320)*
AAA Cincinnati Insurance Svc 513 345-5600
  15 W Central Pkwy Cincinnati (45202) *(G-2959)*
AAA Club Alliance Inc (PA) 419 843-1200
  3201 Meijer Dr Toledo (43617) *(G-17736)*
AAA Club Alliance Inc 937 427-5884
  3321 Dayton Xenia Rd Beavercreek (45432) *(G-1144)*
AAA Flexible Pipe, Cleveland Also called AAA Pipe Cleaning Corporation *(G-4942)*
AAA Flexible Pipe Cleaning 216 341-2900
  7277 Bessemer Ave Cleveland (44127) *(G-4941)*
AAA Home Repair Services 937 748-9988
  535 S Main St Springboro (45066) *(G-17112)*
AAA Massillon Automobile Club, Massillon Also called Massillon Automobile Club *(G-13832)*
AAA Miami Valley (PA) 937 224-2896
  825 S Ludlow St Dayton (45402) *(G-9300)*
AAA Mid-Atlantic, Toledo Also called AAA Club Alliance Inc *(G-17736)*
AAA Ohio Auto Club 614 431-7800
  90 E Wilson Bridge Rd Worthington (43085) *(G-19937)*
AAA Pipe Cleaning Corporation (PA) 216 341-2900
  7277 Bessemer Ave Cleveland (44127) *(G-4942)*
AAA Rental & Sales, Dublin Also called Columbus AAA Corp *(G-10300)*
AAA Shelby County Motor Club 937 492-3167
  920 Wapakoneta Ave Sidney (45365) *(G-16910)*
AAA South Central Ohio Inc 740 354-5614
  1414 12th St Portsmouth (45662) *(G-16262)*

AAA Standard Services Inc 419 535-0274
  4117 South Ave Toledo (43615) *(G-17737)*
AAA Travel Agency, Lebanon Also called AAA Allied Group Inc *(G-12586)*
AAA Travel Agency, Dayton Also called AAA Miami Valley *(G-9300)*
Aaron Landscape Inc 440 838-8875
  14900 York Rd North Royalton (44133) *(G-15479)*
Aarons Inc 330 823-1879
  2102 W State St Alliance (44601) *(G-522)*
Aarons Inc 216 251-4500
  11629 Lorain Ave Cleveland (44111) *(G-4943)*
Aarons Inc 330 385-7201
  16240 Dresden Ave Ste A East Liverpool (43920) *(G-10513)*
Aarons Inc 937 778-3577
  1305 E Ash St Piqua (45356) *(G-16134)*
Aarons Inc 216 587-2745
  5420 Northfield Rd Maple Heights (44137) *(G-13398)*
Aauw Action Fund Inc 330 833-0520
  8400 Milmont St Nw Massillon (44646) *(G-13783)*
Aaz Galvanizing Cincinnati, Cincinnati Also called Witt Glvnzing - Cincinnati Inc *(G-4854)*
AB Marketing LLC 513 385-6158
  1211 Symmes Rd Apt B Fairfield (45014) *(G-10814)*
AB Resources LLC 440 922-1098
  6802 W Snowville Rd Ste E Brecksville (44141) *(G-1810)*
AB Tube Company, Twinsburg Also called Atlas Steel Products Co *(G-18394)*
Aba Insurance Services Inc 800 274-5222
  5910 Landerbrook Dr # 100 Mayfield Heights (44124) *(G-13998)*
Abaco Rhblttion Nursing Fcilty, Columbus Also called Longterm Lodging Inc *(G-8076)*
Abacus Child Care Centers Inc 330 773-4200
  839 S Arlington St Akron (44306) *(G-14)*
Abacus Corporation 614 367-7000
  1676 Brice Rd Reynoldsburg (43068) *(G-16423)*
ABB Inc 614 818-6300
  579 Executive Campus Dr Westerville (43082) *(G-19282)*
ABB Inc 440 585-8500
  23000 Harvard Rd Cleveland (44122) *(G-4944)*
ABB Inc 440 585-7804
  23000 Harvard Rd Beachwood (44122) *(G-1045)*
ABB Industrial Systems, Westerville Also called ABB Inc *(G-19282)*
Abbewood Limited Partnership 440 366-8980
  1210 Abbe Rd S Ofc Elyria (44035) *(G-10591)*
Abbott Electric (PA) 330 452-6601
  1935 Allen Ave Se Canton (44707) *(G-2222)*
Abbott Laboratories 614 624-3191
  585 Cleveland Ave Columbus (43215) *(G-6924)*
Abbott Nutrition, Columbus Also called Abbott Laboratories *(G-6924)*
Abbott Tool Inc 419 476-6742
  405 Dura Ave Toledo (43612) *(G-17738)*
Abbruzzese Brothers Inc (PA) 614 873-1550
  7775 Smith Calhoun Rd Plain City (43064) *(G-16180)*
Abbyshire Place Skilled Nurse, Bidwell Also called Vrable III Inc *(G-1497)*
ABC Appliance Inc 419 693-4414
  3012 Navarre Ave Oregon (43616) *(G-15722)*
ABC Child Care & Learning Ctr 440 964-8799
  2012 W 11th St Ashtabula (44004) *(G-710)*
ABC Day Care, Ashtabula Also called ABC Child Care & Learning Ctr *(G-710)*
ABC Detroit/Toledo, Perrysburg Also called Auction Broadcasting Co LLC *(G-15972)*
ABC Detroit/Toledo Auto Auctn 419 872-0872
  9797 Fremont Pike 3 Perrysburg (43551) *(G-15971)*
ABC Early Childhood Lrng Ctr, Cincinnati Also called Colerain Dry Rdge Chldcare Ltd *(G-3387)*
ABC Fire Inc 440 237-6677
  10250 Royalton Rd North Royalton (44133) *(G-15480)*
ABC Piping Co 216 398-4000
  1277 E Schaaf Rd Ste 5 Brooklyn Heights (44131) *(G-1908)*
Abcd Inc (PA) 330 455-6385
  1225 Gross Ave Ne Canton (44705) *(G-2223)*
Abco Contracting LLC 419 973-4772
  947 Belmont Ave Toledo (43607) *(G-17739)*
Abco Fire LLC 800 875-7200
  510 W Benson St Cincinnati (45215) *(G-2960)*
Abco Fire LLC (HQ) 216 433-7200
  4545 W 160th St Cleveland (44135) *(G-4945)*
Abco Fire Protection, Cleveland Also called Abco Holdings LLC *(G-4946)*
Abco Fire Protection, Cincinnati Also called Abco Fire LLC *(G-2960)*
Abco Holdings LLC (PA) 216 433-7200
  4545 W 160th St Cleveland (44135) *(G-4946)*
Aber's Truck Center, Ashland Also called Abers Garage Inc *(G-649)*
Abercrombie & Fitch Trading Co (HQ) 614 283-6500
  6301 Fitch Path New Albany (43054) *(G-14970)*
Aberdeen Business Park, Cleveland Also called Forest City Enterprises LP *(G-5618)*
Abers Garage Inc (PA) 419 281-5500
  1729 Claremont Ave Ashland (44805) *(G-649)*
ABF Freight System Inc 440 843-4600
  5630 Chevrolet Blvd Cleveland (44130) *(G-4947)*
ABF Freight System Inc 614 294-3537
  1720 Joyce Ave Columbus (43219) *(G-6925)*
ABF Freight System Inc 937 236-2210
  8051 Center Point 70 Blvd Dayton (45424) *(G-9301)*
ABF Freight System Inc 513 779-7888
  6290 Allen Rd West Chester (45069) *(G-19011)*

ABF Freight System Inc 419 525-0118
25 S Mulberry St Mansfield (44902) *(G-13258)*

ABF Freight System Inc 330 549-3800
11000 Market St North Lima (44452) *(G-15395)*

ABG Advisors, Cincinnati *Also called Pension Corporation America (G-4277)*

Abilities First Foundation (PA) 513 423-9496
4710 Timber Trail Dr Middletown (45044) *(G-14411)*

Ability Ctr of Greater Toledo (PA) 419 517-7123
5605 Monroe St Sylvania (43560) *(G-17575)*

Ability Matters LLC 614 214-9652
6058 Heritage View Ct Hilliard (43026) *(G-11875)*

Ability Network Inc 513 943-8888
4357 Ferguson Dr Ste 100 Cincinnati (45245) *(G-2901)*

Ability Works Inc 419 626-1048
3920 Columbus Ave Sandusky (44870) *(G-16723)*

Able, Toledo *Also called Advoctes For Bsic Lgal Eqality (G-17744)*

Able Company Ltd Partnership (PA) 614 444-7663
4777 Westerville Rd Columbus (43231) *(G-6926)*

Able Contracting Group Inc (PA) 440 951-0880
11117 Caddie Ln Painesville (44077) *(G-15832)*

Able Fence & Guard Rail Co, Painesville *Also called Able Contracting Group Inc (G-15832)*

Able Roofing, Columbus *Also called Able Company Ltd Partnership (G-6926)*

Able Roofing LLC 614 444-7663
4777 Westerville Rd Columbus (43231) *(G-6927)*

ABM Engineering, Cincinnati *Also called ABM Facility Services Inc (G-2961)*

ABM Facility Services Inc 859 767-4393
3087 B Terminal Dr Cincinnati (45275) *(G-2961)*

ABM Janitorial Services Inc 216 861-1199
1501 Euclid Ave Ste 320 Cleveland (44115) *(G-4948)*

ABM Janitorial Services Inc 513 731-1418
354 Gest St Cincinnati (45203) *(G-2962)*

ABM Parking Services Inc 937 461-2113
40 N Main St Ste 1540 Dayton (45423) *(G-9302)*

ABM Parking Services Inc 330 747-7678
20 W Federal St Ste M9 Youngstown (44503) *(G-20096)*

ABM Parking Services Inc 216 621-6600
1459 Hamilton Ave Cleveland (44114) *(G-4949)*

Aboutgolf Limited (PA) 419 482-9095
352 Tomahawk Dr Maumee (43537) *(G-13871)*

Above & Beyond Caregivers LLC 614 478-1700
2862 Johnstown Rd Columbus (43219) *(G-6928)*

Abraham Ford LLC 440 233-7402
1115 E Broad St Elyria (44035) *(G-10592)*

Abraxas Foundation of Ohio, Shelby *Also called Cornell Companies Inc (G-16898)*

Abror Health Care, Clyde *Also called Arbors At Clide Asssted Living (G-6808)*

ABS Business Products, Cincinnati *Also called Andrew Belmont Sargent (G-3027)*

Absolute Care Management Llc (PA) 614 846-8053
4618 Sawmill Rd Columbus (43220) *(G-6929)*

Absolute Cleaning Services 440 542-1742
5349 Harper Rd Solon (44139) *(G-16968)*

Absolute Health Services, Canton *Also called Advantage Appliance Services (G-2226)*

Absolute Machine Tools Inc (PA) 440 839-9696
7420 Industrial Pkwy Dr Lorain (44053) *(G-13010)*

Abx Air Inc (HQ) 937 382-5591
145 Hunter Dr Wilmington (45177) *(G-19741)*

Abx Air Inc 937 366-2282
145 Hunter Dr Wilmington (45177) *(G-19742)*

Academic Support Services LLC 740 274-6138
2958 Blossom Ave Columbus (43231) *(G-6930)*

Academy Answering Service Inc 440 442-8500
1446 Som Center Rd Ste 7 Cleveland (44124) *(G-4950)*

Academy Communications, Cleveland *Also called Academy Answering Service Inc (G-4950)*

Academy Court Reporting Inc 216 861-3222
2044 Euclid Ave Lbby Lbby Cleveland (44115) *(G-4951)*

Academy For Young Childrn, Hudson *Also called T L C Child Development Center (G-12146)*

Academy Graphic Comm Inc 216 661-2550
1000 Brookpark Rd Cleveland (44109) *(G-4952)*

Academy Kids Learning Ctr Inc 614 258-5437
289 Woodland Ave Columbus (43203) *(G-6931)*

Academy Medical Staffing Svcs, Columbus *Also called Acloche LLC (G-6938)*

Acadia Solutions Inc 614 505-6135
6751 Burnside Ln Dublin (43016) *(G-10233)*

ACC Automation Co Inc 330 928-3821
475 Wolf Ledges Pkwy Akron (44311) *(G-15)*

ACC-U-Coil, Xenia *Also called Twist Inc (G-20081)*

ACCAA, Ashtabula *Also called Ashtabula County Commnty Actn (G-718)*

Accco Inc 740 697-2005
451 Gordon St Roseville (43777) *(G-16600)*

Accel Inc 614 656-1100
9000 Smiths Mill Rd New Albany (43054) *(G-14971)*

Accel Performance Group LLC (HQ) 216 658-6413
6100 Oak Tree Blvd # 200 Independence (44131) *(G-12177)*

Accelerant Solutions, Genoa *Also called Accelerant Technologies LLC (G-11374)*

Accelerant Technologies LLC 419 236-8768
2257 N Manor Dr Genoa (43430) *(G-11374)*

Accelerated Health Systems LLC 614 334-5135
3780 Ridge Mill Dr Hilliard (43026) *(G-11876)*

Accelerated Moving & Stor Inc 614 836-1007
4001 Refugee Rd Ste 2 Columbus (43232) *(G-6932)*

Accent Drapery Co Inc 614 488-0741
1180 Goodale Blvd Columbus (43212) *(G-6933)*

Accent Drapery Supply Co, Columbus *Also called Accent Drapery Co Inc (G-6933)*

Accentcare Home Health Cal Inc 740 387-4568
458 E Center St Marion (43302) *(G-13522)*

Accentcare Home Health Cal Inc 740 474-7826
119 S Court St Ste A Circleville (43113) *(G-4876)*

Accenture LLP 216 685-1435
1400 W 10th St Cleveland (44113) *(G-4953)*

Accenture LLP 614 629-2000
400 W Nationwide Blvd # 100 Columbus (43215) *(G-6934)*

Accenture LLP 513 455-1000
201 E 4th St Ste 1600 Cincinnati (45202) *(G-2963)*

Accenture LLP 513 651-2444
425 Walnut St Ste 1200 Cincinnati (45202) *(G-2964)*

Access Inc 330 535-2999
230 W Market St Akron (44303) *(G-16)*

Access Catalog Company LLC 440 572-5377
21848 Commerce Pkwy # 100 Strongsville (44149) *(G-17438)*

Access Cleaning Service Inc 937 276-2605
5045 N Main St Ste 100 Dayton (45415) *(G-9303)*

Access Counseling Services LLC 513 649-8008
4464 S Dixie Hwy Middletown (45005) *(G-14472)*

Access Home Care LLC 937 224-9991
2555 S Dixie Dr Ste 100 Dayton (45409) *(G-9304)*

Accessibility, Ashland *Also called Randall R Leab (G-693)*

Accessrn Inc 419 698-1988
1540 S Hlland Sylvania Rd Maumee (43537) *(G-13872)*

Accf Accreditation, Dublin *Also called American Cllege Crdlgy Fndtion (G-10246)*

Accomodaire Total Cleaning LLC 614 367-1347
541 Kasons Way Columbus (43230) *(G-6935)*

Account Temps, Youngstown *Also called Robert Half International Inc (G-20353)*

Accountants To You LLC 513 651-2855
430 Reading Rd Ste 100 Cincinnati (45202) *(G-2965)*

Accounts Payable Department, Columbus *Also called Ohio State University (G-8408)*

Accounts Payable Sso, Cincinnati *Also called Mercy Health (G-4064)*

Accucut, North Royalton *Also called Aaron Landscape Inc (G-15479)*

Acculube, Dayton *Also called Accurate Lubr & Met Wkg Fluids (G-9305)*

Accurate Electric Cnstr Inc 614 863-1844
6901 Americana Pkwy Reynoldsburg (43068) *(G-16424)*

Accurate Group Holdings Inc (PA) 216 520-1740
6000 Freedom Square Dr # 300 Independence (44131) *(G-12178)*

Accurate Healthcare Inc 513 208-6988
4681 Interstate Dr West Chester (45246) *(G-19189)*

Accurate Heating & Cooling 740 775-5005
3001 River Rd Chillicothe (45601) *(G-2807)*

Accurate Inventory and C 800 777-9414
4284 N High St Fl 1 Columbus (43214) *(G-6936)*

Accurate It Services, Columbus *Also called Enviro It LLC (G-7598)*

Accurate Lubr & Met Wkg Fluids (PA) 937 461-9906
403 Homestead Ave Dayton (45417) *(G-9305)*

Accurate Mechanical Inc 740 654-5898
566 Mill Park Dr Lancaster (43130) *(G-12506)*

Accurate Nurse Staffing 419 475-2424
4165 Monroe St Toledo (43606) *(G-17740)*

Accutek Testing Laboratory, Fairfield *Also called McCloy Engineering LLC (G-10877)*

Ace Assembly Packaging Inc 330 866-9117
133 N Mill St Waynesburg (44688) *(G-18979)*

Ace Brokerage, LLC, Cincinnati *Also called Action Engneered Logistics LLC (G-2970)*

Ace Building Maintenance LLC 614 471-2223
2565 Mccutcheon Rd Columbus (43219) *(G-6937)*

Ace Disposal, Dover *Also called Kimble Companies Inc (G-10194)*

Ace Doran Hauling & Rigging Co (HQ) 513 681-7900
1601 Blue Rock St Cincinnati (45223) *(G-2966)*

Ace Hardware, Marysville *Also called Ace Rental Place (G-13605)*

Ace Hardware Corporation 440 333-4223
20200 Detroit Rd Rocky River (44116) *(G-16568)*

Ace Mitchell Bowlers Mart, Cuyahoga Falls *Also called Micnan Inc (G-9209)*

Ace Rental Place 937 642-2891
1299 W 5th St Marysville (43040) *(G-13605)*

Ace Truck Body Inc 614 871-3100
1600 Thrailkill Rd Grove City (43123) *(G-11527)*

Ace-Merit LLC 513 241-3200
30 Garfield Pl Ste 540 Cincinnati (45202) *(G-2967)*

Achievement Ctrs For Children (PA) 216 292-9700
4255 Northfield Rd Cleveland (44128) *(G-4954)*

Achievement Ctrs For Children 440 250-2520
24211 Center Ridge Rd Westlake (44145) *(G-19454)*

Aci Const Co Inc 419 595-4284
2959 S Us Highway 23 Alvada (44802) *(G-567)*

Aci Industries Ltd (PA) 740 368-4160
970 Pittsburgh Dr Delaware (43015) *(G-10065)*

Aci Industries Converting Ltd (HQ) 740 368-4160
970 Pittsburgh Dr Delaware (43015) *(G-10066)*

Aclara Technologies LLC 440 528-7200
30400 Solon Rd Solon (44139) *(G-16969)*

Acloche LLC (PA) 888 608-0889
1800 Watermark Dr Ste 430 Columbus (43215) *(G-6938)*

Acme, Coventry Township *Also called Fred W Albrecht Grocery Co (G-9124)*

Acme, Akron *Also called Fred W Albrecht Grocery Co (G-230)*

Acme Company 330 758-2313
9495 Harvard Blvd Poland (44514) ***(G-16219)***
Acne Bowling Supply, Cuyahoga Falls *Also called Midway Bowling Lanes Inc* ***(G-9210)***
Acock Assoc Architects LLC 614 228-1586
383 N Front St Ste 1 Columbus (43215) ***(G-6939)***
Acord Rk Lumber Company 740 289-3761
125 W 4th St Piketon (45661) ***(G-16108)***
Acorn Distributors Inc 614 294-6444
5310 Crosswind Dr Columbus (43228) ***(G-6940)***
Acorn Farms Inc 614 891-9348
7679 Worthington Rd B Galena (43021) ***(G-11277)***
Acosta Inc 440 498-7370
30600 Aurora Rd Ste 100 Solon (44139) ***(G-16970)***
Acpi Systems Inc 513 738-3840
1440 Kemper Meadow Dr Cincinnati (45240) ***(G-2968)***
Acpx2 ....513 829-2100
1750 Garrett House Ln Fairfield (45014) ***(G-10815)***
Acquisition Logistics Engrg, Worthington *Also called Quality Aero Inc* ***(G-19988)***
Acres of Fun, Wooster *Also called CCJ Enterprises Inc* ***(G-19837)***
Acro Tool & Die Company 330 773-5173
325 Morgan Ave Akron (44311) ***(G-17)***
Acrt Inc (PA) 800 622-2562
1333 Home Ave Akron (44310) ***(G-18)***
Acrt Services Inc 330 945-7500
1333 Home Ave Akron (44310) ***(G-19)***
Acrux Investigation Agency (PA) 937 842-5780
8823 Township Road 239 Lakeview (43331) ***(G-12467)***
ACS Acqco Corp 513 719-2600
201 E 4th St Ste 900 Cincinnati (45202) ***(G-2969)***
ACS Learning Services, Independence *Also called Intellinex LLC* ***(G-12220)***
Act I Temporaries Findlay Inc 419 423-0713
2017 Tiffin Ave Findlay (45840) ***(G-10989)***
Action Coupling & Eqp Inc 330 279-4242
8248 County Road 245 Holmesville (44633) ***(G-12070)***
Action Door, Cleveland *Also called Dortronic Service Inc* ***(G-5506)***
Action Engineered Logistics LLC 513 681-7900
1601 Blue Rock St Cincinnati (45223) ***(G-2970)***
Action For Children Inc (PA) 614 224-0222
78 Jefferson Ave Columbus (43215) ***(G-6941)***
Actionlink LLC 888 737-8757
286 N Cleveland Massillon Akron (44333) ***(G-20)***
Active Chiropractic 440 893-8800
1 S Main St Ste 1 Chagrin Falls (44022) ***(G-2688)***
Active Detective Bureau, Cincinnati *Also called D B A Inc* ***(G-3454)***
Activity Training, Cleveland *Also called County of Cuyahoga* ***(G-5425)***
ACTUARIAL & EMPLOYEE BENEFIT S, Cincinnati *Also called Cai/Insurance Agency Inc* ***(G-3165)***
Acuative Corporation 440 202-4500
8237 Dow Cir Strongsville (44136) ***(G-17439)***
Acuity Healthcare LP 740 283-7499
380 Summit Ave Fl 3 Steubenville (43952) ***(G-17302)***
Acuren Inspection, Dayton *Also called US Inspection Services Inc* ***(G-9958)***
Acuren Inspection Inc 937 228-9729
705 Albany St Dayton (45417) ***(G-9306)***
Acuren Inspection Inc 513 671-7073
502 W Crescentville Rd Cincinnati (45246) ***(G-2971)***
Acuren Inspection Inc 937 228-9729
7333 Paragon Rd Ste 240 Dayton (45459) ***(G-9307)***
Acusport Corporation (PA) 937 593-7010
1 Hunter Pl Bellefontaine (43311) ***(G-1374)***
Acute Care Homenursing Service 216 271-9100
1577 Woodland St Ne Warren (44483) ***(G-18813)***
Acute Care Specialty Hospital 330 363-4860
2600 6th St Sw Canton (44710) ***(G-2224)***
Acxiom Corporation 216 520-3181
5005 Rockside Rd Ste 600 Independence (44131) ***(G-12179)***
Acxiom Info SEC Svcs Inc 216 685-7600
6111 Oak Tree Blvd Independence (44131) ***(G-12180)***
AD Farrow LLC (PA) 614 228-6353
491 W Broad St Columbus (43215) ***(G-6942)***
Ad Investments LLC 614 857-2340
375 N Front St Ste 200 Columbus (43215) ***(G-6943)***
Ada Lberty Joint Ambulance Dst, Ada *Also called County of Hardin* ***(G-5)***
Ada Visiting Nurses, Ada *Also called Community Hlth Prfssionals Inc* ***(G-4)***
Adamhs Bd For Montgomery Cnty, Dayton *Also called Alcohol Drug Addction & Mental* ***(G-9314)***
Adams & Brown Counties Economi 937 695-0316
19211 Main St Winchester (45697) ***(G-19799)***
Adams & Brown Counties Economi (PA) 937 378-6041
406 W Plum St Georgetown (45121) ***(G-11383)***
Adams Brown Wthrzation Program, Winchester *Also called Adams & Brown Counties Economi* ***(G-19799)***
Adams Cnty /Ohio Vly Schl Dst 937 544-2951
555 Lloyd Rd West Union (45693) ***(G-19271)***
Adams County Manor 937 544-2205
10856 State Route 41 West Union (45693) ***(G-19272)***
Adams County Regional Med Ctr 937 386-3001
230 Medical Center Dr Seaman (45679) ***(G-16818)***
Adams County Regional Med Ctr 937 386-3400
230 Medical Center Dr Seaman (45679) ***(G-16819)***
Adams County Senior Citizens 937 544-7459
10835 State Route 41 West Union (45693) ***(G-19273)***
Adams Lane Care Center, Zanesville *Also called Zandex Health Care Corporation* ***(G-20551)***
Adams Lane Care Center, Zanesville *Also called Zandex Inc* ***(G-20548)***
Adams Robinson Construction, Dayton *Also called Adams-Robinson Enterprises Inc* ***(G-9308)***
Adams Rural Electric Coop Inc 937 544-2305
4800 State Route 125 West Union (45693) ***(G-19274)***
Adams Signs, Massillon *Also called Identitek Systems Inc* ***(G-13822)***
Adams-Robinson Enterprises Inc (PA) 937 274-5318
2735 Needmore Rd Dayton (45414) ***(G-9308)***
Adaptive Corporation (PA) 440 257-7460
118 W Streetsboro St Hudson (44236) ***(G-12101)***
Adcom Group Inc 216 574-9100
1370 W 6th St Fl 3 Cleveland (44113) ***(G-4955)***
Addiction Services Council 513 281-7880
2828 Vernon Pl Cincinnati (45219) ***(G-2972)***
Addison Hts Hlth Rhblttion Ctr, Maumee *Also called Swan Pnte Fclty Operations LLC* ***(G-13983)***
Addisonmckee Inc (PA) 513 228-7000
1637 Kingsview Dr Lebanon (45036) ***(G-12587)***
Addus Home Care, Wintersville *Also called Addus Homecare Corporation* ***(G-19807)***
Addus Homecare Corporation 866 684-0385
1406 Cadiz Rd Wintersville (43953) ***(G-19807)***
Adecco Usa Inc 419 720-0111
336 N Superior St 200 Toledo (43604) ***(G-17741)***
Adelman's Truck Sales, Canton *Also called Adelmans Truck Parts Corp* ***(G-2225)***
Adelmans Truck Parts Corp (PA) 330 456-0206
2000 Waynesburg Dr Se Canton (44707) ***(G-2225)***
Adelmos Electric Sewer Clg Co 216 641-2301
4917 Van Epps Rd Brooklyn Heights (44131) ***(G-1909)***
Adelphia, Westlake *Also called Comcast Spotlight* ***(G-19478)***
Adelphia, Cleveland *Also called Comcast Spotlight Inc* ***(G-5373)***
Adena Commercial LLC 614 436-9800
8800 Lyra Dr Ste 650 Columbus (43240) ***(G-6868)***
Adena Corporation 419 529-4456
1310 W 4th St Ontario (44906) ***(G-15682)***
Adena Counseling Center, Chillicothe *Also called Adena Health System* ***(G-2812)***
Adena Dialysis, Chillicothe *Also called Court Dialysis LLC* ***(G-2831)***
Adena Fmly Medicine-Greenfield, Greenfield *Also called Adena Health System* ***(G-11482)***
Adena Health System 740 779-7201
4439 State Route 159 # 120 Chillicothe (45601) ***(G-2808)***
Adena Health System (PA) 740 779-7360
272 Hospital Rd Chillicothe (45601) ***(G-2809)***
Adena Health System 740 779-7500
308 Highland Ave Unit C Wshngtn CT Hs (43160) ***(G-20013)***
Adena Health System 740 420-3000
798 N Court St Circleville (43113) ***(G-4877)***
Adena Health System 937 981-9444
1075 N Washington St Greenfield (45123) ***(G-11482)***
Adena Health System 740 779-8995
85 River Trce Chillicothe (45601) ***(G-2810)***
Adena Health System 740 779-4801
445 Shawnee Ln Chillicothe (45601) ***(G-2811)***
Adena Health System 740 779-4888
455 Shawnee Dr Ln Chillicothe (45601) ***(G-2812)***
Adena Hlth Rehabilitation Ctr, Adena *Also called Adena NH LLC* ***(G-7)***
Adena NH LLC 740 546-3620
213 U S Route 250 Adena (43901) ***(G-7)***
Adena Pckwy-Ross Fmly Physcans 740 779-4500
100 N Walnut St Chillicothe (45601) ***(G-2813)***
Adena Rhblitation Wellness Ctr, Chillicothe *Also called Adena Health System* ***(G-2811)***
Adesa Cleveland, Northfield *Also called Adesa-Ohio Llc* ***(G-15508)***
Adesa Corporation LLC 937 746-5361
4400 William C Good Blvd Franklin (45005) ***(G-11148)***
Adesa-Ohio Llc 330 467-8280
210 E Twinsburg Rd Northfield (44067) ***(G-15508)***
Adex International, Cincinnati *Also called Affinity Disp Expositions Inc* ***(G-2977)***
ADI, Sheffield Village *Also called Advanced Design Industries Inc* ***(G-16883)***
Adler Team Sports, Euclid *Also called R & A Sports Inc* ***(G-10773)***
Adleta Construction, Cincinnati *Also called Adleta Inc* ***(G-2973)***
Adleta Inc 513 554-1469
389 S Wayne Ave Cincinnati (45215) ***(G-2973)***
Administration Services Dept, Cincinnati *Also called University of Cincinnati* ***(G-4761)***
Administrative Service Cons, Findlay *Also called Ebso Inc* ***(G-11021)***
Administrative Service Cons, Cleveland *Also called Ebso Inc* ***(G-5525)***
Administrative Svcs Ohio Dept 614 466-5090
4200 Surface Rd Columbus (43228) ***(G-6944)***
Admiral Truck Parts Inc 330 659-6311
7941 Ranger Rd Bath (44210) ***(G-1033)***
Admirals Pnte Nrsing Rhblttion, Huron *Also called Huron Health Care Center Inc* ***(G-12167)***
Ado Health Services Inc 330 629-2888
1011 Boardman Canfield Rd Youngstown (44512) ***(G-20097)***
Ado Staffing Inc 419 222-8395
2100 Harding Hwy Lima (45804) ***(G-12731)***
Adolph Johnson & Son Co 330 544-8900
3497 Union St Mineral Ridge (44440) ***(G-14635)***
ADP, Cleveland *Also called Automatic Data Processing Inc* ***(G-5082)***

ALPHABETIC

ADP, Westerville *Also called Automatic Data Processing Inc* ***(G-19370)***
Adrian M Schnall MD............216 291-4300
1611 S Green Rd Lbby A Cleveland (44121) ***(G-4956)***
Adriel School Inc (PA)............937 465-0010
414 N Detroit St West Liberty (43357) ***(G-19260)***
ADT Security............440 397-5751
13022 Pearl Rd Strongsville (44136) ***(G-17440)***
Adult Probation Department, Elyria *Also called County of Lorain* ***(G-10611)***
Advance Auto Parts, Brunswick *Also called General Parts Inc* ***(G-1980)***
Advance Auto Parts Inc............440 226-3150
230 Center St Chardon (44024) ***(G-2738)***
Advance Care Inc............513 932-1121
115 Oregonia Rd Lebanon (45036) ***(G-12588)***
Advance Cleaning Contractors, Toledo *Also called Kelli Woods Management Inc* ***(G-17992)***
Advance Door Company............216 883-2424
4555 Willow Pkwy Cleveland (44125) ***(G-4957)***
Advance Home Care LLC (PA)............614 436-3611
1191 S James Rd Ste D Columbus (43227) ***(G-6945)***
Advance Home Care LLC............937 723-6335
1250 W Dorothy Ln Dayton (45409) ***(G-9309)***
Advance Implant Dentistry Inc............513 271-0821
5823 Wooster Pike Cincinnati (45227) ***(G-2974)***
Advance Mechanical Plbg & Htg............937 879-9405
235 Glaser St Ste B Fairborn (45324) ***(G-10782)***
Advance Partners, Beachwood *Also called Advance Payroll Funding Ltd* ***(G-1046)***
Advance Payroll Funding Ltd............216 831-8900
3401 Entp Pkwy Fl 5 Beachwood (44122) ***(G-1046)***
Advance Services, Chillicothe *Also called Dave Pinkerton* ***(G-2834)***
Advance Stores Company Inc............740 369-4491
1675 Us Highway 42 S Delaware (43015) ***(G-10067)***
Advance Trnsp Systems Inc............513 818-4311
10558 Taconic Ter Cincinnati (45215) ***(G-2975)***
Advance Vending Corp............216 587-9500
14600 Industrial Ave S D Cleveland (44137) ***(G-4958)***
Advanced Auto Glass Inc (PA)............412 373-6675
44 N Union St Akron (44304) ***(G-21)***
Advanced Bar Technology, Canton *Also called Gerdau Macsteel Atmosphere Ann* ***(G-2379)***
Advanced Benefit Cons Agcy, Cleveland *Also called Advanced Group Corp* ***(G-4959)***
Advanced Cmpt Connections LLC............419 668-4080
166 Milan Ave Norwalk (44857) ***(G-15561)***
Advanced Computer Graphics............513 936-5060
10895 Indeco Dr Blue Ash (45241) ***(G-1523)***
Advanced Design Industries Inc............440 277-4141
4686 French Creek Rd Sheffield Village (44054) ***(G-16883)***
Advanced Elastomer Systems LP (HQ)............800 352-7866
388 S Main St Ste 600 Akron (44311) ***(G-22)***
Advanced Engrg Solutions Inc............937 743-6900
250 Advanced Dr Springboro (45066) ***(G-17113)***
Advanced Facilities Maint Corp (PA)............614 389-3495
6171 Huntley Rd Ste G Columbus (43229) ***(G-6946)***
Advanced Fastener, Fairfield *Also called Afc Industries Inc* ***(G-10816)***
Advanced Geriatric Education &............888 393-9799
9823 Tulip Tree Ct Loveland (45140) ***(G-13109)***
Advanced Graphite Machining US............216 658-6521
12300 Snow Rd Parma (44130) ***(G-15898)***
Advanced Group Corp (PA)............216 431-8800
3800 Lkside Ave E Ste 400 Cleveland (44114) ***(G-4959)***
Advanced Healthcare Center, Toledo *Also called Healthcare Facility MGT LLC* ***(G-17944)***
Advanced Health Care Center, Toledo *Also called Communi Care Inc* ***(G-17822)***
Advanced Industrial Roofg Inc............330 837-1999
1330 Erie St S Massillon (44646) ***(G-13784)***
Advanced Industrial Svcs LLC............800 846-9094
123 Oakdale Ave Toledo (43605) ***(G-17742)***
Advanced Industrial Svcs LLC (HQ)............419 661-8522
123 Oakdale Ave Toledo (43605) ***(G-17743)***
Advanced Intgrted Slutions LLC............313 724-8600
11140 Deerfield Rd Blue Ash (45242) ***(G-1524)***
Advanced Mechanical Svcs Inc............937 879-7426
575 Sports St Fairborn (45324) ***(G-10783)***
Advanced Medical Equipment Inc (PA)............937 534-1080
2655 S Dixie Dr Kettering (45409) ***(G-12426)***
Advanced Prgrm Resources Inc (PA)............614 761-9994
2715 Tuller Pkwy Dublin (43017) ***(G-10234)***
Advanced Service Tech LLC............937 435-4376
885 Mound Rd Miamisburg (45342) ***(G-14268)***
Advanced Specialty Hosp Toledo, Toledo *Also called Garden II Leasing Co LLC* ***(G-17908)***
Advanced Specialty Products............419 882-6528
428 Clough St Bowling Green (43402) ***(G-1756)***
Advanced Systems Group, Beavercreek Township *Also called Jacobs Technology Inc* ***(G-1271)***
Advanced Tenting Solutions............216 291-3300
10750 Music St Newbury (44065) ***(G-15253)***
Advanced Testing Lab Inc............513 489-8447
6954 Cornell Rd Ste 200 Blue Ash (45242) ***(G-1525)***
Advanced Testing Laboratories, Blue Ash *Also called Advanced Testing Lab Inc* ***(G-1525)***
Advanced Testing MGT Group Inc............513 489-8447
6954 Cornell Rd Ste 200 Blue Ash (45242) ***(G-1526)***
Advanced Tool & Supply Inc............937 278-7337
4530 Wadsworth Rd Dayton (45414) ***(G-9310)***
Advanced Translation/Cnsltng............440 716-0820
3751 Willow Run Westlake (44145) ***(G-19455)***
Advanced Urology Inc (PA)............330 758-9787
904 Sahara Trl Ste 1 Youngstown (44514) ***(G-20098)***
Advanced Welding Division, Tipp City *Also called Daihen Inc* ***(G-17715)***
Advant-E Corporation (PA)............937 429-4288
2434 Esquire Dr Beavercreek (45431) ***(G-1145)***
Advantage Aerotech Inc............614 759-8329
1400 Hollybrier Dr # 121 Columbus (43230) ***(G-6947)***
Advantage Appliance Services............330 498-8101
7235 Whipple Ave Nw Canton (44720) ***(G-2226)***
Advantage Bank, Wshngtn CT Hs *Also called Huntington National Bank* ***(G-20027)***
Advantage Credit Union Inc (PA)............419 529-5603
700 Stumbo Rd Ontario (44906) ***(G-15683)***
Advantage Diagnostic, Beachwood *Also called Advantage Imaging LLC* ***(G-1047)***
Advantage Ford Lincoln Mercury............419 334-9751
885 Hagerty Dr Fremont (43420) ***(G-11182)***
Advantage Home Health Care............800 636-2330
1656 Coles Blvd Portsmouth (45662) ***(G-16263)***
Advantage Home Health Svcs Inc............330 491-8161
7951 Pittsburg Ave Nw North Canton (44720) ***(G-15320)***
Advantage Imaging LLC (PA)............216 292-9998
3733 Park East Dr Ste 100 Beachwood (44122) ***(G-1047)***
Advantage Local, West Chester *Also called Advantage Rn LLC* ***(G-19012)***
Advantage Resourcing Amer Inc (HQ)............781 472-8900
201 E 4th St Ste 800 Cincinnati (45202) ***(G-2976)***
Advantage Rn LLC (PA)............866 301-4045
9021 Meridian Way West Chester (45069) ***(G-19012)***
Advantage Sales & Mktg, Blue Ash *Also called Advantage Sales & Mktg LLC* ***(G-1527)***
Advantage Sales & Mktg LLC............513 841-0500
10300 Alliance Rd Ste 400 Blue Ash (45242) ***(G-1527)***
Advantage Staffing, Cincinnati *Also called Advantage Resourcing Amer Inc* ***(G-2976)***
Advantage Tank Lines Inc (HQ)............330 491-0474
4366 Mount Pleasant St Nw North Canton (44720) ***(G-15321)***
Advantage Tank Lines Inc............330 427-1010
404 12 Pearl St Leetonia (44431) ***(G-12661)***
Advantage Technology Group (PA)............513 563-3560
7723 Tylers Place Blvd # 132 West Chester (45069) ***(G-19013)***
Advantage Waypoint LLC............248 919-3144
9458 Ravenna Rd Twinsburg (44087) ***(G-18389)***
Advantech Corporation............513 742-8895
11380 Reed Hartman Hwy Blue Ash (45241) ***(G-1528)***
Advantech Indus Automtn Group, Blue Ash *Also called Advantech Corporation* ***(G-1528)***
Advent Drilling Inc............330 497-2533
366 Rose Lane St Sw Canton (44720) ***(G-2227)***
Adventure Cmbat Operations LLC............330 818-1029
4501 Hlls Dls Rd Nw A Canton (44708) ***(G-2228)***
Adventure Harley Davidson............330 343-2295
1465 State Route 39 Nw Dover (44622) ***(G-10175)***
Advocare Inc............216 514-1451
25001 Emery Rd Cleveland (44128) ***(G-4960)***
Advocate Property Servic............330 952-1313
620 E Smith Rd Medina (44256) ***(G-14032)***
Advocate Radiology Bil............614 210-1885
10567 Swmill Pkwy Ste 100 Powell (43065) ***(G-16323)***
Advocate Solutions LLC............614 444-5144
762 S Pearl St Columbus (43206) ***(G-6948)***
Advoctes For Bsic Lgal Eqality (PA)............419 255-0814
525 Jefferson Ave Toledo (43604) ***(G-17744)***
Adw, Cleveland *Also called Any Domest Work Inc* ***(G-5045)***
AE Electric Inc............419 392-8468
T483 County Road 1 Grand Rapids (43522) ***(G-11448)***
Aecom............330 253-9741
1300 E 9th St Ste 500 Cleveland (44114) ***(G-4961)***
Aecom Energy & Cnstr Inc............216 622-2300
1300 E 9th St Ste 500 Cleveland (44114) ***(G-4962)***
Aecom Energy & Cnstr Inc............216 523-5600
1500 W 3rd St Ste 200 Cleveland (44113) ***(G-4963)***
Aecom Energy & Cnstr Inc............216 523-5600
1500 W 3rd St Ste 200 Cleveland (44113) ***(G-4964)***
Aecom Energy & Cnstr Inc............216 523-5600
1500 W 3rd St Ste 470 Cleveland (44113) ***(G-4965)***
Aecom Energy & Cnstr Inc............419 698-6277
4001 Cedar Point Rd Oregon (43616) ***(G-15723)***
Aecom Global II LLC............419 774-9862
605 Taylor St Delta (43515) ***(G-10155)***
Aecom Global II LLC............937 233-1230
7333 Paragon Rd Ste 175 Dayton (45459) ***(G-9311)***
Aecom Global II LLC............614 726-3500
5550 Blazer Pkwy Ste 175 Dublin (43017) ***(G-10235)***
Aecom Global II LLC............216 523-5600
1500 W 3rd St Fl 2 Cleveland (44113) ***(G-4966)***
Aecom Technical Services Inc............937 233-1898
4386 Haskell Ln Batavia (45103) ***(G-994)***
Aeea LLC............330 497-5304
4383 Executive Cir Nw Canton (44718) ***(G-2229)***
Aegis Protective Services, Cincinnati *Also called Danson Inc* ***(G-3462)***
Aeilita Div, Dublin *Also called Quest Software Inc* ***(G-10434)***
AEP, Columbus *Also called Ohio Power Company* ***(G-8366)***
AEP, Columbus *Also called Southwestern Electric Power Co* ***(G-8756)***
AEP, Columbus *Also called American Electric Pwr Svc Corp* ***(G-6990)***
AEP, Columbus *Also called Indiana Michigan Power Company* ***(G-7889)***

AEP, Columbus *Also called Public Service Company Okla* ***(G-8578)***

AEP, Columbus *Also called Appalachian Power Company* ***(G-7029)***

AEP, Canton *Also called American Electric Power Co Inc* ***(G-2238)***

AEP Dresden Plant 740 450-1964
9595 Mcglade School Rd Dresden (43821) ***(G-10230)***

AEP Energy Partners Inc 614 716-1000
1 Riverside Plz Columbus (43215) ***(G-6949)***

AEP Energy Services Inc 614 583-2900
155 W Nationwide Blvd Columbus (43215) ***(G-6950)***

AEP Generating Company (HQ) 614 223-1000
1 Riverside Plz Ste 1600 Columbus (43215) ***(G-6951)***

AEP Power Marketing Inc (HQ) 614 716-1000
1 Riverside Plz Fl 1 Columbus (43215) ***(G-6952)***

AEP Pro Serv Rso, Columbus *Also called American Electric Power Co Inc* ***(G-6989)***

AEP Service, Columbus *Also called American Electric Pwr Svc Corp* ***(G-6991)***

AEP Texas North Company, Canton *Also called American Electric Power Co Inc* ***(G-2237)***

Aerco Sandblasting Company 419 224-2464
429 N Jackson St Lima (45801) ***(G-12732)***

Aerie Frtnrl Order Egles 2875 ....419 433-4611
2902 Cleveland Rd W Huron (44839) ***(G-12159)***

Aero Electrical Contractors 614 834-8181
8020 Dove Pkwy Ste A Canal Winchester (43110) ***(G-2152)***

Aero Fulfillment Services Corp (PA) 800 225-7145
3900 Aero Dr Mason (45040) ***(G-13658)***

Aero Fulfillment Services Corp 513 874-4112
6023 Un Centre Blvd Steb West Chester (45069) ***(G-19014)***

Aero-Mark Inc 330 995-0100
10423 Danner Dr Streetsboro (44241) ***(G-17405)***

Aerocon Photogrammetric Svcs (PA) 440 946-6277
4515 Glenbrook Rd Willoughby (44094) ***(G-19641)***

Aerocontrolex Group Inc (HQ) 440 352-6182
313 Gillett St Painesville (44077) ***(G-15833)***

Aerodynamic Concrete & Cnstr 330 906-7477
1726 Massillon Rd Akron (44312) ***(G-23)***

Aerodynmics Inc Ardynamics Inc 404 596-8751
25700 Science Park Dr # 210 Beachwood (44122) ***(G-1048)***

Aeroflex Powell, Hilliard *Also called Star Dynamics Corporation* ***(G-11954)***

Aerospace Simulations, Akron *Also called Lockheed Martin* ***(G-326)***

Aerotek Inc 330 517-7330
1559 Corporate Woods Pkwy # 10 Uniontown (44685) ***(G-18506)***

Aerotek Inc 216 573-5520
5990 W Creek Rd Ste 150 Independence (44131) ***(G-12181)***

Aerotek 58, Independence *Also called Aerotek Inc* ***(G-12181)***

AES, Akron *Also called Advanced Elastomer Systems LP* ***(G-22)***

Aesi, Springboro *Also called Advanced Engrg Solutions Inc* ***(G-17113)***

Aetna Building Maintenance Inc (HQ) 614 476-1818
646 Parsons Ave Columbus (43206) ***(G-6953)***

Aetna Building Maintenance Inc 937 324-5711
525 N Yellow Springs St Springfield (45504) ***(G-17146)***

Aetna Building Maintenance Inc 866 238-6201
2044 Wayne Ave Dayton (45410) ***(G-9312)***

Aetna Health California Inc 614 933-6000
7400 W Campus Rd Ste 100 New Albany (43054) ***(G-14972)***

Aetna Integrated Services, Columbus *Also called Aetna Building Maintenance Inc* ***(G-6953)***

Aetna Life Insurance Company 330 659-8000
4059 Kinros Lake Pkwy # 300 Richfield (44286) ***(G-16493)***

Aey Electric Inc 330 792-5745
801 N Meridian Rd Youngstown (44509) ***(G-20099)***

Afc Cable Systems Inc 740 435-3340
829 Georgetown Rd Cambridge (43725) ***(G-2092)***

Afc Industries Inc (PA) 513 874-7456
3795 Port Union Rd Fairfield (45014) ***(G-10816)***

Affiliate of Nations Roof, Springboro *Also called Nations Roof of Ohio LLC* ***(G-17132)***

Affiliated FM Insurance Co 216 362-4820
25050 Country Club Blvd # 400 North Olmsted (44070) ***(G-15409)***

Affiliated Resource Group Inc 614 889-6555
5700 Perimeter Dr Ste H Dublin (43017) ***(G-10236)***

Affiliates In Oral & Maxlofcl (PA) 513 829-8080
5188 Winton Rd Fairfield (45014) ***(G-10817)***

Affiliates In Oral & Maxlofcl 513 829-8080
7795 Discovery Dr Ste C West Chester (45069) ***(G-19015)***

Affinion Group LLC 614 895-1803
300 W Schrock Rd Westerville (43081) ***(G-19360)***

Affinity Apparel, Fairborn *Also called Affinity Specialty Apparel Inc* ***(G-10784)***

Affinity Disp Expositions Inc 513 771-2339
1301 Glendale Milford Rd Cincinnati (45215) ***(G-2977)***

Affinity Family Physicians, Massillon *Also called Doctors Hosp Physcn Svcs LLC* ***(G-13801)***

Affinity Medical Center, Massillon *Also called Dhsc LLC* ***(G-13800)***

Affinity Specialty Apparel Inc (PA) 866 548-8434
1202 E Dayton Yllow Spgs Fairborn (45324) ***(G-10784)***

Afford-A-Car Inc 937 235-2700
8973 State 201 Tipp City (45371) ***(G-17710)***

Affordable Cars & Finance Inc (PA) 440 777-2424
27932 Lorain Rd North Olmsted (44070) ***(G-15410)***

Afidence Inc 513 234-5822
309 Reading Rd Mason (45040) ***(G-13659)***

Afit Ls Usaf 937 255-3636
2950 Hobson Way Dayton (45433) ***(G-9249)***

AFLAC, Cincinnati *Also called Thomas Gentz* ***(G-4652)***

AFLAC Incorporated 614 410-1696
30 Northwoods Blvd # 100 Columbus (43235) ***(G-6954)***

Afm East Archwood Oil Inc 330 786-1000
745 E Archwood Ave Akron (44306) ***(G-24)***

African Safari Wildlife Park, Port Clinton *Also called Animal Mgt Svcs Ohio Inc* ***(G-16237)***

After Market Products, Avon *Also called North Coast Bearings LLC* ***(G-908)***

Aftermarket Parts Company LLC (HQ) 888 333-6224
3229 Sawmill Pkwy Delaware (43015) ***(G-10068)***

AG Interactive Inc (HQ) 216 889-5000
1 American Rd Cleveland (44144) ***(G-4967)***

AG Trucking Inc 937 497-7770
798 S Vandemark Rd Sidney (45365) ***(G-16911)***

AGC Automotive Americas 937 599-3131
1465 W Sandusky Ave Bellefontaine (43311) ***(G-1375)***

Age Line Inc 216 941-9990
4350 Rocky River Dr Cleveland (44135) ***(G-4968)***

Agee Clymer Mitchell & Laret (PA) 614 221-3318
226 N 5th St Ste 501 Columbus (43215) ***(G-6955)***

Aggressive Mechanical Inc 614 443-3280
638 Greenlawn Ave Columbus (43223) ***(G-6956)***

Agile Global Solutions Inc 916 655-7745
5755 Granger Rd Ste 610 Independence (44131) ***(G-12182)***

Agilysys Inc 440 519-6262
6521 Davis Indus Pkwy Solon (44139) ***(G-16971)***

Agj Kidz LLC 937 350-1001
101 E Alexville 1 Rd 110 Ste 110 1st Centerville (45459) ***(G-2669)***

Agmet LLC (PA) 440 439-7400
7800 Medusa Rd Cleveland (44146) ***(G-4969)***

Agmet LLC 216 662-6939
5463 Dunham Rd Maple Heights (44137) ***(G-13399)***

Agrana Fruit Us Inc 937 693-3821
16197 County Road 25a Anna (45302) ***(G-616)***

Agratronix LLC 330 562-2222
10375 State Route 43 Streetsboro (44241) ***(G-17406)***

Agri Communicators Inc 614 273-0465
1625 Bethel Rd Ste 203 Columbus (43220) ***(G-6957)***

Agridry LLC 419 459-4399
3460 Us Highway 20 Edon (43518) ***(G-10585)***

Agrinomix LLC 440 774-2981
300 Creekside Dr Oberlin (44074) ***(G-15637)***

AGS Custom Graphics Inc 330 963-7770
8107 Bavaria Rd Macedonia (44056) ***(G-13186)***

AH Sturgill Roofing Inc 937 254-2955
4358 Springfield St B Dayton (45431) ***(G-9250)***

Ahern Rentals Inc 440 498-0869
29001 Solon Rd Ste 17 Solon (44139) ***(G-16972)***

Ahf Ohio Inc 330 725-4123
806 E Washinton St Medina (44256) ***(G-14033)***

Ahf Ohio Inc 740 532-6188
2932 S 5th St Ironton (45638) ***(G-12280)***

Ahf Ohio Inc 614 760-8870
4880 Tuttle Rd Dublin (43017) ***(G-10237)***

Ahf Ohio Inc 937 256-4663
264 Wilmington Ave Dayton (45420) ***(G-9313)***

Ahf/Central States Inc 615 383-3570
5920 Venture Dr Ste 100 Dublin (43017) ***(G-10238)***

Ahola Corporation 440 717-7620
6820 W Snowville Rd Brecksville (44141) ***(G-1811)***

Ahoy Transport LLC 740 596-0536
301 E Main St Creola (45622) ***(G-9141)***

Ahsland Cleaning, Ashland *Also called Ashland Cleaning LLC* ***(G-654)***

Ahv Construction, Westerville *Also called Ahv Development LLC* ***(G-19283)***

Ahv Development LLC 614 890-1440
592 Office Pkwy Westerville (43082) ***(G-19283)***

Aic Contracting Inc (PA) 513 881-5900
12100 Mosteller Rd # 100 Cincinnati (45241) ***(G-2978)***

Aidc Solutions, Dayton *Also called Evanhoe & Associates Inc* ***(G-9269)***

Aids Tskfrce Grter Clvland Inc 216 357-3131
2829 Euclid Ave Cleveland (44115) ***(G-4970)***

AIG, Cincinnati *Also called American Gen Lf Insur Co Del* ***(G-3007)***

Aim Integrated Logistics Inc 330 759-0438
1500 Trumbull Ave Girard (44420) ***(G-11406)***

Aim Leasing Company (PA) 330 759-0438
1500 Trumbull Ave Girard (44420) ***(G-11407)***

Aim Mro Holdings Inc (PA) 513 831-2938
375 Center St 175 Miamiville (45147) ***(G-14374)***

Air Comfort Systems Inc 216 587-4125
5108 Richmond Rd Cleveland (44146) ***(G-4971)***

Air Compliance Testing Inc (PA) 216 525-0900
5525 Canal Rd Ste 1 Cleveland (44125) ***(G-4972)***

Air Conditioning Entps Inc 440 729-0900
1370 Ontario St Ste 450 Cleveland (44113) ***(G-4973)***

Air Force Morale Welfare Rec, Dayton *Also called Army & Air Force Exchange Svc* ***(G-9256)***

Air Force US Dept of 937 656-2354
4225 Logistics Ave Dayton (45433) ***(G-9251)***

Air Force US Dept of 937 257-6068
5215 Thurlow St 2 Dayton (45433) ***(G-9252)***

Air Frce Museum Foundation Inc 937 258-1218
1100 Spaatz St Bldg 489 Dayton (45433) ***(G-9253)***

AIR Management Group LLC 330 856-1900
1 American Way Ne 20 Warren (44484) ***(G-18814)***

Air National Guard Med Clinic, Columbus *Also called National Guard Ohio* ***(G-8218)***

ALPHABETIC

Air Systems of Ohio Inc (PA)......216 741-1700
4760 Van Epps Rd Brooklyn Heights (44131) **(G-1910)**
Air Technologies, Columbus *Also called Ohio Transmission Corporation* **(G-8452)**
Air Transport Svcs Group Inc (PA)......937 382-5591
145 Hunter Dr Wilmington (45177) **(G-19743)**
Air Venturi Ltd......216 292-2570
5135 Naiman Pkwy Solon (44139) **(G-16973)**
Air-Temp Climate Control Inc......216 579-1552
3013 Payne Ave Cleveland (44114) **(G-4974)**
Air-Temp Mechanical, Cleveland *Also called Air-Temp Climate Control Inc* **(G-4974)**
Airborn Electronics Inc......330 245-2630
2230 Picton Pkwy Akron (44312) **(G-25)**
Airborne Maint Engrg Svcs Inc......937 366-2559
1111 Airport Rd Wilmington (45177) **(G-19744)**
Airborne Maint Engrg Svcs Inc (HQ)......937 382-5591
145 Hunter Dr Wilmington (45177) **(G-19745)**
Aircraft Wheels and Breaks, Avon *Also called Cleveland Wheels* **(G-890)**
Aire-Tech Inc......614 836-5670
4681 Homer Ohio Ln Groveport (43125) **(G-11621)**
Airgas Inc......866 935-3370
2020 Train Ave Cleveland (44113) **(G-4975)**
Airgas Inc......440 632-1758
14943 Madison Rd Middlefield (44062) **(G-14393)**
Airgas Merchant Gases LLC......800 242-0105
6055 Rckside Woods Blvd N Cleveland (44131) **(G-4976)**
Airgas Safety Inc......513 942-1465
N Park Business Hamilton (45011) **(G-11689)**
Airgas Usa LLC......216 642-6600
6055 Rockside Woods Independence (44131) **(G-12183)**
Airgas Usa LLC......440 786-2864
7600 Oak Leaf Rd Oakwood Village (44146) **(G-15625)**
Airgas Usa LLC......513 563-8070
10031 Cncnnati Dyton Pike Cincinnati (45241) **(G-2979)**
Airgas Usa LLC......440 232-1590
6055 Rocksd Woods Blv 400 Cleveland (44131) **(G-4977)**
Airko Inc......440 333-0133
20160 Center Ridge Rd # 101 Cleveland (44116) **(G-4978)**
Airmate Company......419 636-3184
16280 County Road D Bryan (43506) **(G-2000)**
Airnet Systems Inc (PA)......614 409-4900
7250 Star Check Dr Columbus (43217) **(G-6958)**
Airplaco Equipment Company, Cincinnati *Also called Mesa Industries Inc* **(G-4081)**
Airport Core Hotel LLC (PA)......614 536-0500
2886 Airport Dr Columbus (43219) **(G-6959)**
Airport Pass Park, Cleveland *Also called Parking Company America Inc* **(G-6243)**
Airtron LP......614 274-2345
3021 International St Columbus (43228) **(G-6960)**
Airtron LP......513 860-5959
756 Cincinnati Batavia Pi Cincinnati (45245) **(G-2902)**
Aisling Enterprises LLC......937 203-1757
9747 Crooked Creek Dr Centerville (45458) **(G-2670)**
Aitg, Celina *Also called Ameri Interntl Trade Grp Inc* **(G-2634)**
Aitheras Aviation Group LLC (PA)......216 298-9060
2301 N Marginal Rd Cleveland (44114) **(G-4979)**
Ajax Cleaning Contractors Co......216 881-8484
1561 E 40th St Cleveland (44103) **(G-4980)**
Ajax Commercial Cleaning Inc......330 928-4543
3566 State Rd Ste 5 Cuyahoga Falls (44223) **(G-9158)**
Ajax Tocco Magnethermic Corp (HQ)......330 372-8511
1745 Overland Ave Ne Warren (44483) **(G-18815)**
Ajm Worthington Inc......614 888-5800
6902 N High St Worthington (43085) **(G-19938)**
AK Group Hotels Inc......937 372-9921
300 Xenia Towne Sq Xenia (45385) **(G-20040)**
AK Steel Corporation......513 425-6541
1801 Crawford St Middletown (45044) **(G-14412)**
Aka Wireless Inc......216 213-8040
882 W Maple St Hartville (44632) **(G-11814)**
Ake Marketing......440 232-1661
503 Broadway Ave Bedford (44146) **(G-1293)**
Akil Incorporated......419 625-0857
2525 W Monroe St Sandusky (44870) **(G-16724)**
Akil Industrial Cleaning, Sandusky *Also called Akil Incorporated* **(G-16724)**
Akro-Plastics, Kent *Also called U S Development Corp* **(G-12401)**
Akrochem Corporation......330 535-2108
2845 Newpark Dr Barberton (44203) **(G-949)**
Akron Area Commercial Cleaning......330 434-0767
1264 Copley Rd Akron (44320) **(G-26)**
Akron Art Museum......330 376-9185
1 S High St Akron (44308) **(G-27)**
Akron Auto Auction Inc......330 724-7708
2471 Ley Dr Coventry Township (44319) **(G-9122)**
Akron Automobile Association (PA)......330 762-0631
100 Rosa Parks Dr Akron (44311) **(G-28)**
AKRON AUTOMOBILE CLUB, Akron *Also called Akron Automobile Association* **(G-28)**
Akron Blind Center & Workshop (PA)......330 253-2555
325 E Market St Akron (44304) **(G-29)**
Akron Canton Airport, North Canton *Also called Akron-Canton Regional Airport* **(G-15322)**
Akron Canton Kidney Center, Uniontown *Also called Bio-Mdcal Applcations Ohio Inc* **(G-18507)**
Akron Centl Engrv Mold Mch Inc......330 794-8704
1625 Massillon Rd Akron (44312) **(G-30)**
Akron Children's Hospital, Akron *Also called Childrens Hosp Med Ctr Akron* **(G-135)**
Akron Citicenter Hotel LLC......330 253-8355
20 W Mill St Akron (44308) **(G-31)**
AKRON CITIZEN'S COALITION FOR, Akron *Also called Access Inc* **(G-16)**
Akron City Hospital, Akron *Also called Summa Health System* **(G-459)**
Akron City Hospital Inc......330 253-5046
525 E Market St Akron (44304) **(G-32)**
Akron Cmnty Svc Ctr Urban Leag......234 542-4141
440 Vernon Odom Blvd Akron (44307) **(G-33)**
Akron Coca-Cola Bottling Co......330 784-2653
1560 Triplett Blvd Akron (44306) **(G-34)**
Akron Community Serv Center, Akron *Also called Akron Cmnty Svc Ctr Urban Leag* **(G-33)**
Akron Concrete Corp......330 864-1188
910 White Pond Dr Akron (44320) **(G-35)**
Akron Council of Engineering......330 535-8835
411 Wolf Ledges Pkwy Akron (44311) **(G-36)**
Akron Electric, Barberton *Also called Akron Foundry Co* **(G-950)**
Akron Electric Inc......330 745-8891
1025 Eaton Ave Akron (44303) **(G-37)**
Akron Energy Systems LLC......330 374-0600
226 Opportunity Pkwy Akron (44307) **(G-38)**
Akron Erectors Inc......330 745-7100
8098 W Waterloo Rd Akron (44314) **(G-39)**
Akron Foundry Co (PA)......330 745-3101
2728 Wingate Ave Akron (44314) **(G-40)**
Akron Foundry Co......330 745-3101
1025 Eagon St Barberton (44203) **(G-950)**
Akron Gen Edwin Shaw Rhbltion......330 375-1300
330 Broadway St E Cuyahoga Falls (44221) **(G-9159)**
Akron Gen Hlth & Wellness Ctr, Akron *Also called Akron General Medical Center* **(G-46)**
Akron General Foundation......330 344-6888
400 Wabash Ave Akron (44307) **(G-41)**
AKRON GENERAL HEALTH SYSTEM, Akron *Also called Akron General Foundation* **(G-41)**
Akron General Health System......330 665-8200
4125 Medina Rd Ste 104 Akron (44333) **(G-42)**
Akron General Medical Center (HQ)......330 344-6000
1 Akron General Ave Akron (44307) **(G-43)**
Akron General Medical Center......330 344-1980
224 W Exchange St Ste 330 Akron (44302) **(G-44)**
Akron General Medical Center......330 344-1444
1 Akron General Ave Akron (44307) **(G-45)**
Akron General Medical Center......330 665-8000
4125 Medina Rd Ste 1 Akron (44333) **(G-46)**
Akron Hardware Consultants Inc (PA)......330 644-7167
1100 Killian Rd Akron (44312) **(G-47)**
Akron Health Center, Akron *Also called Planned Prenthood Greater Ohio* **(G-391)**
Akron Inn Limited Partnership......330 336-7692
5 Park Centre Dr Wadsworth (44281) **(G-18745)**
Akron Lead Base Program, Akron *Also called East Akron Neighborhood Dev* **(G-205)**
Akron Management Corp......330 644-8441
452 E Warner Rd Akron (44319) **(G-48)**
Akron Metropolitan Hsing Auth......330 920-1652
500 Hardman Dr Stow (44224) **(G-17350)**
Akron Neonatology Inc......330 379-9473
300 Locust St Akron (44302) **(G-49)**
Akron Plastic Surgeons Inc......330 253-9161
1 Park West Blvd Ste 350 Akron (44320) **(G-50)**
Akron Porcelain & Plastics Co......330 745-2159
83 E State St Barberton (44203) **(G-951)**
Akron Public School Maint Svcs......330 761-2640
515 Grant St Akron (44311) **(G-51)**
Akron Public Schools......330 761-1660
70 N Broadway St Akron (44308) **(G-52)**
Akron Radiology Inc......330 375-3043
525 E Market St Akron (44304) **(G-53)**
Akron Renal Center, Akron *Also called Isd Renal Inc* **(G-284)**
Akron Rubber Dev Lab Inc (PA)......330 794-6600
2887 Gilchrist Rd Akron (44305) **(G-54)**
Akron School Trnsp Svcs......330 761-1390
500 E North St Akron (44304) **(G-55)**
Akron Summit Cmnty Action Agcy......330 572-8532
670 W Exchange St Akron (44302) **(G-56)**
Akron Summit Cmnty Action Agcy......330 733-2290
1335 Massillon Rd Akron (44306) **(G-57)**
Akron Summit Cmnty Action Agcy (PA)......330 376-7730
55 E Mill St Akron (44308) **(G-58)**
AKRON SYMPHONY, Akron *Also called Greater Akron Musical Assn* **(G-246)**
Akron Water Distribution Div, Akron *Also called City of Akron* **(G-139)**
Akron Welding & Spring Co, Akron *Also called Brakefire Incorporated* **(G-107)**
Akron Womans City Club Inc......330 762-6261
732 W Exchange St Akron (44302) **(G-59)**
Akron Zoological Park......330 375-2550
500 Edgewood Ave Akron (44307) **(G-60)**
Akron-Canton Regional Airport......330 499-4059
5400 Lauby Rd Ste 9 North Canton (44720) **(G-15322)**
Akron-Canton Regional Foodbank (PA)......330 535-6900
350 Opportunity Pkwy Akron (44307) **(G-61)**
Akron-Summit Convention......330 374-7560
77 E Mill St Akron (44308) **(G-62)**

Aksm, Columbus *Also called American Kidney Stone MGT Ltd* ***(G-6999)***
Aksm/Genesis Medical Svcs Inc 614 447-0281
100 W 3rd Ave Ste 350 Columbus (43201) ***(G-6961)***
Aksn, Columbus *Also called Allen Khnle Stovall Neuman LLP* ***(G-6967)***
Aktion Associates Incorporated 419 893-7001
1687 Woodlands Dr Maumee (43537) ***(G-13873)***
Akzo Nobel Coatings Inc 614 294-3361
1313 Windsor Ave Columbus (43211) ***(G-6962)***
Al Neyer LLC (PA) 513 271-6400
302 W 3rd St Ste 800 Cincinnati (45202) ***(G-2980)***
Al Neyer LLC 513 271-6400
302 W 3rd St Ste 800 Cincinnati (45202) ***(G-2981)***
Al Peake & Sons Inc 419 243-9284
4949 Stickney Ave Toledo (43612) ***(G-17745)***
Al-Mar Lanes 419 352-4637
1010 N Main St Bowling Green (43402) ***(G-1757)***
Alabama Farmers Coop Inc 419 655-2289
12419 Jerry City Rd Cygnet (43413) ***(G-9238)***
Aladdin Limousines, Westerville *Also called Aladdins Enterprises Inc* ***(G-19361)***
Aladdins Baking Company Inc 216 861-0317
1301 Carnegie Ave Cleveland (44115) ***(G-4981)***
Aladdins Enterprises Inc 614 891-3440
3408 E Dblin Granville Rd Westerville (43081) ***(G-19361)***
Alan Manufacturing Inc 330 262-1555
3927 E Lincoln Way Wooster (44691) ***(G-19825)***
Alan Stone Co Inc 740 448-1100
1324 Ellis Run Rd Cutler (45724) ***(G-9156)***
Alan Stone Company 740 448-1100
1324 Ellis Run Rd Cutler (45724) ***(G-9157)***
Alan Woods Trucking Inc 513 738-3314
3592 Herman Rd Hamilton (45013) ***(G-11690)***
Alano Club Inc 419 335-6211
222 S Brunell St Wauseon (43567) ***(G-18948)***
Alba Manufacturing Inc 513 874-0551
8950 Seward Rd Fairfield (45011) ***(G-10818)***
Albat, Medway *Also called American Line Builders Apprent* ***(G-14140)***
Albco Sales Inc (PA) 330 424-9446
230 Maple St Lisbon (44432) ***(G-12931)***
Albert Freytag Inc 419 628-2018
306 Executive Dr Minster (45865) ***(G-14659)***
Albert Guarnieri & Co 330 794-9834
61 S Seiberling St Akron (44305) ***(G-63)***
Albert M Higley Company (PA) 216 404-5783
2926 Chester Ave Cleveland (44114) ***(G-4982)***
Albert Mike Leasing Inc (PA) 513 563-1400
10340 Evendale Dr Cincinnati (45241) ***(G-2982)***
Albrecht Inc (PA) 513 576-9900
1040 Techne Center Dr Milford (45150) ***(G-14501)***
Albrecht & Company, Milford *Also called Albrecht Inc* ***(G-14501)***
Albright Welding Supply Co Inc (PA) 330 264-2021
3132 E Lincoln Way Wooster (44691) ***(G-19826)***
Albring Vending Company 419 726-8059
702 Galena St Toledo (43611) ***(G-17746)***
Alcatel-Lucent USA Inc 614 860-2000
5475 Rings Rd Ste 101 Dublin (43017) ***(G-10239)***
Alco Inc 740 527-2991
36050 Smith Chapel Rd Logan (43138) ***(G-12967)***
Alco-Chem Inc 330 833-8551
1303 Park Ave Sw Canton (44706) ***(G-2230)***
Alco-Chem Inc (PA) 330 253-3535
45 N Summit St Akron (44308) ***(G-64)***
Alcoa Power & Propulsion, Newburgh Heights *Also called Howmet Corporation* ***(G-15251)***
Alcohlism Chem Dpndncy Program, Newark *Also called Licking Cnty Alcoholism Prvntn* ***(G-15186)***
Alcohol Drug Addiction 330 564-4075
100 W Cedar St Ste 300 Akron (44307) ***(G-65)***
Alcohol and Drug Recovery Ctr, Cleveland *Also called Cleveland Clinic Foundation* ***(G-5298)***
Alcohol Drug Addction & Mental 937 443-0416
409 E Monument Ave # 102 Dayton (45402) ***(G-9314)***
Alcohol/Drug Outpatient T, Cleveland *Also called County of Cuyahoga* ***(G-5418)***
ALCOHOLIC DROP-IN CENTER, Cincinnati *Also called Shelter House Volunteer Group* ***(G-4515)***
Aldi Inc 330 273-7351
1319 W 130th St Hinckley (44233) ***(G-11994)***
Aldo Peraza 614 804-0403
5585 Ranchwood Dr Columbus (43228) ***(G-6963)***
Aldrich Chemical 937 859-1808
3858 Benner Rd Miamisburg (45342) ***(G-14269)***
Aleph Home & Senior Care Inc 216 382-7689
2448 Beachwood Blvd Cleveland (44122) ***(G-4983)***
Alex N Sill Company (PA) 216 524-9999
6000 Lombardo Ctr Ste 600 Seven Hills (44131) ***(G-16825)***
Alex Products Inc 419 399-4500
810 W Gasser Rd Paulding (45879) ***(G-15927)***
Alexander & Associates Co (PA) 513 731-7800
360 Mclean Dr Cincinnati (45237) ***(G-2983)***
Alexander and Bebout Inc 419 238-9567
10098 Lincoln Hwy Van Wert (45891) ***(G-18626)***
Alexander Great Distributing, Steubenville *Also called Mougianis Industries Inc* ***(G-17331)***
Alexander House Inc 513 523-4569
118 Hilltop Rd Oxford (45056) ***(G-15810)***
Alexander J Abernethy 740 432-2107
60755 Southgate Rd Byesville (43723) ***(G-2069)***
Alexander Mann Solutions Corp 216 336-6756
1301 E 9th St Ste 1200 Cleveland (44114) ***(G-4984)***
Alexis Gardens, Toledo *Also called Harvest Facility Holdings LP* ***(G-17937)***
Alexis Medical Center, Toledo *Also called David Lee Grossman MD* ***(G-17844)***
Alexson Services Inc 614 889-5837
525 Metro Pl N Ste 300 Dublin (43017) ***(G-10240)***
Alexson Services Inc 513 874-0423
350 Kolb Dr Fairfield (45014) ***(G-10819)***
Alfons Haar Inc 937 560-2031
150 Advanced Dr Springboro (45066) ***(G-17114)***
Alfred Nickles Bakery Inc 419 332-6418
721 White Rd Fremont (43420) ***(G-11183)***
Alfred Nickles Bakery Inc 330 628-9964
3775 Mogadore Rd Mogadore (44260) ***(G-14669)***
Algart Health Care Inc 216 631-1550
8902 Detroit Ave Cleveland (44102) ***(G-4985)***
Alice Noble Ice Arena 330 345-8686
851 Oldman Rd Wooster (44691) ***(G-19827)***
Alice Training Institute LLC 330 661-0106
2508 Medina Rd Medina (44256) ***(G-14034)***
Alien Technology LLC 408 782-3900
3001 W Tech Blvd Miamisburg (45342) ***(G-14270)***
Alkon Corporation (PA) 419 355-9111
728 Graham Dr Fremont (43420) ***(G-11184)***
Alkon Corporation 614 799-6650
6750 Crosby Ct Dublin (43016) ***(G-10241)***
All About Heating Cooling 513 621-4620
7861 Palace Dr Cincinnati (45249) ***(G-2984)***
All About Home Care Svcs LLC 937 222-2980
1307 E 3rd St Dayton (45403) ***(G-9315)***
All About Kids 937 885-7480
1300 E Social Row Rd Centerville (45458) ***(G-2671)***
All About Kids Daycare N 330 494-8700
6199 Frank Ave Nw North Canton (44720) ***(G-15323)***
All Aerials LLC 330 659-9600
4945 Brecksville Rd Richfield (44286) ***(G-16494)***
All America Insurance Company (HQ) 419 238-1010
800 S Washington St Van Wert (45891) ***(G-18627)***
All American Heating AC, Medina *Also called Gene Tolliver Corp* ***(G-14068)***
All American Sports Corp (HQ) 440 366-8225
7501 Performance Ln North Ridgeville (44039) ***(G-15453)***
All American Trnsp Svcs LLC 419 589-7433
575 Beer Rd Ontario (44906) ***(G-15684)***
All Around Children Montessori 330 928-1444
4117 Bridgewater Pkwy Stow (44224) ***(G-17351)***
All Construction Services Inc 330 225-1653
945 Industrial Pkwy N Brunswick (44212) ***(G-1967)***
All Construction/Mooney Moses, Brunswick *Also called All Construction Services Inc* ***(G-1967)***
All Crane Rental Corp (PA) 614 261-1800
683 Oakland Park Ave Columbus (43224) ***(G-6964)***
All Erection & Crane Rental (PA) 216 524-6550
4700 Acorn Dr Cleveland (44131) ***(G-4986)***
All Erection & Crane Rental 216 524-6550
7809 Old Rockside Rd Cleveland (44131) ***(G-4987)***
All Foils Inc 440 572-3645
16100 Imperial Pkwy Strongsville (44149) ***(G-17441)***
All For Kids Inc 740 435-8050
1405 E Wheeling Ave Cambridge (43725) ***(G-2093)***
All Gone Termite & Pest Ctrl 513 874-7500
9037 Sutton Pl West Chester (45011) ***(G-19016)***
All Heart Home Care LLC 419 298-0034
143 N Michigan Ave Edgerton (43517) ***(G-10581)***
All Hearts Home Health Care 440 342-2026
6009 Landerhaven Dr Ste D Cleveland (44124) ***(G-4988)***
All Industrial Engine Service, Willoughby *Also called All Lift Service Company Inc* ***(G-19642)***
All Industrial Group Inc (PA) 216 441-2000
1555 1/2 Harvard Ave Newburgh Heights (44105) ***(G-15250)***
All Lift Service Company Inc 440 585-1542
4607 Hamann Pkwy Willoughby (44094) ***(G-19642)***
All Metal Sales Inc 440 617-1234
29260 Clemens Rd Ste 3 Westlake (44145) ***(G-19456)***
All My Sons Business Dev Corp 469 461-5000
15224 Neo Pkwy Cleveland (44128) ***(G-4989)***
All My Sons Moving & Storge of 614 405-7202
4401 Lyman Dr Ste D Hilliard (43026) ***(G-11877)***
All Occasions Event Rental 513 563-0600
10629 Reading Rd Cincinnati (45241) ***(G-2985)***
All Ohio Threaded Rod Co Inc 216 426-1800
5349 Saint Clair Ave Cleveland (44103) ***(G-4990)***
All Phase Power and Ltg Inc 419 624-9640
2122 Campbell St Sandusky (44870) ***(G-16725)***
All Pro Cleaning Services Inc 440 519-0055
6001 Cochran Rd Ste 103 Solon (44139) ***(G-16974)***
All Pro Freight Systems Inc (PA) 440 934-2222
1200 Chester Indus Pkwy Avon (44011) ***(G-874)***
All Secured Security Svcs LLC (PA) 614 861-0482
343 E Barthman Ave Columbus (43207) ***(G-6965)***
All Service Glass Company, Lima *Also called Wiechart Enterprises Inc* ***(G-12921)***

A L P H A B E T I C

All Star Training Club ... 330 352-5602
3108 Sparrows Crst Akron (44319) ***(G-66)***
All State Home Mortgage Inc ... 216 261-7700
26250 Euclid Ave Ste 901 Euclid (44132) ***(G-10742)***
All Temp Refrigeration Inc ... 419 692-5016
18996 State Route 66 Delphos (45833) ***(G-10137)***
All-Line Truck Sales, Hubbard *Also called Youngstown-Kenworth Inc* ***(G-12093)***
All-Type Welding & Fabrication ... 440 439-3990
7690 Bond St Cleveland (44139) ***(G-4991)***
Allan Hunter Construction LLC ... 330 634-9882
931 Evans Ave Akron (44305) ***(G-67)***
Allan Miller Insurance Agency ... 513 863-2629
185 N Brookwood Ave Hamilton (45013) ***(G-11691)***
Allan Peace & Associates Inc ... 513 579-1700
2035 Reading Rd Cincinnati (45202) ***(G-2986)***
Allard Excavation LLC ... 740 778-2242
8336 Bennett Schl Hse Rd South Webster (45682) ***(G-17102)***
Allcan Global Services Inc (PA) ... 513 825-1655
11235 Sebring Dr Cincinnati (45240) ***(G-2987)***
Alleen Company, The, Cincinnati *Also called Jbjs Acquisitions LLC* ***(G-3864)***
Allega Recycled Mtls & Sup Co ... 216 447-0814
5585 Canal Rd Cleveland (44125) ***(G-4992)***
Allen Cnty Regional Trnst Auth ... 419 222-2782
200 E High St Ste 2a Lima (45801) ***(G-12733)***
Allen County Childrens Svcs Bd, Lima *Also called County of Allen* ***(G-12765)***
Allen County Eductl Svc Ctr ... 419 222-1836
1920 Slabtown Rd Lima (45801) ***(G-12734)***
Allen County Health Care Ctr, Lima *Also called County of Allen* ***(G-12763)***
Allen County Recyclers Inc ... 419 223-5010
541 S Central Ave Lima (45804) ***(G-12735)***
Allen County Refuse, Lima *Also called Allen County Recyclers Inc* ***(G-12735)***
Allen Est Mangement Ltd ... 419 526-6505
132 Distl Ave Mansfield (44902) ***(G-13259)***
Allen Gardiner Deroberts ... 614 221-1500
777 Goodale Blvd Ste 200 Columbus (43212) ***(G-6966)***
Allen Horizon Center, Elyria *Also called Horizon Education Centers* ***(G-10634)***
Allen Khnle Stovall Neuman LLP ... 614 221-8500
17 S High St Ste 1220 Columbus (43215) ***(G-6967)***
Allen Medical Center ... 440 986-4000
200 W Lorain St Oberlin (44074) ***(G-15638)***
Allen Metro Housinig Auth, Lima *Also called County of Allen* ***(G-12762)***
Allen Metro Hsing MGT Dev Corp ... 419 228-6065
600 S Main St Lima (45804) ***(G-12736)***
Allen Metro Tenants Councel, Lima *Also called Allen Metropolitan Hsing Auth* ***(G-12737)***
Allen Metropolitan Hsing Auth ... 419 228-6065
600 S Main St Lima (45804) ***(G-12737)***
Allen Refractories Company ... 740 927-8000
131 Shackelford Rd Pataskala (43062) ***(G-15920)***
Allen-Keith Construction Co (PA) ... 330 266-2220
2735 Greensburg Rd Canton (44720) ***(G-2231)***
Allergy & Asthma Inc ... 740 654-8623
2405 N Columbus St # 270 Lancaster (43130) ***(G-12507)***
Allergy & Asthma Centre Dayton, Centerville *Also called Allergy & Asthma Centre Dayton* ***(G-2672)***
Allergy & Asthma Centre Dayton (PA) ... 937 435-8999
8039 Wash Vlg Dr Ste 100 Centerville (45458) ***(G-2672)***
Allgeier & Son Inc (PA) ... 513 574-3735
6386 Bridgetown Rd Cincinnati (45248) ***(G-2988)***
Allgood Home Improvements, Fairfield *Also called Eagle Industries Ohio Inc* ***(G-10844)***
Allianalce Hospitalist Group ... 330 823-5626
200 E State St Alliance (44601) ***(G-523)***
Alliance Academy of Cincinnati, Cincinnati *Also called National Heritg Academies Inc* ***(G-4139)***
Alliance Advantage, Columbus *Also called Advantage Aerotech Inc* ***(G-6947)***
Alliance Calibration, Cincinnati *Also called Raitz Inc* ***(G-4384)***
Alliance Citizens Health Assn ... 330 596-6000
200 E State St Alliance (44601) ***(G-524)***
Alliance Data Systems Corp ... 614 729-4000
3075 Loyalty Cir Columbus (43219) ***(G-6968)***
Alliance Data Systems Corp ... 614 729-5000
220 W Schrock Rd Westerville (43081) ***(G-19362)***
Alliance Data Systems Corp ... 614 729-5800
6939 Americana Pkwy Reynoldsburg (43068) ***(G-16425)***
Alliance Fire Dept, Alliance *Also called Interntional Assn Firefighters* ***(G-541)***
Alliance For Womens Health ... 419 228-1000
310 S Cable Rd Lima (45805) ***(G-12738)***
Alliance Franklin Head Start, Alliance *Also called Stark County Cmnty Action Agcy* ***(G-561)***
Alliance Health, Cincinnati *Also called Uc Health Llc* ***(G-4721)***
Alliance Hospitality ... 330 505-2173
801 N Canfield Niles Rd Youngstown (44515) ***(G-20100)***
Alliance Hospitality Inc ... 440 951-7333
7701 Reynolds Rd Mentor (44060) ***(G-14141)***
Alliance Hot Stove Baseball L ... 330 823-7034
1127 Forest Ave Alliance (44601) ***(G-525)***
Alliance Imaging Inc ... 330 493-5100
4825 Higbee Ave Nw # 201 Canton (44718) ***(G-2232)***
Alliance Knife Inc ... 513 367-9000
124 May Dr Harrison (45030) ***(G-11789)***
Alliance Legal Solutions LLC ... 216 525-0100
6161 Oak Tree Blvd # 300 Independence (44131) ***(G-12184)***
Alliance Medical Inc (HQ) ... 800 890-3092
5000 Tuttle Crossing Blvd Dublin (43016) ***(G-10242)***
Alliance Petroleum Corporation (HQ) ... 330 493-0440
4150 Belden Village Mall Canton (44718) ***(G-2233)***
Alliance Solutions Group LLC (PA) ... 216 525-0100
6161 Oak Tree Blvd Independence (44131) ***(G-12185)***
Alliance Towers LLC ... 330 823-1063
350 S Arch Ave Apt 106 Alliance (44601) ***(G-526)***
Allied Barton Security Svcs, Rossford *Also called Alliedbarton Security Svcs LLC* ***(G-16606)***
Allied Builders Inc (PA) ... 937 226-0311
1644 Kuntz Rd Dayton (45404) ***(G-9316)***
Allied Building Products Corp ... 216 362-1764
12800 Brookpark Rd Cleveland (44130) ***(G-4993)***
Allied Building Products Corp ... 513 784-9090
1735 Eastern Ave Cincinnati (45202) ***(G-2989)***
Allied Building Products Corp ... 614 488-0717
1055 Kinnear Rd Columbus (43212) ***(G-6969)***
Allied Car Wash Inc ... 513 559-1733
3330 Central Pkwy Cincinnati (45225) ***(G-2990)***
Allied Cash Advance, Cincinnati *Also called Allied Cash Holdings LLC* ***(G-2991)***
Allied Cash Holdings LLC (PA) ... 305 371-3141
7755 Montgomery Rd # 400 Cincinnati (45236) ***(G-2991)***
Allied Enterprises Inc (PA) ... 440 808-8760
26021 Center Ridge Rd Westlake (44145) ***(G-19457)***
Allied Environmental Svcs Inc ... 419 227-4004
585 Liberty Commons Pkwy Lima (45804) ***(G-12739)***
Allied Erct & Dismantling Co ... 330 744-0808
2100 Poland Ave Youngstown (44502) ***(G-20101)***
Allied Fabricating & Wldg Co ... 614 751-6664
5699 Chantry Dr Columbus (43232) ***(G-6970)***
Allied Fence Builders, Dayton *Also called Allied Builders Inc* ***(G-9316)***
Allied Health Rehab Centers, Ravenna *Also called Portage Physical Therapists* ***(G-16402)***
Allied Home Health Services, Holland *Also called R & F Inc* ***(G-12047)***
Allied Infotech Corporation ... 330 745-8529
2170 Romig Rd Akron (44320) ***(G-68)***
Allied Interstate LLC ... 715 386-1810
P.O. Box 561534 Columbus (43236) ***(G-6971)***
Allied Paving Company, Holland *Also called Allied Paving Inc* ***(G-12006)***
Allied Paving Inc ... 419 666-3100
8406 Airport Hwy Holland (43528) ***(G-12006)***
Allied Restaurant Svc Ohio Inc (PA) ... 419 589-4759
187 Illinois Ave S Mansfield (44905) ***(G-13260)***
Allied Security LLC ... 513 771-3776
110 Boggs Ln Ste 140 Cincinnati (45246) ***(G-2992)***
Allied Supply Company Inc (PA) ... 937 224-9833
1100 E Monument Ave Dayton (45402) ***(G-9317)***
Allied Truck Parts Co ... 330 477-8127
4216 Southway St Sw Canton (44706) ***(G-2234)***
Allied Waste Division, Youngstown *Also called Republic Services Inc* ***(G-20347)***
Allied Waste Division, Dayton *Also called Republic Services Inc* ***(G-9849)***
Allied Waste Industries LLC ... 440 774-3100
43502 Oberlin Elyria Rd Oberlin (44074) ***(G-15639)***
Allied Waste Systems Inc ... 937 268-8110
1577 W River Rd Dayton (45417) ***(G-9318)***
Allied Waste Systems Inc ... 419 925-4592
6141 Depweg Rd Celina (45822) ***(G-2633)***
Allied Waste Systems Inc ... 937 593-3566
2946 Us Highway 68 N Bellefontaine (43311) ***(G-1376)***
Allied Waste Systems Inc ... 419 636-2242
12604 County Road G Bryan (43506) ***(G-2001)***
Allied Wste Svcs Yngstown Coml, Youngstown *Also called Browning-Ferris Inds of Ohio* ***(G-20129)***
Alliedbarton Security Svcs LLC ... 614 225-9061
57 E Wilson Bridge Rd # 300 Worthington (43085) ***(G-19939)***
Alliedbarton Security Svcs LLC ... 419 874-9005
1001 Dixie Hwy Ste F Rossford (43460) ***(G-16606)***
Allmed, Dublin *Also called Alliance Medical Inc* ***(G-10242)***
Alloy Metal Exchange LLC ... 216 478-0200
26000 Corbin Dr Bedford Heights (44128) ***(G-1345)***
Alloyd Insulation Co Inc ... 937 890-7900
5734 Webster St Dayton (45414) ***(G-9319)***
Allpro Parking Ohio LLC ... 614 221-9696
431 E Broad St Columbus (43215) ***(G-6972)***
Allshred Services, Maumee *Also called Recycling Services Inc* ***(G-13968)***
Allstars Travel Group Inc ... 614 901-4100
7775 Walton Pkwy Ste 100 New Albany (43054) ***(G-14973)***
Allstate, Brecksville *Also called Luce Smith & Scott Inc* ***(G-1832)***
Allstate Insurance Company ... 330 650-2917
75 Milford Dr Ste 222 Hudson (44236) ***(G-12102)***
Allstate Insurance Company ... 330 656-6000
75 Executive Pkwy Hudson (44237) ***(G-12103)***
Allstate Painting & Contg Co ... 330 220-5533
1256 Industrial Pkwy N # 2 Brunswick (44212) ***(G-1968)***
Allstate Trk Sls of Estrn OH ... 330 339-5555
327 Stonecreek Rd Nw New Philadelphia (44663) ***(G-15080)***
Alltel Communications Corp (HQ) ... 740 349-8551
66 N 4th St Newark (43055) ***(G-15141)***
Alltel Communications Corp ... 330 656-8000
205 S Hambden St Chardon (44024) ***(G-2739)***
Allwell Behavioral Health Svcs (PA) ... 740 454-9766
2845 Bell St Zanesville (43701) ***(G-20440)***

Allwell Behavioral Health Svcs 740 439-4428
2500 Glenn Hwy Cambridge (43725) ***(G-2094)***
Ally Financial Inc 330 533-7300
3731 Boardman Canfield Rd Canfield (44406) ***(G-2182)***
Almost Family Inc 614 457-1900
445 Hutchinson Ave Columbus (43235) ***(G-6973)***
Almost Family Inc 330 724-7545
1225 E Waterloo Rd Akron (44306) ***(G-69)***
Almost Family Inc 513 662-3400
2135 Dana Ave Ste 220 Cincinnati (45207) ***(G-2993)***
Almost Family Inc 216 464-0443
23611 Chagrin Blvd # 130 Cleveland (44122) ***(G-4994)***
Alois Alzheimer Center, The, Cincinnati *Also called Crystalwood Inc* ***(G-3443)***
Alomie Dialysis LLC 740 941-1688
609 W Emmitt Ave Waverly (45690) ***(G-18965)***
Alorica Customer Care Inc 216 525-3311
9525 Sweet Valley Dr Cleveland (44125) ***(G-4995)***
Alpco, Westlake *Also called Aluminum Line Products Company* ***(G-19459)***
Alpha & Omega Bldg Svcs Inc 513 429-5082
11250 Cornell Park Dr # 200 Blue Ash (45242) ***(G-1529)***
Alpha & Omega Bldg Svcs Inc 937 229-3536
1529 Brown St Rm 223 Dayton (45469) ***(G-9320)***
Alpha & Omega Bldg Svcs Inc (PA) 937 298-2125
2843 Culver Ave Ste B Dayton (45429) ***(G-9321)***
Alpha CHI Omega 614 291-3871
103 E 15th Ave Columbus (43201) ***(G-6974)***
Alpha Epsilon PHI 614 294-5243
200 E 17th Ave Columbus (43201) ***(G-6975)***
Alpha Freight Systems Inc 800 394-9001
5876 Darrow Rd Hudson (44236) ***(G-12104)***
Alpha Group Agency Inc (PA) 216 520-0440
4200 Rockside Rd Ste 300 Cleveland (44131) ***(G-4996)***
Alpha Group of Delaware Inc 614 222-1855
85 Marconi Blvd Columbus (43215) ***(G-6976)***
Alpha Group of Delaware Inc (PA) 740 368-5810
1000 Alpha Dr Delaware (43015) ***(G-10069)***
Alpha Group of Delaware Inc 740 368-5820
1000 Alpha Dr Delaware (43015) ***(G-10070)***
Alpha Imaging LLC (PA) 440 953-3800
4455 Glenbrook Rd Willoughby (44094) ***(G-19643)***
Alpha Investment Partnership (PA) 513 621-1826
525 Vine St Ste 1925 Cincinnati (45202) ***(G-2994)***
Alpha Media LLC 937 294-5858
717 E David Rd Dayton (45429) ***(G-9322)***
Alpha Nursing Homes Inc 740 345-9197
17 Forry St Newark (43055) ***(G-15142)***
Alpha Nursing Homes Inc 740 622-2074
1991 Otsego Ave Coshocton (43812) ***(G-9086)***
Alpha PHI Alpha Homes Inc 330 376-2115
730 Callis Dr Akron (44311) ***(G-70)***
Alpha Security LLC 330 406-2181
87 W Mckinley Way Ste 1 Poland (44514) ***(G-16220)***
Alphamicron Inc 330 676-0648
1950 State Route 59 Kent (44240) ***(G-12351)***
Alphaport Inc 216 619-2400
18013 Cleveland Ste 170 Cleveland (44135) ***(G-4997)***
Alphera Financial Services, Hilliard *Also called BMW Financial Services Na LLC* ***(G-11882)***
Alpine Insulation I LLC 614 221-3399
495 S High St Ste 50 Columbus (43215) ***(G-6977)***
Alpine Nursing Care 216 650-6295
5555 Brecksville Rd Cleveland (44131) ***(G-4998)***
Alpine Structures LLC 330 359-5708
2675 Us Route 62 Dundee (44624) ***(G-10499)***
Alpine Valley Ski Area, Chesterland *Also called Sycamore Lake Inc* ***(G-2804)***
Alps Services Inc 513 671-6300
10653 Chester Rd Cincinnati (45215) ***(G-2995)***
Alro Steel Corporation 330 929-4660
4787 State Rd Cuyahoga Falls (44223) ***(G-9160)***
Alro Steel Corporation 419 720-5300
3003 Airport Hwy Toledo (43609) ***(G-17747)***
Alro Steel Corporation 937 253-6121
821 Springfield St Dayton (45403) ***(G-9323)***
Als Group Usa Corp 513 733-5336
4388 Glendale Milford Rd Blue Ash (45242) ***(G-1530)***
Als Laboratory Group, Cleveland *Also called Als Services Usa Corp* ***(G-4999)***
Als Services Usa Corp 513 582-8277
8961 Steeplechase Way West Chester (45069) ***(G-19017)***
Als Services Usa Corp 604 998-5311
6180 Halle Dr Ste D Cleveland (44125) ***(G-4999)***
Alsan Corporation 330 385-3636
900 W 8th St East Liverpool (43920) ***(G-10514)***
Alside Supply Center, Columbus *Also called Associated Materials LLC* ***(G-7055)***
Alstate-Peterbilt-Trucks, New Philadelphia *Also called Allstate Trk Sls of Estrn OH* ***(G-15080)***
Alstom Grid LLC 330 688-4061
778 Mccauley Rd Unit 110 Stow (44224) ***(G-17352)***
Alstom Signaling Operation LLC 513 552-6485
25 Merchant St Cincinnati (45246) ***(G-2996)***
Alt & Witzig Engineering Inc 513 777-9890
6205 Schumacher Park Dr West Chester (45069) ***(G-19018)***
Alta Care Group Inc 330 793-2487
711 Belmont Ave Youngstown (44502) ***(G-20102)***
Alta Partners LLC 440 808-3654
902 Westpoint Pkwy # 320 Westlake (44145) ***(G-19458)***
Alta360 Research, Maumee *Also called Ritter & Associates Inc* ***(G-13972)***
Altaquip LLC (HQ) 513 674-6464
100 Production Dr Harrison (45030) ***(G-11790)***
Altenheim Foundation Inc 440 238-3361
18627 Shurmer Rd Strongsville (44136) ***(G-17442)***
Altercare Inc 330 335-2555
147 Garfield St Wadsworth (44281) ***(G-18746)***
Altercare Inc (PA) 440 327-5285
35990 Westminister Ave North Ridgeville (44039) ***(G-15454)***
Altercare Hartville, Hartville *Also called GFS Leasing Inc* ***(G-11818)***
Altercare Nobles Pond Inc 330 834-4800
7006 Fulton Dr Nw Canton (44718) ***(G-2235)***
Altercare of Bucyrus Inc 419 562-7644
1929 Whetstone St Bucyrus (44820) ***(G-2023)***
Altercare of Louisville Center 330 875-4224
7187 Saint Francis St Louisville (44641) ***(G-13093)***
Altercare of Mentor, Mentor *Also called Schroer Properties Inc* ***(G-14239)***
Altercare of Mentor Center 440 953-4421
9901 Johnnycake Ridge Rd Mentor (44060) ***(G-14142)***
Altercare of Millersburg 330 674-4444
105 Majora Ln Millersburg (44654) ***(G-14584)***
Altercare of Navarre, North Canton *Also called Schroer Properties Inc* ***(G-15365)***
Altercare of Ohio, Canton *Also called Altercare Nobles Pond Inc* ***(G-2235)***
Altercare of Ravenna, Kent *Also called GFS Leasing Inc* ***(G-12372)***
Altercare of Wadsworth, Wadsworth *Also called Altercare Inc* ***(G-18746)***
Altercrest, Cincinnati *Also called Archdiocese of Cincinnati* ***(G-3042)***
Alternacare Home Health Inc 740 689-1589
1566 Monmouth Dr Ste 103 Lancaster (43130) ***(G-12508)***
Alternate Sltions Private Duty (PA) 937 298-1111
1251 E Dorothy Ln Dayton (45419) ***(G-9324)***
Alternate Solutions First LLC 937 298-1111
1251 E Dorothy Ln Dayton (45419) ***(G-9325)***
Alternate Solutions Healthcare 937 299-1111
1050 Forrer Blvd Dayton (45420) ***(G-9326)***
Alternative Care Mgt Systems 614 761-0035
4789 Rings Rd Dublin (43017) ***(G-10243)***
Alternative Care MGT Systs, Dublin *Also called Alternative Care Mgt Systems* ***(G-10243)***
Alternative Home Care & Stffng 513 794-0571
7759 Montgomery Rd Cincinnati (45236) ***(G-2997)***
Alternative Home Health Care 513 794-0555
5150 E Galbraith Rd # 200 Cincinnati (45236) ***(G-2998)***
Alternative Nursing & HM Care, Wheelersburg *Also called Selective Networking Inc* ***(G-19581)***
Alternative Paths Inc 330 725-9195
246 Northland Dr Ste 200a Medina (44256) ***(G-14035)***
Alternative Residences Two (PA) 740 526-0514
67051 Executive Dr Saint Clairsville (43950) ***(G-16616)***
Alternative Residences Two 330 453-0200
2832 34th St Ne Canton (44705) ***(G-2236)***
Alternative Services Inc 419 861-2121
7710 Hill Ave Holland (43528) ***(G-12007)***
Althans Insurance Agency Inc 440 247-6422
543 Washington St Chagrin Falls (44022) ***(G-2689)***
Altick & Corwin Co Lpa 937 223-1201
1 S Main St Ste 1590 Dayton (45402) ***(G-9327)***
Altimate Care LLC (PA) 614 794-9600
5869 Cleveland Ave Columbus (43231) ***(G-6978)***
Altobelli Realestate (PA) 330 652-0200
304 Vienna Ave Niles (44446) ***(G-15280)***
Altria Group Distribution Co 804 274-2000
4680 Parkway Dr Ste 450 Mason (45040) ***(G-13660)***
Altruism Society Inc 877 283-4001
3695 Green Rd Unit 22896 Beachwood (44122) ***(G-1049)***
Aluchem of Jackson Inc 740 286-2455
14782 Beaver Pike Jackson (45640) ***(G-12306)***
Aluminum Line Products Company (PA) 440 835-8880
24460 Sperry Cir Westlake (44145) ***(G-19459)***
ALUMNI ASSOCIATION, THE, Columbus *Also called Ohio State Univ Alumni Assn* ***(G-8379)***
Alvada Const Inc 419 595-4224
2959 S Us Highway 23 Alvada (44802) ***(G-568)***
Alvada Construction, Alvada *Also called Alvada Const Inc* ***(G-568)***
Alvada Trucking, Alvada *Also called Aci Const Co Inc* ***(G-567)***
Alveo Health LLC 513 557-3502
700 W Pete Rose Way # 426 Cincinnati (45203) ***(G-2999)***
Alvis House, Columbus *Also called Alvis Inc* ***(G-6979)***
Alvis Inc 614 252-1788
844 Bryden Rd Columbus (43205) ***(G-6979)***
Alvis Lndcape Golf Curses Mtls, Harrison *Also called James H Alvis Trucking Inc* ***(G-11803)***
Alzheimer Center, Beachwood *Also called University Hospitals Cleveland* ***(G-1135)***
Alzheimers Disease and 216 721-8457
23215 Commerce Park # 300 Beachwood (44122) ***(G-1050)***
AM Industrial Group LLC (PA) 216 433-7171
16000 Commerce Park Dr Brookpark (44142) ***(G-1935)***
AM Industrial Group LLC 216 267-6783
4680 Grayton Rd Cleveland (44135) ***(G-5000)***
Amalgamated Transit Union 216 861-3350
2428 Saint Clair Ave Ne Cleveland (44114) ***(G-5001)***
Amanda House, Lima *Also called Assisted Living Concepts LLC* ***(G-12742)***

ALPHABETIC

Amandacare Inc

ALPHABETIC SECTION

Amandacare Inc..614 884-8880
2101 S Hamilton Rd # 212 Columbus (43232) *(G-6980)*

Amandacare Home Health, Columbus *Also called Amandacare Inc (G-6980)*

Amaxx Inc..614 486-3481
5975 Wilcox Pl Ste B Dublin (43016) *(G-10244)*

Amazing Portable Circus, The, Cincinnati *Also called Cincinnati Circus Company LLC (G-3292)*

Ambassador Nursing, Hilliard *Also called Lighthouse Medical Staffing (G-11921)*

Amber Gardens, Stow *Also called Tersigni Cargill Entps LLC (G-17396)*

Amber Home Care LLC......................................614 523-0668
2800 Corp Exchange Dr # 100 Columbus (43231) *(G-6981)*

Amberwood Manor...330 339-2151
245 S Broadway St New Philadelphia (44663) *(G-15081)*

Ambius, Brooklyn Heights *Also called Rentokil North America Inc (G-1925)*

Amboy Contractors LLc....................................419 644-2111
424 E Main St Metamora (43540) *(G-14264)*

Ambulatory Medical Care Inc (PA)...................513 831-8555
935 State Route 28 Milford (45150) *(G-14502)*

AMC, Dublin *Also called American Multi-Cinema Inc (G-10250)*

AMC, Cleveland *Also called American Multi-Cinema Inc (G-5015)*

AMC, Rocky River *Also called American Multi-Cinema Inc (G-16569)*

AMC Entertainment Inc.....................................614 846-6575
6360 Busch Blvd Columbus (43229) *(G-6982)*

AMC Entertainment Inc.....................................614 428-5716
275 Easton Town Ctr Columbus (43219) *(G-6983)*

AMC Entertainment Inc.....................................614 429-0100
777 Kinnear Rd Columbus (43212) *(G-6984)*

AMC Entertainment Inc.....................................216 749-0260
4788 Ridge Rd Brooklyn (44144) *(G-1904)*

Amec Fstr Whlr Envrnmnt Infrst.......................513 489-6611
4460 Lake Forest Dr # 200 Blue Ash (45242) *(G-1531)*

Amedisys Inc...740 373-8549
210 N 7th St Marietta (45750) *(G-13430)*

Amelia Davita Dialysis Center.........................513 797-0713
1761 E Ohio Pike Amelia (45102) *(G-572)*

Amenity Home Health Care LLC......................513 931-3689
3025 W Galbraith Rd Cincinnati (45239) *(G-3000)*

Amerathon LLC (HQ)...513 752-7300
671 Ohio Pike Ste K Cincinnati (45245) *(G-2903)*

Ameri Interntl Trade Grp Inc............................419 586-6433
1 Visions Pkwy Celina (45822) *(G-2634)*

Ameri-Line Inc...440 316-4500
27060 Royalton Rd Columbia Station (44028) *(G-6840)*

America Electric Power Texas, Columbus *Also called AEP Power Marketing Inc (G-6952)*

America's Best Medical, Akron *Also called Lincare Inc (G-320)*

Americab Inc..216 429-1134
3380 W 137th St Cleveland (44111) *(G-5002)*

American Air Comfort Tech, Grove City *Also called American Air Furnace Company (G-11528)*

American Air Furnace Company......................614 876-1702
3945 Brookham Dr Grove City (43123) *(G-11528)*

American Airlines Inc.......................................216 706-0702
5300 Riverside Dr Ste 8a Cleveland (44135) *(G-5003)*

American Airlines Inc.......................................937 454-7472
10398 Freight Dr Vandalia (45377) *(G-18656)*

American Airlines Inc.......................................937 890-6668
3600 Terminal Rd Ste 1 Vandalia (45377) *(G-18657)*

American Airlines Inc.......................................216 898-1347
5300 Riverside Dr Ste 1a Cleveland (44135) *(G-5004)*

American Benefits Management, Wadsworth *Also called Masters Agency Inc (G-18764)*

American Boring Inc...740 969-8000
6895 Pickerington Rd Carroll (43112) *(G-2607)*

American Bottling Company...........................614 237-4201
950 Stelzer Rd Columbus (43219) *(G-6985)*

American Brass, Cleveland *Also called Empire Brass Co (G-5537)*

American Broadband Telecom Co...................419 824-5800
1 Seagate Ste 10 Toledo (43604) *(G-17748)*

American Bronzing Company, Columbus *Also called Bron-Shoe Company (G-7150)*

American Brzing Div Paulo Pdts, Willoughby *Also called Paulo Products Company (G-19703)*

American Bulk Commodities Inc (PA).............330 758-0841
8063 Southern Blvd Youngstown (44512) *(G-20103)*

American Bus Personnel Svcs (PA)................513 770-3300
7547 Central Parke Blvd Mason (45040) *(G-13661)*

American Bus Solutions Inc............................614 888-2227
8850 Whitney Dr Lewis Center (43035) *(G-12665)*

American Business Machines, Richfield *Also called Ricoh Usa Inc (G-16527)*

American Cancer Society East.......................800 227-2345
10501 Euclid Ave Cleveland (44106) *(G-5005)*

American Cancer Society East.......................888 227-6446
5555 Frantz Rd Frnt Frnt Dublin (43017) *(G-10245)*

American Centrifuge Plant, Piketon *Also called Centrus Energy Corp (G-16111)*

American Ceramic Society (PA)......................614 890-4700
600 N Cleveland Ave # 210 Westerville (43082) *(G-19284)*

American City Bus Journals Inc.....................937 528-4400
40 N Main St Ste 800 Dayton (45423) *(G-9328)*

American Cllege Crdlgy Fndtion....................614 442-5950
6161 Riverside Dr Dublin (43017) *(G-10246)*

American Coatings Corporation.....................614 335-1000
7510 Montgomery Rd Plain City (43064) *(G-16181)*

American Commerce Insurance Co (HQ).......614 272-6951
3590 Twin Creeks Dr Columbus (43204) *(G-6986)*

American Commodore Tu (PA)........................216 291-4601
4130 Mayfield Rd Cleveland (44121) *(G-5006)*

American Consolidated Inds Inc (PA)............216 587-8000
4650 Johnston Pkwy Cleveland (44128) *(G-5007)*

American Contrs Indemnity Co......................513 688-0800
7794 5 Mile Rd Cincinnati (45230) *(G-3001)*

American Copy Equipment Inc.......................330 722-9555
6599 Granger Rd Cleveland (44131) *(G-5008)*

American Crane Inc...614 496-2268
7791 Taylor Rd Sw Ste A Reynoldsburg (43068) *(G-16426)*

American Crane & Lift Trck Svc, Reynoldsburg *Also called American Crane Inc (G-16426)*

American Custom Industries, Sylvania *Also called Bobbart Industries Inc (G-17576)*

American Cutting Edge Inc.............................937 438-2390
480 Congress Park Dr Centerville (45459) *(G-2673)*

American Eagle Hlth Care Svcs.....................440 428-5103
6831 Chapel Rd Madison (44057) *(G-13220)*

American Eagle Mortgage Co LLC (PA)........440 988-2900
6145 Park Square Dr Ste 4 Lorain (44053) *(G-13011)*

American Electric Power, Brilliant *Also called Cardinal Operating Company (G-1867)*

American Electric Power Co Inc....................419 420-3011
430 Emma St Findlay (45840) *(G-10990)*

American Electric Power Co Inc....................740 829-4129
47201 County Road 273 Conesville (43811) *(G-9035)*

American Electric Power Co Inc....................740 594-1988
9135 State Route 682 Athens (45701) *(G-771)*

American Electric Power Co Inc....................330 438-7024
301 Cleveland Ave Sw Canton (44702) *(G-2237)*

American Electric Power Co Inc....................419 998-5106
369 E Oconnor Ave Lima (45801) *(G-12740)*

American Electric Power Co Inc....................740 779-5261
701 Hardin Dr Chillicothe (45601) *(G-2814)*

American Electric Power Co Inc....................614 856-2750
5900 Refugee Rd Columbus (43232) *(G-6987)*

American Electric Power Co Inc....................614 351-3715
1759 W Mound St Columbus (43223) *(G-6988)*

American Electric Power Co Inc....................740 384-7981
3 W 13th St Wellston (45692) *(G-18997)*

American Electric Power Co Inc....................740 295-3070
405 Brewer Ln Coshocton (43812) *(G-9087)*

American Electric Power Co Inc....................330 580-5085
5300 Navarre Rd Sw Canton (44706) *(G-2238)*

American Electric Power Co Inc....................740 598-4164
306 County Road 7e Brilliant (43913) *(G-1865)*

American Electric Power Co Inc....................614 716-1000
1 Riverside Plz Ste 1600 Columbus (43215) *(G-6989)*

American Electric Pwr Svc Corp (HQ)..........614 716-1000
1 Riverside Plz Fl 1 Columbus (43215) *(G-6990)*

American Electric Pwr Svc Corp...................614 582-1742
825 Tech Center Dr Columbus (43230) *(G-6991)*

American Empire Insurance, Cincinnati *Also called American Empire Surplus Lines (G-3002)*

American Empire Surplus Lines....................513 369-3000
515 Main St Cincinnati (45202) *(G-3002)*

American Emprie Srpls Lines In (HQ)..........513 369-3000
580 Walnut St Cincinnati (45202) *(G-3003)*

American Energy Corporation......................740 926-2430
43521 Mayhugh Hill Rd Beallsville (43716) *(G-1139)*

American Envmtl Group Ltd..........................330 659-5930
3600 Brecksville Rd # 100 Richfield (44286) *(G-16495)*

American Equity Mortgage Inc.....................800 236-2600
6465 Reflections Dr # 240 Dublin (43017) *(G-10247)*

American Family Home Insur Co..................513 943-7100
7000 Midland Blvd Amelia (45102) *(G-573)*

American Federal Bank, Columbus *Also called Congressional Bank (G-7420)*

American Federation of Gov.........................513 861-6047
3200 Vine St Cincinnati (45220) *(G-3004)*

American Federation of State......................937 461-9983
15 Gates St Dayton (45402) *(G-9329)*

American Fidelity Assurance Co..................800 437-1011
90 Northwoods Blvd Ste B Columbus (43235) *(G-6992)*

American Financial Corporation..................513 579-2121
580 Walnut St Fl 9 Cincinnati (45202) *(G-3005)*

American Financial Group Inc (PA)............513 579-2121
301 E 4th St Cincinnati (45202) *(G-3006)*

American Fleet Services, Cleveland *Also called American Nat Fleet Svc Inc (G-5017)*

American Frame Corporation (PA)..............419 893-5595
400 Tomahawk Dr Maumee (43537) *(G-13874)*

American Gen Lf Insur Co Del.....................513 762-7807
250 E 5th St Ste 1500 Cincinnati (45202) *(G-3007)*

American Golf Corporation.........................440 286-9544
13095 Rockhaven Rd Chesterland (44026) *(G-2792)*

American Golf Corporation.........................740 965-5122
3300 Miller Paul Rd Galena (43021) *(G-11278)*

American Golf Corporation.........................310 664-4278
3223 Norton Rd Grove City (43123) *(G-11529)*

American Greetings, Cleveland *Also called AG Interactive Inc (G-4967)*

American Health Group Inc.........................419 891-1212
570 Longbow Dr Maumee (43537) *(G-13875)*

American Health Network Inc...614 794-4500
2500 Corp Exchange Dr # 100 Columbus (43231) **(G-6993)**
American Health Network Inc...740 363-5437
104 N Union St Delaware (43015) **(G-10071)**
American Health Packaging, Columbus *Also called Amerisource Health Svcs LLC* **(G-7012)**
American Heart Assn Ohio Vly...216 791-7500
1375 E 9th St Ste 600 Cleveland (44114) **(G-5009)**
American Heart Association Inc...614 848-6676
5455 N High St Columbus (43214) **(G-6994)**
American Highways Insur Agcy...330 659-8900
3250 Interstate Dr Richfield (44286) **(G-16496)**
American Hlth Netwrk Ohio LLC (HQ)...614 794-4500
2500 Corporate Exchange D Columbus (43231) **(G-6995)**
American Hlth Ntwrk & Fmly PRC...419 524-2212
248 Blymyer Ave Mansfield (44903) **(G-13261)**
American Home Health Care Inc...614 237-1133
861 Taylor Rd Unit I Columbus (43230) **(G-6996)**
American Home Health Services,, Westlake *Also called Infinity Health Services Inc* **(G-19498)**
American Hood Systems Inc...440 365-4567
177 Reaser Ct Elyria (44035) **(G-10593)**
American Hospitality Group Inc (HQ)...330 336-6684
200 Smokerise Dr Wadsworth (44281) **(G-18747)**
American Income Life Insur Co...440 582-0040
12301 Ridge Rd Cleveland (44133) **(G-5010)**
American Institute Research...614 221-8717
41 S High St Ste 2425 Columbus (43215) **(G-6997)**
American Institute Research...614 310-8982
820 Freeway Dr N Columbus (43229) **(G-6998)**
American Insur Administrators...614 486-5388
5455 Rings Rd Ste 200 Dublin (43017) **(G-10248)**
American International Cnstr...440 243-5535
1180 Berea Indus Pkwy Berea (44017) **(G-1445)**
American Italian Golf...614 889-2551
545 Metro Pl S Ste 100 Dublin (43017) **(G-10249)**
American Jersey Cattle Assn (PA)...614 861-3636
6486 E Main St Reynoldsburg (43068) **(G-16427)**
American Kenda Rbr Indus Ltd (HQ)...866 536-3287
7095 Americana Pkwy Reynoldsburg (43068) **(G-16428)**
American Kidney Stone MGT Ltd (PA)...800 637-5188
100 W 3rd Ave Ste 350 Columbus (43201) **(G-6999)**
American Landfill Inc...330 866-3265
7916 Chapel St Se Waynesburg (44688) **(G-18980)**
American Legacy Tours, Cincinnati *Also called Newport Walking Tours LLC* **(G-4161)**
American Legion...330 488-0119
204 Wood St S East Canton (44730) **(G-10502)**
American Legion...440 834-8621
14052 Goodwin St Burton (44021) **(G-2059)**
American Legion Post...330 393-9858
4200 Herner Cnty Line Rd Southington (44470) **(G-17104)**
American Legion Post...330 872-5475
2025 E River Rd Newton Falls (44444) **(G-15272)**
American Legion Post 667, East Canton *Also called American Legion* **(G-10502)**
American Limousine Service, Cleveland *Also called American Livery Service Inc* **(G-5011)**
American Line Builders Apprent...937 849-4177
1900 Lake Rd Medway (45341) **(G-14140)**
American Linehaul Corporation...614 409-8568
1860 Williams Rd Columbus (43207) **(G-7000)**
American Livery Service Inc...216 221-9330
11723 Detroit Ave Cleveland (44107) **(G-5011)**
American Maintenance Svcs Inc...330 744-3400
20 W Federal St Fl 2b Youngstown (44503) **(G-20104)**
American Marine Express Inc...216 268-3005
765 E 140th St Ste A Cleveland (44110) **(G-5012)**
American Maritime Officers...419 255-3940
1 Maritime Plz Fl 2 Toledo (43604) **(G-17749)**
American Mdrn Srpls Lnes Insur, Amelia *Also called American Modern Home Insur Co* **(G-574)**
American Mechanical Group Inc...614 575-3720
5729 Westbourne Ave Columbus (43213) **(G-7001)**
American Med...216 251-5319
13929 W Parkway Rd Cleveland (44135) **(G-5013)**
American Med...330 762-8999
1265 Triplett Blvd Akron (44306) **(G-71)**
American Medical Equipment, Columbus *Also called American Home Health Care Inc* **(G-6996)**
American Midwest Mortgage Corp (PA)...440 882-5210
6363 York Rd Ste 300 Cleveland (44130) **(G-5014)**
American Modern Home Insur Co, Amelia *Also called American Modrn Insur Group Inc* **(G-576)**
American Modern Home Insur Co (HQ)...513 943-7100
7000 Midland Blvd Amelia (45102) **(G-574)**
American Modern Home Svc Co...513 943-7100
7000 Midland Blvd Amelia (45102) **(G-575)**
American Modrn Insur Group Inc (HQ)...800 543-2644
7000 Midland Blvd Amelia (45102) **(G-576)**
American Money Management Corp...513 579-2592
301 E 4th St Fl 27 Cincinnati (45202) **(G-3008)**
American Motorcycle Assn (PA)...614 856-1900
13515 Yarmouth Dr Pickerington (43147) **(G-16083)**
AMERICAN MOTORCYCLIST ASSOCIAT, Pickerington *Also called American Motorcycle Assn* **(G-16083)**
American Multi-Cinema Inc...614 801-9130
4218 Buckeye Pkwy Grove City (43123) **(G-11530)**
American Multi-Cinema Inc...614 889-0580
6700 Village Pkwy Dublin (43017) **(G-10250)**
American Multi-Cinema Inc...216 749-0260
4788 Ridge Rd Cleveland (44144) **(G-5015)**
American Multi-Cinema Inc...440 331-2826
21653 Center Ridge Rd Rocky River (44116) **(G-16569)**
American Municipal Power Inc...614 540-1111
1111 Schrock Rd Ste 100 Columbus (43229) **(G-7002)**
American Mutl Share Insur Corp (PA)...614 764-1900
5656 Frantz Rd Dublin (43017) **(G-10251)**
American Mutual Life Assn (PA)...216 531-1900
19424 S Waterloo Rd Cleveland (44119) **(G-5016)**
American Nat Fleet Svc Inc...216 447-6060
7714 Commerce Park Oval Cleveland (44131) **(G-5017)**
American National Red Cross...216 303-5476
5585 Pearl Rd Parma (44129) **(G-15899)**
American National Red Cross...216 431-3152
3747 Euclid Ave Cleveland (44115) **(G-5018)**
American National Red Cross...419 382-2707
1111 Research Dr Toledo (43614) **(G-17750)**
American National Red Cross...330 535-6131
501 W Market St Akron (44303) **(G-72)**
American Nursing Care Inc...513 731-4600
4750 Wesley Ave Ste Q Cincinnati (45212) **(G-3009)**
American Nursing Care Inc...513 245-1500
4460 Red Bank Rd Ste 100 Cincinnati (45227) **(G-3010)**
American Nursing Care Inc (HQ)...513 576-0262
1700 Edison Dr Ste 300 Milford (45150) **(G-14503)**
American Nursing Care Inc...937 438-3844
5335 Far Hills Ave # 103 Dayton (45429) **(G-9330)**
American Nursing Care Inc...614 847-0555
1206 Brandywine Blvd A Zanesville (43701) **(G-20441)**
American Nursing Care Inc...419 228-0888
658 W Market St Ste 200 Lima (45801) **(G-12741)**
American Nursing Care Inc...740 452-0569
1206 Brandywine Blvd A Zanesville (43701) **(G-20442)**
American Para Prof Systems Inc...513 531-2900
6056 Montgomery Rd Cincinnati (45213) **(G-3011)**
American Posts LLC...419 720-0652
810 Chicago St Toledo (43611) **(G-17751)**
American Power LLC...937 235-0418
1819 Troy St Dayton (45404) **(G-9331)**
American Precast Refractories...614 876-8416
2700 Scioto Pkwy Columbus (43221) **(G-7003)**
American Procomm, Marietta *Also called Davis Pickering & Company Inc* **(G-13441)**
American Producers Sup Co Inc (PA)...740 373-5050
119 2nd St Marietta (45750) **(G-13431)**
American Prprty-Mnagement Corp...330 454-5000
320 Market Ave S Canton (44702) **(G-2239)**
American Prservation Bldrs LLC...216 236-2007
127 Public Sq Ste 1300 Cleveland (44114) **(G-5019)**
American Publishers LLC...419 626-0623
2401 Sawmill Pkwy Ste 10 Huron (44839) **(G-12160)**
American Red Cross (HQ)...513 579-3000
2111 Dana Ave Cincinnati (45207) **(G-3012)**
American Red Cross (HQ)...937 222-0124
370 W 1st St Dayton (45402) **(G-9332)**
American Red Cross...937 376-3111
1080 E Main St Xenia (45385) **(G-20041)**
American Red Cross of Grtr Col (PA)...614 253-7981
995 E Broad St Columbus (43205) **(G-7004)**
American Reprographics Co LLC...614 224-5149
1159 Dublin Rd Columbus (43215) **(G-7005)**
American Residential Svcs LLC...216 561-8880
4547 Hinckley Industrial Cleveland (44109) **(G-5020)**
American Residential Svcs LLC...888 762-7752
3050 Switzer Ave Columbus (43219) **(G-7006)**
American Response Center, Independence *Also called Ohio Alarm Inc* **(G-12241)**
American Retirement Corp...216 291-6140
3 Homewood Way Cleveland (44143) **(G-5021)**
American Retirement Corp...216 321-6331
3151 Mayfield Rd Apt 1105 Cleveland (44118) **(G-5022)**
American Ring & Tool Co, Solon *Also called R L Morrissey & Assoc Inc* **(G-17044)**
American Risk Services LLC...513 772-3712
1130 Congress Ave Ste A Cincinnati (45246) **(G-3013)**
American Roadway Logistics Inc...330 659-2003
3920 Congress Pkwy Richfield (44286) **(G-16497)**
American Rock Mechanics Inc...330 963-0550
9241 Ravenna Rd Ste 6 Twinsburg (44087) **(G-18390)**
American Sales Inc...937 253-9520
1755 Spaulding Rd Dayton (45432) **(G-9254)**
American Sand & Gravel Div, Massillon *Also called Kenmore Construction Co Inc* **(G-13827)**
American Savings Bank (PA)...740 354-3177
503 Chillicothe St Portsmouth (45662) **(G-16264)**
AMERICAN SAVINGS BANK F S B, Portsmouth *Also called American Savings Bank* **(G-16264)**
American Seaway, Bedford Heights *Also called Riser Foods Company* **(G-1359)**

American Security Insurance Co 937 327-7700
1 Assurant Way Springfield (45505) *(G-17147)*
American Select Insurance Co 330 887-0101
1 Park Cir Westfield Center (44251) *(G-19451)*
AMERICAN SHARE INSURANCE, Dublin *Also called American Mutl Share Insur Corp (G-10251)*
AMERICAN SHARE INSURANCE, Dublin *Also called Excess Share Insurance Corp (G-10343)*
American Showa Inc 740 965-4040
677 W Cherry St Sunbury (43074) *(G-17549)*
American Signature Inc (HQ) 614 449-6107
4300 E 5th Ave Columbus (43219) *(G-7007)*
American Society For Nondstctv 614 274-6003
1711 Arlingate Ln Columbus (43228) *(G-7008)*
American Star Painting Co LLC 740 373-5634
201 Mitchells Ln Marietta (45750) *(G-13432)*
American Star Pntg & Coatings, Marietta *Also called American Star Painting Co LLC (G-13432)*
American Svcs & Protection LLC 614 884-0177
2572 Oakstone Dr 8 Columbus (43231) *(G-7009)*
American Systems Cnsulting Inc 614 282-7180
5777 Frantz Rd Ste 150 Dublin (43017) *(G-10252)*
American Tank & Fabricating Co (PA) 216 252-1500
12314 Elmwood Ave Cleveland (44111) *(G-5023)*
American Title of Ohio LLC 303 868-2250
600 Superior Ave E # 1300 Cleveland (44114) *(G-5024)*
American Title Services Inc 330 652-1609
700 Youngstown Warren Rd Niles (44446) *(G-15281)*
American Warming and Vent 419 288-2703
120 Plin St Bradner (43406) *(G-1808)*
American Waste MGT Svcs Inc 330 856-8800
1 American Way Ne Warren (44484) *(G-18816)*
American Way Van & Storage, Vandalia *Also called American Way Van and Stor Inc (G-18658)*
American Way Van and Stor Inc 937 898-7294
1001 S Brown School Rd Vandalia (45377) *(G-18658)*
American Western Home Insur Co 513 943-7100
7000 Midland Blvd Amelia (45102) *(G-577)*
Americas Best Medical Eqp, Akron *Also called Americas Best Medical Eqp Co (G-73)*
Americas Best Medical Eqp Co 330 928-0884
1566 Akron Peninsula Rd # 2 Akron (44313) *(G-73)*
Americas Best Value Inn, Streetsboro *Also called R & H Service Inc (G-17427)*
Americas Best Value Inn 419 626-9890
5608 Milan Rd Sandusky (44870) *(G-16726)*
Americas Dream Homes LLC 614 252-7834
1336 E Main St Ste G Columbus (43205) *(G-7010)*
Americas Floor Source LLC 216 342-4929
26000 Richmond Rd Ste 1 Bedford Heights (44146) *(G-1346)*
Americas Floor Source LLC (PA) 614 808-3915
3442 Millennium Ct Columbus (43219) *(G-7011)*
Americas Urgent Care 614 929-2721
4661 Sawmill Rd Ste 101 Upper Arlington (43220) *(G-18546)*
Americoat, Plain City *Also called American Coatings Corporation (G-16181)*
Americold Logistics LLC 330 834-1742
2140 17th St Sw Massillon (44647) *(G-13785)*
Ameridial Inc 800 445-7128
4877 Higbee Ave Nw Canton (44718) *(G-2240)*
Ameridial Inc 330 479-8044
4535 Strausser St Nw North Canton (44720) *(G-15324)*
Ameridial Inc (PA) 330 497-4888
4535 Strausser St Nw North Canton (44720) *(G-15325)*
Ameridial Inc 330 339-7222
521 W High Ave New Philadelphia (44663) *(G-15082)*
Ameridial Inc 330 868-2000
102 N Market St Minerva (44657) *(G-14641)*
Ameridian Specialty Services 513 769-0150
11520 Rockfield Ct Cincinnati (45241) *(G-3014)*
Amerifirst Financial Corp 216 452-5120
14701 Detroit Ave Ste 750 Lakewood (44107) *(G-12470)*
Amerigroup Ohio Inc 513 733-2300
10123 Alliance Rd Ste 140 Blue Ash (45242) *(G-1532)*
Amerihost Mt. Vernon, Mount Vernon *Also called Emmett Dan House Ltd Partnr (G-14894)*
Amerimark Holdings LLC (PA) 440 325-2000
6864 Engle Rd Cleveland (44130) *(G-5025)*
Amerimed Inc 513 942-3670
9961 Cincinnati Dayton Rd West Chester (45069) *(G-19019)*
Ameripath Cincinnati Inc 513 745-8330
9670 Kenwood Rd Blue Ash (45242) *(G-1533)*
Ameriprise Financial Svcs Inc 330 494-9300
3333 Massillon Rd Ste 110 Akron (44312) *(G-74)*
Ameriprise Financial Svcs Inc 614 846-8723
250 W Old Wlsn Brg Rd # 150 Worthington (43085) *(G-19940)*
Ameriprise Financial Svcs Inc 614 934-4057
655 Metro Pl S Ste 450 Dublin (43017) *(G-10253)*
Ameripro Logistics LLC 410 375-3469
6754 Stovali Dr Dayton (45424) *(G-9333)*
Ameriscape Inc 614 863-5400
6751 Taylor Rd Unit D1 Blacklick (43004) *(G-1499)*
Amerisource Health Svcs LLC 614 492-8177
2550 John Glenn Ave Ste A Columbus (43217) *(G-7012)*
Amerisourcebergen Corporation 610 727-7000
1200 E 5th Ave Columbus (43219) *(G-7013)*
Amerisourcebergen Corporation 614 497-3665
6305 Lasalle Dr Lockbourne (43137) *(G-12944)*
Amerisourcebergen Drug Corp 614 409-0741
6305 Lasalle Dr Lockbourne (43137) *(G-12945)*
Ameristop Food Marts, Cincinnati *Also called Ohio Valley Acquisition Inc (G-4211)*
Ameritas Life Insurance Corp 513 595-2334
1876 Waycross Rd Cincinnati (45240) *(G-3015)*
Ames Material Services Inc 937 382-5591
145 Hunter Dr Wilmington (45177) *(G-19746)*
Ametek Electromechanical Group, Kent *Also called Ametek Tchnical Indus Pdts Inc (G-12352)*
Ametek Tchnical Indus Pdts Inc (HQ) 330 677-3754
100 E Erie St Ste 130 Kent (44240) *(G-12352)*
Amethyst Inc 614 242-1284
455 E Mound St Columbus (43215) *(G-7014)*
AMF Bowling Centers Inc 330 725-4548
201 Harding St Medina (44256) *(G-14036)*
AMF Bowling Centers Inc 614 889-0880
4825 Sawmill Rd Columbus (43235) *(G-7015)*
AMF Facility Services Inc 800 991-2273
844 Oakleaf Dr Dayton (45417) *(G-9334)*
Amg Inc (PA) 937 260-4646
1497 Shoup Mill Rd Dayton (45414) *(G-9335)*
AMG Advertising & PR, Solon *Also called AMG Marketing Resources Inc (G-16975)*
AMG Marketing Resources Inc 216 621-1835
30670 Bnbridge Rd Ste 200 Solon (44139) *(G-16975)*
AMG-Eng, Dayton *Also called Amg Inc (G-9335)*
Amherst Animal Hospital Inc 440 282-5220
1425 Cooper Foster Pk Rd Amherst (44001) *(G-585)*
Amherst Exempted Vlg Schools 440 988-2633
225 Washington St Amherst (44001) *(G-586)*
Amherst Hospital Association 440 988-6000
254 Cleveland Ave Amherst (44001) *(G-587)*
Amherst Maintenance Bldg, Berea *Also called Ohio Tpk & Infrastructure Comm (G-1466)*
Amherst Manor Nursing Home 440 988-4415
175 N Lake St Amherst (44001) *(G-588)*
AMI, Mayfield Heights *Also called Park Place Technologies LLC (G-14005)*
Amica Mutual Insurance Company 866 942-6422
9277 Centre Pointe Dr # 230 West Chester (45069) *(G-19020)*
Amin Turocy & Watson LLP (PA) 216 696-8730
127 Public Sq Fl 57 Cleveland (44114) *(G-5026)*
Amish Door Inc (PA) 330 359-5464
1210 Winesburg St Wilmot (44689) *(G-19797)*
Amish Door Restaurant, Wilmot *Also called Amish Door Inc (G-19797)*
Amish Farm, The, Berlin *Also called Dutch Heritage Farms Inc (G-1478)*
Amish Wedding Foods, Millersburg *Also called Troyer Cheese Inc (G-14625)*
Amitel Beachwood Ltd Partnr 216 831-3030
3628 Park Dr Cleveland (44134) *(G-5027)*
Amitel Limited Partnership 440 234-6688
17525 Rosbough Blvd Cleveland (44130) *(G-5028)*
Amitel Mentor Ltd Partnership 440 392-0800
5660 Emerald Ct Mentor (44060) *(G-14143)*
Amitel Rockside Ltd Partnr 216 520-1450
5101 Independence Cleveland (44131) *(G-5029)*
Amix Inc 513 539-7220
6487 Hankins Rd Middletown (45044) *(G-14413)*
Amko Service Company (HQ) 330 364-8857
3211 Brightwood Rd Midvale (44653) *(G-14489)*
AMLA, Cleveland *Also called American Mutual Life Assn (G-5016)*
Amos Media Company (PA) 937 498-2111
911 S Vandemark Rd Sidney (45365) *(G-16912)*
Amotec Inc (PA) 440 250-4600
1701 E 12th St Apt 10b Cleveland (44114) *(G-5030)*
AMP Advertising Inc 513 333-4100
700 Walnut St Ste 500 Cincinnati (45202) *(G-3016)*
AMP-Ohio, Columbus *Also called American Municipal Power Inc (G-7002)*
Ampac Holdings LLC (HQ) 513 671-1777
12025 Tricon Rd Cincinnati (45246) *(G-3017)*
Ampacet Corporation 513 247-5400
4705 Duke Dr 400 Cincinnati (45249) *(G-3018)*
Ampco System Parking, Cleveland *Also called ABM Parking Services Inc (G-4949)*
Ampersand Group LLC 330 379-0044
1946 S Arlington St Akron (44306) *(G-75)*
Ample Trailer Leasing & Sales 513 563-2550
610 Wayne Park Dr Cincinnati (45215) *(G-3019)*
AMR Eagle, Columbus *Also called Envoy Air Inc (G-7601)*
Amrstrong Distributors Inc 419 483-4840
421 Monroe St Bellevue (44811) *(G-1402)*
AMS, Sidney *Also called Bell Hensley Inc (G-16915)*
Ams Inc 513 244-8500
1608 Elmore St Cincinnati (45223) *(G-3020)*
AMS Construction Inc 513 398-6689
7431 Windsor Park Dr Maineville (45039) *(G-13240)*
AMS Construction Inc (PA) 513 794-0410
10670 Loveland Madeira Rd Loveland (45140) *(G-13110)*
Amsc, Cleveland *Also called Northast Ohio Rgonal Sewer Dst (G-6147)*
Amsdell Construction Inc (PA) 216 458-0670
20445 Emerald Pkwy # 220 Cleveland (44135) *(G-5031)*

ALPHABETIC SECTION
Another Chance Inc

Amstan Logistics, Hamilton *Also called As Logistics Inc* ***(G-11693)***
Amsted Industries Incorporated.....614 836-2323
3900 Bixby Rd Groveport (43125) ***(G-11622)***
Amt, Brecksville *Also called Applied Medical Technology Inc* ***(G-1813)***
Amtrac of Ohio Inc.....330 683-7206
11842 Lincoln Way E Orrville (44667) ***(G-15763)***
Amtrac Railroad Contrs Ohio, Orrville *Also called Amtrac of Ohio Inc* ***(G-15763)***
Amtrak, Toledo *Also called National Railroad Pass Corp* ***(G-18078)***
Amtrust Financial Services, Cleveland *Also called Amtrust North America Inc* ***(G-5032)***
Amtrust North America Inc (HQ).....216 328-6100
800 Superior Ave E # 2100 Cleveland (44114) ***(G-5032)***
AMTS, Brookpark *Also called Credit First NA* ***(G-1941)***
Amusements of America Inc.....614 297-8863
717 E 17th Ave Columbus (43211) ***(G-7016)***
Amvets Post No 6 Inc.....330 833-5935
8417 Audubon St Nw Massillon (44646) ***(G-13786)***
Amx, Cleveland *Also called American Marine Express Inc* ***(G-5012)***
Analytical Pace Services LLC.....937 832-8242
25 Holiday Dr Englewood (45322) ***(G-10696)***
Anark Inc.....513 825-7387
2150 Struble Rd Cincinnati (45231) ***(G-3021)***
Anatrace Products LLC (HQ).....419 740-6600
434 W Dussel Dr Maumee (43537) ***(G-13876)***
Anazao Community Partners (PA).....330 264-9597
2587 Back Orrville Rd Wooster (44691) ***(G-19828)***
Anchor Bronze and Metals Inc.....440 549-5653
11470 Euclid Ave Ste 509 Cleveland (44106) ***(G-5033)***
Anchor Cleaning Contractors.....216 961-7343
1966 W 52nd St Cleveland (44102) ***(G-5034)***
Anchor Lodge Nursing Home Inc.....440 244-2019
3756 W Erie Ave Ofc Lorain (44053) ***(G-13012)***
Anchor Metal Processing Inc (PA).....216 362-1850
11830 Brookpark Rd Cleveland (44130) ***(G-5035)***
ANCHOR TRADER, Upper Arlington *Also called Delta Gamma Fraternity* ***(G-18549)***
Ancillary Medical Investments.....937 456-5520
125 Amelia Dr Eaton (45320) ***(G-10552)***
Ancom Business Products, Brunswick *Also called Symatic Inc* ***(G-1991)***
Andersen & Associates Inc.....330 425-8500
1960 Summit Commerce Park Twinsburg (44087) ***(G-18391)***
Andersen Distribution Inc.....937 898-7844
8569 N Dixie Dr Dayton (45414) ***(G-9336)***
Anderson & Vreeland Inc.....419 636-5002
15348 State Rte 127 E Bryan (43506) ***(G-2002)***
Anderson Aluminum Corporation.....614 476-4877
2816 Morse Rd Columbus (43231) ***(G-7017)***
Anderson and Dubose Inc (PA).....440 248-8800
5300 Tod Ave Sw Warren (44481) ***(G-18817)***
Anderson Ferry, Cincinnati *Also called Consolidated Grain & Barge Co* ***(G-3411)***
Anderson Glass Co Inc.....614 476-4877
2816 Morse Rd Columbus (43231) ***(G-7018)***
Anderson Healthcare Ltd.....513 474-6200
8139 Beechmont Ave Cincinnati (45255) ***(G-3022)***
Anderson Hills Pediatrics Inc.....513 232-8100
7400 Jager Ct Cincinnati (45230) ***(G-3023)***
Anderson Jeffery R RE Inc.....513 241-5800
3805 Edwards Rd Ste 700 Cincinnati (45209) ***(G-3024)***
Anderson Little.....513 474-7800
8516 Beechmont Ave Cincinnati (45255) ***(G-3025)***
Anderson Press Incorporated.....615 370-9922
1840 Baney Rd S Ashland (44805) ***(G-650)***
Anderson Properties, Columbus *Also called Anderson Aluminum Corporation* ***(G-7017)***
Anderson Security Inc (PA).....937 294-1478
4600 S Dixie Dr Moraine (45439) ***(G-14749)***
Anderson Twnship Hstorical Soc.....513 231-2114
6550 Clough Pike Cincinnati (45244) ***(G-3026)***
Anderson Vreeland Midwest, Bryan *Also called Anderson & Vreeland Inc* ***(G-2002)***
Anderson's Farm, Maumee *Also called Andersons Agriculture Group LP* ***(G-13881)***
Anderson's Rail Car Service, Maumee *Also called Andersons Inc* ***(G-13878)***
Anderson, The, Cincinnati *Also called Anderson Healthcare Ltd* ***(G-3022)***
ANDERSON-DUBOSE CO, THE, Warren *Also called Anderson and Dubose Inc* ***(G-18817)***
Andersons Inc.....419 891-6479
1380 Ford St Maumee (43537) ***(G-13877)***
Andersons Inc.....419 891-6634
421 Illinois Ave Maumee (43537) ***(G-13878)***
Andersons Inc (PA).....419 893-5050
1947 Briarfield Blvd Maumee (43537) ***(G-13879)***
Andersons Inc.....419 893-5050
533 Illinois Ave Maumee (43537) ***(G-13880)***
Andersons Agriculture Group LP (HQ).....419 893-5050
1947 Briarfield Blvd Maumee (43537) ***(G-13881)***
Anderzack-Pitzen Cnstr Inc.....419 553-7015
424 E Main St Metamora (43540) ***(G-14265)***
Andover Bancorp Inc (PA).....440 293-7605
19 Public Sq Andover (44003) ***(G-609)***
Andover Floor Covering.....440 293-5339
9950 Belleflower Cir Newbury (44065) ***(G-15254)***
Andover Vlg Retirement Cmnty.....440 293-5416
486 S Main St Andover (44003) ***(G-610)***
Andre Corporation.....574 293-0207
4600 N Masn Montgomery Rd Mason (45040) ***(G-13662)***
Andreas Furniture Company.....330 852-2494
580 Belden Pkwy Ne Sugarcreek (44681) ***(G-17543)***
Andrew Belmont Sargent (PA).....513 769-7800
10855 Medallion Dr Cincinnati (45241) ***(G-3027)***
Andrew Philips Collection, Mason *Also called Millennium Leather LLC* ***(G-13740)***
Andrews Apartments Ltd.....440 946-3600
4420 Sherwin Rd Willoughby (44094) ***(G-19644)***
Andy Frain Services Inc.....419 897-7909
1715 Indian Wood Cir # 200 Maumee (43537) ***(G-13882)***
Andy Mark Inc.....513 248-8000
910 Lila Ave Milford (45150) ***(G-14504)***
Andy's Mirror and Glass, Cincinnati *Also called E J Robinson Glass Co* ***(G-3524)***
Anesthesia Associates Inc.....440 350-0832
7757 Auburn Rd Ste 15 Painesville (44077) ***(G-15834)***
Anesthesiologists, D.O., Inc., Youngstown *Also called Ado Health Services Inc* ***(G-20097)***
Anesthesiology Assoc of Akron.....330 344-6401
224 W Exchange St Ste 220 Akron (44302) ***(G-76)***
Anesthesiology Consultant Inc.....614 566-9983
111 S Grant Ave Columbus (43215) ***(G-7019)***
Anesthesiology Services Netwrk.....937 208-6173
1 Wyoming St Dayton (45409) ***(G-9337)***
Anesthsia Assoc Cincinnati Inc.....513 585-0577
2139 Auburn Ave Cincinnati (45219) ***(G-3028)***
Angel Above Byond Hm Hlth Svcs.....513 553-9955
1041 Old Us Highway 52 New Richmond (45157) ***(G-15124)***
Angel Care Inc.....440 736-7267
7033 Oakes Rd Brecksville (44141) ***(G-1812)***
Angel Hearts Home Health Inc.....937 263-6194
2213 Arbor Blvd Moraine (45439) ***(G-14750)***
Angeline Industries Inc.....419 294-4488
11028 County Highway 44 Upper Sandusky (43351) ***(G-18557)***
Angelo J Colosimo MD, Cincinnati *Also called University Orthopaedic Cnsltnt* ***(G-4783)***
Angelos Caulking & Sealants Co.....614 236-1350
727 N James Rd Columbus (43219) ***(G-7020)***
Angels 4 Life LLC.....513 474-5683
431 Ohio Pike Ste 182s Cincinnati (45255) ***(G-3029)***
Angels Home Care LLC.....419 947-9373
4440 State Route 61 Mount Gilead (43338) ***(G-14851)***
Angels In Waiting Home Care.....440 946-0349
8336 Tyler Blvd Mentor (44060) ***(G-14144)***
Angels On Earth Child Care Co.....216 476-8100
13439 Lorain Ave Cleveland (44111) ***(G-5036)***
Angels Touch Nursing Care.....513 661-4111
3619 Harrison Ave Cincinnati (45211) ***(G-3030)***
Angels Visiting.....419 298-0034
143 N Michigan Ave Edgerton (43517) ***(G-10582)***
Angmar Medical Holdings Inc.....330 835-9663
3480 W Market St Fairlawn (44333) ***(G-10937)***
Angstrom Graphics Inc Midwest (HQ).....216 271-5300
4437 E 49th St Cleveland (44125) ***(G-5037)***
Angstrom Graphics Inc Midwest.....330 225-8950
4437 E 49th St Cleveland (44125) ***(G-5038)***
Anheuser-Busch LLC.....513 381-3927
600 Vine St Ste 1002 Cincinnati (45202) ***(G-3031)***
Animal Ark Pet Resort, Cincinnati *Also called Anark Inc* ***(G-3021)***
Animal Care At Cherry Way, Gahanna *Also called Vma Inc* ***(G-11274)***
Animal Care Unlimited Inc.....614 766-2317
2665 Billingsley Rd Columbus (43235) ***(G-7021)***
Animal Hospital Inc.....440 946-2800
2735 Som Center Rd Willoughby Hills (44094) ***(G-19728)***
Animal Hospital Polaris LLC.....614 888-4050
8928 S Old State Rd Lewis Center (43035) ***(G-12666)***
Animal Medical Center Medina, Medina *Also called Michael T Lee Dvm* ***(G-14105)***
Animal Mgt Svcs Ohio Inc.....248 398-6533
267 S Lightner Rd Port Clinton (43452) ***(G-16237)***
Animal Protective League.....216 771-4616
1729 Willey Ave Cleveland (44113) ***(G-5039)***
Animal Shelter Blemont CN, Saint Clairsville *Also called Belmont County of Ohio* ***(G-16621)***
Anixter Inc.....513 881-4600
4440 Muhlhauser Rd # 200 West Chester (45011) ***(G-19021)***
Ankle and Foot Care Center (PA).....330 385-2413
16844 Saint Clair Ave # 2 East Liverpool (43920) ***(G-10515)***
Ann Arbor Railroad Inc.....419 726-4181
4050 Chrysler Dr Toledo (43008) ***(G-17732)***
Ann Corbett Design Inc.....740 432-2969
534 N 1st St Cambridge (43725) ***(G-2095)***
Anna Maria of Aurora Inc (PA).....330 562-6171
889 N Aurora Rd Aurora (44202) ***(G-824)***
Anna Maria of Aurora Inc.....330 562-3120
849 Rural Rd Aurora (44202) ***(G-825)***
Anna Rescue Squad.....937 394-7377
203 S Linden St Anna (45302) ***(G-617)***
Anne Camm, Psy.d., Company, Middletown *Also called Primary Cr Ntwrk Prmr Hlth Prt* ***(G-14486)***
Anne Grady Corporation.....419 867-7501
1645 Trade Rd Holland (43528) ***(G-12008)***
Anne Grady Corporation (PA).....419 380-8985
1525 Eber Rd Holland (43528) ***(G-12009)***
Annehurst Veterinary Hospital.....614 818-4221
25 Collegeview Rd Westerville (43081) ***(G-19363)***
Another Chance Inc.....614 868-3541
9866 Haverford Pl Pickerington (43147) ***(G-16084)***

ALPHABETIC

Anselmo Rssis Premier Prod Ltd..........800 229-5517
4500 Willow Pkwy Cleveland (44125) ***(G-5040)***
Ansonia Area Emergency Service..........937 337-2651
225 W Elroy Ansonia Rd Ansonia (45303) ***(G-619)***
Anspach Meeks Ellenberger LLP..........614 745-8350
175 S 3rd St Ste 285 Columbus (43215) ***(G-7022)***
Anspach Meeks Ellenberger LLP (PA)..........419 447-6181
300 Madison Ave Ste 1600 Toledo (43604) ***(G-17753)***
Anstine Drywall Inc..........330 784-3867
2215 E Waterloo Rd # 403 Akron (44312) ***(G-77)***
Answer Group, The, Blue Ash *Also called Nielsen Consumer Insights Inc* ***(G-1652)***
Answercare LLC..........855 213-1511
4150 Belden Village St Nw # 307 Canton (44718) ***(G-2241)***
Answering Service Inc..........440 473-1200
5767 Mayfield Rd Rear 1 Cleveland (44124) ***(G-5041)***
Antares Management Solutions, Strongsville *Also called Medical Mutual Services LLC* ***(G-17492)***
Antares Management Solutions, Beachwood *Also called Medical Mutual of Ohio* ***(G-1099)***
Antech Diagnostics Inc..........330 665-4996
1321 Centerview Cir Copley (44321) ***(G-9051)***
Antero Resources Corporation..........740 760-1000
2335 State Route 821 Marietta (45750) ***(G-13433)***
Anthem, Cincinnati *Also called Community Insurance Company* ***(G-3401)***
Anthem Insurance Companies Inc..........614 438-3542
6740 N High St Worthington (43085) ***(G-19941)***
Anthem Insurance Companies Inc..........330 492-2151
4150 Belden Village St Nw # 506 Canton (44718) ***(G-2242)***
Anthem Insurance Companies Inc..........330 783-9800
6000 Lombardo Ctr Lowr 3 Seven Hills (44131) ***(G-16826)***
Anthem Midwest Inc..........614 433-8350
4361 Irwin Simpson Rd Mason (45040) ***(G-13663)***
Anthony Allega, Cleveland *Also called Mid America Trucking Company* ***(G-6051)***
Anthony Allega Cement Contr..........216 447-0814
5585 Canal Rd Cleveland (44125) ***(G-5042)***
Anthony David Salon & Spa..........440 233-8570
6401 S Broadway Lorain (44053) ***(G-13013)***
Anthony Omalley Atty..........216 479-6100
1375 E 9th St Cleveland (44114) ***(G-5043)***
Anthony Roccos Hair Design..........440 646-1925
6255 Highland Rd Cleveland (44143) ***(G-5044)***
Anthony Wayne Local Schools..........419 877-0451
6320 Industrial Pkwy Whitehouse (43571) ***(G-19583)***
Anthony Wayne Trnsp Dept, Whitehouse *Also called Anthony Wayne Local Schools* ***(G-19583)***
Antioch Cnnction Canton MI LLC..........614 531-9285
799 Windmiller Dr Pickerington (43147) ***(G-16085)***
Antioch Salem Fields Frederick..........614 531-9285
799 Windmiller Dr Pickerington (43147) ***(G-16086)***
Antioch University..........937 769-1366
1 Morgan Pl Yellow Springs (45387) ***(G-20088)***
Antonio Sofo Son Importing Co (PA)..........419 476-4211
253 Waggoner Blvd Toledo (43612) ***(G-17754)***
Any Domest Work Inc..........440 845-9911
5735 Pearl Rd Cleveland (44129) ***(G-5045)***
AON Consulting Inc..........614 436-8100
445 Hutchinson Ave # 900 Columbus (43235) ***(G-7023)***
AON Consulting Inc..........614 847-4670
355 E Campus View Blvd Columbus (43235) ***(G-7024)***
AON Consulting Inc..........216 621-8100
1660 W 2nd St Ste 650 Cleveland (44113) ***(G-5046)***
AON Risk Svcs Northeast Inc (HQ)..........216 621-8100
1660 W 2nd St Cleveland (44113) ***(G-5047)***
AP Cchmc..........513 636-4200
3333 Burnet Ave Cincinnati (45229) ***(G-3032)***
Ap/Aim Dublin Suites Trs LLC..........614 790-9000
5100 Upper Metro Pl Dublin (43017) ***(G-10254)***
Ap/Aim Indpndnce Sites Trs LLC..........216 986-9900
5800 Rckside Woods Blvd N Independence (44131) ***(G-12186)***
Ap23 Sports Complex LLC..........614 452-0760
775 Georgesville Rd Columbus (43228) ***(G-7025)***
Apartments of Cedar Hill, Zanesville *Also called Zandex Inc* ***(G-20547)***
Apbn Inc..........724 964-8252
670 Robinson Rd Campbell (44405) ***(G-2138)***
Apc2 Inc (PA)..........513 231-5540
6812 Clough Pike Cincinnati (45244) ***(G-3033)***
Apco Aluminum Awning Co..........614 334-2726
815 Michigan Ave Columbus (43215) ***(G-7026)***
Apco Industries Inc..........614 224-2345
777 Michigan Ave Columbus (43215) ***(G-7027)***
Apco Window & Door Company, Columbus *Also called Apco Industries Inc* ***(G-7027)***
Apelles LLC..........614 899-7322
3700 Corp Dr 2f Ste 240 Columbus (43231) ***(G-7028)***
Apex Academy, Cleveland *Also called National Heritg Academies Inc* ***(G-6109)***
Apex Environmental LLC..........740 543-4389
11 County Road 78 Amsterdam (43903) ***(G-607)***
Apex Environmental Svcs LLC..........513 772-2739
295 Northland Blvd Cincinnati (45246) ***(G-3034)***
Apex Gear..........614 539-3002
2375 Harrisburg Pike Grove City (43123) ***(G-11531)***
Apex Interiors Inc..........330 327-2226
3233 Waterford Way Avon (44011) ***(G-875)***
Apex Restoration Contrs Ltd (PA)..........513 489-1795
6315 Warrick St Cincinnati (45227) ***(G-3035)***
Apg Office Furnishings Inc..........216 621-4590
3615 Superior Ave E 4407a Cleveland (44114) ***(G-5048)***
APL Logistics Ltd..........440 930-2822
32608 Surrey Ln Avon Lake (44012) ***(G-921)***
Apollo Heating and AC Inc..........513 271-3600
1730 Tennessee Ave Cincinnati (45229) ***(G-3036)***
Apollo Property Management LLC (PA)..........216 468-0050
25825 Science Park Dr # 150 Beachwood (44122) ***(G-1051)***
Apostolic Christian Academy, Toledo *Also called First Apostolic Church* ***(G-17891)***
Apostolic Christian Home Inc..........330 927-1010
10680 Steiner Rd Rittman (44270) ***(G-16550)***
Apostolos Group Inc..........330 670-9900
1122 Jacoby Rd Copley (44321) ***(G-9052)***
Appalachia Wood Inc (PA)..........740 596-2551
31310 State Route 93 Mc Arthur (45651) ***(G-14015)***
Appalachian Community Visi..........740 594-8226
444 W Union St Ste C Athens (45701) ***(G-772)***
Appalachian Hardwood Lumber Co..........440 232-6767
5433 Perkins Rd Cleveland (44146) ***(G-5049)***
Appalachian Power Company (HQ)..........614 716-1000
1 Riverside Plz Columbus (43215) ***(G-7029)***
Appalachian Power Company..........330 438-7102
301 Cleveland Ave Sw Canton (44702) ***(G-2243)***
Appalachian Respite Care Ltd..........740 984-4262
501 Pinecrest Dr Beverly (45715) ***(G-1487)***
Appalchian Bhvioral Healthcare, Athens *Also called Mental Health and Addi Serv* ***(G-801)***
Appearance Plus, Cincinnati *Also called Apc2 Inc* ***(G-3033)***
Applause Talent Presentation..........513 844-6788
1525 Singer Ave Hamilton (45011) ***(G-11692)***
Apple A Day Healthcare Svcs, Toledo *Also called Horizons Employment Svcs LLC* ***(G-17960)***
Apple Creek Banking Co (inc) (PA)..........330 698-2631
3 W Main St Apple Creek (44606) ***(G-623)***
Apple Electric, Barberton *Also called Apple Heating Inc* ***(G-952)***
Apple Farm Service Inc (PA)..........937 526-4851
10120 W Versailles Rd Covington (45318) ***(G-9135)***
Apple Farm Service Infc, Covington *Also called Apple Farm Service Inc* ***(G-9135)***
Apple Gate Operating Co Inc..........330 405-4488
8971 Wilcox Dr Twinsburg (44087) ***(G-18392)***
Apple Growth Partners Inc (PA)..........330 867-7350
1540 W Market St Akron (44313) ***(G-78)***
Apple Heating Inc (PA)..........440 997-1212
344 4th St Nw Barberton (44203) ***(G-952)***
Apple Tree Nursery School Inc..........419 530-1070
2801 W Bancroft St 280 Toledo (43606) ***(G-17755)***
Appleseed Cmnty Mntal Hlth Ctr..........419 281-3716
2233 Rocky Ln Ashland (44805) ***(G-651)***
APPLESEED COUNSELING, Ashland *Also called Appleseed Cmnty Mntal Hlth Ctr* ***(G-651)***
Applewood Centers Inc (PA)..........216 696-6815
10427 Detroit Ave Cleveland (44102) ***(G-5050)***
Applewood Centers Inc..........216 521-6511
10427 Detroit Ave Cleveland (44102) ***(G-5051)***
Applewood Centers Inc..........440 324-1300
1865 N Ridge Rd E Ste A Lorain (44055) ***(G-13014)***
Applewood Centers Inc..........216 741-2241
3518 W 25th St Cleveland (44109) ***(G-5052)***
Appliance Recycl Ctrs Amer Inc..........614 876-8771
3700 Parkway Ln Ste D&G Hilliard (43026) ***(G-11878)***
Applied Indus Tech - CA LLC (HQ)..........216 426-4000
1 Applied Plz Cleveland (44115) ***(G-5053)***
Applied Indus Tech - Dixie Inc (HQ)..........216 426-4000
1 Applied Plz Cleveland (44115) ***(G-5054)***
Applied Industrial Tech Inc (PA)..........216 426-4000
1 Applied Plz Cleveland (44115) ***(G-5055)***
Applied Marketing Services..........440 716-9962
28825 Ranney Pkwy Westlake (44145) ***(G-19460)***
Applied Mechanical Systems Inc..........513 825-1800
12082 Champion Way Cincinnati (45241) ***(G-3037)***
Applied Medical Technology Inc (PA)..........440 717-4000
8006 Katherine Blvd Brecksville (44141) ***(G-1813)***
Applied Mint Sups Slutions LLC (HQ)..........216 456-3600
14790 Foltz Pkwy Strongsville (44149) ***(G-17443)***
Applied Optimization Inc..........937 431-5100
3040 Presidential Dr # 100 Beavercreek (45324) ***(G-1146)***
Applied Research Assoc Inc..........937 435-1016
7735 Paragon Rd Dayton (45459) ***(G-9338)***
Applied Research Assoc Inc..........937 873-8166
7735 Paragon Rd Dayton (45459) ***(G-9339)***
Applied Research Solutions Inc (PA)..........937 912-6100
51 Plum St Ste 240 Beavercreek (45440) ***(G-1225)***
Applied Sciences Inc (PA)..........937 766-2020
141 W Xenia Ave Cedarville (45314) ***(G-2631)***
Appraisal Research Corporation (PA)..........419 423-3582
101 E Sandusky St Ste 408 Findlay (45840) ***(G-10991)***
Apprisen, Gahanna *Also called Consumer Credit Coun* ***(G-11237)***
Aprecia Pharmaceuticals Co (PA)..........513 864-4107
10901 Kenwood Rd Blue Ash (45242) ***(G-1534)***
Apria Healthcare LLC..........614 351-5920
4060 Business Park Dr A Columbus (43204) ***(G-7030)***
Apria Healthcare LLC..........937 291-2842
2029 Lyons Rd Miamisburg (45342) ***(G-14271)***

ALPHABETIC SECTION

Apria Healthcare LLC 419 471-1919
4062 Technology Dr Maumee (43537) *(G-13883)*
Apria Healthcare LLC 216 485-1180
5480 Cloverleaf Pkwy # 4 Cleveland (44125) *(G-5056)*
April Enterprises Inc 937 293-7703
5070 Lamme Rd Moraine (45439) *(G-14751)*
APS Medical Billing 419 866-1804
5620 Southwyck Blvd Toledo (43614) *(G-17756)*
Aptim Corp 513 782-4700
5050 Section Ave Cincinnati (45212) *(G-3038)*
Aqua Doc Lake & Pond MGT, Chardon Also called Stat Integrated Tech Inc *(G-2769)*
Aqua Falls Bottled Watrer, Fairborn Also called K & R Distributors Inc *(G-10799)*
Aqua Marine Luxury Apartments, Avon Lake Also called Kopf Construction Corporation *(G-933)*
Aqua Ohio Inc 330 832-5764
870 3rd St Nw Massillon (44647) *(G-13787)*
Aqua Pennsylvania Inc 614 882-6586
5481 Buenos Aires Blvd Westerville (43081) *(G-19364)*
Aqua Tech Envmtl Labs Inc (PA) 740 389-5991
1776 Marion Waldo Rd Marion (43302) *(G-13523)*
Aquarian Pools Inc 513 576-9771
631 Lveland Miamiville Rd Loveland (45140) *(G-13111)*
Aquarius Marine LLC 614 875-8200
250 N Hartford Ave Columbus (43222) *(G-7031)*
Aquasonic Auto & Van Wash, North Olmsted Also called John Atwood Inc *(G-15428)*
Aquasonic Car Wash, Euclid Also called Bp *(G-10745)*
ARA Staffing Services, Cincinnati Also called Healthlinx Inc *(G-3754)*
Aramark Facility Services LLC 216 687-5000
2121 Euclid Ave Cleveland (44115) *(G-5057)*
Aramark Unf & Career AP LLC 513 533-1000
P.O. Box 12131 Cincinnati (45212) *(G-3039)*
Aramark Unf & Career AP LLC 937 223-6667
1200 Webster St Dayton (45404) *(G-9340)*
Aramark Unf & Career AP LLC 614 445-8341
1900 Progress Ave Columbus (43207) *(G-7032)*
Aramark Unf & Career AP LLC 216 341-7400
3600 E 93rd St Cleveland (44105) *(G-5058)*
Arbor Construction Co. 216 360-8989
1350 W 3rd St Cleveland (44113) *(G-5059)*
Arbor Park Phase Two Assoc 561 998-0700
3750 Fleming Ave Cleveland (44115) *(G-5060)*
ARBOR PARK VILLAGE, Cleveland Also called Arbor Pk Phase Three Assoc LP *(G-5061)*
Arbor Park Village, Cleveland Also called Arbor Park Phase Two Assoc *(G-5060)*
Arbor Park Village, Cleveland Also called Longwood Phase One Assoc LP *(G-5951)*
Arbor Pk Phase Three Assoc LP 561 998-0700
3750 Fleming Ave Cleveland (44115) *(G-5061)*
Arbor Rehabilitation & Healtcr 440 423-0206
45125 Fairmount Blvd Gates Mills (44040) *(G-11355)*
Arbor View Family Medicine Inc 740 687-3386
2405 N Columbus St # 200 Lancaster (43130) *(G-12509)*
Arbors At Clide Asssted Living 419 547-7746
700 Coulson St Clyde (43410) *(G-6808)*
ARBORS AT DELAWARE, Delaware Also called Delaware Opco LLC *(G-10090)*
ARBORS AT FAIRLAWN, Fairlawn Also called Fairlawn Opco LLC *(G-10950)*
Arbors At Marietta, Marietta Also called Northpoint Senior Services LLC *(G-13480)*
Arbors At Mifflin, Mansfield Also called Mansfield Opco LLC *(G-13334)*
Arbors At Milfor, The, Milford Also called Northpoint Senior Services LLC *(G-14545)*
Arbors At Stow, Stow Also called Stow Opco LLC *(G-17394)*
Arbors At Streetsboro, Streetsboro Also called Streetsboro Opco LLC *(G-17433)*
ARBORS AT SYLVANIA, Toledo Also called Toledo Opco LLC *(G-18245)*
ARBORS AT WATERVILLE, Waterville Also called Waterville Care LLC *(G-18947)*
Arbors At Woodsfield, Woodsfield Also called Woodsfield Opco LLC *(G-19820)*
Arbors East LLC 614 575-9003
5500 E Broad St Columbus (43213) *(G-7033)*
Arbors of Delaware, Delaware Also called Northpoint Senior Services LLC *(G-10118)*
Arbors West LLC 614 879-7661
375 W Main St West Jefferson (43162) *(G-19247)*
ARBORS WEST SUBACUTE & REHABIL, West Jefferson Also called Arbors West LLC *(G-19247)*
ARC, Columbus Also called American Reprographics Co LLC *(G-7005)*
ARC Abrasives Inc 800 888-4885
2131 Corporate Dr Troy (45373) *(G-18347)*
ARC Document Solutions Inc 216 281-1234
3666 Carnegie Ave Cleveland (44115) *(G-5062)*
ARC Document Solutions Inc 513 326-2300
7157 E Kemper Rd Cincinnati (45249) *(G-3040)*
ARC Document Solutions Inc 937 277-7930
222 N Saint Clair Dayton (45402) *(G-9341)*
ARC Gas & Supply LLC 216 341-5882
4560 Nicky Blvd Ste D Cleveland (44125) *(G-5063)*
ARC Industreis East, Columbus Also called ARC Industries Incorporated O *(G-7036)*
ARC Industries Incorporated O (PA) 614 479-2500
2780 Airport Dr Columbus (43219) *(G-7034)*
ARC Industries Incorporated O 614 436-4800
6633 Doubletree Ave Columbus (43229) *(G-7035)*
ARC Industries Incorporated O 614 864-2406
909 Taylor Station Rd Columbus (43230) *(G-7036)*
ARC Industries Incorporated O 614 267-1207
250 W Dodridge St Columbus (43202) *(G-7037)*
ARC Industries Incorporated O 614 836-0700
4395 Marketing Pl Groveport (43125) *(G-11623)*
ARC Industries Incorporated O 614 836-6050
4200 Bixby Rd Groveport (43125) *(G-11624)*
ARC Industries North, Columbus Also called ARC Industries Incorporated O *(G-7035)*
ARC Industries South, Groveport Also called ARC Industries Incorporated O *(G-11623)*
ARC Industries West, Columbus Also called ARC Industries Incorporated O *(G-7037)*
Arcadia Health Care, Akron Also called Arcadia Services Inc *(G-79)*
Arcadia Services Inc 330 869-9520
1650 W Market St Ste 27 Akron (44313) *(G-79)*
Arcadia Services Inc 937 912-5800
2440 Dayton Xenia Rd C Beavercreek (45434) *(G-1147)*
Arcadis US Inc 216 781-6177
1111 Superior Ave E # 1300 Cleveland (44114) *(G-5064)*
Arcadis US Inc 330 434-1995
222 S Main St Akron (44308) *(G-80)*
Arcadis US Inc 419 473-1121
1 Seagate Ste 700 Toledo (43604) *(G-17757)*
Arch Abraham Nissan & Susuki, Elyria Also called Arch Abraham Susuki Ltd *(G-10594)*
Arch Abraham Susuki Ltd 440 934-6001
1111 E Broad St Elyria (44035) *(G-10594)*
Archbishop Leibold Home, Cincinnati Also called Sisters of Little *(G-4532)*
Archbold Elevator Inc 419 445-2451
3265 County Road 24 Archbold (43502) *(G-632)*
Archbold Hospital, Archbold Also called Community Hsptals Wllness Ctrs *(G-635)*
Archdiocese of Cincinnati 937 323-6507
701 E Columbia St Springfield (45503) *(G-17148)*
Archdiocese of Cincinnati 513 729-1725
9375 Winton Rd Cincinnati (45231) *(G-3041)*
Archdiocese of Cincinnati 513 231-5010
274 Sutton Rd Cincinnati (45230) *(G-3042)*
Archer Corporation 330 455-9995
1917 Henry Ave Sw Canton (44706) *(G-2244)*
Archer Sign, Canton Also called Archer Corporation *(G-2244)*
Archer-Meek-Weiler Agency Inc 614 212-1009
440 Polaris Pkwy Ste 400 Westerville (43082) *(G-19285)*
Archiable Electric Company 513 621-1307
3803 Ford Cir Cincinnati (45227) *(G-3043)*
Architctural Con Solutions Inc 614 940-5399
1997 Harmon Ave Columbus (43223) *(G-7038)*
Architechs Plus, Blue Ash Also called Design Center *(G-1577)*
Architectural Intr Restoration 216 241-2255
2401 Train Ave Cleveland (44113) *(G-5065)*
Architectural Justice, Medina Also called Justice & Co Inc *(G-14088)*
Architectural Metal Erectors 513 242-5106
869 W North Bend Rd Cincinnati (45224) *(G-3044)*
Architectural Systems Inc 614 873-2057
8633 Memorial Dr Plain City (43064) *(G-16182)*
Archway Marketing Services Inc 440 572-0725
20770 Westwood Dr Strongsville (44149) *(G-17444)*
Archways Brookville Inc 513 367-2649
375 Industrial Dr Harrison (45030) *(G-11791)*
Arco Heating & AC Co (PA) 216 663-3211
5325 Naiman Pkwy Ste J Solon (44139) *(G-16976)*
Arctech Fabricating Inc (PA) 937 525-9353
1317 Lagonda Ave Springfield (45503) *(G-17149)*
Arctic Express Inc 614 876-4008
4277 Lyman Dr Hilliard (43026) *(G-11879)*
Arden Courts of Akron Bath, Akron Also called Hcr Manorcare Med Svcs Fla LLC *(G-259)*
Arden Courts of Anderson Twp., Cincinnati Also called Hcr Manorcare Med Svcs Fla LLC *(G-3747)*
Arden Courts of Bainbridge, Chagrin Falls Also called Manor Care of America Inc *(G-2724)*
Arden Courts of Parma, North Royalton Also called Hcr Manorcare Med Svcs Fla LLC *(G-15494)*
Arden Crts Manorcare Hlth Svcs, Westlake Also called Hcr Manorcare Med Svcs Fla LLC *(G-19489)*
Ardent Mills LLC 614 274-2545
4200 Sullivant Ave Columbus (43228) *(G-7039)*
Ardent Technologies Inc 937 312-1345
6234 Far Hills Ave Dayton (45459) *(G-9342)*
Ardmore Inc 330 535-2601
981 E Market St Akron (44305) *(G-81)*
Ardmore Logistics, Westlake Also called Ardmore Power Logistics LLC *(G-19461)*
Ardmore Power Logistics LLC 216 502-0640
24610 Detroit Rd Ste 1200 Westlake (44145) *(G-19461)*
Ardus Medical Inc 855 592-7387
9407 Kenwood Rd Blue Ash (45242) *(G-1535)*
Area Agency On Aging, Reno Also called Buckeye Hills-Hck Vly Reg Dev *(G-16421)*
Area Agency On Aging Planni 800 258-7277
40 W 2nd St Ste 400 Dayton (45402) *(G-9343)*
Area Agency On Aging Dst 7 Inc (PA) 800 582-7277
160 Dorsey Dr Rio Grande (45674) *(G-16546)*
Area Agency On Aging Dst 7 Inc. 740 446-7000
1167 State Route 160 Gallipolis (45631) *(G-11308)*
Area Agency On Aging P S A 2, Dayton Also called Area Agency On Aging Planni *(G-9343)*
Area Agency On Aging Reg 9 Inc 740 439-4478
1730 Southgate Pkwy Cambridge (43725) *(G-2096)*

Area Energy & Electric Inc.....937 642-0386
19255 Smokey Rd Marysville (43040) *(G-13606)*
Area Energy & Electric Inc (PA).....937 498-4784
2001 Commerce Dr Sidney (45365) *(G-16913)*
Area Office On Aging of Nwstrn.....419 382-0624
2155 Arlington Ave Toledo (43609) *(G-17758)*
Area Temps Inc.....216 227-8200
14801 Detroit Ave Lakewood (44107) *(G-12471)*
Area Temps Inc (PA).....216 781-5350
4511 Rockside Rd Ste 190 Independence (44131) *(G-12187)*
Area Temps Inc.....216 518-2000
15689 Broadway Ave Maple Heights (44137) *(G-13400)*
Area Wide Protective, North Canton *Also called Awp Inc (G-15327)*
Area Wide Protective Inc.....513 321-9889
9500 Le Saint Dr Fairfield (45014) *(G-10820)*
Area Wide Protective Inc.....614 272-7840
2439 Scioto Harper Dr Columbus (43204) *(G-7040)*
Arena Management Holdings LLC.....513 421-4111
100 Broadway St Cincinnati (45202) *(G-3045)*
Arensberg Home Health, Newark *Also called George W Arensberg Phrm Inc (G-15169)*
Arett Sales Corp.....937 552-2005
1261 Brukner Dr Troy (45373) *(G-18348)*
Argo-Hytos Inc.....419 353-6070
1835 N Research Dr Bowling Green (43402) *(G-1758)*
Argus International Inc.....513 852-1010
4240 Airport Rd Ste 300 Cincinnati (45226) *(G-3046)*
Aris Horticulture Inc (PA).....330 745-2143
115 3rd St Se Barberton (44203) *(G-953)*
Arise Incorporated.....440 746-8860
7000 S Edgerton Rd # 100 Brecksville (44141) *(G-1814)*
Aristocrat Berea Skilled, Berea *Also called Front Leasing Co LLC (G-1460)*
Aristocrat W Nursing Hm Corp.....216 252-7730
4401 W 150th St Cleveland (44135) *(G-5066)*
Ark Foundation of Dayton.....937 256-2759
2002 S Smithville Rd Dayton (45420) *(G-9344)*
ARKY BOOK STORE, Dayton *Also called Ark Foundation of Dayton (G-9344)*
Arledge Construction Inc (PA).....614 732-4258
2460 Performance Way Columbus (43207) *(G-7041)*
Arlette Child Family Rese, Cincinnati *Also called University of Cincinnati (G-4779)*
Arlington Care Ctr.....740 344-0303
98 S 30th St Newark (43055) *(G-15143)*
Arlington Contact Lens Svc Inc.....614 921-9894
4265 Diplomacy Dr Columbus (43228) *(G-7042)*
Arlington Court Nursing (PA).....614 545-5502
1605 Nw Prof Plz Upper Arlington (43220) *(G-18547)*
Arlington Court Skilled, Upper Arlington *Also called Arlington Court Nursing (G-18547)*
Arlington Memorial Grdns Assn.....513 521-7003
2145 Compton Rd Cincinnati (45231) *(G-3047)*
Arlington Towing Inc.....614 488-2006
2354 Wood Ave Columbus (43221) *(G-7043)*
Arlington-Blaine Lumber Co, Delaware *Also called Khempco Bldg Sup Co Ltd Partnr (G-10113)*
Arlingworth Home Health Inc.....614 659-0961
6479 Reflections Dr # 100 Dublin (43017) *(G-10255)*
Arlitt Child Development Ctr.....513 556-3802
44 W Corry St Cincinnati (45219) *(G-3048)*
Arlo Aluminum & Steel, Dayton *Also called Alro Steel Corporation (G-9323)*
Armada Ltd.....614 505-7256
23 Clairedan Dr Powell (43065) *(G-16324)*
Armaly Brands, London *Also called Armaly LLC (G-12992)*
Armaly LLC.....740 852-3621
110 W 1st St London (43140) *(G-12992)*
Armco Association Park.....513 695-3980
1223 N State Route 741 Lebanon (45036) *(G-12589)*
ARMCO PARK, Lebanon *Also called Armco Association Park (G-12589)*
Armor Paving & Sealing.....614 751-6900
6900 Americana Pkwy Reynoldsburg (43068) *(G-16429)*
Arms Trucking Co Inc (PA).....800 362-1343
14818 Mayfield Rd Huntsburg (44046) *(G-12156)*
Armstrong Cable Services, North Lima *Also called Armstrong Utilities Inc (G-15396)*
Armstrong Steel Erectors Inc.....740 345-4503
50 S 4th St Newark (43055) *(G-15144)*
Armstrong Utilities Inc.....740 894-3886
9651 County Road 1 South Point (45680) *(G-17080)*
Armstrong Utilities Inc.....330 758-6411
9328 Woodworth Rd North Lima (44452) *(G-15396)*
Army & Air Force Exchange Svc.....937 257-2928
2439 Schlatter Dr Dayton (45433) *(G-9255)*
Army & Air Force Exchange Svc.....937 257-7736
5215 Thurlow St Ste 2 Dayton (45433) *(G-9256)*
Arnold's Landscaping, Ontario *Also called Dta Inc (G-15687)*
Arnolds Home Improvement LLC.....734 847-9600
1770 Premainsville Toledo (43613) *(G-17759)*
Around Clock Home Care.....440 350-2547
7757 Auburn Rd Ste 6 Painesville (44077) *(G-15835)*
Arras Group Inc.....216 621-1601
1151 N Marginal Rd Cleveland (44114) *(G-5067)*
Arrow Electronics Inc.....440 498-3617
5440 Naiman Pkwy Solon (44139) *(G-16977)*
Arrow Electronics Inc.....440 498-6400
6675 Parkland Blvd Solon (44139) *(G-16978)*
Arrow Globl Asset Dspstion Inc.....614 328-4100
1120 Morrison Rd Ste A Gahanna (43230) *(G-11233)*
Arrow Industrial Supply, Sunbury *Also called J & J Entps Westerville Inc (G-17557)*
Arrowhead Transport Co.....330 638-2900
2555 Greenville Rd Cortland (44410) *(G-9072)*
ARS Ohio LLC.....513 327-7645
947 Sundance Dr Cincinnati (45233) *(G-3049)*
ARS Rescue Rooter Inc.....440 842-8494
4547 Hinckley Industrial Cleveland (44109) *(G-5068)*
Arslanian Bros Crpt Rug Clg Co.....216 271-6888
19499 Miles Rd Warrensville Heights (44128) *(G-18931)*
Arslanian Brothers Company, Warrensville Heights *Also called Arslanian Bros Crpt Rug Clg Co (G-18931)*
Arszman & Lyons LLC.....513 527-4900
9933 Alliance Rd Ste 2 Blue Ash (45242) *(G-1536)*
Art Hauser Insurance Inc.....513 745-9200
8260 Northcreek Dr # 200 Cincinnati (45236) *(G-3050)*
Art Wall, Strongsville *Also called Dwa Mrkting Prmtional Pdts LLC (G-17457)*
Art-American Printing Plates.....216 241-4420
1138 W 9th St Fl 4 Cleveland (44113) *(G-5069)*
Arthur G James Cancer.....614 293-4878
300 W 10th Ave Ste 519 Columbus (43210) *(G-7044)*
Arthur G James Cancer Hospital.....614 293-3300
300 W 10th Ave Columbus (43210) *(G-7045)*
Arthur J Gallagher & Co.....513 977-3100
201 E 4th St Ste 99 Cincinnati (45202) *(G-3051)*
Arthur Middleton Capital Holdn.....330 966-3033
8000 Freedom Ave Nw Canton (44720) *(G-2245)*
Arthur Middleton Capital Holdn (PA).....330 966-9000
8000 Freedom Ave Nw North Canton (44720) *(G-15326)*
Artis Senior Living.....513 229-7450
6200 Snider Rd Mason (45040) *(G-13664)*
Artistic Dance Enterprises.....614 761-2882
2665 Farmers Dr Columbus (43235) *(G-7046)*
Arts and Exhibitions Intl LLC.....330 995-9300
10145 Philipp Pkwy D Streetsboro (44241) *(G-17407)*
ARTSWAVE, Cincinnati *Also called Cincinnati Institute Fine Arts (G-3312)*
Arvind Sagar Inc.....614 428-8800
2880 Airport Dr Columbus (43219) *(G-7047)*
Arysen Inc.....440 230-4400
5005 Rockside Rd Ste 600 Independence (44131) *(G-12188)*
As Automotive Systems, Valley City *Also called Luk-Aftermarket Service Inc (G-18620)*
As Logistics Inc (HQ).....513 863-4627
101 Knightsbridge Dr Hamilton (45011) *(G-11693)*
ASAP Homecare Inc.....330 674-3306
31 N Mad Anthony St Millersburg (44654) *(G-14585)*
ASAP Homecare Inc.....330 491-0700
4150 Belden Village St Nw Canton (44718) *(G-2246)*
ASAP Homecare Inc (PA).....330 334-7027
1 Park Centre Dr Ste 107 Wadsworth (44281) *(G-18748)*
ASAP Homecare Inc.....330 263-4733
133 Beall Ave Wooster (44691) *(G-19829)*
Asbuilt Construction Ltd.....937 550-4900
29 Eagle Ct Franklin (45005) *(G-11149)*
ASC Group Inc (PA).....614 268-2514
800 Freeway Dr N Ste 101 Columbus (43229) *(G-7048)*
ASC of Cincinnati Inc.....513 886-7100
4028 Binion Way Lebanon (45036) *(G-12590)*
Ascendtech Inc.....216 458-1101
4772 E 355th St Willoughby (44094) *(G-19645)*
Asci, Dublin *Also called American Systems Cnsulting Inc (G-10252)*
Asd Specialty Healthcare LLC.....513 682-3600
9075 Centre Pointe Dr West Chester (45069) *(G-19022)*
Aset Corporation (PA).....937 890-8881
407 Corporate Center Dr Vandalia (45377) *(G-18659)*
Asfoura, Jehad MD, Canton *Also called Luis F Soto MD (G-2441)*
Ash Craft Industries Inc.....440 224-2177
5959 Green Rd Ashtabula (44004) *(G-711)*
Ashford Trs Lessee LLC.....937 436-2400
300 Prestige Pl Miamisburg (45342) *(G-14272)*
Ashland City School District.....419 289-7967
850 Jackson Dr Ashland (44805) *(G-652)*
Ashland Cleaning LLC.....419 281-1747
48 W Main St Ashland (44805) *(G-653)*
Ashland Cleaning LLC.....419 281-1747
48 W Main St Ashland (44805) *(G-654)*
Ashland Cnty Council On Aging.....419 281-1477
240 E 3rd St Ashland (44805) *(G-655)*
Ashland Comfort Control Inc (PA).....419 281-0144
805 E Main St Ashland (44805) *(G-656)*
Ashland Distribution, Twinsburg *Also called Nexeo Solutions LLC (G-18451)*
Ashland Distribution, Dublin *Also called Ashland LLC (G-10256)*
Ashland Distribution, Cleveland *Also called Ashland LLC (G-5070)*
Ashland Distribution, Ashland *Also called Ashland LLC (G-658)*
Ashland Golf Club.....419 289-2917
1333 Center St Ashland (44805) *(G-657)*
Ashland LLC.....614 232-8510
802 Harmon Ave Columbus (43223) *(G-7049)*
Ashland LLC.....614 276-6144
3849 Fisher Rd Columbus (43228) *(G-7050)*

Ashland LLC 614 790-3333
5200 Blazer Pkwy Dublin (43017) ***(G-10256)***
Ashland LLC 216 961-4690
2191 W 110th St Cleveland (44102) ***(G-5070)***
Ashland LLC 216 883-8200
4600 E 71st St Cleveland (44125) ***(G-5071)***
Ashland LLC 419 289-9588
1745 Cottage St Ashland (44805) ***(G-658)***
Ashland Performance Materials, Columbus *Also called Ashland LLC* ***(G-7049)***
Ashland Railway Inc 419 525-2822
803 N Main St Mansfield (44902) ***(G-13262)***
Ashley Enterprises LLC (PA) 330 726-5790
1419 Boardman Canfield Rd Boardman (44512) ***(G-1737)***
Ashley Place Health Care Inc 330 793-3010
5291 Ashley Cir Youngstown (44515) ***(G-20105)***
Ashtabula Area City School Dst 440 992-1221
5921 Gerald Rd Ashtabula (44004) ***(G-712)***
Ashtabula Board of Mental, Ashtabula *Also called Happy Hearts School* ***(G-746)***
Ashtabula Broadcasting Station 440 993-2126
3226 Jefferson Rd Ashtabula (44004) ***(G-713)***
Ashtabula Chemical Corp 440 998-0100
4606 State Rd Ashtabula (44004) ***(G-714)***
Ashtabula Clinic Inc (PA) 440 997-6980
2422 Lake Ave Ashtabula (44004) ***(G-715)***
Ashtabula Cnty Chldren Svcs Bd, Ashtabula *Also called County of Ashtabula* ***(G-739)***
Ashtabula Cnty Eductl Svc Ctr 440 576-4085
4200 State Rd Jefferson (44047) ***(G-12328)***
Ashtabula Community Counseling 440 998-6032
2801 C Ct Unit 2 Ashtabula (44004) ***(G-716)***
Ashtabula County Commissioners 440 576-2816
186 E Satin St Jefferson (44047) ***(G-12329)***
Ashtabula County Commissioners 440 994-1206
2924 Donahoe Dr Ashtabula (44004) ***(G-717)***
Ashtabula County Commnty Actn (PA) 440 997-1721
6920 Austinburg Rd Ashtabula (44004) ***(G-718)***
Ashtabula County Commnty Actn 440 593-6441
327 Mill St Conneaut (44030) ***(G-9037)***
Ashtabula County Commnty Actn 440 576-6911
32 E Jefferson St Jefferson (44047) ***(G-12330)***
Ashtabula County Commnty Actn 440 993-7716
4510 Main Ave Ashtabula (44004) ***(G-719)***
Ashtabula County Commnty Actn 440 997-5957
3215 Lake Ave Ashtabula (44004) ***(G-720)***
Ashtabula County Community 440 997-1721
6920 Austinburg Rd Ashtabula (44004) ***(G-721)***
ASHTABULA COUNTY FAMILY Y, Ashtabula *Also called YMCA of Ashtabula County Inc* ***(G-768)***
Ashtabula County Highway Dept, Jefferson *Also called Ashtabula County Commissioners* ***(G-12329)***
Ashtabula County Medical Ctr (PA) 440 997-2262
2420 Lake Ave Ashtabula (44004) ***(G-722)***
Ashtabula County Medical Ctr 440 997-6960
2422 Lake Ave Ashtabula (44004) ***(G-723)***
Ashtabula County Residential I (PA) 440 593-6404
29 Parrish Rd Conneaut (44030) ***(G-9038)***
Ashtabula County V A Clinic, Ashtabula *Also called Veterans Health Administration* ***(G-766)***
Ashtabula Dental Associates 440 992-3146
5005 State Rd Ashtabula (44004) ***(G-724)***
Ashtabula Job and Family Svcs 440 994-2020
2924 Donahoe Dr Ashtabula (44004) ***(G-725)***
Ashtabula Rgional Hm Hlth Svcs 440 992-4663
3949 Jefferson Rd Ashtabula (44004) ***(G-726)***
Ashtabula Stevedore Company 440 964-7186
1149 E 5th St Ashtabula (44004) ***(G-727)***
Ashtabula Welfare Department, Ashtabula *Also called Ashtabula County Commissioners* ***(G-717)***
Ask Childrens, Akron *Also called Childrens Hosp Med Ctr Akron* ***(G-136)***
Asm International 440 338-5151
9639 Kinsman Rd Novelty (44073) ***(G-15601)***
Aspen Community Living 614 880-6000
2021 E Dublin Granville R Columbus (43229) ***(G-7051)***
Aspen Management Usa LLC (PA) 419 281-3367
1566 County Road 1095 Ashland (44805) ***(G-659)***
Aspen Woodside Village 440 439-8666
19455 Rockside Rd Ofc Cleveland (44146) ***(G-5072)***
Aspire Energy of Ohio LLC (HQ) 330 682-7726
300 Tracy Bridge Rd Orrville (44667) ***(G-15764)***
Aspire Home Healthcare of Ohio, Dublin *Also called Nightingale Home Healthcare* ***(G-10409)***
Asplundh Construction Corp 614 532-5224
481 Schrock Rd Columbus (43229) ***(G-7052)***
Asplundh Tree Expert Co 740 435-4300
4362 Glenn Hwy Cambridge (43725) ***(G-2097)***
Asplundh Tree Expert LLC 740 467-1028
12488 Lancaster St # 94 Millersport (43046) ***(G-14629)***
Assembly Center 800 582-1099
913 Lebanon St Monroe (45050) ***(G-14687)***
Asset Solutions, Cincinnati *Also called Loth Inc* ***(G-3995)***
Assisted Care By Black Stone, Moraine *Also called Black Stone Cincinnati LLC* ***(G-14754)***
Assisted Care By Black Stone, Cincinnati *Also called Black Stone Cincinnati LLC* ***(G-3112)***
Assisted Living Apartments, Lorain *Also called Autumn Aegis Inc* ***(G-13015)***
Assisted Living Concepts Inc 419 586-2484
1506 Meadowview Dr Ofc Celina (45822) ***(G-2635)***
Assisted Living Concepts Inc 740 450-2744
3784 Frazeysburg Rd Ofc Zanesville (43701) ***(G-20443)***
Assisted Living Concepts LLC 419 224-6327
1070 Gloria Ave Ofc Lima (45805) ***(G-12742)***
Assisted Living Facilities, Chillicothe *Also called Traditions of Chillicothe* ***(G-2890)***
Assistnce In Mktg Columbus Inc 614 583-2100
1 Easton Oval Ste 100 Columbus (43219) ***(G-7053)***
Assoc Dvlpmtly Disabled (PA) 614 486-4361
769 Brooksedge Blvd Westerville (43081) ***(G-19365)***
Assoc Dvlpmtly Disabled 614 447-0606
1915 E Cooke Rd Columbus (43224) ***(G-7054)***
Associated Eye Care, Toledo *Also called Regency Park Eye Associates* ***(G-18146)***
Associated Imaging Corporation 419 517-0500
3830 Woodley Rd Ste A Toledo (43606) ***(G-17760)***
Associated Materials LLC 614 985-4611
640 Dearborn Park Ln Columbus (43085) ***(G-7055)***
Associated Materials LLC (HQ) 330 929-1811
3773 State Rd Cuyahoga Falls (44223) ***(G-9161)***
Associated Materials Group Inc (PA) 330 929-1811
3773 State Rd Cuyahoga Falls (44223) ***(G-9162)***
Associated Mtls Holdings LLC 330 929-1811
3773 State Rd Cuyahoga Falls (44223) ***(G-9163)***
Associated Paper Stock Inc (PA) 330 549-5311
11510 South Ave North Lima (44452) ***(G-15397)***
Associated Press 614 885-3444
1103 Schrock Rd Ste 300 Columbus (43229) ***(G-7056)***
Associated Specialists 937 208-7272
7707 Paragon Rd Ste 101 Dayton (45459) ***(G-9345)***
Associated Steel Company Inc 216 475-8000
18200 Miles Rd Cleveland (44128) ***(G-5073)***
Associates In Dermatology Inc (PA) 440 249-0274
26908 Detroit Rd Ste 103 Westlake (44145) ***(G-19462)***
Association For Middle Lvl Edu 614 895-4730
4151 Executive Pkwy # 300 Westerville (43081) ***(G-19366)***
Association of Prosthodontics 614 885-2022
7227 N High St Ste 1 Worthington (43085) ***(G-19942)***
Assocted Ctract Laser Surgeons 419 693-4444
2740 Navarre Ave Oregon (43616) ***(G-15724)***
Assumption Village 330 549-2434
9800 Market St North Lima (44452) ***(G-15398)***
Assuramed Inc (HQ) 330 963-6998
1810 Summit Commerce Park Twinsburg (44087) ***(G-18393)***
Assurant Employee Benefits, Cincinnati *Also called Union Security Insurance Co* ***(G-4727)***
Assured Health Care Inc 937 294-2803
1250 W Dorothy Ln Ste 200 Dayton (45409) ***(G-9346)***
Assured Hlth Care HM Care Svcs, Dayton *Also called Assured Health Care Inc* ***(G-9346)***
Assured Information SEC Inc 937 427-9720
3500 Pentagon Blvd # 310 Beavercreek (45431) ***(G-1148)***
AST, Miamisburg *Also called Advanced Service Tech LLC* ***(G-14268)***
AST Environmental Inc 937 743-0002
70 Commercial Way Springboro (45066) ***(G-17115)***
Aston Oaks Golf Club 513 467-0070
1 Aston Oaks Dr North Bend (45052) ***(G-15317)***
Astoria Place Columbus LLC 614 228-5900
44 S Souder Ave Columbus (43222) ***(G-7057)***
Astoria Place of Barnesville, Barnesville *Also called Barnesville Healthcare Rehab* ***(G-987)***
Astoria Place of Clyde LLC 419 547-9595
700 Helen St Clyde (43410) ***(G-6809)***
Astro Aluminum Enterprises Inc 330 755-1414
65 Main St Struthers (44471) ***(G-17526)***
Astute Inc (PA) 614 508-6100
2400 Corp Exchange Dr # 150 Columbus (43231) ***(G-7058)***
Astute Solutions, Columbus *Also called Astute Inc* ***(G-7058)***
Asurint, Cleveland *Also called One Source Technology LLC* ***(G-6205)***
Asv Services LLC 216 797-1701
27801 Euclid Ave Ste 420 Euclid (44132) ***(G-10743)***
Asw Akron Logistic, Canton *Also called Asw Global LLC* ***(G-2247)***
Asw Global LLC (PA) 330 733-6291
3375 Gilchrist Rd Mogadore (44260) ***(G-14670)***
Asw Global LLC 330 899-1003
2150 International Pkwy Canton (44720) ***(G-2247)***
Asw Global LLC 330 798-5184
3325 Gilchrist Rd Mogadore (44260) ***(G-14671)***
Asw Supply Chain Service, Mogadore *Also called Asw Global LLC* ***(G-14671)***
Asymmetric Technologies LLC 614 725-5310
1395 Grandview Ave Ste 3 Columbus (43212) ***(G-7059)***
At Hospitality LLC 513 527-9962
5375 Medpace Way Cincinnati (45227) ***(G-3052)***
At Systems, Columbus *Also called Garda CL Great Lakes Inc* ***(G-7726)***
At T Broadband & Intern 614 839-4271
P.O. Box 182552 Columbus (43218) ***(G-7060)***
AT&T Corp 937 320-9648
4467 Walnut St Beavercreek (45440) ***(G-1226)***
AT&T Corp 330 337-3505
1098 E State St Ste A Salem (44460) ***(G-16687)***
AT&T Corp 614 223-5318
814 Green Crest Dr Westerville (43081) ***(G-19367)***
AT&T Corp 614 798-3898
7497 Sawmill Rd Dublin (43016) ***(G-10257)***

ALPHABETIC

AT&T Corp......614 271-8911
10654 Brettridge Dr Powell (43065) *(G-16325)*
AT&T Corp......614 539-0165
4108 Buckeye Pkwy Grove City (43123) *(G-11532)*
AT&T Corp......614 223-6513
3419 Indianola Ave Columbus (43214) *(G-7061)*
AT&T Corp......740 455-3042
3575 Maple Ave Ste 502 Zanesville (43701) *(G-20444)*
AT&T Corp......740 549-4546
8601 Columbus Pike Lewis Center (43035) *(G-12667)*
AT&T Corp......330 665-3100
3890 Medina Rd Ste B Akron (44333) *(G-82)*
AT&T Corp......330 505-4200
5412 Youngstown Warren Rd Niles (44446) *(G-15282)*
AT&T Corp......440 951-5309
34808 Euclid Ave Willoughby (44094) *(G-19646)*
AT&T Corp......937 372-9945
767 Industrial Blvd Xenia (45385) *(G-20042)*
AT&T Corp......614 223-8236
150 E Gay St Ste 4a Columbus (43215) *(G-7062)*
AT&T Corp......216 298-1513
45 Erieview Plz Ste 1360 Cleveland (44114) *(G-5074)*
AT&T Corp......614 575-3044
2583 S Hamilton Rd Columbus (43232) *(G-7063)*
AT&T Corp......330 752-7776
45 E Market St Akron (44308) *(G-83)*
AT&T Corp......614 851-2400
1649 Georgesville Sq Dr Columbus (43228) *(G-7064)*
AT&T Corp......513 741-1700
3612 Stonecreek Blvd Cincinnati (45251) *(G-3053)*
AT&T Corp......216 672-0809
3530 Ridge Rd Cleveland (44102) *(G-5075)*
AT&T Corp......513 629-5000
221 E 4th St Cincinnati (45202) *(G-3054)*
AT&T Corp......330 723-1717
1088 N Court St Medina (44256) *(G-14037)*
AT&T Corp......614 337-3902
4300 Appian Way Columbus (43230) *(G-7065)*
AT&T Datacomm LLC......614 223-5799
814 Green Crest Dr Westerville (43081) *(G-19368)*
AT&T Government Solutions Inc......937 306-3030
2940 Presidential Dr # 390 Beavercreek (45324) *(G-1149)*
AT&T Inc......937 320-9648
4467 Walnut St Ste A120 Beavercreek (45440) *(G-1227)*
AT&T Mobility LLC......614 291-2500
1555 Olentangy River Rd Columbus (43212) *(G-7066)*
AT&T Mobility LLC......330 565-5000
8089 South Ave Youngstown (44512) *(G-20106)*
AT&T Mobility LLC......440 846-3232
17970 Royalton Rd Strongsville (44136) *(G-17445)*
AT&T Mobility LLC......216 382-0825
25309 Cedar Rd Cleveland (44124) *(G-5076)*
AT&T Mobility LLC......419 516-0602
2421 Elida Rd Lima (45805) *(G-12743)*
AT&T Mobility LLC......513 381-6800
1605 Western Ave Cincinnati (45214) *(G-3055)*
AT&T Mobility LLC......937 439-4900
199 E Alex Bell Rd # 418 Centerville (45459) *(G-2674)*
AT&T Ohio, Cleveland *Also called Ohio Bell Telephone Company (G-6185)*
AT&T Services Inc......937 456-2330
1338 N Barron St Eaton (45320) *(G-10553)*
Atc Associates, Cincinnati *Also called Atc Group Services LLC (G-3056)*
Atc Group Services LLC......513 771-2112
11121 Canal Rd Cincinnati (45241) *(G-3056)*
Atco Inc......740 592-6659
21 Campbell St Athens (45701) *(G-773)*
Atel, Marion *Also called Aqua Tech Envmtl Labs Inc (G-13523)*
Athens Bicycle Club, Athens *Also called Joey Boyle (G-795)*
ATHENS COUNTRY CLUB, Athens *Also called Athens Golf & Country Club (G-774)*
Athens County Childrens Svcs, Athens *Also called County of Athens (G-781)*
Athens County Emrgncy Med Svcs......740 797-9560
36 N Plains Rd Ste 2 The Plains (45780) *(G-17664)*
Athens Golf & Country Club (PA)......740 592-1655
7606 Country Club Rd Athens (45701) *(G-774)*
Athens Health Partners, The Plains *Also called Lindley Inn (G-17665)*
Athens Medical Associates LLC......740 594-8819
75 Hospital Dr Ste 216 Athens (45701) *(G-775)*
Athens Mold and Machine Inc......740 593-6613
1461 Industrial Pkwy Akron (44310) *(G-84)*
Athens OH 1013 LLC......740 589-5839
924 E State St Athens (45701) *(G-776)*
Athens-Hcking Cnty Recycl Ctrs......740 797-4208
5991 Industrial Park Rd Athens (45701) *(G-777)*
Athletes In Action Sports (HQ)......937 352-1000
651 Taylor Dr Xenia (45385) *(G-20043)*
Athletic Dept, Oberlin *Also called Oberlin College (G-15655)*
Athletics Dept, Cincinnati *Also called University of Cincinnati (G-4771)*
ATI, Toledo *Also called Abbott Tool Inc (G-17738)*
ATI Aviation Services LLC......216 268-4888
12401 Taft Ave Cleveland (44108) *(G-5077)*
Atk Space Systems Inc......937 490-4121
1365 Technology Ct Beavercreek (45430) *(G-1228)*
Atkins & Stang Inc......513 242-8300
1031 Meta Dr Cincinnati (45237) *(G-3057)*
Atlantic Coastal Trucking......201 438-6500
222 E William St Delaware (43015) *(G-10072)*
Atlantic Fish & Distrg Co......330 454-1307
430 6th St Se Canton (44702) *(G-2248)*
Atlantic Food Distributors, Canton *Also called Atlantic Fish & Distrg Co (G-2248)*
Atlantic Foods Corp......513 772-3535
1999 Section Rd Cincinnati (45237) *(G-3058)*
Atlantic Greyhound Lines......513 721-4450
600 Vine St Ste 1400 Cincinnati (45202) *(G-3059)*
Atlantic Hospitality & MGT LLC......216 454-5450
26300 Chagrin Blvd Beachwood (44122) *(G-1052)*
Atlantic Triangle Trucking, Delaware *Also called Atlantic Coastal Trucking (G-10072)*
Atlantis Co Inc (PA)......888 807-3272
105 Ken Mar Indus Pkwy Cleveland (44147) *(G-5078)*
Atlantis Company, The, Cleveland *Also called Atlantis Co Inc (G-5078)*
Atlapac Corp......614 252-2121
2901 E 4th Ave Ste 5 Columbus (43219) *(G-7067)*
Atlas Advisors LLC......888 282-0873
1795 S High St Columbus (43207) *(G-7068)*
Atlas Bolt & Screw Company LLC (HQ)......419 289-6171
1628 Troy Rd Ashland (44805) *(G-660)*
Atlas Butler Heating & Cooling, Columbus *Also called Atlas Capital Services Inc (G-7069)*
Atlas Capital Services Inc (PA)......614 294-7373
4849 Evanswood Dr Columbus (43229) *(G-7069)*
Atlas Construction Company......614 475-4705
4672 Friendship Dr Columbus (43230) *(G-7070)*
Atlas Electrical Construction......440 323-5418
7974 Murray Ridge Rd Elyria (44035) *(G-10595)*
Atlas Fasteners For Cnstr, Ashland *Also called Atlas Bolt & Screw Company LLC (G-660)*
Atlas Home Moving & Storage......614 445-8831
1570 Integrity Dr E Columbus (43209) *(G-7071)*
Atlas Industrial Contrs LLC (HQ)......614 841-4500
5275 Sinclair Rd Columbus (43229) *(G-7072)*
Atlas Industries Inc......419 637-2117
401 Wall St Tiffin (44883) *(G-17671)*
Atlas Machine and Supply Inc......502 584-7262
4985 Provident Dr West Chester (45246) *(G-19190)*
Atlas Recycling Inc......800 837-1520
1420 Burton St Se Warren (44484) *(G-18818)*
Atlas Roofing Company......330 467-7683
4190 E 71st St Cleveland (44105) *(G-5079)*
Atlas Steel Products Co (PA)......330 425-1600
7990 Bavaria Rd Twinsburg (44087) *(G-18394)*
Atlas Towing Service......513 451-1854
5675 Glenway Ave Cincinnati (45238) *(G-3060)*
Atlasbooks, Ashland *Also called Bookmasters Inc (G-665)*
Atm Solutions Inc (PA)......513 742-4900
551 Northland Blvd Cincinnati (45240) *(G-3061)*
Atomic Credit Union Inc (PA)......740 289-5060
711 Beaver Creek Rd Piketon (45661) *(G-16109)*
Atos It Solutions and Svcs Inc......513 336-1000
4705 Duke Dr Mason (45040) *(G-13665)*
Atotech USA Inc......216 398-0550
1000 Harvard Ave Cleveland (44109) *(G-5080)*
Atria Senior Living Group Inc......513 923-3711
9191 Round Top Rd Ofc Cincinnati (45251) *(G-3062)*
Atrium Apparel Corporation......612 889-0959
188 Commerce Blvd Johnstown (43031) *(G-12335)*
Atrium Assembly Corporation, Johnstown *Also called Atrium Apparel Corporation (G-12335)*
Atrium Buying Corporation......740 966-8200
1010 Jackson Hole Dr # 100 Blacklick (43004) *(G-1500)*
Atrium Dialysis, Middletown *Also called Beck Dialysis LLC (G-14415)*
Atrium Health System (HQ)......937 499-5606
1 Medical Center Dr Middletown (45005) *(G-14473)*
Atrium Medical Center......937 499-9596
1 Medical Center Dr Middletown (45005) *(G-14474)*
Atrium Medical Center......513 420-5013
105 Mcknight Dr Middletown (45044) *(G-14414)*
Ats Group LLC......216 744-5757
5845 Harper Rd Solon (44139) *(G-16979)*
Ats Systems Oregon Inc......541 738-0932
425 Enterprise Dr Lewis Center (43035) *(G-12668)*
Ats Transportation Services, Cincinnati *Also called Advance Trnsp Systems Inc (G-2975)*
ATSG, Wilmington *Also called Air Transport Svcs Group Inc (G-19743)*
ATT, Cleveland *Also called AT&T Corp (G-5075)*
Attevo Inc......216 928-2800
24500 Chagrin Blvd # 300 Beachwood (44122) *(G-1053)*
Attitudes New Inc......330 856-1143
1543 Westview Dr Ne Warren (44483) *(G-18819)*
Attorneys-At-Law, Dayton *Also called Porter Wrght Morris Arthur LLP (G-9815)*
Attractions......740 592-5600
19 N Court St Athens (45701) *(G-778)*
Atwood Lake Park, Mineral City *Also called Muskingum Wtrshed Cnsrvncy Dst (G-14634)*
Atwood Mock Post 459, Burton *Also called American Legion (G-2059)*
Atwood Yacht Club Inc......330 735-2135
2637 Lodge Rd Sw Sherrodsville (44675) *(G-16905)*
Auburn Dairy Products Inc......614 488-2536
2200 Cardigan Ave Columbus (43215) *(G-7073)*

Auction Broadcasting Co LLC 419 872-0872
9797 Fremont Pike Perrysburg (43551) ***(G-15972)***
Auction Services Inc 614 497-2000
4700 Groveport Rd Obetz (43207) ***(G-15663)***
Audi Willoughby, Mentor *Also called Stoddard Imported Cars Inc* ***(G-14245)***
Audio-Technica US Inc (HQ) 330 686-2600
1221 Commerce Dr Stow (44224) ***(G-17353)***
Auditor's Ofiice, Coshocton *Also called City of Coshocton* ***(G-9090)***
Auditors Office, Hamilton *Also called Butler County of Ohio* ***(G-11696)***
Audrich Inc 419 483-6225
1 Audrich Sq Bellevue (44811) ***(G-1403)***
Auglaize County Board of Mr/Dd, New Bremen *Also called County of Auglaize* ***(G-15017)***
August Corso Sons Inc 419 626-0765
3404 Milan Rd Sandusky (44870) ***(G-16727)***
August Food & Wine LLC 513 421-2020
1214 Vine St Cincinnati (45202) ***(G-3063)***
August Groh & Sons Inc 513 821-0090
8832 Reading Rd Cincinnati (45215) ***(G-3064)***
Augustine Zeller Group, Perrysburg *Also called Azg Inc* ***(G-15974)***
Aultcare Corp 330 363-6360
2600 6th St Sw Canton (44710) ***(G-2249)***
Aultcare Insurance Company 330 363-6360
2600 6th St Sw Canton (44710) ***(G-2250)***
Aultcomp Inc 330 830-4919
2458 Lincoln Way E Massillon (44646) ***(G-13788)***
Aultman Health Foundation 330 305-6999
6100 Whipple Ave Nw Canton (44720) ***(G-2251)***
Aultman Health Foundation 330 682-3010
832 S Main St Orrville (44667) ***(G-15765)***
Aultman Health Foundation 330 875-6050
1925 Williamsburg Way Ne Louisville (44641) ***(G-13094)***
Aultman Health Foundation (PA) 330 452-9911
2600 6th St Sw Canton (44710) ***(G-2252)***
Aultman Hospital (PA) 330 452-9911
2600 6th St Sw Canton (44710) ***(G-2253)***
Aultman Hospital 330 452-9911
2600 6th St Sw Canton (44710) ***(G-2254)***
Aultman Hospital 330 363-6262
2600 6th St Sw Canton (44710) ***(G-2255)***
Aultman Hospital 330 452-2273
125 Dartmouth Ave Sw Canton (44710) ***(G-2256)***
Aultman North Canton Med Group (PA) 330 433-1200
6046 Whipple Ave Nw Canton (44720) ***(G-2257)***
Aultman North Inc 330 305-6999
6100 Whipple Ave Nw Canton (44720) ***(G-2258)***
AULTMAN ORRVILLE HOSPITAL, Orrville *Also called Orrville Hospital Foundation* ***(G-15779)***
Auman Mahan & Furry A Legal 937 223-6003
110 N Main St Ste 1000 Dayton (45402) ***(G-9347)***
Auntie Jacque Childcare, Steubenville *Also called Jacqueline Kumi-Sakyi* ***(G-17322)***
Aunties Attic 740 548-5059
1550 Lewis Center Rd G Lewis Center (43035) ***(G-12669)***
Aur Group Financial Credit Un 513 737-0508
1401 Nw Washington Blvd Hamilton (45013) ***(G-11694)***
Aurgroup Financial Credit Un 513 942-4422
8811 Holden Blvd Fairfield (45014) ***(G-10821)***
Aurora Hotel Partners LLC 330 562-0767
30 Shawnee Trl Aurora (44202) ***(G-826)***
Aurora Imaging Company 614 761-1390
344 Cramer Creek Ct Dublin (43017) ***(G-10258)***
Aurora Inn and Conference Ctr, Aurora *Also called Cerruti LLC* ***(G-834)***
Aurora Inn Hotel & Event Ctr, Aurora *Also called Aurora Hotel Partners LLC* ***(G-826)***
Aurora Manor Special Care 440 424-4000
101 S Bissell Rd Aurora (44202) ***(G-827)***
Aurora Wholesalers LLC (PA) 440 248-5200
31000 Aurora Rd Solon (44139) ***(G-16980)***
Aussiefit I LLC 614 755-4400
5929 E Main St Columbus (43213) ***(G-7074)***
Austin Building and Design Inc (HQ) 440 544-2600
6095 Parkland Blvd # 100 Cleveland (44124) ***(G-5081)***
Austin Company, The, Cleveland *Also called Austin Building and Design Inc* ***(G-5081)***
Austin Foam Plastics Inc 614 921-0824
2200 International St Columbus (43228) ***(G-7075)***
Austin Wods Rehabilitation Ctr, Youngstown *Also called Austin Woods Nursing Center* ***(G-20107)***
Austin Woods Nursing Center 330 792-7681
4780 Kirk Rd Youngstown (44515) ***(G-20107)***
Austintown Dairy Inc 330 629-6170
780 Bev Rd Youngstown (44512) ***(G-20108)***
Austintown Healthcare Center, Youngstown *Also called Communicare Health Svcs Inc* ***(G-20149)***
Authentic Food LLC 740 369-0377
535 Sunbury Rd Delaware (43015) ***(G-10073)***
Auto Additions Inc 614 899-9100
6001 Westerville Rd Westerville (43081) ***(G-19369)***
Auto Aftermarket Concepts 513 942-2535
1031 Redna Ter Cincinnati (45215) ***(G-3065)***
Auto Body Mill Run, Columbus *Also called Auto Body North Inc* ***(G-7076)***
Auto Body North Inc (PA) 614 436-3700
8675 N High St Columbus (43235) ***(G-7076)***
Auto Center USA Inc 513 683-4900
4544 Kings Water Dr Cincinnati (45249) ***(G-3066)***
Auto Concepts Cincinnatti LLC 513 769-4540
3428 Hauck Rd Ste I Cincinnati (45241) ***(G-3067)***
Auto Crushers, Canton *Also called Slesnick Iron & Metal Co* ***(G-2532)***
Auto Des Sys Inc 614 488-7984
3518 Riverside Dr Upper Arlington (43221) ***(G-18548)***
Auto Plus, Marietta *Also called Ieh Auto Parts LLC* ***(G-13454)***
Auto Warehousing Co Inc 330 824-5149
1950 Halloock Young Warren (44481) ***(G-18820)***
Auto Warehousing Co Inc 419 727-1534
4405 Chrysler Dr Toledo (43608) ***(G-17761)***
Auto-Owners Insurance Company 937 432-6740
1 Prestige Pl Ste 280 Miamisburg (45342) ***(G-14273)***
Auto-Owners Life Insurance Co 419 227-1452
2325 N Cole St Lima (45801) ***(G-12744)***
Autobody Supply Company, Columbus *Also called Finishmaster Inc* ***(G-7657)***
Automatic Data Processing Inc 216 447-1980
7007 E Pleasant Valley Rd Cleveland (44131) ***(G-5082)***
Automatic Data Processing Inc 614 212-4831
713 Brooksedge Plaza Dr Westerville (43081) ***(G-19370)***
Automation & Control Tech Ltd 419 661-6400
28210 Cedar Park Blvd Perrysburg (43551) ***(G-15973)***
Automotive Distributors Co Inc (PA) 614 476-1315
2981 Morse Rd Columbus (43231) ***(G-7077)***
Automotive Distributors Co Inc 330 785-7290
1329 E Archwood Ave Akron (44306) ***(G-85)***
Automotive Distributors Co Inc 216 398-2014
990 Valley Belt Dr Cleveland (44109) ***(G-5083)***
Automotive Distributors Whse, Columbus *Also called Automotive Distributors Co Inc* ***(G-7077)***
Automotive Div Of,, Cincinnati *Also called SGS North America Inc* ***(G-4507)***
Automotive Events Inc 440 356-1383
19111 Detroit Rd Ste 306 Rocky River (44116) ***(G-16570)***
Autonation Ford Amherst, Amherst *Also called Ed Mullinax Ford LLC* ***(G-591)***
Autonation Ford East, Wickliffe *Also called Mullinax East LLC* ***(G-19608)***
Autonation Ford North Canton, Canton *Also called Mullinax Ford North Canton Inc* ***(G-2468)***
Autumn, Bedford *Also called Legacy Consultant Pharmacy* ***(G-1316)***
Autumn Aegis Inc 440 282-6768
1130 Tower Blvd Ste A Lorain (44052) ***(G-13015)***
Autumn Health Care, Newark *Also called Alpha Nursing Homes Inc* ***(G-15142)***
Autumn Health Care, Coshocton *Also called Alpha Nursing Homes Inc* ***(G-9086)***
Autumn Health Care Inc 740 366-2321
23 Forry St Newark (43055) ***(G-15145)***
Autumn Hills Care Center Inc 330 652-2053
2565 Niles Vienna Rd Niles (44446) ***(G-15283)***
Autumn Industries Inc (PA) 330 372-5002
518 Perkins Jones Rd Ne Warren (44483) ***(G-18821)***
Autumn Years Nursing Center, Sabina *Also called Earley & Ross Ltd* ***(G-16615)***
Auxiliary Bd Fairview Gen Hosp 216 476-7000
18101 Lorain Ave Cleveland (44111) ***(G-5084)***
Auxiliary St Lukes Hospital 419 893-5911
5901 Monclova Rd Maumee (43537) ***(G-13884)***
Avalon Foodservice Inc 330 854-4551
1 Avalon Dr Canal Fulton (44614) ***(G-2140)***
Avalon Golf & Country Club 330 539-5008
761 Youngstown Kingsvlle Vienna (44473) ***(G-18735)***
Avalon Golf and Cntry CLB Inc 330 856-8898
1 American Way Ne Warren (44484) ***(G-18822)***
Avalon Holdings Corporation (PA) 330 856-8800
1 American Way Ne Warren (44484) ***(G-18823)***
Avalon Inn and Resort, Warren *Also called AIR Management Group LLC* ***(G-18814)***
Avalon Inn Services Inc 330 856-1900
9519 E Market St Warren (44484) ***(G-18824)***
Avalon Lakes Golf Inc (HQ) 330 856-8898
1 American Way Ne Warren (44484) ***(G-18825)***
Avalon Lakes Pro Shop, Warren *Also called Avalon Lakes Golf Inc* ***(G-18825)***
Avalon Precision Cast Co LLC 216 362-4100
15583 Brookpark Rd Brookpark (44142) ***(G-1936)***
Avalon Precision Metalsmiths, Brookpark *Also called Avalon Precision Cast Co LLC* ***(G-1930)***
Avalon Resort and Spa LLC 330 856-1900
9519 E Market St Warren (44484) ***(G-18826)***
Avanti Salon, Chesterland *Also called Mato Inc* ***(G-2799)***
Avantia Inc 216 901-9366
9655 Sweet Valley Dr # 1 Cleveland (44125) ***(G-5085)***
Avatar Management Services (PA) 330 963-3900
8157 Bavaria Dr E Macedonia (44056) ***(G-13187)***
Avatar Solutions, Macedonia *Also called Avatar Management Services* ***(G-13187)***
Avery Dennison Corporation 440 534-6000
8080 Norton Pkwy Mentor (44060) ***(G-14145)***
Avery Dennison Materials Group, Mentor *Also called Avery Dennison Corporation* ***(G-14145)***
AVI Food Systems Inc (PA) 330 372-6000
2590 Elm Rd Ne Warren (44483) ***(G-18827)***
AVI Food Systems Inc 740 452-9363
333 Richards Rd Zanesville (43701) ***(G-20445)***
AVI Food Systems Inc 440 255-3468
7710 Tyler Blvd Mentor (44060) ***(G-14146)***

ALPHABETIC

ALPHABETIC SECTION

AVI-Spl Employee..937 836-4787
  35 Rockridge Rd Ste B Englewood (45322) *(G-10697)*
Aviation Manufacturing Co Inc............................419 435-7448
  901 S Union St Fostoria (44830) *(G-11122)*
Aviation, Department of, Vandalia *Also called City of Dayton (G-18672)*
Avid Technologies Inc......................................330 487-0770
  2112 Case Pkwy Ste 1 Twinsburg (44087) *(G-18395)*
Avis Administration...937 898-2581
  3300 Valet Dr Vandalia (45377) *(G-18660)*
Avita Health System...419 468-7059
  955 Hosford Rd Galion (44833) *(G-11290)*
Avita Health System (PA)...................................419 468-4841
  269 Portland Way S Galion (44833) *(G-11291)*
Aviva Metals, Lorain *Also called National Bronze Mtls Ohio Inc (G-13063)*
Avizent, Dublin *Also called Frank Gates Service Company (G-10350)*
Avnet Inc...440 479-3607
  34201 Melinz Pkwy Unit D Eastlake (44095) *(G-10544)*
Avnet Inc...614 865-1400
  2800 Corp Exchange Dr # 160 Columbus (43231) *(G-7078)*
Avnet Inc...440 349-7600
  2000 Auburn Dr Ste 200 Beachwood (44122) *(G-1054)*
Avnet Computers, Eastlake *Also called Avnet Inc (G-10544)*
Avnet Computers, Columbus *Also called Avnet Inc (G-7078)*
Avnet Computers, Beachwood *Also called Avnet Inc (G-1054)*
Avon Lake Animal Care Center, Avon Lake *Also called Avon Lake Animal Clinic Inc (G-922)*
Avon Lake Animal Clinic Inc................................440 933-5297
  124 Miller Rd Avon Lake (44012) *(G-922)*
Avon Lake Generating Station, Avon Lake *Also called NRG Power Midwest LP (G-936)*
Avon Lake Sheet Metal Co..................................440 933-3505
  33574 Pin Oak Pkwy Avon Lake (44012) *(G-923)*
Avon Medical Offices, Avon *Also called Kaiser Foundation Hospitals (G-901)*
Avon Oaks Country Club....................................440 892-0660
  32300 Detroit Rd Ste A Avon (44011) *(G-876)*
Avon Oaks Nursing Home, Avon *Also called R & J Investment Co Inc (G-915)*
Avon Properties Inc...440 934-6217
  4141 Center Rd Avon (44011) *(G-877)*
Avondale Golf Club..440 934-4398
  3111 Moon Rd Avon (44011) *(G-878)*
Avondale Youth Center, Zanesville *Also called Muskingum County Adult and CHI (G-20505)*
AW Faber-Castell Usa Inc...................................216 643-4660
  9450 Allen Dr Ste B Cleveland (44125) *(G-5086)*
Aw Farrell Son Inc..513 334-0715
  745 Us Route 50 Milford (45150) *(G-14505)*
Awe Hospitality Group LLC.................................330 888-8836
  9652 N Bedford Rd Macedonia (44056) *(G-13188)*
Awis Designs, Amelia *Also called Interphace Phtgrphy Cmmnctions (G-581)*
Awl Transport Inc...330 899-3444
  4626 State Route 82 Mantua (44255) *(G-13384)*
Awms, Warren *Also called American Waste MGT Svcs Inc (G-18816)*
Awp Inc (PA)...330 677-7401
  4244 Mount Pleasant St Nw # 100 North Canton (44720) *(G-15327)*
Awrs LLC...888 611-2292
  10866 Newmarket Dr Cincinnati (45251) *(G-3068)*
Axa Advisors LLC..513 762-7705
  4000 Smith Rd Ste 300 Cincinnati (45209) *(G-3069)*
Axa Advisors LLC..216 621-7715
  1001 Lakeside Ave E # 1650 Cleveland (44114) *(G-5087)*
Axa Advisors LLC..614 985-3015
  7965 N High St Ste 140 Columbus (43235) *(G-7079)*
Axcess Rcvery Cr Solutions Inc............................513 229-6700
  4540 Cooper Rd Ste 305 Cincinnati (45242) *(G-3070)*
Axesspointe Cmnty Hlth Ctr Inc (PA).....................330 724-5471
  1400 S Arlington St # 38 Akron (44306) *(G-86)*
Axesspointe Community Hlth Ctr, Akron *Also called Axesspointe Cmnty Hlth Ctr Inc (G-86)*
Axia Consulting Inc...614 675-4050
  1391 W 5th Ave Ste 320 Columbus (43212) *(G-7080)*
Axiom Consulting, Blue Ash *Also called Axiom Product Development LLC (G-1537)*
Axiom Product Development LLC.........................513 791-2425
  4370 Creek Rd Blue Ash (45241) *(G-1537)*
Axis Advertising, Columbus *Also called Promohouse Inc (G-8571)*
Ayers Farms Inc...419 938-7707
  820 State Route 39 Perrysville (44864) *(G-16077)*
Ayers Service Group LLC...................................419 678-4811
  5215b State Route 118 Coldwater (45828) *(G-6827)*
Ayers-Sterrett Inc...419 238-5480
  222 N Market St Van Wert (45891) *(G-18628)*
Ayrshire Inc..440 286-9507
  191 Fifth Ave Chardon (44024) *(G-2740)*
Ayrshire Inc..440 992-0743
  1432 E 21st St Ashtabula (44004) *(G-728)*
Azalea Alabama Investment LLC.........................216 520-1250
  8111 Rockside Rd Ste 200 Cleveland (44125) *(G-5088)*
Azg Inc...419 724-3000
  423 E 2nd St Perrysburg (43551) *(G-15974)*
Azimuth Corporation..937 256-8571
  4027 Colonel Glenn Hwy # 230 Beavercreek Township (45431) *(G-1265)*
Aztec Plumbg, Milford *Also called Aztec Plumbing Inc (G-14506)*
Aztec Plumbing Inc...513 732-3320
  5989 Meijer Dr Ste 8 Milford (45150) *(G-14506)*

Aztec Services Group Inc..................................513 541-2002
  3814 William P Dooley Byp Cincinnati (45223) *(G-3071)*
B & A, Cuyahoga Falls *Also called Barrett & Associates Inc (G-9164)*
B & B Contrs & Developers Inc............................330 270-5020
  2781 Salt Springs Rd Youngstown (44509) *(G-20109)*
B & B Industries, Orient *Also called Kmj Leasing Ltd (G-15761)*
B & B Plastics Recyclers Inc................................614 409-2880
  3300 Lockbourne Rd Columbus (43207) *(G-7081)*
B & B Roofing Inc...740 772-4759
  150 Cooks Hill Rd Chillicothe (45601) *(G-2815)*
B & B Wrecking & Excvtg Inc...............................216 429-1700
  4510 E 71st St Ste 6 Cleveland (44105) *(G-5089)*
B & C COMMUNICATIONS, Columbus *Also called Comproducts Inc (G-7416)*
B & D Auto & Towing Inc...................................440 237-3737
  14290 State Rd Ste 1 North Royalton (44133) *(G-15481)*
B & D Concrete Footers Inc................................740 964-2294
  12897 National Rd Sw Etna (43062) *(G-10731)*
B & H Industries Inc...419 485-8373
  14020 Us Highway 20a Montpelier (43543) *(G-14736)*
B & I Hotel Management LLC...............................330 995-0200
  600 N Aurora Rd Aurora (44202) *(G-828)*
B & J Electrical Company Inc...............................513 351-7100
  6316 Wiehe Rd Cincinnati (45237) *(G-3072)*
B & L Agency LLC...740 373-8272
  1001 Pike St Ste 4 Marietta (45750) *(G-13434)*
B & L Transport Inc (PA)...................................866 848-2888
  3149 State Route 39 Millersburg (44654) *(G-14586)*
B & R Railroad Services, Cincinnati *Also called R W Godbey Railroad Services (G-4380)*
B & T Express Inc (PA)......................................330 549-0000
  400 Miley Rd North Lima (44452) *(G-15399)*
B and D Investment Partnership..........................937 233-6698
  7650 Waynetowne Blvd Dayton (45424) *(G-9348)*
B B M, Youngstown *Also called Bechtl Bldng Mntnc Crprtn of (G-20111)*
B C G Systems, Akron *Also called Bcg Systems That Work Inc (G-93)*
B C M, Cleveland *Also called Burton Carol Management (G-5160)*
B D G Wrap-Tite Inc..440 349-5400
  6200 Cochran Rd Solon (44139) *(G-16981)*
B D I, Cleveland *Also called Bearing Distributors Inc (G-5107)*
B D Transportation Inc.....................................937 773-9280
  9590 Looney Rd Piqua (45356) *(G-16135)*
B F G Federal Credit Union (PA)..........................330 374-2990
  445 S Main St Ste B Akron (44311) *(G-87)*
B G News..419 372-2601
  214 W Hall Bgsu Bowling Green (43403) *(G-1759)*
B G Trucking & Construction..............................330 620-8734
  1280 Superior Ave Akron (44307) *(G-88)*
B H C Services Inc..216 289-5300
  26250 Euclid Ave Ste 901 Euclid (44132) *(G-10744)*
B I, Cleveland *Also called Brennan Industries Inc (G-5136)*
B S T, London *Also called Building Systems Trnsp Co (G-12994)*
B W Grinding Co...419 923-1376
  15048 County Road 10 3 Lyons (43533) *(G-13185)*
B W S, Akron *Also called Battered Womens Shelter (G-91)*
B&F Capital Markets Inc...................................216 472-2700
  635 W Lkeside Ave Apt 201 Cleveland (44113) *(G-5090)*
B&N Coal Inc..740 783-3575
  38455 Marietta Rte Dexter City (45727) *(G-10170)*
B-Tek Scales LLC..330 471-8900
  1510 Metric Ave Sw Canton (44706) *(G-2259)*
B2b Power Partners..614 309-6964
  5647 Summer Blvd Galena (43021) *(G-11279)*
Babbage Simmel, Columbus *Also called Babbage-Simmel & Assoc Inc (G-7082)*
Babbage-Simmel & Assoc Inc..............................614 481-6555
  2780 Airport Dr Ste 160 Columbus (43219) *(G-7082)*
Babcock & Wilcox Cnstr Co Inc (HQ).....................330 860-6301
  74 Robinson Ave Barberton (44203) *(G-954)*
Babcock & Wilcox Company (HQ)........................330 753-4511
  20 S Van Buren Ave Barberton (44203) *(G-955)*
Babyphat, Blue Ash *Also called Unirush LLC (G-1712)*
Bachmans Inc...513 943-5300
  4058 Clough Woods Dr Batavia (45103) *(G-995)*
Back In Black Co..419 425-5555
  2100 Fostoria Ave Findlay (45840) *(G-10992)*
Background Information Svcs, Independence *Also called Employeescreeniq (G-12207)*
Backoffice Associates LLC..................................419 660-4600
  16 Executive Dr Ste 200 Norwalk (44857) *(G-15562)*
Backtrack Inc..440 205-8280
  8850 Tyler Blvd Mentor (44060) *(G-14147)*
Bag, The, Lancaster *Also called Dispatch Consumer Services (G-12527)*
Bagel Place Inc (PA)...419 885-1000
  3715 King Rd Toledo (43617) *(G-17762)*
Bailey & Long Inc...614 937-9435
  101 E Town St Ste 115 Columbus (43215) *(G-7083)*
Bailey Associates..614 760-7752
  6836 Caine Rd Columbus (43235) *(G-7084)*
Bailey Cavalieri LLC (PA)...................................614 221-3258
  10 W Broad St Ste 2100 Columbus (43215) *(G-7085)*
Baillie Lumber Co LP..419 462-2000
  3953 County Road 51 Galion (44833) *(G-11292)*

Bajon Salon Montgomery 513 984-8880
7840 Cooper Rd Cincinnati (45242) ***(G-3073)***
Bakemark USA LLC 513 870-0880
9401 Le Saint Dr West Chester (45014) ***(G-19023)***
Baker & Hostetler LLP 216 861-7587
127 Public Sq Ste 2000 Cleveland (44114) ***(G-5091)***
Baker & Hostetler LLP (PA) 216 621-0200
127 Public Sq Ste 2000 Cleveland (44114) ***(G-5092)***
Baker & Hostetler LLP 614 228-1541
65 E State St Ste 2100 Columbus (43215) ***(G-7086)***
Baker & Hostetler LLP 513 929-3400
312 Walnut St Ste 3200 Cincinnati (45202) ***(G-3074)***
Baker & Sons Equipment Co 740 567-3317
45381 State Route 145 Lewisville (43754) ***(G-12714)***
Baker Bnngson Rlty Auctioneers 419 547-7777
1570 W Mcpherson Hwy Clyde (43410) ***(G-6810)***
Baker Concrete Cnstr Inc (PA) 513 539-4000
900 N Garver Rd Monroe (45050) ***(G-14688)***
Baker Dblkar Beck Wley Mathews 330 499-6000
400 S Main St Canton (44720) ***(G-2260)***
Baker Dublikar, Canton *Also called Baker Dblkar Beck Wley Mathews* ***(G-2260)***
Baker Equipment and Mtls Ltd 513 422-6697
990 N Main St Monroe (45050) ***(G-14689)***
Baker Vehicle Systems Inc 330 467-2250
9035 Freeway Dr Macedonia (44056) ***(G-13189)***
Bakers Cllsion Repr Specialist 419 524-1350
595 5th Ave Mansfield (44905) ***(G-13263)***
Bakerwell Inc 614 898-7590
6295 Maxtown Rd Ste 300 Westerville (43082) ***(G-19286)***
Balanced Care Corporation 330 908-1166
997 W Aurora Rd Northfield (44067) ***(G-15509)***
Balanced Care Corporation 937 372-7205
60 Paceline Cir Xenia (45385) ***(G-20044)***
Balancing Company Inc (PA) 937 898-9111
898 Center Dr Vandalia (45377) ***(G-18661)***
Baldwin International, Solon *Also called F I L US Inc* ***(G-17005)***
Baldwin Wallace University 440 826-2285
136 E Bagley Rd Berea (44017) ***(G-1446)***
Ball Bounce and Sport Inc 419 759-3838
211 W Geneva St Dunkirk (45836) ***(G-10501)***
Ball Bounce and Sport Inc 614 662-5381
3275 Alum Creek Dr Columbus (43207) ***(G-7087)***
Ball Bounce and Sport Inc (PA) 419 289-9310
1 Hedstrom Dr Ashland (44805) ***(G-661)***
Ball Bounce and Sport Inc 419 289-9310
100 Hedstrom Dr Ashland (44805) ***(G-662)***
Ballas Egg Products Corp 614 453-0386
40 N 2nd St Zanesville (43701) ***(G-20446)***
Ballet Metropolitan Inc 614 229-4860
322 Mount Vernon Ave Columbus (43215) ***(G-7088)***
Balletmet Columbus, Columbus *Also called Ballet Metropolitan Inc* ***(G-7088)***
Ballreich Bros Inc 419 447-1814
186 Ohio Ave Tiffin (44883) ***(G-17672)***
Ballreichs Potato Chips Snacks, Tiffin *Also called Ballreich Bros Inc* ***(G-17672)***
Balog Steines Hendricks & Manc 330 744-4401
15 Central Sq Ste 300 Youngstown (44503) ***(G-20110)***
Balsara Enterprise Ltd 330 497-7000
6545 Som Center Rd Solon (44139) ***(G-16982)***
Baltic Health Care Corp 330 897-4311
130 Buena Vista St Baltic (43804) ***(G-944)***
Bama Masonry Inc 440 834-4175
14379 Aquilla Rd Burton (44021) ***(G-2060)***
Banc Amer Prctice Slutions Inc 614 794-8247
600 N Cleveland Ave # 300 Westerville (43082) ***(G-19287)***
Banc Certified Merch Svcs LLC 614 850-2740
5006 Cemetery Rd Hilliard (43026) ***(G-11880)***
Banc One Services Corporation (HQ) 614 248-5800
1111 Polaris Pkwy Ste B3 Columbus (43240) ***(G-6869)***
Bankers Life & Casualty Co 614 987-0590
8740 Orion Pl Ste 204 Columbus (43240) ***(G-6870)***
Banquets Unlimited 859 689-4000
1320 Ethan Ave Cincinnati (45225) ***(G-3075)***
Bansal Construction Inc 513 874-5410
3263 Homeward Way Ste A Fairfield (45014) ***(G-10822)***
Banta Electrical Contrs Inc 513 353-4446
5701 Hamilton Cleves Rd Cleves (45002) ***(G-6797)***
Bantam Leasing Inc 513 734-6696
2291 State Route 125 Amelia (45102) ***(G-578)***
Baptist Home and Center 513 662-5880
2373 Harrison Ave Cincinnati (45211) ***(G-3076)***
Bar 145, Columbus *Also called Rcwc Col Inc* ***(G-8592)***
Barb Linden 440 233-1068
1800 Livingston Ave # 200 Lorain (44052) ***(G-13016)***
Barbara Gheens Painting Inc 740 949-0405
50550 Township Road 43 Long Bottom (45743) ***(G-13009)***
Barbara S Desalvo Inc 513 729-2111
800 Compton Rd Unit 18 Cincinnati (45231) ***(G-3077)***
Barberton Area Family Practice 330 615-3205
155 5th St Ne Barberton (44203) ***(G-956)***
Barberton Jaycees 330 745-3733
541 W Tuscarawas Ave # 104 Barberton (44203) ***(G-957)***
Barberton Laundry & Cleaning 330 825-6911
1050 Northview Ave Barberton (44203) ***(G-958)***
Barberton Tree Service Inc 330 848-2344
3307 Clark Mill Rd Norton (44203) ***(G-15554)***
Barbicas Construction Co 330 733-9101
124 Darrow Rd Ste 1 Akron (44305) ***(G-89)***
Barbour Publishing Inc (PA) 740 922-1321
1810 Barbour Dr Se Uhrichsville (44683) ***(G-18487)***
Barbs Graffiti Inc 216 881-5550
3111 Carnegie Ave Cleveland (44115) ***(G-5093)***
Barbs Graffiti Inc (PA) 216 881-5550
3111 Carnegie Ave Cleveland (44115) ***(G-5094)***
Barcus Company Inc 614 451-9000
1601 Bethel Rd Ste 100 Columbus (43220) ***(G-7089)***
Barefoot LLC 513 861-3668
700 W Pete Rose Way Cincinnati (45203) ***(G-3078)***
Bargain Hunter, Millersburg *Also called Graphic Publications Inc* ***(G-14603)***
Baring Distributors, Cleveland *Also called Bdi Inc* ***(G-5104)***
Barkan & Neff Co Lpa (PA) 614 221-4221
250 E Broad St Fl 10 Columbus (43215) ***(G-7090)***
Barkett Fruit Co Inc (PA) 330 364-6645
1213 E 3rd St Dover (44622) ***(G-10176)***
Barkley of Cleveland LLC 440 248-2275
27349 Miles Rd Chagrin Falls (44022) ***(G-2690)***
Barkley Pet Hotel & Day Spa, Chagrin Falls *Also called Barkley of Cleveland LLC* ***(G-2690)***
Barnes Dennig & Co Ltd (PA) 513 241-8313
150 E 4th St Ste 300 Cincinnati (45202) ***(G-3079)***
Barnes Cope, Dayton *Also called Mall Realty Inc* ***(G-9696)***
Barnes Group Inc 419 891-9292
370 W Dussel Dr Ste A Maumee (43537) ***(G-13885)***
Barnes Nursery Inc (PA) 800 421-8722
3511 Cleveland Rd W Huron (44839) ***(G-12161)***
Barnes Wendling Cpas Inc (PA) 216 566-9000
1350 Euclid Ave Ste 1400 Cleveland (44115) ***(G-5095)***
Barnesville Healthcare Rehab 740 425-3648
400 Carrie Ave Barnesville (43713) ***(G-987)***
Barnesville Hospital Assn Inc 740 425-3941
639 W Main St Barnesville (43713) ***(G-988)***
Barnesville Live Stock Ofc, Barnesville *Also called Barnesville Livestock Sales Co* ***(G-989)***
Barnesville Livestock Sales Co 740 425-3611
315 S Gardner St Barnesville (43713) ***(G-989)***
Barnets Inc 937 452-3275
1619 Barnetts Mill Rd Camden (45311) ***(G-2136)***
Barr & Prevost, A Jmt Division, Columbus *Also called Johnson Mirmiran Thompson Inc* ***(G-7944)***
Barr Engineering Incorporated (PA) 614 714-0299
2800 Corp Exchange Dr # 240 Columbus (43231) ***(G-7091)***
Barrett & Associates Inc (PA) 330 928-2323
1060 Graham Rd Ste C Cuyahoga Falls (44224) ***(G-9164)***
Barrett Center For Cancer Prev 513 558-3200
234 Goodman St Cincinnati (45219) ***(G-3080)***
Barrett Paving Materials Inc 513 271-6200
3751 Commerce Dr Middletown (45005) ***(G-14475)***
Barrington Dialysis LLC 740 346-2740
1799 Sinclair Ave Ste 2 Steubenville (43953) ***(G-17303)***
Barrington Golf Club, Aurora *Also called Breezy Point Ltd Partnership* ***(G-831)***
Barrington Golf Club Inc (PA) 330 995-0600
350 N Aurora Rd Aurora (44202) ***(G-829)***
Barrington Golf Club Inc 330 995-0821
680 N Aurora Rd Aurora (44202) ***(G-830)***
Barrington Toledo LLC 419 535-0024
300 S Byrne Rd Toledo (43615) ***(G-17763)***
Barristers of Ohio LLC 330 898-5600
223 Niles Cortland Rd Se # 1 Warren (44484) ***(G-18828)***
Barry Bagel's Place, Toledo *Also called Bagel Place Inc* ***(G-17762)***
Bartha Audio Visual, Columbus *Also called Bkg Holdings LLC* ***(G-7113)***
Bartlett & Co LLC 513 621-4612
600 Vine St Ste 2100 Cincinnati (45202) ***(G-3081)***
Bartley Ambulance, Minerva *Also called C C & S Ambulance Service Inc* ***(G-14642)***
Bartram & Sons Groceries 740 532-5216
2407 S 6th St Ironton (45638) ***(G-12281)***
Bartram Groceries, Ironton *Also called Bartram & Sons Groceries* ***(G-12281)***
Baseline Consulting LLC 440 330-5382
21298 Endsley Ave Cleveland (44116) ***(G-5096)***
Basement Systems Ohio Inc 330 423-4430
8295 Darrow Rd Twinsburg (44087) ***(G-18396)***
BASF Catalysts LLC 216 360-5005
23800 Mercantile Rd Cleveland (44122) ***(G-5097)***
BASF Construction Chem LLC (HQ) 216 831-5500
23700 Chagrin Blvd Cleveland (44122) ***(G-5098)***
Basic Drugs Inc 937 898-4010
300 Corporate Center Dr Vandalia (45377) ***(G-18662)***
Basic Vitamins, Vandalia *Also called Basic Drugs Inc* ***(G-18662)***
Basin Dialysis LLC 937 643-2337
3050 S Dixie Dr Kettering (45409) ***(G-12427)***
Basista & Associates, Cleveland *Also called Profit Recovery of Ohio* ***(G-6310)***
Basista Furniture Inc 216 398-5900
5340 Brookpark Rd Cleveland (44134) ***(G-5099)***
Basol Maintenance Service Inc 419 422-0946
1333 Trenton Ave Findlay (45840) ***(G-10993)***
Bass Lake Inn, Chardon *Also called Bass Lake Tavern Inc* ***(G-2741)***

ALPHABETIC

Bass Lake Tavern Inc 440 285-3100
426 South St Chardon (44024) ***(G-2741)***
Bass Security Services Inc (PA) 216 755-1200
26701 Richmond Rd Bedford Heights (44146) ***(G-1347)***
Bastin Home Inc 513 734-2662
656 W Plane St Bethel (45106) ***(G-1482)***
Batavia Nrsing Cnvalescent Inn, Batavia *Also called Carington Health Systems* ***(G-997)***
Batch Labs Inc 216 901-9366
9655 Sweet Valley Dr # 1 Cleveland (44125) ***(G-5100)***
Bates Bros Amusement Co 740 266-2950
1506 Fernwood Rd Wintersville (43953) ***(G-19808)***
Bates Metal Products Inc 740 498-8371
403 E Mn St Port Washington (43837) ***(G-16260)***
Bath Fitter, Dayton *Also called Bathroom Alternatives Inc* ***(G-9349)***
Bath Manor Limited Partnership 330 836-1006
2330 Smith Rd Akron (44333) ***(G-90)***
BATH MANOR SPECIAL CARE CENTRE, Akron *Also called Bath Manor Limited Partnership* ***(G-90)***
Bathroom Alternatives Inc 937 434-1984
85 Westpark Rd Dayton (45459) ***(G-9349)***
Battelle Dayton Operations, Dayton *Also called Battelle Memorial Institute* ***(G-9257)***
Battelle Memorial Institute (PA) 614 424-6424
505 King Ave Columbus (43201) ***(G-7092)***
Battelle Memorial Institute 937 254-0880
5100 Sprngfeld St Ste 110 Dayton (45431) ***(G-9257)***
Battelle Memorial Institute 614 424-5435
Hc 142 West Jefferson (43162) ***(G-19248)***
Battelle Memorial Institute 614 424-5435
1425 State Route 142 Ne West Jefferson (43162) ***(G-19249)***
Battelle W Jfferson Operations, West Jefferson *Also called Battelle Memorial Institute* ***(G-19249)***
Battelleed 614 859-6433
505 King Ave Columbus (43201) ***(G-7093)***
Battered Womens Shelter 330 723-3900
120 W Washington St 3e1 Medina (44256) ***(G-14038)***
Battered Womens Shelter (PA) 330 374-0740
974 E Market St Akron (44305) ***(G-91)***
Battle Bullying Hotline Inc 216 731-1976
3185 Warren Rd Cleveland (44111) ***(G-5101)***
Bauer Corporation (PA) 800 321-4760
2540 Progress Dr Wooster (44691) ***(G-19830)***
Bauer Ladder, Wooster *Also called Bauer Corporation* ***(G-19830)***
Bauer Lawn Maintenance Inc 419 893-5296
6341 Monclova Rd Maumee (43537) ***(G-13886)***
Baum USA, Sidney *Also called Heidelberg USA Inc* ***(G-16938)***
Bauman Chrysler Jeep Dodge 419 332-8291
2577 W State St Fremont (43420) ***(G-11185)***
Bauman Orchards Inc 330 925-6861
161 Rittman Ave Rittman (44270) ***(G-16551)***
Baumfolder Corporation 937 492-1281
1660 Campbell Rd Sidney (45365) ***(G-16914)***
Baur Leo Century 21 Realty 440 585-2300
32801 Vine St Ste D Willowick (44095) ***(G-19737)***
Bavan & Associates 330 650-0088
10360 Northfield Rd Northfield (44067) ***(G-15510)***
Baxter Burial Vault Service 513 641-1010
909 E Ross Ave Cincinnati (45217) ***(G-3082)***
Baxter Hodell Donnelly Preston (PA) 513 271-1634
302 W 3rd St Ste 500 Cincinnati (45202) ***(G-3083)***
Baxter-Wilbert Burial Vault, Cincinnati *Also called Baxter Burial Vault Service* ***(G-3082)***
Bay Furnace Sheet Metal Co 440 871-3777
24530 Sperry Dr Westlake (44145) ***(G-19463)***
Bay Heating & Air Conditioning, Westlake *Also called Bay Furnace Sheet Metal Co* ***(G-19463)***
Bay Mechanical & Elec Corp 440 282-6816
2221 W Park Dr Lorain (44053) ***(G-13017)***
Bay Park Community Hospital (HQ) 419 690-7900
2801 Bay Park Dr Oregon (43616) ***(G-15725)***
Bay State Gas Company 614 460-4292
200 Civic Center Dr Columbus (43215) ***(G-7094)***
Bay Village City School Dst 440 617-7330
28727 Wolf Rd Cleveland (44140) ***(G-5102)***
Bay Village Montessori Inc 440 871-8773
28370 Bassett Rd Westlake (44145) ***(G-19464)***
Bayer & Becker Inc 513 492-7297
6900 Tylersville Rd Ste A Mason (45040) ***(G-13666)***
Bayer & Becker Inc (PA) 513 492-7401
6900 Tylersville Rd Ste A Mason (45040) ***(G-13667)***
Bayer Heritage Federal Cr Un 740 929-2015
1111 O Neill Dr Hebron (43025) ***(G-11845)***
Bayes Inc 419 661-3933
7414 Ponderosa Rd Perrysburg (43551) ***(G-15975)***
Bayless Pathmark Inc 440 274-2494
19250 Bagley Rd Ste 101 Cleveland (44130) ***(G-5103)***
Bayloff Stmped Pdts Knsman Inc 330 876-4511
8091 State Route 5 Kinsman (44428) ***(G-12452)***
Baymont Inn & Suites, Athens *Also called Motel Partners LLC* ***(G-802)***
Baymont Inn & Suites, Maumee *Also called Sar Biren* ***(G-13974)***
Bayshore Counseling Service (PA) 419 626-9156
1218 Cleveland Rd Ste 3 Sandusky (44870) ***(G-16728)***
Bayshore Obgyn, Sandusky *Also called Northern Ohio Med Spclists LLC* ***(G-16783)***
Bayview Retirees Golf Course 419 726-8081
3900 N Summit St Toledo (43611) ***(G-17764)***
Bazell Oil Co Inc 740 385-5420
14371 State Route 328 Logan (43138) ***(G-12968)***
BBC&m Engineering Inc (PA) 614 793-2226
6190 Enterprise Ct Dublin (43016) ***(G-10259)***
BBDO Worldwide Inc 513 861-3668
700 W Pete Rose Way Cincinnati (45203) ***(G-3084)***
Bbs & Associates Inc 330 665-5227
130 Springside Dr Ste 200 Akron (44333) ***(G-92)***
Bbs Professional Corporation (HQ) 614 888-3100
1103 Schrock Rd Ste 400 Columbus (43229) ***(G-7095)***
Bbt Fleet Services LLC 419 462-7722
549 Russell Rd Mansfield (44903) ***(G-13264)***
Bcbd, West Chester *Also called Cameo Solutions Inc* ***(G-19032)***
Bccp, Chillicothe *Also called Southern Ohio Wns Cancer Prj* ***(G-2887)***
Bcf LLC (PA) 937 746-0721
3160 S Tech Blvd Miamisburg (45342) ***(G-14274)***
Bcg Systems That Work Inc 330 864-4816
1735 Merriman Rd Ste 3000 Akron (44313) ***(G-93)***
BCU Electric Inc 419 281-8944
1019 Us Highway 250 N Ashland (44805) ***(G-663)***
Bd Oil Gathering Corp 740 374-9355
649 Mitchells Ln Marietta (45750) ***(G-13435)***
Bdi Inc (PA) 216 642-9100
8000 Hub Pkwy Cleveland (44125) ***(G-5104)***
Bdo Usa LLP 614 488-3126
300 Spruce St Ste 100 Columbus (43215) ***(G-7096)***
Bdo Usa LLP 513 592-2400
221 E 4th St Ste 2600 Cincinnati (45202) ***(G-3085)***
Bdo Usa LLP 216 325-1700
1422 Euclid Ave Ste 1500 Cleveland (44115) ***(G-5105)***
Bdo Usa LLP 330 668-9696
301 Springside Dr Akron (44333) ***(G-94)***
BDS Inc (PA) 513 921-8441
3500 Southside Ave Cincinnati (45204) ***(G-3086)***
BDS Packaging Inc 937 643-0530
3155 Elbee Rd Ste 201 Moraine (45439) ***(G-14752)***
Bdtk Private Security 937 520-1784
4950 Sweetbirch Dr Dayton (45424) ***(G-9350)***
Beach Golf Course, Arcanum *Also called Mikesell Transportation Broker* ***(G-630)***
Beachwood City Schools 216 464-6609
23757 Commerce Park Cleveland (44122) ***(G-5106)***
Beachwood Nrsing Halthcare Ctr, Beachwood *Also called Ezra Health Care Inc* ***(G-1078)***
Beachwood Prof Fire Fighters C 216 292-1968
P.O. Box 221250 Beachwood (44122) ***(G-1055)***
Beacon Company (PA) 330 733-8322
2350 Gilchrist Rd Akron (44305) ***(G-95)***
Beacon Electric Company 513 851-0711
7815 Redsky Dr Cincinnati (45249) ***(G-3087)***
Beacon Electrical Contractors, Cincinnati *Also called Beacon Electric Company* ***(G-3087)***
Beacon Health 440 354-9924
9220 Mentor Ave Mentor (44060) ***(G-14148)***
Beacon House, The, Saint Clairsville *Also called Zandex Inc* ***(G-16662)***
Beacon of Light Ltd 419 531-9060
360 S Reynolds Rd Ste A Toledo (43615) ***(G-17765)***
Beacon of Light Health Agency, Toledo *Also called Beacon of Light Ltd* ***(G-17765)***
Beacon Point Rehab, Uhrichsville *Also called Uhrichsville Health Care Ctr* ***(G-18494)***
Beacon Sales Acquisition Inc 330 425-3359
2440 Edison Blvd Twinsburg (44087) ***(G-18397)***
Beall Inc 440 974-8719
7875 Johnnycake Ridge Rd Mentor (44060) ***(G-14149)***
Beall Rose Crtif Pub Accntants, Dublin *Also called REA & Associates Inc* ***(G-10438)***
Bearing & Drive Systems Inc (PA) 440 846-9700
14888 Foltz Pkwy Strongsville (44149) ***(G-17446)***
Bearing Distributors Inc (HQ) 216 642-9100
8000 Hub Pkwy Cleveland (44125) ***(G-5107)***
Bearing Technologies Ltd (PA) 440 937-4770
1141 Jaycox Rd Avon (44011) ***(G-879)***
Beary Land, Piqua *Also called Council On Rur Svc Prgrams Inc* ***(G-16141)***
Beatitude House 440 992-0265
3404 Lake Ave Ashtabula (44004) ***(G-729)***
Beauty Bar LLC 419 537-5400
2919 W Central Ave Toledo (43606) ***(G-17766)***
Beauty Systems Group, Greenville *Also called Sally Beauty Supply LLC* ***(G-11518)***
Beaver Clinic, Waverly *Also called Community Action Comm Pike CNT* ***(G-18970)***
Beaver Constructors Inc 330 478-2151
2000 Beaver Place Ave Sw Canton (44706) ***(G-2261)***
Beaver-Vu Bowl 937 426-6771
1238 N Fairfield Rd Beavercreek (45432) ***(G-1150)***
Beavercreek Church of Nazarene 937 426-0079
1850 N Fairfield Rd Beavercreek (45432) ***(G-1151)***
Beavercreek Health Park, Beavercreek *Also called Greene Memorial Hospital Inc* ***(G-1175)***
Beavercreek Medical Center 937 558-3000
2510 Commons Blvd Ste 120 Beavercreek (45431) ***(G-1152)***
Beavercreek Medical Center 937 558-3000
2510 Commons Blvd Ste 120 Beavercreek (45431) ***(G-1153)***
Beavercreek YMCA 937 426-9622
111 W 1st St Ste 207 Dayton (45402) ***(G-9351)***
Beavercreek YMCA Sch's Out I, Dayton *Also called Young Mens Christian Assoc* ***(G-10011)***

Beaverdam Fleet Services Inc 419 643-8880
424 E Main St Beaverdam (45808) *(G-1288)*
Bebley Enterprises Inc (PA) 419 389-9424
2801 W Bancroft St Toledo (43606) *(G-17767)*
Becdel Controls Incorporated 330 652-1386
1869 Warren Ave Niles (44446) *(G-15284)*
Becdir Construction Company 330 547-2134
15764 W Akron Canfield Rd Berlin Center (44401) *(G-1480)*
Bechtl Bldng Mntnc Crprtn of 330 759-2797
3734 Logan Gate Rd Youngstown (44505) *(G-20111)*
Beck Aluminum Intl LLC 440 684-4848
6150 Parkland Blvd # 260 Cleveland (44124) *(G-5108)*
Beck Center For Arts 216 521-2540
17801 Detroit Ave Cleveland (44107) *(G-5109)*
Beck Company 216 883-0909
10701 Broadway Ave Cleveland (44125) *(G-5110)*
Beck Dialysis LLC 513 422-6879
4421 Roosevelt Blvd Ste D Middletown (45044) *(G-14415)*
Becker & Becker, Mason *Also called Bayer & Becker Inc (G-13666)*
Becker Construction Inc 937 859-8308
525 Gargrave Rd Dayton (45449) *(G-9352)*
Becker Electric Supply, Dayton *Also called John A Becker Co (G-9643)*
Becker Electric Supply, Cincinnati *Also called John A Becker Co (G-3876)*
Becker Electric Supply, Columbus *Also called John A Becker Co (G-7942)*
Becker Pumps Corporation 330 928-9966
100 E Ascot Ln Cuyahoga Falls (44223) *(G-9165)*
Beckett House, New Concord *Also called Zandex Inc (G-15040)*
Beckett House At New Concord, New Concord *Also called Zandex Health Care Corporation (G-15041)*
Beckett Ridge Country Club 513 874-2710
5595 Beckett Ridge Blvd # 2 West Chester (45069) *(G-19024)*
Beckett Springs LLC (PA) 513 942-9500
8614 Shepherd Farm Dr West Chester (45069) *(G-19025)*
Beckett Springs Hospital, West Chester *Also called Beckett Springs LLC (G-19025)*
Beckjord Power Station, New Richmond *Also called Duke Energy Ohio Inc (G-15127)*
Beco Legal Systems, Cincinnati *Also called Business Equipment Co Inc (G-3156)*
Bedford Church of Nazarene 440 232-7440
365 Center Rd Bedford (44146) *(G-1294)*
Bedford Heights City Waste 440 439-5343
25301 Solon Rd Bedford (44146) *(G-1295)*
Bedford Heights City Waste Wtr, Bedford *Also called Bedford Heights City Waste (G-1295)*
Bedford Heights Health Center, Bedford Heights *Also called Planned Prenthood Greater Ohio (G-1356)*
Bedford Medical Offices, Brooklyn Heights *Also called Kaiser Foundation Hospitals (G-1918)*
Bedford Nurs Schl Kindergarden, Bedford *Also called Bedford Church of Nazarene (G-1294)*
Beds N Stuff, Grove City *Also called Waterbeds n Stuff Inc (G-11612)*
Beech Acres Parenting Center (PA) 513 231-6630
6881 Beechmont Ave Cincinnati (45230) *(G-3088)*
Beech Acres Thrptic Fster Care, Cincinnati *Also called Beech Acres Parenting Center (G-3088)*
Beechmont Inc 216 831-9100
29600 Chagrin Blvd Cleveland (44122) *(G-5111)*
BEECHMONT COUNTRY CLUB, Cleveland *Also called Beechmont Inc (G-5111)*
Beechmont Ford Inc (PA) 513 752-6611
600 Ohio Pike Cincinnati (45245) *(G-2904)*
Beechmont Motors Inc (PA) 513 388-3883
8639 Beechmont Ave Cincinnati (45255) *(G-3089)*
Beechmont Pet Hospital Inc 513 232-0300
6400 Salem Rd Cincinnati (45230) *(G-3090)*
Beechmont Porsche, Cincinnati *Also called Beechmont Motors Inc (G-3089)*
Beechmont Racquet and Fitness, Cincinnati *Also called Beechmont Racquet Club Inc (G-3091)*
Beechmont Racquet Club Inc 513 528-5700
435 Ohio Pike Cincinnati (45255) *(G-3091)*
Beechmont Toyota Inc 513 388-3800
8667 Beechmont Ave Cincinnati (45255) *(G-3092)*
Beechwold Veterinary Hospital (PA) 614 268-8666
4590 Indianola Ave Columbus (43214) *(G-7097)*
Beechwold Veterinary Hospital 614 766-1222
6924 Riverside Dr Dublin (43017) *(G-10260)*
Beechwood Home 513 321-9294
2140 Pogue Ave Cincinnati (45208) *(G-3093)*
Beechwood Terrace Care Ctr Inc 513 578-6200
8700 Moran Rd Cincinnati (45244) *(G-3094)*
Beeghly Oaks Center For Rehabi, Boardman *Also called Beeghly Oaks Operating LLC (G-1738)*
Beeghly Oaks Operating LLC 330 884-2300
6505 Market St Bldg D Boardman (44512) *(G-1738)*
Beeghly Oaks Skilled, Columbus *Also called V Vrable Inc (G-8929)*
Beem Construction Inc 937 693-3176
225 S Mill St Botkins (45306) *(G-1751)*
Beerco Distributing Co, Fostoria *Also called Hanson Distributing Co Inc (G-11130)*
Behavioral Treatments 614 558-1968
5275 Norwich St Hilliard (43026) *(G-11881)*
Behavorial Healthcare (PA) 740 522-8477
65 Messimer Dr Newark (43055) *(G-15146)*
Behavral Cnnctions WD Cnty Inc (PA) 419 352-5387
280 S Main St Bowling Green (43402) *(G-1760)*
Behavral Cnnctions WD Cnty Inc 419 872-2419
27072 Carronade Dr Ste A Perrysburg (43551) *(G-15976)*
Behavral Cnnctions WD Cnty Inc 419 352-5387
320 W Gypsy Lane Rd Ste A Bowling Green (43402) *(G-1761)*
Behavral Cnnctions WD Cnty Inc 419 352-5387
1010 N Prospect St Bowling Green (43402) *(G-1762)*
Beheydts Auto Wrecking 330 658-6109
15475 Serfass Rd Doylestown (44230) *(G-10223)*
Beiersdorf Inc 513 682-7300
5232 E Provident Dr West Chester (45246) *(G-19191)*
Bekins Van Lines, Cincinnati *Also called Thoman Weil Moving & Stor Co (G-4651)*
Bel Air Care Center 330 821-3939
2350 Cherry Ave Alliance (44601) *(G-527)*
Bel-Park Anesthesia 330 480-3658
1044 Belmont Ave Youngstown (44504) *(G-20112)*
Bel-Wood Country Club Inc 513 899-3361
5873 Ludlum Rd Morrow (45152) *(G-14843)*
Belayusa Corporation 614 878-8200
5197 Trabue Rd Columbus (43228) *(G-7098)*
Belcan LLC 513 645-1509
9100 Centre Pointe Dr West Chester (45069) *(G-19026)*
Belcan LLC (PA) 513 891-0972
10200 Anderson Way Blue Ash (45242) *(G-1538)*
Belcan LLC 513 217-4562
4490 Marie Dr Middletown (45044) *(G-14416)*
Belcan LLC 740 393-8888
105 N Sandusky St Mount Vernon (43050) *(G-14878)*
Belcan Corporation 513 985-7777
10200 Anderson Way Blue Ash (45242) *(G-1539)*
Belcan Corporation 513 891-0972
28999 Aurora Rd Solon (44139) *(G-16983)*
Belcan Corporation 513 277-3100
7785 E Kemper Rd Cincinnati (45249) *(G-3095)*
Belcan Corporation 614 224-6080
519 S High St Columbus (43215) *(G-7099)*
Belcan Engineering Group LLC (HQ) 513 891-0972
10200 Anderson Way Blue Ash (45242) *(G-1540)*
Belcan Engineering Services, Mount Vernon *Also called Belcan LLC (G-14878)*
Belcan Engineering Services, Cincinnati *Also called Belcan Corporation (G-3095)*
Belcan Staffing Services, Dayton *Also called Belcan Svcs Group Ltd Partnr (G-9353)*
Belcan Staffing Solutions, Middletown *Also called Belcan LLC (G-14416)*
Belcan Staffing Solutions, Columbus *Also called Belcan Corporation (G-7099)*
Belcan Svcs Group Ltd Partnr 937 586-5053
832 S Ludlow St Ste 1 Dayton (45402) *(G-9353)*
Belcan Svcs Group Ltd Partnr (HQ) 513 891-0972
10200 Anderson Way Blue Ash (45242) *(G-1541)*
Belcan Svcs Group Ltd Partnr 937 859-8880
3494 Technical Dr Miamisburg (45342) *(G-14275)*
Belcan Techservices, Miamisburg *Also called Belcan Svcs Group Ltd Partnr (G-14275)*
Belco Works Inc 740 695-0500
340 Fox Shannon Pl Saint Clairsville (43950) *(G-16617)*
Belcourt Terracenursing Home, Dublin *Also called Ahf/Central States Inc (G-10238)*
Belden & Blake Corporation 330 602-5551
1748 Saltwell Rd Nw Dover (44622) *(G-10177)*
Belflex Staffing Network LLC (PA) 513 488-8588
11591 Goldcoast Dr Cincinnati (45249) *(G-3096)*
Belfor USA Group Inc 330 916-6468
79 Cuyahoga Fls Indus Par Peninsula (44264) *(G-15947)*
Belfor USA Group Inc 513 860-3111
4710 Interstate Dr Ste L West Chester (45246) *(G-19192)*
Bell Hensley Inc 937 498-1718
804 W Parkwood St Sidney (45365) *(G-16915)*
Bell Moving and Storage Inc (PA) 513 942-7500
4075 Port Union Rd Fairfield (45014) *(G-10823)*
Bell Music Company 330 376-6337
533 W Market St Akron (44303) *(G-96)*
Bella Capelli Inc 440 899-1225
24350 Center Ridge Rd Westlake (44145) *(G-19465)*
Bella Capelli Salon, Westlake *Also called Bella Capelli Inc (G-19465)*
Bellaire Harbor Service LLC 740 676-4305
4102 Jefferson St Bellaire (43906) *(G-1361)*
Bellas Co 740 598-4171
2670 Commercial Ave Mingo Junction (43938) *(G-14653)*
Bellazio Salon & Day Spa 937 432-6722
101 E Alex Bell Rd # 127 Dayton (45459) *(G-9354)*
Bellbrook Rhbltion Healthcare, Bellbrook *Also called Bellbrook Rhbltion Healthcare (G-1370)*
Bellbrook Rhbltion Healthcare 937 848-8421
1957 N Lakeman Dr Bellbrook (45305) *(G-1370)*
Belle Manor Nursing Home, New Carlisle *Also called Bmnh Inc (G-15020)*
Belle Tire 440 735-0800
205 Oak Leaf Oval Bedford (44146) *(G-1296)*
Belle Tire Distributors Inc 419 473-1393
5253 Secor Rd Toledo (43623) *(G-17768)*
Bellefaire Jewish Chld Bur (PA) 216 932-2800
22001 Fairmount Blvd Shaker Heights (44118) *(G-16856)*
Bellefontaine Distribution Ctr, Bellefontaine *Also called Spartannash Company (G-1398)*
Bellefontaine Physical Therapy 937 592-1625
711 Rush Ave Bellefontaine (43311) *(G-1377)*

Belletech Corp (HQ) 937 599-3774
700 W Lake Ave Bellefontaine (43311) ***(G-1378)***
Bellevue Care Center, Bellevue *Also called Saber Healthcare Group LLC* ***(G-1418)***
Bellevue Care Center, Bellevue *Also called Audrich Inc* ***(G-1403)***
Bellevue Four Cnty Ems N Centl 419 483-3322
12513 Us Highway 250 N Milan (44846) ***(G-14492)***
Bellevue Hospital (PA) 419 483-4040
1400 W Main St Unit Front Bellevue (44811) ***(G-1404)***
Bellevue Hospital 419 547-0074
811 Northwest St Bellevue (44811) ***(G-1405)***
Bellman Plumbing Inc 440 324-4477
7520 W Ridge Rd Elyria (44035) ***(G-10596)***
Bellmont County 740 695-9750
210 Fox Shannon Pl Saint Clairsville (43950) ***(G-16618)***
Bellville Hotel Company 419 886-7000
1000 Comfort Plaza Dr Bellville (44813) ***(G-1421)***
Bellwether Entp RE Capitl LLC (PA) 216 820-4500
1360 E 9th St Ste 300 Cleveland (44114) ***(G-5112)***
Belmont & Monroe Lodge 6 of 740 695-2121
72200 Gun Club Rd Saint Clairsville (43950) ***(G-16619)***
Belmont Bhc Pines Hospital Inc 330 759-2700
615 Churchill Hubbard Rd Youngstown (44505) ***(G-20113)***
Belmont Cnty Fire & Squad Offi 740 312-5058
69604 Sunset Hts Bridgeport (43912) ***(G-1859)***
Belmont Community Hlth Ctr, Bellaire *Also called Wheeling Hospital Inc* ***(G-1368)***
Belmont Community Hospital (HQ) 740 671-1200
4697 Harrison St Bellaire (43906) ***(G-1362)***
Belmont Country Club 419 666-1472
29601 Bates Rd Perrysburg (43551) ***(G-15977)***
Belmont County Children Svcs, Saint Clairsville *Also called Belmont County of Ohio* ***(G-16623)***
Belmont County Engineering, Saint Clairsville *Also called Belmont County of Ohio* ***(G-16625)***
Belmont County Home 740 695-4925
100 Pine Ave Saint Clairsville (43950) ***(G-16620)***
Belmont County of Ohio 740 695-4708
45244 National Rd Saint Clairsville (43950) ***(G-16621)***
Belmont County of Ohio 740 695-3144
68325 Bannock Rd Saint Clairsville (43950) ***(G-16622)***
Belmont County of Ohio 740 695-3813
101 N Market St Ste A Saint Clairsville (43950) ***(G-16623)***
Belmont County of Ohio 740 695-0460
68421 Hammond Rd Saint Clairsville (43950) ***(G-16624)***
Belmont County of Ohio 740 695-1580
101 W Maint St Saint Clairsville (43950) ***(G-16625)***
Belmont County Sani Sewer Dst, Saint Clairsville *Also called Belmont County of Ohio* ***(G-16622)***
Belmont Division, Barnesville *Also called South Central Power Company* ***(G-991)***
Belmont Eye Clinic Inc (PA) 330 759-7672
3020 Belmont Ave Youngstown (44505) ***(G-20114)***
Belmont Federal Sav & Ln Assn (PA) 740 676-1165
3301 Guernsey St Bellaire (43906) ***(G-1363)***
Belmont Hills Country Club 740 695-2181
47080 National Rd W Saint Clairsville (43950) ***(G-16626)***
Belmont Manor Nursing Home, Saint Clairsville *Also called Lancia Nursing Home Inc* ***(G-16640)***
Belmont Metro Hsing Auth (PA) 740 633-5085
100 S 3rd St Martins Ferry (43935) ***(G-13599)***
Belmont Metro Hsing Auth A, Martins Ferry *Also called Belmont Metro Hsing Auth* ***(G-13599)***
Belmont Savings Bank 740 695-0140
215 W Main St Saint Clairsville (43950) ***(G-16627)***
Belmore Leasing Co LLC 216 268-3600
1835 Belmore Rd Cleveland (44112) ***(G-5113)***
Belpre Historical Society 740 423-7588
509 Ridge St Belpre (45714) ***(G-1433)***
Belting Company of Cincinnati (PA) 513 621-9050
5500 Ridge Ave Cincinnati (45213) ***(G-3097)***
Belting Company of Cincinnati 937 498-2104
301 Stolle Ave Sidney (45365) ***(G-16916)***
Ben D Imhoff Inc 330 683-4498
315 E Market St Orrville (44667) ***(G-15766)***
Ben El Child Development Ctr 937 465-0010
1150 Scioto St Ste 200 Urbana (43078) ***(G-18573)***
Ben Venue Laboratories, Bedford *Also called Boehringer Ingelheim USA Corp* ***(G-1297)***
Benchmark Craftsman Inc 330 975-4214
4700 Greenwich Rd Seville (44273) ***(G-16837)***
Benchmark Craftsmen, Seville *Also called Benchmark Craftsman Inc* ***(G-16837)***
Benchmark Landscape Cnstr Inc 614 873-8080
9600 Industrial Pkwy Plain City (43064) ***(G-16183)***
Benchmark Masonry Contractors 937 228-1225
2924 Cincinnati Dayton Rd Middletown (45044) ***(G-14417)***
Benchmark National Corporation 419 660-1100
400 N Buckeye St Bellevue (44811) ***(G-1406)***
Benchmark Outfitters, Cincinnati *Also called Rassak LLC* ***(G-4386)***
Benchmark Technologies Corp 419 843-6691
3161 N Republic Blvd Toledo (43615) ***(G-17769)***
Benco Dental Supply Co 513 874-2990
10014 Intl Blvd Bldg 9 Cincinnati (45246) ***(G-3098)***
Benco Dental Supply Co 614 761-1053
4333 Tuller Rd Ste E Dublin (43017) ***(G-10261)***
Bendix Coml Vhcl Systems LLC (HQ) 440 329-9000
901 Cleveland St Elyria (44035) ***(G-10597)***
Bendon Inc (PA) 419 207-3600
1840 Baney Rd S Ashland (44805) ***(G-664)***
Benedict Enterprises Inc (PA) 513 539-9216
750 Lakeview Rd Monroe (45050) ***(G-14690)***
Beneficial Building Services (PA) 330 848-2556
1830 13th St Sw Akron (44314) ***(G-97)***
Benefit ADM Agcy LLC 614 791-1143
5880 Venture Dr Dublin (43017) ***(G-10262)***
Benefit Services Inc (PA) 330 666-0337
3636 Copley Rd Ste 201 Copley (44321) ***(G-9053)***
Benesch Friedlander Coplan & 614 223-9300
41 S High St Ste 2600 Columbus (43215) ***(G-7100)***
Benevento Enterprises Inc 216 621-5890
1384 E 26th St Cleveland (44114) ***(G-5114)***
Benevolent/Protectv Order Elks 440 357-6943
723 Liberty St Painesville (44077) ***(G-15836)***
Benjamin Rose Institute 216 791-8000
850 Euclid Ave Ste 1100 Cleveland (44114) ***(G-5115)***
Benjamin Rose Institute 216 791-3580
2373 Euclid Heights Blvd 2f Cleveland (44106) ***(G-5116)***
Benjamin Rose Institute (PA) 216 791-8000
11890 Fairhill Rd Cleveland (44120) ***(G-5117)***
Benjamin Steel Company Inc 937 233-1212
777 Benjamin Dr Springfield (45502) ***(G-17150)***
Benjamin Steel Company Inc 419 229-8045
3111 Saint Johns Rd Lima (45804) ***(G-12745)***
Benjamin Steel Company Inc 419 522-5500
15 Industrial Pkwy Mansfield (44903) ***(G-13265)***
Benmit Division, North Lawrence *Also called US Tubular Products Inc* ***(G-15394)***
Bennett Enterprises Inc 419 874-3111
10630 Fremont Pike Perrysburg (43551) ***(G-15978)***
Bennett Enterprises Inc 419 893-1004
1409 Reynolds Rd Maumee (43537) ***(G-13887)***
Bennett Supply of Ohio LLC 800 292-5577
8170 Roll And Hold Pkwy Macedonia (44056) ***(G-13190)***
Bennett Venture Academy, Toledo *Also called National Heritg Academies Inc* ***(G-18076)***
Bennington Glen Nursing Home, Marengo *Also called Dearth Management Company* ***(G-13423)***
Bentley Excavating, Painesville *Also called D B Bentley Inc* ***(G-15849)***
Bentley Leasing Co LLC 330 337-9503
2511 Bentley Dr Salem (44460) ***(G-16688)***
Benton School Bus Garage, Oak Harbor *Also called Benton-Carroll-Salem* ***(G-15605)***
Benton-Carroll-Salem 419 898-6214
601 N Benton St Oak Harbor (43449) ***(G-15605)***
Berardi + Partners 614 221-1110
1398 Goodale Blvd Columbus (43212) ***(G-7101)***
Berardis Fresh Roast Inc 440 582-4303
12029 Abbey Rd North Royalton (44133) ***(G-15482)***
Berea Alzheimer's Care Center, Berea *Also called Communicare Health Svcs Inc* ***(G-1453)***
Berea B O E Trnsp Dept 216 898-8300
235 Riveredge Pkwy Berea (44017) ***(G-1447)***
Berea Lake Towers Inc 440 243-9050
4 Berea Commons Ste 1 Berea (44017) ***(G-1448)***
Berea Lk Twers Rtirement Cmnty 440 243-9050
3 Berea Commons Berea (44017) ***(G-1449)***
Berea Service Garage, Berea *Also called City of Berea* ***(G-1451)***
Bergholz 7, Bergholz *Also called Rosebud Mining Company* ***(G-1476)***
Berk Enterprises Inc (PA) 330 369-1192
1554 Thomas Rd Se Warren (44484) ***(G-18829)***
Berk Paper & Supply, Warren *Also called Berk Enterprises Inc* ***(G-18829)***
Berkebile Russell & Associates 440 989-4480
1720 Cooper Foster Park R Lorain (44053) ***(G-13018)***
Berkeley Square Retirement Ctr, Hamilton *Also called Colonial Senior Services Inc* ***(G-11713)***
Berkshire Realty Group, Cincinnati *Also called Brg Realty Group LLC* ***(G-3130)***
Berlin Construction Ltd 330 893-2003
4740 Township Road 356 Millersburg (44654) ***(G-14587)***
Berlin Contractors 330 893-2904
5233 Township Rd 359 Berlin (44610) ***(G-1477)***
Berlin Packaging LLC 614 777-6282
3423 Southpark Pl C Grove City (43123) ***(G-11533)***
Berlin Transportaion LLC 330 674-3395
7576 State Route 241 Millersburg (44654) ***(G-14588)***
Bermex, Columbus *Also called Matvest Inc* ***(G-8130)***
Bermex Inc 330 945-7500
1333 Home Ave Akron (44310) ***(G-98)***
Bernard Busson Builder 330 929-4926
1551 Treetop Trl Akron (44313) ***(G-99)***
Bernard Daniels Lumber Co, Canfield *Also called Daniels Lumber Co Inc* ***(G-2188)***
Berner Trucking, Dover *Also called Knisely Inc* ***(G-10195)***
Berner Trucking 419 476-0207
4310 Lagrange St Toledo (43612) ***(G-17770)***
Berner Trucking Inc 330 343-5812
5885 Crown Rd Nw Dover (44622) ***(G-10178)***
Berns Garden Center, Middletown *Also called Berns Grnhse & Grdn Ctr Inc* ***(G-14418)***
Berns Grnhse & Grdn Ctr Inc (PA) 513 423-5306
825 Greentree Rd Middletown (45044) ***(G-14418)***

ALPHABETIC SECTION
Big Run Urgent Care Center

Berns Oneill SEC & Safety LLC 330 374-9133
1000 N Main St Akron (44310) ***(G-100)***
Bernstein Allergy Group Inc 513 931-0775
8444 Winton Rd Cincinnati (45231) ***(G-3099)***
Beroske Farms & Greenhouse Inc 419 826-4547
12647 County Road 5 Delta (43515) ***(G-10156)***
Berriehill, Dayton *Also called Applied Research Assoc Inc* ***(G-9338)***
Berry Network LLC (HQ) 800 366-1264
3100 Kettering Blvd Moraine (45439) ***(G-14753)***
Bertec Corporation 614 543-0962
6171 Huntley Rd Ste J Columbus (43229) ***(G-7102)***
Bertka, Vicki M MD, Maumee *Also called Fallen Timbers Fmly Physicians* ***(G-13913)***
Bertram Inn, Aurora *Also called B & I Hotel Management LLC* ***(G-828)***
Berwick Electric Company 614 834-2301
6863 Eliza Dr Canal Winchester (43110) ***(G-2153)***
Besl Transfer Co 513 242-3456
5700 Este Ave Cincinnati (45232) ***(G-3100)***
Besse Medical, West Chester *Also called Asd Specialty Healthcare LLC* ***(G-19022)***
Bessemer and Lake Erie RR Co 440 593-1102
950 Ford Ave Conneaut (44030) ***(G-9039)***
Best & Donovan N A Inc 513 791-9180
5570 Creek Rd Blue Ash (45242) ***(G-1542)***
Best Aire Compressor Service (HQ) 419 726-0055
3648 Rockland Cir Millbury (43447) ***(G-14577)***
Best Care Nrsing Rhblttion Ctr 740 574-2558
2159 Dogwood Ridge Rd Wheelersburg (45694) ***(G-19570)***
Best Controls Company, Ashland *Also called Chandler Systems Incorporated* ***(G-673)***
Best Cuts Inc 440 884-6300
7541 W Ridgewood Dr Cleveland (44129) ***(G-5118)***
Best Express Foods Inc 513 531-2378
2368 Victory Pkwy Ste 410 Cincinnati (45206) ***(G-3101)***
Best Lighting Products Inc (HQ) 740 964-0063
1213 Etna Pkwy Etna (43062) ***(G-10732)***
Best One Tire & Svc Lima Inc (PA) 419 229-2380
701 E Hanthorn Rd Lima (45804) ***(G-12746)***
Best Plumbing Limited 614 855-1919
5791 Zarley St Ste A New Albany (43054) ***(G-14974)***
Best Realty Inc 513 932-3948
645 Columbus Ave Ste A Lebanon (45036) ***(G-12591)***
Best Reward Credit Union 216 367-8000
5681 Smith Rd Cleveland (44142) ***(G-5119)***
Best Upon Request Corp Inc 513 605-7800
8170 Corp Pk Dr Ste 300 Cincinnati (45242) ***(G-3102)***
Best Western, Zanesville *Also called Town House Motor Lodge Corp* ***(G-20539)***
Best Western, Englewood *Also called Dayton Hotels LLC* ***(G-10702)***
Best Western Columbus N Hotel 614 888-8230
888 E Dublin Granville Rd Columbus (43229) ***(G-7103)***
Best Western Columbus North, Columbus *Also called Best Western Columbus N Hotel* ***(G-7103)***
Best Western Executive Inn 330 794-1050
2677 Gilchrist Rd Unit 1 Akron (44305) ***(G-101)***
Best Western Falcon Plaza Mtl, Bowling Green *Also called Falcon Plaza LLC* ***(G-1775)***
Best Western Grnd Victoria Inn, Westlake *Also called Northern Tier Hospitality LLC* ***(G-19525)***
Best Western Meander Inn, Youngstown *Also called Meander Inn Inc* ***(G-20276)***
Best Western Wooster Plaza, Wooster *Also called Best Wooster Inc* ***(G-19831)***
Best Wooster Inc 330 264-7750
243 E Liberty St Ste 11 Wooster (44691) ***(G-19831)***
Best Wstn Lawnfield Inn Suites, Mentor *Also called Lawnfield Properties LLC* ***(G-14208)***
Besttransportcom Inc 614 888-2378
400 W Wilson Bridge Rd Worthington (43085) ***(G-19943)***
Bestway Transport Co (PA) 419 687-2000
2040 Sandusky St Plymouth (44865) ***(G-16216)***
Beta Lab & Technical Svcs, Cleveland *Also called First Energy Nuclear Oper Co* ***(G-5595)***
Beta PHI, Celina *Also called Delta Kappa Gamma Society* ***(G-2645)***
Beta RHO House Assoc Kappa 513 221-1280
2801 Clifton Ave Cincinnati (45220) ***(G-3103)***
Beta Theta PI Fraternity (PA) 513 523-7591
5134 Bonham Rd Oxford (45056) ***(G-15811)***
Betco Corporation (PA) 419 241-2156
400 Van Camp Rd Bowling Green (43402) ***(G-1763)***
Beth-El Agape Christian Center 614 445-0674
840 Mansfield Ave Columbus (43219) ***(G-7104)***
Bethany Nursing Home Inc 330 492-7171
626 34th St Nw Canton (44709) ***(G-2262)***
Bethany Village Linden, Dayton *Also called Graceworks Lutheran Services* ***(G-9583)***
Bethesda Butler Hospital, Fairfield Township *Also called Bethesda Hospital Inc* ***(G-10924)***
Bethesda Care, Zanesville *Also called Genesis Healthcare System* ***(G-20481)***
Bethesda Care Center, Fremont *Also called Volunters Amer Care Facilities* ***(G-11226)***
Bethesda Foundation Inc 513 569-6575
619 Oak St Cincinnati (45206) ***(G-3104)***
Bethesda Hospital Inc 513 894-8888
3125 Hamilton Mason Rd Fairfield Township (45011) ***(G-10924)***
Bethesda Hospital Inc (HQ) 513 569-6100
619 Oak St Cincinnati (45206) ***(G-3105)***
Bethesda Hospital Inc 513 745-1111
10500 Montgomery Rd Cincinnati (45242) ***(G-3106)***
Bethesda Hospital Inc 513 563-1505
3801 Hauck Rd Frnt Cincinnati (45241) ***(G-3107)***
Bethesda Hospital Association 740 454-4000
2951 Maple Ave Zanesville (43701) ***(G-20447)***
Bethesda North Hospital, Cincinnati *Also called Trihealth Inc* ***(G-4688)***
Bethesda North Hospital, Cincinnati *Also called Bethesda Hospital Inc* ***(G-3105)***
Bethesda North Hospital, Cincinnati *Also called Bethesda Hospital Inc* ***(G-3106)***
Bethlehem Lutheran Ch Parma 440 845-2230
7500 State Rd Cleveland (44134) ***(G-5120)***
Bettcher Industries Inc (PA) 440 965-4422
6801 State Route 60 Wakeman (44889) ***(G-18774)***
Better Brake Parts Inc 419 227-0685
915 Shawnee Rd Lima (45805) ***(G-12747)***
Better Homes and Gardens, Beavercreek *Also called Big Hill Realty Corp* ***(G-1230)***
Bevan and Associates Lpa, Northfield *Also called Bavan & Associates* ***(G-15510)***
Bevcorp LLC (PA) 440 954-3500
4711 E 355th St Willoughby (44094) ***(G-19647)***
Beverage Distributors Inc 216 431-1600
3800 King Ave Cleveland (44114) ***(G-5121)***
Beverly, Napoleon *Also called Golden Living LLC* ***(G-14941)***
Beverly, Lima *Also called Golden Living LLC* ***(G-12784)***
Beverly, Saint Marys *Also called Golden Living LLC* ***(G-16674)***
Beverly, Columbus *Also called Golden Living LLC* ***(G-7759)***
Beverly, Willoughby *Also called Golden Living LLC* ***(G-19667)***
Beverly, Ravenna *Also called Golden Living LLC* ***(G-16386)***
Beverly, Akron *Also called Golden Living LLC* ***(G-240)***
Beverly, Wadsworth *Also called Golden Living LLC* ***(G-18753)***
Beverly, Medina *Also called Golden Living LLC* ***(G-14071)***
Beverly Hills Inn La Llc 859 494-9151
1830 Us Highway 52 Aberdeen (45101) ***(G-1)***
Bexley, Columbus *Also called Nrt Commercial Utah LLC* ***(G-8301)***
Bexley Plaza Apartments, Columbus *Also called Plaza Properties Inc* ***(G-8552)***
Beyond 2000 Realty Inc 440 842-7200
18332 Bagley Rd Cleveland (44130) ***(G-5122)***
Beyond The Horizons Home Healt 608 630-0617
2645 Fairwood Ave Columbus (43207) ***(G-7105)***
Bfg Supply Co Llc (HQ) 440 834-1883
14500 Kinsman Rd Burton (44021) ***(G-2061)***
BFI Waste Services LLC 800 437-1123
1717 Pennsylvania Ave Salem (44460) ***(G-16689)***
BFR, Bluffton *Also called Bluffton Family Recreation* ***(G-1728)***
Bfs Supply, Cincinnati *Also called Frederick Steel Company LLC* ***(G-3646)***
Bg Holding LLC 513 489-1023
4620 Carlynn Dr Blue Ash (45241) ***(G-1543)***
Bg News, Bowling Green *Also called B G News* ***(G-1759)***
Bh Group LLC (PA) 513 671-3300
4730 Ashley Dr West Chester (45011) ***(G-19027)***
Bh Group LLC 513 671-3300
4730 Ashley Dr West Chester (45011) ***(G-19028)***
Bhatti Enterprises Inc 513 886-6000
8045 Vegas Cir West Chester (45069) ***(G-19029)***
Bhc Fox Run Hospital Inc 740 695-2131
67670 Traco Dr Saint Clairsville (43950) ***(G-16628)***
Bhdp Architecture, Cincinnati *Also called Baxter Hodell Donnelly Preston* ***(G-3083)***
BHF Incorporated 740 945-6410
147 E College St Scio (43988) ***(G-16816)***
Bhfi, Scio *Also called BHF Incorporated* ***(G-16816)***
Bhm CPA Group Inc (PA) 740 474-5210
129 Pinckney St Circleville (43113) ***(G-4878)***
Bico Akron Inc 330 794-1716
3100 Gilchrist Rd Mogadore (44260) ***(G-14672)***
Bico Steel Service Centers, Mogadore *Also called Bico Akron Inc* ***(G-14672)***
Biederman Educational Centers, Cleves *Also called Kindertown Educational Centers* ***(G-6802)***
Bieser Greer & Landis LLP 937 223-3277
6 N Main St Ste 400 Dayton (45402) ***(G-9355)***
Big Blue Trucking Inc 330 372-1421
518 Perkins Jones Rd Ne Warren (44483) ***(G-18830)***
Big Broth and Big Siste of Cen (PA) 614 839-2447
1855 E Dbln Grnvl Rd Fl 1 Columbus (43229) ***(G-7106)***
Big Hill Realty Corp 937 426-4420
4011 Danern Dr Beavercreek (45430) ***(G-1229)***
Big Hill Realty Corp (PA) 937 435-1177
5580 Far Hills Ave Dayton (45429) ***(G-9356)***
Big Hill Realty Corp 937 429-2200
3944 Indian Ripple Rd Beavercreek (45440) ***(G-1230)***
Big Lots Inc 330 726-0796
7110 South Ave Youngstown (44512) ***(G-20115)***
Big Lots Stores Inc (HQ) 614 278-6800
300 Phillipi Rd Columbus (43228) ***(G-7107)***
Big Mat Golf Course, Cleveland *Also called Cleveland Metroparks* ***(G-5331)***
Big O Refuse Inc 740 344-7544
1919 Lancaster Rd Ste B Granville (43023) ***(G-11458)***
Big Red LP 740 548-7799
6025 Cheshire Rd Galena (43021) ***(G-11280)***
Big Red Rooster (HQ) 614 255-0200
121 Thurman Ave Columbus (43206) ***(G-7108)***
Big Run Urgent Care Center 614 871-7130
3000 Meadow Pond Ct # 200 Grove City (43123) ***(G-11534)***

ALPHABETIC

(PA)=Parent Co (HQ)=Headquarters (DH)=Div Headquarters
2018 Harris Ohio
Services Directory
1121

ALPHABETIC SECTION

Big Sandy Distribution Inc (PA) 740 574-2113
   8375 Gallia Pike Franklin Furnace (45629) *(G-11168)*
Big Sandy Furniture Inc (HQ) 740 574-2113
   8375 Gallia Pike Franklin Furnace (45629) *(G-11169)*
Big Sandy Furniture Inc 740 354-3193
   730 10th St Portsmouth (45662) *(G-16265)*
Big Sandy Furniture Inc 740 775-4244
   1404 N Bridge St Chillicothe (45601) *(G-2816)*
Big Sandy Furniture Inc 740 894-4242
   45 County Rd 407 Chesapeake (45619) *(G-2781)*
Big Sandy Furniture Store 5, Portsmouth Also called Big Sandy Furniture Inc *(G-16265)*
Big Sandy Service Company, Franklin Furnace Also called Big Sandy Furniture Inc *(G-11169)*
Big Sandy Superstore, Chesapeake Also called Big Sandy Furniture Inc *(G-2781)*
Big Sandy Superstores, Franklin Furnace Also called Big Sandy Distribution Inc *(G-11168)*
Big Western Lanes, Columbus Also called Big Western Operating Co Inc *(G-7109)*
Big Western Operating Co Inc 614 274-1169
   500 Georgesville Rd Columbus (43228) *(G-7109)*
Bigelow Corporation (PA) 937 339-3315
   1530 Mckaig Ave Troy (45373) *(G-18349)*
Bigger Road Veterinary Clinic (PA) 937 435-3262
   5655 Bigger Rd Dayton (45440) *(G-9357)*
Bigmar Inc 740 966-5800
   9711 Sportsman Club Rd Johnstown (43031) *(G-12336)*
Bilfinger Westcon Inc 330 818-9734
   4525 Vliet St Sw Canton (44710) *(G-2263)*
Bill & Don's Catering, Lorain Also called Lorain Party Center *(G-13057)*
Bill Delord Autocenter Inc 513 932-3000
   917 Columbus Ave Lebanon (45036) *(G-12592)*
Billback Systems LLC 937 433-1844
   8000 Millers Farm Ln Dayton (45458) *(G-9358)*
Billing Connection Inc 740 964-0043
   6422 E Main St Ste 202 Reynoldsburg (43068) *(G-16430)*
Billing Services, Lorain Also called Specialty Medical Services *(G-13076)*
Bills Battery Company Inc 513 922-0100
   5221 Crookshank Rd Cincinnati (45238) *(G-3108)*
Billy Royal, Chagrin Falls Also called Schneider Saddlery LLC *(G-2733)*
Biltimore Towers, Dayton Also called Biltmore Apartments Ltd *(G-9359)*
Biltmore Apartments Ltd 937 461-9695
   210 N Main St Dayton (45402) *(G-9359)*
Bimbo Bakeries Usa Inc 614 868-7565
   1020 Claycraft Rd Ste D Columbus (43230) *(G-7110)*
Bimbo Bakeries Usa Inc 740 446-4552
   1708 Eastern Ave Gallipolis (45631) *(G-11309)*
Bindery & Spc Pressworks Inc 614 873-4623
   351 W Bigelow Ave Plain City (43064) *(G-16184)*
Bindley Western Drug, Dublin Also called Cardinal Health 100 Inc *(G-10276)*
Bindu Associates LLC 440 324-0099
   645 Griswold Rd Elyria (44035) *(G-10598)*
Bingo Division, Youngstown Also called Nannicola Wholesale Co *(G-20293)*
Binkelman Corporation (PA) 419 537-9333
   2601 Hill Ave Toledo (43607) *(G-17771)*
Bio-Blood Components Inc 614 294-3183
   1393 N High St Columbus (43201) *(G-7111)*
Bio-Mdcal Applcations Ohio Inc 937 279-3120
   4100 Salem Ave Trotwood (45416) *(G-18344)*
Bio-Mdcal Applcations Ohio Inc 419 874-3447
   701 Commerce Dr Perrysburg (43551) *(G-15979)*
Bio-Mdcal Applcations Ohio Inc 330 928-4511
   320 Broadway St E Cuyahoga Falls (44221) *(G-9166)*
Bio-Mdcal Applcations Ohio Inc 330 376-4905
   345 Bishop St Akron (44307) *(G-102)*
Bio-Mdcal Applcations Ohio Inc 419 774-0180
   680 Bally Row Mansfield (44906) *(G-13266)*
Bio-Mdcal Applcations Ohio Inc 330 896-6311
   1575 Corp Woods Pkwy # 100 Uniontown (44685) *(G-18507)*
Bio-Mdcal Applcations Ohio Inc 614 338-8202
   4039 E Broad St Columbus (43213) *(G-7112)*
Bio-Mdical Applications RI Inc 740 389-4111
   1730 Marion Waldo Rd Marion (43302) *(G-13524)*
Biolife Plasma Services LP 419 425-8680
   1789 E Melrose Ave Findlay (45840) *(G-10994)*
Biolife Plasma Services LP 419 224-0117
   4299 Elida Rd Lima (45807) *(G-12748)*
Biomat Usa Inc 419 531-3332
   3217 Dorr St Ste B Toledo (43607) *(G-17772)*
Biomedical Laboratory, Hubbard Also called Connie Parks *(G-12084)*
Biomedical Research & Educatn, Cincinnati Also called Cincinnti Educ & RES For Vetrn *(G-3339)*
Bionetics Corporation 757 873-0900
   813 Irving Wick Dr W Heath (43056) *(G-11835)*
Bionix Safety Technologies (HQ) 419 727-0552
   5154 Enterprise Blvd Toledo (43612) *(G-17773)*
Biorx LLC (HQ) 866 442-4679
   7167 E Kemper Rd Cincinnati (45249) *(G-3109)*
Biosortia Pharmaceuticals Inc 614 636-4850
   4266 Tuller Rd Dublin (43017) *(G-10263)*
Biotech Medical Inc 330 494-5504
   7800 Whipple Ave Nw Canton (44767) *(G-2264)*
Birch Manor Apartments I, Medina Also called New Birch Manor I Assoc LLC *(G-14106)*

Birchaven Village 419 424-3000
   415 College St Findlay (45840) *(G-10995)*
Birchaven Village (PA) 419 424-3000
   15100 Birchaven Ln Ofc C Findlay (45840) *(G-10996)*
Birchwood Genetics Inc (PA) 937 678-9313
   465 Stephens Rd West Manchester (45382) *(G-19265)*
Bird Enterprises LLC 330 674-1457
   35 W Jackson St Millersburg (44654) *(G-14589)*
Bishop Ready High School, Columbus Also called Catholic Diocese of Columbus *(G-7210)*
Bistro Off Broadway 937 316-5000
   117 E 5th St Greenville (45331) *(G-11489)*
Bitec, Dayton Also called Sample Machining Inc *(G-9866)*
BITTERSWEET FARMS, Whitehouse Also called Bittersweet Inc *(G-19584)*
Bittersweet Inc (PA) 419 875-6986
   12660 Archbold Whthuse Rd Whitehouse (43571) *(G-19584)*
Bitzel Excavating Inc 330 477-9653
   4141 Southway St Sw Canton (44706) *(G-2265)*
Bixby Living Skills Center, Groveport Also called ARC Industries Incorporated O *(G-11624)*
Biz Com Electric Inc 513 961-7200
   2867 Stanton Ave Cincinnati (45206) *(G-3110)*
Bjaam Environmental Inc 330 854-5300
   472 Elm Ridge Ave Canal Fulton (44614) *(G-2141)*
Bkd LLP 513 621-8300
   312 Walnut St Ste 3000 Cincinnati (45202) *(G-3111)*
Bkg Holdings LLC 614 252-7455
   600 N Cassady Ave Ofc Columbus (43219) *(G-7113)*
Bkg Services Inc 614 476-1800
   3948 Townsfair Way # 230 Columbus (43219) *(G-7114)*
Bkp Ambulance District 419 674-4574
   439 S Main St Kenton (43326) *(G-12408)*
Black & Veatch Corporation 614 473-0921
   4449 Easton Way Ste 150 Columbus (43219) *(G-7115)*
Black Diamond Golf Course 330 674-6110
   7500 Township Road 103 Millersburg (44654) *(G-14590)*
Black Eagle Transfer Company, Ashtabula Also called City Taxicab & Transfer Co *(G-734)*
Black Horse Carriers Inc 330 225-2250
   1319 W 130th St Hinckley (44233) *(G-11995)*
Black River Display, Mansfield Also called D & S Crtive Cmmunications Inc *(G-13289)*
Black River Display Group, Mansfield Also called D & S Crtive Cmmunications Inc *(G-13288)*
Black Sapphire C Columbus Univ 614 297-9912
   1421 Olentangy River Rd Columbus (43212) *(G-7116)*
Black Stone Cincinnati LLC 937 773-8573
   106 W Ash St Ste 504 Piqua (45356) *(G-16136)*
Black Stone Cincinnati LLC 937 424-1370
   3044 Kettering Blvd Moraine (45439) *(G-14754)*
Black Stone Cincinnati LLC (PA) 513 924-1370
   4700 E Galbraith Rd Fl 3 Cincinnati (45236) *(G-3112)*
Black Swamp Equipment LLC (PA) 419 445-0030
   700 E Lugbill Rd Archbold (43502) *(G-633)*
Black Swamp Steel Inc 419 867-8050
   1761 Commerce Rd Holland (43528) *(G-12010)*
Black Tie Affair Inc 330 345-8333
   50 Riffel Rd Wooster (44691) *(G-19832)*
Blackbird Capital Group LLC 513 762-7890
   312 Walnut St Ste 1600 Cincinnati (45202) *(G-3113)*
Blackbrook Country Club Inc 440 951-0010
   8900 Lake Shore Blvd Mentor (44060) *(G-14150)*
Blackburns Fabrication Inc 614 875-0784
   2467 Jackson Pike Columbus (43223) *(G-7117)*
Blacklick Wods Mtro Golf Crses, Reynoldsburg Also called Columbus Frkln Cnty Pk *(G-16440)*
Blackstar Drywall Inc 614 242-4242
   9821 E State Route 37 Sunbury (43074) *(G-17550)*
Blackwell Inn, The, Columbus Also called Ohio State University *(G-8404)*
Bladecutters Lawn and Ldscpg, Dayton Also called Bladecutters Lawn Service Inc *(G-9360)*
Bladecutters Lawn Service Inc 937 274-3861
   5440 N Dixie Dr Dayton (45414) *(G-9360)*
Blakemans Valley Off Eqp Inc 330 729-1000
   8534 South Ave Youngstown (44514) *(G-20116)*
Blanchard Tree and Lawn Inc 419 865-7071
   1530 Kieswetter Rd Holland (43528) *(G-12011)*
Blanchard Valley Health System (PA) 419 423-4500
   1900 S Main St Findlay (45840) *(G-10997)*
Blanchard Valley Health System 419 424-3000
   15100 Birchaven Ln Findlay (45840) *(G-10998)*
Blanchard Valley Hospital, Findlay Also called Blanchard Vly Rgional Hlth Ctr *(G-11004)*
Blanchard Valley Hospital 419 423-4335
   306 Lima Ave Findlay (45840) *(G-10999)*
Blanchard Valley Industries, Findlay Also called County of Hancock *(G-11016)*
Blanchard Valley Industries 419 422-6386
   1700 E Sandusky St Findlay (45840) *(G-11000)*
Blanchard Valley Medical Assoc 419 424-0380
   200 W Pearl St Findlay (45840) *(G-11001)*
Blanchard Valley School, Findlay Also called Blanchard Vly Residential Ctr *(G-11002)*
Blanchard Vly Residential Ctr 419 422-6503
   1705 E Main Cross St Findlay (45840) *(G-11002)*
Blanchard Vly Rgional Hlth Ctr 419 427-0809
   1800 N Blanchard St # 121 Findlay (45840) *(G-11003)*
Blanchard Vly Rgional Hlth Ctr (HQ) 419 423-4500
   1900 S Main St Findlay (45840) *(G-11004)*

Blanchard Vly Rgional Hlth Ctr 419 358-9010
139 Garau St Bluffton (45817) *(G-1727)*
Blast-One International, Columbus *Also called Blastmaster Holdings Usa LLC (G-7118)*
Blastmaster Holdings Usa LLC 877 725-2781
4510 Bridgeway Ave Columbus (43219) *(G-7118)*
Blatchford Inc 937 291-3636
1031 Byers Rd Miamisburg (45342) *(G-14276)*
Blatt Trucking Co Inc (PA) 419 898-0002
1205 Main St Rocky Ridge (43458) *(G-16566)*
Blb Transport Inc 740 474-1341
20615 Us Highway 23 N Circleville (43113) *(G-4879)*
Bleachtech LLC 216 921-1980
320 Ryan Rd Seville (44273) *(G-16838)*
Bleckmann USA LLC 740 809-2645
188 Commerce Blvd Ste B Johnstown (43031) *(G-12337)*
Blendon Gardens Inc 614 840-0500
9590 S Old State Rd Lewis Center (43035) *(G-12670)*
Blendonwoods Metro Park, Westerville *Also called Columbus Frkln Cnty Pk (G-19386)*
Blennerhassett Yacht Club Inc 740 423-9062
800 Oneal St Belpre (45714) *(G-1434)*
Bleux Holdings LLC 859 414-5060
7257 Wooster Pike Cincinnati (45227) *(G-3114)*
Blevins Fabrication, Mansfield *Also called Blevins Metal Fabrication Inc (G-13267)*
Blevins Metal Fabrication Inc 419 522-6082
288 Illinois Ave S Mansfield (44905) *(G-13267)*
Blick Clinic Inc (PA) 330 762-5425
640 W Market St Akron (44303) *(G-103)*
Blick Clinic Inc 330 762-5425
682 W Market St Akron (44303) *(G-104)*
Blind & Son LLC 330 753-7711
344 4th St Nw Barberton (44203) *(G-959)*
Blood Center, Cincinnati *Also called University of Cincinnati (G-4760)*
Blood Courier Inc 216 251-3050
3965 W 130th St Cleveland (44111) *(G-5123)*
Blood Services Centl Ohio Reg (PA) 614 253-7981
995 E Broad St Columbus (43205) *(G-7119)*
Bloomberg Ross MD 740 454-1216
2935 Maple Ave Zanesville (43701) *(G-20448)*
Bloomfield Cottages, Ashland *Also called Brethren Care Inc (G-666)*
Blooms By Plantscaping, Cleveland *Also called Plantscaping Inc (G-6285)*
Blossom Hill Care Center, Huntsburg *Also called Blossom Hills Nursing Home (G-12157)*
Blossom Hill Elderly Housing L 330 385-4310
100 Wilbert Ave East Liverpool (43920) *(G-10516)*
Blossom Hills Nursing Home 440 635-5567
12496 Princeton Rd Huntsburg (44046) *(G-12157)*
Blossom Nrsing Rhblitation Ctr, Salem *Also called Blossom Nursing & Rehab Center (G-16690)*
Blossom Nursing & Rehab Center 330 337-3033
109 Blossom Ln Salem (44460) *(G-16690)*
Blue & Co LLC 513 241-4507
720 E Pete Rose Way # 100 Cincinnati (45202) *(G-3115)*
Blue Ash Business Association 513 253-1006
P.O. Box 429277 Cincinnati (45242) *(G-3116)*
Blue Ash Care Center, Cincinnati *Also called Blue Ash Healthcare Group Inc (G-3118)*
Blue Ash Distribution Ctr LLC 513 699-2279
2135 Dana Ave Ste 200 Cincinnati (45207) *(G-3117)*
Blue Ash Educational Building, Blue Ash *Also called R L B Inc (G-1670)*
Blue Ash Fire Department 513 745-8534
10647 Kenwood Rd Blue Ash (45242) *(G-1544)*
Blue Ash Golf Course, Blue Ash *Also called City of Blue Ash (G-1558)*
Blue Ash Healthcare Group Inc 513 793-3362
4900 Cooper Rd Cincinnati (45242) *(G-3118)*
Blue Ash Roofing Co, Blue Ash *Also called Molloy Roofing Company (G-1645)*
Blue Ash YMCA, Blue Ash *Also called Young Mens Christian (G-1725)*
Blue Beacon of Beaverdam, Beaverdam *Also called Blue Beacon USA LP II (G-1289)*
Blue Beacon of Hubbard Inc 330 534-4419
7044 Truck World Blvd Hubbard (44425) *(G-12082)*
Blue Beacon Truck Wash, Hubbard *Also called Blue Beacon USA LP II (G-12083)*
Blue Beacon Truck Wash, New Paris *Also called Blue Beacon USA LP II (G-15075)*
Blue Beacon USA LP II 330 534-4419
7044 Truck World Blvd Hubbard (44425) *(G-12083)*
Blue Beacon USA LP II 419 643-8146
413 E Main St Beaverdam (45808) *(G-1289)*
Blue Beacon USA LP II 937 437-5533
9787 Us Route 40 W New Paris (45347) *(G-15075)*
Blue Chip 2000 Coml Clg Inc 513 561-2999
7250 Edington Dr Cincinnati (45249) *(G-3119)*
Blue Chip Broadcasting, Cincinnati *Also called Urban One Inc (G-4789)*
Blue Chip Consulting Group LLC 216 503-6001
6000 Lombardo Ctr Ste 650 Seven Hills (44131) *(G-16827)*
Blue Chip Mailing Services Inc 513 541-4800
9933 Alliance Rd Ste 1 Blue Ash (45242) *(G-1545)*
Blue Chip Plumbing Inc 513 941-4010
1950 Waycross Rd Cincinnati (45240) *(G-3120)*
Blue Chip Pros, Cincinnati *Also called Blue Chip 2000 Coml Clg Inc (G-3119)*
Blue Chip, The, Cleveland *Also called Massachusetts Mutl Lf Insur Co (G-5993)*
Blue Chp Srgcl Ctr Ptns LLC 513 561-8900
4760 Red Bank Rd Ste 222 Cincinnati (45227) *(G-3121)*
Blue Cross, Worthington *Also called Anthem Insurance Companies Inc (G-19941)*
Blue Cross, Canton *Also called Anthem Insurance Companies Inc (G-2242)*
Blue Cross, Seven Hills *Also called Anthem Insurance Companies Inc (G-16826)*
Blue Cross & Blue Shield Mich 330 783-3841
2405 Market St Youngstown (44507) *(G-20117)*
Blue Heron Golf Course Inc 330 722-0227
3225 Blue Heron Trce Medina (44256) *(G-14039)*
Blue Ribbon Meats Inc 216 631-8850
3316 W 67th Pl Cleveland (44102) *(G-5124)*
Blue Sky Therapy, Canfield *Also called Wsb Rehabilitation Svcs Inc (G-2216)*
Blue Star Lubrication Tech LLC 847 285-1888
3630 E Kemper Rd Cincinnati (45241) *(G-3122)*
Blue Tech Smart Solutions LLC 216 271-4800
5885 Grant Ave Cleveland (44105) *(G-5125)*
Blue Technologies Inc 330 499-9300
5701 Mayfair Rd Canton (44720) *(G-2266)*
Blue Technologies Inc (PA) 216 271-4800
5885 Grant Ave Cleveland (44105) *(G-5126)*
Blue Water Chamber Orchestra 440 781-6215
3631 Perkins Ave Apt 4cn Cleveland (44114) *(G-5127)*
Blue-Kenwood LLC 513 469-6900
5300 Cornell Rd Blue Ash (45242) *(G-1546)*
Bluebird Retirement Community 740 845-1880
2260 State Route 56 Sw London (43140) *(G-12993)*
Bluefin Media, Perrysburg *Also called Brand Technologies Inc (G-15980)*
Bluefoot Energy Services, Steubenville *Also called Bluefoot Industrial LLC (G-17304)*
Bluefoot Industrial LLC 740 314-5299
224 N 3rd St Steubenville (43952) *(G-17304)*
Bluelinx Corporation 330 794-1141
550 Munroe Falls Rd Akron (44305) *(G-105)*
Bluespring Software Inc (PA) 513 794-1764
10290 Alliance Rd Blue Ash (45242) *(G-1547)*
Bluffton Campus, Bluffton *Also called Blanchard Vly Rgional Hlth Ctr (G-1727)*
Bluffton Family Recreation 419 358-6978
215 Snider Rd Bluffton (45817) *(G-1728)*
Blumenthal, Barry, Cincinnati *Also called Trihealth G LLC (G-4694)*
Bmch Inc 216 642-1300
6100 Rksde Woods Blv N405 Ste 405 Independence (44131) *(G-12189)*
Bmf, Fairlawn *Also called Bober Markey Fedorovich (G-10938)*
Bmi Federal Credit Union 614 707-4000
6165 Emerald Pkwy Dublin (43016) *(G-10264)*
Bmi Federal Credit Union (PA) 614 298-8527
760 Kinnear Rd Frnt Columbus (43212) *(G-7120)*
Bmnh Inc 937 845-3561
1885 N Dayton Lakeview Rd New Carlisle (45344) *(G-15020)*
BMW Financial Services Na LLC (HQ) 614 718-6900
5550 Britton Pkwy Hilliard (43026) *(G-11882)*
BMW Financial Services Na LLC 614 718-6900
5515 Parkcenter Cir Dublin (43017) *(G-10265)*
Bnai Brith Hillel Fdn At Osu 614 294-4797
46 E 16th Ave Columbus (43201) *(G-7121)*
Bnd Rentals Inc 937 898-5061
950 Engle Rd Vandalia (45377) *(G-18663)*
Bnsf Logistics LLC 937 526-3141
611 Marker Rd Versailles (45380) *(G-18723)*
Boak & Sons Inc 330 793-5646
75 Victoria Rd Youngstown (44515) *(G-20118)*
Board Amercn Township Trustees 419 331-8651
102 Pioneer Rd Elida (45807) *(G-10586)*
Board Lucas Cnty Commissioners, Toledo *Also called County of Lucas (G-17837)*
Board Man Frst Untd Methdst Ch 330 758-4527
6809 Market St Youngstown (44512) *(G-20119)*
Board Mental Retardation Dvlpm 740 472-1712
47011 State Route 26 Woodsfield (43793) *(G-19812)*
Board of Delaware County 740 201-3600
7991 Columbus Pike Lewis Center (43035) *(G-12671)*
Board of Dir of Wittenbe 937 327-6231
134 W Ward St Springfield (45504) *(G-17151)*
Board of Dir of Wittenbe 937 327-6310
225 N Fountain Ave Springfield (45504) *(G-17152)*
Board of Mental Retardation, Carrollton *Also called County of Carroll (G-2616)*
Board of Mrdd, Marion *Also called County of Marion (G-13535)*
Boardman Medical Supply Co (HQ) 330 545 6700
300 N State St Girard (44420) *(G-11408)*
Boardman Methodist Daycare, Youngstown *Also called Board Man Frst Untd Methdst Ch (G-20119)*
Boardman Molded Intl LLC 330 788-2400
1110 Thalia Ave Youngstown (44512) *(G-20120)*
Boardman School Bus Garage 330 726-3425
7410 Market St Youngstown (44512) *(G-20121)*
Boardman X-Ray & Mri, Youngstown *Also called Regional Imaging Cons Corp (G-20343)*
Boardman Xray Mri, Youngstown *Also called Medical Imging Diagnostics LLC (G-20279)*
Boars Head Provisions Co Inc 614 662-5300
2225 Spiegel Dr Groveport (43125) *(G-11625)*
Bob Miller Rigging Inc 419 422-7477
11758 Township Road 100 Findlay (45840) *(G-11005)*
Bob Mor Inc 419 485-5555
13508 State Route 15 Montpelier (43543) *(G-14737)*
Bob O Link Golf Course, Avon *Also called Avon Properties Inc (G-877)*
Bob Pulte Chevrolet Inc 513 932-0303
909 Columbus Ave Lebanon (45036) *(G-12593)*

ALPHABETIC

Bob Schmitt Homes Inc 440 327-9495
9095 Gapaston Rd North Ridgeville (44039) ***(G-15455)***
Bob Sumerel Tire Co Inc 513 528-1900
471 Ohio Pike Cincinnati (45255) ***(G-3123)***
Bob Sumerel Tire Co Inc 513 598-2300
5977 Harrison Ave Cincinnati (45248) ***(G-3124)***
Bob Sumerel Tire Co Inc 937 235-0062
7711 Center Point 70 Blvd Dayton (45424) ***(G-9361)***
Bob Sumerel Tire Co Inc 513 792-6600
2540 Annuity Dr Cincinnati (45241) ***(G-3125)***
Bob Sumerel Tire Co Inc 614 527-9700
2807 International St Columbus (43228) ***(G-7122)***
Bob Webb Builders Inc 740 548-5577
7662 N Central Dr Lewis Center (43035) ***(G-12672)***
Bob Webb Homes, Lewis Center *Also called Bob Webb Builders Inc* ***(G-12672)***
Bob-Boyd Ford Inc (PA) 614 860-0606
2840 N Columbus St Lancaster (43130) ***(G-12510)***
Bobb Automotive Inc 614 853-3000
4639 W Broad St Columbus (43228) ***(G-7123)***
Bobb Suzuki, Columbus *Also called Bobb Automotive Inc* ***(G-7123)***
Bobbart Industries Inc 419 350-5477
5035 Alexis Rd Ste 1 Sylvania (43560) ***(G-17576)***
Bobboyd Auto Family, Lancaster *Also called Bob-Boyd Ford Inc* ***(G-12510)***
Bobby Tripodi Foundation Inc (PA) 216 524-3787
5905 Brecksville Rd Independence (44131) ***(G-12190)***
Bobcat Enterprises Inc (PA) 513 874-8945
9605 Prnceton Glendale Rd West Chester (45011) ***(G-19030)***
Bobcat of Dayton Inc (PA) 937 293-3176
2850 E River Rd Unit 1 Moraine (45439) ***(G-14755)***
Bobcat of Pittsburgh, Belmont *Also called Reco Equipment Inc* ***(G-1429)***
Bober Markey Fedorovich (PA) 330 762-9785
3421 Ridgewood Rd Ste 300 Fairlawn (44333) ***(G-10938)***
Bobs Moraine Trucking Inc 937 746-8420
8251 Claude Thomas Rd Franklin (45005) ***(G-11150)***
Boc Water Hydraulics Inc 330 332-4444
12024 Salem Warren Rd Salem (44460) ***(G-16691)***
Bodie Electric Inc 419 435-3672
1109 N Main St Fostoria (44830) ***(G-11123)***
Bodine Perry LLC (PA) 330 702-8100
3711 Strrs Cntre Dr Ste 2 Canfield (44406) ***(G-2183)***
Boehringer Ingelheim USA Corp 440 232-3320
300 Northfield Rd Bedford (44146) ***(G-1297)***
Boeing Company 740 788-4000
801 Irving Wick Dr W Newark (43056) ***(G-15147)***
Boeing Company 740 788-4000
801 Irving Wick Dr W Newark (43056) ***(G-15148)***
Boeing Company 937 431-3503
5200 Vincent Ave Wright Patterson Afb (45433) ***(G-20012)***
Boenning & Scattergood Inc 614 336-8851
9922 Brewster Ln Powell (43065) ***(G-16326)***
Bogie Industries Inc Ltd 330 745-3105
1100 Home Ave Akron (44310) ***(G-106)***
Bogner Construction Company 330 262-6730
305 Mulberry St Wooster (44691) ***(G-19833)***
Bohl Crane Inc (PA) 419 476-7525
534 W Laskey Rd Toledo (43612) ***(G-17774)***
Bohl Equipment Company (PA) 419 476-7525
534 W Laskey Rd Toledo (43612) ***(G-17775)***
Boise Cascade Company 740 382-6766
3007 Harding Hwy E Marion (43302) ***(G-13525)***
Bold, E Luke MD PH D, Willoughby *Also called Nelson & Bold Inc* ***(G-19696)***
Boler Company 330 445-6728
2070 Industrial Pl Se Canton (44707) ***(G-2267)***
Bollin & Sons Inc 419 693-6573
6001 Brent Dr Toledo (43611) ***(G-17776)***
Bollin Label Systems, Toledo *Also called Bollin & Sons Inc* ***(G-17776)***
Bolotin Law Offices 419 424-9800
612 S Main St Ste 201 Findlay (45840) ***(G-11006)***
Bolt Construction Inc 330 549-0349
10422 South Ave Youngstown (44514) ***(G-20122)***
BOLT CONSTRUCTION CO, Youngstown *Also called Bolt Construction Inc* ***(G-20122)***
Bolt Express LLC (PA) 419 729-6698
7255 Crossleigh Ct # 108 Toledo (43617) ***(G-17777)***
Bombeck Family Learning Center 937 229-2158
941 Alberta St Dayton (45409) ***(G-9362)***
Bon Appetit Management Co 614 823-1880
100 W Home St Westerville (43081) ***(G-19371)***
Bon Secours Health System 740 966-3116
8148 Windy Hollow Rd Johnstown (43031) ***(G-12338)***
Bonbright Distributors Inc 937 222-1001
1 Arena Park Dr Dayton (45417) ***(G-9363)***
Bonded Chemicals Inc (HQ) 614 777-9240
2645 Charter St Columbus (43228) ***(G-7124)***
Bonezzi Swtzer Mrphy Plito Lpa (PA) 216 875-2767
1300 E 9th St Ste 1950 Cleveland (44114) ***(G-5128)***
Bonneville International Corp 513 699-5102
2060 Reading Rd Ste 400 Cincinnati (45202) ***(G-3126)***
Bonnie Plant Farm, Cygnet *Also called Alabama Farmers Coop Inc* ***(G-9238)***
Bontrager Excavating Co Inc 330 499-8775
11087 Cleveland Ave Nw Uniontown (44685) ***(G-18508)***
Bookmasters Inc (PA) 419 281-1802
30 Amberwood Pkwy Ashland (44805) ***(G-665)***
Boone Coleman Construction Inc 740 858-6661
32 State Route 239 Portsmouth (45663) ***(G-16266)***
BOONSHOFT MUSEUM OF DISCOVERY, Dayton *Also called Dayton Society Natural History* ***(G-9491)***
Boost Technologies, Dayton *Also called Shumsky Enterprises Inc* ***(G-9880)***
Boost Technologies LLC 800 223-2203
811 E 4th St Dayton (45402) ***(G-9364)***
Booth, Jack B MD, Zanesville *Also called Thomas E Rojewski MD Inc* ***(G-20538)***
Booz Allen Hamilton Inc 937 429-5580
3800 Pentagon Blvd # 110 Beavercreek (45431) ***(G-1154)***
Boral Resources LLC 740 622-8042
48699 County Rd 275 Coshocton (43812) ***(G-9088)***
Borchers Americas Inc (HQ) 440 899-2950
811 Sharon Dr Westlake (44145) ***(G-19466)***
Bordas & Bordas Pllc 740 695-8141
106 E Main St Saint Clairsville (43950) ***(G-16629)***
Borden Dairy Co Cincinnati LLC 513 948-8811
415 John St Cincinnati (45215) ***(G-3127)***
Bosch Rexroth Corporation 614 527-7400
3940 Gantz Rd Ste F Grove City (43123) ***(G-11535)***
Bosco Centre For Senior, Cleveland *Also called Don Bosco Community Center Inc* ***(G-5501)***
Boss Investigations, Akron *Also called Berns Oneill SEC & Safety LLC* ***(G-100)***
Boston Retail Products Inc 330 744-8100
225 Hubbard Rd Youngstown (44505) ***(G-20123)***
Bostwick Design Partnr Inc 216 621-7900
2729 Prospect Ave E Cleveland (44115) ***(G-5129)***
Bostwick-Braun Company (PA) 419 259-3600
7349 Crossleigh Ct Toledo (43617) ***(G-17778)***
Boulevard Motel Corp 440 234-3131
17550 Rosbough Blvd Cleveland (44130) ***(G-5130)***
Bound Tree Medical LLC (HQ) 614 760-5000
5000 Tuttle Crossing Blvd Dublin (43016) ***(G-10266)***
Boundless Flight Inc (PA) 440 610-3683
20226 Detroit Rd Rocky River (44116) ***(G-16571)***
Bowen Engineering Corporation 614 536-0273
22 E Gay St Ste 700 Columbus (43215) ***(G-7125)***
Bowers Insurance Agency Inc 330 638-6146
339 N High St Cortland (44410) ***(G-9073)***
Bowling Green Coop Nurs Schl 419 352-8675
315 S College Dr Bowling Green (43402) ***(G-1764)***
Bowling Green Lincoln Auto SL, Bowling Green *Also called Bowling Green Lncln-Mrcury Inc* ***(G-1765)***
Bowling Green Lncln-Mrcury Inc 419 352-2553
1079 N Main St Bowling Green (43402) ***(G-1765)***
Bowling Green State Univ Fdn 419 372-2551
Mileti Alumni Center Bowling Green (43403) ***(G-1766)***
Bowling Green State University 419 372-8657
120 W Hall Bowling Green (43403) ***(G-1767)***
Bowling Green State University 419 372-2186
516 Admin Bldg Bowling Green (43403) ***(G-1768)***
Bowling Green State University 419 372-2700
245 Troup Ave Bowling Green (43402) ***(G-1769)***
Bowling Transportation Inc (PA) 419 436-9590
1827 Sandusky St Fostoria (44830) ***(G-11124)***
Bowlmor AMF Corp 440 327-1190
38931 Center Ridge Rd North Ridgeville (44039) ***(G-15456)***
Bowman Agricultural RES Ctr, Thornville *Also called Bowman Organic Farms Ltd* ***(G-17666)***
Bowman Organic Farms Ltd 740 246-3936
8100 Blackbird Ln Thornville (43076) ***(G-17666)***
Bowser Morner and Associates, Toledo *Also called Bowser-Morner Inc* ***(G-17779)***
Bowser-Morner Inc 419 691-4800
1419 Miami St Toledo (43605) ***(G-17779)***
Box 21 Rescue Squad Inc 937 223-2821
100 E Helena St 120 Dayton (45404) ***(G-9365)***
BOY SCOUTS OF AMERICA, Columbus *Also called Simon Knton Cncil Byscuts Amer* ***(G-8734)***
Boy Scouts of America (PA) 513 961-2336
10078 Reading Rd Cincinnati (45241) ***(G-3128)***
Boyas Excavating Inc (PA) 216 524-3620
11311 Rockside Rd Cleveland (44125) ***(G-5131)***
Boyd Funeral Home, Cleveland *Also called E F Boyd & Son Inc* ***(G-5516)***
Boyd Property Group LLC 614 725-5228
71 Winner Ave Columbus (43203) ***(G-7126)***
Boyds Kinsman Home Inc 330 876-5581
7929 State Route 5 Kinsman (44428) ***(G-12453)***
Boys & Girls Club of Columbus 614 221-8830
1108 City Park Ave # 301 Columbus (43206) ***(G-7127)***
Boys & Girls Club of Toledo (PA) 419 241-4258
2250 N Detroit Ave Toledo (43606) ***(G-17780)***
Boys Club Camp Association, Toledo *Also called Boys & Girls Club of Toledo* ***(G-17780)***
Bp 216 731-3826
24310 Lakeland Blvd Euclid (44132) ***(G-10745)***
Bp-Ls-Pt Co 614 841-4500
5275 Sinclair Rd Columbus (43229) ***(G-7128)***
Bpf Enterprises Ltd 419 855-2545
1901 Middlesbrough Ct # 2 Maumee (43537) ***(G-13888)***
Bpi Infrmtion Systems Ohio Inc 440 717-4112
6055 W Snowville Rd Brecksville (44141) ***(G-1815)***
Bpm Realty Inc 614 221-6811
195 N Grant Ave Fl 2a Columbus (43215) ***(G-7129)***

ALPHABETIC SECTION

Bpo Elks of USA 740 622-0794
434 Chestnut St Coshocton (43812) *(G-9089)*
Bprex Plastic Packaging Inc 419 423-3271
170 Stanford Pkwy Findlay (45840) *(G-11007)*
Bps Superstore, Blacklick Also called Buckeye Power Sales Co Inc *(G-1502)*
Brackett Builders Inc (PA) 937 339-7505
185 Marybill Dr S Troy (45373) *(G-18350)*
Bracor Inc 216 289-5300
26250 Euclid Ave Ste 901 Euclid (44132) *(G-10746)*
Braden Med Services Inc 740 732-2356
44519 Marietta Rd Caldwell (43724) *(G-2082)*
Bradley Bay Assisted Living 440 871-4509
605 Bradley Rd Bay Village (44140) *(G-1038)*
Bradley Road Nursing Home 440 871-3474
605 Bradley Rd Bay Village (44140) *(G-1039)*
Brady Ware & Schoenfeld Inc 614 885-7407
4249 Easton Way Ste 100 Columbus (43219) *(G-7130)*
Brady Ware & Schoenfeld Inc (PA) 937 223-5247
3601 Rigby Rd Ste 400 Miamisburg (45342) *(G-14277)*
Brady Ware & Schoenfeld Inc 614 825-6277
4249 Easton Way Ste 100 Columbus (43219) *(G-7131)*
Brady Homes Inc 440 937-6255
36741 Chester Rd Avon (44011) *(G-880)*
Brady Plumbing & Heating Inc 440 324-4261
43191 N Ridge Rd Elyria (44035) *(G-10599)*
Brady Ware, Columbus Also called Brady Ware & Schoenfeld Inc *(G-7131)*
Brady Ware & Company, Miamisburg Also called Brady Ware & Schoenfeld Inc *(G-14277)*
Braeview Manor Inc 216 486-9300
20611 Euclid Ave Cleveland (44117) *(G-5132)*
Brakefire Incorporated 330 535-4343
451 Kennedy Rd Akron (44305) *(G-107)*
Bramarjac Inc 419 884-3434
4300 Algire Rd Mansfield (44904) *(G-13268)*
Bramhall Engrg & Surveying Co (PA) 440 934-7878
801 Moore Rd Avon (44011) *(G-881)*
Brampton Inn, Cleveland Also called 1460 Ninth St Assoc Ltd Partnr *(G-4921)*
Branch Clear Chan San Antonio, Mount Vernon Also called W M V O 1300 AM *(G-14924)*
Brand Build Inc 513 579-1950
9933 Alliance Rd Blue Ash (45242) *(G-1548)*
Brand Energy & Infrastructure 419 324-1305
2961 South Ave Toledo (43609) *(G-17781)*
Brand Technologies Inc 419 873-6600
2262 Levis Commons Blvd Perrysburg (43551) *(G-15980)*
Brandmuscle Inc (HQ) 216 464-4342
1100 Superior Ave E # 500 Cleveland (44114) *(G-5133)*
Brands Insurance Agency Inc 513 777-7775
6449 Allen Rd Ste 1 West Chester (45069) *(G-19031)*
Brands' Marina, Port Clinton Also called Tack-Anew Inc *(G-16257)*
Brandywine Country Club Inc 330 657-2525
5555 Akron Peninsula Rd Peninsula (44264) *(G-15948)*
Brandywine Golf Course, Peninsula Also called Brandywine Country Club Inc *(G-15948)*
Brandywine Master Assn 419 866-0135
7705 Pilgrims Lndg Maumee (43537) *(G-13889)*
Brason's Willcare, Euclid Also called B H C Services Inc *(G-10744)*
Brass Ring Golf Club Ltd 740 385-8966
14405 Country Club Ln Logan (43138) *(G-12969)*
Braun & Steidl Architects Inc (HQ) 330 864-7755
1041 W Market St Akron (44313) *(G-108)*
Bravo Wellness LLC (PA) 216 658-9500
20445 Emerald Pkwy # 400 Cleveland (44135) *(G-5134)*
Brawnstone Security LLC 330 800-9006
6986 Fenwick Ave Ne Canton (44721) *(G-2268)*
Brayman Construction Corp 740 237-0000
505 S 3rd St Ironton (45638) *(G-12282)*
Bre Ddr Parker Pavilions LLC 216 755-6451
3300 Enterprise Pkwy Beachwood (44122) *(G-1056)*
Breakthrough Media Ministries, Canal Winchester Also called World Harvest Church Inc *(G-2180)*
Breast Consultation Center, Cincinnati Also called University of Cincinnati *(G-4769)*
Breathing Air Systems Inc 614 864-1235
8855 E Broad St Reynoldsburg (43068) *(G-16431)*
Breathing Association 614 457-4570
1520 Old Henderson Rd # 201 Columbus (43220) *(G-7132)*
Brechbuhler Scales Inc (PA) 330 458-3060
1424 Scales St Sw Canton (44706) *(G-2269)*
Breckenridge Village, Willoughby Also called Ohio Living *(G-19700)*
Brecksville City Service Dept, Brecksville Also called City of Brecksville *(G-1818)*
Brecksville Community Center, Brecksville Also called City of Brecksville *(G-1819)*
Brecksville Leasing Co LLC 330 659-6166
4360 Brecksville Rd Richfield (44286) *(G-16498)*
Brecksvlle Halthcare Group Inc 440 546-0643
8757 Brecksville Rd Brecksville (44141) *(G-1816)*
Brecon Distribution Center, Cincinnati Also called Duke Energy Ohio Inc *(G-3510)*
Breezy Point Ltd Partnership (PA) 440 247-3363
30575 Bnbridge Rd Ste 100 Solon (44139) *(G-16984)*
Breezy Point Ltd Partnership 330 995-0600
350 N Aurora Rd Aurora (44202) *(G-831)*
Breitinger Company 419 526-4255
595 Oakenwaldt St Mansfield (44905) *(G-13269)*
Brenckle Farms Inc 330 877-4426
12434 Duquette Ave Ne Hartville (44632) *(G-11815)*
Brendamour Moving & Stor Inc 800 354-9715
2630 Glendale Milford Rd D Cincinnati (45241) *(G-3129)*
Brenmar Construction Inc 740 286-2151
900 Morton St Jackson (45640) *(G-12307)*
Brenn Field Nursing Center 330 683-4075
1980 Lynn Dr Orrville (44667) *(G-15767)*
Brennan Manna & Diamond LLC (PA) 330 253-5060
75 E Market St Akron (44308) *(G-109)*
Brennan & Associates Inc 216 391-4822
1550 E 33rd St Cleveland (44114) *(G-5135)*
Brennan Electric LLC 513 353-2229
6859 Cemetary Dr Miamitown (45041) *(G-14370)*
Brennan Equipment Services, Holland Also called Brennan Industrial Truck Co *(G-12012)*
Brennan Industrial Truck Co 419 867-6000
6940 Hall St Holland (43528) *(G-12012)*
Brennan Industries Inc (PA) 440 248-1880
6701 Cochran Rd Cleveland (44139) *(G-5136)*
Brennan Industries Inc 440 248-7088
30205 Solon Rd Solon (44139) *(G-16985)*
Brennan-Eberly Team Sports Inc (PA) 419 865-8326
6144 Merger Dr Holland (43528) *(G-12013)*
Brenneman Lumber Co 740 397-0573
51 Parrott St Mount Vernon (43050) *(G-14879)*
Brent Burris Trucking LLC 419 759-2020
2445 County Road 75 Ada (45810) *(G-3)*
Brent Industries Inc 419 382-8693
2922 South Ave Toledo (43609) *(G-17782)*
Brentley Institute Inc 216 225-0087
3143 W 33rd St Ste 2 Cleveland (44109) *(G-5137)*
Brentlinger Enterprises 614 889-2571
6335 Perimeter Loop Rd Dublin (43017) *(G-10267)*
Brentwood Golf Club Inc 440 322-9254
4456 Abbe Rd Sheffield Village (44054) *(G-16884)*
Brentwood Health Care Center, Northfield Also called Brentwood Life Care Company *(G-15511)*
Brentwood Life Care Company 330 468-2273
907 W Aurora Rd Northfield (44067) *(G-15511)*
Brenwood Inc 740 452-7533
1709 Maple Ave Zanesville (43701) *(G-20449)*
Brethren Care Inc 419 289-0803
2140 Center St Ofc Ashland (44805) *(G-666)*
Brethren Care Village LLC 419 289-1585
2140 Center St Ashland (44805) *(G-667)*
Brewer-Garrett Co (PA) 440 243-3535
6800 Eastland Rd Middleburg Heights (44130) *(G-14378)*
Brewster Convalescent Center, Brewster Also called Brewster Parke Inc *(G-1854)*
Brewster Parke Inc 330 767-4179
264 Mohican St Ne Brewster (44613) *(G-1854)*
Brg Realty Group LLC (PA) 513 936-5960
7265 Kenwood Rd Ste 111 Cincinnati (45236) *(G-3130)*
Brian Brocker Dr 330 747-9215
1616 Covington St Youngstown (44510) *(G-20124)*
Brian-Kyles Construction Inc 440 242-0298
875 N Ridge Rd E Lorain (44055) *(G-13019)*
Briar Hill Hlth Care Residence, Middlefield Also called Briar HI Hlth Care Rsdence Inc *(G-14394)*
Briar HI Hlth Care Rsdence Inc 440 632-5241
15950 Pierce St Middlefield (44062) *(G-14394)*
Briar-Gate Realty Inc 614 299-2121
1675 W Mound St Columbus (43223) *(G-7133)*
Briar-Gate Realty Inc 614 299-2122
3655 Brookham Dr Grove City (43123) *(G-11536)*
Briar-Gate Realty Inc 614 299-2121
3827 Brookham Dr Grove City (43123) *(G-11537)*
Briarfield At Ashley Circle, Boardman Also called Ashley Enterprises LLC *(G-1737)*
Briarfield At Ashley Circle 330 793-3010
5291 Ashley Cir Youngstown (44515) *(G-20125)*
BRIARFIELD AT GLANZMAN ROAD, Toledo Also called Concord Care Center of Toledo *(G-17829)*
Briarfield of Sandusky, Sandusky Also called Concord Health Care Inc *(G-16746)*
Briarwood Banquet Center, Cincinnati Also called Banquets Unlimited *(G-3075)*
Briarwood Healthcare Center, Stow Also called Briarwood Ltd *(G-17354)*
Briarwood Ltd 330 688-1828
3700 Englewood Dr Stow (44224) *(G-17354)*
Briarwood Mano, Coldwater Also called Hcf of Briarwood Inc *(G-6829)*
Brice Hotel Inc 614 864-1280
2100 Brice Rd Reynoldsburg (43068) *(G-16432)*
Bricker & Eckler LLP (PA) 614 227-2300
100 S 3rd St Ste B Columbus (43215) *(G-7134)*
Bricker & Eckler LLP 513 870-6700
201 E 5th St Ste 1110 Cincinnati (45202) *(G-3131)*
Brickman Facility Services, New Albany Also called Brightview Landscapes LLC *(G-14975)*
Bridge Counseling Center, Columbus Also called Northland Brdg Franklin Cnty *(G-8291)*
Bridge Home Health & Hostice, Findlay Also called Blanchard Valley Health System *(G-10998)*
Bridge Logistics Inc 513 874-7444
5 Circle Freeway Dr West Chester (45246) *(G-19193)*
Bridge The, Youngstown Also called Siffrin Residential Assn *(G-20375)*

Bridgepoint Risk MGT LLC 419 794-1075
1440 Arrowhead Dr Maumee (43537) ***(G-13890)***
Bridgeport Auto Parts Inc (PA) 740 635-0441
890 National Rd Bridgeport (43912) ***(G-1860)***
Bridgeport Healthcare Center, Portsmouth *Also called Royce Leasing Co LLC* ***(G-16305)***
Bridges To Independence Inc (PA) 740 362-1996
61 W William St Delaware (43015) ***(G-10074)***
Bridges To Independence Inc 740 375-5533
117 N Greenwood St Ste 2 Marion (43302) ***(G-13526)***
Bridgeshome Health Care 330 764-1000
5075 Windfall Rd Medina (44256) ***(G-14040)***
Bridgestone Americas Center, Akron *Also called Bridgestone Research LLC* ***(G-110)***
Bridgestone Research LLC 330 379-7570
1655 S Main St Akron (44301) ***(G-110)***
Bridgestone Ret Operations LLC 513 367-7888
10606 New Haven Rd Harrison (45030) ***(G-11792)***
Bridgestone Ret Operations LLC 513 522-2525
8398 Winton Rd Cincinnati (45231) ***(G-3132)***
Bridgestone Ret Operations LLC 513 741-9701
9820 Colerain Ave Cincinnati (45251) ***(G-3133)***
Bridgestone Ret Operations LLC 330 929-3391
2761 State Rd Cuyahoga Falls (44223) ***(G-9167)***
Bridgestone Ret Operations LLC 419 691-7111
3311 Woodville Rd Northwood (43619) ***(G-15527)***
Bridgestone Ret Operations LLC 513 271-7100
5907 Wooster Pike Cincinnati (45227) ***(G-3134)***
Bridgestone Ret Operations LLC 419 586-1600
1109 N Main St Celina (45822) ***(G-2636)***
Bridgewater Dairy LLC 419 485-8157
14587 County Road 8 50 Montpelier (43543) ***(G-14738)***
Bridgeway Inc (PA) 216 688-4114
2202 Prame Ave Cleveland (44109) ***(G-5138)***
Bridgeway Pointe, Cincinnati *Also called Drake Development Inc* ***(G-3502)***
Bright Beginnings 937 748-2612
60 E North St Springboro (45066) ***(G-17116)***
Bright Beginnings Preschool, Bowling Green *Also called Bowling Green Coop Nurs Schl* ***(G-1764)***
Bright Dental, Sandusky *Also called Smile Brands Inc* ***(G-16795)***
Bright Horizons Battelle, Columbus *Also called Bright Horizons Chld Ctrs LLC* ***(G-7135)***
Bright Horizons Chld Ctrs LLC 614 754-7023
835 Thomas Ln Columbus (43214) ***(G-7135)***
Bright Horizons Chld Ctrs LLC 614 566-9322
111 S Grant Ave Columbus (43215) ***(G-7136)***
Bright Horizons Chld Ctrs LLC 614 227-0550
277 E Town St Columbus (43215) ***(G-7137)***
Bright Horizons Chld Ctrs LLC 614 566-4847
835 Thomas Ln Columbus (43214) ***(G-7138)***
Bright Horizons Chld Ctrs LLC 330 375-7633
475 Ohio St Akron (44304) ***(G-111)***
Brighter Horizons Residential 440 417-1751
1899 Hubbard Rd Madison (44057) ***(G-13221)***
Brighton Gardens of Westlake, Westlake *Also called Sunrise Senior Living Inc* ***(G-19552)***
Brighton Gardens Wash Township, Dayton *Also called Sunrise Senior Living Inc* ***(G-9915)***
Brighton-Best Intl Inc 440 238-1350
16065 Imperial Pkwy Strongsville (44149) ***(G-17447)***
Brightstar Healthcare 513 321-4688
10999 Reed Hartman Hwy # 209 Blue Ash (45242) ***(G-1549)***
Brightview Landscape Svcs Inc 614 801-1712
3001 Innis Rd Columbus (43224) ***(G-7139)***
Brightview Landscape Svcs Inc 614 478-2085
3001 Innis Rd Columbus (43224) ***(G-7140)***
Brightview Landscape Svcs Inc 740 369-4800
3001 Innis Rd Columbus (43224) ***(G-7141)***
Brightview Landscapes LLC 937 235-9595
38 Brandt St Dayton (45404) ***(G-9366)***
Brightview Landscapes LLC 513 874-6484
10139 Transportation Way West Chester (45246) ***(G-19194)***
Brightview Landscapes LLC 216 398-1289
25072 Broadway Ave Oakwood Village (44146) ***(G-15626)***
Brightview Landscapes LLC 440 937-5126
1051 Lear Industrial Pkwy A Avon (44011) ***(G-882)***
Brightview Landscapes LLC 301 987-9200
2323 Performance Way Columbus (43207) ***(G-7142)***
Brightview Landscapes LLC 614 276-5500
2240 Harper Rd Columbus (43204) ***(G-7143)***
Brightview Landscapes LLC 440 729-2302
7901 Old Ranger Rd Chesterland (44026) ***(G-2793)***
Brightview Landscapes LLC 614 741-8233
6530 W Campus Oval # 300 New Albany (43054) ***(G-14975)***
Brilliant Electric Sign Co Ltd 216 741-3800
4811 Van Epps Rd Brooklyn Heights (44131) ***(G-1911)***
Brilligent Solutions Inc (PA) 937 879-4148
1130 Channingway Dr Fairborn (45324) ***(G-10785)***
Brinks Incorporated 614 291-1268
1362 Essex Ave Columbus (43211) ***(G-7144)***
Brinks Incorporated 614 291-0624
506 E Starr Ave Columbus (43201) ***(G-7145)***
Brinks Incorporated 216 621-7493
1422 Superior Ave E Cleveland (44114) ***(G-5139)***
Brinks Incorporated 330 633-5351
1601 Industrial Pkwy Akron (44310) ***(G-112)***
Brinks Incorporated 513 621-9310
1105 Hopkins St Cincinnati (45203) ***(G-3135)***
Brinks Incorporated 937 253-9777
4395 Springfield St Dayton (45431) ***(G-9258)***
Brinks Incorporated 330 832-6130
300 Nova Dr Se Massillon (44646) ***(G-13789)***
Brinks Incorporated 614 761-1205
7293 Sawmill Rd Dublin (43016) ***(G-10268)***
Brinks Incorporated 330 758-7379
6971 Southern Blvd Ste F Youngstown (44512) ***(G-20126)***
Bristol Village Homes 740 947-2118
660 E 5th St Waverly (45690) ***(G-18966)***
Bristol West Casualty Insur Co, Independence *Also called Foremost Insurance Company* ***(G-12212)***
Brite Brazing, Wickliffe *Also called HI Tecmetal Group Inc* ***(G-19601)***
Briteskies LLC 216 369-3600
2306 W 17th St Ste 1 Cleveland (44113) ***(G-5140)***
Britton-Gallagher & Assoc Inc 216 658-7100
1375 E 9th St Fl 30 Cleveland (44114) ***(G-5141)***
Brixx Ice Company 937 222-2257
500 E 1st St Dayton (45402) ***(G-9367)***
Broad & James Inc 614 231-8697
3502 E 7th Ave Columbus (43219) ***(G-7146)***
Broad & James Towing, Columbus *Also called Broad & James Inc* ***(G-7146)***
Broad Street Hotel Assoc LP 614 861-0321
4801 E Broad St Columbus (43213) ***(G-7147)***
Broadband Express Inc 614 823-6464
374 Westdale Ave Ste B Westerville (43082) ***(G-19288)***
Broadband Express LLC 513 834-8085
11359 Mosteller Rd Cincinnati (45241) ***(G-3136)***
Broadband Express LLC 419 536-9127
1915 Nebraska Ave Toledo (43607) ***(G-17783)***
Broadband Hospitality, Youngstown *Also called Great Lakes Telcom Ltd* ***(G-20207)***
Broadspire Services Inc 614 436-8990
445 Hutchinson Ave # 550 Columbus (43235) ***(G-7148)***
Broadview Health Center, Columbus *Also called Generation Health Corp* ***(G-7737)***
Broadview Heights, Broadview Heights *Also called Cleveland Clinic Foundation* ***(G-1874)***
Broadview Mortgage Company (PA) 614 854-7000
3982 Powell Rd Ste 230 Powell (43065) ***(G-16327)***
Broadview Multi-Care Center, Parma *Also called Broadview Nursing Home Inc* ***(G-15900)***
Broadview NH LLC 614 337-1066
5151 N Hamilton Rd Columbus (43230) ***(G-7149)***
Broadview Nursing Home Inc 216 661-5084
5520 Broadview Rd Parma (44134) ***(G-15900)***
Broadvox, Cleveland *Also called Infotelecom Holdings LLC* ***(G-5821)***
Broadvox LLC (HQ) 216 373-4600
75 Erieview Plz Fl 4 Cleveland (44114) ***(G-5142)***
Broadway Care Ctr Mple Hts LLC 216 662-0551
16231 Broadway Ave Maple Heights (44137) ***(G-13401)***
Brock & Associates Builders 330 757-7150
118 Heron Bay Dr Youngstown (44514) ***(G-20127)***
Brock & Sons Inc 513 874-4555
8731 N Gilmore Rd Fairfield (45014) ***(G-10824)***
Brocon Construction Inc 614 871-7300
2120 Hardy Parkway St Grove City (43123) ***(G-11538)***
Brodhead Village Ltd (PA) 614 863-4640
160 W Main St New Albany (43054) ***(G-14976)***
Brohl & Appell, Sandusky *Also called Rexel Usa Inc* ***(G-16789)***
Brokaw Inc 216 241-8003
1213 W 6th St Cleveland (44113) ***(G-5143)***
Broken Arrow Inc 419 562-3480
1649 Marion Rd Bucyrus (44820) ***(G-2024)***
Bron-Shoe Company 614 252-0967
1313 Alum Creek Dr Columbus (43209) ***(G-7150)***
Brondes All Makes Auto Leasing 419 887-1511
1511 Reynolds Rd Maumee (43537) ***(G-13891)***
Brook Beech 216 831-2255
3737 Lander Rd Cleveland (44124) ***(G-5144)***
Brook Haven Home Health Care 937 833-6945
850 Albert Rd Brookville (45309) ***(G-1959)***
Brook Park Recreation Center, Cleveland *Also called City of Brook Park* ***(G-5248)***
Brook Plum Country Club 419 625-5394
3712 Galloway Rd Sandusky (44870) ***(G-16729)***
Brook Willow Chrstn Cmmunities 614 885-3300
55 Lazelle Rd Columbus (43235) ***(G-7151)***
Brookdale Austintown, Austintown *Also called Brookdale Snior Lving Cmmnties* ***(G-868)***
Brookdale Beavercreek, Beavercreek *Also called Brookdale Senior Living Commun* ***(G-1231)***
Brookdale Deer Park 513 745-7600
3801 E Galbraith Rd Ofc Cincinnati (45236) ***(G-3137)***
Brookdale Fox Run, Fairborn *Also called Brookdale Senior Living Inc* ***(G-10786)***
Brookdale Kettering, Beavercreek Township *Also called Brookdale Senior Living Inc* ***(G-1287)***
Brookdale Living Cmnty Ohio, Columbus *Also called Brookdale Lving Cmmunities Inc* ***(G-7152)***
Brookdale Lving Cmmunities Inc 614 734-1000
3500 Trillium Xing Columbus (43235) ***(G-7152)***
Brookdale Lving Cmmunities Inc 330 666-4545
100 Brookmont Rd Ofc Akron (44333) ***(G-113)***
Brookdale Lving Cmmunities Inc 937 399-1216
2981 Vester Ave Springfield (45503) ***(G-17153)***

Brookdale Place Wooster LLC 330 262-1615
1615 Cleveland Rd Wooster (44691) *(G-19834)*
Brookdale Senior Living Commun 330 829-0180
1277 S Sawburg Ave Alliance (44601) *(G-528)*
Brookdale Senior Living Commun 937 203-8443
3839 Indian Ripple Rd Beavercreek (45440) *(G-1231)*
Brookdale Senior Living Commun 937 548-6800
1401 N Broadway St Greenville (45331) *(G-11490)*
Brookdale Senior Living Inc 614 336-3677
7220 Muirfield Dr Dublin (43017) *(G-10269)*
Brookdale Senior Living Inc 937 203-8596
280 Walden Way Ofc Beavercreek Township (45440) *(G-1287)*
Brookdale Senior Living Inc 419 756-5599
1841 Middle Bellville Rd Mansfield (44904) *(G-13270)*
Brookdale Senior Living Inc 513 229-3155
5535 Irwin Simpson Rd Mason (45040) *(G-13668)*
Brookdale Senior Living Inc 855 308-2438
9101 Winton Rd Cincinnati (45231) *(G-3138)*
Brookdale Senior Living Inc 513 745-9292
9090 Montgomery Rd Cincinnati (45242) *(G-3139)*
Brookdale Senior Living Inc 937 294-1772
1701 Far Hills Ave Oakwood (45419) *(G-15620)*
Brookdale Senior Living Inc 330 262-1615
1615 Cleveland Rd Wooster (44691) *(G-19835)*
Brookdale Senior Living Inc 330 666-7011
101 N Clvland Mssillon Rd Akron (44333) *(G-114)*
Brookdale Senior Living Inc 614 277-1200
1305 Lamplighter Dr Grove City (43123) *(G-11539)*
Brookdale Senior Living Inc 216 321-6331
3151 Mayfield Rd Cleveland (44118) *(G-5145)*
Brookdale Senior Living Inc 440 892-4200
28550 Westlake Village Dr Westlake (44145) *(G-19467)*
Brookdale Senior Living Inc 937 864-1500
7800 Dyton Springfield Rd Fairborn (45324) *(G-10786)*
Brookdale Senior Living Inc 614 794-2499
690 Cooper Rd Apt 514 Westerville (43081) *(G-19372)*
Brookdale Senior Living Inc 330 723-5825
49 Leisure Ln A Medina (44256) *(G-14041)*
Brookdale Senior Living Inc 513 745-7600
3801 E Galbraith Rd Ofc Cincinnati (45236) *(G-3140)*
Brookdale Senior Living Inc 419 422-8657
600 Fox Run Rd Ofc Findlay (45840) *(G-11008)*
Brookdale Senior Living Inc 937 738-7342
1565 London Ave Frnt Marysville (43040) *(G-13607)*
Brookdale Snior Lving Cmmnties 740 366-0005
331 Goosepond Rd Newark (43055) *(G-15149)*
Brookdale Snior Lving Cmmnties 937 832-8500
350 Union Blvd Englewood (45322) *(G-10698)*
Brookdale Snior Lving Cmmnties 419 354-5300
121 N Wintergarden Rd Ofc Bowling Green (43402) *(G-1770)*
Brookdale Snior Lving Cmmnties 740 681-9903
241 Whittier Dr S Lancaster (43130) *(G-12511)*
Brookdale Snior Lving Cmmnties 419 423-4440
725 Fox Run Rd Findlay (45840) *(G-11009)*
Brookdale Snior Lving Cmmnties 330 249-1071
1420 S Canfield Niles Rd Austintown (44515) *(G-868)*
Brookdale Snior Lving Cmmnties 419 756-5599
1841 Middle Bellville Rd Mansfield (44904) *(G-13271)*
Brookdale Snior Lving Cmmnties 937 773-0500
1744 W High St Ofc Piqua (45356) *(G-16137)*
Brookdale Snior Lving Cmmnties 330 793-0085
2300 Canfield Rd Ofc Youngstown (44511) *(G-20128)*
Brookdale Willoughby, Willoughby *Also called Emeritus Corporation* *(G-19661)*
Brookeside Ambulance Services 419 476-7442
640 Phillips Ave Toledo (43612) *(G-17784)*
Brookhaven Home Health Care, Brookville *Also called Brook Haven Home Health Care* *(G-1959)*
BROOKHAVEN NURSING & CARE CENT, Brookville *Also called Brookville Enterprises Inc* *(G-1960)*
Brookhill Center Industries 419 876-3932
7989 State Route 108 Ottawa (45875) *(G-15796)*
Brookledge Golf Club, Cuyahoga Falls *Also called City of Cuyahoga Falls* *(G-9174)*
Brooklyn Adult Activity Center, Cleveland *Also called A W S Inc* *(G-4938)*
Brooklyn House, Cleveland *Also called Koinonia Homes Inc* *(G-5907)*
Brookpark Freeway Lanes LLC 216 267-2150
12850 Brookpark Rd Cleveland (44130) *(G-5146)*
Brooks & Stafford Co 216 696-3000
55 Public Sq Ste 1650 Cleveland (44113) *(G-5147)*
Brooksedge Day Care Center 614 529-0077
2185 Hilliard Rome Rd Hilliard (43026) *(G-11883)*
Brookside Country Club Inc 330 477-6505
1800 Canton Ave Nw Canton (44708) *(G-2270)*
Brookside Extended Care Center 513 398-1020
780 Snider Rd Mason (45040) *(G-13669)*
Brookside Golf & Cntry CLB Co 614 889-2581
2770 W Dblin Granville Rd Columbus (43235) *(G-7153)*
Brookside Holdings LLC 419 224-7019
3211 S Dixie Hwy Lima (45804) *(G-12749)*
Brookside Holdings LLC (PA) 419 925-4457
8022 State Route 119 Maria Stein (45860) *(G-13427)*
Brookside Laboratories Inc 419 977-2766
200 White Mountain Dr New Bremen (45869) *(G-15016)*
Brookside Trucking, Lima *Also called Brookside Holdings LLC* *(G-12749)*
Brookside Trucking, Maria Stein *Also called Brookside Holdings LLC* *(G-13427)*
Brookview Healthcare Center, Defiance *Also called Brookview Healthcare Ctr* *(G-10020)*
Brookview Healthcare Ctr 419 784-1014
214 Harding St Defiance (43512) *(G-10020)*
Brookville Enterprises Inc 937 833-2133
1 Country Ln Brookville (45309) *(G-1960)*
Brookville Roadster Inc 937 833-4605
718 Albert Rd Brookville (45309) *(G-1961)*
Brookwood Management Company (PA) 330 497-6565
1201 S Main St Ste 220 Canton (44720) *(G-2271)*
Brookwood Retirement Community, Cincinnati *Also called C Micah Rand Inc* *(G-3162)*
Brotherhd Frtrnl Ordr, Coshocton *Also called Bpo Elks of USA* *(G-9089)*
Brotherhood of Locomotive Engi 740 345-0978
745 Sherman Ave Newark (43055) *(G-15150)*
Brothers Auto Transport LLC 330 824-0082
2188 Lyntz Townline Rd Sw Warren (44481) *(G-18831)*
Brothers Properties Corp 513 381-3000
601 Vine St Ste 1 Cincinnati (45202) *(G-3141)*
Brothers Publishing Co LLC 937 548-3330
5312 Sebring Warner Rd Greenville (45331) *(G-11491)*
Brothers Trading Co Inc (PA) 937 746-1010
400 Victory Ln Springboro (45066) *(G-17117)*
Brothrhood Lcomotive Engineers, Newark *Also called Brotherhood of Locomotive Engi* *(G-15150)*
Brott Mardis & Co 330 762-5022
1540 W Market St Akron (44313) *(G-115)*
Broughton International, Cincinnati *Also called Rippe & Kingston Systems Inc* *(G-4421)*
Brouse McDowell Lpa 216 830-6830
600 Superior Ave E # 1600 Cleveland (44114) *(G-5148)*
Brower Products Inc (HQ) 937 563-1111
401 Northland Blvd Cincinnati (45240) *(G-3142)*
Brown & Brown of Ohio LLC 419 874-1974
360 3 Meadows Dr Perrysburg (43551) *(G-15981)*
Brown and Caldwell 614 410-6144
4700 Lakehurst Ct Ste 100 Dublin (43016) *(G-10270)*
Brown and Margolius Co Lpa 216 621-2034
55 Public Sq Ste 1100 Cleveland (44113) *(G-5149)*
Brown Cnty Bd Mntal Rtardation 937 378-4891
325 W State St Ste A2 Georgetown (45121) *(G-11384)*
Brown Cnty Snior Ctzen Council 937 378-6603
505 N Main St Georgetown (45121) *(G-11385)*
Brown Co Ed Service Center 937 378-6118
9231b Hamer Rd Georgetown (45121) *(G-11386)*
Brown Contracting & Dev LLC 419 341-3939
318 Madison St Port Clinton (43452) *(G-16238)*
Brown County Asphalt Inc 937 446-2481
11254 Hamer Rd Georgetown (45121) *(G-11387)*
Brown County Engineers Office, Georgetown *Also called County of Brown* *(G-11390)*
Brown Derby Roadhouse 330 528-3227
72 N Main St Ste 208 Hudson (44236) *(G-12105)*
Brown Distributing Inc 740 349-7999
51 Swans Rd Ne Newark (43055) *(G-15151)*
Brown Gibbons Lang & Co LLC (PA) 216 241-2800
1 Cleveland C Cleveland (44114) *(G-5150)*
Brown Gibbons Lang Ltd Ptrship 216 241-2800
1111 Superior Ave E # 900 Cleveland (44114) *(G-5151)*
Brown Industrial Inc 937 693-3838
311 W South St Botkins (45306) *(G-1752)*
Brown Medical LLC 740 574-8728
1661 State Route 522 # 3 Wheelersburg (45694) *(G-19571)*
Brown Medical Services, Wheelersburg *Also called Proactive Occptnal Mdicine Inc* *(G-19580)*
Brown Memorial Home Inc 740 474-6238
158 E Mound St Circleville (43113) *(G-4880)*
Brown Memorial Hospital 440 593-1131
158 W Main Rd Conneaut (44030) *(G-9040)*
Brown Motor Sales Co (PA) 419 531-0151
5625 W Central Ave Toledo (43615) *(G-17785)*
Brown Motors, Toledo *Also called Brown Motor Sales Co* *(G-17785)*
Brown WD General Agency Inc 216 241-5840
950 Main Ave Ste 600 Cleveland (44113) *(G-5152)*
Brown, Chris R & Vicki J, Willard *Also called Family Health Partners Inc* *(G-19619)*
Brown, Frank R & Sons, Silver Lake *Also called F B and S Masonry Inc* *(G-16962)*
Browning Mesonic Community (PA) 419 878-4055
8883 Browning Dr Waterville (43566) *(G-18941)*
Browning-Ferris Inds of Ohio (HQ) 330 793-7676
3870 Hendricks Rd Youngstown (44515) *(G-20129)*
Browning-Ferris Inds of Ohio 330 536-8013
8100 S State Line Rd Lowellville (44436) *(G-13170)*
Browning-Ferris Industries Inc 513 899-2942
2420 Mason Morrow Millgro Morrow (45152) *(G-14844)*
Browning-Ferris Industries LLC 440 786-9390
30300 Pettibone Rd Solon (44139) *(G-16986)*
Browning-Ferris Industries LLC 330 393-0385
1901 Pine Ave Se Warren (44483) *(G-18832)*
Browns Run Country Club 513 423-6291
6855 Sloebig Rd Middletown (45042) *(G-14419)*
Brownstone Private Child Care 216 221-1470
18225 Sloane Ave Lakewood (44107) *(G-12472)*

ALPHABETIC

Bruce Klinger — ALPHABETIC SECTION

Bruce Klinger 419 473-2270
   3950 Sunforest Ct Ste 200 Toledo (43623) *(G-17786)*
Bruce M Allman 513 352-6712
   312 Walnut St Ste 1400 Cincinnati (45202) *(G-3143)*
Bruce R Bracken 513 558-3700
   222 Piedmont Ave Cincinnati (45219) *(G-3144)*
Bruder Inc 216 791-9800
   16900 Rockside Rd Maple Heights (44137) *(G-13402)*
Brumbaugh Construction Inc 937 692-5107
   3520 State Route 49 Arcanum (45304) *(G-629)*
Brumbaugh Engrg Surveying LLC 937 698-3000
   1105 S Miami St Ste 1 West Milton (45383) *(G-19268)*
Bruner Corporation (PA) 614 334-9000
   3637 Lacon Rd Hilliard (43026) *(G-11884)*
Brunk Excavating Inc 513 360-0308
   301 Breaden Dr Monroe (45050) *(G-14691)*
Brunk's Stoves, Salem *Also called L B Brunk & Sons Inc (G-16702)*
Bruns Building & Dev Corp Inc 419 925-4095
   1429 Cranberry Rd Saint Henry (45883) *(G-16665)*
Brunswick Center Ridge Lanes, North Ridgeville *Also called Bowlmor AMF Corp (G-15456)*
Brunswick City Schools (PA) 330 225-7731
   3643 Center Rd Brunswick (44212) *(G-1969)*
Brunswick Companies (PA) 330 864-8800
   2857 Riviera Dr Ste 100 Fairlawn (44333) *(G-10939)*
Brunswick Food Pantry Inc 330 225-0395
   2876 Center Rd Brunswick (44212) *(G-1970)*
Brush Contractors Inc 614 850-8500
   5000 Transamerica Dr Columbus (43228) *(G-7154)*
Brush Creek Motorsports 937 515-1353
   720 E Main St West Union (45693) *(G-19275)*
Brust Pipeline, Bryan *Also called Majaac Inc (G-2010)*
Bryan Electric Inc 740 695-9834
   46139 National Rd W Saint Clairsville (43950) *(G-16630)*
Bryan Systems, Montpelier *Also called Bryan Truck Line Inc (G-14739)*
Bryan Truck Line Inc 419 485-8373
   14020 Us Hwy 20 Ste A Montpelier (43543) *(G-14739)*
Bryant Eliza Village 216 361-6141
   7201 Wade Park Ave Cleveland (44103) *(G-5153)*
Bryant Health Center Inc 740 532-6188
   2932 S 5th St Ironton (45638) *(G-12283)*
Bryden Place Inc 614 258-6623
   25201 Chagrin Blvd # 190 Beachwood (44122) *(G-1057)*
BSI Engineering LLC (PA) 513 201-3100
   300 E Bus Way Ste 300 Cincinnati (45241) *(G-3145)*
Bsl - Applied Laser Tech LLC (PA) 216 663-8181
   4560 Johnston Pkwy Cleveland (44128) *(G-5154)*
Bst & G Joint Fire District 740 965-3841
   350 W Cherry St Sunbury (43074) *(G-17551)*
Btas Inc (PA) 937 431-9431
   4391 Dayton Xenia Rd Beavercreek (45432) *(G-1155)*
Buchy Food Service, Cincinnati *Also called Chas G Buchy Packing Company (G-3232)*
Buck and Sons Landscape Svc 614 876-5359
   7147 Hayden Run Rd Hilliard (43026) *(G-11885)*
Buck Equipment Inc 614 539-3039
   1720 Feddern Ave Grove City (43123) *(G-11540)*
Buckeye Ambulance LLC 937 435-1584
   4601 Gateway Cir Kettering (45440) *(G-12428)*
Buckeye Asphalt Paving Co, Toledo *Also called Lucas County Asphalt Inc (G-18016)*
Buckeye Assn Schl Admnstrators 614 846-4080
   8050 N High St Ste 150 Columbus (43235) *(G-7155)*
Buckeye Body and Equipment, Columbus *Also called Buckeye Truck Equipment Inc (G-7162)*
Buckeye Boxes Inc 614 274-8484
   601 N Hague Ave Columbus (43204) *(G-7156)*
Buckeye Cable Systems Inc 419 724-2539
   4212 South Ave Toledo (43615) *(G-17787)*
Buckeye Charter Service Inc (PA) 419 222-2455
   1235 E Hanthorn Rd Lima (45804) *(G-12750)*
Buckeye Charter Service Inc 937 879-3000
   8240 Expansion Way Dayton (45424) *(G-9368)*
Buckeye Charters, Dayton *Also called Buckeye Charter Service Inc (G-9368)*
Buckeye Check Cashing Inc (HQ) 614 798-5900
   6785 Bobcat Way Ste 200 Dublin (43016) *(G-10271)*
Buckeye Cmnty Eighty One LP 614 942-2020
   3021 E Dblin Granville Rd Columbus (43231) *(G-7157)*
Buckeye Cmnty Hope Foundation (PA) 614 942-2014
   3021 E Dblin Grndville Rd Columbus (43231) *(G-7158)*
Buckeye Cmnty Thirty Five LP 614 942-2020
   2228 11th St Sw Akron (44314) *(G-116)*
Buckeye Cmnty Twenty Six LP 614 942-2020
   3021 E Dblin Granville Rd Columbus (43231) *(G-7159)*
Buckeye Commercial Cleaning 614 866-4700
   12936 Stonecreek Dr Ste F Pickerington (43147) *(G-16087)*
Buckeye Community Bank 440 233-8800
   105 Sheffield Ctr Lorain (44055) *(G-13020)*
Buckeye Community Forty Four, Columbus *Also called Kent Place Housing (G-7981)*
Buckeye Community Services Inc 740 941-1639
   207 Remy Ct Waverly (45690) *(G-18967)*
Buckeye Companies (PA) 740 452-3641
   999 Zane St Zanesville (43701) *(G-20450)*
Buckeye Components LLC (PA) 330 482-5163
   1340 State Route 14 Columbiana (44408) *(G-6853)*

Buckeye Dialysis, Kettering *Also called Basin Dialysis LLC (G-12427)*
Buckeye Distributing Inc 440 526-6668
   215 Ken Mar Indus Pkwy Broadview Heights (44147) *(G-1873)*
Buckeye Drag Racing Assn LLC 419 562-0869
   201 Penn Ave Bucyrus (44820) *(G-2025)*
Buckeye Drmtlogy Drmthphthlogy (PA) 614 389-6331
   5720 Blazer Pkwy Dublin (43017) *(G-10272)*
Buckeye Drmtlogy Drmthphthlogy 614 317-9630
   1933 Ohio Dr Grove City (43123) *(G-11541)*
BUCKEYE FASTENERS COMPANY, Streetsboro *Also called Joseph Industries Inc (G-17418)*
Buckeye Golf Club Co Inc 419 636-6984
   10277 County Road D Bryan (43506) *(G-2003)*
Buckeye Heating and AC Sup Inc (PA) 216 831-0066
   5075 Richmond Rd Bedford Heights (44146) *(G-1348)*
Buckeye Hills-Hck Vly Reg Dev 740 373-6400
   P.O. Box 368 Reno (45773) *(G-16421)*
Buckeye Home Health Care 513 791-6446
   10921 Reed Hartman Hwy # 312 Blue Ash (45242) *(G-1550)*
Buckeye Home Health Care (PA) 937 291-3780
   7700 Paragon Rd Ste A Dayton (45459) *(G-9369)*
Buckeye Home Healthcare Inc 614 776-3372
   635 Park Madow Rd Ste 110 Westerville (43081) *(G-19373)*
Buckeye Honda, Hilliard *Also called Spires Motors Inc (G-11953)*
Buckeye Horizon, Mansfield *Also called Horizon Mechanical and Elec (G-13309)*
Buckeye Insurance, Piqua *Also called Home and Farm Insurance Co (G-16149)*
Buckeye Lake Yacht Club Inc 740 929-4466
   5019 Northbank Rd Buckeye Lake (43008) *(G-2021)*
Buckeye Landscape Service Inc 614 866-0088
   6608 Taylor Rd Blacklick (43004) *(G-1501)*
Buckeye Lanes, North Olmsted *Also called Olmsted Lanes Inc (G-15435)*
Buckeye Launderer and Clrs LLC 419 592-2941
   4930 N Holland Sylvania Sylvania (43560) *(G-17577)*
Buckeye Leasing Inc 330 758-0841
   8063 Southern Blvd Youngstown (44512) *(G-20130)*
Buckeye Linen Service Inc 740 345-4046
   76 Jefferson St Newark (43055) *(G-15152)*
Buckeye Mechanical Contg Inc 740 282-0089
   2325 Township Road 370 Toronto (43964) *(G-18334)*
Buckeye Metals, Cleveland *Also called W R G Inc (G-6714)*
Buckeye Paper Co Inc 330 477-5925
   5233 Southway St Sw # 523 Canton (44706) *(G-2272)*
Buckeye Pipe Line Services Co 419 698-8770
   3321 York St Oregon (43616) *(G-15726)*
Buckeye Pool Inc 937 434-7916
   486 Windsor Park Dr Dayton (45459) *(G-9370)*
Buckeye Power Inc (PA) 614 781-0573
   6677 Busch Blvd Columbus (43229) *(G-7160)*
Buckeye Power Inc 740 598-6534
   306 County Road 7e Brilliant (43913) *(G-1866)*
Buckeye Power Sales Co Inc (PA) 513 755-2323
   6850 Commerce Court Dr Blacklick (43004) *(G-1502)*
Buckeye Power Sales Co Inc 937 346-8322
   5238 Cobblegate Blvd Moraine (45439) *(G-14756)*
Buckeye Prof Imaging Inc 800 433-1292
   5143 Stoneham Rd Canton (44720) *(G-2273)*
Buckeye Protective Service 330 456-2671
   2215 6th St Sw Canton (44706) *(G-2274)*
Buckeye Ranch Inc 614 384-7700
   697 E Broad St Columbus (43215) *(G-7161)*
Buckeye Ranch Inc (PA) 614 875-2371
   5665 Hoover Rd Grove City (43123) *(G-11542)*
Buckeye Real Estate, Columbus *Also called Garland Group Inc (G-7730)*
Buckeye Rsdntial Solutions LLC 330 235-9183
   320 E Main St Ste 301 Ravenna (44266) *(G-16374)*
Buckeye Rubber & Packing Co 216 464-8900
   23940 Mercantile Rd Beachwood (44122) *(G-1058)*
Buckeye Rural Elc Coop Inc 740 379-2025
   4848 State Route 325 Patriot (45658) *(G-15926)*
Buckeye State Credit Union (PA) 330 253-9197
   197 E Thornton St Akron (44311) *(G-117)*
Buckeye State Mutual Insur Co (PA) 937 778-5000
   1 Heritage Pl Piqua (45356) *(G-16138)*
Buckeye Supply Company (HQ) 740 452-3641
   999 Zane St Ste A Zanesville (43701) *(G-20451)*
Buckeye Telesystem Inc 419 724-9898
   2700 Oregon Rd Northwood (43619) *(G-15528)*
Buckeye Trils Girl Scout Cncil (PA) 937 275-7601
   450 Shoup Mill Rd Dayton (45415) *(G-9371)*
Buckeye Truck Equipment Inc 614 299-1136
   939 E Starr Ave Columbus (43201) *(G-7162)*
Buckeye Waste Industries Inc 330 645-9900
   2430 S Main St Coventry Township (44319) *(G-9123)*
Buckeye Western Star, Plain City *Also called Sharron Group Inc (G-16206)*
Buckholz Wall Systems, Hilliard *Also called Buckholz Wall Systems LLC (G-11886)*
Buckholz Wall Systems LLC 614 870-1775
   4160 Anson Dr Hilliard (43026) *(G-11886)*
Buckingham Coal Company LLC 740 767-2907
   11 N 4th St Zanesville (43701) *(G-20452)*
Buckingham Dlttle Brroughs LLC (PA) 330 376-5300
   3800 Embassy Pkwy Akron (44333) *(G-118)*

ALPHABETIC SECTION — Busch Development Corporation

Buckingham Dlttle Brroughs LLC 888 811-2825
  4518 Fulton Dr Nw Canton (44718) *(G-2275)*
Buckingham Dlttle Brroughs LLC 330 492-8717
  4518 Fulton Dr Nw Canton (44718) *(G-2276)*
Buckingham Dlttle Brroughs LLC 330 492-8717
  4518 Fulton Dr Nw Canton (44718) *(G-2277)*
Buckingham Dlttle Brroughs LLC 216 621-5300
  1375 E 9th St Ste 1700 Cleveland (44114) *(G-5155)*
Buckingham Doolittle Burroughs, Cleveland Also called Buckingham Dlttle Brroughs LLC *(G-5155)*
Buckner and Sons Masonry Inc 614 279-9777
  3800 Sullivant Ave Ste A Columbus (43228) *(G-7163)*
Bucyrus Community Hospital Inc 419 562-4677
  629 N Sandusky Ave Bucyrus (44820) *(G-2026)*
Bucyrus Community Hospital LLC 419 562-4677
  629 N Sandusky Ave Bucyrus (44820) *(G-2027)*
Bucyrus Community Physicians 419 492-2200
  120 W Main St New Washington (44854) *(G-15133)*
Budco Group Inc (PA) 513 621-6111
  1100 Gest St Cincinnati (45203) *(G-3146)*
Budde Sheet Metal Works Inc (PA) 937 224-0868
  305 Leo St Dayton (45404) *(G-9372)*
Buddies Inc (PA) 216 642-3362
  3888 Pearl Rd Cleveland (44109) *(G-5156)*
Budenheim Usa Inc 614 345-2400
  2219 Westbrooke Dr Columbus (43228) *(G-7164)*
Buderer Drug Company Inc (PA) 419 627-2800
  633 Hancock St Sandusky (44870) *(G-16730)*
Budget Dumpster LLC (PA) 866 284-6164
  830 Canterbury Rd Westlake (44145) *(G-19468)*
Budget Dumpster Rental, Westlake Also called Budget Dumpster LLC *(G-19468)*
Budget Rent A Car System Inc 216 267-2080
  19719 Maplewood Ave Cleveland (44135) *(G-5157)*
Budget Rent A Car System Inc 937 898-1396
  3300 Valet Dr Vandalia (45377) *(G-18664)*
Budget Rent-A-Car, Toledo Also called George P Ballas Buick GMC Trck *(G-17913)*
Budget Rent-A-Car, Cleveland Also called Budget Rent A Car System Inc *(G-5157)*
Budget Rent-A-Car, Vandalia Also called Budget Rent A Car System Inc *(G-18664)*
Budros Ruhlin & Roe Inc 614 481-6900
  1801 Watermark Dr Ste 300 Columbus (43215) *(G-7165)*
Buehler 10, Dover Also called Buehler Food Markets Inc *(G-10179)*
Buehler Food Markets Inc 330 364-3079
  3000 N Wooster Ave Dover (44622) *(G-10179)*
Buffalo Abrasives Inc 614 891-6450
  1093 Smoke Burr Dr Westerville (43081) *(G-19374)*
Buffalo Jacks 937 473-2524
  137 S High St Covington (45318) *(G-9136)*
Buffalo-Gtb Associates LLC 216 831-3735
  3840 Orange Pl Beachwood (44122) *(G-1059)*
Builder Services Group Inc 614 263-9378
  2365 Scioto Harper Dr Columbus (43204) *(G-7166)*
Builder Services Group Inc 513 942-2204
  28 Keisland Ct Hamilton (45015) *(G-11695)*
Builders Exchange Inc (PA) 216 393-6300
  9555 Rockside Rd Ste 300 Cleveland (44125) *(G-5158)*
Builders Firstsource Inc 937 898-1358
  4173 Old Springfield Rd Vandalia (45377) *(G-18665)*
Builders Firstsource Inc 513 874-9950
  10059 Princeton Glendale Cincinnati (45246) *(G-3147)*
Builders Trash Service 614 444-7060
  1575 Harmon Ave Columbus (43223) *(G-7167)*
Building 8 Inc 513 771-8000
  10995 Canal Rd Cincinnati (45241) *(G-3148)*
Building Blocks Child Care Ctr, Maple Heights Also called Robert A Kaufmann Inc *(G-13415)*
Building Integrated Svcs LLC 330 733-9191
  7777 First Pl Oakwood Village (44146) *(G-15627)*
Building Systems Trnsp Co 740 852-9700
  460 E High St London (43140) *(G-12994)*
Building Technicians Corp 440 466-1651
  4500 Clay St Geneva (44041) *(G-11359)*
Bulk Carrier Trnsp Eqp Co 330 339-3333
  2743 Brightwood Rd Se New Philadelphia (44663) *(G-15083)*
Bulk Carriers and Tank Leasing, New Philadelphia Also called Tank Leasing Corp *(G-15117)*
Bulk Transit Corporation (PA) 614 873-4632
  7177 Indl Pkwy Plain City (43064) *(G-16185)*
Bulk Transit Corporation 937 497-9573
  1377 Riverside Dr Sidney (45365) *(G-16917)*
Bulkfoods.com, Toledo Also called Natural Foods Inc *(G-18079)*
Bulkmatic Transport Company 614 497-2372
  2271 Williams Rd Columbus (43207) *(G-7168)*
Bulldawg Holdings LLC (PA) 419 423-3131
  151 Stanford Pkwy Findlay (45840) *(G-11010)*
Bullock, Jos D MD, Columbus Also called Midwest Allergy Associates *(G-8168)*
Bundy Baking Solutions, Urbana Also called Cmbb LLC *(G-18581)*
Buns of Delaware Inc 740 363-2867
  14 W Winter St Delaware (43015) *(G-10075)*
Buns Restaurant & Bakery, Delaware Also called Buns of Delaware Inc *(G-10075)*
Burbank Inc 419 698-3434
  623 Burbank Dr Toledo (43607) *(G-17788)*
Burch Hydro Inc 740 694-9146
  17860 Ankneytown Rd Fredericktown (43019) *(G-11178)*

Burch Hydro Trucking Inc 740 694-9146
  17860 Ankneytown Rd Fredericktown (43019) *(G-11179)*
Burchwood Care Center 513 868-3300
  4070 Hamilton Mason Rd Fairfield Township (45011) *(G-10925)*
Burd Brothers Inc 513 708-7787
  1789 Stanley Ave Dayton (45404) *(G-9373)*
Burd Brothers Inc (PA) 800 538-2873
  4005 Borman Dr Batavia (45103) *(G-996)*
Burdens Machine & Welding 740 345-9246
  94 S 5th St Newark (43055) *(G-15153)*
Bureau Information & Support, Columbus Also called Ohio Department of Health *(G-8328)*
Bureau Labor Market Info, Columbus Also called Ohio Dept of Job & Fmly Svcs *(G-8334)*
Bureau of Sanitation, Perrysburg Also called City of Perrysburg *(G-15987)*
Bureau of Support, Lima Also called County of Allen *(G-12767)*
Bureau Vctional Rehabilitation, Akron Also called Ohio Rehabilitation Svcs Comm *(G-369)*
Bureau Veritas North Amer Inc 330 252-5100
  520 S Main St Ste 2444 Akron (44311) *(G-119)*
Bureau Workers Compensation 614 466-5109
  13430 Yarmouth Dr Pickerington (43147) *(G-16088)*
Buren Insurance Group Inc (PA) 419 281-8060
  1101 Sugarbush Dr Ashland (44805) *(G-668)*
Burge Building Co Inc 440 245-6871
  2626 Broadway Lorain (44052) *(G-13021)*
BURGE SERVICE, Columbus Also called Willglo Services Inc *(G-8994)*
Burge, Ron, Burbank Also called Ron Burge Trucking Inc *(G-2055)*
Burger Plant, Shadyside Also called Ohio Edison Company *(G-16851)*
Burgess & Niple Inc (PA) 502 254-2344
  5085 Reed Rd Columbus (43220) *(G-7169)*
Burgess & Niple Inc 440 354-9700
  100 W Erie St Painesville (44077) *(G-15837)*
Burgess & Niple Inc 513 579-0042
  312 Plum St Ste 1210 Cincinnati (45202) *(G-3149)*
Burgess & Niple / Heapy Engine 614 459-2050
  5085 Reed Rd Columbus (43220) *(G-7170)*
Burke Inc 513 576-5700
  25 Whitney Dr Ste 110 Milford (45150) *(G-14507)*
Burke Inc (PA) 513 241-5663
  500 W 7th St Cincinnati (45203) *(G-3150)*
Burke & Company, Cincinnati Also called Patrick J Burke & Co *(G-4262)*
Burke & Schindler Pllc 859 344-8887
  901 Evans St Cincinnati (45204) *(G-3151)*
Burke Institute, Cincinnati Also called Burke Inc *(G-3150)*
Burke Manley Lpa 513 721-5525
  225 W Court St Cincinnati (45202) *(G-3152)*
Burke Milford, Milford Also called Burke Inc *(G-14507)*
Burkett and Sons Inc 419 242-7377
  28740 Glenwood Rd Perrysburg (43551) *(G-15982)*
Burkett Restaurant Equipment, Perrysburg Also called Burkett and Sons Inc *(G-15982)*
Burkhardt Springfield Neighbor 937 252-7076
  735 Huffman Ave Dayton (45403) *(G-9374)*
Burkhart Excavating Inc 740 896-3312
  9950 State Route 60 Lowell (45744) *(G-13167)*
Burkhart Trucking Inc 740 896-2244
  9950 State Route 60 Lowell (45744) *(G-13168)*
Burkhart Trucking & Excavating, Lowell Also called Burkhart Trucking Inc *(G-13168)*
Burkshire Construction Company 440 885-9700
  6033 State Rd Cleveland (44134) *(G-5159)*
Burlington House Inc 513 851-7888
  2222 Springdale Rd Cincinnati (45231) *(G-3153)*
Burman Wine, Perrysburg Also called Dayton Heidelberg Distrg Co *(G-15994)*
Burnett Pools Inc (PA) 330 372-1725
  2498 State Route 5 Cortland (44410) *(G-9074)*
Burnett Pools and Spas, Cortland Also called Burnett Pools Inc *(G-9074)*
Burns & Scalo Roofing Co Inc 740 383-4639
  2181 Innovation Dr # 101 Marion (43302) *(G-13527)*
Burns Industrial Equipment Inc 330 425-2476
  8155 Roll And Hold Pkwy Macedonia (44056) *(G-13191)*
Burns International Staffing, Mansfield Also called Lexington Court Care Center *(G-13324)*
Burrier Service Company Inc 440 946-6019
  8669 Twinbrook Rd Mentor (44060) *(G-14151)*
Burton Carol Management (PA) 216 464-5130
  4832 Richmond Rd Ste 200 Cleveland (44128) *(G-5160)*
Burton Health Care Center, Burton Also called Windsor House Inc *(G-2066)*
Burton Rubber Processing, Burton Also called Hexpol Compounding LLC *(G-2062)*
Burtons Collision 513 984-3396
  4384 E Galbraith Rd Cincinnati (45236) *(G-3154)*
Burtons Collision & Auto Repr, Cincinnati Also called Burtons Collision *(G-3154)*
Bus Garage, Amherst Also called Amherst Exempted Vlg Schools *(G-586)*
Bus Garage, Liberty Township Also called Lakota Local School District *(G-12722)*
Bus Garage, Geneva Also called Geneva Area City School Dst *(G-11362)*
Bus Garage & Maintenance Dept, Toledo Also called Washington Local Schools *(G-18299)*
Bus Transportation Department, Columbus Also called Gahanna-Jefferson Pub Schl Dst *(G-7724)*
Busam Fairfield LLC 513 771-8100
  6195 Dixie Hwy Fairfield (45014) *(G-10825)*
Busam Subaru/Suzuki, Fairfield Also called Busam Fairfield LLC *(G-10825)*
Busch Development Corporation 440 842-7800
  7501 Ridge Rd Cleveland (44129) *(G-5161)*

Busch Family Chapels, Cleveland *Also called Busch Development Corporation* ***(G-5161)***
Business Admnstrators Cons Inc (PA)..........614 863-8780
6331 E Livingston Ave Reynoldsburg (43068) ***(G-16433)***
Business Aircraft Group Inc (PA)..........216 348-1415
2301 N Marginal Rd Cleveland (44114) ***(G-5162)***
Business Alternatives Inc..........724 325-2777
3458 Massillon Rd Uniontown (44685) ***(G-18509)***
Business Backer LLC..........513 792-6866
10856 Reed Hartman Hwy # 100 Cincinnati (45242) ***(G-3155)***
Business Community Section, Cincinnati *Also called Universal Advertising Assoc* ***(G-4746)***
Business Consultants Limited, Trenton *Also called Cal Crim Inc* ***(G-18340)***
Business Data Systems Inc..........330 633-1221
1267 Southeast Ave Ste 5 Tallmadge (44278) ***(G-17633)***
Business Equipment Co Inc..........513 948-1500
175 Tri County Pkwy # 120 Cincinnati (45246) ***(G-3156)***
Business Furniture LLC..........937 293-1010
8 N Main St Dayton (45402) ***(G-9375)***
Business Research Services..........216 831-5200
26600 Renaissance Pkwy Cleveland (44128) ***(G-5163)***
Business Stationery LLC..........216 514-1192
4944 Commerce Pkwy Cleveland (44128) ***(G-5164)***
Business Tech & Solutions, Beavercreek *Also called Btas Inc* ***(G-1155)***
Busken Bakery Inc (PA)..........513 871-2114
2675 Madison Rd Cincinnati (45208) ***(G-3157)***
Bussines Air Craft Center, Cleveland *Also called Business Aircraft Group Inc* ***(G-5162)***
Busy Bee Electric Inc..........513 353-3553
100 Washington St Hooven (45033) ***(G-12076)***
Butchko Electric Inc..........440 985-3180
7333 S Dewey Rd Amherst (44001) ***(G-589)***
Butler County of Ohio..........513 887-3728
1800 Princeton Rd Fairfield Township (45011) ***(G-10926)***
Butler County of Ohio..........513 887-3154
130 High St Fl 4 Hamilton (45011) ***(G-11696)***
Butler County of Ohio..........513 785-6500
4631 Dixie Hwy Hamilton (45014) ***(G-11697)***
Butler Animal Health Sup LLC (HQ)..........614 761-9095
400 Metro Pl N Ste 100 Dublin (43017) ***(G-10273)***
Butler Animal Health Sup LLC..........614 718-2000
3820 Twin Creeks Dr Columbus (43204) ***(G-7171)***
Butler Animal Hlth Holdg LLC (HQ)..........614 761-9095
400 Metro Pl N Ste 150 Dublin (43017) ***(G-10274)***
Butler Animal Supply, Dublin *Also called Butler Animal Hlth Holdg LLC* ***(G-10274)***
Butler Asphalt Co LLC..........937 890-1141
7500 Johnson Station Rd Vandalia (45377) ***(G-18666)***
Butler Bhavioral Hlth Svcs Inc (PA)..........513 896-7887
1490 University Blvd Hamilton (45011) ***(G-11698)***
Butler Cincione and Dicuccio..........614 221-3151
556 E Town St 100 Columbus (43215) ***(G-7172)***
Butler Cnty Cmnty Hlth Cnsrtm..........513 454-1460
300 High St 4 Hamilton (45011) ***(G-11699)***
Butler County Bd of Mental RE..........513 785-2815
282 N Fair Ave Ste 1 Hamilton (45011) ***(G-11700)***
Butler County Bd of Mental RE..........513 785-2870
5645 Liberty Fairfield Rd Fairfield Township (45011) ***(G-10927)***
Butler County Board of Develop..........513 867-5913
441 Patterson Blvd Fairfield (45014) ***(G-10826)***
Butler County Care Facility, Fairfield Township *Also called Butler County of Ohio* ***(G-10926)***
Butler County Clerk of Courts..........513 887-3282
315 High St Ste 550 Hamilton (45011) ***(G-11701)***
Butler County Courts, Hamilton *Also called Butler County of Ohio* ***(G-11704)***
Butler County Eductl Svc Ctr..........513 737-2817
23 S Front St Fl 3 Hamilton (45011) ***(G-11702)***
Butler County Eductl Svcs Ctr, Hamilton *Also called Butler County Eductl Svc Ctr* ***(G-11702)***
Butler County Engineers Office, Hamilton *Also called Butler County of Ohio* ***(G-11703)***
Butler County Information Svcs, Hamilton *Also called Butler County of Ohio* ***(G-11705)***
Butler County of Ohio..........513 867-5744
1921 Fairgrove Ave Hamilton (45011) ***(G-11703)***
Butler County of Ohio..........513 887-3090
315 High St Fl 5 Hamilton (45011) ***(G-11704)***
Butler County of Ohio..........513 887-3418
315 High St Fl 2 Hamilton (45011) ***(G-11705)***
Butler Institute of Amercn Art (PA)..........330 743-1711
524 Wick Ave Youngstown (44502) ***(G-20131)***
Butler Rural Electric Coop..........513 867-4400
3888 Stillwell Beckett Rd Oxford (45056) ***(G-15812)***
Butt Construction Company Inc..........937 426-1313
3858 Germany Ln Dayton (45431) ***(G-9259)***
Butterfield Co Inc..........330 832-1282
401 26th St Nw Massillon (44647) ***(G-13790)***
Butterfly Inc..........440 892-7777
8200 E Pleasant Valley Rd Independence (44131) ***(G-12191)***
Butts, Charles L II DDS, Lima *Also called K M Clemens DDS Inc* ***(G-12807)***
Buurma Farms Incorporated (PA)..........419 935-6411
3909 Kok Rd Willard (44890) ***(G-19617)***
Buxton Inn Inc..........740 587-0001
313 Broadway E Granville (43023) ***(G-11459)***
Buy Below Retail Inc..........216 292-7805
23600 Mercantile Rd Ste G Cleveland (44122) ***(G-5165)***
Buyers Products Company (PA)..........440 974-8888
9049 Tyler Blvd Mentor (44060) ***(G-14152)***
Bw Enterprises Inc..........937 568-9660
276 Clubhouse Dr South Charleston (45368) ***(G-17075)***
Bw Supply Co., Lyons *Also called B W Grinding Co* ***(G-13185)***
BWC Trucking Company Inc..........740 532-5188
164 State Route 650 Ironton (45638) ***(G-12284)***
Bwi Group NA, Moraine *Also called Bwi North America Inc* ***(G-14757)***
Bwi North America Inc..........937 212-2892
2582 E River Rd Moraine (45439) ***(G-14757)***
Bwxt Nclear Oprtions Group Inc..........216 912-3000
24703 Euclid Ave Cleveland (44117) ***(G-5166)***
Bx Ohio, Cleveland *Also called Builders Exchange Inc* ***(G-5158)***
By-Line Transit Inc..........937 642-2500
17075 White Stone Rd Marysville (43040) ***(G-13608)***
Byer Steel Division, Cincinnati *Also called Byer Steel Recycling Inc* ***(G-3158)***
Byer Steel Recycling Inc (PA)..........513 948-0300
200 W North Bend Rd Cincinnati (45216) ***(G-3158)***
Byrnes-Conway Company..........513 948-8882
21 Byrneslake Ct Cincinnati (45216) ***(G-3159)***
Bzak Landscaping Inc (PA)..........513 831-0907
931 Round Bottom Rd Milford (45150) ***(G-14508)***
Bzak Ldscpg & Maintainance, Milford *Also called Bzak Landscaping Inc* ***(G-14508)***
C & B Buck Bros Asp Maint LLC..........419 536-7325
2742 Victory Ave Toledo (43607) ***(G-17789)***
C & C Industries, Vandalia *Also called Circuits & Cables Inc* ***(G-18671)***
C & G Transportation Inc..........419 288-2653
11100 Wayne Rd Wayne (43466) ***(G-18977)***
C & J Contractors Inc..........216 391-5700
866 Addison Rd Cleveland (44103) ***(G-5167)***
C & K Industrial Services Inc (PA)..........216 642-0055
5617 E Schaaf Rd Independence (44131) ***(G-12192)***
C & K Industrial Services Inc..........513 829-5353
4980 Factory Dr Fairfield (45014) ***(G-10827)***
C & L Supply, Logan *Also called Kilbarger Construction Inc* ***(G-12980)***
C & M Express Logistics Inc..........440 350-0802
342 Blackbrook Rd Painesville (44077) ***(G-15838)***
C & R Inc (PA)..........614 497-1130
5600 Clyde Moore Dr Groveport (43125) ***(G-11626)***
C & S Associates Inc..........440 461-9661
729 Miner Rd Highland Heights (44143) ***(G-11868)***
C & W Tank Cleaning Company..........419 691-1995
50 N Lallendorf Rd Oregon (43616) ***(G-15727)***
C A C Distributing, Cincinnati *Also called Habegger Corporation* ***(G-3725)***
C A E C Inc..........614 337-1091
2975 Morse Rd Ste A Columbus (43231) ***(G-7173)***
C A I Insurance Agency, Cincinnati *Also called Allan Peace & Associates Inc* ***(G-2986)***
C and D Truck Repairs, Leipsic *Also called PGT Trucking Inc* ***(G-12664)***
C C, Mentor *Also called Cardinalcommerce Corporation* ***(G-14153)***
C C & S Ambulance Service Inc..........330 868-4114
207 W Lincolnway Minerva (44657) ***(G-14642)***
C C H, Canton *Also called Canton Christian Home Inc* ***(G-2283)***
C C I, Broadview Heights *Also called Warwick Communications Inc* ***(G-1895)***
C C Mitchell Supply Company..........440 526-2040
3001 E Royalton Rd Cleveland (44147) ***(G-5168)***
C D O, Dayton *Also called Cdo Technologies Inc* ***(G-9260)***
C E I, Canton *Also called Canton Erectors Inc* ***(G-2287)***
C E O, Columbus *Also called Corporate Environments of Ohio* ***(G-7442)***
C E S Credit Union Inc..........561 203-5443
3030 State Route 3 Loudonville (44842) ***(G-13088)***
C E S Credit Union Inc (PA)..........740 397-1136
1215 Yauger Rd Mount Vernon (43050) ***(G-14880)***
C E S Credit Union Inc..........740 892-3323
8 N Main St Utica (43080) ***(G-18610)***
C F N A, Cleveland *Also called Credit First National Assn* ***(G-5434)***
C H Bradshaw Co..........614 871-2087
2004 Hendrix Dr Grove City (43123) ***(G-11543)***
C H Dean Inc (PA)..........937 222-9531
3500 Pentagon Blvd # 200 Beavercreek (45431) ***(G-1156)***
C H T, Cleveland *Also called Compliant Healthcare Tech LLC* ***(G-5389)***
C J & L Construction Inc..........513 769-3600
11980 Runyan Dr Cincinnati (45241) ***(G-3160)***
C K M, Coventry Township *Also called Stanley Stemer of Akron Canton* ***(G-9133)***
C K of Cincinnati Inc..........513 752-5533
7525 State Rd Ste B Cincinnati (45255) ***(G-3161)***
C M Brown Nurseries Inc..........440 259-5403
4906 Middle Ridge Rd Perry (44081) ***(G-15958)***
C M C S, Cincinnati *Also called Comprehensive Managed Care Sys* ***(G-3407)***
C M E F, Canton *Also called Canton Med Educatn Foundation* ***(G-2292)***
C M I Group, Chagrin Falls *Also called Custom Materials Inc* ***(G-2713)***
C M Limited..........614 888-4567
5255 Sinclair Rd Columbus (43229) ***(G-7174)***
C M M Inc..........330 656-3820
546 Meadowridge Way Hudson (44236) ***(G-12106)***
C M S Enterprises Inc (PA)..........740 653-1940
664 S Columbus St Lancaster (43130) ***(G-12512)***
C Micah Rand Inc..........513 605-2000
12100 Reed Hartman Hwy Cincinnati (45241) ***(G-3162)***
C N G, Hilliard *Also called Cache Next Generation LLC* ***(G-11887)***
C P R, Twinsburg *Also called Cleveland Pump Repr & Svcs LLC* ***(G-18402)***

C P W, Brookpark *Also called Car Parts Warehouse Inc (G-1937)*
C R G, Miamisburg *Also called Cornerstone Research Group Inc (G-14287)*
C R G Health Care Systems....330 498-8107
2567 Niles Vienna Rd Ofc Niles (44446) *(G-15285)*
C R M, Clyde *Also called Chaney Roofing Maintenance (G-6811)*
C Ray Wllams Erly Chldhood Ctr, Columbus *Also called Whitehall City Schools (G-8988)*
C S I, Columbus *Also called Clinical Specialties Inc (G-7302)*
C T Columbus, Columbus *Also called C T Corporation System (G-7175)*
C T Communication, Urbana *Also called C T Wireless (G-18574)*
C T Corporation System....614 473-9749
4400 Easton Cmns Ste 300 Columbus (43219) *(G-7175)*
C T I, Akron *Also called Commercial Time Sharing Inc (G-152)*
C T Logistics, Cleveland *Also called Commercial Traffic Company (G-5377)*
C T Logistics, Cleveland *Also called Commercial Traffic Company (G-5378)*
C T Wireless....937 653-2208
731 Scioto St Urbana (43078) *(G-18574)*
C Ted Forsberg....440 992-3145
5005 State Rd Ashtabula (44004) *(G-730)*
C Tucker Cope & Assoc Inc....330 482-4472
170 Duquesne St Columbiana (44408) *(G-6854)*
C V Perry & Co (PA)....614 221-4131
370 S 5th St Columbus (43215) *(G-7176)*
C W A Local 4326....937 322-2227
240 Ludlow Ave Springfield (45505) *(G-17154)*
C W Egg Products LLC....419 375-5800
2360 Wabash Rd Fort Recovery (45846) *(G-11113)*
C&C Clean Team Enterprises LLC....513 321-5100
2016 Madison Rd Cincinnati (45208) *(G-3163)*
C&K Trucking LLC....440 657-5249
41387 Schadden Rd Elyria (44035) *(G-10600)*
C-Auto Glass Inc....216 351-2193
2500 Brookpark Rd # 111 Cleveland (44134) *(G-5169)*
C-N-D Industries Inc....330 478-8811
359 State Ave Nw Massillon (44647) *(G-13791)*
C-Z Realtors, Cambridge *Also called The C-Z Company (G-2131)*
C-Z Trckng Co, Poland *Also called C-Z Trucking Co (G-16221)*
C-Z Trucking Co....330 758-2313
9495 Harvard Blvd Poland (44514) *(G-16221)*
C.C.i, Canton *Also called Consolidated Communications (G-2321)*
C.H. Robinson 123, Columbus *Also called CH Robinson Company Inc (G-7248)*
C.H.P., Columbus *Also called Columbus Housing Partnr Inc (G-7360)*
C2g, Moraine *Also called Legrand North America LLC (G-14798)*
CA Group....419 586-2137
4980 Mud Pike Rd Celina (45822) *(G-2637)*
CA INDUSTRIES, Celina *Also called CA Group (G-2637)*
Ca-Mj Hotel Associates Ltd....330 494-6494
4375 Metro Cir Nw Canton (44720) *(G-2278)*
Cabbage Inc (PA)....440 899-9171
5050 Waterford Dr Sheffield Village (44035) *(G-16885)*
Cabin In The Wood, Dublin *Also called Northwods Cnslting Prtners Inc (G-10410)*
Cabin Restaurant....330 562-9171
34 N Chillicothe Rd Aurora (44202) *(G-832)*
Cabinet and Granite Direct, Cleveland *Also called Direct Import Home Decor Inc (G-5485)*
Cabinet Restylers, Ashland *Also called Thiels Replacement Systems Inc (G-701)*
Cabinet Solutions By Design, Cincinnati *Also called Brower Products Inc (G-3142)*
Cable System, The, Sandusky *Also called Erie County Cablevision Inc (G-16753)*
Cable TV Services Inc....440 816-0033
6400 Kolthoff Dr Cleveland (44142) *(G-5170)*
Cache Next Generation LLC....614 850-9444
3974 Brown Park Dr Ste D Hilliard (43026) *(G-11887)*
Cadle Company II Inc....330 872-0918
100 N Center St Newton Falls (44444) *(G-15273)*
Cadna Automotive, Fairlawn *Also called Cadna Rubber Company Inc (G-10940)*
Cadna Rubber Company Inc....901 566-9090
703 S Clvland Mssillon Rd Fairlawn (44333) *(G-10940)*
Cadre Computer Resources Co (PA)....513 762-7350
201 E 5th St Ste 1800 Cincinnati (45202) *(G-3164)*
Cadre Information Security, Cincinnati *Also called Cadre Computer Resources Co (G-3164)*
Cadx Systems Inc....937 431-1464
2689 Commons Blvd Ste 100 Beavercreek (45431) *(G-1157)*
Caep-Dunlap LLC....330 456-2695
2600 6th St Sw Canton (44710) *(G-2279)*
Caesar Creek Flea Market, Dayton *Also called Ferguson Hills Inc (G-9546)*
Cafaro Co....330 652-6980
5555 Youngstown Warren Rd Niles (44446) *(G-15286)*
Cafaro Peachcreek Co Ltd....419 625-6280
1119 Sandusky Mall Blvd Sandusky (44870) *(G-16731)*
Caffaratti, John MD, Zanesville *Also called Cardiology Associates of (G-20456)*
Cahall Bros Inc (PA)....937 378-4439
50 Cahall Brothers Ln Georgetown (45121) *(G-11388)*
Cahill Corporation....330 724-1224
3951 Creek Wood Ln Uniontown (44685) *(G-18510)*
Cai/Insurance Agency Inc (PA)....513 221-1140
2035 Reading Rd Cincinnati (45202) *(G-3165)*
Cain B M W, Canton *Also called Cain Motors Inc (G-2280)*
Cain Motors Inc....330 494-5588
6527 Whipple Ave Nw Canton (44720) *(G-2280)*
Cal Crim Inc....513 563-5500
384 Deer Run Dr Trenton (45067) *(G-18340)*
Cal-Maine Foods Inc....937 337-9576
3078 Washington Rd Rossburg (45362) *(G-16604)*
Cal-Maine Foods Inc....937 968-4874
1039 Zumbrum Rd Union City (45390) *(G-18500)*
Calabresem Racek & Markos Inc....216 696-5442
1110 Euclid Ave Ste 300 Cleveland (44115) *(G-5171)*
Calafonia Dream By AAC, Cincinnati *Also called Auto Aftermarket Concepts (G-3065)*
Calfee Halter & Griswold LLP (PA)....216 831-2732
1405 E 6th St Ste 1 Cleveland (44114) *(G-5172)*
Calfee Halter & Griswold LLP....513 693-4880
255 E 5th St Cincinnati (45202) *(G-3166)*
Calfee Halter & Griswold LLP....614 621-1500
41 S High St Ste 1200 Columbus (43215) *(G-7177)*
Calfee Halgerr Griswold LLC....614 621-7003
41 S High St Ste 1200 Columbus (43215) *(G-7178)*
Caliber Home Loans Inc....937 435-5363
8534 Yankee St Dayton (45458) *(G-9376)*
Calico Corners, Cleveland *Also called Everfast Inc (G-5557)*
Calico Court....740 455-2541
1101 Colony Dr Zanesville (43701) *(G-20453)*
Call Traditions, Cleveland *Also called Aristocrat W Nursing Hm Corp (G-5066)*
Callahan Hardware, Jackson *Also called Quality Supply & Rental Inc (G-12317)*
Callos Prof Employment II, Youngstown *Also called Callos Resource LLC (G-20132)*
Callos Resource LLC (PA)....330 788-3033
755 Boardman Canfield Rd Youngstown (44512) *(G-20132)*
Calphalon, Bowling Green *Also called Newell Brands Inc (G-1786)*
Calvary Cemetery, Youngstown *Also called Roman Cthlic Docese Youngstown (G-20356)*
Calvary Christian Ch of Ohio....740 828-9000
338 W 3rd St Frazeysburg (43822) *(G-11174)*
Calvary Contracting Inc....937 754-0300
4125 Gibson Dr Tipp City (45371) *(G-17711)*
Calvary Industries Inc (PA)....513 874-1113
9233 Seward Rd Fairfield (45014) *(G-10828)*
Calvert Wire & Cable Corp (HQ)....216 433-7600
17909 Cleve Pkwy Ste 180 Cleveland (44142) *(G-5173)*
Calvin Klein Inc....330 562-2746
549 S Chilcthe Rd Ste C11 Aurora (44202) *(G-833)*
Calvin Lanier....937 952-4221
5363 Birdland Ave Dayton (45417) *(G-9377)*
Calypso Distribution Services, Columbus *Also called Calypso Logistics LLC (G-7179)*
Calypso Logistics LLC....614 262-8911
2035 Innis Rd Columbus (43224) *(G-7179)*
CAM Program. The, Dayton *Also called Consumer Advocacy Model (G-9424)*
Camargo Club....513 561-9292
8605 Shawnee Run Rd Cincinnati (45243) *(G-3167)*
Camargo Construction Company....513 248-1500
6801 Shawnee Run Rd Cincinnati (45243) *(G-3168)*
Camargo Manor Inc....513 605-3000
12100 Reed Hartman Hwy Cincinnati (45241) *(G-3169)*
Camargo Rental Center Inc....513 271-6510
8149 Camargo Rd Cincinnati (45243) *(G-3170)*
Cambria Green Management LLC....330 899-1263
1787 Thorn Dr Uniontown (44685) *(G-18511)*
Cambria Stes Akrn-Canton Arprt, Uniontown *Also called Cambria Green Management LLC (G-18511)*
Cambridge Associates Ltd....740 432-7313
2248 Southgate Pkwy Cambridge (43725) *(G-2098)*
Cambridge Box & Gift Shop, Cambridge *Also called Cambridge Packaging Inc (G-2101)*
Cambridge Counseling Center....740 450-7790
326 Main St Zanesville (43701) *(G-20454)*
Cambridge Country Club, Byesville *Also called Alexander J Abernethy (G-2069)*
Cambridge Country Club Company....740 439-2744
60755 Southgate Rd Byesville (43723) *(G-2070)*
Cambridge Home Healthcare....740 432-6191
1300 Clark St Unit 7 Cambridge (43725) *(G-2099)*
Cambridge NH LLC....740 432-7717
66731 Old Twenty One Rd Cambridge (43725) *(G-2100)*
Cambridge Packaging Inc....740 432-3351
60794 Southgate Rd Cambridge (43725) *(G-2101)*
Cambridge Property Investors....740 432-7313
2248 Southgate Pkwy Cambridge (43725) *(G-2102)*
Camcar Towing, Columbus *Also called Arlington Towing Inc (G-7043)*
Camco Inc....740 477-3682
24685 Us Highway 23 S Circleville (43113) *(G-4881)*
Camden Health Center, Cincinnati *Also called Deaconess Long Term Care of MI (G-3474)*
Camden Management Inc....513 383-1635
463 Ohio Pike Ste 304 Cincinnati (45255) *(G-3171)*
Camelot Hair Tanning & Nails, Holland *Also called Diane Babiuch (G-12020)*
Cameo Solutions Inc....513 645-4220
9078 Union Centre Blvd # 200 West Chester (45069) *(G-19032)*
Cameron Mitchell Rest LLC (PA)....614 621-3663
390 W Nationwide Blvd # 300 Columbus (43215) *(G-7180)*
Camgen Ltd....330 204-8636
1621 Euclid Ave Ste 220-3 Cleveland (44115) *(G-5174)*
Camgen Ltd....330 204-8636
6693 Axtel Dr Canal Winchester (43110) *(G-2154)*
Camillus Villa Inc....440 236-5091
10515 East River Rd Columbia Station (44028) *(G-6841)*

ALPHABETIC

Camp Akita, Logan *Also called First Community Church* ***(G-12972)***
Camp Paradise, Seville *Also called Sociey For Handicapped Citizen* ***(G-16845)***
Camp Patmos Inc 419 746-2214
920 Monagan Rd Kelleys Island (43438) ***(G-12348)***
Camp Pinecliff Inc 614 236-5698
277 S Cassingham Rd Columbus (43209) ***(G-7181)***
Camp Willson, Bellefontaine *Also called Young Mens Christian Assoc* ***(G-1401)***
Campbell Inc (PA) 419 476-4444
2875 Crane Way Northwood (43619) ***(G-15529)***
Campbell Construction Inc (PA) 330 262-5186
1159 Blachleyville Rd Wooster (44691) ***(G-19836)***
Campbell Family Childcare Inc 614 855-4780
5351 New Albany Rd W New Albany (43054) ***(G-14977)***
Campbell Oil Company (PA) 330 833-8555
7977 Hills & Dales Rd Ne Massillon (44646) ***(G-13792)***
Campbell Sales Company 513 697-2900
8805 Governors Hill Dr # 300 Cincinnati (45249) ***(G-3172)***
Campeon Roofg & Waterproofing 513 271-8972
3535 Round Bottom Rd Cincinnati (45244) ***(G-3173)***
Campolo Michael MD 740 522-7600
1930 Tamarack Rd Newark (43055) ***(G-15154)***
Campuseai Inc 216 589-9626
1111 Superior Ave E # 310 Cleveland (44114) ***(G-5175)***
Camtaylor Co Realtors, Worthington *Also called Phil Giessler* ***(G-19984)***
Canal Physician Group 330 344-4000
1 Akron General Ave Akron (44307) ***(G-120)***
Canal Road Partners 216 447-0814
5585 Canal Rd Cleveland (44125) ***(G-5176)***
Canal Square Branch, Akron *Also called Young Mens Christian Assoc* ***(G-517)***
CANAL VILLAGE, Canal Winchester *Also called United Church Residences of* ***(G-2174)***
Canal Winchester Dialysis, Canal Winchester *Also called Vogel Dialysis LLC* ***(G-2175)***
Cancer Care Center, Youngstown *Also called Mahoning Vly Hmtlgy Onclgy Aso* ***(G-20265)***
Cancer Center, Cincinnati *Also called University of Cincinnati* ***(G-4773)***
Cancer Network West Centl Ohio, Lima *Also called Cancer Ntwk of W Cent* ***(G-12751)***
Cancer Ntwk of W Cent 419 226-9085
2615 Fort Amanda Rd Lima (45804) ***(G-12751)***
Candlewood Carrollton, Carrollton *Also called CPX Carrollton Es LLC* ***(G-2617)***
Candlewood Park Healthcare Ctr, Cleveland *Also called Belmore Leasing Co LLC* ***(G-5113)***
Cando Pharmaceutical 513 354-2694
100 Commerce Dr Loveland (45140) ***(G-13112)***
Canfield Healthcare Center, Youngstown *Also called Communicare Health Svcs Inc* ***(G-20150)***
Canfield Metal Coating Corp 330 702-3876
460 W Main St Canfield (44406) ***(G-2184)***
Caniano Bsner Pdiatrics Clinic, Columbus *Also called Nationwide Childrens Hospital* ***(G-8230)***
Cannell Graphics LLC 614 781-9760
5787 Linworth Rd Worthington (43085) ***(G-19944)***
Cannon Group Inc 614 890-0343
5037 Pine Creek Dr Westerville (43081) ***(G-19375)***
Canon Solutions America Inc 937 260-4495
1 Prestige Pl Miamisburg (45342) ***(G-14278)***
Canon Solutions America Inc 216 446-3830
6100 Oak Tree Blvd Independence (44131) ***(G-12193)***
Canon Solutions America Inc 216 750-2980
6161 Oak Tree Blvd # 301 Independence (44131) ***(G-12194)***
Canter Inn Inc (HQ) 740 354-7711
711 2nd St Portsmouth (45662) ***(G-16267)***
Canterbury Golf Club Inc 216 561-1914
22000 S Woodland Rd Cleveland (44122) ***(G-5177)***
Canterbury Villa, Centerburg *Also called Rescare Ohio Inc* ***(G-2667)***
Canterbury Villa of Alliance 330 821-1391
1785 N Freshley Ave Alliance (44601) ***(G-529)***
Canton Allergy Lab, Canton *Also called Ohio Head & Neck Surgeons Inc* ***(G-2480)***
Canton Altman Emrgncy Physcans 330 456-2695
2600 6th St Sw Canton (44710) ***(G-2281)***
Canton Assisted Living 330 492-7131
836 34th St Nw Canton (44709) ***(G-2282)***
Canton Chair Rental, Canton *Also called Maloney & Associates Inc* ***(G-2443)***
Canton Christian Home Inc 330 456-0004
2550 Cleveland Ave Nw Canton (44709) ***(G-2283)***
Canton City School District 330 456-3167
2701 Coventry Blvd Ne Canton (44705) ***(G-2284)***
Canton City School District 330 456-6710
2030 Cleveland Ave Sw Canton (44707) ***(G-2285)***
Canton Country Day School 330 453-8279
3000 Demington Ave Nw Canton (44718) ***(G-2286)***
Canton Erectors Inc 330 453-7363
2009 Quimby Ave Sw Canton (44706) ***(G-2287)***
Canton Floors Inc 330 492-1121
3944 Fulton Dr Nw Canton (44718) ***(G-2288)***
Canton Group Home, Canton *Also called Alternative Residences Two* ***(G-2236)***
Canton Healthcare Center, Canton *Also called Communicare Health Svcs Inc* ***(G-2318)***
Canton Hotel Holdings Inc 330 492-1331
5345 Broadmoor Cir Nw Canton (44709) ***(G-2289)***
Canton Insurance, Canton *Also called Huntington Insurance Inc* ***(G-2409)***
Canton Inventory Service 330 453-1633
2204 38th St Ne Canton (44705) ***(G-2290)***
Canton Jewish Community Center 330 452-6444
432 30th St Nw Canton (44709) ***(G-2291)***
CANTON JEWISH COMMUNITY FEDERA, Canton *Also called Canton Jewish Community Center* ***(G-2291)***
Canton Med Educatn Foundation 330 363-6783
2600 6th St Sw Canton (44710) ***(G-2292)***
Canton Montessori Association 330 452-0148
125 15th St Nw Canton (44703) ***(G-2293)***
Canton Montessori School, Canton *Also called Canton Montessori Association* ***(G-2293)***
Canton Ophthalmology Assoc 330 994-1286
2600 Tuscarawas St W # 200 Canton (44708) ***(G-2294)***
Canton Public Works 330 489-3030
2436 30th St Ne Canton (44705) ***(G-2295)***
Canton Reg Cham of Comm Fdn 330 456-7253
222 Market Ave N Canton (44702) ***(G-2296)***
Canton Rgnal Chmber of Cmmerce 330 456-7253
222 Market Ave N Ste 122 Canton (44702) ***(G-2297)***
Canton S-Group Ltd 419 625-7003
4000 Columbus Ave Sandusky (44870) ***(G-16732)***
Canton School Employees Fed Cr (PA) 330 452-9801
1380 Market Ave N Canton (44714) ***(G-2298)***
Canton School Trnsp Dept, Canton *Also called Canton City School District* ***(G-2285)***
Canton Street Department, Canton *Also called Canton Public Works* ***(G-2295)***
Canton Truck Sales and Service, Midvale *Also called Truck Sales Leasing Inc* ***(G-14491)***
Cantrell Oil Company 937 695-8003
18856 State Route 136 Winchester (45697) ***(G-19800)***
Cantrell's Motel, Winchester *Also called 1st Stop Inc* ***(G-19798)***
Canus Hospitality LLC 937 323-8631
383 E Leffel Ln Springfield (45505) ***(G-17155)***
Canyon Medical Center Inc 614 864-6010
5969 E Broad St Ste 200 Columbus (43213) ***(G-7182)***
Capa, Columbus *Also called Columbus Association For The P* ***(G-7331)***
Capabilities Inc (PA) 419 394-0003
124 S Front St Saint Marys (45885) ***(G-16670)***
Capano & Associates LLC 513 403-6000
8312 Alpine Aster Ct Liberty Township (45044) ***(G-12717)***
Capital Care Women's Center, Columbus *Also called G and H Management* ***(G-7717)***
Capital City Electric LLC 614 933-8700
9798 Karmar Ct Ste B New Albany (43054) ***(G-14978)***
Capital City Indus Systems LLC 614 519-5047
1494 Langram Rd Put In Bay (43456) ***(G-16366)***
Capital City Medical Assoc, Columbus *Also called Central Ohio Primary Care* ***(G-7237)***
Capital Drug, Columbus *Also called Capital Wholesale Drug Company* ***(G-7185)***
Capital Electric, Moraine *Also called MDU Resources Group Inc* ***(G-14801)***
Capital Fire Protection Co (PA) 614 279-9448
3360 Valleyview Dr Columbus (43204) ***(G-7183)***
Capital Health Homecare 740 264-8815
201 Luray Dr 2a Steubenville (43953) ***(G-17305)***
Capital Health Services Inc (PA) 937 278-0404
5040 Philadelphia Dr Dayton (45415) ***(G-9378)***
Capital Investment Group Inc 513 241-5090
226 E 8th St Cincinnati (45202) ***(G-3174)***
Capital Lighting Inc 614 841-1200
901 Polaris Pkwy Columbus (43240) ***(G-6871)***
Capital Partners Realty LLC 614 888-1000
100 E Wilson Bridge Rd # 100 Worthington (43085) ***(G-19945)***
Capital Properties MGT Ltd 216 991-3057
12929 Shaker Blvd Cleveland (44120) ***(G-5178)***
Capital Senior Living (PA) 440 356-5444
22900 Center Ridge Rd Rocky River (44116) ***(G-16572)***
Capital Senior Living Corp 330 748-4204
9633 Valley View Rd Ofc C Macedonia (44056) ***(G-13192)***
Capital Senior Living Corp 419 874-2564
7100 S Wilkinson Way Perrysburg (43551) ***(G-15983)***
Capital Senior Living Corp 216 289-9800
261 Richmond Rd Richmond Heights (44143) ***(G-16536)***
Capital Senior Living Corp 513 829-6200
1400 Corydale Dr Fairfield (45014) ***(G-10829)***
Capital Tire Inc (PA) 419 241-5111
1001 Cherry St Toledo (43608) ***(G-17790)***
Capital Tire Inc 419 865-7151
2220 S Reynolds Rd Toledo (43614) ***(G-17791)***
Capital Transportation Inc 614 258-0400
1170 N Cassady Ave Columbus (43219) ***(G-7184)***
Capital Wholesale Drug Company 614 297-8225
873 Williams Ave Columbus (43212) ***(G-7185)***
Capitol City Cardiology Inc (PA) 614 464-0884
5825 Westbourne Ave Columbus (43213) ***(G-7186)***
Capitol City Trailers Inc 614 491-2616
3960 Groveport Rd Obetz (43207) ***(G-15664)***
Capitol Express Entps Inc (PA) 614 279-2819
3815 Twin Creeks Dr Columbus (43204) ***(G-7187)***
Capitol Tunneling Inc 614 444-0255
2216 Refugee Rd Columbus (43207) ***(G-7188)***
Capitol Varsity Sports Inc 513 523-4126
6723 Ringwood Rd Oxford (45056) ***(G-15813)***
Capri Bowling Lanes Inc 937 832-4000
2727 S Dixie Dr Dayton (45409) ***(G-9379)***
Caprice Health Care Center, North Lima *Also called Caprice Health Care Inc* ***(G-15400)***
Caprice Health Care Inc 330 965-9200
9184 Market St North Lima (44452) ***(G-15400)***

Captain D's, Circleville *Also called James Lafontaine* ***(G-4891)***
Car Paint, Dayton *Also called G & C Finishes From The Future* ***(G-9567)***
Car Parts Warehouse Inc....440 259-2991
3382 N Ridge Rd Perry (44081) ***(G-15959)***
Car Parts Warehouse Inc (PA)....216 281-4500
5200 W 130th St Brookpark (44142) ***(G-1937)***
Car Wash....216 662-6289
5195 Northfield Rd Cleveland (44146) ***(G-5179)***
Car Wash Plus Ltd....513 683-4228
12105 Montgomery Rd Cincinnati (45249) ***(G-3175)***
Car-X Muffler & Brake, Cincinnati *Also called P & M Exhaust Systems Whse* ***(G-4247)***
Caracole Inc....513 761-1480
4138 Hamilton Ave Cincinnati (45223) ***(G-3176)***
Cararo Co Inc....330 652-6980
492 Eastwood Mall Niles (44446) ***(G-15287)***
Caraustar Industries Inc....937 298-9969
2601 E River Rd Moraine (45439) ***(G-14758)***
Caravon Golf Company Ltd....440 937-6018
4400 Nagel Rd Avon (44011) ***(G-883)***
Carbon Products, West Chester *Also called Graphel Corporation* ***(G-19083)***
Carcorp Inc....877 857-2801
2900 Morse Rd Columbus (43231) ***(G-7189)***
Cardiac Vsclar Thrcic Surgeons....513 421-3494
4030 Smith Rd Ste 300 Cincinnati (45209) ***(G-3177)***
Cardida Corporation (PA)....740 439-4359
74978 Broadhead Rd Kimbolton (43749) ***(G-12446)***
Cardinal Builders Inc....614 237-1000
4409 E Main St Columbus (43213) ***(G-7190)***
Cardinal Container Corporation....614 497-3033
3700 Lockbourne Rd Columbus (43207) ***(G-7191)***
Cardinal Environmental Svc Inc....330 252-0220
180 E Miller Ave Akron (44301) ***(G-121)***
Cardinal Health Inc....614 473-0786
2215 Citygate Dr Ste D Columbus (43219) ***(G-7192)***
Cardinal Health Inc (PA)....614 757-5000
7000 Cardinal Pl Dublin (43017) ***(G-10275)***
Cardinal Health Inc....614 497-9552
2320 Mcgaw Rd Obetz (43207) ***(G-15665)***
Cardinal Health Inc....614 757-7690
2088 West Case Rd Ste 110 Columbus (43235) ***(G-7193)***
Cardinal Health 100 Inc (HQ)....614 757-5000
7000 Cardinal Pl Dublin (43017) ***(G-10276)***
Cardinal Health 107 LLC....740 455-2462
3540 East Pike Zanesville (43701) ***(G-20455)***
Cardinal Health 200 LLC....440 349-1247
5260 Naiman Pkwy Cleveland (44139) ***(G-5180)***
Cardinal Health 200 LLC....614 491-0050
1548 Mcgaw Rd Columbus (43207) ***(G-7194)***
Cardinal Health 301 LLC (HQ)....614 757-5000
7000 Cardinal Pl Dublin (43017) ***(G-10277)***
Cardinal Health 414 LLC....419 867-1077
6156 Trust Dr Ste B Holland (43528) ***(G-12014)***
Cardinal Health 414 LLC....937 438-1888
2217 Arbor Blvd Moraine (45439) ***(G-14759)***
Cardinal Health Medical, Cleveland *Also called Cardinal Health 200 LLC* ***(G-5180)***
Cardinal Healthcare....954 202-1883
P.O. Box 183005 Columbus (43218) ***(G-7195)***
Cardinal Maintenance & Svc Co....330 252-0282
180 E Miller Ave Akron (44301) ***(G-122)***
Cardinal Operating Company....740 598-4164
306 County Road 7e Brilliant (43913) ***(G-1867)***
Cardinal Orthopaedic Group Inc....614 759-1186
170 Taylor Station Rd Columbus (43213) ***(G-7196)***
CARDINAL ORTHOPAEDIC INSTITUTE, THE, Columbus *Also called Orthopedic One Inc* ***(G-8485)***
Cardinal Pacelli School....513 321-1048
927 Ellison Ave Cincinnati (45226) ***(G-3178)***
Cardinal Plant, Brilliant *Also called Buckeye Power Inc* ***(G-1866)***
Cardinal Retirement Village, Springfield *Also called Brookdale Lving Cmmunities Inc* ***(G-17153)***
Cardinal Retirement Village....330 928-7888
171 Graham Rd Cuyahoga Falls (44223) ***(G-9168)***
Cardinal Solutions Group Inc (PA)....513 984-6700
7755 Montgomery Rd # 510 Cincinnati (45236) ***(G-3179)***
Cardinal Wds Skilled Nursing, Madison *Also called American Eagle Hlth Care Svcs* ***(G-13220)***
Cardinalcommerce Corporation....877 352-8444
8100 Tyler Blvd Ste 100 Mentor (44060) ***(G-14153)***
Cardio Partners Inc....614 760-5038
5000 Tuttle Crossing Blvd Dublin (43016) ***(G-10278)***
Cardio Thoracic Surgery....614 293-4509
410 W 10th Ave Columbus (43210) ***(G-7197)***
Cardiologist....440 882-0075
6525 Powers Blvd 301 Cleveland (44129) ***(G-5181)***
Cardiologist Clark & Champaign....937 653-8897
900 E Court St Urbana (43078) ***(G-18575)***
Cardiologist of Clark & Champ....937 323-1404
1911 E High St Springfield (45505) ***(G-17156)***
Cardiology Associates of....740 454-6831
751 Forest Ave Ste 301 Zanesville (43701) ***(G-20456)***
Cardiology Center Cincinnati, Cincinnati *Also called Cardiology Ctr of Cincinnati* ***(G-3180)***
Cardiology Consultants Inc....330 454-8076
2600 Tuscarawas St W # 600 Canton (44708) ***(G-2299)***
Cardiology Ctr of Cincinnati (PA)....513 745-9800
10525 Montgomery Rd A Cincinnati (45242) ***(G-3180)***
Cardiology Specialists Inc....330 297-6110
6847 N Chestnut St # 100 Ravenna (44266) ***(G-16375)***
Cardiovascular Associates Inc....330 747-6446
1001 Belmont Ave Youngstown (44504) ***(G-20133)***
Cardiovascular Clinic Inc....440 882-0075
6525 Powers Blvd Rm 301 Cleveland (44129) ***(G-5182)***
Cardiovascular Consultants Inc....330 454-8076
2600 6th St Sw Ste A2710 Canton (44710) ***(G-2300)***
Cardiovascular Medicine Assoc....440 816-2708
7255 Old Oak Blvd C208 Cleveland (44130) ***(G-5183)***
Care & Share of Erie Count....419 624-1411
241 Jackson St Sandusky (44870) ***(G-16733)***
Care Center, Cincinnati *Also called Cincinnati Anml Rfrrl* ***(G-3280)***
Care Connection of Cincinnati....513 842-1101
7265 Kenwood Rd Ste 363 Cincinnati (45236) ***(G-3181)***
Care Information Systems LLC....614 496-4338
5723 Dalymount Dr Dublin (43016) ***(G-10279)***
Care of Trees Inc....800 445-8733
1500 N Mantua St Kent (44240) ***(G-12353)***
Care One LLC....937 236-6707
5440 Charlesgate Rd Dayton (45424) ***(G-9380)***
Career Cnnctions Staffing Svcs....440 471-8210
26260 Center Ridge Rd Westlake (44145) ***(G-19469)***
Career Partners Intl LLC (PA)....919 401-4260
20 S 3rd St Ste 210 Columbus (43215) ***(G-7198)***
Careers Unlimited, Cleveland *Also called Spectrum Supportive Services* ***(G-6518)***
Caregivers Health Network Inc....513 662-3400
2135 Dana Ave Ste 200 Cincinnati (45207) ***(G-3182)***
Careserve (HQ)....740 454-4000
2991 Maple Ave Zanesville (43701) ***(G-20457)***
Careserve Inc....740 962-3761
4114 N State Route 376 Nw McConnelsville (43756) ***(G-14026)***
Caresource Management Group Co (PA)....937 224-3300
230 N Main St Dayton (45402) ***(G-9381)***
Caresource Management Group Co....614 221-3370
3455 Mill Run Dr Hilliard (43026) ***(G-11888)***
Caresource Management Group Co....937 224-3300
230 N Main St Dayton (45402) ***(G-9382)***
Carespring Health Care MGT LLC (PA)....513 943-4000
390 Wards Corner Rd Loveland (45140) ***(G-13113)***
Carestar Inc (PA)....513 618-8300
5566 Cheviot Rd Cincinnati (45247) ***(G-3183)***
Carew Realty Inc....513 241-3888
441 Vine St Ste 3900 Cincinnati (45202) ***(G-3184)***
Careworks of Ohio Inc (PA)....614 792-1085
5555 Glendon Ct Ste 300 Dublin (43016) ***(G-10280)***
Carey Electric Co....937 669-3399
3925 Vanco Ln Vandalia (45377) ***(G-18667)***
Carfagna's Cleve Meats, Columbus *Also called Carfagnas Incorporated* ***(G-7199)***
Carfagnas Incorporated....614 846-6340
1405 E Dblin Granville Rd Columbus (43229) ***(G-7199)***
Cargill Incorporated....216 651-7200
2400 Ships Channel Cleveland (44113) ***(G-5184)***
Cargill Incorporated....440 716-4664
24950 Country Club Blvd # 450 North Olmsted (44070) ***(G-15411)***
Cargill Premix and Nutrition, Brookville *Also called Provimi North America Inc* ***(G-1965)***
Carginal Retirement Village, Cuyahoga Falls *Also called Rv Properties LLC* ***(G-9218)***
Cargotec Services USA Inc....419 482-6866
12233 Williams Rd Perrysburg (43551) ***(G-15984)***
Carillon Historical Park, Dayton *Also called Dayton History* ***(G-9478)***
Caring Hands Inc....330 821-6310
885 S Sawburg Ave Ste 107 Alliance (44601) ***(G-530)***
Caring Hands Home Health Care....740 532-9020
2615 S 3rd St Ironton (45638) ***(G-12285)***
Caring Hearts Home Health Care (PA)....513 339-1237
6677 Summer Field Dr Mason (45040) ***(G-13670)***
Carington Health Systems....513 732-6500
4000 Golden Age Dr Batavia (45103) ***(G-997)***
Carington Health Systems (PA)....513 682-2700
8200 Beckett Park Dr Hamilton (45011) ***(G-11706)***
Carington Health Systems....513 961-8881
3627 Harvey Ave Cincinnati (45229) ***(G-3185)***
Carington Health Systems....937 743-2754
421 Mission Ln Franklin (45005) ***(G-11151)***
CARINGTON PARK, Ashtabula *Also called CHS-Lake Erie Inc* ***(G-733)***
Carington Park, Ashtabula *Also called Salutary Providers Inc* ***(G-762)***
Caritas Inc....419 332-2589
1406 Oak Harbor Rd Fremont (43420) ***(G-11186)***
Carl B Stokes Head Start Ctr, Cleveland *Also called Council For Economic Opport* ***(G-5415)***
Carl E Oeder Sons Sand & Grav....513 494-1555
1000 Mason Morrow Rd Lebanon (45036) ***(G-12594)***
Carl Mills....740 282-2382
1005 Franklin St Toronto (43964) ***(G-18335)***
Carl's Body Shop & Towing, Dayton *Also called Carls Body Shop Inc* ***(G-9383)***
Carles Bratwurst Inc....419 562-7741
1210 E Mansfield St Bucyrus (44820) ***(G-2028)***
Carleton Realty Inc....740 653-5200
826 N Memorial Dr Lancaster (43130) ***(G-12513)***

ALPHABETIC

CARLETON SCHOOL, Syracuse *Also called Meigs Industries Inc* ***(G-17632)***
Carlile Patchen & Murphy LLP (PA) 614 228-6135
366 E Broad St Columbus (43215) ***(G-7200)***
Carlisle McNellie Rini Kram 216 360-7200
24755 Chagrin Blvd Beachwood (44122) ***(G-1060)***
Carlisle Fluid Tech Inc 419 825-5186
320 Phillips Ave Toledo (43612) ***(G-17792)***
Carlisle Health Care Inc 937 746-2662
730 Hillcrest Ave Carlisle (45005) ***(G-2602)***
Carlisle Hotels Inc 614 851-5599
5625 Trabue Rd Columbus (43228) ***(G-7201)***
Carls Body Shop Inc 937 253-5166
1120 Wayne Ave Dayton (45410) ***(G-9383)***
Carlson Amblnce Trnspt Svc Inc 330 225-2400
1642 Pearl Rd Brunswick (44212) ***(G-1971)***
Carlson Hotels Ltd Partnership 740 386-5451
2091 Marion Mt Gilead Rd Marion (43302) ***(G-13528)***
Carlson, L D Company, Kent *Also called Wine-Art of Ohio Inc* ***(G-12406)***
Carmen Steering Committee 330 756-2066
8074 Goodrich Rd Sw Navarre (44662) ***(G-14954)***
Carmichael Equipment Inc (PA) 740 446-2412
668 Pinecrest Dr Bidwell (45614) ***(G-1494)***
Carmike Cinemas Inc 740 264-1680
100 Mall Dr Unit C20 Steubenville (43952) ***(G-17306)***
Carnation Clinic, Alliance *Also called Roger S Palutsis MD* ***(G-557)***
Carnegie Capital Asset MGT LLC 216 595-1349
30300 Chagrin Blvd Cleveland (44124) ***(G-5185)***
Carnegie Companies Inc 440 232-2300
6190 Cochran Rd Ste A Solon (44139) ***(G-16987)***
Carnegie Investment Counsel, Cleveland *Also called Carnegie Capital Asset MGT LLC* ***(G-5185)***
Carnegie Management & Dev Corp 440 892-6800
27500 Detroit Rd Ste 300 Westlake (44145) ***(G-19470)***
Carney McNicholas, Youngstown *Also called Nicholas Carney-Mc Inc* ***(G-20301)***
Carney McNicholas, Sheffield Village *Also called Nicholas Carney-Mc Inc* ***(G-16894)***
Carol A & Ralp V H US B Fdn Tr 513 632-4426
425 Walnut St Fl 11f Cincinnati (45202) ***(G-3186)***
Carol Burton Management LLC 419 666-5120
1800 Miami St Toledo (43605) ***(G-17793)***
Carol Reese 513 347-0252
421 Anderson Ferry Rd Cincinnati (45238) ***(G-3187)***
Carol Scudere 614 839-4357
6912 Keesee Cir New Albany (43054) ***(G-14979)***
Carousel Beauty College, Dayton *Also called Yearwood Corporation* ***(G-10006)***
Carpe Diem Industries LLC (PA) 419 659-5639
4599 Campbell Rd Columbus Grove (45830) ***(G-9029)***
Carpe Diem Industries LLC 419 358-0129
505 E Jefferson St Bluffton (45817) ***(G-1729)***
Carpenter Lipps & Leland LLP (PA) 614 365-4100
280 N High St Ste 1300 Columbus (43215) ***(G-7202)***
Carpet Restoration Plus, Canton *Also called Carpet Services Plus Inc* ***(G-2301)***
Carpet Services Plus Inc 330 458-2409
1807 Allen Ave Se Ste 8 Canton (44707) ***(G-2301)***
Carquest Auto Parts, Columbus *Also called General Parts Inc* ***(G-7734)***
Carrara Companies Inc 330 659-2800
3774 Congress Pkwy Richfield (44286) ***(G-16499)***
Carriage Court Community, Lancaster *Also called Carriage Court Company Inc* ***(G-12514)***
Carriage Court Company Inc 740 654-4422
800 Becks Knob Rd Ofc Lancaster (43130) ***(G-12514)***
Carriage Court of Kenwood, Cincinnati *Also called Hackensack Meridian Health Inc* ***(G-3727)***
Carriage Crt Mrysvlle Ltd Prtn 937 642-2202
717 S Walnut St Marysville (43040) ***(G-13609)***
Carriage House, Norwalk *Also called Fisher-Titus Medical Center* ***(G-15574)***
Carriage House Assisted Living 740 264-7667
63102 Saint Charles Dr Steubenville (43952) ***(G-17307)***
Carriage Inn of Bowerston Inc 740 269-8001
102 Boyce Dr Bowerston (44695) ***(G-1754)***
Carriage Inn of Cadiz Inc 740 942-8084
308 W Warren St Cadiz (43907) ***(G-2073)***
Carriage Inn of Steubenville 740 264-7161
3102 Saint Charles Dr Steubenville (43952) ***(G-17308)***
Carriage Inn of Trotwood Inc 937 854-1180
3500 Shiloh Springs Rd Trotwood (45426) ***(G-18345)***
Carriage Inn of Trotwood Inc 937 277-0505
5020 Philadelphia Dr Dayton (45415) ***(G-9384)***
Carriage Inn Retirement Cmnty 937 278-0404
5040 Philadelphia Dr Dayton (45415) ***(G-9385)***
Carriage Town Chrysler Plymuth 740 369-9611
2815 Stratford Rd Delaware (43015) ***(G-10076)***
Carrie Cerino Restaurants Inc 440 237-3434
8922 Ridge Rd Cleveland (44133) ***(G-5186)***
Carrier Industries Inc 614 851-6363
1700 Georgesville Rd Columbus (43228) ***(G-7203)***
Carroll Electric Coop Inc 330 627-2116
250 Canton Rd Nw Carrollton (44615) ***(G-2611)***
Carroll Golden Age Retreat 330 627-4665
2202 Kensington Rd Ne Carrollton (44615) ***(G-2612)***
Carroll Halliday Inc 740 335-1670
1700 Columbus Ave Wshngtn CT Hs (43160) ***(G-20014)***
Carroll Health Care Center 330 627-5501
648 Longhorn St Nw Carrollton (44615) ***(G-2613)***
Carroll Healthcare Center, Carrollton *Also called Carroll Health Care Center* ***(G-2613)***
Carroll Hills Industries Inc 330 627-5524
540 High St Nw Carrollton (44615) ***(G-2614)***
Carroll Manufacturing & Sales 440 937-3900
35179 Avon Commerce Pkwy Avon (44011) ***(G-884)***
Carroll Properties 513 398-8075
5589 Kings Mills Rd Mason (45040) ***(G-13671)***
Carry Transport Inc 937 236-0026
5536 Brentlinger Dr Dayton (45414) ***(G-9386)***
Carstar, Blue Ash *Also called Cincinnati Collision Center* ***(G-1555)***
Cartemp USA Inc (PA) 440 715-1000
29100 Aurora Rd Solon (44139) ***(G-16988)***
Carter Lumber, Akron *Also called Carter-Jones Lumber Company* ***(G-123)***
Carter Manufacturing Co Inc 513 398-7303
4220 State Route 42 Mason (45040) ***(G-13672)***
Carter-Jones Companies Inc (PA) 330 673-6100
601 Tallmadge Rd Kent (44240) ***(G-12354)***
Carter-Jones Lumber Company (HQ) 330 673-6100
601 Tallmadge Rd Kent (44240) ***(G-12355)***
Carter-Jones Lumber Company 330 784-5441
172 N Case Ave Akron (44305) ***(G-123)***
Carter-Jones Lumber Company 330 674-9060
6139 State Route 39 Millersburg (44654) ***(G-14591)***
Carter-Jones Lumber Company 330 673-6000
601 Tallmadge Rd Kent (44240) ***(G-12356)***
Carts of America, Warren *Also called Hays Enterprises Inc* ***(G-18861)***
Caruso Inc (PA) 513 860-9200
3465 Hauck Rd Cincinnati (45241) ***(G-3188)***
Carvaka Inc 513 381-1531
1404 Race St Ste 302 Cincinnati (45202) ***(G-3189)***
Cas-Ker Company Inc 513 674-7700
2550 Civic Center Dr Cincinnati (45231) ***(G-3190)***
CASA, Cincinnati *Also called Addiction Services Council* ***(G-2972)***
Casa Verde Growers, Columbia Station *Also called Petitti Enterprises Inc* ***(G-6851)***
Casagrande Masonry Inc 740 964-0781
13530 Morse Rd Sw New Albany (43054) ***(G-14980)***
Casal Day Spa and Salon, Canfield *Also called Casals Hair Salon Inc* ***(G-2185)***
Casals Hair Salon Inc (PA) 330 533-6766
4030 Boardman Canfield Rd Canfield (44406) ***(G-2185)***
Casaro Headstart, Niles *Also called W T C S A Headstart Niles Ctr* ***(G-15309)***
Cascade Audi, Cuyahoga Falls *Also called Cascade Group Inc* ***(G-9169)***
Cascade Crossing, Cleveland *Also called Forest City Enterprises LP* ***(G-5615)***
Cascade Group Inc 330 929-1861
4149 State Rd Cuyahoga Falls (44223) ***(G-9169)***
Cascia LLC 440 975-8085
Classic Pk 35300 Vine St Classic Park Willoughby (44095) ***(G-19648)***
Casco Mfg Solutions Inc 513 681-0003
3107 Spring Grove Ave Cincinnati (45225) ***(G-3191)***
Case Farms LLC 330 832-0030
4001 Millennium Blvd Se Massillon (44646) ***(G-13793)***
Case Western Reserve Univ 216 368-2560
2232 Circle Dr Cleveland (44106) ***(G-5187)***
Casegoods Inc 330 825-2461
130 31st St Nw Barberton (44203) ***(G-960)***
Casey Equipment Corporation 330 750-1005
15 Union St Bldg 1 Struthers (44471) ***(G-17527)***
Cash Flow Solutions Inc 513 524-2320
5166 College Corner Pike Oxford (45056) ***(G-15814)***
Cashland Financial Svcs Inc (HQ) 937 253-7842
100 E 3rd St Ste 200 Dayton (45402) ***(G-9387)***
Caskey Cleaners, Columbus *Also called Caskey Cleaning Co* ***(G-7204)***
Caskey Cleaning Co 614 443-7448
47 W Gates St Columbus (43206) ***(G-7204)***
Casleo Corporation 614 252-6508
2741 E 4th Ave Columbus (43219) ***(G-7205)***
Casnet, Akron *Also called High Line Corporation* ***(G-264)***
Casod Industrial Properties, Marion *Also called Graham Investment Co* ***(G-13541)***
Cass Information Systems Inc 614 839-4503
2644 Kirkwood Hyw Newark Columbus (43218) ***(G-7206)***
Cass Information Systems Inc 614 766-2277
2675 Corporate Exchange Columbus (43231) ***(G-7207)***
Cass Logistics, Columbus *Also called Cass Information Systems Inc* ***(G-7207)***
Cassady Alternative Elementary, Columbus *Also called Columbus Public School Dst* ***(G-7377)***
Cassady Schiller & Associates 513 483-6699
4555 Lake Forest Dr # 400 Blue Ash (45242) ***(G-1551)***
Cassady Vlg Aprtments Ohio LLC 216 520-1250
3089 Cassady Village Trl Columbus (43219) ***(G-7208)***
Cassano's Pizza & Subs, Dayton *Also called Cassanos Inc* ***(G-9388)***
Cassanos Inc (PA) 937 294-8400
1700 E Stroop Rd Dayton (45429) ***(G-9388)***
Cassel Hills Golf Course, Vandalia *Also called City of Vandalia* ***(G-18674)***
Cassens Transport Company 937 644-8886
24777 Honda Pkwy Marysville (43040) ***(G-13610)***
Cassens Transport Company 419 727-0520
633 Matzinger Rd Toledo (43612) ***(G-17794)***
Cassidy Trley Coml RE Svcs Inc 513 771-2580
300 E Bus Way Ste 190 Cincinnati (45241) ***(G-3192)***
Cassidy Turley, Norwood *Also called Cushman & Wakefield Inc* ***(G-15598)***

Cassidy Turley, Moraine *Also called Cushman & Wakefield Inc (G-14765)*
Cast Metals Technology Inc 937 968-5460
305 Se Deerfield Rd Union City (45390) *(G-18501)*
Castaway Bay, Sandusky *Also called Cedar Point Park LLC (G-16735)*
Castilian & Co 937 836-9671
848 Union Blvd Englewood (45322) *(G-10699)*
Castilian Hair & Skin Center, Englewood *Also called Castilian & Co (G-10699)*
Castilla, Dr David DDS, Youngstown *Also called Mahoning Valley Dental Service (G-20264)*
Castle Care 440 327-3700
6043 Oakwood Cir North Ridgeville (44039) *(G-15457)*
Castle Care Landscaping, North Ridgeville *Also called Castle Care (G-15457)*
Castle Construction Co Inc 419 289-1122
588 Us Highway 250 E Ashland (44805) *(G-669)*
Castle Heating & Air Inc 216 696-3940
30355 Solon Indus Pkwy Solon (44139) *(G-16989)*
Castle Nursing Homes Inc 330 674-0015
6180 State Route 83 Millersburg (44654) *(G-14592)*
Casto, Columbus *Also called United Management Inc (G-8894)*
Casto Communities Cnstr Ltd 614 228-8545
191 W Nationwide Blvd # 200 Columbus (43215) *(G-7209)*
Casto Health Care, Westerville *Also called Wedgewood Estates (G-19358)*
Casto Health Care 419 884-6400
20 N Mill St Mansfield (44904) *(G-13272)*
Caston Holdings LLC (PA) 440 871-8697
30061 Detroit Rd Westlake (44145) *(G-19471)*
Cat The Rental Store, Cincinnati *Also called Holt Rental Services (G-3776)*
Catalina Marketing Corporation 513 564-8200
525 Vine St Ste 2200 Cincinnati (45202) *(G-3193)*
Catalyst Paper (usa) Inc 937 528-3800
7777 Wash Vlg Dr Ste 210 Dayton (45459) *(G-9389)*
Catamaran Home Dlvry Ohio Inc 440 930-5520
33381 Walker Rd Avon Lake (44012) *(G-924)*
Catawba Island Marina, Port Clinton *Also called Catawba-Cleveland Dev Corp (G-16239)*
Catawba-Cleveland Dev Corp (PA) 419 797-4424
4235 E Beachclub Rd Port Clinton (43452) *(G-16239)*
Caterpillar, Broadview Heights *Also called Ohio Machinery Co (G-1887)*
Caterpillar, Troy *Also called Ohio Machinery Co (G-18370)*
Caterpillar Authorized Dealer, Perrysburg *Also called Ohio Machinery Co (G-16036)*
Caterpillar Authorized Dealer, Broadview Heights *Also called Ohio Machinery Co (G-1886)*
Caterpillar Authorized Dealer, Canton *Also called Ohio Machinery Co (G-2481)*
Caterpillar Authorized Dealer, Girard *Also called Ohio Machinery Co (G-11421)*
Caterpillar Authorized Dealer, Zanesville *Also called Ohio Machinery Co (G-20519)*
Caterpillar Authorized Dealer, Cincinnati *Also called Ohio Machinery Co (G-4209)*
Caterpillar Authorized Dealer, Bolivar *Also called Ohio Machinery Co (G-1750)*
Caterpillar Inc 614 834-2400
8170 Dove Pkwy Canal Winchester (43110) *(G-2155)*
Catherines Care Center Inc 740 282-3605
717 N 6th Ave Steubenville (43952) *(G-17309)*
Catholic Association of The Di (PA) 216 641-7575
10000 Miles Ave Cleveland (44105) *(G-5188)*
Catholic Cemeteries 614 491-2751
6440 S High St Lockbourne (43137) *(G-12946)*
Catholic Charities Corporation 330 723-9615
4210 N Jefferson St Medina (44256) *(G-14042)*
Catholic Charities Corporation 216 939-3713
7800 Detroit Ave Cleveland (44102) *(G-5189)*
Catholic Charities Corporation 216 268-4006
1264 E 123rd St Cleveland (44108) *(G-5190)*
Catholic Charities Corporation 419 289-1903
34 W 2nd St Ste 18 Ashland (44805) *(G-670)*
Catholic Charities Corporation (PA) 216 334-2900
7911 Detroit Ave Cleveland (44102) *(G-5191)*
Catholic Charities of Southwst 937 325-8715
701 E Columbia St Springfield (45503) *(G-17157)*
Catholic Charities of SW Ohio (PA) 513 241-7745
7162 Reading Rd Ste 604 Cincinnati (45237) *(G-3194)*
Catholic Charities Services, Ashland *Also called Catholic Charities Corporation (G-670)*
Catholic Charities Svc Cuyah, Cleveland *Also called Catholic Charities Corporation (G-5189)*
Catholic Chrties Dcese Clvland, Cleveland *Also called Catholic Charities Corporation (G-5191)*
Catholic Chrties Regional Agcy 330 744-3320
319 W Rayen Ave Youngstown (44502) *(G-20134)*
Catholic Club, Toledo *Also called Diocese of Toledo (G-17854)*
Catholic Diocese of Cleveland 419 289-7224
501 Cottage St Ashland (44805) *(G-671)*
Catholic Diocese of Cleveland 216 267-2850
14609 Brookpark Rd Cleveland (44142) *(G-5192)*
Catholic Diocese of Columbus 614 276-5263
707 Salisbury Rd Columbus (43204) *(G-7210)*
Catholic Diocese of Columbus 614 221-5891
197 E Gay St Ste 1 Columbus (43215) *(G-7211)*
Catholic Health Partners, Glandorf *Also called St Ritas Medical Center (G-11432)*
Catholic Healthcare Par, Cincinnati *Also called Mercy Health (G-4065)*
Catholic Healthcare Par..., Springfield *Also called Mercy Health (G-17238)*
Catholic Residential Service 513 784-0400
100 E 8th St Ste 5 Cincinnati (45202) *(G-3195)*
Catholic Social Services Inc 614 221-5891
197 E Gay St Columbus (43215) *(G-7212)*
Catholic Social Svc Miami Vly (PA) 937 223-7217
922 W Riverview Ave Dayton (45402) *(G-9390)*
Catsi Inc 740 574-8417
7991 Ohio River Rd Wheelersburg (45694) *(G-19572)*
Cattrell Companies Inc 740 537-2481
906 Franklin St Toronto (43964) *(G-18336)*
Cavalier Distributing Company 513 247-9222
4650 Lake Forest Dr # 580 Blue Ash (45242) *(G-1552)*
Cavaliers Holdings LLC (PA) 216 420-2000
1 Center Ct Cleveland (44115) *(G-5193)*
Cavaliers Operating Co LLC 216 420-2000
1 Center Ct Cleveland (44115) *(G-5194)*
Caveney Inc 330 497-4600
7801 Cleveland Ave Nw North Canton (44720) *(G-15328)*
Cavins Trucking & Garage LLC (PA) 419 661-9947
100 J St C Perrysburg (43551) *(G-15985)*
Cavitch Familo & Durkin Co Lpa 216 621-7860
1300 E 9th St Cleveland (44114) *(G-5195)*
CB Manufacturing & Sls Co Inc (PA) 937 866-5986
4455 Infirmary Rd Miamisburg (45342) *(G-14279)*
CB Richard Ellis, Toledo *Also called Ellis Richard CB Reichle Klein (G-17864)*
CBA, Perrysburg *Also called Critical Business Analysis Inc (G-15991)*
Cbc Companies Inc 614 222-4343
1691 Nw Professional Plz Columbus (43220) *(G-7213)*
Cbc Companies Inc 614 538-6100
1651 Nw Professional Plz Columbus (43220) *(G-7214)*
Cbc Engineers & Associates Ltd (PA) 937 428-6150
125 Westpark Rd Dayton (45459) *(G-9391)*
Cbcinnovis International Inc (HQ) 614 222-4343
250 E Broad St Fl 21 Columbus (43215) *(G-7215)*
Cbcs, Columbus *Also called Credit Bur Collectn Svcs Inc (G-7458)*
Cbcs, Dayton *Also called Credit Bur Collectn Svcs Inc (G-9444)*
Cbf, Bedford *Also called EBO Inc (G-1305)*
Cbf Industries Inc 216 229-9300
23600 Aurora Rd Bedford (44146) *(G-1298)*
Cbiz Inc 330 644-2044
13680 Cleveland Ave Nw Uniontown (44685) *(G-18512)*
Cbiz Inc (PA) 216 447-9000
6050 Oak Tree Blvd # 500 Cleveland (44131) *(G-5196)*
Cbiz Accounting Tax 330 668-6500
4040 Embassy Pkwy Ste 100 Akron (44333) *(G-124)*
Cbiz Med MGT Professionals Inc 614 771-2222
3455 Mill Run Dr Ste 450 Hilliard (43026) *(G-11889)*
Cbiz Mhm LLC (HQ) 216 447-9000
6050 Oak Tree Blvd Cleveland (44131) *(G-5197)*
Cbl & Associates Prpts Inc 513 424-8517
3461 Towne Blvd Unit 200 Middletown (45005) *(G-14476)*
Cbo LLC 740 598-4121
2680 Commercial Ave Mingo Junction (43938) *(G-14654)*
Cbord Group Inc 330 498-2702
3800 Tabs Dr Uniontown (44685) *(G-18513)*
Cbre Inc 513 369-1300
201 E 5th St Ste 2200 Cincinnati (45202) *(G-3196)*
Cbre Inc 216 687-1800
950 Main Ave Ste 200 Cleveland (44113) *(G-5198)*
Cbre Inc 614 419-7429
860 Taylor Station Rd Blacklick (43004) *(G-1503)*
Cbre Inc 614 438-5488
200 Civic Center Dr Ste 8 Columbus (43215) *(G-7216)*
CBS Corporation 513 749-1035
2060 Reading Rd Fl 34 Cincinnati (45202) *(G-3197)*
CBS Radio Inc 513 699-5105
2060 Reading Rd Cincinnati (45202) *(G-3198)*
CBS Radio Inc 216 861-0100
1041 Huron Rd E Cleveland (44115) *(G-5199)*
Cbt Company, Cincinnati *Also called Belting Company of Cincinnati (G-3097)*
Cbt Company, Sidney *Also called Belting Company of Cincinnati (G-16916)*
Cbts, Cincinnati *Also called Cincinnati Bell Techno (G-3287)*
Ccdc, Dayton *Also called Valentour Education Inc (G-9960)*
Ccems, Coshocton *Also called Coshocton Cnty Emrgncy Med Svc (G-9094)*
Cchs Johnstown Home, Columbus *Also called Columbus Ctr For Humn Svcs Inc (G-7344)*
CCI, Mentor *Also called Cleveland Construction Inc (G-14159)*
CCI Supply Inc 440 953-0045
8620 Tyler Blvd Mentor (44060) *(G-14154)*
Ccj, Wooster *Also called Critchfeld Crtchfield Johnston (G-19859)*
CCJ Enterprises Inc 330 345-4386
3889 Friendsville Rd Wooster (44691) *(G-19837)*
Cd1025 614 221-9923
1036 S Front St Columbus (43206) *(G-7217)*
Cdc Capital Park Head St Ctr, Columbus *Also called Child Dvlpmnt Cncl of Frnkln (G-7259)*
Cdc Management Co 614 781-0216
4949 Freeway Dr E Columbus (43229) *(G-7218)*
Cdc of Shaker Heights 216 295-7000
11717 Euclid Ave Cleveland (44106) *(G-5200)*
Cdc Technologies Inc 937 886-9713
7100 Corporate Way Ste C Dayton (45459) *(G-9392)*
Cdd LLC 905 829-2794
6800 Cintas Blvd Mason (45040) *(G-13673)*
CDM Constructors Inc 740 947-7500
301 E Emmitt Ave Waverly (45690) *(G-18968)*

A L P H A B E T I C

CDM Smith Inc — 740 897-2937
3930 Us Rte 23 S Piketon (45661) *(G-16110)*

CDM SMITH INC — 614 847-8340
445 Hutchinson Ave # 820 Columbus (43235) *(G-7219)*

Cdo Technologies Inc (PA) — 937 258-0022
5200 Sprngfeld St Ste 320 Dayton (45431) *(G-9260)*

Cdw Technologies LLC — 513 677-4100
9349 Waterstone Blvd Cincinnati (45249) *(G-3199)*

Cec Combustion Safety LLC (HQ) — 216 749-2992
2100 Apollo Dr Brookpark (44142) *(G-1938)*

Cec Entertainment Inc — 937 439-1108
30 Prestige Pl Miamisburg (45342) *(G-14280)*

Cecil I Walker Machinery Co — 740 286-7566
1477 Mayhew Rd Jackson (45640) *(G-12308)*

Ceco Concrete Cnstr Del LLC — 513 874-6953
4535 Port Union Rd West Chester (45011) *(G-19033)*

Ceco Concrete Cnstr Del LLC — 734 455-3535
4535 Port Union Rd Ste A West Chester (45011) *(G-19034)*

Cecos International Inc — 513 724-6114
5092 Aber Rd Williamsburg (45176) *(G-19629)*

Cedar Creek Vterinary Svcs Inc — 740 467-2949
12575 Lancaster St Ne Millersport (43046) *(G-14630)*

Cedar Fair LP (PA) — 419 626-0830
1 Cedar Point Dr Sandusky (44870) *(G-16734)*

Cedar Hill Care Center, Zanesville *Also called Zandex Health Care Corporation* *(G-20552)*

Cedar Hill Care Center, Zanesville *Also called Zandex Inc* *(G-20549)*

Cedar House, Cleveland *Also called Rose Mary Johanna Grassell* *(G-6412)*

Cedar Point Park LLC — 419 627-2500
2001 Cleveland Rd Sandusky (44870) *(G-16735)*

Cedar Springs, New Paris *Also called Foundations* *(G-15077)*

Cedar Springs Care Center, New Paris *Also called Heritage Park Rehabilita* *(G-15078)*

Cedar Village, Mason *Also called Jewish Home of Cincinnati* *(G-13726)*

Cedars of Lebanon Nursing Home, Lebanon *Also called Health Care Opportunities Inc* *(G-12609)*

Cedarwood Construction Company — 330 836-9971
1765 Merriman Rd Akron (44313) *(G-125)*

Ceder Hill, Zanesville *Also called Zandex Health Care Corporation* *(G-20550)*

Cefaratti Group, Cleveland *Also called Cefaratti Investigation & Prcs* *(G-5201)*

Cefaratti Investigation & Prcs — 216 696-1161
4608 Saint Clair Ave Cleveland (44103) *(G-5201)*

Cei Physicians Inc — 513 984-5133
1945 Cei Dr Blue Ash (45242) *(G-1553)*

Cei Physicians PSC Inc (PA) — 513 984-5133
1945 Cei Dr Blue Ash (45242) *(G-1554)*

Cei Physicians PSC Inc — 513 233-2700
7794 5 Mile Rd Ste 270 Cincinnati (45230) *(G-3200)*

Cei Physicians PSC Inc — 513 531-2020
4760 Red Bank Rd Ste 108 Cincinnati (45227) *(G-3201)*

Ceiba Enterprises Incorporated — 614 818-3220
159 Baranof W Westerville (43081) *(G-19376)*

Celco Ltd — 330 655-7000
1140 Terex Rd Hudson (44236) *(G-12107)*

Celebrations, Plain City *Also called Made From Scratch Inc* *(G-16197)*

Celebrity Security Inc — 216 671-6425
3408 West Blvd Cleveland (44111) *(G-5202)*

CELINA AREA VISITING NURSES AS, Van Wert *Also called Community Hlth Prfssionals Inc* *(G-18630)*

Celina Insurance Group, Celina *Also called Celina Mutual Insurance Co* *(G-2638)*

Celina Mutual Insurance Co (PA) — 419 586-5181
1 Insurance Sq Celina (45822) *(G-2638)*

Celina Visting Nurses, Celina *Also called Community Hlth Prfssionals Inc* *(G-2641)*

Celina Waste Water Plant, Celina *Also called City of Celina* *(G-2639)*

Cellco Partnership — 330 722-6622
2736 Medina Rd Medina (44256) *(G-14043)*

Cellco Partnership — 614 560-2000
5165 Emerald Pkwy Dublin (43017) *(G-10281)*

Cellco Partnership — 440 984-5200
7566 Oak Point Rd Amherst (44001) *(G-590)*

Cellco Partnership — 330 486-1005
8957 Canyon Falls Blvd Twinsburg (44087) *(G-18398)*

Cellco Partnership — 614 560-8552
7575 Commerce Ct Lewis Center (43035) *(G-12673)*

Cellco Partnership — 513 923-2700
9674 Colerain Ave Cincinnati (45251) *(G-3202)*

Cellco Partnership — 614 476-9786
3985 Morse Xing Columbus (43219) *(G-7220)*

Cellco Partnership — 330 764-7380
1231 N Court St Medina (44256) *(G-14044)*

Cellco Partnership — 330 823-7758
2700 W State St Alliance (44601) *(G-531)*

Cellco Partnership — 419 333-1009
2140 Enterprise St Ste C Fremont (43420) *(G-11187)*

Cellco Partnership — 440 886-5461
7779 Day Dr Parma (44129) *(G-15901)*

Cellco Partnership — 330 928-4382
371 Howe Ave Cuyahoga Falls (44221) *(G-9170)*

Cellco Partnership — 419 353-0904
1530 E Wooster St Bowling Green (43402) *(G-1771)*

Cellco Partnership — 740 652-9540
1926 N Memorial Dr Lancaster (43130) *(G-12515)*

Cellco Partnership — 740 695-3600
50641 Valley Plaza Dr Saint Clairsville (43950) *(G-16631)*

Cellco Partnership — 419 784-3800
1007 N Clinton St Ste 1 Defiance (43512) *(G-10021)*

Cellco Partnership — 740 432-7785
2103 Southgate Pkwy Cambridge (43725) *(G-2103)*

Cellco Partnership — 330 376-8275
50 W Bowery St Akron (44308) *(G-126)*

Cellco Partnership — 513 755-1666
7606 Trailside Dr West Chester (45069) *(G-19035)*

Cellco Partnership — 513 697-1190
8650 Governors Hill Dr Cincinnati (45249) *(G-3203)*

Cellco Partnership — 440 934-0576
36050 Detroit Rd Avon (44011) *(G-885)*

Cellco Partnership — 419 381-1726
1260 S Reynolds Rd Toledo (43615) *(G-17795)*

Cellco Partnership — 216 765-1444
27460 Chagrin Blvd Beachwood (44122) *(G-1061)*

Cellco Partnership — 440 998-3111
3315 N Ridge Rd E Ashtabula (44004) *(G-731)*

Cellco Partnership — 513 422-3437
3663 Towne Blvd Middletown (45005) *(G-14477)*

Cellco Partnership — 740 588-0018
3575 Maple Ave Zanesville (43701) *(G-20458)*

Cellco Partnership — 513 688-1300
482 Ohio Pike Ste 1 Cincinnati (45255) *(G-3204)*

Cellco Partnership — 419 424-2351
15073 E Us Route 224 Findlay (45840) *(G-11011)*

Cellco Partnership — 419 331-4644
2465 Elida Rd Lima (45805) *(G-12752)*

Cellco Partnership — 419 897-9133
1378 Conant St Maumee (43537) *(G-13892)*

Cellco Partnership — 614 759-4400
2406 Taylor Park Dr Reynoldsburg (43068) *(G-16434)*

Cellco Partnership — 419 625-7900
4816 Milan Rd Ste F Sandusky (44870) *(G-16736)*

Cellco Partnership — 440 953-1155
7685 Mentor Ave Mentor (44060) *(G-14155)*

Cellco Partnership — 440 646-9625
5945 Mayfield Rd Cleveland (44124) *(G-5203)*

Cellco Partnership — 440 846-8881
17290 Royalton Rd Strongsville (44136) *(G-17448)*

Cellco Partnership — 740 397-6609
1002 Coshocton Ave 3 Mount Vernon (43050) *(G-14881)*

Cellco Partnership — 614 459-7200
2180 Henderson Rd Columbus (43220) *(G-7221)*

Cellco Partnership — 937 429-4000
2755 Fairfield Cmns Beavercreek (45431) *(G-1158)*

Cellco Partnership — 513 671-2200
55 E Kemper Rd Cincinnati (45246) *(G-3205)*

Cellco Partnership — 513 697-0222
9040 Union Cemetery Rd Cincinnati (45249) *(G-3206)*

Cellco Partnership — 330 665-5220
3750 W Market St Unit C Fairlawn (44333) *(G-10941)*

Cellco Partnership — 440 779-1313
24121 Lorain Rd North Olmsted (44070) *(G-15412)*

Cellco Partnership — 419 843-2995
6710 W Central Ave Ste 20 Toledo (43617) *(G-17796)*

Cellco Partnership — 330 493-7979
4926 Dressler Rd Nw Canton (44718) *(G-2302)*

Cellco Partnership — 937 498-2371
2400 Michigan St Sidney (45365) *(G-16918)*

Cellco Partnership — 216 573-5880
6712 Rockside Rd Independence (44131) *(G-12195)*

Cellco Partnership — 330 922-5997
3490 Hudson Dr Ste 2 Stow (44224) *(G-17355)*

Cellco Partnership — 937 578-0022
1095 Delaware Ave Marysville (43040) *(G-13611)*

Cellco Partnership — 440 542-9631
6440 Som Center Rd Ste C Solon (44139) *(G-16990)*

Cellco Partnership — 330 626-0524
9315 State Route 14 Streetsboro (44241) *(G-17408)*

Cellco Partnership — 330 308-0549
507 Mill Ave Se New Philadelphia (44663) *(G-15084)*

Cellco Partnership — 614 793-8989
5520 Blazer Pkwy Dublin (43016) *(G-10282)*

Cellco Partnership — 740 450-1525
2359 Maple Ave Zanesville (43701) *(G-20459)*

Cellco Partnership — 740 362-2408
1100 Sunbury Rd Ret702 Delaware (43015) *(G-10077)*

Cellco Partnership — 440 324-9479
1621 W River Rd N Elyria (44035) *(G-10601)*

Cellco Partnership — 614 793-8989
5035 Post Rd Dublin (43017) *(G-10283)*

Cellco Partnership — 614 277-2900
3043 Turnberry Ct Grove City (43123) *(G-11544)*

Cellco Partnership — 740 522-6446
668 Hebron Rd Newark (43056) *(G-15155)*

Cellco Partnership — 330 345-6465
4164 Burbank Rd Wooster (44691) *(G-19838)*

Cellular Technology Limited — 216 791-5084
20521 Chagrin Blvd # 200 Shaker Heights (44122) *(G-16857)*

Celtic Healthcare Ne Ohio Inc — 724 742-4360
299 Edwards St Youngstown (44502) *(G-20135)*

Cem-Base Inc 330 963-3101
8530 N Boyle Pkwy Twinsburg (44087) ***(G-18399)***
Cemp, Brooklyn *Also called Victory Capital Management Inc* ***(G-1907)***
Cengage Learning Inc 513 229-1000
5191 Natorp Blvd Lowr Mason (45040) ***(G-13674)***
Centaur Associates, Maumee *Also called Centaur Mail Inc* ***(G-13893)***
Centaur Mail Inc 419 887-5857
4064 Technology Dr Ste A Maumee (43537) ***(G-13893)***
Centaurus Financial Inc 419 756-9747
58 W 3rd St Ste B Mansfield (44902) ***(G-13273)***
Centennial Prsrvtion Group LLC 614 238-0730
600 N Cassady Ave Ste D Columbus (43219) ***(G-7222)***
Centennial Terrace & Quarry 419 885-7106
5773 Centennial Rd Sylvania (43560) ***(G-17578)***
Center 5 330 379-5900
444 N Main St Akron (44310) ***(G-127)***
Center Ed/Train Employmnt, Columbus *Also called Ohio State University* ***(G-8410)***
Center For Balanced Living, Columbus *Also called Center For Eating Disorders* ***(G-7225)***
Center For Chemical Addictions 513 381-6672
830 Ezzard Charles Dr Cincinnati (45214) ***(G-3207)***
Center For Child Development, Akron *Also called University of Akron* ***(G-489)***
Center For Cognitive and Beh (PA) 614 459-4490
4624 Sawmill Rd Columbus (43220) ***(G-7223)***
Center For Cognitv Behav Psych 614 459-4490
4624 Sawmill Rd Columbus (43220) ***(G-7224)***
Center For Community Solutions 216 781-2944
1501 Euclid Ave Ste 311 Cleveland (44115) ***(G-5204)***
Center For Dagnstc Imaging Inc 614 841-0800
2141 Polaris Pkwy Columbus (43240) ***(G-6872)***
Center For Dialysis Care, Cleveland *Also called Cdc of Shaker Heights* ***(G-5200)***
Center For Dialysis Care, Cleveland *Also called Community Dialysis Center* ***(G-5384)***
Center For Dlysis Cre of Cnfld 330 702-3040
3695 Stutz Dr Ste 1 Canfield (44406) ***(G-2186)***
Center For Eating Disorders 614 896-8222
8001 Ravines Edge Ct # 201 Columbus (43235) ***(G-7225)***
Center For Employment Resource, Cincinnati *Also called Great Oaks Inst Tech Creer Dev* ***(G-3704)***
Center For Families & Children 440 888-0300
5955 Ridge Rd Cleveland (44129) ***(G-5205)***
Center For Families & Children (PA) 216 432-7200
4500 Euclid Ave Cleveland (44103) ***(G-5206)***
Center For Families & Children 216 932-9497
1941 S Taylor Rd Ste 225 Cleveland Heights (44118) ***(G-6786)***
Center For Families & Children 216 252-5800
3929 Rocky River Dr Cleveland (44111) ***(G-5207)***
Center For Foot & Ankle Care 513 533-1199
25 Merchant St Ste 220 Cincinnati (45246) ***(G-3208)***
Center For Health Affairs 800 362-2628
1226 Huron Rd E Cleveland (44115) ***(G-5208)***
Center For Human Resource RES, Columbus *Also called Ohio State University* ***(G-8414)***
Center For Individual and Fmly (PA) 419 522-4357
741 Scholl Rd Mansfield (44907) ***(G-13274)***
Center For Prgressive Eye Care, Oregon *Also called Assocted Ctract Laser Surgeons* ***(G-15724)***
Center For Spinal Disorders 419 383-4878
3000 Arlington Ave Toledo (43614) ***(G-17797)***
Center For Srgcal Drmtlogy Inc 614 847-4100
428 County Line Rd W Westerville (43082) ***(G-19289)***
Center For Urologic Health LLC (PA) 330 375-0924
95 Arch St Ste 165 Akron (44304) ***(G-128)***
Center of Hope, Union City *Also called Crotinger Nursing Home Inc* ***(G-18502)***
Center of Voctnl Altrntvs Mntl (PA) 614 294-7117
3770 N High St Columbus (43214) ***(G-7226)***
Center Ridge House, Westlake *Also called Childrens Forever Haven Inc* ***(G-19474)***
Center Ridge Nursing Home Inc 440 327-1295
38600 Center Ridge Rd North Ridgeville (44039) ***(G-15458)***
Center School Association 440 995-7400
6625 Wilson Mills Rd Mayfield Village (44143) ***(G-14010)***
Center Seeds, Sidney *Also called Cover Crop Shop LLC* ***(G-16927)***
Center Service, Cincinnati *Also called Carol Reese* ***(G-3187)***
Center Street Cmnty Clinic Inc 740 751-6380
136 W Center St Marion (43302) ***(G-13529)***
Centerburg Resp & Spclty Rehab, Centerburg *Also called Centerburg Two LLC* ***(G-2666)***
Centerburg Two LLC 740 625-5774
212 Fairview St Centerburg (43011) ***(G-2666)***
Centerpoint Health Inc, Cincinnati *Also called Talbert House Health* ***(G-4622)***
Centerra Co-Op (PA) 419 281-2153
813 Clark Ave Ashland (44805) ***(G-672)***
Centerra Co-Op 800 362-9598
161 E Jefferson St Jefferson (44047) ***(G-12331)***
Centers For Dialysis Care Inc (PA) 216 295-7000
18720 Chagrin Blvd Shaker Heights (44122) ***(G-16858)***
Centerville Child Development 937 434-5949
8095 Garnet Dr Dayton (45458) ***(G-9393)***
Centerville Fitness Inc 937 291-7990
51 E Spring Valley Pike Centerville (45458) ***(G-2675)***
Centerville Washington Pk Dst, Dayton *Also called Washington Township Park Dst* ***(G-9985)***
Centimark Corporation 614 536-1960
7077 Americana Pkwy Reynoldsburg (43068) ***(G-16435)***
Centimark Corporation 937 704-9909
319 Industrial Dr Franklin (45005) ***(G-11152)***
Centimark Corporation 330 920-3560
4665 Allen Rd Ste C Stow (44224) ***(G-17356)***
Centimark Roofing Systems, Franklin *Also called Centimark Corporation* ***(G-11152)***
Central 'travel, Toledo *Also called Central Travel & Ticket Inc* ***(G-17799)***
Central Accounting Systems 513 605-2700
12500 Reed Hartman Hwy Cincinnati (45241) ***(G-3209)***
Central Beverage Group Ltd 614 294-3555
8133 Highfield Dr Lewis Center (43035) ***(G-12674)***
Central Billing Office, Akron *Also called Nationwide Childrens Hospital* ***(G-349)***
Central Bnfits Admnstrtors Inc 614 797-5200
5150 E Dublin Grnvlle 3 Westerville (43081) ***(G-19377)***
Central Business Equipment Co (HQ) 513 891-4430
10321 S Medallion Dr Cincinnati (45241) ***(G-3210)***
Central Cadillac Limited 216 861-5800
2801 Carnegie Ave Cleveland (44115) ***(G-5209)***
Central Cadillac-Hummer, Cleveland *Also called Central Cadillac Limited* ***(G-5209)***
Central Christian School, Kidron *Also called Christian Schools Inc* ***(G-12440)***
Central Cmnty Hse of Columbus (PA) 614 253-7267
1150 E Main St Columbus (43205) ***(G-7227)***
Central Coca-Cola Btlg Co Inc 419 476-6622
3970 Catawba St Toledo (43612) ***(G-17798)***
Central Command Inc 330 723-2062
33891 Henwell Rd Columbia Station (44028) ***(G-6842)***
Central Commnty Hlth Brd of Ha (PA) 513 559-2000
532 Maxwell Ave Cincinnati (45219) ***(G-3211)***
Central Commnty Hlth Brd of Ha 513 559-2981
3020 Vernon Pl Cincinnati (45219) ***(G-3212)***
Central Community 513 559-2000
3007 Vernon Pl Cincinnati (45219) ***(G-3213)***
Central Credit Corp 614 856-5840
2040 Brice Rd Ste 200 Reynoldsburg (43068) ***(G-16436)***
Central Equity Investments Inc 937 454-1270
1280 Industrial Park Dr Vandalia (45377) ***(G-18668)***
Central Exterminating Company (PA) 216 771-0555
3202 Saint Clair Ave Ne Cleveland (44114) ***(G-5210)***
Central Fire Protection Co Inc 937 322-0713
583 Selma Rd Springfield (45505) ***(G-17158)***
Central Hamilton YMCA, Hamilton *Also called Great Miami Valley YMCA* ***(G-11735)***
Central Hospital Services Inc 216 696-6900
1226 Huron Rd E Ste 2 Cleveland (44115) ***(G-5211)***
Central Hummr East 216 514-2700
25975 Central Pkwy Cleveland (44122) ***(G-5212)***
Central Insulation Systems Inc 513 242-0600
300 Murray Rd Cincinnati (45217) ***(G-3214)***
CENTRAL INSURANCE COMPANIES, Van Wert *Also called Central Mutual Insurance Co* ***(G-18629)***
CENTRAL INSURANCE COMPANIES, Van Wert *Also called All America Insurance Company* ***(G-18627)***
Central Mutual Insurance Co (PA) 419 238-1010
800 S Washington St Van Wert (45891) ***(G-18629)***
Central OH Area Agency On Agng 614 645-7250
3776 S High St Columbus (43207) ***(G-7228)***
Central Ohio Associates Ltd 419 342-2045
Central Oh Ind 18 Shelby (44875) ***(G-16897)***
Central Ohio Bandag LP 740 454-9728
1600 S Point Dr Zanesville (43701) ***(G-20460)***
Central Ohio Building Co Inc 614 475-6392
3756 Agler Rd Columbus (43219) ***(G-7229)***
Central Ohio Contractors Inc (PA) 614 539-2579
2879 Jackson Pike Grove City (43123) ***(G-11545)***
Central Ohio Contractors Inc 740 369-7700
888 Us Highway 42 N Delaware (43015) ***(G-10078)***
Central Ohio Custom Contg LLC 614 579-4971
10541 New Delaware Rd Mount Vernon (43050) ***(G-14882)***
Central Ohio Financial Group, Columbus *Also called Northwestern Mutl Lf Insur Co* ***(G-8299)***
Central Ohio Geriatrics LLC 614 530-4077
590 Newark Granville Rd Granville (43023) ***(G-11460)***
Central Ohio Home Help Agency, Columbus *Also called Ssth LLC* ***(G-8769)***
Central Ohio Hospitalists 614 255 6000
3525 Olentangy River Rd # 4330 Columbus (43214) ***(G-7230)***
Central Ohio Ice Rinks Inc 614 475-7575
7001 Dublin Park Dr Dublin (43016) ***(G-10284)***
Central Ohio Medical Textiles 614 453-9274
575 Harmon Ave Columbus (43223) ***(G-7231)***
Central Ohio Mental Health Ctr (PA) 740 368-7831
250 S Henry St Delaware (43015) ***(G-10079)***
Central Ohio Nrlgical Surgeons 614 268-9561
955 Eastwind Dr Ste B Westerville (43081) ***(G-19378)***
Central Ohio Nutrition Center (PA) 614 864-7225
648 Taylor Rd Columbus (43230) ***(G-7232)***
Central Ohio Poison Center 800 222-1222
700 Childrens Dr Columbus (43205) ***(G-7233)***
Central Ohio Poured Walls Inc 614 889-0505
7627 Fishel Dr N Dublin (43016) ***(G-10285)***
Central Ohio Primary Care 614 459-3687
770 Jasonway Ave Ste G2 Columbus (43214) ***(G-7234)***
Central Ohio Primary Care 614 818-9550
285 W Schrock Rd Westerville (43081) ***(G-19379)***

ALPHABETIC

(PA)=Parent Co (HQ)=Headquarters (DH)=Div Headquarters
2018 Harris Ohio Services Directory
1137

Central Ohio Primary Care 614 451-1551
4885 Olentangy River Rd # 2 Columbus (43214) ***(G-7235)***
Central Ohio Primary Care 614 268-6555
4885 Olentangy River Rd Columbus (43214) ***(G-7236)***
Central Ohio Primary Care 614 473-1300
2489 Stelzer Rd 101 Columbus (43219) ***(G-7237)***
Central Ohio Primary Care 614 508-0110
615 Cpland Mill Rd Ste 2d Westerville (43081) ***(G-19380)***
Central Ohio Primary Care 614 552-2300
6488 E Main St Ste C Reynoldsburg (43068) ***(G-16437)***
Central Ohio Primary Care 614 891-9505
507 Executive Campus Dr # 160 Westerville (43082) ***(G-19290)***
Central Ohio Primary Care 614 882-0708
555 W Schrock Rd Ste 110 Westerville (43081) ***(G-19381)***
Central Ohio Primary Care 614 268-8164
3535 Olentangy River Rd Columbus (43214) ***(G-7238)***
Central Ohio Primary Care 614 834-8042
6201 Gender Rd Canal Winchester (43110) ***(G-2156)***
Central Ohio Primary Care 614 540-7339
760 Lakeview Plaza Blvd # 500 Worthington (43085) ***(G-19946)***
Central Ohio Primary Care (PA) 614 326-2672
570 Polaris Pkwy Ste 250 Westerville (43082) ***(G-19291)***
Central Ohio Primary Care 614 442-7550
4030 Henderson Rd Columbus (43220) ***(G-7239)***
Central Ohio Pulmonary Disease, Westerville *Also called Central Ohio Sleep Medicine* ***(G-19292)***
Central Ohio Sleep Medicine 614 475-6700
484 County Line Rd W # 130 Westerville (43082) ***(G-19292)***
Central Ohio Surgical Assoc (PA) 614 222-8000
750 Mount Carmel Mall # 380 Columbus (43222) ***(G-7240)***
Central Ohio Transit Authority 614 275-5800
1333 Fields Ave Columbus (43201) ***(G-7241)***
Central Ohio Transit Authority (PA) 614 275-5800
33 N High St Columbus (43215) ***(G-7242)***
Central Ohio Youth Center, Marysville *Also called Five County Joint Juvenile Det* ***(G-13618)***
Central Ohio Youth For Christ 614 732-5260
5000 Arlington Centre Blv Columbus (43220) ***(G-7243)***
Central Parking System Inc 513 381-2621
303 Broadway St Lot A Cincinnati (45202) ***(G-3215)***
Central Pk W Rhabilitation Ctr, Toledo *Also called Rehabilitation Aquatics* ***(G-18148)***
Central Power Systems, Columbus *Also called Power Distributors LLC* ***(G-8554)***
Central Railroad of Indiana, Cincinnati *Also called Indiana & Ohio Rail Corp* ***(G-3813)***
Central Ready Mix LLC (PA) 513 402-5001
6310 E Kemper Rd Ste 125 Cincinnati (45241) ***(G-3216)***
Central Region, Mason *Also called Dassault Systemes Simulia Corp* ***(G-13694)***
Central Repair Service Inc 513 943-0500
1606 Locust St Point Pleasant (45153) ***(G-16218)***
Central Services Department, Cleveland *Also called County of Cuyahoga* ***(G-5423)***
Central Star 419 756-9449
380 N Main St Ste L102 Mansfield (44902) ***(G-13275)***
Central Star Home Health Svcs, Mansfield *Also called Central Star* ***(G-13275)***
Central Steel and Wire Company 513 242-2233
525 Township Ave Cincinnati (45216) ***(G-3217)***
Central Travel & Ticket Inc (PA) 419 897-2070
4540 Heatherdowns Blvd # 2 Toledo (43614) ***(G-17799)***
Central USA Wireless LLC 513 469-1500
11210 Montgomery Rd Cincinnati (45249) ***(G-3218)***
Central Warehouse Dayton, Vandalia *Also called Central Equity Investments Inc* ***(G-18668)***
Centre Communications Corp 440 454-3262
70 Birch Aly Ste 240 Beavercreek (45440) ***(G-1232)***
Centric Consulting LLC (PA) 888 781-7567
1215 Lyons Rd F Dayton (45458) ***(G-9394)***
Centric Consulting LLC 513 791-3061
9380 Montgomery Rd # 207 Cincinnati (45242) ***(G-3219)***
Centro Properties Group LLC 440 324-6610
3343 Midway Mall Elyria (44035) ***(G-10602)***
Centrus Energy Corp 740 897-2457
3930 Us Rt 23 S Piketon (45661) ***(G-16111)***
Centura Inc 216 593-0226
4381 Renaissance Pkwy Cleveland (44128) ***(G-5213)***
Centura X-Ray, Cleveland *Also called Centura Inc* ***(G-5213)***
Centurion of Akron Inc 330 645-6699
1062 Jacoby Rd Copley (44321) ***(G-9054)***
Century 21, Kent *Also called Wilbur Realty Inc* ***(G-12405)***
Century 21, Mentor *Also called Prudential Select Properties* ***(G-14230)***
Century 21, Lakewood *Also called Prudential Lucien Realty* ***(G-12495)***
Century 21, Columbus *Also called Joseph Walker Inc* ***(G-6887)***
Century 21, Marietta *Also called REO Network Inc* ***(G-13494)***
Century 21, Warren *Also called North Wood Realty* ***(G-18886)***
Century 21 - North Office, Columbus *Also called Century 21-Joe Walker & Assoc* ***(G-6873)***
Century 21 Elite Performance 937 438-8221
2905 River Edge Cir Spring Valley (45370) ***(G-17109)***
Century 21 Trammell Odonnell 440 888-6800
7087 Pearl Rd Cleveland (44130) ***(G-5214)***
Century 21-Joe Walker & Assoc 614 899-1400
8800 Lyra Dr Ste 600 Columbus (43240) ***(G-6873)***
Century Contractors Inc 440 232-2626
26100 Broadway Ave Ste B Cleveland (44146) ***(G-5215)***
Century Equipment Inc (PA) 419 865-7400
5959 Angola Rd Toledo (43615) ***(G-17800)***
Century Equipment Inc 513 285-1800
8650 Bilstein Blvd Hamilton (45015) ***(G-11707)***
Century Equipment Inc 216 292-6911
26565 Miles Rd Ste 200 Cleveland (44128) ***(G-5216)***
Century Federal Credit Union 216 535-3600
10701 East Blvd Cleveland (44106) ***(G-5217)***
Century Glass Co 216 361-7700
6211 Cedar Ave Cleveland (44103) ***(G-5218)***
Century Health Inc (PA) 419 425-5050
1918 N Main St Findlay (45840) ***(G-11012)***
Century Lines Inc 216 271-0700
3184 E 79th St Cleveland (44104) ***(G-5219)***
Century Marketing Corporation (HQ) 419 354-2591
12836 S Dixie Hwy Bowling Green (43402) ***(G-1772)***
Century Mech Solutions Inc 513 681-5700
1554 Chase Ave Cincinnati (45223) ***(G-3220)***
Century National Bank (HQ) 740 454-2521
14 S 5th St Zanesville (43701) ***(G-20461)***
Century National Bank 800 548-3557
33 S 5th St Zanesville (43701) ***(G-20462)***
Century National Bank 740 455-7330
505 Market St Zanesville (43701) ***(G-20463)***
Century Oak Care Center, Cleveland *Also called Swa Inc* ***(G-6560)***
Century Oak Care Center, Cleveland *Also called Southwest Associates* ***(G-6499)***
Century Surety Company (HQ) 614 895-2000
465 N Cleveland Ave Westerville (43082) ***(G-19293)***
Century Tel of Odon Inc (HQ) 440 244-8544
203 W 9th St Lorain (44052) ***(G-13022)***
Centurylabel, Bowling Green *Also called Century Marketing Corporation* ***(G-1772)***
Centurylink, Lorain *Also called Century Tel of Odon Inc* ***(G-13022)***
Centurylink Inc 614 215-4223
4650 Lakehurst Ct Dublin (43016) ***(G-10286)***
Ceogc, Cleveland *Also called Council For Economic Opport* ***(G-5414)***
CER Hotels LLC 330 422-1855
795 Mondial Pkwy Streetsboro (44241) ***(G-17409)***
CEREBRAL PALSY SERVICES CENTER, Cincinnati *Also called United Cerebral Palsy Gr Cinc* ***(G-4729)***
Ceres Enterprises LLC 440 617-9385
835 Sharon Dr Ste 400 Westlake (44145) ***(G-19472)***
Cerni Motor Sales Inc (PA) 330 652-9917
5751 Cerni Pl Youngstown (44515) ***(G-20136)***
Cerruti LLC 330 562-0120
30 Shawnee Trl Aurora (44202) ***(G-834)***
Certanteed Gyps Ciling Mfg Inc 800 233-8990
1192 S Chillicothe Rd Aurora (44202) ***(G-835)***
Certified Angus Beef LLC (HQ) 330 345-2333
206 Riffel Rd Wooster (44691) ***(G-19839)***
Certified Angus Beef LLC 330 345-2333
344 Riffel Rd Wooster (44691) ***(G-19840)***
Certified Oil Inc 614 421-7500
949 King Ave Columbus (43212) ***(G-7244)***
Certified SEC Solutions Inc (PA) 216 785-2986
6050 Oak Tree Blvd Independence (44131) ***(G-12196)***
Certified Service Center, Cincinnati *Also called Service Solutions Group LLC* ***(G-4501)***
Ceso Inc (PA) 937 435-8584
3601 Rigby Rd Ste 310 Miamisburg (45342) ***(G-14281)***
Cessna Aircraft Company 419 866-6761
11591 W Airport Service R Swanton (43558) ***(G-17562)***
Cessna Toledo Citation Svc Ctr, Swanton *Also called Cessna Aircraft Company* ***(G-17562)***
Cetek, Brookpark *Also called Fosbel Inc* ***(G-1945)***
Cetek Ltd 216 362-3900
6779 Engle Rd Ste A Cleveland (44130) ***(G-5220)***
Ceva Freight LLC 614 482-5100
2727 London Groveport Rd Groveport (43125) ***(G-11627)***
Ceva Freight LLC 216 898-6765
18601 Cleveland Pkwy Dr Cleveland (44135) ***(G-5221)***
Ceva Logistics LLC 614 482-5000
2727 London Groveport Rd Groveport (43125) ***(G-11628)***
Ceva Logistics US Inc 614 482-5107
2727 London Groveport Rd Columbus (43207) ***(G-7245)***
Ceva Logistics US Inc 937 578-1160
26230 Stokes Rd East Liberty (43319) ***(G-10507)***
Ceva Ocean Line, Groveport *Also called Ceva Freight LLC* ***(G-11627)***
Ceva Ocean Line, Cleveland *Also called Ceva Freight LLC* ***(G-5221)***
CFI Interiors, Canton *Also called Canton Floors Inc* ***(G-2288)***
CFM Religion Pubg Group LLC (PA) 513 931-4050
8805 Governors Hill Dr # 400 Cincinnati (45249) ***(G-3221)***
CFS Construction Inc 513 559-4500
2170 Gilbert Ave Ste 100 Cincinnati (45206) ***(G-3222)***
CGB -Defiance, Defiance *Also called Consolidated Grain & Barge Co* ***(G-10023)***
Cgh Global, Cincinnati *Also called Cgh-Global Emerg Mngmt Strateg* ***(G-2905)***
Cgh-Glbal Operations Logistics 800 376-0655
4957 Cinnamon Cir Cincinnati (45244) ***(G-3223)***
Cgh-Global Emerg Mngmt Strateg 800 376-0655
851 Ohio Pike Ste 203 Cincinnati (45245) ***(G-2905)***
Cgh-Global Security LLC 800 376-0655
4957 Cinnamon Cir Cincinnati (45244) ***(G-3224)***
Cgh-Global Technologies LLC 800 376-0655
4957 Cinnamon Cir Cincinnati (45244) ***(G-3225)***

ALPHABETIC SECTION

Cgi Technologies Solutions Inc 216 687-1480
   1001 Lakeside Ave E # 800 Cleveland (44114) *(G-5222)*
Cgi Technologies Solutions Inc 614 228-2245
   88 E Broad St Ste 1425 Columbus (43215) *(G-7246)*
Cgi Technologies Solutions Inc 614 880-2200
   2000 Polaris Pkwy Columbus (43240) *(G-6874)*
Ch Relty Iv/Clmbus Partners LP 614 885-3334
   175 Hutchinson Ave Columbus (43235) *(G-7247)*
CH Robinson Company Inc 614 933-5100
   800 Yard St Ste 200 Columbus (43212) *(G-7248)*
CH Robinson Freight Svcs Ltd 440 234-7811
   7261 Engle Rd Ste 400 Cleveland (44130) *(G-5223)*
Ch2m Hill Inc 513 243-5070
   400 E Bus Way Ste 400 Cincinnati (45241) *(G-3226)*
Ch2m Hill Inc 614 888-3100
   2 Easton Oval Ste 125 Columbus (43219) *(G-7249)*
Ch2m Hill Constructors Inc 937 228-4285
   1 S Main St Ste 1100 Dayton (45402) *(G-9395)*
Cha Consulting Inc 216 443-1700
   1501 N Marginal Rd # 200 Cleveland (44114) *(G-5224)*
Chaco Credit Union Inc (PA) 513 785-3500
   100 S 3rd St Hamilton (45011) *(G-11708)*
Chad Downing 614 532-5127
   679 Rose Way Columbus (43230) *(G-7250)*
Chagrin Falls Historical Soc 440 247-4695
   87 E Washington St Chagrin Falls (44022) *(G-2691)*
Chagrin Valley Athletic Club 440 543-5141
   17260 Snyder Rd Chagrin Falls (44023) *(G-2712)*
Chagrin Valley Country Club Co 440 248-4310
   4700 Som Center Rd Chagrin Falls (44022) *(G-2692)*
Chagrin Valley Dispatch 440 247-7321
   88 Center Rd Ste B100 Bedford (44146) *(G-1299)*
Chagrin Valley Hunt Club 440 423-4414
   7620 Old Mill Rd Gates Mills (44040) *(G-11356)*
Chal-Ron LLC 216 383-9050
   15751 Lake Shore Blvd Cleveland (44110) *(G-5225)*
Chalet, Strongsville *Also called Cleveland Metroparks (G-17452)*
Chalk Box Get Fit LLC 440 992-9619
   5521 Main Ave Ashtabula (44004) *(G-732)*
Chalmers P Wylie VA, Columbus *Also called Veterans Health Administration (G-8937)*
Chamber Commerce New Carlisle 937 845-3911
   131 S Main St New Carlisle (45344) *(G-15021)*
Chamberlain Hr 216 589-9280
   36368 Detroit Rd Ste A Avon (44011) *(G-886)*
Chambers Leasing Systems 937 547-9777
   5187 Chld Hm Bradford Rd Greenville (45331) *(G-11492)*
Chambers Leasing Systems Corp (PA) 419 726-9747
   3100 N Summit St Toledo (43611) *(G-17801)*
Champagne National Bank, Urbana *Also called Futura Banc Corp (G-18588)*
Champaign Cnty Board of Dd 937 653-5217
   1250 E Us Highway 36 Urbana (43078) *(G-18576)*
Champaign County Board of Mrdd, Urbana *Also called Champaign Cnty Board of Dd (G-18576)*
Champaign County Engineer, Urbana *Also called County of Champaign (G-18584)*
Champaign Landmark Inc (PA) 937 652-2135
   304 Bloomfield Ave Urbana (43078) *(G-18577)*
Champaign National Bank Urbana 614 798-1321
   6400 Perimeter Loop Rd Dublin (43017) *(G-10287)*
Champaign Premium Grn Growers 937 826-3003
   24320 Woodstock Rd Milford Center (43045) *(G-14575)*
Champaign Realty, Urbana *Also called Richard H Freyhof (G-18599)*
Champaign Residential Services 614 481-5550
   1350 W 5th Ave Ste 230 Columbus (43212) *(G-7251)*
Champaign Residential Svcs Inc (PA) 937 653-1320
   1150 Scioto St Ste 201 Urbana (43078) *(G-18578)*
Champaign Telephone Company (PA) 937 653-4000
   126 Scioto St Urbana (43078) *(G-18579)*
Champion, Cincinnati *Also called Enclosure Suppliers LLC (G-3555)*
Champion Aerie 397, Springfield *Also called Fraternal Order of Eagles (G-17200)*
Champion Clg Specialists Inc 513 871-2333
   8391 Blue Ash Rd Cincinnati (45236) *(G-3227)*
CHAMPION INDUSTRIES DIV, Troy *Also called R T Industries Inc (G-18374)*
Champion One, Beachwood *Also called Champion Optical Network (G 1062)*
Champion Opco LLC (PA) 513 924-4858
   12121 Champion Way Cincinnati (45241) *(G-3228)*
Champion Optical Network 216 831-1800
   23645 Mercantile Rd Ste A Beachwood (44122) *(G-1062)*
Champion Windows Manufacturing, Cincinnati *Also called Champion Opco LLC (G-3228)*
Champions Gym 937 294-8202
   6559 Brantford Rd Dayton (45414) *(G-9396)*
Championship Management Co 740 524-4653
   1150 Wilson Rd Sunbury (43074) *(G-17552)*
Champlain Enterprises LLC (PA) 440 779-4588
   24950 Country Club Blvd # 300 North Olmsted (44070) *(G-15413)*
Champlin Architecture, Cincinnati *Also called Champlin Haupt Architects Inc (G-3229)*
Champlin Haupt Architects Inc (PA) 513 241-4474
   720 E Pete Rose Way # 140 Cincinnati (45202) *(G-3229)*
Champons In Making Daycare LLC 937 728-4886
   160 Park Dr Wilmington (45177) *(G-19747)*
Champs, Cleveland *Also called Healthcomp Inc (G-5738)*

CHAMPS MANAGEMENT SERVICES, Cleveland *Also called Central Hospital Services Inc (G-5211)*
Chander M Kohli MD Facs Inc 330 759-6978
   540 Parmalee Ave Ste 310 Youngstown (44510) *(G-20137)*
Chandler Products LLC 216 481-4400
   1491 Chardon Rd Cleveland (44117) *(G-5226)*
Chandler Systems Incorporated 888 363-9434
   710 Orange St Ashland (44805) *(G-673)*
Chaney Roofing Maintenance 419 639-2761
   7040 State Route 101 N Clyde (43410) *(G-6811)*
Change Healthcare Holdings Inc 330 405-0001
   300 Executive Pkwy W Hudson (44236) *(G-12108)*
Change Healthcare Holdings Inc 216 589-5878
   2060 E 9th St Cleveland (44115) *(G-5227)*
Change Healthcare Tech Enabled 614 566-5861
   3535 Olentangy River Rd Columbus (43214) *(G-7252)*
Changes Hair Designers Inc 614 846-6666
   2054 Polaris Pkwy Columbus (43240) *(G-6875)*
Changes Salon & Day Spa, Columbus *Also called Changes Hair Designers Inc (G-6875)*
Channel 10, Columbus *Also called Wbns Tv Inc (G-8973)*
CHANNEL 48, Cincinnati *Also called Greater Cincinnati TV Educ Fnd (G-3711)*
Chantest Corporation, Cleveland *Also called Charles Rver Labs Clveland Inc (G-5228)*
Chapel Electric Co LLC 937 222-2290
   1985 Founders Dr Dayton (45420) *(G-9397)*
Chapel Electric Co., Dayton *Also called Quebe Holdings Inc (G-9838)*
Chapel Hill Community, Marion *Also called United Church Homes Inc (G-13592)*
CHAPEL HILL COMMUNITY, Kenton *Also called United Church Res of Kenton (G-12425)*
CHAPEL HILL COMMUNITY, Marion *Also called Unite Churc Resid of Oxfor Mis (G-13590)*
Chapel Hill Management Inc 330 633-7100
   2000 Brittain Rd Ste 830 Akron (44310) *(G-129)*
Chapel Hill Medical Offices, Akron *Also called Kaiser Foundation Hospitals (G-299)*
Chapel Hl Chrstn Schl Endwment 330 929-1901
   1090 Howe Ave Cuyahoga Falls (44221) *(G-9171)*
Chapel Steel Corp 800 570-7674
   26400 Richmond Rd Bedford Heights (44146) *(G-1349)*
Chapel-Romanoff Tech LLC 937 222-9840
   1985 Founders Dr Dayton (45420) *(G-9398)*
Chapin Leasing, North Ridgeville *Also called Chapin Logistics Inc (G-15459)*
Chapin Logistics Inc 440 327-1360
   39111 Center Ridge Rd North Ridgeville (44039) *(G-15459)*
Chapman & Chapman Inc 440 934-4102
   36711 American Way Ste 2f Avon (44011) *(G-887)*
Chapman Industrial Cnstr Inc 330 343-1632
   3475 Rue Depaul St Louisville (44641) *(G-13095)*
Charak Ctr For Hlth & Wellness, Cleveland *Also called Rakesh Ranjan MD & Assoc Inc (G-6350)*
Chard Snyder & Associates Inc 513 459-9997
   3510 Irwin Simpson Rd A Mason (45040) *(G-13675)*
Chard Synder, Mason *Also called Chard Snyder & Associates Inc (G-13675)*
Chardon Healthcare Center, Chardon *Also called Water Leasing Co LLC (G-2778)*
Chardon Laboratories Inc 614 860-1000
   7300 Tussing Rd Reynoldsburg (43068) *(G-16438)*
Chardon Lakes Golf Course Inc (PA) 440 285-4653
   470 South St Chardon (44024) *(G-2742)*
Chardon Tool & Supply Co Inc 440 286-6440
   115 Parker Ct Chardon (44024) *(G-2743)*
Chariott Foods Inc 419 243-1101
   6163 Valley Park Dr Toledo (43623) *(G-17802)*
Charity Hospice Inc 740 264-2280
   500 Luray Dr Steubenville (43953) *(G-17310)*
Charles C Smith DDS Inc 937 667-2417
   110 S Tippecanoe Dr Ste A Tipp City (45371) *(G-17712)*
Charles D McIntosh Trckg Inc 937 378-3803
   669 E State St Georgetown (45121) *(G-11389)*
Charles F Jergens Cnstr Inc 937 233-1830
   1280 Brandt Pike Dayton (45404) *(G-9399)*
Charles F Kettering Mem Hosp, Kettering *Also called Kettering Medical Center (G-12431)*
CHARLES F KETTERING MEMORIAL H, Hamilton *Also called Fort Hamilton Hospital (G-11728)*
Charles H Hamilton Co 513 683-2442
   5875 S State Route 48 Maineville (45039) *(G-13241)*
Charles Jergens Contractor 937 233-1830
   1280 Brandt Pike Dayton (45404) *(G-9400)*
Charles L Maccallum MD Inc 330 655-2161
   5778 Darrow Rd Ste D Hudson (44236) *(G-12109)*
Charles Mercy Hlth-St Hospita (PA) 419 696-7200
   2600 Navarre Ave Oregon (43616) *(G-15728)*
Charles Rewinding Div, Canton *Also called Hannon Company (G-2393)*
Charles River Laboratories Inc 419 647-4196
   640 N Elizabeth St Spencerville (45887) *(G-17107)*
Charles River Labs Ashland LLC (HQ) 419 282-8700
   1407 George Rd Ashland (44805) *(G-674)*
Charles Rver Labs Clveland Inc 216 332-1665
   14656 Neo Pkwy Cleveland (44128) *(G-5228)*
Charles Schwab & Co Inc 330 908-4478
   4150 Kinross Lakes Pkwy Richfield (44286) *(G-16500)*
Charles Schwab Corporation 440 617-2301
   2211 Crocker Rd Ste 100 Westlake (44145) *(G-19473)*

Charles Schwab Corporation 216 291-9333
24737 Cedar Rd Cleveland (44124) ***(G-5229)***
Charles V Francis Trust 513 528-5600
19 W Vine St Cincinnati (45215) ***(G-3230)***
Charles W Powers & Assoc Inc 513 721-5353
1 W 4th St Ste 500 Cincinnati (45202) ***(G-3231)***
Charley's Steakery, Columbus *Also called Gosh Enterprises Inc* ***(G-7762)***
Charlie Towing Service Inc 440 234-5300
55 Lou Groza Blvd Berea (44017) ***(G-1450)***
Charlie's Towing Svc, Berea *Also called Charlie Towing Service Inc* ***(G-1450)***
Charnan Div, Ontario *Also called Lake Erie Electric Inc* ***(G-15697)***
Charter Bus Service, Cincinnati *Also called Queen City Transportation LLC* ***(G-4372)***
Charter Hotel Group Ltd Partnr (PA) 216 772-4538
5966 Heisley Rd Mentor (44060) ***(G-14156)***
Charter Vans Inc 937 898-4043
303 Corporate Center Dr # 100 Vandalia (45377) ***(G-18669)***
Charter Vans Tours, Vandalia *Also called Charter Vans Inc* ***(G-18669)***
Chartwell Group LLC (PA) 216 360-0009
1350 Euclid Ave Ste 700 Cleveland (44115) ***(G-5230)***
Chas G Buchy Packing Company 800 762-1060
10510 Evendale Dr Cincinnati (45241) ***(G-3232)***
Chase Bank and Atm, New Philadelphia *Also called Jpmorgan Chase Bank Nat Assn* ***(G-15104)***
Chase Equipment Finance Inc (HQ) 800 678-2601
1111 Polaris Pkwy Ste A3 Columbus (43240) ***(G-6876)***
Chase HM Mrtgages Florence Off, Columbus *Also called Jpmorgan Chase Bank Nat Assn* ***(G-7955)***
Chase Manhattan Mortgage Corp 614 422-7982
200 E Campus View Blvd # 3 Columbus (43235) ***(G-7253)***
Chase Manhattan Mortgage Corp 614 422-6900
3415 Vision Dr Columbus (43219) ***(G-7254)***
Chase Phipps 330 754-0467
2993 Perry Dr Sw Canton (44706) ***(G-2303)***
Chase Suite Hotel, Dublin *Also called Hardage Hotels I LLC* ***(G-10357)***
Chase Transcriptions Inc (PA) 330 650-0539
1737 Georgetown Rd Ste G Hudson (44236) ***(G-12110)***
Chatham Steel Corporation 740 377-9310
235 Commerce Dr South Point (45680) ***(G-17081)***
Chattree and Associates Inc 216 831-1494
3355 Richmond Rd Ste 225 Cleveland (44122) ***(G-5231)***
Chavez Properties, Cincinnati *Also called J & E LLC* ***(G-3850)***
Chb, Solon *Also called Cleveland Harbor Belt RR LLC* ***(G-16993)***
Chcc Home Health Care, East Liverpool *Also called P N P Inc* ***(G-10532)***
Chcc Home Health Care 330 759-4069
60 N Canfield Niles Rd # 50 Austintown (44515) ***(G-869)***
Che International Group LLC (PA) 513 444-2072
9435 Waterstone Blvd # 140 Cincinnati (45249) ***(G-3233)***
Check It Out 4 Me LLC 513 568-4269
7709 Greenland Pl Ste 1 Cincinnati (45237) ***(G-3234)***
Check N Go, Cincinnati *Also called CNG Financial Corporation* ***(G-3375)***
Check N Go of Iowa Inc (HQ) 563 359-7800
7755 Montgomery Rd # 400 Cincinnati (45236) ***(G-3235)***
Checker Distributors, Maumee *Also called Checker Notions Company Inc* ***(G-13894)***
Checker Notions Company Inc (PA) 419 893-3636
400 W Dussel Dr Ste B Maumee (43537) ***(G-13894)***
Checkfree Services Corporation 614 564-3000
6000 Perimeter Dr Dublin (43017) ***(G-10288)***
Checksmart Financial Company (HQ) 614 798-5900
6785 Bobcat Way Ste 200 Dublin (43016) ***(G-10289)***
Cheek-O Inc 513 942-4880
639 Northland Blvd Cincinnati (45240) ***(G-3236)***
Cheers & Lakeside Chalet, Lancaster *Also called Cheers Chalet* ***(G-12516)***
Cheers Chalet 740 654-9036
1211 Coonpath Rd Nw Lancaster (43130) ***(G-12516)***
Cheeseman LLC (HQ) 419 375-4132
2200 State Route 119 Fort Recovery (45846) ***(G-11114)***
Chefs Garden Inc 419 433-4947
9009 Huron Avery Rd Huron (44839) ***(G-12162)***
Chelmsford Apartments Ltd 419 389-0800
5020 Ryan Rd Toledo (43614) ***(G-17803)***
Chelsea Court Apartments, Youngstown *Also called Giffin Management Group Inc* ***(G-20200)***
Chelsea House Fabrics, Columbus *Also called Style-Line Incorporated* ***(G-8798)***
Chemcote Inc 614 792-2683
7599 Fishel Dr N Dublin (43016) ***(G-10290)***
Chemcote Roofing Company 614 792-2683
7599 Fishel Dr N Dublin (43016) ***(G-10291)***
Chemed Corporation (PA) 513 762-6690
255 E 5th St Ste 2600 Cincinnati (45202) ***(G-3237)***
Chemgroup, Columbus *Also called Bonded Chemicals Inc* ***(G-7124)***
Chemical Bank 440 779-0807
25000 Country Club Blvd # 200 North Olmsted (44070) ***(G-15414)***
Chemical Bank 513 232-0800
7373 Beechmont Ave # 100 Cincinnati (45230) ***(G-3238)***
Chemical Bank 330 965-5806
476 Boardman Canfield Rd Youngstown (44512) ***(G-20138)***
Chemical Bank 440 926-2191
351 Main St Grafton (44044) ***(G-11440)***
Chemical Bank 330 314-1395
2 S Main St Poland (44514) ***(G-16222)***
Chemical Bank 440 323-7451
111 Antioch Dr Elyria (44035) ***(G-10603)***
Chemical Bank 330 298-0510
999 E Main St Ravenna (44266) ***(G-16376)***
Chemical Bank 330 314-1380
3900 Market St Youngstown (44512) ***(G-20139)***
Chemical Services Inc 937 898-5566
2600 Thunderhawk Ct Dayton (45414) ***(G-9401)***
Chemical Solvents Inc (PA) 216 741-9310
3751 Jennings Rd Cleveland (44109) ***(G-5232)***
Chemical Solvents Inc 216 741-9310
1010 Denison Ave Cleveland (44109) ***(G-5233)***
Chemimage Filter Tech LLC 330 686-2829
1100 Campus Dr Ste 500 Stow (44224) ***(G-17357)***
Chempower Sheetmetal, Canton *Also called Global Insulation Inc* ***(G-2381)***
Chemsteel Construction Company (PA) 440 234-3930
7850 Freeway Cir Ste 110 Middleburg Heights (44130) ***(G-14379)***
Chemstress Consultant Company (PA) 330 535-5591
39 S Main St Akron (44308) ***(G-130)***
Chemsultants International Inc (PA) 440 974-3080
9079 Tyler Blvd Mentor (44060) ***(G-14157)***
Chemtron Corporation 440 937-6348
35850 Schneider Ct Avon (44011) ***(G-888)***
Cherished Children's Ecdc, Negley *Also called Cherished Childrens Early* ***(G-14959)***
Cherished Childrens Early 330 424-4402
47677 Tomahawk Dr Negley (44441) ***(G-14959)***
Cherokee Hills Golf Club, Valley City *Also called Chgc Inc* ***(G-18614)***
Cherokee Hills Golf Course, Bellefontaine *Also called Vieira Inc* ***(G-1400)***
Cherry Grove Lanes, Cincinnati *Also called Cherry Grove Sports Center* ***(G-3239)***
Cherry Grove Sports Center 513 232-7199
4005 Hopper Hill Rd Cincinnati (45255) ***(G-3239)***
Cherry St Mission Ministries (PA) 419 242-5141
105 17th St Toledo (43604) ***(G-17804)***
Cherry Valley Lodge 740 788-1200
2299 Cherry Valley Rd Se Newark (43055) ***(G-15156)***
Cherry Valley Lodge and Coco, Newark *Also called Cherry Valley Lodge* ***(G-15156)***
Cheryl Ann Special Olympics, Celina *Also called County of Mercer* ***(G-2643)***
Chesapeake Research Review LLC 410 884-2900
9380 Main St Cincinnati (45242) ***(G-3240)***
Chesrown Cadillac, Granville *Also called Chesrown Oldsmobile Cadillac* ***(G-11461)***
Chesrown Oldsmobile Cadillac 740 366-7373
371 Bryn Du Dr Granville (43023) ***(G-11461)***
Chesrown Oldsmobile GMC Inc 614 846-3040
4675 Karl Rd Columbus (43229) ***(G-7255)***
Chessrown Kia Town, Columbus *Also called Chesrown Oldsmobile GMC Inc* ***(G-7255)***
Chester Township Fire Rescue, Chesterland *Also called Township of Chester* ***(G-2805)***
Chester West Dental Group Inc 513 942-8181
5900 W Chester Rd Ste A West Chester (45069) ***(G-19036)***
Chester West Dentistry 330 753-7734
1575 Vernon Odom Blvd Akron (44320) ***(G-131)***
Chester West Holdings Inc 800 647-1900
11500 Canal Rd Cincinnati (45241) ***(G-3241)***
Chester West Medical Center 513 298-3000
7700 University Dr West Chester (45069) ***(G-19037)***
Chester West YMCA 513 779-3917
6703 Yankee Rd Liberty Township (45044) ***(G-12718)***
Chesterfield Steel, Cleveland *Also called Steel Warehouse Cleveland LLC* ***(G-6534)***
Chesterhill Stone Co 740 849-2338
6305 Saltillo Rd East Fultonham (43735) ***(G-10505)***
Chestnut Hill Management Co 614 855-3700
5055 Thompson Rd Columbus (43230) ***(G-7256)***
Cheviot Mutual Holding Company 513 661-0457
3723 Glenmore Ave Cincinnati (45211) ***(G-3242)***
Chevron Ae Resources LLC 330 654-4343
1823 State Route 14 Deerfield (44411) ***(G-10017)***
Chgc Inc 330 225-6122
5740 Center Rd Valley City (44280) ***(G-18614)***
CHI, Dayton *Also called The Maria-Joseph Center* ***(G-9926)***
CHI, Cincinnati *Also called Good Samaritan Hosp Cincinnati* ***(G-3685)***
CHI Health At Home 513 576-0262
1700 Edison Dr Ste 300 Milford (45150) ***(G-14509)***
CHI Health At Home (HQ) 513 576-0262
1700 Edison Dr Ste 300 Milford (45150) ***(G-14510)***
CHI Omega Sorority 937 325-9323
2 Ferncliff Pl Springfield (45504) ***(G-17159)***
CHIC, Cleveland *Also called Consortium For Hlthy & Immunzd* ***(G-5394)***
Chicago Title Insurance Co 330 873-9393
799 White Pond Dr Ste A Akron (44320) ***(G-132)***
Chicago Title Insurance Co 216 241-6045
1111 Superior Ave E # 600 Cleveland (44114) ***(G-5234)***
Chick Master Incubator Company (PA) 330 722-5591
945 Lafayette Rd Medina (44256) ***(G-14045)***
Chicn Fixins Inc 614 929-8431
2041 Pine Needle Ct Columbus (43232) ***(G-7257)***
Chieftain Trucking & Excav Inc 216 485-8034
3926 Valley Rd Ste 300 Cleveland (44109) ***(G-5235)***
Child & Adolescent Speciality 937 667-7711
1483 W Main St Tipp City (45371) ***(G-17713)***
Child & Elder Care Insights 440 356-2900
18500 Lake Rd Ste 200 Rocky River (44116) ***(G-16573)***

Child Adlscent Behavioral Hlth (PA)....330 454-7917
919 2nd St Ne Canton (44704) ***(G-2304)***
Child Adlscent Behavioral Hlth....330 433-6075
4641 Fulton Dr Nw Canton (44718) ***(G-2305)***
Child Care Center, Dayton *Also called Miami Valley Hospital* ***(G-9733)***
Child Care Center, Canton *Also called Aultman Hospital* ***(G-2256)***
Child Care Resource Center (PA)....216 575-0061
4600 Euclid Ave Ste 500 Cleveland (44103) ***(G-5236)***
Child Care Resources Inc (PA)....740 454-6251
1580 Adams Ln Lbby Zanesville (43701) ***(G-20464)***
Child Dev Ctr Jackson Cnty....740 286-3995
692 Pattonsville Rd Jackson (45640) ***(G-12309)***
Child Dvlpmnt Cncl of Frnkln (PA)....614 221-1709
300 E Spring St Columbus (43215) ***(G-7258)***
Child Dvlpmnt Cncl of Frnkln....614 416-5178
2150 Agler Rd Columbus (43224) ***(G-7259)***
Child Focus Inc....513 732-8800
2337 Clermont Center Dr Batavia (45103) ***(G-998)***
Child Focus Inc (PA)....513 752-1555
4629 Aicholtz Rd Ste 2 Cincinnati (45244) ***(G-3243)***
Child Focus Inc....937 444-1613
710 N High St Mount Orab (45154) ***(G-14867)***
Child Sup Dept of Job & Family, Hillsboro *Also called County of Highland* ***(G-11970)***
Child Support, New Philadelphia *Also called County of Tuscarawas* ***(G-15090)***
Child Support, Springfield *Also called County of Clark* ***(G-17182)***
Child Support Agency, Coshocton *Also called County of Coshocton* ***(G-9100)***
Child Support Enforcement Agcy, Toledo *Also called County of Lucas* ***(G-17833)***
Child Support Enforcement Agcy, Cleveland *Also called County of Cuyahoga* ***(G-5422)***
Child Support Enforcement Agcy, Columbus *Also called Franklin Cnty Bd Commissioners* ***(G-7685)***
Child Support Enforcement Agcy, Sandusky *Also called County of Erie* ***(G-16748)***
Child Support Enforcement Agcy, Millersburg *Also called County of Holmes* ***(G-14601)***
Child Support Services, Marion *Also called County of Marion* ***(G-13532)***
Childers Photography....937 256-0501
5616 Burkhardt Rd Dayton (45431) ***(G-9261)***
Children and Family Services, Cleveland *Also called Cuyahoga County* ***(G-5452)***
CHILDREN FIRST DAY CARE, Columbus *Also called Children First Inc* ***(G-7260)***
Children First Inc....614 466-0945
77 S High St Fl 7 Columbus (43215) ***(G-7260)***
Children Medical Group Inc....330 762-9033
3800 Embassy Pkwy Akron (44333) ***(G-133)***
Children Service Unit, Norwalk *Also called County of Huron* ***(G-15569)***
Children Services, Mansfield *Also called County of Richland* ***(G-13280)***
Children Services, West Union *Also called County of Adams* ***(G-19277)***
Children Services, Dayton *Also called County of Montgomery* ***(G-9438)***
Children's Academy, Columbus *Also called Samkel Inc* ***(G-8683)***
Children's Aid Society, Cleveland *Also called Cleveland Municipal School Dst* ***(G-5337)***
Children's Aide Society Campus, Cleveland *Also called Applewood Centers Inc* ***(G-5051)***
Children's Home Healthcare, Cincinnati *Also called Childrens Hospital Medical Ctr* ***(G-3252)***
CHILDREN'S HOME SCHOOL, Cincinnati *Also called Childrens HM of Cncinnati Ohio* ***(G-3244)***
Children's Hospital Northwest, Dublin *Also called Close To Home Health Care Ctr* ***(G-10296)***
CHILDREN'S MEDICAL CENTER, Dayton *Also called Dayton Childrens Hospital* ***(G-9464)***
Children's Outpatient North, Mason *Also called Childrens Hospital Medical Ctr* ***(G-13676)***
CHILDREN'S RESOURCE CENTER, Bowling Green *Also called Wood County Chld Svcs Assn* ***(G-1798)***
Children's Service Board, Bucyrus *Also called Crawford County Children Svcs* ***(G-2035)***
Children's World Learning Cent, Cleveland *Also called Kindercare Education LLC* ***(G-5902)***
Childrens Advocacy Center....740 432-6581
274 Highland Ave Cambridge (43725) ***(G-2104)***
Childrens Aid Society....216 521-6511
10427 Detroit Ave Cleveland (44102) ***(G-5237)***
Childrens Cmprhensive Svcs Inc....419 589-5511
1451 Lucas Rd Mansfield (44903) ***(G-13276)***
Childrens Ctr of Frst Bptst Ch, Cleveland *Also called First Baptist Day Care Center* ***(G-5590)***
Childrens Discovery Center....419 861-1060
1640 Timber Wolf Dr Holland (43528) ***(G-12015)***
Childrens Forever Haven Inc (PA)....440 652-6749
10983 Abbey Rd North Royalton (44133) ***(G-15483)***
Childrens Forever Haven Inc....440 250-9182
28700 Center Ridge Rd Westlake (44145) ***(G-19474)***
Childrens HM of Cncinnati Ohio....513 272-2800
5050 Madison Rd Cincinnati (45227) ***(G-3244)***
Childrens Home Care Dayton....937 641-4663
18 Childrens Plz Dayton (45404) ***(G-9402)***
Childrens Home Care Group....330 543-5000
185 W Cedar St Ste 203 Akron (44307) ***(G-134)***
Childrens Homecare Services....614 355-1100
455 E Mound St Columbus (43215) ***(G-7261)***
Childrens Hosp Guidance Ctrs, Columbus *Also called Nationwide Childrens Hospital* ***(G-8237)***
Childrens Hosp Med Ctr Akron....330 425-3344
8054 Darrow Rd Twinsburg (44087) ***(G-18400)***
Childrens Hosp Med Ctr Akron....330 308-5432
1045 W High Ave New Philadelphia (44663) ***(G-15085)***
Childrens Hosp Med Ctr Akron....330 629-6085
8423 Market St Ste 300 Youngstown (44512) ***(G-20140)***
Childrens Hosp Med Ctr Akron (PA)....330 543-1000
1 Perkins Sq Akron (44308) ***(G-135)***
Childrens Hosp Med Ctr Akron....330 543-8004
1 Perkins Sq Akron (44308) ***(G-136)***
Childrens Hosp Med Ctr Akron....330 676-1020
1951 State Route 59 Ste A Kent (44240) ***(G-12357)***
Childrens Hosp Med Ctr Akron....330 633-2055
143 Northwest Ave Bldg A Tallmadge (44278) ***(G-17634)***
Childrens Hospital, Columbus *Also called Central Ohio Poison Center* ***(G-7233)***
Childrens Hospital....513 636-4051
3373 Burnet Ave Cincinnati (45229) ***(G-3245)***
Childrens Hospital Foundation....614 355-0888
700 Childrens Dr Columbus (43205) ***(G-7262)***
Childrens Hospital Medical Ctr....513 541-4500
2750 Beekman St Cincinnati (45225) ***(G-3246)***
Childrens Hospital Medical Ctr....513 803-9600
7777 Yankee Rd Liberty Township (45044) ***(G-12719)***
Childrens Hospital Medical Ctr....513 636-4200
3333 Burnet Ave Cincinnati (45229) ***(G-3247)***
Childrens Hospital Medical Ctr....513 803-1751
240 Albert Sabin Way Cincinnati (45229) ***(G-3248)***
Childrens Hospital Medical Ctr....513 636-4200
2900 Vernon Pl Cincinnati (45219) ***(G-3249)***
Childrens Hospital Medical Ctr....513 636-4366
2800 Winslow Ave Fl 3 Cincinnati (45206) ***(G-3250)***
Childrens Hospital Medical Ctr....513 636-6100
7495 State Rd Ste 355 Cincinnati (45255) ***(G-3251)***
Childrens Hospital Medical Ctr (PA)....513 636-4200
3333 Burnet Ave Cincinnati (45229) ***(G-3252)***
Childrens Hospital Medical Ctr....513 636-6400
3050 Mack Rd Ste 105 Fairfield (45014) ***(G-10830)***
Childrens Hospital Medical Ctr....513 636-6036
796 Cncnnati Batavia Pike Cincinnati (45245) ***(G-2906)***
Childrens Hospital Medical Ctr....513 636-6800
9560 Children Dr Mason (45040) ***(G-13676)***
Childrens Hospital Medical Ctr....513 636-4200
3350 Elland Ave Cincinnati (45229) ***(G-3253)***
Childrens Hospital Medical Ctr....513 636-8778
3333 Burnet Ave Cincinnati (45229) ***(G-3254)***
Childrens Hospital Medical Ctr....513 636-8778
3333 Burnet Ave Cincinnati (45229) ***(G-3255)***
Childrens Hunger Alliance (PA)....614 341-7700
1105 Schrock Rd Ste 505 Columbus (43229) ***(G-7263)***
Childrens Medical Ctr Toledo....937 641-3000
1 Childrens Plz Dayton (45404) ***(G-9403)***
Childrens Physician Inc....330 494-5600
4575 Everhard Rd Nw Canton (44718) ***(G-2306)***
Childrens Rehabilitation Ctr....330 856-2107
885 Howland Wilson Rd Ne Warren (44484) ***(G-18833)***
Childrens Surgery Center Inc....614 722-2920
700 Childrens Dr Columbus (43205) ***(G-7264)***
Childrens World Learning Ctr, Twinsburg *Also called Kindercare Education LLC* ***(G-18438)***
Childrens World Lrng Ctr 177, Gahanna *Also called Kindercare Education LLC* ***(G-11250)***
Childs Investment Co....330 837-2100
205 Rohr Ave Nw Massillon (44646) ***(G-13794)***
Childtime Childcare Inc....330 723-8697
3550 Octagon Dr Medina (44256) ***(G-14046)***
Childvine Inc....937 748-1260
790 N Main St Springboro (45066) ***(G-17118)***
Chiller LLC (PA)....614 764-1000
7001 Dublin Park Dr Dublin (43016) ***(G-10292)***
Chiller LLC....740 549-0009
8144 Highfield Dr Lewis Center (43035) ***(G-12675)***
Chiller LLC....614 475-7575
3600 Chiller Ln Columbus (43219) ***(G-7265)***
Chillicothe Bowling Lanes Inc....740 773-3300
1680 N Bridge St Chillicothe (45601) ***(G-2817)***
Chillicothe City School Dst....740 775-2936
89 Riverside St Chillicothe (45601) ***(G-2818)***
Chillicothe Country Club Co....740 775-0150
Woodbridge Ave & Arch St Chillicothe (45601) ***(G-2819)***
Chillicothe Cty Sch Trans Off, Chillicothe *Also called Chillicothe City School Dst* ***(G-2818)***
Chillicothe Family Physicians....740 779-4100
60 Capital Dr Chillicothe (45601) ***(G-2820)***
Chillicothe Long Term Care....740 773-6161
230 Cherry St Chillicothe (45601) ***(G-2821)***
Chillicothe Long Term Care (PA)....513 793-8804
7265 Kenwood Rd Ste 300 Cincinnati (45236) ***(G-3256)***
Chillicothe Motel LLC....740 773-3903
20 N Plaza Blvd Chillicothe (45601) ***(G-2822)***
Chillicothe Opco LLC....740 772-5900
60 Marietta Rd Chillicothe (45601) ***(G-2823)***
Chillicothe Racquet Club....740 773-4928
1245 Western Ave Chillicothe (45601) ***(G-2824)***
Chillicothe Telephone Company (HQ)....740 772-8200
68 E Main St Chillicothe (45601) ***(G-2825)***
Chillicothe Telephone Company....740 772-8361
861 Orange St Chillicothe (45601) ***(G-2826)***
Chillicothe VA Medical Center, Chillicothe *Also called Veterans Health Administration* ***(G-2895)***

ALPHABETIC

Chima Travel Bureau Inc (PA) 330 867-4770
55 Merz Blvd Unit B Fairlawn (44333) ***(G-10942)***
Chimney Hill Apartments, Columbus *Also called Real Estate Investors Mgt Inc* ***(G-8594)***
Chimneys Inn 937 567-7850
767 Mmsburg Cnterville Rd Dayton (45459) ***(G-9404)***
Chipmatic Tool & Machine Inc 419 862-2737
212 Ottawa St Elmore (43416) ***(G-10587)***
Chippewa Golf Club, Doylestown *Also called Chippewa Golf Corp* ***(G-10224)***
Chippewa Golf Corp 330 658-2566
12147 Shank Rd Doylestown (44230) ***(G-10224)***
Chippewa Place, Brecksville *Also called Paul Dennis* ***(G-1839)***
Chippewa School District 330 658-4868
165 Brooklyn Ave Doylestown (44230) ***(G-10225)***
Chirst Hospital Surgery Center 513 272-3448
4850 Red Bank Rd Fl 1 Cincinnati (45227) ***(G-3257)***
Chisano Marketing Groups, Miamisburg *Also called Chisano Mktg Cmmunications Inc* ***(G-14282)***
Chisano Mktg Cmmunications Inc 937 847-0607
2000 Byers Rd Miamisburg (45342) ***(G-14282)***
CHN Inc - Adult Day Care 937 548-0506
5420 State Route 571 Greenville (45331) ***(G-11493)***
Choice Healthcare Limited 937 254-6220
1257 N Fairfield Rd Beavercreek (45432) ***(G-1159)***
Choice Hotels Intl Inc 330 656-1252
6625 Dean Memorial Pkwy Hudson (44236) ***(G-12111)***
Choice One Engineering Corp 937 497-0200
440 E Hoewisher Rd Sidney (45365) ***(G-16919)***
Choice Pharmacy Services, Columbus *Also called Pca-Corrections LLC* ***(G-8525)***
Choice Recovery Inc 614 358-9900
1550 Old Henderson Rd S100 Columbus (43220) ***(G-7266)***
Choices Behavioral Healthcare 216 881-4060
3414 Prospect Ave E Cleveland (44115) ***(G-5238)***
Choices For Vctims Dom Volence 614 258-6080
770 E Main St Columbus (43205) ***(G-7267)***
Choices For Vctims Dom Volence 614 224-6617
500 W Wilson Bridge Rd Worthington (43085) ***(G-19947)***
Choices In Community Living (PA) 937 898-3655
1651 Needmore Rd Ste B Dayton (45414) ***(G-9405)***
Chop House Restaurant, Dayton *Also called Connor Concepts Inc* ***(G-9423)***
Chores Unlimited Inc 440 439-5455
26150 Richmond Rd Unit C Bedford Heights (44146) ***(G-1350)***
Chp AP Shared Services 513 981-6704
P.O. Box 5203 Cincinnati (45201) ***(G-3258)***
CHRC, Cincinnati *Also called Cincinnati Humn Relations Comm* ***(G-3310)***
Christ Hospital 513 721-8272
2139 Auburn Ave Cincinnati (45219) ***(G-3259)***
Christ Hospital 513 564-4000
7545 Beechmont Ave Ste F Cincinnati (45255) ***(G-3260)***
Christ Hospital 513 561-7809
11140 Montgomery Rd Cincinnati (45249) ***(G-3261)***
Christ Hospital 513 688-1111
7545 Beechmont Ave Ste E Cincinnati (45255) ***(G-3262)***
Christ Hospital 513 564-1340
4440 Red Bank Rd Ste 100 Cincinnati (45227) ***(G-3263)***
Christ Hospital 513 272-3448
4850 Red Bank Rd Fl 1 Cincinnati (45227) ***(G-3264)***
Christ Hospital 513 585-0050
2123 Auburn Ave Ste 341 Cincinnati (45219) ***(G-3265)***
Christ Hospital 513 755-4700
7589 Tylers Place Blvd West Chester (45069) ***(G-19038)***
Christ Hospital (PA) 513 585-2000
2139 Auburn Ave Cincinnati (45219) ***(G-3266)***
Christ Hospital 513 631-3300
4803 Montgomery Rd # 114 Cincinnati (45212) ***(G-3267)***
Christ Hospital 513 351-0800
2355 Norwood Ave Ste 1 Cincinnati (45212) ***(G-3268)***
Christ Hospital Corporation 513 347-2300
5885 Harrison Ave # 2900 Cincinnati (45248) ***(G-3269)***
CHRIST HOSPITAL HEALTH NETWORK, Cincinnati *Also called Christ Hospital* ***(G-3266)***
Christ Hospital Spine Surgery 513 619-5899
4020 Smith Rd Cincinnati (45209) ***(G-3270)***
Christ Hospital, The, Cincinnati *Also called Christ Hospital* ***(G-3268)***
Christen & Sons Company (PA) 419 243-4161
714 George St Toledo (43608) ***(G-17805)***
Christen Detroit, Toledo *Also called Christen & Sons Company* ***(G-17805)***
Christian Aid Ministries (PA) 330 893-2428
4464 State Route 39 Millersburg (44654) ***(G-14593)***
CHRISTIAN BENEVOLENT ASSOCIATI, Cincinnati *Also called Mt Healthy Christian Home Inc* ***(G-4128)***
Christian Benevolent Assocn (PA) 513 931-5000
8097 Hamilton Ave Cincinnati (45231) ***(G-3271)***
Christian Chld HM Ohio Inc 330 345-7949
2685 Armstrong Rd Wooster (44691) ***(G-19841)***
Christian Community Hlth Svcs 513 381-2247
5 E Liberty St Ste 4 Cincinnati (45202) ***(G-3272)***
Christian Healthcare 330 848-1511
127 Hazelwood Ave Barberton (44203) ***(G-961)***
Christian Missionary Alliance 614 457-4085
3750 Henderson Rd Columbus (43220) ***(G-7268)***
Christian Perry Pre School 330 477-7262
139 Perry Dr Nw Canton (44708) ***(G-2307)***
Christian Rivertree School 330 494-1860
7373 Portage St Nw Massillon (44646) ***(G-13795)***
Christian Schools Inc 330 857-7311
3970 Kidron Rd Kidron (44636) ***(G-12440)***
Christian Twigs Gymnastics CLB 937 866-8356
1900 S Alex Rd Dayton (45449) ***(G-9406)***
Christian Wooster School 330 345-6436
4599 Burbank Rd Ste B Wooster (44691) ***(G-19842)***
Christian Worthington Vlg Inc 614 846-6076
165 Highbluffs Blvd Columbus (43235) ***(G-7269)***
Christopher C Kaeding 614 293-3600
2050 Kenny Rd Ste 3100 Columbus (43221) ***(G-7270)***
Christopher D Cannell, Columbus *Also called Orthoneuro* ***(G-8483)***
CHS Miami Valley Inc 330 204-1040
510 Buckeye Ave Sidney (45365) ***(G-16920)***
CHS Norwood Inc 513 242-1360
1171 Towne St Cincinnati (45216) ***(G-3273)***
CHS of Bowerston Oper Co Inc 937 277-0505
5020 Philadelphia Dr Dayton (45415) ***(G-9407)***
CHS Ohio Valley Inc, Newark *Also called Arlington Care Ctr* ***(G-15143)***
CHS-Lake Erie Inc 440 964-8446
2217 West Ave Ashtabula (44004) ***(G-733)***
Chs-Norwood Inc 513 351-7007
6969 Glenmeadow Ln Cincinnati (45237) ***(G-3274)***
Chu Airport Inn Inc 216 267-5100
16161 Brookpark Rd Brookpark (44142) ***(G-1939)***
Chu Management Co Inc (PA) 330 725-4571
2875 Medina Rd Medina (44256) ***(G-14047)***
Chubb, Cleveland *Also called Federal Insurance Company* ***(G-5581)***
Chubb, Cincinnati *Also called Federal Insurance Company* ***(G-3598)***
Chuck E. Cheese's, Miamisburg *Also called Cec Entertainment Inc* ***(G-14280)***
Chuck Nicholson Inc 330 674-4015
7190 State Route 39 Millersburg (44654) ***(G-14594)***
Chuck Nicholson Leasing, Millersburg *Also called Chuck Nicholson Inc* ***(G-14594)***
Chuck Nicholson Pntc-GMC Trcks 330 343-7781
135 W Broadway St Dover (44622) ***(G-10180)***
Church of God Retirement Cmnty 513 422-5600
4400 Vannest Ave Middletown (45042) ***(G-14420)***
Church of St Mary Catholic, Chardon *Also called Saint Mary Parish* ***(G-2766)***
Chute Gerdeman Inc 614 469-1001
455 S Ludlow St Columbus (43215) ***(G-7271)***
Chwc, Bryan *Also called Community Hsptals Wllness Ctrs* ***(G-2004)***
Ci Disposition Co 216 587-5200
1000 Valley Belt Rd Brooklyn Heights (44131) ***(G-1912)***
Cicar, Dublin *Also called Chemcote Inc* ***(G-10290)***
Cig, Cincinnati *Also called Che International Group LLC* ***(G-3233)***
Cigna Corporation 216 642-1700
3 Summit Park Dr Ste 250 Independence (44131) ***(G-12197)***
Cima Inc 513 682-5900
4416 Dixie Hwy Fairfield (45014) ***(G-10831)***
Cimarron Express Inc 419 855-7713
21611 State Route 51 W Genoa (43430) ***(G-11375)***
Cimcool Industrial Pdts LLC (HQ) 888 246-2665
3000 Disney St Cincinnati (45209) ***(G-3275)***
Cimx LLC 513 248-7700
4625 Red Bank Rd Ste 200 Cincinnati (45227) ***(G-3276)***
Cimx Software, Cincinnati *Also called Cimx LLC* ***(G-3276)***
Cinc 419 663-6644
14006 Bellamy Rd Collins (44826) ***(G-6839)***
Cincilingua Inc 513 721-8782
322 E 4th St Cincinnati (45202) ***(G-3277)***
Cincinatti Chld Hosp Med Ctr, Fairfield *Also called Childrens Hospital Medical Ctr* ***(G-10830)***
Cincinnati, Cleveland *Also called Ohio Transport Inc* ***(G-6196)***
Cincinnati - Vulcan Company 513 242-5300
5353 Spring Grove Ave Cincinnati (45217) ***(G-3278)***
Cincinnati Air Conditioning Co 513 721-5622
2080 Northwest Dr Cincinnati (45231) ***(G-3279)***
Cincinnati Anml Rfrrl 513 530-0911
6995 E Kemper Rd Cincinnati (45249) ***(G-3280)***
Cincinnati Area Chapter, Cincinnati *Also called American Red Cross* ***(G-3012)***
Cincinnati Area Senior Svcs (PA) 513 721-4330
2368 Victory Pkwy Ste 300 Cincinnati (45206) ***(G-3281)***
Cincinnati Art Museum, Cincinnati *Also called Cincinnati Museum Association* ***(G-3318)***
Cincinnati Assn For The Blind 513 221-8558
2045 Gilbert Ave Cincinnati (45202) ***(G-3282)***
Cincinnati Ballet Company Inc 513 621-5219
1555 Central Pkwy Cincinnati (45214) ***(G-3283)***
Cincinnati Bar Association 513 381-8213
225 E 6th St Fl 2 Cincinnati (45202) ***(G-3284)***
Cincinnati Bell Inc (PA) 513 397-9900
221 E 4th St Ste 700 Cincinnati (45202) ***(G-3285)***
Cincinnati Bell Techno 513 841-6700
4600 Montgomery Rd # 400 Cincinnati (45212) ***(G-3286)***
Cincinnati Bell Techno (HQ) 513 841-2287
221 E 4th St Ste 700 Cincinnati (45202) ***(G-3287)***
Cincinnati Bell Tele Co LLC (HQ) 513 565-9402
209 W 7th St Fl 1 Cincinnati (45202) ***(G-3288)***
Cincinnati Bengals Inc (PA) 513 621-3550
1 Paul Brown Stadium Cincinnati (45202) ***(G-3289)***
Cincinnati Better Hearing Ctr, Cincinnati *Also called Cincinnati Head and Neck Inc* ***(G-3308)***

Cincinnati Bulk Terminals LLC....513 621-4800
895 Mehring Way Cincinnati (45203) *(G-3290)*
Cincinnati Casualty Company....513 870-2000
6200 S Gilmore Rd Fairfield (45014) *(G-10832)*
Cincinnati Central Cr Un Inc (PA)....513 241-2050
1717 Western Ave Cincinnati (45214) *(G-3291)*
Cincinnati Children's Hospital, Cincinnati *Also called Childrens Hospital Medical Ctr (G-3253)*
Cincinnati Chld Hosp Med Ctr, Cincinnati *Also called Childrens Hospital Medical Ctr (G-3247)*
Cincinnati Circus Company LLC....513 921-5454
6433 Wiehe Rd Cincinnati (45237) *(G-3292)*
Cincinnati Cnslting Consortium....513 233-0011
220 Wyoming Ave Cincinnati (45215) *(G-3293)*
Cincinnati Collision Center....513 984-4445
9323 Blue Ash Rd Blue Ash (45242) *(G-1555)*
Cincinnati Coml Contg LLC....513 561-6633
4760 Red Bank Rd Ste 226 Cincinnati (45227) *(G-3294)*
Cincinnati Copiers Inc (PA)....513 769-0606
4720 Glendale Milford Rd Blue Ash (45242) *(G-1556)*
Cincinnati Country Club....513 533-5200
2348 Grandin Rd Cincinnati (45208) *(G-3295)*
Cincinnati Ctr/Psychoanalysis....513 961-8484
3001 Highland Ave Cincinnati (45219) *(G-3296)*
Cincinnati Dental Services....513 753-6446
4360 Ferguson Dr Ste 140 Cincinnati (45245) *(G-2907)*
Cincinnati Dental Services....513 741-7779
8111 Cheviot Rd Ste 102 Cincinnati (45247) *(G-3297)*
Cincinnati Dental Services (PA)....513 721-8888
121 E Mcmillan St Cincinnati (45219) *(G-3298)*
Cincinnati Dental Services....513 774-8800
8944 Columbia Rd Ste 300 Loveland (45140) *(G-13114)*
Cincinnati Division, Cincinnati *Also called The Cincinnati Cordage Ppr Co (G-4640)*
Cincinnati Division, Monroe *Also called Terex Utilities Inc (G-14714)*
Cincinnati Drywall Inc....513 321-7322
659 Wilmer Ave Cincinnati (45226) *(G-3299)*
Cincinnati Early Learning Ctr (PA)....513 961-2690
1301 E Mcmillan St Cincinnati (45206) *(G-3300)*
Cincinnati Early Learning Ctr....513 367-2129
498 S State St Harrison (45030) *(G-11793)*
Cincinnati Equitable Insur Co (HQ)....513 621-1826
525 Vine St Ste 1925 Cincinnati (45202) *(G-3301)*
Cincinnati Equitable Insur Co....440 349-2210
5910 Harper Rd Ste 100 Solon (44139) *(G-16991)*
Cincinnati Equitable Insurance, Cincinnati *Also called Alpha Investment Partnership (G-2994)*
Cincinnati Eye Institute, Blue Ash *Also called Cei Physicians PSC Inc (G-1554)*
Cincinnati Eye Institute, Blue Ash *Also called Cei Physicians Inc (G-1553)*
Cincinnati Federal (PA)....513 574-3025
6581 Harrison Ave Cincinnati (45247) *(G-3302)*
Cincinnati Fifth Street Ht LLC....513 579-1234
151 W 5th St Cincinnati (45202) *(G-3303)*
Cincinnati Fill Inc....513 242-7526
900 Kieley Pl Cincinnati (45217) *(G-3304)*
Cincinnati Financial Corp (PA)....513 870-2000
6200 S Gilmore Rd Fairfield (45014) *(G-10833)*
Cincinnati Floor Company Inc (PA)....513 641-4500
5162 Broerman Ave Cincinnati (45217) *(G-3305)*
Cincinnati Gearing Systems Inc....513 527-8600
5757 Mariemont Ave Cincinnati (45227) *(G-3306)*
Cincinnati Group Health, Cincinnati *Also called Trihealth G LLC (G-4693)*
Cincinnati Gutter Supply, West Chester *Also called Mollett Seamless Gutter Co (G-19123)*
Cincinnati Gymnastics Academy....513 860-3082
3635 Woodridge Blvd Fairfield (45014) *(G-10834)*
Cincinnati Hand Surgery Cons (PA)....513 961-4263
10700 Montgomery Rd # 150 Cincinnati (45242) *(G-3307)*
Cincinnati Head and Neck Inc (PA)....513 232-3277
2123 Auburn Ave Cincinnati (45219) *(G-3308)*
Cincinnati Health Network Inc....513 961-0600
2825 Burnet Ave Ste 232 Cincinnati (45219) *(G-3309)*
Cincinnati Humn Relations Comm....513 352-3237
801 Plum St Rm 158 Cincinnati (45202) *(G-3310)*
Cincinnati Hyatt Regency, Cincinnati *Also called Cincinnati Fifth Street Ht LLC (G-3303)*
Cincinnati Hydraulic Svc Inc....513 874-0540
9431 Sutton Pl West Chester (45011) *(G-19039)*
Cincinnati Indeminty Co....513 870-2000
6200 S Gilmore Rd Fairfield (45014) *(G-10835)*
Cincinnati Indus Actoneers Inc....513 241-9701
2020 Dunlap St Cincinnati (45214) *(G-3311)*
Cincinnati Institute Fine Arts (PA)....513 871-2787
20 East Central Pkwy # 2 Cincinnati (45202) *(G-3312)*
Cincinnati Institute Fine Arts....513 241-0343
316 Pike St Cincinnati (45202) *(G-3313)*
Cincinnati Life Insurance Co....513 870-2000
6200 S Gilmore Rd Fairfield (45014) *(G-10836)*
Cincinnati Medical Billing Svc....513 965-8041
8160 Corp Pk Dr Ste 330 Cincinnati (45242) *(G-3314)*
Cincinnati Metro Hsing Auth....513 421-2642
1635 Western Ave Cincinnati (45214) *(G-3315)*
Cincinnati Metro Hsing Auth (PA)....513 421-8190
1635 Western Ave Cincinnati (45214) *(G-3316)*
Cincinnati Metro Hsing Auth....513 333-0670
1627 Western Ave Cincinnati (45214) *(G-3317)*
Cincinnati Mighty Ducks, Cincinnati *Also called Gardens Hockey Inc (G-3663)*
Cincinnati Museum Association (PA)....513 721-5204
953 Eden Park Dr Cincinnati (45202) *(G-3318)*
Cincinnati Museum Center (PA)....513 287-7000
250 W Court St Ste 300e Cincinnati (45202) *(G-3319)*
Cincinnati Netherland Ht LLC....513 421-9100
35 W 5th St Cincinnati (45202) *(G-3320)*
Cincinnati Occupational Therap (PA)....513 791-5688
4440 Carver Woods Dr # 200 Blue Ash (45242) *(G-1557)*
Cincinnati Opera Association....513 768-5500
1243 Elm St Cincinnati (45202) *(G-3321)*
Cincinnati Pool Management Inc....513 777-1444
3461 Mustafa Dr Cincinnati (45241) *(G-3322)*
Cincinnati Public Radio Inc....513 241-8282
1223 Central Pkwy Cincinnati (45214) *(G-3323)*
Cincinnati Reds LLC (PA)....513 765-7000
100 Joe Nuxhall Way Cincinnati (45202) *(G-3324)*
Cincinnati Reds LLC....513 765-7923
100 Main St Cincinnati (45202) *(G-3325)*
Cincinnati Senior Care LLC....513 272-0600
4001 Rosslyn Dr Cincinnati (45209) *(G-3326)*
Cincinnati Shakespeare Company....513 381-2273
217 W 12th St Cincinnati (45202) *(G-3327)*
Cincinnati Speech Hearing Ctr (PA)....513 221-0527
2825 Burnet Ave Ste 401 Cincinnati (45219) *(G-3328)*
Cincinnati Sports Club, Cincinnati *Also called Cincinnati Sports Mall Inc (G-3329)*
Cincinnati Sports Mall Inc....513 527-4000
3950 Red Bank Rd Ste A Cincinnati (45227) *(G-3329)*
Cincinnati Steel Products Co....513 871-4444
4540 Steel Pl Cincinnati (45209) *(G-3330)*
Cincinnati Sub-Zero Pdts LLC....800 989-7373
12011 Mosteller Rd Cincinnati (45241) *(G-3331)*
Cincinnati Symphony Orchestra (PA)....513 621-1919
1241 Elm St Cincinnati (45202) *(G-3332)*
Cincinnati Tae Kwon Do Cntr, Cincinnati *Also called Cincinnati Tae Kwon Do Inc (G-3333)*
Cincinnati Tae Kwon Do Inc....513 271-6900
4325 Red Bank Rd Ste A Cincinnati (45227) *(G-3333)*
Cincinnati USA Rgional Chamber....513 579-3100
3 E 4th St Ste 200 Cincinnati (45202) *(G-3334)*
Cincinnati V A Medical Center, Cincinnati *Also called Veterans Health Administration (G-4812)*
Cincinnati Vending Company, Cincinnati *Also called Walter Alexander Entps Inc (G-4823)*
Cincinnati Voice and Data....513 683-4127
136 Commerce Dr Loveland (45140) *(G-13115)*
Cincinnati Youth Collaborative....513 475-4165
301 Oak St Cincinnati (45219) *(G-3335)*
CINCINNATI ZOO & BOTANICAL GAR, Cincinnati *Also called Zoological Society Cincinnati (G-4874)*
Cincinnatian Hotel....513 381-3000
601 Vine St Cincinnati (45202) *(G-3336)*
Cincinnatian Hotel, The, Cincinnati *Also called Cincinnatian Hotel (G-3336)*
Cincinnatis Optimum RES Envir....513 771-2673
75 Tri County Pkwy Cincinnati (45246) *(G-3337)*
Cincinnatti Processing, West Chester *Also called Empire Packing Company LP (G-19196)*
Cincinnatus Savings & Loan (PA)....513 661-6903
3300 Harrison Ave Cincinnati (45211) *(G-3338)*
Cincinnti Educ & RES For Vetrn....513 861-3100
3200 Vine St Cincinnati (45220) *(G-3339)*
Cinciti Bl Etd Trts LLC....513 397-0963
221 E 4th St Fl 1290 Cincinnati (45202) *(G-3340)*
Cinco Credit Union (PA)....513 281-9988
49 William Howard Taft Rd Cincinnati (45219) *(G-3341)*
CINCO FAMILY FINANCIAL CENTER, Cincinnati *Also called Cinco Credit Union (G-3341)*
Cincom Helpdesk, Cincinnati *Also called Cincom Systems Inc (G-3344)*
Cincom Intrnational Operations (HQ)....513 612-2300
55 Merchant St Ste 100 Cincinnati (45246) *(G-3342)*
Cincom Systems Inc (PA)....513 612-2300
55 Merchant St Ste 100 Cincinnati (45246) *(G-3343)*
Cincom Systems Inc....513 459-1470
4605 Duke Dr Mason (45040) *(G-13677)*
Cincom Systems Inc....513 389-2344
2300 Montana Ave Ste 235 Cincinnati (45211) *(G-3344)*
Cincysmiles Foundation Inc....513 621-0248
635 W 7th St Ste 405 Cincinnati (45203) *(G-3345)*
Cinemark 15, Macedonia *Also called Cinemark Usa Inc (G-13193)*
Cinemark At Valley View, Cleveland *Also called Cinemark Usa Inc (G-5239)*
Cinemark Carriage Pl Movies 12, Columbus *Also called Cinemark Usa Inc (G-7272)*
Cinemark Movies 10, Canton *Also called Cinemark Usa Inc (G-2308)*
Cinemark Movies 10, Wooster *Also called Cinemark Usa Inc (G-19843)*
Cinemark Movies 10, Columbus *Also called Cinemark Usa Inc (G-7273)*
Cinemark Movies 12 At Mill Run, Hilliard *Also called Cinemark Usa Inc (G-11890)*
Cinemark Stnrdge Plz Movies 16, Gahanna *Also called Cinemark Usa Inc (G-11234)*
Cinemark Tinseltown 7, Youngstown *Also called Cinemark Usa Inc (G-20141)*
Cinemark Usa Inc....330 965-2335
7401 Market St Rear Youngstown (44512) *(G-20141)*
Cinemark Usa Inc....216 447-8820
6001 Canal Rd Cleveland (44125) *(G-5239)*

ALPHABETIC

Cinemark Usa Inc 330 908-1005
8161 Macedonia Commons Bl Macedonia (44056) *(G-13193)*
Cinemark Usa Inc 419 589-7300
2355 Walker Lake Rd Ontario (44903) *(G-15685)*
Cinemark Usa Inc 614 538-0403
2570 Bethel Rd Columbus (43220) *(G-7272)*
Cinemark Usa Inc 330 497-9118
6284 Dressler Rd Nw Canton (44720) *(G-2308)*
Cinemark Usa Inc 614 527-3773
3773 Ridge Mill Dr Hilliard (43026) *(G-11890)*
Cinemark Usa Inc 614 471-7620
323 Stoneridge Ln Gahanna (43230) *(G-11234)*
Cinemark Usa Inc 330 345-2610
4108 Burbank Rd Wooster (44691) *(G-19843)*
Cinemark Usa Inc 614 529-8547
5275 Westpointe Plaza Dr Columbus (43228) *(G-7273)*
Cinergy Corp (HQ) 513 421-9500
139 E 4th St Cincinnati (45202) *(G-3346)*
Cinergy Pwr Gneration Svcs LLC 513 421-9500
139 E 4th St Cincinnati (45202) *(G-3347)*
CINFED CREDIT UNION, Cincinnati *Also called Cinfed Federal Credit Union (G-3348)*
Cinfed Federal Credit Union (PA) 513 333-3800
550 Main St Ste 5510 Cincinnati (45202) *(G-3348)*
Cinmar LLC (HQ) 513 603-1000
5566 W Chester Rd West Chester (45069) *(G-19040)*
Cinncinnatian Hotel, The, Cincinnati *Also called Brothers Properties Corp (G-3141)*
Cintas Corporation (PA) 513 459-1200
6800 Cintas Blvd Cincinnati (45262) *(G-3349)*
Cintas Corporation 513 631-5750
5570 Ridge Ave Cincinnati (45213) *(G-3350)*
Cintas Corporation 330 821-2220
12445 Rockhill Ave Ne Alliance (44601) *(G-532)*
Cintas Corporation 513 671-7717
690 E Crscntvlle Rd Ste A Cincinnati (45246) *(G-3351)*
Cintas Corporation No 1 (HQ) 513 459-1200
6800 Cintas Blvd Mason (45040) *(G-13678)*
Cintas Corporation No 2 419 661-8714
28140 Cedar Park Blvd Perrysburg (43551) *(G-15986)*
Cintas Corporation No 2 440 746-7777
1061 Trumbull Ave Girard (44420) *(G-11409)*
Cintas Corporation No 2 440 746-7777
55 Andrews Cir Ste 1a Brecksville (44141) *(G-1817)*
Cintas Corporation No 2 937 401-0098
850 Center Dr Vandalia (45377) *(G-18670)*
Cintas Corporation No 2 513 459-1200
5800 Cintas Blvd Mason (45040) *(G-13679)*
Cintas Corporation No 2 440 238-5565
8221 Dow Cir Strongsville (44136) *(G-17449)*
Cintas Corporation No 2 614 878-7313
1300 Boltonfield St Columbus (43228) *(G-7274)*
Cintas Corporation No 2 440 352-4003
800 Renaissance Pkwy Painesville (44077) *(G-15839)*
Cintas Corporation No 2 740 687-6230
2250 Commerce St Lancaster (43130) *(G-12517)*
Cintas Corporation No 2 513 965-0800
27 Whitney Dr Milford (45150) *(G-14511)*
Cintas Corporation No 2 614 860-9152
1275 Research Rd Blacklick (43004) *(G-1504)*
Cintas Corporation No 2 440 838-8611
1 Andrews Cir Cleveland (44141) *(G-5240)*
Cintas Corporation No 2 330 966-7800
3865 Highland Park Nw Canton (44720) *(G-2309)*
Cintas Corporation No 2 (HQ) 513 459-1200
6800 Cintas Blvd Mason (45040) *(G-13680)*
Cintas Corporation No 2 513 459-1200
6800 Cintas Blvd Mason (45040) *(G-13681)*
Cintas Document Management LLC (HQ) 800 914-1960
6800 Cintas Blvd Mason (45040) *(G-13682)*
Cintas First Aid & Safety, Mason *Also called Cintas Corporation No 2 (G-13680)*
Cintas R US Inc 513 459-1200
6800 Cintas Blvd Cincinnati (45262) *(G-3352)*
Cintas Sales Corporation (HQ) 513 459-1200
6800 Cintas Blvd Cincinnati (45262) *(G-3353)*
Cintas Uniforms AP Fcilty Svcs, Cincinnati *Also called Cintas Corporation (G-3350)*
Cintas-Rus LP (HQ) 513 459-1200
6800 Cintas Blvd Mason (45040) *(G-13683)*
Cintech LLC 513 731-6000
3280 Hageman Ave Cincinnati (45241) *(G-3354)*
Cioffi & Son Construction 330 794-9448
1001 Eastwood Ave Akron (44305) *(G-137)*
CIP International Inc 513 874-9925
9575 Le Saint Dr West Chester (45014) *(G-19041)*
Cipriano Painting 440 892-1827
27387 Hollywood Dr Cleveland (44145) *(G-5241)*
Circle Building Services Inc 614 228-6090
742 Harmon Ave Columbus (43223) *(G-7275)*
Circle Health Services 216 721-4010
12201 Euclid Ave Cleveland (44106) *(G-5242)*
Circle J Home Health Care (PA) 330 482-0877
412 State Route 164 Salineville (43945) *(G-16722)*
Circle Prime Manufacturing 330 923-0019
2114 Front St Cuyahoga Falls (44221) *(G-9172)*
Circle S Farms Inc 614 878-9462
9015 London Groveport Rd Grove City (43123) *(G-11546)*
Circle S Transport Inc 614 207-2184
1008 Arcaro Dr Columbus (43230) *(G-7276)*
Circle T Logistics Inc 740 262-5096
617 W Center St Ste 26 Marion (43302) *(G-13530)*
Circleville Oil Co 740 474-7568
315 Town St Circleville (43113) *(G-4882)*
Circling Hills Golf Course 513 367-5858
10240 Carolina Trace Rd Harrison (45030) *(G-11794)*
Circlvlle Care Rhblitation Ctr, Circleville *Also called Sunbridge Circleville (G-4906)*
Circuits & Cables Inc 937 415-2070
815 S Brown School Rd Vandalia (45377) *(G-18671)*
Cisco Capitol Express, Columbus *Also called Capitol Express Entps Inc (G-7187)*
Cisco Systems Inc 937 427-4264
2661 Commons Blvd Ste 133 Beavercreek (45431) *(G-1160)*
Cisco Systems Inc 330 523-2000
4125 Highlander Pkwy Richfield (44286) *(G-16501)*
Cisco Systems Inc 614 764-4987
5400 Frantz Rd Ste 200 Dublin (43016) *(G-10293)*
Citicorp Credit Services Inc 212 559-1000
1500 Boltonfield St Columbus (43228) *(G-7277)*
Citigroup Global Markets Inc 860 291-4181
4380 Buckeye Ln Ste 200 Beavercreek (45440) *(G-1233)*
Citigroup Global Markets Inc 513 579-8300
4030 Smith Rd Ste 200 Cincinnati (45209) *(G-3355)*
Citigroup Global Markets Inc 419 842-5383
7124 W Central Ave Toledo (43617) *(G-17806)*
Citigroup Global Markets Inc 440 617-2000
2035 Crocker Rd Ste 201 Cleveland (44145) *(G-5243)*
Citigroup Inc 740 548-0594
310 Greif Pkwy Delaware (43015) *(G-10080)*
CITIZENS BANK, Martins Ferry *Also called Unified Bank (G-13602)*
Citizens Bank Company (PA) 740 984-2381
501 5th St Beverly (45715) *(G-1488)*
Citizens Bank National Assn 330 580-1913
400 Tuscarawas St W Ste 1 Canton (44702) *(G-2310)*
Citizens Bank of Ashville Ohio (PA) 740 983-2511
26 Main St E Ashville (43103) *(G-769)*
Citizens Bnk of Logan Ohio Inc (HQ) 740 380-2561
188 W Main St Logan (43138) *(G-12970)*
Citizens Capital Markets Inc 216 589-0900
200 Public Sq Ste 3750 Cleveland (44114) *(G-5244)*
Citizens Federal Sav & Ln Assn 937 593-0015
110 N Main St Bellefontaine (43311) *(G-1379)*
Citizens Financial Svcs Inc 513 385-3200
9620 Colerain Ave # 60 Cincinnati (45251) *(G-3356)*
Citizens Nat Bnk of Bluffton (HQ) 419 358-8040
102 S Main St Bluffton (45817) *(G-1730)*
Citizens Nat Bnk of Bluffton 419 224-0400
201 N Main St Lima (45801) *(G-12753)*
Citizens Nat Bnk Urbana Ohio (HQ) 937 653-1200
1 Monument Sq Urbana (43078) *(G-18580)*
Citizens National Bank (PA) 740 472-1696
143 S Main St Woodsfield (43793) *(G-19813)*
City Alliance Water Sewer Dst 330 823-5216
1015 Walnut Ave Alliance (44601) *(G-533)*
City Architecture Inc 216 881-2444
3636 Euclid Ave Fl 3 Cleveland (44115) *(G-5245)*
City Attorney, Columbus *Also called City of Columbus (G-7284)*
City Beverage Company 419 782-7065
8283 N State Route 66 Defiance (43512) *(G-10022)*
City Casters 937 224-1137
101 Pine St Ste 300 Dayton (45402) *(G-9408)*
City Dash Inc 513 562-2000
949 Laidlaw Ave Cincinnati (45237) *(G-3357)*
City Dayton Water Distribution, Dayton *Also called City of Dayton (G-9413)*
City Dept Streets and Sewers, Hamilton *Also called City of Hamilton (G-11709)*
City Garage, Portsmouth *Also called City of Portsmouth (G-16270)*
City Gospel Mission 513 241-5525
1805 Dalton Ave Cincinnati (45214) *(G-3358)*
City Hospital Association 330 385-7200
425 W 5th St East Liverpool (43920) *(G-10517)*
City Laundry & Dry Cleaning Co, Findlay *Also called Kramer Enterprises Inc (G-11055)*
City Life Inc (PA) 216 523-5899
1382 W 9th St Ste 310 Cleveland (44113) *(G-5246)*
City Machine Technologies Inc 330 740-8186
825 Martin Luther King Jr Youngstown (44502) *(G-20142)*
City Mission (PA) 216 431-3510
5310 Carnegie Ave Cleveland (44103) *(G-5247)*
City of Akron 330 864-0020
530 Nome Ave Akron (44320) *(G-138)*
City of Akron 330 678-0077
1570 Ravenna Rd Kent (44240) *(G-12358)*
City of Akron 330 375-2420
1460 Triplett Blvd Akron (44306) *(G-139)*
City of Akron 330 375-2666
2460 Akron Peninsula Rd Akron (44313) *(G-140)*
City of Akron 330 375-2851
1420 Triplett Blvd Akron (44306) *(G-141)*
City of Akron 330 375-2355
166 S High St Rm 701 Akron (44308) *(G-142)*

City of Aurora....330 562-8662
158 W Pioneer Trl Aurora (44202) ***(G-836)***
City of Avon....440 937-5740
36080 Chester Rd Avon (44011) ***(G-889)***
City of Avon Lake....440 933-6226
201 Miller Rd Avon Lake (44012) ***(G-925)***
City of Beavercreek....937 320-0742
2800 New Germany Trebein Beavercreek (45431) ***(G-1161)***
City of Berea....440 826-5853
400 Barrett Rd Berea (44017) ***(G-1451)***
City of Blue Ash....513 745-8577
4040 Cooper Rd Blue Ash (45241) ***(G-1558)***
City of Brecksville....440 526-1384
9069 Brecksville Rd Brecksville (44141) ***(G-1818)***
City of Brecksville....440 526-4109
1 Community Dr Brecksville (44141) ***(G-1819)***
City of Brook Park....216 433-1545
17400 Holland Rd Cleveland (44142) ***(G-5248)***
City of Brunswick....330 225-9144
4095 Center Rd Brunswick (44212) ***(G-1972)***
City of Bucyrus....419 562-3050
200 S Spring St Bucyrus (44820) ***(G-2029)***
City of Canal Winchester....614 837-8276
22 S Trine St Canal Winchester (43110) ***(G-2157)***
City of Canton....330 489-3080
3530 Central Ave Se Canton (44707) ***(G-2311)***
City of Celina....419 586-2451
1125 S Elm St Celina (45822) ***(G-2639)***
City of Centerville....937 438-3585
10000 Yankee St Dayton (45458) ***(G-9409)***
City of Circleville....740 477-8255
108 E Franklin St Circleville (43113) ***(G-4883)***
City of Cleveland....216 664-2555
1701 Lakeside Ave E Cleveland (44114) ***(G-5249)***
City of Cleveland....216 664-2555
1701 Lakeside Ave E Cleveland (44114) ***(G-5250)***
City of Cleveland....216 664-3121
955 Clague Rd Cleveland (44145) ***(G-5251)***
City of Cleveland....216 664-2941
205 W Saint Clair Ave # 4 Cleveland (44113) ***(G-5252)***
City of Cleveland....216 621-4231
500 Lkeside Ave Ground Fl Cleveland (44114) ***(G-5253)***
City of Cleveland....216 664-2430
205 W Saint Clair Ave # 4 Cleveland (44113) ***(G-5254)***
City of Cleveland....216 664-2620
601 Lakeside Ave E Rm 128 Cleveland (44114) ***(G-5255)***
City of Cleveland....216 348-7210
21400 Chagrin Blvd Cleveland (44122) ***(G-5256)***
City of Cleveland....216 664-6800
3765 Pearl Rd Cleveland (44109) ***(G-5257)***
City of Cleveland....216 664-3922
1300 Lakeside Ave E Cleveland (44114) ***(G-5258)***
City of Cleveland Heights....216 291-2323
40 Severance Cir Cleveland Heights (44118) ***(G-6787)***
City of Cleveland Heights....216 691-7300
14200 Superior Rd Cleveland (44118) ***(G-5259)***
City of Cleveland Heights....216 291-5995
40 Severance Cir Cleveland Heights (44118) ***(G-6788)***
City of Columbus....614 645-7627
3500 Indianola Ave Columbus (43214) ***(G-7278)***
City of Columbus....614 645-7490
910 Dublin Rd Ste 4050 Columbus (43215) ***(G-7279)***
City of Columbus....614 645-1600
3433 Agler Rd Ste 2800 Columbus (43219) ***(G-7280)***
City of Columbus....614 645-3072
1875 Morse Rd 235 Columbus (43229) ***(G-7281)***
City of Columbus....614 645-7417
240 Parsons Ave Columbus (43215) ***(G-7282)***
City of Columbus....614 645-8270
910 Dublin Rd Columbus (43215) ***(G-7283)***
City of Columbus....614 645-6624
375 S High St Fl 7 Columbus (43215) ***(G-7284)***
City of Columbus....614 645-8297
940 Dublin Rd Columbus (43215) ***(G-7285)***
City of Columbus....614 645-3248
6977 S High St Lockbourne (43137) ***(G-12947)***
CITY OF COMPASSION, Perrysburg *Also called A Renewed Mind* ***(G-15970)***
City of Compassion....419 422-7800
1624 Tiffin Ave Findlay (45840) ***(G-11013)***
City of Coshocton....740 622-1763
760 Chestnut St Lbby Coshocton (43812) ***(G-9090)***
City of Cuyahoga Falls....330 971-8000
2550 Bailey Rd Cuyahoga Falls (44221) ***(G-9173)***
City of Cuyahoga Falls....330 971-8416
1621 Bailey Rd Cuyahoga Falls (44221) ***(G-9174)***
City of Cuyahoga Falls....330 971-8130
2310 Second St Cuyahoga Falls (44221) ***(G-9175)***
City of Cuyahoga Falls....330 971-8030
2560 Bailey Rd Cuyahoga Falls (44221) ***(G-9176)***
City of Dayton....937 454-8200
3600 Terminal Rd Ste 300 Vandalia (45377) ***(G-18672)***
City of Dayton....937 333-3725
320 W Monument Ave Dayton (45402) ***(G-9410)***
City of Dayton....937 333-1837
2800 Guthrie Rd Ste A Dayton (45417) ***(G-9411)***
City of Dayton....937 454-8231
3848 Wright Dr Vandalia (45377) ***(G-18673)***
City of Dayton....937 333-6070
3210 Chuck Wagner Ln Dayton (45414) ***(G-9412)***
City of Dayton....937 333-7138
945 Ottawa St Dayton (45402) ***(G-9413)***
City of Delphos....419 695-4010
608 N Canal St Delphos (45833) ***(G-10138)***
City of Dublin....614 410-4750
6555 Shier Rings Rd Dublin (43016) ***(G-10294)***
City of Elyria....440 366-2211
1194 Gulf Rd Elyria (44035) ***(G-10604)***
City of Englewood....937 836-2434
333 W National Rd Ofc Englewood (45322) ***(G-10700)***
City of Euclid....216 289-2800
25500 Lakeland Blvd Cleveland (44132) ***(G-5260)***
City of Findlay....419 424-7179
1201 S River Rd Findlay (45840) ***(G-11014)***
City of Gallipolis....740 441-6003
2501 Ohio Ave Gallipolis (45631) ***(G-11310)***
City of Garfield Heights....216 475-1107
13600 Mccracken Rd Cleveland (44125) ***(G-5261)***
City of Hamilton....513 785-7551
2210 S Erie Hwy Hamilton (45011) ***(G-11709)***
City of Hamilton....513 868-5971
2451 River Rd Hamilton (45015) ***(G-11710)***
City of Hamilton....513 785-7450
960 N 3rd St Hamilton (45011) ***(G-11711)***
City of Hamilton Waste Water, Hamilton *Also called City of Hamilton* ***(G-11710)***
City of Highland Heights....440 461-2441
5827 Highland Rd Cleveland (44143) ***(G-5262)***
City of Hudson Village....330 650-1052
95 Owen Brown St Hudson (44236) ***(G-12112)***
City of Huron....419 433-5000
417 Main St Huron (44839) ***(G-12163)***
City of Independence....216 524-3262
6363 Selig Blvd Cleveland (44131) ***(G-5263)***
City of Independence....216 524-7373
6363 Selig Blvd Cleveland (44131) ***(G-5264)***
City of Kent....330 678-8105
930 Overholt Rd Kent (44240) ***(G-12359)***
City of Kenton (PA)....419 674-4850
111 W Franklin St Kenton (43326) ***(G-12409)***
City of Lakewood....216 252-4322
12920 Berea Rd Cleveland (44111) ***(G-5265)***
City of Lakewood....216 226-0080
2019 Woodward Ave Cleveland (44107) ***(G-5266)***
City of Lakewood....216 529-6170
12650 Detroit Ave Cleveland (44107) ***(G-5267)***
City of Lakewood....216 941-1116
12920 Berea Rd Cleveland (44111) ***(G-5268)***
City of Lakewood....216 521-1515
16024 Madison Ave Lakewood (44107) ***(G-12473)***
City of Lakewood....216 521-1288
16024 Madison Ave Cleveland (44107) ***(G-5269)***
City of Lancaster....740 687-6670
1424 Campground Rd Lancaster (43130) ***(G-12518)***
City of Lima....419 221-5165
900 S Collett St Lima (45804) ***(G-12754)***
City of Lima....419 221-5294
50 Town Sq Fl 3 Lima (45801) ***(G-12755)***
City of Lima....419 221-5175
1405 Reservoir Rd Lima (45804) ***(G-12756)***
City of Lorain....440 288-0281
100 Alabama Ave Lorain (44052) ***(G-13023)***
City of Lorain....440 204-2500
1106 W 1st St Lorain (44052) ***(G-13024)***
City of Louisville (PA)....330 875-3321
215 S Mill St Louisville (44641) ***(G-13096)***
City of Marion....740 382-1479
981 W Center St Marion (43302) ***(G-13531)***
City of Massillon....330 833-3304
100 Dig Indian Dr Sw Massillon (44646) ***(G-13796)***
City of Miamisburg....937 866-4532
10 N 1st St Miamisburg (45342) ***(G-14283)***
City of Miamisburg....937 866-4653
4344 Benner Rd Miamisburg (45342) ***(G-14284)***
City of New Philadelphia....330 339-2121
1234 Commercial Ave Se New Philadelphia (44663) ***(G-15086)***
City of North Olmsted....440 777-8000
5200 Dover Center Rd North Olmsted (44070) ***(G-15415)***
City of North Olmsted....440 734-8200
26000 Lorain Rd North Olmsted (44070) ***(G-15416)***
City of North Olmsted....440 777-0678
5873 Canterbury Rd North Olmsted (44070) ***(G-15417)***
City of North Ridgeville....440 327-8326
35010 Bainbridge Rd North Ridgeville (44039) ***(G-15460)***
City of North Royalton....440 582-3002
11545 Royalton Rd Cleveland (44133) ***(G-5270)***
City of Norwalk....419 663-6715
42 Woodlawn Ave Norwalk (44857) ***(G-15563)***

ALPHABETIC

City of Oberlin (PA).....440 775-1531
85 S Main St Oberlin (44074) ***(G-15640)***
City of Painesville.....440 392-5954
325 Richmond St Painesville (44077) ***(G-15840)***
City of Painesville.....440 392-5795
7 Richmond St Painesville (44077) ***(G-15841)***
City of Parma.....440 885-8983
5680 Chevrolet Blvd Cleveland (44130) ***(G-5271)***
City of Parma.....440 885-8876
6505 Ridge Rd Cleveland (44129) ***(G-5272)***
City of Parma.....440 888-4514
7001 W Ridgewood Dr Cleveland (44129) ***(G-5273)***
City of Perrysburg.....419 872-8020
11980 Route Roached Rd Perrysburg (43551) ***(G-15987)***
City of Pickerington.....614 645-8474
1145 Clubhouse Ln Pickerington (43147) ***(G-16089)***
City of Portsmouth.....740 353-5153
605 Washington St Portsmouth (45662) ***(G-16268)***
City of Portsmouth.....740 353-5419
55 Mary Ann St Portsmouth (45662) ***(G-16269)***
City of Portsmouth.....740 353-3459
55 Mary Ann St Portsmouth (45662) ***(G-16270)***
City of Rocky River.....440 356-5656
21018 Hilliard Blvd Cleveland (44116) ***(G-5274)***
City of Rocky River.....440 356-5630
21012 Hilliard Blvd Cleveland (44116) ***(G-5275)***
City of Sandusky.....419 627-5906
304 Harrison St Sandusky (44870) ***(G-16737)***
City of Sandusky.....419 627-5829
222 Meigs St Sandusky (44870) ***(G-16738)***
City of Sandusky.....419 627-5907
304 Harrison St Sandusky (44870) ***(G-16739)***
City of Seven Hills.....216 524-6262
7777 Summitview Dr Seven Hills (44131) ***(G-16828)***
City of Solon.....440 248-6939
34025 Bainbridge Rd Solon (44139) ***(G-16992)***
City of South Euclid.....216 291-3902
1352 Victory Dr Cleveland (44121) ***(G-5276)***
City of Streetsboro.....330 626-2856
2094 State Route 303 Streetsboro (44241) ***(G-17410)***
City of Sylvania.....419 885-1167
7060 Sylvania Ave Sylvania (43560) ***(G-17579)***
City of Toledo.....419 245-1800
420 Madison Ave Ste 100 Toledo (43604) ***(G-17807)***
City of Toledo.....419 245-1001
1 Government Ctr Ste 2200 Toledo (43604) ***(G-17808)***
City of Toledo.....419 936-2875
2201 Ottawa Dr Toledo (43606) ***(G-17809)***
City of Toledo.....419 936-2924
4032 Creekside Ave Toledo (43612) ***(G-17810)***
City of Toledo.....419 245-1400
1 Government Ctr Ste 1800 Toledo (43604) ***(G-17811)***
City of Toledo.....419 936-2507
555 N Expressway Dr Toledo (43608) ***(G-17812)***
City of Toledo.....419 936-2275
600 Jefferson Ave Ste 300 Toledo (43604) ***(G-17813)***
City of Toledo Div Wtr Dist, Toledo *Also called Toledo Cy Pub Utlty Wtr Distr* ***(G-18235)***
City of Troy.....937 335-1914
1400 Experiment Farm Rd Troy (45373) ***(G-18351)***
City of Vandalia.....937 890-1300
201 Clubhouse Way Vandalia (45377) ***(G-18674)***
City of Wadsworth.....330 334-1581
120 Maple St Wadsworth (44281) ***(G-18749)***
City of Warrensville Heights.....216 587-1230
19700 Miles Rd Cleveland (44128) ***(G-5277)***
City of Wellston.....740 384-2428
203 E Broadway St Wellston (45692) ***(G-18998)***
City of Westerville.....614 901-6500
350 Park Meadow Dr Westerville (43081) ***(G-19382)***
City of Westerville.....614 901-6700
139 E Broadway Ave Westerville (43081) ***(G-19383)***
City of Westlake.....440 871-3441
3200 Crocker Rd Cleveland (44145) ***(G-5278)***
City of Westlake.....440 835-6442
29800 Center Ridge Rd Westlake (44145) ***(G-19475)***
City of Whitehall.....614 237-5478
390 S Yearling Rd Columbus (43213) ***(G-7286)***
City of Willoughby.....440 942-0215
37400 N Industrial Pkwy Willoughby (44094) ***(G-19649)***
City of Willoughby.....440 953-4111
1 Public Sq Willoughby (44094) ***(G-19650)***
City of Willoughby.....440 953-4111
1 Public Sq Willoughby (44094) ***(G-19651)***
City of Willoughby.....440 953-4280
38890 Hodgson Rd Willoughby (44094) ***(G-19652)***
City of Willoughby Hills.....440 942-7207
35455 Chardon Rd Willoughby Hills (44094) ***(G-19729)***
City of Willowick.....440 944-1575
30100 Arnold Rd Willowick (44095) ***(G-19738)***
City of Wilmington.....937 382-7961
260 Charles St Wilmington (45177) ***(G-19748)***
City of Wooster.....330 263-8636
1761 Beall Ave Wooster (44691) ***(G-19844)***
City of Wooster.....330 263-5266
510 N Market St Wooster (44691) ***(G-19845)***
City of Wooster.....330 263-8100
1761 Beall Ave Wooster (44691) ***(G-19846)***
City of Xenia.....937 376-7271
779 Ford Rd Xenia (45385) ***(G-20045)***
City of Xenia.....937 376-7260
966 Towler Rd Xenia (45385) ***(G-20046)***
City of Youngstown (PA).....330 742-8700
26 S Phelps St Bsmt Youngstown (44503) ***(G-20143)***
City of Youngstown.....330 742-8749
26 S Phelps St Fl 3a Youngstown (44503) ***(G-20144)***
City of Zanesville.....740 455-0641
401 Market St Rm 1 Zanesville (43701) ***(G-20465)***
City Scrap & Salvage Co.....330 753-5051
760 Flora Ave Akron (44314) ***(G-143)***
City Service, Loveland *Also called Dill-Elam Inc* ***(G-13123)***
City Springsboro Public Works, Springboro *Also called Springboro Service Center* ***(G-17138)***
City Taxicab & Transfer Co.....440 992-2156
1753 W Prospect Rd Ashtabula (44004) ***(G-734)***
City View Nrsing Rhabilitation, Cleveland *Also called Partners of City View LLC* ***(G-6247)***
City View Nursing & Rehab LLC.....216 361-1414
6606 Carnegie Ave Cleveland (44103) ***(G-5279)***
City Yellow Cab Company.....330 253-3141
650 Home Ave Akron (44310) ***(G-144)***
Citynet Ohio LLC.....614 364-7881
343 N Front St Ste 400 Columbus (43215) ***(G-7287)***
Cityview Nrsing Rhbltation Ctr, Cleveland *Also called City View Nursing & Rehab LLC* ***(G-5279)***
Ciulla Smith & Dale LLP (PA).....440 884-2036
6364 Pearl Rd Ste 4 Cleveland (44130) ***(G-5280)***
Ciuni & Panichi Inc.....216 831-7171
25201 Chagrin Blvd # 200 Cleveland (44122) ***(G-5281)***
Civic Center, Cleveland *Also called City of Independence* ***(G-5264)***
Civica CMI, Englewood *Also called Creative Microsystems Inc* ***(G-10701)***
Civil & Environmental Cons Inc.....513 985-0226
5899 Montclair Blvd Milford (45150) ***(G-14512)***
Civista Bank (HQ).....419 625-4121
100 E Water St Sandusky (44870) ***(G-16740)***
Civista Bank.....419 744-3100
16 Executive Dr Norwalk (44857) ***(G-15564)***
CJ Mahan Construction Co LLC (PA).....614 277-4545
250 N Hartford Ave Columbus (43222) ***(G-7288)***
Cj's Sports Bar, Bowling Green *Also called Al-Mar Lanes* ***(G-1757)***
CL Zimmerman Delaware LLC.....513 860-9300
5115 Excello Ct West Chester (45069) ***(G-19042)***
Claire De Leigh Corp.....614 459-6575
3712 Riverside Dr Columbus (43221) ***(G-7289)***
Claprood Roman J Co.....614 221-5515
242 N Grant Ave Columbus (43215) ***(G-7290)***
Clare-Mar Camp Inc.....440 647-3318
47571 New Lndon Eastrn Rd New London (44851) ***(G-15066)***
Clare-Mar Lakes Rv Sales, New London *Also called Clare-Mar Camp Inc* ***(G-15066)***
Claremont Retirement Village.....614 761-2011
7041 Bent Tree Blvd Columbus (43235) ***(G-7291)***
Clarion Hotel, Hudson *Also called Choice Hotels Intl Inc* ***(G-12111)***
Clarion Hotel, Sandusky *Also called Cafaro Peachcreek Co Ltd* ***(G-16731)***
Clarion Hotel Suites, Blue Ash *Also called 5901 Pfffer Rd Htels Sites LLC* ***(G-1522)***
Clark Schaefer Hackett & Co.....937 399-2000
14 E Main St Ste 500 Springfield (45502) ***(G-17160)***
Clark Schaefer Hackett & Co (PA).....513 241-3111
1 E 4th St Ste 1200 Cincinnati (45202) ***(G-3359)***
Clark Schaefer Hackett & Co.....216 672-5252
600 Superior Ave E # 1300 Cleveland (44114) ***(G-5282)***
Clark Schaefer Hackett & Co.....419 243-0218
3166 N Republic Blvd Toledo (43615) ***(G-17814)***
Clark Schaefer Hackett & Co.....614 885-2208
4449 Easton Way Ste 400 Columbus (43219) ***(G-7292)***
Clark Brands LLC.....330 723-9886
427 N Court St Medina (44256) ***(G-14048)***
Clark County Board of Developm (PA).....937 328-2675
2527 Kenton St Springfield (45505) ***(G-17161)***
Clark County Board of Developm.....937 328-5240
50 W Leffel Ln Springfield (45506) ***(G-17162)***
Clark County Board of Developm.....937 328-5200
110 W Leffel Ln Springfield (45506) ***(G-17163)***
Clark County Human Services, Springfield *Also called County of Clark* ***(G-17179)***
Clark County Mrdd Trnsp, Springfield *Also called Clark County Board of Developm* ***(G-17162)***
Clark County Office, Springfield *Also called Miami Vly Child Dev Ctrs Inc* ***(G-17246)***
Clark Memorial Home Assn.....937 399-4262
106 Kewbury Rd Springfield (45504) ***(G-17164)***
Clark Royster Inc.....740 335-3810
717 Robinson Rd Se Wshngtn CT Hs (43160) ***(G-20015)***
Clark Shawnee Schl Transprtn.....937 328-5382
725 E Leffel Ln Springfield (45505) ***(G-17165)***
Clark Son Actn Liquidation Inc.....330 837-9710
4500 Erie Ave Nw Canal Fulton (44614) ***(G-2142)***

Clark Theders Insurance Agency 513 779-2800
9938 Crescent Park Dr West Chester (45069) ***(G-19043)***

Clark Trucking Inc (HQ) 937 642-0335
11590 Township Road 157 East Liberty (43319) ***(G-10508)***

Clarkdietrich Engineering Serv 513 870-1100
9100 Centre Pointe Dr West Chester (45069) ***(G-19044)***

Clarke Contractors Corp 513 285-7844
4475 Muhlhauser Rd West Chester (45011) ***(G-19045)***

Clarke Power Services Inc (PA) 513 771-2200
3133 E Kemper Rd Cincinnati (45241) ***(G-3360)***

Clarke Power Services Inc 937 684-4402
6061 Executive Blvd Huber Heights (45424) ***(G-12094)***

Clarkwood Granada Apartments, Cleveland *Also called Goldberg Companies Inc* ***(G-5677)***

Clary Trucking Inc 740 702-4242
1177 Eastern Ave Chillicothe (45601) ***(G-2827)***

Classic Accident Repair Center, Mentor *Also called Dcr Systems LLC* ***(G-14167)***

Classic Autobody, Mentor *Also called Jim Brown Chevrolet Inc* ***(G-14198)***

Classic Brands, Chillicothe *Also called Litter Distributing Co Inc* ***(G-2861)***

Classic Buick Olds Cadillac 440 639-4500
1700 Mentor Ave Painesville (44077) ***(G-15842)***

Classic Carriers Inc (PA) 937 604-8118
151 Industrial Pkwy Versailles (45380) ***(G-18724)***

Classic Delight Inc 419 394-7955
310 S Park Dr Saint Marys (45885) ***(G-16671)***

Classic Dental Labs Inc 614 443-0328
1252 S High St Columbus (43206) ***(G-7293)***

Classic Imports Inc (PA) 330 262-5277
2018 Great Trails Dr Wooster (44691) ***(G-19847)***

Classic International Inc (PA) 440 975-1222
8470 Tyler Blvd Mentor (44060) ***(G-14158)***

Classic Lexus, Mentor *Also called Classic International Inc* ***(G-14158)***

Classic Oldsmobile, Painesville *Also called Classic Buick Olds Cadillac* ***(G-15842)***

Classic Papering & Painting 614 221-0505
1061 Goodale Blvd Columbus (43212) ***(G-7294)***

Classic Real Estate Co 937 393-3416
123 W Main St Hillsboro (45133) ***(G-11968)***

Classroom Antics Inc 800 595-3776
10143 Royalton Rd Ste G North Royalton (44133) ***(G-15484)***

Clay Burley Products Co (PA) 740 452-3633
455 Gordon St Roseville (43777) ***(G-16601)***

Clay Distributing Co 419 426-3051
15025 E Us 224 Attica (44807) ***(G-821)***

Clay House, Zanesville *Also called Assisted Living Concepts Inc* ***(G-20443)***

Claypool Electric Inc 740 653-5683
1275 Lncstr Krkrsville Rd Lancaster (43130) ***(G-12519)***

Claypool Electrical Contg, Lancaster *Also called Claypool Electric Inc* ***(G-12519)***

Clays Heritage Carpet Inc (PA) 330 497-1280
1440 N Main St Canton (44720) ***(G-2312)***

Clayton Weaver Trucking Inc 513 896-6932
3043 Lelia Ln Fairfield (45014) ***(G-10837)***

Clayton Railroad Cnstr LLC 937 549-2952
500 Lane Rd West Union (45693) ***(G-19276)***

CLC, Dublin *Also called Construction Labor Contrs LLC* ***(G-10309)***

Cle Transportation Company 567 805-4008
203 Republic St Norwalk (44857) ***(G-15565)***

Clean All Services Inc 937 498-4146
324 Adams St Bldg 1 Sidney (45365) ***(G-16921)***

Clean Break Inc 330 638-5648
300 Muirwood Dr Ne Warren (44484) ***(G-18834)***

Clean Care Inc 419 725-2100
511 Phillips Ave Toledo (43612) ***(G-17815)***

Clean Harbors Envmtl Svcs Inc 216 429-2402
2900 Broadway Ave Cleveland (44115) ***(G-5283)***

Clean Harbors Envmtl Svcs Inc 216 429-2401
2930 Independence Rd Cleveland (44115) ***(G-5284)***

Clean Harbors Envmtl Svcs Inc 513 681-6242
4880 Spring Grove Ave Cincinnati (45232) ***(G-3361)***

Clean Harbors Envmtl Svcs Inc 740 929-3532
581 Milliken Dr Hebron (43025) ***(G-11846)***

Clean Image, Circleville *Also called Camco Inc* ***(G-4881)***

Clean Innovations (PA) 614 299-1187
575 E 11th Ave Columbus (43211) ***(G-7295)***

Clean Living Laundry LLC 513 569-0439
2437 Gilbert Ave Cincinnati (45206) ***(G-3362)***

Cleaner & Dryer Restoration, Toledo *Also called J Schoen Enterprises Inc* ***(G-17981)***

Cleaner Carpet & Jantr Inc 513 469-2070
6516 Bluebird Ct Mason (45040) ***(G-13684)***

Cleaners Extraordinaire Inc 937 324-8488
128 Eagle City Rd Springfield (45502) ***(G-17166)***

Cleaning Authority, Milford *Also called Premier Cleaning Services Inc* ***(G-14555)***

Clear Channel, Dayton *Also called City Casters* ***(G-9408)***

Clear Channel, Lima *Also called Iheartcommunications Inc* ***(G-12803)***

Clear Channel Outdoor Inc 614 276-9781
770 Harrison Dr Columbus (43204) ***(G-7296)***

Clear Vision Engineering LLC 419 478-7151
4401 Jackman Rd Toledo (43612) ***(G-17816)***

Clearcreek Construction 740 420-3568
11050 16th Rd Sw Stoutsville (43154) ***(G-17349)***

Clearfield Ohio Holdings Inc 740 947-5121
300 E 2nd St Waverly (45690) ***(G-18969)***

Clearmont Nursing Convalecent, Milford *Also called Clermont Care Inc* ***(G-14513)***

Clearmount Elementary School 330 497-5640
150 Clearmount Ave Se Canton (44720) ***(G-2313)***

Clearpath HM Hlth Hospice LLC 330 784-2162
475 Wolf Ledges Pkwy Akron (44311) ***(G-145)***

Clearview Cleaning Contractors 216 621-6688
2140 Hamilton Ave Cleveland (44114) ***(G-5285)***

Clearview Lantern Suites, Mineral Ridge *Also called Terre Forme Enterprises Inc* ***(G-14640)***

Clearwater Services Inc 330 836-4946
1411 Vernon Odom Blvd Akron (44320) ***(G-146)***

Clearwater Systems, Akron *Also called Clearwater Services Inc* ***(G-146)***

Cleaveland Seaman's Service, Cleveland *Also called Seamans Services* ***(G-6458)***

Clem Lumber and Distrg Co 330 821-2130
16055 Waverly St Ne Alliance (44601) ***(G-534)***

Clemans Nelson & Assoc Inc (PA) 614 923-7700
485 Metro Pl S Ste 200 Dublin (43017) ***(G-10295)***

Clemente-Mc Kay Ambulance Inc (PA) 330 755-1401
700 5th St Ste 1 Struthers (44471) ***(G-17528)***

Clemson Excavating Inc 440 286-4757
9954 Old State Rd Chardon (44024) ***(G-2744)***

Cleopatra Trucking, Columbus *Also called King Tut Logistics LLC* ***(G-7994)***

Clerac LLC (HQ) 440 345-3999
8249 Mohawk Dr Strongsville (44136) ***(G-17450)***

Clercom Inc 513 724-6101
3710 State Route 133 Williamsburg (45176) ***(G-19630)***

Clermont Care Inc 513 831-1770
934 State Route 28 Milford (45150) ***(G-14513)***

Clermont Cnty Wtr Rsurces Dept 513 732-7970
4400 Haskell Ln Batavia (45103) ***(G-999)***

Clermont Counseling Center 513 345-8555
3730 Glenway Ave Cincinnati (45205) ***(G-3363)***

Clermont Counseling Center (PA) 513 947-7000
43 E Main St Amelia (45102) ***(G-579)***

Clermont County Community, Cincinnati *Also called Veterans Health Administration* ***(G-4813)***

Clermont County Community Svcs (PA) 513 732-2277
3003 Hospital Dr Batavia (45103) ***(G-1000)***

Clermont County Gen Hlth Dst 513 732-7499
2275 Bauer Rd Ste 300 Batavia (45103) ***(G-1001)***

Clermont County Wtr Resources, Batavia *Also called Clermont Cnty Wtr Rsurces Dept* ***(G-999)***

Clermont Hills Co LLC 513 752-4400
4501 Eastgate Blvd Cincinnati (45245) ***(G-2908)***

Clermont Mercy Hospital, Batavia *Also called Sister of Mercy of Clerm Count* ***(G-1024)***

Clermont North East School Dst (PA) 513 625-8283
2792 Us Highway 50 Batavia (45103) ***(G-1002)***

Clermont Recovery Center Inc 513 735-8100
1088 Wasserman Way Ste C Batavia (45103) ***(G-1003)***

Clermont Senior Services, Batavia *Also called Clermont Senior Services Inc* ***(G-1004)***

Clermont Senior Services Inc (PA) 513 724-1255
2085 James E Sauls Sr Dr Batavia (45103) ***(G-1004)***

Clevelan Clinic Hlth Sys W Reg 216 518-3444
5555 Transportation Blvd Cleveland (44125) ***(G-5286)***

Clevelan Clinic Hlth Sys W Reg (HQ) 216 476-7000
18101 Lorain Ave Cleveland (44111) ***(G-5287)***

Clevelan Clinic Hlth Sys W Reg 216 476-7606
18200 Lorain Ave Cleveland (44111) ***(G-5288)***

Clevelan Clinic Hlth Sys W Reg 216 476-7007
15531 Lorain Ave Cleveland (44111) ***(G-5289)***

Cleveland Airport Hospitality 440 871-6000
1100 Crocker Rd Westlake (44145) ***(G-19476)***

Cleveland All Breed Trning CLB 216 398-1118
210 Hayes Dr Ste B Cleveland (44131) ***(G-5290)***

Cleveland Anesthesia Group 216 901-5706
6701 Rockside Rd Ste 200 Independence (44131) ***(G-12198)***

Cleveland Auto Livery Inc 216 421-1101
10802 Cedar Ave Cleveland (44106) ***(G-5291)***

Cleveland Bchwood Hsptlity LLC 216 464-5950
3663 Park East Dr Beachwood (44122) ***(G-1063)***

Cleveland Botanical Garden (PA) 216 721-1600
11030 East Blvd Cleveland (44106) ***(G-5292)***

Cleveland Browns Football LLC 440 891-5000
76 Lou Groza Blvd Berea (44017) ***(G-1452)***

Cleveland Business Furniture, Bedford *Also called Cbf Industries Inc* ***(G-1298)***

Cleveland Cement Contractors, Brooklyn Heights *Also called Cleveland Concrete Cnstr Inc* ***(G-1913)***

Cleveland Center For Etng Dsor 216 765-2535
25550 Chagrin Blvd # 200 Beachwood (44122) ***(G-1064)***

Cleveland Child Care Inc (PA) 216 631-3211
3274 W 58th St Fl 1 Cleveland (44102) ***(G-5293)***

Cleveland Christian Home, Cleveland *Also called National Benevolent Associatio* ***(G-6101)***

Cleveland Christian Home Inc 216 671-0977
4614 Prospect Ave Ste 240 Cleveland (44103) ***(G-5294)***

Cleveland Clinic, Lorain *Also called Kolczun & Kolczun Orthopedics* ***(G-13046)***

Cleveland Clinic Cole Eye Inst 216 444-4508
9500 Euclid Ave Cleveland (44195) ***(G-5295)***

Cleveland Clinic Community Onc 216 447-9747
6100 W Creek Rd Ste 15 Independence (44131) ***(G-12199)***

Cleveland Clinic Coordinating, Cleveland *Also called Cleveland Clinic Foundation* ***(G-5304)***

Cleveland Clinic Foundation 330 505-2280
650 Youngstown Warren Rd Niles (44446) *(G-15288)*
Cleveland Clinic Foundation 330 287-4930
1739 Cleveland Rd Wooster (44691) *(G-19848)*
Cleveland Clinic Foundation (PA) 216 636-8335
9500 Euclid Ave Cleveland (44195) *(G-5296)*
Cleveland Clinic Foundation 440 282-6669
1142 W 37th St Lorain (44052) *(G-13025)*
Cleveland Clinic Foundation 614 451-0489
921 Jasonway Ave Columbus (43214) *(G-7297)*
Cleveland Clinic Foundation 216 444-2820
9500 Euclid Ave Ste P57 Cleveland (44195) *(G-5297)*
Cleveland Clinic Foundation 216 445-8585
9500 Euclid Ave P-47 Cleveland (44195) *(G-5298)*
Cleveland Clinic Foundation 440 988-5651
5700 Cooper Foster Park R Lorain (44053) *(G-13026)*
Cleveland Clinic Foundation 216 444-5000
9500 Euclid Ave Cleveland (44195) *(G-5299)*
Cleveland Clinic Foundation 800 223-2273
2111 E 96th St Cleveland (44106) *(G-5300)*
Cleveland Clinic Foundation 216 444-5755
10300 Carnegie Ave Cleveland (44106) *(G-5301)*
Cleveland Clinic Foundation 440 327-1050
35105 Center Ridge Rd North Ridgeville (44039) *(G-15461)*
Cleveland Clinic Foundation 216 448-0116
25875 Science Park Dr Beachwood (44122) *(G-1065)*
Cleveland Clinic Foundation 216 448-4325
1950 Richmond Rd Cleveland (44124) *(G-5302)*
Cleveland Clinic Foundation 330 287-4500
1740 Cleveland Rd Wooster (44691) *(G-19849)*
Cleveland Clinic Foundation 216 444-2200
6801 Brecksville Rd # 10 Cleveland (44131) *(G-5303)*
Cleveland Clinic Foundation 440 986-4000
2001 E Royalton Rd Broadview Heights (44147) *(G-1874)*
Cleveland Clinic Foundation 440 930-6800
450 Avon Belden Rd Avon Lake (44012) *(G-926)*
Cleveland Clinic Foundation 440 366-9444
303 Chestnut Commons Dr Elyria (44035) *(G-10605)*
Cleveland Clinic Foundation 440 204-7800
5800 Coper Foster Pk Rd W Lorain (44053) *(G-13027)*
Cleveland Clinic Foundation 216 986-4000
6801 Brecksville Rd # 10 Independence (44131) *(G-12200)*
Cleveland Clinic Foundation 216 445-6439
9500 Euclid Ave Cleveland (44195) *(G-5304)*
Cleveland Clinic Foundation 216 444-5757
10000 Cedar Ave Ste 6 Cleveland (44106) *(G-5305)*
Cleveland Clinic Foundation 216 444-2200
9500 Euclid Ave Cleveland (44195) *(G-5306)*
Cleveland Clinic Guesthouse, Cleveland *Also called Clinic Care Inc (G-5364)*
Cleveland Clinic Health System, Cleveland *Also called Cleveland Clinic Foundation (G-5296)*
CLEVELAND CLINIC HEALTH SYSTEM, Euclid *Also called Euclid Hospital (G-10753)*
CLEVELAND CLINIC HEALTH SYSTEM, Cleveland *Also called Fairview Hospital (G-5568)*
Cleveland Clinic Health System, North Ridgeville *Also called Cleveland Clinic Foundation (G-15461)*
CLEVELAND CLINIC HEALTH SYSTEM, Cleveland *Also called Marymount Health Care Systems (G-5990)*
Cleveland Clinic Health System, Independence *Also called Cleveland Clinic Foundation (G-12200)*
Cleveland Clinic Health System 440 449-4500
6780 Mayfield Rd Cleveland (44124) *(G-5307)*
Cleveland Clinic Health System 216 692-7555
18901 Lake Shore Blvd Cleveland (44119) *(G-5308)*
Cleveland Clinic Innovations, Cleveland *Also called Cleveland Clinic Foundation (G-5305)*
Cleveland Clinic Lerner Colleg 216 445-3853
9500 Euclid Ave Cleveland (44195) *(G-5309)*
Cleveland Clinic Star Imaging, Columbus *Also called Cleveland Clinic Foundation (G-7297)*
Cleveland Clinic Wooster, Wooster *Also called Clevelnd Clnc Hlth Systm East (G-19850)*
Cleveland Clinic Wooster, Wooster *Also called Cleveland Clinic Foundation (G-19849)*
Cleveland Clnic HSP Fincl Dept, Cleveland *Also called Cleveland Clinic Foundation (G-5299)*
Cleveland Clnic Lyndhrst Cmpus, Cleveland *Also called Cleveland Clinic Foundation (G-5302)*
Cleveland Coin Mch Exch Inc (HQ) 847 842-6310
3860 Ben Hur Ave Unit 2 Willoughby (44094) *(G-19653)*
Cleveland Concrete Cnstr Inc (PA) 216 741-3954
4823 Van Epps Rd Brooklyn Heights (44131) *(G-1913)*
Cleveland Construction Inc (PA) 440 255-8000
8620 Tyler Blvd Mentor (44060) *(G-14159)*
Cleveland Construction Inc 740 927-9000
6399 Broughton Ave Columbus (43213) *(G-7298)*
Cleveland Construction Inc 440 255-8000
5390 Curseview Dr Ste 200 Mason (45040) *(G-13685)*
Cleveland Corporate Svcs Inc 216 397-1492
2929 Clarkson Rd Cleveland (44118) *(G-5310)*
Cleveland Crane Rental, Twinsburg *Also called Forest City Erectors Inc (G-18417)*
Cleveland Crowne Plaza Airport 440 243-4040
7230 Engle Rd Cleveland (44130) *(G-5311)*
Cleveland Dairy Queen Inc (PA) 440 946-3690
4067 Erie St Ste 2 Willoughby (44094) *(G-19654)*
CLEVELAND DEVELOPMENT FOUNDATI, Cleveland *Also called Greater Cleveland Partnership (G-5698)*
Cleveland Division, Cleveland *Also called Millcraft Paper Company (G-6065)*
Cleveland Ear Nose Throat Ctr 440 550-4179
6770 Mayfield Rd Ste 210 Mayfield Heights (44124) *(G-13999)*
Cleveland East Hotel LLC 216 378-9191
26300 Harvard Rd Cleveland (44122) *(G-5312)*
Cleveland Elc Illuminating Co (HQ) 800 589-3101
76 S Main St Akron (44308) *(G-147)*
Cleveland Elc Illuminating Co 440 953-7650
7755 Auburn Rd Painesville (44077) *(G-15843)*
Cleveland Electric Labs Co (PA) 800 447-2207
1776 Enterprise Pkwy Twinsburg (44087) *(G-18401)*
Cleveland Emergency Med Svc, Cleveland *Also called City of Cleveland (G-5250)*
Cleveland Express Trckg Co Inc 216 348-0922
3091 Rockefeller Ave Cleveland (44115) *(G-5313)*
Cleveland Eye Clinic, Cleveland *Also called Robert Wiley MD Inc (G-6405)*
Cleveland F E S Center 216 231-3257
10701 East Blvd Cleveland (44106) *(G-5314)*
Cleveland Foundation 216 861-3810
1422 Euclid Ave Ste 1300 Cleveland (44115) *(G-5315)*
Cleveland Glass Block Inc (PA) 216 531-6363
4566 E 71st St Cleveland (44105) *(G-5316)*
Cleveland Glass Block Inc 614 252-5888
3091 E 14th Ave Columbus (43219) *(G-7299)*
Cleveland Harbor Belt RR LLC 440 746-0801
29930 Pettibone Rd Solon (44139) *(G-16993)*
Cleveland Heartlab Inc 866 358-9828
6701 Carnegie Ave Ste 500 Cleveland (44103) *(G-5317)*
Cleveland Heights Gospel Choir, Cleveland *Also called Cleveland Heights Highschool (G-5318)*
Cleveland Heights Highschool 216 691-5452
3638 Mount Laurel Rd Cleveland (44121) *(G-5318)*
Cleveland Heights Medical Ctr, Cleveland Heights *Also called Kaiser Foundation Hospitals (G-6792)*
Cleveland Hts Tigers Youth Spo 216 906-4168
3686 Berkeley Rd Cleveland (44118) *(G-5319)*
CLEVELAND HUNGARIAN HERITAGE M, Cleveland *Also called Cleveland Hungarian Heritg Soc (G-5320)*
Cleveland Hungarian Heritg Soc 216 523-3900
1301 E 9th St Ste 2400 Cleveland (44114) *(G-5320)*
Cleveland Indians Baseball Com (PA) 216 420-4487
2401 Ontario St Cleveland (44115) *(G-5321)*
Cleveland Jewish Federation 216 593-2900
25701 Science Park Dr Cleveland (44122) *(G-5322)*
Cleveland Job Corps Center 216 541-2500
13421 Coit Rd Cleveland (44110) *(G-5323)*
Cleveland Magazine, Cleveland *Also called Great Lakes Publishing Company (G-5691)*
Cleveland Marble Mosaic Co (PA) 216 749-2840
4595 Hinckley Indus Pkwy Cleveland (44109) *(G-5324)*
Cleveland Metal Exchange, Twinsburg *Also called Cme Acquisitions LLC (G-18403)*
Cleveland Metro Bar Assn 216 696-3525
1301 E 9th St Cleveland (44114) *(G-5325)*
Cleveland Metroparks 440 526-4285
9445 Brecksville Rd Brecksville (44141) *(G-1820)*
Cleveland Metroparks 216 661-6500
3900 Wildlife Way Cleveland (44109) *(G-5326)*
Cleveland Metroparks 440 331-5530
4600 Valley Pkwy Cleveland (44126) *(G-5327)*
Cleveland Metroparks (PA) 216 635-3200
4101 Fulton Pkwy Cleveland (44144) *(G-5328)*
Cleveland Metroparks 216 661-6500
3900 Wildlife Way Cleveland (44109) *(G-5329)*
Cleveland Metroparks 216 739-6040
9485 Eastland Rd Strongsville (44149) *(G-17451)*
Cleveland Metroparks 440 232-7184
18753 Egbert Rd Cleveland (44146) *(G-5330)*
Cleveland Metroparks 440 572-9990
16200 Valley Pkwy Strongsville (44149) *(G-17452)*
Cleveland Metroparks 440 331-1070
4811 Valley Pkwy Cleveland (44126) *(G-5331)*
Cleveland Metroparks Zoo, Cleveland *Also called Cleveland Metroparks (G-5326)*
CLEVELAND METROPOLITAN SCHOOL, Cleveland *Also called Cleveland Municipal School Dst (G-5335)*
Cleveland Municipal School Dst 216 634-7005
3832 Ridge Rd Cleveland (44144) *(G-5332)*
Cleveland Municipal School Dst 216 432-4600
870 E 79th St Cleveland (44103) *(G-5333)*
Cleveland Municipal School Dst 216 459-4200
5100 Biddulph Ave Cleveland (44144) *(G-5334)*
Cleveland Municipal School Dst (PA) 216 838-0000
1111 Superior Ave E # 1800 Cleveland (44114) *(G-5335)*
Cleveland Municipal School Dst 216 838-8700
11801 Worthington Ave Cleveland (44111) *(G-5336)*
Cleveland Municipal School Dst 216 521-6511
10427 Detroit Ave Cleveland (44102) *(G-5337)*
Cleveland Municipal School Dst 216 459-9818
3518 W 25th St Cleveland (44109) *(G-5338)*
Cleveland Mus Schl Settlement 216 421-5806
11125 Magnolia Dr Cleveland (44106) *(G-5339)*

Cleveland Orchestra, The, Cleveland *Also called Musical Arts Association* ***(G-6093)***
Cleveland Phlhrmonic Orchestra.....216 556-1800
1158 Bates Rd Rocky River (44116) ***(G-16574)***
Cleveland Pick-A-Part Inc.....440 236-5031
12420 Station Rd Columbia Station (44028) ***(G-6843)***
Cleveland Preterm.....216 991-4577
12000 Shaker Blvd Cleveland (44120) ***(G-5340)***
Cleveland Pump Repr & Svcs LLC.....330 963-3100
1761 Highland Rd Twinsburg (44087) ***(G-18402)***
Cleveland Quarries, Vermilion *Also called Irg Operating LLC* ***(G-18711)***
Cleveland Racquet Club Inc.....216 831-2155
29825 Chagrin Blvd Cleveland (44124) ***(G-5341)***
Cleveland Real Estate Partners.....216 623-1600
1801 E 9th St Ste 1700 Cleveland (44114) ***(G-5342)***
Cleveland Research Company LLC.....216 649-7250
1375 E 9th St Ste 2700 Cleveland (44114) ***(G-5343)***
Cleveland Rest Oper Ltd Partnr.....216 328-1121
6000 Fredom Sq Dr Ste 280 Cleveland (44131) ***(G-5344)***
Cleveland S Hospitality LLC.....216 447-1300
6200 Quarry Ln Cleveland (44131) ***(G-5345)***
Cleveland Scrap, Cleveland *Also called Scrap Yard LLC* ***(G-6454)***
Cleveland Sight Center, Cleveland *Also called Cleveland Soc For The Blind* ***(G-5347)***
Cleveland Skating Club.....216 791-2800
2500 Kemper Rd Cleveland (44120) ***(G-5346)***
Cleveland Soc For The Blind.....216 791-8118
1909 E 101st St Cleveland (44106) ***(G-5347)***
Cleveland Southeastern Trails, Chagrin Falls *Also called Garfield Hts Coach Line Inc* ***(G-2697)***
Cleveland State University.....216 687-3786
1860 E 18th St Rm 344 Cleveland (44114) ***(G-5348)***
Cleveland Sysco Inc (HQ).....216 201-3000
4747 Grayton Rd Cleveland (44135) ***(G-5349)***
Cleveland Tank & Supply Inc.....216 771-8265
6560 Juniata Ave Cleveland (44103) ***(G-5350)***
Cleveland Teachers Union Inc.....216 861-7676
1228 Euclid Ave Ste 1100 Cleveland (44115) ***(G-5351)***
Cleveland Thermal LLC.....216 241-3636
1921 Hamilton Ave Cleveland (44114) ***(G-5352)***
Cleveland University, Cleveland *Also called University Rdlgsts of Clveland* ***(G-6668)***
Cleveland VA Medical Research.....216 791-2300
10701 East Blvd Cleveland (44106) ***(G-5353)***
Cleveland Water Department.....216 664-3168
5953 Deering Ave Cleveland (44130) ***(G-5354)***
Cleveland Westlake.....440 892-0333
29690 Detroit Rd Westlake (44145) ***(G-19477)***
Cleveland Wheels.....440 937-6211
1160 Center Rd Avon (44011) ***(G-890)***
Cleveland Works Railway Co.....216 429-7267
3175 Independence Rd Cleveland (44105) ***(G-5355)***
Cleveland Yachting Club Inc.....440 333-1155
200 Yacht Club Dr Cleveland (44116) ***(G-5356)***
Cleveland-Cliffs Inc (PA).....216 694-5700
200 Public Sq Ste 3300 Cleveland (44114) ***(G-5357)***
Clevelnd Clnc Chagrn Flls Fmly.....440 893-9393
551 Washington St Chagrin Falls (44022) ***(G-2693)***
Clevelnd Clnc Hlth Systm East.....330 287-4830
721 E Milltown Rd Wooster (44691) ***(G-19850)***
Clevelnd Clnc Hlth Systm East.....330 468-0190
863 W Aurora Rd Northfield (44067) ***(G-15512)***
Clevelnd Clnc Hlth Systm East.....216 761-3300
13951 Terrace Rd Cleveland (44112) ***(G-5358)***
Clevelnd Museum of Natural His.....216 231-4600
1 Wade Oval Dr Cleveland (44106) ***(G-5359)***
Clgt Solutions LLC.....740 920-4795
1670 Columbus Rd Ste C Granville (43023) ***(G-11462)***
CLI Incorporated.....419 668-8840
306 S Norwalk Rd W Norwalk (44857) ***(G-15566)***
Click Camera & Video.....937 435-3072
2925 Mmsburg Cntrville Rd Miamisburg (45342) ***(G-14285)***
Click4care Inc.....614 431-3700
50 S Liberty St Ste 200 Powell (43065) ***(G-16328)***
Cliff North Consultants Inc.....513 251-4930
3747 Warsaw Ave Cincinnati (45205) ***(G-3364)***
Cliffs Cleveland Foundation.....216 694-5700
1100 Superior Ave E # 1500 Cleveland (44114) ***(G-5360)***
Cliffs Michigan Mining Company, Cleveland *Also called Tilden Mining Company LC* ***(G-6600)***
Cliffs Minnesota Minerals Co.....216 694-5700
1100 Superior Ave E Cleveland (44114) ***(G-5361)***
Cliffs Resources Inc (HQ).....216 694-5700
200 Public Sq Ste 200 Cleveland (44114) ***(G-5362)***
Clifton Care Center Inc.....513 530-1600
463 Warner St Cincinnati (45219) ***(G-3365)***
Clifton Steel Company (PA).....216 662-6111
16500 Rockside Rd Maple Heights (44137) ***(G-13403)***
Cliftonlarsonallen LLP.....330 497-2000
4505 Stephens Cir Nw Canton (44718) ***(G-2314)***
Cliftonlarsonallen LLP.....419 244-3711
1 Seagate Ste 2650 Toledo (43604) ***(G-17817)***
Cliftonlarsonallen LLP.....330 376-0100
388 S Main St Ste 403 Akron (44311) ***(G-148)***
Climaco Lefkwtz Peca Wlcox & (PA).....216 621-8484
55 Public Sq Ste 1950 Cleveland (44113) ***(G-5363)***
Clime Leasing Co LLC.....614 276-4400
4301 Clime Rd N Columbus (43228) ***(G-7300)***
Clinic Care Inc.....216 707-4200
9601 Euclid Ave Cleveland (44106) ***(G-5364)***
Clinic5.....614 598-9960
1466 Northwest Blvd Columbus (43212) ***(G-7301)***
Clinical Health Laboratories, Euclid *Also called Zak Enterprises Ltd* ***(G-10781)***
Clinical Research Center.....513 636-4412
3333 Burnet Ave Rm 3641 Cincinnati (45229) ***(G-3366)***
Clinical Research MGT Inc (HQ).....330 278-2343
1265 Ridge Rd Ste 2 Hinckley (44233) ***(G-11996)***
Clinical Specialties Inc.....614 659-6580
7654 Crosswoods Dr Columbus (43235) ***(G-7302)***
Clinical Technology Inc.....440 526-0160
7005 S Edgerton Rd Brecksville (44141) ***(G-1821)***
Clinicl Otcms Mngmnt Syst LLC.....330 650-9900
9200 S Hills Blvd Ste 200 Broadview Heights (44147) ***(G-1875)***
Clinton Aluminum Dist Inc (PA).....330 882-6743
6270 Van Buren Rd New Franklin (44216) ***(G-15042)***
Clinton County Board of.....937 382-7519
4425 State Route 730 Wilmington (45177) ***(G-19749)***
Clinton County Childrens Svcs, Wilmington *Also called County of Clinton* ***(G-19758)***
Clinton County Community Actn (PA).....937 382-8365
789 N Nelson Ave Wilmington (45177) ***(G-19750)***
Clinton County Community Actn.....937 382-5624
789 N Nelson Ave Wilmington (45177) ***(G-19751)***
Clinton County Dept Jobs/Fmly.....937 382-0963
1025 S South St Ste 200 Wilmington (45177) ***(G-19752)***
Clinton County Head Start, Wilmington *Also called Clinton County Community Actn* ***(G-19751)***
Clinton County Highway Dept, Wilmington *Also called County of Clinton* ***(G-19759)***
Clinton County Offices, Wilmington *Also called Clinton County Board of* ***(G-19749)***
Clinton Memorial Fmly Hlth Ctr, Wilmington *Also called Clinton Memorial Hospital* ***(G-19754)***
Clinton Memorial Hospital, Wilmington *Also called Rchp - Wilmington LLC* ***(G-19781)***
Clinton Memorial Hospital (PA).....937 382-6611
610 W Mn St Wilmington (45177) ***(G-19753)***
Clinton Memorial Hospital.....937 383-3402
825 W Locust St Wilmington (45177) ***(G-19754)***
Clinton-Carvell Inc.....614 351-8858
1131 Harrisburg Pike Columbus (43223) ***(G-7303)***
Clintonville Community Market, Columbus *Also called Clintonville Community Mkt* ***(G-7304)***
Clintonville Community Mkt.....614 261-3663
85 E Gay St Ste 1000 Columbus (43215) ***(G-7304)***
Clippard Instrument Lab Inc (PA).....513 521-4261
7390 Colerain Ave Cincinnati (45239) ***(G-3367)***
Clippard Minimatic, Cincinnati *Also called Clippard Instrument Lab Inc* ***(G-3367)***
Clipper Magazine LLC.....513 794-4100
4601 Malsbary Rd 1 Blue Ash (45242) ***(G-1559)***
Clk Multi-Family MGT LLC.....614 891-0011
5811 Spring Run Dr Columbus (43229) ***(G-7305)***
Clm Pallet Recycling Inc.....614 272-5761
4311 Janitrol Rd Ste 150 Columbus (43228) ***(G-7306)***
Clockwork Logistics Inc.....216 587-5371
4765 E 131st St Garfield Heights (44105) ***(G-11351)***
Clopay Corporation (HQ).....800 282-2260
8585 Duke Blvd Mason (45040) ***(G-13686)***
Clopay Transportation Company.....513 381-4800
312 Walnut St Ste 1600 Cincinnati (45202) ***(G-3368)***
Close To Home Health Care Ctr, Westerville *Also called Nationwide Childrens Hospital* ***(G-19331)***
Close To Home Health Care Ctr, Columbus *Also called Nationwide Childrens Hospital* ***(G-8235)***
Close To Home Health Care Ctr.....614 932-9013
5675 Venture Dr Dublin (43017) ***(G-10296)***
Close To Home III.....740 534-1100
617 Center St Ironton (45638) ***(G-12286)***
Closeout Distribution Inc (HQ).....614 278-6800
300 Phillipi Rd Columbus (43228) ***(G-7307)***
Clossman Catering Incorporated.....513 942-7744
3725 Symmes Rd Hamilton (45015) ***(G-11712)***
Cloudroute LLC.....216 373-4601
59 Alpha Park Cleveland (44143) ***(G-5365)***
Cloverleaf Bowling Center Inc.....216 524-4833
5619 Brecksville Rd Cleveland (44131) ***(G-5366)***
Cloverleaf Cold Storage Co.....330 833-9870
950 Cloverleaf St Se Massillon (44646) ***(G-13797)***
Cloverleaf Cold Storage Co.....419 599-5015
1165 Independence Dr Napoleon (43545) ***(G-14934)***
Cloverleaf Lanes, Cleveland *Also called Cloverleaf Bowling Center Inc* ***(G-5366)***
Cloverleaf Suites, Dublin *Also called Hotel 2345 LLC* ***(G-10365)***
Cloverleaf Transport Co.....419 599-5015
1165 Independence Dr Napoleon (43545) ***(G-14935)***
Clovernook Inc (PA).....513 605-4000
7025 Clovernook Ave Cincinnati (45231) ***(G-3369)***
Clovernook Center For The Bli (PA).....513 522-3860
7000 Hamilton Ave Cincinnati (45231) ***(G-3370)***
Clovernook Country Club.....513 521-0333
2035 W Galbraith Rd Cincinnati (45239) ***(G-3371)***
CLOVERNOOK HEALTH CARE PAVILIO, Cincinnati *Also called Clovernook Inc* ***(G-3369)***

ALPHABETIC

Clovvr LLC 740 653-2224
1275 Kinnear Rd Ste 234 Columbus (43212) *(G-7308)*
Clp Gw Sandusky Tenant LP 419 609-6000
4600 Milan Rd Sandusky (44870) *(G-16741)*
Clp Towne Inc 440 234-3324
5160 W 161st St Brookpark (44142) *(G-1940)*
Cls Facilities Management Svcs, Mentor *Also called Cls Facilities MGT Svcs Inc (G-14160)*
Cls Facilities MGT Svcs Inc 440 602-4600
8061 Tyler Blvd Mentor (44060) *(G-14160)*
Club 51 Fitness, Centerville *Also called Centerville Fitness Inc (G-2675)*
Club At Hillbrook Inc 440 247-4940
14800 Hillbrook Dr Chagrin Falls (44022) *(G-2694)*
Club Life Entertainment LLC 216 831-1134
2000 Auburn Dr Ste 200 Beachwood (44122) *(G-1066)*
Clubcorp Usa Inc 330 724-4444
600 Swartz Rd Akron (44319) *(G-149)*
Clubcorp Usa Inc 216 851-2582
40 Shoreby Dr Cleveland (44108) *(G-5367)*
Clubessential LLC (PA) 800 448-1475
4600 Mcauley Pl Ste 350 Blue Ash (45242) *(G-1560)*
Clubhouse Pub N Grub 440 884-2582
6365 Pearl Rd Cleveland (44130) *(G-5368)*
Clubhouse, The, Cleveland *Also called Clubhouse Pub N Grub (G-5368)*
Clutch Interactive, Columbus *Also called Information Control Corp (G-7897)*
Clyde-Findlay Area Cr Un Inc (PA) 419 547-7781
1455 W Mcpherson Hwy Clyde (43410) *(G-6812)*
Clyo Internal Medicine Inc 937 435-5857
7073 Clyo Rd Centerville (45459) *(G-2676)*
Cm-Gc LLC 513 527-4141
1810 Section Rd Cincinnati (45237) *(G-3372)*
Cmbb LLC 937 652-2151
417 E Water St Urbana (43078) *(G-18581)*
CMC Daymark Corporation 419 354-2591
12830 S Dixie Hwy Bowling Green (43402) *(G-1773)*
Cmdm, Powell *Also called Comprehensive Med Data MGT LLC (G-16331)*
Cme Acquisitions LLC 216 464-4480
1900 Case Pkwy S Twinsburg (44087) *(G-18403)*
Cmha, Cincinnati *Also called Cincinnati Metro Hsing Auth (G-3315)*
Cmp I Blue Ash Owner LLC 513 733-4334
4625 Lake Forest Dr Blue Ash (45242) *(G-1561)*
Cmp I Columbus I Owner LLC 614 764-9393
5175 Post Rd Dublin (43017) *(G-10297)*
Cmp I Columbus II Owner LLC 614 436-7070
7411 Vantage Dr Columbus (43235) *(G-7309)*
Cmp I Owner-T LLC 614 764-9393
5175 Post Rd Dublin (43017) *(G-10298)*
Cmp I Owner-T LLC 614 436-7070
7411 Vantage Dr Columbus (43235) *(G-7310)*
Cmp I Owner-T LLC 513 733-4334
4625 Lake Forest Dr Blue Ash (45242) *(G-1562)*
CMS, Avon *Also called Carroll Manufacturing & Sales (G-884)*
CMS, Stow *Also called Custom Movers Services Inc (G-17358)*
CMS & Co Management Svcs Inc 440 989-5200
3905 Oberlin Ave Lorain (44053) *(G-13028)*
CMS Business Services LLC 740 687-0577
416 N Mount Pleasant Ave Lancaster (43130) *(G-12520)*
CMS Customer Solutions, Columbus *Also called Continntal Mssage Solution Inc (G-7434)*
Cmta Inc 502 326-3085
222 E 14th St Cincinnati (45202) *(G-3373)*
CNB Bank 419 562-7040
105 Washington Sq Bucyrus (44820) *(G-2030)*
Cnd Machine, Massillon *Also called C-N-D Industries Inc (G-13791)*
CNG Financial Corp 513 336-7735
7755 Montgomery Rd # 400 Cincinnati (45236) *(G-3374)*
CNG Financial Corporation (PA) 513 336-7735
7755 Montgomery Rd # 400 Cincinnati (45236) *(G-3375)*
Cnsld Humacare- Employee MGT (PA) 513 605-3522
9435 Waterstone Blvd # 250 Cincinnati (45249) *(G-3376)*
Co Open Options Inc 513 932-0724
19 N Mechanic St Lebanon (45036) *(G-12595)*
Coachs Sports Corner Inc 419 609-3737
1130 Cleveland Rd Sandusky (44870) *(G-16742)*
Coact Associates Ltd 866 646-4400
2748 Centennial Rd Toledo (43617) *(G-17818)*
Coad, Athens *Also called Corporation For OH Appalachian (G-779)*
Coal Grove Long Term Care Inc 740 532-0449
813 1/2 Marion Pike Ironton (45638) *(G-12287)*
Coal Services Inc 740 795-5220
155 Highway 7 S Powhatan Point (43942) *(G-16356)*
Coal Services Group, Powhatan Point *Also called Coal Services Inc (G-16356)*
Coast To Coast Studios LLC 614 861-9800
7522 Blacklick Ridge Blvd Blacklick (43004) *(G-1505)*
Coates Car Care Inc 330 652-4180
59 Youngstown Warren Rd Niles (44446) *(G-15289)*
Coaxial Communications of Sout (PA) 513 797-4400
700 Ackerman Rd Ste 280 Columbus (43202) *(G-7311)*
Coba/Select Sires Inc (PA) 614 878-5333
1224 Alton Darby Creek Rd Columbus (43228) *(G-7312)*
Cobalt Group Inc 614 876-4013
4635 Trueman Blvd Ste 100 Hilliard (43026) *(G-11891)*
Cobblestone Square 20, Elyria *Also called Regal Cinemas Inc (G-10675)*

Coblentz Chocolate Co, Walnut Creek *Also called Walnut Creek Chocolate Company (G-18785)*
Coblentz Distributing Inc 330 852-2888
2641 State R 39 39 R Walnut Creek (44687) *(G-18784)*
Cobos Insurance Centre LLC 440 324-3732
41436 Griswold Rd Elyria (44035) *(G-10606)*
Coca-Cola Bottling Co Cnsld 937 878-5000
1000 Coca Cola Blvd Dayton (45424) *(G-9414)*
Cocca Development Ltd 330 729-1010
100 Debartolo Pl Ste 400 Youngstown (44512) *(G-20145)*
Cochin Technologies LLC 440 941-4856
37854 Briar Lakes Dr Avon (44011) *(G-891)*
Cochran Electric Inc 614 847-0035
90 Grace Dr Powell (43065) *(G-16329)*
Cochran W R Industrial Elc, Powell *Also called Cochran Electric Inc (G-16329)*
Code One Communications Inc 614 338-0321
2785 Castlewood Rd Columbus (43209) *(G-7313)*
Coffee Break Corporation 513 841-1100
1940 Losantiville Ave Cincinnati (45237) *(G-3377)*
Coffman Branch, Springboro *Also called Young Mens Christian Assoc (G-17144)*
Coffman Family Partnership 614 864-5400
5435 Nelsonia Pl Columbus (43213) *(G-7314)*
Cogent-Hmg, Canton *Also called Hospitalists MGT Group LLC (G-2404)*
Cohen & Company Ltd 330 743-1040
201 E Commerce St Ste 400 Youngstown (44503) *(G-20146)*
Cohen & Company Ltd 330 374-1040
3500 Embassy Pkwy Akron (44333) *(G-150)*
COHEN & COMPANY,LTD, Youngstown *Also called Cohen & Company Ltd (G-20146)*
Cohen Electronics Inc 513 425-6911
3110 S Verity Pkwy Middletown (45044) *(G-14421)*
Cohen Middletown, Middletown *Also called Cohen Electronics Inc (G-14421)*
Cohen Todd Kite Stanford LLC 513 205-7286
250 E 5th St Ste 2350 Cincinnati (45202) *(G-3378)*
Coho Creative LLC 513 751-7500
2331 Victory Pkwy Cincinnati (45206) *(G-3379)*
Coilplus Inc 614 866-1338
5677 Alshire Rd Columbus (43232) *(G-7315)*
Coilplus Inc 937 322-4455
4801 Gateway Blvd Springfield (45502) *(G-17167)*
Coilplus Inc 937 778-8884
100 Steelway Dr Piqua (45356) *(G-16139)*
Coilplus Berwick, Piqua *Also called Coilplus Inc (G-16139)*
Coin World, Sidney *Also called Amos Media Company (G-16912)*
Coit, Cincinnati *Also called Velco Inc (G-4805)*
Coit Services of Ohio Inc 216 626-0040
23580 Miles Rd Cleveland (44128) *(G-5369)*
Colaianni Construction Inc 740 769-2362
2141 State Route 150 Dillonvale (43917) *(G-10173)*
Colas Solutions Inc 513 272-5348
7374 Main St Cincinnati (45244) *(G-3380)*
Cold Well Banker Realty, Dayton *Also called David Campbell (G-9451)*
Coldliner Express Inc 614 570-0836
4921 Vulcan Ave Columbus (43228) *(G-7316)*
Coldstream Country Club 513 231-3900
400 Asbury Rd Cincinnati (45255) *(G-3381)*
Coldstream Logistics, Independence *Also called Great Lakes Cold Logistics (G-12215)*
Coldwater Ems, Coldwater *Also called County of Mercer (G-6828)*
Coldwell Banker, Middletown *Also called 1440 Corporation Inc (G-14410)*
Coldwell Banker, Ashland *Also called Ward Realestate Inc (G-707)*
Coldwell Banker, Newark *Also called Mc Mahon Realestate Co (G-15203)*
Coldwell Banker, Cleveland *Also called Hunter Realty Inc (G-5789)*
Coldwell Banker, Dublin *Also called Nrt Commercial Utah LLC (G-10411)*
Coldwell Banker, Canton *Also called Tom Baier & Assoc Inc (G-2563)*
Coldwell Banker, Geneva *Also called Hunter Realty Inc (G-11364)*
Coldwell Banker 513 321-9944
2721 Erie Ave Cincinnati (45208) *(G-3382)*
Coldwell Banker First Place RE 330 726-8161
1275 Boardman Poland Rd # 1 Poland (44514) *(G-16223)*
Coldwell Banker King Thompson 614 759-0808
176 Clint Dr Pickerington (43147) *(G-16090)*
Coldwell Banker West Shell 513 829-4000
9106 W Chester Towne Ctr West Chester (45069) *(G-19046)*
Coldwell Banker West Shell 513 922-9400
3260 Westbourne Dr Cincinnati (45248) *(G-3383)*
Coldwell Banker West Shell 513 385-9300
6700 Ruwes Oak Dr Cincinnati (45248) *(G-3384)*
Coldwell Banker West Shell 513 777-7900
7311 Tylers Corner Pl West Chester (45069) *(G-19047)*
Coldwell Banker West Shell 513 271-7200
7203 Wooster Pike Cincinnati (45227) *(G-3385)*
Coldwell Bnkr Hritg Rltors LLC 937 304-8500
8534 Yankee St Ste 1b Dayton (45458) *(G-9415)*
Coldwell Bnkr Hritg Rltors LLC 937 748-5500
535 N Main St Springboro (45066) *(G-17119)*
Coldwell Bnkr Hritg Rltors LLC (PA) 937 434-7600
2000 Hewitt Ave Dayton (45440) *(G-9416)*
Coldwell Bnkr Hritg Rltors LLC 937 426-6060
4139 Colonel Glenn Hwy Beavercreek Township (45431) *(G-1266)*

Coldwell Bnkr Hritg Rltors LLC..........937 439-4500
8534 Yankee St Ste 1b Dayton (45458) *(G-9417)*
Coldwell Bnkr Hritg Rltors LLC..........937 890-2200
356 N Dixie Dr Ste 1 Vandalia (45377) *(G-18675)*
Cole Selby Funeral Inc..........330 856-4695
3966 Warren Sharon Rd Vienna (44473) *(G-18736)*
Cole + Russell Architects Inc (PA)..........513 721-8080
600 Vine St Ste 2210 Cincinnati (45202) *(G-3386)*
Cole-Valley Motor Co (PA)..........330 372-1665
4111 Elm Rd Ne Warren (44483) *(G-18835)*
Coleeta Daycare Llc (PA)..........614 310-6465
4480 Refugee Rd Ste 201 Columbus (43232) *(G-7317)*
Coleman Data Solutions, Kent *Also called Coleman Professional Svcs Inc (G-12360)*
Coleman Professional Svcs Inc (PA)..........330 673-1347
5982 Rhodes Rd Kent (44240) *(G-12360)*
Coleman Professional Svcs Inc..........330 628-2275
3043 Sanitarium Rd Ste 2 Akron (44312) *(G-151)*
Coleman Professional Svcs Inc..........330 296-8313
3920 Lovers Ln Ravenna (44266) *(G-16377)*
Coleman Spohn Corporation (PA)..........216 431-8070
1775 E 45th St Cleveland (44103) *(G-5370)*
Colerain Dry Rdge Chldcare Ltd..........513 923-4300
3998 Dry Ridge Rd Cincinnati (45252) *(G-3387)*
Colerain Volunteer Fire Co..........740 738-0735
72555 Colerain Rd Dillonvale (43917) *(G-10174)*
Colgan-Davis Inc..........419 893-6116
1682 Lance Pointe Rd Maumee (43537) *(G-13895)*
Colhoc Limited Partnership..........614 246-4625
200 W Nationwide Blvd Columbus (43215) *(G-7318)*
Collaborative Inc..........419 242-7405
1 Seagate Park Level 118 Toledo (43604) *(G-17819)*
Collaborative Pharmacy Svcs, Miamisburg *Also called Kettcor Inc (G-14308)*
Collections Acquisition Co LLC..........614 944-5788
2 Easton Oval Ste 350 Columbus (43219) *(G-7319)*
Collector Wells Intl Inc..........614 888-6263
6360 Huntley Rd Columbus (43229) *(G-7320)*
College Engineering/Aerospace, Columbus *Also called Ohio State University (G-8398)*
College of Dentistry, Columbus *Also called Ohio State University (G-8392)*
College of Musical Arts, Bowling Green *Also called Bowling Green State University (G-1768)*
College Park HM Hlth Care Plus, Coshocton *Also called College Park Inc (G-9091)*
College Park Inc..........740 623-4607
380 Browns Ln Ste 7 Coshocton (43812) *(G-9091)*
College Polymr Science & Engrg, Akron *Also called University of Akron (G-488)*
Collier Nursing Service Inc..........513 791-4357
9844 Zig Zag Rd Montgomery (45242) *(G-14725)*
Colliers International, Columbus *Also called Adena Commercial LLC (G-6868)*
Colliers International, Cincinnati *Also called West Shell Commercial Inc (G-4837)*
Colliers Turley Martin Tucker, Cincinnati *Also called Cassidy Trley Coml RE Svcs Inc (G-3192)*
Collins & Assoc Technical Svcs..........740 574-2320
7991 Ohio River Rd Wheelersburg (45694) *(G-19573)*
Collins Career Center..........740 867-6641
11627 State Route 243 Chesapeake (45619) *(G-2782)*
Collins KAO Inc..........513 948-9000
8911 Rossash Rd Cincinnati (45236) *(G-3388)*
Collins Salon Inc..........513 683-1700
12125 N Lebanon Rd Loveland (45140) *(G-13116)*
Collison Luke Drywall Txturing, Lancaster *Also called Luke Collison (G-12552)*
Collotype Labels Usa Inc..........513 381-1480
4053 Clough Woods Dr Batavia (45103) *(G-1005)*
Colonial Banc Corp (PA)..........937 456-5544
110 W Main St Eaton (45320) *(G-10554)*
Colonial Courier Service Inc..........419 891-0922
409 Osage St Maumee (43537) *(G-13896)*
Colonial Courier Service Inc (PA)..........419 891-0922
413 Osage St Maumee (43537) *(G-13897)*
Colonial Farms, Columbus Grove *Also called Tom Langhals (G-9031)*
Colonial Heating & Cooling Co..........614 837-6100
671 Windmiller Dr Pickerington (43147) *(G-16091)*
Colonial Lf Accident Insur Co..........614 793-8622
485 Metro Pl S Ste 150 Dublin (43017) *(G-10299)*
Colonial Manor Health Care Ctr..........419 994-4191
747 S Mount Vernon Ave Loudonville (44842) *(G-13089)*
Colonial Nursing Home, Rockford *Also called Healthcare Management Cons (G-16563)*
Colonial Sales Inc (PA)..........740 397-4970
8927 Columbus Rd Ste A Mount Vernon (43050) *(G-14883)*
Colonial Senior Services Inc..........513 856-8600
100 Berkley Dr Hamilton (45013) *(G-11713)*
Colonial Senior Services Inc..........513 867-4006
855 Stahlheber Rd Hamilton (45013) *(G-11714)*
Colonial Senior Services Inc..........513 844-8004
855 Stahlheber Rd Hamilton (45013) *(G-11715)*
Colonial Surface Solutions, Columbus Grove *Also called Carpe Diem Industries LLC (G-9029)*
Colonial Terrace, Mount Vernon *Also called Colonial Sales Inc (G-14883)*
Colony Healthcare Center, The, Tallmadge *Also called Communicare Health Svcs Inc (G-17635)*
Colortone Audio Visual (PA)..........216 928-1530
5401 Naiman Pkwy Ste A Cleveland (44139) *(G-5371)*
Colortone Staging & Rentals, Cleveland *Also called Colortone Audio Visual (G-5371)*
Cols Boe Custodial Services, Columbus *Also called Columbus Public School Dst (G-7378)*
Cols Health & Wellness Testing..........614 839-2781
5050 Pine Creek Dr Ste B Westerville (43081) *(G-19384)*
Colt Enterprises Inc..........567 336-6062
133 E John St Maumee (43537) *(G-13898)*
Columbia, Vandalia *Also called Datwyler Sling Sltions USA Inc (G-18676)*
Columbia Energy, Columbus *Also called Columbia Gas Transmission LLC (G-7324)*
Columbia Energy, Cambridge *Also called Columbia Gas Transmission LLC (G-2105)*
Columbia Energy, Springfield *Also called Columbia Gas Transmission LLC (G-17168)*
Columbia Energy, Homer *Also called Columbia Gas Transmission LLC (G-12075)*
Columbia Energy, Sugar Grove *Also called Columbia Gulf Transmission LLC (G-17540)*
Columbia Gas of Ohio Inc (HQ)..........614 460-6000
290 W Nationwide Blvd # 114 Columbus (43215) *(G-7321)*
Columbia Gas of Ohio Inc..........440 891-2458
7080 Fry Rd Cleveland (44130) *(G-5372)*
Columbia Gas of Ohio Inc..........419 435-7725
1800 Broad Ave Findlay (45840) *(G-11015)*
Columbia Gas of Ohio Inc..........740 264-5577
300 Luray Dr Steubenville (43953) *(G-17311)*
Columbia Gas of Ohio Inc..........614 481-1000
290 W Nationwide Blvd Columbus (43215) *(G-7322)*
Columbia Gas of Ohio Inc..........419 539-6046
2901 E Manhattan Blvd Toledo (43611) *(G-17820)*
Columbia Gas Transmission LLC (HQ)..........614 460-6000
200 Cizzic Ctr Dr Columbus (43216) *(G-7323)*
Columbia Gas Transmission LLC..........740 397-8242
8484 Columbus Rd Mount Vernon (43050) *(G-14884)*
Columbia Gas Transmission LLC..........614 460-4704
290 W Nationwide Blvd # 114 Columbus (43215) *(G-7324)*
Columbia Gas Transmission LLC..........740 432-1612
11296 E Pike Rd Cambridge (43725) *(G-2105)*
Columbia Gas Transmission LLC..........937 327-7108
2101 W Main St Springfield (45504) *(G-17168)*
Columbia Gas Transmission LLC..........740 892-2552
1608 Homer Rd Nw Homer (43027) *(G-12075)*
Columbia Gulf Transmission LLC..........740 746-9105
6175 Old Logan Rd Sugar Grove (43155) *(G-17540)*
Columbia Hills Country CLB Inc..........440 236-5051
16200 East River Rd Columbia Station (44028) *(G-6844)*
Columbia Mercy Medical Center, Canton *Also called Columbia-Csa/Hs Greater Canton (G-2315)*
Columbia Properties Lima LLC..........419 222-0004
1920 Roschman Ave Lima (45804) *(G-12757)*
Columbia Recreation Assn..........740 849-2466
5960 Fourth St East Fultonham (43735) *(G-10506)*
Columbia Staffing, Cincinnati *Also called Kilgore Group Inc (G-3922)*
Columbia-Csa/Hs Greater Canton..........330 489-1000
1320 Mercy Dr Nw 30 Canton (44708) *(G-2315)*
Columbian Corporation Mantua..........330 274-2576
11845 State Route 44 Mantua (44255) *(G-13385)*
Columbiana Boiler Company LLC..........330 482-3373
200 W Railroad St Columbiana (44408) *(G-6855)*
Columbiana Service Company LLC..........330 482-5511
338 S Main St Columbiana (44408) *(G-6856)*
Columbs/Worthington Htg AC Inc..........614 771-5381
6363 Fiesta Dr Columbus (43235) *(G-7325)*
Columbus & Ohio River RR Co..........740 622-8092
47849 Papermill Rd Coshocton (43812) *(G-9092)*
Columbus AAA Corp..........614 889-2840
2502 Starford Dr Dublin (43016) *(G-10300)*
Columbus Air Center, Columbus *Also called Industrial Air Centers Inc (G-7893)*
Columbus Airport Ltd Partnr..........614 475-7551
1375 N Cassady Ave Columbus (43219) *(G-7326)*
Columbus Airport Marriott, Columbus *Also called Columbus Airport Ltd Partnr (G-7326)*
Columbus Alzheimers Care Ctr..........614 459-7050
700 Jasonway Ave Columbus (43214) *(G-7327)*
Columbus Area..........614 251-6561
899 E Broad St Ste 100 Columbus (43205) *(G-7328)*
Columbus Area Inc..........614 252-0711
1515 E Broad St Columbus (43205) *(G-7329)*
Columbus Area Community, Columbus *Also called Columbus Area Integrated Hoalt (G-7330)*
Columbus Area Integrated Healt (PA)..........614 252-0711
1515 E Broad St Columbus (43205) *(G-7330)*
Columbus Arthritis Center, Columbus *Also called Columbus Medical Rheumatology (G-7367)*
Columbus Asphalt Paving Inc..........614 759-9800
1196 Technology Dr Gahanna (43230) *(G-11235)*
Columbus Association For The P (PA)..........614 469-1045
55 E State St Columbus (43215) *(G-7331)*
Columbus Association For The P..........614 469-0939
39 E State St Columbus (43215) *(G-7332)*
Columbus Bar Association..........614 221-4112
175 S 3rd St Ste 1100 Columbus (43215) *(G-7333)*
Columbus Blue Jackets, Columbus *Also called Colhoc Limited Partnership (G-7318)*
Columbus Bride..........614 888-4567
34 S 3rd St Columbus (43215) *(G-7334)*
Columbus Car Audio & ACC, Columbus *Also called C A E C Inc (G-7173)*
Columbus Cardiology Cons Inc..........614 224-2281
85 Mcnaughten Rd Ste 300 Columbus (43213) *(G-7335)*

A L P H A B E T I C

Columbus Cardiology Cons Inc (PA)....614 224-2281
745 W State St Ste 750 Columbus (43222) *(G-7336)*
Columbus Childrens Hospital, Columbus *Also called Nationwide Childrens Hospital (G-8233)*
Columbus Christian Center Inc (PA)....614 416-9673
2300 N Cassady Ave Columbus (43219) *(G-7337)*
Columbus City Trnsp Div....614 645-3182
1800 E 17th Ave Columbus (43219) *(G-7338)*
Columbus Clny For Elderly Care....614 891-5055
1150 Colony Dr Westerville (43081) *(G-19385)*
Columbus Club Co....614 224-4131
181 E Broad St Columbus (43215) *(G-7339)*
Columbus Coal & Lime Co (PA)....614 224-9241
1150 Sullivant Ave Columbus (43223) *(G-7340)*
Columbus Col-Weld Corporation....614 276-5303
1515 Harrisburg Pike Columbus (43223) *(G-7341)*
Columbus Cold Storage, Columbus *Also called D & D Investment Co (G-7476)*
Columbus Colony Elderly Care, Westerville *Also called Columbus Clny For Elderly Care (G-19385)*
Columbus Concord Ltd Partnr....614 228-3200
35 W Spring St Columbus (43215) *(G-7342)*
Columbus Country Club....614 861-1332
4831 E Broad St Columbus (43213) *(G-7343)*
Columbus Crew, The, Columbus *Also called Columbus Team Soccer LLC (G-7390)*
Columbus Ctr For Humn Svcs Inc (PA)....614 641-2904
540 Industrial Mile Rd Columbus (43228) *(G-7344)*
Columbus Ctr For Humn Svcs Inc....614 245-8180
6227 Harlem Rd New Albany (43054) *(G-14981)*
Columbus Day Care Center....614 269-8980
3389 Westerville Rd Columbus (43224) *(G-7345)*
Columbus Developmental Center, Columbus *Also called Develpmntal Dsblties Ohio Dept (G-7513)*
Columbus Dialysis, Columbus *Also called Columbus-Rna-Davita LLC (G-7395)*
Columbus Diesel Supply Co Inc....614 445-8391
3100 Delta Marine Dr Reynoldsburg (43068) *(G-16439)*
Columbus Dispatch, Lewis Center *Also called Dispatch Printing Company (G-12684)*
Columbus Dispatch The, Columbus *Also called Dispatch Printing Company (G-7524)*
Columbus Distributing Company (PA)....614 846-1000
4949 Freeway Dr E Columbus (43229) *(G-7346)*
Columbus Distributing Company....740 726-2211
6829 Waldo Delaware Rd Waldo (43356) *(G-18782)*
Columbus Division, Etna *Also called Terex Utilities Inc (G-10739)*
Columbus Division, Columbus *Also called Millcraft Paper Company (G-8175)*
Columbus Drywall & Insulation....614 257-0257
876 N 19th St Columbus (43219) *(G-7347)*
Columbus Drywall Inc....614 257-0257
876 N 19th St Columbus (43219) *(G-7348)*
Columbus Drywall Installation, Columbus *Also called Columbus Drywall Inc (G-7348)*
Columbus Easton Hotel LLC....614 414-1000
3999 Easton Loop W Columbus (43219) *(G-7349)*
Columbus Easton Hotel LLC (PA)....614 414-5000
3900 Chagrin Dr Fl 7 Columbus (43219) *(G-7350)*
Columbus Easton Hotel LLC....614 383-2005
3900 Morse Xing Columbus (43219) *(G-7351)*
Columbus Equipment Company (PA)....614 437-0352
2323 Performance Way Columbus (43207) *(G-7352)*
Columbus Equipment Company....513 771-3922
712 Shepherd Ave Cincinnati (45215) *(G-3389)*
Columbus Equipment Company....330 659-6681
3942 Brecksville Rd Richfield (44286) *(G-16502)*
Columbus Equipment Company....614 443-6541
2323 Performance Way Columbus (43207) *(G-7353)*
Columbus Fair Auto Auction Inc....614 497-2000
4700 Groveport Rd Obetz (43207) *(G-15666)*
Columbus Financial Gr....614 785-5100
8425 Pulsar Pl Ste 450 Columbus (43240) *(G-6877)*
Columbus Foundation....614 251-4000
1234 E Broad St Columbus (43205) *(G-7354)*
Columbus Frkln Cnty Pk....614 895-6219
4265 E Dblin Granville Rd Westerville (43081) *(G-19386)*
Columbus Frkln Cnty Pk (PA)....614 891-0700
1069 W Main St Unit B Westerville (43081) *(G-19387)*
Columbus Frkln Cnty Pk....614 891-0700
1775 Darby Creek Dr Galloway (43119) *(G-11342)*
Columbus Frkln Cnty Pk....614 891-0700
1069 W Main St Westerville (43081) *(G-19388)*
Columbus Frkln Cnty Pk....614 861-3193
7309 E Livingston Ave Reynoldsburg (43068) *(G-16440)*
Columbus Frkln Cnty Pk....614 846-9962
9466 Columbus Pike Lewis Center (43035) *(G-12676)*
Columbus GF Division, Lockbourne *Also called Amerisourcebergen Drug Corp (G-12945)*
Columbus Glass Block, Columbus *Also called Cleveland Glass Block Inc (G-7299)*
Columbus Green Cabs Inc (PA)....614 444-4444
1989 Camaro Ave Columbus (43207) *(G-7355)*
Columbus Gstrntrlogy Group Inc....614 457-1213
3820 Olentangy River Rd Columbus (43214) *(G-7356)*
Columbus Healthcare Center, Columbus *Also called Clime Leasing Co LLC (G-7300)*
Columbus Heating & Vent Co....614 274-1177
182 N Yale Ave Columbus (43222) *(G-7357)*
Columbus Hospitality....614 461-2648
775 Yard St Ste 180 Columbus (43212) *(G-7358)*
Columbus Hotel Partners....513 891-1066
4243 Hunt Rd Blue Ash (45242) *(G-1563)*
Columbus Hotel Partnership LLC....614 890-8600
2700 Corporate Exch Dr Columbus (43231) *(G-7359)*
Columbus Housing Partnr Inc....614 221-8889
3443 Agler Rd Ste 200 Columbus (43219) *(G-7360)*
Columbus Idealease West, Columbus *Also called Rush Truck Leasing Inc (G-8660)*
Columbus Infectious Disease, Westerville *Also called Central Ohio Primary Care (G-19380)*
Columbus Jan Healthnet Svcs, Columbus *Also called Clean Innovations (G-7295)*
Columbus Jewish Federation....614 237-7686
1175 College Ave Columbus (43209) *(G-7361)*
Columbus Landmarks Foundation....614 221-0227
57 Jefferson Ave Fl 1 Columbus (43215) *(G-7362)*
Columbus Leasing LLC....614 885-1885
6500 Doubletree Ave Columbus (43229) *(G-7363)*
Columbus Life Insurance Co....513 361-6700
400 E 4th St Cincinnati (45202) *(G-3390)*
Columbus Maennerchor....614 444-3531
976 S High St Columbus (43206) *(G-7364)*
Columbus Med Assn Foundation....614 240-7420
1390 Dublin Rd Columbus (43215) *(G-7365)*
Columbus Medical Association....614 240-7410
1390 Dublin Rd Columbus (43215) *(G-7366)*
Columbus Medical Rheumatology....614 486-5200
1211 Dublin Rd Fl 1 Columbus (43215) *(G-7367)*
Columbus Metro Federal Cr Un....614 239-0210
4000 E Broad St Columbus (43213) *(G-7368)*
Columbus Metro Federal Cr Un (PA)....614 239-0210
4000 E Broad St Columbus (43213) *(G-7369)*
Columbus Montessori Education....614 231-3790
979 S James Rd Columbus (43227) *(G-7370)*
Columbus Motor Speedway Inc....614 491-1047
1882 Timber Haven Ct Grove City (43123) *(G-11547)*
Columbus Municipal Employees (PA)....614 224-8890
365 S 4th St Columbus (43215) *(G-7371)*
Columbus Museum of Art....614 221-6801
480 E Broad St Columbus (43215) *(G-7372)*
Columbus Neighborhood Health C....614 445-0685
1905 Parsons Ave Columbus (43207) *(G-7373)*
Columbus Obgyn, Columbus *Also called Columbus Obsttrcans Gynclgists (G-7374)*
Columbus Obsttrcans Gynclgists (PA)....614 434-2400
750 Mount Carmel Mall # 100 Columbus (43222) *(G-7374)*
Columbus Oh-16 Airport Gahanna....614 501-4770
665 Taylor Rd Gahanna (43230) *(G-11236)*
Columbus Oncology Associates....614 442-3130
810 Jasonway Ave Ste A Columbus (43214) *(G-7375)*
Columbus Peterbilt, Grove City *Also called Esec Corporation (G-11558)*
Columbus Prescr Phrms Inc....614 294-1600
975 Eastwind Dr Ste 155 Westerville (43081) *(G-19389)*
Columbus Pub Schl Vhcl Maint, Columbus *Also called Columbus Public School Dst (G-7376)*
Columbus Public School Dst....614 365-5263
889 E 17th Ave Columbus (43211) *(G-7376)*
Columbus Public School Dst....614 365-5456
2500 N Cassady Ave Columbus (43219) *(G-7377)*
Columbus Public School Dst....614 365-5043
889 E 17th Ave Columbus (43211) *(G-7378)*
Columbus Public School Dst....614 365-5000
450 E Fulton St Columbus (43215) *(G-7379)*
Columbus Public School Dst....614 365-6542
4001 Appian Way Columbus (43230) *(G-7380)*
Columbus Regional Airport Auth....614 239-4000
4760 E 5th Ave Ste G Columbus (43219) *(G-7381)*
Columbus Regional Airport Auth (PA)....614 239-4015
4600 Intl Gtwy Ste 2 Columbus (43219) *(G-7382)*
Columbus Regional Office, Columbus *Also called Rehabltation Corectn Ohio Dept (G-8608)*
Columbus Rhbilitation Subacute, Columbus *Also called Astoria Place Columbus LLC (G-7057)*
Columbus SAI Motors LLC....614 851-3273
1400 Auto Mall Dr Columbus (43228) *(G-7383)*
Columbus Sail and Pwr Squadron....614 384-0245
8492 Cotter St Lewis Center (43035) *(G-12677)*
Columbus Schl Dst Bus Compound, Columbus *Also called Columbus Public School Dst (G-7380)*
Columbus Serum Company (HQ)....614 444-5211
2025 S High St Columbus (43207) *(G-7384)*
Columbus Southern Power Co, Columbus *Also called American Electric Power Co Inc (G-6988)*
Columbus Southern Power Co (HQ)....614 716-1000
1 Riverside Plz Columbus (43215) *(G-7385)*
Columbus Southern Power Co....740 829-2378
47201 County Road 273 Conesville (43811) *(G-9036)*
Columbus Spech Hearing Ctr Cpd....614 263-5151
510 E North Broadway St Columbus (43214) *(G-7386)*
Columbus Square Bowling Palace....614 895-1122
5707 Forest Hills Blvd Columbus (43231) *(G-7387)*
Columbus Steel Erectors Inc....614 876-5050
1700 Walcutt Rd Columbus (43228) *(G-7388)*

Columbus Surgical Center LLP......614 932-9503
5005 Parkcenter Ave Dublin (43017) *(G-10301)*
Columbus Symphony Orchestra......614 228-9600
55 E State St Fl 5 Columbus (43215) *(G-7389)*
Columbus Team Soccer LLC (PA)......614 447-1301
1 Black And Gold Blvd Columbus (43211) *(G-7390)*
Columbus Urban League Inc......614 257-6300
788 Mount Vernon Ave Columbus (43203) *(G-7391)*
Columbus Vtrinary Emrgncy Svcs......614 846-5800
300 E Wilson Bridge Rd Worthington (43085) *(G-19948)*
Columbus W Hlth Care Co Partnr......614 274-4005
2731 Clime Rd Columbus (43223) *(G-7392)*
Columbus W Hlth Care Co Partnr (PA)......614 274-4222
1700 Heinzerling Dr Columbus (43223) *(G-7393)*
Columbus West Pk Nursing & Reh, Columbus *Also called Columbus W Hlth Care Co Partnr (G-7393)*
Columbus Window Cleaning Co, Columbus *Also called E Wynn Inc (G-7562)*
Columbus Worthington Hospitali......614 885-3334
175 Hutchinson Ave Columbus (43235) *(G-7394)*
COLUMBUS ZOO AND AQUARIUM, Powell *Also called Columbus Zoological Park Assn (G-16330)*
Columbus Zoological Park Assn (PA)......614 645-3400
5220 Powell Rd Powell (43065) *(G-16330)*
Columbus-Gatehouse Inn, Columbus *Also called Island Hospitality MGT LLC (G-7927)*
Columbus-Rna-Davita LLC......614 985-1732
226 Graceland Blvd Columbus (43214) *(G-7395)*
Columbus/Worthington Htg & AC, Columbus *Also called Columbs/Worthington Htg AC Inc (G-7325)*
Com Net Inc......419 739-3100
13888 County Road 25a Wapakoneta (45895) *(G-18792)*
Combined Insurance Co Amer......614 210-6209
150 E Campus View Blvd # 230 Columbus (43235) *(G-7396)*
Combs Interior Specialties Inc......937 879-2047
475 W Funderburg Rd Fairborn (45324) *(G-10787)*
Comcast Cble Cmmunications LLC......503 372-9144
100 Welday Ave Ste A Steubenville (43953) *(G-17312)*
Comcast Corporation......740 633-3437
908 National Rd Bridgeport (43912) *(G-1861)*
Comcast Corporation......419 586-1458
812 N Main St Celina (45822) *(G-2640)*
Comcast Spotlight......440 617-2280
27887 Clemens Rd Ste 3 Westlake (44145) *(G-19478)*
Comcast Spotlight Inc......216 575-8016
3300 Lakeside Ave E Cleveland (44114) *(G-5373)*
Comdoc Inc (HQ)......330 896-2346
3458 Massillon Rd Uniontown (44685) *(G-18514)*
Comdoc Inc......330 539-4822
6790 Belmont Ave Girard (44420) *(G-11410)*
Comenity Servicing LLC......614 729-4000
3095 Loyalty Cir Columbus (43219) *(G-7397)*
Comex Group, Cleveland *Also called Comex North America Inc (G-5374)*
Comex North America Inc (HQ)......303 307-2100
101 W Prospect Ave # 1020 Cleveland (44115) *(G-5374)*
Comey & Shepherd LLC......513 489-2100
7870 E Kemper Rd Ste 100 Cincinnati (45249) *(G-3391)*
Comey & Shepherd LLC (PA)......513 561-5800
6901 Wooster Pike Cincinnati (45227) *(G-3392)*
Comey & Shepherd LLC......513 321-4343
2716 Observatory Ave Cincinnati (45208) *(G-3393)*
Comey & Shepherd LLC......513 231-2800
7333 Beechmont Ave Cincinnati (45230) *(G-3394)*
Comey & Shepherd LLC......513 891-4444
9857 Montgomery Rd Cincinnati (45242) *(G-3395)*
Comey & Shepherd Realtors, Cincinnati *Also called Comey & Shepherd LLC (G-3392)*
Comey Shepherd Realtors Cy Off, Cincinnati *Also called Sweeney Team Inc (G-4606)*
Comforcare Senior Services Inc......513 777-4860
7419 Kingsgate Way West Chester (45069) *(G-19048)*
Comfort Air, Cleveland *Also called Air Comfort Systems Inc (G-4971)*
Comfort Distributors, Cincinnati *Also called Schibi Heating & Cooling Corp (G-4481)*
Comfort Healthcare......216 281-9999
8310 Detroit Ave Cleveland (44102) *(G-5375)*
Comfort Inn, Oxford *Also called Oxford Hospitality Group Inc (G-15828)*
Comfort Inn, Mentor *Also called Alliance Hospitality Inc (G-14141)*
Comfort Inn, Chillicothe *Also called Chillicothe Motel LLC (G-2822)*
Comfort Inn, Piqua *Also called M&C Hotel Interests Inc (G-16151)*
Comfort Inn, Oregon *Also called Northtown Square Ltd Partnr (G-15742)*
Comfort Inn, Seville *Also called Son-Rise Hotels Inc (G-16846)*
Comfort Inn, Cleveland *Also called Peitro Properties Ltd Partnr (G-6260)*
Comfort Inn, Bellville *Also called Valleyview Management Co Inc (G-1426)*
Comfort Inn, Canton *Also called Canton Hotel Holdings Inc (G-2289)*
Comfort Inn, Cleveland *Also called Boulevard Motel Corp (G-5130)*
Comfort Inn......740 454-4144
500 Monroe St Zanesville (43701) *(G-20466)*
Comfort Inn Northeast......513 683-9700
9011 Fields Ertel Rd Cincinnati (45249) *(G-3396)*
Comfort Inns......614 885-4084
1213 E Dblin Granville Rd Columbus (43229) *(G-7398)*
Comfort Keepers, Toledo *Also called Tky Associates LLC (G-18221)*
Comfort Keepers, Cincinnati *Also called C K of Cincinnati Inc (G-3161)*
Comfort Keepers, Hilliard *Also called Quality Life Providers LLC (G-11946)*
Comfort Keepers, Hamilton *Also called Karopa Incorporate (G-11749)*
Comfort Keepers, Springfield *Also called Sdx Home Care Operations LLC (G-17271)*
Comfort Keepers......419 229-1031
1726 Allentown Rd Lima (45805) *(G-12758)*
Comfort Keepers......440 721-0100
368 Blackbrook Rd Painesville (44077) *(G-15844)*
Comfort Keepers Inc......937 322-6288
101 N Fountain Ave Springfield (45502) *(G-17169)*
Comfort Systems USA Ohio Inc (HQ)......440 703-1600
7401 First Pl Ste A Bedford (44146) *(G-1300)*
Comm Ltd Care Dialysis Center......513 784-1800
2109 Reading Rd Cincinnati (45202) *(G-3397)*
Command Alkon Incorporated......614 799-0600
6750 Crosby Ct Dublin (43016) *(G-10302)*
Command Carpet......330 673-7404
1976 Tallmadge Rd Kent (44240) *(G-12361)*
Command Roofing Co......937 298-1155
2485 Arbor Blvd Moraine (45439) *(G-14760)*
Commerce Holdings Inc......513 579-1950
312 Elm St Ste 1150 Cincinnati (45202) *(G-3398)*
Commerce Paper Company......419 241-9101
302 S Byrne Rd Bldg 200 Toledo (43615) *(G-17821)*
Commerce Title Agcy Youngstown......330 743-1171
201 E Commerce St Youngstown (44503) *(G-20147)*
Commercial Cleaning Solutions......937 981-4870
10965 State Route 138 Sw Greenfield (45123) *(G-11483)*
Commercial Comfort Systems Inc......419 481-4444
26610 Eckel Rd Ste 3a Perrysburg (43551) *(G-15988)*
Commercial Debt Cunseling Corp......614 848-9800
445 Hutchinson Ave # 500 Columbus (43235) *(G-7399)*
Commercial Drivers, North Royalton *Also called D C Transportation Service (G-15485)*
Commercial Electric Pdts Corp (PA)......216 241-2886
1821 E 40th St Cleveland (44103) *(G-5376)*
Commercial Electronics Inc......740 281-0180
1294 N 21st St Newark (43055) *(G-15157)*
Commercial Hvac Inc......513 396-6100
5240 Lester Rd Ste 200 Cincinnati (45213) *(G-3399)*
Commercial Interior Products, West Chester *Also called CIP International Inc (G-19041)*
Commercial Maintenance & Repr, Akron *Also called Ohio Maint & Renovation Inc (G-367)*
Commercial Painting Inc......614 298-9963
530 Lkview Plz Blvd Ste F Worthington (43085) *(G-19949)*
Commercial Parts & Ser......614 221-0057
5033 Transamerica Dr Columbus (43228) *(G-7400)*
Commercial Radiator, Columbus *Also called Skinner Diesel Services Inc (G-8741)*
Commercial Svgs Bank Millersbu (HQ)......330 674-9015
91 N Clay St Millersburg (44654) *(G-14595)*
Commercial Time Sharing Inc......330 644-3059
2740 Cory Ave Akron (44314) *(G-152)*
Commercial Traffic Company (PA)......216 267-2000
12487 Plaza Dr Cleveland (44130) *(G-5377)*
Commercial Traffic Company......216 267-2000
12487 Plaza Dr Cleveland (44130) *(G-5378)*
Commercial Truck & Trailer......330 545-9717
313 N State St Girard (44420) *(G-11411)*
Commercial Truck & Trlr Parts, Girard *Also called Commercial Truck & Trailer (G-11411)*
Commercial Warehouse & Cartage......614 409-3901
6295 Commerce Center Dr Groveport (43125) *(G-11629)*
Commission On Partransit, North Olmsted *Also called City of North Olmsted (G-15415)*
Committed To Care Inc......513 245-1190
155 Tri County Pkwy # 220 Cincinnati (45246) *(G-3400)*
Commodore Denig Post No 83......419 625-3274
3615 Hayes Ave Sandusky (44870) *(G-16743)*
Commodore Motel, Port Clinton *Also called Commodore Resorts Inc (G-16241)*
Commodore Prry Inns Suites LLC......419 732-2645
255 W Lakeshore Dr Port Clinton (43452) *(G-16240)*
Commodore Resorts Inc......419 285-3101
255 W Lakeshore Dr Port Clinton (43452) *(G-16241)*
Commons of Providence......419 624-1171
5000 Providence Dr Ste 1 Sandusky (44870) *(G-16744)*
Commonwealth Financial Svcs (PA)......440 449-7709
26451 Curtiss Wright Pkwy Cleveland (44143) *(G-5379)*
Commonwealth Hotels LLC......216 524-5814
5800 Rockside Woods Blvd Cleveland (44131) *(G-5380)*
Commonwealth Hotels LLC......614 790-9000
5100 Upper Metro Pl Dublin (43017) *(G-10303)*
Commquest Services Inc......330 455-0374
625 Cleveland Ave Nw Canton (44702) *(G-2316)*
Commsys Inc......937 220-4990
3055 Kettering Blvd # 415 Moraine (45439) *(G-14761)*
Commu Act Comm of Fayette Cnty (PA)......740 335-7282
1400 Us Highway 22 Nw Wshngtn CT Hs (43160) *(G-20016)*
Commun Mer OCC Healh & Medici, Springfield *Also called Mercy Health (G-17239)*
Communi Care Inc......419 382-2200
955 Garden Lake Pkwy Toledo (43614) *(G-17822)*
Communica Inc (PA)......419 244-7766
31 N Erie St Toledo (43604) *(G-17823)*
Communicare, Akron *Also called Pebble Creek Cnvlscnt Ctr (G-379)*
Communicare Family of Company, Blue Ash *Also called Health Care Facility MGT LLC (G-1608)*

ALPHABETIC

Communicare Health Services, Deshler *Also called East Water Leasing Co LLC (G-10169)*
Communicare Health Svcs Inc....440 234-0454
49 Sheldon Rd Berea (44017) *(G-1453)*
Communicare Health Svcs Inc....330 726-3700
8064 South Ave Youngstown (44512) *(G-20148)*
Communicare Health Svcs Inc....419 485-8307
924 Charlies Way Montpelier (43543) *(G-14740)*
Communicare Health Svcs Inc....330 792-7799
650 S Meridian Rd Youngstown (44509) *(G-20149)*
Communicare Health Svcs Inc....419 394-7611
1209 Indiana Ave Saint Marys (45885) *(G-16672)*
Communicare Health Svcs Inc....330 454-6508
3015 17th St Nw Canton (44708) *(G-2317)*
Communicare Health Svcs Inc....937 399-9217
2317 E Home Rd Springfield (45503) *(G-17170)*
Communicare Health Svcs Inc....330 792-5511
2958 Canfield Rd Youngstown (44511) *(G-20150)*
Communicare Health Svcs Inc....877 366-5306
135 Reichart Ave Wintersville (43953) *(G-19809)*
Communicare Health Svcs Inc....330 454-2152
1223 Market Ave N Canton (44714) *(G-2318)*
Communicare Health Svcs Inc (PA)....513 530-1654
4700 Ashwood Dr Ste 200 Blue Ash (45241) *(G-1564)*
Communicare Health Svcs Inc....740 264-1155
135 Reichart Ave Steubenville (43953) *(G-17313)*
Communicare Health Svcs Inc....330 630-9780
563 Colony Park Dr Tallmadge (44278) *(G-17635)*
Communicare of Clifton, Cincinnati *Also called Clifton Care Center Inc (G-3365)*
Communication Options Inc (HQ)....614 901-7095
4689 Reynoldsburg New Alb New Albany (43054) *(G-14982)*
Communication Svc For Deaf Inc....937 299-0917
2448 W Dorothy Ln Moraine (45439) *(G-14762)*
Communication Svcs For Deaf, Moraine *Also called Communication Svc For Deaf Inc (G-14762)*
Communications III Inc (PA)....614 901-7720
921 Eastwind Dr Ste 104 Westerville (43081) *(G-19390)*
Communications Supply Corp....330 208-1900
4741 Hinckley Indus Pkwy Cleveland (44109) *(G-5381)*
Communiction/Journalism, Columbus *Also called Ohio State University (G-8416)*
Communities In Schools....614 268-2472
510 E North Broadway St Columbus (43214) *(G-7401)*
Community & Rural Health Svcs (PA)....419 334-8943
2221 Hayes Ave Fremont (43420) *(G-11188)*
Community Action, Lisbon *Also called County of Columbiana (G-12934)*
Community Action (PA)....740 354-7541
433 3rd St Portsmouth (45662) *(G-16271)*
Community Action Against Addic....216 881-0765
5209 Euclid Ave Cleveland (44103) *(G-5382)*
Community Action Columbiana CT (PA)....330 424-7221
7880 Lincole Pl Lisbon (44432) *(G-12932)*
Community Action Columbiana CT....330 385-7251
134 E 4th St East Liverpool (43920) *(G-10518)*
Community Action Comm Blmont C, Saint Clairsville *Also called Community Action Comsn Belmont (G-16632)*
Community Action Comm Pike CNT (PA)....740 289-2371
941 Market St Piketon (45661) *(G-16112)*
Community Action Comm Pike CNT....740 961-4011
621 Broadway St Portsmouth (45662) *(G-16272)*
Community Action Comm Pike CNT....740 286-2826
14590 State Route 93 Jackson (45640) *(G-12310)*
Community Action Comm Pike CNT....740 947-7726
227 Valley View Dr Waverly (45690) *(G-18970)*
Community Action Commission, Findlay *Also called Hancock Hardin Wyandot Putnam (G-11042)*
Community Action Commission (PA)....419 626-6540
908 Seavers Way Sandusky (44870) *(G-16745)*
Community Action Comsn Belmont (PA)....740 695-0293
153 1/2 W Main St Saint Clairsville (43950) *(G-16632)*
Community Action Comsn Belmont....740 676-0800
4129 Noble St Bellaire (43906) *(G-1364)*
Community Action Program Comm (PA)....740 653-1711
1743 E Main St Lancaster (43130) *(G-12521)*
Community Action Program Corp (PA)....740 373-3745
218 Putnam St Marietta (45750) *(G-13436)*
Community Action Program Corp....740 373-6016
205 Phillips St Marietta (45750) *(G-13437)*
Community Action Program Inc....937 382-0225
789 N Nelson Ave Wilmington (45177) *(G-19755)*
Community Action-Wayne/Medina (PA)....330 264-8677
905 Pittsburg Ave Wooster (44691) *(G-19851)*
Community Ambulance Service....740 454-6800
952 Linden Ave Zanesville (43701) *(G-20467)*
Community Assesment and Treatm (PA)....216 441-0200
8411 Broadway Ave Cleveland (44105) *(G-5383)*
Community Assisted Living Inc....740 653-2575
500 N Pierce Ave Lancaster (43130) *(G-12522)*
Community Behavioral Hlth Ctr, Cleveland *Also called Chattree and Associates Inc (G-5231)*
Community Behavioral Hlth Inc....513 887-8500
824 S Martin Luther King Hamilton (45011) *(G-11716)*
Community Care Amblance Netwrk (PA)....440 992-1401
115 E 24th St Ashtabula (44004) *(G-735)*
Community Care Hospice....937 382-5400
1669 Rombach Ave Wilmington (45177) *(G-19756)*
Community Caregivers....330 725-9800
230 Quadral Dr Ste D Wadsworth (44281) *(G-18750)*
Community Caregivers....330 533-3427
888 Boardman Canfield Rd D Youngstown (44512) *(G-20151)*
Community Center, Athens *Also called Parks Recreation Athens (G-810)*
Community Center....330 746-7721
1344 5th Ave Youngstown (44504) *(G-20152)*
Community Choice Financial Inc....440 602-9922
34302 Euclid Ave Unit 7 Willoughby (44094) *(G-19655)*
Community Choice Financial Inc (PA)....614 798-5900
6785 Bobcat Way Ste 200 Dublin (43016) *(G-10304)*
Community Choice Home Care....740 574-9900
7318 Ohio River Rd Wheelersburg (45694) *(G-19574)*
Community Concepts & Options, Mason *Also called Community Concepts Inc (G-13687)*
Community Concepts Inc (PA)....513 398-8181
6699 Tri Way Dr Mason (45040) *(G-13687)*
Community Correctional Center, Lebanon *Also called Talbert House (G-12652)*
Community Counseling Services....419 468-8211
2458 Stetzer Rd Bucyrus (44820) *(G-2031)*
Community Counslng Ctr Ashtabu (PA)....440 998-4210
2801 C Ct Unit 2 Ashtabula (44004) *(G-736)*
Community Crime Patrol....614 247-1765
248 E 11th Ave Columbus (43201) *(G-7402)*
Community Dev For All People....614 445-7342
946 Parsons Ave Columbus (43206) *(G-7403)*
Community Dialysis Center....216 229-6170
11717 Euclid Ave Cleveland (44106) *(G-5384)*
Community Dialysis Ctr Mentor....440 255-5999
8900 Tyler Blvd Mentor (44060) *(G-14161)*
Community Drug Board Inc (PA)....330 315-5590
725 E Market St Akron (44305) *(G-153)*
Community Drug Board Inc....330 996-5114
380 S Portage Path Akron (44320) *(G-154)*
Community Education Ctrs Inc....330 424-4065
8473 County Home Rd Lisbon (44432) *(G-12933)*
Community Employment Services, Newark *Also called Licking County Board of Mrdd (G-15188)*
Community Emplyment Svcs WD Ln, Bowling Green *Also called Wood County Ohio (G-1804)*
Community Emrgcy Med Svcs Ohio....614 751-6651
3699 Paragon Dr Columbus (43228) *(G-7404)*
Community Hbilitation Svcs Inc (PA)....234 334-4288
493 Canton Rd Akron (44312) *(G-155)*
Community Health Centers Ohio....216 831-1494
3355 Richmond Rd Ste 225a Beachwood (44122) *(G-1067)*
Community Health Partners Regi (HQ)....440 960-4000
3700 Kolbe Rd Lorain (44053) *(G-13029)*
Community Health Ptnrs Reg Fou (HQ)....440 960-4000
3700 Kolbe Rd Lorain (44053) *(G-13030)*
Community Health Systems Inc....330 841-9011
1350 E Market St Warren (44483) *(G-18836)*
Community Hlth Prfssionals Inc....419 634-7443
1200 S Main St Ada (45810) *(G-4)*
Community Hlth Prfssionals Inc....419 445-5128
230 Westfield Dr Archbold (43502) *(G-634)*
Community Hlth Prfssionals Inc (PA)....419 238-9223
1159 Westwood Dr Van Wert (45891) *(G-18630)*
Community Hlth Prfssionals Inc....419 399-4708
250 Dooley Dr Ste A Paulding (45879) *(G-15928)*
Community Hlth Prfssionals Inc....419 991-1822
3719 Shawnee Rd Lima (45806) *(G-12926)*
Community Hlth Prfssionals Inc....419 586-1999
816 Pro Dr Celina (45822) *(G-2641)*
Community Hlth Prfssionals Inc....419 586-6266
816 Pro Dr Celina (45822) *(G-2642)*
Community Hlth Prfssionals Inc....419 695-8101
602 E 5th St Delphos (45833) *(G-10139)*
Community Hlth Ptnr Reg Hlth S....440 960-4000
3700 Kolbe Rd Lorain (44053) *(G-13031)*
Community Hlth Svcs Dntl Clnic, Fremont *Also called Community & Rural Health Svcs (G-11188)*
Community Home Care....330 971-7011
1900 23rd St Cuyahoga Falls (44223) *(G-9177)*
Community Home Health, Austintown *Also called Chcc Home Health Care (G-869)*
Community Hosp Schl Nursing, Springfield *Also called Community Hospital Springfield (G-17171)*
COMMUNITY HOSPICE, New Philadelphia *Also called Hospice Tuscarawas County Inc (G-15101)*
Community Hospital of Bedford....440 735-3900
44 Blaine Ave Bedford (44146) *(G-1301)*
Community Hospital Springfield (PA)....937 325-0531
100 Medical Center Dr Springfield (45504) *(G-17171)*
Community Hsing Netwrk Dev Co....614 487-6700
1680 Watermark Dr Columbus (43215) *(G-7405)*
Community Hsptals Wllness Ctrs....419 485-3154
909 E Snyder Ave Montpelier (43543) *(G-14741)*
Community Hsptals Wllness Ctrs....419 445-2015
121 Westfield Dr Ste 1 Archbold (43502) *(G-635)*

Community Hsptals Wllness Ctrs (PA)..........419 636-1131
433 W High St Bryan (43506) *(G-2004)*
Community Improvement Corp..........440 466-4675
44 N Forest St Geneva (44041) *(G-11360)*
Community Imprv Corp Nble Cnty..........740 509-0248
44523 Marietta Rd Caldwell (43724) *(G-2083)*
Community Insurance Company..........859 282-7888
1351 Wm Howard Taft Cincinnati (45206) *(G-3401)*
Community Invstors Bancorp Inc..........419 562-7055
119 S Sandusky Ave Bucyrus (44820) *(G-2032)*
Community Isp Inc..........419 867-6060
3035 Moffat Rd Toledo (43615) *(G-17824)*
Community Legal Aid Services..........330 725-1231
120 W Washington St 2c Medina (44256) *(G-14049)*
Community Legal Aid Services (PA)..........330 535-4191
50 S Main St Ste 800 Akron (44308) *(G-156)*
Community Living Experiences..........614 588-0320
2939 Donnylane Blvd Columbus (43235) *(G-7406)*
Community Medical Center, Celina *Also called Mercer Cnty Joint Townshp Hosp (G-2654)*
Community Medicine, Columbus *Also called Ohiohealth Corporation (G-8454)*
Community Memorial Hospital (PA)..........419 542-6692
208 Columbus St Hicksville (43526) *(G-11862)*
Community Mental Health Svc (PA)..........740 695-9344
68353 Bannock Rd Saint Clairsville (43950) *(G-16633)*
Community Mental Health Svcs, Saint Clairsville *Also called Community Mental Health Svc (G-16633)*
Community Mental Healthcare (PA)..........330 343-1811
201 Hospital Dr Dover (44622) *(G-10181)*
Community Mercy Foundation..........937 278-8211
235 W Orchard Springs Dr Dayton (45415) *(G-9418)*
Community Mercy Foundation..........937 390-9000
1500 Villa Rd Springfield (45503) *(G-17172)*
Community Mercy Foundation..........937 328-8134
1 S Limestone St Ste 700 Springfield (45502) *(G-17173)*
Community Mercy Foundation..........937 274-1569
6125 N Main St Dayton (45415) *(G-9419)*
Community Mercy Foundation (HQ)..........937 328-7000
1 S Limestone St Ste 700 Springfield (45502) *(G-17174)*
Community Mercy Foundation..........937 652-3645
904 Scioto St Urbana (43078) *(G-18582)*
Community Mercy Hlth Partners, Springfield *Also called Community Mercy Foundation (G-17173)*
Community Mercy Hlth Partners..........937 653-5432
906 Scioto St Urbana (43078) *(G-18583)*
Community Mercy Hlth Partners (HQ)..........937 523-6670
100 Medical Center Dr Springfield (45504) *(G-17175)*
COMMUNITY NETWORK THE, Xenia *Also called Tcn Behavioral Health Svcs Inc (G-20077)*
Community Prpts Ohio III LLC..........614 253-0984
42 N 17th St Columbus (43203) *(G-7407)*
Community Prpts Ohio MGT Svcs..........614 253-0984
910 E Broad St Columbus (43205) *(G-7408)*
Community Re-Entry Inc..........216 696-2717
4515 Superior Ave Cleveland (44103) *(G-5385)*
Community Refugee & Immigation..........614 235-5747
1925 E Dublin Granville R Columbus (43229) *(G-7409)*
Community Services Inc..........937 667-8631
3 E Main St Tipp City (45371) *(G-17714)*
COMMUNITY SERVICES OF STARK CO, Canton *Also called Commquest Services Inc (G-2316)*
Community Shelter Board..........614 221-9195
111 Liberty St Ste 150 Columbus (43215) *(G-7410)*
Community Skilled Health Care..........330 373-1160
1320 Mahoning Ave Nw Warren (44483) *(G-18837)*
Community Solutions Assn..........330 394-9090
320 High St Ne Warren (44481) *(G-18838)*
Community Srgl Sply Toms Rvr..........614 307-2975
3823 Twin Creeks Dr Columbus (43204) *(G-7411)*
Community Srgl Sply Toms Rvr..........216 475-8440
14500 Broadway Ave Cleveland (44125) *(G-5386)*
Community Support Services Inc (PA)..........330 253-9388
150 Cross St Akron (44311) *(G-157)*
Community Support Services Inc..........330 253-9675
150 Cross St Akron (44311) *(G-158)*
Community Support Services Inc..........330 733-6203
403 Canton Rd Akron (44312) *(G-159)*
Community Supports Services, Fairfield *Also called Butler County Board of Develop (G-10826)*
Community Mntl Hlth Ctr (PA)..........513 228-7800
975 Kingsview Dr Lebanon (45036) *(G-12596)*
Commutair, North Olmsted *Also called Champlain Enterprises LLC (G-15413)*
Como Inc..........614 830-2666
8670 Hill Rd S Pickerington (43147) *(G-16092)*
Compak Inc..........419 207-8888
605 Westlake Dr Ashland (44805) *(G-675)*
Companions of Ashland LLC (PA)..........419 281-2273
1241 E Main St Ashland (44805) *(G-676)*
Company Inc..........216 431-2334
4125 Payne Ave Cleveland (44103) *(G-5387)*
Compass, Toledo *Also called Comprehensive Addiction Svc Sy (G-17826)*
Compass Community Health..........740 355-7102
1634 11th St Portsmouth (45662) *(G-16273)*
Compass Construction Inc..........614 761-7800
7670 Fishel Dr S Dublin (43016) *(G-10305)*
Compass Corp For Recovery Svcs..........419 241-8827
2005 Ashland Ave Toledo (43620) *(G-17825)*
Compass Family and Cmnty Svcs (PA)..........330 743-9275
535 Marmion Ave Youngstown (44502) *(G-20153)*
Compass Family and Cmnty Svcs..........330 743-9275
284 Broadway Ave Youngstown (44504) *(G-20154)*
Compass Health Brands Corp (PA)..........800 947-1728
6753 Engle Rd Ste A Middleburg Heights (44130) *(G-14380)*
Compass Packaging LLC..........330 274-2001
10585 Main St Mantua (44255) *(G-13386)*
Compass Self Storage LLC (PA)..........216 458-0670
20445 Emerald Pkwy Cleveland (44135) *(G-5388)*
Compass Systems & Sales LLC..........330 733-2111
5185 New Haven Cir Norton (44203) *(G-15555)*
Compassionate In Home Care..........614 888-5683
7100 N High St Ste 200 Worthington (43085) *(G-19950)*
Compco Land Company (HQ)..........330 482-0200
85 E Hylda Ave Youngstown (44507) *(G-20155)*
Compdrug (PA)..........614 224-4506
547 E 11th Ave Columbus (43211) *(G-7412)*
Compel Fitness LLC..........216 965-5694
10711 Princeton Pike Ste 341 Cincinnati (45246) *(G-3402)*
Compensation Programs of Ohio..........330 652-9821
33 Fitch Blvd Youngstown (44515) *(G-20156)*
Competitive Interiors Inc..........330 297-1281
625 Enterprise Pkwy Ravenna (44266) *(G-16378)*
Competitive Transportation..........419 529-5300
7086 State Route 546 Bellville (44813) *(G-1422)*
Competitor Swim Products Inc..........800 888-7946
5310 Career Ct Columbus (43213) *(G-7413)*
Complements, Cleveland *Also called Amerimark Holdings LLC (G-5025)*
Complete Building Maint LLC..........513 235-7511
3629 Wabash Ave Cincinnati (45207) *(G-3403)*
Complete General Cnstr Co (PA)..........614 258-9515
1221 E 5th Ave Columbus (43219) *(G-7414)*
Complete Home Care, Massillon *Also called Health Services Inc (G-13818)*
Complete Mechanical Svcs LLC..........513 489-3080
11399 Grooms Rd Blue Ash (45242) *(G-1565)*
Complete Qlty Trnsp Sltons LLC..........513 914-4882
3055 Blue Rock Rd Ste T Cincinnati (45239) *(G-3404)*
Complete Services Inc (PA)..........513 770-5575
6345 Castle Dr Mason (45040) *(G-13688)*
Compliance Testing, Ravenna *Also called Smithers Rapra Inc (G-16413)*
Compliant Healthcare Tech LLC (PA)..........216 255-9607
7123 Pearl Rd Ste 305 Cleveland (44130) *(G-5389)*
Compmanagement Inc (HQ)..........614 376-5300
6377 Emerald Pkwy Dublin (43016) *(G-10306)*
Compmanagement Health Systems..........614 766-5223
6377 Emerald Pkwy Dublin (43016) *(G-10307)*
Composite Tech Amer Inc..........330 562-5201
25201 Chagrin Blvd # 360 Cleveland (44122) *(G-5390)*
Comprehensive Addiction Svc Sy..........419 241-8827
2005 Ashland Ave Toledo (43620) *(G-17826)*
Comprehensive Behavioral Hlth (PA)..........330 797-4050
104 Javit Ct Ste A Youngstown (44515) *(G-20157)*
Comprehensive Cmnty Child Care (PA)..........513 221-0033
2100 Sherman Ave Ste 300 Cincinnati (45212) *(G-3405)*
Comprehensive Counseling Svc..........513 424-0921
1659 S Breiel Blvd Ste A Middletown (45044) *(G-14422)*
Comprehensive Health Care (HQ)..........440 329-7500
630 E River St Elyria (44035) *(G-10607)*
Comprehensive Health Care Inc..........419 238-7777
140 Fox Rd Ste 402 Van Wert (45891) *(G-18631)*
Comprehensive Health Care Svcs, Cincinnati *Also called Comprehensive Health Care Svcs (G-3406)*
Comprehensive Health Care Svcs..........513 245-0100
4580 Springdale Rd Cincinnati (45251) *(G-3406)*
Comprehensive Logistics Co Inc..........330 233-0805
5520 Chevrolet Blvd Parma (44130) *(G-15902)*
Comprehensive Logistics Co Inc..........440 934-0870
5401 Baumhart Rd Lorain (44053) *(G-13032)*
Comprehensive Logistics Co Inc..........330 793-0504
365 Victoria Rd Youngstown (44515) *(G-20158)*
Comprehensive Logistics Co Inc..........330 233-2627
1200 Chester Indus Pkwy Avon Lake (44012) *(G-927)*
Comprehensive Logistics Co Inc (PA)..........800 734-0372
4944 Belmont Ave Ste 202 Youngstown (44505) *(G-20159)*
Comprehensive Managed Care Sys..........513 533-0021
3380 Erie Ave Cincinnati (45208) *(G-3407)*
Comprehensive Med Data MGT LLC..........614 717-9840
9980 Brewster Ln Ste 100 Powell (43065) *(G-16331)*
Comprehensive Pediatrics..........440 835-8270
2001 Crocker Rd Ste 600 Westlake (44145) *(G-19479)*
Comprehensive Services Inc..........614 442-0664
1555 Bethel Rd Columbus (43220) *(G-7415)*
Comprensive Health Network, Greenville *Also called CHN Inc - Adult Day Care (G-11493)*
Comprhensive Cardiologist Cons..........513 936-9191
4760 E Galbraith Rd # 212 Cincinnati (45236) *(G-3408)*
Comprhnsive Care Orthpdics Inc..........419 473-9500
4126 N Hlland Sylvania Rd Toledo (43623) *(G-17827)*

Comproducts Inc (PA) 614 276-5552
1740 Harmon Ave Ste F Columbus (43223) *(G-7416)*
Comptech Computer Tech Inc 937 228-2667
7777 Washington Village D Dayton (45459) *(G-9420)*
Compton Metal Products Inc 937 382-2403
416 Steele Rd Wilmington (45177) *(G-19757)*
Compunet Clinical Labs, Moraine Also called Compunet Clinical Labs LLC *(G-14763)*
Compunet Clinical Labs LLC 937 427-2655
75 Sylvania Dr Beavercreek (45440) *(G-1234)*
Compunet Clinical Labs LLC 937 342-0015
2100 Emmanuel Way Ste C Springfield (45502) *(G-17176)*
Compunet Clinical Labs LLC (HQ) 937 296-0844
2308 Sandridge Dr Moraine (45439) *(G-14763)*
Compunet Clinical Labs LLC 937 208-3555
2508 Sandride Dr Dayton (45439) *(G-9421)*
Computer Helper Publishing 614 939-9094
450 Beecher Rd Columbus (43230) *(G-7417)*
Computer Sciences Corporation 937 904-5113
2435 5th St Bldg 676 Dayton (45433) *(G-9262)*
Computer Sciences Corporation 614 801-2343
3940 Gantz Rd Ste F Grove City (43123) *(G-11548)*
Computer Services, Athens Also called Ohio University *(G-804)*
Computer Solutions, Youngstown Also called GBS Corp *(G-20197)*
Computers Universal Inc 614 543-0473
2850 Presidential Dr # 150 Beavercreek (45324) *(G-1162)*
Comresource Inc 614 221-6348
1159 Dublin Rd Ste 200 Columbus (43215) *(G-7418)*
Coms Interactive, Broadview Heights Also called Clinicl Otcms Mngmnt Syst LLC *(G-1875)*
Comtech Global Inc 614 796-1148
355 E Campus View Blvd # 195 Columbus (43235) *(G-7419)*
COMTEX, Columbus Also called Central Ohio Medical Textiles *(G-7231)*
Comtron Professional Cons, Reynoldsburg Also called Kristi Britton *(G-16464)*
Comunibanc Corp (PA) 419 599-1065
122 E Washington St Napoleon (43545) *(G-14936)*
Con-AG, Saint Marys Also called Conag Inc *(G-16673)*
Conag Inc 419 394-8870
16672 County Road 66a Saint Marys (45885) *(G-16673)*
Concept Freight Service Inc 330 784-1134
4386 Point Comfort Dr New Franklin (44319) *(G-15043)*
Concept Rehab Inc (PA) 419 843-6002
7150 Granite Cir Ste 200 Toledo (43617) *(G-17828)*
Concepts In Community Living (PA) 740 393-0055
700 Wooster Rd Mount Vernon (43050) *(G-14885)*
Conci, Columbus Also called Central Ohio Nutrition Center *(G-7232)*
Concord 614 882-9338
700 Brooksedge Blvd Westerville (43081) *(G-19391)*
Concord Biosciences LLC 440 357-3200
10845 Wellness Way Painesville (44077) *(G-15845)*
Concord Care Center Cortland, Cortland Also called Continent Hlth Co Cortland LLC *(G-9075)*
Concord Care Center of Toledo 419 385-6616
3121 Glanzman Rd Toledo (43614) *(G-17829)*
CONCORD COUNSELING SERVICES, Westerville Also called Concord *(G-19391)*
Concord Dayton Hotel II LLC 937 223-1000
1414 S Patterson Blvd Dayton (45409) *(G-9422)*
Concord Hamiltonian Rvrfrnt Ho 513 896-6200
1 Riverfront Plz Hamilton (45011) *(G-11717)*
Concord Health Care Inc (PA) 330 759-2357
202 Churchill Hubbard Rd Youngstown (44505) *(G-20160)*
Concord Health Care Inc 419 626-5373
620 W Strub Rd Sandusky (44870) *(G-16746)*
Concord Health Center Hartford, Fowler Also called Meadowbrook Manor of Hartford *(G-11144)*
Concord Hlth Rhabilitation Ctr 740 574-8441
1242 Crescent Dr Wheelersburg (45694) *(G-19575)*
Concord Testa Hotel Assoc LLC 330 252-9228
41 Furnace St Akron (44308) *(G-160)*
Concord Therapy Group, Alliance Also called Concorde Therapy Group Inc *(G-535)*
Concorde Therapy Group Inc (PA) 330 493-4210
4645 Belpar St Nw Canton (44718) *(G-2319)*
Concorde Therapy Group Inc 330 478-1752
5156 Whipple Ave Nw Canton (44718) *(G-2320)*
Concorde Therapy Group Inc 330 493-4210
513 E Main St Louisville (44641) *(G-13097)*
Concorde Therapy Group Inc 330 493-4210
2484 W State St Alliance (44601) *(G-535)*
Concordia Care 216 791-3580
2373 Euclid Heights Blvd Cleveland (44106) *(G-5391)*
Concordia Properties LLC 513 671-0120
11700 Princeton Pike B213 Cincinnati (45246) *(G-3409)*
Concordnce Hlthcare Sltons LLC (PA) 419 455-2153
85 Shaffer Park Dr Tiffin (44883) *(G-17673)*
Concrete Coring Company Inc 937 864-7325
400 E Main St Enon (45323) *(G-10726)*
Coney Island Inc 513 232-8230
6201 Kellogg Ave Cincinnati (45230) *(G-3410)*
Conger Construction Group Inc 513 932-1206
2020 Mckinley Blvd Lebanon (45036) *(G-12597)*
Congregate Living of America (PA) 513 899-2801
463 E Pike St Morrow (45152) *(G-14845)*
Congregate Living of America 937 393-6700
141 Willetsville Pike Hillsboro (45133) *(G-11969)*
Congress Lake Club Company 330 877-9318
1 East Dr Hartville (44632) *(G-11816)*
Congressional Bank 614 441-9230
4343 Easton Cmns Ste 150 Columbus (43219) *(G-7420)*
Conie Construction Company, Columbus Also called Jack Conie & Sons Corp *(G-7933)*
Connaissance Consulting LLC 614 289-5200
4071 Easton Way Columbus (43219) *(G-7421)*
Conneaut Senior Services, Conneaut Also called Ashtabula County Commnty Actn *(G-9037)*
Conneaut Telephone Company 440 593-7140
224 State St Conneaut (44030) *(G-9041)*
Connect Call Global LLC 513 348-1800
7560 Central Parke Blvd Mason (45040) *(G-13689)*
Connections Hlth Wlns Advo, Beachwood Also called North East Ohio Health Svcs *(G-1107)*
Connectivity Systems Inc (PA) 740 420-5400
8120 State Route 138 Williamsport (43164) *(G-19637)*
Connectlink Inc 740 867-5095
406 2nd Ave Chesapeake (45619) *(G-2783)*
Connie Parks (PA) 330 759-8334
4504 Logan Way Ste B Hubbard (44425) *(G-12084)*
Connor Concepts Inc 937 291-1661
7727 Washington Vlg Dr Dayton (45459) *(G-9423)*
Connor Evans Hafenstein LLP 614 464-2025
2000 Henderson Rd Ste 460 Columbus (43220) *(G-7422)*
Connor Group A RE Inv Firm LLC 937 434-3095
10510 Springboro Pike Miamisburg (45342) *(G-14286)*
Conrad's Total Car Care, Cleveland Also called Conrads Tire Service Inc *(G-5392)*
Conrads Tire Service Inc (PA) 216 941-3333
14577 Lorain Ave Cleveland (44111) *(G-5392)*
Conserv For Cyhg Vlly Nat Prk 330 657-2909
1403 W Hines Hill Rd Peninsula (44264) *(G-15949)*
Consoldated Graphics Group Inc 216 881-9191
1614 E 40th St Cleveland (44103) *(G-5393)*
Consolidated Care Inc 937 465-8065
501 W Baird St West Liberty (43357) *(G-19261)*
Consolidated Care Inc (PA) 937 465-8065
1521 N Detroit St West Liberty (43357) *(G-19262)*
Consolidated Communications 330 896-3905
7015 Sunset Strip Ave Nw Canton (44720) *(G-2321)*
Consolidated Elec Distrs Inc 614 445-8871
2101 S High St Columbus (43207) *(G-7423)*
Consolidated Electric Coop 740 363-2641
680 Sunbury Rd Delaware (43015) *(G-10081)*
Consolidated Electric Coop Inc 419 947-3055
5255 State Route 95 Mount Gilead (43338) *(G-14852)*
Consolidated Grain & Barge Co 419 785-1941
11859 Krouse Rd Defiance (43512) *(G-10023)*
Consolidated Grain & Barge Co 513 941-4805
4837 River Rd Cincinnati (45233) *(G-3411)*
Consolidated Learning Ctrs Inc 614 791-0050
7100 Muirfield Dr Ste 200 Dublin (43017) *(G-10308)*
Consolidated Lighting Svcs Co, Cincinnati Also called Eco Engineering Inc *(G-3543)*
Consolidated Rail Corporation 440 786-3014
401 Ledge Rd Macedonia (44056) *(G-13194)*
Consolidated Solutions, Cleveland Also called Consoldated Graphics Group Inc *(G-5393)*
Consolidated Utilities, Cincinnati Also called University of Cincinnati *(G-4772)*
Consortium For Hlthy & Immunzd 216 201-2001
10840 Barrington Blvd Cleveland (44130) *(G-5394)*
Constance Care Home Hlth Care 740 477-6360
774 N Court St Circleville (43113) *(G-4884)*
Constant Aviation LLC 216 261-7119
355 Richmond Rd Cleveland (44143) *(G-5395)*
Constant Aviation LLC (PA) 800 440-9004
18601 Cleveland Pkwy Dr 1b Cleveland (44135) *(G-5396)*
Constellations Enterprise LLC (PA) 330 740-8208
1775 Logan Ave Youngstown (44505) *(G-20161)*
Constructconnect, Cincinnati Also called Isqft Inc *(G-3845)*
Construction Biddingcom LLC 440 716-4087
31269 Bradley Rd North Olmsted (44070) *(G-15418)*
Construction First, Columbus Also called Construction One Inc *(G-7424)*
Construction Labor Contrs LLC 614 932-9937
5930 Wilcox Pl Ste F Dublin (43016) *(G-10309)*
Construction One Inc 614 961-1140
101 E Town St Ste 401 Columbus (43215) *(G-7424)*
Construction Resources Inc 440 248-9800
33900 Station St Cleveland (44139) *(G-5397)*
Construction Systems Inc (PA) 614 252-0708
2865 E 14th Ave Columbus (43219) *(G-7425)*
Consulate Healthcare, Wellston Also called Edgewood Manor of Wellston *(G-18999)*
Consulate Healthcare Inc (PA) 419 865-1248
3231 Manley Rd Maumee (43537) *(G-13899)*
Consulate Management Co LLC 330 837-1001
2311 Nave Rd Sw Massillon (44646) *(G-13798)*
Consulate Management Co LLC 740 259-2351
10098 Big Bear Creek Rd Lucasville (45648) *(G-13176)*
Consulate Management Co LLC 419 683-3436
327 W Main St Crestline (44827) *(G-9142)*
Consulate Management Co LLC 419 886-3922
4910 Algire Rd Bellville (44813) *(G-1423)*
Consulate Management Co LLC 440 237-7966
13900 Bennett Rd Cleveland (44133) *(G-5398)*

ALPHABETIC SECTION — Cooper-Smith Advertising LLC

Consulate Management Co LLC 419 683-3255
327 W Main St Crestline (44827) *(G-9143)*
Consulate Management Co LLC 740 259-5536
10098 Big Bear Creek Rd Lucasville (45648) *(G-13177)*
Consulate Management Co LLC 419 867-7926
3600 Butz Rd Maumee (43537) *(G-13900)*
Consultants Collections 330 666-6900
310 N Clvland Mssillon Rd Akron (44333) *(G-161)*
Consultants Laboratory Medici 419 535-9629
3170 W Central Ave Toledo (43606) *(G-17830)*
Consultants To You, Cincinnati *Also called Accountants To You LLC (G-2965)*
Consultnts In Gastroenterology 440 386-2250
7530 Fredle Dr Painesville (44077) *(G-15846)*
Consumer Advocacy Model 937 222-2400
601 S Edwin C Moses Blvd Dayton (45417) *(G-9424)*
Consumer Credit Coun (PA) 614 552-2222
690 Taylor Rd Ste 110 Gahanna (43230) *(G-11237)*
Consumer Credit Counseling (PA) 800 254-4100
1228 Euclid Ave Ste 390 Cleveland (44115) *(G-5399)*
Consumer Foods 440 284-5972
123 Gateway Blvd N Elyria (44035) *(G-10608)*
Consumer Support Services Inc (PA) 740 788-8257
2040 Cherry Valley Rd # 1 Newark (43055) *(G-15158)*
Consumer Support Services Inc 330 764-4785
2575 Medina Rd A Medina (44256) *(G-14050)*
Consumer Support Services Inc 740 522-5464
640 Industrial Pkwy Newark (43056) *(G-15159)*
Consumer Support Services Inc 330 652-8800
1254 Yngstwn Wrrn Rd B Niles (44446) *(G-15290)*
Consumer Support Services Inc 740 344-3600
100 James St Newark (43055) *(G-15160)*
Consumers Bancorp Inc 330 868-7701
614 E Lincolnway Minerva (44657) *(G-14643)*
Consumers Gas Cooperative 330 682-4144
298 Tracy Bridge Rd Orrville (44667) *(G-15768)*
Consumers Life Insurance Co, Cleveland *Also called Medical Mutual of Ohio (G-6015)*
Consumers National Bank (PA) 330 868-7701
614 E Lincolnway Minerva (44657) *(G-14644)*
Container Graphics Corp 419 531-5133
305 Ryder Rd Toledo (43607) *(G-17831)*
CONTAINERPORT GROUP, INC., West Chester *Also called Containerport Group Inc (G-19049)*
Containerport Group Inc 440 333-1330
2400 Creekway Dr Columbus (43207) *(G-7426)*
Containerport Group Inc 513 771-0275
2700 Crescentville Rd West Chester (45069) *(G-19049)*
Containerport Group Inc (HQ) 440 333-1330
1340 Depot St Fl 2 Cleveland (44116) *(G-5400)*
Containerport Group Inc 216 341-4800
5155 Warner Rd Cleveland (44125) *(G-5401)*
Containerport Group Inc 216 692-3124
24881 Rockwell Dr Euclid (44117) *(G-10747)*
Contech Trckg & Logistics LLC 513 645-7000
9025 Centre Pointe Dr # 400 West Chester (45069) *(G-19050)*
Contech-Gdcg 937 426-3577
4197 Research Blvd Beavercreek (45430) *(G-1235)*
Contemporary Arts Center 513 721-0390
44 E 6th St Cincinnati (45202) *(G-3412)*
Continent Hlth Co Cortland LLC 330 637-7906
4250 Sodom Hutchings Rd Cortland (44410) *(G-9075)*
Continental Airlines, Vandalia *Also called United Airlines Inc (G-18703)*
Continental Airlines, Cleveland *Also called United Airlines Inc (G-6633)*
Continental Business Services 614 224-4534
41 S Grant Ave Fl 2 Columbus (43215) *(G-7427)*
Continental Express Inc 937 497-2100
10450 State Route 47 W Sidney (45365) *(G-16922)*
Continental GL Sls & Inv Group 614 679-1201
315 Ashmoore Ct Powell (43065) *(G-16332)*
Continental Group, Powell *Also called Continental GL Sls & Inv Group (G-16332)*
Continental Manor, Blanchester *Also called First Richmond Corp (G-1514)*
Continental Mewthod Solutions, Columbus *Also called Continental Business Services (G-7427)*
Continental Office Furn Corp (PA) 614 262-5010
5061 Freeway Dr E Columbus (43229) *(G-7428)*
Continental Office Furn Corp 614 781-0080
5063 Freeway Dr E Columbus (43229) *(G-7429)*
Continental Products Company 216 531-0710
1150 E 222nd St Cleveland (44117) *(G-5402)*
Continental Properties 614 221-1800
150 E Broad St Ste 700 Columbus (43215) *(G-7430)*
Continental RE Companies (PA) 614 221-1800
150 E Broad St Ste 200 Columbus (43215) *(G-7431)*
Continental Realty Ltd 614 221-6260
180 E Broad St Ste 1708 Columbus (43215) *(G-7432)*
Continental Transport Inc 513 360-2960
997 Platte River Blvd Monroe (45050) *(G-14692)*
Continental/Olentangy Ht LLC 614 297-9912
1421 Olentangy River Rd Columbus (43212) *(G-7433)*
Continntal Mssage Solution Inc 614 224-4534
41 S Grant Ave Fl 2 Columbus (43215) *(G-7434)*
Continntal Office Environments, Columbus *Also called Continental Office Furn Corp (G-7428)*
Continued Care Inc 419 222-2273
920 W Market St Ste 202 Lima (45805) *(G-12759)*
Continuum Home Care Inc 440 964-3332
1100 Lake Ave Ashtabula (44004) *(G-737)*
Contitech North America Inc 440 225-5363
1144 E Market St Ste 543 Akron (44316) *(G-162)*
Contract Freighters Inc 614 577-0447
945 Mahle Dr Reynoldsburg (43068) *(G-16441)*
Contract Lumber Inc (PA) 740 964-3147
3245 Sr 310 Pataskala (43062) *(G-15921)*
Contract Marketing Inc 440 639-9100
9325 Progress Pkwy Mentor (44060) *(G-14162)*
Contract Sweepers & Eqp Co (PA) 614 221-7441
2137 Parkwood Ave Columbus (43219) *(G-7435)*
Contract Transport Services 216 524-8435
3223 Perkins Ave Cleveland (44114) *(G-5403)*
Contractors Materials Company 513 733-3000
10320 S Medallion Dr Cincinnati (45241) *(G-3413)*
Contractors Steel Company 330 425-3050
8383 Boyle Pkwy Twinsburg (44087) *(G-18404)*
Control Cleaning Solutions 330 220-3333
780 Pearl Rd Brunswick (44212) *(G-1973)*
Control Concepts & Design Inc 513 771-7271
5530 Union Centre Dr West Chester (45069) *(G-19051)*
Controlled Credit Corporation 513 921-2600
644 Linn St Ste 1101 Cincinnati (45203) *(G-3414)*
Controls Center Inc (PA) 513 772-2665
1640 E Kemper Rd Ste 2 Cincinnati (45246) *(G-3415)*
Controls Inc 330 239-4345
5204 Portside Dr Medina (44256) *(G-14051)*
Controlsoft Inc 440 443-3900
5387 Avion Park Dr Cleveland (44143) *(G-5404)*
Convalarium At Indian Run, Dublin *Also called Dublin Geriatric Care Co LP (G-10328)*
Convalescent Center Lucasville, Lucasville *Also called Edgewood Manor of Lucasville (G-13178)*
Convenient Food Mart Inc (HQ) 800 860-4844
6078 Pinecone Dr Mentor (44060) *(G-14163)*
Convenient Tire Service, Columbus *Also called W D Tire Warehouse Inc (G-8957)*
Convention & Visitors Bureau, Cleveland *Also called Convention & Visitors Bureau of (G-5405)*
Convention & Vistors Bureau of (PA) 216 875-6603
50 Public Sq Ste 3100 Cleveland (44113) *(G-5405)*
Convergint Technologies LLC 513 771-1717
7812 Redsky Dr Cincinnati (45249) *(G-3416)*
Convergys Corporation (PA) 513 723-7000
201 E 4th St Cincinnati (45202) *(G-3417)*
Convergys Cstmer MGT Group Inc (HQ) 513 723-6104
201 E 4th St Bsmt Cincinnati (45202) *(G-3418)*
Convergys Gvrnment Sltions LLC 513 723-7006
201 E 4th St Ste Bsmt Cincinnati (45202) *(G-3419)*
Conversa Language Center Inc 513 651-5679
817 Main St Ste 600 Cincinnati (45202) *(G-3420)*
Converse Electric Inc 614 808-4377
3783 Gantz Rd Ste A Grove City (43123) *(G-11549)*
Conversion Tech Intl Inc 419 924-5566
700 Oak St West Unity (43570) *(G-19280)*
Convivo Network LLC 216 631-9000
1999 W 58th St Cleveland (44102) *(G-5406)*
Conwed Plas Acquisition V LLC 440 926-2607
61 N Clevlnd Mssiln Rd Akron (44333) *(G-163)*
Cook Paving and Cnstr Co 216 267-7705
4545 Spring Rd Independence (44131) *(G-12201)*
Cooked Foods, Fairfield *Also called Koch Meat Co Inc (G-10871)*
Cookie Cutters Haircutters 614 522-0220
1726 Hill Rd N Pickerington (43147) *(G-16093)*
Coolants Plus Inc (PA) 513 892-4000
2570 Van Hook Ave Hamilton (45015) *(G-11718)*
Coolidge Law 937 223-8177
33 W 1st St Ste 600 Dayton (45402) *(G-9425)*
Coolidge Wall Co LPA (PA) 937 223-8177
33 W 1st St Ste 600 Dayton (45402) *(G-9426)*
Coon Caulking & Restoration, Louisville *Also called Coon Caulking & Sealants Inc (G-13098)*
Coon Caulking & Sealants Inc 330 875-2100
7349 Ravenna Ave Louisville (44641) *(G-13098)*
Cooper Brothers Trucking LLC (PA) 330 784-1717
1355 E Archwood Ave Akron (44306) *(G-164)*
Cooper Farms, Oakwood *Also called Cooper Hatchery Inc (G-15623)*
Cooper Farms Inc (PA) 419 375-4116
2321 State Route 49 Fort Recovery (45846) *(G-11115)*
Cooper Foods, Fort Recovery *Also called V H Cooper & Co Inc (G-11120)*
Cooper Frms Spring Madow Farms 419 375-4119
13243 Cochran Rd Rossburg (45362) *(G-16605)*
Cooper Hatchery Inc (PA) 419 594-3325
22348 Road 140 Oakwood (45873) *(G-15623)*
Cooper Woda Companies Inc (PA) 614 396-3200
500 S Front St Fl 10 Columbus (43215) *(G-7436)*
Cooper-Smith Advertising LLC 419 470-5900
3500 Granite Cir Toledo (43617) *(G-17832)*

Cooper/T Smith Corporation — ALPHABETIC SECTION

Cooper/T Smith Corporation 419 626-0801
2705 W Monroe St Sandusky (44870) *(G-16747)*
Cooperate Screening Services 440 816-0500
16530 Commerce Ct Ste 1 Cleveland (44130) *(G-5407)*
Copart Inc 614 497-1590
1680 Williams Rd Columbus (43207) *(G-7437)*
Copc Hospitals 614 268-8164
3555 Olentangy River Rd Columbus (43214) *(G-7438)*
Cope Farm Equipment Inc (PA) 330 821-5867
24915 State Route 62 Alliance (44601) *(G-536)*
Copeland Access + Inc 937 498-3802
1675 Campbell Rd Sidney (45365) *(G-16923)*
Copeland Oaks 330 938-1050
715 S Johnson Rd Sebring (44672) *(G-16820)*
Copeland Oaks (PA) 330 938-6126
800 S 15th St Sebring (44672) *(G-16821)*
Copley Health Center Inc 330 666-0980
155 Heritage Woods Dr Copley (44321) *(G-9055)*
Copley Ohio Newspapers Inc 330 364-5577
629 Wabash Ave Nw New Philadelphia (44663) *(G-15087)*
Copp Systems Inc 937 228-4188
123 S Keowee St Dayton (45402) *(G-9427)*
Copp Systems Integrator, Dayton *Also called Copp Systems Inc* *(G-9427)*
Copper and Brass Sales Div, Northwood *Also called Thyssenkrupp Logistics Inc* *(G-15545)*
Cora Health Services Inc (PA) 419 221-3004
1110 Shawnee Rd Lima (45805) *(G-12760)*
Coral Company (PA) 216 932-8822
13219 Shaker Sq Cleveland (44120) *(G-5408)*
Corbus LLC (HQ) 937 226-7724
1129 Miamisbrg Cntrvle Rd Ste Dayton (45449) *(G-9428)*
Corcoran and Harnist Htg & AC 513 921-2227
1457 Harrison Ave Cincinnati (45214) *(G-3421)*
Core, Cincinnati *Also called Cincinnatis Optimum RES Envir* *(G-3337)*
Core Resources Inc 513 731-1771
7795 5 Mile Rd Cincinnati (45230) *(G-3422)*
Core-Mark Ohio 650 589-9445
30300 Emerald Valley Pkwy Solon (44139) *(G-16994)*
Corecivic Inc 330 746-3777
2240 Hubbard Rd Youngstown (44505) *(G-20162)*
Cori Care Inc 614 848-4357
1060 Kingsmill Pkwy Columbus (43229) *(G-7439)*
Cork Enterprises Inc 740 654-1842
123 N Broad St Lancaster (43130) *(G-12523)*
Cork Inc 614 253-8400
2006 Kenton St Columbus (43205) *(G-7440)*
Corna Kokosing Construction Co 614 901-8844
6235 Westerville Rd Westerville (43081) *(G-19392)*
Cornelia C Hodgson - Architec (PA) 216 593-0057
23240 Chagrin Blvd # 300 Beachwood (44122) *(G-1068)*
Cornelius Joel Roofing Inc 513 367-4401
9107 Kilby Rd Harrison (45030) *(G-11795)*
Cornell Companies Inc 419 747-3322
2775 State Route 39 Shelby (44875) *(G-16898)*
Corner Cafe, Delaware *Also called Authentic Food LLC* *(G-10073)*
Cornerstone Brands Inc (HQ) 513 603-1000
5568 W Chester Rd West Chester (45069) *(G-19052)*
Cornerstone Brands Group Inc 513 603-1000
5568 W Chester Rd West Chester (45069) *(G-19053)*
Cornerstone Brkrg Ins Svc Agn, Cincinnati *Also called Cornerstone Broker Ins Svcs AG* *(G-3423)*
Cornerstone Broker Ins Svcs AG (PA) 513 241-7675
2101 Florence Ave Cincinnati (45206) *(G-3423)*
Cornerstone Concrete Cnstr Inc 937 442-2805
3166 State Route 321 Sardinia (45171) *(G-16812)*
Cornerstone Managed Prpts LLC 440 263-7708
2147 E 28th St Lorain (44055) *(G-13033)*
Cornerstone Med Svcs Midwest 513 554-0222
4570 Cornell Rd Blue Ash (45241) *(G-1566)*
Cornerstone Medical Associates 330 374-0229
453 S High St Ste 201 Akron (44311) *(G-165)*
Cornerstone Medical Services 513 554-0222
4570 Cornell Rd Blue Ash (45241) *(G-1567)*
CORNERSTONE OF HOPE BEREAVEMEN, Independence *Also called Bobby Tripodi Foundation Inc* *(G-12190)*
Cornerstone Research Group Inc 937 320-1877
510 Earl Blvd Miamisburg (45342) *(G-14287)*
Cornerstone Support Services (PA) 330 339-7850
344 W High Ave New Philadelphia (44663) *(G-15088)*
Cornucopia Inc 216 521-4600
18120 Sloane Ave Lakewood (44107) *(G-12474)*
Cornwell Quality Tools Company 330 628-2627
200 N Cleveland Ave Mogadore (44260) *(G-14673)*
Cornwell Quality Tools Company 330 335-2933
635 Seville Rd Wadsworth (44281) *(G-18751)*
Coroner, Dayton *Also called County of Montgomery* *(G-9440)*
Coroner's Office, Cleveland *Also called County of Cuyahoga* *(G-5420)*
Corporate Cleaning Inc 614 203-6051
781 Northwest Blvd # 103 Columbus (43212) *(G-7441)*
Corporate Electric Company LLC 330 331-7517
378 S Van Buren Ave Barberton (44203) *(G-962)*
Corporate Environments of Ohio 614 358-3375
2899 Morse Rd Columbus (43231) *(G-7442)*
Corporate Exchange Hotel Assoc 614 890-8600
2700 Corporate Exch Dr Columbus (43231) *(G-7443)*
Corporate Fin Assoc of Clumbus 614 457-9219
671 Camden Yard Ct Columbus (43235) *(G-7444)*
Corporate Floors Inc 216 475-3232
15901 Mccracken Rd Cleveland (44128) *(G-5409)*
Corporate Health Benefits 740 348-1401
1915 Tamarack Rd Newark (43055) *(G-15161)*
Corporate Health Dimensions 740 775-6119
311 Caldwell St Chillicothe (45601) *(G-2828)*
Corporate Imageworks LLC 216 292-8800
10375 State Route 43 Streetsboro (44241) *(G-17411)*
Corporate Ladder Search 330 776-4390
1549 Boettler Rd Ste D Uniontown (44685) *(G-18515)*
Corporate One Federal Cr Un (PA) 614 825-9314
8700 Orion Pl Columbus (43240) *(G-6878)*
Corporate Plans Inc 440 542-7800
6830 Cochran Rd Solon (44139) *(G-16995)*
Corporate Screening Svcs Inc (PA) 440 816-0500
16530 Commerce Ct Ste 3 Cleveland (44130) *(G-5410)*
Corporate Support Inc (PA) 419 221-3838
750 Buckeye Rd Lima (45804) *(G-12761)*
Corporate United Inc 440 895-0938
24651 Center Ridge Rd # 527 Westlake (44145) *(G-19480)*
Corporate Wngs - Cleveland LLC 216 261-9000
355 Richmond Rd Ste 8 Cleveland (44143) *(G-5411)*
Corporation For OH Appalachian (PA) 740 594-8499
1 Pinchot Pl Athens (45701) *(G-779)*
Corporation For OH Appalachian 330 364-8882
1260 Monroe St Nw Ste 39s New Philadelphia (44663) *(G-15089)*
Corps Security Agency Inc 513 631-3200
9475 Kenwood Rd Ste 14 Blue Ash (45242) *(G-1568)*
Correction Commission NW Ohio 419 428-3800
3151 County Road 2425 Stryker (43557) *(G-17536)*
Correctons Comm Sthastern Ohio 740 753-4060
16677 Riverside Dr Nelsonville (45764) *(G-14960)*
Corrigan Moving Systems-Ann AR 419 874-2900
12377 Williams Rd Perrysburg (43551) *(G-15989)*
Corrosion Fluid Products Corp (HQ) 248 478-0100
3000 E 14th Ave Columbus (43219) *(G-7445)*
Corrotec Inc 937 325-3585
1125 W North St Springfield (45504) *(G-17177)*
Corrpro Companies Inc (HQ) 330 723-5082
1055 W Smith Rd Medina (44256) *(G-14052)*
Cors & Bassett LLC (PA) 513 852-8200
537 E Pete Rose Way # 400 Cincinnati (45202) *(G-3424)*
Corso's Flower & Garden Center, Sandusky *Also called August Corso Sons Inc* *(G-16727)*
Cort Business Services Corp 513 759-8181
7400 Squire Ct West Chester (45069) *(G-19054)*
Cort Furniture Rental, West Chester *Also called Cort Business Services Corp* *(G-19054)*
CORTLAND BANKS, Cortland *Also called The Cortland Sav & Bnkg Co* *(G-9083)*
Cortland Healthcare Center, Cortland *Also called Saber Healthcare Group LLC* *(G-9082)*
Cos Express Inc 614 276-9000
3616 Fisher Rd Columbus (43228) *(G-7446)*
Coshocton Bowling Center 740 622-6332
775 S 2nd St Coshocton (43812) *(G-9093)*
Coshocton Cnty Emrgncy Med Svc (HQ) 740 622-4294
513 Chestnut St Coshocton (43812) *(G-9094)*
Coshocton County Head Start 740 622-3667
3201 County Road 16 Coshocton (43812) *(G-9095)*
Coshocton Healthcare and, Coshocton *Also called Coshocton Opco LLC* *(G-9096)*
Coshocton Opco LLC 740 622-1220
100 S Whitewoman St Coshocton (43812) *(G-9096)*
Coshocton Trucking South Inc 740 622-1311
2702 S 6th St Coshocton (43812) *(G-9097)*
Coshocton Village Inn & Suites, Coshocton *Also called Coshocton Village Inn Suites* *(G-9098)*
Coshocton Village Inn Suites 740 622-9455
115 N Water St Coshocton (43812) *(G-9098)*
Cosi, Columbus *Also called Franklin County Historical Soc* *(G-7695)*
Cosmax USA Inc Cosmax USA Corp 440 600-5738
30701 Carter St Solon (44139) *(G-16996)*
Cosmic Concepts Ltd 614 228-1104
399 E Main St Ste 140 Columbus (43215) *(G-7447)*
Costello Pntg Bldg Restoration 513 321-3326
1113 Halpin Ave Cincinnati (45208) *(G-3425)*
Costume Specialists Inc (PA) 614 464-2115
211 N 5th St Ste 100 Columbus (43215) *(G-7448)*
Cota, Columbus *Also called Central Ohio Transit Authority* *(G-7242)*
Coti, Blue Ash *Also called Cincinnati Occupational Therap* *(G-1557)*
Cott Systems Inc 614 847-4405
2800 Corp Exchange Dr # 300 Columbus (43231) *(G-7449)*
Cottage Gardens Inc 440 259-2900
4992 Middle Ridge Rd Perry (44081) *(G-15960)*
Cottages of Clayton 937 280-0300
8212 N Main St Dayton (45415) *(G-9429)*
Cotter Mdse Stor of Ohio 330 773-9177
1564 Firestone Pkwy Akron (44301) *(G-166)*
Cotter Moving & Storage Co (PA) 330 535-5115
265 W Bowery St Akron (44308) *(G-167)*
Cottingham Party Savers, Columbus *Also called The Cottingham Paper Co* *(G-8834)*

Cottingham Retirement Cmnty 513 563-3600
3995 Cottingham Dr # 102 Cincinnati (45241) *(G-3426)*

Cottonwd Crk At Spytn-Dyvl, Sylvania *Also called Leisure Sports Inc (G-17599)*

Coughlin Automotive, Newark *Also called Coughlin Chevrolet Toyota Inc (G-15162)*

Coughlin Automotive Group, Pataskala *Also called Coughlin Chevrolet Inc (G-15922)*

Coughlin Chevrolet Inc 740 852-1122
255 Lafayette St London (43140) *(G-12995)*

Coughlin Chevrolet Inc (PA) 740 964-9191
9000 Broad St Sw Pataskala (43062) *(G-15922)*

Coughlin Chevrolet Toyota Inc 740 366-1381
1850 N 21st St Newark (43055) *(G-15162)*

Coughlin Holdings Ltd Partnr 614 847-1002
71 E Wilson Bridge Rd Worthington (43085) *(G-19951)*

Coughlin Realty, Worthington *Also called Coughlin Holdings Ltd Partnr (G-19951)*

Council For Economic Opport 216 541-7878
14209 Euclid Ave Cleveland (44112) *(G-5412)*

Council For Economic Opport 216 476-3201
14402 Puritas Ave Cleveland (44135) *(G-5413)*

Council For Economic Opport (PA) 216 696-9077
1801 Superior Ave E Fl 4 Cleveland (44114) *(G-5414)*

Council For Economic Opport 216 692-4010
1883 Torbenson Dr Cleveland (44112) *(G-5415)*

Council of Child & Adoles, Cleveland *Also called Cleveland Clinic Foundation (G-5297)*

Council of Ecnmc Opprtnts of G 216 651-5154
2220 W 95th St Cleveland (44102) *(G-5416)*

Council On Aging of Southweste 513 721-1025
175 Tri County Pkwy # 200 Cincinnati (45246) *(G-3427)*

Council On Rur Svc Prgrams Inc 937 492-8787
1502 N Main Ave Sidney (45365) *(G-16924)*

Council On Rur Svc Prgrams Inc (PA) 937 778-5220
201 Robert M Davis Pkwy B Piqua (45356) *(G-16140)*

Council On Rur Svc Prgrams Inc 937 773-0773
285 Robert M Davis Pkwy Piqua (45356) *(G-16141)*

Council On Rur Svc Prgrams Inc 937 452-1090
8263 Us Route 127 Camden (45311) *(G-2137)*

Counseling Center Huron County 419 663-3737
292 Benedict Ave Norwalk (44857) *(G-15567)*

COUNSELING CENTER, THE, Portsmouth *Also called Scioto County Counseling Ctr (G-16307)*

Counseling Source Inc 513 984-9838
10921 Reed Hartman Hwy # 134 Blue Ash (45242) *(G-1569)*

Countertop Alternatives Inc 937 254-3334
2325 Woodman Dr Dayton (45420) *(G-9430)*

Countrtops Cabinetry By Design, Mason *Also called Complete Services Inc (G-13688)*

Country Acres of Wayne County 330 698-2031
1240 Wildwood Dr Wooster (44691) *(G-19852)*

Country Club Inc 216 831-9200
2825 Lander Rd Cleveland (44124) *(G-5417)*

Country Club At Muirfield Vlg 614 764-1714
8715 Muirfield Dr Dublin (43017) *(G-10310)*

Country Club Center Homes Inc 330 343-6351
860 E Iron Ave Dover (44622) *(G-10182)*

Country Club Center II Ltd 740 397-2350
1350 Yauger Rd Mount Vernon (43050) *(G-14886)*

Country Club Center III, Ashtabula *Also called Country Club Retirement Center (G-738)*

Country Club of Hudson 330 650-1188
2155 Middleton Rd Hudson (44236) *(G-12113)*

Country Club of North 937 374-5000
1 Club North Dr Xenia (45385) *(G-20047)*

Country Club Retirement Campus, Mount Vernon *Also called Country Club Center II Ltd (G-14886)*

COUNTRY CLUB RETIREMENT CENTER, Dover *Also called Country Club Center Homes Inc (G-10182)*

Country Club Retirement Center 440 992-0022
925 E 26th St Ashtabula (44004) *(G-738)*

Country Club Retirement Center (PA) 740 671-9330
55801 Conno Mara Dr Bellaire (43906) *(G-1365)*

Country Club, The, Dublin *Also called Country Club At Muirfield Vlg (G-10310)*

Country Court Ltd 740 397-4125
1076 Coshocton Ave Mount Vernon (43050) *(G-14887)*

Country Court Nursing Home, Mount Vernon *Also called Country Court Ltd (G-14887)*

Country Gardens 740 522-8810
2326 Newark Granville Rd Granville (43023) *(G-11463)*

Country Living, Columbus *Also called Ohio Rural Electric Coops Inc (G-8371)*

Country Mdow Fclty Oprtons LLC 419 886-3922
4910 Algire Rd Bellville (44813) *(G-1424)*

Country Meadow Care Center, Bellville *Also called Consulate Management Co LLC (G-1423)*

Country Meadow Care Center, Bellville *Also called Country Mdow Fclty Oprtons LLC (G-1424)*

Country Meadow Care Center LLC 419 886-3922
4910 Algire Rd Bellville (44813) *(G-1425)*

Country Meadow Rehabilitation, Bellville *Also called Country Meadow Care Center LLC (G-1425)*

Country Pointe Skilled Nursing 330 264-7881
3071 N Elyria Rd Wooster (44691) *(G-19853)*

Country Saw and Knife Inc 330 332-1611
1375 W State St Salem (44460) *(G-16692)*

Country Suites By Carlson, Elyria *Also called Bindu Associates LLC (G-10598)*

Country Suites By Carlson, Springfield *Also called W2005/Fargo Hotels (pool C) (G-17293)*

Country View of Sunbury, Sunbury *Also called Countryview of Sunbury (G-17553)*

Countryside Cntinuing Care Ctr, Fremont *Also called County of Sandusky (G-11192)*

Countryside Electric Inc 614 478-7960
2920 Switzer Ave Columbus (43219) *(G-7450)*

Countryside Rentals Inc (PA) 740 634-2666
210 S Quarry St Bainbridge (45612) *(G-941)*

Countryside Veterinary Service 330 847-7337
4680 Mahoning Ave Nw Warren (44483) *(G-18839)*

Countryside YMCA Child Dev, Lebanon *Also called Young Mens Christian (G-12660)*

Countryview Assistant Living 740 489-5351
62825 County Home Rd Lore City (43755) *(G-13086)*

Countryview Manor, Carrollton *Also called East Carroll Nursing Home (G-2618)*

Countryview of Sunbury 740 965-3984
14961 N Old 3c Rd Sunbury (43074) *(G-17553)*

County Administrator's Office, Cleveland *Also called County of Cuyahoga (G-5426)*

County Animal Hospital 513 398-8000
1185 Reading Rd Mason (45040) *(G-13690)*

County Engineer, Wshngtn CT Hs *Also called County of Fayette (G-20017)*

County Engineer's Office, Coshocton *Also called County of Coshocton (G-9099)*

County Engineering Office 419 334-9731
2500 W State St Fremont (43420) *(G-11189)*

County Engineers Office, Columbus *Also called Franklin Cnty Bd Commissioners (G-7682)*

County Engineers Office, Athens *Also called County of Athens (G-780)*

County Engineers Office 740 702-3130
755 Fairgrounds Rd Chillicothe (45601) *(G-2829)*

County of Adams 937 544-5067
300 N Wilson Dr West Union (45693) *(G-19277)*

County of Allen 419 228-6065
600 S Main St Lima (45804) *(G-12762)*

County of Allen 419 221-1103
3125 Ada Rd Lima (45801) *(G-12763)*

County of Allen 419 228-2120
1501 S Dixie Hwy Lima (45804) *(G-12764)*

County of Allen 419 227-8590
123 W Spring St Lima (45801) *(G-12765)*

County of Allen 419 221-1226
2450 Ada Rd Lima (45801) *(G-12766)*

County of Allen 419 996-7050
608 W High St Lima (45801) *(G-12767)*

County of Ashtabula 440 998-1811
3914 C Ct Ashtabula (44004) *(G-739)*

County of Athens 740 593-5514
16000 Canineville Rd Athens (45701) *(G-780)*

County of Athens 740 592-3061
18 Stonybrook Dr Athens (45701) *(G-781)*

County of Auglaize 419 738-3816
13093 Infirmary Rd Wapakoneta (45895) *(G-18793)*

County of Auglaize 419 629-2419
20 E 1st St New Bremen (45869) *(G-15017)*

County of Brown 937 378-6456
25 Veterans Blvd Georgetown (45121) *(G-11390)*

County of Brown 937 378-6104
775 Mount Orab Pike Georgetown (45121) *(G-11391)*

County of Carroll 330 627-4866
P.O. Box 98 Carrollton (44615) *(G-2615)*

County of Carroll 330 627-7651
2167 Kensington Rd Ne Carrollton (44615) *(G-2616)*

County of Champaign 937 653-4848
428 Beech St Urbana (43078) *(G-18584)*

County of Clark 937 390-5600
529 E Home Rd Springfield (45503) *(G-17178)*

County of Clark 937 327-1700
1345 Lagonda Ave Springfield (45503) *(G-17179)*

County of Clark 937 390-5615
529 E Home Rd Springfield (45503) *(G-17180)*

County of Clark 937 327-1700
1346 Lagonda Ave Springfield (45503) *(G-17181)*

County of Clark 937 327-1700
1345 Lagonda Ave Springfield (45503) *(G-17182)*

County of Clermont 513 732-7661
2279 Clermont Center Dr Batavia (45103) *(G-1006)*

County of Clermont 513 732-7970
4400 Haskell Ln Batavia (45103) *(G-1007)*

County of Clinton 937 382-2449
1025 S South St Ste 300 Wilmington (45177) *(G-19758)*

County of Clinton 937 382-2078
1326 Fife Ave Wilmington (45177) *(G-19759)*

County of Columbiana 330 424-1386
7880 Lincole Pl Lisbon (44432) *(G-12934)*

County of Coshocton 740 622-2135
23194 County Road 621 Coshocton (43812) *(G-9099)*

County of Coshocton 740 622-1020
725 Pine St Coshocton (43812) *(G-9100)*

County of Crawford 419 562-0015
224 Norton Way Bucyrus (44820) *(G-2033)*

County of Crawford 419 562-7731
815 Whetstone St Bucyrus (44820) *(G-2034)*

County of Cuyahoga 419 399-8260
112 N Williams St Paulding (45879) *(G-15929)*

County of Cuyahoga 216 443-7035
1276 W 3rd St Ste 210 Cleveland (44113) *(G-5418)*

ALPHABETIC

(PA)=Parent Co (HQ)=Headquarters (DH)=Div Headquarters
2018 Harris Ohio Services Directory
1159

County of Cuyahoga ALPHABETIC SECTION

County of Cuyahoga 216 475-7066
14775 Broadway Ave Cleveland (44137) ***(G-5419)***
County of Cuyahoga 216 721-5610
11001 Cedar Ave Ste 400 Cleveland (44106) ***(G-5420)***
County of Cuyahoga 216 443-8011
2079 E 9th St Fl 6 Cleveland (44115) ***(G-5421)***
County of Cuyahoga 216 443-5100
1640 Superior Ave E Cleveland (44114) ***(G-5422)***
County of Cuyahoga 216 443-6954
2079 E 9th St Cleveland (44115) ***(G-5423)***
County of Cuyahoga 216 241-8230
1275 Lakeside Ave E Cleveland (44114) ***(G-5424)***
County of Cuyahoga 216 681-4433
13231 Euclid Ave Cleveland (44112) ***(G-5425)***
County of Cuyahoga 216 443-7181
1219 Ontario St Rm 304 Cleveland (44113) ***(G-5426)***
County of Cuyahoga 216 432-2621
3955 Euclid Ave Rm 344e Cleveland (44115) ***(G-5427)***
County of Cuyahoga 216 443-7265
1276 W 3rd St Ste 319 Cleveland (44113) ***(G-5428)***
County of Darke 937 526-4488
10242 Versailles Se Rd Versailles (45380) ***(G-18725)***
County of Delaware 740 833-2240
50 Channing St Delaware (43015) ***(G-10082)***
County of Delaware 740 657-3945
8647 Columbus Pike Lewis Center (43035) ***(G-12678)***
County of Delaware 740 833-2400
50 Channing St Delaware (43015) ***(G-10083)***
County of Delaware 740 203-2040
1 W Winter St Fl 2 Delaware (43015) ***(G-10084)***
County of Erie 419 433-0617
10102 Hoover Rd Milan (44846) ***(G-14493)***
County of Erie 419 627-8733
3916 Perkins Ave Huron (44839) ***(G-12164)***
County of Erie 419 626-6781
221 W Parish St Sandusky (44870) ***(G-16748)***
County of Erie 419 627-7710
2700 Columbus Ave Sandusky (44870) ***(G-16749)***
County of Fayette 740 335-1541
1600 Robinson Rd Se Wshngtn CT Hs (43160) ***(G-20017)***
County of Fulton 419 335-3816
9120 County Road 14 Wauseon (43567) ***(G-18949)***
County of Gallia 740 446-3222
848 3rd Ave Gallipolis (45631) ***(G-11311)***
County of Gallia 740 446-2665
1107 State Route 160 Gallipolis (45631) ***(G-11312)***
County of Gallia 740 446-4009
1167 State Route 160 Gallipolis (45631) ***(G-11313)***
County of Geauga 440 286-6264
107 South St Ste 5 Chardon (44024) ***(G-2745)***
County of Geauga 440 564-2246
12480 Ravenwood Dr Chardon (44024) ***(G-2746)***
County of Geauga 440 285-9141
12480 Ravenwood Dr Chardon (44024) ***(G-2747)***
County of Guernsey 740 439-5555
274 Highland Ave Cambridge (43725) ***(G-2106)***
County of Guernsey 800 307-8422
324 Highland Ave Cambridge (43725) ***(G-2107)***
County of Guernsey 740 432-2381
324 Highland Ave Cambridge (43725) ***(G-2108)***
County of Guernsey 740 439-6681
1022 Carlisle Ave Cambridge (43725) ***(G-2109)***
County of Hamilton 513 742-1576
2600 Civic Center Dr Cincinnati (45231) ***(G-3428)***
County of Hamilton 513 552-1200
246 Bonham Rd Cincinnati (45215) ***(G-3429)***
County of Hamilton 513 946-4250
138 E Court St Rm 700 Cincinnati (45202) ***(G-3430)***
County of Hamilton 513 598-2965
5884 Bridgetown Rd Cincinnati (45248) ***(G-3431)***
County of Hamilton 513 221-4524
3159 Eden Ave Cincinnati (45219) ***(G-3432)***
County of Hamilton 513 821-6946
7162 Reading Rd Ste 800 Cincinnati (45237) ***(G-3433)***
County of Hancock 419 422-6387
1700 E Sandusky St Findlay (45840) ***(G-11016)***
County of Hancock 419 424-7050
7746 County Road 140 A Findlay (45840) ***(G-11017)***
County of Hancock 419 422-7433
1900 Lima Ave Findlay (45840) ***(G-11018)***
County of Hancock 419 425-7275
1424 E Main Cross St Findlay (45840) ***(G-11019)***
County of Hardin 419 634-7729
530 N Gilbert St Ada (45810) ***(G-5)***
County of Hardin 419 674-4158
705 N Ida St Kenton (43326) ***(G-12410)***
County of Henry 419 592-8075
R858 County Road 15 Napoleon (43545) ***(G-14937)***
County of Highland 937 393-4278
1575 N High St Ste 100 Hillsboro (45133) ***(G-11970)***
County of Holmes 330 279-2801
7260 State Route 83 Holmesville (44633) ***(G-12071)***
County of Holmes 330 674-1926
8478 State Route 39 Millersburg (44654) ***(G-14596)***
County of Holmes 330 674-5035
85 N Grant St B Millersburg (44654) ***(G-14597)***
County of Holmes 330 674-5076
7191 State Route 39 Millersburg (44654) ***(G-14598)***
County of Holmes 330 674-5916
75 E Clinton St Millersburg (44654) ***(G-14599)***
County of Holmes 330 674-1015
981 Wooster Rd Millersburg (44654) ***(G-14600)***
County of Holmes 330 674-1111
85 N Grant St Millersburg (44654) ***(G-14601)***
County of Huron 419 668-8126
185 Shady Lane Dr Norwalk (44857) ***(G-15568)***
County of Huron 419 663-5437
185 Shady Lane Dr Norwalk (44857) ***(G-15569)***
County of Knox 740 392-2200
11660 Upper Gilchrist Rd Mount Vernon (43050) ***(G-14888)***
County of Lake 440 350-5100
8121 Deepwood Blvd Mentor (44060) ***(G-14164)***
County of Lake 440 350-4000
177 Main St Painesville (44077) ***(G-15847)***
County of Lake 440 269-2193
2100 Joseph Lloyd Pkwy Willoughby (44094) ***(G-19656)***
County of Licking 740 967-5951
395 W Jersey St Johnstown (43031) ***(G-12339)***
County of Logan 937 599-7252
101 S Main St Rm 1 Bellefontaine (43311) ***(G-1380)***
County of Logan 937 599-4221
121 S Opera St Rm 12 Bellefontaine (43311) ***(G-1381)***
County of Logan 937 592-2901
2739 County Road 91 Bellefontaine (43311) ***(G-1382)***
County of Logan 937 599-7290
1100 S Detroit St Bellefontaine (43311) ***(G-1383)***
County of Lorain 440 329-5584
247 Hadaway St Elyria (44035) ***(G-10609)***
County of Lorain 440 329-3734
1091 Infirmary Rd Elyria (44035) ***(G-10610)***
County of Lorain 440 326-4700
308 2nd St Elyria (44035) ***(G-10611)***
County of Lorain 440 326-5884
247 Hadaway St Elyria (44035) ***(G-10612)***
County of Lorain 440 647-5803
179 E Herrick Ave Wellington (44090) ***(G-18989)***
County of Lorain 440 284-1830
42495 N Ridge Rd Ste A Elyria (44035) ***(G-10613)***
County of Lorain 440 989-4900
120 East Ave Elyria (44035) ***(G-10614)***
County of Lorain 440 282-3074
4609 Meister Rd Lorain (44053) ***(G-13034)***
County of Lorain 440 326-5880
42100 Russia Rd Elyria (44035) ***(G-10615)***
County of Lorain 440 329-5340
226 Middle Ave Fl 4 Elyria (44035) ***(G-10616)***
County of Lucas 419 213-3000
701 Adams St Toledo (43604) ***(G-17833)***
County of Lucas 419 213-4700
700 Adams St Ste 150 Toledo (43604) ***(G-17834)***
County of Lucas 419 213-8999
3210 Monroe St Toledo (43606) ***(G-17835)***
County of Lucas 419 213-4018
635 N Erie St Toledo (43604) ***(G-17836)***
County of Lucas 419 213-2892
1049 S Mccord Rd Bldg A Holland (43528) ***(G-12016)***
County of Lucas 419 213-4500
1 Government Ctr Ste 800 Toledo (43604) ***(G-17837)***
County of Lucas 419 385-6021
1154 Larc Ln Toledo (43614) ***(G-17838)***
County of Madison 740 852-9404
825 Us Highway 42 Ne London (43140) ***(G-12996)***
County of Marion 740 387-6688
620 Leader St Marion (43302) ***(G-13532)***
County of Marion 740 389-4624
1422 Mount Vernon Ave Marion (43302) ***(G-13533)***
County of Marion 740 389-2317
1680 Marion Waldo Rd Marion (43302) ***(G-13534)***
County of Marion 740 387-1035
2387 Harding Hwy E Marion (43302) ***(G-13535)***
County of Marion 740 382-0624
1775 Mrn Williamsprt Rd E Marion (43302) ***(G-13536)***
County of Medina 330 723-9553
6144 Wedgewood Rd Medina (44256) ***(G-14053)***
County of Medina 330 995-5243
4800 Ledgewood Dr Medina (44256) ***(G-14054)***
County of Medina 330 723-9670
114 Bradway St Medina (44256) ***(G-14055)***
County of Meigs 740 992-6617
Mulburry Heights Stn 11 Pomeroy (45769) ***(G-16231)***
County of Meigs 740 992-2117
175 Race St Middleport (45760) ***(G-14406)***
County of Mercer 419 586-2369
4980 Mud Pike Rd Celina (45822) ***(G-2643)***
County of Mercer 419 586-5106
220 W Livingston St # 10 Celina (45822) ***(G-2644)***
County of Mercer 419 678-8071
510 W Main St Coldwater (45828) ***(G-6828)***

County of Miami...937 335-1314
2100 N County Road 25a Troy (45373) **(G-18352)**
County of Monroe...740 472-0760
47026 Moore Ridge Rd Woodsfield (43793) **(G-19814)**
County of Monroe...740 472-0144
47045 Moore Ridge Rd Woodsfield (43793) **(G-19815)**
County of Montgomery...937 225-4192
345 W 2nd St Dayton (45422) **(G-9431)**
County of Montgomery...937 224-5437
3304 N Main St Dayton (45405) **(G-9432)**
County of Montgomery...937 781-3046
2550 Sandridge Dr Moraine (45439) **(G-14764)**
County of Montgomery...937 854-4576
5625 Little Richmond Rd Dayton (45426) **(G-9433)**
County of Montgomery...937 264-0460
8100 N Main St Dayton (45415) **(G-9434)**
County of Montgomery...937 225-4010
451 W 3rd St Fl 2 Dayton (45422) **(G-9435)**
County of Montgomery...937 225-4804
1111 Edwin C Moses Blvd Dayton (45422) **(G-9436)**
County of Montgomery...937 225-5623
301 W 3rd St Fl 5 Dayton (45402) **(G-9437)**
County of Montgomery...937 224-5437
3501 Merrimac Ave Dayton (45405) **(G-9438)**
County of Montgomery...937 496-3103
41 N Perry St Rm 1 Dayton (45422) **(G-9439)**
County of Montgomery...937 225-4156
361 W 3rd St Dayton (45402) **(G-9440)**
County of Morrow...419 946-2618
27 W High St Mount Gilead (43338) **(G-14853)**
County of Ottawa...419 898-7433
275 N Toussaint South Rd Oak Harbor (43449) **(G-15606)**
County of Ottawa...419 898-6459
8180 W State Route 163 Oak Harbor (43449) **(G-15607)**
County of Ottawa...419 898-2089
8444 W State Route 163 # 102 Oak Harbor (43449) **(G-15608)**
County of Paulding...419 399-3636
501 Mc Donald Pike Paulding (45879) **(G-15930)**
County of Perry...740 342-0416
445 W Broadway St Ste C New Lexington (43764) **(G-15053)**
County of Perry...740 342-2191
2645 Old Somerset Rd New Lexington (43764) **(G-15054)**
County of Pickaway...740 474-7588
110 Island Rd Ste E Circleville (43113) **(G-4885)**
County of Portage...330 296-6411
5000 Newton Falls Rd Ravenna (44266) **(G-16379)**
County of Portage...330 297-3670
449 S Meridian St Fl 3 Ravenna (44266) **(G-16380)**
County of Portage...330 297-3850
466 S Chestnut St Ravenna (44266) **(G-16381)**
County of Preble...937 839-5845
1251 State Route 503 N West Alexandria (45381) **(G-19007)**
County of Richland...419 774-4300
721 Scholl Rd Mansfield (44907) **(G-13277)**
County of Richland...419 774-5676
38 Park St S Ste B Mansfield (44902) **(G-13278)**
County of Richland...419 774-5894
3220 Olivesburg Rd Mansfield (44903) **(G-13279)**
County of Richland...419 774-4100
731 Scholl Rd Mansfield (44907) **(G-13280)**
County of Richland...419 774-5400
171 Park Ave E Mansfield (44902) **(G-13281)**
County of Richland...419 774-5578
411 S Diamond St Mansfield (44902) **(G-13282)**
County of Richland...419 774-5591
77 N Mulberry St Mansfield (44902) **(G-13283)**
County of Richland...419 774-4200
314 Cleveland Ave Mansfield (44902) **(G-13284)**
County of Ross...740 773-4169
182 Cattail Rd Chillicothe (45601) **(G-2830)**
County of Sandusky...419 637-2243
1001 Castalia St Fremont (43420) **(G-11190)**
County of Sandusky...419 334-2602
1865 Countryside Dr Fremont (43420) **(G-11191)**
County of Sandusky...419 334-2602
1865 Countryside Dr Fremont (43420) **(G-11192)**
County of Seneca...419 447-3863
3210 S State Route 100 Tiffin (44883) **(G-17674)**
County of Seneca...419 435-0729
602 S Corporate Dr W Fostoria (44830) **(G-11125)**
County of Seneca...419 447-5011
3362 S Township Rd Tiffin (44883) **(G-17675)**
County of Seneca...419 937-2340
P.O. Box 119 Bascom (44809) **(G-993)**
County of Shelby...937 498-7244
500 Gearhart Rd Sidney (45365) **(G-16925)**
County of Shelby...937 492-6900
2901 Fair Rd Sidney (45365) **(G-16926)**
County of Stark...330 484-4814
3041 Cleveland Ave S Canton (44707) **(G-2322)**
County of Stark...330 477-3609
798 Genoa Ave Nw Massillon (44646) **(G-13799)**
County of Stark...330 451-2303
1701 Mahoning Rd Ne Canton (44705) **(G-2323)**
County of Stark...330 477-6781
5165 Southway St Sw Canton (44706) **(G-2324)**
County of Stark...330 455-6644
121 Cleveland Ave Sw Canton (44702) **(G-2325)**
County of Summit...330 643-2300
25 N Main St Akron (44308) **(G-168)**
County of Summit...330 643-2943
650 Dan St Akron (44310) **(G-169)**
County of Summit...330 634-8193
89 E Howe Rd Tallmadge (44278) **(G-17636)**
County of Summit...330 643-2850
538 E South St Akron (44311) **(G-170)**
County of Summit...330 643-2860
601 E Crosier St Akron (44311) **(G-171)**
County of Summit...330 643-7217
47 N Main St Akron (44308) **(G-172)**
County of Summit Board of Mntl...330 634-8100
636 W Exchange St Akron (44302) **(G-173)**
County of Trumbull...330 675-2640
650 N River Rd Nw Warren (44483) **(G-18840)**
County of Tuscarawas...330 343-0099
154 2nd St Ne New Philadelphia (44663) **(G-15090)**
County of Tuscarawas...330 339-7791
389 16th St Sw New Philadelphia (44663) **(G-15091)**
County of Union...937 645-3018
128 S Main St Ste 203 Marysville (43040) **(G-13612)**
County of Union...937 645-6733
1280 Charles Ln Marysville (43040) **(G-13613)**
County of Union...937 645-4145
128 S Main St Ste 203 Marysville (43040) **(G-13614)**
County of Van Wert...419 968-2141
17872 Lincoln Hwy Middle Point (45863) **(G-14376)**
County of Warren...513 695-1420
416 S East St Unit 1 Lebanon (45036) **(G-12598)**
County of Warren...513 695-1109
300 E Silver St Ste 5 Lebanon (45036) **(G-12599)**
County of Warren...513 925-1377
406 Justice Dr Rm 323 Lebanon (45036) **(G-12600)**
County of Washington...740 376-7430
103 Westview Ave Marietta (45750) **(G-13438)**
County of Washington...740 373-2028
County House Ln Marietta (45750) **(G-13439)**
County of Washington...740 373-5513
1115 Gilman Ave Marietta (45750) **(G-13440)**
County of Wayne...330 262-1786
876 S Geyers Chapel Rd Wooster (44691) **(G-19854)**
County of Wayne...330 264-5060
356 W North St Wooster (44691) **(G-19855)**
County of Wayne...330 345-5340
2534 Burbank Rd Wooster (44691) **(G-19856)**
County of Wayne...330 287-5600
428 W Liberty St Ste 11 Wooster (44691) **(G-19857)**
County of Wayne...330 287-5500
3151 W Old Lincoln Way Wooster (44691) **(G-19858)**
County of Williams...419 485-3141
310 Lincoln Ave Ste A Montpelier (43543) **(G-14742)**
County of Williams...419 636-4508
9876 County Road 16 Bryan (43506) **(G-2005)**
County of Wood...419 686-6951
351 W Main St Portage (43451) **(G-16261)**
County of Wyandot...419 294-1714
7830 State Highway 199 Upper Sandusky (43351) **(G-18558)**
Countyside Continuing Care, Fremont *Also called County of Sandusky* **(G-11191)**
Couple To Couple Leag Intl Inc (PA)...513 471-2000
4290 Delhi Rd Cincinnati (45238) **(G-3434)**
Court Dialysis LLC...740 773-3733
1180 N Bridge St Chillicothe (45601) **(G-2831)**
Court House Manor, Wshngtn CT Hs *Also called Hcf of Court House Inc* **(G-20025)**
Court of Claims of Ohio, Columbus *Also called Supreme Court of Ohio* **(G-8809)**
Court Stret Center Associates...513 241-0415
250 W Court St Ste 200e Cincinnati (45202) **(G-3435)**
Courtesy Ambulance Inc...740 522-8588
1890 W Main St Newark (43055) **(G-15163)**
Courtview Justice Solutions (HQ)...330 497-0033
4825 Higbee Ave Nw # 101 Canton (44718) **(G-2326)**
Courtyard By Marriott, Stow *Also called Hotel Stow LP* **(G-17373)**
Courtyard By Marriott, Hamilton *Also called Concord Hamiltonian Rvrfrnt Ho* **(G-11717)**
Courtyard By Marriott, Cleveland *Also called SDC Unvrsity Cir Developer LLC* **(G-6456)**
Courtyard By Marriott, Akron *Also called Concord Testa Hotel Assoc LLC* **(G-160)**
Courtyard By Marriott, Willoughby *Also called Willoughby Lodging LLC* **(G-19724)**
Courtyard By Marriott, Columbus *Also called Courtyard Management Corp* **(G-7451)**
Courtyard By Marriott, Holland *Also called Marriott International Inc* **(G-12035)**
Courtyard By Marriott, North Olmsted *Also called Marriott International Inc* **(G-15431)**
Courtyard By Marriott, Columbus *Also called Columbus Concord Ltd Partnr* **(G-7342)**
Courtyard By Marriott, Willoughby *Also called Moody Nat Cy Willoughby Mt LLC* **(G-19693)**
Courtyard By Marriott, Mentor *Also called Charter Hotel Group Ltd Partnr* **(G-14156)**
Courtyard By Marriott...216 765-1900
3695 Orange Pl Cleveland (44122) **(G-5429)**
Courtyard By Marriott...513 341-4140
6250 Muhlhauser Rd West Chester (45069) **(G-19055)**

ALPHABETIC

Courtyard By Marriott....440 871-3756
25050 Sperry Dr Westlake (44145) ***(G-19481)***
Courtyard By Marriott....937 433-3131
100 Prestige Pl Miamisburg (45342) ***(G-14288)***
Courtyard By Marriott Canton, Canton *Also called Ca-Mj Hotel Associates Ltd* ***(G-2278)***
Courtyard By Marriott Dayton....937 220-9060
2006 S Edwin C Moses Blvd Dayton (45417) ***(G-9441)***
Courtyard By Marriott Rossford....419 872-5636
9789 Clark Dr Rossford (43460) ***(G-16607)***
Courtyard By Mrt Clmbs Dwntwn, Columbus *Also called Moody Nat Cy Dt Clumbus Mt LLC* ***(G-8186)***
Courtyard Cincinnati Blue Ash, Blue Ash *Also called Cmp I Blue Ash Owner LLC* ***(G-1561)***
Courtyard Cleveland Airport S, Middleburg Heights *Also called Oh-16 Clvlnd Arprt S Prprty Su* ***(G-14383)***
Courtyard Columbus Downtown, Columbus *Also called Hit Swn Trs LLC* ***(G-7841)***
Courtyard Columbus Dublin, Dublin *Also called Cmp I Columbus I Owner LLC* ***(G-10297)***
Courtyard Columbus West, Columbus *Also called Cs Hotels Limited Partnership* ***(G-7470)***
Courtyard Columbus Worthington, Columbus *Also called Cmp I Columbus II Owner LLC* ***(G-7309)***
Courtyard Dayton, Dayton *Also called W2005/Fargo Hotels (pool C)* ***(G-9980)***
Courtyard Easton, Columbus *Also called Olshan Hotel Management Inc* ***(G-8468)***
Courtyard Management Corp....614 475-8530
2901 Airport Dr Columbus (43219) ***(G-7451)***
Courtyard Management Corp....216 901-9988
5051 W Creek Rd Cleveland (44131) ***(G-5430)***
Courtyard Springfield Downtown, Springfield *Also called Crefiii Waramaug* ***(G-17184)***
Cousins Waste Control LLC (PA)....419 726-1500
1701 E Matzinger Rd Toledo (43612) ***(G-17839)***
Cov-Ro Inc....330 856-3176
3900 E Market St Ste 1 Warren (44484) ***(G-18841)***
Cova, Columbus *Also called Center of Voctnl Altrntvs Mntl* ***(G-7226)***
Covelli Enterprises Inc....614 889-7802
6693 Sawmill Rd Dublin (43017) ***(G-10311)***
Covelli Family Ltd Partnership (PA)....330 856-3176
3900 E Market St Warren (44484) ***(G-18842)***
Covenant Care Ohio Inc....419 898-5506
1330 Fulton St Port Clinton (43452) ***(G-16242)***
Covenant Care Ohio Inc....419 531-4201
4420 South Ave Toledo (43615) ***(G-17840)***
Covenant Care Ohio Inc....937 378-0188
8065 Dr Faul Rd Georgetown (45121) ***(G-11392)***
Covenant Care Ohio Inc....937 878-7046
829 Yllow Sprng Frfeld Rd Fairborn (45324) ***(G-10788)***
Covenant Care Ohio Inc....937 399-5551
701 Villa Rd Springfield (45503) ***(G-17183)***
Covenant Care Ohio Inc....937 526-5570
200 Marker Rd Versailles (45380) ***(G-18726)***
Covenant Home Health Care LLC....614 465-2017
5212 W Broad St Ste J Columbus (43228) ***(G-7452)***
Covenant House, Dayton *Also called Jewish Fdrtion of Grter Dayton* ***(G-9641)***
Covenant Transport Inc....423 821-1212
3825 Aries Brook Dr Columbus (43207) ***(G-7453)***
Cover Crop Shop LLC....937 417-3972
739 S Vandemark Rd Sidney (45365) ***(G-16927)***
Covington Car Wash Inc....513 831-6164
5942 Creekview Dr Milford (45150) ***(G-14514)***
Covington Care Center, Covington *Also called Uvmc Nursing Care Inc* ***(G-9140)***
Covington Skilled Nursing, East Palestine *Also called Covington Snf Inc* ***(G-10537)***
Covington Snf Inc....330 426-2920
100 Covington Dr East Palestine (44413) ***(G-10537)***
Covington Square Senior APT....740 623-4603
380 Browns Ln Coshocton (43812) ***(G-9101)***
Cowan Systems LLC....513 769-4774
10801 Evendale Dr Cincinnati (45241) ***(G-3436)***
Cowan Systems LLC....513 721-6444
2751 Crescentville Rd West Chester (45069) ***(G-19056)***
Cowan Systems LLC....330 963-8483
1882 Highland Rd Twinsburg (44087) ***(G-18405)***
Cowen and Company LLC....440 331-3531
20006 Detroit Rd Ste 100 Rocky River (44116) ***(G-16575)***
Cowen Truck Line Inc....419 938-3401
2697 State Route 39 Perrysville (44864) ***(G-16078)***
Cox Automotive Inc....513 874-9310
4969 Muhlhauser Rd West Chester (45011) ***(G-19057)***
Cox Automotive Inc....614 871-2771
3905 Jackson Pike Grove City (43123) ***(G-11550)***
Cox Cable Cleveland Area Inc....216 676-8300
12221 Plaza Dr Cleveland (44130) ***(G-5431)***
Cox Communications Inc....216 712-4500
12221 Plaza Dr Parma (44130) ***(G-15903)***
Cox Communications Inc....937 222-5700
1611 S Main St Dayton (45409) ***(G-9442)***
Cox Institute, Kettering *Also called Wright State University* ***(G-12439)***
Cox Ohio Telcom LLC....216 535-3500
12221 Plaza Dr Parma (44130) ***(G-15904)***
Cox Paving Inc....937 780-3075
2754 Us Highway 22 Nw Wshngtn CT Hs (43160) ***(G-20018)***
Coy Brothers Inc....330 533-6864
433 Fairground Blvd Canfield (44406) ***(G-2187)***
Coyne Graphic Finishing Inc....740 397-6232
1301 Newark Rd Mount Vernon (43050) ***(G-14889)***
CPC Logistics Inc....513 874-5787
8695 Seward Rd Fairfield (45011) ***(G-10838)***
Cpg, Columbus *Also called Containerport Group Inc* ***(G-7426)***
CPG, Columbus *Also called Columbia Gas Transmission LLC* ***(G-7323)***
CPI, Holland *Also called Creative Products Inc* ***(G-12017)***
CPI - Cnstr Polymers Inc (PA)....330 861-5200
7576 Freedom Ave Nw North Canton (44720) ***(G-15329)***
CPI-Hr, Solon *Also called Corporate Plans Inc* ***(G-16995)***
Cpo Managment Services, Columbus *Also called Community Prpts Ohio MGT Svcs* ***(G-7408)***
Cpo3, Columbus *Also called Community Prpts Ohio III LLC* ***(G-7407)***
CPX Canton Airport LLC....330 305-0500
7883 Freedom Ave Nw North Canton (44720) ***(G-15330)***
CPX Carrollton Es LLC....330 627-1200
1296 Canton Rd Nw Carrollton (44615) ***(G-2617)***
Cr Architecture and Design, Cincinnati *Also called Cole + Russell Architects Inc* ***(G-3386)***
Cr Brands Inc (HQ)....513 860-5039
8790 Beckett Rd West Chester (45069) ***(G-19058)***
Crabbe Brown & James LLP (PA)....614 229-4587
500 S Front St Ste 1200 Columbus (43215) ***(G-7454)***
Craft Catalog, Groveport *Also called Craft Wholesalers Inc* ***(G-11630)***
Craft Wholesalers Inc....740 964-6210
4600 S Hamilton Rd Groveport (43125) ***(G-11630)***
Craftsman Electric Inc....513 891-4426
3855 Alta Ave Ste 1 Cincinnati (45236) ***(G-3437)***
Craftsmen Restoration LLC (PA)....877 442-3424
2013 N Clvland Msslion Rd Akron (44333) ***(G-174)***
Craig and Frances Lindner Cent....513 536-4673
4075 Old Western Row Rd Mason (45040) ***(G-13691)***
Craig Smith Auto Group, Galion *Also called Surfside Motors Inc* ***(G-11306)***
Craig Transportation Co....419 874-7981
819 Kingsbury St Ste 102 Maumee (43537) ***(G-13901)***
Crain Communications Inc....330 836-9180
1725 Merriman Rd Ste 300 Akron (44313) ***(G-175)***
Crane 1 Services Inc (PA)....937 704-9900
1027 Byers Rd Miamisburg (45342) ***(G-14289)***
Crane Heating & AC Co....513 641-4700
24 Clay St Cincinnati (45217) ***(G-3438)***
Crane Pro Services, West Chester *Also called Konecranes Inc* ***(G-19104)***
Crane Pumps & Systems Inc....937 773-2442
420 3rd St Piqua (45356) ***(G-16142)***
Cranel Imaging, Columbus *Also called Cranel Incorporated* ***(G-6879)***
Cranel Incorporated (PA)....614 431-8000
8999 Gemini Pkwy Ste A Columbus (43240) ***(G-6879)***
Cranley Surgical Associates....513 961-4335
3747 W Fork Rd Cincinnati (45247) ***(G-3439)***
Crapsey & Gillis Contractors....513 891-6333
8887 Glendale Milford Rd Loveland (45140) ***(G-13117)***
Crawford & Company....440 243-8710
7271 Engle Rd Ste 303 Cleveland (44130) ***(G-5432)***
Crawford & Company....330 652-3296
6752 Brookhollow Dr Sw Warren (44481) ***(G-18843)***
Crawford Cnty Council On Aging, Bucyrus *Also called City of Bucyrus* ***(G-2029)***
Crawford Cnty Job & Fmly Svcs, Bucyrus *Also called County of Crawford* ***(G-2033)***
Crawford Cnty Shared Hlth Svcs....419 468-7985
1220 N Market St Galion (44833) ***(G-11293)***
Crawford County Children Svcs (PA)....419 562-1200
224 Norton Way Bucyrus (44820) ***(G-2035)***
Crawford County Council On Agi....419 562-3050
200 S Spring St Bucyrus (44820) ***(G-2036)***
Crawford Group Inc....419 873-7360
12611 Eckel Junction Rd Perrysburg (43551) ***(G-15990)***
Crawford Group Inc....330 665-5432
3960 Medina Rd Akron (44333) ***(G-176)***
Crawford Hoying Ltd....614 335-2020
6640 Riverside Dr Ste 500 Dublin (43017) ***(G-10312)***
Crawford Manor Healthcare Ctr, Cleveland *Also called Saber Healthcare Group LLC* ***(G-6430)***
Crawford Mechanical Svcs Inc....614 478-9424
3445 Morse Rd Columbus (43231) ***(G-7455)***
Creative Center For Children....513 867-1118
23 Court St Hamilton (45011) ***(G-11719)***
Creative Childrens World LLC (PA)....513 336-7799
7818 S Masn Montgomery Rd Mason (45040) ***(G-13692)***
Creative Crafts Group LLC....303 215-5600
10151 Carver Rd Ste 200 Blue Ash (45242) ***(G-1570)***
Creative Diversified Services....937 376-7810
335 E Market St Xenia (45385) ***(G-20048)***
Creative Foundations Inc (PA)....740 362-5102
57 N Sandusky St Delaware (43015) ***(G-10085)***
Creative Foundations Inc....614 832-2121
127 S Main St Mount Vernon (43050) ***(G-14890)***
Creative Images College of B (PA)....937 478-7922
7535 Poe Ave Dayton (45414) ***(G-9443)***
Creative Imges Inst Csmetology, Dayton *Also called Creative Images College of B* ***(G-9443)***
Creative Learning Child Care....440 729-9001
7654 Sherman Rd Chesterland (44026) ***(G-2794)***
Creative Learning Workshop (PA)....330 393-5929
2460 Elm Rd Ne Ste 500 Warren (44483) ***(G-18844)***

Creative Learning Workshop....937 437-0146
146 N Washington St New Paris (45347) **(G-15076)**
Creative Living Inc....614 421-1131
150 W 10th Ave Columbus (43201) **(G-7456)**
Creative Living Housing Corp....614 421-1226
150 W 10th Ave Ofc Columbus (43201) **(G-7457)**
Creative Marketing Enterprises....419 867-4444
6711 Monroe St Ste 4c Sylvania (43560) **(G-17580)**
Creative Microsystems Inc....937 836-4499
52 Hillside Ct Englewood (45322) **(G-10701)**
Creative Mold and Machine Inc....440 338-5146
10385 Kinsman Rd Newbury (44065) **(G-15255)**
Creative Playroom (PA)....216 475-6464
16574 Broadway Ave Cleveland (44137) **(G-5433)**
Creative Playroom....440 248-3100
32750 Solon Rd Ste 3 Solon (44139) **(G-16997)**
Creative Playrooms, Westlake *Also called Westlake Mntsr Schl & Chld Dv* **(G-19568)**
Creative Playrooms Inc....440 572-9365
16000 Foltz Pkwy Strongsville (44149) **(G-17453)**
Creative Playrooms Inc (PA)....440 349-9111
32750 Solon Rd Ste 3 Solon (44139) **(G-16998)**
Creative Products Inc....419 866-5501
1430 Kieswetter Rd Holland (43528) **(G-12017)**
Creativity For Kids, Cleveland *Also called AW Faber-Castell Usa Inc* **(G-5086)**
Cred-Kap Inc....330 755-1466
400 Sexton St Struthers (44471) **(G-17529)**
Credit Adjustments Inc (PA)....419 782-3709
330 Florence St Defiance (43512) **(G-10024)**
Credit Bur Collectn Svcs Inc (HQ)....614 223-0688
236 E Town St Columbus (43215) **(G-7458)**
Credit Bur Collectn Svcs Inc....937 496-2577
11 W Monument Ave Ste 200 Dayton (45402) **(G-9444)**
Credit First NA....216 362-5000
6275 Eastland Rd Brookpark (44142) **(G-1941)**
Credit First National Assn....216 362-5300
6275 Eastland Rd Cleveland (44142) **(G-5434)**
Credit Infonet Inc....937 235-2546
4540 Honeywell Ct Dayton (45424) **(G-9445)**
Credit Union of Ohio Inc (PA)....614 487-6650
5500 Britton Pkwy Hilliard (43026) **(G-11892)**
Creek At Hicksburg, Hicksville *Also called Hickory Creek Healthcare* **(G-11864)**
Creek Technologies Company....937 272-4581
2372 Lakeview Dr Ste H Beavercreek (45431) **(G-1163)**
CREEKSIDE CONDOMINIUMS, Holland *Also called Lutheran Village At Wolf Creek* **(G-12033)**
Creekside Golf Dome....330 545-5000
1300 N State St Girard (44420) **(G-11412)**
Creekside Golf Ltd....513 785-2999
6090 Golf Club Ln Fairfield Township (45011) **(G-10928)**
Creekside II LLC....614 280-4000
2 Miranova Pl Ste 100 Columbus (43215) **(G-7459)**
Creekside Ltd LLC....513 583-4977
902 Lveland Miamiville Rd Loveland (45140) **(G-13118)**
Crefiii Waramaug....937 322-3600
100 S Fountain Ave Springfield (45502) **(G-17184)**
Cremation Service Inc (PA)....216 861-2334
1612 Leonard St Cleveland (44113) **(G-5435)**
Cremation Service Inc....216 621-6222
1605 Merwin Ave Cleveland (44113) **(G-5436)**
Creme De La Creme Colorado Inc....513 459-4300
5324 Natorp Blvd Mason (45040) **(G-13693)**
Creque's Greenhouse, Sylvania *Also called Jeff Creque Farms Inc* **(G-17596)**
Crescent Park Corporation (PA)....513 759-7000
9817 Crescent Park Dr West Chester (45069) **(G-19059)**
Crest Bending Inc....419 492-2108
108 John St New Washington (44854) **(G-15134)**
Crestline Hospital, Crestline *Also called Medcentral Health System* **(G-9147)**
Crestline Hotels & Resorts LLC....614 846-4355
7490 Vantage Dr Columbus (43235) **(G-7460)**
Crestline Hotels & Resorts LLC....513 489-3666
11435 Reed Hartman Hwy Blue Ash (45241) **(G-1571)**
Crestline Nursing Center, Crestline *Also called Consulate Management Co LLC* **(G-9143)**
Crestline Nursing Home Inc....419 683-3255
327 W Main St Crestline (44827) **(G-9144)**
Crestmont Cadillac Corporation (PA)....216 831-5300
26000 Chagrin Blvd Cleveland (44122) **(G-5437)**
Crestmont North, Lakewood *Also called Crestmont Nursing Home N Corp* **(G-12475)**
Crestmont Nursing Home N Corp (PA)....216 228-9550
13330 Detroit Ave Lakewood (44107) **(G-12475)**
Crestmont Nursing Home N Corp....216 228-9550
13330 Detroit Ave Lakewood (44107) **(G-12476)**
Cresttek LLC (PA)....248 602-2083
565 Metro Pl S Ste 420 Dublin (43017) **(G-10313)**
Crestview Health Care Center....740 695-2500
68637 Bannock Rd Saint Clairsville (43950) **(G-16634)**
CRESTVIEW MANOR I, Lancaster *Also called Crestview Manor Nursing Home* **(G-12524)**
Crestview Manor II, Lancaster *Also called Crestview Manor Nursing Home* **(G-12525)**
Crestview Manor Nursing Home (PA)....740 654-2634
957 Becks Knob Rd Lancaster (43130) **(G-12524)**
Crestview Manor Nursing Home....740 654-2634
925 Becks Knob Rd Lancaster (43130) **(G-12525)**
Crestview Nursing Home, Saint Clairsville *Also called Crestview Health Care Center* **(G-16634)**
Crestview Partners II Gp LP (PA)....216 898-2400
4900 Tiedeman Rd Fl 4 Brooklyn (44144) **(G-1905)**
Crestview Ridge Nursing....937 393-6700
141 Willetsville Pike Hillsboro (45133) **(G-11971)**
Crestwood Mgmt LLC....440 484-2400
23550 Commerce Park # 5000 Cleveland (44122) **(G-5438)**
Crestwood RDG Skilled Nursing, Hillsboro *Also called Congregate Living of America* **(G-11969)**
Crete Carrier Corporation....614 853-4500
5400 Crosswind Dr Columbus (43228) **(G-7461)**
Crew Soccer Stadium LLC....614 447-2739
1 Black And Gold Blvd Columbus (43211) **(G-7462)**
Cridersville Health Care Ctr....419 645-4468
603 E Main St Frnt Cridersville (45806) **(G-9151)**
Cridersville Nursing Home, Cridersville *Also called Cridersville Health Care Ctr* **(G-9151)**
Crisis Center, Chillicothe *Also called Sioto Paintsville Mental Hlth* **(G-2885)**
Crisis Counseling Center, Wilmington *Also called Mental Health & Recovery Ctr* **(G-19773)**
Crisis Intervention & Rcvy Ctr....330 455-9407
832 Mckinley Ave Nw Canton (44703) **(G-2327)**
Crisis Intvntn Ctr Stark Cnty....330 452-9812
2421 13th St Nw Canton (44708) **(G-2328)**
CRISIS NURSERY, Cleveland *Also called Providence House Inc* **(G-6326)**
Crisis Stablization Center, Cincinnati *Also called Central Community* **(G-3213)**
Crispin Iron & Metal Co LLC....740 616-6213
190 Victoria Dr Granville (43023) **(G-11464)**
Criss Cross Directories, North Canton *Also called Haines & Company Inc* **(G-15343)**
Critchfeld Crtchfield Johnston (PA)....330 264-4444
225 N Market St Wooster (44691) **(G-19859)**
Critical Business Analysis Inc....419 874-0800
133 W 2nd St Ste 1 Perrysburg (43551) **(G-15991)**
Critical Care Transport Inc....614 775-0564
2936 E 14th Ave Columbus (43219) **(G-7463)**
Critical Life Inc....419 525-0502
35 Logan Rd Mansfield (44907) **(G-13285)**
Crittenton Family Services....614 251-0103
1414 E Broad St Columbus (43205) **(G-7464)**
Crock Construction Co....740 732-2306
17990 Woodsfield Rd Caldwell (43724) **(G-2084)**
Crogan Colonial Bank....419 483-2541
1 Union Sq Bellevue (44811) **(G-1407)**
Croghan Bancshares Inc....419 794-9399
6465 Wheatstone Ct Maumee (43537) **(G-13902)**
Croghan Colonial Bank (HQ)....419 332-7301
323 Croghan St Fremont (43420) **(G-11193)**
Cronins Inc....513 851-5900
9847 Kings Auto Mall Rd Cincinnati (45249) **(G-3440)**
Crooked Tree Golf Course....513 398-3933
1250 Springfield Pike # 100 Cincinnati (45215) **(G-3441)**
Cross Roads Head Start, Painesville *Also called Crossroads Lake County Adole* **(G-15848)**
Cross Truck Equipment Co Inc....330 477-8151
1801 Perry Dr Sw Canton (44706) **(G-2329)**
Crosschx Inc....800 501-3161
99 E Main St Columbus (43215) **(G-7465)**
Crossgate Bowling Lanes, Blue Ash *Also called Crossgate Lanes Inc* **(G-1572)**
Crossgate Lanes Inc....513 891-0310
4230 Hunt Rd Blue Ash (45242) **(G-1572)**
Crossroad Health Center, Cincinnati *Also called Christian Community Hlth Svcs* **(G-3272)**
Crossroads Center....513 475-5300
311 Mrtin Lther King Dr W Cincinnati (45220) **(G-3442)**
Crossroads Lake County Adole (PA)....440 255-1700
8445 Munson Rd Mentor (44060) **(G-14165)**
Crossroads Lake County Adole....440 358-7370
1083 Mentor Ave Painesville (44077) **(G-15848)**
Crosswoods Ultrascreen Cinema, Columbus *Also called Marcus Theatres Corporation* **(G-8108)**
Croswell of Williamsburg LLC (PA)....513 724-2206
975 W Main St Williamsburg (45176) **(G-19631)**
Croswell of Williamsburg LLC....800 782-8747
4828 Wolf Creek Pike Dayton (45417) **(G-9446)**
Croswell VIP Motor Couch Svc, Williamsburg *Also called Croswell of Williamsburg LLC* **(G-19631)**
Crotinger Nursing Home Inc....937 968-5284
907 E Central St Union City (45390) **(G-18502)**
Crouse Implement....740 892-2086
14149 North St Utica (43080) **(G-18611)**
Crowe Enterprises, Ravenna *Also called Crowe Masonry* **(G-16382)**
Crowe Horwath LLP....614 469-0001
155 W Nationwide Blvd # 500 Columbus (43215) **(G-7466)**
Crowe Horwath LLP....216 623-7500
600 Superior Ave E # 902 Cleveland (44114) **(G-5439)**
Crowe Masonry....330 296-5539
4699 Loomis Pkwy Ravenna (44266) **(G-16382)**
Crown Auto Top Mfg Co, Columbus *Also called Crown Dielectric Inds Inc* **(G-7467)**
Crown Center, Hudson *Also called Laurel Lk Retirement Cmnty Inc* **(G-12130)**
Crown Dielectric Inds Inc....614 224-5161
830 W Broad St Columbus (43222) **(G-7467)**

Crown Equipment Corporation (PA)......419 629-2311
44 S Washington St New Bremen (45869) ***(G-15018)***
Crown Equipment Corporation......419 629-2311
40 S Washington St New Bremen (45869) ***(G-15019)***
Crown Heating & Cooling Inc......330 499-4988
11197 Cleveland Ave Nw Uniontown (44685) ***(G-18516)***
Crown Hill Cemetery, Twinsburg *Also called Stonemor Partners LP* ***(G-18474)***
Crown Lift Trucks, New Bremen *Also called Crown Equipment Corporation* ***(G-15018)***
Crown Logistics, Columbus *Also called MSA Group Inc* ***(G-8204)***
Crown Plaza, Cincinnati *Also called Wph Cincinnati LLC* ***(G-4861)***
Crown Pointe Care Center, Columbus *Also called Franklin Shcp Inc* ***(G-7698)***
Crown Westfalen LLC......614 488-1169
1251 Dublin Rd Columbus (43215) ***(G-7468)***
Crowne Group LLC (PA)......216 589-0198
127 Public Sq Ste 5110 Cleveland (44114) ***(G-5440)***
Crowne Plaza Ci, Cincinnati *Also called Sage Hospitality Resources LLC* ***(G-4469)***
Crowne Plaza Cleveland Airport, Cleveland *Also called Toledo Inns Inc* ***(G-6601)***
Crowne Plaza Clevenland, Independence *Also called Rockside Hospitality LLC* ***(G-12251)***
Crowne Plaza Columbus Downtown, Columbus *Also called Ihg Management (maryland) LLC* ***(G-7883)***
Crowne Plaza Columbus North, Columbus *Also called Columbus Leasing LLC* ***(G-7363)***
Crowne Plaza Dayton, Dayton *Also called Hdi Ltd* ***(G-9602)***
Crowne Plaza Dayton Hotel, Dayton *Also called Integrity Hotel Group* ***(G-9633)***
Crowne Plaza Toledo, Toledo *Also called Paradise Hospitality Inc* ***(G-18116)***
Crowne Plaza Toledo......419 241-1411
444 N Summit St Toledo (43604) ***(G-17841)***
Crowning Food Company......937 323-4699
1966 Commerce Cir Springfield (45504) ***(G-17185)***
Croxton Realty Company......330 492-1697
410 47th St Nw Canton (44709) ***(G-2330)***
Croys Mowing LLC......419 523-5884
440 N Maple St Ottawa (45875) ***(G-15797)***
Crp Contracting......614 338-8501
4477 E 5th Ave Columbus (43219) ***(G-7469)***
CRST International Inc......740 599-0008
16559 Skyline Dr Danville (43014) ***(G-9245)***
Crw Inc......330 264-3785
3716 S Elyria Rd Shreve (44676) ***(G-16907)***
Crystal Arthritis Center Inc......330 668-4045
3975 Embassy Pkwy Ste 101 Akron (44333) ***(G-177)***
Crystal Care Centers Inc......419 281-9595
1251 E Main St Ashland (44805) ***(G-677)***
Crystal Care Centers Inc......419 747-2666
458 Vanderbilt Rd Unit 1 Mansfield (44904) ***(G-13286)***
Crystal Care Centers Inc (PA)......419 747-2666
1159 Wyandotte Ave Mansfield (44906) ***(G-13287)***
Crystal Care Ctr of Portsmouth......740 354-6619
1319 Spring St Portsmouth (45662) ***(G-16274)***
Crystal Care of Mansfield, Mansfield *Also called Crystal Care Centers Inc* ***(G-13287)***
Crystal Clean Parts Washer Svc, Toledo *Also called Heritage Envmtl Svcs LLC* ***(G-17954)***
Crystal Clear Bldg Svcs Inc......440 439-2288
26118 Broadway Ave Ste B Oakwood Village (44146) ***(G-15628)***
Crystal Clinic Surgery Ctr Inc......330 668-4040
3975 Embassy Pkwy Ste 202 Akron (44333) ***(G-178)***
Crystal Clnic Orthpdic Ctr LLC (PA)......330 668-4040
3925 Embassy Pkwy Ste 250 Akron (44333) ***(G-179)***
Crystal Clnic Orthpdic Ctr LLC......330 535-3396
20 Olive St Ste 200 Akron (44310) ***(G-180)***
Crystal Crystal Carpet Care, Columbus *Also called Clinton-Carvell Inc* ***(G-7303)***
Crystalwood Inc......513 605-1000
70 Damon Rd Cincinnati (45218) ***(G-3443)***
Cs Hotels Limited Partnership......614 771-8999
2350 Westbelt Dr Columbus (43228) ***(G-7470)***
Csa, Blue Ash *Also called Corps Security Agency Inc* ***(G-1568)***
Csa America Inc (HQ)......216 524-4990
8501 E Pleasant Valley Rd Cleveland (44131) ***(G-5441)***
Csa America Inc......216 524-4990
8501 E Pleasant Valley Rd Cleveland (44131) ***(G-5442)***
Csa Animal Nutrition LLC......866 615-8084
6640 Poe Ave Ste 225 Dayton (45414) ***(G-9447)***
Csa Group, Cleveland *Also called Csa America Inc* ***(G-5441)***
Csa International Services, Cleveland *Also called Csa America Inc* ***(G-5442)***
CSB, Millersburg *Also called Commercial Svgs Bank Millersbu* ***(G-14595)***
CSB Bancorp Inc (PA)......330 674-9015
91 N Clay St Millersburg (44654) ***(G-14602)***
CSC, Cleveland *Also called Communications Supply Corp* ***(G-5381)***
CSC Insurance Agency Inc......614 895-2000
550 Polaris Pkwy Ste 300 Westerville (43082) ***(G-19294)***
Csh Group......937 226-0070
10100 Innovation Dr # 400 Miamisburg (45342) ***(G-14290)***
Csi Complete, Plain City *Also called Douglas Webb & Associates* ***(G-16188)***
Csi Complete Inc......800 343-0641
8080 Corporate Blvd Plain City (43064) ***(G-16186)***
Csi International, Williamsport *Also called Connectivity Systems Inc* ***(G-19637)***
Csi International Inc......614 781-1571
690 Lkview Plz Blvd Ste C Worthington (43085) ***(G-19952)***
Csi Managed Care Inc......440 717-1700
6955 Treeline Dr Ste A Brecksville (44141) ***(G-1822)***
Csi Network Services, Brecksville *Also called Csi Managed Care Inc* ***(G-1822)***
Csl Plasma Inc......937 331-9186
850 N Main St Dayton (45405) ***(G-9448)***
Csl Plasma Inc......614 267-4982
2650 N High St Columbus (43202) ***(G-7471)***
Csl Plasma Inc......330 535-4338
727 Grant St Lowr Akron (44311) ***(G-181)***
Csl Plasma Inc......216 398-0440
3204 W 25th St Cleveland (44109) ***(G-5443)***
Csr Colortone Staging Rentals......440 914-9500
5401 Naiman Pkwy Ste A Cleveland (44139) ***(G-5444)***
CSRA LLC......937 429-9774
3560 Pentagon Blvd Beavercreek (45431) ***(G-1164)***
Csrc, Chillicothe *Also called Chillicothe Racquet Club* ***(G-2824)***
CSS Publishing Co Inc......419 227-1818
5450 N Dixie Hwy Lima (45807) ***(G-12768)***
Csu/Career Services Center......216 687-2233
2121 Euclid Ave Cleveland (44115) ***(G-5445)***
CSX Corporation......419 225-4121
401 E Robb Ave Lima (45801) ***(G-12769)***
CSX Corporation......614 242-3932
88 E Broad St Ste 1540 Columbus (43215) ***(G-7472)***
CSX Corporation......419 933-5027
2826 Liberty Rd Willard (44890) ***(G-19618)***
CSX Transportation Inc......440 992-0871
1709 E Prospect Rd Ashtabula (44004) ***(G-740)***
CSX Transportation Inc......513 369-5514
3601 Geringer St Cincinnati (45223) ***(G-3444)***
CSX Transportation Inc......614 898-3651
426 Landings Loop E Westerville (43082) ***(G-19295)***
CSX Transportation Inc......937 642-2221
19835 Johnson Rd Marysville (43040) ***(G-13615)***
CSX Transportation Inc......419 257-1225
17000 Deshler Rd North Baltimore (45872) ***(G-15312)***
CSX Transportation Inc......513 422-2031
1003 Forrer St Middletown (45044) ***(G-14423)***
CSX Transportation Inc......419 697-2323
600 Millard Ave Oregon (43616) ***(G-15729)***
CT Communications, Urbana *Also called Champaign Telephone Company* ***(G-18579)***
CT Consultants Inc (PA)......440 951-9000
8150 Sterling Ct Mentor (44060) ***(G-14166)***
CT Consultants Inc......513 791-1700
11120 Kenwood Rd Blue Ash (45242) ***(G-1573)***
CT Logistics Inc......216 267-1636
12487 Plaza Dr Cleveland (44130) ***(G-5446)***
CT Medical Electronics Co......440 526-3551
1 Corporation Ctr Broadview Heights (44147) ***(G-1876)***
Ctd Investments LLC (PA)......614 570-9949
630 E Broad St Columbus (43215) ***(G-7473)***
CTI, Monroe *Also called Continental Transport Inc* ***(G-14692)***
Ctl Analyzers, Shaker Heights *Also called Cellular Technology Limited* ***(G-16857)***
Ctl Engineering Inc (PA)......614 276-8123
2860 Fisher Rd Columbus (43204) ***(G-7474)***
Ctm Integration Incorporated......330 332-1800
1318 Quaker Cir Salem (44460) ***(G-16693)***
Ctpartners Exec Search Inc......216 464-8710
28601 Chagrin Blvd # 600 Beachwood (44122) ***(G-1069)***
Ctrac Inc......440 572-1000
2222 W 110th St Cleveland (44102) ***(G-5447)***
CTS Construction Inc......513 489-8290
6661 Cooper Rd Cincinnati (45242) ***(G-3445)***
CTS Telecommunications, Cincinnati *Also called CTS Construction Inc* ***(G-3445)***
Ctv Media Inc (PA)......614 848-5800
1490 Manning Pkwy Powell (43065) ***(G-16333)***
Cuddy Farms Inc......740 599-7979
15835 Danville Jelloway R Danville (43014) ***(G-9246)***
Cui, Bedford Heights *Also called Chores Unlimited Inc* ***(G-1350)***
Culver Art & Frame Co......740 548-6868
7890 N Central Dr Lewis Center (43035) ***(G-12679)***
Cumberford & Watts, Cleveland *Also called West Side Cardiology Assoc* ***(G-6737)***
Cumberland Gap LLC......513 681-9300
2285 Banning Rd Cincinnati (45239) ***(G-3446)***
Cumberland Trail Golf CLB Crse......740 964-9336
8244 Columbia Rd Sw Etna (43062) ***(G-10733)***
Cummings and Davis Fnrl HM Inc......216 541-1111
13201 Euclid Ave Cleveland (44112) ***(G-5448)***
Cummins Bridgeway Columbus LLC......614 771-1000
4000 Lyman Dr Hilliard (43026) ***(G-11893)***
Cummins Building Maint Inc......740 726-9800
5202 Marion Waldo Rd Prospect (43342) ***(G-16363)***
Cummins Facility Services LLC......740 726-9800
5202 Marion Waldo Rd Prospect (43342) ***(G-16364)***
Cummins Inc......614 771-1000
4000 Lyman Dr Hilliard (43026) ***(G-11894)***
Cumulus Broadcasting LLC......850 243-7676
4805 Montgomery Rd Cincinnati (45212) ***(G-3447)***
Cumulus Broadcasting LLC......330 783-1000
4040 Simon Rd Youngstown (44512) ***(G-20163)***
Cumulus Media Inc......419 725-5700
3225 Arlington Ave Toledo (43614) ***(G-17842)***
Cumulus Media Inc......513 241-9898
4805 Montgomery Rd # 300 Cincinnati (45212) ***(G-3448)***

Cumulus Media Inc......419 240-1000
3225 Arlington Ave Toledo (43614) ***(G-17843)***
Cunningham Paving Company......216 581-8600
20814 Aurora Rd Bedford (44146) ***(G-1302)***
Curator Video LLC......513 842-6605
10250 Alliance Rd Ste 226 Blue Ash (45242) ***(G-1574)***
Curiosity LLC......513 744-6000
35 E 7th St Ste 800 Cincinnati (45202) ***(G-3449)***
Curiosity Advertising, Cincinnati *Also called Curiosity LLC* ***(G-3449)***
Curtiss-Wright Controls......937 252-5601
2600 Paramount Pl Ste 200 Fairborn (45324) ***(G-10789)***
Curtiss-Wright Flow Control......513 735-2538
750 Kent Rd Batavia (45103) ***(G-1008)***
Curtiss-Wright Flow Control......513 528-7900
4600 E Tech Dr Cincinnati (45245) ***(G-2909)***
Curtiss-Wright Flow Control......513 528-7900
4600 E Tech Dr Cincinnati (45245) ***(G-2910)***
Curtiss-Wright Flow Ctrl Corp......513 528-7900
4600 E Tech Dr Cincinnati (45245) ***(G-2911)***
Cusa Ll Inc......216 267-8810
13315 Brookpark Rd Brookpark (44142) ***(G-1942)***
Cushman & Wakefield Inc......513 631-1121
4600 Montgomery Rd Norwood (45212) ***(G-15598)***
Cushman & Wakefield Inc......937 222-7884
3033 Kettering Blvd # 111 Moraine (45439) ***(G-14765)***
Cuso Corporation......513 984-2876
10485 Reading Rd Cincinnati (45241) ***(G-3450)***
Custom AC & Htg Co......614 552-4822
935 Claycraft Rd Gahanna (43230) ***(G-11238)***
Custom Agri Systems Inc......419 209-0940
1289 N Warpole St Upper Sandusky (43351) ***(G-18559)***
Custom Chemical Solutions......800 291-1057
167 Commerce Dr Loveland (45140) ***(G-13119)***
Custom Cleaners, Bryan *Also called George Gardner* ***(G-2006)***
Custom Cleaning and Maint......440 946-7028
38046 2nd St Willoughby (44094) ***(G-19657)***
Custom Cleaning Service LLC......440 774-1222
305 Artino St Unit A Oberlin (44074) ***(G-15641)***
Custom Design Benefits Inc......513 598-2929
5589 Cheviot Rd Cincinnati (45247) ***(G-3451)***
Custom Halthcare Proffessional......216 381-1010
5001 Mayfield Rd Ste 210 Cleveland (44124) ***(G-5449)***
Custom Lawn Care & Ldscpg LLC......740 333-1669
2411 Us Highway 22 Sw Wshngtn CT Hs (43160) ***(G-20019)***
Custom Machine Inc......419 986-5122
3315 W Township Road 158 Tiffin (44883) ***(G-17676)***
Custom Maid Cleaning Services......513 351-6571
3840 Burwood Ave Cincinnati (45212) ***(G-3452)***
Custom Mail Services, Cincinnati *Also called Ngm Inc* ***(G-4168)***
Custom Maint......330 793-2523
73 Country Green Dr Youngstown (44515) ***(G-20164)***
Custom Materials Inc......440 543-8284
16865 Park Circle Dr Chagrin Falls (44023) ***(G-2713)***
Custom Movers Services Inc......330 564-0507
3290 Kent Rd Stow (44224) ***(G-17358)***
Custom Pak, Medina *Also called Industrial Chemical Corp* ***(G-14079)***
Custom Pkg & Inspecting Inc......330 399-8961
5232 Tod Ave Sw Ste 3 Warren (44481) ***(G-18845)***
Custom Products Corporation (PA)......440 528-7100
7100 Cochran Rd Solon (44139) ***(G-16999)***
Custom Staffing Inc (PA)......419 221-3097
505 W Market St Lima (45801) ***(G-12770)***
Custom Trim of America, Akron *Also called Kallas Enterprises Inc* ***(G-300)***
Custom-Pak Inc......330 725-0800
885 W Smith Rd Medina (44256) ***(G-14056)***
Customized Girl, Columbus *Also called E Retailing Associates LLC* ***(G-7561)***
Custompak, Medina *Also called Custom-Pak Inc* ***(G-14056)***
Cuthbert Greenhouse Inc (PA)......614 836-3866
4900 Hendron Rd Groveport (43125) ***(G-11631)***
Cutler and Associates Inc......330 896-1680
971 E Turkeyfoot Lake Rd Akron (44312) ***(G-182)***
Cutler and Associates Inc......330 688-2100
3653 Darrow Rd Ste 1 Stow (44224) ***(G-17359)***
Cutler and Associates Inc (PA)......330 493-9323
4618 Dressler Rd Nw Canton (44718) ***(G-2331)***
Cutler G M A C Real Estate, Canton *Also called Cutler Real Estate* ***(G-2332)***
Cutler Real Estate......330 499-9922
203 Applegrove St Nw North Canton (44720) ***(G-15331)***
Cutler Real Estate (PA)......330 836-9141
2800 W Market St Fairlawn (44333) ***(G-10943)***
Cutler Real Estate......330 688-2100
3653 Darrow Rd Stow (44224) ***(G-17360)***
Cutler Real Estate......330 644-0644
971 E Turkeyfoot Lake Rd A Akron (44312) ***(G-183)***
Cutler Real Estate......330 733-7575
525 N Scranton St Ravenna (44266) ***(G-16383)***
Cutler Real Estate (PA)......330 492-7230
4618 Dressler Rd Nw Canton (44718) ***(G-2332)***
Cutler Real Estate Inc......614 339-4664
6375 Riverside Dr Ste 210 Dublin (43017) ***(G-10314)***
Cutler Realtor, Akron *Also called Cutler and Associates Inc* ***(G-182)***
Cutler/Gmac Real Estate, Canton *Also called Cutler and Associates Inc* ***(G-2331)***
Cuttin' It Close, Mansfield *Also called Tara Flaherty* ***(G-13372)***
Cutting Edge Countertops Inc......419 873-9500
1300 Flagship Dr Perrysburg (43551) ***(G-15992)***
Cuyahoga County......216 420-6750
1701 E 12th St Ste 11 Cleveland (44114) ***(G-5450)***
Cuyahoga County......216 265-3030
12660 Plaza Dr Cleveland (44130) ***(G-5451)***
Cuyahoga County......216 431-4500
3955 Euclid Ave Cleveland (44115) ***(G-5452)***
Cuyahoga County......216 348-3800
2079 E 9th St Cleveland (44115) ***(G-5453)***
Cuyahoga County......216 443-8920
1 W Lakeside Ave Ste 146 Cleveland (44113) ***(G-5454)***
Cuyahoga County AG Soc......440 243-0090
164 Eastland Rd Berea (44017) ***(G-1454)***
Cuyahoga County Board of Menta, Cleveland *Also called County of Cuyahoga* ***(G-5424)***
Cuyahoga County Convention Fac......216 928-1600
1 Saint Clair Ave Ne Cleveland (44114) ***(G-5455)***
Cuyahoga County Dept Pub Works, Cleveland *Also called Cuyahoga County* ***(G-5453)***
Cuyahoga County Fair, Berea *Also called Cuyahoga County AG Soc* ***(G-1454)***
Cuyahoga County Sani Engrg Svc......216 443-8211
6100 W Canal Rd Cleveland (44125) ***(G-5456)***
Cuyahoga Group, The, Maple Heights *Also called Cuyahoga Vending Co Inc* ***(G-13404)***
Cuyahoga Landmark Inc (PA)......440 238-3900
21079 Westwood Dr Strongsville (44149) ***(G-17454)***
Cuyahoga Marketing Service......440 526-5350
375 Treeworth Blvd Cleveland (44147) ***(G-5457)***
Cuyahoga Vending Co Inc (PA)......216 663-1457
14250 Industrial Ave S # 104 Maple Heights (44137) ***(G-13404)***
CV Perry Builders......614 221-4131
370 S 5th St Ste 2 Columbus (43215) ***(G-7475)***
CVNPA, Peninsula *Also called Conserv For Cyhg Vlly Nat Prk* ***(G-15949)***
Cw Financial LLC......941 907-9490
23550 Commerce Park # 5000 Beachwood (44122) ***(G-1070)***
Cw Service, Coldwater *Also called Ayers Service Group LLC* ***(G-6827)***
Cwb Property Managment Inc (PA)......614 793-2244
5775 Perimeter Dr Ste 290 Dublin (43017) ***(G-10315)***
Cwm Envronmental Cleveland LLC......216 663-0808
4450 Johnston Pkwy Ste B Cleveland (44128) ***(G-5458)***
Cy Schwieterman Inc......419 753-2566
10097 Kohler Rd Wapakoneta (45895) ***(G-18794)***
Cyo & Community Services Inc (PA)......330 762-2961
795 Russell Ave Akron (44307) ***(G-184)***
Cypress Communications Inc (HQ)......404 965-7248
75 Erieview Plz Fl 4 Cleveland (44114) ***(G-5459)***
Cypress Companies Inc (PA)......330 849-6500
670 W Market St Akron (44303) ***(G-185)***
Cypress Hospice LLC......440 973-0250
2 Berea Commons Ste 1 Berea (44017) ***(G-1455)***
Cyxtera Data Centers Inc......216 986-2742
6100 Oak Tree Blvd # 200 Cleveland (44131) ***(G-5460)***
D & D Advertising Enterprises......513 921-6827
801 Evans St Ste 203 Cincinnati (45204) ***(G-3453)***
D & D Investment Co......614 272-6567
3080 Valleyview Dr Columbus (43204) ***(G-7476)***
D & D Rv and Auto LLC......937 839-4555
3376 Us Route 35 E West Alexandria (45381) ***(G-19008)***
D & G Focht Construction Co......419 732-2412
2040 E State Rd Port Clinton (43452) ***(G-16243)***
D & J Master Clean Inc......614 847-1181
680 Dearborn Park Ln Columbus (43085) ***(G-7477)***
D & S Crtive Cmmunications Inc (PA)......419 524-6699
140 Park Ave E Mansfield (44902) ***(G-13288)***
D & S Crtive Cmmunications Inc......419 524-4312
195 E 4th St Mansfield (44902) ***(G-13289)***
D & S Properties......614 224-6663
854 E Broad St Columbus (43205) ***(G-7478)***
D & V Trucking Inc......330 482-9440
12803 Clmbana Canfield Rd Columbiana (44408) ***(G-6857)***
D A Peterson Inc......330 821-1111
393 Smyth Ave Alliance (44601) ***(G-537)***
D A R Plumbing, Columbus *Also called Dar Plumbing* ***(G-7489)***
D B A Inc......513 541-6600
4239 Hamilton Ave Cincinnati (45223) ***(G-3454)***
D B Bentley Inc......440 352-8495
2649 Narrows Rd Painesville (44077) ***(G-15849)***
D C Curry Lumber Company......330 264-5223
331 W Henry St Wooster (44691) ***(G-19860)***
D C G, Cleveland *Also called Directconnectgroup Ltd* ***(G-5486)***
D C I, Akron *Also called Digital Color Intl LLC* ***(G-193)***
D C Minnick Contracting Ltd (PA)......937 322-1012
328 Ravenwood Dr Springfield (45504) ***(G-17186)***
D C Transportation Service......440 237-0900
5740 Royalwood Rd Ste C North Royalton (44133) ***(G-15485)***
D E Huddleston Inc......740 773-2130
283 S Paint St Chillicothe (45601) ***(G-2832)***
D E Williams Electric Inc......440 543-1222
168 Solon Rd Ste B Chagrin Falls (44022) ***(G-2695)***
D G M Inc......740 226-1950
1881 Adams Rd Beaver (45613) ***(G-1141)***
D H I Cooperative Inc......614 545-0460
1224 Alton Darby Creek Rd A Columbus (43228) ***(G-7479)***

ALPHABETIC

(PA)=Parent Co (HQ)=Headquarters (DH)=Div Headquarters
2018 Harris Ohio Services Directory 1165

D H Packaging Co (PA)..........513 791-2022
8005 Plainfield Rd Ste 20 Cincinnati (45236) *(G-3455)*
D I S A D E C C Columbus, Columbus *Also called Defense Info Systems Agcy (G-7502)*
D J- Seve Group Inc..........614 888-6600
10030 Columbus Pike Lewis Center (43035) *(G-12680)*
D James Incorporated..........513 574-4550
4320 Bridgetown Rd Cincinnati (45211) *(G-3456)*
D L A Training Center..........614 692-5986
3990 E Brd St Bldg 11 5 Columbus (43213) *(G-7480)*
D L Belknap Trucking Inc..........330 868-7766
3526 Baird Ave Se Paris (44669) *(G-15895)*
D L Ryan Companies LLC..........614 436-6558
440 Polaris Pkwy Ste 350 Westerville (43082) *(G-19296)*
D M I, Reynoldsburg *Also called Dimensional Metals Inc (G-16447)*
D M I Distribution Inc..........765 584-3234
6150 Huntley Rd Ste A Columbus (43229) *(G-7481)*
D S C, Dublin *Also called Dimension Service Corporation (G-10321)*
D W Dickey, Lisbon *Also called D W Dickey and Son Inc (G-12935)*
D W Dickey and Son Inc (PA)..........330 424-1441
7896 Dickey Dr Lisbon (44432) *(G-12935)*
D W F, Toledo *Also called Denver Wholesale Florists Co (G-17850)*
D&D Trucking and Services Inc..........419 692-3205
5191 Kill Rd Delphos (45833) *(G-10140)*
D&M Carter LLC..........513 831-8843
106 Glendale Milford Rd Miamiville (45147) *(G-14375)*
D&T Installed Siding LLC..........614 444-8445
1325 Marion Rd Columbus (43207) *(G-7482)*
D-G Custom Chrome LLC..........513 531-1881
5200 Lester Rd Cincinnati (45213) *(G-3457)*
D-R Training Center & Workshop..........419 289-0470
1256 Center St Ashland (44805) *(G-678)*
D.C.minnick Heating and AC, Springfield *Also called D C Minnick Contracting Ltd (G-17186)*
Da Vinci Group Inc..........614 419-2393
7815 Pembrook Dr Reynoldsburg (43068) *(G-16442)*
Da Vita, Marietta *Also called Davita Inc (G-13442)*
Da Vita, Canton *Also called Davita Inc (G-2335)*
Da Vita, Belpre *Also called Davita Inc (G-1435)*
Dacas Nursing Systems Inc..........330 884-2530
8747 Squires Ln Ne Warren (44484) *(G-18846)*
Dacia R Crum..........513 698-5000
600 Vine St Cincinnati (45202) *(G-3458)*
DAG Construction Co Inc..........513 542-8597
4924 Winton Rd Cincinnati (45232) *(G-3459)*
Dagger Johnston Miller (PA)..........740 653-6464
144 E Main St Lancaster (43130) *(G-12526)*
Dahlberg Learning Center, Columbus *Also called Assoc Dvlpmtly Disabled (G-7054)*
Dahm Brothers Company Inc..........937 461-5627
743 Valley St Dayton (45404) *(G-9449)*
Daifuku America Corporation (HQ)..........614 863-1888
6700 Tussing Rd Reynoldsburg (43068) *(G-16443)*
Daifuku Co, Reynoldsburg *Also called Daifuku America Corporation (G-16443)*
Daihen Inc (HQ)..........937 667-0800
1400 Blauser Dr Tipp City (45371) *(G-17715)*
Daikin Applied Americas Inc..........763 553-5009
2915 Needmore Rd Dayton (45414) *(G-9450)*
Daikin Applied Parts Warehouse, Dayton *Also called Daikin Applied Americas Inc (G-9450)*
Daily Services LLC..........740 326-6130
12 E Gambier St Mount Vernon (43050) *(G-14891)*
Daily Services LLC (PA)..........614 431-5100
1110 Morse Rd Ste B1 Columbus (43229) *(G-7483)*
Dairy Farm, Polk *Also called Falling Star Farm Ltd (G-16230)*
Dairy Farmers America Inc..........330 670-7800
1035 Medina Rd Ste 300 Medina (44256) *(G-14057)*
Dakota Girls LLC..........614 801-2558
2585 London Groveport Rd Grove City (43123) *(G-11551)*
Dakota Software Corporation (PA)..........216 765-7100
1375 Euclid Ave Ste 500 Cleveland (44115) *(G-5461)*
Dalad Group, Independence *Also called Royalton 6001 Ltd (G-12256)*
Dale Ross Trucking Inc..........937 981-2168
11408 State Route 41 S Greenfield (45123) *(G-11484)*
Dale-Roy School & Training Ctr, Ashland *Also called D-R Training Center & Workshop (G-678)*
Dales Truck Parts Inc..........937 766-2551
2891 Us Route 42 E Cedarville (45314) *(G-2632)*
Dalmatian Press, Ashland *Also called Anderson Press Incorporated (G-650)*
Dalton Roofing Co..........513 871-2800
4477 Eastern Ave Cincinnati (45226) *(G-3460)*
Damarc Inc..........330 454-6171
4330 Kirby Ave Ne Canton (44705) *(G-2333)*
Damascus Staffing LLC..........513 954-8941
2263 W Us 22 And 3 Maineville (45039) *(G-13242)*
Damon Tax Service..........513 574-9087
6572 Glenway Ave Cincinnati (45211) *(G-3461)*
Damschroder Roofing Inc..........419 332-5000
2228 Hayes Ave Ste D Fremont (43420) *(G-11194)*
Dan Beard Council, Cincinnati *Also called Boy Scouts of America (G-3128)*
Dan Marchetta Cnstr Co Inc..........330 668-4800
525 N Cleveland Massillon Akron (44333) *(G-186)*
Dan Tobin Pontiac Buick GMC..........614 889-6300
2539 Billingsley Rd Columbus (43235) *(G-7484)*
Dan-Ray Construction LLC..........216 518-8484
4500 Lee Rd Ste 207 Cleveland (44128) *(G-5462)*
Dana & Pariser Attys..........614 253-1010
495 E Mound St Columbus (43215) *(G-7485)*
Dana Companies, LLC, Perrysburg *Also called Dco LLC (G-15996)*
Dana Credit Corporation (HQ)..........419 887-3000
3939 Technology Dr Maumee (43537) *(G-13903)*
Dana Heavy Vehicle Systems..........419 866-3900
6936 Airport Hwy Holland (43528) *(G-12018)*
Dana Lauren Salon & Spa..........440 262-1092
8076 Broadview Rd Broadview Heights (44147) *(G-1877)*
Dana Spicer Service Parts, Holland *Also called Dana Heavy Vehicle Systems (G-12018)*
Danbarry Dollar Svr Cinema, Dayton *Also called B and D Investment Partnership (G-9348)*
Danbarry Linemas Inc..........740 779-6115
119 Pawnee Rd Chillicothe (45601) *(G-2833)*
Danberry Co..........419 866-8888
3555 Briarfield Blvd Maumee (43537) *(G-13904)*
Danbury Woods of Wooster..........330 264-0355
939 Portage Rd Wooster (44691) *(G-19861)*
Danby Products Inc (HQ)..........519 425-8627
1800 Production Dr Findlay (45840) *(G-11020)*
Dancor Inc..........614 340-2155
2155 Dublin Rd Columbus (43228) *(G-7486)*
Daniel A Terreri & Sons Inc..........330 538-2950
1091 N Meridian Rd Youngstown (44509) *(G-20165)*
Daniel Logistics Inc..........614 367-9442
426 Mccormick Blvd Columbus (43213) *(G-7487)*
Daniel Maury Construction Co..........513 984-4096
8960 Glendale Milford Rd Loveland (45140) *(G-13120)*
Daniel's Construction, Berlin Heights *Also called Daniels Basement Waterproofing (G-1481)*
Daniels Basement Waterproofing..........440 965-4332
10407 Main Rd Berlin Heights (44814) *(G-1481)*
Daniels Boarding Kennels..........440 238-7179
21782 Royalton Rd Strongsville (44149) *(G-17455)*
Daniels Lumber Co Inc..........330 533-2211
250 Railroad St Canfield (44406) *(G-2188)*
Danis Building Construction Co (PA)..........937 228-1225
3233 Newmark Dr Miamisburg (45342) *(G-14291)*
Danis Industrial Cnstr Co..........937 228-1225
3233 Newmark Dr Miamisburg (45342) *(G-14292)*
Danite Holdings Ltd..........614 444-3333
1640 Harmon Ave Columbus (43223) *(G-7488)*
Danite Sign Co, Columbus *Also called Danite Holdings Ltd (G-7488)*
Danny Veghs Home Entertainment, Mayfield Heights *Also called Dtv Inc (G-14001)*
Danridge Nursing Home Inc..........330 746-5157
31 Maranatha Ct Youngstown (44505) *(G-20166)*
Danson Inc..........513 948-0066
3033 Robertson Ave Cincinnati (45209) *(G-3462)*
Danton Eye Associates, Beavercreek *Also called Richard L Liston MD (G-1258)*
Dar Plumbing..........614 445-8243
2230 Refugee Rd Columbus (43207) *(G-7489)*
Darana Hybrid Inc..........513 785-7540
345 High St Fl 5 Hamilton (45011) *(G-11720)*
Darby Creek Excavating Inc..........740 477-8600
19524 London Rd Circleville (43113) *(G-4886)*
Darby Creek Golf Course Inc..........937 349-7491
19300 Orchard Rd Marysville (43040) *(G-13616)*
Darby Creek Nursery, Hilliard *Also called R & S Halley & Co Inc (G-11947)*
Darfus..........740 380-1710
1135 W Hunter St Logan (43138) *(G-12971)*
Dari Pizza Enterprises II Inc..........419 534-3000
1683 Woodlands Dr Ste A Maumee (43537) *(G-13905)*
Darice, Strongsville *Also called Lamrite West Inc (G-17482)*
Darice Inc (HQ)..........440 238-9150
13000 Darice Pkwy 82 Strongsville (44149) *(G-17456)*
Darke Cnty Mental Hlth Clinic (PA)..........937 548-1635
212 E Main St Greenville (45331) *(G-11494)*
Darke County Sheriffs Patrol..........937 548-3399
5185 County Home Rd Greenville (45331) *(G-11495)*
Daron Coal Company LLC..........614 643-0337
40580 Cadiz Piedmont Rd Cadiz (43907) *(G-2074)*
Darr Farms, Newcomerstown *Also called George Darr (G-15269)*
Dart Trucking Company Inc (PA)..........330 549-0994
11017 Market St North Lima (44452) *(G-15401)*
Das Dutch Kitchen Inc..........330 683-0530
14278 Lincoln Way E Dalton (44618) *(G-9240)*
Das Dutch Village Inn..........330 482-5050
150 E State Route 14 Columbiana (44408) *(G-6858)*
Dash Logistics Inc..........937 382-9110
259 Olinger Cir Wilmington (45177) *(G-19760)*
Dassault Systemes Simulia Corp..........513 275-1430
5181 Natorp Blvd Ste 205 Mason (45040) *(G-13694)*
DAT, Akron *Also called Downtown Akron Partnership Inc (G-199)*
Data Direction Inc..........216 362-5900
6675 Eastland Rd Ste Bk Cleveland (44130) *(G-5463)*
Data Recovery, Shaker Heights *Also called 1st All File Recovery Usa (G-16855)*
Datacomm Tech..........614 755-5100
6606 Tussing Rd Ste B Reynoldsburg (43068) *(G-16444)*
Datafield Inc..........614 847-9600
25 W New England Ave Worthington (43085) *(G-19953)*
Datalliance, Blue Ash *Also called Enterprise Data Management Inc (G-1588)*

ALPHABETIC SECTION — Day-Met Credit Union Inc (PA)

Datalysys LLC 614 495-0260
6063 Frantz Rd Ste 206 Dublin (43017) *(G-10316)*
Datascan Field Services LLC 440 914-7300
30600 Aurora Rd Ste 180 Solon (44139) *(G-17000)*
Datatrak International Inc 440 443-0082
5900 Landerbrook Dr # 170 Mayfield Heights (44124) *(G-14000)*
Datavantage Corporation (HQ) 440 498-4414
30500 Bruce Industrial Pk Cleveland (44139) *(G-5464)*
Datwyler Sling Sltions USA Inc 937 387-2800
875 Center Dr Vandalia (45377) *(G-18676)*
Datzap LLC 330 785-2100
1520 S Arlington St Akron (44306) *(G-187)*
Daugherty Construction Inc 216 731-9444
22460 Lakeland Blvd Euclid (44132) *(G-10748)*
Daugherty Roofing, Euclid *Also called Daugherty Construction Inc* *(G-10748)*
Daugwood Inc 937 429-9465
3183 Beaver Vu Dr Ste B Beavercreek (45434) *(G-1165)*
Dav Chapter 53, Cheshire *Also called Disabled American Veterans* *(G-2789)*
Dave & Barb Enterprises Inc 513 553-0050
Address Unknonwn New Richmond (45157) *(G-15125)*
Dave Commercial Ground MGT 440 237-5394
9956 Akins Rd North Royalton (44133) *(G-15486)*
Dave Dennis Auto Group, Beavercreek Township *Also called Dave Dnnis Chrysler Jeep Dodge* *(G-1267)*
Dave Dnnis Chrysler Jeep Dodge 937 429-5566
4232 Colonel Glenn Hwy Beavercreek Township (45431) *(G-1267)*
Dave Knapp Ford Lincoln Inc (PA) 937 547-3000
500 Wagner Ave Greenville (45331) *(G-11496)*
Dave Marshall Inc (PA) 937 878-9135
1448 Kauffman Ave Fairborn (45324) *(G-10790)*
Dave Pinkerton 740 477-8888
221 Renick Ave Chillicothe (45601) *(G-2834)*
Dave Sugar Excavating LLC 330 542-1100
11640 S State Line Rd Petersburg (44454) *(G-16081)*
Dave White Chevrolet Inc 419 885-4444
5880 Monroe St Sylvania (43560) *(G-17581)*
Daves Sand & Stone Inc 419 445-9256
19230 County Road F Wauseon (43567) *(G-18950)*
Davey Resource Group Inc 330 673-9511
1500 N Mantua St Kent (44240) *(G-12362)*
Davey Tree & Lawn Care, Stow *Also called Davey Tree Expert Company* *(G-17361)*
Davey Tree & Lawn Care, Milford *Also called Davey Tree Expert Company* *(G-14515)*
Davey Tree & Lawn Care, Cleveland *Also called Davey Tree Expert Company* *(G-5465)*
Davey Tree and Lawn Care, Columbus *Also called Davey Tree Expert Company* *(G-7490)*
Davey Tree Expert Company 330 908-0833
837 Highland Rd E Macedonia (44056) *(G-13195)*
Davey Tree Expert Company 330 628-1499
1437 State Route 43 Mogadore (44260) *(G-14674)*
Davey Tree Expert Company (PA) 330 673-9511
1500 N Mantua St Kent (44240) *(G-12363)*
Davey Tree Expert Company 330 928-4911
4576 Allen Rd Stow (44224) *(G-17361)*
Davey Tree Expert Company 614 471-4144
3603 Westerville Rd Columbus (43224) *(G-7490)*
Davey Tree Expert Company 513 575-1733
6065 Br Hill Guinea Pike Milford (45150) *(G-14515)*
Davey Tree Expert Company 440 439-4770
7625 Bond St Cleveland (44139) *(G-5465)*
David Barber Civic Center 740 498-4383
1066 E State St Newcomerstown (43832) *(G-15266)*
David Campbell 937 266-7064
2000 Hewitt Ave Dayton (45440) *(G-9451)*
David Francis Corporation (PA) 216 524-0900
5005 Rockside Rd Ste 100 Cleveland (44131) *(G-5466)*
David Group (PA) 216 685-4400
1360 E 9th St Ste 830 Cleveland (44114) *(G-5467)*
David Hirsh, Blacklick *Also called Atrium Buying Corporation* *(G-1500)*
David Hummel Building, Cincinnati *Also called Hummel Industries Incorporated* *(G-3798)*
David J Joseph Company, The, Cincinnati *Also called Djj Holding Corporation* *(G-3496)*
David L Barth Lwyr 513 852-8228
537 E Pete Rose Way Cincinnati (45202) *(G-3463)*
David Lee Grossman MD 419 843-8150
1000 Regency Ct Ste 102 Toledo (43623) *(G-17844)*
David M Schneider MD Inc (PA) 513 762 5700
4452 Estgate Blvd Ste 305 Cincinnati (45245) *(G-2912)*
David R White Services Inc (PA) 740 594-8381
5315 Hebbardsville Rd Athens (45701) *(G-782)*
David Scott Salon 440 734-7595
107a Great Northern Mall North Olmsted (44070) *(G-15419)*
David W Milliken (PA) 740 998-5023
2 S Main St Frankfort (45628) *(G-11145)*
David W Steinbach Inc 330 497-5959
6824 Wise Ave Nw Canton (44720) *(G-2334)*
David White Services, Athens *Also called David R White Services Inc* *(G-782)*
Davidson Becker Inc 330 755-2111
11 Spring St Struthers (44471) *(G-17530)*
Davidson Trucking Inc 419 288-2318
1227 Bowling Green Rd E Bradner (43406) *(G-1809)*
Davis 5 Star Holdings LLC (PA) 954 470-8456
14 E Main St Ste 300 Springfield (45502) *(G-17187)*
Davis Beese Nuclear Power Stn, Oak Harbor *Also called Toledo Edison Company* *(G-15617)*

Davis Catering Inc 513 241-3464
30 Garfield Pl Ste 10 Cincinnati (45202) *(G-3464)*
Davis Eye Center 330 923-5676
789 Graham Rd Cuyahoga Falls (44221) *(G-9178)*
Davis H Elliot Cnstr Co Inc 937 847-8025
1 S Gebhart Church Rd Miamisburg (45342) *(G-14293)*
Davis Paul Restoration Dayton 937 436-3411
1960 W Dorothy Ln Ste 207 Moraine (45439) *(G-14766)*
Davis Pickering & Company Inc 740 373-5896
165 Enterprise Dr Marietta (45750) *(G-13441)*
Davis Tobacco Co, Cleveland *Also called The Anter Brothers Company* *(G-6589)*
Davis Tree Farm & Nursery Inc 330 483-3324
6126 Neff Rd Valley City (44280) *(G-18615)*
Davis Young A Legal Prof Assn (PA) 216 348-1700
600 Superior Ave E # 1200 Cleveland (44114) *(G-5468)*
Davita 1620, Cleveland *Also called Davita Inc* *(G-5470)*
Davita Dialysis, Dayton *Also called Davita Inc* *(G-9452)*
Davita Healthcare Partners Inc 216 961-6498
7901 Detroit Ave Cleveland (44102) *(G-5469)*
Davita Healthcare Partners Inc 440 353-0114
35143 Center Ridge Rd North Ridgeville (44039) *(G-15462)*
Davita Inc 513 939-1110
1210 Hicks Blvd Fairfield (45014) *(G-10839)*
Davita Inc 216 712-4700
19133 Hilliard Blvd Rocky River (44116) *(G-16576)*
Davita Inc 440 891-5645
7360 Engle Rd Cleveland (44130) *(G-5470)*
Davita Inc 740 376-2622
1019 Pike St Marietta (45750) *(G-13442)*
Davita Inc 937 456-1174
105 E Wash Jackson Rd Eaton (45320) *(G-10555)*
Davita Inc 330 494-2091
4685 Fulton Dr Nw Canton (44718) *(G-2335)*
Davita Inc 216 525-0990
4801 Acorn Dr Ste 1 Independence (44131) *(G-12202)*
Davita Inc 937 879-0433
1266 N Broad St Fairborn (45324) *(G-10791)*
Davita Inc 937 426-6475
3070 Presidential Dr A Beavercreek (45324) *(G-1166)*
Davita Inc 937 435-4030
5721 Bigger Rd Dayton (45440) *(G-9452)*
Davita Inc 937 376-1453
215 S Allison Ave Ste B Xenia (45385) *(G-20049)*
Davita Inc 440 293-6028
486 S Main St Andover (44003) *(G-611)*
Davita Inc 513 784-1800
2109 Reading Rd Cincinnati (45202) *(G-3465)*
Davita Inc 740 401-0607
2906 Washington Blvd Belpre (45714) *(G-1435)*
Davita Inc 330 335-2300
195 Wadsworth Rd Wadsworth (44281) *(G-18752)*
Davita Inc 440 251-6237
6830 N Ridge Rd Madison (44057) *(G-13222)*
Davita Inc 330 733-1861
73 Massillon Rd Akron (44312) *(G-188)*
Davita Inc 615 341-6311
458 Home St Georgetown (45121) *(G-11393)*
Davita Inc 419 697-2191
3310 Dustin Rd Oregon (43616) *(G-15730)*
Davita Inc 513 624-0400
7502 State Rd Cincinnati (45255) *(G-3466)*
Davita Kidney Dialysis, Andover *Also called Davita Inc* *(G-611)*
Davue Ob-Gyn Associates Inc (PA) 937 277-8988
2200 Philadelphia Dr # 101 Dayton (45406) *(G-9453)*
Dawes Arboretum 740 323-2355
7770 Jacksontown Rd Newark (43056) *(G-15164)*
Dawn Chemical, Willoughby *Also called Dawnchem Inc* *(G-19658)*
Dawn Incorporated (PA) 330 652-7711
106 E Market St Ste 505 Warren (44481) *(G-18847)*
Dawnchem Inc 440 943-3332
30510 Lakeland Blvd Frnt Willoughby (44095) *(G-19658)*
Dawson Companies 440 333-9000
3900 Kinross Lakes Pkwy Richfield (44286) *(G-16503)*
Dawson Personnel, Columbus *Also called Dawson Resources* *(G-7492)*
Dawson Personnel Systems, Columbus *Also called Dawson Resources* *(G-7491)*
Dawson Resources (PA) 614 255-1400
1114 Dublin Rd Columbus (43215) *(G-7491)*
Dawson Resources 614 274-8900
4184 W Broad St Columbus (43228) *(G-7492)*
Day Academy, Springboro *Also called M J J B Ltd* *(G-17127)*
Day Air Credit Union Inc (PA) 937 643-2160
3501 Wilmington Pike Dayton (45429) *(G-9454)*
Day Ketterer Ltd (PA) 330 455-0173
200 Market Ave N Ste 300 Canton (44702) *(G-2336)*
Day Precision Wall Inc 513 353-2999
5715 Hamilton Cleves Rd Cleves (45002) *(G-6798)*
Day Share Ltd 513 451-1100
5915 Glenway Ave Cincinnati (45238) *(G-3467)*
Day Spring Health Care Corp 740 984-4262
501 Pinecrest Dr Beverly (45715) *(G-1489)*
Day-Met Credit Union Inc (PA) 937 236-2562
3199 S Dixie Dr Moraine (45439) *(G-14767)*

Day-Mont Behavioral Hlth Care, Moraine *Also called Day-Mont Bhvoral Hlth Care Inc* ***(G-14768)***
Day-Mont Bhvoral Hlth Care Inc (PA)....937 222-8111
2710 Dryden Rd Moraine (45439) ***(G-14768)***
Daybreak Inc (PA)....937 395-4600
605 S Patterson Blvd Dayton (45402) ***(G-9455)***
Dayhuff Group LLC (PA)....614 854-9999
740 Lakeview Plaza Blvd # 300 Worthington (43085) ***(G-19954)***
Daymark Food Safety Systems....419 353-2458
12830 S Dixie Hwy Bldg B Bowling Green (43402) ***(G-1774)***
Daymark Security Systems, Bowling Green *Also called CMC Daymark Corporation* ***(G-1773)***
Daynas Homecare LLC....216 323-0323
14616 Tabor Ave Maple Heights (44137) ***(G-13405)***
Days Inn, Lewisburg *Also called Janus Hotels and Resorts Inc* ***(G-12711)***
Days Inn, Fremont *Also called Goodnight Inn Inc* ***(G-11203)***
Days Inn, Reynoldsburg *Also called Brice Hotel Inc* ***(G-16432)***
Days Inn....740 695-0100
52601 Holiday Dr Saint Clairsville (43950) ***(G-16635)***
Days Inn Stes Columbus E Arprt, Reynoldsburg *Also called First Hotel Management LLC* ***(G-16453)***
Days of Discovery....937 862-4465
3195 Clear Springs Rd Spring Valley (45370) ***(G-17110)***
Dayspring Health Care Center....937 864-5800
8001 Dyton Springfield Rd Fairborn (45324) ***(G-10792)***
Dayspring Healthcare Center, Beverly *Also called Appalachian Respite Care Ltd* ***(G-1487)***
Dayspring Residential Care, Mansfield *Also called County of Richland* ***(G-13279)***
Daytep Inc....937 456-5860
1816 Alexander Rd Eaton (45320) ***(G-10556)***
Dayton Aerospace Inc....937 426-4300
4141 Colonel Glenn Hwy # 252 Beavercreek Township (45431) ***(G-1268)***
Dayton Animal Hospital Assoc....937 890-4744
8015 N Main St Dayton (45415) ***(G-9456)***
Dayton Anthem....937 428-8000
1222 S Patterson Blvd # 4 Dayton (45402) ***(G-9457)***
Dayton Appliance Parts Co (PA)....937 224-0487
122 Sears St Dayton (45402) ***(G-9458)***
Dayton Area Chamber Commerce....937 226-1444
22 E 5th St Ste 200 Dayton (45402) ***(G-9459)***
Dayton Art Institute....937 223-5277
456 Belmonte Park N Dayton (45405) ***(G-9460)***
Dayton Bag & Burlap Co (PA)....937 258-8000
322 Davis Ave Dayton (45403) ***(G-9461)***
Dayton Business Journal, Dayton *Also called American City Bus Journals Inc* ***(G-9328)***
Dayton Cardiology Consultants (PA)....937 223-3053
1126 S Main St Dayton (45409) ***(G-9462)***
Dayton Children, Dayton *Also called Childrens Medical Ctr Toledo* ***(G-9403)***
Dayton Childrens Hospital....937 641-3376
1 Childrens Plz Dayton (45404) ***(G-9463)***
Dayton Childrens Hospital (PA)....937 641-3000
1 Childrens Plz Dayton (45404) ***(G-9464)***
Dayton Choa....937 278-4871
2301 Wagner Ford Rd Dayton (45414) ***(G-9465)***
Dayton City Parks Golf Maint....937 333-3378
3383 Chuck Wagner Ln Dayton (45414) ***(G-9466)***
Dayton City Water Department, Dayton *Also called City of Dayton* ***(G-9412)***
Dayton Convention Visitors Bur, Dayton *Also called Dayton Cvb* ***(G-9468)***
Dayton Country Club Company....937 294-3352
555 Kramer Rd Dayton (45419) ***(G-9467)***
Dayton Crdiolgy Vascular Cons, Dayton *Also called Dayton Cardiology Consultants* ***(G-9462)***
Dayton Cvb....937 226-8211
1 Chamber Plz Ste A Dayton (45402) ***(G-9468)***
Dayton Digital Media Inc....937 223-8335
2212 Patterson Rd Dayton (45420) ***(G-9469)***
Dayton Digital.com, Dayton *Also called Dayton Digital Media Inc* ***(G-9469)***
Dayton Dmh Inc....937 436-2273
3800 Summit Glen Rd Dayton (45449) ***(G-9470)***
Dayton Dog Training Club Inc....937 293-5219
3040 E River Rd Ste 5 Moraine (45439) ***(G-14769)***
Dayton Door Sales Inc (PA)....937 253-9181
1112 Springfield St Dayton (45403) ***(G-9471)***
Dayton Door Sales Inc....937 253-9181
1112 Springfield St Dayton (45403) ***(G-9472)***
Dayton Dragons Baseball, Dayton *Also called Dayton Prof Basbal CLB LLC* ***(G-9488)***
Dayton Ear Nose Throat Srgeons....937 434-0555
7076 Corporate Way Ste 1 Dayton (45459) ***(G-9473)***
Dayton Eye Surgery Center....937 431-9531
81 Sylvania Dr Beavercreek (45440) ***(G-1236)***
Dayton Foundation Inc....937 222-0410
40 N Main St Ste 500 Dayton (45423) ***(G-9474)***
Dayton Freight Lines Inc....419 589-0350
103 Cairns Rd Mansfield (44903) ***(G-13290)***
Dayton Freight Lines Inc....419 661-8600
28240 Oregon Rd Perrysburg (43551) ***(G-15993)***
Dayton Freight Lines Inc....614 860-1080
1406 Blatt Blvd Columbus (43230) ***(G-7493)***
Dayton Freight Lines Inc....937 236-4880
6265 Executive Blvd Ste A Dayton (45424) ***(G-9475)***
Dayton Freight Lines Inc....330 346-0750
280 Progress Blvd Kent (44240) ***(G-12364)***
Dayton Hara Arena Conf Exhibtn....937 278-4776
1001 Shiloh Springs Rd Dayton (45415) ***(G-9476)***
Dayton Hcri Place Denver....419 247-2800
4500 Dorr St Toledo (43615) ***(G-17845)***
Dayton Heart & Vascular Hosp, Dayton *Also called Heart Hospital of Dto LLC* ***(G-9606)***
Dayton Heart Center Inc (PA)....937 277-4274
1530 Needmore Rd Ste 300 Dayton (45414) ***(G-9477)***
Dayton Heart Hospital, Dayton *Also called Medcath Intermediate Holdings* ***(G-9712)***
Dayton Heidelberg Distrg Co (PA)....937 222-8692
3601 Dryden Rd Moraine (45439) ***(G-14770)***
Dayton Heidelberg Distrg Co....937 220-6450
3601 Dryden Rd Moraine (45439) ***(G-14771)***
Dayton Heidelberg Distrg Co....419 666-9783
912 3rd St Perrysburg (43551) ***(G-15994)***
Dayton Heidelberg Distrg Co....216 520-2626
9101 E Pleasant Vly Cleveland (44131) ***(G-5471)***
Dayton Heidelberg Distrg Co....419 666-9783
912 3rd St Perrysburg (43551) ***(G-15995)***
Dayton Heidelberg Distrg Co....937 220-6450
3601 Dryden Rd Moraine (45439) ***(G-14772)***
Dayton Heidelberg Distrg Co....614 308-0400
3801 Parkwest Dr Columbus (43228) ***(G-7494)***
Dayton Heidelberg Distrg Co....513 421-5000
1518 Dalton Ave Cincinnati (45214) ***(G-3468)***
Dayton History....937 293-2841
1000 Carillon Blvd Dayton (45409) ***(G-9478)***
Dayton Hospice Incorporated (PA)....937 256-4490
324 Wilmington Ave Dayton (45420) ***(G-9479)***
Dayton Hospice Incorporated....513 422-0300
5940 Long Meadow Dr Franklin (45005) ***(G-11153)***
Dayton Hotels LLC....937 832-2222
20 Rockridge Rd Englewood (45322) ***(G-10702)***
Dayton Industrial Drum Inc....937 253-8933
1880 Radio Rd Dayton (45431) ***(G-9263)***
Dayton Mailing Services Inc....937 222-5056
100 S Keowee St Dayton (45402) ***(G-9480)***
Dayton Marriott, Dayton *Also called Concord Dayton Hotel II LLC* ***(G-9422)***
Dayton Marshall Tire Sales Co....937 293-8330
3091 S Dixie Dr Moraine (45439) ***(G-14773)***
Dayton Medical Imaging....937 439-0390
7901 Schatz Pointe Dr Dayton (45459) ***(G-9481)***
Dayton Metro Chapter....937 294-0192
3816 Robertann Dr Dayton (45420) ***(G-9482)***
Dayton Nwborn Care Spclsts Inc....937 641-3329
1 Childrens Plz Rm 4085 Dayton (45404) ***(G-9483)***
Dayton Ob Gyn....937 439-7550
330 N Main St Ste 200 Centerville (45459) ***(G-2677)***
Dayton Osteopathic Hospital (HQ)....937 762-1629
405 W Grand Ave Dayton (45405) ***(G-9484)***
Dayton Outpatien Practice, Dayton *Also called Pain Management Associates Inc* ***(G-9281)***
Dayton Performing Arts Aliance....937 224-3521
126 N Main St Ste 210 Dayton (45402) ***(G-9485)***
Dayton Physicians LLC (PA)....937 280-8400
6680 Poe Ave Ste 200 Dayton (45414) ***(G-9486)***
Dayton Physicians LLC....937 547-0563
1111 Sweitzer St Ste C Greenville (45331) ***(G-11497)***
Dayton Power and Light Company (HQ)....937 224-6000
1065 Woodman Dr Dayton (45432) ***(G-9264)***
Dayton Power and Light Company....937 549-2641
Us Rte 52 Aberdeen (45101) ***(G-2)***
Dayton Power and Light Company....937 549-2641
14869 Us 52 Manchester (45144) ***(G-13255)***
Dayton Power and Light Company....937 331-3032
1 S Gebhart Church Rd Miamisburg (45342) ***(G-14294)***
Dayton Power and Light Company....937 331-4123
1900 Dryden Rd Moraine (45439) ***(G-14774)***
Dayton Precision Services, Dayton *Also called Keaney Investment Group LLC* ***(G-9648)***
Dayton Primary & Urgent Care....937 461-0800
301 W 1st St Ste 100 Dayton (45402) ***(G-9487)***
Dayton Prof Basbal CLB LLC....937 228-2287
220 N Patterson Blvd Dayton (45402) ***(G-9488)***
Dayton Public School District....937 542-3000
115 S Ludlow St Dayton (45402) ***(G-9489)***
Dayton Regional Dialysis Inc (PA)....937 898-5526
8701 Old Troy Pike Ste 10 Dayton (45424) ***(G-9490)***
Dayton Roof & Remodeling Co....937 224-7667
418 Merrick Dr Beavercreek (45434) ***(G-1167)***
Dayton Society Natural History (PA)....937 275-7431
2600 Deweese Pkwy Dayton (45414) ***(G-9491)***
Dayton Society Natural History....513 932-4421
6123 State Route 350 Oregonia (45054) ***(G-15757)***
Dayton South Dialysis, Moraine *Also called Wakoni Dialysis LLC* ***(G-14834)***
Dayton Steel Service, Dayton *Also called Thompson Steel Company Inc* ***(G-9928)***
Dayton Tall Timbers Resort....937 833-3888
7796 Wellbaum Rd Brookville (45309) ***(G-1962)***
Dayton Toro Motorcycle Club....937 723-9133
1536 W 3rd St Dayton (45402) ***(G-9492)***
Dayton Urban League (PA)....937 226-1513
907 W 5th St Dayton (45402) ***(G-9493)***
Dayton V A Medical Center, Dayton *Also called Veterans Affairs US Dept* ***(G-9972)***
Dayton Walls & Ceilings Inc....937 277-0531
4328 Webster St Dayton (45414) ***(G-9494)***

ALPHABETIC SECTION
Del Monde Inc

Dayton Wastewater Trtmnt Plant, Dayton Also called City of Dayton (G-9411)
Dayton Windustrial Co ... 937 461-2603
137 E Helena St Dayton (45404) (G-9495)
Dayton YMCA Camp Kern, Oregonia Also called Young Mens Christian Assoc (G-15759)
Dayton-Dixie Mufflers Inc (PA) ... 419 243-7281
1101 Monroe St Toledo (43604) (G-17846)
Dayton/Cncinnati Tech Svcs LLC (PA) ... 513 892-3940
5757 Cornell Rd Blue Ash (45242) (G-1575)
DB&p Logistics Inc ... 614 491-4035
3544 Watkins Rd Columbus (43232) (G-7495)
Dbi Services LLC ... 410 590-4181
2393 County Road 1 South Point (45680) (G-17082)
Dbp Enterprises LLC ... 740 513-2399
7301 E State Route 37 Sunbury (43074) (G-17554)
DCI, Columbus Also called Digico Imaging Inc (G-7519)
Dco LLC (HQ) ... 419 931-9086
900 E Boundary St Ste 8a Perrysburg (43551) (G-15996)
Dcp Holding Company ... 513 554-1100
100 Crowne Point Pl Sharonville (45241) (G-16881)
Dcr Systems LLC (PA) ... 440 205-9900
8697 Tyler Blvd Mentor (44060) (G-14167)
DCS Sanitation Management Inc (PA) ... 513 891-4980
7864 Camargo Rd Cincinnati (45243) (G-3469)
Dct Telecom Group Inc ... 440 892-0300
27877 Clemens Rd Westlake (44145) (G-19482)
Dcts, Blue Ash Also called Dayton/Cncinnati Tech Svcs LLC (G-1575)
DD&b Inc ... 614 577-0550
4449 Easton Way Columbus (43219) (G-7496)
Ddhew, Columbus Also called Division Drnking Ground Waters (G-7530)
Ddi, Brookpark Also called Distribution Data Incorporated (G-1943)
Ddm Direct of Ohio, Hebron Also called Ddm-Digital Imaging Data (G-11847)
Ddm-Digital Imaging Data ... 740 928-1110
190 Milliken Dr Hebron (43025) (G-11847)
Ddr Corp ... 614 785-6445
445 Hutchinson Ave # 800 Columbus (43235) (G-7497)
Ddr Corp ... 216 755-5547
5539 Dressler Rd Nw Canton (44720) (G-2337)
Ddr Corp (PA) ... 216 755-5500
3300 Enterprise Pkwy Beachwood (44122) (G-1071)
Ddr Tucson Spectrum I LLC ... 216 755-5500
3300 Enterprise Pkwy Beachwood (44122) (G-1072)
De Bra - Kuempel, Cincinnati Also called Debra-Kuempel Inc (G-3476)
DE Foxx & Associates Inc (PA) ... 513 621-5522
324 W 9th St Fl 5 Cincinnati (45202) (G-3470)
De Lucas Place In Park ... 440 233-7272
6075 Middle Ridge Rd Lorain (44053) (G-13035)
De Nora Tech LLC (HQ) ... 440 710-5300
7590 Discovery Ln Painesville (44077) (G-15850)
Deacon 10 ... 216 731-4000
1353 E 260th St Ste 1 Euclid (44132) (G-10749)
Deaconess Associations Inc (PA) ... 513 559-2100
615 Elsinore Pl Bldg B Cincinnati (45202) (G-3471)
Deaconess Hospital of Cincinna (PA) ... 513 559-2100
615 Elsinore Pl Bldg B Cincinnati (45202) (G-3472)
Deaconess Long Term Care Inc (HQ) ... 513 861-0400
330 Straight St Ste 310 Cincinnati (45219) (G-3473)
Deaconess Long Term Care of MI (PA) ... 513 487-3600
330 Straight St Ste 310 Cincinnati (45219) (G-3474)
Deaconis Assocation Inc ... 419 874-9008
27062 Oakmead Dr Perrysburg (43551) (G-15997)
Deaconis Association, Perrysburg Also called Deaconis Assocation Inc (G-15997)
Dealer Supply and Eqp Ltd ... 419 724-8473
1549 Campbell St Toledo (43607) (G-17847)
Dealer Tire LLC (PA) ... 216 432-0088
7012 Euclid Ave Cleveland (44103) (G-5472)
Dealers Group Limited ... 440 352-4970
23240 Chagrin Blvd # 802 Beachwood (44122) (G-1073)
Dealers Supply North Inc (HQ) ... 614 274-6285
2315 Creekside Pkwy # 500 Lockbourne (43137) (G-12948)
Dean Financial Management, Beavercreek Also called C H Dean Inc (G-1156)
Deanhouston Creative Group Inc (PA) ... 513 421-6622
310 Culvert St Ste 300 Cincinnati (45202) (G-3475)
Dearman Moving & Storage Co ... 419 524-3456
961 N Main St Mansfield (44903) (G-13291)
Dearman Moving and Storage, Mansfield Also called J-Trac Inc (G-13315)
Dearth Management Company ... 419 253-0144
825 State Route 61 Marengo (43334) (G-13423)
Dearth Management Company ... 740 389-1214
677 Marion Cardington Rd Marion (43302) (G-13537)
Dearth Management Company (PA) ... 614 847-1070
134 Northwoods Blvd Ste C Columbus (43235) (G-7498)
Dearth Management Company ... 330 339-3595
2594 E High Ave New Philadelphia (44663) (G-15092)
Debello Masonry Inc ... 937 235-2096
30 Eagle Ct Carlisle (45005) (G-2603)
Debra-Kuempel Inc (HQ) ... 513 271-6500
3976 Southern Ave Cincinnati (45227) (G-3476)
Decahealth Inc ... 866 908-3514
7071 W Central Ave Ste C Toledo (43617) (G-17848)
Decision One ... 614 883-0215
3423 Southpark Pl Grove City (43123) (G-11552)
Decisionone Corporation ... 614 883-0228
3425 Urbancrest Indus Dr Urbancrest (43123) (G-18604)
Decker Drilling Inc ... 740 749-3939
11565 State Route 676 Vincent (45784) (G-18743)
Decker Equipment Company Inc ... 866 252-4395
9601 Granger Rd Cleveland (44125) (G-5473)
Decker Forklifts, Cleveland Also called Decker Equipment Company Inc (G-5473)
Deckers Nursery Inc ... 614 836-2130
6239 Rager Rd Groveport (43125) (G-11632)
Decoating Inc ... 419 347-9191
3955 Industrial Pkwy Shelby (44875) (G-16899)
Decorative Flooring Services, Maumee Also called Marble Restoration Inc (G-13939)
Decorative Paint Incorporated ... 419 485-0632
700 Randolph St Montpelier (43543) (G-14743)
Decorative Paving Company ... 513 576-1222
39 Glendale Milford Rd Loveland (45140) (G-13121)
Decosky GM Center, Mount Vernon Also called Decosky Motor Holdings Inc (G-14892)
Decosky Motor Holdings Inc ... 740 397-9122
510 Harcourt Rd 550 Mount Vernon (43050) (G-14892)
Dedicated Logistics Inc ... 513 275-1135
6019 Union Centre Blvd West Chester (45014) (G-19060)
Dedicated Nursing Assoc Inc ... 937 886-4559
228 Byers Rd Ste 103 Miamisburg (45342) (G-14295)
Dedicated Nursing Assoc Inc ... 888 465-6929
70 Birch Aly Ste 240 Beavercreek (45440) (G-1237)
Dedicated Nursing Assoc Inc ... 866 450-5550
11542 Springfield Pike Cincinnati (45246) (G-3477)
Dedicated Nursing Assoc Inc ... 877 411-8350
5672 W Broad St Galloway (43119) (G-11343)
Dedicated Nursing Assoc Inc ... 877 547-9144
1339a Rockside Rd Parma (44134) (G-15905)
Dedicated Tech Services Inc ... 614 309-0059
545 Metro Pl S Ste 100 Dublin (43017) (G-10317)
Dedicated Technologies Inc ... 614 460-3200
580 N 4th St Ste 280 Columbus (43215) (G-7499)
Dedicated Transport LLC (HQ) ... 216 641-2500
700 W Resource Dr Brooklyn Heights (44131) (G-1914)
Dee Jay Cleaners Inc ... 216 731-7060
878 E 222nd St Euclid (44123) (G-10750)
Deed Realty Co ... 330 225-5220
4600 Center Rd Brunswick (44212) (G-1974)
Deemsys Inc ... 614 322-9928
800 Cross Pointe Rd Ste A Gahanna (43230) (G-11239)
Deepwell Energy Services LLC ... 740 685-2253
14764 Clay Pike Rd Senecaville (43780) (G-16823)
Deepwood Center, Mentor Also called County of Lake (G-14164)
Deepwood Industries Inc ... 440 350-5231
8121 Deepwood Blvd Mentor (44060) (G-14168)
Deer Creek Rsort Confrence Ctr, Mount Sterling Also called Xanterra Parks & Resorts Inc (G-14876)
Deer Creek State Park, Mount Sterling Also called Ohio Dept Natural Resources (G-14874)
Deer Park Roofing Inc (PA) ... 513 891-9151
7201 Blue Ash Rd Cincinnati (45236) (G-3478)
Deerfield Construction Co Inc (PA) ... 513 984-4096
8960 Glendale Milford Rd Loveland (45140) (G-13122)
Deerfield Farms ... 330 584-4715
9041 State Route 224 Deerfield (44411) (G-10018)
Deerfield Farms Service Inc (PA) ... 330 584-4715
9041 State Route 224 Deerfield (44411) (G-10019)
Defense Fin & Accounting Svc ... 410 436-9740
3990 E Broad St Columbus (43213) (G-7500)
Defense Fin & Accounting Svc ... 614 693-6700
3990 E Broad St Columbus (43213) (G-7501)
Defense Info Systems Agcy ... 614 692-4433
3990 E Broad St Bldg 20c Columbus (43213) (G-7502)
Defense Research Assoc Inc ... 937 431-1644
3915 Germany Ln Ste 102 Dayton (45431) (G-9265)
Defiance Clinic, Defiance Also called Fauster-Cameron Inc (G-10030)
Defiance Cnty Bd Commissioners ... 419 782-3233
140 E Broadway St Defiance (43512) (G-10025)
Defiance County Senior Center, Defiance Also called Defiance Cnty Bd Commissioners (G-10025)
Defiance Family Physicians ... 419 785-3281
1250 Ralston Ave Ste 104 Defiance (43512) (G-10026)
Defiance Hospital Inc ... 419 782-6955
1200 Ralston Ave Defiance (43512) (G-10027)
DEFIANCE REGIONAL MEDICAL CENTER, Defiance Also called Defiance Hospital Inc (G-10027)
Definitions of Design Inc ... 419 891-0188
467 W Dussel Dr Maumee (43537) (G-13906)
Definitive Solutions Co Inc ... 513 719-9100
8180 Corp Pk Dr Ste 305 Cincinnati (45242) (G-3479)
Definity Partners, West Chester Also called Midwest Mfg Solutions LLC (G-19216)
Deform, Columbus Also called Scientific Forming Tech Corp (G-8705)
Degussa Construction, Cleveland Also called BASF Construction Chem LLC (G-5098)
Dei Fratelli, Northwood Also called Hirzel Canning Company (G-15533)
Dei Incorporated ... 513 825-5800
1550 Kemper Meadow Dr Cincinnati (45240) (G-3480)
Del Monde Inc ... 859 371-7780
2485 Belvo Rd Miamisburg (45342) (G-14296)

ALPHABETIC

Del Monte Fresh Produce NA Inc 614 527-7398
2200 Westbelt Dr Columbus (43228) ***(G-7503)***
Del-Co Water Company Inc (PA) 740 548-7746
6658 Olentangy River Rd Delaware (43015) ***(G-10086)***
Delaneys Tax Accunting Svc Ltd 513 248-2829
1157b State Route 131 Milford (45150) ***(G-14516)***
Delano Foods, Canton *Also called Hiland Group Incorporated* ***(G-2399)***
Delaware City School District 740 363-5901
2462 Liberty Rd Delaware (43015) ***(G-10087)***
Delaware City School Garage, Delaware *Also called Delaware City School District* ***(G-10087)***
Delaware County Engineers, Delaware *Also called County of Delaware* ***(G-10083)***
Delaware County Historical Soc 740 369-3831
2690 Stratford Rd Delaware (43015) ***(G-10088)***
Delaware Court Health Care Ctr, Delaware *Also called Levering Management Inc* ***(G-10115)***
Delaware General Health Dst, Delaware *Also called County of Delaware* ***(G-10084)***
Delaware Golf Club Inc 740 362-2582
3326 Columbus Pike Delaware (43015) ***(G-10089)***
Delaware Opco LLC 502 429-8062
2270 Warrensburg Rd Delaware (43015) ***(G-10090)***
Delhi Township (PA) 513 922-0060
934 Neeb Rd Cincinnati (45233) ***(G-3481)***
Deliass Assets Corp 614 891-0101
780 Brooksedge Plaza Dr Westerville (43081) ***(G-19393)***
Delight Connection, Avon *Also called Cochin Technologies LLC* ***(G-891)***
Delille Oxygen Company (PA) 614 444-1177
772 Marion Rd Columbus (43207) ***(G-7504)***
Delmar Distributing, Columbus *Also called Columbus Distributing Company* ***(G-7346)***
Deloitte & Touche LLP 937 223-8821
220 E Monu Ave Ste 500 Dayton (45402) ***(G-9496)***
Deloitte & Touche LLP 513 784-7100
250 E 5th St Fl 1600 Cincinnati (45202) ***(G-3482)***
Deloitte & Touche LLP 614 221-1000
180 E Broad St Ste 1400 Columbus (43215) ***(G-7505)***
Deloitte & Touche LLP 216 589-1300
127 Public Sq Ste 3300 Cleveland (44114) ***(G-5474)***
Deloitte Consulting, Cincinnati *Also called Deloitte & Touche LLP* ***(G-3482)***
Deloitte Consulting LLP 937 223-8821
711 E Monu Ave Ste 201 Dayton (45402) ***(G-9497)***
Delphi Automotive Systems LLC 248 724-5953
1265 N River Rd Ne Warren (44483) ***(G-18848)***
Delphi Packard Electrical, Warren *Also called Delphi Automotive Systems LLC* ***(G-18848)***
Delphos Ambulatory Care Center 419 692-2662
1800 E 5th St Ste 1 Delphos (45833) ***(G-10141)***
Delphos Plant 2, Delphos *Also called Toledo Molding & Die Inc* ***(G-10152)***
Delta Air Lines Inc 216 265-2400
5300 Riverside Dr Ste 11 Cleveland (44135) ***(G-5475)***
Delta Air Lines Inc 614 239-4440
4600 Intl Gtwy Ste 6 Columbus (43219) ***(G-7506)***
Delta Airlines, Cleveland *Also called Delta Air Lines Inc* ***(G-5475)***
Delta Airlines, Columbus *Also called Delta Air Lines Inc* ***(G-7506)***
Delta Electrical Contrs Ltd 513 421-7744
4890 Gray Rd Cincinnati (45232) ***(G-3483)***
Delta Energy LLC 614 761-3603
5555 Perimeter Dr Dublin (43017) ***(G-10318)***
Delta Gamma Fraternity (PA) 614 481-8169
3250 Riverside Dr Upper Arlington (43221) ***(G-18549)***
Delta Gamma Fraternity 614 487-5599
3220 Riverside Dr Ste A2 Upper Arlington (43221) ***(G-18550)***
Delta Kappa Gamma Society 419 586-6016
1030 Canterbury Dr Celina (45822) ***(G-2645)***
Delta Media Group Inc 330 493-0350
4726 Hills And Dales Rd N Canton (44708) ***(G-2338)***
Delta Railroad Cnstr Inc (PA) 440 992-2997
2648 W Prospect Rd Frnt Ashtabula (44004) ***(G-741)***
Delta Theta Sigma Fraternity, Columbus *Also called Ohio State University* ***(G-8430)***
Deltacraft, Cleveland *Also called Millcraft Group LLC* ***(G-6063)***
Delth Corporation 440 255-7655
6312 Center St Ste C Mentor (44060) ***(G-14169)***
Delventhal Company 419 244-5570
3796 Rockland Cir Millbury (43447) ***(G-14578)***
Demarius Corporation 760 957-5500
5000 Tuttle Crossing Blvd Dublin (43016) ***(G-10319)***
Demmy Construction Inc 937 325-9429
4324 Fairfield Pike Springfield (45502) ***(G-17188)***
Demmy Sand and Gravel LLC 937 325-8840
4324 Fairfield Pike Springfield (45502) ***(G-17189)***
Dempsey Inc 330 758-2309
2803 South Ave Youngstown (44502) ***(G-20167)***
Denier Electric Co Inc (PA) 513 738-2641
10891 State Route 128 Harrison (45030) ***(G-11796)***
Denier Electric Co Inc 614 338-4664
4000 Gantz Rd Ste C Grove City (43123) ***(G-11553)***
Denier Technologies Div, Harrison *Also called Denier Electric Co Inc* ***(G-11796)***
Denmark Consultants Inc 513 530-9984
6000 Cornell Rd Blue Ash (45242) ***(G-1576)***
Dennis & Carol Liederbach 256 582-6200
8651 Wood Hollow Rd Northfield (44067) ***(G-15513)***
Dennis C McCluskey MD & Assoc 330 628-2686
754 S Cleveland Ave # 300 Mogadore (44260) ***(G-14675)***
Dennis Mitsubishi, Columbus *Also called Carcorp Inc* ***(G-7189)***
Dennis Todd Painting Inc 614 879-7952
6055 Us Highway 40 West Jefferson (43162) ***(G-19250)***
Dennis Top Soil & Landscaping 419 865-5656
6340 Dorr St Toledo (43615) ***(G-17849)***
Denny R King 513 917-7968
325 N 10th St Hamilton (45011) ***(G-11721)***
Denso International Amer Inc 937 393-6800
1600 N High St Hillsboro (45133) ***(G-11972)***
Dent Magic, Columbus *Also called Magic Industries Inc* ***(G-8097)***
Dent Magic 614 864-3368
4629 Poth Rd Columbus (43213) ***(G-7507)***
Dental Associates, Columbus *Also called Lawrence M Shell DDS* ***(G-8045)***
DENTAL CARE PLUS GROUP (DCPG), Sharonville *Also called Dcp Holding Company* ***(G-16881)***
Dental Ceramics Inc 330 523-5240
3404 Brecksville Rd Richfield (44286) ***(G-16504)***
Dental Facility 614 292-1472
305 W 12th Ave Rm 1159 Columbus (43210) ***(G-7508)***
DENTAL FACULTY PRACTICE, Columbus *Also called Dental Facility* ***(G-7508)***
Dental Health Group PA 330 630-9222
2000 Brittain Rd Ste 91 Akron (44310) ***(G-189)***
Dental Health Services (PA) 330 864-9090
110 N Miller Rd Ste 200 Fairlawn (44333) ***(G-10944)***
Dental One Inc 216 584-1000
6200 Oak Tree Blvd # 220 Independence (44131) ***(G-12203)***
Dental Services Group, Miamisburg *Also called Sentage Corporation* ***(G-14348)***
Dental Servics of Ohio Daniel 614 863-2222
6323 Tussing Rd Reynoldsburg (43068) ***(G-16445)***
Dentronix Inc 330 916-7300
235 Ascot Pkwy Cuyahoga Falls (44223) ***(G-9179)***
Denture Center 440 964-0542
2010 W 19th St Ashtabula (44004) ***(G-742)***
Denver Wholesale Florists Co 419 241-7241
14 N Erie St Toledo (43604) ***(G-17850)***
Department Children Services, Cleveland *Also called County of Cuyahoga* ***(G-5427)***
Department Information Tech, Cleveland *Also called County of Cuyahoga* ***(G-5421)***
Department Jobs and Fmly Svcs, Marietta *Also called County of Washington* ***(G-13440)***
Department of Anesthetia, Cincinnati *Also called University of Cincinnati* ***(G-4755)***
Department of Aviation, Vandalia *Also called City of Dayton* ***(G-18673)***
Department of Human Nutrition, Columbus *Also called Ohio State University* ***(G-8397)***
Department of Human Services, Georgetown *Also called County of Brown* ***(G-11391)***
Department of Internal Med Div, Columbus *Also called Ohio State University* ***(G-8444)***
Department of Jobs & Family, Cambridge *Also called County of Guernsey* ***(G-2108)***
Department of Neurology, Columbus *Also called Neuroscience Center Inc* ***(G-8269)***
Department of Ob/Gyn, Cleveland *Also called Metrohealth System* ***(G-6040)***
Department of Psychiatry, Cincinnati *Also called University of Cincinnati* ***(G-4758)***
Department of Public Utilities, Circleville *Also called City of Circleville* ***(G-4883)***
Department of Public Utilities, Cleveland *Also called City of Cleveland* ***(G-5258)***
Department of Statistics, Columbus *Also called William I Notz* ***(G-8995)***
Department of Transportation, Marion *Also called County of Marion* ***(G-13536)***
Department Senior Adult S, Cleveland *Also called Cuyahoga County* ***(G-5450)***
Departmental Store, Columbus *Also called Northpointe Plaza* ***(G-8293)***
Dependable Cleaning Contrs 440 953-9191
38230 Glenn Ave Willoughby (44094) ***(G-19659)***
Dependable Painting Co 216 431-4470
4403 Superior Ave Cleveland (44103) ***(G-5476)***
Dependble Bldrs Renovators LLC 614 761-8250
4555 Summit View Rd Dublin (43016) ***(G-10320)***
Deporres, Martin Emrgncy Asst, Cleveland *Also called Catholic Charities Corporation* ***(G-5190)***
Dept of Human Service, Circleville *Also called County of Pickaway* ***(G-4885)***
Dept of Human Services, Mansfield *Also called County of Richland* ***(G-13281)***
Dept of Neighborhoods, Toledo *Also called City of Toledo* ***(G-17811)***
Dept of Public Utilities, Columbus *Also called City of Columbus* ***(G-7279)***
Dept of Public Works R B 216 661-2800
4000 Brookpark Rd Cleveland (44134) ***(G-5477)***
Dept of Streets, North Ridgeville *Also called City of North Ridgeville* ***(G-15460)***
Dept of Surgery, Columbus *Also called Ohio State University* ***(G-8434)***
Depuy Paving Inc 614 272-0256
1850 Mckinley Ave Columbus (43222) ***(G-7509)***
Der Dutchman's Restaurant, Plain City *Also called Dutchman Hospitality Group Inc* ***(G-16189)***
Dermamed Coatings Company LLC 330 634-9449
381 Geneva Ave Tallmadge (44278) ***(G-17637)***
Dermatlgists of Southwest Ohio (PA) 937 435-2094
5300 Far Hills Ave # 100 Dayton (45429) ***(G-9498)***
Desalvo Construction Company 330 759-8145
1491 W Liberty St Hubbard (44425) ***(G-12085)***
Desco Federal Credit Union (PA) 740 354-7791
401 Chillicothe St Portsmouth (45662) ***(G-16275)***
Deshler Amusements Inc 330 532-2922
1894 Campground Rd Wellsville (43968) ***(G-19006)***
Design Center 513 618-3133
10816 Millington Ct # 100 Blue Ash (45242) ***(G-1577)***
Design Central Inc 614 890-0202
6464 Presidential Gtwy Columbus (43231) ***(G-7510)***

Design Concrete Surfaces, Kent *Also called Don Wartko Construction Co* ***(G-12366)***
Design Homes & Development Co....937 438-3667
8534 Yankee St Ste A Dayton (45458) ***(G-9499)***
Design Knowledge Company....937 320-9244
3100 Presidential Dr # 103 Beavercreek (45324) ***(G-1168)***
Design Rstrtion Reconstruction....330 563-0010
4305 Mount Pleasant St Nw # 103 North Canton (44720) ***(G-15332)***
Design Services Cnstr Co, Holland *Also called Douglas Construction Company* ***(G-12022)***
Deskey Associates Inc....513 721-6800
120 E 8th St Cincinnati (45202) ***(G-3484)***
Desoto Dialysis LLC....419 691-1514
2702 Navarre Ave Ste 203 Oregon (43616) ***(G-15731)***
Detillion Landscaping Co Inc....740 775-5305
20337 State Route 104 Chillicothe (45601) ***(G-2835)***
Detmer & Sons Inc (PA)....937 879-2373
1170 Channingway Dr Fairborn (45324) ***(G-10793)***
Detmer & Sons Heating & AC, Fairborn *Also called Detmer & Sons Inc* ***(G-10793)***
Detox Health Care Corp Ohio....513 742-6310
11500 Northlake Dr # 400 Cincinnati (45249) ***(G-3485)***
Detroit Diesel Corporation....330 430-4300
515 11th St Se Canton (44707) ***(G-2339)***
Detroit Dover Animals Hospital....440 871-5220
27366 Detroit Rd Cleveland (44145) ***(G-5478)***
Detroit Royalty Incorporated....216 771-5700
1100 Superior Ave E Fl 10 Cleveland (44114) ***(G-5479)***
Detroit Westfield LLC....330 666-4131
4073 Medina Rd Akron (44333) ***(G-190)***
Deufol Worldwide Packaging LLC....440 232-1100
19800 Alexander Rd Bedford (44146) ***(G-1303)***
Deufol Worldwide Packaging LLC....414 967-8000
4380 Dixie Hwy Fairfield (45014) ***(G-10840)***
Deutsche Bank Securities Inc....440 237-0188
3152 Oakwood Trl Broadview Heights (44147) ***(G-1878)***
Devcare Solutions Ltd....614 221-2277
131 N High St Ste 640 Columbus (43215) ***(G-7511)***
Developmental Disabilities (PA)....513 732-7000
2040 Us Highway 50 Batavia (45103) ***(G-1009)***
Developmental Disabilities....513 732-7015
204 State Rte Hwy 50ben Owensville (45160) ***(G-15809)***
Developmental Disabilities Bd, Tallmadge *Also called County of Summit* ***(G-17636)***
Develpmntal Dsblties Ohio Dept....740 446-1642
2500 Ohio Ave Gallipolis (45631) ***(G-11314)***
Develpmntal Dsblties Ohio Dept....419 385-0231
1101 S Detroit Ave Toledo (43614) ***(G-17851)***
Develpmntal Dsblties Ohio Dept....330 544-2231
30 E Broad St Fl 8 Columbus (43215) ***(G-7512)***
Develpmntal Dsblties Ohio Dept....614 272-0509
1601 W Broad St Columbus (43222) ***(G-7513)***
Develpmntal Dsblties Ohio Dept....937 233-8108
30 E Broad St Fl 8 Columbus (43215) ***(G-7514)***
Develpmntal Dsblties Ohio Dept....513 732-9200
4399 E Bauman Ln Batavia (45103) ***(G-1010)***
Devilbiss Auto Refinishing, Toledo *Also called Carlisle Fluid Tech Inc* ***(G-17792)***
Devirsified Material Handling....419 865-8025
8310 Airport Hwy Holland (43528) ***(G-12019)***
Devry University Inc....614 251-6969
1350 Alum Creek Dr Columbus (43209) ***(G-7515)***
Dexxxon Digital Storage Inc....740 548-7179
7611 Green Meadows Dr Lewis Center (43035) ***(G-12681)***
Deyor Performing Arts Center....330 744-4269
260 W Federal St Youngstown (44503) ***(G-20168)***
Dfs Corporate Services LLC....614 283-2499
6500 New Albany Rd E New Albany (43054) ***(G-14983)***
Dfs Corporate Services LLC....614 777-7020
3311 Mill Meadow Dr Hilliard (43026) ***(G-11895)***
Dhdc, Dayton *Also called Design Homes & Development Co* ***(G-9499)***
Dhl Express (usa) Inc....614 865-8325
570 Polaris Pkwy Ste 110 Westerville (43082) ***(G-19297)***
Dhl Express (usa) Inc....800 225-5345
2315 Creekside Pkwy Lockbourne (43137) ***(G-12949)***
Dhl Express (usa) Inc....440 239-0670
19987 Commerce Pkwy Cleveland (44130) ***(G-5480)***
Dhl Solutions, Lockbourne *Also called Dhl Supply Chain (usa)* ***(G-12951)***
Dhl Supply Chain (usa)....419 727-4318
1717 E Matzinger Rd Toledo (43612) ***(G-17852)***
Dhl Supply Chain (usa)....513 482-6015
401 Murray Rd Cincinnati (45217) ***(G-3486)***
Dhl Supply Chain (usa)....614 836-1265
6390 Commerce Ct Groveport (43125) ***(G-11633)***
Dhl Supply Chain (usa)....229 888-0699
570 Polaris Pkwy Ste 170 Westerville (43082) ***(G-19298)***
Dhl Supply Chain (usa)....614 895-1959
570 Polaris Pkwy Ste 110 Westerville (43082) ***(G-19299)***
Dhl Supply Chain (usa)....614 492-6614
2750 Creekside Pkwy Lockbourne (43137) ***(G-12950)***
Dhl Supply Chain (usa)....740 929-2113
200 Arrowhead Blvd Hebron (43025) ***(G-11848)***
Dhl Supply Chain (usa)....614 662-9247
2829 Rohr Rd Groveport (43125) ***(G-11634)***
Dhl Supply Chain (usa)....513 942-1575
10121 Princtn Glndle Rd B Cincinnati (45246) ***(G-3487)***
Dhl Supply Chain (usa)....513 745-7445
4550 Creek Rd Blue Ash (45242) ***(G-1578)***
Dhl Supply Chain (usa)....614 662-9200
4900 Creekside Pkwy Lockbourne (43137) ***(G-12951)***
Dhl Supply Chain USA, Westerville *Also called Exel Inc* ***(G-19305)***
Dhl Supply Chain USA, Lockbourne *Also called Exel Inc* ***(G-12952)***
Dhr, Strongsville *Also called Massage Envy* ***(G-17490)***
Dhsc LLC (HQ)....330 832-8761
875 8th St Ne Massillon (44646) ***(G-13800)***
Di Feo & Sons Poultry Inc....330 564-8172
1075 Grant St Akron (44301) ***(G-191)***
Di Salle Real Estate Co....419 885-4475
4904 Holland Sylvania Rd Sylvania (43560) ***(G-17582)***
DIA Electric Inc....513 281-0783
3326 Reading Rd Cincinnati (45229) ***(G-3488)***
Dialamerica Marketing Inc....330 836-5293
3090 W Market St Ste 210 Fairlawn (44333) ***(G-10945)***
Dialamerica Marketing Inc....440 234-4410
7271 Engle Rd Ste 400 Cleveland (44130) ***(G-5481)***
Dialysis Center of Dayton East....937 252-1867
1431 Business Center Ct Dayton (45410) ***(G-9500)***
Dialysis Clinic Inc....513 281-0091
499 E Mcmillan St Cincinnati (45206) ***(G-3489)***
Dialysis Clinic Inc....740 351-0596
1207 17th St Portsmouth (45662) ***(G-16276)***
Dialysis Clinic Inc....513 777-0855
7650 University Dr West Chester (45069) ***(G-19061)***
Dialysis Clinic Inc....740 264-6687
4227 Mall Dr Steubenville (43952) ***(G-17314)***
Dialysis Partners of NW Ohio, Toledo *Also called Greenfield Health Systems Corp* ***(G-17923)***
Dialysis Specialists Fairfield....513 863-6331
4750 Dixie Hwy Fairfield (45014) ***(G-10841)***
Diamond Heavy Haul Inc....330 677-8061
123 N Water St Ste A Kent (44240) ***(G-12365)***
Diamond Hill Capital MGT Inc....614 255-3333
325 John H Mcconnell Blvd Columbus (43215) ***(G-7516)***
Diamond Hill Funds....614 255-3333
325 John H Mcconnell Blvd # 200 Columbus (43215) ***(G-7517)***
Diamond Machine and Mfg, Bluffton *Also called Carpe Diem Industries LLC* ***(G-1729)***
Diamond Plastics, Dunkirk *Also called Ball Bounce and Sport Inc* ***(G-10501)***
Diamond Roofing Systems LLP....330 856-2500
8031 E Market St Ste 6 Warren (44484) ***(G-18849)***
DIAMONDS & PEARLS RCH, Cleveland *Also called Diamonds Pearls Hlth Svcs LLC* ***(G-5482)***
Diamonds Pearls Hlth Svcs LLC....216 752-8500
3570 Warrensville Ctr Rd Cleveland (44122) ***(G-5482)***
Diane Babiuch....419 867-8837
7409 International Dr Holland (43528) ***(G-12020)***
Diane Sauer Chevrolet Inc....330 373-1600
700 Niles Rd Se Warren (44483) ***(G-18850)***
Diane Vishnia Rn and Assoc....330 929-1113
2497 State Rd Cuyahoga Falls (44223) ***(G-9180)***
Dick Lavy Trucking Inc....937 448-2104
8848 State Route 121 Bradford (45308) ***(G-1806)***
Dick's Sporting Goods 1021, Heath *Also called Dicks Sporting Goods Inc* ***(G-11836)***
Dick's Sporting Goods 1166, Columbus *Also called Dicks Sporting Goods Inc* ***(G-7518)***
Dickerson Distributing Company....513 539-8483
150 Lawton Ave Monroe (45050) ***(G-14693)***
Dickinson Fleet Services LLC....513 772-3629
11536 Gondola St Ste B Cincinnati (45241) ***(G-3490)***
Dickman Supply Inc (PA)....937 492-6166
1991 St Marys Ave Sidney (45365) ***(G-16928)***
Dickman Supply Inc....937 492-6166
1991 St Mary Ave Sidney (45365) ***(G-16929)***
Dickman Supply Inc....937 492-6166
1425 Sater St Greenville (45331) ***(G-11498)***
Dicks Sporting Goods Inc....740 522-5555
771 S 30th St Ste 9007 Heath (43056) ***(G-11836)***
Dicks Sporting Goods Inc....614 472-4250
4304 Easton Gateway Dr Columbus (43219) ***(G-7518)***
Dickson Industrial Park Inc....740 377-9162
719 County Road 1 South Point (45680) ***(G-17083)***
Didion's Mechanical, Bellevue *Also called Donald E Didion II* ***(G-1408)***
Diebold Incorporated....330 588-3619
217 2nd St Nw Fl 6 Canton (44702) ***(G-2340)***
Diebold Nixdorf Incorporated....513 870-1400
8509 Bilstein Blvd Hamilton (45015) ***(G-11722)***
Diesel-Eagle, Williamsburg *Also called Clercom Inc* ***(G-19630)***
Diet Center Worldwide Inc (PA)....330 665-5861
395 Springside Dr Akron (44333) ***(G-192)***
Dietary Solutions Inc....614 985-6567
171 Green Meadows Dr S Lewis Center (43035) ***(G-12682)***
Diewald & Pope Inc....614 861-6160
245 Connell Ct Reynoldsburg (43068) ***(G-16446)***
Digeronimo Aggregates LLC....216 524-2950
8900 Hemlock Rd Independence (44131) ***(G-12204)***
Digestive Care Inc....937 320-5050
75 Sylvania Dr Beavercreek (45440) ***(G-1238)***
Digestive Disease Consultants....330 225-6468
1299 Industrial Pkwy N # 110 Brunswick (44212) ***(G-1975)***
Digestive Endoscopy Center, Dayton *Also called Digestive Specialists Inc* ***(G-9501)***
Digestive Health Gastrologist, Toledo *Also called Promedica GI Physicians LLC* ***(G-18139)***

ALPHABETIC

Digestive Specialists Inc 937 534-7330
999 Brubaker Dr Ste 1 Dayton (45429) *(G-9501)*

Digico Imaging Inc 614 239-5200
3487 E Fulton St Columbus (43227) *(G-7519)*

Digiknow Inc 888 482-4455
3615 Superior Ave E 4404a Cleveland (44114) *(G-5483)*

Digioia/Suburban Excvtg LLC 440 237-1978
11293 Royalton Rd North Royalton (44133) *(G-15487)*

Digital Color Intl LLC 330 762-6959
1653 Merriman Rd Ste 211 Akron (44313) *(G-193)*

Digital Controls Corporation (PA) 513 746-8118
444 Alexandersville Rd Miamisburg (45342) *(G-14297)*

Digital Management Inc 240 223-4800
4660 Duke Dr Ste 100 Mason (45040) *(G-13695)*

Digitek Software Inc 614 764-8875
650 Radio Dr Lewis Center (43035) *(G-12683)*

Dignity Health 330 493-4443
4535 Dressler Rd Nw Canton (44718) *(G-2341)*

Dill-Elam Inc 513 575-0017
1461 State Route 28 Loveland (45140) *(G-13123)*

Dillard Electric Inc 937 836-5381
106 Quinter Farm Rd Union (45322) *(G-18498)*

Dillin Engineered Systems Corp 419 666-6789
8030 Broadstone Rd Perrysburg (43551) *(G-15998)*

Dillon Group Homes, Fostoria Also called RES-Care Inc *(G-11138)*

Dillon Holdings LLC 513 942-5600
8050 Beckett Center Dr # 103 West Chester (45069) *(G-19062)*

Dillon R D, Fostoria Also called Voca of Ohio *(G-11142)*

Dilly Door Co 419 782-1181
1640 Baltimore St Defiance (43512) *(G-10028)*

Dimech Services Inc 419 727-0111
5505 Enterprise Blvd Toledo (43612) *(G-17853)*

Dimension Service Corporation 614 226-7455
5500 Frantz Rd Ste 100 Dublin (43017) *(G-10321)*

Dimensional Metals Inc (PA) 740 927-3633
58 Klema Dr N Reynoldsburg (43068) *(G-16447)*

Dimensionmark Ltd 513 305-3525
2909 Crescentville Rd West Chester (45069) *(G-19063)*

Dingledine Trucking Company 937 652-3454
1000 Phoenix Dr Urbana (43078) *(G-18585)*

Dinn Hochman and Potter LLC 440 446-1100
5910 Landerbrook Dr # 200 Cleveland (44124) *(G-5484)*

Dino Persichetti 330 821-9600
20040 Hrrsburg Wstvlle Rd Alliance (44601) *(G-538)*

Dinos Catering Inc 440 943-1010
30605 Ridge Rd Wickliffe (44092) *(G-19593)*

Dinsmore & Shohl LLP (PA) 513 977-8200
255 E 5th St Ste 1900 Cincinnati (45202) *(G-3491)*

Diocese of Toledo 419 243-7255
1601 Jefferson Ave Toledo (43604) *(G-17854)*

Diproinduca (usa) Limited LLC 330 722-4442
2528 Medina Rd Medina (44256) *(G-14058)*

Diproinduca USA, Medina Also called Diproinduca (usa) Limited LLC *(G-14058)*

Direct Expediting LLC 513 459-0100
5311 Bentley Oak Dr Mason (45040) *(G-13696)*

Direct Express Delivery Svc 513 541-0600
2841 Colerain Ave Cincinnati (45225) *(G-3492)*

Direct Import Home Decor Inc (PA) 216 898-9758
4979 W 130th St Cleveland (44135) *(G-5485)*

Direct Maintenance LLC 330 744-5211
100 E Federal St Ste 600 Youngstown (44503) *(G-20169)*

Direct Options Inc 513 779-4416
9565 Cncnnati Columbus Rd West Chester (45069) *(G-19064)*

Direct-X, Cincinnati Also called Direct Express Delivery Svc *(G-3492)*

Directconnectgroup Ltd 216 281-2866
5501 Cass Ave Cleveland (44102) *(G-5486)*

Direction Home Akron Canton AR (PA) 330 896-9172
1550 Corporate Woods Pkwy Uniontown (44685) *(G-18517)*

Directions Credit Union Inc (PA) 419 720-4769
5121 Whiteford Rd Sylvania (43560) *(G-17583)*

Directions Credit Union Inc 419 524-7113
777 N Main St Mansfield (44902) *(G-13292)*

Directions For Youth Families 614 258-8043
657 S Ohio Ave Columbus (43205) *(G-7520)*

Directions For Youth Families 614 694-0203
3840 Kimberly Pkwy N Columbus (43232) *(G-7521)*

Directions For Youth Families (PA) 614 294-2661
1515 Indianola Ave Columbus (43201) *(G-7522)*

Directions Research Inc (PA) 513 651-2990
401 E Court St Ste 200 Cincinnati (45202) *(G-3493)*

DISABILITY FOUNDATION THE, Dayton Also called Dayton Foundation Inc *(G-9474)*

Disabillity Rights Ohio, Columbus Also called Ohio Disability Rights Law Pol *(G-8337)*

Disabled American Veterans 330 875-5795
128 Indiana Ave Louisville (44641) *(G-13099)*

Disabled American Veterans 419 526-0203
34 Park Ave W Mansfield (44902) *(G-13293)*

Disabled American Veterans 330 364-1204
824 Hardesty Ave Nw New Philadelphia (44663) *(G-15093)*

Disabled American Veterans 740 367-7973
28051 State Route 7 Cheshire (45620) *(G-2789)*

Disanto Companies 440 442-0600
1960 Caronia Dr Cleveland (44124) *(G-5487)*

Disaster Reconstruction Inc 440 918-1523
33851 Curtis Blvd Ste 202 Eastlake (44095) *(G-10545)*

Discount Drug Mart Inc (PA) 330 725-2340
211 Commerce Dr Medina (44256) *(G-14059)*

Discount Drug Mart Inc 330 343-7700
3015 N Wooster Ave Dover (44622) *(G-10183)*

Discountcontactlenses.com, Columbus Also called Arlington Contact Lens Svc Inc *(G-7042)*

Discover Card Services, Hilliard Also called Dfs Corporate Services LLC *(G-11895)*

Discover Financial Services, New Albany Also called Dfs Corporate Services LLC *(G-14983)*

Discover Training Inc 614 871-0010
4882 Rheims Way Grove City (43123) *(G-11554)*

Discovering The Jewish Jesus, Plain City Also called Shalom Ministries Intl Inc *(G-16205)*

Discovery Express Child Care, Holland Also called Childrens Discovery Center *(G-12015)*

Discovery School 419 756-8880
855 Millsboro Rd Mansfield (44903) *(G-13294)*

Dish Network Corporation 614 534-2001
3315 Mill Meadow Dr Hilliard (43026) *(G-11896)*

Diskcopy Duplication Services 440 460-0800
107 Alpha Park Cleveland (44143) *(G-5488)*

Dismas Distribution Services 614 861-2525
6772 Kilowatt Cir Blacklick (43004) *(G-1506)*

Dispatch Color Press, Columbus Also called Dispatch Consumer Services *(G-7523)*

Dispatch Consumer Services 740 687-1893
3160 W Fair Ave Lancaster (43130) *(G-12527)*

Dispatch Consumer Services (HQ) 740 548-5555
5300 Crosswind Dr Columbus (43228) *(G-7523)*

Dispatch Printing Company (PA) 614 461-5000
62 E Broad St Columbus (43215) *(G-7524)*

Dispatch Printing Company 740 548-5331
7801 N Central Dr Lewis Center (43035) *(G-12684)*

Dispatch Productions Inc 614 460-3700
770 Twin Rivers Dr Columbus (43215) *(G-7525)*

Dist-Trans Inc 614 497-1660
1580 Williams Rd Columbus (43207) *(G-7526)*

Distillata Company (PA) 216 771-2900
1608 E 24th St Cleveland (44114) *(G-5489)*

Distinct Advantage Cabinetry, Toledo Also called Online Mega Sellers Corp *(G-18109)*

Distribution and Trnsp Svc Inc (PA) 937 295-3343
401 S Main St Fort Loramie (45845) *(G-11110)*

Distribution Center, West Chester Also called Martin-Brower Company LLC *(G-19118)*

Distribution Center, Wilmington Also called PC Connection Services *(G-19777)*

Distribution Data Incorporated (PA) 216 362-3009
16101 Snow Rd Ste 200 Brookpark (44142) *(G-1943)*

Distribution Service Company, Wadsworth Also called Cornwell Quality Tools Company *(G-18751)*

District 6, Delaware Also called Ohio Department Transportation *(G-10119)*

District Board Health Mahoning 330 270-2855
50 Westchester Dr Youngstown (44515) *(G-20170)*

District Office, Westerville Also called Columbus Frkln Cnty Pk *(G-19388)*

Distrubution Center, Columbus Also called Ohiohealth Corporation *(G-8458)*

Disttech LLC 800 321-3143
8101 Union Ave Cleveland (44105) *(G-5490)*

Dittman-Adams Company 513 870-7530
4946 Rialto Rd West Chester (45069) *(G-19065)*

Div of Refuse and Recycling, Cleveland Also called City of Lakewood *(G-5265)*

Dival Inc (PA) 216 831-4200
26401 Miles Rd Warrensville Heights (44128) *(G-18932)*

Diver Steel City Auto Crushers 330 744-5083
590 Himrod Ave Youngstown (44506) *(G-20171)*

Diverscare Healthcare Svcs Inc 513 867-4100
1302 Millville Ave Hamilton (45013) *(G-11723)*

Diverscare Healthcare Svcs Inc 937 278-8211
6125 N Main St Dayton (45415) *(G-9502)*

Diverscare Healthcare Svcs Inc 513 271-7010
7010 Rowan Hill Dr Cincinnati (45227) *(G-3494)*

Diversfied Emplyee Sltions Inc 330 764-4125
3745 Medina Rd Medina (44256) *(G-14060)*

Diversicare Leasing Corp 615 771-7575
2159 Dogwood Ridge Rd Wheelersburg (45694) *(G-19576)*

Diversicare of Avon LLC 440 937-6201
4110 Rocky River Dr Cleveland (44135) *(G-5491)*

Diversicare of Mansfield LLC 419 529-6447
2124 Park Ave W Ontario (44906) *(G-15686)*

Diversicare of St. Theresa, Cincinnati Also called Diverscare Healthcare Svcs Inc *(G-3494)*

Diversified Air Systems Inc 330 784-3366
1201 George Wash Blvd Akron (44312) *(G-194)*

Diversified Fall Protection, Westlake Also called Lorad LLC *(G-19511)*

Diversified Health Management 614 338-8888
3569 Refugee Rd Ste C Columbus (43232) *(G-7527)*

Diversified Labor Support LLC 440 234-3090
7050 Engle Rd Ste 101 Cleveland (44130) *(G-5492)*

Diversified Products & Svcs 740 393-6202
1250 Vernonview Dr Mount Vernon (43050) *(G-14893)*

Diversified Systems Inc 614 476-9939
100 Dorchester Sq N # 103 Westerville (43081) *(G-19394)*

Diversipak Inc (PA) 513 321-7884
838 Reedy St Cincinnati (45202) *(G-3495)*

Diversity Search Group LLC 614 352-2988
2600 Corp Exchange Dr # 110 Columbus (43231) *(G-7528)*

Divine Healthcare Services LLC 614 899-6767
2374 E Dublin Granvl Rd Columbus (43229) *(G-7529)*
Division 7 Inc 740 965-1970
72 Holmes St Galena (43021) *(G-11281)*
Division 7 Roofing, Galena *Also called Division 7 Inc (G-11281)*
Division Drnking Ground Waters 614 644-2752
50 W Town St Ste 700 Columbus (43215) *(G-7530)*
Division of Engineering, Columbus *Also called Natural Resources Ohio Dept (G-8249)*
Division of Gastroenterology, Columbus *Also called Ohio State Univ Wexner Med Ctr (G-8387)*
Division of Geological Survey 614 265-6576
2045 Morse Rd Bldg C Columbus (43229) *(G-7531)*
Division of Parks, Saint Marys *Also called Natural Resources Ohio Dept (G-16680)*
Division of Selling Materials, Dover *Also called Smith Concrete Co (G-10214)*
Division of Water Resources, Batavia *Also called County of Clermont (G-1007)*
Division Streets & Utilities, Dublin *Also called City of Dublin (G-10294)*
Dix & Eaton Incorporated 216 241-0405
200 Public Sq Ste 3900 Cleveland (44114) *(G-5493)*
Dixon Builders & Developers 513 887-6400
8050 Beckett Center Dr # 213 West Chester (45069) *(G-19066)*
Dixon Health Care Center, Steubenville *Also called Communicare Health Svcs Inc (G-17313)*
Dizer Corp (PA) 440 368-0200
1912 Mentor Ave Painesville (44077) *(G-15851)*
Dj Neff Enterpeises Inc 440 884-3100
6405 York Rd Cleveland (44130) *(G-5494)*
Djj Holding Corporation (HQ) 513 621-8770
300 Pike St Cincinnati (45202) *(G-3496)*
DKM Construction Inc 740 289-3006
W Perimeter Rd Piketon (45661) *(G-16113)*
Dkmp Consulting Inc 614 733-0979
8000 Corporate Blvd Plain City (43064) *(G-16187)*
Dlc Transport Inc 740 282-1763
320 N 5th St Steubenville (43952) *(G-17315)*
Dlhbowles Inc (PA) 330 478-2503
2422 Leo Ave Sw Canton (44706) *(G-2342)*
Dlr Group Inc 216 522-1350
1422 Euclid Ave Ste 300 Cleveland (44115) *(G-5495)*
Dlr Group Wstlake Reed Lskosky, Cleveland *Also called Dlr Group Inc (G-5495)*
Dlz American Drilling Inc 614 888-0040
6121 Huntley Rd Columbus (43229) *(G-7532)*
Dlz Construction Services Inc 614 888-0040
6121 Huntley Rd Columbus (43229) *(G-7533)*
Dlz National Inc (HQ) 614 888-0040
6121 Huntley Rd Columbus (43229) *(G-7534)*
Dlz Ohio Inc (HQ) 614 888-0040
6121 Huntley Rd Columbus (43229) *(G-7535)*
Dlz Ohio Inc 330 923-0401
1 Canal Square Plz # 1300 Akron (44308) *(G-195)*
DMC Consulting, Toledo *Also called DMC Technology Group (G-17855)*
DMC Technology Group 419 535-2900
7657 Kings Pointe Rd Toledo (43617) *(G-17855)*
DMD Management Inc 330 405-6040
2463 Sussex Blvd Twinsburg (44087) *(G-18406)*
DMD Management Inc 440 944-9400
1919 Bishop Rd Wickliffe (44092) *(G-19594)*
DMD Management Inc (PA) 216 898-8399
12380 Plaza Dr Cleveland (44130) *(G-5496)*
DMD Management Inc 216 371-3600
12504 Cedar Rd Cleveland (44106) *(G-5497)*
Dmh Toyota Lift, Holland *Also called Toyota Industrial Eqp Dlr (G-12064)*
DMR Management Inc 513 771-1700
109 Brookfield Rd Avon Lake (44012) *(G-928)*
Dna Diagnostics Center Inc (HQ) 513 881-7800
1 Ddc Way Fairfield (45014) *(G-10842)*
Dna Technology Park, Fairfield *Also called Dna Diagnostics Center Inc (G-10842)*
Dno Inc 614 231-3601
3650 E 5th Ave Columbus (43219) *(G-7536)*
Dnv GL Healthcare Usa Inc 281 396-1610
400 Techne Center Dr # 100 Milford (45150) *(G-14517)*
Do Cut Sales & Service Inc 330 533-9878
3375 Youngstown Rd Se Warren (44484) *(G-18851)*
Do It Best, Sidney *Also called Lochard Inc (G-16940)*
Do It Best, Lancaster *Also called Slaters Inc (G-12574)*
DO IT BEST, Kent *Also called Carter-Jones Companies Inc (G-12354)*
Do It Best Corp 330 725-3859
444 Independence Dr Medina (44256) *(G-14061)*
Do-Cut True Value, Warren *Also called Do Cut Sales & Service Inc (G-18851)*
Doan Pyramid Electric, Cleveland *Also called Northeast Ohio Electric LLC (G-6155)*
Dobbins Nursing Home Inc 513 553-4139
400 Main St New Richmond (45157) *(G-15126)*
Dobson Cellular Call Center, Youngstown *Also called AT&T Mobility LLC (G-20106)*
Doctor's Urgent Care Offices, Milford *Also called Ambulatory Medical Care Inc (G-14502)*
Doctors Consulting Service 614 793-1980
200 Bradenton Ave Dublin (43017) *(G-10322)*
Doctors Hosp Physcn Svcs LLC 330 834-4725
830 Amherst Rd Ne Ste 201 Massillon (44646) *(G-13801)*
Doctors Hospital Cleveland Inc 740 753-7300
11 John Lloyd Evns Mem Dr Nelsonville (45764) *(G-14961)*
Doctors Hospital Fmly Practice, Grove City *Also called Doctors Hospital Health Center (G-11555)*
Doctors Hospital Health Center 614 544-0101
2030 Stringtown Rd Fl 3 Grove City (43123) *(G-11555)*
Doctors Hospital North, Columbus *Also called Doctors Ohiohealth Corporation (G-7537)*
Doctors Ohiohealth Corporation (HQ) 614 544-5424
5100 W Broad St Columbus (43228) *(G-7537)*
Doctors Urgent Care 419 586-1611
950 S Main St Ste 10 Celina (45822) *(G-2646)*
Doctors Weaver Wallace Conley, Fairfield *Also called Affiliates In Oral & Maxlofcl (G-10817)*
Document Concepts Inc 330 575-5685
607 S Main St A North Canton (44720) *(G-15333)*
Document Imging Spcialists LLC 614 868-9008
5047 Transamerica Dr Columbus (43228) *(G-7538)*
DOCUMENT SOLUTIONS, Xenia *Also called Greene Inc (G-20058)*
Document Solutions Group, Columbus *Also called Document Solutions Ohio LLC (G-7539)*
Document Solutions Ohio LLC 614 846-2400
100 E Campus View Blvd # 105 Columbus (43235) *(G-7539)*
Document Tech Systems Ltd 330 928-5311
525 Portage Trail Ext W Cuyahoga Falls (44223) *(G-9181)*
Dodd Hall Inptent Rhbilitation, Columbus *Also called Ohio State University (G-8388)*
Doepker Group Inc 419 355-1409
1303 W State St Fremont (43420) *(G-11195)*
Dolbey Systems Inc (PA) 440 392-9900
7280 Auburn Rd Painesville (44077) *(G-15852)*
Dold Homes Inc (PA) 419 874-2535
26610 Eckel Rd Perrysburg (43551) *(G-15999)*
Dole Fresh Vegetables Inc 937 525-4300
600 Benjamin Dr Springfield (45502) *(G-17190)*
Dolgencorp LLC 740 588-5700
2505 E Pointe Dr Zanesville (43701) *(G-20468)*
Dolin Supply Co 304 529-4171
702 Solida Rd South Point (45680) *(G-17084)*
Doling & Associates Dental Lab 937 254-0075
3318 Successful Way Dayton (45414) *(G-9503)*
Dollar General, Zanesville *Also called Dolgencorp LLC (G-20468)*
Dollar Paradise (PA) 216 432-0421
1240 E 55th St Cleveland (44103) *(G-5498)*
Domajaparo Inc (PA) 513 742-3600
11400 Winton Rd Cincinnati (45240) *(G-3497)*
Dome Dialysis LLC 614 882-1734
241 W Schrock Rd Westerville (43081) *(G-19395)*
Domestic Connection, New Albany *Also called Carol Scudere (G-14979)*
Domestic Relations 937 225-4063
301 W 3rd St Ste 500 Dayton (45402) *(G-9504)*
Domestic Violence Project Inc 330 445-2000
720 19th St Ne Canton (44714) *(G-2343)*
Domin-8 Entp Solutions Inc (PA) 513 492-5800
4660 Duke Dr Ste 210 Mason (45040) *(G-13697)*
Dominguez Inc 513 425-9955
125 Park St Middletown (45044) *(G-14424)*
Dominion Energy Ohio, Maple Heights *Also called East Ohio Gas Company (G-13406)*
Dominion Energy Ohio, Youngstown *Also called East Ohio Gas Company (G-20175)*
Dominion Energy Ohio, New Franklin *Also called East Ohio Gas Company (G-15044)*
Dominion Energy Ohio, Cleveland *Also called East Ohio Gas Company (G-5520)*
Dominion Energy Ohio, Ashtabula *Also called East Ohio Gas Company (G-743)*
Dominion Energy Ohio, Canton *Also called East Ohio Gas Company (G-2347)*
Dominion Energy Ohio, Wickliffe *Also called East Ohio Gas Company (G-19595)*
Dominion Energy Transm Inc 513 932-5793
1262 W State Route 122 Lebanon (45036) *(G-12601)*
Dominion Homes Inc (HQ) 614 356-5000
4900 Tuttle Crossing Blvd Dublin (43016) *(G-10323)*
Domino Foods Inc 216 432-3222
2075 E 65th St Cleveland (44103) *(G-5499)*
Domino Sugar, Cleveland *Also called Domino Foods Inc (G-5499)*
Domokur Architects Inc 330 666-7878
4651 Medina Rd Copley (44321) *(G-9056)*
Don Bosco Centers, Cleveland *Also called Don Bosco Community Center Inc (G-5500)*
Don Bosco Community Center Inc (PA) 816 421-3160
1763 Wickford Rd Cleveland (44112) *(G-5500)*
Don Bosco Community Center Inc 816 421-3160
1763 Wickford Rd Cleveland (44112) *(G-5501)*
Don Drumm Studios & Gallery 330 253-6840
437 Crouse St Akron (44311) *(G-196)*
Don S Cisle Contractor Inc (PA) 513 867-1400
1714 Fairgrove Ave Hamilton (45011) *(G-11724)*
Don Tester Ford Lincoln Inc 419 668-8233
2800 Route 250 S Norwalk (44857) *(G-15570)*
Don Walter Kitchen Distrs Inc (PA) 330 793-9338
260 Victoria Rd Youngstown (44515) *(G-20172)*
Don Wartko Construction Co (PA) 330 673-5252
975 Tallmadge Rd Kent (44240) *(G-12366)*
Don Wood Bck Oldsmble Pntiac C 740 593-6641
900 E State St Athens (45701) *(G-783)*
Don Wood GMC & Toyota, Athens *Also called Don Wood Inc (G-784)*
Don Wood Inc 740 593-6641
900 E State St Athens (45701) *(G-784)*
Don's Lighthouse Inn, Cleveland *Also called Strang Corporation (G-6545)*

ALPHABETIC

Donald Bowen and Assoc DDS...614 274-0454
2575 W Broad St Unit 3 Columbus (43204) ***(G-7540)***
Donald E Didion II...419 483-2226
1027b County Road 308 Bellevue (44811) ***(G-1408)***
Donald Martens Sons, Cleveland *Also called Martens Donald & Sons* ***(G-5988)***
Donald P Pipino Company Ltd...330 726-8177
7600 Market St Youngstown (44512) ***(G-20173)***
Donald R Kenney & Company (PA)...614 540-2404
470 Olde Worthington Rd # 101 Westerville (43082) ***(G-19300)***
Donauschwaben's Grmnamrcn Cltr, Olmsted Twp *Also called Lenau Park* ***(G-15677)***
Done-Rite Bowling Service Co (PA)...440 232-3280
20434 Krick Rd Bedford (44146) ***(G-1304)***
Donegal Bay, Warrensville Heights *Also called Trickeration Inc* ***(G-18935)***
Donlen Inc (HQ)...216 961-6767
8905 Lake Ave Cleveland (44102) ***(G-5502)***
Donley Concrete Cutting...614 834-0300
151 W Borland St Pickerington (43147) ***(G-16094)***
Donley Ford-Lincoln Inc (PA)...419 281-3673
1641 Claremont Ave Ashland (44805) ***(G-679)***
Donleys Inc (PA)...216 524-6800
5430 Warner Rd Cleveland (44125) ***(G-5503)***
Donnell Ford-Lincoln...330 332-0031
152 Continental Dr Salem (44460) ***(G-16694)***
Donnellon Mc Carthy Inc...937 299-3564
2580 Lance Dr Moraine (45409) ***(G-14775)***
Donnellon Mc Carthy Inc...513 681-3200
4141 Turrill St Cincinnati (45223) ***(G-3498)***
Donnellon Mc Carthy Inc...937 299-0200
2580 Lance Dr Moraine (45409) ***(G-14776)***
Dons Automotive Group LLC...419 337-3010
720 N Shoop Ave Wauseon (43567) ***(G-18951)***
Dons Brooklyn Chevrolet Inc...216 741-1500
4941 Pearl Rd Cleveland (44109) ***(G-5504)***
Donty Horton HM Care Dhhc LLC...513 463-3442
2692 Madison Rd Ste N1192 Cincinnati (45208) ***(G-3499)***
Donzell's, Akron *Also called Donzells Flower & Grdn Ctr Inc* ***(G-197)***
Donzells Flower & Grdn Ctr Inc...330 724-0550
937 E Waterloo Rd Akron (44306) ***(G-197)***
Dooley Heating and AC LLC...614 278-9944
2010 Zettler Rd Columbus (43232) ***(G-7541)***
Door Fabrication Services Inc...937 454-9207
3250 Old Springfield Rd # 1 Vandalia (45377) ***(G-18677)***
Door Shop & Service Inc...614 423-8043
7385 State Route 3 Ste 52 Westerville (43082) ***(G-19301)***
Dorlon Golf Club...440 236-8234
18000 Station Rd Columbia Station (44028) ***(G-6845)***
Dorman, Regina MD, Tallmadge *Also called Northeast Family Health Care* ***(G-17645)***
Dornoch Golf Club Inc...740 369-0863
3329 Columbus Pike Delaware (43015) ***(G-10091)***
Dorothy Love Retirement Cmnty, Sidney *Also called Ohio Presbt Retirement Svcs* ***(G-16945)***
Dorsky Hodgson + Partners Inc (PA)...216 464-8600
23240 Chagrin Blvd # 300 Cleveland (44122) ***(G-5505)***
Dorsky Hodgson Parrish Yue, Cleveland *Also called Dorsky Hodgson + Partners Inc* ***(G-5505)***
Dorsten Industries Inc...419 628-2327
146 N Main St Minster (45865) ***(G-14660)***
Dortronic Service Inc (PA)...216 739-3667
201 E Granger Rd Cleveland (44131) ***(G-5506)***
DOT Diamond Core Drilling Inc (PA)...440 322-6466
780 Sugar Ln Elyria (44035) ***(G-10617)***
DOT Smith LLC...740 245-5105
3607 Garners Ford Rd Thurman (45685) ***(G-17670)***
Dotloop LLC...513 257-0550
700 W Pete Rose Way # 436 Cincinnati (45203) ***(G-3500)***
Dots Market, Dayton *Also called Mary C Enterprises Inc* ***(G-9701)***
Dotson Company...419 877-5176
6848 Providence St Whitehouse (43571) ***(G-19585)***
Double A Trailer Sales Inc (PA)...419 692-7626
1750 E 5th St Delphos (45833) ***(G-10142)***
Double Eagle Club, Galena *Also called Big Red LP* ***(G-11280)***
Double Tree, Columbus *Also called Columbus Worthington Hospitalt* ***(G-7394)***
Double Z Construction Company...614 274-9334
2550 Harrison Rd Columbus (43204) ***(G-7542)***
Doubletree Columbus Hotel, Columbus *Also called Ch Relty Iv/Clmbus Partners LP* ***(G-7247)***
Doubletree Guest Suites Dayton...937 436-2400
300 Prestige Pl Miamisburg (45342) ***(G-14298)***
Doubletree Hotel, Cleveland *Also called SM Double Tree Hotel Lake* ***(G-6491)***
Doubletree Hotel, Cincinnati *Also called 6300 Sharonville Assoc LLC* ***(G-2947)***
Doubletree Hotel, Dayton *Also called Renthotel Dayton LLC* ***(G-9847)***
Doubletree Hotel, Cleveland *Also called Cleveland S Hospitality LLC* ***(G-5345)***
Doubletree Hotel, Miamisburg *Also called Ashford Trs Lessee LLC* ***(G-14272)***
Doubletree Suites by Hilton, Columbus *Also called 50 S Front LLC* ***(G-6914)***
Doug Bigelow Chevrolet Inc...330 644-7500
3281 S Arlington Rd Akron (44312) ***(G-198)***
Doug Chevrolet, Akron *Also called Doug Bigelow Chevrolet Inc* ***(G-198)***
Doug Marine Motors Inc...740 335-3700
1120 Clinton Ave Wshngtn CT Hs (43160) ***(G-20020)***
Douglas Company (PA)...419 865-8600
1716 Prrysburg Holland Rd Holland (43528) ***(G-12021)***
Douglas Construction Company...419 865-8600
1716 Prrysburg Holland Rd Holland (43528) ***(G-12022)***
Douglas R Denny...216 236-2400
6480 Rckside Woods Blvd S Independence (44131) ***(G-12205)***
Douglas Walcher Farms...419 744-2427
866 State Route 162 E North Fairfield (44855) ***(G-15380)***
Douglas Webb & Associates (PA)...614 873-9830
8080 Corporate Blvd Plain City (43064) ***(G-16188)***
Douglass & Associates Co Lpa...216 362-7777
4725 Grayton Rd Cleveland (44135) ***(G-5507)***
Dove Building Services Inc...614 299-4700
1691 Cleveland Ave Columbus (43211) ***(G-7543)***
Dover City Schools...330 343-8880
865 1/2 E Iron Ave Dover (44622) ***(G-10184)***
Dover Cryogenics, Midvale *Also called Amko Service Company* ***(G-14489)***
Dover Hydraulics Inc (PA)...330 364-1617
2996 Progress St Dover (44622) ***(G-10185)***
Dover Hydraulics South, Dover *Also called Dover Hydraulics Inc* ***(G-10185)***
Dover Investments Inc...440 235-5511
7989 Columbia Rd Olmsted Falls (44138) ***(G-15673)***
Dover Nursing Center...330 364-4436
1525 N Crater Ave Dover (44622) ***(G-10186)***
Dover Orthopedic Center, Dover *Also called Teater Orthopedic Surgeons* ***(G-10216)***
Dover Phila Federal Credit Un (PA)...330 364-8874
119 Filmore Ave Dover (44622) ***(G-10187)***
Dover Softies, Dover *Also called L and C Soft Serve Inc* ***(G-10196)***
Dovetail Construction Co Inc (PA)...740 592-1800
26055 Emery Rd Ste G Cleveland (44128) ***(G-5508)***
Dovetail Solar and Wind, Cleveland *Also called Dovetail Construction Co Inc* ***(G-5508)***
Dovin Dairy Farms LLC...440 653-7009
15967 State Route 58 Oberlin (44074) ***(G-15642)***
Dovin Land Company, Oberlin *Also called Dovin Dairy Farms LLC* ***(G-15642)***
Down To Earth Landscaping, Cleveland *Also called A Ressler Inc* ***(G-4935)***
Downtheroad Inc...740 452-4579
3625 Maple Ave Zanesville (43701) ***(G-20469)***
Downtown Akron Partnership Inc...330 374-7676
103 S High St Fl 4 Akron (44308) ***(G-199)***
Downtown Fast Park, Cincinnati *Also called Parking Company America Inc* ***(G-4255)***
Downtown Ford Lincoln Inc...330 456-2781
1423 Tuscarawas St W Canton (44702) ***(G-2344)***
Doylestown Cable, Doylestown *Also called Doylestown Telephone Company* ***(G-10229)***
Doylestown Cable TV, Doylestown *Also called Doylestown Communications* ***(G-10226)***
Doylestown Communications, Doylestown *Also called Doylestown Telephone Company* ***(G-10228)***
Doylestown Communications...330 658-7000
81 N Portage St Doylestown (44230) ***(G-10226)***
Doylestown Health Care Center...330 658-1533
95 Black Dr Doylestown (44230) ***(G-10227)***
Doylestown Telephone Company (PA)...330 658-2121
81 N Portage St Doylestown (44230) ***(G-10228)***
Doylestown Telephone Company...330 658-6666
28 E Marion St Doylestown (44230) ***(G-10229)***
DPL, Aberdeen *Also called Dayton Power and Light Company* ***(G-2)***
DPL Inc (HQ)...937 331-4063
1065 Woodman Dr Dayton (45432) ***(G-9266)***
Dps, Independence *Also called Canon Solutions America Inc* ***(G-12194)***
Dr Darren Adams Dr Grge Pettit, Portsmouth *Also called George P Pettit MD Inc* ***(G-16279)***
Dr Michael J Hulit...330 863-7173
107 N Reed Ave Malvern (44644) ***(G-13250)***
Drake Center LLC...513 418-2500
151 W Galbraith Rd Cincinnati (45216) ***(G-3501)***
Drake Development Inc...513 418-4370
165 W Galbraith Rd Ofc Cincinnati (45216) ***(G-3502)***
Drake State Air...937 472-3740
3711 Ozias Rd Eaton (45320) ***(G-10557)***
Drake State Air Systems Inc...937 472-0640
1417 E Main St Eaton (45320) ***(G-10558)***
Drasc Enterprises Inc...330 852-3254
9060 Bollman Rd Sw Sugarcreek (44681) ***(G-17544)***
Drb Systems LLC (PA)...330 645-3299
3245 Pickle Rd Akron (44312) ***(G-200)***
Drc Holdings Inc...419 230-0188
17623 Road 4 Pandora (45877) ***(G-15889)***
Drees Company...330 899-9554
3906 Kenway Blvd Uniontown (44685) ***(G-18518)***
Dreier & Maller Inc (PA)...614 575-0065
6508 Taylor Rd Sw Reynoldsburg (43068) ***(G-16448)***
Dresch Tolson Dental Labs...419 842-6730
8730 Resource Park Dr Sylvania (43560) ***(G-17584)***
Drew Ag-Transport Inc...937 548-3200
5450 Sebring Warner Rd Greenville (45331) ***(G-11499)***
Drew Medical Inc (PA)...407 363-6700
75 Milford Dr Ste 201 Hudson (44236) ***(G-12114)***
Drew Shoe, Lancaster *Also called Drew Ventures Inc* ***(G-12528)***
Drew Ventures Inc (PA)...740 653-4271
252 Quarry Rd Se Lancaster (43130) ***(G-12528)***
Drop In Babysitting Service, Piqua *Also called West Ohio Conference of* ***(G-16175)***
Drs Hill & Thomas Co...440 944-8887
2785 Som Center Rd Cleveland (44194) ***(G-5509)***

ALPHABETIC SECTION **Dutch Girl Cleaners, Canton**

Drs Paul Boyles & Kennedy ... 614 734-3347
3545 Olentangy River Rd Columbus (43214) ***(G-7544)***
Drs Ravin Birndorf Ravin Inc ... 877 852-8463
3000 Regency Ct Ste 100 Toledo (43623) ***(G-17856)***
Drs Signal Technologies Inc ... 937 429-7470
4393 Dayton Xenia Rd Beavercreek (45432) ***(G-1169)***
Drt Holdings Inc (PA) ... 937 298-7391
618 Greenmount Blvd Dayton (45419) ***(G-9505)***
Drug & Poison Information Ctr, Cincinnati *Also called Poison Information Center* ***(G-4313)***
Drug and Alcohol, Elyria *Also called County of Lorain* ***(G-10614)***
Drury Hotels Company LLC ... 614 798-8802
6170 Parkcenter Cir Dublin (43017) ***(G-10324)***
Drury Hotels Company LLC ... 614 221-7008
88 E Nationwide Blvd Columbus (43215) ***(G-7545)***
Drury Hotels Company LLC ... 937 454-5200
6616 Miller Ln Dayton (45414) ***(G-9506)***
Drury Hotels Company LLC ... 513 771-5601
2265 E Sharon Rd Cincinnati (45241) ***(G-3503)***
Drury Hotels Company LLC ... 614 798-8802
4109 Parkway Centre Dr Grove City (43123) ***(G-11556)***
Drury Inn & Suites Clmbus Conv, Columbus *Also called Drury Hotels Company LLC* ***(G-7545)***
Drury Inn & Suites Columbus NW, Dublin *Also called Drury Hotels Company LLC* ***(G-10324)***
Drury Inn & Suites Columbus S, Grove City *Also called Drury Hotels Company LLC* ***(G-11556)***
Drury Inn & Suites Dayton N, Dayton *Also called Drury Hotels Company LLC* ***(G-9506)***
Drury Inn Suites Cincinnati N, Cincinnati *Also called Drury Hotels Company LLC* ***(G-3503)***
Drw Packing, North Fairfield *Also called Douglas Walcher Farms* ***(G-15380)***
Dry It Rite LLC ... 614 295-8135
4330 Groves Rd Columbus (43232) ***(G-7546)***
Dry Run Limited Partnership ... 513 561-9119
7711 Ivy Hills Dr Cincinnati (45244) ***(G-3504)***
Drywall Barn, The, Youngstown *Also called Meander Tire Company Inc* ***(G-20278)***
DSC Consulting, Cincinnati *Also called Definitive Solutions Co Inc* ***(G-3479)***
DSC Logistics Inc ... 847 390-6800
1260 W Laskey Rd Toledo (43612) ***(G-17857)***
Dsg Canusa, Loveland *Also called Shawcor Pipe Protection LLC* ***(G-13159)***
DSI East ... 330 733-1861
73 Massillon Rd Akron (44312) ***(G-201)***
DSI Systems Inc ... 614 871-1456
3650 Brookham Dr Ste K Grove City (43123) ***(G-11557)***
Dsn, Lockbourne *Also called Dealers Supply North Inc* ***(G-12948)***
Dss Installations Ltd ... 513 761-7000
6717 Montgomery Rd Cincinnati (45236) ***(G-3505)***
Dss/Direct TV, Cincinnati *Also called Dss Installations Ltd* ***(G-3505)***
DSV Solutions LLC ... 740 989-1200
251 Arrowhead Rd Little Hocking (45742) ***(G-12943)***
Dta Inc ... 419 529-2920
3128 Park Ave W Ontario (44906) ***(G-15687)***
DTE Inc ... 419 522-3428
110 Baird Pkwy Mansfield (44903) ***(G-13295)***
Dts, Cuyahoga Falls *Also called Document Tech Systems Ltd* ***(G-9181)***
Dtv Inc (PA) ... 216 226-5465
6505 Mayfield Rd Mayfield Heights (44124) ***(G-14001)***
Dualite Sales & Service Inc (PA) ... 513 724-7100
1 Dualite Ln Williamsburg (45176) ***(G-19632)***
Duane Morris LLP ... 202 577-3075
1614 E 40th St Fl 3 Cleveland (44103) ***(G-5510)***
Duane Morris LLP ... 937 424-7086
200 N High St Columbus (43215) ***(G-7547)***
Dublin, Dublin *Also called Integra Cncinnati/Columbus Inc* ***(G-10377)***
Dublin Building Systems Co ... 614 760-5831
6233 Avery Rd Dublin (43016) ***(G-10325)***
Dublin City Schools ... 614 764-5926
6371 Shier Rings Rd Dublin (43016) ***(G-10326)***
Dublin Cleaners Inc (PA) ... 614 764-9934
6845 Caine Rd Columbus (43235) ***(G-7548)***
Dublin Coml Property Svcs Inc ... 419 732-6732
127 Madison St Port Clinton (43452) ***(G-16244)***
DUBLIN COUNSELING CENTER, Dublin *Also called Syntero Inc* ***(G-10471)***
Dublin Dance Center, Columbus *Also called Artistic Dance Enterprises* ***(G-7046)***
Dublin Family Care Inc ... 614 761-2244
250 W Bridge St Ste 101 Dublin (43017) ***(G-10327)***
Dublin Geriatric Care Co LP ... 614 761-1188
6430 Post Rd Dublin (43016) ***(G-10328)***
Dublin Latchkey Inc ... 614 793-0871
5970 Venture Dr Ste A Dublin (43017) ***(G-10329)***
Dublin Learning Academy ... 614 761-1800
5900 Cromdale Dr Dublin (43017) ***(G-10330)***
Dublin Methodist Hospital, Dublin *Also called Ohiohealth Corporation* ***(G-10416)***
Dublin Millwork Co Inc ... 614 889-7776
7575 Fishel Dr S Dublin (43016) ***(G-10331)***
Dublin Surgical Center LLC ... 614 932-9548
5005 Parkcenter Ave Dublin (43017) ***(G-10332)***
Duckworth Enterprises LLC ... 614 575-2900
2020 Brice Rd Ste 210 Reynoldsburg (43068) ***(G-16449)***
Ducru Spe LLC ... 937 228-2224
1 S Main St Dayton (45402) ***(G-9507)***
Ductbreeze, Cleveland *Also called Rwk Services Inc* ***(G-6423)***
Ducts Inc ... 216 391-2400
883 Addison Rd Cleveland (44103) ***(G-5511)***
Duer Construction Co Inc ... 330 848-9930
70 E North St Akron (44304) ***(G-202)***
Duffy Homes Inc ... 614 410-4100
495 S High St Ste 270 Columbus (43215) ***(G-7549)***
Dufresh Farms, West Mansfield *Also called Heartland Quality Egg Farm* ***(G-19266)***
Dugan & Meyers Construction Co (HQ) ... 513 891-4300
11110 Kenwood Rd Blue Ash (45242) ***(G-1579)***
Dugan & Meyers Construction Co ... 614 257-7430
8740 Orion Pl Ste 220 Columbus (43240) ***(G-6880)***
Dugan & Meyers Interests Inc (PA) ... 513 891-4300
11110 Kenwood Rd Blue Ash (45242) ***(G-1580)***
Dugan & Meyers LLC ... 513 891-4300
11110 Kenwood Rd Blue Ash (45242) ***(G-1581)***
Duke Energy Beckjord LLC ... 513 287-2561
139 E 4th St Cincinnati (45202) ***(G-3506)***
Duke Energy Convention Center, Cincinnati *Also called Global Spectrum* ***(G-3680)***
Duke Energy Kentucky Inc ... 704 594-6200
139 E 4th St Cincinnati (45202) ***(G-3507)***
DUKE ENERGY OHIO, Cincinnati *Also called Duke Energy Kentucky Inc* ***(G-3507)***
Duke Energy Ohio Inc (HQ) ... 704 382-3853
139 E 4th St Cincinnati (45202) ***(G-3508)***
Duke Energy Ohio Inc ... 800 544-6900
5445 Audro Dr Cincinnati (45247) ***(G-3509)***
Duke Energy Ohio Inc ... 513 287-1120
7600 E Kemper Rd Cincinnati (45249) ***(G-3510)***
Duke Energy Ohio Inc ... 513 467-5000
757 Us 52 New Richmond (45157) ***(G-15127)***
Duke Energy Ohio Inc ... 513 421-9500
3300 Central Pkwy Cincinnati (45225) ***(G-3511)***
Duke Enrgy Ohio Cstmer Svc Ctr, Cincinnati *Also called Duke Energy Ohio Inc* ***(G-3511)***
Duke Realty Corporation ... 513 651-3900
5181 Natorp Blvd Ste 600 Mason (45040) ***(G-13698)***
Duke Realty Corporation ... 614 932-6000
6640 Riverside Dr Ste 320 Dublin (43017) ***(G-10333)***
Duke Realty Investors, Mason *Also called Duke Realty Corporation* ***(G-13698)***
Duke-Weeks Realty, Dublin *Also called Duke Realty Corporation* ***(G-10333)***
Dummen Na Inc (PA) ... 614 850-9551
250 S High St Ste 650 Columbus (43215) ***(G-7550)***
Dumouchelle Art Galleries ... 419 255-7606
409 Jefferson Ave Toledo (43604) ***(G-17858)***
Dun Rite Home Improvement Inc ... 330 650-5322
8601 Freeway Dr Macedonia (44056) ***(G-13196)***
Dunbar Armored Inc ... 513 381-8000
1257 W 7th St Cincinnati (45203) ***(G-3512)***
Dunbar Armored Inc ... 614 475-1969
2300 Citygate Dr Unit B Columbus (43219) ***(G-7551)***
Dunbar Armored Inc ... 216 642-5700
5505 Cloverleaf Pkwy Cleveland (44125) ***(G-5512)***
Dunbar Mechanical Inc (PA) ... 734 856-6601
2806 N Reynolds Rd Toledo (43615) ***(G-17859)***
Duncan Aviation Inc ... 513 873-7523
358 Wilmer Ave 121 Cincinnati (45226) ***(G-3513)***
Duncan Falls Assoc ... 740 674-7105
Water St Duncan Falls (43734) ***(G-10498)***
Duncan Oil Co (PA) ... 937 426-5945
849 Factory Rd Dayton (45434) ***(G-9267)***
Dunlap Family Physicians Inc (PA) ... 330 684-2015
830 S Main St Ste Rear Orrville (44667) ***(G-15769)***
Dunlop and Johnston Inc ... 330 220-2700
5498 Innovation Dr Valley City (44280) ***(G-18616)***
Dunnhumby Inc ... 513 579-3400
3825 Edwards Rd Ste 600 Cincinnati (45209) ***(G-3514)***
Dunning Motor Sales Inc ... 740 439-4465
9108 Southgate Rd Cambridge (43725) ***(G-2110)***
Dunsiane Swim Club ... 937 433-7946
600 W Spring Valley Pike Dayton (45458) ***(G-9508)***
Dupont Inc ... 937 268-3411
1515 Nicholas Rd Dayton (45417) ***(G-9509)***
Dupree House, Cincinnati *Also called Episcopal Retirement Homes Inc* ***(G-3568)***
Duquesne Light Company ... 330 385-6103
626 Saint Clair Ave East Liverpool (43920) ***(G-10519)***
Durable Corporation ... 800 537-1603
75 N Pleasant St Norwalk (44857) ***(G-15571)***
Durable Slate Co (PA) ... 614 299-5522
3933 Groves Rd Columbus (43232) ***(G-7552)***
Durable Slate Co ... 216 751-0151
3530 Warrensville Ctr Rd Shaker Heights (44122) ***(G-16859)***
Durable Slate Company, The, Columbus *Also called Durable Slate Co* ***(G-7552)***
Durbin Trucking Inc ... 419 334-2422
10044 Scott St Oak Harbor (43449) ***(G-15609)***
Dure Investments LLC ... 419 697-7800
1761 Meijers Cir Oregon (43616) ***(G-15732)***
Durga Llc ... 513 771-2080
11320 Chester Rd Cincinnati (45246) ***(G-3515)***
Dusk To Dawn Protective Svcs ... 330 837-9992
3554 Lincoln Way E 3 Massillon (44646) ***(G-13802)***
Dutch Creek Foods Inc ... 330 852-2631
1411 Old Route 39 Ne Sugarcreek (44681) ***(G-17545)***
Dutch Girl Cleaners, Canton *Also called Edco Cleaners Inc* ***(G-2351)***

ALPHABETIC

Dutch Heritage Farms Inc 330 893-3232
Hc 39 Berlin (44610) ***(G-1478)***
Dutchess Cleaner, Youngstown *Also called Dutchess Dry Cleaners* ***(G-20174)***
Dutchess Cleaners, Youngstown *Also called Rondinelli Company Inc* ***(G-20358)***
Dutchess Dry Cleaners 330 759-9382
2710 Belmont Ave Ste D Youngstown (44505) ***(G-20174)***
Dutchman Hospitality Group Inc 614 873-3414
445 S Jefferson Ave Plain City (43064) ***(G-16189)***
Dutro Ford Lincoln-Mercury Inc (PA) 740 452-6334
132 S 5th St Zanesville (43701) ***(G-20470)***
Dutro Nissan, Zanesville *Also called Dutro Ford Lincoln-Mercury Inc* ***(G-20470)***
Duty's Towing & Auto Service, Columbus *Also called Dutys Towing* ***(G-7553)***
Dutys Towing 614 252-3336
3288 E Broad St Columbus (43213) ***(G-7553)***
Dva Healthcare - South 513 347-0444
3267 Westbourne Dr Cincinnati (45248) ***(G-3516)***
Dva Renal Healthcare Inc 740 454-2911
3120 Newark Rd Zanesville (43701) ***(G-20471)***
Dw Together LLC 330 225-8200
3698 Center Rd Brunswick (44212) ***(G-1976)***
Dwa Mrkting Prmtional Pdts LLC 216 476-0635
17000 Foltz Pkwy Strongsville (44149) ***(G-17457)***
Dwellworks LLC (PA) 216 682-4200
1317 Euclid Ave Cleveland (44115) ***(G-5513)***
Dwight Spencer & Associates (PA) 614 488-3123
1290 Grandview Ave Columbus (43212) ***(G-7554)***
Dworken & Bernstein Co Lpa (PA) 216 861-4211
1468 W 9th St Ste 135 Cleveland (44113) ***(G-5514)***
Dworken & Bernstein Co Lpa 440 352-3391
60 S Park Pl Fl 2 Painesville (44077) ***(G-15853)***
Dworken and Bernstein, Cleveland *Also called Dworken & Bernstein Co Lpa* ***(G-5514)***
Dworkin Inc (PA) 216 271-5318
5400 Harvard Ave Cleveland (44105) ***(G-5515)***
Dworkin Trucking, Cleveland *Also called Dworkin Inc* ***(G-5515)***
Dwyer Concrete Lifting Inc 614 501-0998
5650 Groveport Rd Groveport (43125) ***(G-11635)***
Dxp Enterprises Inc 513 242-2227
5177 Spring Grove Ave Cincinnati (45217) ***(G-3517)***
Dyn Marine Services Inc 937 427-2663
3040 Presidential Dr Beavercreek (45324) ***(G-1170)***
Dynalectric Company 614 529-7500
1762 Dividend Dr Columbus (43228) ***(G-7555)***
Dynamic Construction Inc 740 927-8898
172 Coors Blvd Pataskala (43062) ***(G-15923)***
Dynamic Currents Corp 419 861-2036
1761 Commerce Rd Holland (43528) ***(G-12023)***
Dynamic Mechanical Systems 513 858-6722
5623 Sigmon Way Fairfield (45014) ***(G-10843)***
Dynamic Metal Services, Bedford Heights *Also called Alloy Metal Exchange LLC* ***(G-1345)***
Dynamic Solution Associates, Independence *Also called Arysen Inc* ***(G-12188)***
Dynamic Structures Inc (PA) 330 892-0164
3790 State Route 7 Ste B New Waterford (44445) ***(G-15137)***
Dynamic Weld Corporation 419 582-2900
242 N St Osgood (45351) ***(G-15791)***
Dynamite Technologies LLC (PA) 614 538-0095
274 Marconi Blvd Ste 300 Columbus (43215) ***(G-7556)***
Dynamix Engineering Ltd 614 443-1178
855 Grandview Ave Ste 300 Columbus (43215) ***(G-7557)***
Dynatech Systems Inc 440 365-1774
161 Reaser Ct Elyria (44035) ***(G-10618)***
Dyncorp 513 942-6500
9266 Meridian Way West Chester (45069) ***(G-19067)***
Dyncorp 513 569-7415
26 W Mrtin Lther King Dr Cincinnati (45220) ***(G-3518)***
Dynegy Inc 513 467-4900
11021 Brower Rd North Bend (45052) ***(G-15318)***
Dynegy Washington II LLC 713 507-6400
859 State Route 83 Beverly (45715) ***(G-1490)***
Dyno Nobel Transportation 740 439-5050
850 Woodlawn Ave Cambridge (43725) ***(G-2111)***
Dyno Transportation, Cambridge *Also called Dyno Nobel Transportation* ***(G-2111)***
Dynotec Inc 614 880-7320
2931 E Dublin Granv Rd Columbus (43231) ***(G-7558)***
E & A Pedco Services Inc (PA) 513 782-4920
11499 Chester Rd Ste 501 Cincinnati (45246) ***(G-3519)***
E & C Div, Cleveland *Also called Greater Cleveland* ***(G-5694)***
E & J Gallo Winery 513 381-4050
125 E Court St Cincinnati (45202) ***(G-3520)***
E & J Trailer Leasing Inc 513 563-7366
610 Wayne Park Dr Ste 5 Cincinnati (45215) ***(G-3521)***
E & J Trailer Sales & Service 513 563-2550
610 Wayne Park Dr Ste 5 Cincinnati (45215) ***(G-3522)***
E & L Premier Corporation 330 836-9901
3250 W Market St Ste 102 Fairlawn (44333) ***(G-10946)***
E & V Ventures Inc (PA) 330 794-6683
1511 E Market St Akron (44305) ***(G-203)***
E A Group, Mentor *Also called Electro-Analytical Inc* ***(G-14171)***
E A Zicka Co 513 451-1440
2714 East Tower Dr Ofc Cincinnati (45238) ***(G-3523)***
E and P Warehouse Services Ltd 330 898-4800
1666 Mcmyler St Nw Warren (44485) ***(G-18852)***
E F Bavis & Associates Inc 513 677-0500
201 Grandin Rd Maineville (45039) ***(G-13243)***
E F Boyd & Son Inc (PA) 216 791-0770
2165 E 89th St Cleveland (44106) ***(G-5516)***
E H Schmidt Executive 419 874-4331
26785 Dixie Hwy Perrysburg (43551) ***(G-16000)***
E H T Company, Euclid *Also called Euclid Heat Treating Co* ***(G-10752)***
E J Links Co The Inc 440 235-0501
26111 John Rd Olmsted Twp (44138) ***(G-15675)***
E J Robinson Glass Co 513 242-9250
5618 Center Hill Ave Cincinnati (45216) ***(G-3524)***
E M Columbus LLC 614 861-3232
2740 Eastland Mall Ste B Columbus (43232) ***(G-7559)***
E M H & T, New Albany *Also called Evans Mechwart Ham* ***(G-14984)***
E M H Regional Medical Center, Amherst *Also called Amherst Hospital Association* ***(G-587)***
E M I, Cleveland *Also called Equipment Manufacturers Intl* ***(G-5548)***
E M I Plastic Equipment, Jackson Center *Also called EMI Corp* ***(G-12322)***
E M S Medical Equipment, Warren *Also called Eastern Medical Equipment Co* ***(G-18853)***
E N T, Columbus *Also called University Otolaryngologists* ***(G-8910)***
E N T Toledo Inc 419 578-7555
2865 N Reynolds Rd # 260 Toledo (43615) ***(G-17860)***
E P Ferris & Associates Inc 614 299-2999
880 King Ave Columbus (43212) ***(G-7560)***
E Q M, Cincinnati *Also called Environmental Quality MGT* ***(G-3562)***
E Retailing Associates LLC 614 300-5785
2282 Westbrooke Dr Columbus (43228) ***(G-7561)***
E S Gallon & Associates 937 586-3100
2621 Dryden Rd Ste 105 Moraine (45439) ***(G-14777)***
E S I Inc (HQ) 513 454-3741
4696 Devitt Dr West Chester (45246) ***(G-19195)***
E S S C, Cincinnati *Also called Cincinnati Sub-Zero Pdts LLC* ***(G-3331)***
E S Wagner Company 419 691-8651
840 Patchen Rd Oregon (43616) ***(G-15733)***
E T B Ltd 740 373-6686
15 Acme St Marietta (45750) ***(G-13443)***
E T Financial Service Inc 937 716-1726
4550 Salem Ave Trotwood (45416) ***(G-18346)***
E Technologies Group, West Chester *Also called Control Concepts & Design Inc* ***(G-19051)***
E W I, Columbus *Also called Edison Welding Institute Inc* ***(G-7578)***
E Wynn Inc 614 444-5288
1851 S High St Columbus (43207) ***(G-7562)***
E Z Cleaners, Englewood *Also called Sunset Carpet Cleaning* ***(G-10721)***
E&I Construction LLC 513 421-2045
1210 Sycamore St Ste 200 Cincinnati (45202) ***(G-3525)***
E&I Solutions LLC 937 912-0288
3610 Pentagon Blvd # 220 Beavercreek (45431) ***(G-1171)***
E-Cycle LLC 614 832-7032
4105 Leap Rd Hilliard (43026) ***(G-11897)***
E-Mek Technologies LLC 937 424-3163
7410 Webster St Dayton (45414) ***(G-9510)***
E-Pallet, Lakewood *Also called Pallet Distributors Inc* ***(G-12494)***
E-Tech Ohio Commision, Columbus *Also called Ohio Education Association* ***(G-8338)***
E.M.s Rams Youth Football Team, Cleveland *Also called EMs Rams Youth Dev Group Inc* ***(G-5538)***
E2b Teknologies Inc (PA) 440 352-4700
521 5th Ave Chardon (44024) ***(G-2748)***
Ea Vica Co 513 481-3500
2714 E Twr Dr Ofc Ste 007 Cincinnati (45238) ***(G-3526)***
Eab Truck Service 216 525-0020
7951 Granger Rd Cleveland (44125) ***(G-5517)***
Eagle Bridge Co 937 492-5654
800 S Vandemark Rd Sidney (45365) ***(G-16930)***
Eagle Burgmann EXT Joint Sol, Cincinnati *Also called Eagleburgmann Ke Inc* ***(G-3529)***
Eagle Creek Golf Club, Norwalk *Also called Norwalk Golf Properties Inc* ***(G-15586)***
Eagle Creek Nursing Center 937 544-5531
141 Spruce Ln West Union (45693) ***(G-19278)***
Eagle Equipment Corporation 937 746-0510
245 Industrial Dr Franklin (45005) ***(G-11154)***
Eagle Financial Bancorp Inc (PA) 513 574-0700
6415 Bridgetown Rd Cincinnati (45248) ***(G-3527)***
Eagle Freight, Berea *Also called L O G Transportation Inc* ***(G-1462)***
Eagle Hardwoods Inc 330 339-8838
6138 Stonecreek Rd Newcomerstown (43832) ***(G-15267)***
Eagle Industrial Painting LLC 330 866-5965
3215 Magnolia Rd Nw Magnolia (44643) ***(G-13239)***
Eagle Industrial Truck Mfg LLC 734 442-1000
1 Air Cargo Pkwy E Swanton (43558) ***(G-17563)***
Eagle Industries Ohio Inc 513 247-2900
275 Commercial Dr Fairfield (45014) ***(G-10844)***
Eagle Protective Services, Willoughby *Also called Ryno 24 Inc* ***(G-19711)***
Eagle Realty Group LLC (HQ) 513 361-7700
421 E 4th St Cincinnati (45202) ***(G-3528)***
Eagle Rock Tours, Coshocton *Also called Muskingum Coach Company* ***(G-9112)***
Eagle Tugs, Swanton *Also called Eagle Industrial Truck Mfg LLC* ***(G-17563)***
Eagle USA Airfreight, Columbus *Also called Ceva Logistics US Inc* ***(G-7245)***
Eagleburgmann Ke Inc (HQ) 859 746-0091
3478 Hauck Rd Cincinnati (45241) ***(G-3529)***

ALPHABETIC SECTION — Eastway Corporation

Eaglewood Care Center 937 399-7195
2000 Villa Rd Springfield (45503) *(G-17191)*

Eaglewood Villa, Springfield *Also called Wallick Construction Co (G-17295)*

Earhart Petroleum Inc (PA) 937 335-2928
1494 Lytle Rd Troy (45373) *(G-18353)*

Earl Twinam 740 820-2654
550 Field Rd Portsmouth (45662) *(G-16277)*

Earle M Jorgensen Company 513 771-3223
601 Redna Ter Cincinnati (45215) *(G-3530)*

Earle M Jorgensen Company 330 425-1500
2060 Enterprise Pkwy Twinsburg (44087) *(G-18407)*

Earley & Ross Ltd 740 634-3301
580 E Washington St Sabina (45169) *(G-16615)*

Early Bird, The, Greenville *Also called Brothers Publishing Co LLC (G-11491)*

Early Childhood Enrichment Ctr 216 991-9761
19824 Sussex Rd Rm 178 Cleveland (44122) *(G-5518)*

Early Childhood Learning Commu 614 451-6418
4141 Rudy Rd Columbus (43214) *(G-7563)*

Early Construction Co 740 894-5150
307 County Road 120 S South Point (45680) *(G-17085)*

Early Construction Company, South Point *Also called Early Construction Co (G-17085)*

Early Express Mail Services, Dayton *Also called Early Express Services Inc (G-9511)*

Early Express Services Inc 937 223-5801
1333 E 2nd St Dayton (45403) *(G-9511)*

Early Learning Tree Chld Ctr (PA) 937 276-3221
2332 N Main St Dayton (45405) *(G-9512)*

Early Learning Tree Chld Ctr 937 293-7907
2332 N Main St Dayton (45405) *(G-9513)*

Earnest Machine Products Co (PA) 440 895-8400
1250 Linda St Ste 301 Rocky River (44116) *(G-16577)*

Earth n Wood Products Inc 330 644-1858
2436 S Arlington Rd Akron (44319) *(G-204)*

Earthbound Holding LLC 972 248-0228
500 Southpark Ctr Strongsville (44136) *(G-17458)*

East Akron Neighborhood Dev 330 773-6838
550 S Arlington St Akron (44306) *(G-205)*

East Butler County YMCA, Fairfield Township *Also called Great Miami Valley YMCA (G-10930)*

East Carroll Nursing Home 330 627-6900
2193 Commerce Dr Carrollton (44615) *(G-2618)*

East Center, Toledo *Also called Unison Behavioral Health Group (G-18268)*

East Central Region, Grove City *Also called Securitas SEC Svcs USA Inc (G-11597)*

East Coast Region, Cleveland *Also called Securitas SEC Svcs USA Inc (G-6462)*

East Dayton Christian School 937 252-5400
999 Spinning Rd Dayton (45431) *(G-9268)*

East Elementary School, Saint Marys *Also called St Marys City Board Education (G-16685)*

East End Community Svcs Corp 937 259-1898
624 Xenia Ave Dayton (45410) *(G-9514)*

East End Neighborhood Hse Assn 216 791-9378
2749 Woodhill Rd Cleveland (44104) *(G-5519)*

East End Ro Burton Inc 440 942-2742
792 Mentor Ave Willoughby (44094) *(G-19660)*

East End Welding Company 330 677-6000
357 Tallmadge Rd Kent (44240) *(G-12367)*

East End YMCA Pre School, Madison *Also called Lake County YMCA (G-13227)*

East Galbraith Health Care Ctr (PA) 513 984-5220
3889 E Galbraith Rd Cincinnati (45236) *(G-3531)*

East Galbraith Nursing Home 513 984-5220
3889 E Galbraith Rd Cincinnati (45236) *(G-3532)*

East Lawn Manor, Marion *Also called County of Marion (G-13533)*

EAST LIVERPOOL CITY HOSPITAL, East Liverpool *Also called City Hospital Association (G-10517)*

East Liverpool Motor Lodge, East Liverpool *Also called Alsan Corporation (G-10514)*

East Liverpool Water Dept 330 385-8812
2220 Michigan Ave East Liverpool (43920) *(G-10520)*

East Manufacturing Corporation (PA) 330 325-9921
1871 State Rte 44 Randolph (44265) *(G-16372)*

East Mentor Recreation Inc 440 354-2000
65 Normandy Dr Mentor (44060) *(G-14170)*

East of Chicago Pizza Inc (PA) 419 225-7116
121 W High St Fl 12 Lima (45801) *(G-12771)*

East Ohio Gas Company (HQ) 800 362-7557
19701 Libby Rd Maple Heights (44137) *(G-13406)*

East Ohio Gas Company 330 742-8121
1165 W Rayen Ave Youngstown (44502) *(G-20175)*

East Ohio Gas Company 330 266-2169
6500 Hampsher Rd New Franklin (44216) *(G-15044)*

East Ohio Gas Company 330 477-9411
4725 Southway St Sw Canton (44706) *(G-2345)*

East Ohio Gas Company 216 736-6959
21200 Miles Rd Cleveland (44128) *(G-5520)*

East Ohio Gas Company 216 736-6120
7001 Center Rd Ashtabula (44004) *(G-743)*

East Ohio Gas Company 330 499-2501
7015 Freedom Ave Nw Canton (44720) *(G-2346)*

East Ohio Gas Company 330 478-1700
332 2nd St Nw Canton (44702) *(G-2347)*

East Ohio Gas Company 216 736-6917
29555 Clayton Ave Wickliffe (44092) *(G-19595)*

East Toledo Family Center (PA) 419 691-1429
1020 Varland Ave Toledo (43605) *(G-17861)*

East Water Leasing Co LLC 419 278-6921
620 E Water St Deshler (43516) *(G-10169)*

East Way Behavioral Hlth Care 937 222-4900
600 Wayne Ave Dayton (45410) *(G-9515)*

Eastbury Bowling Center 330 452-3700
3000 Atl Blvd Ne Unit A Canton (44705) *(G-2348)*

Eastco, Dayton *Also called Eastway Corporation (G-9517)*

Easter Seal, Dayton *Also called Goodwill Ester Seals Miami Vly (G-9579)*

Easter Seal Northwestern Ohio, Fremont *Also called Easter Seals Metro Chicago Inc (G-11196)*

Easter Seal Society of (PA) 330 743-1168
299 Edwards St Youngstown (44502) *(G-20176)*

Easter Seals, Youngstown *Also called Easter Seal Society of (G-20176)*

Easter Seals Center 614 228-5523
3830 Trueman Ct Hilliard (43026) *(G-11898)*

Easter Seals Metro Chicago Inc 419 332-3016
101 S Stone St Fremont (43420) *(G-11196)*

Easter Seals Nothern Ohio Inc 440 324-6600
2173 N Ridge Rd E Ste G Lorain (44055) *(G-13036)*

Easter Seals Tristate (HQ) 513 985-0515
4300 Rossplain Dr Blue Ash (45236) *(G-1582)*

Easter Seals Tristate LLC (PA) 513 281-2316
2901 Gilbert Ave Cincinnati (45206) *(G-3533)*

Easter Seals Tristate LLC 513 475-6791
447 Morgan St Cincinnati (45206) *(G-3534)*

Eastern Community YMCA, Oregon *Also called Young Mens Christian Associat (G-15756)*

Eastern Hill Internal Medicine 513 232-3500
8000 5 Mile Rd Ste 305 Cincinnati (45230) *(G-3535)*

Eastern Hills Pediatric Assoc 513 231-3345
7502 State Rd Ste 3350 Cincinnati (45255) *(G-3536)*

Eastern Hills Pediatrics, Cincinnati *Also called Eastern Hills Pediatric Assoc (G-3536)*

Eastern Horizon Inc 614 253-7000
1640 E 5th Ave Columbus (43219) *(G-7564)*

Eastern Medical Equipment Co 330 394-5555
523 E Market St Warren (44481) *(G-18853)*

Eastern Mumee Bay Arts Council 419 690-5718
595 Sylvandale Ave Oregon (43616) *(G-15734)*

Eastern Ohio P-16 .... 330 675-7623
4314 Mahoning Ave Nw Warren (44483) *(G-18854)*

Eastern Region Department, Dayton *Also called Acuren Inspection Inc (G-9307)*

Eastern Star Hm of Cyhoga Cnty 216 761-0170
2114 Noble Rd Cleveland (44112) *(G-5521)*

Eastgate Advntres Golf G-Karts, Loveland *Also called Recreational Golf Inc (G-13156)*

Eastgate Animal Hospital Inc 513 528-0700
459 Old State Route 74 Cincinnati (45244) *(G-3537)*

Eastgate Graphics, Lebanon *Also called Red Apple Packaging LLC (G-12642)*

Eastgate Health Care Center 513 752-3710
4400 Glen Este Withamsvil Cincinnati (45245) *(G-2913)*

Eastgate Professional Off Pk V 513 943-0050
4357 Ferguson Dr Ste 220 Cincinnati (45245) *(G-2914)*

Eastgate Sod, Maineville *Also called Mike Ward Landscaping Inc (G-13244)*

Eastgate Village 513 753-4400
776 Cincinnati Batavia Pi Cincinnati (45245) *(G-2915)*

Eastgate Woods Apts, Batavia *Also called Edward Rose Associates Inc (G-1012)*

Eastlake Lodging LLC 440 953-8000
35000 Curtis Blvd Eastlake (44095) *(G-10546)*

Eastland Crane & Towing, Columbus *Also called Eastland Crane Service Inc (G-7565)*

Eastland Crane Service Inc 614 868-9750
2190 S Hamilton Rd Columbus (43232) *(G-7565)*

Eastland Lanes Inc 614 868-9866
2666 Old Courtright Rd Columbus (43232) *(G-7566)*

Eastland Mall, Columbus *Also called E M Columbus LLC (G-7559)*

Eastman & Smith Ltd 419 241-6000
1 Seagate Ste 2400 Toledo (43604) *(G-17862)*

Easton Sales and Rental LLC (PA) 440 708-0099
16750 Hilltop Park Pl Chagrin Falls (44023) *(G-2714)*

Easton Town Center Guest Svcs, Columbus *Also called Easton Town Center LLC (G-7568)*

Easton Town Center II LLC 614 416-7000
160 Easton Town Ctr Columbus (43219) *(G-7567)*

Easton Town Center LLC 614 337-2560
4016 Townsfair Way # 201 Columbus (43219) *(G-7568)*

Eastside Body Shop 513 624-1145
7636 Beechmont Ave Cincinnati (45255) *(G-3538)*

Eastside Landscaping Inc 216 381-0070
572 Trebisky Rd Cleveland (44143) *(G-5522)*

Eastside Mri, Cleveland *Also called Drs Hill & Thomas Co (G-5509)*

Eastside Multi Care Inc 216 662-3343
19900 Clare Ave Maple Heights (44137) *(G-13407)*

Eastside Nursery Inc 513 934-1661
2830 Greentree Rd Lebanon (45036) *(G-12602)*

Eastside Roofg Restoration Co 513 471-0434
417 Purcell Ave Cincinnati (45205) *(G-3539)*

Eastway Behavorial Healthcare, Dayton *Also called Eastway Corporation (G-9516)*

Eastway Corporation (PA) 937 496-2000
600 Wayne Ave Dayton (45410) *(G-9516)*

Eastway Corporation 937 531-7000
600 Wayne Ave Dayton (45410) *(G-9517)*

Eastway Supplies Inc...614 252-3650
1561 Alum Creek Dr Columbus (43209) *(G-7569)*
Eastwood Mall, Niles *Also called Cararo Co Inc (G-15287)*
Eastwood Mall, Niles *Also called Marion Plaza Inc (G-15295)*
Eastwood Mall Kids Club, Niles *Also called Cafaro Co (G-15286)*
Eastwood Residential Living...440 417-0608
6261 Chapel Rd Madison (44057) *(G-13223)*
Eastwood Residential Living...440 428-1588
6412 N Ridge Rd Madison (44057) *(G-13224)*
Easy 2 Technologies, Cleveland *Also called Easy2 Technologies Inc (G-5523)*
EASY MONEY, Dublin *Also called Community Choice Financial Inc (G-10304)*
Easy2 Technologies Inc...216 479-0482
1111 Chester Ave Cleveland (44114) *(G-5523)*
Eaton Construction Co Inc...740 474-3414
653 Island Rd Circleville (43113) *(G-4887)*
Eaton Corporation...440 523-5000
1000 Eaton Blvd Beachwood (44122) *(G-1074)*
Eaton Corporation...216 523-5000
1000 Eaton Blvd Beachwood (44122) *(G-1075)*
Eaton Corporation...216 920-2000
333 Babbitt Rd Ste 100 Cleveland (44123) *(G-5524)*
Eaton Fire Division, Eaton *Also called Eaton Rescue Squad (G-10560)*
Eaton Gardens Rehabilitation A...937 456-5537
515 S Maple St Eaton (45320) *(G-10559)*
Eaton Group GMAC Real Estate...330 726-9999
382 Niles Cortland Rd Ne Warren (44484) *(G-18855)*
Eaton Plumbing Inc...614 891-7005
5600 E Walnut St Westerville (43081) *(G-19396)*
Eaton Rescue Squad...937 456-5361
391 W Lexington Rd Eaton (45320) *(G-10560)*
Eaton Tire & Auto Parts, Grafton *Also called Joseph Russo (G-11441)*
Eaton-Aeroquip Llc...419 891-7775
1660 Indian Wood Cir Maumee (43537) *(G-13907)*
Ebenezer Road Corp...513 941-0099
6210 Cleves Warsaw Pike Cincinnati (45233) *(G-3540)*
Ebmc, Dublin *Also called Employee Benefit Management (G-10336)*
Ebnt, Cleveland *Also called Engineering Design and Testing (G-5541)*
EBO Inc (PA)...216 229-9300
23600 Aurora Rd Bedford (44146) *(G-1305)*
Ebony Construction Co...419 841-3455
3510 Centennial Rd Sylvania (43560) *(G-17585)*
Ebs Asset Management, Miamisburg *Also called Eubel Brady Suttman Asset Mgt (G-14300)*
Ebsco Industries Inc...330 478-0281
4150 Belden Village Mall Canton (44718) *(G-2349)*
Ebsco Teleservice, Canton *Also called Ebsco Industries Inc (G-2349)*
Ebso Inc...419 423-3823
215 Stanford Pkwy Findlay (45840) *(G-11021)*
Ebso Inc...440 262-1133
3301 E Royalton Rd Ste 1 Cleveland (44147) *(G-5525)*
EBY-Brown Company LLC...937 324-1036
1982 Commerce Cir Springfield (45504) *(G-17192)*
ECDI, Columbus *Also called Economic & Cmnty Dev Inst Inc (G-7575)*
Ecg Scanning & Medical Svcs (HQ)...888 346-5837
3055 Kettering Blvd 219b Moraine (45439) *(G-14778)*
Echo 24 Inc (PA)...740 964-7081
167 Cypress St Sw Ste A Reynoldsburg (43068) *(G-16450)*
Echo Manor Extended Care Ctr, Pickerington *Also called Home Echo Club Inc (G-16096)*
ECHO Residential Support...614 210-0944
6500 Busch Blvd Ste 215 Columbus (43229) *(G-7570)*
Echo-Tape LLC...614 892-3246
651 Dearborn Park Ln Columbus (43085) *(G-7571)*
Echogen Power Systems Del Inc...234 542-4379
365 Water St Akron (44308) *(G-206)*
Echoing Hills Village Inc...740 594-3541
528 1/2 Richland Ave Athens (45701) *(G-785)*
Echoing Hills Village Inc (PA)...740 327-2311
36272 County Road 79 Warsaw (43844) *(G-18936)*
Echoing Hills Village Inc...937 854-5151
5455 Salem Bend Dr Dayton (45426) *(G-9518)*
Echoing Hills Village Inc...937 237-7881
7040 Union Schoolhouse Rd Dayton (45424) *(G-9519)*
Echoing Hills Village Inc...440 989-1400
3295 Leavitt Rd Lorain (44053) *(G-13037)*
Echoing Hills Village Inc...440 986-3085
235 W Main St South Amherst (44001) *(G-17073)*
Echoing Lake Residential Home, Lorain *Also called Echoing Hills Village Inc (G-13037)*
Echoing Lake/Renouard Home, South Amherst *Also called Echoing Hills Village Inc (G-17073)*
Echoing Meadows, Athens *Also called Echoing Hills Village Inc (G-785)*
Echoing Ridge Residential Ctr, Warsaw *Also called Echoing Hills Village Inc (G-18936)*
Echoing Valley, Dayton *Also called Echoing Hills Village Inc (G-9519)*
Echoing Wood Residential Cntr, Dayton *Also called Echoing Hills Village Inc (G-9518)*
Eci Inc...419 986-5566
2704 County Road 13 Burgoon (43407) *(G-2057)*
Ecke Ranch, Columbus *Also called Dummen Na Inc (G-7550)*
Eckert Fire Protec...513 948-1030
510 W Benson St Cincinnati (45215) *(G-3541)*
Eckinger Construction Company...330 453-2566
2340 Shepler Ch Ave Sw Canton (44706) *(G-2350)*
Eckstein Roofing Company...513 941-1511
264 Stille Dr Cincinnati (45233) *(G-3542)*
Eclipse Blind Systems Inc...330 296-0112
7154 State Route 88 Ravenna (44266) *(G-16384)*
Eclipse Co LLC...440 552-9400
23209 Miles Rd Cleveland (44128) *(G-5526)*
Eclipse Real Estate Group, Columbus *Also called Multicon Construction Co (G-8208)*
Eclipse Resources - Ohio LLC...740 452-4503
4900 Boggs Rd Zanesville (43701) *(G-20472)*
Eclipsecorp LLC...614 626-8536
825 Taylor Rd Columbus (43230) *(G-7572)*
Eco Engineering Inc...513 985-8300
11815 Highway Dr Ste 600 Cincinnati (45241) *(G-3543)*
Eco Global Corp...419 363-2681
10803 Erastus Durbin Rd Rockford (45882) *(G-16561)*
Ecommerce Inc (PA)...800 861-9394
1774 Dividend Dr Columbus (43228) *(G-7573)*
Ecommerce LLC...800 861-9394
1774 Dividend Dr Columbus (43228) *(G-7574)*
Econo Lodge, Toledo *Also called Carol Burton Management LLC (G-17793)*
Econo Lodge, Cincinnati *Also called Msk Hospitality Inc (G-4127)*
Econo Lodge, Elyria *Also called Lodging Industry Inc (G-10645)*
Econo Lodge...419 627-8000
1904 Cleveland Rd Sandusky (44870) *(G-16750)*
Economic & Cmnty Dev Inst Inc...614 559-0104
1655 Old Leonard Ave Columbus (43219) *(G-7575)*
Economy Forms, Columbus *Also called Efco Corp (G-7586)*
Economy Linen & Towel Svc Inc...740 454-6888
508 Howard St Zanesville (43701) *(G-20473)*
Ecoplumbers Inc...614 299-9903
4691 Northwest Pkwy Hilliard (43026) *(G-11899)*
Ecotage...513 782-2229
11700 Princeton Pike # 4 Cincinnati (45246) *(G-3544)*
Ecrm, Solon *Also called Efficient Collaborative Retail (G-17001)*
Ecs Holdco Inc...614 433-0170
705 Lkview Plz Blvd Ste A Worthington (43085) *(G-19955)*
Ed Map Inc...740 753-3439
296 S Harper St Ste 1 Nelsonville (45764) *(G-14962)*
Ed Mullinax Ford LLC...440 984-2431
8000 Leavitt Rd Amherst (44001) *(G-591)*
Ed Schmidt Auto Inc...419 874-4331
26875 Dixie Hwy Perrysburg (43551) *(G-16001)*
Ed Schmidt Chevrolet, Perrysburg *Also called Schmidt Daily Rental Inc (G-16057)*
Ed Schmidt Chevrolet Inc...419 897-8600
1425 Reynolds Rd Maumee (43537) *(G-13908)*
Ed Tomko Chryslr Jep Dge Inc...440 835-5900
33725 Walker Rd Avon Lake (44012) *(G-929)*
Ed Wilson & Son Trucking Inc...330 549-9287
14766 Woodworth Rd New Springfield (44443) *(G-15129)*
Edaptive Computing Inc...937 433-0477
1245 Lyons Rd Ste G Dayton (45458) *(G-9520)*
Edco Cleaners Inc...330 477-3357
2455 Whipple Ave Nw Canton (44708) *(G-2351)*
Eddie Bauer LLC...614 278-9281
4599 Fisher Rd Columbus (43228) *(G-7576)*
Eddie Lane's Diamond Showroom, Cincinnati *Also called Equity Diamond Brokers Inc (G-3570)*
Edelman Plumbing Supply Inc (PA)...216 591-0150
26201 Richmond Rd Ste 4 Bedford Heights (44146) *(G-1351)*
Eden, Cleveland *Also called Emerald Dev Ecnomic Netwrk Inc (G-5533)*
Edendale House, Cleveland *Also called United Cerebral Palsy (G-6636)*
Edge Hair Design & Spa...330 477-2300
4655 Dressler Rd Nw Canton (44718) *(G-2352)*
Edge Plastics Inc...419 522-6696
449 Newman St Mansfield (44902) *(G-13296)*
Edgewood Manor Lucasville II, Lucasville *Also called Consulate Management Co LLC (G-13176)*
Edgewood Manor Nursing Center, Port Clinton *Also called Covenant Care Ohio Inc (G-16242)*
Edgewood Manor of Lucasville...740 259-5536
10098 Big Bear Creek Rd Lucasville (45648) *(G-13178)*
Edgewood Manor of Wellston...740 384-5611
405 N Park Ave Wellston (45692) *(G-18999)*
Edgewood Skate Arena...419 331-0647
2170 Edgewood Dr Lima (45805) *(G-12772)*
Edict Systems Inc...937 429-4288
2434 Esquire Dr Beavercreek (45431) *(G-1172)*
Edison Biotechnology Institute...740 593-4713
101 Konneker The Rdgs Athens (45701) *(G-786)*
Edison Bus Garage, Amsterdam *Also called Edison Local School District (G-608)*
Edison Equipment (PA)...614 883-5710
2225 Mckinley Ave Columbus (43204) *(G-7577)*
Edison Local School District...740 543-4011
8235 Amsterdam Rd Se Amsterdam (43903) *(G-608)*
Edison Welding Institute Inc (PA)...614 688-5000
1250 Arthur E Adams Dr Columbus (43221) *(G-7578)*
EDM Management Inc...330 726-5790
1419 Boardman Poland Rd # 500 Youngstown (44514) *(G-20177)*
Edmond Hotel Investors LLC...614 891-2900
24 E Lincoln St Columbus (43215) *(G-7579)*

Edrich Supply Co...440 238-9440
22700 Royalton Rd Strongsville (44149) *(G-17459)*
Eds Tree & Turf...740 881-5800
5801 S Section Line Rd Delaware (43015) *(G-10092)*
Education Alternatives (PA)...216 332-9360
5445 Smith Rd Brookpark (44142) *(G-1944)*
Education First Credit Un Inc (PA)...614 221-9376
399 E Livingston Ave Columbus (43215) *(G-7580)*
Education Innovations Intl LLC...614 339-3676
655 Metro Pl S Ste 750 Dublin (43017) *(G-10334)*
Education Loan Servicing Corp...216 706-8130
1500 W 3rd St Ste 125 Cleveland (44113) *(G-5527)*
Educational and Community Rdo...513 724-3939
Rr 276 Batavia (45103) *(G-1011)*
Educational Services, Blue Ash *Also called Pcm Sales Inc (G-1663)*
Educational Solutions Co...614 989-4588
1155 Highland St Columbus (43201) *(G-7581)*
Educatonal Svc Ctr Lorain Cnty (PA)...440 244-1659
1885 Lake Ave Elyria (44035) *(G-10619)*
Edw C Levy Co...419 822-8286
6565 County Road 9 Delta (43515) *(G-10157)*
Edward C Hawkins & Co Limited, Cleveland *Also called Hawkins & Co Lpa Ltd (G-5733)*
Edward Howard & Co (PA)...216 781-2400
1100 Superior Ave E # 1600 Cleveland (44114) *(G-5528)*
Edward Rose Associates Inc...513 752-2727
4412 Eastwood Dr Batavia (45103) *(G-1012)*
Edward W Daniel LLC...440 647-1960
46950 State Route 18 S Wellington (44090) *(G-18990)*
Edwards Mooney & Moses...614 351-1439
1320 Mckinley Ave Ste B Columbus (43222) *(G-7582)*
Edwards Creative Learning Ctr...614 492-8977
3858 Alum Creek Dr Ste A Columbus (43207) *(G-7583)*
Edwards Electrical & Mech...614 485-2003
685 Grandview Ave Columbus (43215) *(G-7584)*
Edwards Gem Inc...330 342-8300
5640 Hudson Indus Pkwy Hudson (44236) *(G-12115)*
Edwards Land Clearing Inc...440 988-4477
49090 Cooper Foster Pk Rd Amherst (44001) *(G-592)*
Edwards Land Company...614 241-2070
495 S High St Ste 150 Columbus (43215) *(G-7585)*
Edwards Mooney & Moses of Ohio, Columbus *Also called Edwards Mooney & Moses (G-7582)*
Edwards Tree Service, Amherst *Also called Edwards Land Clearing Inc (G-592)*
Edwin Shaw Rehabilitation Hosp, Akron *Also called Akron General Medical Center (G-43)*
EE, Columbus *Also called Edison Equipment (G-7577)*
Eecutive Directions, Canton *Also called R E Richards Inc (G-2501)*
Eei-Plant, Cincinnati *Also called Environmental Enterprises Inc (G-3561)*
Efco Corp...614 876-1226
3900 Zane Trace Dr Columbus (43228) *(G-7586)*
Efficient Collaborative Retail (PA)...440 498-0500
27070 Miles Rd Ste A Solon (44139) *(G-17001)*
Efficient Electric Corp...614 552-0200
4800 Groves Rd Columbus (43232) *(G-7587)*
Efficient Services Ohio Inc...330 627-4440
277 Steubenville Rd Se Carrollton (44615) *(G-2619)*
Efix Computer Repair & Svc LLC...937 985-4447
1389 E Stroop Rd Kettering (45429) *(G-12429)*
Eger Products Inc (PA)...513 753-4200
1132 Ferris Rd Amelia (45102) *(G-580)*
Eighth Day Sound Systems Inc...440 995-2647
5450 Avion Park Dr Cleveland (44143) *(G-5529)*
Einstruction Corporation (HQ)...330 746-3015
255 W Federal St Youngstown (44503) *(G-20178)*
Eis, Gahanna *Also called Estate Information Svcs LLC (G-11241)*
Eis, Willoughby *Also called Exodus Integrity Service (G-19663)*
Eitel Towing Service Inc...614 877-4139
7111 Stahl Rd Orient (43146) *(G-15760)*
Eitels Amrcas Towing Trnsp Svc, Orient *Also called Eitel Towing Service Inc (G-15760)*
Ej Therapy, Wooster *Also called Herman Bair Enterprise (G-19867)*
EJq Home Health Care Inc...440 323-7004
800 Middle Ave Elyria (44035) *(G-10620)*
Ekomovers USA, Cincinnati *Also called Awrs LLC (G-3068)*
El-Bee, Moraine *Also called Elder Beerman Stores Corp (G-14780)*
Elano Div, Beavercreek *Also called Unison Industries LLC (G-1215)*
Elastizell Systems Inc...937 298-1313
2475 Arbor Blvd Moraine (45439) *(G-14779)*
Elbe Properties (PA)...513 489-1955
8534 E Kemper Rd Cincinnati (45249) *(G-3545)*
Elden & Strauss, Vermilion *Also called Elden Properties Ltd Partnr (G-18709)*
Elden Motels LP (PA)...440 967-8770
15008 Holiday Dr Ste A Vermilion (44089) *(G-18708)*
Elden Properties Ltd Partnr...440 967-0521
15008 Holiday Dr Ste A Vermilion (44089) *(G-18709)*
Elder-Beerman Stores Corp (HQ)...937 296-2700
3155 Elbee Rd Ste 201 Moraine (45439) *(G-14780)*
Eldercare Services Inst LLC...216 791-8000
11890 Fairhill Rd Cleveland (44120) *(G-5530)*
Elderly Day Care Center...419 228-2688
225 E High St Lima (45801) *(G-12773)*
Elderly United of Springfield (PA)...937 323-4948
125 W Main St Springfield (45502) *(G-17193)*
Eldora Enterprises Inc...937 338-3815
13929 State Route 118 New Weston (45348) *(G-15140)*
Eldora Speedway, New Weston *Also called Eldora Enterprises Inc (G-15140)*
Elect General Contractors Inc...740 420-3437
27634 Jackson Rd Circleville (43113) *(G-4888)*
Electra Sound Inc (PA)...216 433-9600
5260 Commerce Pkwy W Parma (44130) *(G-15906)*
Electra Sound Inc...216 433-1050
10779 Brookpark Rd Ste A Cleveland (44130) *(G-5531)*
Electrasound TV & Appl Svc, Parma *Also called Electra Sound Inc (G-15906)*
Electric Connection Inc...614 436-1121
5441 Westerville Rd Westerville (43081) *(G-19397)*
Electric Division, Westerville *Also called City of Westerville (G-19383)*
Electric Motor Tech LLC (PA)...513 821-9999
5217 Beech St Cincinnati (45217) *(G-3546)*
Electric Service Co Inc...513 271-6387
5331 Hetzell St Cincinnati (45227) *(G-3547)*
Electric Services, Cuyahoga Falls *Also called City of Cuyahoga Falls (G-9173)*
Electric Sweeper Service Co, Twinsburg *Also called Merc Acquisitions Inc (G-18448)*
Electrical Appl Repr Svc Inc...216 459-8700
5805 Valley Belt Rd Brooklyn Heights (44131) *(G-1915)*
Electrical Construction, Barberton *Also called Corporate Electric Company LLC (G-962)*
Electrical Corp America Inc...440 245-3007
3807 W Erie Ave Lorain (44053) *(G-13038)*
Electrical Design & Engrg Svcs, Lewis Center *Also called Polaris Automation Inc (G-12704)*
Electrical Service Dept, Wadsworth *Also called City of Wadsworth (G-18749)*
ELECTRICAL TRAINING CENTER, Rossford *Also called Toledo Elec Jint Apprnticeship (G-16612)*
Electro Controls, Sidney *Also called Dickman Supply Inc (G-16929)*
Electro Prime Group LLC (PA)...419 476-0100
4510 Lint Ave Ste B Toledo (43612) *(G-17863)*
Electro-Analytical Inc...440 951-3514
7118 Industrial Park Blvd Mentor (44060) *(G-14171)*
Electrol Systems Inc...513 942-7777
1380 Kemper Meadow Dr Cincinnati (45240) *(G-3548)*
Electromechanical North Amer, Milford *Also called Parker-Hannifin Corporation (G-14550)*
Electronic Merchant Systems, Cleveland *Also called David Francis Corporation (G-5466)*
Electronic Printing Pdts Inc...330 689-3930
4560 Darrow Rd Stow (44224) *(G-17362)*
Electronic Registry Systems...513 771-7330
155 Tri County Pkwy # 110 Cincinnati (45246) *(G-3549)*
Electrovations Inc...330 274-3558
350 Harris Dr Aurora (44202) *(G-837)*
Eleet Cryogenics Inc...330 874-4009
11132 Industrial Pkwy Nw Bolivar (44612) *(G-1746)*
Element Cincinnati...513 984-4112
3701 Port Union Rd Fairfield (45014) *(G-10845)*
Element Mtls Tech Cncnnati Inc (PA)...513 771-2536
3701 Port Union Rd Fairfield (45014) *(G-10846)*
Element Mtrls Tchnlgy Hntngtn...216 643-1208
5405 E Schaaf Rd Cleveland (44131) *(G-5532)*
Eletto Transfer, Moraine *Also called Federated Logistics (G-14784)*
Elevar Design Group Inc...513 721-0600
300 W 4th St Cincinnati (45202) *(G-3550)*
Elford Inc...614 488-4000
1220 Dublin Rd Columbus (43215) *(G-7588)*
Elford Construction Services, Columbus *Also called Elford Inc (G-7588)*
Eliassen Group LLC...781 205-8100
10101 Alliance Rd Ste 195 Blue Ash (45242) *(G-1583)*
Eliokem Inc (HQ)...330 734-1100
175 Ghent Rd Fairlawn (44333) *(G-10947)*
Elite Ambulance Service LLC...888 222-1356
1451 State Route 28 Ste B Loveland (45140) *(G-13124)*
Elite Enclosure Company LLC...937 492-3548
2349 Industrial Dr Sidney (45365) *(G-16931)*
Elite Excavating Company Inc...419 683-4200
4500 Snodgrass Rd Mansfield (44903) *(G-13297)*
Elite Excavating Ohio Company, Mansfield *Also called Elite Excavating Company Inc (G-13297)*
Elite Expediting Corp (PA)...614 279-1181
450 W Wilson Bridge Rd # 345 Worthington (43085) *(G-19956)*
Elite Home Remodeling Inc...614 785-6700
6295a Busch Blvd Ste A Columbus (43229) *(G-7589)*
Elite Investigations SEC Group, Dayton *Also called Elite Isg (G-9521)*
Elite Isg...937 668-6858
7825 N Dixie Dr Ste C Dayton (45414) *(G-9521)*
Elite Logistics Worldwide, Seville *Also called Elite Transportation Svcs LLC (G-16839)*
Elite Proofing, Brookpark *Also called Robert Erney (G-1954)*
Elite Transportation Svcs LLC...330 769-5830
4940 Enterprise Pkwy Seville (44273) *(G-16839)*
Elizabeth H Farbman...330 744-5211
100 E Federal St Youngstown (44503) *(G-20179)*
Elizabeth Place Holdings LLC...323 300-3700
1 Elizabeth Pl Dayton (45417) *(G-9522)*
Elizabeth Scott Inc...419 865-3002
2720 Albon Rd Maumee (43537) *(G-13909)*
Elizabeth Scott Mem Care Ctr, Maumee *Also called Elizabeth Scott Inc (G-13909)*

ALPHABETIC

ELIZABETH'S NEW LIFE WOMEN'S C, Dayton *Also called Elizabeths New Life Center Inc* ***(G-9523)***
Elizabeths New Life Center Inc 937 226-7414
2201 N Main St Dayton (45405) ***(G-9523)***
Elk & Elk Co Lpa (PA) 800 355-6446
6105 Parkland Blvd # 200 Mayfield Heights (44124) ***(G-14002)***
Elks, Portsmouth *Also called Portsmouth Lodge 154 B P O E* ***(G-16299)***
ELKS B P O E, Liberty Twp *Also called Hamilton Lodge 93 Benevolant P* ***(G-12725)***
ELKS LODGE # 1718, Port Clinton *Also called Port Clnton Bpo Elks Ldge 1718* ***(G-16251)***
ELKS LODGE 549, Painesville *Also called Benevolent/Protectv Order Elks* ***(G-15836)***
ELKS OF THE UNITED STATES OF A, Maumee *Also called Maumee Lodge No 1850 Bnvlt* ***(G-13943)***
Elks Run Golf Club, Batavia *Also called Three D Golf LLC* ***(G-1027)***
Ellerbrock Heating & AC 419 782-1834
13055 Dohoney Rd Defiance (43512) ***(G-10029)***
Elliott Auto Bath Inc 513 422-3700
901 Elliott Dr Middletown (45044) ***(G-14425)***
Elliott Davis LLC 513 579-1717
201 E 5th St Ste 2100 Cincinnati (45202) ***(G-3551)***
Elliott Heller Maas Morrow Lpa 330 792-6611
54 Westchester Dr Ste 10 Youngstown (44515) ***(G-20180)***
Elliott Tool Technologies Ltd (PA) 937 253-6133
1760 Tuttle Ave Dayton (45403) ***(G-9524)***
Ellipse Solutions LLC 937 312-1547
7917 Washington Woods Dr Dayton (45459) ***(G-9525)***
Ellis Richard CB Reichle Klein 419 861-1100
1 Seagate Fl 26 Toledo (43604) ***(G-17864)***
Ellison Technologies Inc 440 546-1920
6955 Treeline Dr Ste J Brecksville (44141) ***(G-1823)***
Ellison Technologies Inc 310 323-2121
5333 Muhlhauser Rd Hamilton (45011) ***(G-11725)***
Elm Springs, Green Springs *Also called Elmwood Center Inc* ***(G-11474)***
Elm Valley Fishing Club 937 845-0584
5118 S Dayton Brandt Rd New Carlisle (45344) ***(G-15022)***
Elmco Engineering Oh Inc 419 238-1100
1171 Grill Rd Van Wert (45891) ***(G-18632)***
Elmco Trucking Inc 419 983-2010
30 Railroad St Bloomville (44818) ***(G-1519)***
Elmcroft of Medina, Medina *Also called Senior Care Inc* ***(G-14124)***
Elms Country Club, North Lawrence *Also called Elms of Massillon Inc* ***(G-15393)***
Elms Country Club Inc 330 833-2668
1608 Manchester Ave Sw North Lawrence (44666) ***(G-15392)***
Elms of Massillon Inc 330 833-2668
1608 Manchester Ave Sw North Lawrence (44666) ***(G-15393)***
Elms Retirement Village Inc 440 647-2414
136 S Main St Rear Wellington (44090) ***(G-18991)***
Elmwood At Shawhan, Tiffin *Also called Elmwood Center Inc* ***(G-17677)***
Elmwood At The Springs, Green Springs *Also called Elmwood Center Inc* ***(G-11475)***
Elmwood Center Inc (PA) 419 639-2581
441 N Broadway St Green Springs (44836) ***(G-11474)***
Elmwood Center Inc 419 447-6885
54 S Washington St Tiffin (44883) ***(G-17677)***
Elmwood Center Inc 419 639-2626
401 N Broadway St Green Springs (44836) ***(G-11475)***
Elmwood of Green Springs Ltd 419 639-2626
401 N Broadway St Green Springs (44836) ***(G-11476)***
Elts Broadcasting, Elyria *Also called Elyria-Lorain Broadcasting Co* ***(G-10623)***
Elyria Country Club Company 440 322-6391
41625 Oberlin Elyria Rd Elyria (44035) ***(G-10621)***
Elyria Ford, Elyria *Also called Abraham Ford LLC* ***(G-10592)***
Elyria Foundry Holdings LLC 440 322-4657
120 Filbert St Elyria (44035) ***(G-10622)***
Elyria Waste Water Plant, Elyria *Also called City of Elyria* ***(G-10604)***
Elyria-Lorain Broadcasting Co (HQ) 440 322-3761
538 Broad St 400 Elyria (44035) ***(G-10623)***
Elyria-Lorain Broadcasting Co 440 322-3761
538 Broad St 400 Elyria (44035) ***(G-10624)***
Em Print Group, Elyria *Also called Envelope Mart of North E Ohio* ***(G-10627)***
Embassy Autumnwood MGT LLC 330 927-2060
275 E Sunset Dr Rittman (44270) ***(G-16552)***
Embassy Healthcare Inc 513 868-6500
908 Symmes Rd Fairfield (45014) ***(G-10847)***
Embassy Stes Akrn-Canton Arprt, North Canton *Also called CPX Canton Airport LLC* ***(G-15330)***
Embassy Suites, Cleveland *Also called Commonwealth Hotels LLC* ***(G-5380)***
Embassy Suites, Columbus *Also called Corporate Exchange Hotel Assoc* ***(G-7443)***
Embassy Suites, Dublin *Also called Commonwealth Hotels LLC* ***(G-10303)***
Embassy Suites, Beachwood *Also called IA Urban Htels Bchwood Trs LLC* ***(G-1088)***
Embassy Suites, Independence *Also called Ap/Aim Indpndnce Sites Trs LLC* ***(G-12186)***
Embassy Suites Columbus, Columbus *Also called Columbus Hotel Partnership LLC* ***(G-7359)***
Embassy Suites Columbus, Columbus *Also called Rlj III - Em Clmbus Lessee LLC* ***(G-8638)***
Embassy Suites Columbus Arprt, Columbus *Also called Airport Core Hotel LLC* ***(G-6959)***
Embassy Suites Columbus Dublin, Dublin *Also called Ap/Aim Dublin Suites Trs LLC* ***(G-10254)***
Ember Complete Care (PA) 740 922-6888
1800 N Water Street Ext Uhrichsville (44683) ***(G-18488)***
Ember Home Care 740 922-6968
730 N Water St Uhrichsville (44683) ***(G-18489)***
Embers, Toledo *Also called Robert C Verbon Inc* ***(G-18160)***
Embracing Autism Inc 614 559-0077
2491 W Dblin Granville Rd Columbus (43235) ***(G-7590)***
EMC Corporation 513 794-9624
9825 Kenwood Rd Ste 300 Blue Ash (45242) ***(G-1584)***
EMC Corporation 216 606-2000
6480 Rcksde Wds Blvd S # 330 Independence (44131) ***(G-12206)***
EMC Insurance Companies, Blue Ash *Also called Employers Mutual Casualty Co* ***(G-1585)***
Emco Usa LLC 740 588-1722
1000 Linden Ave Zanesville (43701) ***(G-20474)***
Emcor Facilities Services Inc (HQ) 888 846-9462
9655 Reading Rd Cincinnati (45215) ***(G-3552)***
Emcor Fclities Svcs N Amer Inc 614 430-5078
280 N High St Ste 1700 Columbus (43215) ***(G-7591)***
EMD Millipore Corporation 513 631-0445
2909 Highland Ave Norwood (45212) ***(G-15599)***
Emerald Dev Ecnomic Netwrk Inc 216 961-9690
7812 Madison Ave Cleveland (44102) ***(G-5533)***
Emerald Health Network Inc (HQ) 216 479-2030
3320 W Market St 100 Fairlawn (44333) ***(G-10948)***
Emerald Pediatrics 614 932-5050
5695 Innovation Dr Dublin (43016) ***(G-10335)***
Emerald Woods Golf Course 440 236-8940
11464 Clarke Rd Columbia Station (44028) ***(G-6846)***
Emerge Counseling Service 330 865-8351
900 Mull Ave Akron (44313) ***(G-207)***
Emerge Ministries Inc 330 865-8351
900 Mull Ave Akron (44313) ***(G-208)***
Emergency Medical Group Inc 419 866-6009
5620 Southwyck Blvd 2 Toledo (43614) ***(G-17865)***
Emergency Medical Services, Hammondsville *Also called Saline Township* ***(G-11786)***
Emergency Medical Svcs Billing 216 664-2598
1701 Lakeside Ave E Cleveland (44114) ***(G-5534)***
Emergency Medical Transport 330 484-4000
7100 Whipple Ave Nw Ste A North Canton (44720) ***(G-15334)***
Emergency Medicine Physicians, Canton *Also called Emp Management Group Ltd* ***(G-2355)***
Emergency Medicine Specialists 937 438-8910
8280 Yankee St Dayton (45458) ***(G-9526)***
Emergency Physicians Med Group, Canton *Also called Dignity Health* ***(G-2341)***
Emergency Psychiatric Svc, Akron *Also called Portage Path Behavorial Health* ***(G-398)***
Emergency Response & Trnng 440 349-2700
6001 Cochran Rd Solon (44139) ***(G-17002)***
Emergency Services Inc 614 224-6420
2323 W 5th Ave Ste 220 Columbus (43204) ***(G-7592)***
Emeritus Assisted Living, Canton *Also called Emeritus Corporation* ***(G-2353)***
Emeritus At Brookside Estates, Cleveland *Also called Emeritus Corporation* ***(G-5535)***
Emeritus At Lakeview, Groveport *Also called Emeritus Corporation* ***(G-11636)***
Emeritus At Stow, Stow *Also called Emeritus Corporation* ***(G-17363)***
Emeritus Corporation 330 477-5727
4507 22nd St Nw Apt 33 Canton (44708) ***(G-2353)***
Emeritus Corporation 440 201-9200
15435 Bagley Rd Ste 1 Cleveland (44130) ***(G-5535)***
Emeritus Corporation 440 269-8600
35300 Kaiser Ct Willoughby (44094) ***(G-19661)***
Emeritus Corporation 330 342-0934
5511 Fishcreek Rd Stow (44224) ***(G-17363)***
Emeritus Corporation 614 836-5990
4000 Lakeview Xing Groveport (43125) ***(G-11636)***
Emersion Design LLC 513 841-9100
310 Culvert St Ste 100 Cincinnati (45202) ***(G-3553)***
Emerson Academy, Dayton *Also called National Heritg Academies Inc* ***(G-9769)***
Emerson Process MGT Lllp 877 468-6384
8460 Orion Pl Ste 110 Columbus (43240) ***(G-6881)***
Emery Leasing Co LLC 216 475-8880
20265 Emery Rd Cleveland (44128) ***(G-5536)***
Emh Inc (PA) 330 220-8600
550 Crane Dr Valley City (44280) ***(G-18617)***
Emh Regional Healthcare System, Elyria *Also called Comprehensive Health Care* ***(G-10607)***
Emh Regional Homecare Agency 440 329-7519
90 E Broad St Elyria (44035) ***(G-10625)***
Emh Regional Medical Center 440 988-6800
1997 Healthway Dr Avon (44011) ***(G-892)***
EMI Corp (PA) 937 596-5511
801 W Pike St Jackson Center (45334) ***(G-12322)***
EMI Enterprises Inc 419 666-0012
2639 Tracy Rd Northwood (43619) ***(G-15530)***
EMI Network, Blue Ash *Also called Brand Build Inc* ***(G-1548)***
Emil Pawuk & Associates, Richfield *Also called Empaco Equipment Corporation* ***(G-16505)***
Emily Management Inc 440 354-6713
10280 Pinecrest Rd Painesville (44077) ***(G-15854)***
EMJ Cincinnati, Cincinnati *Also called Earle M Jorgensen Company* ***(G-3530)***
EMJ Cleveland, Twinsburg *Also called Earle M Jorgensen Company* ***(G-18407)***
Emlab P&K LLC (HQ) 330 497-9396
4101 Shuffel St Nw # 200 North Canton (44720) ***(G-15335)***
Emmett Dan House Ltd Partnr 740 392-6886
150 Howard St Mount Vernon (43050) ***(G-14894)***
Emmys Bridal Inc 419 628-7555
336 N Main St Minster (45865) ***(G-14661)***

Emory Rothenbuhler & Sons....740 458-1432
47126 Sunfish Creek Rd Beallsville (43716) ***(G-1140)***
Emp Holdings Ltd....330 493-4443
4535 Dressler Rd Nw Canton (44718) ***(G-2354)***
Emp Management Group Ltd....330 493-4443
4535 Dressler Rd Nw Canton (44718) ***(G-2355)***
Empaco Equipment Corporation (PA)....330 659-9393
2958 Brecksville Rd Richfield (44286) ***(G-16505)***
Empire Brass Co....216 431-6565
5000 Superior Ave Cleveland (44103) ***(G-5537)***
Empire Masonry Company Inc....440 230-2800
12359 Abbey Rd Ste B North Royalton (44133) ***(G-15488)***
Empire One LLC....330 628-9310
1532 State Route 43 Mogadore (44260) ***(G-14676)***
Empire Packing Company LP....513 942-5400
113 Circle Freeway Dr West Chester (45246) ***(G-19196)***
Empire Poured Walls, North Royalton *Also called Empire Masonry Company Inc* ***(G-15488)***
Empire Refractory Services, Toledo *Also called Brand Energy & Infrastructure* ***(G-17781)***
Employee Benefit Management (PA)....614 766-5800
4789 Rings Rd Dublin (43017) ***(G-10336)***
Employeescreeniq Inc....216 514-2800
6111 Oak Tree Blvd # 400 Independence (44131) ***(G-12207)***
Employers Mutual Casualty Co....513 221-6010
11311 Cornell Park Dr # 500 Blue Ash (45242) ***(G-1585)***
Employers Select Plan Agcy Inc....216 642-4200
6480 Rcksde Wds Blvd S # 210 Independence (44131) ***(G-12208)***
Employment Development Inc....330 424-7711
8330 County Home Rd Lisbon (44432) ***(G-12936)***
Employment Network....440 324-5244
42495 N Ridge Rd Elyria (44035) ***(G-10626)***
Employment Relations Board....513 863-0828
3640 Old Oxford Rd Hamilton (45013) ***(G-11726)***
Empower Mediamarketing Inc (PA)....513 871-7779
15 E 14th St Cincinnati (45202) ***(G-3554)***
Empowered For Excellence....567 316-7253
3222 W Central Ave Toledo (43606) ***(G-17866)***
Ems, Cleveland *Also called Energy MGT Specialists Inc* ***(G-5539)***
EMs Rams Youth Dev Group Inc....216 282-4688
1536 E 85th St Cleveland (44106) ***(G-5538)***
Ems Service, Milan *Also called Bellevue Four Cnty Ems N Centl* ***(G-14492)***
Ems Station, Rittman *Also called Rittman City of Inc* ***(G-16555)***
Emsar, Wilmington *Also called Equipment MGT Svc & Repr Inc* ***(G-19761)***
Emsco (PA)....440 238-2100
22350 Royalton Rd Strongsville (44149) ***(G-17460)***
Emsco Inc (HQ)....330 830-7125
1000 Nave Rd Se Massillon (44646) ***(G-13803)***
Emsco Inc....330 833-5600
1000 Nave Rd Se Massillon (44646) ***(G-13804)***
Emsco Distributors, Strongsville *Also called Emsco* ***(G-17460)***
Emt, Cincinnati *Also called Electric Motor Tech LLC* ***(G-3546)***
Emt Ambulance, North Canton *Also called Emergency Medical Transport* ***(G-15334)***
Enabling Partners LLC....440 878-9418
13862 Basswood Cir Strongsville (44136) ***(G-17461)***
Enclosure Suppliers LLC....513 782-3900
12119 Champion Way Cincinnati (45241) ***(G-3555)***
Encompass Health Corporation....513 418-5600
151 W Galbraith Rd Cincinnati (45216) ***(G-3556)***
Encompass Health Corporation....205 970-4869
2685 E High St Springfield (45505) ***(G-17194)***
Encore Healthcare LLC....330 769-2015
83 High St Seville (44273) ***(G-16840)***
Encore Technologies, Cincinnati *Also called Sjn Data Center LLC* ***(G-4534)***
Endeavor Construction Ltd....513 469-1900
6801 Long Spurling Rd Pleasant Plain (45162) ***(G-16214)***
Endevis LLc (PA)....419 482-4848
7643 Kings Pointe Rd # 100 Toledo (43617) ***(G-17867)***
Endo-Surgical Center Fla LLC....440 708-0582
8185 Washington St Chagrin Falls (44023) ***(G-2715)***
Endocrine Lab, Cincinnati *Also called University of Cincinnati* ***(G-4762)***
Endolite, Miamisburg *Also called Blatchford Inc* ***(G-14276)***
Endoscopy Center....419 843-7993
5700 Monroe St Unit 102 Sylvania (43560) ***(G-17586)***
Endoscopy Center of Dayton (PA)....937 320-5050
4200 Indian Ripple Rd Beavercreek (45440) ***(G-1239)***
Enerfab Inc (PA)....513 641-0500
4955 Spring Grove Ave Cincinnati (45232) ***(G-3557)***
Energy MGT Specialists Inc....216 676-9045
15800 Industrial Pkwy Cleveland (44135) ***(G-5539)***
Enertech Electrical Inc....330 536-2131
101 Yngstown Lwllville Rd Lowellville (44436) ***(G-13171)***
Enervise Incorporated (PA)....513 761-6000
4360 Glendale Milford Rd Blue Ash (45242) ***(G-1586)***
Enervise Incorporated....614 885-9800
6663 Huntley Rd Ste K Columbus (43229) ***(G-7593)***
Engaged Health Care Bus Svcs....614 457-8180
4619 Kenny Rd Ste 100 Columbus (43220) ***(G-7594)***
Engineer Department, Delphos *Also called City of Delphos* ***(G-10138)***
Engineer's Office, Millersburg *Also called County of Holmes* ***(G-14598)***
Engineer's Office, Marysville *Also called County of Union* ***(G-13614)***
Engineered Con Structures Corp....216 520-2000
14510 Broadway Ave Cleveland (44125) ***(G-5540)***
Engineered Material Handling, Valley City *Also called Emh Inc* ***(G-18617)***
Engineered Polymer Systems, Medina *Also called Prime Polymers Inc* ***(G-14113)***
Engineering Associates Inc....330 345-6556
1935 Eagle Pass Wooster (44691) ***(G-19862)***
Engineering Chain Div, Sandusky *Also called US Tsubaki Power Transm LLC* ***(G-16807)***
Engineering Department, Dayton *Also called County of Montgomery* ***(G-9433)***
Engineering Design and Testing....440 239-0362
P.O. Box 30160 Cleveland (44130) ***(G-5541)***
Engineering Excellence, Blue Ash *Also called Enervise Incorporated* ***(G-1586)***
Engineering Excellence....972 535-3756
Blue Ash Business Park Blue Ash (45242) ***(G-1587)***
Engisystems Inc....513 229-8860
7588 Central Parke Blvd Mason (45040) ***(G-13699)***
Engle Management Group....513 232-9729
867 Yarger Dr Cincinnati (45230) ***(G-3558)***
Englefield Inc....740 452-2707
1400 Moxahala Ave Zanesville (43701) ***(G-20475)***
Englefield Inc....740 323-2077
10636 Jacksontown Rd Thornville (43076) ***(G-17667)***
Englewood Manor, Englewood *Also called Liberty Nursing Center* ***(G-10712)***
Englewood Square Ltd....937 836-4117
150 Chris Dr Apt 119 Englewood (45322) ***(G-10703)***
Englewood Square Apartments, Englewood *Also called Englewood Square Ltd* ***(G-10703)***
Englewood, City of, Englewood *Also called City of Englewood* ***(G-10700)***
Enhanced Home Health Care LLC....614 433-7266
700 Morse Rd Ste 206 Columbus (43214) ***(G-7595)***
Enhanced Homecare Medina Inc....330 952-2331
3745 Medina Rd Ste E Medina (44256) ***(G-14062)***
Enhanced Software Inc....877 805-8388
625 E North Broadway St Columbus (43214) ***(G-7596)***
Ennis Court, Lakewood *Also called Lakewood Health Care Center* ***(G-12490)***
Enon Firemans Association....937 864-7429
260 E Main St Enon (45323) ***(G-10727)***
Enprotech Industrial Tech LLC (HQ)....216 883-3220
4259 E 49th St Cleveland (44125) ***(G-5542)***
Enrichment Center of Wishing W (PA)....440 237-5000
14574 Ridge Rd Cleveland (44133) ***(G-5543)***
Ensafe Inc....513 621-7233
8187 Fox Knoll Dr West Chester (45069) ***(G-19068)***
ENt and Allergy Health Svcs (PA)....440 779-1112
25761 Lorain Rd Fl 3 North Olmsted (44070) ***(G-15420)***
Entec International Systems, Lakewood *Also called RAD-Con Inc* ***(G-12496)***
Entelco Corporation (PA)....419 872-4620
6528 Weatherfield Ct Maumee (43537) ***(G-13910)***
Enterprise Construction Inc....440 349-3443
30505 Bnbridge Rd Ste 200 Solon (44139) ***(G-17003)***
Enterprise Data Management Inc (HQ)....513 791-7272
4380 Malsbary Rd Ste 250 Blue Ash (45242) ***(G-1588)***
Enterprise Holdings Inc....614 866-1480
6501 Tussing Rd Reynoldsburg (43068) ***(G-16451)***
Enterprise Holdings Inc....937 879-0023
3670 Park 42 Dr Cincinnati (45241) ***(G-3559)***
Enterprise Rent-A-Car, Cincinnati *Also called Enterprise Holdings Inc* ***(G-3559)***
Enterprise Services LLC....740 423-9501
2505 Washington Blvd Frnt Belpre (45714) ***(G-1436)***
Enterprise Systems Sftwr LLC....419 841-3179
4352 W Sylvania Ave Ste M Toledo (43623) ***(G-17868)***
Enterprise Vending Inc....513 772-1373
895 Glendale Milford Rd Cincinnati (45215) ***(G-3560)***
Entertrainment Inc....513 898-8000
7379 Squire Ct West Chester (45069) ***(G-19069)***
Entertrainment Junction, West Chester *Also called Entertrainment Inc* ***(G-19069)***
Enting Water Conditioning Inc (PA)....937 294-5100
3211 Dryden Rd Frnt Frnt Moraine (45439) ***(G-14781)***
Entitle Direct Group Inc (HQ)....216 236-7800
3 Summit Park Dr Ste 525 Independence (44131) ***(G-12209)***
Entrust Healthcare, Columbus *Also called Entrust Solutions LLC* ***(G-7597)***
Entrust Solutions LLC....614 504-4900
20 S 3rd St Ste 210 Columbus (43215) ***(G-7597)***
Entrypoint Consulting LLC....216 674-9070
600 Superior Ave E # 1300 Cleveland (44114) ***(G-5544)***
Envelope Mart, Northwood *Also called EMI Enterprises Inc* ***(G-15530)***
Envelope Mart of North E Ohio....440 322-8862
1540 Lowell St Elyria (44035) ***(G-10627)***
Envelope Mart of Ohio Inc....440 365-8177
1540 Lowell St Elyria (44035) ***(G-10628)***
Envircare Lawn Landscacape LLC....419 874-6779
24112 Lime City Rd Perrysburg (43551) ***(G-16002)***
Envirite of Ohio Inc....330 456-6238
2050 Central Ave Se Canton (44707) ***(G-2356)***
Envirnmental Engrg Systems Inc....937 228-6492
17 Creston Ave Dayton (45404) ***(G-9527)***
Envirnmental Resources MGT Inc....216 593-5200
3333 Richmond Rd Ste 160 Beachwood (44122) ***(G-1076)***
Envirnmental Resources MGT Inc....513 830-9030
9825 Kenwood Rd Ste 100 Blue Ash (45242) ***(G-1589)***
Enviro It LLC....614 453-0709
3854 Fisher Rd Columbus (43228) ***(G-7598)***

ALPHABETIC

Enviro-Flow Companies Ltd......740 453-7980
4830 Northpointe Dr Zanesville (43701) ***(G-20476)***
Envirochemical Inc......440 287-2200
29325 Aurora Rd Solon (44139) ***(G-17004)***
Environment Control of Greater......614 868-9788
2218 Dividend Dr Columbus (43228) ***(G-7599)***
Environment Ctrl Beachwood Inc......330 405-6201
1897 E Aurora Rd Twinsburg (44087) ***(G-18408)***
Environment Ctrl of Miami Cnty......937 669-9900
7939 S County Road 25a A Tipp City (45371) ***(G-17716)***
Environmental Division, Cincinnati *Also called Power Engineers Incorporated* ***(G-4318)***
Environmental Engineering Cons, Cleveland *Also called Vahalla Company Inc* ***(G-6681)***
Environmental Engineering Dept, Marysville *Also called County of Union* ***(G-13612)***
Environmental Enterprises Inc......513 541-1823
4650 Spring Grove Ave Cincinnati (45232) ***(G-3561)***
Environmental Health Dept, Springfield *Also called County of Clark* ***(G-17178)***
Environmental Materials LLC......330 558-9168
2699 Center Rd Hinckley (44233) ***(G-11997)***
Environmental MGT Svcs Inc (PA)......614 876-9988
8220 Industrial Pkwy Plain City (43064) ***(G-16190)***
Environmental Quality MGT (HQ)......513 825-7500
1800 Carillion Blvd 100 Cincinnati (45240) ***(G-3562)***
Environmental Solutions (PA)......513 451-1777
4525 Este Ave Cincinnati (45232) ***(G-3563)***
Environmental Specialists Inc......740 788-8134
55 Builders Dr Newark (43055) ***(G-15165)***
Environmental Stone Works, Hinckley *Also called Environmental Materials LLC* ***(G-11997)***
Environmental Systems Research......614 933-8698
1085 Beecher Xing N Ste A Columbus (43230) ***(G-7600)***
Envirosafe Services of Ohio (HQ)......419 698-3500
876 Otter Creek Rd Oregon (43616) ***(G-15735)***
Enviroscapes......330 875-0768
7727 Paris Ave Louisville (44641) ***(G-13100)***
Enviroscience Inc (PA)......330 688-0111
5070 Stow Rd Stow (44224) ***(G-17364)***
Enviroserve, North Canton *Also called Sunpro Inc* ***(G-15370)***
Envirotest Systems Corp......330 963-4464
2180 Pinnacle Pkwy Twinsburg (44087) ***(G-18409)***
Envirotest Systems Corp......330 963-4464
1291 W Bagley Rd Berea (44017) ***(G-1456)***
Envirotest Systems Corp......330 963-4464
13000 York Delta Dr Cleveland (44133) ***(G-5545)***
Envirotest Systems Corp......330 963-4464
1460t Fairchild Ave Kent (44240) ***(G-12368)***
Envirotest Systems Corp......330 963-4464
128 Reaser Ct Elyria (44035) ***(G-10629)***
Envirotest Systems Corp......330 963-4464
24770 Sperry Dr Cleveland (44145) ***(G-5546)***
Envirotest Systems Corp......330 963-4464
17202 Munn Rd Chagrin Falls (44023) ***(G-2716)***
Envirotest Systems Corp......330 963-4464
1755 N Ridge Rd Painesville (44077) ***(G-15855)***
Envirotest Systems Corp......330 963-4464
770 S Progress Dr Medina (44256) ***(G-14063)***
Envirotest Systems Corp......330 963-4464
10632 Auburn Rd Chardon (44024) ***(G-2749)***
Envirotest Systems Corp......330 963-4464
205 Sandstone Blvd Amherst (44001) ***(G-593)***
Envirotest Systems Corp......330 963-4464
408 E Main St Spencer (44275) ***(G-17105)***
Envirotest Systems Corp......330 963-4464
2180 Pinnacle Pkwy Twinsburg (44087) ***(G-18410)***
Envision Children, Cincinnati *Also called Envision Corporation* ***(G-3564)***
Envision Corporation......513 772-5437
8 Enfield St Ste 4 Cincinnati (45218) ***(G-3564)***
Envision Healthcare Corp......937 534-7330
1530 Needmore Rd Ste 101 Dayton (45414) ***(G-9528)***
Envision Pharmaceutical Svcs, Twinsburg *Also called Rx Options LLC* ***(G-18464)***
Envision Phrm Svcs LLC......330 405-8080
2181 E Aurora Rd Ste 201 Twinsburg (44087) ***(G-18411)***
Envision Rx Options, Twinsburg *Also called Envision Phrm Svcs LLC* ***(G-18411)***
Envision Waste Services LLC......216 831-1818
4451 Renaissance Pkwy Cleveland (44128) ***(G-5547)***
Envoy Air Inc......614 231-4391
4100 E 5th Ave Columbus (43219) ***(G-7601)***
EOPA, Toledo *Also called Pathway Inc* ***(G-18122)***
Epcon Cmmnties Franchising Inc......614 761-1010
500 Stonehenge Pkwy Dublin (43017) ***(G-10337)***
Epcon Communities Inc......614 761-1010
500 Stonehenge Pkwy Dublin (43017) ***(G-10338)***
Epcor Foundries, Cincinnati *Also called Seilkop Industries Inc* ***(G-4492)***
Epilepsy Cntr of Nrthwstrn OH......419 867-5950
1701 Holland Rd Maumee (43537) ***(G-13911)***
Epilogue Inc......440 582-5555
12333 Ridge Rd Ste E North Royalton (44133) ***(G-15489)***
Epiphany Management Group LLC......330 706-4056
283 E Waterloo Rd Akron (44319) ***(G-209)***
Epipheo Incorporated......888 687-7620
700 W Pete Rose Way 450 Cincinnati (45203) ***(G-3565)***
Epipheo Studios, Cincinnati *Also called Epipheo Incorporated* ***(G-3565)***
Epiqurian Inns......614 885-2600
649 High St Worthington (43085) ***(G-19957)***
Episcopal Retirement Homes......513 271-9610
3870 Virginia Ave Ste 2 Cincinnati (45227) ***(G-3566)***
Episcopal Retirement Homes Inc (PA)......513 271-9610
3870 Virginia Ave Ste 2 Cincinnati (45227) ***(G-3567)***
Episcopal Retirement Homes Inc......513 561-6363
3939 Erie Ave Cincinnati (45208) ***(G-3568)***
Episcopal Retirement Homes Inc......513 871-2090
3550 Shaw Ave Ofc Cincinnati (45208) ***(G-3569)***
Epworth Preschool and Daycare......740 387-1062
249 E Center St Marion (43302) ***(G-13538)***
Epworth United Methodist Ch, Marion *Also called Epworth Preschool and Daycare* ***(G-13538)***
Epworth United Methodist Ch......740 387-1062
249 E Center St Marion (43302) ***(G-13539)***
Eq Ohio, Canton *Also called Envirite of Ohio Inc* ***(G-2356)***
Equip Estate Group, Columbus *Also called Schlee Malt House Condo Assn* ***(G-8695)***
Equipment Depot Ohio Inc......513 934-2121
1000 Kingsview Dr Lebanon (45036) ***(G-12603)***
Equipment Depot Ohio Inc (HQ)......513 891-0600
4331 Rossplain Dr Blue Ash (45236) ***(G-1590)***
Equipment Depot Ohio Inc......513 539-8464
101 Lawton Ave Monroe (45050) ***(G-14694)***
Equipment Depot Ohio Inc......513 934-2121
1000 Kingsview Dr Lebanon (45036) ***(G-12604)***
Equipment Maintenance & Repair, Cleves *Also called Equipment Maintenance Inc* ***(G-6799)***
Equipment Maintenance Inc (PA)......513 353-3518
5885 Hamilton Cleves Rd Cleves (45002) ***(G-6799)***
Equipment Manufacturers Intl......216 651-6700
16151 Puritas Ave Cleveland (44135) ***(G-5548)***
Equipment MGT Svc & Repr Inc......937 383-1052
270 Davids Dr Wilmington (45177) ***(G-19761)***
Equipment Yard & Maint Div, Lima *Also called Jacobs Constructors Inc* ***(G-12806)***
Equitable Life Assurance, Solon *Also called Cincinnati Equitable Insur Co* ***(G-16991)***
Equitable Mortgage Corporation (PA)......614 764-1232
3530 Snouffer Rd Ste 100 Columbus (43235) ***(G-7602)***
Equitas Health Inc......614 299-2437
4400 N High St Ste 300 Columbus (43214) ***(G-7603)***
Equitas Health Inc......937 461-2437
15 W 4th St Ste 200 Dayton (45402) ***(G-9529)***
Equitas Health Pharmacy, Dayton *Also called Equitas Health Inc* ***(G-9529)***
Equity Central LLC......614 861-7777
81 Mill St Ste 206 Gahanna (43230) ***(G-11240)***
Equity Consultants LLC......330 659-7600
5800 Lombardo Ctr Ste 202 Seven Hills (44131) ***(G-16829)***
Equity Diamond Brokers Inc (PA)......513 793-4760
9301 Montgomery Rd Cincinnati (45242) ***(G-3570)***
Equity Engineering Group Inc (PA)......216 283-9519
20600 Chagrin Blvd # 1200 Shaker Heights (44122) ***(G-16860)***
Equity Inc (PA)......614 802-2900
4653 Trueman Blvd Ste 100 Hilliard (43026) ***(G-11900)***
Equity Real Estate, Hilliard *Also called Equity Inc* ***(G-11900)***
Equity Residential Properties......216 861-2700
1701 E 12th St Ste 35 Cleveland (44114) ***(G-5549)***
Equity Resources Inc......513 518-6318
130 Tri County Pkwy # 108 Cincinnati (45246) ***(G-3571)***
ERA, Findlay *Also called Noakes Rooney Rlty & Assoc Co* ***(G-11070)***
ERA, Chillicothe *Also called J W Enterprises Inc* ***(G-2856)***
Erb Electric Co......740 633-5055
500 Hall St Ste 1 Bridgeport (43912) ***(G-1862)***
Ergon, Delaware *Also called Alpha Group of Delaware Inc* ***(G-10070)***
Erhal Inc......513 272-5555
3870 Virginia Ave Cincinnati (45227) ***(G-3572)***
Eric Boeppler Fmly Ltd Partnr......513 336-8108
9331 Seward Rd Ste A Fairfield (45014) ***(G-10848)***
Eric Hasemeier Do......740 594-7979
510 W Union St Ste A Athens (45701) ***(G-787)***
Eric Mower and Associates Inc......513 381-8855
830 Main St Fl 10 Cincinnati (45202) ***(G-3573)***
Erie Blacktop Inc......419 625-7374
4507 Tiffin Ave Sandusky (44870) ***(G-16751)***
Erie Co Office of Ed, Huron *Also called North Point Eductl Svc Ctr* ***(G-12168)***
Erie Construction Co, Dayton *Also called Erie Construction Mid-West Inc* ***(G-9530)***
Erie Construction Group Inc......419 625-7374
4507 Tiffin Ave Sandusky (44870) ***(G-16752)***
Erie Construction Mid-West Inc (PA)......419 472-4200
4271 Monroe St Toledo (43606) ***(G-17869)***
Erie Construction Mid-West Inc......937 898-4688
3520 Sudachi Dr Dayton (45414) ***(G-9530)***
Erie County Cablevision Inc......419 627-0800
409 E Market St Sandusky (44870) ***(G-16753)***
Erie County Care Facility, Huron *Also called County of Erie* ***(G-12164)***
Erie County Hwy Dept, Sandusky *Also called County of Erie* ***(G-16749)***
Erie Huron Cac Headstart Inc......419 663-2623
11 E League St Norwalk (44857) ***(G-15572)***
Erie Indemnity Company......330 433-6300
4690 Munson St Nw Canton (44718) ***(G-2357)***
Erie Insurance Exchange......330 568-1802
5676 Everett East Rd Hubbard (44425) ***(G-12086)***

Erie Insurance Exchange....330 479-1010
1120 Valleyview Ave Sw Canton (44710) **(G-2358)**
Erie Insurance Exchange....614 430-8530
445 Hutchinson Ave Columbus (43235) **(G-7604)**
Erie Insurance Exchange....614 436-0224
445 Hutchinson Ave # 350 Columbus (43235) **(G-7605)**
Erie Insurance Exchange....330 433-1925
4690 Munson St Nw Ste A Canton (44718) **(G-2359)**
Erie Island Resort and Marina....419 734-9117
150 E Market St Ste 300 Warren (44481) **(G-18856)**
Erie Lumber Co Division, Hartville *Also called Nilco LLC* **(G-11827)**
ERIE RESIDENTIAL LIVING HOME I, Sandusky *Also called Erie Residential Living Inc* **(G-16754)**
Erie Residential Living Inc....419 625-0060
706 E Park St Sandusky (44870) **(G-16754)**
Erie Shores Credit Union Inc (PA)....419 897-8110
1688 Woodlands Dr Maumee (43537) **(G-13912)**
Erie Shores Golf Club, Madison *Also called Lake Metroparks* **(G-13228)**
Erie Trucking Inc....419 625-7374
4507 Tiffin Ave Sandusky (44870) **(G-16755)**
Erieside Medical Group....440 918-6270
38429 Lake Shore Blvd Willoughby (44094) **(G-19662)**
Erik Balster Hlth Commissioner, Eaton *Also called Preble County General Hlth Dst* **(G-10575)**
Erm Midatlantic, Beachwood *Also called Envirnmental Resources MGT Inc* **(G-1076)**
Ermc II LP....513 424-8517
3461 Towne Blvd Unit 250 Middletown (45005) **(G-14478)**
Ernest Fritsch....614 436-5995
6245 Sunderland Dr Columbus (43229) **(G-7606)**
Ernest V Thomas Jr (PA)....513 961-5311
2323 Park Ave Cincinnati (45206) **(G-3574)**
Ernst & Young LLP....216 861-5000
950 Main Ave Ste 1800 Cleveland (44113) **(G-5550)**
Ernst & Young LLP....216 583-1823
1660 W 2nd St Ste 200 Cleveland (44113) **(G-5551)**
Ernst & Young LLP....614 224-5678
800 Yard St Ste 200 Columbus (43212) **(G-7607)**
Ernst & Young LLP....513 612-1400
312 Walnut St Ste 1900 Cincinnati (45202) **(G-3575)**
Ernst & Young LLP....419 244-8000
1 Seagate Ste 2510 Toledo (43604) **(G-17870)**
Ernst Corporation....513 697-6970
9175 Governors Way Cincinnati (45249) **(G-3576)**
Erp Analysts Inc....614 718-9222
425 Metro Pl N Ste 510 Dublin (43017) **(G-10339)**
Erts, Solon *Also called Emergency Response & Trnng* **(G-17002)**
Es3 Management Inc....440 593-6266
22 Parrish Rd Conneaut (44030) **(G-9042)**
Esber Beverage Company....330 456-4361
2217 Bolivar Rd Sw Canton (44706) **(G-2360)**
Esbi International Salon....330 220-3724
4193 Center Rd Brunswick (44212) **(G-1977)**
Esc and Company Inc....614 794-0568
2000 Toronado Blvd A Columbus (43207) **(G-7608)**
Esc of Cuyahoga County....216 524-3000
6393 Oak Tree Blvd # 300 Independence (44131) **(G-12210)**
Escape Enterprises Inc....614 224-0300
222 Neilston St Columbus (43215) **(G-7609)**
Esd, Toledo *Also called Enterprise Systems Sftwr LLC* **(G-17868)**
Esec Corporation (PA)....330 799-1536
44 Victoria Rd Youngstown (44515) **(G-20181)**
Esec Corporation....614 875-3732
6240 Enterprise Pkwy Grove City (43123) **(G-11558)**
Esj Carrier Corporation....513 728-7388
3240 Production Dr Fairfield (45014) **(G-10849)**
Esko-Graphics Inc (HQ)....937 454-1721
8535 Gander Creek Dr Miamisburg (45342) **(G-14299)**
Eskoartwork, Miamisburg *Also called Esko-Graphics Inc* **(G-14299)**
Eslich Wrecking Company....330 488-8300
3525 Broadway Ave Louisville (44641) **(G-13101)**
Eso, Carrollton *Also called Efficient Services Ohio Inc* **(G-2619)**
Espt Liquidation Inc....330 698-4711
339 Mill St Apple Creek (44606) **(G-624)**
Esri, Columbus *Also called Environmental Systems Research* **(G-7600)**
Essendant Co....330 650-9361
100 E Highland Rd Hudson (44236) **(G-12116)**
Essendant Co....330 425-4001
2100 Highland Rd Twinsburg (44087) **(G-18412)**
Essendant Co....513 942-1354
9775 International Blvd West Chester (45246) **(G-19197)**
Essendant Co....614 876-7774
1634 Westbelt Dr Columbus (43228) **(G-7610)**
Essendant Inc....330 425-4001
2100 Highland Rd Twinsburg (44087) **(G-18413)**
Essential Freight Systems Inc (PA)....330 468-5898
201 E Twinsburg Rd Northfield (44067) **(G-15514)**
Essentialprofile1corp....614 805-4794
735 N Wilson Rd Columbus (43204) **(G-7611)**
Essex and Associates Inc....937 432-1040
7501 Paragon Rd Ste 100 Dayton (45459) **(G-9531)**
Essex Healthcare Corporation (PA)....614 416-0600
2780 Airport Dr Ste 400 Columbus (43219) **(G-7612)**
Essig Research Inc....513 942-7100
497 Circle Freeway Dr # 236 West Chester (45246) **(G-19198)**
Essilor Laboratories Amer Inc....614 274-0840
3671 Interchange Rd Columbus (43204) **(G-7613)**
Essilor of America Inc....614 492-0888
2400 Spiegel Dr Ste A Groveport (43125) **(G-11637)**
Est Analytical, West Chester *Also called Pts Prfssnal Technical Svc Inc* **(G-19134)**
Estabrook Corporation (PA)....440 234-8566
700 W Bagley Rd Berea (44017) **(G-1457)**
Estate Information Svcs LLC....614 729-1700
670 Morrison Rd Ste 300 Gahanna (43230) **(G-11241)**
Estephenson Brenda & John, Maineville *Also called AMS Construction Inc* **(G-13240)**
Estes Express Lines Inc....440 327-3884
38495 Center Ridge Rd North Ridgeville (44039) **(G-15463)**
Estes Express Lines Inc....614 275-6000
1009 Frank Rd Columbus (43223) **(G-7614)**
Estes Express Lines Inc....419 531-1500
5330 Angola Rd Ste B Toledo (43615) **(G-17871)**
Estes Express Lines Inc....937 237-7536
6295 Executive Blvd Huber Heights (45424) **(G-12095)**
Estes Express Lines Inc....419 522-2641
792 5th Ave Mansfield (44905) **(G-13298)**
Estes Express Lines Inc....330 659-9750
2755 Brecksville Rd Richfield (44286) **(G-16506)**
Estes Express Lines Inc....513 779-9581
6459 Allen Rd West Chester (45069) **(G-19070)**
Estes Express Lines Inc....740 401-0410
12140 State Road 7 Belpre (45714) **(G-1437)**
Estes Express Lines 92, Toledo *Also called Estes Express Lines Inc* **(G-17871)**
Esther Marie Nursing Home, Geneva *Also called Nursing Home Management Inc* **(G-11367)**
Estreamz Inc....513 278-7836
1311 Vine St Cincinnati (45202) **(G-3577)**
Esw, Oregon *Also called E S Wagner Company* **(G-15733)**
Et Cetera Services, Westlake *Also called Unpacking Etc* **(G-19561)**
Etb University Properties LLC....440 826-2212
343 W Bagley Rd Berea (44017) **(G-1458)**
Etc Gameco LLC....614 428-7529
157 Easton Town Ctr Columbus (43219) **(G-7615)**
Etech-Systems LLC....216 221-6600
14600 Detroit Ave # 1500 Lakewood (44107) **(G-12477)**
Ethnic Voice of America....440 845-0922
4606 Bruening Dr Cleveland (44134) **(G-5552)**
Etl, Columbus *Also called Intertek Testing Svcs NA Inc* **(G-7920)**
Eubel Brady Suttman Asset Mgt....937 291-1223
10100 Innovation Dr # 410 Miamisburg (45342) **(G-14300)**
Euclid Adult Training Center, Euclid *Also called A W S Inc* **(G-10741)**
Euclid City Schools....216 261-2900
463 Babbitt Rd Euclid (44123) **(G-10751)**
Euclid Finance Division, Euclid *Also called Euclid Hospital* **(G-10754)**
Euclid Fish Company....440 951-6448
7839 Enterprise Dr Mentor (44060) **(G-14172)**
Euclid Health Care Inc (PA)....513 561-4105
6940 Stiegler Ln Cincinnati (45243) **(G-3578)**
Euclid Heat Treating Co....216 481-8444
1408 E 222nd St Euclid (44117) **(G-10752)**
Euclid Hospital, Cleveland *Also called Cleveland Clinic Health System* **(G-5308)**
Euclid Hospital (HQ)....216 531-9000
18901 Lake Shore Blvd Euclid (44119) **(G-10753)**
Euclid Hospital....216 445-6440
18901 Lake Shore Blvd # 4 Euclid (44119) **(G-10754)**
Euclid Indus Maint Clg Contrs....216 361-0288
1561 E 40th St Cleveland (44103) **(G-5553)**
Euclid Medical Products, Apple Creek *Also called Precision Products Group Inc* **(G-626)**
Euclid SC Transportation....216 797-7600
393 Babbitt Rd Cleveland (44123) **(G-5554)**
Eureka Midstream LLC....740 868-1325
27710 State Route 7 Marietta (45750) **(G-13444)**
Euro Usa Inc (PA)....216 714-0500
4481 Johnston Pkwy Cleveland (44128) **(G-5555)**
Eurolink Inc....740 392-1549
106 W Ohio Ave Mount Vernon (43050) **(G-14895)**
Euthenics Inc (PA)....440 260-1555
8235 Mohawk Dr Strongsville (44136) **(G-17462)**
Evangelical Lutheran....419 365-5115
100 Powell Dr Arlington (45814) **(G-647)**
Evangelical Retirement....937 837-5581
5790 Denlinger Rd Dayton (45426) **(G-9532)**
Evanhoe & Associates Inc....937 235-2995
5089 Norman Blvd Dayton (45431) **(G-9269)**
Evans Mechwart Ham (PA)....614 775-4500
5500 New Albany Rd New Albany (43054) **(G-14984)**
Evans Motor Works, Dayton *Also called Volvo BMW Dyton Evans Volkswag* **(G-9975)**
Evanston Bulldogs Youth Footba....513 254-9500
3060 Durrell Ave Cincinnati (45207) **(G-3579)**
Evant (PA)....330 920-1517
4500 Hudson Dr Stow (44224) **(G-17365)**
Event Source, Cleveland *Also called JBK Group Inc* **(G-5854)**
Eventions Ltd....216 952-9898
14925 Shaker Blvd Cleveland (44120) **(G-5556)**

A L P H A B E T I C

Events On Top ALPHABETIC SECTION

Events On Top.....330 757-3786
143 Boardman Canfield Rd Youngstown (44512) ***(G-20182)***
Ever Dry of Cincinnati, West Chester *Also called Riverfront Diversified Inc* ***(G-19142)***
Everdry Waterproofing Toledo, Toledo *Also called Rusk Industries Inc* ***(G-18168)***
Everest Technologies Inc.....614 436-3120
740 Lakeview Plaza Blvd # 250 Worthington (43085) ***(G-19958)***
Everfast Inc.....216 360-9176
24651 Cedar Rd Cleveland (44124) ***(G-5557)***
Evergreen Cooperative Ldry Inc.....216 268-3548
540 E 105th St Ste 206 Cleveland (44108) ***(G-5558)***
Evergreen Healthcare Center, Montpelier *Also called Communicare Health Svcs Inc* ***(G-14740)***
Evergreen Kindervelt Gift Shop, Cincinnati *Also called Williamsburg of Cincinnati Mgt* ***(G-4852)***
Evergreen Pharmaceutical LLC (HQ).....513 719-2600
201 E 4th St Ste 900 Cincinnati (45202) ***(G-3580)***
Evergreen Phrm Cal Inc (HQ).....513 719-2600
201 E 4th St Ste 900 Cincinnati (45202) ***(G-3581)***
Evergreen Plastics, Clyde *Also called Polychem Corporation* ***(G-6820)***
Everris NA Inc (HQ).....614 726-7100
4950 Blazer Pkwy Dublin (43017) ***(G-10340)***
Evers Welding Co Inc.....513 385-7352
4849 Blue Rock Rd Cincinnati (45247) ***(G-3582)***
Everstaff LLC.....440 992-0238
7448 Mentor Ave Mentor (44060) ***(G-14173)***
Everstaff LLC (PA).....877 392-6151
6500 Rockside Rd Ste 385 Cleveland (44131) ***(G-5559)***
Every Child Succeeds.....513 636-2830
3333 Burnet Ave Cincinnati (45229) ***(G-3583)***
Everybodys Inc.....937 293-1010
3050 Springboro Pike Moraine (45439) ***(G-14782)***
Everybodys Workplace Solutions, Moraine *Also called Everybodys Inc* ***(G-14782)***
Everyday Homecare.....937 444-1672
711 S High St Mount Orab (45154) ***(G-14868)***
Evokes LLC.....513 947-8433
8118 Corp Way Ste 212 Mason (45040) ***(G-13700)***
Evolution Ag LLC.....740 363-1341
13275 Us Highway 42 N Plain City (43064) ***(G-16191)***
Evolution Crtive Solutions LLC.....513 681-4450
7107 Shona Dr Ste 110 Cincinnati (45237) ***(G-3584)***
Exact Software North Amer LLC (HQ).....978 539-6186
5455 Rings Rd Ste 100 Dublin (43017) ***(G-10341)***
Exact Software North Amer LLC.....614 410-2600
5455 Rings Rd Ste 100 Dublin (43017) ***(G-10342)***
Excalibur Auto Body Inc (PA).....440 942-5550
30520 Lakeland Blvd Willowick (44095) ***(G-19739)***
Excalibur Body & Frame, Willowick *Also called Excalibur Auto Body Inc* ***(G-19739)***
Excel Decorators Inc.....614 522-0056
3910 Groves Rd Ste A Columbus (43232) ***(G-7616)***
Excel Electrical Contractor.....740 965-3795
7484 Reliance St Worthington (43085) ***(G-19959)***
Excel Health Services LLC.....614 794-0006
163 N Sandusky St Ste 201 Delaware (43015) ***(G-10093)***
Excel Trucking LLC.....614 826-1988
1000 Frank Rd Columbus (43223) ***(G-7617)***
Excelas LLC.....440 442-7310
387 Golfview Ln Ste 200 Cleveland (44143) ***(G-5560)***
Excellence Alliance Group Inc.....513 619-4800
700 Walnut St Ste 210 Cincinnati (45202) ***(G-3585)***
Excellence In Motivation Inc.....763 445-3000
6 N Main St Ste 370 Dayton (45402) ***(G-9533)***
Exceptional Innovation Inc.....614 901-8899
480 Olde Worthington Rd # 350 Westerville (43082) ***(G-19302)***
Excess Share Insurance Corp.....614 764-1900
5656 Frantz Rd Dublin (43017) ***(G-10343)***
Exclusive Homecare Services.....937 236-6750
4699 Salem Ave Ste 1 Dayton (45416) ***(G-9534)***
Executive Insurance Agency (PA).....330 576-1234
130 Springside Dr Ste 300 Akron (44333) ***(G-210)***
Executive Jet Management Inc (HQ).....513 979-6600
4556 Airport Rd Cincinnati (45226) ***(G-3586)***
Executive Management Services.....419 529-8800
1225 Home Rd N Ontario (44906) ***(G-15688)***
EXECUTIVE OFFICE, Berea *Also called Ohio Tpk & Infrastructure Comm* ***(G-1465)***
Executive Properties Inc (PA).....330 376-4037
733 W Market St Ste 102 Akron (44303) ***(G-211)***
Executives Agencies.....614 466-2980
30 E Broad St Fl 26 Columbus (43215) ***(G-7618)***
Exel Freight Connect Inc.....855 393-5378
226 N 5th St Ste 218 Columbus (43215) ***(G-7619)***
Exel Global Logistics Inc.....440 243-5900
21500 Aerospace Pkwy Cleveland (44142) ***(G-5561)***
Exel Global Logistics Inc.....614 409-4500
2144a John Glenn Ave Columbus (43217) ***(G-7620)***
Exel Holdings (usa) Inc (HQ).....614 865-8500
570 Polaris Pkwy Ste 110 Westerville (43082) ***(G-19303)***
Exel Inc.....419 996-7703
635 N Cool Rd Lima (45801) ***(G-12774)***
Exel Inc.....419 226-5500
3875 Reservoir Rd Lima (45801) ***(G-12775)***
Exel Inc.....614 865-8294
570 Polaris Pkwy Ste 110 Westerville (43082) ***(G-19304)***
Exel Inc (HQ).....614 865-8500
570 Polaris Pkwy Westerville (43082) ***(G-19305)***
Exel Inc.....740 927-1762
127 Heritage Dr Etna (43062) ***(G-10734)***
Exel Inc.....614 670-6473
2450 Creekside Pkwy Lockbourne (43137) ***(G-12952)***
Exel Logistics, Groveport *Also called Dhl Supply Chain (usa)* ***(G-11634)***
Exel N Amercn Logistics Inc.....937 854-7900
5522 Little Richmond Rd Dayton (45426) ***(G-9535)***
Exel N Amercn Logistics Inc (HQ).....800 272-1052
570 Players Pkwy Westerville (43081) ***(G-19398)***
Exhibitpro Inc.....614 885-9541
8900 Smiths Mill Rd New Albany (43054) ***(G-14985)***
Exit Two Stop N Go, Montpelier *Also called Ney Oil Company Inc* ***(G-14746)***
Exodus Integrity Service.....440 918-0140
37111 Euclid Ave Ste F Willoughby (44094) ***(G-19663)***
Exonic Systems LLC.....330 315-3100
380 Water St Akron (44308) ***(G-212)***
Expedata LLC.....937 439-6767
8073 Washington Vlg Dr Dayton (45458) ***(G-9536)***
Expeditors Intl Wash Inc.....440 243-9900
18029 Cleveland Pkwy Dr Cleveland (44135) ***(G-5562)***
Expeditors Intl Wash Inc.....614 492-9840
6054 Shook Rd Ste 100 Lockbourne (43137) ***(G-12953)***
Experis Finance Us LLC.....614 223-2300
175 S 3rd St Ste 375 Columbus (43215) ***(G-7621)***
Experis Finance Us LLC.....216 621-0200
6000 Lombardo Ctr Ste 400 Seven Hills (44131) ***(G-16830)***
Experis Us Inc.....614 223-2300
175 S 3rd St Ste 375 Columbus (43215) ***(G-7622)***
Expert System Applications.....440 248-0110
26700 Alsace Ct Apt 302 Beachwood (44122) ***(G-1077)***
Expert Technical Consultants.....614 430-9113
1268 E Ash St Piqua (45356) ***(G-16143)***
Explorer Rv Insurance Agcy Inc.....330 659-8900
3250 Interstate Dr Richfield (44286) ***(G-16507)***
Explorys Inc.....216 767-4700
1111 Superior Ave E Cleveland (44114) ***(G-5563)***
Exponentia US Inc.....614 944-5103
424 Beecher Rd Ste A Columbus (43230) ***(G-7623)***
Express Energy Svcs Oper LP.....740 337-4530
1515 Franklin St Toronto (43964) ***(G-18337)***
Express Packaging Ohio Inc (PA).....740 498-4700
301 Enterprise Dr Newcomerstown (43832) ***(G-15268)***
Express Script, Dublin *Also called Medco Health Solutions Inc* ***(G-10393)***
Express Seed Company.....440 774-2259
51051 Us Highway 20 Oberlin (44074) ***(G-15643)***
Express Twing Recovery Svc Inc.....513 881-1900
9772 Prnceton Glendale Rd West Chester (45246) ***(G-19199)***
Expresso Car Wash 5, Toledo *Also called Expresso Car Wash Systems Inc* ***(G-17873)***
Expresso Car Wash Systems Inc.....419 536-7540
5440 W Central Ave Toledo (43615) ***(G-17872)***
Expresso Car Wash Systems Inc.....419 866-7099
1750 S Reynolds Rd Toledo (43614) ***(G-17873)***
Expressway Pk Softball Complex, Milford *Also called Max Dixons Expressway Park* ***(G-14537)***
Extended Family Concepts Inc.....330 966-2555
913 Pittsburg Ave Nw Canton (44720) ***(G-2361)***
Extreme Detail Clg Cnstr Svcs.....419 392-3243
1724 Barrows St Toledo (43613) ***(G-17874)***
Exxcel Project Management LLC.....614 621-4500
328 Civic Center Dr Columbus (43215) ***(G-7624)***
Ey, Cleveland *Also called Ernst & Young LLP* ***(G-5550)***
Ey, Cleveland *Also called Ernst & Young LLP* ***(G-5551)***
Ey, Columbus *Also called Ernst & Young LLP* ***(G-7607)***
Ey, Cincinnati *Also called Ernst & Young LLP* ***(G-3575)***
Ey, Toledo *Also called Ernst & Young LLP* ***(G-17870)***
Eye Care Associates Inc (PA).....330 746-7691
10 Dutton Dr Youngstown (44502) ***(G-20183)***
Eye Center (PA).....614 228-3937
262 Neil Ave Columbus (43215) ***(G-7625)***
Eye Centers of Ohio Inc.....330 966-1111
6407 Frank Ave Nw North Canton (44720) ***(G-15336)***
Eye Centers of Ohio Inc.....330 966-1111
800 Mckinley Ave Nw Canton (44703) ***(G-2362)***
Eye Inst of Northwestern OH In.....419 865-3866
5555 Airport Hwy Toledo (43615) ***(G-17875)***
Eye Institute of Northwestern, Maumee *Also called Ophthalmology Associates of* ***(G-13953)***
Eye Physicians & Surgeons, Columbus *Also called University Eye Surgeons* ***(G-8908)***
Eye Surgery Center of Wooster, Wooster *Also called Wooster Ophthalmologists Inc* ***(G-19933)***
EZ Grout Corporation Inc.....740 962-2024
1833 N Riverview Rd Malta (43758) ***(G-13249)***
EZ Pack, Cincinnati *Also called SJS Packaging Group Inc* ***(G-4535)***
Ezg Manufacturing, Malta *Also called EZ Grout Corporation Inc* ***(G-13249)***
Ezra Health Care Inc.....440 498-3000
23258 Fernwood Dr Beachwood (44122) ***(G-1078)***
F & M Contractors, Clayton *Also called Ideal Company Inc* ***(G-4911)***
F & M Mafco Inc (PA).....513 367-2151
9149 Dry Fork Rd Harrison (45030) ***(G-11797)***

F A C E, Columbus *Also called Friends of Art For Cultural* **(G-7706)**
F B and S Masonry Inc 330 608-3442
3021 Harriet Rd Silver Lake (44224) **(G-16962)**
F B Wright Co Cincinnati (PA) 513 874-9100
4689 Ashley Dr West Chester (45011) **(G-19071)**
F Dohmen Co 614 757-5000
7000 Cardinal Pl Dublin (43017) **(G-10344)**
F E E, Canal Winchester *Also called Feecorp Corporation* **(G-2158)**
F F A Camp Muskingum, Carrollton *Also called Ohio F F A Camps Inc* **(G-2625)**
F H Bonn 937 323-7024
4300 Gateway Blvd Springfield (45502) **(G-17195)**
F H Bonn Company, Springfield *Also called F H Bonn* **(G-17195)**
F I L US Inc (HQ) 440 248-9500
30403 Bruce Indus Pkwy Solon (44139) **(G-17005)**
F O E, Grove City *Also called Fraternal Order Eagles Inc* **(G-11563)**
F R S Connections 937 393-9662
149 Chillicothe Ave Hillsboro (45133) **(G-11973)**
F S T Express Inc 614 529-7900
1727 Georgesville Rd Columbus (43228) **(G-7626)**
F W Arnold Agency Co Inc 330 832-1556
210 Erie St N Massillon (44646) **(G-13805)**
F+w Media Inc (HQ) 513 531-2690
10151 Carver Rd Ste 200 Blue Ash (45242) **(G-1591)**
Fab Limousines Inc 330 792-6700
3681 Connecticut Ave Youngstown (44515) **(G-20184)**
Fab Tours & Travel, Youngstown *Also called Fab Limousines Inc* **(G-20184)**
Fabco Inc 419 427-0872
616 N Blanchard St Findlay (45840) **(G-11022)**
Fabrizi Trucking & Pav Co Inc (PA) 330 483-3291
20389 1st Ave Cleveland (44130) **(G-5564)**
Facemyer Backhoe and Dozer Svc 740 965-1137
72 Holmes St Sunbury (43074) **(G-17555)**
Facil North America Inc (HQ) 330 487-2500
2242 Pinnacle Pkwy # 100 Twinsburg (44087) **(G-18414)**
Facilities Kahn Management 313 202-7607
121 Springboro Pike Dayton (45449) **(G-9537)**
Facilities MGT Solutions LLC 513 639-2230
250 W Court St Cincinnati (45202) **(G-3587)**
Facilities Operation and Dev, Columbus *Also called Ohio State University* **(G-8445)**
Facility Connect, Twinsburg *Also called French Company LLC* **(G-18418)**
Facility MGT & Support Svcs, East Liberty *Also called MPW Industrial Services Inc* **(G-10511)**
Facility Products & Svcs LLC 330 533-8943
330 Newton St Canfield (44406) **(G-2189)**
Facility Services, Akron *Also called Akron Public School Maint Svcs* **(G-51)**
Facility Svcs & Maint Systems, Middletown *Also called Justin L Paulk* **(G-14481)**
Facilitysource LLC 614 318-1700
200 E Campus View Blvd Columbus (43235) **(G-7627)**
Fackler Country Gardens Inc (PA) 740 522-3128
2326 Newark Granville Rd Granville (43023) **(G-11465)**
Facklers, Granville *Also called Country Gardens* **(G-11463)**
Factory Mutual Insurance Co 440 779-0651
25050 Country Club Blvd # 400 North Olmsted (44070) **(G-15421)**
Factory Mutual Insurance Co 513 742-9516
9 Woodcrest Dr Cincinnati (45246) **(G-3588)**
Facts Management Company 440 892-4272
909 Canterbury Rd Ste P Westlake (44145) **(G-19483)**
Faf Inc 800 496-4696
6800 Port Rd Groveport (43125) **(G-11638)**
Fahlgren Inc (PA) 614 383-1500
4030 Easton Sta Ste 300 Columbus (43219) **(G-7628)**
Fahlgren Inc 614 383-1500
4030 Easton Sta Ste 300 Columbus (43219) **(G-7629)**
Fair Haven Shelby County Home, Sidney *Also called County of Shelby* **(G-16926)**
Fairborn Equipment Company Inc (PA) 419 209-0760
225 Tarhe Trl Upper Sandusky (43351) **(G-18560)**
Fairborn Fish 937 879-1313
101 Mann Ave Fairborn (45324) **(G-10794)**
Fairborn Fish Organization, Fairborn *Also called Fairborn Fish* **(G-10794)**
Fairborn Pre School & Day Care, Fairborn *Also called Fairborn St Luke Untd Mthdst* **(G-10795)**
Fairborn Sftball Offcials Assn 937 902-9920
8740 Cannondale Ln Dayton (45424) **(G-9538)**
Fairborn St Luke Untd Mthdst 937 878-5042
100 N Broad St Fairborn (45324) **(G-10795)**
Fairborn YMCA 937 754-9622
300 S Central Ave Fairborn (45324) **(G-10796)**
Fairchild MD Leasing Co LLC 330 678-4912
1290 Fairchild Ave Kent (44240) **(G-12369)**
Fairfax Health Care Center, Cleveland *Also called Inner City Nursing Home* **(G-5822)**
Fairfeld Bnquet Convention Ctr, Fairfield *Also called Toris Station* **(G-10915)**
Fairfeld Inn Stes Clmbus Arprt 614 237-2100
4300 International Gtwy Columbus (43219) **(G-7630)**
Fairfield Center, Fairfield *Also called Alexson Services Inc* **(G-10819)**
Fairfield Cnty Chld Prtctd, Lancaster *Also called Fairfield County* **(G-12531)**
Fairfield Cnty Job & Fmly Svcs 800 450-8845
239 W Main St Lancaster (43130) **(G-12529)**
Fairfield Community Health Ctr 740 277-6043
1155 E Main St Lancaster (43130) **(G-12530)**
Fairfield County 740 653-4060
239 W Main St Lancaster (43130) **(G-12531)**
Fairfield Diagnstc Imaging LLC 740 654-7559
1241 River Valley Blvd Lancaster (43130) **(G-12532)**
Fairfield Federal Sav Ln Assn (PA) 740 653-3863
111 E Main St Lancaster (43130) **(G-12533)**
Fairfield Gravel, Fairfield *Also called Martin Marietta Materials Inc* **(G-10875)**
Fairfield Homes Inc (PA) 740 653-3583
603 W Wheeling St Lancaster (43130) **(G-12534)**
Fairfield Homes Inc (PA) 740 653-3583
603 W Wheeling St Lancaster (43130) **(G-12535)**
Fairfield Homes Inc 614 873-3533
445 Fairfield Dr Ofc Plain City (43064) **(G-16192)**
Fairfield Industries Inc 740 652-7230
4465 Coonpath Rd Carroll (43112) **(G-2608)**
Fairfield Inn, Westerville *Also called Polaris Innkeepers Inc* **(G-19341)**
Fairfield Inn, Canton *Also called Marriott International Inc* **(G-2449)**
Fairfield Inn, Athens *Also called Athens OH 1013 LLC* **(G-776)**
Fairfield Inn, Stow *Also called Roce Group LLC* **(G-17390)**
Fairfield Inn, Reynoldsburg *Also called First Hospitality Company LLC* **(G-16452)**
Fairfield Inn, Cincinnati *Also called Tharaldson Hospitality MGT* **(G-2935)**
Fairfield Inn, Youngstown *Also called Alliance Hospitality* **(G-20100)**
Fairfield Inn, Willoughby *Also called Tramz Hotels LLC* **(G-19718)**
Fairfield Inn 614 267-1111
3031 Olentangy River Rd Columbus (43202) **(G-7631)**
Fairfield Insul & Drywall Inc 740 654-8811
1655 Election House Rd Nw Lancaster (43130) **(G-12536)**
Fairfield Medical Center, Lancaster *Also called Fairfield Diagnstc Imaging LLC* **(G-12532)**
Fairfield Medical Center (PA) 740 687-8000
401 N Ewing St Lancaster (43130) **(G-12537)**
Fairfield National Bank (HQ) 740 653-7242
143 W Main St Lancaster (43130) **(G-12538)**
Fairfield Tempo Club 513 863-2081
8800 Holden Blvd Fairfield (45014) **(G-10850)**
Fairfield YMCA, Hamilton *Also called Great Miami Valley YMCA* **(G-11733)**
Fairfield YMCA Pre-School, Fairfield *Also called Great Miami Valley YMCA* **(G-10854)**
Fairfld Ctr For Disablts & CER 740 653-1186
681 E 6th Ave Lancaster (43130) **(G-12539)**
Fairhaven Community, Upper Sandusky *Also called United Church Homes Inc* **(G-18568)**
Fairhaven Sheltered Workshop 330 652-1116
6000 Youngstown Warren Rd Niles (44446) **(G-15291)**
Fairhaven Sheltered Workshop 330 847-7275
455 Educational Hwy Nw Warren (44483) **(G-18857)**
Fairhaven Sheltered Workshop (PA) 330 505-3644
45 North Rd Niles (44446) **(G-15292)**
Fairhope Hospice and Palliativ 740 654-7077
282 Sells Rd Lancaster (43130) **(G-12540)**
Fairlawn Associates Ltd 330 867-5000
3180 W Market St Fairlawn (44333) **(G-10949)**
Fairlawn Country Club Company 330 836-5541
200 N Wheaton Rd Akron (44313) **(G-213)**
Fairlawn Medical Offices, Fairlawn *Also called Kaiser Foundation Hospitals* **(G-10961)**
Fairlawn Opco LLC 502 429-8062
575 S Clvland Mssillon Rd Fairlawn (44333) **(G-10950)**
Fairmont Nursing Home Inc 440 338-8220
10190 Fairmount Rd Newbury (44065) **(G-15256)**
Fairmount Elementary School, Canton *Also called Canton City School District* **(G-2284)**
Fairmount Minerals LLC 269 926-9450
8834 Mayfield Rd Ste A Chesterland (44026) **(G-2795)**
Fairmount Montessori Assn 216 321-7571
3380 Fairmount Blvd Cleveland (44118) **(G-5565)**
Fairmount Santrol, Chesterland *Also called Fairmount Minerals LLC* **(G-2795)**
Fairpoint Long Distance, Germantown *Also called Quality One Technologies Inc* **(G-11401)**
Fairpoint Long Distance, Germantown *Also called Orwell Communications Inc* **(G-11400)**
Fairport Enterprises Inc 330 830-9988
2000 Sherman Cir Ne Massillon (44646) **(G-13806)**
Fairview Eye Center Inc 440 333-3060
21375 Lorain Rd Cleveland (44126) **(G-5566)**
Fairview Hlth Sys Fderal Cr Un 216 476-7000
18101 Lorain Ave Cleveland (44111) **(G-5567)**
FAIRVIEW HOMES, Carlisle *Also called Society For Handicapped Citzns* **(G-2606)**
Fairview Hospital, Cleveland *Also called Sabry Hospital* **(G-6431)**
Fairview Hospital (HQ) 216 476-7000
18101 Lorain Ave Cleveland (44111) **(G-5568)**
Fairview Hospital 440 871-1063
850 Columbia Rd Ste 100 Westlake (44145) **(G-19484)**
Fairview Skilled Nursing & Reh, Toledo *Also called Covenant Care Ohio Inc* **(G-17840)**
FAIRVIEW WEST PHYSICIAN CENTER, Cleveland *Also called Auxiliary Bd Fairview Gen Hosp* **(G-5084)**
Fairway Independent Mrtg Corp 513 367-6344
1180 Stone Dr Harrison (45030) **(G-11798)**
Fairway Independent Mrtg Corp 614 930-6552
4215 Worth Ave Ste 220 Columbus (43219) **(G-7632)**
Fairways 440 943-2050
30630 Ridge Rd Wickliffe (44092) **(G-19596)**
Faith Christian Accademy, Columbus *Also called Columbus Christian Center Inc* **(G-7337)**
Faith Mission Inc (HQ) 614 224-6617
245 N Grant Ave Columbus (43215) **(G-7633)**

ALPHABETIC

Faith Mission Inc ALPHABETIC SECTION

Faith Mission Inc 614 224-6617
245 N Grant Ave Columbus (43215) *(G-7634)*
Faithful Companions Inc 440 255-4357
8500 Station St Ste 111 Mentor (44060) *(G-14174)*
Fak Group Inc 440 498-8465
6750 Arnold Miller Pkwy Solon (44139) *(G-17006)*
Falcon Plaza LLC 419 352-4671
1450 E Wooster St Ste 401 Bowling Green (43402) *(G-1775)*
Falcon Transport Co (PA) 330 793-1345
4944 Belmont Ave Ste 201 Youngstown (44505) *(G-20185)*
Falcon Transport Co 330 793-1345
4944 Belmont Ave Ste 201 Youngstown (44505) *(G-20186)*
Fallen Timbers Fmly Physicians 419 893-3321
5705 Monclova Rd Maumee (43537) *(G-13913)*
Falling Leasing Co LLC 440 238-1100
18840 Falling Water Rd Strongsville (44136) *(G-17463)*
Falling Star Farm Ltd 419 945-2651
626 State Route 89 Polk (44866) *(G-16230)*
Falling Water Healthcare Ctr, Strongsville *Also called Falling Leasing Co LLC (G-17463)*
Falls Chrysler Jeep Dodge, Cuyahoga Falls *Also called Falls Motor City Inc (G-9184)*
Falls Dermatology, Cuyahoga Falls *Also called Falls Family Practice Inc (G-9182)*
Falls Family Practice Inc (PA) 330 923-9585
857 Graham Rd Cuyahoga Falls (44221) *(G-9182)*
Falls Heating & Cooling Inc 330 929-8777
461 Munroe Falls Ave Cuyahoga Falls (44221) *(G-9183)*
Falls Motor City Inc 330 929-3066
4100 State Rd Cuyahoga Falls (44223) *(G-9184)*
Falls Stamping & Welding Co (PA) 330 928-1191
2900 Vincent St Cuyahoga Falls (44221) *(G-9185)*
Falls Supersonic Car Wash Inc 330 928-1657
2720 2nd St Cuyahoga Falls (44221) *(G-9186)*
Falls Village Retirement Cmnty 330 945-9797
330 Broadway St E Cuyahoga Falls (44221) *(G-9187)*
Fallsway Equipment Co Inc (PA) 330 633-6000
1277 Devalera St Akron (44310) *(G-214)*
Famicos Foundation 216 791-6476
1325 Ansel Rd Cleveland (44106) *(G-5569)*
FAMILIES THAT WORK, Ravenna *Also called Family Cmnty Svcs Portage Cnty (G-16385)*
Family & Child Abuse (PA) 419 244-3053
2460 Cherry St Toledo (43608) *(G-17876)*
Family Birth Center Lima Mem 419 998-4570
1001 Bellefontaine Ave Lima (45804) *(G-12776)*
Family Child Learning Center, Tallmadge *Also called Childrens Hosp Med Ctr Akron (G-17634)*
Family Cmnty Svcs Portage Cnty 330 297-0078
705 Oakwood St Ravenna (44266) *(G-16385)*
Family Counseling Services, Newark *Also called Woodlnds Srving Centl Ohio Inc (G-15248)*
FAMILY COUNSELING SERVICES OF, Cuyahoga Falls *Also called Trillium Family Solutions Inc (G-9227)*
Family Dental Team Inc (PA) 330 733-7911
620 Ridgewood Xing Ste K Fairlawn (44333) *(G-10951)*
Family Dentistry Inc (PA) 513 932-6991
600 Mound Ct Lebanon (45036) *(G-12605)*
Family Entertainment Services 740 286-8587
780 Rock Run Rd Jackson (45640) *(G-12311)*
Family Ford Lincoln Inc 740 373-9127
909 Pike St Marietta (45750) *(G-13445)*
Family Guidance Center, Ironton *Also called Ironton and Lawrence County (G-12292)*
Family Health Care Center Inc 614 274-4171
2800 W Broad St Ste B Columbus (43204) *(G-7635)*
Family Health Partners Inc 419 935-0196
315 Crestwood Dr Willard (44890) *(G-19619)*
Family Health Plan Inc 419 241-6501
2200 Jefferson Ave Fl 6 Toledo (43604) *(G-17877)*
Family Heritg Lf Insur Co Amer (HQ) 440 922-5200
6001 E Royalton Rd # 200 Broadview Heights (44147) *(G-1879)*
Family Hlth Svcs Drke Cnty Inc (PA) 937 548-3806
5735 Meeker Rd Greenville (45331) *(G-11500)*
Family Home Health Plus, Gallipolis *Also called Ohio Valley Home Health Inc (G-11334)*
Family Life Counseling (PA) 419 774-9969
151 Marion Ave Lowr Lvl Mansfield (44903) *(G-13299)*
Family Lincoln, Marietta *Also called Family Ford Lincoln Inc (G-13445)*
Family Lrng Ctr At Sentinel 419 448-5079
797 E Township Road 201 Tiffin (44883) *(G-17678)*
Family Mdcine Ctr At St Thomas, Akron *Also called Summa Health System (G-460)*
Family Medical Group 513 389-1400
6331 Glenway Ave Cincinnati (45211) *(G-3589)*
Family Medicine Center Minerva 330 868-4184
200 Carolyn Ct Minerva (44657) *(G-14645)*
Family Medicine Stark County 330 499-5600
6512 Whipple Ave Nw Canton (44720) *(G-2363)*
Family Motor Coach Assn Inc (PA) 513 474-3622
8291 Clough Pike Cincinnati (45244) *(G-3590)*
Family Nursing Services Inc 740 775-5463
24 Star Dr Chillicothe (45601) *(G-2836)*
Family Physicans Associates, Cleveland *Also called Terence Isakov MD (G-6583)*
Family Physician Associates 614 901-2273
291 W Schrock Rd Westerville (43081) *(G-19399)*
Family Physicians Associates (PA) 440 442-3866
5187 Mayfield Rd Ste 102 Cleveland (44124) *(G-5570)*
Family Physicians Inc 330 494-7099
4860 Frank Ave Nw Canton (44720) *(G-2364)*
Family Physicians of Coshocton 740 622-0332
440 Browns Ln Coshocton (43812) *(G-9102)*
Family Physicians of Gahanna 614 471-9654
535 Officenter Pl Ste A Columbus (43230) *(G-7636)*
Family Planning Center 740 439-3340
326 Highland Ave Cambridge (43725) *(G-2112)*
Family Plnning Assoc of Ne (PA) 440 352-0608
54 S State St Ste 203 Painesville (44077) *(G-15856)*
Family Practice & Associates 937 399-6650
2701 Moorefield Rd Springfield (45502) *(G-17196)*
Family Practice Center Akron, Akron *Also called Summa Health System (G-457)*
Family Practice Center Inc 330 682-3075
365 S Crown Hill Rd Orrville (44667) *(G-15770)*
Family Practice Ctr Salem Inc 330 332-9961
2370 Southeast Blvd Salem (44460) *(G-16695)*
Family Recovery Center Inc (PA) 330 424-1468
964 N Market St Lisbon (44432) *(G-12937)*
Family Resource Centers, Findlay *Also called Family Rsource Ctr NW Ohio Inc (G-11023)*
Family Rsource Ctr NW Ohio Inc (PA) 419 222-1168
530 S Main St Lima (45804) *(G-12777)*
Family Rsource Ctr NW Ohio Inc 419 422-8616
1941 Carlin St Findlay (45840) *(G-11023)*
Family Senior Care Inc 740 441-1428
859 3rd Ave Gallipolis (45631) *(G-11315)*
Family Service (PA) 513 381-6300
3730 Glenway Ave Cincinnati (45205) *(G-3591)*
FAMILY SERVICE AGENCY, Youngstown *Also called Compass Family and Cmnty Svcs (G-20153)*
Family Service Agency, Youngstown *Also called Rape Information & Counseling (G-20341)*
Family Service Association 937 222-9481
2211 Arbor Blvd Moraine (45439) *(G-14783)*
Family Service of NW Ohio (PA) 419 321-6455
701 Jefferson Ave Ste 301 Toledo (43604) *(G-17878)*
FAMILY SERVICES AND COMMUNITY, Moraine *Also called Family Service Association (G-14783)*
Family Stations Inc 330 783-9986
3930 Sunset Blvd Youngstown (44512) *(G-20187)*
Family Video Movie Club Inc 937 846-1021
401 N Main St New Carlisle (45344) *(G-15023)*
Family YMCA of LANcstr&fairfld 740 277-7373
1180 E Locust St Lancaster (43130) *(G-12541)*
Family YMCA of LANcstr&fairfld (PA) 740 654-0616
465 W 6th Ave Lancaster (43130) *(G-12542)*
Famous Distribution Inc (HQ) 330 762-9621
2620 Ridgewood Rd Ste 200 Akron (44313) *(G-215)*
Famous Distribution Inc 330 434-5194
166 N Union St Akron (44304) *(G-216)*
Famous Enterprises Inc 330 938-6350
350 Courtney Rd Sebring (44672) *(G-16822)*
Famous Enterprises Inc 216 529-1010
11200 Madison Ave Cleveland (44102) *(G-5571)*
Famous Enterprises Inc 419 478-0343
220 Matzinger Rd Toledo (43612) *(G-17879)*
Famous Enterprises Inc (PA) 330 762-9621
2620 Ridgewood Rd Ste 200 Akron (44313) *(G-217)*
Famous II Inc (PA) 330 762-9621
2620 Ridgewood Rd Ste 200 Akron (44313) *(G-218)*
Famous Industries Inc (HQ) 330 535-1811
2620 Ridgewood Rd Ste 200 Akron (44313) *(G-219)*
Famous Industries Inc 330 535-1811
166 N Union St Akron (44304) *(G-220)*
Famous Manufacturing, Akron *Also called Famous Enterprises Inc (G-217)*
Famous Supply Companies, Akron *Also called Famous Distribution Inc (G-215)*
Fanning/Howey Associates Inc 614 764-4661
4930 Bradenton Ave Dublin (43017) *(G-10345)*
Fanning/Howey Associates Inc 919 831-1831
4930 Bradenton Ave Dublin (43017) *(G-10346)*
Fantastic Sams, Oak Hill *Also called Legrand Services Inc (G-15619)*
FANTON Logistics Inc (PA) 216 341-2400
10801 Broadway Ave Cleveland (44125) *(G-5572)*
Far Oaks Orthopedists Inc 937 433-5309
3737 Sthern Blvd Ste 2100 Dayton (45429) *(G-9539)*
Far Oaks Orthopedists Inc 937 298-0452
55 Elva Ct Ste 100 Vandalia (45377) *(G-18678)*
Far Oaks Orthopedists Inc (PA) 937 433-5309
6490 Centervl Bus Pkwy Dayton (45459) *(G-9540)*
Farber Corporation 614 294-1626
800 E 12th Ave Columbus (43211) *(G-7637)*
Farm Credit Mid-America 740 441-9312
2368 Blizzard Ln Albany (45710) *(G-519)*
Farm House Food Distrs Inc 216 791-6948
9000 Woodland Ave Cleveland (44104) *(G-5573)*
Farm Inc 513 922-7020
239 Anderson Ferry Rd Cincinnati (45238) *(G-3592)*
Farmer Smiths Market, Dover *Also called Barkett Fruit Co Inc (G-10176)*
Farmers & Merchants State Bank (HQ) 419 446-2501
307-11 N Defiance St Archbold (43502) *(G-636)*
Farmers Bank & Savings Co Inc (PA) 740 992-0088
211 W 2nd St Pomeroy (45769) *(G-16232)*

FARMERS CASTLE MUSEUM EDUCATIO, Belpre *Also called Belpre Historical Society (G-1433)*
Farmers Citizens Bank (HQ)....419 562-7040
105 Washington Sq Bucyrus (44820) *(G-2037)*
Farmers Equipment Inc....419 339-7000
6008 Elida Rd Lima (45807) *(G-12778)*
Farmers Equipment Inc (PA)....419 339-7000
1749 E Us Highway 36 A Urbana (43078) *(G-18586)*
Farmers Financial Services....937 424-0643
3888 Indian Ripple Rd Beavercreek (45440) *(G-1240)*
Farmers Group Inc....614 406-2424
2500 Farmers Dr Columbus (43235) *(G-7638)*
Farmers Group Inc....330 467-6575
500 W Aurora Rd Ste 115 Northfield (44067) *(G-15515)*
Farmers Group Inc....614 766-6005
7400 Safelite Way Columbus (43235) *(G-7639)*
Farmers Group Inc....614 799-3200
2545 Farmers Dr Ste 440 Columbus (43235) *(G-7640)*
Farmers Group Inc....216 750-4010
5990 W Creek Rd Ste 160 Independence (44131) *(G-12211)*
Farmers Insurance, Columbus *Also called Farmers Group Inc (G-7638)*
Farmers Insurance, Northfield *Also called Farmers Group Inc (G-15515)*
Farmers Insurance, Columbus *Also called Farmers Group Inc (G-7639)*
Farmers Insurance, Columbus *Also called Farmers Group Inc (G-7640)*
Farmers Insurance, Independence *Also called Farmers Group Inc (G-12211)*
Farmers Insurance, Columbus *Also called Farmers New World Lf Insur Co (G-7642)*
Farmers Insurance of Columbus (HQ)....614 799-3200
7400 Skyline Dr E Columbus (43235) *(G-7641)*
Farmers Nat Bnk of Canfield (HQ)....330 533-3341
20 S Broad St Canfield (44406) *(G-2190)*
Farmers National Bank....330 544-7447
51 S Main St Niles (44446) *(G-15293)*
Farmers National Bank....330 682-1010
112 W Market St Orrville (44667) *(G-15771)*
Farmers National Bank....330 385-9200
16924 Saint Clair Ave East Liverpool (43920) *(G-10521)*
Farmers National Bank....330 682-1030
1444 N Main St Orrville (44667) *(G-15772)*
Farmers New World Lf Insur Co....614 764-9975
2500 Farmers Dr Columbus (43235) *(G-7642)*
Farmers Produce Auction, Mount Hope *Also called Mt Hope Auction Inc (G-14866)*
Farmers Savings Bank (PA)....330 648-2441
111 W Main St Spencer (44275) *(G-17106)*
Farmersville Fire Assn Inc....937 696-2863
207 N Elm St Farmersville (45325) *(G-10983)*
Farmersville Fire Department, Farmersville *Also called Farmersville Fire Assn Inc (G-10983)*
Faro Services Inc (PA)....614 497-1700
7070 Pontius Rd Groveport (43125) *(G-11639)*
Farris Enterprises Inc (PA)....614 367-9611
7465 Worthington Galena Worthington (43085) *(G-19960)*
Farris Produce Inc....330 837-4607
2421 Lincoln Way Nw Massillon (44647) *(G-13807)*
Farrish & Farrish Lpa, Cincinnati *Also called Kelly Farrish Lpa (G-3909)*
Farrow Cleaners Co (PA)....216 561-2355
3788 Lee Rd Cleveland (44128) *(G-5574)*
Faruki Ireland & Cox Pllc (PA)....937 227-3700
500 Courthouse Plz 10 Dayton (45402) *(G-9541)*
Fascor Inc....513 421-1777
11260 Chester Rd Ste 100 Cincinnati (45246) *(G-3593)*
Fashion Wallcoverings Inc....216 432-1600
4005 Carnegie Ave Cleveland (44103) *(G-5575)*
Fast Eddys Grounds Maint LLC....740 599-2955
19280 Coshocton Rd Mount Vernon (43050) *(G-14896)*
Fast Switch Ltd....614 336-1122
4900 Blazer Pkwy Dublin (43017) *(G-10347)*
Fast Track Auction Sales, Avon Lake *Also called DMR Management Inc (G-928)*
Fast Traxx Promotions LLC....740 767-3740
17575 Jacksonville Rd Millfield (45761) *(G-14632)*
Fastball Spt Productions LLC....440 746-8000
1333 Lakeside Ave E Cleveland (44114) *(G-5576)*
Fastems LLC....513 779-4614
9850 Windisch Rd West Chester (45069) *(G-19072)*
Fastener Corp of America Inc....440 835-5100
1133 Bassett Rd Westlake (44145) *(G-19485)*
Fastener Industries Inc....440 891-2031
33 Lou Groza Blvd Berea (44017) *(G-1459)*
Faster Inc....419 868-8197
6560 Weatherfield Ct Maumee (43537) *(G-13914)*
Fat Jacks Pizza II Inc (PA)....419 227-1813
1806 N West St Lima (45801) *(G-12779)*
Fathom Online Marketing, Cleveland *Also called Fathom Seo LLC (G-5577)*
Fathom Seo LLC....614 291-8456
1465 Northwest Blvd Columbus (43212) *(G-7643)*
Fathom Seo LLC (PA)....216 525-0510
8200 Sweet Valley Dr Cleveland (44125) *(G-5577)*
Faulkner Grmhsen Keister Shenk (PA)....937 492-1271
100 S Main Ave Sidney (45365) *(G-16932)*
Faurecia Exhaust Systems LLC (HQ)....419 727-5000
543 Matzinger Rd Toledo (43612) *(G-17880)*
Fauster-Cameron Inc (PA)....419 784-1414
1400 E 2nd St Defiance (43512) *(G-10030)*
Favret Company....614 488-5211
1296 Dublin Rd Columbus (43215) *(G-7644)*
Favret Heating & Cooling, Columbus *Also called Favret Company (G-7644)*
Fawcett Center For Tomorrow, Columbus *Also called Ohio State University (G-8427)*
Fay Apartments, Cincinnati *Also called Fay Limited Partnership (G-3594)*
Fay Industries Inc....440 572-5030
17200 Foltz Pkwy Strongsville (44149) *(G-17464)*
Fay Limited Partnership....513 542-8333
3710 President Dr Cincinnati (45225) *(G-3594)*
Fay Limited Partnership (PA)....513 241-1911
36 E 4th St 1320 Cincinnati (45202) *(G-3595)*
Fay Sharpe LLP....216 363-9000
The Halle Bldg 1228e Cleveland (44115) *(G-5578)*
Fayette County Family YMCA, Wshngtn CT Hs *Also called Fayette County Family YMCA (G-20021)*
Fayette County Family YMCA....740 335-0477
100 Civic Dr Wshngtn CT Hs (43160) *(G-20021)*
Fayette County Memorial Hosp (PA)....740 335-1210
1430 Columbus Ave Wshngtn CT Hs (43160) *(G-20022)*
Fayette County Mrdd, Wshngtn CT Hs *Also called Fayette Progressive Industries (G-20023)*
Fayette Parts Service Inc....740 282-4547
1512 Sunset Blvd Steubenville (43952) *(G-17316)*
Fayette Parts Service Inc....724 880-3616
618 Canton Rd Wintersville (43953) *(G-19810)*
Fayette Progressive Industries....740 335-7453
1330 Robinson Rd Se Wshngtn CT Hs (43160) *(G-20023)*
FB Wright of Cincinnati, West Chester *Also called F B Wright Co Cincinnati (G-19071)*
Fc 1346 LLC....330 864-8170
118 Hollywood Ave Akron (44313) *(G-221)*
Fc Continental Landlord LLC....216 621-6060
50 Public Sq Ste 1360 Cleveland (44113) *(G-5579)*
FC Schwendler LLC....330 733-8715
724 Canton Rd Akron (44312) *(G-222)*
FCA US LLC....419 727-2800
4400 Chrysler Dr Toledo (43608) *(G-17881)*
FCA US LLC....419 729-5959
5925 Hagman Rd Toledo (43612) *(G-17882)*
Fchc, Lancaster *Also called Fairfield Community Health Ctr (G-12530)*
Fchs, Dayton *Also called First Community Hlth Svcs LLC (G-9547)*
Fcx Performance Inc (HQ)....614 324-6050
3000 E 14th Ave Columbus (43219) *(G-7645)*
Fdc Enterprises Inc....614 774-9182
5470 Ballentine Pike Springfield (45502) *(G-17197)*
Fdc Machine Repair Inc....216 362-1082
5585 Venture Dr Parma (44130) *(G-15907)*
Feazel Roofing Company....614 898-7663
5855 Chandler Ct Westerville (43082) *(G-19306)*
Fechko Excavating Inc....330 722-2890
865 W Liberty St Ste 120 Medina (44256) *(G-14064)*
Fed Ex Rob Carpenter....419 260-1889
4348 Beck Dr Maumee (43537) *(G-13915)*
Fed/Matrix A Joint Venture LLC....863 665-6363
249 Wayne Ave Dayton (45402) *(G-9542)*
Fedeli Group Inc....216 328-8080
5005 Rockside Rd Ste 500 Cleveland (44131) *(G-5580)*
Federal Equipment Company, Cleveland *Also called Federal Machinery & Eqp Co (G-5582)*
Federal Express Corporation....800 463-3339
2578 Corporate Pl Miamisburg (45342) *(G-14301)*
Federal Express Corporation....800 463-3339
65 Paragon Pkwy Mansfield (44903) *(G-13300)*
Federal Express Corporation....614 492-6106
7066 Cargo Rd Columbus (43217) *(G-7646)*
Federal Express Corporation....800 463-3339
5313 Majestic Pkwy Bedford (44146) *(G-1306)*
Federal Express Corporation....800 463-3339
3499 Saint Johns Rd Lima (45804) *(G-12780)*
Federal Express Corporation....800 463-3339
7600 Caple Blvd Northwood (43619) *(G-15531)*
Federal Express Corporation....800 463-3339
2424 Citygate Dr Columbus (43219) *(G-7647)*
Federal Express Corporation....800 463-3339
2850 International St Columbus (43228) *(G-7648)*
Federal Express Corporation....800 463-3339
3605 Concorde Dr Vandalia (45377) *(G-18679)*
Federal Express Corporation....800 463-3339
3301 Bruening Ave Sw Canton (44706) *(G-2365)*
Federal Express Corporation....937 898-3474
10340 Freight Dr Vandalia (45377) *(G-18680)*
Federal Home Ln Bnk Cincinnati (PA)....513 852-7500
600 Atrium Two # 2 Cincinnati (45201) *(G-3596)*
Federal Home Ln Bnk Cincinnati....513 852-5719
1000 Atrium 2 Cincinnati (45202) *(G-3597)*
Federal Hose Manufacturing, Painesville *Also called First Francis Company Inc (G-15857)*
Federal Insurance Company....216 687-1700
1375 E 9th St Ste 1960 Cleveland (44114) *(G-5581)*
Federal Insurance Company....513 721-0601
312 Walnut St Ste 2100 Cincinnati (45202) *(G-3598)*
Federal Machinery & Eqp Co (PA)....800 652-2466
8200 Bessemer Ave Cleveland (44127) *(G-5582)*
Federal Probation, Columbus *Also called Supreme Court United States (G-8808)*

ALPHABETIC

Federal Rsrve Bnk of Cleveland (HQ).....216 579-2000
1455 E 6th St Cleveland (44114) ***(G-5583)***
Federal Rsrve Bnk of Cleveland.....513 721-4787
150 E 4th St Fl 3 Cincinnati (45202) ***(G-3599)***
FEDERAL SAVINGS BANK, West Chester *Also called Guardian Savings Bank* ***(G-19086)***
Federal-Mogul LLC.....740 432-2393
6420 Glenn Hwy Cambridge (43725) ***(G-2113)***
Federated Logistics.....937 294-3074
2260 Arbor Blvd Moraine (45439) ***(G-14784)***
Federer Homes and Gardens RE, Dayton *Also called Big Hill Realty Corp* ***(G-9356)***
Fedex, Miamisburg *Also called Federal Express Corporation* ***(G-14301)***
Fedex, Mansfield *Also called Federal Express Corporation* ***(G-13300)***
Fedex, Columbus *Also called Federal Express Corporation* ***(G-7646)***
Fedex, Bedford *Also called Federal Express Corporation* ***(G-1306)***
Fedex, Lima *Also called Federal Express Corporation* ***(G-12780)***
Fedex, Northwood *Also called Federal Express Corporation* ***(G-15531)***
Fedex, Columbus *Also called Federal Express Corporation* ***(G-7647)***
Fedex, Columbus *Also called Federal Express Corporation* ***(G-7648)***
Fedex, Vandalia *Also called Federal Express Corporation* ***(G-18679)***
Fedex, Canton *Also called Federal Express Corporation* ***(G-2365)***
Fedex, Vandalia *Also called Federal Express Corporation* ***(G-18680)***
Fedex Corporation.....440 234-0315
17831 Englewood Dr Cleveland (44130) ***(G-5584)***
Fedex Corporation.....614 801-0953
3423 Southpark Pl Grove City (43123) ***(G-11559)***
Fedex Custom Critical Inc (HQ).....234 310-4090
1475 Boettler Rd Uniontown (44685) ***(G-18519)***
Fedex Freight Inc.....330 645-0879
678 Killian Rd Akron (44319) ***(G-223)***
Fedex Freight Inc.....937 233-4826
8101 Terminal Ln Dayton (45424) ***(G-9543)***
Fedex Freight Corporation.....800 979-9232
377 Gateway Dr Chillicothe (45601) ***(G-2837)***
Fedex Freight Corporation.....877 661-8956
7685 Saint Clair Ave Mentor (44060) ***(G-14175)***
Fedex Freight Corporation.....419 729-1755
5657 Enterprise Blvd Toledo (43612) ***(G-17883)***
Fedex Freight Corporation.....800 390-0159
160 Industrial Pkwy Mansfield (44903) ***(G-13301)***
Fedex Freight Corporation.....800 521-3505
2335 Saint Johns Rd Lima (45804) ***(G-12781)***
Fedex Freight Corporation.....800 344-6448
10 Commerce Pkwy West Jefferson (43162) ***(G-19251)***
Fedex Freight Corporation.....800 728-8190
7779 Arbor Dr Northwood (43619) ***(G-15532)***
Fedex Freight Corporation.....800 354-9489
1705 Moxahala Ave Zanesville (43701) ***(G-20477)***
Fedex Ground Package Sys Inc.....800 463-3339
1415 Industrial Dr Chillicothe (45601) ***(G-2838)***
Fedex Ground Package Sys Inc.....800 463-3339
3245 Henry Rd Richfield (44286) ***(G-16508)***
Fedex Ground Package Sys Inc.....412 859-2653
103 Anart St Steubenville (43953) ***(G-17317)***
Fedex Ground Package Sys Inc.....614 863-8000
4600 Poth Rd Columbus (43213) ***(G-7649)***
Fedex Ground Package Sys Inc.....330 244-1534
8033 Pittsburg Ave Nw Canton (44720) ***(G-2366)***
Fedex Ground Package Sys Inc.....800 463-3339
650 S Reynolds Rd Toledo (43615) ***(G-17884)***
Fedex Ground Package Sys Inc.....800 463-3339
3201 Columbia Rd Richfield (44286) ***(G-16509)***
Fedex Ground Package Sys Inc.....513 942-4330
9667 Inter Ocean Dr West Chester (45246) ***(G-19200)***
Fedex Ground Package Sys Inc.....800 463-3339
6120 S Meadows Dr Grove City (43123) ***(G-11560)***
Fedex Office & Print Svcs Inc.....440 946-6353
34800 Euclid Ave Willoughby (44094) ***(G-19664)***
Fedex Office & Print Svcs Inc.....937 436-0677
1189 Mmsburg Cntrville Rd Dayton (45459) ***(G-9544)***
Fedex Office & Print Svcs Inc.....614 621-1100
180 N High St Columbus (43215) ***(G-7650)***
Fedex Office & Print Svcs Inc.....614 538-1429
4516 Kenny Rd Columbus (43220) ***(G-7651)***
Fedex Office & Print Svcs Inc.....614 898-0000
604 W Schrock Rd Westerville (43081) ***(G-19400)***
Fedex Office & Print Svcs Inc.....216 292-2679
27450 Chagrin Blvd Beachwood (44122) ***(G-1079)***
Fedex Smartpost Inc.....800 463-3339
2969 Lewis Centre Way Grove City (43123) ***(G-11561)***
Fedex Sup Chain Dist Sys Inc.....614 277-3970
5765 Green Pointe Dr N Groveport (43125) ***(G-11640)***
Fedex Supply Chain.....412 820-3700
3795 Creekside Prk Way Lockbourne (43137) ***(G-12954)***
Fedex Supply Chain.....614 491-1518
4555 Creekside Pkwy Ste A Lockbourne (43137) ***(G-12955)***
Fedex Truckload Brokerage Inc.....234 310-4090
1475 Boettler Rd Uniontown (44685) ***(G-18520)***
Fedvendor, Alliance *Also called QBS Inc* ***(G-552)***
Feecorp Corporation (PA).....614 837-3010
7995 Allen Rd Nw Canal Winchester (43110) ***(G-2158)***
Feecorp Industrial Services.....740 533-1445
1120 Wyanoke St Ironton (45638) ***(G-12288)***
Feed Lucas County Children Inc.....419 260-1556
1501 Monroe St Ste 27 Toledo (43604) ***(G-17885)***
Feg Consulting LLC.....412 224-2263
3587 Tiffany Ridge Ln Blue Ash (45241) ***(G-1592)***
Fehr Services LLC.....513 829-9333
6200 Pleasant Ave Ste 3 Fairfield (45014) ***(G-10851)***
Feick Contractors Inc.....419 625-3241
224 E Water St Sandusky (44870) ***(G-16756)***
Feinknopf Macioce Schappa ARC.....614 297-1020
995 W 3rd Ave Columbus (43212) ***(G-7652)***
Feintool Equipment Corporation.....513 791-1118
6833 Creek Rd Blue Ash (45242) ***(G-1593)***
Feldkamp Enterprises Inc.....513 347-4500
3642 Muddy Creek Rd Cincinnati (45238) ***(G-3600)***
Feldys.....513 474-2212
8060 Beechmont Ave Cincinnati (45255) ***(G-3601)***
Feller Finch & Associates Inc (PA).....419 893-3680
1683 Woodlands Dr Ste A Maumee (43537) ***(G-13916)***
Fenton Bros Electric Co.....330 343-0093
235 Ray Ave Ne New Philadelphia (44663) ***(G-15094)***
Fenton Rigging & Contg Inc.....513 631-5500
2150 Langdon Farm Rd Cincinnati (45237) ***(G-3602)***
Fenton's Festival of Lights, New Philadelphia *Also called Fenton Bros Electric Co* ***(G-15094)***
Ferfolia Funeral Homes Inc.....216 663-4222
356 W Aurora Rd Northfield (44067) ***(G-15516)***
Ferguson 124, Hilliard *Also called Ferguson Enterprises Inc* ***(G-11901)***
Ferguson Construction Company (PA).....937 498-2381
400 Canal St Sidney (45365) ***(G-16933)***
Ferguson Construction Company.....937 274-1173
2201 Embury Park Rd Dayton (45414) ***(G-9545)***
Ferguson Enterprises Inc.....513 771-6566
2945 Crescentville Rd West Chester (45069) ***(G-19073)***
Ferguson Enterprises Inc.....614 876-8555
4363 Lyman Dr Hilliard (43026) ***(G-11901)***
Ferguson Hills Inc.....513 539-4497
7812 Mcewen Rd Ste 200 Dayton (45459) ***(G-9546)***
Ferguson Integrated Services, West Chester *Also called Ferguson Enterprises Inc* ***(G-19073)***
Feridean Commons LLC.....614 898-7488
6885 Freeman Rd Westerville (43082) ***(G-19307)***
Feridean Group Inc.....614 898-7488
6885 Freeman Rd Westerville (43082) ***(G-19308)***
Fern Exposition Services LLC (PA).....513 621-6111
645 Linn St Cincinnati (45203) ***(G-3603)***
Ferno-Washington Inc (PA).....877 733-0911
70 Weil Way Wilmington (45177) ***(G-19762)***
Ferralloy Inc.....440 250-1900
28001 Ranney Pkwy Cleveland (44145) ***(G-5585)***
Ferrante Wine Farm Inc.....440 466-8466
558 Rte 307 Geneva (44041) ***(G-11361)***
Ferrous Metal Transfer.....216 671-8500
11103 Memphis Ave Brooklyn (44144) ***(G-1906)***
Ferrous Processing and Trading, Cleveland *Also called Fpt Cleveland LLC* ***(G-5628)***
Fersenius Medical Center, Columbus *Also called Mount Carmel E Dialysis Clnc* ***(G-8194)***
Festa Food Company, Cleveland *Also called Pinata Foods Inc* ***(G-6280)***
Fetter and Son LLC.....740 465-2961
2421 Mrral Krkptrick Rd W Morral (43337) ***(G-14840)***
Fetter and Son Farms, Morral *Also called Fetter and Son LLC* ***(G-14840)***
Fetter Son Farms Ltd Lblty Co.....740 465-2961
2421 Mrral Krkptrick Rd W Morral (43337) ***(G-14841)***
Fetters Construction Inc.....419 542-0944
945 E High St Hicksville (43526) ***(G-11863)***
Fh TCH.....614 781-1645
4541 Powell Rd Ste H Powell (43065) ***(G-16334)***
Fhc Enterprises LLC.....614 271-3513
5489 Blue Ash Rd Columbus (43229) ***(G-7653)***
Fiber Systems, Dayton *Also called Industrial Fiberglass Spc Inc* ***(G-9630)***
Fidelitone Inc.....440 260-6523
17851 Englewood Dr Ste I Middleburg Heights (44130) ***(G-14381)***
Fidelity Health Care.....937 208-6400
3170 Kettering Blvd Moraine (45439) ***(G-14785)***
Fidelity National Fincl Inc.....614 865-1562
4111 Executive Pkwy # 304 Westerville (43081) ***(G-19401)***
Fidelity Properties Inc.....330 821-9700
220 E Main St Alliance (44601) ***(G-539)***
Field & Stream Bowhunters.....419 423-9861
1023 Cypress Ave Findlay (45840) ***(G-11024)***
Fields Marketing Research Inc.....513 821-6266
3814 West St Ste 110 Cincinnati (45227) ***(G-3604)***
Fields Research, Cincinnati *Also called Fields Marketing Research Inc* ***(G-3604)***
Fieldstone Farms Theraptic Rid, Chagrin Falls *Also called Therapeutic Riding Center Inc* ***(G-2736)***
Fieldstone Limited Partnership (PA).....937 293-0900
4000 Miller Valentine Ct Moraine (45439) ***(G-14786)***
Fifth Avenue Lumber Co (HQ).....614 294-0068
479 E 5th Ave Columbus (43201) ***(G-7654)***
Fifth Third Bancorp (PA).....800 972-3030
38 Fountain Square Plz Cincinnati (45202) ***(G-3605)***
Fifth Third Bank.....513 574-4457
5830 Harrison Ave Cincinnati (45248) ***(G-3606)***

ALPHABETIC SECTION

Fifth Third Bank..440 984-2402
309 N Leavitt Rd Amherst (44001) *(G-594)*
Fifth Third Bank (HQ)..................................513 579-5203
38 Fountain Square Plz Cincinnati (45202) *(G-3607)*
Fifth Third Bank..419 259-7820
606 Madison Ave Fl 8 Toledo (43604) *(G-17886)*
Fifth Third Bank..513 579-5203
Fifth 3rd Ctr 38 Fountain Cincinnati (45263) *(G-3608)*
Fifth Third Bank..330 686-0511
4070 Fishcreek Rd Cuyahoga Falls (44224) *(G-9188)*
Fifth Third Bank of NW Ohio.......................419 259-7820
1 Seagate Ste 2200 Toledo (43604) *(G-17887)*
Fifth Third Bank of Sthrn OH (HQ)..............937 840-5353
511 N High St Hillsboro (45133) *(G-11974)*
Fifth Third Bnk of Columbus OH.................614 744-7553
21 E State St Fl 4 Columbus (43215) *(G-7655)*
Fifth Third Equipment Fin Co (HQ).............800 972-3030
38 Fountain Square Plz Cincinnati (45202) *(G-3609)*
Figlio Wood Fired Pizza, Columbus *Also called Claire De Leigh Corp* *(G-7289)*
File Sharpening Company Inc.....................937 376-8268
360 W Church St Xenia (45385) *(G-20050)*
Filing Scale Company Inc............................330 425-3092
1500 Enterprise Pkwy Twinsburg (44087) *(G-18415)*
Filling Memorial Home of Mercy (PA)..........419 592-6451
N160 State Route 108 Napoleon (43545) *(G-14938)*
Filltek Fulfillment Services, West Chester *Also called Fulfillment Technologies LLC* *(G-19203)*
Filmco, Aurora *Also called Kapstone Container Corporation* *(G-844)*
Filterfresh Coffee Service Inc.....................513 681-8911
4890 Duff Dr Ste D West Chester (45246) *(G-19201)*
Filtrexx International, Akron *Also called Conwed Plas Acquisition V LLC* *(G-163)*
Finance Dept, Cleveland *Also called City of Cleveland* *(G-5254)*
Finance Dept, Cleveland *Also called City of Cleveland* *(G-5255)*
Finance System of Toledo Inc (PA).............419 578-4300
2821 N Holland Sylvania R Toledo (43615) *(G-17888)*
Financial Bookkeeping Service, Cleveland *Also called Lassiter Corporation* *(G-5927)*
Financial Design Group Inc (PA).................419 843-4737
3230 Central Park W # 100 Toledo (43617) *(G-17889)*
Financial Engines Inc...................................330 726-3100
1449 Boardman Canfield Rd Boardman (44512) *(G-1739)*
Financial Network Group Ltd......................513 469-7500
7890 E Kemper Rd Ste 200 Cincinnati (45249) *(G-3610)*
Financial Perspective Company, Westerville *Also called Thomas Rosser* *(G-19444)*
Financial Plnners of Cleveland...................440 473-1115
6095 Parkland Blvd # 210 Cleveland (44124) *(G-5586)*
Finastra USA Corporation...........................937 435-2335
8555 Gander Creek Dr Miamisburg (45342) *(G-14302)*
Findaway World LLC....................................440 893-0808
31999 Aurora Rd Solon (44139) *(G-17007)*
Findlay Country Club...................................419 422-9263
1500 Country Club Dr Findlay (45840) *(G-11025)*
Findlay Division, Findlay *Also called Shelly Company* *(G-11080)*
Findlay Implement Co (PA).........................419 424-0471
1640 Northridge Rd Findlay (45840) *(G-11026)*
Findlay Inn & Conference Ctr.....................419 422-5682
200 E Main Cross St Findlay (45840) *(G-11027)*
Findlay Laboratory Services, Lima *Also called Lima Pathology Associates Labs* *(G-12826)*
Findlay Publishing Company......................419 422-4545
551 Lake Cascade Pkwy Findlay (45840) *(G-11028)*
Findlay Truck Line Inc..................................419 422-1945
106 W Front St Findlay (45840) *(G-11029)*
Findlay Waste Water Treatment, Findlay *Also called City of Findlay* *(G-11014)*
Findlay Womens Care LLC (PA)..................419 420-0904
1917 S Main St Findlay (45840) *(G-11030)*
Findlay Y M C A Child Dev...........................419 422-3174
231 E Lincoln St Findlay (45840) *(G-11031)*
Findley Davies Inc (PA)................................419 255-1360
1 Seagate Ste 2050 Toledo (43604) *(G-17890)*
Fine Line Graphics Corp (PA)......................614 486-0276
1481 Goodale Blvd Columbus (43212) *(G-7656)*
Fine- Line Communications Inc..................330 562-0731
400 Walnut Ridge Trl Aurora (44202) *(G-838)*
Finishing Touch Cleaning Svcs, Massillon *Also called Butterfield Co Inc* *(G-13790)*
Finichmaster Inc...614 228-4328
212 N Grant Ave Columbus (43215) *(G-7657)*
Finit Group LLC..513 793-4648
8050 Hosbrook Rd Ste 326 Cincinnati (45236) *(G-3611)*
Finit Solutions, Cincinnati *Also called Finit Group LLC* *(G-3611)*
Finlaw Construction Inc..............................330 889-2074
5213 State Route 45 Bristolville (44402) *(G-1871)*
Finley Fire Equipment Co (PA)....................740 962-4328
5255 N State Route 60 Nw McConnelsville (43756) *(G-14027)*
Finneytown Contracting Corp.....................513 482-2700
5151 Fishwick Dr Cincinnati (45216) *(G-3612)*
Fiorilli Construction Co Inc.........................216 696-5845
1247 Medina Rd Medina (44256) *(G-14065)*
Fire Department, Antwerp *Also called Village of Antwerp* *(G-622)*
Fire Department, Willoughby Hills *Also called City of Willoughby Hills* *(G-19729)*
Fire Dept, Cincinnati *Also called Township of Colerain* *(G-4674)*

Fire Foe Corp..330 759-9834
999 Trumbull Ave Girard (44420) *(G-11413)*
Fire Guard LLC...740 625-5181
35 E Granville St Sunbury (43074) *(G-17556)*
Fire Station, Cleveland *Also called City of Cleveland* *(G-5257)*
Firefighters Cmnty Cr Un Inc......................216 621-4644
2300 Saint Clair Ave Ne Cleveland (44114) *(G-5587)*
Fireland Hospital, Norwalk *Also called Counseling Center Huron County* *(G-15567)*
Firelands Ambulance Service.....................419 929-1487
25 James St New London (44851) *(G-15067)*
Firelands Counseling Recovery, Tiffin *Also called Firelands Regional Health Sys* *(G-17679)*
Firelands Federal Credit Union (PA)..........419 483-4180
221 E Main St Bellevue (44811) *(G-1409)*
Firelands Physicians Group, Sandusky *Also called North Coast Prof Co LLC* *(G-16782)*
Firelands Regional Health Sys (PA)...........419 557-7400
1111 Hayes Ave Sandusky (44870) *(G-16757)*
Firelands Regional Health Sys...................419 448-9440
76 Ashwood Dr Tiffin (44883) *(G-17679)*
Firelands Regional Health Sys...................419 332-5524
675 Bartson Rd Fremont (43420) *(G-11197)*
Firelands Regional Health Sys...................419 626-7400
1101 Decatur St Sandusky (44870) *(G-16758)*
Firelands Regional Health Sys...................419 663-3737
292 Benedict Ave Norwalk (44857) *(G-15573)*
FIRELANDS REGIONAL MEDICAL CEN, Sandusky *Also called Firelands Regional Health Sys* *(G-16757)*
Firelands Security Services........................419 627-0562
1210 Sycamore Line Sandusky (44870) *(G-16759)*
FireInds Cnsling Recovery Svcs, Fremont *Also called Firelands Regional Health Sys* *(G-11197)*
FireInds Cnsling Recovery Svcs, Norwalk *Also called Firelands Regional Health Sys* *(G-15573)*
Fireproof Record Center, Grove City *Also called Briar-Gate Realty Inc* *(G-11537)*
Fireproof Records Center, Grove City *Also called Briar-Gate Realty Inc* *(G-11536)*
Firestone, Cuyahoga Falls *Also called Bridgestone Ret Operations LLC* *(G-9167)*
Firestone Country Club, Akron *Also called Akron Management Corp* *(G-48)*
Firm Hahn Law..614 221-0240
65 E State St Ste 1400 Columbus (43215) *(G-7658)*
First 2 Market Products LLC.......................419 874-5444
25671 Fort Meigs Rd Ste A Perrysburg (43551) *(G-16003)*
First Acceptance Corporation.....................614 237-9700
895 S Hamilton Rd Columbus (43213) *(G-7659)*
First Acceptance Corporation.....................937 778-8888
987 E Ash St Piqua (45356) *(G-16144)*
First Acceptance Corporation.....................513 741-0811
6150 Colerain Ave Cincinnati (45239) *(G-3613)*
First Acceptance Corporation.....................614 492-1446
3497 Parsons Ave Columbus (43207) *(G-7660)*
First Acceptance Corporation.....................330 792-7181
4774 Mahoning Ave Ste 5 Youngstown (44515) *(G-20188)*
First Acceptance Corporation.....................614 853-3344
4898 W Broad St Columbus (43228) *(G-7661)*
First American Equity Ln Svcs (HQ)...........800 221-8683
1100 Superior Ave E # 3 Cleveland (44114) *(G-5588)*
First American Title Insur Co......................216 241-1278
1100 Superior Ave E # 200 Cleveland (44114) *(G-5589)*
First American Title Insur Co......................419 625-8505
143 E Water St Sandusky (44870) *(G-16760)*
First American Title Insur Co......................740 450-0006
961 Linden Ave South Zanesville (43701) *(G-17103)*
First Amrcn Cash Advnce SC LLC..............330 644-9144
3100 Manchester Rd Akron (44319) *(G-224)*
First Amrcn Ttle Midland Title, Cleveland *Also called Midland Title Security Inc* *(G-6057)*
First Apostolic Church................................419 885-4888
5701 W Sylvania Ave Toledo (43623) *(G-17891)*
First Assembly Child Care..........................419 529-6501
1000 Mcpherson St Mansfield (44903) *(G-13302)*
First Baptist Day Care Center....................216 371-9394
3630 Fairmount Blvd Cleveland (44118) *(G-5590)*
First Business Fincl Svcs Inc......................216 573-3792
5005 Rockside Rd Ste 600 Cleveland (44131) *(G-5591)*
First Call For Help Inc..................................419 599-1660
600 Freedom Dr Napoleon (43545) *(G-14939)*
First Capital Bancshares Inc.......................740 775-6777
33 W Main St Chillicothe (45601) *(G-2839)*
First Capital Enterprises Inc........................740 773-2166
505 E 7th St Chillicothe (45601) *(G-2840)*
First Choice Cincinnati Branch, Cincinnati *Also called First Choice Medical Staffing* *(G-3614)*
First Choice Med Staff of Ohio....................330 867-1409
3200 W Market St Ste 1 Fairlawn (44333) *(G-10952)*
First Choice Med Staff of Ohio....................419 521-2700
90 W 2nd St Mansfield (44902) *(G-13303)*
First Choice Medical Staffing......................419 861-2722
5445 Sthwyck Blvd Ste 208 Toledo (43614) *(G-17892)*
First Choice Medical Staffing......................513 631-5656
1008 Marshall Ave Frnt Cincinnati (45225) *(G-3614)*
First Choice Medical Staffing......................216 521-2222
1457 W 117th St Cleveland (44107) *(G-5592)*
First Choice Medical Staffing (PA)..............216 521-2222
1457 W 117th St Cleveland (44107) *(G-5593)*

First Choice Medical Staffing 419 626-9740
1164 Cleveland Rd Sandusky (44870) *(G-16761)*
First Choice Packaging Inc (PA) 419 333-4100
1501 W State St Fremont (43420) *(G-11198)*
First Choice Packg Solutions, Fremont *Also called First Choice Packaging Inc (G-11198)*
First Christian Church 330 445-2700
6900 Market Ave N Canton (44721) *(G-2367)*
First Citizens Nat Bnk Inc (PA) 419 294-2351
100 N Sandusky Ave Upper Sandusky (43351) *(G-18561)*
First Class Limos Inc 440 248-1114
31525 Aurora Rd Ste 5 Cleveland (44139) *(G-5594)*
First Command Fincl Plg Inc 937 429-4490
51 Plum St Ste 260 Beavercreek (45440) *(G-1241)*
First Commonwealth Bank 740 548-3340
100 Delaware Xing W Delaware (43015) *(G-10094)*
First Commonwealth Bank 740 369-0048
100 Willow Brook Way S Delaware (43015) *(G-10095)*
First Commonwealth Bank 614 336-2280
10149 Brewster Ln Powell (43065) *(G-16335)*
First Commonwealth Bank 740 657-7000
110 Riverbend Ave Lewis Center (43035) *(G-12685)*
First Communications LLC 330 835-2323
3340 W Market St Fairlawn (44333) *(G-10953)*
First Communications LLC (PA) 330 835-2323
3340 W Market St Fairlawn (44333) *(G-10954)*
First Community Church (PA) 614 488-0681
1320 Cambridge Blvd Columbus (43212) *(G-7662)*
First Community Church 740 385-3827
29746 Logan Horns Mill Rd Logan (43138) *(G-12972)*
First Community Church 614 488-0681
3777 Dublin Rd Columbus (43221) *(G-7663)*
First Community Hlth Svcs LLC 937 247-0400
3634 Watertower Ln Ste 1 Dayton (45449) *(G-9547)*
First Community Mortgage Svcs, Columbus *Also called Union Mortgage Services Inc (G-8889)*
First Community Village 614 324-4455
1800 Riverside Dr Ofc Columbus (43212) *(G-7664)*
First Data Gvrnment Sltions LP 513 489-9599
11311 Cornell Park Dr Blue Ash (45242) *(G-1594)*
First Data Gvrnmnt Solutns Inc (HQ) 513 489-9599
11311 Cornell Park Dr Blue Ash (45242) *(G-1595)*
First Day Fincl Federal Cr Un (PA) 937 222-4546
1030 N Main St Dayton (45405) *(G-9548)*
FIRST DEFIANCE, Defiance *Also called First Federal Bank of Midwest (G-10031)*
First Defiance Financial Corp 419 353-8611
209 W Poe Rd Bowling Green (43402) *(G-1776)*
First Diversity MGT Group, Springfield *Also called 56 Plus Management LLC (G-17145)*
First Diversity Staffing Group 937 323-4114
560 E High St Springfield (45505) *(G-17198)*
First Energy Nuclear Oper Co 440 604-9836
6670 Beta Dr Cleveland (44143) *(G-5595)*
First Fdral Sav Ln Assn Galion 419 468-1518
140 N Columbus St Galion (44833) *(G-11294)*
First Fdral Sav Ln Assn Lkwood (PA) 216 221-7300
14806 Detroit Ave Lakewood (44107) *(G-12478)*
First Fdral Sav Ln Assn Lorain (PA) 440 282-6188
3721 Oberlin Ave Lorain (44053) *(G-13039)*
First Fdral Sav Ln Assn Newark (PA) 740 345-3494
2 N 2nd St Newark (43055) *(G-15166)*
First Fdral Sving Ln Assn Dlta (PA) 419 822-3131
404 Main St Delta (43515) *(G-10158)*
First Federal Bank of Midwest (HQ) 419 782-5015
601 Clinton St Ste 1 Defiance (43512) *(G-10031)*
First Federal Bank of Midwest 419 695-1055
230 E 2nd St Delphos (45833) *(G-10143)*
First Federal Bank of Midwest 419 855-8326
22020 Main St Genoa (43430) *(G-11376)*
First Federal Bank of Ohio (PA) 419 468-1518
140 N Columbus St Galion (44833) *(G-11295)*
First Federal Cmnty Bnk Assn (HQ) 330 364-7777
321 N Wooster Ave Dover (44622) *(G-10188)*
First Federal Credit Control 216 360-2000
24700 Chagrin Blvd # 205 Cleveland (44122) *(G-5596)*
FIRST FEDERAL SAVINGS AND LOAN, Delta *Also called First Fdral Sving Ln Assn Dlta (G-10158)*
First Financial Bancorp 513 551-5640
225 Pictoria Dr Ste 700 Cincinnati (45246) *(G-3615)*
First Financial Bank 513 979-5800
255 E 5th St Ste 2900 Cincinnati (45202) *(G-3616)*
First Financial Bank (HQ) 877 322-9530
255 E 5th St Ste 700 Cincinnati (45202) *(G-3617)*
First Fincl Title Agcy of Ohio 216 664-1920
1500 W 3rd St Ste 400 Cleveland (44113) *(G-5597)*
First Francis Company Inc (HQ) 440 352-8927
25 Florence Ave Painesville (44077) *(G-15857)*
First Fruits Child Dev Ctr I 216 862-4715
21877 Euclid Ave Euclid (44117) *(G-10755)*
First Group America, Cincinnati *Also called First Student Inc (G-3622)*
First Group Investment Partnr (HQ) 513 241-2200
600 Vine St Ste 1200 Cincinnati (45202) *(G-3618)*
First Group of America, Cincinnati *Also called Firstgroup America Inc (G-3626)*
First Hospitality Company LLC 614 864-4555
2826 Taylor Road Ext Reynoldsburg (43068) *(G-16452)*
First Hotel Associates LP 614 228-3800
310 S High St Columbus (43215) *(G-7665)*
First Hotel Management LLC 614 864-1280
2100 Brice Rd Reynoldsburg (43068) *(G-16453)*
First Interstate Properties 216 381-2900
25333 Cedar Rd Ste 300 Cleveland (44124) *(G-5598)*
First Louisville Arden LLC (HQ) 419 252-5500
333 N Summit St Toledo (43604) *(G-17893)*
First Med Urgent & Fmly Ctr 740 756-9238
1201 River Valley Blvd Lancaster (43130) *(G-12543)*
First Mental Retardation, Dayton *Also called Second Mental Retardation (G-9872)*
First Mental Retardation Corp 937 262-3077
3827 W 3rd St Dayton (45417) *(G-9549)*
First Merchants Bank 614 486-9000
2130 Tremont Ctr Columbus (43221) *(G-7666)*
First Miami Student Credit Un 513 529-1251
117 Shriver Ctr Oxford (45056) *(G-15815)*
First Nat Bnk of Nelsonville (PA) 740 753-1941
11 Public Sq Nelsonville (45764) *(G-14963)*
First National Bank Bellevue (HQ) 419 483-7340
120 North St Bellevue (44811) *(G-1410)*
First National Bank of Pandora (HQ) 419 384-3221
102 E Main St Pandora (45877) *(G-15890)*
First National Bank of Waverly (PA) 740 947-2136
107 N Market St Waverly (45690) *(G-18971)*
First National Bank of Waverly 740 493-3372
13256 State Route 124 Piketon (45661) *(G-16114)*
First National Bank PA 330 747-0292
1 W Federal St Youngstown (44503) *(G-20189)*
First National Bnk of Dennison (HQ) 740 922-2532
105 Grant St Dennison (44621) *(G-10163)*
First Ohio Banc & Lending Inc 216 642-8900
6100 Rckside Woods Blvd N Cleveland (44131) *(G-5599)*
First Ohio Home Finance Inc 937 322-3396
1021 N Limestone St Springfield (45503) *(G-17199)*
First Page, Dayton *Also called P & R Communications Svc Inc (G-9796)*
First Realty Property MGT Ltd 440 720-0100
6690 Beta Dr Ste 220 Mayfield Village (44143) *(G-14011)*
First Richmond Corp 937 783-4949
820 E Center St Blanchester (45107) *(G-1514)*
First Scan Imaging, West Chester *Also called Proscan Imaging LLC (G-19133)*
First School Corp 937 433-3455
7659 Mcewen Rd Dayton (45459) *(G-9550)*
First Services Inc 513 241-2200
600 Vine St Ste 1200 Cincinnati (45202) *(G-3619)*
First Settlement Orthopaedics (PA) 740 373-8756
611 2nd St Ste A Marietta (45750) *(G-13446)*
First State Bank (PA) 937 695-0331
19230 State Route 136 Winchester (45697) *(G-19801)*
First Student, Lorain *Also called S B S Transit Inc (G-13075)*
First Student Inc 513 531-6888
1801 Transpark Dr Cincinnati (45229) *(G-3620)*
First Student Inc 937 645-0201
1280 Charles Ln Marysville (43040) *(G-13617)*
First Student Inc 513 761-6100
100 Hamilton Blvd Cincinnati (45215) *(G-3621)*
First Student Inc 513 761-5136
100 Hamilton Blvd Cincinnati (45215) *(G-3622)*
First Student Inc 419 382-9915
419 N Westwood Ave Toledo (43607) *(G-17894)*
First Student Inc (HQ) 513 241-2200
600 Vine St Ste 1400 Cincinnati (45202) *(G-3623)*
First Transit, Cincinnati *Also called Firstgroup Usa Inc (G-3629)*
First Transit Inc 513 732-1206
2040 Us Highway 50 Batavia (45103) *(G-1013)*
First Transit Inc 937 652-4175
2200 S Us Highway 68 Urbana (43078) *(G-18587)*
First Transit Inc (HQ) 513 241-2200
600 Vine St Ste 1400 Cincinnati (45202) *(G-3624)*
First Union Banc Corp 330 896-1222
1559 Corporate Woods Pkwy Uniontown (44685) *(G-18521)*
First Vehicle Services Inc (HQ) 513 241-2200
600 Vine St Ste 1400 Cincinnati (45202) *(G-3625)*
First Virginia, Dublin *Also called Buckeye Check Cashing Inc (G-10271)*
First-Knox National Bank (HQ) 740 399-5500
1 S Main St Mount Vernon (43050) *(G-14897)*
First-Knox National Division, Mount Vernon *Also called First-Knox National Bank (G-14897)*
Firstat Nursing Services 216 295-1500
21825 Chagrin Blvd # 300 Cleveland (44122) *(G-5600)*
Firstenergy, Ashtabula *Also called Jersey Central Pwr & Light Co (G-751)*
Firstenergy, Sandusky *Also called Jersey Central Pwr & Light Co (G-16771)*
Firstenergy, Fairlawn *Also called Jersey Central Pwr & Light Co (G-10960)*
Firstenergy, Springfield *Also called Jersey Central Pwr & Light Co (G-17216)*
Firstenergy, Stratton *Also called Jersey Central Pwr & Light Co (G-17403)*
Firstenergy, Elyria *Also called Jersey Central Pwr & Light Co (G-10637)*
Firstenergy, Cleveland *Also called Jersey Central Pwr & Light Co (G-5860)*
Firstenergy, Brecksville *Also called Jersey Central Pwr & Light Co (G-1829)*
Firstenergy, Cleveland *Also called Jersey Central Pwr & Light Co (G-5861)*

Firstenergy, Painesville *Also called Jersey Central Pwr & Light Co* ***(G-15858)***
Firstenergy, Oak Harbor *Also called Jersey Central Pwr & Light Co* ***(G-15611)***
Firstenergy Corp (PA) 800 736-3402
76 S Main St Bsmt Akron (44308) ***(G-225)***
Firstenergy Nuclear Oper Co 800 646-0400
76 S Main St Bsmt Akron (44308) ***(G-226)***
Firstenterprises Inc 740 369-5100
2000 Nutter Farms Ln Delaware (43015) ***(G-10096)***
Firstgroup America Inc (HQ) 513 241-2200
600 Vine St Ste 1400 Cincinnati (45202) ***(G-3626)***
Firstgroup America Inc 513 419-8611
600 Vine St Ste 1400 Cincinnati (45202) ***(G-3627)***
Firstgroup America Inc 513 241-2200
705 Central Ave Cincinnati (45202) ***(G-3628)***
Firstgroup Usa Inc (HQ) 513 241-2200
600 Vine St Ste 1400 Cincinnati (45202) ***(G-3629)***
Firstmerit, Akron *Also called Huntington National Bank* ***(G-274)***
Firstmerit Mortgage Corp 330 478-3400
4455 Hills & Dales Rd Nw Canton (44708) ***(G-2368)***
Fischer Process Industries, Loveland *Also called Fischer Pump & Valve Company* ***(G-13125)***
Fischer Pump & Valve Company (PA) 513 583-4800
155 Commerce Dr Loveland (45140) ***(G-13125)***
Fiserv, Dublin *Also called Checkfree Services Corporation* ***(G-10288)***
Fiserv Health, Westerville *Also called Harrington Health Services Inc* ***(G-19406)***
Fish Creek Plaza Ltd 330 688-0450
3000 Graham Rd Unit Ofc Stow (44224) ***(G-17366)***
Fishbeck Thmpson Carr Hber Inc 513 469-2370
11353 Reed Hartman Hwy # 500 Blue Ash (45241) ***(G-1596)***
Fishburn Tank Truck Service 419 253-6031
5012 State Route 229 Marengo (43334) ***(G-13424)***
Fishel Company (PA) 614 274-8100
1366 Dublin Rd Columbus (43215) ***(G-7667)***
Fishel Company 614 850-9012
1600 Walcutt Rd Columbus (43228) ***(G-7668)***
Fishel Company 937 233-2268
7651 Center Point 70 Blvd Dayton (45424) ***(G-9551)***
Fishel Company 614 850-4400
1600 Walcutt Rd Columbus (43228) ***(G-7669)***
FISHEL TECHNOLOGIES, Columbus *Also called Fishel Company* ***(G-7667)***
Fisher Design Inc (PA) 513 417-8235
4101 Spring Grove Ave B Cincinnati (45223) ***(G-3630)***
Fisher Foods Marketing Inc (PA) 330 497-3000
4855 Frank Ave Nw North Canton (44720) ***(G-15337)***
Fisher-Titus Medical Center 419 668-4228
175 Shady Lane Dr Off Norwalk (44857) ***(G-15574)***
Fisher-Titus Medical Center (PA) 419 668-8101
272 Benedict Ave Norwalk (44857) ***(G-15575)***
Fit Technologies LLC 216 583-0733
1375 Euclid Ave Ste 310 Cleveland (44115) ***(G-5601)***
Fitch Inc (HQ) 614 885-3453
585 Suth Front St Ste 300 Columbus (43215) ***(G-7670)***
Fitness Center, Avon *Also called Emh Regional Medical Center* ***(G-892)***
Fitness International LLC 513 298-0134
7730 Dudley Dr West Chester (45069) ***(G-19074)***
Fitness International LLC 937 427-0700
2500 N Fairfield Rd Ste F Beavercreek (45431) ***(G-1173)***
Fitness International LLC 419 482-7740
1361 Conant St Maumee (43537) ***(G-13917)***
Fitton Family YMCA, Hamilton *Also called Great Miami Valley YMCA* ***(G-11736)***
Fitworks Fitness & Spt Therapy, Cincinnati *Also called Fitworks Holding LLC* ***(G-3632)***
Fitworks Holding LLC 330 688-2329
4301 Kent Rd Ste 26 Stow (44224) ***(G-17367)***
Fitworks Holding LLC 513 923-9931
5840 Cheviot Rd Cincinnati (45247) ***(G-3631)***
Fitworks Holding LLC 440 333-4141
20001 Center Ridge Rd Rocky River (44116) ***(G-16578)***
Fitworks Holding LLC 513 531-1500
4600 Smith Rd Ste G Cincinnati (45212) ***(G-3632)***
Fitzenrider Inc 419 784-0828
827 Perry St Defiance (43512) ***(G-10032)***
Five & Company Realty Inc 419 423-8004
1621 Tiffin Ave Findlay (45840) ***(G-11032)***
Five County Joint Juvenile Det 937 642-1015
18100 State Route 4 Marysville (43040) ***(G-13618)***
Five Rivers Dialysis, Dayton *Also called Lakeshore Dialysis LLC* ***(G-9670)***
Five Rivers Health Centers (PA) 937 734-6841
2261 Philadelphia Dr # 200 Dayton (45406) ***(G-9552)***
Five Seasons Landscape MGT Inc 740 964-2915
9886 Mink St Sw Rear Etna (43068) ***(G-10728)***
Five Seasons Spt Cntry CLB Inc 513 842-1188
11790 Snider Rd Cincinnati (45249) ***(G-3633)***
Five Seasons Spt Cntry CLB Inc 937 848-9200
4242 Clyo Rd Dayton (45440) ***(G-9553)***
Five Seasons Spt Cntry CLB Inc 440 899-4555
28105 Clemens Rd Cleveland (44145) ***(G-5602)***
Five Star Brand, Cleveland *Also called Storer Meat Co Inc* ***(G-6543)***
Five Star Power Clg & Pntg, Brewster *Also called Mike Morris* ***(G-1856)***
Five Star Senior Living Inc 614 451-6793
4590 Knightsbridge Blvd Columbus (43214) ***(G-7671)***
Five Star Trucking Inc 440 953-9300
4380 Glenbrook Rd Willoughby (44094) ***(G-19665)***
Fixari Family Dental Inc (PA) 614 866-7445
4241 Kimberly Pkwy Columbus (43232) ***(G-7672)***
Flack Global Metals, Cleveland *Also called Flack Steel LLC* ***(G-5603)***
Flack Steel LLC (PA) 216 456-0700
425 W Lkeside Ave Ste 200 Cleveland (44113) ***(G-5603)***
Flag City Auto Wash, Findlay *Also called Napoleon Wash-N-Fill Inc* ***(G-11068)***
Flag City Mack, Findlay *Also called Bulldawg Holdings LLC* ***(G-11010)***
Flagel Huber Flagel & Co (PA) 937 299-3400
3400 S Dixie Dr Moraine (45439) ***(G-14787)***
Flagship Services of Ohio Inc 740 533-1657
82 Township Road 1331 Ironton (45638) ***(G-12289)***
Flairsoft Ltd (PA) 614 888-0700
7720 Rivers Edge Dr Ste 2 Columbus (43235) ***(G-7673)***
Flamos Enterprises Inc 330 478-0009
1501 Raff Rd Sw Ste 1 Canton (44710) ***(G-2369)***
Flanagan Lberman Hoffman Swaim 937 223-5200
15 W 4th St Ste 100 Dayton (45402) ***(G-9554)***
Flash Seats LLC (PA) 216 420-2000
1 Center Ct Cleveland (44115) ***(G-5604)***
Flat Rock Care Center 419 483-7330
7353 County Rd 29 Flat Rock (44828) ***(G-11103)***
Flavik Village Development 216 429-1182
5620 Broadway Ave Rm 200 Cleveland (44127) ***(G-5605)***
Flavorfresh Dispensers Inc 216 641-0200
4705 Van Epps Rd Brooklyn Heights (44131) ***(G-1916)***
FLCC MEALS, Toledo *Also called Feed Lucas County Children Inc* ***(G-17885)***
Fleet Management Institute, Cincinnati *Also called Nuerological & Sleep Disorders* ***(G-4190)***
Fleet Operations, Toledo *Also called City of Toledo* ***(G-17812)***
Fleet Response, Cleveland *Also called Rental Concepts Inc* ***(G-6377)***
Fleetpride West Inc 419 243-3161
200 Indiana Ave Toledo (43604) ***(G-17895)***
Fleetwood Management Inc 614 538-1277
1675 Old Henderson Rd Columbus (43220) ***(G-7674)***
Fleming Construction Co 740 494-2177
5298 Marion Marysville Rd Prospect (43342) ***(G-16365)***
Flex Fund Inc 614 766-7000
6125 Memorial Dr Dublin (43017) ***(G-10348)***
Flex Property Management, Toledo *Also called Flex Realty* ***(G-17896)***
Flex Realty 419 841-6208
5763 Talmadge Rd Ste C2 Toledo (43623) ***(G-17896)***
Flex Spas Cleveland, Cleveland *Also called Flexeco Incorporated* ***(G-5606)***
Flex Technologies Inc 330 897-6311
3430 State Route 93 Baltic (43804) ***(G-945)***
Flex Temp Employment Services 419 355-9675
524 W State St Fremont (43420) ***(G-11199)***
Flexeco Incorporated 216 812-3304
2600 Hamilton Ave Cleveland (44114) ***(G-5606)***
Flexnova Inc 216 288-6961
6100 Oak Tree Blvd Cleveland (44131) ***(G-5607)***
Flexsys America LP (HQ) 330 666-4111
260 Springside Dr Akron (44333) ***(G-227)***
Flick Lumber Co Inc 419 468-6278
340 S Columbus St Galion (44833) ***(G-11296)***
Flick Packaging, Galion *Also called Flick Lumber Co Inc* ***(G-11296)***
Flickinger Piping Company Inc 330 364-4224
439 S Tuscarawas Ave Dover (44622) ***(G-10189)***
Flight Express Inc (HQ) 305 379-8686
7250 Star Check Dr Columbus (43217) ***(G-7675)***
Flight Options Inc (PA) 216 261-3880
26180 Curtiss Wright Pkwy Richmond Heights (44143) ***(G-16537)***
Flight Options LLC (HQ) 216 261-3500
26180 Curtiss Wright Pkwy Cleveland (44143) ***(G-5608)***
Flight Options Intl Inc (HQ) 216 261-3500
355 Richmond Rd Richmond Heights (44143) ***(G-16538)***
Flight Services & Systems Inc (PA) 216 328-0090
5005 Rockside Rd Ste 940 Cleveland (44131) ***(G-5609)***
Flint Ridge Nursing & Rehab, Newark *Also called Generation Health & Rehab Cntr* ***(G-15168)***
Flodraulic Group Incorporated 614 276-8141
765 N Hague Ave Columbus (43204) ***(G-7676)***
Flooring Specialties Div, Cleveland *Also called Frank Novak & Sons Inc* ***(G-5632)***
Floralandscape Inc 419 536-7640
130 Elmdale Rd Toledo (43607) ***(G-17897)***
Florline Group Inc 330 830-3380
800 Vista Ave Se Massillon (44646) ***(G-13808)***
Florline Midwest, Massillon *Also called Florline Group Inc* ***(G-13808)***
Flow-Liner Systems Ltd 800 348-0020
4830 Northpointe Dr Zanesville (43701) ***(G-20478)***
Flower Factory Inc 614 275-6220
4395 Clime Rd Columbus (43228) ***(G-7677)***
Flower Hospital 419 824-1000
5100 Harroun Rd Sylvania (43560) ***(G-17587)***
Flower Hospital (HQ) 419 824-1444
5200 Harroun Rd Sylvania (43560) ***(G-17588)***
Flowerland Garden Centers (PA) 440 439-8636
25018 Broadway Ave Oakwood Village (44146) ***(G-15629)***
Flowers Family Practice Inc 614 277-9631
3667 Marlane Dr Grove City (43123) ***(G-11562)***
Floyd Brown Group, Delaware *Also called Floyd Browne Group Inc* ***(G-10097)***
Floyd Browne Group Inc 740 363-6792
585 Sunbury Rd Delaware (43015) ***(G-10097)***

ALPHABETIC

Floyd P Bucher & Son Inc ALPHABETIC SECTION

Floyd P Bucher & Son Inc...419 867-8792
5743 Larkhall Dr Toledo (43614) *(G-17898)*
Fluid Connector Group, Waterville *Also called Parker-Hannifin Corporation (G-18943)*
Fluid Mechanics LLC (PA)...216 362-7800
760 Moore Rd Avon Lake (44012) *(G-930)*
Fluid Power Components, Franklin *Also called Eagle Equipment Corporation (G-11154)*
Fluidtrols, Westlake *Also called Neff Group Distributors Inc (G-19519)*
Fluor-Bwxt Portsmouth LLC...866 706-6992
1862 Shyville Rd Ste 216 Piketon (45661) *(G-16115)*
Flux A Salon By Hazelton...419 841-5100
131 W Indiana Ave Perrysburg (43551) *(G-16004)*
Flying Colors Public Preschool...740 349-1629
119 Union St Newark (43055) *(G-15167)*
Flypaper Studio Inc...602 801-2208
311 Elm St Ste 200 Cincinnati (45202) *(G-3634)*
Flytz Gymnastics Inc...330 926-2900
2900 State Rd Unit A Cuyahoga Falls (44223) *(G-9189)*
Flytz UAS Training Center, Cuyahoga Falls *Also called Flytz Gymnastics Inc (G-9189)*
FM 91 Point 5, Bainbridge *Also called W K H R Radio (G-943)*
FM Earth, Sunbury *Also called Facemyer Backhoe and Dozer Svc (G-17555)*
FM Global, North Olmsted *Also called Factory Mutual Insurance Co (G-15421)*
FM Global, Cincinnati *Also called Factory Mutual Insurance Co (G-3588)*
FMC Dalysis Svcs Richland Cnty, Mansfield *Also called Bio-Mdcal Applcations Ohio Inc (G-13266)*
FML Resin LLC...440 214-3200
8834 Mayfield Rd Chesterland (44026) *(G-2796)*
FML Terminal Logistics LLC (HQ)...440 214-3200
8834 Mayfield Rd Chesterland (44026) *(G-2797)*
Fmw Rri Opco LLC (PA)...614 744-2659
605 S Front St Ste 150 Columbus (43215) *(G-7678)*
Fnb Inc (PA)...740 922-2532
105 Grant St Dennison (44621) *(G-10164)*
FNB Corporation...330 721-7484
3613 Medina Rd Medina (44256) *(G-14066)*
FNB Corporation...330 425-1818
10071 Darrow Rd Twinsburg (44087) *(G-18416)*
FNB Corporation...440 439-2200
413 Northfield Rd Cleveland (44146) *(G-5610)*
Foam Pac Materials Company, West Chester *Also called Storopack Inc (G-19232)*
Focus Healthcare of Ohio LLC...419 891-9333
1725 Timber Line Rd Maumee (43537) *(G-13918)*
Focus On Youth Inc...513 644-1030
8904 Brookside Ave West Chester (45069) *(G-19075)*
Focus Solutions Inc...513 376-8349
1821 Summit Rd Ste 103 Cincinnati (45237) *(G-3635)*
Focus Staffing, Cincinnati *Also called Focus Solutions Inc (G-3635)*
Foe 2370, Canton *Also called Fraternal Order Eagles Inc (G-2370)*
Foe 4035, Andover *Also called Fraternal Order Eagles Inc (G-612)*
Foe 691, Wapakoneta *Also called Fraternal Order Eagles Inc (G-18795)*
Foe 712, Fremont *Also called Fraternal Order Eagles Inc (G-11200)*
Fojournerf Title Agency, Cincinnati *Also called Reisenfeld & Assoc Lpa LLC (G-4401)*
Folkers Management Corporation (PA)...513 421-0230
7741 Thompson Rd Cincinnati (45247) *(G-3636)*
Food Concepts Intl Inc...513 336-7449
5010 Deerfield Blvd Mason (45040) *(G-13701)*
Food Distributors Inc...740 439-2764
449 N 1st St Cambridge (43725) *(G-2114)*
Food Express US, Groveport *Also called Union Supply Group Inc (G-11680)*
Food For Good Thought Inc...614 447-0424
4185 N High St Columbus (43214) *(G-7679)*
Food Safety Net Services Ltd...614 274-2070
4130 Fisher Rd Columbus (43228) *(G-7680)*
Food Sample Express LLc...330 225-3550
2945 Carquest Dr Brunswick (44212) *(G-1978)*
Food Service, Columbus *Also called Columbus Public School Dst (G-7379)*
Foodliner Inc...563 451-1047
5560 Brentlinger Dr Dayton (45414) *(G-9555)*
Foor Concrete Co Inc (PA)...740 513-4346
5361 State Route 37 E Delaware (43015) *(G-10098)*
Foot & Ankle Care Center...937 492-1211
1000 Michigan St Sidney (45365) *(G-16934)*
Foot & Ankle Clinic, East Liverpool *Also called Ankle and Foot Care Center (G-10515)*
For Hire Carrier, Cincinnati *Also called Hc Transport Inc (G-3744)*
For Kids Sake Inc...330 726-6878
1245 Boardman Canfield Rd Youngstown (44512) *(G-20190)*
For Specialized Alternatives (PA)...419 695-8010
10100 Elida Rd Delphos (45833) *(G-10144)*
For Women Like Me Inc...407 848-7339
8800 Woodland Ave Cleveland (44104) *(G-5611)*
For Women Like Me Inc (PA)...407 848-7339
46 Shopping Plz Ste 155 Chagrin Falls (44022) *(G-2696)*
Ford, Ontario *Also called Graham Chevrolet-Cadillac Co (G-15690)*
Ford Development Corp...513 772-1521
11148 Woodward Ln Cincinnati (45241) *(G-3637)*
Ford Motor Company...513 573-1101
4680 Parkway Dr Ste 420 Mason (45040) *(G-13702)*
Foremost Insurance Company...216 674-7000
5990 W Creek Rd Ste 160 Independence (44131) *(G-12212)*
Foresight Corporation...614 791-1600
655 Metro Pl S Ste 900 Dublin (43017) *(G-10349)*
Forest City Commercial MGT Inc (HQ)...216 621-6060
50 Public Sq Ste 1410 Cleveland (44113) *(G-5612)*
Forest City Enterprises Inc...216 621-6060
50 Public Sq Ste 750 Cleveland (44113) *(G-5613)*
Forest City Enterprises LP (HQ)...216 621-6060
50 Public Sq Ste 1100 Cleveland (44113) *(G-5614)*
Forest City Enterprises LP...216 416-3756
3454 Main St Cleveland (44113) *(G-5615)*
Forest City Enterprises LP...440 888-8664
9233 Independence Blvd # 114 Cleveland (44130) *(G-5616)*
Forest City Enterprises LP...216 416-3780
6880 Ridge Rd Cleveland (44129) *(G-5617)*
Forest City Enterprises LP...216 416-3766
50 Public Sq Ste 1050 Cleveland (44113) *(G-5618)*
Forest City Erectors Inc...330 425-2345
8200 Boyle Pkwy Ste 1 Twinsburg (44087) *(G-18417)*
Forest City Properties LLC (HQ)...216 621-6060
50 Public Sq Ste 1360 Cleveland (44113) *(G-5619)*
Forest City Realty Trust Inc (PA)...216 621-6060
127 Public Sq Ste 3100 Cleveland (44114) *(G-5620)*
Forest City Residential Dev (HQ)...216 621-6060
1170 Trml Twr 50 Pub Sq 1170 Terminal Tower Cleveland (44113) *(G-5621)*
Forest City Washington LLC (HQ)...202 496-6600
50 Public Sq Ste 1360 Cleveland (44113) *(G-5622)*
Forest City Washington, Inc., Cleveland *Also called Forest City Washington LLC (G-5622)*
Forest Cy Residential MGT Inc (HQ)...216 621-6060
50 Public Sq Ste 1200 Cleveland (44113) *(G-5623)*
Forest Fair Mall, Cincinnati *Also called Mills Corporation (G-4099)*
Forest Hill Care Center, Saint Clairsville *Also called Zandex Inc (G-16663)*
Forest Hill Retirement Cmnty, Saint Clairsville *Also called Zandex Health Care Corporation (G-16664)*
Forest Hills Care Center, Cincinnati *Also called Beechwood Terrace Care Ctr Inc (G-3094)*
Forest Hills Center, Columbus *Also called Serenity Center Inc (G-8714)*
Forest Meadow Villas, Medina *Also called Gerspacher Companies (G-14070)*
Forevergreen Lawn Care...440 327-8987
38601 Sugar Ridge Rd North Ridgeville (44039) *(G-15464)*
Forge Industries Inc (PA)...330 782-8301
4450 Market St Youngstown (44512) *(G-20191)*
Forklift of Toledo, Toledo *Also called Towlift Inc (G-18258)*
Formsoft Group Ltd...937 885-5015
10863 Yankee St Dayton (45458) *(G-9556)*
Formu3 International Inc (PA)...330 668-1461
395 Springside Dr Akron (44333) *(G-228)*
Formwork Services LLC...513 539-4000
900 N Garver Rd Monroe (45050) *(G-14695)*
Forrer Development Ltd...937 431-6489
7625 Paragon Rd Ste E Dayton (45459) *(G-9557)*
Forrest Trucking Company...614 879-8642
540 Taylor Blair Rd West Jefferson (43162) *(G-19252)*
Forsythe Solutions Group Inc...513 697-5100
8845 Governors Hill Dr # 201 Cincinnati (45249) *(G-3638)*
Fort Ancient State Memorial, Oregonia *Also called Dayton Society Natural History (G-15757)*
Fort Austin Ltd Partnership...440 892-4200
28550 Westlake Village Dr Cleveland (44145) *(G-5624)*
Fort Dialysis LLC...330 837-7730
2112 Lincoln Way E Massillon (44646) *(G-13809)*
Fort Hamilton Hosp Foundation...513 867-5492
630 Eaton Ave Hamilton (45013) *(G-11727)*
Fort Hamilton Hospital (HQ)...513 867-2000
630 Eaton Ave Hamilton (45013) *(G-11728)*
Fort Hmltn-Hghes Hlthcare Corp (PA)...513 867-2000
630 Eaton Ave Hamilton (45013) *(G-11729)*
Fort Jennings State Bank (PA)...419 286-2527
120 N Water St Fort Jennings (45844) *(G-11108)*
Fort Recovery Equipment Inc...419 375-1006
1201 Industrial Dr Fort Recovery (45846) *(G-11116)*
Fort Recovery Equity Inc (PA)...419 375-4119
2351 Wabash Rd Fort Recovery (45846) *(G-11117)*
Fort Steuben Mall, Steubenville *Also called Goodman Properties Inc (G-17318)*
Fort Wash Inv Advisors Inc (HQ)...513 361-7600
303 Broadway St Ste 1100 Cincinnati (45202) *(G-3639)*
Forte Indus Eqp Systems Inc...513 398-2800
6037 Commerce Ct Mason (45040) *(G-13703)*
Forte Industries, Mason *Also called Forte Indus Eqp Systems Inc (G-13703)*
Fortec Medical Inc (PA)...330 463-1265
6245 Hudson Crossing Pkwy Hudson (44236) *(G-12117)*
Fortec Medical Inc...513 742-9100
2050 Northwest Dr Cincinnati (45231) *(G-3640)*
Forths Foods Inc...740 886-9769
7604 County Road 107 Proctorville (45669) *(G-16358)*
Fortney & Weygandt, North Olmsted *Also called R L Fortney Management Inc (G-15441)*
Fortney & Weygandt Inc...440 716-4000
31269 Bradley Rd North Olmsted (44070) *(G-15422)*
Fortune Brands Windows Inc (HQ)...614 532-3500
3948 Townsfair Way # 200 Columbus (43219) *(G-7681)*
Fortunefavorsthe Bold LLC...216 469-2845
11716 Detroit Ave Lakewood (44107) *(G-12479)*
Forum At Homes, Warren *Also called Dacas Nursing Systems Inc (G-18846)*

Forum At Knightsbridge, Columbus *Also called Sunrise Connecticut Avenue Ass* ***(G-8803)***
Forum At Knightsbridge, Columbus *Also called Five Star Senior Living Inc* ***(G-7671)***
Forum Manufacturing Inc 937 349-8685
77 Brown St Milford Center (43045) ***(G-14576)***
Forwith Logistics LLC 513 386-8310
6129 Guinea Pike Milford (45150) ***(G-14518)***
Fosbel Inc (HQ) 216 362-3900
20600 Sheldon Rd Brookpark (44142) ***(G-1945)***
Fosbel Holding Inc (PA) 216 362-3900
20600 Sheldon Rd Cleveland (44142) ***(G-5625)***
Fosdick & Hilmer Inc 513 241-5640
525 Vine St Ste 1100 Cincinnati (45202) ***(G-3641)***
Foseco Management Inc 440 826-4548
20200 Sheldon Rd Cleveland (44142) ***(G-5626)***
Foster Care To Success, Beachwood *Also called Orphan Foundation of America* ***(G-1113)***
Foster Grandparent Program, Akron *Also called Akron Summit Cmnty Action Agcy* ***(G-56)***
Foster Sales & Delivery Inc 740 245-0200
35 Corporate Dr Bidwell (45614) ***(G-1495)***
Fostoria Community Hospital, Fostoria *Also called Fostoria Hospital Association* ***(G-11126)***
Fostoria Hospital Association (HQ) 419 435-7734
501 Van Buren St Fostoria (44830) ***(G-11126)***
Fostoria Mixing Center, Fostoria *Also called Norfolk Southern Corporation* ***(G-11136)***
Foti Construction Company LLP 440 347-0728
1164 Lloyd Rd Wickliffe (44092) ***(G-19597)***
Foti Contracting LLC 330 656-3454
1164 Lloyd Rd Wickliffe (44092) ***(G-19598)***
Foundation For Communit (PA) 937 461-3450
349 S Main St Dayton (45402) ***(G-9558)***
Foundation For The Family, Cincinnati *Also called Couple To Couple Leag Intl Inc* ***(G-3434)***
Foundation Park Care Center, Toledo *Also called Nursing Care MGT Amer Inc* ***(G-18098)***
Foundation Pk Alzheimers Care, Toledo *Also called Tlevay Inc* ***(G-18223)***
Foundation Software Inc 330 220-8383
17999 Foltz Pkwy Strongsville (44149) ***(G-17465)***
Foundation Steel LLC 419 402-4241
12525 Airport Hwy Swanton (43558) ***(G-17564)***
Foundations 937 437-2311
7739 Us Route 40 New Paris (45347) ***(G-15077)***
Foundations Hlth Solutions Inc 440 793-0200
25000 Country Club Blvd North Olmsted (44070) ***(G-15423)***
Foundtion Behavioral Hlth Svcs 419 584-1000
4761 State Route 29 Celina (45822) ***(G-2647)***
Fountain City Leasing Inc 419 785-3100
2060 E 2nd St Ste 101 Defiance (43512) ***(G-10033)***
Fountain Square MGT Group LLC 513 621-4400
1203 Walnut St Fl 4 Cincinnati (45202) ***(G-3642)***
Fountainhead Nursing Home Inc 740 354-9113
4734 Gallia Pike Franklin Furnace (45629) ***(G-11170)***
Four Bridges Country Club Ltd 513 759-4620
8300 Four Bridges Dr Liberty Township (45044) ***(G-12720)***
Four Corners Cleaning Inc 330 644-0834
3479 E Tuscarawas Ext Barberton (44203) ***(G-963)***
Four County Family Center 800 693-6000
7320 State Route 108 A Wauseon (43567) ***(G-18952)***
Four Oaks Early Intervention 937 562-6779
245 N Valley Rd Xenia (45385) ***(G-20051)***
Four Points By Sheritan, Columbus *Also called Vjp Hospitality Ltd* ***(G-8948)***
Four Season Car Wash 330 372-4163
437 Trumbull Ave Se Warren (44483) ***(G-18858)***
Four Seasons Car Wash, Warren *Also called Four Season Car Wash* ***(G-18858)***
Four Seasons Environmental Inc (PA) 513 539-2978
43 New Garver Rd Monroe (45050) ***(G-14696)***
Four Seasons Washington LLC 740 895-6101
201 Courthouse Pkwy Wshngtn CT Hs (43160) ***(G-20024)***
Four Towers Apts, Cincinnati *Also called Ea Vica Co* ***(G-3526)***
Four Wheel Drive Hardware LLC 330 482-4733
44488 State Route 14 Columbiana (44408) ***(G-6859)***
Four Winds Nursing Facility, Jackson *Also called United Church Homes Inc* ***(G-12320)***
Fowler Electric Co 440 735-2385
26185 Broadway Ave Bedford (44146) ***(G-1307)***
Fowler, Gary J DDS Ms, Lima *Also called Orthodontic Associates LLC* ***(G-12850)***
Fowlers Mill Golf Course, Chesterland *Also called American Golf Corporation* ***(G-2792)***
Fox 8, Cleveland *Also called Fox Television Stations Inc* ***(G-5627)***
Fox Cleaners Inc (PA) 937 276-4171
4333 N Main St Dayton (45405) ***(G-9559)***
Fox Den Fairways Inc 330 678-6792
2770 Call Rd Stow (44224) ***(G-17368)***
Fox Den Golf Course, Stow *Also called Fox Den Fairways Inc* ***(G-17368)***
Fox International Limited Inc (PA) 216 454-1001
23645 Merc Rd Ste B Beachwood (44122) ***(G-1080)***
Fox Run Apartments, Moraine *Also called Fieldstone Limited Partnership* ***(G-14786)***
Fox Run Cntr For Chldrn & Adol, Saint Clairsville *Also called Bhc Fox Run Hospital Inc* ***(G-16628)***
Fox Run Manor, Findlay *Also called Hcf of Findlay Inc* ***(G-11044)***
Fox Run Manor, Findlay *Also called Hcf of Fox Run Inc* ***(G-11045)***
Fox Television Stations Inc 216 432-4278
5800 S Marginal Rd Cleveland (44103) ***(G-5627)***
Foxridge Farms Corp 740 965-1369
7273 Cheshire Rd Galena (43021) ***(G-11282)***
Foxx & Company 513 241-1616
324 W 9th St Fl 5 Cincinnati (45202) ***(G-3643)***
Fpt Cleveland LLC (HQ) 216 441-3800
8550 Aetna Rd Cleveland (44105) ***(G-5628)***
Fraley & Schilling Inc 740 598-4118
708 Dandy Ln Brilliant (43913) ***(G-1868)***
Fram Group Operations LLC 419 661-6700
28399 Cedar Park Blvd Perrysburg (43551) ***(G-16005)***
Frameco, Cleveland *Also called Metal Framing Enterprises LLC* ***(G-6032)***
Frameco Inc 216 433-7080
9005 Bank St Cleveland (44125) ***(G-5629)***
Francis-Schulze Co 937 295-3941
3880 Rangeline Rd Russia (45363) ***(G-16614)***
Franciscan At St Leonard 937 433-0480
8100 Clyo Rd Dayton (45458) ***(G-9560)***
Franciscan Care Ctr Sylvania 419 882-2087
4111 N Hlland Sylvania Rd Toledo (43623) ***(G-17899)***
Franciscan Sisters of Chicago 440 843-7800
6765 State Rd Cleveland (44134) ***(G-5630)***
Franck and Fric Incorporated 216 524-4451
7919 Old Rockside Rd Cleveland (44131) ***(G-5631)***
Frank Gates Service Company (HQ) 614 793-8000
5000 Bradenton Ave # 100 Dublin (43017) ***(G-10350)***
FRANK MESSER & SONS CONSTRUCTI, Cincinnati *Also called Messer Construction Co* ***(G-4083)***
Frank Novak & Sons Inc 216 475-2495
23940 Miles Rd Cleveland (44128) ***(G-5632)***
Frank Paxton Lumber Company, Cincinnati *Also called Paxton Hardwoods LLC* ***(G-4266)***
Frank Santo LLC 216 831-9374
31100 Pinetree Rd Pepper Pike (44124) ***(G-15955)***
Frankes Unlimited Inc 937 642-0706
825 Collins Ave Marysville (43040) ***(G-13619)***
Frankes Wood Products LLC 937 642-0706
825 Collins Ave Marysville (43040) ***(G-13620)***
Franklin & Seidelmann Inc (PA) 216 255-5700
3700 Park East Dr Ste 300 Beachwood (44122) ***(G-1081)***
Franklin & Seidelmann LLC 216 255-5700
3700 Park East Dr Ste 300 Beachwood (44122) ***(G-1082)***
Franklin Boulevard Nursing Hm 216 651-1600
3600 Franklin Blvd Cleveland (44113) ***(G-5633)***
Franklin Cmpt Svcs Group Inc 614 431-3327
6650 Walnut St New Albany (43054) ***(G-14986)***
Franklin Cnty Bd Commissioners 614 462-3030
970 Dublin Rd Columbus (43215) ***(G-7682)***
Franklin Cnty Bd Commissioners 614 275-2571
855 W Mound St Columbus (43223) ***(G-7683)***
Franklin Cnty Bd Commissioners 614 462-3800
373 S High St Fl 2 Columbus (43215) ***(G-7684)***
Franklin Cnty Bd Commissioners 614 462-3275
80 E Fulton St Columbus (43215) ***(G-7685)***
Franklin Cnty Bd Commissioners 614 462-3429
399 S Front St Columbus (43215) ***(G-7686)***
Franklin Cnty Bd Commissioners 614 229-7100
4071 E Main St Columbus (43213) ***(G-7687)***
Franklin Cnty Bd Commissioners 614 462-3194
373 S High St Fl 12 Columbus (43215) ***(G-7688)***
Franklin Cnty Bd Commissioners 614 462-4360
1731 Alum Creek Dr Columbus (43207) ***(G-7689)***
Franklin Cnty Crt Common Pleas 614 525-5775
373 S High St Fl 6 Columbus (43215) ***(G-7690)***
Franklin Communications Inc 614 451-2191
4401 Carriage Hill Ln Columbus (43220) ***(G-7691)***
Franklin Communications Inc 614 459-9769
4401 Carriage Hill Ln Columbus (43220) ***(G-7692)***
Franklin Community Base Correc 614 525-4600
1745 Alum Creek Dr Columbus (43207) ***(G-7693)***
Franklin County Adamh Board 614 224-1057
447 E Broad St Columbus (43215) ***(G-7694)***
Franklin County Childrens Svcs, Columbus *Also called Franklin Cnty Bd Commissioners* ***(G-7687)***
Franklin County Historical Soc 614 228-2674
333 W Broad St Columbus (43215) ***(G-7695)***
Franklin County Pub Defender, Columbus *Also called Franklin Cnty Bd Commissioners* ***(G-7688)***
Franklin County Residential S 614 844-5847
1021 Checkrein Ave Columbus (43229) ***(G-7696)***
Franklin Dental Manufacturing, Dublin *Also called Perio Inc* ***(G-10426)***
Franklin Imaging Llc (PA) 614 885-6894
500 Schrock Rd Columbus (43229) ***(G-7697)***
Franklin Iron & Metal Corp 937 253-8184
1939 E 1st St Dayton (45403) ***(G-9561)***
Franklin Plaza, Cleveland *Also called Franklin Boulevard Nursing Hm* ***(G-5633)***
Franklin Ridge Care Facility, Hamilton *Also called Carington Health Systems* ***(G-11706)***
Franklin Ridge Care Facility, Franklin *Also called Carington Health Systems* ***(G-11151)***
Franklin Shcp Inc 440 614-0160
1850 Crown Park Ct Columbus (43235) ***(G-7698)***
Franklin Specialty Trnspt Inc (HQ) 614 529-7900
2040 Atlas St Columbus (43228) ***(G-7699)***
Franklin Township Fire and Ems 513 876-2996
718 Market St Felicity (45120) ***(G-10985)***

ALPHABETIC

Frans Child Care-Mansfield ... 419 775-2500
750 Scholl Rd Mansfield (44907) ***(G-13304)***
Frantz Medical Group ... 440 974-8522
7740 Metric Dr Mentor (44060) ***(G-14176)***
Frantz Ward LLP ... 216 515-1660
200 Public Sq Ste 3020 Cleveland (44114) ***(G-5634)***
FRATERNAL INSURANCE, Columbus *Also called Order of Unite Commercial Tra* ***(G-8479)***
Fraternal Order Eagles Inc ... 330 477-8059
5024 Monticello Ave Nw Canton (44708) ***(G-2370)***
Fraternal Order Eagles Inc ... 419 738-2582
25 E Auglaize St Wapakoneta (45895) ***(G-18795)***
Fraternal Order Eagles Inc ... 419 332-3961
2570 W State St Fremont (43420) ***(G-11200)***
Fraternal Order Eagles Inc ... 440 293-5997
6210 State Route 85 Andover (44003) ***(G-612)***
Fraternal Order Eagles Inc (HQ) ... 614 883-2200
1623 Gateway Cir Grove City (43123) ***(G-11563)***
Fraternal Order of Eagles ... 937 323-0671
1802 Selma Rd Springfield (45505) ***(G-17200)***
Fraternal Order of Police of O (PA) ... 614 224-5700
222 E Town St Fl 1e Columbus (43215) ***(G-7700)***
Frazeysburg Lions Club Inc ... 740 828-2313
12355 Scout Rd Frazeysburg (43822) ***(G-11175)***
Frazeysburg Restaurant & Bky, Frazeysburg *Also called Calvary Christian Ch of Ohio* ***(G-11174)***
Frch Design Worldwide - Cincin ... 513 241-3000
311 Elm St Ste 600 Cincinnati (45202) ***(G-3644)***
Fred A Nemann Co ... 513 467-9400
6480 Bender Rd Cincinnati (45233) ***(G-3645)***
Fred Christen & Sons Company (PA) ... 419 243-4161
714 George St Toledo (43608) ***(G-17900)***
Fred Martin Nissan LLC ... 330 644-8888
3388 S Arlington Rd Akron (44312) ***(G-229)***
Fred Olivieri Construction Co (PA) ... 330 494-1007
6315 Promway Ave Nw North Canton (44720) ***(G-15338)***
Fred W Albrecht Grocery Co ... 330 645-6222
3235 Manchester Rd Unit A Coventry Township (44319) ***(G-9124)***
Fred W Albrecht Grocery Co ... 330 666-6781
3979 Medina Rd Akron (44333) ***(G-230)***
Frederick C Smith Clinic Inc (PA) ... 740 383-7000
1040 Delaware Ave Marion (43302) ***(G-13540)***
Frederick C Smith Clinic Inc ... 740 363-9021
6 Lexington Blvd Delaware (43015) ***(G-10099)***
Frederick Steel Company LLC ... 513 821-6400
630 Glendale Milford Rd Cincinnati (45215) ***(G-3646)***
Fredericks Landscaping Inc ... 513 821-9407
301 S Cooper Ave Cincinnati (45215) ***(G-3647)***
Fredericks Wine & Dine ... 216 581-5299
22005 Emery Rd Cleveland (44128) ***(G-5635)***
Fredrics Corporation (PA) ... 513 874-2226
7664 Voice Of America Ctr West Chester (45069) ***(G-19076)***
Free Enterprises Incorporated (PA) ... 330 722-2031
241 S State Rd Medina (44256) ***(G-14067)***
Free Store/Food Bank Inc (PA) ... 513 482-4526
1250 Tennessee Ave Cincinnati (45229) ***(G-3648)***
Free Store/Food Bank Inc ... 513 241-1064
1250 Tennessee Ave Cincinnati (45229) ***(G-3649)***
Freedom Center, Columbus *Also called Ohio Department Youth Services* ***(G-8332)***
Freedom Enterprises Inc ... 419 675-1192
11441 County Road 75 Kenton (43326) ***(G-12411)***
Freedom Harley-Davidson Inc ... 330 494-2453
7233 Sunset Strip Ave Nw Canton (44720) ***(G-2371)***
Freedom Rv, Akron *Also called Sirpilla Recrtl Vhcl Ctr Inc* ***(G-439)***
Freedom Specialty Insurance Co (HQ) ... 614 249-1545
1 W Nationwide Blvd Columbus (43215) ***(G-7701)***
Freedom Steel Inc ... 440 266-6800
8200 Tyler Blvd Ste G Mentor (44060) ***(G-14177)***
Freedonia Publishing LLC ... 440 684-9600
767 Beta Dr Cleveland (44143) ***(G-5636)***
Freeland Contracting Co ... 614 443-2718
2100 Integrity Dr S Columbus (43209) ***(G-7702)***
Freeman Manufacturing & Sup Co (PA) ... 440 934-1902
1101 Moore Rd Avon (44011) ***(G-893)***
Freestore/Foodbank ... 513 482-4500
Central Pkwy Cincinnati (45229) ***(G-3650)***
Freeway Lanes Bowl Group LLC ... 440 946-5131
7300 Palisades Pkwy Mentor (44060) ***(G-14178)***
Freeze/Arnold A Freund Legal (PA) ... 937 222-2424
1 S Main St Ste 1800 Dayton (45402) ***(G-9562)***
Freiberg Spine Institute, Blue Ash *Also called Orthopaedic Offices Inc* ***(G-1659)***
Freightlner Trcks of Cncinnati ... 513 772-7171
1 Freightliner Dr Cincinnati (45241) ***(G-3651)***
Freisthler Paving Inc ... 937 498-4802
2323 Campbell Rd Sidney (45365) ***(G-16935)***
Freking Betz ... 513 721-1975
525 Vine St Fl 6 Cincinnati (45202) ***(G-3652)***
Fremont Federal Credit Union (PA) ... 419 334-4434
315 Croghan St Fremont (43420) ***(G-11201)***
Fremont Logistics LLC ... 419 333-0669
1301 Heinz Rd Fremont (43420) ***(G-11202)***
Fremont Plant Operations, Fremont *Also called Goodwill Industries of Erie* ***(G-11205)***
Fremont Regional Dialysis, Fremont *Also called Kinswa Dialysis LLC* ***(G-11209)***
Fremont TMC Head Start, Fremont *Also called W S O S Community A* ***(G-11228)***
French Company LLC ... 330 963-4344
8289 Darrow Rd Twinsburg (44087) ***(G-18418)***
Frencor Inc ... 330 332-1203
409 E 2nd St Ste 6 Salem (44460) ***(G-16696)***
Fresenius Kdney Care W Hmilton, Hamilton *Also called Fresenius Med Care Butler Cty* ***(G-11730)***
Fresenius Kidney Care, Cuyahoga Falls *Also called Bio-Mdcal Applcations Ohio Inc* ***(G-9166)***
Fresenius Med Care Butler Cty ... 513 737-1415
890 Nw Washington Blvd Hamilton (45013) ***(G-11730)***
Fresenius Med Care Cntl Ohio E, Columbus *Also called Bio-Mdcal Applcations Ohio Inc* ***(G-7112)***
Fresenius Med Care Dayton W, Trotwood *Also called Bio-Mdcal Applcations Ohio Inc* ***(G-18344)***
Fresenius Med Care Grove Cy, Grove City *Also called Fresenius Medical Care Vro LLC* ***(G-11564)***
Fresenius Med Care Hldings Inc ... 216 267-1451
14670 Snow Rd Cleveland (44142) ***(G-5637)***
Fresenius Med Care Hldings Inc ... 800 881-5101
2355 S Hamilton Rd Columbus (43232) ***(G-7703)***
Fresenius Med Care Perrysburg, Perrysburg *Also called Bio-Mdcal Applcations Ohio Inc* ***(G-15979)***
Fresenius Medical Care, Marion *Also called Bio-Mdical Applications Rl Inc* ***(G-13524)***
Fresenius Medical Care Vro LLC ... 614 875-2349
3149 Farm Bank Way Grove City (43123) ***(G-11564)***
Fresenius Usa Inc ... 419 691-2475
555 Blue Heron Dr Oregon (43616) ***(G-15736)***
Fresh and Limited, Sidney *Also called Freshway Foods Inc* ***(G-16936)***
Fresh Mark Inc (PA) ... 330 834-3669
1888 Southway St Se Massillon (44646) ***(G-13810)***
Fresh Mark Inc ... 330 833-9870
950 Cloverleaf St Se Massillon (44646) ***(G-13811)***
Fresh Mark Inc ... 330 832-7491
1888 Southway St Sw Massillon (44646) ***(G-13812)***
Fresh Mark Sugardale, Massillon *Also called Fresh Mark Inc* ***(G-13812)***
Freshealth LLC ... 614 231-3601
3650 E 5th Ave Columbus (43219) ***(G-7704)***
Freshway Foods Inc (PA) ... 937 498-4664
601 Stolle Ave Sidney (45365) ***(G-16936)***
Freshway Foods Inc ... 937 498-4664
601 Stolle Ave Sidney (45365) ***(G-16937)***
Freudenberg-Nok General Partnr ... 419 499-2502
11617 State Re 13 Milan (44846) ***(G-14494)***
Frey Electric Inc ... 513 385-0700
5700 Cheviot Rd Ste A Cincinnati (45247) ***(G-3653)***
Friars Club Inc ... 513 488-8777
4300 Vine St Cincinnati (45217) ***(G-3654)***
Friedberg Meyers Roman ... 216 831-0042
28601 Chagrin Blvd # 500 Cleveland (44122) ***(G-5638)***
Friedman Domiano Smith Co Lpa ... 216 621-0070
55 Public Sq Ste 1055 Cleveland (44113) ***(G-5639)***
Friedman Management Company ... 614 224-2424
50 W Broad St Ste 200 Columbus (43215) ***(G-7705)***
Friedman Vlg Retirement Cmnty ... 419 443-1540
175 Saint Francis Ave Tiffin (44883) ***(G-17680)***
Friedman-Swift Associates Inc ... 513 772-9200
110 Boggs Ln Ste 200 Cincinnati (45246) ***(G-3655)***
Friend To Friend Program ... 216 861-1838
4515 Superior Ave Cleveland (44103) ***(G-5640)***
Friend-Ship Child Care Ctr LLC ... 330 484-2051
425 45th St Sw Canton (44706) ***(G-2372)***
Friendly Care Agency, Pickerington *Also called Lbs International Inc* ***(G-16100)***
Friendly Inn Settlement House ... 216 431-7656
2386 Unwin Rd Cleveland (44104) ***(G-5641)***
Friendly Nursing Home Inc ... 937 855-2363
4339 State Route 122 Franklin (45005) ***(G-11155)***
FRIENDLY STREET NEIGHBORHOOD, Cincinnati *Also called Seven Hlls Neighborhood Houses* ***(G-4505)***
Friends Boarding Home, Waynesville *Also called Home The Friends Inc* ***(G-18983)***
Friends Business Source, Findlay *Also called Friends Service Co Inc* ***(G-11033)***
FRIENDS CARE CENTER, Yellow Springs *Also called Friends Health Care Assn* ***(G-20089)***
Friends Health Care Assn (PA) ... 937 767-7363
150 E Herman St Yellow Springs (45387) ***(G-20089)***
Friends of Art For Cultural ... 614 888-9929
191 Melyers Ct Columbus (43235) ***(G-7706)***
Friends of Good Shepherd Manor ... 740 289-2861
374 Good Manor Rd Lucasville (45648) ***(G-13179)***
Friends of The Lib Cyahoga FLS ... 330 928-2117
2015 3rd St Cuyahoga Falls (44221) ***(G-9190)***
Friends Service Co Inc (PA) ... 419 427-1704
2300 Bright Rd Findlay (45840) ***(G-11033)***
Friendship Home, Ashtabula *Also called Ashtabula Community Counseling* ***(G-716)***
Friendship Village of Dayton, Dayton *Also called Evangelical Retirement* ***(G-9532)***
Friendship Vlg of Clmbus Ohio ... 614 890-8287
5757 Ponderosa Dr Columbus (43231) ***(G-7707)***
Friendship Vlg of Clmbus Ohio (PA) ... 614 890-8282
5800 Frest Hills Blvd Ofc Columbus (43231) ***(G-7708)***
Friendship Vlg of Dublin Ohio ... 614 764-1600
6000 Riverside Dr Ofc Ofc Dublin (43017) ***(G-10351)***

Frito-Lay North America Inc....513 874-0112
4696 Devitt Dr West Chester (45246) ***(G-19202)***
Frito-Lay North America Inc....216 491-4000
4580 Hinckley Indus Pkwy Cleveland (44109) ***(G-5642)***
Frito-Lay North America Inc....937 224-8716
49 Kelly Ave Dayton (45404) ***(G-9563)***
Frito-Lay North America Inc....614 508-3004
6611 Broughton Ave Columbus (43213) ***(G-7709)***
Frito-Lay North America Inc....419 893-8171
6501 Monclova Rd Maumee (43537) ***(G-13919)***
Frito-Lay North America Inc....330 786-6000
1460 E Turkeyfoot Lake Rd Akron (44312) ***(G-231)***
Fritz-Rumer-Cooke Co Inc....614 444-8844
635 E Woodrow Ave Columbus (43207) ***(G-7710)***
Frog & Toad Inc....419 877-1180
10835 Waterville St Whitehouse (43571) ***(G-19586)***
Front Leasing Co LLC....440 243-4000
255 Front St Berea (44017) ***(G-1460)***
Frontgate Catalog, West Chester *Also called Cinmar LLC* ***(G-19040)***
Frontier Bassmasters Inc....740 423-9293
904 Boulevard Dr Belpre (45714) ***(G-1438)***
Frontier Power Company....740 622-6755
770 S 2nd St Coshocton (43812) ***(G-9103)***
Frontier Security LLC....937 247-2824
1041 Byers Rd Miamisburg (45342) ***(G-14303)***
Frontier Tank Center Inc....330 659-3888
3800 Congress Pkwy Richfield (44286) ***(G-16510)***
Frontier Technology Inc (PA)....937 429-3302
4141 Colonel Glenn Hwy # 140 Beavercreek Township (45431) ***(G-1269)***
Frontline National LLC....513 528-7823
502 Techne Center Dr G Milford (45150) ***(G-14519)***
Frontline Service, Cleveland *Also called Mental Health Services* ***(G-6025)***
Frost Brown Todd LLC (PA)....513 651-6800
3300 Grt Amrcn Towe 301e Cincinnati (45202) ***(G-3656)***
Frost Brown Todd LLC....614 464-1211
1 Columbus Ste 2300 10 W Columbus (43215) ***(G-7711)***
Frost Roofing Inc....419 739-2701
2 Broadway St Wapakoneta (45895) ***(G-18796)***
Frs Counseling Inc (PA)....937 393-0585
104 Erin Ct Hillsboro (45133) ***(G-11975)***
Frs Counselling, Hillsboro *Also called F R S Connections* ***(G-11973)***
Fruits of The Earth, Grove City *Also called Circle S Farms Inc* ***(G-11546)***
Fruth & Co (PA)....419 435-8541
601 Parkway Dr Ste A Fostoria (44830) ***(G-11127)***
Fryman-Kuck General Contrs Inc....937 274-2892
5150 Webster St Dayton (45414) ***(G-9564)***
FSI Disposal, Clyde *Also called Fultz & Son Inc* ***(G-6813)***
Fsmg, Cincinnati *Also called Fountain Square MGT Group LLC* ***(G-3642)***
FSRc Tanks Inc....234 221-2015
11029 Industrial Pkwy Nw Bolivar (44612) ***(G-1747)***
Fte Networks Inc....502 657-3500
11260 Chester Rd Ste 350 Cincinnati (45246) ***(G-3657)***
Ftech R&D North America Inc (HQ)....937 339-2777
1191 Horizon West Ct Troy (45373) ***(G-18354)***
Fti, Beavercreek Township *Also called Frontier Technology Inc* ***(G-1269)***
FTM Associates LLC....614 846-1834
150 E Campus View Blvd Columbus (43235) ***(G-7712)***
Fts International Inc....330 754-2375
1520 Wood Ave Se East Canton (44730) ***(G-10503)***
Fuchs Franklin Div, Twinsburg *Also called Fuchs Lubricants Co* ***(G-18419)***
Fuchs Lubricants Co....330 963-0400
8036 Bavaria Rd Twinsburg (44087) ***(G-18419)***
Fujiyama International Inc....614 891-2224
5755 Cleveland Ave Columbus (43231) ***(G-7713)***
Fulfillment Technologies LLC....513 346-3100
5389 E Provident Dr West Chester (45246) ***(G-19203)***
Fuller & Henry Ltd (PA)....419 247-2500
1 Seagate Ste 1700 Toledo (43604) ***(G-17901)***
Fullton Mill Services, Delta *Also called Edw C Levy Co* ***(G-10157)***
Fulton County Alano Club, Wauseon *Also called Alano Club Inc* ***(G-18948)***
Fulton County Health Center....419 335-2017
725 S Shoop Ave Wauseon (43567) ***(G-18953)***
Fulton County Health Center....419 337-8661
725 S Shoop Ave Wauseon (43567) ***(G-18954)***
Fulton County Health Center (PA)....419 336 2015
725 S Shoop Ave Wauseon (43567) ***(G-18955)***
Fulton County Health Dept....419 337-6979
606 S Shoop Ave Wauseon (43567) ***(G-18956)***
Fulton County Senior Center....419 337-9299
240 Clinton St Wauseon (43567) ***(G-18957)***
Fulton Manor Nursing Home, Wauseon *Also called Fulton County Health Center* ***(G-18953)***
Fulton Stress Unit, Wauseon *Also called Fulton County Health Center* ***(G-18954)***
Fultz & Son Inc....419 547-9365
100 S Main St Clyde (43410) ***(G-6813)***
Fun Day Events LLC....740 549-9000
947 E Johnstown Rd # 163 Gahanna (43230) ***(G-11242)***
Fun Makers, Tallmadge *Also called Heaven Bound Ascensions* ***(G-17640)***
Fun n Stuff Amusements Inc....330 467-0821
661 Highland Rd E Macedonia (44056) ***(G-13197)***
Funai Service Corporation....614 409-2600
2425 Spiegel Dr Groveport (43125) ***(G-11641)***
Fund Evaluation Group LLC (PA)....513 977-4400
201 E 5th St Ste 1600 Cincinnati (45202) ***(G-3658)***
Funky People, Wooster *Also called Classic Imports Inc* ***(G-19847)***
Funny Bone Comedy Club & Cafe....614 471-5653
145 Easton Town Ctr Columbus (43219) ***(G-7714)***
Funtime Parks Inc....330 562-7131
1060 N Aurora Rd Aurora (44202) ***(G-839)***
Furbay Electric Supply Co (PA)....330 454-3033
208 Schroyer Ave Sw Canton (44702) ***(G-2373)***
Furlong, Lawrence P CPA, Norwalk *Also called Payne Nickles & Co CPA* ***(G-15588)***
Furney Group Home....419 389-0152
4656 Glendale Ave Toledo (43614) ***(G-17902)***
Furniture Bank Central Ohio....614 272-9544
118 S Yale Ave Columbus (43222) ***(G-7715)***
Furniture With A Heart, Columbus *Also called Furniture Bank Central Ohio* ***(G-7715)***
Fusion Alliance LLC....614 852-8000
440 Polaris Pkwy Ste 500 Westerville (43082) ***(G-19309)***
Fusion Alliance LLC....513 563-8444
4555 Lake Forest Dr # 325 Blue Ash (45242) ***(G-1597)***
Fusion Ceramics Inc....330 627-5821
237 High St Sw Carrollton (44615) ***(G-2620)***
Fusion Interior Services Ltd (PA)....513 759-4100
9823 Cincinnati Dayton Rd West Chester (45069) ***(G-19077)***
Futura Banc Corp (PA)....937 653-1167
601 Scioto St Urbana (43078) ***(G-18588)***
Futura Design Service Inc....937 890-5252
6001 N Dixie Dr Dayton (45414) ***(G-9565)***
Future Advantage Inc....330 686-7707
4923 Hudson Dr Stow (44224) ***(G-17369)***
Future Poly Tech Inc (PA)....614 942-1209
2215 Citygate Dr Ste D Columbus (43219) ***(G-7716)***
Future Unlimited Inc....330 273-6677
1407 Jefferson Ave Brunswick (44212) ***(G-1979)***
Fuyao Glass America Inc (HQ)....937 496-5777
2801 W Stroop Rd Dayton (45439) ***(G-9566)***
Fwlm, Chagrin Falls *Also called For Women Like Me Inc* ***(G-2696)***
Fx Digital Media Inc (PA)....216 241-4040
1600 E 23rs St Rs Cleveland (44114) ***(G-5643)***
Fyda Freightliner Youngstown....330 797-0224
5260 76 Dr Youngstown (44515) ***(G-20192)***
Fyda Truck & Equipment, Youngstown *Also called Fyda Freightliner Youngstown* ***(G-20192)***
G & C Finishes From The Future (PA)....937 890-3002
6897 N Dixie Dr Dayton (45414) ***(G-9567)***
G & D Alternative Living Inc....937 446-2803
121 Charles St Sardinia (45171) ***(G-16813)***
G & D Twinsburg, Twinsburg *Also called Giesecke & Devrient Amer Inc* ***(G-18423)***
G & G Investment LLC....513 984-0300
4901 Hunt Rd Ste 300 Blue Ash (45242) ***(G-1598)***
G & J Kartway, Camden *Also called Barnets Inc* ***(G-2136)***
G & J Pepsi-Cola Bottlers Inc....740 354-9191
4587 Gallia Pike Franklin Furnace (45629) ***(G-11171)***
G & J Pepsi-Cola Bottlers Inc....740 774-2148
400 E 7th St Chillicothe (45601) ***(G-2841)***
G & J Pepsi-Cola Bottlers Inc....740 593-3366
2001 E State St Athens (45701) ***(G-788)***
G & J Pepsi-Cola Bottlers Inc....937 393-5744
3500 Progress Way Wilmington (45177) ***(G-19763)***
G & J Pepsi-Cola Bottlers Inc....740 452-2721
335 N 6th St Zanesville (43701) ***(G-20479)***
G & O Resources Ltd....330 253-2525
96 E Crosier St Akron (44311) ***(G-232)***
G & S Metal Products Co Inc....216 831-2388
26840 Fargo Ave Cleveland (44146) ***(G-5644)***
G & S Transfer Inc....330 673-3899
4055a Highway View Dr Kent (44240) ***(G-12370)***
G and H Management....614 268-2273
1243 E Broad St Columbus (43205) ***(G-7717)***
G Big Inc (PA)....740 867-5758
441 Rockwood Ave Chesapeake (45619) ***(G-2784)***
G E G Enterprises Inc....330 494-9160
4080 Fulton Dr Nw Canton (44718) ***(G-2374)***
G E G Enterprises Inc (PA)....330 477-3133
4345 Tuscarawas St W Canton (44708) ***(G-2375)***
G E S, Parma *Also called Ges Graphite Inc* ***(G-15908)***
G F S Marketplace, Ontario *Also called Gordon Food Service Inc* ***(G-15689)***
G F S Marketplace, Lima *Also called Gordon Food Service Inc* ***(G-12786)***
G F S Marketplace, Mentor *Also called Gordon Food Service Inc* ***(G-14181)***
G F S Marketplace, Cleveland *Also called Gordon Food Service Inc* ***(G-5680)***
G G Marck & Associates Inc (PA)....419 478-0900
300 Phillips Ave Toledo (43612) ***(G-17903)***
G H A Inc....440 729-2130
12670 W Geauga Plz Chesterland (44026) ***(G-2798)***
G Herschman Architects Inc (PA)....216 223-3200
25001 Emery Rd Ste 400 Cleveland (44128) ***(G-5645)***
G III Reitter Walls LLC....614 545-4444
1759 Old Leonard Ave Columbus (43219) ***(G-7718)***
G J Goudreau & Co (PA)....216 351-5233
9701 Brookpark Rd Ste 200 Cleveland (44129) ***(G-5646)***
G J Goudreau Operating Co....216 741-7524
9701 Brookpark Rd Ste 200 Cleveland (44129) ***(G-5647)***
G K Packaging, Wshngtn CT Hs *Also called Washington Court Hse Holdg LLC* ***(G-20037)***

A L P H A B E T I C

G M A C Insurance Center, Hudson *Also called Pasco Inc* ***(G-12138)***
G M A Surgery Inc....937 429-7350
3359 Kemp Rd Ste 120 Beavercreek (45431) ***(G-1174)***
G M N Tri Cnty Communty Action (PA)....740 732-2388
615 North St Caldwell (43724) ***(G-2085)***
G M Z, West Chester *Also called CL Zimmerman Delaware LLC* ***(G-19042)***
G Mechanical Inc....614 844-6750
6635 Singletree Dr Columbus (43229) ***(G-7719)***
G P M C, Dublin *Also called Gemini Properties* ***(G-10353)***
G P Properties, Marion *Also called Ted Graham* ***(G-13584)***
G P S Fire Equipment, Cleveland *Also called Gene Ptacek Son Fire Eqp Inc* ***(G-5666)***
G R B Inc (PA)....800 628-9195
6392 Gano Rd West Chester (45069) ***(G-19078)***
G R C, Mason *Also called General Revenue Corporation* ***(G-13707)***
G Robert Toney & Assoc Inc (PA)....954 791-9601
5401 N Marginal Rd Cleveland (44114) ***(G-5648)***
G S M, Batavia *Also called Global Scrap Management Inc* ***(G-1015)***
G S S, Springboro *Also called Graphic Systems Services Inc* ***(G-17120)***
G S Wiring Systems Inc (HQ)....419 423-7111
1801 Production Dr Findlay (45840) ***(G-11034)***
G Stephens Inc....419 241-5188
104 N Summit St Ste 102 Toledo (43604) ***(G-17904)***
G Stephens Inc....614 227-0304
1175 Dublin Rd Ste 2 Columbus (43215) ***(G-7720)***
G W S, West Chester *Also called Global Workplace Solutions LLC* ***(G-19082)***
G&A Marketing Inc, Cincinnati *Also called Gunning & Associates Mktg Inc* ***(G-3719)***
G&K Services Inc....937 873-4500
1202 Dyton Yllow Sprng Rd Fairborn (45324) ***(G-10797)***
G&M Towing and Recovery LLC....216 271-0581
3030 E 55th St Cleveland (44127) ***(G-5649)***
G-Cor Automotive Corp (PA)....614 443-6735
2100 Refugee Rd Columbus (43207) ***(G-7721)***
G. S. I., Vienna *Also called Glowe-Smith Industrial Inc* ***(G-18737)***
G4s Secure Solutions (usa)....614 322-5100
2211 Lake Club Dr Ste 105 Columbus (43232) ***(G-7722)***
G4s Secure Solutions (usa)....513 874-0941
625 Eden Park Dr Ste 700 Cincinnati (45202) ***(G-3659)***
GA Business Purchaser LLC....419 255-8400
1810 Jefferson Ave Toledo (43604) ***(G-17905)***
Gables At Green Pastures....937 642-3893
390 Gables Dr Marysville (43040) ***(G-13621)***
Gables Care Center Inc....740 937-2900
351 Lahm Dr Hopedale (43976) ***(G-12078)***
Gabriel Partners LLC....216 771-1250
200 Public Sq Ste 3100 Cleveland (44114) ***(G-5650)***
Gade Nursing Home 2, Greenville *Also called Village Green Healthcare Ctr* ***(G-11523)***
Gahanna Animal Hospital Inc....614 471-2201
144 W Johnstown Rd Gahanna (43230) ***(G-11243)***
Gahanna Health Care Center....614 475-7222
121 James Rd Columbus (43230) ***(G-7723)***
Gahanna-Jefferson Pub Schl Dst....614 751-7581
782 Science Blvd Columbus (43230) ***(G-7724)***
Galaxie Industrial Svcs LLC....330 503-2334
837 E Western Reserve Rd Youngstown (44514) ***(G-20193)***
Galaxy Associates Inc (HQ)....513 731-6350
3630 E Kemper Rd Cincinnati (45241) ***(G-3660)***
Galaxy Balloons Incorporated....216 476-3360
11750 Berea Rd Ste 3 Cleveland (44111) ***(G-5651)***
Gale Insulation, Hamilton *Also called Truteam LLC* ***(G-11779)***
Gale Insulation, Columbus *Also called Builder Services Group Inc* ***(G-7166)***
Gale Insulation, Hamilton *Also called Builder Services Group Inc* ***(G-11695)***
Galia County Council On Aging, Gallipolis *Also called Area Agency On Aging Dst 7 Inc* ***(G-11308)***
Galion Community Center YMCA....419 468-7754
500 Gill Ave Galion (44833) ***(G-11297)***
Galion Community Hospital....419 468-4841
269 Portland Way S Galion (44833) ***(G-11298)***
Galion Dialysis, Galion *Also called Steele Dialysis LLC* ***(G-11305)***
Galion East Ohio I LP....216 520-1250
1300 Harding Way E Galion (44833) ***(G-11299)***
Gallagher Bassett Services....614 764-7616
545 Metro Pl S Ste 250 Dublin (43017) ***(G-10352)***
Gallagher Benefit Services Inc....216 623-2600
1100 Superior Ave E # 1700 Cleveland (44114) ***(G-5652)***
Gallagher Gams Pryor Tallan....614 228-5151
471 E Broad St Fl 19 Columbus (43215) ***(G-7725)***
Gallagher Sharp....216 241-5310
1501 Euclid Ave Fl 7 Cleveland (44115) ***(G-5653)***
Gallagher Sks, Cincinnati *Also called Arthur J Gallagher & Co* ***(G-3051)***
Gallco Inc....740 446-3775
77 Mill Creek Rd Gallipolis (45631) ***(G-11316)***
GALLCO INDUSTRIES, Gallipolis *Also called Gallco Inc* ***(G-11316)***
Gallery Holdings LLC....773 693-6220
6111 Oak Tree Blvd Independence (44131) ***(G-12213)***
Gallia County Engineer, Gallipolis *Also called County of Gallia* ***(G-11313)***
Gallia County Human Services, Gallipolis *Also called County of Gallia* ***(G-11311)***
Gallia-Meigs Community Action (PA)....740 367-7341
8010 State Route 7 N Cheshire (45620) ***(G-2790)***
Gallipolis Auto Auction Inc....740 446-1576
286 Upper River Rd Gallipolis (45631) ***(G-11317)***
Gallipolis Care LLC....740 446-7112
170 Pinecrest Dr Gallipolis (45631) ***(G-11318)***
Gallipolis Developmental Ctr, Gallipolis *Also called Develpmntal Dsblties Ohio Dept* ***(G-11314)***
Gallipolis Hospitality Inc....740 446-0090
577 State Route 7 N Gallipolis (45631) ***(G-11319)***
Gallipolis Municipal Pool, Gallipolis *Also called City of Gallipolis* ***(G-11310)***
Gallon Takacs Boissoneault & S (PA)....419 843-2001
3516 Granite Cir Toledo (43617) ***(G-17906)***
Gallon, E S Associates, Moraine *Also called E S Gallon & Associates* ***(G-14777)***
Galt Enterprises Inc....216 464-6744
34555 Chagrin Blvd # 100 Moreland Hills (44022) ***(G-14839)***
Gamma PHI Beta Sorority Alpha....937 324-3436
628 Woodlawn Ave Springfield (45504) ***(G-17201)***
Gannet Fleming Engr & Archt, Westerville *Also called Gannett Fleming Inc* ***(G-19402)***
Gannett Fleming Inc....614 794-9424
4151 Executive Pkwy # 350 Westerville (43081) ***(G-19402)***
Gannett Media Tech Intl (HQ)....513 665-3777
312 Elm St Ste 2g Cincinnati (45202) ***(G-3661)***
Ganzfair Investment Inc....614 792-6630
231 Clubhouse Dr Delaware (43015) ***(G-10100)***
Ganzhorn Suites Inc....614 356-9810
10272 Sawmill Pkwy Powell (43065) ***(G-16336)***
Gap Radio Broadcasting LLC....440 992-9700
3226 Jefferson Rd Ashtabula (44004) ***(G-744)***
Garage Door Systems LLC....513 321-9600
858 E Crescentville Rd A West Chester (45246) ***(G-19204)***
Garage, The, Chillicothe *Also called County Engineers Office* ***(G-2829)***
Garber Ag Freight Inc....937 548-8400
4667 Us Route 127 Greenville (45331) ***(G-11501)***
Garber Connect, Englewood *Also called Garber Electrical Contrs Inc* ***(G-10704)***
Garber Electrical Contrs Inc....937 771-5202
100 Rockridge Rd Englewood (45322) ***(G-10704)***
Garbry Ridge Assisted Living....937 778-9385
1567 Garbry Rd Piqua (45356) ***(G-16145)***
Garda CL Great Lakes Inc....614 863-4044
201 Schofield Dr Columbus (43213) ***(G-7726)***
Garda CL Great Lakes Inc....419 385-2411
3635 Marine Rd Toledo (43609) ***(G-17907)***
Garda CL Great Lakes Inc (HQ)....561 939-7000
201 Schofield Dr Columbus (43213) ***(G-7727)***
Garda CL Technical Svcs Inc....937 294-4099
2690 Lance Dr Moraine (45409) ***(G-14788)***
Garden II Leasing Co LLC....419 381-0037
1015 Garden Lake Pkwy Toledo (43614) ***(G-17908)***
Garden Manor Extended Care Cen....513 420-5972
6898 Hmlton Middletown Rd Middletown (45044) ***(G-14426)***
Garden Street Iron & Metal (PA)....513 853-3700
2885 Spring Grove Ave Cincinnati (45225) ***(G-3662)***
Gardeners Edge, Piqua *Also called A M Leonard Inc* ***(G-16133)***
Gardenland, Toledo *Also called Dennis Top Soil & Landscaping* ***(G-17849)***
Gardenlife Inc....440 352-6195
11335 Concord Hambden Rd Concord Twp (44077) ***(G-9033)***
Gardens At Celina The, Celina *Also called Peregrine Health Services Inc* ***(G-2659)***
Gardens At Wapakoneta....419 738-0725
505 Walnut St Wapakoneta (45895) ***(G-18797)***
Gardens Hockey Inc....513 351-3999
2250 Seymour Ave Cincinnati (45212) ***(G-3663)***
Gardens Western Reserve Inc (PA)....330 342-9100
9975 Greentree Pkwy Streetsboro (44241) ***(G-17412)***
Gardens Western Reserve Inc....330 928-4500
45 Chart Rd Cuyahoga Falls (44223) ***(G-9191)***
Gardiner Service Company (PA)....440 248-3400
31200 Bainbridge Rd Ste 1 Solon (44139) ***(G-17008)***
Gardner Inc (PA)....614 456-4000
3641 Interchange Rd Columbus (43204) ***(G-7728)***
Gardner Cement Contractors....419 389-0768
821 Warehouse Rd Toledo (43615) ***(G-17909)***
Gardner Contracting Company....216 881-3800
2662 E 69th St Cleveland (44104) ***(G-5654)***
Gardner-Connell LLC....614 456-4000
3641 Interchange Rd Columbus (43204) ***(G-7729)***
Gareat Sports Complex, Geneva *Also called Geneva Area Recreational* ***(G-11363)***
Garfield Hts Coach Line Inc....440 232-4550
119 Manor Brook Dr Chagrin Falls (44022) ***(G-2697)***
Garick LLC....937 462-8350
11000 Huntington Rd B South Charleston (45368) ***(G-17076)***
Garland Group Inc....614 294-4411
48 E 15th Ave Frnt Columbus (43201) ***(G-7730)***
Garland/Dbs Inc....216 641-7500
3800 E 91st St Cleveland (44105) ***(G-5655)***
Garmann Miller Architects, Minster *Also called Garmann/Miller & Assoc Inc* ***(G-14662)***
Garmann/Miller & Assoc Inc....419 628-4240
38 S Lincoln Dr Minster (45865) ***(G-14662)***
Garner Transportation Group, Findlay *Also called Garner Trucking Inc* ***(G-11035)***
Garner Trucking Inc....419 422-5742
9291 County Road 313 Findlay (45840) ***(G-11035)***
Garretson Firm Resolution (PA)....513 794-0400
6281 Tri Ridge Blvd # 300 Loveland (45140) ***(G-13126)***

Garretson Resolution Group, Loveland *Also called Garretson Firm Resolution* ***(G-13126)***
Garretyson Frm Resolution Grp.....513 794-0400
6281 Tri Ridge Blvd # 300 Loveland (45140) ***(G-13127)***
Gary's Place, Canton *Also called G E G Enterprises Inc* ***(G-2375)***
Gary's Place Salon & Spa, Canton *Also called G E G Enterprises Inc* ***(G-2374)***
Gary's Prescription Pharmacy, Eaton *Also called Ancillary Medical Investments* ***(G-10552)***
Garys Pharmacy Inc.....937 456-5777
125 Amelia Dr Eaton (45320) ***(G-10561)***
Gas Natural Inc., Cleveland *Also called Hearthstone Utilities Inc* ***(G-5744)***
Gaslite Villa Convalescent Ctr.....330 494-4500
7055 High Mill Ave Nw Canal Fulton (44614) ***(G-2143)***
Gaspar Inc.....330 477-2222
1545 Whipple Ave Sw Canton (44710) ***(G-2376)***
Gastrntrlogy Assoc Clvland Inc (PA).....216 593-7700
3700 Park East Dr Ste 100 Cleveland (44122) ***(G-5656)***
Gastroenterology Associates.....330 493-1480
4665 Belpar St Nw Canton (44718) ***(G-2377)***
Gatesair Inc (HQ).....513 459-3400
5300 Kings Island Dr Mason (45040) ***(G-13704)***
Gateway Concrete Forming Svcs.....513 353-2000
5938 Hamilton Cleves Rd Miamitown (45041) ***(G-14371)***
Gateway Distribution Inc (PA).....513 891-4477
11755 Lebanon Rd Cincinnati (45241) ***(G-3664)***
Gateway Electric Incorporated.....216 518-5500
4450 Johnston Pkwy Ste A Cleveland (44128) ***(G-5657)***
Gateway Family House.....216 531-5400
1 Gateway Euclid (44119) ***(G-10756)***
Gateway Health Care Center.....216 486-4949
3 Gateway Cleveland (44119) ***(G-5658)***
Gateway Hospitality Group Inc (PA).....330 405-9800
8921 Canyon Falls Blvd # 140 Twinsburg (44087) ***(G-18420)***
Gateway Products Recycling Inc (PA).....216 341-8777
4223 E 49th St Cleveland (44125) ***(G-5659)***
Gateway Recycling, Cleveland *Also called Gateway Products Recycling Inc* ***(G-5659)***
Gateways To Better Living Inc.....330 480-9870
945 W Rayen Ave Youngstown (44502) ***(G-20194)***
Gateways To Better Living Inc.....330 270-0952
230 Idaho Rd Youngstown (44515) ***(G-20195)***
Gateways To Better Living Inc.....330 797-1764
3220 S Raccoon Rd Canfield (44406) ***(G-2191)***
Gateways To Better Living Inc (PA).....330 792-2854
6000 Mahoning Ave Ste 234 Youngstown (44515) ***(G-20196)***
Gavin AEP Plant.....740 925-3166
7397 State Route 7 N Cheshire (45620) ***(G-2791)***
Gavin Scott Salon & Spa, Hudson *Also called Kristie Warner* ***(G-12129)***
Gaydosh Associates, Cleveland *Also called Royalton Financial Group* ***(G-6419)***
Gaymont Nursing Center, Norwalk *Also called Gaymont Nursing Homes Inc* ***(G-15576)***
Gaymont Nursing Homes Inc.....419 668-8258
66 Norwood Ave Norwalk (44857) ***(G-15576)***
Gb Liquidating Company Inc.....513 248-7600
22 Whitney Dr Milford (45150) ***(G-14520)***
GBA Architectural Pdts Svcs, Medina *Also called Medina Glass Block Inc* ***(G-14100)***
Gbc Design Inc.....330 283-6870
565 White Pond Dr Akron (44320) ***(G-233)***
Gbq Consulting LLC.....614 221-1120
230 West St Ste 700 Columbus (43215) ***(G-7731)***
Gbq Holdings LLC (PA).....614 221-1120
230 West St Ste 700 Columbus (43215) ***(G-7732)***
GBS Corp (PA).....330 494-5330
7233 Freedom Ave Nw North Canton (44720) ***(G-15339)***
GBS Corp.....330 797-2700
1035 N Meridian Rd Youngstown (44509) ***(G-20197)***
GBS Printech Solutions, North Canton *Also called GBS Corp* ***(G-15339)***
Gc At Stonelick Hills.....513 735-4653
3155 Sherilyn Ln Batavia (45103) ***(G-1014)***
Gc Neighborhood Ctrs Assoc Inc.....216 298-4440
3311 Perkins Ave Ste 200 Cleveland (44114) ***(G-5660)***
Gca Services Group Inc (HQ).....800 422-8760
1350 Euclid Ave Ste 1500 Cleveland (44115) ***(G-5661)***
GCCVB, Columbus *Also called Greatr Columbus Conventn & Vis* ***(G-7776)***
GCHA, Cleveland *Also called Greater Clvland Halthcare Assn* ***(G-5701)***
Gcha.....216 696-6900
1226 Huron Rd E Cleveland (44115) ***(G-5662)***
GCI Construction LLC (PA).....216 831-6100
25101 Chagrin Blvd Beachwood (44122) ***(G-1083)***
GE Aviation Systems LLC.....513 786-4555
7831 Ashford Glen Ct West Chester (45069) ***(G-19079)***
GE Aviation Systems LLC.....937 474-9397
111 River Park Dr Dayton (45409) ***(G-9568)***
GE Aviation Systems LLC.....937 898-5881
740 E National Rd Vandalia (45377) ***(G-18681)***
GE Engine Services LLC.....513 243-9404
3024 Symmes Rd Hamilton (45015) ***(G-11731)***
GE Lighting Solutions LLC (HQ).....216 266-4800
1975 Noble Rd Ste 338e Cleveland (44112) ***(G-5663)***
GE Reuter Stokes.....216 749-6332
4710 Elizabeth Ln Cleveland (44144) ***(G-5664)***
Gear's Florists & Garden Ctrs, Cincinnati *Also called Gears Garden Center Inc* ***(G-3665)***
Gearity Early Child Care Ctr.....216 371-7356
2323 Wrenford Rd Cleveland (44118) ***(G-5665)***
Gears Garden Center Inc (PA).....513 931-3800
1579 Goodman Ave Cincinnati (45224) ***(G-3665)***
Geary Family YMCA Fostria.....419 435-6608
154 W Center St Fostoria (44830) ***(G-11128)***
Geauga Cnty Visiting Nurse Svc, Chardon *Also called Visiting Nurse Service Inc* ***(G-2776)***
Geauga County Jobs & Fmly Svcs, Chardon *Also called County of Geauga* ***(G-2747)***
Geauga Mechanical Company.....440 285-2000
12585 Chardon Windsor Rd Chardon (44024) ***(G-2750)***
Geauga Savings Bank (PA).....440 564-9441
10800 Kinsman Rd Newbury (44065) ***(G-15257)***
GECU, Cincinnati *Also called General Electric Credit Union* ***(G-3671)***
Ged Holdings Inc.....330 963-5401
9280 Dutton Dr Twinsburg (44087) ***(G-18421)***
Geddis Paving & Excavating.....419 536-8501
1019 Wamba Ave Toledo (43607) ***(G-17910)***
Geeaa Park Golf Course, Cincinnati *Also called General Electric Employees* ***(G-3672)***
Geeta Hospitality Inc.....937 642-3777
16610 Square Dr Marysville (43040) ***(G-13622)***
Geico General Insurance Co.....513 794-3426
5050 Section Ave Ste 420 Cincinnati (45212) ***(G-3666)***
Geier School Company, Cincinnati *Also called Primrose School of Symmes* ***(G-4330)***
Geis Companies, Streetsboro *Also called Geis Construction Inc* ***(G-17413)***
Geis Company, Streetsboro *Also called Highland Som Development* ***(G-17416)***
Geis Construction Inc.....330 528-3500
10020 Aurora Hudson Rd Streetsboro (44241) ***(G-17413)***
Gem City Home Care LLC.....614 588-0228
4020 Venture Ct Columbus (43228) ***(G-7733)***
Gem City Urologist Inc (PA).....937 832-8400
9000 N Main St Ste 333 Englewood (45415) ***(G-10705)***
Gem City Waterproofing.....937 220-6800
1424 Stanley Ave Dayton (45404) ***(G-9569)***
Gem Electric.....440 286-6200
12577 Gar Hwy Chardon (44024) ***(G-2751)***
Gem Industrial Inc (HQ).....419 467-3287
6842 Commodore Dr Walbridge (43465) ***(G-18775)***
Gem Interiors Inc.....513 831-6535
769 Us Route 50 Milford (45150) ***(G-14521)***
Gemco Medical, Hudson *Also called Edwards Gem Inc* ***(G-12115)***
Gemini Eye Care Center, Huber Heights *Also called James D Egbert Optometrist* ***(G-12096)***
Gemini Properties.....419 531-9211
3501 Executive Pkwy Ofc Toledo (43606) ***(G-17911)***
Gemini Properties.....614 764-2800
6470 Post Rd Ofc Dublin (43016) ***(G-10353)***
Genbanc.....419 855-8381
801 Main St Genoa (43430) ***(G-11377)***
Genco, Lockbourne *Also called Fedex Supply Chain* ***(G-12955)***
Genco Atc, Lockbourne *Also called Fedex Supply Chain* ***(G-12954)***
Genco Marketing Place, Massillon *Also called Genco of Lebanon Inc* ***(G-13813)***
Genco of Lebanon Inc.....330 837-0561
4300 Sterilite St Se Massillon (44646) ***(G-13813)***
Gene Ptacek Son Fire Eqp Inc (PA).....216 651-8300
7310 Associate Ave Cleveland (44144) ***(G-5666)***
Gene Stevens Auto & Truck Ctr.....419 429-2000
1033 Bright Rd Findlay (45840) ***(G-11036)***
Gene Stevens Honda, Findlay *Also called Gene Stevens Auto & Truck Ctr* ***(G-11036)***
Gene Tolliver Corp.....440 324-7727
6222 Norwalk Rd Medina (44256) ***(G-14068)***
General Audit Corp.....419 993-2900
2348 Baton Rouge Ste A Lima (45805) ***(G-12782)***
General Building Maintenance.....330 682-2238
500 Jefferson Ave Orrville (44667) ***(G-15773)***
General Crane Rental LLC.....330 908-0001
9680 Freeway Dr Macedonia (44056) ***(G-13198)***
General Data Company Inc (PA).....513 752-7978
4354 Ferguson Dr Cincinnati (45245) ***(G-2916)***
General Electric Company.....216 883-1000
4477 E 49th St Cleveland (44125) ***(G-5667)***
General Electric Company.....513 977-1500
201 W Crescentville Rd Cincinnati (45246) ***(G-3667)***
General Electric Company.....330 256-5331
2914 Cedar Hill Rd Cuyahoga Falls (44223) ***(G-9192)***
General Electric Company.....937 587-2631
1200 Jaybird Rd Peebles (45660) ***(G-15938)***
General Electric Company.....614 527-1078
3455 Mill Run Dr Hilliard (43026) ***(G-11902)***
General Electric Company.....513 583-3626
4800 Parkway Dr Ste 100 Mason (45040) ***(G-13705)***
General Electric Company.....330 433-5163
4500 Munson St Nw Canton (44718) ***(G-2378)***
General Electric Company.....614 899-8923
4151 Executive Pkwy # 110 Westerville (43081) ***(G-19403)***
General Electric Company.....937 534-6920
950 Forrer Blvd Dayton (45420) ***(G-9570)***
General Electric Company.....513 552-2000
1 Neumann Way Cincinnati (45215) ***(G-3668)***
General Electric Company.....513 583-3500
8700 Governors Hill Dr Cincinnati (45249) ***(G-3669)***
General Electric Company.....513 530-7107
11240 Cornell Park Dr # 114 Blue Ash (45242) ***(G-1599)***
General Electric Company.....440 255-0930
8696 Applewood Ct Mentor (44060) ***(G-14179)***

ALPHABETIC

General Electric Company 937 534-2000
950 Forrer Blvd Dayton (45420) *(G-9571)*
General Electric Company 513 243-9404
2411 Glendale Milford Rd Cincinnati (45241) *(G-3670)*
General Electric Credit Union (PA) 513 243-4328
10485 Reading Rd Cincinnati (45241) *(G-3671)*
General Electric Employees 513 243-2129
12110 Princeton Pike Cincinnati (45246) *(G-3672)*
General Electric Intl Inc (HQ) 617 443-3000
191 Rosa Parks St Cincinnati (45202) *(G-3673)*
General Electric Intl Inc 330 963-2066
8941 Dutton Dr Twinsburg (44087) *(G-18422)*
General Environmental MGT LLC 216 621-3694
16533 Chillicothe Rd Chagrin Falls (44023) *(G-2717)*
General Factory Sups Co Inc 513 864-6007
4811 Winton Rd Cincinnati (45232) *(G-3674)*
General Fncl Tax Cnsulting LLC 888 496-2679
1004 Seabrook Way Cincinnati (45245) *(G-2917)*
General Mills Inc 513 770-0558
5181 Natorp Blvd Ste 540 Mason (45040) *(G-13706)*
General Motors LLC 513 874-0535
9287 Meridian Way West Chester (45069) *(G-19080)*
General Motors LLC 513 603-6600
8752 Jacquemin Dr West Chester (45069) *(G-19081)*
General Parts Inc 330 220-6500
2830 Carquest Dr Brunswick (44212) *(G-1980)*
General Parts Inc 614 267-5197
2825 Silver Dr Columbus (43211) *(G-7734)*
General Pest Control Company 216 252-7140
3561 W 105th St Cleveland (44111) *(G-5668)*
General Plastex Inc 330 745-7775
35 Stuver Pl Barberton (44203) *(G-964)*
General Refrigeration, South Point *Also called Dickson Industrial Park Inc (G-17083)*
General Revenue Corporation (HQ) 513 469-1472
4660 Duke Dr Ste 300 Mason (45040) *(G-13707)*
General Services Cleaning Co 614 840-0562
8111 Blind Brook Ct Columbus (43235) *(G-7735)*
General Temperature Ctrl Inc 614 837-3888
970 W Walnut St Canal Winchester (43110) *(G-2159)*
General Theming Contrs LLC 614 252-6342
3750 Courtright Ct Columbus (43227) *(G-7736)*
General Tool Company (PA) 513 733-5500
101 Landy Ln Cincinnati (45215) *(G-3675)*
General Transport Incorporated 330 786-3400
1100 Jenkins Blvd Akron (44306) *(G-234)*
Generation Health & Rehab Cntr 740 344-9465
1450 W Main St Newark (43055) *(G-15168)*
Generation Health Corp 614 337-1066
5151 N Hamilton Rd Columbus (43230) *(G-7737)*
Generations Coffee Company LLC 440 546-0901
60100 W Snowell Brecksville (44141) *(G-1824)*
Generations Family Medicine 614 337-1282
765 N Hamilton Rd Ste 255 Gahanna (43230) *(G-11244)*
Genes Refrigeration Htg & AC 330 723-4104
6222 Norwalk Rd Medina (44256) *(G-14069)*
Genesis 10, Akron *Also called Genesis Corp (G-235)*
Genesis 10, Columbus *Also called Genesis Corp (G-7738)*
Genesis Caregivers 740 454-1370
2800 Maple Ave Zanesville (43701) *(G-20480)*
Genesis Corp 330 597-4100
1 Cascade Plz Ste 1230 Akron (44308) *(G-235)*
Genesis Corp 614 934-1211
4449 Easton Way Columbus (43219) *(G-7738)*
Genesis Health & Rehab, McConnelsville *Also called Careserve Inc (G-14026)*
Genesis Healthcare System (PA) 740 454-5000
2951 Maple Ave Zanesville (43701) *(G-20481)*
Genesis Healthcare System 740 453-4959
1238 Pfeifer Dr Zanesville (43701) *(G-20482)*
Genesis Hspces Pallitaive Care, Zanesville *Also called Hospice of Genesis Health (G-20488)*
Genesis Logistics, Westerville *Also called Exel Inc (G-19304)*
Genesis Oxygen & Home Med Eqp, Portsmouth *Also called Genesis Respiratory Svcs Inc (G-16278)*
Genesis Respiratory Svcs Inc 740 456-4363
25 E Stimson Ave Athens (45701) *(G-789)*
Genesis Respiratory Svcs Inc (PA) 740 354-4363
4132 Gallia St Portsmouth (45662) *(G-16278)*
Genesis Technology Partners 513 585-5800
3200 Burnet Ave Cincinnati (45229) *(G-3676)*
Genessa Health Marketing, Dayton *Also called Hafenbrack Mktg Cmmnctions Inc (G-9596)*
Genetica Dna Laboratories, Cincinnati *Also called Laboratory Corporation America (G-3956)*
Geneva Area City School Dst 440 466-2684
75 North Ave E Geneva (44041) *(G-11362)*
Geneva Area Recreational 440 466-1002
1822 S Broadway Geneva (44041) *(G-11363)*
Geneva Chervenic Realty Inc 330 686-8400
3589 Darrow Rd Stow (44224) *(G-17370)*
Geneva Liberty Steel Ltd (PA) 330 740-0103
947 Martin Luther King Jr Youngstown (44502) *(G-20198)*
Geneva Pipeline, Geneva *Also called A2 Services LLC (G-11358)*
Genicon Inc 419 491-4478
12150 Monclova Rd Swanton (43558) *(G-17565)*
GENMAK GENEVA LIBERTY, Youngstown *Also called Geneva Liberty Steel Ltd (G-20198)*
Genoa Assembly 107, Elmore *Also called International Ordr of Rnbow Fo (G-10588)*
Genoa Banking Company (PA) 419 855-8381
801 Main St Genoa (43430) *(G-11378)*
Genoa Care Center, Genoa *Also called McClellan Management Inc (G-11381)*
Genoa Legion Post 324 .... 419 855-7049
302 West St Genoa (43430) *(G-11379)*
Genomoncology LLC 216 496-4216
1375 E 9th St Ste 1120 Cleveland (44114) *(G-5669)*
Genox Transportation Inc 419 837-2023
25750 Oregon Rd Perrysburg (43551) *(G-16006)*
Genpak LLC 614 276-5156
845 Kaderly Dr Columbus (43228) *(G-7739)*
Gensuite LLC 513 774-1000
4680 Parkway Dr Ste 400 Mason (45040) *(G-13708)*
Gentiva Health Services Inc 419 887-6700
1745 Indian Wood Cir # 200 Maumee (43537) *(G-13920)*
Gentlebrook Inc (PA) 330 877-3694
880 Sunnyside St Sw Hartville (44632) *(G-11817)*
Genuine Auto Parts 864, Dayton *Also called Hahn Automotive Warehouse Inc (G-9597)*
Genuine Parts Company 614 766-6865
2665 W Dblin Granville Rd Columbus (43235) *(G-7740)*
Geo Byers Sons Holding Inc 614 239-1084
4185 E 5th Ave Columbus (43219) *(G-7741)*
Geo Gradel Co 419 691-7123
3135 Front St Toledo (43605) *(G-17912)*
Geoff Answini 513 792-7800
10506 Montgomery Rd Cincinnati (45242) *(G-3677)*
Geological Department, Cincinnati *Also called University of Cincinnati (G-4770)*
Geopfert Company, The, Akron *Also called J W Geopfert Co Inc (G-287)*
George Darr 740 498-5400
21284 Township Road 257 Newcomerstown (43832) *(G-15269)*
George Fern Company, Cincinnati *Also called Fern Exposition Services LLC (G-3603)*
George G Ellis Jr MD 330 965-0832
910 Boardman Canfield Rd Youngstown (44512) *(G-20199)*
George Gardner 419 636-4277
1420 W High St Bryan (43506) *(G-2006)*
George J Igel & Co Inc 614 445-8421
2040 Alum Creek Dr Columbus (43207) *(G-7742)*
George Knick 937 548-2832
2637 Hllgrove Wdington Rd Greenville (45331) *(G-11502)*
George Kuhn Enterprises Inc 614 481-8838
2200 Mckinley Ave Columbus (43204) *(G-7743)*
George P Ballas Buick GMC Trck (PA) 419 535-1000
5715 W Central Ave Toledo (43615) *(G-17913)*
George P Pettit MD Inc 740 354-1434
1729 27th St Bldg G Portsmouth (45662) *(G-16279)*
George Steel Fabricating Inc 513 932-2887
1207 S Us Route 42 Lebanon (45036) *(G-12606)*
George W Arensberg Phrm Inc 740 344-2195
1272 W Main St Newark (43055) *(G-15169)*
George W Mc Cloy 614 457-6233
921 Chatham Ln Ste 302 Columbus (43221) *(G-7744)*
Georgetown Life Squad 937 378-3082
301 S Main St Unit 1 Georgetown (45121) *(G-11394)*
Georgetown Vineyards Inc 740 435-3222
62920 Georgetown Rd Cambridge (43725) *(G-2115)*
Georgia Boot LLC 740 753-1951
39 E Canal St Nelsonville (45764) *(G-14964)*
Geotex Construction Svcs Inc 614 444-5690
1025 Stimmel Rd Columbus (43223) *(G-7745)*
Gerber Feed Service Inc 330 857-4421
3094 Moser Rd Dalton (44618) *(G-9241)*
Gerdau Macsteel Atmosphere Ann 330 478-0314
1501 Raff Rd Sw Canton (44710) *(G-2379)*
GERIATRICS CENTER OF MANSFIELD, Mansfield *Also called Mansfield Memorial Homes LLC (G-13333)*
Gerlach John J Center For Sen 614 566-5858
180 E Broad St Fl 34 Columbus (43215) *(G-7746)*
Germain & Co Inc 937 885-5827
10552 Success Ln Ste A Dayton (45458) *(G-9572)*
Germain Ford LLC 614 889-7777
7250 Sawmill Rd Columbus (43235) *(G-7747)*
Germain On Scarborough LLC 614 868-0300
5711 Scarborough Blvd Columbus (43232) *(G-7748)*
Germain Toyota, Columbus *Also called Germain On Scarborough LLC (G-7748)*
GERMAN AMERICAN FAMILY SOCIETY, Kent *Also called German Family Society Inc (G-12371)*
German Family Society Inc 330 678-8229
3871 Ranfield Rd Kent (44240) *(G-12371)*
German Mutual Insurance Co 419 599-3993
1000 Westmoreland Ave Napoleon (43545) *(G-14940)*
GERMAN SINGING SOCIETY, Columbus *Also called Columbus Maennerchor (G-7364)*
Germane Solutions, Dayton *Also called Germain & Co Inc (G-9572)*
Gerspacher Companies 330 725-1596
574 Leisure Ln Medina (44256) *(G-14070)*
Gervasi Vineyard, Canton *Also called Vervasi Vineyard & Itln Bistro (G-2576)*
Ges Graphite Inc (PA) 205 838-0820
12300 Snow Rd Parma (44130) *(G-15908)*
Get Help Home, Euclid *Also called Omni Park Health Care LLC (G-10770)*

Getgo Transportation Co LLC 419 666-6850
28500 Lemoyne Rd Millbury (43447) *(G-14579)*
Gethsemane Lutheran Church 614 885-4319
35 E Stanton Ave Columbus (43214) *(G-7749)*
Gexpro, Cleveland *Also called Rexel Usa Inc (G-6388)*
Gfk Custom Research LLC 513 562-1507
11240 Cornell Park Dr Blue Ash (45242) *(G-1600)*
GFS Leasing Inc (PA) 330 296-6415
1463 Tallmadge Rd Kent (44240) *(G-12372)*
GFS Leasing Inc 330 877-2666
1420 Smith Kramer St Ne Hartville (44632) *(G-11818)*
Gfwd Supply, Cincinnati *Also called General Factory Sups Co Inc (G-3674)*
Ghp II LLC 740 681-6825
2893 W Fair Ave Lancaster (43130) *(G-12544)*
Gia USA Inc 216 831-8678
4701 Richmond Rd Cleveland (44128) *(G-5670)*
Giambrone Masonry Inc 216 475-1200
10000 Aurora Hudson Rd Hudson (44236) *(G-12118)*
Giammarco Properties LLC 419 885-4844
5252 Monroe St Toledo (43623) *(G-17914)*
Giant Eagle, Parma *Also called Vala Holdings Ltd (G-15918)*
Giant Eagle Inc 330 364-5301
515 Union Ave Ste 243 Dover (44622) *(G-10190)*
Giant Eagle Inc 216 292-7000
5300 Richmond Rd Bedford Heights (44146) *(G-1352)*
Giant Industries Inc 419 531-4600
900 N Westwood Ave Toledo (43607) *(G-17915)*
Gibsonburg Health Llc 419 637-2104
355 Windsor Ln Gibsonburg (43431) *(G-11402)*
Gideon 800 395-6014
4122 Superior Ave Cleveland (44103) *(G-5671)*
Gideons International 513 932-2857
8 Claridge Ct B Lebanon (45036) *(G-12607)*
Giesecke & Devrient Amer Inc 330 425-1515
2020 Enterprise Pkwy Twinsburg (44087) *(G-18423)*
Giffin Management Group Inc 330 758-4695
6300 South Ave Apt 1200 Youngstown (44512) *(G-20200)*
Giggles & Wiggles Inc (PA) 740 574-4536
1207 Dogwood Ridge Rd Wheelersburg (45694) *(G-19577)*
Gilbane Building Company 614 948-4000
145 E Rich St Fl 4 Columbus (43215) *(G-7750)*
Gilbert Heating & AC 419 625-8875
2121 Cleveland Rd Ste A Sandusky (44870) *(G-16762)*
Gilbert Heating AC & Plumb, Sandusky *Also called Gilbert Heating & AC (G-16762)*
Giles Marathon Inc 440 974-8815
8648 Tyler Blvd Mentor (44060) *(G-14180)*
Gill Podiatry Supply Co, Strongsville *Also called Radebaugh-Fetzer Company (G-17501)*
Gillespie Drug, Caldwell *Also called Braden Med Services Inc (G-2082)*
Gillette Associates LP 330 372-1960
3310 Elm Rd Ne Warren (44483) *(G-18859)*
Gillette Nursing Home Inc 330 372-1960
3310 Elm Rd Ne Warren (44483) *(G-18860)*
Gillmore Security Systems Inc 440 232-1000
26165 Broadway Ave Cleveland (44146) *(G-5672)*
Gilmore Jasion Mahler Ltd (PA) 419 794-2000
1715 Indian Wood Cir # 100 Maumee (43537) *(G-13921)*
Gingerbread Academy, Blue Ash *Also called Gingerbread Inc (G-1601)*
Gingerbread Inc 513 793-4122
4215 Malsbary Rd Blue Ash (45242) *(G-1601)*
Giorgi of Chesapeake Inc 740 256-1724
21019 State Route 7 S Crown City (45623) *(G-9155)*
Girard Technologies Inc 330 783-2495
1101 E Indianola Ave Youngstown (44502) *(G-20201)*
Girl Scouts Lake Erie Council 330 864-9933
1 Girl Scout Way Macedonia (44056) *(G-13199)*
Girl Scouts North East Ohio 216 481-1313
4019 Prospect Ave Cleveland (44103) *(G-5673)*
Girl Scouts North East Ohio (PA) 330 864-9933
1 Girl Scout Way Macedonia (44056) *(G-13200)*
Girl Scouts of The US Amer 614 487-8101
1700 Watermark Dr Columbus (43215) *(G-7751)*
Girl Scouts of Western Ohio (PA) 513 489-1025
4930 Cornell Rd Blue Ash (45242) *(G-1602)*
Girl Scuts Appleseed Ridge Inc 419 225-4085
1870 W Robb Ave Lima (45805) *(G-12783)*
Girl Scuts Ohios Heartland Inc (PA) 614 340-8820
1700 Watermark Dr Columbus (43215) *(G-7752)*
Girl Scuts Wstn Ohio Tledo Div (PA) 419 243-8216
2244 Collingwood Blvd Toledo (43620) *(G-17916)*
Gironda Vito & Bros Inc 330 630-9399
1130 Brittain Rd Akron (44305) *(G-236)*
Giving Tree Inc (HQ) 419 898-0077
11969 W State Route 105 Oak Harbor (43449) *(G-15610)*
GKN Driveline Bowling Green, Bowling Green *Also called GKN Driveline North Amer Inc (G-1777)*
GKN Driveline North Amer Inc 419 354-3955
2223 Wood Bridge Blvd Bowling Green (43402) *(G-1777)*
GKN Freight Services Inc (HQ) 419 232-5623
1202 Industrial Dr Ste 1 Van Wert (45891) *(G-18633)*
GL Nause Co Inc 513 722-9500
1971 Phoenix Dr Loveland (45140) *(G-13128)*
Gladden Community House 614 221-7801
183 Hawkes Ave Columbus (43223) *(G-7753)*
Glass City Federal Credit Un (PA) 419 887-1000
1340 Arrowhead Dr Maumee (43537) *(G-13922)*
Glassrock Plant, Glenford *Also called Pioneer Sands LLC (G-11433)*
Glaucoma Consultants, Columbus *Also called Ohio State University (G-8396)*
Glavan & Accociates Architects 614 205-4060
107 S High St Ste 200 Columbus (43215) *(G-7754)*
Glavin Industries Inc 440 349-0049
6835 Cochran Rd Ste A Solon (44139) *(G-17009)*
Glavin Specialty Co, Solon *Also called Glavin Industries Inc (G-17009)*
Glazer's of Ohio, Columbus *Also called Southern Glzers Dstrs Ohio LLC (G-8754)*
Glazers Distributors Ohio Inc 440 542-7000
7800 Cochran Rd Solon (44139) *(G-17010)*
Gleaming Systems LLC 614 348-7475
2417 Charoe St Lewis Center (43035) *(G-12686)*
Gleason Construction Co Inc 419 865-7480
540 S Centennial Rd Holland (43528) *(G-12024)*
Glemsure Realty Trust 740 522-6620
771 S 30th St Ste 9001 Heath (43056) *(G-11837)*
Glen Arbors Ltd Partnership 937 293-0900
4000 Miller Valentine Ct Moraine (45439) *(G-14789)*
Glen Meadows, Fairfield Township *Also called Glenward Inc (G-10929)*
Glen Surplus Sales Inc (PA) 419 347-1212
14 E Smiley Ave Shelby (44875) *(G-16900)*
Glen Wesley Inc 614 888-7492
5155 N High St Columbus (43214) *(G-7755)*
Glenbeigh Health Sources Inc (PA) 440 951-7000
2863 State Route 45 N Rock Creek (44084) *(G-16558)*
Glenbeigh Hospital (PA) 440 563-3400
2863 State Route 45 N Rock Creek (44084) *(G-16559)*
Glencare Center, Cincinnati *Also called Carington Health Systems (G-3185)*
Glencoe Restoration Group LLC 330 752-1244
575 Canton Rd Akron (44312) *(G-237)*
Glendale Place Care Center LLC 513 771-1779
779 Glendale Milford Rd Cincinnati (45215) *(G-3678)*
Glendale, The, Toledo *Also called Chelmsford Apartments Ltd (G-17803)*
Glendora Health Care Center 330 264-0912
1552 N Honeytown Rd Wooster (44691) *(G-19863)*
Glenellen, North Lima *Also called Lakeside Manor Inc (G-15404)*
Glenlaurel Inc 740 385-4070
14940 Mount Olive Rd Rockbridge (43149) *(G-16560)*
Glenlurel-A Scottish Cntry Inn, Rockbridge *Also called Glenlaurel Inc (G-16560)*
Glenmont 614 876-0084
4599 Avery Rd Hilliard (43026) *(G-11903)*
Glenmoor Country Club Inc 330 966-3600
4191 Glenmoor Rd Nw Lowr Canton (44718) *(G-2380)*
Glenn View Manor Inc 330 652-9901
3379 Main St Star Rt 46 Mineral Ridge (44440) *(G-14636)*
Glennco Systems Inc 740 353-4328
928 16th St Portsmouth (45662) *(G-16280)*
Glenny Glass Company 513 489-2233
209 Castleberry Ct Milford (45150) *(G-14522)*
Glenridge Machine Co 440 975-1055
4610 Beidler Rd Willoughby (44094) *(G-19666)*
Glenview Cntr For Chld Cr & Lr, Cleveland *Also called Bay Village City School Dst (G-5102)*
Glenward Inc 513 863-3100
3472 Hamilton Mason Rd Fairfield Township (45011) *(G-10929)*
Glenway Automotive Service 513 921-2117
4033 Glenway Ave Cincinnati (45205) *(G-3679)*
Glenway Family Medicine, Cincinnati *Also called Christ Hospital Corporation (G-3269)*
Glenwood Assisted Living, Canton *Also called Stone Crossing Assisted Living (G-2551)*
Glenwood Community Inc 740 376-9555
200 Timberline Dr Apt 206 Marietta (45750) *(G-13447)*
Glidden House Associates Ltd 216 231-8900
1901 Ford Dr Cleveland (44106) *(G-5674)*
Glidden House Inn, Cleveland *Also called Glidden House Associates Ltd (G-5674)*
Glimcher Properties Ltd Partnr, Columbus *Also called Washington PRI (G-8967)*
Glm Transport Inc (PA) 419 363-2041
12806 State Route 118 Rockford (45882) *(G-16562)*
Global Cnsld Holdings Inc (PA) 513 703-0965
3965 Marble Ridge Ln Mason (45040) *(G 13709)*
Global Exec Slutions Group LLC 330 666-3354
3505 Embassy Pkwy Ste 200 Akron (44333) *(G-238)*
Global Graphene Group Inc 937 331-9884
1240 Mccook Ave Dayton (45404) *(G-9573)*
Global Ground, Cleveland *Also called Servisair LLC (G-6472)*
Global Gvrnment Edcatn Sltions 937 368-2308
6450 Poe Ave Ste 200 Dayton (45414) *(G-9574)*
Global Insulation Inc (PA) 330 479-3100
4450 Belden Village St Nw # 306 Canton (44718) *(G-2381)*
Global Mall Unlimited 740 533-7203
1423 Missouri Ave Delaware (43015) *(G-10101)*
Global Meals, Columbus *Also called Casleo Corporation (G-7205)*
Global Military Expert Co 800 738-9795
275 Palmetto Ct Beavercreek (45440) *(G-1242)*
Global Risk Consultants Corp 440 746-8861
7000 S Edgerton Rd # 100 Brecksville (44141) *(G-1825)*
Global Scrap Management Inc (PA) 513 576-6600
4340 Batavia Rd Batavia (45103) *(G-1015)*

ALPHABETIC

Global Spectrum — ALPHABETIC SECTION

Global Spectrum 513 419-7300
  525 Elm St Cincinnati (45202) *(G-3680)*
Global Tchnical Recruiters Inc (PA) 216 251-9560
  27887 Clemens Rd Ste 1 Westlake (44145) *(G-19486)*
Global Tchnical Recruiters Inc 440 365-1670
  366 Chestnut Commons Dr Elyria (44035) *(G-10630)*
Global Technology Center, Holland Also called Tekni-Plex Inc *(G-12060)*
Global Telehealth Services, Hudson Also called Integrated Telehealth Inc *(G-12124)*
Global Transportation Services 614 409-0770
  7139 Americana Pkwy Reynoldsburg (43068) *(G-16454)*
Global Workplace Solutions LLC 513 759-6000
  9823 Cincinnati Dayton Rd West Chester (45069) *(G-19082)*
Global-Pak Inc (PA) 330 482-1993
  9636 Elkton Rd Lisbon (44432) *(G-12938)*
Globaltranz Enterprises Inc 513 745-0138
  10945 Reed Hartman Hwy Blue Ash (45242) *(G-1603)*
Globe Food Equipment Company 937 299-5493
  2153 Dryden Rd Moraine (45439) *(G-14790)*
Globe Trucking Inc 419 727-8307
  5261 Stickney Ave Toledo (43612) *(G-17917)*
Glomark-Governan, Columbus Also called Governan LLC *(G-7763)*
Gloria Gadmack Do 216 363-2353
  1730 W 25th St Cleveland (44113) *(G-5675)*
Glow Industries Inc (PA) 419 872-4772
  12962 Eckel Junction Rd Perrysburg (43551) *(G-16007)*
Glowe-Smith Industrial Inc 330 638-5088
  812 Youngstwn Kgsvl Rd Se Vienna (44473) *(G-18737)*
Glt Inc 937 395-0508
  2691 Lance Dr Moraine (45409) *(G-14791)*
Glt Products, Solon Also called Great Lakes Textiles Inc *(G-17012)*
GMAC, Canfield Also called Ally Financial Inc *(G-2182)*
GMAC Insurance, Akron Also called Sbm Business Services Inc *(G-429)*
GMAC Insurance, Richfield Also called Explorer Rv Insurance Agcy Inc *(G-16507)*
GMAC Real Estate, Avon Also called Sweda Sweda Associates Inc *(G-917)*
GMAC Realestate, Warren Also called Eaton Group GMAC Real Estate *(G-18855)*
GMC Excavation & Trucking 419 468-0121
  1859 Biddle Rd Galion (44833) *(G-11300)*
GMI Holdings Inc 330 794-0846
  2850 Gilchrist Rd Akron (44305) *(G-239)*
Gms Inc 937 222-4444
  1509 Stanley Ave Dayton (45404) *(G-9575)*
Gms Management Co Inc Iowa (PA) 216 766-6000
  4645 Richmond Rd Ste 101 Cleveland (44128) *(G-5676)*
Gms Realty, Cleveland Also called Gms Management Co Inc Iowa *(G-5676)*
Gmti, Cincinnati Also called Gannett Media Tech Intl *(G-3661)*
Gng Music Instruction, New Albany Also called Qwaide Enterprises LLC *(G-15003)*
Go 2 It Group, Westlake Also called Career Cnnctions Staffing Svcs *(G-19469)*
Goddard School, Columbus Also called Bailey & Long Inc *(G-7083)*
Goddard School, Grove City Also called Dakota Girls LLC *(G-11551)*
Goddard School, Strongsville Also called Hewlettco Inc *(G-17469)*
Goddard School 513 697-9663
  782 Lveland Miamiville Rd Loveland (45140) *(G-13129)*
Goddard School 614 920-9810
  6405 Canal St Canal Winchester (43110) *(G-2160)*
Goddard School 513 271-6311
  4430 Red Bank Rd Cincinnati (45227) *(G-3681)*
Goddard School of Avon 440 934-3300
  2555 Hale St Avon (44011) *(G-894)*
Goddard School of Landon, The, Mason Also called Krieger Enterprises Inc *(G-13729)*
Goddard School of New Albany, New Albany Also called Campbell Family Childcare Inc *(G-14977)*
Goddard School of Twinsburg 330 487-0394
  2608 Glenwood Dr Twinsburg (44087) *(G-18424)*
Goddard School, The, Westerville Also called Powell Enterprises Inc *(G-19342)*
Goddard School, The, Cincinnati Also called Goddard School *(G-3681)*
Goddard School, The, Mason Also called P J & R J Connection Inc *(G-13744)*
Goddard Schools, Hudson Also called J Nan Enterprises LLC *(G-12125)*
Godfrey & Wing Inc (PA) 330 562-1440
  220 Campus Dr Aurora (44202) *(G-840)*
Godman Guild (PA) 614 294-5476
  303 E 6th Ave Columbus (43201) *(G-7756)*
Goettle Co 513 825-8100
  12071 Hamilton Ave Cincinnati (45231) *(G-3682)*
Goettle Construction, Cincinnati Also called Goettle Holding Company Inc *(G-3683)*
Goettle Holding Company Inc (PA) 513 825-8100
  12071 Hamilton Ave Cincinnati (45231) *(G-3683)*
Goettsch Int Inc (PA) 513 563-6500
  9852 Redhill Dr Blue Ash (45242) *(G-1604)*
Going Home Medical Holding Co 305 340-1034
  15830 Foltz Pkwy Strongsville (44149) *(G-17466)*
Gold Cross, Youngstown Also called Rural/Metro Corporation *(G-20363)*
Gold Cross Ambulance Svcs Inc 330 744-4161
  1122 E Midlothian Blvd Youngstown (44502) *(G-20202)*
Gold Cross Limousine Service 330 757-3053
  26 Sexton St Struthers (44471) *(G-17531)*
Gold Key Homes, Miamisburg Also called Oberer Residential Cnstr *(G-14329)*
Gold Star Chili Inc (PA) 513 231-4541
  650 Lunken Park Dr Cincinnati (45226) *(G-3684)*
Gold Star Insulation L P 614 221-3241
  495 S High St Columbus (43215) *(G-7757)*
Goldberg Companies Inc 440 944-8656
  2252 Par Ln Willoughby Hills (44094) *(G-19730)*
Goldberg Companies Inc 216 475-2600
  4440 Granada Blvd Apt 1 Cleveland (44128) *(G-5677)*
Golden Buckeye Program, Portsmouth Also called Ussa Inc *(G-16319)*
Golden Endings Golden Ret Resc 614 486-0773
  1043 Elmwood Ave Columbus (43212) *(G-7758)*
Golden Hawk Inc 419 683-3304
  4594 Lincoln Hwy 30 Crestline (44827) *(G-9145)*
Golden Hawk Transportation Co (PA) 419 683-3304
  4594 Lincoln Hwy Crestline (44827) *(G-9146)*
Golden Jersey Inn, Yellow Springs Also called Youngs Jersey Dairy Inc *(G-20091)*
Golden Key Ctr For Excptnl Chl 330 493-4400
  1431 30th St Nw Canton (44709) *(G-2382)*
Golden Lamb 513 932-5065
  27 S Broadway St Lebanon (45036) *(G-12608)*
Golden Lamb Rest Ht & Gift Sp, Lebanon Also called Golden Lamb *(G-12608)*
Golden Leaf, Solon Also called Snf Wadsworth LLC *(G-17052)*
Golden Living LLC 419 599-4070
  240 Northcrest Dr Napoleon (43545) *(G-14941)*
Golden Living LLC 419 227-2154
  599 S Shawnee St Lima (45804) *(G-12784)*
Golden Living LLC 419 394-3308
  1140 S Knoxville Ave Saint Marys (45885) *(G-16674)*
Golden Living LLC 440 247-4200
  150 Cleveland St Chagrin Falls (44022) *(G-2698)*
Golden Living LLC 614 861-6666
  1425 Yorkland Rd Columbus (43232) *(G-7759)*
Golden Living LLC 440 256-8100
  9679 Chillicothe Rd Willoughby (44094) *(G-19667)*
Golden Living LLC 330 297-5781
  565 Bryn Mawr St Ravenna (44266) *(G-16386)*
Golden Living LLC 330 762-6486
  721 Hickory St Akron (44303) *(G-240)*
Golden Living LLC 330 335-1558
  365 Johnson Rd Wadsworth (44281) *(G-18753)*
Golden Living LLC 330 725-3393
  555 Springbrook Dr Medina (44256) *(G-14071)*
Golden String Inc 330 503-3894
  16 S Phelps St Youngstown (44503) *(G-20203)*
Golden Years Health Care, Hamilton Also called Golden Years Nursing Home Inc *(G-11732)*
Golden Years Nursing Home Inc 513 893-0471
  2436 Old Oxford Rd Hamilton (45013) *(G-11732)*
Goldfish Swim School 216 364-9090
  4670 Richmond Rd Ste 100 Chagrin Falls (44023) *(G-2718)*
Goldwood Primary School Pta 440 356-6720
  21600 Center Ridge Rd Rocky River (44116) *(G-16579)*
GOLDWOOD PTA, Rocky River Also called Goldwood Primary School Pta *(G-16579)*
Golf and Swim Club, Canton Also called Meadowlake Corporation *(G-2456)*
Golf Center At Kings Island, Mason Also called Grizzly Golf Center Inc *(G-13712)*
Golf Club Co 614 855-7326
  4522 Kitzmiller Rd New Albany (43054) *(G-14987)*
Golf Club of Dublin LLC 614 889-5469
  5805 Eiterman Rd Dublin (43016) *(G-10354)*
Golf Course At Yankee Trace, Dayton Also called City of Centerville *(G-9409)*
Golf Course Maintenance 330 262-9141
  1599 Mechanicsburg Rd Wooster (44691) *(G-19864)*
Golf Galaxy Golfworks Inc 740 328-4193
  4820 Jacksontown Rd Newark (43056) *(G-15170)*
Golfworks, The, Newark Also called Golf Galaxy Golfworks Inc *(G-15170)*
Goliath Contracting Ltd 614 568-7878
  405 Waggoner Rd Reynoldsburg (43068) *(G-16455)*
Good Night Medical Ohio LLC 614 384-7433
  975 Eastwind Dr Ste 165 Westerville (43081) *(G-19404)*
Good Park Golf Course, Akron Also called City of Akron *(G-138)*
Good Samaritan Health Center, Englewood Also called Good Samaritan Hospital *(G-10706)*
Good Samaritan Hosp Cincinnati (HQ) 513 569-6251
  375 Dixmyth Ave Cincinnati (45220) *(G-3685)*
Good Samaritan Hospital 937 224-4646
  1 Elizabeth Pl Dayton (45417) *(G-9576)*
Good Samaritan Hospital (HQ) 937 278-2612
  2222 Philadelphia Dr Dayton (45406) *(G-9577)*
Good Samaritan Hospital 937 276-6784
  9000 N Main St Ofc Englewood (45415) *(G-10706)*
Good Samaritan Hospital 937 734-2612
  40 W 4th St Ste 1202 Dayton (45402) *(G-9578)*
Good Samaritan Hospital Med, Cincinnati Also called Kidney & Hypertension Center *(G-3921)*
Good Samaritan Nursing Home, Cleveland Also called Diversicare of Avon LLC *(G-5491)*
Good Samaritan Soc - Arlington, Arlington Also called Evangelical Lutheran *(G-647)*
Good Samaritan, The, Millersburg Also called Christian Aid Ministries *(G-14593)*
Good Shepard Village LLC 937 322-1911
  422 N Burnett Rd Springfield (45503) *(G-17202)*
Good Shepard, The, Ashland Also called Lutheran Scial Svcs Centl Ohio *(G-686)*
Good Shepherd Home 419 937-1801
  725 Columbus Ave Fostoria (44830) *(G-11129)*
Good Shepherd Home For Aged 614 228-5200
  622 Center St Ashland (44805) *(G-680)*

Good Smaritan Netwrk Ross Cnty 740 774-6303
133 E 7th St Chillicothe (45601) *(G-2842)*
Goodall Complex, Cincinnati *Also called Goodall Properties Ltd (G-3686)*
Goodall Properties Ltd 513 621-5522
324 W 9th St Ste 500 Cincinnati (45202) *(G-3686)*
Goodin Electric Inc 740 522-3113
605 Garfield Ave Ste A Newark (43055) *(G-15171)*
Goodman Beverage Co Inc 440 787-2255
5901 Baumhart Rd Lorain (44053) *(G-13040)*
Goodman Properties Inc 740 264-7781
100 Mall Dr Ofc Ofc Steubenville (43952) *(G-17318)*
Goodnight Inn Inc 419 334-9551
3701 N State Route 53 Fremont (43420) *(G-11203)*
Goodremonts 419 476-1492
1017 W Sylvania Ave Toledo (43612) *(G-17918)*
Goodrich Avionics, Columbus *Also called L3 Aviation Products Inc (G-8025)*
Goodrich Gannett Headstart, Cleveland *Also called Goodrich Gnnett Nghborhood Ctr (G-5678)*
Goodrich Gnnett Nghborhood Ctr 216 432-1717
1400 E 55th St Cleveland (44103) *(G-5678)*
Goodw Indus of Erie, Huron, Ot, Sandusky *Also called Goodwill Industries of Erie (G-16763)*
Goodwill Columbus, Columbus *Also called Goodwill Inds Centl Ohio Inc (G-7760)*
Goodwill Ester Seals Miami Vly (PA) 937 461-4800
660 S Main St Dayton (45402) *(G-9579)*
Goodwill Ester Seals Miami Vly 937 461-4800
660 S Main St Dayton (45402) *(G-9580)*
Goodwill Idstrs Grtr Clvlnd L 330 339-5746
260 Bluebell Dr Nw New Philadelphia (44663) *(G-15095)*
Goodwill Idstrs Grtr Clvlnd L 440 783-1168
16160 Pearl Rd Strongsville (44136) *(G-17467)*
Goodwill Idstrs Grtr Clvlnd L 330 877-7921
864 W Maple St Ste A Hartville (44632) *(G-11819)*
Goodwill Idstrs Grtr Clvlnd L 216 581-6320
12650 Rockside Rd Cleveland (44125) *(G-5679)*
Goodwill Idstrs Grtr Clvlnd L (PA) 330 454-9461
408 9th St Sw Canton (44707) *(G-2383)*
Goodwill Inds Centl Ohio Inc (PA) 614 294-5181
1331 Edgehill Rd Columbus (43212) *(G-7760)*
Goodwill Inds Centl Ohio Inc 740 439-7000
1712 Southgate Pkwy Cambridge (43725) *(G-2116)*
Goodwill Inds Centl Ohio Inc 740 373-1304
1303 Colegate Dr Marietta (45750) *(G-13448)*
Goodwill Inds Centl Ohio Inc 614 274-5296
890 N Hague Ave Columbus (43204) *(G-7761)*
Goodwill Inds Lorain Cnty Inc (PA) 440 242-2124
145 Keep Ct Elyria (44035) *(G-10631)*
Goodwill Inds NW Ohio Inc (PA) 419 255-0070
1120 Madison Ave Toledo (43604) *(G-17919)*
Goodwill Inds of Ashtabula (PA) 440 964-3565
621 Goodwill Dr Ashtabula (44004) *(G-745)*
Goodwill Inds of S Centl Ohio 740 702-4000
457 E Main St Chillicothe (45601) *(G-2843)*
Goodwill Inds of Southern Ohio (PA) 740 353-4394
324 Chillicothe St Portsmouth (45662) *(G-16281)*
Goodwill Inds Rhbilitation Ctr 740 264-6000
131 Main St Steubenville (43953) *(G-17319)*
Goodwill Inds Rhbilitation Ctr (PA) 330 454-9461
408 9th St Sw Canton (44707) *(G-2384)*
Goodwill Industries (PA) 330 264-1300
1034 Nold Ave Wooster (44691) *(G-19865)*
Goodwill Industries Inc 330 724-6995
570 E Waterloo Rd Akron (44319) *(G-241)*
Goodwill Industries of Akron (PA) 330 724-6995
570 E Waterloo Rd Akron (44319) *(G-242)*
Goodwill Industries of Erie 419 355-1579
1040 Oak Harbor Rd Fremont (43420) *(G-11204)*
Goodwill Industries of Erie (PA) 419 625-4744
419 W Market St Sandusky (44870) *(G-16763)*
Goodwill Industries of Erie 419 334-7566
1597 Pontiac Ave Fremont (43420) *(G-11205)*
Goodwill Industries of Lima (PA) 419 228-4821
940 N Cable Rd Ste 1 Lima (45805) *(G-12785)*
Goodwill Industry, Ashtabula *Also called Goodwill Inds of Ashtabula (G-745)*
GOODWILL RETAIL STORE, Zanesville *Also called Zanesvlle Welfre Orgnztn/Goodw (G-20560)*
Goodwill Service Guild 513 771-4800
10600 Springfield Rd Cincinnati (45215) *(G-3687)*
Goodyear Tire & Rubber Company (PA) 330 796-2121
200 E Innovation Way Akron (44316) *(G-243)*
Goodyear Tire & Rubber Company 440 735-9910
7230 Northfield Rd Walton Hills (44146) *(G-18789)*
Goodyear Tire & Rubber Company 614 871-1881
1950 Hendrix Dr Grove City (43123) *(G-11565)*
Goofy Golf II Inc 419 732-6671
1530 S Danbury Rd Port Clinton (43452) *(G-16245)*
Goofy Golf Inc 419 625-1308
3020 Milan Rd Sandusky (44870) *(G-16764)*
Gooseberry Patch, Columbus *Also called H & M Patch Company (G-7788)*
Gorant Chocolatier LLC (PA) 330 726-8821
8301 Market St Boardman (44512) *(G-1740)*
Gorant's Yum Yum Tree, Boardman *Also called Gorant Chocolatier LLC (G-1740)*
Gorbett Enterprises of Solon (PA) 440 248-3950
6531 Cochran Rd Solon (44139) *(G-17011)*
Gordon Bernard Company LLC 513 248-7600
22 Whitney Dr Milford (45150) *(G-14523)*
Gordon Bros Water, Salem *Also called Gordon Brothers Inc (G-16697)*
Gordon Brothers Inc (PA) 800 331-7611
776 N Ellsworth Ave Salem (44460) *(G-16697)*
Gordon Flesch Company Inc 419 884-2031
2756 Lexington Ave Mansfield (44904) *(G-13305)*
Gordon Food Service Inc 419 747-1212
1310 N Lexngtn Sprngmill Ontario (44906) *(G-15689)*
Gordon Food Service Inc 419 225-8983
3447 Elida Rd Lima (45807) *(G-12786)*
Gordon Food Service Inc 440 953-1785
7220 Mentor Ave Mentor (44060) *(G-14181)*
Gordon Food Service Inc 216 573-4900
7575 Granger Rd Cleveland (44125) *(G-5680)*
Gordon Milk Transport, Sugarcreek *Also called Drasc Enterprises Inc (G-17544)*
Gorell Enterprises Inc (PA) 724 465-1800
10250 Philipp Pkwy Streetsboro (44241) *(G-17414)*
Gorell Windows & Doors, Streetsboro *Also called Gorell Enterprises Inc (G-17414)*
Gorilla Glue Company 513 271-3300
2101 E Kemper Rd Cincinnati (45241) *(G-3688)*
Gorjanc Comfort Services Inc 440 449-4411
42 Alpha Park Cleveland (44143) *(G-5681)*
Gorjanc Mechanical, Cleveland *Also called Gorjanc Comfort Services Inc (G-5681)*
Gorsuch Management, Lancaster *Also called Fairfield Homes Inc (G-12534)*
Gorsuch Management, Lancaster *Also called Fairfield Homes Inc (G-12535)*
Gosh Enterprises Inc (PA) 614 923-4700
2500 Farmers Dr 140 Columbus (43235) *(G-7762)*
Gosiger Inc (PA) 937 228-5174
108 Mcdonough St Dayton (45402) *(G-9581)*
Gosiger Inc 937 228-5174
108 Mcdonough St Dayton (45402) *(G-9582)*
Goss Supply Company (PA) 740 454-2571
620 Marietta St Zanesville (43701) *(G-20483)*
Gottlieb Johnson Beam Dal P 740 452-7555
320 Main St Zanesville (43701) *(G-20484)*
Goudreau Management, Cleveland *Also called G J Goudreau & Co (G-5646)*
Goudy Internal Medicine Inc 419 468-8323
270 Portland Way S Rear Galion (44833) *(G-11301)*
Goudy, James A II MD, Galion *Also called Goudy Internal Medicine Inc (G-11301)*
Govana Hospital, Newark *Also called Yeater Alene K MD (G-15249)*
Governan LLC 614 761-2400
4862 Pleasant Valley Dr Columbus (43220) *(G-7763)*
Government Acquisitions Inc 513 721-8700
720 E Pete Rose Way # 360 Cincinnati (45202) *(G-3689)*
Government Resource Partners, Columbus *Also called Fhc Enterprises LLC (G-7653)*
Governor's Room, Oxford *Also called Alexander House Inc (G-15810)*
Governor's Village Assisted Ll, Cleveland *Also called Governors Village LLC (G-5682)*
Governors Pointe LLC 440 205-1570
8506 Hendricks Rd Ofc Mentor (44060) *(G-14182)*
Governors Village LLC 440 449-8788
280 N Cmmons Blvd Apt 101 Cleveland (44143) *(G-5682)*
Gowdy Partners LLC 614 488-4424
1533 Lake Shore Dr Ste 50 Columbus (43204) *(G-7764)*
Goza Dialysis LLC 513 738-0276
3825 Kraus Ln Ste S Fairfield (45014) *(G-10852)*
GP Strategies Corporation 513 583-8810
4770 Duke Dr Ste 120 Mason (45040) *(G-13710)*
GPA, Cincinnati *Also called Gus Perdikakis Associates (G-3721)*
Gpax Ltd 614 501-7622
555 Lancaster Ave Reynoldsburg (43068) *(G-16456)*
Gpc Contracting Company 740 264-6060
500 E Church St Ste 3 Steubenville (43953) *(G-17320)*
Gpd Associates, Akron *Also called Gpd Services Company Inc (G-244)*
Gpd Group, Columbus *Also called Schomer Glaus Pyle (G-8699)*
Gpd Group, Cleveland *Also called Schomer Glaus Pyle (G-6449)*
GPD GROUP, Akron *Also called Schomer Glaus Pyle (G-430)*
Gpd Group, Coventry Township *Also called Schomer Glaus Pyle (G-9132)*
Gpd Services Company Inc (PA) 330 572-2100
520 S Main St Ste 2531 Akron (44311) *(G-244)*
Gprs, Toledo *Also called Ground Penetrating Radar Sys (G-17926)*
Graber Metal Works Inc 440 237-8422
9664 Akins Rd Ste 1 North Royalton (44133) *(G-15490)*
Grabill Plumbing & Heating 330 756-2075
10235 Manchester Ave Sw Beach City (44608) *(G-1043)*
Grace Baptist Church (PA) 937 652-1133
960 Childrens Home Rd Urbana (43078) *(G-18589)*
Grace Baptist Preschool, Urbana *Also called Grace Baptist Church (G-18589)*
Grace Brethren Village Inc 937 836-4011
1010 Taywood Rd Ofc Englewood (45322) *(G-10707)*
Grace Brthren Ch Columbus Ohio (PA) 614 888-7733
8724 Olde Worthington Rd Westerville (43082) *(G-19310)*
Grace Consulting Inc (PA) 440 647-6672
510 Dickson St Lowr Wellington (44090) *(G-18992)*
Grace Hospice LLC 513 458-5545
2100 Sherman Ave Ste 103 Cincinnati (45212) *(G-3690)*

Grace Hospice LLC 937 293-1381
  3033 Kettering Blvd # 220 Moraine (45439) *(G-14792)*
Grace Hospice LLC 216 288-7413
  7314 Industrial Park Blvd Mentor (44060) *(G-14183)*
Grace Hospice LLC 440 826-0350
  16600 W Sprague Rd Ste 35 Cleveland (44130) *(G-5683)*
Grace Hospice of Middleburg, Cleveland *Also called Grace Hospice LLC (G-5683)*
Grace Hospital 216 476-2704
  18101 Lorain Ave Cleveland (44111) *(G-5684)*
Grace Hospital 216 687-1500
  44 Blaine Ave Bedford (44146) *(G-1308)*
Grace Hospital 216 687-1500
  20000 Harvard Ave Warrensville Heights (44122) *(G-18933)*
Grace Hospital 216 687-4013
  254 Cleveland Ave Amherst (44001) *(G-595)*
Grace Polaris Church, Westerville *Also called Grace Brthren Ch Columbus Ohio (G-19310)*
Grace Resurrection Association 937 548-2595
  Grace Rsrrction Cmnty Ctr Greenville (45331) *(G-11503)*
Grace Resurrection Cmnty Ctr, Greenville *Also called Grace Resurrection Association (G-11503)*
Graceworks Lutheran Services 937 436-6850
  6443 Bethany Village Dr Dayton (45459) *(G-9583)*
Graceworks Lutheran Services (PA) 937 433-2140
  6430 Inner Mission Way Dayton (45459) *(G-9584)*
Graceworks Lutheran Services 937 433-2110
  6430 Inner Mission Way Dayton (45459) *(G-9585)*
Gracie Plum Investments Inc 740 355-9029
  609 2nd St Unit 2 Portsmouth (45662) *(G-16282)*
Graco Ohio Inc 330 494-1313
  8400 Port Jackson Ave Nw Canton (44720) *(G-2385)*
Gracor Language Services, Westerville *Also called Ceiba Enterprises Incorporated (G-19376)*
Grady Memorial Hospital (PA) 740 615-1000
  561 W Central Ave Delaware (43015) *(G-10102)*
Grady Rentals LLC 330 627-2022
  4094 Canton Rd Nw Carrollton (44615) *(G-2621)*
Grady Veterinary Hospital Inc 513 931-8675
  9255 Winton Rd Cincinnati (45231) *(G-3691)*
Grae-Con Construction Inc (PA) 740 282-6830
  880 Kingsdale Rd Steubenville (43952) *(G-17321)*
Grae-Con Contructions, Steubenville *Also called Grae-Con Construction Inc (G-17321)*
Graf and Sons Inc 614 481-2020
  2300 International St Columbus (43228) *(G-7765)*
Graf Growers, Akron *Also called White Pond Gardens Inc (G-509)*
Graffiti Co, Cleveland *Also called Barbs Graffiti Inc (G-5094)*
Graffiti Inc 216 881-5550
  3200 Carnegie Ave Cleveland (44115) *(G-5685)*
Graftech Holdings Inc 216 676-2000
  6100 Oak Tree Blvd # 300 Independence (44131) *(G-12214)*
Graham Chevrolet-Cadillac Co (PA) 419 989-4012
  1515 W 4th St Ontario (44906) *(G-15690)*
Graham Investment Co (PA) 740 382-0902
  3007 Harding Hwy E # 203 Marion (43302) *(G-13541)*
Graham Packaging Holdings Co 419 628-1070
  255 Southgate Minster (45865) *(G-14663)*
Graham Packg Plastic Pdts Inc 419 423-3271
  170 Stanford Pkwy Findlay (45840) *(G-11037)*
Grainger 152, Blue Ash *Also called WW Grainger Inc (G-1722)*
Grainger 165, Macedonia *Also called W W Grainger Inc (G-13217)*
Grainger 176, Columbus *Also called WW Grainger Inc (G-9010)*
Grand Aerie of The Fraternal (PA) 614 883-2200
  1623 Gateway Cir Grove City (43123) *(G-11566)*
Grand Central Auto Recycling, Massillon *Also called Greenleaf Ohio LLC (G-13815)*
Grand Court, The, Findlay *Also called Brookdale Senior Living Inc (G-11008)*
Grand Heritage Hotel Portland 440 734-4477
  25105 Country Club Blvd North Olmsted (44070) *(G-15424)*
GRAND LAKE HEALTH SYSTEM, Saint Marys *Also called Joint Township Dst Mem Hosp (G-16676)*
Grand Lake Primary Care, Saint Marys *Also called Joint Township Dst Mem Hosp (G-16675)*
Grand Rapids Care Center, Grand Rapids *Also called Rapids Nursing Homes Inc (G-11453)*
Grand Rapids Care Center, Grand Rapids *Also called Saber Healthcare Group LLC (G-11454)*
Grand River Seafood Supply, Grand River *Also called 101 River Inc (G-11455)*
Grand Valley Country Manor, Windsor *Also called Lynnhaven V LLC (G-19805)*
Grand View Inn Inc 740 377-4388
  154 County Road 450 South Point (45680) *(G-17086)*
Grande Oaks & Grande Pavillion, Cleveland *Also called Oakwood Health Care Svcs Inc (G-6175)*
Grande Pointe Healthcare Cmnty, Cleveland *Also called Merit Leasing Co LLC (G-6027)*
Grandmas Gardens Inc 937 885-2973
  8107 State Route 48 Waynesville (45068) *(G-18982)*
Grandview Avenue Home, Waverly *Also called Buckeye Community Services Inc (G-18967)*
Grandview Family Practice 740 258-9267
  1550 W 5th Ave Lowr Columbus (43212) *(G-7766)*
Grandview Hospital & Med Ctr, Dayton *Also called Dayton Osteopathic Hospital (G-9484)*
Grandview Ht Ltd Partnr Ohio 937 766-5519
  383 E Leffel Ln Springfield (45505) *(G-17203)*

Grandview Inn, South Point *Also called Grand View Inn Inc (G-17086)*
Grange Indemnity Insurance Co 614 445-2900
  671 S High St Columbus (43206) *(G-7767)*
Grange Insurance Companies, Columbus *Also called Grange Mutual Casualty Company (G-7769)*
Grange Life Insurance Company 800 445-3030
  671 S High St Columbus (43206) *(G-7768)*
Grange Mutual Casualty Co 601, Cleveland *Also called Grange Mutual Casualty Company (G-5686)*
Grange Mutual Casualty Co 721, Cincinnati *Also called Grange Mutual Casualty Company (G-3692)*
Grange Mutual Casualty Company, Columbus *Also called Grange Indemnity Insurance Co (G-7767)*
Grange Mutual Casualty Company (PA) 614 445-2900
  671 S High St Columbus (43206) *(G-7769)*
Grange Mutual Casualty Company 614 337-4400
  7271 Engle Rd Ste 400 Cleveland (44130) *(G-5686)*
Grange Mutual Casualty Company 513 671-3722
  12021 Sheraton Ln Cincinnati (45246) *(G-3692)*
Granger Elc Hancock Cnty LLC 517 371-9765
  3763 County Road 140 Findlay (45840) *(G-11038)*
Granger Township 330 239-2111
  3737 Ridge Rd Medina (44256) *(G-14072)*
Granger Township Fire & Rescue, Medina *Also called Granger Township (G-14072)*
Granite Transformations, Dayton *Also called Countertop Alternatives Inc (G-9430)*
Grant Thornton LLP 216 771-1400
  1375 E 9th St Ste 1500 Cleveland (44114) *(G-5687)*
Grant Thornton LLP 513 762-5000
  4000 Smith Rd Ste 500 Cincinnati (45209) *(G-3693)*
Granville Builders Supply, Columbus *Also called Columbus Coal & Lime Co (G-7340)*
Granville Hospitality Llc 740 587-3333
  314 Broadway E Granville (43023) *(G-11466)*
Graphel Corporation 513 779-6166
  6115 Centre Park Dr West Chester (45069) *(G-19083)*
Graphic Cmmnctons Holdings Inc, Hudson *Also called Veritiv Pubg & Print MGT Inc (G-12149)*
Graphic Enterprises Inc 800 553-6616
  3874 Highland Park Nw North Canton (44720) *(G-15340)*
Graphic Entps Off Slutions Inc 800 553-6616
  3874 Highland Park Nw North Canton (44720) *(G-15341)*
Graphic Publications 330 674-2300
  7368 County Road 623 Millersburg (44654) *(G-14603)*
Graphic Systems Services Inc 937 746-0708
  400 S Pioneer Blvd Springboro (45066) *(G-17120)*
Grasan Equipment Company Inc 419 526-4440
  440 S Illinois Ave Mansfield (44907) *(G-13306)*
Gratis Ems 937 787-4285
  405 Harrision St Gratis (45330) *(G-11473)*
Gray & Pape Inc (PA) 513 287-7700
  1318 Main St Fl 1 Cincinnati (45202) *(G-3694)*
Gray Television Group Inc 419 531-1313
  4247 Dorr St Toledo (43607) *(G-17920)*
Graybar Electric Company Inc 216 573-6144
  6161 Halle Dr Cleveland (44125) *(G-5688)*
Graybar Electric Company Inc 513 719-7400
  1022 W 8th St Cincinnati (45203) *(G-3695)*
Graybar Electric Company Inc 614 486-4391
  1200 Kinnear Rd Columbus (43212) *(G-7770)*
Graybar Electric Company Inc 330 799-3220
  1100 Ohio Works Dr Youngstown (44510) *(G-20204)*
Graybar Youngstown Nat Zone, Youngstown *Also called Graybar Electric Company Inc (G-20204)*
Graybill Gallery Kitchens Bath, Beach City *Also called Grabill Plumbing & Heating (G-1043)*
Great American Advisors Inc (HQ) 513 357-3300
  301 E 4th St Fl 8 Cincinnati (45202) *(G-3696)*
Great American Insurance Co (HQ) 513 369-5000
  301 E 4th St Fl 8 Cincinnati (45202) *(G-3697)*
Great American Insurance Co 513 603-2570
  9450 Seward Rd Fairfield (45014) *(G-10853)*
Great American Insurance Co 513 763-7035
  49 E 4th St Bsmt Cincinnati (45202) *(G-3698)*
Great American Life Insur Co (HQ) 513 357-3300
  250 E 5th St Ste 1000 Cincinnati (45202) *(G-3699)*
Great American Woodies, Columbus *Also called Competitor Swim Products Inc (G-7413)*
Great Amrcn Fncl Resources Inc (HQ) 513 333-5300
  250 E 5th St Ste 1000 Cincinnati (45202) *(G-3700)*
Great Amrcn Plan Admin Inc 513 412-2316
  525 Vine St Fl 7 Cincinnati (45202) *(G-3701)*
Great Bear Lodge Sandusky LLC 419 609-6000
  4600 Milan Rd Sandusky (44870) *(G-16765)*
Great Clips, Cincinnati *Also called Image Engineering Inc (G-3808)*
Great Clips, Dayton *Also called R L O Inc (G-9839)*
Great Dane Columbus Inc 614 876-0666
  4080 Lyman Dr Hilliard (43026) *(G-11904)*
Great Dane LLC 614 876-0666
  4080 Lyman Dr Hilliard (43026) *(G-11905)*
Great Dane Trailers, Hilliard *Also called Great Dane LLC (G-11905)*
Great Day Tours Chrtr Bus Svc, Cleveland *Also called Cuyahoga Marketing Service (G-5457)*

Great Eastern Theatre Company........419 691-9668
4500 Navarre Ave Oregon (43616) *(G-15737)*
Great Expectations, Cleveland *Also called Great Southern Video Inc (G-5693)*
Great Expectations D CA Center........330 782-9500
755 Boardman Canfield Rd F8 Youngstown (44512) *(G-20205)*
Great Expressions, Akron *Also called Dental Health Group PA (G-189)*
Great Lakes Cartage Company (PA)........330 702-1930
555 N Meridian Rd Ste 1 Youngstown (44509) *(G-20206)*
Great Lakes Cheese Co Inc (PA)........440 834-2500
17825 Great Lakes Pkwy Hiram (44234) *(G-12002)*
Great Lakes Cold Logistics........216 520-0930
6548 Brecksville Rd Independence (44131) *(G-12215)*
Great Lakes Cold Storage, Solon *Also called Gorbett Enterprises of Solon (G-17011)*
Great Lakes Companies Inc........513 554-0720
925 Laidlaw Ave Cincinnati (45237) *(G-3702)*
Great Lakes Computer Corp........440 937-1100
33675 Lear Indus Pkwy Avon (44011) *(G-895)*
Great Lakes Crushing Ltd........440 944-5500
30831 Euclid Ave Wickliffe (44092) *(G-19599)*
Great Lakes Energy........440 582-4662
332 Clearview Ct Broadview Heights (44147) *(G-1880)*
Great Lakes Fasteners Inc........330 425-4488
2204 E Enterprise Pkwy Twinsburg (44087) *(G-18425)*
Great Lakes Group........216 621-4854
4500 Division Ave Cleveland (44102) *(G-5689)*
Great Lakes Home Hlth Svcs Inc........888 260-9835
3425 Executive Pkwy # 206 Toledo (43606) *(G-17921)*
Great Lakes Home Hlth Svcs Inc........888 260-9835
1530 W Market St Akron (44313) *(G-245)*
Great Lakes Home Hlth Svcs Inc........888 260-9835
5966 Heisley Rd Ste 100 Mentor (44060) *(G-14184)*
Great Lakes Medical Staffing, Perrysburg *Also called Prueter Enterprises Ltd (G-16046)*
Great Lakes Mktg Assoc Inc........419 534-4700
3361 Executive Pkwy # 201 Toledo (43606) *(G-17922)*
Great Lakes Mseum of Scnce Env........216 694-2000
601 Erieside Ave Cleveland (44114) *(G-5690)*
Great Lakes Packers Inc........419 483-2956
400 Great Lakes Pkwy Bellevue (44811) *(G-1411)*
Great Lakes Power Products Inc (PA)........440 951-5111
7455 Tyler Blvd Mentor (44060) *(G-14185)*
Great Lakes Publishing Company (PA)........216 771-2833
1422 Euclid Ave Ste 730 Cleveland (44115) *(G-5691)*
Great Lakes Record Center, Mentor *Also called Moving Solutions Inc (G-14223)*
GREAT LAKES SCIENCE CENTER, Cleveland *Also called Great Lakes Mseum of Scnce Env (G-5690)*
Great Lakes Telcom Ltd........330 629-8848
590 E Western Reserve Rd Youngstown (44514) *(G-20207)*
Great Lakes Textiles Inc (PA)........440 439-1300
6810 Cochran Rd Solon (44139) *(G-17012)*
Great Lakes Towing, Cleveland *Also called Great Lakes Group (G-5689)*
Great Lakes Water Treatment........216 464-8292
4949 Galaxy Pkwy Ste Q Cleveland (44128) *(G-5692)*
Great Lakes Western Star, Toledo *Also called Mizar Motors Inc (G-18065)*
Great Miami Valley YMCA........513 217-5501
5750 Innovation Dr Middletown (45005) *(G-14479)*
Great Miami Valley YMCA (PA)........513 887-0001
105 N 2nd St Hamilton (45011) *(G-11733)*
Great Miami Valley YMCA........513 892-9622
6645 Morris Rd Fairfield Township (45011) *(G-10930)*
Great Miami Valley YMCA........513 867-0600
4803 Augspurger Rd Hamilton (45011) *(G-11734)*
Great Miami Valley YMCA........513 887-0014
105 N 2nd St Hamilton (45011) *(G-11735)*
Great Miami Valley YMCA........513 868-9622
1307 Nw Washington Blvd Hamilton (45013) *(G-11736)*
Great Miami Valley YMCA........513 829-3091
5220 Bibury Rd Fairfield (45014) *(G-10854)*
Great Nthrn Cnsulting Svcs Inc (PA)........614 890-9999
200 E Campus View Blvd # 200 Columbus (43235) *(G-7771)*
Great Oaks Inst Tech Creer Dev (PA)........513 771-8840
3254 E Kemper Rd Cincinnati (45241) *(G-3703)*
Great Oaks Inst Tech Creer Dev........513 771-8840
3254 E Kemper Rd Cincinnati (45241) *(G-3704)*
Great Rivers, Cleveland *Also called American Heart Assn Ohio Vly (G-5009)*
Great Southern Video Inc........216 642-8855
4511 Rockside Rd Ste 210 Cleveland (44131) *(G-5693)*
Great Traditions Homes........513 759-7444
7267 Hamilton Mason Rd West Chester (45069) *(G-19084)*
Great Value Storage........614 848-8420
5301 Tamarack Cir E Columbus (43229) *(G-7772)*
Great Wolf Lodge, Sandusky *Also called Great Bear Lodge Sandusky LLC (G-16765)*
Great Wolf Lodge, Mason *Also called Mason Family Resorts LLC (G-13736)*
Great Wolf Lodge, Sandusky *Also called Clp Gw Sandusky Tenant LP (G-16741)*
Greater Akron Dialysis Center, Akron *Also called Bio-Mdcal Applcations Ohio Inc (G-102)*
Greater Akron Musical Assn........330 535-8131
92 N Main St Akron (44308) *(G-246)*
Greater Andrson Premotes Peace........513 588-8391
7642 Athenia Dr Cincinnati (45244) *(G-3705)*
Greater Cin Cardi Consults In........513 751-4222
2123 Auburn Ave Cincinnati (45219) *(G-3706)*
Greater Cincinnati Behavioral (PA)........513 354-7000
1501 Madison Rd Walnut Hills (45206) *(G-18787)*
Greater Cincinnati Behavioral........513 755-2203
1501 Madison Rd Fl 1 Walnut Hills (45206) *(G-18788)*
Greater Cincinnati Cnvntn/Vstr........513 621-2142
525 Vine St Ste 1200 Cincinnati (45202) *(G-3707)*
Greater Cincinnati Credit Un........513 559-1234
7948 S Masn Montgomery Rd Mason (45040) *(G-13711)*
Greater Cincinnati Dental Labs........513 385-4222
3719 Struble Rd Cincinnati (45251) *(G-3708)*
Greater Cincinnati Gastro Assc (PA)........513 336-8636
2925 Vernon Pl Ste 100 Cincinnati (45219) *(G-3709)*
Greater Cincinnati Ob/Gyn Inc (PA)........513 245-3103
2830 Victory Pkwy Ste 140 Cincinnati (45206) *(G-3710)*
GREATER CINCINNATI ORAL HEALTH, Cincinnati *Also called Cincysmiles Foundation Inc (G-3345)*
Greater Cincinnati Redevelopme, Cincinnati *Also called Port Grter Cincinnati Dev Auth (G-4315)*
Greater Cincinnati TV Educ Fnd........513 381-4033
1223 Central Pkwy Cincinnati (45214) *(G-3711)*
Greater Cleveland........216 566-5107
1240 W 6th St Fl 6 Cleveland (44113) *(G-5694)*
Greater Cleveland Auto Auction........216 433-7777
5801 Engle Rd Cleveland (44142) *(G-5695)*
Greater Cleveland Food Bnk Inc........216 738-2265
15500 S Waterloo Rd Cleveland (44110) *(G-5696)*
Greater Cleveland Hosp Assn, Cleveland *Also called Center For Health Affairs (G-5208)*
Greater Cleveland Hosp Assn........216 696-6900
1226 Huron Rd E Ste 2 Cleveland (44115) *(G-5697)*
Greater Cleveland Partnership (PA)........216 621-3300
1240 Huron Rd E Ste 300 Cleveland (44115) *(G-5698)*
Greater Cleveland Regional........216 575-3932
1240 W 6th St Cleveland (44113) *(G-5699)*
Greater Cleveland Regional........216 781-1110
4601 Euclid Ave Cleveland (44103) *(G-5700)*
Greater Clumbus Convention Ctr, Columbus *Also called Smg Holdings Inc (G-8744)*
Greater Clumbus Convention Ctr........614 827-2500
400 N High St Fl 4 Columbus (43215) *(G-7773)*
Greater Clvland Halthcare Assn........216 696-6900
1226 Huron Rd E Cleveland (44115) *(G-5701)*
Greater Cnti Crdovascular Cons, Cincinnati *Also called Greater Cin Cardi Consults In (G-3706)*
Greater Columbus Chmbr Commrce........614 221-1321
150 S Front St Ste 200 Columbus (43215) *(G-7774)*
Greater Columbus Regional........614 228-9114
285 E State St Ste 170 Columbus (43215) *(G-7775)*
Greater Dayton Cnstr Ltd........937 426-3577
4197 Research Blvd Beavercreek (45430) *(G-1243)*
Greater Dayton Mvg & Stor Co........937 235-0011
3516 Wright Way Rd Ste 2 Dayton (45424) *(G-9586)*
Greater Dayton Public TV (PA)........937 220-1600
110 S Jefferson St Dayton (45402) *(G-9587)*
Greater Dayton Rta........937 425-8400
4 S Main St Dayton (45402) *(G-9588)*
Greater Dayton Surgery Ctr LLC........937 535-2200
1625 Delco Park Dr Dayton (45420) *(G-9589)*
Greater Dyton Rgnal Trnst Auth (PA)........937 425-8310
4 S Main St Ste C Dayton (45402) *(G-9590)*
Greatr Columbus Conventn & Vis (PA)........614 221-6623
277 W Nationwide Blvd Columbus (43215) *(G-7776)*
Green Haines Sgambati Lpa........330 743-5101
100 E Federal St Ste 800 Youngstown (44503) *(G-20208)*
Green Circle Growers Inc (PA)........440 775-1411
51051 Us Highway 20 Oberlin (44074) *(G-15644)*
Green Circle Growers Inc........440 775-1411
15650 State Route 511 Oberlin (44074) *(G-15645)*
Green County Engineer, Xenia *Also called Greene County (G-20054)*
Green County Housing Program, Xenia *Also called American Red Cross (G-20041)*
Green Gate, Cortland *Also called J Gilmore Design Limited (G-9076)*
Green Haven Memorial Gardens........330 533-6811
3495 S Canfield Niles Rd Canfield (44406) *(G-2192)*
Green Hills, West Liberty *Also called West Liberty Care Center Inc (G-19264)*
Green Impressions LLC........440 240-8508
042 Abbe Rd Sheffield Village (44054) *(G-16886)*
Green King Company Inc........614 861-4132
9562 Taylor Rd Sw Reynoldsburg (43068) *(G-16457)*
Green Lawn Cemetery Assn........614 444-1123
1000 Greenlawn Ave Columbus (43223) *(G-7777)*
Green Leaf Motor Express, Ashtabula *Also called Ashtabula Chemical Corp (G-714)*
Green Lines Transportation Inc (PA)........330 863-2111
7089 Alliance Rd Nw Malvern (44644) *(G-13251)*
Green Madows Hlth Wellness Ctr, Louisville *Also called Progressive Green Meadows LLC (G-13105)*
Green Springs Residential Ltd........419 639-2581
430 N Broadway St Green Springs (44836) *(G-11477)*
Green Township Hospitality LLC (PA)........513 574-6000
5505 Rybolt Rd Cincinnati (45248) *(G-3712)*
Greenbriar CONference& Pty Ctr, Wooster *Also called Black Tie Affair Inc (G-19832)*
Greenbriar Healthcare Center, Youngstown *Also called Communicare Health Svcs Inc (G-20148)*

ALPHABETIC

Greenbriar Nursing Center, The, Eaton *Also called October Enterprises Inc* ***(G-10571)***
Greenbriar Retirement Center, Cleveland *Also called Greenbrier Senior Living Cmnty* ***(G-5702)***
Greenbrier Retirement Cmnty, Cleveland *Also called Greenbrier Senior Living Cmnty* ***(G-5703)***
Greenbrier Senior Living Cmnty....440 888-5900
6455 Pearl Rd Cleveland (44130) ***(G-5702)***
Greenbrier Senior Living Cmnty....440 888-0400
6457 Pearl Rd Cleveland (44130) ***(G-5703)***
Greene Cnty Chld Svc Brd Frbrn....937 878-1415
601 Ledbetter Rd Ste A Xenia (45385) ***(G-20052)***
Greene Cnty Combined Hlth Dst....937 374-5600
360 Wilson Dr Xenia (45385) ***(G-20053)***
Greene County....937 562-7500
615 Dayton Xenia Rd Xenia (45385) ***(G-20054)***
Greene County....937 562-6000
541 Ledbetter Rd Xenia (45385) ***(G-20055)***
Greene County....937 562-7800
641 Dayton Xenia Rd Xenia (45385) ***(G-20056)***
Greene County Career Center....937 372-6941
2960 W Enon Rd Xenia (45385) ***(G-20057)***
Greene County Public Health, Xenia *Also called Greene Cnty Combined Hlth Dst* ***(G-20053)***
Greene County Services, Xenia *Also called Greene County* ***(G-20056)***
Greene Inc....937 562-4200
121 Fairground Rd Xenia (45385) ***(G-20058)***
Greene Memorial Hosp Svcs Inc....937 352-2000
1 Prestige Pl Ste 910 Miamisburg (45342) ***(G-14304)***
Greene Memorial Hospital Inc (HQ)....937 352-2000
1141 N Monroe Dr Xenia (45385) ***(G-20059)***
Greene Memorial Hospital Inc....937 458-4500
3359 Kemp Rd Beavercreek (45431) ***(G-1175)***
Greene Oaks....937 352-2800
164 Office Park Dr Xenia (45385) ***(G-20060)***
Greene, The, Beavercreek *Also called Greentown Center LLC* ***(G-1244)***
Greeneview Foods LLC....937 675-4161
96 W Washington St Jamestown (45335) ***(G-12326)***
Greenfield Area Medical Center, Chillicothe *Also called Adena Health System* ***(G-2809)***
Greenfield Area Medical Ctr....937 981-9400
550 Mirabeau St Greenfield (45123) ***(G-11485)***
Greenfield Family Health Ctr, Greenfield *Also called Healthsource of Ohio Inc* ***(G-11487)***
Greenfield Health Systems Corp (PA)....419 389-9681
3401 Glendale Ave Ste 110 Toledo (43614) ***(G-17923)***
Greenfield Hts Oper Group LLC....312 877-1153
1318 Chestnut St Lima (45804) ***(G-12787)***
Greenfield Products Inc....937 981-2696
1230 N Washington St Greenfield (45123) ***(G-11486)***
Greenleaf Auto Recyclers LLC....330 832-6001
12192 Lincoln Way Nw Massillon (44647) ***(G-13814)***
Greenleaf Family Center (PA)....330 376-9494
580 Grant St Akron (44311) ***(G-247)***
Greenleaf Landscapes Inc....740 373-1639
414 Muskingum Dr Marietta (45750) ***(G-13449)***
Greenleaf Ohio LLC....330 832-6001
12192 Lincoln Way Nw Massillon (44647) ***(G-13815)***
Greenline Foods Inc (HQ)....419 354-1149
12700 S Dixie Hwy Bowling Green (43402) ***(G-1778)***
Greenpro Services Inc....937 748-1559
2969 Beal Rd Franklin (45005) ***(G-11156)***
Greens of Lyndhurst The Inc....440 460-1000
1555 Brainard Rd Apt 305 Cleveland (44124) ***(G-5704)***
Greenscapes Landscape Arch, Columbus *Also called Greenscapes Landscape Company* ***(G-7778)***
Greenscapes Landscape Company....614 837-1869
4220 Winchester Pike Columbus (43232) ***(G-7778)***
Greenspace Enterprise Tech Inc....888 309-8517
8401 Claude Thomas Rd # 28 Franklin (45005) ***(G-11157)***
Greenstar Mid-America LLC....330 784-1167
1535 Exeter Rd Akron (44306) ***(G-248)***
Greentech Corporation....937 339-4758
1405 S County Road 25a Troy (45373) ***(G-18355)***
Greentech Lawn and Irrigation, Troy *Also called Greentech Corporation* ***(G-18355)***
Greentown Center LLC....937 490-4990
4452 Buckeye Ln Beavercreek (45440) ***(G-1244)***
Greentown Vlntr Fire Dept Inc....330 494-3002
10100 Cleveland Ave Nw Uniontown (44685) ***(G-18522)***
Greentree Group Inc (PA)....937 490-5500
1360 Tech Ct Ste 100 Dayton (45430) ***(G-9591)***
Greentree Inn, Sandusky *Also called Sortino Management & Dev Co* ***(G-16796)***
Greenville Federal....937 548-4158
690 Wagner Ave Greenville (45331) ***(G-11504)***
Greenville National Bancorp (PA)....937 548-1114
446 S Bwy St Greenville (45331) ***(G-11505)***
Greenville National Bank....937 548-1114
446 S Broadway St Greenville (45331) ***(G-11506)***
Greenville Noland, Moraine *Also called Noland Company* ***(G-14812)***
Greenville Township Rescue....937 548-9339
1401 Sater St Greenville (45331) ***(G-11507)***
Greenwood Chevrolet Inc....330 270-1299
4695 Mahoning Ave Youngstown (44515) ***(G-20209)***
Greenwood's Oldsmobile, Hubbard *Also called Greenwoods Hubbard Chevy-Olds* ***(G-12087)***
Greenwoods Hubbard Chevy-Olds....330 568-4335
2635 N Main St Hubbard (44425) ***(G-12087)***
Greer & Whitehead Cnstr Inc....513 202-1757
510 S State St Ste D Harrison (45030) ***(G-11799)***
Greg Ford Sweet Inc....440 593-7714
4011 E Center St North Kingsville (44068) ***(G-15391)***
Greg Sweet Ford, North Kingsville *Also called Greg Ford Sweet Inc* ***(G-15391)***
Greiner Dental & Associates, Mentor *Also called Raymond A Greiner DDS Inc* ***(G-14232)***
Greiner Dental Association....440 255-2600
7553 Center St Mentor (44060) ***(G-14186)***
Greiser Transportation, Wauseon *Also called Daves Sand & Stone Inc* ***(G-18950)***
Grenada Stamping Assembly Inc (HQ)....419 842-3600
3810 Herr Rd Sylvania (43560) ***(G-17589)***
GREY STONE, Canton *Also called Stone Products Inc* ***(G-2552)***
Greyhound Lines Inc....513 421-7442
1005 Gilbert Ave Cincinnati (45202) ***(G-3713)***
Greyhound Lines Inc....614 221-0577
111 E Town St Ste 100 Columbus (43215) ***(G-7779)***
Greystone Group-Avery Ltd....216 464-3580
30050 Chagrin Blvd # 360 Cleveland (44124) ***(G-5705)***
Greystone Health and, Cambridge *Also called Cambridge NH LLC* ***(G-2100)***
Grgstormpro, Akron *Also called Glencoe Restoration Group LLC* ***(G-237)***
Gribble Foods, Loudonville *Also called Jo Lynn Inc* ***(G-13092)***
Griffin Wheel, Groveport *Also called Amsted Industries Incorporated* ***(G-11622)***
Grimes Aerospace Company....937 484-2001
550 State Route 55 Urbana (43078) ***(G-18590)***
Grimes Seeds, Concord Twp *Also called Gardenlife Inc* ***(G-9033)***
Grippo Foods Inc....513 923-1900
6750 Colerain Ave Cincinnati (45239) ***(G-3714)***
Grismer Tire Company (PA)....937 643-2526
1099 S Main St Centerville (45458) ***(G-2678)***
Grizzly Golf Center Inc....513 398-5200
6042 Fairway Dr Mason (45040) ***(G-13712)***
Grl Engineers Inc (PA)....216 831-6131
30725 Aurora Rd Solon (44139) ***(G-17013)***
Grob Systems Inc....419 358-9015
1070 Navajo Dr Bluffton (45817) ***(G-1731)***
Grocery Outlet Supermarket, Hartville *Also called Sommers Market LLC* ***(G-11831)***
Grogans Towne Chrysler Inc (PA)....419 476-0761
6100 Telegraph Rd Toledo (43612) ***(G-17924)***
Grogg, Terry W MD, Grove City *Also called Southwestern Obstetricians & G* ***(G-11600)***
Grooveryde Cle....323 595-1701
1120 Chester Ave Cleveland (44114) ***(G-5706)***
Gross Builders, Cleveland *Also called I & M J Gross Company* ***(G-5798)***
Gross Electric Inc (PA)....419 537-1818
2807 N Reynolds Rd Toledo (43615) ***(G-17925)***
Gross Lumber Inc....330 683-2055
8848 Ely Rd Apple Creek (44606) ***(G-625)***
Gross Plumbing Incorporated....440 324-9999
6843 Lake Ave Elyria (44035) ***(G-10632)***
Gross Supply, Elyria *Also called Gross Plumbing Incorporated* ***(G-10632)***
Grote Enterprises LLC (PA)....513 731-5700
5240 Lester Rd Cincinnati (45213) ***(G-3715)***
Ground Effects LLC....440 565-5925
31000 Viking Pkwy Westlake (44145) ***(G-19487)***
Ground Penetrating Radar Sys (PA)....419 843-9804
7540 New West Rd Toledo (43617) ***(G-17926)***
Ground Tech Inc....330 270-0700
240 Sinter Ct Youngstown (44510) ***(G-20210)***
Groundsystems Inc (PA)....800 570-0213
11315 Williamson Rd Blue Ash (45241) ***(G-1605)***
Groundsystems Inc....937 903-5325
2929 Northlawn Ave Moraine (45439) ***(G-14793)***
Group Health Associates, Cincinnati *Also called Trihealth G LLC* ***(G-4696)***
Group Management Services Inc (PA)....330 659-0100
3750 Timberlake Dr Richfield (44286) ***(G-16511)***
Group Midwest, North Canton *Also called Midwest Communications Inc* ***(G-15354)***
Group Transportation Svcs Inc (PA)....800 689-6255
5876 Darrow Rd Hudson (44236) ***(G-12119)***
Groupcle LLC....216 251-9641
12500 Berea Rd Cleveland (44111) ***(G-5707)***
Grove City Community Club....614 875-6074
3397 Civic Pl Grove City (43123) ***(G-11567)***
Grove City-Doh, Grove City *Also called Synnex Corporation* ***(G-11603)***
Grove Cy Chrstn Child Care Ctr....614 875-2551
4770 Hoover Rd Grove City (43123) ***(G-11568)***
Grove Walnut Country Club Inc....937 253-3109
5050 Linden Ave Dayton (45432) ***(G-9270)***
Groveport Warehouse, Groveport *Also called Nifco America Corporation* ***(G-11659)***
Grover Musical Products Inc (PA)....216 391-1188
9287 Midwest Ave Cleveland (44125) ***(G-5708)***
Grover Trophy Musical Products, Cleveland *Also called Grover Musical Products Inc* ***(G-5708)***
Grubb Construction Inc....419 293-2316
896 State Route 613 Mc Comb (45858) ***(G-14021)***
Grunwell-Cashero Co....419 476-2426
5212 Tractor Rd Toledo (43612) ***(G-17927)***
Gs Ohio Inc....614 885-5350
8573 Owenfield Dr Powell (43065) ***(G-16337)***

Gs1 Us Inc 609 620-0200
7887 Wash Vlg Dr Ste 300 Dayton (45459) ***(G-9592)***
Gsf North American Jantr Svc 513 733-1451
9850 Prnceton Glendale Rd West Chester (45246) ***(G-19205)***
GTC Artist With Machines, Columbus *Also called General Theming Contrs LLC* ***(G-7736)***
GTE Internet 614 508-6000
6816 Lauffer Rd Columbus (43231) ***(G-7780)***
GTM Service Inc (PA) 440 944-5099
1366 Rockefeller Rd Wickliffe (44092) ***(G-19600)***
GTS, Hudson *Also called Group Transportation Svcs Inc* ***(G-12119)***
Guardian Alarm, Toledo *Also called GA Business Purchaser LLC* ***(G-17905)***
Guardian Angels Senior HM Svc, Sylvania *Also called Guardian Angls Home Hlth Svcs* ***(G-17590)***
Guardian Angls Home Hlth Svcs 419 517-7797
8553 Sylvania Metamora Rd Sylvania (43560) ***(G-17590)***
Guardian Business Services 614 416-6090
3948 Townsfair Way # 220 Columbus (43219) ***(G-7781)***
Guardian Care Services 614 436-8500
665 E Dublin Granville Rd # 330 Columbus (43229) ***(G-7782)***
Guardian Elde 419 225-9040
804 S Mumaugh Rd Lima (45804) ***(G-12788)***
Guardian Elder Care LLC 330 549-0898
9625 Market St North Lima (44452) ***(G-15402)***
Guardian Elder Care Columbus 614 868-9306
2425 Kimberly Pkwy E Columbus (43232) ***(G-7783)***
Guardian Enterprise Group Inc 614 416-6080
3948 Townsfair Way # 220 Columbus (43219) ***(G-7784)***
Guardian Home Technology, Youngstown *Also called Guardian Protection Svcs Inc* ***(G-20211)***
Guardian Life Insur Co of Amer 513 579-1114
419 Plum St Cincinnati (45202) ***(G-3716)***
Guardian Life Insurance, Canton *Also called Sirak Financial Services* ***(G-2529)***
Guardian Protection Svcs Inc 513 422-5319
9852 Windisch Rd West Chester (45069) ***(G-19085)***
Guardian Protection Svcs Inc 330 797-1570
5401 Ashley Cir Ste A Youngstown (44515) ***(G-20211)***
Guardian Savings Bank (PA) 513 942-3535
6100 W Chester Rd West Chester (45069) ***(G-19086)***
Guardian Savings Bank 513 528-8787
560 Ohio Pike Cincinnati (45255) ***(G-3717)***
Guardian Water & Power Inc (PA) 614 291-3141
1160 Goodale Blvd Columbus (43212) ***(G-7785)***
Guardsmark LLC 513 851-5523
4050 Executive Park Dr # 350 Cincinnati (45241) ***(G-3718)***
Guardsmark LLC 419 229-9300
209 N Main St Ste 4a Lima (45801) ***(G-12789)***
Gudenkauf Corporation (PA) 614 488-1776
2679 Mckinley Ave Columbus (43204) ***(G-7786)***
Guenther & Sons Inc 513 738-1448
2578 Long St Ross (45061) ***(G-16603)***
Guenther Mechanical Inc 419 289-6900
1248 Middle Rowsburg Rd Ashland (44805) ***(G-681)***
Guerbet, Cincinnati *Also called Liebel-Flarsheim Company LLC* ***(G-3977)***
Guernsey Cnty Children Svcs Bd, Cambridge *Also called County of Guernsey* ***(G-2106)***
Guernsey Co Public Info Agency, Cambridge *Also called County of Guernsey* ***(G-2107)***
Guernsey County Cdc, Cambridge *Also called Guernsey County Cmnty Dev Corp* ***(G-2117)***
Guernsey County Cmnty Dev Corp 740 439-0020
905 Wheeling Ave Cambridge (43725) ***(G-2117)***
Guernsey County Senior Center, Cambridge *Also called County of Guernsey* ***(G-2109)***
Guernsey Health Enterprises 740 439-3561
1341 Clark St Cambridge (43725) ***(G-2118)***
Guernsey Health Systems Inc (PA) 740 439-3561
1341 Clark St Cambridge (43725) ***(G-2119)***
GUERNSEY INDUSTRIES, Byesville *Also called Ken Harper* ***(G-2071)***
Guernsy Counseling Center, Cambridge *Also called Allwell Behavioral Health Svcs* ***(G-2094)***
Guernsy-Muskingum Elc Coop Inc (PA) 740 826-7661
17 S Liberty St New Concord (43762) ***(G-15034)***
Guess Motors Inc (PA) 866 890-0522
457 Steubenville Rd Se Carrollton (44615) ***(G-2622)***
Guild Associates Inc (PA) 614 798-8215
5750 Shier Rings Rd Dublin (43016) ***(G-10355)***
Guild Biosciences, Dublin *Also called Guild Associates Inc* ***(G-10355)***
Guild Custom Drapery, Cleveland *Also called Farrow Cleaners Co* ***(G-5574)***
Gulf South Medical Supply Inc 614 501-9080
915 Taylor Rd Unit A Gahanna (43230) ***(G-11245)***
Gulfport Energy Corporation 740 251-0407
67185 Executive Dr Saint Clairsville (43950) ***(G-16636)***
Gummer Wholesale Inc (PA) 740 928-0415
1945 James Pkwy Heath (43056) ***(G-11838)***
Gund Sports Marketing Llc 216 420-2000
100 Gateway Plz Cleveland (44115) ***(G-5709)***
Gundlach Sheet Metal Works Inc (PA) 419 626-4525
910 Columbus Ave Sandusky (44870) ***(G-16766)***
Gundlach Sheet Metal Works Inc 419 734-7351
2439 E Gill Rd Port Clinton (43452) ***(G-16246)***
Gunning & Associates Mktg Inc 513 688-1370
1001 Ford Cir Cincinnati (45202) ***(G-3719)***
Gunton Corporation (PA) 216 831-2420
26150 Richmond Rd Cleveland (44146) ***(G-5710)***
Gus Holthaus Signs Inc 513 861-0060
817 Ridgeway Ave Cincinnati (45229) ***(G-3720)***
Gus Perdikakis Associates 513 583-0900
9155 Governors Way Unit A Cincinnati (45249) ***(G-3721)***
Gust Gallucci Co 216 881-0045
6610 Euclid Ave Cleveland (44103) ***(G-5711)***
Gutknecht Construction Company 614 532-5410
2280 Citygate Dr Columbus (43219) ***(G-7787)***
Guy's Party Ctr, Akron *Also called Guys Party Center* ***(G-249)***
Guyler Automotive, Middletown *Also called Pierson Automotive Inc* ***(G-14485)***
Guys Party Center 330 724-6373
500 E Waterloo Rd Akron (44319) ***(G-249)***
Gw Business Solutions LLC 740 645-9861
65 S 5th St Newark (43055) ***(G-15172)***
Gw Sutherland MD 419 578-7200
2865 N Reynolds Rd # 160 Toledo (43615) ***(G-17928)***
Gymnastic World Inc 440 526-2970
6630 Harris Rd Cleveland (44147) ***(G-5712)***
Gymnastics Center, Canton *Also called Y M C A Central Stark County* ***(G-2591)***
Gypc Inc 309 677-0405
475 Stonehaven Rd Dayton (45429) ***(G-9593)***
H & B Window Cleaning Inc 440 934-6158
753 Avon Belden Rd Ste D Avon Lake (44012) ***(G-931)***
H & C Building Supplies, Huron *Also called Huron Cement Products Company* ***(G-12166)***
H & D Steel Service Inc 440 237-3390
9960 York Alpha Dr North Royalton (44133) ***(G-15491)***
H & D Steel Service Center, North Royalton *Also called H & D Steel Service Inc* ***(G-15491)***
H & H Auto Parts Inc (PA) 330 456-4778
300 15th St Sw Canton (44707) ***(G-2386)***
H & H Auto Parts Inc 330 494-2975
6434 Wise Ave Nw Canton (44720) ***(G-2387)***
H & H Green LLC 419 674-4152
13670 Us Highway 68 Kenton (43326) ***(G-12412)***
H & H Retreading Inc 740 682-7721
5400 State Route 93 Oak Hill (45656) ***(G-15618)***
H & M Harley Davidson, Dover *Also called Adventure Harley Davidson* ***(G-10175)***
H & M Patch Company 614 339-8950
2500 Farmers Dr 110 Columbus (43235) ***(G-7788)***
H & M Plumbing Co 614 491-4880
4015 Alum Creek Dr Columbus (43207) ***(G-7789)***
H & M Precision Concrete LLC 937 547-0012
7805 Arcanum Bearsmill Rd Greenville (45331) ***(G-11508)***
H & O Distribution Inc 513 874-2090
325 Osborne Dr Fairfield (45014) ***(G-10855)***
H & R Block, Nevada *Also called Phillip Mc Guire* ***(G-14969)***
H & R Block, Akron *Also called H&R Block Inc* ***(G-250)***
H & R Block, Cleveland *Also called H&R Block Inc* ***(G-5717)***
H & R Block 419 352-9467
241 S Main St Bowling Green (43402) ***(G-1779)***
H & R Block Inc 330 345-1040
2831 Cleveland Rd Wooster (44691) ***(G-19866)***
H & R Block Inc 216 271-7108
5488 Broadway Ave Cleveland (44127) ***(G-5713)***
H & R Block Inc 513 868-1818
2304a Dixie Hwy Hamilton (45015) ***(G-11737)***
H & R Block Brunswick, Brunswick *Also called Dw Together LLC* ***(G-1976)***
H & R Concrete Inc 937 885-2910
9120 State Route 48 Dayton (45458) ***(G-9594)***
H & W Contractors Inc 330 833-0982
1722 1st St Ne Massillon (44646) ***(G-13816)***
H & W Holdings LLC 800 826-3560
341 County Road 120 S South Point (45680) ***(G-17087)***
H A M Landscaping Inc 216 663-6666
4667 Northfield Rd Cleveland (44128) ***(G-5714)***
H B Magruder Memorial Hospital 419 734-4539
611 Fulton St Port Clinton (43452) ***(G-16247)***
H C F Inc 740 289-2528
7143 Us Rte 23 Piketon (45661) ***(G-16116)***
H C R Corp 419 472-0076
4293 Monroe St Toledo (43606) ***(G-17929)***
H Dennert Distributing Corp 513 871-7272
351 Wilmer Ave Cincinnati (45226) ***(G-3722)***
H E R, Westerville *Also called Her Inc* ***(G-19313)***
H E R Realtors, Worthington *Also called Her Inc* ***(G-19963)***
H E R Realtors, Columbus *Also called Her Inc* ***(G-7828)***
H E R Realtors, Columbus *Also called Her Inc* ***(G-7829)***
H E R Realtors, Dublin *Also called Her Inc* ***(G-10359)***
H E R Realtors, Hilliard *Also called Her Inc* ***(G-11907)***
H F A, Akron *Also called Hitchcock Fleming & Assoc Inc* ***(G-266)***
H G C, Cincinnati *Also called Hgc Construction Co* ***(G-3759)***
H G R, Euclid *Also called Hgr Industrial Surplus Inc* ***(G-10759)***
H Hansen Industries, Toledo *Also called Riverside Marine Inds Inc* ***(G-18157)***
H K M, Cleveland *Also called Hkm Drect Mkt Cmmnications Inc* ***(G-5762)***
H L C Trucking Inc 740 676-6181
57245 Ferry Landing Rd Shadyside (43947) ***(G-16849)***
H Leff Electric Company (PA) 216 325-0941
4700 Spring Rd Cleveland (44131) ***(G-5715)***
H M Miller Construction Co 330 628-4811
1225 Waterloo Rd Mogadore (44260) ***(G-14677)***

ALPHABETIC

H M T Dermatology, Medina *Also called Helen M Torok MD* ***(G-14075)***
H M T Dermatology Inc......330 725-0569
5783 Wooster Pike Medina (44256) ***(G-14073)***
H O C J Inc......614 539-4601
2135 Hardy Parkway St Grove City (43123) ***(G-11569)***
H P Products Corporation......513 683-8553
7135 E Kemper Rd Cincinnati (45249) ***(G-3723)***
H R Chally Group, Dayton *Also called SSS Consulting Inc* ***(G-9901)***
H T I Express......419 423-9555
110 Bentley Ct Findlay (45840) ***(G-11039)***
H T V Industries Inc......216 514-0060
30195 Chagrin Blvd 310n Cleveland (44124) ***(G-5716)***
H Wz Contracting-Cinti, West Chester *Also called Bh Group LLC* ***(G-19027)***
H&H Custom Homes LLC......419 994-4070
16573 State Route 3 Loudonville (44842) ***(G-13090)***
H&R Block Inc......330 773-0412
1400 S Arlington St # 18 Akron (44306) ***(G-250)***
H&R Block Inc......440 282-4288
1980 G Coper Foster Pk Rd Amherst (44001) ***(G-596)***
H&R Block Inc......216 861-1185
2068 W 25th St Cleveland (44113) ***(G-5717)***
H. Meyer Dairy, Cincinnati *Also called Borden Dairy Co Cincinnati LLC* ***(G-3127)***
Haag-Streit USA Inc......513 336-7255
5500 Courseview Dr Mason (45040) ***(G-13713)***
Haag-Streit USA Inc (HQ)......513 336-7255
3535 Kings Mills Rd Mason (45040) ***(G-13714)***
Haas Doors, Wauseon *Also called Nofziger Door Sales Inc* ***(G-18960)***
Haasz Automall LLC......330 296-2866
4886 State Route 59 Ravenna (44266) ***(G-16387)***
Habco Tool and Dev Co Inc......440 946-5546
7725 Metric Dr Mentor (44060) ***(G-14187)***
Habegger Corporation (PA)......513 853-6644
4995 Winton Rd Cincinnati (45232) ***(G-3724)***
Habegger Corporation......330 499-4328
7580 Whipple Ave Nw North Canton (44720) ***(G-15342)***
Habegger Corporation......513 612-4700
11413 Enterprise Park Dr Cincinnati (45241) ***(G-3725)***
Habitat For Humanity......216 429-1299
2110 W 110th St Cleveland (44102) ***(G-5718)***
Habitat For Humanity Intl......513 721-4483
4910 Para Dr Cincinnati (45237) ***(G-3726)***
Habitat For Humanity Mid Ohio (PA)......614 422-4828
3140 Westerville Rd Columbus (43224) ***(G-7790)***
Habitec Security Inc (PA)......419 537-6768
1545 Timber Wolf Dr Holland (43528) ***(G-12025)***
Hackensack Meridian Health Inc......513 792-9697
4650 E Galbraith Rd Cincinnati (45236) ***(G-3727)***
Hadassah Dayton Chapter......937 275-0227
880 Fernshire Dr Dayton (45459) ***(G-9595)***
Hadler Company, Columbus *Also called Hadler Realty Company* ***(G-7791)***
Hadler Realty Company......614 457-6650
2000 Henderson Rd Ste 500 Columbus (43220) ***(G-7791)***
Hadler-Zimmerman Inc......614 457-6650
2000 Henderson Rd Ste 500 Columbus (43220) ***(G-7792)***
Hafenbrack Mktg Cmmnctions Inc......937 424-8950
116 E 3rd St Dayton (45402) ***(G-9596)***
Hagglunds Drives Inc (HQ)......614 527-7400
2275 International St Columbus (43228) ***(G-7793)***
Hague Water Conditioning Inc (PA)......614 482-8121
4581 Homer Ohio Ln Groveport (43125) ***(G-11642)***
Hahmooeser & Parks......330 864-5550
200 Public Sq Ste 2000 Cleveland (44114) ***(G-5719)***
Hahn Automotive Warehouse Inc......937 223-1068
32 Franklin St Dayton (45402) ***(G-9597)***
Hahn Loeser & Parks, Columbus *Also called Firm Hahn Law* ***(G-7658)***
Hahn Loeser & Parks LLP (PA)......216 621-0150
200 Public Sq Ste 2800 Cleveland (44114) ***(G-5720)***
Hahs Factory Outlet......330 405-4227
1993 Case Pkwy Twinsburg (44087) ***(G-18426)***
Haid Acquisitions LLC......513 941-8700
1053 Ebenezer Rd Cincinnati (45233) ***(G-3728)***
Haiku......614 294-8168
800 N High St Columbus (43215) ***(G-7794)***
Haines & Company Inc (PA)......330 494-9111
8050 Freedom Ave Nw North Canton (44720) ***(G-15343)***
Hair Forum......513 245-0800
5801 Cheviot Rd Unit 1 Cincinnati (45247) ***(G-3729)***
Hair Removal Center of So, Dayton *Also called Laser Hair Removal Center* ***(G-9674)***
Hair Shoppe Inc......330 497-1651
6460 Wise Ave Nw Canton (44720) ***(G-2388)***
Hairitage, The, Zanesville *Also called Brenwood Inc* ***(G-20449)***
Hairy Cactus Salon Inc......513 771-9335
9437 Civic Centre Blvd B West Chester (45069) ***(G-19087)***
Hajoca Corporation......216 447-0050
6606 Granger Rd Cleveland (44131) ***(G-5721)***
Hal Homes Inc (PA)......513 984-5360
9545 Kenwood Rd Ste 401 Blue Ash (45242) ***(G-1606)***
Halcomb Concrete Construction......513 829-3576
1409 Veterans Dr Fairfield (45014) ***(G-10856)***
Hale Farm & Village, Bath *Also called Western Reserve Historical Soc* ***(G-1036)***
HALE FARM & VILLAGE, Cleveland *Also called Western Reserve Historical Soc* ***(G-6744)***
Halker Drywall & Plastering, Columbus Grove *Also called Halker Drywall Inc* ***(G-9030)***
Halker Drywall Inc......419 646-3679
21457 Road 15u Columbus Grove (45830) ***(G-9030)***
Hall Contracting Services Inc......440 930-0050
33540 Pin Oak Pkwy Avon Lake (44012) ***(G-932)***
Hall Nazareth Inc......419 832-2900
21211 W State Route 65 Grand Rapids (43522) ***(G-11449)***
Halleen Kia, North Olmsted *Also called Affordable Cars & Finance Inc* ***(G-15410)***
Halley Consulting Group LLC......614 899-7325
1224 Oak Bluff Ct Westerville (43081) ***(G-19405)***
Hallmark Home Mortgage LLC......614 568-1960
7965 N High St Ste 100 Columbus (43235) ***(G-7795)***
Hallmark Management Associates (PA)......216 681-0080
1821 Noble Rd Ofc C Cleveland (44112) ***(G-5722)***
Haly Chapter 136, Napoleon *Also called Royal Arch Masons of Ohio* ***(G-14949)***
Hamilton Automotive Warehouse......513 896-4000
630 Maple Ave Ste 36 Hamilton (45011) ***(G-11738)***
Hamilton Automotive Warehouse (PA)......513 896-4100
630 Maple Ave Hamilton (45011) ***(G-11739)***
Hamilton Cnty Auditor Office......513 946-4000
138 E Court St Rm 501 Cincinnati (45202) ***(G-3730)***
HAMILTON COUNSELING CENTER T/S, Hamilton *Also called Butler Bhavioral Hlth Svcs Inc* ***(G-11698)***
Hamilton County Coroner, Cincinnati *Also called County of Hamilton* ***(G-3432)***
Hamilton County Eductl Svc Ctr......513 674-4200
924 Waycross Rd Cincinnati (45240) ***(G-3731)***
Hamilton County Parks District......513 825-3701
10999 Mill Rd Cincinnati (45240) ***(G-3732)***
Hamilton County Society (PA)......513 541-6100
3949 Colerain Ave Cincinnati (45223) ***(G-3733)***
Hamilton Healthcare, Columbus *Also called Hamilton Homecare Inc* ***(G-7796)***
Hamilton Homecare Inc......614 221-0022
309 S 4th St Columbus (43215) ***(G-7796)***
Hamilton Ice Arena, Cleveland *Also called City of Rocky River* ***(G-5274)***
Hamilton Lodge 93 Benevolant P......513 887-4384
4444 Hmlton Middletown Rd Liberty Twp (45011) ***(G-12725)***
Hamilton Manufacturing Corp......419 867-4858
1026 Hamilton Dr Holland (43528) ***(G-12026)***
Hamilton Parks Conservancy......513 785-7055
106 N 2nd St Hamilton (45011) ***(G-11740)***
Hamilton Safe Products Co Inc......614 268-5530
4770 Northwest Pkwy Hilliard (43026) ***(G-11906)***
Hamilton Scrap Processors......513 863-3474
134 Hensel Pl Hamilton (45011) ***(G-11741)***
Hamilton-Parker Company (PA)......614 358-7800
1865 Leonard Ave Columbus (43219) ***(G-7797)***
Hamlet Manor, Chagrin Falls *Also called Golden Living LLC* ***(G-2698)***
Hamlet Nursing Home, Chagrin Falls *Also called Hamlet Village In Chagrin FLS* ***(G-2699)***
Hamlet Village In Chagrin FLS......440 247-4200
150 Cleveland St Chagrin Falls (44022) ***(G-2699)***
Hamlet Village In Chagrin FLS (PA)......216 263-6033
200 Hamlet Hills Dr Ofc Chagrin Falls (44022) ***(G-2700)***
Hammacher Schlemmer & Co Inc......513 860-4570
9180 La Saint Dr West Chester (45069) ***(G-19088)***
Hammer Smith Agency, Massillon *Also called F W Arnold Agency Co Inc* ***(G-13805)***
Hammond Construction Inc......330 455-7039
1278 Park Ave Sw Canton (44706) ***(G-2389)***
Hammond Law Group LLC......513 381-2011
441 Vine St Ste 3200 Cincinnati (45202) ***(G-3734)***
Hammontree & Associates Ltd (PA)......330 499-8817
5233 Stoneham Rd Canton (44720) ***(G-2390)***
Hampson Insurance Agency, Lancaster *Also called Nl of Ky Inc* ***(G-12562)***
Hampton Inn, Rossford *Also called Rossford Hospitality Group Inc* ***(G-16611)***
Hampton Inn, Columbus *Also called Carlisle Hotels Inc* ***(G-7201)***
Hampton Inn, Columbus *Also called Riverview Hotel LLC* ***(G-8637)***
Hampton Inn, Cincinnati *Also called Sree Hotels LLC* ***(G-4570)***
Hampton Inn, Columbus *Also called Indus Airport Hotel II LLC* ***(G-7890)***
Hampton Inn, Marietta *Also called March Investors Ltd* ***(G-13463)***
Hampton Inn, Marysville *Also called Geeta Hospitality Inc* ***(G-13622)***
Hampton Inn, Lima *Also called Roschmans Restaurant ADM* ***(G-12871)***
Hampton Inn, Streetsboro *Also called Meander Hsptality Group II LLC* ***(G-17420)***
Hampton Inn, Maumee *Also called Bennett Enterprises Inc* ***(G-13887)***
Hampton Inn, Bowling Green *Also called R & Y Holding* ***(G-1792)***
Hampton Inn, Saint Clairsville *Also called Somnus Corporation* ***(G-16656)***
Hampton Inn, Columbus *Also called Ntk Hotel Group II LLC* ***(G-8302)***
Hampton Inn, Troy *Also called S P S Inc* ***(G-18378)***
Hampton Inn, Hilliard *Also called Parkins Incorporated* ***(G-11942)***
Hampton Inn & Suite Inc......440 234-0206
7074 Engle Rd Middleburg Heights (44130) ***(G-14382)***
Hampton Inn and Suites, Beachwood *Also called Buffalo-Gtb Associates LLC* ***(G-1059)***
Hampton Inn Cinc Nw/Fairfield, Fairfield *Also called Middletown Innkeepers Inc* ***(G-10882)***
Hampton Inn Cleveland, North Olmsted *Also called Grand Heritage Hotel Portland* ***(G-15424)***
Hampton Inn Columbus Airport, Dublin *Also called Hit Portfolio I Hil Trs LLC* ***(G-10362)***
Hampton Inn Fairborn, Fairborn *Also called W2005/Fargo Hotels (pool C)* ***(G-10810)***
Hampton Inn Stes Clmbus Hllard, Hilliard *Also called Indus Hilliard Hotel LLC* ***(G-11913)***

Hampton Inn Youngstown West, Youngstown *Also called Meander Inn Incorporated* ***(G-20277)***
Hampton Inn-Newark/Heath, Newark *Also called Kribha LLC* ***(G-15180)***
Hampton Inns LLC...330 492-0151
5335 Broadmoor Cir Nw Canton (44709) ***(G-2391)***
Hampton Inns LLC...330 422-0500
800 Mondial Pkwy Streetsboro (44241) ***(G-17415)***
Hampton Woods Nursing Ctr Inc...330 707-1400
1525 E Western Reserve Rd Poland (44514) ***(G-16224)***
Hanby Farms Inc...740 763-3554
10790 Newark Rd Nashport (43830) ***(G-14951)***
Hanco Ambulance Inc...419 423-2912
417 6th St Findlay (45840) ***(G-11040)***
Hanco International...330 456-9407
1605 Waynesburg Dr Se Canton (44707) ***(G-2392)***
Hancock County Engineer, Findlay *Also called County of Hancock* ***(G-11018)***
Hancock County Home, Findlay *Also called County of Hancock* ***(G-11017)***
Hancock Federal Credit Union...419 420-0338
1701 E Melrose Ave Findlay (45840) ***(G-11041)***
Hancock Hardin Wyandot Putnam (PA)...419 423-3755
122 Jefferson St Findlay (45840) ***(G-11042)***
Hancock Hotel, Findlay *Also called 631 South Main Street Dev LLC* ***(G-10987)***
Hancock Job & Family Services...419 424-7022
7814 County Road 140 Findlay (45840) ***(G-11043)***
Hancock Park District, Findlay *Also called County of Hancock* ***(G-11019)***
Hancock-Wood Electric Coop Inc (PA)...419 257-3241
1399 Business Park Dr S North Baltimore (45872) ***(G-15313)***
Hand Ctr At Orthopaedic Inst...937 298-4417
3205 Woodman Dr Dayton (45420) ***(G-9598)***
Hand Rehabilitation Associates...330 668-4055
3925 Embassy Pkwy Ste 200 Akron (44333) ***(G-251)***
Handels Homemade Ice Cream...330 922-4589
2922 State Rd Cuyahoga Falls (44223) ***(G-9193)***
Handl-It Inc...440 439-9400
7120 Krick Rd Ste 1a Bedford (44146) ***(G-1309)***
Handl-It Inc (PA)...330 468-0734
360 Highland Rd E 2 Macedonia (44056) ***(G-13201)***
Handson Central Ohio Inc...614 221-2255
195 N Grant Ave Columbus (43215) ***(G-7798)***
Handy Hubby...419 754-1150
2010 N Reynolds Rd Toledo (43615) ***(G-17930)***
Haney Inc...513 561-1441
5657 Wooster Pike Cincinnati (45227) ***(G-3735)***
Haney PRC, Cincinnati *Also called Haney Inc* ***(G-3735)***
Hanger Inc...419 841-9852
5551 Monroe St Sylvania (43560) ***(G-17591)***
Hanger Prosthetics & (HQ)...330 633-9807
33 North Ave Ste 101 Tallmadge (44278) ***(G-17638)***
Hankook Tire Akron Office, Uniontown *Also called Hankook Tire America Corp* ***(G-18523)***
Hankook Tire America Corp...330 896-6199
3535 Forest Lake Dr Uniontown (44685) ***(G-18523)***
Hanlin-Rainaldi Construction...614 436-4204
6610 Singletree Dr Columbus (43229) ***(G-7799)***
Hanna Cambell & Powell...330 670-7300
3737 Embassy Pkwy Ste 100 Akron (44333) ***(G-252)***
Hanna Chevrolet Cadillac, Steubenville *Also called Transmerica Svcs Technical Sup* ***(G-17338)***
Hanna Commercial LLC...216 861-7200
1350 Euclid Ave Ste 700 Cleveland (44115) ***(G-5723)***
Hanna Commercial Real Estate, Cleveland *Also called Hanna Commercial LLC* ***(G-5723)***
Hanna Holdings Inc...440 971-5600
9485 W Sprague Rd North Royalton (44133) ***(G-15492)***
Hanna Holdings Inc...440 933-6195
2100 Center Rd Ste L Avon (44011) ***(G-896)***
Hanna Holdings Inc...330 707-1000
100 W Mckinley Way Poland (44514) ***(G-16225)***
HANNA PERKIN CENTER, Shaker Heights *Also called Hanna Perkins School* ***(G-16861)***
Hanna Perkins School...216 991-4472
19910 Malvern Rd Shaker Heights (44122) ***(G-16861)***
Hannon Co, The, Canton *Also called Hanco International* ***(G-2392)***
Hannon Company (PA)...330 456-4728
1605 Waynesburg Dr Se Canton (44707) ***(G-2393)***
Hanover House Inc...330 837-1741
435 Avis Ave Nw Massillon (44646) ***(G-13817)***
Hanover Insurance Company...614 408-9000
545 Metro Pl S Ste 380 Dublin (43017) ***(G-10356)***
Hanover Insurance Company...513 829-4555
6061 Winton Rd Fairfield (45014) ***(G-10857)***
Hans Rothenbuhler & Son Inc...440 632-6000
15815 Nauvoo Rd Middlefield (44062) ***(G-14395)***
Hans Truck and Trlr Repr Inc...216 581-0046
14520 Broadway Ave Cleveland (44125) ***(G-5724)***
Hans Zwart MD & Associates (PA)...937 433-4183
1520 S Main St Ste 3 Dayton (45409) ***(G-9599)***
Hans' Freightliner Cleveland, Cleveland *Also called Hans Truck and Trlr Repr Inc* ***(G-5724)***
Hansen-Mueller Co...419 729-5535
1800 N Water St Toledo (43611) ***(G-17931)***
Hanson Aggregates, Sandusky *Also called Wagner Quarries Company* ***(G-16809)***
Hanson Aggregates East LLC...937 364-2311
4281 Roush Rd Hillsboro (45133) ***(G-11976)***
Hanson Aggregates East LLC...740 773-2172
33 Renick Ave Chillicothe (45601) ***(G-2844)***
Hanson Aggregates East LLC...937 587-2671
848 Plum Run Rd Peebles (45660) ***(G-15939)***
Hanson Aggregates East LLC...419 483-4390
9220 Portland Rd Castalia (44824) ***(G-2630)***
Hanson Aggregates East LLC...937 442-6009
13526 Overstake Rd Winchester (45697) ***(G-19802)***
Hanson Concrete Products Ohio...614 443-4846
1500 Haul Rd Columbus (43207) ***(G-7800)***
Hanson Distributing Co Inc...419 435-3214
22116 Township Road 218 Fostoria (44830) ***(G-11130)***
Hanson Pipe & Products, Columbus *Also called Hanson Concrete Products Ohio* ***(G-7800)***
Hanson Productions Inc...419 327-6100
1695 Indian Wood Cir # 200 Maumee (43537) ***(G-13923)***
Hanson Services Inc (PA)...216 226-5425
17017 Madison Ave Lakewood (44107) ***(G-12480)***
Hanson-Faso Sales & Marketing...216 642-4500
372 Ridgeview Dr Cleveland (44131) ***(G-5725)***
Happy Day School, Ravenna *Also called Portage County Board* ***(G-16398)***
Happy Hearts School...440 224-2157
2505 S Ridge Rd E Ashtabula (44004) ***(G-746)***
Harbor (PA)...419 479-3233
6629 W Central Ave Ste 1 Toledo (43617) ***(G-17932)***
Harbor...419 241-6191
123 22nd St Ste 1 Toledo (43604) ***(G-17933)***
Harbor...800 444-3353
5331 Bennett Rd Toledo (43612) ***(G-17934)***
Harbor Court, Rocky River *Also called Capital Senior Living* ***(G-16572)***
Harbor Freight Tools Usa Inc...513 598-4897
5710 Harrison Ave Cincinnati (45248) ***(G-3736)***
Harbor Freight Tools Usa Inc...330 479-9852
2905 Whipple Ave Nw Canton (44708) ***(G-2394)***
Harbor House Inc...740 498-7213
349 E High Ave New Philadelphia (44663) ***(G-15096)***
Harbor Light Hospice, Cleveland *Also called Hospice of Ohio LLC* ***(G-5777)***
Harbor Services, Bellaire *Also called Bellaire Harbor Service LLC* ***(G-1361)***
Harborside Clveland Ltd Partnr...440 871-5900
27601 Westchester Pkwy Westlake (44145) ***(G-19488)***
Harborside Clveland Ltd Partnr...440 526-4770
2801 E Royalton Rd Broadview Heights (44147) ***(G-1881)***
Harborside Healthcare Corp...937 436-6155
3797 Summit Glen Rd Frnt Dayton (45449) ***(G-9600)***
Harborside Healthcare Corp...419 825-1111
401 W Airport Hwy Swanton (43558) ***(G-17566)***
Harborside Healthcare NW Ohio...419 636-5071
1104 Wesley Ave Bryan (43506) ***(G-2007)***
Harborside Healthcarebroadview, Broadview Heights *Also called Harborside Clveland Ltd Partnr* ***(G-1881)***
Harborside Pointe Place LLC...419 727-7870
6101 N Summit St Toledo (43611) ***(G-17935)***
Harborside Sylvania LLC...419 882-1875
5757 Whiteford Rd Sylvania (43560) ***(G-17592)***
Harborside Troy LLC...937 335-7161
512 Crescent Dr Troy (45373) ***(G-18356)***
Harcatus Tri-County Community (PA)...740 922-0933
225 Fair Ave Ne New Philadelphia (44663) ***(G-15097)***
Harcatus Tri-County Community...330 602-5442
504 Bowers Ave Nw New Philadelphia (44663) ***(G-15098)***
Harco Industries Inc...419 674-4159
707 N Ida St Kenton (43326) ***(G-12413)***
Hardage Hotels I LLC...614 766-7762
4130 Tuller Rd Dublin (43017) ***(G-10357)***
Hardin Cnty Cncil On Aging Inc...419 673-1102
100 Memorial Dr Kenton (43326) ***(G-12414)***
Hardin Cnty Dept Mntl Hlth Ret, Kenton *Also called County of Hardin* ***(G-12410)***
Hardin County Engineer...419 673-2232
1040 W Franklin St Kenton (43326) ***(G-12415)***
Hardin County Family YMCA...419 673-6131
918 W Franklin St Kenton (43326) ***(G-12416)***
Hardin County Home...419 673-0961
1211 W Lima St Kenton (43326) ***(G-12417)***
Hardin Hills Health Center, Kenton *Also called Hardin County Home* ***(G-12417)***
Hardin Memorial Hospital (HQ)...419 673-0761
921 E Franklin St Kenton (43326) ***(G-12418)***
Harding Park Cycle, Canton *Also called Damarc Inc* ***(G-2333)***
Hardlines Design Company (PA)...614 784-8733
4608 Indianola Ave Ste D Columbus (43214) ***(G-7801)***
Hardrock Excavating LLC...330 792-9524
2761 Salt Springs Rd Youngstown (44509) ***(G-20212)***
Hardwood Lumber Co, Burton *Also called Stephen M Trudick* ***(G-2065)***
Hardwood Wholesalers Exporters, Lima *Also called T J Ellis Enterprises Inc* ***(G-12898)***
Hardy Diagnostics...937 550-2768
429 S Pioneer Blvd Springboro (45066) ***(G-17121)***
Hargis Industries, West Chester *Also called Hillman Group Inc* ***(G-19207)***
Haribol Haribol Inc (PA)...330 339-7731
145 Bluebell Dr Sw New Philadelphia (44663) ***(G-15099)***
Harley-Dvidson Dlr Systems Inc...216 573-1393
9885 Rockside Rd Ste 100 Cleveland (44125) ***(G-5726)***
Harmer Place, Marietta *Also called United Church Homes Inc* ***(G-13510)***

ALPHABETIC

Harmon Inc

ALPHABETIC SECTION

Harmon Inc 513 645-1550
  4290 Port Union Rd West Chester (45011) *(G-19089)*
Harmon Media Group 330 478-5325
  4501 Hills & Dales Rd Nw Canton (44708) *(G-2395)*
Harmony Court, Cincinnati Also called Chs-Norwood Inc *(G-3274)*
Harmony Home Care Inc 440 243-1332
  12608 State Rd Ste 1a North Royalton (44133) *(G-15493)*
Harnett Vision Transportation, Ashtabula Also called Lt Trucking Inc *(G-754)*
Harold J Becker Company Inc 614 279-1414
  3946 Indian Ripple Rd Beavercreek (45440) *(G-1245)*
Harold K Phllips Rstration Inc 614 443-5699
  972 Harmon Ave Columbus (43223) *(G-7802)*
Harold Tatman & Sons Entps Inc 740 655-2880
  9171 State Route 180 Kingston (45644) *(G-12450)*
Harrington Electric Company 216 361-5101
  3800 Perkins Ave Cleveland (44114) *(G-5727)*
Harrington Health Services Inc (HQ) 614 212-7000
  780 Brooksedge Plaza Dr Westerville (43081) *(G-19406)*
Harrington Hoppe Mitchell Ltd 330 744-1111
  26 Market St Ste 1200 Youngstown (44503) *(G-20213)*
Harris Mackessy & Brennan 614 221-6831
  570 Polaris Pkwy Ste 125 Westerville (43082) *(G-19311)*
Harris & Burgin 513 891-3270
  9545 Kenwood Rd Ste 301 Blue Ash (45242) *(G-1607)*
Harris & Heavener Excavating 740 927-1423
  149 Humphries Dr Etna (43068) *(G-10729)*
Harris Battery Company Inc (PA) 330 874-0205
  10708 Industrial Pkwy Nw Bolivar (44612) *(G-1748)*
Harris Distributing Co 513 541-4222
  4261 Crawford Ave Cincinnati (45223) *(G-3737)*
Harrison Ave Assembly of God 513 367-6100
  949 Harrison Ave Harrison (45030) *(G-11800)*
Harrison Building and Ln Assn (PA) 513 367-2015
  10490 New Haven Rd Harrison (45030) *(G-11801)*
Harrison Co County Home 740 942-3573
  41500 Cadiz Dennison Rd Cadiz (43907) *(G-2075)*
Harrison Community Hosp Inc (PA) 740 942-4631
  951 E Market St Cadiz (43907) *(G-2076)*
Harrison Construction Inc 740 373-7000
  1408 Colegate Dr Marietta (45750) *(G-13450)*
Harrison Contruction, Marietta Also called Harrison Construction Inc *(G-13450)*
Harrison County Coal Company (PA) 740 338-3100
  46226 National Rd Saint Clairsville (43950) *(G-16637)*
Harrison Industries Inc 740 942-2988
  82460 Cadiz Jewett Rd Cadiz (43907) *(G-2077)*
Harrison Pavilion 513 662-5800
  2171 Harrison Ave Cincinnati (45211) *(G-3738)*
Harry C Lobalzo & Sons Inc (PA) 330 666-6758
  61 N Cleveland Ste A Akron (44333) *(G-253)*
Harry Rock & Company 330 644-3748
  8550 Aetna Rd Cleveland (44105) *(G-5728)*
Hart Associates Inc 419 893-9600
  811 Madison Ave Toledo (43604) *(G-17936)*
Hart Industrial Products Div, Middletown Also called Hart Industries Inc *(G-14427)*
Hart Industries Inc (PA) 513 541-4278
  931 Jeanette St Middletown (45044) *(G-14427)*
Hart Roofing Inc 330 452-4055
  437 Mcgregor Ave Nw Canton (44703) *(G-2396)*
Hart-Greer, Bellevue Also called Amrstrong Distributors Inc *(G-1402)*
Harte-Hanks Trnsp Svcs 513 458-7600
  2950 Robinson Ave Cincinnati (45209) *(G-3739)*
Harter Ventures Inc 419 224-4075
  3623 S Buckskin Trl Lima (45807) *(G-12790)*
Hartford Fire Insurance Co 216 447-1000
  7100 E Pleasant Valley Rd # 200 Cleveland (44131) *(G-5729)*
Hartland Petroleum LLC 740 452-3115
  4560 West Pike Zanesville (43701) *(G-20485)*
Hartsfield Atlanta Intl Arprt, Cincinnati Also called Parking Company America Inc *(G-4254)*
Hartung Brothers Inc 419 352-3000
  815 S Dunbridge Rd Bowling Green (43402) *(G-1780)*
Hartville Group Inc (PA) 330 484-8166
  1210 Massillon Rd Akron (44306) *(G-254)*
Hartville Hardware Inc 330 877-4690
  1315 Edison St Nw Hartville (44632) *(G-11820)*
Hartwig Transit Inc 513 563-1765
  11971 Reading Rd Cincinnati (45241) *(G-3740)*
Hartzell Hardwoods (PA) 937 773-7054
  1025 S Roosevelt Ave Piqua (45356) *(G-16146)*
Harvest Facility Holdings LP 419 472-7115
  4560 W Alexis Rd Apt 9 Toledo (43623) *(G-17937)*
Harvest Facility Holdings LP 440 268-9555
  19205 Pearl Rd Ofc Cleveland (44136) *(G-5730)*
Harwick Standard Dist Corp (PA) 330 798-9300
  60 S Seiberling St Akron (44305) *(G-255)*
Hasenstab Architects Inc (PA) 330 434-4464
  190 N Union St Ste 400 Akron (44304) *(G-256)*
Haslett Heating & Cooling Inc 614 299-2133
  7686 Fishel Dr N A Dublin (43016) *(G-10358)*
Hassler Medical Center, Cleveland Also called Clevelan Clinic Hlth Sys W Reg *(G-5288)*
Hastings Home Health Ctr Inc 216 898-3300
  211 Commerce Dr Medina (44256) *(G-14074)*

Hastings Water Works Inc (PA) 440 832-7700
  10331 Brecksville Rd Brecksville (44141) *(G-1826)*
Hat White Management LLC (PA) 800 525-7967
  121 S Main St Ste 201 Akron (44308) *(G-257)*
Hatfield Lincoln Mercury, Columbus Also called Sonic Automotive-1495 Automall *(G-8749)*
Hattenbach Company (PA) 216 881-5200
  5309 Hamilton Ave Cleveland (44114) *(G-5731)*
Hattie Larlham Center For (PA) 330 274-2272
  9772 Diagonal Rd Mantua (44255) *(G-13387)*
Hattie Larlham Center For 330 274-2272
  9772 Diagonal Rd Mantua (44255) *(G-13388)*
Hattie Larlham Community Svcs 330 274-2272
  7996 Darrow Rd Ste 10 Twinsburg (44087) *(G-18427)*
Hattie Larlham Community Svcs 330 274-2272
  9772 Diagonal Rd Mantua (44255) *(G-13389)*
Hatzel & Buehler Inc 740 420-3088
  3381 Congo Dr Circleville (43113) *(G-4889)*
Hauck Hospitality LLC 513 563-8330
  3855 Hauck Rd Cincinnati (45241) *(G-3741)*
Hauser Group, The, Cincinnati Also called Art Hauser Insurance Inc *(G-3050)*
Havar Inc (PA) 740 594-3533
  396 Richland Ave Athens (45701) *(G-790)*
Havar Inc 740 373-7175
  416 3rd St Marietta (45750) *(G-13451)*
Haven Bhavioral Healthcare Inc 937 234-0100
  1 Elizabeth Pl Ste A Dayton (45417) *(G-9601)*
Haven Financial Enterprise 800 265-2401
  675 Alpha Dr Ste E Cleveland (44143) *(G-5732)*
Haven Hill Home, North Royalton Also called Childrens Forever Haven Inc *(G-15483)*
Haven Rest Ministries Inc (PA) 330 535-1563
  175 E Market St Akron (44308) *(G-258)*
Haverhill Coke Company LLC 740 355-9819
  2446 Gallia Pike Franklin Furnace (45629) *(G-11172)*
Havsco Inc 440 439-8900
  5018 Richmond Rd Bedford (44146) *(G-1310)*
Hawa Incorporated (PA) 614 451-1711
  980 Old Henderson Rd C Columbus (43220) *(G-7803)*
Hawkins & Co Lpa Ltd 216 861-1365
  1267 W 9th St Ste 500 Cleveland (44113) *(G-5733)*
Hawkins Markets Inc 330 435-4611
  2800 E Pleasant Home Rd Creston (44217) *(G-9150)*
Hawks Nest Golf Club, Creston Also called Hawkins Markets Inc *(G-9150)*
Hawthorn Glenn Nursing Center, Middletown Also called Semma Enterprises Inc *(G-14457)*
Hawthorne Valley Country Club 440 232-1400
  25250 Rockside Rd Ste 1 Bedford (44146) *(G-1311)*
Haydocy Automotive Inc 614 279-8880
  3895 W Broad St Columbus (43228) *(G-7804)*
Haydocy Automotors, Columbus Also called Haydocy Automotive Inc *(G-7804)*
Hayes Concrete Construction 513 648-9400
  2120 Waycross Rd Cincinnati (45240) *(G-3742)*
Hayes, Rutherford B Pres Lib, Fremont Also called Rthrford B Hayes Prsdntial Ctr *(G-11217)*
Haynes Manufacturing Company, Westlake Also called R and J Corporation *(G-19536)*
Hays & Sons Construction Inc 513 671-9110
  190 Container Pl Cincinnati (45246) *(G-3743)*
Hays Enterprises Inc 330 299-8639
  1901 Ellsworth Bailey Rd Warren (44481) *(G-18861)*
Hayward Distributing Co (PA) 614 272-5953
  4061 Perimeter Dr Columbus (43228) *(G-7805)*
Hbi Payments Ltd 614 944-5788
  3 Easton Oval Ste 210 Columbus (43219) *(G-7806)*
Hbk, Canfield Also called Hill Barth & King LLC *(G-2194)*
Hbk CPA & Consultants, Columbus Also called Hill Barth & King LLC *(G-7835)*
Hbl Automotive, Columbus Also called Lindsey Accura Inc *(G-8070)*
Hc Transport Inc 513 574-1800
  6045 Bridgetown Rd Cincinnati (45248) *(G-3744)*
HCA Holdings Inc 440 826-3240
  19250 Bagley Rd Ste 100 Cleveland (44130) *(G-5734)*
Hccao, Hillsboro Also called Highlnd Cnty Commnty Action or *(G-11981)*
Hcesc Early Learning Program 513 589-3021
  924 Waycross Rd Cincinnati (45240) *(G-3745)*
Hcf Management Inc 740 289-2394
  7143 Us Highway 23 Piketon (45661) *(G-16117)*
Hcf Management Inc 419 435-8112
  25 Christopher Dr Fostoria (44830) *(G-11131)*
Hcf Management Inc (PA) 419 999-2010
  1100 Shawnee Rd Lima (45805) *(G-12791)*
Hcf Management Inc 419 999-2055
  2535 Fort Amanda Rd Lima (45804) *(G-12792)*
Hcf of Bowl Green Care Ctr Inc 419 352-7558
  850 W Poe Rd Bowling Green (43402) *(G-1781)*
Hcf of Bowling Green Inc 419 352-4694
  1021 W Poe Rd Bowling Green (43402) *(G-1782)*
Hcf of Briarwood Inc 419 678-2311
  100 Don Desch Dr D Coldwater (45828) *(G-6829)*
Hcf of Court House Inc 740 335-9290
  555 N Glenn Ave Wshngtn CT Hs (43160) *(G-20025)*
Hcf of Crestview Inc 937 426-5033
  4381 Tonawanda Trl Beavercreek (45430) *(G-1246)*
Hcf of Findlay Inc 419 999-2010
  11745 Township Road 145 Findlay (45840) *(G-11044)*

Hcf of Fox Run Inc 419 424-0832
11745 Township Road 145 Findlay (45840) **(G-11045)**
Hcf of Lima Inc 419 999-2010
1100 Shawnee Rd Lima (45805) **(G-12793)**
Hcf of Perrysburg Inc 419 874-0306
250 Manor Dr Perrysburg (43551) **(G-16008)**
Hcf of Piqua Inc 937 773-0040
1840 W High St Piqua (45356) **(G-16147)**
Hcf of Roselawn Inc 419 647-4115
420 E 4th St Spencerville (45887) **(G-17108)**
Hcf of Shawnee Inc 419 999-2055
2535 Fort Amanda Rd Lima (45804) **(G-12794)**
Hcf of Van Wert Inc 419 999-2010
160 Fox Rd Van Wert (45891) **(G-18634)**
Hcf of Wapakoneta Inc 419 738-3711
1010 Lincoln Hwy Wapakoneta (45895) **(G-18798)**
Hcf of Washington Inc 419 999-2010
555 N Glenn Ave Wshngtn CT Hs (43160) **(G-20026)**
HCFW, Cleveland *Also called Hitchcock Center For Women Inc* **(G-5761)**
Hcg Inc 513 539-9269
203 N Garver Rd Monroe (45050) **(G-14697)**
Hcl of Dayton Inc 937 384-8300
4000 Mmsbrg Ctrvle Rd 4 Ste Miamisburg (45342) **(G-14305)**
Hcr Manor Care, Toledo *Also called Leader Nuring & Rehabilitation* **(G-18002)**
Hcr Manor Care Svc Fla III Inc (HQ) 419 252-5500
333 N Summit St Toledo (43604) **(G-17938)**
Hcr Manorcare Med Svcs Fla LLC 513 745-9600
4580 E Galbraith Rd Cincinnati (45236) **(G-3746)**
Hcr Manorcare Med Svcs Fla LLC 513 233-0831
6870 Clough Pike Cincinnati (45244) **(G-3747)**
Hcr Manorcare Med Svcs Fla LLC 419 252-5500
35 Bierly Rd Ste 2 Portsmouth (45662) **(G-16283)**
Hcr Manorcare Med Svcs Fla LLC 419 531-2127
3450 W Central Ave # 230 Toledo (43606) **(G-17939)**
Hcr Manorcare Med Svcs Fla LLC 330 753-5005
85 3rd St Se Barberton (44203) **(G-965)**
Hcr Manorcare Med Svcs Fla LLC 513 561-4111
4900 Cooper Rd Cincinnati (45242) **(G-3748)**
Hcr Manorcare Med Svcs Fla LLC 614 882-1511
140 Old County Line Rd Westerville (43081) **(G-19407)**
Hcr Manorcare Med Svcs Fla LLC 330 668-6889
171 N Clvland Mssillon Rd Akron (44333) **(G-259)**
Hcr Manorcare Med Svcs Fla LLC (HQ) 419 252-5500
333 N Summit St Ste 100 Toledo (43604) **(G-17940)**
Hcr Manorcare Med Svcs Fla LLC 216 251-3300
4102 Rocky River Dr Cleveland (44135) **(G-5735)**
Hcr Manorcare Med Svcs Fla LLC 440 473-0090
6757 Mayfield Rd Cleveland (44124) **(G-5736)**
Hcr Manorcare Med Svcs Fla LLC 216 486-2300
16101 Euclid Beach Blvd Cleveland (44110) **(G-5737)**
Hcr Manorcare Med Svcs Fla LLC 937 436-9700
1001 E Alex Bell Rd Centerville (45459) **(G-2679)**
Hcr Manorcare Med Svcs Fla LLC 419 691-3088
3953 Navarre Ave Oregon (43616) **(G-15738)**
Hcr Manorcare Med Svcs Fla LLC 440 808-9275
28400 Center Ridge Rd Westlake (44145) **(G-19489)**
Hcr Manorcare Med Svcs Fla LLC 513 591-0400
2250 Banning Rd Cincinnati (45239) **(G-3749)**
Hcr Manorcare Med Svcs Fla LLC 440 887-1442
9205 W Sprague Rd North Royalton (44133) **(G-15494)**
Hctec Partners LLC 513 985-6400
4605 E Galbraith Rd # 200 Cincinnati (45236) **(G-3750)**
Hd Supply Inc 614 771-4849
6200 Commerce Center Dr Groveport (43125) **(G-11643)**
Hd Supply Facilities Maint Ltd 440 542-9188
30311 Emerald Valley Pkwy Solon (44139) **(G-17014)**
Hdi Ltd 937 224-0800
33 E 5th St Dayton (45402) **(G-9602)**
HDR Engineering Inc 614 839-5770
2800 Corp Exchange Dr # 100 Columbus (43231) **(G-7807)**
Hdt Engineered Technologies, Solon *Also called Hunter Defense Tech Inc* **(G-17016)**
He Hari Inc 614 436-0700
7007 N High St Worthington (43085) **(G-19961)**
He Hari Inc (PA) 614 846-6600
600 Enterprise Dr Lewis Center (43035) **(G-12687)**
Head Inc 614 338-8501
4477 E 5th Ave Columbus (43219) **(G-7808)**
Head Mercantile Co Inc 440 847-2700
29065 Clemens Rd Ste 200 Westlake (44145) **(G-19490)**
Head Qaurters Salon & Spa, Lorain *Also called Head Quarters Inc* **(G-13041)**
Head Quarters Inc 440 233-8508
6071 Middle Ridge Rd Lorain (44053) **(G-13041)**
Head Start, Lima *Also called West Ohio Cmnty Action Partnr* **(G-12919)**
Head Start Program, Lorain *Also called Lorain County Community Action* **(G-13052)**
Headstart Program, Circleville *Also called Pickaway County Community Acti* **(G-4895)**
Healing Hands Home Health Ltd 740 385-0710
30605 Stage Coach Rd Logan (43138) **(G-12973)**
Healing Hrts Cunseling Ctr Inc 419 528-5993
680 Park Ave W Mansfield (44906) **(G-13307)**
Healing Touch Healthcare 937 610-5555
627 S Edwin C Moses Blvd 3l Dayton (45417) **(G-9603)**

Health & HM Care Concepts Inc 740 383-4968
353 S State St Marion (43302) **(G-13542)**
Health & Homecare Concepts, Marion *Also called Health & HM Care Concepts Inc* **(G-13542)**
Health Care Dataworks Inc 614 255-5400
4215 Worth Ave Ste 320 Columbus (43219) **(G-7809)**
Health Care Depo of Ohio LLC 614 776-3333
1570 E Dblin Grndville Rd Columbus (43229) **(G-7810)**
Health Care Facilities, Lima *Also called Hcf Management Inc* **(G-12791)**
Health Care Facility MGT LLC (HQ) 513 489-7100
4700 Ashwood Dr Ste 200 Blue Ash (45241) **(G-1608)**
Health Care Management Group, Cincinnati *Also called Central Accounting Systems* **(G-3209)**
Health Care Opportunities Inc (PA) 513 932-0300
102 E Silver St Lebanon (45036) **(G-12609)**
Health Care Opportunities Inc 513 932-4861
220 S Mechanic St Lebanon (45036) **(G-12610)**
Health Care Personnel, Columbus *Also called Prn Nurse Inc* **(G-8562)**
Health Care Plus (HQ) 614 340-7587
1120 Polaris Pkwy Ste 204 Columbus (43240) **(G-6882)**
Health Care Retirement Corp 419 252-5500
333 N Summit St Ste 100 Toledo (43604) **(G-17941)**
Health Care Rtrement Corp Amer (HQ) 419 252-5500
333 N Summit St Ste 103 Toledo (43604) **(G-17942)**
Health Care Rtrement Corp Amer 419 474-6021
4293 Monroe St Toledo (43606) **(G-17943)**
Health Care Rtrement Corp Amer 740 286-5026
8668 State Route 93 Jackson (45640) **(G-12312)**
Health Care Rtrement Corp Amer 419 562-9907
1170 W Mansfield St Bucyrus (44820) **(G-2038)**
Health Care Rtrement Corp Amer 937 298-8084
3313 Wilmington Pike Dayton (45429) **(G-9604)**
Health Care Rtrement Corp Amer 740 373-8920
5001 State Route 60 Marietta (45750) **(G-13452)**
Health Care Rtrement Corp Amer 937 429-1106
1974 N Fairfield Rd Dayton (45432) **(G-9271)**
Health Care Rtrement Corp Amer 937 456-5537
515 S Maple St Eaton (45320) **(G-10562)**
Health Care Rtrement Corp Amer 740 773-5000
1058 Columbus St Chillicothe (45601) **(G-2845)**
Health Care Rtrement Corp Amer 740 354-4505
20 Easter Dr Portsmouth (45662) **(G-16284)**
Health Care Rtrement Corp Amer 614 882-3782
215 Huber Village Blvd Westerville (43081) **(G-19408)**
Health Care Rtrement Corp Amer 937 599-5123
221 School St Bellefontaine (43311) **(G-1384)**
Health Care Rtrement Corp Amer 614 464-2273
920 Thurber Dr W Columbus (43215) **(G-7811)**
Health Care Rtrement Corp Amer 937 390-0005
2615 Derr Rd Springfield (45503) **(G-17204)**
Health Care Rtrement Corp Amer 740 894-3287
7743 County Road 1 South Point (45680) **(G-17088)**
Health Care Rtrement Corp Amer 937 393-5766
1141 Northview Dr Hillsboro (45133) **(G-11977)**
Health Care Rtrement Corp Amer 440 946-1912
8200 Mentor Hills Dr Mentor (44060) **(G-14188)**
Health Care Rtrement Corp Amer 740 635-4600
300 Commercial Dr Bridgeport (43912) **(G-1863)**
Health Care Rtrement Corp Amer 937 773-9346
275 Kienle Dr Piqua (45356) **(G-16148)**
Health Care Rtrement Corp Amer 419 874-3578
10540 Fremont Pike Perrysburg (43551) **(G-16009)**
Health Care Rtrement Corp Amer 937 866-8885
450 Oak Ridge Blvd Miamisburg (45342) **(G-14306)**
Health Care Rtrement Corp Amer 937 548-3141
243 Marion Dr Greenville (45331) **(G-11509)**
Health Care Rtrement Corp Amer 419 337-3050
303 W Leggett St Wauseon (43567) **(G-18958)**
Health Care Rtrement Corp Amer 419 878-8523
8885 Browning Dr Waterville (43566) **(G-18942)**
Health Care Rtrement Corp Amer 513 751-0880
510 Oak St Cincinnati (45219) **(G-3751)**
Health Care Specialists 740 454-4530
945 Bethesda Dr Ste 300 Zanesville (43701) **(G-20486)**
Health Carousel LLC (PA) 866 665-4544
3805 Edwards Rd Ste 700 Cincinnati (45209) **(G-3752)**
Health Center At Renaissance, Olmsted Twp *Also called Olmsted Health and Svc Corp* **(G-15679)**
Health Collaborative 513 618-3600
615 Elsinore Pl Bldg B Cincinnati (45202) **(G-3753)**
Health Data MGT Solutions Inc 216 595-1232
3201 Enterprise Pkwy Beachwood (44122) **(G-1084)**
Health Dept, Columbus *Also called City of Columbus* **(G-7280)**
Health Dept, Columbus *Also called City of Columbus* **(G-7281)**
Health Dept, Cincinnati *Also called County of Hamilton* **(G-3433)**
Health Design Plus Inc 330 656-1072
1755 Georgetown Rd Hudson (44236) **(G-12120)**
Health Force, Eaton *Also called Personal Touch HM Care IPA Inc* **(G-10573)**
HEALTH FOUNDATION OF GREATER C, Cincinnati *Also called Interact For Health* **(G-3831)**
Health Partners Health Clinic 937 645-8488
19900 State Route 739 Marysville (43040) **(G-13623)**

ALPHABETIC

Health Partners Western Ohio....419 679-5994
111 W Espy St Kenton (43326) *(G-12419)*
Health Partners Western Ohio (PA)....419 221-3072
441 E 8th St Lima (45804) *(G-12795)*
Health Recovery Services Inc (PA)....740 592-6720
224 Columbus Rd Ste 102 Athens (45701) *(G-791)*
Health Right, Springboro *Also called Right At Home (G-17137)*
Health Science Campus, Toledo *Also called University of Toledo (G-18280)*
Health Science Campus, Toledo *Also called University of Toledo (G-18282)*
Health Service Preferred, Cincinnati *Also called Integra Group Inc (G-3824)*
Health Services Coshocton Cnty....740 622-7311
230 S 4th St Coshocton (43812) *(G-9104)*
Health Services Inc....330 837-7678
2520 Wales Ave Nw Ste 120 Massillon (44646) *(G-13818)*
Health Smile Center....440 992-2700
2010 W 19th St Ashtabula (44004) *(G-747)*
Health Works Mso Inc (PA)....740 368-5366
561 W Central Ave Delaware (43015) *(G-10103)*
Health, Dept Of- Admin, Columbus *Also called City of Columbus (G-7282)*
Healthcare and Social....614 461-1199
1395 Dublin Rd Columbus (43215) *(G-7812)*
Healthcare Circle Inc....440 331-7347
18149 Williamsburg Oval Strongsville (44136) *(G-17468)*
Healthcare Facility MGT LLC....419 382-2200
955 Garden Lake Pkwy Toledo (43614) *(G-17944)*
Healthcare Facility MGT LLC....330 836-7953
200 Wyant Rd Akron (44313) *(G-260)*
Healthcare Holdings Inc....513 530-1600
4700 Ashwood Dr Ste 200 Blue Ash (45241) *(G-1609)*
Healthcare Management Cons....419 363-2193
201 Buckeye St Rockford (45882) *(G-16563)*
Healthcomp Inc....216 696-6900
1226 Huron Rd E Ste 2 Cleveland (44115) *(G-5738)*
Healthlinx Inc....513 402-2018
602 Main St Ste 300 Cincinnati (45202) *(G-3754)*
Healthpro Medical Billing Inc....419 223-2717
4132 Elida Rd Lima (45807) *(G-12796)*
Healthscope Benefits Inc....614 797-5200
5150 E Dublin Granvll 3 Westerville (43081) *(G-19409)*
Healthsource Inc....330 278-2781
1313 Ridge Rd Hinckley (44233) *(G-11998)*
Healthsource of Ohio Inc....513 707-1997
2055 Hospital Dr Ste 320 Batavia (45103) *(G-1016)*
Healthsource of Ohio Inc....937 392-4381
631 E State St Georgetown (45121) *(G-11395)*
Healthsource of Ohio Inc....937 981-7707
1075 N Washington St Greenfield (45123) *(G-11487)*
HealthSouth, Cincinnati *Also called Encompass Health Corporation (G-3556)*
HealthSouth, Springfield *Also called Encompass Health Corporation (G-17194)*
HealthSouth....937 424-8200
1 Elizabeth Pl Dayton (45417) *(G-9605)*
Healthspan Integrated Care....440 937-2350
36711 American Way Fl 1 Avon (44011) *(G-897)*
Healthspan Integrated Care....216 362-2000
12301 Snow Rd Cleveland (44130) *(G-5739)*
Healthspan Integrated Care....216 621-5600
11203 Stokes Blvd Cleveland (44104) *(G-5740)*
Healthspan Integrated Care....216 524-7377
3733 Park East Dr Cleveland (44122) *(G-5741)*
Healthspan Integrated Care (HQ)....216 621-5600
1001 Lakeside Ave E # 1200 Cleveland (44114) *(G-5742)*
Healthspan Integrated Care....440 572-1000
17406 Royalton Rd Cleveland (44136) *(G-5743)*
Healthspan Integrated Care....330 767-3436
360 Wabash Ave N Brewster (44613) *(G-1855)*
Healthspan Integrated Care....330 486-2800
8920 Canyon Falls Blvd Twinsburg (44087) *(G-18428)*
Healthspan Integrated Care....330 877-4018
900 W Maple St Hartville (44632) *(G-11821)*
Healthspan Integrated Care....330 334-1549
120 High St Wadsworth (44281) *(G-18754)*
Healthspan Integrated Care....330 633-8400
1260 Independence Ave Akron (44310) *(G-261)*
Healthspan Integrated Care....216 362-2277
14600 Detroit Ave Ste 700 Lakewood (44107) *(G-12481)*
Healthspan-Concord Med Offs, Concord Township *Also called Kaiser Foundation Hospitals (G-9032)*
Healthy Advice Networks, Cincinnati *Also called Patientpint Ntwrk Slutions LLC (G-4260)*
Healthy Life HM Healthcare LLC....614 865-3368
5454 Cleveland Ave # 201 Columbus (43231) *(G-7813)*
Healthy Smile Center The, Ashtabula *Also called Health Smile Center (G-747)*
Heap Home Energy Assistance....419 626-6540
908 Seavers Way Sandusky (44870) *(G-16767)*
Hearing Spch Deaf Ctr Grtr Cnc....513 221-0527
2825 Burnet Ave Ste 401 Cincinnati (45219) *(G-3755)*
Heart & HM Assistant Friedman, Tiffin *Also called Friedman Vlg Retirement Cmnty (G-17680)*
Heart Care....614 533-5000
765 N Hamilton Rd Ste 120 Gahanna (43230) *(G-11246)*
Heart Center Northeastern Ohio, Youngstown *Also called Heart Center of N Eastrn Ohio (G-20214)*
Heart Center of N Eastrn Ohio (PA)....330 758-7703
250 Debartolo Pl Ste 2750 Youngstown (44512) *(G-20214)*
Heart Hospital of Dto LLC....937 734-8000
2222 Philadelphia Dr Dayton (45406) *(G-9606)*
Heart of Marion Dialysis, Marion *Also called Tonka Bay Dialysis LLC (G-13585)*
Heart of OH Cncl Bsa (PA)....419 522-8300
3 N Main St Ste 303 Mansfield (44902) *(G-13308)*
Heart Ohio Family Health Ctrs....614 235-5555
882 S Hamilton Rd Columbus (43213) *(G-7814)*
Heart Specialists of Ohio....614 538-0527
3650 Olentangy River Rd # 300 Columbus (43214) *(G-7815)*
Heart To Heart Home Health....330 335-9999
250 Smokerise Dr Apt 302 Wadsworth (44281) *(G-18755)*
Heartbeat International Inc....614 885-7577
5000 Arlington Centre Blv Columbus (43220) *(G-7816)*
Heartbeats To City Inc....330 452-4524
1352 Market Ave S Canton (44707) *(G-2397)*
Hearthstone Utilities Inc (HQ)....440 974-3770
1375 E 9th St Ste 3100 Cleveland (44114) *(G-5744)*
Heartland - Beavercreek, Dayton *Also called Health Care Rtrement Corp Amer (G-9271)*
Heartland - Holly Glen, Toledo *Also called Health Care Rtrement Corp Amer (G-17943)*
Heartland - Lansing, Bridgeport *Also called Health Care Rtrement Corp Amer (G-1863)*
Heartland - Victorian Village, Columbus *Also called Health Care Rtrement Corp Amer (G-7811)*
Heartland Bank (PA)....614 337-4600
850 N Hamilton Rd Gahanna (43230) *(G-11247)*
Heartland Bhavioral Healthcare....330 833-3135
3000 Erie St S Massillon (44646) *(G-13819)*
Heartland Care Partners 3555, Toledo *Also called Hcr Manorcare Med Svcs Fla LLC (G-17939)*
Heartland Employment Svcs LLC....419 252-5500
333 N Summit St Ste 103 Toledo (43604) *(G-17945)*
Heartland Express Inc....614 870-8628
1800 Lone Eagle St Columbus (43228) *(G-7817)*
Heartland Fort Myers Fl LLC (HQ)....419 252-5500
333 N Summit St Toledo (43604) *(G-17946)*
Heartland Healthcare Svcs LLC (PA)....419 535-8435
4755 South Ave Toledo (43615) *(G-17947)*
Heartland HM Hlth Care Hospice, Columbus *Also called Heartland Hospice Services LLC (G-7819)*
Heartland HM Hlth Care Hospice, Lucasville *Also called Heartland Hospice Services LLC (G-13180)*
Heartland HM Hlth Care Hospice, Perrysburg *Also called Heartland Hospice Services LLC (G-16010)*
Heartland HM Hlth Care Hospice, Toledo *Also called In Home Health LLC (G-17972)*
Heartland HM Hlth Care Hospice, Independence *Also called Heartland Hospice Services LLC (G-12216)*
Heartland HM Hlth Care Hospice, Fremont *Also called In Home Health LLC (G-11207)*
Heartland HM Hlth Care Hospice, Dayton *Also called Heartland Hospice Services LLC (G-9607)*
Heartland Holly Glen Care Ctr, Toledo *Also called H C R Corp (G-17929)*
Heartland Home Care LLC (HQ)....419 252-5500
333 N Summit St Toledo (43604) *(G-17948)*
Heartland Home Care LLC....614 433-0423
6500 Busch Blvd Ste 210 Columbus (43229) *(G-7818)*
Heartland Home Health Care, Columbus *Also called Heartland Home Care LLC (G-7818)*
Heartland Hospice Services, Cincinnati *Also called In Home Health LLC (G-3810)*
Heartland Hospice Services, Toledo *Also called Hcr Manor Care Svc Fla III Inc (G-17938)*
Heartland Hospice Services LLC....614 433-0423
6500 Busch Blvd Ste 210 Columbus (43229) *(G-7819)*
Heartland Hospice Services LLC....740 351-0575
35 Bierly Rd Ste 2 Portsmouth (45662) *(G-16285)*
Heartland Hospice Services LLC....740 259-0281
205 North St Lucasville (45648) *(G-13180)*
Heartland Hospice Services LLC....419 531-0440
28555 Starbright Blvd E Perrysburg (43551) *(G-16010)*
Heartland Hospice Services LLC....216 901-1464
4807 Rockside Rd Ste 110 Independence (44131) *(G-12216)*
Heartland Hospice Services LLC....937 299-6980
580 Lincoln Park Blvd # 320 Dayton (45429) *(G-9607)*
Heartland of Bellefontaine, Bellefontaine *Also called Health Care Rtrement Corp Amer (G-1384)*
Heartland of Bucyrus, Bucyrus *Also called Health Care Rtrement Corp Amer (G-2038)*
Heartland of Chillicothe, Chillicothe *Also called Health Care Rtrement Corp Amer (G-2845)*
Heartland of Eaton, Eaton *Also called Health Care Rtrement Corp Amer (G-10562)*
Heartland of Greenville, Greenville *Also called Health Care Rtrement Corp Amer (G-11509)*
Heartland of Hillsboro, Hillsboro *Also called Health Care Rtrement Corp Amer (G-11977)*
Heartland of Jackson, Jackson *Also called Health Care Rtrement Corp Amer (G-12312)*
Heartland of Kettering, Dayton *Also called Health Care Rtrement Corp Amer (G-9604)*
Heartland of Marietta, Marietta *Also called Health Care Rtrement Corp Amer (G-13452)*
Heartland of Mentor, Mentor *Also called Health Care Rtrement Corp Amer (G-14188)*
Heartland of Oak Ridge, Miamisburg *Also called Health Care Rtrement Corp Amer (G-14306)*
Heartland of Oregon, Oregon *Also called Hcr Manorcare Med Svcs Fla LLC (G-15738)*
Heartland of Piqua, Piqua *Also called Health Care Rtrement Corp Amer (G-16148)*

ALPHABETIC SECTION
Her Inc (PA)

Heartland of Portsmouth, Portsmouth *Also called Health Care Rtrement Corp Amer (G-16284)*
Heartland of Riverview, South Point *Also called Health Care Rtrement Corp Amer (G-17088)*
Heartland of Riverview 4148, South Point *Also called Heartlnd-Riverview S Pt OH LLC (G-17089)*
Heartland of Springfield, Springfield *Also called Health Care Rtrement Corp Amer (G-17204)*
Heartland of Waterville, Waterville *Also called Health Care Rtrement Corp Amer (G-18942)*
Heartland of Wauseon, Wauseon *Also called Health Care Rtrement Corp Amer (G-18958)*
Heartland Payment Systems LLC ... 513 518-6125
3455 Steeplechase Ln Loveland (45140) *(G-13130)*
Heartland Petroleum LLC (PA) ... 614 441-4001
4001 E 5th Ave Columbus (43219) *(G-7820)*
Heartland Quality Egg Farm ... 937 355-5103
9800 County Road 26 West Mansfield (43358) *(G-19266)*
Heartland Rhblitation Svcs Inc (HQ) ... 419 537-0764
3425 Executive Pkwy # 128 Toledo (43606) *(G-17949)*
Heartlight Pharmacy Services, Lima *Also called Schaaf Drugs LLC (G-12873)*
Heartlnd-Riverview S Pt OH LLC ... 740 894-3287
7743 County Road 1 South Point (45680) *(G-17089)*
Heartsong Presents, Uhrichsville *Also called Barbour Publishing Inc (G-18487)*
Heartspring Home Hlth Care LLC ... 937 531-6920
1251 E Dorothy Ln Dayton (45419) *(G-9608)*
Heat and Frost Insulators Jatc, Toledo *Also called Toledo Area Insulator Wkrs Jac (G-18226)*
HEat Ttal Fclty Slutions Inc ... 740 965-3005
5064 Red Bank Rd Galena (43021) *(G-11283)*
Heatermeals, Cincinnati *Also called Luxfer Magtech Inc (G-4003)*
Heath Nursing Care Center ... 740 522-1171
717 S 30th St Newark (43056) *(G-15173)*
Heather Hl Rehabilitation Hosp, Chardon *Also called University Hospitals Health (G-2775)*
Heather Knoll Nursing Center, Tallmadge *Also called Heather Knoll Retirement Vlg (G-17639)*
Heather Knoll Retirement Vlg ... 330 688-8600
1134 North Ave Tallmadge (44278) *(G-17639)*
Heather Ridge Commons, Canton *Also called Extended Family Concepts Inc (G-2361)*
Heatherdowns Nursing Center, Columbus *Also called Rossford Grtric Care Ltd Prtnr (G-8651)*
Heathergreene Nursing Homes, Xenia *Also called Liberty Nursing Home Inc (G-20067)*
Heatherhill Care Communities ... 440 285-4040
12340 Bass Lake Rd Chardon (44024) *(G-2752)*
Heatherwoode Golf Course ... 937 748-3222
88 Heatherwoode Blvd Springboro (45066) *(G-17122)*
Heaven Bound Ascensions ... 330 633-3288
66 N Village View Rd Tallmadge (44278) *(G-17640)*
Heavenly Home Health ... 740 859-4735
1800 Old State Route 7 Rayland (43943) *(G-16417)*
Hebco Products Inc ... 419 562-7987
1232 Whetstone St Bucyrus (44820) *(G-2039)*
Heck's Diamond Printing, Toledo *Also called Hecks Direct Mail & Prtg Svc (G-17951)*
Hecks Direct Mail & Prtg Svc (PA) ... 419 697-3505
417 Main St Toledo (43605) *(G-17950)*
Hecks Direct Mail & Prtg Svc ... 419 661-6028
202 W Florence Ave Toledo (43605) *(G-17951)*
Hecla Water Association (PA) ... 740 533-0526
3190 State Route 141 Ironton (45638) *(G-12290)*
Heco Operations Inc ... 614 888-5700
7440 Pingue Dr Worthington (43085) *(G-19962)*
Hector A Buch Jr MD ... 419 227-7399
750 W High St Ste 250 Lima (45801) *(G-12797)*
Hedstrom Fitness, Ashland *Also called Ball Bounce and Sport Inc (G-661)*
Hedstrom Plastics, Ashland *Also called Ball Bounce and Sport Inc (G-662)*
Heery International Inc ... 216 510-4701
5445 West Blvd Cleveland (44137) *(G-5745)*
Heery International Inc ... 216 781-1313
1660 W 2nd St Cleveland (44113) *(G-5746)*
Heidelberg Distributing Div, Moraine *Also called Dayton Heidelberg Distrg Co (G-14770)*
Heidelberg Distributing Lorain, Lorain *Also called Goodman Beverage Co Inc (G-13040)*
Heidelberg USA Inc ... 937 492-1281
1660 Campbell Rd Sidney (45365) *(G-16938)*
Heider Cleaners Inc ... 937 298-6631
3720 Wilmington Pike Dayton (45429) *(G-9609)*
Heidtman Steel Products ... 419 691-4646
2401 Front St Toledo (43605) *(G-17952)*
Heights Emergency Food Center ... 216 381-0707
3663 Mayfield Rd Cleveland (44121) *(G-5747)*
Heights Laundry & Dry Cleaning (PA) ... 216 932-9666
1863 Coventry Rd Cleveland Heights (44118) *(G-6789)*
Heimerl Farms Ltd ... 740 967-0063
3891 Mink St Johnstown (43031) *(G-12340)*
Heinzerling Developmental Ctr, Columbus *Also called Heinzerling Foundation (G-7822)*
Heinzerling Foundation (PA) ... 614 272-8888
1800 Heinzerling Dr Columbus (43223) *(G-7821)*
Heinzerling Foundation ... 614 272-2000
1755 Heinzerling Dr Columbus (43223) *(G-7822)*
Heinzerling Mem Foundation, Columbus *Also called Heinzerling Foundation (G-7821)*
Heiser Staffing Services LLC ... 614 800-4188
330 W Spring St Ste 205 Columbus (43215) *(G-7823)*
Heitmeyer Group LLC ... 614 573-5571
140 Commerce Park Dr C Westerville (43082) *(G-19312)*
Heits Building Services Cincin, Cincinnati *Also called Heits Building Svcs Cnkd LLC (G-3756)*
Heits Building Svcs Cnkd LLC ... 855 464-3487
52 E Crescentville Rd Cincinnati (45246) *(G-3756)*
Helen M Torok MD (PA) ... 330 722-5477
5783 Wooster Pike Medina (44256) *(G-14075)*
Helen Purcell Home ... 740 453-1745
1854 Norwood Blvd Zanesville (43701) *(G-20487)*
Hellandale Community, Fairfield Township *Also called Burchwood Care Center (G-10925)*
Heller Maas Moro & Magill ... 330 393-6602
54 Westchester Dr Ste 10 Youngstown (44515) *(G-20215)*
Heller Mass Morrow and Migue, Youngstown *Also called Elliott Heller Maas Morrow Lpa (G-20180)*
Helm and Associates Inc ... 419 893-1480
501 W Sophia St Unit 8 Maumee (43537) *(G-13924)*
Helmsman Management Svcs LLC ... 614 478-8282
700 Taylor Rd Ste 220 Columbus (43230) *(G-7824)*
Help Foundation Inc ... 216 289-7710
27348 Oak Ct Euclid (44132) *(G-10757)*
Help Foundation Inc ... 216 486-5258
17702 Nottingham Rd Cleveland (44119) *(G-5748)*
Help Foundation Inc (PA) ... 216 432-4810
26900 Euclid Ave Euclid (44132) *(G-10758)*
Help Hotline Crisis Center, Youngstown *Also called Community Center (G-20152)*
Help Hotline Crisis Center ... 330 747-5111
261 E Wood St Youngstown (44503) *(G-20216)*
Help Line of Dlware Mrrow Cnty ... 740 369-3316
11 N Franklin St Delaware (43015) *(G-10104)*
Help ME Grow ... 419 738-4773
214 S Wagner Ave Wapakoneta (45895) *(G-18799)*
Help Network of Northeast Ohio, Youngstown *Also called Help Hotline Crisis Center (G-20216)*
Helping Hands, Lima *Also called Community Hlth Prfssionals Inc (G-12926)*
Helping Hands Health Care Inc ... 513 755-4181
9692 Cncnnati Columbus Rd West Chester (45241) *(G-19206)*
HELPLINE, Delaware *Also called Help Line of Dlware Mrrow Cnty (G-10104)*
Helton Enterprises Inc (PA) ... 419 423-4180
151 Stanford Pkwy Findlay (45840) *(G-11046)*
Hemlock Landscapes Inc ... 440 247-3631
7209 Chagrin Rd Ste A Chagrin Falls (44023) *(G-2719)*
Hemodialysis Services Inc ... 216 378-2691
25550 Chagrin Blvd # 404 Beachwood (44122) *(G-1085)*
Hempstead Manor ... 740 354-8150
727 8th St Portsmouth (45662) *(G-16286)*
Henderson Road Rest Systems (PA) ... 614 442-3310
1615 Old Henderson Rd Columbus (43220) *(G-7825)*
Henderson Trucking, Delaware *Also called Rjw Trucking Company Ltd (G-10124)*
Henderson Trucking Inc ... 740 369-6100
124 Henderson Ct Delaware (43015) *(G-10105)*
Henderson Turf Farm Inc ... 937 748-1559
2969 Beal Rd Franklin (45005) *(G-11158)*
Hendrickson Auxiliary Axles, Hebron *Also called Hendrickson International Corp (G-11849)*
Hendrickson International Corp ... 740 929-5600
277 N High St Hebron (43025) *(G-11849)*
Hendrickson Trailer Commercial, Canton *Also called Boler Company (G-2267)*
Henkel Corporation ... 440 255-8900
7405 Production Dr Mentor (44060) *(G-14189)*
Henkle Schueler Realtors, Lebanon *Also called Henkle-Schueler & Associates (G-12611)*
Henkle-Schueler & Associates (PA) ... 513 932-6070
3000 Henkle Dr G Lebanon (45036) *(G-12611)*
Henley & Assoc SEC Group LLC ... 614 378-3727
967 Jefferson Chase Way Blacklick (43004) *(G-1507)*
Henningson Drham Richardson PC ... 513 984-7500
9987 Carver Rd Ste 200 Blue Ash (45242) *(G-1610)*
Hennis Care Center of Bolivar, Bolivar *Also called Megco Management Inc (G-1749)*
Hennis Care Centre At Dover, Dover *Also called Hennis Nursing Home (G-10191)*
Hennis Nursing Home ... 330 364-8849
1720 N Cross St Dover (44622) *(G-10191)*
Henry Call Inc ... 216 433-5609
308 Pines St Ste 100 Cleveland (44135) *(G-5749)*
Henry County Bank (HQ) ... 419 599-1065
122 E Washington St Napoleon (43545) *(G-14942)*
Henry County Hospital Inc ... 419 592-4015
1600 E Riverview Ave Frnt Napoleon (43545) *(G-14943)*
Henry Gurtzweiler Inc ... 419 729-3955
921 Galena St Toledo (43611) *(G-17953)*
Henry P Thompson Company (PA) ... 513 248-3200
101 Main St Ste 300 Milford (45150) *(G-14524)*
Henry Schein Inc ... 440 349-0891
30600 Aurora Rd Ste 110 Cleveland (44139) *(G-5750)*
Henry Schein Animal Health, Dublin *Also called Butler Animal Health Sup LLC (G-10273)*
Henry Schein Animal Health, Columbus *Also called Butler Animal Health Sup LLC (G-7171)*
Henrys King Touring Company ... 330 628-1886
1369 Burbridge Dr Mogadore (44260) *(G-14678)*
Hensley Industries Inc (PA) ... 513 769-6666
2150 Langdon Farm Rd Cincinnati (45237) *(G-3757)*
Her Inc ... 614 240-7400
583 1/2 S 3rd St Columbus (43215) *(G-7826)*
Her Inc (PA) ... 614 221-7400
4261 Morse Rd Columbus (43230) *(G-7827)*

ALPHABETIC

Her Inc — ALPHABETIC SECTION

Her Inc 614 888-7400
   681 High St Worthington (43085) *(G-19963)*

Her Inc 614 239-7400
   2815 E Main St Columbus (43209) *(G-7828)*

Her Inc 614 878-4734
   4680 W Broad St Columbus (43228) *(G-7829)*

Her Inc 614 864-7400
   1450 Tussing Rd Pickerington (43147) *(G-16095)*

Her Inc 614 889-7400
   5725 Perimeter Dr Dublin (43017) *(G-10359)*

Her Inc 614 771-7400
   3499 Main St Hilliard (43026) *(G-11907)*

Her Inc 614 890-7400
   413 N State St Westerville (43082) *(G-19313)*

Her Real Living, Columbus Also called Her Inc *(G-7826)*

Heraeus Precious Metals North 937 264-1000
   970 Industrial Park Dr Vandalia (45377) *(G-18682)*

Herb Thyme Farms Inc 866 386-0854
   8600 S Wilkinson Way G Perrysburg (43551) *(G-16011)*

Herbert E Orr Company 419 399-4866
   335 W Wall St Paulding (45879) *(G-15931)*

Herbst Electric Company, Cleveland Also called Benevento Enterprises Inc *(G-5114)*

Heritage Administration Svcs, Dublin Also called Heritage Wrranty Insur Rrg Inc *(G-10360)*

Heritage Beverage Company LLC 440 255-5550
   7333 Corporate Blvd Mentor (44060) *(G-14190)*

Heritage Carpet & HM Dctg Ctrs, Canton Also called Clays Heritage Carpet Inc *(G-2312)*

Heritage Club 513 459-7711
   6690 Heritage Club Dr Mason (45040) *(G-13715)*

Heritage Cooperative Inc (PA) 419 294-2371
   11177 Township Road 133 West Mansfield (43358) *(G-19267)*

Heritage Day Health Centers (HQ) 614 451-2151
   2335 N Bank Dr Columbus (43220) *(G-7830)*

Heritage Development, Solon Also called Breezy Point Ltd Partnership *(G-16984)*

Heritage Envmtl Svcs LLC 419 729-1321
   5451 Enterprise Blvd Toledo (43612) *(G-17954)*

Heritage Equipment Company 614 873-3941
   9000 Heritage Dr Plain City (43064) *(G-16193)*

Heritage Golf Club Ltd Partnr 614 777-1690
   3525 Heritage Club Dr Hilliard (43026) *(G-11908)*

Heritage Health Care Services 419 222-2404
   3748 Allentown Rd Lima (45807) *(G-12798)*

Heritage Health Care Services (PA) 419 867-2002
   1745 Indian Wood Cir # 252 Maumee (43537) *(G-13925)*

Heritage Home Health Care 440 333-1925
   20800 Center Ridge Rd # 401 Rocky River (44116) *(G-16580)*

HERITAGE HOUSE NURSING HOME, Columbus Also called Wexner Heritage Village *(G-8984)*

HERITAGE HOUSE NURSING HOME, Columbus Also called Shalom House Inc *(G-8722)*

Heritage Manor, Youngstown Also called Youngstown Area Jwish Fdration *(G-20426)*

Heritage Manor Skilled Nursing, Columbus Also called I Vrable Inc *(G-7878)*

Heritage Marble of Ohio Inc 614 436-1464
   7086 Huntley Rd Columbus (43229) *(G-7831)*

Heritage Marbles, Columbus Also called Heritage Marble of Ohio Inc *(G-7831)*

Heritage Mnr Jwsh HM For Aged, Youngstown Also called Youngstown Area Jwish Fdration *(G-20425)*

Heritage Park Rehabilita 937 437-2311
   7739 Us Route 40 New Paris (45347) *(G-15078)*

Heritage Professional Services 740 456-8245
   3304 Rhodes Ave New Boston (45662) *(G-15011)*

Heritage Sportswear Inc (PA) 740 928-7771
   102 Reliance Dr Hebron (43025) *(G-11850)*

Heritage Square New Boston, New Boston Also called Heritage Professional Services *(G-15011)*

Heritage Truck Equipment Inc 330 699-4491
   1600 E Waterloo Rd Akron (44306) *(G-262)*

Heritage Village of Clyde, Clyde Also called Astoria Place of Clyde LLC *(G-6809)*

Heritage Wrranty Insur Rrg Inc 800 753-5236
   400 Metro Pl N Ste 300 Dublin (43017) *(G-10360)*

Heritage, The, Findlay Also called Manleys Manor Nursing Home Inc *(G-11060)*

Herman Bair Enterprise 330 262-4449
   210 E Milltown Rd A Wooster (44691) *(G-19867)*

Hermann Cahn & Schneider LLP 216 781-5515
   1375 E 9th St Ste 3150 Cleveland (44114) *(G-5751)*

Hermenia Inc 216 795-5710
   1802 Crawford Rd Cleveland (44106) *(G-5752)*

Hernandez Cnstr Svcs Inc 330 796-0500
   33 Merz Blvd Ste 2 Fairlawn (44333) *(G-10955)*

Hernando Zegarra 216 831-5700
   3401 Entp Pkwy Ste 300 Cleveland (44122) *(G-5753)*

Herrnstein Auto Group, Chillicothe Also called Herrnstein Chrysler Inc *(G-2846)*

Herrnstein Chrysler Inc (PA) 740 773-2203
   133 Marietta Rd Chillicothe (45601) *(G-2846)*

Hersh Construction Inc 330 877-1515
   650 S Prospect Ave # 200 Hartville (44632) *(G-11822)*

Hertz, Columbus Also called Geo Byers Sons Holding Inc *(G-7741)*

Hertz Clvland 600 Superior LLC 310 584-8108
   600 Superior Ave E # 100 Cleveland (44114) *(G-5754)*

Hertz Corporation 216 267-8900
   19025 Maplewood Ave Cleveland (44135) *(G-5755)*

Hertz Corporation 513 533-3161
   Cincinnati N Kentucky A P Cincinnati (45275) *(G-3758)*

Hertz Corporation 937 890-2721
   James Cox Intrl Arpt Vandalia (45377) *(G-18683)*

Hertz Corporation 937 898-5806
   3350 S Valet Cir Vandalia (45377) *(G-18684)*

Hertzfeld Poultry Farms Inc 419 832-2070
   15799 Milton Rd Grand Rapids (43522) *(G-11450)*

Herzig-Krall Medical Group 513 896-9595
   5150 Sandy Ln Fairfield (45014) *(G-10858)*

Hester Masonry Co Inc 937 890-2283
   10867 Engle Rd Vandalia (45377) *(G-18685)*

Hewlettco Inc 440 238-4600
   13590 Falling Water Rd Strongsville (44136) *(G-17469)*

Hexpol Compounding LLC 440 834-4644
   14330 Kinsman Rd Burton (44021) *(G-2062)*

Heyburn Dialysis LLC 614 876-3610
   2447 Hilliard Rome Rd Hilliard (43026) *(G-11909)*

Heyman Ralph E Attorney At Law 937 449-2820
   10 N Ludlow St Dayton (45402) *(G-9610)*

Hgc Construction Co (PA) 513 861-8866
   2814 Stanton Ave Cincinnati (45206) *(G-3759)*

Hgcc of Allentown Inc 419 252-5500
   333 N Summit St Toledo (43604) *(G-17955)*

Hgr Industrial Surplus Inc (PA) 216 486-4567
   20001 Euclid Ave Euclid (44117) *(G-10759)*

HHC Ohio Inc 440 953-3000
   35900 Euclid Ave Willoughby (44094) *(G-19668)*

HI Tecmetal Group Inc 440 373-5101
   28910 Lakeland Blvd Wickliffe (44092) *(G-19601)*

HI Tecmetal Group Inc 440 946-2280
   34800 Lakeland Blvd Willoughby (44095) *(G-19669)*

Hi-Five Development Svcs Inc 513 336-9280
   202 W Main St Ste C Mason (45040) *(G-13716)*

Hi-Tek Manufacturing Inc 513 459-1094
   6050 Hi Tek Ct Mason (45040) *(G-13717)*

Hi-Way Distributing Corp Amer 330 645-6633
   3716 E State St Coventry Township (44203) *(G-9125)*

Hi-Way Paving Inc 614 876-1700
   4343 Weaver Ct N Hilliard (43026) *(G-11910)*

Hiab USA Inc (HQ) 419 482-6000
   12233 Williams Rd Perrysburg (43551) *(G-16012)*

Hickey Metal Fabrication Roofg 330 337-9329
   873 Georgetown Rd Salem (44460) *(G-16698)*

Hickman Cancer Center 419 824-1952
   5200 Harroun Rd Sylvania (43560) *(G-17593)*

Hickory Creek Healthcare 419 542-7795
   401 Fountain St Hicksville (43526) *(G-11864)*

Hickory Harvest Foods, Coventry Township Also called Ohio Hickory Harvest Brand Pro *(G-9130)*

Hickory Health Care Inc 330 762-6486
   721 Hickory St Akron (44303) *(G-263)*

Hickory Woods Golf Course Inc 513 575-3900
   1240 Hickory Woods Dr Loveland (45140) *(G-13131)*

Hicks Industrial Roofing, New Philadelphia Also called Hicks Roofing Inc *(G-15100)*

Hicks Roofing Inc 330 364-7737
   2162 Pleasant Vly Rd Ne New Philadelphia (44663) *(G-15100)*

Hicksville Bank Inc (HQ) 419 542-7726
   144 E High St Hicksville (43526) *(G-11865)*

Hicon Inc 513 242-3612
   93 Caldwell Dr A Cincinnati (45216) *(G-3760)*

Hidden Lake Condominiums 614 488-1131
   1363 Lake Shore Dr Columbus (43204) *(G-7832)*

Hide-A-Way Hills Club 740 746-9589
   29042 Hide Away Hills Rd Sugar Grove (43155) *(G-17541)*

Hidy Honda, Dayton Also called Hidy Motors Inc *(G-9272)*

Hidy Motors Inc (PA) 937 426-9564
   2300 Hiller Drv Bevr Crk Beaver Creek Dayton (45434) *(G-9272)*

Higgins Building Company Inc 740 439-5553
   11342 E Pike Rd Cambridge (43725) *(G-2120)*

Higgins Sheltered Workshop, Canton Also called County of Stark *(G-2322)*

High Banks Care Centre, Columbus Also called Provider Services Inc *(G-8575)*

High Line Corporation 330 848-8800
   45 Goodyear Blvd Akron (44305) *(G-264)*

High Point Animal Hospital 419 865-3611
   6020 Manley Rd Maumee (43537) *(G-13926)*

High Power Inc 937 667-1772
   15 Industry Park Ct Tipp City (45371) *(G-17717)*

High TEC Industrial Services, Tipp City Also called Saftek Industrial Service Inc *(G-17726)*

High Voltage Maintenance Corp (HQ) 937 278-0811
   5100 Energy Dr Dayton (45414) *(G-9611)*

High-TEC Industrial Services 937 667-1772
   15 Industry Park Ct Tipp City (45371) *(G-17718)*

High-Tech Pools Inc 440 979-5070
   31330 Industrial Pkwy North Olmsted (44070) *(G-15425)*

Highbanks Care Center LLC 614 888-2021
   111 Lazelle Rd Columbus (43235) *(G-7833)*

Highland County Family YMCA 937 840-9622
   201 Diamond Dr Hillsboro (45133) *(G-11978)*

Highland County Joint 937 393-6100
   1275 N High St Hillsboro (45133) *(G-11979)*

Highland County Water Co Inc (PA) 937 393-4281
6686 Us Highway 50 Hillsboro (45133) ***(G-11980)***

Highland Ctr Early Head Start, Portsmouth *Also called Scioto County C A O Headstart* ***(G-16306)***

Highland District Hospital, Hillsboro *Also called Highland County Joint* ***(G-11979)***

Highland Relief Organization 614 843-5152
2761 Regaldo Dr Columbus (43219) ***(G-7834)***

Highland Som Development (PA) 330 528-3500
10020 Aurora Hudson Rd Streetsboro (44241) ***(G-17416)***

Highland Village Ltd Partnr 614 863-4640
160 W Main St New Albany (43054) ***(G-14988)***

Highlnd Cnty Commnty Action or (PA) 937 393-3060
1487 N High St Ste 500 Hillsboro (45133) ***(G-11981)***

Highpoint Home Healthcare Agcy 330 491-1805
4767 Higbee Ave Nw Canton (44718) ***(G-2398)***

Hightowers Petroleum Company 513 423-4272
3577 Commerce Dr Middletown (45005) ***(G-14480)***

Highway Department, Millersburg *Also called County of Holmes* ***(G-14599)***

Highway Maintenance, Akron *Also called County of Summit* ***(G-171)***

Highway Patrol 740 354-2888
7611 Us Highway 23 Lucasville (45648) ***(G-13181)***

Hiland Group Incorporated (PA) 330 499-8404
7600 Supreme St Nw Canton (44720) ***(G-2399)***

Hill Barth & King LLC (PA) 330 758-8613
6603 Summit Dr Canfield (44406) ***(G-2193)***

Hill Barth & King LLC 614 228-4000
226 N 5th St Ste 500 Columbus (43215) ***(G-7835)***

Hill Barth & King LLC 330 747-1903
6603 Summit Dr Canfield (44406) ***(G-2194)***

Hill Distributing Company 614 276-6533
5080 Tuttle Crossing Blvd # 100 Dublin (43016) ***(G-10361)***

Hill Intl Trcks NA LLC (PA) 330 386-6440
47866 Y And O Rd East Liverpool (43920) ***(G-10522)***

Hill Manor 1 Inc 740 972-3227
3244 Southfield Dr E Columbus (43207) ***(G-7836)***

Hill Side Plaza 216 486-6300
18220 Euclid Ave Cleveland (44112) ***(G-5756)***

Hill View Retirement Center 740 354-3135
1610 28th St Portsmouth (45662) ***(G-16287)***

Hillandale Farms Inc 740 968-3597
72165 Mrrstown Flshing Rd Flushing (43977) ***(G-11104)***

Hillandale Farms Corporation (PA) 330 724-3199
1330 Austin Ave Akron (44306) ***(G-265)***

Hillandale Farms Trnsp 740 893-2232
10513 Croton Rd Johnstown (43031) ***(G-12341)***

Hillandale Healthcare Inc 513 777-1400
8073 Tylersville Rd West Chester (45069) ***(G-19090)***

Hillcrest Ambulance Svc Inc 216 797-4000
26420 Lakeland Blvd Euclid (44132) ***(G-10760)***

Hillcrest Egg & Cheese Co (PA) 216 361-4625
2735 E 40th St Cleveland (44115) ***(G-5757)***

Hillcrest Foodservice, Cleveland *Also called Hillcrest Egg & Cheese Co* ***(G-5757)***

Hillcrest Hospital, Cleveland *Also called Cleveland Clinic Health System* ***(G-5307)***

Hillcrest Training School, Cincinnati *Also called County of Hamilton* ***(G-3429)***

Hillcrest Ymca-Adrian, Cleveland *Also called Young MNS Chrstn Assn Clveland* ***(G-6775)***

Hillebrand Home Health Inc 513 598-6648
4343 Bridgetown Rd Cincinnati (45211) ***(G-3761)***

HILLEBRAND NURSING AND REHABIL, Cincinnati *Also called D James Incorporated* ***(G-3456)***

Hilliard Electric, Cleveland *Also called JZE Electric Inc* ***(G-5878)***

Hilliard Station Dialysis, Hilliard *Also called Heyburn Dialysis LLC* ***(G-11909)***

Hillman Companies Inc 513 851-4900
10590 Hamilton Ave Cincinnati (45231) ***(G-3762)***

Hillman Companies Inc 513 851-4900
1700 Carillion Blvd Cincinnati (45240) ***(G-3763)***

Hillman Companies Inc (HQ) 513 851-4900
10590 Hamilton Ave Cincinnati (45231) ***(G-3764)***

Hillman Group Inc 513 874-5905
9950 Prnceton Glendale Rd West Chester (45246) ***(G-19207)***

Hillman Group Inc (HQ) 513 851-4900
10590 Hamilton Ave Cincinnati (45231) ***(G-3765)***

Hillman Group Anchor Wire, Cincinnati *Also called Hillman Companies Inc* ***(G-3762)***

Hills Communities Inc 513 984-0300
4901 Hunt Rd Ste 300 Blue Ash (45242) ***(G-1611)***

Hills Developers Inc 513 984-0300
4901 Hunt Rd Ste 300 Blue Ash (45242) ***(G-1612)***

Hills Property Management Inc (PA) 513 984-0300
4901 Hunt Rd Ste 300 Blue Ash (45242) ***(G-1613)***

Hills Real Estate Group, Blue Ash *Also called Hills Property Management Inc* ***(G-1613)***

Hills Supply Inc 740 477-8994
8476 Us Highway 22 E Circleville (43113) ***(G-4890)***

Hillsboro Health Center Inc 937 393-5781
1108 Northview Dr Ste 1 Hillsboro (45133) ***(G-11982)***

Hillsboro Transportation Co 513 772-9223
2889 E Crescentville Rd Cincinnati (45246) ***(G-3766)***

Hillside Acres Nursing Home, Willard *Also called Liberty Nursing of Willard* ***(G-19622)***

Hillside Maint Sup Co Inc 513 751-4100
3300 Spring Grove Ave Cincinnati (45225) ***(G-3767)***

Hillside Plaza, Cleveland *Also called Hill Side Plaza* ***(G-5756)***

Hillspring Health Care Center 937 748-1100
325 E Central Ave Springboro (45066) ***(G-17123)***

Hilltop, Columbus *Also called Young Mens Christian Assoc* ***(G-9018)***

Hilltop Basic Resources Inc 513 621-1500
511 W Water St Cincinnati (45202) ***(G-3768)***

Hilltop Concrete, Cincinnati *Also called Hilltop Basic Resources Inc* ***(G-3768)***

Hilltop Nursery School, Harrison *Also called Harrison Ave Assembly of God* ***(G-11800)***

Hilltop Village 216 261-8383
25900 Euclid Ave Ofc Cleveland (44132) ***(G-5758)***

Hilltrux Tank Lines Inc 330 965-1103
6331 Southern Blvd Youngstown (44512) ***(G-20217)***

Hilltrux Tank Lines Inc 330 538-3700
200 Rosemont Rd North Jackson (44451) ***(G-15381)***

Hilscher-Clarke Electric Co (PA) 330 452-9806
519 4th St Nw Canton (44703) ***(G-2400)***

Hilscher-Clarke Electric Co 740 622-5557
572 S 3rd St Coshocton (43812) ***(G-9105)***

Hilton, Cleveland *Also called Park Hotels & Resorts Inc* ***(G-6236)***

Hilton, Cleveland *Also called 1100 Carnegie LP* ***(G-4919)***

Hilton, Cleveland *Also called Park Hotels & Resorts Inc* ***(G-6237)***

Hilton, Westlake *Also called Ceres Enterprises LLC* ***(G-19472)***

Hilton Akron Fairlawn, Fairlawn *Also called Fairlawn Associates Ltd* ***(G-10949)***

Hilton Cleveland/Beachwood, Beachwood *Also called Cleveland Bchwood Hsptlity LLC* ***(G-1063)***

Hilton Cncnnati Netherland Plz, Cincinnati *Also called Cincinnati Netherland Ht LLC* ***(G-3320)***

Hilton Columbus At Easton, Columbus *Also called Columbus Easton Hotel LLC* ***(G-7350)***

Hilton Columbus Polaris, Columbus *Also called Hilton Polaris* ***(G-6884)***

Hilton Garden Blue Ash, Blue Ash *Also called Blue-Kenwood LLC* ***(G-1546)***

Hilton Garden Inn 614 263-7200
3232 Olentangy River Rd Columbus (43202) ***(G-7837)***

Hilton Garden Inn Akron 330 966-4907
5251 Landmark Blvd Canton (44720) ***(G-2401)***

Hilton Garden Inn Beavercreek 937 458-2650
3498 Pentagon Park Blvd Dayton (45431) ***(G-9273)***

Hilton Garden Inn Perrysburg, Perrysburg *Also called Levis Commons Hotel LLC* ***(G-16027)***

Hilton Garden Inn Twinsburg, Twinsburg *Also called Apple Gate Operating Co Inc* ***(G-18392)***

Hilton Grdn Inn Clmbus Polaris 614 846-8884
8535 Lyra Dr Columbus (43240) ***(G-6883)***

Hilton Grdn Inn Columbus Arprt, Columbus *Also called Indus Airport Hotels I LLC* ***(G-7891)***

Hilton Grdn Inn Columbus Arprt 614 231-2869
4265 Sawyer Rd Columbus (43219) ***(G-7838)***

Hilton Homewood Suites, Columbus *Also called Rose Gracias* ***(G-8648)***

Hilton Polaris 614 885-1600
8700 Lyra Dr Columbus (43240) ***(G-6884)***

Hilty Child Care Center 419 384-3220
304 Hilty Dr Pandora (45877) ***(G-15891)***

Hilty Memorial Home Inc 419 384-3218
304 Hilty Dr Pandora (45877) ***(G-15892)***

Hinckley Roofing Inc 330 722-7663
3587 Ridge Rd Medina (44256) ***(G-14076)***

Hiram Maintenance Bldg, Windham *Also called Turnpike and Infrastructure Co* ***(G-19804)***

Hirsch Division, Chagrin Falls *Also called Lake Horry Electric* ***(G-2702)***

Hirsch International Holdings 513 733-4111
4 Kovach Dr Ste 470a Cincinnati (45215) ***(G-3769)***

Hirts Greenhouse and Flowers, Strongsville *Also called Hirts Greenhouse Inc* ***(G-17470)***

Hirts Greenhouse Inc 440 238-8200
14407 Pearl Rd Strongsville (44136) ***(G-17470)***

Hirzel Canning Company (PA) 419 693-0531
411 Lemoyne Rd Northwood (43619) ***(G-15533)***

Hirzel Farms Inc 419 837-2710
20790 Bradner Rd Luckey (43443) ***(G-13183)***

Hirzel Transfer Co 419 287-3288
115 Columbus St Pemberville (43450) ***(G-15941)***

Hispanc Urbn Mnrty Alchlsm DRG 216 398-2333
3305 W 25th St Cleveland (44109) ***(G-5759)***

HISPANIC UMADAOP, Cleveland *Also called Hispanc Urbn Mnrty Alchlsm DRG* ***(G-5759)***

Hit Portfolio I Hil Trs LLC 614 235-0717
3920 Tuller Rd Dublin (43017) ***(G-10362)***

Hit Portfolio I Misc Trs LLC 216 575-1234
420 Superior Ave E Cleveland (44114) ***(G-5760)***

Hit Portfolio I Misc Trs LLC 614 846-4355
7490 Vantage Dr Columbus (43235) ***(G-7839)***

Hit Portfolio I Misc Trs LLC 513 241-3575
151 W 5th St Cincinnati (45202) ***(G-3770)***

Hit Portfolio I Misc Trs LLC 614 228-1234
75 E State St Columbus (43215) ***(G-7840)***

Hit Swn Trs LLC 614 228-3200
35 W Spring St Columbus (43215) ***(G-7841)***

Hitachi Hlthcare Americas Corp 330 425-1313
1959 Summit Commerce Park Twinsburg (44087) ***(G-18429)***

Hitachi Medical Systems Amer, Twinsburg *Also called Hitachi Hlthcare Americas Corp* ***(G-18429)***

Hitchcock Center For Women Inc 216 421-0662
1227 Ansel Rd Cleveland (44108) ***(G-5761)***

Hitchcock Fleming & Assoc Inc 330 376-2111
500 Wolf Ledges Pkwy Akron (44311) ***(G-266)***

Hite Parts Exchange Inc 614 272-5115
2235 Mckinley Ave Columbus (43204) ***(G-7842)***
Hixson Archtcts/Ngnrs/Nteriors, Cincinnati *Also called Hixson Incorporated* ***(G-3771)***
Hixson Incorporated 513 241-1230
659 Van Meter St Ste 300 Cincinnati (45202) ***(G-3771)***
HJ Benken Flor & Greenhouses 513 891-1040
6000 Plainfield Rd Cincinnati (45213) ***(G-3772)***
HJ Ford Associates Inc 937 429-9711
2940 Presidential Dr # 150 Beavercreek (45324) ***(G-1176)***
Hkm Drect Mkt Cmmnications Inc (PA) 216 651-9500
5501 Cass Ave Cleveland (44102) ***(G-5762)***
Hlg Engineering & Survey Inc 614 760-8320
5980 Wilcox Pl Ste G Dublin (43016) ***(G-10363)***
Hman Group Holdings Inc 513 851-4900
10590 Hamilton Ave Cincinnati (45231) ***(G-3773)***
Hmb Information Sys Developers, Westerville *Also called Harris Mackessy & Brennan* ***(G-19311)***
HMC Group Inc 440 847-2720
29065 Clemens Rd Ste 200 Westlake (44145) ***(G-19491)***
HMS Construction & Rental Co 330 628-4811
1225 Waterloo Rd Mogadore (44260) ***(G-14679)***
Hmshost Corporation 419 547-8667
888 N County Road 260 Clyde (43410) ***(G-6814)***
Hntb Corporation 216 522-1140
1100 Superior Ave E # 1701 Cleveland (44114) ***(G-5763)***
Hobart, Troy *Also called ITW Food Equipment Group LLC* ***(G-18359)***
Hobart Bros Stick Electrode 937 332-5375
101 Trade Sq E Troy (45373) ***(G-18357)***
Hobart Sales & Service, Akron *Also called Harry C Lobalzo & Sons Inc* ***(G-253)***
Hobby Lobby Stores Inc 419 861-1862
6645 Airport Hwy Holland (43528) ***(G-12027)***
Hobby Lobby Stores Inc 330 686-1508
4332 Kent Rd Ste 3 Stow (44224) ***(G-17371)***
Hobby Smile Center, Ashtabula *Also called Denture Center* ***(G-742)***
Hobe Lcas Crtif Pub Accntants 216 524-7167
4807 Rockside Rd Ste 510 Cleveland (44131) ***(G-5764)***
Hobsons Inc (HQ) 513 891-5444
50 E-Business Way Ste 300 Cincinnati (45241) ***(G-3774)***
Hoc Transport Company 330 630-0100
1569 Industrial Pkwy Akron (44310) ***(G-267)***
Hochstedler Construction Ltd 740 427-4880
24761 Dennis Church Rd Gambier (43022) ***(G-11347)***
Hockaden & Associates Inc 614 252-0993
883 N Cassady Ave Columbus (43219) ***(G-7843)***
Hocking College Addc 740 541-2221
19234 Taylor Ridge Rd Glouster (45732) ***(G-11434)***
Hocking Valley Community Ho (PA) 740 380-8336
601 State Route 664 N Logan (43138) ***(G-12974)***
Hocking Valley Industries Inc 740 385-2118
1369 E Front St Logan (43138) ***(G-12975)***
Hocking Vly Bnk of Athens Co (PA) 740 592-4441
7 W Stimson Ave Athens (45701) ***(G-792)***
Hockingthensperry Cmnty Action 740 385-6813
1005 C I C Dr Logan (43138) ***(G-12976)***
Hockingthensperry Cmnty Action (PA) 740 767-4500
3 Cardaras Dr Glouster (45732) ***(G-11435)***
Hodell-Natco Industries Inc (PA) 773 472-2305
7825 Hub Pkwy Cleveland (44125) ***(G-5765)***
Hoeting Inc (PA) 513 451-4800
6048 Bridgetown Rd Cincinnati (45248) ***(G-3775)***
Hoeting Realtors, Cincinnati *Also called Hoeting Inc* ***(G-3775)***
Hoffman Group The, Medina *Also called James B Oswald Company* ***(G-14085)***
Hoffman Products, Macedonia *Also called TPC Wire & Cable Corp* ***(G-13213)***
Hogan Services Inc 614 491-8402
1500 Obetz Rd Columbus (43207) ***(G-7844)***
Hogan Truck Leasing Inc 513 454-3500
2001 Ddc Way Fairfield (45014) ***(G-10859)***
Hoge Brush, New Knoxville *Also called Hoge Lumber Company* ***(G-15052)***
Hoge Lumber Company (PA) 419 753-2263
701 S Main St State New Knoxville (45871) ***(G-15052)***
Hoglund Chwlkowski Mrozik Pllc 330 252-8009
520 S Main St Akron (44311) ***(G-268)***
Hoglund Law, Akron *Also called Hoglund Chwlkowski Mrozik Pllc* ***(G-268)***
Hokuto USA Inc 614 782-6200
2200 Southwest Blvd Ste F Grove City (43123) ***(G-11570)***
Holand Management, Sharon Center *Also called Holland Professional Group* ***(G-16875)***
Holbrook & Manter (PA) 740 387-8620
181 E Center St Marion (43302) ***(G-13543)***
Holden Arboretum 440 946-4400
9500 Sperry Rd Willoughby (44094) ***(G-19670)***
Holiday Inn, Wilmington *Also called S & S Management Inc* ***(G-19785)***
Holiday Inn, Cambridge *Also called Cambridge Property Investors* ***(G-2102)***
Holiday Inn, Dayton *Also called S & S Management Inc* ***(G-9861)***
Holiday Inn, Cincinnati *Also called Green Township Hospitality LLC* ***(G-3712)***
Holiday Inn, Sunbury *Also called Dbp Enterprises LLC* ***(G-17554)***
Holiday Inn, Gahanna *Also called Star Group Ltd* ***(G-11269)***
Holiday Inn, Lancaster *Also called Lancaster Host LLC* ***(G-12550)***
Holiday Inn, Vermilion *Also called Elden Motels LP* ***(G-18708)***
Holiday Inn, Worthington *Also called He Hari Inc* ***(G-19961)***
Holiday Inn, Blue Ash *Also called W & H Realty Inc* ***(G-1717)***
Holiday Inn, Springfield *Also called Grandview Ht Ltd Partnr Ohio* ***(G-17203)***
Holiday Inn, Perrysburg *Also called Bennett Enterprises Inc* ***(G-15978)***
Holiday Inn, Gallipolis *Also called Gallipolis Hospitality Inc* ***(G-11319)***
Holiday Inn, Newton Falls *Also called Liberty Ashtabula Holdings* ***(G-15277)***
Holiday Inn, Obetz *Also called Synergy Hotels LLC* ***(G-15671)***
Holiday Inn, Cleveland *Also called Summit Associates Inc* ***(G-6547)***
Holiday Inn, Cleveland *Also called Integrated CC LLC* ***(G-5825)***
Holiday Inn, Beavercreek *Also called PH Fairborn Ht Owner 2800 LLC* ***(G-1197)***
Holiday Inn, Cincinnati *Also called Six Continents Hotels Inc* ***(G-4533)***
Holiday Inn, Cleveland *Also called Seagate Hospitality Group LLC* ***(G-6457)***
Holiday Inn, Cleveland *Also called Jagi Clveland Independence LLC* ***(G-5848)***
Holiday Inn, Cambridge *Also called Cambridge Associates Ltd* ***(G-2098)***
Holiday Inn, Cincinnati *Also called Jagi Juno LLC* ***(G-3858)***
Holiday Inn, Cleveland *Also called Mrn-Newgar Hotel Ltd* ***(G-6085)***
Holiday Inn, Cincinnati *Also called Clermont Hills Co LLC* ***(G-2908)***
Holiday Inn, Youngstown *Also called Rukh Boardman Properties LLC* ***(G-20361)***
Holiday Inn, Akron *Also called Detroit Westfield LLC* ***(G-190)***
Holiday Inn, Marietta *Also called Valley Hospitality Inc* ***(G-13513)***
Holiday Inn, Lima *Also called Columbia Properties Lima LLC* ***(G-12757)***
Holiday Inn, Cincinnati *Also called Hauck Hospitality LLC* ***(G-3741)***
Holiday Inn, Columbus *Also called Town Inn Co LLC* ***(G-8857)***
Holiday Inn, Beavercreek *Also called Wright Executive Ht Ltd Partnr* ***(G-1219)***
Holiday Inn, Lima *Also called Sterling Lodging LLC* ***(G-12892)***
Holiday Inn, Wickliffe *Also called Ridgehills Hotel Ltd Partnr* ***(G-19613)***
Holiday Inn, Wapakoneta *Also called S & S Management Inc* ***(G-18807)***
Holiday Inn, Strongsville *Also called Strongsville Lodging Assoc 1* ***(G-17512)***
Holiday Inn, New Philadelphia *Also called N P Motel System Inc* ***(G-15110)***
Holiday Inn, Cleveland *Also called A C Management Inc* ***(G-4931)***
Holiday Inn, Bedford *Also called Oakwood Hospitality Corp* ***(G-1325)***
Holiday Inn, New Philadelphia *Also called Haribol Haribol Inc* ***(G-15099)***
Holiday Inn 419 691-8800
3154 Navarre Ave Oregon (43616) ***(G-15739)***
Holiday Inn Canton, Canton *Also called Rukh-Jagi Holdings LLC* ***(G-2518)***
Holiday Inn Express 419 332-7700
1501 Hospitality Ct Fremont (43420) ***(G-11206)***
Holiday Inn Express 937 424-5757
5655 Wilmington Pike Dayton (45459) ***(G-9612)***
Holiday Inn Express 614 447-1212
3045 Olentangy River Rd Columbus (43202) ***(G-7845)***
Holiday Inn of Englewood 937 832-1234
10 Rockridge Rd Englewood (45322) ***(G-10708)***
Holiday Lanes Inc 614 861-1600
4589 E Broad St Columbus (43213) ***(G-7846)***
Holland Enterprises Inc 216 671-9333
4538 W 130th St Ste 3 Cleveland (44135) ***(G-5766)***
Holland Management Inc (PA) 330 239-4474
1383 Sharon Copley Rd Sharon Center (44274) ***(G-16874)***
Holland Oil Company (PA) 330 835-1815
1485 Marion Ave Akron (44313) ***(G-269)***
Holland Operations Center, Holland *Also called Toledo Edison Company* ***(G-12062)***
Holland Paving & Seal Coating, Cleveland *Also called Holland Enterprises Inc* ***(G-5766)***
Holland Professional Group 330 239-4474
1343 Sharon Copley Sharon Center (44274) ***(G-16875)***
Holland Roofing Inc 330 963-0237
9221 Ravenna Rd Twinsburg (44087) ***(G-18430)***
Holland Roofing Inc 614 430-3724
3494 E 7th Ave Columbus (43219) ***(G-7847)***
Holland Roofing of Columbus, Columbus *Also called Holland Roofing Inc* ***(G-7847)***
Holly Hill Nursing Home, Newbury *Also called Fairmont Nursing Home Inc* ***(G-15256)***
Hollywood 20, Beavercreek *Also called Regal Cinemas Inc* ***(G-1203)***
Hollywood Casino Toledo 419 661-5200
1968 Miami St Toledo (43605) ***(G-17956)***
Holmes County Board of Dd 330 674-8045
8001 Township Road 574 Holmesville (44633) ***(G-12072)***
Holmes County Fire Department, Millersburg *Also called County of Holmes* ***(G-14596)***
Holmes County Health Dept, Millersburg *Also called County of Holmes* ***(G-14597)***
Holmes County Home, Holmesville *Also called County of Holmes* ***(G-12071)***
HOLMES COUNTY TRAINING CENTER, Holmesville *Also called Lynn Hope Industries Inc* ***(G-12073)***
Holmes Crane, Berlin *Also called Berlin Contractors* ***(G-1477)***
Holmes Lumber & Bldg Ctr Inc 330 674-9060
6139 Hc 39 Millersburg (44654) ***(G-14604)***
Holmes Lumber & Supply, Millersburg *Also called Holmes Lumber & Bldg Ctr Inc* ***(G-14604)***
Holmes Siding Contractors 330 674-2867
6767 County Road 624 Millersburg (44654) ***(G-14605)***
Holmes-Wayne Electric Coop 330 674-1055
6060 State Route 83 Millersburg (44654) ***(G-14606)***
Holo Pundits Inc 614 707-5225
425 Metro Pl N Ste 440 Dublin (43017) ***(G-10364)***
Holt Rental Services (PA) 513 771-0515
11330 Mosteller Rd Cincinnati (45241) ***(G-3776)***
Holthaus Lackner Signs, Cincinnati *Also called Gus Holthaus Signs Inc* ***(G-3720)***

Holthouse Farms of Michigan, Willard *Also called Holthouse Farms of Ohio Inc* ***(G-19620)***
Holthouse Farms of Ohio Inc (PA) 419 935-1041
4373 State Route 103 S Willard (44890) ***(G-19620)***
Holub Iron & Steel Company 330 252-5655
470 N Arlington St Akron (44305) ***(G-270)***
Holy Cross Cemetary, Cleveland *Also called Catholic Diocese of Cleveland* ***(G-5192)***
Holy Family, Lakewood *Also called Lakewood Catholic Academy* ***(G-12486)***
Holy Family Home, Parma *Also called Holy Family Hospice* ***(G-15909)***
Holy Family Hospice 440 888-7722
6707 State Rd Parma (44134) ***(G-15909)***
Holzer Clinic Lawrence County, Proctorville *Also called Holzer Clinic LLC* ***(G-16359)***
Holzer Clinic LLC 304 746-3701
100 Jackson Pike Gallipolis (45631) ***(G-11320)***
Holzer Clinic LLC (HQ) 740 446-5411
90 Jackson Pike Gallipolis (45631) ***(G-11321)***
Holzer Clinic LLC 304 744-2300
100 Jackson Pike Gallipolis (45631) ***(G-11322)***
Holzer Clinic LLC 740 886-9403
98 State St Proctorville (45669) ***(G-16359)***
Holzer Clinic LLC 740 589-3100
2131 E State St Athens (45701) ***(G-793)***
Holzer Clinic LLC 740 446-5412
90 Jackson Pike Gallipolis (45631) ***(G-11323)***
HOLZER CONSOLIDATED HEALTH SYS, Gallipolis *Also called Holzer Health System* ***(G-11324)***
Holzer Health Center, Gallipolis *Also called Holzer Clinic LLC* ***(G-11321)***
Holzer Health System (PA) 740 446-5060
100 Jackson Pike Gallipolis (45631) ***(G-11324)***
Holzer Hospital, Gallipolis *Also called Holzer Clinic LLC* ***(G-11323)***
Holzer Hospital Foundation (HQ) 740 446-5000
100 Jackson Pike Gallipolis (45631) ***(G-11325)***
Holzer Hospital Foundation 740 446-5000
90 Jackson Pike Gallipolis (45631) ***(G-11326)***
Holzer Medical Center, Gallipolis *Also called Holzer Hospital Foundation* ***(G-11325)***
Holzer Medical Ctr - Jackson 740 288-4625
500 Burlington Rd Jackson (45640) ***(G-12313)***
Homan Inc 419 925-4349
6915 Olding Rd Maria Stein (45860) ***(G-13428)***
Homan Transportation Inc 419 465-2626
22 Fort Monroe Pkwy Monroeville (44847) ***(G-14720)***
Home and Farm Insurance Co 937 778-5000
1 Heritage Pl Piqua (45356) ***(G-16149)***
Home Bldrs Assn Grter Cncnnati 513 851-6300
11260 Chester Rd Ste 800 Cincinnati (45246) ***(G-3777)***
Home Care Advantage 330 337-4663
718 E 3rd St Ste C Salem (44460) ***(G-16699)***
Home Care By Black Stone, Piqua *Also called Black Stone Cincinnati LLC* ***(G-16136)***
Home Care By Blackstone, Columbus *Also called Almost Family Inc* ***(G-6973)***
Home Care Network Inc (PA) 937 435-1142
190 E Spring Valley Pike A Dayton (45458) ***(G-9613)***
Home Care Pharmacy LLC (HQ) 513 874-0009
5549 Spellmire Dr West Chester (45246) ***(G-19208)***
Home Care Relief Inc 216 692-2270
753 E 200th St Euclid (44119) ***(G-10761)***
Home City Federal Savings Bank (HQ) 937 390-0470
2454 N Limestone St Springfield (45503) ***(G-17205)***
Home City Ice Company 614 836-2877
4505 S Hamilton Rd Groveport (43125) ***(G-11644)***
Home Depot USA Inc 614 523-0600
6333 Cleveland Ave Columbus (43231) ***(G-7848)***
Home Depot USA Inc 330 965-4790
7001 Southern Blvd Boardman (44512) ***(G-1741)***
Home Depot USA Inc 330 497-1810
4873 Portage St Nw Canton (44720) ***(G-2402)***
Home Depot USA Inc 513 688-1654
520 Ohio Pike Cincinnati (45255) ***(G-3778)***
Home Depot USA Inc 330 922-3448
325 Howe Ave Cuyahoga Falls (44221) ***(G-9194)***
Home Depot USA Inc 937 312-9053
345 N Springboro Pike Dayton (45449) ***(G-9614)***
Home Depot USA Inc 937 312-9076
5860 Wilmington Pike Dayton (45459) ***(G-9615)***
Home Depot USA Inc 216 692-2780
877 E 200th St Euclid (44119) ***(G-10762)***
Home Depot USA Inc 513 360-1100
500 Gateway Blvd Monroe (45050) ***(G-14698)***
Home Depot USA Inc 216 676-9969
10800 Brookpark Rd Cleveland (44130) ***(G-5767)***
Home Depot USA Inc 216 581-6611
21000 Libby Rd Maple Heights (44137) ***(G-13408)***
Home Depot USA Inc 937 431-7346
3775 Presidential Dr Beavercreek (45324) ***(G-1177)***
Home Depot USA Inc 330 245-0280
2811 S Arlington Rd Akron (44312) ***(G-271)***
Home Depot USA Inc 937 837-1551
5200 Salem Ave Unit A Dayton (45426) ***(G-9616)***
Home Depot USA Inc 216 297-1303
3460 Mayfield Rd Cleveland Heights (44118) ***(G-6790)***
Home Depot USA Inc 513 661-2413
6300 Glenway Ave Cincinnati (45211) ***(G-3779)***
Home Depot USA Inc 513 887-1450
6562 Winford Ave Fairfield Township (45011) ***(G-10931)***
Home Depot USA Inc 419 476-4573
1035 W Alexis Rd Toledo (43612) ***(G-17957)***
Home Depot USA Inc 440 357-0428
9615 Diamond Centre Dr Mentor (44060) ***(G-14191)***
Home Depot USA Inc 513 631-1705
3400 Highland Ave Cincinnati (45213) ***(G-3780)***
Home Depot USA Inc 440 684-1343
6199 Wilson Mills Rd Highland Heights (44143) ***(G-11869)***
Home Depot USA Inc 419 537-1920
3200 Secor Rd Toledo (43606) ***(G-17958)***
Home Depot USA Inc 614 878-9150
100 S Grener Ave Columbus (43228) ***(G-7849)***
Home Depot USA Inc 440 826-9092
8199 Pearl Rd Strongsville (44136) ***(G-17471)***
Home Depot USA Inc 614 939-5036
5200 N Hamilton Rd Columbus (43230) ***(G-7850)***
Home Depot USA Inc 440 937-2240
35930 Detroit Rd Avon (44011) ***(G-898)***
Home Depot USA Inc 614 577-1601
2480 Brice Rd Reynoldsburg (43068) ***(G-16458)***
Home Depot USA Inc 330 220-2654
3330 Center Rd Brunswick (44212) ***(G-1981)***
Home Depot USA Inc 419 626-6493
715 Crossings Rd Sandusky (44870) ***(G-16768)***
Home Depot USA Inc 614 876-5558
4101 Trueman Blvd Hilliard (43026) ***(G-11911)***
Home Depot USA Inc 440 324-7222
150 Market Dr Elyria (44035) ***(G-10633)***
Home Depot USA Inc 419 529-0015
2000 August Dr Ontario (44906) ***(G-15691)***
Home Depot USA Inc 216 251-3091
11901 Berea Rd Cleveland (44111) ***(G-5768)***
Home Depot, The, Columbus *Also called Home Depot USA Inc* ***(G-7848)***
Home Depot, The, Boardman *Also called Home Depot USA Inc* ***(G-1741)***
Home Depot, The, Canton *Also called Home Depot USA Inc* ***(G-2402)***
Home Depot, The, Cincinnati *Also called Home Depot USA Inc* ***(G-3778)***
Home Depot, The, Cuyahoga Falls *Also called Home Depot USA Inc* ***(G-9194)***
Home Depot, The, Dayton *Also called Home Depot USA Inc* ***(G-9614)***
Home Depot, The, Dayton *Also called Home Depot USA Inc* ***(G-9615)***
Home Depot, The, Euclid *Also called Home Depot USA Inc* ***(G-10762)***
Home Depot, The, Monroe *Also called Home Depot USA Inc* ***(G-14698)***
Home Depot, The, Cleveland *Also called Home Depot USA Inc* ***(G-5767)***
Home Depot, The, Maple Heights *Also called Home Depot USA Inc* ***(G-13408)***
Home Depot, The, Beavercreek *Also called Home Depot USA Inc* ***(G-1177)***
Home Depot, The, Akron *Also called Home Depot USA Inc* ***(G-271)***
Home Depot, The, Dayton *Also called Home Depot USA Inc* ***(G-9616)***
Home Depot, The, Cleveland Heights *Also called Home Depot USA Inc* ***(G-6790)***
Home Depot, The, Cincinnati *Also called Home Depot USA Inc* ***(G-3779)***
Home Depot, The, Fairfield Township *Also called Home Depot USA Inc* ***(G-10931)***
Home Depot, The, Toledo *Also called Home Depot USA Inc* ***(G-17957)***
Home Depot, The, Mentor *Also called Home Depot USA Inc* ***(G-14191)***
Home Depot, The, Cincinnati *Also called Home Depot USA Inc* ***(G-3780)***
Home Depot, The, Highland Heights *Also called Home Depot USA Inc* ***(G-11869)***
Home Depot, The, Toledo *Also called Home Depot USA Inc* ***(G-17958)***
Home Depot, The, Columbus *Also called Home Depot USA Inc* ***(G-7849)***
Home Depot, The, Strongsville *Also called Home Depot USA Inc* ***(G-17471)***
Home Depot, The, Columbus *Also called Home Depot USA Inc* ***(G-7850)***
Home Depot, The, Avon *Also called Home Depot USA Inc* ***(G-898)***
Home Depot, The, Reynoldsburg *Also called Home Depot USA Inc* ***(G-16458)***
Home Depot, The, Brunswick *Also called Home Depot USA Inc* ***(G-1981)***
Home Depot, The, Sandusky *Also called Home Depot USA Inc* ***(G-16768)***
Home Depot, The, Hilliard *Also called Home Depot USA Inc* ***(G-11911)***
Home Depot, The, Elyria *Also called Home Depot USA Inc* ***(G-10633)***
Home Depot, The, Ontario *Also called Home Depot USA Inc* ***(G-15691)***
Home Depot, The, Cleveland *Also called Home Depot USA Inc* ***(G-5768)***
Home Dialysis of Dayton South, Kettering *Also called Total Renal Care Inc* ***(G-12436)***
Home Echo Club Inc 614 864-1718
10270 Blacklick Eastrn Rd Pickerington (43147) ***(G-16096)***
Home Health Agency, Marietta *Also called Amedisys Inc* ***(G-13430)***
Home Health Care, Ashtabula *Also called Continuum Home Care Inc* ***(G-737)***
Home Health Connection Inc 614 839-4545
6797 N High St Ste 113 Worthington (43085) ***(G-19964)***
Home Helpers 937 393-8600
503 E Main St Hillsboro (45133) ***(G-11983)***
Home Helpers and Direct Link, Hillsboro *Also called Home Helpers* ***(G-11983)***
Home Helpers and Direct Link, New Albany *Also called Loft Services LLC* ***(G-14991)***
Home Helpers In Home Care 330 455-5440
2510 Blake Ave Nw Canton (44708) ***(G-2403)***
Home Hlth Svcs Southwest Hosp, Cleveland *Also called Southwest General Health Ctr* ***(G-6505)***
Home Improvement Center, Harrison *Also called Cornelius Joel Roofing Inc* ***(G-11795)***
Home Instead Senior Care, Toledo *Also called Sar Enterprises LLC* ***(G-18172)***

A L P H A B E T I C

Home Instead Senior Care....330 334-4664
1 Park Centre Dr Ste 15 Wadsworth (44281) ***(G-18756)***

Home Instead Senior Care....740 393-2500
400 W High St Mount Vernon (43050) ***(G-14898)***

Home Instead Senior Care....330 729-1233
5437 Mahoning Ave Ste 22 Youngstown (44515) ***(G-20218)***

Home Instead Senior Care....614 432-8524
3220 Riverside Dr Ste C4 Upper Arlington (43221) ***(G-18551)***

Home Loan Financial Corp (PA)....740 622-0444
413 Main St Ste 1 Coshocton (43812) ***(G-9106)***

Home Loan Savings Bank, Coshocton *Also called Home Loan Financial Corp* ***(G-9106)***

Home Mortgage, Chillicothe *Also called Huntington National Bank* ***(G-2852)***

Home Mortgage, Lima *Also called Huntington National Bank* ***(G-12801)***

Home Mortgage, Cleveland *Also called Huntington National Bank* ***(G-5792)***

Home Moving & Storage Co Inc....614 445-6377
1570 Integrity Dr E Columbus (43209) ***(G-7851)***

Home Nursing Service & Hospice, Marietta *Also called Marietta Memorial Hospital* ***(G-13472)***

Home Run Inc (PA)....800 543-9198
1299 Lavelle Dr Xenia (45385) ***(G-20061)***

Home Savings Bank....330 499-1900
600 S Main St North Canton (44720) ***(G-15344)***

Home The Friends Inc....513 897-6050
514 High St Waynesville (45068) ***(G-18983)***

Home Town Health Network, Massillon *Also called Massillon Cmnty Hosp Hlth Plan* ***(G-13835)***

Home Town Realtors LLC....937 890-9111
9201 N Dixie Dr Dayton (45414) ***(G-9617)***

Home2 By Hilton....513 422-3454
7145 Liberty Centre Dr West Chester (45069) ***(G-19091)***

Home2 Suites, The, Perrysburg *Also called Hoster Hotels LLC* ***(G-16014)***

Homecare Mtters HM Hlth Hspice....419 562-2001
133 S Sandusky Ave Bucyrus (44820) ***(G-2040)***

Homefull....937 293-1945
33 W 1st St Ste 100 Dayton (45402) ***(G-9618)***

Homeland Credit Union Inc (PA)....740 775-3024
310 Caldwell St Chillicothe (45601) ***(G-2847)***

Homeland Credit Union Inc....740 775-3331
25 Consumer Center Dr Chillicothe (45601) ***(G-2848)***

Homeland Defense Solutions....513 333-7800
128 E 6th St Cincinnati (45202) ***(G-3781)***

Homeless Center, Cleveland *Also called Lutheran Metropolitan Ministry* ***(G-5960)***

Homeless Families Foundation....614 461-9427
33 N Grubb St Columbus (43215) ***(G-7852)***

Homelife Companies Inc (PA)....740 369-1297
13 E Winter St Delaware (43015) ***(G-10106)***

Homereach Inc....614 566-0850
7708 Green Meadows Dr D Lewis Center (43035) ***(G-12688)***

Homereach Inc (HQ)....614 566-0850
404 E Wilson Bridge Rd Worthington (43085) ***(G-19965)***

Homereach Healthcare, Lewis Center *Also called Homereach Inc* ***(G-12688)***

Homes By John Hershberger, Hartville *Also called Hersh Construction Inc* ***(G-11822)***

Homes For Kids of Ohio Inc....330 544-8005
165 E Park Ave Niles (44446) ***(G-15294)***

Homestead, Geneva *Also called 599 W Main Corporation* ***(G-11357)***

Homestead Care Rhblitation Ctr, Lancaster *Also called Sunbridge Care Enterprises Inc* ***(G-12578)***

Homestead Golf Course Inc....937 698-4876
5327 Worley Rd Tipp City (45371) ***(G-17719)***

Homestead Healthcare Center, Springfield *Also called Communicare Health Svcs Inc* ***(G-17170)***

Homestead II, Painesville *Also called Multi-Care Inc* ***(G-15867)***

Hometech Healthcare Svcs LLC....216 295-9120
17325 Euclid Ave Ste 3024 Cleveland (44112) ***(G-5769)***

Hometech Transportation Svcs, Cleveland *Also called Hometech Healthcare Svcs LLC* ***(G-5769)***

Hometown Bank (PA)....330 673-9827
142 N Water St Kent (44240) ***(G-12373)***

Hometown Hospital Health Plan....330 834-2200
100 Lillian Gish Blvd Sw # 301 Massillon (44647) ***(G-13820)***

Hometown Improvement Co....614 846-1060
1430 Halfhill Way Columbus (43207) ***(G-7853)***

Hometown Urgent Care....937 372-6012
101 S Orange St Xenia (45385) ***(G-20062)***

Hometown Urgent Care....614 263-4400
4400 N High St Ste 101 Columbus (43214) ***(G-7854)***

Hometown Urgent Care....330 505-9400
1997 Niles Cortland Rd Se Warren (44484) ***(G-18862)***

Hometown Urgent Care....330 629-2300
1305 Boardman Poland Rd Youngstown (44514) ***(G-20219)***

Hometown Urgent Care....937 342-9520
1200 Vester Ave Springfield (45503) ***(G-17206)***

Hometown Urgent Care....740 363-3133
1100 Sunbury Rd Ste 706 Delaware (43015) ***(G-10107)***

Hometown Urgent Care....937 252-2000
4164 Burbank Rd Wooster (44691) ***(G-19868)***

Hometown Urgent Care....614 472-2880
2880 Stelzer Rd Columbus (43219) ***(G-7855)***

Hometown Urgent Care....614 272-1100
4300 Clime Rd Ste 110 Columbus (43228) ***(G-7856)***

Hometown Urgent Care....937 236-8630
6210 Brandt Pike Dayton (45424) ***(G-9619)***

Hometown Urgent Care....937 322-6222
1301 W 1st St Springfield (45504) ***(G-17207)***

Hometown Urgent Care....614 835-0400
3813 S Hamilton Rd Groveport (43125) ***(G-11645)***

Hometown Urgent Care....513 831-5900
1068 State Route 28 Ste C Milford (45150) ***(G-14525)***

Homewood Corporation (PA)....614 898-7200
2700 E Dublin Granville R Columbus (43231) ***(G-7857)***

Homewood Residence At Rockefel, Cleveland *Also called American Retirement Corp* ***(G-5022)***

Homewood Rsdnce At Rchmond Hts, Cleveland *Also called American Retirement Corp* ***(G-5021)***

Homewood Suites, Miamisburg *Also called Req/Jqh Holdings Inc* ***(G-14341)***

Homewood Suites, Columbus *Also called Arvind Sagar Inc* ***(G-7047)***

Homewood Suites, Beavercreek *Also called Wright Executive Ht Ltd Partnr* ***(G-1220)***

Homewood Suites Dublin, Dublin *Also called W2005/Fargo Hotels (pool C)* ***(G-10486)***

Homier & Sons Inc (PA)....419 596-3965
21133 State Route 613 Continental (45831) ***(G-9049)***

Homier Implement Company, Continental *Also called Homier & Sons Inc* ***(G-9049)***

Honda East, Maumee *Also called Randy L Fork Inc* ***(G-13967)***

Honda Federal Credit Union....937 642-6000
24000 Honda Pkwy Marysville (43040) ***(G-13624)***

Honda Logistics North Amer Inc (HQ)....937 642-0335
11590 Township Road 298 East Liberty (43319) ***(G-10509)***

Honda Marysville Location, Raymond *Also called Honda R&D Americas Inc* ***(G-16420)***

Honda North America Inc....937 642-5000
24000 Honda Pkwy Marysville (43040) ***(G-13625)***

Honda of America Mfg Inc....937 644-0724
19900 State Route 739 Marysville (43040) ***(G-13626)***

Honda R&D Americas Inc....937 644-0439
21001 State Route 739 Raymond (43067) ***(G-16420)***

Honda Research Center, Marysville *Also called Sumitomo Elc Wirg Systems Inc* ***(G-13654)***

Honda Support Office, Marysville *Also called Honda of America Mfg Inc* ***(G-13626)***

Honda Trading America Corp....937 644-8004
19900 State Route 739 Marysville (43040) ***(G-13627)***

Honey Run Retreats LLC (PA)....330 674-0011
6920 County Road 203 Millersburg (44654) ***(G-14607)***

Honeywell, Urbana *Also called Grimes Aerospace Company* ***(G-18590)***

Honeywell, Perrysburg *Also called Fram Group Operations LLC* ***(G-16005)***

Honeywell Authorized Dealer, Batavia *Also called Bachmans Inc* ***(G-995)***

Honeywell Authorized Dealer, Cincinnati *Also called Century Mech Solutions Inc* ***(G-3220)***

Honeywell Authorized Dealer, Lima *Also called Timmerman John P Heating AC Co* ***(G-12900)***

Honeywell Authorized Dealer, Cincinnati *Also called Crane Heating & AC Co* ***(G-3438)***

Honeywell Authorized Dealer, Sandusky *Also called Gundlach Sheet Metal Works Inc* ***(G-16766)***

Honeywell Authorized Dealer, Hilliard *Also called Bruner Corporation* ***(G-11884)***

Honeywell Authorized Dealer, Marietta *Also called Morrison Inc* ***(G-13478)***

Honeywell Authorized Dealer, Cincinnati *Also called Cincinnati Air Conditioning Co* ***(G-3279)***

Honeywell Authorized Dealer, Cleveland *Also called Mc Phillips Plbg Htg & AC Co* ***(G-6000)***

Honeywell Authorized Dealer, Columbus *Also called Farber Corporation* ***(G-7637)***

Honeywell Authorized Dealer, Canton *Also called Miracle Plumbing & Heating Co* ***(G-2464)***

Honeywell Authorized Dealer, Cleveland *Also called Gillmore Security Systems Inc* ***(G-5672)***

Honeywell Authorized Dealer, Cincinnati *Also called Feldkamp Enterprises Inc* ***(G-3600)***

Honeywell Authorized Dealer, Coventry Township *Also called Lakes Heating and AC* ***(G-9128)***

Honeywell Authorized Dealer, Dayton *Also called Envirnmental Engrg Systems Inc* ***(G-9527)***

Honeywell Authorized Dealer, Coventry Township *Also called K Company Incorporated* ***(G-9127)***

Honeywell Authorized Dealer, Gahanna *Also called Custom AC & Htg Co* ***(G-11238)***

Honeywell Authorized Dealer, Columbus *Also called Wenger Temperature Control* ***(G-8978)***

Honeywell Authorized Dealer, Cincinnati *Also called Commercial Hvac Inc* ***(G-3399)***

Honeywell Authorized Dealer, Dayton *Also called Trame Mechanical Inc* ***(G-9936)***

Honeywell Authorized Dealer, West Chester *Also called Guardian Protection Svcs Inc* ***(G-19085)***

Honeywell Authorized Dealer, Cincinnati *Also called Corcoran and Harnist Htg & AC* ***(G-3421)***

Honeywell Authorized Dealer, Ashland *Also called Ashland Comfort Control Inc* ***(G-656)***

Honeywell Authorized Dealer, Dayton *Also called Superior Mechanical Svcs Inc* ***(G-9284)***

Honeywell Authorized Dealer, Sidney *Also called Area Energy & Electric Inc* ***(G-16913)***

Honeywell Authorized Dealer, Cincinnati *Also called Mechancal/Industrial Contg Inc* ***(G-4040)***

Honeywell Authorized Dealer, Uniontown *Also called Crown Heating & Cooling Inc* ***(G-18516)***

Honeywell Authorized Dealer, Cincinnati *Also called Perfection Group Inc* ***(G-4279)***

Honeywell Authorized Dealer, Bedford *Also called Smylie One Heating & Cooling* ***(G-1338)***

Honeywell Authorized Dealer, Toledo *Also called Noron Inc* ***(G-18092)***

Honeywell Authorized Dealer, Pickerington *Also called Colonial Heating & Cooling Co* ***(G-16091)***

Honeywell Authorized Dealer, Cuyahoga Falls *Also called Falls Heating & Cooling Inc* ***(G-9183)***
Honeywell Authorized Dealer, Anna *Also called Wells Brother Electric Inc* ***(G-618)***
Honeywell Authorized Dealer, Dublin *Also called Haslett Heating & Cooling Inc* ***(G-10358)***
Honeywell Authorized Dealer, Columbus *Also called American Mechanical Group Inc* ***(G-7001)***
Honeywell Authorized Dealer, Fairborn *Also called Advanced Mechanical Svcs Inc* ***(G-10783)***
Honeywell Authorized Dealer, Canal Winchester *Also called Kessler Heating & Cooling* ***(G-2163)***
Honeywell Authorized Dealer, Cincinnati *Also called TP Mechanical Contractors Inc* ***(G-4675)***
Honeywell International Inc....216 459-6053
925 Keynote Cir Ste 100 Cleveland (44131) ***(G-5770)***
Honeywell International Inc....440 243-8877
8370 Dow Cir Ste 5 Strongsville (44136) ***(G-17472)***
Honeywell International Inc....513 745-7200
1280 Kemper Meadow Dr Cincinnati (45240) ***(G-3782)***
Honeywell International Inc....614 717-2270
2080 Arlingate Ln Columbus (43228) ***(G-7858)***
Honeywell International Inc....937 484-2261
550 State Route 55 Urbana (43078) ***(G-18591)***
Hooberry Associates Inc....330 872-1991
2200 Milton Blvd Newton Falls (44444) ***(G-15274)***
Hoosier Express Inc (PA)....419 436-9590
1827 Sandusky St Fostoria (44830) ***(G-11132)***
Hoover & Wells Inc....419 691-9220
2011 Seaman St Toledo (43605) ***(G-17959)***
Hope Ctr For Cncer Care Warren....330 856-8600
1745 Niles Crtlnd Rd Ne Ste 5 Warren (44484) ***(G-18863)***
Hope Homes Inc....330 688-4935
2044 Bryn Mawr Dr Stow (44224) ***(G-17372)***
Hope Hotel & Conference Center, Fairborn *Also called Visicon Inc* ***(G-10809)***
Hopedale Mining LLC....740 937-2225
86900 Sinfield Rd Hopedale (43976) ***(G-12079)***
Hopes Drams Childcare Lrng Ctr....330 793-8260
33 N Wickliffe Cir Youngstown (44515) ***(G-20220)***
Hopewell (PA)....440 693-4074
9637 State Route 534 Mesopotamia (44439) ***(G-14263)***
Hopewell Day Treatment Center, Cleveland *Also called Positive Education Program* ***(G-6291)***
Hopewell Dental Care....740 522-5000
572 Industrial Pkwy Ste B Newark (43056) ***(G-15174)***
Hopewell Health Centers Inc....740 596-5249
31891 State Route 93 Mc Arthur (45651) ***(G-14016)***
Hopewell Health Centers Inc (PA)....740 773-1006
1049 Western Ave Chillicothe (45601) ***(G-2849)***
Hopewell Health Centers Inc....740 385-6594
541 State Route 664 N C Logan (43138) ***(G-12977)***
Hopewell Industries Inc (PA)....740 622-3563
637 Chestnut St Coshocton (43812) ***(G-9107)***
Hopewell Therapeutic Farm, Mesopotamia *Also called Hopewell* ***(G-14263)***
Hopkin Arprt Lmsine Shttle Svc....216 267-8282
1315 Brookpark Rd Brookpark (44142) ***(G-1946)***
Hopkin S Airport Limosine Svc, Brookpark *Also called Hopkin Arprt Lmsine Shttle Svc* ***(G-1946)***
Hopkins Airport Limousine Svc (PA)....216 267-8810
13315 Brookpark Rd Cleveland (44142) ***(G-5771)***
Hopkins Partners....216 267-1500
5300 Riverside Dr Ste 30 Cleveland (44135) ***(G-5772)***
Hopkins Transportation Svcs, Cleveland *Also called Hopkins Airport Limousine Svc* ***(G-5771)***
Hoppes Construction LLC....580 310-0090
4036 Coral Rd Nw Malvern (44644) ***(G-13252)***
Hord Livestock Company Inc....419 562-0277
887 State Route 98 Bucyrus (44820) ***(G-2041)***
Horenstein Nicho & Blume A L....937 224-7200
124 E 3rd St Fl 5 Dayton (45402) ***(G-9620)***
Horizon Education Centers....440 458-5115
10347 Dewhurst Rd Elyria (44035) ***(G-10634)***
Horizon Education Centers (PA)....440 779-1930
29510 Lorain Rd North Olmsted (44070) ***(G-15426)***
Horizon Freight, Cleveland *Also called Horizon South Inc* ***(G-5775)***
Horizon Freight System Inc....216 341-3322
6600 Bessemer Ave Cleveland (44127) ***(G-5773)***
Horizon Freight System Inc (PA)....216 341-7410
6600 Bessemer Ave Cleveland (44127) ***(G-5774)***
Horizon Health Management LLC....513 793-5220
3889 E Galbraith Rd Cincinnati (45236) ***(G-3783)***
Horizon HM Hlth Care Agcy LLC....614 279-2933
3035 W Broad St Ste 102 Columbus (43204) ***(G-7859)***
Horizon Home Health Care....937 264-3155
410 Corporate Center Dr Vandalia (45377) ***(G-18686)***
Horizon House Apartments LLC....740 354-6393
700 2nd St Portsmouth (45662) ***(G-16288)***
Horizon Mechanical and Elec....419 529-2738
323 N Trimble Rd Mansfield (44906) ***(G-13309)***
Horizon Payroll Services Inc....937 434-8244
2700 Miamisburg Centervil Dayton (45459) ***(G-9621)***
Horizon Pcs Inc (HQ)....740 772-8200
68 E Main St Chillicothe (45601) ***(G-2850)***
Horizon Personnel Resources (PA)....440 585-0031
1516 Lincoln Rd Wickliffe (44092) ***(G-19602)***
Horizon South Inc....800 480-6829
6600 Bessemer Ave Cleveland (44127) ***(G-5775)***
Horizon Telcom Inc (PA)....740 772-8200
68 E Main St Chillicothe (45601) ***(G-2851)***
Horizons Employment Svcs LLC....419 254-9644
2024 W Terrace View St Toledo (43607) ***(G-17960)***
Horizons Imaging & Therapy Ctr, Columbus *Also called Mount Carmel Imaging & Therapy* ***(G-8199)***
Horizons Tuscarawas/Carroll....330 262-4183
527 N Market St Wooster (44691) ***(G-19869)***
Horn Electric Company....330 364-7784
608 S Tuscarawas Ave Dover (44622) ***(G-10192)***
Horn Engineering, Dover *Also called Horn Electric Company* ***(G-10192)***
Horn Nursing and Rehab Center (HQ)....330 262-2951
230 N Market St Wooster (44691) ***(G-19870)***
Horn Nursing and Rehab Center....330 345-9050
4110 E Smithville Wstn Rd Wooster (44691) ***(G-19871)***
Horn Nursing Rehabilitation Ctr, Wooster *Also called Horn Nursing and Rehab Center* ***(G-19870)***
Horner Industrial Services Inc....937 390-6667
5330 Prosperity Dr Springfield (45502) ***(G-17208)***
Horseshoe Cleveland MGT LLC....216 297-4777
100 Public Sq Ste 100 Cleveland (44113) ***(G-5776)***
Horter Investment MGT LLC....513 984-9933
11726 7 Gables Rd Cincinnati (45249) ***(G-3784)***
Hoskins International LLC....419 628-6015
5116 State Route 119 Minster (45865) ***(G-14664)***
Hoskins Intl SEC Invstigations, Minster *Also called Hoskins International LLC* ***(G-14664)***
Hospice Butler and Warren Cnty, Dayton *Also called Dayton Hospice Incorporated* ***(G-9479)***
Hospice Care Ohio (PA)....330 665-1455
3358 Ridgewood Rd Fairlawn (44333) ***(G-10956)***
Hospice Caring Way....419 238-9223
1159 Westwood Dr Van Wert (45891) ***(G-18635)***
Hospice Cincinnati Inc....513 862-1100
2800 Winslow Ave Cincinnati (45206) ***(G-3785)***
Hospice Cincinnati Inc (HQ)....513 891-7700
4360 Cooper Rd Ste 300 Cincinnati (45242) ***(G-3786)***
Hospice of Care, Chardon *Also called Parkside Care Corporation* ***(G-2761)***
Hospice of Central Ohio (PA)....740 344-0311
2269 Cherry Valley Rd Se Newark (43055) ***(G-15175)***
Hospice of Darke County Inc....419 678-4808
230 W Main St Coldwater (45828) ***(G-6830)***
Hospice of Darke County Inc (PA)....937 548-2999
1350 N Broadway St Greenville (45331) ***(G-11510)***
Hospice of Genesis Health....740 454-5381
713 Forest Ave Zanesville (43701) ***(G-20488)***
Hospice of Hamilton....513 895-1270
1010 Eaton Ave Hamilton (45013) ***(G-11742)***
Hospice of Hope Inc....937 444-4900
215 Hughes Blvd Mount Orab (45154) ***(G-14869)***
Hospice of Knox County....740 397-5188
17700 Coshocton Rd Mount Vernon (43050) ***(G-14899)***
Hospice of Memorial Hospita L....419 334-6626
430 S Main St Clyde (43410) ***(G-6815)***
Hospice of Miami County Inc....937 335-5191
550 Summit Ave Ste 101 Troy (45373) ***(G-18358)***
Hospice of Miami Valley LLC (PA)....937 458-6028
46 N Detroit St Ste B Xenia (45385) ***(G-20063)***
Hospice of Middletown....513 424-2273
3909 Central Ave Middletown (45044) ***(G-14428)***
Hospice of North Central Ohio....419 524-9200
2131 Park Ave W Ontario (44906) ***(G-15692)***
Hospice of North Central Ohio (PA)....419 281-7107
1050 Dauch Dr Ashland (44805) ***(G-682)***
Hospice of Northwest Ohio....419 661-4001
800 S Detroit Ave Toledo (43609) ***(G-17961)***
Hospice of Northwest Ohio (PA)....419 661-4001
30000 E River Rd Perrysburg (43551) ***(G-16013)***
Hospice of Ohio LLC (PA)....440 286-2500
677 Alpha Dr Ste H Cleveland (44143) ***(G-5777)***
Hospice of Southern Ohio....740 356-2567
2201 25th St Portsmouth (45662) ***(G-16289)***
Hospice of The Valley Inc (PA)....330 788-1992
5190 Market St Youngstown (44512) ***(G-20221)***
Hospice of The Western Reserve....440 951-8692
5786 Heisley Rd Mentor (44060) ***(G-14192)***
Hospice of The Western Reserve....440 357-5833
5786 Heisley Rd Mentor (44060) ***(G-14193)***
Hospice of The Western Reserve....330 800-2240
5075 Windfall Rd Medina (44256) ***(G-14077)***
Hospice of The Western Reserve....800 707-8921
4670 Richmond Rd Ste 200 Cleveland (44128) ***(G-5778)***
Hospice of The Western Reserve....440 787-2080
2173 N Ridge Rd E Ste H Lorain (44055) ***(G-13042)***
Hospice of The Western Reserve (PA)....216 383-2222
17876 Saint Clair Ave Cleveland (44110) ***(G-5779)***
Hospice of The Western Reserve....440 997-6619
1166 Lake Ave Ashtabula (44004) ***(G-748)***
Hospice of The Western Reserve....800 707-8922
17876 Saint Clair Ave Cleveland (44110) ***(G-5780)***
Hospice of The Western Reserve....216 227-9048
22730 Fairview Center Dr # 100 Cleveland (44126) ***(G-5781)***

ALPHABETIC

Hospice Southwest Ohio Inc 513 770-0820
7625 Camargo Rd Cincinnati (45243) *(G-3787)*
Hospice Tuscarawas County Inc (PA) 330 343-7605
716 Commercial Ave Sw New Philadelphia (44663) *(G-15101)*
Hospice Visiting Nurse Service, Fairlawn *Also called Hospice Care Ohio (G-10956)*
Hospitalists MGT Group LLC (HQ) 866 464-7497
4535 Dressler Rd Nw Canton (44718) *(G-2404)*
Hospitality Home East, Xenia *Also called Xenia East Management Systems (G-20086)*
Hospitality Home West, Xenia *Also called Xenia West Management Systems (G-20087)*
Hospitality House, Massillon *Also called Childs Investment Co (G-13794)*
Hoss, Dayton *Also called Voss Auto Network Inc (G-9976)*
Hoss Value Cars & Trucks Inc (PA) 937 428-2400
766 Mmsburg Cnterville Rd Dayton (45459) *(G-9622)*
Hosser Assisted Living 740 286-8785
101 Markham Dr Jackson (45640) *(G-12314)*
Host Cincinnati Hotel LLC 513 621-7700
21 E 5th St Ste A Cincinnati (45202) *(G-3788)*
Hoster Hotels LLC 419 931-8900
5995 Levis Commons Blvd Perrysburg (43551) *(G-16014)*
Hostexcellence.com, Columbus *Also called Ecommerce Inc (G-7573)*
Hotel 2345 LLC 614 766-7762
4130 Tuller Rd Dublin (43017) *(G-10365)*
Hotel 50 S Front Opco LP 614 228-4600
50 S Front St Columbus (43215) *(G-7860)*
Hotel Dayton, Dayton *Also called Dayton Choa (G-9465)*
Hotel Stow LP 330 945-9722
4047 Bridgewater Pkwy Stow (44224) *(G-17373)*
Hoty Enterprises Inc (PA) 419 609-7000
5500 Milan Rd Ste 220 Sandusky (44870) *(G-16769)*
House Calls LLC 513 841-9800
1936 Elm Ave Cincinnati (45212) *(G-3789)*
House of La Rose Cleveland 440 746-7500
6745 Southpointe Pkwy Brecksville (44141) *(G-1827)*
House of Loreto 330 453-8137
2812 Harvard Ave Nw Canton (44709) *(G-2405)*
House of New Hope 740 345-5437
8135 Mount Vernon Rd Saint Louisville (43071) *(G-16668)*
House of Plastics, Cleveland *Also called HP Manufacturing Company Inc (G-5788)*
Household Centralized Svc Inc 419 474-5754
2052 W Sylvania Ave Toledo (43613) *(G-17962)*
Houston Dick Plbg & Htg Inc 740 763-3961
724 Montgomery Rd Ne Newark (43055) *(G-15176)*
Houston Plumbing & Heating, Newark *Also called Houston Dick Plbg & Htg Inc (G-15176)*
Hovest Construction 419 456-3426
4997 Old State Route 224 Ottawa (45875) *(G-15798)*
Howard Hanna RE & Mrtg Svcs, North Royalton *Also called Hanna Holdings Inc (G-15492)*
Howard Hanna Real Estate, Avon *Also called Hanna Holdings Inc (G-896)*
Howard Hanna Real Estate Svcs, Pepper Pike *Also called Howard Hanna Smythe Cramer (G-15956)*
Howard Hanna Smythe Cramer 440 237-8888
5730 Wallings Rd North Royalton (44133) *(G-15495)*
Howard Hanna Smythe Cramer 330 345-2244
177 W Milltown Rd Unit A Wooster (44691) *(G-19872)*
Howard Hanna Smythe Cramer 440 248-3000
6240 Som Center Rd # 100 Solon (44139) *(G-17015)*
Howard Hanna Smythe Cramer 800 656-7356
4374 Boardman Canfield Rd Canfield (44406) *(G-2195)*
Howard Hanna Smythe Cramer 216 831-0210
28879 Chagrin Blvd Beachwood (44122) *(G-1086)*
Howard Hanna Smythe Cramer (HQ) 216 447-4477
6000 Parkland Blvd Cleveland (44124) *(G-5782)*
Howard Hanna Smythe Cramer 440 333-6500
19204 Detroit Rd Rocky River (44116) *(G-16581)*
Howard Hanna Smythe Cramer 216 447-4477
2603 W Market St Ste 100a Akron (44313) *(G-272)*
Howard Hanna Smythe Cramer 330 468-6833
907 E Aurora Rd Macedonia (44056) *(G-13202)*
Howard Hanna Smythe Cramer 330 725-4137
3565 Medina Rd Medina (44256) *(G-14078)*
Howard Hanna Smythe Cramer 440 835-2800
27115 Knickerbocker Rd Cleveland (44140) *(G-5783)*
Howard Hanna Smythe Cramer 440 282-8002
1711 Cooper Foster Pk Rd Amherst (44001) *(G-597)*
Howard Hanna Smythe Cramer 330 686-1166
3925 Darrow Rd Ste 101 Stow (44224) *(G-17374)*
Howard Hanna Smythe Cramer 440 516-4444
34601 Ridge Rd Ste 3 Willoughby (44094) *(G-19671)*
Howard Hanna Smythe Cramer 440 248-3380
6240 Som Center Rd # 100 Cleveland (44139) *(G-5784)*
Howard Hanna Smythe Cramer 216 751-8550
24465 Greenwich Ln Beachwood (44122) *(G-1087)*
Howard Hanna Smythe Cramer 216 831-9310
3550 Lander Rd Ste 300 Pepper Pike (44124) *(G-15956)*
Howard Hanna Smythe Cramer 330 562-6188
195 Barrington Town Sq Dr Aurora (44202) *(G-841)*
Howard Hanna Smythe Cramer 440 428-1818
2757 Hubbard Rd Madison (44057) *(G-13225)*
Howard Hanna Smythe Cramer 330 493-6555
4758 Dressler Rd Nw Canton (44718) *(G-2406)*
Howard Hanna Smythe Cramer 330 896-3333
3700 Massillon Rd Ste 300 Uniontown (44685) *(G-18524)*
Howard Hanna Smythe Cramer 440 526-1800
8949 Brecksville Rd Cleveland (44141) *(G-5785)*
Howard Hannah Smythe Cramer, Cleveland *Also called Howard Hanna Smythe Cramer (G-5783)*
Howard Johnson, Cincinnati *Also called Johnson Howard International (G-3883)*
Howard Johnson, Girard *Also called Universal Development MGT Inc (G-11428)*
Howard Johnson, Brookpark *Also called 16644 Snow Rd LLC (G-1934)*
Howard Johnson 513 825-3129
400 Glensprin Dr L 275 Sr Cincinnati (45246) *(G-3790)*
Howard Johnson Lima, Lima *Also called R & K Gorby LLC (G-12866)*
Howard Wershbale & Co (PA) 216 831-1200
23240 Chagrin Blvd # 700 Cleveland (44122) *(G-5786)*
Howden American Fan Company 513 874-2400
3235 Homeward Way Fairfield (45014) *(G-10860)*
Howden North America Inc 513 874-2400
2933 Symmes Rd Fairfield (45014) *(G-10861)*
Howland Corners Twn & Ctry Vet 330 856-1862
8000 E Market St Warren (44484) *(G-18864)*
Howley Bread Group Ltd (PA) 440 808-1600
159 Crocker Park Blvd # 290 Westlake (44145) *(G-19492)*
Howmet Corporation (HQ) 800 242-9898
1616 Harvard Ave Newburgh Heights (44105) *(G-15251)*
Hoyer Poured Walls Inc 937 642-6148
18205 Poling Rd Marysville (43040) *(G-13628)*
HP Inc 440 234-7022
5005 Rockside Rd Ste 600 Cleveland (44131) *(G-5787)*
HP Inc 513 983-2817
300 E 6th St Cincinnati (45202) *(G-3791)*
HP Manufacturing Company Inc (PA) 216 361-6500
3705 Carnegie Ave Cleveland (44115) *(G-5788)*
Hpj Industries Inc (PA) 419 278-1000
510 W Broadway St North Baltimore (45872) *(G-15314)*
Hr Associates Personnel Svc, Piqua *Also called S & H Risner Inc (G-16165)*
Hr Butler LLC 614 923-2900
63 Corbins Mill Dr Ste A Dublin (43017) *(G-10366)*
Hr Plus, Independence *Also called Gallery Holdings LLC (G-12213)*
Hr Profile, Cincinnati *Also called Human Resource Profile Inc (G-3795)*
Hr Services Inc 419 224-2462
675 W Market St Ste 200 Lima (45801) *(G-12799)*
Hrh Door Corp 330 893-3233
2589 County Road 168 Dundee (44624) *(G-10500)*
Hrm Enterprises Inc (PA) 330 877-9353
1015 Edison St Nw Hartville (44632) *(G-11823)*
Hrm Leasing, Findlay *Also called Bob Miller Rigging Inc (G-11005)*
Hrnchar's Fairway Ford, Canfield *Also called Paul Hrnchar Ford-Mercury Inc (G-2207)*
HRP Capital Inc 419 865-3111
6855 Spring Valley Dr # 120 Holland (43528) *(G-12028)*
Hs Express LLC 419 729-2400
6003 Benore Rd Toledo (43612) *(G-17963)*
Hs Financial Group LLC 440 871-8484
25651 Detroit Rd Ste 203 Westlake (44145) *(G-19493)*
Hsc Dept of Psychiatry, Toledo *Also called University of Toledo (G-18277)*
Hsi Hemodialysis Services, Beachwood *Also called Hemodialysis Services Inc (G-1085)*
Hsr Business To Business, Cincinnati *Also called Hsr Marketing Communications (G-3792)*
Hsr Marketing Communications 513 671-3811
300 E Bus Way Ste 500 Cincinnati (45241) *(G-3792)*
Hst Lessee Cincinnati LLC 513 852-2702
21 E 5th St Cincinnati (45202) *(G-3793)*
HTI - Hall Trucking Inc 419 423-9555
110 Bentley Ct Findlay (45840) *(G-11047)*
Htp Inc 614 885-1272
8720 Orion Pl Ste 300 Columbus (43240) *(G-6885)*
Hub City Terminals Inc 440 779-2226
27476 Detroit Rd Ste 102 Westlake (44145) *(G-19494)*
Hub City Terminals Inc 419 217-5200
811 Madison Ave Ste 601 Toledo (43604) *(G-17964)*
Hubbard Company 419 784-4455
612 Clinton St Defiance (43512) *(G-10034)*
Hubbard Radio Cincinnati LLC 513 699-5102
2060 Reading Rd Ste 400 Cincinnati (45202) *(G-3794)*
Hubbell Power Systems Inc 330 335-2361
8711 Wadsworth Rd Wadsworth (44281) *(G-18757)*
Huber Heights Dialysis, Huber Heights *Also called Pendster Dialysis LLC (G-12097)*
Huber Heights YMCA 937 236-9622
7251 Shull Rd Dayton (45424) *(G-9623)*
Huber Investment Corporation (PA) 937 233-1122
5550 Huber Rd Dayton (45424) *(G-9624)*
Hubert Company LLC (HQ) 513 367-8600
9555 Dry Fork Rd Harrison (45030) *(G-11802)*
Huckleberry House 614 294-5553
1421 Hamlet St Columbus (43201) *(G-7861)*
Hudec Dental Associates Inc (PA) 216 485-5788
6700 W Snowville Rd Brecksville (44141) *(G-1828)*
Hudson City Engineering Dept 330 342-1770
115 Executive Pkwy # 400 Hudson (44236) *(G-12121)*
Hudson Elms Skilled Nursing, Hudson *Also called Saber Healthcare Group LLC (G-12142)*
Hudson Montessori Association 330 650-0424
7545 Darrow Rd Hudson (44236) *(G-12122)*
HUDSON MONTESSORI SCHOOL, Hudson *Also called Hudson Montessori Association (G-12122)*

ALPHABETIC SECTION Hyde Park Grille, Columbus

Hueston Woods Lodge,, College Corner *Also called Ohio State Parks Inc* ***(G-6838)***
Huffman Health Care Inc......937 476-1000
20 Livingston Ave Dayton (45403) ***(G-9625)***
Huffy Bicycle Company, Springboro *Also called Huffy Corporation* ***(G-17124)***
Huffy Corporation......937 743-5011
901 Pleasant Valley Dr Springboro (45066) ***(G-17124)***
Hugh White Buick, Lancaster *Also called Tbn Acquisition LLC* ***(G-12580)***
Hughes & Knollman Construction......614 237-6167
4601 E 5th Ave Columbus (43219) ***(G-7862)***
Hughes Corporation (PA)......440 238-2550
16900 Foltz Pkwy Strongsville (44149) ***(G-17473)***
Hughes Corporation......440 238-2550
16900 Foltz Pkwy Strongsville (44149) ***(G-17474)***
Hughes Kitchens and Bath LLC......330 455-5269
1258 Cleveland Ave Nw Canton (44703) ***(G-2407)***
Hull & Associates Inc (PA)......614 793-8777
6397 Emerald Pkwy Ste 200 Dublin (43016) ***(G-10367)***
Hull & Associates Inc......419 385-2018
219 S Erie St Toledo (43604) ***(G-17965)***
Hull Bros Inc......419 375-2827
520 E Boundary St Fort Recovery (45846) ***(G-11118)***
Hull Builders Supply Inc......440 967-3159
685 Main St Vermilion (44089) ***(G-18710)***
Human Resource Profile Inc......513 388-4300
8506 Beechmont Ave Cincinnati (45255) ***(G-3795)***
Human Resources Services......740 587-3484
465 Buckstone Pl Westerville (43082) ***(G-19314)***
Human Services, Xenia *Also called Greene County* ***(G-20055)***
Humana Health Plan Ohio Inc......513 784-5200
111 Merchant St Cincinnati (45246) ***(G-3796)***
Humana Inc......330 877-5464
1289 Edison St Nw Hartville (44632) ***(G-11824)***
Humana Inc......216 328-2047
6100 Oak Tree Blvd Independence (44131) ***(G-12217)***
Humana Inc......614 210-1038
485 Metro Pl S Ste 410 Dublin (43017) ***(G-10368)***
Humana Inc......330 498-0537
4690 Munson St Nw Ste C Canton (44718) ***(G-2408)***
Humantics Innovative Solutions......567 265-5200
900 Denton Dr Huron (44839) ***(G-12165)***
Humaserve Hr LLC......513 605-3522
9435 Waterstone Blvd Cincinnati (45249) ***(G-3797)***
Hume Supply Inc......419 991-5751
1359 E Hanthorn Rd Lima (45804) ***(G-12800)***
Humility House......330 505-0144
755 Ohltown Rd Youngstown (44515) ***(G-20222)***
Humility of Mary Info Systems......330 884-6600
250 E Federal St Ste 200 Youngstown (44503) ***(G-20223)***
Hummel Construction Company......330 274-8584
127 E Main St Ravenna (44266) ***(G-16388)***
Hummel Group Inc......330 683-1050
461 Wadsworth Rd Orrville (44667) ***(G-15774)***
Hummel Industries Incorporated......513 242-1321
93 Caldwell Dr B Cincinnati (45216) ***(G-3798)***
Hunt Club LLC......419 885-4647
5600 Alexis Rd Sylvania (43560) ***(G-17594)***
Hunt Products Inc......440 667-2457
3982 E 42nd St Newburgh Heights (44105) ***(G-15252)***
Hunter Defense Tech Inc (PA)......216 438-6111
30500 Aurora Rd Ste 100 Solon (44139) ***(G-17016)***
Hunter Realty Inc......216 831-2911
25101 Chagrin Blvd # 170 Cleveland (44122) ***(G-5789)***
Hunter Realty Inc......440 466-9177
385 S Broadway Geneva (44041) ***(G-11364)***
Huntington Auto Trust 2015-1......302 636-5401
Huntington Ctr 41 S High Columbus (43287) ***(G-7863)***
Huntington Auto Trust 2016-1......302 636-5401
41 S High St Columbus (43215) ***(G-7864)***
Huntington Bancshares Inc (PA)......614 480-8300
41 S High St Columbus (43215) ***(G-7865)***
Huntington Bank, Findlay *Also called Huntington Insurance Inc* ***(G-11048)***
Huntington Hlls Recreation CLB......614 837-0293
6600 Springbrook Dr Pickerington (43147) ***(G-16097)***
Huntington Insurance Inc (HQ)......419 720-7900
519 Madison Ave Toledo (43604) ***(G-17966)***
Huntington Insurance Inc......614 480-3800
7 Easton Oval Columbus (43219) ***(G-7866)***
Huntington Insurance Inc......419 429-4627
236 S Main St Findlay (45840) ***(G-11048)***
Huntington Insurance Inc......216 206-1787
925 Euclid Ave Ste 550 Cleveland (44115) ***(G-5790)***
Huntington Insurance Inc......330 262-6611
121 N Market St Ste 600 Wooster (44691) ***(G-19873)***
Huntington Insurance Inc......614 899-8500
37 W Broad St Ste 1100 Columbus (43215) ***(G-7867)***
Huntington Insurance Inc......330 337-9933
542 E State St Salem (44460) ***(G-16700)***
Huntington Insurance Inc......330 430-1300
220 Market Ave S Ste 40 Canton (44702) ***(G-2409)***
Huntington Insurance Inc......330 674-2931
212 N Washington St Millersburg (44654) ***(G-14608)***
Huntington National Bank......513 762-1860
525 Vine St Ste 14 Cincinnati (45202) ***(G-3799)***
Huntington National Bank......330 742-7013
23 Federal Plaza Central Youngstown (44503) ***(G-20224)***
Huntington National Bank......330 343-6611
232 W 3rd St Ste 207 Dover (44622) ***(G-10193)***
Huntington National Bank......740 773-2681
445 Western Ave Chillicothe (45601) ***(G-2852)***
Huntington National Bank......614 480-0067
4078 Powell Ave Columbus (43213) ***(G-7868)***
Huntington National Bank......614 336-4620
4300 Tuller Rd Dublin (43017) ***(G-10369)***
Huntington National Bank......740 335-3771
134 E Court St Wshngtn CT Hs (43160) ***(G-20027)***
Huntington National Bank......330 996-6300
Iii Cascade Plz Fl 7 Akron (44308) ***(G-273)***
Huntington National Bank (PA)......614 480-4293
17 S High St Fl 1 Columbus (43215) ***(G-7869)***
Huntington National Bank......330 384-7201
106 S Main St Fl 5 Akron (44308) ***(G-274)***
Huntington National Bank......740 452-8444
422 Main St Zanesville (43701) ***(G-20489)***
Huntington National Bank (HQ)......614 480-4293
17 S High St Fl 1 Columbus (43215) ***(G-7870)***
Huntington National Bank......740 695-3323
154 W Main St Saint Clairsville (43950) ***(G-16638)***
Huntington National Bank......330 384-7092
121 S Main St Ste 200 Akron (44308) ***(G-275)***
Huntington National Bank......419 226-8200
631 W Market St Lima (45801) ***(G-12801)***
Huntington National Bank......216 621-1717
101 W Prospect Ave Cleveland (44115) ***(G-5791)***
Huntington National Bank......614 480-8300
2361 Morse Rd Columbus (43229) ***(G-7871)***
Huntington National Bank......216 515-6401
905 Euclid Ave Cleveland (44115) ***(G-5792)***
Huntington National Bank......419 782-5050
405 W 3rd St Defiance (43512) ***(G-10035)***
Huntington Street 16, Medina *Also called Regal Cinemas Inc* ***(G-14120)***
Huntington Technology Finance......614 480-5169
37 W Broad St Columbus (43215) ***(G-7872)***
Huntington Wealth Advisors, Cincinnati *Also called The Huntington Investment Co* ***(G-4643)***
Huntleigh USA Corporation......216 265-3707
11147 Barrington Blvd Cleveland (44130) ***(G-5793)***
Huntsey Corporation......614 568-5030
470 Olde Worthington Rd Westerville (43082) ***(G-19315)***
Huron Cement Products Company (PA)......419 433-4161
617 Main St Huron (44839) ***(G-12166)***
Huron Health Care Center Inc......419 433-4990
1920 Cleveland Rd W Huron (44839) ***(G-12167)***
Huron School of Nursing, Cleveland *Also called Clevelnd Clnc Hlth Systm East* ***(G-5358)***
Husky Energy, Dublin *Also called Husky Marketing and Supply Co* ***(G-10370)***
Husky Marketing and Supply Co......614 210-2300
5550 Blazer Pkwy Ste 200 Dublin (43017) ***(G-10370)***
Hustead Emergency Medical Svc......937 324-3031
6215 Springfield Xenia Rd Springfield (45502) ***(G-17209)***
Huston Nursing Home......740 384-3485
38500 State Route 160 Hamden (45634) ***(G-11687)***
Huttig Building Products Inc......614 492-8248
2160 Mcgaw Rd Obetz (43207) ***(G-15667)***
Huttig Sash & Door Co, Obetz *Also called Huttig Building Products Inc* ***(G-15667)***
Hvac, Mentor *Also called Burrier Service Company Inc* ***(G-14151)***
HWH Archtcts-Ngnrs-Plnners Inc......216 875-4000
600 Superior Ave E # 1100 Cleveland (44114) ***(G-5794)***
Hwy Garage, Wapakoneta *Also called Ohio Department Transportation* ***(G-18805)***
Hwy. Department, Greenville *Also called Ohio Department Transportation* ***(G-11515)***
Hwz Distribution Group LLC (HQ)......513 618-0300
40 W Crescentville Rd West Chester (45246) ***(G-19209)***
Hwz Distribution Group LLC......513 723-1150
3274 Spring Grove Ave Cincinnati (45225) ***(G-3800)***
Hy-Grade Corporation (PA)......216 341-7711
3993 E 93rd St Cleveland (44105) ***(G-5795)***
Hy-Tek Material Handling Inc (PA)......614 497-2500
2222 Rickenbacker Pkwy W Columbus (43217) ***(G-7873)***
Hyatt Corporation......614 463-1234
350 N High St Columbus (43215) ***(G-7074)***
Hyatt Hotel, Cleveland *Also called Hit Portfolio I Misc Trs LLC* ***(G-5760)***
Hyatt Hotel, Columbus *Also called Hyatt Corporation* ***(G-7874)***
Hyatt Hotel, Cincinnati *Also called Hit Portfolio I Misc Trs LLC* ***(G-3770)***
Hyatt Legal Plans Inc......216 241-0022
1111 Superior Ave E # 800 Cleveland (44114) ***(G-5796)***
Hyatt On Capitol Square, Columbus *Also called Hit Portfolio I Misc Trs LLC* ***(G-7840)***
Hyatt Pl Cincinnati-Northeast, Mason *Also called Select Hotels Group LLC* ***(G-13759)***
Hyatt Pl Clveland/Independence, Cleveland *Also called Select Hotels Group LLC* ***(G-6466)***
Hyatt Pl Columbus Worthington, Columbus *Also called Hit Portfolio I Misc Trs LLC* ***(G-7839)***
Hyatt Place Cleveland/, Cleveland *Also called Legacy Village Hospitality LLC* ***(G-5932)***
Hyatt Place Columbus/Dublin, Dublin *Also called Select Hotels Group LLC* ***(G-10451)***
Hyatt Regency Columbus......614 463-1234
350 N High St Columbus (43215) ***(G-7875)***
Hyde Park Golf & Country Club......513 321-3721
3740 Erie Ave Cincinnati (45208) ***(G-3801)***
Hyde Park Grille, Columbus *Also called Henderson Road Rest Systems* ***(G-7825)***

ALPHABETIC

Hyde Park Health Center....513 272-0600
3763 Hopper Hill Rd Cincinnati (45255) ***(G-3802)***
Hyde Park Landscaping, Cincinnati *Also called Hyde Park Ldscp & Tree Svc Inc* ***(G-3803)***
Hyde Park Ldscp & Tree Svc Inc....513 731-1334
5055 Wooster Rd Cincinnati (45226) ***(G-3803)***
Hyde Park Play School....513 631-2095
3846 Drake Ave Cincinnati (45209) ***(G-3804)***
Hydraulic Parts Store Inc....330 364-6667
145 1st Dr Ne New Philadelphia (44663) ***(G-15102)***
Hydraulic Specialists Inc....740 922-3343
5655 Gundy Dr Midvale (44653) ***(G-14490)***
Hydro-Dyne Inc....330 832-5076
225 Wetmore Ave Se Massillon (44646) ***(G-13821)***
Hydrochem LLC....216 861-3949
428 Thacher Ln Youngstown (44515) ***(G-20225)***
Hydrochem LLC....330 792-6569
428 Thacher Ln Youngstown (44515) ***(G-20226)***
Hydrogeologic Inc....330 463-3303
581 Boston Mills Rd # 600 Hudson (44236) ***(G-12123)***
Hyland LLC (HQ)....440 788-5045
28500 Clemens Rd Westlake (44145) ***(G-19495)***
Hyland Software Inc (HQ)....440 788-5000
28500 Clemens Rd Westlake (44145) ***(G-19496)***
Hylant Administrative Services (PA)....419 255-1020
811 Madison Ave Fl 11 Toledo (43604) ***(G-17967)***
Hylant Group, Dublin *Also called Hylant-Maclean Inc* ***(G-10372)***
Hylant Group Inc....513 985-2400
50 E-Business Way Ste 420 Cincinnati (45241) ***(G-3805)***
Hylant Group Inc....614 932-1200
565 Metro Pl S Ste 450 Dublin (43017) ***(G-10371)***
Hylant Group Inc (PA)....419 255-1020
811 Madison Ave Fl 11 Toledo (43604) ***(G-17968)***
Hylant Group Inc....216 447-1050
6000 Fredom Sq Dr Ste 400 Cleveland (44131) ***(G-5797)***
Hylant Group of Cincinnati, Cincinnati *Also called Hylant Group Inc* ***(G-3805)***
Hylant Group of Cleveland, Cleveland *Also called Hylant Group Inc* ***(G-5797)***
Hylant Group of Columbus, Dublin *Also called Hylant Group Inc* ***(G-10371)***
Hylant-Maclean Inc....614 932-1200
565 Metro Pl S Ste 450 Dublin (43017) ***(G-10372)***
Hynes Industries Inc (PA)....330 799-3221
3805 Hendricks Rd Ste A Youngstown (44515) ***(G-20227)***
Hyo OK Inc....614 876-7644
4315 Cosgray Rd Hilliard (43026) ***(G-11912)***
Hyperlogistics Group Inc (PA)....614 497-0800
9301 Intermodal Ct N Columbus (43217) ***(G-7876)***
Hyperquake LLC....513 563-6555
205 W 4th St Ste 1010 Cincinnati (45202) ***(G-3806)***
Hyway Trucking Company....419 423-7145
10060 W Us Route 224 Findlay (45840) ***(G-11049)***
Hzw Environmental Cons LLC (PA)....800 804-8484
6105 Heisley Rd Mentor (44060) ***(G-14194)***
I & M J Gross Company (PA)....440 237-1681
14300 Ridge Rd Ste 100 Cleveland (44133) ***(G-5798)***
I A R Inc (PA)....740 432-3371
220 N 8th St Cambridge (43725) ***(G-2121)***
I C S, Cincinnati *Also called Industrial Comm & Sound Inc* ***(G-3816)***
I C S, Groveport *Also called Innovtive Crtive Solutions LLC* ***(G-11647)***
I H S Services Inc....419 224-8811
3225 W Elm St Ste D Lima (45805) ***(G-12802)***
I H Schlezinger Inc....614 252-1188
1041 Joyce Ave Columbus (43219) ***(G-7877)***
I L S, Cleveland *Also called Supply Technologies LLC* ***(G-6556)***
I L T Diversified Mtl Hdlg....419 865-8025
8310 Airport Hwy Holland (43528) ***(G-12029)***
I P S, Cincinnati *Also called Integrated Protection Svcs Inc* ***(G-3827)***
I P S, Rossford *Also called Industrial Power Systems Inc* ***(G-16608)***
I P S Interior Landscaping, Canal Winchester *Also called Rentokil North America Inc* ***(G-2168)***
I Supply Co....937 878-5240
1255 Spangler Rd Fairborn (45324) ***(G-10798)***
I T E LLC....513 576-6200
424 Wards Corner Rd # 300 Loveland (45140) ***(G-13132)***
I V C, Lebanon *Also called Industrial Vibrations Cons* ***(G-12612)***
I Vrable Inc....614 545-5500
3248 Henderson Rd Columbus (43220) ***(G-7878)***
I-Force LLC....614 431-5100
1110 Morse Rd Ste 200 Columbus (43229) ***(G-7879)***
I-Tran Inc....330 659-0801
4100 Congress Pkwy W Richfield (44286) ***(G-16512)***
I-X Center Corporation....216 265-2675
6200 Riverside Dr Cleveland (44135) ***(G-5799)***
IA Urban Htels Bchwood Trs LLC....216 765-8066
3775 Park East Dr Beachwood (44122) ***(G-1088)***
Iacominis Papa Joes Inc....330 923-7999
1561 Akron Peninsula Rd Akron (44313) ***(G-276)***
Iacovetta Builders Inc....614 272-6464
2525 Fisher Rd Columbus (43204) ***(G-7880)***
Iaitam, Canton *Also called International Association of* ***(G-2413)***
Iap Government Services Group, Columbus *Also called Innovative Architectural* ***(G-7900)***
Iarc, Ontario *Also called Intercity Amateur Rdo CLB Inc* ***(G-15693)***
Ibeda Inc Sprflash Gas Equip, Westlake *Also called Applied Marketing Services* ***(G-19460)***
IBH, Coventry Township *Also called Interval Brotherhood Homes* ***(G-9126)***
Ibi, Chillicothe *Also called Ingle-Barr Inc* ***(G-2853)***
IBM, Beavercreek *Also called International Bus Mchs Corp* ***(G-1179)***
IBP Columbus, Columbus *Also called Installed Building Pdts LLC* ***(G-7909)***
Ic Roofing, Mason *Also called Interstate Contractors LLC* ***(G-13723)***
Ice Land USA Lakewood....216 529-1200
14740 Lakewood Hts Blvd Lakewood (44107) ***(G-12482)***
Ice Land USA Ltd....440 268-2800
15381 Royalton Rd Strongsville (44136) ***(G-17475)***
Ice Miller LLP....614 462-2700
250 West St Ste 700 Columbus (43215) ***(G-7881)***
Ice Zone Ltd....330 965-1423
2445 Belmont Ave Youngstown (44505) ***(G-20228)***
ICM, Bedford Heights *Also called Intergrated Consulting* ***(G-1353)***
ICM Distributing Company Inc....234 212-3030
1755 Entp Pkwy Ste 200 Twinsburg (44087) ***(G-18431)***
Icon Environmental Group LLC....513 426-6767
24 Whitney Dr Ste D Milford (45150) ***(G-14526)***
Icon Property Rescue, Milford *Also called Icon Environmental Group LLC* ***(G-14526)***
Icr Engineering, Mason *Also called Icr Inc* ***(G-13718)***
Icr Inc....513 900-7007
4770 Duke Dr Ste 370 Mason (45040) ***(G-13718)***
Ics Electrical Services, Cincinnati *Also called Instrmntation Ctrl Systems Inc* ***(G-3822)***
Icx Corporation (HQ)....330 656-3611
2 Summit Park Dr Ste 105 Cleveland (44131) ***(G-5800)***
ID Networks Inc....440 992-0062
7720 Jefferson Rd Ashtabula (44004) ***(G-749)***
Iddings Trucking Inc....740 568-1780
741 Blue Knob Rd Marietta (45750) ***(G-13453)***
Ideal Company Inc (PA)....937 836-8683
8313 Kimmel Rd Ste A Clayton (45315) ***(G-4911)***
Ideal Image Inc....937 832-1660
115 Haas Dr Englewood (45322) ***(G-10709)***
Ideal Setech LLC....419 782-5522
24862 Elliott Rd Defiance (43512) ***(G-10036)***
Idealease Miami Valley Intl, Cincinnati *Also called Miami Valley Intl Trcks Inc* ***(G-4087)***
Ideastream (PA)....216 916-6100
1375 Euclid Ave Cleveland (44115) ***(G-5801)***
Identitek Systems Inc....330 832-9844
1100 Industrial Ave Sw Massillon (44647) ***(G-13822)***
Idexx Laboratories Inc....330 629-6076
945 Boardman Canfield Rd Youngstown (44512) ***(G-20229)***
Ieh Auto Parts LLC....740 373-8327
123 Tennis Center Dr Marietta (45750) ***(G-13454)***
Ieh Auto Parts LLC....740 732-2395
218 West St Caldwell (43724) ***(G-2086)***
Ieh Auto Parts LLC....216 351-2560
4565 Hinckley Indus Pkwy Cleveland (44109) ***(G-5802)***
Ieh Auto Parts LLC....740 373-8151
121 Tennis Center Dr Marietta (45750) ***(G-13455)***
Ies Infrstrcture Solutions LLC (HQ)....330 830-3500
800 Nave Rd Se Massillon (44646) ***(G-13823)***
Ies Systems Inc....330 533-6683
464 Lisbon St Canfield (44406) ***(G-2196)***
Iet Inc....419 385-1233
3539 Glendale Ave Ste C Toledo (43614) ***(G-17969)***
Iewc Corp....440 835-5601
1991 Crocker Rd Ste 110 Westlake (44145) ***(G-19497)***
Iforce, Columbus *Also called I-Force LLC* ***(G-7879)***
Ifs Financial Services Inc (HQ)....513 362-8000
370 S Cleveland Ave Westerville (43081) ***(G-19410)***
Igh II Inc....419 874-3575
110 Industrial Dr Mansfield (44904) ***(G-13310)***
Igs Solar LLC....844 447-7652
6100 Emerald Pkwy Dublin (43016) ***(G-10373)***
Iheartcommunications Inc....419 625-1010
1640 Cleveland Rd Sandusky (44870) ***(G-16770)***
Iheartcommunications Inc....937 224-1137
101 Pine St Dayton (45402) ***(G-9626)***
Iheartcommunications Inc....614 486-6101
2323 W 5th Ave Ste 200 Columbus (43204) ***(G-7882)***
Iheartcommunications Inc....937 224-1137
101 Pine St Ste 300 Dayton (45402) ***(G-9627)***
Iheartcommunications Inc....216 520-2600
6200 Oak Tree Blvd Fl 4 Cleveland (44131) ***(G-5803)***
Iheartcommunications Inc....419 289-2605
1197 Us Highway 42 Ashland (44805) ***(G-683)***
Iheartcommunications Inc....419 529-2211
1400 Radio Ln Mansfield (44906) ***(G-13311)***
Iheartcommunications Inc....330 965-0057
7461 South Ave Youngstown (44512) ***(G-20230)***
Iheartcommunications Inc....216 409-9673
310 W Lakeside Ave Fl 6 Cleveland (44113) ***(G-5804)***
Iheartcommunications Inc....513 763-5500
1906 Highland Ave Cincinnati (45219) ***(G-3807)***
Iheartcommunications Inc....419 782-9336
2110 Radio Dr Defiance (43512) ***(G-10037)***
Iheartcommunications Inc....419 223-2060
667 W Market St Lima (45801) ***(G-12803)***

Ihg Management (maryland) LLC 614 461-4100
33 E Nationwide Blvd Columbus (43215) **(G-7883)**
IHNWC, Lebanon *Also called Interfaith Hosptlty Ntwrk of W* **(G-12613)**
Ijus LLC (PA) 614 470-9882
690 Taylor Rd Ste 100 Gahanna (43230) **(G-11248)**
Ikps, Fredericktown *Also called Integrity Kokosing Pipeline Sv* **(G-11180)**
Ilead LLC 440 846-2346
20376 Kelsey Ln Strongsville (44149) **(G-17476)**
Ilead Marketing, Strongsville *Also called Ilead LLC* **(G-17476)**
Illinois & Midland RR Inc (HQ) 217 670-1242
4349 Easton Way Ste 110 Columbus (43219) **(G-7884)**
Illinois Central Railroad Co 419 726-6028
4820 Schwartz Rd Toledo (43611) **(G-17970)**
Illinois Tool Works Inc 216 292-7161
26101 Fargo Ave Bedford (44146) **(G-1312)**
Illinois Tool Works Inc 513 891-7474
10125 Carver Rd Blue Ash (45242) **(G-1614)**
Illumetek Corp 330 342-7582
121 E Ascot Ln Cuyahoga Falls (44223) **(G-9195)**
Illumination Research Inc 513 774-9531
5947 Drfield Blvd Ste 203 Mason (45040) **(G-13719)**
Illumination Works LLC 937 938-1321
2689 Cmmons Blvd Ste 120 Beavercreek (45431) **(G-1178)**
Illusion Unlimited, Cleveland *Also called Merle-Holden Enterprises Inc* **(G-6029)**
Ilpea Industries Inc 330 562-2916
1300 Danner Dr Aurora (44202) **(G-842)**
Ils Technology LLC 800 695-8650
6065 Parkland Blvd Cleveland (44124) **(G-5805)**
Ilt Toyota-Lift, Cleveland *Also called Interstate Lift Trucks Inc* **(G-5835)**
Image By J & K LLC 888 667-6929
1575 Henthorne Dr Maumee (43537) **(G-13927)**
Image Consulting Services Inc (PA) 440 951-9919
1775 Donwell Dr Cleveland (44121) **(G-5806)**
Image Engineering Inc 513 541-8544
7038 Golfway Dr Cincinnati (45239) **(G-3808)**
Image Pavement Maintenance 937 833-9200
425 Carr Dr Brookville (45309) **(G-1963)**
Imagepace LLC 513 579-9911
5375 Medpace Way Cincinnati (45227) **(G-3809)**
IMAGINATION STATION, Toledo *Also called Toledo Science Center* **(G-18248)**
Imagistics International, Dayton *Also called Mike Rennie* **(G-9746)**
Imam WD Mohammed Comm Devt, Springfield *Also called Lateef Elmin Mhammad Inv Group* **(G-17220)**
Imcd Us LLC (HQ) 216 228-8900
14725 Detroit Ave Ste 300 Lakewood (44107) **(G-12483)**
Imco Carbide Tool Inc 419 661-6313
28170 Cedar Park Blvd Perrysburg (43551) **(G-16015)**
Imco Recycling of Ohio LLC 740 922-2373
7335 Newport Rd Se Uhrichsville (44683) **(G-18490)**
Imflux Inc 513 488-1017
3550 Symmes Rd Ste 100 Hamilton (45015) **(G-11743)**
Imhoff Construction, Orrville *Also called Ben D Imhoff Inc* **(G-15766)**
Immaculate Interiors 440 324-9300
123 Brace Ave Elyria (44035) **(G-10635)**
Immediate Health Associates 614 794-0481
575 Cpland Mill Rd Ste 1d Westerville (43081) **(G-19411)**
Immediate Medical Service Inc 330 823-0400
2461 W State St Ste E Alliance (44601) **(G-540)**
Impact Ceramics LLC 440 554-3624
17000 Saint Clair Ave # 3 Cleveland (44110) **(G-5807)**
Impact Community Action 614 252-2799
700 Bryden Rd Fl 2 Columbus (43215) **(G-7885)**
Impact Medical Mgt Group 440 365-7014
1120 E Broad St Elyria (44035) **(G-10636)**
Impact Products LLC (HQ) 419 841-2891
2840 Centennial Rd Toledo (43617) **(G-17971)**
Impact Sales Inc 937 274-1905
2501 Neff Rd Dayton (45414) **(G-9628)**
Imperial Alum - Minerva LLC 330 868-7765
217 Roosevelt St Minerva (44657) **(G-14646)**
Imperial Express Inc 937 399-9400
202 N Limestone St # 300 Springfield (45503) **(G-17210)**
Imperial Foods, Cleveland *Also called Gust Gallucci Co* **(G-5711)**
Imperial Heating and Coolg Inc (PA) 440 498-1788
30685 Solon Industrial Pk Solon (44139) **(G-17017)**
Imperial Lumber, Eaton *Also called Maronda Homes Inc Florida* **(G-10566)**
Impressive Packaging Inc 419 368-6808
627 County Rd 30 A Hayesville (44838) **(G-11834)**
Improve It Home Remodeling Inc (PA) 614 297-5121
40 W 1st Ave Columbus (43201) **(G-7886)**
Improvedge LLC 614 793-1738
9878 Brewster Ln 210 Powell (43065) **(G-16338)**
Impullitti & Sons Landscaping, Burton *Also called Impullitti Landscaping Inc* **(G-2063)**
Impullitti Landscaping Inc 440 834-1866
14659 Ravenna Rd Burton (44021) **(G-2063)**
IMS Company 440 543-1615
10373 Stafford Rd Chagrin Falls (44023) **(G-2720)**
IMT, Brunswick *Also called Integrated Marketing Tech Inc* **(G-1982)**
In His Prsence Ministries Intl 614 516-1812
5757 Karl Rd Columbus (43229) **(G-7887)**
In Home Health LLC 419 531-0440
3450 W Central Ave # 132 Toledo (43606) **(G-17972)**
In Home Health LLC 513 831-5800
3960 Red Bank Rd Ste 140 Cincinnati (45227) **(G-3810)**
In Home Health LLC 419 355-9209
907 W State St Ste A Fremont (43420) **(G-11207)**
In Terminal Services Corp 216 518-8407
5300 Greenhurst Ext Maple Heights (44137) **(G-13409)**
In-Plas Recycling Inc 513 541-9800
4211 Crawford Ave Cincinnati (45223) **(G-3811)**
Inacomp Computer Centers, Lewis Center *Also called Pcm Sales Inc* **(G-12702)**
Inc Research LLC 513 381-5550
441 Vine St Ste 1200 Cincinnati (45202) **(G-3812)**
Inc/Ballew A Head Joint Ventr 614 338-5801
4477 E 5th Ave Columbus (43219) **(G-7888)**
Incentisoft Solutions LLC 877 562-4461
20445 Emerald Pkwy # 400 Cleveland (44135) **(G-5808)**
Incept Corporation 330 649-8000
4150 Belden Village St Nw # 205 Canton (44718) **(G-2410)**
Incubit LLC 740 362-1401
40 N Sandusky St Ste 200 Delaware (43015) **(G-10108)**
Indecon Solutions LLC 614 799-1850
655 Metro Pl S Ste 740 Dublin (43017) **(G-10374)**
Independence 10, Akron *Also called Regal Cinemas Inc* **(G-407)**
Independence Bank 216 447-1444
4401 Rockside Rd Cleveland (44131) **(G-5809)**
Independence Business Supply, Cleveland *Also called Indepndence Office Bus Sup Inc* **(G-5815)**
Independence Capital Corp 440 888-7000
5579 Pearl Rd Ste 100 Cleveland (44129) **(G-5810)**
Independence Care Community 419 435-8505
1000 Independence Ave Fostoria (44830) **(G-11133)**
Independence Equipment Lsg Co 216 642-3408
4401 Rockside Rd Cleveland (44131) **(G-5811)**
Independence Excavating Inc (PA) 216 524-1700
5720 E Schaaf Rd Independence (44131) **(G-12218)**
Independence Foundation Inc 330 296-2851
161 E Main St Ravenna (44266) **(G-16389)**
Independence House, Fostoria *Also called Independence Care Community* **(G-11133)**
Independence Local Schools 216 642-5865
6111 Archwood Rd Independence (44131) **(G-12219)**
Independence of Portage County (PA) 330 296-2851
161 E Main St Ravenna (44266) **(G-16390)**
Independence Oncology 216 524-7979
6100 W Creek Rd Ste 16 Cleveland (44131) **(G-5812)**
Independence Place II, Cleveland *Also called Forest City Enterprises LP* **(G-5616)**
Independence Travel 216 447-9950
5000 Rockside Rd Ste 240 Cleveland (44131) **(G-5813)**
Independent Evaluators Inc 419 872-5650
27457 Holiday Ln Ste B Perrysburg (43551) **(G-16016)**
Independent Hotel Partners LLC 216 524-0700
5300 Rockside Rd Cleveland (44131) **(G-5814)**
Independent Living of Ohio 937 323-8400
530 S Burnett Rd Springfield (45505) **(G-17211)**
Independent Order Odd Fellows 740 548-5038
5230 Cypress Dr Lewis Center (43035) **(G-12689)**
Independent Order-Odd Fellows, Conneaut *Also called Odd Fellows Hall* **(G-9045)**
Independent Radio Taxi Inc 330 746-8844
308 And One Half W Youngstown (44503) **(G-20231)**
Independent Steel Company LLC 330 225-7741
615 Liverpool Dr Valley City (44280) **(G-18618)**
Indepndence Office Bus Sup Inc 216 398-8880
4550 Hinckley Indus Pkwy Cleveland (44109) **(G-5815)**
Indian Hills Senior Community 216 486-7700
1541 E 191st St Euclid (44117) **(G-10763)**
Indian Learning Head Start, Bellaire *Also called Community Action Comsn Belmont* **(G-1364)**
Indian Mound Mall, Heath *Also called Glemsure Realty Trust* **(G-11837)**
Indian Nation Inc 740 532-6143
1051 Skyline Cir Se North Canton (44709) **(G-15345)**
Indian Ridge Golf Club L L C 513 524-4653
2600 Oxford Millville Rd Oxford (45056) **(G-15816)**
Indiana & Ohio Central RR 740 385-3127
665 E Front St Logan (43138) **(G-12978)**
Indiana & Ohio Rail, Logan *Also called Indiana & Ohio Central RR* **(G-12978)**
Indiana & Ohio Rail Corp (HQ) 513 860-1000
2856 Cypress Way Cincinnati (45212) **(G-3813)**
Indiana & Ohio Rail Corp 419 229-1010
1750 N Sugar St Lima (45801) **(G-12804)**
Indiana & Ohio Railway Company 513 860-1000
2856 Cypress Way Cincinnati (45212) **(G-3814)**
Indiana Michigan Power Company (HQ) 614 716-1000
1 Riverside Plz Columbus (43215) **(G-7889)**
Indico LLC (HQ) 440 775-7777
528 E Lorain St Oberlin (44074) **(G-15646)**
Indigo Group 513 557-8794
4645 Stonehaven Dr Liberty Twp (45011) **(G-12726)**
Indrolect Co 513 821-4788
630 W Wyoming Ave Cincinnati (45215) **(G-3815)**
Indus Airport Hotel II LLC 614 235-0717
4280 International Gtwy Columbus (43219) **(G-7890)**
Indus Airport Hotels I LLC 614 231-2869
4265 Sawyer Rd Columbus (43219) **(G-7891)**

ALPHABETIC

Indus Hilliard Hotel LLC 614 334-1800
3950 Lyman Dr Hilliard (43026) ***(G-11913)***
Indus Trade & Technology LLC 614 527-0257
2249 Westbrooke Dr Bldg H Columbus (43228) ***(G-7892)***
Indus Valley Consultants Inc (PA) 937 660-4748
1430 Yankee Park Pl Ste A Dayton (45458) ***(G-9629)***
Industrial Air Centers Inc 614 274-9171
2840 Fisher Rd Ste E Columbus (43204) ***(G-7893)***
Industrial Air Control Inc 330 772-6422
1276 Brookfield Rd Hubbard (44425) ***(G-12088)***
Industrial Chemical Corp (PA) 330 725-0800
885 W Smith Rd Medina (44256) ***(G-14079)***
Industrial Cleaning, Canton *Also called MPW Industrial Services Inc* ***(G-2467)***
Industrial Cleaning, Lorain *Also called MPW Industrial Services Inc* ***(G-13062)***
Industrial Comm & Sound Inc 614 276-8123
2105 Schappelle Ln Cincinnati (45240) ***(G-3816)***
Industrial Controls Distrs LLC 513 733-5200
9407 Meridian Way West Chester (45069) ***(G-19092)***
Industrial Energy Systems Inc 216 267-9590
15828 Industrial Pkwy # 3 Cleveland (44135) ***(G-5816)***
Industrial Fiberglass Spc Inc 937 222-9000
521 Kiser St Dayton (45404) ***(G-9630)***
Industrial First Inc (PA) 216 991-8605
25840 Miles Rd Ste 2 Bedford (44146) ***(G-1313)***
Industrial Fluid Management, Mc Clure *Also called Poggemeyer Design Group Inc* ***(G-14020)***
Industrial Insul Coatings LLC 800 506-1399
142 E 2nd St Girard (44420) ***(G-11414)***
Industrial Maint Svcs Inc 440 729-2068
9824 Washington St Ste A Chagrin Falls (44023) ***(G-2721)***
Industrial Mill Maintenance 330 746-1155
1609 Wilson Ave Ste 2 Youngstown (44506) ***(G-20232)***
Industrial Origami Inc 440 260-0000
6755 Engle Rd Ste A Cleveland (44130) ***(G-5817)***
Industrial Parts & Service Co 330 966-5025
6440 Promler St Nw Canton (44720) ***(G-2411)***
Industrial Parts and Service, Canton *Also called Industrial Parts & Service Co* ***(G-2411)***
Industrial Power Systems Inc 419 531-3121
146 Dixie Hwy Rossford (43460) ***(G-16608)***
Industrial Repair & Mfg Inc (PA) 419 822-4232
1140 E Main St Ste A Delta (43515) ***(G-10159)***
Industrial Sorting Svcs Inc 513 772-6501
2599 Commerce Blvd Cincinnati (45241) ***(G-3817)***
Industrial Tube and Steel Corp (PA) 330 474-5530
4658 Crystal Pkwy Kent (44240) ***(G-12374)***
Industrial Vibrations Cons (PA) 513 932-4678
210 S West St Lebanon (45036) ***(G-12612)***
Industrial Waste Control Inc 330 270-9900
240 Sinter Ct Youngstown (44510) ***(G-20233)***
Industry Insights Inc 614 389-2100
6235 Emerald Pkwy Columbus (43235) ***(G-7894)***
Industry Products Co (PA) 937 778-0585
500 W Statler Rd Piqua (45356) ***(G-16150)***
Inertial Aerospace Services, Cleveland *Also called Inertial Airline Services Inc* ***(G-5818)***
Inertial Airline Services Inc 440 995-6555
375 Alpha Park Cleveland (44143) ***(G-5818)***
Inet Interactive LLC 513 322-5600
9100 W Chester Towne Ctr # 200 West Chester (45069) ***(G-19093)***
Infectious Diseases Department, Columbus *Also called Ohio State University* ***(G-8415)***
Infinite SEC Solutions LLC 419 720-5678
663 Gawil Ave Toledo (43609) ***(G-17973)***
Infinite Shares LLC 216 317-1601
9401 Mentor Ave 167 Mentor (44060) ***(G-14195)***
Infinity, Cleveland *Also called Aleph Home & Senior Care Inc* ***(G-4983)***
Infinity Health Services Inc (PA) 440 614-0145
975 Crocker Rd A Westlake (44145) ***(G-19498)***
Influent, Dublin *Also called Pccw Teleservices (us) Inc* ***(G-10424)***
Info Line Inc 330 252-8064
703 S Main St Ste 200 Akron (44311) ***(G-277)***
Info Trak &, Mansfield *Also called Info Trak Incorporated* ***(G-13312)***
Info Trak Incorporated 419 747-9296
165 Marion Ave Mansfield (44903) ***(G-13312)***
Infoaccessnet LLC 216 328-0100
8801 E Pleasant Valley Rd Cleveland (44131) ***(G-5819)***
Infocision Management Corp (PA) 330 668-1411
325 Springside Dr Akron (44333) ***(G-278)***
Infocision Management Corp 330 726-0872
6951 Southern Blvd Ste E Youngstown (44512) ***(G-20234)***
Infocision Management Corp 419 529-8685
1404 Park Ave E Mansfield (44905) ***(G-13313)***
Infocision Management Corp 330 668-6615
250 N Clvland Mssillon Rd Akron (44333) ***(G-279)***
Infocision Management Corp 937 259-2400
101 Woodman Dr Dayton (45431) ***(G-9274)***
Infocision Management Corp 330 544-1400
5740 Interstate Blvd Youngstown (44515) ***(G-20235)***
Infoquest Information Services 614 761-3003
2000 Henderson Rd Ste 300 Columbus (43220) ***(G-7895)***
Infor (us) Inc 678 319-8000
2800 Corp Exchange Dr # 350 Columbus (43231) ***(G-7896)***
Infor (us) Inc 614 781-2325
8760 Orion Pl Ste 300 Columbus (43240) ***(G-6886)***
Information & Referral Center, Lima *Also called County of Allen* ***(G-12764)***
Information Builders Inc 513 891-2338
1 Financial Way Ste 307 Montgomery (45242) ***(G-14726)***
Information Control Corp 614 523-3070
2500 Corporate Exch Dr Columbus (43231) ***(G-7897)***
Information Management Svcs, Columbus *Also called Document Imging Spcialists LLC* ***(G-7538)***
Information Systems Dept, Batavia *Also called County of Clermont* ***(G-1006)***
Infoscitex Corporation 937 429-9008
4027 Colonel Glenn Hwy # 210 Beavercreek Township (45431) ***(G-1270)***
Infostore LLC 216 749-4636
1200 E Granger Rd Cleveland (44131) ***(G-5820)***
Infotelecom Holdings LLC (PA) 216 373-4811
75 Erieview Plz Fl 4 Cleveland (44114) ***(G-5821)***
Infoverity LLC 614 327-5173
5131 Post Rd Ste 220 Dublin (43017) ***(G-10375)***
Infovision 21 Inc 614 761-8844
6077 Frantz Rd Ste 105 Dublin (43017) ***(G-10376)***
Infra-Metals Co 740 353-1350
1 Sturgill Way Portsmouth (45662) ***(G-16290)***
Infusion Partners Inc (HQ) 513 396-6060
4623 Wesley Ave Ste H Cincinnati (45212) ***(G-3818)***
Ingersoll-Rand Company 419 633-6800
209 N Main St Bryan (43506) ***(G-2008)***
Ingle-Barr Inc (PA) 740 702-6117
20 Plyleys Ln Chillicothe (45601) ***(G-2853)***
Ingleside Investments Inc 614 221-1025
1036 S Front St Columbus (43206) ***(G-7898)***
Ingram Entrmt Holdings Inc 419 662-3132
668 1st St Perrysburg (43551) ***(G-16017)***
Initial Tropical Plant Svcs, Groveport *Also called Rentokil North America Inc* ***(G-11666)***
Injection Molders Supply, Chagrin Falls *Also called IMS Company* ***(G-2720)***
Inland Products Inc (PA) 614 443-3425
599 Frank Rd Columbus (43223) ***(G-7899)***
Inland Waters of Ohio, Youngstown *Also called Hydrochem LLC* ***(G-20225)***
Inliner American Inc 614 529-6440
4143 Weaver Ct S Hilliard (43026) ***(G-11914)***
Inloes Heating and Cooling, Hamilton *Also called Inloes Mechanical Inc* ***(G-11744)***
Inloes Mechanical Inc 513 896-9499
157 N B St Hamilton (45013) ***(G-11744)***
Inman Nationwide Shipping, Cleveland *Also called Cremation Service Inc* ***(G-5436)***
Inn At Chestnut Hill, The, Columbus *Also called Chestnut Hill Management Co* ***(G-7256)***
Inn At Christine Valley 330 270-3347
3150 S Schenley Ave Youngstown (44511) ***(G-20236)***
Inn At Hillenvale Ltd 740 392-8245
1615 Yauger Rd Ste B26 Mount Vernon (43050) ***(G-14900)***
Inn At Honey Run, Millersburg *Also called Honey Run Retreats LLC* ***(G-14607)***
Inn At Lakeview 614 836-2866
4000 Lakeview Xing Ofc Groveport (43125) ***(G-11646)***
Inn At Marietta Ltd 740 373-9600
150 Browns Rd Ofc Marietta (45750) ***(G-13456)***
Inn At Medina Limited LLC 330 723-0110
100 High Point Dr Ofc Medina (44256) ***(G-14080)***
Inn At Medina The, Medina *Also called Inn At Medina Limited LLC* ***(G-14080)***
Inn At North Hills, Zanesville *Also called North Hills Management Company* ***(G-20517)***
Inn At Univ Vlg MGT Co LLC 330 837-3000
2650 Ohio State Dr Se Massillon (44646) ***(G-13824)***
Inn At Wickliffe LLC 440 585-0600
28600 Ridgehills Dr Wickliffe (44092) ***(G-19603)***
Inn On The Square, Newark *Also called Longaberger Company* ***(G-15197)***
Inn, The, Versailles *Also called Renaissance Corporation* ***(G-18729)***
Inner City Nursing Home 216 795-1363
9014 Cedar Ave Cleveland (44106) ***(G-5822)***
Inner-Space Cleaning Corp 440 646-0701
6151 Wilson Mills Rd # 240 Cleveland (44143) ***(G-5823)***
Innerworkings Inc 513 984-9500
7141 E Kemper Rd Cincinnati (45249) ***(G-3819)***
Inno-Pak LLC (PA) 740 363-0090
1932 Pittsburgh Dr Delaware (43015) ***(G-10109)***
Innomark Communications, Fairfield *Also called Pakmark LLC* ***(G-10892)***
Innomark Communications LLC 937 425-6152
12080 Mosteller Rd Sharonville (45241) ***(G-16882)***
Innosource, West Chester *Also called Vallen Distribution Inc* ***(G-19177)***
Innovairre Communications LLC 330 869-8500
3200 W Market St Ste 302 Fairlawn (44333) ***(G-10957)***
Innovative Architectural 614 416-0614
2740 Airport Dr Ste 300 Columbus (43219) ***(G-7900)***
Innovative Concept, Girard *Also called Boardman Medical Supply Co* ***(G-11408)***
Innovative Controls Corp 419 691-6684
1354 E Broadway St Toledo (43605) ***(G-17974)***
Innovative Dialysis of Toledo 419 473-9900
3829 Woodley Rd Ste 12 Toledo (43606) ***(G-17975)***
Innovative Enrgy Solutions LLC 937 228-3044
3680 Symmes Rd Hamilton (45015) ***(G-11745)***
Innovative Joint Utility Svcs, Gahanna *Also called Ijus LLC* ***(G-11248)***
Innovative Logistics Group Inc 937 832-9350
30 Lau Pkwy Englewood (45315) ***(G-10710)***
Innovative Logistics Svcs Inc 330 468-6422
201 E Twinsburg Rd Northfield (44067) ***(G-15517)***

Innovative Studnt Ln Solutions, Cincinnati *Also called Student Loan Strategies LLC* ***(G-4597)***
Innovative Technologies Corp (PA)....937 252-2145
1020 Woodman Dr Ste 100 Dayton (45432) ***(G-9275)***
Innovel Solutions Inc....614 878-2092
5330 Crosswind Dr Columbus (43228) ***(G-7901)***
Innovel Solutions Inc....614 492-5304
4100 Lockbourne Industria Columbus (43207) ***(G-7902)***
Innovis Data Solutions Inc....614 222-4343
250 E Broad St Columbus (43215) ***(G-7903)***
Innovtive Cllectn Concepts Inc....513 489-5500
11353 Reed Hartman Hwy # 100 Blue Ash (45241) ***(G-1615)***
Innovtive Crtive Solutions LLC....614 491-9638
5835 Green Pointe Dr S B Groveport (43125) ***(G-11647)***
Innovtive Sltons Unlimited LLC (PA)....740 289-3282
1862 Shyville Rd Piketon (45661) ***(G-16118)***
Innovtive Sltons Unlimited LLC....740 289-3282
1862 Shyville Rd Piketon (45661) ***(G-16119)***
Inovative Facility Svcs LLC....419 861-1710
1573 Henthorne Dr Maumee (43537) ***(G-13928)***
Inprem Hlstic Cmnty Rsurce Ctr, Columbus *Also called In His Prsence Ministries Intl* ***(G-7887)***
Inquiry Systems Inc....614 464-3800
1195 Goodale Blvd Columbus (43212) ***(G-7904)***
Inreality LLC....513 218-9603
403 Vine St Ste 200 Cincinnati (45202) ***(G-3820)***
Inside Foodland, Gallipolis *Also called Ohio Valley Bank Company* ***(G-11330)***
Inside Out (PA)....937 525-7880
501 S Wittenberg Ave Springfield (45506) ***(G-17212)***
Inside Out Child Care, Springfield *Also called Inside Out* ***(G-17212)***
Inside Outfitters, Lewis Center *Also called Lumenomics Inc* ***(G-12693)***
Insight Communications, Columbus *Also called Time Warner Cable Inc* ***(G-8847)***
Insight Communications of Co....614 236-1200
3770 E Livingston Ave Columbus (43227) ***(G-7905)***
Insight Direct Usa Inc....614 456-0423
375 N Front St Columbus (43215) ***(G-7906)***
Insight Ohio, Columbus *Also called Insight Communications of Co* ***(G-7905)***
Insight Technical Services, Sandusky *Also called All Phase Power and Ltg Inc* ***(G-16725)***
Inspection Group Incorporated....614 891-3606
440 Polaris Pkwy Ste 170 Westerville (43082) ***(G-19316)***
Installed Building Pdts II LLC....626 812-6070
495 S High St Ste 50 Columbus (43215) ***(G-7907)***
Installed Building Pdts Inc (PA)....614 221-3399
495 S High St Ste 50 Columbus (43215) ***(G-7908)***
Installed Building Pdts LLC....614 308-9900
1320 Mckinley Ave Ste A Columbus (43222) ***(G-7909)***
Installed Building Pdts LLC....330 798-9640
2783 Gilchrist Rd Unit B Akron (44305) ***(G-280)***
Installed Building Pdts LLC....419 662-4524
6412 Fairfield Dr Ste A Northwood (43619) ***(G-15534)***
Installed Products & Services, West Chester *Also called Reading Rock Residential LLC* ***(G-19223)***
Instanceworkplace, Columbus *Also called M J S Holding* ***(G-8092)***
Instant Tax Service, Beavercreek *Also called Its Financial LLC* ***(G-1247)***
Instantwhip Foods Inc....330 688-8825
4870 Hudson Dr Stow (44224) ***(G-17375)***
Instantwhip-Akron Inc....614 488-2536
4870 Hudson Dr Stow (44224) ***(G-17376)***
Instantwhip-Columbus Inc (HQ)....614 871-9447
3855 Marlane Dr Grove City (43123) ***(G-11571)***
Institute Environmental Health, Cincinnati *Also called University of Cincinnati* ***(G-4766)***
Institute For Human Services (PA)....614 251-6000
1706 E Broad St Columbus (43203) ***(G-7910)***
Institute For Orthpdic Surgery, Lima *Also called West Central Ohio Group Ltd* ***(G-12915)***
Institute/Reproductive Health....513 585-2355
2123 Auburn Ave Ste A44 Cincinnati (45219) ***(G-3821)***
Institutional Care Pharmacy (PA)....419 447-6216
1815 W County Road 54 Tiffin (44883) ***(G-17681)***
Institutional Foods, Warren *Also called J V Hansel Inc* ***(G-18866)***
Instrmntation Ctrl Systems Inc....513 662-2600
11355 Sebring Dr Cincinnati (45240) ***(G-3822)***
Insulating Sales Co Inc....513 742-2600
11430 Sebring Dr Cincinnati (45240) ***(G-3823)***
Insulation Northwest, Columbus *Also called Installed Building Pdts II LLC* ***(G-7907)***
Insurance Intermediaries Inc....614 846-1111
280 N High St Ste 300 Columbus (43215) ***(G-7911)***
Integer Holdings Corporation....216 937-2800
1771 E 30th St Cleveland (44114) ***(G-5824)***
Integra Cncinnati/Columbus Inc....614 764-8040
6241 Riverside Dr Dublin (43017) ***(G-10377)***
Integra Group Inc....513 326-5600
16 Triangle Park Dr # 1600 Cincinnati (45246) ***(G-3824)***
Integra Ohio Inc....513 378-5214
4900 Charlemar Dr Bldg A Cincinnati (45227) ***(G-3825)***
Integra Realty Resources - Cin....513 561-2305
8241 Cornell Rd Ste 210 Cincinnati (45249) ***(G-3826)***
Integrated AG Services, Milford Center *Also called Champaign Premium Grn Growers* ***(G-14575)***
Integrated CC LLC....216 707-4132
8650 Euclid Ave Cleveland (44106) ***(G-5825)***
Integrated Data Services Inc....937 656-5496
111 Harries St Apt 202 Dayton (45402) ***(G-9631)***
Integrated Marketing Tech Inc....330 225-3550
2945 Carquest Dr Brunswick (44212) ***(G-1982)***
Integrated Power Services LLC....216 433-7808
5325 W 130th St Cleveland (44130) ***(G-5826)***
Integrated Power Services LLC....513 863-8816
2175a Schlichter Dr Hamilton (45015) ***(G-11746)***
Integrated Prj Resources LLC....330 272-0998
600 E 2nd St Salem (44460) ***(G-16701)***
Integrated Protection Svcs Inc (PA)....513 631-5505
5303 Lester Rd Cincinnati (45213) ***(G-3827)***
Integrated Services of Appala....740 594-6807
11 Graham Dr Athens (45701) ***(G-794)***
Integrated Solutions and....513 826-1932
1430 Yankee Park Pl Dayton (45458) ***(G-9632)***
Integrated Telehealth Inc....216 373-2221
75 Milford Dr Ste 201 Hudson (44236) ***(G-12124)***
Integrated Youth Services Inc....937 427-3837
1055 E High St Springfield (45505) ***(G-17213)***
Integres Fast Forward Shipping, Medina *Also called Integres Global Logistics Inc* ***(G-14081)***
Integres Global Logistics Inc (HQ)....866 347-2101
84 Medina Rd Medina (44256) ***(G-14081)***
Integrity Enterprizes (PA)....216 289-8801
27801 Euclid Ave Ste 440 Euclid (44132) ***(G-10764)***
Integrity Ex Logistics LLC....888 374-5138
4420 Cooper Rd Cincinnati (45242) ***(G-3828)***
Integrity Global Marketing LLC....330 492-9989
4735 Belpar St Nw Canton (44718) ***(G-2412)***
Integrity Gymnstics Chrleading....614 733-0818
8185 Business Way Plain City (43064) ***(G-16194)***
Integrity Hotel Group....937 224-0800
33 E 5th St Dayton (45402) ***(G-9633)***
Integrity Information Tech Inc....937 846-1769
2742 N Dayton Lakeview Rd New Carlisle (45344) ***(G-15024)***
Integrity It, New Carlisle *Also called Integrity Information Tech Inc* ***(G-15024)***
Integrity Kokosing Pipeline Sv....740 694-6315
17531 Waterford Rd Fredericktown (43019) ***(G-11180)***
Integrity Processing LLC....330 285-6937
1055 Wooster Rd N Barberton (44203) ***(G-966)***
Integrity Stainless, Streetsboro *Also called Olympic Steel Inc* ***(G-17423)***
Integrity Stainless, Streetsboro *Also called Is Acquisition Inc* ***(G-17417)***
Integrity Wall & Ceiling Inc....419 381-1855
5242 Angola Rd Ste 180 Toledo (43615) ***(G-17976)***
Integrted Prcision Systems Inc....330 963-0064
9321 Ravenna Rd Ste C Twinsburg (44087) ***(G-18432)***
Intelisol Inc....614 409-0052
4555 Creekside Pkwy Lockbourne (43137) ***(G-12956)***
Intellicorp Records Inc....216 450-5200
3000 Auburn Dr Ste 410 Beachwood (44122) ***(G-1089)***
Intelligent Information Inc....513 860-4233
4838 Duff Dr Ste C West Chester (45246) ***(G-19210)***
Intelligrated Systems Inc (HQ)....866 936-7300
7901 Innovation Way Mason (45040) ***(G-13720)***
Intelligrated Systems LLC....513 701-7300
7901 Innovation Way Mason (45040) ***(G-13721)***
Intelligrated Systems Ohio LLC (HQ)....513 701-7300
7901 Innovation Way Mason (45040) ***(G-13722)***
Intellinet Corporation (PA)....216 289-4100
1111 Chester Ave Ste 200 Cleveland (44114) ***(G-5827)***
Intellinex LLC....216 685-6000
6000 Fredom Sq Dr Ste 100 Independence (44131) ***(G-12220)***
Intelliq Health....513 489-8838
5050 Section Ave Ste 320 Cincinnati (45212) ***(G-3829)***
Intellitarget Marketing Svcs, Coshocton *Also called ITM Marketing Inc* ***(G-9108)***
Inter Distr Svcs of Cleve....330 468-4949
8055 Highland Pointe Pkwy Macedonia (44056) ***(G-13203)***
Inter Healt Care of Cambr Zane (PA)....614 436-9404
960 Checkrein Ave Ste A Columbus (43229) ***(G-7912)***
Inter Healt Care of Cambr Zane....513 984-1110
8050 Hosbrook Rd Ste 406 Cincinnati (45236) ***(G-3830)***
Inter Healt Care of North OH I....740 453-5130
2806 Bell St Zanesville (43701) ***(G-20490)***
Inter Healt Care of North OH I....419 422-5328
2129 Stephen Ave Ste 3 Ste 2 Findlay (45840) ***(G-11050)***
Inter Tel, West Chester *Also called Mitel (delaware) Inc* ***(G-19122)***
Interact For Health....513 458-6600
3805 Edwards Rd Ste 500 Cincinnati (45209) ***(G-3831)***
Interact One Inc....513 469-7042
4665 Cornell Rd Ste 255 Blue Ash (45241) ***(G-1616)***
Interactive Bus Systems Inc....513 984-2205
130 Tri County Pkwy # 208 Cincinnati (45246) ***(G-3832)***
Interactive Engineering Corp....330 239-6888
884 Medina Rd Medina (44256) ***(G-14082)***
Interactive Solutions Intl LLC....513 619-5100
155 Tri County Pkwy 111 Cincinnati (45246) ***(G-3833)***
Interbake Foods LLC....614 294-4931
1740 Joyce Ave Columbus (43219) ***(G-7913)***
Interbake Foods LLC....614 294-4931
1700 E 17th Ave Columbus (43219) ***(G-7914)***

ALPHABETIC

Interbrand Design Forum Inc — ALPHABETIC SECTION

Interbrand Design Forum Inc 937 439-4400
700 W Pete Rose Way # 460 Cincinnati (45203) *(G-3834)*

Interbrand Hulefeld Inc 513 421-2210
700 W Pete Rose Way Cincinnati (45203) *(G-3835)*

Interchez Lgistics Systems Inc 330 923-5080
600 Alpha Pkwy Stow (44224) *(G-17377)*

Intercity Amateur Rdo CLB Inc 419 989-3429
120 Homewood Rd Ontario (44906) *(G-15693)*

Intercnnect Cbling Netwrk Svcs 440 891-0465
125 Pelret Indus Pkwy Berea (44017) *(G-1461)*

Intercntnntal Ht Group Rsurces 216 707-4300
8800 Euclid Ave Cleveland (44106) *(G-5828)*

Intercoastal Trnsp Systems 513 829-1287
5284 Winton Rd Fairfield (45014) *(G-10862)*

Intercontinental Hotels Group 216 707-4100
9801 Carnegie Ave Cleveland (44106) *(G-5829)*

Interdesign Inc 440 248-0136
30725 Solon Indus Pkwy Solon (44139) *(G-17018)*

Interdyne Corporation 419 229-8192
931 N Jefferson St Lima (45801) *(G-12805)*

Interfaith Hosptlty Ntwrk of W 513 934-5250
203 E Warren St Lebanon (45036) *(G-12613)*

Intergrated Consulting 216 214-7547
5311 Northfield Rd Bedford Heights (44146) *(G-1353)*

Interim Halthcare Columbus Inc (HQ) 614 888-3130
784 Morrison Rd Gahanna (43230) *(G-11249)*

Interim Halthcare Columbus Inc 330 836-5571
3040 W Market St Ste 1 Fairlawn (44333) *(G-10958)*

Interim Halthcare Columbus Inc 740 349-8700
900 Sharon Valley Rd Newark (43055) *(G-15177)*

INTERIM HEALTHCARE, Columbus *Also called Salo Inc* *(G-8679)*

Interim Healthcare, Zanesville *Also called Inter Healt Care of North OH I* *(G-20490)*

Interim Healthcare (PA) 740 354-5550
4130 Gallia St Portsmouth (45662) *(G-16291)*

Interim Healthcare of Dayton 937 291-5330
30 W Rahn Rd Ste 2 Dayton (45429) *(G-9634)*

Interim Healthcare SE Ohio Inc 740 373-3800
1017 Pike St Marietta (45750) *(G-13457)*

Interim Services, Fairlawn *Also called Interim Hlthcare Columbus Inc* *(G-10958)*

Interim Services, Findlay *Also called Inter Healt Care of North OH I* *(G-11050)*

Interim Services, Newark *Also called Interim Hlthcare Columbus Inc* *(G-15177)*

Interim Services, Columbus *Also called Inter Healt Care of Cambr Zane* *(G-7912)*

Interim Services, Cincinnati *Also called Inter Healt Care of Cambr Zane* *(G-3830)*

Interior Supply Cincinnati LLC 614 424-6611
481 E 11th Ave Columbus (43211) *(G-7915)*

Internal Mdcine Cons of Clmbus 614 878-6413
104 N Murray Hill Rd Columbus (43228) *(G-7916)*

Internal Medical Center, Akron *Also called Summa Health System* *(G-458)*

Internal Medical Physicians 330 868-3711
1168 Alliance Rd Nw Minerva (44657) *(G-14647)*

Internal Medicine, Columbus *Also called Ohio State University* *(G-8390)*

Internal Medicine of Akron 330 376-2728
150 Springside Dr 320c Akron (44333) *(G-281)*

Internash Global Svc Group LLC 513 772-0430
4621 Interstate Dr West Chester (45246) *(G-19211)*

International Assn Lions 740 986-6502
24920 Locust Grove Rd Williamsport (43164) *(G-19638)*

International Assn Lions Clubs, Newark *Also called Licking Valley Lions Club* *(G-15195)*

International Association of (PA) 330 628-3012
4848 Munson St Nw Canton (44718) *(G-2413)*

International Bus Mchs Corp 917 406-7400
3000 Presidential Dr # 300 Beavercreek (45324) *(G-1179)*

International Chem Wkrs Cr Un (PA) 330 926-1444
1655 W Market St Fl 6 Akron (44313) *(G-282)*

International Data MGT Inc (PA) 330 869-8500
3200 W Market St Ste 302 Fairlawn (44333) *(G-10959)*

International Exposition Ctr, Cleveland *Also called I-X Center Corporation* *(G-5799)*

International Frat of Del 330 922-5959
2735 Elmwood St Cuyahoga Falls (44221) *(G-9196)*

International Healthcare Corp 513 731-3338
2837 Burnet Ave Cincinnati (45219) *(G-3836)*

International Management Group (PA) 216 522-1200
1360 E 9th St Ste 100 Cleveland (44114) *(G-5830)*

International Masonry Inc 614 469-8338
135 Spruce St Columbus (43215) *(G-7917)*

International Mdsg Corp (HQ) 216 522-1200
1360 E 9th St Ste 100 Cleveland (44114) *(G-5831)*

International Merchants, Blue Ash *Also called Req/Jqh Holdings Inc* *(G-1681)*

International MGT Counsel, Sandusky *Also called YMCA of Sandusky Ohio Inc* *(G-16811)*

International Ordr of Rnbow Fo 419 862-3009
18706 W State Route 105 Elmore (43416) *(G-10588)*

International Paper, Toledo *Also called Veritiv Operating Company* *(G-18289)*

International Paper, Fairfield *Also called Veritiv Operating Company* *(G-10922)*

International Paper Compa 513 248-6000
6283 Tri Ridge Blvd Loveland (45140) *(G-13133)*

International Steel Group 330 841-2800
2234 Main Street Ext Sw Warren (44481) *(G-18865)*

International Technegroup Inc (PA) 513 576-3900
5303 Dupont Cir Milford (45150) *(G-14527)*

International Truck & Eng Corp 937 390-4045
6125 Urbana Rd Springfield (45502) *(G-17214)*

International Un Elev Constrs 614 291-5859
23 W 2nd Ave Ste C Columbus (43201) *(G-7918)*

International Union United Au 216 447-6080
5000 Rockside Rd Ste 300 Cleveland (44131) *(G-5832)*

International Union United Au 513 897-4939
8137 Lytle Trails Rd Waynesville (45068) *(G-18984)*

International Union United Au 513 563-1252
10708 Reading Rd Cincinnati (45241) *(G-3837)*

International Union United Au 419 893-4677
1691 Woodlands Dr Maumee (43537) *(G-13929)*

International Union Elvtor Cns, Columbus *Also called International Un Elev Constrs* *(G-7918)*

Internatl Un Oper Eng 18 (PA) 216 432-3131
3515 Prospect Ave E Fl 1 Cleveland (44115) *(G-5833)*

Interntional Assn Firefighters 330 823-5222
63 E Broadway St Alliance (44601) *(G-541)*

Interntional Molasses Corp Ltd 937 276-7980
4744 Wolf Creek Pike Dayton (45417) *(G-9635)*

Interntional Towers I Ohio Ltd 216 520-1250
25 Market St Youngstown (44503) *(G-20237)*

Interntnal Pckg Pallets Crates, Sidney *Also called Wappoo Wood Products Inc* *(G-16960)*

Interntnal Spcial Adit Systems, Cleveland *Also called First Federal Credit Control* *(G-5596)*

Interntonal Aliance Thea Stage 440 734-4883
4689 Georgette Ave North Olmsted (44070) *(G-15427)*

Interphace Phtgrphy Cmmnctions 254 289-6270
1365 Meadowlark Ln Amelia (45102) *(G-581)*

Interscope Manufacturing Inc 513 423-8866
2901 Carmody Blvd Middletown (45042) *(G-14429)*

Interstate Coml GL & Door, Northwood *Also called A E D Inc* *(G-15526)*

Interstate Construction Inc 614 539-1188
3511 Farm Bank Way Grove City (43123) *(G-11572)*

Interstate Contractors LLC 513 372-5393
762 Reading Rd G Mason (45040) *(G-13723)*

Interstate Diesel Service Inc (PA) 216 881-0015
5300 Lakeside Ave E Cleveland (44114) *(G-5834)*

Interstate Fire & SEC Systems 330 453-9495
3271 Bruening Ave Sw Canton (44706) *(G-2414)*

Interstate Gas Supply Inc (PA) 614 659-5000
6100 Emerald Pkwy Dublin (43016) *(G-10378)*

Interstate Lanes of Ohio Ltd 419 666-2695
819 Lime City Rd Rossford (43460) *(G-16609)*

Interstate Lift Truck, Holland *Also called Devirsified Material Handling* *(G-12019)*

Interstate Lift Trucks Inc 216 328-0970
5667 E Schaaf Rd Cleveland (44131) *(G-5835)*

Interstate McBee, Cleveland *Also called McBee Supply Corporation* *(G-6001)*

Interstate Optical Co (HQ) 419 529-6800
680 Lindaire Ln E Ontario (44906) *(G-15694)*

Interstate Shredding LLC 330 545-5477
27 Furnace Ln Girard (44420) *(G-11415)*

Interstate Truckway Inc 614 771-1220
5440 Renner Rd Columbus (43228) *(G-7919)*

Interstate Truckway Inc (PA) 513 542-5500
1755 Dreman Ave Cincinnati (45223) *(G-3838)*

Interstate Warehousing VA LLC 513 874-6500
110 Distribution Dr Fairfield (45014) *(G-10863)*

Interstate-Mcbee, Cleveland *Also called Interstate Diesel Service Inc* *(G-5834)*

Intertec Corporation 419 537-9711
3400 Executive Pkwy Toledo (43606) *(G-17977)*

Intertek Testing Svcs NA Inc 614 279-8090
1717 Arlingate Ln Columbus (43228) *(G-7920)*

Interval Brotherhood Homes 330 644-4095
3445 S Main St Coventry Township (44319) *(G-9126)*

Intervention For Peace Inc 330 725-1298
689 W Liberty St Ste 7 Medina (44256) *(G-14083)*

Intex Supply Company 216 535-4300
26301 Curtiss Wright Pkwy Richmond Heights (44143) *(G-16539)*

Intgrted Bridge Communications 513 381-1380
302 W 3rd St Ste 900 Cincinnati (45202) *(G-3839)*

Intitle Agency Inc 513 241-8780
120 E 4th St Ste 400 Cincinnati (45202) *(G-3840)*

Intl Europa Salon & Spa 216 292-6969
24700 Chagrin Blvd # 101 Cleveland (44122) *(G-5836)*

Intown Suites Management Inc 937 433-9038
8981 Kingsridge Dr Dayton (45458) *(G-9636)*

Intralot Inc 440 268-2900
13500 Darice Pkwy Ste C Strongsville (44149) *(G-17477)*

Intren Inc 815 482-0651
1267 Tennessee Ave Cincinnati (45229) *(G-3841)*

Intrepid USA Healthcare Svcs, Elyria *Also called NC Hha Inc* *(G-10658)*

Intrigue Salon & Day Spa 330 493-7003
4762 Dressler Rd Nw Canton (44718) *(G-2415)*

Intrust It, Blue Ash *Also called Lan Solutions Inc* *(G-1624)*

Inventory Controlled Mdsg, Twinsburg *Also called ICM Distributing Company Inc* *(G-18431)*

Inverness Club 419 578-9000
4601 Dorr St Ste 1 Toledo (43615) *(G-17978)*

Invest, Tiffin *Also called Old Fort Banking Company* *(G-17692)*

Investek Management Svcs F/C 419 873-1236
1090 W South Boundary St # 100 Perrysburg (43551) *(G-16018)*

Investek Realty LLC...419 873-1236
1090 W South Boundary St # 100 Perrysburg (43551) ***(G-16019)***
Investmerica limited...216 618-3296
547 Washington St Ste 10 Chagrin Falls (44022) ***(G-2701)***
Invotec Engineering Inc...937 886-3232
10909 Industry Ln Miamisburg (45342) ***(G-14307)***
Ionno Properties s Corp...330 479-9267
4412 Pleasant Vly Rd Se Dennison (44621) ***(G-10165)***
Ioof Home of Ohio Inc (PA)...937 399-8631
404 E Mccreight Ave Springfield (45503) ***(G-17215)***
Iowa 80 Group, Hebron *Also called Truckomat Corporation* ***(G-11861)***
Ipi, Hayesville *Also called Impressive Packaging Inc* ***(G-11834)***
Ips, Avon Lake *Also called Catamaran Home Dlvry Ohio Inc* ***(G-924)***
Ipsos-Asi LLC...513 872-4300
3505 Columbia Pkwy # 300 Cincinnati (45226) ***(G-3842)***
Ipsos-Asi, Inc., Cincinnati *Also called Ipsos-Asi LLC* ***(G-3842)***
Ipsos-Insight LLC...513 552-1100
11499 Chester Rd Ste 401 Cincinnati (45246) ***(G-3843)***
Iq Innovations LLC...614 222-0882
580 N 4th St Ste 560 Columbus (43215) ***(G-7921)***
Irace Inc...330 836-7247
2265 W Market St Akron (44313) ***(G-283)***
Irace Automotive, Akron *Also called Irace Inc* ***(G-283)***
Ireland Cancer Center, Cleveland *Also called University Hospitals* ***(G-6657)***
Irg Operating LLC...440 963-4008
850 W River Rd Vermilion (44089) ***(G-18711)***
Irg Realty Advisors LLC (PA)...330 659-4060
4020 Kinross Lakes Pkwy Richfield (44286) ***(G-16513)***
Irish Envy LLC...440 808-8000
30307 Detroit Rd Westlake (44145) ***(G-19499)***
Iron City Distributing, Mingo Junction *Also called Bellas Co* ***(G-14653)***
Iron Mountain Incorporated...513 874-3535
9247 Meridian Way West Chester (45069) ***(G-19094)***
Iron Mountain Incorporated...614 801-0151
3250 Urbancrest Indus Dr Urbancrest (43123) ***(G-18605)***
Iron Mountain Info MGT LLC...513 297-3268
5845 Highland Ridge Dr Cincinnati (45232) ***(G-3844)***
Iron Mountain Info MGT LLC...513 942-7300
3790 Symmes Rd Hamilton (45015) ***(G-11747)***
Iron Mountain Info MGT LLC...513 297-1906
9247 Meridian Way West Chester (45069) ***(G-19095)***
Iron Mountain Info MGT LLC...614 840-9321
4848 Evanswood Dr Columbus (43229) ***(G-7922)***
Iron Mountain Info MGT LLC...440 248-0999
5101 Naiman Pkwy Ste B Solon (44139) ***(G-17019)***
Iron Mountain Info MGT LLC...513 247-2183
11350 Deerfield Rd Blue Ash (45242) ***(G-1617)***
Irongate Inc (PA)...937 433-3300
122 N Main St Centerville (45459) ***(G-2680)***
Irongate Inc...937 298-6000
4461 Far Hills Ave Dayton (45429) ***(G-9637)***
Irongate Inc...937 432-3432
1353 Lyons Rd Dayton (45458) ***(G-9638)***
Irongate Inc Realtors, Dayton *Also called Irongate Inc* ***(G-9637)***
Irongate Realtors, Centerville *Also called Irongate Inc* ***(G-2680)***
Irons Fruit Farm...513 932-2853
1640 Stubbs Mill Rd Lebanon (45036) ***(G-12614)***
Ironton and Lawrence County (PA)...740 532-3534
305 N 5th St Ironton (45638) ***(G-12291)***
Ironton and Lawrence County...740 532-7855
1518 S 3rd St Ironton (45638) ***(G-12292)***
Irth Solutions Inc (PA)...614 459-2328
5009 Horizons Dr Ste 100 Columbus (43220) ***(G-7923)***
Is Acquisition Inc (HQ)...440 287-0150
3000 Crane Centre Dr Streetsboro (44241) ***(G-17417)***
Isaac Brant Ledman Teetor LLP...614 221-2121
2 Miranova Pl Ste 700 Columbus (43215) ***(G-7924)***
Isaac Wiles Burkholder & Teeto...614 221-5216
2 Miranova Pl Ste 700 Columbus (43215) ***(G-7925)***
Isaacs Company (PA)...513 336-8500
6091 Commerce Ct Mason (45040) ***(G-13724)***
Isaacs Fluid Power Eqp Co, Mason *Also called Isaacs Company* ***(G-13724)***
Isabelle Ridgway Care Ctr Inc...614 252-4931
1520 Hawthorne Ave Columbus (43203) ***(G-7926)***
Isd Renal Inc...330 375-6848
525 E Market St Bldg 50 Akron (44304) ***(G-284)***
Ishikawa Gasket America Inc...419 353-7300
828 Van Camp Rd Bowling Green (43402) ***(G-1783)***
ISI Systems Inc (PA)...740 942-0050
43029 Industrial Park Rd Cadiz (43907) ***(G-2078)***
Island Bike Rental Inc...419 285-2016
2071 Langram Rd Put In Bay (43456) ***(G-16367)***
Island Hospitality MGT LLC...614 864-8844
2084 S Hamilton Rd Columbus (43232) ***(G-7927)***
Island House Inc...419 734-0100
102 Madison St Port Clinton (43452) ***(G-16248)***
Island House Inn, Port Clinton *Also called Island House Inc* ***(G-16248)***
Island Service Company...419 285-3695
341 Bayview Ave Put In Bay (43456) ***(G-16368)***
ISLAND VIEW GIFTS, Put In Bay *Also called Miller Boat Line Inc* ***(G-16369)***
Islander Apartments, Cleveland *Also called Islander Company* ***(G-5837)***
Islander Company...440 243-0593
7711 Normandie Blvd Cleveland (44130) ***(G-5837)***
Isomedix Operations Inc...614 836-5757
4405 Marketing Pl Groveport (43125) ***(G-11648)***
Isomedix Operations Inc (HQ)...440 354-2600
5960 Heisley Rd Mentor (44060) ***(G-14196)***
Isqft Inc (HQ)...513 645-8004
3825 Edwards Rd Ste 800 Cincinnati (45209) ***(G-3845)***
Israel Adath (PA)...513 793-1800
3201 E Galbraith Rd Cincinnati (45236) ***(G-3846)***
It Services, Kettering *Also called Efix Computer Repair & Svc LLC* ***(G-12429)***
Itc, Dayton *Also called Innovative Technologies Corp* ***(G-9275)***
Itcube LLC...513 891-7300
10999 Reed Hartman Hwy # 136 Blue Ash (45242) ***(G-1618)***
Itelligence Inc (HQ)...513 956-2000
10856 Reed Hartman Hwy Cincinnati (45242) ***(G-3847)***
Itelligence Outsourcing Inc (HQ)...513 956-2000
10856 Reed Hartman Hwy Cincinnati (45242) ***(G-3848)***
Iticketscom...614 410-4140
700 Taylor Rd Ste 210 Columbus (43230) ***(G-7928)***
ITM Marketing Inc...740 295-3575
470 Downtowner Plz Coshocton (43812) ***(G-9108)***
Its Financial LLC...937 425-6889
51 Plum St Ste 260 Beavercreek (45440) ***(G-1247)***
Its Technologies Inc (PA)...419 842-2100
7060 Spring Meadows Dr W D Holland (43528) ***(G-12030)***
Its Traffic Systems Inc...440 892-4500
28915 Clemens Rd Ste 200 Westlake (44145) ***(G-19500)***
ITW Food Equipment Group LLC (HQ)...937 332-2396
701 S Ridge Ave Troy (45374) ***(G-18359)***
Ivan Law Inc...330 533-5000
2200 Hubbard Rd Youngstown (44505) ***(G-20238)***
Ivan Weaver Construction Co (PA)...330 695-3461
124 N Mill St Fredericksburg (44627) ***(G-11177)***
Ivory Services Inc...216 344-3094
2122 Saint Clair Ave Ne Cleveland (44114) ***(G-5838)***
Ivy Health Care Inc (PA)...513 251-2557
2025 Wyoming Ave Cincinnati (45205) ***(G-3849)***
Ivy Hills Country Club, Cincinnati *Also called Dry Run Limited Partnership* ***(G-3504)***
Ivy House Care Center, Painesville *Also called United Rest Homes Inc* ***(G-15884)***
Ivy Woods Care Center, Cincinnati *Also called Ivy Health Care Inc* ***(G-3849)***
Iwi Incorporated (PA)...440 585-5900
1399 Rockefeller Rd Wickliffe (44092) ***(G-19604)***
J & B Classical Glass & Mirror, Mansfield *Also called J & B Equipment & Supply Inc* ***(G-13314)***
J & B Equipment & Supply Inc...419 884-1155
2750 Lexington Ave Mansfield (44904) ***(G-13314)***
J & B Leasing Inc of Ohio...419 269-1440
435 Dura Ave Toledo (43612) ***(G-17979)***
J & B Systems Company Inc...513 732-2000
5055 State Route 276 Batavia (45103) ***(G-1017)***
J & C Ambulance Services Inc (PA)...330 899-0022
7100 Whipple Ave Nw Ste G North Canton (44720) ***(G-15346)***
J & D Basement Sytems, Reynoldsburg *Also called J & D Home Improvement Inc* ***(G-16459)***
J & D Home Improvement Inc (PA)...740 927-0722
13659 E Main St Reynoldsburg (43068) ***(G-16459)***
J & D Mining Inc...330 339-4935
3497 University Dr Ne New Philadelphia (44663) ***(G-15103)***
J & E LLC...513 241-0429
250 W Court St Ste 200e Cincinnati (45202) ***(G-3850)***
J & F Construction and Dev Inc...419 562-6662
2141 State Route 19 Bucyrus (44820) ***(G-2042)***
J & H Erectors, Portsmouth *Also called J&H Rnfrcing Strl Erectors Inc* ***(G-16292)***
J & J, Dayton *Also called Joe and Jill Lewis Inc* ***(G-9642)***
J & J Carriers LLC...614 447-2615
2572 Cleveland Ave Ste 5 Columbus (43211) ***(G-7929)***
J & J Entps Westerville Inc...614 898-5997
660 Kintner Pkwy Sunbury (43074) ***(G-17557)***
J & J General Maintenance Inc...740 533-9729
2430 S 3rd St Ironton (45638) ***(G-12293)***
J & J Schlaegel Inc...937 652-2045
1250 E Us Highway 36 Urbana (43078) ***(G-18592)***
J & N, Cincinnati *Also called Building 8 Inc* ***(G-3148)***
J & R Associates...440 250-4080
14803 Holland Rd Brookpark (44142) ***(G-1947)***
J & S Industrial Mch Pdts Inc...419 691-1380
123 Oakdale Ave Toledo (43605) ***(G-17980)***
J & T Washes Inc...614 486-9093
1319 W 5th Ave Columbus (43212) ***(G-7930)***
J A A Interior & Coml Cnstr...216 431-7633
3615 Superior Ave E 3103h Cleveland (44114) ***(G-5839)***
J A Donadee Corporation (PA)...330 533-3305
535 N Broad St Ste 5 Canfield (44406) ***(G-2197)***
J A G Black Gold Management Co...614 565-3246
6301 S High St Lockbourne (43137) ***(G-12957)***
J A Guy Inc...937 642-3415
13116 Weaver Rd Marysville (43040) ***(G-13629)***
J and J Environmental Inc...513 398-4521
7611 Easy St Mason (45040) ***(G-13725)***
J and J Sales, Delaware *Also called Aci Industries Converting Ltd* ***(G-10066)***

ALPHABETIC

J and S Tool Incorporated — 216 676-8330
15330 Brookpark Rd Cleveland (44135) *(G-5840)*

J B Express Inc — 740 702-9830
27311 Old Route 35 Chillicothe (45601) *(G-2854)*

J B Hunt Transport Inc — 440 786-8436
26235 Cannon Rd Bedford Heights (44146) *(G-1354)*

J B Hunt Transport Inc — 419 547-2777
600 N Woodland Ave Clyde (43410) *(G-6816)*

J B M Cleaning & Supply Co — 330 837-8805
3106 Sheila St Nw Massillon (44646) *(G-13825)*

J C Construction, Alliance Also called J C Masonry Construction Inc *(G-542)*

J C Direct Mail Inc — 614 836-4848
4241 Williams Rd Groveport (43125) *(G-11649)*

J C Masonry Construction Inc — 330 823-9795
7450 Parks Ave Ne Alliance (44601) *(G-542)*

J Cherie LLC — 216 453-1051
3645 Norwood Rd Shaker Heights (44122) *(G-16862)*

J D Byrider, Youngstown Also called Midwest Motors Inc *(G-20286)*

J D Drilling Co — 740 949-2512
107 S 3rd St Racine (45771) *(G-16371)*

J D S Leasing Inc — 440 236-6575
27230 Royalton Rd Columbia Station (44028) *(G-6847)*

J D Williamson Cnstr Co Inc — 330 633-1258
441 Geneva Ave Tallmadge (44278) *(G-17641)*

J Daniel & Company Inc — 513 575-3100
1975 Phoenix Dr Loveland (45140) *(G-13134)*

J E Davis Corporation — 440 377-4700
5187 Smith Ct Ste 100 Sheffield Village (44054) *(G-16887)*

J E F Inc — 513 921-4130
1857 Grand Ave Cincinnati (45214) *(G-3851)*

J F Bernard Inc — 330 785-3830
359 Stanton Ave Akron (44301) *(G-285)*

J F Good Co, Akron Also called Famous Industries Inc *(G-220)*

J F Painting Co, Columbus Also called Johnson & Fischer Inc *(G-7943)*

J Feldkamp Design Build Ltd — 513 870-0601
3239 Profit Dr Fairfield (45014) *(G-10864)*

J G Martin Inc — 216 491-1584
4159 Lee Rd Cleveland (44128) *(G-5841)*

J Gilmore Design Limited — 330 638-8224
3172 Niles Cortland Rd Ne Cortland (44410) *(G-9076)*

J K Enterprises Inc — 614 481-8838
2200 Mckinley Ave Columbus (43204) *(G-7931)*

J K Meurer Corp — 513 831-7500
33 Glendale Milford Rd Loveland (45140) *(G-13135)*

J L Swaney Inc — 740 884-4450
975 Vigo Rd Chillicothe (45601) *(G-2855)*

J M T Cartage Inc — 330 478-2430
4925 Southway St Sw Canton (44706) *(G-2416)*

J M T Freight Specialists, Seville Also called Jarrells Moving & Transport Co *(G-16841)*

J M Towning Inc — 614 876-7335
3690 Lacon Rd Hilliard (43026) *(G-11915)*

J McCoy Lumber Co Ltd (PA) — 937 587-3423
6 N Main St Peebles (45660) *(G-15940)*

J Nan Enterprises LLC — 330 653-3766
5601 Darrow Rd Hudson (44236) *(G-12125)*

J P Farley Corporation (PA) — 440 250-4300
29055 Clemens Rd Westlake (44145) *(G-19501)*

J P Jenks Inc — 440 428-4500
4493 S Madison Rd Madison (44057) *(G-13226)*

J P Sand & Gravel Company — 614 497-0083
5911 Lockbourne Rd Lockbourne (43137) *(G-12958)*

J P Transportation Company — 513 424-6978
2518 Oxford State Rd Middletown (45044) *(G-14430)*

J Peterman Company LLC — 888 647-2555
5345 Creek Rd Blue Ash (45242) *(G-1619)*

J R Johnson Engineering Inc — 440 234-9972
6673 Eastland Rd Cleveland (44130) *(G-5842)*

J R Mead Industrial Contrs — 614 891-4466
6606 Lake Of The Woods Pt Galena (43021) *(G-11284)*

J R Metals, West Chester Also called Misa Metals Inc *(G-19120)*

J Rayl Transport Inc — 330 940-1668
24881 Rockwell Dr Euclid (44117) *(G-10765)*

J Russell Construction — 330 633-6462
180 Southwest Ave Tallmadge (44278) *(G-17642)*

J Rutledge Enterprises Inc — 502 241-4100
3512 Spring Grove Ave Cincinnati (45223) *(G-3852)*

J S N Holdings — 216 447-0070
6055 Rockside Woods Blvd # 100 Cleveland (44131) *(G-5843)*

J S P A Inc — 407 957-6664
2717 Burnaby Dr Columbus (43209) *(G-7932)*

J Schoen Enterprises Inc (PA) — 419 536-0970
5056 Angola Rd Toledo (43615) *(G-17981)*

J T Adams Co Inc — 216 641-3290
4520 Willow Pkwy Cleveland (44125) *(G-5844)*

J T Express Inc — 513 727-8185
1200 N Main St Monroe (45050) *(G-14699)*

J V Hansel Inc — 330 716-0806
6055 Louise Ct Nw Warren (44481) *(G-18866)*

J V Janitorial Services Inc — 216 749-1150
1230 E Schaaf Rd Ste 1 Cleveland (44131) *(G-5845)*

J W Didado Electric Inc — 330 374-0070
1033 Kelly Ave Akron (44306) *(G-286)*

J W Enterprises Inc (PA) — 740 774-4500
159 E Main St Chillicothe (45601) *(G-2856)*

J W Geopfert Co Inc — 330 762-2293
1024 Home Ave Akron (44310) *(G-287)*

J W J Investments Inc — 419 643-3161
7400 Sweeney Rd Bluffton (45817) *(G-1732)*

J Way Leasing Ltd — 440 934-1020
1284 Miller Rd Avon (44011) *(G-899)*

J&B Sprafka Enterprises Inc (PA) — 330 733-4212
1430 Goodyear Blvd Akron (44305) *(G-288)*

J&B Steel Contractors, West Chester Also called J&B Steel Erectors Inc *(G-19096)*

J&B Steel Erectors Inc — 513 874-1722
9430 Sutton Pl West Chester (45011) *(G-19096)*

J&H Rnfrcing Strl Erectors Inc — 740 355-0141
55 River Ave Portsmouth (45662) *(G-16292)*

J&J Precision Machine Ltd — 330 923-5783
1474 Main St Cuyahoga Falls (44221) *(G-9197)*

J-C-R Tech Inc — 937 783-2296
936 Cherry St Blanchester (45107) *(G-1515)*

J-Mak Industries, Columbus Also called Panacea Products Corporation *(G-8513)*

J-Trac Inc — 419 524-3456
961 N Main St Mansfield (44903) *(G-13315)*

J-Vac Industries Inc — 740 384-2155
202 S Pennsylvania Ave Wellston (45692) *(G-19000)*

J. Peterman, Blue Ash Also called J Peterman Company LLC *(G-1619)*

J.L.L., Brecksville Also called Jones Lang Lsalle Americas Inc *(G-1831)*

Jac-Lin Manor — 419 994-5700
695 S Mount Vernon Ave Loudonville (44842) *(G-13091)*

Jack & Jill Babysitter Serv, Cincinnati Also called Jack & Jill Babysitting Svc *(G-3853)*

Jack & Jill Babysitting Svc — 513 731-5261
6252 Beechmont Ave Apt 11 Cincinnati (45230) *(G-3853)*

Jack A Hamilton & Assoc Inc — 740 968-4947
342 High St Flushing (43977) *(G-11105)*

Jack Conie & Sons Corp — 614 291-5931
1340 Windsor Ave Columbus (43211) *(G-7933)*

Jack Cooper Transport Co Inc — 440 949-2044
5211 Oster Rd Sheffield Village (44054) *(G-16888)*

Jack Entertainment, Cleveland Also called Horseshoe Cleveland MGT LLC *(G-5776)*

Jack Gibson Construction Co — 330 394-5280
2460 Parkman Rd Nw Warren (44485) *(G-18867)*

Jack Matia Honda, Elyria Also called Matia Motors Inc *(G-10650)*

Jack Thistledown Racino LLC (PA) — 216 662-8600
21501 Emery Rd Cleveland (44128) *(G-5846)*

Jackson Co Bd of Dd — 740 384-7938
202 S Pennsylvania Ave Wellston (45692) *(G-19001)*

Jackson Comfort Htg Coolg Sys, Northfield Also called Jackson Comfort Systems Inc *(G-15518)*

Jackson Comfort Systems Inc — 330 468-3111
499 E Twinsburg Rd Northfield (44067) *(G-15518)*

Jackson Community YMCA, Massillon Also called Y M C A Central Stark County *(G-13862)*

Jackson County Board On Aging (PA) — 740 286-2909
25 E Mound St Jackson (45640) *(G-12315)*

Jackson County Hlth Facilities — 740 384-0722
142 Jenkins Memorial Rd Wellston (45692) *(G-19002)*

JACKSON COUNTY SENIOR CITIZENS, Jackson Also called Jackson County Board On Aging *(G-12315)*

Jackson Hewitt Tax Service, Trotwood Also called E T Financial Service Inc *(G-18346)*

Jackson I-94 Ltd Partnership — 614 793-2244
6059 Frantz Rd Ste 205 Dublin (43017) *(G-10379)*

Jackson Kelly Pllc — 330 252-9060
17 S Main St 1 Akron (44308) *(G-289)*

Jackson Kohrman & Pll Krantz — 216 696-8700
1375 E 9th St Fl 29 Cleveland (44114) *(G-5847)*

JACKSON VINTON COMMUNITY ACTIO, Wellston Also called Jackson-Vinton Cmnty Action *(G-19003)*

Jackson-Vinton Cmnty Action (PA) — 740 384-3722
118 S New York Ave Wellston (45692) *(G-19003)*

Jaco Waterproofing LLC — 513 738-0084
4350 Wade Mill Rd Fairfield (45014) *(G-10865)*

Jacob Neal Salon, Columbus Also called Salon Communication Services *(G-8680)*

Jacobs Constructors Inc — 419 226-1344
1840 Buckeye Rd Gatew Lima (45804) *(G-12806)*

Jacobs Constructors Inc — 513 595-7900
1880 Waycross Rd Cincinnati (45240) *(G-3854)*

Jacobs Dwelling Nursing Home — 740 824-3635
25680 Bethlehem Township Coshocton (43812) *(G-9109)*

Jacobs Engineering Group Inc — 513 595-7500
1880 Waycross Rd Cincinnati (45240) *(G-3855)*

Jacobs Engineering Group Inc — 513 595-7500
1880 Waycross Rd Cincinnati (45240) *(G-3856)*

Jacobs Mechanical Co — 513 681-6800
4500 W Mitchell Ave Cincinnati (45232) *(G-3857)*

Jacobs Real Estate Services — 216 514-9830
2000 Auburn Dr Ste 120 Beachwood (44122) *(G-1090)*

Jacobs Technology Inc — 937 429-5056
4027 Colonel Glenn Hwy Beavercreek Township (45431) *(G-1271)*

Jacobson Warehouse Company Inc — 614 314-1091
3880 Groveport Rd Obetz (43207) *(G-15668)*

Jacobson Warehouse Company Inc — 614 409-0003
2450 Spiegel Dr Ste H Groveport (43125) *(G-11650)*

Jacobson Warehouse Company Inc 614 497-6300
6600 Port Rd Ste 200 Groveport (43125) *(G-11651)*
Jacor LLC 330 441-4182
1011 Lake Rd Medina (44256) *(G-14084)*
Jacqueline Kumi-Sakyi 740 282-5955
1609 Moreland Dr Steubenville (43952) *(G-17322)*
Jada Inc 419 512-1713
303 N Main St Mount Vernon (43050) *(G-14901)*
Jade Investments 330 425-3141
2300 E Aurora Rd Twinsburg (44087) *(G-18433)*
Jade-Sterling Steel Co Inc (PA) 330 425-3141
2300 E Aurora Rd Twinsburg (44087) *(G-18434)*
Jae Co 2, Westerville *Also called Mark Humrichouser (G-19327)*
Jaekle Group Inc 330 405-9353
1410 Highland Rd E Macedonia (44056) *(G-13204)*
Jag Healthcare Inc 440 385-4370
220 Buckingham Rd Rocky River (44116) *(G-16582)*
Jagi Clveland Independence LLC 216 524-8050
6001 Rockside Rd Cleveland (44131) *(G-5848)*
Jagi Juno LLC (PA) 513 489-1955
8534 E Kemper Rd Cincinnati (45249) *(G-3858)*
Jagi Springhill LLC 216 264-4190
6060 Rockside Pl Independence (44131) *(G-12221)*
Jaguar Volvo, Canton *Also called Kempthorn Automall (G-2422)*
Jainco International Inc 440 519-0100
30405 Solon Rd Ste 9 Solon (44139) *(G-17020)*
Jaincotech, Solon *Also called Jainco International Inc (G-17020)*
Jake Sweeney Automotive Inc 513 782-2800
33 W Kemper Rd Cincinnati (45246) *(G-3859)*
Jake Sweeney Body Shop 513 782-1100
169 Northland Blvd Ste 1 Cincinnati (45246) *(G-3860)*
Jake Sweeney Chevrolet Imports, Cincinnati *Also called Jake Sweeney Body Shop (G-3860)*
James Advantage Funds 937 426-7640
1349 Fairground Rd Xenia (45385) *(G-20064)*
James Air Cargo Inc 440 243-9095
6519 Eastland Rd Ste 6 Cleveland (44142) *(G-5849)*
James B Oswald Company 330 723-3637
5000 Foote Rd Medina (44256) *(G-14085)*
James C Sass Atty 419 843-3545
3230 Central Park W # 200 Toledo (43617) *(G-17982)*
James Cancer Center, Columbus *Also called Ohio State University (G-8436)*
James D Egbert Optometrist (PA) 937 236-1770
6557 Brandt Pike Huber Heights (45424) *(G-12096)*
James H Alvis Trucking Inc 513 623-8121
9570 State Route 128 Harrison (45030) *(G-11803)*
James Hunt Construction Co 513 721-0559
1865 Summit Rd Cincinnati (45237) *(G-3861)*
James L Jacobson 937 223-1130
40 N Main St Ste 2700 Dayton (45423) *(G-9639)*
James Lafontaine 740 474-5052
25050 Us Highway 23 S Circleville (43113) *(G-4891)*
James Powers 614 566-9397
340 E Town St Ste 8700 Columbus (43215) *(G-7934)*
James Ray Lozier 419 884-2656
84 Foxcroft Rd Mansfield (44904) *(G-13316)*
James Recker 419 837-5378
1446 Ottawa Rd Genoa (43430) *(G-11380)*
Janat Clemmons Center, Hamilton *Also called Butler County Bd of Mental RE (G-11700)*
Jancoa Janitorial Services Inc 513 351-7200
5235 Montgomery Rd Cincinnati (45212) *(G-3862)*
Jani-Source Inc 740 374-6298
478 Bramblewood Hts Rd Marietta (45750) *(G-13458)*
Janik LLP (PA) 440 838-7600
9200 S Hills Blvd Ste 300 Cleveland (44147) *(G-5850)*
Janiking, Cincinnati *Also called Jenkins Enterprises LLC (G-2920)*
Janitec Building Service, New Richmond *Also called Dave & Barb Enterprises Inc (G-15125)*
Janitorial Management Services, Greenville *Also called Ktm Enterprises Inc (G-11512)*
Janitorial Services Inc 216 341-8601
8555 Sweet Valley Dr H Cleveland (44125) *(G-5851)*
Janitorial Support Services, Columbus *Also called Academic Support Services LLC (G-6930)*
Janotta & Herner, Monroeville *Also called Jhi Group Inc (G-14721)*
Janson Industries 330 455-7029
1200 Garfield Ave Sw Canton (44706) *(G-2417)*
Jantech Building Services Inc 216 661-6102
4963 Schaaf Ln Brooklyn Heights (44131) *(G-1917)*
Janus Hotel and Resort, Cincinnati *Also called Elbe Properties (G-3545)*
Janus Hotels and Resorts Inc 513 631-8500
6840 State Route 503 N Lewisburg (45338) *(G-12711)*
Jared Galleria of Jewelery 614 476-6532
4159 Morse Xing Columbus (43219) *(G-7935)*
Jaro Transportation Svcs Inc (PA) 330 393-5659
975 Post Rd Nw Warren (44483) *(G-18868)*
Jarrells Moving & Transport Co 330 952-1240
1155 Industrial Pkwy Medina (44256) *(G-14086)*
Jarrells Moving & Transport Co (PA) 330 764-4333
5076 Park Ave W Seville (44273) *(G-16841)*
Jarrett Logistics Systems Inc 330 682-0099
1347 N Main St Orrville (44667) *(G-15775)*
Jarvis Mechanical Constrs Inc (PA) 513 831-0055
803 Us Route 50 Milford (45150) *(G-14528)*
Jasar Recycling Inc 864 233-5421
183 Edgeworth Ave East Palestine (44413) *(G-10538)*
Jason Wilson 937 604-8209
5575 Ross Rd Tipp City (45371) *(G-17720)*
Javitch Block LLC 513 381-3051
700 Walnut St Ste 300 Cincinnati (45202) *(G-3863)*
Javitch Block LLC (PA) 216 623-0000
1100 Superior Ave E Fl 19 Cleveland (44114) *(G-5852)*
Javitch Block LLC 216 623-0000
140 E Town St Ste 1250 Columbus (43215) *(G-7936)*
Jay Blue Communications 216 661-2828
7500 Associate Ave Cleveland (44144) *(G-5853)*
Jay-Mac, Canton *Also called Young Truck Sales Inc (G-2592)*
JB Hunt Transport Svcs Inc 614 335-6681
5435 Crosswind Dr Columbus (43228) *(G-7937)*
JB Management Inc 419 841-2596
6540 W Central Ave Ste A Toledo (43617) *(G-17983)*
JB Roofing, Tiffin *Also called Tecta America Corp (G-17703)*
Jbentley Studio & Spa LLC 614 790-8828
8882 Moreland St Powell (43065) *(G-16339)*
Jbj Enterprises Inc 440 992-6051
2450 W Prospect Rd Ashtabula (44004) *(G-750)*
Jbjs Acquisitions LLC 513 769-0393
11939 Tramway Dr Cincinnati (45241) *(G-3864)*
JBK Group Inc (PA) 216 901-0000
6001 Towpath Dr Cleveland (44125) *(G-5854)*
Jbm Cleaning, Massillon *Also called J B M Cleaning & Supply Co (G-13825)*
Jbo Holding Company 216 367-8787
1100 Superior Ave E # 1500 Cleveland (44114) *(G-5855)*
JC Penney, Akron *Also called JC Penney Corporation Inc (G-290)*
JC Penney Corporation Inc 330 633-7700
2000 Brittain Rd Ste 600 Akron (44310) *(G-290)*
Jc's 5 Star Outlet, Columbus *Also called Sb Capital Acquisitions LLC (G-8690)*
Jcc, Sylvania *Also called Jewish Cmnty Ctr of Toledo (G-17597)*
JD Equipment Inc 740 450-7446
4394 Northpointe Dr Zanesville (43701) *(G-20491)*
JD Equipment Inc (PA) 614 527-8800
5850 Zarley St New Albany (43054) *(G-14989)*
JD Music Tile Co 740 420-9611
105 E Ohio St Circleville (43113) *(G-4892)*
Jdel Inc 614 436-2418
200 W Nationwide Blvd # 1 Columbus (43215) *(G-7938)*
Jdi Group Inc 419 725-7161
360 W Dussel Dr Maumee (43537) *(G-13930)*
Jdrm Engineering Inc 419 824-2400
5604 Main St Ste 200 Sylvania (43560) *(G-17595)*
JE Carsten Company (PA) 330 794-4440
61 S Seiberling St Akron (44305) *(G-291)*
Jean R Wagner 614 430-0065
470 Olde Worthington Rd Westerville (43082) *(G-19317)*
Jed Industries Inc 440 639-9973
320 River St Grand River (44045) *(G-11456)*
Jedson Engineering Inc (PA) 513 965-5999
705 Central Ave Ste 300 Cincinnati (45202) *(G-3865)*
Jeff Creque Farms Inc 419 829-2941
9700 Sylvania Ave Sylvania (43560) *(G-17596)*
Jeff Plumber Inc (PA) 330 940-2600
1100 Tower Dr Akron (44305) *(G-292)*
Jeff Wyler Automotive Fmly Inc (PA) 513 752-7450
829 Eastgate South Dr Cincinnati (45245) *(G-2918)*
Jeff Wyler Chevrolet Inc 513 752-3447
1117 State Route 32 Batavia (45103) *(G-1018)*
Jeff Wyler Ft Thomas Inc 513 752-7450
829 Eastgate South Dr Cincinnati (45245) *(G-2919)*
Jeff Wyler Mazda, Batavia *Also called Jeff Wyler Chevrolet Inc (G-1018)*
Jefferey Anderson Real Estate, Cincinnati *Also called Pfh Partners LLC (G-4289)*
Jeffers Crane Service Inc (HQ) 419 693-0421
5421 Navarre Ave Oregon (43616) *(G-15740)*
Jefferson Golf & Country Club 614 759-7500
7271 Jefferson Meadows Dr Blacklick (43004) *(G-1508)*
Jefferson Invstgtors Scurities 740 283-3681
1439 Sunset Blvd Steubenville (43952) *(G-17323)*
Jefferson Medical Co 216 443-9000
950 Main Ave Ste 500 Cleveland (44113) *(G-5856)*
Jeffrey Carr Construction Inc 330 879-5210
4164 Erie Ave Sw Massillon (44646) *(G-13826)*
Jeffrey W Smith 740 532-9000
411 Center St Ironton (45638) *(G-12294)*
Jeg's High-Performance Center, Delaware *Also called Jegs Automotive Inc (G-10110)*
Jegs Automotive Inc (PA) 614 294-5050
101 Jegs Pl Delaware (43015) *(G-10110)*
Jelly Bean Junction Lrng Ctr, Dublin *Also called Consolidated Learning Ctrs Inc (G-10308)*
Jenkins Enterprises LLC 513 752-7896
849 Locust Corner Rd Cincinnati (45245) *(G-2920)*
JENKINS MEMORIAL HEALTH FACILI, Wellston *Also called Jackson County Hlth Facilities (G-19002)*
Jenne Inc 440 835-0040
33665 Chester Rd Avon (44011) *(G-900)*
Jennings Eliza Home Inc (HQ) 216 226-0282
10603 Detroit Ave Cleveland (44102) *(G-5857)*

ALPHABETIC

(PA)=Parent Co (HQ)=Headquarters (DH)=Div Headquarters
2018 Harris Ohio Services Directory
1227

Jennings Eliza Senior Care (PA) 216 226-5000
26376 John Rd Ofc C Olmsted Twp (44138) ***(G-15676)***
Jennings & Associates 740 369-4426
26 Northwood Dr Delaware (43015) ***(G-10111)***
Jennings Ctr For Older Adults 216 581-2900
10204 Granger Rd 232 Cleveland (44125) ***(G-5858)***
Jennings Hall Nursing Facility, Cleveland *Also called Jennings Ctr For Older Adults* ***(G-5858)***
Jennings Heating & Cooling, Akron *Also called Jennings Heating Company Inc* ***(G-293)***
Jennings Heating Company Inc 330 784-1286
1671 E Market St Akron (44305) ***(G-293)***
Jennite Co 419 531-1791
4694 W Bancroft St Toledo (43615) ***(G-17984)***
Jergens Inc (PA) 216 486-5540
15700 S Waterloo Rd Cleveland (44110) ***(G-5859)***
Jericho Investments Company, Etna *Also called William D Taylor Sr Inc* ***(G-10740)***
Jerl Machine Inc 419 873-0270
11140 Avenue Rd Perrysburg (43551) ***(G-16020)***
Jerry Haag Motors Inc 937 402-2090
1475 N High St Hillsboro (45133) ***(G-11984)***
Jerry L Garver Branch, Canal Winchester *Also called Young Mens Christian Assoc* ***(G-2181)***
Jersey Central Pwr & Light Co (HQ) 800 736-3402
76 S Main St Akron (44308) ***(G-294)***
Jersey Central Pwr & Light Co 440 994-8271
2210 S Ridge W Ashtabula (44004) ***(G-751)***
Jersey Central Pwr & Light Co 419 366-2915
2508 W Perkins Ave Sandusky (44870) ***(G-16771)***
Jersey Central Pwr & Light Co 330 315-6713
395 Ghent Rd Rm 407 Fairlawn (44333) ***(G-10960)***
Jersey Central Pwr & Light Co 937 327-1218
420 York St Springfield (45505) ***(G-17216)***
Jersey Central Pwr & Light Co 740 537-6308
29503 State Route 7 Stratton (43961) ***(G-17403)***
Jersey Central Pwr & Light Co 440 326-3222
6326 Lake Ave Elyria (44035) ***(G-10637)***
Jersey Central Pwr & Light Co 216 432-6330
6800 S Marginal Rd Cleveland (44103) ***(G-5860)***
Jersey Central Pwr & Light Co 440 546-8609
6896 Miller Rd Brecksville (44141) ***(G-1829)***
Jersey Central Pwr & Light Co 330 336-9884
9681 Silvercreek Rd Wadsworth (44281) ***(G-18758)***
Jersey Central Pwr & Light Co 216 479-1132
2423 Payne Ave Cleveland (44114) ***(G-5861)***
Jersey Central Pwr & Light Co 440 953-7651
7755 Auburn Rd Painesville (44077) ***(G-15858)***
Jersey Central Pwr & Light Co 419 321-7207
5501 N State Route 2 Oak Harbor (43449) ***(G-15611)***
Jess Hauer Masonry Inc 513 521-2178
7430 Roettele Pl Cincinnati (45231) ***(G-3866)***
Jess Howard Electric Company 614 864-2167
6630 Taylor Rd Blacklick (43004) ***(G-1509)***
Jet Express Inc (PA) 937 274-7033
4518 Webster St Dayton (45414) ***(G-9640)***
Jet Machine & Manufacturing, Cincinnati *Also called Wulco Inc* ***(G-4862)***
Jet Mintenance Consulting Corp 937 205-2406
1113 Airport Rd Ste Jmcc Wilmington (45177) ***(G-19764)***
Jet Rubber Company 330 325-1821
4457 Tallmadge Rd Rootstown (44272) ***(G-16597)***
Jetro Cash and Carry Entps LLC 216 525-0101
6150 Halle Dr Cleveland (44125) ***(G-5862)***
Jetselect LLC (PA) 614 338-4380
4130 E 5th Ave Columbus (43219) ***(G-7939)***
Jetson Engineering 513 965-5999
705 Central Ave Cincinnati (45202) ***(G-3867)***
Jewish Cmnty Ctr of Toledo 419 885-4485
6465 Sylvania Ave Sylvania (43560) ***(G-17597)***
Jewish Community Care At Home, Cleveland *Also called Jewish Family Services Associa* ***(G-5863)***
Jewish Community Center Inc 513 761-7500
8485 Ridge Rd Cincinnati (45236) ***(G-3868)***
Jewish Community Ctr Cleveland 216 831-0700
26001 S Woodland Rd Beachwood (44122) ***(G-1091)***
Jewish Day Schl Assoc Grtr Clv (PA) 216 763-1400
27601 Fairmount Blvd Pepper Pike (44124) ***(G-15957)***
Jewish Edcatn Ctr of Cleveland 216 371-0446
2030 S Taylor Rd Cleveland Heights (44118) ***(G-6791)***
Jewish Family Service of The C 513 469-1188
8487 Ridge Rd Cincinnati (45236) ***(G-3869)***
Jewish Family Services 614 231-1890
1070 College Ave Ste A Columbus (43209) ***(G-7940)***
Jewish Family Services Associa (PA) 216 292-3999
3659 Green Rd Ste 322 Cleveland (44122) ***(G-5863)***
Jewish Family Services Associa 216 292-3999
24075 Commerce Park # 105 Cleveland (44122) ***(G-5864)***
Jewish Fderation of Cincinnati 513 985-1500
8499 Ridge Rd Cincinnati (45236) ***(G-3870)***
Jewish Fdrtion of Grter Dayton 937 837-2651
4911 Covenant House Dr Dayton (45426) ***(G-9641)***
Jewish Home of Cincinnati 513 754-3100
5467 Cedar Village Dr Mason (45040) ***(G-13726)***
Jewish Hospital LLC 513 686-3000
4777 E Galbraith Rd Cincinnati (45236) ***(G-3871)***
Jewish Hospital Cincinnati Inc 513 686-3303
4777 E Galbraith Rd Cincinnati (45236) ***(G-3872)***
Jh Instruments, Columbus *Also called Fcx Performance Inc* ***(G-7645)***
Jhi Group Inc (PA) 419 465-4611
309 Monroe St Monroeville (44847) ***(G-14721)***
Jiffy Products America Inc 440 282-2818
5401 Baumhart Rd Ste B Lorain (44053) ***(G-13043)***
Jilco Industries Inc (PA) 330 698-0280
11234 Hackett Rd Kidron (44636) ***(G-12441)***
Jim Brown Chevrolet Inc (PA) 440 255-5511
6877 Center St Mentor (44060) ***(G-14197)***
Jim Brown Chevrolet Inc 440 255-5511
8490 Tyler Blvd Mentor (44060) ***(G-14198)***
Jim Hayden Inc 513 563-8828
3154 Exon Ave Cincinnati (45241) ***(G-3873)***
Jim Keim Ford 614 888-3333
5575 Keim Cir Columbus (43228) ***(G-7941)***
Jim May Auto Sales & Svc Ctr, Findlay *Also called May Jim Auto Sales LLC* ***(G-11063)***
Jimmy's Limousine Service, West Chester *Also called Jls Enterprises Inc* ***(G-19097)***
Jims Electric Inc 440 327-8800
39221 Center Ridge Rd North Ridgeville (44039) ***(G-15465)***
Jit Packaging Aurora Inc 330 562-8080
1250 Page Rd Aurora (44202) ***(G-843)***
JJO Construction Inc 440 255-1515
9045 Osborne Dr Mentor (44060) ***(G-14199)***
Jjr Solutions LLC 937 912-0288
3610 Pentagon Blvd # 220 Beavercreek (45431) ***(G-1180)***
Jk-Co LLC 419 422-5240
16960 E State Route 12 Findlay (45840) ***(G-11051)***
Jke, Westlake *Also called Jordan Kyli Enterprises Inc* ***(G-19502)***
JKL Construction Inc 513 553-3333
620 Hamilton St New Richmond (45157) ***(G-15128)***
JKL Development Company (PA) 937 390-0358
2101 E Home Rd Springfield (45503) ***(G-17217)***
Jls Enterprises Inc 513 769-1888
8167 Regal Ln Ste A West Chester (45069) ***(G-19097)***
JLW Marketing LLC 513 260-8418
4240 Airport Rd Ste 106 Cincinnati (45226) ***(G-3874)***
Jma Healthcare LLC 440 439-7976
24579 Broadway Ave Cleveland (44146) ***(G-5865)***
Jmt, Columbus *Also called Johnson Mirmiran Thompson Inc* ***(G-7945)***
JMw Welding and Mfg 330 484-2428
512 45th St Sw Canton (44706) ***(G-2418)***
Jo Lin Health Center Inc 740 532-0860
1050 Clinton St Ironton (45638) ***(G-12295)***
Jo Lynn Inc 419 994-3204
430 N Jefferson St Loudonville (44842) ***(G-13092)***
Job & Family Svcs Clinton Cnty, Wilmington *Also called Clinton County Dept Jobs/Fmly* ***(G-19752)***
Job 1 USA (HQ) 419 255-5005
701 Jefferson Ave Ste 202 Toledo (43604) ***(G-17985)***
Job and Family Service, Chardon *Also called County of Geauga* ***(G-2746)***
Job and Family Services, Norwalk *Also called County of Huron* ***(G-15568)***
Job and Family Services Dept, Toledo *Also called County of Lucas* ***(G-17835)***
Job Service of Ohio, Akron *Also called Ohio Dept of Job & Fmly Svcs* ***(G-364)***
Job1usa, Toledo *Also called Rumpf Corporation* ***(G-18167)***
Jobar Enterprise Inc 216 561-5184
3361 E 147th St Cleveland (44120) ***(G-5866)***
Jobes Henderson & Assoc Inc 740 344-5451
59 Grant St Newark (43055) ***(G-15178)***
Jobs On Site, Mansfield *Also called Edge Plastics Inc* ***(G-13296)***
Joe and Jill Lewis Inc 937 718-8829
716 N Broadway St Dayton (45402) ***(G-9642)***
Joe Dickey Electric Inc 330 549-3976
180 W South Range Rd North Lima (44452) ***(G-15403)***
Joe Dodge Kidd Inc 513 752-1804
1065 Ohio Pike Cincinnati (45245) ***(G-2921)***
Joe Lasita & Sons Inc 513 241-5288
940 W 5th St Cincinnati (45203) ***(G-3875)***
Joe McClelland Inc (PA) 740 452-3036
98 E La Salle St Zanesville (43701) ***(G-20492)***
Joel Pomerene Memorial Hosp, Millersburg *Also called County of Holmes* ***(G-14600)***
Joel Pomerene Memorial Hosp (PA) 330 674-1015
981 Wooster Rd Millersburg (44654) ***(G-14609)***
Joes Ldscpg Beavercreek Inc 937 427-1133
2500 National Rd Beavercreek Township (45324) ***(G-1272)***
Joey Boyle 216 273-8317
11 Garfield Ave Athens (45701) ***(G-795)***
John & Hester Powell Grimm, Findlay *Also called University of Findlay* ***(G-11097)***
John A Becker Co (PA) 937 226-1341
1341 E 4th St Dayton (45402) ***(G-9643)***
John A Becker Co 513 771-2550
11310 Mosteller Rd Cincinnati (45241) ***(G-3876)***
John A Becker Co 614 272-8800
3825 Business Park Dr Columbus (43204) ***(G-7942)***
John Atwood Inc 440 777-4147
28800 Lorain Rd North Olmsted (44070) ***(G-15428)***
John Brown Trucking Inc 330 758-0841
8063 Southern Blvd Youngstown (44512) ***(G-20239)***
John Deere Authorized Dealer, Alliance *Also called Cope Farm Equipment Inc* ***(G-536)***

John Deere Authorized Dealer, Coldwater *Also called Lefeld Implement Inc* ***(G-6831)***
John Deere Authorized Dealer, Georgetown *Also called Cahall Bros Inc* ***(G-11388)***
John Deere Authorized Dealer, Bloomingdale *Also called Kuester Implement Company Inc* ***(G-1517)***
John Deere Authorized Dealer, North Royalton *Also called Shearer Farm Inc* ***(G-15502)***
John Deere Authorized Dealer, Wooster *Also called Shearer Farm Inc* ***(G-19915)***
John Deere Authorized Dealer, Monroeville *Also called Shearer Farm Inc* ***(G-14722)***
John Deere Authorized Dealer, Upper Sandusky *Also called Wyandot Tractor & Implement Co* ***(G-18571)***
John Deere Authorized Dealer, Findlay *Also called Findlay Implement Co* ***(G-11026)***
John Deere Authorized Dealer, Mentor *Also called Great Lakes Power Products Inc* ***(G-14185)***
John Deere Authorized Dealer, Copley *Also called Shetlers Sales & Service Inc* ***(G-9064)***
John Deere Authorized Dealer, Zanesville *Also called JD Equipment Inc* ***(G-20491)***
John Deere Authorized Dealer, Canton *Also called Western Branch Diesel Inc* ***(G-2585)***
John Deere Authorized Dealer, Hartville *Also called Hartville Hardware Inc* ***(G-11820)***
John Deere Authorized Dealer, Ontario *Also called Shearer Farm Inc* ***(G-15712)***
John Deere Authorized Dealer, New Albany *Also called JD Equipment Inc* ***(G-14989)***
John Deere Authorized Dealer, Cincinnati *Also called Murphy Tractor & Eqp Co Inc* ***(G-4132)***
John Deere Authorized Dealer, Marietta *Also called E T B Ltd* ***(G-13443)***
John Deere Authorized Dealer, Tipp City *Also called Koenig Equipment Inc* ***(G-17721)***
John Dellagnese & Assoc Inc.....330 668-4000
4000 Embassy Pkwy Ste 400 Akron (44333) ***(G-295)***
John Eramo & Sons Inc.....614 777-0020
3670 Lacon Rd Hilliard (43026) ***(G-11916)***
John F Gallagher Plumbing Co.....440 946-4256
36360 Lakeland Blvd Eastlake (44095) ***(G-10547)***
John F Stambaugh & Co.....419 687-6833
5063 Bevier Rd Plymouth (44865) ***(G-16217)***
John Glenn Columbus Intl Arprt, Columbus *Also called Columbus Regional Airport Auth* ***(G-7382)***
John H Cooper Elec Contg Co.....513 271-5000
1769 Elmore St Cincinnati (45223) ***(G-3877)***
John H Kappus Co (PA).....216 367-6677
4755 W 150th St Cleveland (44135) ***(G-5867)***
John O Bostock Jr.....937 263-8540
5107 Midway Ave Dayton (45417) ***(G-9644)***
John P Novatny Electric Co.....330 630-8900
955 Evans Ave Akron (44305) ***(G-296)***
John Rbrts Hair Studio Spa Inc (PA).....216 839-1430
673 Alpha Dr Ste F Cleveland (44143) ***(G-5868)***
John S Knight Center, Akron *Also called Akron-Summit Convention* ***(G-62)***
John Stewart Company.....513 703-5412
6819 Montgomery Rd Cincinnati (45236) ***(G-3878)***
John W. Schaeffer, M.d, Lorain *Also called North Ohio Heart Center* ***(G-13069)***
John Zidian Co Inc (PA).....330 743-6050
574 Mcclurg Rd Youngstown (44512) ***(G-20240)***
Johnny Appleseed Broadcasting.....419 529-5900
2900 Park Ave W Ontario (44906) ***(G-15695)***
Johnnys Carwash.....513 474-6603
7901 Beechmont Ave Cincinnati (45255) ***(G-3879)***
Johns Manville Corporation.....419 784-7000
600 Jackson Ave Defiance (43512) ***(G-10038)***
Johnson Adams & Protrouski.....419 238-6251
1178 Professional Dr Van Wert (45891) ***(G-18636)***
Johnson & Fischer Inc.....614 276-8868
5303 Trabue Rd Columbus (43228) ***(G-7943)***
Johnson Bros Greenwich, Greenwich *Also called Johnson Bros Rubber Co Inc* ***(G-11526)***
Johnson Bros Rubber Co Inc (PA).....419 853-4122
42 W Buckeye St West Salem (44287) ***(G-19270)***
Johnson Bros Rubber Co Inc.....419 752-4814
41 Center St Greenwich (44837) ***(G-11526)***
Johnson Cntrls SEC Sltions LLC.....330 497-0850
5590 Lauby Rd Ste 6 Canton (44720) ***(G-2419)***
Johnson Cntrls SEC Sltions LLC.....440 262-1084
6650 W Snowville Rd Ste K Brecksville (44141) ***(G-1830)***
Johnson Cntrls SEC Sltions LLC.....561 988-3600
6175 Shamrock Ct Ste S Dublin (43016) ***(G-10380)***
Johnson Cntrls SEC Sltions LLC.....513 277-4966
4750 Wesley Ave Ste Q Cincinnati (45212) ***(G-3880)***
Johnson Cntrls SEC Sltions LLC.....419 243-8400
1722 Indian Wood Cir F Maumee (43537) ***(G-13931)***
Johnson Contrls Authorized Dlr, Dayton *Also called Allied Supply Company Inc* ***(G-9317)***
Johnson Contrls Authorized Dlr, Canton *Also called Morrow Control and Supply Inc* ***(G-2465)***
Johnson Contrls Authorized Dlr, Akron *Also called Famous Industries Inc* ***(G-219)***
Johnson Contrls Authorized Dlr, Cincinnati *Also called Habegger Corporation* ***(G-3724)***
Johnson Contrls Authorized Dlr, Cincinnati *Also called Controls Center Inc* ***(G-3415)***
Johnson Contrls Authorized Dlr, Northwood *Also called Yanfeng US Automotive* ***(G-15553)***
Johnson Contrls Authorized Dlr, Toledo *Also called Famous Enterprises Inc* ***(G-17879)***
Johnson Contrls Authorized Dlr, Akron *Also called Famous Distribution Inc* ***(G-216)***
Johnson Controls.....513 874-1227
9685 Cincinnati Dayton Rd West Chester (45069) ***(G-19098)***
Johnson Controls.....614 602-2000
6175 Shamrock Ct Ste S Dublin (43016) ***(G-10381)***
Johnson Controls.....614 717-9079
6175 Shamrock Ct Dublin (43016) ***(G-10382)***
Johnson Controls.....440 268-1160
17295 Foltz Pkwy Ste G Strongsville (44149) ***(G-17478)***
Johnson Controls Inc.....614 895-6600
835 Green Crest Dr Westerville (43081) ***(G-19412)***
Johnson Controls Inc.....330 270-4385
1044 N Meridian Rd Ste A Youngstown (44509) ***(G-20241)***
Johnson Controls Inc.....513 489-0950
7863 Palace Dr Cincinnati (45249) ***(G-3881)***
Johnson Electric Supply Co (PA).....513 421-3700
1841 Riverside Dr Cincinnati (45202) ***(G-3882)***
Johnson Howard International.....513 825-3129
400 Glensprings Dr Cincinnati (45246) ***(G-3883)***
Johnson Institutional MGT, Cincinnati *Also called Johnson Trust Co* ***(G-3884)***
Johnson Mirmiran Thompson Inc.....614 714-0270
2800 Corp Exchange Dr # 250 Columbus (43231) ***(G-7944)***
Johnson Mirmiran Thompson Inc.....614 714-0270
4600 Mcauley Pl Ste 150 Blue Ash (45242) ***(G-1620)***
Johnson Mirmiran Thompson Inc.....614 714-0270
2800 Corp Exchange Dr Columbus (43231) ***(G-7945)***
Johnson Mirmiran Thompson Inc.....614 714-0270
959 W Saint Clair Ave # 300 Cleveland (44113) ***(G-5869)***
Johnson Trust Co.....513 598-8859
3777 W Fork Rd Fl 2 Cincinnati (45247) ***(G-3884)***
Joint Emergency Med Svc Inc.....937 746-3471
201 E 6th St Franklin (45005) ***(G-11159)***
Joint Implant Surgeons Inc.....614 221-6331
7727 Smiths Mill Rd 200 New Albany (43054) ***(G-14990)***
Joint Township Dst Mem Hosp.....419 394-9959
1040 Hager St Saint Marys (45885) ***(G-16675)***
Joint Township Dst Mem Hosp (PA).....419 394-3335
200 Saint Clair Ave Saint Marys (45885) ***(G-16676)***
Joint Township Dst Mem Hosp.....419 394-9992
975 Hager St Saint Marys (45885) ***(G-16677)***
Jolly Tots Too Inc.....614 471-0688
5511 N Hamilton Rd Columbus (43230) ***(G-7946)***
Jon R Dvorak MD.....419 872-7700
1090 W South Boundary St # 5 Perrysburg (43551) ***(G-16021)***
Jonathon R Johnson & Assoc.....216 932-6529
1489 Rydalmount Rd Cleveland (44118) ***(G-5870)***
Jones & Henry Engineers Ltd (PA).....419 473-9611
3103 Executive Pkwy # 300 Toledo (43606) ***(G-17986)***
Jones Cochenour & Co Inc (PA).....740 653-9581
125 W Mulberry St Lancaster (43130) ***(G-12545)***
Jones Day Limited Partnership.....614 469-3939
325 John H Mcconnell Blvd # 600 Columbus (43215) ***(G-7947)***
Jones Day Limited Partnership (PA).....216 586-3939
901 Lakeside Ave E Ste 2 Cleveland (44114) ***(G-5871)***
Jones Group Interiors Inc.....330 253-9180
701 S Broadway St Ste 200 Akron (44311) ***(G-297)***
Jones Home, The, Cleveland *Also called Cleveland Municipal School Dst* ***(G-5338)***
Jones Lang Lsalle Americas Inc.....216 447-5276
9921 Brecksville Rd Brecksville (44141) ***(G-1831)***
Jones Law Group LLC.....614 545-9998
513 E Rich St Ste 100 Columbus (43215) ***(G-7948)***
Jones Metal Products Company.....740 545-6341
305 N Center St West Lafayette (43845) ***(G-19257)***
Jones Potato Chip Co (PA).....419 529-9424
823 Bowman St Mansfield (44903) ***(G-13317)***
Jones Truck & Spring Repr Inc.....614 443-4619
350 Frank Rd Columbus (43207) ***(G-7949)***
Jonle Co Inc.....513 662-2282
4117 Bridgetown Rd Cincinnati (45211) ***(G-3885)***
Jonle Heating & Cooling, Cincinnati *Also called Jonle Co Inc* ***(G-3885)***
Jordan Kyli Enterprises Inc.....216 256-3773
24650 Center Ridge Rd Westlake (44145) ***(G-19502)***
Jordan Realtors Inc.....513 791-0281
7658 Montgomery Rd Cincinnati (45236) ***(G-3886)***
Joseph A Girgis MD Inc (PA).....440 930-6095
5334 Meadow Lane Ct Sheffield Village (44035) ***(G-16889)***
Joseph and Florence Mandel.....216 464-4055
26500 Shaker Blvd Beachwood (44122) ***(G-1092)***
Joseph Chevrolet Oldsmobile Co.....513 741-6700
8733 Colerain Ave Cincinnati (45251) ***(G-3887)***
Joseph Industries Inc.....330 528-0091
10039 Aurora Hudson Rd Streetsboro (44241) ***(G-17418)***
Joseph Northland Porsche Audi, Cincinnati *Also called Cronins Inc* ***(G-3440)***
Joseph R Harrison Company Lpa.....330 666-6900
36 37th St Sw Barberton (44203) ***(G-967)***
Joseph Russo.....440 748-2690
12044 Island Rd Grafton (44044) ***(G-11441)***
Joseph S Mischell.....513 542-9800
5109 Winton Rd Cincinnati (45232) ***(G-3888)***
Joseph Schmidt Realty Inc.....330 225-6688
47 Pearl Rd Brunswick (44212) ***(G-1983)***
Joseph T Ryerson & Son Inc.....513 542-5800
555 N Yearling Rd Columbus (43213) ***(G-7950)***
Joseph T Ryerson & Son Inc.....513 896-4600
1108 Central Ave Hamilton (45011) ***(G-11748)***
Joseph Walker Inc.....614 895-3840
8800 Lyra Dr Ste 600 Columbus (43240) ***(G-6887)***
Joseph, Mann & Creed, Twinsburg *Also called Media Collections Inc* ***(G-18447)***
Joshen Paper & Packaging Co (PA).....216 441-5600
5800 Grant Ave Cleveland (44105) ***(G-5872)***

ALPHABETIC

Joshua Homes, Columbus *Also called Joshua Investment Company Inc* ***(G-7951)***
Joshua Investment Company Inc 614 428-5555
3065 Mcctcheon Crssing Dr Columbus (43219) ***(G-7951)***
Josina Lott Foundation 419 866-9013
120 S Holland Sylvania Rd Toledo (43615) ***(G-17987)***
JOSINA LOTT RESIDENTIAL HOME, Toledo *Also called Josina Lott Foundation* ***(G-17987)***
Joslin Diabetes Center Inc 937 401-7575
1989 Miambrg Ctrvl Rd 2 Ste Dayton (45459) ***(G-9645)***
Jostin Construction Inc 513 559-9390
2335 Florence Ave Cincinnati (45206) ***(G-3889)***
Joyce Buick Inc 419 529-3211
1400 Park Ave W Ontario (44906) ***(G-15696)***
Joyce Buick GMC of Mansfield, Ontario *Also called Joyce Buick Inc* ***(G-15696)***
JP Flooring Systems Inc 513 346-4300
9097 Union Centre Blvd West Chester (45069) ***(G-19099)***
JP Recovery Services Inc 440 356-5048
20220 Center Ridge Rd # 370 Rocky River (44116) ***(G-16583)***
Jpmorgan Chase Bank Nat Assn 614 759-8955
8445 E Main St Reynoldsburg (43068) ***(G-16460)***
Jpmorgan Chase Bank Nat Assn 614 876-7650
6364 Scioto Darby Rd Hilliard (43026) ***(G-11917)***
Jpmorgan Chase Bank Nat Assn 614 248-2410
2025 Brice Rd Reynoldsburg (43068) ***(G-16461)***
Jpmorgan Chase Bank Nat Assn (HQ) 614 436-3055
1111 Polaris Pkwy Columbus (43240) ***(G-6888)***
Jpmorgan Chase Bank Nat Assn 614 794-7398
340 S Cleveland Ave Westerville (43081) ***(G-19413)***
Jpmorgan Chase Bank Nat Assn 614 476-1910
4000 Morse Xing Columbus (43219) ***(G-7952)***
Jpmorgan Chase Bank Nat Assn 513 221-1040
4805 Montgomery Rd Cincinnati (45212) ***(G-3890)***
Jpmorgan Chase Bank Nat Assn 513 826-2317
9019 Plainfield Rd Blue Ash (45236) ***(G-1621)***
Jpmorgan Chase Bank Nat Assn 419 358-4055
135 S Main St Bluffton (45817) ***(G-1733)***
Jpmorgan Chase Bank Nat Assn 216 781-2127
3415 Vision Dr Columbus (43219) ***(G-7953)***
Jpmorgan Chase Bank Nat Assn 740 423-4111
321 Main St Belpre (45714) ***(G-1439)***
Jpmorgan Chase Bank Nat Assn 614 248-5391
100 E Broad St Ste 2460 Columbus (43215) ***(G-7954)***
Jpmorgan Chase Bank Nat Assn 513 985-5120
822 Delta Ave Cincinnati (45226) ***(G-3891)***
Jpmorgan Chase Bank Nat Assn 513 784-0770
45 E 4th St Cincinnati (45202) ***(G-3892)***
Jpmorgan Chase Bank Nat Assn 740 363-8032
61 N Sandusky St Delaware (43015) ***(G-10112)***
Jpmorgan Chase Bank Nat Assn 330 364-7242
141 E High Ave New Philadelphia (44663) ***(G-15104)***
Jpmorgan Chase Bank Nat Assn 740 382-7362
165 W Center St Marion (43302) ***(G-13544)***
Jpmorgan Chase Bank Nat Assn 419 394-2358
125 W Spring St Saint Marys (45885) ***(G-16678)***
Jpmorgan Chase Bank Nat Assn 419 294-4944
335 N Sandusky Ave Upper Sandusky (43351) ***(G-18562)***
Jpmorgan Chase Bank Nat Assn 740 676-2671
3201 Belmont St Ste 100 Bellaire (43906) ***(G-1366)***
Jpmorgan Chase Bank Nat Assn 330 972-1905
2647 Bailey Rd Cuyahoga Falls (44221) ***(G-9198)***
Jpmorgan Chase Bank Nat Assn 513 985-5350
967 Lila Ave Milford (45150) ***(G-14529)***
Jpmorgan Chase Bank Nat Assn 513 595-6450
11745 Princeton Pike Cincinnati (45246) ***(G-3893)***
Jpmorgan Chase Bank Nat Assn 440 442-7800
5332 Mayfield Rd Cleveland (44124) ***(G-5873)***
Jpmorgan Chase Bank Nat Assn 330 972-1735
5638 Manchester Rd New Franklin (44319) ***(G-15045)***
Jpmorgan Chase Bank Nat Assn 330 287-5101
601 Portage Rd Wooster (44691) ***(G-19874)***
Jpmorgan Chase Bank Nat Assn 330 650-0476
136 W Streetsboro St Hudson (44236) ***(G-12126)***
Jpmorgan Chase Bank Nat Assn 440 352-5491
2772 N Ridge Rd Perry (44081) ***(G-15961)***
Jpmorgan Chase Bank Nat Assn 419 424-7570
1971 Broad Ave Findlay (45840) ***(G-11052)***
Jpmorgan Chase Bank Nat Assn 937 534-8218
950 Forrer Blvd Dayton (45420) ***(G-9646)***
Jpmorgan Chase Bank Nat Assn 330 225-1330
3191 Center Rd Brunswick (44212) ***(G-1984)***
Jpmorgan Chase Bank Nat Assn 843 679-3653
3415 Vision Dr Columbus (43219) ***(G-7955)***
Jpmorgan Chase Bank Nat Assn 330 325-7855
4000 Waterloo Rd Randolph (44265) ***(G-16373)***
Jpmorgan Chase Bank Nat Assn 330 287-5101
601 Portage Rd Wooster (44691) ***(G-19875)***
Jpmorgan Chase Bank Nat Assn 419 946-3015
16 N Main St Mount Gilead (43338) ***(G-14854)***
Jpmorgan Chase Bank Nat Assn 419 586-6668
205 W Market St Celina (45822) ***(G-2648)***
Jpmorgan Chase Bank Nat Assn 440 352-5969
30 S Park Pl Ste 100 Painesville (44077) ***(G-15859)***
Jpmorgan Chase Bank Nat Assn 330 545-2551
43 W Liberty St Girard (44420) ***(G-11416)***
Jpmorgan Chase Bank Nat Assn 440 286-6111
100 Center St Ste 100 Chardon (44024) ***(G-2753)***
Jpmorgan Chase Bank Nat Assn 330 972-1915
1805 Brittain Rd Akron (44310) ***(G-298)***
Jpmorgan Chase Bank Nat Assn 330 759-1750
3999 Belmont Ave Youngstown (44505) ***(G-20242)***
Jpmorgan Chase Bank Nat Assn 419 424-7512
500 S Main St Findlay (45840) ***(G-11053)***
Jpmorgan Chase Bank Nat Assn 614 248-5800
275 W Schrock Rd Westerville (43081) ***(G-19414)***
Jpmorgan Chase Bank Nat Assn 614 920-4182
6314 Gender Rd Canal Winchester (43110) ***(G-2161)***
Jpmorgan Chase Bank Nat Assn 614 834-3120
7915 Refugee Rd Pickerington (43147) ***(G-16098)***
Jpmorgan Chase Bank Nat Assn 614 853-2999
5684 W Broad St Galloway (43119) ***(G-11344)***
Jpmorgan Chase Bank Nat Assn 614 248-3315
4066 Powell Rd Powell (43065) ***(G-16340)***
Jpmorgan Chase Bank Nat Assn 740 657-8906
8681 Columbus Pike Lewis Center (43035) ***(G-12690)***
Jpmorgan Chase Bank Nat Assn 216 524-0600
7703 Broadview Rd Seven Hills (44131) ***(G-16831)***
Jpmorgan Chase Bank Nat Assn 740 374-2263
125 Putnam St Marietta (45750) ***(G-13459)***
Jpmorgan Chase Bank Nat Assn 614 248-7505
713 Brooksedge Plaza Dr Westerville (43081) ***(G-19415)***
Jpmorgan Chase Bank Nat Assn 614 248-5800
800 Brooksedge Blvd Westerville (43081) ***(G-19416)***
Jpmorgan Chase Bank Nat Assn 440 277-1038
1882 E 29th St Lorain (44055) ***(G-13044)***
Jpmorgan Chase Bank Nat Assn 419 739-3600
801 Defiance St Wapakoneta (45895) ***(G-18800)***
Jpmorgan Chase Bank Nat Assn 330 722-6626
3626 Medina Rd Medina (44256) ***(G-14087)***
Jpmorgan Chase Bank Nat Assn 614 248-2083
1199 Corrugated Way Columbus (43201) ***(G-7956)***
Jpmorgan Chase Bank Nat Assn 216 781-4437
1300 E 9th St Fl 13 Cleveland (44114) ***(G-5874)***
Jpmorgan High Yield Fund 614 248-7017
1111 Polaris Pkwy Columbus (43240) ***(G-6889)***
Jpmorgan Inv Advisors Inc (HQ) 614 248-5800
1111 Polaris Pkwy Columbus (43240) ***(G-6890)***
Jr Engineering Inc 330 848-0960
123 9th St Nw Barberton (44203) ***(G-968)***
Jrb Industries LLC 567 825-7022
3425 State Route 571 Greenville (45331) ***(G-11511)***
JS Bova Excavating LLC 234 254-4040
235 State St Struthers (44471) ***(G-17532)***
JS Paris Excavating Inc 330 538-3048
12240 Commissioner Dr North Jackson (44451) ***(G-15382)***
Jtc Contracting Inc 216 635-0745
7635 Hub Pkwy Ste C Cleveland (44125) ***(G-5875)***
Jtc Office Services, Cleveland *Also called Jtc Contracting Inc* ***(G-5875)***
Jtd Health Systems Inc 419 394-3335
200 Saint Clair Ave Saint Marys (45885) ***(G-16679)***
Jtekt Auto Tenn Morristown 440 835-1000
29570 Clemens Rd Westlake (44145) ***(G-19503)***
Jtf Construction Inc 513 860-9835
4235 Muhlhauser Rd Fairfield (45014) ***(G-10866)***
Jti Transportation Inc 419 661-9360
5601 Cherry St Stony Ridge (43463) ***(G-17347)***
Jto Club Corp 440 352-1900
6011 Heisley Rd Mentor (44060) ***(G-14200)***
Jubilee Academy, Cleveland *Also called Chal-Ron LLC* ***(G-5225)***
Judson (PA) 216 791-2004
2181 Ambleside Dr Apt 411 Cleveland (44106) ***(G-5876)***
Judson 216 791-2555
1890 E 107th St Cleveland (44106) ***(G-5877)***
Judson Care Center Inc 216 292-5706
2373 Harrison Ave Cincinnati (45211) ***(G-3894)***
Judson Manor, Cleveland *Also called Judson* ***(G-5877)***
Judson Palmer Home Corp 419 422-9656
2911 N Main St Findlay (45840) ***(G-11054)***
JUDSON UNIVERSITY CIRCLE, Cleveland *Also called Judson* ***(G-5876)***
Judson Village, Cincinnati *Also called Baptist Home and Center* ***(G-3076)***
Judy Mills Company Inc (PA) 513 271-4241
3360 Red Bank Rd Cincinnati (45227) ***(G-3895)***
Juice Technologies Inc 800 518-5576
350 E 1st Ave Ste 210 Columbus (43201) ***(G-7957)***
Julian & Grube Inc 614 846-1899
333 County Line Rd W A Westerville (43082) ***(G-19318)***
Julian Speer Co 614 261-6331
5255 Sinclair Rd Columbus (43229) ***(G-7958)***
Julius Zorn Inc 330 923-4999
3690 Zorn Dr Cuyahoga Falls (44223) ***(G-9199)***
Jumplinecom Inc 614 859-1170
5000 Arlngton Centre Blvd Columbus (43220) ***(G-7959)***
Junior Achvment Mhning Vly Inc 330 539-5268
1601 Motor Inn Dr Ste 305 Girard (44420) ***(G-11417)***
Juniper Networks Inc 614 932-1432
545 Metro Pl S Ste 164 Dublin (43017) ***(G-10383)***
Jurus Stanley R Atty At Law 614 486-0297
1375 Dublin Rd Columbus (43215) ***(G-7960)***

ALPHABETIC SECTION Kalmbach Pork Finishing LLC

Jurus Law Office, Columbus *Also called Jurus Stanley R Atty At Law* ***(G-7960)***
Just 4 Kidz Childcare....440 285-2221
13896 Gar Hwy Chardon (44024) ***(G-2754)***
Just In Time Care Inc....614 985-3555
5320 E Main St Ste 200 Columbus (43213) ***(G-7961)***
Just In Time Care Services, Columbus *Also called Just In Time Care Inc* ***(G-7961)***
Justice & Business Svcs LLC....740 423-5005
210 Florence St Belpre (45714) ***(G-1440)***
Justice & Co Inc....330 225-6000
2462 Pearl Rd Medina (44256) ***(G-14088)***
Justin L Paulk....513 422-7060
3641 Commerce Dr Middletown (45005) ***(G-14481)***
Juvenile Court Cnty Muskingum....740 453-0351
1860 East Pike Zanesville (43701) ***(G-20493)***
Juvenile Detention Center, Columbus *Also called Franklin Cnty Bd Commissioners* ***(G-7686)***
Juzo, Cuyahoga Falls *Also called Julius Zorn Inc* ***(G-9199)***
Jvc Sports Corp....330 726-1757
8249 South Ave Youngstown (44512) ***(G-20243)***
JWF Technologies Llc (PA)....513 769-9611
6820 Fairfield Bus Ctr Fairfield (45014) ***(G-10867)***
Jyg Innovations LLC....937 630-3858
6450 Poe Ave Ste 103 Dayton (45414) ***(G-9647)***
JZE Electric Inc (PA)....440 243-7600
6800 Eastland Rd Cleveland (44130) ***(G-5878)***
K & D Enterprises Inc....440 946-3600
4420 Sherwin Rd Ste 1 Willoughby (44094) ***(G-19672)***
K & K Interiors Inc....419 627-0039
2230 Superior St Sandusky (44870) ***(G-16772)***
K & L Floormasters LLC....330 493-0869
1518 Cadney St Ne Canton (44714) ***(G-2420)***
K & L Trucking Inc....419 822-3836
490 W Main St Delta (43515) ***(G-10160)***
K & M Construction Company....330 723-3681
230 E Smith Rd Medina (44256) ***(G-14089)***
K & M Contracting Ohio Inc....330 759-1090
5635 Sampson Dr Girard (44420) ***(G-11418)***
K & M International Inc (PA)....330 425-2550
1955 Midway Dr Ste A Twinsburg (44087) ***(G-18435)***
K & M Kleening Service Inc....614 737-3750
4429 Professional Pkwy Groveport (43125) ***(G-11652)***
K & M Tire Inc (PA)....419 695-1061
965 Spencerville Rd Delphos (45833) ***(G-10145)***
K & M Tire Inc....419 695-1060
502 N Main St Delphos (45833) ***(G-10146)***
K & P Trucking LLC....419 935-8646
3862 State Route 103 S Willard (44890) ***(G-19621)***
K & R Distributors Inc....937 864-5495
7606 Dayton Rd Fairborn (45324) ***(G-10799)***
K & W Roofing Inc....740 927-3122
8356 National Rd Sw Etna (43062) ***(G-10735)***
K - O - I Warehouse Inc....937 323-5585
622 W Main St Springfield (45504) ***(G-17218)***
K - O - I Warehouse Inc (HQ)....513 357-2400
2701 Spring Grove Ave Cincinnati (45225) ***(G-3896)***
K 100 Radio Station, Toledo *Also called Cumulus Media Inc* ***(G-17843)***
K A P C O, Kent *Also called Kent Adhesive Products Co* ***(G-12376)***
K Amalia Enterprises Inc....614 733-3800
8025 Corporate Blvd Plain City (43064) ***(G-16195)***
K and R, Fairlawn *Also called Kenneth Zerrusen* ***(G-10962)***
K and W Roofing, Etna *Also called K & W Roofing Inc* ***(G-10735)***
K C M Consulting, Toledo *Also called Knight Crockett Miller Ins* ***(G-17996)***
K Company Incorporated....330 773-5125
2234 S Arlington Rd Coventry Township (44319) ***(G-9127)***
K F T Inc....513 241-5910
726 Mehring Way Cincinnati (45203) ***(G-3897)***
K H F Inc....330 928-0694
3884 State Rd Cuyahoga Falls (44223) ***(G-9200)***
K Hovnanian Summit Homes LLC (HQ)....330 454-4048
2000 10th St Ne Canton (44705) ***(G-2421)***
K M & M....216 651-3333
9715 Clinton Rd Cleveland (44144) ***(G-5879)***
K M B Inc....330 889-3451
1306 State Route 88 Bristolville (44402) ***(G-1872)***
K M C Corporation (PA)....740 598-4171
2670 Commercial Ave Mingo Junction (43938) ***(G-14655)***
K M Clemens DDS Inc....419 228-4036
2115 Allentown Rd Ste C Lima (45805) ***(G-12807)***
K M I, Columbus *Also called Knowledge MGT Interactive Inc* ***(G-8005)***
K M T Service....614 777-7770
3786 Fishinger Blvd Hilliard (43026) ***(G-11918)***
K O I, Cincinnati *Also called KOI Enterprises Inc* ***(G-3939)***
K O I Auto Parts, Cincinnati *Also called K - O - I Warehouse Inc* ***(G-3896)***
K R Drenth Trucking Inc....708 983-6340
119 E Court St Cincinnati (45202) ***(G-3898)***
K Ray Holding Co....614 861-4738
3121 Brice Rd Brice (43109) ***(G-1858)***
K S Bandag Inc....330 264-9237
737 Industrial Blvd Wooster (44691) ***(G-19876)***
K W Zellers & Son Inc....330 877-9371
13494 Duquette Ave Ne Hartville (44632) ***(G-11825)***

K West Group LLC....972 722-3874
8305 Fremont Pike Perrysburg (43551) ***(G-16022)***
K&D Group Inc (PA)....440 946-3600
4420 Sherwin Rd Ste 1 Willoughby (44094) ***(G-19673)***
K&K Technical Group Inc....513 202-1300
10053 Simonson Rd Ste 2 Harrison (45030) ***(G-11804)***
K-Limited Carrier Ltd (PA)....419 269-0002
131 Matzinger Rd Toledo (43612) ***(G-17988)***
K-M-S Industries Inc....440 243-6680
6519 Eastland Rd Ste 1 Brookpark (44142) ***(G-1948)***
K-Y Residential Coml Indus Dev....330 448-4055
505 Bedford Rd Se Brookfield (44403) ***(G-1897)***
K.M.S., Brookpark *Also called K-M-S Industries Inc* ***(G-1948)***
K4 Architecture LLC....513 455-5005
555 Gest St Cincinnati (45203) ***(G-3899)***
Ka Architecture, Seven Hills *Also called Ka Inc* ***(G-16832)***
KA Bergquist Inc (PA)....419 865-4196
1100 King Rd Toledo (43617) ***(G-17989)***
Ka Inc....216 781-9144
6000 Lombardo Ctr Ste 500 Seven Hills (44131) ***(G-16832)***
Kace Logistics LLC....419 273-3388
1515 Matzinger Rd Toledo (43612) ***(G-17990)***
Kademenos Wisehart Hines (PA)....419 524-6011
6 W 3rd St Ste 200 Mansfield (44902) ***(G-13318)***
Kaffenbarger Truck Eqp Co (PA)....937 845-3804
10100 Ballentine Pike New Carlisle (45344) ***(G-15025)***
Kaffenbarger Truck Eqp Co....513 772-6800
3260 E Kemper Rd Cincinnati (45241) ***(G-3900)***
Kahan & Kahan, Cleveland *Also called Shapiro Shapiro & Shapiro* ***(G-6477)***
Kaiser Consulting LLC....614 378-5361
818 Riverbend Ave Powell (43065) ***(G-16341)***
Kaiser Foundation Health Plan, Avon *Also called Healthspan Integrated Care* ***(G-897)***
Kaiser Foundation Health Plan, Cleveland *Also called Healthspan Integrated Care* ***(G-5739)***
Kaiser Foundation Health Plan, Cleveland *Also called Healthspan Integrated Care* ***(G-5740)***
Kaiser Foundation Health Plan, Cleveland *Also called Healthspan Integrated Care* ***(G-5741)***
Kaiser Foundation Health Plan, Cleveland *Also called Healthspan Integrated Care* ***(G-5743)***
Kaiser Foundation Health Plan, Brewster *Also called Healthspan Integrated Care* ***(G-1855)***
Kaiser Foundation Health Plan, Twinsburg *Also called Healthspan Integrated Care* ***(G-18428)***
Kaiser Foundation Health Plan, Hartville *Also called Healthspan Integrated Care* ***(G-11821)***
Kaiser Foundation Health Plan, Wadsworth *Also called Healthspan Integrated Care* ***(G-18754)***
Kaiser Foundation Health Plan, Akron *Also called Healthspan Integrated Care* ***(G-261)***
Kaiser Foundation Health Plan, Lakewood *Also called Healthspan Integrated Care* ***(G-12481)***
Kaiser Foundation Hospitals....440 350-3614
7536 Fredle Dr Concord Township (44077) ***(G-9032)***
Kaiser Foundation Hospitals....330 633-8400
1260 Independence Ave Akron (44310) ***(G-299)***
Kaiser Foundation Hospitals....216 524-7377
36711 American Way Avon (44011) ***(G-901)***
Kaiser Foundation Hospitals....800 524-7377
10 Severance Cir Cleveland Heights (44118) ***(G-6792)***
Kaiser Foundation Hospitals....216 524-7377
5400 Lancaster Dr Brooklyn Heights (44131) ***(G-1918)***
Kaiser Foundation Hospitals....800 524-7377
4914 Portage Rd North Canton (44720) ***(G-15347)***
Kaiser Foundation Hospitals....800 524-7377
3443 Medina Rd Medina (44256) ***(G-14090)***
Kaiser Foundation Hospitals....800 524-7377
4055 Embassy Pkwy Ste 110 Fairlawn (44333) ***(G-10961)***
Kaiser Foundation Hospitals....800 524-7377
7695 Mentor Ave Mentor (44060) ***(G-14201)***
Kaiser Foundation Hospitals....800 524-7377
2500 State Route 59 Kent (44240) ***(G-12375)***
Kaiser Foundation Hospitals....216 524-7377
20575 Ctr Ridgerd Ste 500 Rocky River (44116) ***(G-16584)***
Kaiser Foundation Hospitals....800 524-7377
5400 Lancaster Dr Brooklyn Heights (44131) ***(G-1919)***
Kaiser Foundation Hospitals....216 524-7377
17406 Royalton Rd Strongsville (44136) ***(G-17479)***
Kaiser Foundation Hospitals....330 486-2800
8920 Canyon Falls Blvd Twinsburg (44087) ***(G-18436)***
Kaiser Foundation Hospitals....216 524-7377
5105 S O M Center Rd Willoughby (44094) ***(G-19674)***
Kaiser Logistics LLC....937 534-0213
201 Lawton Ave Monroe (45050) ***(G-14700)***
Kaiser Wells Pharmacy, Norwalk *Also called Kaiser-Wells Inc* ***(G-15577)***
Kaiser-Wells Inc....419 668-7651
251 Benedict Ave Norwalk (44857) ***(G-15577)***
Kajima International Inc (HQ)....440 544-2600
6095 Parkland Blvd Cleveland (44124) ***(G-5880)***
Kal Electric Inc....740 593-8720
5265 Hebbardsville Rd Athens (45701) ***(G-796)***
Kalahari Resort, Sandusky *Also called Lmn Development LLC* ***(G-16775)***
Kallas Enterprises Inc....330 253-6893
916 E Buchtel Ave Akron (44305) ***(G-300)***
Kalmbach Pork Finishing LLC....419 294-3838
7148 State Highway 199 Upper Sandusky (43351) ***(G-18563)***

ALPHABETIC

Kalypso LP (PA).....216 378-4290
3659 Green Rd Ste 100 Beachwood (44122) ***(G-1093)***
Kaman Corporation.....330 468-1811
7900 Empire Pkwy Macedonia (44056) ***(G-13205)***
Kandy Kane Childrens Lrng Ctr (PA).....330 864-6642
1010 S Hawkins Ave Akron (44320) ***(G-301)***
Kandy Kane Chrstn Day Care Ctr, Akron *Also called Kandy Kane Childrens Lrng Ctr* ***(G-301)***
Kangaroo Pouch Daycare Inc.....440 473-4725
488 Leverett Ln Cleveland (44143) ***(G-5881)***
Kansas City Hardwood Corp.....913 621-1975
17717 Hilliard Rd Lakewood (44107) ***(G-12484)***
KAO Collins Inc (PA).....513 948-9000
1201 Edison Dr Cincinnati (45216) ***(G-3901)***
Kaplan Trucking Company (PA).....216 341-3322
6600 Bessemer Ave Cleveland (44127) ***(G-5882)***
Kapp Construction Inc.....937 324-0134
329 Mount Vernon Ave Springfield (45503) ***(G-17219)***
Kappa House Corp of Delta.....614 487-9461
3220 Riverside Dr Ste A2 Upper Arlington (43221) ***(G-18552)***
Kappa Kappa Gamma Foundation (PA).....614 228-6515
530 E Town St Columbus (43215) ***(G-7962)***
Kappa Kappa Gamma Fraternity, Columbus *Also called Kappa Kappa Gamma Foundation* ***(G-7962)***
Kappus Company, Cleveland *Also called John H Kappus Co* ***(G-5867)***
Kapstone Container Corporation.....330 562-6111
1450 S Chillicothe Rd Aurora (44202) ***(G-844)***
Kapton Caulking & Building.....440 526-0670
6500 Harris Rd Cleveland (44147) ***(G-5883)***
Kar Products.....216 416-7200
1301 E 9th St Ste 700 Cleveland (44114) ***(G-5884)***
Karam & Simon Realty Inc.....330 929-0707
207 Portage Trail Ext W # 101 Cuyahoga Falls (44223) ***(G-9201)***
Karamu House Inc (PA).....216 795-7070
2355 E 89th St Cleveland (44106) ***(G-5885)***
KARAMU THEATRE, Cleveland *Also called Karamu House Inc* ***(G-5885)***
Karcher Group Inc.....330 493-6141
5590 Lauby Rd Ste 8 North Canton (44720) ***(G-15348)***
Kare A Lot.....614 298-8933
1030 King Ave Columbus (43212) ***(G-7963)***
Kare A Lot Child Care Center, Columbus *Also called Kare A Lot Infnt Tddlr Dev Ctr* ***(G-7964)***
Kare A Lot Infnt Tddlr Dev Ctr.....614 481-7532
3164 Riverside Dr Columbus (43221) ***(G-7964)***
Kare Medical Trnspt Svcs LLP.....937 578-0263
1002 Columbus Ave Marysville (43040) ***(G-13630)***
Karl Hc LLC.....614 846-5420
5700 Karl Rd Columbus (43229) ***(G-7965)***
Karlsberger Companies (PA).....614 461-9500
99 E Main St Columbus (43215) ***(G-7966)***
Karopa Incorporate.....513 860-1616
3987 Hmiltn Mddltwn Rd Hamilton (45011) ***(G-11749)***
Karpinski Engineering Inc.....614 430-9820
8800 Lyra Dr Ste 530 Columbus (43240) ***(G-6891)***
Karpinski Engineering Inc (PA).....216 391-3700
3135 Euclid Ave Ste 200 Cleveland (44115) ***(G-5886)***
Karrington Operating Co Inc (HQ).....614 324-5951
919 Old Henderson Rd Columbus (43220) ***(G-7967)***
Karst & Sons Inc.....614 501-9530
6496 Taylor Rd Sw Reynoldsburg (43068) ***(G-16462)***
Kassouf Company.....216 651-3333
2231 Lilac Ln Avon (44011) ***(G-902)***
Kastle Electric Co LLC.....937 254-2681
4501 Kettering Blvd Moraine (45439) ***(G-14794)***
Kastle Electric Company.....937 254-2681
4501 Kettering Blvd Moraine (45439) ***(G-14795)***
Kastle Electric Company.....513 360-2901
100 Cart Path Dr Monroe (45050) ***(G-14701)***
Kastle Technologies, Monroe *Also called Kastle Electric Company* ***(G-14701)***
Kastle Technologies Co LLC (HQ).....513 360-2901
100 Cart Path Dr Monroe (45050) ***(G-14702)***
Kastle Technologies Co LLC.....614 433-9860
185-H Huntley Rd Columbus (43229) ***(G-7968)***
Kathleen K Karol MD.....419 878-7992
2865 N Reynolds Rd # 170 Toledo (43615) ***(G-17991)***
Kathman Electric Co Inc.....513 353-3365
8969 Harrison Pike Cleves (45002) ***(G-6800)***
Katz Teller, Cincinnati *Also called Katz Teller Brant Hild Co Lpa* ***(G-3902)***
Katz Teller Brant Hild Co Lpa.....513 721-4532
255 E 5th St Fl 24 Cincinnati (45202) ***(G-3902)***
Kaufman Container Company (PA).....216 898-2000
1000 Keystone Pkwy # 100 Cleveland (44135) ***(G-5887)***
Kaval-Levine Management Co.....440 944-5402
34500 Chardon Rd Ste 5 Willoughby Hills (44094) ***(G-19731)***
Kbec Sugarcreek Health Center, Dayton *Also called Kettering Medical Center* ***(G-9655)***
Kbj-Summit LLC.....440 232-3334
7817 First Pl Bedford (44146) ***(G-1314)***
Kcbs LLC.....513 421-9422
7800 E Kemper Rd Ste 160 Cincinnati (45249) ***(G-3903)***
Kdb, Columbus *Also called Etc Gameco LLC* ***(G-7615)***
Ke Gutridge LLC.....614 252-0420
1111 Rarig Ave Columbus (43219) ***(G-7969)***
Keaney Investment Group LLC.....937 263-6429
1440 Nicholas Rd Dayton (45417) ***(G-9648)***
Keating Muething & Klekamp Pll (PA).....513 579-6400
1 E 4th St Ste 1400 Cincinnati (45202) ***(G-3904)***
Keebler Hall, Akron *Also called Community Support Services Inc* ***(G-159)***
Keen & Cross Envmtl Svcs Inc.....513 674-1700
504 Northland Blvd Cincinnati (45240) ***(G-3905)***
Keeptryan Inc.....330 319-1866
55 E Exchange St Akron (44308) ***(G-302)***
Kegler Brown Hl Ritter Co Lpa (PA).....614 462-5400
65 E State St Ste 1800 Columbus (43215) ***(G-7970)***
Kegler Brown Hl Ritter Co Lpa.....216 586-6650
600 Superior Ave E # 2500 Cleveland (44114) ***(G-5888)***
Keidel Supply Company Inc (PA).....513 351-1600
1150 Tennessee Ave Cincinnati (45229) ***(G-3906)***
Keihin Thermal Tech Amer Inc.....740 869-3000
10500 Oday Harrison Rd Mount Sterling (43143) ***(G-14873)***
Keim Concrete LLC.....330 264-5313
4175 W Old Lincoln Way Wooster (44691) ***(G-19877)***
Keim Lumber Company.....330 893-2251
State Rte 557 Baltic (43804) ***(G-946)***
Keim, Jim Ford Sales, Columbus *Also called Jim Keim Ford* ***(G-7941)***
Keith D Weiner & Assoc Lpa, Cleveland *Also called Weiner Keith D Co L P A Inc* ***(G-6729)***
Keithley Instruments LLC (HQ).....440 248-0400
28775 Aurora Rd Solon (44139) ***(G-17021)***
Keithley Instruments Intl Corp.....440 248-0400
28775 Aurora Rd Cleveland (44139) ***(G-5889)***
Kelchner Inc (HQ).....937 704-9890
50 Advanced Dr Springboro (45066) ***(G-17125)***
Keller Farms Landscape & Nurs, Columbus *Also called Keller Group Limited* ***(G-7971)***
Keller Group Limited.....614 866-9551
3909 Groves Rd Columbus (43232) ***(G-7971)***
Keller Logistics Group Inc.....419 784-4805
24862 Elliott Rd Ste 101 Defiance (43512) ***(G-10039)***
Keller Logistics Group Inc (PA).....866 276-9486
24862 Elliott Rd Ste 101 Defiance (43512) ***(G-10040)***
Keller Ochs Koch Inc.....419 332-8288
416 S Arch St Fremont (43420) ***(G-11208)***
Keller Warehousing & Dist LLC.....419 784-4805
1160 Carpenter Rd Defiance (43512) ***(G-10041)***
Keller Williams Advisors LLC.....513 766-9200
3505 Columbia Pkwy # 125 Cincinnati (45226) ***(G-3907)***
Keller Williams Advisory Rlty.....513 372-6500
8276 Beechmont Ave Cincinnati (45255) ***(G-3908)***
Keller Williams Classic Pro.....614 451-8500
1510 W Lane Ave Columbus (43221) ***(G-7972)***
Keller Williams Realtors, Beachwood *Also called Murwood Real Estate Group LLC* ***(G-1106)***
Keller Williams Rlty M Walker.....330 571-2020
3589 Darrow Rd Stow (44224) ***(G-17378)***
Kellermyer Bergensons Svcs LLC (PA).....419 867-4300
1575 Henthorne Dr Maumee (43537) ***(G-13932)***
Kelley & Ferraro LLP.....216 575-0777
950 Main Ave Ste 1300 Cleveland (44113) ***(G-5890)***
Kelley Brothers Roofing Inc.....513 829-7717
4905 Factory Dr Fairfield (45014) ***(G-10868)***
Kelley Companies.....330 668-6100
190 Montrose West Ave # 200 Copley (44321) ***(G-9057)***
Kelley Steel Erectors Inc (PA).....440 232-1573
7220 Division St Cleveland (44146) ***(G-5891)***
Kelleys Isle Ferry Boat Lines.....419 798-9763
510 W Main St Marblehead (43440) ***(G-13421)***
Kelli Woods Management Inc.....419 478-1200
4708 Angola Rd Toledo (43615) ***(G-17992)***
Kellison & Co (PA).....216 464-5160
4925 Galaxy Pkwy Ste U Cleveland (44128) ***(G-5892)***
Kelly Farrish Lpa.....513 621-8700
810 Sycamore St Fl 6 Cincinnati (45202) ***(G-3909)***
KElly Youth Services Inc.....513 761-0700
800 Compton Rd Unit 11 Cincinnati (45231) ***(G-3910)***
Kemba Credit Union Inc (PA).....513 762-5070
8763 Union Centre Blvd # 101 West Chester (45069) ***(G-19100)***
Kemba Financial Credit Un Inc.....614 235-2395
4311 N High St Columbus (43214) ***(G-7973)***
Kemba Financial Credit Un Inc.....614 853-9774
55 Office Centre Pl Columbus (43228) ***(G-7974)***
Kemba Financial Credit Union.....614 235-2395
4220 E Broad St Columbus (43213) ***(G-7975)***
Kemper Company.....440 846-1100
10890 Prospect Rd Strongsville (44149) ***(G-17480)***
Kemper House of Strongsville, Strongsville *Also called Kemper Company* ***(G-17480)***
Kemper Insurance, Canton *Also called Sirak-Moore Insurance Agcy Inc* ***(G-2531)***
Kemper Shuttle Services, Blue Ash *Also called Universal Work and Power LLC* ***(G-1714)***
Kempthorn Automall (PA).....800 451-3877
1449 Cleveland Ave Nw Canton (44703) ***(G-2422)***
Kempthorn Automall.....330 456-8287
1449 Cleveland Ave Nw Canton (44703) ***(G-2423)***
Kempthorn Motors Inc.....330 452-6511
1449 Cleveland Ave Nw Canton (44703) ***(G-2424)***
Kemron Environmental Svcs Inc.....740 373-4071
2343 State Route 821 Marietta (45750) ***(G-13460)***
Ken Harper.....740 439-4452
60772 Southgate Rd Byesville (43723) ***(G-2071)***
Ken Heiberger Paving Inc.....614 837-0290
458 W Waterloo St Canal Winchester (43110) ***(G-2162)***

ALPHABETIC SECTION
Kettering Tennis Center

Ken Miller Supply Inc ... 330 264-9146
1537 Blachleyville Rd Wooster (44691) ***(G-19878)***
Ken Neyer Plumbing Inc ... 513 353-3311
4895 Hamilton Cleves Rd Cleves (45002) ***(G-6801)***
Ken-Ray Electric, Brice *Also called K Ray Holding Co* ***(G-1858)***
Kenakore Solutions, Perrysburg *Also called TRT Management Corporation* ***(G-16065)***
Kenan Advantage Group Inc (PA) ... 877 999-2524
4366 Mount Pleasant St Nw North Canton (44720) ***(G-15349)***
Kenco Group Inc ... 614 409-8754
5235 Westpoint Dr Bldg 1 Groveport (43125) ***(G-11653)***
Kencor Properties Inc ... 513 984-3870
7565 Kenwood Rd Ste 100 Cincinnati (45236) ***(G-3911)***
Kenda USA, Reynoldsburg *Also called American Kenda Rbr Indus Ltd* ***(G-16428)***
Kendal At Granville ... 740 321-0400
2158 Columbus Rd Granville (43023) ***(G-11467)***
Kendal At Oberlin ... 440 775-0094
600 Kendal Dr Oberlin (44074) ***(G-15647)***
Kendall Holdings Ltd (PA) ... 614 486-4750
2111 Builders Pl Columbus (43204) ***(G-7976)***
Kendis & Associates Co Lpa ... 216 579-1818
614 W Superior Ave # 1500 Cleveland (44113) ***(G-5893)***
Kendle International Inc ... 513 763-1414
441 Vine St Ste 500 Cincinnati (45202) ***(G-3912)***
Kendrick-Mollenauer Pntg Co ... 614 443-7037
1099 Stimmel Rd Columbus (43223) ***(G-7977)***
Kenexis Consulting Corporation ... 614 451-7031
3366 Riverside Dr Ste 200 Upper Arlington (43221) ***(G-18553)***
Kenmar Landscaping Company, Medina *Also called Kenmar Lawn & Grdn Care Co LLC* ***(G-14091)***
Kenmar Lawn & Grdn Care Co LLC ... 330 239-2924
3665 Ridge Rd Medina (44256) ***(G-14091)***
Kenmarc Electrical Contractors, Cincinnati *Also called Kenmarc Inc* ***(G-3913)***
Kenmarc Inc ... 513 541-2791
1055 Heywood St Cincinnati (45225) ***(G-3913)***
Kenmore Construction Co Inc (PA) ... 330 762-8936
700 Home Ave Akron (44310) ***(G-303)***
Kenmore Construction Co Inc ... 330 832-8888
9500 Forty Corners Rd Nw Massillon (44647) ***(G-13827)***
Kenmore Research Company ... 330 297-1407
935 N Freedom St Ravenna (44266) ***(G-16391)***
Kennametal Inc ... 216 898-6120
18105 Cleveland Pkwy Dr Cleveland (44135) ***(G-5894)***
Kennedy Graphics, Cleveland *Also called Kennedy Mint Inc* ***(G-5895)***
Kennedy Group Enterprises Inc ... 440 879-0078
13370 Prospect Rd 2c Strongsville (44149) ***(G-17481)***
Kennedy Mint Inc ... 440 572-3222
12102 Pearl Rd Rear Cleveland (44136) ***(G-5895)***
Kenneth G Myers Cnstr Co Inc ... 419 639-2051
201 Smith St Green Springs (44836) ***(G-11478)***
Kenneth Zerrusen ... 330 869-9007
3412 W Market St Fairlawn (44333) ***(G-10962)***
Kenneth's Design Group, Columbus *Also called Kenneths Hair Salons & Day Sp* ***(G-7978)***
Kenneths Hair Salons & Day Sp (PA) ... 614 457-7712
5151 Reed Rd Ste 250b Columbus (43220) ***(G-7978)***
Kenny Obayashi Joint Venture V ... 703 969-0611
144 Cuyahoga St Akron (44304) ***(G-304)***
Kenoil Inc ... 330 262-1144
1537 Blachleyville Rd Wooster (44691) ***(G-19879)***
Kenosha Beef International Ltd ... 614 771-1330
1821 Dividend Dr Columbus (43228) ***(G-7979)***
Kens Beverage Inc ... 513 874-8200
3219 Homeward Way Fairfield (45014) ***(G-10869)***
Kens Flower Shop Inc ... 419 841-9590
140 W South Boundary St Perrysburg (43551) ***(G-16023)***
Kensington Care Center, Aurora *Also called Anna Maria of Aurora Inc* ***(G-824)***
Kensington Place Inc ... 614 252-5276
1001 Parkview Blvd Columbus (43219) ***(G-7980)***
Kensington Prep Plant, Carrollton *Also called Rosebud Mining Company* ***(G-2627)***
Kent Adhesive Products Co ... 330 678-1626
1000 Cherry St Kent (44240) ***(G-12376)***
Kent Automotive Inc ... 330 678-5520
1080 W Main St Kent (44240) ***(G-12377)***
Kent Healthcare Center, Kent *Also called Fairchild MD Leasing Co LLC* ***(G-12369)***
Kent Lincoln-Mercury Sales, Kent *Also called Kent Automotive Inc* ***(G-12377)***
Kent Medical Offices, Kent *Also called Kaiser Foundation Hospitals* ***(G-12375)***
Kent Place Housing ... 614 942-2020
1414 Gault St Columbus (43205) ***(G-7981)***
Kent Ridge At Golden Pond Ltd ... 330 677-4040
5241 Sunnybrook Rd Kent (44240) ***(G-12378)***
Kent State University ... 330 672-2607
237 Schwartz Ste 237 Kent (44242) ***(G-12379)***
Kent State University ... 330 672-3114
1613 E Summit St Kent (44240) ***(G-12380)***
Kenthworth of Dayton, Dayton *Also called Palmer Trucks Inc* ***(G-9799)***
Kenton Auto and Truck Wrecking ... 419 673-8234
13188 Us Highway 68 Kenton (43326) ***(G-12420)***
Kenton Community Health Center, Kenton *Also called Health Partners Western Ohio* ***(G-12419)***
Kenton Motor Sales, Kenton *Also called Kenton Auto and Truck Wrecking* ***(G-12420)***
Kentucky Heart Institute Inc ... 740 353-8100
2001 Scioto Trl Ste 200 Portsmouth (45662) ***(G-16293)***
Kentucky Window Cleaning, Tipp City *Also called Ohio Window Cleaning Inc* ***(G-17723)***
Kenwood Country Club Inc ... 513 527-3590
6501 Kenwood Rd Cincinnati (45243) ***(G-3914)***
Kenwood Management, Cincinnati *Also called Urban Retail Properties LLC* ***(G-4790)***
Kenwood Office, Cincinnati *Also called Sibcy Cline Inc* ***(G-4520)***
Kenwood Ter Hlth Care Ctr Inc ... 513 793-2255
7450 Keller Rd Cincinnati (45243) ***(G-3915)***
Kenwood Terrace Care Center, Cincinnati *Also called Kenwood Ter Hlth Care Ctr Inc* ***(G-3915)***
Kenworth of Cincinnati Inc ... 513 771-5831
65 Partnership Way Cincinnati (45241) ***(G-3916)***
Kenworth Truck Co, Chillicothe *Also called Rumpke/Kenworth Contract* ***(G-2883)***
Kenyon Co, Coshocton *Also called Novelty Advertising Co Inc* ***(G-9113)***
Kenyon College ... 740 427-2202
100 W Wegan St Gambier (43022) ***(G-11348)***
Kenyon Inn, Gambier *Also called Kenyon College* ***(G-11348)***
Kerkan Roofing Inc ... 513 821-0556
721 W Wyoming Ave Cincinnati (45215) ***(G-3917)***
Kerns Chevrolet Buick GMC, Celina *Also called Kerns Chevrolet-Buick-Gmc Inc* ***(G-2649)***
Kerns Chevrolet-Buick-Gmc Inc ... 419 586-5131
218 S Walnut St Celina (45822) ***(G-2649)***
Kerr House Inc ... 419 832-1733
17777 Beaver St Grand Rapids (43522) ***(G-11451)***
Kerrington Health Systems Inc ... 513 863-0360
2923 Hamilton Mason Rd Fairfield Township (45011) ***(G-10932)***
Kerry Ford Inc (PA) ... 513 671-6400
155 W Kemper Rd Cincinnati (45246) ***(G-3918)***
Kerry Mitsubishi, Cincinnati *Also called Kerry Ford Inc* ***(G-3918)***
Kessler Heating & Cooling ... 614 837-9961
9793 Basil Western Rd Nw Canal Winchester (43110) ***(G-2163)***
Kessler Outdoor Advertising, Zanesville *Also called Kessler Sign Company* ***(G-20494)***
Kessler Sign Company (PA) ... 740 453-0668
2669 National Rd Zanesville (43701) ***(G-20494)***
Kettcor Inc ... 937 458-4949
4301 Lyons Rd Miamisburg (45342) ***(G-14308)***
Kettenring Country Club Inc ... 419 782-2101
1124 Powell View Dr Defiance (43512) ***(G-10042)***
Kettering Adventist Healthcare ... 937 534-4651
5350 Lamme Rd Moraine (45439) ***(G-14796)***
Kettering Adventist Healthcare ... 937 298-3399
3533 Southern Blvd Kettering (45429) ***(G-12430)***
Kettering Adventist Healthcare ... 937 878-8644
1045 Channingway Dr Fairborn (45324) ***(G-10800)***
Kettering Adventist Healthcare ... 937 401-6306
1989 Miamisbg Cntrvll Rd Centerville (45459) ***(G-2681)***
Kettering Adventist Healthcare ... 513 867-3166
7117 Dutchland Pkwy Liberty Township (45044) ***(G-12721)***
Kettering Adventist Healthcare ... 937 298-4331
3965 Southern Blvd Dayton (45429) ***(G-9649)***
Kettering Adventist Healthcare ... 937 395-8816
2110 Leiter Rd Miamisburg (45342) ***(G-14309)***
Kettering Anesthesia Assoc Inc ... 937 298-4331
3533 Sthern Blvd Ste 5200 Dayton (45429) ***(G-9650)***
Kettering Animal Hospital Inc ... 937 294-5211
1600 Delco Park Dr Dayton (45420) ***(G-9651)***
Kettering City School District ... 937 297-1990
2636 Wilmington Pike Dayton (45419) ***(G-9652)***
Kettering City School District ... 937 499-1770
2640 Wilmington Pike Dayton (45419) ***(G-9653)***
Kettering College Medical Art, Dayton *Also called Kettering Medical Center* ***(G-9654)***
Kettering Health Network, Kettering *Also called Kettering Adventist Healthcare* ***(G-12430)***
Kettering Health Network, Liberty Township *Also called Kettering Adventist Healthcare* ***(G-12721)***
Kettering Health Network, Dayton *Also called Kettering Medical Center* ***(G-9656)***
Kettering Health Network Khn, Miamisburg *Also called Kettering Adventist Healthcare* ***(G-14309)***
Kettering Hospital Youth Svcs, Moraine *Also called Kettering Adventist Healthcare* ***(G-14796)***
Kettering Medical Center ... 937 702-4000
3535 Pentagon Park Blvd Beavercreek (45431) ***(G-1181)***
Kettering Medical Center (HQ) ... 937 298-4331
3535 Southern Blvd Kettering (45429) ***(G-12431)***
Kettering Medical Center ... 937 866-0551
4000 Mmsburg Cntrville Rd Miamisburg (45342) ***(G-14310)***
Kettering Medical Center ... 937 298-4331
3535 Southern Blvd Dayton (45429) ***(G-9654)***
Kettering Medical Center ... 937 866-2984
317 Sycamore Glen Dr Ofc Miamisburg (45342) ***(G-14311)***
Kettering Medical Center ... 937 299-0099
580 Lincoln Park Blvd # 200 Dayton (45429) ***(G-9655)***
Kettering Medical Center ... 937 384-8750
1251 E Dorothy Ln Dayton (45419) ***(G-9656)***
Kettering Recreation Center ... 937 296-2587
2900 Glengarry Dr Dayton (45420) ***(G-9657)***
Kettering School Maintainence, Dayton *Also called Kettering City School District* ***(G-9652)***
Kettering Tennis Center ... 937 434-6602
4565 Gateway Cir Dayton (45440) ***(G-9658)***

ALPHABETIC

Keuchel & Associates Inc — ALPHABETIC SECTION

Keuchel & Associates Inc 330 945-9455
175 Muffin Ln Cuyahoga Falls (44223) *(G-9202)*

Kevin C McDonnell MD 330 344-6401
224 W Exchange St Ste 220 Akron (44302) *(G-305)*

Kevin D Arnold, Columbus *Also called Center For Cognitive and Beh* *(G-7223)*

Kevin Kennedy Associates Inc 317 536-7000
275 Outerbelt St Columbus (43213) *(G-7982)*

Key Blue Prints Inc (PA) 614 228-3285
195 E Livingston Ave Columbus (43215) *(G-7983)*

Key Career Place 216 987-3029
2415 Woodland Ave Cleveland (44115) *(G-5896)*

Key Center Properties LP 216 687-0500
127 Public Sq Ste 2727 Cleveland (44114) *(G-5897)*

Key Color, Columbus *Also called Key Blue Prints Inc* *(G-7983)*

Key II Security Inc 937 339-8530
110 W Main St Troy (45373) *(G-18360)*

Key Office Services 419 747-9749
1999 Leppo Rd Mansfield (44903) *(G-13319)*

Key Realty Ltd 419 270-7445
130 Fountain Dr Holland (43528) *(G-12031)*

Keybanc Capital Markets Inc (HQ) 800 553-2240
127 Public Sq Cleveland (44114) *(G-5898)*

Keybank National Association (HQ) 800 539-2968
127 Public Sq Ste 5600 Cleveland (44114) *(G-5899)*

Keybank National Association 216 689-8481
100 Public Sq Ste 600 Cleveland (44113) *(G-5900)*

Keybank National Association 216 813-0000
4910 Tiedeman Rd Cleveland (44144) *(G-5901)*

Keybridge Medical Revenue MGT, Lima *Also called General Audit Corp* *(G-12782)*

Keynes Bros Inc (PA) 740 385-6824
1 W Front St Logan (43138) *(G-12979)*

Keysource Acquisition LLC 513 469-7881
7820 Palace Dr Cincinnati (45249) *(G-3919)*

Keysource Medical, Cincinnati *Also called Keysource Acquisition LLC* *(G-3919)*

Keystone Automotive Inds Inc 513 961-5500
2831 Stanton Ave Cincinnati (45206) *(G-3920)*

Keystone Automotive Inds Inc 330 759-8019
1282 Trumbull Ave Ste C Girard (44420) *(G-11419)*

Keystone Business Solutions, Akron *Also called Keystone Technology Cons* *(G-306)*

Keystone Foods LLC 419 843-3009
4763 High Oaks Blvd Toledo (43623) *(G-17993)*

Keystone Freight Corp 614 542-0320
2545 Parsons Ave Columbus (43207) *(G-7984)*

Keystone Technology Cons 330 666-6200
787 Wye Rd Akron (44333) *(G-306)*

Keyw Corporation 937 702-9512
1415 Research Park Dr Beavercreek (45432) *(G-1182)*

Kf Construction and Excvtg LLC 419 547-7555
220 Norwest St Clyde (43410) *(G-6817)*

KF Express LLC 614 258-8858
10440 Delwood Pl Powell (43065) *(G-16342)*

Kforce Inc 614 436-4027
200 E Campus View Blvd # 225 Columbus (43235) *(G-7985)*

Kforce Inc 216 643-8141
3 Summit Park Dr Ste 550 Independence (44131) *(G-12222)*

Kgbo Holdings Inc 800 580-3101
6525 Centervl Bus Pkwy Centerville (45459) *(G-2682)*

Kgbo Holdings Inc 800 580-3101
8630 Jacquemin Dr West Chester (45069) *(G-19101)*

Kgbo Holdings Inc (PA) 513 831-2600
4289 Ivy Pointe Blvd Cincinnati (45245) *(G-2922)*

Kgk Gardening Design Corp 330 656-1709
1975 Norton Rd Hudson (44236) *(G-12127)*

Khempco Bldg Sup Co Ltd Partnr (PA) 740 549-0465
130 Johnson Dr Delaware (43015) *(G-10113)*

Khm Consulting Inc 330 460-5635
1152 Pearl Rd Brunswick (44212) *(G-1985)*

Khm Travel Group, Brunswick *Also called Khm Consulting Inc* *(G-1985)*

Kiddie Kollege & Academy, Zanesville *Also called Genesis Healthcare System* *(G-20482)*

Kiddie Kollege Inc 440 327-5435
33169 Center Ridge Rd North Ridgeville (44039) *(G-15466)*

Kiddie Korral, Sandusky *Also called Kiddle Korral* *(G-16773)*

Kiddie Party Company LLC 440 273-7680
1690 Lander Rd Mayfield Heights (44124) *(G-14003)*

Kiddie West Pediatric Center 614 276-7733
4766 W Broad St Columbus (43228) *(G-7986)*

Kiddle Korral 419 626-9082
315 W Follett St Sandusky (44870) *(G-16773)*

Kidney & Hypertension Center (PA) 513 861-0800
3219 Clifton Ave Ste 325 Cincinnati (45220) *(G-3921)*

Kidney & Hypertension Con 330 649-9400
4689 Fulton Dr Nw Canton (44718) *(G-2425)*

Kidney Center of Bexley LLC 614 231-2200
1151 College Ave Columbus (43209) *(G-7987)*

Kidney Center Partnership 330 799-1150
139 Javit Ct Youngstown (44515) *(G-20244)*

Kidney Group Inc 330 746-1488
1340 Belmont Ave Ste 2300 Youngstown (44504) *(G-20245)*

Kidney Services W Centl Ohio 419 227-0918
750 W High St Ste 100 Lima (45801) *(G-12808)*

Kidron Auction Inc 330 857-2641
4885 Kidron Rd Kidron (44636) *(G-12442)*

Kidron Electric Inc 330 857-2871
5358 Kidron Rd Kidron (44636) *(G-12443)*

Kidron Electric & Mech Contrs, Kidron *Also called Kidron Electric Inc* *(G-12443)*

Kids 'r' Kids 3 OH, Springboro *Also called Childvine Inc* *(G-17118)*

Kids Ahead Inc 330 628-7404
726 S Cleveland Ave Mogadore (44260) *(G-14680)*

Kids Country, Medina *Also called Medina Advantage Inc* *(G-14096)*

Kids Country, Stow *Also called Future Advantage Inc* *(G-17369)*

Kids Country 330 899-0909
1801 Town Park Blvd Uniontown (44685) *(G-18525)*

Kids First Learning Centers 440 235-2500
26184 Bagley Rd Olmsted Falls (44138) *(G-15674)*

Kids Kastle Day Care 419 586-0903
6783 Staeger Rd Celina (45822) *(G-2650)*

Kids Play Green, Uniontown *Also called Kids-Play Inc* *(G-18526)*

Kids R Kids 2 Ohio 513 860-3197
9077 Union Centre Blvd West Chester (45069) *(G-19102)*

Kids R Kids Schools Qulty Lrng 937 748-1260
790 N Main St Springboro (45066) *(G-17126)*

Kids World 614 473-9229
2812 Morse Rd Columbus (43231) *(G-7988)*

Kids-Play Inc 330 896-2400
1651 Boettler Rd Uniontown (44685) *(G-18526)*

Kids-Play Inc 330 896-2400
1651 Boettler Rd Canton (44721) *(G-2426)*

Kidstown LLC 330 502-4484
55 Stadium Dr Youngstown (44512) *(G-20246)*

Kidz By Riverside Inc 330 392-0700
421 Main Ave Sw Warren (44481) *(G-18869)*

Kidz Watch, Centerville *Also called Agj Kidz LLC* *(G-2669)*

Kiemle-Hankins Company (PA) 419 661-2430
94 H St Perrysburg (43551) *(G-16024)*

Kil Kare Inc 937 429-2961
1166 Dayton Xenia Rd Xenia (45385) *(G-20065)*

Kil-Kare Speedway & Drag Strip, Xenia *Also called Kil Kare Inc* *(G-20065)*

Kilbarger Construction Inc 740 385-5531
450 Gallagher Ave Logan (43138) *(G-12980)*

Kilgore Group Inc 513 684-3721
201 E 4th St Cincinnati (45202) *(G-3922)*

Killbuck Savings Bank Co Inc (HQ) 330 276-4881
165 N Main St Killbuck (44637) *(G-12445)*

Killer Creative Media, Cincinnati *Also called Killer Spotscom Inc* *(G-3923)*

Killer Spotscom Inc 513 201-1380
463 Ohio Pike Ste 301 Cincinnati (45255) *(G-3923)*

Kimball Midwest, Columbus *Also called Midwest Motor Supply Co* *(G-8170)*

Kimberly Williford Attorney 419 241-1220
900 Adams St Toledo (43604) *(G-17994)*

Kimble Companies Inc 330 963-5493
8500 Chamberlin Rd Twinsburg (44087) *(G-18437)*

Kimble Companies Inc (PA) 330 343-5665
3596 State Route 39 Nw Dover (44622) *(G-10194)*

Kimes Convalescent Center 740 593-3391
75 Kimes Ln Athens (45701) *(G-797)*

Kimmel Cleaners Inc (PA) 419 294-1959
225 N Sandusky Ave Upper Sandusky (43351) *(G-18564)*

Kin Care, Lima *Also called Comfort Keepers* *(G-12758)*

Kinane Inc 513 459-0177
7440 S Masn Montgomery Rd Mason (45040) *(G-13727)*

Kinder Care Learning Center, Fairfield Township *Also called Kindercare Education LLC* *(G-10933)*

Kinder Garden School 513 791-4300
10969 Reed Hartman Hwy Blue Ash (45242) *(G-1622)*

Kinder Kare Day Nursery 740 886-6905
627 County Road 411 Proctorville (45669) *(G-16360)*

Kinder Mrgan Lqds Trminals LLC 513 841-0500
5297 River Rd Cincinnati (45233) *(G-3924)*

Kindercare Center 1480, Dayton *Also called Kindercare Learning Ctrs Inc* *(G-9659)*

Kindercare Child Care Network, Solon *Also called Kindercare Learning Ctrs LLC* *(G-17022)*

Kindercare Child Care Network, Cincinnati *Also called Kindercare Learning Ctrs LLC* *(G-3925)*

Kindercare Child Care Network, Worthington *Also called Kindercare Learning Ctrs Inc* *(G-19966)*

Kindercare Child Care Network, Cleveland *Also called Kindercare Learning Ctrs LLC* *(G-5903)*

Kindercare Child Care Network, Cincinnati *Also called Kindercare Learning Ctrs LLC* *(G-3926)*

Kindercare Child Care Network, Cincinnati *Also called Kindercare Learning Ctrs LLC* *(G-3927)*

Kindercare Education LLC 513 896-4769
7939 Morris Rd Fairfield Township (45011) *(G-10933)*

Kindercare Education LLC 330 405-5556
2572 Glenwood Dr Twinsburg (44087) *(G-18438)*

Kindercare Education LLC 614 337-2035
4885 Cherry Bottom Rd Gahanna (43230) *(G-11250)*

Kindercare Education LLC 440 442-3360
679 Alpha Dr Cleveland (44143) *(G-5902)*

Kindercare Learning Ctrs Inc 937 435-2353
951 E Rahn Rd Dayton (45429) *(G-9659)*

Kindercare Learning Ctrs Inc ... 614 888-9696
77 Caren Ave Worthington (43085) *(G-19966)*
Kindercare Learning Ctrs LLC ... 440 248-5437
6140 Kruse Dr Solon (44139) *(G-17022)*
Kindercare Learning Ctrs LLC ... 513 771-8787
1459 E Kemper Rd Cincinnati (45246) *(G-3925)*
Kindercare Learning Ctrs LLC ... 740 549-0264
96 Neverland Dr Lewis Center (43035) *(G-12691)*
Kindercare Learning Ctrs LLC ... 440 442-8067
5684 Mayfield Rd Cleveland (44124) *(G-5903)*
Kindercare Learning Ctrs LLC ... 614 866-4446
6601 Bartlett Rd Reynoldsburg (43068) *(G-16463)*
Kindercare Learning Ctrs LLC ... 513 961-3164
2850 Winslow Ave Cincinnati (45206) *(G-3926)*
Kindercare Learning Ctrs LLC ... 614 759-6622
5959 E Broad St Columbus (43213) *(G-7989)*
Kindercare Learning Ctrs LLC ... 513 791-4712
10580 Montgomery Rd Cincinnati (45242) *(G-3927)*
Kindertown Educational Centers (PA) ... 859 344-8802
8720 Bridgetown Rd Cleves (45002) *(G-6802)*
Kindred At Home, Dayton *Also called Kindred Healthcare Inc (G-9661)*
Kindred At Home, Bedford Heights *Also called Kindred Healthcare Inc (G-1355)*
Kindred Healthcare Inc ... 937 222-5963
707 S Edwin C Moses Blvd Dayton (45417) *(G-9660)*
Kindred Healthcare Inc ... 513 336-0178
411 Western Row Rd Mason (45040) *(G-13728)*
Kindred Healthcare Inc ... 419 224-1888
730 W Market St Lima (45801) *(G-12809)*
Kindred Healthcare Inc ... 937 433-2400
7887 Washington Vlg Dr Dayton (45459) *(G-9661)*
Kindred Healthcare Inc ... 216 593-2200
23333 Harvard Rd Beachwood (44122) *(G-1094)*
Kindred Healthcare Inc ... 440 232-1800
5386 Majestic Pkwy Ste 1 Bedford Heights (44146) *(G-1355)*
Kindred Healthcare Inc ... 937 222-5963
601 S Edwin C Moses Blvd Dayton (45417) *(G-9662)*
Kindred Healthcare Oper Inc ... 740 545-6355
620 E Main St West Lafayette (43845) *(G-19258)*
Kindred Healthcare Oper Inc ... 614 882-2490
5460 Cleveland Ave Columbus (43231) *(G-7990)*
Kindred Healthcare Oper Inc ... 740 387-7537
175 Community Dr Marion (43302) *(G-13545)*
Kindred Healthcare Oper Inc ... 740 439-4437
1471 Wills Creek Vly Dr Cambridge (43725) *(G-2122)*
Kindred Healthcare Operating ... 330 762-0901
145 Olive St Akron (44310) *(G-307)*
Kindred Healthcare Operating ... 419 877-5338
11239 Waterville St Whitehouse (43571) *(G-19587)*
Kindred Hosp - Clveland - Gtwy, Cleveland *Also called Specialty Hosp Cleveland Inc (G-6515)*
Kindred Hospital, Dayton *Also called Kindred Healthcare Inc (G-9660)*
Kindred Hospital - Cleveland, Cleveland *Also called Select Medical Corporation (G-6467)*
Kindred Hospital Central Ohio ... 419 526-0777
730 W Market St Lima (45801) *(G-12810)*
Kindred Hospital-Dayton, Dayton *Also called Kindred Healthcare Inc (G-9662)*
Kindred Nrsing Rhbltton- Cmnty, Marion *Also called Kindred Healthcare Oper Inc (G-13545)*
Kindred Nrsing Rhbltton- Lbnon, Lebanon *Also called Kindred Nursing Centers E LLC (G-12615)*
Kindred Nursing, Cambridge *Also called Kindred Healthcare Oper Inc (G-2122)*
Kindred Nursing Centers E LLC ... 740 772-5900
60 Marietta Rd Chillicothe (45601) *(G-2857)*
Kindred Nursing Centers E LLC ... 513 932-0105
700 Monroe Rd Lebanon (45036) *(G-12615)*
Kindred Nursing Centers E LLC ... 614 276-8222
2770 Clime Rd Columbus (43223) *(G-7991)*
Kindred Nursing Centers E LLC ... 614 837-9666
36 Lehman Dr Canal Winchester (43110) *(G-2164)*
Kindred Nursing Centers E LLC ... 314 631-3000
1300 Hill Rd N Pickerington (43147) *(G-16099)*
Kindred Nursing Centers E LLC ... 740 344-0357
75 Mcmillen Dr Newark (43055) *(G-15179)*
Kindred Nursing Centers E LLC ... 502 596-7300
300 Arlington Ave Logan (43138) *(G-12981)*
Kindred Transitional, Chillicothe *Also called Kindred Nursing Centers E LLC (G-2857)*
Kindred Transitional, Newark *Also called Kindred Nursing Centers E LLC (G-15179)*
Kindred Transitional Care, Columbus *Also called Kindred Nursing Centers E LLC (G-7991)*
Kindred Transitional Care, Pickerington *Also called Kindred Nursing Centers E LLC (G-16099)*
Kindred Transitional Care, Logan *Also called Kindred Nursing Centers E LLC (G-12981)*
Kindred Transitional Care and, Painesville *Also called Personacare of Ohio Inc (G-15873)*
King Bros Feed & Supply, Bristolville *Also called K M B Inc (G-1872)*
King Business Interiors Inc ... 614 430-0020
1400 Goodale Blvd Ste 102 Columbus (43212) *(G-7992)*
King Collision (PA) ... 330 729-0525
8020 Market St Youngstown (44512) *(G-20247)*
King Collision Inc ... 330 372-3242
2000 N River Rd Ne Warren (44483) *(G-18870)*
King Group Inc ... 216 831-9330
25550 Chagrin Blvd # 300 Beachwood (44122) *(G-1095)*
King James Group, Westlake *Also called King James Park Ltd (G-19505)*
King James Group IV Ltd ... 440 250-1851
24700 Center Ridge Rd G50 Westlake (44145) *(G-19504)*
King James Park Ltd ... 440 835-1100
24700 Center Ridge Rd G50 Westlake (44145) *(G-19505)*
King Kold Inc ... 937 836-2731
331 N Main St Englewood (45322) *(G-10711)*
King Memory LLC ... 614 418-6044
380 Morrison Rd Ste A Columbus (43213) *(G-7993)*
King Saver, Marion *Also called Sack n Save Inc (G-13578)*
King Tree Leasing Co LLC ... 937 278-0723
1390 King Tree Dr Dayton (45405) *(G-9663)*
King Tut Logistics LLC ... 614 538-0509
3600 Enterprise Ave Columbus (43228) *(G-7994)*
King's Electric Services, Lebanon *Also called Kween Industries Inc (G-12617)*
Kingdom Kids Inc ... 513 851-6400
6106 Havenwood Ct Hamilton (45011) *(G-11750)*
Kings Cove Automotive LLC ... 513 677-0177
5726 Dixie Hwy Fairfield (45014) *(G-10870)*
Kings Island Company ... 513 754-5700
6300 Kings Island Dr Kings Mills (45034) *(G-12448)*
Kings Island Park LLC ... 513 754-5901
6300 Kings Island Dr Kings Mills (45034) *(G-12449)*
Kings Mazda Kia, Cincinnati *Also called Auto Center USA Inc (G-3066)*
Kings Medical Company ... 330 653-3968
1920 Georgetown Rd A Hudson (44236) *(G-12128)*
Kings Toyota Inc ... 513 583-4333
4700 Fields Ertel Rd Cincinnati (45249) *(G-3928)*
Kings Toyota Scion, Cincinnati *Also called Kings Toyota Inc (G-3928)*
Kings Welding and Fabg Inc ... 330 738-3592
5259 Bane Rd Ne Mechanicstown (44651) *(G-14031)*
Kings-Mason Properties,, Lebanon *Also called Kingsmason Properties Ltd (G-12616)*
Kingsbury Tower I Ltd ... 216 795-3950
8925 Hough Ave Cleveland (44106) *(G-5904)*
Kingsmason Properties Ltd ... 513 932-6010
3000 Henkle Dr Ste G Lebanon (45036) *(G-12616)*
Kingston Healthcare Company ... 937 866-9089
1120 Dunaway St Miamisburg (45342) *(G-14312)*
Kingston Healthcare Company ... 419 824-4200
4125 King Rd Sylvania (43560) *(G-17598)*
Kingston Healthcare Company ... 440 967-1800
4210 Telegraph Ln Vermilion (44089) *(G-18712)*
Kingston Healthcare Company ... 740 389-2311
464 James Way Ofc Marion (43302) *(G-13546)*
Kingston Healthcare Company ... 419 289-3859
20 Amberwood Pkwy Ashland (44805) *(G-684)*
Kingston Healthcare Company (PA) ... 419 247-2880
1 Seagate Ste 1960 Toledo (43604) *(G-17995)*
Kingston National Bank Inc (PA) ... 740 642-2191
2 N Main St Kingston (45644) *(G-12451)*
Kingston of Ashland, Ashland *Also called Kingston Healthcare Company (G-684)*
Kingston of Miamisburg, Miamisburg *Also called Kingston Healthcare Company (G-14312)*
Kingston of Vermilion, Vermilion *Also called Kingston Healthcare Company (G-18712)*
Kingston Residence, Toledo *Also called Kingston Healthcare Company (G-17995)*
Kingston Residence of Marion, Marion *Also called Kingston Healthcare Company (G-13546)*
Kingston Rsdnce Perrysburg LLC ... 419 872-6200
345 E Boundary St Perrysburg (43551) *(G-16025)*
Kingwood Center ... 419 522-0211
900 Park Ave W Mansfield (44906) *(G-13320)*
Kinker Eveleigh Insurance, Loveland *Also called Wilmared Inc (G-13166)*
Kinsale Golf & Fitnes CLB LLC ... 740 881-6500
3737 Village Club Dr Powell (43065) *(G-16343)*
Kinswa Dialysis LLC ... 419 332-0310
100 Pinnacle Dr Fremont (43420) *(G-11209)*
Kirby Vacuum Cleaner, Westlake *Also called Scott Fetzer Company (G-19544)*
Kirila Contractors Inc ... 330 448-4055
505 Bedford Rd Se Brookfield (44403) *(G-1898)*
Kirila Fire Trning Fclties Inc ... 724 854-5207
509 Bedford Rd Se Brookfield (44403) *(G-1899)*
Kirila Realty, Brookfield *Also called K-Y Residential Coml Indus Dev (G-1897)*
Kirk & Blum Manufacturing Co (HQ) ... 513 458-2600
4625 Red Bank Rd Ste 200 Cincinnati (45227) *(G-3929)*
Kirk & Blum Manufacturing Co ... 419 782-9885
24220 Bowman Rd Defiance (43512) *(G-10043)*
Kirk and Blum, Defiance *Also called Kirk & Blum Manufacturing Co (G-10043)*
Kirk Bros Co Inc ... 419 595-4020
11942 Us Highway 224 Alvada (44802) *(G-569)*
Kirk Key Interlock Company LLC ... 330 833-8223
9048 Meridian Cir Nw North Canton (44720) *(G-15350)*
Kirk NationaLease Co (PA) ... 937 498-1151
3885 Michigan St Sidney (45365) *(G-16939)*
Kirk Williams Company Inc ... 614 875-9023
2734 Home Rd Grove City (43123) *(G-11573)*
Kirtland Country Club ... 440 942-4400
39438 Kirtland Rd Willoughby (44094) *(G-19675)*
Kirtland Country Club Company ... 440 942-4400
39438 Kirtland Rd Willoughby (44094) *(G-19676)*
Kissel Bros Shows Inc ... 513 741-1080
6104 Rose Petal Dr Cincinnati (45247) *(G-3930)*
Kitchen Collection LLC ... 740 773-9150
133 Redd St Chillicothe (45601) *(G-2858)*

ALPHABETIC

(PA)=Parent Co (HQ)=Headquarters (DH)=Div Headquarters
2018 Harris Ohio Services Directory
1235

Kitchen Katering Inc...216 481-8080
24111 Rockwell Dr Euclid (44117) *(G-10766)*
Kittyhawk Golf Course, Dayton *Also called Dayton City Parks Golf Maint (G-9466)*
Kiwanis International Inc...740 385-5887
13519 Lakefront Dr Logan (43138) *(G-12982)*
Kiwiplan Inc...513 554-1500
7870 E Kemper Rd Ste 200 Cincinnati (45249) *(G-3931)*
Klaben Auto Group, Kent *Also called Klaben Lincoln Ford Inc (G-12383)*
Klaben Auto Group, Kent *Also called 1106 West Main Inc (G-12350)*
Klaben Family Dodge Inc...330 673-9971
1338 W Main St Kent (44240) *(G-12381)*
Klaben Leasing and Sales Inc...330 673-9971
1338 W Main St Kent (44240) *(G-12382)*
Klaben Lincoln Ford Inc (PA)...330 673-3139
1089 W Main St Kent (44240) *(G-12383)*
Klais and Company Inc (PA)...330 867-8443
3320 W Market St 100 Fairlawn (44333) *(G-10963)*
Klarna Inc...614 615-4705
629 N High St Ste 300 Columbus (43215) *(G-7995)*
Klase Enterprises Inc (PA)...330 452-6300
713 12th St Ne Canton (44704) *(G-2427)*
Klassic Hardwood Flooring, Cuyahoga Falls *Also called K H F Inc (G-9200)*
Klean A Kar Inc (PA)...614 221-3145
8251 Windsong Ct Columbus (43235) *(G-7996)*
Klein Associates Inc...937 873-8166
1750 Commerce Center Blvd Fairborn (45324) *(G-10801)*
Kleingers Group Inc...614 882-4311
350 Worthington Rd Ste B Westerville (43082) *(G-19319)*
Kleingers Group Inc (PA)...513 779-7851
6305 Centre Park Dr West Chester (45069) *(G-19103)*
Kleman Services LLC...419 339-0871
2150 Baty Rd Lima (45807) *(G-12811)*
Klingbeil Capital MGT LLC (PA)...614 396-4919
500 W Wilson Bridge Rd Worthington (43085) *(G-19967)*
Klingbeil Management Group Co (PA)...614 220-8900
21 W Broad St Fl 10 Columbus (43215) *(G-7997)*
Klingbeil Multifamilty Fund IV...415 398-0106
21 W Broad St Fl 11 Columbus (43215) *(G-7998)*
Klingshirn & Sons Trucking...937 338-5000
14884 St Rt 118 S Burkettsville (45310) *(G-2058)*
Klingshirn, Tom & Sons Trckng, Burkettsville *Also called Klingshirn & Sons Trucking (G-2058)*
Kllee Trucking Inc...740 867-6454
1714 Township Road 278 Chesapeake (45619) *(G-2785)*
Kloeckner Metals Corporation...513 769-4000
11501 Reading Rd Cincinnati (45241) *(G-3932)*
Klosterman Baking Co...513 242-1004
1000 E Ross Ave Cincinnati (45217) *(G-3933)*
Km2 Solutions LLC...610 213-1408
2400 Corp Exchange Dr # 210 Columbus (43231) *(G-7999)*
Kmart Corporation...614 836-5000
4400 S Hamilton Rd Groveport (43125) *(G-11654)*
Kmart Corporation...330 372-6688
541 Perkins Jones Rd Ne Warren (44483) *(G-18871)*
Kmb Management Services Corp...330 263-2660
801 E Wayne Ave Wooster (44691) *(G-19880)*
Kmh Systems Inc...513 469-9400
675 Redna Ter Cincinnati (45215) *(G-3934)*
Kmi Inc...614 326-6304
5025 Arlington Centre Blv Columbus (43220) *(G-8000)*
Kmj Leasing Ltd...614 871-3883
7001 Harrisburg Pike Orient (43146) *(G-15761)*
Kmk, Cincinnati *Also called Keating Muething & Klekamp Pll (G-3904)*
Kmon Inc...419 873-0029
1401 Arrowhead Dr Maumee (43537) *(G-13933)*
KMu Trucking & Excvtg Inc...440 934-1008
4436 Center Rd Avon (44011) *(G-903)*
Knall Beverage Inc...216 252-2500
4550 Tiedeman Rd Ste 1 Cleveland (44144) *(G-5905)*
Knapp Veterinary Hospital Inc...614 267-3124
596 Oakland Park Ave Columbus (43214) *(G-8001)*
Kneisel Contracting Corp...513 615-8816
3461 Mustafa Dr Cincinnati (45241) *(G-3935)*
Knight Crockett Miller Ins...419 254-2400
22 N Erie St Ste A Toledo (43604) *(G-17996)*
Knight Transportation Inc...614 308-4900
4275 Westward Ave Columbus (43228) *(G-8002)*
Knight-Swift Trnsp Hldings Inc...614 274-5204
4141 Parkwest Dr Columbus (43228) *(G-8003)*
Knights Inn, Mansfield *Also called Mansfield Hotel Partnership (G-13331)*
Knights Inn, Maumee *Also called Maumee Lodging Enterprises (G-13944)*
Knights of Columbus...937 890-2971
6050 Dog Leg Rd Dayton (45415) *(G-9664)*
Knights of Columbus...419 628-2089
40 N Main St Minster (45865) *(G-14665)*
Knights of Columbus...740 382-3671
1242 E Center St Marion (43302) *(G-13547)*
KNIGHTS OF COLUMBUS #3766, Mantua *Also called Columbian Corporation Mantua (G-13385)*
Knisely Inc...330 343-5812
5885 Crown Rd Nw Dover (44622) *(G-10195)*
Kno-Ho-Co- Ashland Community A (PA)...740 622-9801
120 N 4th St Coshocton (43812) *(G-9110)*
Knoch Corporation...330 244-1440
1015 Schneider St Se 1a Canton (44720) *(G-2428)*
Knollman Construction LLC...614 841-0130
4601 E 5th Ave Columbus (43219) *(G-8004)*
Knollwood Florists Inc...937 426-0861
3766 Dayton Xenia Rd Beavercreek (45432) *(G-1183)*
Knollwood Florists Inc...937 426-0861
3766 Dayton Xenia Rd Beavercreek (45432) *(G-1184)*
Knollwood Garden Center, Beavercreek *Also called Knollwood Florists Inc (G-1183)*
Knotice LLC...800 801-4194
526 S Main St Ste 705 Akron (44311) *(G-308)*
Know Theatre of Cincinnati...513 300-5669
1120 Jackson St Cincinnati (45202) *(G-3936)*
Knowledge MGT Interactive Inc...614 224-0664
330 W Spring St Ste 320 Columbus (43215) *(G-8005)*
Knowledgeworks Foundation (PA)...513 241-1422
1 W 4th St Ste 200 Cincinnati (45202) *(G-3937)*
Knox Area Transit...740 392-7433
25 Columbus Rd Mount Vernon (43050) *(G-14902)*
Knox Area Transit Kat, Mount Vernon *Also called Knox Area Transit (G-14902)*
Knox Community Hosp Foundation...740 393-9814
1330 Coshocton Ave Mount Vernon (43050) *(G-14903)*
Knox Community Hospital...740 393-9000
1330 Coshocton Ave Mount Vernon (43050) *(G-14904)*
Knox County Engineer...740 397-1590
422 Columbus Rd Mount Vernon (43050) *(G-14905)*
Knox County Head Start Inc (PA)...740 397-1344
11700 Upper Gilchrist Rd B Mount Vernon (43050) *(G-14906)*
Knox County Health Department, Mount Vernon *Also called County of Knox (G-14888)*
Knox New Hope Industries Inc...740 397-4601
1375 Newark Rd Mount Vernon (43050) *(G-14907)*
Knoxbi Company LLC...440 892-6800
27500 Detroit Rd Westlake (44145) *(G-19506)*
KOA Dayton Tall Timbers Resort, Brookville *Also called Dayton Tall Timbers Resort (G-1962)*
Koch Aluminum Mfg Inc...419 625-5956
1615 E Perkins Ave Sandusky (44870) *(G-16774)*
Koch Knight LLC (HQ)...330 488-1651
5385 Orchardview Dr Se East Canton (44730) *(G-10504)*
Koch Meat Co Inc...513 874-3500
4100 Port Union Rd Fairfield (45014) *(G-10871)*
Koehlke Components Inc...937 435-5435
1201 Commerce Center Dr Franklin (45005) *(G-11160)*
Koenig Equipment Inc...937 877-1920
5695 S County Road 25a Tipp City (45371) *(G-17721)*
Koester Pavilion Nursing Home, Troy *Also called Uvmc Nursing Care Inc (G-18386)*
Kohler Catering, Dayton *Also called Kohler Foods Inc (G-9665)*
Kohler Day Care, Cleveland *Also called Phillis Wheat Association Inc (G-6274)*
Kohler Foods Inc (PA)...937 291-3600
4572 Presidential Way Dayton (45429) *(G-9665)*
Kohlmyer Sporting Goods Inc...440 277-8296
5000 Grove Ave Lorain (44055) *(G-13045)*
Kohlmyer Sports, Lorain *Also called Kohlmyer Sporting Goods Inc (G-13045)*
Kohnen & Patton...513 381-0656
201 E 5th St Ste 800 Cincinnati (45202) *(G-3938)*
Kohr Royer Griffith Dev Co LLC...614 228-2471
1480 Dublin Rd Columbus (43215) *(G-8006)*
KOI Enterprises Inc (HQ)...513 357-2400
2701 Spring Grove Ave Cincinnati (45225) *(G-3939)*
Koi Siferd Hossellman (PA)...419 228-1221
700 N Main St Lima (45801) *(G-12812)*
Koinonia Homes Inc...216 588-8777
6161 Oak Tree Blvd # 400 Cleveland (44131) *(G-5906)*
Koinonia Homes Inc...216 351-5361
4248 W 35th St Cleveland (44109) *(G-5907)*
Kokosing Construction Inc...330 263-4168
1516 Timken Rd Wooster (44691) *(G-19881)*
Kokosing Construction Co Inc (HQ)...614 228-1029
886 Mckinley Ave Columbus (43222) *(G-8007)*
Kokosing Construction Co Inc...440 323-9346
1539 Lowell St Elyria (44035) *(G-10638)*
Kokosing Construction Co Inc...614 228-1029
886 Mckinley Ave Columbus (43222) *(G-8008)*
Kokosing Inc (PA)...614 212-5700
6235 Wstrville Rd Ste 200 Westerville (43081) *(G-19417)*
Kokosing Industrial Inc (HQ)...614 212-5700
6235 Westerville Rd Westerville (43081) *(G-19418)*
Kolbus America Inc (HQ)...216 931-5100
812 Huron Rd E Ste 750 Cleveland (44115) *(G-5908)*
Kolczun & Kolczun Orthopedics...440 985-3113
5800 Coper Foster Pk Rd W Lorain (44053) *(G-13046)*
Kollander World Travel Inc...216 692-1000
761 E 200th St Cleveland (44119) *(G-5909)*
Koltcz Concrete Block Co...440 232-3630
7660 Oak Leaf Rd Bedford (44146) *(G-1315)*
Komar Plumbing Co...330 758-5073
49 Roche Way Youngstown (44512) *(G-20248)*
Kone Inc...330 762-8886
6670 W Snowville Rd Ste 7 Cleveland (44141) *(G-5910)*
Kone Inc...614 866-1751
735 Cross Pointe Rd Ste G Gahanna (43230) *(G-11251)*

ALPHABETIC SECTION L A Fitness Intl LLC

Konecranes Inc ... 513 755-2800
9879 Crescent Park Dr West Chester (45069) ***(G-19104)***
Konica Minolta Business Soluti ... 910 990-5837
2 Summit Park Dr Ste 450 Cleveland (44131) ***(G-5911)***
Konica Minolta Business Soluti ... 440 546-5795
9150 S Hills Blvd Ste 100 Broadview Heights (44147) ***(G-1882)***
Koorsen Fire & Security Inc ... 614 878-2228
727 Manor Park Dr Columbus (43228) ***(G-8009)***
Koorsen Fire & Security Inc ... 614 878-2228
727 Manor Park Dr Columbus (43228) ***(G-8010)***
Koorsen Fire & Security Inc ... 937 324-9405
3577 Concorde Dr Vandalia (45377) ***(G-18687)***
Kopf Construction Corporation ... 440 933-0250
750 Aqua Marine Blvd Avon Lake (44012) ***(G-933)***
Korman Construction Corp ... 614 274-2170
3695 Interchange Rd Columbus (43204) ***(G-8011)***
Koroseal Interior Products LLC ... 855 753-5474
700 Bf Goodrich Rd Marietta (45750) ***(G-13461)***
Kottler Metal Products Co Inc ... 440 946-7473
1595 Lost Nation Rd Willoughby (44094) ***(G-19677)***
Kovachy Auto Parts, Cleveland *Also called Ieh Auto Parts LLC* ***(G-5802)***
Kozmic Korner ... 330 494-4148
8282 Port Jackson Ave Nw Canton (44720) ***(G-2429)***
Kpmg LLP ... 513 421-6430
312 Walnut Strste 3400 Cincinnati (45202) ***(G-3940)***
Kpmg LLP ... 614 249-2300
191 W Nationwide Blvd # 500 Columbus (43215) ***(G-8012)***
Kpmg LLP ... 216 696-9100
1375 E 9th St Ste 2600 Cleveland (44114) ***(G-5912)***
Kraft Electrical & Telecom Svs, Cincinnati *Also called Kraft Electrical Contg Inc* ***(G-3941)***
Kraft Electrical Contg Inc (PA) ... 513 467-0500
5710 Hillside Ave Cincinnati (45233) ***(G-3941)***
Kraft Electrical Contg Inc ... 614 836-9300
4407 Professional Pkwy Groveport (43125) ***(G-11655)***
Kraftmaid Trucking Inc (PA) ... 440 632-2531
16052 Industrial Pkwy Middlefield (44062) ***(G-14396)***
Krajewski Corp ... 740 522-2000
2825 Hallie Ln Granville (43023) ***(G-11468)***
Krakowski Trucking Inc ... 330 722-7935
1100 W Smith Rd Medina (44256) ***(G-14092)***
Kramer & Feldman Inc ... 513 821-7444
7636 Production Dr Cincinnati (45237) ***(G-3942)***
Kramer & Kramer Inc ... 937 456-1101
420 N Barron St Eaton (45320) ***(G-10563)***
Kramer & Kramer Realtors, Eaton *Also called Kramer & Kramer Inc* ***(G-10563)***
Kramer Enterprises Inc (PA) ... 419 422-7924
116 E Main Cross St Findlay (45840) ***(G-11055)***
Kramig Co ... 513 761-4010
323 S Wayne Ave Cincinnati (45215) ***(G-3943)***
Kraton Polymers US LLC ... 740 423-7571
2419 State Rd 618 Belpre (45714) ***(G-1441)***
Kreative Communication Network ... 330 743-1612
951 Cameron Ave Youngstown (44502) ***(G-20249)***
Kreber Graphics Inc (PA) ... 614 529-5701
2580 Westbelt Dr Columbus (43228) ***(G-8013)***
Krebs Steve BP Oil Co ... 513 641-0150
930 Tennessee Ave Cincinnati (45229) ***(G-3944)***
Kreller Bus Info Group Inc ... 513 723-8900
817 Main St Ste 300 Cincinnati (45202) ***(G-3945)***
Kreller Group, Cincinnati *Also called Kreller Bus Info Group Inc* ***(G-3945)***
Kreps Ron Drywall & Plst Co ... 330 726-8252
6042 Market St Youngstown (44512) ***(G-20250)***
Kribha LLC ... 740 788-8991
1008 Hebron Rd Newark (43056) ***(G-15180)***
Krieger Enterprises Inc ... 513 573-9132
3613 Scialville Foster Rd Mason (45040) ***(G-13729)***
Krieger Ford Inc (PA) ... 614 888-3320
1800 Morse Rd Columbus (43229) ***(G-8014)***
Kristi Britton ... 614 868-7612
6400 E Main St Ste 203 Reynoldsburg (43068) ***(G-16464)***
Kristie Warner ... 330 650-4450
4960 Darrow Rd Hudson (44224) ***(G-12129)***
Kroger Co ... 513 782-3300
150 Tri County Pkwy Cincinnati (45246) ***(G-3946)***
Kroger Co ... 740 335-4030
548 Clinton Ave Wshngtn CT Hs (43160) ***(G-20020)***
Kroger Co ... 937 294-7210
2917 W Alex Bell Rd Dayton (45459) ***(G-9666)***
Kroger Co ... 614 898-3200
4111 Executive Pkwy # 100 Westerville (43081) ***(G-19419)***
Kroger Co ... 740 363-4398
1840 Columbus Pike Delaware (43015) ***(G-10114)***
Kroger Co ... 614 759-2745
850 S Hamilton Rd Columbus (43213) ***(G-8015)***
Kroger Co ... 937 376-7962
1700 W Park Sq Xenia (45385) ***(G-20066)***
Kroger Co ... 937 848-5990
6480 Wilmington Pike Dayton (45459) ***(G-9667)***
Kroger Co Foundation ... 513 762-4000
1014 Vine St Ste 1000 Cincinnati (45202) ***(G-3947)***
Kroger Refill Center ... 614 333-5017
2270 Rickenbacker Pkwy W Columbus (43217) ***(G-8016)***
Krohn Conservatory Gift Shop, Cincinnati *Also called Park Cincinnati Board* ***(G-4252)***
Kronis Coatings, Mansfield *Also called Systems Jay LLC Nanogate* ***(G-13371)***
Kross Acquisition Company LLC ... 513 554-0555
10690 Loveland Madeira Rd Loveland (45140) ***(G-13136)***
Krugliak Wilkins Grifiyhd & ... 330 364-3472
158 N Broadway St New Philadelphia (44663) ***(G-15105)***
Krugliak Wilkins Grifiyhd & (PA) ... 330 497-0700
4775 Munson St Nw Canton (44718) ***(G-2430)***
Krumroy-Cozad Cnstr Corp ... 330 376-4136
376 W Exchange St Akron (44302) ***(G-309)***
Krush Technology, Kettering *Also called Oovoo LLC* ***(G-12434)***
Krystowski Ford Tractor Sales, Wellington *Also called Krystowski Tractor Sales Inc* ***(G-18993)***
Krystowski Tractor Sales Inc ... 440 647-2015
47117 State Route 18 Wellington (44090) ***(G-18993)***
KS Associates Inc ... 440 365-4730
260 Burns Rd Ste 100 Elyria (44035) ***(G-10639)***
Kst Security Inc ... 614 878-2228
727 Manor Park Dr Columbus (43228) ***(G-8017)***
Ktc Quell, Dayton *Also called Kettering Tennis Center* ***(G-9658)***
Ktib Inc ... 330 722-7935
1100 W Smith Rd Medina (44256) ***(G-14093)***
Ktm Enterprises Inc ... 937 548-8357
120 W 3rd St Greenville (45331) ***(G-11512)***
Ktm North America Inc (PA) ... 855 215-6360
1119 Milan Ave Amherst (44001) ***(G-598)***
Kubota Authorized Dealer, Columbus *Also called Columbus Equipment Company* ***(G-7352)***
Kubota Authorized Dealer, Fort Recovery *Also called Hull Bros Inc* ***(G-11118)***
Kubota Authorized Dealer, Plain City *Also called Evolution Ag LLC* ***(G-16191)***
Kubota Authorized Dealer, Granville *Also called Fackler Country Gardens Inc* ***(G-11465)***
Kubota Authorized Dealer, Urbana *Also called Farmers Equipment Inc* ***(G-18586)***
Kubota Authorized Dealer, Findlay *Also called Streacker Tractor Sales Inc* ***(G-11087)***
Kucera International Inc (PA) ... 440 975-4230
38133 Western Pkwy Willoughby (44094) ***(G-19678)***
Kuehne + Nagel Inc ... 419 635-4051
Erie Industrial Park # 2 Port Clinton (43452) ***(G-16249)***
Kuempel Service Inc ... 513 271-6500
3976 Southern Ave Cincinnati (45227) ***(G-3948)***
Kuester Implement Company Inc ... 740 944-1502
1436 State Route 152 Bloomingdale (43910) ***(G-1517)***
Kuhlman Construction Products, Maumee *Also called Kuhlman Corporation* ***(G-13934)***
Kuhlman Corporation (PA) ... 419 897-6000
1845 Indian Wood Cir Maumee (43537) ***(G-13934)***
Kuhnle Bros Trucking, Newbury *Also called Kuhnle Brothers Inc* ***(G-15258)***
Kuhnle Brothers Inc ... 440 564-7168
14905 Cross Creek Pkwy Newbury (44065) ***(G-15258)***
Kumler Automotive, Lancaster *Also called Kumler Collision Inc* ***(G-12546)***
Kumler Collision Inc ... 740 653-4301
2313 E Main St Lancaster (43130) ***(G-12546)***
Kunesh Eye Center Inc ... 937 298-1703
2601 Far Hills Ave Ste 2 Oakwood (45419) ***(G-15621)***
Kunkel Apothecary, Cincinnati *Also called Kunkel Pharmaceuticals Inc* ***(G-3949)***
Kunkel Pharmaceuticals Inc ... 513 231-1943
7717 Beechmont Ave Cincinnati (45255) ***(G-3949)***
Kunkle Farm Limited ... 419 237-2748
20674 Us Highway 20 Alvordton (43501) ***(G-570)***
Kuno Creative Group LLC ... 440 225-4144
36901 American Way Ste 2a Avon (44011) ***(G-904)***
Kuntzman Trucking Inc (PA) ... 330 821-9160
13515 Oyster Rd Alliance (44601) ***(G-543)***
Kurtz Bros Compost Services ... 330 864-2621
2677 Riverview Rd Akron (44313) ***(G-310)***
Kurzhals Inc ... 513 941-4624
6847 Menz Ln Cincinnati (45233) ***(G-3950)***
Kusan Inc ... 614 262-1818
4060 Indianola Ave Columbus (43214) ***(G-8018)***
Kween Industries Inc ... 513 932-2293
2964 S State Route 42 Lebanon (45036) ***(G-12617)***
Kwik Parking ... 419 246-0454
709 Madison Ave Ste 205 Toledo (43604) ***(G-17997)***
Kyocera SGS Precision Tools (PA) ... 330 688-6667
55 S Main St Munroe Falls (44262) ***(G-14931)***
Kyocera SGS Precision Tools ... 330 686-4151
22 Marc Dr Cuyahoga Falls (44223) ***(G-9203)***
Kyocera SGS Precision Tools ... 330 922-1953
238 Marc Dr Cuyahoga Falls (44223) ***(G-9204)***
KZF Bwsc Joint Venture ... 513 621-6211
700 Broadway St Cincinnati (45202) ***(G-3951)***
KZF Design Inc ... 513 621-6211
700 Broadway St Cincinnati (45202) ***(G-3952)***
L & H Wholesale & Supply, Sheffield Village *Also called Luxury Heating Co* ***(G-16890)***
L & I Custom Walls Inc ... 513 683-2045
10369 Cones Rd Loveland (45140) ***(G-13137)***
L & J Fasteners Inc ... 614 876-7313
3636 Lacon Rd Hilliard (43026) ***(G-11919)***
L & M Products Inc ... 937 456-7141
1407 N Barron St Eaton (45320) ***(G-10564)***
L & W Supply Corporation ... 614 276-6391
1150 Mckinley Ave Columbus (43222) ***(G-8019)***
L A Fitness Intl LLC ... 937 439-2795
45 W Alex Bell Rd Washington Township (45459) ***(G-18938)***

ALPHABETIC

L A Hair Force 419 756-3101
  1509 Lexington Ave Mansfield (44907) *(G-13321)*
L A King Trucking Inc 419 727-9398
  434 Matzinger Rd Toledo (43612) *(G-17998)*
L and C Soft Serve Inc 330 364-3823
  717 N Wooster Ave Dover (44622) *(G-10196)*
L and M Investment Co 740 653-3583
  603 W Wheeling St Lancaster (43130) *(G-12547)*
L B & B Associates Inc 216 451-2672
  555 E 88th St Cleveland (44108) *(G-5913)*
L B Brunk & Sons Inc 330 332-0359
  10460 Salem Warren Rd Salem (44460) *(G-16702)*
L B Foster Company 330 652-1461
  1193 Salt Springs Rd Mineral Ridge (44440) *(G-14637)*
L B Industries Inc 330 750-1002
  534 Lowellville Rd Struthers (44471) *(G-17533)*
L Brands, Columbus Also called Mast Industries Inc *(G-8124)*
L Brands Service Company LLC 614 415-7000
  3 Limited Pkwy Columbus (43230) *(G-8020)*
L Brands Store Dsign Cnstr Inc 614 415-7000
  3 Ltd Pkwy Columbus (43230) *(G-8021)*
L C A D A, Lorain Also called Lorain County Alcohol and Drug *(G-13051)*
L Calvin Jones & Company 330 533-1195
  3744 Starrs Centre Dr Canfield (44406) *(G-2198)*
L J F Management Inc 513 688-0104
  4719 Alma Ave Ofc 200 Blue Ash (45242) *(G-1623)*
L J Navy Trucking Company 614 754-8929
  2365 Performance Way Columbus (43207) *(G-8022)*
L Jack Ruscilli 614 876-9484
  2041 Arlingate Ln Columbus (43228) *(G-8023)*
L M Berry and Company (PA) 937 296-2121
  3170 Kettering Blvd Moraine (45439) *(G-14797)*
L M Berry and Company 513 768-7700
  312 Plum St Ste 600 Cincinnati (45202) *(G-3953)*
L O G Transportation Inc 440 891-0850
  120 Blaze Industrial Pkwy Berea (44017) *(G-1462)*
L O M Inc 216 363-6009
  1370 Ontario St Ste 2000 Cleveland (44113) *(G-5914)*
L P K, Cincinnati Also called Libby Prszyk Kthman Hldngs Inc *(G-3974)*
L R G Inc 937 890-0510
  3795 Wyse Rd Dayton (45414) *(G-9668)*
L S C Service Corp 216 521-7260
  14306 Detroit Ave Apt 237 Lakewood (44107) *(G-12485)*
L S R, Cincinnati Also called Lerner Sampson & Rothfuss *(G-3969)*
L S R, Hebron Also called Legend Smelting and Recycl Inc *(G-11851)*
L T O B, Grove City Also called Little Theater Off Broadway *(G-11578)*
L V I, Dayton Also called Lion-Vallen Ltd Partnership *(G-9686)*
L V Trckng, Columbus Also called L V Trucking Inc *(G-8024)*
L V Trucking Inc 614 275-4994
  2440 Harrison Rd Columbus (43204) *(G-8024)*
L&T Technology Services Ltd 732 688-4402
  5550 Blazer Pkwy Ste 125 Dublin (43017) *(G-10384)*
L'U Vabella, Lowellville Also called M & M Wine Cellar Inc *(G-13172)*
L-3 Cmmncations Nova Engrg Inc 877 282-1168
  4393 Digital Way Mason (45040) *(G-13730)*
L3 Aviation Products Inc 614 825-2001
  1105 Schrock Rd Ste 800 Columbus (43229) *(G-8025)*
La Fitness West Chester, West Chester Also called Fitness International LLC *(G-19074)*
La Force Inc 614 875-2545
  3940 Gantz Rs Unit E Grove City (43123) *(G-11574)*
La Force Inc 513 772-0783
  2851 E Kemper Rd Cincinnati (45241) *(G-3954)*
La France Crystal Dry Cleaners, Youngstown Also called La France South Inc *(G-20251)*
La France South Inc (PA) 330 782-1400
  2607 Glenwood Ave Youngstown (44511) *(G-20251)*
La King Trucking Inc 419 225-9039
  1516 Findlay Rd Lima (45801) *(G-12813)*
La Piazza Pasta & Grill, Troy Also called Leos La Piazza Inc *(G-18361)*
La Quinta Inn, Reynoldsburg Also called Lq Management LLC *(G-16467)*
La Quinta Inn, Cincinnati Also called Lq Management LLC *(G-4002)*
La Quinta Inn, Cleveland Also called Lq Management LLC *(G-5954)*
La Quinta Inn, Cleveland Also called Lq Management LLC *(G-5955)*
La Villa Cnference Banquet Ctr 216 265-9305
  11500 Brookpark Rd Cleveland (44130) *(G-5915)*
La-Z-Boy Incorporated 614 478-0898
  4228 Easton Gateway Dr Columbus (43219) *(G-8026)*
Lab Care, Barberton Also called Summa Health *(G-980)*
Lab Care, Stow Also called Summa Health *(G-17395)*
Labcare 330 753-3649
  165 5th St Se Ste A Barberton (44203) *(G-969)*
Labelle Hmhealth Care Svcs LLC 440 842-3005
  5500 Ridge Rd Ste 138 Cleveland (44129) *(G-5916)*
Labelle Hmhealth Care Svcs LLC 740 392-1405
  314 S Main St Ste B Mount Vernon (43050) *(G-14908)*
Labelle News Agency Inc 740 282-9731
  814 University Blvd Steubenville (43952) *(G-17324)*
Labone Inc 513 585-9000
  3200 Burnet Ave Cincinnati (45229) *(G-3955)*
Labor Ready, Steubenville Also called Trueblue Inc *(G-17345)*

Laboratory Corporation America 614 475-7852
  941 E Johnstown Rd Columbus (43230) *(G-8027)*
Laboratory Corporation America 937 383-6964
  630 W Main St Wilmington (45177) *(G-19765)*
Laboratory Corporation America 330 865-3624
  1 Park West Blvd Ste 290 Akron (44320) *(G-311)*
Laboratory Corporation America 440 951-6841
  38429 Lake Shore Blvd Willoughby (44094) *(G-19679)*
Laboratory Corporation America 614 882-6278
  5888 Cleveland Ave Columbus (43231) *(G-8028)*
Laboratory Corporation America 513 242-6800
  1737 Tennessee Ave Cincinnati (45229) *(G-3956)*
Laboratory Corporation America 419 281-7100
  53 Sugarbush Ct Ashland (44805) *(G-685)*
Laboratory Corporation America 937 866-8188
  415 Byers Rd Ste 100 Miamisburg (45342) *(G-14313)*
Laboratory Corporation America 614 336-3993
  5920 Wilcox Pl Ste F Dublin (43016) *(G-10385)*
Laboratory Corporation America 440 328-3275
  418 E Broad St Mansfield (44907) *(G-13322)*
Laboratory Corporation America 440 884-1591
  6789 Ridge Rd Ste 210 Cleveland (44129) *(G-5917)*
Laboratory Corporation America 740 522-2034
  95 S Terrace Ave Newark (43055) *(G-15181)*
Laboratory Corporation America 330 686-0194
  4482 Darrow Rd Stow (44224) *(G-17379)*
Laboratory Corporation America 440 205-8299
  8300 Tyler Blvd Mentor (44060) *(G-14202)*
Laboratory Corporation America 440 838-0404
  2525 E Royalton Rd Ste 3 Cleveland (44147) *(G-5918)*
Laboratory of Dermatopathology 937 434-2351
  7835 Paragon Rd Dayton (45459) *(G-9669)*
Lacaisse Inc 513 621-6211
  700 Broadway St Cincinnati (45202) *(G-3957)*
Lacca, Lima Also called West Ohio Cmnty Action Partnr *(G-12918)*
Lacp St Ritas Medical Ctr LLC 419 324-4075
  708 W Spring St Lima (45801) *(G-12814)*
Ladan Learning Center 614 426-4306
  6028 Cleveland Ave Columbus (43231) *(G-8029)*
Ladd Distribution LLC (HQ) 937 438-2646
  4849 Hempstead Station Dr Kettering (45429) *(G-12432)*
Ladder Man Inc 614 784-1120
  1505 E Bowman St Wooster (44691) *(G-19882)*
Ladera Healthcare Company 614 459-1313
  1661 Old Henderson Rd Columbus (43220) *(G-8030)*
Lads and Lasses, Warren Also called Wee Care Daycare *(G-18926)*
Lafarge North America Inc 419 798-4486
  831 S Quarry Rd Marblehead (43440) *(G-13422)*
Lafarge North America Inc 330 393-5656
  6205 Newton Fls Bailey Rd Warren (44481) *(G-18872)*
Lafayette Life Insurance Co (HQ) 800 443-8793
  400 Broadway St Cincinnati (45202) *(G-3958)*
Laibe Electric Co 419 724-8200
  404 N Byrne Rd Toledo (43607) *(G-17999)*
Laidlaw Education Services, Cincinnati Also called First Student Inc *(G-3621)*
Laidlaw Educational Services, Cincinnati Also called Firstgroup America Inc *(G-3627)*
Laidlaw Transit Services Inc (HQ) 513 241-2200
  600 Vine St Ste 1400 Cincinnati (45202) *(G-3959)*
Lairson Trucking LLC 513 894-0452
  99 N Riverside Dr Hamilton (45011) *(G-11751)*
Lake Center Depot, Cleveland Also called Cleveland Municipal School Dst *(G-5333)*
Lake Cnty Captains Prof Basbal, Willoughby Also called Cascia LLC *(G-19648)*
Lake Cnty Deptmntl Retrdtn/Dvl, Willoughby Also called County of Lake *(G-19656)*
Lake County Council On Aging (PA) 440 205-8111
  8520 East Ave Mentor (44060) *(G-14203)*
Lake County Family Practice 440 352-4880
  9500 Mentor Ave Ste 100 Mentor (44060) *(G-14204)*
Lake County Job and Fmly Svcs, Painesville Also called County of Lake *(G-15847)*
Lake County Local Hazmat 440 350-5499
  8505 Garfield Rd Mentor (44060) *(G-14205)*
Lake County Nursery, Madison Also called Lcn Holdings Inc *(G-13229)*
Lake County YMCA (PA) 440 352-3303
  933 Mentor Ave Fl 2 Painesville (44077) *(G-15860)*
Lake County YMCA 440 946-1160
  37100 Euclid Ave Willoughby (44094) *(G-19680)*
Lake County YMCA 440 259-2724
  4540 River Rd Perry (44081) *(G-15962)*
Lake County YMCA 440 428-5125
  730 N Lake St Madison (44057) *(G-13227)*
Lake Data Center Inc 440 944-2020
  800 Lloyd Rd Wickliffe (44092) *(G-19605)*
Lake Erie Construction Co 419 668-3302
  25 S Norwalk Rd E Norwalk (44857) *(G-15578)*
Lake Erie Correctional Fcilty, Conneaut Also called Management & Training Corp *(G-9043)*
Lake Erie Electric Inc (PA) 440 835-5565
  25730 1st St Westlake (44145) *(G-19507)*
Lake Erie Electric Inc 330 724-1241
  1888 Brown St Akron (44301) *(G-312)*
Lake Erie Electric Inc 419 529-4611
  539 Home Rd N Ontario (44906) *(G-15697)*
Lake Erie Home Repair 419 871-0687
  257 Milan Ave Norwalk (44857) *(G-15579)*

Lake Erie Med Surgical Sup Inc 734 847-3847
6920 Hall St Holland (43528) ***(G-12032)***
Lake Erie Nature & Science Ctr 440 871-2900
28728 Wolf Rd Bay Village (44140) ***(G-1040)***
Lake Farm Park, Kirtland *Also called Lake Metroparks* ***(G-12457)***
Lake Front II Inc 330 337-8033
12688 Salem Warren Rd Salem (44460) ***(G-16703)***
Lake Health, Painesville *Also called Tripoint Medical Center* ***(G-15883)***
Lake Horry Electric (PA) 440 808-8791
255 Bramley Ct Chagrin Falls (44022) ***(G-2702)***
Lake Hospital System Inc 440 953-9600
36000 Euclid Ave Willoughby (44094) ***(G-19681)***
Lake Hospital System Inc 440 632-3024
15050 S Springdale Ave Middlefield (44062) ***(G-14397)***
Lake Hospital System Inc (PA) 440 375-8100
7590 Auburn Rd Painesville (44077) ***(G-15861)***
Lake Hospital Systems, Madison *Also called Madison Medical Campus* ***(G-13232)***
Lake Isabella Recreation Assn, East Fultonham *Also called Columbia Recreation Assn* ***(G-10506)***
Lake Local Board of Education 330 877-9383
13188 Kent Ave Ne Hartville (44632) ***(G-11826)***
Lake Metroparks 440 428-3164
7298 Lake Rd Madison (44057) ***(G-13228)***
Lake Metroparks 440 256-2122
8800 Chardon Rd Kirtland (44094) ***(G-12457)***
Lake Metroparks 440 256-1404
8668 Kirtland Chardon Rd Willoughby (44094) ***(G-19682)***
Lake Mhawk Prperty Owners Assn 330 863-0000
1 N Mohawk Dr Malvern (44644) ***(G-13253)***
Lake Park At Flower Hospital, Sylvania *Also called Flower Hospital* ***(G-17587)***
Lake Pnte Rhbltion Nrsing Ctr, Conneaut *Also called Es3 Management Inc* ***(G-9042)***
Lake Side Building Maintenance 216 589-9900
200 Public Sq Cleveland (44114) ***(G-5919)***
Lake Univ Ireland Cancer Ctr, Mentor *Also called University Hospitals Cleveland* ***(G-14252)***
Lake Urgent & Family Med Ctr (PA) 440 255-6400
6965 Center St Mentor (44060) ***(G-14206)***
Lake Urgent Care Centers, Mentor *Also called Lake Urgent & Family Med Ctr* ***(G-14206)***
Lake Wynoka Prprty Owners Assn 937 446-3774
1 Waynoka Dr Lake Waynoka (45171) ***(G-12463)***
Lake-West Hospital, Willoughby *Also called Lake Hospital System Inc* ***(G-19681)***
Lakefront Lines Inc (HQ) 216 267-8810
13315 Brookpark Rd Brookpark (44142) ***(G-1949)***
Lakefront Lines Inc 419 537-0677
3152 Hill Ave Toledo (43607) ***(G-18000)***
Lakefront Lines Inc 614 476-1113
3152 E 17th Ave Columbus (43219) ***(G-8031)***
Lakefront Lines Inc 513 829-8290
4991 Factory Dr Fairfield (45014) ***(G-10872)***
Lakefront Trailways, Toledo *Also called Lakefront Lines Inc* ***(G-18000)***
Lakefront Trailways, Columbus *Also called Lakefront Lines Inc* ***(G-8031)***
Lakefront Trailways, Fairfield *Also called Lakefront Lines Inc* ***(G-10872)***
Lakeland Foundation 440 525-7094
7700 Clocktower Dr C2089 Willoughby (44094) ***(G-19683)***
Lakeland Glass Co (PA) 440 277-4527
4994 Grove Ave Lorain (44055) ***(G-13047)***
Lakes Country Club Inc 614 882-4167
7129 Africa Rd Galena (43021) ***(G-11285)***
Lakes Golf & Country Club Inc 614 882-2582
6740 Worthington Rd Westerville (43082) ***(G-19320)***
Lakes Golf and Country Club, Galena *Also called Lakes Country Club Inc* ***(G-11285)***
Lakes Heating and AC 330 644-7811
2476 N Turkeyfoot Rd Coventry Township (44319) ***(G-9128)***
Lakeshore Dialysis LLC 937 278-0516
4750 N Main St Dayton (45405) ***(G-9670)***
Lakeside Association 419 798-4461
236 Walnut Ave Lakeside (43440) ***(G-12464)***
Lakeside Manor Inc 330 549-2545
9661 Market St North Lima (44452) ***(G-15404)***
Lakeside Realty LLC 330 793-4200
1749 S Raccoon Rd Youngstown (44515) ***(G-20252)***
Lakeside Sand & Gravel Inc 330 274-2569
3498 Frost Rd Mantua (44255) ***(G-13390)***
Lakeside Supply Co 216 941-6800
3000 W 117th St Cleveland (44111) ***(G-5920)***
Lakeside Title Escrow Agcy Inc 216 503-5600
29550 Detroit Rd Ste 301 Westlake (44145) ***(G-19508)***
Laketec Communications Inc 440 892-2001
27881 Lorain Rd North Olmsted (44070) ***(G-15429)***
Laketran 440 350-1000
555 Lakeshore Blvd Painesville (44077) ***(G-15862)***
Lakewood Acceptance Corp 216 658-1234
15200 Lorain Ave Cleveland (44111) ***(G-5921)***
Lakewood Catholic Academy 216 521-4352
14808 Lake Ave Lakewood (44107) ***(G-12486)***
Lakewood Chrysler-Plymouth 216 521-1000
13001 Brookpark Rd Brookpark (44142) ***(G-1950)***
Lakewood City School District 216 529-4400
14740 Lakewood Hts Blvd Lakewood (44107) ***(G-12487)***
Lakewood Clveland Fmly Med Ctr 216 227-2162
16215 Madison Ave Lakewood (44107) ***(G-12488)***
Lakewood Community Care Center, Cleveland *Also called City of Lakewood* ***(G-5266)***
Lakewood Community Care Center 216 226-0080
2019 Woodward Ave Lakewood (44107) ***(G-12489)***
Lakewood Country Club Company 440 871-0400
2613 Bradley Rd Cleveland (44145) ***(G-5922)***
Lakewood Greenhouse Inc 419 691-3541
909 Lemoyne Rd Northwood (43619) ***(G-15535)***
Lakewood Health Care Center 216 226-3103
13315 Detroit Ave Lakewood (44107) ***(G-12490)***
Lakewood Hospital Association (HQ) 216 529-7160
14519 Detroit Ave Lakewood (44107) ***(G-12491)***
Lakewood Hospital Association 216 228-5437
1450 Belle Ave Cleveland (44107) ***(G-5923)***
Lakewood Police Dept, Cleveland *Also called City of Lakewood* ***(G-5267)***
Lakewood Y, Lakewood *Also called Young MNS Chrstn Assn Clveland* ***(G-12502)***
Lakewoods II Ltd 937 254-6141
980 Wilmington Ave Dayton (45420) ***(G-9671)***
Lakota Bus Garage 419 986-5558
5186 Sandusky Cty Rd 13 Kansas (44841) ***(G-12347)***
Lakota Local School District 513 777-2150
6947 Yankee Rd Liberty Township (45044) ***(G-12722)***
Lally Pipe & Tube, Struthers *Also called L B Industries Inc* ***(G-17533)***
Lamalfa Party Center, Mentor *Also called Michaels Inc* ***(G-14217)***
Lamar Advertising Company 216 676-4321
12222 Plaza Dr Cleveland (44130) ***(G-5924)***
Lamar Advertising Company 740 699-0000
52610 Holiday Dr Saint Clairsville (43950) ***(G-16639)***
Lamrite West Inc (HQ) 440 238-7318
14225 Pearl Rd Strongsville (44136) ***(G-17482)***
Lamrite West Inc 440 572-9946
17647 Foltz Pkwy Strongsville (44149) ***(G-17483)***
Lamrite West Inc 440 268-0634
14225 Pearl Rd Strongsville (44136) ***(G-17484)***
Lan Solutions Inc 513 469-6500
9850 Redhill Dr Blue Ash (45242) ***(G-1624)***
Lancaster Bingo Company, Lancaster *Also called Lancaster Bingo Company Inc* ***(G-12548)***
Lancaster Bingo Company Inc (PA) 740 681-4759
200 Quarry Rd Se Lancaster (43130) ***(G-12548)***
Lancaster Commercial Pdts LLC 740 286-5081
2353 Westbrooke Dr Columbus (43228) ***(G-8032)***
Lancaster Country Club 740 654-3535
3100 Country Club Rd Sw Lancaster (43130) ***(G-12549)***
Lancaster Host LLC 740 654-4445
1861 Riverway Dr Lancaster (43130) ***(G-12550)***
Lancaster Municipal Gas, Lancaster *Also called City of Lancaster* ***(G-12518)***
Lancaster Pollard & Co LLC (HQ) 614 224-8800
65 E State St Ste 1600 Columbus (43215) ***(G-8033)***
Lancaster Pollard Mrtg Co LLC (PA) 614 224-8800
65 E State St Ste 1600 Columbus (43215) ***(G-8034)***
Lancaster Transportation, Cincinnati *Also called Mv Transportation Inc* ***(G-4134)***
LANCASTER-FAIRFIELD COMMUNITY, Lancaster *Also called Community Action Program Comm* ***(G-12521)***
Lance A1 Cleaning Services LLC 614 370-0550
342 Hanton Way Columbus (43213) ***(G-8035)***
Lancer Insurance Company 440 473-1634
734 Alfa Dr Ste L Cleveland (44143) ***(G-5925)***
Lancia Nursing Home Inc 740 695-4404
51999 Guirino Dr Saint Clairsville (43950) ***(G-16640)***
Lancia Nursing Home Inc (PA) 740 264-7101
1852 Sinclair Ave Steubenville (43953) ***(G-17325)***
Lancia Villa Royal, Steubenville *Also called Lancia Nursing Home Inc* ***(G-17325)***
Lanco Global Systems Inc 937 660-8090
1430c Yankee Park Pl Dayton (45458) ***(G-9672)***
Land Art Inc (PA) 419 666-5296
7728 Ponderosa Rd Perrysburg (43551) ***(G-16026)***
Land Design Consultants 440 255-8463
9025 Osborne Dr Mentor (44060) ***(G-14207)***
Land OLakes Inc 330 879-2158
8485 Navarre Rd Sw Massillon (44646) ***(G-13828)***
Landes Fresh Meats Inc 937 836-3613
9476 Haber Rd Clayton (45315) ***(G-4912)***
Landing Gear Test Facility 937 255-5740
1981 5th St Dayton (45433) ***(G-9276)***
Landmark America Inc (PA) 330 372-6800
1268 N River Rd Ne Ste 1 Warren (44483) ***(G-18873)***
Landrum & Brown Incorporated (PA) 513 530-5333
11279 Cornell Park Dr Blue Ash (45242) ***(G-1625)***
Landscape & Christmas Tree, Akron *Also called Acro Tool & Die Company* ***(G-17)***
Landscping Rclmtion Spcialists 330 339-4900
3497 University Dr Ne New Philadelphia (44663) ***(G-15106)***
Landsel Title Agency Inc (PA) 614 337-1928
961 N Hamilton Rd Ste 100 Gahanna (43230) ***(G-11252)***
Lane Alton & Horst LLC 614 228-6885
2 Miranova Pl Ste 220 Columbus (43215) ***(G-8036)***
Lane Aviation Corporation 614 237-3747
4389 International Gtwy # 228 Columbus (43219) ***(G-8037)***
Lane Chevrolet 937 426-2313
635 S Orchard Ln Beavercreek Township (45434) ***(G-1273)***
Lane Life Corp (PA) 330 799-1002
5801 Mahoning Ave Youngstown (44515) ***(G-20253)***
Lane Life Trans, Youngstown *Also called Lane Life Corp* ***(G-20253)***

ALPHABETIC

Lane Wood Industries......419 352-5059
991 S Main St Bowling Green (43402) ***(G-1784)***
Lane's Moving & Storage, Lima *Also called Lanes Transfer Inc* ***(G-12815)***
Lanes Transfer Inc......419 222-8692
245 E Murphy St Lima (45801) ***(G-12815)***
Lang Chevrolet Co......937 426-2313
635 Orchard Ln Beavercreek Township (45434) ***(G-1274)***
Lang Chevrolet Geo, Beavercreek Township *Also called Lang Chevrolet Co* ***(G-1274)***
Lang Financial Group Inc......513 699-2966
4225 Malsbary Rd Ste 100 Blue Ash (45242) ***(G-1626)***
Lang Masonry Contractors Inc......740 749-3512
405 Watertown Rd Waterford (45786) ***(G-18939)***
Lang Stone Company Inc (PA)......614 235-4099
4099 E 5th Ave Columbus (43219) ***(G-8038)***
Langdon Inc......513 733-5955
9865 Wayne Ave Cincinnati (45215) ***(G-3960)***
Language Logic......513 241-9112
600 Vine St Ste 2020 Cincinnati (45202) ***(G-3961)***
Lanhan Contractors Inc......440 918-1099
2220 Lost Nation Rd Willoughby (44094) ***(G-19684)***
Lannings Foods, Mount Vernon *Also called S and S Gilardi Inc* ***(G-14921)***
Lanxess Corporation......440 279-2367
145 Parker Ct Chardon (44024) ***(G-2755)***
Lap Technology LLC......937 415-5794
6101 Webster St Dayton (45414) ***(G-9673)***
Lapham-Hickey Steel Corp......614 443-4881
753 Marion Rd Columbus (43207) ***(G-8039)***
Larchwood Health Group LLC......216 941-6100
4110 Rcky Rver Dr Ste 251 Cleveland (44135) ***(G-5926)***
Larchwood Village Independent, Cleveland *Also called Larchwood Health Group LLC* ***(G-5926)***
Laria Chevrolet-Buick Inc......330 925-2015
112 E Ohio Ave Rittman (44270) ***(G-16553)***
Lariche Chevrolet-Cadillac, Findlay *Also called Lariche Subaru Inc* ***(G-11056)***
Lariche Subaru Inc......419 422-1855
215 E Main Cross St Findlay (45840) ***(G-11056)***
Larlham Care Hattie Group......330 274-2272
9772 Diagonal Rd Mantua (44255) ***(G-13391)***
Larlham Center For Children, Twinsburg *Also called Hattie Larlham Community Svcs* ***(G-18427)***
Larosas Inc (PA)......513 347-5660
2334 Boudinot Ave Cincinnati (45238) ***(G-3962)***
Larrimer & Larrimer LLC......419 222-6266
165 N High St Columbus (43215) ***(G-8040)***
Larrimer & Larrimer LLC (PA)......614 221-7548
165 N High St Fl 3 Columbus (43215) ***(G-8041)***
Larrimer & Larrimer LLC......740 366-0184
2000 Newark Granville Rd # 200 Granville (43023) ***(G-11469)***
Larry L Minges......513 738-4901
4396 Wade Mill Rd Hamilton (45014) ***(G-11752)***
Larry Lang Excavating Inc......740 984-4750
19371 State Route 60 Beverly (45715) ***(G-1491)***
Larry Smith Contractors Inc......513 367-0218
5737 Dry Fork Rd Cleves (45002) ***(G-6803)***
Larry Smith Plumbing, Cleves *Also called Larry Smith Contractors Inc* ***(G-6803)***
Larue Enterprises Inc......937 438-5711
3331 Seajay Dr Beavercreek (45430) ***(G-1248)***
Laser Craft Inc......440 327-4300
38900 Taylor Pkwy North Ridgeville (44035) ***(G-15467)***
Laser Hair Removal Center......937 433-7536
5300 Far Hills Ave # 250 Dayton (45429) ***(G-9674)***
Laser Label Technologies, Stow *Also called Electronic Printing Pdts Inc* ***(G-17362)***
Laserflex Corporation (HQ)......614 850-9600
3649 Parkway Ln Hilliard (43026) ***(G-11920)***
Lash Paving Inc......740 635-4335
70700 Swingle Rd Bridgeport (43912) ***(G-1864)***
Lasik Plus Vision Center......513 794-9964
7840 Montgomery Rd Cincinnati (45236) ***(G-3963)***
Lassiter Corporation......216 391-4800
3700 Kelley Ave Cleveland (44114) ***(G-5927)***
Lasting Impressions Event......614 252-5400
5080 Sinclair Rd Ste 200 Columbus (43229) ***(G-8042)***
Lasting Imprssions Event Rentl, Columbus *Also called Lasting Impressions Event* ***(G-8042)***
Lata, Westerville *Also called Los Alamos Technical Assoc Inc* ***(G-19420)***
Lateef Elmin Mhammad Inv Group......937 450-3388
524 W Liberty St Springfield (45506) ***(G-17220)***
Lathrop Company Inc (HQ)......419 893-7000
28 N Saint Clair St Toledo (43604) ***(G-18001)***
Latrobe Spcialty Mtls Dist Inc (HQ)......330 609-5137
1551 Vienna Pkwy Vienna (44473) ***(G-18738)***
Laudan Properties LLC......234 212-3225
2204 E Enterprise Pkwy Twinsburg (44087) ***(G-18439)***
Laughlin Music & Vending Svc (PA)......740 593-7778
148 W Union St Athens (45701) ***(G-798)***
Laughlin Music and Vending Svc, Athens *Also called Laughlin Music & Vending Svc* ***(G-798)***
Laukhuf, Gary DDS, Ashtabula *Also called Ashtabula Dental Associates* ***(G-724)***
Laurel Development Corporation......614 794-8800
8181 Worthington Rd Westerville (43082) ***(G-19321)***
Laurel Health Care Company......740 264-5042
500 Stanton Blvd Steubenville (43952) ***(G-17326)***
Laurel Health Care Company (HQ)......614 794-8800
8181 Worthington Rd Uppr Westerville (43082) ***(G-19322)***
Laurel Health Care Company......614 888-4553
6830 N High St Worthington (43085) ***(G-19968)***
Laurel Health Care Company......614 885-0408
1030 High St Worthington (43085) ***(G-19969)***
Laurel Healthcare......419 782-7879
1701 Jefferson Ave Defiance (43512) ***(G-10044)***
Laurel Hlth Care Battle Creek (HQ)......614 794-8800
8181 Worthington Rd Westerville (43082) ***(G-19323)***
Laurel Hlth Care of Mt Plasant (HQ)......614 794-8800
8181 Worthington Rd # 2 Westerville (43082) ***(G-19324)***
Laurel Lk Retirement Cmnty Inc......330 650-0681
200 Laurel Lake Dr Rear Hudson (44236) ***(G-12130)***
Laurel School (PA)......216 464-1441
1 Lyman Cir Cleveland (44122) ***(G-5928)***
Laurels of Bedford, The, Westerville *Also called Laurel Hlth Care Battle Creek* ***(G-19323)***
Laurels of Defiance, The, Westerville *Also called Oak Health Care Investors* ***(G-19335)***
Laurels of Hillsboro......937 393-1925
175 Chillicothe Ave Hillsboro (45133) ***(G-11985)***
Laurels of Massillon, The, Massillon *Also called Fairport Enterprises Inc* ***(G-13806)***
Laurels of Mt Pleasant, Westerville *Also called Laurel Hlth Care of Mt Plasant* ***(G-19324)***
Laurels of Mt Vernon, Mount Vernon *Also called Oak Health Care Investors* ***(G-14916)***
Laurels of Norworth, Worthington *Also called Laurel Health Care Company* ***(G-19968)***
Laurels of Steubenville, The, Steubenville *Also called Laurel Health Care Company* ***(G-17326)***
LAURELWOOD CENTER FOR BEHAVIOU, Willoughby *Also called Laurelwood Hospital* ***(G-19685)***
Laurelwood Hospital (PA)......440 953-3000
35900 Euclid Ave Willoughby (44094) ***(G-19685)***
Laurelwood, The, Dayton *Also called Harborside Healthcare Corp* ***(G-9600)***
Laurie Ann Home Health Care......330 872-7512
2200 Milton Blvd Newton Falls (44444) ***(G-15275)***
Laurie Ann Nursing Home, Newton Falls *Also called Hooberry Associates Inc* ***(G-15274)***
Laurito & Laurito LLC......937 743-4878
7550 Paragon Rd Dayton (45459) ***(G-9675)***
Laurrels of Defiance, Defiance *Also called Laurel Healthcare* ***(G-10044)***
Lavery Buick, Alliance *Also called Lavery Chevrolet-Buick Inc* ***(G-544)***
Lavery Chevrolet-Buick Inc (PA)......330 823-1100
1096 W State St Alliance (44601) ***(G-544)***
Lavy Concrete Construction......937 606-4754
7277 W Piqua Clayton Rd Covington (45318) ***(G-9137)***
Law Excavating Inc......740 745-3420
9128 Mount Vernon Rd Saint Louisville (43071) ***(G-16669)***
Law Offces Rbert A Schrger Lpa......614 824-5731
81 S 5th St Ste 400 Columbus (43215) ***(G-8043)***
Law Offices of John D Clunk C......330 436-0300
4500 Courthouse Blvd # 400 Stow (44224) ***(G-17380)***
Lawhon and Associates Inc (PA)......614 481-8600
1441 King Ave Columbus (43212) ***(G-8044)***
Lawn & Garden Equipment, Moraine *Also called Buckeye Power Sales Co Inc* ***(G-14756)***
Lawn Management Sprinkler Co......513 272-3808
3828 Round Bottom Rd F Cincinnati (45244) ***(G-3964)***
Lawnfield Properties LLC......440 974-3572
8434 Mentor Ave Mentor (44060) ***(G-14208)***
Lawnmark, Stow *Also called Prusa Inc* ***(G-17387)***
Lawnview Industries Inc......937 653-5217
1250 E Us Highway 36 Urbana (43078) ***(G-18593)***
Lawo, Toledo *Also called Legal Aid Western Ohio Inc* ***(G-18003)***
Lawrence A Cervino MD......330 668-4065
3975 Embassy Pkwy Ste 203 Akron (44333) ***(G-313)***
Lawrence Cnty Bd Dev Dsblities......740 377-2356
1749 County Road 1 South Point (45680) ***(G-17090)***
Lawrence Cnty Early Chldhd Ctr, South Point *Also called Lawrence Cnty Bd Dev Dsblities* ***(G-17090)***
Lawrence Cnty Hstorical Museum......740 532-1222
506 S 6th St Ironton (45638) ***(G-12296)***
Lawrence Industries Inc (PA)......216 518-7000
4500 Lee Rd Ste 120 Cleveland (44128) ***(G-5929)***
Lawrence M Shell DDS......614 235-3444
2862 E Main St Ste A Columbus (43209) ***(G-8045)***
Lawrence Saltis Plaza, Stow *Also called Fish Creek Plaza Ltd* ***(G-17366)***
Lawyers Title Cincinnati Inc (HQ)......513 421-1313
3500 Red Bank Rd Cincinnati (45227) ***(G-3965)***
Lawyers Title Company......330 376-0000
799 White Pond Dr Ste A Akron (44320) ***(G-314)***
Layh & Associates......937 767-9171
416 Xenia Ave Yellow Springs (45387) ***(G-20090)***
Layton Inc (PA)......740 349-7101
169 Dayton Rd Ne Newark (43055) ***(G-15182)***
Layton Services, Newark *Also called Layton Trucking Inc* ***(G-15183)***
Layton Trucking Inc......740 366-1447
1384 E Main St Newark (43055) ***(G-15183)***
Lazar Brothers Inc......440 585-9333
30030 Lakeland Blvd Wickliffe (44092) ***(G-19606)***
Lazer Kraze......513 339-1030
6075 Braymoore Dr Galena (43021) ***(G-11286)***
Lbi Starbucks DC 3......614 415-6363
3 Limited Pkwy Columbus (43230) ***(G-8046)***

ALPHABETIC SECTION

Lbs International Inc 614 866-3688
12920 Sheffield Dr Pickerington (43147) *(G-16100)*

Lc, Cleveland Also called Logan Clutch Corporation *(G-5950)*

Lca-Vision Inc (HQ) 513 792-9292
7840 Montgomery Rd Cincinnati (45236) *(G-3966)*

Lccaa-Hopkins Locke-Head Start, Lorain Also called Lorain County Community Action *(G-13053)*

Lcd Home Health Agency LLC 513 497-0441
6 S 2nd St Ste 409 Hamilton (45011) *(G-11753)*

Lcd Nurse Aide Academy, Hamilton Also called Lcd Home Health Agency LLC *(G-11753)*

Lcn Holdings Inc 440 259-5571
5052 S Ridge Rd Madison (44057) *(G-13229)*

Lcnb National Bank (HQ) 513 932-1414
2 N Broadway St Lowr Lebanon (45036) *(G-12618)*

Lcnb National Bank 740 775-6777
33 W Main St Frnt Chillicothe (45601) *(G-2859)*

Lcnb National Bank 937 456-5544
110 W Main St Eaton (45320) *(G-10565)*

Lcs, Loveland Also called London Computer Systems Inc *(G-13140)*

Lcs Inc 419 678-8600
411 Stachler Dr Saint Henry (45883) *(G-16666)*

Le Chaperon Rouge (PA) 440 934-0296
1504 Travelers Pt Avon (44011) *(G-905)*

Le Chaperon Rouge Company 440 899-9477
27390 Center Ridge Rd Westlake (44145) *(G-19509)*

Le Nails (PA) 440 846-1866
1144 Southpark Ctr Cleveland (44136) *(G-5930)*

LE Smith Company (PA) 419 636-4555
1030 E Wilson St Bryan (43506) *(G-2009)*

Leadec Corp (HQ) 513 731-3590
9395 Kenwood Rd Ste 200 Blue Ash (45242) *(G-1627)*

Leader Nuring & Rehabilitation (HQ) 419 252-5718
333 N Summit St Toledo (43604) *(G-18002)*

Leader Promotions Inc (PA) 614 416-6565
790 E Johnstown Rd Columbus (43230) *(G-8047)*

Leader Technologies Inc (PA) 614 890-1986
674 Enterprise Dr Lewis Center (43035) *(G-12692)*

Leaderpromos.com, Columbus Also called Leader Promotions Inc *(G-8047)*

Leaders Family Farms 419 599-1570
0064 County Rd 16 Napoleon (43545) *(G-14944)*

Leaders Moving & Storage Co, Worthington Also called Leaders Moving Company *(G-19970)*

Leaders Moving Company 614 785-9595
7455 Alta View Blvd Worthington (43085) *(G-19970)*

Leadership Circle LLC 801 518-2980
10918 Springbrook Ct Whitehouse (43571) *(G-19588)*

LEADS COMMUNITY ACTION AGENCY, Newark Also called Leads Inc *(G-15184)*

Leads Inc (PA) 740 349-8606
159 Wilson St Newark (43055) *(G-15184)*

Leaffilter North LLC (PA) 330 655-7950
1595 Georgetown Rd Ste G Hudson (44236) *(G-12131)*

LEAP, Cleveland Also called Linking Employment Abilities *(G-5944)*

Learning Express Toys, Westlake Also called Caston Holdings LLC *(G-19471)*

Learning Trails School, Solon Also called Balsara Enterprise Ltd *(G-16982)*

Learning Tree Childcare Ctr 419 229-5484
775 S Thayer Rd Lima (45806) *(G-12927)*

Leather Gallery Inc 513 312-1722
50 Farnese Ct Lebanon (45036) *(G-12619)*

Leatherman Nursing Ctrs Corp (PA) 330 336-6684
200 Smokerise Dr Ste 300 Wadsworth (44281) *(G-18759)*

Lebanon Chrysler - Plymuth Inc 513 932-2717
518 W Main St Lebanon (45036) *(G-12620)*

Lebanon Ford, Lebanon Also called Lebanon Ford Inc *(G-12621)*

Lebanon Ford Inc 513 932-1010
770 Columbus Ave Lebanon (45036) *(G-12621)*

Lebanon Health Care Center, Lebanon Also called Advance Care Inc *(G-12588)*

Lebanon Nursing & Rehab Ctr 513 932-1121
115 Oregonia Rd Lebanon (45036) *(G-12622)*

Lebanon Nursing Home, Lebanon Also called Health Care Opportunities Inc *(G-12610)*

Lebanon Presbyterian Church 513 932-0369
123 N East St Lebanon (45036) *(G-12623)*

Led Transportation 330 484-2772
4645 Monica Ave Sw Canton (44706) *(G-2431)*

Lee & Associates - Columbus, Dublin Also called Lee & Associates Inc *(G-10386)*

Lee & Associates Inc 614 923-3300
5100 Prkcnter Ave Ste 100 Dublin (43017) *(G-10386)*

Lee Personnel Inc 513 744-6780
621 E Mehring Way # 807 Cincinnati (45202) *(G-3967)*

Leeda Services Inc (PA) 330 392-6006
1441 Parkman Rd Nw Warren (44485) *(G-18874)*

Lees Roby Inc 330 872-0983
425 Ridge Rd Newton Falls (44444) *(G-15276)*

Lefco Worthington LLC 216 432-4422
18451 Euclid Ave Cleveland (44112) *(G-5931)*

Lefeld Implement Inc (PA) 419 678-2375
5228 State Route 118 Coldwater (45828) *(G-6831)*

Lefeld Supplies Rental, Coldwater Also called Lefeld Welding & Stl Sups Inc *(G-6832)*

Lefeld Welding & Stl Sups Inc (PA) 419 678-2397
600 N 2nd St Coldwater (45828) *(G-6832)*

Legacy Commercial Finishes, Columbus Also called Legacy Commercial Flooring Ltd *(G-8048)*

Legacy Commercial Flooring Ltd (PA) 614 476-1043
800 Morrison Rd Columbus (43230) *(G-8048)*

Legacy Consultant Pharmacy 336 760-1670
26691 Richmond Rd Bedford (44146) *(G-1316)*

Legacy Freedom Treatment Ctr 614 741-2100
751 Northwest Blvd # 200 Columbus (43212) *(G-8049)*

Legacy Health Services, Wickliffe Also called DMD Management Inc *(G-19594)*

Legacy Health Services, Cleveland Also called DMD Management Inc *(G-5496)*

Legacy Industrial Services LLC 606 584-8953
9272 Scoffield Rd Ripley (45167) *(G-16547)*

Legacy Place, Twinsburg Also called DMD Management Inc *(G-18406)*

Legacy Village Hospitality LLC 216 382-3350
24665 Cedar Rd Cleveland (44124) *(G-5932)*

Legacy Village Management Off 216 382-3871
25333 Cedar Rd Ste 303 Cleveland (44124) *(G-5933)*

Legal Aid Society Cincinnati (PA) 513 241-9400
215 E 9th St Ste 200 Cincinnati (45202) *(G-3968)*

Legal Aid Society of Cleveland (PA) 216 861-5500
1223 W 6th St Fl 4 Cleveland (44113) *(G-5934)*

Legal Aid Society of Columbus (PA) 614 737-0139
1108 City Park Ave # 100 Columbus (43206) *(G-8050)*

LEGAL AID SOCIETY OF GREATER C, Cincinnati Also called Legal Aid Society Cincinnati *(G-3968)*

Legal Aid Western Ohio Inc 419 724-0030
525 Jefferson Ave 400 Toledo (43604) *(G-18003)*

Legal Hair and Day Spa, Steubenville Also called Philip Icuss Jr *(G-17333)*

Legend Equities Corporation 216 741-3113
5755 Granger Rd Ste 910 Independence (44131) *(G-12223)*

Legend Lake Golf Club Inc 440 285-3110
11135 Auburn Rd Chardon (44024) *(G-2756)*

Legend Smelting and Recycl Inc (PA) 740 928-0139
717 Oneill Dr Hebron (43025) *(G-11851)*

Legends Care Center, Massillon Also called Consulate Management Co LLC *(G-13798)*

Legndary Cleaners LLC 216 374-1205
1215 W 10th St Apt 1003 Cleveland (44113) *(G-5935)*

Legrand North America LLC 937 224-0639
3555 Kettering Blvd Moraine (45439) *(G-14798)*

Legrand North America LLC 937 224-0639
1501 Webster St Dayton (45404) *(G-9676)*

Legrand Services Inc 740 682-6046
230 W Hill St Oak Hill (45656) *(G-15619)*

Lehigh Outfitters LLC (HQ) 740 753-1951
39 E Canal St Nelsonville (45764) *(G-14965)*

Lehn Painting Inc (PA) 513 732-1515
4175 Taylor Rd Batavia (45103) *(G-1019)*

Lei Cbus LLC 614 302-8830
7492 Sancus Blvd Worthington (43085) *(G-19971)*

Leidos Inc 330 405-9810
8866 Commons Blvd Ste 201 Twinsburg (44087) *(G-18440)*

Leidos Inc 858 826-6000
4449 Easton Way Ste 150 Columbus (43219) *(G-8051)*

Leidos Inc 937 431-2220
3745 Pentagon Blvd Beavercreek (45431) *(G-1185)*

Leidos Engineering LLC 330 405-9810
8866 Commons Blvd Ste 201 Twinsburg (44087) *(G-18441)*

Leidos Technical Services Inc 513 672-8400
497 Circle Freeway Dr # 236 West Chester (45246) *(G-19212)*

Leikin Motor Companies Inc 440 946-6900
38750 Mentor Ave Willoughby (44094) *(G-19686)*

Leisure Sports Inc 419 829-2891
9501 Central Ave Sylvania (43560) *(G-17599)*

Lemmon & Lemmon Inc 330 497-8686
1201 S Main St Ste 200 North Canton (44720) *(G-15351)*

Lenau Park 440 235-2646
7370 Columbia Rd Olmsted Twp (44138) *(G-15677)*

Lencyk Masonry Co Inc 330 729-9780
7671 South Ave Youngstown (44512) *(G-20254)*

Lennox Industries Inc 614 871-3017
3750 Brookham Dr Ste A Grove City (43123) *(G-11575)*

Lenny's Collision Center, Barberton Also called Lennys Auto Sales Inc *(G-970)*

Lennys Auto Sales Inc 330 848-2993
893 Wooster Rd N Barberton (44203) *(G-970)*

Lenz Inc 937 277-9364
3301 Klepinger Rd Dayton (45406) *(G-9677)*

Lenz Company, Dayton Also called Lenz Inc *(G-9677)*

Leo A Dick & Sons Co (PA) 330 452-5010
935 Mckinley Ave Nw Canton (44703) *(G-2432)*

Leo Yannenoff Jewish Community (PA) 614 231-2731
1125 College Ave Columbus (43209) *(G-8052)*

Leonard Insur Svcs Agcy Inc (HQ) 330 266-1904
4244 Mount Pleasant St Nw Canton (44720) *(G-2433)*

Leos La Piazza Inc 937 339-5553
2 N Market St Troy (45373) *(G-18361)*

Lepi Enterprises Inc 740 453-2980
630 Gw Morse St Zanesville (43701) *(G-20495)*

Leppo Inc (PA) 330 633-3999
176 West Ave Tallmadge (44278) *(G-17643)*

Leppo Inc 330 456-2930
1534 Shepler Ch Ave Sw Canton (44706) *(G-2434)*

LEPPO EQUIPMENT, Tallmadge *Also called Leppo Inc* ***(G-17643)***

Leppo Equipment, Canton *Also called Leppo Inc* ***(G-2434)***

Lerner Sampson & Rothfuss (PA)....513 241-3100
120 E 4th St Cincinnati (45202) ***(G-3969)***

Leroy Twp Fire Dept....440 254-4124
13028 Leroy Center Rd Painesville (44077) ***(G-15863)***

Lesaint Logistics Inc....513 874-3900
4487 Le Saint Ct West Chester (45014) ***(G-19105)***

Lesaint Logistics LLC....513 988-0101
5564 Alan B Shepherd St Trenton (45067) ***(G-18341)***

Lesaint Logistics LLC....513 874-3900
4487 Le Saint Ct West Chester (45014) ***(G-19106)***

Lesco Inc (HQ)....216 706-9250
1385 E 36th St Cleveland (44114) ***(G-5936)***

Level 3 Communications Inc....330 256-8999
520 S Main St Ste 2435 Akron (44311) ***(G-315)***

Level 3 Telecom LLC....614 255-2000
250 W Old Wilson Brg 13 Worthington (43085) ***(G-19972)***

Level 3 Telecom LLC....234 542-6279
1019 E Turkeyfoot Lake Rd Akron (44312) ***(G-316)***

Level 3 Telecom LLC....513 841-0000
3268 Highland Ave Cincinnati (45213) ***(G-3970)***

Level 3 Telecom LLC....513 841-0000
3268 Highland Ave Cincinnati (45213) ***(G-3971)***

Level 3 Telecom LLC....513 682-7806
9490 Meridian Way West Chester (45069) ***(G-19107)***

Level 3 Telecom LLC....513 682-7806
9490 Meridian Way West Chester (45069) ***(G-19108)***

Level 3 Telecom LLC....513 682-7806
9490 Meridian Way West Chester (45069) ***(G-19109)***

Level 3 Telecom LLC....513 841-0000
3268 Highland Ave Cincinnati (45213) ***(G-3972)***

Level Seven....216 524-9055
4807 Rockside Rd Ste 700 Independence (44131) ***(G-12224)***

Levering Management Inc....419 768-2401
115 N Portland St Chesterville (43317) ***(G-2806)***

Levering Management Inc....740 369-6400
4 New Market Dr Delaware (43015) ***(G-10115)***

Levering Management Inc....740 387-9545
195 Executive Dr Marion (43302) ***(G-13548)***

Levering Management Inc....419 756-4747
70 Winchester Rd Mansfield (44907) ***(G-13323)***

Levine Arnold S Law Offices....513 241-6748
324 Reading Rd Cincinnati (45202) ***(G-3973)***

Levis Commons Hotel LLC....419 873-3573
6165 Levis Commons Blvd Perrysburg (43551) ***(G-16027)***

Levy & Associates LLC....614 898-5200
4645 Executive Dr Columbus (43220) ***(G-8053)***

Lewaro Contsruction, Dayton *Also called LEWaro-D&j-A Joint Venture Co* ***(G-9678)***

LEWaro-D&j-A Joint Venture Co....937 443-0000
1436 Yankee Park Pl Ste A Dayton (45458) ***(G-9678)***

Lewis Adkins W Jr....216 623-0501
1375 E 9th St Ste 900 Cleveland (44114) ***(G-5937)***

Lewis & Michael Inc (PA)....937 252-6683
1827 Woodman Dr Dayton (45420) ***(G-9679)***

Lewis & Michael Mvg & Stor Co....614 275-2997
845 Harrisburg Pike Columbus (43223) ***(G-8054)***

Lewis and Michael SEC Stor, Cincinnati *Also called Security Storage Co Inc* ***(G-4490)***

Lewis Landscaping Inc....330 666-2655
3606 Minor Rd Copley (44321) ***(G-9058)***

Lewis P C Jackson....216 750-0404
6100 Oak Tree Blvd # 400 Independence (44131) ***(G-12225)***

Lewis P C Jackson....937 306-6304
70 Birch Aly Beavercreek (45440) ***(G-1249)***

Lewis Price Realty Co....330 856-1911
8031 E Market St Warren (44484) ***(G-18875)***

Lexamed....419 693-5307
705 Front St Toledo (43605) ***(G-18004)***

Lexington Court Care Center, Mansfield *Also called Casto Health Care* ***(G-13272)***

Lexington Court Care Center....419 884-2000
250 Delaware Ave Mansfield (44904) ***(G-13324)***

Lexis Nexis, Miamisburg *Also called PNC Bank-Atm* ***(G-14336)***

Lexis Nexis, Miamisburg *Also called Relx Inc* ***(G-14340)***

Lexisnexis Group (HQ)....937 865-6800
9443 Springboro Pike Miamisburg (45342) ***(G-14314)***

Lexmark Enterprise Sftwr LLC, Westlake *Also called Hyland LLC* ***(G-19495)***

Lextant Corporation....614 228-9711
250 S High St Ste 600 Columbus (43215) ***(G-8055)***

Lexus Financial Services, Blue Ash *Also called Toyota Motor Credit Corp* ***(G-1698)***

Lexus of Dayton, Dayton *Also called Team Rahal of Dayton Inc* ***(G-9921)***

Lg Fuel Cell Systems Inc....330 491-4800
6065 Strip Ave Nw Canton (44720) ***(G-2435)***

Lgstx Services Inc....866 931-2337
145 Hunter Dr Wilmington (45177) ***(G-19766)***

Lha Developments....330 785-3219
910 Eller Ave Akron (44306) ***(G-317)***

Libby Przyk Kthman Hldngs Inc (PA)....513 241-6330
19 Garfield Pl Fl 5 Cincinnati (45202) ***(G-3974)***

Liberty Ashtabula Holdings....330 872-6000
4185 State Route 5 Newton Falls (44444) ***(G-15277)***

Liberty Bible Academy Assn....513 754-1234
4900 Old Irwin Simpson Rd Mason (45040) ***(G-13731)***

Liberty Capital Inc (PA)....937 382-1000
3435 Airborne Rd Ste B Wilmington (45177) ***(G-19767)***

Liberty Capital Services LLC....614 505-0620
438 E Wilson Bridge Rd Worthington (43085) ***(G-19973)***

Liberty Casting Company LLC....740 363-1941
407 Curtis St Delaware (43015) ***(G-10116)***

Liberty Center AC By Marriott, Liberty Township *Also called Liberty Ctr Lodging Assoc LLC* ***(G-12723)***

Liberty Comm Sftwr Sltions Inc....614 318-5000
1050 Kingsmill Pkwy Columbus (43229) ***(G-8056)***

Liberty Ctr Lodging Assoc LLC....608 833-4100
7505 Gibson St Liberty Township (45069) ***(G-12723)***

Liberty Dlysis Md-Mrica Dlysis, Columbus *Also called Fresenius Med Care Hldings Inc* ***(G-7703)***

Liberty Ems Services LLC....216 630-6626
1294 W 70th St Cleveland (44102) ***(G-5938)***

Liberty Ford Southwest Inc....440 888-2600
6600 Pearl Rd Cleveland (44130) ***(G-5939)***

Liberty Health Care Center, Youngstown *Also called Windsor House Inc* ***(G-20416)***

Liberty Health Care Center Inc....937 296-1550
4336 W Franklin St 100 Bellbrook (45305) ***(G-1371)***

Liberty Healthshare Inc....855 585-4237
4845 Fulton Dr Nw Ste 1 Canton (44718) ***(G-2436)***

Liberty Insulation Co Inc (PA)....513 621-0108
2903 Kant Pl Beavercreek (45431) ***(G-1186)***

Liberty Insulation Co Inc....513 621-0108
5782 Deerfield Rd Milford (45150) ***(G-14530)***

Liberty Maintenance Inc....330 755-7711
777 N Meridian Rd Youngstown (44509) ***(G-20255)***

Liberty Mortgage Company Inc....614 224-4000
473 E Rich St Columbus (43215) ***(G-8057)***

Liberty Mutual, Fairfield *Also called Ohio Casualty Insurance Co* ***(G-10887)***

Liberty Mutual Insurance Co....614 864-4100
630 Morrison Rd Ste 300 Gahanna (43230) ***(G-11253)***

Liberty Mutual Insurance Co....614 855-6193
440 Polaris Pkwy Ste 150 Westerville (43082) ***(G-19325)***

Liberty Mutual Insurance Co....513 984-0550
4747 Lake Forest Dr # 150 Blue Ash (45242) ***(G-1628)***

Liberty Nrsing Ctr of Jmestown....937 675-3311
4960 Old Us Route 35 E Jamestown (45335) ***(G-12327)***

Liberty Nrsing Ctr Rvrside LLC....513 557-3621
315 Lilienthal St Cincinnati (45204) ***(G-3975)***

Liberty Nursing Center....937 836-5143
425 Lauricella Ct Englewood (45322) ***(G-10712)***

Liberty Nursing Center of Thre....513 941-0787
7800 Jandaracres Dr Cincinnati (45248) ***(G-3976)***

Liberty Nursing Home Inc....937 376-2121
126 Wilson Dr Xenia (45385) ***(G-20067)***

Liberty Nursing of Willard....419 935-0148
370 E Howard St Willard (44890) ***(G-19622)***

Liberty Residence II....330 334-3262
1054 Freedom Dr Apt 115 Wadsworth (44281) ***(G-18760)***

Liberty Savings Bank FSB (HQ)....937 382-1000
2251 Rombach Ave Wilmington (45177) ***(G-19768)***

Liberty Steel Products Inc (PA)....330 538-2236
11650 Mahoning Ave North Jackson (44451) ***(G-15383)***

Liberty Steel Products Inc....330 534-7998
7193 Masury Rd Hubbard (44425) ***(G-12089)***

Liberty Tax Inc....614 853-1090
942 Galloway Rd Galloway (43119) ***(G-11345)***

Liberty Tire Recycling LLC....614 871-8097
3041 Jackson Pike Grove City (43123) ***(G-11576)***

Liberty Township, Liberty Township *Also called Four Bridges Country Club Ltd* ***(G-12720)***

Liberty Village Manor, Dublin *Also called Liberty Vlg Senior Communities* ***(G-10387)***

Liberty Vlg Senior Communities....614 889-5002
4248 Tuller Rd Ste 201 Dublin (43017) ***(G-10387)***

Liberty West Nursing Center, Toledo *Also called Parkview Manor Inc* ***(G-18119)***

Liberty-Alpha III JV....330 755-7711
24 Madison St Campbell (44405) ***(G-2139)***

Licco Inc....740 522-8345
600 Industrial Pkwy Newark (43056) ***(G-15185)***

Licensing Section, Columbus *Also called Public Safety Ohio Department* ***(G-8577)***

Licking Cnty Alcoholism Prvntn....740 281-3639
62 E Stevens St Newark (43055) ***(G-15186)***

Licking County Aging Program....740 345-0821
1058 E Main St Newark (43055) ***(G-15187)***

Licking County Board of Mrdd....740 349-6588
116 N 22nd St Newark (43055) ***(G-15188)***

Licking County Players Inc....740 349-2287
131 W Main St Newark (43055) ***(G-15189)***

Licking Knox Labor Council....740 345-1765
34 N 4th St Newark (43055) ***(G-15190)***

LICKING MEMORIAL HEALTH SYSTEMS, Newark *Also called Licking Memorial Hospital* ***(G-15192)***

Licking Memorial Hlth Systems (PA)....220 564-4000
1320 W Main St Newark (43055) ***(G-15191)***

Licking Memorial Hospital (HQ)....740 348-4137
1320 W Main St Newark (43055) ***(G-15192)***

Licking Muskingum Cmnty Correc....740 349-6980
20 S 2nd St Newark (43055) ***(G-15193)***

Licking Rhabilitation Svcs Inc....740 345-2837
11177 Lambs Ln Newark (43055) *(G-15194)*
Licking Rural Electrification (PA)....740 892-2071
11339 Mount Vernon Rd Utica (43080) *(G-18612)*
Licking Valley Lions Club....740 763-3733
3187 Licking Valley Rd Newark (43055) *(G-15195)*
Licking-Knox Goodwill Inds Inc (PA)....740 345-9861
65 S 5th St Newark (43055) *(G-15196)*
Licking-Knox Goodwill Inds Inc....740 397-0051
60 Parrott St Mount Vernon (43050) *(G-14909)*
Licking-Knox Goodwill Inds Inc....614 235-7675
3990 E Broad St Columbus (43213) *(G-8058)*
Liebel-Flarsheim Company LLC....513 761-2700
2111 E Galbraith Rd Cincinnati (45237) *(G-3977)*
Lieben Wooster LP....330 390-5722
6834 County Road 672 # 102 Millersburg (44654) *(G-14610)*
Liebert Corporation (HQ)....614 888-0246
1050 Dearborn Dr Columbus (43085) *(G-8059)*
Liebert Corporation....614 841-6104
6700 Huntley Rd Ste A Columbus (43229) *(G-8060)*
Liebert Field Services Inc....614 841-5763
610 Executive Campus Dr Westerville (43082) *(G-19326)*
Liebert Learning Center, Columbus *Also called Liebert Corporation (G-8060)*
Liechty Inc (HQ)....419 445-1565
1701 S Defiance St Archbold (43502) *(G-637)*
Life Care Center of Cleveland, Westlake *Also called Life Care Centers America Inc (G-19510)*
Life Care Center of Medina, Medina *Also called Medina Medical Investors Ltd (G-14104)*
Life Care Centers America Inc....440 365-5200
1212 Abbe Rd S Elyria (44035) *(G-10640)*
Life Care Centers America Inc....440 871-3030
26520 Center Ridge Rd Westlake (44145) *(G-19510)*
Life Care Centers America Inc....614 889-6320
3000 Bethel Rd Columbus (43220) *(G-8061)*
Life Care Centers America Inc....330 483-3131
2400 Columbia Rd Valley City (44280) *(G-18619)*
Life Care Centers of Medina, Valley City *Also called Life Care Centers America Inc (G-18619)*
Life Care Medical Services, North Canton *Also called J & C Ambulance Services Inc (G-15346)*
Life Center Adult Day Care....614 866-7212
2225 State Route 256 Reynoldsburg (43068) *(G-16465)*
LIFE CENTER AT WESLEY RIDGE, Reynoldsburg *Also called Life Center Adult Day Care (G-16465)*
Life Connection of Ohio....419 893-4891
3661 Brrfeld Blvd Ste 105 Maumee (43537) *(G-13935)*
Life Connection of Ohio Inc....937 223-8223
40 Wyoming St Dayton (45409) *(G-9680)*
Life Enriching Communities (PA)....513 719-3510
6279 Tri Ridge Blvd # 320 Loveland (45140) *(G-13138)*
Life Insurance Mktg Co Inc....330 867-1707
91 Mayfield Ave Akron (44313) *(G-318)*
Life Line Screening....216 581-6556
6150 Oak Tree Blvd # 200 Independence (44131) *(G-12226)*
Life Line Screening Amer Ltd (PA)....216 581-6556
6150 Oak Tree Blvd Independence (44131) *(G-12227)*
Life Skills Center, Akron *Also called Hat White Management LLC (G-257)*
Life Star Rescue Inc....419 238-2507
1171 Production Dr Van Wert (45891) *(G-18637)*
Life Time Fitness Inc....513 234-0660
8310 Wilkens Blvd Mason (45040) *(G-13732)*
Life Time Fitness Inc....952 229-7158
3825 Hard Rd Dublin (43016) *(G-10388)*
Life Time Fitness Inc....614 428-6000
3900 Easton Sta Columbus (43219) *(G-8062)*
Lifebanc....216 752-5433
4775 Richmond Rd Cleveland (44128) *(G-5940)*
Lifecare Alliance....614 278-3130
1699 W Mound St Columbus (43223) *(G-8063)*
Lifecare Ambulance Inc....440 323-2527
598 Cleveland St Elyria (44035) *(G-10641)*
Lifecare Ambulance Inc (PA)....440 323-6111
640 Cleveland St Elyria (44035) *(G-10642)*
Lifecare Fmly Hlth & Dntl Ctr....330 454-2000
2725 Lincoln St E Canton (44707) *(G-2437)*
Lifecare Hospice (PA)....330 264-4899
1900 Akron Rd Wooster (44691) *(G-19883)*
Lifecare Hospice....330 336-6595
102 Main St Wadsworth (44281) *(G-18761)*
Lifecare Medical Services....614 258-2545
3065 E 14th Ave Columbus (43219) *(G-8064)*
Lifecare Pallivative Medicine, Wooster *Also called Lifecare Hospice (G-19883)*
Lifecare Pallivative Medicine, Wadsworth *Also called Lifecare Hospice (G-18761)*
Lifecenter Organ Donor Network (PA)....513 558-5555
615 Elsinore Pl Ste 400 Cincinnati (45202) *(G-3978)*
Lifecycle Solutions Jv LLC....937 938-1321
2689 Cmmons Blvd Ste 120 Beavercreek (45431) *(G-1187)*
Lifeline Hospital, Steubenville *Also called Ltac Investors LLC (G-17328)*
Lifeline Systems Company....330 762-5627
703 S Main St Ste 211 Akron (44311) *(G-319)*
Lifepoint Solutions, Amelia *Also called Clermont Counseling Center (G-579)*
Lifeservices Development Corp....440 257-3866
7685 Lake Shore Blvd Mentor (44060) *(G-14209)*
Lifeshare Cmnty Blood Svcs Inc (PA)....440 322-6159
105 Cleveland St Ste 101 Elyria (44035) *(G-10643)*
Lifeshare Community Blood Svcs....440 322-6573
105 Cliffland St Elyria (44035) *(G-10644)*
Lifespan Incorporated (PA)....513 868-3210
1900 Fairgrove Ave Hamilton (45011) *(G-11754)*
Lifestar Ambulance Inc....419 245-6210
1402 Lagrange St Toledo (43608) *(G-18005)*
Lifestges Smrtan Ctr For Women....937 277-8988
2200 Philadelphia Dr # 101 Dayton (45406) *(G-9681)*
Lifestgs-Smrtan Ctrs For Women, Dayton *Also called Lifestges Smrtan Ctr For Women (G-9681)*
Lifestyle Communities Ltd (PA)....614 918-2000
230 West St Ste 200 Columbus (43215) *(G-8065)*
Lifestyle Landscaping Inc....440 353-0333
34613 Center Ridge Rd North Ridgeville (44039) *(G-15468)*
Lifeteam Ambulance Service, East Liverpool *Also called Lifeteam Ems Inc (G-10523)*
Lifeteam Ems Inc....330 386-9284
740 Dresden Ave Ste A East Liverpool (43920) *(G-10523)*
Lifetime, Mason *Also called Life Time Fitness Inc (G-13732)*
Lifetime Fitness, Columbus *Also called Life Time Fitness Inc (G-8062)*
Lifetouch Inc....419 435-2646
922 Springville Ave Ste B Fostoria (44830) *(G-11134)*
Lifetouch Inc....937 298-6275
3701 Wilmington Pike Dayton (45429) *(G-9682)*
Lifetouch Nat Schl Studios Inc....419 483-8200
102 Commerce Park Dr Bellevue (44811) *(G-1412)*
Lifetouch Nat Schl Studios Inc....330 497-1291
1300 S Main St Ste 300 Canton (44720) *(G-2438)*
Lifetouch Nat Schl Studios Inc....513 772-2110
11815 Highway Dr Ste 100 Cincinnati (45241) *(G-3979)*
Lifeworks At Southwest General, Cleveland *Also called Southwest General Health Ctr (G-6502)*
Light of Hearts Villa....440 232-1991
283 Union St Ofc Cleveland (44146) *(G-5941)*
Lighthouse Insurance Group LLC (PA)....216 503-2439
6150 Oak Tree Blvd # 210 Independence (44131) *(G-12228)*
Lighthouse Medical Staffing....614 937-6259
3970 Brown Park Dr Ste B Hilliard (43026) *(G-11921)*
Lighthouse Youth Services Inc....513 221-1017
3603 Washington Ave Cincinnati (45229) *(G-3980)*
Lighthouse Youth Services Inc....513 861-1111
2522 Highland Ave Cincinnati (45219) *(G-3981)*
Lighthouse Youth Services Inc (PA)....513 221-3350
401 E Mcmillan St Cincinnati (45206) *(G-3982)*
Lighthouse Youth Services Inc....740 634-3094
1071 Tong Hollow Rd Bainbridge (45612) *(G-942)*
Lighting Maint Harmon Sign....419 841-6658
7844 W Central Ave Toledo (43617) *(G-18006)*
Lighting Services Inc....330 405-4879
9001 Dutton Dr Twinsburg (44087) *(G-18442)*
Lightwell Inc (PA)....614 310-2700
565 Metro Pl S Ste 220 Dublin (43017) *(G-10389)*
Lillian and Betty Ratner Schl....216 464-0033
27575 Shaker Blvd Cleveland (44124) *(G-5942)*
Lima Auto Mall Inc....419 993-6000
2200 N Cable Rd Lima (45807) *(G-12816)*
Lima Cdllac Pntiac Olds Nissan, Lima *Also called Lima Auto Mall Inc (G-12816)*
Lima City School Central Svcs, Lima *Also called Lima City School District (G-12817)*
Lima City School District....419 996-3450
600 E Wayne St Lima (45801) *(G-12817)*
Lima Cnvlscent HM Fndation Inc (PA)....419 227-5450
1650 Allentown Rd Lima (45805) *(G-12818)*
Lima Communications Corp....419 228-8835
1424 Rice Ave Lima (45805) *(G-12819)*
Lima Community Health Center, Lima *Also called Health Partners Western Ohio (G-12795)*
Lima Dental Assoc Risolvato Lt....419 228-4036
2115 Allentown Rd Ste C Lima (45805) *(G-12820)*
Lima Distribution Center, Lima *Also called Spartannash Company (G-12880)*
Lima Division, Lima *Also called Benjamin Steel Company Inc (G-12745)*
Lima Family YMCA (PA)....419 223-6045
345 S Elizabeth St Lima (45801) *(G-12821)*
Lima Mall Inc....419 331-6255
2400 Elida Rd Ste 166 Lima (45805) *(G-12822)*
Lima Manor, Lima *Also called Hcf of Lima Inc (G-12793)*
Lima Medical Supplies Inc....419 226-9581
770 W North St Lima (45801) *(G-12823)*
Lima Memorial Health System, Lima *Also called Lima Memorial Hospital (G-12824)*
Lima Memorial Hospital (HQ)....419 228-3335
1001 Bellefontaine Ave Lima (45804) *(G-12824)*
Lima Memorial Hospital La....419 738-5151
1251 Lincoln Hwy Wapakoneta (45895) *(G-18801)*
Lima Memorial Joint Oper Co (PA)....419 228-5165
1001 Belelfontaine Ave Lima (45804) *(G-12825)*
Lima Pathology Associates Labs (PA)....419 226-9595
415 W Market St Ste B Lima (45801) *(G-12826)*
Lima Sheet Metal Machine & Mfg....419 229-1161
1001 Bowman Rd Lima (45804) *(G-12827)*
Lima Superior Federal Cr Un....419 738-4512
202 Willipie St Wapakoneta (45895) *(G-18802)*

ALPHABETIC

Lima Superior Federal Cr Un (PA) 419 223-9746
  4230 Elida Rd Lima (45807) *(G-12828)*
Lima-Allen County Paramedics, Lima Also called Harter Ventures Inc *(G-12790)*
Limbach Company LLC 614 299-2175
  851 Williams Ave Columbus (43212) *(G-8066)*
Limbach Company LLC 614 299-2175
  822 Cleveland Ave Columbus (43201) *(G-8067)*
Limited, Columbus Also called L Brands Store Dsign Cnstr Inc *(G-8021)*
Limited Services Corporation, Columbus Also called L Brands Service Company LLC *(G-8020)*
Limited Technology Svcs Inc, Columbus Also called Mast Technology Services Inc *(G-8126)*
Limitless Solutions Inc 614 577-1550
  600 Claycraft Rd Columbus (43230) *(G-8068)*
Lin R Rogers Elec Contrs Inc 614 876-9336
  5050 Nike Dr Ste C Hilliard (43026) *(G-11922)*
Lincare Inc 330 928-0884
  1566 Akron Peninsula Rd # 2 Akron (44313) *(G-320)*
Lincoln Crawford Nrsg/Rehab CT 513 861-2044
  1346 Lincoln Ave Cincinnati (45206) *(G-3983)*
Lincoln Fincl Advisors Corp 216 765-7400
  28601 Chagrin Blvd # 300 Beachwood (44122) *(G-1096)*
Lincoln Fincl Advisors Corp 614 888-6516
  7650 Rivers Edge Dr # 200 Columbus (43235) *(G-8069)*
Lincoln Hts Hlth Connection, Cincinnati Also called The Healthcare Connection Inc *(G-4642)*
Lincoln Moving & Storage Co 216 741-5500
  8686 Brookpark Rd Cleveland (44129) *(G-5943)*
Lincoln Mrcury Kings Auto Mall (PA) 513 683-3800
  9600 Kings Auto Mall Rd Cincinnati (45249) *(G-3984)*
Lincoln Park Associates II LP 937 297-4300
  694 Isaac Prugh Way Dayton (45429) *(G-9683)*
Lincoln Park Manor, Dayton Also called Lincoln Park Associates II LP *(G-9683)*
LINCOLN PARK MEDICAL CENTER, Chillicothe Also called Hopewell Health Centers Inc *(G-2849)*
Lincolnview Local Schools (PA) 419 968-2226
  15945 Middle Point Rd Van Wert (45891) *(G-18638)*
Lincolnway Home, Middle Point Also called County of Van Wert *(G-14376)*
Linda Cpers Idntity Hair Dsign 513 791-2555
  7800 Montgomery Rd Cincinnati (45236) *(G-3985)*
Linde Gas, Cincinnati Also called Airgas Usa LLC *(G-2979)*
Linden Home Dialysis, Dayton Also called Total Renal Care Inc *(G-9933)*
Linden Industries Inc 330 928-4064
  137 Ascot Pkwy Cuyahoga Falls (44223) *(G-9205)*
Linden Medical Center, Columbus Also called Family Health Care Center Inc *(G-7635)*
LINDER CENTER OF HOPE, Mason Also called Craig and Frances Lindner Cent *(G-13691)*
Lindhorst & Dreidame Co Lpa 513 421-6630
  312 Walnut St Ste 3100 Cincinnati (45202) *(G-3986)*
Lindley Inn 740 797-9701
  9000 Hocking Hills Dr The Plains (45780) *(G-17665)*
Lindner Clinical Trial Center 513 585-1777
  2123 Auburn Ave Ste 424 Cincinnati (45219) *(G-3987)*
Lindsey Accura Inc 800 980-8199
  5880 Scarborough Blvd Columbus (43232) *(G-8070)*
Lindsey Cnstr & Design Inc 330 785-9931
  2151 S Arlington Rd Akron (44306) *(G-321)*
Lineage Logistics LLC 937 328-3349
  1985 Airpark Dr Springfield (45502) *(G-17221)*
Linemaster Services LLC 614 507-9945
  5736 Buckeye Pkwy Grove City (43123) *(G-11577)*
Liniform Service, Barberton Also called Barberton Laundry & Cleaning *(G-958)*
Link & Reneissance Inc 440 235-0501
  26111 John Rd Olmsted Twp (44138) *(G-15678)*
Link Construction Group Inc 937 292-7774
  895 County Road 32 N Bellefontaine (43311) *(G-1385)*
Link Iq LLC (PA) 859 983-6080
  125 Westpark Rd Dayton (45459) *(G-9684)*
Linking Employment Abilities (PA) 216 696-2716
  2545 Lorain Ave Cleveland (44113) *(G-5944)*
Linkmedia 360, Independence Also called National Yllow Pages Media LLC *(G-12237)*
Links 937 644-9988
  200 Gallery Dr Marysville (43040) *(G-13631)*
Links At The Renaissance, Olmsted Twp Also called E J Links Co The Inc *(G-15675)*
Links At Windy Knoll LLC 937 631-3744
  500 Roscommon Dr Springfield (45503) *(G-17222)*
Links Golf Course, Olmsted Twp Also called Link & Reneissance Inc *(G-15678)*
Linn Street Holdings LLC 513 699-8825
  2135 Dana Ave Ste 200 Cincinnati (45207) *(G-3988)*
Linsalata Capital Partners Fun 440 684-1400
  5900 Landerbrook Dr # 280 Cleveland (44124) *(G-5945)*
Linwood Park Company 440 963-0481
  4920 Liberty Ave Vermilion (44089) *(G-18713)*
Lion Group Inc (HQ) 937 898-1949
  7200 Poe Ave Ste 400 Dayton (45414) *(G-9685)*
Lion Uniform Group, Fairborn Also called G&K Services Inc *(G-10797)*
Lion's Den, Worthington Also called Mile Inc *(G-19978)*
Lion's Gate Trning SEC Sltions, Euclid Also called Lions Gate SEC Solutions Inc *(G-10767)*
Lion-Vallen Ltd Partnership (PA) 937 898-1949
  7200 Poe Ave Ste 400 Dayton (45414) *(G-9686)*
Lions Club International Inc 330 424-3490
  38240 Industrial Park Rd Lisbon (44432) *(G-12939)*

Lions Gate SEC Solutions Inc 440 539-8382
  295 E 208th St Euclid (44123) *(G-10767)*
Lippincott Plumbing-Heating AC 419 222-0856
  872 Saint Johns Ave Lima (45804) *(G-12829)*
Liqui-Box International Inc 614 888-9280
  480 Schrock Rd Ste G Columbus (43229) *(G-8071)*
Liquid Transport Corp 513 769-4777
  10711 Evendale Dr Cincinnati (45241) *(G-3989)*
Lisbon Lions Club, Lisbon Also called Lions Club International Inc *(G-12939)*
Lisnr Inc 513 322-8400
  920 Race St Ste 4 Cincinnati (45202) *(G-3990)*
Litco International Inc (PA) 330 539-5433
  1 Litco Dr Vienna (44473) *(G-18739)*
Literature Fulfillment Svcs 513 774-8600
  11400 Grooms Rd Ste 112 Blue Ash (45242) *(G-1629)*
Lithko Contracting LLC 614 733-0300
  8065 Corporate Blvd Plain City (43064) *(G-16196)*
Lithko Contracting LLC (PA) 513 564-2000
  2958 Crescentville Rd West Chester (45069) *(G-19110)*
Lithko Contracting LLC 513 863-5100
  900 N Garver Rd Monroe (45050) *(G-14703)*
Lithko Restoration Tech LLC (PA) 513 863-5500
  990 N Main St Monroe (45050) *(G-14704)*
Lithko Restoration Tech LLC 614 221-0711
  1059 Cable Ave Columbus (43222) *(G-8072)*
Lithuanian World Community 513 542-0076
  5927 Monticello Ave Cincinnati (45224) *(G-3991)*
Litigation Management Inc 440 484-2000
  6000 Parkland Blvd # 100 Mayfield Heights (44124) *(G-14004)*
Litigation Support Svcs Inc 513 241-5605
  817 Main St Ste 400 Cincinnati (45202) *(G-3992)*
Litter Bob Fuel & Heating Co (HQ) 740 773-2196
  524 Eastern Ave Chillicothe (45601) *(G-2860)*
Litter Distributing Co Inc 740 774-2831
  656 Hospital Rd Chillicothe (45601) *(G-2861)*
Litter Quality Propane, Chillicothe Also called Litter Bob Fuel & Heating Co *(G-2860)*
Little Bark View Limited (PA) 216 520-1250
  8111 Rockside Rd Ste 200 Cleveland (44125) *(G-5946)*
Little Dreamers Big Believers 614 294-2922
  1077 N High St Columbus (43201) *(G-8073)*
Little Lambs Childrens Center 614 471-9269
  425 S Hamilton Rd Gahanna (43230) *(G-11254)*
Little Miami Home Care Inc 513 248-8988
  5371 S Milford Rd Apt 16 Milford (45150) *(G-14531)*
Little Miami River Catering Co 937 848-2464
  80 E Franklin St Bellbrook (45305) *(G-1372)*
Little Mountain Country Club, Painesville Also called Madison Route 20 LLC *(G-15864)*
Little Squirt Sports Park 419 227-6200
  1996 W Robb Ave Lima (45805) *(G-12830)*
Little Theater Off Broadway 614 875-3919
  3981 Broadway Grove City (43123) *(G-11578)*
Little Turtle Golf Club, Westerville Also called Turtle Golf Management Ltd *(G-19446)*
Littler Mendelson PC 216 696-7600
  1100 Superior Ave E Fl 20 Cleveland (44114) *(G-5947)*
Live Technologies Holdings Inc 614 278-7777
  3445 Millennium Ct Columbus (43219) *(G-8074)*
Livin Care Alter of Kirke Inc 740 927-3209
  205 E Main St Kirkersville (43033) *(G-12455)*
Living Assistance Services 330 733-1532
  22 Northwest Ave Tallmadge (44278) *(G-17644)*
Living Care Alternatives 740 927-3209
  205 E Main St Kirkersville (43033) *(G-12456)*
Living Care Altrntves of Utica 740 892-3414
  233 N Main St Utica (43080) *(G-18613)*
Living In Family Environment 614 475-5305
  142 N High St Gahanna (43230) *(G-11255)*
Living Matters LLC 866 587-8074
  13613 Caine Ave Cleveland (44105) *(G-5948)*
Livinginston Court Flea Market, Columbus Also called Rainbow Flea Market Inc *(G-8585)*
Livingston Care Center, Dayton Also called Huffman Health Care Inc *(G-9625)*
Livingston Painting, Union City Also called Rl Painting and Mfg Inc *(G-18503)*
Lkq Corporation 614 575-8200
  5830 Green Pointe Dr S A Groveport (43125) *(G-11656)*
Lkq Corporation 330 733-6333
  1435 Triplett Blvd Akron (44306) *(G-322)*
Lkq Triplettasap Inc (HQ) 330 733-6333
  1435 Triplett Blvd Akron (44306) *(G-323)*
Llanfair Retirement Community, Cincinnati Also called Ohio Living *(G-4208)*
LLP Ziegler Metzger 216 781-5470
  1111 Superior Ave E # 1000 Cleveland (44114) *(G-5949)*
Lm Constrction Trry Lvrini Inc 740 695-9604
  67682 Clark Rd Saint Clairsville (43950) *(G-16641)*
Lmn Development LLC (PA) 419 433-7200
  7000 Kalahari Dr Sandusky (44870) *(G-16775)*
Lmt Enterprises Maumee Inc 419 891-7325
  1772 Indian Wood Cir Maumee (43537) *(G-13936)*
Lns America Inc (HQ) 513 528-5674
  4621 E Tech Dr Cincinnati (45245) *(G-2923)*
Lobby Shoppes Inc (PA) 937 324-0002
  200 N Murray St Springfield (45503) *(G-17223)*
Lobby Shoppes Inc-Springfield, Springfield Also called Lobby Shoppes Inc *(G-17223)*
LOCAL 17A, Canton Also called United Food & Commercial Wkr *(G-2567)*

LOCAL 18 I.U.O.E., Cleveland *Also called Internatl Un Oper Eng 18* ***(G-5833)***
Local 268, Cleveland *Also called Amalgamated Transit Union* ***(G-5001)***
Local 5-689, Piketon *Also called Pace International Union* ***(G-16123)***
Local 883, North Olmsted *Also called Interntonal Aliance Thea Stage* ***(G-15427)***
Local 911 United Mine Workers....740 256-6083
5102 State Route 218 Gallipolis (45631) ***(G-11327)***
Local Union 856 Uaw Bldg Corp....330 733-6231
1155 George Wash Blvd Akron (44312) ***(G-324)***
Lochard Inc....937 492-8811
903 Wapakoneta Ave Sidney (45365) ***(G-16940)***
Locker Moving & Storage Inc (PA)....330 784-0477
131 Perry Dr Nw Canton (44708) ***(G-2439)***
Lockes Garden Center Inc....440 774-6981
461 E Lorain St Oberlin (44074) ***(G-15648)***
Lockhart Concrete Co (PA)....330 745-6520
800 W Waterloo Rd Akron (44314) ***(G-325)***
Lockheed Martin, West Chester *Also called Leidos Technical Services Inc* ***(G-19212)***
Lockheed Martin....330 796-2800
1210 Massillon Rd Akron (44315) ***(G-326)***
Lockheed Martin Corporation....937 429-0100
2940 Presidential Dr # 290 Beavercreek (45324) ***(G-1188)***
Locktooth Division, Cleveland *Also called Hodell-Natco Industries Inc* ***(G-5765)***
Locum Medical Group LLC....216 464-2125
6100 Oak Tree Blvd Independence (44131) ***(G-12229)***
Locust Dental Center....330 535-7876
300 Locust St Ste 430 Akron (44302) ***(G-327)***
Locust Dental Ctr, Akron *Also called Locust Dental Center* ***(G-327)***
Locust Hills Golf Course, Springfield *Also called Locust Hills Golf Inc* ***(G-17224)***
Locust Hills Golf Inc....937 265-5152
5575 N River Rd Springfield (45502) ***(G-17224)***
Locust Ridge Nursing Home Inc (PA)....937 444-2920
12745 Elm Corner Rd Williamsburg (45176) ***(G-19633)***
Lodge At Saw Mill Creek, The, Huron *Also called Saw Mill Creek Ltd* ***(G-12170)***
Lodge Care Center Inc....513 683-9966
9370 Union Cemetery Rd Loveland (45140) ***(G-13139)***
Lodge Stone Wood....513 769-4325
11350 Swing Rd Blue Ash (45241) ***(G-1630)***
Lodging First LLC....614 792-2770
94 N High St Ste 250 Dublin (43017) ***(G-10390)***
Lodging Industry Inc....440 323-7488
7704 Milan Rd Sandusky (44870) ***(G-16776)***
Lodging Industry Inc....419 732-2929
1723 E Perry St Port Clinton (43452) ***(G-16250)***
Lodging Industry Inc....440 324-3911
523 Griswold Rd Elyria (44035) ***(G-10645)***
Lodi Community Hospital (PA)....330 948-1222
225 Elyria St Lodi (44254) ***(G-12964)***
Loeb Electric Company (PA)....614 294-6351
1800 E 5th Ave Ste A Columbus (43219) ***(G-8075)***
Lofino's Investment, Beavercreek *Also called Lofinos Inc* ***(G-1250)***
Lofinos Inc....937 431-1662
3255 Seajay Dr Beavercreek (45430) ***(G-1250)***
Loft Services LLC....614 855-2452
8010 Morse Rd New Albany (43054) ***(G-14991)***
Logan Acres, Bellefontaine *Also called County of Logan* ***(G-1382)***
Logan Clutch Corporation....440 808-4258
28855 Ranney Pkwy Cleveland (44145) ***(G-5950)***
Logan Cnty Prbate Juvenile Crt, Bellefontaine *Also called County of Logan* ***(G-1380)***
Logan County Board of Mrdd, Bellefontaine *Also called Logan Housing Corp Inc* ***(G-1387)***
Logan County Childrens Svcs, Bellefontaine *Also called County of Logan* ***(G-1383)***
Logan County Engineering Off....937 592-2791
1991 County Road 13 Bellefontaine (43311) ***(G-1386)***
Logan Health Care Center....740 385-2155
300 Arlington Ave Logan (43138) ***(G-12983)***
Logan Healthcare Leasing LLC....216 367-1214
300 Arlington Ave Logan (43138) ***(G-12984)***
Logan Housing Corp Inc....937 592-2009
1973 State Route 47 W Bellefontaine (43311) ***(G-1387)***
Logan Logistics, Canton *Also called W L Logan Trucking Company* ***(G-2580)***
Logan-Hocking School District....740 385-7844
13483 Mysville William Rd Logan (43138) ***(G-12985)***
Logic Soft Inc....614 884-5544
5900 Sawmill Rd Ste 200 Dublin (43017) ***(G-10391)***
Logikor LLC....513 762-7678
463 Ohio Pike Ste 105 Cincinnati (45255) ***(G-3993)***
Logistics Department, Dayton *Also called Wright Brothers Aero Inc* ***(G-10004)***
Logistics Inc....419 478-1514
6010 Skyview Dr Toledo (43612) ***(G-18007)***
Lolly The Trolley, Cleveland *Also called Trolley Tours of Cleveland* ***(G-6619)***
London City Admin Offices....740 852-3243
6 E 2nd St London (43140) ***(G-12997)***
London Computer Systems Inc....513 583-0840
1007 Cottonwood Dr Loveland (45140) ***(G-13140)***
Long-Stanton Mfg Company....513 874-8020
9388 Sutton Pl West Chester (45011) ***(G-19111)***
Longaberger Company....740 349-8411
50 N 2nd St Newark (43055) ***(G-15197)***
Longbow Research LLC (PA)....216 986-0700
6050 Oak Tree Blvd # 350 Independence (44131) ***(G-12230)***
Longmeadow Care Center Inc....330 297-5781
565 Bryn Mawr St Ravenna (44266) ***(G-16392)***
Longterm Lodging Inc....614 224-0614
721 S Souder Ave Columbus (43223) ***(G-8076)***
Longwood Family YMCA, Macedonia *Also called Young Mens Christian Assoc* ***(G-13219)***
Longwood Phase One Assoc LP....561 998-0700
3750 Fleming Ave Cleveland (44115) ***(G-5951)***
Longworth Enterprises Inc....513 738-4663
8050 Beckett Center Dr West Chester (45069) ***(G-19112)***
Lorad LLC....216 265-2862
24400 Sperry Dr Westlake (44145) ***(G-19511)***
Lorain Cnty Brd Mntl Rtrdtn, Elyria *Also called County of Lorain* ***(G-10610)***
Lorain Cnty Bys Girls CLB Inc (PA)....440 775-2582
4111 Pearl Ave Lorain (44055) ***(G-13048)***
Lorain Cnty Elderly Hsing Corp....440 288-1600
1600 Kansas Ave Lorain (44052) ***(G-13049)***
Lorain Cnty Sty Off Eqp Co Inc....440 960-7070
1953 Cooper Foster Pk Rd Amherst (44001) ***(G-599)***
Lorain Country Job & Fmly Svcs, Elyria *Also called County of Lorain* ***(G-10613)***
Lorain County Alcohol and Drug....440 246-0109
305 W 20th St Lorain (44052) ***(G-13050)***
Lorain County Alcohol and Drug (PA)....440 989-4900
2115 W Park Dr Lorain (44053) ***(G-13051)***
Lorain County Board....440 329-3734
1091 Infirmary Rd Elyria (44035) ***(G-10646)***
Lorain County Childrens Svcs, Elyria *Also called County of Lorain* ***(G-10616)***
Lorain County Community Action (PA)....440 245-2009
936 Broadway Lorain (44052) ***(G-13052)***
Lorain County Community Action....440 246-0480
1050 Reid Ave Lorain (44052) ***(G-13053)***
Lorain County Engineers, Elyria *Also called County of Lorain* ***(G-10612)***
Lorain County Garage, Elyria *Also called County of Lorain* ***(G-10615)***
Lorain County Landfill, Oberlin *Also called Republic Services Inc* ***(G-15659)***
Lorain County Sani Engineers, Elyria *Also called County of Lorain* ***(G-10609)***
Lorain Family Hlth & RES Ctrs, Lorain *Also called Cleveland Clinic Foundation* ***(G-13026)***
Lorain Glass Co Inc....440 277-6004
1865 N Ridge Rd E Ste E Lorain (44055) ***(G-13054)***
Lorain Life Care Ambulance Svc....440 244-6467
109 W 23rd St Lorain (44052) ***(G-13055)***
Lorain Lifecare Ambulance, Elyria *Also called Lifecare Ambulance Inc* ***(G-10642)***
Lorain National Bank (HQ)....440 244-6000
457 Broadway Lorain (44052) ***(G-13056)***
Lorain Party Center....440 282-5599
5900 S Mayflower Dr Lorain (44053) ***(G-13057)***
Loraine Cnty Bd Mntal Rtrdtion, Lorain *Also called County of Lorain* ***(G-13034)***
Lorantffy Care Center Inc....330 666-2631
2631 Copley Rd Copley (44321) ***(G-9059)***
Lordstown Cnstr Recovery, Warren *Also called Lafarge North America Inc* ***(G-18872)***
Lorenz Corporation (PA)....937 228-6118
501 E 3rd St Dayton (45402) ***(G-9687)***
Lori Holding Co (PA)....740 342-3230
1400 Commerce Dr New Lexington (43764) ***(G-15055)***
Lorraine Elyria Broadcasting, Elyria *Also called Weol* ***(G-10688)***
Lory Dialysis LLC....740 522-2955
65 S Terrace Ave Newark (43055) ***(G-15198)***
Los Alamos Technical Assoc Inc....614 508-1200
756 Park Meadow Rd Westerville (43081) ***(G-19420)***
Losantiville Country Club....513 631-4133
3097 Losantiville Ave Cincinnati (45213) ***(G-3994)***
Lost Creek Care Center, Lima *Also called Volunters Amer Care Facilities* ***(G-12911)***
Lost Creek Country Club Inc....419 229-2026
2409 Lost Creek Blvd Lima (45804) ***(G-12831)***
Lost Creek Health C, Lima *Also called Guardian Elde* ***(G-12788)***
Lost Nation Golf Course, Willoughby *Also called City of Willoughby* ***(G-19652)***
Lost Nation Sports Park....440 602-4000
38630 Jet Center Pl Willoughby (44094) ***(G-19687)***
Loth Inc (PA)....513 554-4900
3574 E Kemper Rd Cincinnati (45241) ***(G-3995)***
Loth Inc....614 487-4000
855 Grandview Ave Ste 2 Columbus (43215) ***(G-8077)***
Loth Inc....614 225-1933
855 Grandview Ave Ste 2 Columbus (43215) ***(G-8078)***
Lott Industries Incorporated....419 476-2516
5500 Telegraph Rd Toledo (43612) ***(G-18008)***
Lott Industries Incorporated....419 891-5215
1645 Holland Rd Maumee (43537) ***(G-13937)***
Lott Industries Incorporated....419 534-4980
3350 Hill Ave Toledo (43607) ***(G-18009)***
Lou Ritenour Decorators Inc....330 425-3232
2066 Case Pkwy S Twinsburg (44087) ***(G-18443)***
Lou-Ray Associates Inc....330 220-1999
1378 Pearl Rd Ste 201 Brunswick (44212) ***(G-1986)***
Louderback Fmly Invstments Inc....937 845-1762
3545 S Dayton Lakeview Rd New Carlisle (45344) ***(G-15026)***
Louieville Title Agncy For Nrt....419 248-4611
626 Madison Ave Ste 100 Toledo (43604) ***(G-18010)***
Louis Arthur Steel Company (PA)....440 997-5545
185 Water St Geneva (44041) ***(G-11365)***
Louis Perry & Associates Inc....330 334-1585
165 Smokerise Dr Wadsworth (44281) ***(G-18762)***

A L P H A B E T I C

(PA)=Parent Co (HQ)=Headquarters (DH)=Div Headquarters
2018 Harris Ohio Services Directory
1245

Louis Stokes Cleveland Vamc, Cleveland *Also called Veterans Health Administration* ***(G-6691)***
Louis Stokes Head Start....216 295-0854
4075 E 173rd St Cleveland (44128) ***(G-5952)***
Louis Trauth Dairy LLC (HQ)....859 431-7553
9991 Commerce Park Dr West Chester (45246) ***(G-19213)***
Louisville Child Care Center....330 875-4303
3477 Elmhurst Cir Uniontown (44685) ***(G-18527)***
Louisville Frternal Order of E....330 875-2113
306 W Main St Louisville (44641) ***(G-13102)***
Louisville YMCA, Louisville *Also called Y M C A Central Stark County* ***(G-13108)***
Louisvlle Title Agcy For NW OH (PA)....419 248-4611
626 Madison Ave Ste 100 Toledo (43604) ***(G-18011)***
LOURIES OF HILLSBORO, Hillsboro *Also called Laurels of Hillsboro* ***(G-11985)***
Love N Comfort Home Care....740 450-7658
2814 Maple Ave Zanesville (43701) ***(G-20496)***
Loveland & Brosius LLC....614 488-4092
3300 Riverside Dr Ste 125 Upper Arlington (43221) ***(G-18554)***
Loveland Excavating Inc....513 965-6600
260 Osborne Dr Fairfield (45014) ***(G-10873)***
Loveland Excavating and Paving, Fairfield *Also called Loveland Excavating Inc* ***(G-10873)***
Loveland Health Care Ctr LLC....513 605-6000
501 N 2nd St Loveland (45140) ***(G-13141)***
Loveman Steel Corporation....440 232-6200
5455 Perkins Rd Bedford (44146) ***(G-1317)***
Loves Travel Stops....419 837-0071
26530 Baker Dr Perrysburg (43551) ***(G-16028)***
Loves Travel Stops....419 643-8482
416 Village Ave Beaverdam (45808) ***(G-1290)***
Loves Travel Stops....937 325-2961
4725 S Charleston Pike Springfield (45502) ***(G-17225)***
Loves Trvl Stops Cntry Stores, Springfield *Also called Loves Travel Stops* ***(G-17225)***
Loving Care Hospice Inc (PA)....740 852-7755
56 S Oak St London (43140) ***(G-12998)***
Loving Family Home Care Inc....888 469-2178
2600 N Reynolds Rd 101a Toledo (43615) ***(G-18012)***
Loving Hands Home Care Inc....330 792-7032
4179 Nottingham Ave Youngstown (44511) ***(G-20256)***
Low Country Metal, Richfield *Also called I-Tran Inc* ***(G-16512)***
Lowe's Greenhouses Flor Ldscp, Chagrin Falls *Also called Lowes Greenhouse & Gift Shop* ***(G-2722)***
Lower Great Lakes Kenworth Inc....419 874-3511
12650 Eckel Junction Rd Perrysburg (43551) ***(G-16029)***
Lowes Greenhouse & Gift Shop....440 543-5123
16540 Chillicothe Rd Chagrin Falls (44023) ***(G-2722)***
Lowes Home Centers LLC....216 351-4723
7327 Northcliff Ave Cleveland (44144) ***(G-5953)***
Lowes Home Centers LLC....419 739-1300
1340 Bellefontaine St Wapakoneta (45895) ***(G-18803)***
Lowes Home Centers LLC....937 235-2920
8421 Old Troy Pike Dayton (45424) ***(G-9688)***
Lowes Home Centers LLC....740 574-6200
7915 Ohio River Rd Wheelersburg (45694) ***(G-19578)***
Lowes Home Centers LLC....330 665-9356
186 N Clvland Mssillon Rd Akron (44333) ***(G-328)***
Lowes Home Centers LLC....330 829-2700
2595 W State St Alliance (44601) ***(G-545)***
Lowes Home Centers LLC....937 599-4000
2168 Us Highway 68 S Bellefontaine (43311) ***(G-1388)***
Lowes Home Centers LLC....419 420-7531
1077 Bright Rd Findlay (45840) ***(G-11057)***
Lowes Home Centers LLC....330 832-1901
101 Massillon Marketplace Massillon (44646) ***(G-13829)***
Lowes Home Centers LLC....513 741-0585
10235 Colerain Ave Cincinnati (45251) ***(G-3996)***
Lowes Home Centers LLC....614 433-9957
1465 Polaris Pkwy Columbus (43240) ***(G-6892)***
Lowes Home Centers LLC....740 389-9737
1840 Marion Mt Gilead Rd Marion (43302) ***(G-13549)***
Lowes Home Centers LLC....740 450-5500
3755 Frazeysburg Rd Zanesville (43701) ***(G-20497)***
Lowes Home Centers LLC....513 598-7050
6150 Harrison Ave Cincinnati (45247) ***(G-3997)***
Lowes Home Centers LLC....614 769-9940
8231 E Broad St Reynoldsburg (43068) ***(G-16466)***
Lowes Home Centers LLC....614 853-6200
1675 Georgesville Sq Dr Columbus (43228) ***(G-8079)***
Lowes Home Centers LLC....440 937-3500
1445 Center Rd Avon (44011) ***(G-906)***
Lowes Home Centers LLC....513 445-1000
575 Corwin Nixon Blvd South Lebanon (45065) ***(G-17078)***
Lowes Home Centers LLC....216 831-2860
24500 Miles Rd Bedford (44146) ***(G-1318)***
Lowes Home Centers LLC....937 327-6000
1601 N Bechtle Ave Springfield (45504) ***(G-17226)***
Lowes Home Centers LLC....419 331-3598
2411 N Eastown Rd Lima (45807) ***(G-12832)***
Lowes Home Centers LLC....740 681-3464
2240 Lowes Dr Lancaster (43130) ***(G-12551)***
Lowes Home Centers LLC....614 659-0530
6555 Dublin Center Dr Dublin (43017) ***(G-10392)***
Lowes Home Centers LLC....614 238-2601
3616 E Broad St Columbus (43213) ***(G-8080)***
Lowes Home Centers LLC....740 522-0003
888 Hebron Rd Newark (43056) ***(G-15199)***
Lowes Home Centers LLC....740 773-7777
867 N Bridge St Chillicothe (45601) ***(G-2862)***
Lowes Home Centers LLC....440 998-6555
2416 Dillon Dr Ashtabula (44004) ***(G-752)***
Lowes Home Centers LLC....513 753-5094
618 Mount Moriah Dr Cincinnati (45245) ***(G-2924)***
Lowes Home Centers LLC....614 497-6170
3899 S High St Columbus (43207) ***(G-8081)***
Lowes Home Centers LLC....513 731-6127
5385 Ridge Ave Cincinnati (45213) ***(G-3998)***
Lowes Home Centers LLC....330 287-2261
3788 Burbank Rd Wooster (44691) ***(G-19884)***
Lowes Home Centers LLC....937 339-2544
2000 W Main St Troy (45373) ***(G-18362)***
Lowes Home Centers LLC....440 392-0027
9600 Mentor Ave Mentor (44060) ***(G-14210)***
Lowes Home Centers LLC....440 942-2759
36300 Euclid Ave Willoughby (44094) ***(G-19688)***
Lowes Home Centers LLC....740 374-2151
842 Pike St Marietta (45750) ***(G-13462)***
Lowes Home Centers LLC....419 874-6758
10295 Fremont Pike Perrysburg (43551) ***(G-16030)***
Lowes Home Centers LLC....330 626-2980
1210 State Route 303 Streetsboro (44241) ***(G-17419)***
Lowes Home Centers LLC....419 389-9464
5501 Airport Hwy Toledo (43615) ***(G-18013)***
Lowes Home Centers LLC....419 843-9758
7000 W Central Ave Toledo (43617) ***(G-18014)***
Lowes Home Centers LLC....614 447-2851
2345 Silver Dr Columbus (43211) ***(G-8082)***
Lowes Home Centers LLC....330 245-4300
940 Interstate Pkwy Akron (44312) ***(G-329)***
Lowes Home Centers LLC....513 965-3280
5694 Romar Dr Milford (45150) ***(G-14532)***
Lowes Home Centers LLC....330 908-2750
8224 Golden Link Blvd Northfield (44067) ***(G-15519)***
Lowes Home Centers LLC....419 470-2491
1136 W Alexis Rd Toledo (43612) ***(G-18015)***
Lowes Home Centers LLC....513 336-9741
9380 S Masn Montgomery Rd Mason (45040) ***(G-13733)***
Lowes Home Centers LLC....937 498-8400
2700 W Michigan St Sidney (45365) ***(G-16941)***
Lowes Home Centers LLC....740 699-3000
50421 Valley Plaza Dr Saint Clairsville (43950) ***(G-16642)***
Lowes Home Centers LLC....330 920-9280
3570 Hudson Dr Stow (44224) ***(G-17381)***
Lowes Home Centers LLC....740 589-3750
983 E State St Athens (45701) ***(G-799)***
Lowes Home Centers LLC....740 393-5350
1010 Coshocton Ave Mount Vernon (43050) ***(G-14910)***
Lowes Home Centers LLC....419 429-5700
12700 County Road 212 Findlay (45840) ***(G-11058)***
Lowes Home Centers LLC....937 547-2400
1550 Wagner Ave Greenville (45331) ***(G-11513)***
Lowes Home Centers LLC....330 335-1900
1065 Wlliams Reserve Blvd Wadsworth (44281) ***(G-18763)***
Lowes Home Centers LLC....937 347-4000
126 Hospitality Dr Xenia (45385) ***(G-20068)***
Lowes Home Centers LLC....440 239-2630
9149 Pearl Rd Strongsville (44136) ***(G-17485)***
Lowes Home Centers LLC....513 755-4300
7975 Tylersville Sq Rd West Chester (45069) ***(G-19113)***
Lowes Home Centers LLC....513 671-2093
505 E Kemper Rd Cincinnati (45246) ***(G-3999)***
Lowes Home Centers LLC....440 331-1027
20639 Center Ridge Rd Rocky River (44116) ***(G-16585)***
Lowes Home Centers LLC....330 677-3040
218 Nicholas Way Kent (44240) ***(G-12384)***
Lowes Home Centers LLC....419 747-1920
940 N Lexington Spring Rd Ontario (44906) ***(G-15698)***
Lowes Home Centers LLC....330 339-1936
495 Mill Rd New Philadelphia (44663) ***(G-15107)***
Lowes Home Centers LLC....440 985-5700
7500 Oak Point Rd Lorain (44053) ***(G-13058)***
Lowes Home Centers LLC....419 447-4101
1025 W Market St Tiffin (44883) ***(G-17682)***
Lowes Home Centers LLC....937 578-4440
15775 Us Highway 36 Marysville (43040) ***(G-13632)***
Lowes Home Centers LLC....440 324-5004
646 Midway Blvd Elyria (44035) ***(G-10647)***
Lowes Home Centers LLC....937 438-4900
2900 Martins Dr Dayton (45449) ***(G-9689)***
Lowes Home Centers LLC....937 427-1110
2850 Centre Dr Ste I Beavercreek (45324) ***(G-1189)***
Lowes Home Centers LLC....937 848-5600
6300 Wilmington Pike Dayton (45459) ***(G-9690)***
Lowes Home Centers LLC....614 529-5900
3600 Park Mill Run Dr Hilliard (43026) ***(G-11923)***
Lowes Home Centers LLC....513 737-3700
1495 Main St Hamilton (45013) ***(G-11755)***

ALPHABETIC SECTION — M & A Distribution, Solon

Lowes Home Centers LLC 740 894-7120
294 County Road 120 S South Point (45680) *(G-17091)*
Lowes Home Centers LLC 513 727-3900
3125 Towne Blvd Middletown (45044) *(G-14431)*
Lowes Home Centers LLC 419 355-0221
1952 N State Route 53 Fremont (43420) *(G-11210)*
Lowes Home Centers LLC 419 624-6000
5500 Milan Rd Ste 304 Sandusky (44870) *(G-16777)*
Lowes Home Centers LLC 419 782-9000
1831 N Clinton St Defiance (43512) *(G-10045)*
Lowes Home Centers LLC 330 609-8000
940 Niles Cortland Rd Se Warren (44484) *(G-18876)*
Lowes Home Centers LLC 330 965-4500
1100 Doral Dr Youngstown (44514) *(G-20257)*
Lowes Home Centers LLC 937 383-7000
1175 Rombach Ave Wilmington (45177) *(G-19769)*
Lowes Home Centers LLC 937 854-8200
5252 Salem Ave Dayton (45426) *(G-9691)*
Lowes Home Centers LLC 740 636-2100
1895 Lowes Blvd Wshngtn CT Hs (43160) *(G-20029)*
Lowes Home Centers LLC 330 497-2720
6375 Strip Ave Nw Canton (44720) *(G-2440)*
Lowes Home Centers LLC 740 266-3500
4115 Mall Dr Steubenville (43952) *(G-17327)*
Lowes Home Centers LLC 614 476-7100
4141 Morse Xing Columbus (43219) *(G-8083)*
Lowry Controls Inc 513 583-0182
273 E Kemper Rd Loveland (45140) *(G-13142)*
Loyal American Life Insur Co (HQ) 800 633-6752
250 E 5th St Fl 8 Cincinnati (45202) *(G-4000)*
Loyal Oak Golf Course Inc 330 825-2904
2909 Clvland Massillon Rd Barberton (44203) *(G-971)*
Lpl Financial Holdings Inc 513 772-2592
11260 Chester Rd Ste 250 Cincinnati (45246) *(G-4001)*
Lq Management LLC 614 866-6456
2447 Brice Rd Reynoldsburg (43068) *(G-16467)*
Lq Management LLC 513 771-0300
11029 Dowlin Dr Cincinnati (45241) *(G-4002)*
Lq Management LLC 216 447-1133
6161 Quarry Ln Cleveland (44131) *(G-5954)*
Lq Management LLC 216 251-8500
4222 W 150th St Cleveland (44135) *(G-5955)*
LSI Adl Techonology LLC 614 345-9040
2727 Scioto Pkwy Columbus (43221) *(G-8084)*
LSI Industries Inc 913 281-1100
10000 Alliance Rd Blue Ash (45242) *(G-1631)*
LT Harnett Trucking Inc 440 997-5528
2440 State Rd Ashtabula (44004) *(G-753)*
Lt Land Development LLC 937 382-0072
94 N South St Ste A Wilmington (45177) *(G-19770)*
Lt Trucking Inc 440 997-5528
2440 State Rd Ashtabula (44004) *(G-754)*
Ltac Investors LLC 740 346-2600
200 School St Steubenville (43953) *(G-17328)*
Ltc Nursing, North Royalton Also called Epilogue Inc *(G-15489)*
Ltc Pharmacy, Twinsburg Also called Pharmerica Long-Term Care Inc *(G-18454)*
Lti Inc 614 278-7777
3445 Millennium Ct Columbus (43219) *(G-8085)*
Lu-Jean Feng Clinic LLC 216 831-7007
31200 Pinetree Rd Cleveland (44124) *(G-5956)*
Lubrizol Advanced Mtls Inc 440 933-0400
550 Moore Rd Avon Lake (44012) *(G-934)*
Luburgh Inc (PA) 740 452-3668
4174 East Pike Zanesville (43701) *(G-20498)*
Lucas & Clark Family Dentistry 937 393-3494
624 S High St Hillsboro (45133) *(G-11986)*
Lucas Building Mainenance LLC 740 479-1800
323 Mastin Ave Ironton (45638) *(G-12297)*
Lucas County Asphalt Inc 419 476-0705
7540 Hollow Creek Dr Toledo (43617) *(G-18016)*
Lucas County Board of Developm 419 380-4000
1154 Larc Ln Toledo (43614) *(G-18017)*
Lucas County Engineer, Holland Also called County of Lucas *(G-12016)*
Lucas County Home Training, Oregon Also called Desoto Dialysis LLC *(G-15731)*
Lucas County Prosecution, Toledo Also called County of Lucas *(G-17834)*
Lucas County Regional Hlth Dst, Toledo Also called County of Lucas *(G-17836)*
Lucas County Tasc, Toledo Also called Tasc of Northwest Ohio Inc *(G-18214)*
Lucas Metropolitan Hsing Auth 419 259-9457
435 Nebraska Ave Toledo (43604) *(G-18018)*
Lucas Plumbing & Heating Inc 440 282-4567
2125 W Park Dr Lorain (44053) *(G-13059)*
Lucas Precision LLC 216 451-5588
13020 Saint Clair Ave Cleveland (44108) *(G-5957)*
Luce Smith & Scott Inc 440 746-1700
6860 W Snwvlle Rd Ste 110 Brecksville (44141) *(G-1832)*
Lucien Realty 440 331-8500
18630 Detroit Ave Cleveland (44107) *(G-5958)*
Ludy Greenhouse Mfg Corp (PA) 800 255-5839
122 Railroad St New Madison (45346) *(G-15072)*
Luis F Soto MD 330 649-9400
4689 Fulton Dr Nw Canton (44718) *(G-2441)*

Luk Transmission System LLC (PA) 330 464-4184
3177 Old Airport Rd Wooster (44691) *(G-19885)*
Luk-Aftermarket Service Inc 330 273-4383
5370 Wegman Dr Valley City (44280) *(G-18620)*
Luke Collison 740 969-2283
565 Rainbow Dr Nw Lancaster (43130) *(G-12552)*
Luke Immediate Care Center 419 227-2245
825 W Market St Ste 205 Lima (45805) *(G-12833)*
Luke Medical Center, Lima Also called Luke Immediate Care Center *(G-12833)*
Luke Theis Contractors, Findlay Also called Luke Theis Enterprises Inc *(G-11059)*
Luke Theis Enterprises Inc 419 422-2040
14120 State Route 568 Findlay (45840) *(G-11059)*
Lumber Craft, Columbus Also called Fifth Avenue Lumber Co *(G-7654)*
Lumberjack's Creative Bldg Ctr, Akron Also called Lumberjacks Inc *(G-330)*
Lumberjacks Inc (PA) 330 762-2401
723 E Tallmadge Ave Ste 1 Akron (44310) *(G-330)*
Lumenance LLC (PA) 319 541-6811
4449 Easton Way Fl 2 Columbus (43219) *(G-8086)*
Lumenomics Inc 614 798-3500
8333 Green Meadows Dr N Lewis Center (43035) *(G-12693)*
Luminex HD& f Company, Blue Ash Also called Luminex Home Decor *(G-1632)*
Luminex Home Decor (PA) 513 563-1113
10521 Millington Ct Blue Ash (45242) *(G-1632)*
Luper Neidental & Logan A Leg 614 221-7663
1160 Dublin Rd Ste 400 Columbus (43215) *(G-8087)*
Lusk & Harkin Ltd 614 221-3707
35 N 4th St Fl 5 Columbus (43215) *(G-8088)*
Lusk Hrkin Architects Planners, Columbus Also called Lusk & Harkin Ltd *(G-8088)*
Lute Supply Inc (PA) 740 353-1447
3920 Us Highway 23 Portsmouth (45662) *(G-16294)*
Luther Home of Mercy 419 836-3918
5810 N Main St Williston (43468) *(G-19639)*
Lutheran Home 419 724-1414
131 N Wheeling St Ofc Toledo (43605) *(G-18019)*
Lutheran Home 440 871-0090
2116 Dover Center Rd Cleveland (44145) *(G-5959)*
Lutheran Hospital, Solon Also called Lutheran Medical Center *(G-17023)*
Lutheran Housing Services Inc 419 861-4990
2021 N Mccord Rd Ste B Toledo (43615) *(G-18020)*
Lutheran Medical Center (HQ) 216 696-4300
33001 Solon Rd Ste 112 Solon (44139) *(G-17023)*
Lutheran Memorial Home Inc 419 502-5700
2021 N Mccord Rd Toledo (43615) *(G-18021)*
Lutheran Metropolitan Ministry 216 658-4638
2100 Lakeside Ave E Cleveland (44114) *(G-5960)*
Lutheran Scial Svcs Centl Ohio (PA) 419 289-3523
500 W Wilson Bridge Rd Worthington (43085) *(G-19974)*
Lutheran Scial Svcs Centl Ohio 419 289-3523
622 Center St Ashland (44805) *(G-686)*
Lutheran Senior City Inc (HQ) 614 228-5200
935 N Cassady Ave Columbus (43219) *(G-8089)*
Lutheran Social 419 229-2222
205 W Market St Ste 500 Lima (45801) *(G-12834)*
Lutheran Social Services of 614 228-5200
500 W Wilson Bridge Rd # 245 Worthington (43085) *(G-19975)*
Lutheran Village At Wolf Creek 419 861-2233
2001 Prrysbrg Hllnd Ofc Holland (43528) *(G-12033)*
Lutheran Village Courtyard, Columbus Also called Lutheran Senior City Inc *(G-8089)*
Luxfer Magtech Inc (HQ) 513 772-3066
2940 Highland Ave Ste 210 Cincinnati (45212) *(G-4003)*
Luxury Heating Co 440 366-0971
5327 Ford Rd Sheffield Village (44035) *(G-16890)*
Lyden Company 419 868-6800
310 S Reynolds Rd Ste A Toledo (43615) *(G-18022)*
Lyden Oil Company 330 792-1100
3711 Leharps Dr Ste A Youngstown (44515) *(G-20258)*
Lykins Companies Inc (PA) 513 831-8820
5163 Wlfpn Plsnt Hl Rd Milford (45150) *(G-14533)*
Lykins Energy Solutions, Milford Also called Lykins Companies Inc *(G-14533)*
Lykins Oil Company (HQ) 513 831-8820
5163 Wlfpn Plsnt Hl Rd Milford (45150) *(G-14534)*
Lykins Transportation Inc 513 831-8820
5163 Wlfpn Plsnt Hl Rd Milford (45150) *(G-14535)*
Lyman W Iiggins Urban Affairs 419 385-2532
2155 Arlington Ave Toledo (43609) *(G-18023)*
Lyndco Inc 740 671-9098
56805 Ferry Landing Rd 8a Shadyside (43947) *(G-16850)*
Lynn Hope Industries Inc 330 674-8045
8001 Township Rd Ste 574 Holmesville (44633) *(G-12073)*
Lynnhaven V LLC 440 272-5600
5165 State Route 322 Windsor (44099) *(G-19805)*
Lynnhaven Xii LLC 419 756-7111
535 Lexington Ave Mansfield (44907) *(G-13325)*
Lyondell Chemical Company 513 530-4000
11530 Northlake Dr Cincinnati (45249) *(G-4004)*
Lyons Doughty & Veldhuis PC 614 229-3888
471 E Broad St Fl 12 Columbus (43215) *(G-8090)*
M & A Distributing Co Inc (PA) 440 703-4580
31031 Diamond Pkwy Solon (44139) *(G-17024)*
M & A Distributing Co Inc 614 294-3555
871 Michigan Ave Columbus (43215) *(G-8091)*
M & A Distribution, Solon Also called M & A Distributing Co Inc *(G-17024)*

(PA)=Parent Co (HQ)=Headquarters (DH)=Div Headquarters

M & B Trucking Express Corp — 440 236-8820
27457 Royalton Rd Columbia Station (44028) *(G-6848)*

M & D Blacktop Sealing, Grove City *Also called Pavement Protectors Inc* *(G-11590)*

M & L Electric Inc — 937 833-5154
4439a New Market Banta Rd Lewisburg (45338) *(G-12712)*

M & L Leasing Co — 330 343-8910
8999 Bay Dr Ne Mineral City (44656) *(G-14633)*

M & M Heating & Cooling, Toledo *Also called M&M Heating & Cooling Inc* *(G-18024)*

M & M Metals International Inc — 513 221-4411
840 Dellway St Cincinnati (45229) *(G-4005)*

M & M Wine Cellar Inc — 330 536-6450
259 Bedford Rd Lowellville (44436) *(G-13172)*

M & M Wintergreens Inc — 216 398-1288
3728 Fulton Rd Cleveland (44109) *(G-5961)*

M & R Amusement Services Inc (PA) — 937 525-0404
1100 Lagonda Ave Springfield (45503) *(G-17227)*

M & R Electric Motor Svc Inc — 937 222-6282
1516 E 5th St Dayton (45403) *(G-9692)*

M & R Fredericktown Ltd Inc — 440 801-1563
895 Home Ave Akron (44310) *(G-331)*

M & S Drywall Inc — 513 738-1510
10999 State Route 128 Harrison (45030) *(G-11805)*

M & W Construction Entps LLC — 419 227-2000
1201 Crestwood Dr Lima (45805) *(G-12835)*

M A Folkes Company Inc — 513 785-4200
3095 Mcbride Ct Hamilton (45011) *(G-11756)*

M C Hair Consultants Inc — 234 678-3987
833 Portage Trl Cuyahoga Falls (44221) *(G-9206)*

M C M & One Com, Dayton *Also called McM Electronics Inc* *(G-9708)*

M C Trucking Company LLC — 937 584-2486
228 Melvin Rd Wilmington (45177) *(G-19771)*

M Conley Company (PA) — 330 456-8243
1312 4th St Se Canton (44707) *(G-2442)*

M Consultants LLC — 614 839-4639
750 Brooksedge Blvd Westerville (43081) *(G-19421)*

M E Theaters Inc — 937 596-6424
106 W Pike St Jackson Center (45334) *(G-12323)*

M G Management, Blue Ash *Also called Murray Guttman* *(G-1649)*

M G Q Inc — 419 992-4236
1525 W County Road 42 Tiffin (44883) *(G-17683)*

M H EBY Inc — 614 879-6901
4435 State Route 29 West Jefferson (43162) *(G-19253)*

M H Equipment, Hudson *Also called MH Logistics Corp* *(G-12134)*

M H Equipment - Ohio, Dayton *Also called Mh Equipment Company* *(G-9725)*

M J Baumann, Columbus *Also called Mj Baumann Co Inc* *(G-8180)*

M J J B Ltd — 937 748-4414
505 N Main St Springboro (45066) *(G-17127)*

M J Lanese Landscaping Inc — 440 942-3444
37115 Code Ave Willoughby (44094) *(G-19689)*

M J S Holding — 614 410-2512
226 N 5th St Columbus (43215) *(G-8092)*

M K Moore & Sons Inc — 937 236-1812
5150 Wagner Ford Rd Dayton (45414) *(G-9693)*

M L S, Columbus *Also called Microwave Leasing Services LLC* *(G-8161)*

M M Construction — 513 553-0106
1924 St Routee 222 Bethel (45106) *(G-1483)*

M P & A Fibers Inc — 440 926-1074
1024 Commerce Dr Grafton (44044) *(G-11442)*

M P Dory Co — 614 444-2138
2001 Integrity Dr S Columbus (43209) *(G-8093)*

M R C, Cincinnati *Also called MRC Global (us) Inc* *(G-4126)*

M R I Center, Toledo *Also called Associated Imaging Corporation* *(G-17760)*

M R S I, Cincinnati *Also called Marketing Research Svcs Inc* *(G-4023)*

M R T, Middletown *Also called Maintenance & Repair Tech Inc* *(G-14432)*

M Retail Engineering Inc — 614 818-2323
750 Brooksedge Blvd Westerville (43081) *(G-19422)*

M S, Twinsburg *Also called The Mau-Sherwood Supply Co* *(G-18475)*

M S G, Maumee *Also called Mannik & Smith Group Inc* *(G-13938)*

M S I Design, Columbus *Also called Myers/Schmalenberger Inc* *(G-8211)*

M T Business Technologies, Holland *Also called Office Products Toledo Inc* *(G-12044)*

M T Business Technologies — 440 933-7682
33588 Pin Oak Pkwy Avon Lake (44012) *(G-935)*

M T Golf Course Managment Inc (PA) — 513 923-1188
9799 Prechtel Rd Cincinnati (45252) *(G-4006)*

M&C Hotel Interests Inc — 440 543-1331
17021 Chillicothe Rd Chagrin Falls (44023) *(G-2723)*

M&C Hotel Interests Inc — 937 778-8100
987 E Ash St Ste 171 Piqua (45356) *(G-16151)*

M&J Fox Investments, Cleveland *Also called Wtb Inc* *(G-6761)*

M&M Heating & Cooling Inc — 419 243-3005
1515 Washington St Toledo (43604) *(G-18024)*

M-A Building and Maint Co — 216 391-5577
5515 Old Brecksville Rd Independence (44131) *(G-12231)*

M-E Companies Inc (HQ) — 614 818-4900
635 Brooksedge Blvd Westerville (43081) *(G-19423)*

M-E Companies Inc — 513 942-3141
23 Triangle Park Dr # 2300 Cincinnati (45246) *(G-4007)*

M-Engineering, Westerville *Also called M Consultants LLC* *(G-19421)*

M-V Rlty Mller Valentine Group, Cincinnati *Also called Miller-Valentine Partners Ltd* *(G-4097)*

M.O.M., Blue Ash *Also called Modern Office Methods Inc* *(G-1644)*

M/I Financial LLC (HQ) — 614 418-8650
3 Easton Oval Ste 340 Columbus (43219) *(G-8094)*

M/I Homes Inc (PA) — 614 418-8000
3 Easton Oval Ste 500 Columbus (43219) *(G-8095)*

M/I Homes of Austin LLC — 614 418-8000
3 Easton Oval Ste 500 Columbus (43219) *(G-8096)*

MA Architects, Columbus *Also called Meacham & Apel Architects Inc* *(G-8139)*

Maag Automatik Inc — 330 677-2225
235 Progress Blvd Kent (44240) *(G-12385)*

Maag Reduction Engineering, Kent *Also called Maag Automatik Inc* *(G-12385)*

Mac Group, The, Strongsville *Also called Hughes Corporation* *(G-17474)*

Mac Kenzie Nursery Supply Inc — 440 259-3517
3891 Shepard Rd Perry (44081) *(G-15963)*

Mac Manufacturing Inc (PA) — 330 823-9900
14599 Commerce St Ne Alliance (44601) *(G-546)*

Mac Manufacturing Inc — 330 829-1680
1453 Allen Rd Salem (44460) *(G-16704)*

Mac Mechanical Corporation — 216 531-0444
1441 Dille Rd Cleveland (44117) *(G-5962)*

Mac Queen Orchards Inc — 419 865-2916
7605 Garden Rd Holland (43528) *(G-12034)*

Mac Trailer Manufacturing Inc (PA) — 330 823-9900
14599 Commerce St Ne Alliance (44601) *(G-547)*

Mac Trailer Service Inc — 330 823-9190
14504 Commerce St Ne Alliance (44601) *(G-548)*

Macair Aviation LLC — 937 347-1302
140 N Valley Rd Xenia (45385) *(G-20069)*

Macaulay-Brown Inc (PA) — 937 426-3421
4021 Executive Dr Beavercreek (45430) *(G-1251)*

Macb, Beavercreek *Also called Macaulay-Brown Inc* *(G-1251)*

Macdonald Mott LLC — 216 535-3640
18013 Cleveland Pkwy Dr # 200 Cleveland (44135) *(G-5963)*

Mace Personal Def & SEC Inc (HQ) — 440 424-5321
4400 Carnegie Ave Cleveland (44103) *(G-5964)*

Machine Tool Division, Bluffton *Also called Grob Systems Inc* *(G-1731)*

Mack Industries — 419 353-7081
507 Derby Ave Bowling Green (43402) *(G-1785)*

Macke Brothers Inc — 513 771-7500
10355 Spartan Dr Cincinnati (45215) *(G-4008)*

Mackil Inc — 937 833-3310
705 Arlington Rd Brookville (45309) *(G-1964)*

Macmillan Sobanski & Todd LLC (PA) — 419 255-5900
1 Maritime Plz Fl 5 Toledo (43604) *(G-18025)*

Maco Construction Services — 330 482-4472
170 Duquesne St Columbiana (44408) *(G-6860)*

Maco Inc — 740 472-5445
47013 State Route 26 Woodsfield (43793) *(G-19816)*

Macomb Group Inc — 419 666-6899
2830 Crane Way Northwood (43619) *(G-15536)*

Macomb Group Toledo Division, Northwood *Also called Macomb Group Inc* *(G-15536)*

Macys Cr & Customer Svcs Inc — 513 881-9950
9249 Meridian Way West Chester (45069) *(G-19114)*

Macys Cr & Customer Svcs Inc (HQ) — 513 398-5221
9111 Duke Blvd Mason (45040) *(G-13734)*

Made From Scratch Inc (PA) — 614 873-3344
7500 Montgomery Rd Plain City (43064) *(G-16197)*

Madeira Health Care Center, Cincinnati *Also called Euclid Health Care Inc* *(G-3578)*

Madeira Health Care Center — 513 561-4105
6940 Stiegler Ln Cincinnati (45243) *(G-4009)*

Madison Avenue Mktg Group Inc — 419 473-9000
1600 Madison Ave Toledo (43604) *(G-18026)*

Madison Bowl Inc — 513 271-2700
4761 Madison Rd Cincinnati (45227) *(G-4010)*

Madison Care Inc — 440 428-1492
7600 S Ridge Rd Madison (44057) *(G-13230)*

Madison Cnty Lndon Cy Hlth Dst — 740 852-3065
306 Lafayette St Ste B London (43140) *(G-12999)*

Madison County Engineer, London *Also called County of Madison* *(G-12996)*

Madison Family Health Corp — 740 845-7000
210 N Main St London (43140) *(G-13000)*

Madison Health Care, Madison *Also called Madison Care Inc* *(G-13230)*

Madison House Inc — 740 845-0145
351 Keny Blvd London (43140) *(G-13001)*

Madison Local School, Mansfield *Also called SC Madison Bus Garage* *(G-13362)*

Madison Local School District (PA) — 419 589-2600
1379 Grace St Mansfield (44905) *(G-13326)*

Madison Local School District — 440 428-5111
92 E Main St Madison (44057) *(G-13231)*

Madison Medical Campus — 440 428-6800
6270 N Ridge Rd Madison (44057) *(G-13232)*

Madison Motor Service Inc — 419 332-0727
2921 W State St Fremont (43420) *(G-11211)*

Madison Route 20 LLC — 440 358-7888
7667 Hermitage Rd Painesville (44077) *(G-15864)*

Madison Square Apartments, Plain City *Also called Fairfield Homes Inc* *(G-16192)*

Madison Tree & Landscape Co — 614 207-5422
3180 Glade Run Rd West Jefferson (43162) *(G-19254)*

Madison Tree Care & Ldscpg Inc — 513 576-6391
636 Round Bottom Rd Milford (45150) *(G-14536)*

Mae Holding Company (PA).......513 751-2424
7290 Deaconsbench Ct Cincinnati (45244) **(G-4011)**
Magic Castle Inc.......937 434-4911
4990 Wilmington Pike Dayton (45440) **(G-9694)**
Magic Industries Inc.......614 759-8422
4651 Poth Rd Columbus (43213) **(G-8097)**
Magnetech, Massillon *Also called 3-D Service Ltd* **(G-13780)**
Magnetech Industrial Svcs Inc (HQ).......330 830-3500
800 Nave Rd Se Massillon (44646) **(G-13830)**
Magnetech Industrial Svcs Inc.......330 830-3500
800 Nave Rd Se Massillon (44646) **(G-13831)**
Magnetic Springs Water Company (PA).......614 421-1780
1917 Joyce Ave Columbus (43219) **(G-8098)**
Magnum Management Corporation.......419 627-2334
1 Cedar Point Dr Sandusky (44870) **(G-16778)**
Magnum Medical Overseas JV LLC.......979 848-8169
2936 Vernon Pl 3 Cincinnati (45219) **(G-4012)**
Magolius Margolius & Assoc Lpa.......216 621-2034
55 Public Sq Ste 1100 Cleveland (44113) **(G-5965)**
Maguire & Schneider LLP.......614 224-1222
1650 Lake Shore Dr # 150 Columbus (43204) **(G-8099)**
Mahajan Tita & Katra, Toledo *Also called R I D Inc* **(G-18145)**
Mahalls 20 Lanes.......216 521-3280
13200 Madison Ave Cleveland (44107) **(G-5966)**
Mahoney Dialysis LLC.......937 642-0676
491 Colemans Xing Marysville (43040) **(G-13633)**
Mahoning Clmbana Training Assn.......330 747-5639
20 W Federal St Ste 604 Youngstown (44503) **(G-20259)**
Mahoning Country Club Inc.......330 545-2517
710 E Liberty St Girard (44420) **(G-11420)**
Mahoning County.......330 793-5514
761 Industrial Rd Youngstown (44509) **(G-20260)**
Mahoning County.......330 799-1581
940 Bears Den Rd Youngstown (44511) **(G-20261)**
Mahoning County.......330 797-2837
4795 Woodridge Dr Youngstown (44515) **(G-20262)**
Mahoning County Childrens Svcs.......330 941-8888
222 W Federal St Fl 4 Youngstown (44503) **(G-20263)**
Mahoning County Engineers, Youngstown *Also called Mahoning County* **(G-20261)**
Mahoning Valley Dental Service (PA).......330 759-1771
5100 Belmont Ave Ste 1 Youngstown (44505) **(G-20264)**
MAHONING VALLEY HOSPITAL, Youngstown *Also called Vibra Hosp Mahoning Vly LLC* **(G-20405)**
Mahoning Valley Scrappers, Niles *Also called Palisdes Bsbal A Cal Ltd Prtnr* **(G-15302)**
Mahoning Vly Hmtlgy Onclgy Aso.......330 318-1100
500 Gypsy Ln Youngstown (44504) **(G-20265)**
Mahoning Vly Hmtology Oncology, Warren *Also called Trumbull Mem Hosp Foundation* **(G-18915)**
Mahoning Vly Infusioncare Inc (PA).......330 759-9487
4891 Belmont Ave Youngstown (44505) **(G-20266)**
Mahoning Youngstown Community.......330 747-5661
737 N Garland Ave Youngstown (44506) **(G-20267)**
Mahoning Youngstown Community (PA).......330 747-7921
1325 5th Ave Youngstown (44504) **(G-20268)**
MAI Capital Management LLC.......216 920-4800
1360 E 9th St Ste 1100 Cleveland (44114) **(G-5967)**
MAI Capital Management LLC.......216 920-4913
1360 E 9th St Ste 1100 Cleveland (44114) **(G-5968)**
MAI Manufacturing, Marysville *Also called Straight 72 Inc* **(G-13652)**
Maids Home Service of Cincy.......513 396-6900
1830 Sherman Ave Cincinnati (45212) **(G-4013)**
Mail Contractors America Inc.......513 769-5967
3065 Cresecentville Rd Cincinnati (45262) **(G-4014)**
Mail It Corp.......419 249-4848
380 S Erie St Toledo (43604) **(G-18027)**
Mailender Inc.......513 942-5453
9500 Glades Dr West Chester (45011) **(G-19115)**
Main Line Supply Co Inc (PA).......937 254-6910
300 N Findlay St Dayton (45403) **(G-9695)**
Main Lite Electric Co Inc.......330 369-8333
3000 Sferra Ave Nw Warren (44483) **(G-18877)**
Main Place Inc (PA).......740 345-6246
112 S 3rd St Newark (43055) **(G-15200)**
Main Sail LLC.......216 472-5100
20820 Chagrin Blvd # 102 Cleveland (44122) **(G-5969)**
Main Sequence Technology Inc (PA).......440 946-5214
5370 Pinehill Dr Mentor On The Lake (44060) **(G-14261)**
Main Street Fmly Medicine LLC.......614 253-8537
881 E Main St Columbus (43205) **(G-8100)**
Main Street Terrace Care Ctr.......740 653-8767
1318 E Main St Lancaster (43130) **(G-12553)**
Maines Collision Repr & Bdy Sp.......937 322-4618
1717 E Pleasant St Springfield (45505) **(G-17228)**
Maines Paper & Food Svc Inc.......216 643-7500
199 Oak Leaf Oval Bedford (44146) **(G-1319)**
Maines Towing & Recovery Svc, Springfield *Also called Maines Collision Repr & Bdy Sp* **(G-17228)**
Maintenance & Repair Tech Inc.......513 422-1198
408 Vanderveer St Middletown (45044) **(G-14432)**
Maintenance Department, Logan *Also called Logan-Hocking School District* **(G-12985)**
Maintenance Systems Nthrn Ohio, Elyria *Also called Purple Marlin Inc* **(G-10672)**
Maintenance Systerms of N Ohio.......440 323-1291
42208 Albrecht Rd Ste 1 Elyria (44035) **(G-10648)**
Maintenance Unlimited Inc.......440 238-1162
12351 Prospect Rd Strongsville (44149) **(G-17486)**
Mainthia Technologies Inc.......216 433-2198
21000 Brookpark Rd Cleveland (44135) **(G-5970)**
Majaac Inc.......419 636-5678
820 E Edgerton St Bryan (43506) **(G-2010)**
Majastan Group LLC.......216 231-6400
12200 Fairhill Rd B201 Cleveland (44120) **(G-5971)**
Majestic Manufacturing Inc.......330 457-2447
4536 State Route 7 New Waterford (44445) **(G-15138)**
Majestic Steel Properties Inc.......440 786-2666
31099 Chagrin Blvd # 150 Cleveland (44124) **(G-5972)**
Majestic Steel Service, Cleveland *Also called Majestic Steel Usa Inc* **(G-5973)**
Majestic Steel Usa Inc (PA).......440 786-2666
31099 Chagrin Blvd # 150 Cleveland (44124) **(G-5973)**
Majestic Tool and Machine Inc.......440 248-5058
30700 Carter St Ste C Solon (44139) **(G-17025)**
Majidzadeh Enterprises Inc (PA).......614 823-4949
6350 Presidential Gtwy Columbus (43231) **(G-8101)**
Major Electronix Corp.......440 942-0054
33801 Curtis Blvd Ste 110 Eastlake (44095) **(G-10548)**
Major Legal Services, Independence *Also called Alliance Legal Solutions LLC* **(G-12184)**
Major Metals Company.......419 886-4600
844 Kochheiser Rd Mansfield (44904) **(G-13327)**
Maketewah Country Club Company.......513 242-9333
5401 Reading Rd Cincinnati (45237) **(G-4015)**
Making Evrlasting Memories LLC.......513 864-0100
11475 Northlake Dr Cincinnati (45249) **(G-4016)**
Makoy Center Inc.......614 777-1211
5462 Center St Hilliard (43026) **(G-11924)**
Malavite Excavating Inc.......330 484-1274
5508 Ridge Ave Se East Sparta (44626) **(G-10540)**
Malik Punam.......513 636-1333
3333 Burnet Ave Cincinnati (45229) **(G-4017)**
Mall Park Southern.......330 758-4511
7401 Market St Rm 267 Youngstown (44512) **(G-20269)**
Mall Realty Inc.......937 866-3700
862 Watertower Ln Dayton (45449) **(G-9696)**
Mallard Cove Senior Dev LLC.......513 772-6655
1410 Mallard Cove Dr Ofc Cincinnati (45246) **(G-4018)**
Mallard Cove Senior Living, Cincinnati *Also called Mallard Cove Senior Dev LLC* **(G-4018)**
Malley's Chocolates, Cleveland *Also called Malleys Candies Inc* **(G-5974)**
Malleys Candies Inc.......216 529-6262
13400 Brookpark Rd Cleveland (44135) **(G-5974)**
Malone Warehouse Tire Inc.......740 592-2893
5239 Hebbardsville Rd Athens (45701) **(G-800)**
Maloney & Associates Inc.......330 479-7084
4850 Southway St Sw Canton (44706) **(G-2443)**
Maloney + Novotny LLC (PA).......216 363-0100
1111 Superior Ave E # 700 Cleveland (44114) **(G-5975)**
Mammana Custom Woodworking Inc.......216 581-9059
14400 Industrial Ave N Maple Heights (44137) **(G-13410)**
Mammoth Restoration and Clg, Worthington *Also called Farris Enterprises Inc* **(G-19960)**
Mammovan Inc.......330 726-2064
61 Midgewood Dr Youngstown (44512) **(G-20270)**
Man Golf Ohio LLC.......440 635-5178
14107 Mayfield Rd Huntsburg (44046) **(G-12158)**
Man-Tansky Inc.......740 454-2512
3260 Maple Ave Zanesville (43701) **(G-20499)**
Managed Technology Svcs LLC.......937 247-8915
3366 S Tech Blvd Miamisburg (45342) **(G-14315)**
Management & Training Corp.......801 693-2600
501 Thompson Rd Conneaut (44030) **(G-9043)**
Management Information Svcs, Dayton *Also called County of Montgomery* **(G-9439)**
Management Recruiters Intl, Columbus *Also called Management Recruiters Intl Inc* **(G-8102)**
Management Recruiters Intl Inc.......614 252-6200
800 E Broad St Columbus (43205) **(G-8102)**
Manary Pool, Willowick *Also called City of Willowick* **(G-19738)**
Manatron Inc (HQ).......937 431-4000
4105 Executive Dr Beavercreek (45430) **(G-1252)**
Manatron Sabre Systems and Svc (HQ).......937 431-4000
4105 Executive Dr Beavercreek (45430) **(G-1253)**
Mancan Inc.......440 884-9675
13500 Pearl Rd Ste 109 Strongsville (44136) **(G-17487)**
Manchester Bennett Towers & Ul.......330 743-1171
201 E Commerce St Ste 200 Youngstown (44503) **(G-20271)**
Mandalay Inc.......937 294-6600
2700 E River Rd Moraine (45439) **(G-14799)**
Mandalay Banquet Center, Moraine *Also called Mandalay Inc* **(G-14799)**
MANDEL JEWISH COMMUNITY OF CLE, Beachwood *Also called Jewish Community Ctr Cleveland* **(G-1091)**
Manfield Living Center Ltd.......419 512-1711
73 Madison Rd Mansfield (44905) **(G-13328)**
Manhattan Associates Inc.......440 878-0771
10153 S Bexley Cir Strongsville (44136) **(G-17488)**
Manhattan Mortgage Group Ltd.......614 933-8955
6833 Clark State Rd Blacklick (43004) **(G-1510)**
Manifest Software, Upper Arlington *Also called Manifest Solutions Corp* **(G-18555)**

ALPHABETIC

Manifest Solutions Corp 614 930-2800
2035 Riverside Dr Upper Arlington (43221) *(G-18555)*
Manley Deas & Kochalski LLC (PA) 614 220-5611
1555 Lake Shore Dr Columbus (43204) *(G-8103)*
Manleys Manor Nursing Home Inc 419 424-0402
2820 Greenacre Dr Findlay (45840) *(G-11060)*
Mannik & Smith Group Inc (PA) 419 891-2222
1800 Indian Wood Cir Maumee (43537) *(G-13938)*
Mannik & Smith Group Inc 740 942-4222
104 S Main St Cadiz (43907) *(G-2079)*
Mannik Smith Group, The, Cadiz *Also called Mannik & Smith Group Inc* *(G-2079)*
Mannion & Gray Co LpA 216 344-9422
1375 E 9th St Ste 1600 Cleveland (44114) *(G-5976)*
Mannon Pipeline LLC 740 643-1534
9160 State Route 378 Willow Wood (45696) *(G-19736)*
Mano Logistics LLC 330 454-1307
1934 Navarre Rd Sw Canton (44706) *(G-2444)*
Manor 1, Orrville *Also called Orrvilla Retirement Community* *(G-15777)*
Manor At Perrysburg, The, Perrysburg *Also called Hcf of Perrysburg Inc* *(G-16008)*
Manor At Whitehall, The, Columbus *Also called Shg Whitehall Holdings LLC* *(G-8726)*
Manor Care, Cincinnati *Also called Hcr Manorcare Med Svcs Fla LLC* *(G-3746)*
Manor Care, Barberton *Also called Hcr Manorcare Med Svcs Fla LLC* *(G-965)*
Manor Care, Cincinnati *Also called Hcr Manorcare Med Svcs Fla LLC* *(G-3748)*
Manor Care, Toledo *Also called Hcr Manorcare Med Svcs Fla LLC* *(G-17940)*
Manor Care Inc (HQ) 419 252-5500
333 N Summit St Ste 103 Toledo (43604) *(G-18028)*
Manor Care Hlth Svcs Cntrville, Centerville *Also called Hcr Manorcare Med Svcs Fla LLC* *(G-2679)*
Manor Care Nursing Center (HQ) 419 252-5500
333 N Summit St Ste 100 Toledo (43604) *(G-18029)*
Manor Care of America Inc 440 543-6766
8100 Washington St Chagrin Falls (44023) *(G-2724)*
Manor Care of America Inc 330 867-8530
1211 W Market St Akron (44313) *(G-332)*
Manor Care of America Inc 330 492-7835
5005 Higbee Ave Nw Canton (44718) *(G-2445)*
Manor Care of America Inc 440 779-6900
23225 Lorain Rd North Olmsted (44070) *(G-15430)*
Manor Care of America Inc 440 951-5551
37603 Euclid Ave Willoughby (44094) *(G-19690)*
Manor Care of America Inc 440 345-9300
9055 W Sprague Rd North Royalton (44133) *(G-15496)*
Manor Care of Boynton Beach (HQ) 419 252-5500
333 N Summit St Ste 103 Toledo (43604) *(G-18030)*
Manor Care of Kansas Inc (HQ) 419 252-5500
333 N Summit St Ste 100 Toledo (43604) *(G-18031)*
Manor Care of North Olmsted 419 252-5500
333 N Summit St Ste 100 Toledo (43604) *(G-18032)*
Manor Care of Plantation Inc 419 252-5500
333 N Summit St Ste 100 Toledo (43604) *(G-18033)*
Manor Care of York North Inc 419 252-5500
333 N Summit St Ste 100 Toledo (43604) *(G-18034)*
Manor Care Wilmington Inc (HQ) 419 252-5500
333 N Summit St Ste 100 Toledo (43604) *(G-18035)*
Manor Care York (south) Inc 419 252-5500
333 N Summit St Ste 100 Toledo (43604) *(G-18036)*
Manor Care-North, Toledo *Also called Manor Care of York North Inc* *(G-18034)*
Manor Cr-Mprial Rchmond VA LLC (HQ) 419 252-5000
333 N Summit St Toledo (43604) *(G-18037)*
Manor Hse Bnquet Cnference Ctr, Mason *Also called Kinane Inc* *(G-13727)*
Manor, The, Niles *Also called C R G Health Care Systems* *(G-15285)*
Manor, The, Euclid *Also called Kitchen Katering Inc* *(G-10766)*
Manorcare Health Services LLC (HQ) 419 252-5500
333 N Summit St Ste 100 Toledo (43604) *(G-18038)*
Manorcare Health Svcs VA Inc (HQ) 419 252-5500
333 N Summit St Ste 100 Toledo (43604) *(G-18039)*
Manorcare Hlth Svcs Lakeshore, Cleveland *Also called Hcr Manorcare Med Svcs Fla LLC* *(G-5737)*
Manorcare Hlth Svcs Rcky River, Cleveland *Also called Hcr Manorcare Med Svcs Fla LLC* *(G-5735)*
Manorcare Hlth Svcs Wsterville, Westerville *Also called Hcr Manorcare Med Svcs Fla LLC* *(G-19407)*
Manorcare Hlth Svcs-Mayfield H, Cleveland *Also called Hcr Manorcare Med Svcs Fla LLC* *(G-5736)*
Manorcare of Kingston Court 419 252-5500
333 N Summit St Ste 100 Toledo (43604) *(G-18040)*
Manorcare of Willoughby Inc 419 252-5500
333 N Summit St Ste 100 Toledo (43604) *(G-18041)*
Mansfield Ambulance Inc 419 525-3311
369 Marion Ave Mansfield (44903) *(G-13329)*
Mansfield City Building Maint 419 755-9698
30 N Diamond St Mansfield (44902) *(G-13330)*
Mansfield Distributing Co Div, Mansfield *Also called The Maple City Ice Company* *(G-13373)*
Mansfield Express, Ontario *Also called Mansfield Whsng & Dist Inc* *(G-15699)*
Mansfield Family Practice, Mansfield *Also called American Hlth Ntwrk & Fmly PRC* *(G-13261)*
Mansfield Hotel Partnership 419 529-2100
555 N Trimble Rd Mansfield (44906) *(G-13331)*
Mansfield Hotel Partnership (PA) 419 529-1000
500 N Trimble Rd Mansfield (44906) *(G-13332)*
Mansfield Memorial Homes LLC (PA) 419 774-5100
50 Blymyer Ave Mansfield (44903) *(G-13333)*
Mansfield Opco LLC 502 429-8062
1600 Crider Rd Mansfield (44903) *(G-13334)*
Mansfield Plumbing Pdts LLC (HQ) 419 938-5211
150 E 1st St Perrysville (44864) *(G-16079)*
Mansfield Plumbing Pdts LLC 330 496-2301
13211 State Route 226 Big Prairie (44611) *(G-1498)*
Mansfield Truck Sales & Svc 419 522-9811
85 Longview Ave E Mansfield (44903) *(G-13335)*
Mansfield Whsng & Dist Inc (HQ) 419 522-3510
222 Tappan Dr N Ontario (44906) *(G-15699)*
MANSION HOMES, Bryan *Also called Manufactured Housing Entps Inc* *(G-2011)*
Mansuetto Roofing Company, Martins Ferry *Also called N F Mansuetto & Sons Inc* *(G-13600)*
Manta Media Inc 888 875-5833
8760 Orion Pl Ste 200 Columbus (43240) *(G-6893)*
Mantaline Corporation 330 274-2264
4754 E High St Mantua (44255) *(G-13392)*
MANTUA BED FRAMES, Bedford *Also called Mantua Manufacturing Co* *(G-1320)*
Mantua Manufacturing Co (PA) 800 333-8333
7900 Northfield Rd Bedford (44146) *(G-1320)*
Manufactured Assemblies Corp 937 898-2060
7482 Webster St Vandalia (45377) *(G-18688)*
Manufactured Comfort, Athens *Also called White & Chambers Partnership* *(G-820)*
Manufactured Housing Entps Inc 419 636-4511
9302 Us Highway 6 Bryan (43506) *(G-2011)*
Manufacturing Services Intl 937 299-9922
15 W Dorothy Ln Dayton (45429) *(G-9697)*
Manzano Dialysis LLC 937 879-0433
1266 N Broad St Fairborn (45324) *(G-10802)*
MAP SYSTEMS AND SOLUTIONS, Columbus *Also called Mapsys Inc* *(G-8104)*
Maple Crest, Bluffton *Also called Mennonite Memorial Home Inc* *(G-1735)*
Maple Crest Assisted Living, Bucyrus *Also called Maplecrst Asistd Lvg Intl Ordr* *(G-2043)*
Maple Crest Builders, Delaware *Also called Eds Tree & Turf* *(G-10092)*
Maple Crest Nrsing HM For Aged, Struthers *Also called Cred-Kap Inc* *(G-17529)*
MAPLE CREST SENIOR LIVING VILL, Bluffton *Also called Mennonite Memorial Home Inc* *(G-1734)*
Maple Gardens Rehab, Eaton *Also called Eaton Gardens Rehabilitation A* *(G-10559)*
Maple Grove Companies, Tiffin *Also called M G Q Inc* *(G-17683)*
Maple Heights Atc, Cleveland *Also called County of Cuyahoga* *(G-5419)*
Maple Knoll Communities Inc 513 524-7990
6727 Contreras Rd Oxford (45056) *(G-15817)*
Maple Knoll Communities Inc (PA) 513 782-2400
11100 Springfield Pike Cincinnati (45246) *(G-4019)*
Maple Knoll Village, Cincinnati *Also called Maple Knoll Communities Inc* *(G-4019)*
Maple Lee Greenhouse, Powell *Also called Gs Ohio Inc* *(G-16337)*
Maple Mountain Industries Inc 330 948-2510
312 Bank St Lodi (44254) *(G-12965)*
Maplecrst Asistd Lvg Intl Ordr 419 562-4988
717 Rogers St Bucyrus (44820) *(G-2043)*
Mapleside Bakery, Brunswick *Also called Mapleside Valley LLC* *(G-1987)*
Mapleside Valley LLC (PA) 330 225-5576
294 Pearl Rd Brunswick (44212) *(G-1987)*
Mapleview Farms Inc (PA) 419 826-3671
2425 S Fulton Lucas Rd Swanton (43558) *(G-17567)*
Maplewood At Bath Creek LLC 234 208-9872
190 W Bath Rd Cuyahoga Falls (44223) *(G-9207)*
Maplewood At Cuyahoga Falls, Cuyahoga Falls *Also called Maplewood At Bath Creek LLC* *(G-9207)*
Maplewood Nursing Center Inc 740 383-2126
409 Bellefontaine Ave Marion (43302) *(G-13550)*
Mapother & Mapother Attorneys, Cincinnati *Also called Javitch Block LLC* *(G-3863)*
Mapp Building Service LLC 513 253-3990
11367 Deerfield Rd 200 Blue Ash (45242) *(G-1633)*
Mapsys Inc (PA) 614 255-7258
920 Michigan Ave Columbus (43215) *(G-8104)*
Marathon Mfg & Sup Co 330 343-2656
5165 Main St Ne New Philadelphia (44663) *(G-15108)*
Marathon Petroleum Company LP 330 479-5688
3500 21st St Sw Canton (44706) *(G-2446)*
Marathon Petroleum Company LP 614 274-1125
Lincoln Village Sta Columbus (43228) *(G-8105)*
Marathon Petroleum Company LP 513 932-6007
999 W State Route 122 Lebanon (45036) *(G-12624)*
Marathon Petroleum Corporation (PA) 419 422-2121
539 S Main St Findlay (45840) *(G-11061)*
Marathon Pipe Line LLC (HQ) 419 422-2121
539 S Main St Ste 7614 Findlay (45840) *(G-11062)*
Marble Cliff Block & Bldrs Sup, Lockbourne *Also called J P Sand & Gravel Company* *(G-12958)*
Marble Restoration Inc 419 865-9000
6539 Weatherfield Ct Maumee (43537) *(G-13939)*
Marc Glassman Inc 216 265-7700
19101 Snow Rd Cleveland (44142) *(G-5977)*

Marc Glassman Inc 330 995-9246
300 Aurora Commons Cir Aurora (44202) *(G-845)*
Marc's 45, Aurora *Also called Marc Glassman Inc (G-845)*
Marc's Distribution Center, Cleveland *Also called Marc Glassman Inc (G-5977)*
Marca Industries Inc 740 387-1035
2387 Harding Hwy E Marion (43302) *(G-13551)*
Marca Terrace Widows 937 252-1661
50 S Findlay St Dayton (45403) *(G-9698)*
March Investors Ltd 740 373-5353
508 Pike St Marietta (45750) *(G-13463)*
Marco Photo Service Inc 419 529-9010
1655 Nussbaum Pkwy Ontario (44906) *(G-15700)*
Marco's Pizza, Toledo *Also called Marcos Inc (G-18042)*
Marcos Inc 419 885-4844
5252 Monroe St Toledo (43623) *(G-18042)*
Marcum Conference Center, Oxford *Also called Miami University (G-15821)*
Marcums Don Pool Care Inc 513 561-7050
6841 Main St Ste 1 Cincinnati (45244) *(G-4020)*
Marcus Hotels Inc 614 228-3800
310 S High St Columbus (43215) *(G-8106)*
Marcus Mllchap RE Inv Svcs Inc 614 360-9800
230 West St Ste 100 Columbus (43215) *(G-8107)*
Marcus Theatres Corporation 614 759-6500
1776 Hill Rd N Pickerington (43147) *(G-16101)*
Marcus Theatres Corporation 614 436-9818
200 Hutchinson Ave Columbus (43235) *(G-8108)*
Marcus Thomas Llc (PA) 216 292-4700
4781 Richmond Rd Cleveland (44128) *(G-5978)*
Marcus Thomas Llc 330 793-3000
5212 Mahoning Ave Ste 311 Youngstown (44515) *(G-20272)*
Marcy Industries Company LLC 740 943-2343
1836 Likens Rd Marion (43302) *(G-13552)*
Marfo Company (PA) 614 276-3352
799 N Hague Ave Columbus (43204) *(G-8109)*
Marfre Inc 513 321-3377
4785 Morse St Cincinnati (45226) *(G-4021)*
Margaret B Shipley Child Hlth (PA) 330 478-6333
919 2nd St Ne Canton (44704) *(G-2447)*
Margret Wagner House, Cleveland *Also called Benjamin Rose Institute (G-5116)*
Maria Child Care, Toledo *Also called Sisters of Notre D (G-18189)*
Maria Gardens Inc (PA) 440 238-7637
20465 Royalton Rd Strongsville (44149) *(G-17489)*
Marian Living Center, North Lima *Also called Assumption Village (G-15398)*
Marietta Aquatic Center 740 373-2445
233 Pennsylvania Ave Marietta (45750) *(G-13464)*
Marietta Bantam Baseball Leag 740 350-9844
103 Chalet Ln Marietta (45750) *(G-13465)*
Marietta Center For Health & 740 373-1867
117 Bartlett St Marietta (45750) *(G-13466)*
Marietta Coal Co (PA) 740 695-2197
67705 Friends Church Rd Saint Clairsville (43950) *(G-16643)*
Marietta College 740 376-4790
213 4th St Marietta (45750) *(G-13467)*
Marietta Community Based, Marietta *Also called Veterans Health Administration (G-13514)*
Marietta Country Club Inc 740 373-7722
705 Pike St Marietta (45750) *(G-13468)*
MARIETTA FAMILY YMCA, Marietta *Also called Young Mens Christian Assn (G-13520)*
Marietta Gynecologic Assoc 740 374-3622
410 2nd St Marietta (45750) *(G-13469)*
Marietta Industrial Entps Inc (PA) 740 373-2252
17943 State Route 7 Marietta (45750) *(G-13470)*
Marietta Memorial Hospital 740 401-0362
809 Farson St Belpre (45714) *(G-1442)*
Marietta Memorial Hospital (PA) 740 374-1400
401 Matthew St Marietta (45750) *(G-13471)*
Marietta Memorial Hospital 740 373-8549
210 N 7th St Ste 300 Marietta (45750) *(G-13472)*
Marietta Nursing and Rehab Ctr, Marietta *Also called Marietta Center For Health & (G-13466)*
Marietta Silos LLC 740 373-2822
2417 Waterford Rd Marietta (45750) *(G-13473)*
Marietta Transfer Company 740 896-3565
11569 State Route 60 Lowell (45744) *(G-13169)*
Marilyn Wagner, Uniontown *Also called Louisville Child Care Center (G-18527)*
Marimor Industries, Lima *Also called County of Allen (G-12766)*
Marimor Industries Inc 419 221-1226
2450 Ada Rd Lima (45801) *(G-12836)*
Mario's Beauty Salon, Aurora *Also called Marios International Spa & Ht (G-846)*
Marion Area Counseling Ctr (PA) 740 387-5210
320 Executive Dr Marion (43302) *(G-13553)*
Marion Area Health Center, Marion *Also called Frederick C Smith Clinic Inc (G-13540)*
Marion Cnty Bd Dev Dsabilities 740 387-1035
2387 Harding Hwy E Marion (43302) *(G-13554)*
Marion Country Club Company 740 387-0974
2415 Crissinger Rd Marion (43302) *(G-13555)*
Marion Country Club, The, Marion *Also called Marion Country Club Company (G-13555)*
Marion Country Inn & Suites, Marion *Also called Carlson Hotels Ltd Partnership (G-13528)*
Marion County Board of Mr Dd, Marion *Also called Marion Cnty Bd Dev Dsabilities (G-13554)*
Marion District, Marion *Also called Ohio-American Water Co Inc (G-13570)*
Marion Family YMCA 740 725-9622
645 Barks Rd E Marion (43302) *(G-13556)*
Marion Gen Social Work Dept 740 383-8788
1000 Mckinley Park Dr Marion (43302) *(G-13557)*
Marion General Hosp HM Hlth 740 383-8770
278 Barks Rd W Marion (43302) *(G-13558)*
Marion General Hospital, Marion *Also called Marion Gen Social Work Dept (G-13557)*
Marion General Hospital Inc (HQ) 740 383-8400
1000 Mckinley Park Dr Marion (43302) *(G-13559)*
Marion Goodwill Industries (PA) 740 387-7023
340 W Fairground St Marion (43302) *(G-13560)*
Marion Head Start Center 740 382-6858
2387 Harding Hwy E Marion (43302) *(G-13561)*
Marion Manor 740 387-9545
195 Executive Dr Marion (43302) *(G-13562)*
Marion Manor Nursing Home, Marion *Also called Levering Management Inc (G-13548)*
Marion Plaza Inc 330 747-2661
5577 Youngstown Warren Rd Niles (44446) *(G-15295)*
Marion Road Enterprises 614 228-6525
477 S Front St Columbus (43215) *(G-8110)*
Marios International Spa & Ht (PA) 330 562-5141
34 N Chillicothe Rd Aurora (44202) *(G-846)*
Marios International Spa & Ht 440 845-7373
7155 W Pleasant Valley Rd Cleveland (44129) *(G-5979)*
Maritz Travel Company 660 626-1501
1740 Indian Wood Cir Maumee (43537) *(G-13940)*
Maritzcx Research LLC 419 725-4000
1740 Indian Wood Cir Maumee (43537) *(G-13941)*
Marjorie P Lee Rtirement Cmnty, Cincinnati *Also called Episcopal Retirement Homes Inc (G-3569)*
Mark Andy Comco, Milford *Also called Andy Mark Inc (G-14504)*
Mark Dura Inc 330 995-0883
11384 Chamberlain Rd Aurora (44202) *(G-847)*
Mark Feldstein & Assoc Inc 419 867-9500
6703 Monroe St Sylvania (43560) *(G-17600)*
Mark Humrichouser 614 324-5231
6295 Maxtown Rd Ste 100 Westerville (43082) *(G-19327)*
Mark Luikart Inc 330 339-9141
715 Cookson Ave Se New Philadelphia (44663) *(G-15109)*
Mark Sweeney Burick, Cincinnati *Also called Sweeny Walt Pntc GMC Trck Sles (G-4607)*
Mark Thomas Ford Inc 330 638-1010
3098 State Route 5 Cortland (44410) *(G-9077)*
Mark-L Inc 614 863-8832
1180 Claycraft Rd Gahanna (43230) *(G-11256)*
Mark-L Construction, Gahanna *Also called Mark-L Inc (G-11256)*
Market Inquiry Llc 513 794-1088
5825 Creek Rd Blue Ash (45242) *(G-1634)*
Market Ready Services, Columbus *Also called Mrap LLC (G-8202)*
Marketing Comm Resource Inc 440 484-3010
4800 E 345th St Willoughby (44094) *(G-19691)*
Marketing Indus Solutions Corp (HQ) 513 703-0965
3965 Marble Ridge Ln Mason (45040) *(G-13735)*
Marketing Research Svcs Inc 513 772-7580
110 Boggs Ln Ste 380 Cincinnati (45246) *(G-4022)*
Marketing Research Svcs Inc (HQ) 513 579-1555
310 Culvert St Fl 2 Cincinnati (45202) *(G-4023)*
Marketing Results Ltd 614 575-9300
3985 Groves Rd Columbus (43232) *(G-8111)*
Marketing Support Services Inc (PA) 513 752-1200
4921 Para Dr Cincinnati (45237) *(G-4024)*
Marketvision Research Inc 513 603-6340
5426 W Chester Rd West Chester (45069) *(G-19116)*
Marketvision Research Inc (PA) 513 791-3100
5151 Pfeiffer Rd Ste 300 Blue Ash (45242) *(G-1635)*
Markfrank Hair Salons, Cleveland *Also called Z A F Inc (G-6778)*
Markowitz Rosenberg Assoc Drs 440 646-2200
5850 Landerbrook Dr # 100 Cleveland (44124) *(G-5980)*
Marks Cleaning Service Inc 330 725-5702
325 S Elmwood Ave Medina (44256) *(G-14094)*
Marlin Mechanical LLC 800 669-2645
6600 Grant Ave Cleveland (44105) *(G-5981)*
Marmon Highway Tech LLC 330 878-5595
6332 Columbia Rd Nw Dover (44622) *(G-10197)*
Maronda Homes Inc Florida 937 472-3907
1050 S Barron St Eaton (45320) *(G-10566)*
Marous Brothers Cnstr Inc 440 951-3904
1702 Joseph Lloyd Pkwy Willoughby (44094) *(G-19692)*
Marquette Group, Dayton *Also called Gypc Inc (G-9593)*
Marquis Mobility Inc 330 497-5373
4051 Whipple Ave Nw Ste E Canton (44718) *(G-2448)*
Marriage License Bureau, Cleveland *Also called Cuyahoga County (G-5454)*
Marriott, Columbus *Also called Columbus Easton Hotel LLC (G-7349)*
Marriott, Clyde *Also called Hmshost Corporation (G-6814)*
Marriott, Dublin *Also called Winegardner & Hammons Inc (G-10493)*
Marriott, Cleveland *Also called Cleveland East Hotel LLC (G-5312)*
Marriott, West Chester *Also called Union Centre Hotel LLC (G-19173)*
Marriott 440 542-2375
31225 Bainbridge Rd Ste A Solon (44139) *(G-17026)*
Marriott Columbus Univ Area, Columbus *Also called Uph Holdings LLC (G-8913)*
Marriott Hotel Services Inc 216 252-5333
4277 W 150th St Cleveland (44135) *(G-5982)*

ALPHABETIC

Marriott International Inc 614 861-1400
695 Taylor Rd Columbus (43230) *(G-8112)*
Marriott International Inc 330 484-0300
4025 Greentree Ave Sw Canton (44706) *(G-2449)*
Marriott International Inc 513 487-3800
151 Goodman St Cincinnati (45219) *(G-4025)*
Marriott International Inc 216 696-9200
127 Public Sq Fl 1 Cleveland (44114) *(G-5983)*
Marriott International Inc 614 228-5050
50 N 3rd St Columbus (43215) *(G-8113)*
Marriott International Inc 614 436-7070
7411 Vantage Dr Columbus (43235) *(G-8114)*
Marriott International Inc 614 475-8530
2901 Airport Dr Columbus (43219) *(G-8115)*
Marriott International Inc 614 864-8844
2084 S Hamilton Rd Columbus (43232) *(G-8116)*
Marriott International Inc 614 222-2610
36 E Gay St Columbus (43215) *(G-8117)*
Marriott International Inc 614 885-0799
7300 Huntington Park Dr Columbus (43235) *(G-8118)*
Marriott International Inc 330 666-4811
120 Montrose West Ave Copley (44321) *(G-9060)*
Marriott International Inc 419 866-1001
1435 E Mall Dr Holland (43528) *(G-12035)*
Marriott International Inc 440 716-9977
24901 Country Club Blvd North Olmsted (44070) *(G-15431)*
Marriott International Inc 513 530-5060
11401 Reed Hartman Hwy Blue Ash (45241) *(G-1636)*
Marriott McKinley Grande Hotel, Canton *Also called American Prprty-Mnagement Corp (G-2239)*
Mars Electric Company (PA) 440 946-2250
6655 Beta Dr Ste 200 Cleveland (44143) *(G-5984)*
Marsam Metalfab Inc 330 405-1520
1870 Enterprise Pkwy Twinsburg (44087) *(G-18444)*
Marsh Berry & Company Inc (PA) 440 354-3230
28601 Chagrin Blvd # 400 Beachwood (44122) *(G-1097)*
Marsh Inc (PA) 513 421-1234
333 E 8th St Cincinnati (45202) *(G-4026)*
Marsh & McLennan Agency LLC 513 248-4888
6279 Tri Ridge Blvd # 400 Loveland (45140) *(G-13143)*
Marsh & McLennan Agency LLC 937 228-4135
409 E Monu Ave Ste 400 Dayton (45402) *(G-9699)*
Marsh Building Products Inc (PA) 937 222-3321
2030 Winners Cir Dayton (45404) *(G-9700)*
Marsh Foundation 419 238-1695
1229 Lincoln Hwy Van Wert (45891) *(G-18639)*
Marsh USA Inc 216 937-1700
200 Public Sq Ste 3760 Cleveland (44114) *(G-5985)*
Marsh USA Inc 513 287-1600
525 Vine St Ste 1600 Cincinnati (45202) *(G-4027)*
Marsh USA Inc 614 227-6200
325 John H Mcconnell Blvd # 350 Columbus (43215) *(G-8119)*
Marsh USA Inc 216 830-8000
200 Public Sq Ste 900 Cleveland (44114) *(G-5986)*
Marshall & Associates Inc 513 683-6396
1537 Durango Dr Loveland (45140) *(G-13144)*
Marshall & Melhorn LLC 419 249-7100
4 Seagate Ste 800 Toledo (43604) *(G-18043)*
Marshall Ford, Cleveland *Also called Sorbir Inc (G-6495)*
Marshall Information Svcs LLC 614 430-0355
6665 Busch Blvd Columbus (43229) *(G-8120)*
Marshallville Packing Co Inc 330 855-2871
50 E Market St Marshallville (44645) *(G-13597)*
Marsol Apartments 440 449-5800
6503 1/2 Marsol Rd Cleveland (44124) *(G-5987)*
Martens Donald & Sons (PA) 216 265-4211
10830 Brookpark Rd Cleveland (44130) *(G-5988)*
Martin + WD Apprisal Group Ltd 419 241-4998
43 S Saint Clair St Toledo (43604) *(G-18044)*
Martin Altmeyer Funeral Home 330 385-3650
15872 Saint Clair Ave East Liverpool (43920) *(G-10524)*
Martin Carpet Cleaning Company 614 443-4655
795 S Wall St Columbus (43206) *(G-8121)*
Martin Chevrolet Inc 937 849-1381
2135 S Dayton Lakeview Rd New Carlisle (45344) *(G-15027)*
Martin Greg Excavating Inc 513 727-9300
1501 S University Blvd Middletown (45044) *(G-14433)*
Martin Healthcare Group, The, Solon *Also called Physician Staffing Inc (G-17039)*
Martin Logistics Inc 330 456-8000
4526 Louisville St Ne Canton (44705) *(G-2450)*
Martin Ls DDS Ms (PA) 513 829-8999
1211 Nilles Rd Fairfield (45014) *(G-10874)*
Martin Marietta Aggragate, West Chester *Also called Martin Marietta Materials Inc (G-19117)*
Martin Marietta Aggregates, Grove City *Also called Martin Marietta Materials Inc (G-11579)*
Martin Marietta Materials Inc 513 701-1140
9277 Centre Pointe Dr # 250 West Chester (45069) *(G-19117)*
Martin Marietta Materials Inc 513 353-1400
10905 Us 50 North Bend (45052) *(G-15319)*
Martin Marietta Materials Inc 513 829-6446
107 River Cir Bldg 1 Fairfield (45014) *(G-10875)*
Martin Marietta Materials Inc 614 871-6708
3300 Jackson Pike Grove City (43123) *(G-11579)*
Martin Periodontics, Fairfield *Also called Martin Ls DDS Ms (G-10874)*
Martin Trnsp Systems Inc 419 726-1348
320 Matzinger Rd Toledo (43612) *(G-18045)*
Martin-Brower Company LLC 513 773-2301
4260 Port Union Rd West Chester (45011) *(G-19118)*
Martinez Construction Services, Lorain *Also called Stevens Engineers Constrs Inc (G-13079)*
Marucci and Gaffney Excvtg Co (PA) 330 743-8170
18 Hogue St Youngstown (44502) *(G-20273)*
Marvel Consultants (PA) 216 292-2855
28601 Chagrin Blvd # 210 Cleveland (44122) *(G-5989)*
Marvin W Mielke Inc 330 725-8845
1040 Industrial Pkwy Medina (44256) *(G-14095)*
Marxent Labs LLC 937 999-5005
3100 Res Blvd Ste 360 Kettering (45420) *(G-12433)*
Mary C Enterprises Inc (PA) 937 253-6169
2274 Patterson Rd Dayton (45420) *(G-9701)*
Mary Evans Childcare Center, Columbus *Also called First Community Church (G-7663)*
Mary Hammond Center, McConnelsville *Also called Mary Hmmond Adult Actvties Ctr (G-14028)*
Mary Hmmond Adult Actvties Ctr 740 962-4200
900 S Riverside Dr Ne McConnelsville (43756) *(G-14028)*
Mary Kelley's Restaurant, Columbus *Also called Mary Kelleys Inc (G-8122)*
Mary Kelleys Inc 614 760-7041
1013 Highland St Columbus (43201) *(G-8122)*
Mary Rtan Hlth Assn Logan Cnty (PA) 937 592-4015
205 E Palmer Rd Bellefontaine (43311) *(G-1389)*
Mary Rutan Hospital, Bellefontaine *Also called Mary Rtan Hlth Assn Logan Cnty (G-1389)*
Mary Rutan Hospital (HQ) 937 592-4015
205 E Palmer Rd Bellefontaine (43311) *(G-1390)*
Mary Scott Nursing Home Inc 937 278-0761
3109 Campus Dr Dayton (45406) *(G-9702)*
Maryann McEowen 330 638-6385
272 Wae Trl Cortland (44410) *(G-9078)*
Maryhaven Inc (PA) 614 449-1530
1791 Alum Creek Dr Columbus (43207) *(G-8123)*
Maryhaven Inc 937 644-9192
715 S Plum St Marysville (43040) *(G-13634)*
Maryhaven Inc 419 946-6734
245 Neal Ave Ste A Mount Gilead (43338) *(G-14855)*
Marymount Health Care Systems 216 332-1100
13900 Mccracken Rd Cleveland (44125) *(G-5990)*
Marymount Hospital Inc (HQ) 216 581-0500
9500 Euclid Ave Cleveland (44195) *(G-5991)*
Marysville Food Pantry 937 644-3248
333 Ash St Marysville (43040) *(G-13635)*
Marysville Steel Inc 937 642-5971
323 E 8th St Marysville (43040) *(G-13636)*
Marysvlle Obsttrics Gynecology (PA) 937 644-1244
150 Morey Dr Marysville (43040) *(G-13637)*
Marysvlle Ohio Srgical Ctr LLC (PA) 937 642-6622
122 Professional Pkwy Marysville (43040) *(G-13638)*
Marysvlle Ohio Srgical Ctr LLC 937 578-4200
17853 State Route 31 Marysville (43040) *(G-13639)*
Marzetti Distribution Center, Grove City *Also called Tmarzetti Company (G-11605)*
Mas Inc (PA) 330 659-3333
2718 Brecksville Rd Richfield (44286) *(G-16514)*
Mascals Contracting Services, Columbus *Also called United Insulation Co Inc (G-8893)*
Masco Inc 330 797-2904
160 Marwood Cir Youngstown (44512) *(G-20274)*
Maslyk Landscaping Inc 440 748-3635
12289 Eaton Commerce Pkwy Columbia Station (44028) *(G-6849)*
Mason Family Resorts LLC 513 339-0141
2501 Great Wolf Dr Mason (45040) *(G-13736)*
Mason Health Care Center 513 398-2881
5640 Cox Smith Rd Mason (45040) *(G-13737)*
Mason Steel, Walton Hills *Also called Mason Structural Steel Inc (G-18790)*
Mason Steel Erecting Inc 440 439-1040
7500 Northfield Rd Cleveland (44146) *(G-5992)*
Mason Structural Steel Inc 440 439-1040
7500 Northfield Rd Walton Hills (44146) *(G-18790)*
Masonic Healthcare Inc 937 525-3001
3 Masonic Dr Springfield (45504) *(G-17229)*
Massachusetts Mutl Lf Insur Co 513 579-8555
1 W 4th St Ste 1000 Cincinnati (45202) *(G-4028)*
Massachusetts Mutl Lf Insur Co 216 592-7359
1660 W 2nd St Ste 850 Cleveland (44113) *(G-5993)*
Massage Envy, Westlake *Also called Irish Envy LLC (G-19499)*
Massage Envy 440 878-0500
6 Southpark Ctr Strongsville (44136) *(G-17490)*
Massey's Pizza, Columbus *Also called Premier Broadcasting Co Inc (G-8555)*
Massillon Automobile Club 330 833-1084
1972 Wales Rd Ne Ste 1 Massillon (44646) *(G-13832)*
Massillon Cable TV Inc (PA) 330 833-4134
814 Cable Ct Nw Massillon (44647) *(G-13833)*
Massillon City School Bus Gar 330 830-1849
1 George Red Bird Dr Se Massillon (44646) *(G-13834)*
Massillon Cmnty Hosp Hlth Plan 330 837-6880
100 Lillian Gish Blvd Sw Massillon (44647) *(G-13835)*
Massillon Community Dialysis, Massillon *Also called Fort Dialysis LLC (G-13809)*
Massillon Feed Mill, Massillon *Also called Case Farms LLC (G-13793)*

Massillon Health System LLC 330 837-7200
400 Austin Ave Nw Massillon (44646) ***(G-13836)***
Mast Global Fashions, Reynoldsburg *Also called Mast Industries Inc* ***(G-16468)***
Mast Industries Inc (HQ) 614 415-7000
2 Limited Pkwy Columbus (43230) ***(G-8124)***
Mast Industries Inc 614 856-6000
8655 E Broad St Reynoldsburg (43068) ***(G-16468)***
Mast Logistics Services Inc 614 415-7500
2 Limited Pkwy Columbus (43230) ***(G-8125)***
Mast Technology Services Inc 614 415-7000
3 Limited Pkwy Columbus (43230) ***(G-8126)***
Mast Trucking Inc 330 674-8913
6471 County Road 625 Millersburg (44654) ***(G-14611)***
Master Clean Carpet & Uphlstry, Columbus *Also called D & J Master Clean Inc* ***(G-7477)***
Master Maintenance Co, Lima *Also called Nicholas D Starr Inc* ***(G-12843)***
Master-Halco Inc 513 869-7600
620 Commerce Center Dr Fairfield (45011) ***(G-10876)***
Masterpiece Painting Company 330 395-9900
546 Washington St Ne Warren (44483) ***(G-18878)***
Masterplan, Cincinnati *Also called Genesis Technology Partners* ***(G-3676)***
Masters Agency Inc 330 805-5985
1108 Ledgestone Dr Wadsworth (44281) ***(G-18764)***
Masters Drug Company Inc 800 982-7922
3600 Pharma Way Lebanon (45036) ***(G-12625)***
Masters Pharmaceutical Inc (PA) 513 354-2690
3600 Pharma Way Lebanon (45036) ***(G-12626)***
Masters Pharmaceutical Inc 800 982-7922
3600 Pharma Way Lebanon (45036) ***(G-12627)***
Masur Trucking Inc 513 860-9600
11825 Reading Rd Ste 1 Cincinnati (45241) ***(G-4029)***
Mat, Lima *Also called Allen Metro Hsing MGT Dev Corp* ***(G-12736)***
Mat Innovative Solutions LLC 216 398-8010
153 Hayes Dr Independence (44131) ***(G-12232)***
Matandy Steel & Metal Pdts LLC 513 844-2277
1200 Central Ave Hamilton (45011) ***(G-11757)***
Matandy Steel Sales, Hamilton *Also called Matandy Steel & Metal Pdts LLC* ***(G-11757)***
Matco Industries Inc 740 852-7054
204 Maple St London (43140) ***(G-13002)***
Matco Properties Inc 440 366-5501
823 Leona St Elyria (44035) ***(G-10649)***
MATCO SERVICES, London *Also called Matco Industries Inc* ***(G-13002)***
Matco Tools Corporation (HQ) 330 929-4949
4403 Allen Rd Stow (44224) ***(G-17382)***
Material Management, Columbus *Also called Ohio Department Transportation* ***(G-8330)***
Material Suppliers Inc 419 298-2440
2444 State Route 49 Edgerton (43517) ***(G-10583)***
Matern Ohio Management Inc 614 457-7660
1241 Dublin Rd Ste 200 Columbus (43215) ***(G-8127)***
Maternohio Clinical Assoicates 614 457-7660
1241 Dublin Rd Ste 102 Columbus (43215) ***(G-8128)***
Maternohio Management Services, Columbus *Also called Matern Ohio Management Inc* ***(G-8127)***
Matesich Distributing Co 740 349-8686
1190 E Main St Newark (43055) ***(G-15201)***
Matheson Tri-Gas Inc 614 771-1311
4579 Sutphen Ct Hilliard (43026) ***(G-11925)***
Mathews Josiah 567 204-8818
602 E 5th St Lima (45804) ***(G-12837)***
Mathews Auto Group, Marion *Also called Mathews Kennedy Ford L-M Inc* ***(G-13564)***
Mathews Dodge Chrysler Jeep 740 389-2341
1866 Marion Waldo Rd Marion (43302) ***(G-13563)***
Mathews Ford Inc 740 522-2181
500 Hebron Rd Newark (43056) ***(G-15202)***
Mathews Ford-Oregon, Oregon *Also called Oregon Ford Inc* ***(G-15746)***
Mathews Kennedy Ford L-M Inc (PA) 740 387-3673
1155 Delaware Ave Marion (43302) ***(G-13564)***
Matia Motors Inc 440 365-7311
823 Leona St Elyria (44035) ***(G-10650)***
Matlock Electric Co Inc (PA) 513 731-9600
2780 Highland Ave Cincinnati (45212) ***(G-4030)***
Mato Inc 440 729-9008
8027 Mayfield Rd Chesterland (44026) ***(G-2799)***
Matrix Management Solutions 330 470-3700
5200 Stoneham Rd Canton (44720) ***(G-2451)***
Matrix Media Services Inc 614 228-2200
463 E Town St Ste 200 Columbus (43215) ***(G-8129)***
Matrix Pointe Software LLC 216 333-1263
30400 Detroit Rd Ste 400 Westlake (44145) ***(G-19512)***
Matrix Research Inc (PA) 937 427-8433
1300 Research Park Dr Beavercreek (45432) ***(G-1190)***
Matrix Research & Engineering, Beavercreek *Also called Matrix Research Inc* ***(G-1190)***
Matrix Sys Auto Finishes LLC 248 668-8135
600 Nova Dr Se Massillon (44646) ***(G-13837)***
Matrix Technologies Inc (PA) 419 897-7200
1760 Indian Wood Cir Maumee (43537) ***(G-13942)***
Matt Construction Services 216 641-0030
6600 Grant Ave Cleveland (44105) ***(G-5994)***
Mattingly Foods Inc (PA) 740 454-0136
302 State St Zanesville (43701) ***(G-20500)***
Mattlin Construction Inc 513 598-5402
5835 Hamilton Cleves Rd Cleves (45002) ***(G-6804)***

Mattress Warehouse, Independence *Also called Mat Innovative Solutions LLC* ***(G-12232)***
Matvest Inc 614 487-8720
1380 Dublin Rd Ste 200 Columbus (43215) ***(G-8130)***
Maumee Bay Golf Course, Oregon *Also called TW Recreational Services* ***(G-15754)***
Maumee Bay State Park Resort, Oregon *Also called Xanterra Parks & Resorts Inc* ***(G-15755)***
Maumee Lodge No 1850 Bnvlt 419 893-7272
137 W Wayne St Maumee (43537) ***(G-13943)***
Maumee Lodging Enterprises 419 865-1380
1520 S Hlland Sylvania Rd Maumee (43537) ***(G-13944)***
Maumee Ob Gyn Assoc 419 891-6201
660 Beaver Creek Cir # 200 Maumee (43537) ***(G-13945)***
Maumee Plumbing & Htg Sup Inc (PA) 419 874-7991
12860 Eckel Junction Rd Perrysburg (43551) ***(G-16031)***
Maumee Valley Guidance Center (PA) 419 782-8856
211 Biede Ave Defiance (43512) ***(G-10046)***
Maumee Youth Center, Liberty Center *Also called Youth Services Ohio Department* ***(G-12716)***
Mauser Usa LLC 740 397-1762
219 Commerce Dr Mount Vernon (43050) ***(G-14911)***
Mauser Usa LLC 740 397-1762
219 Commerce Dr Mount Vernon (43050) ***(G-14912)***
Maval Industries LLC 330 405-1600
1555 Enterprise Pkwy Twinsburg (44087) ***(G-18445)***
Maval Manufacturing, Twinsburg *Also called Maval Industries LLC* ***(G-18445)***
Maverick Media (PA) 419 331-1600
57 Town Sq Lima (45801) ***(G-12838)***
Max Dixons Expressway Park 513 831-2273
689 Us Route 50 Milford (45150) ***(G-14537)***
Maxim Healthcare Services Inc 740 522-6094
96 Integrity Dr Ste A Hebron (43025) ***(G-11852)***
Maxim Healthcare Services Inc 740 772-4100
220 N Plaza Blvd Chillicothe (45601) ***(G-2863)***
Maxim Healthcare Services Inc 216 606-3000
6155 Rockside Rd Independence (44131) ***(G-12233)***
Maxim Healthcare Services Inc 614 986-3001
735 Taylor Rd Gahanna (43230) ***(G-11257)***
Maxim Technologies Inc 614 457-6325
3960 Brown Park Dr Ste D Hilliard (43026) ***(G-11926)***
Maximation LLC 614 526-2260
2257 A Wstbroke Dr Bldg H Columbus (43228) ***(G-8131)***
Maximum Call Center, Cincinnati *Also called Maximum Communications Inc* ***(G-4031)***
Maximum Communications Inc 513 489-3414
117 Williams St Cincinnati (45215) ***(G-4031)***
Maxwell Lightning Protection 937 228-7250
621 Pond St Dayton (45402) ***(G-9703)***
May Jim Auto Sales LLC 419 422-9797
3690 Speedway Dr Findlay (45840) ***(G-11063)***
Mayer Laminates MA, Hudson *Also called Meyer Decorative Surfaces USA* ***(G-12133)***
Mayers Electric Co Inc 513 272-2900
4004 Erie Ct Ste B Cincinnati (45227) ***(G-4032)***
Mayfair Country Club Inc 330 699-2209
2229 Raber Rd Uniontown (44685) ***(G-18528)***
Mayfair Nursing Care Centers 614 889-6320
3000 Bethel Rd Columbus (43220) ***(G-8132)***
Mayfair School, Toledo *Also called Harbor* ***(G-17934)***
Mayfair Village, Columbus *Also called Mayfair Nursing Care Centers* ***(G-8132)***
Mayfare Village, Columbus *Also called Life Care Centers America Inc* ***(G-8061)***
Mayfield Clinic Inc (PA) 513 221-1100
3825 Edwards Rd Ste 300 Cincinnati (45209) ***(G-4033)***
Mayfield Sand Ridge Club 216 381-0826
1545 Sheridan Rd Cleveland (44121) ***(G-5995)***
Mayfield Village, Cleveland *Also called Skoda Minotti Holdings LLC* ***(G-6484)***
Mayflower Nursing Home Inc 330 492-7131
836 34th St Nw Canton (44709) ***(G-2452)***
Maza Inc 614 760-0003
7635 Commerce Pl Plain City (43064) ***(G-16198)***
Mazanec Raskin & Ryder, Cleveland *Also called Mazanec Raskin & Ryder Co Lpa* ***(G-5996)***
Mazanec Raskin & Ryder Co Lpa (PA) 440 248-7906
34305 Solon Rd Ste 100 Cleveland (44139) ***(G-5996)***
Mazda Saab of Bedford, Bedford *Also called Partners Auto Group Bdford Inc* ***(G-1329)***
Mazel Company, The, Solon *Also called Aurora Wholesalers LLC* ***(G-16980)***
Mazella Companies, Cleveland *Also called Mazzella Holding Company Inc* ***(G-5997)***
Mazzella Holding Company Inc (PA) 513 772-4466
21000 Aerospace Pkwy Cleveland (44142) ***(G-5997)***
MB Financial Inc 937 283-2027
2251 Rombach Ave Wilmington (45177) ***(G-19772)***
MBC Cardiologist Inc 937 223-4461
122 Wyoming St Dayton (45409) ***(G-9704)***
MBC Holdings Inc (PA) 419 445-1015
1613 S Defiance St Archbold (43502) ***(G-638)***
MBI Solutions Inc 937 619-4000
332 Congress Park Dr Dayton (45459) ***(G-9705)***
MBI Tree Service LLC 513 926-9857
872 Franklin Rd Waynesville (45068) ***(G-18985)***
Mbs Acquisition, Mason *Also called Remtec Engineering* ***(G-13756)***
Mc Alarney Pool Spas and Billd 740 373-6698
908 Pike St Marietta (45750) ***(G-13474)***
Mc Auley Center 937 653-5432
906 Scioto St Urbana (43078) ***(G-18594)***

ALPHABETIC

Mc Cloy Financial Services 614 457-6233
921 Chatham Ln Ste 300 Columbus (43221) **(G-8133)**
Mc Clurg & Creamer Inc 419 866-7080
7450 Hill Ave Holland (43528) **(G-12036)**
Mc Cormack Advisors Intl 216 522-1200
1360 E 9th St Ste 100 Cleveland (44114) **(G-5998)**
Mc Daniel Motor Co (Inc) 740 389-2355
1111 Mount Vernon Ave Marion (43302) **(G-13565)**
Mc Fadden Construction Inc 419 668-4165
4426 Old State Rd N Norwalk (44857) **(G-15580)**
Mc Graw-Hill Educational Pubg, Ashland *Also called McGraw-Hill School Education H* **(G-687)**
Mc Gregor Family Enterprises (PA) 513 583-0040
9990 Kings Auto Mall Rd Cincinnati (45249) **(G-4034)**
Mc Mahon Realestate Co (PA) 740 344-2250
591 Country Club Dr Newark (43055) **(G-15203)**
Mc Meechan Construction Co 216 581-9373
17633 S Miles Rd Cleveland (44128) **(G-5999)**
Mc Neal Industries Inc 440 721-0400
835 Richmond Rd Painesville (44077) **(G-15865)**
Mc Phillips Plbg Htg & AC Co 216 481-1400
16115 Waterloo Rd Cleveland (44110) **(G-6000)**
Mc Sign Company (PA) 440 209-6200
8959 Tyler Blvd Mentor (44060) **(G-14211)**
McAfee Air Duct Cleaning, Dayton *Also called McAfee Heating & AC Co Inc* **(G-9706)**
McAfee Heating & AC Co Inc 937 438-1976
4750 Hempstead Station Dr Dayton (45429) **(G-9706)**
McAlarney Pols Spas Billd More, Marietta *Also called Mc Alarney Pool Spas and Billd* **(G-13474)**
McArthur Lumber and Post, Mc Arthur *Also called Appalachia Wood Inc* **(G-14015)**
McAuley Center, Urbana *Also called Mercy Mem Hosp Urbana Ohio* **(G-18596)**
McBee Supply Corporation 216 881-0015
5300 Lakeside Ave E Cleveland (44114) **(G-6001)**
McCad, Mount Gilead *Also called Morrow County Council On Drugs* **(G-14858)**
McCafferty Community Based, Cleveland *Also called Veterans Health Administration* **(G-6692)**
McCallisters Landscaping & Sup 440 259-3348
2519 N Ridge Rd Perry (44081) **(G-15964)**
McCarthy Burgess & Wolff Inc (PA) 440 735-5100
26000 Cannon Rd Bedford (44146) **(G-1321)**
McCc Sportswear Inc 513 583-9210
9944 Prnceton Glendale Rd West Chester (45246) **(G-19214)**
McCdp, Youngstown *Also called Meridian Healthcare* **(G-20285)**
McClellan Management Inc 419 855-7755
300 Cherry St Genoa (43430) **(G-11381)**
McClintock Electric Inc 330 264-6380
402 E Henry St Wooster (44691) **(G-19886)**
McCloy Engineering LLC 513 984-4112
3701 Port Union Rd Fairfield (45014) **(G-10877)**
McCluskey Automotive, Cincinnati *Also called McCluskey Chevrolet Inc* **(G-4035)**
McCluskey Chevrolet Inc (PA) 513 761-1111
8525 Reading Rd Cincinnati (45215) **(G-4035)**
McCo, Portsmouth *Also called Mechanical Construction Co* **(G-16295)**
MCCO, Cleveland *Also called Medical Center Co (inc)* **(G-6014)**
McConnell Excavating Ltd 440 774-4578
15804 State Route 58 Oberlin (44074) **(G-15649)**
McCormick Equipment Co Inc (PA) 513 677-8888
112 Northeast Dr Loveland (45140) **(G-13145)**
McCoy Landscape Services Inc 740 375-2730
2391 Likens Rd Marion (43302) **(G-13566)**
McCrate Delaet & Co 937 492-3161
100 S Main Ave Ste 203 Sidney (45365) **(G-16942)**
McCrate Delaet & Co Cpa's, Sidney *Also called McCrate Delaet & Co* **(G-16942)**
McCullough-Hyde Mem Hosp Inc (PA) 513 523-2111
110 N Poplar St Oxford (45056) **(G-15818)**
McCullough-Hyde Mem Hosp Inc 513 863-2215
1390 Eaton Ave Hamilton (45013) **(G-11758)**
McDaniels Cnstr Corp Inc 614 252-5852
1069 Woodland Ave Columbus (43219) **(G-8134)**
McDermott International Inc 740 687-4292
2600 E Main St Lancaster (43130) **(G-12554)**
McDonald Finanacial Group, Cleveland *Also called Keybanc Capital Markets Inc* **(G-5898)**
MCDONALD HOPKINS LLC (PA) 216 348-5400
600 Superior Ave E # 2100 Cleveland (44114) **(G-6002)**
McDonald's, Mount Gilead *Also called Pam Johnsonident* **(G-14861)**
McDonald's, Lewis Center *Also called D J- Seve Group Inc* **(G-12680)**
McDonalds 3490 ....330 762-7747
578 E Market St Akron (44304) **(G-333)**
McDonalds Corporation 614 682-1128
2600 Corporate Exch Dr Columbus (43231) **(G-8135)**
McDonalds Design & Build Inc 419 782-4191
101 Clinton St Ste 2200 Defiance (43512) **(G-10047)**
McElvain Group Home 419 589-6697
634 Mcbride Rd Mansfield (44905) **(G-13336)**
McEp, Dayton *Also called Medical Center At Elizabeth Pl* **(G-9713)**
McGill Airclean LLC 614 829-1200
1777 Refugee Rd Columbus (43207) **(G-8136)**
McGill Smith Punshon Inc 513 759-0004
3700 Park 42 Dr Ste 190b Cincinnati (45241) **(G-4036)**
McGinnis Inc (HQ) 740 377-4391
502 2nd St E South Point (45680) **(G-17092)**
McGinnis Inc 513 941-8070
5525 River Rd Cincinnati (45233) **(G-4037)**
McGohan Brabender, Moraine *Also called McGohan/Brabender Agency Inc* **(G-14800)**
McGohan/Brabender Agency Inc (PA) 937 293-1600
3931 S Dixie Dr Moraine (45439) **(G-14800)**
McGowan & Company Inc (PA) 800 545-1538
20595 Lorain Rd Ste 300 Cleveland (44126) **(G-6003)**
McGowan Program Administrators, Cleveland *Also called McGowan & Company Inc* **(G-6003)**
McGraw-Hill School Education H 419 207-7400
1250 George Rd Ashland (44805) **(G-687)**
McGraw/Kokosing Inc 614 212-5700
101 Clark Blvd Monroe (45044) **(G-14705)**
McGregor Senior Ind Hsing 216 851-8200
14900 Private Dr Cleveland (44112) **(G-6004)**
Mch Services Inc 260 432-9699
190 E Spring Valley Pike Dayton (45458) **(G-9707)**
MCI Communications Svcs Inc 216 265-9953
21000 Brookpark Rd Cleveland (44135) **(G-6005)**
MCI Communications Svcs Inc 440 635-0418
12956 Taylor Wells Rd Chardon (44024) **(G-2757)**
McKeen Security Inc 740 699-1301
69100 Bayberry Dr Ste 200 Saint Clairsville (43950) **(G-16644)**
McKeever & Niekamp Elc Inc 937 431-9363
1834 Woods Dr Beavercreek (45432) **(G-1191)**
McKesson Corporation 740 636-3500
3000 Kenskill Ave Wshngtn CT Hs (43160) **(G-20030)**
McKesson Medical-Surgical Inc 614 539-2600
3500 Centerpoint Dr Urbancrest (43123) **(G-18606)**
McKesson Medical-Surgical Top 513 985-0525
12074 Champion Way Cincinnati (45241) **(G-4038)**
McKinley Air Transport Inc 330 497-6956
5430 Lauby Rd Bldg 4 Canton (44720) **(G-2453)**
McKinley Early Childhood Ctr (PA) 330 454-4800
1350 Cherry Ave Ne Canton (44714) **(G-2454)**
McKinley Early Childhood Ctr 330 252-2552
440 Vernon Odom Blvd Akron (44307) **(G-334)**
McKinley Hall Inc 937 328-5300
2624 Lexington Ave Springfield (45505) **(G-17230)**
McKinley Life Care Center LLC 330 456-1014
800 Market Ave N Ste 1560 Canton (44702) **(G-2455)**
MCKINLEY NATIONAL MEMORIAL, Canton *Also called Stark Cnty Historical Soc Inc* **(G-2542)**
McKinsey & Company Inc 216 274-4000
950 Main Ave Ste 1200 Cleveland (44113) **(G-6006)**
McKinsey & Company Inc 216 274-4000
950 Main Ave Ste 1200 Cleveland (44113) **(G-6007)**
McKirnan Bros Inc 419 586-2428
530 Schunk Rd Celina (45822) **(G-2651)**
McKirnan Bros. Inc., Celina *Also called McKirnan Bros Inc* **(G-2651)**
McM Capital Partners 216 514-1840
25201 Chagrin Blvd # 360 Beachwood (44122) **(G-1098)**
McM Electronics Inc 937 434-0031
650 Congress Park Dr Dayton (45459) **(G-9708)**
McM General Properties Ltd 216 851-8000
13829 Euclid Ave Cleveland (44112) **(G-6008)**
McMaster Farms 330 482-2913
345 Old Fourteen Rd Columbiana (44408) **(G-6861)**
McMicken College of Asa, Cincinnati *Also called University of Cincinnati* **(G-4764)**
McMullen Transportation LLC 937 981-4455
11350 State Route 41 Greenfield (45123) **(G-11488)**
McNational Inc (PA) 740 377-4391
502 2nd St E South Point (45680) **(G-17093)**
McNaughton-Mckay Elc Ohio Inc (HQ) 614 476-2800
2255 Citygate Dr Columbus (43219) **(G-8137)**
McNaughton-Mckay Elc Ohio Inc 419 422-2984
1950 Industrial Dr Findlay (45840) **(G-11064)**
McNaughton-Mckay Elc Ohio Inc 419 891-0262
355 Tomahawk Dr Unit 1 Maumee (43537) **(G-13946)**
McNaughton-Mckay Electric Ohio, Columbus *Also called McNaughton-Mckay Elc Ohio Inc* **(G-8137)**
McNeil Industries Inc 440 951-7756
835 Richmond Rd Painesville (44077) **(G-15866)**
McNerney & Associates LLC (PA) 513 241-9951
440 Northland Blvd Cincinnati (45240) **(G-4039)**
McNerney & Son Inc 419 666-0200
1 Maritime Plz Uppr Toledo (43604) **(G-18046)**
McPaul Corp 419 447-6313
981 S Morgan St Tiffin (44883) **(G-17684)**
McPc Inc (PA) 440 238-0102
21500 Aerospace Pkwy Brookpark (44142) **(G-1951)**
McPc Tech Pdts & Solutions, Brookpark *Also called McPc Inc* **(G-1951)**
McR LLC 937 879-5055
2601 Missi Point Blvd Ste Beavercreek (45431) **(G-1192)**
MCR Services Inc 614 421-0860
638 E 5th Ave Columbus (43201) **(G-8138)**
McSteen & Associates Inc 440 585-9800
1415 E 286th St Wickliffe (44092) **(G-19607)**
McTech Corp (PA) 216 391-7700
8100 Grand Ave Ste 100 Cleveland (44104) **(G-6009)**

McV Health Care Facilities....513 398-1486
411 Western Row Rd Mason (45040) *(G-13738)*
McWane Inc....740 622-6651
2266 S 6th St Coshocton (43812) *(G-9111)*
MD Business Solutions Inc....513 872-4500
9825 Kenwood Rd Ste 108 Blue Ash (45242) *(G-1637)*
Mds Foods Inc (PA)....330 879-9780
4676 Erie Ave Sw Ste A Navarre (44662) *(G-14955)*
MDU Resources Group Inc....937 424-2550
3150 Encrete Ln Moraine (45439) *(G-14801)*
Me/Ibi Group, Westerville *Also called M-E Companies Inc (G-19423)*
Meacham & Apel Architects Inc....614 764-0407
775 Yard St Ste 325 Columbus (43212) *(G-8139)*
Mead Family Medical Ctr, Chillicothe *Also called Corporate Health Dimensions (G-2828)*
Meadbrook Care Center, Cincinnati *Also called Trinity Healthcare Corporation (G-4700)*
Meade Construction Inc (PA)....740 694-5525
13 N Mill St Lexington (44904) *(G-12715)*
Meade Construction Company, Lexington *Also called Meade Construction Inc (G-12715)*
Meaden & Moore LLP (PA)....216 241-3272
1375 E 9th St Ste 1800 Cleveland (44114) *(G-6010)*
Meadow Wind Hlth Care Ctr Inc....330 833-2026
300 23rd St Ne Massillon (44646) *(G-13838)*
Meadowbrook Country Club....937 836-5186
6001 Salem Ave Clayton (45315) *(G-4913)*
Meadowbrook Country Club....937 836-5186
6001 Salem Ave Clayton (45315) *(G-4914)*
Meadowbrook Mall Company (PA)....330 747-2661
2445 Belmont Ave Youngstown (44505) *(G-20275)*
Meadowbrook Manor of Hartford....330 772-5253
3090 Five Pnts Hrtford Rd Fowler (44418) *(G-11144)*
Meadowbrook Meat Company Inc....614 771-9660
4300 Diplomacy Dr Columbus (43228) *(G-8140)*
Meadowhawk Dialysis, Marysville *Also called Mahoney Dialysis LLC (G-13633)*
Meadowlake Corporation....330 492-2010
1211 39th St Ne Ste A Canton (44714) *(G-2456)*
Meadowood Golf Course, Westlake *Also called City of Westlake (G-19475)*
Meadows Healthcare, Cincinnati *Also called Mkjb Inc (G-4108)*
Meadowview Care Center, Seville *Also called Encore Healthcare LLC (G-16840)*
MEALS ON WHEELS, Columbus *Also called Lifecare Alliance (G-8063)*
Meals On Wheels, Dayton *Also called Senior Resource Connection (G-9875)*
Meals On Wheels-Older Adult Al....740 681-5050
253 Boving Rd Lancaster (43130) *(G-12555)*
Meander Hospitality Group Inc....330 702-0226
6599 Seville Dr Ste 100 Canfield (44406) *(G-2199)*
Meander Hsptality Group II LLC....330 422-0500
800 Mondial Pkwy Streetsboro (44241) *(G-17420)*
Meander Inn Inc....330 544-2378
870 N Canfield Niles Rd Youngstown (44515) *(G-20276)*
Meander Inn Incorporated....330 544-0660
880 N Canfield Niles Rd Youngstown (44515) *(G-20277)*
Meander Tire Company Inc....330 750-6155
408 N Meridian Rd Youngstown (44509) *(G-20278)*
Meat Packers Outlet, Massillon *Also called Steaks & Such Inc (G-13858)*
Mecco Inc....513 422-3651
2100 S Main St Middletown (45044) *(G-14434)*
Mechancal/Industrial Contg Inc....513 489-8282
11863 Solzman Rd Cincinnati (45249) *(G-4040)*
Mechanical Cnstr Managers LLC (PA)....937 274-1987
5245 Wadsworth Rd Dayton (45414) *(G-9709)*
Mechanical Construction Co....740 353-5668
2302 8th St Portsmouth (45662) *(G-16295)*
Mechanical Contractors, Marysville *Also called J A Guy Inc (G-13629)*
Mechanical Support Svcs Inc....614 777-8808
4641 Northwest Pkwy Hilliard (43026) *(G-11927)*
Mechanical Systems Dayton Inc....937 254-3235
4401 Springfield St Dayton (45431) *(G-9277)*
Mechanics Bank (PA)....419 524-0831
2 S Main St Mansfield (44902) *(G-13337)*
Med -Center/Med Partners....440 349-6400
34055 Solon Rd Ste 106 Cleveland (44139) *(G-6011)*
Med America Hlth Systems Corp (PA)....937 223-6192
1 Wyoming St Dayton (45409) *(G-9710)*
Med Assist Prgram of Info Line....330 762 0609
703 S Main St Ste 211 Akron (44311) *(G-335)*
Med Center, Cleveland *Also called Med -Center/Med Partners (G-6011)*
Med Center One Streetsboro....330 626-3455
9318 State Route 14 Streetsboro (44241) *(G-17421)*
Med Central HM Hlth & Hospice, Mansfield *Also called Medcentral Health System (G-13338)*
Med Clean....614 207-3317
5725 Westbourne Ave Columbus (43213) *(G-8141)*
Med Cntral Hlth Sys Child Care, Mansfield *Also called Medcentral Health System (G-13341)*
Med Ride Ems....614 747-9744
2741 E 4th Ave Columbus (43219) *(G-8142)*
Med Star Emgncy Mdcl Srv (PA)....330 394-6611
1600 Youngstown Rd Se Warren (44484) *(G-18879)*
Med Star Ems, Warren *Also called Med Star Emgncy Mdcl Srv (G-18879)*
Med Vet Associates, Worthington *Also called Medvet Associates Inc (G-19976)*
Med-Pass Incorporated....937 438-8884
1 Reynolds Way Dayton (45430) *(G-9711)*
Med-Trans Inc (PA)....937 325-4926
714 W Columbia St Springfield (45504) *(G-17231)*
Med-Trans Inc....937 293-9771
3510 Encrete Ln Moraine (45439) *(G-14802)*
Med3000 Group Inc....937 291-7850
3131 Newmark Dr Ste 100 Miamisburg (45342) *(G-14316)*
Meda-Care Transportation Inc....513 521-4799
270 Northland Blvd # 227 Cincinnati (45246) *(G-4041)*
Medallion Club (PA)....614 794-6999
5000 Club Dr Westerville (43082) *(G-19328)*
Medben Companies, Newark *Also called Medical Benefits Mutl Lf Insur (G-15204)*
MEDBEN COMPANIES, Newark *Also called Medical Bnfits Admnstrtors Inc (G-15205)*
Medcare Ambulance, Columbus *Also called Community Emrgcy Med Svcs Ohio (G-7404)*
Medcath Intermediate Holdings....937 221-8016
707 S Edwin Moses Blvd Dayton (45408) *(G-9712)*
Medcentral Health System....419 526-8900
1750 W 4th St Ste 1 Ontario (44906) *(G-15701)*
Medcentral Health System....419 526-8442
335 Glessner Ave Mansfield (44903) *(G-13338)*
Medcentral Health System (HQ)....419 526-8000
335 Glessner Ave Mansfield (44903) *(G-13339)*
Medcentral Health System....419 526-8970
770 Balgreen Dr Ste 105 Mansfield (44906) *(G-13340)*
Medcentral Health System....419 683-1040
291 Heiser Ct Crestline (44827) *(G-9147)*
Medcentral Health System....419 342-5015
199 W Main St Shelby (44875) *(G-16901)*
Medcentral Health System....419 526-8043
160 S Linden Rd Mansfield (44906) *(G-13341)*
Medcentral Hlth Sys Spt Mdcine, Ontario *Also called Medcentral Health System (G-15701)*
Medcentral Workable....419 526-8444
1750 W 4th St Ste 5 Ontario (44906) *(G-15702)*
Medco Health Solutions Inc....614 822-2000
5151 Blazer Pkwy Ste B Dublin (43017) *(G-10393)*
Medcorp Inc....419 425-9700
330 N Cory St Findlay (45840) *(G-11065)*
Medcorp Inc (PA)....419 727-7000
745 Medcorp Dr Toledo (43608) *(G-18047)*
Mede America of Ohio LLC....330 425-3241
2045 Midway Dr Twinsburg (44087) *(G-18446)*
MEDFLIGHT OF OHIO, Columbus *Also called Ohio Medical Trnsp Inc (G-8360)*
Medhurst Mason Contractors Inc....440 543-8885
17111 Munn Rd Ste 1 Chagrin Falls (44023) *(G-2725)*
Medi Home Care, Gallipolis *Also called Medi Home Health Agency Inc (G-11328)*
Medi Home Health Agency Inc (HQ)....740 266-3977
105 Main St Steubenville (43953) *(G-17329)*
Medi Home Health Agency Inc....740 441-1779
412 2nd Ave Gallipolis (45631) *(G-11328)*
Medi-Home Care, Steubenville *Also called Medi Home Health Agency Inc (G-17329)*
Media Collections Inc....216 831-5626
8948 Canyon Falls Blvd # 200 Twinsburg (44087) *(G-18447)*
Media Group At Michael's, The, Dayton *Also called Mfh Inc (G-9723)*
Media Source Inc (PA)....614 873-7635
7858 Industrial Pkwy Plain City (43064) *(G-16199)*
Media-Com Inc....330 673-2323
2449 State Route 59 Kent (44240) *(G-12386)*
Mediadvertiser Company....513 651-0265
337 Lorelei Dr Fayetteville (45118) *(G-10984)*
Medic Home Health Care LLC....440 449-7727
701 Beta Dr Ste 7 Cleveland (44143) *(G-6012)*
Medic Management Group LLC (PA)....330 670-5316
275 Springside Dr Akron (44333) *(G-336)*
Medic Response Service Inc (PA)....419 522-1998
98 S Diamond St Mansfield (44902) *(G-13342)*
Medical Account Services Inc....937 297-6072
3131 S Dixie Dr Ste 535 Moraine (45439) *(G-14803)*
Medical Administrators Inc....440 899-2229
28301 Ranney Pkwy Westlake (44145) *(G-19513)*
Medical Arts Physician Center....216 431-1500
2475 E 22nd St Ste 120 Cleveland (44115) *(G-6013)*
Medical Assoc Cambridge Inc....740 439-3515
1515 Maple Dr Ste 1 Cambridge (43725) *(G-2123)*
Medical Associates of Mid-Ohio....419 289 1331
2109 Claremont Ave Ashland (44805) *(G-688)*
Medical Benefits Mutl Lf Insur (PA)....740 522-8425
1975 Tamarack Rd Newark (43055) *(G-15204)*
Medical Bnfits Admnstrtors Inc....740 522-8425
1975 Tamarack Rd Newark (43055) *(G-15205)*
Medical Care PSC Inc....513 281-4400
2950 Robertson Ave Fl 2 Cincinnati (45209) *(G-4042)*
Medical Care Reimbursement....513 281-4400
2950 Robertson Ave Fl 2 Cincinnati (45209) *(G-4043)*
Medical Center, Columbus *Also called Ohio State University (G-8395)*
Medical Center, Columbus *Also called Ohio State University (G-8403)*
Medical Center, Columbus *Also called Ohio State University (G-8422)*
Medical Center At Elizabeth Pl....937 223-6237
1 Elizabeth Pl Dayton (45417) *(G-9713)*
Medical Center Co (inc)....216 368-4256
2250 Circle Dr Cleveland (44106) *(G-6014)*
Medical Center Security, Columbus *Also called Ohio State University (G-8441)*
Medical College of Ohio, Toledo *Also called Stephen R Saddemi MD (G-18201)*

(PA)=Parent Co (HQ)=Headquarters (DH)=Div Headquarters
2018 Harris Ohio
Services Directory
1255

Medical College of Ohio...419 383-7100
3355 Glendale Ave Fl 3 Toledo (43614) ***(G-18048)***
Medical Diagnostic Lab Inc (PA)...440 333-1375
24651 Center Ridge Rd # 350 Westlake (44145) ***(G-19514)***
Medical Flight 2, Marysville *Also called Ohio Medical Trnsp Inc* ***(G-13643)***
Medical Group Associates Inc...740 283-4773
114 Brady Cir E Steubenville (43952) ***(G-17330)***
Medical Imaging Equipment, Cleveland *Also called Philips Medical Systems Clevel* ***(G-6273)***
Medical Imging Diagnostics LLC...330 726-0322
819 Mckay Ct Ste B103 Youngstown (44512) ***(G-20279)***
Medical Mutual of Ohio (PA)...216 687-7000
2060 E 9th St Frnt Ste Cleveland (44115) ***(G-6015)***
Medical Mutual of Ohio...440 878-4800
15885 W Sprague Rd Strongsville (44136) ***(G-17491)***
Medical Mutual of Ohio...419 473-7100
3737 W Sylvania Ave Toledo (43623) ***(G-18049)***
Medical Mutual of Ohio...216 292-0400
23700 Commerce Park Beachwood (44122) ***(G-1099)***
Medical Mutual of Ohio...614 621-4585
10 W Broad St Ste 1400 Columbus (43215) ***(G-8143)***
Medical Mutual Services LLC (HQ)...440 878-4800
17800 Royalton Rd Strongsville (44136) ***(G-17492)***
Medical Office, Athens *Also called Ohio University* ***(G-807)***
Medical Onclgy-Hematology Assn...937 223-2183
3737 Sthern Blvd Ste 4200 Dayton (45429) ***(G-9714)***
Medical Prsnnel Pool of Dayton, Dayton *Also called Interim Healthcare of Dayton* ***(G-9634)***
Medical Radiation Physics, Milford *Also called Mrp Inc* ***(G-14543)***
Medical Records, Steubenville *Also called Trinity Health System* ***(G-17341)***
Medical Records Department, Columbus *Also called Ohio State University* ***(G-8437)***
Medical Recovery Systems Inc...513 872-7000
3372 Central Pkwy Cincinnati (45225) ***(G-4044)***
Medical Reimbursement, Cincinnati *Also called Medical Care Reimbursement* ***(G-4043)***
Medical Reimbursment, Cincinnati *Also called Medical Care PSC Inc* ***(G-4042)***
Medical Service Company (PA)...440 232-3000
24000 Broadway Ave Bedford (44146) ***(G-1322)***
Medical Solutions LLC...513 936-3468
9987 Carver Rd Ste 510 Blue Ash (45242) ***(G-1638)***
Medical Specialties Distrs LLC...440 232-0320
26350 Broadway Ave Oakwood Village (44146) ***(G-15630)***
Medical Specialties Distrs LLC...614 888-7939
400 Lazelle Rd Ste 13 Columbus (43240) ***(G-6894)***
Medical Surgical Associates...740 522-7600
1930 Tamarack Rd Newark (43055) ***(G-15206)***
Medical Transport Systems Inc...330 837-9818
909 Las Olas Blvd Nw North Canton (44720) ***(G-15352)***
Medicine Midwest LLC (PA)...513 533-1199
4700 Smith Rd Ste A Cincinnati (45212) ***(G-4045)***
Medicine Midwest LLC...937 435-8786
979 Congress Park Dr Dayton (45459) ***(G-9715)***
Medicount Management Inc...513 772-4465
10361 Spartan Dr Cincinnati (45215) ***(G-4046)***
Medigistics Inc (PA)...614 430-5700
1111 Schrock Rd Ste 200 Columbus (43229) ***(G-8144)***
Medill Elemntary Sch of Volntr...740 687-7352
1160 Sheridan Dr Lancaster (43130) ***(G-12556)***
Medina Advantage Inc...330 723-8697
3550 Octagon Dr Medina (44256) ***(G-14096)***
Medina Automall, Medina *Also called Medina Management Company LLC* ***(G-14102)***
Medina Cnty Jvnile Dtntion Ctr...330 764-8408
655 Independence Dr Medina (44256) ***(G-14097)***
Medina County Health Dept, Medina *Also called County of Medina* ***(G-14054)***
Medina County Home, Medina *Also called County of Medina* ***(G-14053)***
Medina County Sanitary...330 273-3610
791 W Smith Rd Medina (44256) ***(G-14098)***
Medina County Sheltered Inds...330 334-4491
150 Quadral Dr Ste D Wadsworth (44281) ***(G-18765)***
Medina Creative Accessibility...330 220-2112
232 N Court St Medina (44256) ***(G-14099)***
Medina Glass Block Inc...330 239-0239
1213 Medina Rd Medina (44256) ***(G-14100)***
Medina Hospital...330 723-3117
1000 E Washington St Medina (44256) ***(G-14101)***
Medina Management Company LLC...330 723-3291
3205 Medina Rd Medina (44256) ***(G-14102)***
Medina Meadows...330 725-1550
550 Miner Dr Medina (44256) ***(G-14103)***
Medina Medical Investors Ltd...330 483-3131
2400 Columbia Rd Medina (44256) ***(G-14104)***
Medina Medical Offices, Medina *Also called Kaiser Foundation Hospitals* ***(G-14090)***
Medina World Cars Inc...330 725-4901
11800 Pearl Rd Strongsville (44136) ***(G-17493)***
Mediquant Inc...440 746-2300
6900 S Edgerton Rd # 100 Brecksville (44141) ***(G-1833)***
Medisync Midwest Ltd Lblty Co...513 533-1199
25 Merchant St Ste 220 Cincinnati (45246) ***(G-4047)***
Medline Diamed LLC (HQ)...330 484-1450
3800 Commerce St Sw Canton (44706) ***(G-2457)***
Medlink of Ohio Inc (HQ)...216 751-5900
20600 Chagrin Blvd # 290 Cleveland (44122) ***(G-6016)***
Medlink of Ohio Inc...330 773-9434
1225 E Waterloo Rd Akron (44306) ***(G-337)***
Medohio Family Care Center, Columbus *Also called Ohio State University* ***(G-8394)***
Medone Hospital Physicians...314 255-6900
3525 Olentangy River Rd Columbus (43214) ***(G-8145)***
Medpace Inc...513 366-3220
5355 Medpace Way Cincinnati (45227) ***(G-4048)***
Medpace Inc (HQ)...513 579-9911
5375 Medpace Way Cincinnati (45227) ***(G-4049)***
Medpace Bioanalytical Labs LLC...513 366-3260
5365 Medpace Way Cincinnati (45227) ***(G-4050)***
Medport Inc...216 244-6832
8104 Madison Ave Cleveland (44102) ***(G-6017)***
Medpro LLC...937 336-5586
251 W Lexington Rd Eaton (45320) ***(G-10567)***
Medsearch Staffing Service (PA)...440 243-6363
7530 Lucerne Dr Ste 208 Cleveland (44130) ***(G-6018)***
Medvet Associates Inc...937 293-2714
2714 Springboro W Moraine (45439) ***(G-14804)***
Medvet Associates Inc (PA)...614 846-5800
300 E Wilson Bridge Rd # 100 Worthington (43085) ***(G-19976)***
Medwork LLC...937 449-0800
1435 Cincinnati St # 100 Dayton (45417) ***(G-9716)***
Medwork Occupational Hlth Care, Dayton *Also called Medwork LLC* ***(G-9716)***
Meeder Asset Management Inc...614 760-2112
6125 Memor Dr Dublin (43017) ***(G-10394)***
Mees Distributors Inc (PA)...513 541-2311
1541 W Fork Rd Cincinnati (45223) ***(G-4051)***
Mega Techway Inc...440 605-0700
760 Beta Dr Ste F Cleveland (44143) ***(G-6019)***
Megacity Fire Protection Inc (PA)...937 335-0775
8210 Expansion Way Dayton (45424) ***(G-9717)***
Megco Management Inc...330 874-9999
300 Yant St Bolivar (44612) ***(G-1749)***
Megen Construction Company Inc (PA)...513 742-9191
11130 Ashburn Rd Cincinnati (45240) ***(G-4052)***
Mehler & Hagestrom, Cleveland *Also called Mehler and Hagestrom Inc* ***(G-6020)***
Mehler and Hagestrom Inc (PA)...216 621-4984
1660 W 2nd St Ste 780 Cleveland (44113) ***(G-6020)***
MEI Hotels Incorporated...216 589-0441
1375 E 9th St Ste 2800 Cleveland (44114) ***(G-6021)***
Meigs Center Ltd...740 992-6472
333 Page St Middleport (45760) ***(G-14407)***
Meigs Cnty Dept Jobs Fmly Svcs, Middleport *Also called County of Meigs* ***(G-14406)***
Meigs County Council On Aging...740 992-2161
112 E Memorial Dr Fl 1 Pomeroy (45769) ***(G-16233)***
Meigs County Emrgncy Med Svcs, Pomeroy *Also called County of Meigs* ***(G-16231)***
Meigs Industries Inc...740 992-6681
1310 Carleton St Syracuse (45779) ***(G-17632)***
Meigs Local School District...740 742-2990
36895 State Route 124 Middleport (45760) ***(G-14408)***
Mel Lanzer Co...419 592-2801
2266 Scott St Napoleon (43545) ***(G-14945)***
Melamed Riley Advertising LLC...216 241-2141
1375 Euclid Ave Ste 410 Cleveland (44115) ***(G-6022)***
Mellott & Mellott Pll...513 241-2940
12 Walnut St Ste 2500 Cincinnati (45216) ***(G-4053)***
Melo International Inc...440 519-0526
3700 Kelley Ave Cleveland (44114) ***(G-6023)***
Mels Auto Glass Inc...513 563-7771
11775 Reading Rd Cincinnati (45241) ***(G-4054)***
Melvin Stone, Wilmington *Also called M C Trucking Company LLC* ***(G-19771)***
Memorial Complex, Madison *Also called Madison Local School District* ***(G-13231)***
Memorial Hospital (PA)...419 334-6657
715 S Taft Ave Fremont (43420) ***(G-11212)***
Memorial Hospital...419 547-6419
430 S Main St Clyde (43410) ***(G-6818)***
MEMORIAL HOSPITAL HEALTHLINK, Fremont *Also called Memorial Hospital* ***(G-11212)***
Memorial Hospital Union County...937 644-1001
660 London Ave Marysville (43040) ***(G-13640)***
Memorial Hospital Union County (PA)...937 644-6115
500 London Ave Marysville (43040) ***(G-13641)***
Memorial Tournament, The, Dublin *Also called Muirfield Village Golf Club* ***(G-10402)***
Menard Inc...937 630-3550
8480 Springboro Pike Miamisburg (45342) ***(G-14317)***
Menard Inc...513 737-2204
2865 Princeton Rd Fairfield Township (45011) ***(G-10934)***
Menard Inc...614 501-1654
6800 E Broad St Columbus (43213) ***(G-8146)***
Menards Contractor Sales...419 726-4029
1415 E Alexis Rd Toledo (43612) ***(G-18050)***
Mended Reeds Home...740 533-1883
803 Vernon St Ironton (45638) ***(G-12298)***
Mendelson Electronics Co Inc...937 461-3525
340 E 1st St Dayton (45402) ***(G-9718)***
Mendelson Liquidation Outlet, Dayton *Also called Mendelson Electronics Co Inc* ***(G-9718)***
Mendelson Realty Ltd...937 461-3525
340 E 1st St Dayton (45402) ***(G-9719)***
Menke Bros Construction Co...419 286-2086
24266 Road T Delphos (45833) ***(G-10147)***
Menlo Logistics Inc...740 963-1154
107 Heritage Dr Etna (43062) ***(G-10736)***
Mennonite Memorial Home Inc (PA)...419 358-1015
410 W Elm St Bluffton (45817) ***(G-1734)***

Mennonite Memorial Home Inc....419 358-7654
700 Maple Crest Ct Bluffton (45817) *(G-1735)*
Menorah Park Center For Senio (PA)....216 831-6500
27100 Cedar Rd Cleveland (44122) *(G-6024)*
Menorah Park Center For Senio....216 831-6515
27200 Cedar Rd Beachwood (44122) *(G-1100)*
Menorah Park Center For Senio....330 867-2143
960 Graham Rd 3 Cuyahoga Falls (44221) *(G-9208)*
Mental Health & Recovery Ctr (PA)....937 383-3031
953 S South St Wilmington (45177) *(G-19773)*
Mental Health and Addi Serv....419 381-1881
930 S Detroit Ave Toledo (43614) *(G-18051)*
Mental Health and Addi Serv....513 948-3600
1101 Summit Rd Cincinnati (45237) *(G-4055)*
Mental Health and Addi Serv....614 752-0333
2200 W Broad St Columbus (43223) *(G-8147)*
Mental Health and Addi Serv....330 467-7131
1756 Sagamore Rd Northfield (44067) *(G-15520)*
Mental Health and Addi Serv....614 752-0333
2200 W Broad St Columbus (43223) *(G-8148)*
Mental Health and Addi Serv....740 594-5000
100 Hospital Dr Athens (45701) *(G-801)*
MENTAL HEALTH RECOVERY CENTERS, Lebanon *Also called Communty Mntl Hlth Ctr (G-12596)*
Mental Health Service....937 399-9500
474 N Yellow Springs St Springfield (45504) *(G-17232)*
Mental Health Services (PA)....216 623-6555
1744 Payne Ave Cleveland (44114) *(G-6025)*
Mental Hlth Serv For CL & Mad....937 390-7980
1086 Mound St Springfield (45505) *(G-17233)*
Mental Hlth Serv For CL & Mad (PA)....937 399-9500
474 N Yellow Springs St Springfield (45504) *(G-17234)*
Mental Hlth Serv For CL & Mad....740 852-6256
210 N Main St London (43140) *(G-13003)*
Mental Retardation & Dev, Cincinnati *Also called County of Hamilton (G-3428)*
Mental Retardation & Dev, Cincinnati *Also called County of Hamilton (G-3431)*
Mental Rtrdtion Preble Cnty Bd (PA)....937 456-5891
201 E Lexington Rd Ste A Eaton (45320) *(G-10568)*
Mentor Exempted Vlg Schl Dst....440 974-5260
7060 Hopkins Rd Mentor (44060) *(G-14212)*
Mentor Hsley Rcquet Fitnes CLB, Mentor *Also called Jto Club Corp (G-14200)*
Mentor Lagoons Yacht Club Inc....440 205-3625
8365 Harbor Dr Mentor (44060) *(G-14213)*
Mentor Lumber and Supply Co (PA)....440 255-8814
7180 Center St Mentor (44060) *(G-14214)*
Mentor Medical Offices, Mentor *Also called Kaiser Foundation Hospitals (G-14201)*
Mentor School Service Trnsp, Mentor *Also called Mentor Exempted Vlg Schl Dst (G-14212)*
Mentor Surgery Center Ltd....440 205-5725
9485 Mentor Ave Ste 1 Mentor (44060) *(G-14215)*
Mentor Way Nursing & Rehab Cen....440 255-9309
8881 Schaeffer St Mentor (44060) *(G-14216)*
Mentor Wholesale Lumber, Mentor *Also called Mentor Lumber and Supply Co (G-14214)*
Mentoring Ctr For Centl Ohio, Columbus *Also called Big Broth and Big Siste of Cen (G-7106)*
Menzies Aviation (texas) Inc....216 362-6565
5921 Cargo Rd Cleveland (44135) *(G-6026)*
Merc Acquisitions Inc....216 925-5918
1933 Highland Rd Twinsburg (44087) *(G-18448)*
Mercelina Mobile Home Park....419 586-5407
424 Elmgrove Dr Celina (45822) *(G-2652)*
Mercer (us) Inc....513 632-2600
525 Vine St Ste 1600 Cincinnati (45202) *(G-4056)*
Mercer Cnty Joint Townshp Hosp....419 584-0143
909 E Wayne St Ste 126 Celina (45822) *(G-2653)*
Mercer Cnty Joint Townshp Hosp....419 678-2341
800 W Main St Coldwater (45828) *(G-6833)*
Mercer Cnty Joint Townshp Hosp....419 586-1611
950 S Main St Celina (45822) *(G-2654)*
Mercer County Community Hosp, Coldwater *Also called Mercer Cnty Joint Townshp Hosp (G-6833)*
Mercer Landmark Inc....419 586-7443
417 W Market St Celina (45822) *(G-2655)*
Mercer Residential Services....419 586-4709
334 Godfrey Ave Celina (45822) *(G-2656)*
Mercer Residential Svcs Inc....419 586-4709
420 S Sugar St Celina (45822) *(G-2657)*
Merchandise Inc....513 353-2200
5929 State Rte 128 Miamitown (45041) *(G-14372)*
Merchandising Services Co....866 479-8246
10999 Reed Hartman Hwy Blue Ash (45242) *(G-1639)*
Merchant Data Service Inc....937 847-6585
2275 E Central Ave Miamisburg (45342) *(G-14318)*
Merchants 5 Star Ltd....740 373-0313
18192 State Route 7 Marietta (45750) *(G-13475)*
Merchants National Bank (HQ)....937 393-1134
100 N High St Hillsboro (45133) *(G-11987)*
Merchants Scrty Srvc of Dayton....937 256-9373
2015 Wayne Ave Dayton (45410) *(G-9720)*
Mercier's Tree Experts, South Point *Also called Merciers Incorporated (G-17094)*
Merciers Incorporated....410 590-4181
2393 County Road 1 South Point (45680) *(G-17094)*
Mercy Allen Hospital, Oberlin *Also called Mercy Health (G-15652)*
Mercy Anderson Ambulatory Ctr, Cincinnati *Also called Mercy Health Anderson Hospital (G-4068)*
Mercy Anderson Cancer Center, Cincinnati *Also called Mercy Health Anderson Hospital (G-4069)*
Mercy Clinic, Toledo *Also called Mercy Hlth St Vincent Med LLC (G-18058)*
Mercy Ctr For Hlth Promtn St, Oregon *Also called Sisters of Mercy Amer Reg Comm (G-15750)*
Mercy Franciscan Hosp Mt Airy, Cincinnati *Also called Mercy Health Partners (G-4073)*
Mercy Franciscan Hosp Mt Airy (PA)....513 853-5101
2446 Kipling Ave Cincinnati (45239) *(G-4057)*
Mercy Franciscan Hospital, Cincinnati *Also called Mercy Health Partners (G-4072)*
Mercy Franciscan Senior Netwrk, Cincinnati *Also called Mercy Health Partners (G-4074)*
Mercy Frncscan Hosp Wstn Hills....513 389-5000
3131 Queen City Ave Cincinnati (45238) *(G-4058)*
Mercy Hamilton Hospital....513 603-8600
3000 Mack Rd Fairfield (45014) *(G-10878)*
Mercy Health....937 323-4585
160 Tuttle Rd Springfield (45503) *(G-17235)*
Mercy Health....330 729-1372
250 Debartolo Pl Youngstown (44512) *(G-20280)*
Mercy Health....419 935-0187
218 S Myrtle Ave Willard (44890) *(G-19623)*
Mercy Health....330 792-7418
6252 Mahoning Ave Youngstown (44515) *(G-20281)*
Mercy Health....513 829-1700
2960 Mack Rd Ste 201 Fairfield (45014) *(G-10879)*
Mercy Health....513 686-5392
4750 E Galbraith Rd # 207 Cincinnati (45236) *(G-4059)*
Mercy Health....330 841-4406
8600 E Market St Ste 5 Warren (44484) *(G-18880)*
Mercy Health....513 639-0250
P.O. Box 5203 Cincinnati (45201) *(G-4060)*
Mercy Health....419 492-1300
202 W Mansfield St New Washington (44854) *(G-15135)*
Mercy Health....513 981-5750
3301 Mercy Health Blvd Cincinnati (45211) *(G-4061)*
Mercy Health....440 355-4206
105 Opportunity Way Lagrange (44050) *(G-12460)*
Mercy Health....937 390-1700
211 Northparke Dr Ste 101 Springfield (45503) *(G-17236)*
Mercy Health....937 390-9665
100 W Mccreight Ave # 400 Springfield (45504) *(G-17237)*
Mercy Health....513 248-0100
201 Old Bank Rd Ste 103 Milford (45150) *(G-14538)*
Mercy Health (PA)....513 639-2800
1701 Mercy Health Pl Cincinnati (45237) *(G-4062)*
Mercy Health....513 232-7100
8094 Beechmont Ave Cincinnati (45255) *(G-4063)*
Mercy Health....440 988-1009
578 N Leavitt Rd Amherst (44001) *(G-600)*
Mercy Health....937 653-3445
1300 S Us Highway 68 Urbana (43078) *(G-18595)*
Mercy Health....513 686-8100
9403 Kenwood Rd Ste D203 Blue Ash (45242) *(G-1640)*
Mercy Health....937 390-5515
2615 E High St Springfield (45505) *(G-17238)*
Mercy Health....440 937-4600
1480 Center Rd Ste A Avon (44011) *(G-907)*
Mercy Health....440 336-2239
1120 E Broad St Fl 2 Elyria (44035) *(G-10651)*
Mercy Health....440 327-7372
6115 Emerald St North Ridgeville (44039) *(G-15469)*
Mercy Health....440 775-1881
319 W Lorain St Oberlin (44074) *(G-15650)*
Mercy Health....440 934-8344
5054 Waterford Dr Sheffield Village (44035) *(G-16891)*
Mercy Health....440 967-8713
1607 State Route 50 Ste 6 Vermilion (44089) *(G-18714)*
Mercy Health....513 639-2800
P.O. Box 5203 Cincinnati (45201) *(G-4064)*
Mercy Health....513 233-6736
7500 State Rd Cincinnati (45255) *(G-4065)*
Mercy Health....419 251-2659
2213 Cherry St Toledo (43608) *(G-18052)*
Mercy Health....513 870-7008
3000 Mack Rd Fairfield (45014) *(G-10880)*
Mercy Health....419 264-5800
106 N Wilhelm St Holgate (43527) *(G-12003)*
Mercy Health....440 324-0400
41201 Schadden Rd Elyria (44035) *(G-10652)*
Mercy Health....440 366-5577
39263 Center Ridge Rd North Ridgeville (44039) *(G-15470)*
Mercy Health....419 407-3990
3930 Sunforest Ct Ste 100 Toledo (43623) *(G-18053)*
Mercy Health....440 775-1211
200 W Lorain St Oberlin (44074) *(G-15651)*
Mercy Health....330 746-7211
1044 Belmont Ave Youngstown (44504) *(G-20282)*
Mercy Health....513 585-9600
10475 Reading Rd Ste 209 Cincinnati (45241) *(G-4066)*
Mercy Health....419 475-4666
3425 Executive Pkwy 200nw Toledo (43606) *(G-18054)*

ALPHABETIC

Mercy Health 419 226-9064
959 W North St Lima (45805) *(G-12839)*
Mercy Health 937 328-8700
2501 E High St Springfield (45505) *(G-17239)*
Mercy Health 440 233-1000
3700 Kolbe Rd Lorain (44053) *(G-13060)*
Mercy Health 937 390-5075
2600 N Limestone St Springfield (45503) *(G-17240)*
Mercy Health 440 774-6800
200 W Lorain St Oberlin (44074) *(G-15652)*
Mercy Health 419 476-2124
723 Phillips Ave Ste 201 Toledo (43612) *(G-18055)*
Mercy Health - Springfield C 937 323-5001
148 W North St Springfield (45504) *(G-17241)*
Mercy Health - St 419 696-7465
2600 Navarre Ave Oregon (43616) *(G-15741)*
Mercy Health Anderson Hospital (HQ) 513 624-4500
7500 State Rd Cincinnati (45255) *(G-4067)*
Mercy Health Anderson Hospital 513 624-1950
7520 State Rd Cincinnati (45255) *(G-4068)*
Mercy Health Anderson Hospital 513 624-4025
8000 5 Mile Rd Ste 105 Cincinnati (45230) *(G-4069)*
Mercy Health Cincinnati LLC (HQ) 513 952-5000
1701 Mercy Health Pl Cincinnati (45237) *(G-4070)*
Mercy Health Partners 513 233-2444
8000 5 Mile Rd Ste 350 Cincinnati (45230) *(G-4071)*
Mercy Health Partners 513 389-5000
3301 Mercy Health Blvd # 100 Cincinnati (45211) *(G-4072)*
Mercy Health Partners 513 853-5101
2446 Kipling Ave Cincinnati (45239) *(G-4073)*
Mercy Health Partners 513 451-8900
2950 West Park Dr Ofc Cincinnati (45238) *(G-4074)*
Mercy Health Partners 513 981-5056
4600 Mcauley Pl Ste A Blue Ash (45242) *(G-1641)*
Mercy Health Partners 513 686-4800
4750 E Galbraith Rd # 207 Cincinnati (45236) *(G-4075)*
MERCY HEALTH PARTNERS OF SOUTHWEST OHIO, Cincinnati *Also called Mercy Health Partners (G-4071)*
Mercy Health Sys - Nthrn Reg (HQ) 419 251-1359
2200 Jefferson Ave Toledo (43604) *(G-18056)*
Mercy Health Tiffin Center, Tiffin *Also called Mercy Hospital Tiffin Ohio (G-17685)*
Mercy Health West Park 513 451-8900
2950 West Park Dr Cincinnati (45238) *(G-4076)*
Mercy Health Youngstown LLC 330 729-1420
8401 Market St Youngstown (44512) *(G-20283)*
Mercy Health Youngstown LLC (HQ) 330 746-7211
1044 Belmont Ave Youngstown (44504) *(G-20284)*
Mercy Health Youngstown LLC 330 841-4000
667 Eastland Ave Se Warren (44484) *(G-18881)*
Mercy Healthplexm LLC 513 870-7101
3050 Mack Rd Ste 210 Fairfield (45014) *(G-10881)*
Mercy Hlth St Vincent Med LLC (PA) 419 251-3232
2213 Cherry St Toledo (43608) *(G-18057)*
Mercy Hlth St Vincent Med LLC 419 251-0580
2200 Jefferson Ave Toledo (43604) *(G-18058)*
Mercy Hospital Anderson, Cincinnati *Also called Mercy Health Anderson Hospital (G-4067)*
Mercy Hospital of Defiance 419 782-8444
1400 E 2nd St Defiance (43512) *(G-10048)*
Mercy Hospital of Willard, Willard *Also called Sisters of Mrcy of Wllard Ohio (G-19627)*
Mercy Hospital Tiffin Ohio 419 455-8101
40 Fair Ln Tiffin (44883) *(G-17685)*
Mercy Hospital Tiffin Ohio (PA) 419 455-7000
45 St Lawrence Dr Tiffin (44883) *(G-17686)*
Mercy House Partners, Cincinnati *Also called West Park Retirement Community (G-4836)*
Mercy McAuley Center, Urbana *Also called Community Mercy Hlth Partners (G-18583)*
Mercy Medical Associates 513 686-4840
4750 E Galbraith Rd # 207 Cincinnati (45236) *(G-4077)*
Mercy Medical Center 937 390-5000
1343 N Fountain Blvd Springfield (45504) *(G-17242)*
Mercy Medical Center Inc 330 649-4380
4369 Whipple Ave Nw Canton (44718) *(G-2458)*
Mercy Medical Center Inc (HQ) 330 489-1000
1320 Mercy Dr Nw Canton (44708) *(G-2459)*
Mercy Medical Center Inc 330 627-7641
125 Canton Rd Nw Carrollton (44615) *(G-2623)*
Mercy Medical Center Hospice, Canton *Also called Mercy Medical Center Inc (G-2458)*
Mercy Mem Hosp Urbana Ohio 937 653-5231
904 Scioto St Urbana (43078) *(G-18596)*
Mercy Professional Care 330 832-2280
2859 Aaronwood Ave Ne Massillon (44646) *(G-13839)*
Mercy Siena Woods, Dayton *Also called Community Mercy Foundation (G-9418)*
Mercy Sienna Spring II, Dayton *Also called Community Mercy Foundation (G-9419)*
Mercy St Theresa Center Inc 513 271-7010
7010 Rowan Hill Dr # 200 Cincinnati (45227) *(G-4078)*
Mergis Group, The, Maumee *Also called Randstad Professionals Us LLC (G-13966)*
Mergis Group, The, Blue Ash *Also called Randstad Professionals Us LP (G-1675)*
Meridian Healthcare (PA) 330 797-0070
527 N Meridian Rd Youngstown (44509) *(G-20285)*
Meriprise Financial, Canton *Also called Aeea LLC (G-2229)*
Merit House LLC 419 478-5131
4645 Lewis Ave Toledo (43612) *(G-18059)*
Merit Leasing Co LLC 216 261-9592
3 Merit Dr Cleveland (44143) *(G-6027)*
Meritech Inc 216 459-8333
4577 Hinckley Indus Pkwy Cleveland (44109) *(G-6028)*
Merle-Holden Enterprises Inc (PA) 216 661-6887
5715 Broadview Rd Cleveland (44134) *(G-6029)*
Merlene Enterprises Inc 440 593-6771
734 Harbor St Conneaut (44030) *(G-9044)*
Merrick Body Shop 440 243-6700
520 Front St Berea (44017) *(G-1463)*
Merrick Chevrolet Co 440 878-6700
15303 Royalton Rd Strongsville (44136) *(G-17494)*
Merrill Lynch Pierce Fenner 614 225-3152
65 E State St Ste 2600 Columbus (43215) *(G-8149)*
Merrill Lynch Pierce Fenner 419 891-2091
3292 Levis Commons Blvd Perrysburg (43551) *(G-16032)*
Merrill Lynch Pierce Fenner 740 335-2930
209 E Court St Wshngtn CT Hs (43160) *(G-20031)*
Merrill Lynch Pierce Fenner 614 475-2798
2 Easton Oval Ste 100 Columbus (43219) *(G-8150)*
Merrill Lynch Pierce Fenner 740 452-3681
905 Zane St Ste 3 Zanesville (43701) *(G-20501)*
Merrill Lynch Pierce Fenner 614 225-3197
1155 Scanlon Ln Springfield (45503) *(G-17243)*
Merrill Lynch Pierce Fenner 937 847-4000
10100 Innovation Dr # 300 Miamisburg (45342) *(G-14319)*
Merrill Lynch Pierce Fenner 614 225-3000
4661 Sawmill Rd Ste 200 Columbus (43220) *(G-8151)*
Merrill Lynch Pierce Fenner 330 670-2400
4000 Embassy Pkwy Ste 300 Akron (44333) *(G-338)*
Merrill Lynch Pierce Fenner 216 363-6500
1375 E 9th St Ste 1400 Cleveland (44114) *(G-6030)*
Merrill Lynch Pierce Fenner 330 670-2400
4000 Embassy Pkwy Ste 300 Akron (44333) *(G-339)*
Merrill Lynch Pierce Fenner 614 825-0350
8425 Pulsar Pl Ste 200 Columbus (43240) *(G-6895)*
Merrill Lynch Pierce Fenner 513 579-3600
425 Walnut St Ste 2500 Cincinnati (45202) *(G-4079)*
Merrill Lynch Pierce Fenner 216 292-8000
30195 Chagrin Blvd # 120 Cleveland (44124) *(G-6031)*
Merrill Lynch Pierce Fenner 513 562-2100
312 Walnut St Ste 2400 Cincinnati (45202) *(G-4080)*
Merrill Lynch Pierce Fenner 614 798-4354
555 Metro Pl N Ste 550 Dublin (43017) *(G-10395)*
Merrill Lynch Pierce Fenner 330 497-6600
4678 Munson St Nw Canton (44718) *(G-2460)*
Merrill Lynch Pierce Fenner 330 702-7300
4137 Boardman Canfield Rd Canfield (44406) *(G-2200)*
Merrill Lynch Pierce Fenner 330 702-0535
4137 Boardman Canfield Rd # 201 Canfield (44406) *(G-2201)*
Merrill Lynch Pierce Fenner 330 655-2312
10 W Streetsboro St # 305 Hudson (44236) *(G-12132)*
Merrill Lynch Pierce Fenner 330 670-2400
4000 Embassy Pkwy Ste 210 Bath (44210) *(G-1034)*
Merrill Lynch Business 513 791-5700
5151 Pfeiffer Rd Ste 100 Blue Ash (45242) *(G-1642)*
Merry Maids, Beavercreek *Also called Larue Enterprises Inc (G-1248)*
Merry Moppets Early Learning 614 529-1730
5075 Britton Pkwy Hilliard (43026) *(G-11928)*
Mershon Center For Education, Columbus *Also called Ohio State University (G-8402)*
Mes, Sunbury *Also called Mine Equipment Services LLC (G-17558)*
Mes Inc (PA) 740 201-8112
625 Bear Run Ln Lewis Center (43035) *(G-12694)*
Mesa Industries Inc (PA) 513 321-2950
4027 Eastern Ave Cincinnati (45226) *(G-4081)*
Mesi, South Point *Also called Mike Enyart & Sons Inc (G-17095)*
Mesilla Dialysis LLC 937 484-4600
1430 E Us Highway 36 Urbana (43078) *(G-18597)*
Messer Construction Co 513 672-5000
2495 Langdon Farm Rd Cincinnati (45237) *(G-4082)*
Messer Construction Co (PA) 513 242-1541
643 W Court St Cincinnati (45203) *(G-4083)*
Messer Construction Co 937 291-1300
4801 Hempstead Station Dr A Dayton (45429) *(G-9721)*
Messer Construction Co 614 275-0141
3705 Business Park Dr Columbus (43204) *(G-8152)*
Met Group 330 864-1916
2640 W Market St Fairlawn (44333) *(G-10964)*
MET-ED, Akron *Also called Metropolitan Edison Company (G-342)*
Meta Manufacturing Corporation 513 793-6382
8901 Blue Ash Rd Ste 1 Blue Ash (45242) *(G-1643)*
Metacarta Incorporated 937 458-0345
250 Veronia Dr Ste 300 Springfield (45505) *(G-17244)*
Metal Conversions Ltd (PA) 419 525-0011
849 Crawford Ave N Mansfield (44905) *(G-13343)*
Metal Framing Enterprises LLC 216 433-7080
9005 Bank St Cleveland (44125) *(G-6032)*
Metal Management Ohio Inc 419 782-7791
27063 State Route 281 Defiance (43512) *(G-10049)*
Metal Masters Inc 330 343-3515
125 Williams Dr Nw Dover (44622) *(G-10198)*
Metal Shredders Inc 937 866-0777
5101 Farmersville W Miamisburg (45342) *(G-14320)*

Metalico Akron Inc (HQ) 330 376-1400
943 Hazel St Akron (44305) **(G-340)**

Metalico Annaco, Akron *Also called Metalico Akron Inc* **(G-340)**

Metals USA Crbn Flat Rlled Inc 937 882-6354
5750 Lower Valley Pike Springfield (45502) **(G-17245)**

Metals USA Crbn Flat Rlled Inc (HQ) 330 264-8416
1070 W Liberty St Wooster (44691) **(G-19887)**

Metamateria Partners LLC 614 340-1690
1275 Kinnear Rd Columbus (43212) **(G-8153)**

Metcalf & Eddy Inc 216 910-2000
1375 E 9th St Ste 2801 Cleveland (44114) **(G-6033)**

Metcon Ltd (PA) 937 447-9200
6730 Greentree Rd Bradford (45308) **(G-1807)**

Metcut Research Associates Inc (PA) 513 271-5100
3980 Rosslyn Dr Cincinnati (45209) **(G-4084)**

Methodist Elder Care Services, Reynoldsburg *Also called Wesley Ridge Inc* **(G-16489)**

MetLife, Broadview Heights *Also called Metropolitan Life Insur Co* **(G-1883)**

MetLife, Dublin *Also called Metropolitan Life Insur Co* **(G-10396)**

MetLife Auto HM Insur Agcy Inc (HQ) 815 266-5301
9797 Springboro Pike Dayton (45448) **(G-9722)**

Metro Air, Hilliard *Also called Metro Heating and AC Co* **(G-11929)**

Metro Health Dental Associates 216 778-4982
2500 Metrohealth Dr Cleveland (44109) **(G-6034)**

Metro Health System 330 669-2249
6022 N Honeytown Rd Smithville (44677) **(G-16966)**

Metro Heating and AC Co 614 777-1237
4731 Northwest Pkwy Hilliard (43026) **(G-11929)**

Metro Parks, Westerville *Also called Columbus Frkln Cnty Pk* **(G-19387)**

Metro Recycling, Cincinnati *Also called Charles V Francis Trust* **(G-3230)**

Metro Regional Transit Auth (PA) 330 762-0341
416 Kenmore Blvd Akron (44301) **(G-341)**

Metro Safety and Security LLC 614 792-2770
5785 Emporium Sq Columbus (43231) **(G-8154)**

Metrohealth Beachwood Hlth Ctr, Beachwood *Also called Metrohealth System* **(G-1101)**

Metrohealth Broadway Hlth Ctr, Cleveland *Also called Metrohealth System* **(G-6041)**

Metrohealth Buckeye Health Ctr, Cleveland *Also called Metrohealth System* **(G-6039)**

Metrohealth Dept of Dentistry 216 778-4739
2500 Metrohealth Dr Cleveland (44109) **(G-6035)**

Metrohealth Medical Center (PA) 216 778-7800
2500 Metrohealth Dr Cleveland (44109) **(G-6036)**

Metrohealth Premier Health Ctr, Westlake *Also called Metrohealth System* **(G-19515)**

Metrohealth System 216 957-5000
3838 W 150th St Cleveland (44111) **(G-6037)**

Metrohealth System (PA) 216 398-6000
2500 Metrohealth Dr Cleveland (44109) **(G-6038)**

Metrohealth System 216 957-4000
2816 E 116th St Cleveland (44120) **(G-6039)**

Metrohealth System 216 778-8446
2500 Metrohealth Dr Cleveland (44109) **(G-6040)**

Metrohealth System 216 957-1500
6835 Broadway Ave Cleveland (44105) **(G-6041)**

Metrohealth System 216 778-3867
2500 Metrohealth Dr Cleveland (44109) **(G-6042)**

Metrohealth System 216 765-0733
3609 Park East Dr Ste 300 Beachwood (44122) **(G-1101)**

Metrohealth System 216 957-2100
4229 Pearl Rd Cleveland (44109) **(G-6043)**

Metrohealth System 216 957-3200
25200 Center Ridge Rd Westlake (44145) **(G-19515)**

Metrohealth System 216 591-0523
29125 Chagrin Blvd # 110 Beachwood (44122) **(G-1102)**

Metrohealth System The, Cleveland *Also called Metrohealth Medical Center* **(G-6036)**

Metrohealth West Park Hlth Ctr, Cleveland *Also called Metrohealth System* **(G-6037)**

Metrohlth Pepper Pike Hlth Ctr, Beachwood *Also called Metrohealth System* **(G-1102)**

Metropltan Vterinary Med Group 330 253-2544
1053 S Clvland Msslion Rd Copley (44321) **(G-9061)**

Metropolitan Armored Car, Toledo *Also called Garda CL Great Lakes Inc* **(G-17907)**

Metropolitan Cleaners, Dayton *Also called Rentz Corp* **(G-9848)**

Metropolitan Edison Company (HQ) 800 736-3402
76 S Main St Akron (44308) **(G-342)**

Metropolitan Envmtl Svcs Inc 614 771-1881
5055 Nike Dr Hilliard (43026) **(G-11930)**

Metropolitan Family Care, Reynoldsburg *Also called Metropolitian Family Care Inc* **(G-16469)**

Metropolitan Life Insur Co 440 746-8699
9200 S Hills Blvd Ste 100 Broadview Heights (44147) **(G-1883)**

Metropolitan Life Insur Co 614 792-1463
5600 Blazer Pkwy Ste 100 Dublin (43017) **(G-10396)**

Metropolitan Pool Service Co 216 741-9451
3427 Brookpark Rd Parma (44134) **(G-15910)**

Metropolitan Pools, Parma *Also called Metropolitan Pool Service Co* **(G-15910)**

Metropolitan Security Svcs Inc 216 298-4076
801 W Superior Ave Cleveland (44113) **(G-6044)**

Metropolitan Security Svcs Inc 330 253-6459
2 S Main St Akron (44308) **(G-343)**

Metropolitan Veterinary Hosp, Copley *Also called Metropltan Vterinary Med Group* **(G-9061)**

Metropolitan YMCA, Englewood *Also called Young Mens Christian Assoc* **(G-10725)**

Metropolitian Family Care Inc 614 237-1067
7094 E Main St Reynoldsburg (43068) **(G-16469)**

Metzenbaum Sheltered Inds 440 729-1919
8090 Cedar Rd Chesterland (44026) **(G-2800)**

Meyer Decorative Surfaces USA (HQ) 800 776-3900
300 Executive Pkwy W # 100 Hudson (44236) **(G-12133)**

Meyer Hill Lynch Corporation 419 897-9797
1771 Indian Wood Cir Maumee (43537) **(G-13947)**

Meyerpt, Hudson *Also called Wbc Group LLC* **(G-12150)**

Meyers + Associates Arch LLC 614 221-9433
232 N 3rd St Ste 300 Columbus (43215) **(G-8155)**

Meyers Ldscp Svcs & Nurs Inc 614 210-1194
6081 Columbus Pike Lewis Center (43035) **(G-12695)**

Mff Somerset LLc 216 752-5600
3550 Northfield Rd Shaker Heights (44122) **(G-16863)**

Mfh Inc (PA) 937 435-4701
241 E Alex Bell Rd Dayton (45459) **(G-9723)**

Mfh Inc 937 435-4701
241 E Alex Bell Rd Dayton (45459) **(G-9724)**

Mgc, Dublin *Also called Midwest Gymnstics Cheerleading* **(G-10398)**

MGF Sourcing Us LLC (HQ) 614 904-3300
4200 Regent St Ste 205 Columbus (43219) **(G-8156)**

MGM Health Care Winchstr, Canal Winchester *Also called Kindred Nursing Centers E LLC* **(G-2164)**

Mh Equipment Company 937 890-6800
3000 Production Ct Dayton (45414) **(G-9725)**

Mh Equipment Company 614 871-1571
2055 Hardy Parkway St Grove City (43123) **(G-11580)**

Mh Equipment Company 513 681-2200
2650 Spring Grove Ave Cincinnati (45214) **(G-4085)**

MH Logistics Corp 330 425-2476
1892 Georgetown Rd Hudson (44236) **(G-12134)**

Mhrs Board of Stark County, Canton *Also called County of Stark* **(G-2325)**

MI, Miamitown *Also called Merchandise Inc* **(G-14372)**

MI - De - Con Inc 740 532-2277
3331 S 3rd St Ironton (45638) **(G-12299)**

Miami Cnty Cmnty Action Cuncil 937 335-7921
1695 Troy Sidney Rd Troy (45373) **(G-18363)**

Miami Co Highway Dept, Troy *Also called County of Miami* **(G-18352)**

Miami Co YMCA Child Care 937 778-5241
325 W Ash St Piqua (45356) **(G-16152)**

Miami Corporation (PA) 513 451-6700
720 Anderson Ferry Rd Cincinnati (45238) **(G-4086)**

Miami County Childrens Svcs Bd 937 335-4103
510 W Water St Ste 210 Troy (45373) **(G-18364)**

Miami County Park District 937 335-6273
2645 E State Route 41 Troy (45373) **(G-18365)**

Miami Industrial Trucks Inc (PA) 937 293-4194
2830 E River Rd Moraine (45439) **(G-14805)**

Miami Industrial Trucks Inc 419 424-0042
130 Stanford Pkwy Findlay (45840) **(G-11066)**

Miami Metropolitan Hsing Auth, Troy *Also called Miami Cnty Cmnty Action Cuncil* **(G-18363)**

Miami Rifle Pistol Club 513 732-9943
P.O. Box 235 Milford (45150) **(G-14539)**

Miami University 513 529-2232
801 S Patterson Ave Oxford (45056) **(G-15819)**

Miami University 513 727-3200
4200 E University Blvd Middletown (45042) **(G-14435)**

Miami University 513 529-8380
410 E Spring St Oxford (45056) **(G-15820)**

Miami University 513 529-6911
Fisher Dr Oxford (45056) **(G-15821)**

Miami University 513 529-1251
701 E Spring St Ste 117 Oxford (45056) **(G-15822)**

Miami University 513 529-1230
725 E Chestnut St Oxford (45056) **(G-15823)**

Miami University-Middletown, Middletown *Also called Miami University* **(G-14435)**

Miami Valley, Dayton *Also called Premier Health Partners* **(G-9820)**

Miami Valley Bekins Inc 937 278-4296
5941 Milo Rd Dayton (45414) **(G-9726)**

Miami Valley Broadcasting Corp (HQ) 937 259-2111
1611 S Main St Dayton (45409) **(G-9727)**

Miami Valley Cap, Dayton *Also called Miami Valley Community Action* **(G-9728)**

Miami Valley Community Action (PA) 937 222-1009
719 S Main St Dayton (45402) **(G-9728)**

Miami Valley Community Action 937 456-2800
308 Eaton Lewisburg Rd Eaton (45320) **(G-10569)**

Miami Valley Community Action 937 548-8143
1469 Sweitzer St Greenville (45331) **(G-11514)**

Miami Valley Family Care Ctr, Dayton *Also called Catholic Social Svc Miami Vly* **(G-9390)**

Miami Valley Family Care Ctr 937 268-0336
4100 W 3rd St Dayton (45428) **(G-9729)**

Miami Valley Gaming & Racg LLC 513 934-7070
6000 W State Route 63 Lebanon (45036) **(G-12628)**

Miami Valley Golf Club (PA) 937 278-7381
3311 Salem Ave Dayton (45406) **(G-9730)**

Miami Valley Hospital 937 436-5200
2400 Miami Valley Dr Dayton (45459) **(G-9731)**

Miami Valley Hospital 937 208-7065
211 Kenbrook Dr Vandalia (45377) **(G-18689)**

Miami Valley Hospital (HQ) 937 208-8000
1 Wyoming St Dayton (45409) **(G-9732)**

ALPHABETIC

(PA)=Parent Co (HQ)=Headquarters (DH)=Div Headquarters

2018 Harris Ohio Services Directory

1259

Miami Valley Hospital....937 224-3916
28 Hill St Dayton (45409) ***(G-9733)***
Miami Valley Hospitalist Group....937 208-8394
30 E Apple St Ste 3300 Dayton (45409) ***(G-9734)***
Miami Valley Hsing Assn I Inc....937 263-4449
907 W 5th St Dayton (45402) ***(G-9735)***
Miami Valley Insurance Assoc, Dayton *Also called Norman-Spencer Agency Inc* ***(G-9775)***
Miami Valley Intl Trcks Inc....513 733-8500
11775 Highway Dr Ste D Cincinnati (45241) ***(G-4087)***
Miami Valley Memory Grdns Assn (HQ)....937 885-7779
1639 E Lytle 5 Points Rd Dayton (45458) ***(G-9736)***
Miami Valley Moving & Storage, Dayton *Also called Miami Valley Bekins Inc* ***(G-9726)***
Miami Valley Regional Plg Comm....937 223-6323
10 N Ludlow St Ste 700 Dayton (45402) ***(G-9737)***
Miami Valley School....937 434-4444
5151 Denise Dr Dayton (45429) ***(G-9738)***
Miami Valley South Campus, Dayton *Also called Miami Valley Hospital* ***(G-9731)***
Miami Valley Steel Service Inc....937 773-7127
201 Fox Dr Piqua (45356) ***(G-16153)***
Miami Valley Urgent Care....937 252-2000
6229 Troy Pike Dayton (45424) ***(G-9739)***
Miami View Head Start, Dayton *Also called Miami Vly Child Dev Ctrs Inc* ***(G-9741)***
Miami Vly Child Dev Ctrs Inc (PA)....937 226-5664
215 Horace St Dayton (45402) ***(G-9740)***
Miami Vly Child Dev Ctrs Inc....937 325-2559
1450 S Yellow Springs St Springfield (45506) ***(G-17246)***
Miami Vly Child Dev Ctrs Inc....937 228-1644
215 Horace St Dayton (45402) ***(G-9741)***
Miami Vly Fandom For Literacy....513 933-0452
222 S Mechanic St Lebanon (45036) ***(G-12629)***
Miami Vly Hsing Oprtunties Inc (PA)....937 263-4449
907 W 5th St Dayton (45402) ***(G-9742)***
Miami Vly Jvnile Rhblttion Ctr....937 562-4000
2100 Greene Way Blvd Xenia (45385) ***(G-20070)***
Miami-Luken Inc (PA)....937 743-7775
265 S Pioneer Blvd Springboro (45066) ***(G-17128)***
Miamisburg City School Dst....937 866-1283
200 N 12th St Miamisburg (45342) ***(G-14321)***
Miamisburg Dialysis, Miamisburg *Also called Morro Dialysis LLC* ***(G-14324)***
Miamisburg Family Practice....937 866-2494
415 Byers Rd Ste 300 Miamisburg (45342) ***(G-14322)***
Miamisburg Pk Recreation Dept, Miamisburg *Also called City of Miamisburg* ***(G-14283)***
Miamisburg Transportation Dept, Miamisburg *Also called Miamisburg City School Dst* ***(G-14321)***
Miarer Transportation Inc....419 665-2334
2930 County Road 69 Gibsonburg (43431) ***(G-11403)***
Miceli Dairy Products Co (PA)....216 791-6222
2721 E 90th St Cleveland (44104) ***(G-6045)***
Micha Ltd....740 653-6464
144 E Main St Lancaster (43130) ***(G-12557)***
Michael A Garcia Salon....614 235-1605
2440 E Main St Columbus (43209) ***(G-8157)***
Michael Baker Intl Inc....330 453-3110
101 Cleveland Ave Nw # 106 Canton (44702) ***(G-2461)***
Michael Baker Intl Inc....412 269-6300
1111 Superior Ave E # 2300 Cleveland (44114) ***(G-6046)***
Michael Baker Intl Inc....614 418-1773
250 West St Ste 420 Columbus (43215) ***(G-8158)***
Michael Benza and Assoc Inc....440 526-4206
6860 W Snowville Rd # 100 Brecksville (44141) ***(G-1834)***
Michael Brothers Inc....419 332-5716
3728 Hayes Ave Fremont (43420) ***(G-11213)***
Michael Christopher Salon Inc....440 449-0999
6255 Wilson Mills Rd Cleveland (44143) ***(G-6047)***
Michael G Lawley....513 793-3933
8099 Cornell Rd Cincinnati (45249) ***(G-4088)***
Michael Schuster Associates....513 241-5666
316 W 4th St Ste 600 Cincinnati (45202) ***(G-4089)***
Michael T Lee Dvm....330 722-5076
1060 S Court St Medina (44256) ***(G-14105)***
Michael's Bakery & Deli, Cleveland *Also called Michaels Bakery Inc* ***(G-6048)***
Michael's Cafe & Bakery, Toledo *Also called Michaels Gourmet Catering* ***(G-18060)***
Michaels Inc....440 357-0384
5783 Heisley Rd Mentor (44060) ***(G-14217)***
Michaels Bakery Inc....216 351-7530
4478 Broadview Rd Cleveland (44109) ***(G-6048)***
Michaels For Hair, Dayton *Also called Mfh Inc* ***(G-9724)***
Michaels Gourmet Catering....419 698-2988
101 Main St Ste 7 Toledo (43605) ***(G-18060)***
Michel Tires Plus 227550, Cincinnati *Also called Bridgestone Ret Operations LLC* ***(G-3132)***
Michel Tires Plus 227553, Cincinnati *Also called Bridgestone Ret Operations LLC* ***(G-3134)***
Michel Tires Plus 227554, Cincinnati *Also called Bridgestone Ret Operations LLC* ***(G-3133)***
Michel Tires Plus 227571, Celina *Also called Bridgestone Ret Operations LLC* ***(G-2636)***
Michel Tires Plus 227574, Northwood *Also called Bridgestone Ret Operations LLC* ***(G-15527)***
Michel Tires Plus 227925, Harrison *Also called Bridgestone Ret Operations LLC* ***(G-11792)***
Mickis Creative Options Inc....419 526-4254
327 Park Ave W Mansfield (44906) ***(G-13344)***
Micnan Inc (PA)....330 920-6200
3365 Cavalier Trl Cuyahoga Falls (44224) ***(G-9209)***
Micro Center, Hilliard *Also called Micro Electronics Inc* ***(G-11932)***
Micro Center, Cincinnati *Also called Micro Electronics Inc* ***(G-4090)***
Micro Center Inc....614 850-3000
4119 Leap Rd Hilliard (43026) ***(G-11931)***
Micro Center Online Inc....614 326-8500
747 Bethel Rd Columbus (43214) ***(G-8159)***
Micro Construction LLC....740 862-0751
8675 Lncster Newark Rd Ne Baltimore (43105) ***(G-948)***
Micro Electronics Inc....614 334-1430
2701 Charter St Ste B Columbus (43228) ***(G-8160)***
Micro Electronics Inc (PA)....614 850-3000
4119 Leap Rd Hilliard (43026) ***(G-11932)***
Micro Electronics Inc....614 850-3500
4055 Leap Rd Hilliard (43026) ***(G-11933)***
Micro Electronics Inc....440 449-7000
1349 Som Center Rd Cleveland (44124) ***(G-6049)***
Micro Electronics Inc....513 782-8500
11755 Mosteller Rd Rear Cincinnati (45241) ***(G-4090)***
Micro Industries Corporation (PA)....740 548-7878
8399 Green Meadows Dr N Westerville (43081) ***(G-19424)***
Micro Products Co Inc....440 943-0258
26653 Curtiss Wright Pkwy Willoughby Hills (44092) ***(G-19732)***
Micro Roll Off Containers, Baltimore *Also called Micro Construction LLC* ***(G-948)***
Micro Thinner, Hilliard *Also called Micro Electronics Inc* ***(G-11933)***
Microanalysis Society Inc....614 256-8063
3405 Scioto Run Blvd Hilliard (43026) ***(G-11934)***
Microcenter DC, Columbus *Also called Micro Electronics Inc* ***(G-8160)***
Microman Inc (PA)....614 923-8000
4393 Tuller Rd Ste A Dublin (43017) ***(G-10397)***
Microplex Inc....330 498-0600
7568 Whipple Ave Nw North Canton (44720) ***(G-15353)***
Micros Retail, Cleveland *Also called Datavantage Corporation* ***(G-5464)***
Microsoft Corporation....614 719-5900
8800 Lyra Dr Ste 400 Columbus (43240) ***(G-6896)***
Microsoft Corporation....216 986-1440
6050 Oak Tree Blvd # 300 Cleveland (44131) ***(G-6050)***
Microsoft Corporation....513 339-2800
4605 Duke Dr Ste 800 Mason (45040) ***(G-13739)***
Microwave Leasing Services LLC....614 308-5433
2860 Fisher Rd Columbus (43204) ***(G-8161)***
Mid America Glass Block, Cleveland *Also called Cleveland Glass Block Inc* ***(G-5316)***
Mid America Trucking Company....216 447-0814
5585 Canal Rd Cleveland (44125) ***(G-6051)***
Mid Atlantic Stor Systems Inc....740 335-2019
1551 Robinson Rd Se Wshngtn CT Hs (43160) ***(G-20032)***
Mid County Ems....419 898-9366
222 W Washington St Oak Harbor (43449) ***(G-15612)***
Mid Ohio Dialysis, Ontario *Also called Wallowa Dialysis LLC* ***(G-15719)***
Mid Ohio Emergency Svcs LLC....614 566-5070
3525 Olentangy Blvd # 4330 Columbus (43214) ***(G-8162)***
Mid Ohio Employment Services (PA)....419 747-5466
2282 Village Mall Dr # 2 Ontario (44906) ***(G-15703)***
Mid Ohio Home Health Ltd....419 529-3883
1332 W 4th St Ontario (44906) ***(G-15704)***
Mid Ohio Vly Bulk Trnspt Inc....740 373-2481
16380 State Route 7 Marietta (45750) ***(G-13476)***
Mid State Systems Inc....740 928-1115
9455 Lancaster Rd Hebron (43025) ***(G-11853)***
Mid-America Gutters Inc (PA)....513 671-4000
862 E Crescentville Rd West Chester (45246) ***(G-19215)***
Mid-America Stainless, Cleveland *Also called Mid-America Steel Corp* ***(G-6052)***
Mid-America Steel Corp....800 282-3466
20900 Saint Clair Ave Cleveland (44117) ***(G-6052)***
Mid-American Clg Contrs Inc....937 859-6222
360 Gargrave Rd Ste E Dayton (45449) ***(G-9743)***
Mid-American Clg Contrs Inc....419 429-6222
1648 Tiffin Ave Findlay (45840) ***(G-11067)***
Mid-American Clg Contrs Inc (PA)....419 229-3899
447 N Elizabeth St Lima (45801) ***(G-12840)***
Mid-American Clg Contrs Inc....614 291-7170
1046 King Ave Columbus (43212) ***(G-8163)***
Mid-Amrica Cnsulting Group Inc....216 432-6925
3700 Euclid Ave 2 Cleveland (44115) ***(G-6053)***
Mid-Continent Construction Co....440 439-6100
7235 Free Ave Ste A Oakwood Village (44146) ***(G-15631)***
Mid-Ohio Air Conditioning....614 291-4664
456 E 5th Ave Columbus (43201) ***(G-8164)***
Mid-Ohio Contracting Inc....330 343-2925
1817 Horns Ln Nw Dover (44622) ***(G-10199)***
Mid-Ohio Development Corp (PA)....614 836-0606
4393 Arbor Lake Dr Groveport (43125) ***(G-11657)***
Mid-Ohio Electric Co....614 274-8000
1170 Mckinley Ave Columbus (43222) ***(G-8165)***
Mid-Ohio Energy Cooperative....419 568-5321
1210 W Lima St Kenton (43326) ***(G-12421)***
Mid-Ohio Foodbank....614 317-9400
3960 Brookham Dr Grove City (43123) ***(G-11581)***
Mid-Ohio Forklifts Inc....330 633-1230
1336 Home Ave Akron (44310) ***(G-344)***
Mid-Ohio Harley-Davidson Inc....937 322-3590
2100 Quality Ln Springfield (45505) ***(G-17247)***
Mid-Ohio Heart Clinic Inc....419 524-8151
680 Park Ave W Ste 100 Mansfield (44906) ***(G-13345)***

ALPHABETIC SECTION

Mid-Ohio Mechanical Inc 740 587-3362
1844 Lancaster Rd Granville (43023) *(G-11470)*
Mid-Ohio Pdiatrics Adolescents 614 899-0000
595 Cpland Mill Rd Ste 2a Westerville (43081) *(G-19425)*
Mid-Ohio Pipeline Company Inc 419 884-3772
2270 Eckert Rd Mansfield (44904) *(G-13346)*
Mid-Ohio Pipeline Services, Mansfield Also called Mid-Ohio Pipeline Company Inc *(G-13346)*
Mid-Ohio Properties, Groveport Also called Mid-Ohio Development Corp *(G-11657)*
Mid-Ohio Psychlogical Svcs Inc (PA) 740 687-0042
624 E Main St Lancaster (43130) *(G-12558)*
Mid-Ohio Valley Lime Inc (PA) 740 373-1006
State Rt 7 S Marietta (45750) *(G-13477)*
Mid-Ohio Wines Inc 440 989-1011
5901 Baumhart Rd Lorain (44053) *(G-13061)*
Mid-State Bolt and Nut Co Inc (PA) 614 253-8631
1575 Alum Creek Dr Columbus (43209) *(G-8166)*
Mid-West Materials Inc 440 259-5200
3687 Shepard Rd Perry (44081) *(G-15965)*
Mid-Western Childrens Home 513 877-2141
4585 Long Spurling Rd Pleasant Plain (45162) *(G-16215)*
Midas Muffler, Toledo Also called Dayton-Dixie Mufflers Inc *(G-17846)*
Middle Bass Ferry Company, The, Put In Bay Also called Island Service Company *(G-16368)*
Middletown City Divison Fire 513 425-7996
2300 Roosevelt Blvd Middletown (45044) *(G-14436)*
Middletown Innkeepers Inc 513 942-3440
430 Kolb Dr Fairfield (45014) *(G-10882)*
Middletown School Vhcl Svc Ctr 513 420-4568
2951 Cincinnati Dayton Rd Middletown (45044) *(G-14437)*
Middltown Area Senior Citizens 513 423-1734
3907 Central Ave Middletown (45044) *(G-14438)*
Middltown Crdvscular Assoc Inc 513 217-6400
103 Mcknight Dr Ste A Middletown (45044) *(G-14439)*
Middough Inc (PA) 216 367-6000
1901 E 13th St Ste 400 Cleveland (44114) *(G-6054)*
Mideast Baptist Conference 440 834-8984
14282 Butternut Rd Burton (44021) *(G-2064)*
Midfitz Inc 216 663-8816
23800 Corbin Dr Cleveland (44128) *(G-6055)*
Midland Atlantic Prpts LLC (PA) 513 792-5000
8044 Montgomery Rd # 710 Cincinnati (45236) *(G-4091)*
Midland Hardware Company (PA) 216 228-7721
1521 W 117th St Cleveland (44107) *(G-6056)*
Midland Title Security Inc (HQ) 216 241-6045
1111 Superior Ave E # 700 Cleveland (44114) *(G-6057)*
Midland-Guardian Co (HQ) 513 943-7100
7000 Midland Blvd Amelia (45102) *(G-582)*
Midlands Millroom Supply Inc 330 453-9100
1911 36th St Ne Canton (44705) *(G-2462)*
Midohio Crdiolgy Vascular Cons (PA) 614 262-6772
3705 Olentangy River Rd # 100 Columbus (43214) *(G-8167)*
MIDOHIO ENERGY COOPERATIVE, Kenton Also called Mid-Ohio Energy Cooperative *(G-12421)*
Midpark Animal Hospital 216 362-6622
6611 Smith Rd Cleveland (44130) *(G-6058)*
Midusa Credit Union (PA) 513 420-8640
1201 Crawford St Middletown (45044) *(G-14440)*
Midusa Credit Union 513 420-8640
3600 Towne Blvd Ste A Middletown (45005) *(G-14482)*
Midway Bowling Lanes Inc 330 762-7477
1925 20th St Cuyahoga Falls (44223) *(G-9210)*
Midway Delivery Service 216 391-0700
4699 Commerce Ave Cleveland (44103) *(G-6059)*
Midway Garage Inc 740 345-0699
140 Everett Ave Newark (43055) *(G-15207)*
Midway Mall Merchants Assoc 440 244-1245
3343 Midway Mall Elyria (44035) *(G-10653)*
Midway Realty Company 440 324-2404
1800 Lorain Blvd Elyria (44035) *(G-10654)*
Midwest Allergy Associates (PA) 614 846-5944
8080 Ravines Edge Ct # 100 Columbus (43235) *(G-8168)*
Midwest Behavioral Care Ltd 937 454-0092
3821 Little York Rd Dayton (45414) *(G-9744)*
Midwest Church Cnstr Ltd 419 874-0838
634 Eckel Rd Ste A Perrysburg (43551) *(G-16033)*
Midwest Cmnty Federal Cr Un 419 782-9856
1481 Deerwood Dr Defiance (43512) *(G-10050)*
Midwest Cmnty Hlth Assoc Inc (HQ) 419 633-4034
442 W High St Ste 3 Bryan (43506) *(G-2012)*
Midwest Communications Inc 800 229-4756
4721 Eagle St Nw North Canton (44720) *(G-15354)*
Midwest Contracting Inc 419 866-4560
1428 Albon Rd Holland (43528) *(G-12037)*
Midwest Curtainwalls Inc 216 641-7900
5171 Grant Ave Cleveland (44125) *(G-6060)*
Midwest Digital Inc 330 966-4744
4721 Eagle St Nw North Canton (44720) *(G-15355)*
Midwest Division - Brunswick, Brunswick Also called W W Williams Company LLC *(G-1995)*
Midwest East Division, Cincinnati Also called Intren Inc *(G-3841)*
Midwest Emergency Services LLC 586 294-2700
3585 Ridge Park Dr Fairlawn (44333) *(G-10965)*
Midwest Environmental Inc 419 382-9200
28757 Glenwood Rd Perrysburg (43551) *(G-16034)*
Midwest Equipment Co 216 441-1400
9800 Broadway Ave Cleveland (44125) *(G-6061)*
Midwest Express Inc (HQ) 937 642-0335
11590 Township Road 298 East Liberty (43319) *(G-10510)*
Midwest Eye Center, Cincinnati Also called David M Schneider MD Inc *(G-2912)*
Midwest Fairborn Dialysis, Fairborn Also called Manzano Dialysis LLC *(G-10802)*
Midwest Fresh Foods Inc 614 469-1492
38 N Glenwood Ave Columbus (43222) *(G-8169)*
Midwest Gymnstics Cheerleading 614 764-0775
9361 Pratolino Villa Dr Dublin (43016) *(G-10398)*
Midwest Health Services Inc 330 828-0779
107 Tommy Henrich Dr Nw Massillon (44647) *(G-13840)*
Midwest Heating & Cooling, Columbus Also called Midwest Roofing & Furnace Co *(G-8172)*
MIDWEST HOME INFUSION, Xenia Also called Greene Oaks *(G-20060)*
Midwest Industrial Supply Inc 800 321-0699
1929 E Manhattan Blvd Toledo (43608) *(G-18061)*
Midwest Iron and Metal Co 937 222-5992
461 Homestead Ave Dayton (45417) *(G-9745)*
Midwest Laundry Inc 513 563-5560
10110 Cncnnati Dyton Pike Cincinnati (45241) *(G-4092)*
Midwest Liquidators Inc 614 433-7355
6827 N High St Ste 109 Worthington (43085) *(G-19977)*
Midwest Logistics Systems 419 584-1414
8779 State Route 703 Celina (45822) *(G-2658)*
Midwest Mfg Solutions LLC 513 381-7200
5474 Spellmire Dr West Chester (45246) *(G-19216)*
Midwest Mosaic Inc 419 377-3894
2268 Robinwood Ave Toledo (43620) *(G-18062)*
Midwest Motor Supply Co (PA) 800 233-1294
4800 Roberts Rd Columbus (43228) *(G-8170)*
Midwest Motors Inc 330 758-5800
7871 Market St Youngstown (44512) *(G-20286)*
Midwest Optoelectronics LLC 419 724-0565
2801 W Bancroft St 230 Toledo (43606) *(G-18063)*
Midwest Painting, Dayton Also called Muha Construction Inc *(G-9760)*
Midwest Physcans Ansthsia Svcs 614 884-0641
5151 Reed Rd Ste 225c Columbus (43220) *(G-8171)*
Midwest Physicians, Columbus Also called Change Healthcare Tech Enabled *(G-7252)*
Midwest Poultry Services Lp 419 375-4417
374 New Wston Ft Lrmie Rd Fort Recovery (45846) *(G-11119)*
Midwest Rehab Inc 419 238-3405
118 E Highland Ave Ada (45810) *(G-6)*
Midwest Reinforcing Contrs 937 390-8998
1839 N Fountain Blvd Springfield (45504) *(G-17248)*
Midwest Retina Inc 614 233-9500
2935 Maple Ave Zanesville (43701) *(G-20502)*
Midwest Roofing & Furnace Co 614 252-5241
646 S Nelson Rd Columbus (43205) *(G-8172)*
Midwest Seafood Inc (PA) 937 746-8856
475 Victory Ln Springboro (45066) *(G-17129)*
Midwest Service Center, Grove City Also called Safety Today Inc *(G-11595)*
Midwest Tape LLC 419 868-9370
1417 Timber Wolf Dr Holland (43528) *(G-12038)*
Midwest Trailer Sales & Svc 513 772-2818
3000 Crescentville Rd West Chester (45069) *(G-19119)*
Midwest Trmnals Tledo Intl Inc 419 698-8171
3518 Saint Lawrence Dr Toledo (43605) *(G-18064)*
Midwest Ultrasound Inc 513 936-0444
237 Wlliam Howard Taft Rd Cincinnati (45219) *(G-4093)*
Midwest Ultrasound Inc (PA) 513 248-8885
50 W Techne Center Dr D Milford (45150) *(G-14540)*
Midwest Urbana Dialysis, Urbana Also called Mesilla Dialysis LLC *(G-18597)*
Midwestern Auto Group, Dublin Also called Brentlinger Enterprises *(G-10267)*
Midwestern Plumbing Service 513 753-0050
3984 Bach Buxton Rd Cincinnati (45202) *(G-4094)*
Mie, Marietta Also called Marietta Industrial Entps Inc *(G-13470)*
Miencorp Inc 330 978-8511
706 Robbins Ave Niles (44446) *(G-15296)*
Migrant Head Start 937 846-0699
476 N Dayton Lakeview Rd New Carlisle (45344) *(G-15028)*
Mike Castrucci Ford 513 831-7010
1020 State Route 28 Milford (45150) *(G-14541)*
Mike Coates Cnstr Co Inc 330 652-0190
800 Summit Ave Niles (44446) *(G-15297)*
Mike Enyart & Sons Inc 740 523-0235
77 Private Drive 615 South Point (45680) *(G-17095)*
Mike George Excavating 419 855-4147
24366 W Hellwig Rd Genoa (43430) *(G-11382)*
Mike Morris 330 767-4122
505 Wabash Ave N Brewster (44613) *(G-1856)*
Mike Pusateri Excavating Inc 330 385-5221
16363 Saint Clair Ave East Liverpool (43920) *(G-10525)*
Mike Rennie 513 830-0020
300 E Bus Way Ste 270 Dayton (45401) *(G-9746)*
Mike Sikora Realty Inc 440 255-7777
7340 Center St Mentor (44060) *(G-14218)*
Mike Ward Landscaping Inc 513 683-6436
424 E Us Highway 22 And 3 Maineville (45039) *(G-13244)*
Mike's Truck & Trailer, West Chester Also called Midwest Trailer Sales & Svc *(G-19119)*

Mike-Sells Potato Chip Co (HQ)..........937 228-9400
333 Leo St Dayton (45404) ***(G-9747)***
Mikes Carwash Inc (PA)..........513 677-4700
100 Northeast Dr Loveland (45140) ***(G-13146)***
Mikes Trucking Ltd..........614 879-8808
570 Plain City Grgsvlle Galloway (43119) ***(G-11346)***
Mikesell Transportation Broker..........937 996-5731
1476 State Route 503 Arcanum (45304) ***(G-630)***
Mikouis Enterprise Inc..........330 424-1418
38655 Saltwell Rd Lisbon (44432) ***(G-12940)***
Milcon Concrete Inc..........937 339-6274
1360 S County Road 25a 25 A Troy (45373) ***(G-18366)***
Mildred Byer Clnic For Hmeless, Toledo *Also called Toledo Family Health Center* ***(G-18236)***
Mile Inc (PA)..........614 794-2203
110 E Wilson Bridge Rd # 100 Worthington (43085) ***(G-19978)***
Miles Alloy Inc..........216 245-8893
13800 Miles Ave Cleveland (44105) ***(G-6062)***
Miles Farmers Market Inc..........440 248-5222
28560 Miles Rd Solon (44139) ***(G-17027)***
Miles-Mcclellan Cnstr Co Inc (PA)..........614 487-7744
2100 Builders Pl Columbus (43204) ***(G-8173)***
Milestone, Cleveland *Also called Clean Harbors Envmtl Svcs Inc* ***(G-5283)***
Milestone Ventures LLC..........317 908-2093
1776 Tamarack Rd Newark (43055) ***(G-15208)***
Milford Coml Clg Svcs Inc..........513 575-5678
701 Us Highway 50 Ste A Milford (45150) ***(G-14542)***
Military Resources LLC..........330 263-1040
1036 Burbank Rd Wooster (44691) ***(G-19888)***
Military Resources LLC (PA)..........330 309-9970
1834 Cleveland Rd Ste 301 Wooster (44691) ***(G-19889)***
Mill Creek Golf Club, Ostrander *Also called Mill Creek Golf Course Corp* ***(G-15793)***
Mill Creek Golf Course, Youngstown *Also called Mill Creek Metropolitan Park* ***(G-20287)***
Mill Creek Golf Course Corp..........740 666-7711
7259 Penn Rd Ostrander (43061) ***(G-15793)***
Mill Creek Metropolitan Park..........330 740-7112
Boardman Canfield Rd Youngstown (44502) ***(G-20287)***
Mill Creek Nursing..........419 468-4046
900 Wedgewood Cir Galion (44833) ***(G-11302)***
Mill Distributors Inc..........330 995-9200
45 Aurora Industrial Pkwy Aurora (44202) ***(G-848)***
Mill Manor Nursing Home Inc..........440 967-6614
983 Exchange St Vermilion (44089) ***(G-18715)***
Mill Pond Family Physicians..........330 928-3111
265 Portage Trail Ext W Cuyahoga Falls (44223) ***(G-9211)***
Mill Rose Laboratories Inc..........440 974-6730
7310 Corp Blvd Mentor (44060) ***(G-14219)***
Mill Run Care Center LLC..........614 527-3000
3399 Mill Run Dr Hilliard (43026) ***(G-11935)***
Mill Run Gardens & Care Center, Hilliard *Also called Mill Run Care Center LLC* ***(G-11935)***
Mill-Rose Company (PA)..........440 255-9171
7995 Tyler Blvd Mentor (44060) ***(G-14220)***
Millar Elevator Service, Cleveland *Also called Schindler Elevator Corporation* ***(G-6446)***
Millcraft Group LLC (PA)..........216 441-5500
6800 Grant Ave Cleveland (44105) ***(G-6063)***
Millcraft Paper Company (HQ)..........216 441-5505
6800 Grant Ave Cleveland (44105) ***(G-6064)***
Millcraft Paper Company..........740 924-9470
4311 Janitrol Rd Ste 600 Columbus (43228) ***(G-8174)***
Millcraft Paper Company..........937 222-7829
1200 Leo St Dayton (45404) ***(G-9748)***
Millcraft Paper Company..........614 675-4800
4311 Janitrol Rd Ste 600 Columbus (43228) ***(G-8175)***
Millcraft Paper Company..........216 441-5500
6800 Grant Ave Cleveland (44105) ***(G-6065)***
Millenium Control Systems LLC..........440 510-0050
34525 Melinz Pkwy Ste 205 Eastlake (44095) ***(G-10549)***
Millennia Housing MGT Ltd (PA)..........216 520-1250
127 Public Sq Ste 1300 Cleveland (44114) ***(G-6066)***
Millennium Cpitl Recovery Corp..........330 528-1450
95 Executive Pkwy Ste 100 Hudson (44236) ***(G-12135)***
Millennium Leather LLC..........201 541-7121
4680 Parkway Dr Ste 200 Mason (45040) ***(G-13740)***
Miller & Co Portable Toil Svcs..........330 453-9472
2400 Shepler Ch Ave Sw Canton (44706) ***(G-2463)***
Miller Boat Line Inc (PA)..........419 285-2421
535 Bayview Ave Put In Bay (43456) ***(G-16369)***
Miller Bros Const Inc..........419 445-1015
1613 S Defiance St Archbold (43502) ***(G-639)***
Miller Bros Paint & Decorating, Cincinnati *Also called Miller Bros Wallpaper Company* ***(G-4095)***
Miller Bros Wallpaper Company..........513 231-4470
8460 Beechmont Ave Ste A Cincinnati (45255) ***(G-4095)***
Miller Brothers Cnstr Dem LLC..........513 257-1082
3685 Oxford Millville Rd Oxford (45056) ***(G-15824)***
Miller Cable Company..........419 639-2091
210 S Broadway St Green Springs (44836) ***(G-11479)***
Miller Cnfeld Pddock Stone PLC..........513 394-5252
511 Walnut St Cincinnati (45202) ***(G-4096)***
Miller Consolidated Industries (PA)..........937 294-2681
2221 Arbor Blvd Moraine (45439) ***(G-14806)***
Miller Contracting Group Inc..........419 453-3825
17359 S Rt E 66 Ottoville (45876) ***(G-15808)***
Miller Engineering, Marietta *Also called Thomas L Miller* ***(G-13503)***
Miller Fireworks Company Inc (PA)..........419 865-7329
501 Glengary Rd Holland (43528) ***(G-12039)***
Miller Fireworks Novelty, Holland *Also called Miller Fireworks Company Inc* ***(G-12039)***
Miller Homes of Kidron LLC..........330 857-0161
6397 Kidron Rd Kidron (44636) ***(G-12444)***
Miller House, Celina *Also called Assisted Living Concepts Inc* ***(G-2635)***
Miller Logging Inc..........330 279-4721
8373 State Route 83 Holmesville (44633) ***(G-12074)***
Miller Pipeline LLC..........937 506-8837
11990 Peters Rd Tipp City (45371) ***(G-17722)***
Miller Pipeline LLC..........614 777-8377
5000 Scioto Darby Rd Hilliard (43026) ***(G-11936)***
Miller Products Inc..........330 238-4200
1421 W Main St Alliance (44601) ***(G-549)***
Miller Supply of WvA Inc (PA)..........330 264-9146
1537 Blachleyville Rd Wooster (44691) ***(G-19890)***
Miller Transfer and Rigging Co (HQ)..........330 325-2521
3833 State Route 183 Rootstown (44272) ***(G-16598)***
Miller Valentin Construction, Dayton *Also called Mv Commercial Construction LLC* ***(G-9763)***
Miller Valentine Group, Dayton *Also called Miller-Vlentine Operations Inc* ***(G-9750)***
Miller Valentine Group, Dayton *Also called Miller-Vlentine Operations Inc* ***(G-9751)***
Miller Yount Paving Inc..........330 372-4408
2295 Hagland Blackstub Rd Cortland (44410) ***(G-9079)***
Miller's Textiles, Springfield *Also called Springfeld Unfrm-Linen Sup Inc* ***(G-17278)***
Miller-Valentine Construction..........937 293-0900
137 N Main St Ste 900 Dayton (45402) ***(G-9749)***
Miller-Valentine Partners..........937 293-0900
4000 Miller Valentine Ct Moraine (45439) ***(G-14807)***
Miller-Valentine Partners Ltd..........513 588-1000
9349 Waterstone Blvd # 200 Cincinnati (45249) ***(G-4097)***
Miller-Vlentine Operations Inc (PA)..........937 293-0900
137 N Main St Ste 900 Dayton (45402) ***(G-9750)***
Miller-Vlentine Operations Inc..........513 771-0900
9435 Waterstone Blvd Dayton (45409) ***(G-9751)***
Miller-Vlntine Partners Ltd Lc..........513 588-1000
9349 Waterstone Blvd # 200 Cincinnati (45249) ***(G-4098)***
Millers Rental and Sls Co Inc (PA)..........330 753-8600
2023 Romig Rd Akron (44320) ***(G-345)***
Millers Rental and Sls Co Inc..........216 642-1447
5410 Warner Rd Cleveland (44125) ***(G-6067)***
Millers Textile Services Inc..........419 738-3552
1002 Bellefontaine St Wapakoneta (45895) ***(G-18804)***
Millers Textile Services Inc..........614 262-1206
540 E Columbia St Springfield (45503) ***(G-17249)***
Millersburg Hotel, Millersburg *Also called Bird Enterprises LLC* ***(G-14589)***
Millersburg Tire Service Inc..........330 674-1085
7375 State Route 39 Millersburg (44654) ***(G-14612)***
Milliken Millwork Inc..........513 874-6771
400 Circle Freeway Dr West Chester (45246) ***(G-19217)***
Milliken's Dairy Cone, Frankfort *Also called David W Milliken* ***(G-11145)***
Millikin & Fitton, Hamilton *Also called Millikin and Fitton Law Firm* ***(G-11759)***
Millikin and Fitton Law Firm (PA)..........513 829-6700
232 High St Hamilton (45011) ***(G-11759)***
Milliron Iron & Metal, Mansfield *Also called Milliron Recycling Inc* ***(G-13347)***
Milliron Recycling Inc..........419 747-6522
2384 Springmill Rd Mansfield (44903) ***(G-13347)***
Millis Transfer Inc..........513 863-0222
1982 Jackson Rd Hamilton (45011) ***(G-11760)***
Mills Corporation..........513 671-2882
600 Cincinnati Mills Dr Cincinnati (45240) ***(G-4099)***
Mills Creek Association..........440 327-5336
5175 Mills Creek Ln North Ridgeville (44039) ***(G-15471)***
Mills Fence Co Inc (PA)..........513 631-0333
6315 Wiehe Rd Cincinnati (45237) ***(G-4100)***
Mills James Productions, Hilliard *Also called Mills/James Inc* ***(G-11937)***
Mills Security Alarm Systems..........513 921-4600
490 Mount Hope Ave Cincinnati (45204) ***(G-4101)***
Mills Transfer, Lowell *Also called Marietta Transfer Company* ***(G-13169)***
Mills/James Inc..........614 777-9933
3545 Fishinger Blvd Hilliard (43026) ***(G-11937)***
Milltown Family Physicians..........330 345-8016
128 E Milltown Rd Ste 105 Wooster (44691) ***(G-19891)***
Millwood Inc..........440 914-0540
30311 Emerald Valley Pkwu Solon (44139) ***(G-17028)***
Millwood Inc (PA)..........330 393-4400
3708 International Blvd Vienna (44473) ***(G-18740)***
Millwood Natural LLC..........330 393-4400
3708 International Blvd Vienna (44473) ***(G-18741)***
Millwood Plant, Howard *Also called Pioneer Sands LLC* ***(G-12081)***
Mim Software Inc (PA)..........216 896-9798
25800 Science Park Dr # 180 Beachwood (44122) ***(G-1103)***
Mimis Cafe 112, Columbus *Also called Swh Mimis Cafe LLC* ***(G-6908)***
Mimrx Co Inc..........614 850-6672
2787 Charter St Columbus (43228) ***(G-8176)***
Minamyer Residential Mr/Dd Svc..........614 802-0190
967 Worthington Woods Loo Columbus (43085) ***(G-8177)***
Minature Society Cincinnati..........513 931-9708
6718 Siebern Ave Cincinnati (45236) ***(G-4102)***
Mine Equipment Services LLC (PA)..........740 936-5427
3958 State Route 3 Sunbury (43074) ***(G-17558)***

Minerva Elder Care Inc..........330 868-4147
1035 E Lincolnway Minerva (44657) ***(G-14648)***
Minerva Elderly Care, Minerva *Also called Minerva Elder Care Inc* ***(G-14648)***
Minerva Medical Center, Minerva *Also called Family Medicine Center Minerva* ***(G-14645)***
Minerva Park, Columbus *Also called Kindred Healthcare Oper Inc* ***(G-7990)***
Minerva Welding and Fabg Inc..........330 868-7731
22133 Us Route 30 Minerva (44657) ***(G-14649)***
Minford Retirement Center LLC..........740 820-2821
9641 State Route 335 Minford (45653) ***(G-14652)***
Minges Drywall, Hamilton *Also called Larry L Minges* ***(G-11752)***
Mini University, Dayton *Also called Wright State University* ***(G-9290)***
Mini University Inc..........513 275-5184
401 Western College Dr Oxford (45056) ***(G-15825)***
Mini University Inc (PA)..........937 426-1414
115 Harbert Dr Ste A Beavercreek (45440) ***(G-1254)***
Ministerial Dare Care, Cleveland *Also called Ministerial Day Care-Headstart* ***(G-6068)***
Ministerial Day Care-Headstart (PA)..........216 541-7400
7020 Superior Ave Cleveland (44103) ***(G-6068)***
Minnesota Limited LLC..........330 343-4612
2198 Donald Dr Dover (44622) ***(G-10200)***
Minster Bank (PA)..........419 628-2351
95 W 4th St Minster (45865) ***(G-14666)***
Minute Men Inc (PA)..........216 426-2225
3740 Carnegie Ave Ste 201 Cleveland (44115) ***(G-6069)***
Minute Men of FL, Cleveland *Also called Minute Men Inc* ***(G-6069)***
Miracle Health Care, Columbus *Also called Svh Holdings LLC* ***(G-8813)***
Miracle Method of Columbus, Columbus *Also called Sayles Company LLC* ***(G-8689)***
Miracle Plumbing & Heating Co..........330 477-2402
2121 Whipple Ave Nw Canton (44708) ***(G-2464)***
Miracle Renovations..........513 371-0750
2786 Shaffer Ave Cincinnati (45211) ***(G-4103)***
Miracle Spirtl Retrst Orgnsizn..........216 324-4287
11609 Wade Park Ave Cleveland (44106) ***(G-6070)***
Miraclecorp Products (PA)..........937 293-9994
2425 W Dorothy Ln Moraine (45439) ***(G-14808)***
Mircale Health Care..........614 237-7702
3245 E Livingston Ave # 108 Columbus (43227) ***(G-8178)***
Mirifex Systems LLC (PA)..........440 891-1210
1383 Sharon Copley Rd Sharon Center (44274) ***(G-16876)***
Mirka USA Inc..........330 963-6421
2375 Edison Blvd Twinsburg (44087) ***(G-18449)***
Misa Metals Inc (HQ)..........212 660-6000
9050 Centre Pointe Dr West Chester (45069) ***(G-19120)***
Misa Metals Inc..........440 892-4944
26926 Kenley Ct Ste 200 Westlake (44145) ***(G-19516)***
Mispace Inc..........614 626-2602
5954 Rockland Ct Columbus (43221) ***(G-8179)***
Mission Essntial Personnel LLC (PA)..........614 416-2345
6525 W Campus Oval # 101 New Albany (43054) ***(G-14992)***
Mission Pride Inc..........216 759-7404
3011 Berkshire Rd Cleveland Heights (44118) ***(G-6793)***
Mistras Group Inc..........419 836-5904
3094 Moline Martin Rd Millbury (43447) ***(G-14580)***
Mistras Group Inc..........740 788-9188
1480 James Pkwy Heath (43056) ***(G-11839)***
Mistras Group Inc..........330 244-1541
413 Applegrove St Nw North Canton (44720) ***(G-15356)***
Mistras Group Inc..........419 227-4100
3157 Harding Hwy Bldg Lima (45804) ***(G-12841)***
Mitchell & Sons Moving & Stor..........419 289-3311
1217 Township Road 1153 Ashland (44805) ***(G-689)***
Mitchells Salon & Day Spa (PA)..........513 793-0900
5901 E Galbraith Rd # 230 Cincinnati (45236) ***(G-4104)***
Mitchells Salon & Day Spa..........513 793-0900
7795 University Ct Ste A West Chester (45069) ***(G-19121)***
Mitchells Salon & Day Spa..........513 772-3200
11330 Princeton Pike Cincinnati (45246) ***(G-4105)***
Mitchells Salon & Day Spa..........513 731-0600
2692 Madison Rd Cincinnati (45208) ***(G-4106)***
Mitel (delaware) Inc..........513 733-8000
9100 W Chester Towne Ctr West Chester (45069) ***(G-19122)***
Miter Masonry Contractors..........513 821-3334
421 Maple Ave Arlington Heights (45215) ***(G-648)***
Mitosis LLC..........937 557-3440
14 W 1st St Ste 302 Dayton (45402) ***(G-9752)***
Mitsubshi Intl Fd Ingrdnts Inc (HQ)..........614 652-1111
5080 Tuttle Crossing Blvd Dublin (43016) ***(G-10399)***
Mizar Motors Inc (HQ)..........419 729-2400
6003 Benore Rd Toledo (43612) ***(G-18065)***
MJ Auto Parts Inc (PA)..........440 205-6272
7900 Tyler Blvd Mentor (44060) ***(G-14221)***
Mj Baumann Co Inc..........614 759-7100
6400 Broughton Ave Columbus (43213) ***(G-8180)***
MJ Design Associates Inc..........614 873-7333
8463 Estates Ct Plain City (43064) ***(G-16200)***
Mj-6 LLC..........419 517-7725
2621 Liverpool Ct Toledo (43617) ***(G-18066)***
Mjr Sales, Plain City *Also called K Amalia Enterprises Inc* ***(G-16195)***
Mjr-Construction Co..........216 523-8050
3101 W 25th St Ste 100 Cleveland (44109) ***(G-6071)***
Mk Childcare Warsaw Ave LLC..........513 922-6279
3711 Warsaw Ave Cincinnati (45205) ***(G-4107)***
Mkjb Inc..........513 851-8400
11760 Pellston Ct Cincinnati (45240) ***(G-4108)***
Mkm Distribution Services Inc..........330 549-9670
100 Eastgate Dr North Lima (44452) ***(G-15405)***
Mlm Childcare LLC..........513 623-8243
16 Beaufort Hunt Ln Cincinnati (45242) ***(G-4109)***
Mmi II, West Chester *Also called Milliken Millwork Inc* ***(G-19217)***
Mmi of Kentucky, Cincinnati *Also called Contractors Materials Company* ***(G-3413)***
Mmi-Cpr LLC..........216 674-0645
7100 E Pleasant Valley Rd Independence (44131) ***(G-12234)***
Mmic Inc..........513 697-0445
6867 Obannon Blf Loveland (45140) ***(G-13147)***
Mobilcomm Inc..........513 742-5555
1211 W Sharon Rd Cincinnati (45240) ***(G-4110)***
Mobile Analytical Services..........614 873-1710
8426 Industrial Pkwy Plain City (43064) ***(G-16201)***
Mobile Cardiac Imaging LLC..........419 251-3711
2409 Cherry St Ste 100 Toledo (43608) ***(G-18067)***
Mobile Instr Svc & Repr Inc (PA)..........937 592-5025
333 Water Ave Bellefontaine (43311) ***(G-1391)***
Mobile Meals Inc (PA)..........330 376-7717
1357 Home Ave Akron (44310) ***(G-346)***
Mobile Meals of Salem Inc..........330 332-2160
1995 E State St Salem (44460) ***(G-16705)***
Mobilex USA, Columbus *Also called Trident USA Health Svcs LLC* ***(G-8870)***
MOBILITY WORKS FOUNDATION, THE, Richfield *Also called Wmk Inc* ***(G-16533)***
Moca Cleveland, Cleveland *Also called Museum Cntmprary Art Cleveland* ***(G-6092)***
Mocha House Inc (PA)..........330 392-3020
467 High St Ne Warren (44481) ***(G-18882)***
Modal Shop Inc..........513 351-9919
3149 E Kemper Rd Cincinnati (45241) ***(G-4111)***
Model Group Inc..........513 559-0048
2170 Gilbert Ave Ste 100 Cincinnati (45206) ***(G-4112)***
Modern Builders Supply Inc..........330 726-7000
500 Victoria Rd Youngstown (44515) ***(G-20288)***
Modern Builders Supply Inc (PA)..........330 729-2690
302 Mcclurg Rd Youngstown (44512) ***(G-20289)***
Modern Builders Supply Inc..........937 222-2627
2627 Stanley Ave Dayton (45404) ***(G-9753)***
Modern Builders Supply Inc..........513 531-1000
6225 Wiehe Rd Cincinnati (45237) ***(G-4113)***
Modern Builders Supply Inc..........419 241-3961
3500 Phillips Ave Toledo (43608) ***(G-18068)***
Modern Day Concrete Cnstr..........513 738-1026
9773 Crosby Rd Harrison (45030) ***(G-11806)***
Modern Glass Pnt & Tile Co Inc..........740 454-1253
933 Linden Ave Zanesville (43701) ***(G-20503)***
Modern Medical Inc..........800 547-3330
250 Progressive Way Westerville (43082) ***(G-19329)***
Modern Office Methods Inc (PA)..........513 791-0909
4747 Lake Forest Dr # 200 Blue Ash (45242) ***(G-1644)***
Modern Office Methods Inc..........614 891-3693
929 Eastwind Dr Ste 220 Westerville (43081) ***(G-19426)***
Modern Poured Walls Inc..........440 647-6661
41807 State Route 18 Wellington (44090) ***(G-18994)***
Modern Tech Solutions Inc..........937 426-9025
4141 Colonel Glenn Hwy # 115 Beavercreek Township (45431) ***(G-1275)***
Modern Welding Co Ohio Inc..........740 344-9425
1 Modern Way Newark (43055) ***(G-15209)***
Modlich Stone Works, Columbus *Also called Modlich Stoneworks Inc* ***(G-8181)***
Modlich Stoneworks Inc..........614 276-2848
2255 Harper Rd Columbus (43204) ***(G-8181)***
Modular Systems Technicians..........216 459-2630
15708 Industrial Pkwy Cleveland (44135) ***(G-6072)***
Moeller Trucking Inc..........419 925-4799
8100 Industrial Dr Maria Stein (45860) ***(G-13429)***
Mohawk Fine Papers Inc..........440 969-2049
6642 Center Rd Ashtabula (44004) ***(G-755)***
Mohawk Golf Club..........419 447-5876
4399 S State Route 231 Tiffin (44883) ***(G-17687)***
Mohawk RE-Bar Services Inc..........440 268-0780
15110 Foltz Pkwy Ste 106 Strongsville (44149) ***(G-17495)***
Mohican Hills Golf Club Inc..........419 368-4700
25 County Road 1950 Jeromesville (44840) ***(G-12333)***
Mohican State Park Lodge & Con, Perrysville *Also called Natural Resources Ohio Dept* ***(G-16080)***
Mohun Health Care Center..........614 416-6132
2320 Airport Dr Columbus (43219) ***(G-8182)***
MOHUN HEALTH CARE CENTER GIFT, Columbus *Also called Mohun Health Care Center* ***(G-8182)***
Moisture Guard Corporation..........330 928-7200
4370 Allen Rd Stow (44224) ***(G-17383)***
Molina Healthcare Inc..........800 642-4168
3000 Corp Exchange Dr # 100 Columbus (43231) ***(G-8183)***
Molina Healthcare Inc..........216 606-1400
6161 Oak Tree Blvd Independence (44131) ***(G-12235)***
Molina Healthcare of Ohio, Columbus *Also called Molina Healthcare Inc* ***(G-8183)***
Molina Healthcare of Ohio, Independence *Also called Molina Healthcare Inc* ***(G-12235)***
Mollett Seamless Gutter Co..........513 825-0500
9345 Prnceton Glendale Rd West Chester (45011) ***(G-19123)***

ALPHABETIC

Molloy Roofing Company....513 791-7400
11099 Deerfield Rd Blue Ash (45242) ***(G-1645)***
Molly Maid of Lorain County....440 327-0000
753 Leona St Elyria (44035) ***(G-10655)***
Molyet Crop Production Inc....419 992-4288
546 E County Road 51 Tiffin (44883) ***(G-17688)***
Monaco Palace Inc....614 475-4817
4869 Rock Haven Rd Newark (43055) ***(G-15210)***
Monacos Place Bnquet Spcalists, Newark *Also called Monaco Palace Inc* ***(G-15210)***
Monarch, Cleveland *Also called Integrated Power Services LLC* ***(G-5826)***
Monarch Construction Company....513 351-6900
1654 Sherman Ave Cincinnati (45212) ***(G-4114)***
Monarch Electric Service Co (HQ)....216 433-7800
5325 W 130th St Cleveland (44130) ***(G-6073)***
Monarch Steel Company Inc....216 587-8000
4650 Johnston Pkwy Cleveland (44128) ***(G-6074)***
Monco Enterprises Inc (PA)....937 461-0034
700 Liberty Ln Dayton (45449) ***(G-9754)***
Mondelez Global LLC....330 626-6500
545 Mondial Pkwy Streetsboro (44241) ***(G-17422)***
Mondo Polymer Technologies Inc....740 376-9396
27620 State Rte 7 Reno (45773) ***(G-16422)***
Monesi Trucking & Eqp Repr Inc....614 921-9183
1715 Atlas St Columbus (43228) ***(G-8184)***
Monode Marking Products Inc (PA)....440 975-8802
9200 Tyler Blvd Mentor (44060) ***(G-14222)***
Monro Inc....440 835-2393
29778 Detroit Rd Westlake (44145) ***(G-19517)***
Monro Inc....614 360-3883
4570 W Broad St Columbus (43228) ***(G-8185)***
Monro Muffler Brake, Westlake *Also called Monro Inc* ***(G-19517)***
Monro Muffler Brake, Columbus *Also called Monro Inc* ***(G-8185)***
Monro Muffler Brake Inc....937 999-3202
4 Remick Blvd Springboro (45066) ***(G-17130)***
Monroe Achievement Center, Woodsfield *Also called Board Mental Retardation Dvlpm* ***(G-19812)***
MONROE ADULT CRAFTS ORGANIZATI, Woodsfield *Also called Maco Inc* ***(G-19816)***
Monroe County Association For....740 472-1712
47011 State Route 26 Woodsfield (43793) ***(G-19817)***
Monroe County Care Center, Woodsfield *Also called County of Monroe* ***(G-19815)***
Monroe County Engineers Dept, Woodsfield *Also called County of Monroe* ***(G-19814)***
Monroe Family Health Center....740 472-0757
37984 Airport Rd Woodsfield (43793) ***(G-19818)***
Monroe Heating and AC, Monroe *Also called Monroe Mechanical Incorporated* ***(G-14706)***
Monroe Mechanical Incorporated....513 539-7555
150 Breaden Dr B Monroe (45050) ***(G-14706)***
Monsoon Lagoon Water Park, Port Clinton *Also called Goofy Golf II Inc* ***(G-16245)***
Monster Worldwide Inc....513 719-3331
10296 Springfield Pike # 500 Cincinnati (45215) ***(G-4115)***
Montefiore Home....216 360-9080
1 David N Myers Pkwy Beachwood (44122) ***(G-1104)***
Monterey Care Center, Grove City *Also called Whetstone Care Center LLC* ***(G-11616)***
MONTESSORI CHILDREN SCHOOL, Westlake *Also called Bay Village Montessori Inc* ***(G-19464)***
Montessori Community School....740 344-9411
621 Country Club Dr Newark (43055) ***(G-15211)***
Montford Heights, Cincinnati *Also called Duke Energy Ohio Inc* ***(G-3509)***
Montgmery Cnty Prosecutors Off, Dayton *Also called County of Montgomery* ***(G-9437)***
Montgomery Care Center, Cincinnati *Also called Nursing Care MGT Amer Inc* ***(G-4194)***
Montgomery Cnty Children Svcs, Dayton *Also called County of Montgomery* ***(G-9432)***
Montgomery County Dept of Job, Dayton *Also called County of Montgomery* ***(G-9436)***
Montgomery County N Incertr, Moraine *Also called County of Montgomery* ***(G-14764)***
Montgomery Developmental Ctr, Columbus *Also called Develpmntal Dsblties Ohio Dept* ***(G-7514)***
Montgomery Iron & Paper Co Inc....937 222-4059
400 E 4th St Dayton (45402) ***(G-9755)***
Montgomery Jeep Eagle, Cincinnati *Also called Lincoln Mrcury Kings Auto Mall* ***(G-3984)***
Montgomery Paper Co Div, Dayton *Also called Montgomery Iron & Paper Co Inc* ***(G-9755)***
Montgomery Swim & Tennis Club....513 793-6433
9941 Orchard Club Dr Montgomery (45242) ***(G-14727)***
Montgomery Trucking Company....740 384-2138
103 E 13th St Wellston (45692) ***(G-19004)***
Montpelier Auto Auction Ohio....419 485-1691
14125 County Road M50 Montpelier (43543) ***(G-14744)***
Montpelier Gardens, Columbus *Also called Buckeye Cmnty Twenty Six LP* ***(G-7159)***
Montpelier Hospital, Montpelier *Also called Community Hsptals Wllness Ctrs* ***(G-14741)***
Montpelier Senior Center....419 485-3218
325 N Jonesville St Montpelier (43543) ***(G-14745)***
Montrose Cinema 12, Akron *Also called Regal Cinemas Inc* ***(G-406)***
Montrose Ford Inc (PA)....330 666-0711
3960 Medina Rd Fairlawn (44333) ***(G-10966)***
Montrose Sheffield LLC....440 934-6699
5033 Detroit Rd Sheffield Village (44054) ***(G-16892)***
Moo Moo Carwash, Etna *Also called Moo Moo North Hamilton LLC* ***(G-10730)***
Moo Moo North Hamilton LLC (PA)....614 751-9274
13375 National Rd Sw D Etna (43068) ***(G-10730)***
Moody Nat Cy Dt Clmbus Mt LLC....614 228-3200
35 W Spring St Columbus (43215) ***(G-8186)***
Moody Nat Cy Willoughby Mt LLC....440 530-1100
35103 Maplegrove Rd Willoughby (44094) ***(G-19693)***
Moody-Nolan Inc (PA)....614 461-4664
300 Spruce St Ste 300 Columbus (43215) ***(G-8187)***
Moodys of Dayton Inc (PA)....614 443-3898
4359 Infirmary Rd Miamisburg (45342) ***(G-14323)***
Moon Co-Op Services....513 523-3990
1 Oakhill Dr Oxford (45056) ***(G-15826)***
Moonlight Security Inc....937 252-1600
2710 Dryden Rd Moraine (45439) ***(G-14809)***
Moore Self Storage, Cleveland *Also called Compass Self Storage LLC* ***(G-5388)***
Moore Trnspt Tulsa Ltd Lblty....419 726-4499
4015 Stickney Ave Toledo (43612) ***(G-18069)***
Moose Fmly Ctr 501 Middletown, Middletown *Also called Moose International Inc* ***(G-14441)***
Moose International Inc....513 422-6776
3009 S Main St Middletown (45044) ***(G-14441)***
Moraine Country Club....937 294-6200
4075 Southern Blvd Unit 1 Dayton (45429) ***(G-9756)***
Morelia Consultants LLC....513 469-1500
11210 Montgomery Rd Cincinnati (45249) ***(G-4116)***
Morelia Group LLC....513 469-1500
8600 Governors Hill Dr # 160 Cincinnati (45249) ***(G-4117)***
Morgan & Sons Moving & Storage, Dayton *Also called Van Howards Lines Inc* ***(G-9963)***
Morgan Bank National Assn, Hudson *Also called Northwest Bank* ***(G-12137)***
Morgan County Public Transit....740 962-1322
37 S 5th St McConnelsville (43756) ***(G-14029)***
Morgan Services Inc....419 243-2214
34 10th St Toledo (43604) ***(G-18070)***
Morgan Services Inc....216 241-3107
2013 Columbus Rd Cleveland (44113) ***(G-6075)***
Morgan Services Inc....937 223-5241
817 Webster St Dayton (45404) ***(G-9757)***
Morgan Stanley....513 721-2000
221 E 4th St Ste 2200 Cincinnati (45202) ***(G-4118)***
Morgan Stanley....440 835-6750
159 Crocker Park Blvd # 460 Westlake (44145) ***(G-19518)***
Morgan Stanley....216 523-3000
1301 E 9th St Ste 3100 Cleveland (44114) ***(G-6076)***
Morgan Stanley....330 670-4600
3700 Embassy Pkwy Ste 340 Akron (44333) ***(G-347)***
Morgan Stanley....614 473-2086
4449 Easton Way Ste 300 Columbus (43219) ***(G-8188)***
Morgan Stanley & Co LLC....614 798-3100
545 Metro Pl S Ste 300 Dublin (43017) ***(G-10400)***
Morgan Stanley & Co LLC....614 228-0600
41 S High St Ste 2700 Columbus (43215) ***(G-8189)***
Morgan Stnley Smith Barney LLC....216 360-4900
31099 Chagrin Blvd Fl 3 Cleveland (44124) ***(G-6077)***
Morgan Uniforms & Linen Rental, Cleveland *Also called Morgan Services Inc* ***(G-6075)***
Moring View Care Center, New Philadelphia *Also called Dearth Management Company* ***(G-15092)***
Morning View Care Center, Marion *Also called Dearth Management Company* ***(G-13537)***
Morning View Care Center, Columbus *Also called Dearth Management Company* ***(G-7498)***
Morphick Inc....844 506-6774
4555 Lake Forest Dr # 150 Blue Ash (45242) ***(G-1646)***
Morral Companies LLC (HQ)....740 465-3251
132 Postle Ave Morral (43337) ***(G-14842)***
Morris Cadillac Buick GMC (PA)....440 327-4181
26100 Lorain Rd North Olmsted (44070) ***(G-15432)***
Morris Schneider Wittstadt LLC....440 942-5168
35110 Euclid Ave Ste 2 Willoughby (44094) ***(G-19694)***
Morris Technologies Inc....513 733-1611
11988 Tramway Dr Cincinnati (45241) ***(G-4119)***
Morrison Inc....740 373-5869
410 Colegate Dr Marietta (45750) ***(G-13478)***
Morro Dialysis LLC....937 865-0633
290 Alexandersville Rd Miamisburg (45342) ***(G-14324)***
Morrow Cnty Fire Fighter....419 946-7976
140 S Main St Mount Gilead (43338) ***(G-14856)***
Morrow Co Ed Service Center, Mount Gilead *Also called County of Morrow* ***(G-14853)***
Morrow Control and Supply Inc (PA)....330 452-9791
810 Marion Motley Ave Ne Canton (44705) ***(G-2465)***
Morrow County Child Care Ctr....419 946-5007
406 Bank St Mount Gilead (43338) ***(G-14857)***
Morrow County Council On Drugs....419 947-4055
950 Meadow Dr Mount Gilead (43338) ***(G-14858)***
Morrow County Emergency Squad, Mount Gilead *Also called Morrow Cnty Fire Fighter* ***(G-14856)***
Morrow County Hospital....419 949-3085
651 W Marion Rd Mount Gilead (43338) ***(G-14859)***
Morrow County Hospital (PA)....419 947-9127
651 W Marion Rd Mount Gilead (43338) ***(G-14860)***
MORROW COUNTY HOSPITAL HOME HE, Mount Gilead *Also called Morrow County Hospital* ***(G-14860)***
Morrow County Hospital MCH At, Mount Gilead *Also called Morrow County Hospital* ***(G-14859)***
Morrow Gravel Company Inc (PA)....513 771-0820
11641 Mosteller Rd Ste 2 Cincinnati (45241) ***(G-4120)***

Morrow Manor Nursing Home, Chesterville *Also called Levering Management Inc* (G-2806)
Morse Van Line, Painesville *Also called William R Morse* (G-15887)
Mortgage Information Services (PA)....216 514-7480
4877 Galaxy Pkwy Ste I Cleveland (44128) (G-6078)
Mortgage Now Inc (PA)....800 245-1050
9700 Rockside Rd Ste 295 Cleveland (44125) (G-6079)
Mortgage Service Center, Canton *Also called Security Savings Mortgage Corp* (G-2524)
Morton Buildings Inc....419 675-2311
14483 State Route 31 Kenton (43326) (G-12422)
Morton Buildings Plant, Kenton *Also called Morton Buildings Inc* (G-12422)
Morton Landscape Dev Co, Columbia Station *Also called Mortons Lawn Service Inc* (G-6850)
Morton Salt Inc....330 925-3015
151 Industrial Ave Rittman (44270) (G-16554)
Mortons Lawn Service Inc....440 236-3550
11564 Station Rd Columbia Station (44028) (G-6850)
Mosier Industrial Services....419 683-4000
900 S Wiley St Crestline (44827) (G-9148)
Moskowitz Bros Inc....513 242-2100
5300 Vine St Cincinnati (45217) (G-4121)
Moskowitz Family Ltd....513 729-2300
7220 Pippin Rd Cincinnati (45239) (G-4122)
Moskowitz Family Trust, Cincinnati *Also called Moskowitz Family Ltd* (G-4122)
Mosley Pfundt & Glick Inc....419 861-1120
6455 Wheatstone Ct Maumee (43537) (G-13948)
Moss Affiliate Marketing, Solon *Also called Paul Moss LLC* (G-17038)
Motel 6, Troy *Also called R P L Corporation* (G-18373)
Motel 6 Operating LP....614 431-2525
7474 N High St Columbus (43235) (G-8190)
Motel Investments Marietta Inc....740 374-8190
700 Pike St Marietta (45750) (G-13479)
Motel Partners LLC....740 594-3000
20 Home St Athens (45701) (G-802)
Moti Corporation....440 734-4500
22115 Brookpark Rd Cleveland (44126) (G-6080)
Motion Controls Robotics Inc....419 334-5886
1500 Walter Ave Fremont (43420) (G-11214)
Moto Franchise Corporation (PA)....937 291-1900
7086 Corporate Way Ste 2 Dayton (45459) (G-9758)
Motophoto, Dayton *Also called Moto Franchise Corporation* (G-9758)
Motor Carrier Service Inc....419 693-6207
815 Lemoyne Rd Northwood (43619) (G-15537)
Motorists Coml Mutl Insur Co (PA)....614 225-8211
471 E Broad St Bsmt Columbus (43215) (G-8191)
MOTORISTS INSURANCE GROUP, Columbus *Also called Motorists Mutual Insurance Co* (G-8193)
MOTORISTS INSURANCE GROUP, Columbus *Also called Motorists Life Insurance Co* (G-8192)
MOTORISTS INSURANCE GROUP, Columbus *Also called Motorists Coml Mutl Insur Co* (G-8191)
Motorists Life Ins Co, Dayton *Also called Motorists Mutual Insurance Co* (G-9759)
Motorists Life Insurance Co....614 225-8211
471 E Broad St Ste 200 Columbus (43215) (G-8192)
Motorists Mutual Insurance Co (PA)....614 225-8211
471 E Broad St Ste 200 Columbus (43215) (G-8193)
Motorists Mutual Insurance Co....440 779-8900
28111 Lorain Rd North Olmsted (44070) (G-15433)
Motorists Mutual Insurance Co....330 896-9311
3532 Massillon Rd Uniontown (44685) (G-18529)
Motorists Mutual Insurance Co....937 435-5540
8255 Yankee St Dayton (45458) (G-9759)
Motz Group Inc (PA)....513 533-6452
3607 Church St Ste 300 Cincinnati (45244) (G-4123)
Mougianis Industries Inc....740 264-6372
1626 Cadiz Rd Steubenville (43953) (G-17331)
Mound Builders Guidance Center....740 522-2828
65 Messimer Dr Unit 2 Newark (43055) (G-15212)
Mound Technologies Inc....937 748-2937
25 Mound Park Dr Springboro (45066) (G-17131)
Moundbuilders Country Club Co....740 344-4500
125 N 33rd St Newark (43055) (G-15213)
Moundbuilders Guidance Ctr Inc....740 397-0442
8402 Blackjack Rd Mount Vernon (43050) (G-14913)
Mount Aloysius Corp....740 342-3343
5375 Tile Plant Rd Se New Lexington (43704) (G-15056)
Mount Alverna Home, Cleveland *Also called Franciscan Sisters of Chicago* (G-5630)
Mount Auburn Community Hdo....513 659-4514
2236 Burnet Ave Cincinnati (45219) (G-4124)
Mount Carmel E Dialysis Clnc....614 322-0433
85 Mcnaughten Rd Columbus (43213) (G-8194)
Mount Carmel East Hospital....614 234-6000
6001 E Broad St Columbus (43213) (G-8195)
Mount Carmel Health (HQ)....614 234-5000
793 W State St Columbus (43222) (G-8196)
Mount Carmel Health....614 234-8170
730 W Rich St Columbus (43222) (G-8197)
Mount Carmel Health....614 855-4878
55 N High St Ste A New Albany (43054) (G-14993)
Mount Carmel Health....614 234-0100
501 W Schrock Rd Ste 350 Westerville (43081) (G-19427)
Mount Carmel Health System (HQ)....614 234-6000
6150 E Broad St Columbus (43213) (G-8198)
Mount Carmel Health System....614 775-6600
7333 Smiths Mill Rd New Albany (43054) (G-14994)
Mount Carmel Health System....614 898-4000
500 S Cleveland Ave Westerville (43081) (G-19428)
Mount Carmel Home Care, Westerville *Also called Mount Carmel Health* (G-19427)
Mount Carmel Imaging & Therapy....614 234-8080
5969 E Broad St Ste 100 Columbus (43213) (G-8199)
Mount Carmel Kindercare, Columbus *Also called Kindercare Learning Ctrs LLC* (G-7989)
Mount Carmel/Walnut Hills, Columbus *Also called Walnut Hills Physical Therapy* (G-8964)
Mount Crmel Hospice Evrgrn Ctr....614 234-0200
1144 Dublin Rd Columbus (43215) (G-8200)
Mount Orab Ems, Mount Orab *Also called Mt Orab Fire Department Inc* (G-14870)
MOUNT ST JOSEPH NURSING HOME, Euclid *Also called Sisters Od Saint Joseph of SAI* (G-10776)
Mount Vernon NH LLC....740 392-1099
1135 Gambier Rd Mount Vernon (43050) (G-14914)
Mount Vrnon Hlth Rhblttion Ctr, Mount Vernon *Also called Mount Vernon NH LLC* (G-14914)
Mountain Foods Inc....440 286-7177
9761 Ravenna Rd Chardon (44024) (G-2758)
Movers and Shuckers LLC....740 263-2164
11275 Lovers Ln Mount Vernon (43050) (G-14915)
Moving Solutions Inc....440 946-9300
8001 Moving Way Mentor (44060) (G-14223)
Mowerys Collision Inc....614 274-6072
155 Phillipi Rd Columbus (43228) (G-8201)
Mowry Construction & Engrg Inc....419 289-2262
2105 Claremont Ave Ashland (44805) (G-690)
Moyal and Petroff MD....440 461-6477
730 Som Center Rd Ste 230 Cleveland (44143) (G-6081)
Moyer Industries Inc....937 832-7283
7555 Jacks Ln Clayton (45315) (G-4915)
Mp Biomedicals LLC....440 337-1200
29525 Fountain Pkwy Solon (44139) (G-17029)
Mpf Sales and Mktg Group LLC....513 793-6241
11243 Cornell Park Dr Blue Ash (45242) (G-1647)
Mpg Transport, Toledo *Also called United Road Services Inc* (G-18272)
Mpi Label Systems Eqp Rfid Div, Alliance *Also called Miller Products Inc* (G-549)
Mplx Terminals LLC....440 526-4653
10439 Brecksville Rd Cleveland (44141) (G-6082)
Mplx Terminals LLC....330 479-5539
2408 Gambrinus Ave Sw Canton (44706) (G-2466)
Mplx Terminals LLC....504 252-8064
840 Heath Rd Heath (43056) (G-11840)
Mplx Terminals LLC....513 451-0485
4015 River Rd Cincinnati (45204) (G-4125)
Mpower Inc....614 783-0478
4643 Winery Way Gahanna (43230) (G-11258)
MPS Group Inc....937 746-2117
512 Linden Ave Carlisle (45005) (G-2604)
MPW Construction Services....440 647-6661
41807 State Route 18 Wellington (44090) (G-18995)
MPW Container Management Corp....216 362-8400
4848 W 130th St Cleveland (44135) (G-6083)
MPW Industrial Services Inc....330 454-1898
907 Belden Ave Se Canton (44707) (G-2467)
MPW Industrial Services Inc (HQ)....800 827-8790
9711 Lancaster Rd Hebron (43025) (G-11854)
MPW Industrial Services Inc....740 774-5251
65 Kenworth Dr Chillicothe (45601) (G-2864)
MPW Industrial Services Inc....740 345-2431
150 S 29th St Newark (43055) (G-15214)
MPW Industrial Services Inc....937 644-0200
11000 State Route 347 East Liberty (43319) (G-10511)
MPW Industrial Services Inc....440 277-9072
1930 E 28th St Lorain (44055) (G-13062)
MPW Industrial Svcs Group Inc (PA)....740 927-8790
9711 Lancaster Rd Hebron (43025) (G-11855)
MPW Industrial Water Svcs Inc....800 827-8790
9711 Lancaster Rd Hebron (43025) (G-11856)
Mr Box, Mansfield *Also called Skybox Packaging LLC* (G-13364)
Mr Excavator Inc....440 256-2008
8616 Euclid Chardon Rd Kirtland (44094) (G-12458)
Mr Magic Car Wash & Detail Ctr, Beachwood *Also called Mr Magic Carnegie Inc* (G-1105)
Mr Magic Carnegie Inc....440 461-7572
23511 Chagrin Blvd # 306 Beachwood (44122) (G-1105)
Mr Rooter Plumbing Corporation....419 625-4444
8200 E Pleasant Valley Rd Independence (44131) (G-12236)
Mr. Beams, Mayfield Village *Also called Wireless Environment LLC* (G-14014)
Mrap LLC....614 545-3190
1721 Westbelt Dr Columbus (43228) (G-8202)
MRC Global (us) Inc....419 324-0039
3110 Frenchmens Rd Toledo (43607) (G-18071)
MRC Global (us) Inc....513 489-6922
7275 Edington Dr Cincinnati (45249) (G-4126)
Mrdd, Sandusky *Also called Ability Works Inc* (G-16723)
Mreto, Cincinnati *Also called Southwest OH Trans Auth* (G-4554)
Mri Network, Akron *Also called Global Exec Slutions Group LLC* (G-238)

ALPHABETIC

Mri Software LLC (PA) — ALPHABETIC SECTION

Mri Software LLC (PA) 800 327-8770
28925 Fountain Pkwy Solon (44139) *(G-17030)*
Mrivera Construction, Cleveland *Also called Mjr-Construction Co (G-6071)*
MRM Construction Inc 740 388-0079
110 Bellomy Dr Gallipolis (45631) *(G-11329)*
Mrn Limited Partnership 216 589-5631
629 Euclid Ave Cleveland (44114) *(G-6084)*
Mrn-Newgar Hotel Ltd 216 443-1000
629 Euclid Ave Lbby 1 Cleveland (44114) *(G-6085)*
Mroeki Inc 330 318-3926
8571 Foxwood Ct Ste A Youngstown (44514) *(G-20290)*
Mrp Inc 513 965-9700
5632 Sugar Camp Rd Milford (45150) *(G-14543)*
Mrs Dennis Potato Farm Inc 419 335-2778
15370 County Road K Wauseon (43567) *(G-18959)*
Mrsi, Cincinnati *Also called Medical Recovery Systems Inc (G-4044)*
Ms Consultants Inc (PA) 330 744-5321
333 E Federal St Youngstown (44503) *(G-20291)*
Ms Consultants Inc 614 898-7100
2221 Schrock Rd Columbus (43229) *(G-8203)*
Ms Consultants Inc. 216 522-1926
600 Superior Ave E # 1300 Cleveland (44114) *(G-6086)*
MSA Architects, Cincinnati *Also called Michael Schuster Associates (G-4089)*
MSA Group Inc 614 334-0400
2839 Charter St Columbus (43228) *(G-8204)*
Msab Park Creek LLC 440 842-5100
20375 Center Ridge Rd # 204 Rocky River (44116) *(G-16586)*
Msd, Dayton *Also called Mechanical Systems Dayton Inc (G-9277)*
MSI, Chesterland *Also called Metzenbaum Sheltered Inds (G-2800)*
MSI International LLC 330 869-6459
6100 Oak Tree Blvd # 200 Cleveland (44131) *(G-6087)*
Msk Hospitality Inc 513 771-0370
11620 Chester Rd Cincinnati (45246) *(G-4127)*
Mssl Consolidated Inc 330 766-5510
8640 E Market St Warren (44484) *(G-18883)*
Msstaff LLC 419 868-8536
5950 Airport Hwy Ste 12 Toledo (43615) *(G-18072)*
Mt Business Technologies, Avon Lake *Also called M T Business Technologies (G-935)*
Mt Business Technologies, Cleveland *Also called Office Products Inc/Cleveland (G-6181)*
Mt Business Technologies Inc (HQ) 419 529-6100
1150 National Pkwy Mansfield (44906) *(G-13348)*
Mt Healthy Christian Home Inc 513 931-5000
8097 Hamilton Ave Cincinnati (45231) *(G-4128)*
Mt Hope Auction Inc (PA) 330 674-6188
8076 State Rte 241 Mount Hope (44660) *(G-14866)*
Mt Orab Fire Department Inc 937 444-3945
113 Spice St Mount Orab (45154) *(G-14870)*
Mt Royal Villa Care Center, Cleveland *Also called Consulate Management Co LLC (G-5398)*
Mt Texas LLC 513 853-4400
3055 Colerain Ave Cincinnati (45225) *(G-4129)*
Mt View Terrace, Blue Ash *Also called Sycamore Senior Center (G-1692)*
Mt Washington Care Center Inc 513 231-4561
6900 Beechmont Ave Cincinnati (45230) *(G-4130)*
MTA Leasing, Fairlawn *Also called Montrose Ford Inc (G-10966)*
Mtd Acceptance Corp Inc 330 225-2600
5965 Grafton Rd Valley City (44280) *(G-18621)*
Mtd Holdings Inc (PA) 330 225-2600
5965 Grafton Rd Valley City (44280) *(G-18622)*
MTI, Cleveland *Also called Mainthia Technologies Inc (G-5970)*
Mtm Technologies (texas) Inc 513 786-6600
10653 Techwood Cir # 100 Blue Ash (45242) *(G-1648)*
Mto Suncoke, Middletown *Also called Suncoke Energy Nc (G-14463)*
Mtsi, Beavercreek Township *Also called Modern Tech Solutions Inc (G-1275)*
Mud Pike Group Home The, Celina *Also called Mercer Residential Services (G-2656)*
Mueller Art Cover & Binding Co 440 238-3303
12005 Alameda Dr Strongsville (44149) *(G-17496)*
Muetzel Plumbing & Heating Co 614 299-7700
1661 Kenny Rd Columbus (43212) *(G-8205)*
Muha Construction Inc 937 435-0678
855 Congress Park Dr # 101 Dayton (45459) *(G-9760)*
Muirfield Association Inc 614 889-0922
8372 Muirfield Dr Dublin (43017) *(G-10401)*
Muirfield Village Golf Club 614 889-6700
5750 Memorial Dr Dublin (43017) *(G-10402)*
Mulberry Garden A L S 330 630-3980
395 S Main St Apt 210 Munroe Falls (44262) *(G-14932)*
Mull Iron, Rittman *Also called Rittman Inc (G-16556)*
Mullett Company 440 564-9000
14980 Cross Creek Pkwy Newbury (44065) *(G-15259)*
Mullinax East LLC 440 296-3020
28825 Euclid Ave Wickliffe (44092) *(G-19608)*
Mullinax Ford North Canton Inc 330 238-3206
5900 Whipple Ave Nw Canton (44720) *(G-2468)*
Mullins International Sls Corp 937 233-4213
2949 Valley Pike Dayton (45404) *(G-9761)*
Multi Builders Inc 216 831-1400
27800 Cedar Rd Cleveland (44122) *(G-6088)*
Multi Cntry SEC Slutions Group 216 973-0291
3459 W 117th St Cleveland (44111) *(G-6089)*

Multi County Juvenile Det Ctr 740 652-1525
923 Liberty Dr Lancaster (43130) *(G-12559)*
Multi Flow Transport Inc 216 641-0200
4705 Van Epps Rd Brooklyn Heights (44131) *(G-1920)*
Multi Products Company 330 674-5981
7188 State Route 39 Millersburg (44654) *(G-14613)*
Multi-Care Inc 440 352-0788
60 Wood St Painesville (44077) *(G-15867)*
Multi-Cnty Jvnile Attntion Sys (PA) 330 484-6471
815 Faircrest St Sw Canton (44706) *(G-2469)*
Multi-Flow Dispensers Ohio Inc (PA) 216 641-0200
4705 Van Epps Rd Brooklyn Heights (44131) *(G-1921)*
Multi-Plastics Inc (PA) 740 548-4894
7770 N Central Dr Lewis Center (43035) *(G-12696)*
Multicare Home Health Services 216 731-8900
27691 Euclid Ave Ste B-1 Euclid (44132) *(G-10768)*
Multicare Management Group 513 868-6500
908 Symmes Rd Fairfield (45014) *(G-10883)*
Multicon Builders Inc (PA) 614 241-2070
495 S High St Ste 150 Columbus (43215) *(G-8206)*
Multicon Builders Inc 614 463-1142
503 S High St Columbus (43215) *(G-8207)*
Multicon Construction, Columbus *Also called Multicon Builders Inc (G-8207)*
Multicon Construction Co 614 351-2683
1320 Mckinley Ave Ste C Columbus (43222) *(G-8208)*
Multifab, Elyria *Also called Multilink Inc (G-10656)*
Multilink Inc 440 366-6966
580 Ternes Ln Elyria (44035) *(G-10656)*
Munich Reinsurance America Inc 614 221-7123
471 E Broad St Fl 17 Columbus (43215) *(G-8209)*
Municipal Garage, Cleveland *Also called City of Lakewood (G-5268)*
Municipal Golf Course, Pickerington *Also called City of Pickerington (G-16089)*
Municipal Government, Toledo *Also called City of Toledo (G-17808)*
Municipal Power Plant, Hamilton *Also called City of Hamilton (G-11711)*
Municipal Water Supply, Kent *Also called City of Akron (G-12358)*
Municpal Cntrs Saling Pdts Inc 513 482-3300
7740 Reinhold Dr Cincinnati (45237) *(G-4131)*
Mural & Son Inc 216 267-3322
11340 Brookpark Rd Cleveland (44130) *(G-6090)*
Murphy Contracting Co 330 743-8915
285 Andrews Ave Youngstown (44505) *(G-20292)*
Murphy Tractor & Eqp Co Inc 513 772-3232
11441 Mosteller Rd Cincinnati (45241) *(G-4132)*
Murray & Murray Co Lpa (PA) 419 624-3000
111 E Shoreline Dr Ste 2 Sandusky (44870) *(G-16779)*
Murray American Energy Inc 740 338-3100
46226 National Rd Saint Clairsville (43950) *(G-16645)*
Murray Guttman 513 984-0300
4901 Hunt Rd Ste 300 Blue Ash (45242) *(G-1649)*
Murray Kentucky Energy Inc (HQ) 740 338-3100
46226 National Rd Saint Clairsville (43950) *(G-16646)*
Murray Leasing Inc 330 386-4757
14778 E Liverpool Rd East Liverpool (43920) *(G-10526)*
Murray Ridge Production Center 440 329-3734
1091 Infirmary Rd Elyria (44035) *(G-10657)*
Murray Wells Wendeln & Robinsn, Piqua *Also called Murray Wlls Wndeln Rbnson Cpas (G-16154)*
Murray Wlls Wndeln Rbnson Cpas (PA) 937 773-6373
326 N Wayne St Piqua (45356) *(G-16154)*
Murtech Consulting LLC 216 328-8580
4700 Rockside Rd Ste 310 Cleveland (44131) *(G-6091)*
Murwood Real Estate Group LLC 216 839-5500
29225 Chagrin Blvd # 360 Beachwood (44122) *(G-1106)*
Museum Cntmprary Art Cleveland 216 421-8671
11400 Euclid Ave Cleveland (44106) *(G-6092)*
Musical Arts Association (PA) 216 231-7300
11001 Euclid Ave Cleveland (44106) *(G-6093)*
Muskingum Cnty Ctr For Seniors 740 454-9761
160 Nth St Zanesville (43701) *(G-20504)*
Muskingum Coach Company (PA) 740 622-2545
1662 S 2nd St Coshocton (43812) *(G-9112)*
Muskingum County Adult and CHI 740 849-2344
4155 Roseville Rd Zanesville (43701) *(G-20505)*
Muskingum County Engineers Off, Zanesville *Also called Muskingum County Ohio (G-20508)*
MUSKINGUM COUNTY HEADSTART, Zanesville *Also called Child Care Resources Inc (G-20464)*
Muskingum County Home, Zanesville *Also called Muskingum County Ohio (G-20507)*
Muskingum County Ohio 740 452-0678
160 N 4th St Zanesville (43701) *(G-20506)*
Muskingum County Ohio 740 454-1911
401 Main St Zanesville (43701) *(G-20507)*
Muskingum County Ohio 740 453-0381
155 Rehl Rd Zanesville (43701) *(G-20508)*
Muskingum Iron & Metal Co 740 452-9351
345 Arthur St Zanesville (43701) *(G-20509)*
Muskingum Livestock Auction, Zanesville *Also called Muskingum Livestock Sales Inc (G-20510)*
Muskingum Livestock Sales Inc 740 452-9984
944 Malinda St Zanesville (43701) *(G-20510)*

Muskingum Residentials Inc 740 453-5350
1900 Montgomery Ave Zanesville (43701) *(G-20511)*
Muskingum Starlight Industries (PA) 740 453-4622
1304 Newark Rd Zanesville (43701) *(G-20512)*
Muskingum Starlight Industries 740 453-4622
1330 Newark Rd Zanesville (43701) *(G-20513)*
Muskingum Vly Nrsing Rhblttion 740 984-4262
501 Pinecrest Dr Beverly (45715) *(G-1492)*
Muskingum Vly Symphonic Winds 740 826-8095
163 Stormont St New Concord (43762) *(G-15035)*
Muskingum Wtrshed Cnsrvncy Dst 740 685-6013
22172 Park Rd Senecaville (43780) *(G-16824)*
Muskingum Wtrshed Cnsrvncy Dst 330 343-6780
4956 Shop Rd Ne Mineral City (44656) *(G-14634)*
Mustard Seed Health Fd Mkt Inc 440 519-3663
6025 Kruse Dr Ste 100 Solon (44139) *(G-17031)*
Muth Lumber Company Inc 740 533-0800
1301 Adams Ln Ironton (45638) *(G-12300)*
Mutual Electric Company 937 254-6211
3660 Dayton Park Dr Dayton (45414) *(G-9762)*
Mutual Health Services Company 216 687-7000
2060 E 9th St Cleveland (44115) *(G-6094)*
Mutual Holding Company, Cleveland *Also called Mutual Health Services Company (G-6094)*
Mutual Shareholder Svcs LLC 440 922-0067
8000 Town Centre Dr # 400 Broadview Heights (44147) *(G-1884)*
Mv Commercial Construction LLC 937 293-0900
137 N Main St Ste 900 Dayton (45402) *(G-9763)*
Mv Communities, Cincinnati *Also called Miller-Vlntine Partners Ltd Lc (G-4098)*
Mv Land Development Company 937 293-0900
137 N Main St Ste 900 Dayton (45402) *(G-9764)*
Mv Residential Cnstr Inc 513 588-1000
9349 Waterstone Blvd # 200 Cincinnati (45249) *(G-4133)*
Mv Residential Development LLC 937 293-0900
4000 Miller Valentine Ct Moraine (45439) *(G-14810)*
Mv Transportation Inc 419 627-0740
1230 N Depot St Sandusky (44870) *(G-16780)*
Mv Transportation Inc 740 681-5086
1801 Transpark Dr Cincinnati (45229) *(G-4134)*
MVCDC, Dayton *Also called Miami Vly Child Dev Ctrs Inc (G-9740)*
Mvd Communications LLC (PA) 513 683-4711
5188 Cox Smith Rd Mason (45040) *(G-13741)*
Mvd Connect, Mason *Also called Mvd Communications LLC (G-13741)*
Mvfl, Lebanon *Also called Miami Vly Fandom For Literacy (G-12629)*
Mvhe Inc (HQ) 937 499-8211
110 N Main St Ste 370 Dayton (45402) *(G-9765)*
MVHO, Dayton *Also called Miami Vly Hsing Oprtunties Inc (G-9742)*
Mvi Home Care, Youngstown *Also called Mahoning Vly Infusioncare Inc (G-20266)*
Mw Mielke, Medina *Also called Marvin W Mielke Inc (G-14095)*
Mw Mosaic, Toledo *Also called Midwest Mosaic Inc (G-18062)*
Mwa Enterprises Ltd 419 599-3835
900 American Rd Napoleon (43545) *(G-14946)*
Mwd Logistics Inc 419 522-3510
222 Tappan Dr N Ontario (44906) *(G-15705)*
Mxd Group Inc 614 801-0621
1650 Watermark Dr Ste 100 Columbus (43215) *(G-8210)*
Mxd Group Inc (HQ) 866 711-3129
7795 Walton Pkwy New Albany (43054) *(G-14995)*
Mxd Group, Inc., New Albany *Also called Mxd Group Inc (G-14995)*
Mxr Sourceone, Mentor *Also called Sourceone Healthcare Tech Inc (G-14244)*
My Lawn Ldscp & Irrigation Co, Spring Valley *Also called Tim Mundy (G-17111)*
My Place Child Care 740 349-3505
1335 E Main St Newark (43055) *(G-15215)*
Myca Mltmdia Trning Sltons LLC 513 544-2379
4555 Lake Forest Dr # 650 Blue Ash (45242) *(G-1650)*
MYCAP, Youngstown *Also called Mahoning Youngstown Community (G-20268)*
Mycity Transporatation Co 216 591-1900
16781 Shgrin Blvd Ste 283 Shaker Heights (44120) *(G-16864)*
Myers Bus Parts and Sups Co 330 533-2275
8860 Akron Canfield Rd Canfield (44406) *(G-2202)*
Myers Equipment, Canfield *Also called Myers Bus Parts and Sups Co (G-2202)*
Myers Equipment Corporation 330 533-5556
8860 Akron Canfield Rd Canfield (44406) *(G-2203)*
Myers Industries Inc (PA) 330 253-5592
1293 S Main St Akron (44301) *(G-348)*
Myers Industries Inc 440 632-0230
15150 Madison Rd Middlefield (44062) *(G-14398)*
Myers Machinery Movers Inc 614 871-5052
2210 Hardy Parkway St Grove City (43123) *(G-11582)*
Myers/Schmalenberger Inc (PA) 614 621-2796
462 S Ludlow St Columbus (43215) *(G-8211)*
Myocare Nursing Home Inc 216 252-7555
24340 Sperry Dr Cleveland (44145) *(G-6095)*
Mzf Inc 216 464-3910
27629 Chagrin Blvd 101b Cleveland (44122) *(G-6096)*
N & C Active Learning LLC 937 545-1342
1380 N Fairfield Rd Beavercreek (45432) *(G-1193)*
N A A C P, Youngstown *Also called Natio Assoc For The Advan of (G-20295)*
N A L C, Northwood *Also called National Assn Ltr Carriers (G-15538)*
N A S, Cleveland *Also called Nas Rcrtment Cmmunications LLC (G-6100)*
N C B International Department 216 488-7990
23000 Millcreek Blvd # 7350 Cleveland (44122) *(G-6097)*
N C B-F S B, Hillsboro *Also called National Cooperative Bank NA (G-11989)*
N C R Employee Benefit Assn 937 299-3571
4435 Dogwood Trl Dayton (45429) *(G-9766)*
N Cook Inc 513 275-9872
5762 Argus Rd Cincinnati (45224) *(G-4135)*
N E C Columbus, Columbus *Also called National Electric Coil Inc (G-8217)*
N F Mansuetto & Sons Inc 740 633-7320
116 Wood St Martins Ferry (43935) *(G-13600)*
N L C, Independence *Also called Nations Lending Corporation (G-12238)*
N P I, Cleveland *Also called Neighborhood Progress Inc (G-6117)*
N P I Audio Video Solutions, Cleveland *Also called Northeast Projections Inc (G-6156)*
N P Motel System Inc 330 339-7731
145 Bluebell Dr Sw New Philadelphia (44663) *(G-15110)*
N R I, Columbus *Also called Nationwide Rlty Investors Ltd (G-8248)*
N Safe Sound Security Inc 888 317-7233
5555 County Road 203 Millersburg (44654) *(G-14614)*
N Services Inc 513 793-2000
10901 Reed Hartman Hwy Blue Ash (45242) *(G-1651)*
N W O, Northwood *Also called Nwo Beverage Inc (G-15541)*
N Wasserstrom & Sons Inc (HQ) 614 228-5550
2300 Lockbourne Rd Columbus (43207) *(G-8212)*
N-T Steel, Cleveland *Also called Associated Steel Company Inc (G-5073)*
N. S. Farrington & Co., New Albany *Also called Norm Sharlotte Inc (G-15002)*
Nabisco, Streetsboro *Also called Mondelez Global LLC (G-17422)*
Nacco Industries Inc (PA) 440 229-5151
5875 Landerbrook Dr # 220 Cleveland (44124) *(G-6098)*
Nadler Nadler & Burdman Co Lpa 330 533-6195
6550 Seville Dr Ste B Canfield (44406) *(G-2204)*
Naf Wright Patterson Afb, Dayton *Also called Air Force US Dept of (G-9252)*
Nahhas, Ahed T MD, Toledo *Also called Toledo Cardiology Inc (G-18230)*
Nai Ohio Equities, Realtors, Columbus *Also called Ohio Equities LLC (G-8341)*
Nam Showcase Cinemas Milford, Milford *Also called National Amusements Inc (G-14544)*
Nami of Preble County Ohio 937 456-4947
800 E Saint Clair St Eaton (45320) *(G-10570)*
Namru-Dayton, Dayton *Also called United States Dept of Navy (G-9286)*
Namsa, Northwood *Also called North Amercn Science Assoc Inc (G-15539)*
Namsa Sterilzation Products, Northwood *Also called North Amercn Science Assoc Inc (G-15540)*
Nanaeles Day Care Inc 216 991-6139
3685 Lee Rd Cleveland (44120) *(G-6099)*
Nannicola Wholesale Co 330 799-0888
2750 Salt Springs Rd Youngstown (44509) *(G-20293)*
NAPA Auto Parts, Mentor *Also called MJ Auto Parts Inc (G-14221)*
NAPA Distribution Center, Columbus *Also called Genuine Parts Company (G-7740)*
Napoleon Wash-N-Fill Inc (PA) 419 422-7216
339 E Main Cross St Findlay (45840) *(G-11068)*
Napoleon Wash-N-Fill Inc (PA) 419 592-0851
485 N Perry St Napoleon (43545) *(G-14947)*
Naragon Companies Inc 330 745-7700
2197 Wadsworth Rd Norton (44203) *(G-15556)*
Narrow Way Custom Technology 937 743-1611
100 Industry Dr Carlisle (45005) *(G-2605)*
Nas Rcrtment Cmmunications LLC (HQ) 216 478-0300
9700 Rockside Rd Ste 170 Cleveland (44125) *(G-6100)*
Nas Ventures 614 338-8501
4477 E 5th Ave Columbus (43219) *(G-8213)*
NASA-Trmi Group Inc 937 387-6517
7918 N Main St Dayton (45415) *(G-9767)*
Nasco Roofing and Cnstr Inc 330 746-3566
1900 Mccartney Rd Youngstown (44505) *(G-20294)*
Nassief Automotive Inc 440 997-5151
2920 Gh Dr Austinburg (44010) *(G-865)*
Nassief Honda, Austinburg *Also called Nassief Automotive Inc (G-865)*
Nat'l Rglartory RES Institutue, Columbus *Also called Ohio State University (G-8435)*
Nate, Cincinnati *Also called August Food & Wine LLC (G-3063)*
Natio Assoc For The Advan of 330 782-9777
1350 5th Ave Youngstown (44504) *(G-20295)*
National Administative Svc LLC 614 358-3607
400 Metro Pl N Ste 360 Dublin (43017) *(G-10403)*
National All-Jersey Inc (PA) 614 861-3636
6486 E Main St Reynoldsburg (43068) *(G-16470)*
National Alliance SEC Agcy Inc 937 387-6517
7918 N Main St Dayton (45415) *(G-9768)*
National Amusements Inc 513 699-1500
500 Rivers Edge Milford (45150) *(G-14544)*
National Amusements Inc 513 699-1500
760 Cincinnati Mills Dr Cincinnati (45240) *(G-4136)*
National Amusements Inc 419 215-3095
2300 Village Dr W # 1700 Maumee (43537) *(G-13949)*
National Assn Ltr Carriers 419 289-8359
530 Claremont Ave Ashland (44805) *(G-691)*
National Assn Ltr Carriers 419 693-8392
4437 Woodville Rd Northwood (43619) *(G-15538)*
National Auto Care Corporation 800 548-1875
440 Polaris Pkwy Ste 250 Westerville (43082) *(G-19330)*

ALPHABETIC

National Auto Experts LLC 440 274-5114
8370 Dow Cir Ste 100 Strongsville (44136) ***(G-17497)***
National Benevolent Associatio 216 476-0333
4614 Prospect Ave Ste 240 Cleveland (44103) ***(G-6101)***
National Blanking LLC 419 385-0636
135 N Fearing Blvd Toledo (43607) ***(G-18073)***
National Board of Boiler (PA) 614 888-8320
1055 Crupper Ave Columbus (43229) ***(G-8214)***
National Bronze Mtls Ohio Inc 440 277-1226
5311 W River Rd Lorain (44055) ***(G-13063)***
National Car Mart III Inc 216 398-2228
9255 Brookpark Rd Cleveland (44129) ***(G-6102)***
National Car Rental, Strongsville *Also called Clerac LLC* ***(G-17450)***
National Center For Space Expl, Cleveland *Also called Universities Space Res Assn* ***(G-6651)***
National Ch Rsdnces Brstol Vlg, Waverly *Also called Waverly Care Center Inc* ***(G-18976)***
National Ch Rsdnces Stygler Rd, Columbus *Also called Traditions At Stygler Road* ***(G-8863)***
National Ch Rsidences Mill Run, Hilliard *Also called Traditions At Mill Run* ***(G-11960)***
National Child Support Center, Blue Ash *Also called Innovtive Cllectn Concepts Inc* ***(G-1615)***
National Church, Cuyahoga Falls *Also called Traditions At Bath Rd Inc* ***(G-9226)***
National Church Residences (PA) 614 451-2151
2335 N Bank Dr Columbus (43220) ***(G-8215)***
National Church Residences 614 451-2151
2335 N Bank Dr Columbus (43220) ***(G-8216)***
NATIONAL CHURCH RESIDENCES CENTER FOR SENIOR HEALTH, Columbus *Also called Heritage Day Health Centers* ***(G-7830)***
NATIONAL CHURCH RESIDENCES FIRST COMMUNITY VILLAGE, Columbus *Also called First Community Village* ***(G-7664)***
National City Bank, Akron *Also called PNC Bank National Association* ***(G-394)***
National City Bank, Newark *Also called PNC Bank National Association* ***(G-15228)***
National City Bank, Sandusky *Also called PNC Bank National Association* ***(G-16785)***
National City Bank, Toledo *Also called PNC Bank National Association* ***(G-18129)***
National City Cmnty Dev Corp 216 575-2000
1900 E 9th St Cleveland (44114) ***(G-6103)***
National City Mortgage 614 401-5030
545 Metro Pl S Ste 100 Dublin (43017) ***(G-10404)***
National City Mortgage Inc (HQ) 937 910-1200
3232 Newmark Dr Miamisburg (45342) ***(G-14325)***
National Colloid Company 740 282-1171
906 Adams St Steubenville (43952) ***(G-17332)***
National Compressor Svcs LLC (PA) 419 868-4980
10349 Industrial St Holland (43528) ***(G-12040)***
National Concession Company 216 881-9911
4582 Willow Pkwy Cleveland (44125) ***(G-6104)***
National Consumer Coop Bnk 937 393-4246
139 S High St Hillsboro (45133) ***(G-11988)***
National Cooperative Bank NA (HQ) 937 393-4246
139 S High St Ste 1 Hillsboro (45133) ***(G-11989)***
National Dentex LLC 216 671-0577
3873 Rocky River Dr Cleveland (44111) ***(G-6105)***
National Electric Coil Inc (PA) 614 488-1151
800 King Ave Columbus (43212) ***(G-8217)***
National Electro-Coatings Inc 216 898-0080
15655 Brookpark Rd Cleveland (44142) ***(G-6106)***
National Engrg & Contg Co 440 238-3331
50 Public Sq Ste 2175 Cleveland (44113) ***(G-6107)***
National Engrg Archtctral Svcs, Columbus *Also called Barr Engineering Incorporated* ***(G-7091)***
National Entp Systems Inc (PA) 440 542-1360
29125 Solon Rd Solon (44139) ***(G-17032)***
National Exchange Club 419 535-3232
3050 W Central Ave Toledo (43606) ***(G-18074)***
National Exchange Club Foundat 419 535-3232
3050 W Central Ave Toledo (43606) ***(G-18075)***
National Express Transit Corp 513 322-6214
8041 Hosbrook Rd Ste 330 Cincinnati (45236) ***(G-4137)***
National Flight Services Inc (HQ) 419 865-2311
10971 E Airport Svc Rd Swanton (43558) ***(G-17568)***
National Football Museum Inc 330 456-8207
2121 George Halas Dr Nw Canton (44708) ***(G-2470)***
National Gas & Oil Corporation (HQ) 740 344-2102
1500 Granville Rd Newark (43055) ***(G-15216)***
National Gas & Oil Corporation 740 454-7252
1423 Lake Dr Zanesville (43701) ***(G-20514)***
National Gas Oil Corp 740 348-1243
120 O Neill Dr Hebron (43025) ***(G-11857)***
National General Insurance 212 380-9462
800 Superior Ave E Cleveland (44114) ***(G-6108)***
National Golf Links, South Charleston *Also called Bw Enterprises Inc* ***(G-17075)***
National Ground Water Assn Inc 614 898-7791
601 Dempsey Rd Westerville (43081) ***(G-19429)***
National Guard Ohio 614 492-3166
7370 Minuteman Way Columbus (43217) ***(G-8218)***
National Heat Exch Clg Corp 330 482-0893
8397 Southern Blvd Youngstown (44512) ***(G-20296)***
National Heritg Academies Inc 937 223-2889
501 Hickory St Dayton (45410) ***(G-9769)***
National Heritg Academies Inc 513 251-6000
1798 Queen City Ave Cincinnati (45214) ***(G-4138)***
National Heritg Academies Inc 419 269-2247
5130 Bennett Rd Toledo (43612) ***(G-18076)***
National Heritg Academies Inc 513 751-5555
1712 Duck Creek Rd Cincinnati (45207) ***(G-4139)***
National Heritg Academies Inc 419 531-3285
305 Wenz Rd Toledo (43615) ***(G-18077)***
National Heritg Academies Inc 937 235-5498
173 Avondale Dr Dayton (45404) ***(G-9770)***
National Heritg Academies Inc 937 278-6671
3901 Turner Rd Dayton (45415) ***(G-9771)***
National Heritg Academies Inc 216 731-0127
860 E 222nd St Euclid (44123) ***(G-10769)***
National Heritg Academies Inc 216 451-1725
16005 Terrace Rd Cleveland (44112) ***(G-6109)***
National Heritg Academies Inc 330 792-4806
2420 Donald Ave Youngstown (44509) ***(G-20297)***
National Highway Equipment Co 614 459-4900
971 Old Henderson Rd Columbus (43220) ***(G-8219)***
National Hot Rod Association 740 928-5706
2650 National Rd Sw Ste B Hebron (43025) ***(G-11858)***
National Housing Corporation (PA) 614 481-8106
45 N 4th St Ste 200 Columbus (43215) ***(G-8220)***
National Housing Tr Ltd Partnr 614 451-9929
2335 N Bank Dr Columbus (43220) ***(G-8221)***
National Interstate Corp (HQ) 330 659-8900
3250 Interstate Dr Richfield (44286) ***(G-16515)***
National Interstate Insur Co (HQ) 330 659-8900
3250 Interstate Dr Richfield (44286) ***(G-16516)***
National Labor Relations Board 216 522-3716
1240 E 9th St Rm 1695 Cleveland (44199) ***(G-6110)***
National Lien Digest, Highland Heights *Also called C & S Associates Inc* ***(G-11868)***
National Lime and Stone Co 419 396-7671
370 N Patterson St Carey (43316) ***(G-2596)***
National Lime and Stone Co 740 548-4206
2406 S Section Line Rd Delaware (43015) ***(G-10117)***
National Lime and Stone Co 419 562-0771
4580 Bethel Rd Bucyrus (44820) ***(G-2044)***
National Lime and Stone Co 419 423-3400
9860 County Road 313 Findlay (45840) ***(G-11069)***
National Lime and Stone Co 614 497-0083
5911 Lockbourne Rd Lockbourne (43137) ***(G-12959)***
National Lime Stone Clmbus Reg, Delaware *Also called National Lime and Stone Co* ***(G-10117)***
National Liquidators, Cleveland *Also called G Robert Toney & Assoc Inc* ***(G-5648)***
National Marketshare Group (PA) 513 921-0800
2155 W 8th St Cincinnati (45204) ***(G-4140)***
National Mentor Inc 216 525-1885
9800 Rockside Rd Ste 800 Cleveland (44125) ***(G-6111)***
National Mentor Holdings Inc 513 221-0175
2245 Gilbert Ave Cincinnati (45206) ***(G-4141)***
National Mentor Holdings Inc 419 443-0867
526 Plaza Dr Fostoria (44830) ***(G-11135)***
National Mentor Holdings Inc 330 491-4331
100 Debartolo Pl Ste 330 Youngstown (44512) ***(G-20298)***
National Mentor Holdings Inc 330 835-1468
3085 W Market St Fairlawn (44333) ***(G-10967)***
National Mentor Holdings Inc 234 806-5361
4451 Mahoning Ave Nw Warren (44483) ***(G-18884)***
National Metal Trading LLC 440 487-9771
3950 Ben Hur Ave Willoughby (44094) ***(G-19695)***
National Multiple Sclerosis 330 759-9066
4300 Belmont Ave Youngstown (44505) ***(G-20299)***
National Office, Cleveland *Also called National Electro-Coatings Inc* ***(G-6106)***
National Railroad Pass Corp 419 246-0159
415 Emerald Ave Toledo (43604) ***(G-18078)***
National Realty Services Inc (HQ) 614 798-0971
2261 Sandover Rd Columbus (43220) ***(G-8222)***
National Registry-Emergency, Columbus *Also called National Rgstry Emrgncy Mdcl* ***(G-8224)***
National Rent A Car, Vandalia *Also called National Rental (us) Inc* ***(G-18690)***
National Rent A Car, Columbus *Also called National Rental (us) Inc* ***(G-8223)***
National Rental (us) Inc 937 890-0100
3600 Terminal Rd Vandalia (45377) ***(G-18690)***
National Rental (us) Inc 614 239-3270
4600 International Gtwy Columbus (43219) ***(G-8223)***
National Rgstry Emrgncy Mdcl 614 888-4484
6610 Busch Blvd Columbus (43229) ***(G-8224)***
National Safety Tech LLC, Toledo *Also called Bionix Safety Technologies* ***(G-17773)***
National Service Club, Toledo *Also called National Exchange Club Foundat* ***(G-18075)***
National Service Information 740 387-6806
145 Baker St Marion (43302) ***(G-13567)***
National Smallwares, Columbus *Also called Wasserstrom Company* ***(G-8970)***
National Staffing Alternative, Lima *Also called Rkpl Inc* ***(G-12869)***
National Staffing Group Ltd 440 546-0800
8221 Brecksville Rd # 202 Brecksville (44141) ***(G-1835)***
National Testing Laboratories (PA) 440 449-2525
6571 Wilson Mills Rd # 3 Cleveland (44143) ***(G-6112)***
National Trail Raceway, Hebron *Also called National Hot Rod Association* ***(G-11858)***
National Trnsp Solutions Inc 330 405-2660
1831 Highland Rd Twinsburg (44087) ***(G-18450)***
National Underground Railroad 513 333-7500
250 W Court St Ste 300e Cincinnati (45202) ***(G-4142)***

National Valuation Consultants...513 929-4100
441 Vine St Cincinnati (45202) *(G-4143)*
National Veterinary Assoc Inc...330 652-0055
1007 Youngstown Warren Rd Niles (44446) *(G-15298)*
National Weather Service...937 383-0031
1901 S State Route 134 Wilmington (45177) *(G-19774)*
National Weather Service...216 265-2370
5301 W Hngr Fdral Fclties Cleveland (44135) *(G-6113)*
National Weather Service...419 522-1375
2101 Harrington Mem Rd Mansfield (44903) *(G-13349)*
National Yllow Pages Media LLC...216 447-9400
2 Summit Park Dr Ste 630 Independence (44131) *(G-12237)*
National Youth Advocate Progra...740 349-7511
15 N 3rd St Fl 3 Newark (43055) *(G-15217)*
National Youth Advocate Progra (PA)...614 487-8758
1801 Watermark Dr Ste 200 Columbus (43215) *(G-8225)*
National Youth Advocate Progra...614 252-6927
1303 E Main St Columbus (43205) *(G-8226)*
NationaLease, Girard *Also called Aim Leasing Company* *(G-11407)*
NationaLease, Girard *Also called Aim Integrated Logistics Inc* *(G-11406)*
Nations Lending Corporation...440 842-4817
4 Summit Park Dr Ste 200 Independence (44131) *(G-12238)*
Nations Roof of Ohio LLC...937 439-4160
275 S Pioneer Blvd Springboro (45066) *(G-17132)*
Nations Title Agency of Ohio (HQ)...614 839-3848
3700 Corporate Dr Ste 200 Columbus (43231) *(G-8227)*
Nationstar Mortgage LLC...614 985-9500
150 E Campus View Blvd Columbus (43235) *(G-8228)*
Nationwide, Cincinnati *Also called Rick Blazing Insurance Agency* *(G-4417)*
Nationwide Biweekly ADM Inc...937 376-5800
855 Lower Bellbrook Rd Xenia (45385) *(G-20071)*
Nationwide Childrens Hospital...614 722-2700
700 Childrens Dr Columbus (43205) *(G-8229)*
Nationwide Childrens Hospital...614 722-5750
555 S 18th St Ste 6g Columbus (43205) *(G-8230)*
Nationwide Childrens Hospital (PA)...614 722-2000
700 Childrens Dr Columbus (43205) *(G-8231)*
Nationwide Childrens Hospital...513 636-6000
796 Old State Route 74 # 200 Cincinnati (45245) *(G-2925)*
Nationwide Childrens Hospital...330 253-5200
1 Canal Square Plz # 110 Akron (44308) *(G-349)*
Nationwide Childrens Hospital...614 722-2000
700 Childrens Dr Columbus (43205) *(G-8232)*
Nationwide Childrens Hospital...614 355-8300
433 N Cleveland Ave Westerville (43082) *(G-19331)*
Nationwide Childrens Hospital...614 722-8200
655 E Livingston Ave Columbus (43205) *(G-8233)*
Nationwide Childrens Hospital...614 864-9216
1310 Hill Rd N Pickerington (43147) *(G-16102)*
Nationwide Childrens Hospital...614 355-0802
3433 Agler Rd Ste 1400 Columbus (43219) *(G-8234)*
Nationwide Childrens Hospital...614 355-8100
6435 E Broad St Columbus (43213) *(G-8235)*
Nationwide Childrens Hospital...614 355-9200
1125 E Main St Columbus (43205) *(G-8236)*
Nationwide Childrens Hospital...614 355-8000
495 E Main St Columbus (43215) *(G-8237)*
Nationwide Corporation (HQ)...614 249-7111
1 Nationwide Plz Columbus (43215) *(G-8238)*
Nationwide Corporation...614 249-4302
1 Nationwide Plz Columbus (43215) *(G-8239)*
Nationwide Corporation...330 452-8705
1000 Market Ave N Canton (44702) *(G-2471)*
Nationwide Corporation...614 277-5103
3400 Southpark Pl Ste A Grove City (43123) *(G-11583)*
Nationwide Energy Partners LLC...614 918-2031
230 West St Ste 150 Columbus (43215) *(G-8240)*
Nationwide Fin Inst Dis Agency...614 249-6825
1 Nationwide Plz 2-0501 Columbus (43215) *(G-8241)*
Nationwide Financial Svcs Inc (HQ)...614 249-7111
1 Nationwide Plz Columbus (43215) *(G-8242)*
Nationwide General Insur Co...614 249-7111
1 W Nationwide Blvd # 100 Columbus (43215) *(G-8243)*
Nationwide Health MGT LLC...440 888-8888
5700 Chevrolet Blvd Parma (44130) *(G-15911)*
Nationwide Inv Svcs Corp...614 249-7111
2 Nationwide Plz Columbus (43215) *(G-8244)*
Nationwide Life Insur Co Amer...800 688-5177
P.O. Box 182928 Columbus (43218) *(G-8245)*
Nationwide Mutl Fire Insur Co (HQ)...614 249-7111
1 W Nationwide Blvd # 100 Columbus (43215) *(G-8246)*
Nationwide Mutual Insurance Co (PA)...614 249-7111
1 Nationwide Plz Columbus (43215) *(G-8247)*
Nationwide Mutual Insurance Co...330 489-5000
1000 Market Ave N Canton (44702) *(G-2472)*
Nationwide Mutual Insurance Co...614 948-4153
955 County Line Rd W Westerville (43082) *(G-19332)*
Nationwide Mutual Insurance Co...614 430-3047
9243 Columbus Pike Lewis Center (43035) *(G-12697)*
Nationwide Rlty Investors Ltd (HQ)...614 857-2330
375 N Front St Ste 200 Columbus (43215) *(G-8248)*
Nationwide Rtirement Solutions (HQ)...614 854-8300
5900 Parkwood Pl Dublin (43016) *(G-10405)*
Nationwide Transport Llc...513 554-0203
4445 Lk Frest Dr Ste 475 Cincinnati (45242) *(G-4144)*
Nationwide Truck Brokers Inc...937 335-9229
3355 S County Road 25a Troy (45373) *(G-18367)*
Natl City Coml Capitol LLC...513 455-9746
995 Dalton Ave Cincinnati (45203) *(G-4145)*
Natorps Inc (PA)...513 398-4769
8601 Snider Rd Mason (45040) *(G-13742)*
Natrop Inc...513 242-1375
4400 Reading Rd Cincinnati (45229) *(G-4146)*
Natural Foods Inc (PA)...419 537-1713
3040 Hill Ave Toledo (43607) *(G-18079)*
Natural Resources Ohio Dept...419 394-3611
834 Edgewater Dr Saint Marys (45885) *(G-16680)*
Natural Resources Ohio Dept...419 938-5411
1098 Ashlnd Cnty Rd 300 Ste 3006 Perrysville (44864) *(G-16080)*
Natural Resources Ohio Dept...614 265-6948
2045 Morse Rd Bldg C Columbus (43229) *(G-8249)*
Natural Resources Ohio Dept...614 265-6852
1894 Fountain Square Ct Columbus (43224) *(G-8250)*
Nature Fresh Farms Usa Inc...419 330-5080
9250 Us Highway 20a Delta (43515) *(G-10161)*
Nature Stone, Bedford *Also called Ohio Concrete Resurfacing Inc* *(G-1326)*
NATURES BIN, Lakewood *Also called Cornucopia Inc* *(G-12474)*
Nautica Queen, Cleveland *Also called Paul A Ertel* *(G-6252)*
Navigtor MGT Prtners Ltd Lblty...614 796-0090
1400 Goodale Blvd Ste 100 Columbus (43212) *(G-8251)*
Navistar Intl Trnsp Corp...937 390-4242
5975 Urbana Rd Springfield (45502) *(G-17250)*
Nayak, Naresh K MD, Marietta *Also called First Settlement Orthopaedics* *(G-13446)*
Nb and T Insurance Agency Inc...937 393-1985
111 Governor Foraker Pl Hillsboro (45133) *(G-11990)*
Nb Trucking Inc...740 335-9331
1659 Rte 22 E Washington Court Hou (43160) *(G-18937)*
Nba, Xenia *Also called Nationwide Biweekly ADM Inc* *(G-20071)*
NBBJ Construction Services, Columbus *Also called NBBJ LLC* *(G-8252)*
NBBJ LLC (PA)...206 223-5026
250 S High St Ste 300 Columbus (43215) *(G-8252)*
Nbdc II LLC...513 681-5439
2127 W North Bend Rd Cincinnati (45224) *(G-4147)*
Nbw Inc...216 377-1700
4556 Industrial Pkwy Cleveland (44135) *(G-6114)*
NC Hha Inc...216 593-7750
1170 E Broad St Ste 101 Elyria (44035) *(G-10658)*
Nca Financial Planners, Cleveland *Also called Financial Plnners of Cleveland* *(G-5586)*
NCC ASSOCIATES, Columbus *Also called North Cntl Mntal Hlth Svcs Inc* *(G-8288)*
Ncmf, Canton *Also called Aultman North Canton Med Group* *(G-2257)*
Ncop LLC...419 599-4070
240 Northcrest Dr Napoleon (43545) *(G-14948)*
NCR At Home Health & Wellness...614 451-2151
2335 N Bank Dr Columbus (43220) *(G-8253)*
NCR Country Club, Dayton *Also called N C R Employee Benefit Assn* *(G-9766)*
Ncs Healthcare of Ohio LLC...330 364-5011
219 W 12th St Dover (44622) *(G-10201)*
Ncs Healthcare of Ohio LLC (HQ)...513 719-2600
201 E 4th St Ste 900 Cincinnati (45202) *(G-4148)*
Ncs Healthcare of Ohio LLC...614 534-0400
2305 Westbrooke Dr Bldg C Columbus (43228) *(G-8254)*
Ncs Incorporated...440 684-9455
729 Miner Rd Cleveland (44143) *(G-6115)*
Nds, Ravenna *Also called Neighborhood Development Svcs* *(G-16393)*
Neace Assoc Insur Agcy of Ohio...614 224-0772
285 Cozzins St Columbus (43215) *(G-8255)*
Neace Lukens, Rocky River *Also called Nl of Ky Inc* *(G-16587)*
Neace Lukens, Columbus *Also called Nl of Ky Inc* *(G-8283)*
Neals Construction Company...513 489-7700
7770 E Kemper Rd Cincinnati (45249) *(G-4149)*
Neals Design Remodel, Cincinnati *Also called Neals Construction Company* *(G-4149)*
Nearly New Shop, Findlay *Also called Blanchard Valley Hospital* *(G-10999)*
Necco Center...740 534-1386
115 Private Road 977 Pedro (45659) *(G-15937)*
Needmore Road Primary Care, Dayton *Also called Primary Cr Ntwrk Prmr Hlth Prt* *(G-9823)*
Neff & Associates, Cleveland *Also called T J Neff Holdings Inc* *(G-6564)*
Neff and Associates, Cleveland *Also called Dj Neff Enterpeises Inc* *(G-5494)*
Neff Group Distributors Inc...440 835-7010
909 Canterbury Rd Ste G Westlake (44145) *(G-19519)*
Neff Machinery and Supplies...740 454-0128
112 S Shawnee Ave Zanesville (43701) *(G-20515)*
Neff Parts, Zanesville *Also called Neff Machinery and Supplies* *(G-20515)*
Neff Paving Ltd (PA)...740 453-3063
6575 West Pike Zanesville (43701) *(G-20516)*
Nehemiah Manufacturing Co LLC...513 351-5700
1130 Findlay St Cincinnati (45214) *(G-4150)*
Neighborcare Inc (HQ)...513 719-2600
201 E 4th St Ste 900 Cincinnati (45202) *(G-4151)*
NEIGHBORHOOD CENTERS, Cleveland *Also called Gc Neighborhood Ctrs Assoc Inc* *(G-5660)*
Neighborhood Development Svcs...330 296-2003
120 E Main St Ravenna (44266) *(G-16393)*

ALPHABETIC

Neighborhood Family Practice, Cleveland *Also called Neighborhood Health Care Inc* ***(G-6116)***
Neighborhood Health Asso (PA) 419 720-7883
313 Jefferson Ave Toledo (43604) ***(G-18080)***
Neighborhood Health Care Inc (PA) 216 281-8945
4115 Bridge Ave 300 Cleveland (44113) ***(G-6116)***
Neighborhood Health Care Inc (PA) 513 221-4949
2415 Auburn Ave Cincinnati (45219) ***(G-4152)***
Neighborhood House (PA) 614 252-4941
1000 Atcheson St Columbus (43203) ***(G-8256)***
Neighborhood Hsg Servs Toledo 419 691-2900
704 2nd St Toledo (43605) ***(G-18081)***
Neighborhood Logistics Co Inc 440 466-0020
5449 Bishop Rd Geneva (44041) ***(G-11366)***
Neighborhood Progress Inc (PA) 216 830-2770
11327 Shaker Blvd Ste 500 Cleveland (44104) ***(G-6117)***
Neighborhood Properties Inc 419 473-2604
2753 W Central Ave Toledo (43606) ***(G-18082)***
NEIL KENNEDY RECOVERY CLINIC, Youngstown *Also called Youngstown Committee On Alchol* ***(G-20429)***
Neil Kravitz Group Sales Inc 513 961-8697
412 S Cooper Ave Cincinnati (45215) ***(G-4153)***
Nelsen Corporation (PA) 330 745-6000
3250 Barber Rd Norton (44203) ***(G-15557)***
Nelson & Bold Inc 440 975-1422
36060 Euclid Ave Ste 201 Willoughby (44094) ***(G-19696)***
Nelson Financial Group 513 686-7800
3195 Dayton Xenia Rd # 900 Dayton (45434) ***(G-9278)***
Nelson Manufacturing Company 419 523-5321
6448 State Route 224 Ottawa (45875) ***(G-15799)***
Nelson Packaging Company Inc 419 229-3471
1801 Reservoir Rd Lima (45804) ***(G-12842)***
Nelson Park Apartments, Beachwood *Also called Npa Associates* ***(G-1109)***
Nelson Stark Company 513 489-0866
7685 Fields Ertel Rd D2 Cincinnati (45241) ***(G-4154)***
Nelson Stud Welding Inc 440 250-9242
821 Sharon Dr Westlake (44145) ***(G-19520)***
Nelson Tree Service Inc (HQ) 937 294-1313
3300 Office Park Dr # 205 Dayton (45439) ***(G-9772)***
Nemco Inc 419 542-7751
301 Meuse Argonne St Hicksville (43526) ***(G-11866)***
Nemco Food Equipment, Hicksville *Also called Nemco Inc* ***(G-11866)***
Nentwick Convalescent Home 330 385-5001
500 Selfridge St East Liverpool (43920) ***(G-10527)***
Neo-Pet LLC 440 893-9949
1894 E 123rd St Apt 1 Cleveland (44106) ***(G-6118)***
Neocap/Cbcf 330 675-2669
411 Pine Ave Se Warren (44483) ***(G-18885)***
Neocom, Warren *Also called Northeast Ohio Communic* ***(G-18888)***
Neopost USA Inc 440 526-3196
6670 W Snowville Rd Ste 2 Brecksville (44141) ***(G-1836)***
Nephrology Department, Cincinnati *Also called University of Cincinnati* ***(G-4774)***
Neptune Plumbing & Heating Co 216 475-9100
23860 Miles Rd Ste G Cleveland (44128) ***(G-6119)***
Nerone & Sons Inc 216 662-2235
19501 S Miles Rd Ste 1 Cleveland (44128) ***(G-6120)***
Nes, Solon *Also called National Entp Systems Inc* ***(G-17032)***
Nest Tenders Limited 614 901-1570
5083 Westerville Rd Columbus (43231) ***(G-8257)***
Nestle Product Technology Ctr, Marysville *Also called R & D Nestle Center Inc* ***(G-13646)***
Nestle Quality Assurance Ctr, Dublin *Also called Nestle Usa Inc* ***(G-10406)***
Nestle Usa Inc 513 576-4930
6279 Tri Ridge Blvd # 100 Loveland (45140) ***(G-13148)***
Nestle Usa Inc 614 526-5300
6625 Eiterman Rd Dublin (43016) ***(G-10406)***
Netcare Access, Columbus *Also called Netcare Corporation* ***(G-8258)***
Netcare Corporation (PA) 614 274-9500
199 S Cent Ave Columbus (43223) ***(G-8258)***
Netcare Corporation 614 274-9500
741 E Broad St Columbus (43205) ***(G-8259)***
Netco, Cleveland *Also called National Engrg & Contg Co* ***(G-6107)***
Neteam Systems LLC 330 523-5100
1111 Superior Ave E # 1111 Cleveland (44114) ***(G-6121)***
Netjets Assn Shred Arcft Plots 614 863-2008
2740 Airport Dr Columbus (43219) ***(G-8260)***
Netjets Aviation Inc 614 239-5501
760 Morrison Rd Ste 250 Gahanna (43230) ***(G-11259)***
Netjets Inc (HQ) 614 239-5500
4111 Bridgeway Ave Columbus (43219) ***(G-8261)***
Netjets International Inc (HQ) 614 239-5500
4111 Bridgeway Ave Columbus (43219) ***(G-8262)***
Netjets Large Aircraft Inc 614 239-4853
4111 Bridgeway Ave Columbus (43219) ***(G-8263)***
Netjets Sales Inc 614 239-5500
4111 Bridgeway Ave Columbus (43219) ***(G-8264)***
Netmap Analytics, Worthington *Also called Verisk Crime Analytics Inc* ***(G-20005)***
Netrada North America LLC 866 345-5835
5389 E Provident Dr West Chester (45246) ***(G-19218)***
Netsmart Technologies Inc 440 942-4040
30775 Bnbridge Rd Ste 200 Solon (44139) ***(G-17033)***
Netsmart Technologies Inc 614 764-0143
5455 Rings Rd Dublin (43017) ***(G-10407)***
Nettleton Steel Treating Div, Cleveland *Also called Thermal Treatment Center Inc* ***(G-6591)***
Netwave Corporation 614 850-6300
6457 Reflections Dr # 130 Dublin (43017) ***(G-10408)***
Network, Canton *Also called M Conley Company* ***(G-2442)***
Network Housing 2005 Inc 614 487-6700
1680 Watermark Dr Columbus (43215) ***(G-8265)***
Network Restorations II 614 253-0984
129 E 7th Ave Columbus (43201) ***(G-8266)***
Network Restorations III LLC 614 253-0984
910 E Broad St Columbus (43205) ***(G-8267)***
Neundorfer Inc 440 942-8990
4590 Hamann Pkwy Willoughby (44094) ***(G-19697)***
Neundorfer Engineering Service, Willoughby *Also called Neundorfer Inc* ***(G-19697)***
Neurological Associates Inc 614 544-4455
931 Chatham Ln Ste 200 Columbus (43221) ***(G-8268)***
Neurology Nroscience Assoc Inc (PA) 330 572-1011
701 White Pond Dr Akron (44320) ***(G-350)***
Neuroscience Center Inc 614 293-8930
1654 Upham Dr Fl 4 Columbus (43210) ***(G-8269)***
Neurosurgical Network Inc 419 251-1155
3909 Woodley Rd Ste 600 Toledo (43606) ***(G-18083)***
Neutral Telecom Corporation 440 377-4700
6472 Monroe Ln Ste 200 North Ridgeville (44039) ***(G-15472)***
New Albany Athc Booster CLB 614 413-8325
7600 Fodor Rd New Albany (43054) ***(G-14996)***
New Albany Care Center LLC 614 855-8866
5691 Thompson Rd Columbus (43230) ***(G-8270)***
New Albany Cleaning Services 614 855-9990
108 N High St Ste B New Albany (43054) ***(G-14997)***
New Albany Country Club Comm A 614 939-8500
1 Club Ln New Albany (43054) ***(G-14998)***
New Albany Links Dev Co Ltd 614 939-5914
7100 New Albany Links Dr New Albany (43054) ***(G-14999)***
New Albany Plain Loc SC Transp 614 855-2033
55 N High St Ste A New Albany (43054) ***(G-15000)***
New Albany Surgery Center LLC 614 775-1616
5040 Forest Dr Ste 100 New Albany (43054) ***(G-15001)***
New Avenues To Independence (PA) 216 481-1907
17608 Euclid Ave Cleveland (44112) ***(G-6122)***
New Avenues To Independence 216 671-8224
12131 Bennington Ave Cleveland (44135) ***(G-6123)***
New Avenues To Independence 888 853-8905
4230 Lake Ave Ashtabula (44004) ***(G-756)***
New Beginnings Pediatrics Inc 419 483-4122
1400 W Main St Ste G Bellevue (44811) ***(G-1413)***
New Bgnnngs Assembly of God Ch 614 497-2658
492 Williams Rd Columbus (43207) ***(G-8271)***
New Birch Manor I Assoc LLC 330 723-3404
23875 Miner Dr Medina (44256) ***(G-14106)***
New Boston Aerie 2271 FOE 740 456-0171
3200 Rhodes Ave New Boston (45662) ***(G-15012)***
New Boston Eagles, New Boston *Also called New Boston Aerie 2271 FOE* ***(G-15012)***
New Carlisle Spt & Fitnes Ctr 937 846-1000
524 N Dayton Lakeview Rd New Carlisle (45344) ***(G-15029)***
New Channel Direct, Cleveland *Also called Angstrom Graphics Inc Midwest* ***(G-5038)***
New Concepts, Toledo *Also called Philio Inc* ***(G-18124)***
New Concord Health Center 740 826-4135
1280 Friendship Dr New Concord (43762) ***(G-15036)***
New Dawn Child Care Center, Dover *Also called Dover City Schools* ***(G-10184)***
New Dawn Health Care Inc 330 343-5521
865 E Iron Ave Dover (44622) ***(G-10202)***
New Dawn Retirement Community, Dover *Also called New Dawn Health Care Inc* ***(G-10202)***
New Diamond Line Cont Corp 330 644-9993
760 Killian Rd Ste B Coventry Township (44319) ***(G-9129)***
New Directions Inc 216 591-0324
30800 Chagrin Blvd Cleveland (44124) ***(G-6124)***
New England Life Insurance Co 614 457-6233
921 Chatham Ln Ste 300 Columbus (43221) ***(G-8272)***
New England Motor Freight Inc 513 782-0017
11101 Mosteller Rd Ste 1 Cincinnati (45241) ***(G-4155)***
New England Rms Inc 401 384-6759
402 E Wilson Bridge Rd A Worthington (43085) ***(G-19979)***
New England Securities, Columbus *Also called New England Life Insurance Co* ***(G-8272)***
New Enland Life Ins Co, Columbus *Also called Mc Cloy Financial Services* ***(G-8133)***
New Flyer, Delaware *Also called Aftermarket Parts Company LLC* ***(G-10068)***
New Haven Estates Inc (PA) 419 933-2181
2744 E State Highway 224 New Haven (44850) ***(G-15051)***
New Holland Lions Club, Williamsport *Also called International Assn Lions* ***(G-19638)***
New Hope & Horizons 513 761-7999
4055 Executive Park Dr # 100 Cincinnati (45241) ***(G-4156)***
New Hope Center, Mansfield *Also called County of Richland* ***(G-13284)***
New Hope Christian Academy 740 477-6427
2264 Walnut Creek Pike Circleville (43113) ***(G-4893)***
New Hope Vocational Services, Mentor *Also called Richcreek Bailey Rehabilitatio* ***(G-14237)***
New Horizon Youth Center Co 740 782-0092
40060 National Rd Bethesda (43719) ***(G-1485)***
New Horizon Youth Family Ctr (PA) 740 687-0835
1592 Granville Pike Lancaster (43130) ***(G-12560)***

New Horizons Surgery Center...740 375-5854
1167 Independence Ave Marion (43302) *(G-13568)*
New Innovations Inc...330 899-9954
3540 Forest Lake Dr Uniontown (44685) *(G-18530)*
New Jersey Aquarium LLC...614 414-7300
4016 Townsfair Way # 201 Columbus (43219) *(G-8273)*
New Lexington City of...740 342-1633
215 S Main St New Lexington (43764) *(G-15057)*
New Lexington Mncpl Water Plnt, New Lexington *Also called New Lexington City of (G-15057)*
New Lfcare Hspitals Dayton LLC...937 384-8300
4000 Mmsburg Cntrville Rd Miamisburg (45342) *(G-14326)*
New Life Christian Center...740 687-1572
2642 Clumbus Lancaster Rd Lancaster (43130) *(G-12561)*
New Life Hospice Ctr St Joseph, Lorain *Also called New Life Hospice Inc (G-13064)*
New Life Hospice Inc...440 934-1458
3500 Kolbe Rd Lorain (44053) *(G-13064)*
New Life Hospice Inc (HQ)...440 934-1458
5255 N Abbe Rd Ste 2 Sheffield Village (44035) *(G-16893)*
New London Area Historical Soc...419 929-3674
210 E Main St New London (44851) *(G-15068)*
New Lxngton Care Rhblttion Ctr, New Lexington *Also called Sunbridge Healthcare LLC (G-15064)*
New Nghbors Rsdential Svcs Inc...937 717-5731
4230 E National Rd Springfield (45505) *(G-17251)*
New NV Co LLC...330 896-7611
3777 Boettler Oaks Dr Uniontown (44685) *(G-18531)*
New Path International LLC...614 410-3974
1476 Manning Pkwy Ste A Powell (43065) *(G-16344)*
New Philadelphia General Svcs, New Philadelphia *Also called City of New Philadelphia (G-15086)*
New Pittsburgh Fire & Rescue F...330 264-1230
3311 N Elyria Rd Wooster (44691) *(G-19892)*
New Pros Communications Inc...740 201-0410
155 Hidden Ravines Dr Powell (43065) *(G-16345)*
New River Electrical Corp...614 891-1142
6005 Westerville Rd Westerville (43081) *(G-19430)*
New School Inc...513 281-7999
3 Burton Woods Ln Cincinnati (45229) *(G-4157)*
New Tech West High School, Cleveland *Also called Cleveland Municipal School Dst (G-5336)*
New Technology Steel LLC...419 385-0636
135 N Fearing Blvd Toledo (43607) *(G-18084)*
New Technology Steel LLC (PA)...419 385-0636
2401 Front St Toledo (43605) *(G-18085)*
New Vision Medical Labs, Lima *Also called St Ritas Medical Center (G-12886)*
New Vulco Mfg & Sales Co LLC...513 242-2672
5353 Spring Grove Ave Cincinnati (45217) *(G-4158)*
New Waterford Fireman...330 457-2363
3766 E Main St New Waterford (44445) *(G-15139)*
New Wembley LLC...440 543-8171
8345 Woodberry Blvd Chagrin Falls (44023) *(G-2726)*
New World Energy Resources (PA)...740 344-4087
1500 Granville Rd Newark (43055) *(G-15218)*
New World Van Lines Ohio Inc...614 836-5720
4633 Homer Ohio Ln Groveport (43125) *(G-11658)*
New Wrld Cmmunications of Ohio...216 432-4041
5800 S Marginal Rd Cleveland (44103) *(G-6125)*
New York Community Bank...440 734-7040
4800 Great Northern Blvd North Olmsted (44070) *(G-15434)*
New York Community Bank...216 741-7333
5767 Broadview Rd Cleveland (44134) *(G-6126)*
New York Life Insurance Co...216 520-1345
6100 Oak Tree Blvd # 300 Independence (44131) *(G-12239)*
New York Life Insurance Co...513 621-9999
5905 E Galbraith Rd # 4000 Cincinnati (45236) *(G-4159)*
New York Life Insurance Co...216 221-1100
14600 Detroit Ave Ste 900 Lakewood (44107) *(G-12492)*
Newark Care Center LLC...740 366-2321
151 Price Rd Newark (43055) *(G-15219)*
Newark Corporation...330 523-4457
4180 Highlander Pkwy Richfield (44286) *(G-16517)*
Newark Drywall Inc...740 763-3572
18122 Nashport Rd Nashport (43830) *(G-14952)*
Newark Electronics Corporation...330 523-4912
4180 Highlander Pkwy Richfield (44286) *(G-16518)*
Newark Hlls Hlth Rhblttion Ctr, Newark *Also called Newark NH LLC (G-15221)*
Newark Management Partners LLC...740 322-6455
50 N 2nd St Newark (43055) *(G-15220)*
Newark Metropolitan Hotel, Newark *Also called Newark Management Partners LLC (G-15220)*
Newark NH LLC...740 345-9197
17 Forry St Newark (43055) *(G-15221)*
Newark Parcel Service Company...614 253-3777
640 N Cassady Ave Columbus (43219) *(G-8274)*
Newark Resident Homes Inc...740 345-7231
15 W Saint Clair St Apt C Newark (43055) *(G-15222)*
Newark Sleep Diagnostic Center...740 522-9499
1900 Tamarack Rd Ste 1908 Newark (43055) *(G-15223)*
Newbold Technologies, East Liverpool *Also called Soaring Eagle Inc (G-10535)*
Newcome Corp...614 848-5688
9005 Antares Ave Columbus (43240) *(G-6897)*
Newcome Electronic Systems, Columbus *Also called Newcome Corp (G-6897)*
Newcomer Concrete Services Inc (PA)...419 668-2789
646 Townline Road 151 Norwalk (44857) *(G-15581)*
Newcomer Funeral Svc Group Inc...513 521-1971
7830 Hamilton Ave Cincinnati (45231) *(G-4160)*
Newcomerstown Development Inc...740 498-5165
1100 E State Rd Newcomerstown (43832) *(G-15270)*
Newcomerstown Progress Corp...740 498-5165
1100 E State Rd Newcomerstown (43832) *(G-15271)*
Newell Brands Inc...419 662-2225
20750 Midstar Dr Bowling Green (43402) *(G-1786)*
Newfound Technologies, Columbus *Also called Liberty Comm Sftwr Sltions Inc (G-8056)*
Newlex Classic Riders Inc...740 342-3885
810 N Main St New Lexington (43764) *(G-15058)*
Newman International Inc...513 932-7379
964 W Main St Lebanon (45036) *(G-12630)*
Newman Sanitary Gasket, Lebanon *Also called Newman International Inc (G-12630)*
Newmark & Company RE Inc...216 453-3000
1350 Euclid Ave Ste 300 Cleveland (44115) *(G-6127)*
Newmark Grubb Knight Frank, Cleveland *Also called Newmark & Company RE Inc (G-6127)*
Newport Walking Tours LLC...859 951-8560
6292 Eagles Lake Dr Cincinnati (45248) *(G-4161)*
Newstart Loan , The, Cincinnati *Also called 722 Redemption Funding Inc (G-2948)*
Newtown Nine Inc (PA)...440 781-0623
8155 Roll And Hold Pkwy Macedonia (44056) *(G-13206)*
Newtown Nine Inc...330 376-7741
568 E Crosier St Akron (44311) *(G-351)*
Nex Transport Inc...937 645-3761
13900 State Route 287 East Liberty (43319) *(G-10512)*
Nexeo Solutions LLC...330 405-0461
1842 Enterprise Pkwy Twinsburg (44087) *(G-18451)*
Nexgen Building Supply, Cincinnati *Also called Nexgen Enterprises Inc (G-4162)*
Nexgen Building Supply, West Chester *Also called Hwz Distribution Group LLC (G-19209)*
Nexgen Building Supply, Cincinnati *Also called Hwz Distribution Group LLC (G-3800)*
Nexgen Enterprises Inc (PA)...513 618-0300
3274 Spring Grove Ave Cincinnati (45225) *(G-4162)*
Nexstar Broadcasting Inc...614 263-4444
3165 Olentangy River Rd Columbus (43202) *(G-8275)*
Nexstar Broadcasting Inc...937 293-2101
4595 S Dixie Dr Moraine (45439) *(G-14811)*
Nexstep Healthcare LLC...216 797-4040
673 Alpha Dr Ste G Cleveland (44143) *(G-6128)*
Next Generation, Columbus *Also called Rcs Enterprises Inc (G-8591)*
Nextel Communications Inc...513 891-9200
7878 Montgomery Rd Cincinnati (45236) *(G-4163)*
Nextel Communications Inc...614 801-9267
1727 Stringtown Rd Grove City (43123) *(G-11584)*
Nextel Partners Operating Corp...330 305-1365
6791 Strip Ave Nw North Canton (44720) *(G-15357)*
Nextel Partners Operating Corp...419 380-2000
5350 Airport Hwy Ste 110 Toledo (43615) *(G-18086)*
Nextmed Systems Inc (PA)...216 674-0511
16 Triangle Park Dr Cincinnati (45246) *(G-4164)*
Nextt Corp...513 813-6398
106 Koehler Ave Apt 4 Cincinnati (45215) *(G-4165)*
Nexus Communications Inc...740 549-1092
2631 Morse Rd Columbus (43231) *(G-8276)*
Nexus Engineering Group LLC (PA)...216 404-7867
1422 Euclid Ave Ste 1400 Cleveland (44115) *(G-6129)*
Nexxtshow Exposition Svcs LLC...877 836-3131
645 Linn St Cincinnati (45203) *(G-4166)*
Ney Oil Company Inc...419 485-4009
13441 State Route 15 Montpelier (43543) *(G-14746)*
Neyer Management, Cincinnati *Also called Neyer Real Estate MGT LLC (G-4167)*
Neyer Real Estate MGT LLC...513 618-6000
3927 Brotherton Rd # 200 Cincinnati (45209) *(G-4167)*
Nf Il Cleveland Op Co LLC...216 443-9043
527 Prospect Ave E Cleveland (44115) *(G-6130)*
Nfm/Welding Engineers Inc...330 837-3868
1339 Duncan St Sw Massillon (44647) *(G-13841)*
Ngic, Cleveland *Also called National General Insurance (G-6108)*
Ngm Inc...513 821-7363
7676 Reinhold Dr Cincinnati (45237) *(G-4168)*
Ngn Electric Corp...330 923-2777
10310 Brecksville Rd Brecksville (44141) *(G-1837)*
Ngts, Beavercreek Township *Also called Northrop Grumman Technical (G-1276)*
NGWA, Westerville *Also called National Ground Water Assn Inc (G-19429)*
Nhs - Totco Inc...419 691-2900
704 2nd St Toledo (43605) *(G-18087)*
NHS WEATHERIZATION PROGRAM, Toledo *Also called Neighborhood Hsg Servs Toledo (G-18081)*
Nht, Columbus *Also called National Housing Tr Ltd Partnr (G-8221)*
Niagara Health Corporation (HQ)...614 898-4000
6150 E Broad St Columbus (43213) *(G-8277)*
Nichalex Inc...330 726-1422
801 Kentwood Dr Youngstown (44512) *(G-20300)*
Nicholas Carney-Mc Inc (PA)...330 792-5460
100 Victoria Rd Youngstown (44515) *(G-20301)*
Nicholas Carney-Mc Inc...440 243-8560
2931 Abbe Rd Sheffield Village (44054) *(G-16894)*

ALPHABETIC

Nicholas D Starr Inc (PA)..........419 229-3192
301 W Elm St Lima (45801) ***(G-12843)***
Nicholas E Davis..........937 228-2838
40 N Main St Ste 1700 Dayton (45423) ***(G-9773)***
Nicholson Builders Inc..........614 846-8621
6525 Busch Blvd Ste 101 Columbus (43229) ***(G-8278)***
Nick Amster Inc (PA)..........330 264-9667
1700b Old Mansfield Rd Wooster (44691) ***(G-19893)***
Nick Amster Inc..........330 264-9667
326 N Hillcrest Dr Ste C Wooster (44691) ***(G-19894)***
Nick Mayer Lincoln-Mercury Inc..........440 835-3700
24400 Center Ridge Rd Westlake (44145) ***(G-19521)***
Nick Strimbu Inc (PA)..........330 448-4046
3500 Parkway Dr Brookfield (44403) ***(G-1900)***
Nick Strimbu Inc..........330 448-4046
303 Oxford St Dover (44622) ***(G-10203)***
Nickle Bakery, Washington Court Hou *Also called Nb Trucking Inc* ***(G-18937)***
Nickolas Rsidential Trtmnt Ctr..........937 496-7100
5581 Dayton Liberty Rd Dayton (45417) ***(G-9774)***
Nicola Gudbranson & Cooper LLC..........216 621-7227
25 W Prospect Ave # 1400 Cleveland (44115) ***(G-6131)***
Nicoles Child Care Center (PA)..........216 751-6668
4035 E 141st St Cleveland (44128) ***(G-6132)***
Nicolozakes Trckg & Cnstr Inc..........740 432-5648
8555 Georgetown Rd Cambridge (43725) ***(G-2124)***
Niederst Management Ltd (PA)..........440 331-8800
21400 Lorain Rd Cleveland (44126) ***(G-6133)***
Nielsen Consumer Insights Inc..........513 489-9000
4665 Cornell Rd Ste 160 Blue Ash (45241) ***(G-1652)***
Nieman Plumbing Inc..........513 851-5588
2030 Stapleton Ct Cincinnati (45240) ***(G-4169)***
Niese Leasing, Ottawa *Also called Niese Transport Inc* ***(G-15800)***
Niese Transport Inc..........419 523-4400
418 N Agner St Ottawa (45875) ***(G-15800)***
Nifco America Corporation..........614 836-8733
2435 Spiegel Dr Groveport (43125) ***(G-11659)***
Nightingale Holdings LLC (PA)..........330 645-0200
670 Jarvis Rd Akron (44319) ***(G-352)***
Nightingale Home Care..........614 457-6006
3380 Tremont Rd Ste 270 Columbus (43221) ***(G-8279)***
Nightingale Home Healthcare..........614 408-0104
5945 Wilcox Pl Ste C Dublin (43016) ***(G-10409)***
Nightingale Montessori Inc..........937 324-0336
1106 E High St Springfield (45505) ***(G-17252)***
NIGHTINGALE MONTESSORI SCHOOL, Springfield *Also called Nightingale Montessori Inc* ***(G-17252)***
Nightngl-Alan Med Eqp Svcs LLC..........513 247-8200
11418 Deerfield Rd Bldg 1 Blue Ash (45242) ***(G-1653)***
Nightrider Overnite Copy Svc, Cleveland *Also called Ricoh Usa Inc* ***(G-6394)***
Nightrider Overnite Copy Svc, Akron *Also called Ricoh Usa Inc* ***(G-416)***
Nilco LLC (HQ)..........888 248-5151
1221 W Maple St Ste 100 Hartville (44632) ***(G-11827)***
Nilco LLC..........330 538-3386
489 Rosemont Rd North Jackson (44451) ***(G-15384)***
Niles Generating Station, Niles *Also called NRG Power Midwest LP* ***(G-15301)***
Niles Historical Society..........330 544-2143
503 Brown St Niles (44446) ***(G-15299)***
Niles Iron & Metal Company LLC (PA)..........330 652-2262
700 S Main St Niles (44446) ***(G-15300)***
Niles Scrap Iron & Metal Co, Niles *Also called Niles Iron & Metal Company LLC* ***(G-15300)***
Nimishillen & Tuscarawas LLC..........330 438-5821
2633 8th St Ne Canton (44704) ***(G-2473)***
Nippon Express USA Inc..........614 801-5695
3705 Urbancrest Indus Dr Grove City (43123) ***(G-11585)***
Nisbet Corporation..........513 563-1111
11575 Reading Rd Cincinnati (45241) ***(G-4170)***
Nisonger Center, Columbus *Also called Ohio State University* ***(G-8401)***
Nisource Inc..........614 460-4878
290 W Nationwide Blvd Columbus (43215) ***(G-8280)***
Nissin Intl Trnspt USA Inc..........937 644-2644
16940 Square Dr Marysville (43040) ***(G-13642)***
Nitschke Sampson Dietz Inc..........614 464-1933
990 W 3rd Ave Columbus (43212) ***(G-8281)***
NJ Executive Services Inc..........614 239-2996
4111 Bridgeway Ave Columbus (43219) ***(G-8282)***
Njasap, Columbus *Also called Netjets Assn Shred Arcft Plots* ***(G-8260)***
Nk Parts Industries Inc..........937 493-4651
2640 Campbell Rd Sidney (45365) ***(G-16943)***
Nkp West, Sidney *Also called Nk Parts Industries Inc* ***(G-16943)***
Nl of Ky Inc..........740 689-9876
2680 Kull Rd Lancaster (43130) ***(G-12562)***
Nl of Ky Inc..........216 643-7100
1340 Depot St Ste 300 Rocky River (44116) ***(G-16587)***
Nl of Ky Inc..........614 224-0772
285 Cozzins St Columbus (43215) ***(G-8283)***
NM Residential, Cleveland *Also called Niederst Management Ltd* ***(G-6133)***
Nms Inc Certif Pub Accountants (PA)..........440 286-5222
121 South St Chardon (44024) ***(G-2759)***
No Cages Harley-Davidson..........614 764-2453
7610 Commerce Pl Plain City (43064) ***(G-16202)***
Noaca, Cleveland *Also called Northeast Ohio Areawide* ***(G-6153)***
Noah's Ark After School Care, Rootstown *Also called Noahs Ark Child Care Inc* ***(G-16599)***
Noahs Ark Child Care Inc (PA)..........330 325-7236
4524 Lynn Rd Rootstown (44272) ***(G-16599)***
Noahs Ark Child Dev Ctr..........513 988-0921
3259 Wayne Madison Rd Trenton (45067) ***(G-18342)***
Noahs Ark Creative Care..........740 323-3664
1255 Nadine Dr Newark (43056) ***(G-15224)***
Noahs Ark Learning Center..........740 965-1668
100 Tippett Ct Ste 103 Sunbury (43074) ***(G-17559)***
Noakes Rooney Rlty & Assoc Co..........419 423-4861
2113 Tiffin Ave Ste 103 Findlay (45840) ***(G-11070)***
Nobel Learning Center..........740 732-4722
44135 Marietta Rd Caldwell (43724) ***(G-2087)***
Noble Cnty Nble Cnty Cmmsoners..........740 732-4958
44069 Marietta Rd Caldwell (43724) ***(G-2088)***
Noble County Health Department, Caldwell *Also called Noble Cnty Nble Cnty Cmmsoners* ***(G-2088)***
Noble Technologies Corp (PA)..........330 287-1530
2020 Noble Dr Wooster (44691) ***(G-19895)***
Noble-Davis Consulting Inc..........440 519-0850
6190 Cochran Rd Ste D Solon (44139) ***(G-17034)***
Nobletek, Wooster *Also called Noble Technologies Corp* ***(G-19895)***
Noco Company..........216 464-8131
30339 Diamond Pkwy # 102 Solon (44139) ***(G-17035)***
Nofziger Door Sales Inc (PA)..........419 337-9900
320 Sycamore St Wauseon (43567) ***(G-18960)***
Noggins Hair Design Inc..........513 474-4405
8556 Beechmont Ave # 450 Cincinnati (45255) ***(G-4171)***
Noic, Sylvania *Also called Northern Ohio Investment Co* ***(G-17601)***
Noland Company (HQ)..........937 396-7980
3110 Kettering Blvd Moraine (45439) ***(G-14812)***
Nollenberger Truck Center (PA)..........419 837-5996
5320 Fremont Pike Stony Ridge (43463) ***(G-17348)***
Non Emergency Ambulance Svc..........330 296-4541
4830 Harding Ave Ravenna (44266) ***(G-16394)***
Noneman Real Estate Company..........419 531-4020
3519 Secor Rd Toledo (43606) ***(G-18088)***
Nooney & Moses, Akron *Also called Installed Building Pdts LLC* ***(G-280)***
Noor Home Health Care..........216 320-0803
2490 Lee Blvd Ste 110 Cleveland Heights (44118) ***(G-6794)***
NOR Corp..........440 366-0099
10247 Dewhurst Rd Ste 101 Elyria (44035) ***(G-10659)***
Noramco, Carrollton *Also called North American Plas Chem Inc* ***(G-2624)***
Noramco Transport Corp (PA)..........513 245-9050
9252 Colerain Ave Ste 4 Cincinnati (45251) ***(G-4172)***
Norandex Bldg Mtls Dist Inc..........330 656-8924
300 Executive Park Ste 100 Hudson (44236) ***(G-12136)***
Norandex Building Mtls Dist, Hudson *Also called Norandex Bldg Mtls Dist Inc* ***(G-12136)***
Norcare Enterprises Inc (PA)..........440 233-7232
6140 S Broadway Lorain (44053) ***(G-13065)***
Norcia Bakery..........330 454-1077
624 Belden Ave Ne Canton (44704) ***(G-2474)***
Nord Center..........440 233-7232
6140 S Broadway Lorain (44053) ***(G-13066)***
Nord Center Associates Inc (HQ)..........440 233-7232
6140 S Broadway Lorain (44053) ***(G-13067)***
Nord Center Associates Inc..........440 233-7232
3150 Clifton Ave Lorain (44055) ***(G-13068)***
Nord Rehabilitation Center, Lorain *Also called Nord Center Associates Inc* ***(G-13068)***
Nordmann Roofing Co Inc..........419 691-5737
1722 Starr Ave Toledo (43605) ***(G-18089)***
Norfab, Elyria *Also called Northern Ohio Roofg Shtmtl Inc* ***(G-10664)***
Norfolk Southern Corporation..........419 436-2408
3101 N Township Road 47 Fostoria (44830) ***(G-11136)***
Norfolk Southern Corporation..........614 251-2684
3329 Thoroughbred Dr Columbus (43217) ***(G-8284)***
Norfolk Southern Corporation..........419 381-5505
2101 Hill Ave Toledo (43607) ***(G-18090)***
Norfolk Southern Corporation..........419 254-1562
341 Emerald Ave Toledo (43604) ***(G-18091)***
Norfolk Southern Corporation..........440 992-2274
645 E 6th St Ashtabula (44004) ***(G-757)***
Norfolk Southern Corporation..........440 992-2215
2886 Harbor Sta Ashtabula (44004) ***(G-758)***
Norfolk Southern Corporation..........513 271-0972
5555 Wooster Pike Cincinnati (45227) ***(G-4173)***
Norfolk Southern Corporation..........216 362-6087
6409 Clark Ave Cleveland (44102) ***(G-6134)***
Norfolk Southern Corporation..........419 529-4574
2586 Park Ave W Ontario (44906) ***(G-15706)***
Norfolk Southern Corporation..........419 483-1423
24424 N Prairie Rd Bellevue (44811) ***(G-1414)***
Norfolk Southern Corporation..........419 485-3510
701 Linden St Montpelier (43543) ***(G-14747)***
Norfolk Southern Corporation..........740 535-4102
200 Wabash Ave Mingo Junction (43938) ***(G-14656)***
Norfolk Southern Corporation..........216 518-8407
5300 Greenhurst Ext Maple Heights (44137) ***(G-13411)***
Norfolk Southern Corporation..........216 362-6087
4860 W 150th St Cleveland (44135) ***(G-6135)***
Norfolk Southern Corporation..........419 626-4323
2234 Tiffin Ave Sandusky (44870) ***(G-16781)***

ALPHABETIC SECTION

Northcoast Behavior Healthcare, Toledo

Norfolk Southern Corporation..................................740 353-4529
  2435 8th St Portsmouth (45662) *(G-16296)*
Norfolk Southern Corporation..................................937 297-5420
  3101 Springboro Pike Moraine (45439) *(G-14813)*
Norfolk Southern Corporation..................................513 977-3246
  1410 Gest St Fl 2 Cincinnati (45203) *(G-4174)*
Norfolk Southern Corporation..................................740 574-8491
  914 Hayport Rd Wheelersburg (45694) *(G-19579)*
Norfolk Southern Railway Co...................................440 439-1827
  7847 Northfield Rd Bedford (44146) *(G-1323)*
Norfolk Sthern Ashtbula Cltock, Ashtabula *Also called Norfolk Southern Corporation* *(G-758)*
Norhteast Ohio Museum..330 336-7657
  6807 Boneta Rd Medina (44256) *(G-14107)*
Norm Sharlotte Inc..336 788-7705
  5101 Forest Dr Ste C New Albany (43054) *(G-15002)*
Norman Jones Enlow & Co (PA)................................614 228-4000
  226 N 5th St Ste 500 Columbus (43215) *(G-8285)*
Norman Noble Inc...216 761-2133
  6120 Parkland Blvd # 306 Cleveland (44124) *(G-6136)*
Norman-Spencer Agency Inc (PA)..............................937 432-1600
  8075 Washington Vlg Dr Dayton (45458) *(G-9775)*
Normandy Group LLC...513 745-0990
  5151 Pfeiffer Rd Ste 210 Blue Ash (45242) *(G-1654)*
Normandy Manor of Rocky River................................440 333-5401
  22709 Lake Rd Rocky River (44116) *(G-16588)*
Normandy Office Associates.....................................513 381-8696
  1055 Saint Paul Pl Cincinnati (45202) *(G-4175)*
Normanity Town, Cincinnati *Also called Normandy Office Associates* *(G-4175)*
Noron Inc..419 726-2677
  5465 Enterprise Blvd Toledo (43612) *(G-18092)*
Norris Brothers Co Inc...216 771-2233
  2138 Davenport Ave Cleveland (44114) *(G-6137)*
Norstar Aluminum Molds Inc....................................440 632-0853
  15986 Valplast St Middlefield (44062) *(G-14399)*
North Amercn Science Assoc Inc (PA).........................419 666-9455
  6750 Wales Rd Northwood (43619) *(G-15539)*
North Amercn Science Assoc Inc................................419 666-9455
  2261 Tracy Rd Northwood (43619) *(G-15540)*
North American Broadcasting....................................614 481-7800
  1458 Dublin Rd Columbus (43215) *(G-8286)*
North American Plas Chem Inc..................................330 627-2210
  750 Garfield Ave Nw Carrollton (44615) *(G-2624)*
North American Properties Inc..................................513 721-2744
  212 E 3rd St Ste 300 Cincinnati (45202) *(G-4176)*
North American Van Lines, West Chester *Also called University Moving & Storage Co* *(G-19174)*
North Bay Construction Inc......................................440 835-1898
  25800 1st St Ste 1 Westlake (44145) *(G-19522)*
North Branch Nursery Inc..419 287-4679
  3359 Kesson Rd Pemberville (43450) *(G-15942)*
North Broadway Childrens Ctr...................................614 262-6222
  48 E North Broadway St Columbus (43214) *(G-8287)*
North Canton City School Dst...................................330 497-5615
  387 Pershing Ave Ne Canton (44720) *(G-2475)*
North Canton Medical Offices, North Canton *Also called Kaiser Foundation Hospitals* *(G-15347)*
North Canton Schl Transprtatn, Canton *Also called North Canton City School Dst* *(G-2475)*
North Cape Manufacturing, Streetsboro *Also called Technology House Ltd* *(G-17434)*
NORTH CENTER, THE, Lorain *Also called Norcare Enterprises Inc* *(G-13065)*
North Central Elc Coop Inc......................................800 426-3072
  350 Stump Pike Rd Attica (44807) *(G-822)*
North Central Ems, Milan *Also called Norwalk Area Health Services* *(G-14495)*
North Central Sales Inc...216 481-2418
  528 E 200th St Cleveland (44119) *(G-6138)*
North Cntl Mntal Hlth Svcs Inc (PA)............................614 227-6865
  1301 N High St Columbus (43201) *(G-8288)*
North Coast Auto Mall, Bedford *Also called 1st Gear Auto Inc* *(G-1291)*
North Coast Bearings LLC.......................................440 930-7600
  1050 Jaycox Rd Avon (44011) *(G-908)*
North Coast Center, Willoughby *Also called Signature Health Inc* *(G-19713)*
North Coast Coml Roofg Systems, Twinsburg *Also called Beacon Sales Acquisition Inc* *(G-18397)*
North Coast Concrete Inc..216 642-1114
  6061 Carey Dr Cleveland (44125) *(G-6139)*
North Coast Logistics Inc (PA)..................................216 362-7159
  18901 Snow Rd Frnt Brookpark (44142) *(G-1952)*
North Coast Perennials Inc......................................440 428-1277
  3754 Dayton Rd Madison (44057) *(G-13233)*
North Coast Prof Co LLC..419 557-5541
  1031 Pierce St Sandusky (44870) *(G-16782)*
North Coast Sales...440 632-0793
  15200 Madison Rd 101c Middlefield (44062) *(G-14400)*
North Community Counseling Ctr (PA).........................614 846-2588
  4897 Karl Rd Columbus (43229) *(G-8289)*
North Dayton School Discovery, Dayton *Also called National Heritg Academies Inc* *(G-9771)*
North East Family Healthcare, Tallmadge *Also called Pioneer Physicians Networking* *(G-17647)*
North East Mechanical Inc.......................................440 871-7525
  26200 1st St Westlake (44145) *(G-19523)*

North East Ohio Health Svcs (PA)..............................216 831-6466
  24200 Chagrin Blvd # 126 Beachwood (44122) *(G-1107)*
North Electric Inc..216 331-4141
  12117 Bennington Ave # 200 Cleveland (44135) *(G-6140)*
North Gateway Tire Co Inc.......................................330 725-8473
  4001 Pearl Rd Medina (44256) *(G-14108)*
North Hills Management Company..............................740 450-9999
  1575 Bowers Ln Apt C13 Zanesville (43701) *(G-20517)*
North Lima Dairy Queen Inc (PA)...............................330 549-3220
  10067 Market St North Lima (44452) *(G-15406)*
North Main Animal Clinic, Dayton *Also called Dayton Animal Hospital Assoc* *(G-9456)*
North Ohio Heart Center..440 204-4000
  3600 Kolbe Rd Ste 127 Lorain (44053) *(G-13069)*
North Ohio Heart Center Inc....................................440 414-9500
  7255 Old Oak Blvd C408 Cleveland (44130) *(G-6141)*
North Ohio Heart Center Inc....................................440 366-3600
  10325 Dewhurst Rd Elyria (44035) *(G-10660)*
North Ohio Heart Center Inc....................................440 204-4000
  1220 Moore Rd Ste B Avon (44011) *(G-909)*
North Ohio Heart Center Inc (PA)..............................440 204-4000
  3600 Kolbe Rd Ste 127 Lorain (44053) *(G-13070)*
North Ohio Heart Center Inc....................................440 326-4120
  125 E Broad St Ste 305 Elyria (44035) *(G-10661)*
North Park Care Center LLC....................................440 250-4080
  14803 Holland Rd Brookpark (44142) *(G-1953)*
North Park Retirement Cmnty (PA).............................216 267-0555
  14801 Holland Rd Lbby Cleveland (44142) *(G-6142)*
North Point Eductl Svc Ctr.......................................440 967-0904
  710 Cleveland Rd W Huron (44839) *(G-12168)*
North Randall Village (PA)..216 663-1112
  21937 Miles Rd Side Cleveland (44128) *(G-6143)*
North Ridge Veterinary Hosp....................................440 428-5166
  6336 N Ridge Rd Madison (44057) *(G-13234)*
North Shore Door Co Inc..800 783-6112
  162 Edgewood St Elyria (44035) *(G-10662)*
North Shore Gastroenterology &, Westlake *Also called North Shore Gstrenterology Inc* *(G-19524)*
North Shore Gstrenterology Inc.................................440 808-1212
  850 Columbia Rd Ste 200 Westlake (44145) *(G-19524)*
North Shore Retirement Cmnty..................................419 798-8203
  9400 E Northshore Blvd Lakeside (43440) *(G-12465)*
North Side Bank and Trust Co (PA)............................513 542-7800
  4125 Hamilton Ave Cincinnati (45223) *(G-4177)*
North Side Bank and Trust Co..................................513 533-8000
  2739 Madison Rd Cincinnati (45209) *(G-4178)*
North Star Asphalt, Dalton *Also called Wenger Asphalt Inc* *(G-9243)*
North Star Critical Care LLC....................................330 386-9110
  16356 State Route 267 East Liverpool (43920) *(G-10528)*
North Star Golf Club, Sunbury *Also called Championship Management Co* *(G-17552)*
North Star Painting Co Inc.......................................330 743-2333
  3526 Mccartney Rd Youngstown (44505) *(G-20302)*
North Star Realty Incorporated..................................513 737-1700
  3501 Tylersville Rd Ste G Fairfield (45011) *(G-10884)*
North Valley Bank (PA)...740 452-7920
  2775 Maysville Pike Zanesville (43701) *(G-20518)*
North Wood Realty (PA)..330 423-0837
  1315 Boardman Poland Rd # 7 Youngstown (44514) *(G-20303)*
North Wood Realty..330 856-3915
  1985 Niles Cortland Rd Se Warren (44484) *(G-18886)*
Northast Ohio Eye Surgeons Inc (PA)..........................330 678-0201
  2013 State Route 59 Kent (44240) *(G-12387)*
Northast Ohio Eye Surgeons Inc................................330 836-8545
  1 Park West Blvd Ste 310 Akron (44320) *(G-353)*
Northast Ohio Med Rserve Corps...............................216 789-6653
  3612 Ridge Park Dr Broadview Heights (44147) *(G-1885)*
Northast Ohio Orthpedics Assoc................................330 344-1980
  224 W Exchange St Ste 440 Akron (44302) *(G-354)*
Northast Ohio Rgonal Sewer Dst (PA).........................216 881-6600
  3900 Euclid Ave Cleveland (44115) *(G-6144)*
Northast Ohio Rgonal Sewer Dst................................216 641-3200
  6000 Canal Rd Cleveland (44125) *(G-6145)*
Northast Ohio Rgonal Sewer Dst................................216 961-2187
  5800 Cleveland Mem Shr Cleveland (44102) *(G-6146)*
Northast Ohio Rgonal Sewer Dst................................216 641-6000
  4747 E 49th St Cleveland (44125) *(G-6147)*
Northast Ohio Rgonal Sewer Dst................................216 531-4892
  14021 Lake Shore Blvd Cleveland (44110) *(G-6148)*
Northast Ohio Sstnble Cmmnties................................216 410-7698
  146 S High St Ste 800 Akron (44308) *(G-355)*
Northast Ohio Trnching Svc Inc.................................216 663-6006
  17900 Miles Rd Cleveland (44128) *(G-6149)*
Northast Srgical Assoc of Ohio (PA)............................216 643-2780
  6100 Rckside Woods Blvd N Independence (44131) *(G-12240)*
Northastern Eductl TV Ohio Inc.................................330 677-4549
  1750 W Campus Center Dr Kent (44240) *(G-12388)*
Northastern Ohio Alzheimer Ctr, Columbiana *Also called Windsor House Inc* *(G-6867)*
Northbend Archtctural Pdts Inc..................................513 577-7988
  2080 Waycross Rd Cincinnati (45240) *(G-4179)*
Northcast Bhvral Hlathcare Sys, Northfield *Also called Mental Health and Addi Serv* *(G-15520)*
Northcoast Behavior Healthcare, Toledo *Also called Mental Health and Addi Serv* *(G-18051)*

(PA)=Parent Co (HQ)=Headquarters (DH)=Div Headquarters

Northcoast Duplicating Inc....216 573-6681
7850 Hub Pkwy Cleveland (44125) ***(G-6150)***
Northcoast Healthcare MGT Inc....216 591-2000
23611 Chagrin Blvd # 380 Beachwood (44122) ***(G-1108)***
Northcoast Moving Enterprising....440 943-3900
1420 Lloyd Rd Wickliffe (44092) ***(G-19609)***
Northcutt Trucking Inc....440 458-5139
40259 Butternut Ridge Rd Elyria (44035) ***(G-10663)***
Northeast Cincinnati Hotel LLC....513 459-9800
9664 S Masn Montgomery Rd Mason (45040) ***(G-13743)***
Northeast Concrete & Cnstr....614 898-5728
7243 Saddlewood Dr Westerville (43082) ***(G-19333)***
Northeast Family Health Care....330 630-2332
65 Community Rd Ste C Tallmadge (44278) ***(G-17645)***
Northeast Furniture Rental, Akron *Also called Beacon Company* ***(G-95)***
Northeast Lubricants Ltd (PA)....216 478-0507
4500 Renaissance Pkwy Cleveland (44128) ***(G-6151)***
Northeast OH Neighborhood Heal (PA)....216 231-2323
8300 Hough Ave Cleveland (44103) ***(G-6152)***
Northeast Ohio Adoption Svcs....330 856-5582
5000 E Market St Ste 26 Warren (44484) ***(G-18887)***
Northeast Ohio Areawide....216 621-3055
1299 Superior Ave E Cleveland (44114) ***(G-6153)***
Northeast Ohio Cardiology Svcs....330 253-8195
95 Arch St Ste 300350 Akron (44304) ***(G-356)***
Northeast Ohio Chapter Natnl (PA)....216 696-8220
6155 Rockside Rd Ste 202 Cleveland (44131) ***(G-6154)***
Northeast Ohio Communic....330 399-2700
2910 Youngstown Rd Se Warren (44484) ***(G-18888)***
Northeast Ohio Community Alter, Warren *Also called Neocap/Cbcf* ***(G-18885)***
Northeast Ohio Corrections, Youngstown *Also called Corecivic Inc* ***(G-20162)***
Northeast Ohio Dukes....330 360-0968
4289 N Park Ave Warren (44483) ***(G-18889)***
Northeast Ohio Electric LLC (PA)....216 587-9510
5069 Corbin Dr Cleveland (44128) ***(G-6155)***
Northeast Ohio Orthopedics....330 856-1070
1552 North Rd Se Ste 101 Warren (44484) ***(G-18890)***
Northeast Professional Hm Care (PA)....330 966-2311
1177 S Main St Ste 11 Canton (44720) ***(G-2476)***
Northeast Projections Inc....330 375-9444
8600 Sweet Valley Dr Cleveland (44125) ***(G-6156)***
Northeast Scene Inc....216 241-7550
737 Bolivar Rd Cleveland (44115) ***(G-6157)***
Northern Automotive Inc (PA)....614 436-2001
8600 N High St Columbus (43235) ***(G-8290)***
Northern Bckeye Edcatn Council, Archbold *Also called Northwest Ohio Computer Assn* ***(G-640)***
Northern Datacomm Corp....330 665-0344
3700 Embassy Pkwy Ste 141 Akron (44333) ***(G-357)***
Northern Frozen Foods Inc....440 439-0600
21500 Alexander Rd Cleveland (44146) ***(G-6158)***
Northern Haserot, Cleveland *Also called Northern Frozen Foods Inc* ***(G-6158)***
Northern Management & Leasing....216 676-4600
5231 Engle Rd Cleveland (44142) ***(G-6159)***
Northern Ohio Explosives, Forest *Also called Wampum Hardware Co* ***(G-11107)***
Northern Ohio Investment Co....419 885-8300
6444 Monroe St Ste 6 Sylvania (43560) ***(G-17601)***
Northern Ohio Med Spclists LLC....419 625-2841
2500 W Strub Rd Ste 210 Sandusky (44870) ***(G-16783)***
Northern Ohio Plumbing Co....440 951-3370
35601 Curtis Blvd Unit 1 Eastlake (44095) ***(G-10550)***
Northern Ohio Printing Inc....216 398-0000
4721 Hinckley Indus Pkwy Cleveland (44109) ***(G-6160)***
Northern Ohio Realty, Elyria *Also called NOR Corp* ***(G-10659)***
Northern Ohio Recovery Assn (PA)....216 391-6672
3746 Prospect Ave E Cleveland (44115) ***(G-6161)***
Northern Ohio Roofg Shtmtl Inc....440 322-8262
880 Infirmary Rd Elyria (44035) ***(G-10664)***
Northern Ohio Rural Water....419 668-7213
2205 Us Highway 20 E Norwalk (44857) ***(G-15582)***
Northern Plumbing Systems....513 831-5111
1708 State Route 28 Goshen (45122) ***(G-11437)***
Northern Style Cnstr LLC....330 412-9594
344 Lease St Ste 104 Akron (44306) ***(G-358)***
Northern Tier Hospitality LLC....570 888-7711
1100 Crocker Rd Westlake (44145) ***(G-19525)***
Northfield Presbt Ch Day Care....330 467-4411
7755 S Boyden Rd Northfield (44067) ***(G-15521)***
Northfield Presbt Day Care Ctr....330 467-4411
7755 S Boyden Rd Northfield (44067) ***(G-15522)***
Northgate Chrysler Jeep Inc....513 385-3900
8536 Colerain Ave Cincinnati (45251) ***(G-4180)***
Northgate Pk Retirement Cmnty, Cincinnati *Also called Atria Senior Living Group Inc* ***(G-3062)***
Northgate Pk Retirement Cmnty....513 923-3711
9191 Round Top Rd Ofc Cincinnati (45251) ***(G-4181)***
Northland Brdg Franklin Cnty....614 846-2588
4897 Karl Rd Columbus (43229) ***(G-8291)***
Northland Hotel Inc....614 885-1601
1078 E Dblin Granville Rd Columbus (43229) ***(G-8292)***
Northland Lanes Inc....419 224-1961
721 N Cable Rd Lima (45805) ***(G-12844)***
Northmont Service Center....937 832-5050
7277 Hoke Rd Englewood (45315) ***(G-10713)***
Northpoint Senior Services LLC....740 369-9614
2270 Warrensburg Rd Delaware (43015) ***(G-10118)***
Northpoint Senior Services LLC....740 373-3597
400 N 7th St Marietta (45750) ***(G-13480)***
Northpoint Senior Services LLC....513 248-1655
5900 Meadow Creek Dr Milford (45150) ***(G-14545)***
Northpointe Plaza....614 744-2229
191 W Nationwide Blvd # 200 Columbus (43215) ***(G-8293)***
Northpointe Property MGT LLC....614 579-9712
3250 Henderson Rd Ste 103 Columbus (43220) ***(G-8294)***
Northridge Health Center, North Ridgeville *Also called Altercare Inc* ***(G-15454)***
Northrop Grumman Systems Corp....937 429-6450
4020 Executive Dr Beavercreek (45430) ***(G-1255)***
Northrop Grumman Technical....937 320-3100
4065 Colonel Glenn Hwy Beavercreek Township (45431) ***(G-1276)***
Northside Baptist Church, Lebanon *Also called Northside Baptst Child Dev Ctr* ***(G-12631)***
Northside Baptst Child Dev Ctr....513 932-5642
161 Miller Rd Lebanon (45036) ***(G-12631)***
Northside Internal Medicine, Westerville *Also called Central Ohio Primary Care* ***(G-19381)***
Northstar Alloys & Machine Co....440 234-3069
631 Wyleswood Dr Berea (44017) ***(G-1464)***
Northstar Asphalt Inc....330 497-0936
7345 Sunset Strip Ave Nw North Canton (44720) ***(G-15358)***
Northtown Square Ltd Partnr....419 691-8911
2930 Navarre Ave Oregon (43616) ***(G-15742)***
Northview Senior Living Center, Johnstown *Also called Zandex Inc* ***(G-12344)***
Northview Senior Living Center, Johnstown *Also called Zandex Health Care Corporation* ***(G-12345)***
Northwest Bank....330 342-4018
178 W Streetsboro St # 1 Hudson (44236) ***(G-12137)***
Northwest Building Resources (HQ)....419 286-5400
23734 State Route 189 Fort Jennings (45844) ***(G-11109)***
Northwest Child Development An....937 559-9565
2823 Campus Dr Dayton (45406) ***(G-9776)***
Northwest Cmmuntiy Action Comm, Bryan *Also called Pulaski Head Start* ***(G-2019)***
Northwest Columbus Urology....937 342-9260
1164 E Home Rd Ste J Springfield (45503) ***(G-17253)***
Northwest Counseling Services, Columbus *Also called Northwest Mental Health Svcs* ***(G-8297)***
Northwest Country Place Inc....440 488-2700
9223 Amber Wood Dr Willoughby (44094) ***(G-19698)***
Northwest Electrical Contg Inc....419 865-4757
1617 Shanrock Dr Holland (43528) ***(G-12041)***
Northwest Eye Surgeons Inc (PA)....614 451-7550
2250 N Bank Dr Columbus (43220) ***(G-8295)***
Northwest Fam Svc Dda Fam Rsou, Lima *Also called Family Rsource Ctr NW Ohio Inc* ***(G-12777)***
Northwest Fire Ambulance....937 437-8354
135 N Washington St New Paris (45347) ***(G-15079)***
Northwest Firestop Inc....419 517-4777
328 21st St Toledo (43604) ***(G-18093)***
Northwest Hts Title Agcy LLC....614 451-6313
4200 Regent St Ste 210 Columbus (43219) ***(G-8296)***
Northwest Limousine Inc....440 322-5804
642 Sugar Ln Ste 207 Elyria (44035) ***(G-10665)***
Northwest Local School Dst....513 923-1000
3308 Compton Rd Cincinnati (45251) ***(G-4182)***
Northwest Local School Dst (PA)....330 854-2291
2309 Locust St S Canal Fulton (44614) ***(G-2144)***
Northwest Mental Health Svcs....614 457-7876
1560 Fishinger Rd Ste 100 Columbus (43221) ***(G-8297)***
Northwest Ohio Cardiology Cons (PA)....419 842-3000
2121 Hughes Dr Ste 850 Toledo (43606) ***(G-18094)***
Northwest Ohio Chapter Cfma....419 891-1040
145 Chesterfield Ln Maumee (43537) ***(G-13950)***
Northwest Ohio Computer Assn (PA)....419 267-5565
209 Nolan Pkwy Archbold (43502) ***(G-640)***
Northwest Ohio Dvlopmental Ctr, Toledo *Also called Develpmntal Dsblties Ohio Dept* ***(G-17851)***
Northwest Ohio Orthopedic & Sp....419 427-1984
7595 County Road 236 Findlay (45840) ***(G-11071)***
Northwest Ohio Orthopedics....419 885-2553
6444 Monroe St Ste 1 Sylvania (43560) ***(G-17602)***
Northwest Ohio Practice, Maumee *Also called William Vaughan Company* ***(G-13995)***
Northwest Ohio Urgent Care Inc....419 720-7363
1421 S Reynolds Rd Toledo (43615) ***(G-18095)***
NORTHWEST PRODUCTS, Stryker *Also called Quadco Rehabilitation Center* ***(G-17537)***
Northwest Products Div, Archbold *Also called Quadco Rehabilitation Center* ***(G-642)***
Northwest Swim Club Inc....614 442-8716
1064 Bethel Rd Columbus (43220) ***(G-8298)***
Northwest Ttl Agy of OH MI In (PA)....419 241-8195
328 N Erie St Toledo (43604) ***(G-18096)***
Northwesterly Assisted Living, Cleveland *Also called Northwesterly Ltd* ***(G-6162)***
Northwesterly Ltd....216 228-2266
1341 Marlowe Ave Cleveland (44107) ***(G-6162)***
Northwestern Healthcare Center, Berea *Also called Rocky River Leasing Co LLC* ***(G-1468)***

ALPHABETIC SECTION Nvr Inc

Northwestern Mutl Fincl Netwrk, Cleveland *Also called Brown WD General Agency Inc* ***(G-5152)***
Northwestern Mutl Lf Insur Co.......513 366-3600
3805 Edwards Rd Ste 200 Cincinnati (45209) ***(G-4183)***
Northwestern Mutl Lf Insur Co.......614 221-5287
800 Yard St Ste 300 Columbus (43212) ***(G-8299)***
Northwestern Mutual Inv Svcs, Toledo *Also called Bruce Klinger* ***(G-17786)***
Northwestern Mutual Life, Copley *Also called Kelley Companies* ***(G-9057)***
NORTHWESTERN OHIO ADMINISTRATO, Holland *Also called Union Cnstr Wkrs Hlth Plan* ***(G-12065)***
Northwestern Ohio SEC Systems (PA).......419 227-1655
121 E High St Lima (45801) ***(G-12845)***
Northwestern Water & Sewer Dst.......419 354-9090
12560 Middleton Pike Bowling Green (43402) ***(G-1787)***
Northwestrn Natl Insur Company.......513 425-5899
709 Curtis St Middletown (45044) ***(G-14442)***
Northwestrn OH Communty Action (PA).......419 784-2150
1933 E 2nd St Defiance (43512) ***(G-10051)***
Northwind Industries Inc.......216 433-0666
15500 Commerce Park Dr Cleveland (44142) ***(G-6163)***
Northwods Cnslting Prtners Inc.......614 781-7800
5815 Wall St Dublin (43017) ***(G-10410)***
Northwstern Ohio Admnistrators.......419 248-2401
7142 Nightingale Dr 1 Holland (43528) ***(G-12042)***
Nortone Service Inc.......740 527-2057
164 Slocum Ave Buckeye Lake (43008) ***(G-2022)***
Norvell Landscaping Inc.......513 423-9009
218 Old Oxford St Rd Middletown (45044) ***(G-14443)***
Norwalk Area Health Services.......419 499-2515
12513 State Route 250 Milan (44846) ***(G-14495)***
Norwalk Area Health Services (HQ).......419 668-8101
272 Benedict Ave Norwalk (44857) ***(G-15583)***
Norwalk Area Hlth Systems Inc (PA).......419 668-8101
272 Benedict Ave Norwalk (44857) ***(G-15584)***
Norwalk Clinic Inc.......419 668-4851
257 Benedict Ave Ste C1 Norwalk (44857) ***(G-15585)***
Norwalk Golf Properties Inc.......419 668-8535
2406 New State Rd Norwalk (44857) ***(G-15586)***
Norwich Elementary Pto.......614 921-6000
4454 Davidson Rd Hilliard (43026) ***(G-11938)***
Norwood Endoscopy Center.......513 731-5600
4746 Montgomery Rd # 100 Cincinnati (45212) ***(G-4184)***
Norwood Hardware & Supply Co (PA).......513 733-1175
2906 Glendale Milford Rd Cincinnati (45241) ***(G-4185)***
Norwood Health Care Center LLC.......513 351-0153
1578 Sherman Ave Cincinnati (45212) ***(G-4186)***
Norwood School, Marietta *Also called Community Action Program Corp* ***(G-13437)***
Notoweega Nation Inc.......740 777-1480
38494 Mysvlle Grendale Rd Logan (43138) ***(G-12986)***
Notre Dame Academy Apartments.......216 707-1590
1325 Ansel Rd Cleveland (44106) ***(G-6164)***
Notre Dame College of Ohio.......440 279-1127
13000 Auburn Rd Chardon (44024) ***(G-2760)***
Notre Dame Pre-School, Chardon *Also called Notre Dame College of Ohio* ***(G-2760)***
Nottingham Home, Cleveland *Also called Help Foundation Inc* ***(G-5748)***
Nottingham-Spirk Des.......216 800-5782
2200 Overlook Rd Cleveland (44106) ***(G-6165)***
Nova Technology Solutions LLC.......937 426-2596
3100 Presidential Dr # 310 Beavercreek (45324) ***(G-1194)***
Novco, Ashville *Also called Noxious Vegetation Control Inc* ***(G-770)***
Novel Writing Workshop, Blue Ash *Also called F+w Media Inc* ***(G-1591)***
Novelart Manufacturing Company (PA).......513 351-7700
2121 Section Rd Cincinnati (45237) ***(G-4187)***
Novelty Advertising Co Inc.......740 622-3113
1148 Walnut St Coshocton (43812) ***(G-9113)***
Novotec Recycling LLC.......614 231-8326
3960 Groves Rd Columbus (43232) ***(G-8300)***
Novus Clinic.......330 630-9699
518 West Ave Tallmadge (44278) ***(G-17646)***
Now Security Group, Cincinnati *Also called US Protection Service LLC* ***(G-4796)***
Noxious Vegetation Control Inc.......614 486-8994
14923 State Route 104 Ashville (43103) ***(G-770)***
Npa Associates.......614 258-4053
23875 Commerce Park # 120 Beachwood (44122) ***(G-1109)***
Npc Group Inc.......312 627-6000
8500 Governors Hill Dr Symmes Twp (45249) ***(G-17629)***
Npk Construction Equipment Inc (HQ).......440 232-7900
7550 Independence Dr Bedford (44146) ***(G-1324)***
Nr2, Columbus *Also called Network Restorations II* ***(G-8266)***
Nr3, Columbus *Also called Network Restorations III LLC* ***(G-8267)***
NRG Power Midwest LP.......440 930-6401
33570 Lake Rd Avon Lake (44012) ***(G-936)***
NRG Power Midwest LP.......330 505-4327
1047 Belmont Ave Niles (44446) ***(G-15301)***
Nri Global Inc.......905 790-2828
3401 Rodgers Rd Delta (43515) ***(G-10162)***
Nrp Contractors LLC (PA).......216 475-8900
5309 Transportation Blvd Cleveland (44125) ***(G-6166)***
Nrp Group LLC (PA).......216 475-8900
5309 Transportation Blvd Cleveland (44125) ***(G-6167)***
Nrp Holdings LLC.......216 475-8900
5309 Transportation Blvd Cleveland (44125) ***(G-6168)***
Nrt Commercial Utah LLC.......614 239-0808
2288 E Main St Columbus (43209) ***(G-8301)***
Nrt Commercial Utah LLC.......614 889-0808
4535 W Dblin Granville Rd Dublin (43017) ***(G-10411)***
Nsa Technologies LLC.......330 576-4600
3867 Medina Rd Ste 256 Akron (44333) ***(G-359)***
Nsb Retail Systems Inc.......614 840-1421
400 Venture Dr Lewis Center (43035) ***(G-12698)***
Nsd, Elyria *Also called North Shore Door Co Inc* ***(G-10662)***
Nsl Analytical Services Inc (PA).......216 438-5200
4450 Cranwood Pkwy Cleveland (44128) ***(G-6169)***
Ntk Hotel Group II LLC.......614 559-2000
501 N High St Columbus (43215) ***(G-8302)***
Ntt Data Inc.......513 794-1400
3284 North Bend Rd # 107 Cincinnati (45239) ***(G-4188)***
Nu Waves Ltd.......513 360-0800
132 Edison Dr Middletown (45044) ***(G-14444)***
Nu-Di Corporation, Cleveland *Also called Nu-Di Products Co Inc* ***(G-6170)***
Nu-Di Products Co Inc.......216 251-9070
12730 Triskett Rd Cleveland (44111) ***(G-6170)***
Nucentury Textile Services LLC (PA).......419 241-2267
1 Southard Ave Toledo (43604) ***(G-18097)***
Nuclear Reactor Laboratory, Columbus *Also called Ohio State University* ***(G-8425)***
Nucon International Inc.......614 846-5710
6800 Huntley Rd Columbus (43229) ***(G-8303)***
Nucor Corporation.......407 855-2990
P.O. Box 5810 Cincinnati (45201) ***(G-4189)***
Nuerocare Center Inc.......330 494-2917
4105 Holiday St Nw Canton (44718) ***(G-2477)***
Nuerological & Sleep Disorders.......513 721-7533
8250 Kenwood Crossing Way # 225 Cincinnati (45236) ***(G-4190)***
Nueterra Holdings LLC.......614 451-0500
930 Bethel Rd Columbus (43214) ***(G-8304)***
Nugrowth Solutions LLC (PA).......800 747-9273
4181 Arlingate Plz Columbus (43228) ***(G-8305)***
Nulife Music Group.......216 870-3720
16781 Chagrin Blvd # 174 Cleveland (44120) ***(G-6171)***
Number 1 Landscaping, Medina *Also called South Star Corp* ***(G-14128)***
Numotion, Maumee *Also called United Seating & Mobility LLC* ***(G-13991)***
Nuray Radiologists Inc.......513 965-8059
8160 Corp Pk Dr Ste 330 Cincinnati (45242) ***(G-4191)***
Nurenberg Plevin Heller.......440 423-0750
600 Superior Ave E # 1200 Cleveland (44114) ***(G-6172)***
Nurotoco Massachusetts Inc.......513 762-6690
255 E 5th St Cincinnati (45202) ***(G-4192)***
Nurse Medical Healthcare Svcs.......614 801-1300
3421 Farm Bank Way Grove City (43123) ***(G-11586)***
Nursefinders, Akron *Also called Medlink of Ohio Inc* ***(G-337)***
Nurses Care Inc (PA).......513 424-1141
9009 Springboro Pike Miamisburg (45342) ***(G-14327)***
Nurses Care Inc.......513 424-1141
1083 Hicks Blvd Ste 140 Fairfield (45014) ***(G-10885)***
Nurses Care Inc.......513 791-0233
9200 Montgomery Rd 13b Cincinnati (45242) ***(G-4193)***
Nurses Heart Med Staffing LLC.......614 648-5111
1100 Morse Rd Ste 104 Columbus (43229) ***(G-8306)***
Nursing Care MGT Amer Inc.......740 927-9888
144 E Broad St Pataskala (43062) ***(G-15924)***
Nursing Care MGT Amer Inc.......513 793-5092
7777 Cooper Rd Cincinnati (45242) ***(G-4194)***
Nursing Care MGT Amer Inc.......419 385-3958
1621 S Byrne Rd Toledo (43614) ***(G-18098)***
Nursing Home & Assisted Living, Lorain *Also called Sprenger Entrprises Inc* ***(G-13078)***
Nursing Home Management Inc.......440 466-1181
60 West St Geneva (44041) ***(G-11367)***
Nursing Resources Corp.......419 333-3000
3600 Brrfeld Blvd Ste 100 Maumee (43537) ***(G-13951)***
Nurtur Holdings LLC (PA).......614 487-3033
6279 Tri Ridge Blvd # 250 Loveland (45140) ***(G-13149)***
Nurtury.......330 723-1800
250 N Spring Grove St Medina (44256) ***(G-14109)***
Nutls Press Inc (PA).......614 237-8626
3540 E Fulton St Columbus (43227) ***(G-8307)***
Nutrition Program, Toledo *Also called Lyman W Liggins Urban Affairs* ***(G-18023)***
Nutrition Trnsp Svcs LLC.......937 962-2661
6531 State Route 503 N Lewisburg (45338) ***(G-12713)***
Nuwaves Engineering, Middletown *Also called Nu Waves Ltd* ***(G-14444)***
Nuway Incorporated.......740 587-2452
996 Thornwood Dr Heath (43056) ***(G-11841)***
Nvr Inc.......440 933-7734
2553 Palmer Ln Avon (44011) ***(G-910)***
Nvr Inc.......440 584-4200
4034 Willow Way Kent (44240) ***(G-12389)***
Nvr Inc.......440 639-0525
408 Greenfield Ln Painesville (44077) ***(G-15868)***
Nvr Inc.......513 494-0167
5153 Riverview Dr South Lebanon (45065) ***(G-17079)***
Nvr Inc.......513 202-0323
9439 Tebbs Ct Harrison (45030) ***(G-11807)***

ALPHABETIC

ALPHABETIC SECTION

Nvr Inc 937 529-7000
2094 Northwest Pkwy Dayton (45426) *(G-9777)*
Nvr Inc 440 584-4250
6770 W Snowville Rd 100 Brecksville (44141) *(G-1838)*
Nwd Arena District II LLC 614 857-2330
375 N Front St Ste 200 Columbus (43215) *(G-8308)*
Nwo Beverage Inc 419 725-2162
6700 Wales Rd Northwood (43619) *(G-15541)*
Nwo Gastroenterology Assoc Inc 419 471-1317
4841 Monroe St Ste 110 Toledo (43623) *(G-18099)*
Nye F A & Sons Enterprises 419 986-5400
7443 N Township Road 70 Tiffin (44883) *(G-17689)*
Nyman Construction Co 216 475-7800
23209 Miles Rd Fl 2 Cleveland (44128) *(G-6173)*
Nzr Retail of Toledo Inc 419 724-0005
4820 Monroe St Toledo (43623) *(G-18100)*
O A I, Cleveland *Also called Ohio Aerospace Institute (G-6184)*
O A R D C, Wooster *Also called Ohio State University (G-19898)*
O B M, Cleveland *Also called Ohio Business Machines LLC (G-6187)*
O C I, Cincinnati *Also called Oncolgy/Hmatology Care Inc PSC (G-4226)*
O C I Construction Co Inc 440 338-3166
8560 Pekin Rd Novelty (44072) *(G-15602)*
O C P, Holland *Also called OCP Contractors Inc (G-12043)*
O D Miller Electric Co Inc 330 875-1651
1115 W Main St Louisville (44641) *(G-13103)*
O D W, Columbus *Also called Odw Logistics Inc (G-8313)*
O E Meyer Co (PA) 419 625-1256
3303 Tiffin Ave Sandusky (44870) *(G-16784)*
O K Coal & Concrete, Zanesville *Also called Joe McClelland Inc (G-20492)*
O N Equity Sales Company 513 794-6794
1 Financial Way Ste 100 Montgomery (45242) *(G-14728)*
O S U Faculty Club 614 292-2262
181 S Oval Mall Columbus (43210) *(G-8309)*
O S U Telephone Service, Columbus *Also called Ohio State University (G-8413)*
O T I, Columbus *Also called Optimum Technology Inc (G-8474)*
O-Heil Irrigation, Dayton *Also called Ohio Irrigation Lawn Sprinkler (G-9786)*
O.C.S.E.a, Westerville *Also called Ohio Civil Service Employees A (G-19337)*
O/B Leasing Company, Cincinnati *Also called Budco Group Inc (G-3146)*
Oad, Grove City *Also called Ohio Auto Delivery Inc (G-11587)*
Oak Associates Ltd 330 666-5263
3875 Embassy Pkwy Ste 250 Akron (44333) *(G-360)*
Oak Brook Garden Apartments, North Royalton *Also called Oak Brook Gardens (G-15497)*
Oak Brook Gardens 440 237-3613
13911 Oakbrook Dr Apt 205 North Royalton (44133) *(G-15497)*
Oak Creek Terrace Inc 937 439-1454
2316 Springmill Rd Dayton (45440) *(G-9778)*
Oak Creek United Church 937 434-3941
5280 Bigger Rd Dayton (45440) *(G-9779)*
Oak Grove Manor Inc 419 589-6222
1670 Crider Rd Mansfield (44903) *(G-13350)*
Oak Harbor Lions Club 419 898-3828
101 S Brookside Dr Oak Harbor (43449) *(G-15613)*
Oak Health Care Investor (HQ) 614 794-8800
8181 Worthington Rd Westerville (43082) *(G-19334)*
Oak Health Care Investors 740 397-3200
13 Avalon Rd Mount Vernon (43050) *(G-14916)*
Oak Health Care Investors (HQ) 614 794-8800
8181 Worthington Rd Westerville (43082) *(G-19335)*
Oak Hills Swim & Racquet 513 922-1827
5850 Muddy Creek Rd Cincinnati (45233) *(G-4195)*
Oak Hlls Nrsing Rehabilitation, Cincinnati *Also called Oaktree LLC (G-4196)*
Oak Park Health Care Center, Cleveland *Also called Jma Healthcare LLC (G-5865)*
Oak Pavilion Nursing & Rehabil, Cincinnati *Also called Health Care Rtrement Corp Amer (G-3751)*
Oakhill Manor Care Center 330 875-5060
4466 Lynnhaven Ave Louisville (44641) *(G-13104)*
Oakhill Medical Associates 937 599-1411
4879 Us Highway 68 S West Liberty (43357) *(G-19263)*
Oakhurst Country Club, Grove City *Also called American Golf Corporation (G-11529)*
Oakland Nursery Inc (PA) 614 268-3834
1156 Oakland Park Ave Columbus (43224) *(G-8310)*
Oakleaf Toledo Ltd Partnership 419 885-3934
4220 N Hllnd Sylvina Ofc Toledo (43623) *(G-18101)*
Oakleaf Village, Toledo *Also called Oakleaf Toledo Ltd Partnership (G-18101)*
Oakleaf Village Ltd 614 431-1739
5500 Karl Rd Apt 113 Columbus (43229) *(G-8311)*
Oakponte Nrsing Rehabilitation, Baltic *Also called Baltic Health Care Corp (G-944)*
Oaks of Brecksville, The, Brecksville *Also called Saber Healthcare Group LLC (G-1848)*
Oaks of Brecksville, The, Brecksville *Also called Brecksvlle Hlthcare Group Inc (G-1816)*
Oaks of West Kettering Inc 937 293-1152
1150 W Dorothy Ln Dayton (45409) *(G-9780)*
Oaktree LLC 513 598-8000
4307 Bridgetown Rd Cincinnati (45211) *(G-4196)*
Oakwood Club Inc 216 381-7755
1545 Sheridan Rd Cleveland (44121) *(G-6174)*
Oakwood Health Care Svcs Inc 440 439-7976
24579 Broadway Ave Cleveland (44146) *(G-6175)*

Oakwood Hospitality Corp 440 786-1998
23303 Oakwood Commons Dr Bedford (44146) *(G-1325)*
Oakwood Management Company 740 774-3570
402 W Main St Chillicothe (45601) *(G-2865)*
Oakwood Management Company (PA) .. 614 866-8702
6950 Americana Pkwy Ste A Reynoldsburg (43068) *(G-16471)*
Oakwood Optical, Oakwood *Also called Kunesh Eye Center Inc (G-15621)*
Oakwood Village, Springfield *Also called Community Mercy Foundation (G-17172)*
Oapse, Dayton *Also called Ohio Assn Pub Schl Employees (G-9279)*
Oapse-Local 4, Columbus *Also called Ohio Assn Pub Schl Employees (G-8317)*
Oarnet, Columbus *Also called Ohio State University (G-8432)*
Oasis Golf Club, Loveland *Also called Creekside Ltd LLC (G-13118)*
Oasis Systems Inc 937 426-1295
4141 Colonel Glenn Hwy Beavercreek Township (45431) *(G-1277)*
Oasis Thrptic Fster Care Ntwrk 740 698-0340
34265 State Route 681 S Albany (45710) *(G-520)*
Oasis Turf & Tree Inc 513 697-9090
8900 Glendl Milford Rd A4 Loveland (45140) *(G-13150)*
Oatey Company, Cleveland *Also called Oatey Supply Chain Svcs Inc (G-6176)*
Oatey Distribution Center, Cleveland *Also called Oatey Supply Chain Svcs Inc (G-6177)*
Oatey Supply Chain Svcs Inc (HQ) 216 267-7100
20600 Emerald Pkwy Cleveland (44135) *(G-6176)*
Oatey Supply Chain Svcs Inc 216 267-7100
4565 Industrial Pkwy Cleveland (44135) *(G-6177)*
Ob Gyn Associates of Lancaster 740 653-5088
1532 Wesley Way Lancaster (43130) *(G-12563)*
Ob-Gyn Specialists Lima Inc 419 227-0610
830 W High St Ste 101 Lima (45801) *(G-12846)*
Obaco, Bowling Green *Also called Ohio Biliffs Crt Officers Assn (G-1788)*
OBannon Creek Golf Club 513 683-5657
6842 Oakland Rd Loveland (45140) *(G-13151)*
Oberer Companies, Miamisburg *Also called Oberer Development Co (G-14328)*
Oberer Development Co (PA) 937 910-0851
3445 Newmark Dr Miamisburg (45342) *(G-14328)*
Oberer Residential Cnstr 937 278-0851
3475 Newmark Dr Miamisburg (45342) *(G-14329)*
Oberer Thompson Co, Beavercreek *Also called Greater Dayton Cnstr Ltd (G-1243)*
Oberers Flowers Inc (PA) 937 223-1253
1448 Troy St Dayton (45404) *(G-9781)*
Oberlanders Tree & Ldscp Ltd 419 562-8733
1874 E Mansfield St Bucyrus (44820) *(G-2045)*
Oberlin Clinic Inc 440 774-7337
224 W Lorain St Ste P Oberlin (44074) *(G-15653)*
Oberlin College 440 775-8519
200 Woodland St Oberlin (44074) *(G-15654)*
Oberlin College 440 775-8500
200 Woodland St Oberlin (44074) *(G-15655)*
Oberlin College 440 935-1475
10 E College St Oberlin (44074) *(G-15656)*
Oberlin College Recreation Ctr, Oberlin *Also called Oberlin College (G-15654)*
Oberlin Early Childhood Center 440 774-8193
317 E College St Oberlin (44074) *(G-15657)*
Oberlin Inn, Oberlin *Also called Oberlin College (G-15656)*
OBERLIN MUNICIPAL LIGHT & POWE, Oberlin *Also called City of Oberlin (G-15640)*
Obr Cooling Towers Inc 419 243-3443
9665 S Compass Dr Rossford (43460) *(G-16610)*
OBrien Cut Stone Company (PA) 216 663-7800
19100 Miles Rd Cleveland (44128) *(G-6178)*
OBrien Law Firm Company Lpa 216 685-7500
29550 Detroit Rd Westlake (44145) *(G-19526)*
Obstetrics & Gynecology Assoc (PA) 513 221-3800
3050 Mack Rd Ste 375 Fairfield (45014) *(G-10886)*
Obstetrics & Gynecology S Inc (PA) 937 296-0167
3533 Sthern Blvd Ste 4600 Dayton (45429) *(G-9782)*
Obstetrics Gynclogy of Reserve 330 666-1166
799 Wye Rd Akron (44333) *(G-361)*
Occasions Party Centre 330 882-5113
6800 Manchester Rd New Franklin (44216) *(G-15046)*
Occupational Health Center, Lorain *Also called Barb Linden (G-13016)*
Occupational Health Link (PA) 614 885-0039
445 Hutchinson Ave # 205 Columbus (43235) *(G-8312)*
Occupational Health Services 937 492-7296
915 Michigan St Sidney (45365) *(G-16944)*
Occupational Hlth Safety Dept, Independence *Also called Sterling Infosystems Inc (G-12262)*
Ocean Prime, Columbus *Also called Cameron Mitchell Rest LLC (G-7180)*
Ocean Wide Seafood Company 937 610-5740
2601 W 8th St Apt 10 Cincinnati (45204) *(G-4197)*
Oclc Inc (PA) 614 764-6000
6565 Kilgour Pl Dublin (43017) *(G-10412)*
OConnor Acciani & Levy LLC (PA) 513 241-7111
600 Vine St Ste 1600 Cincinnati (45202) *(G-4198)*
OCP Contractors Inc (PA) 419 865-7168
1740 Commerce Rd Holland (43528) *(G-12043)*
Ocr Services Corporation 513 719-2600
201 E 4th St Ste 900 Cincinnati (45202) *(G-4199)*
October Enterprises Inc 937 456-9535
501 W Lexington Rd Eaton (45320) *(G-10571)*
Odd Fellows Hall 440 599-7973
253 Liberty St Conneaut (44030) *(G-9045)*

Odnr Computer Communication, Columbus *Also called Natural Resources Ohio Dept (G-8250)*
Odot District 4, Canfield *Also called Ohio Department Transportation (G-2205)*
Odw Logistics Inc (PA)......614 549-5000
400 W Nationwide Blvd # 200 Columbus (43215) **(G-8313)**
Odyssey Consulting Services......614 523-4248
2531 Oakstone Dr Columbus (43231) **(G-8314)**
Odyssey Healthcare Inc......614 414-0500
540 Officenter Pl Ste 295 Gahanna (43230) **(G-11260)**
Odyssey Healthcare Inc......937 298-2800
3085 Woodman Dr Ste 200 Dayton (45420) **(G-9783)**
Odyssey Healthcare of Columbus, Gahanna *Also called Odyssey Healthcare Inc (G-11260)*
Oeconnection LLC......888 776-5792
4205 Highlander Pkwy Richfield (44286) **(G-16519)**
Oeder Carl E Sons Sand & Grav......513 494-1238
1000 Mason Mrrow Mlgrv Rd Lebanon (45036) **(G-12632)**
OEM Parts Outlet......419 472-2237
1815 W Sylvania Ave Toledo (43613) **(G-18102)**
Oesterlen-Services For Youth......937 399-6101
1918 Mechanicsburg Rd Springfield (45503) **(G-17254)**
Ofeq Institute Inc......440 943-1497
2620 Bishop Rd Wickliffe (44092) **(G-19610)**
Office Depot Inc......800 463-3768
9880 Sweet Valley Dr # 2 Cleveland (44125) **(G-6179)**
Office For Children Fmly Svcs, Columbus *Also called Ohio Dept of Job & Fmly Svcs (G-8335)*
Office Furniture Resources Inc......216 781-8200
1213 Prospect Ave E Cleveland (44115) **(G-6180)**
Office Furniture Solution, North Canton *Also called Document Concepts Inc (G-15333)*
Office Furniture USA, Columbus *Also called Thomas W Ruff and Company (G-8838)*
Office of Divisional Support, Oxford *Also called Miami University (G-15823)*
Office of Procurement Services, Columbus *Also called Administrative Svcs Ohio Dept (G-6944)*
Office Products Inc/Cleveland......919 754-3700
1239 W 6th St Cleveland (44113) **(G-6181)**
Office Products Toledo Inc......419 865-7001
1205 Corporate Dr Holland (43528) **(G-12044)**
Office World Inc (PA)......419 991-4694
3820 S Dixie Hwy Lima (45806) **(G-12928)**
OfficeMax Contract Inc......216 898-2400
18673 Sheldon Rd B Cleveland (44130) **(G-6182)**
OfficeMax North America Inc......614 899-6186
87 Huber Village Blvd Westerville (43081) **(G-19431)**
OfficeMax North America Inc......330 666-4550
37 N Clvland Massillon Rd Akron (44333) **(G-362)**
Official Investigations Inc......844 263-3424
3284 North Bend Rd # 310 Cincinnati (45239) **(G-4200)**
Ofori, Jason MD, Toledo *Also called Vision Associates Inc (G-18292)*
OFSWCD, Reynoldsburg *Also called Ohio Federation of Soil and WA (G-16472)*
OGara Group Inc (PA)......513 338-0660
9113 Le Street Dr Cincinnati (45249) **(G-4201)**
Oglethorpe Middlepoint LLC......419 968-2950
17872 Lincoln Hwy Middle Point (45863) **(G-14377)**
Ogrinc Mechanical Corporation......216 765-8010
26650 Rnohance Pkwy Ste 1 Cleveland (44128) **(G-6183)**
Ogs Industries, Akron *Also called Ohio Gasket and Shim Co Inc (G-366)*
OH St Trans Dist 02 Outpost......419 693-8870
200 Lemoyne Rd Northwood (43619) **(G-15542)**
Oh-16 Clvlnd Arprt S Prprty Su......440 243-8785
7345 Engle Rd Middleburg Heights (44130) **(G-14383)**
Ohashi Technica USA Inc (HQ)......740 965-5115
111 Burrer Dr Sunbury (43074) **(G-17560)**
Oherbein Kpsic Rtirement Cmnty, Leipsic *Also called Otterbein Snior Lfstyle Chices (G-12663)*
Ohic Insurance Company (HQ)......614 221-7777
155 E Broad St Fl 10 Columbus (43215) **(G-8315)**
Ohigro Inc (PA)......740 726-2429
6720 Gillette Rd Waldo (43356) **(G-18783)**
Ohio & Indiana Roofing......937 339-8768
17 S Market St Troy (45373) **(G-18368)**
Ohio & Michigan Paper Company......419 666-1500
350 4th St Perrysburg (43551) **(G-16035)**
Ohio Academy of Science......614 488-2228
1500 W 3rd Ave Ste 228 Columbus (43212) **(G-8316)**
Ohio Aerospace Institute (PA)......440 962-3000
22800 Cedar Point Rd Cleveland (44142) **(G-6184)**
Ohio Agriculture RES & Dev Ctr, Wooster *Also called Ohio State University (G-19899)*
Ohio Alarm Inc......216 692-1204
750 W Resource Dr Ste 200 Independence (44131) **(G-12241)**
Ohio and Indiana Roofing Co, Saint Henry *Also called Bruns Building & Dev Corp Inc (G-16665)*
Ohio Anestisia, Canton *Also called Russell D Ens Do (G-2520)*
Ohio Assn Pub Schl Employees (PA)......614 890-4770
6805 Oak Creek Dr Ste 1 Columbus (43229) **(G-8317)**
Ohio Assn Pub Schl Employees......937 253-5100
1675 Woodman Dr Dayton (45432) **(G-9279)**
Ohio Assn Pub Schl Employees......330 659-7335
3380 Brecksville Rd # 101 Richfield (44286) **(G-16520)**
Ohio Assn Pub Treasurers......937 415-2237
333 James Bohanan Dr Vandalia (45377) **(G-18691)**
Ohio Association of Foodbanks......614 221-4336
101 E Town St Ste 540 Columbus (43215) **(G-8318)**
Ohio Association Realtors Inc......614 228-6675
200 E Town St Columbus (43215) **(G-8319)**
Ohio Auto Auction, Grove City *Also called Cox Automotive Inc (G-11550)*
Ohio Auto Delivery Inc......614 277-1445
1700 Feddern Ave Grove City (43123) **(G-11587)**
Ohio Auto Supply Company......330 454-5105
1128 Tuscarawas St W Canton (44702) **(G-2478)**
Ohio Automobile Club (PA)......614 431-7901
90 E Wilson Bridge Rd # 1 Worthington (43085) **(G-19980)**
Ohio Automobile Club......614 559-0000
2400 Sobeck Rd Columbus (43232) **(G-8320)**
Ohio Automobile Club......614 277-1310
4750 Big Run South Rd B Grove City (43123) **(G-11588)**
Ohio Automobile Club......513 870-0951
8210 Highland Pointe Dr West Chester (45069) **(G-19124)**
Ohio Automotive Supply Co......419 422-1655
525 W Main Cross St Findlay (45840) **(G-11072)**
Ohio Ballet, Akron *Also called Ohio Chamber Ballet (G-363)*
Ohio Bell Telephone Company (HQ)......216 822-3439
45 Erieview Plz Cleveland (44114) **(G-6185)**
Ohio Biliffs Crt Officers Assn......419 354-9302
1 Court House Sq Bowling Green (43402) **(G-1788)**
Ohio Blow Pipe Company (PA)......216 681-7379
446 E 131st St Cleveland (44108) **(G-6186)**
Ohio Board of Cosmetology, Grove City *Also called State of Ohio (G-11602)*
Ohio Bridge Corporation......740 432-6334
201 Wheeling Ave Cambridge (43725) **(G-2125)**
Ohio Broach & Machine Company......440 946-1040
35264 Topps Indus Pkwy Willoughby (44094) **(G-19699)**
Ohio Builders Resources LLC......614 865-0306
5901 Chandler Ct Ste D Westerville (43082) **(G-19336)**
Ohio Building Service Inc......513 761-0268
2212 Losantiville Ave Cincinnati (45237) **(G-4202)**
Ohio Business Machines LLC (PA)......216 485-2000
1111 Superior Ave E # 105 Cleveland (44114) **(G-6187)**
Ohio Camp Cherith Inc......330 725-4202
3854 Remsen Rd Medina (44256) **(G-14110)**
Ohio Cancer Specialists (PA)......419 756-2122
1125 Aspira Ct Mansfield (44906) **(G-13351)**
Ohio Carriers Corp......330 878-5311
6531 Mckracken Dr Nw Dover (44622) **(G-10204)**
Ohio Carts, Mentor *Also called Omni Cart Services Inc (G-14225)*
Ohio Casualty Insurance, Montgomery *Also called Ohio National Life Insur Co (G-14732)*
Ohio Casualty Insurance Co (HQ)......800 843-6446
9450 Seward Rd Fairfield (45014) **(G-10887)**
Ohio Casualty Insurance Co......513 867-3000
136 N 3rd St Hamilton (45011) **(G-11761)**
Ohio Cat, Cadiz *Also called Ohio Machinery Co (G-2080)*
Ohio Catholic Federal Cr Un (PA)......216 663-6800
13623 Rockside Rd Cleveland (44125) **(G-6188)**
Ohio Chamber Ballet......330 972-7900
354 E Market St Akron (44325) **(G-363)**
Ohio Chamber of Commerce Inc......614 228-4201
230 E Town St Ste 300 Columbus (43215) **(G-8321)**
Ohio Check Cashers Inc......513 559-0220
3513 Reading Rd Cincinnati (45229) **(G-4203)**
Ohio Citizen Action (PA)......216 861-5200
614 W Superior Ave # 1200 Cleveland (44113) **(G-6189)**
Ohio Citrus Juices Inc......614 539-0030
2201 Hardy Parkway St Grove City (43123) **(G-11589)**
Ohio Civil Service Employees A......614 865-4700
390 Worthington Rd Ste A Westerville (43082) **(G-19337)**
Ohio Cle Institute, Columbus *Also called Ohio State Bar Association (G-8377)*
Ohio Clinic Aesthc Plstc Srgy......440 808-9315
2237 Crocker Rd Ste 140 Westlake (44145) **(G-19527)**
Ohio Cllbrtive Lrng Sltons Inc (PA)......216 595-5289
24700 Chagrin Blvd # 104 Beachwood (44122) **(G-1110)**
Ohio Con Sawing & Drlg Inc (PA)......419 841-1330
8534 Central Ave Sylvania (43560) **(G-17603)**
Ohio Con Sawing & Drlg Inc......614 252-1122
2935 E 14th Ave Ste 200 Columbus (43219) **(G-8322)**
Ohio Concrete Resurfacing Inc (PA)......440 786-9100
15 N Park St Bedford (44146) **(G-1326)**
Ohio Custodial Maintenance......614 443-1232
1291 S High St Columbus (43206) **(G-8323)**
Ohio Custodial Management, Columbus *Also called Ohio Custodial Maintenance (G-8323)*
Ohio Department of Aging......614 466-5500
246 N High St Fl 1 Columbus (43215) **(G-8324)**
Ohio Department of Commerce......614 644-7381
77 S High St Fl 22 Columbus (43215) **(G-8325)**
Ohio Department of Commerce......614 728-8400
77 S High St Fl 21 Columbus (43215) **(G-8326)**
Ohio Department of Education......740 289-2908
175 Beaver Creek Rd Piketon (45661) **(G-16120)**
Ohio Department of Health......330 792-2397
50 Westchester Dr Ste 202 Austintown (44515) **(G-870)**
Ohio Department of Health......614 645-3621
3850 Sullivant Ave # 102 Columbus (43228) **(G-8327)**

ALPHABETIC

Ohio Department of Health 614 466-1521
246 N High St Columbus (43215) ***(G-8328)***
Ohio Department of Health 937 285-6250
1323 W 3rd St Dayton (45402) ***(G-9784)***
Ohio Department of Health 419 447-1450
600 N River Rd Tiffin (44883) ***(G-17690)***
Ohio Department of Health 614 438-1255
400 E Campus View Blvd Columbus (43235) ***(G-8329)***
Ohio Department Transportation 740 363-1251
400 E William St Delaware (43015) ***(G-10119)***
Ohio Department Transportation 937 548-3015
1144 Martin St Greenville (45331) ***(G-11515)***
Ohio Department Transportation 419 738-4214
511 Converse Dr Wapakoneta (45895) ***(G-18805)***
Ohio Department Transportation 614 275-1324
1600 W Broad St Columbus (43223) ***(G-8330)***
Ohio Department Transportation 330 533-4351
501 W Main St Canfield (44406) ***(G-2205)***
Ohio Department Transportation 330 637-5951
310 2nd St Cortland (44410) ***(G-9080)***
Ohio Department Veterans Svcs 614 644-0898
77 S High St Fl 7 Columbus (43215) ***(G-8331)***
Ohio Department Youth Services 740 881-3337
51 N High St Fl 5 Columbus (43215) ***(G-8332)***
Ohio Dept Amvet Svc Foundation (PA) 614 431-6990
1395 E Dublin Granville R Columbus (43229) ***(G-8333)***
Ohio Dept Natural Resources 740 869-3124
20635 State Park Road 20 Mount Sterling (43143) ***(G-14874)***
Ohio Dept of Job & Fmly Svcs 614 752-9494
4300 Kimberly Pkwy N Columbus (43232) ***(G-8334)***
Ohio Dept of Job & Fmly Svcs 330 484-5402
161 S High St Ste 300 Akron (44308) ***(G-364)***
Ohio Dept of Job & Fmly Svcs 419 334-3891
2511 Countryside Dr Fremont (43420) ***(G-11215)***
Ohio Dept of Job & Fmly Svcs 614 466-1213
255 E Main St Fl 3 Columbus (43215) ***(G-8335)***
Ohio Dept Rhbilitation Corectn 614 274-9000
770 W Broad St Columbus (43222) ***(G-8336)***
Ohio Design Centre 216 831-1245
23533 Mercantile Rd Beachwood (44122) ***(G-1111)***
Ohio Desk Co 216 623-0600
4851 Van Epps Rd Ste B Brooklyn Heights (44131) ***(G-1922)***
Ohio Disability Rights Law Pol 614 466-7264
200 Civic Center Dr Columbus (43215) ***(G-8337)***
Ohio District 5 Area 419 522-5612
2131 Park Ave W Ontario (44906) ***(G-15707)***
Ohio Drilling Company (PA) 330 832-1521
2405 Bostic Blvd Sw Massillon (44647) ***(G-13842)***
Ohio E Check, Painesville *Also called Envirotest Systems Corp* ***(G-15855)***
Ohio E-Check, Cleveland *Also called Envirotest Systems Corp* ***(G-5546)***
Ohio Eastern Star Home 740 397-1706
1451 Gambier Rd Ofc Mount Vernon (43050) ***(G-14917)***
Ohio Edison Company (HQ) 800 736-3402
76 S Main St Bsmt Akron (44308) ***(G-365)***
Ohio Edison Company 330 747-2071
100 E Federal St Ste 100 Youngstown (44503) ***(G-20304)***
Ohio Edison Company 740 671-2900
57246 Ferry Landing Rd Shadyside (43947) ***(G-16851)***
Ohio Edison Company 330 740-7754
730 South Ave Youngstown (44502) ***(G-20305)***
Ohio Edison Company 330 336-9880
9681 Silvercreek Rd Wadsworth (44281) ***(G-18766)***
Ohio Education Association 614 485-6000
2470 North Star Rd Columbus (43221) ***(G-8338)***
Ohio Education Association (PA) 614 228-4526
225 E Broad St Fl 2 Columbus (43215) ***(G-8339)***
Ohio Educational Credit Union (PA) 216 621-6296
4141 Rockside Rd Ste 400 Seven Hills (44131) ***(G-16833)***
Ohio Entertainment Security 937 325-7216
3749 Mahar Rd South Vienna (45369) ***(G-17100)***
Ohio Equities LLC 614 207-1805
6210 Busch Blvd Columbus (43229) ***(G-8340)***
Ohio Equities LLC 614 469-0058
17 S High St Ste 799 Columbus (43215) ***(G-8341)***
Ohio Exposition Center 614 644-4000
717 E 17th Ave Columbus (43211) ***(G-8342)***
Ohio Exterminating Co Inc 614 294-6311
1347 N High St Columbus (43201) ***(G-8343)***
Ohio Eye Alliance (PA) 330 823-1680
985 S Sawburg Ave Alliance (44601) ***(G-550)***
Ohio Eye Associates, Columbus *Also called Eye Center* ***(G-7625)***
Ohio Eye Specialists Inc 800 948-3937
50 N Plaza Blvd Chillicothe (45601) ***(G-2866)***
Ohio Eyecare Specialists Inc (PA) 937 222-3937
105 Sugar Camp Cir # 200 Oakwood (45409) ***(G-15622)***
Ohio F F A Camps Inc 330 627-2208
3266 Dyewood Rd Sw Carrollton (44615) ***(G-2625)***
Ohio Fabricators Inc (PA) 216 391-2400
883 Addison Rd Cleveland (44103) ***(G-6190)***
Ohio Fair Plan Undwrt Assn 614 839-6446
2500 Corp Exchange Dr # 250 Columbus (43231) ***(G-8344)***
Ohio Farm Bur Federation Inc (PA) 614 249-2400
280 N High St Fl 6 Columbus (43215) ***(G-8345)***
Ohio Farmers Insurance Company (PA) 800 243-0210
1 Park Cir Westfield Center (44251) ***(G-19452)***
Ohio Farmers Insurance Company 330 484-5660
1801 Faircrest St Se Canton (44707) ***(G-2479)***
Ohio Farmers Insurance Company 614 848-6174
2000 Polaris Pkwy Ste 202 Columbus (43240) ***(G-6898)***
Ohio Federation of Soil and WA 614 784-1900
8995 E Main St Reynoldsburg (43068) ***(G-16472)***
Ohio Field Office, Dublin *Also called The Nature Conservancy* ***(G-10476)***
Ohio Fresh Eggs LLC (PA) 740 893-7200
11212 Croton Rd Croton (43013) ***(G-9154)***
Ohio Fresh Eggs LLC 937 354-2233
20449 County Road 245 Mount Victory (43340) ***(G-14929)***
Ohio Gas Company (HQ) 419 636-1117
200 W High St Bryan (43506) ***(G-2013)***
Ohio Gas Company 419 636-3642
715 E Wilson St Bryan (43506) ***(G-2014)***
Ohio Gasket and Shim Co Inc (PA) 330 630-0626
976 Evans Ave Akron (44305) ***(G-366)***
Ohio Gstroenterology Group Inc 614 221-8355
815 W Broad St Ste 220 Columbus (43222) ***(G-8346)***
Ohio Gstroenterology Group Inc 614 754-5500
85 Mcnaughten Rd Ste 320 Columbus (43213) ***(G-8347)***
Ohio Gstroenterology Group Inc (PA) 614 754-5500
3400 Olentangy River Rd Columbus (43202) ***(G-8348)***
Ohio Gypsum Supply, Springfield *Also called Robinson Insulation Co Inc* ***(G-17264)***
Ohio Head & Neck Surgeons Inc (PA) 330 492-2844
4912 Higbee Ave Nw # 200 Canton (44718) ***(G-2480)***
Ohio Health, Columbus *Also called Gerlach John J Center For Sen* ***(G-7746)***
Ohio Health, Nelsonville *Also called Doctors Hospital Cleveland Inc* ***(G-14961)***
Ohio Health Care Employees, Columbus *Also called Healthcare and Social* ***(G-7812)***
Ohio Health Choice Inc (HQ) 800 554-0027
6000 Parkland Blvd # 100 Cleveland (44124) ***(G-6191)***
Ohio Health Council 614 221-7614
155 E Broad St Ste 301 Columbus (43215) ***(G-8349)***
Ohio Health Group LLC 614 566-0010
155 E Broad St Ste 1700 Columbus (43215) ***(G-8350)***
Ohio Healthcare Federal Cr Un (PA) 614 737-6034
3955 W Dblin Granville Rd Dublin (43017) ***(G-10413)***
Ohio Heart 513 206-1320
7545 Beechmont Ave Ste E Cincinnati (45255) ***(G-4204)***
Ohio Heart and Vascular 513 206-1800
5885 Harrison Ave # 1900 Cincinnati (45248) ***(G-4205)***
Ohio Heart Health Center Inc (PA) 513 351-9900
237 William Howard Taft Rd Cincinnati (45219) ***(G-4206)***
Ohio Heart Instit, Youngstown *Also called Cardiovascular Associates Inc* ***(G-20133)***
Ohio Heart Institute Inc (PA) 330 747-6446
1001 Belmont Ave Youngstown (44504) ***(G-20306)***
Ohio Heating and Refrigeration 614 863-6666
1465 Clara St Columbus (43211) ***(G-8351)***
Ohio Heavy Equipment Lsg LLC (PA) 513 965-6600
9520 Le Saint Dr Fairfield (45014) ***(G-10888)***
Ohio Hi Point Career Center 937 599-3010
412 N Main St Urbana (43078) ***(G-18598)***
Ohio Hickory Harvest Brand Pro 330 644-6266
90 Logan Pkwy Coventry Township (44319) ***(G-9130)***
Ohio High School Football Coac 419 673-1286
138 Purple Finch Loop Etna (43062) ***(G-10737)***
Ohio Hills Health Service, Woodsfield *Also called Monroe Family Health Center* ***(G-19818)***
Ohio Hills Health Services (PA) 740 425-5165
101 E Main St Barnesville (43713) ***(G-990)***
Ohio Historical Society (PA) 614 297-2300
800 E 17th Ave Columbus (43211) ***(G-8352)***
OHIO HISTORY CONNECTION, Columbus *Also called Ohio Historical Society* ***(G-8352)***
Ohio Home Health Care Inc 937 853-0271
5050 Nebraska Ave Ste 5 Dayton (45424) ***(G-9785)***
Ohio Hospital Association 614 221-7614
155 E Broad St Ste 301 Columbus (43215) ***(G-8353)***
Ohio Hospital For Psychiatry 877 762-9026
880 Greenlawn Ave Columbus (43223) ***(G-8354)***
Ohio Hrtland Cmnty Action Comm (PA) 740 387-1039
372 E Center St Marion (43302) ***(G-13569)***
Ohio Hrtland Cmnty Action Comm 419 468-5121
124 Buehler St Galion (44833) ***(G-11303)***
Ohio Hydraulics Inc 513 771-2590
2510 E Sharon Rd Ste 1 Cincinnati (45241) ***(G-4207)***
Ohio Indemnity Company 614 228-1601
250 E Broad St Fl 7 Columbus (43215) ***(G-8355)***
Ohio Inns Inc 937 440-9303
87 Troy Town Dr Troy (45373) ***(G-18369)***
Ohio Institute of Cardiac Care (PA) 937 322-1700
2200 N Limestone St # 100 Springfield (45503) ***(G-17255)***
Ohio Irrigation Lawn Sprinkler (PA) 937 432-9911
2109 E Social Row Rd Dayton (45458) ***(G-9786)***
Ohio Kepro Inc 216 447-9604
5700 Lombardo Ctr Ste 100 Seven Hills (44131) ***(G-16834)***
Ohio Laminating & Binding Inc 614 771-4868
4364 Reynolds Dr Hilliard (43026) ***(G-11939)***
Ohio Laundry, Columbus *Also called Super Laundry Inc* ***(G-8804)***
Ohio Lbrers Frnge Bneft Prgram 614 898-9006
800 Hillsdowne Rd Westerville (43081) ***(G-19432)***

Ohio Legal Rights Service 614 466-7264
50 W Broad St Ste 1400 Columbus (43215) *(G-8356)*
Ohio Light Opera 330 263-2345
1189 Beall Ave Wooster (44691) *(G-19896)*
Ohio Living 330 638-2420
303 N Mecca St Cortland (44410) *(G-9081)*
Ohio Living 614 224-1651
645 Neil Ave Ofc Columbus (43215) *(G-8357)*
Ohio Living 513 681-4230
1701 Llanfair Ave Cincinnati (45224) *(G-4208)*
Ohio Living 440 942-4342
36855 Ridge Rd Willoughby (44094) *(G-19700)*
Ohio Living (PA) 614 888-7800
1001 Kingsmill Pkwy Columbus (43229) *(G-8358)*
Ohio Machinery Co 419 874-7975
25970 Dixie Hwy Perrysburg (43551) *(G-16036)*
Ohio Machinery Co 740 942-4626
1016 E Market St Cadiz (43907) *(G-2080)*
Ohio Machinery Co (PA) 440 526-6200
3993 E Royalton Rd Broadview Heights (44147) *(G-1886)*
Ohio Machinery Co 330 478-6525
4731 Corporate St Sw Canton (44706) *(G-2481)*
Ohio Machinery Co 330 530-9010
1 Ohio Machinery Blvd Girard (44420) *(G-11421)*
Ohio Machinery Co 740 453-0563
3415 East Pike Zanesville (43701) *(G-20519)*
Ohio Machinery Co 513 771-0515
11330 Mosteller Rd Cincinnati (45241) *(G-4209)*
Ohio Machinery Co 614 878-2287
5252 Walcutt Ct Columbus (43228) *(G-8359)*
Ohio Machinery Co 330 874-1003
10955 Industrial Pkwy Nw Bolivar (44612) *(G-1750)*
Ohio Machinery Co 440 526-0520
900 Ken Mar Indus Pkwy Broadview Heights (44147) *(G-1887)*
Ohio Machinery Co 937 335-7660
1281 Brukner Dr Troy (45373) *(G-18370)*
Ohio Maint & Renovation Inc (PA) 330 315-3101
124 Darrow Rd Akron (44305) *(G-367)*
Ohio Masonic Retirement Vlg 937 525-1743
4 Masonic Dr Springfield (45504) *(G-17256)*
Ohio Materials Handling, Macedonia *Also called Newtown Nine Inc* *(G-13206)*
Ohio Medical Group, Cleveland *Also called North Ohio Heart Center Inc* *(G-6141)*
Ohio Medical Group, Avon *Also called North Ohio Heart Center Inc* *(G-909)*
Ohio Medical Group (PA) 440 414-9400
29325 Health Campus Dr # 3 Westlake (44145) *(G-19528)*
Ohio Medical Trnsp Inc 937 747-3540
22758 Wilbur Rd Marysville (43040) *(G-13643)*
Ohio Medical Trnsp Inc 740 962-2055
975 E Airport Rd Ne McConnelsville (43756) *(G-14030)*
Ohio Medical Trnsp Inc (PA) 614 791-4400
2827 W Dblin Granville Rd Columbus (43235) *(G-8360)*
Ohio Metal Processing Inc 740 286-6457
16064 Beaver Pike Jackson (45640) *(G-12316)*
Ohio Mulch Supply Inc (PA) 614 445-4455
1600 Universal Rd Columbus (43207) *(G-8361)*
Ohio Mutual Insurance Company (PA) 419 562-3011
1725 Hopley Ave Bucyrus (44820) *(G-2046)*
Ohio Nat Mutl Holdings Inc (PA) 513 794-6100
1 Financial Way Ste 100 Montgomery (45242) *(G-14729)*
Ohio National Fincl Svcs Inc (HQ) 513 794-6100
1 Financial Way Ste 100 Montgomery (45242) *(G-14730)*
Ohio National Life Assurance 513 794-6100
1 Financial Way Ste 100 Montgomery (45242) *(G-14731)*
Ohio National Life Insur Co (HQ) 513 794-6100
1 Financial Way Ste 100 Montgomery (45242) *(G-14732)*
Ohio News Network 614 460-3700
770 Twin Rivers Dr Columbus (43215) *(G-8362)*
Ohio News Network 216 367-7493
3001 Euclid Ave Cleveland (44115) *(G-6192)*
Ohio News Network, The, Columbus *Also called Ohio News Network* *(G-8362)*
Ohio North E Hlth Systems Inc 330 747-9551
726 Wick Ave Youngstown (44505) *(G-20307)*
Ohio North E Hlth Systems Inc (PA) 330 747-9551
726 Wick Ave Youngstown (44505) *(G-20308)*
Ohio Northern University 419 227-0061
306 N Main St Lima (45801) *(G-12847)*
Ohio Nthrn Univ Legal Clinic, Lima *Also called Ohio Northern University* *(G-12847)*
Ohio Nut & Bolt Company Div, Berea *Also called Fastener Industries Inc* *(G-1459)*
Ohio Oil Gathering Corporation (HQ) 740 828-2892
9320 Blackrun Rd Nashport (43830) *(G-14953)*
Ohio Operating Engineers Apprn 614 487-6531
1184 Dublin Rd Columbus (43215) *(G-8363)*
Ohio Orthopedic Center, Lancaster *Also called River Vly Orthpdics Spt Mdcine* *(G-12570)*
Ohio Orthpd Surgery Inst LLC 614 827-8777
4605 Sawmill Rd Columbus (43220) *(G-8364)*
Ohio Osteopathic Hospital Assn 614 299-2107
52 W 3rd Ave Columbus (43201) *(G-8365)*
Ohio Paving & Cnstr Co Inc 440 975-8929
38220 Willoughby Pkwy Willoughby (44094) *(G-19701)*
Ohio Paving Group LLC 216 475-1700
4873 Osborn Rd Cleveland (44128) *(G-6193)*
Ohio Pediatrics Inc 937 299-2339
7200 Poe Ave Ste 201 Dayton (45414) *(G-9787)*
Ohio Pediatrics Inc (PA) 937 299-2743
1775 Delco Park Dr Dayton (45420) *(G-9788)*
Ohio Pia Service Corporation 614 552-8000
600 Cross Pointe Rd Gahanna (43230) *(G-11261)*
Ohio Pizza Products Inc (HQ) 937 294-6969
201 Lawton Ave Monroe (45050) *(G-14707)*
Ohio Pools & Spas Inc (PA) 330 494-7755
6815 Whipple Ave Nw Canton (44720) *(G-2482)*
Ohio Power Company (HQ) 614 716-1000
1 Riverside Plz Columbus (43215) *(G-8366)*
Ohio Power Company 330 264-1616
500 Maple St Wooster (44691) *(G-19897)*
Ohio Power Company 614 836-2570
4500 S Hamilton Rd Groveport (43125) *(G-11660)*
Ohio Power Company 888 216-3523
1 Riverside Plz Canton (44701) *(G-2483)*
Ohio Power Company 419 443-4634
2622 S State Route 100 Tiffin (44883) *(G-17691)*
Ohio Power Company 614 836-2570
700 Morrison Rd Gahanna (43230) *(G-11262)*
Ohio Power Company 614 836-2570
215 N Front St Columbus (43215) *(G-8367)*
Ohio Power Company 740 695-7800
47687 National Rd Saint Clairsville (43950) *(G-16647)*
Ohio Presbt Retirement Svcs 330 746-2944
1216 5th Ave Youngstown (44504) *(G-20309)*
Ohio Presbt Retirement Svcs 330 867-2150
1150 W Market St Akron (44313) *(G-368)*
Ohio Presbt Retirement Svcs 937 498-2391
3003 Cisco Rd Sidney (45365) *(G-16945)*
Ohio Presbt Retirement Svcs 513 539-7391
225 Britton Ln Monroe (45050) *(G-14708)*
Ohio Presbt Retirement Svcs 937 415-5666
6520 Poe Ave Dayton (45414) *(G-9789)*
Ohio Presbt Retirement Svcs 614 228-8888
717 Neil Ave Columbus (43215) *(G-8368)*
Ohio Presbt Retirement Vlg, Monroe *Also called Ohio Presbt Retirement Svcs* *(G-14708)*
Ohio Presbyterian Rtr Svcs 614 888-7800
1001 Kingsmill Pkwy Columbus (43229) *(G-8369)*
Ohio Pressure Grouting, Cuyahoga Falls *Also called Technical Construction Spc* *(G-9224)*
Ohio Pub Employees Rtrement Sys 614 228-8471
277 E Town St Columbus (43215) *(G-8370)*
Ohio Real Title Agency LLC (PA) 216 373-9900
1213 Prospect Ave E # 200 Cleveland (44115) *(G-6194)*
Ohio Rehabilitation Svcs Comm 330 643-3080
161 S High St Ste 103 Akron (44308) *(G-369)*
Ohio Renal Care Group LLC 440 974-3459
8840 Tyler Blvd Mentor (44060) *(G-14224)*
Ohio Renal Care Grp Mentor Dia, Mentor *Also called Ohio Renal Care Group LLC* *(G-14224)*
Ohio Republican Party, Columbus *Also called Republican State Central Execu* *(G-8616)*
Ohio Resources, Westerville *Also called Ohio Builders Resources LLC* *(G-19336)*
Ohio Retina Associates Inc (PA) 330 966-9800
4690 Munson St Nw Ste D Canton (44718) *(G-2484)*
Ohio River Forecast, Wilmington *Also called National Weather Service* *(G-19774)*
Ohio Rural Electric Coops, Columbus *Also called Buckeye Power Inc* *(G-7160)*
Ohio Rural Electric Coops Inc 614 846-5757
6677 Busch Blvd Columbus (43229) *(G-8371)*
Ohio Rver Vly Wtr Snttion Comm 513 231-7719
5735 Kellogg Ave Cincinnati (45230) *(G-4210)*
Ohio School Boards Association 614 540-4000
8050 N High St Ste 100 Columbus (43235) *(G-8372)*
Ohio School Boards Association 614 540-4000
8050 N High St Ste 100 Columbus (43235) *(G-8373)*
Ohio School Pictures, Bellevue *Also called Royal Color Inc* *(G-1417)*
Ohio School Psychologists Assn 614 414-5980
4449 Easton Way Fl 2offi Columbus (43219) *(G-8374)*
Ohio Seed Improvement Assn 614 889-1136
6150 Avery Rd Dublin (43016) *(G-10414)*
Ohio Senior Home Hlth Care LLC 614 470-6070
6004 Cleveland Ave Columbus (43231) *(G-8375)*
Ohio Skate Inc (PA) 419 476-2808
5735 Opportunity Dr Toledo (43612) *(G-18103)*
Ohio Soc of Crtif Pub Accntnts 614 764-2727
4249 Easton Way Ste 150 Columbus (43219) *(G-8376)*
Ohio Soceity of Cpas, Columbus *Also called Ohio Soc of Crtif Pub Accntnts* *(G-8376)*
Ohio State Bar Association 614 487-2050
1700 Lake Shore Dr Columbus (43204) *(G-8377)*
Ohio State Bar Association 614 487-2050
1700 Lake Shore Dr Columbus (43204) *(G-8378)*
Ohio State Home Services Inc (PA) 330 467-1055
365 Highland Rd E Macedonia (44056) *(G-13207)*
Ohio State Home Services Inc 614 850-5600
4271 Weaver Ct N Hilliard (43026) *(G-11940)*
Ohio State Medical Association (PA) 614 527-6762
5115 Prkcnter Ave Ste 200 Dublin (43017) *(G-10415)*
Ohio State Parks Inc 513 664-3504
5201 Lodge Rd College Corner (45003) *(G-6838)*
Ohio State Univ Alumni Assn 614 292-2200
2200 Olentangy River Rd Columbus (43210) *(G-8379)*
Ohio State Univ Child Care, Columbus *Also called Ohio State University* *(G-8405)*

(PA)=Parent Co (HQ)=Headquarters (DH)=Div Headquarters
2018 Harris Ohio Services Directory
1279

Ohio State Univ Managed Health 614 292-8405
1900 Kenny Rd Columbus (43210) ***(G-8380)***
Ohio State Univ Res Foundation 614 292-3815
1960 Kenny Rd Columbus (43210) ***(G-8381)***
Ohio State Univ Spt Mdcine Ctr, Columbus *Also called Ohio State University* ***(G-8433)***
Ohio State Univ Vtrnarian Hosp, Columbus *Also called Ohio State University* ***(G-8428)***
Ohio State Univ Wexner Med Ctr 614 293-2663
369 Grenadine Way Columbus (43235) ***(G-8382)***
Ohio State Univ Wexner Med Ctr 614 227-0562
915 Olentangy River Rd # 5000 Columbus (43212) ***(G-8383)***
Ohio State Univ Wexner Med Ctr (PA) 614 293-8000
410 W 10th Ave Columbus (43210) ***(G-8384)***
Ohio State Univ Wexner Med Ctr 614 293-7521
320 W 10th Ave Columbus (43210) ***(G-8385)***
Ohio State Univ Wexner Med Ctr 614 366-3687
1492 E Broad St Columbus (43205) ***(G-8386)***
Ohio State Univ Wexner Med Ctr 614 293-6255
410 W 10th Ave Columbus (43210) ***(G-8387)***
Ohio State University 614 366-3692
480 Medical Center Dr Columbus (43210) ***(G-8388)***
Ohio State University 614 688-3939
555 Borror Dr Columbus (43210) ***(G-8389)***
Ohio State University 614 293-8045
410 W 10th Ave Rm 205 Columbus (43210) ***(G-8390)***
Ohio State University 614 293-2800
2050 Kenny Rd Ste 1010 Columbus (43221) ***(G-8391)***
Ohio State University 614 292-5578
305 W 12th Ave Columbus (43210) ***(G-8392)***
Ohio State University 614 257-3000
300 W 10th Ave Columbus (43210) ***(G-8393)***
Ohio State University 614 293-7417
1615 Fishinger Rd Columbus (43221) ***(G-8394)***
Ohio State University 614 293-8750
480 W 9th Ave Columbus (43210) ***(G-8395)***
Ohio State University 614 293-8116
915 Olentangy River Rd Columbus (43212) ***(G-8396)***
Ohio State University 330 263-3700
1680 Madison Ave Wooster (44691) ***(G-19898)***
Ohio State University 614 292-5504
350 Campbell Hl Columbus (43210) ***(G-8397)***
Ohio State University 740 376-7431
202 Davis Ave Marietta (45750) ***(G-13481)***
Ohio State University 614 292-5491
2300 West Case Rd Columbus (43235) ***(G-8398)***
Ohio State University 614 292-4139
1248 Arthur E Adams Dr Columbus (43221) ***(G-8399)***
Ohio State University 614 292-2624
555 Borror Dr Ste 1030 Columbus (43210) ***(G-8400)***
Ohio State University 614 685-3192
1581 Dodd Dr Ste 321 Columbus (43210) ***(G-8401)***
Ohio State University 614 292-1681
1501 Neil Ave Columbus (43201) ***(G-8402)***
Ohio State University 740 593-2657
1 Park Pl Athens (45701) ***(G-803)***
Ohio State University 614 293-3860
1375 Perry St Columbus (43201) ***(G-8403)***
Ohio State University 614 247-4000
2110 Tuttle Park Pl Columbus (43210) ***(G-8404)***
Ohio State University 614 292-4453
725 Ackerman Rd Columbus (43202) ***(G-8405)***
Ohio State University 614 292-4510
2400 Olentangy River Rd Columbus (43210) ***(G-8406)***
Ohio State University 330 263-3701
1680 Madison Ave Wooster (44691) ***(G-19899)***
Ohio State University 614 292-4843
1121 Kinnear Rd Bldg E Columbus (43212) ***(G-8407)***
Ohio State University 614 292-6831
901 Woody Hayes Dr Columbus (43210) ***(G-8408)***
Ohio State University 614 257-5200
420 N James Rd Columbus (43219) ***(G-8409)***
Ohio State University 614 292-4353
1900 Kenny Rd Columbus (43210) ***(G-8410)***
Ohio State University 614 293-4997
395 W 12th Ave Columbus (43210) ***(G-8411)***
Ohio State University 614 293-2494
2130 Neil Ave Columbus (43210) ***(G-8412)***
Ohio State University 614 292-7788
320 W 8th Ave Columbus (43201) ***(G-8413)***
Ohio State University 614 442-7300
921 Chatham Ln Ste 100 Columbus (43221) ***(G-8414)***
Ohio State University 614 293-8732
N.1135 Doan Hl Columbus (43210) ***(G-8415)***
Ohio State University 614 292-6291
3007 Derby Rd Columbus (43221) ***(G-8416)***
Ohio State University 614 293-8158
410 W 10th Ave Rm 130 Columbus (43210) ***(G-8417)***
Ohio State University 614 292-0110
1875 Millikin Rd Fl 3 Columbus (43210) ***(G-8418)***
Ohio State University 614 292-6741
Ps Pschology Rm 225 Columbus (43210) ***(G-8419)***
Ohio State University 614 292-5144
305 W 12th Ave Ste 2131 Columbus (43210) ***(G-8420)***
Ohio State University 330 263-3725
5119 Lauby Rd Canton (44720) ***(G-2485)***
Ohio State University 614 293-8732
456 W 10th Ave Rm 4725 Columbus (43210) ***(G-8421)***
Ohio State University 614 293-8588
410 W 10th Ave Columbus (43210) ***(G-8422)***
Ohio State University 614 688-5721
29 W Woodruff Ave Ofc 121 Columbus (43210) ***(G-8423)***
Ohio State University 614 293-3737
650 Ackerman Rd Ste 135 Columbus (43202) ***(G-8424)***
Ohio State University 614 688-8220
1298 Kinnear Rd Columbus (43212) ***(G-8425)***
Ohio State University 614 292-6122
2578 Kenny Rd Columbus (43210) ***(G-8426)***
Ohio State University 614 292-3238
2400 Olentangy River Rd Columbus (43210) ***(G-8427)***
Ohio State University 614 292-6661
601 Vernon Tharp St Columbus (43210) ***(G-8428)***
Ohio State University 614 292-5990
930 Kinnear Rd Columbus (43212) ***(G-8429)***
Ohio State University 614 294-2635
80 E 13th Ave Columbus (43201) ***(G-8430)***
Ohio State University 614 292-6251
1070 Carmack Rd Columbus (43210) ***(G-8431)***
Ohio State University 614 728-8100
1224 Kinnear Rd Columbus (43212) ***(G-8432)***
Ohio State University 614 293-2222
2050 Kenny Rd Fl 3 Columbus (43221) ***(G-8433)***
Ohio State University 614 293-8133
410 W 10th Ave Fl 7 Columbus (43210) ***(G-8434)***
Ohio State University 614 292-9404
1080 Carmack Rd Columbus (43210) ***(G-8435)***
Ohio State University 614 293-5066
300 W 10th Ave 924 Columbus (43210) ***(G-8436)***
Ohio State University 614 293-8419
410 W 10th Ave Rm 140 Columbus (43210) ***(G-8437)***
Ohio State University 614 292-0476
191 W Woodruff Ave Columbus (43210) ***(G-8438)***
Ohio State University 614 292-1472
305 W 12th Ave Columbus (43210) ***(G-8439)***
Ohio State University 614 293-8196
N924 Doan Hall 410 W 10 Columbus (43210) ***(G-8440)***
Ohio State University 614 293-8333
450 W 10th Ave Columbus (43210) ***(G-8441)***
Ohio State University 614 293-8000
450 W 10th Ave Columbus (43210) ***(G-8442)***
Ohio State University 614 292-2751
305 W 12th Ave Columbus (43210) ***(G-8443)***
Ohio State University 614 293-4967
473 W 12th Ave Columbus (43210) ***(G-8444)***
Ohio State University 614 292-6158
2003 Millikin Rd Rm 150 Columbus (43210) ***(G-8445)***
Ohio State University 614 293-4925
2050 Kenny Rd Ste 2200 Columbus (43221) ***(G-8446)***
Ohio State University 614 293-8074
915 Olentangy River Rd Columbus (43212) ***(G-8447)***
Ohio State University EXT, Marietta *Also called Ohio State University* ***(G-13481)***
OHIO STATE UNIVERSITY FACULTY, Columbus *Also called O S U Faculty Club* ***(G-8309)***
Ohio State Waterproofing, Macedonia *Also called Ohio State Home Services Inc* ***(G-13207)***
Ohio Steel Sheet & Plate Inc 800 827-2401
7845 Chestnut Ridge Rd Hubbard (44425) ***(G-12090)***
Ohio Steel Slitters Inc 330 477-6741
1401 Raff Rd Sw Canton (44710) ***(G-2486)***
Ohio Structures Inc (HQ) 330 533-0084
535 N Broad St Ste 5 Canfield (44406) ***(G-2206)***
Ohio Support Services Corp (PA) 614 443-0291
1291 S High St Columbus (43206) ***(G-8448)***
Ohio Surgery Center, Columbus *Also called Nueterra Holdings LLC* ***(G-8304)***
Ohio Surgery Center Ltd 614 451-0500
930 Bethel Rd Columbus (43214) ***(G-8449)***
Ohio Technical College Inc 216 881-1700
1374 E 51st St Cleveland (44103) ***(G-6195)***
Ohio Technical Services Inc 614 372-0829
1949 Camaro Ave Columbus (43207) ***(G-8450)***
Ohio Textile Service Inc 740 450-4900
2270 Fairview Rd Zanesville (43701) ***(G-20520)***
Ohio Tool Systems Inc (PA) 330 659-4181
3863 Congress Pkwy Richfield (44286) ***(G-16521)***
Ohio Tpk & Infrastructure Comm (HQ) 440 234-2081
682 Prospect St Berea (44017) ***(G-1465)***
Ohio Tpk & Infrastructure Comm 419 826-4831
8891 County Road 1 Swanton (43558) ***(G-17569)***
Ohio Tpk & Infrastructure Comm 440 234-2081
682 Prospect St Berea (44017) ***(G-1466)***
Ohio Transmission Corporation (HQ) 614 342-6247
1900 Jetway Blvd Columbus (43219) ***(G-8451)***
Ohio Transmission Corporation 419 468-7866
1311 Freese Works Pl Galion (44833) ***(G-11304)***
Ohio Transmission Corporation 513 539-8411
400 Wright Dr Middletown (45044) ***(G-14445)***
Ohio Transmission Corporation 614 342-6247
1900 Jetway Blvd Columbus (43219) ***(G-8452)***

Ohio Transport Corporation (PA)....513 539-0576
5593 Hmlton Middletown Rd Middletown (45044) ***(G-14446)***
Ohio Transport Inc....216 741-8000
3750 Valley Rd Ste A Cleveland (44109) ***(G-6196)***
Ohio University....740 593-1000
3 Station St Apt D Athens (45701) ***(G-804)***
Ohio University....740 593-1771
Woub 35 S Cllg St 395 Athens (45701) ***(G-805)***
Ohio University....740 593-1771
35 S College St Athens (45701) ***(G-806)***
Ohio University....740 593-2195
227 W Washington St Apt 1 Athens (45701) ***(G-807)***
Ohio University....740 593-1660
2 Health Center Dr Rm 110 Athens (45701) ***(G-808)***
Ohio Utilities Protection Svc....330 759-0050
4740 Belmont Ave Youngstown (44505) ***(G-20310)***
Ohio Valley Acquisition Inc....513 553-0768
250 E 5th St Ste 1200 Cincinnati (45202) ***(G-4211)***
Ohio Valley Bank Company....740 446-2168
236 2nd Ave Gallipolis (45631) ***(G-11330)***
Ohio Valley Bank Company (HQ)....740 446-2631
420 3rd Ave Gallipolis (45631) ***(G-11331)***
Ohio Valley Bank Company....740 446-1646
100 Jackson Pike Gallipolis (45631) ***(G-11332)***
Ohio Valley Bank Company....740 446-2631
143 3rd Ave Gallipolis (45631) ***(G-11333)***
Ohio Valley Coal, Saint Clairsville *Also called Ohio Valley Resources Inc* ***(G-16649)***
Ohio Valley Coal Company (HQ)....740 926-1351
46226 National Rd Saint Clairsville (43950) ***(G-16648)***
Ohio Valley Elec Svcs LLC....513 771-2410
4585 Cornell Rd Blue Ash (45241) ***(G-1655)***
Ohio Valley Electric Corp (PA)....740 289-7200
3932 Us Rte 23 Piketon (45661) ***(G-16121)***
Ohio Valley Electric Corp....740 289-7225
3932 Us Rt 23 Piketon (45661) ***(G-16122)***
Ohio Valley Flooring Inc (PA)....513 271-3434
5555 Murray Ave Cincinnati (45227) ***(G-4212)***
Ohio Valley Group Inc....440 543-0500
16965 Park Circle Dr Chagrin Falls (44023) ***(G-2727)***
Ohio Valley Home Care LLC....330 385-2333
425 W 5th St East Liverpool (43920) ***(G-10529)***
Ohio Valley Home Health Inc....740 249-4219
2097 E State St Ste B1 Athens (45701) ***(G-809)***
Ohio Valley Home Health Inc (PA)....740 441-1393
1480 Jackson Pike Gallipolis (45631) ***(G-11334)***
Ohio Valley Home Hlth Svcs Inc (PA)....330 385-2333
425 W 5th St East Liverpool (43920) ***(G-10530)***
Ohio Valley Integration Svcs....937 492-0008
2005 Commerce Dr Sidney (45365) ***(G-16946)***
Ohio Valley Manor Inc....937 392-4318
5280 Us Highway 62 And 68 Ripley (45167) ***(G-16548)***
Ohio Valley Medical Center LLC....937 521-3900
100 E Main St Springfield (45502) ***(G-17257)***
Ohio Valley Resources Inc....740 795-5220
46226 National Rd Saint Clairsville (43950) ***(G-16649)***
Ohio Valley Technical Services, Cincinnati *Also called Clean Harbors Envmtl Svcs Inc* ***(G-3361)***
Ohio Valley Transloading Co....740 795-4967
46226 National Rd Saint Clairsville (43950) ***(G-16650)***
Ohio Valley Wine & Beer, Cincinnati *Also called Ohio Valley Wine Company* ***(G-4213)***
Ohio Valley Wine Company (PA)....513 771-9370
10975 Medallion Dr Cincinnati (45241) ***(G-4213)***
Ohio Vally Ambulatory Surgery....740 423-4684
608 Washington Blvd Belpre (45714) ***(G-1443)***
Ohio Vision of Toledo Inc Opt, Oregon *Also called Optivue Inc* ***(G-15743)***
Ohio Window Cleaning Inc....937 877-0832
4582 Us Route 40 Tipp City (45371) ***(G-17723)***
Ohio Yuth Advocate Program Inc....614 252-6927
1303 E Main St Columbus (43205) ***(G-8453)***
Ohio's Country Journal, Columbus *Also called Agri Communicators Inc* ***(G-6957)***
Ohio-American Water Co Inc (HQ)....740 382-3993
365 E Center St Marion (43302) ***(G-13570)***
Ohio-Kentucky Steel Corp....937 743-4600
2001 Commerce Center Dr Franklin (45005) ***(G-11161)***
Ohio-Kentucky-Indiana Regional....513 621-6300
720 E Pete Rose Way # 420 Cincinnati (45202) ***(G-4214)***
Ohio/Oklahoma Hearst TV Inc....513 412-5000
1700 Young St Cincinnati (45202) ***(G-4215)***
Ohio/Oklahoma Hearst TV Inc....513 412-5000
1700 Young St Cincinnati (45202) ***(G-4216)***
Ohioans Home Health Care Inc....419 843-4422
28315 Kensington Ln Perrysburg (43551) ***(G-16037)***
Ohiocare Ambulatory Surgery....419 897-5501
5959 Monclova Rd Maumee (43537) ***(G-13952)***
Ohioguidestone (PA)....440 234-2006
434 Eastland Rd Berea (44017) ***(G-1467)***
Ohioguidestone....440 260-8900
3500 Carnegie Ave Cleveland (44115) ***(G-6197)***
Ohiohealth, Kenton *Also called Hardin Memorial Hospital* ***(G-12418)***
Ohiohealth Corporation....614 566-5456
3595 Olentangy River Rd Columbus (43214) ***(G-8454)***
Ohiohealth Corporation....614 544-8000
7500 Hospital Dr Dublin (43016) ***(G-10416)***
Ohiohealth Corporation....614 566-2124
180 E Broad St Columbus (43215) ***(G-8455)***
Ohiohealth Corporation....614 566-3500
3333 Chippewa St Columbus (43204) ***(G-8456)***
Ohiohealth Corporation (PA)....614 788-8860
180 E Broad St Columbus (43215) ***(G-8457)***
Ohiohealth Corporation....614 566-5977
2601 Silver Dr Columbus (43211) ***(G-8458)***
Ohiohealth Corporation....614 566-4800
755 Thomas Ln Columbus (43214) ***(G-8459)***
Ohiohealth Corporation....614 566-5414
697 Thomas Ln Columbus (43214) ***(G-8460)***
OHIOHEALTH MANSFIELD HOSPITAL, Mansfield *Also called Medcentral Health System* ***(G-13339)***
OHIOHEALTH O'BLENESS HOSPITAL, Athens *Also called Sheltering Arms Hospital Found* ***(G-811)***
Ohiohealth Research Institute....614 566-4297
3545 Olentangy River Rd # 328 Columbus (43214) ***(G-8461)***
Ohiohlth Rverside Methdst Hosp....614 566-5000
3535 Olentangy River Rd Columbus (43214) ***(G-8462)***
Ohiosolutions.org, Beachwood *Also called A+ Solutions LLC* ***(G-1044)***
Ohs LLC....513 252-2249
11427 Reed Hartman Hwy Blue Ash (45241) ***(G-1656)***
Ohs Media Group, Blue Ash *Also called Ohs LLC* ***(G-1656)***
Oicc, Springfield *Also called Ohio Institute of Cardiac Care* ***(G-17255)***
Oid Associates....330 666-3161
215 Springside Dr Akron (44333) ***(G-370)***
OK Industries Inc....419 435-2361
2307 W Corporate Dr W Fostoria (44830) ***(G-11137)***
OK Interiors Corp....513 742-3278
11100 Ashburn Rd Cincinnati (45240) ***(G-4217)***
Oki Rgonal Council Governments, Cincinnati *Also called Ride Share Information* ***(G-4419)***
OKL Can Line Inc....513 825-1655
11235 Sebring Dr Cincinnati (45240) ***(G-4218)***
Ol' Smokehaus, Clayton *Also called Landes Fresh Meats Inc* ***(G-4912)***
Old Barn Out Back Inc....419 999-3989
3175 W Elm St Lima (45805) ***(G-12848)***
Old Barn Out Back Restaurant, Lima *Also called Old Barn Out Back Inc* ***(G-12848)***
Old Dominion Freight Line Inc....330 545-8628
1730 N State St Girard (44420) ***(G-11422)***
Old Dominion Freight Line Inc....937 235-1596
3100 Transportation Rd Dayton (45404) ***(G-9790)***
Old Dominion Freight Line Inc....513 771-1486
6431 Centre Park Dr West Chester (45069) ***(G-19125)***
Old Dominion Freight Line Inc....419 726-4032
5950 Stickney Ave Toledo (43612) ***(G-18104)***
Old Dominion Freight Line Inc....614 491-3903
2885 Alum Creek Dr Columbus (43207) ***(G-8463)***
Old Dominion Freight Line Inc....216 641-5566
8055 Old Granger Rd Cleveland (44125) ***(G-6198)***
Old Fort Banking Company....419 447-4790
33 E Market St Tiffin (44883) ***(G-17692)***
Old Rpblic Ttle Nthrn Ohio LLC....216 524-5700
6480 Rckside Woods Blvd S Independence (44131) ***(G-12242)***
Old Time Pottery Inc....513 825-5211
1191 Smiley Ave Cincinnati (45240) ***(G-4219)***
Old Time Pottery Inc....440 842-1244
7011 W 130th St Ste 1 Cleveland (44130) ***(G-6199)***
Old Time Pottery Inc....614 337-1258
2200 Morse Rd Columbus (43229) ***(G-8464)***
Old Towne Windows & Doors, Milan *Also called Olde Towne Windows Inc* ***(G-14496)***
Old Trail School....330 666-1118
2315 Ira Rd Bath (44210) ***(G-1035)***
Olde Towne Windows Inc....419 626-9613
9501 Us Highway 250 N # 1 Milan (44846) ***(G-14496)***
Older Wiser Life Services LLC....330 659-2111
4028 Broadview Rd Ste 1 Richfield (44286) ***(G-16522)***
Oldies 95, Dayton *Also called Miami Valley Broadcasting Corp* ***(G-9727)***
Olentangy Village Apartments, Columbus *Also called Olentangy Village Associates* ***(G-8465)***
Olentangy Village Associates....614 515-4680
2907 N High St Columbus (43202) ***(G-8465)***
Oliver House Rest Complex....419 243-1302
27 Broadway St Ste A Toledo (43604) ***(G-18105)***
Oliver Steel Plate, Bedford *Also called A M Castle & Co* ***(G-1292)***
Olmsted Health and Svc Corp....440 235-7100
26376 John Rd Ofc Olmsted Twp (44138) ***(G-15679)***
Olmsted Lanes Inc....440 777-6363
24488 Lorain Rd North Olmsted (44070) ***(G-15435)***
Olmsted Manor Nursing Home....440 250-4080
27500 Mill Rd North Olmsted (44070) ***(G-15436)***
Olmsted Manor Retirement Prpts....440 250-4080
26612 Center Ridge Rd Westlake (44145) ***(G-19529)***
Olmsted Mnor Rtrment Cmnty Ltd....440 779-8886
27420 Mill Rd North Olmsted (44070) ***(G-15437)***
Olmsted Parks and Recreation, North Olmsted *Also called City of North Olmsted* ***(G-15416)***
Olmsted Residence Corporation....440 235-7100
26376 John Rd Ofc Olmsted Twp (44138) ***(G-15680)***

A L P H A B E T I C

Ologie LLC ... 614 221-1107
447 E Main St Ste 122 Columbus (43215) *(G-8466)*

Olon Ricerca Bioscience LLC ... 440 357-3300
7528 Auburn Rd Painesville (44077) *(G-15869)*

Olshan Hotel Management Inc ... 614 414-1000
3999 Easton Loop W Columbus (43219) *(G-8467)*

Olshan Hotel Management Inc ... 614 416-8000
3900 Morse Xing Columbus (43219) *(G-8468)*

Olympia Candies, Strongsville Also called Robert E McGrath Inc *(G-17503)*

Olympic Steel Inc (PA) ... 216 292-3800
22901 Millcreek Blvd # 650 Cleveland (44122) *(G-6200)*

Olympic Steel Inc ... 216 292-3800
5092 Richmond Rd Cleveland (44146) *(G-6201)*

Olympic Steel Inc ... 440 287-0150
3000 Crane Centre Dr Streetsboro (44241) *(G-17423)*

Olympic Steel Inc ... 216 292-3800
5080 Richmond Rd Bedford (44146) *(G-1327)*

Om Group, Westlake Also called Borchers Americas Inc *(G-19466)*

Omega Laboratories Inc ... 330 628-5748
400 N Cleveland Ave Mogadore (44260) *(G-14681)*

Omega Sea LLC ... 440 639-2372
1000 Bacon Rd Painesville (44077) *(G-15870)*

Omega Title Agency LLC ... 330 436-0600
4500 Courthouse Blvd # 100 Stow (44224) *(G-17384)*

Omegasea Ltd Liability Co ... 440 639-2372
1000 Bacon Rd Painesville (44077) *(G-15871)*

OMI Transportation Inc ... 419 241-8711
1600 Water St Toledo (43604) *(G-18106)*

Omni Cart Services Inc ... 440 205-8363
7370 Production Dr Mentor (44060) *(G-14225)*

Omni Fasteners Inc ... 440 838-1800
909 Towpath Trl Broadview Heights (44147) *(G-1888)*

Omni Fireproofing Co LLC ... 513 870-9115
9305 Le Saint Dr West Chester (45014) *(G-19126)*

Omni Interglobal Inc ... 216 239-3833
600 Superior Ave E # 1300 Cleveland (44114) *(G-6202)*

Omni Manor Inc (PA) ... 330 545-1550
101 W Liberty St Girard (44420) *(G-11423)*

Omni Manor Inc ... 330 793-5648
3245 Vestal Rd Youngstown (44509) *(G-20311)*

Omni Nursing Home, Youngstown Also called Omni Manor Inc *(G-20311)*

Omni Park Health Care LLC ... 216 289-8963
27801 Euclid Ave Ste 600 Euclid (44132) *(G-10770)*

Omnicare Inc (HQ) ... 513 719-2600
900 Omnicare Ctr 201e4t Cincinnati (45202) *(G-4220)*

Omnicare Distribution Ctr LLC ... 419 720-8200
201 E 4th St Ste 1 Cincinnati (45202) *(G-4221)*

Omnicare Management Company ... 513 719-1535
201 E 4th St Ste 900 Cincinnati (45202) *(G-4222)*

Omnicare of Central Ohio, Columbus Also called Ncs Healthcare of Ohio LLC *(G-8254)*

Omnicare of Cincinnati, West Chester Also called Home Care Pharmacy LLC *(G-19208)*

Omnicare of Dover, Dover Also called Ncs Healthcare of Ohio LLC *(G-10201)*

Omnicare of Northwest Ohio, Perrysburg Also called Westhaven Services Co LLC *(G-16073)*

Omnicare of St. George, Cincinnati Also called Superior Care Pharmacy Inc *(G-4603)*

Omnicare Phrm of Midwest LLC (HQ) ... 513 719-2600
201 E 4th St Ste 900 Cincinnati (45202) *(G-4223)*

Omnicare Purch Ltd Partner Inc ... 800 990-6664
201 E 4th St Ste 900 Cincinnati (45202) *(G-4224)*

Omnisource LLC ... 419 537-1631
2453 Hill Ave Toledo (43607) *(G-18107)*

Omnisource LLC ... 419 227-3411
1610 E 4th St Lima (45804) *(G-12849)*

Omnisource LLC ... 419 394-3351
04575 County Road 33a Saint Marys (45885) *(G-16681)*

Omnisource LLC ... 419 537-9400
5130 N Detroit Ave Toledo (43612) *(G-18108)*

Omnova Solutions Inc ... 330 794-6300
2990 Gilchrist Rd Akron (44305) *(G-371)*

Omya Industries Inc (HQ) ... 513 387-4600
9987 Carver Rd Ste 300 Blue Ash (45242) *(G-1657)*

On Call Medical, Athens Also called Eric Hasemeier Do *(G-787)*

On Search Partners LLC ... 440 318-1006
6240 Som Center Rd # 230 Solon (44139) *(G-17036)*

On Site Instruments LLC ... 614 846-1900
403 Venture Dr Lewis Center (43035) *(G-12699)*

On-Call Nursing Inc ... 216 577-8890
15644 Madison Ave Lakewood (44107) *(G-12493)*

On-Power Inc ... 513 228-2100
3525 Grant Ave Ste A Lebanon (45036) *(G-12633)*

Oncall LLC ... 513 381-4320
8044 Montgomery Rd # 420 Cincinnati (45236) *(G-4225)*

Oncodiagnostic Laboratory Inc ... 216 861-5846
812 Huron Rd E Ste 520 Cleveland (44115) *(G-6203)*

Oncolgy/Hmatology Care Inc PSC (PA) ... 513 751-2145
5053 Wooster Rd Cincinnati (45226) *(G-4226)*

Oncology Partners Network, Cincinnati Also called Trihealth Oncology Inst LLC *(G-4697)*

One Call Now, Dayton Also called Swn Communications Inc *(G-9917)*

One Lincoln Park ... 937 298-0550
590 Isaac Prugh Way Dayton (45429) *(G-9791)*

One Sky Flight LLC ... 877 703-2348
26180 Curtiss Wright Pkwy Cleveland (44143) *(G-6204)*

One Source Technology LLC ... 216 420-1700
1111 Superior Ave E # 2000 Cleveland (44114) *(G-6205)*

One Stop Remodeling, Columbus Also called Wingler Construction Corp *(G-9000)*

One Way Express Incorporated ... 440 439-9182
380 Solon Rd Ste 5 Cleveland (44146) *(G-6206)*

ONE WAY FARM CHILDREN'S HOME, Fairfield Also called One Way Farm of Fairfield Inc *(G-10889)*

One Way Farm of Fairfield Inc ... 513 829-3276
6131 E River Rd Fairfield (45014) *(G-10889)*

One10 LLC ... 763 445-3000
130 W 2nd St Ste 500 Dayton (45402) *(G-9792)*

Oneeighty Inc ... 330 263-6021
104 Spink St Wooster (44691) *(G-19900)*

ONeil & Associates Inc (PA) ... 937 865-0800
495 Byers Rd Miamisburg (45342) *(G-14330)*

ONeil Awning and Tent Inc ... 614 837-6352
895 W Walnut St Canal Winchester (43110) *(G-2165)*

ONeill Senior Center Inc (PA) ... 740 373-3914
333 4th St Marietta (45750) *(G-13482)*

Onesco, Montgomery Also called O N Equity Sales Company *(G-14728)*

Onestaff Inc ... 859 815-1345
2358 Harrison Ave Apt 20 Cincinnati (45211) *(G-4227)*

Onex Construction Inc ... 330 995-9015
1430 Miller Pkwy Streetsboro (44241) *(G-17424)*

Online Imaging Solutions, Cleveland Also called American Copy Equipment Inc *(G-5008)*

Online Mega Sellers Corp (PA) ... 888 384-6468
4236 W Alexis Rd Toledo (43623) *(G-18109)*

Ontario Commons, Ontario Also called Diversicare of Mansfield LLC *(G-15686)*

Ontario Local School District ... 419 529-3814
3644 Pearl St Ontario (44906) *(G-15708)*

Ontario Mechanical LLC ... 419 529-2578
2880 Park Ave W Ontario (44906) *(G-15709)*

Onx USA LLC (HQ) ... 440 569-2300
5910 Landerbrook Dr # 250 Cleveland (44124) *(G-6207)*

Ooh Ooh Drive Thru, Springfield Also called M & R Amusement Services Inc *(G-17227)*

Oovoo LLC ... 917 515-2074
1700 S Patterson Blvd Kettering (45409) *(G-12434)*

Open Arms Health Systems LLC ... 614 385-8354
868 Freeway Dr N Columbus (43229) *(G-8469)*

Open Door Christian School ... 440 322-6386
8287 W Ridge Rd Elyria (44035) *(G-10666)*

Open Online LLC (PA) ... 614 481-6999
1650 Lake Shore Dr # 350 Columbus (43204) *(G-8470)*

Open Text Inc ... 614 658-3588
3671 Ridge Mill Dr Hilliard (43026) *(G-11941)*

Openonline, Columbus Also called Open Online LLC *(G-8470)*

Operation Thank You ... 513 899-3134
2467 Ford Rd Morrow (45152) *(G-14846)*

Opers Legal Dept ... 614 227-0550
277 E Town St Columbus (43215) *(G-8471)*

Ophthalmology Associates of ... 419 865-3866
3509 Briarfield Blvd Maumee (43537) *(G-13953)*

Ophthlmic Srgeons Cons of Ohio ... 614 221-7464
262 Neil Ave Ste 430 Columbus (43215) *(G-8472)*

Opinions Ltd (PA) ... 440 893-0300
33 River St Chagrin Falls (44022) *(G-2703)*

Oppenheimer & Co Inc ... 513 723-9200
5905 E Galbraith Rd # 6200 Cincinnati (45236) *(G-4228)*

Opportunities For Ohioans (HQ) ... 614 438-1200
400 E Campus View Blvd Columbus (43235) *(G-8473)*

Opportunities For Ohioans ... 513 852-3260
895 Central Ave Fl 7 Cincinnati (45202) *(G-4229)*

Opportunity Homes Inc ... 330 424-1411
7891 State Route 45 Lisbon (44432) *(G-12941)*

OPRS FOUNDATION, Columbus Also called Ohio Presbyterian Rtr Svcs *(G-8369)*

Optima 777 LLC ... 216 771-7700
777 Saint Clair Ave Ne Cleveland (44114) *(G-6208)*

Optimal Life Intgrtve Mdcne PA ... 419 474-3657
4103 Stonehenge Dr Sylvania (43560) *(G-17604)*

Optimetrics Inc ... 937 306-7180
4027 Colonel Glenn Hwy Beavercreek Township (45431) *(G-1278)*

Optimist International ... 419 238-5086
1008 Woodland Ave Van Wert (45891) *(G-18640)*

Optimum Graphics, Westerville Also called Optimum System Products Inc *(G-19433)*

Optimum System Products Inc (PA) ... 614 885-4464
921 Eastwind Dr Ste 133 Westerville (43081) *(G-19433)*

Optimum Technology Inc (PA) ... 614 785-1110
100 E Campus View Blvd # 380 Columbus (43235) *(G-8474)*

Optio-Vision By Kahn & Diehl, Oregon Also called Ottivue *(G-15747)*

Option Care Enterprises Inc ... 513 576-8400
50 W Techne Center Dr J Milford (45150) *(G-14546)*

Option Care Infusion Svcs Inc ... 614 431-6453
7654 Crosswoods Dr Columbus (43235) *(G-8475)*

Option Care Infusion Svcs Inc ... 513 576-8400
25 Whitney Dr Ste 114 Milford (45150) *(G-14547)*

Option Line ... 614 586-1380
665 E Dublin Granville Rd # 290 Columbus (43229) *(G-8476)*

Options Flight Support Inc ... 216 261-3500
26180 Curtiss Wright Pkwy Cleveland (44143) *(G-6209)*

ALPHABETIC SECTION Osborne Co

Options For Family & Youth 216 267-7070
11351 Pearl Rd Ste 103 Strongsville (44136) ***(G-17498)***
Optis Solutions 513 948-2070
6705 Steger Dr Cincinnati (45237) ***(G-4230)***
Optivue Inc 419 891-1391
2740 Navarre Ave Oregon (43616) ***(G-15743)***
Optumrx Inc 614 794-3300
250 Progressive Way Westerville (43082) ***(G-19338)***
OR Colan Associates LLC 440 827-6116
22710 Fairview Center Dr Cleveland (44126) ***(G-6210)***
Oracle Corporation 513 826-5632
3610 Pentagon Blvd # 205 Beavercreek (45431) ***(G-1195)***
Oracle Systems Corporation 513 826-6000
9987 Carver Rd Ste 250 Blue Ash (45242) ***(G-1658)***
Oracle Systems Corporation 216 328-9100
3333 Richmond Rd Ste 420 Beachwood (44122) ***(G-1112)***
Oral & Maxillofacial Surgeons (PA) 419 385-5743
1850 Eastgate Rd Ste A Toledo (43614) ***(G-18110)***
Oral & Maxillofacial Surgeons 419 471-0300
4646 Nantuckett Dr Ste A Toledo (43623) ***(G-18111)***
Orange Barrel Media LLC 614 294-4898
250 N Hartford Ave Columbus (43222) ***(G-8477)***
Orbit Industries Inc (PA) 440 243-3311
6840 Lake Abrams Dr Cleveland (44130) ***(G-6211)***
Orbit Movers & Erectors Inc 937 277-8080
1101 Negley Pl Dayton (45402) ***(G-9793)***
Orbit Systems Inc 614 504-8011
615 Carle Ave Lewis Center (43035) ***(G-12700)***
Orc International Inc 419 893-0029
1900 Indian Wood Cir # 200 Maumee (43537) ***(G-13954)***
Orc International Inc 513 579-1555
310 Culvert St Fl 2 Cincinnati (45202) ***(G-4231)***
Orca House 216 231-3772
1905 E 89th St Cleveland (44106) ***(G-6212)***
Orcha of North Livin & Rehab C, Napoleon *Also called Ncop LLC* ***(G-14948)***
Orchard Hill Swim Club 513 385-0211
8601 Cheviot Rd Cincinnati (45251) ***(G-4232)***
Orchard Hills Country Club, Bryan *Also called Buckeye Golf Club Co Inc* ***(G-2003)***
Orchard Hiltz & McCliment Inc 614 418-0600
580 N 4th St Ste 610 Columbus (43215) ***(G-8478)***
Orchard Phrm Svcs LLC 330 491-4200
7835 Freedom Ave Nw North Canton (44720) ***(G-15359)***
Orchard Villa Inc 419 697-4100
2841 Munding Dr Oregon (43616) ***(G-15744)***
Orchards of Ridgewood Livin, Fairlawn *Also called Rwdop LLC* ***(G-10970)***
Order of Symposiarchs America 740 387-9713
704 Vernon Heights Blvd Marion (43302) ***(G-13571)***
Order of Unite Commercial Tra (PA) 614 487-9680
1801 Watermark Dr Ste 100 Columbus (43215) ***(G-8479)***
Ordms, Blue Ash *Also called Oscar Rbrtsn Doc Mgmt Svcs* ***(G-1661)***
Oregon Clean Energy Center 419 566-9466
816 N Lallendorf Rd Oregon (43616) ***(G-15745)***
Oregon Ford Inc 419 698-4444
2811 Navarre Ave Oregon (43616) ***(G-15746)***
OReilly Automotive Inc 216 642-7591
7621 Broadview Rd Seven Hills (44131) ***(G-16835)***
OReilly Automotive Inc 937 660-3040
2381 Beechwood Dr Germantown (45327) ***(G-11399)***
OReilly Automotive Inc 330 494-0042
1233 N Main St North Canton (44720) ***(G-15360)***
OReilly Automotive Inc 419 324-2077
7417 W Central Ave Toledo (43617) ***(G-18112)***
OReilly Automotive Inc 419 630-0811
1116 S Main St Bryan (43506) ***(G-2015)***
OReilly Automotive Inc 330 318-3136
8308 Market St Boardman (44512) ***(G-1742)***
OReilly Automotive Inc 740 845-1016
229 Lafayette St London (43140) ***(G-13004)***
OReilly Automotive Inc 614 444-5352
1455 Parsons Ave Columbus (43207) ***(G-8480)***
OReilly Automotive Inc 513 731-7700
4630 Ridge Ave Cincinnati (45209) ***(G-4233)***
OReilly Automotive Inc 213 332-0427
5489 Warrensville Ctr Rd Maple Heights (44137) ***(G-13412)***
OReilly Automotive Inc 330 238-1416
1805 W State St Alliance (44601) ***(G-551)***
OReilly Automotive Inc 330 267-4383
1196 W Maple St Hartville (44632) ***(G-11828)***
Organizational Horizons Inc 614 268-6013
5721 N High St Ste Lla Worthington (43085) ***(G-19981)***
Oriana House Inc 330 374-9610
941 Sherman St Akron (44311) ***(G-372)***
Oriana House Inc (PA) 330 535-8116
885 E Buchtel Ave Akron (44305) ***(G-373)***
Oriana House Inc 330 996-7730
15 Frederick Ave Akron (44310) ***(G-374)***
Oriana House Inc 216 881-5440
1829 E 55th St Cleveland (44103) ***(G-6213)***
Oriana House Inc 216 361-9655
3540 Croton Ave Cleveland (44115) ***(G-6214)***
Oriana House Inc 330 643-2171
205 E Crosier St Akron (44311) ***(G-375)***
Original Hartstone Pottery Inc 740 452-9999
1719 Dearborn St Zanesville (43701) ***(G-20521)***
Original Partners Ltd Partnr (PA) 513 381-8696
1055 Saint Paul Pl Cincinnati (45202) ***(G-4234)***
Orin Group LLC 330 630-3937
537 N Clvland Mssillon Rd Akron (44333) ***(G-376)***
Orion Academy, Cincinnati *Also called National Heritg Academies Inc* ***(G-4138)***
Orion Care Services LLC 216 752-3600
18810 Harvard Ave Cleveland (44122) ***(G-6215)***
Orkin, Columbus *Also called Steve Shaffer* ***(G-8787)***
Orkin LLC 614 888-5811
6230 Huntley Rd Columbus (43229) ***(G-8481)***
Orkin Pest Control 561, Columbus *Also called Orkin LLC* ***(G-8481)***
ORourke Wrecking Company 513 871-1400
660 Lunken Park Dr Cincinnati (45226) ***(G-4235)***
Orphan Foundation of America 571 203-0270
23811 Chagrin Blvd # 210 Beachwood (44122) ***(G-1113)***
Orrvilla Inc 330 683-4455
333 E Sassafras St Orrville (44667) ***(G-15776)***
Orrvilla Retirement Community 330 683-4455
333 E Sassafras St Orrville (44667) ***(G-15777)***
Orrville Boys and Girls Club 330 683-4888
820 N Ella St Orrville (44667) ***(G-15778)***
Orrville Hospital Foundation 330 684-4700
832 S Main St Orrville (44667) ***(G-15779)***
Orrville Trucking & Grading Co (PA) 330 682-4010
475 Orr St Orrville (44667) ***(G-15780)***
Ors Nasco Inc 918 781-5300
9901 Princeton Glendale West Chester (45246) ***(G-19219)***
Orsanco, Cincinnati *Also called Ohio Rver Vly Wtr Snttion Comm* ***(G-4210)***
Ortho Neuro, Westerville *Also called Orthoneuro* ***(G-19434)***
Orthodontic Associates LLC (PA) 419 229-8771
260 S Eastown Rd Lima (45807) ***(G-12850)***
Orthodontic Association 419 523-4014
1020 N Perry St Ottawa (45875) ***(G-15801)***
Ortholink Physicians, New Albany *Also called Joint Implant Surgeons Inc* ***(G-14990)***
Orthoneuro (PA) 614 890-6555
70 S Cleveland Ave Westerville (43081) ***(G-19434)***
Orthoneuro 614 890-6555
4420 Refugee Rd Columbus (43232) ***(G-8482)***
Orthoneuro 614 890-6555
1313 Olentangy River Rd Columbus (43212) ***(G-8483)***
Orthopaedic & Spine Center At 614 468-0300
6810 Perimeter Dr 200a Dublin (43016) ***(G-10417)***
Orthopaedic Institute Ohio Inc (PA) 419 222-6622
801 Medical Dr Ste A Lima (45804) ***(G-12851)***
Orthopaedic Offices Inc 513 221-5500
9825 Kenwood Rd Ste 200 Blue Ash (45242) ***(G-1659)***
Orthopdic Spt Mdicine Cons Inc 513 777-7714
275 N Breiel Blvd Middletown (45042) ***(G-14447)***
Orthopedic Assoc of Zanesville 740 454-3273
2854 Bell St Zanesville (43701) ***(G-20522)***
Orthopedic Associates (PA) 937 415-9100
7677 Yankee St Ste 110 Centerville (45459) ***(G-2683)***
Orthopedic Associates Dayton 937 280-4988
7980 N Main St Dayton (45415) ***(G-9794)***
Orthopedic Associates Inc 440 892-1440
24723 Detroit Rd Westlake (44145) ***(G-19530)***
Orthopedic Cons Cincinnati (PA) 513 733-8894
4701 Creek Rd Ste 110 Blue Ash (45242) ***(G-1660)***
Orthopedic Cons Cincinnati 513 753-7488
4440 Glnste Wthmsville Rd Cincinnati (45245) ***(G-2926)***
Orthopedic Cons Cincinnati 513 232-6677
7575 5 Mile Rd Cincinnati (45230) ***(G-4236)***
Orthopedic Cons Cincinnati 513 245-2500
7663 5 Mile Rd Cincinnati (45230) ***(G-4237)***
Orthopedic Cons Cincinnati 513 347-9999
6909 Good Samaritan Dr Cincinnati (45247) ***(G-4238)***
Orthopedic Diagnstc Trtmnt Ctr 513 791-6611
10547 Montgomery Rd 400a Montgomery (45242) ***(G-14733)***
Orthopedic Diagnstc Trtmnt Ctr 513 221-4848
4600 Smith Rd Ste B Cincinnati (45212) ***(G-4239)***
Orthopedic One Inc 614 827-8700
4605 Sawmill Rd Columbus (43220) ***(G-8484)***
Orthopedic One Inc (PA) 614 545-7900
170 Taylor Station Rd Columbus (43213) ***(G-8485)***
Orthorpdics Mltspcialty Netwrk (PA) 330 493-1630
4760 Belpar St Nw Canton (44718) ***(G-2487)***
Orton Edward Jr Crmic Fndation 614 895-2663
6991 S Old 3c Hwy Westerville (43082) ***(G-19339)***
Orville Pet Spa & Resort 330 683-3335
1669 N Main St Orrville (44667) ***(G-15781)***
Orwell Communications Inc 937 855-6511
48130102 Germantown (45327) ***(G-11400)***
Os Hill Leasing Inc 330 386-6440
47866 Y And O Rd East Liverpool (43920) ***(G-10531)***
Osborn Engineering Company (PA) 216 861-2020
1100 Superior Ave E # 300 Cleveland (44114) ***(G-6216)***
Osborn Marketing Research Corp 440 871-1047
1818 Century Oaks Dr Westlake (44145) ***(G-19531)***
Osborne Co 440 942-7000
7954 Reynolds Rd Mentor (44060) ***(G-14226)***

ALPHABETIC

ALPHABETIC SECTION

Osborne Materials Company (PA) 440 357-7026
  1 Williams St Grand River (44045) *(G-11457)*
Osborne Trucking Company (PA) 513 874-2090
  325 Osborne Dr Fairfield (45014) *(G-10890)*
Oscar Rbrtsn Doc Mgmt Svcs 800 991-4611
  10999 Reed Hartman Hwy # 208 Blue Ash (45242) *(G-1661)*
Osf International Inc 513 942-6620
  6320 S Gilmore Rd Fairfield (45014) *(G-10891)*
Osgood State Bank (inc) (PA) 419 582-2681
  275 W Main St Osgood (45351) *(G-15792)*
OSMA, Dublin Also called Ohio State Medical Association *(G-10415)*
Ostendorf-Morris Properties 216 861-7200
  1100 Superior Ave E # 800 Cleveland (44114) *(G-6217)*
Osterfeld Champion Service 937 254-8437
  121 Commerce Park Dr Dayton (45404) *(G-9795)*
Osterwisch Company Inc 513 791-3282
  6755 Highland Ave Cincinnati (45236) *(G-4240)*
Osu Cnter For Wllness Prvntion, Columbus Also called Ohio State University *(G-8391)*
Osu Dept Psychology, Columbus Also called Ohio State University *(G-8419)*
Osu Division of Pulmonary, Columbus Also called Ohio State University *(G-8446)*
Osu Emergency Medicine LLC 614 947-3700
  700 Ackerman Rd Ste 270 Columbus (43202) *(G-8486)*
Osu Faculty Practice, Columbus Also called Ohio State University *(G-8439)*
Osu Hospitals, Columbus Also called Ohio State University *(G-8442)*
Osu Industrial Welding Sy, Columbus Also called Ohio State University *(G-8399)*
Osu Internal Medicine LLC (PA) 614 293-0080
  3900 Stoneridge Ln Ste B Dublin (43017) *(G-10418)*
Osu Medical Staff ADM, Columbus Also called Ohio State University *(G-8417)*
Osu Nephrology Medical Ctr 614 293-8300
  410 W 10th Ave Columbus (43210) *(G-8487)*
Osu Obgyn, Columbus Also called Ohio State University *(G-8411)*
Osu Orthodontic Clinic 614 292-1058
  2010 901 Woody Hayes Dr Columbus (43210) *(G-8488)*
Osu Pathology Services LLC 614 293-5905
  410 W 10th Ave Columbus (43210) *(G-8489)*
Osu Pathology Services LLC 614 247-6461
  1645 Neil Ave Rm 129 Columbus (43210) *(G-8490)*
Osu Personnel, Columbus Also called Ohio State University *(G-8412)*
Osu Physical Medicine LLC 614 366-6398
  480 Medical Center Dr # 1036 Columbus (43210) *(G-8491)*
Osu Physics Dept, The, Columbus Also called Ohio State University *(G-8438)*
Osu Psychiatry LLC 614 794-1818
  700 Ackerman Rd Ste 600 Columbus (43202) *(G-8492)*
Osu Radiology LLC 614 293-8315
  395 W 12th Ave Columbus (43210) *(G-8493)*
OSu Spt Mdcine Physcians Inc 614 293-3600
  2835 Fred Taylor Dr Columbus (43202) *(G-8494)*
Osu Surgery LLC 614 293-8116
  915 Olentangy River Rd # 2100 Columbus (43212) *(G-8495)*
Osu Surgery LLC (PA) 614 261-1141
  700 Ackerman Rd Ste 350 Columbus (43202) *(G-8496)*
Osu Value City Arena, Columbus Also called Ohio State University *(G-8400)*
Osu-Infectious Diseases, Columbus Also called Ohio State University *(G-8421)*
Osup Community Outreach LLC 614 685-1542
  700 Ackerman Rd Ste 600 Columbus (43202) *(G-8497)*
Oswald Companies, Cleveland Also called Jbo Holding Company *(G-5855)*
Oswald Company Inc (PA) 513 745-4424
  308 E 8th St Ste 500 Cincinnati (45202) *(G-4241)*
Otis Elevator Company 513 531-7888
  2463 Crowne Point Dr Cincinnati (45241) *(G-4242)*
Otis Elevator Company 614 777-6500
  777 Dearborn Park Ln L Columbus (43085) *(G-8498)*
Otis Elevator Company 216 573-2333
  9800 Rockside Rd Ste 1200 Cleveland (44125) *(G-6218)*
Otis Wright & Sons Inc 419 227-4400
  1601 E 4th St Lima (45804) *(G-12852)*
Otolaryngology Department, Columbus Also called Ohio State Univ Wexner Med Ctr *(G-8386)*
Otp Industrial Solutions, Columbus Also called Ohio Transmission Corporation *(G-8451)*
Otp Industrial Solutions, Middletown Also called Ohio Transmission Corporation *(G-14445)*
Ots-NJ LLC 732 833-0600
  21 Traxler St Butler (44822) *(G-2067)*
Ottawa Cnty Sr Healthcare, Oak Harbor Also called County of Ottawa *(G-15607)*
Ottawa County Board M R D D 419 734-6650
  235 N Toussaint St Oak Harbor (43449) *(G-15614)*
Ottawa County Dept Human Svcs, Oak Harbor Also called County of Ottawa *(G-15608)*
Ottawa County Transit Board 419 898-7433
  275 N Toussaint South Rd Oak Harbor (43449) *(G-15615)*
Ottawa Hills Memorial Park 419 539-0218
  4210 W Central Ave Ste 1 Ottawa Hills (43606) *(G-15806)*
Ottawa House, Toledo Also called Zepf Housing Corp One Inc *(G-18333)*
Otterbein Cridersville, Cridersville Also called Otterbein Snior Lfstyle Chices *(G-9152)*
Otterbein Homes 513 933-5439
  580 N State Route 741 Lebanon (45036) *(G-12634)*
Otterbein Lebanon 513 933-5465
  585 N State Route 741 Lebanon (45036) *(G-12635)*
OTTERBEIN NORTH SHORE, Lakeside Also called North Shore Retirement Cmnty *(G-12465)*

Otterbein Portage Valley Inc 888 749-4950
  20311 Pemberville Rd Ofc Pemberville (43450) *(G-15943)*
OTTERBEIN SENIOR LIFESTYLE CHO, Lebanon Also called Otterbein Homes *(G-12634)*
Otterbein Snior Lfstyle Chices 513 260-7690
  105 Atrium Dr Middletown (45005) *(G-14483)*
Otterbein Snior Lfstyle Chices (PA) 513 933-5400
  585 N State Route 741 Lebanon (45036) *(G-12636)*
Otterbein Snior Lfstyle Chices 419 645-5114
  100 Red Oak Dr Cridersville (45806) *(G-9152)*
Otterbein Snior Lfstyle Chices 419 943-4376
  901 E Main St Leipsic (45856) *(G-12663)*
Otterbein Snior Lfstyle Chices 419 394-2366
  11230 State Route 364 Saint Marys (45885) *(G-16682)*
OTTERBEIN ST MARY'S, Pemberville Also called Otterbein Portage Valley Inc *(G-15943)*
Otterbein St Mary's, Lebanon Also called Otterbein Snior Lfstyle Chices *(G-12636)*
Otterbein St Marys Retrmnt, Saint Marys Also called Otterbein Snior Lfstyle Chices *(G-16682)*
Ottivue (PA) 419 693-4444
  2740 Navarre Ave Oregon (43616) *(G-15747)*
Otto Falkenberg Excavating 330 626-4215
  9350 Coit Rd Mantua (44255) *(G-13393)*
Our House Inc 440 835-2110
  27633 Bassett Rd Westlake (44145) *(G-19532)*
Our Lady of Bethlehem Schools 614 459-8285
  4567 Olentangy River Rd Columbus (43214) *(G-8499)*
Our Lady of Wayside Inc (PA) 440 934-6152
  38135 Colorado Ave Avon (44011) *(G-911)*
Our Lady Prptul Hlp Cnmty Bngo 513 742-3200
  9908 Shellbark Ln Cincinnati (45231) *(G-4243)*
Our Ohio Communications, Columbus Also called Ohio Farm Bur Federation Inc *(G-8345)*
Ourday At Messiah Preschool 614 882-4416
  51 N State St Westerville (43081) *(G-19435)*
Out Patient, Sandusky Also called Firelands Regional Health Sys *(G-16758)*
Outdoor Family Center, Perry Also called Lake County YMCA *(G-15962)*
Outlook Point At Xenia, Xenia Also called Balanced Care Corporation *(G-20044)*
Outlook Pointe, Northfield Also called Balanced Care Corporation *(G-15509)*
Outpatient Anderson, Cincinnati Also called Childrens Hospital Medical Ctr *(G-3251)*
Outreach Cmnty Living Svcs Inc 330 263-0862
  337 W North St Wooster (44691) *(G-19901)*
Outreach Professional Svcs Inc 216 472-4094
  2351 E 22nd St Cleveland (44115) *(G-6219)*
Ovations 216 687-9292
  2000 Prospect Ave E Cleveland (44115) *(G-6220)*
Ovations Food Services LP 513 419-7254
  525 Elm St Cincinnati (45202) *(G-4244)*
OVEC, Piketon Also called Ohio Valley Electric Corp *(G-16121)*
Overbrook Center, Middleport Also called Meigs Center Ltd *(G-14407)*
Overbrook Park, Chillicothe Also called Overbrook Park Ltd *(G-2867)*
Overbrook Park Ltd 740 773-1159
  2179 Anderson Station Rd Chillicothe (45601) *(G-2867)*
Overcashier and Horst Htg & AC 419 841-3333
  3745 Centennial Rd Sylvania (43560) *(G-17605)*
Overhead Door Co of Dayton, Dayton Also called Dayton Door Sales Inc *(G-9471)*
Overhead Door Co of Toledo, Toledo Also called Overhead Inc *(G-18113)*
Overhead Door Co Springfield, Dayton Also called Dayton Door Sales Inc *(G-9472)*
Overhead Door Co- Cincinnati 513 346-4000
  9345 Prnceton Glendale Rd West Chester (45011) *(G-19127)*
Overhead Door Company, Columbus Also called Graf and Sons Inc *(G-7765)*
Overhead Inc (PA) 419 476-7811
  340 New Towne Square Dr Toledo (43612) *(G-18113)*
Overland Xpress LLC (PA) 513 528-1158
  431 Ohio Pike Ste 311 Cincinnati (45255) *(G-4245)*
Overlook House 216 795-3550
  2187 Overlook Rd Cleveland (44106) *(G-6221)*
Ovm Investment Group LLC 937 392-0145
  5280 Us Hwy 62 & 88 Ripley (45167) *(G-16549)*
Owens Corning Basement Finishi, Columbus Also called US Home Center LLC *(G-8924)*
Owens Corning Sales LLC (HQ) 419 248-8000
  1 Owens Corning Pkwy Toledo (43659) *(G-18114)*
Owens Corning Sales LLC 740 587-3562
  2790 Columbus Rd Granville (43023) *(G-11471)*
Owners Management 440 439-3800
  25250 Rockside Rd Ste 1 Cleveland (44146) *(G-6222)*
Owners Management Company 440 439-3800
  25250 Rockside Rd Bedford (44146) *(G-1328)*
Owv Exc, Shadyside Also called Virginia Ohio-West Excvtg Co *(G-16852)*
Oxcyon Inc 440 239-3345
  17520 Engle Lake Dr Ste 1 Cleveland (44130) *(G-6223)*
Oxford Blazer Company Inc 614 792-2220
  5700 Blazer Pkwy Ste B Dublin (43017) *(G-10419)*
Oxford Country Club Inc 513 524-0801
  6200 Contreras Rd Oxford (45056) *(G-15827)*
Oxford Hospitality Group Inc 513 524-0114
  5056 College Corner Pike Oxford (45056) *(G-15828)*
Oxford Min Cmpany-Kentucky LLC 740 622-6302
  544 Chestnut St Coshocton (43812) *(G-9114)*
Oxford Mining Company Inc 740 342-7666
  2500 Township Rd 205 New Lexington (43764) *(G-15059)*
Oxford Square, Blue Ash Also called L J F Management Inc *(G-1623)*

Oyer Electric Inc 740 773-2828
14650 Pleasant Valley Rd Chillicothe (45601) *(G-2868)*
Ozanne Construction Co Inc 216 696-2876
1635 E 25th St Cleveland (44114) *(G-6224)*
P & D Removal Service 513 226-7687
400 N Wayne Ave Cincinnati (45215) *(G-4246)*
P & D Transportation Inc 614 577-1130
4274 Groves Rd Columbus (43232) *(G-8500)*
P & D Transportation Inc (PA) 740 454-1221
1705 Moxahala Ave Zanesville (43701) *(G-20523)*
P & M Exhaust Systems Whse 513 825-2660
11843 Kemper Springs Dr Cincinnati (45240) *(G-4247)*
P & R Communications Svc Inc (PA) 937 222-0861
700 E 1st St Dayton (45402) *(G-9796)*
P & W Painting Contractors Inc 419 698-2209
3031 Front St Toledo (43605) *(G-18115)*
P B S Animal Health, Massillon *Also called Robert J Matthews Company (G-13849)*
P C B, New Albany *Also called Rossman (G-15006)*
P C C Refrigerated Ex Inc 614 754-8929
2365 Performance Way Columbus (43207) *(G-8501)*
P C S, Akron *Also called Pastoral Counseling Svc Summit (G-378)*
P C Vpa 937 293-2133
3033 Kettering Blvd # 319 Moraine (45439) *(G-14814)*
P C Vpa 440 826-0500
16600 W Sprague Rd Ste 80 Cleveland (44130) *(G-6225)*
P C Workshop Inc 419 399-4805
900 W Caroline St Paulding (45879) *(G-15932)*
P D I, Springboro *Also called Pdi Communication Systems Inc (G-17133)*
P E I, Akron *Also called Power Engineers Incorporated (G-399)*
P E Miller & Assoc 614 231-4743
1341 S Hamilton Rd Columbus (43227) *(G-8502)*
P E Miller & Associates Inc 614 231-4743
1341 S Hamilton Rd Columbus (43227) *(G-8503)*
P E Systems Inc 937 258-0141
5100 Sprngfeld St Ste 510 Dayton (45431) *(G-9280)*
P I & I Motor Express Inc (PA) 330 448-4035
908 Broadway St Masury (44438) *(G-13866)*
P I C C A, Circleville *Also called Pickaway County Community Acti (G-4894)*
P J & R J Connection Inc 513 398-2777
754 Reading Rd Mason (45040) *(G-13744)*
P J McNerney & Associates, Cincinnati *Also called McNerney & Associates LLC (G-4039)*
P JS Hair Styling Shoppe 440 333-1244
20400 Lorain Rd Cleveland (44126) *(G-6226)*
P K Wadsworth Heating & Coolg 440 248-4821
34280 Solon Rd Frnt Solon (44139) *(G-17037)*
P N P Inc 330 386-1231
48444 Bell School Rd East Liverpool (43920) *(G-10532)*
P P I, Cleveland *Also called Project Packaging Inc (G-6323)*
P R Machine Works Inc 419 529-5748
1825 Nussbaum Pkwy Ontario (44906) *(G-15710)*
P S G, Youngstown *Also called Phoenix Systems Group Inc (G-20320)*
P T I, Walbridge *Also called Professional Transportation (G-18776)*
P T I Inc 419 445-2800
421 Commercial Pettisville (43553) *(G-16082)*
P&S Bakery Inc 330 707-4141
3279 E Western Reserve Rd Youngstown (44514) *(G-20312)*
P-Americas LLC 419 227-3541
1750 Greely Chapel Rd Lima (45804) *(G-12853)*
P-Americas LLC 330 746-7652
500 Pepsi Pl Youngstown (44502) *(G-20313)*
P-Americas LLC 216 252-7377
4561 Industrial Pkwy Cleveland (44135) *(G-6227)*
P-N-D Communications Inc 419 683-1922
7900 Middletown Rd Crestline (44827) *(G-9149)*
P3 Infrastructure Inc 330 686-1129
3105 Preakness Dr Stow (44224) *(G-17385)*
Pac Manufacturing, Middletown *Also called Pac Worldwide Corporation (G-14448)*
Pac Worldwide Corporation 800 610-9367
3131 Cincinnati Dayton Rd Middletown (45044) *(G-14448)*
Paccar Leasing Corporation 937 235-2589
7740 Center Point 70 Blvd Dayton (45424) *(G-9797)*
Pace Analytical Services Inc 614 486-5421
4860 Blazer Pkwy Dublin (43017) *(G-10420)*
Pace International Union 419 929-1335
100 New London Ave New London (44851) *(G-15069)*
Pace International Union 740 772-2038
170 S Hickory St Chillicothe (45601) *(G-2869)*
Pace International Union 740 289-2368
2288 Wakefield Mound Rd Piketon (45661) *(G-16123)*
Pace Sankar Landscaping Inc 330 343-0858
4005 Johnstown Rd Ne Dover (44622) *(G-10205)*
Pace-Sankar Landscaping, Dover *Also called Pace Sankar Landscaping Inc (G-10205)*
Pacer, Dublin *Also called Xpo Intermodal Solutions Inc (G-10495)*
Pacer Stacktrain, Dublin *Also called Xpo Stacktrain LLC (G-10496)*
Pache Management Company Inc 614 451-9236
5026 Dierker Rd Ofc Columbus (43220) *(G-8504)*
Pacific Heritg Inn Polaris LLC 614 880-9080
9090 Lyra Dr Columbus (43240) *(G-6899)*
Pacific MGT Holdings LLC 440 324-3339
250 Warden Ave Elyria (44035) *(G-10667)*
Pacific Valve, Piqua *Also called Crane Pumps & Systems Inc (G-16142)*
Packaging & Pads R Us LLC (PA) 419 499-2905
12406 Us Highway 250 N C Milan (44846) *(G-14497)*
Packship Usa Inc (PA) 330 682-7225
1347 N Main St Orrville (44667) *(G-15782)*
PacLease, Cincinnati *Also called Kenworth of Cincinnati Inc (G-3916)*
PacLease, Dayton *Also called Paccar Leasing Corporation (G-9797)*
Pactiv LLC 614 771-5400
2120 Westbelt Dr Columbus (43228) *(G-8505)*
Pactiv LLC 614 777-4019
1999 Dividend Dr Columbus (43228) *(G-8506)*
Padgett-Young & Associates, Ashland *Also called Buren Insurance Group Inc (G-668)*
Pae & Associates Inc 937 833-0013
7925 Paragon Rd Dayton (45459) *(G-9798)*
Pagan, Fremont *Also called Flex Temp Employment Services (G-11199)*
Pager Plus One Inc 513 748-3788
927 Old State Rt 28 Ste G Milford (45150) *(G-14548)*
Pagetech Ltd 614 238-0518
951 Robinwood Ave Ste F Columbus (43213) *(G-8507)*
Pain Control Consultants Inc 614 430-5727
1680 Watermark Dr 100 Columbus (43215) *(G-8508)*
Pain Management Associates Inc 937 252-2000
1010 Woodman Dr Ste 100 Dayton (45432) *(G-9281)*
Pain Net Inc 614 481-5960
99 N Brice Rd Ste 270 Columbus (43213) *(G-8509)*
Painesville Dental Group Inc (PA) 440 354-2183
128 Mentor Ave Painesville (44077) *(G-15872)*
Painesville Municipal Electric, Painesville *Also called City of Painesville (G-15840)*
Paint Creek Youth Center, Bainbridge *Also called Lighthouse Youth Services Inc (G-942)*
Painters District Council 6 ....440 239-4575
8257 Dow Cir Cleveland (44136) *(G-6228)*
Painters Local Union 555 ....740 353-1431
2101 7th St Portsmouth (45662) *(G-16297)*
Painting Company 614 873-1334
6969 Industrial Pkwy Plain City (43064) *(G-16203)*
Paisley House For Aged Women 330 799-9431
1408 Mahoning Ave Youngstown (44509) *(G-20314)*
Pajka Eye Center Inc 419 228-7432
855 W Market St Ste A Lima (45805) *(G-12854)*
Pak Lab 513 735-4777
5069 State Route 276 Batavia (45103) *(G-1020)*
Paklab, Batavia *Also called Universal Packg Systems Inc (G-1029)*
Paklab, Cincinnati *Also called Universal Packg Systems Inc (G-4748)*
Pakmark LLC 513 285-1040
420 Distribution Cir Fairfield (45014) *(G-10892)*
Pakteem Technical Services 513 772-1515
1201 Glendale Milford Rd Cincinnati (45215) *(G-4248)*
Paladin Professional Sound, Cleveland *Also called Paladin Protective Systems Inc (G-6229)*
Paladin Protective Systems Inc 216 441-6500
7680 Hub Pkwy Cleveland (44125) *(G-6229)*
Palazzo Brothers Electric Inc 419 668-1100
2811 State Route 18 Norwalk (44857) *(G-15587)*
Palestine Chld Relief Fund 330 678-2645
1340 Morris Rd Kent (44240) *(G-12390)*
Palisdes Bsbal A Cal Ltd Prtnr 330 505-0000
111 Eastwood Mall Blvd Niles (44446) *(G-15302)*
Palladium Healthcare LLC 216 644-4383
16910 Harvard Ave Cleveland (44128) *(G-6230)*
Pallet Distributors Inc (PA) 888 805-9670
14701 Detroit Ave Ste 610 Lakewood (44107) *(G-12494)*
Palliative Care of Ohio, Newark *Also called Hospice of Central Ohio (G-15175)*
Palm Crest East Inc 440 322-0726
1251 East Ave Elyria (44035) *(G-10668)*
Palm Crest Nursing Homes, Elyria *Also called Palm Crest East Inc (G-10668)*
Palmer Associates, Toledo *Also called Clear Vision Engineering LLC (G-17816)*
Palmer Express Incorporated 440 942-3333
34799 Curtis Blvd Ste A Willoughby (44095) *(G-19702)*
Palmer Holland Inc 440 686-2300
25000 Country Club Blvd # 444 North Olmsted (44070) *(G-15438)*
Palmer Trucks Inc 937 235-3318
7740 Center Point 70 Blvd Dayton (45424) *(G-9799)*
Palmer Volkema Thomas Inc 614 221-4400
140 E Town St Ste 1100 Columbus (43215) *(G-8510)*
Palmer-Donavin Mfg Co (PA) 614 486-0975
3210 Centerpoint Dr Columbus (43212) *(G-8511)*
Palmer-Donavin Mfg Co 419 692-5000
911 Spencerville Rd Delphos (45833) *(G-10148)*
Palmer-Donavin Mfg Co 614 277-2777
3210 Centerpoint Dr Urbancrest (43123) *(G-18607)*
Palmetto Construction Svcs LLC 614 503-7150
892 Scott St Columbus (43222) *(G-8512)*
Pam Johnsonident 419 946-4551
535 W Marion Rd Mount Gilead (43338) *(G-14861)*
PAm Transportation Svcs Inc 330 270-7900
12274 Mahoning Ave North Jackson (44451) *(G-15385)*
PAm Transportation Svcs Inc 419 935-9501
2501 Miller Rd Willard (44890) *(G-19624)*
Pan-Glo of St Louis, Urbana *Also called Russell T Bundy Associates Inc (G-18600)*
Panacea Products Corporation (PA) 614 850-7000
2711 International St Columbus (43228) *(G-8513)*
Panache Hair Salon, Youngstown *Also called Vlp Inc (G-20407)*

ALPHABETIC

Panasonic Corp North America....513 770-9294
6402 Thornberry Ct Mason (45040) ***(G-13745)***
Panasonic Corp North America....201 392-6872
1400 W Market St Troy (45373) ***(G-18371)***
Pandora Bancshares Inc (HQ)....419 384-3221
102 E Main St Pandora (45877) ***(G-15893)***
Pandora Manufacturing Llc (PA)....419 384-3241
157 W Main St Ottawa (45875) ***(G-15802)***
Panelmatic Inc....330 782-8007
1125 Meadowbrook Ave Youngstown (44512) ***(G-20315)***
Panelmatic Youngstown, Youngstown *Also called Panelmatic Inc* ***(G-20315)***
Panera Bread, Westlake *Also called Howley Bread Group Ltd* ***(G-19492)***
Panera Bread, Warren *Also called Covelli Family Ltd Partnership* ***(G-18842)***
Panini North America Inc....937 291-2195
577 Congress Park Dr Dayton (45459) ***(G-9800)***
Panther II Transportation Inc (HQ)....800 685-0657
84 Medina Rd Medina (44256) ***(G-14111)***
Panther Premium Logistics Inc (HQ)....800 685-0657
84 Medina Rd Medina (44256) ***(G-14112)***
Paper Alied Indus Chem & Enrgy, Chillicothe *Also called Pace International Union* ***(G-2869)***
Pappas Leah....614 621-7007
41 S High St Fl 12 Columbus (43215) ***(G-8514)***
Par International Inc....614 529-1300
2160 Mcgaw Rd Obetz (43207) ***(G-15669)***
Paradigm Industrial LLC....937 224-4415
1345 Stanley Ave Dayton (45404) ***(G-9801)***
Paradise Hospitality Inc....419 255-6190
2 Seagate Toledo (43604) ***(G-18116)***
Paragon Consulting Inc....440 684-3101
5900 Landerbrook Dr # 205 Cleveland (44124) ***(G-6231)***
Paragon Machine Company, Bedford *Also called Done-Rite Bowling Service Co* ***(G-1304)***
Paragon Salons Inc (PA)....513 574-7610
6775 Harrison Ave Cincinnati (45247) ***(G-4249)***
Paragon Salons Inc....513 651-4600
441 Race St Cincinnati (45202) ***(G-4250)***
Paragon Salons Inc....513 683-6700
12064 Montgomery Rd Cincinnati (45249) ***(G-4251)***
Paragon Tec Inc....216 361-5555
3740 Carnegie Ave Ste 302 Cleveland (44115) ***(G-6232)***
Parallel Technologies Inc....614 798-9700
4868 Blazer Pkwy Dublin (43017) ***(G-10421)***
Paramount Care Inc (HQ)....419 887-2500
1901 Indian Wood Cir Maumee (43537) ***(G-13955)***
Paramount Confection Co, Springboro *Also called Miami-Luken Inc* ***(G-17128)***
Paramount Health Care, Maumee *Also called Paramount Care Inc* ***(G-13955)***
Paramount Lawn Service Inc....513 984-5200
8900 Glendale Milford Rd A1 Loveland (45140) ***(G-13152)***
Paramount Plumbing Inc (PA)....330 336-1096
3080 S Medina Line Rd Norton (44203) ***(G-15558)***
Paramount Support Service....740 526-0540
252 W Main St Ste H Saint Clairsville (43950) ***(G-16651)***
Paran Management Company Ltd....216 921-5663
2720 Van Aken Blvd # 200 Cleveland (44120) ***(G-6233)***
Paris Cleaners Inc....330 296-3300
650 Enterprise Pkwy Ravenna (44266) ***(G-16395)***
Paris Healthcare Linen, Ravenna *Also called Paris Cleaners Inc* ***(G-16395)***
Park Pet and Play LLC....877 907-6222
7471 Tyler Blvd Ste N Mentor (44060) ***(G-14227)***
Park Arrowhead Golf Club Inc....419 628-2444
2211 Dirksen Rd Minster (45865) ***(G-14667)***
Park Centre Lanes Inc....330 499-0555
7313 Whipple Ave Nw Canton (44720) ***(G-2488)***
Park Cincinnati Board....513 421-4086
1501 Eden Park Dr Cincinnati (45202) ***(G-4252)***
Park Corporation (PA)....216 267-4870
6200 Riverside Dr Cleveland (44135) ***(G-6234)***
Park Creek Center, Rocky River *Also called Msab Park Creek LLC* ***(G-16586)***
Park Creek Rtirement Cmnty Inc....440 842-5100
10064 N Church Dr Cleveland (44130) ***(G-6235)***
Park Dist Maintenance, Massillon *Also called County of Stark* ***(G-13799)***
Park Group Co of America Inc....440 238-9440
22700 Royalton Rd Strongsville (44149) ***(G-17499)***
Park Haven Home, Ashtabula *Also called Park Haven Inc* ***(G-759)***
Park Haven Inc....440 992-9441
6434 Lee Road Ext Ashtabula (44004) ***(G-759)***
Park Health Center, Saint Clairsville *Also called Belmont County Home* ***(G-16620)***
Park Hotels & Resorts Inc....216 447-0020
6200 Quarry Ln Cleveland (44131) ***(G-6236)***
Park Hotels & Resorts Inc....216 464-5950
3663 Park East Dr Cleveland (44122) ***(G-6237)***
Park Hotels & Resorts Inc....937 436-2400
300 Prestige Pl Miamisburg (45342) ***(G-14331)***
Park Inn....419 241-3000
101 N Summit St Toledo (43604) ***(G-18117)***
Park International Theme Svcs....513 381-6131
2195 Victory Pkwy Cincinnati (45206) ***(G-4253)***
Park Management Specialist (PA)....419 893-4879
216 W Wayne St Maumee (43537) ***(G-13956)***
Park n Fly Inc....404 264-1000
19000 Snow Rd Cleveland (44142) ***(G-6238)***
Park National Bank (HQ)....740 349-8451
50 N 3rd St Newark (43055) ***(G-15225)***
Park National Bank....614 228-0063
140 E Town St Ste 1400 Columbus (43215) ***(G-8515)***
Park National Bank....740 349-8451
21 S 1st St Ste Front Newark (43055) ***(G-15226)***
Park National Bank....937 324-6800
40 S Limestone St Springfield (45502) ***(G-17258)***
Park Place Airport Parking, Cleveland *Also called Park Place Management Inc* ***(G-6239)***
Park Place International LLC....877 991-1991
8401 Chagrin Rd Ste 15a Chagrin Falls (44023) ***(G-2728)***
Park Place Management Inc....216 362-1080
18975 Snow Rd Cleveland (44142) ***(G-6239)***
Park Place Nursery, Cleveland *Also called T L C Landscaping Inc* ***(G-6565)***
Park Place Technologies LLC....610 544-0571
5910 Landerbrook Dr # 300 Mayfield Heights (44124) ***(G-14005)***
Park Place Technologies LLC (PA)....877 778-8707
5910 Landerbrook Dr # 300 Mayfield Heights (44124) ***(G-14006)***
Park Raceway Inc....419 476-7751
777 Hollywood Blvd Dayton (45414) ***(G-9802)***
Park Side Dialysis, Westerville *Also called Dome Dialysis LLC* ***(G-19395)***
Park View Nursing Center, Edgerton *Also called Peregrine Health Services Inc* ***(G-10584)***
Park Village Health Care Ctr, Dover *Also called Dover Nursing Center* ***(G-10186)***
Park Vista Retirement Cmnty, Youngstown *Also called Ohio Presbt Retirement Svcs* ***(G-20309)***
Park-N-Go Inc....937 890-7275
1140 W National Rd Vandalia (45377) ***(G-18692)***
Park-N-Go Airport Parking, Vandalia *Also called Park-N-Go Inc* ***(G-18692)***
Parkcliffe Development....419 381-9447
4226 Parkcliff Ln Toledo (43615) ***(G-18118)***
Parker Marketing Research LLC....513 248-8100
5405 Dupont Cir Ste B Milford (45150) ***(G-14549)***
Parker Steel Company, Maumee *Also called Parker Steel International Inc* ***(G-13957)***
Parker Steel International Inc (PA)....419 473-2481
1625 Indian Wood Cir Maumee (43537) ***(G-13957)***
Parker, Michael G MD, Akron *Also called Akron Plastic Surgeons Inc* ***(G-50)***
Parker-Hannifin Corporation....937 456-5571
725 N Beech St Eaton (45320) ***(G-10572)***
Parker-Hannifin Corporation....513 831-2340
50 W Techne Center Dr H Milford (45150) ***(G-14550)***
Parker-Hannifin Corporation....614 279-7070
3885 Gateway Blvd Columbus (43228) ***(G-8516)***
Parker-Hannifin Corporation....216 896-3000
6035 Parkland Blvd Cleveland (44124) ***(G-6240)***
Parker-Hannifin Corporation....419 878-7000
1290 Wtrville Monclova Rd Waterville (43566) ***(G-18943)***
Parker-Hannifin Corporation....216 531-3000
6035 Parkland Blvd Cleveland (44124) ***(G-6241)***
Parker-Hannifin Intl Corp (HQ)....216 896-3000
6035 Parkland Blvd Cleveland (44124) ***(G-6242)***
Parking Company America Inc....513 241-0415
250 W Court St Ste 200e Cincinnati (45202) ***(G-4254)***
Parking Company America Inc....216 265-0500
18899 Snow Rd Cleveland (44142) ***(G-6243)***
Parking Company America Inc....513 381-2179
250 W Court St Ste 100e Cincinnati (45202) ***(G-4255)***
Parking Company of America, Cincinnati *Also called Court Stret Center Associates* ***(G-3435)***
Parking Sltions For Healthcare, Columbus *Also called Parking Solutions Inc* ***(G-8517)***
Parking Solutions Inc (HQ)....614 469-7000
353 W Nationwide Blvd Columbus (43215) ***(G-8517)***
Parkins Incorporated....614 334-1800
3950 Lyman Dr Hilliard (43026) ***(G-11942)***
Parklane Manor of Akron Inc....330 724-3315
744 Colette Dr Akron (44306) ***(G-377)***
Parkmead Apartments, Grove City *Also called Wallick Properties Midwest LLC* ***(G-11610)***
Parkops Columbus LLC....877 499-9155
56 E Long St Columbus (43215) ***(G-8518)***
Parks Drilling Company (PA)....614 761-7707
5745 Avery Rd Dublin (43016) ***(G-10422)***
Parks Ob Gyn Assoc, Chillicothe *Also called Adena Health System* ***(G-2808)***
Parks Recreation & Prpts Dept, Cleveland *Also called City of Cleveland* ***(G-5256)***
Parks Recreation Athens....740 592-0046
701 E State St Athens (45701) ***(G-810)***
Parks Recreation Division....937 496-7135
455 Infirmary Rd Dayton (45417) ***(G-9803)***
Parkside Behavioral Healthcare....614 471-2552
349 Olde Ridenour Rd Gahanna (43230) ***(G-11263)***
Parkside Care Corporation....440 286-2273
831 South St Chardon (44024) ***(G-2761)***
Parkside Health Care Center, Columbiana *Also called Windsor House Inc* ***(G-6866)***
PARKSIDE MANOR, Maumee *Also called Consulate Healthcare Inc* ***(G-13899)***
Parkside Nrsing Rehabilitation, Fairfield *Also called Embassy Healthcare Inc* ***(G-10847)***
Parkside Nrsing Rhbltation Ctr, Fairfield *Also called Multicare Management Group* ***(G-10883)***
PARKVIEW CARE CENTER, Fremont *Also called Caritas Inc* ***(G-11186)***
Parkview Health Care, Sandusky *Also called United Church Homes Inc* ***(G-16805)***
Parkview Manor Inc (PA)....937 296-1550
425 Lauricella Ct Englewood (45322) ***(G-10714)***
Parkview Manor Inc....419 243-5191
2051 Collingwood Blvd Toledo (43620) ***(G-18119)***

Parkview Physicians Group, Bryan *Also called Midwest Cmnty Hlth Assoc Inc* ***(G-2012)***
Parkway Surgery Center Inc....419 531-7860
2120 W Central Ave Toledo (43606) ***(G-18120)***
Parkwood Apartments, Toledo *Also called Lucas Metropolitan Hsing Auth* ***(G-18018)***
Parkwood Corporation (PA)....216 875-6500
1000 Lakeside Ave E Cleveland (44114) ***(G-6244)***
Parma Adult Training Center, Cleveland *Also called Cuyahoga County* ***(G-5451)***
Parma Care Center Inc....216 661-6800
5553 Broadview Rd Cleveland (44134) ***(G-6245)***
Parma Care Nursing & Rehab, Cleveland *Also called Parma Care Center Inc* ***(G-6245)***
Parma Clinic Cancer Center....440 743-4747
6525 Parma Blvd Fl 2 Cleveland (44129) ***(G-6246)***
Parma Communirty Hospital, Cleveland *Also called Parma Clinic Cancer Center* ***(G-6246)***
Parma Community General Hosp (PA)....440 743-3000
7007 Powers Blvd Parma (44129) ***(G-15912)***
Parma Community General Hosp....440 743-4280
7007 Powers Blvd Parma (44129) ***(G-15913)***
Parma Medical Center, Brooklyn Heights *Also called Kaiser Foundation Hospitals* ***(G-1919)***
Parma Service Garage, Cleveland *Also called City of Parma* ***(G-5271)***
Parman Group Inc (PA)....513 673-0077
4501 Hilton Corporate Dr Columbus (43232) ***(G-8519)***
Parmatown South, Cleveland *Also called Forest City Enterprises LP* ***(G-5617)***
PARMAUTO FEDERAL CREDIT UNION, Cleveland *Also called Best Reward Credit Union* ***(G-5119)***
Parole & Community Services, Columbus *Also called Ohio Dept Rhbilitation Corectn* ***(G-8336)***
Parrish McIntyre Tire, Mogadore *Also called Parrish Tire Company of Akron* ***(G-14682)***
Parrish Tire Company of Akron....330 628-6800
3833 Mogadore Indus Pkwy Mogadore (44260) ***(G-14682)***
Parsec Inc (PA)....513 621-6111
1100 Gest St Cincinnati (45203) ***(G-4256)***
Parsec Intermodal Cannada, Cincinnati *Also called Parsec Inc* ***(G-4256)***
Parta, Kent *Also called Portage Area Rgonal Trnsp Auth* ***(G-12391)***
Partners Auto Group Bdford Inc....440 439-2323
11 Broadway Ave Bedford (44146) ***(G-1329)***
Partners of City View LLC....216 361-1414
6606 Carnegie Ave Cleveland (44103) ***(G-6247)***
Partners of Marion Care, Marion *Also called Sunbrdge Marion Hlth Care Corp* ***(G-13582)***
Partnership LLC....440 471-8310
29077 Clemens Rd Cleveland (44145) ***(G-6248)***
Parts Plus, West Chester *Also called Smyth Automotive Inc* ***(G-19157)***
Parts Pro Automotive Warehouse, Wickliffe *Also called GTM Service Inc* ***(G-19600)***
Partssource Inc....330 562-9900
777 Lena Dr Aurora (44202) ***(G-849)***
Pas Technologies Inc....937 840-1000
214 Hobart Dr Hillsboro (45133) ***(G-11991)***
Pasco Inc....330 650-0613
1140 Terex Rd Hudson (44236) ***(G-12138)***
Passion To Heal Healthcare....216 849-0180
4228 W 58th St Cleveland (44144) ***(G-6249)***
Passport, Columbus *Also called Central OH Area Agency On Agng* ***(G-7228)***
Passport, Cleveland *Also called Western Reserve Area Agency* ***(G-6743)***
Pastoral Care Management Svcs....513 205-1398
1240 Rosemont Ave Cincinnati (45205) ***(G-4257)***
Pastoral Counseling Svc Summit....330 996-4600
611 W Market St Akron (44303) ***(G-378)***
Pat Catan's, Strongsville *Also called Lamrite West Inc* ***(G-17484)***
Pat Catan's Craft Centers, Strongsville *Also called Darice Inc* ***(G-17456)***
Pat Henry Group LLC (PA)....216 447-0831
6046 Bridgehaven Dr Milford (45150) ***(G-14551)***
Pat Young Service Co Inc (PA)....216 447-8550
6100 Hillcrest Dr Cleveland (44125) ***(G-6250)***
Pat Young Service Co Inc....440 891-1550
1260 Moore Rd Ste K Avon (44011) ***(G-912)***
Pataskala Oaks Care Center, Pataskala *Also called Nursing Care MGT Amer Inc* ***(G-15924)***
Patella Carpet & Tile, Youngstown *Also called Patellas Floor Center Inc* ***(G-20316)***
Patellas Floor Center Inc....330 758-4099
6620 Market St Youngstown (44512) ***(G-20316)***
Patented Acquisition Corp (PA)....937 353-2299
2490 Cross Pointe Dr Miamisburg (45342) ***(G-14332)***
Path Forward It, Cincinnati *Also called Recker Consulting LLC* ***(G-4393)***
Pathlabs, Toledo *Also called Pathology Laboratories Inc* ***(G-18121)***
Pathology Laboratories Inc (HQ)....419 255-4600
1946 N 13th St Ste 301 Toledo (43604) ***(G-18121)***
Pathway Inc....419 242-7304
505 Hamilton St Toledo (43604) ***(G-18122)***
Pathway 2 Hope Inc....866 491-3040
3036 Gilbert Ave Cincinnati (45206) ***(G-4258)***
Pathway Caring For Children (PA)....330 493-0083
4895 Dressler Rd Nw Ste A Canton (44718) ***(G-2489)***
Pathway House LLC....872 223-9797
15539 Saranac Rd Cleveland (44110) ***(G-6251)***
Pathway School of Discovery, Dayton *Also called National Heritg Academies Inc* ***(G-9770)***
Pathways Center, Columbus *Also called Columbus Area Inc* ***(G-7329)***
Pathways of Central Ohio....740 345-6166
1627 Bryn Mawr Dr Newark (43055) ***(G-15227)***
Patient Account MGT Svcs LLC....614 575-0044
950 Taylor Station Rd I Columbus (43230) ***(G-8520)***
Patient Financial Services, Rocky River *Also called JP Recovery Services Inc* ***(G-16583)***
Patientpint Hosp Solutions LLC....513 936-6800
8230 Montgomery Rd # 300 Cincinnati (45236) ***(G-4259)***
Patientpint Ntwrk Slutions LLC (HQ)....513 936-6800
5901 E Galbraith Rd Cincinnati (45236) ***(G-4260)***
Patientpoint LLC (PA)....513 936-6800
5901 E Galbraith Rd Cincinnati (45236) ***(G-4261)***
Patricia A Dickerson MD....937 436-1117
1299 E Alex Bell Rd Dayton (45459) ***(G-9804)***
Patrick J Burke & Co....513 455-8200
901 Adams Crossing Fl 1 Cincinnati (45202) ***(G-4262)***
Patrick Mahoney....614 292-5766
1223 Neil Ave Columbus (43201) ***(G-8521)***
Patrick Staffing Inc (PA)....937 743-5585
1200 E 2nd St Ste B Franklin (45005) ***(G-11162)***
Patriot Emergency Med Svcs Inc....740 532-2222
2914 S 4th St Ironton (45638) ***(G-12301)***
Patriot Indus Contg Svcs LLC....513 248-8222
200 Olympic Dr Milford (45150) ***(G-14552)***
Patriot Ridge Community, Fairborn *Also called United Church Homes Inc* ***(G-10806)***
Patriot Roofing & Restoration, Blue Ash *Also called Patriot Roofing Company Inc* ***(G-1662)***
Patriot Roofing Company Inc (PA)....513 469-7663
11524 Grooms Rd Ste A Blue Ash (45242) ***(G-1662)***
Patrol Urban Services LLC....614 620-4672
4563 E Walnut St Westerville (43081) ***(G-19436)***
Patterson Pope, Cincinnati *Also called Central Business Equipment Co* ***(G-3210)***
Patterson Pope Inc....513 891-4430
10321 S Medallion Dr Cincinnati (45241) ***(G-4263)***
Patterson-Uti Drilling Co LLC....724 239-2812
67090 Executive Dr Saint Clairsville (43950) ***(G-16652)***
Pattie Group Inc (PA)....440 338-1288
15533 Chillicothe Rd Novelty (44072) ***(G-15603)***
Pattie's Landscaping, Novelty *Also called Pattie Group Inc* ***(G-15603)***
Paul A Ertel....216 696-8888
1153 Main Ave Cleveland (44113) ***(G-6252)***
Paul Davis Restoration, Moraine *Also called Davis Paul Restoration Dayton* ***(G-14766)***
Paul Dennis....440 746-8600
7005 Stadium Dr Ofc Brecksville (44141) ***(G-1839)***
Paul Hrnchar Ford-Mercury Inc....330 533-3673
366 W Main St Canfield (44406) ***(G-2207)***
Paul Moss LLC....216 765-1580
5895 Harper Rd Solon (44139) ***(G-17038)***
Paul Paratto, Willoughby *Also called Howard Hanna Smythe Cramer* ***(G-19671)***
Paul Peterson Company (PA)....614 486-4375
950 Dublin Rd Columbus (43215) ***(G-8522)***
Paul Peterson Safety Div Inc....614 486-4375
950 Dublin Rd Columbus (43215) ***(G-8523)***
Paul R Young Funeral Homes (PA)....513 521-9303
7345 Hamilton Ave Cincinnati (45231) ***(G-4264)***
Paul Werth Associates Inc (PA)....614 224-8114
10 N High St Ste 300 Columbus (43215) ***(G-8524)***
Paul, Elaine MD, Columbus *Also called Drs Paul Boyles & Kennedy* ***(G-7544)***
Paula Jo Moore....330 894-2910
10990 Myers Rd Kensington (44427) ***(G-12349)***
Paulding Area Visiting Nurses, Paulding *Also called Community Hlth Prfssionals Inc* ***(G-15928)***
Paulding County Hospital....419 399-4080
1035 W Wayne St Paulding (45879) ***(G-15933)***
Paulding Exempted Vlg Schl Dst (PA)....419 594-3309
405 N Water St Paulding (45879) ***(G-15934)***
PAULDING PUTNAM ELECTRIC COOPE, Paulding *Also called Paulding-Putnam Electric Coop* ***(G-15935)***
Paulding-Putnam Electric Coop (PA)....419 399-5015
401 Mc Donald Pike Paulding (45879) ***(G-15935)***
Paulo Products Company....440 942-0153
4428 Hamann Pkwy Willoughby (44094) ***(G-19703)***
Pauls Bus Service Inc....513 851-5089
3561 W Kemper Rd Cincinnati (45251) ***(G-4265)***
Pavement Protectors Inc....614 875-9989
2020 Longwood Ave Grove City (43123) ***(G-11590)***
Pavillion At Camargo, The, Cincinnati *Also called Camargo Manor Inc* ***(G-3169)***
Pawnee Maintenance Inc....740 373-6861
101 Rathbone Rd Marietta (45750) ***(G-13483)***
Paws Inn Inc....937 435-1500
8926 Kingsridge Dr Dayton (45458) ***(G-9805)***
Pax Steel Products Inc....419 678-1481
104 E Vine St Coldwater (45828) ***(G-6834)***
Paxton Hardwoods LLC....513 984-8200
7455 Dawson Rd Cincinnati (45243) ***(G-4266)***
Paychex Inc....614 781-6143
600 Lkview Plz Blvd Ste G Worthington (43085) ***(G-19982)***
Paychex Inc....330 342-0530
100 E Hines Hill Rd Hudson (44236) ***(G-12139)***
Paychex Inc....513 727-9182
3420 Atrium Blvd Ste 200 Middletown (45005) ***(G-14484)***
Paychex Inc....800 939-2462
675 W Market St Lima (45801) ***(G-12855)***
Paychex Inc....614 210-0400
5080 Tuttle Crossing Blvd # 450 Dublin (43016) ***(G-10423)***

ALPHABETIC

Paycom Software Inc 888 678-0796
255 E 5th St Cincinnati (45202) *(G-4267)*
Paycor Inc 614 985-6140
250 E Wilson Bridge Rd # 110 Worthington (43085) *(G-19983)*
Paycor Inc 216 447-7913
4500 Rockside Rd Ste 320 Cleveland (44131) *(G-6253)*
Paycor Inc (PA) 513 381-0505
4811 Montgomery Rd Cincinnati (45212) *(G-4268)*
Paygro, South Charleston *Also called Garick LLC (G-17076)*
Payne Nickles & Co CPA (PA) 419 668-2552
257 Benedict Ave Ste D Norwalk (44857) *(G-15588)*
Payroll Services Unlimited 740 653-9581
125 W Mulberry St Lancaster (43130) *(G-12564)*
Pazco Inc 216 447-9581
4500 Rockside Rd Ste 420 Cleveland (44131) *(G-6254)*
Pbsi, Cincinnati *Also called Positive Bus Solutions Inc (G-4317)*
PC Connection Inc 937 382-4800
3336 Progress Way Bldg 11 Wilmington (45177) *(G-19775)*
PC Connection Sales Corp 937 382-4800
2870 Old State 1 Wilmington (45177) *(G-19776)*
PC Connection Services 937 382-4800
2870 Old State Route 73 # 1 Wilmington (45177) *(G-19777)*
Pca-Corrections LLC 614 297-8244
4014 Venture Ct Columbus (43228) *(G-8525)*
PCC, Columbus *Also called Producers Credit Corporation (G-8565)*
PCC Transportation, Columbus *Also called P C C Refrigerated Ex Inc (G-8501)*
Pccw Teleservices (us) Inc (PA) 614 652-6300
5200 Rings Rd Dublin (43017) *(G-10424)*
Pcm Inc 614 854-1399
8337 Green Meadows Dr N Lewis Center (43035) *(G-12701)*
Pcm Logistics, Lewis Center *Also called Pcm Inc (G-12701)*
Pcm Sales Inc 501 342-1000
8200 Sweet Valley Dr # 108 Cleveland (44125) *(G-6255)*
Pcm Sales Inc 513 842-3500
4600 Mcauley Pl Ste 200 Blue Ash (45242) *(G-1663)*
Pcm Sales Inc 740 548-2222
8337 Green Meadows Dr N Lewis Center (43035) *(G-12702)*
Pcm Sales Inc 937 885-6444
3020 S Tech Blvd Miamisburg (45342) *(G-14333)*
Pcms Datafit Inc 513 587-3100
25 Merchant St Ste 135 Cincinnati (45246) *(G-4269)*
Pcrf, The, Kent *Also called Palestine Chld Relief Fund (G-12390)*
Pcs Cost 216 771-1090
1360 E 9th St Ste 910 Cleveland (44114) *(G-6256)*
Pcy Enterprises Inc 513 241-5566
3111 Spring Grove Ave Cincinnati (45225) *(G-4270)*
PDG, Bowling Green *Also called Poggemeyer Design Group Inc (G-1791)*
Pdi Communication Systems Inc (PA) 937 743-6010
40 Greenwood Ln Springboro (45066) *(G-17133)*
Pdi Plastics, Westerville *Also called Cannon Group Inc (G-19375)*
Pdk Construction Inc 740 992-6451
34070 Crew Rd Pomeroy (45769) *(G-16234)*
Pds, Fairfield *Also called CPC Logistics Inc (G-10838)*
Pdsi Technical Services, Dayton *Also called Production Design Services Inc (G-9832)*
Pe, Westlake *Also called North Bay Construction Inc (G-19522)*
Peabody Coal Company 740 450-2420
2810 East Pike Apt 3 Zanesville (43701) *(G-20524)*
Peabody Landscape Cnstr Inc 614 488-2877
2253 Dublin Rd Columbus (43228) *(G-8526)*
Peabody Landscape Group, Columbus *Also called Peabody Landscape Cnstr Inc (G-8526)*
Peace Foundation, Medina *Also called Intervention For Peace Inc (G-14083)*
Peak 10 Inc 513 645-2900
5307 Muhlhauser Rd Hamilton (45011) *(G-11762)*
Peak Performance Center Inc 440 838-5600
1 Eagle Valley Ct Broadview Heights (44147) *(G-1889)*
Peak Transportation Inc 419 874-5201
26624 Glenwood Rd Perrysburg (43551) *(G-16038)*
Pearl Crossing, Cleveland *Also called Harvest Facility Holdings LP (G-5730)*
Pearl Interactive Network Inc 614 258-2943
1103 Schrock Rd Ste 109 Columbus (43229) *(G-8527)*
Pearne & Gordon LLP 216 579-1700
1801 E 9th St Ste 1200 Cleveland (44114) *(G-6257)*
Pearne Gordon McCoy & Granger, Cleveland *Also called Pearne & Gordon LLP (G-6257)*
Pease & Associates LLC (PA) 216 348-9600
1422 Euclid Ave Ste 801 Cleveland (44115) *(G-6258)*
Pebble Creek, Akron *Also called Nightingale Holdings LLC (G-352)*
Pebble Creek Cnvlscnt Ctr 330 645-0200
670 Jarvis Rd Akron (44319) *(G-379)*
Pebble Creek Golf Club, Mansfield *Also called Bramarjac Inc (G-13268)*
Pebble Creek Golf Course, Cincinnati *Also called M T Golf Course Managment Inc (G-4006)*
Peck Distributors Inc 216 587-6814
17000 Rockside Rd Maple Heights (44137) *(G-13413)*
Peck Food Service, Maple Heights *Also called Peck Distributors Inc (G-13413)*
Peck Hannaford Briggs Service, Cincinnati *Also called Peck-Hannaford Briggs Svc Corp (G-4271)*
Peck-Hannaford Briggs Svc Corp 513 681-1200
4673 Spring Grove Ave Cincinnati (45232) *(G-4271)*
Peco II Inc 614 431-0694
7060 Huntley Rd Columbus (43229) *(G-8528)*
Pedersen Insulation Company 614 471-3788
2901 Johnstown Rd Columbus (43219) *(G-8529)*
Pediatric Assoc Cincinnati 513 791-1222
4360 Cooper Rd Ste 201 Cincinnati (45242) *(G-4272)*
Pediatric Assoc of Fairfield 513 874-9460
5502 Dixie Hwy Ste A Fairfield (45014) *(G-10893)*
Pediatric Assoc of Springfield 937 328-2320
1640 N Limestone St Springfield (45503) *(G-17259)*
Pediatric Associates Inc (PA) 614 501-7337
1021 Country Club Rd A Columbus (43213) *(G-8530)*
Pediatric Associates of Dayton (PA) 937 832-7337
9000 N Main St Ste 332 Englewood (45415) *(G-10715)*
Pediatric Care Inc (PA) 513 931-6357
800 Compton Rd Unit 25 Cincinnati (45231) *(G-4273)*
Pediatric Services Inc (PA) 440 845-1500
6707 Powers Blvd Ste 203 Cleveland (44129) *(G-6259)*
Pediatrics Assoc of Mt Carmel 513 752-3650
4371 Ferguson Dr Cincinnati (45245) *(G-2927)*
Pediatrics of Akron Inc 330 253-7753
300 Locust St Ste 200 Akron (44302) *(G-380)*
Pediatrics of Lima Inc 419 222-4045
830 W High St Ste 102 Lima (45801) *(G-12856)*
Peerless Technologies Corp 937 490-5000
2300 National Rd Beavercreek Township (45324) *(G-1279)*
Pegasus Technical Services Inc 513 793-0094
46 E Hollister St Cincinnati (45219) *(G-4274)*
Peitro Properties Ltd Partnr 216 328-7777
6191 Quarry Ln Cleveland (44131) *(G-6260)*
Pel LLC 216 267-5775
4666 Manufacturing Ave Cleveland (44135) *(G-6261)*
Pella Corporation 513 948-8480
145 B Colwell Dr Cincinnati (45216) *(G-4275)*
Pella Window & Door, Cleveland *Also called Gunton Corporation (G-5710)*
Pembrooke Place Skilled, Columbus *Also called Vrable IV Inc (G-8956)*
Pemco North Canton Division, Canton *Also called Powell Electrical Systems Inc (G-2491)*
Pen Brands LLC (HQ) 216 447-1199
220 Eastview Dr Ste 102 Brooklyn Heights (44131) *(G-1923)*
Pendster Dialysis LLC 937 237-0769
7769 Old Country Ct Huber Heights (45424) *(G-12097)*
Penn Mutual Life Insurance Co 330 668-9065
130 Springside Dr Ste 100 Akron (44333) *(G-381)*
Penn Ohio Electrical Contrs, Masury *Also called Penn-Ohio Electrical Company (G-13867)*
PENN POWER, Akron *Also called Pennsylvania Power Company (G-383)*
Penn Tool, Youngstown *Also called Pennsylvania Tl Sls & Svc Inc (G-20317)*
Penn-Ohio Electrical Company 330 448-1234
1370 Sharon Hogue Rd Masury (44438) *(G-13867)*
Pennington International Inc 513 631-2130
1977 Section Rd Ste 1 Cincinnati (45237) *(G-4276)*
Pennington Seed Inc 513 642-8980
9530 Le Saint Dr Fairfield (45014) *(G-10894)*
Pennsylvania Electric Company (HQ) 800 545-7741
76 S Main St Bsmt Akron (44308) *(G-382)*
Pennsylvania Power Company (HQ) 800 720-3600
76 S Main St Bsmt Akron (44308) *(G-383)*
Pennsylvania Tl Sls & Svc Inc (PA) 330 758-0845
625 Bev Rd Youngstown (44512) *(G-20317)*
Pension Corporation America 513 281-3366
2133 Luray Ave Cincinnati (45206) *(G-4277)*
Penske Logistics LLC 216 765-5475
3000 Auburn Dr Ste 100 Beachwood (44122) *(G-1114)*
Penske Logistics LLC 330 626-7623
9777 Mopar Dr Streetsboro (44241) *(G-17425)*
Penske Logistics LLC 419 547-2615
600 N Woodland Ave Clyde (43410) *(G-6819)*
Penske Logistics LLC 440 232-5811
7600 First Pl Cleveland (44146) *(G-6262)*
Penske Truck Leasing Co LP 419 873-8611
12222 Williams Rd Perrysburg (43551) *(G-16039)*
Penske Truck Leasing Co LP 614 658-0000
2470 Westbelt Dr Columbus (43228) *(G-8531)*
Penske Truck Leasing Co LP 513 771-7701
2528 Commodity Cir Cincinnati (45241) *(G-4278)*
Penske Truck Leasing Co LP 330 645-3100
3000 Fortuna Dr Akron (44312) *(G-384)*
Penske Truck Leasing Co LP 440 232-5811
7600 First Pl Bedford (44146) *(G-1330)*
Pentaflex Inc 937 325-5551
4981 Gateway Blvd Springfield (45502) *(G-17260)*
Pentair Rsdntial Fltration LLC 440 286-4116
220 Park Dr Chardon (44024) *(G-2762)*
People To My Site LLC 614 452-8179
580 N 4th St Ste 500 Columbus (43215) *(G-8532)*
People To Site, Columbus *Also called People To My Site LLC (G-8532)*
Peoplefacts LLC 800 849-1071
135 Chesterfield Ln # 100 Maumee (43537) *(G-13958)*
Peoples Bancorp Inc (PA) 740 373-3155
138 Putnam St Marietta (45750) *(G-13484)*
Peoples Bank 937 748-0067
95 Edgebrooke Dr Springboro (45066) *(G-17134)*
Peoples Bank (HQ) 740 373-3155
138 Putnam St Marietta (45750) *(G-13485)*

ALPHABETIC SECTION — Petermann Ltd

Peoples Bank 740 286-6773
101 E A St Wellston (45692) *(G-19005)*

Peoples Bank 937 382-1441
48 N South St Wilmington (45177) *(G-19778)*

Peoples Bank National Assn 937 746-5733
1400 E 2nd St Franklin (45005) *(G-11163)*

Peoples Banking and Trust Co (HQ) 740 373-3155
138 Putnam St Marietta (45750) *(G-13486)*

Peoples Banking and Trust Co 740 439-2767
845 Wheeling Ave Cambridge (43725) *(G-2126)*

Peoples Cartage Inc 330 833-8571
8045 Navarre Rd Sw Massillon (44648) *(G-13843)*

Peoples Federal Sav & Ln Assn (HQ) 937 492-6129
101 E Court St Sidney (45365) *(G-16947)*

PEOPLES HOSPITAL, Ashland Also called Samaritan Regional Health Sys *(G-698)*

Peoples Nat Bnk of New Lxngton (PA) 740 342-5111
110 N Main St New Lexington (43764) *(G-15060)*

Peoples Services Inc (PA) 330 453-3709
2207 Kimball Rd Se Canton (44707) *(G-2490)*

Peopletomysitecom LLC (PA) 800 295-4519
580 N 4th St Ste 500 Columbus (43215) *(G-8533)*

Peopleworks Dev of Hr LLC 419 636-4637
3440 County Road 9 Bryan (43506) *(G-2016)*

Pep Boys - Manny Moe & Jack 614 864-2092
2830 S Hamilton Rd Columbus (43232) *(G-8534)*

Pepco, Toledo Also called Professional Electric Pdts Co *(G-18137)*

Pepper Cnstr Co Ohio LLC 614 793-4477
495 Metro Pl S Ste 350 Dublin (43017) *(G-10425)*

Pepper Pike Club Company Inc 216 831-9400
2800 Som Center Rd Cleveland (44124) *(G-6263)*

PEPPER PIKE GOLF CLUB, Cleveland Also called Pepper Pike Club Company Inc *(G-6263)*

Pepperl + Fuchs Inc (HQ) 330 425-3555
1600 Enterprise Pkwy Twinsburg (44087) *(G-18452)*

Pepsi-Cola Metro Btlg Co Inc 330 336-3553
904 Seville Rd Wadsworth (44281) *(G-18767)*

Pepsi-Cola Metro Btlg Co Inc 937 461-4664
526 Milburn Ave Dayton (45404) *(G-9806)*

Pepsi-Cola Metro Btlg Co Inc 440 323-5524
925 Lorain Blvd Elyria (44035) *(G-10669)*

Pepsi-Cola Metro Btlg Co Inc 330 963-0426
1999 Enterprise Pkwy Twinsburg (44087) *(G-18453)*

Pepsico, Franklin Furnace Also called G & J Pepsi-Cola Bottlers Inc *(G-11171)*

Pepsico, Chillicothe Also called G & J Pepsi-Cola Bottlers Inc *(G-2841)*

Pepsico, Zanesville Also called G & J Pepsi-Cola Bottlers Inc *(G-20479)*

Pepsico, Youngstown Also called P-Americas LLC *(G-20313)*

Peq Services + Solutions Inc (HQ) 937 610-4800
1 Prestige Pl Ste 900 Miamisburg (45342) *(G-14334)*

Per Diem Nurse Staffing LLT 419 878-8880
18 N 3rd St Lowr Waterville (43566) *(G-18944)*

Perceptionist Inc 614 384-7500
1010 Taylor Station Rd A Columbus (43230) *(G-8535)*

Perceptis LLC 216 458-4122
1250 Old River Rd Ste 300 Cleveland (44113) *(G-6264)*

Perco Inc 740 342-5156
2235 State Route 13 Ne New Lexington (43764) *(G-15061)*

Perduco Group Inc 937 401-0271
3610 Pentagon Blvd # 110 Beavercreek (45431) *(G-1196)*

Peregrine Health Services Inc 419 586-4135
1301 Myers Rd Celina (45822) *(G-2659)*

Peregrine Health Services Inc 419 298-2321
328 W Vine St Edgerton (43517) *(G-10584)*

Perfect Cut-Off Inc 440 943-0000
29201 Anderson Rd Wickliffe (44092) *(G-19611)*

Perfection Group Inc (PA) 513 772-7545
2649 Commerce Blvd Cincinnati (45241) *(G-4279)*

Perfection Mechanical Svcs Inc 513 772-7545
2649 Commerce Blvd Cincinnati (45241) *(G-4280)*

Perfection Services Inc 513 772-7545
2649 Commerce Blvd Cincinnati (45241) *(G-4281)*

Performance Automotive Network, Fairfield Also called Performance Autoplex LLC *(G-10895)*

Performance Autoplex LLC 513 870-5033
5726 Dixie Hwy Fairfield (45014) *(G-10895)*

Performance Lexus, Fairfield Also called Kings Cove Automotive LLC *(G-10870)*

Performance Painting LLC 440 735-3340
7603 First Pl Oakwood Village (44146) *(G-15632)*

Performance Pontc-Oldmbl GM Tr 330 264-1113
1363 W Old Lincoln Way Wooster (44691) *(G-19902)*

Performance Toyota Volkswagen, Wooster Also called Performance Pontc-Oldmbl GM Tr *(G-19902)*

Performnce Fodservice - Presto, Monroe Also called Ohio Pizza Products Inc *(G-14707)*

Perinatal Partners, Dayton Also called Primary Cr Ntwrk Prmr Hlth Prt *(G-9826)*

Perio Inc (PA) 614 791-1207
6156 Wilcox Rd Dublin (43016) *(G-10426)*

Perk Company Inc (PA) 216 391-1444
8100 Grand Ave Ste 300 Cleveland (44104) *(G-6265)*

Perkfect Design Solutions 614 778-3560
308 E 9th Ave Columbus (43201) *(G-8536)*

Perkinelmer Hlth Sciences Inc 330 825-4525
520 S Main St Ste 2423 Akron (44311) *(G-385)*

Perkins Family Restaurant, Alliance Also called Dino Persichetti *(G-538)*

Perkins Motor Service Ltd (PA) 440 277-1256
1864 E 28th St Lorain (44055) *(G-13071)*

Perma-Fix of Dayton Inc 937 268-6501
300 Cherokee Dr Dayton (45417) *(G-9807)*

Permanent Family Solutions, Columbus Also called Buckeye Ranch Inc *(G-7161)*

Permanent Gen Asrn Corp Ohio 216 986-3000
9700 Rockside Rd Cleveland (44125) *(G-6266)*

Permedion Inc 614 895-9900
350 Worthington Rd Ste H Westerville (43082) *(G-19340)*

Permian Oil & Gas Division, Newark Also called National Gas & Oil Corporation *(G-15216)*

Perram Electric Inc 330 239-2661
6882 Ridge Rd Wadsworth (44281) *(G-18768)*

Perrin Asphalt Co Inc 330 253-1020
525 Dan St Akron (44310) *(G-386)*

Perry Contract Services Inc 614 274-4350
2319 Scioto Harper Dr Columbus (43204) *(G-8537)*

Perry County Engineer, New Lexington Also called County of Perry *(G-15054)*

Perry Interiors Inc 513 761-9333
4054 Clough Woods Dr Batavia (45103) *(G-1021)*

Perry Kelly Plumbing Inc 513 528-6554
4498 Mt Carmel Tobasco Rd Cincinnati (45244) *(G-4282)*

Perry Pro Tech Inc (PA) 419 228-1360
545 W Market St Lowr Lowr Lima (45801) *(G-12857)*

Perry Pro Tech Inc 419 475-9030
1270 Flagship Dr Perrysburg (43551) *(G-16040)*

Perry Transportation Dept 440 259-3005
3829 Main St Perry (44081) *(G-15966)*

Perrysburg Board of Education 419 874-3127
25715 Fort Meigs Rd Perrysburg (43551) *(G-16041)*

Perrysburg Bus Garage, Perrysburg Also called Perrysburg Board of Education *(G-16041)*

Perrysburg Pediatrics 419 872-7700
1601 Brigham Dr Ste 200 Perrysburg (43551) *(G-16042)*

Perrysburg Rsdntial Seal Cting 419 872-7325
26651 Eckel Rd Perrysburg (43551) *(G-16043)*

Persistent Systems Inc 727 786-0379
145 Baker St Marion (43302) *(G-13572)*

Personacare of Ohio Inc 440 357-1311
70 Normandy Dr Painesville (44077) *(G-15873)*

Personal & Fmly Counseling Svc 330 343-8171
1433 5th St Nw New Philadelphia (44663) *(G-15111)*

Personal Lawn Care Inc 440 934-5296
3910 Long Rd Avon (44011) *(G-913)*

Personal Service Insurance Co 800 282-9416
2760 Airport Dr Ste 130 Columbus (43219) *(G-8538)*

Personal Touch HM Care IPA Inc 216 986-0885
4500 Rockside Rd Ste 460 Cleveland (44131) *(G-6267)*

Personal Touch HM Care IPA Inc 937 456-4447
302 Eaton Lewisburg Rd Eaton (45320) *(G-10573)*

Personal Touch HM Care IPA Inc 513 868-2272
7924 Jessies Way C Hamilton (45011) *(G-11763)*

Personal Touch HM Care IPA Inc 513 984-9600
8260 Northcreek Dr # 140 Cincinnati (45236) *(G-4283)*

Personal Touch HM Care IPA Inc 614 227-6952
454 E Main St Ste 227 Columbus (43215) *(G-8539)*

Personal Touch HM Care IPA Inc 330 263-1112
543 Riffel Rd Ste F Wooster (44691) *(G-19903)*

Personalized Data Corporation 216 289-2200
26155 Euclid Ave Uppr Cleveland (44132) *(G-6268)*

Personalized Data Entry & Word, Cleveland Also called Personalized Data Corporation *(G-6268)*

Perspectus Architecture LLC (PA) 216 752-1800
13212 Shaker Sq Ste 204 Cleveland (44120) *(G-6269)*

Pet Central Lodge & Grooming 440 282-1811
1425 C Foster Pk Rd C Amherst (44001) *(G-601)*

Pet Food Holdings Inc (HQ) 419 394-3374
1601 Mckinley Rd Saint Marys (45885) *(G-16683)*

Pete Baur Buick Gmc Inc (PA) 440 238-5600
14000 Pearl Rd Cleveland (44136) *(G-6270)*

Peter A Wimberg Company Inc 513 271-2332
5401 Hetzell St Cincinnati (45227) *(G-4284)*

Peter Graham Dunn Inc. 330 816-0035
1417 Zuercher Rd Dalton (44618) *(G-9242)*

Peter M Kostoff 330 849-6681
222 S Main St Fl 4 Akron (44308) *(G-387)*

Peterbilt of Cincinnati 513 772-1740
2550 Annuity Dr Cincinnati (45241) *(G-4285)*

Peterbilt of Northwest Ohio 419 423-3441
1330 Trenton Ave Findlay (45840) *(G-11073)*

Peterj Brodhead 216 696-3232
1001 Lakeside Ave E Cleveland (44114) *(G-6271)*

Peterman 513 722-2229
6757 Linton Rd Goshen (45122) *(G-11438)*

Peterman Associates Inc 419 722-9566
3480 N Main St Findlay (45840) *(G-11074)*

Peterman Plumbing and Htg Inc 330 364-4497
525 W 15th St Dover (44622) *(G-10206)*

Petermann 513 539-0324
505 Yankee Rd Monroe (45050) *(G-14709)*

Petermann Ltd 330 653-3323
91 Owen Brown St Hudson (44236) *(G-12140)*

Petermann Northeast LLC ... 513 351-7383
8041 Hosbrook Rd Ste 330 Cincinnati (45236) ***(G-4286)***
Peters Main Street Photography (PA) ... 740 852-2731
314 N Main St London (43140) ***(G-13005)***
Peters Tschantz & Assoc Inc ... 330 666-3702
275 Springside Dr Ste 300 Akron (44333) ***(G-388)***
Peterson Construction Company ... 419 941-2233
18817 State Route 501 Wapakoneta (45895) ***(G-18806)***
Petitti Enterprises Inc ... 440 236-5055
10310 East River Rd Columbia Station (44028) ***(G-6851)***
Petitti Garden Centers, Oakwood Village *Also called Flowerland Garden Centers* ***(G-15629)***
Petland Inc (PA) ... 740 775-2464
250 Riverside St Chillicothe (45601) ***(G-2870)***
Petro Cells, Cincinnati *Also called Petro Environmental Tech* ***(G-4287)***
Petro Environmental Tech (PA) ... 513 489-6789
8160 Corp Pk Dr Ste 300 Cincinnati (45242) ***(G-4287)***
Petro Stopping Center, Westlake *Also called Ta Operating LLC* ***(G-19553)***
Petro-Com Corp (PA) ... 440 327-6900
32523 Lorain Rd North Ridgeville (44039) ***(G-15473)***
Petros Homes Inc ... 440 546-9000
10474 Broadview Rd Cleveland (44147) ***(G-6272)***
Petsmart Inc ... 513 336-0365
8175 Arbor Square Dr Mason (45040) ***(G-13746)***
Petsmart Inc ... 419 423-6869
2330 Tiffin Ave Findlay (45840) ***(G-11075)***
Petsmart Inc ... 614 433-9361
1184 Polaris Pkwy Columbus (43240) ***(G-6900)***
Petsmart Inc ... 419 747-4544
2275 Walker Lake Rd Ontario (44903) ***(G-15711)***
Petsmart Inc ... 513 248-4954
245 Rivers Edge Milford (45150) ***(G-14553)***
Petsmart Inc ... 419 865-3941
1450 Spring Meadows Dr Holland (43528) ***(G-12045)***
Petsmart Inc ... 513 752-8463
650 Eastgate South Dr B Cincinnati (45245) ***(G-2928)***
Petsmart Inc ... 937 236-1335
8281 Old Troy Pike Huber Heights (45424) ***(G-12098)***
Petsmart Inc ... 614 418-9389
3713 Easton Market Columbus (43219) ***(G-8540)***
Petsmart Inc ... 330 922-4114
355 Howe Ave Cuyahoga Falls (44221) ***(G-9212)***
Petsmart Inc ... 330 629-2479
1101 Doral Dr Youngstown (44514) ***(G-20318)***
Petsmart Inc ... 330 544-1499
5812 Youngstown Warren Rd Niles (44446) ***(G-15303)***
Petsmart Inc ... 614 497-3001
6499 Adelaide Ct Groveport (43125) ***(G-11661)***
Petsmart Inc ... 440 974-1100
9122 Mentor Ave Mentor (44060) ***(G-14228)***
Petsuites of America Inc ... 513 554-4408
3701 Hauck Rd Cincinnati (45241) ***(G-4288)***
Pf Holdings LLC ... 740 549-3558
8522 Cotter St Lewis Center (43035) ***(G-12703)***
Pfg Ventures LP (PA) ... 216 520-8400
8800 E Pleasant Valley Rd # 1 Independence (44131) ***(G-12243)***
Pfh Partners LLC ... 513 241-5800
3805 Edwards Rd Ste 700 Cincinnati (45209) ***(G-4289)***
Pfpc Enterprises Inc ... 513 941-6200
5750 Hillside Ave Cincinnati (45233) ***(G-4290)***
Pgim Inc ... 419 331-6604
3435 W Elm St Lima (45807) ***(G-12858)***
PGT Trucking Inc ... 419 943-3437
6302 Road 5 Leipsic (45856) ***(G-12664)***
Pgw Auto Glass LLC ... 419 993-2421
2599 Ft Shawnee Ind Dr Lima (45804) ***(G-12859)***
PH B, Cincinnati *Also called The Peck-Hannaford Briggs Co* ***(G-4645)***
PH Fairborn Ht Owner 2800 LLC ... 937 426-7800
2800 Presidential Dr Beavercreek (45324) ***(G-1197)***
Phantom Photography LLC ... 419 215-8060
1630 Avondale Ave Ste 1 Toledo (43607) ***(G-18123)***
Phantom Technical Services Inc ... 614 868-9920
111 Outerbelt St Columbus (43213) ***(G-8541)***
Pharmaceutical Repackaging, Zanesville *Also called Cardinal Health 107 LLC* ***(G-20455)***
Pharmacy Benefit Direct, Youngstown *Also called Pharmacy Data Management Inc* ***(G-20319)***
Pharmacy Data Management Inc (PA) ... 330 757-1500
1170 E Western Reserve Rd Youngstown (44514) ***(G-20319)***
Pharmacy-Lite Packaging, Elyria *Also called Pacific MGT Holdings LLC* ***(G-10667)***
Pharmed Corporation ... 440 250-5400
24340 Sperry Dr Westlake (44145) ***(G-19533)***
Pharmed Institutional Pharmacy, Westlake *Also called Pharmed Corporation* ***(G-19533)***
Pharmerica Long-Term Care Inc ... 330 425-4450
1750 Highland Rd Ste F Twinsburg (44087) ***(G-18454)***
PHC Foundation, Cincinnati *Also called Private HM Care Foundation Inc* ***(G-4335)***
Phelan Insurance Agency Inc (PA) ... 800 843-3069
863 E Main St Versailles (45380) ***(G-18727)***
Phg Retail Services, Milford *Also called Pat Henry Group LLC* ***(G-14551)***
Phil Giessler ... 614 888-0307
882 High St Ste A Worthington (43085) ***(G-19984)***
Phil Wagler Construction Inc ... 330 899-0316
3710 Tabs Dr Uniontown (44685) ***(G-18532)***
Philio Inc ... 419 531-5544
5301 Reynolds Rd Toledo (43615) ***(G-18124)***
Philip Icuss Jr ... 740 264-4647
2311 Sunset Blvd Steubenville (43952) ***(G-17333)***
Philips Healthcare Cleveland ... 440 483-3235
595 Miner Rd Highland Heights (44143) ***(G-11870)***
Philips Medical Systems Clevel (HQ) ... 440 247-2652
595 Miner Rd Cleveland (44143) ***(G-6273)***
Phillip Mc Guire ... 740 482-2701
1585 County Highway 62 Nevada (44849) ***(G-14969)***
Phillips Companies ... 937 426-5461
620 Phillips Dr Beavercreek Township (45434) ***(G-1280)***
Phillips Edison & Company LLC (HQ) ... 513 554-1110
11501 Northlake Dr Fl 1 Cincinnati (45249) ***(G-4291)***
Phillips Mfg and Tower Co (PA) ... 419 347-1720
5578 State Route 61 N Shelby (44875) ***(G-16902)***
Phillips Ready Mix Co ... 937 426-5151
620 Phillips Dr Beavercreek Township (45434) ***(G-1281)***
Phillips Sand & Gravel Co, Beavercreek Township *Also called Phillips Companies* ***(G-1280)***
Phillips Supply Company (PA) ... 513 579-1762
1230 Findlay St Cincinnati (45214) ***(G-4292)***
Phillis Wheat Association Inc ... 216 391-4443
4450 Cedar Ave Ste 1 Cleveland (44103) ***(G-6274)***
Phillis Wheatley Association, Cleveland *Also called Phyllis Wheatley Assn Dev* ***(G-6278)***
Philo Band Boosters ... 740 221-3023
1359 Wheeling Ave Zanesville (43701) ***(G-20525)***
Phinney Industrial Roofing ... 614 308-9000
700 Hadley Dr Columbus (43228) ***(G-8542)***
Phisical Plant, Marietta *Also called Marietta College* ***(G-13467)***
Phoenix ... 513 721-8901
812 Race St Cincinnati (45202) ***(G-4293)***
Phoenix Corporation ... 513 727-4763
1211 Hook Dr Middletown (45042) ***(G-14449)***
Phoenix Cosmopolitan Group LLC ... 814 746-4863
36550 Chester Rd Apt 1505 Avon (44011) ***(G-914)***
Phoenix Golf Links ... 614 539-3636
4239 London Groveport Rd Grove City (43123) ***(G-11591)***
Phoenix Group Holding Co ... 937 704-9850
4 Sycamore Creek Dr Ste A Springboro (45066) ***(G-17135)***
Phoenix Homes Inc (PA) ... 419 692-2421
238 N Main St Delphos (45833) ***(G-10149)***
Phoenix International Frt Svcs, Cleveland *Also called CH Robinson Freight Svcs Ltd* ***(G-5223)***
Phoenix Metals, Middletown *Also called Phoenix Corporation* ***(G-14449)***
Phoenix Residential Centers ... 440 887-6097
6465 Pearl Rd Ste 1 Cleveland (44130) ***(G-6275)***
Phoenix Resource Network LLC ... 800 990-4948
602 Main St Ste 202 Cincinnati (45202) ***(G-4294)***
Phoenix School Program, Akron *Also called Young Mens Christian Assoc* ***(G-515)***
Phoenix Steel Service Inc ... 216 332-0600
4679 Johnston Pkwy Cleveland (44128) ***(G-6276)***
Phoenix Systems Group Inc ... 330 726-6500
755 Brdmn Cnfeld Rd Ste G Youngstown (44512) ***(G-20320)***
Phoenix Technologies Intl LLC ... 419 353-7738
1098 Fairview Ave Bowling Green (43402) ***(G-1789)***
Phpk Technologies, Columbus *Also called Kendall Holdings Ltd* ***(G-7976)***
Phycal Inc ... 440 460-2477
51 Alpha Park Cleveland (44143) ***(G-6277)***
PhyCor, Holland *Also called HRP Capital Inc* ***(G-12028)***
Phyllis At Madison ... 513 321-1300
2324 Madison Rd Ste 1 Cincinnati (45208) ***(G-4295)***
Phyllis Wheatley Assn Dev ... 216 391-4443
4450 Cedar Ave Ste 1 Cleveland (44103) ***(G-6278)***
Physical Thrapy Consulting Svc, Columbus *Also called Patrick Mahoney* ***(G-8521)***
Physician Hospital Alliance ... 937 558-3456
10050 Innovation Dr # 240 Miamisburg (45342) ***(G-14335)***
Physician Providers North, Columbus *Also called Provider Physicians Inc* ***(G-8574)***
Physician Sales & Service, Cincinnati *Also called McKesson Medical-Surgical Top* ***(G-4038)***
Physician Staffing Inc ... 440 542-1950
30680 Bainbridge Rd Lowr Solon (44139) ***(G-17039)***
Physicians Ambulance Svc Inc (PA) ... 216 332-1667
4495 Cranwood Pkwy Cleveland (44128) ***(G-6279)***
Physicians Care of Marietta (PA) ... 740 373-2519
800 Pike St Ste 2 Marietta (45750) ***(G-13487)***
Physicians Care of Marrita, Marietta *Also called Physicians Care of Marietta* ***(G-13487)***
Physicians Choice Inc ... 513 844-1608
5130 Prnceton Glendale Rd Liberty Twp (45011) ***(G-12727)***
Physicians In Family Practice ... 440 775-1881
319 W Lorain St Oberlin (44074) ***(G-15658)***
Physicians Medical Trnspt Team, Cleveland *Also called Physicians Ambulance Svc Inc* ***(G-6279)***
Physicians Surgeons For Women ... 937 323-7340
1821 E High St Springfield (45505) ***(G-17261)***
Physicians Urology Centre, Akron *Also called Center For Urologic Health LLC* ***(G-128)***
Physicians Weight Ls Ctr Amer (PA) ... 330 666-7952
395 Springside Dr Akron (44333) ***(G-389)***
Piasans Mill Inc ... 419 448-0100
255 Riverside Dr Tiffin (44883) ***(G-17693)***
Piatt Park Ltd Partnership ... 513 381-8696
1055 Saint Paul Pl # 300 Cincinnati (45202) ***(G-4296)***

ALPHABETIC SECTION Places Inc

Pic, Akron *Also called Goodwill Industries Inc* **(G-241)**
Pickaway County Community Acti (PA)..........740 477-1655
469 E Ohio St Circleville (43113) **(G-4894)**
Pickaway County Community Acti..........740 474-7411
145 E Corwin St Circleville (43113) **(G-4895)**
Pickaway County Community Acti..........740 477-1655
590 E Ohio St Circleville (43113) **(G-4896)**
Pickaway Diversfied Industries..........740 474-1522
548 Lancaster Pike Circleville (43113) **(G-4897)**
Pickaway Diversified..........740 474-1522
548 Lancaster Pike Circleville (43113) **(G-4898)**
Pickaway Manor Care Center, Circleville *Also called Whetstone Care Center LLC* **(G-4908)**
Pickaway Manor Inc..........740 474-5400
391 Clark Dr Circleville (43113) **(G-4899)**
Pickaway Plains Ambulance Svc (PA)..........740 474-4180
1950 Stoneridge Dr Circleville (43113) **(G-4900)**
Pickaway Senior Citizen Center, Circleville *Also called Pickaway County Community Acti* **(G-4896)**
Pickerington Marcus Cinemas, Pickerington *Also called Marcus Theatres Corporation* **(G-16101)**
Pickerngton Area Cunseling Ctr, Lancaster *Also called New Horizon Youth Family Ctr* **(G-12560)**
Pickett Concrete, Chesapeake *Also called G Big Inc* **(G-2784)**
Picklesimer Trucking Inc..........937 642-1091
360 Palm Dr Marysville (43040) **(G-13644)**
Pickrel Brothers Inc..........937 461-5960
901 S Perry St Dayton (45402) **(G-9808)**
Pickrel Schaeffer Ebeling Lpa..........937 223-1130
40 N Main St Ste 2700 Dayton (45423) **(G-9809)**
Pics Produce Inc..........513 381-1239
4756 Paddock Rd Cincinnati (45229) **(G-4297)**
Pier n Port Travel Inc..........513 841-9900
2692 Madison Rd Ste H1 Cincinnati (45208) **(G-4298)**
Pierce Cleaners Inc..........614 888-4225
5205 N High St Columbus (43214) **(G-8543)**
Pierceton Trucking Co Inc..........740 446-0114
4311 State Route 160 Gallipolis (45631) **(G-11335)**
Pierson Automotive Inc..........513 424-1881
3456 S Dixie Hwy Middletown (45005) **(G-14485)**
Pike Cnty Adult Activities Ctr..........740 947-7503
301 Clough St Waverly (45690) **(G-18972)**
Pike Cnty Recovery Council Inc (PA)..........740 835-8437
218 E North St Waverly (45690) **(G-18973)**
Pike County Dialysis, Waverly *Also called Alomie Dialysis LLC* **(G-18965)**
Pike County Head Start Inc..........740 289-2371
941 Market St Piketon (45661) **(G-16124)**
Pike County YMCA..........740 947-8862
400 Pride Dr Waverly (45690) **(G-18974)**
Pike Run Golf Club Inc..........419 538-7000
10807 Road H Ottawa (45875) **(G-15803)**
Piketon Nursing Center Inc..........740 289-4074
300 Overlook Dr Piketon (45661) **(G-16125)**
Pilgrim United Church Christ..........513 574-4208
4418 Bridgetown Rd Cincinnati (45211) **(G-4299)**
Piling & Shoring Services, Columbus *Also called Righter Construction Svcs Inc* **(G-8630)**
Pillar of Fire..........513 542-1212
6275 Collegevue Pl Cincinnati (45224) **(G-4300)**
Pillar Technology Group LLC..........614 535-7868
580 N 4th St Columbus (43215) **(G-8544)**
Pilot Dogs Incorporated..........614 221-6367
625 W Town St Columbus (43215) **(G-8545)**
Pinata Foods Inc..........216 281-8811
3590 W 58th St Cleveland (44102) **(G-6280)**
Pine Brook Golf Club Inc..........440 748-2939
11043 Durkee Rd Grafton (44044) **(G-11443)**
Pine Hills Continuing Care Ctr..........740 753-1931
1950 Mount Saint Marys Dr # 2 Nelsonville (45764) **(G-14966)**
Pine Hills Golf Club Inc..........330 225-4477
433 W 130th St Hinckley (44233) **(G-11999)**
Pine Kirk Nursing Home, Kirkersville *Also called Livin Care Alter of Kirke Inc* **(G-12455)**
Pine Lake Trout Club, Chagrin Falls *Also called M&C Hotel Interests Inc* **(G-2723)**
Pine Ridge Pine Vllg Resdntl H..........513 724-3460
146 N 3rd St Williamsburg (45176) **(G-19634)**
Pine Ridge Valley Apartments, Willoughby Hills *Also called Goldberg Companies Inc* **(G-19730)**
Pine Valley Care Center, Richfield *Also called Brecksville Leasing Co LLC* **(G-16498)**
Pinecraft Land Holdings LLC..........330 390-5722
6834 County Road 672 # 102 Millersburg (44654) **(G-14615)**
Pines At Glenwood, Marietta *Also called Glenwood Community Inc* **(G-13447)**
Pines Golf Club..........330 684-1414
1319 N Millborne Rd Orrville (44667) **(G-15783)**
Pines Healthcare Center, The, Canton *Also called Communicare Health Svcs Inc* **(G-2317)**
Pines Manufacturing Inc (PA)..........440 835-5553
29100 Lakeland Blvd Westlake (44145) **(G-19534)**
Pines Technology, Westlake *Also called Pines Manufacturing Inc* **(G-19534)**
Pinewood Home, Sardinia *Also called G & D Alternative Living Inc* **(G-16813)**
Pinewood Place Apartments..........419 243-1413
1210 Collingwood Blvd Toledo (43604) **(G-18125)**
Pinnacle Academy, Euclid *Also called National Heritg Academies Inc* **(G-10769)**
Pinnacle Building Services Inc..........614 871-6190
776 Rinkliff Ln Chillicothe (45601) **(G-2871)**
Pinnacle Recycling LLC..........330 745-3700
2330 Romig Rd Akron (44320) **(G-390)**
Pinney Doc Co, Ashtabula *Also called Ashtabula Stevedore Company* **(G-727)**
Pinney Dock & Transport LLC..........440 964-7186
1149 E 5th St Ashtabula (44004) **(G-760)**
Pins & Needles Inc (PA)..........440 243-6400
7300 Pearl Rd Cleveland (44130) **(G-6281)**
Pioneer Automotive Tech Inc (HQ)..........937 746-2293
100 S Pioneer Blvd Springboro (45066) **(G-17136)**
Pioneer Cldding Glzing Systems..........216 816-4242
5615 Cloverleaf Pkwy Cleveland (44125) **(G-6282)**
Pioneer Cldding Glzing Systems (PA)..........513 583-5925
4074 Bethany Rd Mason (45040) **(G-13747)**
Pioneer Hi-Bred Intl Inc..........740 657-6120
59 Greif Pkwy Ste 200 Delaware (43015) **(G-10120)**
Pioneer Hi-Bred Intl Inc..........419 748-8051
15180 Henry Wood Rd Grand Rapids (43522) **(G-11452)**
Pioneer Packing Co..........419 352-5283
510 Napoleon Rd Bowling Green (43402) **(G-1790)**
Pioneer Physicians Networking..........330 633-6601
65 Community Rd Ste C Tallmadge (44278) **(G-17647)**
Pioneer Pipe Inc..........740 376-2400
2021 Hanna Rd Marietta (45750) **(G-13488)**
Pioneer Pipe Fabricating, Marietta *Also called Pioneer Pipe Inc* **(G-13488)**
Pioneer Rural Electric Coop (PA)..........800 762-0997
344 W Us Route 36 Piqua (45356) **(G-16155)**
Pioneer Sands LLC..........740 659-2241
2446 State Route 204 Glenford (43739) **(G-11433)**
Pioneer Sands LLC..........740 599-7773
26900 Coshocton Rd Howard (43028) **(G-12081)**
Pioneer Solutions LLC..........216 383-3400
24800 Rockwell Dr Euclid (44117) **(G-10771)**
Pioneer Trails Inc..........330 674-1234
7572 State Route 241 Millersburg (44654) **(G-14616)**
Pipeline Packaging Corporation (HQ)..........440 349-3200
30310 Emerald Valley Pkwy Solon (44139) **(G-17040)**
Piper Plumbing Inc..........330 274-0160
2480 Bartlett Rd Mantua (44255) **(G-13394)**
Pipestone Golf Course, Miamisburg *Also called City of Miamisburg* **(G-14284)**
Pipino Management Company (PA)..........330 629-2261
1275 Boardman Poland Rd Youngstown (44514) **(G-20321)**
Piqua Country Club Holding Co..........937 773-7744
9812 Country Club Rd Piqua (45356) **(G-16156)**
PIQUA COUNTRY CLUB POOL, Piqua *Also called Piqua Country Club Holding Co* **(G-16156)**
Piqua Industrial Cut & Sew..........937 773-7397
727 E Ash St Piqua (45356) **(G-16157)**
Piqua Manor, Piqua *Also called Hcf of Piqua Inc* **(G-16147)**
Piqua Materials Inc..........937 773-4824
1750 W Statler Rd Piqua (45356) **(G-16158)**
Piqua Materials Inc (PA)..........513 771-0820
11641 Mosteller Rd Ste 1 Cincinnati (45241) **(G-4301)**
Piqua Mineral Division, Piqua *Also called Piqua Materials Inc* **(G-16158)**
Piqua Steel Co..........937 773-3632
4243 W Us Route 36 Piqua (45356) **(G-16159)**
Piqua Transfer & Storage Co..........937 773-3743
9782 Looney Rd Piqua (45356) **(G-16160)**
Pirhl Contractors LLC..........216 378-9690
800 W Saint Clair Ave 4 Cleveland (44113) **(G-6283)**
Pitmark Services Inc..........330 876-2217
7925 State Route 5 Kinsman (44428) **(G-12454)**
Pitney Bowes Inc..........203 426-7025
6910 Treeline Dr Ste C Brecksville (44141) **(G-1840)**
Pitney Bowes Inc..........740 374-5535
111 Marshall Rd Marietta (45750) **(G-13489)**
Pitney Bowes Presort Svcs Inc..........513 860-3607
10085 International Blvd West Chester (45246) **(G-19220)**
Pitt-Ohio Express LLC..........614 801-1064
2101 Hardy Parkway St Grove City (43123) **(G-11592)**
Pitt-Ohio Express LLC..........419 726-6523
5200 Stickney Ave Toledo (43612) **(G-18126)**
Pitt-Ohio Express LLC..........513 860-3424
5000 Duff Dr West Chester (45246) **(G-19221)**
Pitt-Ohio Express LLC..........419 729-8173
5200 Stickney Ave Toledo (43612) **(G-18127)**
Pitt-Ohio Express LLC..........216 433-9000
15225 Industrial Pkwy Cleveland (44135) **(G-6284)**
Pittsburgh & Conneaut Dock, Conneaut *Also called Bessemer and Lake Erie RR Co* **(G-9039)**
Pittsburgh Plumbing & Htg Sup, Akron *Also called Famous II Inc* **(G-218)**
Pivotek LLC..........513 372-6205
8910 Le Saint Dr West Chester (45014) **(G-19128)**
Pizzuti, Columbus *Also called Creekside II LLC* **(G-7459)**
Pizzuti Builders LLC..........614 280-4000
2 Miranova Pl Ste 800 Columbus (43215) **(G-8546)**
Pizzuti Inc (PA)..........614 280-4000
629 N High St 500 Columbus (43215) **(G-8547)**
Pk Management LLC (PA)..........216 472-1870
26301 Curtiss Wright Pkwy Richmond Heights (44143) **(G-16540)**
Places Inc..........937 461-4300
11 W Monument Ave Ste 700 Dayton (45402) **(G-9810)**

ALPHABETIC

(PA)=Parent Co (HQ)=Headquarters (DH)=Div Headquarters

Plane Detail LLC 614 734-1201
5707 State Route 61 Mount Gilead (43338) ***(G-14862)***
Planes Companies, West Chester *Also called Planes Moving & Storage Inc* ***(G-19129)***
Planes Moving & Storage Inc (PA) 513 759-6000
9823 Cincinnati Dayton Rd West Chester (45069) ***(G-19129)***
Planes Mvg & Stor Co Columbus 614 777-9090
2000 Dividend Dr Columbus (43228) ***(G-8548)***
Planned Parenthood Association (PA) 937 226-0780
224 N Wilkinson St Dayton (45402) ***(G-9811)***
Planned Parenthood NW Ohio Inc 419 255-1115
1301 Jefferson Ave Toledo (43604) ***(G-18128)***
Planned Parenthood of SW OH (PA) 513 721-7635
2314 Auburn Ave Cincinnati (45219) ***(G-4302)***
Planned Prenthood Greater Ohio (PA) 614 224-2235
206 E State St Columbus (43215) ***(G-8549)***
Planned Prenthood Greater Ohio 330 535-2671
444 W Exchange St Akron (44302) ***(G-391)***
Planned Prenthood Greater Ohio 216 961-8804
25350 Rockside Rd Bedford Heights (44146) ***(G-1356)***
Planned Prenthood Greater Ohio 330 788-2487
77 E Midlothian Blvd Youngstown (44507) ***(G-20322)***
Planned Prnthood of Grter Mami, Dayton *Also called Planned Parenthood Association* ***(G-9811)***
Planned Prnthood of Mhning Vly 330 788-6506
77 E Midlothian Blvd Youngstown (44507) ***(G-20323)***
Plantscaping Inc 216 367-1200
1865 E 40th St Cleveland (44103) ***(G-6285)***
Plastic Recycling Tech Inc (PA) 937 615-9286
9054 N County Road 25a Piqua (45356) ***(G-16161)***
Plastic Recycling Tech Inc 419 238-9395
7600 Us Route 127 Van Wert (45891) ***(G-18641)***
Plastic Surgery Group Inc (PA) 513 791-4440
4050 Red Bank Rd Ste 42 Cincinnati (45227) ***(G-4303)***
Plastic Technologies Inc (PA) 419 867-5400
1440 Timber Wolf Dr Holland (43528) ***(G-12046)***
Platform Cement Inc 440 602-9750
7503 Tyler Blvd Mentor (44060) ***(G-14229)***
Platform Lab, Columbus *Also called Rev1 Ventures* ***(G-8627)***
Platinum Express Inc 937 235-9540
2549 Stanley Ave Dayton (45404) ***(G-9812)***
Platinum Prestige Property 614 705-2251
4120 Beechbank Rd Columbus (43213) ***(G-8550)***
Platinum RE Professionals LLC 440 942-2100
10 Public Sq Willoughby (44094) ***(G-19704)***
Platinum Restoration Contrs 440 327-0699
104 Reaser Ct Elyria (44035) ***(G-10670)***
Platinum Restoration Inc 440 327-0699
104 Reaser Ct Elyria (44035) ***(G-10671)***
Platinum Technologies 216 926-1080
121 S Main St Ste 200 Akron (44308) ***(G-392)***
Play It Again Sports, Cincinnati *Also called Mc Gregor Family Enterprises* ***(G-4034)***
Play Time Day Nursery Inc 513 385-8281
9550 Colerain Ave Cincinnati (45251) ***(G-4304)***
Playhouse Square Foundation 216 771-4444
1501 Euclid Ave Ste 200 Cleveland (44115) ***(G-6286)***
Playhouse Square Holdg Co LLC (PA) 216 771-4444
1501 Euclid Ave Ste 200 Cleveland (44115) ***(G-6287)***
Playtime Preschool LLC 614 975-1005
1030 Alum Creek Dr Columbus (43209) ***(G-8551)***
Plaz-Way Inc 330 264-9025
1983 E Lincoln Way Wooster (44691) ***(G-19904)***
Plaza Inn Foods Inc 937 354-2181
491 S Main St Mount Victory (43340) ***(G-14930)***
Plaza Inn Restaurant, Mount Victory *Also called Plaza Inn Foods Inc* ***(G-14930)***
Plaza Properties Inc (PA) 614 237-3726
3016 Maryland Ave Columbus (43209) ***(G-8552)***
Pleasant Hill Golf Club, Middletown *Also called Amix Inc* ***(G-14413)***
Pleasant Hill Leasing LLC 740 289-2394
7143 Us Rte 23 S Piketon (45661) ***(G-16126)***
Pleasant Hill Manor, Piketon *Also called Pleasant Hill Leasing LLC* ***(G-16126)***
Pleasant Hl Otptent Thrapy Ctr, Piketon *Also called H C F Inc* ***(G-16116)***
Pleasant Lake Apartments Ltd 440 845-2694
10129 S Lake Blvd Cleveland (44130) ***(G-6288)***
Pleasant Lake Nursing Home 440 842-2273
7260 Ridge Rd Cleveland (44129) ***(G-6289)***
Pleasant Lake Villa, Cleveland *Also called Pleasant Lake Nursing Home* ***(G-6289)***
Pleasant Ridge Care Center Inc (PA) 513 631-1310
5501 Verulam Ave Cincinnati (45213) ***(G-4305)***
Pleasant View Health Care Ctr, Barberton *Also called Pleasant View Nursing Home* ***(G-972)***
Pleasant View Nursing Home (PA) 330 745-6028
401 Snyder Ave Barberton (44203) ***(G-972)***
Pleasant View Nursing Home 330 848-5028
220 3rd St Se Barberton (44203) ***(G-973)***
Pleasantview Nursing Home, Cleveland *Also called Ridge Pleasant Valley Inc* ***(G-6395)***
Plettner Hart Management, Cincinnati *Also called Sheakley Med MGT Resources LLC* ***(G-4512)***
Plevniak Construction Inc 330 718-1600
1235 Townsend Ave Youngstown (44505) ***(G-20324)***
Ploger Transportation LLC (PA) 419 465-2100
15581 County Road 46 Bellevue (44811) ***(G-1415)***
Pls Protective Services 513 521-3581
8263 Clara Ave Cincinnati (45239) ***(G-4306)***
Plug Smart, Columbus *Also called Juice Technologies Inc* ***(G-7957)***
Plumbing Contractor, Westerville *Also called Eaton Plumbing Inc* ***(G-19396)***
Plumbline Solutions Inc 419 581-2963
1219 W Main Cross St # 101 Findlay (45840) ***(G-11076)***
Plus Management Services Inc (PA) 419 225-9018
2440 Baton Rouge Ofc C Lima (45805) ***(G-12860)***
Plus One Communications LLC 330 255-4500
1115 S Main St Akron (44301) ***(G-393)***
Plus Realty Cincinnati Inc 513 575-4500
1160 State Route 28 Milford (45150) ***(G-14554)***
Ply-Trim Enterprises Inc 330 799-7876
550 N Meridian Rd Youngstown (44509) ***(G-20325)***
Ply-Trim South Inc 330 799-7876
550 N Meridian Rd Youngstown (44509) ***(G-20326)***
PMC Systems Limited 330 538-2268
12155 Commissioner Dr North Jackson (44451) ***(G-15386)***
PMI Supply Inc 760 598-1128
5000 Tuttle Crossing Blvd Dublin (43016) ***(G-10427)***
Pmwi LLC 614 975-5004
3177 Overbridge Dr Hilliard (43026) ***(G-11943)***
PNC Banc Corp Ohio (HQ) 513 651-8738
201 E 5th St Cincinnati (45202) ***(G-4307)***
PNC Bank, Cincinnati *Also called PNC Banc Corp Ohio* ***(G-4307)***
PNC Bank National Association 330 375-8342
1 Cascade Plz Ste 200 Akron (44308) ***(G-394)***
PNC Bank National Association 740 349-8431
68 W Church St Fl 1 Newark (43055) ***(G-15228)***
PNC Bank National Association 513 721-2500
5 Main Dr Cincinnati (45231) ***(G-4308)***
PNC Bank National Association 330 742-4426
100 E Federal St Ste 100 Youngstown (44503) ***(G-20327)***
PNC Bank National Association 330 562-9700
7044 N Aurora Rd Aurora (44202) ***(G-850)***
PNC Bank National Association 513 455-9522
995 Dalton Ave Cincinnati (45203) ***(G-4309)***
PNC Bank National Association 419 621-2930
129 W Perkins Ave Sandusky (44870) ***(G-16785)***
PNC Bank National Association 330 854-0974
420 Beverly Ave Canal Fulton (44614) ***(G-2145)***
PNC Bank National Association 440 546-6760
6750 Miller Rd Brecksville (44141) ***(G-1841)***
PNC Bank National Association 419 259-5466
405 Madison Ave Ste 4 Toledo (43604) ***(G-18129)***
PNC Bank-Atm 937 865-6800
9333 Springboro Pike Miamisburg (45342) ***(G-14336)***
PNC Equipment Finance LLC 513 421-9191
995 Dalton Ave Cincinnati (45203) ***(G-4310)***
PNC Mortgage Company (HQ) 412 762-2000
3232 Newmark Dr Bldg 2 Miamisburg (45342) ***(G-14337)***
Png Telecommunications Inc (PA) 513 942-7900
8805 Governors Hill Dr # 250 Cincinnati (45249) ***(G-4311)***
Pnk (ohio) LLC 513 232-8000
6301 Kellogg Rd Cincinnati (45230) ***(G-4312)***
Poelking Bowling Centers 937 435-3855
8871 Kingsridge Dr Dayton (45458) ***(G-9813)***
Poelking Lanes Inc (PA) 937 299-5573
1403 Wilmington Ave Dayton (45420) ***(G-9814)***
Poggemeyer Design Group Inc (PA) 419 244-8074
1168 N Main St Bowling Green (43402) ***(G-1791)***
Poggemeyer Design Group Inc 419 748-7438
2926 Us Highway 6 Mc Clure (43534) ***(G-14020)***
Point Place, Toledo *Also called Harborside Pointe Place LLC* ***(G-17935)***
Point Plus Personnel, Columbus *Also called Chad Downing* ***(G-7250)***
Pointclickcare, Milford *Also called Wescom Solutions Inc* ***(G-14574)***
Poison & Toxic Control Center, Lorain *Also called Mercy Health* ***(G-13060)***
Poison Information Center 513 636-5111
3333 Burnet Ave Fl 3 Cincinnati (45229) ***(G-4313)***
Polaris Automation Inc 614 431-0170
8333 Green Meadows Dr N A Lewis Center (43035) ***(G-12704)***
Polaris Innkeepers Inc 614 568-0770
9000 Worthington Rd Westerville (43082) ***(G-19341)***
Polaris Kindercare, Lewis Center *Also called Kindercare Learning Ctrs LLC* ***(G-12691)***
Polaris Technologies, Youngstown *Also called Modern Builders Supply Inc* ***(G-20289)***
Polaris Towne Center LLC 614 456-0123
1500 Polaris Pkwy # 3000 Columbus (43240) ***(G-6901)***
Polish American Citizens Club 330 253-0496
472 E Glenwood Ave Akron (44310) ***(G-395)***
Polish-American Club, Akron *Also called Polish American Citizens Club* ***(G-395)***
Pollak Distributing Co Inc 216 851-9911
1200 Babbitt Rd Euclid (44132) ***(G-10772)***
Pollak Foods, Euclid *Also called Pollak Distributing Co Inc* ***(G-10772)***
Pollock Research & Design Inc 330 332-3300
1134 Salem Pkwy Salem (44460) ***(G-16706)***
Poly Flex, Baltic *Also called Flex Technologies Inc* ***(G-945)***
Polychem Corporation 419 547-1400
202 Watertower Dr Clyde (43410) ***(G-6820)***
Polycom Inc 937 245-1853
35 Rockridge Rd Ste A Englewood (45322) ***(G-10716)***

Polymer Packaging Inc (PA) ... 330 832-2000
8333 Navarre Rd Se Massillon (44646) ***(G-13844)***
Polymer Protective Packaging, Massillon *Also called Polymer Packaging Inc* ***(G-13844)***
Polymershapes LLC ... 937 877-1903
1480 Blauser Dr Tipp City (45371) ***(G-17724)***
Polyone Corporation ... 440 930-1000
733 E Water St North Baltimore (45872) ***(G-15315)***
Polyone Corporation (PA) ... 440 930-1000
33587 Walker Rd Avon Lake (44012) ***(G-937)***
POMERENE HOSPITAL, Millersburg *Also called Joel Pomerene Memorial Hosp* ***(G-14609)***
Pomeroy It Solutions Sls Inc ... 440 717-1364
6670 W Snowville Rd Ste 3 Brecksville (44141) ***(G-1842)***
Pond-Woolpert LLC ... 937 461-5660
4454 Idea Center Blvd Beavercreek (45430) ***(G-1256)***
Pontiac Bill Delord Autocenter, Lebanon *Also called Bill Delord Autocenter Inc* ***(G-12592)***
Pontoon Solutions Inc ... 855 881-1533
1695 Indian Wood Cir # 200 Maumee (43537) ***(G-13959)***
Pope & Associates Inc ... 513 671-1277
11800 Conrey Rd Ste 240 Cincinnati (45249) ***(G-4314)***
Pope Consulting, Cincinnati *Also called Pope & Associates Inc* ***(G-4314)***
Poppees Popcorn Inc ... 440 327-0775
38727 Taylor Pkwy North Ridgeville (44035) ***(G-15474)***
Popper & Associates Msrp LLC ... 614 798-8991
7153 Timberview Dr Dublin (43017) ***(G-10428)***
Port Clnton Bpo Elks Ldge 1718 ... 419 734-1900
231 Buckeye Blvd Port Clinton (43452) ***(G-16251)***
Port Grter Cincinnati Dev Auth ... 513 621-3000
3 E 4th St Ste 300 Cincinnati (45202) ***(G-4315)***
Port Lawrence Title and Tr Co (HQ) ... 419 244-4605
4 Seagate Ste 101 Toledo (43604) ***(G-18130)***
Porta-Kleen, Lancaster *Also called Pro-Kleen Industrial Svcs Inc* ***(G-12566)***
Portage Animal Clinic, Kent *Also called Stow-Kent Animal Hospital Inc* ***(G-12397)***
Portage Area Rgonal Trnsp Auth ... 330 678-1287
2000 Summit Rd Kent (44240) ***(G-12391)***
Portage Bancshares Inc (PA) ... 330 296-8090
1311 E Main St Ravenna (44266) ***(G-16396)***
Portage Community Bank, Ravenna *Also called Portage Bancshares Inc* ***(G-16396)***
Portage Community Bank Inc (HQ) ... 330 296-8090
1311 E Main St Ravenna (44266) ***(G-16397)***
Portage Country Club Company ... 330 836-8565
240 N Portage Path Akron (44303) ***(G-396)***
Portage County Board ... 330 678-2400
2500 Brady Lake Rd Ravenna (44266) ***(G-16398)***
Portage County Board (PA) ... 330 297-6209
2606 Brady Lake Rd Ravenna (44266) ***(G-16399)***
Portage County Engineer Office, Ravenna *Also called County of Portage* ***(G-16379)***
Portage Family Medicine ... 330 626-5566
9480 Rosemont Dr Streetsboro (44241) ***(G-17426)***
Portage Group Werner Home, Portage *Also called County of Wood* ***(G-16261)***
Portage Industries Inc ... 330 296-2839
7008 State Route 88 Ravenna (44266) ***(G-16400)***
PORTAGE LEARNING CENTERS, Ravenna *Also called Portage Private Industry* ***(G-16403)***
Portage Path Behavorial Health (PA) ... 330 253-3100
340 S Broadway St Akron (44308) ***(G-397)***
Portage Path Behavorial Health ... 330 762-6110
10 Penfield Ave Akron (44310) ***(G-398)***
Portage Pediatrics ... 330 297-8824
6847 N Chestnut St # 200 Ravenna (44266) ***(G-16401)***
Portage Physical Therapists (PA) ... 330 297-9020
771 N Freedom St Ravenna (44266) ***(G-16402)***
Portage Private Industry ... 330 297-7795
145 N Chestnut St Lowr Ravenna (44266) ***(G-16403)***
Porter Drywall Inc ... 614 890-2111
297 Old County Line Rd Westerville (43081) ***(G-19437)***
Porter Wrght Morris Arthur LLP ... 513 381-4700
250 E 5th St Ste 2200 Cincinnati (45202) ***(G-4316)***
Porter Wrght Morris Arthur LLP ... 216 443-2506
950 Main Ave Ste 500 Cleveland (44113) ***(G-6290)***
Porter Wrght Morris Arthur LLP ... 937 449-6810
1 S Main St Ste 1600 Dayton (45402) ***(G-9815)***
Portman Material Handling, Monroe *Also called Equipment Depot Ohio Inc* ***(G-14694)***
Portsmouth Ambulance ... 740 289-2932
2796 Gallia St Portsmouth (45662) ***(G-16298)***
Portsmouth Health Department, Portsmouth *Also called City of Portsmouth* ***(G-16268)***
Portsmouth Lodge 154 B P O E (PA) ... 740 353-1013
544 4th St Portsmouth (45662) ***(G-16299)***
Portsmouth Metro Hsing Auth (PA) ... 740 354-4547
410 Court St Portsmouth (45662) ***(G-16300)***
Portsmouth Raceway Park Inc ... 740 354-3278
Highway 52 Portsmouth (45662) ***(G-16301)***
Portsmuth Emrgncy Amblance Svc ... 740 354-3122
2796 Gallia St Portsmouth (45662) ***(G-16302)***
Positions, Lima *Also called Hector A Buch Jr MD* ***(G-12797)***
Positive Bus Solutions Inc ... 513 772-2255
200 Northland Blvd 100 Cincinnati (45246) ***(G-4317)***
Positive Education Program ... 216 227-2730
11500 Franklin Blvd Cleveland (44102) ***(G-6291)***
Positive Education Program ... 440 471-8200
4320 W 220th St Cleveland (44126) ***(G-6292)***
Positive Electric Inc ... 937 428-0606
4738 Gateway Cir Ste C Dayton (45440) ***(G-9816)***
Post Browning, Cincinnati *Also called Convergint Technologies LLC* ***(G-3416)***
Post-Up Stand, Maple Heights *Also called Suntwist Corp* ***(G-13420)***
Postal Mail Sort Inc ... 330 747-1515
1024 Mahoning Ave Ste 8 Youngstown (44502) ***(G-20328)***
Postema Insurance & Investment ... 419 782-2500
2014 Baltimore St Defiance (43512) ***(G-10052)***
Potter Inc (PA) ... 419 636-5624
630 Commerce Dr Bryan (43506) ***(G-2017)***
Potter Technologies LLC ... 419 380-8404
843 Warehouse Rd Toledo (43615) ***(G-18131)***
Pottery Barn Inc ... 216 378-1211
26300 Cedar Rd Ste 1010 Cleveland (44122) ***(G-6293)***
Pottery Barn Inc ... 614 478-3154
3945 Easton Square Pl W H-1 Columbus (43219) ***(G-8553)***
POTTERY MAKING ILLUSTRATE, Westerville *Also called American Ceramic Society* ***(G-19284)***
Poultry Service Associates ... 937 968-3339
9317 Young Rd Dayton (45390) ***(G-9248)***
Powel Crosley Jr Branch, Cincinnati *Also called Young Mens Christian Associat* ***(G-4865)***
Powell Company Ltd (PA) ... 419 228-3552
3255 Saint Johns Rd Lima (45804) ***(G-12861)***
Powell Electrical Systems Inc ... 330 966-1750
8967 Pleasantwood Ave Nw Canton (44720) ***(G-2491)***
Powell Enterprises Inc ... 614 882-0111
8750 Olde Worthington Rd Westerville (43082) ***(G-19342)***
Power Direct, Cleveland *Also called R D D Inc* ***(G-6339)***
Power Distributors LLC (PA) ... 614 876-3533
3700 Paragon Dr Columbus (43228) ***(G-8554)***
Power Engineers Incorporated ... 513 326-1500
11733 Chesterdale Rd Cincinnati (45246) ***(G-4318)***
Power Engineers Incorporated ... 234 678-9875
1 S Main St Ste 501 Akron (44308) ***(G-399)***
Power Management Inc (PA) ... 937 222-2909
420 Davis Ave Dayton (45403) ***(G-9817)***
Power Scheduling Group, Piketon *Also called Ohio Valley Electric Corp* ***(G-16122)***
Power System Engineering Inc ... 740 568-9220
2349a State Route 821 Marietta (45750) ***(G-13490)***
Power Train Components Inc ... 419 636-4430
509 E Edgerton St Bryan (43506) ***(G-2018)***
Power-Pack Conveyor Company ... 440 975-9955
38363 Airport Pkwy Willoughby (44094) ***(G-19705)***
Powernet Global Communications, Cincinnati *Also called Png Telecommunications Inc* ***(G-4311)***
Powers Agency, Cincinnati *Also called Charles W Powers & Assoc Inc* ***(G-3231)***
Powers Equipment ... 740 746-8220
7265 Sugar Grove Rd Sugar Grove (43155) ***(G-17542)***
PPG Architectural Finishes Inc ... 440 826-5100
16651 W Sprague Rd Strongsville (44136) ***(G-17500)***
PPG Industries, Lima *Also called Pgw Auto Glass LLC* ***(G-12859)***
Ppmc, Columbus *Also called Engaged Health Care Bus Svcs* ***(G-7594)***
Pps Holding LLC ... 513 985-6400
4605 E Galbraith Rd # 200 Cincinnati (45236) ***(G-4319)***
PQ Systems, Dayton *Also called Productivity Qulty Systems Inc* ***(G-9833)***
Practical Solution, Dayton *Also called Centric Consulting LLC* ***(G-9394)***
Prasco LLC (PA) ... 513 204-1100
6125 Commerce Ct Mason (45040) ***(G-13748)***
Prasco Laboratories, Mason *Also called Prasco LLC* ***(G-13748)***
Praxair Distribution Inc ... 330 376-2242
1760 E Market St Akron (44305) ***(G-400)***
PRC Medical LLC (PA) ... 330 493-9004
111 Stow Ave Ste 200 Cuyahoga Falls (44221) ***(G-9213)***
Pre-Clinical Services, Spencerville *Also called Charles River Laboratories Inc* ***(G-17107)***
Pre-Fore Inc ... 740 467-2206
410 Blacklick Rd Millersport (43046) ***(G-14631)***
Preble County Council On Aging ... 937 456-4947
800 E Saint Clair St Eaton (45320) ***(G-10574)***
Preble County General Hlth Dst ... 937 472-0087
615 Hillcrest Dr Eaton (45320) ***(G-10575)***
Precesion Finning Bending Inc ... 330 382-9351
1250 Saint George St # 6 East Liverpool (43920) ***(G-10533)***
Precious Angels Child Care I, Cleveland *Also called Precious Angels Lrng Ctr Inc* ***(G-6294)***
Precious Angels Lrng Ctr Inc ... 440 886-1919
5574 Pearl Rd Cleveland (44129) ***(G-6294)***
Precious Cargo Transportation ... 440 564-8039
15050 Cross Creek Pkwy Newbury (44065) ***(G-15260)***
Precision Broadbnd Installatns ... 614 523-2917
7642 Red Bank Rd Westerville (43082) ***(G-19343)***
Precision Coatings Systems ... 937 642-4727
948 Columbus Ave Marysville (43040) ***(G-13645)***
Precision Electrical Services ... 740 474-4490
201 W Main St Circleville (43113) ***(G-4901)***
Precision Endoscopy Amer Inc (PA) ... 410 527-9598
4575 Hudson Dr Stow (44224) ***(G-17386)***
Precision Environmental Co (HQ) ... 216 642-6040
5500 Old Brecksville Rd Independence (44131) ***(G-12244)***
Precision Funding Corp ... 330 405-1313
2132 Case Pkwy Ste A Twinsburg (44087) ***(G-18455)***
Precision Geophysical Inc (PA) ... 330 674-2198
2695 State Route 83 Millersburg (44654) ***(G-14617)***

ALPHABETIC

(PA)=Parent Co (HQ)=Headquarters (DH)=Div Headquarters
2018 Harris Ohio Services Directory 1293

Precision Metalforming Assn (PA)....216 241-1482
6363 Oak Tree Blvd Independence (44131) *(G-12245)*
Precision Mtal Fabrication Inc (PA)....937 235-9261
191 Heid Ave Dayton (45404) *(G-9818)*
Precision Paving Inc....419 499-7283
3414 State Route 113 E Milan (44846) *(G-14498)*
Precision Pipeline Svcs LLC....740 652-1679
10 Whiley Rd Lancaster (43130) *(G-12565)*
Precision Products Group Inc....330 698-4711
339 Mill St Apple Creek (44606) *(G-626)*
Precision Steel Services Inc (PA)....419 476-5702
31 E Sylvania Ave Toledo (43612) *(G-18132)*
Precision Strip Inc....937 667-6255
315 Park Ave Tipp City (45371) *(G-17725)*
Precision Strip Inc (HQ)....419 628-2343
86 S Ohio St Minster (45865) *(G-14668)*
Precision Strip Inc....419 661-1100
7401 Ponderosa Rd Perrysburg (43551) *(G-16044)*
Precision Strip Inc....513 423-4166
4400 Oxford State Rd Middletown (45044) *(G-14450)*
Precision Supply Company Inc....330 225-5530
2845 Interstate Pkwy Brunswick (44212) *(G-1988)*
Precision Vhcl Solutions LLC....513 651-9444
559 Liberty Hl Cincinnati (45202) *(G-4320)*
Precision Welding Corporation....216 524-6110
7900 Exchange St Cleveland (44125) *(G-6295)*
Predator Trucking Company....419 849-2601
1121 State Route 105 Woodville (43469) *(G-19823)*
Predator Trucking Company (PA)....330 530-0712
3181 Trumbull Ave Mc Donald (44437) *(G-14024)*
Predict Technologies Div, Cleveland *Also called Reid Asset Management Company (G-6368)*
Predictive Service LLC (PA)....866 772-6770
25200 Chagrin Blvd # 300 Cleveland (44122) *(G-6296)*
Preemptive Solutions LLC....440 443-7200
767 Beta Dr Cleveland (44143) *(G-6297)*
Preferred Acquisition Co LLC (PA)....216 587-0957
4871 Neo Pkwy Cleveland (44128) *(G-6298)*
Preferred Airparts, Kidron *Also called Jilco Industries Inc (G-12441)*
Preferred Capital Lending Inc....216 472-1391
200 Public Sq Ste 160 Cleveland (44114) *(G-6299)*
Preferred Living, Westerville *Also called Preferred RE Investments LLC (G-19344)*
Preferred Medical Group Inc....404 403-8310
23600 Commerce Park Beachwood (44122) *(G-1115)*
Preferred RE Investments LLC....614 901-2400
470 Olde Worthington Rd # 470 Westerville (43082) *(G-19344)*
Preferred Roofing Ohio Inc....216 587-0957
4871 Neo Pkwy Cleveland (44128) *(G-6300)*
Preferred Roofing Services LLC....216 587-0957
4871 Neo Pkwy Cleveland (44128) *(G-6301)*
Preferred Temporary Services....330 494-5502
4791 Munson St Nw Canton (44718) *(G-2492)*
Pregnancy Care of Cincinnati....513 487-7777
2415 Auburn Ave Cincinnati (45219) *(G-4321)*
Premier Asphalt Paving Co Inc....440 237-6600
10519 Royalton Rd North Royalton (44133) *(G-15498)*
Premier Broadcasting Co Inc....614 866-0700
5310 E Main St Ste 101 Columbus (43213) *(G-8555)*
Premier Care....614 431-0599
500 W Wilson Bridge Rd # 235 Worthington (43085) *(G-19985)*
Premier Cleaning Services Inc....513 831-2492
5866 Wlfpen Plasant Hl Rd Milford (45150) *(G-14555)*
Premier Construction Company....513 874-2611
9361 Seward Rd Fairfield (45014) *(G-10896)*
Premier Estate of Three Rivers, Cincinnati *Also called Premier Estates 521 LLC (G-4322)*
Premier Estates 521 LLC....765 288-2488
7800 Jandacres Dr Cincinnati (45248) *(G-4322)*
Premier Estates 525 LLC....513 631-6800
1578 Sherman Ave Cincinnati (45212) *(G-4323)*
Premier Estates 526 LLC....513 922-1440
5999 Bender Rd Cincinnati (45233) *(G-4324)*
Premier Esttes Cncnnt-Rverside, Cincinnati *Also called Pristine Senior Living (G-4334)*
Premier Esttes Cncnnt-Rverview, Cincinnati *Also called Premier Estates 526 LLC (G-4324)*
Premier Feeds LLC....937 584-2411
238 Melvin Rd Wilmington (45177) *(G-19779)*
Premier Health Care MGT Inc....248 644-5522
4750 Ashwood Dr Ste 300 Blue Ash (45241) *(G-1664)*
Premier Health Group LLC....937 535-4100
110 N Main St Ste 350 Dayton (45402) *(G-9819)*
Premier Health Partners (PA)....937 499-9596
110 N Main St Ste 450 Dayton (45402) *(G-9820)*
Premier Health Partners....937 526-3235
471 Marker Rd Versailles (45380) *(G-18728)*
Premier Health Specialists Inc (HQ)....937 223-4518
110 N Main St Ste 350 Dayton (45402) *(G-9821)*
Premier Heart Associates Inc....937 832-2425
6251 Good Samaritan Way # 220 Dayton (45424) *(G-9822)*
Premier Heart Inc....937 832-2425
9000 N Main St Ste 101 Englewood (45415) *(G-10717)*
Premier Integrated Med Assoc (PA)....937 291-6813
6520 Acro Ct Centerville (45459) *(G-2684)*
Premier Integration....330 545-8690
50 Harry St Girard (44420) *(G-11424)*
Premier Management Co Inc....740 867-2144
805 3rd Ave Chesapeake (45619) *(G-2786)*
Premier Physican Centers, Westlake *Also called Medical Diagnostic Lab Inc (G-19514)*
Premier Physicians, Cleveland *Also called Gloria Gadmack Do (G-5675)*
Premier Physicians Centers Inc (PA)....440 895-5085
24651 Center Ridge Rd # 350 Westlake (44145) *(G-19535)*
Premier Prpts Centl Ohio Inc....614 755-4275
5674 Westbourne Ave Columbus (43213) *(G-8556)*
Premier Radiology Group Inc....937 431-9729
2145 N Fairfield Rd Ste A Beavercreek (45431) *(G-1198)*
Premier Rstrtion Mech Svcs LLC....513 420-1600
2890 S Main St Middletown (45044) *(G-14451)*
Premier System Integrators Inc....513 217-7294
2660 Towne Blvd Middletown (45044) *(G-14452)*
Premier Truck Parts Inc....216 642-5000
5800 W Canal Rd Cleveland (44125) *(G-6302)*
Premier Truck Sls & Rentl Inc....216 642-5000
5800 W Canal Rd Cleveland (44125) *(G-6303)*
Premiere Kidney Center Newark, Newark *Also called Lory Dialysis LLC (G-15198)*
Premiere Produce, Cleveland *Also called Anselmo Rssis Premier Prod Ltd (G-5040)*
Premiere Service Mortgage Corp (PA)....513 546-9895
6266 Centre Park Dr West Chester (45069) *(G-19130)*
Premierfirst Home Health Care....614 443-3110
1430 S High St Columbus (43207) *(G-8557)*
Premium Beverage Supply Ltd....614 777-1007
3701 Lacon Rd Hilliard (43026) *(G-11944)*
Premium Trnsp Logistics LLC (PA)....419 861-3430
5445 Sthwyck Blvd Ste 210 Toledo (43614) *(G-18133)*
Premix Holding Company....330 666-3751
3637 Ridgewood Rd Fairlawn (44333) *(G-10968)*
Prengers, Oregonia *Also called Roger Shawn Houck (G-15758)*
Presbyterian Child Center....740 852-3190
211 Garfield Ave London (43140) *(G-13006)*
Prescription Supply Inc....419 661-6600
2233 Tracy Rd Northwood (43619) *(G-15543)*
Presidio Infrastructure....419 241-8303
20 N Saint Clair St Toledo (43604) *(G-18134)*
Presidio Infrastructure....614 381-1400
5025 Bradenton Ave Ste B Dublin (43017) *(G-10429)*
Presort America Ltd....614 836-5120
4227 Williams Rd Groveport (43125) *(G-11662)*
Press Wood Management, Beachwood *Also called Cw Financial LLC (G-1070)*
Pressley Ridge Foundation....513 752-4548
4355 Ferguson Dr Ste 125 Cincinnati (45245) *(G-2929)*
Pressley Ridge Foundation....513 737-0400
734 Dayton St Hamilton (45011) *(G-11764)*
Pressley Ridge Pryde....513 559-1402
7162 Reading Rd Ste 300 Cincinnati (45237) *(G-4325)*
Prestige Audio Visual Inc....513 641-1600
4835 Para Dr Cincinnati (45237) *(G-4326)*
Prestige AV & Creative Svcs, Cincinnati *Also called Prestige Audio Visual Inc (G-4326)*
Prestige Delivery Systems LLC (HQ)....216 332-8000
9535 Midwest Ave Ste 104 Cleveland (44125) *(G-6304)*
Prestige Delivery Systems LLC....614 836-8980
4279 Directors Blvd Groveport (43125) *(G-11663)*
PRESTIGE HEALTHCARE, Gallipolis *Also called Gallipolis Care LLC (G-11318)*
Prestige Interiors Inc....330 425-1690
2239 E Enterprise Pkwy Twinsburg (44087) *(G-18456)*
Prestige Technical Svcs Inc (PA)....513 779-6800
7908 Cincinnati Dayton Rd T West Chester (45069) *(G-19131)*
Prestige Valet Inc....513 871-4220
4220 Appleton St Cincinnati (45209) *(G-4327)*
Prevent Blindness - Ohio....614 464-2020
1500 W 3rd Ave Ste 200 Columbus (43212) *(G-8558)*
Price Rd Hlth Rhbilitation Ctr, Newark *Also called Newark Care Center LLC (G-15219)*
Price Thrice Supply, Columbus *Also called Valley Interior Systems Inc (G-8930)*
Price Woods Products Inc....513 722-1200
6507 Snider Rd Loveland (45140) *(G-13153)*
Pricewaterhousecoopers LLP....216 875-3000
200 Public Sq Fl 18 Cleveland (44114) *(G-6305)*
Pricewaterhousecoopers LLP....419 254-2500
406 Washington St Ste 200 Toledo (43604) *(G-18135)*
Pricewaterhousecoopers LLP....513 723-4700
201 E 5th St Ste 2300 Cincinnati (45202) *(G-4328)*
Pricewaterhousecoopers LLP....614 225-8700
41 S High St Ste 25 Columbus (43215) *(G-8559)*
Pride -N- Joy Preschool Inc....740 522-3338
1319 W Main St Newark (43055) *(G-15229)*
Pride Transportation Inc....419 424-2145
611 Howard St Findlay (45840) *(G-11077)*
Pridecraft Enterprises, Cincinnati *Also called Standard Textile Co Inc (G-4579)*
Primary Care Nursing Services....614 764-0960
3140 Lilly Mar Ct Dublin (43017) *(G-10430)*
Primary Care Physicians Assn....330 499-9944
4575 Stephens Cir Nw Canton (44718) *(G-2493)*
Primary Cr Ntwrk Prmr Hlth Prt....513 492-5940
4859 Nixon Park Dr Ste A Mason (45040) *(G-13749)*
Primary Cr Ntwrk Prmr Hlth Prt....937 890-6644
900 S Dixie Dr Ste 40 Vandalia (45377) *(G-18693)*
Primary Cr Ntwrk Prmr Hlth Prt....937 278-5854
1530 Needmore Rd Ste 200 Dayton (45414) *(G-9823)*

Primary Cr Ntwrk Prmr Hlth Prt....937 208-9090
1222 S Patterson Blvd # 120 Dayton (45402) ***(G-9824)***

Primary Cr Ntwrk Prmr Hlth Prt....937 208-7000
722 N Fairfield Rd Beavercreek (45434) ***(G-1199)***

Primary Cr Ntwrk Prmr Hlth Prt....937 743-5965
8401 Claude Thomas Rd Franklin (45005) ***(G-11164)***

Primary Cr Ntwrk Prmr Hlth Prt....513 420-5233
1 Medical Center Dr Middletown (45005) ***(G-14486)***

Primary Cr Ntwrk Prmr Hlth Prt....513 204-5785
7450 S Masn Montgomery Rd Mason (45040) ***(G-13750)***

Primary Cr Ntwrk Prmr Hlth Prt (PA)....937 226-7085
110 N Main St Ste 350 Dayton (45402) ***(G-9825)***

Primary Cr Ntwrk Prmr Hlth Prt....937 424-9800
2350 Miami Valley Dr # 410 Dayton (45459) ***(G-9826)***

Primary Dayton Innkeepers LLC....937 938-9550
7701 Washington Vlg Dr Dayton (45459) ***(G-9827)***

Primary Eyecare Associates (PA)....937 492-2351
1086 Fairington Dr Sidney (45365) ***(G-16948)***

Primary Solutions, Columbus *Also called Marshall Information Svcs LLC* ***(G-8120)***

Primatech Inc (PA)....614 841-9800
50 Northwoods Blvd Ste A Columbus (43235) ***(G-8560)***

Primax Marketing Group....513 443-2797
2300 Montana Ave Ste 102 Cincinnati (45211) ***(G-4329)***

Prime Ae Group Inc....614 839-0250
8415 Pulsar Pl Ste 300 Columbus (43240) ***(G-6902)***

Prime Communications LP....281 240-7800
4232 Belden Village Mall Canton (44718) ***(G-2494)***

Prime Home Care LLC (PA)....513 340-4183
2775 W Us Hwy 22 3 Ste 1 Maineville (45039) ***(G-13245)***

Prime Home Care LLC....419 535-1414
3454 Oak Alley Ct Ste 304 Toledo (43606) ***(G-18136)***

Prime Polymers Inc....330 662-4200
2600 Medina Rd Medina (44256) ***(G-14113)***

Prime Prodata Inc....330 497-2578
800 N Main St North Canton (44720) ***(G-15361)***

Prime Time Delivery & Whse, Cleveland *Also called Prime Time Enterprises Inc* ***(G-6306)***

Prime Time Enterprises Inc....440 891-8855
6410 Eastland Rd Ste A Cleveland (44142) ***(G-6306)***

Prime Time Party Rental Inc....937 296-9262
5225 Springboro Pike Moraine (45439) ***(G-14815)***

Primecare Sutheastern Ohio Inc....740 454-8551
1210 Ashland Ave Zanesville (43701) ***(G-20526)***

Primed....937 435-9013
979 Congress Park Dr Dayton (45459) ***(G-9828)***

Primed At Congress Park, Dayton *Also called Medicine Midwest LLC* ***(G-9715)***

Primed Physicians, Dayton *Also called Primed Premier Integrated Med* ***(G-9830)***

Primed Physicians, Centerville *Also called Premier Integrated Med Assoc* ***(G-2684)***

Primed Physicians....937 298-8058
540 Lincoln Park Blvd # 390 Dayton (45429) ***(G-9829)***

Primed Premier Integrated Med (PA)....937 291-6893
6520 Acro Ct Dayton (45459) ***(G-9830)***

Primehalth Wns Hlth Specialist....440 918-4630
35040 Chardon Rd Ste 205 Willoughby Hills (44094) ***(G-19733)***

Primerica, Canton *Also called Rick Allman* ***(G-2514)***

Primero Home Loans LLC....877 959-2921
4725 Lakehurst Ct Ste 400 Dublin (43016) ***(G-10431)***

Primetals Technologies USA LLC....419 929-1554
81 E Washburn St New London (44851) ***(G-15070)***

Primetech Communications Inc....513 942-6000
4505 Muhlhauser Rd West Chester (45011) ***(G-19132)***

Primetime, Canton *Also called Aultman Hospital* ***(G-2255)***

Primo Properties LLC....330 606-6746
5555 Cerni Pl Austintown (44515) ***(G-871)***

Primrose Rtrment Cmmnities LLC....419 224-1200
3500 W Elm St Lima (45807) ***(G-12862)***

Primrose School At Golf Vlg....740 881-5830
8771 Moreland St Powell (43065) ***(G-16346)***

Primrose School At Polaris....614 899-2588
561 Westar Blvd Westerville (43082) ***(G-19345)***

Primrose School of Symmes....513 697-6970
9175 Governors Way Cincinnati (45249) ***(G-4330)***

Primrose School of Worthington, Worthington *Also called Ajm Worthington Inc* ***(G-19938)***

Printed Resources, Columbus *Also called Nutis Press Inc* ***(G-8307)***

Printing Concepts, Stow *Also called Traxium LLC* ***(G-17397)***

Printing Services....440 708-1999
16750 Park Circle Dr Chagrin Falls (44023) ***(G-2729)***

Printpack Inc....513 891-7886
8044 Montgomery Rd # 600 Cincinnati (45236) ***(G-4331)***

Priority 1 Construction Svcs....513 922-0203
5178 Crookshank Rd Cincinnati (45238) ***(G-4332)***

Priority Building Services Inc....937 233-7030
2370 National Rd Beavercreek Township (45324) ***(G-1282)***

Priority Designs Inc....614 337-9979
100 S Hamilton Rd Columbus (43213) ***(G-8561)***

Priority Dispatch Inc (PA)....513 791-3900
4665 Malsbary Rd Blue Ash (45242) ***(G-1665)***

Priority Dispatch Inc....216 332-9852
5385 Naiman Pkwy Solon (44139) ***(G-17041)***

Priority III Contracting Inc....513 922-0203
5178 Crookshank Rd Cincinnati (45238) ***(G-4333)***

Priority Mortgage Corp....614 431-1141
150 E Wilson Bridge Rd # 350 Worthington (43085) ***(G-19986)***

Pristine Senior Living, Cincinnati *Also called Premier Estates 525 LLC* ***(G-4323)***

Pristine Senior Living....513 471-8667
315 Lilienthal St Cincinnati (45204) ***(G-4334)***

Pristine Senior Living and, Willard *Also called Pristine Senior Living of* ***(G-19625)***

Pristine Senior Living of....419 935-0148
370 E Howard St Willard (44890) ***(G-19625)***

Pristine Snior Lving Englewood....937 836-5143
425 Lauricella Ct Englewood (45322) ***(G-10718)***

Private Duty & Visiting Nurses, Celina *Also called Community Hlth Prfssionals Inc* ***(G-2642)***

Private Duty Services Inc....419 238-3714
1157 Westwood Dr Van Wert (45891) ***(G-18642)***

Private HM Care Foundation Inc....513 662-8999
3808 Applegate Ave Cincinnati (45211) ***(G-4335)***

Private Practice Nurses Inc....216 481-1305
403 Cary Jay Blvd Cleveland (44143) ***(G-6307)***

Private School Aid Service, Westlake *Also called Facts Management Company* ***(G-19483)***

Prn Health Services Inc....513 792-2217
8044 Montgomery Rd # 700 Cincinnati (45236) ***(G-4336)***

Prn Nurse Inc....614 864-9292
6161 Radekin Rd Columbus (43232) ***(G-8562)***

Pro Care Janitor Supply....937 778-2275
317 N Main St Piqua (45356) ***(G-16162)***

Pro Care Medical Trnsp Svc, Circleville *Also called Pickaway Plains Ambulance Svc* ***(G-4900)***

Pro Century, Westerville *Also called CSC Insurance Agency Inc* ***(G-19294)***

Pro Ed Communications Inc....216 595-7919
25101 Chagrin Blvd # 230 Cleveland (44122) ***(G-6308)***

Pro Health Care Services Ltd....614 856-9111
270 Main St Ste A Groveport (43125) ***(G-11664)***

Pro Kids & Families Program, Cleveland *Also called Ohioguidestone* ***(G-6197)***

Pro Oncall Technologies LLC (PA)....513 489-7660
6902 E Kemper Rd Cincinnati (45249) ***(G-4337)***

Pro Seniors Inc....513 345-4160
7162 Reading Rd Ste 1150 Cincinnati (45237) ***(G-4338)***

Pro-Kleen Industrial Svcs Inc....740 689-1886
1030 Mill Park Dr Lancaster (43130) ***(G-12566)***

Pro-Lam, Milford *Also called Professonal Laminate Mllwk Inc* ***(G-14556)***

Pro-Touch, Columbus *Also called T&L Global Management LLC* ***(G-8818)***

Pro-Touch Inc....614 586-0303
721 N Rose Ave Columbus (43219) ***(G-8563)***

Pro-Tow Inc....614 444-8697
1669 Harmon Ave Columbus (43223) ***(G-8564)***

Proactive Occpational Medicine, Wheelersburg *Also called Brown Medical LLC* ***(G-19571)***

Proactive Occptnal Mdicine Inc....740 574-8728
1661 State Route 522 # 2 Wheelersburg (45694) ***(G-19580)***

Proampac, Cincinnati *Also called Ampac Holdings LLC* ***(G-3017)***

Procamps Inc....513 745-5855
4600 Mcauley Pl Fl 4 Blue Ash (45242) ***(G-1666)***

Process Construction Inc....513 251-2211
2128 State Ave Cincinnati (45214) ***(G-4339)***

Process Plus LLC (PA)....513 742-7590
135 Merchant St Ste 300 Cincinnati (45246) ***(G-4340)***

Process Pump & Seal Inc....513 988-7000
2993 Woodsdale Rd Trenton (45067) ***(G-18343)***

Procter & Gamble Distrg LLC....513 945-7960
2 P&G Plz Tn8 235 Cincinnati (45202) ***(G-4341)***

Procter & Gamble Distrg LLC....937 387-5189
1800 Union Park Blvd Union (45377) ***(G-18499)***

Procter & Gamble Distrg LLC....513 626-2500
11510 Reed Hartman Hwy Blue Ash (45241) ***(G-1667)***

Procterville Food Fair, Proctorville *Also called Forths Foods Inc* ***(G-16358)***

Procurement Payments, Kent *Also called Kent State University* ***(G-12379)***

Prodrivers, Columbus *Also called Professional Drivers GA Inc* ***(G-8566)***

Produce One Inc....931 253-4749
904 Woodley Rd Dayton (45403) ***(G-9831)***

Producer Group LLC (PA)....440 871-7700
19111 Detroit Rd Ste 304 Rocky River (44116) ***(G-16589)***

Producers Credit Corporation....614 433-2150
8351 N High St Ste 250 Columbus (43235) ***(G-8565)***

Production Design Services Inc (PA)....937 866-3377
313 Mound St Dayton (45402) ***(G-9832)***

Production Services Unlimited....513 695-1658
575 Columbus Ave Lebanon (45036) ***(G-12637)***

Productivity Qulty Systems Inc (PA)....937 885-2255
210b E Spring Valley Pike Dayton (45458) ***(G-9833)***

Professional Building Maint, Dayton *Also called Space Management Inc* ***(G-9894)***

Professional Contract Systems....513 469-8800
11804 Conrey Rd Ste 100 Cincinnati (45249) ***(G-4342)***

Professional Detailing Pdts, Canton *Also called Ohio Auto Supply Company* ***(G-2478)***

Professional Drivers GA Inc....614 529-8282
4251 Diplomacy Dr Columbus (43228) ***(G-8566)***

Professional Electric Pdts Co....419 269-3790
501 Phillips Ave Toledo (43612) ***(G-18137)***

Professional Hse Clg Svcs Inc....440 729-7866
8228 Mayfield Rd Ste 1b Chesterland (44026) ***(G-2801)***

Professional Maint Dayton....937 461-5259
223 E Helena St Dayton (45404) ***(G-9834)***

Professional Maint of Columbus....614 443-6528
541 Stimmel Rd Columbus (43223) ***(G-8567)***

Professional Maint of Columbus..........513 579-1762
1 Crosley Field Ln Cincinnati (45214) *(G-4343)*
Professional Nursing Service, Cuyahoga Falls *Also called Diane Vishnia Rn and Assoc (G-9180)*
Professional Nursing Service, Cuyahoga Falls *Also called Vishnia & Associates Inc (G-9233)*
Professional Plumbing Services..........740 454-1066
3570 Old Wheeling Rd Zanesville (43701) *(G-20527)*
Professional Property Maint, New Carlisle *Also called Louderback Fmly Invstments Inc (G-15026)*
Professional Refrigeration, Millersport *Also called Pre-Fore Inc (G-14631)*
Professional Restoration Svc..........330 825-1803
1170 Industrial Pkwy Medina (44256) *(G-14114)*
Professional Sales Associates..........330 299-7343
5045 Park Ave W Ste 1b Seville (44273) *(G-16842)*
Professional Service Inds, Columbus *Also called Professional Service Inds Inc (G-8568)*
Professional Service Inds Inc..........614 876-8000
4960 Vulcan Ave Ste C Columbus (43228) *(G-8568)*
Professional Service Inds Inc..........216 447-1335
5555 Canal Rd Cleveland (44125) *(G-6309)*
Professional Services, Cleveland *Also called Jewish Family Services Associa (G-5864)*
Professional Telecom Svcs..........513 232-7700
2119 Beechmont Ave Cincinnati (45230) *(G-4344)*
Professional Transportation..........419 661-0576
30801 Drouillard Rd Walbridge (43465) *(G-18776)*
Professional Travel Inc (PA)..........440 734-8800
25000 Country Club Blvd # 170 North Olmsted (44070) *(G-15439)*
Professionals For Womens Hlth (PA)..........614 268-8800
921 Jasonway Ave Ste B Columbus (43214) *(G-8569)*
Professnal Glfers Assn of Amer..........419 882-3197
5201 Corey Rd Sylvania (43560) *(G-17606)*
Professnal Mint Cincinnati Inc..........513 579-1161
1230 Findlay St Cincinnati (45214) *(G-4345)*
Professnal Mint Lttle Ohio Div, Cincinnati *Also called Professional Maint of Columbus (G-4343)*
Professonal Data Resources Inc (PA)..........513 792-5100
4555 Lake Forest Dr # 220 Blue Ash (45242) *(G-1668)*
Professonal Football Hall Fame, Canton *Also called National Football Museum Inc (G-2470)*
Professonal Laminate Mllwk Inc..........513 891-7858
1003 Tech Dr Milford (45150) *(G-14556)*
Profile Digital Printing LLC..........937 866-4241
5449 Marina Dr Dayton (45449) *(G-9835)*
Profiol, Canton *Also called Graco Ohio Inc (G-2385)*
Profit Recovery of Ohio..........440 243-1743
16510 Webster Rd Cleveland (44130) *(G-6310)*
Proforma, Independence *Also called Pfg Ventures LP (G-12243)*
Progressive Agency Inc..........440 461-5000
6300 Wilson Mills Rd Cleveland (44143) *(G-6311)*
Progressive Bayside Insur Co..........440 395-4460
6300 Wilson Mills Rd Cleveland (44143) *(G-6312)*
Progressive Casualty Insur Co (HQ)..........440 461-5000
6300 Wilson Mills Rd Mayfield Village (44143) *(G-14012)*
Progressive Casualty Insur Co..........440 683-8164
651 Beta Dr 150 Cleveland (44143) *(G-6313)*
Progressive Casualty Insur Co..........440 603-4033
747 Alpha Dr Ste A21 Cleveland (44143) *(G-6314)*
Progressive Choice Insur Co..........440 461-5000
6300 Wilson Mills Rd Cleveland (44143) *(G-6315)*
Progressive Corporation..........800 925-2886
600 Mills Rd Cleveland (44101) *(G-6316)*
Progressive Corporation..........440 461-5000
300 N Commons Blvd Cleveland (44143) *(G-6317)*
Progressive Dodge, Massillon *Also called Progrssive Oldsmobile Cadillac (G-13845)*
Progressive Entps Holdings Inc..........614 794-3300
250 Progressive Way Westerville (43082) *(G-19346)*
Progressive Fishing Assn..........419 877-9909
8050 Schadel Rd Whitehouse (43571) *(G-19589)*
Progressive Flooring Svcs Inc..........614 868-9005
100 Heritage Dr Etna (43062) *(G-10738)*
Progressive Furniture Inc (HQ)..........419 446-4500
502 Middle St Archbold (43502) *(G-641)*
Progressive Green Meadows LLC..........330 875-1456
7770 Columbus Rd Louisville (44641) *(G-13105)*
Progressive Hawaii Insurance C..........440 461-5000
6300 Wilson Mills Rd Cleveland (44143) *(G-6318)*
Progressive Insurance, Cleveland *Also called Progressive Corporation (G-6316)*
PROGRESSIVE INSURANCE, Mayfield Village *Also called Progressive Casualty Insur Co (G-14012)*
PROGRESSIVE INSURANCE, Cleveland *Also called Progressive Bayside Insur Co (G-6312)*
Progressive Insurance, Youngstown *Also called Progressive Max Insurance Co (G-20329)*
Progressive Insurance, Cleveland *Also called Progressive Casualty Insur Co (G-6313)*
PROGRESSIVE INSURANCE, Cleveland *Also called Progressive Northwestern Insur (G-6319)*
PROGRESSIVE INSURANCE, Cleveland *Also called Progressive Hawaii Insurance C (G-6318)*
PROGRESSIVE INSURANCE, Cleveland *Also called Progressive Premier Insurance (G-6321)*
Progressive Insurance, Cleveland *Also called Progressive Corporation (G-6317)*
Progressive Insurance, Cleveland *Also called Progressive Agency Inc (G-6311)*
Progressive International, Archbold *Also called Progressive Furniture Inc (G-641)*
Progressive Max Insurance Co..........330 533-8733
120 Westchester Dr Ste 1 Youngstown (44515) *(G-20329)*
Progressive Medical Intl, Dublin *Also called PMI Supply Inc (G-10427)*
Progressive Medical Intl, Dublin *Also called Demarius Corporation (G-10319)*
Progressive Northwestern Insur..........440 461-5000
6300 Wilson Mills Rd Cleveland (44143) *(G-6319)*
Progressive Park LLC..........330 434-4514
5553 Broadview Rd Cleveland (44134) *(G-6320)*
Progressive Premier Insurance..........440 461-5000
6300 Wilson Mills Rd W33 Cleveland (44143) *(G-6321)*
Progressive Quality Care Inc (PA)..........216 661-6800
5553 Broadview Rd Parma (44134) *(G-15914)*
Progressive Select Insur Co..........440 461-5000
6300 Wilson Mills Rd Cleveland (44143) *(G-6322)*
Progressive Womens Care..........330 629-8466
6505 Market St Ste C112 Youngstown (44512) *(G-20330)*
Progrssive Oldsmobile Cadillac..........330 833-8585
7966 Hills & Dales Rd Ne Massillon (44646) *(G-13845)*
Progrssive Sweeping Contrs Inc (PA)..........419 464-0130
5202 Enterprise Blvd Toledo (43612) *(G-18138)*
Prohealth Partners Inc..........419 491-7150
12661 Eckel Junction Rd Perrysburg (43551) *(G-16045)*
Project C U R E Inc..........937 262-3500
200 Daruma Pkwy Dayton (45439) *(G-9836)*
Project Packaging Inc..........216 451-7878
17877 Saint Clair Ave # 6 Cleveland (44110) *(G-6323)*
Project Rebuild Inc..........330 639-1559
406 Shorb Ave Nw Canton (44703) *(G-2495)*
Projetech Inc..........513 481-4900
3815 Harrison Ave Cincinnati (45211) *(G-4346)*
Prokids Inc..........513 281-2000
2605 Burnet Ave Cincinnati (45219) *(G-4347)*
Prolift Industrial Equipment, West Chester *Also called Toyota Industries N Amer Inc (G-19164)*
Prolift Industrial Equipment, Dayton *Also called Toyota Industries N Amer Inc (G-9935)*
Proline Electric Inc..........740 687-4571
301 Cedar Hill Rd Lancaster (43130) *(G-12567)*
Proline Xpress Inc..........440 777-8120
24371 Lorain Rd Ste 206 North Olmsted (44070) *(G-15440)*
Prologue Research Intl Inc..........614 324-1500
580 N 4th St Ste 270 Columbus (43215) *(G-8570)*
Promanco Inc..........740 374-2120
27823 State Route 7 Marietta (45750) *(G-13491)*
Prome Conti Care Serv Corpo..........419 885-1715
5855 Monroe St Ste 200 Sylvania (43560) *(G-17607)*
PROMEDICA, Oregon *Also called Bay Park Community Hospital (G-15725)*
PROMEDICA, Maumee *Also called St Lukes Hospital (G-13980)*
Promedica, Toledo *Also called Toledo Hospital (G-18239)*
Promedica..........419 291-3450
1695 Indian Wood Cir # 100 Maumee (43537) *(G-13960)*
Promedica GI Physicians LLC..........419 843-7996
3439 Granite Cir Toledo (43617) *(G-18139)*
Promedica Gnt-Urinary Surgeons (PA)..........419 531-8558
3500 Executive Pkwy Toledo (43606) *(G-18140)*
Promedica Health Systems Inc (PA)..........567 585-7454
100 Madison Ave Toledo (43604) *(G-18141)*
Promedica Health Systems Inc..........419 891-6201
660 Beaver Creek Cir # 200 Maumee (43537) *(G-13961)*
PROMEDICA HOME HEALTH CARE, Sylvania *Also called Prome Conti Care Serv Corpo (G-17607)*
Promedica Physcn Cntinuum Svcs..........419 824-7200
5855 Monroe St Fl 1 Sylvania (43560) *(G-17608)*
Promedica Physician, Toledo *Also called Sunforest Ob Gyn Associates (G-18208)*
PROMEDICA PHYSICIAN GROUP, Sylvania *Also called Promedica Physcn Cntinuum Svcs (G-17608)*
Promedica Toledo Hospital, Toledo *Also called Toledo Hospital (G-18238)*
Promedidcal Heath Syytem, Maumee *Also called Promedica Health Systems Inc (G-13961)*
Promerus LLC..........440 922-0300
9921 Brecksville Rd Brecksville (44141) *(G-1843)*
Promohouse Inc..........614 324-9200
515 Park St Columbus (43215) *(G-8571)*
PROP SHOP, Cleveland *Also called Playhouse Square Holdg Co LLC (G-6287)*
Property 3, Cleveland *Also called Weston Inc (G-6748)*
Property Estate Management LLC..........513 684-0418
1526 Elm St Ste 1 Cincinnati (45202) *(G-4348)*
Pros Freight Corporation..........440 543-7555
16687 Hilltop Park Pl Chagrin Falls (44023) *(G-2730)*
Proscan Imaging LLC (PA)..........513 281-3400
5400 Kennedy Ave Ste 1 Cincinnati (45213) *(G-4349)*
Proscan Imaging LLC..........513 759-7350
7307 Tylers Corner Pl West Chester (45069) *(G-19133)*
Prosource, Blue Ash *Also called Cincinnati Copiers Inc (G-1556)*
Prospect Mold & Die Company..........330 929-3311
1100 Main St Cuyahoga Falls (44221) *(G-9214)*
Prosperity Care Service..........614 430-8626
2021 Dublin Rd Columbus (43228) *(G-8572)*
Protech Alarm Systems, Canton *Also called Protech Security Inc (G-2496)*

ALPHABETIC SECTION
Pure Led Solutions, Cleveland

Protech Security Inc...330 499-3555
7026 Sunset Strip Ave Nw Canton (44720) *(G-2496)*
Protem Homecare LLC...216 663-8188
3535 Lee Rd Cleveland (44120) *(G-6324)*
Proterra Inc (PA)...216 383-8449
29103 Euclid Ave Wickliffe (44092) *(G-19612)*
Protiviti Inc...216 696-6010
1001 Lakeside Ave E Cleveland (44114) *(G-6325)*
Prout Boiler Htg & Wldg Inc...330 744-0293
3124 Temple St Youngstown (44510) *(G-20331)*
Provantage LLC...330 494-3781
7576 Freedom Ave Nw North Canton (44720) *(G-15362)*
Provato LLC...440 546-0768
8748 Brecksville Rd # 125 Brecksville (44141) *(G-1844)*
Provenitfinance LLC...888 958-1060
195 Fox Glen Dr W Pickerington (43147) *(G-16103)*
Provia - Heritage Stone, Sugarcreek *Also called Provia Holdings Inc (G-17546)*
Provia Holdings Inc (PA)...330 852-4711
2150 State Route 39 Sugarcreek (44681) *(G-17546)*
Providence Care Center...419 627-2273
2025 Hayes Ave Sandusky (44870) *(G-16786)*
PROVIDENCE CARE CENTERS, Sandusky *Also called Commons of Providence (G-16744)*
Providence Health Partners LLC...937 297-8999
2912 Springboro W Ste 201 Moraine (45439) *(G-14816)*
Providence Hospital (PA)...513 853-5000
2446 Kipling Ave Cincinnati (45239) *(G-4350)*
Providence House Inc...216 651-5982
2050 W 32nd St Cleveland (44113) *(G-6326)*
Providence Medical Group Inc...937 297-8999
2912 Springboro W Ste 201 Moraine (45439) *(G-14817)*
Providence Rees Inc...614 833-6231
2111 Builders Pl Columbus (43204) *(G-8573)*
Provident Travel Corporation...513 247-1100
11309 Montgomery Rd Ste B Cincinnati (45249) *(G-4351)*
Provider Physicians Inc...614 755-3000
6096 E Main St Ste 112 Columbus (43213) *(G-8574)*
Provider Services, North Olmsted *Also called Foundations Hlth Solutions Inc (G-15423)*
Provider Services Inc...614 888-2021
111 Lazelle Rd Columbus (43235) *(G-8575)*
Providian Med Field Svc LLC...440 833-0460
5335 Avion Park Dr Unit A Highland Heights (44143) *(G-11871)*
Provimi North America Inc (HQ)...937 770-2400
10 Collective Way Brookville (45309) *(G-1965)*
Province Kent OH LLC...330 673-3808
609 S Lincoln St Ste F Kent (44240) *(G-12392)*
Province of St John The Baptis...513 241-5615
28 W Liberty St Cincinnati (45202) *(G-4352)*
Proware, Cincinnati *Also called Sadler-Necamp Financial Svcs (G-4466)*
Prt, Piqua *Also called Plastic Recycling Tech Inc (G-16161)*
Prudential, Columbus *Also called Residential One Realty Inc (G-8620)*
Prudential, Lima *Also called Pgim Inc (G-12858)*
Prudential Calhoon Co Realtors...614 777-1000
3535 Fishinger Blvd # 100 Hilliard (43026) *(G-11945)*
Prudential Insur Co of Amer...513 612-6400
3 Crowne Point Ct Ste 100 Cincinnati (45241) *(G-4353)*
Prudential Insur Co of Amer...330 896-7200
3515 Massillon Rd Ste 200 Uniontown (44685) *(G-18533)*
Prudential Insur Co of Amer...440 684-4409
5875 Landerbrook Dr # 110 Cleveland (44124) *(G-6327)*
Prudential Insur Co of Amer...419 893-6227
1705 Indian Wood Cir # 115 Maumee (43537) *(G-13962)*
Prudential Lucien Realty...216 226-4673
18630 Detroit Ave Lakewood (44107) *(G-12495)*
Prudential Select Properties (PA)...440 255-1111
7395 Center St Mentor (44060) *(G-14230)*
Prudential Welsh Realty...440 974-3100
7400 Center St Mentor (44060) *(G-14231)*
Prueter Enterprises Ltd...419 872-5343
25660 Dixie Hwy Ste 2 Perrysburg (43551) *(G-16046)*
Prus Construction Company...513 321-7774
5325 Wooster Pike Cincinnati (45226) *(G-4354)*
Prusa Inc...330 688-8500
1049 Mccauley Rd Stow (44224) *(G-17387)*
PS Lifestyle LLC...440 600-1595
55 Public Sq Ste 1180 Cleveland (44113) *(G-6328)*
Psa Airlines Inc...937 454-9338
3634 Cargo Rd Vandalia (45377) *(G-18694)*
Psa Airlines Inc (HQ)...937 454-1116
3400 Terminal Rd Vandalia (45377) *(G-18695)*
PSC Crane & Rigging, Piqua *Also called Piqua Steel Co (G-16159)*
PSC Metals Inc...330 455-0212
237 Tuscarawas St E Canton (44702) *(G-2497)*
PSC Metals Inc...614 299-4175
1283 Joyce Ave Columbus (43219) *(G-8576)*
PSC Metals Inc...234 208-2331
284 7th St Nw Barberton (44203) *(G-974)*
PSC Metals Inc...330 794-8300
701 W Hopocan Ave Barberton (44203) *(G-975)*
PSC Metals Inc...330 745-4437
701 W Hopocan Ave Barberton (44203) *(G-976)*
PSC Metals Inc...330 484-7610
3101 Varley Ave Sw Canton (44706) *(G-2498)*
PSC Metals Inc...216 341-3400
4250 E 68th Berdelle Cleveland (44105) *(G-6329)*
PSC Metals - Wooster LLC...330 264-8956
972 Columbus Rd Wooster (44691) *(G-19905)*
Pse, Marietta *Also called Power System Engineering Inc (G-13490)*
Pse Credit Union Inc (PA)...440 843-8300
5255 Regency Dr Cleveland (44129) *(G-6330)*
PSI Associates Inc...330 425-8474
2112 Case Pkwy Ste 10 Twinsburg (44087) *(G-18457)*
PSI Supply Chain Solutions LLC...614 389-4717
5050 Bradenton Ave Dublin (43017) *(G-10432)*
PSI Testing and Engineering, Cleveland *Also called Professional Service Inds Inc (G-6309)*
Psp Operations Inc...614 888-5700
7440 Pingue Dr Worthington (43085) *(G-19987)*
Psy-Care Inc...330 856-6663
8577 E Market St Warren (44484) *(G-18891)*
Psycare Inc (PA)...330 759-2310
2980 Belmont Ave Youngstown (44505) *(G-20332)*
Psychiatric Psychological Svcs, Elyria *Also called Santantonio Diana and Assoc (G-10677)*
Psychiatric Solutions Inc...440 953-3000
35900 Euclid Ave Willoughby (44094) *(G-19706)*
Psychiatric Solutions Inc...330 759-2700
615 Churchill Hubbard Rd Youngstown (44505) *(G-20333)*
Psychiatric Solutions Inc...419 891-9333
1725 Timber Line Rd Maumee (43537) *(G-13963)*
Psychiatric Solutions Inc...740 695-2131
67670 Traco Dr Saint Clairsville (43950) *(G-16653)*
Psychlgcal Behavioral Cons LLC (PA)...216 456-8123
25101 Chagrin Blvd # 100 Beachwood (44122) *(G-1116)*
Psychology Consultants Inc...330 764-7916
3591 Reserve Commons Dr # 301 Medina (44256) *(G-14115)*
Psychpros Inc...513 651-9500
2404 Auburn Ave Cincinnati (45219) *(G-4355)*
Ptc Holdings Inc...216 771-6960
1422 Euclid Ave Ste 1130 Cleveland (44115) *(G-6331)*
Pti, Holland *Also called Plastic Technologies Inc (G-12046)*
Pti, Bowling Green *Also called Phoenix Technologies Intl LLC (G-1789)*
Pti Qcs, Warren *Also called Pti Qlity Cntnment Sltions LLC (G-18892)*
Pti Qlity Cntnment Sltions LLC...313 304-8677
5655 Opportunity Dr Ste 4 Toledo (43612) *(G-18142)*
Pti Qlity Cntnment Sltions LLC...330 306-0125
5232 Tod Ave Sw Warren (44481) *(G-18892)*
Ptmj Enterprises...440 543-8000
32000 Aurora Rd Solon (44139) *(G-17042)*
Pts Prfssnal Technical Svc Inc (PA)...513 642-0111
503 Commercial Dr West Chester (45014) *(G-19134)*
PTX Flooring Inc...419 726-1775
2701 128th St Toledo (43611) *(G-18143)*
Pubco Corporation (PA)...216 881-5300
3830 Kelley Ave Cleveland (44114) *(G-6332)*
Public Broadcasting Found NW (PA)...419 380-4600
1270 S Detroit Ave Toledo (43614) *(G-18144)*
Public Safety, Cleveland *Also called City of Cleveland (G-5249)*
Public Safety Ohio Department...937 335-6209
1275 Experiment Farm Rd Troy (45373) *(G-18372)*
Public Safety Ohio Department...419 768-3955
3980 County Road 172 Mount Gilead (43338) *(G-14863)*
Public Safety Ohio Department...614 752-7600
1970 W Broad St Columbus (43223) *(G-8577)*
Public Service Company Okla (HQ)...614 716-1000
1 Riverside Plz Columbus (43215) *(G-8578)*
Public Service Dept, Portsmouth *Also called City of Portsmouth (G-16269)*
Public Services Department, Westerville *Also called City of Westerville (G-19382)*
Public Storage...216 220-7978
22800 Miles Rd Bedford Heights (44128) *(G-1357)*
Public Utilities- Water Div, Columbus *Also called City of Columbus (G-7285)*
Public Utilities- Water Div, Lockbourne *Also called City of Columbus (G-12947)*
Public Utlties-Electricity Div, Columbus *Also called City of Columbus (G-7278)*
Pulaski Head Start...419 636-8862
6678 Us Highway 127 Bryan (43506) *(G-2019)*
Pulmonary & Medicine Dayton (PA)...937 439-3600
4000 Miamisburg Centervil Miamisburg (45342) *(G-14338)*
Pulmonary Crtcal Care Spcalist...419 843-7800
1661 Holland Rd Ste 200 Maumee (43537) *(G-13964)*
Pulmonary Division, Cincinnati *Also called University of Cincinnati (G-4777)*
Pulte Homes Inc...330 239-1587
387 Medina Rd Ste 1700 Medina (44256) *(G-14116)*
Pump House Ministries...419 207-3900
400 Orange St Ashland (44805) *(G-692)*
Punderson Manor Resort, Newbury *Also called TW Recreational Services Inc (G-15262)*
Punderson Manor State Park, Newbury *Also called Xanterra Parks & Resorts Inc (G-15265)*
Puppy Pals Rescue Inc...937 426-2643
4241 Country Glen Cir Beavercreek (45432) *(G-1200)*
Pups Paradise...419 873-6115
12615 Roachton Rd Perrysburg (43551) *(G-16047)*
Pure Concept Ecosalon & Spa, Mason *Also called Pure Concept Salon Inc (G-13751)*
Pure Concept Salon Inc...513 770-2120
5625 Deerfield Cir Mason (45040) *(G-13751)*
Pure Led Solutions, Cleveland *Also called C-Auto Glass Inc (G-5169)*

ALPHABETIC

Pure Romance LLC (PA) ...513 248-8656
655 Plum St Ste 3 Cincinnati (45202) ***(G-4356)***
Purepay, Columbus *Also called Hbi Payments Ltd* ***(G-7806)***
Purina Animal Nutrition LLC ...419 224-2015
1111 N Cole St Lima (45805) ***(G-12863)***
Purina Animal Nutrition LLC ...330 682-1951
635 Collins Blvd Orrville (44667) ***(G-15784)***
Purina Animal Nutrition LLC ...330 879-2158
8485 Navarre Rd Sw Massillon (44646) ***(G-13846)***
Purple Marlin Inc ...440 323-1291
42208 Albrecht Rd Ste 1 Elyria (44035) ***(G-10672)***
Put In Bay Transportation ...419 285-4855
2009 Langram Rd Put In Bay (43456) ***(G-16370)***
Putman Janitorial Service Inc ...513 942-1900
4836 Duff Dr Ste D West Chester (45246) ***(G-19222)***
Putnam Cnty Amblatory Care Ctr, Lima *Also called St Ritas Medical Center* ***(G-12885)***
Putnam Cnty Amblatory Care Ctr, Lima *Also called St Ritas Medical Center* ***(G-12888)***
Putnam County Y M C A, Ottawa *Also called Young Mens Christian Assoc* ***(G-15805)***
Putnam Logistics, Columbus *Also called P & D Transportation Inc* ***(G-8500)***
Putnam Truck Load Direct, Zanesville *Also called P & D Transportation Inc* ***(G-20523)***
Pxp Ohio ...614 575-4242
6800 Tussing Rd Reynoldsburg (43068) ***(G-16473)***
Pymatuning Ambulance Service ...440 293-7991
153 Station St Andover (44003) ***(G-613)***
Pyramid Control Systems Inc ...513 679-7400
5546 Fair Ln Cincinnati (45227) ***(G-4357)***
Pyramid Controls, Cincinnati *Also called Pyramid Control Systems Inc* ***(G-4357)***
Pyramyd Air Ltd (PA) ...216 896-0893
5135 Naiman Pkwy Solon (44139) ***(G-17043)***
Pyxis Data Systems, Dublin *Also called Cardinal Health 301 LLC* ***(G-10277)***
Q Fact Marketing Research Inc (PA) ...513 891-2271
11767 Thayer Ln Cincinnati (45249) ***(G-4358)***
Q Laboratories, Cincinnati *Also called Q Labs LLC* ***(G-4359)***
Q Labs LLC (PA) ...513 471-1300
1400 Harrison Ave Cincinnati (45214) ***(G-4359)***
Q, The, Cleveland *Also called Cavaliers Operating Co LLC* ***(G-5194)***
Qbase LLC (PA) ...888 458-0345
3725 Pentagon Blvd # 100 Beavercreek (45431) ***(G-1201)***
QBS Inc ...330 821-8801
1548 S Linden Ave Alliance (44601) ***(G-552)***
Qes Pressure Control LLC ...724 324-2391
64201 Wintergreen Rd Lore City (43755) ***(G-13087)***
Qh Management Company LLC ...440 497-1100
11080 Concord Hambden Rd Concord Twp (44077) ***(G-9034)***
Qsr Parent Co ...330 425-8472
1700 Highland Rd Twinsburg (44087) ***(G-18458)***
QT Equipment Company (PA) ...330 724-3055
151 W Dartmore Ave Akron (44301) ***(G-401)***
Quad Ambulance District ...330 866-9847
6930 Minerva Rd Se Waynesburg (44688) ***(G-18981)***
Quad/Graphics Inc ...614 276-4800
4051 Fondorf Dr Columbus (43228) ***(G-8579)***
Quadax Inc ...330 759-4600
17 Colonial Dr Ste 101 Youngstown (44505) ***(G-20334)***
Quadax Inc (PA) ...440 777-6300
7500 Old Oak Blvd Middleburg Heights (44130) ***(G-14384)***
Quadax Inc ...614 882-1200
4151 Executive Pkwy # 360 Westerville (43081) ***(G-19438)***
Quadco Rehabilitation Center (PA) ...419 682-1011
427 N Defiance St Stryker (43557) ***(G-17537)***
Quadco Rehabilitation Center ...419 445-1950
600 Oak St Archbold (43502) ***(G-642)***
Quail Hollow Management Inc ...440 639-4000
11295 Quail Hollow Dr Painesville (44077) ***(G-15874)***
Quail Hollow Resort, Concord Twp *Also called Qh Management Company LLC* ***(G-9034)***
Quail Hollow Resort Cntry CLB, Painesville *Also called Quail Hollow Management Inc* ***(G-15874)***
Quaker Heights Care Community, Waynesville *Also called Quaker Heights Nursing HM Inc* ***(G-18986)***
Quaker Heights Nursing HM Inc ...513 897-6050
514 High St Waynesville (45068) ***(G-18986)***
Quaker Steak & Lube, Westlake *Also called Travelcenters of America LLC* ***(G-19557)***
Quaker Steak and Lube, Westlake *Also called Travelcenters of America LLC* ***(G-19556)***
Qualchoice Inc ...330 656-1231
3605 Warrensville Ctr Rd Beachwood (44122) ***(G-1117)***
Quality Aero Inc (PA) ...614 436-1609
6797 N High St Ste 324 Worthington (43085) ***(G-19988)***
Quality Air Heating and AC, Columbus *Also called Kusan Inc* ***(G-8018)***
Quality Assured Cleaning Inc ...614 798-1505
6407 Nicholas Dr Columbus (43235) ***(G-8580)***
Quality Block & Supply Inc (HQ) ...330 364-4411
Rr 250 Mount Eaton (44659) ***(G-14850)***
Quality Care Nursing Svc Inc ...740 377-9095
501 Washington St Ste 13 South Point (45680) ***(G-17096)***
Quality Carriers Inc ...419 222-6800
1586 Findlay Rd Lima (45801) ***(G-12864)***
Quality Cement Inc ...216 676-8838
10840 Brookpark Rd Cleveland (44130) ***(G-6333)***
Quality Cleaners of Ohio Inc ...330 688-5616
3773 Darrow Rd Stow (44224) ***(G-17388)***
Quality Cleaning Systems LLC ...330 567-2050
7945 Shreve Rd Shreve (44676) ***(G-16908)***
Quality Clg Svc of NW Ohio ...419 335-9105
861 N Fulton St Wauseon (43567) ***(G-18961)***
Quality Control Inspection (PA) ...440 359-1900
40 Tarbell Ave Cleveland (44146) ***(G-6334)***
Quality Electrical & Mech Inc ...419 294-3591
1190 E Kibby St Lima (45804) ***(G-12865)***
Quality Fabricated Metals Inc ...330 332-7008
14000 W Middletown Rd Salem (44460) ***(G-16707)***
Quality Inn, Bellville *Also called Bellville Hotel Company* ***(G-1421)***
Quality Inn, Montpelier *Also called Bob Mor Inc* ***(G-14737)***
Quality Inn, Port Clinton *Also called Lodging Industry Inc* ***(G-16250)***
Quality Inn, Tiffin *Also called McPaul Corp* ***(G-17684)***
Quality Inn, Brookpark *Also called Chu Airport Inn Inc* ***(G-1939)***
Quality Inn, Richfield *Also called Richfield Banquet & Confer* ***(G-16526)***
Quality Inn, Mansfield *Also called Mansfield Hotel Partnership* ***(G-13332)***
Quality Inn, Marietta *Also called Motel Investments Marietta Inc* ***(G-13479)***
Quality Life Providers LLC ...614 527-9999
3974 Brown Park Dr Ste E Hilliard (43026) ***(G-11946)***
Quality Lines Inc ...740 815-1165
2440 Bright Rd Findlay (45840) ***(G-11078)***
Quality Maintenance Company, Marion *Also called Quality Masonry Company Inc* ***(G-13573)***
Quality Masonry Company Inc ...740 387-6720
1001 S Prospect St # 101 Marion (43302) ***(G-13573)***
Quality Mechanical Services, Lima *Also called Quality Electrical & Mech Inc* ***(G-12865)***
Quality One Technologies Inc ...937 855-6511
36 N Plum St Germantown (45327) ***(G-11401)***
Quality Plant Productions Inc ...440 526-8711
4586 Newton Rd Richfield (44286) ***(G-16523)***
Quality Plus, Painesville *Also called Emily Management Inc* ***(G-15854)***
Quality Restaurant Supply, Cincinnati *Also called Quality Supply Co* ***(G-4360)***
Quality Solutions Inc ...440 933-9946
P.O. Box 40147 Cleveland (44140) ***(G-6335)***
Quality Steels Corp (HQ) ...937 294-4133
2221 Arbor Blvd Moraine (45439) ***(G-14818)***
Quality Supply & Rental Inc (PA) ...740 286-7517
720 Veterans Dr Jackson (45640) ***(G-12317)***
Quality Supply Chain Co-Op Inc ...614 764-3124
1 Dave Thomas Blvd Dublin (43017) ***(G-10433)***
Quality Supply Co (PA) ...937 890-6114
4020 Rev Dr Cincinnati (45232) ***(G-4360)***
Quality Towing, West Chester *Also called Sprandel Enterprises Inc* ***(G-19158)***
Quality Trailers of Oh Inc ...330 332-9630
1664 Salem Pkwy W Salem (44460) ***(G-16708)***
Quality Welding Inc ...419 483-6067
104 Ronald Ln Bellevue (44811) ***(G-1416)***
Qualtech NP, Batavia *Also called Curtiss-Wright Flow Control* ***(G-1008)***
Qualtech NP, Cincinnati *Also called Curtiss-Wright Flow Control* ***(G-2910)***
Qualtech NP, Cincinnati *Also called Curtiss-Wright Flow Ctrl Corp* ***(G-2911)***
Quandel Construction Group Inc ...717 657-0909
774 Park Meadow Rd Westerville (43081) ***(G-19439)***
Quandel Group Main Office, Westerville *Also called Quandel Construction Group Inc* ***(G-19439)***
Quanexus Inc ...937 885-7272
571 Congress Park Dr Dayton (45459) ***(G-9837)***
Quantech Services Inc ...937 490-8461
4141 Colonel Glenn Hwy # 273 Beavercreek Township (45431) ***(G-1283)***
Quantum Construction Company ...513 351-6903
1654 Sherman Ave Cincinnati (45212) ***(G-4361)***
Quantum Health Inc ...614 846-4318
7450 Huntington Park Dr Columbus (43235) ***(G-8581)***
Quantum Metals Inc ...513 573-0144
3675 Taft Rd Lebanon (45036) ***(G-12638)***
Quantum Services, Columbus *Also called Accurate Inventory and C* ***(G-6936)***
Quasonix Inc (PA) ...513 942-1287
6025 Schumacher Park Dr West Chester (45069) ***(G-19135)***
Quebe Holdings Inc (PA) ...937 222-2290
1985 Founders Dr Dayton (45420) ***(G-9838)***
Queen City Blacktop Company ...513 251-8400
2130 Osterfeld St Cincinnati (45214) ***(G-4362)***
Queen City Electric Inc ...513 591-2600
4015 Cherry St Ste 2 Cincinnati (45223) ***(G-4363)***
Queen City General & Vascular (PA) ...513 232-8181
10506 Montgomery Rd # 101 Cincinnati (45242) ***(G-4364)***
Queen City Generl Consultants, Cincinnati *Also called Queen City General & Vascular* ***(G-4364)***
Queen City Hospice LLC ...513 510-4406
8250 Kenwood Crossing Way # 200 Cincinnati (45236) ***(G-4365)***
Queen City Jobs, Cincinnati *Also called Hubbard Radio Cincinnati LLC* ***(G-3794)***
Queen City Mechanicals Inc ...513 353-1430
1950 Waycross Rd Cincinnati (45240) ***(G-4366)***
Queen City Medical Group ...513 528-5600
7991 Beechmont Ave Cincinnati (45255) ***(G-4367)***
Queen City of Physicians, Cincinnati *Also called Queen City Physicians* ***(G-4368)***
Queen City Physicians ...513 872-2061
2475 W Galbraith Rd Ste 3 Cincinnati (45239) ***(G-4368)***

Queen City Physicians Ltd 513 791-6992
7825 Laurel Ave Cincinnati (45243) *(G-4369)*
Queen City Polymers Inc (PA) 513 779-0990
6101 Schumacher Park Dr West Chester (45069) *(G-19136)*
Queen City Racquet Club LLC 513 771-2835
11275 Chester Rd Cincinnati (45246) *(G-4370)*
Queen City Reprographics 513 326-2300
2863 E Sharon Rd Cincinnati (45241) *(G-4371)*
Queen City Transportation LLC 513 941-8700
211 Township Ave Ste 2 Cincinnati (45216) *(G-4372)*
Queen Cy Hspice Plliative Care, Cincinnati *Also called Queen City Hospice LLC (G-4365)*
Queen Cy Spt Mdcine Rhbltation 513 561-1111
3950 Red Bank Rd Cincinnati (45227) *(G-4373)*
Queensgate Food Group LLC 513 721-5503
619 Linn St Cincinnati (45203) *(G-4374)*
Queensgate Food Service, Cincinnati *Also called Queensgate Food Group LLC (G-4374)*
Quest Ase, Cincinnati *Also called Quest Global Services-Na Inc (G-4376)*
Quest Diagnostics, Beavercreek *Also called Wright State University (G-1222)*
Quest Global Services-Na Inc 513 563-8855
11499 Chester Rd Ste 600 Cincinnati (45246) *(G-4375)*
Quest Global Services-Na Inc (HQ) 513 648-4900
11499 Chester Rd Ste 600 Cincinnati (45246) *(G-4376)*
Quest Quality Services LLC 419 704-7407
8036 Joshua Ln Maumee (43537) *(G-13965)*
Quest Recovery Prevention Svcs (PA) 330 453-8252
1341 Market Ave N Canton (44714) *(G-2499)*
Quest Software Inc 614 336-9223
6500 Emerald Pkwy Ste 400 Dublin (43016) *(G-10434)*
Questar Solutions LLC 330 966-2070
7948 Freedom Ave Nw North Canton (44720) *(G-15363)*
Questar, Inc., North Canton *Also called Questar Solutions LLC (G-15363)*
Questmark, Cincinnati *Also called Diversipak Inc (G-3495)*
Questmark, Stow *Also called Centimark Corporation (G-17356)*
Quick Delivery Service Inc (HQ) 330 453-3709
2207 Kimball Rd Se Canton (44707) *(G-2500)*
Quick Solutions Inc 614 825-8000
440 Polaris Pkwy Ste 500 Westerville (43082) *(G-19347)*
Quick Tab II Inc (PA) 419 448-6622
241 Heritage Dr Tiffin (44883) *(G-17694)*
Quicken Loans Arena, Cleveland *Also called Cavaliers Holdings LLC (G-5193)*
Quicken Loans Inc 216 586-8900
100 Public Sq Ste 400 Cleveland (44113) *(G-6336)*
Quickslide, Springboro *Also called Hardy Diagnostics (G-17121)*
Quilalea Corporation 330 487-0777
3861 Sawbridge Dr Richfield (44286) *(G-16524)*
Quilter Cvlian Cnsrvation Camp, Green Springs *Also called W S O S Community A (G-11480)*
Quincy Amusements Inc 419 874-2154
2005 Hollenbeck Dr Perrysburg (43551) *(G-16048)*
Quincy Mall Inc (PA) 614 228-5331
191 W Nationwide Blvd # 200 Columbus (43215) *(G-8582)*
Quintus Technologies LLC 614 891-2732
8270 Green Meadows Dr N Lewis Center (43035) *(G-12705)*
Quotient Technology Inc 513 229-8659
5191 Natorp Blvd Ste 420 Mason (45040) *(G-13752)*
Qvidian Corporation 513 631-1155
10260 Alliance Rd Ste 210 Blue Ash (45242) *(G-1669)*
Qwaide Enterprises LLC 614 209-0551
6044 Phar Lap Dr New Albany (43054) *(G-15003)*
Qwest Corporation 614 793-9258
4650 Lakehurst Ct Ste 100 Dublin (43016) *(G-10435)*
R & A Sports Inc 216 289-2254
23780 Lakeland Blvd Euclid (44132) *(G-10773)*
R & B Contractors LLC 513 738-0954
3730 Schloss Ln Shandon (45063) *(G-16873)*
R & D Nestle Center Inc 937 642-7015
809 Collins Ave Marysville (43040) *(G-13646)*
R & E Joint Venture Inc 614 891-9404
6843 Regency Dr Westerville (43082) *(G-19348)*
R & F Inc 419 868-2909
6228 Merger Dr Holland (43528) *(G-12047)*
R & H Service Inc 330 626-2888
9420 State Route 14 Streetsboro (44241) *(G-17427)*
R & J Investment Co Inc 440 934-5204
37800 French Creek Rd Avon (44011) *(G-915)*
R & J Trucking, Youngstown *Also called American Bulk Commodities Inc (G-20103)*
R & J Trucking Inc (HQ) 800 262-9365
8063 Southern Blvd Youngstown (44512) *(G-20335)*
R & J Trucking Inc 330 758-0841
147 Curtis Dr Shelby (44875) *(G-16903)*
R & J Trucking Inc 740 374-3050
14530 Sr 7 Marietta (45750) *(G-13492)*
R & J Trucking Inc 440 960-1508
5250 Baumhart Rd Lorain (44053) *(G-13072)*
R & J Trucking Inc 419 837-9937
3423 Genoa Rd Perrysburg (43551) *(G-16049)*
R & K Gorby LLC 419 222-0004
1920 Roschman Ave Lima (45804) *(G-12866)*
R & L Carriers, Norwalk *Also called R & L Transfer Inc (G-15589)*
R & L Carriers Inc 419 874-5976
134 W South Boundary St Perrysburg (43551) *(G-16050)*
R & L Transfer Inc 216 531-3324
1403 State Route 18 Norwalk (44857) *(G-15589)*
R & L Transfer Inc 330 743-3609
5550 Dunlap Rd Youngstown (44515) *(G-20336)*
R & L Transfer Inc 330 482-5800
1320 Springfield Rd Columbiana (44408) *(G-6862)*
R & M, Springfield *Also called R&M Materials Handling Inc (G-17262)*
R & M Delivery 740 574-2113
8375 Gallia Pike Franklin Furnace (45629) *(G-11173)*
R & M Fluid Power Inc 330 758-2766
7953 Southern Blvd Youngstown (44512) *(G-20337)*
R & R Inc (PA) 330 799-1536
44 Victoria Rd Youngstown (44515) *(G-20338)*
R & R Cleveland Mack Sales, Youngstown *Also called R & R Inc (G-20338)*
R & R Hvac Systems 419 861-0266
1650 Eber Rd Ste E Holland (43528) *(G-12048)*
R & R Pipeline Inc (PA) 740 345-3692
155 Dayton Rd Ne Newark (43055) *(G-15230)*
R & R Sanitation Inc 330 325-2311
1447 Martin Rd Mogadore (44260) *(G-14683)*
R & R Truck Sales Inc 330 784-5881
1650 E Waterloo Rd Akron (44306) *(G-402)*
R & R Wiring Contractors Inc 513 752-6304
1269 Clough Pike Batavia (45103) *(G-1022)*
R & S Halley & Co Inc 614 771-0388
6368 Scioto Darby Rd Hilliard (43026) *(G-11947)*
R & S Lines Inc 419 682-7807
102 Ellis St Stryker (43557) *(G-17538)*
R & Y Holding 419 353-3464
142 Campbell Hill Rd Bowling Green (43402) *(G-1792)*
R A Hermes Inc 513 251-5200
4015 Cherry St Ste 27 Cincinnati (45223) *(G-4377)*
R A I, Cleveland *Also called Research Associates Inc (G-6381)*
R and G Enterprises of Ohio 440 845-6870
9213 Harrow Dr Cleveland (44129) *(G-6337)*
R and J Corporation 440 871-6009
24142 Detroit Rd Westlake (44145) *(G-19536)*
R B C Apollo Equity Partners (HQ) 216 875-2626
600 Superior Ave E # 2300 Cleveland (44114) *(G-6338)*
R B Development Company Inc 513 829-8100
5200 Camelot Dr Fairfield (45014) *(G-10897)*
R B Jergens Contractors Inc 937 669-9799
11418 N Dixie Dr Vandalia (45377) *(G-18696)*
R B Stout Inc 330 666-8811
1285 N Clvland Msslion Rd Akron (44333) *(G-403)*
R C Enterprises Inc 330 782-2111
5234 Southern Blvd Ste C Youngstown (44512) *(G-20339)*
R C Hemm Glass Shops Inc (PA) 937 773-5591
514 S Main St Piqua (45356) *(G-16163)*
R C M, Akron *Also called Rubber City Machinery Corp (G-419)*
R D D Inc (PA) 216 781-5858
4719 Blythin Rd Cleveland (44125) *(G-6339)*
R D Jergens Contractors Inc (PA) 937 669-9799
11418 N Dixie Dr Vandalia (45377) *(G-18697)*
R D Jones Excavating Inc 419 648-5870
10225 Alger Rd Harrod (45850) *(G-11813)*
R Dorsey & Company Inc 614 486-8900
400 W Wilson Bridge Rd # 105 Worthington (43085) *(G-19989)*
R E Kramig & Co Inc 513 761-4010
323 S Wayne Ave Cincinnati (45215) *(G-4378)*
R E Richards Inc 330 499-1001
9701 Cleveland Ave Nw # 100 Canton (44720) *(G-2501)*
R E Warner & Associates Inc 440 835-9400
25777 Detroit Rd Ste 200 Westlake (44145) *(G-19537)*
R E Watson Inc 513 863-0070
2728 Hamilton Cleves Rd Hamilton (45013) *(G-11765)*
R G Seller Co, Moraine *Also called R G Sellers Company (G-14819)*
R G Sellers Company (PA) 937 299-1545
3185 Elbee Rd Moraine (45439) *(G-14819)*
R G Smith Company 419 524-4778
166 W 6th St Mansfield (44902) *(G-13352)*
R I D Inc 419 251-4790
2222 Cherry St Ste 1400 Toledo (43608) *(G-18145)*
R J Martin Elec Svcs Inc 216 662-7100
22841 Aurora Rd Bedford Heights (44146) *(G-1358)*
R J W, Cleveland *Also called Total Transportation Trckg Inc (G-6604)*
R K Campf Corp 330 332-7089
465 Newgarden Ave Salem (44460) *(G-16709)*
R K Hydro-Vac Inc (PA) 937 773-8600
322 Wyndham Way Piqua (45356) *(G-16164)*
R K Industries Inc 419 523-5001
725 N Locust St Ottawa (45875) *(G-15804)*
R Kelly Inc 513 631-8488
7645 Production Dr Cincinnati (45237) *(G-4379)*
R L B Inc (PA) 513 793-3758
10149 Kenwood Rd Blue Ash (45242) *(G-1670)*
R L Baugher, Dvm, Warren *Also called Countryside Veterinary Service (G-18839)*
R L Fortney Management Inc (PA) 440 716-4000
31269 Bradley Rd North Olmsted (44070) *(G-15441)*
R L King Insurance Agency 419 255-9947
7723 Airport Hwy Ste F Holland (43528) *(G-12049)*

ALPHABETIC

(PA)=Parent Co (HQ)=Headquarters (DH)=Div Headquarters
2018 Harris Ohio Services Directory
1299

R L Lipton Distributing LLC....800 321-6553
425 Victoria Rd Ste B Austintown (44515) ***(G-872)***
R L Lipton Distributing Co....216 475-4150
5900 Pennsylvania Ave Maple Heights (44137) ***(G-13414)***
R L Morrissey & Assoc Inc (PA)....440 498-3730
30450 Bruce Indus Pkwy Solon (44139) ***(G-17044)***
R L O Inc (PA)....937 620-9998
466 Windsor Park Dr Dayton (45459) ***(G-9839)***
R L S Corporation....740 773-1440
990 Eastern Ave Chillicothe (45601) ***(G-2872)***
R L S Recycling, Chillicothe *Also called R L S Corporation* ***(G-2872)***
R M X, Roseville *Also called Rmx Freight Systems Inc* ***(G-16602)***
R N R Consulting, Cleveland *Also called Rahim Inc* ***(G-6349)***
R P Cunningham DDS Inc....614 885-2022
7227 N High St Ste 1 Worthington (43085) ***(G-19990)***
R P L Corporation....937 335-0021
1375 W Market St Troy (45373) ***(G-18373)***
R P Marketing Public Relations....419 241-2221
1500 Timber Wolf Dr Holland (43528) ***(G-12050)***
R S Sewing Inc....330 478-3360
1387 Clarendon Ave Sw # 10 Canton (44710) ***(G-2502)***
R Square Inc....216 328-2077
6100 Oak Tree Blvd # 200 Cleveland (44131) ***(G-6340)***
R T A, Lima *Also called Allen Cnty Regional Trnst Auth* ***(G-12733)***
R T A, Dayton *Also called Greater Dyton Rgnal Trnst Auth* ***(G-9590)***
R T Industries Inc (PA)....937 335-5784
110 Foss Way Troy (45373) ***(G-18374)***
R T Industries Inc....937 339-8313
1625 Troy Sidney Rd Troy (45373) ***(G-18375)***
R T Vernal Paving Inc....330 549-3189
11299 South Ave North Lima (44452) ***(G-15407)***
R W Earhart Company....937 753-1191
700 Mote Dr Covington (45318) ***(G-9138)***
R W Godbey Railroad Services....513 651-3800
2815 Spring Grove Ave Cincinnati (45225) ***(G-4380)***
R W Sauder Inc....330 359-5440
2648 Us Rt 62 Winesburg (44690) ***(G-19806)***
R W Sidley Incorporated (PA)....440 352-9343
436 Casement Ave Painesville (44077) ***(G-15875)***
R W Sidley Incorporated....440 352-9343
436 Casement Ave Painesville (44077) ***(G-15876)***
R W Sidley Incorporated....330 793-7374
3424 Oregon Ave Youngstown (44509) ***(G-20340)***
R&F Erectors Inc....513 574-8273
5763 Snyder Rd Cincinnati (45247) ***(G-4381)***
R&M Materials Handling Inc....937 328-5100
4501 Gateway Blvd Springfield (45502) ***(G-17262)***
R+l Pramount Trnsp Systems Inc....937 382-1494
600 Gilliam Rd Wilmington (45177) ***(G-19780)***
R-3 Enterprises, Sidney *Also called Roe Transport Inc* ***(G-16951)***
R-Cap Security LLC....216 761-6355
7800 Superior Ave Cleveland (44103) ***(G-6341)***
R-K-Campf Transport, Salem *Also called R K Campf Corp* ***(G-16709)***
R.dorsey & Company, Worthington *Also called R Dorsey & Company Inc* ***(G-19989)***
Ra Consultants LLC....513 469-6600
10856 Kenwood Rd Blue Ash (45242) ***(G-1671)***
RA Staff Company Inc....440 891-9900
16500 W Sprague Rd Cleveland (44130) ***(G-6342)***
Racaza International LLC....614 973-9266
555 N Metro Pls Ste 245 Dublin (43017) ***(G-10436)***
Raceway Foods Inc....513 932-2457
665 N Brdway Lbnon Rceway Lebanon (45036) ***(G-12639)***
Rack & Ballauer Excvtg Co Inc....513 738-7000
11321 Paddys Run Rd Hamilton (45013) ***(G-11766)***
Rack Seven Paving Co Inc....513 271-4863
7208 Main St Cincinnati (45244) ***(G-4382)***
Racksquared LLC....614 737-8812
325 E Spring St Columbus (43215) ***(G-8583)***
Raco Industries LLC (HQ)....513 984-2101
5481 Creek Rd Blue Ash (45242) ***(G-1672)***
Raco Wireless LLC (HQ)....513 870-6480
4460 Carver Woods Dr # 100 Blue Ash (45242) ***(G-1673)***
Racquet Club At Harper's Point, Cincinnati *Also called Towne Properties Assoc Inc* ***(G-4670)***
RAD-Con Inc (PA)....440 871-5720
13001 Athens Ave Ste 300 Lakewood (44107) ***(G-12496)***
Radebaugh-Fetzer Company....440 878-4700
22400 Ascoa Ct Strongsville (44149) ***(G-17501)***
Radial South LP....678 584-4047
6360-6440 Port Rd Groveport (43125) ***(G-11665)***
Radio Page Leasing, Cleveland *Also called Answering Service Inc* ***(G-5041)***
Radio Promotions....513 381-5000
2518 Spring Grove Ave Cincinnati (45214) ***(G-4383)***
Radio Seaway Inc....216 916-6100
1375 Euclid Ave Ste 450 Cleveland (44115) ***(G-6343)***
Radio Station Wclv, Cleveland *Also called Radio Seaway Inc* ***(G-6343)***
Radiohio Incorporated....614 460-3850
605 S Front St Fl 3 Columbus (43215) ***(G-8584)***
Radiology & Imaging Services....330 864-0832
2603 W Market St Ste 110 Akron (44313) ***(G-404)***
Radiology Assoc Canton Inc....330 363-2842
2600 6th St Sw Canton (44710) ***(G-2503)***
Radiology Department, Steubenville *Also called Trinity Health System* ***(G-17339)***
Radiology Physicians Inc....614 717-9840
3769 Columbus Pike # 220 Delaware (43015) ***(G-10121)***
Radiometer America Inc....440 925-2977
810 Sharon Dr Westlake (44145) ***(G-19538)***
Radisson Eastlake, Eastlake *Also called Eastlake Lodging LLC* ***(G-10546)***
Radisson Hotel Cleve....440 734-5060
25070 Country Club Blvd North Olmsted (44070) ***(G-15442)***
Radisson Hotel Cleveland Gtwy....216 377-9000
651 Huron Rd E Cleveland (44115) ***(G-6344)***
Radisson Inn, Cleveland *Also called Radisson Hotel Cleveland Gtwy* ***(G-6344)***
Radius Hospitality MGT LLC....330 735-2211
2650 Lodge Rd Sw Sherrodsville (44675) ***(G-16906)***
Radix Wire Co (PA)....216 731-9191
26000 Lakeland Blvd Cleveland (44132) ***(G-6345)***
Radix Wire Company, The, Cleveland *Also called Radix Wire Co* ***(G-6345)***
Rae Ann West Lake, Westlake *Also called Rae-Ann Holdings Inc* ***(G-19539)***
Rae-Ann Center, Cleveland *Also called Raeann Inc* ***(G-6348)***
Rae-Ann Enterprises Inc....440 249-5092
27310 W Oviatt Rd Cleveland (44140) ***(G-6346)***
Rae-Ann Geneva Skld Nrsng/Rehb, Geneva *Also called Raeann Inc* ***(G-11368)***
Rae-Ann Holdings Inc....440 871-0500
28303 Detroit Rd Westlake (44145) ***(G-19539)***
Rae-Ann Holdings Inc....440 871-5181
29505 Detroit Rd Cleveland (44145) ***(G-6347)***
Rae-Ann Suburban, Cleveland *Also called Rae-Ann Enterprises Inc* ***(G-6346)***
Rae-Ann Suburban Inc....440 871-5181
29505 Detroit Rd Westlake (44145) ***(G-19540)***
Rae-Suburban, Cleveland *Also called Rae-Ann Holdings Inc* ***(G-6347)***
Raeann Inc....440 466-5733
839 W Main St Geneva (44041) ***(G-11368)***
Raeann Inc (PA)....440 871-5181
P.O. Box 40175 Bay Village (44140) ***(G-6348)***
Raf Automation, Solon *Also called Fak Group Inc* ***(G-17006)***
Raf Celina LLC....216 464-6626
1915-1955 Haveman Rd Celina (45822) ***(G-2660)***
Rahal Land and Racing, Hilliard *Also called Team Rahal Inc* ***(G-11957)***
Rahf IV Kent LLC....216 621-6060
1546 S Water St Kent (44240) ***(G-12393)***
Rahim Inc....216 621-8977
1111 Superior Ave E # 1330 Cleveland (44114) ***(G-6349)***
Rahn Dental Group Inc....937 435-0324
5660 Far Hills Ave Dayton (45429) ***(G-9840)***
Rail Logistics Inc (PA)....440 933-6500
32861 Pin Oak Pkwy Ste D Avon Lake (44012) ***(G-938)***
Railway Equipment Lsg & Maint, Solon *Also called RELAM Inc* ***(G-17046)***
Railwork Track Services, North Jackson *Also called Railworks Corporation* ***(G-15387)***
Railworks Corporation....330 538-2261
1550 N Bailey Rd North Jackson (44451) ***(G-15387)***
Rain Tree, The, Mansfield *Also called County of Richland* ***(G-13277)***
Rainbow Bowling Lanes, Columbus *Also called Rainbow Lanes Inc* ***(G-8586)***
Rainbow Connection Day Care, Mentor *Also called Delth Corporation* ***(G-14169)***
Rainbow Data Systems Inc....937 431-8000
2358 Lakeview Dr Ste A Beavercreek (45431) ***(G-1202)***
Rainbow Flea Market Inc (PA)....614 291-3133
865 King Ave Columbus (43212) ***(G-8585)***
Rainbow Lanes Inc....614 491-7155
3224 S High St Columbus (43207) ***(G-8586)***
Rainbow Station Day Care Inc (PA)....614 759-8667
226 Durand St Pickerington (43147) ***(G-16104)***
Rainforest At Zoo, Cleveland *Also called Cleveland Metroparks* ***(G-5329)***
Raintree Country Club Inc....330 699-3232
4350 Mayfair Rd Uniontown (44685) ***(G-18534)***
Raise, Chesterland *Also called RES-Care Inc* ***(G-2802)***
Raisin Rack Inc (PA)....614 882-5886
2545 W Schrock Rd Westerville (43081) ***(G-19440)***
Raisin Rack Natural Food Mkt, Westerville *Also called Raisin Rack Inc* ***(G-19440)***
Raitz Inc....513 769-1200
11402 Reading Rd Cincinnati (45241) ***(G-4384)***
Rak Corrosion Control Inc....440 985-2171
7455 S Dewey Rd Amherst (44001) ***(G-602)***
Rakesh Ranjan MD & Assoc Inc (PA)....216 375-9897
12395 Mccracken Rd Ste A Cleveland (44125) ***(G-6350)***
Ram Construction Services....440 740-0100
100 Corporation Ctr # 4 Broadview Heights (44147) ***(G-1890)***
Ram Construction Services of....513 297-1857
4710 Ashley Dr West Chester (45011) ***(G-19137)***
Ram Resources, Dayton *Also called Ram Restoration LLC* ***(G-9841)***
Ram Restoration LLC....937 347-7418
11125 Yankee St Ste A Dayton (45458) ***(G-9841)***
Rama Inc....614 473-9888
2890 Airport Dr Columbus (43219) ***(G-8587)***
Rama Tika Developers LLC....419 806-6446
719 Earick Rd Mansfield (44903) ***(G-13353)***
Ramada Hotel & Conference Ctr, Toledo *Also called Westgate Limited Partnership* ***(G-18307)***
Ramada Inn, Dublin *Also called Sb Hotel LLC* ***(G-10449)***
Ramada Inn, Portsmouth *Also called Canter Inn Inc* ***(G-16267)***
Ramada Inn, Sandusky *Also called Americas Best Value Inn* ***(G-16726)***

Ramada Inn, Wadsworth *Also called Akron Inn Limited Partnership* ***(G-18745)***
Ramada Inn, Cleveland *Also called Moti Corporation* ***(G-6080)***
Ramada Inn, Wickliffe *Also called Inn At Wickliffe LLC* ***(G-19603)***
Ramada Inn Cumberland Hotel, Cincinnati *Also called Cumberland Gap LLC* ***(G-3446)***
Ramada Inn East - Airport, Columbus *Also called Broad Street Hotel Assoc LP* ***(G-7147)***
Ramada Plaza Akron, Akron *Also called Akron Citicenter Hotel LLC* ***(G-31)***
Ramada Xenia, Xenia *Also called AK Group Hotels Inc* ***(G-20040)***
Ramar-Genesis, Akron *Also called Community Drug Board Inc* ***(G-154)***
Rambus Inc 440 397-2549
6611 W Snowville Rd Brecksville (44141) ***(G-1845)***
Ramos Trucking Corporation 216 781-0770
2890 W 3rd St Cleveland (44113) ***(G-6351)***
Ran Temps Inc 216 991-5500
12800 Shaker Blvd Cleveland (44120) ***(G-6352)***
Ranac Computer Corporation 317 844-0141
3460 S Dixie Dr Moraine (45439) ***(G-14820)***
Rand Loveland, Loveland *Also called Loveland Health Care Ctr LLC* ***(G-13141)***
Randall Mortgage Services (PA) 614 336-7948
655 Metro Pl S Ste 600 Dublin (43017) ***(G-10437)***
Randall R Leab 330 689-6263
1895 Township Road 1215 Ashland (44805) ***(G-693)***
Randolph & Assoc Real Estate, Columbus *Also called Randolph and Associates RE* ***(G-8588)***
Randolph and Associates RE 614 269-8418
239 Buttonwood Ct Columbus (43230) ***(G-8588)***
Rands Trucking Inc 740 397-1144
1201 Gambier Rd Mount Vernon (43050) ***(G-14918)***
Randstad Engineering, Blue Ash *Also called Randstad Professionals Us LLC* ***(G-1674)***
Randstad Professionals Us LLC 419 893-2400
1745 Indian Wood Cir # 150 Maumee (43537) ***(G-13966)***
Randstad Professionals Us LLC 513 792-6658
4555 Lake Forest Dr # 300 Blue Ash (45242) ***(G-1674)***
Randstad Professionals Us LP 513 791-8600
5151 Pfeiffer Rd Ste 120 Blue Ash (45242) ***(G-1675)***
Randstad Technologies LLC 614 436-0961
8415 Pulsar Pl Ste 110 Columbus (43240) ***(G-6903)***
Randstad Technologies LLC 216 520-0206
6100 Oak Tree Blvd # 110 Independence (44131) ***(G-12246)***
Randstad Technologies LP 614 552-3280
3750 Fishinger Blvd Hilliard (43026) ***(G-11948)***
Randy L Fork Inc 419 891-1230
1230 Conant St Maumee (43537) ***(G-13967)***
Range Rsurces - Appalachia LLC 330 866-3301
1748 Saltwell Rd Nw Dover (44622) ***(G-10207)***
Rankin & Rankin Inc 740 452-7575
806 Market St Zanesville (43701) ***(G-20528)***
Rape Information & Counseling 330 782-3936
535 Marmion Ave Youngstown (44502) ***(G-20341)***
Raphaels Schl Buty Culture Inc (PA) 330 782-3395
615 Boardman Canfield Rd Boardman (44512) ***(G-1743)***
Rapid Aerial Imaging, Dayton *Also called Rapid Mortgage Company* ***(G-9842)***
Rapid Delivery Service Co Inc 513 733-0500
529 N Wayne Ave Cincinnati (45215) ***(G-4385)***
Rapid Mortgage Company 937 748-8888
9537 Gem Stone Dr Dayton (45458) ***(G-9842)***
Rapid Plumbing Inc 513 575-1509
1407 State Route 28 Loveland (45140) ***(G-13154)***
Rapids Nursing Homes Inc 216 292-5706
24201 W 3rd St Grand Rapids (43522) ***(G-11453)***
Rapier Electric Inc 513 868-9087
4845 Augspurger Rd Hamilton (45011) ***(G-11767)***
Rapistan Systems, Brecksville *Also called Siemens Industry Inc* ***(G-1850)***
Raritan National, New Springfield *Also called Ruritan* ***(G-15130)***
Rascal House Pizza, Cleveland *Also called S R Restaurant Corp* ***(G-6427)***
Rassak LLC 513 791-9453
7680 Demar Rd Cincinnati (45243) ***(G-4386)***
Rathbone Group LLC 800 870-5521
1100 Superior Ave E # 1850 Cleveland (44114) ***(G-6353)***
Rave - Rlable Audio Video Elec, Dayton *Also called Reliable Contractors Inc* ***(G-9846)***
Ravenna Assembly of God Inc 330 297-1493
6401 State Route 14 Ravenna (44266) ***(G-16404)***
Ravenwood Health, Chardon *Also called Ravenwood Mental Hlth Ctr Inc* ***(G-2763)***
Ravenwood Mental Health Center 440 632-5355
16030 E High St Middlefield (44062) ***(G-14401)***
Ravenwood Mental Hlth Ctr Inc (PA) 440 285-3568
12557 Ravenwood Dr Chardon (44024) ***(G-2763)***
Rawiga Country Club Inc 330 336-2220
10353 Rawiga Rd Seville (44273) ***(G-16843)***
Ray Bertolini Trucking Co 330 867-0666
2070 Wright Rd Akron (44320) ***(G-405)***
Ray Esser & Sons Inc 440 324-2018
830 Walnut St Ste 1 Elyria (44035) ***(G-10673)***
Ray Fogg Building Methods Inc 216 351-7976
981 Keynote Cir Ste 15 Cleveland (44131) ***(G-6354)***
Ray Hamilton Companies 513 641-5400
11083 Kenwood Rd Blue Ash (45242) ***(G-1676)***
Ray Hamilton Company, Cincinnati *Also called Wnb Group LLC* ***(G-4855)***
Ray Hamilton Company, Blue Ash *Also called Ray Hamilton Companies* ***(G-1676)***
Ray Meyer Sign Company Inc 513 984-5446
8942 Glendale Milford Rd Loveland (45140) ***(G-13155)***
Ray St Clair Roofing Inc 513 874-1234
3810 Port Union Rd Fairfield (45014) ***(G-10898)***
Raycom Media Inc 216 367-7300
1717 E 12th St Cleveland (44114) ***(G-6355)***
Raycom Media Inc 513 421-1919
635 W 7th St Ste 200 Cincinnati (45203) ***(G-4387)***
Raymond A Greiner DDS Inc 440 951-6688
7553 Center St Mentor (44060) ***(G-14232)***
Raymond James Fincl Svcs Inc 513 287-6777
255 E 5th St Ste 2210 Cincinnati (45202) ***(G-4388)***
Raymond James Fincl Svcs Inc 419 586-5121
225 N Main St Celina (45822) ***(G-2661)***
Raymond Recepton House 614 276-6127
3860 Trabue Rd Columbus (43228) ***(G-8589)***
Raymond Storage Concepts Inc (PA) 513 891-7290
5480 Creek Rd Unit 1 Blue Ash (45242) ***(G-1677)***
Rbm Environmental and Cnstr 419 693-5840
4526 Bayshore Rd Oregon (43616) ***(G-15748)***
Rbp Atlanta LLC 614 246-2522
4100 Regent St Ste G Columbus (43219) ***(G-8590)***
Rcf Group, West Chester *Also called River City Furniture LLC* ***(G-19141)***
Rchp - Wilmington LLC (PA) 937 382-6611
610 W Main St Wilmington (45177) ***(G-19781)***
Rcr East Inc (PA) 513 793-2090
6922 Ohio Ave Cincinnati (45236) ***(G-4389)***
Rcr East Inc 513 231-8292
6164 Salem Rd Cincinnati (45230) ***(G-4390)***
Rcs Enterprises Inc 614 337-8520
139 W Johnstown Rd Columbus (43230) ***(G-8591)***
RCT Engineering Inc (PA) 561 684-7534
24880 Shaker Blvd Beachwood (44122) ***(G-1118)***
Rcwc Col Inc 614 564-9344
955 W 5th Ave Ste 7 Columbus (43212) ***(G-8592)***
Rde System Corp 513 933-8000
986 Winzig Ln Lebanon (45036) ***(G-12640)***
Rde System Corporation 513 933-8000
986 Windsor Ave Dayton (45402) ***(G-9843)***
RDF Logistics, Lorain *Also called RDF Trucking Corporation* ***(G-13073)***
RDF Trucking Corporation 440 282-9060
7425 Industrial Pkwy Dr Lorain (44053) ***(G-13073)***
Rdi Corporation 513 524-3320
110 S Locust St Ste A Oxford (45056) ***(G-15829)***
Rdl Architects Inc 216 752-4300
16102 Chagrin Blvd # 200 Cleveland (44120) ***(G-6356)***
Rdp Foodservice Ltd 614 261-5661
620 Oakland Park Ave Columbus (43214) ***(G-8593)***
Rdsi Banking Systems, Defiance *Also called Rurbanc Data Services Inc* ***(G-10055)***
RE Middleton Cnstr LLC 513 398-9255
503 W Main St Mason (45040) ***(G-13753)***
Re/Max 937 477-4997
51 Plum St Ste 220 Beavercreek (45440) ***(G-1257)***
Re/Max Consultant Group 614 855-2822
6650 Walnut St New Albany (43054) ***(G-15004)***
RE/Max Experts Realty 330 364-7355
720 N Wooster Ave Dover (44622) ***(G-10208)***
RE/Max Real Estate Experts 440 255-6505
8444 Mentor Ave Mentor (44060) ***(G-14233)***
Re/Max Realty/Findlay, Findlay *Also called Five & Company Realty Inc* ***(G-11032)***
REA & Associates Inc 330 722-8222
694 E Washington St Medina (44256) ***(G-14117)***
REA & Associates Inc (PA) 330 339-6651
419 W High Ave New Philadelphia (44663) ***(G-15112)***
REA & Associates Inc 419 331-1040
2579 Shawnee Rd Lima (45806) ***(G-12929)***
REA & Associates Inc 330 674-6055
212 N Washington St # 100 Millersburg (44654) ***(G-14618)***
REA & Associates Inc 440 266-0077
122 4th St Nw New Philadelphia (44663) ***(G-15113)***
REA & Associates Inc 614 889-8725
5775 Perimeter Dr Ste 200 Dublin (43017) ***(G-10438)***
Reachout Wireless, Columbus *Also called Nexus Communications Inc* ***(G-8276)***
Reading Family Practice 513 563-6934
9400 Reading Rd Ste 2 Cincinnati (45215) ***(G-4391)***
Reading Rock Residential LLC 513 874-4770
4677 Devitt Dr West Chester (45246) ***(G-19223)***
Ready Set Grow 614 855-5100
5200 New Albany Rd New Albany (43054) ***(G-15005)***
Reagan Elementary School, Ashland *Also called Ashland City School District* ***(G-652)***
Real America Inc 216 261-1177
24555 Lake Shore Blvd Cleveland (44123) ***(G-6357)***
Real Art Design Group Inc (PA) 937 223-9955
520 E 1st St Dayton (45402) ***(G-9844)***
Real Estate, Cincinnati *Also called Camden Management Inc* ***(G-3171)***
Real Estate Capital Fund LLC 216 491-3990
20820 Chagrin Blvd # 300 Cleveland (44122) ***(G-6358)***
Real Estate II Inc 937 390-3119
1140 E Home Rd Springfield (45503) ***(G-17263)***
Real Estate Investors Mgt Inc (PA) 614 777-2444
4041 Roberts Rd Columbus (43228) ***(G-8594)***

A L P H A B E T I C

Real Estate Mortgage Corp......440 356-5373
200 Jackson Dr Chagrin Falls (44022) ***(G-2704)***
Real Estate Showcase......740 389-2000
731 E Center St Marion (43302) ***(G-13574)***
Real Living Inc......614 560-9942
379 W Olentangy St Powell (43065) ***(G-16347)***
Real Living Title Agency Ltd......440 974-7810
7470b Auburn Rd Painesville (44077) ***(G-15877)***
Real Living Title Agency Ltd (PA)......614 459-7400
77 E Nationwide Blvd Columbus (43215) ***(G-8595)***
Real Property Management, Columbus *Also called Hidden Lake Condominiums* ***(G-7832)***
Real Property Management Inc (PA)......614 766-6500
5550 Blazer Pkwy Ste 175 Dublin (43017) ***(G-10439)***
Real Time Systems, Cincinnati *Also called Tyco International MGT Co LLC* ***(G-4712)***
Realm Technologies LLC......513 297-3095
954 Greengate Dr Lebanon (45036) ***(G-12641)***
Realty Corporation of America......216 522-0020
3048 Meadowbrook Blvd Cleveland Heights (44118) ***(G-6795)***
Realty One Inc......330 686-1166
3925 Darrow Rd Ste 101 Stow (44224) ***(G-17389)***
Realty One Inc......440 951-2123
8396 Mentor Ave Mentor (44060) ***(G-14234)***
Realty One Inc......216 221-6585
1495 Warren Rd Ste 201 Lakewood (44107) ***(G-12497)***
Realty One Inc......440 526-2900
8805 Brecksville Rd Brecksville (44141) ***(G-1846)***
Realty One Inc......440 888-8600
9225 W Sprague Rd North Royalton (44133) ***(G-15499)***
Realty One Inc......330 896-5225
4016 Massillon Rd Ste A Uniontown (44685) ***(G-18535)***
Realty One Inc......440 238-1400
12333 Pearl Rd Cleveland (44136) ***(G-6359)***
Realty One Inc......440 365-8392
1240 Abbe Rd N Elyria (44035) ***(G-10674)***
Realty One Inc......440 333-8700
20800 Center Ridge Rd # 203 Rocky River (44116) ***(G-16590)***
Realty One Inc......330 562-2277
195 Barrington Town Sq Dr Aurora (44202) ***(G-851)***
Realty One Inc......330 262-7200
177 W Milltown Rd Unit A Wooster (44691) ***(G-19906)***
Realty One Inc......440 282-8002
1711 Cooper Foster Park Amherst (44001) ***(G-603)***
Realty One Inc......440 835-6500
600 Dover Center Rd Ste C Bay Village (44140) ***(G-1041)***
Realty One Amherst 59, Amherst *Also called Realty One Inc* ***(G-603)***
Realty One Bay Village, Bay Village *Also called Realty One Inc* ***(G-1041)***
Realty One Stowe Fall, Stow *Also called Realty One Inc* ***(G-17389)***
Rebiz LLC......844 467-3249
1925 Saint Clair Ave Ne Cleveland (44114) ***(G-6360)***
Rebman Recreation Inc......440 282-6761
5300 Oberlin Ave Lorain (44053) ***(G-13074)***
Rebman Truck Service Inc......419 589-8161
1004 Vanderbilt Rd Mansfield (44904) ***(G-13354)***
Recaro Child Safety LLC......248 904-1570
4921 Para Dr Cincinnati (45237) ***(G-4392)***
Receivable MGT Svcs Corp......330 659-1000
4836 Brecksville Rd Richfield (44286) ***(G-16525)***
Recker & Boerger Appliances, West Chester *Also called Recker and Boerger Inc* ***(G-19224)***
Recker and Boerger Inc......513 942-9663
10115 Transportation Way West Chester (45246) ***(G-19224)***
Recker Brothers, Genoa *Also called James Recker* ***(G-11380)***
Recker Consulting LLC......513 924-5500
6900 Steger Dr Cincinnati (45237) ***(G-4393)***
Reco Equipment Inc (PA)......740 619-8071
41245 Reco Rd Belmont (43718) ***(G-1429)***
Reconstructive Ortho Sports, Cincinnati *Also called Reconstructive Orthopedics* ***(G-4394)***
Reconstructive Orthopedics (PA)......513 793-3933
10615 Montgomery Rd # 200 Cincinnati (45242) ***(G-4394)***
Record Express LLC......513 685-7329
4295 Armstrong Blvd Batavia (45103) ***(G-1023)***
Recording Workshop......740 663-1000
455 Massieville Rd Chillicothe (45601) ***(G-2873)***
Recording Workshop, The, Chillicothe *Also called Recording Workshop* ***(G-2873)***
Recovery Center......740 687-4500
201 S Columbus St Lancaster (43130) ***(G-12568)***
Recovery One LLC......614 336-4207
3240 Henderson Rd Ste A Columbus (43220) ***(G-8596)***
Recovery Prv RES of Del & Mor......740 369-6811
118 Stover Dr Delaware (43015) ***(G-10122)***
Recovery Resources (PA)......216 431-4131
3950 Chester Ave Cleveland (44114) ***(G-6361)***
Recovery Resources......216 431-4131
4269 Pearl Rd Ste 300 Cleveland (44109) ***(G-6362)***
Recovery Works Healing Ctr LLC......937 384-0580
100 Elmwood Park Dr West Carrollton (45449) ***(G-19009)***
Recreation Dept, Cleveland *Also called City of Independence* ***(G-5263)***
Recreational Golf Inc......513 677-0347
203 Glen Lake Rd Loveland (45140) ***(G-13156)***
Recreational Sports & Svc, Berea *Also called Baldwin Wallace University* ***(G-1446)***
Recruitmilitary, Loveland *Also called Rvet Operating LLC* ***(G-13157)***
Recycled Systems Furniture Inc......614 880-9110
401 E Wilson Bridge Rd Worthington (43085) ***(G-19991)***
Recycling Services Inc (PA)......419 381-7762
3940 Technology Dr Maumee (43537) ***(G-13968)***
Red Apple Packaging LLC......513 228-5522
611 Norgal Dr Lebanon (45036) ***(G-12642)***
Red Barn, Willoughby *Also called Red Oak Camp* ***(G-19707)***
Red Brick Property MGT LLC......513 524-9340
21 N Poplar St Oxford (45056) ***(G-15830)***
Red Capital Advisors, Columbus *Also called Red Capital Partners LLC* ***(G-8598)***
Red Capital Markets LLC......614 857-1400
10 W Broad St Ste 1800 Columbus (43215) ***(G-8597)***
Red Capital Partners LLC (HQ)......614 857-1400
10 W Broad St Fl 8 Columbus (43215) ***(G-8598)***
Red Carpet Car Wash Inc......330 477-5772
4546 Tuscarawas St W Canton (44708) ***(G-2504)***
Red Carpet Health Care Center......740 439-4401
8420 Georgetown Rd Cambridge (43725) ***(G-2127)***
Red Carpet Janitorial Service (PA)......513 242-7575
3478 Hauck Rd Ste D Cincinnati (45241) ***(G-4395)***
Red Dog Pet Resort & Spa......513 733-3647
4975 Babson Pl Cincinnati (45227) ***(G-4396)***
Red Mortgage Capital LLC (HQ)......614 857-1400
10 W Broad St Ste 1800 Columbus (43215) ***(G-8599)***
Red Oak Camp......440 256-0716
9057 Kirtland Chardon Rd Willoughby (44094) ***(G-19707)***
Red Robin Gourmet Burgers Inc......330 305-1080
6522 Strip Ave Nw Canton (44720) ***(G-2505)***
Red Roof Inn, Columbus *Also called Fmw Rri Opco LLC* ***(G-7678)***
Red Roof Inns Inc (HQ)......614 744-2600
605 S Front St Ste 150 Columbus (43215) ***(G-8600)***
Red Roof Inns Inc......614 224-6539
111 Nationwide Plz Columbus (43215) ***(G-8601)***
Red Roof Inns Inc......440 892-7920
29595 Clemens Rd Cleveland (44145) ***(G-6363)***
Red Roof Inns Inc......740 695-4057
68301 Red Roof Ln Saint Clairsville (43950) ***(G-16654)***
Red Roof Inns Inc......440 243-5166
17555 Bagley Rd Cleveland (44130) ***(G-6364)***
Red Squirrel, Fairfield Township *Also called Robiden Inc* ***(G-10935)***
Red Tail Golf Club, Avon *Also called Caravon Golf Company Ltd* ***(G-883)***
Reddy Electric Co......937 372-8205
1145 Bellbrook Ave Xenia (45385) ***(G-20072)***
Redefine Enterprises LLC......330 952-2024
3839 Pearl Rd Medina (44256) ***(G-14118)***
Redwood Living Inc......216 360-9441
7510 E Pleasant Valley Rd Independence (44131) ***(G-12247)***
Reece-Campbell Inc......513 542-4600
10839 Chester Rd Cincinnati (45246) ***(G-4397)***
Reed Hartman Corporate Center......513 984-3030
10925 Reed Hartman Hwy # 200 Blue Ash (45242) ***(G-1678)***
Reed Westlake Leskosky Ltd (PA)......216 522-0449
1422 Euclid Ave Ste 300 Cleveland (44115) ***(G-6365)***
Reese Pyle Drake & Meyer (PA)......740 345-3431
36 N 2nd St Newark (43055) ***(G-15231)***
Refectory Restaurant Inc......614 451-9774
1092 Bethel Rd Columbus (43220) ***(G-8602)***
Reflections Hair Studio Inc......330 725-5782
3605 Medina Rd Medina (44256) ***(G-14119)***
Reflektions Ltd......614 560-6994
560 Sunbury Rd Ste 1 Delaware (43015) ***(G-10123)***
Refrigeration Systems Company (HQ)......614 263-0913
1770 Genessee Ave Columbus (43211) ***(G-8603)***
Refuse / Recycling, Athens *Also called Athens-Hcking Cnty Recycl Ctrs* ***(G-777)***
Regal Carpet Center Inc......216 475-1844
5411 Northfield Rd Cleveland (44146) ***(G-6366)***
Regal Carpet Co, Cleveland *Also called Regal Carpet Center Inc* ***(G-6366)***
Regal Cinema South 10, Youngstown *Also called Regal Cinemas Inc* ***(G-20342)***
Regal Cinemas Inc......614 853-0850
1800 Georgesville Sq Columbus (43228) ***(G-8604)***
Regal Cinemas Inc......330 723-4416
200 W Reagan Pkwy Medina (44256) ***(G-14120)***
Regal Cinemas Inc......440 975-8820
36655 Euclid Ave Willoughby (44094) ***(G-19708)***
Regal Cinemas Inc......937 431-9418
2651 Fairfield Cmns Beavercreek (45431) ***(G-1203)***
Regal Cinemas Inc......440 934-3356
5500 Abbe Rd Elyria (44035) ***(G-10675)***
Regal Cinemas Inc......330 666-9373
4020 Medina Rd Ste 100 Akron (44333) ***(G-406)***
Regal Cinemas Inc......440 871-4546
30147 Detroit Rd Westlake (44145) ***(G-19541)***
Regal Cinemas Inc......330 758-0503
7420 South Ave Youngstown (44512) ***(G-20342)***
Regal Cinemas Inc......330 633-7668
1210 Independence Ave Akron (44310) ***(G-407)***
Regal Cinemas Corporation......513 770-0713
5500 Deerfield Blvd Mason (45040) ***(G-13754)***
Regal Cinemas Corporation......440 720-0500
631 Richmond Rd Richmond Heights (44143) ***(G-16541)***
Regal Cinemas Inc......440 891-9845
18348 Bagley Rd Cleveland (44130) ***(G-6367)***

Regal Entertainment Group, Columbus *Also called Regal Cinemas Inc* ***(G-8604)***
Regal Entertainment Group, Westlake *Also called Regal Cinemas Inc* ***(G-19541)***
Regal Hospitality LLC 614 436-0004
201 Hutchinson Ave Columbus (43235) ***(G-8605)***
Regal Plumbing & Heating Co 937 492-2894
9303 State Route 29 W Sidney (45365) ***(G-16949)***
Regency Hospital Toledo LLC 419 318-5700
5220 Alexis Rd Sylvania (43560) ***(G-17609)***
Regency Leasing Co LLC 614 542-3100
2000 Regency Manor Cir Columbus (43207) ***(G-8606)***
Regency Manor Rehab, Columbus *Also called Regency Leasing Co LLC* ***(G-8606)***
Regency Office Furniture, Akron *Also called Regency Seating Inc* ***(G-408)***
Regency Park 330 682-2273
230 S Crown Hill Rd Orrville (44667) ***(G-15785)***
Regency Park Eye Associates (PA) 419 882-0588
1000 Regency Ct Ste 100 Toledo (43623) ***(G-18146)***
Regency Park Nursing & Rehab 330 682-2273
230 S Crown Hill Rd Orrville (44667) ***(G-15786)***
Regency Roofing Companies Inc (PA) 330 468-1021
576 Highland Rd E Ste A Macedonia (44056) ***(G-13208)***
Regency Seating Inc 330 848-3700
2375 Romig Rd Akron (44320) ***(G-408)***
Regency Technologies, Twinsburg *Also called RSR Partners LLC* ***(G-18463)***
Regency Windows Corporation 330 963-4077
2288 E Aurora Rd Twinsburg (44087) ***(G-18459)***
Regency, The, Cincinnati *Also called 2444 Mdson Rd Cndo Owners Assn* ***(G-2943)***
Regensis Stna Training Program 614 849-0115
415 E Mound St Columbus (43215) ***(G-8607)***
Regent Electric Inc 419 476-8333
5235 Tractor Rd Toledo (43612) ***(G-18147)***
Regent Systems Inc 937 640-8010
7590 Paragon Rd Dayton (45459) ***(G-9845)***
Region 2b, Maumee *Also called International Union United Au* ***(G-13929)***
Region 8, Cleveland *Also called National Labor Relations Board* ***(G-6110)***
Regional Food Program, Logan *Also called Tri-County Community Act* ***(G-12991)***
Regional Imaging Cons Corp 330 726-9006
819 Mckay Ct Ste B103 Youngstown (44512) ***(G-20343)***
Registered Contractors Inc 440 205-0873
8425 Station St Mentor (44060) ***(G-14235)***
Rehab & Nursing Ctr Sprng Crk, Dayton *Also called 5440 Charlesgate Rd Oper LLC* ***(G-9293)***
Rehab Center 330 297-2770
6847 N Chestnut St Ravenna (44266) ***(G-16405)***
Rehab Continuum Inc 513 984-8070
10921 Reed Hartman Hwy # 133 Blue Ash (45242) ***(G-1679)***
Rehab Continuum, The, Blue Ash *Also called Rehab Continuum Inc* ***(G-1679)***
Rehab Continuum, The, Blue Ash *Also called Counseling Source Inc* ***(G-1569)***
Rehab Medical Inc 513 381-3740
1150 W 8th St Ste 110 Cincinnati (45203) ***(G-4398)***
Rehab Nursing Ctr At Firelands, New London *Also called 204 W Main Street Oper Co LLC* ***(G-15065)***
Rehab Resources 513 474-4123
8595 Beechmont Ave # 204 Cincinnati (45255) ***(G-4399)***
Rehabcare Group MGT Svcs Inc 740 779-6732
230 Cherry St Chillicothe (45601) ***(G-2874)***
Rehabcare Group MGT Svcs Inc 740 356-6160
1202 18th St Portsmouth (45662) ***(G-16303)***
Rehabcenter, Ravenna *Also called Rehab Center* ***(G-16405)***
Rehabilitation Aquatics 419 843-2500
3130 Central Park W Ste A Toledo (43617) ***(G-18148)***
Rehabilitation Services, Columbus *Also called Ohio Department of Health* ***(G-8329)***
REHABILITATION SERVICES OF NOR, Mansfield *Also called Center For Individual and Fmly* ***(G-13274)***
Rehabltation Corectn Ohio Dept 614 752-0800
1030 Alum Creek Dr Columbus (43209) ***(G-8608)***
Rehablttion Ctr At Mrietta Mem 740 374-1407
401 Matthew St Marietta (45750) ***(G-13493)***
Rehablttion Ctr At Mrtta Mmori, Marietta *Also called Rehablttion Ctr At Mrietta Mem* ***(G-13493)***
Rehmann LLC 419 865-8118
7124 W Central Ave Toledo (43617) ***(G-18149)***
Rehrig Penn Logistics Inc 614 833-2564
8200 Dove Pkwy Canal Winchester (43110) ***(G-2166)***
Rei Telecom Inc (PA) 614 255-3100
7890 Robinett Way Canal Winchester (43110) ***(G-2167)***
Reichard Industries, LLC, Columbiana *Also called Columbiana Service Company LLC* ***(G-6856)***
Reid Asset Management Company 216 642-3223
9555 Rockside Rd Ste 350 Cleveland (44125) ***(G-6368)***
Reid Physician Associates Inc 937 456-4400
109b Wash Jackson Rd Eaton (45320) ***(G-10576)***
Reid Physicians Associates, Eaton *Also called Reid Physician Associates Inc* ***(G-10576)***
Reilly Painting Co 216 371-8160
1899 S Taylor Rd Cleveland Heights (44118) ***(G-6796)***
Reilly Sweeping Inc 440 786-8400
20350 Hannan Pkwy Cleveland (44146) ***(G-6369)***
Reimer Law Co 440 600-5500
30455 Solon Rd Ste 1 Solon (44139) ***(G-17045)***
Reinhart Foodservice LLC 513 421-9184
535 Shepherd Ave Cincinnati (45215) ***(G-4400)***
Reinnovations Contracting Inc 330 505-9035
3711 Main St Mineral Ridge (44440) ***(G-14638)***
Reis Trucking Inc 513 353-1960
10080 Valley Junction Rd Cleves (45002) ***(G-6805)***
Reisenfeld & Assoc Lpa LLC (PA) 513 322-7000
3962 Red Bank Rd Cincinnati (45227) ***(G-4401)***
Reitter Stucco Inc 614 291-2212
1100 King Ave Columbus (43212) ***(G-8609)***
Reitter Wall Systems Inc 614 545-4444
1178 Joyce Ave Columbus (43219) ***(G-8610)***
Reladyne LLC (HQ) 513 489-6000
8280 Montgomery Rd # 101 Cincinnati (45236) ***(G-4402)***
RELAM Inc 440 232-3354
7695 Bond St Solon (44139) ***(G-17046)***
Relay Gear Ltd 888 735-2943
3738 Paragon Dr Columbus (43228) ***(G-8611)***
Relay Rail Div., Mineral Ridge *Also called L B Foster Company* ***(G-14637)***
Relentless Recovery Inc 216 621-8333
1898 Scranton Rd Uppr Cleveland (44113) ***(G-6370)***
Reliability First Corporation 216 503-0600
3 Summit Park Dr Ste 600 Cleveland (44131) ***(G-6371)***
Reliable Appl Installation Inc 614 246-6840
3736 Paragon Dr Columbus (43228) ***(G-8612)***
Reliable Appl Installation Inc 330 784-7474
2850 Gilchrist Rd Ste 1b Akron (44305) ***(G-409)***
Reliable Contractors Inc 937 433-0262
94 Compark Rd Ste 200 Dayton (45459) ***(G-9846)***
Reliable Polymer Services LP 800 321-0954
300 1st St Wadsworth (44281) ***(G-18769)***
Reliable Rnners Curier Svc Inc 440 578-1011
8624 Station St Mentor (44060) ***(G-14236)***
Reliable Trnsp Solutions LLC 937 378-2700
642 E State St Georgetown (45121) ***(G-11396)***
Reliance Financial Services NA 419 783-8007
401 Clinton St Defiance (43512) ***(G-10053)***
Reliant Capital Solutions LLC 614 452-6100
670 Cross Pointe Rd Gahanna (43230) ***(G-11264)***
Reliant Recovery Solutions, Gahanna *Also called Reliant Capital Solutions LLC* ***(G-11264)***
Relmec Mechanical LLC 216 391-1030
4975 Hamilton Ave Cleveland (44114) ***(G-6372)***
Relx Inc 937 865-6800
9443 Springboro Pike Miamisburg (45342) ***(G-14339)***
Relx Inc 937 865-6800
9443 Springboro Pike Miamisburg (45342) ***(G-14340)***
REM Corp 740 828-2601
26 E 3rd St Frazeysburg (43822) ***(G-11176)***
REM Electronics Supply Co Inc (PA) 330 373-1300
525 S Park Ave Warren (44483) ***(G-18893)***
REM Ohio Waivered Services, Reynoldsburg *Also called REM-Ohio Inc* ***(G-16474)***
REM-Ohio Inc 937 335-8267
721 Lincoln Ave Troy (45373) ***(G-18376)***
REM-Ohio Inc 440 986-3337
214 W Main St South Amherst (44001) ***(G-17074)***
REM-Ohio Inc 330 644-9730
470 Portage Lakes Dr # 207 Coventry Township (44319) ***(G-9131)***
REM-Ohio Inc 614 367-1370
6402 E Main St Ste 103 Reynoldsburg (43068) ***(G-16474)***
Remax Homesource 440 951-2500
3500 Kaiser Ct Ste 300 Willoughby (44095) ***(G-19709)***
Remax Results Plus, Milford *Also called Plus Realty Cincinnati Inc* ***(G-14554)***
Remax Traditions, Chagrin Falls *Also called Western Reserve Realty LLC* ***(G-2710)***
Remco Security, Youngstown *Also called R C Enterprises Inc* ***(G-20339)***
Remedi Seniorcare of Ohio LLC (HQ) 800 232-4239
962 S Dorset Rd Troy (45373) ***(G-18377)***
Remedy Intelligent Staffing, West Chester *Also called Select Staffing* ***(G-19149)***
Remel Products, Oakwood Village *Also called Thermo Fisher Scientific Inc* ***(G-15635)***
Reminger Co LPA (PA) 216 687-1311
101 W Prospect Ave # 1400 Cleveland (44115) ***(G-6373)***
Reminger Co LPA 419 254-1311
405 Madison Ave Ste 2300 Toledo (43604) ***(G-18150)***
Reminger Co LPA 513 721-1311
525 Vine St Ste 1700 Cincinnati (45202) ***(G-4403)***
Remington Steel, Springfield *Also called Westfield Steel Inc* ***(G-17299)***
Remote Support Services, Green Springs *Also called Wynn-Reeth Inc* ***(G-11481)***
Remtec Automation LLC 877 759-8151
6049 Hi Tek Ct Mason (45040) ***(G-13755)***
Remtec Engineering 513 860-4299
6049 Hi Tek Ct Mason (45040) ***(G-13756)***
Renaissance Cleveland Hotel, Cleveland *Also called Skyline Clvland Rnaissance LLC* ***(G-6487)***
Renaissance Corporation (PA) 937 526-3672
21 W Main St Versailles (45380) ***(G-18729)***
Renaissance Home Health Care 216 662-8702
5311 Northfield Rd Bedford (44146) ***(G-1331)***
Renaissance Hotel Operating Co 216 696-5600
24 Public Sq Fl 1 Cleveland (44113) ***(G-6374)***
Renaissance House Inc 419 663-1316
48 Executive Dr Ste 1 Norwalk (44857) ***(G-15590)***

ALPHABETIC

Renaissance House Inc...419 626-1110
158 E Market St Ste 805 Sandusky (44870) ***(G-16787)***
Renaissance, The, Olmsted Twp *Also called Olmsted Residence Corporation* ***(G-15680)***
Renal Life Link Inc...937 383-3338
1675 Alex Dr Wilmington (45177) ***(G-19782)***
Rendigs Fry Kiely & Dennis LLP (PA)...513 381-9200
600 Vine St Ste 2602 Cincinnati (45202) ***(G-4404)***
Renhill Stffing Srvces-America (HQ)...419 254-2800
28315 Kensington Ln Ste B Perrysburg (43551) ***(G-16051)***
Renier Construction Corp...614 866-4580
2164 Citygate Dr Columbus (43219) ***(G-8613)***
Renner Kenner Grieve Bobak (PA)...330 376-1242
106 S Main St Akron (44308) ***(G-410)***
Renner Otto Boiselle & Sklar...216 621-1113
1621 Euclid Ave Ste 1900 Cleveland (44115) ***(G-6375)***
Rennie & Jonson Montgomery...513 241-4722
36 E 7th St Ste 2100 Cincinnati (45202) ***(G-4405)***
Renovo Neural Inc...216 445-4252
10000 Cedar Ave Cleveland (44106) ***(G-6376)***
Rent To Own, Bainbridge *Also called Countryside Rentals Inc* ***(G-941)***
Rent-A-Center Inc...330 337-1107
2870 E State St Ste 500 Salem (44460) ***(G-16710)***
Rent-A-Center Inc...419 382-8585
3418 Glendale Ave Toledo (43614) ***(G-18151)***
Rent-N-Roll...513 528-6929
7841 Laurel Ave Cincinnati (45243) ***(G-4406)***
Rental Concepts Inc (PA)...216 525-3870
6450 Rockside Woods Blvd Cleveland (44131) ***(G-6377)***
Rentech Solutions Inc...216 398-1111
4934 Campbell Rd Ste C Willoughby (44094) ***(G-19710)***
Renthotel Dayton LLC...937 461-4700
11 S Ludlow St Dayton (45402) ***(G-9847)***
Rentokil Initial PLC, Youngstown *Also called Rentokil North America Inc* ***(G-20344)***
Rentokil North America Inc...330 797-9090
5560 W Webb Rd Youngstown (44515) ***(G-20344)***
Rentokil North America Inc...216 328-0700
1240 Valley Belt Rd Brooklyn Heights (44131) ***(G-1924)***
Rentokil North America Inc...216 739-0200
1240 Valley Belt Rd Brooklyn Heights (44131) ***(G-1925)***
Rentokil North America Inc...614 837-0099
6300 Commerce Center Dr G Groveport (43125) ***(G-11666)***
Rentokil North America Inc...614 837-0099
6300 Cmmerce Ctr Dr Ste G Canal Winchester (43110) ***(G-2168)***
Rentwear Inc...330 535-2301
7944 Whipple Ave Nw Canton (44720) ***(G-2506)***
Rentz Corp (PA)...937 434-2774
759 Grants Trl Dayton (45459) ***(G-9848)***
REO Network Inc...740 374-8900
203 Pike St Marietta (45750) ***(G-13494)***
Repro Acquisition Company LLC...216 738-3800
25001 Rockwell Dr Cleveland (44117) ***(G-6378)***
Reprocenter, The, Cleveland *Also called Repro Acquisition Company LLC* ***(G-6378)***
Reproductive Gynecology Inc...330 375-7722
95 Arch St Ste 250 Akron (44304) ***(G-411)***
Reproductive Gynecology Inc...330 452-6010
2600 Tuscarawas St W # 560 Canton (44708) ***(G-2507)***
Reps Resource LLC...513 874-0500
9120 Union Centre Blvd # 300 West Chester (45069) ***(G-19138)***
Reptiles By Mack LLC...937 372-9570
37 S Detroit St Ste 101 Xenia (45385) ***(G-20073)***
Republic Bank...513 793-7666
9683 Kenwood Rd Blue Ash (45242) ***(G-1680)***
Republic N&T Railroad Inc...330 438-5826
2633 8th St Ne Canton (44704) ***(G-2508)***
Republic Parking System Inc...937 415-0016
3600 Terminal Rd Vandalia (45377) ***(G-18698)***
Republic Services, Solon *Also called Browning-Ferris Industries LLC* ***(G-16986)***
Republic Services Inc...937 593-3566
2946 Us Rt 68 N Bellefontaine (43311) ***(G-1392)***
Republic Services Inc...330 536-8013
8100 S State Line Rd Lowellville (44436) ***(G-13173)***
Republic Services Inc...419 925-4592
6141 Depweg Rd Celina (45822) ***(G-2662)***
Republic Services Inc...419 626-2454
4005 Tiffin Ave Sandusky (44870) ***(G-16788)***
Republic Services Inc...216 741-4013
8123 Jones Rd Cleveland (44105) ***(G-6379)***
Republic Services Inc...216 741-4013
8123 Jones Rd Cleveland (44105) ***(G-6380)***
Republic Services Inc...440 458-5191
40195 Butternut Ridge Rd Elyria (44035) ***(G-10676)***
Republic Services Inc...330 830-9050
2800 Erie St S Massillon (44646) ***(G-13847)***
Republic Services Inc...330 793-7676
450 Thacher Ln Youngstown (44515) ***(G-20345)***
Republic Services Inc...330 793-7676
3870 Hendricks Rd Youngstown (44515) ***(G-20346)***
Republic Services Inc...330 793-7676
3870 Henricks Rd Youngstown (44515) ***(G-20347)***
Republic Services Inc...419 636-5109
12359 County Road G Bryan (43506) ***(G-2020)***
Republic Services Inc...440 774-4060
43502 Oberlin Elyria Rd Oberlin (44074) ***(G-15659)***
Republic Services Inc...513 554-0237
10751 Evendale Dr Cincinnati (45241) ***(G-4407)***
Republic Services Inc...937 268-8110
1577 W River Rd Dayton (45417) ***(G-9849)***
Republic Services Inc...513 771-4200
11563 Mosteller Rd Cincinnati (45241) ***(G-4408)***
Republic Services Inc...614 308-3000
933 Frank Rd Columbus (43223) ***(G-8614)***
Republic Services Inc...740 969-4487
933 Frank Rd Columbus (43223) ***(G-8615)***
Republic Services Inc...800 247-3644
2800 Erie St S Massillon (44646) ***(G-13848)***
Republic Services Inc...330 434-9183
964 Hazel St Akron (44305) ***(G-412)***
Republic Services Inc...800 331-0988
97 Hubbard Ave Gallipolis (45631) ***(G-11336)***
Republic Services Inc...419 396-3581
11164 County Highway 4 Carey (43316) ***(G-2597)***
Republic Services Inc...419 635-2367
530 N Camp Rd Port Clinton (43452) ***(G-16252)***
Republic Services Inc...419 726-9465
6196 Hagman Rd Toledo (43612) ***(G-18152)***
Republic Services Inc...937 492-3470
1600 Riverside Dr Sidney (45365) ***(G-16950)***
Republic Telcom Worldwide LLC...330 244-8285
8000 Freedom Ave Nw North Canton (44720) ***(G-15364)***
Republic Telcom Worldwide LLC (HQ)...330 966-4586
3939 Everhard Rd Nw Canton (44709) ***(G-2509)***
Republic/Construction...330 747-1510
460 E Federal St Youngstown (44503) ***(G-20348)***
Republican Headquarters...330 343-6131
203 S Wooster Ave Dover (44622) ***(G-10209)***
Republican State Central Execu...614 228-2481
211 S 5th St Columbus (43215) ***(G-8616)***
Req/Jqh Holdings Inc (PA)...513 891-1066
4243 Hunt Rd Ste 2 Blue Ash (45242) ***(G-1681)***
Req/Jqh Holdings Inc...937 432-0000
3100 Contemporary Ln Miamisburg (45342) ***(G-14341)***
RES Care, Waverly *Also called RES-Care Inc* ***(G-18975)***
RES Care OH, Carrollton *Also called RES-Care Inc* ***(G-2626)***
RES-Care Inc...740 782-1476
39555 National Rd Bethesda (43719) ***(G-1486)***
RES-Care Inc...740 526-0285
66387 Airport Rd Saint Clairsville (43950) ***(G-16655)***
RES-Care Inc...440 729-2432
8228 Mayfield Rd Ste 5b Chesterland (44026) ***(G-2802)***
RES-Care Inc...513 858-4550
7908 Cincinnati Dayton Rd West Chester (45069) ***(G-19139)***
RES-Care Inc...740 968-0181
41743 Mount Hope Rd Flushing (43977) ***(G-11106)***
RES-Care Inc...330 627-7552
520 S Lisbon St Carrollton (44615) ***(G-2626)***
RES-Care Inc...740 941-1178
212 Saint Anns Ln Waverly (45690) ***(G-18975)***
RES-Care Inc...419 435-6620
1016 Dillon Cir Fostoria (44830) ***(G-11138)***
RES-Care Inc...740 446-7549
8204 Carla Dr Gallipolis (45631) ***(G-11337)***
RES-Care Inc...330 453-4144
2915 33rd St Ne Canton (44705) ***(G-2510)***
Rescare...740 867-3051
11090 County Road 1 Chesapeake (45619) ***(G-2787)***
Rescare Ohio Inc...330 479-9841
2821 Whipple Ave Nw # 100 Canton (44708) ***(G-2511)***
Rescare Ohio Inc...740 625-6873
80 Miller St Centerburg (43011) ***(G-2667)***
Rescare Ohio Inc...740 867-4568
1107 Us Hwy 52 Chesapeake (45619) ***(G-2788)***
Rescare Ohio Inc (HQ)...513 724-1177
348 W Main St Williamsburg (45176) ***(G-19635)***
Rescare Ohio Inc...513 829-8992
5099 Camelot Dr Hamilton (45014) ***(G-11768)***
Rescue Incorporated...419 255-9585
3350 Collingwood Blvd # 2 Toledo (43610) ***(G-18153)***
Rescue Mission of Mahoning Val (PA)...330 744-5485
962 Martin L King Jr Blvd Youngstown (44510) ***(G-20349)***
Rescue Mission of Mahoning Val...330 744-5485
2246 Glenwood Ave Youngstown (44511) ***(G-20350)***
Rescue Rooter of Columbus, Columbus *Also called American Residential Svcs LLC* ***(G-7006)***
Rescue Squad, Greenville *Also called Greenville Township Rescue* ***(G-11507)***
Research & Investigation Assoc...419 526-1299
186 Sturges Ave Mansfield (44903) ***(G-13355)***
Research and Education The, Cincinnati *Also called Lindner Clinical Trial Center* ***(G-3987)***
Research Associates Inc (PA)...440 892-1000
27999 Clemens Rd Frnt Cleveland (44145) ***(G-6381)***
Research Institute, Dayton *Also called University of Dayton* ***(G-9955)***
Research Institute At Nation...614 722-2700
700 Childrens Dr Columbus (43205) ***(G-8617)***
Research Institute Univ Hosp, Cleveland *Also called University Hospitals Cleveland* ***(G-6659)***
Resers Fine Foods Inc...216 231-7112
1921 E 119th St Cleveland (44106) ***(G-6382)***

ALPHABETIC SECTION

Reynoldsburg Kindercare, Reynoldsburg

Reserve 330 666-1166
3636 Yellow Creek Rd Akron (44333) *(G-413)*
Reserve Ftl LLC 440 519-1768
1831 Highland Rd Twinsburg (44087) *(G-18460)*
Reserve Ftl LLC 773 721-8740
1451 Trump Ave Ne Canton (44730) *(G-2512)*
Reserve Iron Ohio, Canton *Also called Reserve Ftl LLC (G-2512)*
Reserve Management Group, Twinsburg *Also called Reserve Ftl LLC (G-18460)*
Reserve Square Apts, Cleveland *Also called Equity Residential Properties (G-5549)*
Reserves Network Inc (PA) 440 779-1400
22021 Brookpark Rd # 220 Cleveland (44126) *(G-6383)*
Residence Artists Inc 440 286-8822
220 5th Ave Chardon (44024) *(G-2764)*
Residence At Garden Gate, Cincinnati *Also called Rcr East Inc (G-4389)*
Residence At Huntington Court, Hamilton *Also called Residence At Kensington Place (G-11769)*
Residence At Kensington Place 513 863-4218
350 Hancock Ave Hamilton (45011) *(G-11769)*
Residence At Salem Woods, Cincinnati *Also called Rcr East Inc (G-4390)*
Residence Inn 614 222-2610
36 E Gay St Columbus (43215) *(G-8618)*
Residence Inn By Marriott, Mentor *Also called Amitel Mentor Ltd Partnership (G-14143)*
Residence Inn By Marriott, Troy *Also called Ohio Inns Inc (G-18369)*
Residence Inn By Marriott, Cleveland *Also called Summit Hotel Trs 144 LLC (G-6548)*
Residence Inn By Marriott, Cleveland *Also called Amitel Limited Partnership (G-5028)*
Residence Inn By Marriott, Columbus *Also called Olshan Hotel Management Inc (G-8467)*
Residence Inn By Marriott, Columbus *Also called Marriott International Inc (G-8116)*
Residence Inn By Marriott, Columbus *Also called Marriott International Inc (G-8117)*
Residence Inn By Marriott, Columbus *Also called Marriott International Inc (G-8118)*
Residence Inn By Marriott, Copley *Also called Marriott International Inc (G-9060)*
Residence Inn By Marriott, Blue Ash *Also called Marriott International Inc (G-1636)*
Residence Inn By Marriott, Columbus *Also called 5 Star Hotel Management IV LP (G-6913)*
Residence Inn By Marriott, Columbus *Also called Residence Inn (G-8618)*
Residence Inn By Marriott, Cleveland *Also called Amitel Beachwood Ltd Partnr (G-5027)*
Residence Inn By Marriott, Cleveland *Also called Amitel Rockside Ltd Partnr (G-5029)*
Residence Inn By Marriott Beav 937 427-3914
2779 Frfield Commons Blvd Beavercreek (45431) *(G-1204)*
Residence Inn Cleveland Dwntwn, Cleveland *Also called Nf II Cleveland Op Co LLC (G-6130)*
Residence of Chardon 440 286-2277
501 Chardon Windsor Rd Chardon (44024) *(G-2765)*
Resident Home Association 937 278-0791
3661 Salem Ave Dayton (45406) *(G-9850)*
RESIDENT HOME, THE, Cincinnati *Also called Rhc Inc (G-4413)*
Residential Concepts Inc 513 724-6067
117 Kermit Ave Williamsburg (45176) *(G-19636)*
Residential Finance Corp (PA) 614 324-4700
1 Easton Oval Ste 400 Columbus (43219) *(G-8619)*
Residential Hm Assn of Marion (PA) 740 387-9999
205 W Center St Ste 100 Marion (43302) *(G-13575)*
Residential Home For The Devlp (PA) 740 622-9778
925 Chestnut St Coshocton (43812) *(G-9115)*
Residential Home For The Devlp 740 452-5133
3484 Old Wheeling Rd Zanesville (43701) *(G-20529)*
Residential Inc 740 342-4158
226 S Main St New Lexington (43764) *(G-15062)*
Residential Management Systems 419 222-8806
1555 Allentown Rd Lima (45805) *(G-12867)*
Residential Management Systems (PA) 614 880-6014
402 E Wilson Bridge Rd Worthington (43085) *(G-19992)*
Residential Management Systems 419 255-6060
1446 Reynolds Rd Ste 100 Maumee (43537) *(G-13969)*
Residential One Realty Inc (PA) 614 436-9830
8351 N High St Ste 150 Columbus (43235) *(G-8620)*
Residents of Chardon, Chardon *Also called Residence of Chardon (G-2765)*
Residnce Inn Cincinnati Dwntwn, Cincinnati *Also called 506 Phelps Holdings LLC (G-2946)*
Residntial Coml Rnovations Inc 330 815-1476
7686 S Clvland Mssllon Rd Clinton (44216) *(G-6807)*
Resilience Capitl Partners LLC (PA) 216 292-0200
25101 Chagrin Blvd # 350 Cleveland (44122) *(G-6384)*
Resilience Management, Cleveland *Also called Resilience Capitl Partners LLC (G-6384)*
Resolute Bank 419 868-1750
3425 Brrfeld Blvd Ste 100 Maumee (43537) *(G-13970)*
Resolvit Resources LLC 513 619-5900
895 Central Ave Ste 350 Cincinnati (45202) *(G-4409)*
Resource America Inc 330 896-8510
3500 Massillon Rd Ste 100 Uniontown (44685) *(G-18536)*
Resource Energy Inc 330 896-8510
3500 Massillon Rd Ste 100 Uniontown (44685) *(G-18537)*
Resource Interactive, Columbus *Also called Resource Ventures Ltd (G-8623)*
Resource Interactive 614 621-2888
250 S High St Ste 400 Columbus (43215) *(G-8621)*
Resource International, Columbus *Also called Majidzadeh Enterprises Inc (G-8101)*
Resource International 513 769-6998
4480 Lake Forest Dr # 308 Blue Ash (45242) *(G-1682)*
Resource International Inc (HQ) 614 823-4949
6350 Presidential Gtwy Columbus (43231) *(G-8622)*

Resource One Cmpt Systems Inc 614 485-4800
651 Lkview Plz Blvd Ste E Worthington (43085) *(G-19993)*
Resource Title Agency Inc (PA) 216 520-0050
7100 E Pleasant Vly # 100 Cleveland (44131) *(G-6385)*
Resource Title Nat Agcy Inc 216 520-0050
7100 E Pleasant Valley Rd # 100 Independence (44131) *(G-12248)*
Resource Ventures Ltd (HQ) 614 621-2888
250 S High St Ste 400 Columbus (43215) *(G-8623)*
Rest Haven Nursing Home, Mc Dermott *Also called Voiers Enterprises Inc (G-14023)*
Rest Haven Nursing Home Inc 937 548-1138
1096 N Ohio St Greenville (45331) *(G-11516)*
Restaurant Depot, Cleveland *Also called Jetro Cash and Carry Entps LLC (G-5862)*
Restaurant Depot LLC 216 525-0101
6150 Halle Dr Cleveland (44125) *(G-6386)*
Restaurant Equippers Inc 614 358-6622
635 W Broad St Columbus (43215) *(G-8624)*
Restaurant On The Dam, Stockport *Also called Stockport Mill Country Inn Inc (G-17346)*
Restaurant Refreshment Service, Cincinnati *Also called Coffee Break Corporation (G-3377)*
Restaurant Specialties Inc 614 885-9707
801 W Cherry St Ste 200 Sunbury (43074) *(G-17561)*
Restoration Resources Inc 330 650-4486
1546 Georgetown Rd Hudson (44236) *(G-12141)*
Retail 4 Less, Columbus *Also called Sb Capital Group LLC (G-8691)*
Retail Distribution Center, Maumee *Also called Andersons Inc (G-13877)*
Retail Forward Inc 614 355-4000
2 Easton Oval Ste 500 Columbus (43219) *(G-8625)*
Retail Renovations Inc (PA) 330 334-4501
7530 State Rd Wadsworth (44281) *(G-18770)*
Retalix Inc 937 384-2277
2490 Technical Dr Miamisburg (45342) *(G-14342)*
Retalix Usa Inc 937 384-2277
2490 Technical Dr Miamisburg (45342) *(G-14343)*
Retina Associate of Cleveland (PA) 216 831-5700
3401 Entp Pkwy Ste 300 Beachwood (44122) *(G-1119)*
Retina Associate of Cleveland 216 221-2878
14725 Detroit Ave Ste 200 Lakewood (44107) *(G-12498)*
Retina Group Inc (PA) 614 464-3937
262 Neil Ave Ste 220 Columbus (43215) *(G-8626)*
Retina Vitreous Associates (PA) 419 517-6599
6591 W Central Ave # 202 Toledo (43617) *(G-18154)*
Retrobox.com, Gahanna *Also called Arrow Globl Asset Dspstion Inc (G-11233)*
Return Polymers Inc 419 289-1998
400 Westlake Dr Ashland (44805) *(G-694)*
Reuben Co (PA) 419 241-3400
24 S Huron St Toledo (43604) *(G-18155)*
Reupert Heating and AC Co Inc 513 922-5050
5137 Crookshank Rd Cincinnati (45238) *(G-4410)*
Rev1 Ventures 614 487-3700
1275 Kinnear Rd Columbus (43212) *(G-8627)*
Revenue Assistance Corporation 216 763-2100
4780 Hinckley Indstrl 2 Cleveland (44109) *(G-6387)*
Revenue Group, Cleveland *Also called Revenue Assistance Corporation (G-6387)*
Reverse Center Clinic 419 885-8800
5465 Main St Sylvania (43560) *(G-17610)*
Reves Salon & Spa 419 885-1140
5633 Main St Sylvania (43560) *(G-17611)*
Reville Tire Co (PA) 330 468-1900
8044 Olde 8 Rd Northfield (44067) *(G-15523)*
Reville Wholesale Distributing, Northfield *Also called Reville Tire Co (G-15523)*
Revlocal Inc 740 392-9246
895 Harcourt Rd Ste C Mount Vernon (43050) *(G-14919)*
Revolution Group Inc 614 212-1111
600 N Cleveland Ave # 110 Westerville (43082) *(G-19349)*
Rex Reliable, Canton *Also called Rexs Air Conditioning Company (G-2513)*
Rexel Usa Inc 216 778-6400
5605 Granger Rd Cleveland (44131) *(G-6388)*
Rexel Usa Inc 440 248-3800
2699 Solon Sales 30310 Solon (44139) *(G-17047)*
Rexel Usa Inc 419 625-6761
140 Lane St Sandusky (44870) *(G-16789)*
Rexel Usa Inc 614 771-7373
3670 Parkway Ln Ste A Hilliard (43026) *(G-11949)*
Rexs Air Conditioning Company 330 499-8733
7801 Freedom Ave Nw Canton (44720) *(G-2513)*
Reynolds & Co Inc 740 353-1040
839 Gallia St Portsmouth (45662) *(G-16304)*
Reynolds & Company Cpa's, Portsmouth *Also called Reynolds & Co Inc (G-16304)*
Reynolds and Reynolds Company (HQ) 937 485-2000
1 Reynolds Way Kettering (45430) *(G-12435)*
Reynolds Electric Company Inc 419 228-5448
413 Flanders Ave Lima (45801) *(G-12868)*
Reynolds Industries Inc 330 889-9466
380 W Main St West Farmington (44491) *(G-19246)*
Reynolds Road Surgical Ctr LLC 419 578-7500
2865 N Reynolds Rd # 190 Toledo (43615) *(G-18156)*
Reynolds, De Witt Securities, Cincinnati *Also called Sena Weller Rohs Williams (G-4495)*
Reynoldsburg City Schools 614 501-1041
7932 E Main St Reynoldsburg (43068) *(G-16475)*
Reynoldsburg Kindercare, Reynoldsburg *Also called Kindercare Learning Ctrs LLC (G-16463)*

(PA)=Parent Co (HQ)=Headquarters (DH)=Div Headquarters

Reynoldsburg Swim Club Inc 614 866-3211
7215 E Main St Reynoldsburg (43068) ***(G-16476)***
Rez Stone, Toledo *Also called Hoover & Wells Inc* ***(G-17959)***
Rezod, Columbus *Also called Trubuilt Construction Svcs LLC* ***(G-8875)***
RG Barry Corporation (HQ) 614 864-6400
13405 Yarmouth Rd Nw Pickerington (43147) ***(G-16105)***
RGI Inc 513 221-2121
2245 Gilbert Ave Ste 103 Cincinnati (45206) ***(G-4411)***
Rgis LLC 216 447-1744
4500 Rockside Rd Ste 340 Independence (44131) ***(G-12249)***
Rgis LLC 330 799-1566
5423 Mahoning Ave Ste C Youngstown (44515) ***(G-20351)***
Rgis LLC 248 651-2511
6488 E Main St Ste B Reynoldsburg (43068) ***(G-16477)***
Rgis LLC 330 896-9802
767 E Turkey Foot Lake Rd Akron (44319) ***(G-414)***
Rgis LLC 513 772-5990
4000 Executive Park Dr # 105 Cincinnati (45241) ***(G-4412)***
Rh Meyers Apartments, Beachwood *Also called Menorah Park Center For Senio* ***(G-1100)***
Rham, Marion *Also called Residential Hm Assn of Marion* ***(G-13575)***
Rhc Inc (PA) 513 389-7501
3030 W Fork Rd Cincinnati (45211) ***(G-4413)***
Rhdd, Zanesville *Also called Residential Home For The Devlp* ***(G-20529)***
Rhenium Alloys Inc (PA) 440 365-7388
38683 Taylor Pkwy North Ridgeville (44035) ***(G-15475)***
Rhiel Supply Co Inc (PA) 330 799-7777
3735 Oakwood Ave Austintown (44515) ***(G-873)***
Rhiel Supply Co, The, Austintown *Also called Rhiel Supply Co Inc* ***(G-873)***
Rhinegeist LLC 513 381-1367
1910 Elm St Cincinnati (45202) ***(G-4414)***
Rhinegeist Brewery, Cincinnati *Also called Rhinegeist LLC* ***(G-4414)***
Rhodes Hs-Sch of Leadership, Cleveland *Also called Cleveland Municipal School Dst* ***(G-5334)***
Ricart Automotive, Groveport *Also called Ricart Ford Inc* ***(G-11667)***
Ricart Ford Inc 614 836-5321
4255 S Hamilton Rd Groveport (43125) ***(G-11667)***
Ricco Enterprises Incorporated 216 883-7775
6010 Fleet Ave Frnt Ste Cleveland (44105) ***(G-6389)***
Rich Crites & Dittmer LLC 614 228-5822
6400 Rverside Dr Ste D100 Dublin (43017) ***(G-10440)***
Richard A Broock 937 449-2840
10 N Ludlow St Dayton (45402) ***(G-9851)***
Richard E Jacobs Group LLC 440 871-4800
25425 Center Ridge Rd Cleveland (44145) ***(G-6390)***
Richard Goettle Inc 513 825-8100
12071 Hamilton Ave Cincinnati (45231) ***(G-4415)***
Richard H Freyhof (PA) 937 653-5837
1071 S Main St Urbana (43078) ***(G-18599)***
Richard J Nelson MD 419 578-7555
6005 Monclova Rd Ste 320 Maumee (43537) ***(G-13971)***
Richard L Bowen & Assoc Inc (PA) 216 491-9300
13000 Shaker Blvd Ste 1 Cleveland (44120) ***(G-6391)***
Richard L Liston MD 937 320-2020
89 Sylvania Dr Beavercreek (45440) ***(G-1258)***
Richard R Jencen & Associates 216 781-0131
2850 Euclid Ave Cleveland (44115) ***(G-6392)***
Richard Tomm MD 216 297-3060
1611 S Green Rd Ste 213 Cleveland (44121) ***(G-6393)***
Richard Wolfe Trucking Inc 740 392-2445
7299 Newark Rd Mount Vernon (43050) ***(G-14920)***
RICHARD'S FENCE COMPANY, Akron *Also called Richards Whl Fence Co Inc* ***(G-415)***
Richards Electric Sup Co Inc (PA) 513 242-8800
4620 Reading Rd Cincinnati (45229) ***(G-4416)***
Richards Whl Fence Co Inc 330 773-0423
1600 Firestone Pkwy Akron (44301) ***(G-415)***
Richardson Glass Service Inc (PA) 740 366-5090
1165 Mount Vernon Rd Newark (43055) ***(G-15232)***
RICHARDSON GLASS SERVICE INC DBA LEE'S GLASS SERVICE, Newark *Also called Richardson Glass Service Inc* ***(G-15232)***
Richardson Printing Corp (PA) 740 373-5362
201 Acme St Marietta (45750) ***(G-13495)***
Richcreek Bailey Rehabilitatio 440 527-8610
7600 Tyler Blvd Mentor (44060) ***(G-14237)***
Richfield Banquet & Confer 330 659-6151
4742 Brecksville Rd Richfield (44286) ***(G-16526)***
Richfield Financial Group Inc 440 546-4288
8223 Brecksville Rd # 201 Brecksville (44141) ***(G-1847)***
Richfield Labs, Blue Ash *Also called Ameripath Cincinnati Inc* ***(G-1533)***
Richland Co & Associates Inc (PA) 419 782-0141
101 Clinton St Ste 2200 Defiance (43512) ***(G-10054)***
Richland County Child Support 419 774-5700
161 Park Ave E Mansfield (44902) ***(G-13356)***
Richland County Engineers, Mansfield *Also called County of Richland* ***(G-13283)***
Richland County Prosectors Off, Mansfield *Also called County of Richland* ***(G-13278)***
Richland Mall Shopping Ctr 419 529-4003
2209 Lexington Ave Mansfield (44907) ***(G-13357)***
Richland Manor, Bluffton *Also called J W J Investments Inc* ***(G-1732)***
Richland Newhope Industries (PA) 419 774-4400
150 E 4th St Mansfield (44902) ***(G-13358)***
Richland Newhope Industries 419 774-4200
314 Cleveland Ave Mansfield (44902) ***(G-13359)***
Richland Newhope Industries 419 774-4496
985 W Longview Ave Mansfield (44906) ***(G-13360)***
Richland Township Fire Dept 740 536-7313
3150 Market St Rushville (43150) ***(G-16613)***
Richland Trust Company (HQ) 419 525-8700
3 N Main St Ste 1 Mansfield (44902) ***(G-13361)***
Richmond Medical Center (PA) 440 585-6500
27100 Chardon Rd Richmond Heights (44143) ***(G-16542)***
Richs Towing & Service Inc (PA) 440 234-3435
20531 1st Ave Middleburg Heights (44130) ***(G-14385)***
Richter Landscaping 513 539-0300
240 Senate Dr Monroe (45050) ***(G-14710)***
Richwood Banking Co (PA) 740 943-2317
28 N Franklin St Richwood (43344) ***(G-16544)***
Rick Allman 330 699-1660
4450 Belden Village St Nw Nw800 Canton (44718) ***(G-2514)***
Rick Blazing Insurance Agency 513 677-8300
300 E Bus Way Ste 200 Cincinnati (45241) ***(G-4417)***
Rick Eplion Paving 740 446-3000
7159 State Route 7 S Gallipolis (45631) ***(G-11338)***
Rick Kuntz Trucking Inc 330 296-9311
9056 State Route 88 Windham (44288) ***(G-19803)***
Rickerier and Eckler 513 870-6565
9277 Centre Pointe Dr # 100 West Chester (45069) ***(G-19140)***
Ricketts Excavating Inc 740 687-0338
230 Hamburg Rd Sw Lancaster (43130) ***(G-12569)***
Ricking Paper and Specialty Co 513 825-3551
525 Northland Blvd Cincinnati (45240) ***(G-4418)***
Ricks Hair Center 330 545-5120
27 Churchill Rd Girard (44420) ***(G-11425)***
Ricoh Usa Inc 513 984-9898
10300 Alliance Rd Ste 350 Blue Ash (45242) ***(G-1683)***
Ricoh Usa Inc 614 310-6500
300 W Wilson Bridge Rd # 110 Worthington (43085) ***(G-19994)***
Ricoh Usa Inc 216 574-9111
1360 E 9th St Bsmt 1 Cleveland (44114) ***(G-6394)***
Ricoh Usa Inc 330 523-3900
4125 Highlander Pkwy # 175 Richfield (44286) ***(G-16527)***
Ricoh Usa Inc 330 384-9111
80 W Center St Akron (44308) ***(G-416)***
Riddell Inc 440 366-8225
7501 Performance Ln North Ridgeville (44039) ***(G-15476)***
Riddell All American Sport, North Ridgeville *Also called All American Sports Corp* ***(G-15453)***
Riddle, Kevin L MD, Miamisburg *Also called Miamisburg Family Practice* ***(G-14322)***
Ride Share Information 513 621-6300
720 E Pete Rose Way # 420 Cincinnati (45202) ***(G-4419)***
Riders 1812 Inn 440 354-0922
792 Mentor Ave Painesville (44077) ***(G-15878)***
Riders Inn, Willoughby *Also called East End Ro Burton Inc* ***(G-19660)***
Ridge Manor Nuseries Inc 440 466-5781
7925 N Ridge Rd Madison (44057) ***(G-13235)***
Ridge Murray Prod Ctr Oberlin 440 774-7400
285 Artino St Oberlin (44074) ***(G-15660)***
Ridge Pleasant Valley Inc (PA) 440 845-0200
7377 Ridge Rd Cleveland (44129) ***(G-6395)***
Ridge Road Depot, Cleveland *Also called Cleveland Municipal School Dst* ***(G-5332)***
Ridgehills Hotel Ltd Partnr 440 585-0600
28600 Ridgehills Dr Wickliffe (44092) ***(G-19613)***
Ridgepark Center, Akron *Also called Kindred Healthcare Operating* ***(G-307)***
Ridgepark Medical Associates 216 749-8256
7575 Northcliff Ave # 307 Cleveland (44144) ***(G-6396)***
Ridgeview Hospital, Middle Point *Also called Oglethorpe Middlepoint LLC* ***(G-14377)***
Ridgeville Community Choir 419 267-3820
633 First St Ridgeville Corners (43555) ***(G-16545)***
Ridgewood At Friendship Vlg 614 890-8285
5675 Ponderosa Dr Ofc Columbus (43231) ***(G-8628)***
Ridgewood Golf Course, Cleveland *Also called City of Parma* ***(G-5272)***
Ridgewood YMCA, North Royalton *Also called Young MNS Chrstn Assn Clveland* ***(G-15507)***
Rieck Services, Dayton *Also called Mechanical Cnstr Managers LLC* ***(G-9709)***
Rieman Arszman Cstm Distrs Inc 513 874-5444
9190 Seward Rd Fairfield (45014) ***(G-10899)***
Riepenhoff Landscape Ltd 614 876-4683
3872 Scoto Darby Creek Rd Hilliard (43026) ***(G-11950)***
Riggs School Buses, Cincinnati *Also called Marfre Inc* ***(G-4021)***
Right At Home, Maumee *Also called Colt Enterprises Inc* ***(G-13898)***
Right At Home, Beavercreek *Also called Daugwood Inc* ***(G-1165)***
Right At Home 937 291-2244
15 Dinsley Pl Springboro (45066) ***(G-17137)***
Right At Home LLC 614 734-1110
8828 Commerce Loop Dr Columbus (43240) ***(G-6904)***
Righter Co Inc 614 272-9700
2424 Harrison Rd Columbus (43204) ***(G-8629)***
Righter Construction Svcs Inc 614 272-9700
2424 Harrison Rd Columbus (43204) ***(G-8630)***
Rightthing LLC (HQ) 419 420-1830
3401 Technology Dr Findlay (45840) ***(G-11079)***
Rightthing, The, Findlay *Also called Rightthing LLC* ***(G-11079)***
Rightway Food Service, Lima *Also called Powell Company Ltd* ***(G-12861)***

Rightway Investments LLC 216 854-7697
1959 Edgewood Dr Twinsburg (44087) ***(G-18461)***
Rii, Columbus *Also called Resource International Inc* ***(G-8622)***
Rilco Industrial Controls Inc (HQ) 513 530-0055
5012 Calvert St Cincinnati (45209) ***(G-4420)***
Riley's Restaurant, Cincinnati *Also called William Royce Inc* ***(G-4850)***
Ringler Feedlots LLC 419 253-5300
461 State Route 61 Marengo (43334) ***(G-13425)***
Ringler Inc 419 253-5300
461 State Route 61 Marengo (43334) ***(G-13426)***
Rinkov Eyecare Center (PA) 614 224-2414
81 E Gay St Columbus (43215) ***(G-8631)***
Rinkov, Mark H Od, Columbus *Also called Rinkov Eyecare Center* ***(G-8631)***
Ripcho Studio 216 631-0664
7630 Lorain Ave Cleveland (44102) ***(G-6397)***
Rippe & Kingston Systems Inc (PA) 513 241-1375
1077 Celestial St Ste 124 Cincinnati (45202) ***(G-4421)***
Rise Fitness, Medina *Also called Redefine Enterprises LLC* ***(G-14118)***
Riser Foods Company (HQ) 216 292-7000
5300 Richmond Rd Bedford Heights (44146) ***(G-1359)***
Risi, Akron *Also called Radiology & Imaging Services* ***(G-404)***
Rising Sun Express, Jackson Center *Also called Rse Group Inc* ***(G-12325)***
Rising Sun Express LLC 937 596-6167
1003 S Main St Jackson Center (45334) ***(G-12324)***
Risk International Svcs Inc (HQ) 216 255-3400
4055 Embassy Pkwy Ste 100 Fairlawn (44333) ***(G-10969)***
Ritchies Food Distributors Inc 740 443-6303
527 S West St Piketon (45661) ***(G-16127)***
Rite Rug Co 614 478-3365
5465 N Hamilton Rd Columbus (43230) ***(G-8632)***
Rite Rug Co 614 882-4322
6083 Chandler Ct Westerville (43082) ***(G-19350)***
Rite Rug Co 937 318-9197
2015 Commerce Center Blvd Fairborn (45324) ***(G-10803)***
Rite Rug Co 440 945-4100
20036 Progress Dr Strongsville (44149) ***(G-17502)***
Rite Rug Co 614 552-1190
6574 E Broadstreet Reynoldsburg (43068) ***(G-16478)***
Rite Rug Co 513 942-0010
9974 International Blvd West Chester (45246) ***(G-19225)***
Rite Way Restoration, Columbus *Also called Dry It Rite LLC* ***(G-7546)***
Riten Industries 740 335-5353
1110 Lakeview Ave Wshngtn CT Hs (43160) ***(G-20033)***
Ritenour Industrial, Twinsburg *Also called Lou Ritenour Decorators Inc* ***(G-18443)***
Rittenhouse 513 423-2322
3000 Mcgee Ave Middletown (45044) ***(G-14453)***
Ritter & Associates Inc 419 535-5757
1690 Woodlands Dr Ste 103 Maumee (43537) ***(G-13972)***
Ritter & Randolph LLC 513 381-5700
1 E 4th St Ste 700 Cincinnati (45202) ***(G-4422)***
Rittman City of Inc 330 925-2065
25 N State St Rittman (44270) ***(G-16555)***
Rittman Inc 330 927-6855
10 Mull Dr Rittman (44270) ***(G-16556)***
Rivals Sports Grille LLC 216 267-0005
6710 Smith Rd Middleburg Heights (44130) ***(G-14386)***
River City Furniture LLC (PA) 513 612-7303
6454 Centre Park Dr West Chester (45069) ***(G-19141)***
River City Pharma 513 870-1680
8695 Seward Rd Fairfield (45011) ***(G-10900)***
River Consulting LLC (HQ) 614 797-2480
445 Hutchinson Ave # 740 Columbus (43235) ***(G-8633)***
River Downs, Cincinnati *Also called Pnk (ohio) LLC* ***(G-4312)***
River Downs Race Course, Cincinnati *Also called River Downs Turf Club Inc* ***(G-4423)***
River Downs Turf Club Inc 513 232-8000
6301 Kellogg Rd Cincinnati (45230) ***(G-4423)***
River Greens Golf Course Inc 740 545-7817
22749 State Route 751 West Lafayette (43845) ***(G-19259)***
River Plumbing & Supply, Avon *Also called River Plumbing Inc* ***(G-916)***
River Plumbing Inc 440 934-3720
1756 Moore Rd Avon (44011) ***(G-916)***
River Recycling Entps Ltd (PA) 216 459-2100
4195 Bradley Rd Cleveland (44109) ***(G-6398)***
River Road Family Physicians 419 872-7745
1601 Brigham Dr Ste 250 Perrysburg (43551) ***(G-16052)***
River Road Hotel Corp 614 267-7461
3110 Olentangy River Rd Columbus (43202) ***(G-8634)***
River Rock Rehabilitation 740 382-4035
990 S Prospect St Ste 4 Marion (43302) ***(G-13576)***
River Rose Obstetrics & Gyneco, Athens *Also called Athens Medical Associates LLC* ***(G-775)***
River Valley Credit Union Inc (PA) 937 859-1970
505 Earl Blvd Miamisburg (45342) ***(G-14344)***
River View Surgery Center, Lancaster *Also called Riverview Surgery Center* ***(G-12571)***
River Vly Orthpdics Spt Mdcine (PA) 740 687-3346
2405 N Columbus St # 120 Lancaster (43130) ***(G-12570)***
Rivera, Mary, Cincinnati *Also called Reading Family Practice* ***(G-4391)***
Riverain Technologies LLC 937 425-6811
3020 S Tech Blvd Miamisburg (45342) ***(G-14345)***
Riverbend Music Center, Cincinnati *Also called Cincinnati Symphony Orchestra* ***(G-3332)***
Riverfront Diversified Inc 513 874-7200
9814 Harwood Ct West Chester (45014) ***(G-19142)***
Riverfront Steel Inc 513 769-9999
10310 S Medallion Dr Cincinnati (45241) ***(G-4424)***
Riverhills Bank (HQ) 513 553-6700
553 Chamber Dr Milford (45150) ***(G-14557)***
Riverhills Healthcare Inc (PA) 513 241-2370
111 Wellington Pl Lowr Cincinnati (45219) ***(G-4425)***
Riverhills Healthcare Inc 513 791-6400
4805 Montgomery Rd # 150 Cincinnati (45212) ***(G-4426)***
Rivers Bend Health Care LLC 740 894-3476
335 Township Road 1026 South Point (45680) ***(G-17097)***
Riverside Care Center LLC 740 962-5303
856 Riverside Dr S Mc Connelsville (43756) ***(G-14022)***
Riverside Cmnty Urban Redev 330 929-3000
1989 Front St Cuyahoga Falls (44221) ***(G-9215)***
Riverside Cnstr Svcs Inc 513 723-0900
218 W Mcmicken Ave Cincinnati (45214) ***(G-4427)***
Riverside Commons Ltd Partnr 614 863-4640
6880 Tussing Rd Reynoldsburg (43068) ***(G-16479)***
Riverside Company, The, Cleveland *Also called Riverside Partners LLC* ***(G-6400)***
Riverside Drives Inc 216 362-1211
4509 W 160th St Cleveland (44135) ***(G-6399)***
Riverside Drives Disc, Cleveland *Also called Riverside Drives Inc* ***(G-6399)***
Riverside Drv Animal Care Ctr 614 414-2668
6924 Riverside Dr Dublin (43017) ***(G-10441)***
Riverside Manor, Newcomerstown *Also called Newcomerstown Progress Corp* ***(G-15271)***
Riverside Marine Inds Inc 419 729-1621
2824 N Summit St Toledo (43611) ***(G-18157)***
Riverside Medical Inc 513 936-5360
111 Wellington Pl Cincinnati (45219) ***(G-4428)***
Riverside Mnor Nrsing Rhab Ctr, Newcomerstown *Also called Newcomerstown Development Inc* ***(G-15270)***
Riverside Nephrology Assoc Inc 614 538-2250
929 Jasonway Ave Columbus (43214) ***(G-8635)***
Riverside Nrsing Rhabilitation, Dayton *Also called King Tree Leasing Co LLC* ***(G-9663)***
Riverside of Miami County, Troy *Also called R T Industries Inc* ***(G-18375)***
Riverside Partners LLC 216 344-1040
50 Public Sq Ste 2900 Cleveland (44113) ***(G-6400)***
Riverside Radiology and (PA) 614 340-7747
100 E Campus View Blvd # 100 Columbus (43235) ***(G-8636)***
Riverside Research Institute 937 431-3810
2640 Hibiscus Way Beavercreek (45431) ***(G-1205)***
Riverside Veterinary Hospital, Dublin *Also called Beechwold Veterinary Hospital* ***(G-10260)***
Rivertreechristian.com, Massillon *Also called Christian Rivertree School* ***(G-13795)***
Riverview Community, Cincinnati *Also called United Church Homes Inc* ***(G-4730)***
Riverview Health Institute 937 222-5390
1 Elizabeth Pl Dayton (45417) ***(G-9852)***
Riverview Hotel LLC 614 268-8700
3160 Olentangy River Rd Columbus (43202) ***(G-8637)***
Riverview Industries Inc 419 898-5250
8380 W State Route 163 Oak Harbor (43449) ***(G-15616)***
Riverview Surgery Center 740 681-2700
2401 N Columbus St Lancaster (43130) ***(G-12571)***
Riviera Country Club, Dublin *Also called American Italian Golf* ***(G-10249)***
RJ Runge Company Inc 419 740-5781
3539 Ne Catawba Rd Port Clinton (43452) ***(G-16253)***
Rjw Inc (PA) 216 398-6090
5755 Granger Rd Ste 400 Independence (44131) ***(G-12250)***
Rjw Trucking Company Ltd 740 363-5343
124 Henderson Ct Delaware (43015) ***(G-10124)***
Rk Express International LLC 513 574-2400
5474 Sanrio Ct Cincinnati (45247) ***(G-4429)***
Rk Family Inc 740 389-2674
233 America Blvd Marion (43302) ***(G-13577)***
Rk Family Inc 513 737-0436
1416 Main St Hamilton (45013) ***(G-11770)***
Rk Family Inc 419 443-1663
2300 W Market St Tiffin (44883) ***(G-17695)***
Rk Family Inc 419 355-8230
1800 E State St Fremont (43420) ***(G-11216)***
Rk Family Inc 330 264-5475
3541 E Lincoln Way Wooster (44691) ***(G-19907)***
Rk Family Inc 513 934-0015
1879 Deerfield Rd Lebanon (45036) ***(G-12643)***
Rkpl Inc 419 224-2121
216 N Elizabeth St Lima (45801) ***(G-12869)***
RL Best Company 330 758-8601
723 Bev Rd Boardman (44512) ***(G-1744)***
Rl Global Services, Wilmington *Also called R+l Pramount Trnsp Systems Inc* ***(G-19780)***
Rl Painting and Mfg Inc 937 968-5526
10001 Oh In State Line Union City (45390) ***(G-18503)***
RL Trucking Inc 419 732-4177
62 Grande Lake Dr Port Clinton (43452) ***(G-16254)***
Rla Investments Inc 513 554-1470
389 Wade St Cincinnati (45214) ***(G-4430)***
Rlj III - Em Clmbus Lessee LLC 614 890-8600
2700 Corporate Exch Dr Columbus (43231) ***(G-8638)***
Rlj Management Co Inc (PA) 614 942-2020
3021 E Dblin Granville Rd Columbus (43231) ***(G-8639)***

A L P H A B E T I C

(PA)=Parent Co (HQ)=Headquarters (DH)=Div Headquarters

RLM Fabricating Inc 419 729-6130
4801 Bennett Rd Toledo (43612) ***(G-18158)***

RLR Investments LLC 937 382-1494
600 Gilliam Rd Wilmington (45177) ***(G-19783)***

Rls Disposal Company Inc 740 773-1440
990 Eastern Ave Chillicothe (45601) ***(G-2875)***

Rmb Enterprises Inc 513 539-3431
2742 Oxford State Rd Middletown (45044) ***(G-14454)***

Rmf Nooter Inc 419 727-1970
915 Matzinger Rd Toledo (43612) ***(G-18159)***

Rmi International Inc 937 642-5032
24500 Honda Pwky Marysville (43040) ***(G-13647)***

RMS Aquaculture Inc (PA) 216 433-1340
6629 Engle Rd Ste 108 Cleveland (44130) ***(G-6401)***

RMS Management, Westlake *Also called RMS of Ohio Inc* ***(G-19542)***

RMS of Ohio Inc 440 617-6605
24651 Center Ridge Rd # 300 Westlake (44145) ***(G-19542)***

RMS of Ohio Inc 513 841-0990
7162 Reading Rd Ste 1010 Cincinnati (45237) ***(G-4431)***

RMS of Ohio Inc 937 291-3622
5335 Far Hills Ave # 306 Dayton (45429) ***(G-9853)***

Rmx Freight Systems Inc (PA) 740 849-2374
4550 Roseville Rd Roseville (43777) ***(G-16602)***

Rnw Holdings Inc 330 792-0600
200 Division Street Ext Youngstown (44510) ***(G-20352)***

Roadrunner Trnsp Systems Inc 330 920-4101
89 Cuyhoga Fls Indus Pkwy Peninsula (44264) ***(G-15950)***

Roadtrippers Inc 917 688-9887
131 E Mcmicken Ave Cincinnati (45202) ***(G-4432)***

Roadway Express, Toledo *Also called Yrc Inc* ***(G-18327)***

Rob's Restaurant & Catering, Brookville *Also called Mackil Inc* ***(G-1964)***

Robbins Kelly Patterson Tucker 513 721-3330
7 W 7th St Ste 1400 Cincinnati (45202) ***(G-4433)***

Robeck Fluid Power Co 330 562-1140
350 Lena Dr Aurora (44202) ***(G-852)***

Robert A Kaufmann Inc 216 663-1150
5210 Northfield Rd Maple Heights (44137) ***(G-13415)***

Robert C Verbon Inc 419 867-6868
4964 Forest Hill Dr Toledo (43623) ***(G-18160)***

Robert E Kose 419 843-7800
1661 Holland Rd Ste 200 Maumee (43537) ***(G-13973)***

Robert E Lubow MD 513 961-8861
3001 Highland Ave Cincinnati (45219) ***(G-4434)***

Robert E McGrath Inc 440 572-7747
11606 Pearl Rd Strongsville (44136) ***(G-17503)***

Robert Ellis 513 821-0275
305 Crescent Ave Cincinnati (45215) ***(G-4435)***

Robert Erney 312 788-9005
14830 Larkfield Dr Brookpark (44142) ***(G-1954)***

Robert F Arrom Md Inc 513 893-4107
1020 Symmes Rd Fairfield (45014) ***(G-10901)***

Robert F Lindsay Co (PA) 419 476-6221
4268 Rose Garden Dr Toledo (43623) ***(G-18161)***

Robert G Owen Trucking Inc (PA) 330 756-1013
9260 Erie Ave Sw Navarre (44662) ***(G-14956)***

Robert Half International Inc 937 224-7376
1 S Main St Ste 300 Dayton (45402) ***(G-9854)***

Robert Half International Inc 330 629-9494
970 Windham Ct Ste 1a Youngstown (44512) ***(G-20353)***

Robert Half International Inc 513 563-0770
10300 Alliance Rd Ste 220 Blue Ash (45242) ***(G-1684)***

Robert Half International Inc 614 221-8326
277 W Nationwide Blvd Columbus (43215) ***(G-8640)***

Robert Half International Inc 614 602-0505
5550 Blazer Pkwy Ste 250 Dublin (43017) ***(G-10442)***

Robert Half International Inc 513 621-8367
201 E 5th St Ste 2000a Cincinnati (45202) ***(G-4436)***

Robert Half International Inc 216 621-4253
1001 Lakeside Ave E 1320a Cleveland (44114) ***(G-6402)***

Robert Half International Inc 614 221-1544
277 W Nationwide Blvd # 200 Columbus (43215) ***(G-8641)***

Robert J Matthews Company (PA) 330 834-3000
2780 Richville Dr Se Massillon (44646) ***(G-13849)***

ROBERT K FOX FAMILY WIDE, Lancaster *Also called Family YMCA of LANcstr&fairfld* ***(G-12542)***

Robert L Dawson M.D., James, Galion *Also called Avita Health System* ***(G-11290)***

Robert L Stark Enterprises Inc 216 292-0242
1350 W 3rd St Cleveland (44113) ***(G-6403)***

Robert Lucke Homes Inc 513 683-3300
8825 Chapelsquare Ln B Cincinnati (45249) ***(G-4437)***

Robert M Neff Inc 614 444-1562
711 Stimmel Rd Columbus (43223) ***(G-8642)***

Robert McConnell, Shandon *Also called R & B Contractors LLC* ***(G-16873)***

Robert Neff & Son Inc 740 454-0128
132 S Shawnee Ave Zanesville (43701) ***(G-20530)***

Robert Stough Ventures Corp 419 882-4073
5409 Monroe St Toledo (43623) ***(G-18162)***

Robert W Baird & Co Inc 216 737-7330
200 Public Sq Ste 1650 Cleveland (44114) ***(G-6404)***

Robert Wiley MD Inc 216 621-3211
2740 Carnegie Ave Cleveland (44115) ***(G-6405)***

Robert Winner Sons Inc (PA) 419 582-4321
8544 State Route 705 Yorkshire (45388) ***(G-20092)***

ROBERTSON BEREAVEMENT CENTER, Medina *Also called Bridgeshome Health Care* ***(G-14040)***

Robertson Cnstr Svcs Inc 740 929-1000
1801 Thornwood Dr Heath (43056) ***(G-11842)***

Robertson Heating Sup Co Ohio (PA) 800 433-9532
2155 W Main St Alliance (44601) ***(G-553)***

Robertson Htg Sup Aliance Ohio (PA) 330 821-9180
2155 W Main St Alliance (44601) ***(G-554)***

Robertson Htg Sup Canton Ohio (PA) 330 821-9180
2155 W Main St Alliance (44601) ***(G-555)***

Robertson Htg Sup Clmbus Ohio (PA) 330 821-9180
2155 W Main St Alliance (44601) ***(G-556)***

Robiden Inc 513 421-0000
6059 Creekside Way Fairfield Township (45011) ***(G-10935)***

Robinson Health System Inc 330 678-4100
6847 N Chestnut St Ravenna (44266) ***(G-16406)***

Robinson Health System Inc (HQ) 330 297-0811
6847 N Chestnut St Ravenna (44266) ***(G-16407)***

Robinson Health System Inc 330 297-0811
1993 State Route 59 Kent (44240) ***(G-12394)***

Robinson Hlth Affl Med Ctr One, Streetsboro *Also called Robinson Memorial Hospital* ***(G-17428)***

Robinson Htg Air-Conditioning 513 422-6812
1208 2nd Ave Middletown (45044) ***(G-14455)***

Robinson Insulation Co Inc 937 323-9599
4715 Urbana Rd Springfield (45502) ***(G-17264)***

Robinson Investments Ltd 937 593-1849
811 N Main St Bellefontaine (43311) ***(G-1393)***

Robinson Memorial Hospital 330 626-3455
9424 State Route 14 Streetsboro (44241) ***(G-17428)***

Robinson Surgery Center, Ravenna *Also called Robinson Health System Inc* ***(G-16406)***

Robinson Visitn Nrs Asoc/Hospc 330 297-8899
6847 N Chestnut St Ravenna (44266) ***(G-16408)***

Robots and Pencils LP 587 350-4095
24245 Mercantile Rd Beachwood (44122) ***(G-1120)***

Roby Lees Restaurant & Catrg, Newton Falls *Also called Lees Roby Inc* ***(G-15276)***

Roce Group LLC 330 969-2627
4170 Steels Pointe Stow (44224) ***(G-17390)***

Rock and Roll of Fame and Muse 216 781-7625
1100 Rock And Roll Blvd Cleveland (44114) ***(G-6406)***

Rock Creek Medical Center, Rock Creek *Also called Glenbeigh Hospital* ***(G-16559)***

Rock House Entrmt Group Inc 440 232-7625
7809 First Pl Oakwood Village (44146) ***(G-15633)***

Rockbridge Capital LLC (PA) 614 246-2400
4100 Regent St Ste G Columbus (43219) ***(G-8643)***

Rockfish Interactive Corp 513 381-1583
659 Van Meter St Ste 520 Cincinnati (45202) ***(G-4438)***

Rockford Homes Inc (PA) 614 785-0015
999 Polaris Pkwy Ste 200 Columbus (43240) ***(G-6905)***

Rocking Horse Chld Hlth Ctr (PA) 937 328-7266
651 S Limestone St Springfield (45505) ***(G-17265)***

Rocknstarr Holdings LLC 330 509-9086
112 S Meridian Rd Youngstown (44509) ***(G-20354)***

Rockport Early Childhood Ctr, Cleveland *Also called Rockport United Methodist Ch* ***(G-6407)***

Rockport United Methodist Ch 440 331-9434
3301 Wooster Rd Cleveland (44116) ***(G-6407)***

Rockside Center Ltd 216 447-0070
6055 Rockside Woods Blvd Cleveland (44131) ***(G-6408)***

Rockside Hospitality LLC 216 524-0700
5300 Rockside Rd Independence (44131) ***(G-12251)***

Rockwell Automation Ohio Inc (HQ) 513 576-6151
1700 Edison Dr Milford (45150) ***(G-14558)***

Rockwell Springs Trout Club (PA) 419 684-7971
1581 County Road 310 Clyde (43410) ***(G-6821)***

Rockwood Dry Cleaners Corp 614 471-3700
171 Granville St Gahanna (43230) ***(G-11265)***

Rockwood Equity Partners LLC (PA) 216 378-9326
3201 Entp Pkwy Ste 370 Cleveland (44122) ***(G-6409)***

Rocky Creek Hlth Rhabilitation, Columbus *Also called Gahanna Health Care Center* ***(G-7723)***

Rocky River Leasing Co LLC 440 243-5688
570 N Rocky River Dr Berea (44017) ***(G-1468)***

Rocky River Medical Offices, Rocky River *Also called Kaiser Foundation Hospitals* ***(G-16584)***

ROCKY RIVER RIDING, Cleveland *Also called Valley Riding* ***(G-6684)***

Rockynol, Fairlawn *Also called Senior Independence* ***(G-10975)***

Rockynol Retirement Community, Akron *Also called Ohio Presbt Retirement Svcs* ***(G-368)***

Rod Lightning Mutual Insur Co (PA) 330 262-9060
1685 Cleveland Rd Wooster (44691) ***(G-19908)***

Rodbat Security Services, Marysville *Also called Rmi International Inc* ***(G-13647)***

Roddy Group Inc 216 763-0088
24500 Chagrin Blvd # 200 Beachwood (44122) ***(G-1121)***

Rodem Inc (PA) 513 922-6140
5095 Crookshank Rd Cincinnati (45238) ***(G-4439)***

Rodem Process Equipment, Cincinnati *Also called Rodem Inc* ***(G-4439)***

Roderick Linton Belfance LLP 330 434-3000
50 S Main St Fl 10 Akron (44308) ***(G-417)***

Rodeway Inn, Dublin *Also called Jackson I-94 Ltd Partnership* ***(G-10379)***

Roe Dental Laboratory Inc ... 216 663-2233
7165 E Pleasant Valley Rd Independence (44131) *(G-12252)*
Roe Transport Inc ... 937 497-7161
3680 Michigan St Sidney (45365) *(G-16951)*
Roeder Cartage Company Inc (PA) ... 419 221-1600
1979 N Dixie Hwy Lima (45801) *(G-12870)*
Roediger Realty Inc ... 937 322-0352
331 Mount Vernon Ave Springfield (45503) *(G-17266)*
Roehrenbeck Electric Inc ... 614 443-9709
2525 English Rd Columbus (43207) *(G-8644)*
Roemer Land Investment Co ... 419 475-5151
3912 Sunforest Ct Ste A Toledo (43623) *(G-18163)*
Roetzel and Andress A Legal P (PA) ... 330 376-2700
222 S Main St Ste 400 Akron (44308) *(G-418)*
Roetzel and Andress A Legal P ... 614 463-9489
41 S High St Fl 21 Columbus (43215) *(G-8645)*
Roetzel and Andress A Legal P ... 216 623-0150
1375 E 9th St Fl 10 Cleveland (44114) *(G-6410)*
Roger Bettis Trucking Inc ... 330 863-2111
7089 Alliance Rd Nw Malvern (44644) *(G-13254)*
Roger Kreps Drywall & Plst Inc ... 330 726-6090
939 Augusta Dr Youngstown (44512) *(G-20355)*
Roger S Palutsis MD ... 330 821-0201
1401 S Arch Ave Alliance (44601) *(G-557)*
Roger Shawn Houck ... 513 933-0563
7887 Wilmington Rd Oregonia (45054) *(G-15758)*
Roger Zatkoff Company ... 248 478-2400
2475 Edison Blvd Twinsburg (44087) *(G-18462)*
Rogosin Institute Inc ... 937 374-3116
740 Birch Rd Xenia (45385) *(G-20074)*
Roholt Vision Institute Inc ... 330 702-8755
25 Manor Hill Dr Canfield (44406) *(G-2208)*
Rohrs Farms ... 419 757-0110
810 Courtright St Mc Guffey (45859) *(G-14025)*
Roll Formed Products Co Div, Youngstown *Also called Hynes Industries Inc (G-20227)*
Rollandia Golf & Magic Castle, Dayton *Also called A To Z Golf Managment Co (G-9299)*
Rolling Hocevar & Associa ... 614 760-8320
5980 Wilcox Pl Ste G Dublin (43016) *(G-10443)*
Rolling Acres Care Center, North Lima *Also called Guardian Elder Care LLC (G-15402)*
Rolling Hlls Rhab Wellness Ctr ... 330 225-9121
4426 Homestead Dr Brunswick (44212) *(G-1989)*
Rollins Moving and Storage Inc ... 937 525-4013
1050 Wheel St Springfield (45503) *(G-17267)*
Rolls Realty ... 614 792-5662
6706 Harriott Rd Powell (43065) *(G-16348)*
Rolta Advizex Technologies LLC (HQ) ... 216 901-1818
6480 S Rockside Woods Independence (44131) *(G-12253)*
Roman Cthlic Docese Youngstown ... 330 875-5562
2308 Reno Dr Louisville (44641) *(G-13106)*
Roman Cthlic Docese Youngstown ... 330 792-4721
248 S Belle Vista Ave Youngstown (44509) *(G-20356)*
Roman Plumbing Company ... 330 455-5155
2411 Shepler Ch Ave Sw Canton (44706) *(G-2515)*
Roman/Peshoff Inc ... 419 241-2221
1500 Timber Wolf Dr Holland (43528) *(G-12051)*
Romanelli & Hughes Building Co ... 614 891-2042
148 W Schrock Rd Westerville (43081) *(G-19441)*
Romanelli & Hughes Contractors, Westerville *Also called Romanelli & Hughes Building Co (G-19441)*
Romanoff Electric Inc (PA) ... 614 755-4500
1288 Research Rd Gahanna (43230) *(G-11266)*
Romanoff Electric Co LLC ... 419 726-2627
5570 Enterprise Blvd Toledo (43612) *(G-18164)*
Romanoff Electric Co LLC ... 937 640-7925
5570 Enterprise Blvd Toledo (43612) *(G-18165)*
Romaster Corp ... 330 825-1945
3013 Wadsworth Rd Norton (44203) *(G-15559)*
Rometrics Too Hair Nail Gllery ... 440 808-1391
26155 Detroit Rd Westlake (44145) *(G-19543)*
Romitech Inc (PA) ... 937 297-9529
2000 Composite Dr Dayton (45420) *(G-9855)*
Ron Burge Trucking Inc ... 330 624-5373
1876 W Britton Rd Burbank (44214) *(G-2055)*
Ron Carrocce Trucking Company ... 330 758-0841
8063 Southern Blvd Youngstown (44512) *(G-20357)*
Ron Foth Advertising, Columbus *Also called Ron Foth Retail Inc (G-8646)*
Ron Foth Retail Inc ... 614 888-7771
8100 N High St Columbus (43235) *(G-8646)*
Ron Johnson Plumbing and Htg ... 419 433-5365
14805 Shawmill Rd Norwalk (44857) *(G-15591)*
Ron Marhofer Automall Inc ... 330 835-6707
1260 Main St Cuyahoga Falls (44221) *(G-9216)*
Ron Marhofer Automall Inc (PA) ... 330 923-5059
1350 Main St Cuyahoga Falls (44221) *(G-9217)*
Ron Marhofer Collision Center ... 330 686-2262
1585 Commerce Dr Stow (44224) *(G-17391)*
Ron Marhofer Lincoln Mercury, Cuyahoga Falls *Also called Ron Marhofer Automall Inc (G-9217)*
Ron Neff Her Realtors, Chillicothe *Also called Ron Neff Real Estate (G-2876)*
Ron Neff Real Estate (PA) ... 740 773-4670
153 S Paint St Chillicothe (45601) *(G-2876)*
Ronald McDonald Hse Grtr Cinci ... 513 636-5591
350 Erkenbrecher Ave Cincinnati (45229) *(G-4440)*
Rondinelli Company Inc (PA) ... 330 726-7643
207 Boardman Canfield Rd Youngstown (44512) *(G-20358)*
Rondinellis Tuxedo ... 330 726-7768
207 Boardman Canfield Rd Youngstown (44512) *(G-20359)*
Rondy & Co., Barberton *Also called Tahoma Rubber & Plastics Inc (G-983)*
Rondy Fleet Services Inc ... 330 745-9016
255 Wooster Rd N Barberton (44203) *(G-977)*
Rood Trucking Company Inc (PA) ... 330 652-3519
3505 Union St Mineral Ridge (44440) *(G-14639)*
Roofing By Insulation Inc ... 937 315-5024
1727 Dalton Dr New Carlisle (45344) *(G-15030)*
Roofing Supply Group LLC ... 614 239-1111
1288 Essex Ave Columbus (43201) *(G-8647)*
Root Inc (PA) ... 419 874-0077
5470 Main St Ste 100 Sylvania (43560) *(G-17612)*
Root Map Module, Sylvania *Also called Root Inc (G-17612)*
Rootstown Township ... 330 296-8240
4268 Sandy Lake Rd Ravenna (44266) *(G-16409)*
Roppe Distribution, Fostoria *Also called Roppe Holding Company (G-11139)*
Roppe Holding Company ... 419 435-9335
1500 Sandusky St Fostoria (44830) *(G-11139)*
Roricks Inc ... 330 497-6888
4701 Eagle St Nw Canton (44720) *(G-2516)*
Roricks Ceiling Center, Canton *Also called Roricks Inc (G-2516)*
Rosary Care Center ... 419 824-3600
6832 Convent Blvd Sylvania (43560) *(G-17613)*
Rosby Brothers Grnhse & Grnhse, Cleveland *Also called Rosby Brothers Inc (G-6411)*
Rosby Brothers Inc ... 216 351-0850
42 E Schaaf Rd Cleveland (44131) *(G-6411)*
Roschmans Restaurant ADM ... 419 225-8300
1933 Roschman Ave Lima (45804) *(G-12871)*
Roscoe Medical, Middleburg Heights *Also called Compass Health Brands Corp (G-14380)*
Roscoe Village Foundation ... 740 622-2222
200 N Whitewoman St Coshocton (43812) *(G-9116)*
Rose & Dobyns An Ohio Partnr (PA) ... 937 382-2838
97 N South St Wilmington (45177) *(G-19784)*
Rose City Manufacturing Inc ... 937 325-5561
900 W Leffel Ln Springfield (45506) *(G-17268)*
Rose Community Management LLC (PA) ... 917 542-3600
6000 Fredom Sq Dr Ste 500 Independence (44131) *(G-12254)*
Rose Garden Nursing Home, Mount Vernon *Also called Jada Inc (G-14901)*
Rose Gracias ... 614 785-0001
115 Hutchinson Ave 101-136 Columbus (43235) *(G-8648)*
Rose Lane Inc, Massillon *Also called Rose Ln Hlth Rhabilitation Inc (G-13850)*
Rose Ln Hlth Rhabilitation Inc ... 330 833-3174
5425 High Mill Ave Nw Massillon (44646) *(G-13850)*
Rose Mary Johanna Grassell (PA) ... 216 481-4823
2346 W 14th St Cleveland (44113) *(G-6412)*
Rose Metal Industries, Cleveland *Also called Rose Properties Inc (G-6413)*
Rose Products and Services Inc ... 614 443-7647
545 Stimmel Rd Columbus (43223) *(G-8649)*
Rose Properties Inc ... 216 881-6000
1536 E 43rd St Cleveland (44103) *(G-6413)*
Rose Transport Inc ... 614 864-4004
6747 Taylor Rd Sw Reynoldsburg (43068) *(G-16480)*
Rosebud Mining Company ... 740 658-4217
28490 Birmingham Rd Freeport (43973) *(G-11181)*
Rosebud Mining Company ... 740 768-2097
9076 County Road 53 Bergholz (43908) *(G-1476)*
Rosebud Mining Company ... 740 922-9122
5600 Pleasant Vly Rd Se Uhrichsville (44683) *(G-18491)*
Rosebud Mining Company ... 330 222-2334
95 N Lisbon St Carrollton (44615) *(G-2627)*
Roseland Lanes Inc ... 440 439-0097
26383 Broadway Ave Bedford (44146) *(G-1332)*
Roselawn Health Services Corp ... 330 823-0618
11999 Klinger Ave Ne Alliance (44601) *(G-558)*
Roselawn Terrace, Alliance *Also called Roselawn Health Services Corp (G-558)*
Rosemary Center ... 216 481-4823
19350 Euclid Ave Euclid (44117) *(G-10774)*
Roseville Motor Express Inc ... 614 921-2121
2720 Westbelt Dr Columbus (43228) *(G-8650)*
Rosewood Manor ... 740 859-7673
212 4th St Yorkville (43971) *(G-20093)*
Rosewood Manor Nursing Home, Yorkville *Also called Rosewood Manor (G-20093)*
Ross Sinclaire & Assoc LLC (PA) ... 513 381-3939
700 Walnut St Ste 600 Cincinnati (45202) *(G-4441)*
Ross Brittain Schonberg Lpa ... 216 447-1551
6480 Rckside Woods Blvd S Independence (44131) *(G-12255)*
Ross Cnty Cmmittee For Elderly ... 740 773-3544
1824 Western Ave Chillicothe (45601) *(G-2877)*
Ross Cnty Job & Family Svcs, Chillicothe *Also called Ross County Children Svcs Ctr (G-2878)*
Ross Consolidated Corp (PA) ... 440 748-5800
36790 Giles Rd Grafton (44044) *(G-11444)*
Ross County Children Svcs Ctr (PA) ... 740 773-2651
150 E 2nd St Chillicothe (45601) *(G-2878)*
Ross County Community (PA) ... 740 702-7222
603 Central Ctr Chillicothe (45601) *(G-2879)*

A L P H A B E T I C

Ross County Health District.....740 775-1114
150 E 2nd St Chillicothe (45601) *(G-2880)*
Ross County Water Company Inc.....740 774-4117
663 Fairgrounds Rd Chillicothe (45601) *(G-2881)*
Ross County YMCA.....740 772-4340
100 Mill St Chillicothe (45601) *(G-2882)*
Ross Dialysis, Fairfield *Also called Goza Dialysis LLC (G-10852)*
Ross Incineration Services Inc.....440 366-2000
36790 Giles Rd Grafton (44044) *(G-11445)*
Ross Training Center Inc.....937 592-0025
36 County Road 32 S Bellefontaine (43311) *(G-1394)*
Ross Transportation Svcs Inc.....440 748-5900
36790 Giles Rd Grafton (44044) *(G-11446)*
Rossford Grtric Care Ltd Prtnr.....614 459-0445
1661 Old Henderson Rd Columbus (43220) *(G-8651)*
Rossford Hospitality Group Inc.....419 874-2345
9753 Clark Dr Rossford (43460) *(G-16611)*
Rossman.....614 523-4150
7795 Walton Pkwy New Albany (43054) *(G-15006)*
Roth Bros Inc (HQ).....330 793-5571
3847 Crum Rd Youngstown (44515) *(G-20360)*
Rothert Farm Inc.....419 467-0095
1084 S Opfer Lentz Rd Elmore (43416) *(G-10589)*
Roto Group LLC.....614 760-8690
7001 Discovery Blvd Fl 2 Dublin (43017) *(G-10444)*
Roto-Rooter, Cincinnati *Also called Nurotoco Massachusetts Inc (G-4192)*
Roto-Rooter Development Co (HQ).....513 762-6690
255 E 5th St Ste 2500 Cincinnati (45202) *(G-4442)*
Roto-Rooter Group Inc (HQ).....513 762-6690
2500 Chemed Ctr Cincinnati (45202) *(G-4443)*
Roto-Rooter Services Company.....614 238-8006
4480 Bridgeway Ave Ste B Columbus (43219) *(G-8652)*
Roto-Rooter Services Company (HQ).....513 762-6690
255 E 5th St Ste 2500 Cincinnati (45202) *(G-4444)*
Roto-Rooter Services Company.....513 541-3840
2125 Montana Ave Cincinnati (45211) *(G-4445)*
Roto-Rooter Services Company.....216 429-1928
5375 Naiman Pkwy Solon (44139) *(G-17048)*
Rouen Chrysler Plymouth Dodge.....419 837-6228
1091 Fremont Pike Woodville (43469) *(G-19824)*
Rouen Dodge, Woodville *Also called Rouen Chrysler Plymouth Dodge (G-19824)*
Rough Brothers Mfg Inc.....513 242-0310
5513 Vine St Ste 1 Cincinnati (45217) *(G-4446)*
Roulston Research Corp.....216 431-3000
1350 Euclid Ave Ste 400 Cleveland (44115) *(G-6414)*
Round Room LLC.....330 880-0660
3 Massillon Mrktplc Dr Sw Massillon (44646) *(G-13851)*
Round Room LLC.....440 888-0322
9253 W Sprague Rd North Royalton (44133) *(G-15500)*
Round Room LLC.....937 429-2230
3301 Dayton Xenia Rd Beavercreek (45432) *(G-1206)*
Roundstone Management Ltd.....440 617-0333
15422 Detroit Ave Lakewood (44107) *(G-12499)*
Roundtable Online Learning LLC.....440 220-5252
8401 Chagrin Rd Ste 6 Chagrin Falls (44023) *(G-2731)*
Roundtower Technologies LLC (PA).....513 247-7900
5905 E Galbraith Rd # 3000 Cincinnati (45236) *(G-4447)*
Roush Equipment Inc (PA).....614 882-1535
100 W Schrock Rd Westerville (43081) *(G-19442)*
Roush Honda, Westerville *Also called Roush Equipment Inc (G-19442)*
Rovisys Building Tech LLC (PA).....330 954-7600
260 Campus Dr Aurora (44202) *(G-853)*
Rovisys Building Tech Rbt, Aurora *Also called Rovisys Building Tech LLC (G-853)*
Rovisys Company (PA).....330 562-8600
1455 Danner Dr Aurora (44202) *(G-854)*
Roy J Miller.....330 674-2405
6739 State Route 241 Millersburg (44654) *(G-14619)*
Royal American Links Golf Club, Galena *Also called American Golf Corporation (G-11278)*
Royal Appliance Manufacturing, Solon *Also called TTI Floor Care North Amer Inc (G-17061)*
Royal Appliance Mfg Co (HQ).....440 996-2000
7005 Cochran Rd Cleveland (44139) *(G-6415)*
Royal Arch Masons of Ohio.....419 762-5565
109 E School St Napoleon (43545) *(G-14949)*
Royal Building Cleaning Svcs, Toledo *Also called W David Maupin Inc (G-18294)*
Royal Car Wash, Canton *Also called Royal Sheen Service Center (G-2517)*
Royal Car Wash Inc.....513 385-2777
6925 Colerain Ave Cincinnati (45239) *(G-4448)*
Royal Color Inc.....440 234-1337
550 Goodrich Rd Bellevue (44811) *(G-1417)*
Royal Electric Cnstr Corp.....614 253-6600
1250 Memory Ln N Columbus (43209) *(G-8653)*
Royal Health Services LLC.....614 826-1316
3556 Sullivant Ave # 203 Columbus (43204) *(G-8654)*
Royal Manor Health Care Inc (PA).....216 752-3600
18810 Harvard Ave Cleveland (44122) *(G-6416)*
Royal Manor Homes, Cleveland *Also called Royal Oak Nrsing Rhbltion Ctr (G-6417)*
Royal Oak Nrsing Rhbltion Ctr.....440 884-9191
6973 Pearl Rd Cleveland (44130) *(G-6417)*
Royal Paper Stock Company Inc (PA).....614 851-4714
1300 Norton Rd Columbus (43228) *(G-8655)*
Royal Paper Stock Company Inc.....513 870-5780
339 Circle Freeway Dr West Chester (45246) *(G-19226)*
Royal Redeemer Lutheran Church.....440 237-7958
11680 Royalton Rd Cleveland (44133) *(G-6418)*
Royal Redeemer Lutheran School, Cleveland *Also called Royal Redeemer Lutheran Church (G-6418)*
Royal Sheen Service Center.....330 966-7200
6857 Whipple Ave Nw Canton (44720) *(G-2517)*
Royalton 6001 Ltd.....216 447-0070
6055 Rockside Woods Blvd # 100 Independence (44131) *(G-12256)*
Royalton Financial Group.....440 582-3020
13374 Ridge Rd Ste 1 Cleveland (44133) *(G-6419)*
Royalton Senior Living Inc.....440 582-4111
14277 State Rd North Royalton (44133) *(G-15501)*
Royalton Woods, North Royalton *Also called Royalton Senior Living Inc (G-15501)*
Royalty Mooney & Moses, Northwood *Also called Installed Building Pdts LLC (G-15534)*
Royce Leasing Co LLC.....740 354-1240
2125 Royce St Portsmouth (45662) *(G-16305)*
Royce Security Services, Cleveland *Also called Sam-Tom Inc (G-6441)*
Royce-Rollins Fuel Cell System, Canton *Also called Lg Fuel Cell Systems Inc (G-2435)*
RPC Electronics Inc.....877 522-7927
749 Miner Rd Ste 4 Cleveland (44143) *(G-6420)*
RPC Mechanical Services (HQ).....513 733-1641
5301 Lester Rd Cincinnati (45213) *(G-4449)*
Rpf Consulting LLC.....678 494-8030
7870 E Kemper Rd Ste 300 Cincinnati (45249) *(G-4450)*
Rpg Inc.....419 289-2757
400 Westlake Dr Ashland (44805) *(G-695)*
RPM Midwest LLC.....513 762-9000
352 Gest St Cincinnati (45203) *(G-4451)*
RR Donnelley & Sons Company.....614 539-5527
3801 Gantz Rd Ste A Grove City (43123) *(G-11593)*
Rrp Packaging.....419 666-6119
327 5th St Perrysburg (43551) *(G-16053)*
Rrr Express LLC.....800 723-3424
6432 Centre Park Dr West Chester (45069) *(G-19143)*
Rrr Logistics, West Chester *Also called Rrr Express LLC (G-19143)*
Rse Group Inc.....937 596-6167
1003 S Main St Jackson Center (45334) *(G-12325)*
Rsfi Office Furniture, Worthington *Also called Recycled Systems Furniture Inc (G-19991)*
RSI, Dayton *Also called Regent Systems Inc (G-9845)*
RSI Construction, Sunbury *Also called Restaurant Specialties Inc (G-17561)*
RSM US LLP.....937 298-0201
2000 W Dorothy Ln Moraine (45439) *(G-14821)*
RSM US LLP.....614 224-7722
250 West St Ste 200 Columbus (43215) *(G-8656)*
RSM US LLP.....216 523-1900
1001 Lakeside Ave E # 200 Cleveland (44114) *(G-6421)*
RSR Partners LLC.....440 519-1768
1831 Highland Rd Twinsburg (44087) *(G-18463)*
Rss, Cleveland *Also called Dwellworks LLC (G-5513)*
Rt80 Express Inc.....330 706-0900
4409 Clvland Massillon Rd Barberton (44203) *(G-978)*
RTC EMPLOYMENT SERVICES, Bellefontaine *Also called RTC Industries Inc (G-1395)*
RTC Industries Inc.....937 592-0534
36 County Road 32 S Bellefontaine (43311) *(G-1395)*
Rthrford B Hayes Prsdntial Ctr.....419 332-2081
Spiegel Grv Fremont (43420) *(G-11217)*
Rti, Akron *Also called Parklane Manor of Akron Inc (G-377)*
RTS, Georgetown *Also called Reliable Trnsp Solutions LLC (G-11396)*
Rtw Inc.....614 594-9217
544 W Walnut St Columbus (43215) *(G-8657)*
Rubber & Plastics News, Akron *Also called Crain Communications Inc (G-175)*
Rubber City Machinery Corp.....330 434-3500
1 Thousand Sweitzer Ave Akron (44311) *(G-419)*
Rubber City Radio Group (PA).....330 869-9800
1795 W Market St Akron (44313) *(G-420)*
Rubber City Realty Inc.....330 745-9034
942 Kenmore Blvd Akron (44314) *(G-421)*
Rubber Seal Products, Dayton *Also called Teknol Inc (G-9922)*
Rubin Erb.....330 852-4423
2149 Dutch Valley Dr Nw Sugarcreek (44681) *(G-17547)*
Rubini Enterprises Inc.....419 729-7010
5015 Enterprise Blvd Toledo (43612) *(G-18166)*
Rudolph Brothers & Co.....614 833-0707
6550 Oley Speaks Way Canal Winchester (43110) *(G-2169)*
Rudolph Libbe Inc (HQ).....419 241-5000
6494 Latcha Rd Walbridge (43465) *(G-18777)*
RUDOLPH/LIBBE, Walbridge *Also called Rudolph Libbe Inc (G-18777)*
RUDOLPH/LIBBE, Walbridge *Also called Gem Industrial Inc (G-18775)*
Rudolph/Libbe Companies Inc (PA).....419 241-5000
6494 Latcha Rd Walbridge (43465) *(G-18778)*
Rudzik Excavating Inc.....330 755-1540
401 Lowellville Rd Struthers (44471) *(G-17534)*
Ruffing Care Inc.....419 447-4662
2320 W County Road 6 Tiffin (44883) *(G-17696)*
Ruffing Family Care Ctr Tiffin, Tiffin *Also called Ruffing Care Inc (G-17696)*
RUFFING MONTESSORI SCHOOL, Cleveland *Also called Fairmount Montessori Assn (G-5565)*
Ruffing Montessori School.....440 333-2250
1285 Orchard Park Dr Rocky River (44116) *(G-16591)*

Ruhl Electric Co...330 823-7230
6428 Union Ave Ne Alliance (44601) *(G-559)*
Ruhlin Company (PA)...330 239-2800
6931 Ridge Rd Sharon Center (44274) *(G-16877)*
Rukh Boardman Properties LLC...330 726-5472
7410 South Ave Youngstown (44512) *(G-20361)*
Rukh-Jagi Holdings LLC...330 494-2770
4520 Everhard Rd Nw Canton (44718) *(G-2518)*
Rumpf Ambulance, Toledo *Also called Brookeside Ambulance Services (G-17784)*
Rumpf Corporation (PA)...419 255-5005
701 Jefferson Ave Ste 201 Toledo (43604) *(G-18167)*
Rumpke Amusements Inc...513 738-2646
10795 Hughes Rd Cincinnati (45251) *(G-4452)*
Rumpke Cnsld Companies Inc (PA)...513 738-0800
3963 Kraus Ln Hamilton (45014) *(G-11771)*
Rumpke Container Service, Dayton *Also called Rumpke Transportation Co LLC (G-9856)*
Rumpke Container Service, Cincinnati *Also called Rumpke Transportation Co LLC (G-4454)*
Rumpke Recycling, Cincinnati *Also called Rumpke Waste Inc (G-4456)*
Rumpke Recycling, Circleville *Also called Rumpke Waste Inc (G-4902)*
Rumpke Sanitary Landfill Inc...513 851-0122
10795 Hughes Rd Cincinnati (45251) *(G-4453)*
Rumpke Softball Park, Cincinnati *Also called Rumpke Amusements Inc (G-4452)*
Rumpke Transportation Co LLC...937 461-0004
1932 E Monument Ave Dayton (45402) *(G-9856)*
Rumpke Transportation Co LLC...513 242-4600
553 Vine St Cincinnati (45202) *(G-4454)*
Rumpke Waste Inc (HQ)...513 851-0122
10795 Hughes Rd Cincinnati (45251) *(G-4455)*
Rumpke Waste Inc...937 548-1939
5474 Jaysville St John Rd Greenville (45331) *(G-11517)*
Rumpke Waste Inc...937 378-4126
9427 Beyers Rd Georgetown (45121) *(G-11397)*
Rumpke Waste Inc...513 242-4401
5535 Vine St Cincinnati (45217) *(G-4456)*
Rumpke Waste Inc...740 474-9790
819 Island Rd Circleville (43113) *(G-4902)*
Rumpke Waste and Recycl Svcs, Hamilton *Also called Rumpke Cnsld Companies Inc (G-11771)*
Rumpke/Kenworth Contract...740 774-5111
65 Kenworth Dr Chillicothe (45601) *(G-2883)*
Run Jump-N-Play...513 701-7529
5897 Pfeiffer Rd Blue Ash (45242) *(G-1685)*
Runt Ware & Sanitary Service...330 494-5776
7944 Whipple Ave Nw Canton (44720) *(G-2519)*
Runyon & Sons Roofing Inc...440 974-6810
8745 Munson Rd Mentor (44060) *(G-14238)*
Rural Lorain County Water Auth...440 355-5121
42401 State Route 303 Lagrange (44050) *(G-12461)*
RURAL WATER UTILITY, Chillicothe *Also called Ross County Water Company Inc (G-2881)*
Rural/Metro Corporation...216 749-2211
1122 E Midlothian Blvd Youngstown (44502) *(G-20362)*
Rural/Metro Corporation...330 744-4161
1122 E Midlothian Blvd Youngstown (44502) *(G-20363)*
Rural/Metro Corporation...440 543-3313
8401 Chagrin Rd Ste 15a Chagrin Falls (44023) *(G-2732)*
Ruralogic Inc...419 630-0500
24500 Chagrin Blvd # 300 Beachwood (44122) *(G-1122)*
Rurbanc Data Services Inc...419 782-2530
7622 N State Route 66 Defiance (43512) *(G-10055)*
Ruritan...330 542-2308
3814 Columbiana Rd New Springfield (44443) *(G-15130)*
Ruscilli Construction Co Inc (PA)...614 876-9484
5000 Arlngtn Ctr Blvd # 300 Columbus (43220) *(G-8658)*
Ruscilli Investment Co, Columbus *Also called L Jack Ruscilli (G-8023)*
Rush Expediting Inc...937 885-0894
2619 Needmore Rd Dayton (45414) *(G-9857)*
Rush Lincoln Mercury, Columbus *Also called Rush Motor Sales Inc (G-8659)*
Rush Motor Sales Inc...614 471-9980
2350 Morse Rd Columbus (43229) *(G-8659)*
Rush Package Delivery Inc (PA)...937 224-7874
2619 Needmore Rd Dayton (45414) *(G-9858)*
Rush Package Delivery Inc...937 297-6182
2619 Needmore Rd Dayton (45414) *(G-9859)*
Rush Package Delivery Inc...513 771-7874
10091 Moteller Ln Cincinnati (45201) *(G-4457)*
Rush Trans, Cincinnati *Also called Rush Package Delivery Inc (G-4457)*
Rush Trnsp & Logistics, Dayton *Also called Rush Package Delivery Inc (G-9858)*
Rush Trnsp & Logistics, Dayton *Also called Rush Package Delivery Inc (G-9859)*
Rush Truck Center, Cincinnati, Cincinnati *Also called Rush Truck Centers Ohio Inc (G-4458)*
Rush Truck Center, Lima, Lima *Also called Rush Truck Centers Ohio Inc (G-12872)*
Rush Truck Centers Ohio Inc (HQ)...513 733-8500
11775 Highway Dr Cincinnati (45241) *(G-4458)*
Rush Truck Centers Ohio Inc...419 224-6045
2655 Saint Johns Rd Lima (45804) *(G-12872)*
Rush Truck Leasing Inc (HQ)...614 876-3500
4200 Currency Dr Columbus (43228) *(G-8660)*
Rushcard, Blue Ash *Also called Unifund Corporation (G-1710)*
Rusk Industries Inc...419 841-6055
2930 Centennial Rd Toledo (43617) *(G-18168)*
Russell D Ens Do...330 499-5700
4665 Douglas Cir Nw # 101 Canton (44718) *(G-2520)*
Russell Hawk Enterprises Inc...330 343-4612
2198 Donald Dr Dover (44622) *(G-10210)*
Russell T Bundy Associates Inc (PA)...937 652-2151
417 E Water St Ste 1 Urbana (43078) *(G-18600)*
Russell Weisman Jr MD...216 844-3127
11100 Euclid Ave Cleveland (44106) *(G-6422)*
Rusty Oak Nursery Ltd...330 225-7704
1547 Marks Rd Valley City (44280) *(G-18623)*
Rustys Towing Service Inc...614 491-6288
4845 Obetz Reese Rd Columbus (43207) *(G-8661)*
Ruth McMillan Cancer Center, Xenia *Also called US Oncology Inc (G-20082)*
Rutherford Funeral Home Inc (PA)...614 451-0593
2383 N High St Columbus (43202) *(G-8662)*
Ruthman Pump and Engineering...937 783-2411
459 E Fancy St Blanchester (45107) *(G-1516)*
Rutland Bus Garage, Middleport *Also called Meigs Local School District (G-14408)*
Rutledge Environmental Svcs, Cincinnati *Also called J Rutledge Enterprises Inc (G-3852)*
Rv Properties LLC...330 928-7888
171 Graham Rd Cuyahoga Falls (44223) *(G-9218)*
Rvet Operating LLC...513 683-5020
422 W Loveland Ave Loveland (45140) *(G-13157)*
Rwb Properties and Cnstr LLC...513 541-0900
611 Shepherd Dr Unit 6 Cincinnati (45215) *(G-4459)*
Rwc Inc...614 890-0600
6210 Frost Rd Westerville (43082) *(G-19351)*
Rwdop LLC...330 666-3776
3558 Ridgewood Rd Fairlawn (44333) *(G-10970)*
Rwk Services Inc (PA)...440 526-2144
4700 Rockside Rd Ste 330 Cleveland (44131) *(G-6423)*
RWS Enterprises LLC...513 598-6770
9019 Colerain Ave Cincinnati (45251) *(G-4460)*
Rx Options LLC (HQ)...330 405-8080
2181 E Aurora Rd Ste 101 Twinsburg (44087) *(G-18464)*
Rxoc Information Operations...937 255-1151
2977 Hobson Way Dayton (45433) *(G-9282)*
Rxp Ohio LLC...614 937-2844
630 E Broad St Columbus (43215) *(G-8663)*
Rxp Wireless, Columbus *Also called Rxp Ohio LLC (G-8663)*
Rxp Wireless LLC...330 264-1500
3417 Cleveland Rd Wooster (44691) *(G-19909)*
Ryan Logistics Inc...937 642-4158
711 Clymer Rd Marysville (43040) *(G-13648)*
Ryan Partnership, Westerville *Also called D L Ryan Companies LLC (G-19296)*
Ryan Sheridan...330 270-2380
45 N Canfield Niles Rd Youngstown (44515) *(G-20364)*
Ryan, Charles R MD Facog, Lima *Also called Ob-Gyn Specialists Lima Inc (G-12846)*
Ryans All-Glass Incorporated (PA)...513 771-4440
9884 Springfield Pike Cincinnati (45215) *(G-4461)*
Rybac Inc...614 228-3578
407 E Livingston Ave Columbus (43215) *(G-8664)*
Ryder Truck Rental Inc...614 409-6550
6500 Port Rd Groveport (43125) *(G-11668)*
Ryder Truck Rental Inc...614 846-6780
775 Schrock Rd Columbus (43229) *(G-8665)*
Ryder Truck Rental Inc...513 241-7736
1190 Gest St Cincinnati (45203) *(G-4462)*
Ryder Truck Rental Inc...419 666-9833
1380 4th St Perrysburg (43551) *(G-16054)*
Ryder Truck Rental Inc...614 876-0405
2600 Westbelt Dr Columbus (43228) *(G-8666)*
Ryder Truck Rental Inc...937 236-1650
3580 Needmore Rd Dayton (45414) *(G-9860)*
Ryder Truck Rental Inc...513 772-0223
2575 Commodity Cir Cincinnati (45241) *(G-4463)*
Ryder Truck Rental Inc...216 433-4700
11250 Brookpark Rd Cleveland (44130) *(G-6424)*
Ryerson Coil Processing, Hamilton *Also called Joseph T Ryerson & Son Inc (G-11748)*
Ryno 24 Inc...440 946-7700
4429 Hamann Pkwy Frnt Willoughby (44094) *(G-19711)*
S & B Enterprises LLC...740 753-2646
668 Poplar St Nelsonville (45764) *(G-14967)*
S & B Trucking Inc (PA)...614 554-4090
3045 Gale Dr Hubbard (44425) *(G-12091)*
S & D Application LLC (PA)...419 288-3660
158 Church St Wayne (43466) *(G-18978)*
S & E Electric Inc...330 425-7866
1521 Highland Rd Twinsburg (44087) *(G-18465)*
S & H Risner Inc...937 778-8563
314 N Wayne St Piqua (45356) *(G-16165)*
S & K Asphalt & Concrete...330 848-6284
2275 Manchester Rd Akron (44314) *(G-422)*
S & P Solutions Inc...440 918-9111
35000 Chardon Rd Ste 110 Willoughby Hills (44094) *(G-19734)*
S & S Inc...216 383-1880
21300 Saint Clair Ave Cleveland (44117) *(G-6425)*
S & S Halthcare Strategies Ltd...513 772-8866
1385 Kemper Meadow Dr Cincinnati (45240) *(G-4464)*
S & S Management Inc...937 382-5858
155 Holiday Dr Wilmington (45177) *(G-19785)*

ALPHABETIC

(PA)=Parent Co (HQ)=Headquarters (DH)=Div Headquarters
2018 Harris Ohio Services Directory
1311

S & S Management Inc 937 235-2000
5612 Merily Way Dayton (45424) ***(G-9861)***
S & S Management Inc 567 356-4151
1510 Saturn Dr Wapakoneta (45895) ***(G-18807)***
S & S Real Estate Managers LLC 937 256-7000
4996 Woodman Park Dr # 13 Dayton (45432) ***(G-9283)***
S & T Truck and Auto Svc Inc 614 272-8163
3150 Valleyview Dr Rm 8 Columbus (43204) ***(G-8667)***
S & W Properties, Columbus *Also called D & S Properties* ***(G-7478)***
S A, Columbus *Also called Safe Auto Insurance Company* ***(G-8668)***
S A F Y, Delphos *Also called For Specialized Alternatives* ***(G-10144)***
S A I, New Albany *Also called Shremshock Architects Inc* ***(G-15007)***
S A Storer and Sons Company 419 843-3133
3135 Centennial Rd Sylvania (43560) ***(G-17614)***
S A T Landscaping, Columbus *Also called Spray A Tree Inc* ***(G-8764)***
S A W - Rocky River Adult Trai, Rocky River *Also called A W S Inc* ***(G-16567)***
S A W Adult Training Center, Cleveland *Also called A W S Inc* ***(G-4937)***
S and R Leasing 330 276-3061
9705 Township Rd Millersburg (44654) ***(G-14620)***
S and S Gilardi Inc 740 397-2751
1033 Newark Rd Mount Vernon (43050) ***(G-14921)***
S B Morabito Trucking Inc 216 441-3070
3560 E 55th St Cleveland (44105) ***(G-6426)***
S B S Transit Inc 440 288-2222
1800 Colorado Ave Lorain (44052) ***(G-13075)***
S C A T, Tiffin *Also called Seneca-Crawford Area Trnsp* ***(G-17702)***
S C E, Brookpark *Also called Standard Contg & Engrg Inc* ***(G-1955)***
S C O R E, Cleveland *Also called Service Corps Retired Execs* ***(G-6471)***
S C O R E, Toledo *Also called Service Corps Retired Execs* ***(G-18180)***
S C O R E 81, Akron *Also called Service Corps Retired Execs* ***(G-434)***
S C R, Mentor On The Lake *Also called Strategic Consumer Research* ***(G-14262)***
S C Wooster Bus Garage 330 264-4060
1494 Old Mansfield Rd Wooster (44691) ***(G-19910)***
S D Myers Inc 330 630-7000
180 South Ave Tallmadge (44278) ***(G-17648)***
S E S, West Chester *Also called Superior Envmtl Sltons SES Inc* ***(G-19234)***
S E S, West Chester *Also called Superior Envmtl Solutions LLC* ***(G-19235)***
S E T Inc 330 536-6724
235 E Water St Ste C Lowellville (44436) ***(G-13174)***
S F S, Clyde *Also called Spader Freight Services Inc* ***(G-6824)***
S G I, Cincinnati *Also called The Sheakley Group Inc* ***(G-4646)***
S G Loewendick and Sons Inc 614 539-2582
2877 Jackson Pike Grove City (43123) ***(G-11594)***
S M C, Upper Sandusky *Also called Schmidt Machine Company* ***(G-18566)***
S M E, Columbus *Also called Settle Muter Electric Ltd* ***(G-8718)***
S O R T A, Cincinnati *Also called Southwest OH Trans Auth* ***(G-4553)***
S P C A Cincinnati, Cincinnati *Also called Hamilton County Society* ***(G-3733)***
S P Richards Company 614 497-2270
2410 Mcgaw Rd Obetz (43207) ***(G-15670)***
S P S & Associates Inc 330 283-4267
2926 Ivanhoe Rd Silver Lake (44224) ***(G-16963)***
S P S Inc 937 339-7801
45 Troy Town Dr Troy (45373) ***(G-18378)***
S R Door Inc (PA) 740 927-3558
1120 O Neill Dr Hebron (43025) ***(G-11859)***
S R Restaurant Corp 216 781-6784
1836 Euclid Ave Ste 800 Cleveland (44115) ***(G-6427)***
S S Kemp & Company (HQ) 216 271-7062
4567 Willow Pkwy Cleveland (44125) ***(G-6428)***
S W S, Akron *Also called Sws Equipment Services Inc* ***(G-470)***
S&D/Osterfeld Mech Contrs Inc 937 277-1700
1101 Negley Pl Dayton (45402) ***(G-9862)***
S&Me Inc 614 793-2226
6190 Enterprise Ct Dublin (43016) ***(G-10445)***
S&P Data Ohio LLC 216 965-0018
1500 W 3rd St Ste 130 Cleveland (44113) ***(G-6429)***
S&P Global Inc 614 835-2444
6405 Commerce Ct Groveport (43125) ***(G-11669)***
S&P Global Inc 330 482-9544
41438 Kings Ct Leetonia (44431) ***(G-12662)***
S&S Car Care Inc 330 494-9535
5340 Mayfair Rd Canton (44720) ***(G-2521)***
S&V Industries Inc (PA) 330 666-1986
5054 Paramount Dr Medina (44256) ***(G-14121)***
S-L Distribution Company Inc 740 676-6932
3157 Guernsey St Bellaire (43906) ***(G-1367)***
S. B. Stone & Company, Independence *Also called Level Seven* ***(G-12224)***
S. Rose Company, Cleveland *Also called Office Furniture Resources Inc* ***(G-6180)***
S.E.I., New Philadelphia *Also called Starlight Enterprises Inc* ***(G-15116)***
S.E.S., Alliance *Also called Steel Eqp Specialists Inc* ***(G-563)***
S.O.S., Cleveland *Also called Senior Outreach Services* ***(G-6470)***
S.O.S. Electric, Chillicothe *Also called Oyer Electric Inc* ***(G-2868)***
Sabco Industries Inc 419 531-5347
4511 South Ave Toledo (43615) ***(G-18169)***
Saber Healthcare Group LLC 330 369-4672
1926 Ridge Ave Se Warren (44484) ***(G-18894)***
Saber Healthcare Group LLC 330 297-4564
6831 N Chestnut St Ravenna (44266) ***(G-16410)***
Saber Healthcare Group LLC 937 382-1621
75 Hale St Wilmington (45177) ***(G-19786)***
Saber Healthcare Group LLC 440 546-0643
8757 Brecksville Rd Brecksville (44141) ***(G-1848)***
Saber Healthcare Group LLC 513 631-6800
1500 Sherman Ave Cincinnati (45212) ***(G-4465)***
Saber Healthcare Group LLC 216 486-5736
1500 E 191st St Euclid (44117) ***(G-10775)***
Saber Healthcare Group LLC 216 795-5710
1802 Crawford Rd Cleveland (44106) ***(G-6430)***
Saber Healthcare Group LLC 216 662-3343
19900 Clare Ave Maple Heights (44137) ***(G-13416)***
Saber Healthcare Group LLC 937 826-3351
1649 Park Rd Woodstock (43084) ***(G-19821)***
Saber Healthcare Group LLC 419 483-6225
1 Audrich Sq Bellevue (44811) ***(G-1418)***
Saber Healthcare Group LLC 330 638-4015
369 N High St Cortland (44410) ***(G-9082)***
Saber Healthcare Group LLC 419 484-1111
24201 W 3rd St Grand Rapids (43522) ***(G-11454)***
Saber Healthcare Group LLC (PA) 216 292-5706
26691 Richmond Rd Frnt Bedford (44146) ***(G-1333)***
Saber Healthcare Group LLC 216 292-5706
120 Brookmont Rd Akron (44333) ***(G-423)***
Saber Healthcare Group LLC 330 650-0436
563 W Streetsboro St Hudson (44236) ***(G-12142)***
Sable Creek Golf Course Inc 330 877-9606
5942 Edison St Ne Hartville (44632) ***(G-11829)***
Sabroske Electric Inc 419 332-6444
115 Lincoln St Fremont (43420) ***(G-11218)***
Sabry Hospital 216 476-7052
18101 Lorain Ave Cleveland (44111) ***(G-6431)***
Sack n Save Inc 740 382-2464
725 Richmond Ave Marion (43302) ***(G-13578)***
Sacs Cnslting Invstigative Svc, Akron *Also called Sacs Cnslting Training Ctr Inc* ***(G-424)***
Sacs Cnslting Training Ctr Inc 330 255-1101
520 S Main St Ste 2516 Akron (44311) ***(G-424)***
Sadguru Krupa LLC 330 644-2111
897 Arlington Rdg E Akron (44312) ***(G-425)***
Sadler-Necamp Financial Svcs 513 489-5477
7621 E Kemper Rd Cincinnati (45249) ***(G-4466)***
Saec/Kinetic Vision Inc 513 793-4959
10255 Evendale Commons Dr Cincinnati (45241) ***(G-4467)***
Safe Auto Insurance Company 740 472-1900
47060 Black Walnut Pkwy Woodsfield (43793) ***(G-19819)***
Safe Auto Insurance Company (HQ) 614 231-0200
4 Easton Oval Columbus (43219) ***(G-8668)***
Safe Auto Insurance Group Inc (PA) 614 231-0200
4 Easton Oval Columbus (43219) ***(G-8669)***
Safe-N-Sound Security Inc 330 491-1148
5555 County Road 203 Millersburg (44654) ***(G-14621)***
Safegard Bckgrund Screning LLC 216 370-7345
3711 Chester Ave Cleveland (44114) ***(G-6432)***
Safeguard Properties LLC (HQ) 216 739-2900
7887 Safeguard Cir Cleveland (44125) ***(G-6433)***
Safeguard Properties MGT LLC (PA) 216 739-2900
7887 Hub Pkwy Cleveland (44125) ***(G-6434)***
Safelite Autoglass, Columbus *Also called Safelite Fulfillment Inc* ***(G-8670)***
Safelite Autoglass, Cleveland *Also called Safelite Fulfillment Inc* ***(G-6435)***
Safelite Autoglass, Columbus *Also called Safelite Group Inc* ***(G-8672)***
Safelite Fulfillment Inc 614 781-5449
760 Dearborn Park Ln Columbus (43085) ***(G-8670)***
Safelite Fulfillment Inc 216 475-7781
6050 Towpath Dr Ste A Cleveland (44125) ***(G-6435)***
Safelite Fulfillment Inc 614 210-9050
7400 Safelite Way Columbus (43235) ***(G-8671)***
Safelite Glass Corp 614 431-4936
600 Lkview Plz Blvd Ste A Worthington (43085) ***(G-19995)***
Safelite Group Inc (HQ) 614 210-9000
7400 Safelite Way Columbus (43235) ***(G-8672)***
Safelite Solutions LLC 614 210-9000
7400 Safelite Way Columbus (43235) ***(G-8673)***
Safely Home Inc 440 232-9310
121 Center Rd Ofc Bedford (44146) ***(G-1334)***
Safety and Hygiene, Pickerington *Also called Bureau Workers Compensation* ***(G-16088)***
Safety and Sustainment Branch, Dayton *Also called Landing Gear Test Facility* ***(G-9276)***
Safety Grooving & Grinding LP 419 592-8666
13226 County Road R Napoleon (43545) ***(G-14950)***
Safety Resources Company Ohio 330 477-1100
4650 Southway St Sw Canton (44706) ***(G-2522)***
Safety Solutions Inc (HQ) 614 799-9900
6161 Shamrock Ct Dublin (43016) ***(G-10446)***
Safety Today Inc (HQ) 614 409-7200
3287 Southwest Blvd Grove City (43123) ***(G-11595)***
Safety-Kleen Systems Inc 513 563-0931
4120 Thunderbird Ln Fairfield (45014) ***(G-10902)***
Safety-Kleen Systems Inc 740 929-3532
581 Milliken Dr Hebron (43025) ***(G-11860)***
Safety-Kleen Systems Inc 440 992-8665
1302 W 38th St Ashtabula (44004) ***(G-761)***

Safeway Electric Company Inc........614 443-7672
1973 Lockbourne Rd Columbus (43207) *(G-8674)*
Safran Humn Rsrces Support Inc (HQ)........513 552-3230
111 Merchant St Cincinnati (45246) *(G-4468)*
Safran Power Usa LLC........330 487-2000
8380 Darrow Rd Twinsburg (44087) *(G-18466)*
Saftek Industrial Service Inc........937 667-1772
15 Industry Park Ct Tipp City (45371) *(G-17726)*
Safway Services LLC........513 860-2626
9536 Glades Dr West Chester (45011) *(G-19144)*
Safy, Delphos *Also called Specialized Alternatives For F (G-10151)*
Safy of Cleveland, Shaker Heights *Also called Specialized Alternatives For F (G-16867)*
Saga Communications Neng Inc........614 451-2191
4401 Carriage Hill Ln Columbus (43220) *(G-8675)*
Sagamore Hills Medical Center, Northfield *Also called Clevelnd Clnc Hlth Systm East (G-15512)*
Sagar Satyavolu MD........937 323-1404
1911 E High St Springfield (45505) *(G-17269)*
Sage Hospitality Resources LLC........513 771-2080
11320 Chester Rd Cincinnati (45246) *(G-4469)*
Saia Motor Freight Line LLC........419 726-9761
1919 E Manhattan Blvd Toledo (43608) *(G-18170)*
Saia Motor Freight Line LLC........330 659-4277
2920 Brecksville Rd Ste B Richfield (44286) *(G-16528)*
Saia Motor Freight Line LLC........614 870-8778
1717 Krieger St Columbus (43228) *(G-8676)*
Saini, Hari MD, Miamisburg *Also called Schuster Cardiology (G-14346)*
Saint Cecilia Church........614 878-5353
440 Norton Rd Columbus (43228) *(G-8677)*
Saint Edward Housing Corp........330 668-2828
3125 Smith Rd Ofc Fairlawn (44333) *(G-10971)*
Saint Edward's Church, Ashland *Also called Catholic Diocese of Cleveland (G-671)*
Saint Francis De Sales Church........440 884-2319
3434 George Ave Cleveland (44134) *(G-6436)*
Saint James Day Care Center........513 662-2287
3929 Boudinot Ave Cincinnati (45211) *(G-4470)*
Saint Johns Villa........330 627-4662
701 Crest St Nw Carrollton (44615) *(G-2628)*
Saint Joseph Orphanage........513 231-5010
274 Sutton Rd Cincinnati (45230) *(G-4471)*
Saint Joseph Orphanage (PA)........513 741-3100
5400 Edalbert Dr Cincinnati (45239) *(G-4472)*
Saint Joseph Orphanage........937 643-0398
3131 S Dixie Dr Ste 220 Moraine (45439) *(G-14822)*
Saint Mary Parish........440 285-7051
401 North St Chardon (44024) *(G-2766)*
Saint Marys Cy Schools-Bus Gar, Saint Marys *Also called St Marys City Board Education (G-16684)*
Saint Marys Living Center, Saint Marys *Also called Communicare Health Svcs Inc (G-16672)*
Saint Moritz Security Services, Youngstown *Also called St Moritz Security Svcs Inc (G-20381)*
Saint Rtas Bhavioral Hlth Svcs, Lima *Also called St Ritas Medical Center (G-12884)*
Sairb, Blue Ash *Also called Schulman Assocs Instl Review (G-1687)*
Saleh, Hady DMD, Tipp City *Also called Charles C Smith DDS Inc (G-17712)*
Salem Area Vsiting Nurse Assoc........330 332-9986
718 E 3rd St Ste A Salem (44460) *(G-16711)*
Salem Church of God Inc........937 836-6500
6500 Southway Rd Unit 2 Clayton (45315) *(G-4916)*
Salem Community Center Inc........330 332-5885
1098 N Ellsworth Ave Salem (44460) *(G-16712)*
Salem Community Hospital (PA)........330 332-1551
1995 E State St Salem (44460) *(G-16713)*
Salem Dental Laboratory, Cleveland *Also called National Dentex LLC (G-6105)*
Salem Healthcare MGT LLC........330 332-1588
1985 E Pershing St Salem (44460) *(G-16714)*
Salem Hills Golf and Cntry CLB, Salem *Also called Lake Front II Inc (G-16703)*
Salem Historical Soc Museum........330 337-6733
208 S Broadway Ave Salem (44460) *(G-16715)*
SALEM HOME MEDICAL, Salem *Also called Salem Community Hospital (G-16713)*
Salem Internal Medicine Assoc........330 332-5232
564 E 2nd St Salem (44460) *(G-16716)*
Salem Media Group Inc........216 901-0921
4 Summit Park Dr Ste 150 Cleveland (44131) *(G-6437)*
Salem West Healthcare Center, Salem *Also called Bentley Leasing Co LLC (G-16688)*
Salem West Healthcare Center, Wintersville *Also called Communicare Health Svcs Inc (G-19809)*
Sales Building Systems, Mentor *Also called Contract Marketing Inc (G-14162)*
Salidawoods, Mentor *Also called Lifeservices Development Corp (G-14209)*
Saline Township........330 532-2195
164 Main St Hammondsville (43930) *(G-11786)*
Sally Beauty Supply 9927, Columbus *Also called Sally Beauty Supply LLC (G-8678)*
Sally Beauty Supply LLC........937 548-7684
5805 Jaysville St John Rd Greenville (45331) *(G-11518)*
Sally Beauty Supply LLC........614 278-1691
4309 Janitrol Rd Columbus (43228) *(G-8678)*
Salo Inc........740 623-2331
232 Chestnut St Coshocton (43812) *(G-9117)*
Salo Inc (PA)........614 436-9404
960 Checkrein Ave Ste A Columbus (43229) *(G-8679)*
Salo Incorporated........740 964-2904
350 S Main St B Pataskala (43062) *(G-15925)*
Saloma Intl Co Since 1978........440 941-1527
430 Grant St Akron (44311) *(G-426)*
Salomanetics, Akron *Also called Saloma Intl Co Since 1978 (G-426)*
Salon Alexandre Inc........513 207-8406
9755 Cncnnati Columbus Rd West Chester (45241) *(G-19227)*
Salon Communication Services........614 233-8500
650 N High St Columbus (43215) *(G-8680)*
Salon Hazelton........419 874-9404
131 W Indiana Ave Perrysburg (43551) *(G-16055)*
Salon La........513 784-1700
2711 Edmondson Rd Cincinnati (45209) *(G-4473)*
Salon PS, Cleveland *Also called PS Lifestyle LLC (G-6328)*
Salon Spa & Wellness Center, West Chester *Also called Hairy Cactus Salon Inc (G-19087)*
Salon Success Intl LLC........330 468-0476
420 Highland Rd E Macedonia (44056) *(G-13209)*
Salon Ware Inc........330 665-2244
1298 Centerview Cir Copley (44321) *(G-9062)*
Sals Heating and Cooling Inc........216 676-4949
11701 Royalton Rd Cleveland (44133) *(G-6438)*
Salt Fork Resort Club Inc........740 498-8116
74978 Broadhead Rd Kimbolton (43749) *(G-12447)*
Salt Fork Rsort Conference Ctr, Cambridge *Also called Xanterra Parks & Resorts Inc (G-2134)*
Salutary Providers Inc........440 964-8446
2217 West Ave Ashtabula (44004) *(G-762)*
Salvagedata Recovery LLC (PA)........914 600-2434
43 Alpha Park Cleveland (44143) *(G-6439)*
Salvagnini America Inc (HQ)........513 874-8284
27 Bicentennial Ct Hamilton (45015) *(G-11772)*
Salvation Army, Galion *Also called Ohio Hrtland Cmnty Action Comm (G-11303)*
Salvation Army........614 252-7171
966 E Main St Columbus (43205) *(G-8681)*
Salvation Army........937 528-5100
1000 N Keowee St Dayton (45404) *(G-9863)*
Salvation Army........419 447-2252
505 E Market St Tiffin (44883) *(G-17697)*
Salvation Army........859 255-5791
2250 Park Ave Cincinnati (45212) *(G-4474)*
Salvation Army........330 762-8481
190 S Maple St Akron (44302) *(G-427)*
Salvation Army........800 728-7825
1675 S High St Columbus (43207) *(G-8682)*
Salvation Army........513 762-5600
114 East Central Pkwy Cincinnati (45202) *(G-4475)*
Salvation Army........216 861-8185
2507 E 22nd St Cleveland (44115) *(G-6440)*
Salvation Army........330 773-3331
1006 Grant St Akron (44311) *(G-428)*
Salvation Army........330 735-2671
5037 Edgewood Rd Sw Carrollton (44615) *(G-2629)*
Sam BS Restaurant........419 353-2277
163 S Main St Bowling Green (43402) *(G-1793)*
Sam's Distribution Center, Westerville *Also called Dhl Supply Chain (usa) (G-19299)*
Sam-Tom Inc........216 426-7752
3740 Euclid Ave Ste 102 Cleveland (44115) *(G-6441)*
Samanritan Family Care, Dayton *Also called Primary Cr Ntwrk Prmr Hlth Prt (G-9825)*
Samaritan Behavioral Health (HQ)........937 276-8333
601 Enid Ave Dayton (45429) *(G-9864)*
Samaritan Care Center & Villa, Medina *Also called Ahf Ohio Inc (G-14033)*
Samaritan Care Center & Villa........330 725-4123
806 E Washington St Medina (44256) *(G-14122)*
Samaritan Crisiscare, Dayton *Also called Good Samaritan Hospital (G-9576)*
Samaritan Health & Rehab Ctr, Ashland *Also called Samaritan Regional Health Sys (G-697)*
Samaritan Health Partners (HQ)........937 208-8400
2222 Philadelphia Dr Dayton (45406) *(G-9865)*
Samaritan N Surgery Ctr Ltd........937 567-6100
9000 N Main St Englewood (45415) *(G-10719)*
Samaritan Professional Corp........419 289-0491
1025 Center St Ashland (44805) *(G-696)*
Samaritan Regional Health Sys........419 281-1330
2163 Claremont Ave Ashland (44805) *(G-697)*
Samaritan Regional Health Sys (PA)........419 289-0491
1025 Center St Ashland (44805) *(G-698)*
Sami S Rafidi........330 799-9508
2000 Canfield Rd Youngstown (44511) *(G-20365)*
Samkel Inc........614 491-3270
100 Obetz Rd Columbus (43207) *(G-8683)*
Sammy's, Cleveland *Also called City Life Inc (G-5246)*
Sample Machining Inc........937 258-3338
220 N Jersey St Dayton (45403) *(G-9866)*
Samples Chuck-General Contr........419 586-1434
1460 E Wayne St Celina (45822) *(G-2663)*
Samron Inc........330 782-6539
674 Bev Rd Youngstown (44512) *(G-20366)*
Samsel Rope & Marine Supply Co (PA)........216 241-0333
1285 Old River Rd Uppr Cleveland (44113) *(G-6442)*
Samsel Supply Company, Cleveland *Also called Samsel Rope & Marine Supply Co (G-6442)*

ALPHABETIC

(PA)=Parent Co (HQ)=Headquarters (DH)=Div Headquarters
2018 Harris Ohio
Services Directory
1313

Samuel Son & Co Inc 419 470-7070
  1500 Coining Dr Toledo (43612) *(G-18171)*
Samuel Steel Pickling Company (PA) 330 963-3777
  1400 Enterprise Pkwy Twinsburg (44087) *(G-18467)*
Samuel Strapping Systems Inc 740 522-2500
  1455 James Pkwy Heath (43056) *(G-11843)*
Samuels Products Inc 513 891-4456
  9851 Redhill Dr Blue Ash (45242) *(G-1686)*
Sanborn Vending, Nelsonville Also called S & B Enterprises LLC *(G-14967)*
Sanctuary At The Ohio Valley, Ironton Also called Ahf Ohio Inc *(G-12280)*
Sanctuary At Tuttle Crossing 614 408-0182
  4880 Tuttle Rd Dublin (43017) *(G-10447)*
Sanctuary At Wilmington Place 937 256-4663
  264 Wilmington Ave Dayton (45420) *(G-9867)*
Sanctuary of The Ohio Valley, Ironton Also called Bryant Health Center Inc *(G-12283)*
Sanctuary Software Studio Inc 330 666-9690
  3560 W Market St Ste 100 Fairlawn (44333) *(G-10972)*
Sand Ridge Golf Club 440 285-8088
  12150 Mayfield Rd Chardon (44024) *(G-2767)*
Sand Run Supports LLC 330 256-2127
  2695 Sand Run Pkwy Fairlawn (44333) *(G-10973)*
Sand T Nursing Home, Brunswick Also called Willowood Care Center *(G-1997)*
Sandco Industries 419 334-9090
  567 Premier Dr Clyde (43410) *(G-6822)*
Sandel Corp 614 475-5898
  152 N High St Gahanna (43230) *(G-11267)*
Sander Woody Ford (PA) 513 541-5586
  235 W Mitchell Ave Cincinnati (45232) *(G-4476)*
Sandridge Food Corporation 330 725-8883
  133 Commerce Dr Medina (44256) *(G-14123)*
Sandridge Gourmet Salads, Medina Also called Sandridge Food Corporation *(G-14123)*
Sands Decker Cps Llc (PA) 614 459-6992
  1495 Old Henderson Rd Columbus (43220) *(G-8684)*
Sands Hill Coal Hauling Co Inc (PA) 740 384-4211
  38701 State Route 160 Hamden (45634) *(G-11688)*
Sandusky Area YMCA Foundation 419 621-9622
  2101 W Perkins Ave Sandusky (44870) *(G-16790)*
Sandusky Cnty Job & Fmly Svcs, Fremont Also called Ohio Dept of Job & Fmly Svcs *(G-11215)*
Sandusky County Engr & Hwy Gar 419 334-9731
  2500 W State St Fremont (43420) *(G-11219)*
Sandusky Harbor Marina Inc 419 627-1201
  1 Huron St Sandusky (44870) *(G-16791)*
Sandusky Harbour Marina, Sandusky Also called Sandusky Harbor Marina Inc *(G-16791)*
Sandusky Newspapers Inc (PA) 419 625-5500
  314 W Market St Sandusky (44870) *(G-16792)*
Sandusky Register 419 625-5500
  314 W Market St Sandusky (44870) *(G-16793)*
Sandusky Rotary Club Charitabl 419 625-1707
  1722 Sandpiper Ct Huron (44839) *(G-12169)*
Sandusky Yacht Club Inc 419 625-6567
  529 E Water St Sandusky (44870) *(G-16794)*
Sandusky YMCA, Sandusky Also called Sandusky Area YMCA Foundation *(G-16790)*
Sandy Creek Joint Fire Dst 330 868-5193
  505 E Lincolnway Minerva (44657) *(G-14650)*
Sandys Auto & Truck Svc Inc 937 461-4980
  3053 Springboro W Moraine (45439) *(G-14823)*
Sandys Towing (PA) 937 461-4980
  3053 Springboro W Moraine (45439) *(G-14824)*
Sanese Services Inc (PA) 614 436-1234
  2590 Elm Rd Ne Warren (44483) *(G-18895)*
Sanfillipos Automotive Service, Cincinnati Also called Glenway Automotive Service *(G-3679)*
Sanfrey Freight Services Inc 330 372-1883
  695 Summit St Nw Ste 1 Warren (44485) *(G-18896)*
Sanico Inc 440 439-5686
  7601 First Pl Ste 12 Cleveland (44146) *(G-6443)*
Sanitation & Garage Services, Marion Also called City of Marion *(G-13531)*
Sanoh America Inc 740 392-9200
  7905 Industrial Park Dr Mount Vernon (43050) *(G-14922)*
Santa Maria Community Svcs Inc (PA) 513 557-2720
  617 Steiner St Cincinnati (45204) *(G-4477)*
Santantonio Diana and Assoc 440 323-5121
  750 Abbe Rd S Elyria (44035) *(G-10677)*
Santas Hide Away Hollow Inc 440 632-5000
  15400 Bundysburg Rd Middlefield (44062) *(G-14402)*
Santmyer Oil Co Inc (PA) 330 262-6501
  3000 Old Airport Rd Wooster (44691) *(G-19911)*
Santo Salon & Spa, Pepper Pike Also called Frank Santo LLC *(G-15955)*
Sap America Inc 513 762-7630
  312 Walnut St Ste 1600 Cincinnati (45202) *(G-4478)*
Sar Biren 419 865-0407
  6425 Kit Ln Maumee (43537) *(G-13974)*
Sar Enterprises LLC 419 472-8181
  2631 W Central Ave Toledo (43606) *(G-18172)*
Sarah Jane Living Center Ltd 419 692-6618
  328 W 2nd St Delphos (45833) *(G-10150)*
SARAH MOORE COMMUNITY, Delaware Also called Sarah Moore Hlth Care Ctr Inc *(G-10125)*
Sarah Moore Hlth Care Ctr Inc 740 362-9641
  26 N Union St Delaware (43015) *(G-10125)*

Saras Garden 419 335-7272
  620 W Leggett St Wauseon (43567) *(G-18962)*
Sardinia Life Squad 937 446-2178
  159 Winchester St Sardinia (45171) *(G-16814)*
Sargus Juvenille Center, Saint Clairsville Also called Bellmont County *(G-16618)*
Sarnova Inc (PA) 614 760-5000
  5000 Tuttle Crossing Blvd Dublin (43016) *(G-10448)*
Saro Truck Dispatch Inc 419 873-1358
  26180 Glenwood Rd Perrysburg (43551) *(G-16056)*
Sarta, Canton Also called Stark Area Regional Trnst Auth *(G-2539)*
Sasi, Toledo Also called Substance Abuse Services Inc *(G-18206)*
Sasi, Toledo Also called Compass Corp For Recovery Svcs *(G-17825)*
Satcom Service LLC 614 863-6470
  7052 Americana Pkwy Reynoldsburg (43068) *(G-16481)*
Sateri Home Inc (PA) 330 758-8106
  7246 Ronjoy Pl Youngstown (44512) *(G-20367)*
Sattlerpearson Inc 419 698-3822
  3055 E Plaza Blvd Northwood (43619) *(G-15544)*
Saturn Electric Inc 937 278-2580
  2628 Nordic Rd Dayton (45414) *(G-9868)*
Saturn of Toledo Inc 419 841-9070
  6141 W Central Ave Toledo (43615) *(G-18173)*
Saturn-West, Columbus Also called Northern Automotive Inc *(G-8290)*
Sauder Haritage Inn 419 445-6408
  22611 State Route 2 Archbold (43502) *(G-643)*
Sauder Village 419 446-2541
  22611 State Route 2 Archbold (43502) *(G-644)*
Sauder Woodworking Co (PA) 419 446-3828
  502 Middle St Archbold (43502) *(G-645)*
Sauder's Quality Eggs, Winesburg Also called R W Sauder Inc *(G-19806)*
Sauer Group Inc 614 853-2500
  1801 Lone Eagle St Columbus (43228) *(G-8685)*
Sauer Incorporated 614 853-2500
  1801 Lone Eagle St Columbus (43228) *(G-8686)*
Savage and Associates Inc (PA) 419 475-8665
  4427 Talmadge Rd Bldg 2 Toledo (43623) *(G-18174)*
Savage and Associates Inc 419 731-4441
  104 E Wyandot Ave Upper Sandusky (43351) *(G-18565)*
Savage Auto Supply Div, Hamilton Also called Hamilton Automotive Warehouse *(G-11738)*
Savage Auto Supply Div, Hamilton Also called Hamilton Automotive Warehouse *(G-11739)*
Savare Corporation (HQ) 770 517-3749
  230 West St Ste 700 Columbus (43215) *(G-8687)*
Save Edge USA, Xenia Also called File Sharpening Company Inc *(G-20050)*
Savings Bank (PA) 740 474-3191
  118 N Court St 120 Circleville (43113) *(G-4903)*
Saw Mill Creek Ltd 419 433-3800
  400 Sawmill Creek Dr W Huron (44839) *(G-12170)*
Saw Service and Supply Company 216 252-5600
  11925 Zelis Rd Cleveland (44135) *(G-6444)*
Sawdey Solution Services Inc (PA) 937 490-4060
  1430 Oak Ct Ste 304 Beavercreek (45430) *(G-1259)*
Sawmill Creek Golf Racquet CLB, Huron Also called Sawmill Greek Golf Racquet CLB *(G-12173)*
Sawmill Creek Golf Racquet CLB 419 433-4945
  2401 Cleveland Rd W Huron (44839) *(G-12171)*
Sawmill Creek Resort Ltd 419 433-3800
  400 Sawmill Creek Dr W Huron (44839) *(G-12172)*
Sawmill Creek Shops, Huron Also called Sawmill Creek Golf Racquet CLB *(G-12171)*
Sawmill Greek Golf Racquet CLB 419 433-3789
  300 Sawmill Creek Dr W Huron (44839) *(G-12173)*
Sawmill Road Management Co LLC (PA) 937 342-9071
  1990 Kingsgate Rd Ste A Springfield (45502) *(G-17270)*
Sawyer Realtors 513 423-6521
  1505 S Breiel Blvd Middletown (45044) *(G-14456)*
Sawyer Steel Erectors Inc 419 867-8050
  1761 Commerce Rd Holland (43528) *(G-12052)*
Sax 5th Ave Car Wash Inc (PA) 614 486-9093
  1319 W 5th Ave Columbus (43212) *(G-8688)*
Sax Car Wash, Columbus Also called Sax 5th Ave Car Wash Inc *(G-8688)*
Saxon House Condo 440 333-8675
  3167 Linden Rd Cleveland (44116) *(G-6445)*
Saxton Real Estate Co (PA) 614 875-2327
  3703 Broadway Grove City (43123) *(G-11596)*
Sayles Company LLC 614 801-0432
  1575 Integrity Dr E Columbus (43209) *(G-8689)*
Sb Capital Acquisitions LLC 614 443-4080
  4010 E 5th Ave Columbus (43219) *(G-8690)*
Sb Capital Group LLC (PA) 516 829-2400
  4300 E 5th Ave Columbus (43219) *(G-8691)*
Sb Financial Group Inc (PA) 419 783-8950
  401 Clinton St Defiance (43512) *(G-10056)*
Sb Hotel LLC (PA) 614 793-2244
  5775 Perimeter Dr Ste 290 Dublin (43017) *(G-10449)*
SBC Advertising Ltd 614 891-7070
  333 W Nationwide Blvd Columbus (43215) *(G-8692)*
SBC Recycling, Centerburg Also called Shredded Bedding Corporation *(G-2668)*
Sbh I & II, Columbus Also called Spruce Bough Homes LLC *(G-8768)*
Sbm Business Services Inc (HQ) 330 396-7000
  333 S Main St Ste 200 Akron (44308) *(G-429)*
SC Chippewa Preschool, Doylestown Also called Chippewa School District *(G-10225)*

SC Madison Bus Garage...419 589-3373
600 Esley Ln Mansfield (44905) *(G-13362)*
Scanner Applications LLC...513 248-5588
400 Milford Pkwy Milford (45150) *(G-14559)*
Scanner Applications, Inc., Milford *Also called Scanner Applications LLC (G-14559)*
Scarbrough E Tennis Fitnes CLB, Columbus *Also called Scarbrough E Tennis Fitnes Ctr (G-8693)*
Scarbrough E Tennis Fitnes Ctr...614 751-2597
5641 Alshire Rd Columbus (43232) *(G-8693)*
Scared Heart Nursing Home, Oregon *Also called Sisters of Little (G-15749)*
Scarffs Nursery Inc...937 845-3130
411 N Dayton Lakeview Rd New Carlisle (45344) *(G-15031)*
Scarlet & Gray Cleaning Svc...513 661-4483
3247 Glenmore Ave Apt 1 Cincinnati (45211) *(G-4479)*
Scci Hospital Lima, Lima *Also called Kindred Healthcare Inc (G-12809)*
Scene Magazine, Cleveland *Also called Northeast Scene Inc (G-6157)*
Scenic Ridge Fruit Farms...419 368-3353
2031 State Route 89 Jeromesville (44840) *(G-12334)*
Scg Fields LLC...440 546-1200
10303 Brecksville Rd Brecksville (44141) *(G-1849)*
Schaaf Drugs LLC (PA)...419 879-4327
1331 N Cole St Lima (45801) *(G-12873)*
Schaffer Mark Excvtg & Trcking...419 668-5990
1623 Old State Rd N Norwalk (44857) *(G-15592)*
Schauer Group Incorporated...330 453-7721
200 Market Ave N Ste 100 Canton (44702) *(G-2523)*
Schauer Indpendence Insur Agcy, Canton *Also called Steele W W Jr Agency Inc (G-2549)*
Schawk, Cincinnati *Also called Sgk LLC (G-4506)*
Schechter, Gross Day School, Pepper Pike *Also called Jewish Day Schl Assoc Grtr Clv (G-15957)*
Scheeser Buckley Mayfield LLC...330 896-4664
1540 Corporate Woods Pkwy Uniontown (44685) *(G-18538)*
Scheiderer Transport Inc...614 873-5103
8520 State Route 161 E Plain City (43064) *(G-16204)*
Schenker Inc...614 662-7217
2842 Spiegel Dr Groveport (43125) *(G-11670)*
Schenker Inc...614 257-8365
2525 Rohr Rd Ste C Lockbourne (43137) *(G-12960)*
Schenker Inc...419 491-1055
2 Air Cargo Pkwy E Swanton (43558) *(G-17570)*
Scher Group, Beachwood *Also called Dealers Group Limited (G-1073)*
Scherer Industrial Group, Springfield *Also called Horner Industrial Services Inc (G-17208)*
Scherzinger Corp...513 531-7848
10557 Medallion Dr Cincinnati (45241) *(G-4480)*
Scherzinger Drilling Inc...513 738-2000
9629 State Route 128 Harrison (45030) *(G-11808)*
Scherzinger Trmt & Pest Ctrl, Cincinnati *Also called Scherzinger Corp (G-4480)*
Schibi Heating & Cooling Corp...513 385-3344
5025 Hubble Rd Cincinnati (45247) *(G-4481)*
Schiff Agency, Fairfield *Also called Schiff John J & Thomas R & Co (G-10903)*
Schiff John J & Thomas R & Co...513 870-2580
6200 S Gilmore Rd Fairfield (45014) *(G-10903)*
Schill Grounds Management, North Ridgeville *Also called Schill Landscaping and Lawn CA (G-15477)*
Schill Landscaping and Lawn CA (PA)...440 327-3030
5000 Mills Indus Pkwy North Ridgeville (44039) *(G-15477)*
Schimpf Ginocchio Mullins Lpa...513 977-5570
36 E 7th St Ste 2600 Cincinnati (45202) *(G-4482)*
Schindewolf Express Inc...937 585-5919
200 S Boggs St De Graff (43318) *(G-10016)*
Schindler Elevator Corporation...216 391-8600
1100 E 55th St Cleveland (44103) *(G-6446)*
Schindler Elevator Corporation...419 867-5100
1530 Timber Wolf Dr Holland (43528) *(G-12053)*
Schindler Elevator Corporation...419 861-5900
1530 Timber Wolf Dr Holland (43528) *(G-12054)*
Schindler Elevator Corporation...614 573-2777
3607 Interchange Rd Columbus (43204) *(G-8694)*
Schindler Elevator Corporation...216 370-9524
18013 Clvlnd Pkw Dr 140 Cleveland (44135) *(G-6447)*
Schirmer Construction Co...440 716-4900
31350 Industrial Pkwy North Olmsted (44070) *(G-15443)*
Schlabach Wood Design Inc...330 897-2600
52567 State Route 651 Baltic (43804) *(G-947)*
Schlee Malt House Condo Assn...614 463-1999
495 S High St Ste 10 Columbus (43215) *(G-8695)*
Schlessman Seed Co (PA)...419 499-2572
11513 Us Highway 250 N Milan (44846) *(G-14499)*
Schlezinger Metals, Columbus *Also called I H Schlezinger Inc (G-7877)*
Schlosser, David W DDS, Stow *Also called Stow Dental Group Inc (G-17393)*
Schmid Mechanical Inc...330 264-3633
207 N Hillcrest Dr Wooster (44691) *(G-19912)*
Schmid Mechanical Co...614 261-6331
5255 Sinclair Rd Columbus (43229) *(G-8696)*
Schmids Service Now Inc...330 264-2040
258 S Columbus Ave Wooster (44691) *(G-19913)*
Schmidt Bros Inc...419 826-3671
420 N Hallett Ave Swanton (43558) *(G-17571)*
Schmidt Daily Rental Inc...419 874-4331
26875 Dixie Hwy Perrysburg (43551) *(G-16057)*
Schmidt Machine Company...419 294-3814
7013 State Highway 199 Upper Sandusky (43351) *(G-18566)*
Schmidt-Vogel Consulting, Cincinnati *Also called Itelligence Outsourcing Inc (G-3848)*
Schneder Elc Bldngs Amrcas Inc...513 398-9800
1770 Masn Mrrw Millgrv Rd Lebanon (45036) *(G-12644)*
Schneider Downs & Co Inc...614 621-4060
65 E State St Ste 2000 Columbus (43215) *(G-8697)*
Schneider Elc Systems USA Inc...440 234-3900
6745 Engle Rd Ste 205 Cleveland (44130) *(G-6448)*
Schneider Electric 324, Richfield *Also called Schneider Electric Usa Inc (G-16529)*
Schneider Electric Usa Inc...440 526-9070
3623 Brecksville Rd Ste A Richfield (44286) *(G-16529)*
Schneider Electric Usa Inc...513 755-5000
9870 Crescent Park Dr West Chester (45069) *(G-19145)*
Schneider Home Equipment Co (PA)...513 522-1200
7948 Pippin Rd Cincinnati (45239) *(G-4483)*
Schneider Nat Carriers Inc...740 362-6910
600 London Rd Delaware (43015) *(G-10126)*
Schneider National Inc...419 673-0254
808 Fontaine St Kenton (43326) *(G-12423)*
Schneider Saddlery LLC...440 543-2700
8255 Washington St Chagrin Falls (44023) *(G-2733)*
Schneller Heating and AC Co...859 341-1200
1079 Ohio Pike Cincinnati (45245) *(G-2930)*
Schneller LLC...330 673-1299
6019 Powdermill Rd Kent (44240) *(G-12395)*
Schnippel Construction Inc...937 693-3831
302 N Main St Botkins (45306) *(G-1753)*
Schoch Tile & Carpet Inc...513 922-3466
5282 Crookshank Rd Cincinnati (45238) *(G-4484)*
Schodorf Truck Body & Eqp Co...614 228-6793
885 Harmon Ave Columbus (43223) *(G-8698)*
Schoenbrunn Healthcare...330 339-3595
2594 E High Ave New Philadelphia (44663) *(G-15114)*
Schoenbrunn Landscaping Inc...330 364-3688
1505 State Route 39 Nw Dover (44622) *(G-10211)*
Schoenbrunn Ldscp & Lawn Svc, Dover *Also called Schoenbrunn Landscaping Inc (G-10211)*
Scholastic Book Fairs Inc...513 714-1000
5459 W Chester Rd Ste C West Chester (45069) *(G-19146)*
Scholastic Book Fairs Inc...440 572-4880
12850 Darice Pkwy Ste A Strongsville (44149) *(G-17504)*
Schomer Glaus Pyle...614 210-0751
1801 Watermark Dr Ste 210 Columbus (43215) *(G-8699)*
Schomer Glaus Pyle...216 518-5544
5595 Transportation Blvd Cleveland (44125) *(G-6449)*
Schomer Glaus Pyle (PA)...330 572-2100
520 S Main St Ste 2531 Akron (44311) *(G-430)*
Schomer Glaus Pyle...330 645-2131
470 Portage Lakes Dr Coventry Township (44319) *(G-9132)*
Schoner Chevrolet Inc...330 877-6731
720 W Maple St Hartville (44632) *(G-11830)*
School Age Child Care, Columbus *Also called Upper Arlington City Schl Dst (G-8914)*
School Bus Garage, Reynoldsburg *Also called Reynoldsburg City Schools (G-16475)*
School Bus Garage, Goshen *Also called Peterman (G-11438)*
School Choice Ohio Inc...614 223-1555
88 E Broad St Ste 640 Columbus (43215) *(G-8700)*
School Edctl Policy Leadership, Columbus *Also called Ohio State University (G-8423)*
School Employees Lorain County...440 324-3400
340 Griswold Rd Elyria (44035) *(G-10678)*
School Employees Retirement...614 222-5853
300 E Broad St Ste 100 Columbus (43215) *(G-8701)*
School of Hope, Fremont *Also called County of Sandusky (G-11190)*
Schooley Caldwell Associates...614 628-0300
300 Marconi Blvd Ste 100 Columbus (43215) *(G-8702)*
Schottenstein Center, The, Columbus *Also called Ohio State University (G-8389)*
Schottenstein Property Group, Columbus *Also called Schottenstein Realty LLC (G-8704)*
Schottenstein RE Group LLC...614 418-8900
2 Easton Oval Ste 510 Columbus (43219) *(G-8703)*
Schottenstein Realty LLC...614 445-8461
4300 E 5th Ave Columbus (43219) *(G-8704)*
Schroedel Scullin & Bestic LLC...330 533-1131
196 N Broad St Ste A Canfield (44406) *(G-2209)*
Schroeder Associates Inc (PA)...419 258-5075
5554 County Road 424 Antwerp (45813) *(G-620)*
Schroeder Company (PA)...419 473-3139
4668 Talmadge Rd Toledo (43623) *(G-18175)*
Schroer Properties Inc...740 687-5100
1590 Chartwell St Ofc Lancaster (43130) *(G-12572)*
Schroer Properties Inc (PA)...330 498-8200
339 E Maple St North Canton (44720) *(G-15365)*
Schroer Properties Inc...440 357-7900
9901 Johnnycake Ridge Rd Mentor (44060) *(G-14239)*
Schroer Properties of Lanfair, Lancaster *Also called Schroer Properties Inc (G-12572)*
Schrudder Prfmce Group LLC...513 652-7675
7723 Tylers Place Blvd West Chester (45069) *(G-19147)*
Schulman Assocs Instl Review (PA)...513 761-4100
4445 Lake Forest Dr # 300 Blue Ash (45242) *(G-1687)*
Schumacher & Co Inc...859 655-9000
920 Lila Ave Milford (45150) *(G-14560)*
Schumacher Homes, Belmont *Also called 50 X 20 Holding Company Inc (G-1428)*

ALPHABETIC

Schumacher Homes, Canton *Also called 50 X 20 Holding Company Inc* ***(G-2220)***
Schumm Plumbing & Heating, Van Wert *Also called Schumm Richard A Plbg & Htg* ***(G-18643)***
Schumm Richard A Plbg & Htg.....419 238-4994
9883 Liberty Union Rd Van Wert (45891) ***(G-18643)***
Schuster Cardiology.....937 866-0637
4000 Miamisburg Ctr Ste Miamisburg (45342) ***(G-14346)***
Schuster Electronics Inc.....330 425-8134
2057d E Aurora Rd Twinsburg (44087) ***(G-18468)***
Schuster/Cleveland, Twinsburg *Also called Schuster Electronics Inc* ***(G-18468)***
Schusters Greenhouse Ltd.....440 235-2440
9165 Columbia Rd Cleveland (44138) ***(G-6450)***
Schwebel Baking Co-Solon Bky, Solon *Also called Schwebel Baking Company* ***(G-17049)***
Schwebel Baking Company.....440 248-1500
6250 Camp Industrial Rd Solon (44139) ***(G-17049)***
Schweitzer Construction Co.....513 761-4980
325 Clark Rd Ste 1 Cincinnati (45215) ***(G-4485)***
Schweizer Dipple Inc.....440 786-8090
7227 Division St Cleveland (44146) ***(G-6451)***
Schwendeman Agency Inc (PA).....740 373-6793
109 Putnam St Marietta (45750) ***(G-13496)***
Schwendeman Sigafoos Agcy, Marietta *Also called Schwendeman Agency Inc* ***(G-13496)***
SCI, Fremont *Also called Keller Ochs Koch Inc* ***(G-11208)***
SCI, Miamisburg *Also called Shawntech Communications Inc* ***(G-14350)***
SCI Direct LLC.....330 494-5504
7800 Whipple Ave Nw North Canton (44720) ***(G-15366)***
Scientific Forming Tech Corp (PA).....614 451-8330
2545 Farmers Dr Ste 200 Columbus (43235) ***(G-8705)***
Scioto County C A O Headstart.....740 354-3333
1511 Hutchins St Portsmouth (45662) ***(G-16306)***
Scioto County Child Services, New Boston *Also called Scioto County Ohio* ***(G-15013)***
Scioto County Counseling Ctr (PA).....740 354-6685
1634 11th St Portsmouth (45662) ***(G-16307)***
Scioto County Ohio.....740 456-4164
3940 Gallia St New Boston (45662) ***(G-15013)***
Scioto County Region Wtr Dst 1.....740 259-2301
326 Robert Lucas Rd Lucasville (45648) ***(G-13182)***
Scioto Downs Inc.....614 295-4700
6000 S High St Columbus (43207) ***(G-8706)***
SCIOTO MEMORIAL HOSPITAL CAMPU, Portsmouth *Also called Southern Ohio Medical Center* ***(G-16311)***
Scioto Packaging Inc.....614 491-1500
6969 Alum Creek Dr Columbus (43217) ***(G-8707)***
Scioto Pnt Vly Mental Hlth Ctr, Wshngtn CT Hs *Also called Scioto Pnt Vly Mental Hlth Ctr* ***(G-20034)***
Scioto Pnt Vly Mental Hlth Ctr (PA).....740 775-1260
4449 State Route 159 Chillicothe (45601) ***(G-2884)***
Scioto Pnt Vly Mental Hlth Ctr.....740 335-6935
1300 E Paint St Wshngtn CT Hs (43160) ***(G-20034)***
Scioto Reserve Inc (PA).....740 881-9082
7383 Scioto Pkwy Powell (43065) ***(G-16349)***
Scioto Reserve Inc.....740 881-6500
3982 Powell Rd Ste 332 Powell (43065) ***(G-16350)***
Scioto Reserve Country Club, Powell *Also called Scioto Reserve Inc* ***(G-16350)***
Scioto Reserve Golf & Athc CLB, Powell *Also called Scioto Reserve Inc* ***(G-16349)***
Scioto Residential Services.....740 353-0288
2333 Vinton Ave Portsmouth (45662) ***(G-16308)***
Scioto Sand & Gravel, Prospect *Also called Fleming Construction Co* ***(G-16365)***
Scioto Services LLc (HQ).....937 644-0888
405 S Oak St Marysville (43040) ***(G-13649)***
Scioto-Darby Concrete Inc.....614 876-3114
4540 Edgewyn Ave Hilliard (43026) ***(G-11951)***
Scores Fun Center, Mentor *Also called East Mentor Recreation Inc* ***(G-14170)***
Scot Burton Contractors LLC.....440 564-1011
11330 Kinsman Rd Newbury (44065) ***(G-15261)***
Scot Industries Inc.....330 262-7585
6578 Ashland Rd Wooster (44691) ***(G-19914)***
Scott D Phillips.....513 870-8200
9277 Centre Pointe Dr West Chester (45069) ***(G-19148)***
Scott Fetzer Co, Cleveland *Also called Scott Fetzer Financial Group* ***(G-6453)***
Scott Fetzer Company (HQ).....440 892-3000
28800 Clemens Rd Westlake (44145) ***(G-19544)***
Scott Fetzer Company.....216 267-9000
4801 W 150th St Cleveland (44135) ***(G-6452)***
Scott Fetzer Financial Group.....440 892-3000
28800 Clemens Rd Cleveland (44145) ***(G-6453)***
Scott Industrial Systems Inc (PA).....937 233-8146
4433 Interpoint Blvd Dayton (45424) ***(G-9869)***
Scott Scriven & Wahoff LLP.....614 222-8686
250 E Broad St Ste 900 Columbus (43215) ***(G-8708)***
Scotts Commercial Truck Svcs, Toledo *Also called Scotts Towing Co* ***(G-18176)***
Scotts Company LLC (HQ).....937 644-3729
14111 Scottslawn Rd Marysville (43040) ***(G-13650)***
Scotts Miracle-Gro Company (PA).....937 644-0011
14111 Scottslawn Rd Marysville (43040) ***(G-13651)***
Scotts Miracle-Gro Products, Marysville *Also called Scotts Company LLC* ***(G-13650)***
Scotts Towing Co.....419 729-7888
5930 Benore Rd Toledo (43612) ***(G-18176)***
Scrap Yard LLC.....216 271-5825
15000 Miles Ave Cleveland (44128) ***(G-6454)***
Screen Works Inc (PA).....937 264-9111
3970 Image Dr Dayton (45414) ***(G-9870)***
Scribes & Scrbblr Chld Dev Ctr.....440 884-5437
14101 Uhlin Dr Cleveland (44130) ***(G-6455)***
Scrip Pharmacy, Columbus *Also called Mimrx Co Inc* ***(G-8176)***
Scrogginsgrear Inc.....513 672-4281
200 Northland Blvd Cincinnati (45246) ***(G-4486)***
Scs Construction Services Inc.....513 929-0260
2130 Western Ave Cincinnati (45214) ***(G-4487)***
Scwashtan, Reynoldsburg *Also called Duckworth Enterprises LLC* ***(G-16449)***
SD Myers LLC.....330 630-7000
180 South Ave Tallmadge (44278) ***(G-17649)***
SDA, Dublin *Also called Sunny Day Academy LLC* ***(G-10465)***
SDC Unvrsity Cir Developer LLC.....216 791-5333
2021 Cornell Rd Cleveland (44106) ***(G-6456)***
Sdr Services LLC.....513 625-0695
2109 State Route 28 B Goshen (45122) ***(G-11439)***
SDS Earth Moving Inc.....330 358-2132
3966 Wayland Rd Diamond (44412) ***(G-10172)***
Sdx Home Care Operations LLC.....877 692-0345
101 N Fountain Ave Springfield (45502) ***(G-17271)***
Sea Ltd (PA).....614 888-4160
7001 Buffalo Pkwy Columbus (43229) ***(G-8709)***
Sea-Land Chemical Co (PA).....440 871-7887
821 Westpoint Pkwy Westlake (44145) ***(G-19545)***
Seacrist Landscaping and Cnstr.....440 946-2731
9442 Mercantile Dr Mentor (44060) ***(G-14240)***
Seagate Hospitality Group LLC.....216 252-7700
4181 W 150th St Cleveland (44135) ***(G-6457)***
Seagate Office Products Inc.....419 861-6161
1044 Hamilton Dr Holland (43528) ***(G-12055)***
Seagate Roofg & Waterproofing, Toledo *Also called Burbank Inc* ***(G-17788)***
Seal Mayfield LLC.....440 684-4100
6103 Landerhaven Dr Mayfield Heights (44124) ***(G-14007)***
Seal-Rite Door, Hebron *Also called S R Door Inc* ***(G-11859)***
Seals Construction Inc.....614 836-7200
10283 Busey Rd Nw Canal Winchester (43110) ***(G-2170)***
Seamans Services.....216 621-4107
1050 W 3rd St Cleveland (44114) ***(G-6458)***
Seapine Software Inc (HQ).....513 754-1655
6960 Cintas Blvd Mason (45040) ***(G-13757)***
Seaport Division, Toledo *Also called Toledo-Lucas County Port Auth* ***(G-18255)***
Search 2 Close Columbus Ltd (PA).....614 389-5353
10254 Sawmill Pkwy Powell (43065) ***(G-16351)***
Searidge, Madison *Also called Eastwood Residential Living* ***(G-13224)***
Sears, Columbus *Also called Innovel Solutions Inc* ***(G-7901)***
Sears, Columbus *Also called Innovel Solutions Inc* ***(G-7902)***
Sears Roebuck and Co.....614 797-2095
1280 Polaris Pkwy Columbus (43240) ***(G-6906)***
Sears Roebuck and Co.....937 427-8528
2727 Fairfield Cmns Beavercreek (45431) ***(G-1207)***
Sears Roebuck and Co.....419 226-4172
2400 Elida Rd Ste 100 Lima (45805) ***(G-12874)***
Sears Roebuck and Co.....614 760-7195
4975 Tuttle Crossing Blvd Dublin (43016) ***(G-10450)***
Sears Roebuck and Co.....330 629-7700
7401 Market St Rm 7 Youngstown (44512) ***(G-20368)***
Sears Roebuck and Co.....330 652-5128
5555 Youngstown Warren Rd # 120 Niles (44446) ***(G-15304)***
Sears Roebuck and Co.....440 846-3595
17271 Southpark Ctr Cleveland (44136) ***(G-6459)***
Sears Auto Center, Beavercreek *Also called Sears Roebuck and Co* ***(G-1207)***
Sears Auto Center, Niles *Also called Sears Roebuck and Co* ***(G-15304)***
Sears Auto Center, Cleveland *Also called Sears Roebuck and Co* ***(G-6459)***
Sears Product Service 1474, Youngstown *Also called Sears Roebuck and Co* ***(G-20368)***
Season Contractors Inc.....440 717-0188
55 Eagle Valley Ct Broadview Heights (44147) ***(G-1891)***
Seaway Building Services, Toledo *Also called Seaway Sponge & Chamois Co* ***(G-18177)***
Seaway Cash N Carry, Cleveland *Also called Total Wholesale Inc* ***(G-6605)***
Seaway Sponge & Chamois Co (PA).....419 691-4694
458 2nd St Toledo (43605) ***(G-18177)***
Seaworld Entertainment Inc.....330 562-8101
1100 Squires Rd Aurora (44202) ***(G-855)***
Sebaly Shillito & Dyer Lpa (PA).....937 222-2500
1900 Kettering Tower 40n Dayton (45423) ***(G-9871)***
Sebastiani Trucking Inc.....330 286-0059
61 Railroad St Canfield (44406) ***(G-2210)***
Sebesta Inc.....216 351-7621
2802 Tuxedo Ave Parma (44134) ***(G-15915)***
Sechkar Company.....740 385-8900
4831 2nd St Nelsonville (45764) ***(G-14968)***
Second Harvest Food Bank, Springfield *Also called Archdiocese of Cincinnati* ***(G-17148)***
Second Mental Retardation.....937 262-3077
3827 W 3rd St Dayton (45417) ***(G-9872)***
Second National Bank (HQ).....937 548-2122
499 S Broadway St Greenville (45331) ***(G-11519)***
Second Phase Inc.....330 797-9930
191 S Four Mile Run Rd Youngstown (44515) ***(G-20369)***

Section 8, Cincinnati *Also called Cincinnati Metro Hsing Auth* ***(G-3317)***
Section 8 Housing Assistance, Portsmouth *Also called Portsmouth Metro Hsing Auth* ***(G-16300)***
Secura Fact, Lakewood *Also called Security Hut Inc* ***(G-12500)***
Secure Trnsp Co Ohio LLC....800 856-9994
777 Dearborn Park Ln S Worthington (43085) ***(G-19996)***
Securestate LLC....216 927-0115
23340 Miles Rd Cleveland (44128) ***(G-6460)***
Securitas Electronic SEC Inc (HQ)....855 331-0359
3800 Tabs Dr Uniontown (44685) ***(G-18539)***
Securitas SEC Svcs USA Inc....216 431-3139
3747 Euclid Ave Cleveland (44115) ***(G-6461)***
Securitas SEC Svcs USA Inc....513 639-7615
655 Plum St 150 Cincinnati (45202) ***(G-4488)***
Securitas SEC Svcs USA Inc....937 224-7432
118 W 1st St Dayton (45402) ***(G-9873)***
Securitas SEC Svcs USA Inc....614 871-6051
2180 Southwest Blvd Grove City (43123) ***(G-11597)***
Securitas SEC Svcs USA Inc....440 887-6800
12000 Snow Rd Ste 5 Cleveland (44130) ***(G-6462)***
Securitas SEC Svcs USA Inc....216 503-2021
9885 Rockside Rd Ste 155 Cleveland (44125) ***(G-6463)***
Security Check LLC (PA)....614 944-5788
2 Easton Oval Ste 350 Columbus (43219) ***(G-8710)***
Security Fence Group Inc (PA)....513 681-3700
4260 Dane Ave Cincinnati (45223) ***(G-4489)***
Security Hut Inc (PA)....216 226-0461
18614 Detroit Ave Lakewood (44107) ***(G-12500)***
Security Investments LLC....614 441-4601
4807 Smoketalk Ln Westerville (43081) ***(G-19443)***
Security Nat Auto Accptnce LLC....513 459-8118
6951 Cintas Blvd Mason (45040) ***(G-13758)***
Security National Bank & Tr Co (HQ)....740 426-6384
50 N 3rd St Newark (43055) ***(G-15233)***
Security National Bank & Tr Co....937 324-6800
40 S Limestone St Springfield (45502) ***(G-17272)***
Security Savings Mortgage Corp....330 455-2833
300 Tuscarawas St W Fl 8 Canton (44702) ***(G-2524)***
Security Storage Co Inc....513 961-2700
706 Oak St Cincinnati (45206) ***(G-4490)***
Security Title Guarantee Agcy....513 651-3393
150 E 4th St Fl 4 Cincinnati (45202) ***(G-4491)***
Sedlak Management Cons Inc....216 206-4700
22901 Millcreek Blvd # 600 Cleveland (44122) ***(G-6464)***
Seed Consultants Inc (HQ)....740 333-8644
648 Miami Trace Rd Sw Wshngtn CT Hs (43160) ***(G-20035)***
Seeley Enterprises Company (PA)....440 293-6600
104 Parker Dr Andover (44003) ***(G-614)***
Seeley Medical, Andover *Also called Seeley Enterprises Company* ***(G-614)***
Seeley Medical Oxygen Co (HQ)....440 255-7163
104 Parker Dr Andover (44003) ***(G-615)***
Seeley Svdge Ebert Gourash Lpa....216 566-8200
26600 Detroit Rd Fl 3 Cleveland (44145) ***(G-6465)***
Seg of Ohio Inc (PA)....614 414-7300
4016 Townsfair Way # 201 Columbus (43219) ***(G-8711)***
Segmint Inc....330 594-5379
365 Water St Akron (44308) ***(G-431)***
Sehlhorst Equipment Svcs Inc....513 353-9300
4450 Monroe Ave Hooven (45033) ***(G-12077)***
SEI Cincinnati, Cincinnati *Also called Systems Evolution Inc* ***(G-4610)***
Seibert-Keck Insurance Agency (PA)....330 867-3140
2950 W Market St Ste A Fairlawn (44333) ***(G-10974)***
Seifert & Group Inc....330 833-2700
2323 Nave Rd Se Massillon (44646) ***(G-13852)***
Seifert Technologies Inc (PA)....330 833-2700
2323 Nave Rd Se Massillon (44646) ***(G-13853)***
Seilkop Industries Inc (PA)....513 761-1035
425 W North Bend Rd Cincinnati (45216) ***(G-4492)***
Selby General Hospital....740 568-2037
1338 Colegate Dr Marietta (45750) ***(G-13497)***
Selby General Hospital (PA)....740 568-2000
1106 Colegate Dr Marietta (45750) ***(G-13498)***
Select Genetics LLC....740 599-7979
15835 Dnville Jelloway Rd Danville (43014) ***(G-9247)***
Select Hotels Group LLC....513 754-0003
5070 Natorp Blvd Mason (45040) ***(G-13759)***
Select Hotels Group LLC....216 328-1060
6025 Jefferson Dr Cleveland (44131) ***(G-6466)***
Select Hotels Group LLC....614 799-1913
6161 Parkcenter Cir Dublin (43017) ***(G-10451)***
Select Industries Corp....937 233-9191
60 Heid Ave Dayton (45404) ***(G-9874)***
Select Medical Corporation....216 983-8030
11900 Fairhill Rd Ste 100 Cleveland (44120) ***(G-6467)***
Select Medical Corporation....330 761-7500
200 E Market St Akron (44308) ***(G-432)***
Select Spclty Hsptal-Akron LLC....330 761-7500
200 E Market St Akron (44308) ***(G-433)***
Select Specialty Hosp Columbus....614 291-8467
1087 Dennison Ave Columbus (43201) ***(G-8712)***
Select Specialty Hospital....513 862-4700
375 Dixmyth Ave Fl 15 Cincinnati (45220) ***(G-4493)***
Select Staffing....513 247-9772
7682 Overglen Dr West Chester (45069) ***(G-19149)***
Select Steel Inc....330 652-1756
1825 Hunter Ave Niles (44446) ***(G-15305)***
Select-Arc Inc....937 295-5215
600 Enterprise Dr Fort Loramie (45845) ***(G-11111)***
Selection MGT Systems Inc....513 522-8764
155 Tri County Pkwy # 150 Cincinnati (45246) ***(G-4494)***
Selection.com, Cincinnati *Also called Selection MGT Systems Inc* ***(G-4494)***
Selective Networking Inc....740 574-2682
8407 Hayport Rd Wheelersburg (45694) ***(G-19581)***
Selecttech Services Corp....937 438-9905
8045 Washington Vlg Dr Centerville (45458) ***(G-2685)***
Self Reliance Inc....937 525-0809
3674 E National Rd Ste 3 Springfield (45505) ***(G-17273)***
Self-Funded Plans Inc (PA)....216 566-1455
1432 Hamilton Ave Cleveland (44114) ***(G-6468)***
Selinsky Force LLC....330 477-4527
4015 23rd St Sw Canton (44706) ***(G-2525)***
Selman & Company (PA)....440 646-9336
6110 Parkland Blvd Cleveland (44124) ***(G-6469)***
SEM Villa Inc....513 831-3262
6409 Small House Cir Loveland (45140) ***(G-13158)***
Sem Villa Retirement Community, Loveland *Also called SEM Villa Inc* ***(G-13158)***
Seminole 8 Theaters, Avon Lake *Also called Seminole Theater Co LLC* ***(G-939)***
Seminole Theater Co LLC....440 934-6998
32818 Walker Rd Avon Lake (44012) ***(G-939)***
Semma Enterprises Inc....513 863-7775
5414 Hankins Rd Middletown (45044) ***(G-14457)***
Sena Weller Rohs Williams....513 241-6443
300 Main St Fl 4 Cincinnati (45202) ***(G-4495)***
Seneca County Dialysis, Tiffin *Also called Seneca Dialysis LLC* ***(G-17700)***
Seneca County Ems....419 447-0266
126 Hopewell Ave Tiffin (44883) ***(G-17698)***
Seneca County Firemens Assn....419 447-7909
1070 S County Road 17 Tiffin (44883) ***(G-17699)***
Seneca County Highway Dept, Tiffin *Also called County of Seneca* ***(G-17674)***
Seneca County Human Services, Tiffin *Also called County of Seneca* ***(G-17675)***
Seneca Dialysis LLC....419 443-1051
10 St Lawrence Dr Tiffin (44883) ***(G-17700)***
Seneca Lake Park, Senecaville *Also called Muskingum Wtrshed Cnsrvncy Dst* ***(G-16824)***
Seneca Medical, Tiffin *Also called Concordnce Hlthcare Sltons LLC* ***(G-17673)***
Seneca Medical LLC (HQ)....419 447-0236
85 Shaffer Park Dr Tiffin (44883) ***(G-17701)***
Seneca RE ADS Ind Fostoria Div....419 435-0729
602 S Corporate Dr W Fostoria (44830) ***(G-11140)***
Seneca Steel Erectors Inc (PA)....740 385-0517
975 E Main St Logan (43138) ***(G-12987)***
Seneca-Crawford Area Trnsp (PA)....419 937-2428
3446 S Township Road 151 Tiffin (44883) ***(G-17702)***
Senior Behaviroal Health, Cincinnati *Also called Trihealth Inc* ***(G-4689)***
Senior Care Inc....937 372-1530
60 Paceline Cir Xenia (45385) ***(G-20075)***
Senior Care Inc....330 721-2000
1046 N Jefferson St Medina (44256) ***(G-14124)***
Senior Care Inc....937 291-3211
8630 Washington Church Rd Miamisburg (45342) ***(G-14347)***
Senior Care Inc....419 516-4788
2075 N Eastown Rd Lima (45807) ***(G-12875)***
Senior Care Management Inc....419 578-7000
3501 Executive Pkwy # 219 Toledo (43606) ***(G-18178)***
Senior Center, Chillicothe *Also called Ross Cnty Cmmittee For Elderly* ***(G-2877)***
Senior Center West, Lakewood *Also called City of Lakewood* ***(G-12473)***
SENIOR CITIZENS CENTER, Portsmouth *Also called United Scoto Senior Activities* ***(G-16316)***
Senior Help Solutions, Mount Vernon *Also called Home Instead Senior Care* ***(G-14898)***
Senior Independence....330 873-3468
83 N Miller Rd Ste 101 Fairlawn (44333) ***(G-10975)***
Senior Independence....330 744-5071
1110 5th Ave Youngstown (44504) ***(G-20370)***
Senior Independence Adult....440 954-8372
36855 Ridge Rd Willoughby (44094) ***(G-19712)***
Senior Independence Adult....513 681-8174
25 Indiana Ave Monroe (45050) ***(G-14711)***
Senior Independence Adult....513 539-2697
27 Indiana Ave Monroe (45050) ***(G-14712)***
Senior Lifestyle Corporation....513 777-4457
7222 Heritagespring Dr West Chester (45069) ***(G-19150)***
Senior Lifestyle Evergreen Ltd....513 948-2308
230 W Galbraith Rd Cincinnati (45215) ***(G-4496)***
Senior Nutrition, Zanesville *Also called Muskingum County Ohio* ***(G-20506)***
Senior Outreach Services....216 421-6900
2390 E 79th St Cleveland (44104) ***(G-6470)***
Senior Resource Connection (PA)....937 223-8246
222 Salem Ave Dayton (45406) ***(G-9875)***
Senior Select Home Health Care....330 665-4663
3009 Smith Rd Ste 25 Fairlawn (44333) ***(G-10976)***
Senior Star Management Company....513 271-1747
5435 Kenwood Rd Cincinnati (45227) ***(G-4497)***

ALPHABETIC

Sensation Research 513 602-1611
1159 Chaucer Pl Maineville (45039) *(G-13246)*

Sensi Care 3 ..... 440 323-6310
1243 East Ave Elyria (44035) *(G-10679)*

Sensor Technology Systems, Miamisburg Also called Steiner Eoptics Inc *(G-14354)*

Sentage Corporation 937 865-5900
1037 Byers Rd Miamisburg (45342) *(G-14348)*

Sentinel Fluid Controls LLC (HQ) 419 478-9086
5702 Opportunity Dr Toledo (43612) *(G-18179)*

Sequent Inc (PA) 614 436-5880
8415 Pulsar Pl Ste 200 Columbus (43240) *(G-6907)*

SEQUENT INFORMATION SOLUTIONS, Columbus Also called Sequent Inc *(G-6907)*

Sequoia Pro Bowl 614 885-7043
5501 Sandalwood Blvd Columbus (43229) *(G-8713)*

Serenity Center Inc 614 891-1111
2841 E Dblin Granville Rd Columbus (43231) *(G-8714)*

Serenity HM Halthcare Svcs LLC 937 222-0002
33 White Allen Ave Dayton (45405) *(G-9876)*

Serex Corporation (PA) 330 726-6062
55 Victoria Rd Youngstown (44515) *(G-20371)*

Serv Pro of Barberton/Norton, Medina Also called Professional Restoration Svc *(G-14114)*

Serv-A-Lite Products Inc (HQ) 309 762-7741
10590 Hamilton Ave Cincinnati (45231) *(G-4498)*

Servall Electric Company Inc 513 771-5584
11697 Lebanon Rd Cincinnati (45241) *(G-4499)*

Servatii Inc (PA) 513 271-5040
3888 Virginia Ave Cincinnati (45227) *(G-4500)*

Servatii Pastry and Dealey, Cincinnati Also called Servatii Inc *(G-4500)*

Service Building, Dayton Also called Dayton Public School District *(G-9489)*

Service Center Title Agency 937 312-3080
6718 Loop Rd Dayton (45459) *(G-9877)*

Service Center Warehouse, Euclid Also called Euclid City Schools *(G-10751)*

Service Corporation Intl, Cleveland Also called Cummings and Davis Fnrl HM Inc *(G-5448)*

Service Corps Retired Execs 216 522-4194
1350 Euclid Ave Ste 216 Cleveland (44115) *(G-6471)*

Service Corps Retired Execs 330 379-3163
1 Cascade Plz Fl 18 Akron (44308) *(G-434)*

Service Corps Retired Execs 419 259-7598
2200 Jefferson Ave Fl 1 Toledo (43604) *(G-18180)*

Service Department, Hudson Also called City of Hudson Village *(G-12112)*

Service Dept, Cleveland Also called City of Warrensville Heights *(G-5277)*

Service Dept, Streetsboro Also called City of Streetsboro *(G-17410)*

Service Experts Htg & AC LLC 937 426-3444
2600 S Limestone St Springfield (45505) *(G-17274)*

Service Experts Htg & AC LLC 513 489-3361
4610 Carlynn Dr Blue Ash (45241) *(G-1688)*

Service Experts Htg & AC LLC 614 859-6993
1751 Dividend Dr Columbus (43228) *(G-8715)*

Service Experts LLC 330 577-3918
847 Home Ave Akron (44310) *(G-435)*

Service Experts of Columbus, Columbus Also called Service Experts Htg & AC LLC *(G-8715)*

Service Garage, Cleveland Also called City of Garfield Heights *(G-5261)*

Service Master By Allen Keith, Canton Also called Allen-Keith Construction Co *(G-2231)*

Service Master By Ameri Steam, Cleveland Also called A Team LLC *(G-4936)*

Service Plus, Akron Also called Yrs Inc *(G-518)*

Service Pronet Inc 614 874-4300
1535 Georgesville Rd Columbus (43228) *(G-8716)*

Service Solutions Group LLC 513 772-6600
890 Redna Ter Cincinnati (45215) *(G-4501)*

Service Steel Div, Cincinnati Also called Van Pelt Corporation *(G-4803)*

Service-Tech, Cleveland Also called A Bee C Service Inc *(G-4930)*

Servicelink Field Services LLC 440 424-0058
30825 Aurora Rd Ste 140 Solon (44139) *(G-17050)*

ServiceMaster, Lima Also called Kleman Services LLC *(G-12811)*

ServiceMaster, Youngstown Also called Dempsey Inc *(G-20167)*

ServiceMaster, Lebanon Also called A 1 Janitorial Cleaning Svc *(G-12585)*

ServiceMaster, Lancaster Also called C M S Enterprises Inc *(G-12512)*

ServiceMaster, Berea Also called T & L Enterprises Inc *(G-1471)*

ServiceMaster By McCastle, Bedford Also called ServiceMaster Clean *(G-1335)*

ServiceMaster By Sidwell Inc 740 687-1077
430 E Mulberry St Lancaster (43130) *(G-12573)*

ServiceMaster By Steinbach 330 497-5959
6824 Wise Ave Nw Canton (44720) *(G-2526)*

ServiceMaster Clean 440 349-0979
26496 Broadway Ave Bedford (44146) *(G-1335)*

ServiceMaster of Defiance Inc 419 784-5570
1255 Carpenter Rd Defiance (43512) *(G-10057)*

Services & Support ADM, Oak Harbor Also called Ottawa County Board M R D D *(G-15614)*

Services On Deck Inc (PA) 513 759-2854
8263 Kyles Station Rd # 1 Liberty Township (45044) *(G-12724)*

Services On Mark Inc 614 846-5400
705 Lkview Plz Blvd Ste L Worthington (43085) *(G-19997)*

Servicmaster By Disaster Recon, Eastlake Also called Disaster Reconstruction Inc *(G-10545)*

Servicmster Coml Clg Advantage, Lancaster Also called CMS Business Services LLC *(G-12520)*

Servisair LLC (HQ) 216 267-9910
5851 Cargo Rd Cleveland (44135) *(G-6472)*

SERVPRO, Worthington Also called Heco Operations Inc *(G-19962)*

SERVPRO, Hudson Also called Restoration Resources Inc *(G-12141)*

SERVPRO, North Canton Also called Caveney Inc *(G-15328)*

Sesco, Brooklyn Heights Also called Specialty Equipment Sales Co *(G-1927)*

Setco Sales Company (HQ) 513 941-5110
5880 Hillside Ave Cincinnati (45233) *(G-4502)*

Setiawan Associates LLC 614 285-5815
50 W Broad St Ste 1800 Columbus (43215) *(G-8717)*

Seton Catholic School Hudson 330 342-4200
6923 Stow Rd Hudson (44236) *(G-12143)*

Settle Muter Electric Ltd (PA) 614 866-7554
711 Claycraft Rd Columbus (43230) *(G-8718)*

Seven Hills Fireman Assn 216 524-3321
7195 Broadview Rd Seven Hills (44131) *(G-16836)*

Seven Hills Obgyn Associates 513 922-6666
6350 Glenway Ave Ste 205 Cincinnati (45211) *(G-4503)*

Seven Hills Womens Health Ctrs (PA) 513 721-3200
2060 Reading Rd Ste 150 Cincinnati (45202) *(G-4504)*

Seven Hlls Neighborhood Houses (PA) 513 407-5362
901 Findlay St Cincinnati (45214) *(G-4505)*

Seven Secured Inc 281 362-2887
15830 Foltz Pkwy Strongsville (44149) *(G-17505)*

Seven Seventeen Credit Un Inc (PA) 330 372-8100
3181 Larchmont Ave Ne Warren (44483) *(G-18897)*

Seven Seventeen Credit Un Inc. 330 372-8100
100 Brewster Dr Se Warren (44484) *(G-18898)*

Sewell Motor Express Co (PA) 937 382-3847
370 Davids Dr Wilmington (45177) *(G-19787)*

Sewer & Drainage Services, Toledo Also called City of Toledo *(G-17810)*

Sewer Department, Sandusky Also called City of Sandusky *(G-16739)*

Sewer Rodding Equipment Co 419 991-2065
3434 S Dixie Hwy Lima (45804) *(G-12876)*

Sewer Savors, Cincinnati Also called Municpal Cntrs Saling Pdts Inc *(G-4131)*

Sexton Industrial Inc 513 530-5555
366 Circle Freeway Dr West Chester (45246) *(G-19228)*

Seymour & Associates 419 517-7079
1760 Manley Rd Maumee (43537) *(G-13975)*

Sfa Architects, Cincinnati Also called Elevar Design Group Inc *(G-3550)*

Sfa Architects Inc 937 281-0600
120 W 2nd St Ste 1800 Dayton (45402) *(G-9878)*

Sfc Graphics Inc 419 255-1283
110 E Woodruff Ave Toledo (43604) *(G-18181)*

Sfd Company LLC 216 662-8000
16625 Granite Rd Maple Heights (44137) *(G-13417)*

Sfn Group Inc 419 727-4104
1212 E Alexis Rd Toledo (43612) *(G-18182)*

Sfr Group, Youngstown Also called Sami S Rafidi *(G-20365)*

Sgi Matrix LLC (PA) 937 438-9033
1041 Byers Rd Miamisburg (45342) *(G-14349)*

Sgk LLC 513 569-9900
537 E Pete Rose Way # 100 Cincinnati (45202) *(G-4506)*

Sgl Carbon Technic LLC 440 572-3600
21945 Drake Rd Strongsville (44149) *(G-17506)*

SGS North America Inc 513 674-7048
650 Northland Blvd # 600 Cincinnati (45240) *(G-4507)*

Sgt Inc 216 433-3982
21000 Brookpark Rd Cleveland (44135) *(G-6473)*

SH Bell Company 412 963-9910
2217 Michigan Ave East Liverpool (43920) *(G-10534)*

Sh-91 Limited Partnership 330 535-1581
1221 Everton Dr Akron (44307) *(G-436)*

Shadco Inc 310 217-8777
100 Titanium Way Toronto (43964) *(G-18338)*

Shade Tree Cool Living LLC 614 844-5990
6317 Busch Blvd Columbus (43229) *(G-8719)*

Shadoart Productions Inc 614 227-6125
503 S Front St Ste 260 Columbus (43215) *(G-8720)*

Shadow Valley Tennis & Fitness 419 861-3986
1661 N Hlland Sylvania Rd Toledo (43615) *(G-18183)*

Shadow Valley Tennis Club 419 865-1141
1661 S Hlland Sylvania Rd Maumee (43537) *(G-13976)*

SHADOWBOX, Columbus Also called Shadoart Productions Inc *(G-8720)*

Shady Hollow Cntry CLB Co Inc 330 832-1581
4865 Wales Ave Nw Massillon (44646) *(G-13854)*

Shady Lawn Nursing Home, Dalton Also called A Provide Care Inc *(G-9239)*

Shadyside Care Center, Shadyside Also called Zandex Inc *(G-16854)*

Shadyside Health Center, Shadyside Also called Wheeling Hospital Inc *(G-16853)*

Shafer Confession 419 399-4662
411 E Jackson St Paulding (45879) *(G-15936)*

Shaffer Distributing Company (PA) 614 421-6800
1100 W 3rd Ave Columbus (43212) *(G-8721)*

Shaffer Pomeroy Ltd 419 756-7302
909 S Main St Mansfield (44907) *(G-13363)*

Shaias Parking Inc 216 621-0328
812 Huron Rd E Ste 701 Cleveland (44115) *(G-6474)*

Shakemasters, Macedonia Also called Regency Roofing Companies Inc *(G-13208)*

Shaker Grdns Nursing Rehab Ctr, Shaker Heights Also called Mff Somerset LLc *(G-16863)*

Shaker Heights Country Club Co 216 991-3324
3300 Courtland Blvd Shaker Heights (44122) *(G-16865)*
Shaker House 216 991-6000
3700 Northfield Rd Ste 3 Cleveland (44122) *(G-6475)*
Shaker Run Golf Club 513 727-0007
1320 Golf Club Dr Lebanon (45036) *(G-12645)*
Shaker Valley Foods Inc 216 961-8600
3304 W 67th Pl Cleveland (44102) *(G-6476)*
Shaklee Corporation 614 409-2953
5650 Green Pointe Dr N A Groveport (43125) *(G-11671)*
Shalom House Inc (HQ) 614 239-1999
1135 College Ave Columbus (43209) *(G-8722)*
Shalom Ministries Intl Inc (PA) 614 504-6052
9018 Heritage Dr Plain City (43064) *(G-16205)*
Shamas Ltd 419 872-9908
102 W Indiana Ave Perrysburg (43551) *(G-16058)*
Shamrock Acquisition Company, Westlake *Also called Shamrock Companies Inc (G-19546)*
Shamrock Companies Inc (PA) 440 899-9510
24090 Detroit Rd Westlake (44145) *(G-19546)*
Shamrock Golf Club, Delaware *Also called Ganzfair Investment Inc (G-10100)*
Shamrock Moving & Storage Co, Strongsville *Also called Tersher Corporation (G-17516)*
Shamrock Taxi Ltd 614 263-8294
P.O. Box 360363 Columbus (43236) *(G-8723)*
Shamrock Towing Inc (PA) 614 882-3555
6333 Frost Rd Westerville (43082) *(G-19352)*
Shancliff Investments Ltd 330 883-5560
1358 Meadowood Cir Youngstown (44514) *(G-20372)*
Shane Security Services Inc 330 757-4001
7217 Pennsylvania Ave Poland (44514) *(G-16226)*
Shapiro Shapiro & Shapiro 216 927-2030
4469 Renaissance Pkwy Cleveland (44128) *(G-6477)*
Shared PET Imaging Llc 330 491-0480
4825 Higbee Ave Nw # 201 Canton (44718) *(G-2527)*
Shared Services, Cleveland *Also called Securitas SEC Svcs USA Inc (G-6463)*
Shared Services LLC 513 821-4278
5905 E Galbraith Rd # 8000 Cincinnati (45236) *(G-4508)*
Sharon Twnship Frfighters Assn 330 239-4992
1274 Sharon Copley Rd Sharon Center (44274) *(G-16878)*
Sharonview Nursing Home, South Vienna *Also called Vienna Enterprises Inc (G-17101)*
Sharonville Car Wash 513 769-4219
11727 Lebanon Rd Cincinnati (45241) *(G-4509)*
Sharonville Mthdist Wkdays Nrs 513 563-8278
3751 Creek Rd Cincinnati (45241) *(G-4510)*
Sharp Edge LLC 440 255-5917
8855 Twinbrook Rd Mentor (44060) *(G-14241)*
Sharp's Valet Parkg, Fairfield *Also called Sharps Valet Parking (G-10904)*
Sharpnack Chevrolet Co (PA) 440 967-3144
5401 Portage Dr Vermilion (44089) *(G-18716)*
Sharpnack Chvrlet Bick Cdillac 419 935-0194
1330 S Conwell Ave Willard (44890) *(G-19626)*
Sharps Valet Parking 513 863-1777
843 Southwind Dr Fairfield (45014) *(G-10904)*
Sharron Group Inc (PA) 614 873-5856
7605 Commerce Pl Plain City (43064) *(G-16206)*
Shaw Group Inc 937 593-2022
2946 Us Highway 68 N Bellefontaine (43311) *(G-1396)*
Shaw Jewish Community Center 330 867-7850
750 White Pond Dr Akron (44320) *(G-437)*
Shaw's Inn, Lancaster *Also called Cork Enterprises Inc (G-12523)*
Shawcor Pipe Protection LLC 513 683-7800
173 Commerce Dr Loveland (45140) *(G-13159)*
Shawnee Animal Clinic Inc 740 353-5758
101 Bierly Rd Portsmouth (45662) *(G-16309)*
Shawnee Country Club 419 227-7177
1700 Shawnee Rd Lima (45805) *(G-12877)*
Shawnee Hills Golf Course, Cleveland *Also called Cleveland Metroparks (G-5330)*
Shawnee Manor, Lima *Also called Hcf of Shawnee Inc (G-12794)*
Shawnee Manor Nursing Home, Lima *Also called Hcf Management Inc (G-12792)*
Shawnee Optical Inc 440 997-2020
3705 State Rd Ashtabula (44004) *(G-763)*
Shawnee Trophies & Sptg Gds, Chillicothe *Also called Chillicothe Bowling Lanes Inc (G-2817)*
Shawnee Weekday Early Lrng Ctr 419 991 4806
2600 Zurmehly Rd Lima (45806) *(C-12930)*
Shawneespring Hlth Cre Cntr Rl 513 943-4000
390 Wards Corner Rd Loveland (45140) *(G-13160)*
Shawntech Communications Inc (PA) 937 898-4900
8521 Gander Creek Dr Miamisburg (45342) *(G-14350)*
Sheakley Cente 513 487-7106
401 E Mcmillan St Cincinnati (45206) *(G-4511)*
Sheakley Med MGT Resources LLC 513 891-1006
8212 Blue Ash Rd Cincinnati (45236) *(G-4512)*
Sheakley Unicomp Inc 513 771-2277
1 Sheakley Way Ste 100 Cincinnati (45246) *(G-4513)*
Sheakley-Uniservice Inc 513 771-2277
1 Sheakley Way Ste 100 Cincinnati (45246) *(G-4514)*
Shearer Farm Inc 440 237-4806
11204 Royalton Rd North Royalton (44133) *(G-15502)*
Shearer Farm Inc (PA) 330 345-9023
7762 Cleveland Rd Wooster (44691) *(G-19915)*
Shearer Farm Inc 419 465-4622
13 Fort Monroe Pkwy Monroeville (44847) *(G-14722)*
Shearer Farm Inc 419 529-6160
2715 W 4th St Ontario (44906) *(G-15712)*
Shearer's Snacks, Massillon *Also called Shearers Foods LLC (G-13855)*
Shearers Foods LLC (PA) 330 834-4030
100 Lincoln Way E Massillon (44646) *(G-13855)*
Sheedy Paving Inc 614 252-2111
730 N Rose Ave Columbus (43219) *(G-8724)*
Sheer Professionals Inc 330 345-8666
2912 Cleveland Rd Wooster (44691) *(G-19916)*
Shelby County Child Care, Sidney *Also called Council On Rur Svc Prgrams Inc (G-16924)*
Shelby County Highway Dept, Sidney *Also called County of Shelby (G-16925)*
Shelby County Mem Hosp Assn (PA) 937 498-2311
915 Michigan St Sidney (45365) *(G-16952)*
Shelby County Mem Hosp Assn 937 492-9591
705 Fulton St Sidney (45365) *(G-16953)*
Shelby Welded Tube Div, Shelby *Also called Phillips Mfg and Tower Co (G-16902)*
Sheldon Harry E Calvary Camp 440 593-4381
4411 Lake Rd Conneaut (44030) *(G-9046)*
Shells Inc (PA) 330 808-5558
1245 S Cleveland Massillo Copley (44321) *(G-9063)*
Shelly and Sands Inc 740 859-2104
1731 Old State Route 7 Rayland (43943) *(G-16418)*
Shelly and Sands Inc 740 453-6260
3840 Durant Rd Zanesville (43701) *(G-20531)*
Shelly and Sands Inc 614 444-5100
1515 Harmon Ave Columbus (43223) *(G-8725)*
Shelly and Sands Inc 419 529-8455
1300 W 4th St Rear Ontario (44906) *(G-15713)*
Shelly and Sands Inc 740 453-0721
3570 S River Rd Zanesville (43701) *(G-20532)*
Shelly Company 419 396-7641
1794 County Highway 99 Carey (43316) *(G-2598)*
Shelly Company 740 441-1714
24537 Canal Rd Circleville (43113) *(G-4904)*
Shelly Company 419 422-8854
1700 Fostoria Ave Ste 200 Findlay (45840) *(G-11080)*
Shelly Company 330 425-7861
8920 Canyon Falls Blvd # 3 Twinsburg (44087) *(G-18469)*
Shelly Company, The, Thornville *Also called Shelly Materials Inc (G-17668)*
Shelly Materials, East Fultonham *Also called Chesterhill Stone Co (G-10505)*
Shelly Materials Inc 740 666-5841
8328 Watkins Rd Ostrander (43061) *(G-15794)*
Shelly Materials Inc (HQ) 740 246-6315
80 Park Dr Thornville (43076) *(G-17668)*
Shelter House Volunteer Group (PA) 513 721-0643
411 Gest St Cincinnati (45203) *(G-4515)*
Shelter Moving & Storage, West Chester *Also called Shetler Moving & Stor of Ohio (G-19151)*
Sheltering Arms Hospital Found 740 592-9300
55 Hospital Dr Athens (45701) *(G-811)*
Shepards Meadows, Poland *Also called Shepherd of The Valley Luthera (G-16227)*
Shepards Wood Nursing, Youngstown *Also called Shepherd of The Valley Luthera (G-20374)*
Shepherd Excavating Inc 614 889-1115
6295 Cosgray Rd Dublin (43016) *(G-10452)*
Shepherd of The Valley Luthera (PA) 330 530-4038
5525 Silica Rd Youngstown (44515) *(G-20373)*
Shepherd of The Valley Luthera 330 726-9061
7148 West Blvd Youngstown (44512) *(G-20374)*
Shepherd of The Valley Luthera 330 726-7110
301 W Western Reserve Rd Poland (44514) *(G-16227)*
Sheraton Airport Hotel, Cleveland *Also called Hopkins Partners (G-5772)*
Sheraton Clmbus At Capitol Sq, Columbus *Also called 75 East State LLC (G-6916)*
Sheraton Suites Akron, Cuyahoga Falls *Also called Riverside Cmnty Urban Redev (G-9215)*
Sheraton Suites Columbus, Columbus *Also called Regal Hospitality LLC (G-8605)*
Shereton Hotel Independance, Cleveland *Also called Independent Hotel Partners LLC (G-5814)*
Sheriff's Office, Dayton *Also called County of Montgomery (G-9431)*
Sherman Financial Group LLC 513 707-3000
8600 Governors Hill Dr # 201 Cincinnati (45249) *(G-4516)*
Sherman Thompson Oh Tc LP 216 520-1250
275 N 3rd St Ironton (45638) *(G-12302)*
Shermco Industries Inc 614 836-8556
4383 Professional Pkwy Groveport (43125) *(G-11672)*
Sherwood Fd Dstrs Clveland Div, Maple Heights *Also called Sfd Company LLC (G-13417)*
Sherwood Food Distributors LLC 216 662-6794
16625 Granite Rd Maple Heights (44137) *(G-13418)*
SHERWOOD FOOD DISTRIBUTORS, L.L.C., Maple Heights *Also called Sherwood Food Distributors LLC (G-13418)*
Shetler Moving & Stor of Ohio 513 755-0700
9917 Charter Park Dr West Chester (45069) *(G-19151)*
Shetlers Sales & Service Inc 330 760-3358
3500 Copley Rd Copley (44321) *(G-9064)*
Shg Whitehall Holdings LLC 216 292-5706
4805 Langley Ave Columbus (43213) *(G-8726)*
Shield Security Service 330 650-2001
P.O. Box 1001 Hudson (44236) *(G-12144)*

ALPHABETIC

(PA)=Parent Co (HQ)=Headquarters (DH)=Div Headquarters
2018 Harris Ohio Services Directory
1319

Shields Capital Corporation.......216 767-1340
20600 Chagrin Blvd # 800 Beachwood (44122) ***(G-1123)***
Shilling AC Heating & Plumbing, Port Clinton *Also called Gundlach Sheet Metal Works Inc* ***(G-16246)***
Shiloh Group.......937 833-2219
14336 Amity Rd Brookville (45309) ***(G-1966)***
Shiloh Manufacturing LLC (HQ).......330 558-2693
880 Steel Dr Valley City (44280) ***(G-18624)***
SHILOH SPRINGS CARE CENTER, Trotwood *Also called Carriage Inn of Trotwood Inc* ***(G-18345)***
Shiloh Springs Care Center, Dayton *Also called Carriage Inn of Trotwood Inc* ***(G-9384)***
Shiloh Springs Care Center, Brookville *Also called Shiloh Group* ***(G-1966)***
Shima Limousine Services Inc.......440 918-6400
7555 Tyler Blvd Ste 12 Mentor (44060) ***(G-14242)***
Shindler Neff Holmes Schlag.......419 243-6281
300 Madison Ave Ste 1200 Toledo (43604) ***(G-18184)***
Shining Company.......614 588-4115
3739 Wynds Dr Columbus (43232) ***(G-8727)***
Ship Shape Marine Inc.......419 734-1554
410 W Perry St Port Clinton (43452) ***(G-16255)***
Ship-Paq Inc.......513 860-0700
3845 Port Union Rd Fairfield (45014) ***(G-10905)***
Shippers Cartage & Dist, Cleveland *Also called Shippers Consolidated Dist* ***(G-6478)***
Shippers Consolidated Dist.......216 579-9303
1840 Carter Rd Cleveland (44113) ***(G-6478)***
Shipping & Receiving Dept, Cleveland *Also called Case Western Reserve Univ* ***(G-5187)***
Shipyard, The, Columbus *Also called Peopletomysitecom LLC* ***(G-8533)***
Shirleys Gourmet Popcorn Co, Pandora *Also called Drc Holdings Inc* ***(G-15889)***
Shiv Hotels LLC.......740 374-8190
700 Pike St Marietta (45750) ***(G-13499)***
Shiver Security Systems Inc.......513 719-4000
6404 Thornberry Ct # 410 Mason (45040) ***(G-13760)***
Shoemaker Electric Company.......614 294-5626
831 Bonham Ave Columbus (43211) ***(G-8728)***
Shoemaker Industrial Solutions, Columbus *Also called Shoemaker Electric Company* ***(G-8728)***
Shoptech Industrial Sftwr.......513 985-9900
400 E Bus Way Ste 300 Cincinnati (45241) ***(G-4517)***
Shoreby Club, Cleveland *Also called Clubcorp Usa Inc* ***(G-5367)***
Shoreby Club Inc.......216 851-2587
40 Shoreby Dr Cleveland (44108) ***(G-6479)***
Shoreline Company, Strongsville *Also called Shoreline Transportation Inc* ***(G-17508)***
Shoreline Express Inc.......440 878-3750
20137 Progress Dr Strongsville (44149) ***(G-17507)***
Shoreline Transportation Inc.......440 878-2000
20137 Progress Dr Strongsville (44149) ***(G-17508)***
Short and Sweet, Columbus *Also called Nationwide Childrens Hospital* ***(G-8229)***
Short Freight Lines Inc.......419 729-1691
6180 Benore Rd Toledo (43612) ***(G-18185)***
Shotstop Ballistics LLC.......330 686-0020
4319 Lorwood Dr Ste 102 Stow (44224) ***(G-17392)***
Shoupes Constuction.......937 352-6457
1410 Ludlow Rd Xenia (45385) ***(G-20076)***
Show What You Know, Dayton *Also called Lorenz Corporation* ***(G-9687)***
Showcase Cinemas, Maumee *Also called National Amusements Inc* ***(G-13949)***
Showe Builders Inc (HQ).......614 481-8106
45 N 4th St Columbus (43215) ***(G-8729)***
Shp Leading Design (PA).......513 381-2112
312 Plum St Ste 700 Cincinnati (45202) ***(G-4518)***
Shr Management Resources Corp.......937 274-1546
2222 Philadelphia Dr Dayton (45406) ***(G-9879)***
Shrader Tire & Oil Inc (PA).......419 472-2128
2045 W Sylvania Ave # 51 Toledo (43613) ***(G-18186)***
Shred It, Columbus *Also called TDS Document Management Ltd* ***(G-8826)***
Shred-It USA LLC.......847 288-0377
6838 Firfield Bus Ctr Dr Fairfield (45014) ***(G-10906)***
Shred-It USA LLC (HQ).......800 697-4733
6838 Firfield Bus Ctr Dr Fairfield (45014) ***(G-10907)***
Shredded Bedding Corporation (PA).......740 893-3567
6589 Bennington Chapel Rd Centerburg (43011) ***(G-2668)***
Shremshock Architects Inc (PA).......614 545-4550
7400 W Campus Rd Ste 150 New Albany (43054) ***(G-15007)***
Shriners Hspitals For Children.......513 872-6000
3229 Burnet Ave Cincinnati (45229) ***(G-4519)***
Shumaker Loop & Kendrick LLP (PA).......419 241-9000
1000 Jackson St Toledo (43604) ***(G-18187)***
Shumsky Enterprises Inc (PA).......937 223-2203
811 E 4th St Dayton (45402) ***(G-9880)***
Shumsky Promotional, Dayton *Also called Boost Technologies LLC* ***(G-9364)***
Shurmer Place At Altenheim.......440 238-9001
18821 Shurmer Rd Strongsville (44136) ***(G-17509)***
Sibcy Cline Inc.......937 610-3404
8353 Yankee St Dayton (45458) ***(G-9881)***
Sibcy Cline Inc.......513 752-4000
792 Eastgate South Dr # 800 Cincinnati (45245) ***(G-2931)***
Sibcy Cline Inc.......513 793-2121
8040 Montgomery Rd Cincinnati (45236) ***(G-4520)***
Sibcy Cline Inc.......513 385-3330
600 Wessel Dr Fairfield (45014) ***(G-10908)***
Sibcy Cline Inc (PA).......513 984-4100
8044 Montgomery Rd # 300 Cincinnati (45236) ***(G-4521)***
Sibcy Cline Inc.......513 829-0044
600 Wessel Dr Fairfield (45014) ***(G-10909)***
Sibcy Cline Inc.......513 777-8100
7677 Voice Of Amer Ctr Dr West Chester (45069) ***(G-19152)***
Sibcy Cline Inc.......513 793-2700
9979 Montgomery Rd Cincinnati (45242) ***(G-4522)***
Sibcy Cline Inc.......513 931-7700
9250 Winton Rd Cincinnati (45231) ***(G-4523)***
Sibcy Cline Inc.......513 677-1830
7395 Mason Montgomery Rd Mason (45040) ***(G-13761)***
Sibcy Cline Inc.......937 429-2101
2476 Commons Blvd Ste E Beavercreek (45431) ***(G-1208)***
Sibcy Cline Inc.......513 932-6334
103 Oregonia Rd Lebanon (45036) ***(G-12646)***
Sibcy Cline Mortgage Services.......513 984-6776
8044 Montgomery Rd # 301 Cincinnati (45236) ***(G-4524)***
Sibcy Cline Realtors, Cincinnati *Also called Sibcy Cline Inc* ***(G-4521)***
Sibcy Cline Realtors, West Chester *Also called Sibcy Cline Inc* ***(G-19152)***
Sibcy Cline Realtors, Cincinnati *Also called Sibcy Cline Inc* ***(G-4523)***
Sibcy Cline Realtors, Mason *Also called Sibcy Cline Inc* ***(G-13761)***
Sibcy, Cline Realtors, Lebanon *Also called Sibcy Cline Inc* ***(G-12646)***
Sickle Cell Awaremess Grp.......513 281-4450
3458 Reading Rd Cincinnati (45229) ***(G-4525)***
Sidaris Italian Foods, Cleveland *Also called Resers Fine Foods Inc* ***(G-6382)***
Side Effects Inc.......937 704-9696
259 Industrial Dr Franklin (45005) ***(G-11165)***
Sidle Transit Service Inc.......330 683-2807
5454 N Crown Hill Rd Orrville (44667) ***(G-15787)***
Sidney Care Center, Sidney *Also called CHS Miami Valley Inc* ***(G-16920)***
Sidney Electric Company (PA).......419 222-1109
840 S Vandemark Rd Sidney (45365) ***(G-16954)***
Sidney-Shelby County YMCA (PA).......937 492-9134
300 E Parkwood St Sidney (45365) ***(G-16955)***
Sidwell Materials Inc.......740 849-2394
4200 Maysville Pike Zanesville (43701) ***(G-20533)***
Siebenthaler Company (PA).......937 427-4110
3001 Catalpa Dr Dayton (45405) ***(G-9882)***
Siebenthaler's Garden Center, Dayton *Also called Siebenthaler Company* ***(G-9882)***
Siegel Siegel J & Jennings Co (PA).......216 763-1004
23425 Commerce Park # 103 Beachwood (44122) ***(G-1124)***
Siemens Energy Inc.......740 393-8897
105 N Sandusky St Mount Vernon (43050) ***(G-14923)***
Siemens Fire Safety, Cleveland *Also called Siemens Industry Inc* ***(G-6480)***
Siemens Industry Inc.......216 365-7030
5350 Trnsp Blvd Ste 9 Cleveland (44125) ***(G-6480)***
Siemens Industry Inc.......440 526-2770
6930 Treeline Dr Ste A Brecksville (44141) ***(G-1850)***
Siemens Industry Inc.......513 742-5590
1310 Kemper Meadow Dr # 500 Cincinnati (45240) ***(G-4526)***
Siemens PLM Software.......513 576-2400
2000 Eastman Dr Milford (45150) ***(G-14561)***
Siemens Product Life Mgmt Sftw.......513 576-2400
2000 Eastman Dr Milford (45150) ***(G-14562)***
Siemer Distributing, New Lexington *Also called Lori Holding Co* ***(G-15055)***
Siemer Distributing Company.......740 342-3230
1400 Commerce Dr New Lexington (43764) ***(G-15063)***
Siena Springs II.......513 639-2800
6217 N Main St Dayton (45415) ***(G-9883)***
Sienna Hills Nursing & Rehab.......740 546-3013
73841 Pleasant Grove Rd Adena (43901) ***(G-8)***
Sierra Lobo Inc (PA).......419 332-7101
102 Pinnacle Dr Fremont (43420) ***(G-11220)***
Sievers Security Systems Inc (PA).......216 383-1234
18210 Saint Clair Ave Cleveland (44110) ***(G-6481)***
Siffrin Residential Assn.......330 799-8932
136 Westchester Dr Ste 1 Youngstown (44515) ***(G-20375)***
Sight Resource Corporation (PA).......513 942-4423
8100 Beckett Center Dr West Chester (45069) ***(G-19153)***
Sigma CHI Frat.......614 297-8783
260 E 15th Ave Columbus (43201) ***(G-8730)***
Sigma T E K, Cincinnati *Also called Sigmatek Systems LLC* ***(G-4527)***
Sigma Technologies Ltd.......419 874-9262
27096 Oakmead Dr Perrysburg (43551) ***(G-16059)***
Sigma-Aldrich, Miamisburg *Also called Aldrich Chemical* ***(G-14269)***
Sigmatek Systems LLC (PA).......513 674-0005
1445 Kemper Meadow Dr Cincinnati (45240) ***(G-4527)***
Sign America Incorporated.......740 765-5555
3887 State Route 43 Richmond (43944) ***(G-16535)***
Sign Source USA Inc.......419 224-1130
1700 S Dixie Hwy Lima (45804) ***(G-12878)***
Signal Office Supply Inc.......513 821-2280
415 W Benson St Cincinnati (45215) ***(G-4528)***
Signal Productions Inc.......323 382-0000
1267 W 9th St Cleveland (44113) ***(G-6482)***
Signature Inc.......614 734-0010
5115 Prkcnter Ave Ste 200 Dublin (43017) ***(G-10453)***
Signature Assoc-A Cushman, Toledo *Also called Signature Associates Inc* ***(G-18188)***
Signature Associates Inc.......419 244-7505
4 Seagate Ste 608 Toledo (43604) ***(G-18188)***

Signature Boutique Hotel LP...216 595-0900
1010 Eaton Blvd Beachwood (44122) *(G-1125)*
Signature Concrete Inc...937 723-8435
517 Windsor Park Dr Dayton (45459) *(G-9884)*
Signature Control Systems LLC...614 864-2222
2228 Citygate Dr Columbus (43219) *(G-8731)*
Signature Controls, Columbus *Also called Signature Control Systems LLC (G-8731)*
Signature Health Inc...440 953-9999
38882 Mentor Ave Willoughby (44094) *(G-19713)*
Signature Health Services LLC...740 522-6017
675 Hopewell Dr Heath (43056) *(G-11844)*
Signature Healthcare LLC...330 372-1977
2473 North Rd Ne Warren (44483) *(G-18899)*
Signature Healthcare LLC...440 232-1800
5386 Majestic Pkwy Bedford (44146) *(G-1336)*
Signature Optical Inc...216 831-6299
2000 Auburn Dr Ste 140 Beachwood (44122) *(G-1126)*
Signature Salon, Cleveland *Also called Best Cuts Inc (G-5118)*
Signature Solon Golf Course, Solon *Also called Weymouth Valley Inc (G-17067)*
Signet Management Co Ltd...330 762-9102
19 N High St Akron (44308) *(G-438)*
Signum LLC...440 248-2233
32000 Aurora Rd Ste C Solon (44139) *(G-17051)*
Sika Corporation...740 387-9224
1682 Mrn Williamsprt Rd E Marion (43302) *(G-13579)*
Siler Excavation Services...513 400-8628
6025 Catherine Dr Milford (45150) *(G-14563)*
Silliker Laboratories Ohio Inc...614 486-0150
2057 Builders Pl Columbus (43204) *(G-8732)*
Silvan Trucking Company Ohio, Columbus *Also called S & T Truck and Auto Svc Inc (G-8667)*
Silver Lake Country Club...330 688-6066
1325 Graham Rd Silver Lake (44224) *(G-16964)*
Silver Lake Management Corp...330 688-6066
1325 Graham Rd Silver Lake (44224) *(G-16965)*
Sima Marine Sales Inc (PA)...440 269-3200
200 Forest Dr Willoughby (44095) *(G-19714)*
Simco Controls, Columbus *Also called Simco Supply Co (G-8733)*
Simco Supply Co...614 253-1999
3000 E 14th Ave Columbus (43219) *(G-8733)*
Simmons Brothers Corporation...330 722-1415
780 W Smith Rd Ste A Medina (44256) *(G-14125)*
Simms Metal Management Ohio, Defiance *Also called Metal Management Ohio Inc (G-10049)*
Simon Knton Cncil Byscuts Amer (PA)...614 436-7200
807 Kinnear Rd Columbus (43212) *(G-8734)*
Simon Property Group...614 717-9300
5043 Tuttle Crossing Blvd Dublin (43016) *(G-10454)*
Simon Roofing and Shtmtl Corp (PA)...330 629-7392
70 Karago Ave Youngstown (44512) *(G-20376)*
Simone Health Management Inc...614 224-1347
750 E Broad St Ste 300 Columbus (43205) *(G-8735)*
Simonson Construction Svcs Inc...419 281-8299
2112 Troy Rd Ashland (44805) *(G-699)*
Simonton Windows, Columbus *Also called Fortune Brands Windows Inc (G-7681)*
Simplex Time Recorder 514, West Chester *Also called Simplex Time Recorder LLC (G-19229)*
Simplex Time Recorder LLC...800 746-7539
8910 Beckett Rd West Chester (45069) *(G-19154)*
Simplex Time Recorder LLC...513 874-1227
10182 International Blvd West Chester (45246) *(G-19229)*
Simplifi Eso LLC...614 635-8679
2 Miranova Pl Ste 500 Columbus (43215) *(G-8736)*
Simplified Logistics LLC...440 250-8912
28915 Clemens Rd Ste 220 Westlake (44145) *(G-19547)*
Simply Money, Cincinnati *Also called Financial Network Group Ltd (G-3610)*
Simply Youth LLC...330 284-2537
123 Cleveland Ave Nw Canton (44702) *(G-2528)*
Simpson Strong-Tie Company Inc...614 876-8060
2600 International St Columbus (43228) *(G-8737)*
Sims Buick-G M C Truck Inc...330 372-3500
3100 Elm Rd Ne Warren (44483) *(G-18900)*
Sims GMC Trucks, Warren *Also called Sims Buick-G M C Truck Inc (G-18900)*
Sims-Lohman Inc (PA)...513 651-3510
6325 Este Ave Cincinnati (45232) *(G-4529)*
Sims-Lohman Fine Kitchens Gran, Cincinnati *Also called Sims-Lohman Inc (G-4529)*
Sinclair Broadcast Group Inc...513 641-4400
1906 Highland Ave Cincinnati (45219) *(G-4530)*
Sinclair Broadcast Group Inc...513 641-4400
1906 Highland Ave Cincinnati (45219) *(G-4531)*
Sinclair Media II Inc...614 481-6666
1261 Dublin Rd Columbus (43215) *(G-8738)*
Sinclair Media II Inc...614 481-6666
1261 Dublin Rd Columbus (43215) *(G-8739)*
Sinclair Media II Inc...614 481-6666
1261 Dublin Rd Columbus (43215) *(G-8740)*
Sines Inc...440 352-6572
1744 N Ridge Rd Painesville (44077) *(G-15879)*
Singleton Health Care Center...216 231-0076
1867 E 82nd St Cleveland (44103) *(G-6483)*
Sioto Paintsville Mental Hlth...740 775-1260
4449 State Route 159 Chillicothe (45601) *(G-2885)*
Sirak Financial Companies, Canton *Also called Sirak Financial Services Inc (G-2530)*
Sirak Financial Services...330 493-3211
4700 Dressler Rd Nw Canton (44718) *(G-2529)*
Sirak Financial Services Inc (PA)...330 493-0642
4700 Dressler Rd Nw Canton (44718) *(G-2530)*
Sirak-Moore Insurance Agcy Inc...330 493-3211
4700 Dressler Rd Nw Canton (44718) *(G-2531)*
Sirna & Sons Inc (PA)...330 298-2222
7176 State Route 88 Ravenna (44266) *(G-16411)*
Sirna's Market & Deli, Ravenna *Also called Sirna & Sons Inc (G-16411)*
Sirpilla Recrtl Vhcl Ctr Inc...330 494-2525
1005 Interstate Pkwy Akron (44312) *(G-439)*
Sirva Inc...216 606-4000
6200 Oak Tree Blvd # 300 Independence (44131) *(G-12257)*
Sirva Mortgage Inc...800 531-3837
6200 Oak Tree Blvd # 300 Independence (44131) *(G-12258)*
Sirva Relocation LLC (HQ)...216 606-4000
6200 Oak Tree Blvd # 300 Independence (44131) *(G-12259)*
Sirva Worldwide Relocation Mvg, Independence *Also called Sirva Relocation LLC (G-12259)*
SIS, Columbus *Also called Strategic Insurance Sftwr Inc (G-8794)*
Sisler Heating & Cooling Inc...330 722-7101
249 S State Rd Medina (44256) *(G-14126)*
Sister of Mercy of Clerm Count (HQ)...513 732-8200
3000 Hospital Dr Batavia (45103) *(G-1024)*
Sisters Charity Mother House, Mount Saint Joseph *Also called Sisters of Charity of Cinc (G-14872)*
Sisters Od Saint Joseph of SAI...216 531-7426
21800 Chardon Rd Euclid (44117) *(G-10776)*
Sisters of Charity of Cinc (HQ)...513 347-5200
5900 Delhi Rd Mount Saint Joseph (45051) *(G-14871)*
Sisters of Charity of Cinc...513 347-5436
5900 Delhi Rd Mount Saint Joseph (45051) *(G-14872)*
Sisters of Little...216 464-1222
4291 Richmond Rd Warrensville Heights (44122) *(G-18934)*
Sisters of Little...419 698-4331
930 S Wynn Rd Oregon (43616) *(G-15749)*
Sisters of Little...513 281-8001
476 Riddle Rd Cincinnati (45220) *(G-4532)*
Sisters of Mercy...419 332-8208
1220 Tiffin St Fremont (43420) *(G-11221)*
Sisters of Mercy Amer Reg Comm...419 696-7203
1001 Isaac Streets Dr Oregon (43616) *(G-15750)*
Sisters of Mercy Fremont, Ohio, Fremont *Also called Sisters of Mercy (G-11221)*
Sisters of Mrcy of Wllard Ohio (HQ)...419 964-5000
1100 Neal Zick Rd Willard (44890) *(G-19627)*
Sisters of Notre D...419 471-0170
3912 Sunforest Ct Ste B Toledo (43623) *(G-18189)*
Sisters of The Transfiguration, Cincinnati *Also called Society of The Transfiguration (G-4548)*
Site 046, Bellefontaine *Also called Allied Waste Systems Inc (G-1376)*
Site 091b, Bryan *Also called Allied Waste Systems Inc (G-2001)*
Site K62, Williamsburg *Also called Cecos International Inc (G-19629)*
Site L10, Morrow *Also called Browning-Ferris Industries Inc (G-14844)*
Site R24, Oberlin *Also called Allied Waste Industries LLC (G-15639)*
Site Worx LLC...513 229-0295
3980 Turtlecreek Rd Lebanon (45036) *(G-12647)*
Siteworx, Lebanon *Also called Site Worx LLC (G-12647)*
Six C Fabrication Inc...330 296-5594
5245 S Prospect St Ravenna (44266) *(G-16412)*
Six Continents Hotels Inc...513 563-8330
3855 Hauck Rd Cincinnati (45241) *(G-4533)*
Six Disciplines LLC (PA)...419 424-6647
1219 W Main Cross St # 205 Findlay (45840) *(G-11081)*
Six Flags Ohio, Aurora *Also called Funtime Parks Inc (G-839)*
Sjn Data Center LLC (PA)...513 386-7871
4620 Wesley Ave Cincinnati (45212) *(G-4534)*
SJS Packaging Group Inc...513 841-1351
6545 Wiehe Rd Cincinnati (45237) *(G-4535)*
Sk Rigging Co Inc...513 771-7766
11515 Rockfield Ct Cincinnati (45241) *(G-4536)*
Skally's Restaurant, Cincinnati *Also called Skallys Old World Bakery Inc (G-4537)*
Skallys Old World Bakery Inc...513 931-1411
1933 W Galbraith Rd Cincinnati (45239) *(G-4537)*
Skanska USA Building Inc...513 421-0082
201 E 5th St Ste 2020 Cincinnati (45202) *(G-4538)*
Skate Town U S A...513 874-9855
8730 N Pavillion West Chester (45069) *(G-19155)*
Skateworld Inc (PA)...937 294-4032
1601 E David Rd Dayton (45429) *(G-9885)*
Skateworld of Kettering, Dayton *Also called Skateworld Inc (G-9885)*
Skidmore Sales & Distrg Co Inc (PA)...513 755-4200
9889 Cincinnati Dayton Rd West Chester (45069) *(G-19156)*
Skilled Care Pharmacy Inc (PA)...513 459-7626
6175 Hi Tek Ct Mason (45040) *(G-13762)*
Skilled Nurse Ctr of...330 615-3717
155 5th St Ne Barberton (44203) *(G-979)*
Skillsoft Corporation...216 524-5200
6645 Acres Dr Independence (44131) *(G-12260)*

ALPHABETIC

ALPHABETIC SECTION

Skinner Diesel Services Inc (PA).................................614 491-8785
  2440 Lockbourne Rd Columbus (43207) *(G-8741)*
Skipco Financial Adjusters (PA)....................................330 854-4800
  2306 Locust St S Canal Fulton (44614) *(G-2146)*
Skoda Minotti Holdings LLC (PA)...................................440 449-6800
  6685 Beta Dr Cleveland (44143) *(G-6484)*
Skoda Mntti Crtif Pub Accntnts (HQ)...............................440 449-6800
  6685 Beta Dr Mayfield Village (44143) *(G-14013)*
SKW Management LLC...937 382-7938
  3841 Panhandle Rd Lynchburg (45142) *(G-13184)*
Sky Climber Twr Solutions LLC......................................740 203-3900
  1800 Pittsburgh Dr Delaware (43015) *(G-10127)*
Sky Financial Capital Tr III..614 480-3278
  41 S High St Columbus (43215) *(G-8742)*
Sky Lane Drive-Thru, Garrettsville *Also called Skylane LLC (G-11352)*
Sky Zone Boston Heights, Hudson *Also called Wonderworker Inc (G-12155)*
Sky Zone Indoor Trampoline Pk, Cincinnati *Also called Sky Zone Indoor Trampoline Pk (G-4539)*
Sky Zone Indoor Trampoline Pk......................................614 302-6093
  11745 Commons Dr Cincinnati (45246) *(G-4539)*
Skybox Packaging LLC..419 525-7209
  1275 Pollock Pkwy Mansfield (44905) *(G-13364)*
Skycasters LLC..330 785-2100
  1520 S Arlington St # 100 Akron (44306) *(G-440)*
Skye Development Company LLC......................................216 223-0160
  25001 Emery Rd Ste 420 Cleveland (44128) *(G-6485)*
Skylane LLC...330 527-9999
  8311 Windham St Garrettsville (44231) *(G-11352)*
Skylight Financial Group LLC.......................................216 621-5680
  2012 W 25th St Ste 900 Cleveland (44113) *(G-6486)*
Skyline Chili Inc (PA)..513 874-1188
  4180 Thunderbird Ln Fairfield (45014) *(G-10910)*
Skyline Clvland Rnaissance LLC.....................................216 696-5600
  24 Public Sq Cleveland (44113) *(G-6487)*
Skyview Baptist Ranch Inc..330 674-7511
  7241 Township Road 319 Millersburg (44654) *(G-14622)*
SL Wellspring LLC...513 948-2339
  8000 Evergreen Ridge Dr Cincinnati (45215) *(G-4540)*
Slagle Mechanical Contractors......................................937 492-4151
  877 W Russell Rd Sidney (45365) *(G-16956)*
Slaters Inc...740 654-2204
  1141 N Memorial Dr Lancaster (43130) *(G-12574)*
Slavic Village Development...216 429-1182
  5620 Broadway Ave Uppr Ste 200 Cleveland (44127) *(G-6488)*
Slawson Equipment Co Inc...216 391-7263
  7851 Freeway Cir Cleveland (44130) *(G-6489)*
Slay Transportation Co Inc...740 865-2910
  Rr 7 Box 34684 Sardis (43946) *(G-16815)*
SLC Custom Packaging, Macedonia *Also called Specialty Lubricants Corp (G-13210)*
Sleep Care Inc..614 901-8989
  985 Schrock Rd Columbus (43229) *(G-8743)*
Sleep Inn, Oregon *Also called Dure Investments LLC (G-15732)*
Sleep Network Inc (PA)...419 535-9282
  3450 W Central Ave # 118 Toledo (43606) *(G-18190)*
Sleepy Hollow Golf Course, Brecksville *Also called Cleveland Metroparks (G-1820)*
Slesnick Iron & Metal Co...330 453-8475
  927 Warner Rd Se Canton (44707) *(G-2532)*
Slick Automated Solutions Inc......................................567 247-1080
  1825 Nussbaum Pkwy Ontario (44906) *(G-15714)*
Slimans Chrysler Plymuth Dodge, Amherst *Also called Slimans Sales & Service Inc (G-604)*
Slimans Sales & Service Inc..440 988-4484
  7498 Leavitt Rd Amherst (44001) *(G-604)*
Slipgrips, Nelsonville *Also called Lehigh Outfitters LLC (G-14965)*
Sliver Lake Country Club, Silver Lake *Also called Silver Lake Management Corp (G-16965)*
Slovene Home For The Aged..216 486-0268
  18621 Neff Rd Cleveland (44119) *(G-6490)*
Slush Puppie..513 771-0940
  44 Carnegie Way West Chester (45246) *(G-19230)*
SM Double Tree Hotel Lake..216 241-5100
  1111 Lakeside Ave E Cleveland (44114) *(G-6491)*
Small Sand & Gravel Inc..740 427-3130
  10229 Killduff Rd Gambier (43022) *(G-11349)*
Smalls Asphalt Paving Inc..740 427-4096
  10229 Killduff Rd Gambier (43022) *(G-11350)*
Smart (PA)..216 228-9400
  24950 Country Club Blvd # 340 North Olmsted (44070) *(G-15444)*
Smart - Transportation Div, North Olmsted *Also called Smart (G-15444)*
Smart Ed Services, Cleveland *Also called Cleveland Corporate Svcs Inc (G-5310)*
Smart Solutions, Beachwood *Also called Ohio Cllbrtive Lrng Sltons Inc (G-1110)*
Smb Construction Co Inc (PA).......................................419 269-1473
  5120 Jackman Rd Toledo (43613) *(G-18191)*
SMG AGENT FOR CLEVELAND CONVEN, Cleveland *Also called Cuyahoga County Convention Fac (G-5455)*
Smg Holdings Inc...614 827-2500
  400 N High St Fl 2 Columbus (43215) *(G-8744)*
Smgoa, Columbus *Also called Sports Medicine Grant Inc (G-8763)*
Smile Brands Inc...419 627-1255
  1313 W Bogart Rd Ste D Sandusky (44870) *(G-16795)*
Smile Development Inc..419 882-7187
  5860 Alexis Rd Ste 1 Sylvania (43560) *(G-17615)*

Smink Electric Inc..440 322-5518
  215 Winckles St Elyria (44035) *(G-10680)*
Smith & Associates Excavating......................................740 362-3355
  2765 Drake Rd Columbus (43219) *(G-8745)*
Smith & English II Inc..513 697-9300
  12191 State Route 22 3 Loveland (45140) *(G-13161)*
Smith & Oby Company..440 735-5333
  7676 Northfield Rd Walton Hills (44146) *(G-18791)*
Smith & Oby Service Co...440 735-5322
  7676 Northfield Rd Bedford (44146) *(G-1337)*
Smith Ambulance Service Inc..330 825-0205
  214 W 3rd St Dover (44622) *(G-10212)*
Smith Ambulance Service Inc (PA)..................................330 602-0050
  214 W 3rd St Dover (44622) *(G-10213)*
Smith Barney, Beavercreek *Also called Citigroup Global Markets Inc (G-1233)*
Smith Barney, Toledo *Also called Citigroup Global Markets Inc (G-17806)*
Smith Barney, Cleveland *Also called Citigroup Global Markets Inc (G-5243)*
Smith Brothers Erection Inc..740 373-3575
  101 Industry Rd Marietta (45750) *(G-13500)*
Smith Clinic, Delaware *Also called Women Health Partners (G-10136)*
Smith Concrete Co (PA)...740 373-7441
  2301 Progress St Dover (44622) *(G-10214)*
Smith Construction Group Inc.......................................937 426-0500
  731 Orchard Ln Beavercreek Township (45434) *(G-1284)*
Smith Peter Kalail Co Lpa..216 503-5055
  6480 Rcksde Wds Blvd S # 300 Independence (44131) *(G-12261)*
Smith Rolfes & Skazdahl Lpa (PA)..................................513 579-0080
  600 Vine St Ste 2600 Cincinnati (45202) *(G-4541)*
Smith Tandy Company..614 224-9255
  555 City Park Ave Columbus (43215) *(G-8746)*
Smith Trucking Inc..419 841-8676
  3775 Centennial Rd Sylvania (43560) *(G-17616)*
Smith, Matthew J Co Lpa, Cincinnati *Also called Smith Rolfes & Skazdahl Lpa (G-4541)*
Smith, R G of Mansfield, Mansfield *Also called R G Smith Company (G-13352)*
Smithbarney, Cincinnati *Also called Citigroup Global Markets Inc (G-3355)*
Smithers Group Inc (PA)..330 762-7441
  121 S Main St Ste 300 Akron (44308) *(G-441)*
Smithers Quality Assessments.......................................330 762-4231
  121 S Main St Ste 300 Akron (44308) *(G-442)*
Smithers Rapra Inc..330 297-1495
  1150 N Freedom St Ravenna (44266) *(G-16413)*
Smithers Rapra Inc (HQ)...330 762-7441
  425 W Market St Akron (44303) *(G-443)*
Smithers Tire & Auto Testng TX.....................................330 762-7441
  425 W Market St Akron (44303) *(G-444)*
Smithers Trnsp Test Ctrs, Akron *Also called Smithers Tire & Auto Testng TX (G-444)*
Smithfield Packaged Meats Corp.....................................513 782-3805
  801 E Kemper Rd Cincinnati (45246) *(G-4542)*
Smithfoods Orrville Inc..740 389-4643
  135 Sara Ave Marion (43302) *(G-13580)*
Smithfoods Trucking Inc..330 684-6502
  1201 Sterling Ave Orrville (44667) *(G-15788)*
Smithpearlman & Co..513 248-9210
  100 Techne Center Dr # 200 Milford (45150) *(G-14564)*
Smithville Western Commons, Wooster *Also called Horn Nursing and Rehab Center (G-19871)*
Smoky Row Childrens Center...614 766-2122
  8615 Smoky Row Rd Powell (43065) *(G-16352)*
Smoot Construction Co Ohio (PA)...................................614 257-0032
  1907 Leonard Ave Ste 200 Columbus (43219) *(G-8747)*
SMS, Alliance *Also called Stark Metal Sales Inc (G-562)*
SMS Technical Services LLC...330 426-4126
  49560 State Route 14 East Palestine (44413) *(G-10539)*
SMS Transport LLC...937 813-8897
  8235 Old Troy Pike 272 Dayton (45424) *(G-9886)*
Smylie One Heating & Cooling.......................................440 449-4328
  5108 Richmond Rd Bedford (44146) *(G-1338)*
Smyth Automotive Inc (PA)..513 528-2800
  4275 Mt Carmel Tobasco Rd Cincinnati (45244) *(G-4543)*
Smyth Automotive Inc...513 528-0061
  4271 Mt Carmel Tobasco Rd Cincinnati (45244) *(G-4544)*
Smyth Automotive Inc...513 777-6400
  8868 Cincinnati Columbus West Chester (45069) *(G-19157)*
Smythe Cramer Co, Uniontown *Also called Howard Hanna Smythe Cramer (G-18524)*
Smythe Cramer Reltrs, Cleveland *Also called Howard Hanna Smythe Cramer (G-5784)*
Smythe-Cramer Co Madison, Madison *Also called Howard Hanna Smythe Cramer (G-13225)*
Snapblox Hosted Solutions LLC.....................................866 524-7707
  131 Eight Mile Rd Cincinnati (45255) *(G-4545)*
Snavely Building Company (PA).....................................440 585-9091
  7139 Pine St Ste 110 Chagrin Falls (44022) *(G-2705)*
Snavely Development Company (PA).................................440 585-9091
  7139 Pine St Chagrin Falls (44022) *(G-2706)*
Snelling, Fairlawn *Also called E & L Premier Corporation (G-10946)*
Snf Wadsworth LLC..330 336-3472
  5625 Emerald Ridge Pkwy Solon (44139) *(G-17052)*
Snl Designs Ltd...440 247-2344
  13 N Franklin St Chagrin Falls (44022) *(G-2707)*
Snow Hill Country Club Inc...937 987-2491
  11093 State Route 73 New Vienna (45159) *(G-15132)*

(G-0000) Company's Geographic Section entry number

Snows Lakeside Tavern 513 954-5626
4344 Dry Ridge Rd Cincinnati (45252) *(G-4546)*
Snpj Recreation Farm 440 256-3423
10946 Heath Rd Willoughby (44094) *(G-19715)*
Snyder Brick and Block, Moraine *Also called Snyder Concrete Products Inc (G-14825)*
Snyder Concrete Products Inc (PA) 937 885-5176
2301 W Dorothy Ln Moraine (45439) *(G-14825)*
Snyder's Potato Chips, Bellaire *Also called S-L Distribution Company Inc (G-1367)*
Snyder's Service Now, Wooster *Also called Schmids Service Now Inc (G-19913)*
Snyders Antique Auto Parts Inc 330 549-5313
12925 Woodworth Rd New Springfield (44443) *(G-15131)*
Soaring Eagle Inc 330 385-5579
114 W 5th St East Liverpool (43920) *(G-10535)*
Soccer Centre Inc 419 893-5419
1620 Market Place Dr # 1 Maumee (43537) *(G-13977)*
Soccer Centre Owners Ltd 419 893-5425
1620 Market Place Dr Maumee (43537) *(G-13978)*
SOCIAL MINISTRY ORGANIZATION, Springfield *Also called Oesterlen-Services For Youth (G-17254)*
Social Services of Allen, Augl, Lima *Also called Lutheran Social (G-12834)*
Society For Handicapped Citzns 937 746-4201
624 Fairview Dr Carlisle (45005) *(G-2606)*
Society For Prsrvtion Encurage, Dayton *Also called Dayton Metro Chapter (G-9482)*
Society For Rehabilitation 440 209-0135
9290 Lake Shore Blvd Mentor (44060) *(G-14243)*
Society Handicapped Citz Medin (PA) 330 722-1900
4283 Paradise Rd Seville (44273) *(G-16844)*
Society Handicapped Citz Medin 330 722-1710
5810 Deerview Ln Medina (44256) *(G-14127)*
Society of St Vincent De Paul 513 421-2273
1125 Bank St Cincinnati (45214) *(G-4547)*
Society of The Transfiguration (PA) 513 771-7462
555 Albion Ave Cincinnati (45246) *(G-4548)*
Society Plastics Engineers Inc 419 287-4898
15520 S River Rd Pemberville (43450) *(G-15944)*
Society Rehabilitation, Mentor *Also called Society For Rehabilitation (G-14243)*
Society St Vincent De Paul Cle (PA) 216 696-6525
6610 Biddulph Rd Cleveland (44144) *(G-6492)*
Sociey For Handicapped Citizen 330 725-7041
4283 Paradise Rd Seville (44273) *(G-16845)*
Socius1 LLC (PA) 614 280-9880
5747 Perimeter Dr Ste 200 Dublin (43017) *(G-10455)*
Sodexo Inc 330 425-0709
2333 Sandalwood Dr Twinsburg (44087) *(G-18470)*
Sofco Erectors Inc (PA) 513 771-1600
10360 Wayne Ave Cincinnati (45215) *(G-4549)*
Sofo Importing Company, Toledo *Also called Antonio Sofo Son Importing Co (G-17754)*
Soft Touch Wood LLC 330 545-4204
1560 S State St Girard (44420) *(G-11426)*
Soft Tuch Furn Repr Rfinishing, Girard *Also called Soft Touch Wood LLC (G-11426)*
Software Answers Inc 440 526-0095
6770 W Snowville Rd 200 Brecksville (44141) *(G-1851)*
Software Info Systems LLC 513 791-7777
8805 Governors Hill Dr # 210 Cincinnati (45249) *(G-4550)*
Software Management Group 513 618-2165
1128 Main St Fl 6 Cincinnati (45202) *(G-4551)*
Software Solutions Inc (PA) 513 932-6667
420 E Main St Lebanon (45036) *(G-12648)*
Software Support Group Inc 216 566-0555
22211 Westchester Rd Shaker Heights (44122) *(G-16866)*
Sogeti USA LLC 614 847-4477
579 Executive Campus Dr # 300 Westerville (43082) *(G-19353)*
Sogeti USA LLC 937 433-3334
6494 Centervl Bus Pkwy Dayton (45459) *(G-9887)*
Sogeti USA LLC (HQ) 937 291-8100
10100 Innovation Dr # 200 Miamisburg (45342) *(G-14351)*
Sogeti USA LLC 216 654-2230
6055 Rockside Woods # 170 Cleveland (44131) *(G-6493)*
Sogeti USA LLC 513 824-3000
4445 Lake Forest Dr # 550 Blue Ash (45242) *(G-1689)*
Soho Development Company 614 207-3261
501 Cole Dr Johnstown (43031) *(G-12342)*
Soin Medical Center, Beavercreek *Also called Kettering Medical Center (G-1181)*
Sojourn Lodging Inc 330 422-1855
795 Mondial Pkwy Streetsboro (44241) *(G-17429)*
Sojourner Home, Hamilton *Also called Sojourner Recovery Services (G-11773)*
Sojourner Recovery Services (PA) 513 868-7654
294 N Fair Ave Hamilton (45011) *(G-11773)*
Solar Imaging LLC 614 626-8536
825 Taylor Rd Gahanna (43230) *(G-11268)*
Solar Testing Laboratories Inc (PA) 216 741-7007
1125 Valley Belt Rd Brooklyn Heights (44131) *(G-1926)*
Solenis LLC 614 336-1101
5200 Blazer Pkwy Dublin (43017) *(G-10456)*
Solid Waste Auth Centl Ohio 614 871-5100
4239 London Groveport Rd Grove City (43123) *(G-11598)*
Solidarity Health Network Inc 216 831-1220
4853 Galaxy Pkwy Ste K Cleveland (44128) *(G-6494)*
Solomon Cloud Solutions, Findlay *Also called Plumbline Solutions Inc (G-11076)*
Solomon Lei & Associates Inc 419 246-6931
947 Belmont Ave Toledo (43607) *(G-18192)*
Solomon, Lei & Associates, Toledo *Also called Solomon Lei & Associates Inc (G-18192)*
Solon Branch, Solon *Also called Agilysys Inc (G-16971)*
Solon Creative Playroom Center, Solon *Also called Creative Playroom (G-16997)*
Solon Crtive Plyroom Mntessori, Cleveland *Also called Creative Playroom (G-5433)*
Solon Fire Department, Solon *Also called City of Solon (G-16992)*
Solon Lodging Associates LLC 440 248-9600
30100 Aurora Rd Solon (44139) *(G-17053)*
Solon Pnte At Emrald Ridge LLC 440 498-3000
5625 Emerald Ridge Pkwy Solon (44139) *(G-17054)*
Solupay Consulting Inc 216 535-9016
1900 Entp Pkwy Ste A Twinsburg (44087) *(G-18471)*
Solutions Through Innovative T 937 320-9994
3152 Presidential Dr Beavercreek (45324) *(G-1209)*
Somc, Portsmouth *Also called Southern Ohio Medical Center (G-16313)*
Somc Foundation Inc 740 356-5000
1805 27th St Portsmouth (45662) *(G-16310)*
Somc Hospice, Portsmouth *Also called Hospice of Southern Ohio (G-16289)*
Somc Speech and Hearing Svcs, Portsmouth *Also called Rehabcare Group MGT Svcs Inc (G-16303)*
Somc Urgent Care Ctr Prtsmouth, Portsmouth *Also called Southern Ohio Medical Center (G-16312)*
Somerset Hlth Rhbilitation Ctr, Somerset *Also called Somerset NH LLC (G-17070)*
Somerset NH LLC 740 743-2924
411 S Columbus St Somerset (43783) *(G-17070)*
Something Special Lrng Ctr Inc 419 422-1400
655 Fox Run Rd Ste J Findlay (45840) *(G-11082)*
Something Special Lrng Ctr Inc (PA) 419 878-4190
8251 Wterville Swanton Rd Waterville (43566) *(G-18945)*
Sommers Market LLC (PA) 330 352-7470
214 Market Ave Sw Hartville (44632) *(G-11831)*
Sommers Mobil Leasing, Elyria *Also called Midway Realty Company (G-10654)*
Sommerset Development Ltd 440 286-6194
10585 Somerset Dr Chardon (44024) *(G-2768)*
Somnus Corporation 740 695-3961
51130 National Rd Saint Clairsville (43950) *(G-16656)*
Son-Rise Hotels Inc 330 769-4949
4949 Park Ave W Seville (44273) *(G-16846)*
Sonesta Intl Hotels Corp 614 791-8554
435 Metro Pl S Dublin (43017) *(G-10457)*
Sonic Automotive 614 870-8200
1500 Auto Mall Dr Columbus (43228) *(G-8748)*
Sonic Automotive 1400, Columbus *Also called Columbus SAI Motors LLC (G-7383)*
Sonic Automotive-1495 Automall 614 317-4326
1495 Auto Mall Dr Columbus (43228) *(G-8749)*
Sonit Systems LLC 419 446-2151
130 Westfield Dr Archbold (43502) *(G-646)*
Sonitrol of South West Ohio, Mason *Also called Shiver Security Systems Inc (G-13760)*
Sonitrol Security Systems, Mansfield *Also called Research & Investigation Assoc (G-13355)*
Sonoco Products Company 513 381-2088
4747 Lake Forest Dr # 100 Blue Ash (45242) *(G-1690)*
Sonoco Products Company 937 429-0040
761 Space Dr Beavercreek Township (45434) *(G-1285)*
Sonoco Prtective Solutions Inc 937 890-7628
6061 Milo Rd Dayton (45414) *(G-9888)*
Sons of Un Vtrans of Civil War 740 992-6144
600 Grant St Middleport (45760) *(G-14409)*
Sonshine Commercial Cleaning, Dayton *Also called Rde System Corporation (G-9843)*
Sophisticated Systems Inc (PA) 614 418-4600
2191 Citygate Dr Columbus (43219) *(G-8750)*
Sorbir Inc (PA) 440 449-1000
6200 Mayfield Rd Cleveland (44124) *(G-6495)*
Sordyl & Associates Inc 419 866-6811
2962 W Course Rd Maumee (43537) *(G-13979)*
Sortino Management & Dev Co 419 626-6761
1935 Cleveland Rd Sandusky (44870) *(G-16796)*
Sos2000, Cincinnati *Also called Signal Office Supply Inc (G-4528)*
Soto Salon & Spa 419 872-5555
580 Craig Dr Ste 6 Perrysburg (43551) *(G-16060)*
Sound Com Corporation 440 234-2604
227 Depot St Berea (44017) *(G-1469)*
Sound Com System, Berea *Also called Sound Com Corporation (G-1469)*
Soundtrack Printing 330 606-7117
1400 Sackett Ave Cuyahoga Falls (44223) *(G-9219)*
Source Diagnostics LLC (PA) 440 542-9481
5275 Naiman Pkwy Ste E Solon (44139) *(G-17055)*
Sourcelink Ohio LLC 937 885-8000
3303 W Tech Blvd Miamisburg (45342) *(G-14352)*
Sourceone Healthcare Tech Inc (HQ) 440 701-1200
8020 Tyler Blvd Mentor (44060) *(G-14244)*
Sourcepoint 740 363-6677
800 Cheshire Rd Delaware (43015) *(G-10128)*
South Beach Grille, Cincinnati *Also called Waterfront & Associates Inc (G-4824)*
South Beach Resort 419 798-4900
8620 E Bayshore Rd Lakeside Marblehead (43440) *(G-12466)*
South Central Ohio Cmpt Assn, Piketon *Also called Ohio Department of Education (G-16120)*
South Central Ohio Eductl Ctr 740 456-0517
522 Glenwood Ave New Boston (45662) *(G-15014)*

ALPHABETIC

South Central Power Company...740 474-6045
2100 Chickasaw Dr Circleville (43113) ***(G-4905)***
South Central Power Company (PA)...740 653-4422
2780 Coonpath Rd Ne Lancaster (43130) ***(G-12575)***
South Central Power Company...614 837-4351
10229 Busey Rd Nw Canal Winchester (43110) ***(G-2171)***
South Central Power Company...740 425-4018
37801 Brnsvlle Bthesda Rd Barnesville (43713) ***(G-991)***
South Cmty Family YMCA Cdc, Dayton *Also called Young Mens Christian Assoc* ***(G-10010)***
South Cntrl OH Rgnl Juv Dtn CT, Chillicothe *Also called County of Ross* ***(G-2830)***
South Community Inc (PA)...937 293-8300
3095 Kettering Blvd Ste 1 Moraine (45439) ***(G-14826)***
South Community Inc...937 252-0100
2745 S Smthvlle Rd Ste 14 Dayton (45420) ***(G-9889)***
South Dayton Acute Care Cons...937 433-8990
33 W Rahn Rd Dayton (45429) ***(G-9890)***
South Dyton Urlgcal Asscations (PA)...937 294-1489
10 Southmoor Cir Nw Ste 1 Dayton (45429) ***(G-9891)***
South E Harley Davidson Sls Co (PA)...440 439-5300
23105 Aurora Rd Cleveland (44146) ***(G-6496)***
South E Harley Davidson Sls Co...440 439-3013
23165 Aurora Rd Cleveland (44146) ***(G-6497)***
South East Chevrolet Co...440 585-9300
2810 Bishop Rd Willoughby Hills (44092) ***(G-19735)***
South Eastern Erectors, Cincinnati *Also called R&F Erectors Inc* ***(G-4381)***
South Franklin Circle...440 247-1300
16575 S Franklin St Chagrin Falls (44023) ***(G-2734)***
South Lrrain Cnty Amblance Dst, Wellington *Also called County of Lorain* ***(G-18989)***
South Mill Pet Care Center...330 758-6479
8105 South Ave Youngstown (44512) ***(G-20377)***
South Shore Cable Cnstr Inc...440 816-0033
6400 Kolthoff Dr Cleveland (44142) ***(G-6498)***
South Shore Controls Inc...440 259-2500
4485 N Ridge Rd Perry (44081) ***(G-15967)***
South Shore Electric Inc...440 366-6289
589 Ternes Ln Elyria (44035) ***(G-10681)***
South Shore Marine Services...419 433-5798
1611 Sawmill Pkwy Huron (44839) ***(G-12174)***
South Star Corp...330 239-5466
3775 Ridge Rd Medina (44256) ***(G-14128)***
South Town Painting Inc...937 847-1600
320 E Linden Ave Miamisburg (45342) ***(G-14353)***
South Western Head Start, Grove City *Also called South- Western City School Dst* ***(G-11599)***
South- Western City School Dst...614 801-8438
4308 Haughn Rd Grove City (43123) ***(G-11599)***
Southast Cmnty Mental Hlth Ctr (PA)...614 225-0980
16 W Long St Columbus (43215) ***(G-8751)***
Southast Cmnty Mental Hlth Ctr...614 444-0800
1455 S 4th St Columbus (43207) ***(G-8752)***
Southast Cmnty Mental Hlth Ctr...614 445-6832
1705 S High St Columbus (43207) ***(G-8753)***
Southast Cmnty Mental Hlth Ctr...614 293-9613
445 E Granville Rd Worthington (43085) ***(G-19998)***
Southbrook Care Center, Springfield *Also called Southbrook Health Care Ctr Inc* ***(G-17275)***
Southbrook Health Care Ctr Inc...937 322-3436
2299 S Yellow Springs St Springfield (45506) ***(G-17275)***
Southeast, New Philadelphia *Also called Cornerstone Support Services* ***(G-15088)***
Southeast Area Law Enforcement...216 475-1234
165 Center Rd Bedford (44146) ***(G-1339)***
Southeast Area Transit (PA)...740 454-8574
375 Fairbanks St Zanesville (43701) ***(G-20534)***
Southeast Asia Collection, Athens *Also called Ohio State University* ***(G-803)***
Southeast Counseling, Worthington *Also called Southast Cmnty Mental Hlth Ctr* ***(G-19998)***
Southeast Diversified Inds...740 432-4241
1401 Burgess Ave Cambridge (43725) ***(G-2128)***
Southeast Golf Cars, Cleveland *Also called South E Harley Davidson Sls Co* ***(G-6496)***
Southeast Golf Cars, Cleveland *Also called South E Harley Davidson Sls Co* ***(G-6497)***
Southeast Security Corporation...330 239-4600
1385 Wolf Creek Trl Sharon Center (44274) ***(G-16879)***
Southeastern Equipment Co Inc...614 889-1073
6390 Shier Rings Rd Dublin (43016) ***(G-10458)***
Southeastern Med, Cambridge *Also called Southstern Ohio Rgonal Med Ctr* ***(G-2129)***
Southeastern Ohio Brdcstg Sys...740 452-5431
629 Downard Rd Zanesville (43701) ***(G-20535)***
Southeastern Ohio Symphony Orc...740 826-8197
163 Stormont St New Concord (43762) ***(G-15037)***
Southeastern Ohio TV Sys (PA)...740 452-5431
629 Downard Rd Zanesville (43701) ***(G-20536)***
Southeastern Rehabilitation...740 679-2111
62222 Frankfort Rd Salesville (43778) ***(G-16720)***
Southerly Waste Water Plant, Cleveland *Also called Northast Ohio Rgonal Sewer Dst* ***(G-6148)***
Southern Care Inc...419 774-0555
41 Briggs Dr Ontario (44906) ***(G-15715)***
Southern Center, Tallmadge *Also called Weaver Industries Inc* ***(G-17661)***
Southern Glazers Wine and Sp...330 422-9463
9450 Rosemont Dr Streetsboro (44241) ***(G-17430)***
Southern Glzers Dstrs Ohio LLC (HQ)...614 552-7900
4800 Poth Rd Columbus (43213) ***(G-8754)***
Southern Graphic Systems Inc...419 662-9873
9648 Grassy Creek Dr Perrysburg (43551) ***(G-16061)***
Southern Hills Skilled, Columbus *Also called Vrable II Inc* ***(G-8955)***
Southern Mill Creek Pdts Ohio, Eastlake *Also called Univar Inc* ***(G-10551)***
Southern Ohio Bhvoral Hlth LLC...740 533-0055
2113 S 7th St Ironton (45638) ***(G-12303)***
Southern Ohio Door Contrls Inc (PA)...513 353-4793
8080 Furlong Dr Miamitown (45041) ***(G-14373)***
Southern Ohio Eye Assoc LLC (PA)...740 773-6347
159 E 2nd St Chillicothe (45601) ***(G-2886)***
Southern Ohio Gun Distrs Inc...513 932-8148
240 Harmon Ave Lebanon (45036) ***(G-12649)***
Southern Ohio Health, Georgetown *Also called Healthsource of Ohio Inc* ***(G-11395)***
Southern Ohio Medical Center (PA)...740 354-5000
1805 27th St Portsmouth (45662) ***(G-16311)***
Southern Ohio Medical Center...740 356-5000
1248 Kinneys Ln Portsmouth (45662) ***(G-16312)***
Southern Ohio Medical Center...740 354-5000
1805 27th St Portsmouth (45662) ***(G-16313)***
Southern Ohio Wns Cancer Prj...740 775-7332
150 E 2nd St Chillicothe (45601) ***(G-2887)***
Southern Park Limo Service, Youngstown *Also called Sutton Motor Coach Tours Inc* ***(G-20386)***
Southern Title of Ohio Ltd (PA)...419 525-4600
58 W 3rd St Ste D Mansfield (44902) ***(G-13365)***
Southgate Corp...740 522-2151
1499 W Main St Newark (43055) ***(G-15234)***
Southrly Wstwater Trtmnt Plant, Cleveland *Also called Northast Ohio Rgonal Sewer Dst* ***(G-6145)***
Southside Envmtl Group LLC...330 299-0027
1806 Warren Ave Niles (44446) ***(G-15306)***
Southside Learning & Dev Ctr...614 444-1529
280 Reeb Ave Columbus (43207) ***(G-8755)***
Southstern Ohio Rgional Fd Ctr...740 385-6813
1005 C I C Dr Logan (43138) ***(G-12988)***
Southstern Ohio Rgonal Med Ctr (PA)...740 439-3561
1341 Clark St Cambridge (43725) ***(G-2129)***
Southtown Heating & Cooling...937 320-9900
3024 Springboro W Unit A Moraine (45439) ***(G-14827)***
Southway Fence Company...330 477-5251
5156 Southway St Sw Canton (44706) ***(G-2533)***
Southwest Associates...440 243-7888
7250 Old Oak Blvd Cleveland (44130) ***(G-6499)***
Southwest Cmnty Hlth Systems...440 816-8000
18697 Bagley Rd Cleveland (44130) ***(G-6500)***
Southwest Community Center, Urbancrest *Also called Young Mens Christian Assoc* ***(G-18609)***
Southwest Family Physicians...440 816-2750
7225 Old Oak Blvd A210 Cleveland (44130) ***(G-6501)***
Southwest Financial Svcs Ltd...513 621-6699
537 E Pete Rose Way Ste 3 Cincinnati (45202) ***(G-4552)***
Southwest Gastroenterology, Cleveland *Also called Southwest Urology LLC* ***(G-6507)***
Southwest General Health Ctr, Cleveland *Also called Southwest General Health Ctr* ***(G-6503)***
Southwest General Health Ctr...440 816-4202
7390 Old Oak Blvd Cleveland (44130) ***(G-6502)***
Southwest General Health Ctr...440 816-4900
18181 Pearl Rd Ste B104 Strongsville (44136) ***(G-17510)***
Southwest General Health Ctr...440 816-8200
18697 Oak Vw Cleveland (44130) ***(G-6503)***
Southwest General Health Ctr (PA)...440 816-8000
18697 Bagley Rd Cleveland (44130) ***(G-6504)***
Southwest General Health Ctr...440 816-8005
17951 Jefferson Park Rd Cleveland (44130) ***(G-6505)***
Southwest General Hospital, Cleveland *Also called Southwest Cmnty Hlth Systems* ***(G-6500)***
Southwest Healthcare of Brown...937 378-7800
425 Home St Georgetown (45121) ***(G-11398)***
Southwest Internal Medicine...440 816-2777
7255 Old Oak Blvd C209 Cleveland (44130) ***(G-6506)***
Southwest OH Trans Auth (PA)...513 621-4455
602 Main St Ste 1100 Cincinnati (45202) ***(G-4553)***
Southwest OH Trans Auth...513 632-7511
1401 Bank St Cincinnati (45214) ***(G-4554)***
Southwest Ohio Amblatry Srgery...513 425-0930
295 N Breiel Blvd Middletown (45042) ***(G-14458)***
Southwest Ohio Dvlopmental Ctr, Batavia *Also called Develpmntal Dsblties Ohio Dept* ***(G-1010)***
Southwest Ohio Ent Spclsts Inc (PA)...937 496-2600
1222 S Patterson Blvd # 400 Dayton (45402) ***(G-9892)***
Southwest Regional Medical Ctr, Georgetown *Also called Southwest Healthcare of Brown* ***(G-11398)***
Southwest Urology LLC (PA)...440 845-0900
6900 Pearl Rd Ste 200 Cleveland (44130) ***(G-6507)***
Southwestern Electric Power Co (HQ)...614 716-1000
1 Riverside Plz Columbus (43215) ***(G-8756)***
Southwestern Obstetricians & G...614 875-0444
4461 Broadway 200 Grove City (43123) ***(G-11600)***
Southwestern Tile and MBL Co...614 464-1257
1030 Cable Ave Columbus (43222) ***(G-8757)***
Southwood Auto Sales...330 788-8822
5334 South Ave Youngstown (44512) ***(G-20378)***

Southwoods Surgical Hospital......330 729-8000
7630 Southern Blvd Youngstown (44512) ***(G-20379)***
Southwstern PCF Spclty Fin Inc (HQ)......513 336-7735
7755 Montgomery Rd # 400 Cincinnati (45236) ***(G-4555)***
Sovereign Healthcare, Cleveland *Also called North Park Retirement Cmnty* ***(G-6142)***
Sowder Concrete Contractors, Dayton *Also called Sowder Concrete Corporation* ***(G-9893)***
Sowder Concrete Corporation......937 890-1633
8510 N Dixie Dr Dayton (45414) ***(G-9893)***
Sp Medical, Cleveland *Also called Superior Products Llc* ***(G-6554)***
Sp Plus Corporation......216 444-2255
9500 Euclid Ave Wb1 Cleveland (44195) ***(G-6508)***
Sp Plus Corporation......216 687-0141
1301 E 9th St Ste 1050 Cleveland (44114) ***(G-6509)***
Sp Plus Corporation......216 267-7275
5300 Riverside Dr Cleveland (44135) ***(G-6510)***
Sp Plus Corporation......216 267-5030
5300 Riverside Dr Cleveland (44135) ***(G-6511)***
Spa At River Ridge Salon, The, Dublin *Also called Urban Oassis Inc* ***(G-10480)***
Spa Fitness Centers Inc (PA)......419 476-6018
343 New Towne Square Dr Toledo (43612) ***(G-18193)***
Space Management Inc......937 254-6622
2109 S Smithville Rd Dayton (45420) ***(G-9894)***
Spader Freight Carriers Inc......419 547-1117
1134 E Mcpherson Hwy Clyde (43410) ***(G-6823)***
Spader Freight Services Inc (PA)......419 547-1117
1134 E Mcpherson Hwy Clyde (43410) ***(G-6824)***
Spagnas......740 376-9245
301 Gilman Ave Marietta (45750) ***(G-13501)***
Spall Autoc Syste / US Millwr, Lima *Also called Spallinger Millwright Svc Co* ***(G-12879)***
Spallinger Millwright Svc Co......419 225-5830
1155 E Hanthorn Rd Lima (45804) ***(G-12879)***
Spangenberg Law Firm, Cleveland *Also called Spangenberg Shibley Liber LLP* ***(G-6512)***
Spangenberg Shibley Liber LLP......216 215-7445
1001 Lakeside Ave E # 1700 Cleveland (44114) ***(G-6512)***
Spanish American Committee (PA)......216 961-2100
4407 Lorain Ave Fl 1 Cleveland (44113) ***(G-6513)***
Spanish Portugese Translation, Westlake *Also called Advanced Translation/Cnsltng* ***(G-19455)***
Spano Brothers Cnstr Co......330 645-1544
2595 Pressler Rd Akron (44312) ***(G-445)***
Sparkbase Inc......216 867-0877
3615 Superior Ave E 4403d Cleveland (44114) ***(G-6514)***
Spartan Construction Co Inc......419 389-1854
3001 South Ave Toledo (43609) ***(G-18194)***
Spartan Logistics, Columbus *Also called Spartan Whse & Dist Co Inc* ***(G-8758)***
Spartan Supply Co Inc......513 932-6954
942 Old 122 Rd Lebanon (45036) ***(G-12650)***
Spartan Whse & Dist Co Inc (PA)......614 497-1777
4140 Lockbourne Rd Columbus (43207) ***(G-8758)***
Spartannash Company......937 599-1110
4067 County Road 130 Bellefontaine (43311) ***(G-1397)***
Spartannash Company......419 228-3141
1100 Prosperity Rd Lima (45801) ***(G-12880)***
Spartannash Company......419 998-2562
1257 Neubrecht Rd Lima (45801) ***(G-12881)***
Spartannash Company......937 599-1110
4067 County Road 130 Bellefontaine (43311) ***(G-1398)***
Spartannash Company......513 793-6300
1 Sheakley Way Ste 160 Cincinnati (45246) ***(G-4556)***
Spaulding Construction Co Inc......330 494-1776
7640 Whipple Ave Nw Canton (44720) ***(G-2534)***
Specialty Care Vision, Newark *Also called Surgicenter Ltd* ***(G-15237)***
Spears Transf & Expediting Inc......937 275-2443
2637 Nordic Rd Dayton (45414) ***(G-9895)***
Special Touch Homecare LLC......937 549-1843
207 Pike St Manchester (45144) ***(G-13256)***
Specialized Alternatives For F......216 295-7239
20600 Chagrin Blvd # 900 Shaker Heights (44122) ***(G-16867)***
Specialized Alternatives For F (PA)......419 695-8010
10100 Elida Rd Delphos (45833) ***(G-10151)***
Specialized Pharmacy Svcs - N, Cincinnati *Also called Specialized Pharmacy Svcs LLC* ***(G-4557)***
Specialized Pharmacy Svcs LLC (HQ)......513 719-2600
201 E 4th St Ste 900 Cincinnati (45202) ***(G-4557)***
Specialized Services Inc......330 448-4035
908 Broadway St Masury (44438) ***(G-13668)***
Specialty Equipment Engrg Div, Solon *Also called Belcan Corporation* ***(G-16983)***
Specialty Equipment Sales Co......216 351-2559
5705 Valley Belt Rd Brooklyn Heights (44131) ***(G-1927)***
Specialty Hosp Cleveland Inc......216 592-2830
2351 E 22nd St Fl 7 Cleveland (44115) ***(G-6515)***
Specialty Logistics Inc (PA)......513 421-2041
1440 W 8th St Cincinnati (45203) ***(G-4558)***
Specialty Lubricants Corp......330 425-2567
8300 Corporate Park Dr Macedonia (44056) ***(G-13210)***
Specialty Medical Services......440 245-8010
221 W 8th St Lorain (44052) ***(G-13076)***
Specialty Steel Co Inc......800 321-8500
18250 Miles Rd Cleveland (44128) ***(G-6516)***
Speck Sales Incorporated......419 353-8312
17746 N Dixie Hwy Bowling Green (43402) ***(G-1794)***
Spectra Medical Distribution, Akron *Also called M & R Fredericktown Ltd Inc* ***(G-331)***
Spectrum Eye Care Inc......419 423-8665
15840 Medical Dr S Ste A Findlay (45840) ***(G-11083)***
Spectrum MGT Holdg Co LLC......614 481-5408
3760 Interchange Rd Columbus (43204) ***(G-8759)***
Spectrum MGT Holdg Co LLC......740 455-9705
737 Howard St Zanesville (43701) ***(G-20537)***
Spectrum MGT Holdg Co LLC......330 856-2343
8600 E Market St Ste 4 Warren (44484) ***(G-18901)***
Spectrum MGT Holdg Co LLC......419 386-0040
2853 East Harbor Rd Ste A Port Clinton (43452) ***(G-16256)***
Spectrum MGT Holdg Co LLC......740 762-0291
32 Enterprise Pl Chillicothe (45601) ***(G-2888)***
Spectrum MGT Holdg Co LLC......513 469-1112
3290 Westbourne Dr Cincinnati (45248) ***(G-4559)***
Spectrum MGT Holdg Co LLC......614 344-4159
1015 Olentangy River Rd Columbus (43212) ***(G-8760)***
Spectrum MGT Holdg Co LLC......937 552-5760
75 W Main St Springfield (45502) ***(G-17276)***
Spectrum MGT Holdg Co LLC......740 200-3385
28 Station St Athens (45701) ***(G-812)***
Spectrum MGT Holdg Co LLC......614 503-4153
3652 Main St Hilliard (43026) ***(G-11952)***
Spectrum MGT Holdg Co LLC......440 319-3271
2904 State Rd Ashtabula (44004) ***(G-764)***
Spectrum MGT Holdg Co LLC......419 775-9292
1280 Park Ave W Mansfield (44906) ***(G-13366)***
Spectrum MGT Holdg Co LLC......330 208-9028
530 Suth Main St Ste 1751 Akron (44311) ***(G-446)***
Spectrum MGT Holdg Co LLC......937 684-8891
275 Leo St Dayton (45404) ***(G-9896)***
Spectrum MGT Holdg Co LLC......740 772-7809
1315 Granville Pike Ne Lancaster (43130) ***(G-12576)***
Spectrum MGT Holdg Co LLC......937 294-6800
3691 Turner Rd Dayton (45415) ***(G-9897)***
Spectrum MGT Holdg Co LLC......937 306-6082
614 N Main St Piqua (45356) ***(G-16166)***
Spectrum Networks Inc......513 697-2000
9145 Governors Way Cincinnati (45249) ***(G-4560)***
Spectrum Orthpedics Inc Canton (PA)......330 455-5367
7442 Frank Ave Nw North Canton (44720) ***(G-15367)***
Spectrum Rehabilitation, Cincinnati *Also called Christ Hospital* ***(G-3262)***
Spectrum Supportive Services, Cleveland *Also called Spectrum Supportive Services* ***(G-6517)***
Spectrum Supportive Services......216 875-0460
4269 Pearl Rd Ste 300 Cleveland (44109) ***(G-6517)***
Spectrum Supportive Services (PA)......216 761-2388
2900 Detroit Ave Fl 3 Cleveland (44113) ***(G-6518)***
Speech Center, Saint Marys *Also called Jtd Health Systems Inc* ***(G-16679)***
Speech Language Hearing Clinic, Columbus *Also called Ohio State University* ***(G-8431)***
Speedeon Data LLC......440 264-2100
5875 Landerbrook Dr # 130 Cleveland (44124) ***(G-6519)***
Speedie Auto Salvage Ltd......330 878-9961
6995 Eberhart Rd Nw Dover (44622) ***(G-10215)***
Speelman Electric Inc......330 633-1410
358 Commerce St Tallmadge (44278) ***(G-17650)***
Speer Industries Incorporated (PA)......614 261-6331
5255 Sinclair Rd Columbus (43229) ***(G-8761)***
Speer Mechanical, Columbus *Also called Julian Speer Co* ***(G-7958)***
Speer Mechanical, Columbus *Also called Speer Industries Incorporated* ***(G-8761)***
Spellacys Turf-Lawn Inc......740 965-5508
6555 Plumb Rd Galena (43021) ***(G-11287)***
Spencer Research, Columbus *Also called Dwight Spencer & Associates* ***(G-7554)***
Spengler Nathanson PLL......419 241-2201
4 Seagate Ste 400 Toledo (43604) ***(G-18195)***
Sperian Protection Usa Inc......614 539-5056
3325 Lewis Centre Way Grove City (43123) ***(G-11601)***
Sphere, The, Fairfield *Also called AB Marketing LLC* ***(G-10814)***
Spherion of Lima Inc (PA)......419 224-8367
216 N Elizabeth St Lima (45801) ***(G-12882)***
Spherion Outsourcing Group, Toledo *Also called Sfn Group Inc* ***(G-18182)***
Spieker Company......419 872-7000
8350 Fremont Pike Perrysburg (43551) ***(G-16062)***
Spillman Company......614 444-2184
1701 Muler Rd Columbus (43207) ***(G-8762)***
Spires Motors Inc......614 771-2345
3820 Parkway Ln Hilliard (43026) ***(G-11953)***
Spirit Health, Cincinnati *Also called Spirit Women Health Netwrk LLC* ***(G-2932)***
Spirit Medical Transport LLC......937 548-2800
5484 S State Route 49 Greenville (45331) ***(G-11520)***
Spirit Services, Solon *Also called Van Dyne-Crotty Co* ***(G-17064)***
Spirit Services Company, Columbus *Also called Van Dyne-Crotty Co* ***(G-8932)***
Spirit Services Company, Columbus *Also called Van Dyne-Crotty Co* ***(G-8933)***
Spirit Women Health Netwrk LLC......561 544-2004
4270 Ivy Pointe Blvd # 220 Cincinnati (45245) ***(G-2932)***
Spitzer Auto World Amherst......440 988-4444
200 N Leavitt Rd Amherst (44001) ***(G-605)***
Spitzer Chevrolet Company......330 966-9524
7111 Sunset Strip Ave Nw Canton (44720) ***(G-2535)***
Spitzer Chevrolet Inc......330 467-4141
333 E Aurora Rd Northfield (44067) ***(G-15524)***

ALPHABETIC

Spitzer Lakewood, Brookpark *Also called Lakewood Chrysler-Plymouth* ***(G-1950)***
Spitzer Motor City Inc......567 307-7119
1777 W 4th St Ontario (44906) ***(G-15716)***
Spitzer Motors of Mansfield, Ontario *Also called Spitzer Motor City Inc* ***(G-15716)***
Splish Splash Auto Bath, Springfield *Also called JKL Development Company* ***(G-17217)***
Split Rock Golf Club Inc......614 877-9755
10210 Scioto Darby Rd Orient (43146) ***(G-15762)***
Sponseller Group Inc (PA)......419 861-3000
1600 Timber Wolf Dr Holland (43528) ***(G-12056)***
Sports Care Rehabilitation......419 578-7530
2865 N Reynolds Rd # 110 Toledo (43615) ***(G-18196)***
Sports Construction Group, Brecksville *Also called Sports Surfaces Cnstr LLC* ***(G-1852)***
Sports Facility Acoustics Inc......440 323-1400
801 Bond St Elyria (44035) ***(G-10682)***
Sports Medicine and Spine Ctr, Middletown *Also called Atrium Medical Center* ***(G-14414)***
Sports Medicine Grant Inc......614 461-8199
417 Hill Rd N Ste 401 Pickerington (43147) ***(G-16106)***
Sports Medicine Grant Inc (PA)......614 461-8174
323 E Town St Ste 100 Columbus (43215) ***(G-8763)***
Sports Surfaces Cnstr LLC......440 546-1200
10303 Brecksville Rd Brecksville (44141) ***(G-1852)***
Sports Therapy Inc......513 671-5841
11729 Springfield Pike Cincinnati (45246) ***(G-4561)***
Sports Therapy Inc......513 531-1698
4600 Smith Rd Rear Rear Cincinnati (45212) ***(G-4562)***
Sportsman Gun & Reel Club Inc......440 233-8287
44165 Middle Ridge Rd Lorain (44053) ***(G-13077)***
Sportsmans Market Inc......513 735-9100
2001 Sportys Dr Batavia (45103) ***(G-1025)***
Sportstime Ohio, Cleveland *Also called Fastball Spt Productions LLC* ***(G-5576)***
Sportsworld, Youngstown *Also called Jvc Sports Corp* ***(G-20243)***
Sporty Events......440 342-5046
8430 Mayfield Rd Chesterland (44026) ***(G-2803)***
SPORTY'S WRIGHT BROTHERS COLLE, Batavia *Also called Sportsmans Market Inc* ***(G-1025)***
Spotlight Labs, Beavercreek *Also called Global Military Expert Co* ***(G-1242)***
Sprandel Enterprises Inc......513 777-6622
6467 Gano Rd West Chester (45069) ***(G-19158)***
Spray A Tree Inc......614 457-8257
1585 Pemberton Dr Columbus (43221) ***(G-8764)***
Sprayworks Equipment Group LLC......330 587-4141
215 Navarre Rd Sw Canton (44707) ***(G-2536)***
Spread Eagle Tavern Inc......330 223-1583
10150 Plymouth St Hanoverton (44423) ***(G-11787)***
Sprenger Entrprises Inc......440 244-2019
3756 W Erie Ave Apt 201 Lorain (44053) ***(G-13078)***
Sprenger Retirement Centers, Lorain *Also called CMS & Co Management Svcs Inc* ***(G-13028)***
Spring Creek Apts, Columbus *Also called Clk Multi-Family MGT LLC* ***(G-7305)***
Spring Creek Nursing Center, Dayton *Also called Care One LLC* ***(G-9380)***
Spring Grove Center, Cincinnati *Also called Talbert House* ***(G-4617)***
Spring Grove Cmtry & Arboretum (PA)......513 681-7526
4521 Spring Grove Ave Cincinnati (45232) ***(G-4563)***
Spring Grove Funeral Homes Inc......513 681-7526
4389 Spring Grove Ave Cincinnati (45223) ***(G-4564)***
Spring Grove Rsrce Rcovery Inc......513 681-6242
4879 Spring Grove Ave Cincinnati (45232) ***(G-4565)***
Spring Hill Apartments, Akron *Also called Sh-91 Limited Partnership* ***(G-436)***
Spring Hills At Middletown, Middletown *Also called Springhills LLC* ***(G-14487)***
Spring Hills At Singing Woods, Dayton *Also called Springhills LLC* ***(G-9899)***
Spring Hills Golf Club......740 543-3270
99 Corder Dr East Springfield (43925) ***(G-10543)***
Spring Hills Golf Club......330 825-2439
6571 Clvland Massillon Rd New Franklin (44216) ***(G-15047)***
Spring Meadow Extended Care Ce (PA)......419 866-6124
1125 Clarion Ave Holland (43528) ***(G-12057)***
Spring Meadow Extended Care Ce......419 866-6124
105 S Main St Mansfield (44902) ***(G-13367)***
Spring Meadows Care Center, Woodstock *Also called Woodstock Care Center Inc* ***(G-19822)***
Spring Meadows Care Center, Woodstock *Also called Saber Healthcare Group LLC* ***(G-19821)***
Spring Valley Golf & Athc CLB......440 365-1411
257 Crocker Park Blvd Westlake (44145) ***(G-19548)***
Springboro Service Center......937 748-0020
220 E Mill St Springboro (45066) ***(G-17138)***
Springcar Company LLC......440 892-6800
27500 Detroit Rd Ste 300 Westlake (44145) ***(G-19549)***
Springdale Family Medicine PC......513 771-7213
212 W Sharon Rd Cincinnati (45246) ***(G-4566)***
Springdale Ice Cream Beverage......513 699-4984
11801 Chesterdale Rd Cincinnati (45246) ***(G-4567)***
Springdot Inc......513 542-4000
2611 Colerain Ave Cincinnati (45214) ***(G-4568)***
Springfeld Rgnal Cncer Ctr LLC, Springfield *Also called Mercy Health - Springfield C* ***(G-17241)***
Springfeld Rgnal Otpatient Ctr......937 390-8310
2610 N Limestone St Springfield (45503) ***(G-17277)***
Springfeld Unfrm-Linen Sup Inc......937 323-5544
141 N Murray St Springfield (45503) ***(G-17278)***
Springfield Business Eqp Co (PA)......937 322-3828
3783 W National Rd Springfield (45504) ***(G-17279)***
Springfield Cartage LLC......937 222-2120
1546 Stanley Ave Dayton (45404) ***(G-9898)***
Springfield Country Club Co......937 399-4215
2315 Signal Hill Rd Springfield (45504) ***(G-17280)***
Springfield Family Y M C A......937 323-3781
300 S Limestone St Springfield (45505) ***(G-17281)***
Springfield Little Tigers Foot......330 549-2359
49 Philrose Ln Youngstown (44514) ***(G-20380)***
Springfield Regional Med Ctr, Springfield *Also called Community Mercy Hlth Partners* ***(G-17175)***
Springfield Urology, Springfield *Also called Northwest Columbus Urology* ***(G-17253)***
Springhill Suites, Columbus *Also called Black Sapphire C Columbus Univ* ***(G-7116)***
Springhill Suites, Gahanna *Also called Columbus Oh-16 Airport Gahanna* ***(G-11236)***
Springhill Suites, Solon *Also called Solon Lodging Associates LLC* ***(G-17053)***
Springhill Suites Independence, Independence *Also called Jagi Springhill LLC* ***(G-12221)***
Springhills LLC......937 274-1400
140 E Woodbury Dr Dayton (45415) ***(G-9899)***
Springhills LLC......513 424-9999
3851 Towne Blvd Middletown (45005) ***(G-14487)***
Springmeade, Tipp City *Also called Uvmc Nursing Care Inc* ***(G-17731)***
Springs Window Fashions LLC......614 492-6770
6295 Commerce Center Dr Groveport (43125) ***(G-11673)***
Springside Racquet Fitnes CLB, Akron *Also called Oid Associates* ***(G-370)***
Springvale Golf Crse Ballroom, North Olmsted *Also called City of North Olmsted* ***(G-15417)***
Springview Manor Nursing Home......419 227-3661
883 W Spring St Lima (45805) ***(G-12883)***
Sprint, North Canton *Also called Nextel Partners Operating Corp* ***(G-15357)***
Sprint, Toledo *Also called Nextel Partners Operating Corp* ***(G-18086)***
Sprint Communications Co LP......419 725-2444
1708 W Alexis Rd Toledo (43613) ***(G-18197)***
Sprint Spectrum LP......440 686-2600
25363 Lorain Rd North Olmsted (44070) ***(G-15445)***
Sprint Spectrum LP......614 575-5500
2367 S Hamilton Rd Columbus (43232) ***(G-8765)***
Sprint Spectrum LP......614 793-2500
6614 Sawmill Rd Columbus (43235) ***(G-8766)***
Sprint Spectrum LP......614 428-2300
3918 Townsfair Way Columbus (43219) ***(G-8767)***
Spruce Bough Homes LLC......614 253-0984
18 E 3rd Ave Columbus (43201) ***(G-8768)***
Spryance Inc......678 808-0600
3101 Executive Pkwy # 600 Toledo (43606) ***(G-18198)***
Spunfab, Cuyahoga Falls *Also called Keuchel & Associates Inc* ***(G-9202)***
Spurlock Truck Service......937 268-6100
129 Lincoln Park Blvd Dayton (45429) ***(G-9900)***
Sqa, Akron *Also called Smithers Quality Assessments* ***(G-442)***
Squire Patton Boggs (us) LLP......513 361-1200
221 E 4th St Ste 2900 Cincinnati (45202) ***(G-4569)***
Squires Construction Company......216 252-0300
20800 Center Ridge Rd Ll15 Rocky River (44116) ***(G-16592)***
Squires Roofing Company, Rocky River *Also called Squires Construction Company* ***(G-16592)***
Sr Improvements Services LLC......567 207-6488
1485 County Road 268 Vickery (43464) ***(G-18733)***
Sreco Flexible, Lima *Also called Sewer Rodding Equipment Co* ***(G-12876)***
Sree Hotels LLC......513 354-2430
617 Vine St Ste A Cincinnati (45202) ***(G-4570)***
Srinsoft Inc......614 893-6535
7243 Sawmill Rd Ste 205 Dublin (43016) ***(G-10459)***
Ssg, Shaker Heights *Also called Software Support Group Inc* ***(G-16866)***
Ssi Fabricated Inc......513 217-3535
2860 Cincinnati Dayton Rd Middletown (45044) ***(G-14459)***
Ssoe Inc......330 821-7198
22831 State Route 62 Alliance (44601) ***(G-560)***
SSP Fittings Corp (PA)......330 425-4250
8250 Boyle Pkwy Twinsburg (44087) ***(G-18472)***
SSS Consulting Inc......937 259-1200
3123 Res Blvd Ste 250 Dayton (45420) ***(G-9901)***
Ssth LLC......614 884-0793
739 S James Rd Ste 100 Columbus (43227) ***(G-8769)***
St Aloysius Services Inc......513 482-1745
4721 Reading Rd Cincinnati (45237) ***(G-4571)***
St Anne Mercy Hospital......419 407-2663
3404 W Sylvania Ave Toledo (43623) ***(G-18199)***
St Anthony Messenger Press, Cincinnati *Also called Province of St John The Baptis* ***(G-4352)***
St Augustine Corporation......216 939-7600
1341 Nicholson Ave Lakewood (44107) ***(G-12501)***
St Augustine Towers......216 634-7444
7821 Lake Ave Apt 304 Cleveland (44102) ***(G-6520)***
St Bartholomew Cons School, Cincinnati *Also called Archdiocese of Cincinnati* ***(G-3041)***
St Catherine's Manor, Fostoria *Also called St Catherines Care Centers O* ***(G-11141)***
St Catherines Care Centers O......419 435-8112
25 Christopher Dr Fostoria (44830) ***(G-11141)***
St Catherines Care Ctr Findlay......419 422-3978
8455 County Road 140 Findlay (45840) ***(G-11084)***

ALPHABETIC SECTION — Stanley Steemer Intl Inc

St Cecilia School, Columbus *Also called Saint Cecilia Church* (G-8677)
St Charles Child Dev Center, Oregon *Also called Mercy Health - St* (G-15741)
St Clair Auto Body 216 531-7300
  13608 Saint Clair Ave Cleveland (44110) (G-6521)
St Clair Auto Body Shop, Cleveland *Also called St Clair Auto Body* (G-6521)
St Clairsville V A Primary, Saint Clairsville *Also called Veterans Health Administration* (G-16659)
St Edward Home 330 668-2828
  3131 Smith Rd Fairlawn (44333) (G-10977)
St Elizabeth Boardman Hospital, Youngstown *Also called Mercy Health Youngstown LLC* (G-20283)
St Elizabeth Health Center, Youngstown *Also called Mercy Health Youngstown LLC* (G-20284)
ST FRANCIS FRIARY, Cincinnati *Also called Friars Club Inc* (G-3654)
St George & Co Inc 330 733-7528
  2586 Robindale Ave Akron (44312) (G-447)
St George Company, Akron *Also called St George & Co Inc* (G-447)
St John Medical Center 440 835-8000
  29000 Center Ridge Rd Westlake (44145) (G-19550)
St Joseph Care Center, Louisville *Also called Roman Cthlic Docese Youngstown* (G-13106)
St Joseph Infant Maternity Hm 513 563-2520
  10722 Wyscarver Rd Cincinnati (45241) (G-4572)
ST JOSEPH`S HOME, Cincinnati *Also called St Joseph Infant Maternity Hm* (G-4572)
St Jude Social Concern Hot 440 365-7971
  636 Sycamore St Elyria (44035) (G-10683)
St Lawrence Steel Corporation 330 562-9000
  2500 Crane Centre Dr Streetsboro (44241) (G-17431)
St Luke Lutheran Community 330 868-5600
  4301 Woodale Ave Se Minerva (44657) (G-14651)
St Luke Lutheran Community 330 644-3914
  615 Latham Ln New Franklin (44319) (G-15048)
St Luke Lutheran Community 330 644-3914
  615 Latham Ln New Franklin (44319) (G-15049)
St Lukes Gift Shop, Maumee *Also called Auxiliary St Lukes Hospital* (G-13884)
St Lukes Hospital 419 893-5911
  5901 Monclova Rd Maumee (43537) (G-13980)
St Mary & Joseph Home, Warrensville Heights *Also called Sisters of Little* (G-18934)
St Marys City Board Education 419 394-1116
  1445 Celina Rd Saint Marys (45885) (G-16684)
St Marys City Board Education 419 394-2616
  650 Armstrong St Saint Marys (45885) (G-16685)
St Moritz Security Svcs Inc 330 270-5922
  32 N Four Mile Run Rd Youngstown (44515) (G-20381)
St Moritz Security Svcs Inc 614 351-8798
  705 Lkview Plz Blvd Ste G Worthington (43085) (G-19999)
St Pauls Catholic Church (PA) 330 724-1263
  433 Mission Dr Akron (44301) (G-448)
St Pauls Community Center 419 255-5520
  230 13th St Toledo (43604) (G-18200)
St Regis Investment LLC 216 520-1250
  8111 Rockside Rd Cleveland (44125) (G-6522)
St Rita's Homecare, Lima *Also called St Ritas Medical Center* (G-12887)
St Ritas Medical Center 419 226-9067
  730 W Market St Lima (45801) (G-12884)
St Ritas Medical Center (HQ) 419 227-3361
  730 W Market St Lima (45801) (G-12885)
St Ritas Medical Center 419 538-6288
  601 Us 224 Glandorf (45848) (G-11432)
St Ritas Medical Center 419 226-9229
  750 W High St Ste 400 Lima (45801) (G-12886)
St Ritas Medical Center 419 538-7025
  959 W North St Lima (45805) (G-12887)
St Ritas Medical Center 419 227-3361
  4357 Ottawa Rd Lima (45801) (G-12888)
St Ritas Medical Center 419 996-5895
  967 Bellefontaine Ave # 201 Lima (45804) (G-12889)
St Ritas Medical Center 419 228-1535
  830 W High St Ste 150 Lima (45801) (G-12890)
St Ritas Work Ornted Rhblttion, Lima *Also called St Ritas Medical Center* (G-12890)
St Stephen United Church Chrst 419 624-1814
  905 E Perkins Ave Sandusky (44870) (G-16797)
St Stephens Community House 614 294-6347
  1500 E 17th Ave Columbus (43219) (G-8770)
ST STEPHENS COMMUNITY SERVICE, Columbus *Also called St Stephens Community House* (G-8770)
St Thomas Episcopal Church 513 831-6908
  100 Miami Ave Terrace Park (45174) (G-17662)
St Thomas Nursery School, Terrace Park *Also called St Thomas Episcopal Church* (G-17662)
St Vincent Charity Med Ctr (PA) 216 861-6200
  2351 E 22nd St Cleveland (44115) (G-6523)
St Vincent De Paul Scl Svs 937 222-7349
  1133 S Edwin C Moses Blvd Dayton (45417) (G-9902)
St Vincent De Paul Society, Cleveland *Also called Society St Vincent De Paul Cle* (G-6492)
St Vincent Family Centers (PA) 614 252-0731
  1490 E Main St Columbus (43205) (G-8771)
St Vincent Medical Group, Cleveland *Also called Medical Arts Physician Center* (G-6013)
St. Cthrnes Manor Wash Crt Hse, Wshngtn CT Hs *Also called Hcf of Washington Inc* (G-20026)
St. Elizabeth Youngstown Hosp, Youngstown *Also called Mercy Health* (G-20282)
St. Joseph Warren Hospital, Warren *Also called Mercy Health Youngstown LLC* (G-18881)
St. Rita's Home Care, Lima *Also called Mercy Health* (G-12839)
ST. VINCENT HOSPITAL AND MEDIA, Toledo *Also called Mercy Hlth St Vincent Med LLC* (G-18057)
St. Vincent Medical Group, Cleveland *Also called Outreach Professional Svcs Inc* (G-6219)
Staarmann Concrete Inc 513 756-9191
  4316 Stahlheber Rd Hamilton (45013) (G-11774)
Stachler Concrete Inc 419 678-3867
  431 Stachler Dr Saint Henry (45883) (G-16667)
Stack Constructyion Technology, Mason *Also called To Scale Software LLC* (G-13769)
Stack Container Service Inc 216 531-7555
  24881 Rockwell Dr Euclid (44117) (G-10777)
Stafast Products Inc (PA) 440 357-5546
  505 Lakeshore Blvd Painesville (44077) (G-15880)
Stafast West, Painesville *Also called Stafast Products Inc* (G-15880)
Staffco-Campisano, Cleveland *Also called RA Staff Company Inc* (G-6342)
Staffmark Holdings Inc (HQ) 513 651-1111
  201 E 4th St Ste 800 Cincinnati (45202) (G-4573)
Staffmark Investment LLC (HQ) 513 651-3600
  201 E 4th St Ste 800 Cincinnati (45202) (G-4574)
Stage Works 513 522-3118
  7800 Perry St Cincinnati (45231) (G-4575)
Stagnaro Saba Patterson Co Lpa (PA) 513 533-2700
  2623 Erie Ave Cincinnati (45208) (G-4576)
Stagnaro Saba Patterson Co Lpa 513 533-2700
  7373 Beechmont Ave Cincinnati (45230) (G-4577)
Stahlheber & Sons Inc 513 726-4446
  4205 Hamilton Eaton Rd Hamilton (45011) (G-11775)
Stahlheber Excavating, Hamilton *Also called Stahlheber & Sons Inc* (G-11775)
Staid Logic LLC (PA) 309 807-0575
  595 E Broad St Ste 206 Columbus (43215) (G-8772)
Staley Inc 614 552-2333
  8040 Corporate Blvd Plain City (43064) (G-16207)
Staley Technologies Inc (PA) 330 339-2898
  1035 Front Ave Sw New Philadelphia (44663) (G-15115)
Stallion Oilfield Cnstr LLC 330 868-2083
  3361 Baird Ave Se Paris (44669) (G-15896)
Stambaugh Charter Academy, Youngstown *Also called National Heritg Academies Inc* (G-20297)
Stamm Contracting Co Inc 330 274-8230
  4566 Orchard St Mantua (44255) (G-13395)
Stan Hywet Hall and Grdns Inc 330 836-5533
  714 N Portage Path Akron (44303) (G-449)
Stand Energy Corporation 513 621-1113
  1077 Celestial St Ste 110 Cincinnati (45202) (G-4578)
Standard Contg & Engrg Inc 440 243-1001
  6356 Eastland Rd Brookpark (44142) (G-1955)
Standard Laboratories Inc 513 422-1088
  2601 S Verity Pkwy Middletown (45044) (G-14460)
Standard Parking, Cleveland *Also called Sp Plus Corporation* (G-6508)
Standard Plumbing & Heating Co (PA) 330 453-5150
  435 Walnut Ave Se Canton (44702) (G-2537)
Standard Register Inc 937 221-1000
  600 Albany St Dayton (45417) (G-9903)
Standard Retirement Svcs Inc 440 808-2724
  24610 Detroit Rd Ste 2000 Westlake (44145) (G-19551)
Standard Textile Co Inc (PA) 513 761-9255
  1 Knollcrest Dr Cincinnati (45237) (G-4579)
Standard Welding & Lift Truck, Lorain *Also called Perkins Motor Service Ltd* (G-13071)
Standards Testing Labs Inc (PA) 330 833-8548
  1845 Harsh Ave Se Massillon (44646) (G-13856)
Standex Electronics, Cincinnati *Also called Standex International Corp* (G-4580)
Standex International Corp 513 871-3777
  4538 Camberwell Rd Cincinnati (45209) (G-4580)
Standing Stone National Bank (PA) 740 653-5115
  137 W Wheeling St Lancaster (43130) (G-12577)
Standley Law Group LLP 614 792-5555
  6300 Riverside Dr Dublin (43017) (G-10460)
Standrdaero Component Svcs Inc 513 618-9588
  11550 Mosteller Rd Cincinnati (45241) (G-4581)
Stanley Miller Construction Co 330 484-2229
  2250 Howenstine Dr Se East Sparta (44626) (G-10541)
Stanley Steemer, Youngstown *Also called Samron Inc* (G-20366)
Stanley Steemer, Wickliffe *Also called Lazar Brothers Inc* (G-19606)
Stanley Steemer, Conneaut *Also called Merlene Enterprises Inc* (G-9044)
Stanley Steemer Carpet Cleaner, Dublin *Also called Stanley Steemer Intl Inc* (G-10461)
Stanley Steemer Carpet Clr 05, Dublin *Also called Stanley Steemer Intl Inc* (G-10462)
Stanley Steemer Carpet Clr 07, Cincinnati *Also called Stanley Steemer Intl Inc* (G-4582)
Stanley Steemer Carpet Clr 09, Beavercreek Township *Also called Stanley Steemer Intl Inc* (G-1286)
Stanley Steemer Intl Inc (PA) 614 764-2007
  5800 Innovation Dr Dublin (43016) (G-10461)
Stanley Steemer Intl Inc 419 227-1212
  1253 N Cole St Lima (45801) (G-12891)

Stanley Steemer Intl Inc...513 771-0213
637 Redna Ter Cincinnati (45215) ***(G-4582)***
Stanley Steemer Intl Inc...614 652-2241
5500 Stanley Steemer Pkwy Dublin (43016) ***(G-10462)***
Stanley Steemer Intl Inc...937 431-3205
824 Space Dr Beavercreek Township (45434) ***(G-1286)***
Stanley Stemer of Akron Canton...330 785-5005
76 Hanna Pkwy Coventry Township (44319) ***(G-9133)***
Stansley Mineral Resources Inc (PA)...419 843-2813
3793 Silica Rd B Sylvania (43560) ***(G-17617)***
Stantec Arch & Engrg PC...216 454-2150
3700 Park East Dr Ste 200 Cleveland (44122) ***(G-6524)***
Stantec Arch & Engrg PC...614 486-4383
1500 Lake Shore Dr # 100 Columbus (43204) ***(G-8773)***
Stantec Architecture Inc...216 454-2150
3700 Park East Dr Ste 200 Cleveland (44122) ***(G-6525)***
Stantec Consulting Svcs Inc...614 210-2000
6465 Reflections Dr # 150 Dublin (43017) ***(G-10463)***
Stantec Consulting Svcs Inc...216 454-2150
3700 Park East Dr Ste 200 Cleveland (44122) ***(G-6526)***
Stantec Consulting Svcs Inc...513 842-8200
11687 Lebanon Rd Cincinnati (45241) ***(G-4583)***
Stantec Consulting Svcs Inc...614 486-4383
1500 Lake Shore Dr # 100 Columbus (43204) ***(G-8774)***
Stantec Consulting Svcs Inc...216 621-2407
1300 E 9th St Ste 1100 Cleveland (44114) ***(G-6527)***
Staples Inc...740 845-5600
500 E High St London (43140) ***(G-13007)***
Staples Inc...614 472-2014
700 Taylor Rd Ste 100 Columbus (43230) ***(G-8775)***
Star 64, Cincinnati *Also called Sinclair Broadcast Group Inc* ***(G-4531)***
Star 93.3 FM, Cincinnati *Also called Pillar of Fire* ***(G-4300)***
Star Beauty Plus LLC (PA)...216 662-9750
20900 Libby Rd Maple Heights (44137) ***(G-13419)***
Star Builders Inc...440 986-5951
46405 Telegraph Rd Amherst (44001) ***(G-606)***
Star County Home Consortium...330 451-7395
201 3rd St Ne Fl 2201 Canton (44702) ***(G-2538)***
Star Dist & Manufacturring LLC...513 860-3573
9818 Prnceton Glendale Rd West Chester (45246) ***(G-19231)***
Star Dynamics Corporation (PA)...614 334-4510
4455 Reynolds Dr Hilliard (43026) ***(G-11954)***
Star Group Ltd...614 428-8678
460 Waterbury Ct Gahanna (43230) ***(G-11269)***
Star Inc...740 354-1517
2625 Gallia St Portsmouth (45662) ***(G-16314)***
Star Leasing Co (PA)...614 278-9999
4080 Business Park Dr Columbus (43204) ***(G-8776)***
Star One Holdings Inc...513 474-9100
8118 Beechmont Ave Cincinnati (45255) ***(G-4584)***
Star One Holdings Inc...513 779-9500
6875 Fountains Blvd Ste A West Chester (45069) ***(G-19159)***
Star One Holdings Inc...513 300-6663
9722 Montgomery Rd Cincinnati (45242) ***(G-4585)***
Star Packaging Inc...614 564-9936
1796 Frebis Ave Columbus (43206) ***(G-8777)***
Star-Ex Inc...937 473-2397
1600 Mote Dr Covington (45318) ***(G-9139)***
Starfire, Hamilton *Also called Coolants Plus Inc* ***(G-11718)***
Starforce National Corporation...513 979-3600
455 Delta Ave Ste 410 Cincinnati (45226) ***(G-4586)***
Stark and Summit Regional EXT, Canton *Also called Ohio State University* ***(G-2485)***
Stark Area Regional Trnst Auth (PA)...330 477-2782
1600 Gateway Blvd Se Canton (44707) ***(G-2539)***
Stark Cnty Dept Job Fmly Svcs...330 451-8400
221 3rd St Se Canton (44702) ***(G-2540)***
Stark Cnty Emrgncy Physicians...330 492-7950
5154 Fulton Dr Nw Canton (44718) ***(G-2541)***
Stark Cnty Historical Soc Inc...330 455-7043
800 Mckinley Monu Dr Nw Canton (44708) ***(G-2542)***
Stark County Board of Developm...330 477-5200
2950 Whipple Ave Nw Canton (44708) ***(G-2543)***
Stark County Cmnty Action Agcy...330 821-5977
321 Franklin Ave Alliance (44601) ***(G-561)***
Stark County Engineer, Canton *Also called County of Stark* ***(G-2324)***
Stark County Neurologists Inc...330 494-2097
4105 Holiday St Nw Canton (44718) ***(G-2544)***
Stark County Park District...330 477-3552
5300 Tyner Ave Nw Canton (44708) ***(G-2545)***
Stark County Sewer Dept, Canton *Also called County of Stark* ***(G-2323)***
Stark County Womens Clinic Inc...330 493-0313
5000 Higbee Ave Nw Canton (44718) ***(G-2546)***
Stark Federal Credit Union (PA)...330 493-8325
4100 Dressler Rd Nw Canton (44718) ***(G-2547)***
Stark Industrial LLC...330 493-9773
5103 Stoneham Rd North Canton (44720) ***(G-15368)***
Stark Knoll...330 376-3300
3475 Richwood Rd Akron (44333) ***(G-450)***
Stark Medical Specialties Inc (PA)...330 837-1111
323 Marion Ave Nw Ste 200 Massillon (44646) ***(G-13857)***
Stark Metal Sales Inc...330 823-7383
432 Keystone St Alliance (44601) ***(G-562)***
Stark Sandblasting & Pntg Co, Canton *Also called Flamos Enterprises Inc* ***(G-2369)***
Stark Summit Ambulance, North Canton *Also called Medical Transport Systems Inc* ***(G-15352)***
Starlight Enterprises Inc...330 339-2020
400 E High Ave New Philadelphia (44663) ***(G-15116)***
Starlight Special School, Zanesville *Also called Muskingum Starlight Industries* ***(G-20513)***
Start, Cleveland *Also called Support To At Risk Teens* ***(G-6557)***
Start-Black Servicesjv LLC...740 598-4891
797 Cool Spring Rd Mingo Junction (43938) ***(G-14657)***
Startek Inc...419 528-7801
850 W 4th St Ontario (44906) ***(G-15717)***
Starting Point, Cleveland *Also called Child Care Resource Center* ***(G-5236)***
Starwin Industries Inc...937 293-8568
3387 Woodman Dr Dayton (45429) ***(G-9904)***
Starwood, Middlefield *Also called Norstar Aluminum Molds Inc* ***(G-14399)***
Starwood Hotels & Resorts, Cincinnati *Also called Host Cincinnati Hotel LLC* ***(G-3788)***
Starwood Hotels & Resorts...614 345-9291
3030 Plaza Prpts Blvd Columbus (43219) ***(G-8778)***
Starwood Hotels & Resorts...614 888-8230
888 E Dublin Granville Rd Columbus (43229) ***(G-8779)***
Stat Communications, Columbus *Also called Universal Recovery Systems* ***(G-8907)***
Stat Express Delivery LLC (PA)...614 880-7828
705 Lkview Plz Blvd Ste M Worthington (43085) ***(G-20000)***
Stat Integrated Tech Inc (PA)...440 286-7663
10779 Mayfield Rd Chardon (44024) ***(G-2769)***
State 8 Motorcycle & Atv, Peninsula *Also called Wholecycle Inc* ***(G-15953)***
State Alarm Inc (PA)...330 726-8111
5956 Market St Youngstown (44512) ***(G-20382)***
State Alarm Systems, Youngstown *Also called State Alarm Inc* ***(G-20382)***
State Auto Financial Corp (HQ)...614 464-5000
518 E Broad St Columbus (43215) ***(G-8780)***
State Auto Insurance Co, Strongsville *Also called State Auto Prperty Cslty Insur* ***(G-17511)***
State Auto Insurance Companies, Columbus *Also called State Automobile Mutl Insur Co* ***(G-8781)***
STATE AUTO INSURANCE COMPANIES, Columbus *Also called State Auto Financial Corp* ***(G-8780)***
State Auto Prperty Cslty Insur...440 842-6200
14843 W Sprague Rd Ste F Strongsville (44136) ***(G-17511)***
State Automobile Mutl Insur Co (PA)...833 724-3577
518 E Broad St Columbus (43215) ***(G-8781)***
State Bank and Trust Company (HQ)...419 783-8950
401 Clinton St Defiance (43512) ***(G-10058)***
State Bank and Trust Company...419 485-5521
1201 E Main St Montpelier (43543) ***(G-14748)***
State Chemical, Cleveland *Also called Zucker Building Company* ***(G-6785)***
State Chemical Manufacturing, Cleveland *Also called State Industrial Products Corp* ***(G-6530)***
State Crest Carpet & Flooring (PA)...440 232-3980
5400 Perkins Rd Bedford (44146) ***(G-1340)***
State Farm General Insur Co...740 364-5000
1440 Granville Rd Newark (43055) ***(G-15235)***
State Farm Insurance, Newark *Also called State Farm General Insur Co* ***(G-15235)***
State Farm Insurance, Perrysburg *Also called State Farm Mutl Auto Insur Co* ***(G-16063)***
State Farm Insurance, Cleveland *Also called State Farm Mutl Auto Insur Co* ***(G-6528)***
State Farm Insurance, Dayton *Also called State Farm Life Insurance Co* ***(G-9905)***
State Farm Insurance, New Albany *Also called State Farm Mutl Auto Insur Co* ***(G-15008)***
State Farm Insurance, Newark *Also called State Farm Mutl Auto Insur Co* ***(G-15236)***
State Farm Insurance, Cleveland *Also called State Farm Mutl Auto Insur Co* ***(G-6529)***
State Farm Life Insurance Co...937 276-1900
1436 Needmore Rd Dayton (45414) ***(G-9905)***
State Farm Mutl Auto Insur Co...419 873-0100
13001 Roachton Rd Perrysburg (43551) ***(G-16063)***
State Farm Mutl Auto Insur Co...216 621-3723
2700 W 25th St Cleveland (44113) ***(G-6528)***
State Farm Mutl Auto Insur Co...614 775-2001
5400 New Albany Rd New Albany (43054) ***(G-15008)***
State Farm Mutl Auto Insur Co...740 364-5000
1440 Granville Rd Newark (43055) ***(G-15236)***
State Farm Mutl Auto Insur Co...216 321-1422
2245 Warrensville Ctr Rd Cleveland (44118) ***(G-6529)***
State Highway Dept Gallia, Gallipolis *Also called County of Gallia* ***(G-11312)***
State Highway Garage, Chillicothe *Also called Transportation Ohio Department* ***(G-2891)***
State Industrial Products Corp (PA)...877 747-6986
5915 Landerbrook Dr # 300 Cleveland (44124) ***(G-6530)***
State Industrial Products Corp...216 861-6363
12420 Plaza Dr Cleveland (44130) ***(G-6531)***
State of Heart HM Hlth Hospice, Coldwater *Also called Hospice of Darke County Inc* ***(G-6830)***
State of Ohio...614 466-3455
4200 Surface Rd Columbus (43228) ***(G-8782)***
State of Ohio...614 466-3834
1929 Gateway Cir Grove City (43123) ***(G-11602)***
STATE OF THE HEART HOSPICE, Greenville *Also called Hospice of Darke County Inc* ***(G-11510)***
State Park Motors Inc...740 264-3113
766 Canton Rd Steubenville (43953) ***(G-17334)***

ALPHABETIC SECTION

State Tchers Rtrement Sys Ohio (HQ) 614 227-4090
275 E Broad St Columbus (43215) *(G-8783)*
State Valley Dental Center 330 920-8060
63 Graham Rd Ste 3 Cuyahoga Falls (44223) *(G-9220)*
State-Wide Express Inc 216 676-4600
5231 Engle Rd Cleveland (44142) *(G-6532)*
Stateco Financial Services 614 464-5000
518 E Broad St Columbus (43215) *(G-8784)*
Status Solutions LLC 866 846-7272
999 County Line Rd W A Westerville (43082) *(G-19354)*
Staufs Coffee Roasters II Inc (PA) 614 487-6050
705 Hadley Dr Columbus (43228) *(G-8785)*
Stautberg Family LLC 513 941-5070
3871 Deerpath Ln Cincinnati (45248) *(G-4587)*
Staybrdge Sites Columbus Arprt, Columbus *Also called Rama Inc (G-8587)*
Staybridge Suites, Canfield *Also called Meander Hospitality Group Inc (G-2199)*
Staybridge Suites, Mayfield Heights *Also called Seal Mayfield LLC (G-14007)*
Stb Enterprises 330 478-0044
4417 17th St Nw Canton (44708) *(G-2548)*
STC Transporation Inc 216 441-6217
8806 Crane Ave Cleveland (44105) *(G-6533)*
Steak Escape, Columbus *Also called Escape Enterprises Inc (G-7609)*
Steaks & Such Inc 330 837-9296
244 Federal Ave Nw Massillon (44647) *(G-13858)*
Stearns Companies LLC 419 422-0241
4404 Township Road 142 Findlay (45840) *(G-11085)*
Stedman Floor Co Inc 614 836-3190
420 Lowery Ct Groveport (43125) *(G-11674)*
Steel Eqp Specialists Inc (PA) 330 823-8260
1507 Beeson St Ne Alliance (44601) *(G-563)*
Steel Plate LLC 888 894-8818
8333 Boyle Pkwy Twinsburg (44087) *(G-18473)*
Steel Valley Construction Co 330 392-8391
135 Pine Ave Se Ste 203 Warren (44481) *(G-18902)*
Steel Warehouse Cleveland LLC 888 225-3760
3193 Independence Rd Cleveland (44105) *(G-6534)*
Steele Dialysis LLC 419 462-1028
865 Harding Way W Galion (44833) *(G-11305)*
Steele W W Jr Agency Inc 330 453-7721
200 Market Ave N Ste 100 Canton (44702) *(G-2549)*
Steele, George R Co, Hillsboro *Also called Nb and T Insurance Agency Inc (G-11990)*
Steelial Cnstr Met Fabrication, Vinton *Also called Steelial Wldg Met Fbrction Inc (G-18744)*
Steelial Wldg Met Fbrction Inc 740 669-5300
70764 State Route 124 Vinton (45686) *(G-18744)*
Steelsummit Holdings Inc 513 825-8550
11150 Southland Rd Cincinnati (45240) *(G-4588)*
Steelsummit Ohio, Jackson *Also called Ohio Metal Processing Inc (G-12316)*
Stein Inc 216 883-4277
1034 Holmden Ave Cleveland (44109) *(G-6535)*
Stein Hospice Services Inc 419 447-0475
1200 Sycamore Line Sandusky (44870) *(G-16798)*
Stein Hospice Services Inc 419 502-0019
126 Columbus Ave Sandusky (44870) *(G-16799)*
Stein Hospice Services Inc (PA) 800 625-5269
1200 Sycamore Line Sandusky (44870) *(G-16800)*
Stein Hospice Services Inc 419 663-3222
150 Milan Ave Norwalk (44857) *(G-15593)*
Steinbach Painiting, Canton *Also called David W Steinbach Inc (G-2334)*
Steiner Associates, Columbus *Also called Easton Town Center II LLC (G-7567)*
Steiner Eoptics Inc (PA) 937 426-2341
3475 Newmark Dr Miamisburg (45342) *(G-14354)*
Steingass Mechanical Contg 330 725-6090
754 S Progress Dr Medina (44256) *(G-14129)*
Stella Maris Inc 216 781-0550
1320 Washington Ave Cleveland (44113) *(G-6536)*
Stella Mris Detoxification Ctr, Cleveland *Also called Stella Maris Inc (G-6536)*
Stellar Automotive Group, Seville *Also called Stellar Srkg Acquisition LLC (G-16847)*
Stellar Srkg Acquisition LLC 330 769-8484
4935 Enterprise Pkwy Seville (44273) *(G-16847)*
Stembanc Inc 440 332-4279
100 7th Ave Ste 200 Chardon (44024) *(G-2770)*
Step By Step Emplyment Trining 440 967-9042
664 Exchange St Vermilion (44089) *(G-18717)*
Stephen A Rudolph Inc 210 381-1367
1011 S Green Rd Ste 260 Cleveland (44121) *(G-6537)*
Stephen M Trudick 440 834-1891
13813 Station Rd Burton (44021) *(G-2065)*
Stephen R Saddemi MD 419 578-7200
2865 N Reynolds Rd # 160 Toledo (43615) *(G-18201)*
Stephens-Matthews Mktg Inc 740 984-8011
605 Center St Beverly (45715) *(G-1493)*
Stepping Stones Child Care, Cleveland *Also called Gearity Early Child Care Ctr (G-5665)*
Steps At Liberty Center, Wooster *Also called Oneeighty Inc (G-19900)*
Stepstone Group Real Estate LP 216 522-0330
127 Public Sq Ste 5050 Cleveland (44114) *(G-6538)*
Stericycle Inc 330 393-0370
1901 Pine Ave Se Warren (44483) *(G-18903)*
Stericycle Inc 513 539-6213
4495 Salzman Rd Middletown (45044) *(G-14461)*
Stericycle Inc 419 729-1934
1301 E Alexis Rd Toledo (43612) *(G-18202)*

Steriltek Inc (PA) 615 627-0241
11910 Briarwyck Woods Dr Painesville (44077) *(G-15881)*
Steris Isomedix, Groveport *Also called Isomedix Operations Inc (G-11648)*
Sterling Buying Group LLC 513 564-9000
3802 Ford Cir Cincinnati (45227) *(G-4589)*
Sterling Heights Gsa Prpts Ltd 419 609-7000
5500 Milan Rd Ste 220 Sandusky (44870) *(G-16801)*
Sterling House Bowling Green, Bowling Green *Also called Brookdale Snior Lving Cmmnties (G-1770)*
Sterling House of Alliance, Alliance *Also called Brookdale Senior Living Commun (G-528)*
Sterling House of Findlay, Findlay *Also called Brookdale Snior Lving Cmmnties (G-11009)*
Sterling House of Greenville, Greenville *Also called Brookdale Senior Living Commun (G-11490)*
Sterling House of Lancaster, Lancaster *Also called Brookdale Snior Lving Cmmnties (G-12511)*
Sterling House of Mansfield, Mansfield *Also called Brookdale Senior Living Inc (G-13270)*
Sterling House of Mansfield, Mansfield *Also called Brookdale Snior Lving Cmmnties (G-13271)*
Sterling House of Newark, Newark *Also called Brookdale Snior Lving Cmmnties (G-15149)*
Sterling House of Piqua, Piqua *Also called Brookdale Snior Lving Cmmnties (G-16137)*
Sterling House of Youngstown, Youngstown *Also called Brookdale Snior Lving Cmmnties (G-20128)*
Sterling Infosystems Inc 216 685-7600
6111 Oak Tree Blvd Independence (44131) *(G-12262)*
Sterling Joint Ambulance Dst 740 869-3006
24 S London St Mount Sterling (43143) *(G-14875)*
Sterling Land Title Agency 937 438-2000
7016 Corporate Way Ste B Dayton (45459) *(G-9906)*
Sterling Land Title Agency 513 755-3700
7594 Cox Ln West Chester (45069) *(G-19160)*
Sterling Lodging LLC 419 879-4000
803 S Leonard Ave Lima (45804) *(G-12892)*
Sterling Ltd Co 216 464-8850
3550 Lander Rd Ste 200 Cleveland (44124) *(G-6539)*
Sterling Med Staffing Group, Cincinnati *Also called Sterling Medical Corporation (G-4592)*
Sterling Medical Associates 513 984-1800
411 Oak St Cincinnati (45219) *(G-4590)*
Sterling Medical Corporation 513 984-1800
411 Oak St Cincinnati (45219) *(G-4591)*
Sterling Medical Corporation (PA) 513 984-1800
411 Oak St Cincinnati (45219) *(G-4592)*
Sterling Paper Co (HQ) 614 443-0303
1845 Progress Ave Columbus (43207) *(G-8786)*
Stern Advertising Inc (PA) 216 464-4850
950 Main Ave Ste 700 Cleveland (44113) *(G-6540)*
Steubenville Country CLB Manor 740 266-6118
575 Lovers Ln Steubenville (43953) *(G-17335)*
Steubenville Country Club Inc 740 264-0521
413 Lovers Ln Steubenville (43953) *(G-17336)*
Steubenville Home Training, Steubenville *Also called Barrington Dialysis LLC (G-17303)*
Steubenville Truck Center Inc 740 282-2711
620 South St Steubenville (43952) *(G-17337)*
Steve Austin Auto Group 937 592-3015
2500 S Main St Bellefontaine (43311) *(G-1399)*
Steve Austins of Hardin County, Bellefontaine *Also called Steve Austin Auto Group (G-1399)*
Steve Brown 937 436-2700
1353 Lyons Rd Dayton (45458) *(G-9907)*
Steve Byerly Masonry, Columbus *Also called Steven H Byerly Inc (G-8788)*
Steve S Towing and Recovery 513 422-0254
6475 Trenton Franklin Rd Middletown (45042) *(G-14462)*
Steve Shaffer 614 276-6355
3905 Sullivant Ave Columbus (43228) *(G-8787)*
Steven H Byerly Inc 614 882-0092
4890 Cleveland Ave Columbus (43231) *(G-8788)*
Steven L Sawdai 513 829-3830
6120 Pleasant Ave Fairfield (45014) *(G-10911)*
Steven Schaefer Associates Inc (PA) 513 542-3300
10411 Medallion Dr # 121 Cincinnati (45241) *(G-4593)*
Stevens Aviation Inc 937 890-0189
3500 Hangar Dr Vandalia (45377) *(G-18699)*
Stevens Engineers Constrs Inc 440 277-6207
1515 E 28th St Lorain (44055) *(G-13079)*
Stevenson Service Experts, Blue Ash *Also called Service Experts Htg & AC LLC (G-1688)*
Steward Northside Med Ctr Inc 330 884-1000
500 Gypsy Ln Youngstown (44504) *(G-20383)*
Steward Trumbull Mem Hosp Inc 330 841-9011
1350 E Market St Warren (44483) *(G-18904)*
Stewart Advnced Land Title Ltd (PA) 513 753-2800
4355 Ferguson Dr Ste 190 Cincinnati (45245) *(G-2933)*
Stewart Lodge Inc 440 417-1898
7774 Warner Rd Madison (44057) *(G-13236)*
Stewart Title Company 440 520-7130
4212 State Route 306 Willoughby (44094) *(G-19716)*
Stg Communication Services Inc 330 482-0500
1401 Wardingsley Ave Columbiana (44408) *(G-6863)*
Stg Communication Services Inc 330 482-0500
1401 Wardingsley Ave Columbiana (44408) *(G-6864)*
STI Technologies, Beavercreek *Also called Solutions Through Innovative T (G-1209)*

(PA)=Parent Co (HQ)=Headquarters (DH)=Div Headquarters

Stickelman Schneider Assoc LLC (HQ) — ALPHABETIC SECTION

Stickelman Schneider Assoc LLC (HQ) 513 475-6000
  1130 Channingway Dr Fairborn (45324) *(G-10804)*
Still Water Family Care, Versailles Also called Premier Health Partners *(G-18728)*
Stillwater Center, Dayton Also called County of Montgomery *(G-9434)*
Stilson & Associates Inc 614 847-0300
  6121 Huntley Rd Columbus (43229) *(G-8789)*
Stingray Pressure Pumping LLC (PA) 405 648-4177
  42739 National Rd Belmont (43718) *(G-1430)*
Stock Equipment Company, Chagrin Falls Also called Stock Fairfield Corporation *(G-2735)*
Stock Fairfield Corporation 440 543-6000
  16490 Chillicothe Rd Chagrin Falls (44023) *(G-2735)*
Stockmeister Enterprises Inc 740 286-1619
  700 E Main St Jackson (45640) *(G-12318)*
Stockport Mill Country Inn Inc 740 559-2822
  1995 Broadway St Stockport (43787) *(G-17346)*
Stoddard Imported Cars Inc 440 951-1040
  8599 Market St Mentor (44060) *(G-14245)*
Stofcheck Ambulance Inc 740 383-2787
  314 W Center St Marion (43302) *(G-13581)*
Stofcheck Ambulance Service, Marion Also called Stofcheck Ambulance Inc *(G-13581)*
Stofcheck Ambulance Svc Inc (PA) 740 499-2200
  220 S High St La Rue (43332) *(G-12459)*
Stohen Group LLC 513 448-6288
  3965 Marble Ridge Ln Mason (45040) *(G-13763)*
Stokes Fruit Farm 937 382-4004
  3182 Center Rd Wilmington (45177) *(G-19788)*
Stoll Farms Inc 330 682-5786
  15040 Fox Lake Rd Marshallville (44645) *(G-13598)*
Stolle Machinery Company LLC 330 493-0444
  4150 Belden Village St Nw Canton (44718) *(G-2550)*
Stolle Machinery Company LLC 330 453-2015
  4337 Excel St North Canton (44720) *(G-15369)*
Stolly Financial Planning, Lima Also called Stolly Insurance Agency Inc *(G-12893)*
Stolly Insurance Agency Inc 419 227-2570
  1730 Allentown Rd Lima (45805) *(G-12893)*
Stone Coffman Company LLC 614 861-4668
  6015 Taylor Rd Gahanna (43230) *(G-11270)*
Stone Crossing Assisted Living 330 492-7131
  820 34th St Nw Canton (44709) *(G-2551)*
Stone Gardens 216 292-0070
  27090 Cedar Rd Cleveland (44122) *(G-6541)*
Stone Mart, Columbus Also called Indus Trade & Technology LLC *(G-7892)*
Stone Oak Country Club 419 867-0969
  100 Stone Oak Blvd Holland (43528) *(G-12058)*
Stone Products Inc (HQ) 800 235-6088
  3105 Varley Ave Sw Canton (44706) *(G-2552)*
Stone Ridge Golf Club, Bowling Green Also called Wryneck Development LLC *(G-1805)*
Stoneco Inc (HQ) 419 422-8854
  1700 Fostoria Ave Ste 200 Findlay (45840) *(G-11086)*
Stoneco Inc 419 393-2555
  13762 Road 179 Oakwood (45873) *(G-15624)*
Stonegate Construction Inc 740 423-9170
  1378 Way Rd Belpre (45714) *(G-1444)*
Stonehedge Enterprises Inc 330 928-2161
  580 E Cuyahoga Falls Ave Akron (44310) *(G-451)*
Stonehedge Place, Akron Also called Stonehedge Enterprises Inc *(G-451)*
Stonehenge Capital Company LLC 614 246-2456
  191 W Nationwide Blvd Columbus (43215) *(G-8790)*
Stonehenge Fincl Holdings Inc (PA) 614 246-2500
  191 W Nationwide Blvd # 600 Columbus (43215) *(G-8791)*
Stonemor Partners LP 330 491-8001
  4450 Belden Village St Nw # 802 Canton (44718) *(G-2553)*
Stonemor Partners LP 937 866-4135
  6722 Hemple Rd Dayton (45439) *(G-9908)*
Stonemor Partners LP 330 425-8128
  8592 Darrow Rd Twinsburg (44087) *(G-18474)*
Stonewood Residential Inc (PA) 216 267-9777
  6320 Smith Rd Cleveland (44142) *(G-6542)*
Stoney Hollow Tire Inc 740 635-5200
  1st & Hanover Sts Martins Ferry (43935) *(G-13601)*
Stoney Lodge Inc 419 837-6409
  3491 Latcha Rd Millbury (43447) *(G-14581)*
Stoney Ridge Inn South Ltd 513 539-9247
  1250 Hmilton Lebanon Rd E Monroe (45050) *(G-14713)*
Stoney Ridge Truck Plaza, Monroe Also called Stoney Ridge Inn South Ltd *(G-14713)*
Stoops Freightliner of Dayton, Dayton Also called Stoops Frghtlnr-Qlity Trlr Inc *(G-9909)*
Stoops Frghtlnr-Qlity Trlr Inc 937 236-4092
  7800 Center Point 70 Blvd Dayton (45424) *(G-9909)*
Stoops of Lima Inc 419 228-4334
  598 E Hanthorn Rd Lima (45804) *(G-12894)*
Store & Haul Inc 419 238-4284
  1165 Grill Rd Van Wert (45891) *(G-18644)*
Store & Haul Trucking, Van Wert Also called Store & Haul Inc *(G-18644)*
Storer Meat Co Inc 216 621-7538
  3700 Clark Ave Cleveland (44109) *(G-6543)*
Stork Herron Cleveland, Cleveland Also called Element Mtrls Tchnlgy Hntngtn *(G-5532)*
Stork Studios Inc 419 841-7766
  3830 Woodley Rd Ste A Toledo (43606) *(G-18203)*
Storopack Inc (HQ) 513 874-0314
  4758 Devitt Dr West Chester (45246) *(G-19232)*

Stouffer Realty Inc (PA) 330 835-4900
  130 N Miller Rd Ste A Fairlawn (44333) *(G-10978)*
Stout Lori Cleaning & Such 419 637-7644
  503 N Main St Gibsonburg (43431) *(G-11404)*
Stout Risius Ross LLC 216 685-5000
  600 Superior Ave E # 1700 Cleveland (44114) *(G-6544)*
Stover Excavating Inc 614 873-5865
  7500 Industrial Pkwy Plain City (43064) *(G-16208)*
Stover Transportation Inc 614 777-4184
  3710 Lacon Rd Hilliard (43026) *(G-11955)*
Stow Dental Group Inc 330 688-6456
  3506 Darrow Rd Stow (44224) *(G-17393)*
Stow Montessori Center, Stow Also called All Around Children Montessori *(G-17351)*
Stow Opco LLC 502 429-8062
  2910 Lermitage Pl Stow (44224) *(G-17394)*
Stow-Kent Animal Hospital Inc (PA) 330 673-0049
  4559 Kent Rd Kent (44240) *(G-12396)*
Stow-Kent Animal Hospital Inc 330 673-1002
  4148 State Route 43 Kent (44240) *(G-12397)*
Strader's Green House, Columbus Also called Straders Garden Centers Inc *(G-8792)*
Straders Garden Centers Inc (PA) 614 889-1314
  5350 Riverside Dr Columbus (43220) *(G-8792)*
Straders Nrthwst Schwinn 614 889-2453
  5350 Riverside Dr Columbus (43220) *(G-8793)*
Straight 72 Inc 740 943-5730
  20078 State Route 4 Marysville (43040) *(G-13652)*
Stranahan Theatre & Great Hall, Toledo Also called Stranahan Theatre Trust *(G-18204)*
Stranahan Theatre Trust 419 381-8851
  4645 Heatherdowns Blvd # 2 Toledo (43614) *(G-18204)*
Strand Associates Inc 513 861-5600
  615 Elsinore Pl Ste 320 Cincinnati (45202) *(G-4594)*
Strand Associates Inc 614 835-0460
  4433 Professional Pkwy Groveport (43125) *(G-11675)*
Strang Corporation (PA) 216 961-6767
  8905 Lake Ave Fl 1 Cleveland (44102) *(G-6545)*
Stratacache Inc (PA) 937 224-0485
  2 Emmet St Ste 200 Dayton (45405) *(G-9910)*
Stratacache Products, Dayton Also called Stratacache Inc *(G-9910)*
Stratagraph Ne Inc 740 373-3091
  116 Ellsworth Ave Marietta (45750) *(G-13502)*
Strategic Consumer Research 216 261-0308
  8050 Harbor Creek Dr # 2102 Mentor On The Lake (44060) *(G-14262)*
Strategic Data Systems Inc 513 772-7374
  11260 Chester Rd Ste 425 Cincinnati (45246) *(G-4595)*
Strategic Insurance Sftwr Inc 614 915-9769
  4181 Arlingate Plz Columbus (43228) *(G-8794)*
Strategic Insurance Software, Columbus Also called Nugrowth Solutions LLC *(G-8305)*
Strategic Research Group Inc 614 220-8860
  995 Goodale Blvd Ste 1 Columbus (43212) *(G-8795)*
Strategic Systems Inc 614 717-4774
  485 Metro Pl S Ste 270 Dublin (43017) *(G-10464)*
Stratford Commons Inc 440 914-0900
  7000 Cochran Rd Solon (44139) *(G-17056)*
Stratos Wealth Partners Ltd 440 519-2500
  3750 Park East Dr Beachwood (44122) *(G-1127)*
Stratton Chevrolet Co 330 537-3151
  16050 State Route 14a Beloit (44609) *(G-1432)*
Strawser Construction Inc (HQ) 614 276-5501
  1392 Dublin Rd Columbus (43215) *(G-8796)*
Strawser Equipment & Lsg Inc 614 444-2521
  1235 Stimmel Rd Columbus (43223) *(G-8797)*
Streacker Tractor Sales Inc 419 422-6973
  1218 Trenton Ave Findlay (45840) *(G-11087)*
Streamline Technical Svcs LLC 614 441-7448
  4555 Creekside Pkwy Lockbourne (43137) *(G-12961)*
Street and Service Department, Cleveland Also called City of North Royalton *(G-5270)*
Street Deparment, Norwalk Also called City of Norwalk *(G-15563)*
Street Department, Cuyahoga Falls Also called City of Cuyahoga Falls *(G-9176)*
Streets & Sewer Departments, Cleveland Also called City of Euclid *(G-5260)*
Streetsboro Board Education 330 626-4909
  1901 Annalane Dr Streetsboro (44241) *(G-17432)*
Streetsboro Bus Garage, Streetsboro Also called Streetsboro Board Education *(G-17432)*
Streetsboro Opco LLC 502 429-8062
  1645 Maplewood Dr Streetsboro (44241) *(G-17433)*
Streetsboro Operations, Twinsburg Also called Facil North America Inc *(G-18414)*
Stress Engineering Svcs Inc 513 336-6701
  7030 Stress Engrg Way Mason (45040) *(G-13764)*
Stricker Auto Sales, Batavia Also called Stricker Bros Inc *(G-1026)*
Stricker Bros Inc 513 732-1152
  4955 Benton Rd Batavia (45103) *(G-1026)*
Strike Logistics, Toledo Also called Bolt Express LLC *(G-17777)*
Strike Zone Inc 440 235-4420
  8501 Stearns Rd Olmsted Twp (44138) *(G-15681)*
Strollo Architects Inc 330 743-1177
  201 W Federal St Youngstown (44503) *(G-20384)*
Strongsville Lodging Assoc 1 .... 440 238-8800
  15471 Royalton Rd Strongsville (44136) *(G-17512)*
Strongsville Medical Offices, Strongsville Also called Kaiser Foundation Hospitals *(G-17479)*
Strongville Recreation Complex 440 580-3230
  18688 Royalton Rd Strongsville (44136) *(G-17513)*

Strs Ohio, Columbus *Also called State Tchers Rtrement Sys Ohio* ***(G-8783)***
Structural Building Systems 330 656-9353
5802 Akron Cleveland Rd Hudson (44236) ***(G-12145)***
STS Logistics Inc 419 294-1498
13863 County Highway 119 Upper Sandusky (43351) ***(G-18567)***
STS Management, Toledo *Also called STS Restaurant Management Inc* ***(G-18205)***
STS Operating Inc 513 941-6200
5750 Hillside Ave Cincinnati (45233) ***(G-4596)***
STS Restaurant Management Inc 419 246-0730
420 Madison Ave Ste 103 Toledo (43604) ***(G-18205)***
Studebaker Electric Company 937 890-9510
8459 N Main St Ste 114 Dayton (45415) ***(G-9911)***
Studebaker Nurseries Inc 800 845-0584
11140 Milton Carlisle Rd New Carlisle (45344) ***(G-15032)***
Studebaker Wholesale Nurseries, New Carlisle *Also called Studebaker Nurseries Inc* ***(G-15032)***
Student Loan Strategies LLC 513 645-5400
151 W 4th St Frnt Cincinnati (45202) ***(G-4597)***
Student Wilce Health Center, Columbus *Also called Ohio State University* ***(G-8418)***
Studer-Obringer Inc 419 492-2121
525 S Kibler St New Washington (44854) ***(G-15136)***
Studio Mz Hair Design, Cleveland *Also called Mzf Inc* ***(G-6096)***
Studio of Prime Ae Group, Akron *Also called Braun & Steidl Architects Inc* ***(G-108)***
Stykemain Pntiac-Buick-Gmc Ltd (PA) 419 784-5252
25124 Elliott Rd Defiance (43512) ***(G-10059)***
Style Crest Inc 419 332-7369
605 Hagerty Dr Fremont (43420) ***(G-11222)***
Style Crest Inc (HQ) 419 332-7369
2450 Enterprise St Fremont (43420) ***(G-11223)***
Style Crest Enterprises Inc (PA) 419 355-8586
2450 Enterprise St Fremont (43420) ***(G-11224)***
Style Crest Transport Inc 419 332-7369
2450 Enterprise St Fremont (43420) ***(G-11225)***
Style-Line Incorporated (PA) 614 291-0600
901 W 3rd Ave Ste A Columbus (43212) ***(G-8798)***
Su-Jon Enterprises 330 372-1100
2448 Weir Rd Ne Warren (44483) ***(G-18905)***
Suarez Corporation Industries 330 494-4282
7800 Whipple Ave Nw Canton (44767) ***(G-2554)***
Substance Abuse Services Inc 419 243-7274
2005 Ashland Ave Toledo (43620) ***(G-18206)***
Suburban Collision Centers 440 243-5533
1151 W Bagley Rd Berea (44017) ***(G-1470)***
Suburban Gala Lanes Inc (PA) 419 468-7488
975 Hopley Ave Bucyrus (44820) ***(G-2047)***
Suburban Maint & Cnstr Inc 440 237-7765
16330 York Rd Ste 2 North Royalton (44133) ***(G-15503)***
Suburban Maint Contrs Inc 440 237-7765
16330 York Rd North Royalton (44133) ***(G-15504)***
Suburban Medical Laboratory 330 929-7992
26300 Euclid Ave Ste 810 Euclid (44132) ***(G-10778)***
SUBURBAN PAVILION NURSING AND, Cleveland *Also called Emery Leasing Co LLC* ***(G-5536)***
Suburban School, Brunswick *Also called Suburban Transportation Co Inc* ***(G-1990)***
Suburban Transportation Co Inc 440 846-9291
1289 Pearl Rd Brunswick (44212) ***(G-1990)***
Suburban Veterinarian Clinic 937 433-2160
102 E Spring Valley Pike Dayton (45458) ***(G-9912)***
Success Kidz 24-Hr Enrchmt Ctr 614 419-2276
1800 Parsons Ave Columbus (43207) ***(G-8799)***
Successful Eductl Seminars, Dayton *Also called Nelson Financial Group* ***(G-9278)***
Sue Smedley 937 399-5155
417 Wildwood Dr Springfield (45504) ***(G-17282)***
Sugar Creek Packing Co 513 551-5255
4360 Creek Rd Blue Ash (45241) ***(G-1691)***
Sugar Valley Meats, Sugarcreek *Also called Rubin Erb* ***(G-17547)***
Sugarbush Golf Club, Garrettsville *Also called Sugarbush Golf Inc* ***(G-11353)***
Sugarbush Golf Inc 330 527-4202
11186 State Route 88 Garrettsville (44231) ***(G-11353)***
Suite 224 Internet 440 593-7113
224 State St Conneaut (44030) ***(G-9047)***
Suite224 and Cablesuite541, Conneaut *Also called Conneaut Telephone Company* ***(G-9041)***
Suma Health Sys St Thomas Hosp, Akron *Also called Center 5* ***(G-127)***
Sumaria Systems Inc 937 429-6070
3164 Presidential Dr Beavercreek (45324) ***(G-1210)***
Sumitomo Demag Plstc Machinery 440 876-8960
11792 Alameda Dr Strongsville (44149) ***(G-17514)***
Sumitomo Elc Wirg Systems Inc 937 642-7579
14800 Industrial Pkwy Marysville (43040) ***(G-13653)***
Sumitomo Elc Wirg Systems Inc 937 642-7579
16960 Square Dr Marysville (43040) ***(G-13654)***
Summa Akron City Hospital, Akron *Also called Summa Health System* ***(G-456)***
Summa Barberton Hospital, Barberton *Also called Summa Health* ***(G-981)***
Summa Care, Akron *Also called Summa Health System* ***(G-453)***
Summa Health 330 873-1518
1 Park West Blvd Ste 130 Akron (44320) ***(G-452)***
Summa Health 330 926-0384
2345 4th St Cuyahoga Falls (44221) ***(G-9221)***
Summa Health 330 753-3649
165 5th St Se Ste A Barberton (44203) ***(G-980)***
Summa Health 330 688-4531
3869 Darrow Rd Ste 208 Stow (44224) ***(G-17395)***
Summa Health 330 615-3000
155 5th St Ne Barberton (44203) ***(G-981)***
Summa Health Center Lk Medina 330 952-0014
3780 Medina Rd Ste 220 Medina (44256) ***(G-14130)***
Summa Health System 330 535-7319
168 E Market St Ste 208 Akron (44308) ***(G-453)***
Summa Health System 330 836-9023
750 White Pond Dr Ste 500 Akron (44320) ***(G-454)***
Summa Health System 330 252-0095
1077 Gorge Blvd Akron (44310) ***(G-455)***
Summa Health System 330 375-3000
525 E Market St Akron (44304) ***(G-456)***
Summa Health System 330 334-1504
195 Wadsworth Rd Wadsworth (44281) ***(G-18771)***
Summa Health System 330 630-9726
182 East Ave Tallmadge (44278) ***(G-17651)***
Summa Health System 330 375-3584
75 Arch St Ste 303 Akron (44304) ***(G-457)***
Summa Health System 330 375-3315
75 Arch St Ste 302 Akron (44304) ***(G-458)***
Summa Health System 330 375-3315
55 Arch St Ste 1b Akron (44304) ***(G-459)***
Summa Health System 330 375-3000
444 N Main St Akron (44310) ***(G-460)***
Summa Health System 330 864-8060
1 Park West Blvd Ste 130 Akron (44320) ***(G-461)***
Summa Insurance Company Inc (HQ) 800 996-8411
10 N Main St Akron (44308) ***(G-462)***
Summa Park West, Akron *Also called Summa Health System* ***(G-461)***
Summa Physicians, Tallmadge *Also called Summa Health System* ***(G-17651)***
Summa Rehab Hospital LLC 330 572-7300
29 N Adams St Akron (44304) ***(G-463)***
Summa Rehabilitation Services, Akron *Also called Summa Health System* ***(G-454)***
Summacare, Akron *Also called Summa Insurance Company Inc* ***(G-462)***
Summacare Inc 330 996-8410
10 N Main St Unit 1 Akron (44308) ***(G-464)***
Summerfield Homes LLC 614 253-0984
27 Linwood Ave Columbus (43205) ***(G-8800)***
Summers Acquisition Corp (HQ) 216 941-7700
12555 Berea Rd Cleveland (44111) ***(G-6546)***
Summers Rubber Company, Cleveland *Also called Summers Acquisition Corp* ***(G-6546)***
Summerville At Mentor, Mentor *Also called Summerville Senior Living Inc* ***(G-14246)***
Summerville Senior Living Inc 440 354-5499
5700 Emerald Ct Mentor (44060) ***(G-14246)***
Summit Acres Inc (PA) 740 732-2364
44565 Sunset Rd Caldwell (43724) ***(G-2089)***
Summit Acres Nursing Home, Caldwell *Also called Summit Acres Inc* ***(G-2089)***
Summit Advantage LLC 330 835-2453
3340 W Market St Ste 100 Fairlawn (44333) ***(G-10979)***
Summit Associates Inc 216 831-3300
3750 Orange Pl Cleveland (44122) ***(G-6547)***
Summit At Park Hills LLC 317 462-8048
2270 Park Hills Dr Ofc Fairborn (45324) ***(G-10805)***
Summit Bhvioral Healthcare Ctr, Cincinnati *Also called Mental Health and Addi Serv* ***(G-4055)***
Summit Claim Services LLC 330 706-9898
5511 Manchester Rd C New Franklin (44319) ***(G-15050)***
Summit Cnty Dept Job Fmly Svcs 330 643-8200
1180 S Main St Ste 102 Akron (44301) ***(G-465)***
Summit Cnty Internists & Assoc (PA) 330 375-3690
55 Arch St Ste 1a Akron (44304) ***(G-466)***
Summit Cnty Juvenile CT, Akron *Also called County of Summit* ***(G-169)***
Summit County Jail, Akron *Also called Oriana House Inc* ***(G-375)***
Summit County Probation Offs, Akron *Also called County of Summit* ***(G-168)***
Summit Environmental Tech Inc (PA) 330 253-8211
3310 Win St Cuyahoga Falls (44223) ***(G-9222)***
Summit Facility Operations LLC 330 633-0555
330 Southwest Ave Tallmadge (44278) ***(G-17652)***
Summit Financial Strategies 614 885-1115
7965 N High St Ste 350 Columbus (43235) ***(G-8801)***
Summit Funding Group Inc (PA) 513 489-1222
4680 Parkway Dr Ste 300 Mason (45040) ***(G-13765)***
Summit Hand Center Inc 330 668-4055
3975 Embassy Pkwy Ste 201 Akron (44333) ***(G-467)***
Summit Home Health Care Svcs, Cuyahoga Falls *Also called Menorah Park Center For Senio* ***(G-9208)***
Summit Hotel Trs 144 LLC 216 443-9043
527 Prospect Ave E Cleveland (44115) ***(G-6548)***
Summit Management Services Inc 330 723-0864
201 Northland Dr Ofc Medina (44256) ***(G-14131)***
Summit Opthomology Optical 330 864-8060
1 Park West Blvd Ste 150 Akron (44320) ***(G-468)***
Summit Quest, Dayton *Also called Summit Solutions Inc* ***(G-9913)***
Summit Quest Academy, Dublin *Also called Viaquest Behavioral Health LLC* ***(G-10482)***
Summit Solutions Inc 937 291-4333
446 Windsor Park Dr Dayton (45459) ***(G-9913)***
Summit Towing, Dayton *Also called Spurlock Truck Service* ***(G-9900)***
Summit Villa Care Center, Tallmadge *Also called Summit Facility Operations LLC* ***(G-17652)***

ALPHABETIC

Summithotel ALPHABETIC SECTION

Summithotel.....513 527-9900
5345 Medpace Way Cincinnati (45227) *(G-4598)*
Summitt Ohio Leasing Co LLC.....937 436-2273
3800 Summit Glen Rd Dayton (45449) *(G-9914)*
Sumner Home For The Aged Inc (PA).....330 666-2952
4327 Cobblestone Dr Copley (44321) *(G-9065)*
Sumner On Merriman, Copley *Also called Sumner Home For The Aged Inc (G-9065)*
Sumner On Ridgewood.....330 664-1360
970 Sumner Pkwy Copley (44321) *(G-9066)*
Sumner Solutions Inc.....513 531-6382
3610 Sherbrooke Dr Cincinnati (45241) *(G-4599)*
Sumser Health Care Center, Canton *Also called Mayflower Nursing Home Inc (G-2452)*
Sumtotal Systems LLC.....352 264-2800
100 E Campus View Blvd # 250 Columbus (43235) *(G-8802)*
Sun Coke Energy, Franklin Furnace *Also called Haverhill Coke Company LLC (G-11172)*
Sun Federal Credit Union.....419 537-0200
3341 Executive Pkwy Toledo (43606) *(G-18207)*
Sun Federal Credit Union (PA).....800 786-0945
1625 Holland Rd Maumee (43537) *(G-13981)*
Sun Healthcare Group Inc.....419 784-1450
395 Harding St Defiance (43512) *(G-10060)*
Sun Valley Infosys LLC.....937 267-6435
1750 N Fountain Blvd Springfield (45504) *(G-17283)*
Sunbelt Rentals Inc.....216 362-0300
13800 Brookpark Rd Cleveland (44135) *(G-6549)*
Sunbrdge Marion Hlth Care Corp.....740 389-6306
524 James Way Marion (43302) *(G-13582)*
Sunbridge Care Enterprises Inc.....740 653-8630
1900 E Main St Lancaster (43130) *(G-12578)*
Sunbridge Circleville.....740 477-1695
1155 Atwater Ave Circleville (43113) *(G-4906)*
Sunbridge Healthcare LLC.....740 342-5161
920 S Main St New Lexington (43764) *(G-15064)*
Suncoke Energy Nc.....513 727-5571
3353 Yankee Rd Middletown (45044) *(G-14463)*
Suncrest Gardens Inc.....330 650-4969
5157 Akron Cleveland Rd Peninsula (44264) *(G-15951)*
Sunesis Construction Company.....513 326-6000
2610 Crescentville Rd West Chester (45069) *(G-19161)*
Sunesis Environmental LLC.....513 326-6000
325 Commercial Dr Fairfield (45014) *(G-10912)*
Sunforest Ob Gyn Associates.....419 473-6622
3740 W Sylvania Ave # 103 Toledo (43623) *(G-18208)*
Sunny Border Ohio Inc.....440 858-9660
3637 State Route 167 Jefferson (44047) *(G-12332)*
Sunny Day Academy LLC (PA).....614 718-1717
255 Bradenton Ave Dublin (43017) *(G-10465)*
Sunny Side Farms, Fort Recovery *Also called Midwest Poultry Services Lp (G-11119)*
Sunny Slope Nursing Home, Dayton *Also called CHS of Bowerston Oper Co Inc (G-9407)*
Sunny Slope Nursing Home, Bowerston *Also called Carriage Inn of Bowerston Inc (G-1754)*
Sunny View Nursing Home, Zanesville *Also called Careserve (G-20457)*
Sunnyside Toyota Inc.....440 777-9911
27000 Lorain Rd North Olmsted (44070) *(G-15446)*
Sunplus HM Care - Circleville, Circleville *Also called Accentcare Home Health Cal Inc (G-4876)*
Sunplus Home Health - Marion, Marion *Also called Accentcare Home Health Cal Inc (G-13522)*
Sunpoint Senior Living Hamlet.....440 247-4200
150 Cleveland St Chagrin Falls (44022) *(G-2708)*
Sunpower Inc.....740 594-2221
2005 E State St Ste 104 Athens (45701) *(G-813)*
Sunpro Inc (HQ).....330 966-0910
7640 Whipple Ave Nw North Canton (44720) *(G-15370)*
Sunrise At Finneytown, Cincinnati *Also called Sunrise Senior Living LLC (G-4600)*
Sunrise At Parma, Cleveland *Also called Sunrise Senior Living LLC (G-6552)*
Sunrise At Shaker Heights, Cleveland *Also called Sunrise Senior Living Inc (G-6551)*
Sunrise Connecticut Avenue Ass.....614 451-6766
4590 Knightsbridge Blvd Columbus (43214) *(G-8803)*
Sunrise Cooperative Inc.....937 462-8341
149 N Chillicothe St South Charleston (45368) *(G-17077)*
Sunrise Cooperative Inc.....937 575-6780
215 Looney Rd Piqua (45356) *(G-16167)*
Sunrise Cooperative Inc.....937 382-1633
1425 Rombach Ave Wilmington (45177) *(G-19789)*
Sunrise Cooperative Inc.....937 323-7536
821 N Belmont Ave Springfield (45503) *(G-17284)*
Sunrise Homes, Lisbon *Also called Mikouis Enterprise Inc (G-12940)*
Sunrise Industries Harps Jantr, Warren *Also called Turn Around Group Inc (G-18917)*
Sunrise Land Co (HQ).....216 621-6060
1250 Trml Twr 50 Pub Sq 1250 Terminal Tower Cleveland (44113) *(G-6550)*
Sunrise Manor Convalescent Ctr.....513 797-5144
3434 State Route 132 Amelia (45102) *(G-583)*
Sunrise Mortgage Services Inc.....614 989-5412
3596 Ringling Ln Gahanna (43230) *(G-11271)*
Sunrise of Cuyahoga Falls, Cuyahoga Falls *Also called Sunrise Senior Living LLC (G-9223)*
Sunrise of Dublin, Dublin *Also called Sunrise Senior Living LLC (G-10466)*
Sunrise of Findlay, Findlay *Also called Sunrise Senior Living LLC (G-11088)*
Sunrise of Gahanna, Gahanna *Also called Sunrise Senior Living Inc (G-11272)*
Sunrise of Hamilton, Hamilton *Also called Sunrise Senior Living LLC (G-11776)*
Sunrise of Poland, Poland *Also called Sunrise Senior Living LLC (G-16228)*
Sunrise of Rocky River, Rocky River *Also called Sunrise Senior Living Inc (G-16593)*
Sunrise of Wooster, Wooster *Also called Sunrise Senior Living LLC (G-19917)*
Sunrise On The Scioto, Upper Arlington *Also called Sunrise Senior Living Inc (G-18556)*
Sunrise Pl For Memory Impaired, Worthington *Also called Sunrise Senior Living Inc (G-20001)*
Sunrise Pointe, Maple Heights *Also called Eastside Multi Care Inc (G-13407)*
Sunrise Pointe, Maple Heights *Also called Saber Healthcare Group LLC (G-13416)*
Sunrise Senior Living Inc.....614 846-6500
6525 N High St Worthington (43085) *(G-20001)*
Sunrise Senior Living Inc.....937 438-0054
6800 Paragon Rd Ofc Dayton (45459) *(G-9915)*
Sunrise Senior Living Inc.....614 418-9775
775 E Johnstown Rd Gahanna (43230) *(G-11272)*
Sunrise Senior Living Inc.....440 895-2383
21600 Detroit Rd Rocky River (44116) *(G-16593)*
Sunrise Senior Living Inc.....440 808-0074
27819 Center Ridge Rd Ofc Westlake (44145) *(G-19552)*
Sunrise Senior Living Inc.....614 457-3500
3500 Riverside Dr Upper Arlington (43221) *(G-18556)*
Sunrise Senior Living Inc.....216 751-0930
16333 Chagrin Blvd Cleveland (44120) *(G-6551)*
Sunrise Senior Living LLC.....937 836-9617
95 W Wenger Rd Englewood (45322) *(G-10720)*
Sunrise Senior Living LLC.....330 262-1615
1615 Cleveland Rd Wooster (44691) *(G-19917)*
Sunrise Senior Living LLC.....419 425-3440
401 Lake Cascade Pkwy Findlay (45840) *(G-11088)*
Sunrise Senior Living LLC.....330 707-1313
335 W Mckinley Way Poland (44514) *(G-16228)*
Sunrise Senior Living LLC.....513 729-5233
9101 Winton Rd Cincinnati (45231) *(G-4600)*
Sunrise Senior Living LLC.....330 929-8500
1500 State Rd Cuyahoga Falls (44223) *(G-9223)*
Sunrise Senior Living LLC.....216 447-8909
7766 Broadview Rd Cleveland (44134) *(G-6552)*
Sunrise Senior Living LLC.....614 718-2062
4175 Stoneridge Ln Dublin (43017) *(G-10466)*
Sunrise Senior Living LLC.....513 893-9000
896 Nw Washington Blvd Hamilton (45013) *(G-11776)*
Sunrise Television Corp.....937 293-2101
4595 S Dixie Dr Moraine (45439) *(G-14828)*
Sunrise Television Corp.....740 282-9999
9 Red Donely Plz Mingo Junction (43938) *(G-14658)*
Sunrise Television Corp.....419 244-2197
4 Seagate Ste 101 Toledo (43604) *(G-18209)*
Sunrush Construction Co Inc (PA).....740 775-1300
1988 Western Ave Chillicothe (45601) *(G-2889)*
Sunset Carpet Cleaning.....937 836-5531
9 Beckenham Rd Englewood (45322) *(G-10721)*
Sunset Hills Cemetery Corp.....330 494-2051
5001 Everhard Rd Nw Canton (44718) *(G-2555)*
Sunset House Inc.....419 536-4645
4020 Indian Rd Toledo (43606) *(G-18210)*
Sunset Memorial Park Assn.....440 777-0450
6265 Columbia Rd North Olmsted (44070) *(G-15447)*
Sunset Nursing Center, Ironton *Also called Coal Grove Long Term Care Inc (G-12287)*
Sunset Nursing Home, Cleveland *Also called Hermenia Inc (G-5752)*
Sunset Rtrment Communities Inc (PA).....419 724-1200
4040 Indian Rd Ottawa Hills (43606) *(G-15807)*
Sunshine Communities (PA).....419 865-0251
7223 Maumee Western Rd Maumee (43537) *(G-13982)*
Sunshine Homecare.....419 207-9900
320 Pleasant St Ashland (44805) *(G-700)*
Sunshine Housekeeping, Lebanon *Also called Rde System Corp (G-12640)*
Sunshine Inc. Northwest Ohio, Maumee *Also called Sunshine Communities (G-13982)*
Sunshine Nursery School, Columbus *Also called Christian Missionary Alliance (G-7268)*
Sunsource Inc.....513 941-6200
5750 Hillside Ave Cincinnati (45233) *(G-4601)*
Sunsource Pabco, Cincinnati *Also called STS Operating Inc (G-4596)*
Sunstorm Games LLC.....216 403-4820
23245a Mercantile Rd Beachwood (44122) *(G-1128)*
Suntwist Corp.....800 935-3534
5461 Dunham Rd Maple Heights (44137) *(G-13420)*
Super 8 Motel, Millbury *Also called Stoney Lodge Inc (G-14581)*
Super 8 Motel, Sandusky *Also called Lodging Industry Inc (G-16776)*
Super 8 Motel Columbus North, Columbus *Also called Northland Hotel Inc (G-8292)*
Super Laundry, Cincinnati *Also called Clean Living Laundry LLC (G-3362)*
Super Laundry Inc.....614 258-5147
2268 Westbrooke Dr Columbus (43228) *(G-8804)*
Super Shine Inc.....513 423-8999
1549 S Breiel Blvd Ste A Middletown (45044) *(G-14464)*
Super Systems Inc (PA).....513 772-0060
7205 Edington Dr Cincinnati (45249) *(G-4602)*
Super Tan.....330 722-2799
1110 N Court St Medina (44256) *(G-14132)*
Superior Apartments.....216 861-6405
1850 Superior Ave E 102a Cleveland (44114) *(G-6553)*

ALPHABETIC SECTION Sws Environmental Services

Superior Bev Group Centl Ohio, Lewis Center *Also called Central Beverage Group Ltd* **(G-12674)**
Superior Beverage Company Inc 440 703-4580
31031 Diamond Pkwy Solon (44139) **(G-17057)**
Superior Beverage Group Ltd 614 294-3555
8133 Highfield Dr Lewis Center (43035) **(G-12706)**
Superior Beverage Group Ltd (PA) 440 703-4580
31031 Diamond Pkwy Solon (44139) **(G-17058)**
Superior Bulk Logistics Inc 513 874-3440
4963 Provident Dr West Chester (45246) **(G-19233)**
Superior Care Pharmacy Inc 513 719-2600
201 E 4th St Ste 900 Cincinnati (45202) **(G-4603)**
Superior Carriers, West Chester *Also called Superior Bulk Logistics Inc* **(G-19233)**
Superior Clay Corp 740 922-4122
6566 Superior Rd Se Uhrichsville (44683) **(G-18492)**
Superior Dental Care Inc 937 438-0283
6683 Centervl Bus Pkwy Dayton (45459) **(G-9916)**
Superior Envmtl Sltons SES Inc 513 874-6910
9976 Joseph James Dr West Chester (45246) **(G-19234)**
Superior Envmtl Solutions LLC (PA) 513 874-8355
9996 Joseph James Dr West Chester (45246) **(G-19235)**
Superior Financial Services, Wapakoneta *Also called Lima Superior Federal Cr Un* **(G-18802)**
Superior Group 614 488-8035
740 Waterman Ave Columbus (43215) **(G-8805)**
Superior Kraft Homes LLC 740 947-7710
3404 Rhodes Ave New Boston (45662) **(G-15015)**
Superior Linen & AP Svcs Inc 513 751-1345
481 Wayne St Cincinnati (45206) **(G-4604)**
Superior Linen & Apparel Svcs, Cincinnati *Also called Superior Linen & AP Svcs Inc* **(G-4604)**
Superior Marine Ways Inc 740 894-6224
5852 County Rd 1 Suoth Pt Proctorville (45669) **(G-16361)**
Superior Mechanical Svcs Inc 937 259-0082
3100 Plainfield Rd Ste C Dayton (45432) **(G-9284)**
Superior Med Inc (PA) 740 439-8839
1251 Clark St Cambridge (43725) **(G-2130)**
Superior Medical Care, Sheffield Village *Also called Joseph A Girgis MD Inc* **(G-16889)**
Superior Medical Care Inc 440 282-7420
5172 Leavitt Rd Ste B Lorain (44053) **(G-13080)**
Superior Packaging Toledo LLC 419 380-3335
2970 Airport Hwy Toledo (43609) **(G-18211)**
Superior Paving & Materials 330 499-5849
5947 Whipple Ave Nw Canton (44720) **(G-2556)**
Superior Products Llc 216 651-9400
3786 Ridge Rd Cleveland (44144) **(G-6554)**
Superior Products LLC 216 651-9400
3786 Ridge Rd Cleveland (44144) **(G-6555)**
Superior Street Partners LLC 216 862-0058
19010 Shaker Blvd Shaker Heights (44122) **(G-16868)**
Superior Water Conditioning Co, Moraine *Also called Enting Water Conditioning Inc* **(G-14781)**
SUPERIOR WHOLESALE DISTRIBUTOR, Lima *Also called Swd Corporation* **(G-12896)**
Superior's Brand Meats, Massillon *Also called Fresh Mark Inc* **(G-13810)**
Supermedia LLC 740 369-2391
19 E Central Ave Fl 1 Marion (43302) **(G-13583)**
Superr-Spdie Portable Svcs Inc 330 733-9000
1050 Killian Rd Akron (44312) **(G-469)**
Supers Landscaping Inc 440 775-0027
48211 State Route 511 Oberlin (44074) **(G-15661)**
Supply Network Inc 614 527-5800
2353 International St Columbus (43228) **(G-8806)**
Supply Tech of Columbus LLC 614 299-0184
5197 Trabue Rd Columbus (43228) **(G-8807)**
Supply Technologies LLC (HQ) 440 947-2100
6065 Parkland Blvd Ste 1 Cleveland (44124) **(G-6556)**
Support Fincl Resources Inc 800 444-5465
830 E Franklin St Ste A Centerville (45459) **(G-2686)**
Support Insur Systems Agcy Inc (PA) 937 434-5700
830 E Franklin St Ste A Centerville (45459) **(G-2687)**
Support To At Risk Teens 216 696-5507
4515 Superior Ave Cleveland (44103) **(G-6557)**
Supportcare Inc 216 446-2650
4700 Rockside Rd Ste 100 Independence (44131) **(G-12263)**
Supportcare Inc (PA) 614 889-5837
525 Metro Pl N Ste 350 Dublin (43017) **(G-10467)**
Supportcare Ohio, Dublin *Also called Supportcare Inc* **(G-10467)**
Supreme Court United States 419 213-5800
1946 N 13th St Ste 292 Toledo (43604) **(G-18212)**
Supreme Court United States 614 719-3107
85 Marconi Blvd Rm 546 Columbus (43215) **(G-8808)**
Supreme Court United States 513 564-7575
100 E 5th St Rm 110 Cincinnati (45202) **(G-4605)**
Supreme Court United States 216 357-7300
801 W Superior Ave 20-100 Cleveland (44113) **(G-6558)**
Supreme Court of Ohio 937 898-3996
245 James Bohanan Dr Vandalia (45377) **(G-18700)**
Supreme Court of Ohio 614 387-9800
65 S Front St Fl 1 Columbus (43215) **(G-8809)**
Supreme Touch Home Health Svcs 614 783-1115
2547 W Broad St Columbus (43204) **(G-8810)**
Surburan Collision Ctr, Berea *Also called Suburban Collision Centers* **(G-1470)**
Sure Home Improvments LLC 614 586-0610
6031 E Main St Ste 222 Columbus (43213) **(G-8811)**
Suresite Consulting Group LLC (PA) 216 593-0400
3659 Green Rd Ste 214 Beachwood (44122) **(G-1129)**
Surface Combustion Inc 419 878-8444
1270 Wtrville Monclova Rd Waterville (43566) **(G-18946)**
Surfside Motors Inc (PA) 419 462-1746
7459 State Route 309 Galion (44833) **(G-11306)**
Surgere Inc 330 526-7971
5399 Lauby Rd Ste 200 North Canton (44720) **(G-15371)**
Surgery and Gynecology Inc (PA) 614 294-1603
114r W 3rd Ave Columbus (43201) **(G-8812)**
Surgery Center, Cincinnati *Also called Christ Hospital* **(G-3264)**
Surgery Center Cincinnati LLC 513 947-1130
4415 Aicholtz Rd Cincinnati (45245) **(G-2934)**
Surgery Center Howland Ltd 330 609-7874
1934 Niles Cortland Rd Ne Warren (44484) **(G-18906)**
Surgery Center, The, Cleveland *Also called Surgery Ctr An Ohio Ltd Partnr* **(G-6559)**
Surgery Ctr An Ohio Ltd Partnr 440 826-3240
19250 Bagley Rd Cleveland (44130) **(G-6559)**
Surgi Care Ambulatory, Maumee *Also called Ohiocare Ambulatory Surgery* **(G-13952)**
Surgical Hosp At Southwoods 330 729-8000
7630 Southern Blvd Youngstown (44512) **(G-20385)**
Surgical Oncology Division, Columbus *Also called Ohio State University* **(G-8440)**
Surgicenter Ltd 740 522-3937
1651 W Main St Newark (43055) **(G-15237)**
Surgicenter of Mansfield 419 774-9410
1030 Cricket Ln Mansfield (44906) **(G-13368)**
Surmount Solutions Group LLC 937 842-5780
8823 Township Road 239 Lakeview (43331) **(G-12468)**
Surreal Entertainment LLC 330 262-5277
2018 Great Trails Dr Wooster (44691) **(G-19918)**
Susan A Smith Crystal Care 419 747-2666
5375 Teeter Rd Butler (44822) **(G-2068)**
Suter Produce Inc 419 384-3665
12200 Pandora Rd Pandora (45877) **(G-15894)**
Sutphen Corporation (PA) 800 726-7030
6450 Eiterman Rd Dublin (43016) **(G-10468)**
Sutton Motor Coach Tours Inc 330 726-2800
7338 Southern Blvd Youngstown (44512) **(G-20386)**
Suzie Roselius Real Estate, Beavercreek *Also called Big Hill Realty Corp* **(G-1229)**
Svh Holdings LLC 844 560-7775
4322 N Hamilton Rd Columbus (43230) **(G-8813)**
Swa Inc 440 243-7888
7250 Old Oak Blvd Cleveland (44130) **(G-6560)**
Swaco, Grove City *Also called Solid Waste Auth Centl Ohio* **(G-11598)**
Swagelok Company 440 349-5934
31400 Aurora Rd Solon (44139) **(G-17059)**
Swan Pnte Fclty Operations LLC 419 867-7926
3600 Butz Rd Maumee (43537) **(G-13983)**
Swan Point Care Center, Maumee *Also called Consulate Management Co LLC* **(G-13900)**
Swan Sales 513 422-3100
2910 Oxford State Rd Middletown (45044) **(G-14465)**
Swanton Hlth Care Rtrement Ctr 419 825-1145
214 S Munson Rd Swanton (43558) **(G-17572)**
Swanton Maintenance Building, Swanton *Also called Ohio Tpk & Infrastructure Comm* **(G-17569)**
Swanton Vly Care Rhblttion Ctr, Swanton *Also called Harborside Healthcare Corp* **(G-17566)**
Swartz Contracting, Lima *Also called Swartz Enterprises Inc* **(G-12895)**
Swartz Enterprises Inc 419 331-1024
2622 Baty Rd Lima (45807) **(G-12895)**
Swd Corporation 419 227-2436
435 N Main St Lima (45801) **(G-12896)**
Sweda Sweda Associates Inc 419 433-4841
5329 N Abbey Avon (44011) **(G-917)**
Sweeney Chrysler Dodge Jeep, Lebanon *Also called Lebanon Chrysler - Plymuth Inc* **(G-12620)**
Sweeney Chrysler Dodge Jeep, Lebanon *Also called Walt Sweeney Fleet Sales* **(G-12657)**
Sweeney Robert E Co Lpa 216 696-0606
55 Public Sq Ste 1500 Cleveland (44113) **(G-6561)**
Sweeney Team Inc 513 934-0700
576 Mound Ct Ste A Lebanon (45036) **(G-12651)**
Sweeney Team Inc (PA) 513 241-3400
1440 Main St Cincinnati (45202) **(G-4606)**
Sweeny Walt Pntc GMC Trck Sles 513 621-4888
3365 Highland Ave Cincinnati (45213) **(G-4607)**
Swh Mimis Cafe LLC 614 433-0441
1428 Polaris Pkwy Columbus (43240) **(G-6908)**
Swift Filters Inc (PA) 440 735-0995
24040 Forbes Rd Oakwood Village (44146) **(G-15634)**
Swim Incorporated 614 885-1619
400 W Dublin Granville Rd Worthington (43085) **(G-20002)**
Swings N Things Family Fun Pk, Olmsted Twp *Also called Strike Zone Inc* **(G-15681)**
Swiss Tech Products, Solon *Also called Interdesign Inc* **(G-17018)**
Swn Communications Inc 877 698-3262
6450 Poe Ave Ste 500 Dayton (45414) **(G-9917)**
Sws Environmental Services 254 629-1718
3820 Ventura Dr Findlay (45840) **(G-11089)**

ALPHABETIC

(PA)=Parent Co (HQ)=Headquarters (DH)=Div Headquarters
2018 Harris Ohio Services Directory
1333

Sws Equipment Services Inc......330 806-2767
712 Palisades Dr Akron (44303) *(G-470)*
Swx Enterprises Inc......216 676-4600
5231 Engle Rd Brookpark (44142) *(G-1956)*
Sycamore Board of Education......513 489-3937
9609 Montgomery Rd Cincinnati (45242) *(G-4608)*
Sycamore Creek Country Club......937 748-0791
8300 Country Club Ln Springboro (45066) *(G-17139)*
Sycamore Glen Retirement Cmnty, Miamisburg *Also called Kettering Medical Center (G-14311)*
Sycamore Hills Golf Club, Fremont *Also called Michael Brothers Inc (G-11213)*
Sycamore Lake Inc......440 729-9775
10620 Mayfield Rd Chesterland (44026) *(G-2804)*
Sycamore Medical Center, Miamisburg *Also called Kettering Medical Center (G-14310)*
Sycamore Run Nursing, Millersburg *Also called Castle Nursing Homes Inc (G-14592)*
Sycamore Senior Center (PA)......513 984-1234
4455 Carver Woods Dr Blue Ash (45242) *(G-1692)*
Sydney ASC, Piqua *Also called Valley Regional Surgery Center (G-16174)*
Sygma Network Inc......614 734-2500
5550 Blazer Pkwy Ste 300 Dublin (43017) *(G-10469)*
Sygma Network Inc (HQ)......614 734-2500
5550 Blazer Pkwy Ste 300 Dublin (43017) *(G-10470)*
Sygma Network Inc......614 771-3801
2400 Harrison Rd Columbus (43204) *(G-8814)*
Sylvania Center, Sylvania *Also called Harborside Sylvania LLC (G-17592)*
Sylvania Community Svcs Ctr......419 885-2451
4747 N Hlland Sylvania Rd Sylvania (43560) *(G-17618)*
Sylvania Country Club......419 392-0530
5201 Corey Rd Sylvania (43560) *(G-17619)*
Sylvania Franciscan Health (HQ)......419 882-8373
1715 Indian Wood Cir # 200 Maumee (43537) *(G-13984)*
Sylvania Lighting Svcs Corp......440 742-8208
35405 Spatterdock Ln Solon (44139) *(G-17060)*
Sylvania Ultrasound Institute, Toledo *Also called Stork Studios Inc (G-18203)*
Sylvania Veterinary Hospital (PA)......419 885-4421
4801 N Hlland Sylvania Rd Sylvania (43560) *(G-17620)*
Sylvester Materials Co......419 841-3874
7901 Sylvania Ave Sylvania (43560) *(G-17621)*
Symantec Corporation......216 643-6700
6100 Oak Tree Blvd Independence (44131) *(G-12264)*
Symatic Inc......330 225-1510
2831 Center Rd Brunswick (44212) *(G-1991)*
Symcox Grinding & Steele Co......330 678-1080
825 Tallmadge Rd Kent (44240) *(G-12398)*
Synergy Consulting Group Inc......330 899-9301
3700 Massillon Rd Ste 300 Uniontown (44685) *(G-18540)*
Synergy Health North Amer Inc......513 398-6406
7086 Industrial Row Dr Mason (45040) *(G-13766)*
Synergy Homecare, Westerville *Also called Huntsey Corporation (G-19315)*
Synergy Homecare South Dayton......937 610-0555
501 Windsor Park Dr Dayton (45459) *(G-9918)*
Synergy Hotels LLC......614 492-9000
4870 Old Rathmell Ct Obetz (43207) *(G-15671)*
Synnex Corporation......614 539-6995
4001 Gantz Rd Ste A Grove City (43123) *(G-11603)*
Synoran......614 236-4014
2389 Bryden Rd Columbus (43209) *(G-8815)*
Syntero Inc (PA)......614 889-5722
299 Cramer Creek Ct Dublin (43017) *(G-10471)*
Synthetic Stucco Corporation......513 897-9227
4571 Isaac Ct Waynesville (45068) *(G-18987)*
Syracuse Water Dept......740 992-7777
2581 3rd St Pomeroy (45769) *(G-16235)*
Sysco Central Ohio Inc......614 272-0658
2400 Harrison Rd Columbus (43204) *(G-8816)*
Sysco Cincinnati LLC......513 563-6300
10510 Evendale Dr Cincinnati (45241) *(G-4609)*
System EDM of Ohio, Mason *Also called Hi-Tek Manufacturing Inc (G-13717)*
System Optics Csmt Srgcal Arts......330 630-9699
518 West Ave Tallmadge (44278) *(G-17653)*
System Optics Laser Vision Ctr......330 630-2451
518 West Ave Tallmadge (44278) *(G-17654)*
System Seals Inc (HQ)......440 735-0200
9505 Midwest Ave Cleveland (44125) *(G-6562)*
Systemax Manufacturing Inc......937 368-2300
6450 Poe Ave Ste 200 Dayton (45414) *(G-9919)*
Systems Alternatives Intl......419 891-1100
1705 Indian Wood Cir # 100 Maumee (43537) *(G-13985)*
Systems Evolution Inc......513 459-1992
7870 E Kemper Rd Ste 400 Cincinnati (45249) *(G-4610)*
Systems Evolution Inc (PA)......513 459-1992
7870 E Kemper Rd Ste 400 Cincinnati (45249) *(G-4611)*
Systems Jay LLC Nanogate (HQ)......419 524-3778
150 Longview Ave E Mansfield (44903) *(G-13369)*
Systems Jay LLC Nanogate......419 747-4161
1595 W Longview Ave Mansfield (44906) *(G-13370)*
Systems Jay LLC Nanogate......419 747-6639
1575 W Longview Ave Mansfield (44906) *(G-13371)*
Systems Pack Inc......330 467-5729
649 Highland Rd E Macedonia (44056) *(G-13211)*
Systems Temoptics Coop Opt Un......330 633-4321
518 West Ave Tallmadge (44278) *(G-17655)*
Sytronics Inc......937 431-6100
4433 Dayton Xenia Rd # 1 Beavercreek (45432) *(G-1211)*
Syvania Pediatric Dental Care, Sylvania *Also called Smile Development Inc (G-17615)*
T & B Electric Ltd......740 881-5696
7464 Watkins Rd Ostrander (43061) *(G-15795)*
T & F Systems Inc......216 881-3525
1599 E 40th St Cleveland (44103) *(G-6563)*
T & L Enterprises Inc......440 234-5900
1060 W Bagley Rd Ste 101 Berea (44017) *(G-1471)*
T & L Transport Inc......330 674-0655
4395 County Road 58 Millersburg (44654) *(G-14623)*
T & R Properties (PA)......614 923-4000
3895 Stoneridge Ln Dublin (43017) *(G-10472)*
T & R Property Management, Dublin *Also called T & R Properties (G-10472)*
T Allen Inc......440 234-2366
200 Depot St Berea (44017) *(G-1472)*
T and D Interiors Incorporated......419 331-4372
3626 Allentown Rd Lima (45807) *(G-12897)*
T C P, Aurora *Also called Technical Consumer Pdts Inc (G-856)*
T C Rumpke Waste Collection......513 385-7627
5665 Dunlap Rd Cincinnati (45252) *(G-4612)*
T E S - East, Versailles *Also called Bnsf Logistics LLC (G-18723)*
T H Winston Company......513 271-2123
4817 Glenshade Ave Cincinnati (45227) *(G-4613)*
T J D Industrial Clg & Maint......419 425-5025
12340 Township Road 109 Findlay (45840) *(G-11090)*
T J Ellis Enterprises Inc (PA)......419 999-5026
1505 Neubrecht Rd Lima (45801) *(G-12898)*
T J Neff Holdings Inc......440 884-3100
6405 York Rd Cleveland (44130) *(G-6564)*
T J Williams Electric Co......513 738-5366
7925 New Haven Rd Harrison (45030) *(G-11809)*
T K Edwards LLC......614 406-8064
782 N High St Columbus (43215) *(G-8817)*
T K Holdings, Piqua *Also called Tk Holdings Inc (G-16168)*
T L C Child Development Center......330 655-2797
187 Ravenna St Hudson (44236) *(G-12146)*
T L C Landscaping Inc......440 248-4852
38000 Aurora Rd Cleveland (44139) *(G-6565)*
T L Express, Mantua *Also called Triple Ladys Agency Inc (G-13396)*
T M C Systems LLC......440 740-1234
7655 Town Centre Dr Broadview Heights (44147) *(G-1892)*
T M I, Columbus *Also called Team Management Inc (G-8827)*
T M R, Brunswick *Also called Total Marketing Resources LLC (G-1993)*
T M S, Cincinnati *Also called Modal Shop Inc (G-4111)*
T N C Construction Inc......614 554-5330
6058 Winnebago St Grove City (43123) *(G-11604)*
T N C Recovery and Maintenance, Grove City *Also called T N C Construction Inc (G-11604)*
T O J Inc (PA)......440 352-1900
6011 Heisley Rd Mentor (44060) *(G-14247)*
T P McHncal Cntrs Svc Fbrction, Columbus *Also called TP Mechanical Contractors Inc (G-8859)*
T R L Inc......330 448-4071
3500 Parkway Dr Brookfield (44403) *(G-1901)*
T W I International Inc (HQ)......440 439-1830
24460 Aurora Rd Cleveland (44146) *(G-6566)*
T W Ruff, Columbus *Also called Loth Inc (G-8077)*
T X I, Greenville *Also called Telecom Expertise Inds Inc (G-11521)*
T&B Manufacturing, Miamiville *Also called Aim Mro Holdings Inc (G-14374)*
T&L Global Management LLC......614 586-0303
1572 Lafayette Dr Columbus (43220) *(G-8818)*
T&T Enterprises of Ohio Inc......513 942-1141
5100 Duff Dr West Chester (45246) *(G-19236)*
T-Shirt City, Cincinnati *Also called TSC Apparel LLC (G-4703)*
Ta Operating LLC (HQ)......440 808-9100
24601 Center Ridge Rd # 200 Westlake (44145) *(G-19553)*
Tab Construction Company Inc......330 454-5228
530 Walnut Ave Ne Canton (44702) *(G-2557)*
TAC Enterprises, Springfield *Also called TAC Industries Inc (G-17285)*
TAC Industries Inc (PA)......937 328-5200
2160 Old Selma Rd Springfield (45505) *(G-17285)*
TAC Industries Inc......937 328-5200
2160 Old Selma Rd Springfield (45505) *(G-17286)*
Tacg LLC (PA)......937 203-8201
3725 Pentagon Blvd # 110 Beavercreek (45431) *(G-1212)*
Tack-Anew Inc......419 734-4212
451 W Lakeshore Dr Port Clinton (43452) *(G-16257)*
Tafaro John......513 381-0656
1 W 4th St Ste 800 Cincinnati (45202) *(G-4614)*
Taft Law, Dayton *Also called Nicholas E Davis (G-9773)*
Taft Museum, Cincinnati *Also called Cincinnati Institute Fine Arts (G-3313)*
Taft Museum of Art......513 241-0343
316 Pike St Cincinnati (45202) *(G-4615)*
Taft Stettinius Hollister LLP (PA)......513 381-2838
425 Walnut St Ste 1800 Cincinnati (45202) *(G-4616)*
Taft Stettinius Hollister LLP......614 221-4000
65 E State St Ste 1000 Columbus (43215) *(G-8819)*
Taft Stettinius Hollister LLP......216 241-3141
200 Public Sq Ste 3500 Cleveland (44114) *(G-6567)*

Tahoma Enterprises Inc (PA)....330 745-9016
255 Wooster Rd N Barberton (44203) *(G-982)*
Tahoma Rubber & Plastics Inc (HQ)....330 745-9016
255 Wooster Rd N Barberton (44203) *(G-983)*
Tailored Healthcare Staffing, Cincinnati *Also called Health Carousel LLC (G-3752)*
Tailored Management Services (PA)....614 859-1500
1165 Dublin Rd Columbus (43215) *(G-8820)*
Taitech Inc (PA)....937 431-1007
1430 Oak Ct Ste 301 Beavercreek (45430) *(G-1260)*
Takkt America Holding Inc (PA)....513 367-8600
9555 Dry Fork Rd Harrison (45030) *(G-11810)*
Talbert House....513 541-0127
3129 Spring Grove Ave Cincinnati (45225) *(G-4617)*
Talbert House....513 751-7747
5837 Hamilton Ave Cincinnati (45224) *(G-4618)*
Talbert House....513 541-1184
1611 Emerson Ave Cincinnati (45239) *(G-4619)*
Talbert House (PA)....513 872-5863
2600 Victory Pkwy Cincinnati (45206) *(G-4620)*
Talbert House....513 684-7968
328 Mcgregor Ave Ste 106 Cincinnati (45219) *(G-4621)*
Talbert House....513 933-9304
5234 W State Route 63 Lebanon (45036) *(G-12652)*
Talbert House Health (HQ)....513 541-7577
5837 Hamilton Ave Unit 3 Cincinnati (45224) *(G-4622)*
Talemed LLC....513 774-7300
6279 Tri Ridge Blvd # 110 Loveland (45140) *(G-13162)*
Taleris Credit Union Inc....216 739-2300
1250 E Granger Rd Cleveland (44131) *(G-6568)*
Tallmadge Asphalt & Pav Co Inc....330 677-0000
741 Tallmadge Rd Kent (44240) *(G-12399)*
Tallmadge Board of Education....330 633-2215
89 W Overdale Dr Tallmadge (44278) *(G-17656)*
Tallmadge Collision Center (PA)....330 630-2188
195 Northeast Ave Tallmadge (44278) *(G-17657)*
Tallmadge Schools Bus Garage, Tallmadge *Also called Tallmadge Board of Education (G-17656)*
Talmage N Porter MD....937 435-9013
979 Congress Park Dr Dayton (45459) *(G-9920)*
Talmer Bank and Trust....330 726-3396
2 S Broad St Canfield (44406) *(G-2211)*
Talon Title Agency LLC (PA)....614 818-0500
570 Polaris Pkwy Ste 140 Westerville (43082) *(G-19355)*
Talx Corporation....614 527-9404
3455 Mill Run Dr Hilliard (43026) *(G-11956)*
Tam-O-Shanter Sports Complex, Sylvania *Also called City of Sylvania (G-17579)*
Tamaron Country Club, Toledo *Also called Tamaron Golf LLC (G-18213)*
Tamaron Golf LLC....419 474-5067
2162 W Alexis Rd Toledo (43613) *(G-18213)*
Tamer Win Golf & Country Club, Cortland *Also called Win Tamer Corporation (G-9085)*
Tangoe Inc....614 842-9918
200 E Campus View Blvd # 150 Columbus (43235) *(G-8821)*
Tank Leasing Corp....330 339-3333
2743 Brightwood Rd Se New Philadelphia (44663) *(G-15117)*
Tank Services Company, Dennison *Also called Ionno Properties s Corp (G-10165)*
Tanner Heating & AC Inc....937 299-2500
2238 E River Rd Moraine (45439) *(G-14829)*
Tanos Salon....216 831-7880
24225 Chagrin Blvd Cleveland (44122) *(G-6569)*
Tansky Honda, Zanesville *Also called Man-Tansky Inc (G-20499)*
Tansky Motors Inc (PA)....650 322-7069
297 E Main St Logan (43138) *(G-12989)*
Tanyas Image & Wellness Salon, Cincinnati *Also called Tanyas Image LLC (G-4623)*
Tanyas Image LLC (PA)....513 386-9981
2716 Erie Ave Ste 3 Cincinnati (45208) *(G-4623)*
Tape Products Company (PA)....513 489-8840
11630 Deerfield Rd Cincinnati (45242) *(G-4624)*
Tappan Lake Marina Inc....740 269-2031
33315 Cadiz Dennison Rd Scio (43988) *(G-16817)*
Tappan Marina, Scio *Also called Tappan Lake Marina Inc (G-16817)*
Tara Flaherty....419 565-1334
1872 White Pine Dr Mansfield (44904) *(G-13372)*
Taragon Advisors, Cleveland *Also called Real Estate Capital Fund LLC (G-6358)*
Target Auto Body Inc....216 391-1942
5005 Carnegie Ave Cleveland (44103) *(G-6570)*
Target Corporation....513 671-8603
900 E Kemper Rd Cincinnati (45246) *(G-4625)*
Target Corporation....614 801-6700
1 Walker Way West Jefferson (43162) *(G-19255)*
Target Stores Inc....614 279-4224
3720 Soldano Blvd Columbus (43228) *(G-8822)*
Target Trans-Logic, Austintown *Also called 44444 LLC (G-867)*
Tarrier Foods Corp....614 876-8594
2700 International St # 100 Columbus (43228) *(G-8823)*
Tarsec, Columbus *Also called Norfolk Southern Corporation (G-8284)*
Tarta, Toledo *Also called Toledo Area Rgional Trnst Auth (G-18227)*
Tartan Fields Golf Club Ltd....614 792-0900
8070 Tartan Fields Dr Dublin (43017) *(G-10473)*
Tasc of Northwest Ohio Inc (PA)....419 242-9955
701 Jefferson Ave Ste 101 Toledo (43604) *(G-18214)*
Tasc of Southeast Ohio....740 594-2276
86 Columbus Rd Athens (45701) *(G-814)*
Tasco Inc Ohio, Cleveland *Also called Telemessaging Services Inc (G-6579)*
Tasty Pure Food Company (PA)....330 434-8141
1557 Industrial Pkwy Akron (44310) *(G-471)*
Tata America Intl Corp....513 677-6500
1000 Summit Dr Unit 1 Milford (45150) *(G-14565)*
Tata Consultancy Services, Milford *Also called Tata America Intl Corp (G-14565)*
Tatman, Harold & Sons, Kingston *Also called Harold Tatman & Sons Entps Inc (G-12450)*
Tax Department, Coldwater *Also called Village of Coldwater (G-6837)*
Taylor - Winfield Corporation....330 797-0300
3200 Innovation Pl Youngstown (44509) *(G-20387)*
Taylor Chevrolet Inc....740 653-2091
2510 N Memorial Dr Lancaster (43130) *(G-12579)*
Taylor Communications, Dayton *Also called Standard Register Inc (G-9903)*
Taylor Construction Company....330 628-9310
1532 State Route 43 Mogadore (44260) *(G-14684)*
Taylor Corporation....419 420-0790
1920 Breckenridge Rd # 110 Findlay (45840) *(G-11091)*
Taylor Dealership, Lancaster *Also called Taylor Chevrolet Inc (G-12579)*
Taylor Distributing Company....513 771-1850
2875 E Sharon Rd Cincinnati (45241) *(G-4626)*
Taylor House, Findlay *Also called Taylor Corporation (G-11091)*
Taylor Made Graphics....440 882-6318
7921 Hollenbeck Cir Cleveland (44129) *(G-6571)*
Taylor Murtis Human Svcs Sys....216 283-4400
12395 Mccracken Rd Cleveland (44125) *(G-6572)*
Taylor Murtis Human Svcs Sys (PA)....216 283-4400
13422 Kinsman Rd Cleveland (44120) *(G-6573)*
Taylor Murtis Human Svcs Sys....216 281-7192
3167 Fulton Rd Cleveland (44109) *(G-6574)*
Taylor Stn Surgical Ctr Ltd....614 751-4466
275 Taylor Station Rd Ab Columbus (43213) *(G-8824)*
Taylor Strategy Partners LLC (PA)....614 436-6650
8000 Ravines Edge Ct # 200 Columbus (43235) *(G-8825)*
Taylor Telecommunications Inc....330 628-5501
3470 Gilchrist Rd Mogadore (44260) *(G-14685)*
Taylor Warehouse Corporation....513 771-2956
2875 E Sharon Rd Cincinnati (45241) *(G-4627)*
Taylors Staffing....740 446-3305
37817 State Route 124 Pomeroy (45769) *(G-16236)*
Tazmanian Freight Fwdg Inc (PA)....216 265-7881
6640 Engle Rd Ste A Middleburg Heights (44130) *(G-14387)*
Tazmanian Freight Systems, Middleburg Heights *Also called Tazmanian Freight Fwdg Inc (G-14387)*
Tbn Acquisition LLC....740 653-2091
2480 N Memorial Dr Lancaster (43130) *(G-12580)*
TCI, Cincinnati *Also called Technical Consultants Inc (G-4629)*
TCI 214, Pemberville *Also called Tire Centers LLC (G-15945)*
Tcn Behavioral Health Svcs Inc (PA)....937 376-8700
452 W Market St Xenia (45385) *(G-20077)*
TCS, Cincinnati *Also called Trans-Continental Systems Inc (G-4678)*
Tdci, Columbus *Also called Infor (us) Inc (G-6886)*
Tdk Refrigeration Leasing, Delphos *Also called All Temp Refrigeration Inc (G-10137)*
TDS Document Management Ltd....614 367-9633
161 Jackson St Columbus (43206) *(G-8826)*
Team Green Lawn LLC....937 673-4315
1070 Union Rd Xenia (45385) *(G-20078)*
Team Industrial Services Inc....440 498-9494
5901 Harper Rd Cleveland (44139) *(G-6575)*
Team Management Inc....614 486-0864
2018 N 4th St Columbus (43201) *(G-8827)*
Team NEO....216 363-5400
1111 Superior Ave E # 1600 Cleveland (44114) *(G-6576)*
Team Rahal Inc....614 529-7000
4601 Lyman Dr Hilliard (43026) *(G-11957)*
Team Rahal of Dayton Inc (PA)....937 438-3800
8111 Yankee St Dayton (45458) *(G-9921)*
Team Sports LLC....419 865-8326
6232 Merger Dr Holland (43528) *(G-12059)*
Teasdale Fenton Carpet Cleanin....513 797-0900
12145 Centron Pl Cincinnati (45246) *(G-4628)*
Teater Orthopedic Surgeons....330 343-3335
515 Union Ave Ste 167 Dover (44622) *(G-10216)*
Tebo Financial Services Inc....234 207-2500
4740 Belpar St Nw Ste A Canton (44718) *(G-2558)*
Tech Center Inc....330 762-6212
265 S Main St Ste 200 Akron (44308) *(G-472)*
Tech International, Johnstown *Also called Technical Rubber Company Inc (G-12343)*
Tech Mahindra (americas) Inc....216 912-2002
200 W Prospect Ave Cleveland (44113) *(G-6577)*
Tech Pro Inc....330 923-3546
3030 Gilchrist Rd Akron (44305) *(G-473)*
Tech Products Corporation (HQ)....937 438-1100
2215 Lyons Rd Miamisburg (45342) *(G-14355)*
Techdisposal, Reynoldsburg *Also called Datacomm Tech (G-16444)*
Techna Glass Inc....513 685-3800
904 State Route 28 Milford (45150) *(G-14566)*
Techncal Sltons Spcialists Inc....513 792-8930
4250 Creek Rd Blue Ash (45241) *(G-1693)*

ALPHABETIC

Technical Assurance Inc......440 953-3147
38112 2nd St Willoughby (44094) ***(G-19717)***
Technical Construction Spc......330 929-1088
3341 Cavalier Trl Cuyahoga Falls (44224) ***(G-9224)***
Technical Consultants Inc......513 521-2696
8228 Winton Rd Ste 200a Cincinnati (45231) ***(G-4629)***
Technical Consumer Pdts Inc......800 324-1496
325 Campus Dr Aurora (44202) ***(G-856)***
Technical Rubber Company Inc (PA)......740 967-9015
200 E Coshocton St Johnstown (43031) ***(G-12343)***
Technicolor Entertainment Svcs, Wilmington *Also called Technicolor Thomson Group* ***(G-19790)***
Technicolor Thomson Group......937 383-6000
3418 Progress Way Wilmington (45177) ***(G-19790)***
Technology House Ltd (PA)......440 248-3025
10036 Aurora Hudson Rd Streetsboro (44241) ***(G-17434)***
Technology Hub, Columbus *Also called Km2 Solutions LLC* ***(G-7999)***
Technology Recovery Group Ltd (PA)......440 250-9970
31390 Viking Pkwy Westlake (44145) ***(G-19554)***
Techsoft Systems Inc......513 772-5010
10296 Springfield Pike Cincinnati (45215) ***(G-4630)***
Techsolve Inc......513 948-2000
6705 Steger Dr Cincinnati (45237) ***(G-4631)***
Tecta America Corp......419 447-1716
1480 S County Road 594 Tiffin (44883) ***(G-17703)***
Tecta America Zero Company LLC (HQ)......513 541-1848
6225 Wiehe Rd Cincinnati (45237) ***(G-4632)***
Ted Graham......740 223-3509
3007 Harding Hwy E Marion (43302) ***(G-13584)***
Ted Ruck Co Inc......419 738-2613
101 N Wood St Wapakoneta (45895) ***(G-18808)***
Tegam Inc (PA)......440 466-6100
10 Tegam Way Geneva (44041) ***(G-11369)***
Tek Systems......614 789-6200
5115 Prkcnter Ave Ste 170 Dublin (43017) ***(G-10474)***
Tek-Collect Incorporated......614 299-2766
871 Park St Columbus (43215) ***(G-8828)***
Tekmar-Dohrmann, Mason *Also called Teledyne Tekmar Company* ***(G-13768)***
Tekni-Plex Inc......419 491-2407
1445 Timber Wolf Dr Holland (43528) ***(G-12060)***
Teknobility LLC......216 255-9433
3013 Gary Kyle Ct Medina (44256) ***(G-14133)***
Teknol Inc (PA)......937 264-0190
5751 Webster St Dayton (45414) ***(G-9922)***
Teksystems Inc......216 606-3600
5990 W Creek Rd Ste 175 Independence (44131) ***(G-12265)***
Teksystems Inc......513 719-3950
3825 Edwards Rd Ste 500 Cincinnati (45209) ***(G-4633)***
Teksystems 611, Cincinnati *Also called Teksystems Inc* ***(G-4633)***
Telamon Corporation......937 254-2004
600 N Irwin St Dayton (45403) ***(G-9923)***
Telarc International Corp (PA)......216 464-2313
23412 Commerce Park Beachwood (44122) ***(G-1130)***
Telcom Construction Svcs Inc......330 239-6900
5067 Paramount Dr Medina (44256) ***(G-14134)***
Tele-Solutions Inc (PA)......330 782-2888
6001 Suthern Blvd Ste 102 Youngstown (44512) ***(G-20388)***
Tele-Vac Environmental, Mason *Also called J and J Environmental Inc* ***(G-13725)***
Telecmmnctons Stffing Slutions......614 799-9300
8191 Glencree Pl Dublin (43016) ***(G-10475)***
Telecom Expertise Inds Inc (PA)......937 548-5254
5879 Jysville St Johns Rd Greenville (45331) ***(G-11521)***
Teledyne Instruments Inc......513 229-7000
4736 Scialville Foster Rd Mason (45040) ***(G-13767)***
Teledyne Tekmar, Mason *Also called Teledyne Instruments Inc* ***(G-13767)***
Teledyne Tekmar Company (HQ)......513 229-7000
4736 Scialville Foster Rd Mason (45040) ***(G-13768)***
Telemaxx Communications LLC (PA)......216 371-8800
2150 Lee Rd Cleveland (44118) ***(G-6578)***
Telemessaging Services Inc......440 845-5400
7441 W Ridgewood Dr # 130 Cleveland (44129) ***(G-6579)***
Telepage Communication Systems, Marietta *Also called Twin Comm Inc* ***(G-13508)***
Teleperformance USA, Akron *Also called Tpusa Inc* ***(G-479)***
Teleperformance USA, Columbus *Also called Tpusa Inc* ***(G-8860)***
Telephone & Cmpt Contrs Inc......419 726-8142
5560 308th St Toledo (43611) ***(G-18215)***
Telephone Service Company, Wapakoneta *Also called TSC Communications Inc* ***(G-18810)***
Telephony & Data Solutions, Dublin *Also called Microman Inc* ***(G-10397)***
Teletronic Services Inc (PA)......216 778-6500
22550 Ascoa Ct Strongsville (44149) ***(G-17515)***
Teletronics Communications, Strongsville *Also called Teletronic Services Inc* ***(G-17515)***
Telhio Credit Union Inc (PA)......614 221-3233
96 N 4th St Columbus (43215) ***(G-8829)***
Telhio Credit Union Inc......614 221-3233
201 Outerbelt St Columbus (43213) ***(G-8830)***
Telinx Solutions LLC......330 819-0657
961 Mallet Hill Ct Medina (44256) ***(G-14135)***
Telligen Tech Inc......614 934-1554
2740 Airport Dr Ste 190 Columbus (43219) ***(G-8831)***
Tembec Btlsr Inc......419 244-5856
2112 Sylvan Ave Toledo (43606) ***(G-18216)***
Tems, Toronto *Also called Toronto Emergency Medical Svc* ***(G-18339)***
Ten Thusand Villages Cleveland......216 575-1058
12425 Cedar Rd Cleveland (44106) ***(G-6580)***
Tenable Protective Svcs Inc (PA)......216 361-0002
2423 Payne Ave Cleveland (44114) ***(G-6581)***
Tenable Protective Svcs Inc......513 741-3560
5643 Cheviot Rd Ste 5 Cincinnati (45247) ***(G-4634)***
Tender Mercies Inc (PA)......513 721-8666
27 W 12th St Cincinnati (45202) ***(G-4635)***
Tender Nursing Care......614 856-3508
7668 Slate Ridge Blvd Reynoldsburg (43068) ***(G-16482)***
Tendon Manufacturing Inc......216 663-3200
20805 Aurora Rd Cleveland (44146) ***(G-6582)***
Tennis Unlimited Inc......330 928-8763
2108 Akron Peninsula Rd Akron (44313) ***(G-474)***
Tensile Testing, Cleveland *Also called J T Adams Co Inc* ***(G-5844)***
Teradata Corporation (PA)......866 548-8348
10000 Innovation Dr Miamisburg (45342) ***(G-14356)***
Teradata Operations Inc (HQ)......937 242-4030
10000 Innovation Dr Miamisburg (45342) ***(G-14357)***
Terence Isakov MD......440 449-1014
5187 Mayfield Rd Ste 102 Cleveland (44124) ***(G-6583)***
Terex Utilities Inc......614 444-7373
110 Venture Dr Etna (43062) ***(G-10739)***
Terex Utilities Inc......937 293-6526
4401 Gateway Blvd Springfield (45502) ***(G-17287)***
Terex Utilities Inc......513 539-9770
920 Deneen Ave Monroe (45050) ***(G-14714)***
Terik Roofing Inc......330 785-0060
72 Hanna Pkwy Coventry Township (44319) ***(G-9134)***
Terminal Ready-Mix Inc......440 288-0181
524 Colorado Ave Lorain (44052) ***(G-13081)***
Terminal Warehouse Inc......330 453-3709
2207 Kimball Rd Se Canton (44707) ***(G-2559)***
Terminal Warehouse Inc (HQ)......330 773-2056
1779 Marvo Dr Akron (44306) ***(G-475)***
Terminix Intl Co Ltd Partnr......513 942-6670
4305 Muhlhauser Rd Ste 2 Fairfield (45014) ***(G-10913)***
Terminix Intl Co Ltd Partnr......216 518-1091
5350 Transportation Blvd Cleveland (44125) ***(G-6584)***
Terminix Intl Co Ltd Partnr......419 868-8290
6541 Weatherfield Ct Maumee (43537) ***(G-13986)***
Terminix Intl Co Ltd Partnr......513 539-7846
4455 Salman Rd Middletown (45044) ***(G-14466)***
Terminix Intl Co Ltd Partnr......978 744-2402
2680 Roberts Ave Nw Ste A Canton (44709) ***(G-2560)***
Terminix Intl Coml Xenia......513 539-7846
4455 Salzman Rd Middletown (45044) ***(G-14467)***
Terrace Construction Co Inc......216 739-3170
3965 Pearl Rd Cleveland (44109) ***(G-6585)***
Terrace Park Country Club Inc......513 965-4061
5341 S Milford Rd Milford (45150) ***(G-14567)***
Terracon Consultants Inc......513 321-5816
611 Lunken Park Dr Cincinnati (45226) ***(G-4636)***
Terracon Consultants Inc......614 863-3113
800 Morrison Rd Gahanna (43230) ***(G-11273)***
Terracon Consultants N1, Cincinnati *Also called Terracon Consultants Inc* ***(G-4636)***
Terracon Consultants N4, Gahanna *Also called Terracon Consultants Inc* ***(G-11273)***
Terrafirm Construction LLC......913 433-2998
250 N Hartford Ave Columbus (43222) ***(G-8832)***
Terre Forme Enterprises Inc......330 847-6800
3000 Austintown Warren Rd Mineral Ridge (44440) ***(G-14640)***
Terry Asphalt Materials Inc (HQ)......513 874-6192
8600 Bilstein Blvd Hamilton (45015) ***(G-11777)***
Terry J Reppa & Associates......440 888-8533
7029 Pearl Rd Ste 350 Cleveland (44130) ***(G-6586)***
Tersher Corporation......440 439-8383
17000 Foltz Pkwy Strongsville (44149) ***(G-17516)***
Tersigni Cargill Entps LLC......330 351-0942
4315 Hudson Dr Stow (44224) ***(G-17396)***
Tesar Industrial Contrs Inc (PA)......216 741-8008
3920 Jennings Rd Cleveland (44109) ***(G-6587)***
Tesco-Transportion Eqp Sls......419 836-2835
6401 Seaman Rd Oregon (43616) ***(G-15751)***
Test America, North Canton *Also called Emlab P&K LLC* ***(G-15335)***
Testa Enterprises Inc......330 926-9060
2335 2nd St Ste A Cuyahoga Falls (44221) ***(G-9225)***
Testamerica Laboratories Inc (HQ)......800 456-9396
4101 Shuffel St Nw North Canton (44720) ***(G-15372)***
Testamerica Laboratories Inc......513 733-5700
11416 Reading Rd Cincinnati (45241) ***(G-4637)***
Testamerica Laboratories Inc......937 294-6856
2017 Springboro W Moraine (45439) ***(G-14830)***
Testing and Inspection Fcilty, Troy *Also called Public Safety Ohio Department* ***(G-18372)***
Tetra Tech Inc......513 251-2730
250 W Court St Ste 200w Cincinnati (45202) ***(G-4638)***
Teva Womens Health Inc (HQ)......513 731-9900
5040 Duramed Rd Cincinnati (45213) ***(G-4639)***
Texas Eastern Transmission LP......513 932-1816
1157 W State Route 122 Lebanon (45036) ***(G-12653)***
Texas Infusion Partners, Cincinnati *Also called Infusion Partners Inc* ***(G-3818)***

Texo International Inc........513 731-6350
2828 Highland Ave Norwood (45212) *(G-15600)*
Tfh-Eb Inc........614 253-7246
550 Schrock Rd Columbus (43229) *(G-8833)*
Tfi Transportation Inc........330 332-4655
10370 W South Range Rd Salem (44460) *(G-16717)*
TH Martin Inc........216 741-2020
8500 Brookpark Rd Cleveland (44129) *(G-6588)*
Th Services........740 258-9054
12151 Bolen Rd Ne Newark (43055) *(G-15238)*
Tharaldson Hospitality MGT........513 947-9402
4521 Eastgate Blvd Cincinnati (45245) *(G-2935)*
Thayer Power & Comm Line, Reynoldsburg *Also called Thayer Pwr Comm Line Cnstr LLC (G-16483)*
Thayer Pwr Comm Line Cnstr LLC (PA)........814 474-1174
117 Cypress St Sw Reynoldsburg (43068) *(G-16483)*
The Abbewood, Elyria *Also called Abbewood Limited Partnership (G-10591)*
The Anter Brothers Company (PA)........216 252-4555
12501 Elmwood Ave Cleveland (44111) *(G-6589)*
The C-Z Company (PA)........740 432-6334
201 Wheeling Ave Cambridge (43725) *(G-2131)*
The Cadle Company (PA)........330 872-0918
100 N Center St Newton Falls (44444) *(G-15278)*
The Cincinnati Cordage Ppr Co........513 242-3600
800 E Ross Ave Cincinnati (45217) *(G-4640)*
The Cleveland-Cliffs Iron Co........216 694-5700
1100 Superior Ave E # 1500 Cleveland (44114) *(G-6590)*
The Columbia Oil Co........513 868-8700
4951 Hmlton Middletown Rd Liberty Twp (45011) *(G-12728)*
The Cortland Sav & Bnkg Co (HQ)........330 637-8040
194 W Main St Cortland (44410) *(G-9083)*
The Cottingham Paper Co........614 294-6444
324 E 2nd Ave Columbus (43201) *(G-8834)*
The Daimler Group Inc........614 488-4424
1533 Lake Shore Dr Columbus (43204) *(G-8835)*
The Famous Manufacturing Co........330 762-9621
2620 Ridgewood Rd Ste 200 Akron (44313) *(G-476)*
The First Central National Bnk (PA)........937 663-4186
103 S Springfield St Saint Paris (43072) *(G-16686)*
The Foodbank Inc........937 461-0265
56 Armor Pl Dayton (45417) *(G-9924)*
The For Cincinnati Association (PA)........513 744-3344
650 Walnut St Cincinnati (45202) *(G-4641)*
The For National Association........937 470-1059
4215 Breezewood Ave Dayton (45406) *(G-9925)*
The Fountain On The Greens, Cleveland *Also called Greens of Lyndhurst The Inc (G-5704)*
The Good Shepherd, Ashland *Also called Good Shepherd Home For Aged (G-680)*
The Healthcare Connection Inc (PA)........513 588-3623
1401 Steffen Ave Cincinnati (45215) *(G-4642)*
The Huntington Investment Co (HQ)........614 480-3600
41 S High St Fl 7 Columbus (43215) *(G-8836)*
The Huntington Investment Co........513 351-2555
525 Vine St Ste 2100 Cincinnati (45202) *(G-4643)*
The In Cincinnati Playhouse........513 421-3888
962 Mount Adams Cir Cincinnati (45202) *(G-4644)*
The Interlake Steamship Co........440 260-6900
7300 Engle Rd Middleburg Heights (44130) *(G-14388)*
The Liberty Nat Bankof Ada........419 673-1217
100 E Franklin St Kenton (43326) *(G-12424)*
The Maids........440 735-6243
23480 Aurora Rd Ste 1 Bedford Heights (44146) *(G-1360)*
The Maple City Ice Company (PA)........419 668-2531
371 Cleveland Rd Norwalk (44857) *(G-15594)*
The Maple City Ice Company........419 747-4777
1245 W Longview Ave Mansfield (44906) *(G-13373)*
The Maria-Joseph Center........937 278-2692
4830 Salem Ave Dayton (45416) *(G-9926)*
The Mau-Sherwood Supply Co (PA)........330 405-1200
8400 Darrow Rd Ste 1 Twinsburg (44087) *(G-18475)*
The Middlefield Banking Co (HQ)........440 632-1666
15985 E High St Middlefield (44062) *(G-14403)*
The Nature Conservancy........614 717-2770
6375 Riverside Dr Ste 100 Dublin (43017) *(G-10476)*
The Oaks Lodge........330 769-2601
5878 Longacre Ln Chippewa Lake (44215) *(G-2899)*
The Pavilion, Sidney *Also called Shelby County Mem Hosp Assn (G-16953)*
The Peck-Hannaford Briggs Co (PA)........513 681-4600
4670 Chester Ave Cincinnati (45232) *(G-4645)*
The Peoples Bank Co Inc (PA)........419 678-2385
112 W Main St 114 Coldwater (45828) *(G-6835)*
The Peoples Bank Co Inc........419 678-2385
112 W Main St Coldwater (45828) *(G-6836)*
The Peoples Savings and Ln Co (PA)........937 653-1600
10 Monument Sq Urbana (43078) *(G-18601)*
The Sheakley Group Inc (PA)........513 771-2277
1 Sheakley Way Ste 100 Cincinnati (45246) *(G-4646)*
The Surgery Center, Cleveland *Also called HCA Holdings Inc (G-5734)*
The Villa At Lake MGT Co........440 599-1999
48 Parrish Rd Ofc Conneaut (44030) *(G-9048)*
Theatre Management Corporation........513 723-1180
125 E Court St Ste 1000 Cincinnati (45202) *(G-4647)*

Thelen Associates Inc........513 825-4350
1780 Carillion Blvd Cincinnati (45240) *(G-4648)*
Theodore C Rumpke, Cincinnati *Also called T C Rumpke Waste Collection (G-4612)*
Therapeutic Riding Center Inc........440 708-0013
16497 Snyder Rd Chagrin Falls (44023) *(G-2736)*
Therapy In Motion LLC........216 459-2846
5000 Rockside Rd Ste 500 Independence (44131) *(G-12266)*
Therapy Support Inc........513 469-6999
4351 Creek Rd Blue Ash (45241) *(G-1694)*
Theratrust........740 345-7688
23 Forry St Newark (43055) *(G-15239)*
Thermal Solutions Inc........513 742-2836
9491 Seward Rd Fairfield (45014) *(G-10914)*
Thermal Solutions Inc........740 886-2861
9329 County Road 107 Proctorville (45669) *(G-16362)*
Thermal Treatment Center Inc (HQ)........216 881-8100
1101 E 55th St Cleveland (44103) *(G-6591)*
Thermaltech Engineering Inc (PA)........513 561-2271
3960 Red Bank Rd Ste 250 Cincinnati (45227) *(G-4649)*
Thermo Fisher Scientific Inc........800 871-8909
1 Thermo Fisher Way Oakwood Village (44146) *(G-15635)*
Thermo King, Cincinnati *Also called Transport Specialists Inc (G-4680)*
Thermo-TEC Insulation Inc........216 663-3842
1415 E 222nd St Euclid (44117) *(G-10779)*
Thiels Replacement Systems Inc........419 289-6139
419 E 8th St Ashland (44805) *(G-701)*
Things Remembered Inc (PA)........440 473-2000
5500 Avion Park Dr Highland Heights (44143) *(G-11872)*
Think Patented, Miamisburg *Also called Patented Acquisition Corp (G-14332)*
THINK TV, Dayton *Also called Greater Dayton Public TV (G-9587)*
Think-Ability LLC........419 589-2238
1256 Warner Ave Mansfield (44905) *(G-13374)*
Thinkpath Engineering Svcs LLC (PA)........937 291-8374
9080 Springboro Pike # 300 Miamisburg (45342) *(G-14358)*
Thinktv Network........937 220-1600
110 S Jefferson St Dayton (45402) *(G-9927)*
Thinkware Incorporated........513 598-3300
7611 Cheviot Rd Ste 2 Cincinnati (45247) *(G-4650)*
Third Dimension Inc (PA)........877 926-3223
633 Pleasant Ave Geneva (44041) *(G-11370)*
Third Federal Savings (HQ)........800 844-7333
7007 Broadway Ave Cleveland (44105) *(G-6592)*
Third Federal Savings........440 885-4900
5950 Ridge Rd Cleveland (44129) *(G-6593)*
Third Federal Savings........440 716-1865
26949 Lorain Rd North Olmsted (44070) *(G-15448)*
Third Federal Savings........440 843-6300
6849 Pearl Rd Cleveland (44130) *(G-6594)*
Third Federal Savings & Loan, Cleveland *Also called Third Federal Savings (G-6594)*
Third Savings, Piqua *Also called Unity National Bank (G-16171)*
Thistledown Inc........216 662-8600
21501 Emery Rd Cleveland (44128) *(G-6595)*
Thistledown Racetrack, Cleveland *Also called Thistledown Inc (G-6595)*
Thoman Weil Moving & Stor Co........513 251-5000
5151 Fischer Ave Cincinnati (45217) *(G-4651)*
Thomarios, Copley *Also called Apostolos Group Inc (G-9052)*
Thomas & Thomas, Cincinnati *Also called Ernest V Thomas Jr (G-3574)*
Thomas A Wildey School, Owensville *Also called Developmental Disabilities (G-15809)*
Thomas and Associates........330 494-2111
1421 Portage St Nw Ste C Canton (44720) *(G-2561)*
Thomas and King Inc........614 527-0571
5561 Wstchster Woods Blvd Hilliard (43026) *(G-11958)*
Thomas Do-It Center Inc (PA)........740 446-2002
176 Mccormick Rd Gallipolis (45631) *(G-11339)*
Thomas Door Controls Inc........614 263-1756
4196 Indianola Ave Columbus (43214) *(G-8837)*
Thomas E Anderson DDS Inc........330 467-6466
147 E Aurora Rd Northfield (44067) *(G-15525)*
Thomas E Keller Trucking Inc........419 784-4805
24862 Elliott Rd Defiance (43512) *(G-10061)*
Thomas E Rojewski MD Inc........740 454-0158
2945 Maple Ave Zanesville (43701) *(G-20538)*
Thomas Gentz........513 247-7300
10284 Falling Waters Ln Cincinnati (45241) *(G-4652)*
Thomas Glass Company Inc (PA)........614 268-8611
400 E Wilson Bridge Rd A Worthington (43085) *(G-20003)*
Thomas J Dyer Company (PA)........513 321-8100
5240 Lester Rd Cincinnati (45213) *(G-4653)*
Thomas L Miller........740 374-3041
111 Strecker Hl Marietta (45750) *(G-13503)*
Thomas L Stover Inc........330 665-8060
754 S Cleveland Ave # 300 Mogadore (44260) *(G-14686)*
Thomas Packer & Co (PA)........330 533-9777
6601 Westford Pl Ste 101 Canfield (44406) *(G-2212)*
Thomas R Truitt Od........937 644-8637
1001 W 5th St Marysville (43040) *(G-13655)*
Thomas Rental, Gallipolis *Also called Thomas Do-It Center Inc (G-11339)*
Thomas Rosser........614 890-2900
855 S Sunbury Rd Westerville (43081) *(G-19444)*
Thomas Transport Delivery Inc........330 908-3100
9055 Freeway Dr Unit 1 Macedonia (44056) *(G-13212)*

(PA)=Parent Co (HQ)=Headquarters (DH)=Div Headquarters
2018 Harris Ohio Services Directory
1337

Thomas Trucking Inc ...513 731-8411
2558 Apple Ridge Ln Cincinnati (45236) ***(G-4654)***
Thomas W Ruff and Company ...800 828-0234
855 Grandview Ave Ste 2 Columbus (43215) ***(G-8838)***
Thompkins Child Adlescent Svcs ...740 622-4470
1199 S 2nd St Coshocton (43812) ***(G-9118)***
Thompson Capri Lanes Inc ...614 888-3159
5860 Roche Dr Columbus (43229) ***(G-8839)***
Thompson Concrete Ltd ...740 756-7256
6182 Winchester Rd Carroll (43112) ***(G-2609)***
Thompson Electric Inc ...330 686-2300
49 Northmoreland Ave Munroe Falls (44262) ***(G-14933)***
Thompson Hall & Jordan Fnrl HM, Cincinnati *Also called Domajaparo Inc* ***(G-3497)***
Thompson Hall & Jordan Fnrl HM ...513 761-8881
400 N Wayne Ave Cincinnati (45215) ***(G-4655)***
Thompson Heating & Cooling ...513 242-4450
800 E Ross Ave Cincinnati (45217) ***(G-4656)***
Thompson Heating Corporation ...513 769-7696
6 N Commerce Park Dr Cincinnati (45215) ***(G-4657)***
Thompson Hine LLP ...614 469-3200
10 W Broad St Ste 700 Columbus (43215) ***(G-8840)***
Thompson Hine LLP ...614 469-3200
41 S High St Ste 1700 Columbus (43215) ***(G-8841)***
Thompson Hine LLP ...937 443-6859
10050 Innovation Dr # 400 Miamisburg (45342) ***(G-14359)***
Thompson Hine LLP (PA) ...216 566-5500
127 Public Sq Cleveland (44114) ***(G-6596)***
Thompson Plumbing Htg Coolg, Cincinnati *Also called Thompson Heating Corporation* ***(G-4657)***
Thompson Steel Company Inc ...937 236-6940
3911 Dayton Park Dr Dayton (45414) ***(G-9928)***
Thomsons Landscaping ...740 374-9353
26130 State Route 7 Marietta (45750) ***(G-13504)***
Thor Construction, Columbus *Also called Central Ohio Building Co Inc* ***(G-7229)***
Thornton Landscape Inc ...513 683-8100
424 E Us Highway 22 And 3 Maineville (45039) ***(G-13247)***
Thornville NH LLC ...740 246-5253
14100 Zion Rd Thornville (43076) ***(G-17669)***
Thornvlle Hlth Rhblitation Ctr, Thornville *Also called Thornville NH LLC* ***(G-17669)***
Thorsens Greenhouse LLC ...740 363-5069
2069 Hyatts Rd Delaware (43015) ***(G-10129)***
Thorson Baker & Assoc Inc (PA) ...330 659-6688
3030 W Streetsboro Rd Richfield (44286) ***(G-16530)***
Thos A Lupica ...419 252-6298
608 Madison Ave Ste 1000 Toledo (43604) ***(G-18217)***
Thp Limited Inc ...513 241-3222
100 E 8th St Ste 3 Cincinnati (45202) ***(G-4658)***
Thrasher Dinsmore & Dolan (PA) ...440 285-2242
100 7th Ave Ste 150 Chardon (44024) ***(G-2771)***
Thrasher Disnmore & Doland, Chardon *Also called Thrasher Dinsmore & Dolan* ***(G-2771)***
Thread Information Design Inc ...419 887-6801
4635 W Alexis Rd Toledo (43623) ***(G-18218)***
Thread Marketing Group, Toledo *Also called Thread Information Design Inc* ***(G-18218)***
Three C Body Shop Inc (PA) ...614 274-9700
2300 Briggs Rd Columbus (43223) ***(G-8842)***
Three C Body Shop Inc ...614 885-0900
8321 N High St Columbus (43235) ***(G-8843)***
Three D Golf LLC ...513 732-0295
2000 Elklick Rd Batavia (45103) ***(G-1027)***
Three D Metals Inc (PA) ...330 220-0451
5462 Innovation Dr Valley City (44280) ***(G-18625)***
Three M Associates ...330 674-9646
7488 State Route 241 Millersburg (44654) ***(G-14624)***
Three Rivers Energy LLC ...740 623-3035
18137 County Road 271 Coshocton (43812) ***(G-9119)***
Three Rivers Heating & Air, Cincinnati *Also called Apollo Heating and AC Inc* ***(G-3036)***
Three Village Condominium ...440 461-1483
5150 Three Village Dr Cleveland (44124) ***(G-6597)***
Three-D Transport Inc ...419 924-5368
14237 Us Highway 127 West Unity (43570) ***(G-19281)***
Thrifty Car Rental, Cleveland *Also called Thrifty Rent-A-Car System Inc* ***(G-6598)***
Thrifty Rent-A-Car System Inc ...440 842-1660
7701 Day Dr Cleveland (44129) ***(G-6598)***
Thriverx, Cincinnati *Also called Biorx LLC* ***(G-3109)***
Thurns Bakery & Deli ...614 221-9246
541 S 3rd St Columbus (43215) ***(G-8844)***
Thyssen Krupp Logistics, Northwood *Also called Tkx Logistics* ***(G-15546)***
Thyssenkrupp Bilstein Amer Inc (HQ) ...513 881-7600
8685 Bilstein Blvd Hamilton (45015) ***(G-11778)***
Thyssenkrupp Bilstein Amer Inc ...513 881-7600
4440 Muhlhauser Rd West Chester (45011) ***(G-19162)***
Thyssenkrupp Elevator Corp ...440 717-0080
9200 Market Pl Broadview Heights (44147) ***(G-1893)***
Thyssenkrupp Elevator Corp ...513 241-6000
934 Dalton Ave Cincinnati (45203) ***(G-4659)***
Thyssenkrupp Elevator Corp ...614 895-8930
929 Eastwind Dr Ste 218 Westerville (43081) ***(G-19445)***
Thyssenkrupp Logistics Inc (HQ) ...419 662-1800
8001 Thyssenkrupp Pkwy Northwood (43619) ***(G-15545)***
Thyssenkrupp Materials NA Inc ...216 883-8100
6050 Oak Tree Blvd # 110 Independence (44131) ***(G-12267)***
Thyssenkrupp Materials NA Inc ...937 898-7400
10100 Innovation Dr # 210 Miamisburg (45342) ***(G-14360)***
Thyssenkrupp Materials NA Inc ...440 234-7500
17901 Englewood Dr Cleveland (44130) ***(G-6599)***
Tier One Distribution LLC ...937 323-6325
2105 Sheridan Ave Springfield (45505) ***(G-17288)***
Tiffany's Banquet Center, Brookfield *Also called A Tara Tiffanys Property* ***(G-1896)***
Tiffin Cmnty YMCA Rcration Ctr (PA) ...419 447-8711
180 Summit St Tiffin (44883) ***(G-17704)***
Tiffin Developmental Center, Tiffin *Also called Ohio Department of Health* ***(G-17690)***
Tiffin Loader Crane Company ...419 448-8156
4151 W State Route 18 Tiffin (44883) ***(G-17705)***
Tiffin Paper Company (PA) ...419 447-2121
265 6th Ave Tiffin (44883) ***(G-17706)***
Tiffin Womens Care, Findlay *Also called Findlay Womens Care LLC* ***(G-11030)***
Tiger 2010 LLC (PA) ...330 236-5100
6929 Portage St Nw North Canton (44720) ***(G-15373)***
Tiki Bowling Lanes Inc ...740 654-4513
1521 Tiki Ln Lancaster (43130) ***(G-12581)***
Tiki Lounge & Restaurant, Lancaster *Also called Tiki Bowling Lanes Inc* ***(G-12581)***
Tilden Mining Company LC (HQ) ...216 694-5700
200 Public Sq Ste 3300 Cleveland (44114) ***(G-6600)***
Tim Mundy ...937 862-8686
3159 State Route 42 Spring Valley (45370) ***(G-17111)***
Timbertop Apartments, Akron *Also called Bernard Busson Builder* ***(G-99)***
Timco Rubber Products Inc (PA) ...216 267-6242
125 Blaze Industrial Pkwy Berea (44017) ***(G-1473)***
Time Staffing, Fremont *Also called Doepker Group Inc* ***(G-11195)***
Time Warner, Columbus *Also called Spectrum MGT Holdg Co LLC* ***(G-8759)***
Time Warner, Zanesville *Also called Spectrum MGT Holdg Co LLC* ***(G-20537)***
Time Warner, Warren *Also called Spectrum MGT Holdg Co LLC* ***(G-18901)***
Time Warner, Port Clinton *Also called Spectrum MGT Holdg Co LLC* ***(G-16256)***
Time Warner, Chillicothe *Also called Spectrum MGT Holdg Co LLC* ***(G-2888)***
Time Warner, Columbus *Also called Spectrum MGT Holdg Co LLC* ***(G-8760)***
Time Warner, Springfield *Also called Spectrum MGT Holdg Co LLC* ***(G-17276)***
Time Warner, Lancaster *Also called Spectrum MGT Holdg Co LLC* ***(G-12576)***
Time Warner, Dayton *Also called Spectrum MGT Holdg Co LLC* ***(G-9897)***
Time Warner Cable, Akron *Also called Level 3 Telecom LLC* ***(G-316)***
Time Warner Cable, Cincinnati *Also called Level 3 Telecom LLC* ***(G-3970)***
Time Warner Cable, Cincinnati *Also called Level 3 Telecom LLC* ***(G-3971)***
Time Warner Cable, Akron *Also called TW Telecom Inc* ***(G-482)***
Time Warner Cable, Cincinnati *Also called Level 3 Telecom LLC* ***(G-3972)***
Time Warner Cable Entps LLC ...614 255-6289
1600 Dublin Rd Columbus (43215) ***(G-8845)***
Time Warner Cable Entps LLC ...513 489-5000
11325 Reed Hartman Hwy # 110 Blue Ash (45241) ***(G-1695)***
Time Warner Cable Entps LLC ...614 481-5072
1125 Chambers Rd Columbus (43212) ***(G-8846)***
Time Warner Cable Inc ...513 354-1100
9825 Kenwood Rd Ste 102 Blue Ash (45242) ***(G-1696)***
Time Warner Cable Inc ...614 236-1200
3770 E Livingston Ave Columbus (43227) ***(G-8847)***
Time Warner Cable Inc ...440 366-0416
578 Ternes Ln Elyria (44035) ***(G-10684)***
Time Warner Cable Inc ...419 331-1111
3100 Elida Rd Lima (45805) ***(G-12899)***
Time Warner Cable Inc ...614 481-5050
1980 Alum Creek Dr Columbus (43207) ***(G-8848)***
Time Warner Cable Inc ...330 800-3874
1919 Brittain Rd Akron (44310) ***(G-477)***
Time Warner Cable Inc ...614 481-5000
1266 Dublin Rd Columbus (43215) ***(G-8849)***
Time Warner Cable Inc ...330 494-9200
5520 Whipple Ave Nw Canton (44720) ***(G-2562)***
Time Warner Cable Inc ...330 633-9203
755 Wick Ave Youngstown (44505) ***(G-20389)***
Time Warner Cable Inc ...513 489-5000
11252 Cornell Park Dr Blue Ash (45242) ***(G-1697)***
Time Warner Cable Inc ...937 471-1572
419 S Barron St Eaton (45320) ***(G-10577)***
Time Warner Cable Inc ...513 523-6333
114 S Locust St Oxford (45056) ***(G-15831)***
Time Warner Cable Inc ...937 483-5152
1450 Experiment Farm Rd Troy (45373) ***(G-18379)***
Time Warner Cable Inc ...740 345-4329
111 N 11th St Newark (43055) ***(G-15240)***
Time Warner Cable Inc ...937 667-8302
1440 Commerce Park Dr Tipp City (45371) ***(G-17727)***
Time Warner Cable Inc ...937 492-4145
1602 Wapakoneta Ave Sidney (45365) ***(G-16957)***
Time Warner Telecom, West Chester *Also called Level 3 Telecom LLC* ***(G-19107)***
Time Warner Telecom, West Chester *Also called Level 3 Telecom LLC* ***(G-19108)***
Time Warner Telecom, West Chester *Also called Level 3 Telecom LLC* ***(G-19109)***
Times Reporter/Midwest Offset, New Philadelphia *Also called Copley Ohio Newspapers Inc* ***(G-15087)***
Timeware Inc ...330 963-2700
9329 Ravenna Rd Ste D Twinsburg (44087) ***(G-18476)***

Timken Corporation (HQ)....330 471-3378
4500 Mount Pleasant St Nw North Canton (44720) ***(G-15374)***
Timken Mercy Health Center, Carrollton *Also called Mercy Medical Center Inc* ***(G-2623)***
Timmerman John P Heating AC Co (PA)....419 229-4015
4563 Elida Rd Lima (45807) ***(G-12900)***
Timothy Sinfield....740 685-3684
54962 Marietta Rd Pleasant City (43772) ***(G-16213)***
Tiny Tots Day Nursery....330 755-6473
310 Argonne St Struthers (44471) ***(G-17535)***
Tipharah Designs, Dayton *Also called Tipharah Group Corp* ***(G-9929)***
Tipharah Group Corp (PA)....937 430-6266
252 Burgess Ave Dayton (45415) ***(G-9929)***
Tipharah Group Corp....937 430-6266
252 Burgess Ave Dayton (45415) ***(G-9930)***
Tipharah Hospitality, Dayton *Also called Tipharah Group Corp* ***(G-9930)***
Tipp City Veterinary Hosp Inc....937 667-8489
4900 S County Road 25a Tipp City (45371) ***(G-17728)***
Tipp Machine & Tool Inc....937 890-8428
4201 Little York Rd Dayton (45414) ***(G-9931)***
Tipp-Monroe Community Svcs Inc....937 667-8631
3 E Main St Tipp City (45371) ***(G-17729)***
Tippecanoe Country Club Inc....330 758-7518
5870 Tippecanoe Rd Canfield (44406) ***(G-2213)***
TIPPECANOE PRO SHOP, Canfield *Also called Tippecanoe Country Club Inc* ***(G-2213)***
Tire Centers LLC....419 287-3227
4004 State Route 105 Pemberville (43450) ***(G-15945)***
Tire Waste Transport Inc....419 363-2681
10803 Erastus Durbin Rd Rockford (45882) ***(G-16564)***
Titan Transfer Inc....513 458-4233
6432 Centre Park Dr West Chester (45069) ***(G-19163)***
Title Division, Lewis Center *Also called County of Delaware* ***(G-12678)***
Title First Agency Inc (PA)....614 224-9207
3650 Olentangy River Rd # 400 Columbus (43214) ***(G-8850)***
Tj Metzgers Inc....419 861-8611
207 Arco Dr Toledo (43607) ***(G-18219)***
Tjm Clmbus LLC Tjm Clumbus LLC....614 885-1885
6500 Doubletree Ave Columbus (43229) ***(G-8851)***
Tk Gas Services Inc....740 826-0303
2303 John Glenn Hwy New Concord (43762) ***(G-15038)***
Tk Holdings Inc....937 778-9713
1401 Innovation Pkwy Piqua (45356) ***(G-16168)***
Tk Homecare Llc....419 517-7000
7110 W Central Ave Ste A Toledo (43617) ***(G-18220)***
Tkf Conveyor Systems LLC....513 621-5260
5298 River Rd Cincinnati (45233) ***(G-4660)***
Tkx Logistics....419 662-1800
8001 Thyssenkrupp Pkwy Northwood (43619) ***(G-15546)***
Tky Associates LLC....419 535-7777
2451 N Reynolds Rd Toledo (43615) ***(G-18221)***
TL Industries Inc (PA)....419 666-8144
2541 Tracy Rd Northwood (43619) ***(G-15547)***
TLC Eyecare....419 882-2020
3000 Regency Ct Ste 100 Toledo (43623) ***(G-18222)***
TLC Health Wellness & Fitness....330 527-4852
1 Memory Ln Garrettsville (44231) ***(G-11354)***
TLC Home Health Care Inc....740 732-5211
43 Kennedy Dr Caldwell (43724) ***(G-2090)***
Tlevay Inc....419 385-3958
1621 S Byrne Rd Toledo (43614) ***(G-18223)***
Tm Wallick Rsdntl Prpts I Ltd....614 863-4640
6880 Tussing Rd Reynoldsburg (43068) ***(G-16484)***
Tmarzetti Company....614 277-3577
5800 N Meadows Dr Grove City (43123) ***(G-11605)***
TMR Inc....330 220-8564
2945 Carquest Dr Brunswick (44212) ***(G-1992)***
Tms International LLC....419 747-5500
1344 Bowman St Mansfield (44903) ***(G-13375)***
Tmt Inc....419 592-1041
655 D St Perrysburg (43551) ***(G-16064)***
Tmt Logistics, Perrysburg *Also called Tmt Inc* ***(G-16064)***
Tmw Systems Inc (HQ)....216 831-6606
6085 Parkland Blvd Mayfield Heights (44124) ***(G-14008)***
Tnr Properties, Delaware *Also called Delaware Golf Club Inc* ***(G-10089)***
Tns Global, Cincinnati *Also called Tns North America Inc* ***(G-4661)***
Tns North America Inc....513 621-7887
600 Vine St Ste 300 Cincinnati (45202) ***(G-4661)***
Tns Retail Forward, Columbus *Also called Retail Forward Inc* ***(G-8625)***
TNT Equipment Company (PA)....614 882-1549
6677 Broughton Ave Columbus (43213) ***(G-8852)***
TNT Mobile Powerwash Inc....614 402-7474
260 Pfeifer Dr Canal Winchester (43110) ***(G-2172)***
TNT Power Wash Inc....614 662-3110
3220 Toy Rd Groveport (43125) ***(G-11676)***
TNT Power Wash Inc (PA)....614 662-3110
3220 Toy Rd Groveport (43125) ***(G-11677)***
TNT Services, Groveport *Also called TNT Power Wash Inc* ***(G-11676)***
TNT Services, Groveport *Also called TNT Power Wash Inc* ***(G-11677)***
To Scale Software LLC....513 253-0053
6398 Thornberry Ct Mason (45040) ***(G-13769)***
TOA Technologies Inc (PA)....216 360-8106
3333 Richmond Rd Ste 420 Beachwood (44122) ***(G-1131)***

Tobh, Cleveland *Also called Tours of Black Heritage Inc* ***(G-6606)***
Tobin, Dan Pontiac, Columbus *Also called Dan Tobin Pontiac Buick GMC* ***(G-7484)***
Todd A Ruck Inc....614 527-9927
5100 Harvest Meadow Ct Hilliard (43026) ***(G-11959)***
Todd Alspaugh & Associates....419 476-8126
415 E State Line Rd Toledo (43612) ***(G-18224)***
Todd Associates Inc (PA)....440 461-1101
23825 Commerce Park Ste A Beachwood (44122) ***(G-1132)***
Todd Organization, The, Rocky River *Also called Producer Group LLC* ***(G-16589)***
Toddler's School, Toledo *Also called Young Services Inc* ***(G-18324)***
Todds Enviroscapes Inc....330 875-0768
7727 Paris Ave Louisville (44641) ***(G-13107)***
Tolco Corporation....419 241-1113
1920 Linwood Ave Toledo (43604) ***(G-18225)***
Toledo Area Insulator Wkrs Jac....419 531-5911
4535 Hill Ave Toledo (43615) ***(G-18226)***
Toledo Area Rgional Trnst Auth (PA)....419 243-7433
1127 W Central Ave Toledo (43610) ***(G-18227)***
Toledo Assembly Complex, Toledo *Also called FCA US LLC* ***(G-17881)***
Toledo Building Services Co....419 241-3101
2121 Adams St Toledo (43604) ***(G-18228)***
Toledo Cardiology Cons Inc (PA)....419 251-6183
2409 Cherry St Ste 100 Toledo (43608) ***(G-18229)***
Toledo Cardiology Inc....419 479-5690
4235 Secor Rd Toledo (43623) ***(G-18230)***
Toledo Childrens Hosp Fdn....419 824-9072
2142 N Cove Blvd Toledo (43606) ***(G-18231)***
Toledo City Parks, Toledo *Also called City of Toledo* ***(G-17809)***
Toledo Clinic Inc....419 865-3111
6135 Trust Dr Ste 230 Holland (43528) ***(G-12061)***
Toledo Clinic Inc (PA)....419 473-3561
4235 Secor Rd Toledo (43623) ***(G-18232)***
Toledo Clinic Inc....419 381-9977
1414 S Byrne Rd Toledo (43614) ***(G-18233)***
Toledo Club....419 243-2200
235 14th St Toledo (43604) ***(G-18234)***
Toledo Ctr For Eting Disorders, Sylvania *Also called Reverse Center Clinic* ***(G-17610)***
Toledo Cutting Tools, Perrysburg *Also called Imco Carbide Tool Inc* ***(G-16015)***
Toledo Cy Pub Utlity Wtr Distr....419 936-2506
401 S Erie St Toledo (43604) ***(G-18235)***
Toledo District Nurses Assn....419 255-0983
5520 Monroe St Sylvania (43560) ***(G-17622)***
Toledo Ear Nose and Throat, Maumee *Also called Richard J Nelson MD* ***(G-13971)***
Toledo Edison Company (HQ)....800 447-3333
76 S Main St Bsmt Akron (44308) ***(G-478)***
Toledo Edison Company....419 321-8488
5501 N State Route 2 Oak Harbor (43449) ***(G-15617)***
Toledo Edison Company....419 249-5364
6099 Angola Rd Holland (43528) ***(G-12062)***
Toledo Elec Jint Apprnticeship....419 666-8088
803 Lime City Rd Rossford (43460) ***(G-16612)***
Toledo Express Airport, Swanton *Also called Toledo-Lucas County Port Auth* ***(G-17573)***
Toledo Family Health Center, Toledo *Also called Neighborhood Health Asso* ***(G-18080)***
Toledo Family Health Center....419 241-1554
313 Jefferson Ave Toledo (43604) ***(G-18236)***
Toledo Glass LLC (PA)....419 241-3151
103 Avondale Ave Toledo (43604) ***(G-18237)***
Toledo Hospital (HQ)....419 291-4000
2142 N Cove Blvd Toledo (43606) ***(G-18238)***
Toledo Hospital....419 291-2273
5520 Monroe St Sylvania (43560) ***(G-17623)***
Toledo Hospital....419 291-8701
2150 W Central Ave Ste A Toledo (43606) ***(G-18239)***
Toledo Inns Inc....440 243-4040
7230 Engle Rd Cleveland (44130) ***(G-6601)***
Toledo Jewelers Supply Co....419 241-4181
245 23rd St Toledo (43604) ***(G-18240)***
Toledo Legal Aid Society....419 720-3048
520 Madison Ave Ste 640 Toledo (43604) ***(G-18241)***
Toledo Maintance Center, Toledo *Also called Toledo Public Schools* ***(G-18247)***
Toledo Medical Equipment Co (PA)....419 866-7120
4060 Technology Dr Maumee (43537) ***(G-13987)***
Toledo Memorial Pk & Mausoleum....419 882-7151
6382 Monroe St Sylvania (43560) ***(G-17624)***
Toledo Metro Area Cncl Gvrnmnt....419 241-9155
300 M Luther King Jr Dr Toledo (43604) ***(G-18242)***
Toledo Mirror & Glass, Toledo *Also called Toledo Glass LLC* ***(G-18237)***
Toledo Molding & Die Inc....419 354-6050
515 E Gypsy Lane Rd Bowling Green (43402) ***(G-1795)***
Toledo Molding & Die Inc....419 692-6022
24086 State Route 697 Delphos (45833) ***(G-10152)***
Toledo Mud Hens Basbal CLB Inc....419 725-4367
406 Washington St Fl 5 Toledo (43604) ***(G-18243)***
Toledo Museum of Art (PA)....419 255-8000
2445 Monroe St Toledo (43620) ***(G-18244)***
Toledo Opco LLC....502 429-8062
7120 Port Sylvania Dr Toledo (43617) ***(G-18245)***
Toledo Optical Laboratory Inc....419 248-3384
1201 Jefferson Ave Toledo (43604) ***(G-18246)***
Toledo Public Schools....419 243-6422
130 S Hawley St Toledo (43609) ***(G-18247)***

A L P H A B E T I C

(PA)=Parent Co (HQ)=Headquarters (DH)=Div Headquarters
2018 Harris Ohio Services Directory
1339

Toledo Railways and Light Co, Akron *Also called Toledo Edison Company* ***(G-478)***
Toledo Refining Company LLC (HQ)....419 698-6600
1819 Woodville Rd Oregon (43616) ***(G-15752)***
Toledo Science Center....419 244-2674
1 Discovery Way Toledo (43604) ***(G-18248)***
Toledo Shredding LLC....419 698-1153
275 Millard Ave Bldg 3 Toledo (43605) ***(G-18249)***
Toledo Sign Company Inc (PA)....419 244-4444
2021 Adams St Toledo (43604) ***(G-18250)***
Toledo Sports Center Inc....419 693-0687
1516 Starr Ave Toledo (43605) ***(G-18251)***
Toledo Springs Service, Toledo *Also called Rubini Enterprises Inc* ***(G-18166)***
Toledo Swiss Singers....419 693-4110
3860 Starr Ave Oregon (43616) ***(G-15753)***
Toledo Television Investors LP....419 535-0024
300 S Byrne Rd Toledo (43615) ***(G-18252)***
Toledo V A Outpatient Clinic, Toledo *Also called Veterans Health Administration* ***(G-18290)***
Toledo Zoo....419 385-5721
2700 Broadway St Toledo (43609) ***(G-18253)***
Toledo Zoological Society (PA)....419 385-4040
2 Hippo Way Toledo (43609) ***(G-18254)***
Toledo-Lucas County Port Auth (PA)....419 243-8251
1 Maritime Plz Ste 701 Toledo (43604) ***(G-18255)***
Toledo-Lucas County Port Auth....419 865-2351
11013 Airport Hwy Ste 11 Swanton (43558) ***(G-17573)***
Tolson Enterprises Inc....419 843-6465
6591 W Central Ave # 100 Toledo (43617) ***(G-18256)***
Tolson Investment Property, Toledo *Also called Tolson Enterprises Inc* ***(G-18256)***
Tom Ahl Chryslr-Plymouth-Dodge....419 227-0202
617 King Ave Lima (45805) ***(G-12901)***
Tom Baier & Assoc Inc....330 497-3115
4686 Douglas Cir Nw Canton (44718) ***(G-2563)***
Tom Langhals....419 659-5629
4599 Campbell Rd Columbus Grove (45830) ***(G-9031)***
Tom Paige Catering Company....216 431-4236
2275 E 55th St Cleveland (44103) ***(G-6602)***
Tom Properties LLC....614 781-0055
777 Dearborn Park Ln A Columbus (43085) ***(G-8853)***
Tomita USA Inc (HQ)....614 873-6509
7801 Corp Blvd Unit G Plain City (43064) ***(G-16209)***
Tomm, Richard MD, Cleveland *Also called Richard Tomm MD* ***(G-6393)***
Tommy Bahama Group Inc....614 750-9668
4185 The Strand Columbus (43219) ***(G-8854)***
Toms Installation Co Inc....419 584-1218
5349 State Route 29 Celina (45822) ***(G-2664)***
Tomson Steel Company....513 420-8600
1400 Made Industrial Dr Middletown (45044) ***(G-14468)***
Toni & Marie Bader....937 339-3621
831 E Main St Troy (45373) ***(G-18380)***
Tonka Bay Dialysis LLC....740 375-0849
1221 Delaware Ave Marion (43302) ***(G-13585)***
Tony Packo's Food Company, Toledo *Also called Tony Packos Toledo LLC* ***(G-18257)***
Tony Packos Toledo LLC (PA)....419 691-6054
1902 Front St Toledo (43605) ***(G-18257)***
Tonys Pizza Service, Middletown *Also called Swan Sales* ***(G-14465)***
Tool Testing Lab Inc....937 898-5696
11601 N Dixie Dr Tipp City (45371) ***(G-17730)***
Tooling Components Division, Cleveland *Also called Jergens Inc* ***(G-5859)***
Top Dawg Group LLC....216 398-1066
220 Eastview Dr Ste 103 Brooklyn Heights (44131) ***(G-1928)***
Top Echelon Contracting Inc....330 454-3508
4883 Dressler Rd Nw # 200 Canton (44718) ***(G-2564)***
Top Gun Sales Performance Inc....513 770-0870
5155 Financial Way Ste 1 Mason (45040) ***(G-13770)***
Top Network, Columbus *Also called Essilor Laboratories Amer Inc* ***(G-7613)***
Top Performance, Ashtabula *Also called Jbj Enterprises Inc* ***(G-750)***
Top Tier Soccer LLC....937 903-6114
1268 Walnut Valley Ln Dayton (45458) ***(G-9932)***
TOPICZ, Cincinnati *Also called Novelart Manufacturing Company* ***(G-4187)***
Topmind/Planex Construction....248 719-0474
831 Elliott Dr Middletown (45044) ***(G-14469)***
Toris Station....513 829-7815
74 Donald Dr Fairfield (45014) ***(G-10915)***
Toronto Emergency Medical Svc....740 537-3891
201 S 4th St Toronto (43964) ***(G-18339)***
Toshiba Amer Bus Solutions Inc....216 642-7555
7850 Hub Pkwy Cleveland (44125) ***(G-6603)***
Tosoh America Inc (HQ)....614 539-8622
3600 Gantz Rd Grove City (43123) ***(G-11606)***
Total Carpet & Cleaning Svc, Dayton *Also called John O Bostock Jr* ***(G-9644)***
Total Fleet Solutions LLC....419 868-8853
7050 Spring Meadows Dr W A Holland (43528) ***(G-12063)***
Total Loop Inc....888 614-5667
1790 Town Park Blvd Ste A Uniontown (44685) ***(G-18541)***
Total Marketing Resources LLC....330 220-1275
2811 Carquest Dr Brunswick (44212) ***(G-1993)***
Total Package Express Inc (PA)....513 741-5500
5871 Cheviot Rd Ste 1 Cincinnati (45247) ***(G-4662)***
Total Quality Logistics LLC....513 831-2600
1701 Edison Dr Milford (45150) ***(G-14568)***
Total Quality Logistics LLC....513 831-2600
5130 Glncrssing Way Ste 3 Cincinnati (45238) ***(G-4663)***
Total Quality Logistics LLC....513 831-2600
1701 Edison Dr Milford (45150) ***(G-14569)***
Total Quality Logistics LLC (HQ)....513 831-2600
4289 Ivy Pointe Blvd Cincinnati (45245) ***(G-2936)***
Total Renal Care Inc....937 294-6711
3030 S Dixie Dr Kettering (45409) ***(G-12436)***
Total Renal Care Inc....937 252-1867
1431 Business Center Ct Dayton (45410) ***(G-9933)***
Total Rhabilitation Specialist....440 236-8527
23050 Louise Ln Columbia Station (44028) ***(G-6852)***
Total Solutions, Northwood *Also called Campbell Inc* ***(G-15529)***
Total Transportation Trckg Inc....216 398-6090
5755 Granger Rd Ste 400 Cleveland (44131) ***(G-6604)***
Total Warehousing Services....419 562-2878
115 Crossroads Blvd Bucyrus (44820) ***(G-2048)***
Total Wholesale Inc....216 361-5757
3900 Woodland Ave Cleveland (44115) ***(G-6605)***
Toth Renovation LLC....614 542-9683
444 Siebert St Columbus (43206) ***(G-8855)***
Touchmark, Dublin *Also called Advanced Prgrm Resources Inc* ***(G-10234)***
Touchstone Group Assoc LLC....513 791-1717
9675 Montgomery Rd # 201 Cincinnati (45242) ***(G-4664)***
Touchstone Mdse Group LLC (HQ)....513 741-0400
7200 Industrial Row Dr Mason (45040) ***(G-13771)***
Toula Industries Ltd LLC....937 689-1818
1019 Valley Vista Way Dayton (45429) ***(G-9934)***
Tour De Force Crm Inc....419 425-4800
14601 County Road 212 # 1 Findlay (45840) ***(G-11092)***
Tours of Black Heritage Inc....440 247-2737
8800 Woodland Ave Cleveland (44104) ***(G-6606)***
Toward Independence Inc (PA)....937 376-3996
81 E Main St Xenia (45385) ***(G-20079)***
Towards Employment Inc....216 696-5750
1255 Euclid Ave Ste 300 Cleveland (44115) ***(G-6607)***
Towe & Associates Inc....937 275-0900
415 S Miami St Ste 415 West Milton (45383) ***(G-19269)***
Towe and Associates, West Milton *Also called Towe & Associates Inc* ***(G-19269)***
Towers Perrin, Cincinnati *Also called Towers Watson Pennsylvania Inc* ***(G-4665)***
Towers Watson Pennsylvania Inc....513 345-4200
255 E 5th St Ste 2120 Cincinnati (45202) ***(G-4665)***
Towlift Inc (PA)....216 749-6800
1395 Valley Belt Rd Brooklyn Heights (44131) ***(G-1929)***
Towlift Inc....419 666-1333
2860 Crane Way Northwood (43619) ***(G-15548)***
Towlift Inc....614 851-1001
1200 Milepost Dr Columbus (43228) ***(G-8856)***
Towlift Inc....419 531-6110
140 N Byrne Rd Toledo (43607) ***(G-18258)***
Town & Country Adult Services, Springfield *Also called TAC Industries Inc* ***(G-17286)***
Town & Country School, Springfield *Also called Clark County Board of Developm* ***(G-17161)***
Town House Motor Lodge Corp....740 452-4511
135 N 7th St Zanesville (43701) ***(G-20539)***
Town Inn Co LLC....614 221-3281
175 E Town St Columbus (43215) ***(G-8857)***
Town of Canal Fulton (PA)....330 854-9448
155 Market St E Ste A Canal Fulton (44614) ***(G-2147)***
Towne & Country Vet Clinic, Warren *Also called Howland Corners Twn & Ctry Vet* ***(G-18864)***
Towne Air Freight, Brookpark *Also called Clp Towne Inc* ***(G-1940)***
Towne Building Group Inc (PA)....513 381-8696
1055 Saint Paul Pl Cincinnati (45202) ***(G-4666)***
Towne Construction Svcs LLC....513 561-3700
500 Kent Rd Ste A Batavia (45103) ***(G-1028)***
Towne Development Group Ltd....513 381-8696
1055 Saint Paul Pl # 300 Cincinnati (45202) ***(G-4667)***
Towne Investment Company LP....513 381-8696
1055 Saint Paul Pl Cincinnati (45202) ***(G-4668)***
Towne Mall, Middletown *Also called Ermc II LP* ***(G-14478)***
Towne Mall, Middletown *Also called Cbl & Associates Prpts Inc* ***(G-14476)***
Towne Management Realty, Cincinnati *Also called Towne Properties Assoc Inc* ***(G-4671)***
Towne Properties, Cincinnati *Also called Original Partners Ltd Partnr* ***(G-4234)***
Towne Properties Asset MGT, Cincinnati *Also called Towne Properties Asset MGT* ***(G-4669)***
Towne Properties Asset MGT (PA)....513 381-8696
1055 Saint Paul Pl # 100 Cincinnati (45202) ***(G-4669)***
Towne Properties Assoc Inc....513 489-9700
8675 E Kemper Rd Cincinnati (45249) ***(G-4670)***
Towne Properties Assoc Inc....513 489-4059
11340 Montgomery Rd # 202 Cincinnati (45249) ***(G-4671)***
Towne Properties Assoc Inc....513 874-3737
11840 Kemper Springs Dr C Cincinnati (45240) ***(G-4672)***
Towne Properties Machine Group, Batavia *Also called Towne Construction Svcs LLC* ***(G-1028)***
TownePlace Suites By Marriott, Streetsboro *Also called CER Hotels LLC* ***(G-17409)***
TownePlace Suites By Marriott, Streetsboro *Also called Sojourn Lodging Inc* ***(G-17429)***
TownePlace Suites By Marriott....419 425-9545
2501 Tiffin Ave Findlay (45840) ***(G-11093)***
TownePlace Suites By Marriott....513 774-0610
9369 Waterstone Blvd Cincinnati (45249) ***(G-4673)***

Townhall 2 .... 330 678-3006
155 N Water St Kent (44240) *(G-12400)*
TOWNHALL 2 24 HOUR HELPLINE, Kent Also called Townhall 2 *(G-12400)*
Townhomes Management Inc 614 228-3578
407 E Livingston Ave Columbus (43215) *(G-8858)*
Township of Chester 440 729-9951
8552 Parkside Dr Chesterland (44026) *(G-2805)*
Township of Colerain 513 741-7551
3360 W Galbraith Rd Cincinnati (45239) *(G-4674)*
Township of Copley 330 666-1853
1540 S Clvlnd Mssillon Rd Copley (44321) *(G-9067)*
TOWPATH RACQUET CLUB, Akron Also called Tennis Unlimited Inc *(G-474)*
Toyota Industrial Eqp Dlr 419 865-8025
8310 Airport Hwy Holland (43528) *(G-12064)*
Toyota Industries N Amer Inc 513 779-7500
9890 Charter Park Dr West Chester (45069) *(G-19164)*
Toyota Industries N Amer Inc 937 237-0976
6254 Executive Blvd Dayton (45424) *(G-9935)*
Toyota Material Hdlg Ohio Inc (PA) 216 328-0970
5667 E Schaaf Rd Independence (44131) *(G-12268)*
Toyota Motor Credit Corp 513 984-7100
1945 Cei Dr Blue Ash (45242) *(G-1698)*
Toyota of Bedford 440 439-8600
18151 Rockside Rd Bedford (44146) *(G-1341)*
Toyota of Logan, Logan Also called Tansky Motors Inc *(G-12989)*
Toyota West, Columbus Also called Sonic Automotive *(G-8748)*
Toys r Us Inc 614 759-7744
2686 Taylor Road Ext Reynoldsburg (43068) *(G-16485)*
TP Mechanical Contractors Inc (PA) 513 851-8881
1500 Kemper Meadow Dr Cincinnati (45240) *(G-4675)*
TP Mechanical Contractors Inc 614 253-8556
2130 Franklin Rd Columbus (43209) *(G-8859)*
TPC Food Service, Tiffin Also called Tiffin Paper Company *(G-17706)*
TPC Wire & Cable Corp (HQ) 800 521-7935
9600 Valley View Rd Macedonia (44056) *(G-13213)*
Tpg Noramco LLC 513 245-9050
9252 Colerain Ave Ste 4 Cincinnati (45251) *(G-4676)*
Tpusa Inc 330 374-1232
150 E Market St Akron (44308) *(G-479)*
Tpusa Inc 614 621-5512
4335 Equity Dr Columbus (43228) *(G-8860)*
Tql, Milford Also called Total Quality Logistics LLC *(G-14568)*
Tql, Cincinnati Also called Total Quality Logistics LLC *(G-2936)*
TRAC, Athens Also called Tri County Mental Health Svcs *(G-815)*
Tracy Appliance, Lima Also called Tracy Refrigeration Inc *(G-12902)*
Tracy Refrigeration Inc 419 223-4786
4064 Elida Rd Lima (45807) *(G-12902)*
Tradeglobal, West Chester Also called Netrada North America LLC *(G-19218)*
Trademark Games, Lorain Also called Trademark Global LLC *(G-13082)*
Trademark Global LLC (HQ) 440 960-6226
7951 W Erie Ave Lorain (44053) *(G-13082)*
Trader Buds Westside Dodge 614 272-0000
4000 W Broad St Columbus (43228) *(G-8861)*
Traders World Inc 513 424-2052
601 Union Rd Monroe (45050) *(G-14715)*
Tradesmen Group Inc 614 799-0889
8465 Rausch Dr Plain City (43064) *(G-16210)*
Tradesmen International LLC 419 502-9140
2419 E Perkins Ave Sandusky (44870) *(G-16802)*
Tradesmen International LLC 513 771-1115
4398 Glendale Milford Rd Blue Ash (45242) *(G-1699)*
Tradesmen International LLC (PA) 440 349-3432
9760 Shepard Rd Macedonia (44056) *(G-13214)*
Tradesmen Services LLC 440 349-3432
9760 Shepard Rd Macedonia (44056) *(G-13215)*
Tradesmen Services, Inc., Macedonia Also called Tradesmen Services LLC *(G-13215)*
Tradesource Inc 216 801-4944
5504 State Rd Parma (44134) *(G-15916)*
Tradesource Inc 614 824-3883
1550 Old Henderson Rd Columbus (43220) *(G-8862)*
Trading Corp of America, Columbus Also called Marfo Company *(G-8109)*
Traditions At Bath Rd Inc 330 929-6272
300 E Bath Rd Cuyahoga Falls (44223) *(G-9226)*
Traditions At Mill Run 614 771-0100
3550 Fishinger Blvd Hilliard (43026) *(G-11960)*
Traditions At Stygler Road 614 475-8778
167 N Stygler Rd Columbus (43230) *(G-8863)*
Traditions of Chillicothe 740 773-8107
142 University Dr Ofc Chillicothe (45601) *(G-2890)*
Traffic Ctrl Safety Svcs LLC 330 904-2732
8970 Allen Dr Ne Alliance (44601) *(G-564)*
Traffic Engineering, Akron Also called City of Akron *(G-141)*
Trafftech Inc 216 361-8808
7000 Hubbard Ave Cleveland (44127) *(G-6608)*
Trafzer Excavating Inc 740 383-2616
1560 Likens Rd Marion (43302) *(G-13586)*
Traichal Construction Company (PA) 800 255-3667
332 Plant St Niles (44446) *(G-15307)*
Trak Staffing Services Inc (PA) 513 333-4199
625 Eden Park Dr Ste 300 Cincinnati (45202) *(G-4677)*

Trak-1 Technology Inc 513 204-5530
4770 Duke Dr Ste 200 Mason (45040) *(G-13772)*
Trame Mechanical Inc 937 258-1000
2721 Timber Ln Dayton (45414) *(G-9936)*
Tramz Hotels LLC 440 975-9922
35110 Maplegrove Rd Willoughby (44094) *(G-19718)*
Trane Cleveland, Mentor Also called Trane Inc *(G-14248)*
Trane Inc 440 946-7823
7567 Tyler Blvd Mentor (44060) *(G-14248)*
Trans Con Buildings, Cleveland Also called Owners Management *(G-6222)*
Trans Core, Cleveland Also called Transcore Its LLC *(G-6610)*
Trans Healthcare, Wapakoneta Also called Gardens At Wapakoneta *(G-18797)*
Trans Vac Inc 419 229-8192
931 N Jefferson St Lima (45801) *(G-12903)*
Trans World Alloys, Toronto Also called Shadco Inc *(G-18338)*
Trans-Continental Systems Inc (PA) 513 769-4774
10801 Evendale Dr Ste 105 Cincinnati (45241) *(G-4678)*
Trans-States Express Inc 513 679-7100
7750 Reinhold Dr Cincinnati (45237) *(G-4679)*
Transamerica Premier Lf Insur 614 488-5983
1335 Dublin Rd Ste 200c Columbus (43215) *(G-8864)*
Transamerica Premier Lf Insur 216 524-1436
6480 Rockside Woods S 1 Independence (44131) *(G-12269)*
Transco Railway Products Inc 419 726-3383
4800 Schwartz Rd Toledo (43611) *(G-18259)*
Transcon Builders Inc (PA) 440 439-3400
25250 Rockside Rd Ste 2 Cleveland (44146) *(G-6609)*
Transcore Its LLC 440 243-2222
6930 Engle Rd Ste Y Cleveland (44130) *(G-6610)*
Transcriptiongear Inc 888 834-2392
7280 Auburn Rd Painesville (44077) *(G-15882)*
Transcriptiongear.com, Painesville Also called Transcriptiongear Inc *(G-15882)*
Transdigm Group Incorporated (PA) 216 706-2960
1301 E 9th St Ste 3000 Cleveland (44114) *(G-6611)*
Transforce Inc 513 860-4402
8080 Beckett Center Dr # 202 West Chester (45069) *(G-19165)*
Transformation Network (PA) 419 207-1188
1310 Claremont Ave Unit A Ashland (44805) *(G-702)*
Transfreight Inc 937 332-0366
3355 S County Road 25a B Troy (45373) *(G-18381)*
Transit Service Company 330 782-3343
1130 Prfmce Pl Unit A Youngstown (44502) *(G-20390)*
Transitional Living Inc (HQ) 513 863-6383
2052 Princeton Rd Fairfield Township (45011) *(G-10936)*
Transitworks LLC 330 861-1118
1090 W Wilbeth Rd Akron (44314) *(G-480)*
Transmerica Svcs Technical Sup 740 282-3695
4404 Scioto Dr Steubenville (43953) *(G-17338)*
Transport Corp America Inc 330 538-3328
1951 N Bailey Rd North Jackson (44451) *(G-15388)*
Transport Services Inc 440 582-4900
10499 Royalton Rd Cleveland (44133) *(G-6612)*
Transport Specialists Inc (PA) 513 771-2220
12130 Best Pl Cincinnati (45241) *(G-4680)*
Transportatin Office, Youngstown Also called Mahoning County *(G-20262)*
Transportation Center, Warren Also called Warren City Board Education *(G-18923)*
Transportation Department, Ontario Also called Ontario Local School District *(G-15708)*
Transportation Department, Ashtabula Also called Ashtabula Area City School Dst *(G-712)*
Transportation Department, Columbus Also called Ohio State University *(G-8426)*
Transportation Dept, Dayton Also called Kettering City School District *(G-9653)*
Transportation Group, Mantua Also called Mantaline Corporation *(G-13392)*
Transportation Ohio Department 614 275-1300
1600 W Broad St Columbus (43223) *(G-8865)*
Transportation Ohio Department 740 773-3191
255 Larrick Ln Chillicothe (45601) *(G-2891)*
Transportation Unlimited Inc (PA) 216 426-0088
3740 Carnegie Ave Ste 101 Cleveland (44115) *(G-6613)*
Transtar Electric Inc 419 385-7573
767 Warehouse Rd Ste B Toledo (43615) *(G-18260)*
Transworld News, Cleveland Also called Windy Hill Ltd Inc *(G-6753)*
Transystems Corporation 614 433-7800
400 W Nationwide Blvd # 225 Columbus (43215) *(G-8866)*
Transystems Corporation 216 861-1780
55 Public Sq Ste 1900 Cleveland (44113) *(G-6614)*
Travel Authority (PA) 513 272-2887
6800 Wooster Pike Cincinnati (45227) *(G-4681)*
Travelcenters America Inc (HQ) 440 808-9100
24601 Center Ridge Rd # 200 Westlake (44145) *(G-19555)*
Travelcenters of America Inc 330 769-2053
Junction Of I 71 And I 76 Lodi (44254) *(G-12966)*
Travelcenters of America LLC 724 981-9464
24601 Center Ridge Rd # 200 Westlake (44145) *(G-19556)*
Travelcenters of America LLC (PA) 440 808-9100
24601 Center Ridge Rd # 200 Westlake (44145) *(G-19557)*
Travelcenters of America LLC 330 793-4426
I 80 Rte 46 Exit 223 A Rt 46 Youngstown (44515) *(G-20391)*
Travelers Insurance, Columbus Also called Freedom Specialty Insurance Co *(G-7701)*
Travelers Insurance, Cincinnati Also called Travelers Property Cslty Corp *(G-4682)*
Travelers Insurance, Cleveland Also called Travelers Property Cslty Corp *(G-6615)*

Travelers Property Cslty Corp.......513 639-5300
615 Elsinore Pl Bldg B Cincinnati (45202) ***(G-4682)***
Travelers Property Cslty Corp.......216 643-2100
6150 Oak Tree Blvd # 400 Cleveland (44131) ***(G-6615)***
Traxium LLC.......330 572-8200
4246 Hudson Dr Stow (44224) ***(G-17397)***
Treasure Island Gift Shop, Cincinnati *Also called Goodwill Service Guild* ***(G-3687)***
Treasurers Office, Dayton *Also called County of Montgomery* ***(G-9435)***
Tremco Incorporated (HQ).......216 292-5000
3735 Green Rd Beachwood (44122) ***(G-1133)***
Tremor LLC.......513 983-1100
9545 Kenwood Rd Ste 303 Blue Ash (45242) ***(G-1700)***
Trend Construction, Cincinnati *Also called Ford Development Corp* ***(G-3637)***
Trend Consulting Services, Solon *Also called Netsmart Technologies Inc* ***(G-17033)***
Trepanier Daniels & Trepanier.......740 286-1288
80 Dixon Run Rd Ste 80 Jackson (45640) ***(G-12319)***
Treu House of Munch Inc.......419 666-7770
8000 Arbor Dr Northwood (43619) ***(G-15549)***
Trg Maintenance LLC.......614 891-4850
514 N State St Ste B Westerville (43082) ***(G-19356)***
Trg Repair, Westlake *Also called Technology Recovery Group Ltd* ***(G-19554)***
Tri Area Electric Co Inc.......330 744-0151
37 Wayne Ave Youngstown (44502) ***(G-20392)***
Tri County Assembly of God.......513 874-8575
7350 Dixie Hwy Fairfield (45014) ***(G-10916)***
Tri County Concrete Inc (PA).......330 425-4464
9423 Darrow Rd Twinsburg (44087) ***(G-18477)***
Tri County Eggs, Versailles *Also called Weaver Bros Inc* ***(G-18731)***
Tri County Extended Care Ctr.......513 829-3555
5200 Camelot Dr Fairfield (45014) ***(G-10917)***
Tri County Family Physicians.......614 837-6363
11925 Lithopolis Rd Nw Canal Winchester (43110) ***(G-2173)***
Tri County Help Center Inc (PA).......740 695-5441
104 1/2 N Marietta St Saint Clairsville (43950) ***(G-16657)***
Tri County Mall Promotion Fund, Cincinnati *Also called Concordia Properties LLC* ***(G-3409)***
Tri County Mental Health Svcs (PA).......740 592-3091
90 Hospital Dr Athens (45701) ***(G-815)***
Tri County Mental Health Svcs.......740 594-5045
90 Hospital Dr Athens (45701) ***(G-816)***
Tri County Nite Hunter Assn Ci.......740 385-7341
2940 Laurel Run Rd Logan (43138) ***(G-12990)***
Tri County Tower Service.......330 538-9874
8900 Mahoning Ave North Jackson (44451) ***(G-15389)***
Tri County Visitng Nrs Prvt.......419 738-7430
803 Brewfield Dr Wapakoneta (45895) ***(G-18809)***
Tri Green Interstate Equipment.......614 879-7731
1499 Us Highway 42 Ne London (43140) ***(G-13008)***
Tri Modal Service Inc.......614 876-6325
2015 Walcutt Rd Columbus (43228) ***(G-8867)***
Tri State Corporation.......513 763-0215
923 Glenwood Ave Cincinnati (45229) ***(G-4683)***
Tri State Forest Products, Springfield *Also called Tier One Distribution LLC* ***(G-17288)***
Tri State Urlogic Svcs PSC Inc (PA).......513 841-7400
2000 Joseph E Sanker Blvd Cincinnati (45212) ***(G-4684)***
Tri Tech Service Systems Inc.......937 787-4664
9501 Pleasant Valley Rd Somerville (45064) ***(G-17071)***
Tri Village Joint Ambulance, New Madison *Also called Tri Village Rescue Service* ***(G-15073)***
Tri Village Rescue Service.......937 996-3155
320 N Main St New Madison (45346) ***(G-15073)***
Tri Zob Inc.......216 252-4500
4117 Rocky River Dr Cleveland (44135) ***(G-6616)***
Tri-America Contractors Inc (PA).......740 574-0148
1664 State Route 522 Wheelersburg (45694) ***(G-19582)***
Tri-Anim Health Services Inc (HQ).......614 760-5000
5000 Tuttle Crossing Blvd Dublin (43016) ***(G-10477)***
Tri-City Industrial Power Inc (PA).......937 866-4099
915 N Main St Miamisburg (45342) ***(G-14361)***
Tri-Con Incorporated.......513 530-9844
11160 Kenwood Rd Ste 200 Blue Ash (45242) ***(G-1701)***
Tri-County Community Act.......740 385-6812
1005 C I C Dr Logan (43138) ***(G-12991)***
Tri-County Heating & Cooling, Barberton *Also called Blind & Son LLC* ***(G-959)***
Tri-County Mulch, Akron *Also called Tri-County Pallet Recycl Inc* ***(G-481)***
Tri-County Pallet Recycl Inc.......330 848-0313
900 Flora Ave Akron (44314) ***(G-481)***
Tri-Mor Corp.......330 963-3101
8530 N Boyle Pkwy Twinsburg (44087) ***(G-18478)***
Tri-State Aluminium Inc (HQ).......419 666-0100
1663 Tracy St Toledo (43605) ***(G-18261)***
Tri-State Amblnce Pramedic Svc.......304 233-2331
7100 Whipple Ave Nw Ste C North Canton (44720) ***(G-15375)***
Tri-State Asphalt Co, Rayland *Also called Shelly and Sands Inc* ***(G-16418)***
Tri-State Beef Co Inc.......513 579-1722
2124 Baymiller St Cincinnati (45214) ***(G-4685)***
Tri-State Forest Products Inc (PA).......937 323-6325
2105 Sheridan Ave Springfield (45505) ***(G-17289)***
Tri-State Industries Inc.......740 532-0406
606 Carlton Davidson Ln Coal Grove (45638) ***(G-6826)***
Tri-State Mobile Notaries, Cincinnati *Also called Official Investigations Inc* ***(G-4200)***
Tri-State Trailer Sales Inc.......412 747-7777
5230 Duff Dr West Chester (45246) ***(G-19237)***
Triad Data Processing, New Concord *Also called Triplett & Adams Entps Inc* ***(G-15039)***
Triad Energy Corporation.......740 374-2940
125 Putnam St Marietta (45750) ***(G-13505)***
Triad Engineering & Contg Co (PA).......440 786-1000
9715 Clinton Rd Cleveland (44144) ***(G-6617)***
Triad Governmental Systems.......937 376-5446
358 S Monroe St Xenia (45385) ***(G-20080)***
Triad Group Inc (PA).......419 228-8800
855 W Market St Lowr Lima (45805) ***(G-12904)***
Triad Oil & Gas Engineering.......740 374-2940
27724 State Route 7 Marietta (45750) ***(G-13506)***
Triad Pll.......740 374-2940
27724 State Route 7 Marietta (45750) ***(G-13507)***
Triad Residential (PA).......419 482-0711
1605 Holland Rd Ste A4 Maumee (43537) ***(G-13988)***
Triad Staffing, Independence *Also called Bmch Inc* ***(G-12189)***
Triad Technologies LLC (PA).......937 832-2861
985 Falls Creek Dr Vandalia (45377) ***(G-18701)***
Triad Transport Inc.......614 491-9497
1484 Williams Rd Columbus (43207) ***(G-8868)***
Triangle Commercial Properties, Westerville *Also called Donald R Kenney & Company* ***(G-19300)***
Triangle Label, West Chester *Also called G R B Inc* ***(G-19078)***
Triangle Office Park LLC.......513 563-7555
2135 Dana Ave Ste 200 Cincinnati (45207) ***(G-4686)***
Triangle Precision Industries.......937 299-6776
1650 Delco Park Dr Dayton (45420) ***(G-9937)***
Tribute Contracting & Cons LLC.......740 451-1010
2125 County Road 1 South Point (45680) ***(G-17098)***
Trickeration Inc.......216 360-9966
26055 Emery Rd Ste E Warrensville Heights (44128) ***(G-18935)***
Tricont Trucking Company.......614 527-7398
2200 Westbelt Dr Columbus (43228) ***(G-8869)***
Tricor Emplyment Screening Ltd.......800 818-5116
110 Blaze Industrial Pkwy Berea (44017) ***(G-1474)***
Tricor Industrial, Wooster *Also called Tricor Metals* ***(G-19920)***
Tricor Industrial Inc (PA).......330 264-3299
3225 W Old Lincoln Way Wooster (44691) ***(G-19919)***
Tricor Metals, Wooster *Also called Tricor Industrial Inc* ***(G-19919)***
Tricor Metals.......330 264-3299
3225 W Old Lincoln Way Wooster (44691) ***(G-19920)***
Tricor Pacific Capital Partner, Burton *Also called Bfg Supply Co Llc* ***(G-2061)***
Tricounty Ambulance Service.......440 951-4600
7000 Spinach Dr Mentor (44060) ***(G-14249)***
Tridec Technologies LLC.......937 938-8160
4764 Fishburg Rd Ste D Huber Heights (45424) ***(G-12099)***
Trident USA Health Svcs LLC.......614 888-2226
6185 Huntley Rd Ste Q Columbus (43229) ***(G-8870)***
Triec Electrical Services Inc.......937 323-3721
1630 Progress Rd Springfield (45505) ***(G-17290)***
Trihealth Inc.......513 929-0020
415 W Court St Ste 100 Cincinnati (45203) ***(G-4687)***
Trihealth Inc.......513 865-1111
10506 Montgomery Rd Cincinnati (45242) ***(G-4688)***
Trihealth Inc.......513 569-6777
375 Dixmyth Ave Cincinnati (45220) ***(G-4689)***
Trihealth Inc.......513 891-1627
11121 Kenwood Rd Blue Ash (45242) ***(G-1702)***
Trihealth Inc (HQ).......513 569-6111
619 Oak St Cincinnati (45206) ***(G-4690)***
Trihealth Inc.......513 871-2340
2753 Erie Ave Cincinnati (45208) ***(G-4691)***
Trihealth Evendale Hospital (HQ).......513 454-2222
3155 Glendale Milford Rd Cincinnati (45241) ***(G-4692)***
Trihealth Fitnes Hlth Pavilion, Montgomery *Also called Trihealth Inc* ***(G-14734)***
Trihealth G LLC (HQ).......513 732-0700
4600 Wesley Ave Ste N Cincinnati (45212) ***(G-4693)***
Trihealth G LLC.......513 346-5000
55 Progress Pl Cincinnati (45246) ***(G-4694)***
Trihealth G LLC.......513 624-5535
7691 5 Mile Rd Ste 214 Cincinnati (45230) ***(G-4695)***
Trihealth G LLC.......513 922-1200
2001 Anderson Ferry Rd Cincinnati (45238) ***(G-4696)***
Trihealth Hf LLC.......513 398-3445
7423 S Mason Mntgomery Mason (45040) ***(G-13773)***
Trihealth Inc.......513 985-0900
6200 Pfeiffer Rd Ste 330 Montgomery (45242) ***(G-14734)***
Trihealth Oncology Inst LLC.......513 451-4033
5520 Cheviot Rd Cincinnati (45247) ***(G-4697)***
Trihealth Orthpd & Spine Inst, Montgomery *Also called Trihealth Os LLC* ***(G-14735)***
Trihealth Os LLC.......513 791-6611
10547 Montgomery Rd 400a Montgomery (45242) ***(G-14735)***
Trihealth Rehabilitation Hosp.......513 601-0600
2155 Dana Ave Cincinnati (45207) ***(G-4698)***
Trihealth Work Capacity Center, Cincinnati *Also called Hospice Cincinnati Inc* ***(G-3785)***
Trillium Creek Dermatology, Medina *Also called H M T Dermatology Inc* ***(G-14073)***
Trillium Family Solutions Inc.......330 454-7066
111 Stow Ave Ste 100 Cuyahoga Falls (44221) ***(G-9227)***
Trilogy Fulfillment LLC.......614 491-0553
6600 Alum Creek Dr Groveport (43125) ***(G-11678)***

Trilogy Health Services LLC 419 935-6511
1050 Neal Zick Rd Willard (44890) ***(G-19628)***
Trilogy Healthcare Allen LLC 419 643-3161
7400 Swaney Rd Bluffton (45817) ***(G-1736)***
Trilogy Healthcare Putnam LLC 419 532-2961
755 Ottawa St Kalida (45853) ***(G-12346)***
Trilogy Rehab Services LLC 740 452-3000
2991 Maple Ave Zanesville (43701) ***(G-20540)***
Trimark Ss Kemp, Cleveland *Also called S S Kemp & Company* ***(G-6428)***
Trimark Usa LLC 216 271-7700
4567 Willow Pkwy Cleveland (44125) ***(G-6618)***
Trimat Construction Inc 740 388-9515
13621 State Route 554 Bidwell (45614) ***(G-1496)***
Trimble & Julian, Westerville *Also called Julian & Grube Inc* ***(G-19318)***
Trimble Engineering & Cnstr 937 233-8921
5475 Kellenburger Rd Dayton (45424) ***(G-9938)***
Trimor, Twinsburg *Also called Tri-Mor Corp* ***(G-18478)***
Trimor, Twinsburg *Also called Cem-Base Inc* ***(G-18399)***
Trinity Action Partnership 937 456-2800
308 Eaton Lewisburg Rd Eaton (45320) ***(G-10578)***
Trinity Community, Beavercreek *Also called United Church Homes Inc* ***(G-1261)***
Trinity Contracting Inc 614 905-4410
4878 Mgnolia Blossom Blvd Columbus (43230) ***(G-8871)***
Trinity Credit Counseling Inc 513 769-0621
11229 Reading Rd Ste 1 Cincinnati (45241) ***(G-4699)***
TRINITY DEBT MANAGEMENT, Cincinnati *Also called Trinity Credit Counseling Inc* ***(G-4699)***
Trinity Health Corporation 614 846-5420
5700 Karl Rd Columbus (43229) ***(G-8872)***
Trinity Health Corporation 419 448-3124
485 W Market St Tiffin (44883) ***(G-17707)***
Trinity Health Group Ltd 614 899-4830
827 Yard St Columbus (43212) ***(G-8873)***
Trinity Health System 740 283-7848
380 Summit Ave Steubenville (43952) ***(G-17339)***
Trinity Health System 740 264-8000
4000 Johnson Rd Fl 1 Steubenville (43952) ***(G-17340)***
Trinity Health System 740 264-8101
4000 Johnson Rd Fl 1 Steubenville (43952) ***(G-17341)***
Trinity Health System (HQ) 740 283-7000
380 Summit Ave Steubenville (43952) ***(G-17342)***
Trinity Health West, Steubenville *Also called Trinity Health System* ***(G-17340)***
Trinity Healthcare Corporation 513 489-2444
8211 Weller Rd Cincinnati (45242) ***(G-4700)***
Trinity Home Builders Inc 614 889-7830
2700 E Dublin Granville Columbus (43231) ***(G-8874)***
Trinity Hospital Holding Co (HQ) 740 264-8000
380 Summit Ave Steubenville (43952) ***(G-17343)***
Trinity Hospital Twin City 740 922-2800
819 N 1st St Dennison (44621) ***(G-10166)***
Trinity Luth Child Care 419 289-2126
508 Center St Ashland (44805) ***(G-703)***
Trinity Lutheran Church of Ash, Ashland *Also called Trinity Luth Child Care* ***(G-703)***
Trinity Medical Center East, Steubenville *Also called Trinity Hospital Holding Co* ***(G-17343)***
Trinity Medical Center East, Steubenville *Also called Trinity Health System* ***(G-17342)***
Trinity United Methodist Ch 419 224-2909
301 W Market St Lima (45801) ***(G-12905)***
Trinity United Methodist Ctr, Lima *Also called Trinity United Methodist Ch* ***(G-12905)***
Trinity West 740 264-8000
4000 Johnson Rd Fl 1 Steubenville (43952) ***(G-17344)***
Trio Trucking Inc 513 679-7100
7750 Reinhold Dr Cincinnati (45237) ***(G-4701)***
Tripack LLC 859 282-7914
401 Milford Pkwy Ste B Milford (45150) ***(G-14570)***
Tripack Sleever, Milford *Also called Tripack LLC* ***(G-14570)***
Triple Ladys Agency Inc (PA) 330 274-1100
4626 State Route 82 Mantua (44255) ***(G-13396)***
Triple Q Foundations Co Inc 513 932-3121
139 Harmon Ave Lebanon (45036) ***(G-12654)***
Triple T Transport Inc (PA) 740 657-3244
433 Lewis Center Rd Lewis Center (43035) ***(G-12707)***
Triplefin LLC (PA) 855 877-5346
11333 Cornell Park Dr Blue Ash (45242) ***(G-1703)***
Triplefin LLC 513 794-9870
11333 Cornell Park Dr Blue Ash (45242) ***(G-1704)***
Triplett & Adams Entps Inc 816 221-1024
140 S Friendship Dr New Concord (43762) ***(G-15039)***
Triplett ASAP, Akron *Also called Lkq Triplettasap Inc* ***(G-323)***
Tripoint Medical Center, Painesville *Also called Lake Hospital System Inc* ***(G-15861)***
Tripoint Medical Center 440 375-8100
7590 Auburn Rd Painesville (44077) ***(G-15883)***
Trippe, Glen MD, Bellevue *Also called New Beginnings Pediatrics Inc* ***(G-1413)***
Trisco Systems Incorporated 419 339-9912
2000 Baty Rd Lima (45807) ***(G-12906)***
Tristate Concrete, Metamora *Also called Tscs Inc* ***(G-14266)***
Triton Services Inc 513 679-6800
8162 Duke Blvd Mason (45040) ***(G-13774)***
Triumph Energy Corporation 513 367-9900
9171 Dry Fork Rd Harrison (45030) ***(G-11811)***
Triumph Hospital Mansfield 419 526-0777
335 Glessner Ave Mansfield (44903) ***(G-13376)***
Triversity Construction Co LLC 513 733-0046
5050 Section Ave Ste 330 Cincinnati (45212) ***(G-4702)***
Troilo & Associates, New Albany *Also called Allstars Travel Group Inc* ***(G-14973)***
Trolley Tours of Cleveland 216 771-4484
1790 Columbus Rd Cleveland (44113) ***(G-6619)***
Troutwine Auto Sales Inc 937 692-8373
9 N Main St Arcanum (45304) ***(G-631)***
Troy Bowl, Troy *Also called Bigelow Corporation* ***(G-18349)***
Troy Built Building LLC 419 425-1093
1001 Fishlock Ave Findlay (45840) ***(G-11094)***
Troy Center, Troy *Also called Harborside Troy LLC* ***(G-18356)***
Troy Christian School 937 339-5692
1586 Mckaig Rd Troy (45373) ***(G-18382)***
Troy City Water Distribution, Troy *Also called City of Troy* ***(G-18351)***
Troy Country Club Inc 937 335-5691
1830 Peters Rd Troy (45373) ***(G-18383)***
Troyer Cheese Inc 330 893-2479
6597 County Road 625 Millersburg (44654) ***(G-14625)***
Troyers Home Pantry (PA) 330 698-4182
668 W Main St Apple Creek (44606) ***(G-627)***
TRT Management Corporation (PA) 419 661-1233
487 J St Perrysburg (43551) ***(G-16065)***
Tru Green-Chemlawn, Hilliard *Also called Trugreen Limited Partnership* ***(G-11961)***
Tru Green-Chemlawn, Springboro *Also called Trugreen Limited Partnership* ***(G-17140)***
Tru Green-Chemlawn, Mansfield *Also called Trugreen Limited Partnership* ***(G-13377)***
Tru Green-Chemlawn, Bedford *Also called Trugreen Limited Partnership* ***(G-1342)***
Tru Green-Chemlawn, Fairfield *Also called Trugreen Limited Partnership* ***(G-10918)***
Tru Green-Chemlawn, Mentor *Also called Trugreen Limited Partnership* ***(G-14250)***
Tru Green-Chemlawn, Lewis Center *Also called Trugreen Limited Partnership* ***(G-12708)***
Tru Green-Chemlawn, Elyria *Also called Trugreen Limited Partnership* ***(G-10685)***
Tru Green-Chemlawn, Lima *Also called Trugreen Limited Partnership* ***(G-12908)***
Tru Green-Chemlawn, Groveport *Also called Trugreen Limited Partnership* ***(G-11679)***
Tru Green-Chemlawn, Brilliant *Also called Trugreen Limited Partnership* ***(G-1869)***
Tru Green-Chemlawn, Canton *Also called Trugreen Limited Partnership* ***(G-2565)***
Tru Green-Chemlawn, Dayton *Also called Trugreen Limited Partnership* ***(G-9939)***
Tru Green-Chemlawn, Vandalia *Also called Trugreen Limited Partnership* ***(G-18702)***
Tru-Gro Landscaping, Dayton *Also called Woody Tree Medics* ***(G-10003)***
Trubuilt Construction Svcs LLC 614 279-4800
777 Harrison Dr Columbus (43204) ***(G-8875)***
Trucco Construction Co Inc 740 417-9010
3531 Airport Rd Delaware (43015) ***(G-10130)***
Truck Country Indiana Inc 419 228-4334
598 E Hanthorn Rd Lima (45804) ***(G-12907)***
Truck Sales Leasing Inc (PA) 330 343-5581
3429 Brightwood Rd Midvale (44653) ***(G-14491)***
Trucking and Logistics, South Point *Also called H & W Holdings LLC* ***(G-17087)***
Trucking Division, Toledo *Also called FCA US LLC* ***(G-17882)***
Truckmen, Geneva *Also called Neighborhood Logistics Co Inc* ***(G-11366)***
Truckomat Corporation 740 467-2818
10707 Lancaster Rd Ste 37 Hebron (43025) ***(G-11861)***
Truckstops of America, Lodi *Also called Travelcenters of America LLC* ***(G-12966)***
Truckway Leasing, Cincinnati *Also called Interstate Truckway Inc* ***(G-3838)***
True Core Federal Credit Union 740 345-6608
215 Deo Dr Newark (43055) ***(G-15241)***
True North Energy LLC 614 222-0198
631 S High St Columbus (43215) ***(G-8876)***
True North Energy LLC 440 442-0060
6411 Mayfield Rd Mayfield Heights (44124) ***(G-14009)***
True North Energy LLC (PA) 877 245-9336
10346 Brecksville Rd Brecksville (44141) ***(G-1853)***
True North Trucking, Toledo *Also called Lyden Company* ***(G-18022)***
True Value, Hartville *Also called Hrm Enterprises Inc* ***(G-11823)***
True2form Collision Repair Ctr (PA) 330 399-6659
3924 Youngstown Rd Se Warren (44484) ***(G-18907)***
Trueblue Inc 740 282-1079
2125 Sunset Blvd Steubenville (43952) ***(G-17345)***
Truechoicepack Corp 937 630-3832
5155 Financial Way Ste 6 Mason (45040) ***(G-13775)***
Truenorth Cultural Arts 440 949-5200
4530 Colorado Ave Sheffield Village (44054) ***(G-16895)***
Truenorth Energy, Mayfield Heights *Also called True North Energy LLC* ***(G-14009)***
Truepoint Inc 513 792-6648
4901 Hunt Rd Ste 200 Blue Ash (45242) ***(G-1705)***
Trugreen Chemlawn, Mansfield *Also called Igh II Inc* ***(G-13310)***
Trugreen Limited Partnership 614 527-7070
5150 Nike Dr Hilliard (43026) ***(G-11961)***
Trugreen Limited Partnership 937 557-0060
760 Pleasant Valley Dr Springboro (45066) ***(G-17140)***
Trugreen Limited Partnership 419 884-3636
110 Industrial Dr Mansfield (44904) ***(G-13377)***
Trugreen Limited Partnership 440 786-7200
20375 Hannan Pkwy Bedford (44146) ***(G-1342)***
Trugreen Limited Partnership 513 223-3707
4041 Thunderbird Ln Fairfield (45014) ***(G-10918)***
Trugreen Limited Partnership 440 290-3340
7460 Clover Ave Mentor (44060) ***(G-14250)***

Trugreen Limited Partnership 614 285-3721
461 Enterprise Dr Lewis Center (43035) *(G-12708)*
Trugreen Limited Partnership 440 540-4209
151 Keep Ct Elyria (44035) *(G-10685)*
Trugreen Limited Partnership 419 516-4200
2083 N Dixie Hwy Lima (45801) *(G-12908)*
Trugreen Limited Partnership 614 610-4142
4045 Lakeview Xing Groveport (43125) *(G-11679)*
Trugreen Limited Partnership 740 598-4724
198 Penn St Brilliant (43913) *(G-1869)*
Trugreen Limited Partnership 330 409-2861
6302 Promway Ave Nw Canton (44720) *(G-2565)*
Trugreen Limited Partnership 937 866-8399
767 Liberty Ln Dayton (45449) *(G-9939)*
Trugreen Limited Partnership 937 410-4055
800 Center Dr Vandalia (45377) *(G-18702)*
Trugreen-Chem Lawn 330 533-2839
8529 South Ave Poland (44514) *(G-16229)*
Truitt Thos R & Truitt Susan M, Marysville *Also called Thomas R Truitt Od (G-13655)*
Trumball Cnty Fire Chiefs Assn 330 675-6602
640 N River Rd Nw Warren (44483) *(G-18908)*
Trumball Cnty Hzardous Mtl Bur, Warren *Also called Trumball Cnty Fire Chiefs Assn (G-18908)*
Trumbll-Mhoning Med Group Phrm, Cortland *Also called Trumbull-Mahoning Med Group (G-9084)*
Trumbull Cmnty Action Program (PA) 330 393-2507
1230 Palmyra Rd Sw Warren (44485) *(G-18909)*
Trumbull County Engineering (PA) 330 675-2640
650 N River Rd Nw Warren (44483) *(G-18910)*
Trumbull County Engineers, Warren *Also called County of Trumbull (G-18840)*
Trumbull County One Stop 330 675-2000
280 N Park Ave Warren (44481) *(G-18911)*
Trumbull Housing Dev Corp 330 369-1533
4076 Youngstown Rd Se # 101 Warren (44484) *(G-18912)*
Trumbull Industries Inc 330 393-6624
850 Bronze Rd Ne Warren (44483) *(G-18913)*
Trumbull Industries Inc 330 799-3333
1040 N Meridian Rd Youngstown (44509) *(G-20393)*
Trumbull Manufacturing Inc 330 393-6624
400 Dietz Rd Ne Warren (44483) *(G-18914)*
Trumbull Mem Hosp Foundation 330 841-9376
1350 E Market St Warren (44483) *(G-18915)*
Trumbull Special Courier Inc 330 841-0074
346 Willard Ave Se Warren (44483) *(G-18916)*
Trumbull-Mahoning Med Group 330 372-8800
2600 State Route 5 Cortland (44410) *(G-9084)*
Trupointe Cooperative Inc 937 575-6780
215 Looney Rd Piqua (45356) *(G-16169)*
Trustaff Management Inc 513 272-3999
4675 Cornell Rd Blue Ash (45241) *(G-1706)*
Trustaff Travel Nurses, Blue Ash *Also called Trustaff Management Inc (G-1706)*
Trusted Homecare Solutions 937 506-7063
2324 Stanley Ave Ste 115 Dayton (45404) *(G-9940)*
Truteam LLC 513 942-2204
28 Kiesland Ct Hamilton (45015) *(G-11779)*
Trx Great Plains Inc 855 259-9259
6600 Bessemer Ave Cleveland (44127) *(G-6620)*
TS Tech Americas Inc 740 593-5958
10 Kenny Dr Athens (45701) *(G-817)*
TS Tech Americas Inc (HQ) 614 575-4100
8458 E Broad St Reynoldsburg (43068) *(G-16486)*
TSA Inspections, Mansfield *Also called James Ray Lozier (G-13316)*
TSC Apparel LLC (PA) 513 771-1138
Centennial Plaza Iii 895 Cincinnati (45202) *(G-4703)*
TSC Communications Inc 419 739-2200
2 Willipie St Wapakoneta (45895) *(G-18810)*
TSC Television Inc 419 941-6001
2 Willipie St Wapakoneta (45895) *(G-18811)*
Tscs Inc 419 644-3921
14293 State Route 64 Metamora (43540) *(G-14266)*
Tsg Resources Inc 330 498-8200
339 E Maple St Ste 110 North Canton (44720) *(G-15376)*
Tsg-Cincinnati LLC 513 793-6241
11243 Cornell Park Dr Blue Ash (45242) *(G-1707)*
Tsi Inc 419 468-1855
1263 State Route 598 Galion (44833) *(G-11307)*
Tsk Assisted Living Services 330 297-2000
240 W Riddle Ave Ravenna (44266) *(G-16414)*
Tsl Ltd (PA) 419 843-3200
5217 Monroe St Ste A1 Toledo (43623) *(G-18262)*
Tsm Logistics LLC 419 234-6074
4567 Old Town Run Rd Rockford (45882) *(G-16565)*
TSS Medical, West Chester *Also called TSS Technologies Inc (G-19166)*
TSS Real Estate Ltd 513 772-7000
1201 Hill Smith Dr Cincinnati (45215) *(G-4704)*
TSS Resources, Dublin *Also called Telecmmnctons Stffing Slutions (G-10475)*
TSS Technologies Inc (PA) 513 772-7000
8800 Global Way West Chester (45069) *(G-19166)*
TTI Floor Care North Amer Inc (HQ) 440 996-2000
7005 Cochran Rd Solon (44139) *(G-17061)*
TTI Floor Care North America, Cleveland *Also called Royal Appliance Mfg Co (G-6415)*
Ttl Associates Inc (PA) 419 241-4556
1915 N 12th St Toledo (43604) *(G-18263)*
Tube Fittings Division, Columbus *Also called Parker-Hannifin Corporation (G-8516)*
Tucker Ellis LLP 720 897-4400
950 Main Ave Ste 1100 Cleveland (44113) *(G-6621)*
Tucker Ellis LLP (PA) 216 592-5000
950 Main Ave Ste 1100 Cleveland (44113) *(G-6622)*
Tucker Ellis LLP 614 358-9717
175 S 3rd St Ste 520 Columbus (43215) *(G-8877)*
Tucson Inc 330 339-4935
3497 University Dr Ne New Philadelphia (44663) *(G-15118)*
Tuffy Associates Corp (PA) 419 865-6900
7150 Granite Cir Ste 100 Toledo (43617) *(G-18264)*
Tuffy Auto Service Centers, Toledo *Also called Tuffy Associates Corp (G-18264)*
Tunnell Hill Reclamation, New Lexington *Also called Oxford Mining Company Inc (G-15059)*
Turbo Parts LLC 740 223-1695
1676 Cascade Dr Marion (43302) *(G-13587)*
Turfscape Inc 330 405-0741
8490 Tower Dr Twinsburg (44087) *(G-18479)*
Turn Around Group Inc 330 372-0064
1512 Phoenix Rd Ne Warren (44483) *(G-18917)*
Turn-Key Industrial Svcs LLC 614 274-1128
820 Distribution Dr Columbus (43228) *(G-8878)*
Turner Construction Company 513 721-4224
250 W Court St Ste 300w Cincinnati (45202) *(G-4705)*
Turner Construction Company 216 522-1180
1422 Euclid Ave Ste 1400 Cleveland (44115) *(G-6623)*
Turner Construction Company 513 363-0883
2315 Iowa Ave Cincinnati (45206) *(G-4706)*
Turner Construction Company 614 984-3000
262 Hanover St Columbus (43215) *(G-8879)*
Turney's, Chesterland *Also called G H A Inc (G-2798)*
Turning Pt Counseling Svcs Inc (PA) 330 744-2991
611 Belmont Ave Youngstown (44502) *(G-20394)*
Turning Technologies LLC (PA) 330 746-3015
255 W Federal St Youngstown (44503) *(G-20395)*
Turnkey Network Solutions LLC 614 876-9944
3450 Millikin Ct Ste A Columbus (43228) *(G-8880)*
Turnpike and Infrastructure Co 330 527-2169
9196 State Route 700 Windham (44288) *(G-19804)*
Turpin Hills Swim Racquet CLB 513 231-3242
3814 West St Ste 311 Cincinnati (45227) *(G-4707)*
Turtle Golf Management Ltd (HQ) 614 882-5920
5400 Little Turtle Way W Westerville (43081) *(G-19446)*
Tuscany Spa Salon 513 489-8872
11355 Montgomery Rd Cincinnati (45249) *(G-4708)*
Tuscarawas Cnty Job Fmly Svcs, New Philadelphia *Also called County of Tuscarawas (G-15091)*
Tuscarawas County Commitee 330 364-6611
425 Prospect St Dover (44622) *(G-10217)*
Tuscarawas County Help ME Grow 330 339-3493
1433 5th St Nw New Philadelphia (44663) *(G-15119)*
TUSCARAWAS COUNTY SENIOR CENTE, Dover *Also called Tuscarawas County Commitee (G-10217)*
Tusco Grocers Inc 740 922-8721
30 S 4th St Dennison (44621) *(G-10167)*
Tusco Imaa Chapter No 602 ....330 878-7369
6607 Cherry Run Rd Nw Strasburg (44680) *(G-17401)*
Tusco RC Club, Strasburg *Also called Tusco Imaa Chapter No 602 (G-17401)*
Tusing Builders Ltd 419 465-3100
2596 Us Route 20 E Monroeville (44847) *(G-14723)*
Tuttle Crossing Associates, Dublin *Also called Simon Property Group (G-10454)*
Tuttle Landscaping & Grdn Ctr 419 756-7555
1295 S Trimble Rd Mansfield (44907) *(G-13378)*
TV Minority Company Inc 937 832-9350
30 Lau Pkwy Englewood (45315) *(G-10722)*
TV Minority Company Inc 937 226-1559
1700 E Monument Ave Dayton (45402) *(G-9941)*
TVC Home Health Care 330 755-1110
70 W Mckinley Way Ste 8 Youngstown (44514) *(G-20396)*
TW Recreational Services 419 836-1466
1750 State Park Rd 2 Oregon (43616) *(G-15754)*
TW Recreational Services Inc 440 564-9144
11755 Kinsman Rd Newbury (44065) *(G-15262)*
TW Telecom Inc 234 542-6279
1019 E Turkeyfoot Lake Rd Akron (44312) *(G-482)*
TWC Concrete Services LLC 513 771-8192
10737 Medallion Dr Cincinnati (45241) *(G-4709)*
Twelve Inc (PA) 330 837-3555
619 Tremont Ave Sw Massillon (44647) *(G-13859)*
TWELVE OF OHIO, THE, Massillon *Also called Twelve Inc (G-13859)*
Twh, Hicksville *Also called Wholesale House Inc (G-11867)*
Twigs Kids, Dayton *Also called Christian Twigs Gymnastics CLB (G-9406)*
Twilight Gardens Healthcare 419 668-2086
196 W Main St Norwalk (44857) *(G-15595)*
Twin Cedars Services Inc 513 932-0399
935 Old Ralph 122 Lebanon (45036) *(G-12655)*
Twin Comm Inc 740 774-4701
2349 State Route 821 Marietta (45750) *(G-13508)*
Twin Haven Reception Hall 330 425-1616
10439 Ravenna Rd Twinsburg (44087) *(G-18480)*

Twin Maples Home Health Care...740 596-1022
63044 Us Highway 50 Mc Arthur (45651) *(G-14017)*
Twin Maples Nursing Home...740 596-5955
31054 State Route 93 Mc Arthur (45651) *(G-14018)*
Twin Oaks Care Center Inc...419 524-1205
73 Madison Rd Mansfield (44905) *(G-13379)*
Twin Pines Retreat Care Center...330 688-5553
456 Seasons Rd Stow (44224) *(G-17398)*
Twin Rvers Care Rhbltation Ctr, Defiance *Also called Sun Healthcare Group Inc (G-10060)*
Twin Towers...513 853-2000
5343 Hamilton Ave Apt 513 Cincinnati (45224) *(G-4710)*
Twin Vly Behavioral Healthcare, Columbus *Also called Mental Health and Addi Serv (G-8147)*
Twin Vly Behavioral Hlth Care, Columbus *Also called Mental Health and Addi Serv (G-8148)*
Twinbrook Hills Baptist Church...513 863-3107
40 Wrenwood Dr Hamilton (45013) *(G-11780)*
Twinoaks Living and Lrng Ctr, Mansfield *Also called Manfield Living Center Ltd (G-13328)*
Twinsburg Medical Offices, Twinsburg *Also called Kaiser Foundation Hospitals (G-18436)*
Twism Enterprises LLC...513 800-1098
12110 Regency Run Ct # 9 Cincinnati (45240) *(G-4711)*
Twist Inc...937 675-9581
1380 Lavelle Dr Xenia (45385) *(G-20081)*
Two Happy Frogs Incorporated...330 633-1666
165 Northeast Ave Tallmadge (44278) *(G-17658)*
Two K General Company, Delaware *Also called Twok General Co (G-10131)*
Two M Precision Co Inc...440 946-2120
1747 Joseph Lloyd Pkwy # 3 Willoughby (44094) *(G-19719)*
Two Men & A Truck, Columbus *Also called Nest Tenders Limited (G-8257)*
Two Men & A Vacuum LLC...614 300-7970
81 S 4th St Ste 100 Columbus (43215) *(G-8881)*
Two Men & Truck Inc...419 882-1002
2800 Tremainsville Rd A Toledo (43613) *(G-18265)*
Two Men and A Truck, Toledo *Also called Two Men & Truck Inc (G-18265)*
Two Men and A Truck, Akron *Also called E & V Ventures Inc (G-203)*
Two Men and A Truck/Cleveland, Wickliffe *Also called Northcoast Moving Enterprising (G-19609)*
Two-X Engners Constructers LLC...330 995-0592
570 Club Dr Aurora (44202) *(G-857)*
Twok General Co...740 417-9195
19 Gruber St Bldg B Delaware (43015) *(G-10131)*
Tyco International MGT Co LLC...888 787-8324
2884 E Kemper Rd Cincinnati (45241) *(G-4712)*
Tycor Roofing Inc...330 452-8150
1704 Warner Rd Se Canton (44707) *(G-2566)*
Tyler Technologies Inc...937 276-5261
4100 Miller Valentine Ct Moraine (45439) *(G-14831)*
Tylinter Inc (HQ)...800 321-6188
8570 Tyler Blvd Mentor (44060) *(G-14251)*
Tyrone Townhouses PA Inv LLC...216 520-1250
8111 Rockside Rd Cleveland (44125) *(G-6624)*
U A W Region 2 Headquarters, Cleveland *Also called International Union United Au (G-5832)*
U C Child Care Center Inc...513 961-2825
3310 Ruther Ave Cincinnati (45220) *(G-4713)*
U C Health Dermatology, West Chester *Also called Uc Health Llc (G-19168)*
U C M Residential Services...937 643-3757
400 Gade Ave Union City (45390) *(G-18504)*
U D F, Cincinnati *Also called United Dairy Farmers Inc (G-4731)*
U H Ahuja Medical Center, Cleveland *Also called University Hospitals (G-6654)*
U Haul Co of Northwestern Ohio (HQ)...419 478-1101
50 W Alexis Rd Toledo (43612) *(G-18266)*
U S A Concrete Specialists...330 482-9150
145 Nulf Dr Columbiana (44408) *(G-6865)*
U S A Plumbing Company...614 882-6402
1425 Community Park Dr Columbus (43229) *(G-8882)*
U S A Waterproofing Inc...330 425-2440
1632 Enterprise Pkwy Twinsburg (44087) *(G-18481)*
U S Army Corps of Engineers...740 269-2681
86801 Eslick Rd Uhrichsville (44683) *(G-18493)*
U S Army Corps of Engineers...740 767-3527
23560 Jenkins Dam Rd Glouster (45732) *(G-11436)*
U S Army Corps of Engineers...513 684-3048
550 Main St Ste 10022 Cincinnati (45202) *(G-4714)*
U S Associates Realty Inc...216 663-3400
4700 Rockside Rd Ste 150 Cleveland (44131) *(G-6625)*
U S Bank Arena, Cincinnati *Also called Arena Management Holdings LLC (G-3045)*
U S C, Miamisburg *Also called Ulliman Schutte Cnstr LLC (G-14363)*
U S Cargo, Cleveland *Also called United States Cargo & Courier (G-6646)*
U S Dental Care, Columbus *Also called US Dental Care/M D Gelender (G-8923)*
U S Dept of Labor Occupational...216 447-4194
6393 Oak Tree Blvd # 203 Independence (44131) *(G-12270)*
U S Development Corp (PA)...330 673-6900
900 W Main St Kent (44240) *(G-12401)*
U S Diagnostics, Dayton *Also called Dayton Medical Imaging (G-9481)*
U S Laboratories Inc...440 248-1223
33095 Bainbridge Rd Cleveland (44139) *(G-6626)*
U S Protective Services, Independence *Also called United States Protective (G-12271)*
U S Title Agency Inc...216 621-1424
1213 Prospect Ave E # 400 Cleveland (44115) *(G-6627)*
U S Xpress Inc...937 328-4100
825 W Leffel Ln Springfield (45506) *(G-17291)*
U S Xpress Inc...740 363-0700
2000 Nutter Farms Ln Delaware (43015) *(G-10132)*
U S Xpress Inc...740 452-4153
2705 E Pointe Dr Zanesville (43701) *(G-20541)*
U Save Auto Rental...330 925-2015
112 E Ohio Ave Rittman (44270) *(G-16557)*
U T C, Beavercreek *Also called Universal Technology Corp (G-1216)*
U Z Engineered Products Co, Cleveland *Also called State Industrial Products Corp (G-6531)*
U-Co Industries Inc...937 644-3021
16900 Square Dr Ste 110 Marysville (43040) *(G-13656)*
U-Haul, Toledo *Also called U Haul Co of Northwestern Ohio (G-18266)*
U-Haul Neighborhood Dealer -Ce...419 929-3724
1005 Us Highway 250 S New London (44851) *(G-15071)*
U-Save Auto Rental, Rittman *Also called U Save Auto Rental (G-16557)*
U.S. Bridge, Cambridge *Also called Ohio Bridge Corporation (G-2125)*
U.S.t Environmental Contractor, Logan *Also called Alco Inc (G-12967)*
Uahs Heather Hill Home Health...440 285-5098
12340 Bass Lake Rd Chardon (44024) *(G-2772)*
Uasi, Cincinnati *Also called United Audit Systems Inc (G-4728)*
Uaw Local 863, Cincinnati *Also called International Union United Au (G-3837)*
UBS Financial Services Inc...330 655-8319
43 Village Way Ste 201 Hudson (44236) *(G-12147)*
UBS Financial Services Inc...440 414-2740
2055 Crocker Rd Ste 201 Westlake (44145) *(G-19558)*
UBS Financial Services Inc...419 624-6800
111 E Shoreline Dr Ste 3 Sandusky (44870) *(G-16803)*
UBS Financial Services Inc...740 336-7823
324 3rd St Marietta (45750) *(G-13509)*
UBS Financial Services Inc...513 576-5000
312 Walnut St Ste 3300 Cincinnati (45202) *(G-4715)*
UBS Financial Services Inc...419 318-5525
5757 Monroe St Sylvania (43560) *(G-17625)*
UBS Financial Services Inc...937 428-1300
7887 Wash Vlg Dr Ste 100 Dayton (45459) *(G-9942)*
UBS Financial Services Inc...513 792-2146
8044 Montgomery Rd # 200 Cincinnati (45236) *(G-4716)*
UBS Financial Services Inc...216 831-3400
2000 Auburn Dr Ste 100 Cleveland (44122) *(G-6628)*
UBS Financial Services Inc...614 460-6559
41 S High St Ste 3300 Columbus (43215) *(G-8883)*
UBS Financial Services Inc...614 442-6240
5025 Arlngtn Ctr Blvd # 120 Columbus (43220) *(G-8884)*
UBS Financial Services Inc...937 223-3141
3601 Rigby Rd Ste 500 Miamisburg (45342) *(G-14362)*
UBS Financial Services Inc...513 792-2100
8044 Montgomery Rd # 200 Cincinnati (45236) *(G-4717)*
Uc Health, Cincinnati *Also called University Radiology Assoc (G-4784)*
Uc Health Llc...513 584-6999
9313 S Mason Montgomery R Mason (45040) *(G-13776)*
Uc Health Llc...513 475-7458
7700 University Ct # 1800 West Chester (45069) *(G-19167)*
Uc Health Llc...513 475-7630
7690 Discovery Dr # 1700 West Chester (45069) *(G-19168)*
Uc Health Llc...513 475-7880
222 Piedmont Ave Ste 6000 Cincinnati (45219) *(G-4718)*
Uc Health Llc...513 475-8881
7700 University Ct West Chester (45069) *(G-19169)*
Uc Health Llc...513 585-7600
3200 Burnet Ave Cincinnati (45229) *(G-4719)*
Uc Health Llc...513 298-3000
7798 Discovery Dr Ste F West Chester (45069) *(G-19170)*
Uc Health Llc...513 475-7777
7710 University Ct West Chester (45069) *(G-19171)*
Uc Health Llc...513 648-9077
11590 Century Blvd # 102 Cincinnati (45246) *(G-4720)*
Uc Health Llc...513 584-8600
3120 Burnet Ave Ste 203 Cincinnati (45229) *(G-4721)*
Uc Health Llc...513 475-7500
7798 Discovery Dr Ste E West Chester (45069) *(G-19172)*
Uc Health Llc (PA)...513 585-6000
3200 Burnet Ave Cincinnati (45229) *(G-4722)*
Uc Health Dermatology, Cincinnati *Also called Univ Dermatology (G-4745)*
Uc Health Primary Care Mason, Mason *Also called Uc Health Llc (G-13776)*
Uc Physician, Cincinnati *Also called Bruce R Bracken (G-3144)*
Uc Physicians, Cincinnati *Also called University of Cincinnati Phys (G-4780)*
Uc Physicians At Univ Pointe, West Chester *Also called University of Cincinnati Phys (G-19175)*
Ucb, Toledo *Also called United Collection Bureau Inc (G-18269)*
Ucc Childrens Center...513 217-5501
5750 Innovation Dr Middletown (45005) *(G-14488)*
UCI, Cleveland *Also called University Circle Incorporated (G-6653)*
Uct Property Inc...614 228-3276
1801 Watermark Dr Ste 100 Columbus (43215) *(G-8885)*
Ucvp For Research, Cincinnati *Also called University of Cincinnati (G-4765)*
Ues Inc (PA)...937 426-6900
4401 Dayton Xenia Rd Beavercreek (45432) *(G-1213)*
Ues Metals Group...937 255-9340
4401 Dayton Xenia Rd Beavercreek (45432) *(G-1214)*

A
L
P
H
A
B
E
T
I
C

Ufcw 75 Real Estate Corp 937 677-0075
7250 Poe Ave Ste 400 Dayton (45414) ***(G-9943)***
UFCW LOCAL 1059, Columbus *Also called United Food Comml Wrkrs Un* ***(G-8890)***
Ufcw Local No. 75, Dayton *Also called United Food and Coml Wkrs* ***(G-9946)***
Uhhs Westlake Medical Center 440 250-2070
960 Clague Rd Ste 3201 Westlake (44145) ***(G-19559)***
Uhhs-Geauga Regional Hospital, Chardon *Also called University Hospitals* ***(G-2774)***
Uhhs-Memorial Hosp of Geneva 440 466-1141
870 W Main St Geneva (44041) ***(G-11371)***
Uhl's Jamestown Market, Jamestown *Also called Greeneview Foods LLC* ***(G-12326)***
Uhmg Department of Urologist (PA) 216 844-3009
11100 Euclid Ave Cleveland (44106) ***(G-6629)***
Uhrichsville Health Care Ctr 740 922-2208
5166 Spanson Dr Se Uhrichsville (44683) ***(G-18494)***
UIC General Contractors, Ashtabula *Also called Union Industrial Contractors* ***(G-765)***
Uima, Cincinnati *Also called University of Cincinnati* ***(G-4768)***
Ull Inc (PA) 440 543-5195
9812 Washington St Chagrin Falls (44023) ***(G-2737)***
Ulliman Schutte Cnstr LLC (PA) 937 247-0375
9111 Springboro Pike Miamisburg (45342) ***(G-14363)***
Ulmer & Berne, Cincinnati *Also called Dacia R Crum* ***(G-3458)***
Ulmer & Berne Illinois, Cleveland *Also called Ulmer & Berne LLP* ***(G-6630)***
Ulmer & Berne LLP (PA) 216 583-7000
1660 W 2nd St Ste 1100 Cleveland (44113) ***(G-6630)***
Ulmer & Berne LLP 513 698-5000
600 Vine St Ste 2800 Cincinnati (45202) ***(G-4723)***
Ulmer & Berne LLP 513 698-5058
600 Vine St Ste 2800 Cincinnati (45202) ***(G-4724)***
Ulmer & Berne LLP 614 229-0000
65 E State St Ste 1100 Columbus (43215) ***(G-8886)***
Ulrich Professional Group 330 673-9501
401 Devon Pl Ste 215 Kent (44240) ***(G-12402)***
Ulta Beauty Inc 513 752-1472
700 Estgate S Dr Ste 250 Cincinnati (45245) ***(G-2937)***
Ulta Beauty Inc 419 621-1345
4020 Milan Rd Unit 915 Sandusky (44870) ***(G-16804)***
Ulta Beauty Inc 440 248-5618
6025 Kruse Dr Solon (44139) ***(G-17062)***
Ultimate Air Center, North Canton *Also called Ultimate Jetcharters LLC* ***(G-15377)***
Ultimate Building Maintenance 330 369-9771
3229 Youngstown Rd Se Warren (44484) ***(G-18918)***
Ultimate Health Care, South Point *Also called Quality Care Nursing Svc Inc* ***(G-17096)***
Ultimate Jetcharters LLC 330 497-3344
6061 W Airport Dr North Canton (44720) ***(G-15377)***
Ultimate Rehab Ltd 513 563-8777
11305 Reed Hartman Hwy # 226 Blue Ash (45241) ***(G-1708)***
Ultimus Fund Solutions LLC (PA) 513 587-3400
225 Pictoria Dr Ste 450 Cincinnati (45246) ***(G-4725)***
Ultra Tech Machinery Inc 330 929-5544
297 Ascot Pkwy Cuyahoga Falls (44223) ***(G-9228)***
Ulysses Caremark Holding Corp 440 542-4214
29100 Aurora Rd Solon (44139) ***(G-17063)***
Underground Utilities Inc 419 465-2587
416 Monroe St Monroeville (44847) ***(G-14724)***
UNI-Facs, Columbus *Also called Universal Fabg Cnstr Svcs Inc* ***(G-8905)***
Unico Alloys & Metals Inc 614 299-0545
1177 Joyce Ave Ste B Columbus (43219) ***(G-8887)***
Unicon International Inc (PA) 614 861-7070
241 Outerbelt St Columbus (43213) ***(G-8888)***
Unicustom Inc 513 874-9806
3263 Homeward Way Fairfield (45014) ***(G-10919)***
Unified Bank (HQ) 740 633-0445
201 S 4th St Martins Ferry (43935) ***(G-13602)***
Unified Cnstr Systems Ltd (PA) 330 773-2511
1920 S Main St Akron (44301) ***(G-483)***
Unifirst Corporation 614 575-9999
211 Reynoldsburg New Albn Blacklick (43004) ***(G-1511)***
Unifirst Corporation 937 746-0531
265 Industrial Dr Franklin (45005) ***(G-11166)***
Unifund Ccr LLC 513 489-8877
10625 Techwood Cir Blue Ash (45242) ***(G-1709)***
Unifund Corporation 513 489-8877
10625 Techwood Cir Blue Ash (45242) ***(G-1710)***
Union Bank Company 740 387-2265
111 S Main St Marion (43302) ***(G-13588)***
Union Central Life Insur Co (HQ) 866 696-7478
1876 Waycross Rd Cincinnati (45240) ***(G-4726)***
Union Centre Hotel LLC 513 874-7335
6189 Muhlhauser Rd West Chester (45069) ***(G-19173)***
Union Christel Manor Inc 937 968-6265
400 S Melvin Eley Ave Union City (45390) ***(G-18505)***
Union City Crystal Manor, Union City *Also called Union Christel Manor Inc* ***(G-18505)***
Union Club Company 216 621-4230
1211 Euclid Ave Cleveland (44115) ***(G-6631)***
Union Cnstr Wkrs Hlth Plan 419 248-2401
7142 Nightingale Dr Ste 1 Holland (43528) ***(G-12065)***
Union Cnty Board of Devlpmt, Marysville *Also called County of Union* ***(G-13613)***
Union Country Club 330 343-5544
1000 N Bellevue Ave Dover (44622) ***(G-10218)***
Union Home Mortgage Corp (PA) 440 234-4300
8241 Dow Cir Strongsville (44136) ***(G-17517)***
Union Hospital Association (PA) 330 343-3311
659 Boulevard St Dover (44622) ***(G-10219)***
Union Hospital Association 330 602-0719
500 Medical Park Dr Dover (44622) ***(G-10220)***
Union Hospital Home Hlth Care 330 343-6909
659 Boulevard St Dover (44622) ***(G-10221)***
Union Industrial Contractors 440 998-7871
1800 E 21st St Ashtabula (44004) ***(G-765)***
Union Mortgage Services Inc (PA) 614 457-4815
1080 Fishinger Rd Columbus (43221) ***(G-8889)***
Union Rural Electric Coop Inc (PA) 937 642-1826
15461 Us Highway 36 Marysville (43040) ***(G-13657)***
Union Savings Bank 937 434-1254
5651 Far Hills Ave Dayton (45429) ***(G-9944)***
Union Security Insurance Co 513 621-1924
312 Elm St Ste 1500 Cincinnati (45202) ***(G-4727)***
Union Supply Group Inc 614 409-1444
3321 Toy Rd Groveport (43125) ***(G-11680)***
Union Tank Car Company 419 864-7216
939 Holland Rd W Marion (43302) ***(G-13589)***
Unique Construction Svcs Inc 513 608-1363
10999 Reed Hartman Hwy # 313 Blue Ash (45242) ***(G-1711)***
Unirush LLC (HQ) 866 766-2229
4701 Creek Rd Ste 200 Blue Ash (45242) ***(G-1712)***
Uniserv, Brookfield *Also called United Steel Service LLC* ***(G-1902)***
Unison Behavioral Health Group (PA) 419 242-9577
544 E Woodruff Ave Toledo (43604) ***(G-18267)***
Unison Behavioral Health Group 419 693-0631
1425 Starr Ave Toledo (43605) ***(G-18268)***
Unison Industries LLC 937 426-0621
2455 Dayton Xenia Rd Dayton (45434) ***(G-9285)***
Unison Industries LLC 937 427-0550
2070 Heller Dr Beavercreek (45434) ***(G-1215)***
Unistrut-Columbus, Columbus *Also called Loeb Electric Company* ***(G-8075)***
Unite Churc Resid of Oxfor Mis (HQ) 740 382-4885
170 E Center St Marion (43302) ***(G-13590)***
United Agencies Inc 216 696-8044
1422 Euclid Ave Ste 510 Cleveland (44115) ***(G-6632)***
United Airlines Inc 937 454-2009
3600 Terminal Rd Ste 213 Vandalia (45377) ***(G-18703)***
United Airlines Inc 216 501-4700
5970 Cargo Rd Cleveland (44135) ***(G-6633)***
United Alloys and Metals, Columbus *Also called Unico Alloys & Metals Inc* ***(G-8887)***
United Amblnce Svc of Cmbridge (HQ) 740 439-7787
1331 Campbell Ave Cambridge (43725) ***(G-2132)***
United Ambulance Service 740 732-5653
523 Main St Caldwell (43724) ***(G-2091)***
United American Insurance Co 440 265-9200
10749 Pearl Rd Ste D Strongsville (44136) ***(G-17518)***
United Architectural Mtls Inc 330 433-9220
7830 Cleveland Ave Nw North Canton (44720) ***(G-15378)***
United Armored Services, Columbus *Also called Garda CL Great Lakes Inc* ***(G-7727)***
United Art and Education Inc 800 322-3247
799 Lyons Rd Dayton (45459) ***(G-9945)***
United Atmtc Htng Spply of Clv (PA) 216 621-5571
2125 Superior Ave E Cleveland (44114) ***(G-6634)***
United Audit Systems Inc 513 723-1122
1924 Dana Ave Cincinnati (45207) ***(G-4728)***
United Bank N A, Bucyrus *Also called United Bank National Assn* ***(G-2049)***
United Bank National Assn (HQ) 419 562-3040
401 S Sandusky Ave Bucyrus (44820) ***(G-2049)***
United Building Materials, Dayton *Also called Gms Inc* ***(G-9575)***
United Cerebral Palsy (PA) 216 791-8363
10011 Euclid Ave Cleveland (44106) ***(G-6635)***
United Cerebral Palsy 216 381-9993
1374 Edendale St Cleveland (44121) ***(G-6636)***
United Cerebral Palsy Gr Cinc 513 221-4606
2300 Drex Ave Cincinnati (45212) ***(G-4729)***
United Church Homes 740 382-4885
170 E Center St Marion (43302) ***(G-13591)***
United Church Homes Inc 513 922-1440
5999 Bender Rd Cincinnati (45233) ***(G-4730)***
United Church Homes Inc 937 878-0262
789 Stoneybrook Trl Fairborn (45324) ***(G-10806)***
United Church Homes Inc 330 854-4177
12200 Strausser St Nw Canal Fulton (44614) ***(G-2148)***
United Church Homes Inc 937 426-8481
3218 Indian Ripple Rd Beavercreek (45440) ***(G-1261)***
United Church Homes Inc (PA) 740 382-4885
170 E Center St Marion (43302) ***(G-13592)***
United Church Homes Inc 740 376-5600
401 Harmar St Marietta (45750) ***(G-13510)***
United Church Homes Inc 740 286-7551
215 Seth Ave Jackson (45640) ***(G-12320)***
United Church Homes Inc 419 294-4973
850 Marseilles Ave Upper Sandusky (43351) ***(G-18568)***
United Church Homes Inc 419 621-1900
3800 Boardwalk Blvd Sandusky (44870) ***(G-16805)***
United Church Res of Kenton 740 382-4885
900 E Columbus St Kenton (43326) ***(G-12425)***
United Church Residences of 614 837-2008
85 Covenant Way Canal Winchester (43110) ***(G-2174)***

United Collection Bureau Inc (PA) 419 866-6227
5620 Southwyck Blvd Toledo (43614) *(G-18269)*
United Collection Bureau Inc 419 866-6227
1345 Ford St Maumee (43537) *(G-13989)*
United Community Fincl Corp (PA) 330 742-0500
275 W Federal St Youngstown (44503) *(G-20397)*
United Consumer Fincl Svcs Co 440 835-3230
865 Bassett Rd Cleveland (44145) *(G-6637)*
United Dairy Farmers Inc (PA) 513 396-8700
3955 Montgomery Rd Cincinnati (45212) *(G-4731)*
United Dental Laboratories (PA) 330 253-1810
261 South Ave Akron (44302) *(G-484)*
United Disability Services Inc (PA) 330 374-1169
701 S Main St Akron (44311) *(G-485)*
United Discount, Cleveland *Also called Dollar Paradise* *(G-5498)*
United Electric Company Inc 502 459-5242
1309 Ethan Ave Cincinnati (45225) *(G-4732)*
United Electric Motor Repair, Cleveland *Also called United Atmtc Htng Spply of Clv* *(G-6634)*
United Engraving, Cincinnati *Also called Wood Graphics Inc* *(G-4858)*
United Fd & Coml Wkrs Intl Un 216 241-2828
9199 Market Pl Broadview Heights (44147) *(G-1894)*
United Fd Coml Wkrs Local 880 (PA) 216 241-5930
2828 Euclid Ave Cleveland (44115) *(G-6638)*
United Food & Commercial Wkr 330 452-4850
1800 Cleveland Ave Nw Canton (44709) *(G-2567)*
United Food and Coml Wkrs 937 665-0075
7250 Poe Ave Ste 400 Dayton (45414) *(G-9946)*
United Food Comml Wrkrs Un 614 235-3635
4150 E Main St Fl 2 Columbus (43213) *(G-8890)*
United Garage & Service Corp (PA) 216 623-1550
2069 W 3rd St Cleveland (44113) *(G-6639)*
United GL & Panl Systems Inc 330 244-9745
4250 Strausser St Nw Canton (44720) *(G-2568)*
United Grinding North Amer Inc (HQ) 937 859-1975
2100 United Grinding Blvd Miamisburg (45342) *(G-14364)*
United Group Services Inc (PA) 800 633-9690
9740 Near Dr West Chester (45246) *(G-19238)*
United Health Network Ltd 330 492-2102
4455 Dressler Rd Nw Canton (44718) *(G-2569)*
United Healthcare, Cincinnati *Also called Unitedhealth Group Inc* *(G-4744)*
United Healthcare Ohio Inc 216 694-4080
1001 Lkeside Ave Ste 1000 Cleveland (44114) *(G-6640)*
United Healthcare Ohio Inc (HQ) 614 410-7000
9200 Worthington Rd Columbus (43085) *(G-8891)*
United Healthcare Ohio Inc 513 603-6200
5151 Pfeiffer Rd Ste 400 Blue Ash (45242) *(G-1713)*
United Home Health Services 614 880-8686
297 Woodland Ave Columbus (43203) *(G-8892)*
United Hsptality Solutions LLC 800 238-0487
11998 Clay Pike Rd Buffalo (43722) *(G-2053)*
United Hydraulics, Willoughby *Also called Two M Precision Co Inc* *(G-19719)*
United Insulation Co Inc 614 263-9378
1985 Oakland Park Ave Columbus (43224) *(G-8893)*
United Insurance Company Amer 513 771-6771
135 Merchant St Ste 120 Cincinnati (45246) *(G-4733)*
United Insurance Company Amer 419 531-4289
1650 N Reynolds Rd Toledo (43615) *(G-18270)*
United Insurance Company Amer 216 514-1904
23215 Commerce Park # 310 Beachwood (44122) *(G-1134)*
United Labor Agency Inc 216 664-3446
1020 Bolivar Rd Fl 3 Cleveland (44115) *(G-6641)*
United Mail LLC 513 482-7429
1221 Harrison Ave Cincinnati (45214) *(G-4734)*
United Management Inc (PA) 614 228-5331
250 Civic Center Dr Columbus (43215) *(G-8894)*
United Management Inc 513 936-8568
8280 Montgomery Rd # 303 Cincinnati (45236) *(G-4735)*
United McGill Corporation (HQ) 614 829-1200
1 Mission Park Groveport (43125) *(G-11681)*
United Mercantile Corporation 513 831-1300
575 Chamber Dr Milford (45150) *(G-14571)*
United Methodist Camps, Worthington *Also called West Ohio Conference of* *(G-20007)*
United Methodist Childrens (PA) 614 885-5020
1033 High St Worthington (43085) *(G-20004)*
United Methodist Childrens HM, Worthington *Also called United Methodist Childrens* *(G-20004)*
United Methodist Community Ctr 330 743-5149
2401 Belmont Ave Youngstown (44505) *(G-20398)*
United Ohio Insurance Company 419 562-3011
1725 Hopley Ave Bucyrus (44820) *(G-2050)*
United Omaha Life Insurance Co 216 573-6900
6060 Rockside Woods # 330 Cleveland (44131) *(G-6642)*
United Parcel Service Inc 614 385-9100
1711 Georgesville Rd Columbus (43228) *(G-8895)*
United Parcel Service Inc 440 826-2591
17940 Englewood Dr Cleveland (44130) *(G-6643)*
United Parcel Service Inc 937 859-2314
225 S Alex Rd West Carrollton (45449) *(G-19010)*
United Parcel Service Inc 800 742-5877
1536 N Bridge St Chillicothe (45601) *(G-2892)*
United Parcel Service Inc 440 243-3344
6940 Engle Rd Ste C Middleburg Heights (44130) *(G-14389)*
United Parcel Service Inc 614 431-0600
118 Graceland Blvd Columbus (43214) *(G-8896)*
United Parcel Service Inc 440 846-6000
13500 Pearl Rd Ste 139 Strongsville (44136) *(G-17519)*
United Parcel Service Inc OH 419 747-3080
875 W Longview Ave Mansfield (44906) *(G-13380)*
United Parcel Service Inc OH 513 852-6135
500 Gest St Cincinnati (45203) *(G-4736)*
United Parcel Service Inc OH 800 742-5877
4300 E 68th St Cleveland (44105) *(G-6644)*
United Parcel Service Inc OH 740 373-0772
105 Industry Rd Marietta (45750) *(G-13511)*
United Parcel Service Inc OH 419 222-7399
801 Industry Ave Lima (45804) *(G-12909)*
United Parcel Service Inc OH 216 676-4560
18685 Sheldon Rd Cleveland (44130) *(G-6645)*
United Parcel Service Inc OH 740 363-0636
1675 Us Highway 42 S Delaware (43015) *(G-10133)*
United Parcel Service Inc OH 440 826-3320
3250 Old Airport Rd Wooster (44691) *(G-19921)*
United Parcel Service Inc OH 419 891-6776
1550 Holland Rd Maumee (43537) *(G-13990)*
United Parcel Service Inc OH 419 424-9494
1301 Commerce Pkwy Findlay (45840) *(G-11095)*
United Parcel Service Inc OH 330 545-0177
800 Trumbull Ave Girard (44420) *(G-11427)*
United Parcel Service Inc OH 440 275-3301
1553 State Route 45 Austinburg (44010) *(G-866)*
United Parcel Service Inc OH 330 339-6281
241 8th Street Ext Sw New Philadelphia (44663) *(G-15120)*
United Parcel Service Inc OH 740 598-4293
500 Labelle St Brilliant (43913) *(G-1870)*
United Parcel Service Inc OH 740 592-4570
1 Kenny Dr Athens (45701) *(G-818)*
United Parcel Service Inc OH 614 277-3300
3500 Centerpoint Dr Urbancrest (43123) *(G-18608)*
United Parcel Service Inc OH 740 968-3508
44191 Lafferty Rd Saint Clairsville (43950) *(G-16658)*
United Parcel Service Inc OH 614 841-7159
100 E Campus View Blvd # 300 Columbus (43235) *(G-8897)*
United Parcel Service Inc OH 800 742-5877
1507 Augusta St Zanesville (43701) *(G-20542)*
United Parcel Service Inc OH 419 891-6841
1212 E Alexis Rd Toledo (43612) *(G-18271)*
United Parcel Service Inc OH 330 478-1007
4850 Navarre Rd Sw Canton (44706) *(G-2570)*
United Parcel Service Inc OH 419 586-8556
1851 Industrial Dr Celina (45822) *(G-2665)*
United Parcel Service Inc OH 513 241-5289
640 W 3rd St Cincinnati (45202) *(G-4737)*
United Parcel Service Inc OH 614 383-4580
1476 Likens Rd Marion (43302) *(G-13593)*
United Parcel Service Inc OH 513 782-4000
11141 Canal Rd Cincinnati (45241) *(G-4738)*
United Parcel Service Inc OH 513 241-5316
644 Linn St Ste 325 Cincinnati (45203) *(G-4739)*
United Parcel Service Inc OH 419 872-0211
12171 Eckel Rd Perrysburg (43551) *(G-16066)*
United Parcel Service Inc OH 614 272-8500
2450 Rathmell Rd Obetz (43207) *(G-15672)*
United Parcel Service Inc OH 614 870-4111
5101 Trabue Rd Columbus (43228) *(G-8898)*
United Parcel Service Inc OH 513 863-1681
1951 Logan Ave Hamilton (45015) *(G-11781)*
United Parcel Service Inc OH 937 773-4762
8460 Industry Park Dr Piqua (45356) *(G-16170)*
United Parcel Service Inc OH 419 782-3552
820 Carpenter Rd Defiance (43512) *(G-10062)*
United Parcel Service Inc OH 937 382-0658
2500 S Us Highway 68 Wilmington (45177) *(G-19791)*
United Parcel Service Inc OH 740 962-7971
21 Gingersnap Rd Portsmouth (45662) *(G-16315)*
United Parcel Service Inc OH 800 742-5877
95 Karago Ave Ste 4 Youngstown (44512) *(G-20399)*
United Performance Metals Inc (HQ) 513 860-6500
3475 Symmes Rd Hamilton (45015) *(G-11782)*
United Producers Inc 937 456-4161
617 S Franklin St Eaton (45320) *(G-10579)*
United Producers Inc (PA) 614 433-2150
8351 N High St Ste 250 Columbus (43235) *(G-8899)*
United Rehabilitation Services 937 233-1230
4710 Troy Pike Dayton (45424) *(G-9947)*
United Rentals North Amer Inc 800 877-3687
620 Eckel Rd Perrysburg (43551) *(G-16067)*
United Rest Homes Inc 440 354-2131
308 S State St Painesville (44077) *(G-15884)*
United Road Services Inc 419 837-2703
27400 Luckey Rd Toledo (43605) *(G-18272)*
United Sales Co, Canton *Also called Klase Enterprises Inc* *(G-2427)*
United Scoto Senior Activities (PA) 740 354-6672
117 Market St 119 Portsmouth (45662) *(G-16316)*
United Seating & Mobility LLC 567 302-4000
412 W Dussel Dr Maumee (43537) *(G-13991)*

ALPHABETIC

United Senior Services, Springfield *Also called Elderly United of Springfield* ***(G-17193)***
United Skates America Inc 440 944-5300
30325 Palisades Pkwy Wickliffe (44092) ***(G-19614)***
United Srgcal Prtners Intl Inc 330 702-1489
4147 Westford Dr Canfield (44406) ***(G-2214)***
United States Cargo & Courier 216 325-0483
4735 W 150th St Ste D Cleveland (44135) ***(G-6646)***
United States Cargo & Courier 614 449-2854
2036 Williams Rd Columbus (43207) ***(G-8900)***
United States Commemrtv Art GA 330 494-5504
7800 Whipple Ave Nw Canton (44767) ***(G-2571)***
United States Dept Agriculture 419 626-8439
2900 Columbus Ave Sandusky (44870) ***(G-16806)***
United States Dept of Navy 937 938-3926
2624 Q St Bldg 851 Area B Dayton (45433) ***(G-9286)***
United States Enrichment Corp 740 897-2331
3930 Us Highway 23 Anx Piketon (45661) ***(G-16128)***
United States Enrichment Corp 740 897-2457
3930 Us Rte 23 S Piketon (45661) ***(G-16129)***
United States Protective (PA) 216 475-8550
750 W Resource Dr Ste 200 Independence (44131) ***(G-12271)***
United States Trotting Assn (PA) 614 224-2291
6130 S Sunbury Rd Westerville (43081) ***(G-19447)***
United States Trotting Assn 614 224-2291
800 Michigan Ave Columbus (43215) ***(G-8901)***
United Stationers, Twinsburg *Also called Essendant Inc* ***(G-18413)***
United Steel Service LLC (PA) 330 448-4057
4500 Parkway Dr Brookfield (44403) ***(G-1902)***
United Steelworkers 740 772-5988
196 Burbridge Ave Chillicothe (45601) ***(G-2893)***
United Steelworkers 740 928-0157
2100 James Pkwy Newark (43056) ***(G-15242)***
United Steelworkers 440 979-1050
24371 Lorain Rd Ste 207 North Olmsted (44070) ***(G-15449)***
United Steelworkers 419 238-7980
351 Pleasant St Ste 1 Van Wert (45891) ***(G-18645)***
United Steelworkers 740 633-0899
705 Main St Martins Ferry (43935) ***(G-13603)***
United Steelworkers 440 244-1358
2501 Broadway Lorain (44052) ***(G-13083)***
United Steelworkers 440 354-2328
50 Branch Ave Painesville (44077) ***(G-15885)***
United Steelworkers 614 272-8609
4467 Village Park Dr Columbus (43228) ***(G-8902)***
United Steelworkers 740 622-8860
1048 S 6th St Coshocton (43812) ***(G-9120)***
United Steelworkers 513 793-0272
8968 Blue Ash Rd Cincinnati (45242) ***(G-4740)***
United Steelworkers of America 330 493-7721
4069 Bradley Cir Nw Canton (44718) ***(G-2572)***
United Sttes Bowl Congress Inc 740 922-3120
710 Gorley St Uhrichsville (44683) ***(G-18495)***
United Sttes Bowl Congress Inc 513 761-3338
520 W Wyoming Ave Cincinnati (45215) ***(G-4741)***
United Sttes Bowl Congress Inc 419 531-4058
5062 Dorr St Toledo (43615) ***(G-18273)***
United Sttes Bowl Congress Inc 440 327-0102
38931 Center Ridge Rd North Ridgeville (44039) ***(G-15478)***
United Sttes Bowl Congress Inc 614 237-3716
643 S Hamilton Rd Columbus (43213) ***(G-8903)***
United Studios of America, Canton *Also called Usam Inc* ***(G-2575)***
United Technical Support Svcs 330 562-3330
206 E Garfield Rd Aurora (44202) ***(G-858)***
United Technical Support Svcs 330 562-3330
206 E Garfield Rd Aurora (44202) ***(G-859)***
United Telemanagement Corp 937 454-1888
6450 Poe Ave Ste 401 Dayton (45414) ***(G-9948)***
United Telephone Company Ohio 419 227-1660
122 S Elizabeth St Lima (45801) ***(G-12910)***
United Way, Cincinnati *Also called Family Service* ***(G-3591)***
United Way Central Ohio Inc 614 227-2700
360 S 3rd St Columbus (43215) ***(G-8904)***
United Way Greater Cincinnati (PA) 513 762-7100
2400 Reading Rd Cincinnati (45202) ***(G-4742)***
United Way Greater Cleveland (PA) 216 436-2100
1331 Euclid Ave Cleveland (44115) ***(G-6647)***
United Way Greater Stark Cnty 330 491-0445
401 Market Ave N Ste 300 Canton (44702) ***(G-2573)***
United Way of Greater Toledo (PA) 419 254-4742
424 Jackson St Toledo (43604) ***(G-18274)***
United Way of Summit County 330 762-7601
90 N Prospect St Akron (44304) ***(G-486)***
United Way of The Greater Dayt (PA) 937 225-3060
33 W 1st St Ste 500 Dayton (45402) ***(G-9949)***
United-Maier Signs Inc 513 681-6600
1030 Straight St Cincinnati (45214) ***(G-4743)***
Unitedhealth Group Inc 513 603-6200
400 E Bus Way Ste 100 Cincinnati (45241) ***(G-4744)***
Unity Health Network LLC 330 655-3820
5655 Hudson Dr Ste 110 Hudson (44236) ***(G-12148)***
Unity Health Network LLC (PA) 330 923-5899
3033 State Rd Cuyahoga Falls (44223) ***(G-9229)***
Unity Health Network LLC 330 626-0549
9150 Market Square Dr Streetsboro (44241) ***(G-17435)***
Unity Health Network LLC 330 678-7782
307 W Main St Kent (44240) ***(G-12403)***
Unity Health Network LLC 330 633-7782
116 East Ave Tallmadge (44278) ***(G-17659)***
Unity I Home Healthcare LLC 740 351-0500
221 Market St Portsmouth (45662) ***(G-16317)***
Unity National Bank (HQ) 937 773-0752
215 N Wayne St Piqua (45356) ***(G-16171)***
Univ Dermatology 513 475-7630
3012 Glenmore Ave Ste 307 Cincinnati (45238) ***(G-4745)***
Univ Hospital, The, Cincinnati *Also called University of Cincinnati* ***(G-4776)***
Univar Inc 440 510-1259
33851 Curtis Blvd Ste 208 Eastlake (44095) ***(G-10551)***
Univar USA Inc 513 714-5264
4600 Dues Dr West Chester (45246) ***(G-19239)***
Univar USA Inc 419 666-7880
30450 Tracy Rd Walbridge (43465) ***(G-18779)***
Univar USA Inc 330 425-4330
1686 Highland Rd Twinsburg (44087) ***(G-18482)***
Univar USA Inc 513 870-4050
12 Standen Dr Hamilton (45015) ***(G-11783)***
Univar USA Inc 440 238-8550
21600 Drake Rd Strongsville (44149) ***(G-17520)***
Univenture Inc (PA) 937 645-4600
4266 Tuller Rd Ste 101 Dublin (43017) ***(G-10478)***
Univenture Inc 937 645-4600
4266 Tuller Rd Ste 101 Dublin (43017) ***(G-10479)***
Univenture CD Packg & Systems, Dublin *Also called Univenture Inc* ***(G-10478)***
Universal 1 Credit Union Inc (PA) 800 762-9555
1 River Park Dr Dayton (45409) ***(G-9950)***
Universal Advertising Assoc 513 522-5000
2530 Civic Center Dr Cincinnati (45231) ***(G-4746)***
Universal Contracting, Cincinnati *Also called Finneytown Contracting Corp* ***(G-3612)***
Universal Contracting Corp 513 482-2700
5151 Fishwick Dr Cincinnati (45216) ***(G-4747)***
Universal Development MGT Inc (PA) 330 759-7017
1607 Motor Inn Dr Ste 1 Girard (44420) ***(G-11428)***
Universal Disposal Inc 440 286-3153
9954 Old State Rd Chardon (44024) ***(G-2773)***
Universal Enterprises Inc (PA) 419 529-3500
545 Beer Rd Ontario (44906) ***(G-15718)***
Universal Fabg Cnstr Svcs Inc 614 274-1128
1241 Mckinley Ave Columbus (43222) ***(G-8905)***
Universal Green Energy Solutio 844 723-7768
2086 Belltree Dr Reynoldsburg (43068) ***(G-16487)***
Universal Grinding Corporation 216 631-9410
1234 W 78th St Cleveland (44102) ***(G-6648)***
Universal Health Care Svcs Inc 614 547-0282
2873 Suwanee Rd Columbus (43224) ***(G-8906)***
Universal Marketing Group LLC 419 720-9696
5454 Airport Hwy Toledo (43615) ***(G-18275)***
Universal Nursing Services (PA) 330 434-7318
483 Augusta Dr Akron (44333) ***(G-487)***
Universal Oil Inc 216 771-4300
265 Jefferson Ave Cleveland (44113) ***(G-6649)***
Universal Packg Systems Inc 513 732-2000
5055 State Route 276 Batavia (45103) ***(G-1029)***
Universal Packg Systems Inc 513 674-9400
470 Northland Blvd Cincinnati (45240) ***(G-4748)***
Universal Packg Systems Inc 513 735-4777
5069 State Route 276 Batavia (45103) ***(G-1030)***
Universal Recovery Systems 614 299-0184
5197 Trabue Rd Columbus (43228) ***(G-8907)***
Universal Refrigeration Div, Ontario *Also called Universal Enterprises Inc* ***(G-15718)***
Universal Steel Company 216 883-4972
6600 Grant Ave Cleveland (44105) ***(G-6650)***
Universal Technology Corp (PA) 937 426-2808
1270 N Fairfield Rd Beavercreek (45432) ***(G-1216)***
Universal Transportation Syste 513 539-9491
220 Senate Dr Monroe (45050) ***(G-14716)***
Universal Transportation Syste (PA) 513 829-1287
5284 Winton Rd Fairfield (45014) ***(G-10920)***
Universal Veneer, Granville *Also called Krajewski Corp* ***(G-11468)***
Universal Veneer Mill Corp 740 522-1147
1776 Tamarack Rd Newark (43055) ***(G-15243)***
Universal Work and Power LLC 513 981-1111
4620 Carlynn Dr Blue Ash (45241) ***(G-1714)***
Universial Transportation, Fairfield *Also called Intercoastal Trnsp Systems* ***(G-10862)***
Universities Space Res Assn 216 368-0750
10900 Euclid Ave Cleveland (44106) ***(G-6651)***
UNIVERSITY ADVANCEMENT, Bowling Green *Also called Bowling Green State Univ Fdn* ***(G-1766)***
University Anesthesiologists 216 844-3777
11100 Euclid Ave Ste 2517 Cleveland (44106) ***(G-6652)***
University Cincinnati Book Str, Cincinnati *Also called University of Cincinnati* ***(G-4767)***
University Circle Incorporated (PA) 216 791-3900
10831 Magnolia Dr Cleveland (44106) ***(G-6653)***
University Club Inc 513 721-2600
401 E 4th St Cincinnati (45202) ***(G-4749)***
University Dayton RES Inst, Dayton *Also called University of Dayton* ***(G-9954)***

ALPHABETIC SECTION University Radiology Assoc

University Dermatology Cons......513 584-4775
234 Goodman St A3 Cincinnati (45219) ***(G-4750)***
University Dermatology Cons......513 475-7630
222 Piedmont Ave Ste 5300 Cincinnati (45219) ***(G-4751)***
University Eye Surgeons......614 293-5635
456 W 10th Ave Ste 5241 Columbus (43210) ***(G-8908)***
University Family Physicians......513 929-0104
2123 Auburn Ave Cincinnati (45219) ***(G-4752)***
University Family Physicians......513 475-7505
305 Crescent Ave Cincinnati (45215) ***(G-4753)***
University GYN&ob Cnsltnts Inc (PA)......614 293-8697
1654 Upham Dr Rm N500 Columbus (43210) ***(G-8909)***
University Hosp A & MBL Care, Cincinnati *Also called University of Cincinnati* ***(G-4756)***
University Hosp Hlth Sys Inc, Conneaut *Also called Brown Memorial Hospital* ***(G-9040)***
University Hosp Hlth Sys Shake, Willoughby *Also called University Prmry Care Prctices* ***(G-19720)***
University Hosp Prtage Med Ctr, Ravenna *Also called Robinson Health System Inc* ***(G-16407)***
University Hosp Rdilology Dept, Cincinnati *Also called University of Cincinnati* ***(G-4763)***
University Hospital, Cleveland *Also called University Orthpedic Assoc Inc* ***(G-6667)***
University Hospital, Cincinnati *Also called University of Cincinnati* ***(G-4778)***
University Hospitals......440 250-2001
960 Clague Rd Ste 2410 Westlake (44145) ***(G-19560)***
University Hospitals......216 593-5500
3999 Richmond Rd Cleveland (44122) ***(G-6654)***
University Hospitals......216 536-3020
2915 Ludlow Rd Cleveland (44120) ***(G-6655)***
University Hospitals......440 285-6000
13207 Ravenna Rd Chardon (44024) ***(G-2774)***
University Hospitals (PA)......216 767-8900
3605 Warrensville Ctr Rd Shaker Heights (44122) ***(G-16869)***
University Hospitals......440 743-3000
7007 Powers Blvd Parma (44129) ***(G-15917)***
University Hospitals......216 844-6400
12200 Fairhill Rd Frnt Cleveland (44120) ***(G-6656)***
University Hospitals......216 844-8797
11100 Euclid Ave Wrn5065 Cleveland (44106) ***(G-6657)***
University Hospitals......216 767-8500
11001 Euclid Ave Cleveland (44106) ***(G-6658)***
University Hospitals Cleveland......216 844-1000
11100 Euclid Ave Cleveland (44106) ***(G-6659)***
University Hospitals Cleveland......440 205-5755
9485 Mentor Ave Ste 102 Mentor (44060) ***(G-14252)***
University Hospitals Cleveland (HQ)......216 844-1000
11100 Euclid Ave Cleveland (44106) ***(G-6660)***
University Hospitals Cleveland......216 844-4663
4510 Richmond Rd Cleveland (44128) ***(G-6661)***
University Hospitals Cleveland......216 844-3323
3605 Warrensville Ctr Rd Shaker Heights (44122) ***(G-16870)***
University Hospitals Cleveland......216 721-8457
23215 Commerce Park # 300 Beachwood (44122) ***(G-1135)***
University Hospitals Cleveland......216 844-3528
11100 Euclid Ave Cleveland (44106) ***(G-6662)***
University Hospitals He......216 844-4663
4510 Richmond Rd Cleveland (44128) ***(G-6663)***
University Hospitals Health (PA)......440 285-4040
12340 Bass Lake Rd Chardon (44024) ***(G-2775)***
University Hospitals Health Sy......216 844-4663
11100 Euclid Ave Cleveland (44106) ***(G-6664)***
University Hospitals Hlth Sys, Bedford *Also called Community Hospital of Bedford* ***(G-1301)***
University Hospitals Hlth Sys, Beachwood *Also called Qualchoice Inc* ***(G-1117)***
University Hospitals Parma, Parma *Also called University Hospitals* ***(G-15917)***
University Hsptl-Uc Physicians, Cincinnati *Also called University of Cincinnati* ***(G-4759)***
University Manor Hlth Care Ctr......216 721-1400
2186 Ambleside Dr Cleveland (44106) ***(G-6665)***
University Medical Assoc Inc......740 593-0753
350 Parks Hall Athens (45701) ***(G-819)***
University Mednet (PA)......216 383-0100
18599 Lake Shore Blvd Euclid (44119) ***(G-10780)***
University Mednet......440 255-0800
9000 Mentor Ave Ste 101 Mentor (44060) ***(G-14253)***
University Mednet......440 285-9079
22750 Rockside Rd Ste 210 Bedford (44146) ***(G-1343)***
University Moving & Storage Co......248 615-7000
8735 Rite Track Way West Chester (45069) ***(G-19174)***
University Neurology Inc......513 475-8730
222 Piedmont Ave Ste 3200 Cincinnati (45219) ***(G-4754)***
University of Akron......330 972-6008
170 University Ave Akron (44325) ***(G-488)***
University of Akron......330 972-8210
108 Fir Hl Akron (44325) ***(G-489)***
University of Cincinnati......513 558-4194
231 Albert Sabin Way Cincinnati (45267) ***(G-4755)***
University of Cincinnati......513 584-7522
3200 Burnet Ave Cincinnati (45229) ***(G-4756)***
University of Cincinnati......513 558-4516
231 Albert Sabin Way Cincinnati (45267) ***(G-4757)***
University of Cincinnati......513 558-7700
260 Stetson St Ste 3200 Cincinnati (45219) ***(G-4758)***
University of Cincinnati......513 475-8771
222 Piedmont Ave Ste 7000 Cincinnati (45219) ***(G-4759)***
University of Cincinnati......513 558-1200
3130 Highland Ave Fl 3 Cincinnati (45219) ***(G-4760)***
University of Cincinnati......513 556-6381
51 Goodman St Cincinnati (45219) ***(G-4761)***
University of Cincinnati......513 558-4444
3125 Eden Ave Cincinnati (45219) ***(G-4762)***
University of Cincinnati......513 584-4396
234 Goodman St 761 Cincinnati (45219) ***(G-4763)***
University of Cincinnati......513 556-5087
146 Mcmicken Hall Cincinnati (45221) ***(G-4764)***
University of Cincinnati......513 556-4054
2614 Mecken Cir Cincinnati (45221) ***(G-4765)***
University of Cincinnati......513 558-5439
3223 Eden Avenue Cincinnati (45267) ***(G-4766)***
University of Cincinnati......513 556-4200
51 W Goodman Dr Cincinnati (45221) ***(G-4767)***
University of Cincinnati......513 558-4231
231 Albert Sabin Way Cincinnati (45267) ***(G-4768)***
University of Cincinnati......513 584-5331
234 Goodman St Cincinnati (45219) ***(G-4769)***
University of Cincinnati......513 556-3732
500 Geo Physics Bldg 5f Cincinnati (45221) ***(G-4770)***
University of Cincinnati......513 556-4603
2751 O'vrsity Way Ste 880 Cincinnati (45221) ***(G-4771)***
University of Cincinnati......513 558-1799
3001 Short Vine St Cincinnati (45219) ***(G-4772)***
University of Cincinnati......513 584-3200
234 Goodman St Cincinnati (45219) ***(G-4773)***
University of Cincinnati......513 558-5471
231 Albert Sabin Way G258 Cincinnati (45267) ***(G-4774)***
University of Cincinnati......513 475-8524
222 Piedmont Ave Ste 6000 Cincinnati (45219) ***(G-4775)***
University of Cincinnati......513 584-1000
331 Albert Sabin Way Cincinnati (45229) ***(G-4776)***
University of Cincinnati......513 558-4831
231 Albert Sabin Way Cincinnati (45267) ***(G-4777)***
University of Cincinnati......513 584-1000
234 Goodman St Cincinnati (45219) ***(G-4778)***
University of Cincinnati......513 556-3803
Edwards 1 Bldg Cincinnati (45221) ***(G-4779)***
University of Cincinnati Phys......513 475-8000
7700 University Ct # 1800 West Chester (45069) ***(G-19175)***
University of Cincinnati Phys (PA)......513 475-8521
222 Piedmont Ave Ste 2200 Cincinnati (45219) ***(G-4780)***
University of Cincinnati Phys......513 475-7934
2830 Victory Pkwy Ste 320 Cincinnati (45206) ***(G-4781)***
University of Cncnnati Srgeons (PA)......513 245-3300
2830 Victory Pkwy Ste 320 Cincinnati (45206) ***(G-4782)***
University of Dayton......937 255-3141
300 College Park Ave Dayton (45469) ***(G-9951)***
University of Dayton (PA)......937 229-2919
300 College Park Ave Dayton (45469) ***(G-9952)***
University of Dayton......937 229-2113
300 College St Dayton (45402) ***(G-9953)***
University of Dayton......937 229-3822
711 E Monu Ave Ste 101 Dayton (45469) ***(G-9954)***
University of Dayton......937 229-3913
1529 Brown St Dayton (45469) ***(G-9955)***
University of Dyton Schl Engrg, Dayton *Also called University of Dayton* ***(G-9953)***
University of Findlay......419 434-4516
1015 N Main St Findlay (45840) ***(G-11096)***
University of Findlay......419 434-4531
1000 N Main St Findlay (45840) ***(G-11097)***
University of Individuality, Akron *Also called Community Hbilitation Svcs Inc* ***(G-155)***
University of Tledo Foundation......419 530-7730
2801 W Bancroft St 1002 Toledo (43606) ***(G-18276)***
University of Toledo......419 534-3770
3120 Glendale Ave Ste 79 Toledo (43614) ***(G-18277)***
University of Toledo......419 383-3556
4430 N Hllnd Sylvnia Rd Apt 7101 Toledo (43623) ***(G-18278)***
University of Toledo......419 383-4000
3000 Arlington Ave Toledo (43614) ***(G-18279)***
University of Toledo......419 383-5322
3000 Arlington Ave Toledo (43614) ***(G-18280)***
University of Toledo......419 383-3759
3000 Arlington Ave Toledo (43614) ***(G-18281)***
University of Toledo......419 383-4229
3000 Arlington Ave Toledo (43614) ***(G-18282)***
University of Toledo Med Ctr, Toledo *Also called University of Toledo* ***(G-18279)***
University Ophthalmology Assoc......216 382-8022
1611 S Green Rd Ste 306c Cleveland (44121) ***(G-6666)***
University Orthopaedic Cnsltnt......513 475-8690
222 Piedmont Ave Ste 2200 Cincinnati (45219) ***(G-4783)***
University Orthpedic Assoc Inc (PA)......216 844-1000
11100 Euclid Ave Ste 3001 Cleveland (44106) ***(G-6667)***
University Otolaryngologists (PA)......614 273-2241
810 Mackenzie Dr Columbus (43220) ***(G-8910)***
University Park Nursing Home, Cleveland *Also called Progressive Park LLC* ***(G-6320)***
University Plz Ht Cnfrence Ctr, Columbus *Also called River Road Hotel Corp* ***(G-8634)***
University Prmry Care Prctices (HQ)......440 946-7391
4212 State Route 306 # 304 Willoughby (44094) ***(G-19720)***
University Radiology Assoc......513 475-8760
222 Piedmont Ave Ste 2100 Cincinnati (45219) ***(G-4784)***

ALPHABETIC

University Rdlgsts of Clveland....216 844-1700
2485 Euclid Ave Cleveland (44115) ***(G-6668)***
University Settlement Inc (PA)....216 641-8948
4800 Broadway Ave Cleveland (44127) ***(G-6669)***
University Suburban Health Ctr (PA)....216 382-8920
1611 S Green Rd Ste A61 Cleveland (44121) ***(G-6670)***
University Surgeons Inc....216 844-3021
11100 Euclid Ave 7002 Cleveland (44106) ***(G-6671)***
University Tech Service, Columbus *Also called Ohio State University* ***(G-8407)***
University Toledo Medical Ctr, Toledo *Also called University of Toledo* ***(G-18278)***
University Toledo Physicians, Toledo *Also called Medical College of Ohio* ***(G-18048)***
University Womens Healthcare....937 208-2948
627 S Edwin C Moses Blvd Dayton (45417) ***(G-9956)***
Universty of Cincinnti Medcl C (PA)....513 584-1000
234 Goodman St Cincinnati (45219) ***(G-4785)***
Universty of Cincinnti Medcl C....513 475-8000
222 Piedmont Ave Cincinnati (45219) ***(G-4786)***
Universty of Cincinnti Medcl C....513 475-8300
7690 Discovery Dr # 3000 West Chester (45069) ***(G-19176)***
Unknown, Massillon *Also called Round Room LLC* ***(G-13851)***
Unknown, Canton *Also called Prime Communications LP* ***(G-2494)***
Unknown, Beavercreek *Also called Round Room LLC* ***(G-1206)***
Unpacking Etc....440 871-0506
787 Bassett Rd Westlake (44145) ***(G-19561)***
UNUM Life Insurance Co Amer....614 807-2500
445 Hutchinson Ave # 300 Columbus (43235) ***(G-8911)***
Upgrade Homes....614 975-8532
586 Blenheim Rd Columbus (43214) ***(G-8912)***
Uph Holdings LLC....614 447-9777
3100 Olentangy River Rd Columbus (43202) ***(G-8913)***
Upper Arlington City Schl Dst....614 487-5133
4770 Burbank Dr Columbus (43220) ***(G-8914)***
Upper Arlington Lutheran Ch (PA)....614 451-3736
2300 Lytham Rd Columbus (43220) ***(G-8915)***
Upper Arlington Surgery Center....614 442-6515
2240 N Bank Dr Columbus (43220) ***(G-8916)***
Upper Valley Family Care....937 339-5355
200 Kienle Dr Piqua (45356) ***(G-16172)***
Upreach LLC....614 442-7702
4488 Mobile Dr Columbus (43220) ***(G-8917)***
UPS, Mansfield *Also called United Parcel Service Inc OH* ***(G-13380)***
UPS, Cincinnati *Also called United Parcel Service Inc OH* ***(G-4736)***
UPS, Cleveland *Also called United Parcel Service Inc OH* ***(G-6644)***
UPS, Marietta *Also called United Parcel Service Inc OH* ***(G-13511)***
UPS, Lima *Also called United Parcel Service Inc OH* ***(G-12909)***
UPS, Cleveland *Also called United Parcel Service Inc OH* ***(G-6645)***
UPS, Delaware *Also called United Parcel Service Inc OH* ***(G-10133)***
UPS, Wooster *Also called United Parcel Service Inc OH* ***(G-19921)***
UPS, Maumee *Also called United Parcel Service Inc OH* ***(G-13990)***
UPS, Findlay *Also called United Parcel Service Inc OH* ***(G-11095)***
UPS, Girard *Also called United Parcel Service Inc OH* ***(G-11427)***
UPS, Columbus *Also called United Parcel Service Inc* ***(G-8895)***
UPS, Austinburg *Also called United Parcel Service Inc OH* ***(G-866)***
UPS, New Philadelphia *Also called United Parcel Service Inc OH* ***(G-15120)***
UPS, Brilliant *Also called United Parcel Service Inc OH* ***(G-1870)***
UPS, Cleveland *Also called United Parcel Service Inc* ***(G-6643)***
UPS, Athens *Also called United Parcel Service Inc OH* ***(G-818)***
UPS, West Carrollton *Also called United Parcel Service Inc* ***(G-19010)***
UPS, Urbancrest *Also called United Parcel Service Inc OH* ***(G-18608)***
UPS, Saint Clairsville *Also called United Parcel Service Inc OH* ***(G-16658)***
UPS, Chillicothe *Also called United Parcel Service Inc* ***(G-2892)***
UPS, Columbus *Also called United Parcel Service Inc OH* ***(G-8897)***
UPS, Zanesville *Also called United Parcel Service Inc OH* ***(G-20542)***
UPS, Toledo *Also called United Parcel Service Inc OH* ***(G-18271)***
UPS, Canton *Also called United Parcel Service Inc OH* ***(G-2570)***
UPS, Celina *Also called United Parcel Service Inc OH* ***(G-2665)***
UPS, Cincinnati *Also called United Parcel Service Inc OH* ***(G-4737)***
UPS, Middleburg Heights *Also called United Parcel Service Inc* ***(G-14389)***
UPS, Marion *Also called United Parcel Service Inc OH* ***(G-13593)***
UPS, Cincinnati *Also called United Parcel Service Inc OH* ***(G-4738)***
UPS, Cincinnati *Also called United Parcel Service Inc OH* ***(G-4739)***
UPS, Perrysburg *Also called United Parcel Service Inc OH* ***(G-16066)***
UPS, Obetz *Also called United Parcel Service Inc OH* ***(G-15672)***
UPS, Columbus *Also called United Parcel Service Inc OH* ***(G-8898)***
UPS, Hamilton *Also called United Parcel Service Inc OH* ***(G-11781)***
UPS, Piqua *Also called United Parcel Service Inc OH* ***(G-16170)***
UPS, Defiance *Also called United Parcel Service Inc OH* ***(G-10062)***
UPS, Wilmington *Also called United Parcel Service Inc OH* ***(G-19791)***
UPS, Columbus *Also called United Parcel Service Inc* ***(G-8896)***
UPS, Portsmouth *Also called United Parcel Service Inc OH* ***(G-16315)***
UPS, Youngstown *Also called United Parcel Service Inc OH* ***(G-20399)***
UPS, Strongsville *Also called United Parcel Service Inc* ***(G-17519)***

UPS Ground Freight Inc....330 659-6693
3495 Brecksville Rd Richfield (44286) ***(G-16531)***
UPS Ground Freight Inc....937 236-4700
3730 Valley St Dayton (45424) ***(G-9957)***
UPS Ground Freight Inc....330 448-0440
7945 3rd St Masury (44438) ***(G-13869)***
Uptime Corporation....216 661-1655
4820 Van Epps Rd Brooklyn Heights (44131) ***(G-1930)***
Uptown Hair & Day Spa, Englewood *Also called Uptown Hair Studio Inc* ***(G-10723)***
Uptown Hair Studio Inc....937 832-2111
390 W National Rd Englewood (45322) ***(G-10723)***
Uranium Disposition Svcs LLC....740 289-3620
3930 Us Highway 23 Anx Piketon (45661) ***(G-16130)***
Urban Craft, Grove City *Also called Young Mens Christian Assoc* ***(G-11620)***
Urban Express Transportation, Columbus *Also called Eastern Horizon Inc* ***(G-7564)***
Urban Leagu of Greater Clevlnd....216 622-0999
2930 Prospect Ave E Cleveland (44115) ***(G-6672)***
Urban League of Greater Southw....513 281-9955
3458 Reading Rd Cincinnati (45229) ***(G-4787)***
Urban Oassis Inc....614 766-9946
5555 Wall St Dublin (43017) ***(G-10480)***
Urban One Inc....216 579-1111
6555 Carnegie Ave Cleveland (44103) ***(G-6673)***
Urban One Inc....513 749-1009
1821 Summit Rd Ste 400 Cincinnati (45237) ***(G-4788)***
Urban One Inc....614 487-1444
350 E 1st Ave Ste 100 Columbus (43201) ***(G-8918)***
Urban One Inc....216 861-0100
1041 Huron Rd E Cleveland (44115) ***(G-6674)***
Urban One Inc....513 679-6000
705 Central Ave Ste 200 Cincinnati (45202) ***(G-4789)***
Urban Retail Properties LLC....513 346-4482
7875 Montgomery Rd Cincinnati (45236) ***(G-4790)***
Urbancrest Affrdbl Hsing LLC....614 228-3578
3443 Agler Rd Ste 200 Columbus (43219) ***(G-8919)***
Urological Associates Inc....614 221-5189
750 Mount Carmel Mall # 350 Columbus (43222) ***(G-8920)***
Urology Group, Cincinnati *Also called Tri State Urlogic Svcs PSC Inc* ***(G-4684)***
URS, Cleveland *Also called Aecom Energy & Cnstr Inc* ***(G-4963)***
URS, Cleveland *Also called Aecom Energy & Cnstr Inc* ***(G-4964)***
URS, Cleveland *Also called Aecom Energy & Cnstr Inc* ***(G-4965)***
URS Group Inc....330 836-9111
564 White Pond Dr Akron (44320) ***(G-490)***
URS Group Inc....216 622-2300
1300 E 9th St Ste 500 Cleveland (44114) ***(G-6675)***
URS Group Inc....614 464-4500
277 W Nationwide Blvd Columbus (43215) ***(G-8921)***
URS Group Inc....513 651-3440
525 Vine St Ste 1900 Cincinnati (45202) ***(G-4791)***
URS-Smith Group VA Idiq Joint....614 464-4500
277 W Nationwide Blvd Columbus (43215) ***(G-8922)***
Ursuline Center, Toledo *Also called Ursuline Convent Sacred Heart* ***(G-18283)***
Ursuline Convent Sacred Heart....419 531-8990
4035 Indian Rd Toledo (43606) ***(G-18283)***
US Airways, Cleveland *Also called American Airlines Inc* ***(G-5003)***
US Airways, Vandalia *Also called American Airlines Inc* ***(G-18656)***
US Airways Express, Vandalia *Also called Psa Airlines Inc* ***(G-18695)***
US Bank, Cincinnati *Also called US Bank National Association* ***(G-4792)***
US Bank, Portsmouth *Also called US Bank National Association* ***(G-16318)***
US Bank, Cincinnati *Also called US Bank National Association* ***(G-4793)***
US Bank, Cincinnati *Also called US Bank National Association* ***(G-4794)***
US Bank, Fairborn *Also called US Bank National Association* ***(G-10807)***
US Bank, Troy *Also called US Bank National Association* ***(G-18384)***
US Bank, Sidney *Also called US Bank National Association* ***(G-16958)***
US Bank National Association (HQ)....513 632-4234
425 Walnut St Fl 1 Cincinnati (45202) ***(G-4792)***
US Bank National Association....740 353-4151
602 Chillicothe St Frnt Portsmouth (45662) ***(G-16318)***
US Bank National Association....513 979-1000
5065 Wooster Rd Cincinnati (45226) ***(G-4793)***
US Bank National Association....513 458-2844
2300 Wall St Ste A Cincinnati (45212) ***(G-4794)***
US Bank National Association....937 873-7845
1 W Main St Fairborn (45324) ***(G-10807)***
US Bank National Association....937 335-8351
910 W Main St Troy (45373) ***(G-18384)***
US Bank National Association....937 498-1131
115 E Court St Sidney (45365) ***(G-16958)***
US Bronco Services Inc....513 829-9880
280 Donald Dr Fairfield (45014) ***(G-10921)***
US Communications and Elc Inc....440 519-0880
4933 Neo Pkwy Cleveland (44128) ***(G-6676)***
US Dental Care/M D Gelender....614 252-3181
949 E Livingston Ave Columbus (43205) ***(G-8923)***
US Dept of the Air Force....937 257-0837
4881 Sug Mple Dr Bldg 830 Dayton (45433) ***(G-9287)***
US Dept of the Air Force....937 255-5150
2856 G St Dayton (45433) ***(G-9288)***
US Expediting Logistics LLC....937 235-1014
4311 Old Springfield Rd Vandalia (45377) ***(G-18704)***

ALPHABETIC SECTION — Valley Hospice Inc (PA)

US Federal District Court, Dayton *Also called 6th Circuit Court* (G-9294)
US Foods Inc 330 963-6789
  8000 Bavaria Rd Twinsburg (44087) (G-18483)
US Foods Inc 614 539-7993
  5445 Spellmire Dr West Chester (45246) (G-19240)
US Home Center LLC (PA) 614 737-9000
  2050 Integrity Dr S Columbus (43209) (G-8924)
US Inspection Services Inc (HQ) 937 660-9879
  7333 Paragon Rd Ste 240 Dayton (45459) (G-9958)
US Inspection Services Inc 513 671-7073
  502 W Crescentville Rd Cincinnati (45246) (G-4795)
US Molding Machinery Co Inc 440 918-1701
  38294 Pelton Rd Willoughby (44094) (G-19721)
US Oncology Inc 937 352-2140
  1141 N Monroe Dr Xenia (45385) (G-20082)
US Probation, Toledo *Also called Supreme Court United States* (G-18212)
US Probation & Parole Svc., Cincinnati *Also called Supreme Court United States* (G-4605)
US Probation Office, Cleveland *Also called Supreme Court United States* (G-6558)
US Probation Office, Columbus *Also called 6th Circuit Court* (G-6915)
US Protection Service LLC 513 422-7910
  1850 W Galbraith Rd Cincinnati (45239) (G-4796)
US Safetygear Inc (PA) 330 898-1344
  5001 Enterprise Dr Nw Warren (44481) (G-18919)
US Security Associates Inc 513 381-7033
  230 Northland Blvd # 307 Cincinnati (45246) (G-4797)
US Security Associates Inc 937 454-9035
  69 N Dixie Dr Ste F Vandalia (45377) (G-18705)
US Security Holdings Inc 614 488-6110
  1350 W 5th Ave Ste 300 Columbus (43212) (G-8925)
US Swimming Lake Erie Swimming 330 423-0485
  301 Rockledge Dr Bay Village (44140) (G-1042)
US Tech Arospc Engrg Corp (PA) 330 455-1181
  4200 Munson St Nw Canton (44718) (G-2574)
US Technology Aerospace, Canton *Also called US Tech Arospc Engrg Corp* (G-2574)
US Tsubaki Power Transm LLC 419 626-4560
  1010 Edgewater Ave Sandusky (44870) (G-16807)
US Tubular Products Inc 330 832-1734
  14852 Lincoln Way W North Lawrence (44666) (G-15394)
USA Parking Systems Inc 216 621-9255
  1325 Carnegie Ave Frnt Cleveland (44115) (G-6677)
Usaf Sctt 937 257-0228
  4180 Watson Way Dayton (45433) (G-9289)
Usaf-Medical Center, Dayton *Also called US Dept of the Air Force* (G-9287)
Usam Inc 330 244-8782
  4450 Belden Village St Nw # 305 Canton (44718) (G-2575)
Usavinyl LLC 614 771-4805
  5795 Green Pointe Dr S Groveport (43125) (G-11682)
Usec, Piketon *Also called United States Enrichment Corp* (G-16128)
USF Holland Inc 740 441-1200
  95 Holland Dr Gallipolis (45631) (G-11340)
USF Holland LLC 513 874-8960
  10074 Prncton Glendale Rd West Chester (45246) (G-19241)
USF Holland LLC 419 354-6633
  20820 Midstar Dr Bowling Green (43402) (G-1796)
USF Holland LLC 614 529-9300
  4800 Journal St Columbus (43228) (G-8926)
USF Holland LLC 937 233-7600
  2700 Valley Pike Dayton (45404) (G-9959)
USF Holland LLC 216 941-4340
  10720 Memphis Ave Cleveland (44144) (G-6678)
USF Holland LLC 330 549-2917
  10855 Market St North Lima (44452) (G-15408)
USFreightways, West Chester *Also called USF Holland LLC* (G-19241)
USFreightways, Columbus *Also called USF Holland LLC* (G-8926)
USFreightways, Dayton *Also called USF Holland LLC* (G-9959)
USFreightways, Cleveland *Also called USF Holland LLC* (G-6678)
USFreightways, North Lima *Also called USF Holland LLC* (G-15408)
USFreightways, Gallipolis *Also called USF Holland Inc* (G-11340)
Ushc Physicians Inc 216 382-2036
  1611 S Green Rd Ste 260 Cleveland (44121) (G-6679)
Usher Transport Inc 614 875-0528
  2040 Hendrix Dr Grove City (43123) (G-11607)
Usi Inc 419 243-1191
  1120 Madison Ave Toledo (43604) (G-18284)
USI Cable Corp 937 606-2636
  102 Fox Dr Piqua (45356) (G-16173)
USI Insurance Services Nat 614 228-5565
  580 N 4th St Ste 400 Columbus (43215) (G-8927)
USI Midwest LLC (HQ) 513 852-6300
  312 Elm St Ste 24 Cincinnati (45202) (G-4798)
Usic Locating Services LLC 330 733-9393
  441 Munroe Falls Rd Akron (44312) (G-491)
Usic Locating Services LLC 419 874-9988
  12769 Eagleville Rd B North Baltimore (45872) (G-15316)
Usic Locating Services LLC 513 554-0456
  3478 Hauck Rd Ste D Cincinnati (45241) (G-4799)
Ussa Inc 740 354-6672
  117 119 Market St Portsmouth (45662) (G-16319)
Uswa, Chillicothe *Also called United Steelworkers* (G-2893)
Uswa, Newark *Also called United Steelworkers* (G-15242)
Uswa, North Olmsted *Also called United Steelworkers* (G-15449)
Uswa, Van Wert *Also called United Steelworkers* (G-18645)
Uswa, Martins Ferry *Also called United Steelworkers* (G-13603)
Uswa, Lorain *Also called United Steelworkers* (G-13083)
Uswa, Painesville *Also called United Steelworkers* (G-15885)
Uswa, Columbus *Also called United Steelworkers* (G-8902)
Uswa, Coshocton *Also called United Steelworkers* (G-9120)
Uswa, Cincinnati *Also called United Steelworkers* (G-4740)
Uswa, Canton *Also called United Steelworkers of America* (G-2572)
Utah Spas, Toledo *Also called Spa Fitness Centers Inc* (G-18193)
Utica East Ohio Midstream LLC 740 431-4168
  8349 Azalea Rd Sw Dennison (44621) (G-10168)
Utica National Insurance Group 614 823-5300
  2600 Corp Exchange Dr # 200 Columbus (43231) (G-8928)
Utica Nursing Home, Utica *Also called Living Care Altrntves of Utica* (G-18613)
Utilicon Corporation 216 391-8500
  888 E 70th St Cleveland (44103) (G-6680)
Utilities Department, Toledo *Also called City of Toledo* (G-17807)
Utilities Dept, Painesville *Also called City of Painesville* (G-15841)
Utility Field Services, Lima *Also called City of Lima* (G-12756)
Utility Technologies Intl Corp 614 879-7624
  4700 Homer Ohio Ln Groveport (43125) (G-11683)
Utility Trailer Mfg Co 513 436-2600
  4225 Curliss Ln Batavia (45103) (G-1031)
Uts, Fairfield *Also called Universal Transportation Syste* (G-10920)
Uts Inc 513 332-9000
  P.O. Box 36342 Cincinnati (45236) (G-4800)
Utter Construction Inc 513 876-2246
  1302 State Route 133 Bethel (45106) (G-1484)
Uvmc Management Corporation (HQ) 937 440-4000
  3130 N County Road 25a Troy (45373) (G-18385)
Uvmc Nursing Care Inc 937 440-7663
  3232 N County Road 25a Troy (45373) (G-18386)
Uvmc Nursing Care Inc 937 473-2075
  75 Mote Dr Covington (45318) (G-9140)
Uvmc Nursing Care Inc 937 667-7500
  4375 S County Road 25a Tipp City (45371) (G-17731)
V and V Appliance Parts Inc (PA) 330 743-5144
  27 W Myrtle Ave Youngstown (44507) (G-20400)
V Clew LLC 740 687-2273
  1201 River Valley Blvd Lancaster (43130) (G-12582)
V F, Portsmouth *Also called Valley Wholesale Foods Inc* (G-16320)
V H Cooper & Co Inc (HQ) 419 375-4116
  2321 State Route 49 Fort Recovery (45846) (G-11120)
V M Systems Inc 419 535-1044
  3125 Hill Ave Toledo (43607) (G-18285)
V N A, Cleveland *Also called Visiting Nrse Assn of Clveland* (G-6702)
V Vrable Inc 614 545-5500
  3248 Henderson Rd Ste 104 Columbus (43220) (G-8929)
V Westaar Inc 740 803-2803
  6249 Westwick Pl Lewis Center (43035) (G-12709)
VA Medical Center Automated RE 740 772-7118
  17273 State Route 104 Chillicothe (45601) (G-2894)
Vacationland Federal Credit Un 440 967-5155
  2911 Hayes Ave Sandusky (44870) (G-16808)
Vadakin Inc 740 373-7518
  110 Industry Rd Marietta (45750) (G-13512)
Vahalla Company Inc 216 326-2245
  3257 E 139th St Cleveland (44120) (G-6681)
Vala Holdings Ltd 216 398-2980
  1825 Snow Rd Ste 1 Parma (44134) (G-15918)
Valentine Buick Gmc Inc 937 878-7371
  1105 N Central Ave Fairborn (45324) (G-10808)
Valentine Group, Dayton *Also called Mv Land Development Company* (G-9764)
Valentour Education Inc 937 434-5949
  8095 Garnet Dr Dayton (45458) (G-9960)
Valicor Environmental Svcs LLC (HQ) 513 733-4666
  1045 Reed Dr Ste A Monroe (45050) (G-14717)
Validex, Cincinnati *Also called DE Foxx & Associates Inc* (G-3470)
Valleaire Golf Club Inc 440 237-9191
  6969 Boston Rd Hinckley (44233) (G-12000)
Vallejo Company 216 741-3933
  4429 State Rd Ste 1 Cleveland (44109) (G-6682)
Vallen Distribution Inc 513 942-9100
  9407 Meridian Way West Chester (45069) (G-19177)
Valley Acoustics Inc 330 799-1894
  1203 N Meridian Rd Youngstown (44509) (G-20401)
Valley Care Health System, Warren *Also called Community Health Systems Inc* (G-18836)
Valley Electrical Cnsld Inc 330 539-4044
  977 Tibbetts Wick Rd Girard (44420) (G-11429)
Valley Fleet, Ashland *Also called Valley Transportation Inc* (G-704)
Valley Ford Truck Inc (PA) 216 524-2400
  5715 Canal Rd Cleveland (44125) (G-6683)
Valley Gstrnterology Endoscopy, Martins Ferry *Also called Wheeling Hospital Inc* (G-13604)
Valley Harley Davidson Co (PA) 740 695-9591
  41255 Reco Rd Belmont (43718) (G-1431)
Valley Harley Davidson-Buell, Belmont *Also called Valley Harley Davidson Co* (G-1431)
Valley Hospice Inc (PA) 740 859-5041
  10686 State Route 150 Rayland (43943) (G-16419)

Valley Hospitality Inc 740 374-9660
701 Pike St Marietta (45750) ***(G-13513)***
Valley Industrial Trucks Inc (PA) 330 788-4081
1152 Meadowbrook Ave Youngstown (44512) ***(G-20402)***
Valley Interior Systems Inc 937 890-7319
2760 Thunderhawk Ct Dayton (45414) ***(G-9961)***
Valley Interior Systems Inc (PA) 513 961-0400
2203 Fowler St Cincinnati (45206) ***(G-4801)***
Valley Interior Systems Inc 614 351-8440
3840 Fisher Rd Columbus (43228) ***(G-8930)***
Valley Machine Tool Co Inc 513 899-2737
9773 Morrow Cozaddale Rd Morrow (45152) ***(G-14847)***
Valley Regional Surgery Center 877 858-5029
283 Looney Rd Piqua (45356) ***(G-16174)***
Valley Riding 216 267-2525
19901 Puritas Ave Cleveland (44135) ***(G-6684)***
Valley Roofing LLC 513 831-9444
5293 Tech Valley Dr Milford (45150) ***(G-14572)***
Valley Sterling of Cleveland, Cleveland *Also called Valley Ford Truck Inc* ***(G-6683)***
Valley Title & Escro Agency 330 392-6171
2833 Elm Rd Ne Warren (44483) ***(G-18920)***
Valley Title & Escrow Agency 440 632-9833
15985 E High St Ste 203 Middlefield (44062) ***(G-14404)***
Valley Transportation Inc 419 289-6200
1 Valley Dr Ashland (44805) ***(G-704)***
Valley View Alzhimers Care Ctr 740 998-2948
3363 Ragged Ridge Rd Frankfort (45628) ***(G-11146)***
Valley View Fire Dept 216 524-7200
6899 Hathaway Rd Cleveland (44125) ***(G-6685)***
Valley View Golf Club Inc 330 928-9034
3600 Haas Rd Cuyahoga Falls (44223) ***(G-9230)***
Valley View Health Center, Portsmouth *Also called Community Action Comm Pike CNT* ***(G-16272)***
Valley View Health Center, Jackson *Also called Community Action Comm Pike CNT* ***(G-12310)***
Valley View Place 740 454-7720
3200 Shale Dr Zanesville (43701) ***(G-20543)***
Valley Wholesale Foods Inc (PA) 740 354-5216
415 Market St Portsmouth (45662) ***(G-16320)***
Valleyview Management Co Inc 419 886-4000
855 Comfort Plaza Dr Bellville (44813) ***(G-1426)***
Valleywood Golf Club Inc 419 826-3991
13501 Airport Hwy Swanton (43558) ***(G-17574)***
Valmark Insurance Agency LLC 330 576-1234
130 Springside Dr Ste 300 Akron (44333) ***(G-492)***
Valmark Securities Inc (HQ) 330 576-1234
130 Springside Dr Ste 300 Akron (44333) ***(G-493)***
Valmer Land Title Agency (PA) 614 860-0005
2227 State Route 256 B Reynoldsburg (43068) ***(G-16488)***
Valmer Land Title Agency 614 875-7001
3383 Farm Bank Way Grove City (43123) ***(G-11608)***
Valucadd Solutions, Cincinnati *Also called Twism Enterprises LLC* ***(G-4711)***
Value Auto Auction LLC 740 982-3030
3776 Hc 93 Crooksville (43731) ***(G-9153)***
Value City, Columbus *Also called American Signature Inc* ***(G-7007)***
Value City Furniture Inc 330 929-2111
790 Howe Ave Cuyahoga Falls (44221) ***(G-9231)***
Value Recovery Group Inc (PA) 614 324-5959
919 Old Henderson Rd Columbus (43220) ***(G-8931)***
Valvoline Instant Oil Change 937 548-0123
661 Wagner Ave Greenville (45331) ***(G-11522)***
Valvoline LLC 513 557-3100
3901 River Rd Cincinnati (45204) ***(G-4802)***
Van Buren Dental Associates 937 253-9115
1950 S Smithville Rd Kettering (45420) ***(G-12437)***
Van Con Inc 937 890-8400
8535 N Dixie Dr Ste B Dayton (45414) ***(G-9962)***
Van Devere Inc (PA) 330 253-6137
300 W Market St Akron (44303) ***(G-494)***
Van Devere Buick, Akron *Also called Van Devere Inc* ***(G-494)***
Van Dyk Mortgage Corporation 513 429-2122
4680 Parkway Dr Ste 100 Mason (45040) ***(G-13777)***
Van Dyne-Crotty Co (PA) 614 684-0048
2150 Fairwood Ave Columbus (43207) ***(G-8932)***
Van Dyne-Crotty Co 614 491-3903
2150 Fairwood Ave Columbus (43207) ***(G-8933)***
Van Dyne-Crotty Co 440 248-6935
30400 Bruce Indus Pkwy Solon (44139) ***(G-17064)***
Van Howards Lines Inc 937 235-0007
3516 Wright Way Rd Ste 2 Dayton (45424) ***(G-9963)***
Van Mayberrys & Storage Inc 937 298-8800
1850 Cardington Rd Moraine (45409) ***(G-14832)***
Van Mills Lines Inc 440 846-0200
14675 Foltz Pkwy Strongsville (44149) ***(G-17521)***
Van Ness Stone Inc 440 564-1111
10500 Kinsman Rd Newbury (44065) ***(G-15263)***
Van Pelt Corporation 513 242-6000
5170 Broerman Ave Cincinnati (45217) ***(G-4803)***
Van Rue Incorporated 419 238-0715
10357 Van Wert Decatur Rd Van Wert (45891) ***(G-18646)***
Van Stevens Lines Inc 419 729-8871
64 N Fearing Blvd Toledo (43607) ***(G-18286)***
Van Tassel Construction Corp 419 873-0188
25591 Fort Meigs Rd Ste A Perrysburg (43551) ***(G-16068)***
Van Wert County Day Care Inc 419 238-9918
10485 Van Wert Decatur Rd Van Wert (45891) ***(G-18647)***
Van Wert County Engineers 419 238-0210
1192 Grill Rd Van Wert (45891) ***(G-18648)***
Van Wert County Hospital Assn (PA) 419 238-2390
1250 S Washington St Van Wert (45891) ***(G-18649)***
Van Wert County Hospital Assn 419 232-2077
140 Fox Rd Ste 201 Van Wert (45891) ***(G-18650)***
Van Wert Manor, Van Wert *Also called Hcf of Van Wert Inc* ***(G-18634)***
Van Wert Medical Services Ltd 419 238-7727
140 Fox Rd Ste 105 Van Wert (45891) ***(G-18651)***
Vana Solutions LLC 937 242-6399
4027 Col Glenn Hwy 110 Beavercreek (45431) ***(G-1217)***
Vancare Inc 937 898-4202
208 N Cassel Rd Vandalia (45377) ***(G-18706)***
Vance Property Management LLC 419 467-9548
4200 South Ave Toledo (43615) ***(G-18287)***
Vance Property Management LLC (PA) 419 887-1878
4200 South Ave Toledo (43615) ***(G-18288)***
Vance Road Enterprises Inc 937 268-6953
1431 N Gettysburg Ave Dayton (45417) ***(G-9964)***
Vancrest Ltd 419 695-2871
1425 E 5th St Delphos (45833) ***(G-10153)***
Vancrest Ltd 419 749-2194
510 E Tully St Convoy (45832) ***(G-9050)***
Vancrest Ltd 937 456-3010
1600 Park Ave Eaton (45320) ***(G-10580)***
Vancrest Apts 419 695-7335
310 Elida Rd Delphos (45833) ***(G-10154)***
Vancrest Health Care Center, Van Wert *Also called Van Rue Incorporated* ***(G-18646)***
Vancrest Health Care Center 419 264-0700
600 Joe E Brown Ave Holgate (43527) ***(G-12004)***
Vancrest Healthcare Cntr, Delphos *Also called Vancrest Ltd* ***(G-10153)***
Vancrest Healthcare Cntr Eaton, Eaton *Also called Vancrest Ltd* ***(G-10580)***
Vancrest of Convoy, Convoy *Also called Vancrest Ltd* ***(G-9050)***
Vand Corp 216 481-3788
1301 E 9th St Ste 1900 Cleveland (44114) ***(G-6686)***
Vandalia Blacktop Seal Coating 937 454-0571
6740 Webster St Dayton (45414) ***(G-9965)***
Vandalia Municipal Court, Vandalia *Also called Supreme Court of Ohio* ***(G-18700)***
Vandalia Park, Vandalia *Also called Vancare Inc* ***(G-18706)***
Vandalia Rental, Vandalia *Also called Bnd Rentals Inc* ***(G-18663)***
Vandra Bros Construction Inc 440 232-3030
24629 Broadway Ave Cleveland (44146) ***(G-6687)***
Vanguard Imaging Partners 937 236-4780
6251 Good Samaritan Way # 140 Dayton (45424) ***(G-9966)***
Vanguard Wines LLC (PA) 614 291-3493
1020 W 5th Ave Columbus (43212) ***(G-8934)***
Vans Express Inc 216 224-5388
222 Concord Ln Hinckley (44233) ***(G-12001)***
Vantage Aging 440 324-3588
42495 N Ridge Rd Elyria (44035) ***(G-10686)***
Vantage Aging (PA) 330 253-4597
2279 Romig Rd Akron (44320) ***(G-495)***
Vantage Aging 330 785-9770
1155 E Tallmadge Ave Akron (44310) ***(G-496)***
Vantage Financial Group, Cleveland *Also called 6200 Rockside LLC* ***(G-4927)***
Vantage Land Title, Dayton *Also called Service Center Title Agency* ***(G-9877)***
Vantage Partners LLC 216 925-1302
3000 Aerospace Pkwy Brookpark (44142) ***(G-1957)***
Vantiv LLC (HQ) 877 713-5964
8500 Governors Hill Dr Symmes Twp (45249) ***(G-17630)***
Varco LP 440 277-8696
1807 E 28th St Lorain (44055) ***(G-13084)***
Vargo Integrated Systems Inc 614 876-1163
3709 Parkway Ln Hilliard (43026) ***(G-11962)***
Various Views Research Inc 513 489-9000
11353 Reed Hartman Hwy # 200 Blue Ash (45241) ***(G-1715)***
Varney Dispatch Inc 513 682-4200
4 Triangle Park Dr # 404 Cincinnati (45246) ***(G-4804)***
Varo Engineers Inc 513 729-9313
6039 Schumacher Park Dr West Chester (45069) ***(G-19178)***
Varo Engineers Inc 740 587-2228
2790 Columbus Rd Granville (43023) ***(G-11472)***
Vartek Services Inc 937 438-3550
4770 Hempstead Station Dr Dayton (45429) ***(G-9967)***
Vasconcellos Inc 513 576-1250
400 Techne Center Dr # 406 Milford (45150) ***(G-14573)***
Vaughn Industries LLC (PA) 419 396-3900
1201 E Findlay St Carey (43316) ***(G-2599)***
Vaughn Industries LLC 740 548-7100
7749 Green Meadows Dr Lewis Center (43035) ***(G-12710)***
VCA Animal Hospitals Inc 419 423-7232
2141 Bright Rd Findlay (45840) ***(G-11098)***
VCA Findlay Animal Hospital, Findlay *Also called VCA Animal Hospitals Inc* ***(G-11098)***
VCA Green Animal Hospital, Uniontown *Also called VCA Green Animal Medical Ctr* ***(G-18542)***
VCA Green Animal Medical Ctr 330 896-4040
1620 Corporate Woods Cir Uniontown (44685) ***(G-18542)***

Vds, Columbus *Also called Video Duplication Services Inc* ***(G-8940)***
Vec Inc 330 539-4044
977 Tibbetts Wick Rd Girard (44420) ***(G-11430)***
Vecmar Computer Solutions, Mentor *Also called Vecmar Corporation* ***(G-14254)***
Vecmar Corporation 440 953-1119
7595 Jenther Dr Mentor (44060) ***(G-14254)***
Vector Security Inc 440 466-7233
50 E Main St Geneva (44041) ***(G-11372)***
Vector Security Inc 330 726-9841
970 Windham Ct Ste 2 Boardman (44512) ***(G-1745)***
Vector Technical Inc 440 946-8800
38033 Euclid Ave Ste T9 Willoughby (44094) ***(G-19722)***
Vediscovery LLC 216 241-3443
1382 W 9th St Ste 400 Cleveland (44113) ***(G-6688)***
Velco Inc 513 772-4226
10280 Chester Rd Cincinnati (45215) ***(G-4805)***
Velocity Grtest Phone Ever Inc 419 868-9983
7130 Spring Meadows Dr W Holland (43528) ***(G-12066)***
Velocys Inc 614 733-3300
7950 Corporate Blvd Plain City (43064) ***(G-16211)***
Velotta Company 330 239-1211
6740 Ridge Rd Sharon Center (44274) ***(G-16880)***
Venator Holdings LLC 248 792-9209
1690 Woodlands Dr Ste 220 Maumee (43537) ***(G-13992)***
Venco Venturo Industries LLC (PA) 513 772-8448
12110 Best Pl Cincinnati (45241) ***(G-4806)***
Venco/Venturo Div, Cincinnati *Also called Venco Venturo Industries LLC* ***(G-4806)***
Vendor Supply of Ohio, West Chester *Also called Vendors Supply Inc* ***(G-19179)***
Vendors Supply Inc 513 755-2111
6448 Gano Rd West Chester (45069) ***(G-19179)***
Venezia Hauling, New Middletown *Also called Venezia Transport Service Inc* ***(G-15074)***
Venezia Transport Service Inc 330 542-9735
6017 E Calla Rd New Middletown (44442) ***(G-15074)***
Ventech Solutions Inc (PA) 614 757-1167
8425 Pulsar Pl Ste 300 Columbus (43240) ***(G-6909)***
Ventra Salem LLC 330 337-8002
800 Pennsylvania Ave Salem (44460) ***(G-16718)***
Venture Plastics Inc 330 872-6262
4325 Warren Ravenna Rd Newton Falls (44444) ***(G-15279)***
Venture Productions Inc 937 544-2823
11516 State Route 41 West Union (45693) ***(G-19279)***
Venturo Manufacturing Inc 513 772-8448
12110 Best Pl Cincinnati (45241) ***(G-4807)***
Veolia Es Industrial Svcs Inc 937 425-0512
6151 Executive Blvd Dayton (45424) ***(G-9968)***
Veolia Es Tchncal Slutions LLC 937 859-6101
4301 Infirmary Rd Miamisburg (45342) ***(G-14365)***
Ver-A-Fast Corp 440 331-0250
20545 Center Ridge Rd # 300 Rocky River (44116) ***(G-16594)***
Verantis Corporation (HQ) 440 243-0700
7251 Engle Rd Ste 300 Middleburg Heights (44130) ***(G-14390)***
Verified Person Inc 901 767-6121
4511 Rockside Rd Ste 400 Independence (44131) ***(G-12272)***
Verisk Crime Analytics Inc 614 865-6000
250 Old Wilson Brg Worthington (43085) ***(G-20005)***
Veritiv Operating Company 614 251-7100
525 N Nelson Rd Columbus (43219) ***(G-8935)***
Veritiv Operating Company 216 573-7400
7575 E Pleasant Valley Rd # 200 Independence (44131) ***(G-12273)***
Veritiv Operating Company 419 243-6100
1320 Locust St Toledo (43608) ***(G-18289)***
Veritiv Operating Company 513 285-0999
6120 S Gilmore Rd Fairfield (45014) ***(G-10922)***
Veritiv Operating Company 216 901-5700
9797 Sweet Valley Dr Cleveland (44125) ***(G-6689)***
Veritiv Pubg & Print MGT Inc (HQ) 330 650-5522
5700 Darrow Rd Ste 110 Hudson (44236) ***(G-12149)***
Verizon, Dublin *Also called Cellco Partnership* ***(G-10281)***
Verizon, Cincinnati *Also called Cellco Partnership* ***(G-3202)***
Verizon, Medina *Also called Cellco Partnership* ***(G-14044)***
Verizon, Alliance *Also called Cellco Partnership* ***(G-531)***
Verizon, Fremont *Also called Cellco Partnership* ***(G-11187)***
Verizon, Marion *Also called Supermedia LLC* ***(G-13583)***
Verizon, Cincinnati *Also called Cellco Partnership* ***(G-3204)***
Verizon, Findlay *Also called Cellco Partnership* ***(G-11011)***
Verizon, Lima *Also called Cellco Partnership* ***(G-12752)***
Verizon, Maumee *Also called Cellco Partnership* ***(G-13892)***
Verizon, Reynoldsburg *Also called Cellco Partnership* ***(G-16434)***
Verizon, Sandusky *Also called Cellco Partnership* ***(G-16736)***
Verizon, Mentor *Also called Cellco Partnership* ***(G-14155)***
Verizon, Cleveland *Also called Cellco Partnership* ***(G-5203)***
Verizon, Strongsville *Also called Cellco Partnership* ***(G-17448)***
Verizon, Mount Vernon *Also called Cellco Partnership* ***(G-14881)***
Verizon, Columbus *Also called Cellco Partnership* ***(G-7221)***
Verizon, Beavercreek *Also called Cellco Partnership* ***(G-1158)***
Verizon, Cincinnati *Also called Cellco Partnership* ***(G-3205)***
Verizon, Cincinnati *Also called Cellco Partnership* ***(G-3206)***
Verizon, Fairlawn *Also called Cellco Partnership* ***(G-10941)***
Verizon, Toledo *Also called Cellco Partnership* ***(G-17796)***
Verizon, Canton *Also called Cellco Partnership* ***(G-2302)***
Verizon, Sidney *Also called Cellco Partnership* ***(G-16918)***
Verizon, Stow *Also called Cellco Partnership* ***(G-17355)***
Verizon, Elyria *Also called Cellco Partnership* ***(G-10601)***
Verizon, Dublin *Also called Cellco Partnership* ***(G-10283)***
Verizon, Newark *Also called Cellco Partnership* ***(G-15155)***
Verizon, Wooster *Also called Cellco Partnership* ***(G-19838)***
Verizon Bus Netwrk Svcs Inc 513 897-1501
9073 Lytle Ferry Rd Waynesville (45068) ***(G-18988)***
Verizon Business, Cleveland *Also called MCI Communications Svcs Inc* ***(G-6005)***
Verizon Business, Chardon *Also called MCI Communications Svcs Inc* ***(G-2757)***
Verizon Business Global LLC 440 457-4049
12300 Ridge Rd North Royalton (44133) ***(G-15505)***
Verizon Business Global LLC 330 505-2368
5185 Youngstown Warren Rd Niles (44446) ***(G-15308)***
Verizon Business Global LLC 614 219-2317
5000 Britton Pkwy Hilliard (43026) ***(G-11963)***
Verizon Communications Inc 419 281-1714
1041 Commerce Pkwy Ashland (44805) ***(G-705)***
Verizon Communications Inc 330 334-1268
1114 Williams Reserve Wadsworth (44281) ***(G-18772)***
Verizon Communications Inc 440 892-4504
30171 Detroit Rd Westlake (44145) ***(G-19562)***
Verizon Communications Inc 740 383-0527
550 Leader St Marion (43302) ***(G-13594)***
Verizon Communications Inc 419 874-3933
1130 Levis Commons Blvd Perrysburg (43551) ***(G-16069)***
Verizon New York Inc 330 364-0508
715 Commercial Pkwy Dover (44622) ***(G-10222)***
Verizon New York Inc 740 383-0411
100 Executive Dr Marion (43302) ***(G-13595)***
Verizon New York Inc 614 301-2498
5000 Britton Pkwy Hilliard (43026) ***(G-11964)***
Verizon North Inc 740 942-2566
994 E Market St Cadiz (43907) ***(G-2081)***
Verizon North Inc 937 382-6961
215 E Main St Wilmington (45177) ***(G-19792)***
Verizon North Inc 419 734-5000
1971 E State Rd Port Clinton (43452) ***(G-16258)***
Verizon North Inc 330 339-7733
1121 Tuscarawas Ave Nw New Philadelphia (44663) ***(G-15121)***
Verizon Select Services Inc 908 559-2054
12300 Ridge Rd North Royalton (44133) ***(G-15506)***
Verizon South Inc 740 354-0544
1121 Robinson Ave Portsmouth (45662) ***(G-16321)***
Verizon Wireless, Wooster *Also called Rxp Wireless LLC* ***(G-19909)***
Verizon Wireless, Amherst *Also called Cellco Partnership* ***(G-590)***
Verizon Wireless, Lewis Center *Also called Cellco Partnership* ***(G-12673)***
Verizon Wireless, Columbus *Also called Cellco Partnership* ***(G-7220)***
Verizon Wireless, Parma *Also called Cellco Partnership* ***(G-15901)***
Verizon Wireless, Cuyahoga Falls *Also called Cellco Partnership* ***(G-9170)***
Verizon Wireless, Bowling Green *Also called Cellco Partnership* ***(G-1771)***
Verizon Wireless, Lancaster *Also called Cellco Partnership* ***(G-12515)***
Verizon Wireless, Saint Clairsville *Also called Cellco Partnership* ***(G-16631)***
Verizon Wireless, Defiance *Also called Cellco Partnership* ***(G-10021)***
Verizon Wireless, Cambridge *Also called Cellco Partnership* ***(G-2103)***
Verizon Wireless, Akron *Also called Cellco Partnership* ***(G-126)***
Verizon Wireless, West Chester *Also called Cellco Partnership* ***(G-19035)***
Verizon Wireless, Avon *Also called Cellco Partnership* ***(G-885)***
Verizon Wireless, Toledo *Also called Cellco Partnership* ***(G-17795)***
Verizon Wireless, Beachwood *Also called Cellco Partnership* ***(G-1061)***
Verizon Wireless, Ashtabula *Also called Cellco Partnership* ***(G-731)***
Verizon Wireless, Middletown *Also called Cellco Partnership* ***(G-14477)***
Verizon Wireless, Zanesville *Also called Cellco Partnership* ***(G-20458)***
Verizon Wireless, North Olmsted *Also called Cellco Partnership* ***(G-15412)***
Verizon Wireless, Independence *Also called Cellco Partnership* ***(G-12195)***
Verizon Wireless, Marysville *Also called Cellco Partnership* ***(G-13611)***
Verizon Wireless, Solon *Also called Cellco Partnership* ***(G-16990)***
Verizon Wireless, Streetsboro *Also called Cellco Partnership* ***(G-17408)***
Verizon Wireless, New Philadelphia *Also called Cellco Partnership* ***(G-15084)***
Verizon Wireless, Dublin *Also called Cellco Partnership* ***(G-10282)***
Verizon Wireless, Zanesville *Also called Cellco Partnership* ***(G-20459)***
Verizon Wireless, Delaware *Also called Cellco Partnership* ***(G-10077)***
Verizon Wireless, Grove City *Also called Cellco Partnership* ***(G-11544)***
Verizon Wireless 330 963-1300
2000 Highland Rd Twinsburg (44087) ***(G-18484)***
Verizon Wireless Inc 937 434-2355
2799 Mmsburg Cntrville Rd Dayton (45459) ***(G-9969)***
Vermeer Sales & Service Inc (PA) 330 723-8383
2389 Medina Rd Medina (44256) ***(G-14136)***
Vermilion Board of Education 440 204-1700
1065 Decatur St Vermilion (44089) ***(G-18718)***
Vermilion Boat Club Inc 440 967-6634
5416 Liberty Ave Vermilion (44089) ***(G-18719)***

ALPHABETIC

Vermilion Family YMCA 440 967-4208
320 Aldrich Rd Vermilion (44089) *(G-18720)*
Vermilion Farm Market 440 967-9666
2901 Liberty Ave Vermilion (44089) *(G-18721)*
Vermilion School Bus Garage, Vermilion *Also called Vermilion Board of Education (G-18718)*
Vernon F Glaser & Associates 937 298-5536
3085 Woodman Dr Ste 250 Dayton (45420) *(G-9970)*
Versailles Gardens Apts, Canton *Also called Brookwood Management Company (G-2271)*
Versailles Health Care Center, Versailles *Also called Covenant Care Ohio Inc (G-18726)*
Versailles Util Dept, Versailles *Also called Village of Versailles (G-18730)*
Versatex LLC 513 639-3119
324 W 9th St Cincinnati (45202) *(G-4808)*
Verst Group Logistics Inc 513 782-1725
98 Glendale Milford Rd Cincinnati (45215) *(G-4809)*
Verst Group Logistics Inc 513 772-2494
11880 Enterprise Dr Cincinnati (45241) *(G-4810)*
Verti Insurance Company 844 448-3784
3590 Twin Creeks Dr Columbus (43204) *(G-8936)*
Vertical Knowledge LLC (PA) 216 920-7790
8 E Washington St Ste 200 Chagrin Falls (44022) *(G-2709)*
Vertiv, Columbus *Also called Liebert Corporation (G-8059)*
Vertiv, Dayton *Also called High Voltage Maintenance Corp (G-9611)*
Vertiv, Westerville *Also called Liebert Field Services Inc (G-19326)*
Vertiv Energy Systems Inc 440 288-1122
1510 Kansas Ave Lorain (44052) *(G-13085)*
Vervasi Vineyard & Itln Bistro 330 497-1000
1700 55th St Ne Canton (44721) *(G-2576)*
Vesco Oil Corporation 614 367-1412
254 Business Center Dr Blacklick (43004) *(G-1512)*
Vet Path Services Inc 513 469-0777
6450 Castle Dr Mason (45040) *(G-13778)*
Veteran Security Patrol Co 937 222-7333
601 S E C Moses Blvd # 170 Dayton (45417) *(G-9971)*
Veteran Security Patrol Co 513 381-4482
36 E 7th St Ste 2201 Cincinnati (45202) *(G-4811)*
Veterans ADM Out Ptient Clinic, Columbus *Also called Ohio State University (G-8409)*
Veterans Affairs US Dept 937 268-6511
4100 W 3rd St Dayton (45428) *(G-9972)*
Veterans Clinic, Canton *Also called Veterans Health Administration (G-2577)*
Veterans Fgn Wars Post 2850 ....216 631-2585
3296 W 61st St Cleveland (44102) *(G-6690)*
Veterans Health Administration 740 568-0412
418 Colegate Dr Marietta (45750) *(G-13514)*
Veterans Health Administration 202 461-4800
17273 State Route 104 Chillicothe (45601) *(G-2895)*
Veterans Health Administration 513 861-3100
3200 Vine St Cincinnati (45220) *(G-4812)*
Veterans Health Administration 513 943-3680
4600 Beechwood Rd Cincinnati (45244) *(G-4813)*
Veterans Health Administration 216 791-3800
10701 East Blvd Cleveland (44106) *(G-6691)*
Veterans Health Administration 614 257-5524
420 N James Rd Columbus (43219) *(G-8937)*
Veterans Health Administration 866 463-0912
4314 Main Ave Frnt Ashtabula (44004) *(G-766)*
Veterans Health Administration 740 695-9321
103 Plaza Dr Ste A Saint Clairsville (43950) *(G-16659)*
Veterans Health Administration 419 259-2000
3333 Glendale Ave Toledo (43614) *(G-18290)*
Veterans Health Administration 330 740-9200
2031 Belmont Ave Youngstown (44505) *(G-20403)*
Veterans Health Administration 216 939-0699
4242 Lorain Ave Cleveland (44113) *(G-6692)*
Veterans Health Administration 330 489-4600
733 Market Ave S Canton (44702) *(G-2577)*
Veterinary RFRrl&emer Ctr of 330 665-4996
1321 Centerview Cir Copley (44321) *(G-9068)*
Vexor Technology Inc (PA) 330 721-9773
955 W Smith Rd Medina (44256) *(G-14137)*
Veyance Industrial Svcs Inc (PA) 307 682-7855
703 S Clvland Mssillon Rd Fairlawn (44333) *(G-10980)*
Vgs Inc 216 431-7800
2239 E 55th St Cleveland (44103) *(G-6693)*
Via Quest, Dublin *Also called Alexson Services Inc (G-10240)*
Viaquest Inc (PA) 614 889-5837
525 Metro Pl N Ste 300 Dublin (43017) *(G-10481)*
Viaquest Behavioral Health LLC (PA) 614 339-0868
525 Metro Pl N Ste 450 Dublin (43017) *(G-10482)*
Viaquest Home Health LLC (HQ) 800 645-3267
525 Metro Pl N Dublin (43017) *(G-10483)*
Vibo Construction Inc 614 210-6780
266 N 4th St Ste 100 Columbus (43215) *(G-8938)*
Vibra Healthcare LLC 330 675-5555
1350 E Market St Warren (44483) *(G-18921)*
Vibra Healthcare LLC 330 726-5050
8049 South Ave Youngstown (44512) *(G-20404)*
Vibra Hosp Mahoning Vly LLC 330 726-5000
8049 South Ave Youngstown (44512) *(G-20405)*
Viconsi Company, Cleveland *Also called Visconsi Management Inc (G-6701)*
Victor McKenzie Drilling Co 740 453-0834
3596 Maple Ave Ste A Zanesville (43701) *(G-20544)*
Victoria Retirement Community, Cincinnati *Also called Saber Healthcare Group LLC (G-4465)*
Victorian Oaks Asst Lvng/Demta, Cambridge *Also called Victorian Oaks LLC (G-2133)*
Victorian Oaks LLC 740 432-2262
1480 Deerpath Dr Cambridge (43725) *(G-2133)*
Victory Capital Management Inc (HQ) 216 898-2400
4900 Tiedeman Rd Fl 4 Brooklyn (44144) *(G-1907)*
Victory Ftnes Ctrs of Columbus (PA) 614 351-1688
3427 South Blvd Columbus (43204) *(G-8939)*
Victory Lanes Inc 937 323-8684
1906 Commerce Cir Springfield (45504) *(G-17292)*
Victory Machine and Fab 937 693-3171
920 S Vandemark Rd Sidney (45365) *(G-16959)*
Victory Pool, Cleveland *Also called City of South Euclid (G-5276)*
Victory Sq Aprtmnts Ltd Partnr 330 455-8035
1206 Lppert Rd Ne Apt 211 Canton (44705) *(G-2578)*
Victory White Metal Company (PA) 216 271-1400
6100 Roland Ave Cleveland (44127) *(G-6694)*
Victory White Metal Company 216 271-7200
3027 E 55th St Cleveland (44127) *(G-6695)*
Victory Wholesale Grocery, Springboro *Also called Brothers Trading Co Inc (G-17117)*
Video Duplication Services Inc (PA) 614 871-3827
3777 Busineoh Pk Dr Ste A Columbus (43204) *(G-8940)*
Video Works 419 865-6800
336 Hayes Rd Toledo (43615) *(G-18291)*
Vieira Inc 937 599-3221
4622 County Road 49 Bellefontaine (43311) *(G-1400)*
Vienna Enterprises Inc 937 568-4524
125 E National Rd South Vienna (45369) *(G-17101)*
Vietnam Veterans America Inc 330 877-6017
874 Marigold St Nw Hartville (44632) *(G-11832)*
Viewray Incorporated 440 703-3210
2 Thermo Fisher Way Oakwood Village (44146) *(G-15636)*
Vig Property Development LLC 888 384-5970
201 E 5th St 19001065 Cincinnati (45202) *(G-4814)*
Vigilant Defense 513 309-0672
8366 Princeton Glendale West Chester (45069) *(G-19180)*
Vigilant Global Trade Svcs LLC (PA) 260 417-1825
3140 Courtland Blvd # 3400 Shaker Heights (44122) *(G-16871)*
Vigilant Technology Solutions, West Chester *Also called Vigilant Defense (G-19180)*
Viking Explosives LLC 218 263-8845
25800 Science Park Dr Cleveland (44122) *(G-6696)*
Viking Fabricators Inc 740 374-5246
2021 Hanna Rd Marietta (45750) *(G-13515)*
Viking Office Products Inc 513 881-7200
4700 Muhlhauser Rd West Chester (45011) *(G-19181)*
Villa Angela Care Center, Columbus *Also called Karl Hc LLC (G-7965)*
Villa Georgetown, Georgetown *Also called Covenant Care Ohio Inc (G-11392)*
Villa Milano Inc 614 882-2058
1630 Schrock Rd Columbus (43229) *(G-8941)*
Villa Mlano Bnquet Cnfrnce Ctr, Columbus *Also called Villa Milano Inc (G-8941)*
Villa Restaurant, Carrollton *Also called Saint Johns Villa (G-2628)*
Villa Springfield, Springfield *Also called Covenant Care Ohio Inc (G-17183)*
VILLAGE AT SAINT EDWARD, Fairlawn *Also called St Edward Home (G-10977)*
Village At St Edward Ind Lving, Fairlawn *Also called Saint Edward Housing Corp (G-10971)*
Village At The Greene, Beavercreek *Also called Hcf of Crestview Inc (G-1246)*
Village At Wstrvlle Retiremnt, Westerville *Also called Health Care Rtrement Corp Amer (G-19408)*
Village Christian Schools, Pleasant Plain *Also called Mid-Western Childrens Home (G-16215)*
Village Chrysler-Dodge, Millersburg *Also called Village Motors Inc (G-14626)*
Village Communities LLC 614 540-2400
470 Olde Worthington Rd # 100 Westerville (43082) *(G-19357)*
Village Green Healthcare Ctr 937 548-1993
405 Chestnut St Greenville (45331) *(G-11523)*
Village Handyman, The, Akron *Also called Craftsmen Restoration LLC (G-174)*
Village Inn Restaurant, Coshocton *Also called Roscoe Village Foundation (G-9116)*
Village Motors Inc 330 674-2055
784 Wooster Rd Millersburg (44654) *(G-14626)*
Village Network (PA) 330 264-0650
2000 Noble Dr Wooster (44691) *(G-19922)*
Village of Antwerp (PA) 419 258-7422
118 N Main St Antwerp (45813) *(G-621)*
Village of Antwerp 419 258-6631
203 S Cleveland St Antwerp (45813) *(G-622)*
Village of Byesville 740 685-5901
221 Main St Byesville (43723) *(G-2072)*
Village of Coldwater 419 678-2685
610 W Sycamore St Coldwater (45828) *(G-6837)*
Village of Cuyahoga Heights (PA) 216 641-7020
4863 E 71st St Frnt Cleveland (44125) *(G-6697)*
Village of Groveport 614 830-2060
655 Blacklick St Groveport (43125) *(G-11684)*
Village of Strasburg 330 878-7115
358 5th St Sw Strasburg (44680) *(G-17402)*
Village of Valley View 216 524-6511
6848 Hathaway Rd Cleveland (44125) *(G-6698)*
Village of Versailles 937 526-4191
177 N Center St Versailles (45380) *(G-18730)*

Vimas Painting Company Inc 330 536-2222
4328 Mccartney Rd Lowellville (44436) *(G-13175)*
Vin Devers (PA) 888 847-9535
5570 Monroe St Sylvania (43560) *(G-17626)*
Vincent Ltg Systems Co Inc (PA) 216 475-7600
6161 Cochran Rd Ste D Solon (44139) *(G-17065)*
Vindicator Printing Company 330 744-8611
101 W Boardman St Youngstown (44503) *(G-20406)*
Vinifera Imports Ltd 440 942-9463
7551 Clover Ave Mentor (44060) *(G-14255)*
Vintage Wine Distributor Inc 614 876-2580
2277 Westbrooke Dr Columbus (43228) *(G-8942)*
VINTON CO NATIONAL BANK, Mc Arthur *Also called Vinton County Nat Bnk McArthur (G-14019)*
Vinton County Nat Bnk McArthur (HQ) 740 596-2525
112 W Main St Mc Arthur (45651) *(G-14019)*
Vinyl Design Corporation 419 283-4009
7856 Hill Ave Holland (43528) *(G-12067)*
Viox Services, Cincinnati *Also called Emcor Facilities Services Inc (G-3552)*
VIP Building Exteriors Contrs, Cuyahoga Falls *Also called VIP Restoration Inc (G-9232)*
VIP Electric Company 440 255-0180
8358 Mentor Ave Mentor (44060) *(G-14256)*
VIP Home Care, Akron *Also called VIP Homecare Inc (G-497)*
VIP Homecare Inc 330 929-2838
545 E Cuyahoga Falls Ave Akron (44310) *(G-497)*
VIP Restoration Inc 216 426-9500
1375 E 55th St Cleveland (44103) *(G-6699)*
VIP Restoration Inc (PA) 216 426-9500
650 Graham Rd Ste 106 Cuyahoga Falls (44221) *(G-9232)*
Virginia Ohio-West Excvtg Co 740 676-7464
56461 Ferry Landing Rd Shadyside (43947) *(G-16852)*
Virginia T'S, Hebron *Also called Heritage Sportswear Inc (G-11850)*
Virginia Tile Company 216 741-8400
4749 Spring Rd Brooklyn Heights (44131) *(G-1931)*
Virtual Hold Technology LLC (PA) 330 666-1181
3875 Embassy Pkwy Ste 350 Akron (44333) *(G-498)*
Virtual Pc's, Lima *Also called Office World Inc (G-12928)*
Virtuoso, Cincinnati *Also called Pier n Port Travel Inc (G-4298)*
Visconsi Companies Ltd 216 464-5550
30050 Chagrin Blvd # 360 Cleveland (44124) *(G-6700)*
Visconsi Management Inc 216 464-5550
30050 Chagrin Blvd # 360 Cleveland (44124) *(G-6701)*
Vishnia & Associates Inc 330 929-5512
2497 State Rd Cuyahoga Falls (44223) *(G-9233)*
Visicon Inc 937 879-2696
Area A Bldg 823 Fairborn (45324) *(G-10809)*
Vision & Vocational Services (PA) 614 294-5571
1393 N High St Columbus (43201) *(G-8943)*
Vision America of Ohio, Chillicothe *Also called Ohio Eye Specialists Inc (G-2866)*
Vision Associates Inc (PA) 419 578-7598
2865 N Reynolds Rd # 170 Toledo (43615) *(G-18292)*
Vision Express Inc 740 922-8848
801 W 1st St Uhrichsville (44683) *(G-18496)*
Vision Service Plan 614 471-7511
3400 Morris Xing Columbus (43219) *(G-8944)*
Visions Matter LLC 513 934-1934
838 W State Route 122 Lebanon (45036) *(G-12656)*
Visiting Angels, Cincinnati *Also called RWS Enterprises LLC (G-4460)*
Visiting Angels, Toledo *Also called Tk Homecare Llc (G-18220)*
Visiting Angels, Ravenna *Also called Tsk Assisted Living Services (G-16414)*
Visiting Angels, Tallmadge *Also called Living Assistance Services (G-17644)*
Visiting Angels, Salem *Also called Frencor Inc (G-16696)*
Visiting Angels, Cleveland *Also called Majastan Group LLC (G-5971)*
Visiting Angels Lvng Asst, West Chester *Also called Dillon Holdings LLC (G-19062)*
Visiting Nrse Assn of Clveland 419 281-2480
1165 E Main St Ashland (44805) *(G-706)*
Visiting Nrse Assn of Clveland 419 522-4969
40 W 4th St Mansfield (44902) *(G-13381)*
Visiting Nrse Assn of Clveland (PA) 216 931-1400
2500 E 22nd St Cleveland (44115) *(G-6702)*
Visiting Nrse Assn of Mid-Ohio 216 931-1300
2500 E 22nd St Cleveland (44115) *(G-6703)*
Visiting Nurse Assn Ashland, Ashland *Also called Visiting Nrse Assn of Clveland (G-706)*
Visiting Nurse Associal (PA) 513 345-8000
2400 Reading Rd Ste 207 Cincinnati (45202) *(G-4815)*
Visiting Nurse Association 216 931-1300
2500 E 22nd St Cleveland (44115) *(G-6704)*
Visiting Nurse Service Inc (PA) 330 745-1601
1 Home Care Pl Akron (44320) *(G-499)*
Visiting Nurse Service Inc 440 286-9461
13221 Ravenna Rd Ste 1 Chardon (44024) *(G-2776)*
Visiting Nurses Association, Sylvania *Also called Toledo District Nurses Assn (G-17622)*
VISON SUPPORT SERVICES, Akron *Also called Akron Blind Center & Workshop (G-29)*
Vista Centre 330 424-5852
100 Vista Dr Lisbon (44432) *(G-12942)*
Vista Color Imaging Inc 216 651-2830
4770 Van Epps Rd Ste 1 Brooklyn Heights (44131) *(G-1932)*
Vista Industrial Packaging LLC 800 454-6117
4700 Fisher Rd Columbus (43228) *(G-8945)*
Vista Packaging & Logistics, Columbus *Also called Vista Industrial Packaging LLC (G-8945)*
Vistacare USA Inc 614 975-3230
540 Officenter Pl Ste 100 Columbus (43230) *(G-8946)*
Visual Art Graphic Services 330 274-2775
5244 Goodell Rd Mantua (44255) *(G-13397)*
Visual Edge Technology Inc (PA) 330 494-9694
3874 Highland Park Nw Canton (44720) *(G-2579)*
Visual Evidence/E-Discovery, Cleveland *Also called Vediscovery LLC (G-6688)*
Vita Pup, Akron *Also called JE Carsten Company (G-291)*
Vital Resources Inc 440 614-5150
1119 Sheltered Brook Dr Huron (44839) *(G-12175)*
Vitalyst 216 201-9070
3615 Superior Ave E 4406a Cleveland (44114) *(G-6705)*
Vitamin Shoppe Inc 440 238-5987
17893 Southpark Ctr Strongsville (44136) *(G-17522)*
Vitas Healthcare Corp of Ohio, Cincinnati *Also called Detox Health Care Corp Ohio (G-3485)*
Vitas Healthcare Corporation 513 742-6310
11500 Northlake Dr # 400 Cincinnati (45249) *(G-4816)*
Vitas Healthcare Corporation 216 706-2100
600 E Granger Rd Ste 100 Cleveland (44131) *(G-6706)*
Vitran Express Inc 614 870-2255
5075 Krieger Ct Columbus (43228) *(G-8947)*
Vitran Express Inc 216 426-8584
5300 Crayton Ave Cleveland (44104) *(G-6707)*
Vitran Express Inc 513 771-4894
2789 Crescentville Rd West Chester (45069) *(G-19182)*
Vivial Media LLC 513 768-7800
720 E Pete Rose Way # 350 Cincinnati (45202) *(G-4817)*
Vivial Media LLC 937 610-4100
3100 Res Blvd Ste 250 Dayton (45420) *(G-9973)*
Vizmeg Landscape Inc 330 686-0901
778 Mccauley Rd Unit 100 Stow (44224) *(G-17399)*
Vjp Hospitality Ltd 614 475-8383
3030 Plaza Prpts Blvd Columbus (43219) *(G-8948)*
Vloan, Strongsville *Also called Union Home Mortgage Corp (G-17517)*
Vlp Inc 330 758-8811
7301 West Blvd Ste A3 Youngstown (44512) *(G-20407)*
Vma Inc 614 475-7300
1353 Cherry Way Dr Gahanna (43230) *(G-11274)*
Vmi Group Inc 330 405-4146
8854 Valley View Rd Macedonia (44056) *(G-13216)*
Vna, Cleveland *Also called Visiting Nrse Assn of Mid-Ohio (G-6703)*
Vna of Mid Ohio, Mansfield *Also called Visiting Nrse Assn of Clveland (G-13381)*
Voc Works Ltd 614 760-3515
5555 Glendon Ct Ste 300 Dublin (43016) *(G-10484)*
Voca of Ohio 419 435-5836
1021 Dillon Rd Fostoria (44830) *(G-11142)*
Vocalink Inc 937 223-1415
405 W 1st St Ste A Dayton (45402) *(G-9974)*
Vocational Guidance Services (PA) 216 431-7800
2239 E 55th St Cleveland (44103) *(G-6708)*
Vocational Guidance Services 440 322-1123
359 Lowell St Elyria (44035) *(G-10687)*
Vocational Rehabilitation, Cincinnati *Also called Opportunities For Ohioans (G-4229)*
Vocational Services, Elyria *Also called Vocational Guidance Services (G-10687)*
Vocational Services Inc 216 431-8085
2239 E 55th St Cleveland (44103) *(G-6709)*
Vocon Design Inc (PA) 216 588-0800
3142 Prospect Ave E Cleveland (44115) *(G-6710)*
Vocworks, Dublin *Also called Careworks of Ohio Inc (G-10280)*
Voestlpine Precision Strip LLC (HQ) 330 220-7800
3052 Interstate Pkwy Brunswick (44212) *(G-1994)*
Vogel Dialysis LLC 614 834-3564
3568 Gender Rd Canal Winchester (43110) *(G-2175)*
Vogt Warehouse, Cincinnati *Also called Specialty Logistics Inc (G-4558)*
Voiers Enterprises Inc 740 259-2838
2274 Mc Dermott Pond Crk Mc Dermott (45652) *(G-14023)*
Volk Optical Inc 440 942-6161
7893 Enterprise Dr Mentor (44060) *(G-14257)*
Volpone Enterprises Inc 440 969-1141
5223 N Ridge Rd W Ste 2 Ashtabula (44004) *(G-767)*
Volt Management Corp 513 791-2000
8044 Montgomery Rd # 630 Cincinnati (45236) *(G-4818)*
Volt Workforce Solutions, Cincinnati *Also called Volt Management Corp (G-4818)*
Volunteer Energy Services Inc (PA) 614 856-3128
790 Windmiller Dr Ste A Pickerington (43147) *(G-16107)*
Volunteer of Amer Autemwood CA, Tiffin *Also called Volunters Amer Care Facilities (G-17708)*
Volunteers of America NW Ohio 419 248-3733
701 Jefferson Ave Ste 203 Toledo (43604) *(G-18293)*
Volunters Amer Care Facilities 419 447-7151
670 E State Route 18 Tiffin (44883) *(G-17708)*
Volunters Amer Care Facilities 419 225-9040
804 S Mumaugh Rd Lima (45804) *(G-12911)*
Volunters Amer Care Facilities 419 334-9521
600 N Brush St Fremont (43420) *(G-11226)*
Volunters of Amer Greater Ohio 614 861-8551
4280 Macsway Ave Columbus (43232) *(G-8949)*
Volunters of Amer Greater Ohio 216 541-9000
775 E 152nd St Cleveland (44110) *(G-6711)*

ALPHABETIC

Volunters of Amer Greater Ohio....614 372-3120
2335 N Bank Dr Columbus (43220) ***(G-8950)***
Volunters of Amer Greater Ohio (PA)....614 253-6100
1776 E Broad St Columbus (43203) ***(G-8951)***
Volunters of Amer Greater Ohio....419 524-5013
921 N Main St Mansfield (44903) ***(G-13382)***
Volunters of Amer Greater Ohio....614 263-9134
3620 Indianola Ave Columbus (43214) ***(G-8952)***
Volunters of America Cntl Ohio....614 801-1655
4026 Mcdowell Rd Grove City (43123) ***(G-11609)***
Volvo BMW Dyton Evans Volkswag....937 890-6200
7124 Poe Ave Dayton (45414) ***(G-9975)***
Vora Ventures LLC....513 792-5100
10290 Alliance Rd Blue Ash (45242) ***(G-1716)***
Vorys Sater Seymour Pease LLP....216 479-6100
200 Public Sq Ste 1400 Cleveland (44114) ***(G-6712)***
Vorys Sater Seymour Pease LLP....513 723-4000
301 E 4th St Ste 3410 Cincinnati (45202) ***(G-4819)***
Voss Auto Network Inc (PA)....937 428-2447
766 Mmsburg Cnterville Rd Dayton (45459) ***(G-9976)***
Voss Auto Network Inc....937 433-1444
100 Loop Rd Dayton (45459) ***(G-9977)***
Voss Chevrolet Inc....937 428-2500
100 Loop Rd Dayton (45459) ***(G-9978)***
Voss Dodge (PA)....937 435-7800
90 Loop Rd Dayton (45459) ***(G-9979)***
Voss Hyundai, Dayton *Also called Hoss Value Cars & Trucks Inc* ***(G-9622)***
Voss Toyota Inc....937 427-3700
2110 Heller Dr Beavercreek (45434) ***(G-1218)***
Vox Mobile....800 536-9030
6100 Rockside Woods # 100 Independence (44131) ***(G-12274)***
Voya Financial Inc....614 431-5000
7965 N High St Columbus (43235) ***(G-8953)***
Vps, Inc., Mason *Also called Vet Path Services Inc* ***(G-13778)***
Vrable Healthcare Inc (PA)....614 545-5500
3248 Henderson Rd Columbus (43220) ***(G-8954)***
Vrable II Inc....614 545-5502
3248 Henderson Rd Columbus (43220) ***(G-8955)***
Vrable III Inc....740 446-7150
311 Buck Ridge Rd Bidwell (45614) ***(G-1497)***
Vrable IV Inc (HQ)....614 545-5502
3248 Henderson Rd Columbus (43220) ***(G-8956)***
Vsm Sewing Inc (HQ)....440 808-6550
31000 Viking Pkwy Westlake (44145) ***(G-19563)***
Vsync, Columbus *Also called Enhanced Software Inc* ***(G-7596)***
Vulcan Enterprises Inc....419 396-3535
2600 State Highway 568 A Carey (43316) ***(G-2600)***
Vulcan Feg....937 332-2763
750 Lincoln Ave Troy (45373) ***(G-18387)***
Vulcan Fire Protection, Carey *Also called Vulcan Enterprises Inc* ***(G-2600)***
Vulcan Machinery Corporation....330 376-6025
20 N Case Ave Akron (44305) ***(G-500)***
Vulcan Oil Company, Cincinnati *Also called New Vulco Mfg & Sales Co LLC* ***(G-4158)***
Vwc Liquidation Company LLC....330 372-6776
1701 Henn Pkwy Sw Warren (44481) ***(G-18922)***
VWR Chemicals LLC....330 425-2522
220 Lena Dr Aurora (44202) ***(G-860)***
VWR International, Aurora *Also called VWR Chemicals LLC* ***(G-860)***
W & H Realty Inc (PA)....513 891-1066
4243 Hunt Rd Blue Ash (45242) ***(G-1717)***
W B Mason Co Inc....216 267-5000
12985 Snow Rd Cleveland (44130) ***(G-6713)***
W B N X T V 55....330 922-5500
2690 State Rd Cuyahoga Falls (44223) ***(G-9234)***
W C National Mailing Corp....614 836-5703
4241 Williams Rd Groveport (43125) ***(G-11685)***
W C P O - T V, Cincinnati *Also called Wfts* ***(G-4847)***
W D Tire Warehouse Inc (PA)....614 461-8944
3805 E Livingston Ave Columbus (43227) ***(G-8957)***
W David Maupin Inc....419 389-0458
3564 Marine Rd Toledo (43609) ***(G-18294)***
W E Quicksall and Assoc Inc (PA)....330 339-6676
554 W High Ave New Philadelphia (44663) ***(G-15122)***
W F Bolin Company Inc....614 276-6397
4100 Fisher Rd Columbus (43228) ***(G-8958)***
W F H M - F M 95.5, Cleveland *Also called Salem Media Group Inc* ***(G-6437)***
W G Lockhart Construction Co....330 745-6520
800 W Waterloo Rd Akron (44314) ***(G-501)***
W G U C-FM Radio, Cincinnati *Also called Cincinnati Public Radio Inc* ***(G-3323)***
W H O T Inc (PA)....330 783-1000
4040 Simon Rd Ste 1 Youngstown (44512) ***(G-20408)***
W J Alarm Service, Warren *Also called Wj Service Co Inc* ***(G-18928)***
W K H R Radio....440 708-0915
17425 Snyder Rd Bainbridge (45612) ***(G-943)***
W K S, Cleves *Also called Wm Kramer and Sons Inc* ***(G-6806)***
W K Y C Channel 3, Cleveland *Also called Wkyc-Tv Inc* ***(G-6756)***
W L Logan Trucking Company....330 478-1404
3224 Navarre Rd Sw Canton (44706) ***(G-2580)***
W L W T T V 5....513 412-5000
1700 Young St Cincinnati (45202) ***(G-4820)***
W M V O 1300 AM....740 397-1000
17421 Coshocton Rd Mount Vernon (43050) ***(G-14924)***
W N W O, Toledo *Also called Barrington Toledo LLC* ***(G-17763)***
W O I O, Cleveland *Also called Raycom Media Inc* ***(G-6355)***
W P Dolle LLC....513 421-6515
201 E 5th St Ste 1000 Cincinnati (45202) ***(G-4821)***
W Pol Contracting Inc....330 325-7177
4188 Ohio 14 Ravenna (44266) ***(G-16415)***
W R G Inc....216 351-8494
3961 Pearl Rd Cleveland (44109) ***(G-6714)***
W R Shepherd Inc (PA)....614 889-2896
390 W Olentangy St Powell (43065) ***(G-16353)***
W S E M, Cleveland *Also called West Side Ecumenical Ministry* ***(G-6740)***
W S N Y F M Sunny 95, Columbus *Also called Franklin Communications Inc* ***(G-7691)***
W S O S Community A....419 729-8035
1500 N Superior St # 303 Toledo (43604) ***(G-18295)***
W S O S Community A (PA)....419 333-6068
109 S Front St Fremont (43420) ***(G-11227)***
W S O S Community A....419 639-2802
1518 E County Road 113 Green Springs (44836) ***(G-11480)***
W S O S Community A....419 334-8511
765 S Buchanan St Fremont (43420) ***(G-11228)***
W S T R, Cincinnati *Also called Sinclair Broadcast Group Inc* ***(G-4530)***
W T C S A Headstart Niles Ctr....330 652-0338
309 N Rhodes Ave Niles (44446) ***(G-15309)***
W T Sports Inc....740 654-0035
5288 Aryshire Dr Dublin (43017) ***(G-10485)***
W U P W, Toledo *Also called Sunrise Television Corp* ***(G-18209)***
W W Grainger Inc....330 425-8387
8211 Bavaria Dr E Macedonia (44056) ***(G-13217)***
W W Schaub Electric Co....330 494-3560
501 Applegrove St Nw Canton (44720) ***(G-2581)***
W W W M....419 240-1055
3225 Arlington Ave Toledo (43614) ***(G-18296)***
W W Williams Company LLC....419 837-5067
3325 Libbey Rd Perrysburg (43551) ***(G-16070)***
W W Williams Company LLC....330 534-1161
7125 Masury Rd Hubbard (44425) ***(G-12092)***
W W Williams Company LLC....419 837-5067
3325 Libbey Rd Perrysburg (43551) ***(G-16071)***
W W Williams Company LLC....800 336-6651
4806 Interstate Dr West Chester (45246) ***(G-19242)***
W W Williams Company LLC (HQ)....614 228-5000
835 Goodale Blvd Columbus (43212) ***(G-8959)***
W W Williams Company LLC....330 225-7751
1176 Industrial Pkwy N Brunswick (44212) ***(G-1995)***
W W Williams Company LLC....614 228-5000
835 Goodale Blvd Columbus (43212) ***(G-8960)***
W W Williams Company LLC....614 527-9400
3535 Parkway Ln Hilliard (43026) ***(G-11965)***
W W Wllams Company-Midwest Div, Hilliard *Also called W W Williams Company LLC* ***(G-11965)***
W X I X, Cincinnati *Also called Raycom Media Inc* ***(G-4387)***
W. W. Wllams LLC - Lgstics Div, Columbus *Also called W W Williams Company LLC* ***(G-8960)***
W.F. Hann & Sons, Warrensville Heights *Also called Dival Inc* ***(G-18932)***
W.G. Nord Cmnty Mntal Hlth Ctr, Lorain *Also called Nord Center Associates Inc* ***(G-13067)***
W2005/Fargo Hotels (pool C)....937 890-6112
7087 Miller Ln Dayton (45414) ***(G-9980)***
W2005/Fargo Hotels (pool C)....614 791-8675
5300 Parkcenter Ave Dublin (43017) ***(G-10486)***
W2005/Fargo Hotels (pool C)....937 322-2200
1751 W 1st St Springfield (45504) ***(G-17293)***
W2005/Fargo Hotels (pool C)....937 429-5505
2550 Paramount Pl Fairborn (45324) ***(G-10810)***
Wabe Maquaw Holdings Inc....419 243-1191
17 Corey Creek Rd Toledo (43623) ***(G-18297)***
Wabush Mines Cliffs Mining Co....216 694-5700
200 Public Sq Ste 3300 Cleveland (44114) ***(G-6715)***
Wachter Inc....513 777-0701
10186 International Blvd West Chester (45246) ***(G-19243)***
Wackenhut, Columbus *Also called G4s Secure Solutions (usa)* ***(G-7722)***
Wade & Gatton Nurseries....419 883-3191
1288 Gatton Rock Rd Bellville (44813) ***(G-1427)***
Wade Trim....216 363-0300
1100 Superior Ave E # 1710 Cleveland (44114) ***(G-6716)***
Wadell Village Children Svcs, Marion *Also called County of Marion* ***(G-13534)***
Wadsworth Galaxy Rest Inc....330 334-3663
201 Park Centre Dr Wadsworth (44281) ***(G-18773)***
Wadsworth Service Inc....419 861-8181
7851 Freeway Cir Middleburg Heights (44130) ***(G-14391)***
Wadsworth Solutions Northeast, Perrysburg *Also called Wadsworth-Slawson Inc* ***(G-16072)***
Wadsworth-Slawson Inc....216 391-7263
1500 Michael Owens Way Perrysburg (43551) ***(G-16072)***
Waelzholz North America LLC....216 267-5500
5221 W 164th St Cleveland (44142) ***(G-6717)***
Wagler Homes, Uniontown *Also called Phil Wagler Construction Inc* ***(G-18532)***
Wagner Industrial Electric Inc (HQ)....937 298-7481
3178 Encrete Ln Moraine (45439) ***(G-14833)***

ALPHABETIC SECTION Warren City Board Education

Wagner Lincoln-Mercury Inc 419 435-8131
1200 S Vance St Carey (43316) ***(G-2601)***

Wagner Quarries Company 419 625-8141
4203 Milan Rd Sandusky (44870) ***(G-16809)***

Wagner Smith Company, Moraine *Also called Wagner Industrial Electric Inc* ***(G-14833)***

Waibel Heating Company 614 837-7615
2840 Cedar Hill Rd Nw Canal Winchester (43110) ***(G-2176)***

Waids Rainbow Rental Inc 216 524-3736
1050 Killian Rd Akron (44312) ***(G-502)***

Wakoni Dialysis LLC 937 294-7188
4700 Springboro Pike A Moraine (45439) ***(G-14834)***

Walden Club 330 995-7162
1119 Aurora Hudson Rd Aurora (44202) ***(G-861)***

Walden Company Ltd 330 562-7145
1119 Aurora Hudson Rd Aurora (44202) ***(G-862)***

Walden Country Club, Aurora *Also called Walden Company Ltd* ***(G-862)***

Walden Ponds Golf Club, Fairfield Township *Also called Creekside Golf Ltd* ***(G-10928)***

Walden Security, Cleveland *Also called Metropolitan Security Svcs Inc* ***(G-6044)***

Walden Security, Akron *Also called Metropolitan Security Svcs Inc* ***(G-343)***

Walden Turf Center 330 995-0023
375 Deer Island Dr Aurora (44202) ***(G-863)***

Waldon Management Corp (PA) 330 792-7688
111 Westchester Dr Youngstown (44515) ***(G-20409)***

Waldorf Marking Devices Div, Mentor *Also called Monode Marking Products Inc* ***(G-14222)***

Walgreen Co 937 433-5314
6485 Wilmington Pike Dayton (45459) ***(G-9981)***

Walgreen Co 614 236-8622
3015 E Livingston Ave Columbus (43209) ***(G-8961)***

Walgreen Co 330 677-5650
320 S Water St Kent (44240) ***(G-12404)***

Walgreen Co 330 745-2674
900 Wooster Rd N Barberton (44203) ***(G-984)***

Walgreen Co 937 396-1358
4497 Far Hills Ave Kettering (45429) ***(G-12438)***

Walgreen Co 937 781-9561
2600 S Smithville Rd Dayton (45420) ***(G-9982)***

Walgreen Co 330 733-4237
302 Canton Rd Akron (44312) ***(G-503)***

Walgreen Co 937 277-6022
2710 Salem Ave Dayton (45406) ***(G-9983)***

Walgreen Co 740 368-9380
19 London Rd Delaware (43015) ***(G-10134)***

Walgreen Co 614 336-0431
6805 Hospital Dr Dublin (43016) ***(G-10487)***

Walgreen Co 937 859-3879
1260 E Central Ave Miamisburg (45342) ***(G-14366)***

Walgreen Co 216 595-1407
25221 Miles Rd Unit H Cleveland (44128) ***(G-6718)***

Walgreen Co 330 928-5444
2645 State Rd Cuyahoga Falls (44223) ***(G-9235)***

Walgreens, Dayton *Also called Walgreen Co* ***(G-9981)***

Walgreens, Columbus *Also called Walgreen Co* ***(G-8961)***

Walgreens, Kent *Also called Walgreen Co* ***(G-12404)***

Walgreens, Barberton *Also called Walgreen Co* ***(G-984)***

Walgreens, Kettering *Also called Walgreen Co* ***(G-12438)***

Walgreens, Dayton *Also called Walgreen Co* ***(G-9982)***

Walgreens, Akron *Also called Walgreen Co* ***(G-503)***

Walgreens, Dayton *Also called Walgreen Co* ***(G-9983)***

Walgreens, Delaware *Also called Walgreen Co* ***(G-10134)***

Walgreens, Dublin *Also called Walgreen Co* ***(G-10487)***

Walgreens, Miamisburg *Also called Walgreen Co* ***(G-14366)***

Walgreens, Cleveland *Also called Walgreen Co* ***(G-6718)***

Walgreens, Cuyahoga Falls *Also called Walgreen Co* ***(G-9235)***

Walker Auto Group Inc 937 433-4950
8457 Springboro Pike Miamisburg (45342) ***(G-14367)***

Walker Machinery and Lift, Jackson *Also called Cecil I Walker Machinery Co* ***(G-12308)***

Walker Mitsubishi, Miamisburg *Also called Walker Auto Group Inc* ***(G-14367)***

Walker National Inc 614 492-1614
2195 Wright Brothers Ave Columbus (43217) ***(G-8962)***

Wall St Recycling LLC 330 296-8657
6751 Wall St Ravenna (44266) ***(G-16416)***

Wall Street Recycling, Ravenna *Also called Wall St Recycling LLC* ***(G-16416)***

Wall2wall Soccer LLC 513 573-9898
846 Reading Rd Mason (45040) ***(G-13770)***

Wallace, Grove City *Also called RR Donnelley & Sons Company* ***(G-11593)***

Wallace & Turner Insurance Inc 937 324-8492
30 Warder St Ste 200 Springfield (45504) ***(G-17294)***

Wallace F Ackley Co (PA) 614 231-3661
695 Kenwick Rd Columbus (43209) ***(G-8963)***

Wallick Co., New Albany *Also called Highland Village Ltd Partnr* ***(G-14988)***

Wallick Companies Cnstr Prpts, New Albany *Also called Wallick Enterprises Inc* ***(G-15009)***

Wallick Company, The, New Albany *Also called Brodhead Village Ltd* ***(G-14976)***

Wallick Construction Co 937 399-7009
3001 Middle Urbana Rd Springfield (45502) ***(G-17295)***

Wallick Enterprises Inc 614 863-4640
160 W Main St New Albany (43054) ***(G-15009)***

Wallick Properties Midwest LLC 614 539-9041
4243 Farr Ct Grove City (43123) ***(G-11610)***

Wallick Properties Midwest LLC (PA) 614 863-4640
160 W Main St Ste 200 New Albany (43054) ***(G-15010)***

Wallover Enterprises Inc (HQ) 440 238-9250
21845 Drake Rd Strongsville (44149) ***(G-17523)***

Wallowa Dialysis LLC 419 747-4039
2148 W 4th St Ontario (44906) ***(G-15719)***

Walman Optical Company 419 248-3384
1201 Jefferson Ave Toledo (43604) ***(G-18298)***

Walmart Inc 937 843-3681
11040 Pear Ln Belle Center (43310) ***(G-1373)***

Walmart Inc 740 636-5400
1400 Old Chllicothe Rd Se Wshngtn CT Hs (43160) ***(G-20036)***

Walmart Inc 937 399-0370
2100 N Bechtle Ave Springfield (45504) ***(G-17296)***

Walmart Inc 614 871-7094
3880 Southwest Blvd Grove City (43123) ***(G-11611)***

Walmart Inc 740 765-5700
843 State Route 43 Wintersville (43952) ***(G-19811)***

Walmart Inc 740 286-8203
100 Walmart Dr Jackson (45640) ***(G-12321)***

Walmart Inc 614 409-5500
2525 Rohr Rd Ste A Lockbourne (43137) ***(G-12962)***

Walnut Creek Chocolate Company 330 893-2995
4917 State Rte 515 Walnut Creek (44687) ***(G-18785)***

Walnut Creek Foods, Walnut Creek *Also called Coblentz Distributing Inc* ***(G-18784)***

Walnut Creek Nursing Facility, Moraine *Also called April Enterprises Inc* ***(G-14751)***

Walnut Hills Apartments, Cincinnati *Also called Walnut Hills Preservation LP* ***(G-4822)***

Walnut Hills Center Location, Cincinnati *Also called Easter Seals Tristate LLC* ***(G-3534)***

Walnut Hills Inc 330 852-2457
4748 Olde Pump St Walnut Creek (44687) ***(G-18786)***

Walnut Hills Physical Therapy 614 234-8000
5965 E Broad St Ste 390 Columbus (43213) ***(G-8964)***

Walnut Hills Preservation LP 513 281-1288
861 Beecher St Ofc Ofc Cincinnati (45206) ***(G-4822)***

Walnut Ridge Management 234 678-3900
520 S Main St Ste 2457 Akron (44311) ***(G-504)***

Walt Sweeney Fleet Sales 513 932-2717
518 W Main St Lebanon (45036) ***(G-12657)***

Waltek Inc 614 469-0156
399 W State St Columbus (43215) ***(G-8965)***

Walter Alexander Entps Inc 513 841-1100
1940 Losantiville Ave Cincinnati (45237) ***(G-4823)***

Walter F Stephens Jr Inc 937 746-0521
415 South Ave Franklin (45005) ***(G-11167)***

Walter Haverfield LLP (PA) 216 781-1212
1301 E 9th St Ste 3500 Cleveland (44114) ***(G-6719)***

Walthall LLP (PA) 216 573-2330
6300 Rockside Rd Ste 100 Cleveland (44131) ***(G-6720)***

Walton Manor Health Care Ctr 440 439-4433
19859 Alexander Rd Cleveland (44146) ***(G-6721)***

Wampum Hardware Co 740 685-2585
60711 Dynamite Rd Salesville (43778) ***(G-16721)***

Wampum Hardware Co 419 273-2542
17507 Township Road 50 Forest (45843) ***(G-11107)***

Wannemacher Enterprises Inc (PA) 419 225-9060
400 E Hanthorn Rd Lima (45804) ***(G-12912)***

Wannemacher Truck Lines, Lima *Also called Wannemacher Enterprises Inc* ***(G-12912)***

Wapakoneta Manor, Wapakoneta *Also called Hcf of Wapakoneta Inc* ***(G-18798)***

Wapakoneta YMCA 419 739-9622
1100 Defiance St Wapakoneta (45895) ***(G-18812)***

Wappoo Wood Products Inc 937 492-1166
12877 Kirkwood Rd Sidney (45365) ***(G-16960)***

Ward & Werner Co 614 885-0741
6620 Plesenton Dr W Worthington (43085) ***(G-20006)***

Ward Realestate Inc 419 281-2000
600 E Main St Ashland (44805) ***(G-707)***

Ward Trucking LLC 330 659-6658
2800 Brecksville Rd Richfield (44286) ***(G-16532)***

Ward Trucking LLC 614 275-3800
1601 Mckinley Ave Columbus (43222) ***(G-8966)***

Warehouse, Columbus *Also called Restaurant Equippers Inc* ***(G-8624)***

Warehouse, Cleveland *Also called Basista Furniture Inc* ***(G-5099)***

Warehouse Services Group Llc 419 868-6400
6145 Merger Dr Holland (43528) ***(G-12060)***

Warm 98, Cincinnati *Also called Cumulus Media Inc* ***(G-3448)***

Warner Buick-Nissan Inc 419 423-7161
1060 County Road 95 Findlay (45840) ***(G-11099)***

Warner Dennehey Marshall 216 912-3787
127 Public Sq Ste 3510 Cleveland (44114) ***(G-6722)***

Warner Mechanical Corporation 419 332-7116
1609 Dickinson St Fremont (43420) ***(G-11229)***

Warner Nissan, Findlay *Also called Warner Buick-Nissan Inc* ***(G-11099)***

Warner Nurseries Inc 440 946-0880
6190 Middle Ridge Rd Madison (44057) ***(G-13237)***

Warner Nursery, Madison *Also called Warner Nurseries Inc* ***(G-13237)***

Warnock Tanner & Assoc Inc 419 897-6999
959 Illinois Ave Ste C Maumee (43537) ***(G-13993)***

Warren Bros & Sons Inc (PA) 740 373-1430
108b S 7th St Marietta (45750) ***(G-13516)***

Warren City Board Education 330 841-2265
600 Roanoke Ave Sw Warren (44483) ***(G-18923)***

ALPHABETIC

Warren Co Human Services Dept, Lebanon ALPHABETIC SECTION

Warren Co Human Services Dept, Lebanon Also called County of Warren *(G-12598)*
Warren County Board Devlpmntal 513 925-1813
42 Kings Way Lebanon (45036) *(G-12658)*
Warren County Community Svcs (PA) 513 695-2100
570 N State Route 741 Lebanon (45036) *(G-12659)*
WARREN COUNTY OF PRODUCTION SE, Lebanon Also called Production Services Unlimited *(G-12637)*
Warren County Park District, Lebanon Also called County of Warren *(G-12599)*
Warren County Wtr & Sewer Dept, Lebanon Also called County of Warren *(G-12600)*
Warren Dermatology and Allergy, Warren Also called Warren Drmatology Allergies PC *(G-18924)*
Warren Door, Niles Also called Traichal Construction Company *(G-15307)*
Warren Drilling Co Inc 740 783-2775
305 Smithson St Dexter City (45727) *(G-10171)*
Warren Drmatology Allergies PC 330 856-6365
735 Niles Cortland Rd Se Warren (44484) *(G-18924)*
Warren Guillard Brick Layers, Tallmadge Also called Warren Guillard Bricklayers *(G-17660)*
Warren Guillard Bricklayers 330 633-3855
107 Potomac Ave Tallmadge (44278) *(G-17660)*
Warren Housing Development 330 369-1533
4076 Youngstown Rd Se # 101 Warren (44484) *(G-18925)*
Warren Trucking, Dexter City Also called Warren Drilling Co Inc *(G-10171)*
Warren Twnship Vlntr Fire Dept 740 373-2424
17305 State Route 550 Marietta (45750) *(G-13517)*
Warrens IGA, Marietta Also called Warren Bros & Sons Inc *(G-13516)*
Warrenton Copper LLC 636 456-3488
1240 Marquette St Cleveland (44114) *(G-6723)*
Warsteiner Importers Agency 513 942-9872
9359 Allen Rd West Chester (45069) *(G-19183)*
Warsteiner USA, West Chester Also called Warsteiner Importers Agency *(G-19183)*
Warstler Brothers Landscaping 330 492-9500
4125 Salway Ave Nw Canton (44718) *(G-2582)*
Warwick Communications Inc (PA) 216 787-0300
405 Ken Mar Indus Pkwy Broadview Heights (44147) *(G-1895)*
Wasco Inc (PA) 740 373-3418
340 Muskingum Dr Marietta (45750) *(G-13518)*
Washing Systems LLC (PA) 800 272-1974
167 Commerce Dr Loveland (45140) *(G-13163)*
Washington Cnty Engineers Off, Marietta Also called County of Washington *(G-13438)*
Washington County Home, Marietta Also called County of Washington *(G-13439)*
Washington Court Hse Holdg LLC 614 873-7733
1850 Lowes Blvd Wshngtn CT Hs (43160) *(G-20037)*
Washington Group, Cleveland Also called Aecom Energy & Cnstr Inc *(G-4962)*
Washington Group, Oregon Also called Aecom Energy & Cnstr Inc *(G-15723)*
Washington Local Schools 419 473-8356
5201 Douglas Rd Toledo (43613) *(G-18299)*
Washington Manor Inc (PA) 937 433-3441
7300 Mcewen Rd Dayton (45459) *(G-9984)*
Washington Manor Nursing Ctr, Dayton Also called Washington Manor Inc *(G-9984)*
Washington PRI (HQ) 614 621-9000
180 E Broad St Fl 22 Columbus (43215) *(G-8967)*
Washington Prime Group LP (HQ) 614 621-9000
180 E Broad St Columbus (43215) *(G-8968)*
Washington Prime Group Inc (PA) 614 621-9000
180 E Broad St Fl 21 Columbus (43215) *(G-8969)*
Washington Square Apartments 740 349-8353
340 Eastern Ave Ofc Newark (43055) *(G-15244)*
Washington Township Park Dst (PA) 937 433-5155
221 S Main St Dayton (45402) *(G-9985)*
Washington Twnship Mntgomery 937 433-0130
895 Mmsburg Cnterville Rd Dayton (45459) *(G-9986)*
Washington Twnship Rcrtion Ctr, Dayton Also called Washington Twnship Mntgomery *(G-9986)*
Wasiniak Construction Inc 419 668-8624
2519 State Route 61 Norwalk (44857) *(G-15596)*
Wassarstrom Rest Sup Super Str, Columbus Also called Wasserstrom Company *(G-8971)*
Wasserstom Disrtributing Ofc, Columbus Also called Marion Road Enterprises *(G-8110)*
Wasserstrom Company (PA) 614 228-6525
4500 E Broad St Columbus (43213) *(G-8970)*
Wasserstrom Company 614 228-6525
2777 Silver Dr Columbus (43211) *(G-8971)*
Wasserstrom Holdings Inc 614 228-6525
477 S Front St Columbus (43215) *(G-8972)*
Wasserstrom Marketing Division, Columbus Also called N Wasserstrom & Sons Inc *(G-8212)*
Waste Management, Waynesburg Also called American Landfill Inc *(G-18980)*
Waste Management of Lima, Lima Also called Waste Management Ohio Inc *(G-12913)*
Waste Management Ohio Inc 440 201-1235
6705 Richmond Rd Solon (44139) *(G-17066)*
Waste Management Ohio Inc 800 356-5235
675 Chamber Dr Chillicothe (45601) *(G-2896)*
Waste Management Ohio Inc 800 910-2831
116 N Bauer Rd Wooster (44691) *(G-19923)*
Waste Management Ohio Inc 330 452-9000
1800 9th St Ne Canton (44705) *(G-2583)*
Waste Management Ohio Inc 614 382-6342
1006 W Walnut St Canal Winchester (43110) *(G-2177)*
Waste Management Ohio Inc 419 547-7791
3956 State Route 412 Vickery (43464) *(G-18734)*
Waste Management Ohio Inc 866 797-9018
12201 Council Dr North Jackson (44451) *(G-15390)*
Waste Management Ohio Inc 800 343-6047
1700 N Broad St Fairborn (45324) *(G-10811)*
Waste Management Ohio Inc 866 409-4671
6525 Wales Rd Northwood (43619) *(G-15550)*
Waste Management Ohio Inc 440 286-7116
10237 Cutts Rd Chardon (44024) *(G-2777)*
Waste Management Ohio Inc 740 345-1212
100 Ecology Row Newark (43055) *(G-15245)*
Waste Management Ohio Inc 419 221-3644
1550 E 4th St Lima (45804) *(G-12913)*
Waste Management Ohio Inc 614 833-5290
1046 W Walnut St Canal Winchester (43110) *(G-2178)*
Waste Management Ohio Inc (HQ) 800 343-6047
1700 N Broad St Fairborn (45324) *(G-10812)*
Waste Management Ohio Inc 440 285-6767
4339 Tuttle Rd Geneva (44041) *(G-11373)*
Waste Management Ohio Inc 419 221-2029
1550 E 4th St Lima (45804) *(G-12914)*
Waste Management Ohio NW, Northwood Also called Waste Management Ohio Inc *(G-15550)*
Waste Parchment Inc 330 674-6868
4510 Township Road 307 Millersburg (44654) *(G-14627)*
Waste Water Treatment Plant, Massillon Also called City of Massillon *(G-13796)*
Waste Water Treatment Plant, Zanesville Also called City of Zanesville *(G-20465)*
Wastren - Energx Mission 740 897-3724
1571 Shyville Rd Piketon (45661) *(G-16131)*
Wastren Advantage Inc (PA) 970 254-1277
1571 Shyville Rd Piketon (45661) *(G-16132)*
Water & Sewer Department, Johnstown Also called County of Licking *(G-12339)*
Water & Sewer Department, Avon Lake Also called City of Avon Lake *(G-925)*
Water 1, Lucasville Also called Scioto County Region Wtr Dst 1 *(G-13182)*
Water Department, Dayton Also called City of Dayton *(G-9410)*
Water Department, Cuyahoga Falls Also called City of Cuyahoga Falls *(G-9175)*
Water Leasing Co LLC 440 285-9400
620 Water St Chardon (44024) *(G-2778)*
Water Pollution Control, Lorain Also called City of Lorain *(G-13023)*
Water Pollution Control, Sandusky Also called City of Sandusky *(G-16737)*
Water Pollution Control Ctrl, Canton Also called City of Canton *(G-2311)*
Water Transport LLC 740 937-2199
100 Sammi Dr Hopedale (43976) *(G-12080)*
Waterbeds n Stuff Inc (PA) 614 871-1171
3933 Brookham Dr Grove City (43123) *(G-11612)*
Waterfront & Associates Inc 859 581-1414
700 Walnut St Ste 200 Cincinnati (45202) *(G-4824)*
Waterhouse Bath and Kit Studio, Perrysburg Also called Maumee Plumbing & Htg Sup Inc *(G-16031)*
Watertown Steel Company LLC 740 749-3512
405 Watertown Rd Waterford (45786) *(G-18940)*
Waterville Care LLC 419 878-3901
555 Anthony Wayne Trl Waterville (43566) *(G-18947)*
Waterway Gas & Wash Company 330 995-2900
7010 N Aurora Rd Aurora (44202) *(G-864)*
Waterworks America Inc 440 526-4815
5005 Rcksde Rd Crwn Cn 6f Crown Centre Cleveland (44131) *(G-6724)*
Waterworks Crystals, Cleveland Also called Waterworks America Inc *(G-6724)*
Waterworks, The, Columbus Also called Tfh-Eb Inc *(G-8833)*
Watkins Mechanical Inc (PA) 937 748-0220
10 Parker Dr Springboro (45066) *(G-17141)*
Watkins Mechanical Services, Springboro Also called Watkins Mechanical Inc *(G-17141)*
Watson Gravel Inc (PA) 513 863-0070
2728 Hamilton Cleves Rd Hamilton (45013) *(G-11784)*
Watteredge LLC (HQ) 440 933-6110
567 Miller Rd Avon Lake (44012) *(G-940)*
Wauseon Dialysis LLC 419 335-0695
721 S Shoop Ave Wauseon (43567) *(G-18963)*
Wauseon Machine & Mfg Inc (PA) 419 337-0940
995 Enterprise Ave Wauseon (43567) *(G-18964)*
Waverly Care Center Inc 740 947-2113
444 Cherry St Frnt Waverly (45690) *(G-18976)*
Waxman Consumer Pdts Group Inc 614 491-0500
5920 Green Pointe Dr S A Groveport (43125) *(G-11686)*
Waxman Consumer Pdts Group Inc (HQ) 440 439-1830
24455 Aurora Rd Cleveland (44146) *(G-6725)*
Waxman Industries Inc (PA) 440 439-1830
24460 Aurora Rd Cleveland (44146) *(G-6726)*
Waycraft Inc (PA) 419 563-0550
118 River St Bucyrus (44820) *(G-2051)*
Waycraft Inc 419 562-3321
118 River St Bucyrus (44820) *(G-2052)*
Wayne - Dalton, Dundee Also called Hrh Door Corp *(G-10500)*
Wayne County Care Center, Wooster Also called County of Wayne *(G-19854)*
Wayne County Child Support, Wooster Also called County of Wayne *(G-19857)*
Wayne County Childrens Svcs, Wooster Also called County of Wayne *(G-19856)*
Wayne County Engineers Wooster, Wooster Also called County of Wayne *(G-19858)*

ALPHABETIC SECTION
Wells Fargo Clearing Svcs LLC

Wayne Employment Training Ctr, Wooster *Also called County of Wayne* ***(G-19855)***
Wayne Healthcare (PA) 937 548-1141
835 Sweitzer St Greenville (45331) ***(G-11524)***
Wayne Homes, Uniontown *Also called Wh Midwest LLC* ***(G-18543)***
Wayne Industries Inc 937 548-6025
5844 Jysville St Johns Rd Greenville (45331) ***(G-11525)***
Wayne Lanes, Wooster *Also called Plaz-Way Inc* ***(G-19904)***
Wayne Mutual Insurance Co 330 345-8100
3873 Cleveland Rd Wooster (44691) ***(G-19924)***
Wayne Savings Bancshares Inc (PA) 330 264-5767
151 N Market St Wooster (44691) ***(G-19925)***
Wayne Savings Community Bank (HQ) 330 264-5767
151 N Market St Wooster (44691) ***(G-19926)***
Wayne Street Development LLC 740 373-5455
424 2nd St Marietta (45750) ***(G-13519)***
Wayne Trail Technologies Inc 937 295-2120
203 E Park St Fort Loramie (45845) ***(G-11112)***
Wayne Water Systems, Harrison *Also called Wayne/Scott Fetzer Company* ***(G-11812)***
Wayne/Scott Fetzer Company 800 237-0987
101 Production Dr Harrison (45030) ***(G-11812)***
Waypoint Aviation LLC 800 769-4765
4765 Airport Rd Cincinnati (45226) ***(G-4825)***
Wayside Farms Inc 330 666-7716
4557 Quick Rd Peninsula (44264) ***(G-15952)***
Wayside Farms Nursing, Peninsula *Also called Wayside Farms Inc* ***(G-15952)***
Wb Services Inc 330 390-5722
6834 County Road 672 # 102 Millersburg (44654) ***(G-14628)***
Wbc Group LLC (PA) 866 528-2144
6333 Hudson Crossing Pkwy Hudson (44236) ***(G-12150)***
Wbgu FM 88 1, Bowling Green *Also called Bowling Green State University* ***(G-1767)***
Wbns Tv Inc 614 460-3700
770 Twin Rivers Dr Columbus (43215) ***(G-8973)***
Wbns-AM Sports Radio 1460 Fan, Columbus *Also called Radiohio Incorporated* ***(G-8584)***
Wbnx TV 55, Cuyahoga Falls *Also called Winston Brdcstg Netwrk Inc* ***(G-9236)***
WCCS, Lebanon *Also called Warren County Community Svcs* ***(G-12659)***
Wcdp, Fremont *Also called Wsos Child Development Program* ***(G-11230)***
WCH, Bowling Green *Also called Wood County Hospital Assoc* ***(G-1800)***
Wckx-FM, Columbus *Also called Urban One Inc* ***(G-8918)***
Wcm Holdings Inc (PA) 513 705-2100
11500 Canal Rd Cincinnati (45241) ***(G-4826)***
Wcmh, Columbus *Also called Nexstar Broadcasting Inc* ***(G-8275)***
Wcoil, Lima *Also called West Central Ohio Internet* ***(G-12916)***
WD Partners Inc 614 634-7000
7007 Discovery Blvd Dublin (43017) ***(G-10488)***
Wdpn, Alliance *Also called D A Peterson Inc* ***(G-537)***
Wdtn, Moraine *Also called Sunrise Television Corp* ***(G-14828)***
Wdtn, Moraine *Also called Nexstar Broadcasting Inc* ***(G-14811)***
Weastec, Hillsboro *Also called Denso International Amer Inc* ***(G-11972)***
Weatherables, Groveport *Also called Usavinyl LLC* ***(G-11682)***
Weatherproofing Tech Inc (HQ) 216 292-5000
3735 Green Rd Beachwood (44122) ***(G-1136)***
Weatherproofing Tech Inc 281 480-7900
3735 Green Rd Beachwood (44122) ***(G-1137)***
Weatherwax, Middletown *Also called Wmvh LLC* ***(G-14471)***
Weaver Bros Inc (PA) 937 526-3907
895 E Main St Versailles (45380) ***(G-18731)***
Weaver Bros Inc 937 526-4777
10638 State Route 47 Versailles (45380) ***(G-18732)***
Weaver Brothers Farm, Versailles *Also called Weaver Bros Inc* ***(G-18732)***
Weaver Custom Homes Inc 330 264-5444
124 E Liberty St Ste A Wooster (44691) ***(G-19927)***
Weaver Fab & Finishing, Akron *Also called Bogie Industries Inc Ltd* ***(G-106)***
Weaver Industries Inc 330 379-3606
636 W Exchange St Akron (44302) ***(G-505)***
Weaver Industries Inc (PA) 330 379-3660
520 S Main St Ste 2441 Akron (44311) ***(G-506)***
Weaver Industries Inc 330 666-5114
340 N Clvland Mssillon Rd Akron (44333) ***(G-507)***
Weaver Industries Inc 330 733-2431
89 E Howe Rd Tallmadge (44278) ***(G-17661)***
Weaver Industries Inc 330 745-2400
2337 Romig Rd Ste 2 Akron (44320) ***(G-508)***
Weaver Secure Shred, Akron *Also called Weaver Industries Inc* ***(G-508)***
Web Yoga Inc 937 428-0000
938 Senate Dr Dayton (45459) ***(G-9987)***
Webb, Barry W, Cincinnati *Also called Springdale Family Medicine PC* ***(G-4566)***
Weber Associates, Columbus *Also called Weber Partners Ltd* ***(G-8974)***
Weber Health Care Center Inc 440 647-2088
214 E Herrick Ave Wellington (44090) ***(G-18996)***
Weber Obrien Ltd 419 885-8338
5580 Monroe St Ste 210 Sylvania (43560) ***(G-17627)***
Weber Partners Ltd (PA) 614 222-6806
775 Yard St Ste 350 Columbus (43212) ***(G-8974)***
Webert & Co, Sylvania *Also called Weber Obrien Ltd* ***(G-17627)***
Webmd Health Corp 330 425-3241
2045 Midway Dr Twinsburg (44087) ***(G-18485)***
Wedgewood Estates 419 756-7400
730 N Spring Rd Unit 356 Westerville (43082) ***(G-19358)***
Wedgewood Golf & Country Club 614 793-9600
9600 Wedgewood Blvd Powell (43065) ***(G-16354)***
Wedgewood Lanes Inc 330 792-1949
1741 S Raccoon Rd Youngstown (44515) ***(G-20410)***
Wedgewood Urgent Care, Westerville *Also called Immediate Health Associates* ***(G-19411)***
Wednesday Auto Auction, Obetz *Also called Columbus Fair Auto Auction Inc* ***(G-15666)***
Wee Care Day Care Lrng Centre, Youngstown *Also called Nichalex Inc* ***(G-20300)***
Wee Care Daycare 330 856-1313
1145 Niles Cortland Rd Se Warren (44484) ***(G-18926)***
Wee Care Learning Center, Van Wert *Also called Van Wert County Day Care Inc* ***(G-18647)***
Wee Care Learning Center 937 454-9363
9675 N Dixie Dr Dayton (45414) ***(G-9988)***
Weeber-Morse, Carmen MD, Perrysburg *Also called Jon R Dvorak MD* ***(G-16021)***
Weed Man Lawncare LLC 513 683-6310
12100 Phanpion Way Cincinnati (45241) ***(G-4827)***
Weekleys Mailing Service Inc 440 234-4325
1420 W Bagley Rd Berea (44017) ***(G-1475)***
Wege, Lima *Also called Maverick Media* ***(G-12838)***
Wegman Hessler Vanderburg 216 642-3342
6055 Rockside Woods Blvd # 200 Cleveland (44131) ***(G-6727)***
Wegman Company, Cincinnati *Also called Wegman Construction Company* ***(G-4828)***
Wegman Construction Company 513 381-1111
1101 York St Ste 500 Cincinnati (45214) ***(G-4828)***
Weiffenbach Marble & Tile Co 937 832-7055
150 Lau Pkwy Englewood (45315) ***(G-10724)***
Weiland's Gourmet Market, Columbus *Also called Weilands Fine Meats Inc* ***(G-8975)***
Weilands Fine Meats Inc 614 267-9910
3600 Indianola Ave Columbus (43214) ***(G-8975)***
Weiler Welding Company Inc (PA) 937 222-8312
2400 Sandridge Dr Moraine (45439) ***(G-14835)***
Weinberg Capital Group Inc (PA) 216 503-8307
5005 Rockside Rd Ste 1140 Cleveland (44131) ***(G-6728)***
Weiner Keith D Co L P A Inc 216 771-6500
75 Public Sq Ste 600 Cleveland (44113) ***(G-6729)***
Weinstein and Associates, Painesville *Also called Weinstein Donald Jay PHD* ***(G-15886)***
Weinstein Donald Jay PHD 216 831-1040
54 S State St Painesville (44077) ***(G-15886)***
Welch Holdings Inc 513 353-3220
8953 E Miami River Rd Cincinnati (45247) ***(G-4829)***
Welch Packaging LLC 937 223-3958
321 Hopeland St Dayton (45417) ***(G-9989)***
Welcome Nursing Home, Oberlin *Also called Wessell Generations Inc* ***(G-15662)***
Weld Plus Inc 513 941-4411
4790 River Rd Cincinnati (45233) ***(G-4830)***
Welker-Mckee Div, Cleveland *Also called Hajoca Corporation* ***(G-5721)***
Well Point Anthem, Dayton *Also called Dayton Anthem* ***(G-9457)***
Welles Bowen Realty Inc 419 535-0011
2460 N Reynolds Rd Toledo (43615) ***(G-18300)***
Wellington F Roemer Insurance 419 473-0258
3912 Sunforest Ct Ste A Toledo (43623) ***(G-18301)***
Wellington Group LLC 216 525-2200
6133 Rockside Rd Ste 205 Independence (44131) ***(G-12275)***
Wellington Manor, Fairfield Township *Also called Kerrington Health Systems Inc* ***(G-10932)***
Wellington Orthopedics, Cincinnati *Also called Orthopedic Cons Cincinnati* ***(G-4236)***
Wellington Orthpd Spt Medicine, Blue Ash *Also called Orthopedic Cons Cincinnati* ***(G-1660)***
Wellington Orthpd Spt Medicine, Cincinnati *Also called Orthopedic Cons Cincinnati* ***(G-4237)***
Wellington Orthpd Spt Medicine, Cincinnati *Also called Orthopedic Cons Cincinnati* ***(G-4238)***
Wellington Place LLC 440 734-9933
4800 Clague Rd Apt 108 North Olmsted (44070) ***(G-15450)***
Wellington Technologies Inc 440 238-4377
802 Sharon Dr Westlake (44145) ***(G-19564)***
Wells & Sons Janitorial Svc 937 878-4375
1877 S Maple Ave Ste 250 Fairborn (45324) ***(G-10813)***
Wells Brother Electric Inc 937 394-7559
105 Shue Dr Anna (45302) ***(G-618)***
Wells Fargo Advisors, Dublin *Also called Wells Fargo Clearing Svcs LLC* ***(G-10489)***
Wells Fargo Advisors, Cleveland *Also called Wells Fargo Clearing Svcs LLC* ***(G-6730)***
Wells Fargo Advisors, Columbus *Also called Wells Fargo Clearing Svcs LLC* ***(G-8976)***
Wells Fargo Advisors, Toledo *Also called Wells Fargo Clearing Svcs LLC* ***(G-18302)***
Wells Fargo Advisors, Westlake *Also called Wells Fargo Clearing Svcs LLC* ***(G-19565)***
Wells Fargo Advisors, Toledo *Also called Wells Fargo Clearing Svcs LLC* ***(G-18303)***
Wells Fargo Advisors, Cincinnati *Also called Wells Fargo Clearing Svcs LLC* ***(G-4831)***
Wells Fargo Advisors, Cleveland *Also called Wells Fargo Clearing Svcs LLC* ***(G-6731)***
Wells Fargo Bank National Assn 513 424-6640
1076 Summitt Dr Middletown (45042) ***(G-14470)***
Wells Fargo Clearing Svcs LLC 614 764-2040
485 Metro Pl S Ste 300 Dublin (43017) ***(G-10489)***
Wells Fargo Clearing Svcs LLC 216 378-2722
30100 Chagrin Blvd # 200 Cleveland (44124) ***(G-6730)***
Wells Fargo Clearing Svcs LLC 614 221-8371
41 S High St Ste 1550 Columbus (43215) ***(G-8976)***
Wells Fargo Clearing Svcs LLC 419 356-3272
3450 W Central Ave # 130 Toledo (43606) ***(G-18302)***
Wells Fargo Clearing Svcs LLC 440 835-9250
25 Main St Fl 2 Westlake (44145) ***(G-19565)***
Wells Fargo Clearing Svcs LLC 419 720-9700
7335 Crossleigh Ct # 100 Toledo (43617) ***(G-18303)***

ALPHABETIC

Wells Fargo Clearing Svcs LLC 513 241-9900
255 E 5th St Ste 1400 Cincinnati (45202) ***(G-4831)***
Wells Fargo Clearing Svcs LLC 216 574-7300
950 Main Ave Ste 300 Cleveland (44113) ***(G-6731)***
Wells Fargo Home Mortgage Inc 614 781-8847
485 Metro Pl S Ste 300 Dublin (43017) ***(G-10490)***
Wells, Mark D MD, Akron *Also called Lawrence A Cervino MD* ***(G-313)***
Wellspring Health Care, Cincinnati *Also called SL Wellspring LLC* ***(G-4540)***
Wellston Auditor's Office, Wellston *Also called City of Wellston* ***(G-18998)***
Welltower Inc (PA) 419 247-2800
4500 Dorr St Toledo (43615) ***(G-18304)***
WELSH HOME FOR THE AGED, Rocky River *Also called Womens Welsh Clubs of America* ***(G-16596)***
Welspun Usa Inc 614 945-5100
3901 Gantz Rd Ste A Grove City (43123) ***(G-11613)***
Weltman Weinberg & Reis Co Lpa 216 739-5100
965 Keynote Cir Brooklyn Heights (44131) ***(G-1933)***
Weltman Weinberg & Reis Co Lpa (PA) 216 685-1000
323 W Lkeside Ave Ste 200 Cleveland (44113) ***(G-6732)***
Weltman Weinberg & Reis Co Lpa 614 801-2600
3705 Marlane Dr Grove City (43123) ***(G-11614)***
Weltman Weinberg & Reis Co Lpa 513 723-2200
525 Vine St Ste 800 Cincinnati (45202) ***(G-4832)***
Weltman Weinberg & Reis Co Lpa 216 459-8633
981 Keynote Cir Cleveland (44131) ***(G-6733)***
Welty Building Company Ltd (PA) 330 867-2400
3421 Ridgewood Rd Ste 200 Fairlawn (44333) ***(G-10981)***
Wembley Club, The, Chagrin Falls *Also called New Wembley LLC* ***(G-2726)***
Wems, Piketon *Also called Wastren - Energx Mission* ***(G-16131)***
Wenco Inc 937 849-6002
1807 Dalton Dr New Carlisle (45344) ***(G-15033)***
Wendel Poultry Service Inc 419 375-2439
1860 Union City Rd Fort Recovery (45846) ***(G-11121)***
Wendt-Bristol Health Services (PA) 614 403-9966
921 Jasonway Ave Ste B Columbus (43214) ***(G-8977)***
Wendys Company (PA) 614 764-3100
1 Dave Thomas Blvd Dublin (43017) ***(G-10491)***
Wendys Restaurants LLC (HQ) 614 764-3100
1 Dave Thomas Blvd Dublin (43017) ***(G-10492)***
Wenger Asphalt Inc 330 837-4767
26 N Cochran St Dalton (44618) ***(G-9243)***
Wenger Excavating Inc 330 837-4767
26 N Cochran St Dalton (44618) ***(G-9244)***
Wenger Temperature Control 614 586-4016
2005 Progress Ave Columbus (43207) ***(G-8978)***
Wenzler Daycare & Learning Ctr, Dayton *Also called Wenzler Daycare Learning Ctr* ***(G-9990)***
Wenzler Daycare Learning Ctr 937 435-8200
4535 Presidential Way Dayton (45429) ***(G-9990)***
Weol 440 236-9283
538 Broad St Elyria (44035) ***(G-10688)***
Weol/Wnwv Radio, Elyria *Also called Elyria-Lorain Broadcasting Co* ***(G-10624)***
Were-AM, Cleveland *Also called Urban One Inc* ***(G-6674)***
Werlor Inc 419 784-4285
1420 Ralston Ave Defiance (43512) ***(G-10063)***
Werlor Waste Control, Defiance *Also called Werlor Inc* ***(G-10063)***
Wern-Rausch Locke Advertising 330 493-8866
4470 Dressler Rd Nw Canton (44718) ***(G-2584)***
Werner Enterprises Inc 937 325-5403
4395 Laybourne Rd Springfield (45505) ***(G-17297)***
Wernli Realty Inc 937 258-7878
1300 Grange Hall Rd Beavercreek (45430) ***(G-1262)***
Wesbanco Inc 614 208-7298
2000 Henderson Rd Ste 100 Columbus (43220) ***(G-8979)***
Wesbanco Inc 740 532-0263
311 S 5th St Ironton (45638) ***(G-12304)***
Wesbanco Bank Inc 740 425-1927
230 E Main St Barnesville (43713) ***(G-992)***
Wesbanco Bank Inc 513 741-5766
5511 Cheviot Rd Cincinnati (45247) ***(G-4833)***
Weschler Instruments, Strongsville *Also called Hughes Corporation* ***(G-17473)***
Wesco Distribution Inc 216 741-0441
4741 Hinckley Indus Pkwy Cleveland (44109) ***(G-6734)***
Wesco Distribution Inc 937 228-9668
2080 Winners Cir Dayton (45404) ***(G-9991)***
Wesco Distribution Inc 419 666-1670
6519 Fairfield Dr Northwood (43619) ***(G-15551)***
Wescom Solutions Inc 513 831-1207
300 Techne Center Dr A Milford (45150) ***(G-14574)***
Wesley Community Center Inc 937 263-3556
3730 Delphos Ave Dayton (45417) ***(G-9992)***
Wesley Educ Cntr For Chldrn 513 569-1840
525 Hale Ave Cincinnati (45229) ***(G-4834)***
WESLEY RIDGE, Columbus *Also called Glen Wesley Inc* ***(G-7755)***
Wesley Ridge Inc 614 759-0023
2225 Taylor Park Dr Reynoldsburg (43068) ***(G-16489)***
Wesleyan Senior Living (PA) 440 284-9000
807 West Ave Elyria (44035) ***(G-10689)***
WESLEYAN VILLAGE, Elyria *Also called Wesleyan Senior Living* ***(G-10689)***
Wesleyan Village 440 284-9000
807 West Ave Elyria (44035) ***(G-10690)***
Wessell Generations Inc 440 775-1491
417 S Main St Oberlin (44074) ***(G-15662)***
West Bay Care Rhbilitation Ctr, Westlake *Also called Harborside Clveland Ltd Partnr* ***(G-19488)***
West Central Ohio Group Ltd 419 224-7586
801 Medical Dr Ste B Lima (45804) ***(G-12915)***
West Central Ohio Internet 419 229-2645
215 N Elizabeth St Lima (45801) ***(G-12916)***
West Central Ohio Surgery & En 419 226-8700
770 W High St Ste 100 Lima (45801) ***(G-12917)***
West Chester Chrstn Chld 513 777-6300
7951 Tylersville Rd West Chester (45069) ***(G-19184)***
West Chester Hospital, West Chester *Also called Chester West Medical Center* ***(G-19037)***
West Chester Protective Gear, Cincinnati *Also called Chester West Holdings Inc* ***(G-3241)***
West Chester, Barrington of, West Chester *Also called Senior Lifestyle Corporation* ***(G-19150)***
West Corporation 330 574-0510
5185 Youngstown Warren Rd Niles (44446) ***(G-15310)***
West Denison Baseball League 216 251-5790
3556 W 105th St Cleveland (44111) ***(G-6735)***
West End Branch, Willoughby *Also called Lake County YMCA* ***(G-19680)***
West End Health Center Inc 513 621-2726
1413 Linn St Cincinnati (45214) ***(G-4835)***
West End YMCA, Cincinnati *Also called Young Mens Christian Associat* ***(G-4868)***
West Entitlement Operations, Columbus *Also called Defense Fin & Accounting Svc* ***(G-7501)***
West Jefferson Plbg Htg Coolin, West Jefferson *Also called West Jefferson Plumbing Htg* ***(G-19256)***
West Jefferson Plumbing Htg 614 879-9606
174 E Main St West Jefferson (43162) ***(G-19256)***
West Lafytt Rehabltion, West Lafayette *Also called Kindred Healthcare Oper Inc* ***(G-19258)***
West Liberty Care Center Inc 937 465-5065
6557 Us Highway 68 S West Liberty (43357) ***(G-19264)***
West Market Optical Service, Akron *Also called Summit Opthomology Optical* ***(G-468)***
West Memory Gardens, Dayton *Also called Stonemor Partners LP* ***(G-9908)***
West Montrose Properties (PA) 330 867-4013
2841 Riviera Dr Ste 300 Fairlawn (44333) ***(G-10982)***
West Ohio Cmnty Action Partnr 419 227-2586
540 S Central Ave Lima (45804) ***(G-12918)***
West Ohio Cmnty Action Partnr (PA) 419 227-2586
540 S Central Ave Lima (45804) ***(G-12919)***
West Ohio Conference of (PA) 614 844-6200
32 Wesley Blvd Worthington (43085) ***(G-20007)***
West Ohio Conference of 937 773-5313
415 W Greene St Piqua (45356) ***(G-16175)***
West Park Animal Hospital, Cleveland *Also called Tri Zob Inc* ***(G-6616)***
West Park Family Physician 419 472-1124
3425 Executive Pkwy # 100 Toledo (43606) ***(G-18305)***
West Park Health Partners, Toledo *Also called West Park Family Physician* ***(G-18305)***
West Park Healthcare, Cleveland *Also called Myocare Nursing Home Inc* ***(G-6095)***
West Park Place, Toledo *Also called Gemini Properties* ***(G-17911)***
West Park Retirement Community, Cincinnati *Also called Mercy Health West Park* ***(G-4076)***
West Park Retirement Community 513 451-8900
2950 West Park Dr Ofc Cincinnati (45238) ***(G-4836)***
West Roofing Systems Inc (PA) 800 356-5748
121 Commerce Dr Lagrange (44050) ***(G-12462)***
West Shell Coml Encore Intl, Cincinnati *Also called Nisbet Corporation* ***(G-4170)***
West Shell Commercial Inc 513 721-4200
425 Walnut St Ste 1200 Cincinnati (45202) ***(G-4837)***
West Shell Gale Schnetzer 513 683-3833
748 Wards Corner Rd Loveland (45140) ***(G-13164)***
West Shore Child Care Center 440 333-2040
20401 Hilliard Blvd Cleveland (44116) ***(G-6736)***
West Shore Day Treatment Ctr, Cleveland *Also called Positive Education Program* ***(G-6292)***
West Side Cardiology Assoc 440 333-8600
20455 Lorain Rd Fl 2 Cleveland (44126) ***(G-6737)***
West Side Cardiology Assoc 440 333-8600
20455 Lorain Rd Fl 2 Cleveland (44126) ***(G-6738)***
West Side Community House 216 771-7297
9300 Lorain Ave Cleveland (44102) ***(G-6739)***
West Side Dtscher Fruen Verein 440 238-3361
18627 Shurmer Rd Strongsville (44136) ***(G-17524)***
West Side Ecumenical Ministry (PA) 216 325-9369
5209 Detroit Ave Cleveland (44102) ***(G-6740)***
West Side Montessori 419 866-1931
7115 W Bancroft St Toledo (43615) ***(G-18306)***
West Side Pediatrics Inc (PA) 513 922-8200
663 Anderson Ferry Rd # 1 Cincinnati (45238) ***(G-4838)***
West Union Elementary School, West Union *Also called Adams Cnty /Ohio Vly Schl Dst* ***(G-19271)***
West View Manor Inc 330 264-8640
1715 Mechanicsburg Rd Wooster (44691) ***(G-19928)***
West View Manor Retirement Ctr, Wooster *Also called West View Manor Inc* ***(G-19928)***
West-Way Management Company 440 250-1851
24700 Center Ridge Rd G50 Westlake (44145) ***(G-19566)***
Westark Family Services Inc 330 832-5043
42 1st St Ne Massillon (44646) ***(G-13860)***
Westerly Wstwater Trtmnt Plant, Cleveland *Also called Northast Ohio Rgonal Sewer Dst* ***(G-6146)***

Western & Southern Lf Insur Co (HQ).....513 629-1800
400 Broadway St Cincinnati (45202) *(G-4839)*
Western & Southern Lf Insur Co.....614 277-4800
1931 Ohio Dr Grove City (43123) *(G-11615)*
Western & Southern Lf Insur Co.....234 380-4525
85 Executive Pkwy Ste 200 Hudson (44236) *(G-12151)*
Western & Southern Lf Insur Co.....440 324-2626
347 Midway Blvd Ste 101 Elyria (44035) *(G-10691)*
Western & Southern Lf Insur Co.....330 792-6818
320 S Canfield Niles Rd Youngstown (44515) *(G-20411)*
Western & Southern Lf Insur Co.....330 825-9935
4172 Clvland Massillon Rd Barberton (44203) *(G-985)*
Western & Southern Lf Insur Co.....937 435-1964
1964 E Whipp Rd Dayton (45440) *(G-9993)*
Western & Southern Lf Insur Co.....740 653-3210
1583 Victor Rd Nw Lancaster (43130) *(G-12583)*
Western & Southern Lf Insur Co.....513 891-0777
6281 Tri Ridge Blvd # 310 Loveland (45140) *(G-13165)*
Western & Southern Lf Insur Co.....614 898-1066
8425 Pulsar Pl Ste 310 Columbus (43240) *(G-6910)*
Western & Southern Lf Insur Co.....937 773-5303
1255 E Ash St Ste 2 Piqua (45356) *(G-16176)*
Western & Southern Lf Insur Co.....937 399-7696
30 Warder St Ste 130 Springfield (45504) *(G-17298)*
Western & Southern Lf Insur Co.....740 354-2848
35 Bierly Rd Ste 1 Portsmouth (45662) *(G-16322)*
Western & Southern Lf Insur Co.....937 393-1969
902 N High St Ste B Hillsboro (45133) *(G-11992)*
Western & Southern Lf Insur Co.....419 524-1800
1989 W 4th St Ontario (44906) *(G-15720)*
Western Branch Diesel Inc.....330 454-8800
1616 Metric Ave Sw Canton (44706) *(G-2585)*
Western Family Physicians.....513 853-4900
3425 North Bend Rd Ste A Cincinnati (45239) *(G-4840)*
Western Hills Care Center.....513 941-0099
6210 Cleves Warsaw Pike Cincinnati (45233) *(G-4841)*
Western Hills Country Club.....513 922-0011
5780 Cleves Warsaw Pike Cincinnati (45233) *(G-4842)*
Western Hills Dialysis, Cincinnati *Also called Dva Healthcare - South (G-3516)*
Western Hills Retirement Vlg, Cincinnati *Also called Ebenezer Road Corp (G-3540)*
Western Hills Sportsplex Inc (PA).....513 451-4900
2323 Ferguson Rd Ste 1 Cincinnati (45238) *(G-4843)*
Western KY Coal Resources LLC.....740 338-3100
46226 National Rd Saint Clairsville (43950) *(G-16660)*
Western Management Inc (PA).....216 941-3333
14577 Lorain Ave Cleveland (44111) *(G-6741)*
Western Reserve Area Agency (PA).....216 621-0303
925 Euclid Ave Ste 600 Cleveland (44115) *(G-6742)*
Western Reserve Area Agency.....216 621-0303
925 Euclid Ave Ste 600 Cleveland (44115) *(G-6743)*
Western Reserve Group (PA).....330 262-9060
1685 Cleveland Rd Wooster (44691) *(G-19929)*
Western Reserve Historical Soc.....330 666-3711
2686 Oak Hill Dr Bath (44210) *(G-1036)*
Western Reserve Historical Soc (PA).....216 721-5722
10825 East Blvd Cleveland (44106) *(G-6744)*
Western Reserve Interiors Inc.....216 447-1081
7777 Exchange St Ste 7 Cleveland (44125) *(G-6745)*
Western Reserve Legal Services, Akron *Also called Community Legal Aid Services (G-156)*
Western Reserve Mechanical Inc.....330 652-3888
3041 S Main St Niles (44446) *(G-15311)*
Western Reserve Public Media, Kent *Also called Northastern Eductl TV Ohio Inc (G-12388)*
Western Reserve Racquet Club.....330 653-3103
11013 Aurora Hudson Rd Streetsboro (44241) *(G-17436)*
Western Reserve Realty LLC.....440 247-3707
26 S Main St Ste 100 Chagrin Falls (44022) *(G-2710)*
Western Reserve Transit Auth (PA).....330 744-8431
604 Mahoning Ave Youngstown (44502) *(G-20412)*
Western Rsrve Girl Scout Cncil.....330 864-9933
1 Girl Scout Way Macedonia (44056) *(G-13218)*
Western Rsrve Land Conservancy (PA).....440 729-9621
3850 Chagrin River Rd Chagrin Falls (44022) *(G-2711)*
Western Rsrve Msonic Cmnty Inc.....330 721-3000
4931 Nettleton Rd # 4318 Medina (44256) *(G-14138)*
Western Southern Life Incur, Ontario *Also called Western & Southern Lf Insur Co (G-15720)*
Western Southern Mutl Holdg Co (PA).....866 832-7719
400 Broadway St Cincinnati (45202) *(G-4844)*
Western Sports Mall, Cincinnati *Also called Western Hills Sportsplex Inc (G-4843)*
Western States Envelope Co.....419 666-7480
6859 Commodore Dr Walbridge (43465) *(G-18780)*
Western States Envelope Label, Walbridge *Also called Western States Envelope Co (G-18780)*
Western Sthern Fincl Group Inc (HQ).....866 832-7719
400 Broadway St Cincinnati (45202) *(G-4845)*
Western Tradewinds Inc (PA).....937 859-4300
521 Byers Rd Miamisburg (45342) *(G-14368)*
Western-Southern Life, Cincinnati *Also called Western & Southern Lf Insur Co (G-4839)*
Western-Southern Life Insur, Grove City *Also called Western & Southern Lf Insur Co (G-11615)*
Westerville Dermatology Inc.....614 895-0400
235 W Schrock Rd Westerville (43081) *(G-19448)*
Westerville-Worthington Learni.....614 891-4105
149 Charring Cross Dr S Westerville (43081) *(G-19449)*
Westfall Aggregate & Mtls Inc.....740 420-9090
19522 London Rd Circleville (43113) *(G-4907)*
Westfield Bank Fsb (HQ).....800 368-8930
2 Park Cir Westfield Center (44251) *(G-19453)*
Westfield Belden Village.....330 494-5490
4230 Belden Village Mall Canton (44718) *(G-2586)*
Westfield Electric Inc.....419 862-0078
2995 State Route 51 Gibsonburg (43431) *(G-11405)*
Westfield Group, Westfield Center *Also called Ohio Farmers Insurance Company (G-19452)*
Westfield Group, Columbus *Also called Ohio Farmers Insurance Company (G-6898)*
Westfield Services Inc (PA).....614 796-7700
2000 Polaris Pkwy Ste 202 Columbus (43240) *(G-6911)*
Westfield Steel Inc.....937 322-2414
1120 S Burnett Rd Springfield (45505) *(G-17299)*
Westgate Lanes Incorporated.....419 229-3845
721 N Cable Rd Lima (45805) *(G-12920)*
Westgate Limited Partnership.....419 535-7070
457 S Reynolds Rd Toledo (43615) *(G-18307)*
Westhafer Trucking Inc.....330 698-3030
6333 E Messner Rd Apple Creek (44606) *(G-628)*
Westhaven Services Co LLC.....419 661-2200
7643 Ponderosa Rd Perrysburg (43551) *(G-16073)*
Westin Cincinnati, The, Cincinnati *Also called Hst Lessee Cincinnati LLC (G-3793)*
Westin Cleveland, Cleveland *Also called Optima 777 LLC (G-6208)*
Westin Columbus, Columbus *Also called Wm Columbus Hotel LLC (G-9001)*
Westin Columbus, Columbus *Also called Marcus Hotels Inc (G-8106)*
Westin Hotel, Columbus *Also called First Hotel Associates LP (G-7665)*
Westlake Cab Service.....440 331-5000
2069 W 3rd St Cleveland (44113) *(G-6746)*
Westlake Fire Dept, Cleveland *Also called City of Westlake (G-5278)*
Westlake Marriott.....440 892-6887
30100 Clemens Rd Westlake (44145) *(G-19567)*
Westlake Mntsr Schl & Chld Dv.....440 835-5858
26830 Detroit Rd Westlake (44145) *(G-19568)*
Westlake Village, Cleveland *Also called Fort Austin Ltd Partnership (G-5624)*
Westlake Village Inc.....440 892-4200
28550 Westlake Village Dr Cleveland (44145) *(G-6747)*
Westland Heating & AC, Westlake *Also called North East Mechanical Inc (G-19523)*
Westminster Financial Company.....937 898-5010
125 N Wilkinson St Dayton (45402) *(G-9994)*
Westminster Fincl Companies, Dayton *Also called Westmnster Fncl Securities Inc (G-9995)*
Westminster Management Company.....614 274-5154
2731 Clime Rd Columbus (43223) *(G-8980)*
Westminster Thurber, Columbus *Also called Ohio Living (G-8357)*
Westminster Thurber Community, Columbus *Also called Ohio Presbt Retirement Svcs (G-8368)*
Westmnster Fncl Securities Inc.....937 898-5010
40 N Main St Ste 2400 Dayton (45423) *(G-9995)*
Westmoreland Place, Chillicothe *Also called Chillicothe Long Term Care (G-2821)*
Westmoreland Place, Cincinnati *Also called Chillicothe Long Term Care (G-3256)*
Weston Brands LLC.....216 901-6801
7575 E Pleasant Valley Rd # 100 Independence (44131) *(G-12276)*
Weston Group Inc.....740 454-2741
1575 Bowers Ln Zanesville (43701) *(G-20545)*
Weston Inc (PA).....440 349-9000
4760 Richmond Rd Ste 200 Cleveland (44128) *(G-6748)*
Westover Preparatory School, Hamilton *Also called Colonial Senior Services Inc (G-11714)*
Westover Retirement Community, Hamilton *Also called Colonial Senior Services Inc (G-11715)*
Westpatrick Corp.....614 875-8200
250 N Hartford Ave 300 Columbus (43222) *(G-8981)*
Westpost Columbus LLC.....614 885-1885
6500 Doubletree Ave Columbus (43229) *(G-8982)*
Westrock CP LLC.....770 448-2193
1010 Mead St Wshngtn CT Hs (43160) *(G-20038)*
Westshore Prmry Care Assoc Inc.....440 934-0276
5323 Meadow Lane Ct Sheffield Village (44035) *(G-16896)*
Westshore Ymca/Westlake Chrn, Westlake *Also called Young MNS Chrstn Assn Clveland (G-19569)*
Westside Family Practice Inc.....614 878-4541
5206 Chaps Ct Columbus (43221) *(G-8983)*
Westside Health Care, Cincinnati *Also called J E F Inc (G-3851)*
Westview Apartments Ohio LLC.....216 520-1250
3111 Leo Ave Youngstown (44509) *(G-20413)*
Westview-Youngstown Ltd.....330 799-2787
3111 Leo Ave Youngstown (44509) *(G-20414)*
Westwat Management, Westlake *Also called King James Group IV Ltd (G-19504)*
Westway Trml Cincinnati LLC.....513 921-8441
3500 Southside Ave Cincinnati (45204) *(G-4846)*
Westwood Behavioral Health Ctr.....419 238-3434
1158 Westwood Dr Van Wert (45891) *(G-18652)*
Westwood Bhvioural Hlth Centre, Paulding *Also called County of Paulding (G-15930)*
Westwood Country Club Company.....440 331-3016
22625 Detroit Rd Rocky River (44116) *(G-16595)*
Wetherngton Golf Cntry CLB Inc (PA).....513 755-2582
7337 Country Club Ln West Chester (45069) *(G-19185)*

Wexner Heritage Village (PA)...614 231-4900
1151 College Ave Columbus (43209) **(G-8984)**
Wexner Research Institute, Columbus *Also called Nationwide Childrens Hospital* **(G-8232)**
Weymouth Valley Inc...440 498-8888
39000 Signature Dr Solon (44139) **(G-17067)**
Wf Services, Canton *Also called Workforce Services Inc* **(G-2589)**
Wfin AM, Findlay *Also called Findlay Publishing Company* **(G-11028)**
Wfmj Television Inc...330 744-8611
101 W Boardman St Youngstown (44503) **(G-20415)**
Wfmj-Tv21, Youngstown *Also called Vindicator Printing Company* **(G-20406)**
Wfts...216 431-5555
3001 Euclid Ave Cleveland (44115) **(G-6749)**
Wfts...513 721-9900
1720 Gilbert Ave Cincinnati (45202) **(G-4847)**
WGTE-TV-FM, Toledo *Also called Public Broadcasting Found NW* **(G-18144)**
Wh Midwest LLC (PA)...330 896-7611
3777 Boettler Oaks Dr Uniontown (44685) **(G-18543)**
Whalen & Co CPA, Worthington *Also called Whalen and Company Inc* **(G-20008)**
Whalen and Company Inc...614 396-4200
250 W Old Wlsn Brg Rd # 300 Worthington (43085) **(G-20008)**
Wheatland Tube Company, Cambridge *Also called Zekelman Industries Inc* **(G-2135)**
Wheaton & Sprague Engineering (PA)...330 923-5560
1151 Campus Dr Ste 100 Stow (44224) **(G-17400)**
Wheaton Sprague Bldg Envelope, Stow *Also called Wheaton & Sprague Engineering* **(G-17400)**
Wheeler Cleaning LLC...614 818-0981
159 Drakewood Rd Westerville (43081) **(G-19450)**
Wheeling & Lake Erie Rlwy Co (HQ)...330 767-3401
100 1st St Se Brewster (44613) **(G-1857)**
Wheeling Hospital Inc...740 695-2090
107 Plaza Dr Ste D Saint Clairsville (43950) **(G-16661)**
Wheeling Hospital Inc...740 671-0850
3801 Lincoln Ave Shadyside (43947) **(G-16853)**
Wheeling Hospital Inc...740 633-4765
90 N 4th St Martins Ferry (43935) **(G-13604)**
Wheeling Hospital Inc...740 676-4623
3000 Guernsey St Bellaire (43906) **(G-1368)**
Whelco Industrial Ltd...419 873-6134
28210 Cedar Park Blvd Perrysburg (43551) **(G-16074)**
Whetstone Care Center LLC...614 875-7700
3929 Hoover Rd Grove City (43123) **(G-11616)**
Whetstone Care Center LLC...614 457-1100
3710 Olentangy River Rd Columbus (43214) **(G-8985)**
Whetstone Care Center LLC...740 474-6036
391 Clark Dr Circleville (43113) **(G-4908)**
Whetstone Center, Columbus *Also called Whetstone Care Center LLC* **(G-8985)**
Whetstone Industries Inc...419 947-9222
440 Douglas St Mount Gilead (43338) **(G-14864)**
WHETSTONE SCHOOL, Mount Gilead *Also called Whetstone Industries Inc* **(G-14864)**
Whirlpool Corporation...740 383-7122
1300 Marion Agosta Rd Marion (43302) **(G-13596)**
Whirlpool Corporation...419 423-6097
4325 County Road 86 Findlay (45840) **(G-11100)**
Whirlpool Corporation...419 547-2610
1081 W Mcpherson Hwy Clyde (43410) **(G-6825)**
Whisler Plumbing & Heating Inc...330 833-2875
2521 Lincoln Way E Massillon (44646) **(G-13861)**
Whispering Hills Care Center...740 392-3982
416 Wooster Rd Mount Vernon (43050) **(G-14925)**
Whitaker Masonry Inc...330 225-7970
4910 Grafton Rd Brunswick (44212) **(G-1996)**
Whitcomb & Hess Inc...419 289-7007
1020 Cleveland Ave Ashland (44805) **(G-708)**
White & Chambers Partnership...740 594-8381
5315 Hebbardsville Rd Athens (45701) **(G-820)**
White Allen Chevrolet, Dayton *Also called White Family Companies Inc* **(G-9996)**
White Barn Candle Co...614 856-6000
7 Limited Pkwy E Reynoldsburg (43068) **(G-16490)**
White Cars, Sylvania *Also called Dave White Chevrolet Inc* **(G-17581)**
White Castle System Inc (PA)...614 228-5781
555 W Goodale St Columbus (43215) **(G-8986)**
White Family Collision Center...419 885-8885
5328 Alexis Rd Sylvania (43560) **(G-17628)**
White Family Companies Inc...937 222-3701
442 N Main St Dayton (45405) **(G-9996)**
White Glove Executive Services...614 226-2553
2647 Bryan Cir Grove City (43123) **(G-11617)**
White House Fruit Farm Inc...330 533-4161
9249 Youngstown Salem Rd Canfield (44406) **(G-2215)**
White Oak Investments Inc...614 491-1000
3730 Lockbourne Rd Columbus (43207) **(G-8987)**
White Oak Manor, Warren *Also called Saber Healthcare Group LLC* **(G-18894)**
White Pond Gardens Inc...330 836-2727
1015 White Pond Dr Akron (44320) **(G-509)**
White Rock Quarry L P...419 855-8388
3800 N Bolander Rd Clay Center (43408) **(G-4910)**
White' S Ford, Urbana *Also called Whites Service Center Inc* **(G-18602)**
Whited Seigneur Sams & Rahe...740 702-2600
213 S Paint St Chillicothe (45601) **(G-2897)**

Whiteford Greenhouse...419 882-4110
4554 Whiteford Rd Toledo (43623) **(G-18308)**
Whiteford Kenworth, Perrysburg *Also called Lower Great Lakes Kenworth Inc* **(G-16029)**
Whitehall City Schools...614 417-5680
4738 Kae Ave Columbus (43213) **(G-8988)**
Whitehall Division of Fire, Columbus *Also called City of Whitehall* **(G-7286)**
Whitehall Frmens Bnvlence Fund...614 237-5478
390 S Yearling Rd Columbus (43213) **(G-8989)**
Whitehouse Country Manor, Whitehouse *Also called Whitehouse Operator LLC* **(G-19590)**
Whitehouse Inn, Whitehouse *Also called Frog & Toad Inc* **(G-19586)**
Whitehouse Operator LLC...419 877-5338
11239 Waterville St Whitehouse (43571) **(G-19590)**
Whitehurst Company (PA)...419 865-0799
6325 Garden Rd Maumee (43537) **(G-13994)**
Whites Service Center Inc...937 653-5279
1246 N Main St Urbana (43078) **(G-18602)**
Whitespace Creative, Akron *Also called Whitespace Design Group Inc* **(G-510)**
Whitespace Design Group Inc...330 762-9320
243 Furnace St Akron (44304) **(G-510)**
Whitestone Group Inc...614 501-7007
4100 Regent St Ste C Columbus (43219) **(G-8990)**
Whitewater Car & Van Wash Co, Toledo *Also called Robert Stough Ventures Corp* **(G-18162)**
Whitford Woods Co Inc...440 693-4344
16192 Bundysburg Rd Middlefield (44062) **(G-14405)**
Whiting-Turner Contracting Co...614 459-6515
250 W Old Wilson Bridge R Worthington (43085) **(G-20009)**
Whiting-Turner Contracting Co...440 449-9200
5875 Landerbrook Dr # 100 Cleveland (44124) **(G-6750)**
Whitt Inc...513 753-7707
1152 Ferris Rd Amelia (45102) **(G-584)**
Whitt Plumbing, Amelia *Also called Whitt Inc* **(G-584)**
Whittguard Security Services...440 288-7233
37435 Colorado Ave Avon (44011) **(G-918)**
Whiz Am-FM, Zanesville *Also called Southeastern Ohio Brdcstg Sys* **(G-20535)**
Whiz-TV, Zanesville *Also called Southeastern Ohio TV Sys* **(G-20536)**
Whole Health Management Inc (HQ)...216 921-8601
1375 E 9th St Ste 2500 Cleveland (44114) **(G-6751)**
Wholecycle Inc...330 929-8123
100 Cyhoga Fls Indus Pkwy Peninsula (44264) **(G-15953)**
Wholesale Decor LLC...330 587-7100
650 S Prospect Ave # 200 Hartville (44632) **(G-11833)**
Wholesale House Inc (PA)...419 542-1315
503 W High St Hicksville (43526) **(G-11867)**
Wholesale Tire Division, Toledo *Also called Capital Tire Inc* **(G-17790)**
Wholesale Tire Division, Toledo *Also called Capital Tire Inc* **(G-17791)**
Wic, Columbus *Also called Ohio Department of Health* **(G-8327)**
Wic Program, Austintown *Also called Ohio Department of Health* **(G-870)**
Wic Womens Infants Program, Youngstown *Also called Mahoning Youngstown Community* **(G-20267)**
Wicked Woods Golf Club, Newbury *Also called Wicked Woods Gulf Club Inc* **(G-15264)**
Wicked Woods Gulf Club Inc...440 564-7960
14085 Ravenna Rd Newbury (44065) **(G-15264)**
Wickens Hrzer Pnza Cook Btista...440 695-8000
35765 Chester Rd Avon (44011) **(G-919)**
Wickertree Tnnis Ftnes CLB LLC...614 882-5724
5760 Maple Canyon Ave Columbus (43229) **(G-8991)**
Wickliffe Associates Partnr...440 585-3505
30315 Euclid Ave Wickliffe (44092) **(G-19615)**
Wickliffe Country Place, Parma *Also called 3g Operating Company LLC* **(G-15897)**
Wickliffe Country Place Ltd...440 944-9400
1919 Bishop Rd Wickliffe (44092) **(G-19616)**
Wickliffe Lanes, Wickliffe *Also called Wickliffe Associates Partnr* **(G-19615)**
Wickline Floral & Garden Ctr, Xenia *Also called Wickline Landscaping Inc* **(G-20083)**
Wickline Landscaping Inc (PA)...937 372-0521
1625 N Detroit St Xenia (45385) **(G-20083)**
Widepint Intgrted Sltions Corp...614 410-1587
8351 N High St Ste 200 Columbus (43235) **(G-8992)**
Widmer's, Cincinnati *Also called C&C Clean Team Enterprises LLC* **(G-3163)**
Widmer's Drycleaners, Cincinnati *Also called Widmers LLC* **(G-4848)**
Widmers LLC (HQ)...513 321-5100
2016 Madison Rd Cincinnati (45208) **(G-4848)**
Widows Home of Dayton Ohio...937 252-1661
50 S Findlay St Dayton (45403) **(G-9997)**
Wiechart Enterprises Inc...419 227-0027
4511 Elida Rd Lima (45807) **(G-12921)**
Wiegands Lake Park Inc...440 338-5795
9390 Kinsman Rd Novelty (44072) **(G-15604)**
Wiggins Clg & Crpt Svc Inc (PA)...937 279-9080
4699 Salem Ave Ste 2 Dayton (45416) **(G-9998)**
Wilbert Inc...419 483-2300
635 Southwest St Bellevue (44811) **(G-1419)**
Wilbert Plastic Services, Bellevue *Also called Wilbert Inc* **(G-1419)**
Wilbur Realty Inc (PA)...330 673-5883
548 S Water St Kent (44240) **(G-12405)**
Wild Republic, Twinsburg *Also called K & M International Inc* **(G-18435)**
WILDWOOD SURGICAL CENTER, Toledo *Also called Reynolds Road Surgical Ctr LLC* **(G-18156)**

ALPHABETIC SECTION Windsorwood Place Inc

Wildwood Yacht Club Inc...216 531-9052
P.O. Box 19001 Cleveland (44119) ***(G-6752)***
Wiles Boyle Burkholder &...614 221-5216
2 Miranova Pl Ste 700 Columbus (43215) ***(G-8993)***
Wiles Doucher, Columbus *Also called Wiles Boyle Burkholder &* ***(G-8993)***
Wiley Avenue Group Home, Saint Clairsville *Also called Alternative Residences Two* ***(G-16616)***
Wiley Homes Inc...419 535-3988
4011 Angola Rd Toledo (43615) ***(G-18309)***
Wilkes & Company Inc...419 433-2325
205 Sprowl Rd Huron (44839) ***(G-12176)***
Wilkris Company...513 271-9344
411 Terrace Pl Terrace Park (45174) ***(G-17663)***
Will-Burt Company (PA)...330 682-7015
169 S Main St Orrville (44667) ***(G-15789)***
Will-Burt Company...330 682-7015
312 Collins Blvd Orrville (44667) ***(G-15790)***
Willard Head Start Day Care, Cleveland *Also called Council of Ecnmc Opprtnts of G* ***(G-5416)***
Willcare, Euclid *Also called Bracor Inc* ***(G-10746)***
Willglo Services Inc...614 443-3020
995 Thurman Ave Columbus (43206) ***(G-8994)***
William & Clippard YMCA, Cincinnati *Also called Young Mens Christian Associat* ***(G-4869)***
William D Taylor Sr Inc (PA)...614 653-6683
263 Trail E Etna (43062) ***(G-10740)***
William Hafer Drayage Inc...513 771-5000
11320 Mosteller Rd Ste 1 Cincinnati (45241) ***(G-4849)***
William I Notz...614 292-3154
1958 Neil Ave Rm 319 Columbus (43210) ***(G-8995)***
William Kerfoot Masonry Inc...330 772-6460
4948 State Route 7 Burghill (44404) ***(G-2056)***
William R Morse...440 352-2600
83 S State St Painesville (44077) ***(G-15887)***
William Royce Inc...513 771-3361
11568 Springfield Pike Cincinnati (45246) ***(G-4850)***
William Sydney Druen...614 444-7655
85 E Deshler Ave Columbus (43206) ***(G-8996)***
William Thomas Group Inc...800 582-3107
10795 Hughes Rd Cincinnati (45251) ***(G-4851)***
William Vaughan Company...419 891-1040
145 Chesterfield Ln Maumee (43537) ***(G-13995)***
William Wood...740 543-4052
8392 County Road 39 Bloomingdale (43910) ***(G-1518)***
William X Greene Bus Advisor, Cincinnati *Also called Scrogginsgrear Inc* ***(G-4486)***
William Zamarelli Realtors...330 856-2299
8700 E Market St Ste 6 Warren (44484) ***(G-18927)***
Williams Bros Builders Inc...440 365-3261
686 Sugar Ln Elyria (44035) ***(G-10692)***
Williams Bros Roofg & Siding...937 434-3838
3600 Valley Pike Piqua (45356) ***(G-16177)***
Williams Bros Roofg Siding Co...937 434-3838
3600 Valley St Dayton (45424) ***(G-9999)***
Williams Concrete Cnstr Co Inc...330 745-6388
2959 Barber Rd Ste 100 Norton (44203) ***(G-15560)***
Williams Conty Hllsd Cntry Lvg, Bryan *Also called County of Williams* ***(G-2005)***
Williams County Health Dept, Montpelier *Also called County of Williams* ***(G-14742)***
Williams County Landfill, Bryan *Also called Republic Services Inc* ***(G-2020)***
Williams Homes LLC...419 472-1005
1841 Eastgate Rd Toledo (43614) ***(G-18310)***
Williams Partners LP...330 966-3674
7235 Whipple Ave Nw North Canton (44720) ***(G-15379)***
Williams Street Apartments, Columbus *Also called Buckeye Cmnty Eighty One LP* ***(G-7157)***
Williams Super Service Inc...330 733-7750
9462 Main Ave Se East Sparta (44626) ***(G-10542)***
Williams Toyota Lift, East Sparta *Also called Williams Super Service Inc* ***(G-10542)***
Williamsburg of Cincinnati Mgt...513 948-2308
230 W Galbraith Rd Cincinnati (45215) ***(G-4852)***
Willimsburg Rsdntial Altrntves, Williamsburg *Also called Rescare Ohio Inc* ***(G-19635)***
Willis Day Management Inc (PA)...419 476-8000
4100 Bennett Rd Ste 1 Toledo (43612) ***(G-18311)***
Willis Day Storage Co (HQ)...419 470-6255
4100 Bennett Rd Ste 1 Toledo (43612) ***(G-18312)***
Willis of Ohio Inc (HQ)...614 457-7000
775 Yard St Ste 200 Columbus (43212) ***(G-8997)***
Willis One Hour Heating & AC...513 752-2512
756 Cncnnati Batavia Pike Cincinnati (45245) ***(G-2938)***
Willis Towers Watson, Cleveland *Also called Wtw Delaware Holdings LLC* ***(G-6762)***
Williston Luther Home of Mercy, Williston *Also called Luther Home of Mercy* ***(G-19639)***
Willo Maintenance, Willoughby *Also called Dependable Cleaning Contrs* ***(G-19659)***
Willo Security Inc...614 481-9456
1989 W 5th Ave Ste 3 Columbus (43212) ***(G-8998)***
Willo Security Inc (PA)...440 953-9191
38230 Glenn Ave Willoughby (44094) ***(G-19723)***
Willo Transportation, Willoughby *Also called Palmer Express Incorporated* ***(G-19702)***
Willory LLC...330 576-5486
1970 N Cleveland Mssilln Bath (44210) ***(G-1037)***
Willoughby City Garage, Willoughby *Also called City of Willoughby* ***(G-19649)***
Willoughby Commons 16, Willoughby *Also called Regal Cinemas Inc* ***(G-19708)***
Willoughby Lodging LLC...440 530-1100
35103 Maplegrove Rd Fl 3 Willoughby (44094) ***(G-19724)***
Willoughby Medical Offices, Willoughby *Also called Kaiser Foundation Hospitals* ***(G-19674)***
Willoughby Montessori Day Schl...440 942-5602
5543 Som Center Rd Willoughby (44094) ***(G-19725)***
Willoughby Supply Company (PA)...440 942-7939
7433 Clover Ave Mentor (44060) ***(G-14258)***
Willow & Cane, Springboro *Also called Willow and Cane LLC* ***(G-17142)***
Willow and Cane LLC...609 280-1150
1110 Lakemont Dr Springboro (45066) ***(G-17142)***
Willow Brook Christian Home, Columbus *Also called Brook Willow Chrstn Cmmunities* ***(G-7151)***
Willow Brook Christian Village, Delaware *Also called Willow Brook Chrstn Cmmunities* ***(G-10135)***
Willow Brook Chrstn Cmmunities (PA)...740 369-0048
100 Delaware Xing W Delaware (43015) ***(G-10135)***
Willow Dialysis Cntr, Wilmington *Also called Renal Life Link Inc* ***(G-19782)***
Willow Haven Nursing Home, Zanesville *Also called Zandex Health Care Corporation* ***(G-20553)***
Willow Knoll Nursing Center, Middletown *Also called Church of God Retirement Cmnty* ***(G-14420)***
Willow Ridge Nursery, Madison *Also called Ridge Manor Nuseries Inc* ***(G-13235)***
Willoway Nurseries Inc (PA)...440 934-4435
4534 Center Rd Avon (44011) ***(G-920)***
Willowbend Nurseries LLC...440 259-3121
4654 Davis Rd Perry (44081) ***(G-15968)***
Willowood Care Center...330 225-3156
1186 Hadcock Rd Brunswick (44212) ***(G-1997)***
Willows At Willard, The, Willard *Also called Trilogy Health Services LLC* ***(G-19628)***
Willows Health and Rehab Ctr, Euclid *Also called Saber Healthcare Group LLC* ***(G-10775)***
Wilmared Inc...513 891-6615
6279 Tri Ridge Blvd Loveland (45140) ***(G-13166)***
Wilmer Cutler Pick Hale Dorr...937 395-2100
3139 Research Blvd Dayton (45420) ***(G-10000)***
Wilmerhale, Dayton *Also called Wilmer Cutler Pick Hale Dorr* ***(G-10000)***
Wilmingtn Nursng/Rehab Resdidn...937 382-1621
75 Hale St Wilmington (45177) ***(G-19793)***
Wilmington City Cab Service, Wilmington *Also called City of Wilmington* ***(G-19748)***
Wilmington Iron and Met Co Inc...937 382-3867
2149 S Us Highway 68 Wilmington (45177) ***(G-19794)***
Wilmington Medical Associates...937 382-1616
1184 W Locust St Wilmington (45177) ***(G-19795)***
Wilmington Nursing, Wilmington *Also called Saber Healthcare Group LLC* ***(G-19786)***
Wilson Shannon & Snow Inc...740 345-6611
10 W Locust St Newark (43055) ***(G-15246)***
Wilson Enterprises Inc...614 444-8873
1600 Universal Rd Columbus (43207) ***(G-8999)***
Wilson Health, Sidney *Also called Shelby County Mem Hosp Assn* ***(G-16952)***
Wilson Mem Hosp Occptnal Clnic, Sidney *Also called Occupational Health Services* ***(G-16944)***
Wilson's Garden Center, Newark *Also called Wilsons Hillview Farm Inc* ***(G-15247)***
Wilson's Turf, Columbus *Also called Wilson Enterprises Inc* ***(G-8999)***
Wilsons Hillview Farm Inc...740 763-2873
10923 Lambs Ln Newark (43055) ***(G-15247)***
Wimberg Lansdscaping, Cincinnati *Also called Peter A Wimberg Company Inc* ***(G-4284)***
Win Tamer Corporation...330 637-2881
2940 Niles Cortland Rd Ne Cortland (44410) ***(G-9085)***
Winchester Care Rehabilitation, Canal Winchester *Also called Winchester Place Leasing LLC* ***(G-2179)***
Winchester Place Leasing LLC...614 834-2273
36 Lehman Dr Canal Winchester (43110) ***(G-2179)***
Winchester Terrace, Mansfield *Also called Levering Management Inc* ***(G-13323)***
Winchester Wholesale, Winchester *Also called Cantrell Oil Company* ***(G-19800)***
WINDFALL INDUSTRIES, Wadsworth *Also called Medina County Sheltered Inds* ***(G-18765)***
Window Factory of America (PA)...440 439-3050
21600 Alexander Rd Bedford (44146) ***(G-1344)***
Winds Laure Cente For Behav ME, Willoughby *Also called HHC Ohio Inc* ***(G-19668)***
Windsong Care Center, Akron *Also called Saber Healthcare Group LLC* ***(G-423)***
Windsor Companies (PA)...740 653-8822
1430 Collins Rd Nw Lancaster (43130) ***(G-12584)***
Windsor Construction, Brookpark *Also called J & R Associates* ***(G-1947)***
Windsor Health Care, Youngstown *Also called Windsor House Inc* ***(G-20417)***
Windsor House Inc...330 759-7858
1355 Churchill Hubbard Rd Youngstown (44505) ***(G-20416)***
Windsor House Inc...330 743-1393
1735 Belmont Ave Youngstown (44504) ***(G-20417)***
Windsor House Inc...330 482-1375
930 E Park Ave Columbiana (44408) ***(G-6866)***
Windsor House Inc...330 549-9259
1899 W Garfield Rd Columbiana (44408) ***(G-6867)***
Windsor House Inc...440 834-0544
14095 E Center St Burton (44021) ***(G-2066)***
Windsor Lane Health Care, Gibsonburg *Also called Gibsonburg Health Llc* ***(G-11402)***
Windsor Medical Center Inc...330 499-8300
1454 E Maple St Canton (44720) ***(G-2587)***
Windsorwood Place Inc...740 623-4600
255 Browns Ln Coshocton (43812) ***(G-9121)***

A L P H A B E T I C

Windstream Ohio LLC (HQ)....440 329-4000
363 3rd St Elyria (44035) **(G-10693)**
Windstream Ohio LLC....330 650-8436
100 Owen Brown St Hudson (44236) **(G-12152)**
Windstream Western Reserve LLC....330 650-8000
245 N Main St Hudson (44236) **(G-12153)**
Windwood Swim & Tennis Club....513 777-2552
6649 N Windwood Dr West Chester (45069) **(G-19186)**
Windy Hill Ltd Inc (PA)....216 391-4800
3700 Kelley Ave Cleveland (44114) **(G-6753)**
Windy Knoll Golf Club, Springfield *Also called Links At Windy Knoll LLC* **(G-17222)**
Wine Trends Inc....216 520-2626
9101 E Pleasant Valley Rd Independence (44131) **(G-12277)**
Wine-Art of Ohio Inc....330 678-7733
463 Portage Blvd Kent (44240) **(G-12406)**
Winegardner & Hammons Inc....614 791-1000
5605 Paul G Blzr Mmrl Pkw Dublin (43017) **(G-10493)**
Winelco Inc....513 755-8050
6141 Centre Park Dr West Chester (45069) **(G-19187)**
Wing-FM, Dayton *Also called Alpha Media LLC* **(G-9322)**
Wingler Construction Corp....614 626-8546
771 S Hamilton Rd Columbus (43213) **(G-9000)**
Wings Investors Company Ltd....513 241-5800
3805 Edwards Rd Ste 200 Cincinnati (45209) **(G-4853)**
Wingspan Care Group (PA)....216 932-2800
22001 Fairmount Blvd Shaker Heights (44118) **(G-16872)**
Winking Lizard Inc....330 220-9944
3634 Center Rd Brunswick (44212) **(G-1998)**
Winking Lizard Inc....330 467-1002
1615 Main St Peninsula (44264) **(G-15954)**
Winkle Electric Company Inc (PA)....330 744-5303
1900 Hubbard Rd Youngstown (44505) **(G-20418)**
Winkle Industries Inc....330 823-9730
2080 W Main St Alliance (44601) **(G-565)**
Winn-Scapes Inc....614 866-9466
6079 Taylor Rd Gahanna (43230) **(G-11275)**
Winncom Technologies Corp (HQ)....440 498-9510
28900 Ftn Pkwy Unit B Solon (44139) **(G-17068)**
Winner Aviation Corporation....330 856-5000
1453 Youngstown Kingsvill Vienna (44473) **(G-18742)**
Winner's Meat Service, Yorkshire *Also called Robert Winner Sons Inc* **(G-20092)**
Winnscapes Inc/Schmidt Nurs Co, Gahanna *Also called Winn-Scapes Inc* **(G-11275)**
Winston Brdcstg Netwrk Inc (PA)....330 928-5711
2690 State Rd Cuyahoga Falls (44223) **(G-9236)**
Winston Products LLC....440 478-1418
30339 Diamond Pkwy # 105 Cleveland (44139) **(G-6754)**
Winsupply Inc (PA)....937 294-5331
3110 Kettering Blvd Moraine (45439) **(G-14836)**
Winsupply Inc....937 865-0796
9300 Byers Rd Miamisburg (45342) **(G-14369)**
Winter Drive In Theater, Toledo *Also called A and S Ventures Inc* **(G-17734)**
Winterfield Venture Academy, Toledo *Also called National Heritg Academies Inc* **(G-18077)**
Winterhurst Ice Rink, Lakewood *Also called Lakewood City School District* **(G-12487)**
Wintersong Village of Delaware, Delaware *Also called A L K Inc* **(G-10064)**
Wireless Center Inc (PA)....216 503-3777
1925 Saint Clair Ave Ne Cleveland (44114) **(G-6755)**
Wireless Connections, Norwalk *Also called Advanced Cmpt Connections LLC* **(G-15561)**
Wireless Environment LLC....216 455-0192
600 Beta Dr Ste 100 Mayfield Village (44143) **(G-14014)**
Wireless Source Entps LLC....419 266-5556
16545 Euler Rd Bowling Green (43402) **(G-1797)**
Wirtzberger Enterprises Corp....440 428-1901
136 W Main St Madison (44057) **(G-13238)**
Wise Choices In Learning Ltd....440 324-6056
352 Griswold Rd Elyria (44035) **(G-10694)**
Wise Medical Staffing Inc (PA)....740 775-4108
80 E 2nd St Chillicothe (45601) **(G-2898)**
Wise Services Inc....937 854-0281
1705 Guenther Rd Dayton (45417) **(G-10001)**
Witmers Inc....330 427-2147
39821 Salem Unity Rd Salem (44460) **(G-16719)**
Witt Glvnzing - Cincinnati Inc....513 871-5700
4454 Steel Pl Cincinnati (45209) **(G-4854)**
Wittenberg University, Springfield *Also called Board of Dir of Wittenbe* **(G-17152)**
Wize-AM, Dayton *Also called Iheartcommunications Inc* **(G-9626)**
Wizf-FM, Cincinnati *Also called Urban One Inc* **(G-4788)**
Wj Service Co Inc (PA)....330 372-5040
2592 Elm Rd Ne Warren (44483) **(G-18928)**
Wjcb LLC....513 631-3200
9475 Kenwood Rd Ste 14 Blue Ash (45242) **(G-1718)**
Wjw TV, Cleveland *Also called New Wrld Cmmunications of Ohio* **(G-6125)**
Wkrc-Tv/Cbs, Cincinnati *Also called Iheartcommunications Inc* **(G-3807)**
Wksu FM Natl Public Radio, Kent *Also called Kent State University* **(G-12380)**
Wkyc-Tv Inc....216 344-3300
1333 Lakeside Ave E Cleveland (44114) **(G-6756)**
Wlio Television-Channel 35, Lima *Also called Lima Communications Corp* **(G-12819)**
Wlwt, Cincinnati *Also called Ohio/Oklahoma Hearst TV Inc* **(G-4216)**
Wm Columbus Hotel LLC....614 228-3800
310 S High St Columbus (43215) **(G-9001)**
Wm Kramer and Sons Inc....513 353-1142
9171 Harrison Pike # 12 Cleves (45002) **(G-6806)**
Wman, Mansfield *Also called Iheartcommunications Inc* **(G-13311)**
Wmji-FM, Cleveland *Also called Iheartcommunications Inc* **(G-5804)**
Wmjk FM, Sandusky *Also called Iheartcommunications Inc* **(G-16770)**
Wmk Inc....630 782-1900
4199 Kinross Lakes Pkwy Richfield (44286) **(G-16533)**
Wmvh LLC....513 425-7886
4616 Manchester Rd Middletown (45042) **(G-14471)**
Wmvx Radio, Cleveland *Also called Iheartcommunications Inc* **(G-5803)**
Wnb Group LLC....513 641-5400
4817 Section Ave Cincinnati (45212) **(G-4855)**
Wnir/FM, Kent *Also called Media-Com Inc* **(G-12386)**
Wnwo-TV, Toledo *Also called Toledo Television Investors LP* **(G-18252)**
Wober Muster, Springfield *Also called Crowning Food Company* **(G-17185)**
Woda Construction Inc....614 396-3200
500 S Front St Fl 10 Columbus (43215) **(G-9002)**
Wojos Heating & AC Inc....419 693-3220
5523 Woodville Rd Northwood (43619) **(G-15552)**
Wolcott Group....330 666-5900
1684 Medina Rd Ste 204 Medina (44256) **(G-14139)**
Wolf Group, The, Blue Ash *Also called Wolf Sensory Inc* **(G-1720)**
Wolf Machine Company (PA)....513 791-5194
5570 Creek Rd Blue Ash (45242) **(G-1719)**
Wolf Sensory Inc....513 891-9100
10860 Kenwood Rd Blue Ash (45242) **(G-1720)**
Wolfes Roofing Inc....419 666-6233
6568 State Route 795 Walbridge (43465) **(G-18781)**
Wolff Bros Supply Inc....419 425-8511
6000 Fostoria Ave Findlay (45840) **(G-11101)**
Wolff Bros Supply Inc....330 400-5990
2800 W Strub Rd Sandusky (44870) **(G-16810)**
Wolff Bros Supply Inc....330 264-5900
565 N Applecreek Rd Wooster (44691) **(G-19930)**
Wolff Bros Supply Inc....330 786-4140
1200 Kelly Ave Akron (44306) **(G-511)**
Wolters Kluwer Clinical Drug....330 650-6506
1100 Terex Rd Hudson (44236) **(G-12154)**
Wolverton Inc....330 220-3320
3048 Nationwide Pkwy Brunswick (44212) **(G-1999)**
Wolves Club Inc....419 476-4418
5930 Dalton Rd Toledo (43612) **(G-18313)**
Womans Health Center, Wooster *Also called Cleveland Clinic Foundation* **(G-19848)**
Women Health Partners....740 363-9021
6 Lexington Blvd Delaware (43015) **(G-10136)**
Women Physicans of Ob/Gyn Inc (PA)....614 734-3340
3525 Olentangy River Rd # 6350 Columbus (43214) **(G-9003)**
Womens Care Inc....419 756-6000
500 S Trimble Rd Mansfield (44906) **(G-13383)**
Womens Centers-Dayton....937 228-2222
359 Forest Ave Ste 106 Dayton (45405) **(G-10002)**
Womens Civic Club Grove City....614 871-0145
3881 Tamara Dr Grove City (43123) **(G-11618)**
Womens Recovery Center....937 562-2400
515 Martin Dr Xenia (45385) **(G-20084)**
Womens Welsh Clubs of America....440 331-0420
22199 Center Ridge Rd Rocky River (44116) **(G-16596)**
Wonderworker Inc....234 249-3030
6217 Chittenden Rd Hudson (44236) **(G-12155)**
Wong Margaret W Assoc Co Lpa (PA)....313 527-9989
3150 Chester Ave Cleveland (44114) **(G-6757)**
Wood Herron & Evans LLP (PA)....513 241-2324
441 Vine St Ste 2700 Cincinnati (45202) **(G-4856)**
Wood & Lamping LLP....513 852-6000
600 Vine St Ste 2500 Cincinnati (45202) **(G-4857)**
Wood County Chld Svcs Assn....419 352-7588
1045 Klotz Rd Bowling Green (43402) **(G-1798)**
Wood County Committee On Aging (PA)....419 353-5661
305 N Main St Bowling Green (43402) **(G-1799)**
Wood County Health Department, Bowling Green *Also called Wood County Ohio* **(G-1803)**
Wood County Hospital Assoc (PA)....419 354-8900
960 W Wooster St Bowling Green (43402) **(G-1800)**
Wood County Ohio....419 354-9201
1 Court House Sq Bowling Green (43402) **(G-1801)**
Wood County Ohio....419 353-8411
1965 E Gypsy Lane Rd Bowling Green (43402) **(G-1802)**
Wood County Ohio....419 353-6914
1840 E Gypsy Lane Rd Bowling Green (43402) **(G-1803)**
Wood County Ohio....419 352-5059
705 W Newton Rd Bowling Green (43402) **(G-1804)**
Wood Electric Inc....330 339-7002
210 11th St Nw New Philadelphia (44663) **(G-15123)**
Wood Glen Alzheimers Community, Dayton *Also called Summitt Ohio Leasing Co LLC* **(G-9914)**
Wood Glenn Nursing Center, Dayton *Also called Dayton Dmh Inc* **(G-9470)**
Wood Graphics Inc (HQ)....513 771-6300
8075 Reading Rd Ste 301 Cincinnati (45237) **(G-4858)**
Wood Haven Health Care, Bowling Green *Also called Wood County Ohio* **(G-1802)**
Woodard Photographic Inc (HQ)....419 483-3364
550 Goodrich Rd Bellevue (44811) **(G-1420)**

Woodcraft Supply LLC....513 407-8371
11711 Princeton Pike # 251 Cincinnati (45246) ***(G-4859)***
Woodhill Supply Inc (PA)....440 269-1100
4665 Beidler Rd Willoughby (44094) ***(G-19726)***
Woodhull LLC (PA)....937 294-5311
125 Commercial Way Springboro (45066) ***(G-17143)***
Woodland Assisted Living Resi....614 755-7591
5380 E Broad St Ofc Columbus (43213) ***(G-9004)***
Woodland Centers Inc (PA)....740 446-5500
3086 State Route 160 Gallipolis (45631) ***(G-11341)***
Woodland Country Manor Inc....513 523-4449
4166 Somerville Rd Somerville (45064) ***(G-17072)***
Woodland Run Equin Vet Facilty....614 871-4919
1474 Borror Rd Grove City (43123) ***(G-11619)***
Woodlands At Hampton, Poland *Also called Hampton Woods Nursing Ctr Inc* ***(G-16224)***
Woodlands At Robinson, The, Ravenna *Also called Saber Healthcare Group LLC* ***(G-16410)***
Woodlands At Sunset House, Toledo *Also called Sunset House Inc* ***(G-18210)***
Woodlands of Columbus, Columbus *Also called Woodland Assisted Living Resi* ***(G-9004)***
Woodlawn Nursing Home, Mansfield *Also called Lynnhaven Xii LLC* ***(G-13325)***
Woodlnds Srving Centl Ohio Inc....740 349-7051
68 W Church St Ste 318 Newark (43055) ***(G-15248)***
Woodpeckers Inc....440 238-1824
13700 Prospect Rd Strongsville (44149) ***(G-17525)***
Woodrow Manufacturing Co....937 399-9333
4300 River Rd Springfield (45502) ***(G-17300)***
Woodruff Enterprises Inc....937 399-9300
4951 Gateway Blvd Springfield (45502) ***(G-17301)***
WOODS EDGE POINT, Cincinnati *Also called CHS Norwood Inc* ***(G-3273)***
Woodsfield Opco LLC....502 429-8062
37930 Airport Rd Woodsfield (43793) ***(G-19820)***
Woodside Village Care Center....419 947-2015
841 W Marion Rd Mount Gilead (43338) ***(G-14865)***
Woodstock Care Center Inc....937 826-3351
1649 Park Rd Woodstock (43084) ***(G-19822)***
Woodward Construction Inc....513 247-9241
11425 Deerfield Rd Blue Ash (45242) ***(G-1721)***
Woodward Excavating Co....614 866-4384
7340 Tussing Rd Reynoldsburg (43068) ***(G-16491)***
Woodworkers Outlet....440 286-3942
510 Center St Chardon (44024) ***(G-2779)***
Woody Tree Medics....937 298-5316
4350 Delco Dell Rd Dayton (45429) ***(G-10003)***
Woolace Electric Corp....419 428-3161
1978 County Road 22a Stryker (43557) ***(G-17539)***
Woolpert Inc....614 476-6000
1 Easton Oval Ste 310 Columbus (43219) ***(G-9005)***
Woolprt-Mrrick Joint Ventr LLP....937 461-5660
4454 Idea Center Blvd Beavercreek (45430) ***(G-1263)***
Wooster Clinic Inc....330 264-1512
1740 Cleveland Rd Wooster (44691) ***(G-19931)***
Wooster Community Hospital, Wooster *Also called City of Wooster* ***(G-19846)***
Wooster Division Fire, Wooster *Also called City of Wooster* ***(G-19845)***
Wooster Inn, The, Wooster *Also called Kmb Management Services Corp* ***(G-19880)***
Wooster Motor Ways Inc (PA)....330 264-9557
3501 W Old Lincoln Way Wooster (44691) ***(G-19932)***
Wooster Ophthalmologists Inc....330 345-7800
3519 Friendsville Rd Wooster (44691) ***(G-19933)***
Wooster Products Inc....330 264-2844
3503 Old Airport Rd Wooster (44691) ***(G-19934)***
Work Connections Intl LLC....419 448-4655
525 Wall St Ste A Tiffin (44883) ***(G-17709)***
Work Leads To Independence, Bowling Green *Also called Lane Wood Industries* ***(G-1784)***
Work Solutions Group LLC....440 205-8297
8324 Tyler Blvd Mentor (44060) ***(G-14259)***
Work Tech, Akron *Also called Community Support Services Inc* ***(G-158)***
Workers Compensation Ohio Bur....800 644-6292
30 W Spring St Columbus (43215) ***(G-9006)***
Workers Compensation Ohio Bur (HQ)....614 644-6292
30 W Spring St Fl 2-29 Columbus (43215) ***(G-9007)***
Workforce Initiative Assn (PA)....330 433-9675
822 30th St Nw Canton (44709) ***(G-2588)***
Workforce One, Hamilton *Also called Butler County of Ohio* ***(G-11697)***
Workforce Services Inc (PA)....330 484-2566
6245 Sherman Ch Ave Sw Canton (44706) ***(G-2589)***
Working Community Services, Columbus *Also called Goodwill Inds Centl Ohio Inc* ***(G-7761)***
Workplace Media Inc....440 392-2171
9325 Progress Pkwy Mentor (44060) ***(G-14260)***
Workshops of David T Smith....513 932-2472
3600 Shawhan Rd Morrow (45152) ***(G-14848)***
Workshops, The, Canton *Also called Stark County Board of Developm* ***(G-2543)***
Workspeed Management LLC....917 369-9025
28925 Fountain Pkwy Solon (44139) ***(G-17069)***
World Auto Parts Inc....216 781-8418
1240 Carnegie Ave Cleveland (44115) ***(G-6758)***
World Harvest Church Inc (PA)....614 837-1990
4595 Gender Rd Canal Winchester (43110) ***(G-2180)***
World Shipping Inc (PA)....440 356-7676
1340 Depot St Ste 200 Cleveland (44116) ***(G-6759)***
World Tableware Inc (HQ)....419 325-2608
300 Madison Ave Fl 4 Toledo (43604) ***(G-18314)***
World Trck Towing Recovery Inc....330 723-1116
4970 Park Ave W Seville (44273) ***(G-16848)***
World Wide Travel Service, Cincinnati *Also called AAA Allied Group Inc* ***(G-2958)***
World Wide Travel Service, Sidney *Also called AAA Shelby County Motor Club* ***(G-16910)***
Worldpay Inc (PA)....513 900-5250
8500 Governors Hill Dr Symmes Twp (45249) ***(G-17631)***
Worlds of Worthington, Worthington *Also called Laurel Health Care Company* ***(G-19969)***
Worldwide Equipment Inc....513 563-6363
10649 Evendale Dr Cincinnati (45241) ***(G-4860)***
Worldwide of Cincinnati, Cincinnati *Also called Worldwide Equipment Inc* ***(G-4860)***
Worly Plumbing Supply Inc (PA)....614 445-1000
400 Greenlawn Ave Columbus (43223) ***(G-9008)***
Worthington Industries Inc....513 539-9291
350 Lawton Ave Monroe (45050) ***(G-14718)***
Worthington Inn, The, Worthington *Also called Epiqurian Inns* ***(G-19957)***
Worthington Public Library....614 807-2626
820 High St Worthington (43085) ***(G-20010)***
WORTHINGTON SWIMMING POOL, Worthington *Also called Swim Incorporated* ***(G-20002)***
Worthington United Methdst Ch....614 885-5365
600 High St Worthington (43085) ***(G-20011)***
Worthlington Dental Group, Worthington *Also called Association of Prosthodontics* ***(G-19942)***
Worthngton Stelpac Systems LLC (HQ)....614 438-3205
1205 Dearborn Dr Columbus (43085) ***(G-9009)***
Wosu Am-FM TV, Columbus *Also called Ohio State University* ***(G-8406)***
Woub Channel 20 & 44, Athens *Also called Ohio University* ***(G-806)***
Woub Public Media, Athens *Also called Ohio University* ***(G-805)***
Wph Cincinnati LLC....513 771-2080
11320 Chester Rd Cincinnati (45246) ***(G-4861)***
Wqio 93q Request....740 392-9370
17421 Coshocton Rd Mount Vernon (43050) ***(G-14926)***
Wqkt/Wkvx, Wooster *Also called Wwst Corporation LLC* ***(G-19935)***
Wqmx 94.9 FM, Akron *Also called Rubber City Radio Group* ***(G-420)***
Wqmx Love Fund....330 869-9800
1795 W Market St Akron (44313) ***(G-512)***
Wraaa, Cleveland *Also called Western Reserve Area Agency* ***(G-6742)***
Wrap & Send Services Co., Cincinnati *Also called D H Packaging Co* ***(G-3455)***
Wrench Ltd Company (PA)....740 654-5304
4805 Scooby Ln Carroll (43112) ***(G-2610)***
Wrg Services Inc....440 942-8650
38585 Apollo Pkwy Willoughby (44094) ***(G-19727)***
Wright Brothers Aero Inc....937 454-8475
3700 Mccall St Dayton (45417) ***(G-10004)***
Wright Brothers Aero Inc (PA)....937 890-8900
3700 Mccauley Dr Ste C Vandalia (45377) ***(G-18707)***
Wright Center....216 382-1868
1611 S Green Rd Ste 124 Cleveland (44121) ***(G-6760)***
Wright Distribution Centers....419 227-7621
1000 E Hanthorn Rd Lima (45804) ***(G-12922)***
Wright Executive Ht Ltd Partnr....937 283-3200
123 Gano Rd Wilmington (45177) ***(G-19796)***
Wright Executive Ht Ltd Partnr (PA)....937 426-7800
2800 Presidential Dr Beavercreek (45324) ***(G-1219)***
Wright Executive Ht Ltd Partnr....937 429-0600
2750 Presidential Dr Beavercreek (45324) ***(G-1220)***
Wright Harvey House, The, Northwood *Also called Sattlerpearson Inc* ***(G-15544)***
Wright Nutrition Inc....614 873-0418
8000 Memorial Dr Plain City (43064) ***(G-16212)***
Wright Patterson Afb Lodging, Dayton *Also called Army & Air Force Exchange Svc* ***(G-9255)***
Wright State Physcans Drmtlogy (PA)....937 224-7546
725 University Blvd Beavercreek (45324) ***(G-1221)***
Wright State University....937 775-4070
3640 Colonel Glenn Hwy Dayton (45435) ***(G-9290)***
Wright State University....937 298-4331
3525 Southern Blvd Kettering (45429) ***(G-12439)***
Wright State University....937 775-3333
3640 Colonel Glenn Hwy Beavercreek (45324) ***(G-1222)***
Wright Surgery Center, Cleveland *Also called Wright Center* ***(G-6760)***
Wright-Patt Credit Union Inc (PA)....937 912-7000
3560 Pentagon Blvd Beavercreek (45431) ***(G-1223)***
Wrightway Fd Svc Rest Sup Inc....419 222-7911
3255 Saint Johns Rd Lima (45804) ***(G-12923)***
Wrkz, Columbus *Also called North American Broadcasting* ***(G-8286)***
Wrl Advertising, Canton *Also called Wern-Rausch Locke Advertising* ***(G-2584)***
Wrwk 1065....419 725-5700
3225 Arlington Ave Toledo (43614) ***(G-18315)***
Wryneck Development LLC....419 354-2535
1553 Muirfield Dr Bowling Green (43402) ***(G-1805)***
Wsb Rehabilitation Svcs Inc....330 847-7819
4329 Mahoning Ave Nw B Warren (44483) ***(G-18929)***
Wsb Rehabilitation Svcs Inc (PA)....330 533-1338
510 W Main St Ste B Canfield (44406) ***(G-2216)***
Wsny FM, Columbus *Also called Franklin Communications Inc* ***(G-7692)***
Wsny Radio Station, Columbus *Also called Saga Communications Neng Inc* ***(G-8675)***
Wsos Child Development Program....419 334-8511
765 S Buchanan St Fremont (43420) ***(G-11230)***
Wss- Dayton, Moraine *Also called Winsupply Inc* ***(G-14836)***
Wssr Cpas, Chillicothe *Also called Whited Seigneur Sams & Rahe* ***(G-2897)***

ALPHABETIC

Wsyx and ABC 6, Columbus *Also called Sinclair Media II Inc (G-8739)*
Wta Consulting, Maumee *Also called Warnock Tanner & Assoc Inc (G-13993)*
Wtb Inc....216 298-1895
815 Superior Ave E Cleveland (44114) *(G-6761)*
Wtov TV 9, Mingo Junction *Also called Sunrise Television Corp (G-14658)*
Wtvg-TV, Toledo *Also called Gray Television Group Inc (G-17920)*
Wtw Delaware Holdings LLC....216 937-4000
1001 Lakeside Ave E Cleveland (44114) *(G-6762)*
Wulco Inc (PA)....513 679-2600
6899 Steger Dr Ste A Cincinnati (45237) *(G-4862)*
Wunderlich Securities Inc....440 646-1400
5885 Landerbrook Dr # 304 Cleveland (44124) *(G-6763)*
Wupw LLC....419 244-3600
730 N Summit St Toledo (43604) *(G-18316)*
Wurtec Incorporated (PA)....419 726-1066
6200 Brent Dr Toledo (43611) *(G-18317)*
Wviz/Pbs Hd, Cleveland *Also called Ideastream (G-5801)*
Wvno-FM, Ontario *Also called Johnny Appleseed Broadcasting (G-15695)*
Wvxu Radio, Cincinnati *Also called Xavier University (G-4863)*
Ww CD Radio, Columbus *Also called Ingleside Investments Inc (G-7898)*
WW Grainger Inc....513 563-7100
4420 Glendale Milford Rd Blue Ash (45242) *(G-1722)*
WW Grainger Inc....614 276-5231
3640 Interchange Rd Columbus (43204) *(G-9010)*
WW&r, Cleveland *Also called Weltman Weinberg & Reis Co Lpa (G-6732)*
WWCD, Columbus *Also called Cd1025 (G-7217)*
Wwho TV, Columbus *Also called Sinclair Media II Inc (G-8738)*
Wws Associates Inc (PA)....513 761-5333
11093 Kenwood Rd Ste 7 Blue Ash (45242) *(G-1723)*
Wwst Corporation LLC....330 264-5122
186 S Hillcrest Dr Wooster (44691) *(G-19935)*
Www.logicsoftusa.com, Dublin *Also called Logic Soft Inc (G-10391)*
Wxeg-FM, Dayton *Also called Iheartcommunications Inc (G-9627)*
Wxkr, Toledo *Also called Cumulus Media Inc (G-17842)*
Wyandot County AG Soc....419 294-4320
10171 State Highway 53 N Upper Sandusky (43351) *(G-18569)*
Wyandot County Fair, Upper Sandusky *Also called Wyandot County AG Soc (G-18569)*
Wyandot County Home, Upper Sandusky *Also called County of Wyandot (G-18558)*
Wyandot Memorial Hospital....419 294-4991
885 N Sandusky Ave Upper Sandusky (43351) *(G-18570)*
Wyandot Tractor & Implement Co....419 294-2349
10264 County Highway 121 Upper Sandusky (43351) *(G-18571)*
Wyandotte Athletic Club....614 861-6303
5198 Riding Club Ln Columbus (43213) *(G-9011)*
Wyant Leasing Co LLC....330 836-7953
200 Wyant Rd Akron (44313) *(G-513)*
Wyant Woods Care Center, Akron *Also called Healthcare Facility MGT LLC (G-260)*
Wyant Woods Care Center, Akron *Also called Wyant Leasing Co LLC (G-513)*
Wyfm FM, Youngstown *Also called Cumulus Broadcasting LLC (G-20163)*
Wyle Laboratories Inc....937 912-3470
2601 Mission Point Blvd # 300 Beavercreek (45431) *(G-1224)*
Wyle Laboratories Inc....937 320-2712
2700 Indian Ripple Rd Beavercreek (45440) *(G-1264)*
Wyler, Jeff, Dealer Group, Cincinnati *Also called Jeff Wyler Automotive Fmly Inc (G-2918)*
Wyndham Hotels & Resorts, Cleveland *Also called Wyndham International Inc (G-6764)*
Wyndham International Inc....330 666-9300
200 Montrose West Ave Copley (44321) *(G-9069)*
Wyndham International Inc....216 615-7500
1260 Euclid Ave Cleveland (44115) *(G-6764)*
Wynn-Reeth Inc....419 639-2094
137 S Broadway St Green Springs (44836) *(G-11481)*
Wyoming Family Practice Center, Cincinnati *Also called University Family Physicians (G-4753)*
Wyse Advertising Inc (PA)....216 696-2424
668 Euclid Ave Ste 100 Cleveland (44114) *(G-6765)*
Wz Management Inc....330 628-4881
3417 E Waterloo Rd Akron (44312) *(G-514)*
Wzak, Cleveland *Also called Urban One Inc (G-6673)*
Wzoo-FM, Ashtabula *Also called Ashtabula Broadcasting Station (G-713)*
Wzrx....419 223-2060
667 W Market St Lima (45801) *(G-12924)*
X F Construction Svcs Inc....614 575-2700
1120 Claycraft Rd Columbus (43230) *(G-9012)*
X F Petroleum Equipment, Columbus *Also called X F Construction Svcs Inc (G-9012)*
X-Ray Industries Inc....216 642-0100
5403 E Schaaf Rd Cleveland (44131) *(G-6766)*
X-S Merchandise Inc (PA)....216 524-5620
7000 Granger Rd Ste 2 Independence (44131) *(G-12278)*
Xact, Xenia *Also called Xenia Area Cmnty Theater Inc (G-20085)*
Xanterra Parks & Resorts Inc....740 439-2751
Us Rte 22 E Cambridge (43725) *(G-2134)*
Xanterra Parks & Resorts Inc....419 836-1466
1750 State Park Rd 2 Oregon (43616) *(G-15755)*
Xanterra Parks & Resorts Inc....740 869-2020
22300 State Park 20 Rd Mount Sterling (43143) *(G-14876)*
Xanterra Parks & Resorts Inc....440 564-9144
11755 Kinsman Rd Newbury (44065) *(G-15265)*
Xavier University....513 745-3335
3800 Victory Pkwy Unit 1 Cincinnati (45207) *(G-4863)*
Xenia Area Cmnty Theater Inc....937 372-0516
45 E 2nd St Xenia (45385) *(G-20085)*
Xenia East Management Systems....937 372-4495
1301 N Monroe Dr Xenia (45385) *(G-20086)*
Xenia Waster Water, Xenia *Also called City of Xenia (G-20045)*
Xenia West Management Systems....937 372-8081
1384 N Monroe Dr Xenia (45385) *(G-20087)*
Xentry Systems Integration LLC (HQ)....614 452-7300
771 Dearborn Park Ln N Columbus (43085) *(G-9013)*
Xerox Corporation....419 418-6500
600 Jefferson Ave Ste 200 Toledo (43604) *(G-18318)*
Xerox Corporation....216 642-7806
6000 Fredom Sq Dr Ste 100 Cleveland (44131) *(G-6767)*
Xerox Corporation....513 554-3200
10560 Ashview Pl Blue Ash (45242) *(G-1724)*
Xo Communications LLC....216 619-3200
3 Summit Park Dr Ste 250 Cleveland (44131) *(G-6768)*
Xpedx, Cleveland *Also called Veritiv Operating Company (G-6689)*
Xpo Cnw Inc....440 716-8971
5498 Dorothy Dr North Olmsted (44070) *(G-15451)*
Xpo Intermodal Inc (HQ)....614 923-1400
5165 Emerald Pkwy 300 Dublin (43017) *(G-10494)*
Xpo Intermodal Solutions Inc (HQ)....614 923-1400
5165 Emerald Pkwy Dublin (43017) *(G-10495)*
Xpo Logistics, Obetz *Also called Jacobson Warehouse Company Inc (G-15668)*
Xpo Logistics, Groveport *Also called Jacobson Warehouse Company Inc (G-11650)*
Xpo Logistics, Groveport *Also called Jacobson Warehouse Company Inc (G-11651)*
Xpo Logistics Freight Inc....513 870-0044
5289 Duff Dr West Chester (45246) *(G-19244)*
Xpo Logistics Freight Inc....614 876-7100
2625 Westbelt Dr Columbus (43228) *(G-9014)*
Xpo Logistics Freight Inc....937 898-9808
3410 Stop 8 Rd Dayton (45414) *(G-10005)*
Xpo Logistics Freight Inc....419 499-8888
12518 State Route 250 Milan (44846) *(G-14500)*
Xpo Logistics Freight Inc....216 433-1000
12901 Snow Rd Parma (44130) *(G-15919)*
Xpo Logistics Freight Inc....740 894-3859
96 Private Drive 339 South Point (45680) *(G-17099)*
Xpo Logistics Freight Inc....330 824-2242
6700 Muth Rd Sw Warren (44481) *(G-18930)*
Xpo Logistics Freight Inc....419 294-5728
1850 E Wyandot Ave Upper Sandusky (43351) *(G-18572)*
Xpo Logistics Freight Inc....419 666-3022
28291 Glenwood Rd Perrysburg (43551) *(G-16075)*
Xpo Logistics Freight Inc....937 364-2361
5215 Us Route 50 Hillsboro (45133) *(G-11993)*
Xpo Logistics Freight Inc....740 922-5614
2401 N Water Street Ext Uhrichsville (44683) *(G-18497)*
Xpo Logistics Freight Inc....330 896-7300
3733 Massillon Rd Uniontown (44685) *(G-18544)*
Xpo Logistics Freight Inc....937 492-3899
2021 Campbell Rd Sidney (45365) *(G-16961)*
Xpo Stacktrain LLC....614 923-1400
5165 Emerald Pkwy Dublin (43017) *(G-10496)*
Xpress Loan Servicing, Cleveland *Also called Education Loan Servicing Corp (G-5527)*
Xri Testing, Cleveland *Also called X-Ray Industries Inc (G-6766)*
Xto Energy Inc....740 671-9901
2358 W 23rd St Bellaire (43906) *(G-1369)*
Xtreme Contracting Ltd....614 568-7030
7600 Asden Ct Reynoldsburg (43068) *(G-16492)*
Xzamcorp....330 629-2218
4119 Logans Way Perry (44081) *(G-15969)*
Y M C A, Cincinnati *Also called Young Mens Christian Associat (G-4866)*
Y M C A, Circleville *Also called Young Mens Christian Assoc (G-4909)*
Y M C A, Middletown *Also called Ucc Childrens Center (G-14488)*
Y M C A, Versailles *Also called County of Darke (G-18725)*
Y M C A, Shelby *Also called Young Mens Christn Assn Shelby (G-16904)*
Y M C A, Toledo *Also called Young Mens Christian Associat (G-18323)*
Y M C A Central Stark County....330 305-5437
200 Charlotte St Nw Canton (44720) *(G-2590)*
Y M C A Central Stark County....330 875-1611
1421 S Nickelplate St Louisville (44641) *(G-13108)*
Y M C A Central Stark County....330 877-8933
11928 King Church Ave Nw Uniontown (44685) *(G-18545)*
Y M C A Central Stark County....330 830-6275
7389 Caritas Cir Nw Massillon (44646) *(G-13862)*
Y M C A Central Stark County....330 498-4082
7241 Whipple Ave Nw Canton (44720) *(G-2591)*
Y M C A of Ashland Ohio Inc....419 289-0626
207 Miller St Ashland (44805) *(G-709)*
Y M C A-Head Start, East Liverpool *Also called Community Action Columbiana CT (G-10518)*
Y Town Realty Inc....330 743-8844
1641 5th Ave Youngstown (44504) *(G-20419)*
Y W C A, Hamilton *Also called YWCA of Hamilton (G-11785)*
Yanfeng US Automotive....419 662-4905
7560 Arbor Dr Northwood (43619) *(G-15553)*

ALPHABETIC SECTION — Young Mens Christian Assoc

Yankee Run Golf Course 330 448-8096
  7610 Warren Sharon Rd Brookfield (44403) *(G-1903)*
Yardmaster Inc (PA) 440 357-8400
  1447 N Ridge Rd Painesville (44077) *(G-15888)*
Yardmaster of Columbus Inc 614 863-4510
  570 Reynldsbrg New Albany Blacklick (43004) *(G-1513)*
Yark Automotive Group Inc (PA) 419 841-7771
  6019 W Central Ave Toledo (43615) *(G-18319)*
Yark Subaru, Toledo *Also called Yark Automotive Group Inc (G-18319)*
Yashco Systems Inc 614 467-4600
  3974 Brown Park Dr Hilliard (43026) *(G-11966)*
Yearwood Corporation (PA) 937 223-3572
  125 E 2nd St Dayton (45402) *(G-10006)*
Yeater Alene K MD 740 348-4694
  15 Messimer Dr Newark (43055) *(G-15249)*
Yeck Brothers Company 937 294-4000
  2222 Arbor Blvd Moraine (45439) *(G-14837)*
Yellow Cab Co of Cleveland 216 623-1500
  2069 W 3rd St Cleveland (44113) *(G-6769)*
Yellow Cabs, Columbus *Also called Columbus Green Cabs Inc (G-7355)*
Yellow Transportation, West Chester *Also called Yrc Inc (G-19245)*
Yellow Transportation, Richfield *Also called Yrc Inc (G-16534)*
Yellow Transportation, Columbus *Also called Yrc Inc (G-9023)*
Yerman & Young Painting Inc 330 861-0022
  811 Brady Ave Barberton (44203) *(G-986)*
YMCA, Lockbourne *Also called Young Mens Christian Assoc (G-12963)*
YMCA, Mansfield *Also called Frans Child Care-Mansfield (G-13304)*
YMCA, Fremont *Also called Young Mens Christian Assn (G-11231)*
YMCA, Columbus *Also called Young Mens Christian Assoc (G-9017)*
YMCA, Akron *Also called Young Mens Christian Assoc (G-516)*
YMCA, Ashland *Also called Y M C A of Ashland Ohio Inc (G-709)*
YMCA, Gahanna *Also called Young Mens Christian Assoc (G-11276)*
YMCA, Powell *Also called Young Mens Christian Assoc (G-16355)*
YMCA, Hilliard *Also called Young Mens Christian Assoc (G-11967)*
YMCA, Van Wert *Also called Young Mens Christian Assn (G-18653)*
YMCA, Columbus *Also called Young Mens Christian Assoc (G-9019)*
YMCA, Uniontown *Also called Y M C A Central Stark County (G-18545)*
YMCA, Chardon *Also called Young MNS Chrstn Assn Clveland (G-2780)*
YMCA, Mount Vernon *Also called Young Mens Christian Mt Vernon (G-14927)*
YMCA, Columbus *Also called Young Mens Christian Assoc (G-9020)*
YMCA 330 823-1930
  205 S Union Ave Alliance (44601) *(G-566)*
YMCA 937 653-9622
  191 Community Dr Urbana (43078) *(G-18603)*
YMCA Camp Campbell Gard, Hamilton *Also called Great Miami Valley YMCA (G-11734)*
YMCA Child Care, Canton *Also called Y M C A Central Stark County (G-2590)*
YMCA Crayon Club Chld Care, Dayton *Also called Young Mens Christian Assoc (G-10012)*
YMCA Cuyahoga Falls Branch, Cuyahoga Falls *Also called Young Mens Christian Assoc (G-9237)*
YMCA Inc 330 385-6400
  15655 State Route 170 A2 East Liverpool (43920) *(G-10536)*
YMCA of Ashtabula County Inc 440 997-5321
  263 W Prospect Rd Ashtabula (44004) *(G-768)*
YMCA of Clermont County Inc 513 724-9622
  2075 James E Sauls Sr Dr Batavia (45103) *(G-1032)*
YMCA of East Liverpool Ohio, East Liverpool *Also called YMCA Inc (G-10536)*
YMCA OF FINDLAY, Findlay *Also called Young MNS Chrstn Assn Findlay (G-11102)*
YMCA of Greater Dayton, Dayton *Also called Young Mens Christian Assoc (G-10009)*
YMCA of Greater Toledo, Toledo *Also called Young Mens Christian Associat (G-18320)*
YMCA of Greater Toledo, Perrysburg *Also called Young Mens Christian Associat (G-16076)*
YMCA of Massillon (PA) 330 837-5116
  131 Tremont Ave Se Massillon (44646) *(G-13863)*
YMCA of Massillon 330 879-0800
  1226 Market St Ne Navarre (44662) *(G-14957)*
YMCA of Sandusky Ohio Inc 419 621-9622
  2101 W Perkins Ave Sandusky (44870) *(G-16811)*
YMCA OF THE USA, Wooster *Also called Young Mens Christian Assoc (G-19936)*
YMCA OF WESTERN STARK COUNTY, Massillon *Also called YMCA of Massillon (G-13863)*
YMCA OF YOUNGSTOWN, Youngstown *Also called Young Mens Christian Assn (G-20421)*
YMCA West Park, Cleveland *Also called Young MNS Chrstn Assn Clveland (G-6773)*
Ymca/M.e.lions, Cincinnati *Also called Young Mens Christian Associat (G-4867)*
Yndc, Youngstown *Also called Youngstown Neighborhood Dev (G-20432)*
Yockey Group Inc 513 899-2188
  6344 E Us Hwy 22 And 3 Morrow (45152) *(G-14849)*
Yocum Realty Company 419 222-3040
  421 S Cable Rd Lima (45805) *(G-12925)*
Yoder Drilling and Geothermal 330 852-4342
  997 State Route 93 Nw Sugarcreek (44681) *(G-17548)*
Yoder Industries Inc (PA) 937 278-5769
  2520 Needmore Rd Dayton (45414) *(G-10007)*
Yoder Machinery Sales Company 419 865-5555
  1500 Holloway Rd Holland (43528) *(G-12069)*
Yoder Trading Company, Barberton *Also called Aris Horticulture Inc (G-953)*
York Building Maintenance Inc 216 398-8100
  4748 Broadview Rd Cleveland (44109) *(G-6770)*

YORK GOLF CLUB, Columbus *Also called York Temple Country Club Inc (G-9015)*
York Risk Services Group Inc 866 391-9675
  5555 Glendon Ct Dublin (43016) *(G-10497)*
York Risk Services Group Inc 440 863-2500
  16560 Commerce Ct Ste 100 Cleveland (44130) *(G-6771)*
York Rite 216 751-1417
  13512 Kinsman Rd Cleveland (44120) *(G-6772)*
York Temple Country Club Inc 614 885-5459
  7459 N High St Columbus (43235) *(G-9015)*
York-Mahoning Mech Contrs Inc 330 788-7011
  724 Canfield Rd Youngstown (44511) *(G-20420)*
Yorkland Health Care Inc 614 751-2525
  1425 Yorkland Rd Columbus (43232) *(G-9016)*
Yorkland Park Care Center, Columbus *Also called Yorkland Health Care Inc (G-9016)*
Young & Alexander Co Lpa (PA) 937 224-9291
  130 W 2nd St Ste 1500 Dayton (45402) *(G-10008)*
Young & Bertke Air Systems, Cincinnati *Also called Pcy Enterprises Inc (G-4270)*
Young & Rubicam Inc 513 419-2300
  110 Shillito Pl Cincinnati (45202) *(G-4864)*
Young and Associates Inc 330 678-0524
  121 E Main St Kent (44240) *(G-12407)*
Young Chemical Co LLC (HQ) 330 486-4210
  1755 Entp Pkwy Ste 400 Twinsburg (44087) *(G-18486)*
Young Medical, Maumee *Also called Apria Healthcare LLC (G-13883)*
Young Medical Services, Maumee *Also called Toledo Medical Equipment Co (G-13987)*
Young Mens Christian 513 791-5000
  5000 Ymca Dr Blue Ash (45242) *(G-1725)*
Young Mens Christian 513 932-1424
  1699 Deerfield Rd Lebanon (45036) *(G-12660)*
Young Mens Christian Assn, Mount Vernon *Also called Young MNS Chrstn Assn Grter NY (G-14928)*
Young Mens Christian Assn 419 332-9622
  1000 North St Fremont (43420) *(G-11231)*
Young Mens Christian Assn (PA) 330 744-8411
  17 N Champion St Youngstown (44503) *(G-20421)*
Young Mens Christian Assn 740 373-2250
  300 N 7th St Marietta (45750) *(G-13520)*
Young Mens Christian Assn 419 238-0443
  241 W Main St Van Wert (45891) *(G-18653)*
Young Mens Christian Assoc 614 491-0980
  1570 Rohr Rd Lockbourne (43137) *(G-12963)*
Young Mens Christian Assoc 614 871-9622
  3600 Discovery Dr Grove City (43123) *(G-11620)*
Young Mens Christian Assoc (PA) 937 223-5201
  118 W St Ste 300 Dayton (45402) *(G-10009)*
Young Mens Christian Assoc 330 923-5223
  544 Broad Blvd Cuyahoga Falls (44221) *(G-9237)*
Young Mens Christian Assoc 330 467-8366
  8761 Shepard Rd Macedonia (44056) *(G-13219)*
Young Mens Christian Assoc 330 264-3131
  680 Woodland Ave Wooster (44691) *(G-19936)*
Young Mens Christian Assoc 330 784-0408
  888 Jonathan Ave Akron (44306) *(G-515)*
Young Mens Christian Assoc 740 477-1661
  440 Nicholas Dr Circleville (43113) *(G-4909)*
Young Mens Christian Assoc 614 885-4252
  1640 Sandalwood Pl Columbus (43229) *(G-9017)*
Young Mens Christian Assoc 330 724-1255
  350 E Wilbeth Rd Akron (44301) *(G-516)*
Young Mens Christian Assoc 330 376-1335
  80 W Center St Akron (44308) *(G-517)*
Young Mens Christian Assoc 614 416-9622
  555 Ymca Pl Gahanna (43230) *(G-11276)*
Young Mens Christian Assoc 740 881-1058
  7798 Liberty Rd N Powell (43065) *(G-16355)*
Young Mens Christian Assoc 614 334-9622
  4515 Cosgray Rd Hilliard (43026) *(G-11967)*
Young Mens Christian Assoc 937 312-1810
  4545 Marshall Rd Dayton (45429) *(G-10010)*
Young Mens Christian Assoc 614 539-1770
  3500 1st Ave Urbancrest (43123) *(G-18609)*
Young Mens Christian Assoc 614 276-8224
  2879 Valleyview Dr Columbus (43204) *(G-9018)*
Young Mens Christian Assoc 513 932-3756
  5291 State Route 350 Oregonia (45054) *(G-15759)*
Young Mens Christian Assoc 614 252-3166
  130 Woodland Ave Columbus (43203) *(G-9019)*
Young Mens Christian Assoc 937 426-9622
  111 W 1st St Ste 207 Dayton (45402) *(G-10011)*
Young Mens Christian Assoc 937 836-9622
  1200 W National Rd Englewood (45315) *(G-10725)*
Young Mens Christian Assoc 419 523-5233
  101 Putnam Pkwy Ottawa (45875) *(G-15805)*
Young Mens Christian Assoc 937 228-9622
  316 N Wilkinson St Dayton (45402) *(G-10012)*
Young Mens Christian Assoc 937 223-5201
  88 Remick Blvd Springboro (45066) *(G-17144)*
Young Mens Christian Assoc 614 878-7269
  600 Fox Ridge St Columbus (43228) *(G-9020)*
Young Mens Christian Assoc 937 593-9001
  2732 County Road 11 Bellefontaine (43311) *(G-1401)*

Young Mens Christian Assoc 614 834-9622
6767 Refugee Rd Canal Winchester (43110) ***(G-2181)***
Young Mens Christian Associat (PA) 419 729-8135
1500 N Superior St Fl 2 Toledo (43604) ***(G-18320)***
Young Mens Christian Associat 419 475-3496
2110 Tremainsville Rd Toledo (43613) ***(G-18321)***
Young Mens Christian Associat 419 794-7304
716 Askin St Maumee (43537) ***(G-13996)***
Young Mens Christian Associat 513 521-7112
9601 Winton Rd Cincinnati (45231) ***(G-4865)***
Young Mens Christian Associat 419 251-9622
13415 Eckel Junction Rd Perrysburg (43551) ***(G-16076)***
Young Mens Christian Associat 513 731-0115
2039 Sherman Ave Cincinnati (45212) ***(G-4866)***
Young Mens Christian Associat 513 474-1400
8108 Clough Pike Fl 1 Cincinnati (45244) ***(G-4867)***
Young Mens Christian Associat 513 241-9622
1425b Linn St Cincinnati (45214) ***(G-4868)***
Young Mens Christian Associat 513 923-4466
8920 Cheviot Rd Cincinnati (45251) ***(G-4869)***
Young Mens Christian Associat 419 474-3995
1500 N Superior St Fl 2 Toledo (43604) ***(G-18322)***
Young Mens Christian Associat 419 866-9622
2100 S Hlland Sylvania Rd Maumee (43537) ***(G-13997)***
Young Mens Christian Associat 419 475-3496
2020 Tremainsville Rd Toledo (43613) ***(G-18323)***
Young Mens Christian Associat 419 691-3523
2960 Pickle Rd Oregon (43616) ***(G-15756)***
Young Mens Christian Mt Vernon 740 392-9622
103 N Main St Mount Vernon (43050) ***(G-14927)***
Young Mens Christn Assn Shelby 419 347-1312
111 W Smiley Ave Shelby (44875) ***(G-16904)***
Young Mens Christn Assosiation, Fairborn *Also called Fairborn YMCA* ***(G-10796)***
Young MNS Christn Assn Findlay (PA) 419 422-4424
300 E Lincoln St Findlay (45840) ***(G-11102)***
Young MNS Chrstn Assn Clveland 216 521-8400
16915 Detroit Ave Lakewood (44107) ***(G-12502)***
Young MNS Chrstn Assn Clveland 216 941-4654
15501 Lorain Ave Cleveland (44111) ***(G-6773)***
Young MNS Chrstn Assn Clveland 440 842-5200
11409 State Rd North Royalton (44133) ***(G-15507)***
Young MNS Chrstn Assn Clveland 216 731-7454
631 Babbitt Rd Cleveland (44123) ***(G-6774)***
Young MNS Chrstn Assn Clveland 216 382-4300
5000 Mayfield Rd Cleveland (44124) ***(G-6775)***
Young MNS Chrstn Assn Clveland 440 285-7543
12460 Bass Lake Rd Chardon (44024) ***(G-2780)***
Young MNS Chrstn Assn Clveland 440 808-8150
1575 Columbia Rd Westlake (44145) ***(G-19569)***
Young MNS Chrstn Assn Grter NY 740 392-9622
103 N Main St Mount Vernon (43050) ***(G-14928)***
Young Services Inc (PA) 419 704-2009
806 Starr Ave Toledo (43605) ***(G-18324)***
Young Truck Sales Inc (PA) 330 477-6271
4970 Southway St Sw Canton (44706) ***(G-2592)***
Young Womens Christian 419 241-3235
1018 Jefferson Ave Toledo (43604) ***(G-18325)***
Young Womens Christian 937 461-5550
141 W 3rd St Dayton (45402) ***(G-10013)***
Young Womens Christian 419 238-6639
408 E Main St Van Wert (45891) ***(G-18654)***
Young Womens Christian Assn (PA) 614 224-9121
65 S 4th St Columbus (43215) ***(G-9021)***
Young Womens Christian Assn 330 746-6361
25 W Rayen Ave Youngstown (44503) ***(G-20422)***
Young Womens Christian Associ (PA) 216 881-6878
4019 Prospect Ave Cleveland (44103) ***(G-6776)***
Young Womns Chrstn Assc Canton (PA) 330 453-7644
231 6th St Ne Canton (44702) ***(G-2593)***
Young Womns Chrstn Assc Canton 330 453-0789
1700 Gateway Blvd Se Canton (44707) ***(G-2594)***
Young Womns Chrstn Assc Lima 419 241-3230
1018 Jefferson Ave Toledo (43604) ***(G-18326)***
Youngs Jersey Dairy Inc 937 325-0629
6880 Springfield Xenia Rd Yellow Springs (45387) ***(G-20091)***
Youngstown ARC Engraving Co 330 793-2471
380 Victoria Rd Youngstown (44515) ***(G-20423)***
Youngstown Area (PA) 330 759-7921
2747 Belmont Ave Youngstown (44505) ***(G-20424)***
Youngstown Area Jwish Fdration (PA) 330 746-3251
505 Gypsy Ln Youngstown (44504) ***(G-20425)***
Youngstown Area Jwish Fdration 330 746-1076
517 Gypsy Ln Youngstown (44504) ***(G-20426)***
Youngstown Automatic Door Co 330 747-3135
1223 Gibson St Youngstown (44502) ***(G-20427)***
Youngstown Club 330 744-3111
201 E Commerce St Ste 400 Youngstown (44503) ***(G-20428)***
Youngstown Committee On Alchol 330 744-1181
2151 Rush Blvd Youngstown (44507) ***(G-20429)***
Youngstown Community Hlth Ctr, Youngstown *Also called Ohio North E Hlth Systems Inc* ***(G-20308)***
Youngstown Country Club 330 759-1040
1402 Country Club Dr Youngstown (44505) ***(G-20430)***
Youngstown Developmental Ctr, Columbus *Also called Develpmntal Dsblties Ohio Dept* ***(G-7512)***
Youngstown Health Center, Youngstown *Also called Planned Prenthood Greater Ohio* ***(G-20322)***
Youngstown Hearing Speech Ctr (PA) 330 726-8391
299 Edwards St Youngstown (44502) ***(G-20431)***
Youngstown Lithographing Co, Youngstown *Also called Youngstown ARC Engraving Co* ***(G-20423)***
Youngstown Neighborhood Dev 330 480-0423
820 Canfield Rd Youngstown (44511) ***(G-20432)***
Youngstown Ohio Otpatient Svcs 330 884-2020
6426 Market St Youngstown (44512) ***(G-20433)***
Youngstown Orthopaedic Assoc 330 726-1466
6470 Tippecanoe Rd Ste A Canfield (44406) ***(G-2217)***
Youngstown Plastic Tooling (PA) 330 782-7222
1209 Velma Ct Youngstown (44512) ***(G-20434)***
Youngstown Propane Inc (PA) 330 792-6571
810 N Meridian Rd Youngstown (44509) ***(G-20435)***
Youngstown V A Otptient Clinic, Youngstown *Also called Veterans Health Administration* ***(G-20403)***
Youngstown Water Dept, Youngstown *Also called City of Youngstown* ***(G-20144)***
Youngstown Window Cleaning Co 330 743-3880
1057 Trumbull Ave Ste G Girard (44420) ***(G-11431)***
Youngstown-Kenworth Inc (PA) 330 534-9761
7255 Hubbard Masury Rd Hubbard (44425) ***(G-12093)***
Youngstown-Warren Reg Chamber (PA) 330 744-2131
11 Central Sq Ste 1600 Youngstown (44503) ***(G-20436)***
Youth Advocate Services 614 258-9927
825 Grandview Ave Columbus (43215) ***(G-9022)***
Youth Development Center, Cincinnati *Also called Lighthouse Youth Services Inc* ***(G-3980)***
Youth Mntrng & At Rsk Intrvntn 216 324-2451
2092 Washington Dr Richmond Heights (44143) ***(G-16543)***
Youth Opportunities Unlimited 216 566-5445
1361 Euclid Ave Cleveland (44115) ***(G-6777)***
Youth Partial Hospitalization, Dayton *Also called South Community Inc* ***(G-9889)***
Youth Services, Cleveland *Also called County of Cuyahoga* ***(G-5428)***
Youth Services Ohio Department 419 875-6965
Township Rd 1 D U 469 Liberty Center (43532) ***(G-12716)***
YOUTH TO YOUTH, Columbus *Also called Compdrug* ***(G-7412)***
Yowell Transportation Svc Inc 937 294-5933
1840 Cardington Rd Moraine (45409) ***(G-14838)***
Yp, Youngstown *Also called Youngstown Propane Inc* ***(G-20435)***
Yrc Inc 513 874-9320
10074 Prncton Glendale Rd West Chester (45246) ***(G-19245)***
Yrc Inc 330 659-4151
5250 Brecksville Rd Richfield (44286) ***(G-16534)***
Yrc Inc 419 729-0631
4431 South Ave Toledo (43615) ***(G-18327)***
Yrc Inc 330 665-0274
1275 Oh Ave Copley (44321) ***(G-9070)***
Yrc Inc 614 878-9281
5400 Fisher Rd Columbus (43228) ***(G-9023)***
Yrc Inc 913 344-5174
1275 Oh Ave Copley (44321) ***(G-9071)***
Yrc Ubc Cargo Claim Dept, Copley *Also called Yrc Inc* ***(G-9071)***
Yrs Inc 330 665-3906
4100 Embassy Pkwy Akron (44333) ***(G-518)***
Ysd Industries Inc 330 792-6521
3710 Henricks Rd Youngstown (44515) ***(G-20437)***
Yund Car Care Center, Massillon *Also called Yund Inc* ***(G-13864)***
Yund Inc 330 837-9358
205 1st St Nw Massillon (44647) ***(G-13864)***
YWCA, Columbus *Also called Young Womens Christian Assn* ***(G-9021)***
YWCA, Toledo *Also called Young Womns Chrstn Assc Lima* ***(G-18326)***
YWCA, Youngstown *Also called Young Womens Christian Assn* ***(G-20422)***
YWCA, Van Wert *Also called Young Womens Christian* ***(G-18654)***
YWCA OF CANTON, Canton *Also called Young Womns Chrstn Assc Canton* ***(G-2593)***
YWCA of Cleveland, Cleveland *Also called Young Womens Christian Associ* ***(G-6776)***
YWCA of Dayton, Dayton *Also called Young Womens Christian* ***(G-10013)***
YWCA of Greater Cincinnati (PA) 513 241-7090
898 Walnut St Fl 1 Cincinnati (45202) ***(G-4870)***
YWCA of Hamilton 513 856-9800
244 Dayton St Hamilton (45011) ***(G-11785)***
YWCA Shelter & Housing Network 937 222-6333
141 W 3rd St Dayton (45402) ***(G-10014)***
Z A F Inc 216 291-1234
2165 S Green Rd Cleveland (44121) ***(G-6778)***
Z L B, Cleveland *Also called Csl Plasma Inc* ***(G-5443)***
Z Produce Co Inc 614 224-4373
720 Harmon Ave Columbus (43223) ***(G-9024)***
Z Snow Removal Inc 513 683-7719
8177 S State Route 48 Maineville (45039) ***(G-13248)***
Z Wireless, Hartville *Also called Aka Wireless Inc* ***(G-11814)***
Z-Bus, Zanesville *Also called Southeast Area Transit* ***(G-20534)***
Zack Pack, Monroe *Also called Hcg Inc* ***(G-14697)***
Zak Enterprises Ltd (PA) 216 261-9700
26250 Euclid Ave Ste 810 Euclid (44132) ***(G-10781)***

ALPHABETIC SECTION Zvn Properties Inc

Zamarelli William Relators, Warren *Also called William Zamarelli Realtors* **(G-18927)**
Zandex Inc....740 695-3281
100 Reservoir Rd Ofc 2 Saint Clairsville (43950) **(G-16662)**
Zandex Inc....740 676-8381
60583 State Route 7 Shadyside (43947) **(G-16854)**
Zandex Inc (PA)....740 454-1400
1122 Taylor St Zanesville (43701) **(G-20546)**
Zandex Inc....740 452-2087
1126 Adair Ave Zanesville (43701) **(G-20547)**
Zandex Inc....740 454-9769
1856 Adams Ln Zanesville (43701) **(G-20548)**
Zandex Inc....740 695-7233
100 Reservoir Rd Ofc 1 Saint Clairsville (43950) **(G-16663)**
Zandex Inc....740 967-1111
267 N Main St Johnstown (43031) **(G-12344)**
Zandex Inc....740 454-6823
1136 Adair Ave Zanesville (43701) **(G-20549)**
Zandex Inc....740 872-0809
1280 Friendship Dr New Concord (43762) **(G-15040)**
Zandex Health Care, Zanesville *Also called Zandex Inc* **(G-20546)**
Zandex Health Care Corporation....740 452-4636
1136 Adair Ave Zanesville (43701) **(G-20550)**
Zandex Health Care Corporation....740 454-9769
1856 Adams Ln Zanesville (43701) **(G-20551)**
Zandex Health Care Corporation....740 695-7233
100 Reservoir Rd Saint Clairsville (43950) **(G-16664)**
Zandex Health Care Corporation (HQ)....740 454-1400
1122 Taylor St Zanesville (43701) **(G-20552)**
Zandex Health Care Corporation....740 454-9747
1020 Taylor St Zanesville (43701) **(G-20553)**
Zandex Health Care Corporation....740 454-1400
267 N Main St Johnstown (43031) **(G-12345)**
Zandex Health Care Corporation....740 454-1400
1280 Friendship Dr New Concord (43762) **(G-15041)**
Zaner-Bloser Inc (HQ)....614 486-0221
1400 Goodale Blvd Ste 200 Columbus (43212) **(G-9025)**
Zanesville, Zanesville *Also called Cambridge Counseling Center* **(G-20454)**
Zanesville Bulk, Zanesville *Also called Englefield Inc* **(G-20475)**
Zanesville Chevrolet Cadillac....740 452-3611
3657 Maple Ave Zanesville (43701) **(G-20554)**
Zanesville Country Club....740 452-2726
1300 Country Club Dr Zanesville (43701) **(G-20555)**
Zanesville Dialysis, Zanesville *Also called Dva Renal Healthcare Inc* **(G-20471)**
Zanesville Metro Hsing Auth (PA)....740 454-9714
407 Pershing Rd Zanesville (43701) **(G-20556)**
Zanesville NH LLC....740 452-4351
4200 Harrington Dr Zanesville (43701) **(G-20557)**
Zanesville Surgery Center LLC....740 453-5713
2907 Bell St Zanesville (43701) **(G-20558)**
Zanesville Welfare Organizatio....740 450-6060
3610 West Pike Zanesville (43701) **(G-20559)**
Zanesvlle Hlth Rhblitation Ctr, Zanesville *Also called Zanesville NH LLC* **(G-20557)**
Zanesvlle Welfre Orgnztn/Goodw (PA)....740 450-6060
3610 West Pike Zanesville (43701) **(G-20560)**
Zarcal Zanesville LLC....216 226-2132
14600 Detroit Ave # 1500 Lakewood (44107) **(G-12503)**
Zaremba Group Incorporated....216 221-6600
14600 Detroit Ave # 1500 Cleveland (44107) **(G-6779)**
Zaremba Group LLC....216 221-6600
14600 Detroit Ave Lakewood (44107) **(G-12504)**
Zaremba LLC....216 221-6600
14600 Detroit Ave # 1500 Cleveland (44107) **(G-6780)**
Zaremba Zanesville LLC....216 221-6600
14600 Detroit Ave # 1500 Lakewood (44107) **(G-12505)**
Zashin & Rich Co LPA (PA)....216 696-4441
950 Main Ave Fl 4 Cleveland (44113) **(G-6781)**
Zatkoff Seals & Packings, Twinsburg *Also called Roger Zatkoff Company* **(G-18462)**
Zavarella Brothers Cnstr Co....440 232-2243
5381 Erie St Ste B Cleveland (44146) **(G-6782)**
Zebec of North America Inc....513 829-5533
210 Donald Dr Fairfield (45014) **(G-10923)**
Zebo Productions....937 339-0397
1875 Barnhart Rd Troy (45373) **(G-18388)**
Zeiger Tigges & Little LLP....614 365-9900
41 S High St Ste 3500 Columbus (43215) **(G-9026)**
Zeiter Leasing, Norwalk *Also called Zeiter Trucking Inc* **(G-15597)**
Zeiter Trucking Inc....419 668-2229
2590 State Route 18 Norwalk (44857) **(G-15597)**
Zekelman Industries Inc....740 432-2146
9208 Jeffrey Dr Cambridge (43725) **(G-2135)**
Zemba Bros Inc....740 452-1880
3401 East Pike Zanesville (43701) **(G-20561)**
Zender Electric....419 436-1538
966 Springville Ave Fostoria (44830) **(G-11143)**
Zenith Systems LLC (PA)....216 587-9510
5055 Corbin Dr Cleveland (44128) **(G-6783)**
Zenith Systems LLC....216 406-7916
9627 Price St Ne Atwater (44201) **(G-823)**
Zep Inc....440 239-1580
6777 Engle Rd Ste A Cleveland (44130) **(G-6784)**
Zepf Center....419 255-4050
905 Nebraska Ave Toledo (43607) **(G-18328)**
Zepf Center (PA)....419 841-7701
6605 W Central Ave # 100 Toledo (43617) **(G-18329)**
Zepf Center....419 213-5627
6605 W Central Ave # 100 Toledo (43617) **(G-18330)**
Zepf Center....419 255-4050
525 Hamilton St Ste 101a Toledo (43604) **(G-18331)**
Zepf Center....419 213-5627
1301 Monroe St Toledo (43604) **(G-18332)**
Zepf Housing Corp One Inc....419 531-0019
5310 Hill Ave Toledo (43615) **(G-18333)**
Zicka Development, Cincinnati *Also called Zicka Walker Builders Ltd* **(G-4871)**
Zicka Walker Builders Ltd....513 247-3500
7861 E Kemper Rd Cincinnati (45249) **(G-4871)**
Zide Screen Printing, Marietta *Also called Zide Sport Shop of Ohio Inc* **(G-13521)**
Zide Sport Shop of Ohio Inc (PA)....740 373-6446
253 2nd St Marietta (45750) **(G-13521)**
Ziebart, Fairborn *Also called Dave Marshall Inc* **(G-10790)**
Ziegler Bolt & Nut House, Canton *Also called Ziegler Bolt & Parts Co* **(G-2595)**
Ziegler Bolt & Parts Co (PA)....330 478-2542
4848 Corporate St Sw Canton (44706) **(G-2595)**
Ziegler Tire and Supply Co (PA)....330 353-1499
4150 Millennium Blvd Se Massillon (44646) **(G-13865)**
Ziegler Tire and Supply Co....513 539-7574
1100 Reed Dr Monroe (45050) **(G-14719)**
Ziggler Heating, Ashtabula *Also called Volpone Enterprises Inc* **(G-767)**
Ziks Family Pharmacy 100....937 225-9350
1130 W 3rd St Dayton (45402) **(G-10015)**
Zin Technologies Inc (PA)....440 625-2200
6745 Engle Rd Ste 105 Middleburg Heights (44130) **(G-14392)**
Zincks Inn (PA)....330 893-6600
4703 State Rt 39 Berlin (44610) **(G-1479)**
Zink Calls....419 732-6171
30 Park Dr Port Clinton (43452) **(G-16259)**
Zink Commercial, Westerville *Also called Zink Foodservice Group* **(G-19359)**
Zink Foodservice Group....800 492-7400
420 Westdale Ave Westerville (43082) **(G-19359)**
Zinner & Co....216 831-0733
3201 Entp Pkwy Ste 410 Beachwood (44122) **(G-1138)**
Zinni Golf Co Inc....330 533-7155
9866 Lisbon Rd Canfield (44406) **(G-2218)**
Zinz Cnstr & Restoration....330 332-7939
6487 Mahoning Ave Youngstown (44515) **(G-20438)**
Zion Christian School....330 792-4066
3300 Canfield Rd Youngstown (44511) **(G-20439)**
Zip Center, The-Division, Marietta *Also called Richardson Printing Corp* **(G-13495)**
Zipline Logistics LLC....888 469-4754
2300 W 5th Ave Columbus (43215) **(G-9027)**
Zipscene LLC....513 201-5174
615 Main St Fl 5 Cincinnati (45202) **(G-4872)**
Zoff Heating & Plumbing, Akron *Also called A To Zoff Co Inc* **(G-12)**
Zone Transportation Co....440 324-3544
41670 Schadden Rd Elyria (44035) **(G-10695)**
Zoo Cincinnati....513 961-0041
3400 Vine St Cincinnati (45220) **(G-4873)**
Zoological Society Cincinnati....513 281-4700
3400 Vine St Cincinnati (45220) **(G-4874)**
Zucker Building Company....216 861-7114
5915 Landerbrook Dr # 300 Cleveland (44124) **(G-6785)**
Zurich American Insurance Co....216 328-9400
5005 Rockside Rd Ste 200 Independence (44131) **(G-12279)**
Zusman Community Hospice....614 559-0350
1151 College Ave Columbus (43209) **(G-9028)**
Zvn Properties Inc....330 854-5890
957 Cherry St E Canal Fulton (44614) **(G-2149)**

ALPHABETIC

SERVICES INDEX

• Service categories are listed in alphabetical order.

A

ABORTION CLINIC
ABRASIVES
ACADEMIC TUTORING SVCS
ACADEMY
ACCELERATORS: Linear
ACCIDENT & HEALTH INSURANCE CARRIERS
ACCIDENT INSURANCE CARRIERS
ACCOUNTING SVCS, NEC
ACCOUNTING SVCS: Certified Public
ACUPUNCTURISTS' OFFICES
ADDRESSING SVCS
ADHESIVES
ADHESIVES & SEALANTS
ADJUSTMENT BUREAU, EXC INSURANCE
ADOPTION SVCS
ADULT DAYCARE CENTERS
ADULT EDUCATION SCHOOLS, PUBLIC
ADVERTISING AGENCIES
ADVERTISING AGENCIES: Consultants
ADVERTISING COPY WRITING SVCS
ADVERTISING MATERIAL DISTRIBUTION
ADVERTISING REPRESENTATIVES: Electronic Media
ADVERTISING REPRESENTATIVES: Media
ADVERTISING REPRESENTATIVES: Newspaper
ADVERTISING REPRESENTATIVES: Printed Media
ADVERTISING REPRESENTATIVES: Radio
ADVERTISING REPRESENTATIVES: Television & Radio Time Sales
ADVERTISING SPECIALTIES, WHOLESALE
ADVERTISING SVCS, NEC
ADVERTISING SVCS: Billboards
ADVERTISING SVCS: Coupon Distribution
ADVERTISING SVCS: Direct Mail
ADVERTISING SVCS: Display
ADVERTISING SVCS: Outdoor
ADVERTISING SVCS: Sample Distribution
ADVERTISING SVCS: Transit
ADVERTISING: Aerial
ADVOCACY GROUP
AGENTS, BROKERS & BUREAUS: Personal Service
AGRICULTURAL EQPT: BARN, SILO, POULTRY, DAIRY/LIVESTOCK MACH
AGRICULTURAL EQPT: Fertilizing Machinery
AGRICULTURAL MACHINERY & EQPT: Wholesalers
AGRICULTURAL PROG REG OFFICES, GOVT: Agriculture Fair Board
AID TO FAMILIES WITH DEPENDENT CHILDREN OR AFDC
AIR CONDITIONING & VENTILATION EQPT & SPLYS: Wholesales
AIR CONDITIONING EQPT
AIR CONDITIONING EQPT, WHOLE HOUSE: Wholesalers
AIR CONDITIONING REPAIR SVCS
AIR DUCT CLEANING SVCS
AIR POLLUTION CONTROL EQPT & SPLYS WHOLESALERS
AIR POLLUTION MEASURING SVCS
AIR PURIFICATION EQPT
AIR TRAFFIC CONTROL SVCS
AIR, WATER & SOLID WASTE PROGRAMS ADMINISTRATION SVCS
AIR-CONDITIONING SPLY SVCS
AIRCRAFT & HEAVY EQPT REPAIR SVCS
AIRCRAFT CLEANING & JANITORIAL SVCS
AIRCRAFT DEALERS
AIRCRAFT ELECTRICAL EQPT REPAIR SVCS
AIRCRAFT ENGINES & PARTS
AIRCRAFT EQPT & SPLYS WHOLESALERS
AIRCRAFT FLIGHT INSTRUMENTS
AIRCRAFT FUELING SVCS
AIRCRAFT HANGAR OPERATION SVCS
AIRCRAFT MAINTENANCE & REPAIR SVCS
AIRCRAFT PARTS & EQPT, NEC
AIRCRAFT PARTS WHOLESALERS
AIRCRAFT SERVICING & REPAIRING
AIRLINE TRAINING
AIRPORT
AIRPORT TERMINAL SVCS
AIRPORTS & FLYING FIELDS
AIRPORTS, FLYING FIELDS & SVCS
ALARM SYSTEMS WHOLESALERS
ALCOHOL TREATMENT CLINIC, OUTPATIENT
ALCOHOLISM COUNSELING, NONTREATMENT
ALKALIES & CHLORINE
ALLOYS: Additive, Exc Copper Or Made In Blast Furnaces
ALUMINUM
ALUMINUM: Coil & Sheet
ALUMINUM: Slabs, Primary
AMBULANCE SVCS
AMBULANCE SVCS: Air
AMBULATORY SURGICAL CENTERS
AMUSEMENT & REC SVCS: Attractions, Concessions & Rides
AMUSEMENT & REC SVCS: Baseball Club, Exc Pro & Semi-Pro
AMUSEMENT & REC SVCS: Flying Field, Maintained By Av Clubs
AMUSEMENT & RECREATION SVCS, NEC
AMUSEMENT & RECREATION SVCS: Agricultural Fair
AMUSEMENT & RECREATION SVCS: Amusement Arcades
AMUSEMENT & RECREATION SVCS: Amusement Mach Rental, Coin-Op
AMUSEMENT & RECREATION SVCS: Amusement Ride
AMUSEMENT & RECREATION SVCS: Arcades
AMUSEMENT & RECREATION SVCS: Boating Club, Membership
AMUSEMENT & RECREATION SVCS: Bowling Instruction
AMUSEMENT & RECREATION SVCS: Carnival Operation
AMUSEMENT & RECREATION SVCS: Concession Operator
AMUSEMENT & RECREATION SVCS: Exhibition Operation
AMUSEMENT & RECREATION SVCS: Exposition Operation
AMUSEMENT & RECREATION SVCS: Festival Operation
AMUSEMENT & RECREATION SVCS: Fishing Lakes & Piers, Op
AMUSEMENT & RECREATION SVCS: Gambling & Lottery Svcs
AMUSEMENT & RECREATION SVCS: Gambling, Coin Machines
AMUSEMENT & RECREATION SVCS: Golf Club, Membership
AMUSEMENT & RECREATION SVCS: Golf Professionals
AMUSEMENT & RECREATION SVCS: Golf Svcs & Professionals
AMUSEMENT & RECREATION SVCS: Gun & Hunting Clubs
AMUSEMENT & RECREATION SVCS: Gun Club, Membership
AMUSEMENT & RECREATION SVCS: Hockey Club, Exc Pro/Semi-Pro
AMUSEMENT & RECREATION SVCS: Hunting Club, Membership
AMUSEMENT & RECREATION SVCS: Ice Skating Rink
AMUSEMENT & RECREATION SVCS: Indoor Court Clubs
AMUSEMENT & RECREATION SVCS: Instruction Schools, Camps
AMUSEMENT & RECREATION SVCS: Kiddie Park
AMUSEMENT & RECREATION SVCS: Lottery Tickets, Sales
AMUSEMENT & RECREATION SVCS: Outdoor Field Clubs
AMUSEMENT & RECREATION SVCS: Picnic Ground Operation
AMUSEMENT & RECREATION SVCS: Pool Parlor
AMUSEMENT & RECREATION SVCS: Racquetball Club, Membership
AMUSEMENT & RECREATION SVCS: Recreation Center
AMUSEMENT & RECREATION SVCS: Recreation SVCS
AMUSEMENT & RECREATION SVCS: Soccer Club, Exc Pro/Semi-Pro
AMUSEMENT & RECREATION SVCS: Swimming Club, Membership
AMUSEMENT & RECREATION SVCS: Swimming Pool, Non-Membership
AMUSEMENT & RECREATION SVCS: Tennis & Professionals
AMUSEMENT & RECREATION SVCS: Tennis Club, Membership
AMUSEMENT & RECREATION SVCS: Theme Park
AMUSEMENT & RECREATION SVCS: Tourist Attraction, Commercial
AMUSEMENT & RECREATION SVCS: Trampoline Operation
AMUSEMENT & RECREATION SVCS: Video Game Arcades
AMUSEMENT ARCADES
AMUSEMENT PARK DEVICES & RIDES: Carnival Mach & Eqpt, NEC
AMUSEMENT PARKS
AMUSEMENT/REC SVCS: Ticket Sales, Sporting Events, Contract
ANATOMICAL SPECIMENS & RESEARCH MATERIAL, WHOLESALE
ANIMAL & REPTILE EXHIBIT
ANIMAL FEED & SUPPLEMENTS: Livestock & Poultry
ANIMAL FEED: Wholesalers
ANIMAL FOOD & SUPPLEMENTS: Bird Food, Prepared
ANIMAL FOOD & SUPPLEMENTS: Dog & Cat
ANIMAL FOOD & SUPPLEMENTS: Livestock
ANIMAL FOOD & SUPPLEMENTS: Poultry
ANTENNA REPAIR & INSTALLATION SVCS
ANTENNAS: Radar Or Communications
ANTIPOVERTY BOARD
APARTMENT LOCATING SVCS
APPAREL DESIGNERS: Commercial
APPLIANCES, HOUSEHOLD OR COIN OPERATED: Laundry Dryers
APPLIANCES, HOUSEHOLD: Kitchen, Major, Exc Refrigs & Stoves
APPLIANCES: Household, Refrigerators & Freezers
APPLIANCES: Major, Cooking
APPLIANCES: Small, Electric
APPLICATIONS SOFTWARE PROGRAMMING
APPRAISAL SVCS, EXC REAL ESTATE
ARBORETUM
ARCHEOLOGICAL EXPEDITIONS
ARCHITECTURAL SVCS
ARCHITECTURAL SVCS: Engineering
ARCHITECTURAL SVCS: Engineering
ARCHITECTURAL SVCS: House Designer
ARMATURE REPAIRING & REWINDING SVC
ARMORED CAR SVCS
ART & ORNAMENTAL WARE: Pottery
ART DESIGN SVCS
ART GALLERIES
ART GOODS & SPLYS WHOLESALERS
ART GOODS, WHOLESALE
ART RELATED SVCS
ART SCHOOL, EXC COMMERCIAL
ART SPLY STORES
ARTS & CRAFTS SCHOOL
ARTS OR SCIENCES CENTER
ASPHALT & ASPHALT PRDTS
ASPHALT COATINGS & SEALERS
ASPHALT MIXTURES WHOLESALERS
ASSOCIATION FOR THE HANDICAPPED
ASSOCIATIONS: Alumni
ASSOCIATIONS: Bar
ASSOCIATIONS: Business
ASSOCIATIONS: Engineering
ASSOCIATIONS: Fraternal
ASSOCIATIONS: Homeowners
ASSOCIATIONS: Parent Teacher
ASSOCIATIONS: Real Estate Management
ASSOCIATIONS: Trade
ATHLETIC CLUB & GYMNASIUMS, MEMBERSHIP
ATHLETIC EQPT INSPECTION SVCS
ATHLETIC ORGANIZATION
ATOMIZERS
AUCTION SVCS: Livestock
AUCTION SVCS: Motor Vehicle
AUCTIONEERS: Fee Basis
AUDIO & VIDEO EQPT, EXC COMMERCIAL
AUDIO-VISUAL PROGRAM PRODUCTION SVCS
AUDITING SVCS
AUTO & HOME SUPPLY STORES: Auto & Truck Eqpt & Parts
AUTO & HOME SUPPLY STORES: Automotive Access
AUTO & HOME SUPPLY STORES: Automotive parts

SERVICES INDEX

AUTO & HOME SUPPLY STORES: Batteries, Automotive & Truck
AUTO & HOME SUPPLY STORES: Truck Eqpt & Parts
AUTO SPLYS & PARTS, NEW, WHSLE: Exhaust Sys, Mufflers, Etc
AUTOMATED TELLER MACHINE NETWORK
AUTOMATED TELLER MACHINE OR ATM REPAIR SVCS
AUTOMATIC REGULATING CONTROL: Building Svcs Monitoring, Auto
AUTOMOBILE FINANCE LEASING
AUTOMOBILE RECOVERY SVCS
AUTOMOBILE STORAGE GARAGE
AUTOMOBILES & OTHER MOTOR VEHICLES WHOLESALERS
AUTOMOBILES: Wholesalers
AUTOMOTIVE & TRUCK GENERAL REPAIR SVC
AUTOMOTIVE BATTERIES WHOLESALERS
AUTOMOTIVE BODY SHOP
AUTOMOTIVE BODY, PAINT & INTERIOR REPAIR & MAINTENANCE SVC
AUTOMOTIVE BRAKE REPAIR SHOPS
AUTOMOTIVE COLLISION SHOPS
AUTOMOTIVE CUSTOMIZING SVCS, NONFACTORY BASIS
AUTOMOTIVE DEALERS, NEC
AUTOMOTIVE EMISSIONS TESTING SVCS
AUTOMOTIVE GLASS REPLACEMENT SHOPS
AUTOMOTIVE LETTERING & PAINTING SVCS
AUTOMOTIVE PAINT SHOP
AUTOMOTIVE PARTS, ACCESS & SPLYS
AUTOMOTIVE PRDTS: Rubber
AUTOMOTIVE RADIATOR REPAIR SHOPS
AUTOMOTIVE REPAIR SHOPS: Brake Repair
AUTOMOTIVE REPAIR SHOPS: Diesel Engine Repair
AUTOMOTIVE REPAIR SHOPS: Electrical Svcs
AUTOMOTIVE REPAIR SHOPS: Engine Repair, Exc Diesel
AUTOMOTIVE REPAIR SHOPS: Frame & Front End Repair Svcs
AUTOMOTIVE REPAIR SHOPS: Frame Repair Shops
AUTOMOTIVE REPAIR SHOPS: Machine Shop
AUTOMOTIVE REPAIR SHOPS: Muffler Shop, Sale/Rpr/Installation
AUTOMOTIVE REPAIR SHOPS: Rebuilding & Retreading Tires
AUTOMOTIVE REPAIR SHOPS: Tire Recapping
AUTOMOTIVE REPAIR SHOPS: Trailer Repair
AUTOMOTIVE REPAIR SHOPS: Truck Engine Repair, Exc Indl
AUTOMOTIVE REPAIR SHOPS: Turbocharger & Blower Repair
AUTOMOTIVE REPAIR SHOPS: Wheel Alignment
AUTOMOTIVE REPAIR SVC
AUTOMOTIVE REPAIR SVCS, MISCELLANEOUS
AUTOMOTIVE RUSTPROOFING & UNDERCOATING SHOPS
AUTOMOTIVE SPLYS & PARTS, NEW, WHOL: Auto Servicing Eqpt
AUTOMOTIVE SPLYS & PARTS, NEW, WHOL: Testing Eqpt, Electric
AUTOMOTIVE SPLYS & PARTS, NEW, WHOLESALE: Bumpers
AUTOMOTIVE SPLYS & PARTS, NEW, WHOLESALE: Engines/Eng Parts
AUTOMOTIVE SPLYS & PARTS, NEW, WHOLESALE: Seat Covers
AUTOMOTIVE SPLYS & PARTS, NEW, WHOLESALE: Splys
AUTOMOTIVE SPLYS & PARTS, NEW, WHOLESALE: Tools & Eqpt
AUTOMOTIVE SPLYS & PARTS, NEW, WHOLESALE: Trailer Parts
AUTOMOTIVE SPLYS & PARTS, NEW, WHOLESALE: Wheels
AUTOMOTIVE SPLYS & PARTS, USED, WHOLESALE
AUTOMOTIVE SPLYS & PARTS, USED, WHOLESALE: Dry Cell Batt
AUTOMOTIVE SPLYS & PARTS, WHOLESALE, NEC
AUTOMOTIVE SPLYS, USED, WHOLESALE & RETAIL
AUTOMOTIVE SPLYS/PART, NEW, WHOL: Spring, Shock Absorb/Strut
AUTOMOTIVE SPLYS/PARTS, NEW, WHOL: Body Rpr/Paint Shop Splys
AUTOMOTIVE SVCS, EXC REPAIR & CARWASHES: Customizing
AUTOMOTIVE SVCS, EXC REPAIR & CARWASHES: Insp & Diagnostic
AUTOMOTIVE SVCS, EXC REPAIR & CARWASHES: Lubrication
AUTOMOTIVE SVCS, EXC REPAIR & CARWASHES: Maintenance
AUTOMOTIVE SVCS, EXC REPAIR & CARWASHES: Road Svc
AUTOMOTIVE SVCS, EXC REPAIR: Carwash, Automatic
AUTOMOTIVE SVCS, EXC REPAIR: Carwash, Self-Service
AUTOMOTIVE SVCS, EXC REPAIR: Truck Wash
AUTOMOTIVE SVCS, EXC REPAIR: Washing & Polishing
AUTOMOTIVE SVCS, EXC RPR/CARWASHES: High Perf Auto Rpr/Svc
AUTOMOTIVE TOWING & WRECKING SVC
AUTOMOTIVE TOWING SVCS
AUTOMOTIVE TRANSMISSION REPAIR SVC
AUTOMOTIVE UPHOLSTERY SHOPS
AUTOMOTIVE WELDING SVCS
AUTOMOTIVE: Seat Frames, Metal
AVIATION PROPELLER & BLADE REPAIR SVCS
AVIATION SCHOOL

B

BABYSITTING BUREAU
BADGES, WHOLESALE
BAGS: Plastic
BAGS: Plastic, Made From Purchased Materials
BAGS: Shopping, Made From Purchased Materials
BAIL BONDING SVCS
BAKERIES, COMMERCIAL: On Premises Baking Only
BAKERIES: On Premises Baking & Consumption
BAKERY PRDTS: Cookies & crackers
BAKERY PRDTS: Wholesalers
BAKERY: Wholesale Or Wholesale & Retail Combined
BAKING PAN GLAZING & CLEANING SVCS
BALLET PRODUCTION SVCS
BANKS: Commercial, NEC
BANKS: Federal Reserve
BANKS: Federal Reserve Branches
BANKS: Mortgage & Loan
BANKS: National Commercial
BANKS: State Commercial
BANQUET HALL FACILITIES
BAR
BARBER SHOPS
BARGES BUILDING & REPAIR
BARS: Concrete Reinforcing, Fabricated Steel
BASKETS, WHOLESALE
BATTERY CHARGERS
BATTERY REPAIR & SVCS
BEADS, WHOLESALE
BEARINGS & PARTS Ball
BEAUTY & BARBER SHOP EQPT
BEAUTY CULTURE SCHOOL
BEAUTY SALONS
BED & BREAKFAST INNS
BEDDING & BEDSPRINGS STORES
BEDDING, BEDSPREADS, BLANKETS & SHEETS: Comforters & Quilts
BEER & ALE WHOLESALERS
BEER & ALE, WHOLESALE: Beer & Other Fermented Malt Liquors
BEER, WINE & LIQUOR STORES: Beer, Packaged
BEER, WINE & LIQUOR STORES: Wine
BELTING: Plastic
BELTS: Seat, Automotive & Aircraft
BEVERAGE STORES
BEVERAGES, ALCOHOLIC: Near Beer
BEVERAGES, ALCOHOLIC: Wines
BEVERAGES, BEER & ALE, WHOLESALE: Ale
BEVERAGES, NONALCOHOLIC: Bottled & canned soft drinks
BEVERAGES, NONALCOHOLIC: Carbonated
BEVERAGES, NONALCOHOLIC: Carbonated, Canned & Bottled, Etc
BEVERAGES, NONALCOHOLIC: Flavoring extracts & syrups, nec
BEVERAGES, NONALCOHOLIC: Soft Drinks, Canned & Bottled, Etc
BEVERAGES, WINE & DISTILLED ALCOHOLIC, WHOLESALE: Wine
BEVERAGES, WINE/DISTILLED ALCOH, WHOL: Brandy/Brandy Spirits
BIBLE CAMPS
BICYCLE REPAIR SHOP
BICYCLE SHOPS
BICYCLES, PARTS & ACCESS
BILLIARD & POOL PARLORS
BILLIARD EQPT & SPLYS WHOLESALERS
BILLIARD TABLE REPAIR SVCS
BILLING & BOOKKEEPING SVCS
BINDING SVC: Books & Manuals
BINDING SVC: Pamphlets
BINGO HALL
BIOFEEDBACK CENTERS
BIOLOGICAL PRDTS: Exc Diagnostic
BIRTH CONTROL CLINIC
BLASTING SVC: Sand, Metal Parts
BLOCK & BRICK: Sand Lime
BLOCKS: Standard, Concrete Or Cinder
BLOOD BANK
BLOOD DONOR STATIONS
BLOOD RELATED HEALTH SVCS
BLOWERS & FANS
BLUEPRINTING SVCS
BOARDING SCHOOL
BOAT BUILDING & REPAIR
BOAT DEALERS
BOAT DEALERS: Motor
BOAT REPAIR SVCS
BOAT YARD: Boat yards, storage & incidental repair
BODIES: Truck & Bus
BOILER & HEATING REPAIR SVCS
BOILER REPAIR SHOP
BOND & MORTGAGE COMPANIES
BOOK STORES
BOOK STORES: Religious
BOOKS, WHOLESALE
BOTANICAL GARDENS
BOTTLED GAS DEALERS: Propane
BOTTLED WATER DELIVERY
BOTTLES: Plastic
BOUTIQUE STORES
BOWLING CENTERS
BOWLING EQPT & SPLY STORES
BOWLING EQPT & SPLYS
BOXES & SHOOK: Nailed Wood
BOXES: Corrugated
BOXES: Wooden
BOYS' CAMPS
BOYS' TOWNS
BRAKES & BRAKE PARTS
BRAZING SVCS
BRICK, STONE & RELATED PRDTS WHOLESALERS
BRIDAL SHOPS
BROACHING MACHINES
BROADCASTING & COMMS EQPT: Antennas, Transmitting/Comms
BROADCASTING STATIONS, RADIO: Educational
BROADCASTING STATIONS, RADIO: Exc Music Format
BROADCASTING STATIONS, RADIO: Music Format
BROADCASTING STATIONS, RADIO: Sports
BROADCASTING STATIONS, TELEVISION: Translator Station
BROKERS & DEALERS: Mortgages, Buying & Selling
BROKERS & DEALERS: Securities
BROKERS & DEALERS: Security
BROKERS & DEALERS: Stock
BROKERS' SVCS
BROKERS, MARINE TRANSPORTATION
BROKERS: Business
BROKERS: Food
BROKERS: Loan
BROKERS: Mortgage, Arranging For Loans
BROKERS: Printing
BROKERS: Security
BRONZING SVCS: Baby Shoes
BROOMS & BRUSHES
BROOMS & BRUSHES: Household Or Indl
BUCKETS: Plastic
BUILDING & OFFICE CLEANING SVCS
BUILDING & STRUCTURAL WOOD MEMBERS
BUILDING CLEANING & MAINTENANCE SVCS
BUILDING CLEANING SVCS
BUILDING COMPONENT CLEANING SVCS
BUILDING COMPONENTS: Structural Steel
BUILDING INSPECTION SVCS
BUILDING MAINTENANCE SVCS, EXC REPAIRS
BUILDING PRDTS & MATERIALS DEALERS
BUILDING SCALES MODELS
BUILDINGS & COMPONENTS: Prefabricated Metal

SERVICES INDEX

BUILDINGS, PREFABRICATED: Wholesalers
BUILDINGS: Farm & Utility
BUILDINGS: Prefabricated, Metal
BUILDINGS: Prefabricated, Wood
BURGLAR ALARM MAINTENANCE & MONITORING SVCS
BURIAL VAULTS: Concrete Or Precast Terrazzo
BURLAP WHOLESALERS
BUS BARS: Electrical
BUS CHARTER SVC: Local
BUS CHARTER SVC: Long-Distance
BUS TERMINALS & SVC FACILITIES
BUSES: Wholesalers
BUSHINGS & BEARINGS
BUSINESS & SECRETARIAL SCHOOLS
BUSINESS ACTIVITIES: Non-Commercial Site
BUSINESS FORMS WHOLESALERS
BUSINESS FORMS: Printed, Manifold
BUSINESS MACHINE REPAIR, ELECTRIC
BUSINESS SUPPORT SVCS
BUSINESS TRAINING SVCS
BUTTER WHOLESALERS

C

CABINETS: Entertainment
CABINETS: Entertainment Units, Household, Wood
CABINETS: Kitchen, Wood
CABINETS: Office, Wood
CABINETS: Show, Display, Etc, Wood, Exc Refrigerated
CABLE & OTHER PAY TELEVISION DISTRIBUTION
CABLE & PAY TELEVISION SVCS: Closed Circuit
CABLE & PAY TELEVISION SVCS: Direct Broadcast Satellite
CABLE & PAY TELEVISION SVCS: Multipoint Distribution Sys/MDS
CABLE & PAY TV SVCS: Satellite Master Antenna Sys/SMATV
CABLE TELEVISION
CABLE WIRING SETS: Battery, Internal Combustion Engines
CABLE: Noninsulated
CABS, FOR HIRE: Horse Drawn
CAFES
CAFETERIAS
CALENDARS, WHOLESALE
CALIBRATING SVCS, NEC
CAMERA & PHOTOGRAPHIC SPLYS STORES
CAMPGROUNDS
CAMPSITES
CANDLES
CANDLES: Wholesalers
CANDY & CONFECTIONS: Chocolate Covered Dates
CANDY & CONFECTIONS: Cough Drops, Exc Pharmaceutical Preps
CANDY MAKING GOODS & SPLYS, WHOLESALE
CANDY, NUT & CONFECTIONERY STORE: Popcorn, Incl Caramel Corn
CANDY, NUT & CONFECTIONERY STORES: Candy
CANDY, NUT & CONFECTIONERY STORES: Produced For Direct Sale
CANDY: Chocolate From Cacao Beans
CANNED SPECIALTIES
CANS: Fiber
CANVAS PRDTS
CANVAS PRDTS: Convertible Tops, Car/Boat, Fm Purchased Mtrl
CANVAS PRDTS: Shades, Made From Purchased Materials
CAR LOADING SVCS
CAR WASH EQPT
CAR WASHES
CARBON & GRAPHITE PRDTS, NEC
CARBON PAPER & INKED RIBBONS
CARDS: Beveled
CARNIVAL & AMUSEMENT PARK EQPT WHOLESALERS
CARPET & RUG CLEANING PLANTS
CARPET & UPHOLSTERY CLEANING SVCS
CARPET & UPHOLSTERY CLEANING SVCS: Carpet/Furniture, On Loc
CARPET & UPHOLSTERY CLEANING SVCS: On Customer Premises
CARTONS: Egg, Molded Pulp, Made From Purchased Materials
CASH REGISTERS WHOLESALERS
CASINO HOTELS & MOTELS
CASTINGS: Commercial Investment, Ferrous
CASTINGS: Die, Aluminum
CASTINGS: Die, Nonferrous
CASTINGS: Machinery, Aluminum

CASTINGS: Precision
CATALOG & MAIL-ORDER HOUSES
CATALOG SALES
CATAPULTS
CATERERS
CEMENT & CONCRETE RELATED PRDTS & EQPT: Bituminous
CEMENT ROCK: Crushed & Broken
CEMENT: Hydraulic
CEMETERIES
CEMETERIES: Real Estate Operation
CEMETERY ASSOCIATION
CEMETERY MEMORIAL DEALERS
CENTRAL RESERVE DEPOSITORY: Federal Home Loan Banks
CERAMIC FLOOR & WALL TILE WHOLESALERS
CHAINS: Power Transmission
CHAMBERS OF COMMERCE
CHARGE ACCOUNT SVCS
CHARTER FLYING SVC
CHASSIS: Motor Vehicle
CHECK CASHING SVCS
CHECK CLEARING SVCS
CHECK VALIDATION SVCS
CHEESE WHOLESALERS
CHEMICAL CLEANING SVCS
CHEMICAL PROCESSING MACHINERY & EQPT
CHEMICAL SPLYS FOR FOUNDRIES
CHEMICALS & ALLIED PRDTS WHOLESALERS, NEC
CHEMICALS & ALLIED PRDTS, WHOL: Chemicals, Swimming Pool/Spa
CHEMICALS & ALLIED PRDTS, WHOL: Food Additives/Preservatives
CHEMICALS & ALLIED PRDTS, WHOL: Gases, Compressed/Liquefied
CHEMICALS & ALLIED PRDTS, WHOLESALE: Alkalines & Chlorine
CHEMICALS & ALLIED PRDTS, WHOLESALE: Anti-Corrosion Prdts
CHEMICALS & ALLIED PRDTS, WHOLESALE: Caustic Soda
CHEMICALS & ALLIED PRDTS, WHOLESALE: Chemicals, Indl
CHEMICALS & ALLIED PRDTS, WHOLESALE: Chemicals, Indl & Heavy
CHEMICALS & ALLIED PRDTS, WHOLESALE: Compressed Gas
CHEMICALS & ALLIED PRDTS, WHOLESALE: Concrete Additives
CHEMICALS & ALLIED PRDTS, WHOLESALE: Detergent/Soap
CHEMICALS & ALLIED PRDTS, WHOLESALE: Detergents
CHEMICALS & ALLIED PRDTS, WHOLESALE: Dry Ice
CHEMICALS & ALLIED PRDTS, WHOLESALE: Essential Oils
CHEMICALS & ALLIED PRDTS, WHOLESALE: Glue
CHEMICALS & ALLIED PRDTS, WHOLESALE: Oxygen
CHEMICALS & ALLIED PRDTS, WHOLESALE: Plastics Film
CHEMICALS & ALLIED PRDTS, WHOLESALE: Plastics Materials, NEC
CHEMICALS & ALLIED PRDTS, WHOLESALE: Plastics Prdts, NEC
CHEMICALS & ALLIED PRDTS, WHOLESALE: Plastics Sheets & Rods
CHEMICALS & ALLIED PRDTS, WHOLESALE: Plastics, Basic Shapes
CHEMICALS & ALLIED PRDTS, WHOLESALE: Resins
CHEMICALS & ALLIED PRDTS, WHOLESALE: Resins, Plastics
CHEMICALS & ALLIED PRDTS, WHOLESALE: Rubber, Synthetic
CHEMICALS & ALLIED PRDTS, WHOLESALE: Salts & Polishes, Indl
CHEMICALS & ALLIED PRDTS, WHOLESALE: Sanitation Preparations
CHEMICALS & ALLIED PRDTS, WHOLESALE: Sealants
CHEMICALS & ALLIED PRDTS, WHOLESALE: Spec Clean/Sanitation
CHEMICALS & ALLIED PRDTS, WHOLESALE: Syn Resin, Rub/Plastic
CHEMICALS, AGRICULTURE: Wholesalers
CHEMICALS: Agricultural
CHEMICALS: Bleaching Powder, Lime Bleaching Compounds
CHEMICALS: High Purity, Refined From Technical Grade
CHEMICALS: Inorganic, NEC
CHEMICALS: Isotopes, Radioactive
CHEMICALS: NEC

CHEMICALS: Organic, NEC
CHICKEN SLAUGHTERING & PROCESSING
CHILD & YOUTH SVCS, NEC
CHILD DAY CARE SVCS
CHILD GUIDANCE SVCS
CHILD RESTRAINT SEATS, AUTOMOTIVE, WHOLESALE
CHILDBIRTH PREPARATION CLINIC
CHILDREN'S & INFANTS' CLOTHING STORES
CHILDREN'S AID SOCIETY
CHILDREN'S BOARDING HOME
CHILDREN'S DANCING SCHOOL
CHILDREN'S HOME
CHINAWARE WHOLESALERS
CHIROPRACTORS' OFFICES
CHOCOLATE, EXC CANDY FROM BEANS: Chips, Powder, Block, Syrup
CHURCHES
CIGARETTE STORES
CIRCUIT BOARD REPAIR SVCS
CLAIMS ADJUSTING SVCS
CLEANING & DESCALING SVC: Metal Prdts
CLEANING & DYEING PLANTS, EXC RUGS
CLEANING EQPT: Commercial
CLEANING EQPT: Floor Washing & Polishing, Commercial
CLEANING OR POLISHING PREPARATIONS, NEC
CLEANING PRDTS: Specialty
CLEANING SVCS
CLEANING SVCS: Industrial Or Commercial
CLEARINGHOUSE ASSOCIATIONS: Bank Or Check
CLOTHING & ACCESS, WOMEN, CHILD & INFANT, WHOL: Diapers
CLOTHING & ACCESS, WOMEN, CHILD & INFANT, WHSLE: Sportswear
CLOTHING & ACCESS, WOMEN, CHILDREN & INFANT, WHOL: Handbags
CLOTHING & ACCESS, WOMEN, CHILDREN & INFANT, WHOL: Uniforms
CLOTHING & ACCESS, WOMEN, CHILDREN/INFANT, WHOL: Baby Goods
CLOTHING & ACCESS: Costumes, Theatrical
CLOTHING & ACCESS: Hospital Gowns
CLOTHING & FURNISHINGS, MEN'S & BOYS', WHOLESALE: Gloves
CLOTHING & FURNISHINGS, MEN'S & BOYS', WHOLESALE: Uniforms
CLOTHING & FURNISHINGS, MENS & BOYS, WHOL: Sportswear/Work
CLOTHING & FURNISHINGS, MENS & BOYS, WHOLESALE: Apprl Belts
CLOTHING STORES, NEC
CLOTHING STORES: Dancewear
CLOTHING STORES: Designer Apparel
CLOTHING STORES: Formal Wear
CLOTHING STORES: Lingerie & Corsets, Underwear
CLOTHING STORES: T-Shirts, Printed, Custom
CLOTHING/ACCESS, WOMEN, CHILDREN/INFANT, WHOL: Hosp Gowns
CLOTHING/FURNISHINGS, MEN/BOY, WHOL: Furnishings, Exc Shoes
CLOTHING: Caps, Baseball
CLOTHING: Hospital, Men's
CLOTHING: T-Shirts & Tops, Knit
CLOTHING: Uniforms & Vestments
CLOTHING: Uniforms, Ex Athletic, Women's, Misses' & Juniors'
CLOTHING: Uniforms, Military, Men/Youth, Purchased Materials
CLOTHING: Uniforms, Work
CLUTCHES, EXC VEHICULAR
COAL & OTHER MINERALS & ORES WHOLESALERS
COAL MINING SERVICES
COAL MINING SVCS: Bituminous, Contract Basis
COAL MINING: Anthracite
COAL MINING: Bituminous & Lignite Surface
COAL MINING: Bituminous Coal & Lignite-Surface Mining
COAL MINING: Bituminous Underground
COAL MINING: Bituminous, Strip
COAL MINING: Bituminous, Surface, NEC
COAL MINING: Lignite, Surface, NEC
COATING SVC: Aluminum, Metal Prdts
COATING SVC: Metals & Formed Prdts
COATING SVC: Metals, With Plastic Or Resins
COATINGS: Epoxy
COCKTAIL LOUNGE
COFFEE SVCS

SERVICES INDEX

COIN COUNTERS
COIN-OPERATED LAUNDRY
COIN-OPERATED LAUNDRY MACHINE ROUTES
COINS, WHOLESALE
COLD STORAGE MACHINERY WHOLESALERS
COLLECTION AGENCIES
COLLECTION AGENCY, EXC REAL ESTATE
COLLEGE, EXC JUNIOR
COLLEGES, UNIVERSITIES & PROFESSIONAL SCHOOLS
COLOR SEPARATION: Photographic & Movie Film
COMBINATION UTILITIES, NEC
COMBINED ELEMENTARY & SECONDARY SCHOOLS, PRIVATE
COMMERCIAL & INDL SHELVING WHOLESALERS
COMMERCIAL & OFFICE BUILDINGS RENOVATION & REPAIR
COMMERCIAL ART & GRAPHIC DESIGN SVCS
COMMERCIAL ART & ILLUSTRATION SVCS
COMMERCIAL CONTAINERS WHOLESALERS
COMMERCIAL EQPT & SPLYS, WHOLESALE: Price Marking
COMMERCIAL EQPT WHOLESALERS, NEC
COMMERCIAL EQPT, WHOLESALE: Bakery Eqpt & Splys
COMMERCIAL EQPT, WHOLESALE: Coffee Brewing Eqpt & Splys
COMMERCIAL EQPT, WHOLESALE: Comm Cooking & Food Svc Eqpt
COMMERCIAL EQPT, WHOLESALE: Restaurant, NEC
COMMERCIAL EQPT, WHOLESALE: Scales, Exc Laboratory
COMMERCIAL EQPT, WHOLESALE: Teaching Machines, Electronic
COMMERCIAL EQPT, WHOLESALE: Vending Machines, Coin-Operated
COMMERCIAL PHOTOGRAPHIC STUDIO
COMMERCIAL PRINTING & NEWSPAPER PUBLISHING COMBINED
COMMODITIES SAMPLING SVC
COMMODITY CONTRACT POOL OPERATORS
COMMODITY CONTRACTS BROKERS, DEALERS
COMMODITY INVESTORS
COMMON SAND MINING
COMMUNICATIONS CARRIER: Wired
COMMUNICATIONS EQPT REPAIR & MAINTENANCE
COMMUNICATIONS EQPT WHOLESALERS
COMMUNICATIONS SVCS
COMMUNICATIONS SVCS: Cellular
COMMUNICATIONS SVCS: Data
COMMUNICATIONS SVCS: Electronic Mail
COMMUNICATIONS SVCS: Internet Connectivity Svcs
COMMUNICATIONS SVCS: Internet Host Svcs
COMMUNICATIONS SVCS: Nonvocal Message
COMMUNICATIONS SVCS: Online Svc Providers
COMMUNICATIONS SVCS: Radio Pager Or Beeper
COMMUNICATIONS SVCS: Signal Enhancement Network Svcs
COMMUNICATIONS SVCS: Telegram
COMMUNICATIONS SVCS: Telephone Or Video
COMMUNICATIONS SVCS: Telephone, Broker
COMMUNICATIONS SVCS: Telephone, Data
COMMUNICATIONS SVCS: Telephone, Local
COMMUNICATIONS SVCS: Telephone, Local & Long Distance
COMMUNICATIONS SVCS: Telephone, Long Distance
COMMUNICATIONS SVCS: Television Antenna Construction & Rent
COMMUNITY ACTION AGENCY
COMMUNITY CENTER
COMMUNITY CENTERS: Adult
COMMUNITY CENTERS: Youth
COMMUNITY COLLEGE
COMMUNITY DEVELOPMENT GROUPS
COMMUNITY SVCS EMPLOYMENT TRAINING PROGRAM
COMMUNITY THEATER PRODUCTION SVCS
COMMUTATORS: Electronic
COMPACT DISCS OR CD'S, WHOLESALE
COMPOST
COMPRESSORS, AIR CONDITIONING: Wholesalers
COMPRESSORS: Air & Gas, Including Vacuum Pumps
COMPRESSORS: Repairing
COMPRESSORS: Wholesalers
COMPUTER & COMPUTER SOFTWARE STORES
COMPUTER & COMPUTER SOFTWARE STORES: Peripheral Eqpt
COMPUTER & COMPUTER SOFTWARE STORES: Personal Computers
COMPUTER & COMPUTER SOFTWARE STORES: Software & Access
COMPUTER & COMPUTER SOFTWARE STORES: Software, Bus/Non-Game
COMPUTER & DATA PROCESSING EQPT REPAIR & MAINTENANCE
COMPUTER & OFFICE MACHINE MAINTENANCE & REPAIR
COMPUTER DATA ESCROW SVCS
COMPUTER FACILITIES MANAGEMENT SVCS
COMPUTER GRAPHICS SVCS
COMPUTER INTERFACE EQPT: Indl Process
COMPUTER PERIPHERAL EQPT REPAIR & MAINTENANCE
COMPUTER PERIPHERAL EQPT, NEC
COMPUTER PERIPHERAL EQPT, WHOLESALE
COMPUTER PERIPHERAL EQPT: Decoders
COMPUTER PROGRAMMING SVCS
COMPUTER PROGRAMMING SVCS: Custom
COMPUTER RELATED MAINTENANCE SVCS
COMPUTER RELATED SVCS, NEC
COMPUTER SOFTWARE DEVELOPMENT
COMPUTER SOFTWARE DEVELOPMENT & APPLICATIONS
COMPUTER SOFTWARE SYSTEMS ANALYSIS & DESIGN: Custom
COMPUTER SOFTWARE WRITERS
COMPUTER SOFTWARE WRITERS: Freelance
COMPUTER STORAGE DEVICES, NEC
COMPUTER SYSTEM SELLING SVCS
COMPUTER SYSTEMS ANALYSIS & DESIGN
COMPUTER TERMINALS
COMPUTER TRAINING SCHOOLS
COMPUTER-AIDED DESIGN SYSTEMS SVCS
COMPUTER-AIDED ENGINEERING SYSTEMS SVCS
COMPUTERS, NEC
COMPUTERS, NEC, WHOLESALE
COMPUTERS, PERIPHERAL & SOFTWARE, WHOLESALE: Word Processing
COMPUTERS, PERIPHERALS & SOFTWARE, WHOLESALE: Printers
COMPUTERS, PERIPHERALS & SOFTWARE, WHOLESALE: Software
COMPUTERS, PERIPHERALS & SOFTWARE, WHOLESALE: Terminals
CONCERT MANAGEMENT SVCS
CONCRETE CURING & HARDENING COMPOUNDS
CONCRETE PRDTS
CONCRETE: Asphaltic, Not From Refineries
CONCRETE: Dry Mixture
CONCRETE: Ready-Mixed
CONDENSERS: Heat Transfer Eqpt, Evaporative
CONES, PYROMETRIC: Earthenware
CONFECTIONERY PRDTS WHOLESALERS
CONFECTIONS & CANDY
CONFINEMENT SURVEILLANCE SYS MAINTENANCE & MONITORING SVCS
CONNECTORS: Electronic
CONSERVATION PROGRAMS ADMINISTRATION SVCS
CONSTRUCTION & MINING MACHINERY WHOLESALERS
CONSTRUCTION EQPT REPAIR SVCS
CONSTRUCTION EQPT: Cranes
CONSTRUCTION EQPT: Roofing Eqpt
CONSTRUCTION MATERIALS, WHOLESALE: Aggregate
CONSTRUCTION MATERIALS, WHOLESALE: Air Ducts, Sheet Metal
CONSTRUCTION MATERIALS, WHOLESALE: Awnings
CONSTRUCTION MATERIALS, WHOLESALE: Block, Concrete & Cinder
CONSTRUCTION MATERIALS, WHOLESALE: Brick, Exc Refractory
CONSTRUCTION MATERIALS, WHOLESALE: Building Stone
CONSTRUCTION MATERIALS, WHOLESALE: Building Stone, Granite
CONSTRUCTION MATERIALS, WHOLESALE: Building Stone, Marble
CONSTRUCTION MATERIALS, WHOLESALE: Building, Exterior
CONSTRUCTION MATERIALS, WHOLESALE: Building, Interior
CONSTRUCTION MATERIALS, WHOLESALE: Ceiling Systems & Prdts
CONSTRUCTION MATERIALS, WHOLESALE: Cement
CONSTRUCTION MATERIALS, WHOLESALE: Ceramic, Exc Refractory
CONSTRUCTION MATERIALS, WHOLESALE: Door Frames
CONSTRUCTION MATERIALS, WHOLESALE: Doors, Garage
CONSTRUCTION MATERIALS, WHOLESALE: Drywall Materials
CONSTRUCTION MATERIALS, WHOLESALE: Eavestroughing, Part/Sply
CONSTRUCTION MATERIALS, WHOLESALE: Glass
CONSTRUCTION MATERIALS, WHOLESALE: Gravel
CONSTRUCTION MATERIALS, WHOLESALE: Hardboard
CONSTRUCTION MATERIALS, WHOLESALE: Joists
CONSTRUCTION MATERIALS, WHOLESALE: Lime, Exc Agricultural
CONSTRUCTION MATERIALS, WHOLESALE: Limestone
CONSTRUCTION MATERIALS, WHOLESALE: Masons' Materials
CONSTRUCTION MATERIALS, WHOLESALE: Metal Buildings
CONSTRUCTION MATERIALS, WHOLESALE: Millwork
CONSTRUCTION MATERIALS, WHOLESALE: Molding, All Materials
CONSTRUCTION MATERIALS, WHOLESALE: Pallets, Wood
CONSTRUCTION MATERIALS, WHOLESALE: Particleboard
CONSTRUCTION MATERIALS, WHOLESALE: Prefabricated Structures
CONSTRUCTION MATERIALS, WHOLESALE: Roof, Asphalt/Sheet Metal
CONSTRUCTION MATERIALS, WHOLESALE: Roofing & Siding Material
CONSTRUCTION MATERIALS, WHOLESALE: Sand
CONSTRUCTION MATERIALS, WHOLESALE: Septic Tanks
CONSTRUCTION MATERIALS, WHOLESALE: Sewer Pipe, Clay
CONSTRUCTION MATERIALS, WHOLESALE: Siding, Exc Wood
CONSTRUCTION MATERIALS, WHOLESALE: Stone, Crushed Or Broken
CONSTRUCTION MATERIALS, WHOLESALE: Trim, Sheet Metal
CONSTRUCTION MATERIALS, WHOLESALE: Veneer
CONSTRUCTION MATERIALS, WHOLESALE: Windows
CONSTRUCTION MATLS, WHOL: Lumber, Rough, Dressed/Finished
CONSTRUCTION MATLS, WHOLESALE: Soil Erosion Cntrl Fabrics
CONSTRUCTION MTRLS, WHOL: Exterior Flat Glass, Plate/Window
CONSTRUCTION SAND MINING
CONSTRUCTION SITE PREPARATION SVCS
CONSTRUCTION: Agricultural Building
CONSTRUCTION: Airport Runway
CONSTRUCTION: Apartment Building
CONSTRUCTION: Athletic Field
CONSTRUCTION: Bridge
CONSTRUCTION: Commercial & Institutional Building
CONSTRUCTION: Commercial & Office Building, New
CONSTRUCTION: Commercial & Office Buildings, Prefabricated
CONSTRUCTION: Concrete Patio
CONSTRUCTION: Condominium
CONSTRUCTION: Curb
CONSTRUCTION: Dams, Waterways, Docks & Other Marine
CONSTRUCTION: Drainage System
CONSTRUCTION: Electric Power Line
CONSTRUCTION: Elevated Highway
CONSTRUCTION: Fire Station
CONSTRUCTION: Food Prdts Manufacturing or Packing Plant
CONSTRUCTION: Garage
CONSTRUCTION: Gas Main
CONSTRUCTION: Golf Course
CONSTRUCTION: Grain Elevator
CONSTRUCTION: Greenhouse
CONSTRUCTION: Guardrails, Highway
CONSTRUCTION: Heavy
CONSTRUCTION: Heavy Highway & Street
CONSTRUCTION: Hospital
CONSTRUCTION: Hotel & Motel, New
CONSTRUCTION: Indl Building & Warehouse
CONSTRUCTION: Indl Building, Prefabricated
CONSTRUCTION: Indl Buildings, New, NEC
CONSTRUCTION: Indl Plant
CONSTRUCTION: Institutional Building
CONSTRUCTION: Irrigation System

SERVICES INDEX

CONSTRUCTION: Land Preparation
CONSTRUCTION: Marine
CONSTRUCTION: Multi-Family Housing
CONSTRUCTION: Multi-family Dwellings, New
CONSTRUCTION: Nonresidential Buildings, Custom
CONSTRUCTION: Oil & Gas Line & Compressor Station
CONSTRUCTION: Oil & Gas Pipeline Construction
CONSTRUCTION: Pharmaceutical Manufacturing Plant
CONSTRUCTION: Pipeline, NEC
CONSTRUCTION: Pond
CONSTRUCTION: Power & Communication Transmission Tower
CONSTRUCTION: Power Plant
CONSTRUCTION: Railroad & Subway
CONSTRUCTION: Railway Roadbed
CONSTRUCTION: Refineries
CONSTRUCTION: Religious Building
CONSTRUCTION: Residential, Nec
CONSTRUCTION: Restaurant
CONSTRUCTION: Scaffolding
CONSTRUCTION: School Building
CONSTRUCTION: Sewer Line
CONSTRUCTION: Shopping Center & Mall
CONSTRUCTION: Silo, Agricultural
CONSTRUCTION: Single-Family Housing
CONSTRUCTION: Single-family Housing, New
CONSTRUCTION: Steel Buildings
CONSTRUCTION: Street Sign Installation & Mntnce
CONSTRUCTION: Street Surfacing & Paving
CONSTRUCTION: Svc Station
CONSTRUCTION: Swimming Pools
CONSTRUCTION: Telephone & Communication Line
CONSTRUCTION: Tennis Court
CONSTRUCTION: Transmitting Tower, Telecommunication
CONSTRUCTION: Tunnel
CONSTRUCTION: Utility Line
CONSTRUCTION: Warehouse
CONSTRUCTION: Waste Disposal Plant
CONSTRUCTION: Waste Water & Sewage Treatment Plant
CONSTRUCTION: Water & Sewer Line
CONSTRUCTION: Water Main
CONSULTING SVC: Actuarial
CONSULTING SVC: Business, NEC
CONSULTING SVC: Computer
CONSULTING SVC: Data Processing
CONSULTING SVC: Educational
CONSULTING SVC: Engineering
CONSULTING SVC: Executive Placement & Search
CONSULTING SVC: Financial Management
CONSULTING SVC: Human Resource
CONSULTING SVC: Management
CONSULTING SVC: Marketing Management
CONSULTING SVC: New Business Start Up
CONSULTING SVC: Online Technology
CONSULTING SVC: Personnel Management
CONSULTING SVC: Productivity Improvement
CONSULTING SVC: Telecommunications
CONSULTING SVCS, BUSINESS: Agricultural
CONSULTING SVCS, BUSINESS: City Planning
CONSULTING SVCS, BUSINESS: Communications
CONSULTING SVCS, BUSINESS: Economic
CONSULTING SVCS, BUSINESS: Employee Programs Administration
CONSULTING SVCS, BUSINESS: Energy Conservation
CONSULTING SVCS, BUSINESS: Environmental
CONSULTING SVCS, BUSINESS: Indl Development Planning
CONSULTING SVCS, BUSINESS: Lighting
CONSULTING SVCS, BUSINESS: Safety Training Svcs
CONSULTING SVCS, BUSINESS: Sys Engnrg, Exc Computer/Prof
CONSULTING SVCS, BUSINESS: Systems Analysis & Engineering
CONSULTING SVCS, BUSINESS: Test Development & Evaluation
CONSULTING SVCS, BUSINESS: Testing, Educational Or Personnel
CONSULTING SVCS, BUSINESS: Traffic
CONSULTING SVCS, BUSINESS: Urban Planning & Consulting
CONSULTING SVCS: Nuclear
CONSULTING SVCS: Physics
CONSULTING SVCS: Psychological
CONSULTING SVCS: Scientific
CONSUMER BUYING SVCS
CONSUMER CREDIT REPORTING BUREAU
CONSUMER PURCHASING SVCS
CONTAINERS: Cargo, Wood
CONTAINERS: Corrugated
CONTAINERS: Metal
CONTAINERS: Plastic
CONTAINERS: Shipping, Bombs, Metal Plate
CONTAINERS: Shipping, Wood
CONTAINMENT VESSELS: Reactor, Metal Plate
CONTRACTOR: Dredging
CONTRACTOR: Framing
CONTRACTOR: Rigging & Scaffolding
CONTRACTORS: Access Control System Eqpt
CONTRACTORS: Access Flooring System Installation
CONTRACTORS: Acoustical & Ceiling Work
CONTRACTORS: Acoustical & Insulation Work
CONTRACTORS: Antenna Installation
CONTRACTORS: Artificial Turf Installation
CONTRACTORS: Asbestos Removal & Encapsulation
CONTRACTORS: Asphalt
CONTRACTORS: Awning Installation
CONTRACTORS: Banking Machine Installation & Svc
CONTRACTORS: Bathtub Refinishing
CONTRACTORS: Boiler Maintenance Contractor
CONTRACTORS: Boiler Setting
CONTRACTORS: Bricklaying
CONTRACTORS: Bridge Painting
CONTRACTORS: Building Board-up
CONTRACTORS: Building Eqpt & Machinery Installation
CONTRACTORS: Building Fireproofing
CONTRACTORS: Building Sign Installation & Mntnce
CONTRACTORS: Building Site Preparation
CONTRACTORS: Cable Laying
CONTRACTORS: Cable Splicing Svcs
CONTRACTORS: Cable TV Installation
CONTRACTORS: Caisson Drilling
CONTRACTORS: Carpentry Work
CONTRACTORS: Carpentry, Cabinet & Finish Work
CONTRACTORS: Carpentry, Cabinet Building & Installation
CONTRACTORS: Carpet Laying
CONTRACTORS: Chimney Construction & Maintenance
CONTRACTORS: Closet Organizers, Installation & Design
CONTRACTORS: Coating, Caulking & Weather, Water & Fire
CONTRACTORS: Commercial & Office Building
CONTRACTORS: Communications Svcs
CONTRACTORS: Computer Installation
CONTRACTORS: Concrete
CONTRACTORS: Concrete Pumping
CONTRACTORS: Concrete Reinforcement Placing
CONTRACTORS: Concrete Repair
CONTRACTORS: Concrete Structure Coating, Plastic
CONTRACTORS: Construction Caulking
CONTRACTORS: Construction Site Cleanup
CONTRACTORS: Construction Site Metal Structure Coating
CONTRACTORS: Core Drilling & Cutting
CONTRACTORS: Countertop Installation
CONTRACTORS: Demolition, Building & Other Structures
CONTRACTORS: Diamond Drilling & Sawing
CONTRACTORS: Directional Oil & Gas Well Drilling Svc
CONTRACTORS: Drapery Track Installation
CONTRACTORS: Driveway
CONTRACTORS: Drywall
CONTRACTORS: Earthmoving
CONTRACTORS: Electric Power Systems
CONTRACTORS: Electrical
CONTRACTORS: Electronic Controls Installation
CONTRACTORS: Energy Management Control
CONTRACTORS: Epoxy Application
CONTRACTORS: Erection & Dismantling, Poured Concrete Forms
CONTRACTORS: Excavating
CONTRACTORS: Exterior Concrete Stucco
CONTRACTORS: Exterior Painting
CONTRACTORS: Fence Construction
CONTRACTORS: Fiber Optic Cable Installation
CONTRACTORS: Fire Detection & Burglar Alarm Systems
CONTRACTORS: Fire Sprinkler System Installation Svcs
CONTRACTORS: Floor Laying & Other Floor Work
CONTRACTORS: Flooring
CONTRACTORS: Food Concessions
CONTRACTORS: Food Svcs Eqpt Installation
CONTRACTORS: Foundation & Footing
CONTRACTORS: Foundation Building
CONTRACTORS: Fountain Installation
CONTRACTORS: Garage Doors
CONTRACTORS: Gas Field Svcs, NEC
CONTRACTORS: General Electric
CONTRACTORS: Glass Tinting, Architectural & Automotive
CONTRACTORS: Glass, Glazing & Tinting
CONTRACTORS: Gutters & Downspouts
CONTRACTORS: Heating & Air Conditioning
CONTRACTORS: Heating Systems Repair & Maintenance Svc
CONTRACTORS: Highway & Street Construction, General
CONTRACTORS: Highway & Street Paving
CONTRACTORS: Highway & Street Resurfacing
CONTRACTORS: Home & Office Intrs Finish, Furnish/Remodel
CONTRACTORS: Hotel & Motel Renovation
CONTRACTORS: Hotel, Motel/Multi-Family Home Renovtn/Remodel
CONTRACTORS: Hydraulic Eqpt Installation & Svcs
CONTRACTORS: Hydronics Heating
CONTRACTORS: Indl Building Renovation, Remodeling & Repair
CONTRACTORS: Insulation Installation, Building
CONTRACTORS: Kitchen & Bathroom Remodeling
CONTRACTORS: Lighting Conductor Erection
CONTRACTORS: Lighting Syst
CONTRACTORS: Lightweight Steel Framing Installation
CONTRACTORS: Machine Rigging & Moving
CONTRACTORS: Machinery Dismantling
CONTRACTORS: Machinery Installation
CONTRACTORS: Maintenance, Parking Facility Eqpt
CONTRACTORS: Marble Installation, Interior
CONTRACTORS: Marble Masonry, Exterior
CONTRACTORS: Masonry & Stonework
CONTRACTORS: Mechanical
CONTRACTORS: Millwrights
CONTRACTORS: Mosaic Work
CONTRACTORS: Multi-Family Home Remodeling
CONTRACTORS: Nonresidential Building Design & Construction
CONTRACTORS: Nuclear Power Refueling
CONTRACTORS: Office Furniture Installation
CONTRACTORS: Oil & Gas Field Fire Fighting Svcs
CONTRACTORS: Oil & Gas Field Geological Exploration Svcs
CONTRACTORS: Oil & Gas Field Geophysical Exploration Svcs
CONTRACTORS: Oil & Gas Well Drilling Svc
CONTRACTORS: Oil & Gas Well Flow Rate Measurement Svcs
CONTRACTORS: Oil & Gas Well On-Site Foundation Building Svcs
CONTRACTORS: Oil & Gas Well Redrilling
CONTRACTORS: Oil Field Haulage Svcs
CONTRACTORS: Oil Field Mud Drilling Svcs
CONTRACTORS: Oil Field Pipe Testing Svcs
CONTRACTORS: Oil Sampling Svcs
CONTRACTORS: Oil/Gas Field Casing,Tube/Rod Running,Cut/Pull
CONTRACTORS: Oil/Gas Well Construction, Rpr/Dismantling Svcs
CONTRACTORS: On-Site Welding
CONTRACTORS: Ornamental Metal Work
CONTRACTORS: Paint & Wallpaper Stripping
CONTRACTORS: Painting & Wall Covering
CONTRACTORS: Painting, Commercial
CONTRACTORS: Painting, Commercial, Exterior
CONTRACTORS: Painting, Commercial, Interior
CONTRACTORS: Painting, Indl
CONTRACTORS: Painting, Residential
CONTRACTORS: Parking Facility Eqpt Installation
CONTRACTORS: Parking Lot Maintenance
CONTRACTORS: Patio & Deck Construction & Repair
CONTRACTORS: Pavement Marking
CONTRACTORS: Pile Driving
CONTRACTORS: Pipe & Boiler Insulating
CONTRACTORS: Pipe Laying
CONTRACTORS: Plastering, Plain or Ornamental
CONTRACTORS: Plumbing
CONTRACTORS: Pollution Control Eqpt Installation
CONTRACTORS: Post Disaster Renovations
CONTRACTORS: Power Generating Eqpt Installation
CONTRACTORS: Precast Concrete Struct Framing & Panel Placing
CONTRACTORS: Prefabricated Window & Door Installation
CONTRACTORS: Process Piping
CONTRACTORS: Refractory or Acid Brick Masonry
CONTRACTORS: Refrigeration

SERVICES INDEX

CONTRACTORS: Resilient Floor Laying
CONTRACTORS: Roof Repair
CONTRACTORS: Roofing
CONTRACTORS: Roofing & Gutter Work
CONTRACTORS: Safety & Security Eqpt
CONTRACTORS: Sandblasting Svc, Building Exteriors
CONTRACTORS: Septic System
CONTRACTORS: Sheet Metal Work, NEC
CONTRACTORS: Sheet metal Work, Architectural
CONTRACTORS: Shoring & Underpinning
CONTRACTORS: Sidewalk
CONTRACTORS: Siding
CONTRACTORS: Single-Family Home Fire Damage Repair
CONTRACTORS: Single-family Home General Remodeling
CONTRACTORS: Skylight Installation
CONTRACTORS: Solar Energy Eqpt
CONTRACTORS: Sound Eqpt Installation
CONTRACTORS: Special Trades, NEC
CONTRACTORS: Specialized Public Building
CONTRACTORS: Spraying, Nonagricultural
CONTRACTORS: Sprinkler System
CONTRACTORS: Steam Cleaning, Building Exterior
CONTRACTORS: Stone Masonry
CONTRACTORS: Storage Tank Erection, Metal
CONTRACTORS: Store Fixture Installation
CONTRACTORS: Structural Iron Work, Structural
CONTRACTORS: Structural Steel Erection
CONTRACTORS: Svc Station Eqpt
CONTRACTORS: Svc Station Eqpt Installation, Maint & Repair
CONTRACTORS: Tile Installation, Ceramic
CONTRACTORS: Trenching
CONTRACTORS: Tuck Pointing & Restoration
CONTRACTORS: Underground Utilities
CONTRACTORS: Ventilation & Duct Work
CONTRACTORS: Wall Covering
CONTRACTORS: Wall Covering, Commercial
CONTRACTORS: Warm Air Heating & Air Conditioning
CONTRACTORS: Water Well Drilling
CONTRACTORS: Water Well Servicing
CONTRACTORS: Waterproofing
CONTRACTORS: Window Treatment Installation
CONTRACTORS: Windows & Doors
CONTRACTORS: Wood Floor Installation & Refinishing
CONTRACTORS: Wrecking & Demolition
CONTROL EQPT: Electric
CONTROL EQPT: Noise
CONTROL PANELS: Electrical
CONTROLS & ACCESS: Indl, Electric
CONTROLS: Environmental
CONTROLS: Relay & Ind
CONVALESCENT HOME
CONVALESCENT HOMES
CONVENIENCE STORES
CONVENTION & TRADE SHOW SVCS
CONVERTERS: Data
CONVERTERS: Phase Or Rotary, Electrical
CONVEYOR SYSTEMS: Belt, General Indl Use
CONVEYOR SYSTEMS: Robotic
CONVEYORS & CONVEYING EQPT
COOKING & FOOD WARMING EQPT: Commercial
COPPER ORE MINING
COPY MACHINES WHOLESALERS
CORK PRDTS, FABRICATED, WHOLESALE
CORRECTIONAL FACILITY OPERATIONS
CORRECTIONAL INSTITUTIONS
CORRECTIONAL INSTITUTIONS, GOVERNMENT: Detention Center
CORRECTIONAL INSTITUTIONS, GOVERNMENT: Prison, government
CORRECTIONAL INSTITUTIONS, GOVERNMENT: State
CORRESPONDENCE SCHOOLS
CORRUGATED PRDTS: Boxes, Partition, Display Items, Sheet/Pad
COSMETIC PREPARATIONS
COSMETICS & TOILETRIES
COSMETICS WHOLESALERS
COSMETOLOGIST
COSMETOLOGY & PERSONAL HYGIENE SALONS
COSMETOLOGY SCHOOL
COUNCIL FOR SOCIAL AGENCY
COUNTERS & COUNTING DEVICES
COUNTRY CLUBS
COURIER OR MESSENGER SVCS
COURIER SVCS, AIR: Letter Delivery, Private
COURIER SVCS, AIR: Package Delivery, Private
COURIER SVCS, AIR: Parcel Delivery, Private
COURIER SVCS: Air
COURIER SVCS: Ground
COURIER SVCS: Package By Vehicle
COURIER SVCS: Parcel By Vehicle
COURT REPORTING SVCS
COURTS
COURTS OF LAW: County Government
COURTS OF LAW: Federal
COURTS OF LAW: Local
COURTS OF LAW: State
COVERS: Automobile Seat
CRANE & AERIAL LIFT SVCS
CRANES & MONORAIL SYSTEMS
CRANES: Indl Plant
CRANES: Indl Truck
CRANES: Overhead
CRANKSHAFTS & CAMSHAFTS: Machining
CRATING SVCS: Shipping
CREATIVE SVCS: Advertisers, Exc Writers
CREDIT & OTHER FINANCIAL RESPONSIBILITY INSURANCE
CREDIT AGENCIES: Federal & Federally Sponsored
CREDIT AGENCIES: Federal Home Loan Mortgage Corporation
CREDIT AGENCIES: National Consumer Cooperative Bank
CREDIT BUREAUS
CREDIT CARD PROCESSING SVCS
CREDIT CARD SVCS
CREDIT INST, SHORT-TERM BUSINESS: Financing Dealers
CREDIT INSTITUTIONS, SHORT-TERM BUS: Buying Install Notes
CREDIT INSTITUTIONS, SHORT-TERM BUS: Wrkg Capital Finance
CREDIT INSTITUTIONS: Personal
CREDIT INSTITUTIONS: Short-Term Business
CREDIT INVESTIGATION SVCS
CREDIT UNIONS: Federally Chartered
CREDIT UNIONS: State Chartered
CREMATORIES
CRISIS CENTER
CRISIS INTERVENTION CENTERS
CRUDE PETROLEUM & NATURAL GAS PRODUCTION
CRUDE PETROLEUM & NATURAL GAS PRODUCTION
CRUDE PETROLEUM PRODUCTION
CRYSTAL GOODS, WHOLESALE
CUPS: Paper, Made From Purchased Materials
CURTAIN & DRAPERY FIXTURES: Poles, Rods & Rollers
CURTAIN WALLS: Building, Steel
CURTAINS: Window, From Purchased Materials
CUSTODIAL SVCS: School, Contract Basis
CUSTOMIZING SVCS
CUSTOMS CLEARANCE OF FREIGHT
CUT STONE & STONE PRODUCTS
CUTLERY
CYLINDER & ACTUATORS: Fluid Power
Convents

D

DAIRY PRDTS STORE: Ice Cream, Packaged
DAIRY PRDTS STORES
DAIRY PRDTS WHOLESALERS: Fresh
DAIRY PRDTS: Butter
DAIRY PRDTS: Cheese
DAIRY PRDTS: Dietary Supplements, Dairy & Non-Dairy Based
DAIRY PRDTS: Frozen Desserts & Novelties
DAIRY PRDTS: Ice Cream & Ice Milk
DAIRY PRDTS: Milk, Condensed & Evaporated
DAIRY PRDTS: Milk, Fluid
DAIRY PRDTS: Milk, Processed, Pasteurized, Homogenized/Btld
DAIRY PRDTS: Natural Cheese
DAIRY PRDTS: Whipped Topping, Exc Frozen Or Dry Mix
DANCE HALL OR BALLROOM OPERATION
DANCE HALL SVCS
DANCE INSTRUCTOR & SCHOOL
DATA ENTRY SVCS
DATA PROCESSING & PREPARATION SVCS
DATA PROCESSING SVCS
DATABASE INFORMATION RETRIEVAL SVCS
DATING SVCS
DEBT COUNSELING OR ADJUSTMENT SVCS: Individuals
DECORATIVE WOOD & WOODWORK
DEGREASING MACHINES
DELIVERY SVCS, BY VEHICLE
DENTAL EQPT & SPLYS
DENTAL EQPT & SPLYS WHOLESALERS
DENTAL EQPT & SPLYS: Orthodontic Appliances
DENTISTS' OFFICES & CLINICS
DEPARTMENT STORES
DEPARTMENT STORES: Non-Discount
DEPARTMENT STORES: Surplus & Salvage
DEPOSIT INSURANCE
DESALTER KITS: Sea Water
DESIGN SVCS, NEC
DESIGN SVCS: Commercial & Indl
DESIGN SVCS: Computer Integrated Systems
DETECTIVE & ARMORED CAR SERVICES
DETECTIVE AGENCY
DETECTIVE SVCS
DETOXIFICATION CENTERS, OUTPATIENT
DIAGNOSTIC SUBSTANCES
DICE & DICE CUPS
DIES & TOOLS: Special
DIET & WEIGHT REDUCING CENTERS
DIETICIANS' OFFICES
DIODES: Light Emitting
DIRECT SELLING ESTAB: Coffee, Soda/Beer, Etc, Door-To-Door
DIRECT SELLING ESTABLISHMENTS: Appliances, House-To-House
DIRECT SELLING ESTABLISHMENTS: Telemarketing
DISASTER SVCS
DISC JOCKEYS
DISCOUNT DEPARTMENT STORES
DISINFECTING SVCS
DISKETTE DUPLICATING SVCS
DISPLAY FIXTURES: Wood
DISPLAY ITEMS: Solid Fiber, Made From Purchased Materials
DISPLAY LETTERING SVCS
DOCK EQPT & SPLYS, INDL
DOCUMENT DESTRUCTION SVC
DOCUMENT STORAGE SVCS
DOMESTIC HELP SVCS
DOMICILIARY CARE FACILITY
DOOR & WINDOW REPAIR SVCS
DOORS & WINDOWS WHOLESALERS: All Materials
DOORS & WINDOWS: Storm, Metal
DOORS: Garage, Overhead, Metal
DOORS: Garage, Overhead, Wood
DOORS: Glass
DOORS: Wooden
DRAFTING SPLYS WHOLESALERS
DRAFTING SVCS
DRAGSTRIP OPERATION
DRAPERIES & CURTAINS
DRAPERIES & DRAPERY FABRICS, COTTON
DRAPERIES: Plastic & Textile, From Purchased Materials
DRAPERY & UPHOLSTERY STORES: Draperies
DRAPES & DRAPERY FABRICS, FROM MANMADE FIBER
DRIED FRUITS WHOLESALERS
DRINKING PLACES: Alcoholic Beverages
DRINKING PLACES: Bars & Lounges
DRINKING PLACES: Tavern
DRIVE-A-WAY AUTOMOBILE SVCS
DRUG ABUSE COUNSELOR, NONTREATMENT
DRUG CLINIC, OUTPATIENT
DRUG STORES
DRUGS & DRUG PROPRIETARIES, WHOL: Biologicals/Allied Prdts
DRUGS & DRUG PROPRIETARIES, WHOLESALE
DRUGS & DRUG PROPRIETARIES, WHOLESALE: Antiseptics
DRUGS & DRUG PROPRIETARIES, WHOLESALE: Biotherapeutics
DRUGS & DRUG PROPRIETARIES, WHOLESALE: Blood Plasma
DRUGS & DRUG PROPRIETARIES, WHOLESALE: Druggists' Sundries
DRUGS & DRUG PROPRIETARIES, WHOLESALE: Patent Medicines
DRUGS & DRUG PROPRIETARIES, WHOLESALE: Pharmaceuticals
DRUGS & DRUG PROPRIETARIES, WHOLESALE: Vitamins & Minerals
DRYCLEANING & LAUNDRY SVCS: Commercial & Family
DRYCLEANING PLANTS

SERVICES INDEX

DRYCLEANING SVC: Drapery & Curtain
DRYERS & REDRYERS: Indl
DUCTS: Sheet Metal
DURABLE GOODS WHOLESALERS, NEC
DYES & PIGMENTS: Organic

E

EARTH SCIENCE SVCS
EATING PLACES
ECONOMIC PROGRAMS ADMINISTRATION SVCS, NEC
EDUCATIONAL PROGRAM ADMINISTRATION, GOVERNMENT: County
EDUCATIONAL PROGRAMS ADMINISTRATION SVCS
EDUCATIONAL SVCS
EDUCATIONAL SVCS, NONDEGREE GRANTING: Continuing Education
EGG WHOLESALERS
ELECTRIC & OTHER SERVICES COMBINED
ELECTRIC FENCE CHARGERS
ELECTRIC MOTOR REPAIR SVCS
ELECTRIC POWER DISTRIBUTION TO CONSUMERS
ELECTRIC POWER GENERATION: Fossil Fuel
ELECTRIC POWER, COGENERATED
ELECTRIC SERVICES
ELECTRIC SVCS, NEC Power Broker
ELECTRIC SVCS, NEC Power Transmission
ELECTRIC SVCS, NEC: Power Generation
ELECTRICAL APPARATUS & EQPT WHOLESALERS
ELECTRICAL APPLIANCES, TELEVISIONS & RADIOS WHOLESALERS
ELECTRICAL CONSTRUCTION MATERIALS WHOLESALERS
ELECTRICAL CURRENT CARRYING WIRING DEVICES
ELECTRICAL DISCHARGE MACHINING, EDM
ELECTRICAL EQPT & SPLYS
ELECTRICAL EQPT FOR ENGINES
ELECTRICAL EQPT REPAIR & MAINTENANCE
ELECTRICAL EQPT REPAIR SVCS
ELECTRICAL EQPT REPAIR SVCS: High Voltage
ELECTRICAL EQPT: Automotive, NEC
ELECTRICAL GOODS, WHOLESALE: Alarms & Signaling Eqpt
ELECTRICAL GOODS, WHOLESALE: Batteries, Storage, Indl
ELECTRICAL GOODS, WHOLESALE: Boxes & Fittings
ELECTRICAL GOODS, WHOLESALE: Burglar Alarm Systems
ELECTRICAL GOODS, WHOLESALE: Cable Conduit
ELECTRICAL GOODS, WHOLESALE: Clothes Dryers, Electric & Gas
ELECTRICAL GOODS, WHOLESALE: Connectors
ELECTRICAL GOODS, WHOLESALE: Electrical Appliances, Major
ELECTRICAL GOODS, WHOLESALE: Electronic Parts
ELECTRICAL GOODS, WHOLESALE: Facsimile Or Fax Eqpt
ELECTRICAL GOODS, WHOLESALE: Fire Alarm Systems
ELECTRICAL GOODS, WHOLESALE: Generators
ELECTRICAL GOODS, WHOLESALE: Household Appliances, NEC
ELECTRICAL GOODS, WHOLESALE: Intercommunication Eqpt
ELECTRICAL GOODS, WHOLESALE: Light Bulbs & Related Splys
ELECTRICAL GOODS, WHOLESALE: Lighting Fittings & Access
ELECTRICAL GOODS, WHOLESALE: Lighting Fixtures, Comm & Indl
ELECTRICAL GOODS, WHOLESALE: Mobile telephone Eqpt
ELECTRICAL GOODS, WHOLESALE: Modems, Computer
ELECTRICAL GOODS, WHOLESALE: Motor Ctrls, Starters & Relays
ELECTRICAL GOODS, WHOLESALE: Motors
ELECTRICAL GOODS, WHOLESALE: Paging & Signaling Eqpt
ELECTRICAL GOODS, WHOLESALE: Radio Parts & Access, NEC
ELECTRICAL GOODS, WHOLESALE: Security Control Eqpt & Systems
ELECTRICAL GOODS, WHOLESALE: Semiconductor Devices
ELECTRICAL GOODS, WHOLESALE: Sound Eqpt
ELECTRICAL GOODS, WHOLESALE: Switchgear
ELECTRICAL GOODS, WHOLESALE: Telephone & Telegraphic Eqpt
ELECTRICAL GOODS, WHOLESALE: Telephone Eqpt
ELECTRICAL GOODS, WHOLESALE: Vacuum Cleaners, Household
ELECTRICAL GOODS, WHOLESALE: Washing Machines
ELECTRICAL GOODS, WHOLESALE: Wire & Cable
ELECTRICAL GOODS, WHOLESALE: Wire & Cable, Ctrl & Sig
ELECTRICAL GOODS, WHOLESALE: Wire & Cable, Electronic
ELECTRICAL HOUSEHOLD APPLIANCE REPAIR
ELECTRICAL MEASURING INSTRUMENT REPAIR & CALIBRATION SVCS
ELECTRICAL SPLYS
ELECTRODES: Thermal & Electrolytic
ELECTROMEDICAL EQPT
ELECTROMETALLURGICAL PRDTS
ELECTRONIC EQPT REPAIR SVCS
ELECTRONIC PARTS & EQPT WHOLESALERS
ELECTRONIC SHOPPING
ELEMENTARY & SECONDARY PRIVATE DENOMINATIONAL SCHOOLS
ELEMENTARY & SECONDARY SCHOOLS, COMBINED CATHOLIC
ELEMENTARY & SECONDARY SCHOOLS, PRIVATE NEC
ELEMENTARY & SECONDARY SCHOOLS, PUBLIC
ELEMENTARY & SECONDARY SCHOOLS, SPECIAL EDUCATION
ELEMENTARY SCHOOLS, CATHOLIC
ELEMENTARY SCHOOLS, NEC
ELEMENTARY SCHOOLS, PRIVATE
ELEMENTARY SCHOOLS, PUBLIC
ELEVATOR: Grain, Storage Only
ELEVATORS & EQPT
ELEVATORS WHOLESALERS
ELEVATORS: Installation & Conversion
EMBROIDERING & ART NEEDLEWORK FOR THE TRADE
EMBROIDERY ADVERTISING SVCS
EMERGENCY & RELIEF SVCS
EMERGENCY SHELTERS
EMPLOYEE LEASING SVCS
EMPLOYMENT AGENCY SVCS
EMPLOYMENT SVCS: Labor Contractors
EMPLOYMENT SVCS: Nurses' Registry
ENGINEERING HELP SVCS
ENGINEERING SVCS
ENGINEERING SVCS: Acoustical
ENGINEERING SVCS: Aviation Or Aeronautical
ENGINEERING SVCS: Civil
ENGINEERING SVCS: Construction & Civil
ENGINEERING SVCS: Electrical Or Electronic
ENGINEERING SVCS: Fire Protection
ENGINEERING SVCS: Heating & Ventilation
ENGINEERING SVCS: Industrial
ENGINEERING SVCS: Machine Tool Design
ENGINEERING SVCS: Mechanical
ENGINEERING SVCS: Mining
ENGINEERING SVCS: Pollution Control
ENGINEERING SVCS: Professional
ENGINEERING SVCS: Sanitary
ENGINEERING SVCS: Structural
ENGINES: Internal Combustion, NEC
ENGRAVING SVCS
ENTERTAINERS
ENTERTAINERS & ENTERTAINMENT GROUPS
ENTERTAINMENT PROMOTION SVCS
ENTERTAINMENT SVCS
ENVELOPES
ENVELOPES WHOLESALERS
ENVIRON QUALITY PROGS ADMIN, GOVT: Sanitary Engineering
ENVIRON QUALITY PROGS ADMIN, GOVT: Water Control & Quality
ENVIRONMENTAL QUALITY PROGS ADMIN, GOVT: Recreational
ENVIRONMENTAL QUALITY PROGS ADMIN, GOVT: Waste Mgmt
ENZYMES
EQUIPMENT & VEHICLE FINANCE LEASING COMPANIES
EQUIPMENT: Rental & Leasing, NEC
ETCHING SVC: Metal
EXCAVATING MACHINERY & EQPT WHOLESALERS
EXECUTIVE OFFICES: Federal, State & Local
EXHIBITORS, ITINERANT, MOTION PICTURE
EXPLOSIVES
EXPLOSIVES, EXC AMMO & FIREWORKS WHOLESALERS
EXTENDED CARE FACILITY
EXTERMINATING & FUMIGATING SVCS
EYEGLASSES

F

FABRICS: Broadwoven, Synthetic Manmade Fiber & Silk
FABRICS: Metallized
FABRICS: Trimmings
FABRICS: Woven, Narrow Cotton, Wool, Silk
FACIAL SALONS
FACILITIES SUPPORT SVCS
FACILITY RENTAL & PARTY PLANNING SVCS
FAMILY COUNSELING SVCS
FAMILY OR MARRIAGE COUNSELING
FAMILY PLANNING CENTERS
FAMILY PLANNING CLINIC
FAMILY SVCS AGENCY
FARM & GARDEN MACHINERY WHOLESALERS
FARM MACHINERY REPAIR SVCS
FARM PRDTS, RAW MATERIAL, WHOLESALE: Tobacco & Tobacco Prdts
FARM PRDTS, RAW MATERIALS, WHOLESALE: Farm Animals
FARM PRDTS, RAW MATERIALS, WHOLESALE: Hides
FARM SPLY STORES
FARM SPLYS WHOLESALERS
FARM SPLYS, WHOLESALE: Feed
FARM SPLYS, WHOLESALE: Flower & Field Bulbs
FARM SPLYS, WHOLESALE: Garden Splys
FARM SPLYS, WHOLESALE: Greenhouse Eqpt & Splys
FARM SPLYS, WHOLESALE: Herbicides
FARM SPLYS, WHOLESALE: Seed, Grass
FASTENERS WHOLESALERS
FASTENERS: Metal
FASTENERS: Notions, NEC
FEDERAL SAVINGS & LOAN ASSOCIATIONS
FEDERAL SAVINGS BANKS
FENCING DEALERS
FENCING: Chain Link
FERRALLOY ORES, EXC VANADIUM
FERTILIZER MINERAL MINING
FERTILIZER, AGRICULTURAL: Wholesalers
FERTILIZERS: NEC
FERTILIZERS: Phosphatic
FIBER & FIBER PRDTS: Synthetic Cellulosic
FIBER OPTICS
FIELD WAREHOUSING SVCS
FILE FOLDERS
FILM & SHEET: Unsuppported Plastic
FILM DEVELOPING & PRINTING SVCS
FILM: Rubber
FILTER ELEMENTS: Fluid & Hydraulic Line
FILTERS
FILTERS & SOFTENERS: Water, Household
FINANCIAL INVESTMENT ACTIVITIES, NEC: Security Transfer
FINANCIAL INVESTMENT ADVICE
FINANCIAL SVCS
FINGERPRINTING SVCS
FIRE ALARM MAINTENANCE & MONITORING SVCS
FIRE CONTROL EQPT REPAIR SVCS, MILITARY
FIRE EXTINGUISHER SVC
FIRE EXTINGUISHERS, WHOLESALE
FIRE OR BURGLARY RESISTIVE PRDTS
FIRE PROTECTION EQPT
FIRE PROTECTION SVCS: Contracted
FIRE PROTECTION, EXC CONTRACT
FIRE PROTECTION, GOVERNMENT: County
FIRE PROTECTION, GOVERNMENT: Fire Department, Volunteer
FIRE PROTECTION, GOVERNMENT: Local
FIREARMS & AMMUNITION, EXC SPORTING, WHOLESALE
FIREARMS, EXC SPORTING, WHOLESALE
FIREWOOD, WHOLESALE
FIREWORKS SHOPS
FIREWORKS: Wholesalers
FISH & SEAFOOD WHOLESALERS
FISH, PACKAGED FROZEN: Wholesalers
FISHING CAMPS
FITTINGS & ASSEMBLIES: Hose & Tube, Hydraulic Or Pneumatic
FITTINGS: Pipe
FLAT GLASS: Construction
FLEA MARKET
FLIGHT TRAINING SCHOOLS
FLOATING DRY DOCKS
FLOOR COVERING STORES
FLOOR COVERING STORES: Carpets

SERVICES INDEX

FLOOR COVERING STORES: Floor Tile
FLOOR COVERING: Plastic
FLOOR COVERINGS WHOLESALERS
FLOOR WAXING SVCS
FLORIST: Flowers, Fresh
FLORIST: Plants, Potted
FLORISTS
FLORISTS' SPLYS, WHOLESALE
FLOTATION COMPANIES: Securities
FLOWERS & FLORISTS' SPLYS WHOLESALERS
FLOWERS & NURSERY STOCK, WHOLESALE
FLOWERS, ARTIFICIAL, WHOLESALE
FLOWERS, FRESH, WHOLESALE
FLUID POWER PUMPS & MOTORS
FLUID POWER VALVES & HOSE FITTINGS
FLUXES
FOAMS & RUBBER, WHOLESALE
FOIL & LEAF: Metal
FOOD PRDTS, CANNED: Chili
FOOD PRDTS, CANNED: Ethnic
FOOD PRDTS, CANNED: Fruits
FOOD PRDTS, CANNED: Tomatoes
FOOD PRDTS, CONFECTIONERY, WHOLESALE: Candy
FOOD PRDTS, CONFECTIONERY, WHOLESALE: Nuts, Salted/Roasted
FOOD PRDTS, CONFECTIONERY, WHOLESALE: Potato Chips
FOOD PRDTS, CONFECTIONERY, WHOLESALE: Snack Foods
FOOD PRDTS, CONFECTIONERY, WHOLESALE: Syrups, Fountain
FOOD PRDTS, FISH & SEAFOOD, WHOLESALE: Fresh
FOOD PRDTS, FISH & SEAFOOD, WHOLESALE: Frozen, Unpackaged
FOOD PRDTS, FISH & SEAFOOD, WHOLESALE: Seafood
FOOD PRDTS, FROZEN: NEC
FOOD PRDTS, FRUITS & VEG, FRESH, WHOL: Banana Ripening Svc
FOOD PRDTS, FRUITS & VEGETABLES, FRESH, WHOLESALE
FOOD PRDTS, FRUITS & VEGETABLES, FRESH, WHOLESALE: Potatoes
FOOD PRDTS, FRUITS & VEGETABLES, FRESH, WHOLESALE: Vegetable
FOOD PRDTS, FRUITS & VEGETABLES, FRESH, WHOLESALE: Vegetable
FOOD PRDTS, MEAT & MEAT PRDTS, WHOLESALE: Brokers
FOOD PRDTS, MEAT & MEAT PRDTS, WHOLESALE: Cured Or Smoked
FOOD PRDTS, MEAT & MEAT PRDTS, WHOLESALE: Fresh
FOOD PRDTS, MEAT & MEAT PRDTS, WHOLESALE: Lard
FOOD PRDTS, POULTRY, WHOLESALE: Live/Dressed/Frozen, Unpkgd
FOOD PRDTS, WHOL: Canned Goods, Fruit, Veg, Seafood/Meats
FOOD PRDTS, WHOLESALE: Baking Splys
FOOD PRDTS, WHOLESALE: Beverage Concentrates
FOOD PRDTS, WHOLESALE: Beverages, Exc Coffee & Tea
FOOD PRDTS, WHOLESALE: Chocolate
FOOD PRDTS, WHOLESALE: Coffee & Tea
FOOD PRDTS, WHOLESALE: Coffee, Green Or Roasted
FOOD PRDTS, WHOLESALE: Corn
FOOD PRDTS, WHOLESALE: Dried or Canned Foods
FOOD PRDTS, WHOLESALE: Grain Elevators
FOOD PRDTS, WHOLESALE: Grains
FOOD PRDTS, WHOLESALE: Health
FOOD PRDTS, WHOLESALE: Juices
FOOD PRDTS, WHOLESALE: Molasses, Indl
FOOD PRDTS, WHOLESALE: Natural & Organic
FOOD PRDTS, WHOLESALE: Pizza Splys
FOOD PRDTS, WHOLESALE: Salt, Edible
FOOD PRDTS, WHOLESALE: Sauces
FOOD PRDTS, WHOLESALE: Spaghetti
FOOD PRDTS, WHOLESALE: Specialty
FOOD PRDTS, WHOLESALE: Starch
FOOD PRDTS, WHOLESALE: Water, Mineral Or Spring, Bottled
FOOD PRDTS, WHOLESALE: Wine Makers' Eqpt & Splys
FOOD PRDTS: Coffee
FOOD PRDTS: Dried & Dehydrated Fruits, Vegetables & Soup Mix
FOOD PRDTS: Eggs, Processed
FOOD PRDTS: Eggs, Processed, Frozen
FOOD PRDTS: Flour

FOOD PRDTS: Flour & Other Grain Mill Products
FOOD PRDTS: Mixes, Flour
FOOD PRDTS: Potato & Corn Chips & Similar Prdts
FOOD PRDTS: Potato Chips & Other Potato-Based Snacks
FOOD PRDTS: Poultry, Processed, Frozen
FOOD PRDTS: Preparations
FOOD PRDTS: Salads
FOOD PRDTS: Sugar
FOOD PRDTS: Turkey, Processed, NEC
FOOD PRODUCTS MACHINERY
FOOD STORES: Convenience, Chain
FOOD STORES: Convenience, Independent
FOOD STORES: Delicatessen
FOOD STORES: Grocery, Chain
FOOD STORES: Grocery, Independent
FOOD STORES: Supermarket, More Than 100K Sq Ft, Hypermrkt
FOOD STORES: Supermarkets
FOOD STORES: Supermarkets, Chain
FOOD STORES: Supermarkets, Independent
FOOTWEAR, WHOLESALE: Athletic
FOOTWEAR, WHOLESALE: Shoes
FORGINGS
FORGINGS: Iron & Steel
FORGINGS: Nonferrous
FORGINGS: Plumbing Fixture, Nonferrous
FORMS: Concrete, Sheet Metal
FOUNDRIES: Aluminum
FOUNDRIES: Brass, Bronze & Copper
FOUNDRIES: Nonferrous
FOUNDRIES: Steel
FOUNDRY MACHINERY & EQPT
FRAMES & FRAMING WHOLESALE
FRANCHISES, SELLING OR LICENSING
FREIGHT CAR LOADING & UNLOADING SVCS
FREIGHT CONSOLIDATION SVCS
FREIGHT FORWARDING ARRANGEMENTS
FREIGHT FORWARDING ARRANGEMENTS: Domestic
FREIGHT FORWARDING ARRANGEMENTS: Foreign
FREIGHT HANDLING SVCS: Air
FREIGHT TRANSPORTATION ARRANGEMENTS
FROZEN FRUITS WHOLESALERS
FRUIT & VEGETABLE MARKETS
FRUIT STANDS OR MARKETS
FRUITS & VEGETABLES WHOLESALERS: Fresh
FUEL OIL DEALERS
FUND RAISING ORGANIZATION, NON-FEE BASIS
FUNDRAISING SVCS
FUNERAL DIRECTOR
FUNERAL HOME
FUNERAL HOMES & SVCS
FUNGICIDES OR HERBICIDES
FURNACES & OVENS: Indl
FURNACES: Indl, Electric
FURNACES: Warm Air, Electric
FURNITURE & CABINET STORES: Custom
FURNITURE REFINISHING SVCS
FURNITURE REFINISHING SVCS
FURNITURE REPAIR & MAINTENANCE SVCS
FURNITURE STORES
FURNITURE STORES: Office
FURNITURE STORES: Outdoor & Garden
FURNITURE WHOLESALERS
FURNITURE, MATTRESSES: Wholesalers
FURNITURE, OFFICE: Wholesalers
FURNITURE, WHOLESALE: Bedsprings
FURNITURE, WHOLESALE: Filing Units
FURNITURE, WHOLESALE: Tables, Occasional
FURNITURE: Bed Frames & Headboards, Wood
FURNITURE: Frames, Box Springs Or Bedsprings, Metal
FURNITURE: Household, Upholstered, Exc Wood Or Metal
FURNITURE: Household, Wood
FURNITURE: Institutional, Exc Wood
FURNITURE: Mattresses & Foundations
FURNITURE: Office, Exc Wood
FURNITURE: Office, Wood
FURNITURE: Play Pens, Children's, Wood

G

GAMES & TOYS: Child Restraint Seats, Automotive
GARAGE DOOR REPAIR SVCS
GARMENT: Pressing & cleaners' agents
GAS & OIL FIELD EXPLORATION SVCS
GAS & OIL FIELD SVCS, NEC
GAS & OTHER COMBINED SVCS

GAS FIELD MACHINERY & EQPT
GAS PRODUCTION & DISTRIBUTION
GAS PRODUCTION & DISTRIBUTION: Liq Petroleum, Distrib-Mains
GAS STATIONS
GAS SYSTEM CONVERSION SVCS
GASES: Acetylene
GASES: Indl
GASKETS
GASKETS & SEALING DEVICES
GASOLINE FILLING STATIONS
GASOLINE WHOLESALERS
GATES: Ornamental Metal
GEARS: Power Transmission, Exc Auto
GENERAL & INDUSTRIAL LOAN INSTITUTIONS
GENERAL COUNSELING SVCS
GENERAL MERCHANDISE, NONDURABLE, WHOLESALE
GERIATRIC RESIDENTIAL CARE FACILITY
GERIATRIC SOCIAL SVCS
GIFT SHOP
GIFT WRAPPING SVCS
GIFT, NOVELTY & SOUVENIR STORES: Party Favors
GIFTS & NOVELTIES: Wholesalers
GIRLS CAMPS
GLASS FABRICATORS
GLASS PRDTS, FROM PURCHASED GLASS: Windshields
GLASS PRDTS, PRESSED OR BLOWN: Glass Fibers, Textile
GLASS STORES
GLASS, AUTOMOTIVE: Wholesalers
GLASS: Fiber
GLASS: Flat
GLASS: Pressed & Blown, NEC
GLASS: Structural
GLOVES: Work
GO-CART DEALERS
GOLF CARTS: Powered
GOLF CARTS: Wholesalers
GOLF COURSES: Public
GOLF DRIVING RANGES
GOLF EQPT
GOLF GOODS & EQPT
GOURMET FOOD STORES
GOVERNMENT, EXECUTIVE OFFICES: City & Town Managers' Offices
GOVERNMENT, EXECUTIVE OFFICES: County Supervisor/Exec Office
GOVERNMENT, EXECUTIVE OFFICES: Local
GOVERNMENT, EXECUTIVE OFFICES: Mayors'
GOVERNMENT, GENERAL: Administration
GOVERNMENT, GENERAL: Administration, County
GOVERNMENT, GENERAL: Administration, State
GOVERNMENT, GENERAL: Supply Agency
GOVERNMENT, LEGISLATIVE BODIES: County
GOVERNMENT, LEGISLATIVE BODIES: County Commissioner
GOVERNMENT, LEGISLATIVE BODIES: Town Council
GRADING SVCS
GRAIN & FIELD BEANS WHOLESALERS
GRANITE: Crushed & Broken
GRANITE: Cut & Shaped
GRANTMAKING FOUNDATIONS
GRAPHIC ARTS & RELATED DESIGN SVCS
GRAPHITE MINING SVCS
GRAVEL MINING
GREASES & INEDIBLE FATS, RENDERED
GREENHOUSES: Prefabricated Metal
GREETING CARD SHOPS
GRINDING SVC: Precision, Commercial Or Indl
GROCERIES WHOLESALERS, NEC
GROCERIES, GENERAL LINE WHOLESALERS
GROUP DAY CARE CENTER
GROUP FOSTER HOME
GROUP HOSPITALIZATION PLANS
GUARD PROTECTIVE SVCS
GUARD SVCS
GUIDED MISSILES & SPACE VEHICLES
GYMNASTICS INSTRUCTION

H

HAIRDRESSERS
HALFWAY GROUP HOME, PERSONS WITH SOCIAL OR PERSONAL PROBLEMS
HALFWAY HOME FOR DELINQUENTS & OFFENDERS
HAND TOOLS, NEC: Wholesalers
HANDYMAN SVCS

SERVICES INDEX

HANGARS & OTHER AIRCRAFT STORAGE FACILITIES
HARDWARE
HARDWARE & BUILDING PRDTS: Plastic
HARDWARE & EQPT: Stage, Exc Lighting
HARDWARE STORES
HARDWARE STORES: Door Locks & Lock Sets
HARDWARE STORES: Pumps & Pumping Eqpt
HARDWARE STORES: Tools
HARDWARE WHOLESALERS
HARDWARE, WHOLESALE: Bolts
HARDWARE, WHOLESALE: Builders', NEC
HARDWARE, WHOLESALE: Casters & Glides
HARDWARE, WHOLESALE: Garden Tools, Hand
HARDWARE, WHOLESALE: Nuts
HARDWARE, WHOLESALE: Power Tools & Access
HARDWARE, WHOLESALE: Saw Blades
HARDWARE, WHOLESALE: Screws
HARDWARE: Rubber
HARNESS ASSEMBLIES: Cable & Wire
HEAD START CENTER, EXC IN CONJUNCTION WITH SCHOOL
HEALTH & ALLIED SERVICES, NEC
HEALTH & WELFARE COUNCIL
HEALTH CLUBS
HEALTH FOOD & SUPPLEMENT STORES
HEALTH INSURANCE CARRIERS
HEALTH MAINTENANCE ORGANIZATION: Insurance Only
HEALTH PRACTITIONERS' OFFICES, NEC
HEALTH SCREENING SVCS
HEALTH SYSTEMS AGENCY
HEARING TESTING SVCS
HEAT TREATING: Metal
HEATERS: Room & Wall, Including Radiators
HEATING & AIR CONDITIONING EQPT & SPLYS WHOLESALERS
HEATING EQPT & SPLYS
HELP SUPPLY SERVICES
HELPING HAND SVCS, INCLUDING BIG BROTHER, ETC
HIGHWAY & STREET MAINTENANCE SVCS
HIGHWAY BRIDGE OPERATION
HISTORICAL SOCIETY
HOBBY, TOY & GAME STORES: Arts & Crafts & Splys
HOBBY, TOY & GAME STORES: Children's Toys & Games, Exc Dolls
HOBBY, TOY & GAME STORES: Toys & Games
HOGS WHOLESALERS
HOLDING COMPANIES, NEC
HOLDING COMPANIES: Banks
HOLDING COMPANIES: Investment, Exc Banks
HOLDING COMPANIES: Personal, Exc Banks
HOME CENTER STORES
HOME FOR THE DESTITUTE
HOME FOR THE EMOTIONALLY DISTURBED
HOME FOR THE MENTALLY HANDICAPPED
HOME FOR THE MENTALLY RETARDED
HOME FOR THE MENTALLY RETARDED, EXC SKILLED OR INTERMEDIATE
HOME FOR THE PHYSICALLY HANDICAPPED
HOME FURNISHINGS WHOLESALERS
HOME HEALTH CARE SVCS
HOME IMPROVEMENT & RENOVATION CONTRACTOR AGENCY
HOMEBUILDERS & OTHER OPERATIVE BUILDERS
HOMEFURNISHING STORES: Fireplaces & Wood Burning Stoves
HOMEFURNISHING STORES: Lighting Fixtures
HOMEFURNISHING STORES: Metalware
HOMEFURNISHING STORES: Pottery
HOMEFURNISHINGS & SPLYS, WHOLESALE: Decorative
HOMEFURNISHINGS, WHOLESALE: Blankets
HOMEFURNISHINGS, WHOLESALE: Blinds, Venetian
HOMEFURNISHINGS, WHOLESALE: Carpets
HOMEFURNISHINGS, WHOLESALE: Draperies
HOMEFURNISHINGS, WHOLESALE: Grills, Barbecue
HOMEFURNISHINGS, WHOLESALE: Kitchenware
HOMEFURNISHINGS, WHOLESALE: Mirrors/Pictures, Framed/Unframd
HOMEFURNISHINGS, WHOLESALE: Pottery
HOMEFURNISHINGS, WHOLESALE: Rugs
HOMEFURNISHINGS, WHOLESALE: Wood Flooring
HOMES FOR THE ELDERLY
HOSE: Automobile, Rubber
HOSE: Flexible Metal
HOSES & BELTING: Rubber & Plastic
HOSPITAL EQPT REPAIR SVCS
HOSPITALS: AMA Approved Residency
HOSPITALS: Cancer
HOSPITALS: Children's
HOSPITALS: Chronic Disease
HOSPITALS: Hospital, Professional Nursing School
HOSPITALS: Medical & Surgical
HOSPITALS: Medical School Affiliated With Nursing
HOSPITALS: Medical School Affiliated with Residency
HOSPITALS: Medical School Affiliation
HOSPITALS: Mental Retardation
HOSPITALS: Mental, Exc For The Mentally Retarded
HOSPITALS: Orthopedic
HOSPITALS: Professional Nursing School With AMA Residency
HOSPITALS: Psychiatric
HOSPITALS: Rehabilitation, Alcoholism
HOSPITALS: Rehabilitation, Drug Addiction
HOSPITALS: Specialty, NEC
HOSPITALS: Substance Abuse
HOTEL: Franchised
HOTELS & MOTELS
HOTLINE
HOUSEHOLD APPLIANCE PARTS: Wholesalers
HOUSEHOLD APPLIANCE REPAIR SVCS
HOUSEHOLD APPLIANCE STORES
HOUSEHOLD APPLIANCE STORES: Air Cond Rm Units, Self-Contnd
HOUSEHOLD APPLIANCE STORES: Appliance Parts
HOUSEHOLD APPLIANCE STORES: Electric
HOUSEHOLD APPLIANCE STORES: Electric Household, Major
HOUSEHOLD APPLIANCE STORES: Gas Appliances
HOUSEHOLD FURNISHINGS, NEC
HOUSEHOLD SEWING MACHINES WHOLESALERS: Electric
HOUSEKEEPING & MAID SVCS
HOUSES: Fraternity & Sorority
HOUSES: Lodging, Organization
HOUSES: Rooming & Boarding
HOUSEWARE STORES
HOUSEWARES, ELECTRIC: Cooking Appliances
HOUSING AUTHORITY OPERATOR
HOUSING PROGRAM ADMIN, GOVT: Housing Authority, Nonoperating
HOUSING PROGRAM ADMINISTRATION, GOVT: Planning & Development
HOUSING PROGRAMS ADMINISTRATION SVCS
HUMAN RESOURCE, SOCIAL WORK & WELFARE ADMINISTRATION SVCS
HUMANE SOCIETIES
HYDRAULIC EQPT REPAIR SVC

I

ICE
ICE CREAM & ICES WHOLESALERS
ICE WHOLESALERS
IGNEOUS ROCK: Crushed & Broken
INCUBATORS & BROODERS: Farm
INDL & PERSONAL SVC PAPER WHOLESALERS
INDL & PERSONAL SVC PAPER, WHOL: Bags, Paper/Disp Plastic
INDL & PERSONAL SVC PAPER, WHOL: Boxes, Corrugtd/Solid Fiber
INDL & PERSONAL SVC PAPER, WHOL: Container, Paper/Plastic
INDL & PERSONAL SVC PAPER, WHOL: Paper, Wrap/Coarse/Prdts
INDL & PERSONAL SVC PAPER, WHOLESALE: Boxes & Containers
INDL & PERSONAL SVC PAPER, WHOLESALE: Disposable
INDL & PERSONAL SVC PAPER, WHOLESALE: Paper Tubes & Cores
INDL & PERSONAL SVC PAPER, WHOLESALE: Patterns, Paper
INDL & PERSONAL SVC PAPER, WHOLESALE: Press Sensitive Tape
INDL & PERSONAL SVC PAPER, WHOLESALE: Shipping Splys
INDL & PERSONAL SVC PAPER, WHOLESALE: Towels, Paper
INDL CONTRACTORS: Exhibit Construction
INDL DIAMONDS WHOLESALERS
INDL EQPT CLEANING SVCS
INDL EQPT SVCS
INDL GASES WHOLESALERS
INDL HELP SVCS
INDL MACHINERY & EQPT WHOLESALERS
INDL MACHINERY REPAIR & MAINTENANCE
INDL PROCESS INSTRUMENTS: Controllers, Process Variables
INDL SPLYS WHOLESALERS
INDL SPLYS, WHOL: Fasteners, Incl Nuts, Bolts, Screws, Etc
INDL SPLYS, WHOLESALE: Abrasives
INDL SPLYS, WHOLESALE: Adhesives, Tape & Plasters
INDL SPLYS, WHOLESALE: Barrels, New Or Reconditioned
INDL SPLYS, WHOLESALE: Bearings
INDL SPLYS, WHOLESALE: Bottler Splys
INDL SPLYS, WHOLESALE: Drums, New Or Reconditioned
INDL SPLYS, WHOLESALE: Electric Tools
INDL SPLYS, WHOLESALE: Fasteners & Fastening Eqpt
INDL SPLYS, WHOLESALE: Fittings
INDL SPLYS, WHOLESALE: Gaskets
INDL SPLYS, WHOLESALE: Gaskets & Seals
INDL SPLYS, WHOLESALE: Gears
INDL SPLYS, WHOLESALE: Hydraulic & Pneumatic Pistons/Valves
INDL SPLYS, WHOLESALE: Knives, Indl
INDL SPLYS, WHOLESALE: Mill Splys
INDL SPLYS, WHOLESALE: Plastic, Pallets
INDL SPLYS, WHOLESALE: Power Transmission, Eqpt & Apparatus
INDL SPLYS, WHOLESALE: Rubber Goods, Mechanical
INDL SPLYS, WHOLESALE: Seals
INDL SPLYS, WHOLESALE: Signmaker Eqpt & Splys
INDL SPLYS, WHOLESALE: Tools
INDL SPLYS, WHOLESALE: Tools, NEC
INDL SPLYS, WHOLESALE: Valves & Fittings
INDL TOOL GRINDING SVCS
INDL TRUCK REPAIR SVCS
INDOOR PARKING SVCS
INDUSTRIAL & COMMERCIAL EQPT INSPECTION SVCS
INFORMATION BUREAU SVCS
INFORMATION RETRIEVAL SERVICES
INFORMATION SVCS: Consumer
INNS
INSPECTION & TESTING SVCS
INSPECTION SVCS, TRANSPORTATION
INSTRUMENTS, MEASURING & CNTRL: Testing, Abrasion, Etc
INSTRUMENTS, MEASURING & CONTROLLING: Cable Testing
INSTRUMENTS: Analytical
INSTRUMENTS: Eye Examination
INSTRUMENTS: Indl Process Control
INSTRUMENTS: Measurement, Indl Process
INSTRUMENTS: Measuring & Controlling
INSTRUMENTS: Measuring Electricity
INSTRUMENTS: Measuring, Electrical Energy
INSTRUMENTS: Medical & Surgical
INSTRUMENTS: Power Measuring, Electrical
INSTRUMENTS: Test, Electrical, Engine
INSTRUMENTS: Test, Electronic & Electric Measurement
INSTRUMENTS: Test, Electronic & Electrical Circuits
INSULATION & CUSHIONING FOAM: Polystyrene
INSULATION MATERIALS WHOLESALERS
INSULATION: Fiberglass
INSULATORS & INSULATION MATERIALS: Electrical
INSURANCE AGENCIES & BROKERS
INSURANCE AGENTS, NEC
INSURANCE BROKERS, NEC
INSURANCE CARRIERS: Automobile
INSURANCE CARRIERS: Bank Deposit
INSURANCE CARRIERS: Direct Accident & Health
INSURANCE CARRIERS: Hospital & Medical
INSURANCE CARRIERS: Life
INSURANCE CARRIERS: Pet, Health
INSURANCE CARRIERS: Property & Casualty
INSURANCE CARRIERS: Title
INSURANCE CARRIERS: Worker's Compensation
INSURANCE CLAIM ADJUSTERS, NOT EMPLOYED BY INSURANCE COMPANY
INSURANCE CLAIM PROCESSING, EXC MEDICAL
INSURANCE EDUCATION SVCS
INSURANCE INFORMATION & CONSULTING SVCS
INSURANCE RESEARCH SVCS
INSURANCE: Agents, Brokers & Service
INTERCOMMUNICATIONS SYSTEMS: Electric
INTERIOR DECORATING SVCS
INTERIOR DESIGN SVCS, NEC
INTERIOR DESIGNING SVCS

SERVICES INDEX

INTERMEDIATE CARE FACILITY
INTERMEDIATE INVESTMENT BANKS
INVENTORY COMPUTING SVCS
INVESTMENT ADVISORY SVCS
INVESTMENT BANKERS
INVESTMENT COUNSELORS
INVESTMENT FIRM: General Brokerage
INVESTMENT FUNDS, NEC
INVESTMENT FUNDS: Open-Ended
INVESTMENT OFFICES: Management, Closed-End
INVESTMENT OFFICES: Money Market Mutual
INVESTMENT RESEARCH SVCS
INVESTORS, NEC
INVESTORS: Real Estate, Exc Property Operators
IRON ORE MINING
IRON ORES
IRRIGATION SYSTEMS, NEC Water Distribution Or Sply Systems

J

JANITORIAL & CUSTODIAL SVCS
JANITORIAL EQPT & SPLYS WHOLESALERS
JEWELRY APPAREL
JEWELRY REPAIR SVCS
JEWELRY STORES
JEWELRY, WHOLESALE
JOB COUNSELING
JOB TRAINING & VOCATIONAL REHABILITATION SVCS
JOB TRAINING SVCS
JUICE, FROZEN: Wholesalers
JUNIOR HIGH SCHOOLS, PUBLIC
JUNIOR OR SENIOR HIGH SCHOOLS, NEC
JUVENILE CORRECTIONAL FACILITIES
JUVENILE CORRECTIONAL HOME

K

KEY DUPLICATING SHOP
KIDNEY DIALYSIS CENTERS
KINDERGARTEN
KITCHEN CABINET STORES, EXC CUSTOM
KITCHEN CABINETS WHOLESALERS
KITCHEN TOOLS & UTENSILS WHOLESALERS
KITCHENWARE STORES
KNIVES: Agricultural Or Indl

L

LABELS: Paper, Made From Purchased Materials
LABOR RESOURCE SVCS
LABOR UNION
LABORATORIES, TESTING: Automobile Proving & Testing Ground
LABORATORIES, TESTING: Food
LABORATORIES, TESTING: Hazardous Waste
LABORATORIES, TESTING: Hydrostatic
LABORATORIES, TESTING: Industrial Sterilization
LABORATORIES, TESTING: Metallurgical
LABORATORIES, TESTING: Pollution
LABORATORIES, TESTING: Prdt Certification, Sfty/Performance
LABORATORIES, TESTING: Product Testing
LABORATORIES, TESTING: Product Testing, Safety/Performance
LABORATORIES, TESTING: Soil Analysis
LABORATORIES, TESTING: Water
LABORATORIES: Biological
LABORATORIES: Biological Research
LABORATORIES: Biotechnology
LABORATORIES: Blood Analysis
LABORATORIES: Commercial Nonphysical Research
LABORATORIES: Dental
LABORATORIES: Dental & Medical X-Ray
LABORATORIES: Dental, Artificial Teeth Production
LABORATORIES: Dental, Crown & Bridge Production
LABORATORIES: Dental, Denture Production
LABORATORIES: Electronic Research
LABORATORIES: Environmental Research
LABORATORIES: Medical
LABORATORIES: Medical Pathology
LABORATORIES: Noncommercial Research
LABORATORIES: Physical Research, Commercial
LABORATORIES: Testing
LABORATORIES: Testing
LABORATORIES: Testing, Assaying
LABORATORIES: Ultrasound

LABORATORY APPARATUS & FURNITURE
LABORATORY EQPT, EXC MEDICAL: Wholesalers
LABORATORY EQPT: Clinical Instruments Exc Medical
LABORATORY INSTRUMENT REPAIR SVCS
LADDERS: Metal
LAMINATED PLASTICS: Plate, Sheet, Rod & Tubes
LAMINATING SVCS
LAND SUBDIVIDERS & DEVELOPERS: Commercial
LAND SUBDIVIDERS & DEVELOPERS: Residential
LAND SUBDIVISION & DEVELOPMENT
LANGUAGE SCHOOLS
LAUNDRIES, EXC POWER & COIN-OPERATED
LAUNDRY & DRYCLEANER AGENTS
LAUNDRY & DRYCLEANING SVCS, EXC COIN-OPERATED: Pickup
LAUNDRY & GARMENT SVCS, NEC: Accy/Non-Garment Cleaning/Rpr
LAUNDRY & GARMENT SVCS, NEC: Garment Alteration & Repair
LAUNDRY & GARMENT SVCS, NEC: Garment Making, Alter & Repair
LAUNDRY SVC: Mat & Rug Sply
LAUNDRY SVC: Safety Glove Sply
LAUNDRY SVC: Work Clothing Sply
LAUNDRY SVCS: Indl
LAWN & GARDEN EQPT
LAWN & GARDEN EQPT STORES
LAWN MOWER REPAIR SHOP
LEASING & RENTAL SVCS: Cranes & Aerial Lift Eqpt
LEASING & RENTAL SVCS: Earth Moving Eqpt
LEASING & RENTAL SVCS: Oil Field Eqpt
LEASING & RENTAL: Computers & Eqpt
LEASING & RENTAL: Construction & Mining Eqpt
LEASING & RENTAL: Medical Machinery & Eqpt
LEASING & RENTAL: Mobile Home Sites
LEASING & RENTAL: Office Machines & Eqpt
LEASING & RENTAL: Other Real Estate Property
LEASING & RENTAL: Trucks, Indl
LEASING & RENTAL: Trucks, Without Drivers
LEASING & RENTAL: Utility Trailers & RV's
LEASING: Passenger Car
LEASING: Railroad Property
LEASING: Residential Buildings
LEATHER & CUT STOCK WHOLESALERS
LEATHER GOODS, EXC FOOTWEAR, GLOVES, LUGGAGE/BELTING, WHOL
LEATHER GOODS: Coin Purses
LEATHER, LEATHER GOODS & FURS, WHOLESALE
LEGAL AID SVCS
LEGAL COUNSEL & PROSECUTION: Attorney General's Office
LEGAL COUNSEL & PROSECUTION: County Government
LEGAL COUNSEL & PROSECUTION: Local Government
LEGAL COUNSEL & PROSECUTION: Public Prosecutors' Office
LEGAL OFFICES & SVCS
LEGAL SVCS: Administrative & Government Law
LEGAL SVCS: Bankruptcy Law
LEGAL SVCS: Criminal Law
LEGAL SVCS: Debt Collection Law
LEGAL SVCS: General Practice Attorney or Lawyer
LEGAL SVCS: General Practice Law Office
LEGAL SVCS: Labor & Employment Law
LEGAL SVCS: Real Estate Law
LEGAL SVCS: Specialized Law Offices, Attorney
LEGISLATIVE BODIES: Federal, State & Local
LEGITIMATE LIVE THEATER PRODUCERS
LESSORS: Farm Land
LESSORS: Landholding Office
LIABILITY INSURANCE
LIFE INSURANCE AGENTS
LIFE INSURANCE CARRIERS
LIFE INSURANCE: Fraternal Organizations
LIFE INSURANCE: Mutual Association
LIFEGUARD SVC
LIGHTING EQPT: Motor Vehicle
LIGHTING FIXTURES WHOLESALERS
LIGHTING FIXTURES, NEC
LIGHTING FIXTURES: Indl & Commercial
LIGHTING FIXTURES: Motor Vehicle
LIGHTING MAINTENANCE SVC
LIME
LIME ROCK: Ground
LIMESTONE: Crushed & Broken
LIMESTONE: Dimension

LIMESTONE: Ground
LIMOUSINE SVCS
LINEN SPLY SVC
LINEN SPLY SVC: Towel
LINEN SPLY SVC: Uniform
LIQUEFIED PETROLEUM GAS WHOLESALERS
LIQUIDATORS
LIVESTOCK LOAN COMPANIES
LIVESTOCK WHOLESALERS, NEC
LOADS: Electronic
LOGGING
LOOSELEAF BINDERS
LOTIONS OR CREAMS: Face
LUBRICATING OIL & GREASE WHOLESALERS
LUGGAGE & LEATHER GOODS STORES: Leather, Exc Luggage & Shoes
LUMBER & BLDG MATLS DEALER, RET: Garage Doors, Sell/Install
LUMBER & BLDG MATRLS DEALERS, RET: Bath Fixtures, Eqpt/Sply
LUMBER & BLDG MATRLS DEALERS, RETAIL: Doors, Wood/Metal
LUMBER & BLDG MTRLS DEALERS, RET: Planing Mill Prdts/Lumber
LUMBER & BLDG MTRLS DEALERS, RET: Windows, Storm, Wood/Metal
LUMBER & BUILDING MATERIAL DEALERS, RETAIL: Roofing Material
LUMBER & BUILDING MATERIALS DEALER, RET: Door & Window Prdts
LUMBER & BUILDING MATERIALS DEALER, RET: Masonry Matls/Splys
LUMBER & BUILDING MATERIALS DEALERS, RETAIL: Brick
LUMBER & BUILDING MATERIALS DEALERS, RETAIL: Cement
LUMBER & BUILDING MATERIALS DEALERS, RETAIL: Countertops
LUMBER & BUILDING MATERIALS DEALERS, RETAIL: Siding
LUMBER & BUILDING MATLS DEALERS, RET: Concrete/Cinder Block
LUMBER & BUILDING MTRLS DEALERS, RET: Insulation Mtrl, Bldg
LUMBER: Dimension, Hardwood
LUMBER: Fiberboard
LUMBER: Hardwood Dimension & Flooring Mills
LUMBER: Plywood, Hardwood
LUMBER: Plywood, Softwood
LUMBER: Treated
LUNCHROOMS & CAFETERIAS

M

MACHINE PARTS: Stamped Or Pressed Metal
MACHINE SHOPS
MACHINE TOOL ACCESS: Cutting
MACHINE TOOL ACCESS: Diamond Cutting, For Turning, Etc
MACHINE TOOL ACCESS: Drill Bushings, Drilling Jig
MACHINE TOOL ACCESS: Knives, Metalworking
MACHINE TOOLS & ACCESS
MACHINE TOOLS, METAL CUTTING: Home Workshop
MACHINE TOOLS, METAL CUTTING: Sawing & Cutoff
MACHINE TOOLS, METAL CUTTING: Tool Replacement & Rpr Parts
MACHINE TOOLS, METAL FORMING: Bending
MACHINE TOOLS, METAL FORMING: Marking
MACHINE TOOLS, METAL FORMING: Mechanical, Pneumatic Or Hyd
MACHINE TOOLS: Metal Cutting
MACHINE TOOLS: Metal Forming
MACHINERY & EQPT FINANCE LEASING
MACHINERY & EQPT, AGRICULTURAL, WHOL: Farm Eqpt Parts/Splys
MACHINERY & EQPT, AGRICULTURAL, WHOLESALE: Agricultural, NEC
MACHINERY & EQPT, AGRICULTURAL, WHOLESALE: Dairy
MACHINERY & EQPT, AGRICULTURAL, WHOLESALE: Farm Implements
MACHINERY & EQPT, AGRICULTURAL, WHOLESALE: Landscaping Eqpt
MACHINERY & EQPT, AGRICULTURAL, WHOLESALE: Lawn
MACHINERY & EQPT, AGRICULTURAL, WHOLESALE: Lawn & Garden
MACHINERY & EQPT, AGRICULTURAL, WHOLESALE: Livestock Eqpt

SERVICES INDEX

MACHINERY & EQPT, AGRICULTURAL, WHOLESALE: Tractors
MACHINERY & EQPT, INDL, WHOL: Brewery Prdts Mfrg, Commercial
MACHINERY & EQPT, INDL, WHOL: Controlling Instruments/Access
MACHINERY & EQPT, INDL, WHOL: Environ Pollution Cntrl, Air
MACHINERY & EQPT, INDL, WHOL: Meters, Consumption Registerng
MACHINERY & EQPT, INDL, WHOL: Oil Field Tool Joints, Re-built
MACHINERY & EQPT, INDL, WHOLESALE: Cement Making
MACHINERY & EQPT, INDL, WHOLESALE: Chemical Process
MACHINERY & EQPT, INDL, WHOLESALE: Conveyor Systems
MACHINERY & EQPT, INDL, WHOLESALE: Cranes
MACHINERY & EQPT, INDL, WHOLESALE: Dairy Prdts Manufacturing
MACHINERY & EQPT, INDL, WHOLESALE: Drilling Bits
MACHINERY & EQPT, INDL, WHOLESALE: Engines & Parts, Diesel
MACHINERY & EQPT, INDL, WHOLESALE: Engines, Gasoline
MACHINERY & EQPT, INDL, WHOLESALE: Engs & Parts, Air-Cooled
MACHINERY & EQPT, INDL, WHOLESALE: Fans
MACHINERY & EQPT, INDL, WHOLESALE: Food Manufacturing
MACHINERY & EQPT, INDL, WHOLESALE: Food Product Manufacturng
MACHINERY & EQPT, INDL, WHOLESALE: Heat Exchange
MACHINERY & EQPT, INDL, WHOLESALE: Hoists
MACHINERY & EQPT, INDL, WHOLESALE: Hydraulic Systems
MACHINERY & EQPT, INDL, WHOLESALE: Indl Machine Parts
MACHINERY & EQPT, INDL, WHOLESALE: Instruments & Cntrl Eqpt
MACHINERY & EQPT, INDL, WHOLESALE: Lift Trucks & Parts
MACHINERY & EQPT, INDL, WHOLESALE: Machine Tools & Access
MACHINERY & EQPT, INDL, WHOLESALE: Machine Tools & Metalwork
MACHINERY & EQPT, INDL, WHOLESALE: Noise Control
MACHINERY & EQPT, INDL, WHOLESALE: Packaging
MACHINERY & EQPT, INDL, WHOLESALE: Paper Manufacturing
MACHINERY & EQPT, INDL, WHOLESALE: Petroleum Industry
MACHINERY & EQPT, INDL, WHOLESALE: Plastic Prdts Machinery
MACHINERY & EQPT, INDL, WHOLESALE: Pneumatic Tools
MACHINERY & EQPT, INDL, WHOLESALE: Processing & Packaging
MACHINERY & EQPT, INDL, WHOLESALE: Propane Conversion
MACHINERY & EQPT, INDL, WHOLESALE: Recycling
MACHINERY & EQPT, INDL, WHOLESALE: Robots
MACHINERY & EQPT, INDL, WHOLESALE: Safety Eqpt
MACHINERY & EQPT, INDL, WHOLESALE: Tanks, Storage
MACHINERY & EQPT, INDL, WHOLESALE: Trailers, Indl
MACHINERY & EQPT, WHOLESALE: Construction & Mining, Ladders
MACHINERY & EQPT, WHOLESALE: Construction, Cranes
MACHINERY & EQPT, WHOLESALE: Construction, General
MACHINERY & EQPT, WHOLESALE: Contractors Materials
MACHINERY & EQPT, WHOLESALE: Drilling, Wellpoints
MACHINERY & EQPT, WHOLESALE: Logging
MACHINERY & EQPT, WHOLESALE: Masonry
MACHINERY & EQPT, WHOLESALE: Oil Field Eqpt
MACHINERY & EQPT, WHOLESALE: Road Construction & Maintenance
MACHINERY & EQPT: Electroplating
MACHINERY & EQPT: Farm
MACHINERY & EQPT: Gas Producers, Generators/Other Rltd Eqpt
MACHINERY BASES
MACHINERY CLEANING SVCS
MACHINERY, MAILING: Postage Meters
MACHINERY, METALWORKING: Assembly, Including Robotic
MACHINERY, METALWORKING: Cutting & Slitting
MACHINERY, OFFICE: Paper Handling
MACHINERY, PACKAGING: Wrapping
MACHINERY, WOODWORKING: Pattern Makers'
MACHINERY/EQPT, INDL, WHOL: Cleaning, High Press, Sand/Steam
MACHINERY: Ammunition & Explosives Loading
MACHINERY: Assembly, Exc Metalworking
MACHINERY: Automotive Related
MACHINERY: Binding
MACHINERY: Bottling & Canning
MACHINERY: Construction
MACHINERY: Custom
MACHINERY: Glassmaking
MACHINERY: Logging Eqpt
MACHINERY: Metalworking
MACHINERY: Mining
MACHINERY: Packaging
MACHINERY: Paper Industry Miscellaneous
MACHINERY: Plastic Working
MACHINERY: Printing Presses
MACHINERY: Recycling
MACHINERY: Road Construction & Maintenance
MACHINERY: Rubber Working
MACHINERY: Textile
MACHINERY: Wire Drawing
MAGAZINES, WHOLESALE
MAGNETS: Permanent
MAIL PRESORTING SVCS
MAIL-ORDER HOUSE, NEC
MAIL-ORDER HOUSES: Arts & Crafts Eqpt & Splys
MAIL-ORDER HOUSES: Automotive Splys & Eqpt
MAIL-ORDER HOUSES: Books, Exc Book Clubs
MAIL-ORDER HOUSES: Cheese
MAIL-ORDER HOUSES: Computer Software
MAIL-ORDER HOUSES: Computers & Peripheral Eqpt
MAIL-ORDER HOUSES: Educational Splys & Eqpt
MAIL-ORDER HOUSES: Gift Items
MAILBOX RENTAL & RELATED SVCS
MAILING & MESSENGER SVCS
MAILING LIST: Brokers
MAILING LIST: Compilers
MAILING SVCS, NEC
MANAGEMENT CONSULTING SVCS: Administrative
MANAGEMENT CONSULTING SVCS: Automation & Robotics
MANAGEMENT CONSULTING SVCS: Banking & Finance
MANAGEMENT CONSULTING SVCS: Business
MANAGEMENT CONSULTING SVCS: Business Planning & Organizing
MANAGEMENT CONSULTING SVCS: Compensation & Benefits Planning
MANAGEMENT CONSULTING SVCS: Construction Project
MANAGEMENT CONSULTING SVCS: Corporation Organizing
MANAGEMENT CONSULTING SVCS: Distribution Channels
MANAGEMENT CONSULTING SVCS: Food & Beverage
MANAGEMENT CONSULTING SVCS: Franchising
MANAGEMENT CONSULTING SVCS: General
MANAGEMENT CONSULTING SVCS: Hospital & Health
MANAGEMENT CONSULTING SVCS: Industrial & Labor
MANAGEMENT CONSULTING SVCS: Industry Specialist
MANAGEMENT CONSULTING SVCS: Information Systems
MANAGEMENT CONSULTING SVCS: Maintenance
MANAGEMENT CONSULTING SVCS: Management Engineering
MANAGEMENT CONSULTING SVCS: Manufacturing
MANAGEMENT CONSULTING SVCS: Merchandising
MANAGEMENT CONSULTING SVCS: New Products & Svcs
MANAGEMENT CONSULTING SVCS: Planning
MANAGEMENT CONSULTING SVCS: Public Utilities
MANAGEMENT CONSULTING SVCS: Quality Assurance
MANAGEMENT CONSULTING SVCS: Real Estate
MANAGEMENT CONSULTING SVCS: Restaurant & Food
MANAGEMENT CONSULTING SVCS: Retail Trade Consultant
MANAGEMENT CONSULTING SVCS: Training & Development
MANAGEMENT CONSULTING SVCS: Transportation
MANAGEMENT SERVICES
MANAGEMENT SVCS, FACILITIES SUPPORT: Environ Remediation
MANAGEMENT SVCS, FACILITIES SUPPORT: Jails, Privately Ops
MANAGEMENT SVCS: Administrative
MANAGEMENT SVCS: Business
MANAGEMENT SVCS: Circuit, Motion Picture Theaters
MANAGEMENT SVCS: Construction
MANAGEMENT SVCS: Financial, Business
MANAGEMENT SVCS: Hospital
MANAGEMENT SVCS: Hotel Or Motel
MANAGEMENT SVCS: Nursing & Personal Care Facility
MANAGEMENT SVCS: Personnel
MANAGEMENT SVCS: Restaurant
MANAGERS: Athletes
MANPOWER POOLS
MANPOWER TRAINING
MANUFACTURED & MOBILE HOME DEALERS
MANUFACTURING INDUSTRIES, NEC
MARBLE, BUILDING: Cut & Shaped
MARINAS
MARINE CARGO HANDLING SVCS
MARINE CARGO HANDLING SVCS: Loading & Unloading
MARINE CARGO HANDLING SVCS: Marine Terminal
MARINE SPLYS WHOLESALERS
MARINE SVC STATIONS
MARKETS: Meat & fish
MARKING DEVICES: Embossing Seals & Hand Stamps
MARKING DEVICES: Screens, Textile Printing
MARRIAGE BUREAU
MARTIAL ARTS INSTRUCTION
MASSAGE PARLORS
MATERIALS HANDLING EQPT WHOLESALERS
MATS OR MATTING, NEC: Rubber
MATS, MATTING & PADS: Auto, Floor, Exc Rubber Or Plastic
MATS, MATTING & PADS: Nonwoven
MEAL DELIVERY PROGRAMS
MEAT & MEAT PRDTS WHOLESALERS
MEAT CUTTING & PACKING
MEAT MARKETS
MEAT PRDTS: Cooked Meats, From Purchased Meat
MEAT PRDTS: Frozen
MEAT PRDTS: Pork, From Slaughtered Meat
MEAT PRDTS: Prepared Beef Prdts From Purchased Beef
MEAT PROCESSED FROM PURCHASED CARCASSES
MEATS, PACKAGED FROZEN: Wholesalers
MECHANICAL INSTRUMENT REPAIR SVCS
MEDIA BUYING AGENCIES
MEDICAL & HOSPITAL EQPT WHOLESALERS
MEDICAL & SURGICAL SPLYS: Bandages & Dressings
MEDICAL & SURGICAL SPLYS: Clothing, Fire Resistant & Protect
MEDICAL & SURGICAL SPLYS: Hosiery, Support
MEDICAL CENTERS
MEDICAL EQPT REPAIR SVCS, NON-ELECTRIC
MEDICAL FIELD ASSOCIATION
MEDICAL HELP SVCS
MEDICAL INSURANCE CLAIM PROCESSING: Contract Or Fee Basis
MEDICAL RESCUE SQUAD
MEDICAL SVCS ORGANIZATION
MEDICAL TRAINING SERVICES
MEDICAL X-RAY MACHINES & TUBES WHOLESALERS
MEDICAL, DENTAL & HOSP EQPT, WHOLESALE: X-ray Film & Splys
MEDICAL, DENTAL & HOSPITAL EQPT, WHOL: Dentists' Prof Splys
MEDICAL, DENTAL & HOSPITAL EQPT, WHOL: Hospital Eqpt & Splys
MEDICAL, DENTAL & HOSPITAL EQPT, WHOL: Hosptl Eqpt/Furniture
MEDICAL, DENTAL & HOSPITAL EQPT, WHOL: Physician Eqpt/Splys
MEDICAL, DENTAL & HOSPITAL EQPT, WHOL: Surgical Eqpt & Splys
MEDICAL, DENTAL & HOSPITAL EQPT, WHOLESALE: Artificial Limbs
MEDICAL, DENTAL & HOSPITAL EQPT, WHOLESALE: Diagnostic, Med
MEDICAL, DENTAL & HOSPITAL EQPT, WHOLESALE: Med Eqpt & Splys
MEDICAL, DENTAL & HOSPITAL EQPT, WHOLESALE: Medical Lab
MEDICAL, DENTAL & HOSPITAL EQPT, WHOLESALE: Safety
MEDICAL, DENTAL & HOSPITAL EQPT, WHOLESALE: Therapy
MEDICAL, DENTAL/HOSPITAL EQPT, WHOL: Tech Aids, Handicapped
MEDICAL, DENTAL/HOSPITAL EQPT, WHOL: Veterinarian Eqpt/Sply
MEMBER ORGS, CIVIC, SOCIAL & FRATERNAL: Bars & Restaurants

SERVICES INDEX

MEMBERSHIP HOTELS
MEMBERSHIP ORGANIZATIONS, BUSINESS: Community Affairs & Svcs
MEMBERSHIP ORGANIZATIONS, BUSINESS: Contractors' Association
MEMBERSHIP ORGANIZATIONS, BUSINESS: Merchants' Association
MEMBERSHIP ORGANIZATIONS, BUSINESS: Public Utility Assoc
MEMBERSHIP ORGANIZATIONS, CIVIC, SOCIAL/FRAT: Boy Scout Org
MEMBERSHIP ORGANIZATIONS, CIVIC, SOCIAL/FRAT: Rec Assoc
MEMBERSHIP ORGANIZATIONS, CIVIC, SOCIAL/FRAT: Social Assoc
MEMBERSHIP ORGANIZATIONS, CIVIC, SOCIAL/FRAT: Youth Orgs
MEMBERSHIP ORGANIZATIONS, LABOR UNIONS & SIMILAR: Trade
MEMBERSHIP ORGANIZATIONS, NEC: Amateur Sports Promotion
MEMBERSHIP ORGANIZATIONS, NEC: Art Council
MEMBERSHIP ORGANIZATIONS, NEC: Automobile Owner Association
MEMBERSHIP ORGANIZATIONS, NEC: Bowling club
MEMBERSHIP ORGANIZATIONS, NEC: Charitable
MEMBERSHIP ORGANIZATIONS, NEC: Food Co-Operative
MEMBERSHIP ORGANIZATIONS, NEC: Historical Club
MEMBERSHIP ORGANIZATIONS, NEC: Personal Interest
MEMBERSHIP ORGANIZATIONS, PROF: Education/Teacher Assoc
MEMBERSHIP ORGANIZATIONS, PROFESSIONAL: Accounting Assoc
MEMBERSHIP ORGANIZATIONS, PROFESSIONAL: Health Association
MEMBERSHIP ORGANIZATIONS, REL: Christian & Reformed Church
MEMBERSHIP ORGANIZATIONS, REL: Churches, Temples & Shrines
MEMBERSHIP ORGANIZATIONS, RELIGIOUS: Apostolic Church
MEMBERSHIP ORGANIZATIONS, RELIGIOUS: Assembly Of God Church
MEMBERSHIP ORGANIZATIONS, RELIGIOUS: Baptist Church
MEMBERSHIP ORGANIZATIONS, RELIGIOUS: Brethren Church
MEMBERSHIP ORGANIZATIONS, RELIGIOUS: Catholic Church
MEMBERSHIP ORGANIZATIONS, RELIGIOUS: Church Of Christ
MEMBERSHIP ORGANIZATIONS, RELIGIOUS: Church Of God
MEMBERSHIP ORGANIZATIONS, RELIGIOUS: Community Church
MEMBERSHIP ORGANIZATIONS, RELIGIOUS: Lutheran Church
MEMBERSHIP ORGANIZATIONS, RELIGIOUS: Methodist Church
MEMBERSHIP ORGANIZATIONS, RELIGIOUS: Nonchurch
MEMBERSHIP ORGANIZATIONS, RELIGIOUS: Pentecostal Church
MEMBERSHIP ORGANIZATIONS, RELIGIOUS: Presbyterian Church
MEMBERSHIP ORGS, BUSINESS: Junior Chamber Of Commerce
MEMBERSHIP ORGS, CIVIC, SOCIAL & FRAT: Comm Member Club
MEMBERSHIP ORGS, CIVIC, SOCIAL & FRAT: Dwelling-Related
MEMBERSHIP ORGS, CIVIC, SOCIAL & FRAT: Girl Scout
MEMBERSHIP ORGS, CIVIC, SOCIAL & FRATERNAL: Civic Assoc
MEMBERSHIP ORGS, CIVIC, SOCIAL & FRATERNAL: Condo Assoc
MEMBERSHIP ORGS, CIVIC, SOCIAL & FRATERNAL: Protection
MEMBERSHIP ORGS, CIVIC, SOCIAL & FRATERNAL: Singing Society
MEMBERSHIP ORGS, CIVIC, SOCIAL & FRATERNAL: University Club
MEMBERSHIP ORGS, CIVIC, SOCIAL/FRAT: Business Persons Club
MEMBERSHIP ORGS, CIVIC, SOCIAL/FRAT: Educator's Assoc
MEMBERSHIP ORGS, LABOR UNIONS/SIMILAR: Employees' Assoc
MEMBERSHIP ORGS, RELIGIOUS: Non-Denominational Church
MEMBERSHIP SPORTS & RECREATION CLUBS
MEN'S & BOYS' CLOTHING STORES
MEN'S & BOYS' CLOTHING WHOLESALERS, NEC
MEN'S & BOYS' SPORTSWEAR WHOLESALERS
MENTAL HEALTH CLINIC, OUTPATIENT
MENTAL HEALTH PRACTITIONERS' OFFICES
MERCHANDISING MACHINE OPERATORS: Vending
METAL & STEEL PRDTS: Abrasive
METAL COMPONENTS: Prefabricated
METAL CUTTING SVCS
METAL FABRICATORS: Architechtural
METAL FABRICATORS: Plate
METAL FABRICATORS: Sheet
METAL MINING SVCS
METAL SERVICE CENTERS & OFFICES
METAL SLITTING & SHEARING
METAL STAMPING, FOR THE TRADE
METAL STAMPINGS: Patterned
METALS SVC CENTERS & WHOL: Semifinished Prdts, Iron/Steel
METALS SVC CENTERS & WHOL: Structural Shapes, Iron Or Steel
METALS SVC CENTERS & WHOLESALERS: Cable, Wire
METALS SVC CENTERS & WHOLESALERS: Casting, Rough,Iron/Steel
METALS SVC CENTERS & WHOLESALERS: Concrete Reinforcing Bars
METALS SVC CENTERS & WHOLESALERS: Copper
METALS SVC CENTERS & WHOLESALERS: Ferroalloys
METALS SVC CENTERS & WHOLESALERS: Ferrous Metals
METALS SVC CENTERS & WHOLESALERS: Flat Prdts, Iron Or Steel
METALS SVC CENTERS & WHOLESALERS: Foundry Prdts
METALS SVC CENTERS & WHOLESALERS: Iron & Steel Prdt, Ferrous
METALS SVC CENTERS & WHOLESALERS: Nonferrous Sheets, Etc
METALS SVC CENTERS & WHOLESALERS: Pipe & Tubing, Steel
METALS SVC CENTERS & WHOLESALERS: Plates, Metal
METALS SVC CENTERS & WHOLESALERS: Rope, Wire, Exc Insulated
METALS SVC CENTERS & WHOLESALERS: Sheets, Galvanized/Coated
METALS SVC CENTERS & WHOLESALERS: Sheets, Metal
METALS SVC CENTERS & WHOLESALERS: Stampings, Metal
METALS SVC CENTERS & WHOLESALERS: Steel
METALS SVC CENTERS & WHOLESALERS: Strip, Metal
METALS SVC CENTERS & WHOLESALERS: Tubing, Metal
METALS SVC CNTRS & WHOL: Metal Wires, Ties, Cables/Screening
METALS SVC CTRS & WHOLESALERS: Aluminum Bars, Rods, Etc
METALS: Primary Nonferrous, NEC
METALWORK: Miscellaneous
METER READERS: Remote
MGMT CONSULTING SVCS: Matls, Incl Purch, Handle & Invntry
MGT SVCS, FACIL SUPPT: Base Maint Or Provide Personnel
MICROFILM EQPT WHOLESALERS
MICROFILM SVCS
MILK, FLUID: Wholesalers
MILLING: Cereal Flour, Exc Rice
MILLWORK
MINE & QUARRY SVCS: Nonmetallic Minerals
MINERALS: Ground or Treated
MINIATURE GOLF COURSES
MINING MACHINES & EQPT: Crushers, Stationary
MISC FINAN INVEST ACTIVITY: Mutual Fund, Ind Salesperson
MIXTURES & BLOCKS: Asphalt Paving
MOBILE HOME REPAIR SVCS
MOBILE HOMES, EXC RECREATIONAL
MODELS
MODELS: General, Exc Toy
MOLDED RUBBER PRDTS
MOLDING COMPOUNDS
MOLDING SAND MINING
MOLDS: Indl
MOLDS: Plastic Working & Foundry
MONEY ORDER ISSUANCE SVCS
MONTESSORI CHILD DEVELOPMENT CENTER
MOPS: Floor & Dust
MORTGAGE BANKERS
MORTGAGE COMPANIES: Urban
MOTEL
MOTION PICTURE & VIDEO DISTRIBUTION
MOTION PICTURE & VIDEO PRODUCTION SVCS
MOTION PICTURE DISTRIBUTION SVCS
MOTION PICTURE PRODUCTION & DISTRIBUTION
MOTION PICTURE PRODUCTION & DISTRIBUTION: Television
MOTION PICTURE PRODUCTION ALLIED SVCS
MOTOR INN
MOTOR REBUILDING SVCS, EXC AUTOMOTIVE
MOTOR SCOOTERS & PARTS
MOTOR VEHICLE ASSEMBLY, COMPLETE: Autos, Incl Specialty
MOTOR VEHICLE ASSEMBLY, COMPLETE: Fire Department Vehicles
MOTOR VEHICLE DEALERS: Automobiles, New & Used
MOTOR VEHICLE DEALERS: Cars, Used Only
MOTOR VEHICLE DEALERS: Pickups & Vans, Used
MOTOR VEHICLE DEALERS: Pickups, New & Used
MOTOR VEHICLE DEALERS: Trucks, Tractors/Trailers, New & Used
MOTOR VEHICLE PARTS & ACCESS: Body Components & Frames
MOTOR VEHICLE PARTS & ACCESS: Booster Cables, Jump-Start
MOTOR VEHICLE PARTS & ACCESS: Clutches
MOTOR VEHICLE PARTS & ACCESS: Engines & Parts
MOTOR VEHICLE PARTS & ACCESS: Fuel Systems & Parts
MOTOR VEHICLE PARTS & ACCESS: Mufflers, Exhaust
MOTOR VEHICLE PARTS & ACCESS: Power Steering Eqpt
MOTOR VEHICLE PARTS & ACCESS: Pumps, Hydraulic Fluid Power
MOTOR VEHICLE PARTS & ACCESS: Wiring Harness Sets
MOTOR VEHICLE RACING & DRIVER SVCS
MOTOR VEHICLE SPLYS & PARTS WHOLESALERS: New
MOTOR VEHICLE SPLYS & PARTS WHOLESALERS: Used
MOTOR VEHICLE: Shock Absorbers
MOTOR VEHICLES & CAR BODIES
MOTOR VEHICLES, WHOLESALE: Ambulances
MOTOR VEHICLES, WHOLESALE: Commercial
MOTOR VEHICLES, WHOLESALE: Trailers, Truck, New & Used
MOTOR VEHICLES, WHOLESALE: Truck bodies
MOTOR VEHICLES, WHOLESALE: Truck tractors
MOTOR VEHICLES, WHOLESALE: Trucks, commercial
MOTOR VEHICLES, WHOLESALE: Vans, commercial
MOTORCYCLE DEALERS
MOTORCYCLE DEALERS
MOTORCYCLE REPAIR SHOPS
MOTORCYCLES: Wholesalers
MOTORS: Electric
MOTORS: Generators
MOVIE THEATERS, EXC DRIVE-IN
MOVING SVC & STORAGE: Local
MOVING SVC: Local
MOVING SVC: Long-Distance
MULTI-SVCS CENTER
MUSEUMS
MUSEUMS & ART GALLERIES
MUSIC BROADCASTING SVCS
MUSIC RECORDING PRODUCER
MUSIC SCHOOLS
MUSICAL ENTERTAINERS
MUSICAL INSTRUMENT PARTS & ACCESS, WHOLESALE
MUSICAL INSTRUMENTS & ACCESS: NEC
MUSICIAN
MUTUAL ACCIDENT & HEALTH ASSOCIATIONS
MUTUAL FUND MANAGEMENT

N

NAIL SALONS
NATIONAL SECURITY FORCES
NATIONAL SECURITY, GOVERNMENT: Air Force
NATIONAL SECURITY, GOVERNMENT: Army
NATIONAL SECURITY, GOVERNMENT: National Guard
NATIONAL SECURITY, GOVERNMENT: Navy
NATURAL GAS DISTRIBUTION TO CONSUMERS
NATURAL GAS PRODUCTION
NATURAL GAS TRANSMISSION
NATURAL GAS TRANSMISSION & DISTRIBUTION

SERVICES INDEX

NATURAL GASOLINE PRODUCTION
NATURAL RESOURCE PRESERVATION SVCS
NAUTICAL & NAVIGATIONAL INSTRUMENT REPAIR SVCS
NAUTICAL REPAIR SVCS
NEIGHBORHOOD CENTER
NEIGHBORHOOD DEVELOPMENT GROUP
NEW & USED CAR DEALERS
NEWS SYNDICATES
NEWSPAPERS & PERIODICALS NEWS REPORTING SVCS
NEWSSTAND
NONCURRENT CARRYING WIRING DEVICES
NONMETALLIC MINERALS DEVELOPMENT & TEST BORING SVC
NONMETALLIC MINERALS: Support Activities, Exc Fuels
NOTARIES PUBLIC
NOVELTIES, PAPER, WHOLESALE
NOVELTY SHOPS
NURSERIES & LAWN & GARDEN SPLY STORE, RET: Lawn/Garden Splys
NURSERIES & LAWN & GARDEN SPLY STORES, RETAIL
NURSERIES & LAWN & GARDEN SPLY STORES, RETAIL: Fertilizer
NURSERIES & LAWN & GARDEN SPLY STORES, RETAIL: Top Soil
NURSERIES & LAWN/GARDEN SPLY STORE, RET: Lawnmowers/Tractors
NURSERIES & LAWN/GARDEN SPLY STORES, RET: Garden Splys/Tools
NURSERIES/LAWN/GARDEN SPLY STORES, RET: Hydroponic Eqpt/Sply
NURSERIES/LAWN/GRDN SPLY STORE, RET: Nursery Stck, Seed/Bulb
NURSERY & GARDEN CENTERS
NURSERY SCHOOLS
NURSERY STOCK, WHOLESALE
NURSING & PERSONAL CARE FACILITIES, NEC
NURSING CARE FACILITIES: Skilled
NURSING HOME, EXC SKILLED & INTERMEDIATE CARE FACILITY
NUTRITION SVCS
NUTS: Metal

O

OFC/CLINIC OF MED DRS: Special, Phys Or Surgeon, Eye Or ENT
OFC/CLINIC OF MED DRS: Specl, Phys Or Surgeon, Occup & Indl
OFC/CLINIC, MED DRS: Specl, Phys Or Surgeon, Infect Disease
OFCS & CLINICS, MEDICAL DRS: Specl, Physician Or Surgn, ENT
OFFICE CLEANING OR CHARRING SVCS
OFFICE EQPT & ACCESSORY CUSTOMIZING SVCS
OFFICE EQPT WHOLESALERS
OFFICE EQPT, WHOLESALE: Blueprinting
OFFICE EQPT, WHOLESALE: Duplicating Machines
OFFICE EQPT, WHOLESALE: Photocopy Machines
OFFICE FURNITURE REPAIR & MAINTENANCE SVCS
OFFICE MANAGEMENT SVCS
OFFICE SPLY & STATIONERY STORES
OFFICE SPLY & STATIONERY STORES: Office Forms & Splys
OFFICE SPLY & STATIONERY STORES: School Splys
OFFICE SPLYS, NEC, WHOLESALE
OFFICES & CLINICS DOCTORS OF MED: Intrnl Med Practitioners
OFFICES & CLINICS DRS OF MED: Psychiatrists/Psychoanalysts
OFFICES & CLINICS HLTH PRACTITNRS: Psychiatric Social Wrkr
OFFICES & CLINICS OF DENTISTS: Dental Clinic
OFFICES & CLINICS OF DENTISTS: Dental Surgeon
OFFICES & CLINICS OF DENTISTS: Dentists' Office
OFFICES & CLINICS OF DENTISTS: Group & Corporate Practice
OFFICES & CLINICS OF DENTISTS: Prosthodontist
OFFICES & CLINICS OF DENTISTS: Specialist, Practitioners
OFFICES & CLINICS OF DOCTORS OF MEDICINE: Allergist
OFFICES & CLINICS OF DOCTORS OF MEDICINE: Anesthesiologist
OFFICES & CLINICS OF DOCTORS OF MEDICINE: Dermatologist
OFFICES & CLINICS OF DOCTORS OF MEDICINE: Dispensary
OFFICES & CLINICS OF DOCTORS OF MEDICINE: Endocrinologist
OFFICES & CLINICS OF DOCTORS OF MEDICINE: Gastronomist
OFFICES & CLINICS OF DOCTORS OF MEDICINE: Group Health Assoc
OFFICES & CLINICS OF DOCTORS OF MEDICINE: Gynecologist
OFFICES & CLINICS OF DOCTORS OF MEDICINE: Hematologist
OFFICES & CLINICS OF DOCTORS OF MEDICINE: Med Insurance Plan
OFFICES & CLINICS OF DOCTORS OF MEDICINE: Nephrologist
OFFICES & CLINICS OF DOCTORS OF MEDICINE: Neurologist
OFFICES & CLINICS OF DOCTORS OF MEDICINE: Neurosurgeon
OFFICES & CLINICS OF DOCTORS OF MEDICINE: Obstetrician
OFFICES & CLINICS OF DOCTORS OF MEDICINE: Oncologist
OFFICES & CLINICS OF DOCTORS OF MEDICINE: Ophthalmologist
OFFICES & CLINICS OF DOCTORS OF MEDICINE: Pathologist
OFFICES & CLINICS OF DOCTORS OF MEDICINE: Pediatrician
OFFICES & CLINICS OF DOCTORS OF MEDICINE: Psychiatric Clinic
OFFICES & CLINICS OF DOCTORS OF MEDICINE: Psychiatrist
OFFICES & CLINICS OF DOCTORS OF MEDICINE: Radiologist
OFFICES & CLINICS OF DOCTORS OF MEDICINE: Surgeon
OFFICES & CLINICS OF DOCTORS OF MEDICINE: Surgeon, Plastic
OFFICES & CLINICS OF DOCTORS OF MEDICINE: Urologist
OFFICES & CLINICS OF DOCTORS, MEDICINE: Gen & Fam Practice
OFFICES & CLINICS OF DRS OF MED: Cardiologist & Vascular
OFFICES & CLINICS OF DRS OF MED: Clinic, Op by Physicians
OFFICES & CLINICS OF DRS OF MED: Em Med Ctr, Freestanding
OFFICES & CLINICS OF DRS OF MED: Health Maint Org Or HMO
OFFICES & CLINICS OF DRS OF MED: Physician/Surgeon, Int Med
OFFICES & CLINICS OF DRS OF MED: Physician/Surgeon, Phy Med
OFFICES & CLINICS OF DRS OF MED: Specialist/Phy, Fertility
OFFICES & CLINICS OF DRS OF MEDICINE: Geriatric
OFFICES & CLINICS OF DRS OF MEDICINE: Med Clinic, Pri Care
OFFICES & CLINICS OF DRS OF MEDICINE: Med Insurance Assoc
OFFICES & CLINICS OF DRS OF MEDICINE: Physician, Orthopedic
OFFICES & CLINICS OF DRS OF MEDICINE: Pulmonary
OFFICES & CLINICS OF DRS OF MEDICINE: Rheumatology
OFFICES & CLINICS OF DRS OF MEDICINE: Sports Med
OFFICES & CLINICS OF DRS, MED: Specialized Practitioners
OFFICES & CLINICS OF HEALTH PRACTITIONERS: Coroner
OFFICES & CLINICS OF HEALTH PRACTITIONERS: Nurse & Med Asst
OFFICES & CLINICS OF HEALTH PRACTITIONERS: Nutrition
OFFICES & CLINICS OF HEALTH PRACTITIONERS: Nutritionist
OFFICES & CLINICS OF HEALTH PRACTITIONERS: Occu Therapist
OFFICES & CLINICS OF HEALTH PRACTITIONERS: Paramedic
OFFICES & CLINICS OF HEALTH PRACTITIONERS: Physical Therapy
OFFICES & CLINICS OF HEALTH PRACTITIONERS: Physiotherapist
OFFICES & CLINICS OF HEALTH PRACTITIONERS: Speech Pathology
OFFICES & CLINICS OF HEALTH PRACTITIONERS: Speech Therapist
OFFICES & CLINICS OF HEALTH PRACTRS: Clinical Psychologist
OFFICES & CLINICS OF HLTH PRACTITIONERS: Reg/Practical Nurse
OFFICES & CLINICS OF OPTOMETRISTS: Group & Corporate
OFFICES & CLINICS OF OPTOMETRISTS: Specialist, Contact Lens
OFFICES & CLINICS OF OPTOMETRISTS: Specialist, Optometrists
OIL & GAS FIELD EQPT: Drill Rigs
OIL FIELD MACHINERY & EQPT
OIL FIELD SVCS, NEC
OILS & GREASES: Blended & Compounded
OILS & GREASES: Lubricating
OILS: Lubricating
OLD AGE ASSISTANCE
OLEFINS
ON-LINE DATABASE INFORMATION RETRIEVAL SVCS
OPERATIVE BUILDERS: Condominiums
OPERATIVE BUILDERS: Townhouse
OPERATOR TRAINING, COMPUTER
OPERATOR: Apartment Buildings
OPERATOR: Nonresidential Buildings
OPHTHALMIC GOODS
OPHTHALMIC GOODS WHOLESALERS
OPHTHALMIC GOODS, NEC, WHOLESALE: Lenses
OPHTHALMIC GOODS: Lenses, Ophthalmic
OPTICAL GOODS STORES
OPTICAL GOODS STORES: Contact Lenses, Prescription
OPTICAL INSTRUMENTS & LENSES
OPTICAL SCANNING SVCS
OPTOMETRIC EQPT & SPLYS WHOLESALERS
OPTOMETRISTS' OFFICES
ORCHESTRAS & BANDS
ORGAN BANK
ORGANIZATIONS & UNIONS: Labor
ORGANIZATIONS, NEC
ORGANIZATIONS: Civic & Social
ORGANIZATIONS: Educational Research Agency
ORGANIZATIONS: Medical Research
ORGANIZATIONS: Noncommercial Social Research
ORGANIZATIONS: Physical Research, Noncommercial
ORGANIZATIONS: Political
ORGANIZATIONS: Political Campaign
ORGANIZATIONS: Professional
ORGANIZATIONS: Religious
ORGANIZATIONS: Research Institute
ORGANIZATIONS: Scientific Research Agency
ORGANIZATIONS: Veterans' Membership
ORPHANAGE
ORTHODONTIST
OUTDOOR PARKING SVCS
OUTREACH PROGRAM
OXYGEN TENT SVCS

P

PACKAGE DESIGN SVCS
PACKAGED FROZEN FOODS WHOLESALERS, NEC
PACKAGING & LABELING SVCS
PACKAGING MATERIALS, INDL: Wholesalers
PACKAGING MATERIALS, WHOLESALE
PACKAGING MATERIALS: Paper
PACKAGING MATERIALS: Plastic Film, Coated Or Laminated
PACKAGING MATERIALS: Polystyrene Foam
PACKAGING: Blister Or Bubble Formed, Plastic
PACKING & CRATING SVC
PACKING & CRATING SVCS: Containerized Goods For Shipping
PACKING SVCS: Shipping
PADS: Athletic, Protective
PAGING SVCS
PAINT STORE
PAINTING SVC: Metal Prdts
PAINTS & ADDITIVES
PAINTS & ALLIED PRODUCTS
PAINTS, VARNISHES & SPLYS WHOLESALERS
PAINTS, VARNISHES & SPLYS, WHOLESALE: Paints
PALLET REPAIR SVCS
PALLETIZERS & DEPALLETIZERS
PALLETS & SKIDS: Wood
PALLETS: Plastic
PALLETS: Wooden

SERVICES INDEX

PANELS: Building, Wood
PAPER & BOARD: Die-cut
PAPER CONVERTING
PAPER NAPKINS WHOLESALERS
PAPER PRDTS: Sanitary
PAPER PRDTS: Towels, Napkins/Tissue Paper, From Purchd Mtrls
PAPER, WHOLESALE: Fine
PAPER, WHOLESALE: Printing
PAPER: Adhesive
PAPER: Cloth, Lined, Made From Purchased Materials
PAPER: Coated & Laminated, NEC
PAPER: Wrapping & Packaging
PAPERBOARD
PARKING GARAGE
PARKING LOTS
PARKING LOTS & GARAGES
PAROLE OFFICE
PARTITIONS & FIXTURES: Except Wood
PARTITIONS WHOLESALERS
PARTITIONS: Wood & Fixtures
PARTS: Metal
PARTY & SPECIAL EVENT PLANNING SVCS
PASSENGER AIRLINE SVCS
PATENT OWNERS & LESSORS
PATIENT MONITORING EQPT WHOLESALERS
PATROL SVCS: Electric Transmission Or Gas Lines
PATTERNS: Indl
PAYROLL SVCS
PENSION & RETIREMENT PLAN CONSULTANTS
PENSION FUNDS
PERFORMING ARTS CENTER PRODUCTION SVCS
PERIODICALS, WHOLESALE
PERSONAL APPEARANCE SVCS
PERSONAL CARE FACILITY
PERSONAL CREDIT INSTITUTIONS: Auto Loans, Incl Insurance
PERSONAL CREDIT INSTITUTIONS: Auto/Consumer Finance Co's
PERSONAL CREDIT INSTITUTIONS: Consumer Finance Companies
PERSONAL CREDIT INSTITUTIONS: Finance Licensed Loan Co's, Sm
PERSONAL CREDIT INSTITUTIONS: Financing, Autos, Furniture
PERSONAL CREDIT INSTITUTIONS: Install Sales Finance
PERSONAL DOCUMENT & INFORMATION SVCS
PERSONAL FINANCIAL SVCS
PERSONAL INVESTIGATION SVCS
PERSONAL SHOPPING SVCS
PERSONAL SVCS
PERSONAL SVCS, NEC
PEST CONTROL IN STRUCTURES SVCS
PEST CONTROL SVCS
PESTICIDES WHOLESALERS
PET & PET SPLYS STORES
PET FOOD WHOLESALERS
PET SPLYS
PET SPLYS WHOLESALERS
PETROLEUM & PETROLEUM PRDTS, WHOL Svc Station Splys, Petro
PETROLEUM & PETROLEUM PRDTS, WHOLESALE Crude Oil
PETROLEUM & PETROLEUM PRDTS, WHOLESALE Diesel Fuel
PETROLEUM & PETROLEUM PRDTS, WHOLESALE Fuel Oil
PETROLEUM & PETROLEUM PRDTS, WHOLESALE Petroleum Brokers
PETROLEUM & PETROLEUM PRDTS, WHOLESALE: Bulk Stations
PETROLEUM PRDTS WHOLESALERS
PHARMACEUTICAL PREPARATIONS: Proprietary Drug PRDTS
PHARMACEUTICALS
PHARMACEUTICALS: Mail-Order Svc
PHARMACIES & DRUG STORES
PHOSPHATES
PHOTOCOPY MACHINE REPAIR SVCS
PHOTOCOPY MACHINES
PHOTOCOPY SPLYS WHOLESALERS
PHOTOCOPYING & DUPLICATING SVCS
PHOTOENGRAVING SVC
PHOTOFINISHING LABORATORIES
PHOTOFINISHING LABORATORIES
PHOTOGRAMMATIC MAPPING SVCS
PHOTOGRAPH DEVELOPING & RETOUCHING SVCS
PHOTOGRAPHIC EQPT & SPLYS WHOLESALERS
PHOTOGRAPHY SVCS: Commercial
PHOTOGRAPHY SVCS: Portrait Studios
PHOTOGRAPHY SVCS: School
PHOTOGRAPHY SVCS: Still Or Video
PHOTOGRAPHY: Aerial
PHOTOTYPESETTING SVC
PHYSICAL EXAMINATION & TESTING SVCS
PHYSICAL EXAMINATION SVCS, INSURANCE
PHYSICAL FITNESS CENTERS
PHYSICAL FITNESS CLUBS WITH TRAINING EQPT
PHYSICIANS' OFFICES & CLINICS: Medical
PHYSICIANS' OFFICES & CLINICS: Medical doctors
PHYSICIANS' OFFICES & CLINICS: Osteopathic
PICTURE FRAMING SVCS, CUSTOM
PIECE GOODS, NOTIONS & DRY GOODS, WHOL: Textiles, Woven
PIECE GOODS, NOTIONS & DRY GOODS, WHOLESALE: Fabrics
PIECE GOODS, NOTIONS & DRY GOODS, WHOLESALE: Tape, Textile
PIECE GOODS, NOTIONS/DRY GOODS, WHOL: Drapery Mtrl, Woven
PIECE GOODS, NOTIONS/DRY GOODS, WHOL: Sewing Splys/Notions
PILOT SVCS: Aviation
PIPE & FITTING: Fabrication
PIPE & FITTINGS: Cast Iron
PIPE FITTINGS: Plastic
PIPE SECTIONS, FABRICATED FROM PURCHASED PIPE
PIPE: Seamless Steel
PIPELINE & POWER LINE INSPECTION SVCS
PIPELINE TERMINAL FACILITIES: Independent
PIPELINES, EXC NATURAL GAS: Gasoline, Common Carriers
PIPELINES: Crude Petroleum
PIPELINES: Natural Gas
PIPELINES: Refined Petroleum
PIPES & TUBES: Steel
PIPES OR FITTINGS: Sewer, Clay
PISTONS & PISTON RINGS
PLANETARIUMS
PLANNING & DEVELOPMENT ADMIN, GOVT: Urban & Community, Local
PLANNING & DEVELOPMENT ADMIN, GOVT: Urban/Community, County
PLANNING & DEVELOPMENT ADMINISTRATION, GOVT: County Agency
PLANT CARE SVCS
PLANTING MACHINERY & EQPT WHOLESALERS
PLANTS, POTTED, WHOLESALE
PLAQUES: Picture, Laminated
PLASMAPHEROUS CENTER
PLASTIC COLORING & FINISHING
PLASTIC PRDTS REPAIR SVCS
PLASTICS FILM & SHEET
PLASTICS MATERIAL & RESINS
PLASTICS MATERIALS, BASIC FORMS & SHAPES WHOLESALERS
PLASTICS PROCESSING
PLASTICS SHEET: Packing Materials
PLASTICS: Cast
PLASTICS: Extruded
PLASTICS: Injection Molded
PLASTICS: Molded
PLASTICS: Polystyrene Foam
PLASTICS: Thermoformed
PLATE WORK: For Nuclear Industry
PLATES
PLATES: Sheet & Strip, Exc Coated Prdts
PLATING & POLISHING SVC
PLATING COMPOUNDS
PLATING SVC: NEC
PLEATING & STITCHING SVC
PLUMBING & HEATING EQPT & SPLY, WHOLESALE: Hydronic Htg Eqpt
PLUMBING & HEATING EQPT & SPLYS WHOLESALERS
PLUMBING & HEATING EQPT & SPLYS, WHOL: Fireplaces, Prefab
PLUMBING & HEATING EQPT & SPLYS, WHOL: Pipe/Fitting, Plastic
PLUMBING & HEATING EQPT & SPLYS, WHOL: Plumbing Fitting/Sply
PLUMBING & HEATING EQPT & SPLYS, WHOL: Water Purif Eqpt
PLUMBING FIXTURES
PLUMBING FIXTURES: Plastic
PLUMBING FIXTURES: Vitreous
PODIATRISTS' OFFICES
POLICE PROTECTION
POLICE PROTECTION: Local Government
POLICE PROTECTION: Sheriffs' Office
POLICE PROTECTION: State Highway Patrol
POLICYHOLDERS' CONSULTING SVCS
POLITICAL ACTION COMMITTEES
POLYETHYLENE CHLOROSULFONATED RUBBER
POLYVINYLIDENE CHLORIDE RESINS
POPCORN & SUPPLIES WHOLESALERS
POSTERS, WHOLESALE
POULTRY & POULTRY PRDTS WHOLESALERS
POULTRY & SMALL GAME SLAUGHTERING & PROCESSING
POWDER: Metal
POWER MOWERS WHOLESALERS
POWER SUPPLIES: Transformer, Electronic Type
POWER TOOL REPAIR SVCS
POWER TRANSMISSION EQPT WHOLESALERS
POWER TRANSMISSION EQPT: Mechanical
POWER TRANSMISSION EQPT: Vehicle
PRACTICAL NURSING SCHOOL
PRECIPITATORS: Electrostatic
PRESCHOOL CENTERS
PRESSED FIBER & MOLDED PULP PRDTS, EXC FOOD PRDTS
PRINTED CIRCUIT BOARDS
PRINTERS' SVCS: Folding, Collating, Etc
PRINTING & WRITING PAPER WHOLESALERS
PRINTING MACHINERY
PRINTING MACHINERY, EQPT & SPLYS: Wholesalers
PRINTING TRADES MACHINERY & EQPT REPAIR SVCS
PRINTING, COMMERCIAL: Labels & Seals, NEC
PRINTING, COMMERCIAL: Screen
PRINTING, LITHOGRAPHIC: Calendars
PRINTING, LITHOGRAPHIC: Forms & Cards, Business
PRINTING, LITHOGRAPHIC: Forms, Business
PRINTING, LITHOGRAPHIC: Offset & photolithographic printing
PRINTING, LITHOGRAPHIC: On Metal
PRINTING: Books
PRINTING: Commercial, NEC
PRINTING: Flexographic
PRINTING: Gravure, Color
PRINTING: Gravure, Rotogravure
PRINTING: Laser
PRINTING: Letterpress
PRINTING: Lithographic
PRINTING: Offset
PRINTING: Photolithographic
PRINTING: Screen, Fabric
PRINTING: Screen, Manmade Fiber & Silk, Broadwoven Fabric
PRIVATE INVESTIGATOR SVCS
PROBATION OFFICE
PRODUCT STERILIZATION SVCS
PROFESSIONAL DANCE SCHOOLS
PROFESSIONAL EQPT & SPLYS, WHOLESALE: Analytical Instruments
PROFESSIONAL EQPT & SPLYS, WHOLESALE: Bank
PROFESSIONAL EQPT & SPLYS, WHOLESALE: Engineers', NEC
PROFESSIONAL EQPT & SPLYS, WHOLESALE: Optical Goods
PROFESSIONAL EQPT & SPLYS, WHOLESALE: Precision Tools
PROFESSIONAL SCHOOLS
PROFESSIONAL STANDARDS REVIEW BOARDS
PROFILE SHAPES: Unsupported Plastics
PROGRAM ADMINISTRATION, GOVERNMENT: Social & Human Resources
PROGRAM ADMINISTRATION, GOVERNMENT: Social & Manpower, State
PROGRAM ADMINISTRATION, GOVT: Social & Manpower, County
PROMOTION SVCS
PROOFREADING SVCS
PROPERTY & CASUALTY INSURANCE AGENTS
PROPERTY DAMAGE INSURANCE

SERVICES INDEX

PUBLIC FINANCE, TAX/MONETARY POLICY OFFICES, GOVT: Taxation
PUBLIC FINANCE, TAXATION & MONETARY POLICY OFFICES
PUBLIC HEALTH PROGRAM ADMIN, GOVT: Health Statistics Ctr
PUBLIC HEALTH PROGRAM ADMIN, GOVT: Mental Health Agency
PUBLIC HEALTH PROGRAM ADMINISTRATION, GOVERNMENT: County
PUBLIC HEALTH PROGRAM ADMINISTRATION, GOVERNMENT: Local
PUBLIC HEALTH PROGRAM ADMINISTRATION, GOVERNMENT: State
PUBLIC HEALTH PROGRAM ADMINISTRATION, GOVT: Cancer Detection
PUBLIC HEALTH PROGRAM ADMINISTRATION, GOVT: Child Health
PUBLIC HEALTH PROGRAMS ADMINISTRATION SVCS
PUBLIC LIBRARY
PUBLIC ORDER & SAFETY ACTIVITIES, NEC
PUBLIC ORDER & SAFETY OFFICES, GOVERNMENT: County
PUBLIC ORDER & SAFETY OFFICES, GOVT: Emergency Mgmt Office
PUBLIC RELATIONS & PUBLICITY SVCS
PUBLIC RELATIONS SVCS
PUBLIC WELFARE CENTER
PUBLISHERS: Book
PUBLISHERS: Books, No Printing
PUBLISHERS: Magazines, No Printing
PUBLISHERS: Miscellaneous
PUBLISHERS: Music, Sheet
PUBLISHERS: Newspaper
PUBLISHERS: Newspapers, No Printing
PUBLISHERS: Periodical, With Printing
PUBLISHERS: Periodicals, Magazines
PUBLISHERS: Periodicals, No Printing
PUBLISHERS: Technical Manuals
PUBLISHERS: Telephone & Other Directory
PUBLISHERS: Trade journals, No Printing
PUBLISHING & BROADCASTING: Internet Only
PUBLISHING & PRINTING: Books
PUBLISHING & PRINTING: Directories, NEC
PUBLISHING & PRINTING: Magazines: publishing & printing
PUBLISHING & PRINTING: Newsletters, Business Svc
PUBLISHING & PRINTING: Newspapers
PUBLISHING & PRINTING: Trade Journals
PULP MILLS
PUMPS
PUMPS & PARTS: Indl
PUMPS & PUMPING EQPT REPAIR SVCS
PUMPS & PUMPING EQPT WHOLESALERS
PUMPS: Domestic, Water Or Sump
PUMPS: Measuring & Dispensing
PUMPS: Oil Well & Field
PURCHASING SVCS

R

RACE TRACK OPERATION
RACETRACKS: Auto
RACETRACKS: Horse
RACKS: Display
RADIO & TELEVISION COMMUNICATIONS EQUIPMENT
RADIO & TELEVISION OR TV ANNOUNCING SVCS
RADIO & TELEVISION REPAIR
RADIO BROADCASTING & COMMUNICATIONS EQPT
RADIO BROADCASTING STATIONS
RADIO COMMUNICATIONS: Airborne Eqpt
RADIO COMMUNICATIONS: Carrier Eqpt
RADIO REPAIR & INSTALLATION SVCS
RADIO REPAIR SHOP, NEC
RADIO, TELEVISION & CONSUMER ELECTRONICS STORES: Eqpt, NEC
RADIO, TV & CONSUMER ELEC STORES: Automotive Sound Eqpt
RADIO, TV & CONSUMER ELEC STORES: High Fidelity Stereo Eqpt
RADIO, TV/CONSUMER ELEC STORES: Antennas, Satellite Dish
RADIOS WHOLESALERS
RAILROAD CAR CUSTOMIZING SVCS
RAILROAD CAR RENTING & LEASING SVCS
RAILROAD CAR REPAIR SVCS
RAILROAD CARGO LOADING & UNLOADING SVCS

RAILROAD EQPT
RAILROAD EQPT & SPLYS WHOLESALERS
RAILROAD EQPT: Cars, Rebuilt
RAILROAD FREIGHT AGENCY
RAILROAD MAINTENANCE & REPAIR SVCS
RAILROAD SWITCHING & TERMINAL SVCS
RAILROADS: Long Haul
REAL ESTATE AGENCIES & BROKERS
REAL ESTATE AGENCIES: Buying
REAL ESTATE AGENCIES: Commercial
REAL ESTATE AGENCIES: Leasing & Rentals
REAL ESTATE AGENCIES: Multiple Listing Svc
REAL ESTATE AGENCIES: Rental
REAL ESTATE AGENCIES: Residential
REAL ESTATE AGENCIES: Selling
REAL ESTATE AGENTS & MANAGERS
REAL ESTATE APPRAISERS
REAL ESTATE AUCTION
REAL ESTATE ESCROW AGENCIES
REAL ESTATE INVESTMENT TRUSTS
REAL ESTATE MANAGERS: Cemetery
REAL ESTATE MANAGERS: Condominium
REAL ESTATE MANAGERS: Cooperative Apartment
REAL ESTATE OPERATORS, EXC DEVEL: Prprty, Auditorium/Theater
REAL ESTATE OPERATORS, EXC DEVEL: Theater Bldg, Owner & Op
REAL ESTATE OPERATORS, EXC DEVELOPERS: Apartment Hotel
REAL ESTATE OPERATORS, EXC DEVELOPERS: Auditorium & Hall
REAL ESTATE OPERATORS, EXC DEVELOPERS: Bank Building
REAL ESTATE OPERATORS, EXC DEVELOPERS: Commercial/Indl Bldg
REAL ESTATE OPERATORS, EXC DEVELOPERS: Property, Retail
REAL ESTATE OPERATORS, EXC DEVELOPERS: Residential Hotel
REAL ESTATE OPERATORS, EXC DEVELOPERS: Retirement Hotel
REAL ESTATE OPERATORS, EXC DEVELOPERS: Shopping Ctr
REAL ESTATE OPERATORS, EXC DEVELOPERS: Shopping Ctr, Commnty
REAL ESTATE OPS, EXC DEVELOPER: Residential Bldg, 4 Or Less
REALTY INVESTMENT TRUSTS
RECLAIMED RUBBER: Reworked By Manufacturing Process
RECOVERY SVCS: Solvents
RECREATIONAL & SPORTING CAMPS
RECREATIONAL CAMPS
RECREATIONAL DAY CAMPS
RECREATIONAL SPORTING EQPT REPAIR SVCS
RECREATIONAL VEHICLE DEALERS
RECREATIONAL VEHICLE PARKS
RECREATIONAL VEHICLE PARKS & CAMPGROUNDS
RECYCLABLE SCRAP & WASTE MATERIALS WHOLESALERS
REFERRAL SVCS, PERSONAL & SOCIAL PROBLEMS
REFINERS & SMELTERS: Aluminum
REFINERS & SMELTERS: Lead, Secondary
REFINERS & SMELTERS: Nonferrous Metal
REFINING: Petroleum
REFRACTORIES: Nonclay
REFRACTORY MATERIALS WHOLESALERS
REFRIGERATION & HEATING EQUIPMENT
REFRIGERATION EQPT & SPLYS WHOLESALERS
REFRIGERATION EQPT & SPLYS, WHOL: Refrig Units, Motor Veh
REFRIGERATION EQPT & SPLYS, WHOLESALE: Commercial Eqpt
REFRIGERATION REPAIR SVCS
REFRIGERATION SVC & REPAIR
REFUGEE SVCS
REFUSE SYSTEMS
REGULATION & ADMIN, GOVT: Public Svc Commission, Exc Transp
REGULATION & ADMINISTRATION, GOVT: Transp Dept, Nonoperating
REGULATORS: Power
REHABILITATION CENTER, OUTPATIENT TREATMENT
REHABILITATION CTR, RESIDENTIAL WITH HEALTH CARE INCIDENTAL
REHABILITATION SVCS

REINSURANCE CARRIERS: Accident & Health
REINSURANCE CARRIERS: Surety
RELOCATION SVCS
REMOTE DATABASE INFORMATION RETRIEVAL SVCS
RENT-A-CAR SVCS
RENTAL CENTERS: Furniture
RENTAL CENTERS: General
RENTAL CENTERS: Party & Banquet Eqpt & Splys
RENTAL CENTERS: Tools
RENTAL SVCS: Aircraft
RENTAL SVCS: Appliance
RENTAL SVCS: Audio-Visual Eqpt & Sply
RENTAL SVCS: Beach & Water Sports Eqpt
RENTAL SVCS: Bicycle
RENTAL SVCS: Business Machine & Electronic Eqpt
RENTAL SVCS: Clothing
RENTAL SVCS: Costume
RENTAL SVCS: Dress Suit
RENTAL SVCS: Electronic Eqpt, Exc Computers
RENTAL SVCS: Golf Cart, Power
RENTAL SVCS: Home Cleaning & Maintenance Eqpt
RENTAL SVCS: Invalid Splys
RENTAL SVCS: Mobile Communication Eqpt
RENTAL SVCS: Office Facilities & Secretarial Svcs
RENTAL SVCS: Oil Eqpt
RENTAL SVCS: Recreational Vehicle
RENTAL SVCS: Sound & Lighting Eqpt
RENTAL SVCS: Sporting Goods, NEC
RENTAL SVCS: Stores & Yards Eqpt
RENTAL SVCS: Television
RENTAL SVCS: Tent & Tarpaulin
RENTAL SVCS: Trailer
RENTAL SVCS: Tuxedo
RENTAL SVCS: Vending Machine
RENTAL SVCS: Video Disk/Tape, To The General Public
RENTAL SVCS: Work Zone Traffic Eqpt, Flags, Cones, Etc
RENTAL: Passenger Car
RENTAL: Portable Toilet
RENTAL: Trucks, With Drivers
RENTAL: Video Tape & Disc
REPOSSESSION SVCS
REPRODUCTION SVCS: Video Tape Or Disk
RESEARCH & DEVELOPMENT SVCS, COMMERCIAL: Engineering Lab
RESEARCH, DEV & TESTING SVCS, COMM: Chem Lab, Exc Testing
RESEARCH, DEVELOPMENT & TEST SVCS, COMM: Business Analysis
RESEARCH, DEVELOPMENT & TEST SVCS, COMM: Cmptr Hardware Dev
RESEARCH, DEVELOPMENT & TEST SVCS, COMM: Research, Exc Lab
RESEARCH, DEVELOPMENT & TESTING SVCS, COMM: Agricultural
RESEARCH, DEVELOPMENT & TESTING SVCS, COMM: Bus Economic Svc
RESEARCH, DEVELOPMENT & TESTING SVCS, COMM: Natural Resource
RESEARCH, DEVELOPMENT & TESTING SVCS, COMM: Research Lab
RESEARCH, DEVELOPMENT & TESTING SVCS, COMM: Sociological
RESEARCH, DEVELOPMENT & TESTING SVCS, COMMERCIAL: Business
RESEARCH, DEVELOPMENT & TESTING SVCS, COMMERCIAL: Economic
RESEARCH, DEVELOPMENT & TESTING SVCS, COMMERCIAL: Education
RESEARCH, DEVELOPMENT & TESTING SVCS, COMMERCIAL: Energy
RESEARCH, DEVELOPMENT & TESTING SVCS, COMMERCIAL: Food
RESEARCH, DEVELOPMENT & TESTING SVCS, COMMERCIAL: Medical
RESEARCH, DEVELOPMENT & TESTING SVCS, COMMERCIAL: Physical
RESEARCH, DVLPT & TEST SVCS, COMM: Mkt Analysis or Research
RESEARCH, DVLPT & TESTING SVCS, COMM: Mkt, Bus & Economic
RESEARCH, DVLPT & TESTING SVCS, COMM: Survey, Mktg
RESIDENTIAL CARE FOR CHILDREN
RESIDENTIAL CARE FOR THE HANDICAPPED

SERVICES INDEX

RESIDENTIAL MENTAL HEALTH & SUBSTANCE ABUSE FACILITIES
RESIDENTIAL MENTALLY HANDICAPPED FACILITIES
RESIDENTIAL REMODELERS
RESINS: Custom Compound Purchased
RESORT HOTEL: Franchised
RESORT HOTELS
RESPIRATORY THERAPY CLINIC
REST HOME, WITH HEALTH CARE INCIDENTAL
RESTAURANT EQPT REPAIR SVCS
RESTAURANTS: Fast Food
RESTAURANTS:Full Svc, American
RESTAURANTS:Full Svc, Diner
RESTAURANTS:Full Svc, Ethnic Food
RESTAURANTS:Full Svc, Family
RESTAURANTS:Full Svc, Family, Chain
RESTAURANTS:Full Svc, Family, Independent
RESTAURANTS:Full Svc, French
RESTAURANTS:Full Svc, Italian
RESTAURANTS:Full Svc, Mexican
RESTAURANTS:Full Svc, Seafood
RESTAURANTS:Full Svc, Steak
RESTAURANTS:Full Svc, Steak & Barbecue
RESTAURANTS:Limited Svc, Box Lunch Stand
RESTAURANTS:Limited Svc, Carry-Out Only, Exc Pizza
RESTAURANTS:Limited Svc, Chicken
RESTAURANTS:Limited Svc, Coffee Shop
RESTAURANTS:Limited Svc, Fast-Food, Chain
RESTAURANTS:Limited Svc, Fast-Food, Independent
RESTAURANTS:Limited Svc, Grill
RESTAURANTS:Limited Svc, Ice Cream Stands Or Dairy Bars
RESTAURANTS:Limited Svc, Lunch Counter
RESTAURANTS:Limited Svc, Pizza
RESTAURANTS:Limited Svc, Pizzeria, Chain
RESTAURANTS:Limited Svc, Pizzeria, Independent
RESTAURANTS:Ltd Svc, Ice Cream, Soft Drink/Fountain Stands
RESTROOM CLEANING SVCS
RETAIL BAKERY: Bagels
RETAIL BAKERY: Bread
RETAIL FIREPLACE STORES
RETAIL LUMBER YARDS
RETAIL STORES: Alarm Signal Systems
RETAIL STORES: Alcoholic Beverage Making Eqpt & Splys
RETAIL STORES: Audio-Visual Eqpt & Splys
RETAIL STORES: Business Machines & Eqpt
RETAIL STORES: Christmas Lights & Decorations
RETAIL STORES: Communication Eqpt
RETAIL STORES: Concrete Prdts, Precast
RETAIL STORES: Educational Aids & Electronic Training Mat
RETAIL STORES: Electronic Parts & Eqpt
RETAIL STORES: Farm Eqpt & Splys
RETAIL STORES: Farm Machinery, NEC
RETAIL STORES: Fiberglass Materials, Exc Insulation
RETAIL STORES: Fire Extinguishers
RETAIL STORES: Hair Care Prdts
RETAIL STORES: Hearing Aids
RETAIL STORES: Hospital Eqpt & Splys
RETAIL STORES: Ice
RETAIL STORES: Incontinent Care Prdts
RETAIL STORES: Medical Apparatus & Splys
RETAIL STORES: Mobile Telephones & Eqpt
RETAIL STORES: Orthopedic & Prosthesis Applications
RETAIL STORES: Pet Food
RETAIL STORES: Pet Splys
RETAIL STORES: Photocopy Machines
RETAIL STORES: Picture Frames, Ready Made
RETAIL STORES: Plumbing & Heating Splys
RETAIL STORES: Police Splys
RETAIL STORES: Religious Goods
RETAIL STORES: Safety Splys & Eqpt
RETAIL STORES: Telephone & Communication Eqpt
RETAIL STORES: Telephone Eqpt & Systems
RETAIL STORES: Theatrical Eqpt & Splys
RETAIL STORES: Tropical Fish
RETAIL STORES: Typewriters & Business Machines
RETAIL STORES: Water Purification Eqpt
RETAIL STORES: Welding Splys
RETIREMENT COMMUNITIES WITH NURSING
REUPHOLSTERY & FURNITURE REPAIR
RIDING APPAREL STORES
RIDING STABLES
ROBOTS: Assembly Line
RODS: Steel & Iron, Made In Steel Mills
ROLL FORMED SHAPES: Custom
ROLLING MILL MACHINERY
ROOFING MATERIALS: Asphalt
ROOFING MATERIALS: Sheet Metal
ROOMING & BOARDING HOUSES: Dormitory, Commercially Operated
RUBBER
RUBBER PRDTS: Mechanical
RUBBER PRDTS: Reclaimed
RUBBER, CRUDE, WHOLESALE

S

SADDLERY STORES
SAFETY EQPT & SPLYS WHOLESALERS
SAFETY INSPECTION SVCS
SALES PROMOTION SVCS
SALT MINING: Common
SAND & GRAVEL
SAND MINING
SAND: Hygrade
SANDBLASTING SVC: Building Exterior
SANDSTONE: Dimension
SANITARY SVC, NEC
SANITARY SVCS: Disease Control
SANITARY SVCS: Environmental Cleanup
SANITARY SVCS: Hazardous Waste, Collection & Disposal
SANITARY SVCS: Incinerator, Operation Of
SANITARY SVCS: Medical Waste Disposal
SANITARY SVCS: Nonhazardous Waste Disposal Sites
SANITARY SVCS: Oil Spill Cleanup
SANITARY SVCS: Refuse Collection & Disposal Svcs
SANITARY SVCS: Rubbish Collection & Disposal
SANITARY SVCS: Sanitary Landfill, Operation Of
SANITARY SVCS: Sewage Treatment Facility
SANITARY SVCS: Toxic Or Hazardous Waste Cleanup
SANITARY SVCS: Waste Materials, Disposal At Sea
SANITARY SVCS: Waste Materials, Recycling
SANITATION CHEMICALS & CLEANING AGENTS
SATELLITES: Communications
SAVINGS & LOAN ASSOCIATIONS, NOT FEDERALLY CHARTERED
SAVINGS INSTITUTIONS: Federally Chartered
SAW BLADES
SAWING & PLANING MILLS
SCAFFOLDING WHOLESALERS
SCALE REPAIR SVCS
SCHOOL BUS SVC
SCHOOL FOR PHYSICALLY HANDICAPPED, NEC
SCHOOL FOR RETARDED, NEC
SCHOOL SPLYS, EXC BOOKS: Wholesalers
SCHOOLS & EDUCATIONAL SVCS, NEC
SCHOOLS: Elementary & Secondary
SCHOOLS: Vocational, NEC
SCRAP & WASTE MATERIALS, WHOLESALE: Auto Wrecking For Scrap
SCRAP & WASTE MATERIALS, WHOLESALE: Ferrous Metal
SCRAP & WASTE MATERIALS, WHOLESALE: Junk & Scrap
SCRAP & WASTE MATERIALS, WHOLESALE: Metal
SCRAP & WASTE MATERIALS, WHOLESALE: Nonferrous Metals Scrap
SCRAP & WASTE MATERIALS, WHOLESALE: Oil
SCRAP & WASTE MATERIALS, WHOLESALE: Paper
SCRAP & WASTE MATERIALS, WHOLESALE: Rags
SCRAP & WASTE MATERIALS, WHOLESALE: Rubber Scrap
SCRAP STEEL CUTTING
SCREW MACHINE PRDTS
SEALANTS
SEALING COMPOUNDS: Sealing, synthetic rubber or plastic
SEARCH & NAVIGATION SYSTEMS
SEARCH & RESCUE SVCS
SEAT BELTS: Automobile & Aircraft
SECRETARIAL SVCS
SECURE STORAGE SVC: Document
SECURE STORAGE SVC: Household & Furniture
SECURITY GUARD SVCS
SECURITY PROTECTIVE DEVICES MAINTENANCE & MONITORING SVCS
SECURITY SYSTEMS SERVICES
SECURITY UNDERWRITERS
SELF-HELP GROUP HOME
SELF-HELP ORGANIZATION, NEC
SELF-PROPELLED AIRCRAFT DEALER
SEMICONDUCTOR CIRCUIT NETWORKS
SEMICONDUCTORS & RELATED DEVICES
SENIOR HIGH SCHOOLS, PUBLIC
SEPTIC TANK CLEANING SVCS
SERVICE STATION EQPT REPAIR SVCS
SERVICES, NEC
SETTLEMENT HOUSE
SEWAGE & WATER TREATMENT EQPT
SEWAGE FACILITIES
SEWER CLEANING & RODDING SVC
SEWING CONTRACTORS
SEWING MACHINE STORES
SEWING, NEEDLEWORK & PIECE GOODS STORE: Quilting Matls/Splys
SEWING, NEEDLEWORK & PIECE GOODS STORES: Knitting Splys
SHAPES & PILINGS, STRUCTURAL: Steel
SHEET METAL SPECIALTIES, EXC STAMPED
SHEETING: Laminated Plastic
SHELTERED WORKSHOPS
SHELVING: Office & Store, Exc Wood
SHIMS: Metal
SHIPBUILDING & REPAIR
SHIPPING AGENTS
SHOE STORES
SHOE STORES: Men's
SHOES & BOOTS WHOLESALERS
SHOES: Men's
SHOES: Plastic Or Rubber
SHOES: Women's
SHOPPING CART REPAIR SVCS
SHOPPING CENTERS & MALLS
SIDING: Plastic
SIGN PAINTING & LETTERING SHOP
SIGNALS: Traffic Control, Electric
SIGNS & ADVERTISING SPECIALTIES
SIGNS & ADVERTISING SPECIALTIES: Signs
SIGNS & ADVERTSG SPECIALTIES: Displays/Cutouts Window/Lobby
SIGNS, ELECTRICAL: Wholesalers
SIGNS, EXC ELECTRIC, WHOLESALE
SIGNS: Electrical
SILK SCREEN DESIGN SVCS
SKATING RINKS: Roller
SKI LODGE
SKILL TRAINING CENTER
SNACK & NONALCOHOLIC BEVERAGE BARS
SNOW PLOWING SVCS
SOAPS & DETERGENTS
SOCIAL CHANGE ASSOCIATION
SOCIAL CLUBS
SOCIAL SERVICES INFORMATION EXCHANGE
SOCIAL SERVICES, NEC
SOCIAL SVCS CENTER
SOCIAL SVCS, HANDICAPPED
SOCIAL SVCS: Individual & Family
SOCIAL WORKER
SOFT DRINKS WHOLESALERS
SOFTWARE PUBLISHERS: Application
SOFTWARE PUBLISHERS: Business & Professional
SOFTWARE PUBLISHERS: Education
SOFTWARE PUBLISHERS: Home Entertainment
SOFTWARE PUBLISHERS: NEC
SOFTWARE PUBLISHERS: Publisher's
SOFTWARE TRAINING, COMPUTER
SOLDERS
SORORITY HOUSES
SOUND EFFECTS & MUSIC PRODUCTION: Motion Picture
SOUND RECORDING STUDIOS
SOYBEAN PRDTS
SPACE RESEARCH & TECHNOLOGY, GOVERNMENT: Federal
SPACE VEHICLE EQPT
SPARK PLUGS: Internal Combustion Engines
SPAS
SPECIAL EDUCATION SCHOOLS, PRIVATE
SPECIAL EDUCATION SCHOOLS, PUBLIC
SPECIAL EVENTS DECORATION SVCS
SPECIALIZED LIBRARIES
SPECIALTY FOOD STORES: Coffee
SPECIALTY FOOD STORES: Eggs & Poultry
SPECIALTY FOOD STORES: Health & Dietetic Food
SPECIALTY FOOD STORES: Juices, Fruit Or Vegetable
SPECIALTY OUTPATIENT CLINICS, NEC
SPECULATIVE BUILDERS: Multi-Family Housing
SPECULATIVE BUILDERS: Single-Family Housing
SPEECH DEFECT CLINIC
SPEED CHANGERS

SERVICES INDEX

SPICE & HERB STORES
SPONGES, ANIMAL, WHOLESALE
SPORTING & ATHLETIC GOODS: Basketball Eqpt & Splys, NEC
SPORTING & RECREATIONAL GOODS & SPLYS WHOLESALERS
SPORTING & RECREATIONAL GOODS, WHOL: Water Slides, Rec Park
SPORTING & RECREATIONAL GOODS, WHOLESALE: Athletic Goods
SPORTING & RECREATIONAL GOODS, WHOLESALE: Boat Access & Part
SPORTING & RECREATIONAL GOODS, WHOLESALE: Bowling
SPORTING & RECREATIONAL GOODS, WHOLESALE: Fitness
SPORTING & RECREATIONAL GOODS, WHOLESALE: Golf
SPORTING & RECREATIONAL GOODS, WHOLESALE: Gymnasium
SPORTING & RECREATIONAL GOODS, WHOLESALE: Hunting
SPORTING FIREARMS WHOLESALERS
SPORTING GOODS
SPORTING GOODS STORES, NEC
SPORTING GOODS STORES: Firearms
SPORTING GOODS STORES: Gymnasium Eqpt, NEC
SPORTING GOODS STORES: Pool & Billiard Tables
SPORTING GOODS STORES: Skating Eqpt
SPORTING GOODS STORES: Specialty Sport Splys, NEC
SPORTING GOODS STORES: Tennis Goods & Eqpt
SPORTS APPAREL STORES
SPORTS CLUBS, MANAGERS & PROMOTERS
SPORTS TEAMS & CLUBS: Baseball
SPORTS TEAMS & CLUBS: Basketball
SPORTS TEAMS & CLUBS: Football
SPORTS TEAMS & CLUBS: Ice Hockey
SPORTS TEAMS & CLUBS: Soccer
SPRAYS: Self-Defense
SPRINGS: Steel
SPRINGS: Wire
SPRINKLING SYSTEMS: Fire Control
STADIUM EVENT OPERATOR SERVICES
STAFFING, EMPLOYMENT PLACEMENT
STAINLESS STEEL
STAMPINGS: Automotive
STAMPINGS: Metal
STATE CREDIT UNIONS, NOT FEDERALLY CHARTERED
STATE SAVINGS BANKS, NOT FEDERALLY CHARTERED
STATIONARY & OFFICE SPLYS, WHOL: Computer/Photocopying Splys
STATIONARY & OFFICE SPLYS, WHOLESALE: Laser Printer Splys
STATIONARY & OFFICE SPLYS, WHOLESALE: Stationery
STATIONERY & OFFICE SPLYS WHOLESALERS
STEAM HEATING SYSTEMS SPLY SVCS
STEAM SPLY SYSTEMS SVCS INCLUDING GEOTHERMAL
STEAM, HEAT & AIR CONDITIONING DISTRIBUTION SVC
STEEL FABRICATORS
STEEL MILLS
STEEL, COLD-ROLLED: Flat Bright, From Purchased Hot-Rolled
STEEL, COLD-ROLLED: Sheet Or Strip, From Own Hot-Rolled
STEEL, HOT-ROLLED: Sheet Or Strip
STEEL: Cold-Rolled
STITCHING SVCS: Custom
STONE: Dimension, NEC
STONE: Quarrying & Processing, Own Stone Prdts
STONEWARE PRDTS: Pottery
STORE FIXTURES, EXC REFRIGERATED: Wholesalers
STORE FIXTURES: Wood
STORES: Auto & Home Supply
STUDIOS: Artists & Artists' Studios
STUDIOS: Sculptor's
STUDS & JOISTS: Sheet Metal
SUB-LESSORS: Real Estate
SUBSCRIPTION FULFILLMENT SVCS: Magazine, Newspaper, Etc
SUBSTANCE ABUSE CLINICS, OUTPATIENT
SUBSTANCE ABUSE COUNSELING
SUMMER CAMPS, EXC DAY & SPORTS INSTRUCTIONAL
SUPERMARKETS & OTHER GROCERY STORES
SURGICAL APPLIANCES & SPLYS
SURGICAL EQPT: See Also Instruments
SURGICAL INSTRUMENT REPAIR SVCS

SURVEYING & MAPPING: Land Parcels
SVC ESTABLISHMENT EQPT & SPLYS WHOLESALERS
SVC ESTABLISHMENT EQPT, WHOL: Cleaning & Maint Eqpt & Splys
SVC ESTABLISHMENT EQPT, WHOL: Concrete Burial Vaults & Boxes
SVC ESTABLISHMENT EQPT, WHOL: Laundry/Dry Cleaning Eqpt/Sply
SVC ESTABLISHMENT EQPT, WHOLESALE : Barber Shop Eqpt & Splys
SVC ESTABLISHMENT EQPT, WHOLESALE: Beauty Parlor Eqpt & Sply
SVC ESTABLISHMENT EQPT, WHOLESALE: Firefighting Eqpt
SVC ESTABLISHMENT EQPT, WHOLESALE: Laundry Eqpt & Splys
SVC ESTABLISHMENT EQPT, WHOLESALE: Locksmith Eqpt & Splys
SVC ESTABLISHMENT EQPT, WHOLESALE: Restaurant Splys
SVC ESTABLISHMENT EQPT, WHOLESALE: Vending Machines & Splys
SWIMMING INSTRUCTION
SWIMMING POOL & HOT TUB CLEANING & MAINTENANCE SVCS
SWIMMING POOL SPLY STORES
SWIMMING POOLS, EQPT & SPLYS: Wholesalers
SWITCHGEAR & SWITCHBOARD APPARATUS
SYMPHONY ORCHESTRA
SYNAGOGUES
SYRUPS, DRINK
SYSTEMS ENGINEERING: Computer Related
SYSTEMS INTEGRATION SVCS
SYSTEMS INTEGRATION SVCS: Local Area Network
SYSTEMS INTEGRATION SVCS: Office Computer Automation
SYSTEMS SOFTWARE DEVELOPMENT SVCS

T

TABULATING SVCS
TAGS & LABELS: Paper
TANK & BOILER CLEANING SVCS
TANK REPAIR & CLEANING SVCS
TANK REPAIR SVCS
TANKS: Cryogenic, Metal
TANKS: Lined, Metal
TANKS: Standard Or Custom Fabricated, Metal Plate
TANNING SALONS
TAPES: Pressure Sensitive
TAX RETURN PREPARATION SVCS
TAXI CABS
TECHNICAL & TRADE SCHOOLS, NEC
TECHNICAL INSTITUTE
TECHNICAL MANUAL PREPARATION SVCS
TECHNICAL WRITING SVCS
TELECOMMUNICATION EQPT REPAIR SVCS, EXC TELEPHONES
TELECOMMUNICATION SYSTEMS & EQPT
TELECOMMUNICATIONS CARRIERS & SVCS: Wired
TELECOMMUNICATIONS CARRIERS & SVCS: Wireless
TELEMARKETING BUREAUS
TELEPHONE ANSWERING SVCS
TELEPHONE COUNSELING SVCS
TELEPHONE EQPT INSTALLATION
TELEPHONE EQPT: NEC
TELEPHONE SET REPAIR SVCS
TELEPHONE SVCS
TELEVISION BROADCASTING & COMMUNICATIONS EQPT
TELEVISION BROADCASTING STATIONS
TELEVISION FILM PRODUCTION SVCS
TELEVISION REPAIR SHOP
TEMPORARY HELP SVCS
TEN PIN CENTERS
TENANT SCREENING SVCS
TERMITE CONTROL SVCS
TEST BORING, METAL MINING
TESTERS: Gas, Exc Indl Process
TESTING SVCS
TEXTILE & APPAREL SVCS
THEATER COMPANIES
THEATRICAL PRODUCERS & SVCS
THERMOCOUPLES: Indl Process
THERMOPLASTIC MATERIALS
TICKET OFFICES & AGENCIES: Theatrical
TICKET OFFICES & AGENCIES: Travel

TIRE & TUBE REPAIR MATERIALS, WHOLESALE
TIRE CORD & FABRIC
TIRE DEALERS
TIRE RECAPPING & RETREADING
TIRE SUNDRIES OR REPAIR MATERIALS: Rubber
TIRES & INNER TUBES
TIRES & TUBES WHOLESALERS
TIRES & TUBES, WHOLESALE: Automotive
TIRES & TUBES, WHOLESALE: Truck
TITLE & TRUST COMPANIES
TITLE ABSTRACT & SETTLEMENT OFFICES
TITLE INSURANCE AGENTS
TITLE INSURANCE: Guarantee Of Titles
TITLE INSURANCE: Real Estate
TITLE SEARCH COMPANIES
TOBACCO & PRDTS, WHOLESALE: Cigarettes
TOBACCO & TOBACCO PRDTS WHOLESALERS
TOILETRIES, COSMETICS & PERFUME STORES
TOILETRIES, WHOLESALE: Hair Preparations
TOILETRIES, WHOLESALE: Razor Blades
TOILETRIES, WHOLESALE: Toiletries
TOILETS, PORTABLE, WHOLESALE
TOLL BRIDGE OPERATIONS
TOLL ROAD OPERATIONS
TOOL REPAIR SVCS
TOOLS: Hand
TOOLS: Hand, Plumbers'
TOOLS: Hand, Power
TOUR OPERATORS
TOURIST INFORMATION BUREAU
TOURIST LODGINGS
TOWELS: Fabric & Nonwoven, Made From Purchased Materials
TOWERS: Cooling, Sheet Metal
TOWING & TUGBOAT SVC
TOWING SVCS: Marine
TOYS
TOYS & HOBBY GOODS & SPLYS, WHOLESALE: Arts/Crafts Eqpt/Sply
TOYS & HOBBY GOODS & SPLYS, WHOLESALE: Balloons, Novelty
TOYS & HOBBY GOODS & SPLYS, WHOLESALE: Bingo Games & Splys
TOYS & HOBBY GOODS & SPLYS, WHOLESALE: Educational Toys
TOYS & HOBBY GOODS & SPLYS, WHOLESALE: Toys & Games
TOYS & HOBBY GOODS & SPLYS, WHOLESALE: Toys, NEC
TOYS & HOBBY GOODS & SPLYS, WHOLESALE: Video Games
TOYS, HOBBY GOODS & SPLYS WHOLESALERS
TRADE SHOW ARRANGEMENT SVCS
TRAFFIC CONTROL FLAGGING SVCS
TRAILERS & PARTS: Truck & Semi's
TRAILERS & TRAILER EQPT
TRAILERS: Bodies
TRAILERS: Semitrailers, Truck Tractors
TRAINING SCHOOL FOR DELINQUENTS
TRANS PROG REG & ADMIN, GOVT: Motor Vehicle Licensing & Insp
TRANSFORMERS: Electric
TRANSFORMERS: Furnace, Electric
TRANSFORMERS: Power Related
TRANSLATION & INTERPRETATION SVCS
TRANSPORTATION AGENTS & BROKERS
TRANSPORTATION ARRANGEMENT SVCS, PASSENGER: Carpool/Vanpool
TRANSPORTATION ARRANGEMENT SVCS, PASSENGER: Tours, Conducted
TRANSPORTATION ARRANGEMNT SVCS, PASS: Travel Tour Pkgs, Whol
TRANSPORTATION BROKERS: Truck
TRANSPORTATION EQPT & SPLYS, WHOL: Aircraft Engs/Eng Parts
TRANSPORTATION EQPT & SPLYS, WHOLESALE: Acft/Space Vehicle
TRANSPORTATION EQPT & SPLYS, WHOLESALE: Nav Eqpt & Splys
TRANSPORTATION EQPT & SPLYS, WHOLESALE: Tanks & Tank Compnts
TRANSPORTATION EQPT & SPLYS WHOLESALERS, NEC
TRANSPORTATION EQUIPMENT, NEC
TRANSPORTATION INSPECTION SVCS

SERVICES INDEX

TRANSPORTATION PROG REG & ADMIN, GOVT: Bureau, Public Roads
TRANSPORTATION PROGRAM REGULATION & ADMIN GOVT: Local
TRANSPORTATION PROGRAM REGULATION & ADMIN, GOVT: Federal
TRANSPORTATION PROGRAMS REGULATION & ADMINISTRATION SVCS
TRANSPORTATION SVCS, NEC
TRANSPORTATION SVCS, WATER: Boat Cleaning
TRANSPORTATION SVCS, WATER: Canal Barge Operations
TRANSPORTATION SVCS, WATER: Cleaning
TRANSPORTATION SVCS: Airport
TRANSPORTATION SVCS: Airport Limousine, Scheduled Svcs
TRANSPORTATION SVCS: Airport, Regular Route
TRANSPORTATION SVCS: Bus Line Operations
TRANSPORTATION SVCS: Bus Line, Interstate
TRANSPORTATION SVCS: Maint Facilities, Vehicle Passenger
TRANSPORTATION SVCS: Maintenance Facilities, Buses
TRANSPORTATION SVCS: Railroad Terminals
TRANSPORTATION SVCS: Railroad, Passenger
TRANSPORTATION SVCS: Railroads, Interurban
TRANSPORTATION SVCS: Rental, Local
TRANSPORTATION SVCS: Vanpool Operation
TRANSPORTATION: Air, Nonscheduled Passenger
TRANSPORTATION: Air, Nonscheduled, NEC
TRANSPORTATION: Air, Scheduled Freight
TRANSPORTATION: Air, Scheduled Passenger
TRANSPORTATION: Bus Transit Systems
TRANSPORTATION: Bus Transit Systems
TRANSPORTATION: Deep Sea Foreign Freight
TRANSPORTATION: Deep Sea Passenger
TRANSPORTATION: Great Lakes Domestic Freight
TRANSPORTATION: Local Passenger, NEC
TRANSPORTATION: Passenger Ferries
TRANSPORTATION: Transit Systems, NEC
TRAVEL AGENCIES
TRAVEL CLUBS
TRAVEL TRAILER DEALERS
TRAVEL TRAILERS & CAMPERS
TRAVELER ACCOMMODATIONS, NEC
TRAVELERS' CHECK ISSUANCE SVCS
TROPHIES, NEC
TROPHY & PLAQUE STORES
TRUCK & BUS BODIES: Ambulance
TRUCK & BUS BODIES: Truck, Motor Vehicle
TRUCK & BUS BODIES: Utility Truck
TRUCK & FREIGHT TERMINALS & SUPPORT ACTIVITIES
TRUCK BODIES: Body Parts
TRUCK BODY SHOP
TRUCK DRIVER SVCS
TRUCK GENERAL REPAIR SVC
TRUCK PAINTING & LETTERING SVCS
TRUCK PARTS & ACCESSORIES: Wholesalers
TRUCK STOPS
TRUCKING & HAULING SVCS: Animal & Farm Prdt
TRUCKING & HAULING SVCS: Baggage Transfer Svcs
TRUCKING & HAULING SVCS: Building Materials
TRUCKING & HAULING SVCS: Coal, Local
TRUCKING & HAULING SVCS: Contract Basis
TRUCKING & HAULING SVCS: Draying, Local, Without Storage
TRUCKING & HAULING SVCS: Furniture Moving & Storage, Local
TRUCKING & HAULING SVCS: Furniture, Local W/out Storage
TRUCKING & HAULING SVCS: Garbage, Collect/Transport Only
TRUCKING & HAULING SVCS: Haulage & Cartage, Light, Local
TRUCKING & HAULING SVCS: Hazardous Waste
TRUCKING & HAULING SVCS: Heavy Machinery, Local
TRUCKING & HAULING SVCS: Heavy, NEC
TRUCKING & HAULING SVCS: Liquid Petroleum, Exc Local
TRUCKING & HAULING SVCS: Liquid, Local
TRUCKING & HAULING SVCS: Live Poultry
TRUCKING & HAULING SVCS: Lumber & Timber
TRUCKING & HAULING SVCS: Machinery, Heavy
TRUCKING & HAULING SVCS: Mail Carriers, Contract
TRUCKING & HAULING SVCS: Petroleum, Local
TRUCKING & HAULING SVCS: Safe Moving, Local
TRUCKING & HAULING SVCS: Trailer/Container On Flat Car
TRUCKING, AUTOMOBILE CARRIER
TRUCKING, DUMP
TRUCKING, REFRIGERATED: Long-Distance
TRUCKING: Except Local
TRUCKING: Local, With Storage
TRUCKING: Local, Without Storage
TRUCKING: Long-Distance, Less Than Truckload
TRUCKS & TRACTORS: Industrial
TRUCKS, INDL: Wholesalers
TRUSSES: Wood, Floor
TRUSSES: Wood, Roof
TRUST COMPANIES: National With Deposits, Commercial
TRUST COMPANIES: State Accepting Deposits, Commercial
TRUST MANAGEMENT SVCS: Charitable
TRUST MANAGEMENT SVCS: Personal Investment
TUBE & TUBING FABRICATORS
TUBES: Steel & Iron
TUBING: Flexible, Metallic
TUBING: Plastic
TUGBOAT SVCS
TUNGSTEN MILL PRDTS
TURBINES & TURBINE GENERATOR SETS
TURBINES: Gas, Mechanical Drive
TURNKEY VENDORS: Computer Systems
TYPESETTING SVC
TYPESETTING SVC: Computer

U

UNIFORM SPLY SVCS: Indl
UNIFORM STORES
UNISEX HAIR SALONS
UNITED FUND COUNCILS
UNIVERSITY
UPHOLSTERY WORK SVCS
URANIUM ORE MINING, NEC
USED CAR DEALERS
USED CLOTHING STORES
USED MERCHANDISE STORES
USED MERCHANDISE STORES: Clothing & Shoes
USED MERCHANDISE STORES: Furniture
USHER SVC
UTILITIES REGULATION & ADMINISTRATION

V

VACATION LODGES
VACUUM CLEANER STORES
VACUUM CLEANERS: Household
VALET PARKING SVCS
VALUE-ADDED RESELLERS: Computer Systems
VALVE REPAIR SVCS, INDL
VALVES & PIPE FITTINGS
VALVES: Aerosol, Metal
VALVES: Aircraft, Hydraulic
VALVES: Indl
VALVES: Nuclear Power Plant, Ferrous
VARIETY STORE MERCHANDISE, WHOLESALE
VARIETY STORES
VEGETABLE STANDS OR MARKETS
VEHICLES: All Terrain
VENDING MACHINE OPERATORS: Beverage
VENDING MACHINE OPERATORS: Food
VENDING MACHINE OPERATORS: Sandwich & Hot Food
VENDING MACHINE REPAIR SVCS
VENDING MACHINES & PARTS
VENTILATING EQPT: Metal
VENTURE CAPITAL COMPANIES
VESSELS: Process, Indl, Metal Plate
VETERANS AFFAIRS ADMINISTRATION SVCS
VETERANS' AFFAIRS ADMINISTRATION, GOVERNMENT: Federal
VETERINARY PRDTS: Instruments & Apparatus
VIDEO & AUDIO EQPT, WHOLESALE
VIDEO PRODUCTION SVCS
VIDEO REPAIR SVCS
VIDEO TAPE PRODUCTION SVCS
VIDEO TAPE WHOLESALERS, RECORDED
VINYL RESINS, NEC
VISITING NURSE
VISUAL COMMUNICATIONS SYSTEMS
VITAMINS: Pharmaceutical Preparations
VOCATIONAL OR TECHNICAL SCHOOLS, PUBLIC
VOCATIONAL REHABILITATION AGENCY
VOCATIONAL TRAINING AGENCY

W

WALL COVERINGS WHOLESALERS
WALLS: Curtain, Metal
WAREHOUSING & STORAGE FACILITIES, NEC
WAREHOUSING & STORAGE, REFRIGERATED: Cold Storage Or Refrig
WAREHOUSING & STORAGE, REFRIGERATED: Frozen Or Refrig Goods
WAREHOUSING & STORAGE: Automobile, Dead Storage
WAREHOUSING & STORAGE: General
WAREHOUSING & STORAGE: General
WAREHOUSING & STORAGE: Liquid
WAREHOUSING & STORAGE: Miniwarehouse
WAREHOUSING & STORAGE: Refrigerated
WAREHOUSING & STORAGE: Self Storage
WARM AIR HEATING & AC EQPT & SPLYS, WHOLESALE Air Filters
WARM AIR HEATING & AC EQPT & SPLYS, WHOLESALE Furnaces
WARM AIR HEATING & AC EQPT & SPLYS, WHOLESALE Furnaces, Elec
WARM AIR HEATING/AC EQPT/SPLYS, WHOL Warm Air Htg Eqpt/Splys
WARM AIR HEATING/AC EQPT/SPLYS, WHOL: Ventilating Eqpt/Sply
WARRANTY INSURANCE: Automobile
WASHERS: Metal
WASTE CLEANING SVCS
WATCH REPAIR SVCS
WATCHES & PARTS, WHOLESALE
WATER SOFTENER SVCS
WATER SOFTENING WHOLESALERS
WATER SPLY: Irrigation
WATER SUPPLY
WATER: Distilled
WATERBEDS & ACCESS STORES
WEATHER FORECASTING SVCS
WEDDING CHAPEL: Privately Operated
WELDING EQPT
WELDING EQPT & SPLYS WHOLESALERS
WELDING REPAIR SVC
WELDING SPLYS, EXC GASES: Wholesalers
WELDMENTS
WELFARE PENSIONS
WHEELBARROWS
WHEELS
WHEELS & BRAKE SHOES: Railroad, Cast Iron
WINDOW & DOOR FRAMES
WINDOW CLEANING SVCS
WINDOW FRAMES & SASHES: Plastic
WINDOW FRAMES, MOLDING & TRIM: Vinyl
WINE & DISTILLED ALCOHOLIC BEVERAGES WHOLESALERS
WINE CELLARS, BONDED: Wine, Blended
WIRE & WIRE PRDTS
WIRE FENCING & ACCESS WHOLESALERS
WIRE MATERIALS: Steel
WIRE WINDING OF PURCHASED WIRE
WIRE, FLAT: Strip, Cold-Rolled, Exc From Hot-Rolled Mills
WIRE: Nonferrous
WOMEN'S & CHILDREN'S CLOTHING WHOLESALERS, NEC
WOMEN'S & GIRLS' SPORTSWEAR WHOLESALERS
WOMEN'S CLOTHING STORES
WOOD & WOOD BY-PRDTS, WHOLESALE
WOOD CHIPS, PRODUCED AT THE MILL
WOOD PRDTS: Moldings, Unfinished & Prefinished
WOOD PRDTS: Mulch, Wood & Bark
WOOD PRDTS: Survey Stakes
WOODWORK & TRIM: Interior & Ornamental
WORK EXPERIENCE CENTER

X

X-RAY EQPT & TUBES
X-RAY EQPT REPAIR SVCS

Y

YACHT CLUBS
YOUTH CAMPS
YOUTH SELF-HELP AGENCY

Z

ZOOLOGICAL GARDEN, NONCOMMERCIAL
ZOOS & BOTANICAL GARDENS

SERVICES SECTION

> **BOXES: Folding**
> Service category → **BOXES: Folding**
> Edgar & Son Paperboard ....G...... 999 999-9999
> Yourtown *(G-11480)*
> Ready Box Co ....E...... 999 999-9999
> City → Anytown *(G-7097)*
>
> Indicates approximate employment figure
> A = Over 500 employees, B = 251-500
> C = 101-250, D = 51-100, E = 25-50
>
> → Business phone
>
> → Geographic Section entry number where full company information appears.

See footnotes for symbols and codes identification.
- Refer to the Services Index preceding this section to locate service headings.

ABORTION CLINIC
Cleveland Preterm ....E...... 216 991-4577
 Cleveland *(G-5340)*

ABRASIVES
ARC Abrasives Inc ....D...... 800 888-4885
 Troy *(G-18347)*
Lawrence Industries Inc ....C...... 216 518-7000
 Cleveland *(G-5929)*
Mill-Rose Company ....C...... 440 255-9171
 Mentor *(G-14220)*
National Lime and Stone Co ....C...... 419 396-7671
 Carey *(G-2596)*

ACADEMIC TUTORING SVCS
Academic Support Services LLC ....E...... 740 274-6138
 Columbus *(G-6930)*

ACADEMY
Ohio Academy of Science ....E...... 614 488-2228
 Columbus *(G-8316)*

ACCELERATORS: Linear
Ci Disposition Co ....E...... 216 587-5200
 Brooklyn Heights *(G-1912)*

ACCIDENT & HEALTH INSURANCE CARRIERS
American Modrn Insur Group Inc ....C...... 800 543-2644
 Amelia *(G-576)*
Medical Mutual of Ohio ....B...... 216 292-0400
 Beachwood *(G-1099)*
Noor Home Health Care ....D...... 216 320-0803
 Cleveland Heights *(G-6794)*
Royal Health Services LLC ....E...... 614 826-1316
 Columbus *(G-8654)*

ACCIDENT INSURANCE CARRIERS
Liberty Mutual Insurance Co ....E...... 614 855-6193
 Westerville *(G-19325)*
Nationwide Corporation ....E...... 614 249-7111
 Columbus *(G-8238)*
Nationwide Mutual Insurance Co ....A...... 614 249-7111
 Columbus *(G-8247)*
Paramount Care Inc ....B...... 419 887-2500
 Maumee *(G-13955)*
Progressive Casualty Insur Co ....D...... 440 603-4033
 Cleveland *(G-6314)*

ACCOUNTING SVCS, NEC
American Electric Pwr Svc Corp ....B...... 614 716-1000
 Columbus *(G-6990)*
Brott Mardis & Co ....E...... 330 762-5022
 Akron *(G-115)*
C H Dean Inc ....D...... 937 222-9531
 Beavercreek *(G-1156)*
Cliftonlarsonallen LLP ....E...... 330 376-0100
 Akron *(G-148)*
Defense Fin & Accounting Svc ....A...... 614 693-6700
 Columbus *(G-7501)*
Deloitte & Touche LLP ....C...... 614 221-1000
 Columbus *(G-7505)*
Elliott Davis LLC ....E...... 513 579-1717
 Cincinnati *(G-3551)*
Fehr Services LLC ....E...... 513 829-9333
 Fairfield *(G-10851)*

Flex Fund Inc ....E...... 614 766-7000
 Dublin *(G-10348)*
Klingbeil Management Group Co ....E...... 614 220-8900
 Columbus *(G-7997)*
Kpmg LLP ....C...... 614 249-2300
 Columbus *(G-8012)*
Mutual Shareholder Svcs LLC ....E...... 440 922-0067
 Broadview Heights *(G-1884)*
Ohio State University ....E...... 614 292-6831
 Columbus *(G-8408)*
Pease & Associates LLC ....E...... 216 348-9600
 Cleveland *(G-6258)*
Rlj Management Co Inc ....C...... 614 942-2020
 Columbus *(G-8639)*

ACCOUNTING SVCS: Certified Public
415 Group Inc ....E...... 330 492-0094
 Canton *(G-2219)*
Apple Growth Partners Inc ....D...... 330 867-7350
 Akron *(G-78)*
Barnes Dennig & Co Ltd ....D...... 513 241-8313
 Cincinnati *(G-3079)*
Barnes Wendling Cpas Inc ....E...... 216 566-9000
 Cleveland *(G-5095)*
Bhm CPA Group Inc ....D...... 740 474-5210
 Circleville *(G-4878)*
Bkd LLP ....D...... 513 621-8300
 Cincinnati *(G-3111)*
Blue & Co LLC ....C...... 513 241-4507
 Cincinnati *(G-3115)*
Bober Markey Fedorovich ....D...... 330 762-9785
 Fairlawn *(G-10938)*
Bodine Perry LLC ....E...... 330 702-8100
 Canfield *(G-2183)*
Brady Ware & Schoenfeld Inc ....D...... 614 885-7407
 Columbus *(G-7130)*
Brady Ware & Schoenfeld Inc ....D...... 937 223-5247
 Miamisburg *(G-14277)*
Brady Ware & Schoenfeld Inc ....D...... 614 825-6277
 Columbus *(G-7131)*
Burke & Schindler Pllc ....E...... 859 344-8887
 Cincinnati *(G-3151)*
Cassady Schiller & Associates ....E...... 513 483-6699
 Blue Ash *(G-1551)*
Ciulla Smith & Dale LLP ....E...... 440 884-2036
 Cleveland *(G-5280)*
Ciuni & Panichi Inc ....D...... 216 831-7171
 Cleveland *(G-5281)*
Clark Schaefer Hackett & Co ....E...... 937 399-2000
 Springfield *(G-17160)*
Clark Schaefer Hackett & Co ....E...... 513 241-3111
 Cincinnati *(G-3359)*
Clark Schaefer Hackett & Co ....E...... 216 672-5252
 Cleveland *(G-5282)*
Clark Schaefer Hackett & Co ....D...... 419 243-0218
 Toledo *(G-17814)*
Clark Schaefer Hackett & Co ....E...... 614 885-2208
 Columbus *(G-7292)*
Cliftonlarsonallen LLP ....D...... 330 497-2000
 Canton *(G-2314)*
Cliftonlarsonallen LLP ....E...... 419 244-3711
 Toledo *(G-17817)*
Cohen & Company Ltd ....D...... 330 743-1040
 Youngstown *(G-20146)*
Cohen & Company Ltd ....D...... 330 374-1040
 Akron *(G-150)*
Crowe Horwath LLP ....C...... 614 469-0001
 Columbus *(G-7466)*
Crowe Horwath LLP ....E...... 216 623-7500
 Cleveland *(G-5439)*
Csh Group ....E...... 937 226-0070
 Miamisburg *(G-14290)*

Deloitte & Touche LLP ....D...... 937 223-8821
 Dayton *(G-9496)*
Deloitte & Touche LLP ....B...... 513 784-7100
 Cincinnati *(G-3482)*
Ernst & Young LLP ....D...... 216 861-5000
 Cleveland *(G-5550)*
Ernst & Young LLP ....E...... 216 583-1823
 Cleveland *(G-5551)*
Ernst & Young LLP ....E...... 614 224-5678
 Columbus *(G-7607)*
Ernst & Young LLP ....E...... 513 612-1400
 Cincinnati *(G-3575)*
Ernst & Young LLP ....E...... 419 244-8000
 Toledo *(G-17870)*
Essex and Associates Inc ....E...... 937 432-1040
 Dayton *(G-9531)*
Flagel Huber Flagel & Co ....E...... 937 299-3400
 Moraine *(G-14787)*
Foundations Hlth Solutions Inc ....D...... 440 793-0200
 North Olmsted *(G-15423)*
Foxx & Company ....E...... 513 241-1616
 Cincinnati *(G-3643)*
Fruth & Co ....E...... 419 435-8541
 Fostoria *(G-11127)*
Grant Thornton LLP ....C...... 216 771-1400
 Cleveland *(G-5687)*
Grant Thornton LLP ....D...... 513 762-5000
 Cincinnati *(G-3693)*
Hill Barth & King LLC ....E...... 330 758-8613
 Canfield *(G-2193)*
Hill Barth & King LLC ....D...... 614 228-4000
 Columbus *(G-7835)*
Hill Barth & King LLC ....E...... 330 747-1903
 Canfield *(G-2194)*
Hobe Lcas Crtif Pub Accntants ....E...... 216 524-7167
 Cleveland *(G-5764)*
Holbrook & Manter ....E...... 740 387-8620
 Marion *(G-13543)*
Howard Wershbale & Co ....D...... 216 831-1200
 Cleveland *(G-5786)*
Jones Cochenour & Co Inc ....E...... 740 653-9581
 Lancaster *(G-12545)*
Julian & Grube Inc ....E...... 614 846-1899
 Westerville *(G-19318)*
Kpmg LLP ....C...... 513 421-6430
 Cincinnati *(G-3940)*
Kpmg LLP ....C...... 216 696-9100
 Cleveland *(G-5912)*
Maloney + Novotny LLC ....D...... 216 363-0100
 Cleveland *(G-5975)*
McCrate Delaet & Co ....E...... 937 492-3161
 Sidney *(G-16942)*
Meaden & Moore LLP ....D...... 216 241-3272
 Cleveland *(G-6010)*
Mellott & Mellott Pll ....E...... 513 241-2940
 Cincinnati *(G-4053)*
Mosley Pfundt & Glick Inc ....E...... 419 861-1120
 Maumee *(G-13948)*
Murray Wlls Wndeln Rbnson Cpas ....E...... 937 773-6373
 Piqua *(G-16154)*
Nms Inc Certif Pub Accountants ....E...... 440 286-5222
 Chardon *(G-2759)*
Norman Jones Enlow & Co ....E...... 614 228-4000
 Columbus *(G-8285)*
Patrick J Burke & Co ....E...... 513 455-8200
 Cincinnati *(G-4262)*
Payne Nickles & Co CPA ....E...... 419 668-2552
 Norwalk *(G-15588)*
Pricewaterhousecoopers LLP ....B...... 216 875-3000
 Cleveland *(G-6305)*
Pricewaterhousecoopers LLP ....E...... 419 254-2500
 Toledo *(G-18135)*

ACCOUNTING SVCS: Certified Public

Pricewaterhousecoopers LLP ....D 513 723-4700
  Cincinnati *(G-4328)*
Pricewaterhousecoopers LLP ....C 614 225-8700
  Columbus *(G-8559)*
REA & Associates Inc ....E 330 722-8222
  Medina *(G-14117)*
REA & Associates Inc ....D 330 339-6651
  New Philadelphia *(G-15112)*
REA & Associates Inc ....E 419 331-1040
  Lima *(G-12929)*
REA & Associates Inc ....E 330 674-6055
  Millersburg *(G-14618)*
REA & Associates Inc ....D 440 266-0077
  New Philadelphia *(G-15113)*
REA & Associates Inc ....E 614 889-8725
  Dublin *(G-10438)*
Rehmann LLC ....D 419 865-8118
  Toledo *(G-18149)*
Reynolds & Co Inc ....E 740 353-1040
  Portsmouth *(G-16304)*
RSM US LLP ....C 937 298-0201
  Moraine *(G-14821)*
RSM US LLP ....E 614 224-7722
  Columbus *(G-8656)*
Schneider Downs & Co Inc ....D 614 621-4060
  Columbus *(G-8697)*
Schroedel Scullin & Bestic LLC ....E 330 533-1131
  Canfield *(G-2209)*
Skoda Mntti Crtif Pub Accntnts ....D 440 449-6800
  Mayfield Village *(G-14013)*
Smithpearlman & Co ....E 513 248-9210
  Milford *(G-14564)*
Thomas Packer & Co ....E 330 533-9777
  Canfield *(G-2212)*
Walthall LLP ....E 216 573-2330
  Cleveland *(G-6720)*
Weber Obrien Ltd ....E 419 885-8338
  Sylvania *(G-17627)*
Whalen and Company Inc ....E 614 396-4200
  Worthington *(G-20008)*
Whitcomb & Hess Inc ....E 419 289-7007
  Ashland *(G-708)*
Whited Seigneur Sams & Rahe ....E 740 702-2600
  Chillicothe *(G-2897)*
William Vaughan Company ....D 419 891-1040
  Maumee *(G-13995)*
Wilson Shannon & Snow Inc ....E 740 345-6611
  Newark *(G-15246)*
Zinner & Co ....E 216 831-0733
  Beachwood *(G-1138)*

ACUPUNCTURISTS' OFFICES

Central Ohio Primary Care ....D 614 818-9550
  Westerville *(G-19379)*
Central Ohio Primary Care ....E 614 268-6555
  Columbus *(G-7236)*
Central Ohio Primary Care ....E 614 442-7550
  Columbus *(G-7239)*
Mercy Health ....D 937 328-8700
  Springfield *(G-17239)*
Ohio Presbt Retirement Svcs ....C 614 228-8888
  Columbus *(G-8368)*
Primary Cr Ntwrk Prmr Hlth Prt ....D 937 208-7000
  Beavercreek *(G-1199)*

ADDRESSING SVCS

Hecks Direct Mail & Prtg Svc ....E 419 697-3505
  Toledo *(G-17950)*

ADHESIVES

Conversion Tech Intl Inc ....E 419 924-5566
  West Unity *(G-19280)*

ADHESIVES & SEALANTS

Cincinnati Assn For The Blind ....C 513 221-8558
  Cincinnati *(G-3282)*
Continental Products Company ....E 216 531-0710
  Cleveland *(G-5402)*
Hexpol Compounding LLC ....C 440 834-4644
  Burton *(G-2062)*
Hoover & Wells Inc ....C 419 691-9220
  Toledo *(G-17959)*
Sonoco Products Company ....D 937 429-0040
  Beavercreek Township *(G-1285)*
United McGill Corporation ....E 614 829-1200
  Groveport *(G-11681)*

ADJUSTMENT BUREAU, EXC INSURANCE

Roddy Group Inc ....E 216 763-0088
  Beachwood *(G-1121)*

ADOPTION SVCS

Beech Acres Parenting Center ....C 513 231-6630
  Cincinnati *(G-3088)*
County of Lorain ....C 440 329-5340
  Elyria *(G-10616)*
Heartbeat International Inc ....E 614 885-7577
  Columbus *(G-7816)*
Mahoning County Childrens Svcs ....C 330 941-8888
  Youngstown *(G-20263)*
Northeast Ohio Adoption Svcs ....E 330 856-5582
  Warren *(G-18887)*
Options For Family & Youth ....E 216 267-7070
  Strongsville *(G-17498)*
United Methodist Childrens ....D 614 885-5020
  Worthington *(G-20004)*

ADULT DAYCARE CENTERS

2100 Lakeside Shelter For Men ....E 216 566-0047
  Cleveland *(G-4924)*
CA Group ....E 419 586-2137
  Celina *(G-2637)*
CHN Inc - Adult Day Care ....E 937 548-0506
  Greenville *(G-11493)*
Consumer Support Services Inc ....D 740 344-3600
  Newark *(G-15160)*
DMD Management Inc ....A 216 371-3600
  Cleveland *(G-5497)*
Gardens Western Reserve Inc ....D 330 342-9100
  Streetsboro *(G-17412)*
Horizon Education Centers ....E 440 458-5115
  Elyria *(G-10634)*
Inn At Christine Valley ....E 330 270-3347
  Youngstown *(G-20236)*
Life Center Adult Day Care ....E 614 866-7212
  Reynoldsburg *(G-16465)*
ONeill Senior Center Inc ....E 740 373-3914
  Marietta *(G-13482)*
Senior Independence Adult ....E 440 954-8372
  Willoughby *(G-19712)*
Senior Independence Adult ....E 513 681-8174
  Monroe *(G-14711)*
Senior Independence Adult ....E 513 539-2697
  Monroe *(G-14712)*

ADULT EDUCATION SCHOOLS, PUBLIC

Cleveland Municipal School Dst ....D 216 459-4200
  Cleveland *(G-5334)*
Great Oaks Inst Tech Creer Dev ....E 513 771-8840
  Cincinnati *(G-3704)*

ADVERTISING AGENCIES

AMP Advertising Inc ....E 513 333-4100
  Cincinnati *(G-3016)*
Arras Group Inc ....E 216 621-1601
  Cleveland *(G-5067)*
Barefoot LLC ....E 513 861-3668
  Cincinnati *(G-3078)*
BBDO Worldwide Inc ....E 513 861-3668
  Cincinnati *(G-3084)*
Bbs & Associates Inc ....E 330 665-5227
  Akron *(G-92)*
Chisano Mktg Cmmunications Inc ......E 937 847-0607
  Miamisburg *(G-14282)*
Commerce Holdings Inc ....E 513 579-1950
  Cincinnati *(G-3398)*
D & S Crtive Cmmunications Inc ....D 419 524-6699
  Mansfield *(G-13288)*
Detroit Royalty Incorporated ....D 216 771-5700
  Cleveland *(G-5479)*
Dix & Eaton Incorporated ....E 216 241-0405
  Cleveland *(G-5493)*
Epiphen Incorporated ....E 888 687-7620
  Cincinnati *(G-3565)*
Hsr Marketing Communications ....D 513 671-3811
  Cincinnati *(G-3792)*
Inquiry Systems Inc ....E 614 464-3800
  Columbus *(G-7904)*
Kuno Creative Group LLC ....E 440 225-4144
  Avon *(G-904)*
L M Berry and Company ....A 937 296-2121
  Moraine *(G-14797)*
Madison Avenue Mktg Group Inc ....E 419 473-9000
  Toledo *(G-18026)*
Marketing Support Services Inc ....D 513 752-1200
  Cincinnati *(G-4024)*
Melamed Riley Advertising LLC ....E 216 241-2141
  Cleveland *(G-6022)*
Monster Worldwide Inc ....D 513 719-3331
  Cincinnati *(G-4115)*
People To My Site LLC ....E 614 452-8179
  Columbus *(G-8532)*
Quad/Graphics Inc ....C 614 276-4800
  Columbus *(G-8579)*
Rockfish Interactive Corp ....E 513 381-1583
  Cincinnati *(G-4438)*
Roman/Peshoff Inc ....E 419 241-2221
  Holland *(G-12051)*
Sgk LLC ....E 513 569-9900
  Cincinnati *(G-4506)*
Thread Information Design Inc ....E 419 887-6801
  Toledo *(G-18218)*
Touchstone Mdse Group LLC ....D 513 741-0400
  Mason *(G-13771)*
Vivial Media LLC ....D 937 610-4100
  Dayton *(G-9973)*
Wern-Rausch Locke Advertising ....E 330 493-8866
  Canton *(G-2584)*
Whitespace Design Group Inc ....E 330 762-9320
  Akron *(G-510)*

ADVERTISING AGENCIES: Consultants

Airmate Company ....D 419 636-3184
  Bryan *(G-2000)*
AMG Marketing Resources Inc ....E 216 621-1835
  Solon *(G-16975)*
Brand Build Inc ....E 513 579-1950
  Blue Ash *(G-1548)*
Brokaw Inc ....E 216 241-8003
  Cleveland *(G-5143)*
Charles W Powers & Assoc Inc ....E 513 721-5353
  Cincinnati *(G-3231)*
Cooper-Smith Advertising LLC ....E 419 470-5900
  Toledo *(G-17832)*
Curiosity LLC ....D 513 744-6000
  Cincinnati *(G-3449)*
D & D Advertising Enterprises ....E 513 921-6827
  Cincinnati *(G-3453)*
David Group ....E 216 685-4400
  Cleveland *(G-5467)*
Deanhouston Creative Group Inc ....E 513 421-6622
  Cincinnati *(G-3475)*
Eric Mower and Associates Inc ....E 513 381-8855
  Cincinnati *(G-3573)*
Fahlgren Inc ....E 614 383-1500
  Columbus *(G-7628)*
Fahlgren Inc ....D 614 383-1500
  Columbus *(G-7629)*
Guardian Enterprise Group Inc ....E 614 416-6080
  Columbus *(G-7784)*
Gypc Inc ....C 309 677-0405
  Dayton *(G-9593)*
Hart Associates Inc ....D 419 893-9600
  Toledo *(G-17936)*
Hitchcock Fleming & Assoc Inc ....D 330 376-2111
  Akron *(G-266)*
Kreber Graphics Inc ....D 614 529-5701
  Columbus *(G-8013)*
Marcus Thomas Llc ....D 216 292-4700
  Cleveland *(G-5978)*
Marcus Thomas Llc ....D 330 793-3000
  Youngstown *(G-20272)*
Matrix Media Services Inc ....E 614 228-2200
  Columbus *(G-8129)*
Nas Rcrtment Cmmunications LLC .....C 216 478-0300
  Cleveland *(G-6100)*
Real Art Design Group Inc ....E 937 223-9955
  Dayton *(G-9844)*
Ron Foth Retail Inc ....D 614 888-7771
  Columbus *(G-8646)*
SBC Advertising Ltd ....C 614 891-7070
  Columbus *(G-8692)*
Stern Advertising Inc ....E 216 464-4850
  Cleveland *(G-6540)*
Universal Advertising Assoc ....E 513 522-5000
  Cincinnati *(G-4746)*
Wyse Advertising Inc ....E 216 696-2424
  Cleveland *(G-6765)*

ADVERTISING COPY WRITING SVCS

Madison Avenue Mktg Group Inc ....E 419 473-9000
  Toledo *(G-18026)*

SERVICES SECTION

AGENTS, BROKERS & BUREAUS: Personal Service

ADVERTISING MATERIAL DISTRIBUTION

Company	Code	Phone
Berry Network LLC — Moraine (G-14753)	C	800 366-1264
Dispatch Consumer Services — Lancaster (G-12527)	D	740 687-1893
Dispatch Consumer Services — Columbus (G-7523)	E	740 548-5555

ADVERTISING REPRESENTATIVES: Electronic Media

Company	Code	Phone
Ctv Media Inc — Powell (G-16333)	E	614 848-5800
Madison Avenue Mktg Group Inc — Toledo (G-18026)	E	419 473-9000
Segmint Inc — Akron (G-431)	E	330 594-5379

ADVERTISING REPRESENTATIVES: Media

Company	Code	Phone
Agri Communicators Inc — Columbus (G-6957)	E	614 273-0465
Creative Crafts Group LLC — Blue Ash (G-1570)	D	303 215-5600
Maverick Media — Lima (G-12838)	E	419 331-1600

ADVERTISING REPRESENTATIVES: Newspaper

Company	Code	Phone
American City Bus Journals Inc — Dayton (G-9328)	E	937 528-4400
B G News — Bowling Green (G-1759)	E	419 372-2601
Copley Ohio Newspapers Inc — New Philadelphia (G-15087)	C	330 364-5577
Sandusky Register — Sandusky (G-16793)	E	419 625-5500

ADVERTISING REPRESENTATIVES: Printed Media

Company	Code	Phone
Manta Media Inc — Columbus (G-6893)	E	888 875-5833

ADVERTISING REPRESENTATIVES: Radio

Company	Code	Phone
Iheartcommunications Inc — Dayton (G-9627)	C	937 224-1137
Killer Spotscom Inc — Cincinnati (G-3923)	D	513 201-1380

ADVERTISING REPRESENTATIVES: Television & Radio Time Sales

Company	Code	Phone
Thinktv Network — Dayton (G-9927)	E	937 220-1600

ADVERTISING SPECIALTIES, WHOLESALE

Company	Code	Phone
Boost Technologies LLC — Dayton (G-9364)	D	800 223-2203
Corporate Imageworks LLC — Streetsboro (G-17411)	E	216 292-8800
Dayton Heidelberg Distrg Co — Moraine (G-14771)	D	937 220-6450
Evolution Crtive Solutions LLC — Cincinnati (G-3584)	E	513 681-4450
Galaxy Balloons Incorporated — Cleveland (G-5651)	C	216 476-3360
L M Berry and Company — Cincinnati (G-3953)	D	513 768-7700
Leader Promotions Inc — Columbus (G-8047)	E	614 416-6565
Marathon Mfg & Sup Co — New Philadelphia (G-15108)	D	330 343-2050
Novelty Advertising Co Inc — Coshocton (G-9113)	E	740 622-3113
Nutis Press Inc — Columbus (G-8307)	C	614 237-8626
Peter Graham Dunn Inc — Dalton (G-9242)	E	330 816-0035
Relay Gear Ltd — Columbus (G-8611)	E	888 735-2943
Screen Works Inc — Dayton (G-9870)	E	937 264-9111
Shamrock Companies Inc — Westlake (G-19546)	C	440 899-9510
Shumsky Enterprises Inc — Dayton (G-9880)	D	937 223-2203

Company	Code	Phone
Traichal Construction Company — Niles (G-15307)	E	800 255-3667

ADVERTISING SVCS, NEC

Company	Code	Phone
Ohs LLC — Blue Ash (G-1656)	E	513 252-2249

ADVERTISING SVCS: Billboards

Company	Code	Phone
Clear Channel Outdoor Inc — Columbus (G-7296)	E	614 276-9781

ADVERTISING SVCS: Coupon Distribution

Company	Code	Phone
Catalina Marketing Corporation — Cincinnati (G-3193)	E	513 564-8200

ADVERTISING SVCS: Direct Mail

Company	Code	Phone
A W S Inc — Rocky River (G-16567)	C	440 333-1791
A W S Inc — Cleveland (G-4937)	B	216 749-0356
Amerimark Holdings LLC — Cleveland (G-5025)	B	440 325-2000
Angstrom Graphics Inc Midwest — Cleveland (G-5037)	B	216 271-5300
Atco Inc — Athens (G-773)	C	740 592-6659
Clipper Magazine LLC — Blue Ash (G-1559)	D	513 794-4100
Consolidated Graphics Group Inc — Cleveland (G-5393)	C	216 881-9191
Ddm-Digital Imaging Data — Hebron (G-11847)	D	740 928-1110
Deepwood Industries Inc — Mentor (G-14168)	C	440 350-5231
Digital Color Intl LLC — Akron (G-193)	E	330 762-6959
Directconnectgroup Ltd — Cleveland (G-5486)	A	216 281-2866
Hecks Direct Mail & Prtg Svc — Toledo (G-17951)	E	419 661-6028
Hkm Drect Mkt Cmmnications Inc — Cleveland (G-5762)	C	216 651-9500
Pickaway Diversfied Industries — Circleville (G-4897)	D	740 474-1522
Popper & Associates Msrp LLC — Dublin (G-10428)	E	614 798-8991
Resource Interactive — Columbus (G-8621)	E	614 621-2888
Sourcelink Ohio LLC — Miamisburg (G-14352)	C	937 885-8000
TMR Inc — Brunswick (G-1992)	C	330 220-8564
Traxium LLC — Stow (G-17397)	E	330 572-8200
Yeck Brothers Company — Moraine (G-14837)	E	937 294-4000

ADVERTISING SVCS: Display

Company	Code	Phone
Digital Color Intl LLC — Akron (G-193)	E	330 762-6959
Groupcle LLC — Cleveland (G-5707)	E	216 251-9641
Innomark Communications LLC — Sharonville (G-16882)	E	937 425-6152
Team Management Inc — Columbus (G-8827)	C	614 486-0864

ADVERTISING SVCS: Outdoor

Company	Code	Phone
Kessler Sign Company — Zanesville (G-20494)	E	740 453-0668
Lamar Advertising Company — Cleveland (G-5924)	E	216 676-4321
Lamar Advertising Company — Saint Clairsville (G-16639)	E	740 699-0000
Matrix Media Services Inc — Columbus (G-8129)	E	614 228-2200
Orange Barrel Media LLC — Columbus (G-8477)	E	614 294-4898

ADVERTISING SVCS: Sample Distribution

Company	Code	Phone
Dismas Distribution Services — Blacklick (G-1506)	E	614 861-2525
Signum LLC — Solon (G-17051)	D	440 248-2233

ADVERTISING SVCS: Transit

Company	Code	Phone
Paul Werth Associates Inc — Columbus (G-8524)	E	614 224-8114

ADVERTISING: Aerial

Company	Code	Phone
Hillman Group Inc — West Chester (G-19207)	E	513 874-5905

ADVOCACY GROUP

Company	Code	Phone
Center For Community Solutions — Cleveland (G-5204)	E	216 781-2944
Childrens Hunger Alliance — Columbus (G-7263)	D	614 341-7700
Choices For Vctims Dom Volence — Worthington (G-19947)	E	614 224-6617
Cleveland Municipal School Dst — Cleveland (G-5335)	B	216 838-0000
Cleveland Municipal School Dst — Cleveland (G-5336)	E	216 838-8700
Columbus Landmarks Foundation — Columbus (G-7362)	E	614 221-0227
Lincare Inc — Akron (G-320)	E	330 928-0884
Mahoning Youngstown Community — Youngstown (G-20268)	D	330 747-7921
Miami Vly Fandom For Literacy — Lebanon (G-12629)	E	513 933-0452
Nationwide Childrens Hospital — Columbus (G-8233)	B	614 722-8200
Ohio Legal Rights Service — Columbus (G-8356)	E	614 466-7264
Phyllis Wheatley Assn Dev — Cleveland (G-6278)	E	216 391-4443
Salvation Army — Akron (G-427)	E	330 762-8481
Salvation Army — Cincinnati (G-4475)	D	513 762-5600
Salvation Army — Columbus (G-8681)	D	614 252-7171
Scioto Residential Services — Portsmouth (G-16308)	E	740 353-0288
United Methodist Community Ctr — Youngstown (G-20398)	E	330 743-5149

AGENTS, BROKERS & BUREAUS: Personal Service

Company	Code	Phone
Abraham Ford LLC — Elyria (G-10592)	E	440 233-7402
Aecom Energy & Cnstr Inc — Cleveland (G-4963)	A	216 523-5600
Aecom Energy & Cnstr Inc — Cleveland (G-4964)	A	216 523-5600
Another Chance Inc — Pickerington (G-16084)	E	614 868-3541
Canon Solutions America Inc — Independence (G-12193)	D	216 446-3830
Canton S-Group Ltd — Sandusky (G-16732)	B	419 625-7003
Cass Information Systems Inc — Columbus (G-7207)	C	614 766-2277
Coast To Coast Studios LLC — Blacklick (G-1505)	E	614 861-9800
Corporate United Inc — Westlake (G-19480)	E	440 895-0938
Covelli Enterprises Inc — Dublin (G-10311)	D	614 889-7802
Douglas R Denny — Independence (G-12205)	E	216 236-2400
Essilor of America Inc — Groveport (G-11637)	C	614 492-0888
Finastra USA Corporation — Miamisburg (G-14302)	E	937 435-2335
Genesis Respiratory Svcs Inc — Athens (G-789)	E	740 456-4363
Hamilton Cnty Auditor Office — Cincinnati (G-3730)	C	513 946-4000
Legend Equities Corporation — Independence (G-12223)	D	216 741-3113
Limitless Solutions Inc — Columbus (G-8068)	E	614 577-1550
Oriana House Inc — Akron (G-372)	A	330 374-9610
Progressive Quality Care Inc — Parma (G-15914)	E	216 661-6800
Promohouse Inc — Columbus (G-8571)	E	614 324-9200
Return Polymers Inc — Ashland (G-694)	D	419 289-1998

Employee Codes: A=Over 500 employees, B=251-500, C=101-250, D=51-100, E=25-50

AGENTS, BROKERS & BUREAUS: Personal Service

Riverside Medical Inc .... E 513 936-5360
Cincinnati (G-4428)
Sander Woody Ford .... D 513 541-5586
Cincinnati (G-4476)
Southern Graphic Systems Inc .... B 419 662-9873
Perrysburg (G-16061)
United Parcel Service Inc OH .... B 740 962-7971
Portsmouth (G-16315)
Verizon New York Inc .... C 614 301-2498
Hilliard (G-11964)

AGRICULTURAL EQPT: BARN, SILO, POULTRY, DAIRY/LIVESTOCK MACH

Fort Recovery Equipment Inc .... E 419 375-1006
Fort Recovery (G-11116)

AGRICULTURAL EQPT: Fertilizing Machinery

Shearer Farm Inc .... E 330 345-9023
Wooster (G-19915)

AGRICULTURAL MACHINERY & EQPT: Wholesalers

Baker & Sons Equipment Co .... E 740 567-3317
Lewisville (G-12714)
Buckeye Companies .... E 740 452-3641
Zanesville (G-20450)
Deerfield Farms Service Inc .... D 330 584-4715
Deerfield (G-10019)
JD Equipment Inc .... D 614 527-8800
New Albany (G-14989)
Liechty Inc .... E 419 445-1565
Archbold (G-637)
Wyandot Tractor & Implement Co .... E 419 294-2349
Upper Sandusky (G-18571)

AGRICULTURAL PROG REG OFFICES, GOVT: Agriculture Fair Board

United States Dept Agriculture .... D 419 626-8439
Sandusky (G-16806)

AID TO FAMILIES WITH DEPENDENT CHILDREN OR AFDC

Shelter House Volunteer Group .... E 513 721-0643
Cincinnati (G-4515)

AIR CONDITIONING & VENTILATION EQPT & SPLYS: Wholesales

Gardiner Service Company .... C 440 248-3400
Solon (G-17008)
Lute Supply Inc .... E 740 353-1447
Portsmouth (G-16294)
Thompson Heating Corporation .... D 513 769-7696
Cincinnati (G-4657)
Wolff Bros Supply Inc .... E 419 425-8511
Findlay (G-11101)

AIR CONDITIONING EQPT

Liebert Corporation .... A 614 888-0246
Columbus (G-8059)

AIR CONDITIONING EQPT, WHOLE HOUSE: Wholesalers

Controls Center Inc .... D 513 772-2665
Cincinnati (G-3415)
Habegger Corporation .... D 513 612-4700
Cincinnati (G-3725)
Industrial Controls Distrs LLC .... E 513 733-5200
West Chester (G-19092)
Noland Company .... C 937 396-7980
Moraine (G-14812)
United Atmtc Htng Spply of Clv .... E 216 621-5571
Cleveland (G-6634)

AIR CONDITIONING REPAIR SVCS

Columbs/Worthington Htg AC Inc .... E 614 771-5381
Columbus (G-7325)
Cov-Ro Inc .... E 330 856-3176
Warren (G-18841)
Mid-Ohio Air Conditioning .... E 614 291-4664
Columbus (G-8164)
Osterfeld Champion Service .... E 937 254-8437
Dayton (G-9795)

Smith & Oby Service Co .... E 440 735-5322
Bedford (G-1337)

AIR DUCT CLEANING SVCS

A Bee C Service Inc .... E 440 735-1505
Cleveland (G-4930)
Southtown Heating & Cooling .... E 937 320-9900
Moraine (G-14827)

AIR POLLUTION CONTROL EQPT & SPLYS WHOLESALERS

Verantis Corporation .... E 440 243-0700
Middleburg Heights (G-14390)

AIR POLLUTION MEASURING SVCS

Terminix Intl Co Ltd Partnr .... E 513 539-7846
Middletown (G-14466)

AIR PURIFICATION EQPT

Verantis Corporation .... E 440 243-0700
Middleburg Heights (G-14390)

AIR TRAFFIC CONTROL SVCS

Corporate Wngs - Cleveland LLC .... E 216 261-9000
Cleveland (G-5411)

AIR, WATER & SOLID WASTE PROGRAMS ADMINISTRATION SVCS

City of Cleveland .... E 216 664-3121
Cleveland (G-5251)
City of Columbus .... E 614 645-8297
Columbus (G-7285)
City of Columbus .... D 614 645-3248
Lockbourne (G-12947)
County of Hamilton .... E 513 946-4250
Cincinnati (G-3430)

AIR-CONDITIONING SPLY SVCS

Marketing Comm Resource Inc .... D 440 484-3010
Willoughby (G-19691)

AIRCRAFT & HEAVY EQPT REPAIR SVCS

Airborne Maint Engrg Svcs Inc .... A 937 366-2559
Wilmington (G-19744)
Airborne Maint Engrg Svcs Inc .... D 937 382-5591
Wilmington (G-19745)
Cincinnati Hydraulic Svc Inc .... E 513 874-0540
West Chester (G-19039)
Constant Aviation LLC .... E 216 261-7119
Cleveland (G-5395)
Equipment Maintenance Inc .... E 513 353-3518
Cleves (G-6799)
Grimes Aerospace Company .... B 937 484-2001
Urbana (G-18590)
McNational Inc .... E 740 377-4391
South Point (G-17093)
Mt Texas LLC .... E 513 853-4400
Cincinnati (G-4129)
Ohio Machinery Co .... C 440 526-6200
Broadview Heights (G-1886)
Pas Technologies Inc .... D 937 840-1000
Hillsboro (G-11991)
Terex Utilities Inc .... C 937 293-6526
Springfield (G-17287)

AIRCRAFT CLEANING & JANITORIAL SVCS

Legndary Cleaners LLC .... E 216 374-1205
Cleveland (G-5935)
McKinley Air Transport Inc .... E 330 497-6956
Canton (G-2453)
Plane Detail LLC .... E 614 734-1201
Mount Gilead (G-14862)

AIRCRAFT DEALERS

Options Flight Support Inc .... C 216 261-3500
Cleveland (G-6209)

AIRCRAFT ELECTRICAL EQPT REPAIR SVCS

General Electric Company .... B 513 977-1500
Cincinnati (G-3667)

SERVICES SECTION

Honeywell International Inc .... D 440 243-8877
Strongsville (G-17472)

AIRCRAFT ENGINES & PARTS

General Electric Company .... A 513 552-2000
Cincinnati (G-3668)
Hi-Tek Manufacturing Inc .... C 513 459-1094
Mason (G-13717)
Pas Technologies Inc .... D 937 840-1000
Hillsboro (G-11991)

AIRCRAFT EQPT & SPLYS WHOLESALERS

Cleveland Wheels .... D 440 937-6211
Avon (G-890)
GE Engine Services LLC .... B 513 243-9404
Hamilton (G-11731)
NJ Executive Services Inc .... E 614 239-2996
Columbus (G-8282)
Sportsmans Market Inc .... C 513 735-9100
Batavia (G-1025)
Transdigm Group Incorporated .... C 216 706-2960
Cleveland (G-6611)

AIRCRAFT FLIGHT INSTRUMENTS

L3 Aviation Products Inc .... D 614 825-2001
Columbus (G-8025)

AIRCRAFT FUELING SVCS

McKinley Air Transport Inc .... E 330 497-6956
Canton (G-2453)
Winner Aviation Corporation .... D 330 856-5000
Vienna (G-18742)

AIRCRAFT HANGAR OPERATION SVCS

General Electric Company .... A 513 552-2000
Cincinnati (G-3668)

AIRCRAFT MAINTENANCE & REPAIR SVCS

Aitheras Aviation Group LLC .... E 216 298-9060
Cleveland (G-4979)
ATI Aviation Services LLC .... E 216 268-4888
Cleveland (G-5077)
Constant Aviation LLC .... E 800 440-9004
Cleveland (G-5396)
Duncan Aviation Inc .... D 513 873-7523
Cincinnati (G-3513)
Flight Options Inc .... B 216 261-3880
Richmond Heights (G-16537)
Flight Options Intl Inc .... E 216 261-3500
Richmond Heights (G-16538)
Netjets Large Aircraft Inc .... D 614 239-4853
Columbus (G-8263)

AIRCRAFT PARTS & EQPT, NEC

General Electric Company .... B 513 977-1500
Cincinnati (G-3667)
Schneller LLC .... D 330 673-1299
Kent (G-12395)
Transdigm Group Incorporated .... C 216 706-2960
Cleveland (G-6611)
Unison Industries LLC .... B 937 426-0621
Dayton (G-9285)
Unison Industries LLC .... B 937 427-0550
Beavercreek (G-1215)
Wayne Trail Technologies Inc .... D 937 295-2120
Fort Loramie (G-11112)

AIRCRAFT PARTS WHOLESALERS

Abx Air Inc .... B 937 382-5591
Wilmington (G-19741)
Airborne Maint Engrg Svcs Inc .... A 937 366-2559
Wilmington (G-19744)
Airborne Maint Engrg Svcs Inc .... D 937 382-5591
Wilmington (G-19745)
Grimes Aerospace Company .... B 937 484-2001
Urbana (G-18590)
Jilco Industries Inc .... E 330 698-0280
Kidron (G-12441)
Netjets Inc .... E 614 239-5500
Columbus (G-8261)
Netjets Sales Inc .... C 614 239-5500
Columbus (G-8264)

SERVICES SECTION

AIRCRAFT SERVICING & REPAIRING

Abx Air Inc .... B 937 382-5591
  Wilmington (G-19741)
Cessna Aircraft Company .... D 419 866-6761
  Swanton (G-17562)
Huntleigh USA Corporation .... B 216 265-3707
  Cleveland (G-5793)
Lane Aviation Corporation .... C 614 237-3747
  Columbus (G-8037)
National Flight Services Inc .... D 419 865-2311
  Swanton (G-17568)
Unison Industries LLC .... B 937 426-0621
  Dayton (G-9285)
Unison Industries LLC .... B 937 427-0550
  Beavercreek (G-1215)

AIRLINE TRAINING

Macair Aviation LLC .... E 937 347-1302
  Xenia (G-20069)

AIRPORT

Akron-Canton Regional Airport .... E 330 499-4059
  North Canton (G-15322)
City of Dayton .... C 937 454-8200
  Vandalia (G-18672)
City of Dayton .... E 937 454-8231
  Vandalia (G-18673)
Columbus Regional Airport Auth .... E 614 239-4000
  Columbus (G-7381)
Columbus Regional Airport Auth .... B 614 239-4015
  Columbus (G-7382)
Park-N-Go Inc .... E 937 890-7275
  Vandalia (G-18692)
Ultimate Jetcharters LLC .... D 330 497-3344
  North Canton (G-15377)

AIRPORT TERMINAL SVCS

American Airlines Inc .... E 216 706-0702
  Cleveland (G-5003)
American Airlines Inc .... D 937 454-7472
  Vandalia (G-18656)
American Airlines Inc .... E 216 898-1347
  Cleveland (G-5004)
Servisair LLC .... C 216 267-9910
  Cleveland (G-6472)
Stevens Aviation Inc .... D 937 890-0189
  Vandalia (G-18699)
Wright Brothers Aero Inc .... D 937 890-8900
  Vandalia (G-18707)

AIRPORTS & FLYING FIELDS

Macair Aviation LLC .... E 937 347-1302
  Xenia (G-20069)

AIRPORTS, FLYING FIELDS & SVCS

Aviation Manufacturing Co Inc .... D 419 435-7448
  Fostoria (G-11122)
Boeing Company .... A 740 788-4000
  Newark (G-15147)
Executive Jet Management Inc .... B 513 979-6600
  Cincinnati (G-3586)
GE Aviation Systems LLC .... B 513 786-4555
  West Chester (G-19079)

ALARM SYSTEMS WHOLESALERS

Ohio Alarm Inc .... E 216 692-1204
  Independence (G-12241)

ALCOHOL TREATMENT CLINIC, OUTPATIENT

Behavral Cnnctions WD Cnty Inc .... C 419 352-5387
  Bowling Green (G-1760)
Behavral Cnnctions WD Cnty Inc .... E 419 872-2419
  Perrysburg (G-15976)
Behavral Cnnctions WD Cnty Inc .... E 419 352-5387
  Bowling Green (G-1761)
Century Health Inc .... D 419 425-5050
  Findlay (G-11012)
County of Lorain .... E 440 989-4900
  Elyria (G-10614)
Firelands Regional Health Sys .... E 419 663-3737
  Norwalk (G-15573)
Hitchcock Center For Women Inc ...... E 216 421-0662
  Cleveland (G-5761)
Maryhaven Inc .... E 419 946-6734
  Mount Gilead (G-14855)
Mental Health & Recovery Ctr .... E 937 383-3031
  Wilmington (G-19773)
Orca House .... E 216 231-3772
  Cleveland (G-6212)
Recovery Prv RES of Del & Mor .... E 740 369-6811
  Delaware (G-10122)

ALCOHOLISM COUNSELING, NONTREATMENT

Addiction Services Council .... E 513 281-7880
  Cincinnati (G-2972)
Amethyst Inc .... D 614 242-1284
  Columbus (G-7014)
Licking Cnty Alcoholism Prvntn .... E 740 281-3639
  Newark (G-15186)
Northern Ohio Recovery Assn .... E 216 391-6672
  Cleveland (G-6161)
Oriana House Inc .... A 330 535-8116
  Akron (G-373)
Oriana House Inc .... C 330 643-2171
  Akron (G-375)
Scioto County Counseling Ctr .... D 740 354-6685
  Portsmouth (G-16307)
Sojourner Recovery Services .... E 513 868-7654
  Hamilton (G-11773)
Turning Pt Counseling Svcs Inc .... D 330 744-2991
  Youngstown (G-20394)

ALKALIES & CHLORINE

National Colloid Company .... E 740 282-1171
  Steubenville (G-17332)
National Lime and Stone Co .... C 419 396-7671
  Carey (G-2596)

ALLOYS: Additive, Exc Copper Or Made In Blast Furnaces

Morris Technologies Inc .... E 513 733-1611
  Cincinnati (G-4119)

ALUMINUM

Benjamin Steel Company Inc .... E 937 233-1212
  Springfield (G-17150)

ALUMINUM: Coil & Sheet

Monarch Steel Company Inc .... E 216 587-8000
  Cleveland (G-6074)

ALUMINUM: Slabs, Primary

Imperial Alum - Minerva LLC .... D 330 868-7765
  Minerva (G-14646)

AMBULANCE SVCS

1st Advanced Ems LLC .... D 614 348-9991
  Gahanna (G-11232)
American Med .... C 216 251-5319
  Cleveland (G-5013)
American Med .... B 330 762-8999
  Akron (G-71)
Americas Urgent Care .... E 614 929-2721
  Upper Arlington (G-18546)
Anna Rescue Squad .... E 937 394-7377
  Anna (G-617)
Athens County Emrgncy Med Svcs ... D 740 797-9560
  The Plains (G-17664)
Bellevue Four Cnty Fms N Centl .... C 419 403-0322
  Milan (G-14492)
Bkp Ambulance District .... E 419 674-4574
  Kenton (G-12408)
Brookeside Ambulance Services .... E 419 476-7442
  Toledo (G-17784)
Buckeye Ambulance LLC .... D 937 435-1584
  Kettering (G-12428)
C C & S Ambulance Service Inc .... E 330 868-4114
  Minerva (G-14642)
Carlson Ambince Trnspt Svc Inc .... E 330 225-2400
  Brunswick (G-1971)
City of Cleveland .... B 216 664-2555
  Cleveland (G-5249)
City of Cleveland .... B 216 664-2555
  Cleveland (G-5250)
City of Westlake .... E 440 871-3441
  Westlake (G-5278)
Clemente-Mc Kay Ambulance Inc ...... E 330 755-1401
  Struthers (G-17528)
Community Ambulance Service .... D 740 454-6800
  Zanesville (G-20467)
Community Care Ambulance Netwrk .. D 440 992-1401
  Ashtabula (G-735)
Coshocton Cnty Emrgncy Med Svc ... E 740 622-4294
  Coshocton (G-9094)
County of Hardin .... E 419 634-7729
  Ada (G-5)
County of Lorain .... E 440 647-5803
  Wellington (G-18989)
County of Meigs .... E 740 992-6617
  Pomeroy (G-16231)
County of Seneca .... E 419 937-2340
  Bascom (G-993)
Courtesy Ambulance Inc .... E 740 522-8588
  Newark (G-15163)
Critical Care Transport Inc .... D 614 775-0564
  Columbus (G-7463)
Eaton Rescue Squad .... E 937 456-5361
  Eaton (G-10560)
Elite Ambulance Service LLC .... E 888 222-1356
  Loveland (G-13124)
Emergency Medical Transport .... D 330 484-4000
  North Canton (G-15334)
Firelands Ambulance Service .... E 419 929-1487
  New London (G-15067)
Franklin Township Fire and Ems .... E 513 876-2996
  Felicity (G-10985)
Georgetown Life Squad .... E 937 378-3082
  Georgetown (G-11394)
Gold Cross Ambulance Svcs Inc .... C 330 744-4161
  Youngstown (G-20202)
Greenville Township Rescue .... E 937 548-9339
  Greenville (G-11507)
Guernsey Health Enterprises .... A 740 439-3561
  Cambridge (G-2118)
Hanco Ambulance Inc .... E 419 423-2912
  Findlay (G-11040)
Harter Ventures Inc .... D 419 224-4075
  Lima (G-12790)
Hillcrest Ambulance Svc Inc .... C 216 797-4000
  Euclid (G-10760)
Hustead Emergency Medical Svc ...... E 937 324-3031
  Springfield (G-17209)
J & C Ambulance Services Inc .... C 330 899-0022
  North Canton (G-15346)
Kare Medical Trnspt Svcs LLP .... E 937 578-0263
  Marysville (G-13630)
Lacp St Ritas Medical Ctr LLC .... D 419 324-4075
  Lima (G-12814)
Lane Life Corp .... E 330 799-1002
  Youngstown (G-20253)
Lifecare Ambulance Inc .... E 440 323-2527
  Elyria (G-10641)
Lifecare Ambulance Inc .... E 440 323-6111
  Elyria (G-10642)
Lifecare Medical Services .... E 614 258-2545
  Columbus (G-8064)
Lifestar Ambulance Inc .... C 419 245-6210
  Toledo (G-18005)
Lifeteam Ems Inc .... E 330 386-9284
  East Liverpool (G-10523)
Lorain Life Care Ambulance Svc .... D 440 244-6467
  Lorain (G-13055)
Mansfield Ambulance Inc .... E 419 525-3311
  Mansfield (G-13329)
Martens Donald & Sons .... D 216 265-4211
  Cleveland (G-5988)
Med Ride Ems .... D 614 747-9744
  Columbus (G-8142)
Med Star Emgncy Mdcl Srv .... E 330 394-6611
  Warren (G-18879)
Med-Trans Inc .... D 937 325-4926
  Springfield (G-17231)
Med-Trans Inc .... E 937 293-9771
  Moraine (G-14802)
Medcorp Inc .... C 419 425-9700
  Findlay (G-11065)
Medcorp Inc .... D 419 727-7000
  Toledo (G-18047)
Medic Response Service Inc .... E 419 522-1998
  Mansfield (G-13342)
Mercy Health .... E 440 775-1211
  Oberlin (G-15651)
Metrohealth System .... E 216 778-3867
  Cleveland (G-6042)
Metrohealth System .... C 216 957-4000
  Cleveland (G-6039)

Employee Codes: A=Over 500 employees, B=251-500
C=101-250, D=51-100, E=25-50

AMBULANCE SVCS

Company	Type	Phone
Mid County Ems	E	419 898-9366
Oak Harbor (G-15612)		
Morgan County Public Transit	E	740 962-1322
McConnelsville (G-14029)		
Morrow Cnty Fire Fighter	D	419 946-7976
Mount Gilead (G-14856)		
Mt Orab Fire Department Inc	E	937 444-3945
Mount Orab (G-14870)		
Non Emergency Ambulance Svc	E	330 296-4541
Ravenna (G-16394)		
North Star Critical Care LLC	E	330 386-9110
East Liverpool (G-10528)		
Northwest Fire Ambulance	E	937 437-8354
New Paris (G-15079)		
Norwalk Area Health Services	C	419 499-2515
Milan (G-14495)		
Norwalk Area Health Services	C	419 668-8101
Norwalk (G-15583)		
Ohio Medical Trnsp Inc	C	614 791-4400
Columbus (G-8360)		
Patriot Emergency Med Svcs Inc	E	740 532-2222
Ironton (G-12301)		
Physicians Ambulance Svc Inc	E	216 332-1667
Cleveland (G-6279)		
Pickaway Plains Ambulance Svc	C	740 474-4180
Circleville (G-4900)		
Portage Path Behavorial Health	D	330 762-6110
Akron (G-398)		
Portsmouth Ambulance	C	740 289-2932
Portsmouth (G-16298)		
Portsmuth Emrgncy Amblance Svc	B	740 354-3122
Portsmouth (G-16302)		
Pymatuning Ambulance Service	E	440 293-7991
Andover (G-613)		
Quad Ambulance District	E	330 866-9847
Waynesburg (G-18981)		
Rittman City of Inc	E	330 925-2065
Rittman (G-16555)		
Rural/Metro Corporation	C	216 749-2211
Youngstown (G-20362)		
Rural/Metro Corporation	C	330 744-4161
Youngstown (G-20363)		
Rural/Metro Corporation	C	440 543-3313
Chagrin Falls (G-2732)		
Sardinia Life Squad	E	937 446-2178
Sardinia (G-16814)		
Smith Ambulance Service Inc	E	330 825-0205
Dover (G-10212)		
Smith Ambulance Service Inc	E	330 602-0050
Dover (G-10213)		
Spirit Medical Transport LLC	D	937 548-2800
Greenville (G-11520)		
Sterling Joint Ambulance Dst	E	740 869-3006
Mount Sterling (G-14875)		
Stofcheck Ambulance Inc	C	740 383-2787
Marion (G-13581)		
Stofcheck Ambulance Svc Inc	E	740 499-2200
La Rue (G-12459)		
Toronto Emergency Medical Svc	E	740 537-3891
Toronto (G-18339)		
Tri Village Rescue Service	E	937 996-3155
New Madison (G-15073)		
Tri-State Amblnce Pramedic Svc	E	304 233-2331
North Canton (G-15375)		
Tricounty Ambulance Service	D	440 951-4600
Mentor (G-14249)		
United Amblnce Svc of Cmbridge	E	740 439-7787
Cambridge (G-2132)		
United Ambulance Service	E	740 732-5653
Caldwell (G-2091)		
Village of Antwerp	E	419 258-6631
Antwerp (G-622)		

AMBULANCE SVCS: Air

Company	Type	Phone
Ohio Medical Trnsp Inc	D	740 962-2055
McConnelsville (G-14030)		
Ohio Medical Trnsp Inc	C	614 791-4400
Columbus (G-8360)		

AMBULATORY SURGICAL CENTERS

Company	Type	Phone
Childrens Surgery Center Inc	D	614 722-2920
Columbus (G-7264)		
Columbus Surgical Center LLP	E	614 932-9503
Dublin (G-10301)		
Dublin Surgical Center LLC	E	614 932-9548
Dublin (G-10332)		
Endoscopy Center	E	419 843-7993
Sylvania (G-17586)		
Ohio Surgery Center Ltd	D	614 451-0500
Columbus (G-8449)		
Ohio Valley Medical Center LLC	D	937 521-3900
Springfield (G-17257)		
Ohio Vally Ambulatory Surgery	E	740 423-4684
Belpre (G-1443)		
Ohiocare Ambulatory Surgery	E	419 897-5501
Maumee (G-13952)		
Riverview Surgery Center	E	740 681-2700
Lancaster (G-12571)		
Southwest Ohio Amblatry Srgery	E	513 425-0930
Middletown (G-14458)		
Surgery Center Howland Ltd	E	330 609-7874
Warren (G-18906)		
The Healthcare Connection Inc	E	513 588-3623
Cincinnati (G-4642)		
United Srgcal Prtners Intl Inc	E	330 702-1489
Canfield (G-2214)		
Valley Regional Surgery Center	E	877 858-5029
Piqua (G-16174)		
West Central Ohio Surgery & En	E	419 226-8700
Lima (G-12917)		
Zanesville Surgery Center LLC	D	740 453-5713
Zanesville (G-20558)		

AMUSEMENT & REC SVCS: Attractions, Concessions & Rides

Company	Type	Phone
Coney Island Inc	E	513 232-8230
Cincinnati (G-3410)		
Dayton History	C	937 293-2841
Dayton (G-9478)		
M & R Amusement Services Inc	E	937 525-0404
Springfield (G-17227)		

AMUSEMENT & REC SVCS: Baseball Club, Exc Pro & Semi-Pro

Company	Type	Phone
Cascia LLC	E	440 975-8085
Willoughby (G-19648)		

AMUSEMENT & REC SVCS: Flying Field, Maintained By Av Clubs

Company	Type	Phone
Macair Aviation LLC	E	937 347-1302
Xenia (G-20069)		

AMUSEMENT & RECREATION SVCS, NEC

Company	Type	Phone
Kettering Recreation Center	E	937 296-2587
Dayton (G-9657)		
Leaders Family Farms	E	419 599-1570
Napoleon (G-14944)		

AMUSEMENT & RECREATION SVCS: Agricultural Fair

Company	Type	Phone
Cuyahoga County AG Soc	E	440 243-0090
Berea (G-1454)		
Wyandot County AG Soc	E	419 294-4320
Upper Sandusky (G-18569)		

AMUSEMENT & RECREATION SVCS: Amusement Arcades

Company	Type	Phone
Entertrainment Inc	E	513 898-8000
West Chester (G-19069)		

AMUSEMENT & RECREATION SVCS: Amusement Mach Rental, Coin-Op

Company	Type	Phone
S & B Enterprises LLC	E	740 753-2646
Nelsonville (G-14967)		

AMUSEMENT & RECREATION SVCS: Amusement Ride

Company	Type	Phone
Bates Bros Amusement Co	D	740 266-2950
Wintersville (G-19808)		
Kissel Bros Shows Inc	E	513 741-1080
Cincinnati (G-3930)		
Know Theatre of Cincinnati	E	513 300-5669
Cincinnati (G-3936)		

AMUSEMENT & RECREATION SVCS: Arcades

Company	Type	Phone
16 Bit Bar	E	513 381-1616
Cincinnati (G-2939)		

AMUSEMENT & RECREATION SVCS: Boating Club, Membership

Company	Type	Phone
Columbus Sail and Pwr Squadron	C	614 384-0245
Lewis Center (G-12677)		
Island Service Company	C	419 285-3695
Put In Bay (G-16368)		
Sandusky Yacht Club Inc	D	419 625-6567
Sandusky (G-16794)		
Vermilion Boat Club Inc	E	440 967-6634
Vermilion (G-18719)		

AMUSEMENT & RECREATION SVCS: Bowling Instruction

Company	Type	Phone
Beaver-Vu Bowl	E	937 426-6771
Beavercreek (G-1150)		

AMUSEMENT & RECREATION SVCS: Carnival Operation

Company	Type	Phone
Amusements of America Inc	C	614 297-8863
Columbus (G-7016)		
Deshler Amusements Inc	E	330 532-2922
Wellsville (G-19006)		

AMUSEMENT & RECREATION SVCS: Concession Operator

Company	Type	Phone
Flash Seats LLC	E	216 420-2000
Cleveland (G-5604)		
National Concession Company	E	216 881-9911
Cleveland (G-6104)		

AMUSEMENT & RECREATION SVCS: Exhibition Operation

Company	Type	Phone
Asm International	D	440 338-5151
Novelty (G-15601)		
Roto Group LLC	D	614 760-8690
Dublin (G-10444)		

AMUSEMENT & RECREATION SVCS: Exposition Operation

Company	Type	Phone
Ohio Exposition Center	D	614 644-4000
Columbus (G-8342)		
Park Corporation	B	216 267-4870
Cleveland (G-6234)		
Relx Inc	E	937 865-6800
Miamisburg (G-14340)		

AMUSEMENT & RECREATION SVCS: Festival Operation

Company	Type	Phone
Circle S Farms Inc	E	614 878-9462
Grove City (G-11546)		

AMUSEMENT & RECREATION SVCS: Fishing Lakes & Piers, Op

Company	Type	Phone
Snows Lakeside Tavern	E	513 954-5626
Cincinnati (G-4546)		

AMUSEMENT & RECREATION SVCS: Gambling & Lottery Svcs

Company	Type	Phone
Miami Valley Gaming & Racg LLC	D	513 934-7070
Lebanon (G-12628)		

AMUSEMENT & RECREATION SVCS: Gambling, Coin Machines

Company	Type	Phone
Jack Thistledown Racino LLC	E	216 662-8600
Cleveland (G-5846)		

AMUSEMENT & RECREATION SVCS: Golf Club, Membership

Company	Type	Phone
797 Elks Golf Club Inc	E	937 382-2666
Wilmington (G-19740)		
Akron Management Corp	B	330 644-8441
Akron (G-48)		
American Golf Corporation	E	740 965-5122
Galena (G-11278)		
American Italian Golf	D	614 889-2551
Dublin (G-10249)		
Ashland Golf Club	E	419 289-2917
Ashland (G-657)		

SERVICES SECTION

AMUSEMENT & RECREATION SVCS: Recreation SVCS

Avalon Golf and Cntry CLB Inc .... D 330 856-8898
 Warren *(G-18822)*
Barrington Golf Club Inc .... D 330 995-0600
 Aurora *(G-829)*
Barrington Golf Club Inc .... D 330 995-0821
 Aurora *(G-830)*
Big Red LP .... D 740 548-7799
 Galena *(G-11280)*
Brass Ring Golf Club Ltd .... E 740 385-8966
 Logan *(G-12969)*
Breezy Point Ltd Partnership .... E 330 995-0600
 Aurora *(G-831)*
Breezy Point Ltd Partnership .... C 440 247-3363
 Solon *(G-16984)*
Canterbury Golf Club Inc .... D 216 561-1914
 Cleveland *(G-5177)*
Caravon Golf Company Ltd .... E 440 937-6018
 Avon *(G-883)*
City of Parma .... E 440 885-8876
 Cleveland *(G-5272)*
Congress Lake Club Company .... E 330 877-9318
 Hartville *(G-11816)*
Cumberland Trail Golf CLB Crse .... E 740 964-9336
 Etna *(G-10733)*
Dornoch Golf Club Inc .... E 740 369-0863
 Delaware *(G-10091)*
Golf Club Co .... E 614 855-7326
 New Albany *(G-14987)*
Heritage Club .... D 513 459-7711
 Mason *(G-13715)*
Jefferson Golf & Country Club .... E 614 759-7500
 Blacklick *(G-1508)*
Lakes Country Club Inc .... C 614 882-4167
 Galena *(G-11285)*
Legend Lake Golf Club Inc .... E 440 285-3110
 Chardon *(G-2756)*
Leisure Sports Inc .... E 419 829-2891
 Sylvania *(G-17599)*
Lost Creek Country Club Inc .... E 419 229-2026
 Lima *(G-12831)*
Madison Route 20 LLC .... E 440 358-7888
 Painesville *(G-15864)*
Michael Brothers Inc .... E 419 332-5716
 Fremont *(G-11213)*
Mill Creek Golf Course Corp .... E 740 666-7711
 Ostrander *(G-15793)*
Mohawk Golf Club .... E 419 447-5876
 Tiffin *(G-17687)*
Muirfield Village Golf Club .... E 614 889-6700
 Dublin *(G-10402)*
New Albany Links Dev Co Ltd .... D 614 939-5914
 New Albany *(G-14999)*
OBannon Creek Golf Club .... E 513 683-5657
 Loveland *(G-13151)*
Pepper Pike Golf Company Inc .... D 216 831-9400
 Cleveland *(G-6263)*
Pike Run Golf Club Inc .... E 419 538-7000
 Ottawa *(G-15803)*
Quail Hollow Management Inc .... D 440 639-4000
 Painesville *(G-15874)*
Radius Hospitality MGT LLC .... D 330 735-2211
 Sherrodsville *(G-16906)*
Sand Ridge Golf Club .... D 440 285-8088
 Chardon *(G-2767)*
Sawmill Creek Golf Racquet CLB .... D 419 433-4945
 Huron *(G-12171)*
Sawmill Greek Golf Racquet CLB .... D 419 433-3789
 Huron *(G-12173)*
Spring Valley Golf & Athc CLB .... D 440 365-1411
 Westlake *(G-19548)*
Stone Oak Country Club .... E 419 867-0969
 Holland *(G-12058)*
Tartan Fields Golf Club Ltd .... D 614 792-0900
 Dublin *(G-10473)*
Valleaire Golf Club Inc .... E 440 237-9191
 Hinckley *(G-12000)*
Valleywood Golf Club Inc .... E 419 826-3991
 Swanton *(G-17574)*
Walden Club .... D 330 995-7162
 Aurora *(G-861)*

AMUSEMENT & RECREATION SVCS: Golf Professionals

Meadowbrook Country Club .... D 937 836-5186
 Clayton *(G-4913)*

AMUSEMENT & RECREATION SVCS: Golf Svcs & Professionals

Avalon Holdings Corporation .... D 330 856-8800
 Warren *(G-18823)*
Creekside Golf Dome .... E 330 545-5000
 Girard *(G-11412)*
Delaware Golf Club Inc .... E 740 362-2582
 Delaware *(G-10089)*
Magic Castle Inc .... E 937 434-4911
 Dayton *(G-9694)*
Man Golf Ohio LLC .... E 440 635-5178
 Huntsburg *(G-12158)*
Spring Hills Golf Club .... E 740 543-3270
 East Springfield *(G-10543)*

AMUSEMENT & RECREATION SVCS: Gun & Hunting Clubs

Field & Stream Bowhunters .... D 419 423-9861
 Findlay *(G-11024)*

AMUSEMENT & RECREATION SVCS: Gun Club, Membership

Sportsman Gun & Reel Club Inc .... C 440 233-8287
 Lorain *(G-13077)*

AMUSEMENT & RECREATION SVCS: Hockey Club, Exc Pro/Semi-Pro

Gardens Hockey Inc .... E 513 351-3999
 Cincinnati *(G-3663)*

AMUSEMENT & RECREATION SVCS: Hunting Club, Membership

Columbia Recreation Assn .... E 740 849-2466
 East Fultonham *(G-10506)*
Elm Valley Fishing Club .... D 937 845-0584
 New Carlisle *(G-15022)*
Tri County Nite Hunter Assn Ci .... E 740 385-7341
 Logan *(G-12990)*

AMUSEMENT & RECREATION SVCS: Ice Skating Rink

Alice Noble Ice Arena .... E 330 345-8686
 Wooster *(G-19827)*
Central Ohio Ice Rinks Inc .... E 614 475-7575
 Dublin *(G-10284)*
Chiller LLC .... D 614 764-1000
 Dublin *(G-10292)*
Chiller LLC .... E 740 549-0009
 Lewis Center *(G-12675)*
Chiller LLC .... E 614 475-7575
 Columbus *(G-7265)*
City of Sylvania .... E 419 885-1167
 Sylvania *(G-17579)*
Ice Land USA Lakewood .... E 216 529-1200
 Lakewood *(G-12482)*
Ice Land USA Ltd .... D 440 268-2800
 Strongsville *(G-17475)*
Ice Zone Ltd .... E 330 965-1423
 Youngstown *(G-20228)*
Lakewood City School District .... E 216 529-4400
 Lakewood *(G-12487)*

AMUSEMENT & RECREATION SVCS: Indoor Court Clubs

Soccer Centre Owners Ltd .... E 419 893-5425
 Maumee *(G-13978)*
Western Hills Sportsplex Inc .... D 513 451-4900
 Cincinnati *(G-4843)*

AMUSEMENT & RECREATION SVCS: Instruction Schools, Camps

Integrity Gymnstics Chrleading .... E 614 733-0818
 Plain City *(G-16194)*

AMUSEMENT & RECREATION SVCS: Kiddie Park

Little Squirt Sports Park .... E 419 227-6200
 Lima *(G-12830)*

AMUSEMENT & RECREATION SVCS: Lottery Tickets, Sales

Fat Jacks Pizza II Inc .... E 419 227-1813
 Lima *(G-12779)*

AMUSEMENT & RECREATION SVCS: Outdoor Field Clubs

Frontier Bassmasters Inc .... E 740 423-9293
 Belpre *(G-1438)*
West Denison Baseball League .... E 216 251-5790
 Cleveland *(G-6735)*

AMUSEMENT & RECREATION SVCS: Picnic Ground Operation

Wiegands Lake Park Inc .... E 440 338-5795
 Novelty *(G-15604)*

AMUSEMENT & RECREATION SVCS: Pool Parlor

S & S Management Inc .... E 567 356-4151
 Wapakoneta *(G-18807)*

AMUSEMENT & RECREATION SVCS: Racquetball Club, Membership

Beechmont Racquet Club Inc .... E 513 528-5700
 Cincinnati *(G-3091)*
Western Reserve Racquet Club .... E 330 653-3103
 Streetsboro *(G-17436)*

AMUSEMENT & RECREATION SVCS: Recreation Center

Baldwin Wallace University .... E 440 826-2285
 Berea *(G-1446)*
CCJ Enterprises Inc .... E 330 345-4386
 Wooster *(G-19837)*
City of Brook Park .... E 216 433-1545
 Cleveland *(G-5248)*
City of Miamisburg .... E 937 866-4532
 Miamisburg *(G-14283)*
City of North Olmsted .... D 440 734-8200
 North Olmsted *(G-15416)*
City of Rocky River .... E 440 356-5656
 Cleveland *(G-5274)*
City of Seven Hills .... C 216 524-6262
 Seven Hills *(G-16828)*
Community Action Columbiana CT .... E 330 385-7251
 East Liverpool *(G-10518)*
Goofy Golf Inc .... E 419 625-1308
 Sandusky *(G-16764)*
Makoy Center Inc .... E 614 777-1211
 Hilliard *(G-11924)*
Max Dixons Expressway Park .... E 513 831-2273
 Milford *(G-14537)*
Oberlin College .... C 440 775-8519
 Oberlin *(G-15654)*
Society of The Transfiguration .... E 513 771-7462
 Cincinnati *(G-4548)*
Washington Twnship Mntgomery .... C 937 433-0130
 Dayton *(G-9986)*
YMCA .... D 937 653-9622
 Urbana *(G-18603)*
Young Mens Christian Assoc .... D 330 264-3131
 Wooster *(G-19936)*
Young Mens Christian Assoc .... D 614 276-8224
 Columbus *(G-9018)*
Young Mens Christian Assoc .... D 740 477-1661
 Circleville *(G-4909)*
Young Mens Christian Assoc .... C 614 885-4252
 Columbus *(G-9017)*
Young Mens Christian Assoc .... E 937 228-9622
 Dayton *(G-10012)*
YWCA of Hamilton .... E 513 856-9800
 Hamilton *(G-11785)*

AMUSEMENT & RECREATION SVCS: Recreation SVCS

Army & Air Force Exchange Svc .... A 937 257-7736
 Dayton *(G-9256)*
City of Independence .... E 216 524-3262
 Cleveland *(G-5263)*
Cleveland Metroparks .... D 440 331-5530
 Cleveland *(G-5327)*

AMUSEMENT & RECREATION SVCS: Recreation SVCS

Cleveland Metroparks............................B........ 216 635-3200
  Cleveland *(G-5328)*
Cleveland Metroparks............................B........ 216 739-6040
  Strongsville *(G-17451)*
Cleveland Metroparks............................E........ 440 572-9990
  Strongsville *(G-17452)*
Columbus Frkln Cnty Pk..........................E........ 614 891-0700
  Westerville *(G-19387)*
County of Hancock..................................E........ 419 425-7275
  Findlay *(G-11019)*
Goodrich Gnnett Nghborhood Ctr..........E........ 216 432-1717
  Cleveland *(G-5678)*
Lake Metroparks......................................D........ 440 256-2122
  Kirtland *(G-12457)*
Lake Metroparks......................................E........ 440 256-1404
  Willoughby *(G-19682)*
Stark County Park District......................D........ 330 477-3552
  Canton *(G-2545)*
Strike Zone Inc..D........ 440 235-4420
  Olmsted Twp *(G-15681)*
Washington Township Park Dst..............E........ 937 433-5155
  Dayton *(G-9985)*

AMUSEMENT & RECREATION SVCS: Soccer Club, Exc Pro/Semi-Pro

Soccer Centre Inc....................................E........ 419 893-5419
  Maumee *(G-13977)*

AMUSEMENT & RECREATION SVCS: Swimming Club, Membership

Dunsiane Swim Club................................E........ 937 433-7946
  Dayton *(G-9508)*
Lancaster Country Club..........................D........ 740 654-3535
  Lancaster *(G-12549)*
Northwest Swim Club Inc........................E........ 614 442-8716
  Columbus *(G-8298)*
Oak Hills Swim & Racquet......................E........ 513 922-1827
  Cincinnati *(G-4195)*
Orchard Hill Swim Club..........................D........ 513 385-0211
  Cincinnati *(G-4232)*
Reynoldsburg Swim Club Inc..................E........ 614 866-3211
  Reynoldsburg *(G-16476)*
Swim Incorporated..................................E........ 614 885-1619
  Worthington *(G-20002)*
Turpin Hills Swim Racquet CLB..............E........ 513 231-3242
  Cincinnati *(G-4707)*
US Swimming Lake Erie Swimming........E........ 330 423-0485
  Bay Village *(G-1042)*
Young Mens Christian Assoc..................E........ 614 878-7269
  Columbus *(G-9020)*

AMUSEMENT & RECREATION SVCS: Swimming Pool, Non-Membership

Alliance Hospitality Inc..........................E........ 440 951-7333
  Mentor *(G-14141)*
Centennial Terrace & Quarry..................E........ 419 885-7106
  Sylvania *(G-17578)*
City of Gallipolis....................................E........ 740 441-6003
  Gallipolis *(G-11310)*
City of South Euclid...............................E........ 216 291-3902
  Cleveland *(G-5276)*
City of Willowick....................................D........ 440 944-1575
  Willowick *(G-19738)*
Huntington Hlls Recreation CLB............E........ 614 837-0293
  Pickerington *(G-16097)*
Marietta Aquatic Center........................E........ 740 373-2445
  Marietta *(G-13464)*

AMUSEMENT & RECREATION SVCS: Tennis & Professionals

Heaven Bound Ascensions.....................E........ 330 633-3288
  Tallmadge *(G-17640)*

AMUSEMENT & RECREATION SVCS: Tennis Club, Membership

Chillicothe Racquet Club........................E........ 740 773-4928
  Chillicothe *(G-2824)*
Cleveland Racquet Club Inc...................D........ 216 831-2155
  Cleveland *(G-5341)*
Kettering Tennis Center.........................E........ 937 434-6602
  Dayton *(G-9658)*
Scarbrough E Tennis Fitnes Ctr.............E........ 614 751-2597
  Columbus *(G-8693)*
Shadow Valley Tennis Club....................E........ 419 865-1141
  Maumee *(G-13976)*

Tennis Unlimited Inc..............................E........ 330 928-8763
  Akron *(G-474)*
Western Hills Sportsplex Inc.................D........ 513 451-4900
  Cincinnati *(G-4843)*
Wickertree Tnnis Ftnes CLB LLC............E........ 614 882-5724
  Columbus *(G-8991)*

AMUSEMENT & RECREATION SVCS: Theme Park

Cedar Fair LP..A........ 419 626-0830
  Sandusky *(G-16734)*
Cedar Point Park LLC..............................D........ 419 627-2500
  Sandusky *(G-16735)*
Columbus Frkln Cnty Pk..........................E........ 614 846-9962
  Lewis Center *(G-12676)*
Fun n Stuff Amusements Inc..................D........ 330 467-0821
  Macedonia *(G-13197)*
Funtime Parks Inc..................................C........ 330 562-7131
  Aurora *(G-839)*
Kings Island Park LLC.............................C........ 513 754-5901
  Kings Mills *(G-12449)*
Linwood Park Company..........................E........ 440 963-0481
  Vermilion *(G-18713)*
Lodge Stone Wood..................................E........ 513 769-4325
  Blue Ash *(G-1630)*
Seaworld Entertainment Inc..................E........ 330 562-8101
  Aurora *(G-855)*
Strongville Recreation Complex.............C........ 440 580-3230
  Strongsville *(G-17513)*

AMUSEMENT & RECREATION SVCS: Tourist Attraction, Commercial

Dutch Heritage Farms Inc......................E........ 330 893-3232
  Berlin *(G-1478)*

AMUSEMENT & RECREATION SVCS: Trampoline Operation

Sky Zone Indoor Trampoline Pk..............D........ 614 302-6093
  Cincinnati *(G-4539)*
Wonderworker Inc...................................D........ 234 249-3030
  Hudson *(G-12155)*

AMUSEMENT & RECREATION SVCS: Video Game Arcades

Strike Zone Inc..D........ 440 235-4420
  Olmsted Twp *(G-15681)*

AMUSEMENT ARCADES

Bell Music Company................................E........ 330 376-6337
  Akron *(G-96)*
Magic Castle Inc.....................................E........ 937 434-4911
  Dayton *(G-9694)*
Pnk (ohio) LLC..A........ 513 232-8000
  Cincinnati *(G-4312)*
Stonehedge Enterprises Inc..................E........ 330 928-2161
  Akron *(G-451)*

AMUSEMENT PARK DEVICES & RIDES: Carnival Mach & Eqpt, NEC

Majestic Manufacturing Inc...................E........ 330 457-2447
  New Waterford *(G-15138)*

AMUSEMENT PARKS

Columbus Frkln Cnty Pk..........................E........ 614 895-6219
  Westerville *(G-19386)*
Columbus Frkln Cnty Pk..........................E........ 614 891-0700
  Galloway *(G-11342)*
Kings Island Company............................C........ 513 754-5700
  Kings Mills *(G-12448)*
Lmn Development LLC............................D........ 419 433-7200
  Sandusky *(G-16775)*
Lost Nation Sports Park.........................E........ 440 602-4000
  Willoughby *(G-19687)*
Magnum Management Corporation.......A........ 419 627-2334
  Sandusky *(G-16778)*
Muskingum Wtrshed Cnsrvncy Dst.......E........ 740 685-6013
  Senecaville *(G-16824)*
Muskingum Wtrshed Cnsrvncy Dst.......E........ 330 343-6780
  Mineral City *(G-14634)*
Rumpke Amusements Inc......................E........ 513 738-2646
  Cincinnati *(G-4452)*

AMUSEMENT/REC SVCS: Ticket Sales, Sporting Events, Contract

Iticketscom...E........ 614 410-4140
  Columbus *(G-7928)*

ANATOMICAL SPECIMENS & RESEARCH MATERIAL, WHOLESALE

Labelle News Agency Inc.......................E........ 740 282-9731
  Steubenville *(G-17324)*

ANIMAL & REPTILE EXHIBIT

Toledo Zoo...E........ 419 385-5721
  Toledo *(G-18253)*

ANIMAL FEED & SUPPLEMENTS: Livestock & Poultry

Cooper Hatchery Inc..............................C........ 419 594-3325
  Oakwood *(G-15623)*
Provimi North America Inc....................B........ 937 770-2400
  Brookville *(G-1965)*

ANIMAL FEED: Wholesalers

Land OLakes Inc.....................................E........ 330 879-2158
  Massillon *(G-13828)*
Provimi North America Inc....................B........ 937 770-2400
  Brookville *(G-1965)*

ANIMAL FOOD & SUPPLEMENTS: Bird Food, Prepared

Centerra Co-Op..E........ 800 362-9598
  Jefferson *(G-12331)*
Centerra Co-Op..E........ 419 281-2153
  Ashland *(G-672)*

ANIMAL FOOD & SUPPLEMENTS: Dog & Cat

Land OLakes Inc.....................................E........ 330 879-2158
  Massillon *(G-13828)*

ANIMAL FOOD & SUPPLEMENTS: Livestock

Hanby Farms Inc....................................E........ 740 763-3554
  Nashport *(G-14951)*
Land OLakes Inc.....................................E........ 330 879-2158
  Massillon *(G-13828)*

ANIMAL FOOD & SUPPLEMENTS: Poultry

Cooper Farms Inc...................................D........ 419 375-4116
  Fort Recovery *(G-11115)*

ANTENNA REPAIR & INSTALLATION SVCS

Central USA Wireless LLC......................E........ 513 469-1500
  Cincinnati *(G-3218)*
Dss Installations Ltd.............................E........ 513 761-7000
  Cincinnati *(G-3505)*

ANTENNAS: Radar Or Communications

Circle Prime Manufacturing...................E........ 330 923-0019
  Cuyahoga Falls *(G-9172)*
Quasonix Inc...E........ 513 942-1287
  West Chester *(G-19135)*

ANTIPOVERTY BOARD

Akron Summit Cmnty Action Agcy........C........ 330 572-8532
  Akron *(G-56)*
Akron Summit Cmnty Action Agcy........D........ 330 733-2290
  Akron *(G-57)*
Akron Summit Cmnty Action Agcy........B........ 330 376-7730
  Akron *(G-58)*
Ashtabula County Commnty Actn.........C........ 440 997-1721
  Ashtabula *(G-718)*
Ashtabula County Commnty Actn.........D........ 440 593-6441
  Conneaut *(G-9037)*
Ashtabula County Commnty Actn.........E........ 440 576-6911
  Jefferson *(G-12330)*
Ashtabula County Commnty Actn.........E........ 440 993-7716
  Ashtabula *(G-719)*
Council For Economic Opport................D........ 216 541-7878
  Cleveland *(G-5412)*
Council For Economic Opport................E........ 216 696-9077
  Cleveland *(G-5414)*
Council For Economic Opport................E........ 216 692-4010
  Cleveland *(G-5415)*

SERVICES SECTION

ARCHITECTURAL SVCS: Engineering

Warren County Community Svcs ....C...... 513 695-2100
 Lebanon (G-12659)

APARTMENT LOCATING SVCS

Akron Metropolitan Hsing Auth ....C...... 330 920-1652
 Stow (G-17350)
Alpha PHI Alpha Homes Inc ....D...... 330 376-2115
 Akron (G-70)

APPAREL DESIGNERS: Commercial

Tommy Bahama Group Inc ....C...... 614 750-9668
 Columbus (G-8854)

APPLIANCES, HOUSEHOLD OR COIN OPERATED: Laundry Dryers

Whirlpool Corporation ....C...... 740 383-7122
 Marion (G-13596)

APPLIANCES, HOUSEHOLD: Kitchen, Major, Exc Refrigs & Stoves

ABC Appliance Inc ....E...... 419 693-4414
 Oregon (G-15722)
New Path International LLC ....E...... 614 410-3974
 Powell (G-16344)

APPLIANCES: Household, Refrigerators & Freezers

Whirlpool Corporation ....C...... 740 383-7122
 Marion (G-13596)

APPLIANCES: Major, Cooking

Nacco Industries Inc ....E...... 440 229-5151
 Cleveland (G-6098)

APPLIANCES: Small, Electric

Johnson Bros Rubber Co Inc ....E...... 419 752-4814
 Greenwich (G-11526)

APPLICATIONS SOFTWARE PROGRAMMING

1 Edi Source Inc ....C...... 440 519-7800
 Solon (G-16967)
B-Tek Scales LLC ....E...... 330 471-8900
 Canton (G-2259)
Campuseai Inc ....C...... 216 589-9626
 Cleveland (G-5175)
Foundation Software Inc ....D...... 330 220-8383
 Strongsville (G-17465)
Jenne Inc ....C...... 440 835-0040
 Avon (G-900)
Managed Technology Svcs LLC ....D...... 937 247-8915
 Miamisburg (G-14315)
Manhattan Associates Inc ....D...... 440 878-0771
 Strongsville (G-17488)
Synoran ....E...... 614 236-4014
 Columbus (G-8815)
Teradata Corporation ....B...... 866 548-8348
 Miamisburg (G-14356)

APPRAISAL SVCS, EXC REAL ESTATE

Amos Media Company ....B...... 937 498-2111
 Sidney (G-16912)

ARBORETUM

Dawes Arboretum ....E...... 740 323-2355
 Newark (G-15164)
Holden Arboretum ....D...... 440 946-4400
 Willoughby (G-19670)

ARCHEOLOGICAL EXPEDITIONS

ASC Group Inc ....E...... 614 268-2514
 Columbus (G-7048)

ARCHITECTURAL SVCS

Arcadis US Inc ....E...... 216 781-6177
 Cleveland (G-5064)
ASC Group Inc ....E...... 614 268-2514
 Columbus (G-7048)
Big Red Rooster ....D...... 614 255-0200
 Columbus (G-7108)
Burgess & Niple Inc ....D...... 440 354-9700
 Painesville (G-15837)

Burgess & Niple / Heapy Engine ....D...... 614 459-2050
 Columbus (G-7170)
Ceso Inc ....D...... 937 435-8584
 Miamisburg (G-14281)
Cha Consulting Inc ....C...... 216 443-1700
 Cleveland (G-5224)
Chemstress Consultant Company ....C...... 330 535-5591
 Akron (G-130)
Chute Gerdeman Inc ....D...... 614 469-1001
 Columbus (G-7271)
City Architecture Inc ....E...... 216 881-2444
 Cleveland (G-5245)
CT Consultants Inc ....C...... 440 951-9000
 Mentor (G-14166)
Delphi Automotive Systems LLC ....E...... 248 724-5953
 Warren (G-18848)
Design Center ....E...... 513 618-3133
 Blue Ash (G-1577)
Dlr Group Inc ....D...... 216 522-1350
 Cleveland (G-5495)
Dlz Ohio Inc ....C...... 614 888-0040
 Columbus (G-7535)
Emersion Design LLC ....E...... 513 841-9100
 Cincinnati (G-3553)
Fanning/Howey Associates Inc ....D...... 919 831-1831
 Dublin (G-10346)
Garland/Dbs Inc ....C...... 216 641-7500
 Cleveland (G-5655)
Gbc Design Inc ....E...... 330 283-6870
 Akron (G-233)
Glavan & Accociates Architects ....E...... 614 205-4060
 Columbus (G-7754)
Gpd Services Company Inc ....D...... 330 572-2100
 Akron (G-244)
Heery International Inc ....E...... 216 510-4701
 Cleveland (G-5745)
Heery International Inc ....E...... 216 781-1313
 Cleveland (G-5746)
Holland Professional Group ....D...... 330 239-4474
 Sharon Center (G-16875)
HWH Archtcts-Ngnrs-Plnners Inc ....E...... 216 875-4000
 Cleveland (G-5794)
Ka Inc ....C...... 216 781-9144
 Seven Hills (G-16832)
Karlsberger Companies ....E...... 614 461-9500
 Columbus (G-7966)
KZF Bwsc Joint Venture ....E...... 513 621-6211
 Cincinnati (G-3951)
Loth Inc ....C...... 513 554-4900
 Cincinnati (G-3995)
Louis Perry & Associates Inc ....C...... 330 334-1585
 Wadsworth (G-18762)
Meyers + Associates Arch LLC ....E...... 614 221-9433
 Columbus (G-8155)
Ms Consultants Inc ....C...... 330 744-5321
 Youngstown (G-20291)
Nitschke Sampson Dietz Inc ....E...... 614 464-1933
 Columbus (G-8281)
Orchard Hiltz & McCliment Inc ....D...... 614 418-0600
 Columbus (G-8478)
Perkfect Design Solutions ....E...... 614 778-3560
 Columbus (G-8536)
Poggemeyer Design Group Inc ....C...... 419 244-8074
 Bowling Green (G-1791)
Rdl Architects Inc ....E...... 216 752-4300
 Cleveland (G-6356)
Reed Westlake Leskosky Ltd ....D...... 216 522-0449
 Cleveland (G-6365)
Richard R Jencen & Associates ....E...... 216 781-0131
 Cleveland (G-6392)
Schomer Glaus Pyle ....D...... 614 210-0751
 Columbus (G-8699)
Schomer Glaus Pyle ....E...... 216 518-5544
 Cleveland (G-6449)
Schomer Glaus Pyle ....B...... 330 572-2100
 Akron (G-430)
Shp Leading Design ....D...... 513 381-2112
 Cincinnati (G-4518)
Shremshock Architects Inc ....D...... 614 545-4550
 New Albany (G-15007)
Simonson Construction Svcs Inc ....D...... 419 281-8299
 Ashland (G-699)
Stantec Arch & Engrg PC ....E...... 216 454-2150
 Cleveland (G-6524)
Stantec Arch & Engrg PC ....D...... 614 486-4383
 Columbus (G-8773)
Stantec Architecture Inc ....E...... 216 454-2150
 Cleveland (G-6525)
Stantec Consulting Svcs Inc ....E...... 216 454-2150
 Cleveland (G-6526)

Stantec Consulting Svcs Inc ....D...... 513 842-8200
 Cincinnati (G-4583)
Stantec Consulting Svcs Inc ....C...... 614 486-4383
 Columbus (G-8774)
Stilson & Associates Inc ....E...... 614 847-0300
 Columbus (G-8789)
Trinity Health Group Ltd ....E...... 614 899-4830
 Columbus (G-8873)
United Architectural Mtls Inc ....E...... 330 433-9220
 North Canton (G-15378)
URS Group Inc ....E...... 614 464-4500
 Columbus (G-8921)
WD Partners Inc ....E...... 614 634-7000
 Dublin (G-10488)

ARCHITECTURAL SVCS: Engineering

Aecom Global II LLC ....B...... 614 726-3500
 Dublin (G-10235)
Dei Incorporated ....D...... 513 825-5800
 Cincinnati (G-3480)
E & A Pedco Services Inc ....D...... 513 782-4920
 Cincinnati (G-3519)
Fed/Matrix A Joint Venture LLC ....E...... 863 665-6363
 Dayton (G-9542)
Johnson Mirmiran Thompson Inc ....E...... 614 714-0270
 Columbus (G-7944)
Prime Ae Group Inc ....D...... 614 839-0250
 Columbus (G-6902)
Technical Assurance Inc ....E...... 440 953-3147
 Willoughby (G-19717)
Twism Enterprises LLC ....E...... 513 800-1098
 Cincinnati (G-4711)

ARCHITECTURAL SVCS: Engineering

A D A Architects Inc ....E...... 216 521-5134
 Cleveland (G-4932)
Acock Assoc Architects LLC ....E...... 614 228-1586
 Columbus (G-6939)
Aecom Global II LLC ....D...... 216 523-5600
 Cleveland (G-4966)
Austin Building and Design Inc ....C...... 440 544-2600
 Cleveland (G-5081)
Balog Steines Hendricks & Manc ....E...... 330 744-4401
 Youngstown (G-20110)
Baxter Hodell Donnelly Preston ....C...... 513 271-1634
 Cincinnati (G-3083)
Berardi + Partners ....E...... 614 221-1110
 Columbus (G-7101)
Bostwick Design Partnr Inc ....E...... 216 621-7900
 Cleveland (G-5129)
Braun & Steidl Architects Inc ....E...... 330 864-7755
 Akron (G-108)
Burgess & Niple ....C...... 513 579-0042
 Cincinnati (G-3149)
Burgess & Niple Inc ....B...... 502 254-2344
 Columbus (G-7169)
Champlin Haupt Architects Inc ....D...... 513 241-4474
 Cincinnati (G-3229)
Cole + Russell Architects Inc ....E...... 513 721-8080
 Cincinnati (G-3386)
Collaborative Inc ....E...... 419 242-7405
 Toledo (G-17819)
Cornelia C Hodgson - Architec ....E...... 216 593-0057
 Beachwood (G-1068)
CT Consultants Inc ....E...... 513 791-1700
 Blue Ash (G-1573)
Domokur Architects Inc ....E...... 330 666-7878
 Copley (G-9056)
Dorsky Hodgson + Partners Inc ....D...... 216 464-8600
 Cleveland (G-5505)
Elevar Design Group Inc ....E...... 513 721-0600
 Cincinnati (G-3550)
Fanning/Howey Associates Inc ....D...... 614 764-4661
 Dublin (G-10345)
Feinknopf Macioce Schappa ARC ....E...... 614 297-1020
 Columbus (G-7652)
G Herschman Architects Inc ....D...... 216 223-3200
 Cleveland (G-5645)
Garmann/Miller & Assoc Inc ....E...... 419 628-4240
 Minster (G-14662)
Hardlines Design Company ....E...... 614 784-8733
 Columbus (G-7801)
Hasenstab Architects Inc ....E...... 330 434-4464
 Akron (G-256)
Hixson Incorporated ....C...... 513 241-1230
 Cincinnati (G-3771)
Jdi Group Inc ....D...... 419 725-7161
 Maumee (G-13930)
K4 Architecture LLC ....D...... 513 455-5005
 Cincinnati (G-3899)

Employee Codes: A=Over 500 employees, B=251-500
C=101-250, D=51-100, E=25-50

ARCHITECTURAL SVCS: Engineering

KZF Design Inc .... D 513 621-6211
  Cincinnati *(G-3952)*
Lacaisse Inc .... D 513 621-6211
  Cincinnati *(G-3957)*
Lusk & Harkin Ltd .... E 614 221-3707
  Columbus *(G-8088)*
McGill Smith Punshon Inc .... E 513 759-0004
  Cincinnati *(G-4036)*
Meacham & Apel Architects Inc .... D 614 764-0407
  Columbus *(G-8139)*
Michael Schuster Associates .... E 513 241-5666
  Cincinnati *(G-4089)*
Middough Inc .... B 216 367-6000
  Cleveland *(G-6054)*
Moody-Nolan Inc .... E 614 461-4664
  Columbus *(G-8187)*
NBBJ LLC .... C 206 223-5026
  Columbus *(G-8252)*
Osborn Engineering Company .... D 216 861-2020
  Cleveland *(G-6216)*
Perspectus Architecture LLC .... E 216 752-1800
  Cleveland *(G-6269)*
Pond-Woolpert LLC .... D 937 461-5660
  Beavercreek *(G-1256)*
R E Warner & Associates Inc .... D 440 835-9400
  Westlake *(G-19537)*
Richard L Bowen & Assoc Inc .... D 216 491-9300
  Cleveland *(G-6391)*
Schooley Caldwell Associates .... D 614 628-0300
  Columbus *(G-8702)*
Sfa Architects Inc .... E 937 281-0600
  Dayton *(G-9878)*
Ssoe Inc .... E 330 821-7198
  Alliance *(G-560)*
Strollo Architects Inc .... E 330 743-1477
  Youngstown *(G-20384)*
URS Group Inc .... D 330 836-9111
  Akron *(G-490)*
Woolprt-Mrrick Joint Ventr LLP .... E 937 461-5660
  Beavercreek *(G-1263)*

ARCHITECTURAL SVCS: House Designer

Frch Design Worldwide - Cincin .... B 513 241-3000
  Cincinnati *(G-3644)*

ARMATURE REPAIRING & REWINDING SVC

City Machine Technologies Inc .... E 330 740-8186
  Youngstown *(G-20142)*
Dolin Supply Co .... E 304 529-4171
  South Point *(G-17084)*
Integrated Power Services LLC .... E 216 433-7808
  Cleveland *(G-5826)*
Setco Sales Company .... D 513 941-5110
  Cincinnati *(G-4502)*

ARMORED CAR SVCS

Brinks Incorporated .... E 614 291-1268
  Columbus *(G-7144)*
Brinks Incorporated .... E 614 291-0624
  Columbus *(G-7145)*
Brinks Incorporated .... D 216 621-7493
  Cleveland *(G-5139)*
Brinks Incorporated .... E 330 633-5351
  Akron *(G-112)*
Brinks Incorporated .... D 513 621-9310
  Cincinnati *(G-3135)*
Brinks Incorporated .... E 937 253-9777
  Dayton *(G-9258)*
Brinks Incorporated .... E 330 832-6130
  Massillon *(G-13789)*
Brinks Incorporated .... E 614 761-1205
  Dublin *(G-10268)*
Brinks Incorporated .... E 330 758-7379
  Youngstown *(G-20126)*
Dunbar Armored Inc .... D 513 381-8000
  Cincinnati *(G-3512)*
Dunbar Armored Inc .... E 614 475-1969
  Columbus *(G-7551)*
Dunbar Armored Inc .... E 216 642-5700
  Cleveland *(G-5512)*
Garda CL Great Lakes Inc .... E 614 863-4044
  Columbus *(G-7726)*
Garda CL Great Lakes Inc .... E 419 385-2411
  Toledo *(G-17907)*
Garda CL Great Lakes Inc .... B 561 939-7000
  Columbus *(G-7727)*
Garda CL Technical Svcs Inc .... E 937 294-4099
  Moraine *(G-14788)*

ART & ORNAMENTAL WARE: Pottery

J-Vac Industries Inc .... D 740 384-2155
  Wellston *(G-19000)*

ART DESIGN SVCS

Shamrock Companies Inc .... C 440 899-9510
  Westlake *(G-19546)*

ART GALLERIES

Columbus Museum of Art .... D 614 221-6801
  Columbus *(G-7372)*
Dumouchelle Art Galleries .... E 419 255-7606
  Toledo *(G-17858)*

ART GOODS & SPLYS WHOLESALERS

Checker Notions Company Inc .... D 419 893-3636
  Maumee *(G-13894)*
Distribution Data Incorporated .... E 216 362-3009
  Brookpark *(G-1943)*
Earthbound Holding LLC .... E 972 248-0228
  Strongsville *(G-17458)*
Lamrite West Inc .... E 440 572-9946
  Strongsville *(G-17483)*
Lamrite West Inc .... C 440 238-7318
  Strongsville *(G-17482)*

ART GOODS, WHOLESALE

Cannell Graphics LLC .... E 614 781-9760
  Worthington *(G-19944)*
Don Drumm Studios & Gallery .... E 330 253-6840
  Akron *(G-196)*

ART RELATED SVCS

Grenada Stamping Assembly Inc ..... E 419 842-3600
  Sylvania *(G-17589)*

ART SCHOOL, EXC COMMERCIAL

Cincinnati Museum Association .... C 513 721-5204
  Cincinnati *(G-3318)*
Cleveland Mus Schl Settlement .... C 216 421-5806
  Cleveland *(G-5339)*

ART SPLY STORES

Don Drumm Studios & Gallery .... E 330 253-6840
  Akron *(G-196)*
Lamrite West Inc .... C 440 238-7318
  Strongsville *(G-17482)*
United Art and Education Inc .... E 800 322-3247
  Dayton *(G-9945)*

ARTS & CRAFTS SCHOOL

South Central Ohio Eductl Ctr .... C 740 456-0517
  New Boston *(G-15014)*

ARTS OR SCIENCES CENTER

Contemporary Arts Center .... E 513 721-0390
  Cincinnati *(G-3412)*
Deyor Performing Arts Center .... E 330 744-4269
  Youngstown *(G-20168)*

ASPHALT & ASPHALT PRDTS

Lucas County Asphalt Inc .... E 419 476-0705
  Toledo *(G-18016)*
Morrow Gravel Company Inc .... C 513 771-0820
  Cincinnati *(G-4120)*
Shelly and Sands Inc .... E 740 453-0721
  Zanesville *(G-20532)*
Shelly Materials Inc .... E 740 666-5841
  Ostrander *(G-15794)*
Stoneco Inc .... D 419 422-8854
  Findlay *(G-11086)*

ASPHALT COATINGS & SEALERS

Hy-Grade Corporation .... E 216 341-7711
  Cleveland *(G-5795)*
Owens Corning Sales LLC .... A 419 248-8000
  Toledo *(G-18114)*
Simon Roofing and Shtmtl Corp .... C 330 629-7392
  Youngstown *(G-20376)*
State Industrial Products Corp .... B 877 747-6986
  Cleveland *(G-6530)*
Terry Asphalt Materials Inc .... E 513 874-6192
  Hamilton *(G-11777)*

ASPHALT MIXTURES WHOLESALERS

Barrett Paving Materials Inc .... C 513 271-6200
  Middletown *(G-14475)*
Hy-Grade Corporation .... E 216 341-7711
  Cleveland *(G-5795)*

ASSOCIATION FOR THE HANDICAPPED

Cincinnati Assn For The Blind .... C 513 221-8558
  Cincinnati *(G-3282)*
Cleveland Soc For The Blind .... C 216 791-8118
  Cleveland *(G-5347)*
County of Mercer .... D 419 586-2369
  Celina *(G-2643)*
Hattie Larlham Community Svcs ..... E 330 274-2272
  Twinsburg *(G-18427)*
Medina Creative Accessibility .... D 330 220-2112
  Medina *(G-14099)*
Northeast Ohio Chapter Natnl .... E 216 696-8220
  Cleveland *(G-6154)*
Southeast Diversified Inds .... D 740 432-4241
  Cambridge *(G-2128)*
Spectrum Supportive Services .... E 216 875-0460
  Cleveland *(G-6517)*

ASSOCIATIONS: Alumni

Ohio State Univ Alumni Assn .... D 614 292-2200
  Columbus *(G-8379)*
University of Findlay .... C 419 434-4516
  Findlay *(G-11096)*

ASSOCIATIONS: Bar

Cincinnati Bar Association .... E 513 381-8213
  Cincinnati *(G-3284)*
Columbus Bar Association .... E 614 221-4112
  Columbus *(G-7333)*
Ohio State Bar Association .... D 614 487-2050
  Columbus *(G-8378)*

ASSOCIATIONS: Business

A Fox Construction .... E 614 506-1685
  Canal Winchester *(G-2150)*
American Legion Post .... E 330 872-5475
  Newton Falls *(G-15272)*
Blue Ash Business Association .... D 513 253-1006
  Cincinnati *(G-3116)*
Certified Angus Beef LLC .... D 330 345-2333
  Wooster *(G-19839)*
Certified Angus Beef LLC .... E 330 345-2333
  Wooster *(G-19840)*
City of Kenton .... E 419 674-4850
  Kenton *(G-12409)*
City of Louisville .... D 330 875-3321
  Louisville *(G-13096)*
City of Oberlin .... E 440 775-1531
  Oberlin *(G-15640)*
City of Toledo .... A 419 245-1001
  Toledo *(G-17808)*
City of Toledo .... D 419 245-1400
  Toledo *(G-17811)*
Consolidated Electric Coop Inc .... D 419 947-3055
  Mount Gilead *(G-14852)*
County of Montgomery .... E 937 225-4010
  Dayton *(G-9435)*
Enon Firemans Association .... E 937 864-7429
  Enon *(G-10727)*
Hirzel Canning Company .... D 419 693-0531
  Northwood *(G-15533)*
Interstate Contractors LLC .... E 513 372-5393
  Mason *(G-13723)*
Longaberger Company .... D 740 349-8411
  Newark *(G-15197)*
Mahoning Clmbana Training Assn ... E 330 747-5639
  Youngstown *(G-20259)*
National Hot Rod Association .... C 740 928-5706
  Hebron *(G-11858)*
Odd Fellows Hall .... E 440 599-7973
  Conneaut *(G-9045)*
Ohio Assn Pub Treasurers .... C 937 415-2237
  Vandalia *(G-18691)*
Ohio Biliffs Crt Officers Assn .... D 419 354-9302
  Bowling Green *(G-1788)*
Ohio Civil Service Employees A .... D 614 865-4700
  Westerville *(G-19337)*
Ohio Department of Commerce .... C 614 728-8400
  Columbus *(G-8326)*
Ross County YMCA .... D 740 772-4340
  Chillicothe *(G-2882)*

SERVICES SECTION

ATHLETIC ORGANIZATION

Service Corps Retired Execs ....E....... 216 522-4194
   Cleveland *(G-6471)*
Service Corps Retired Execs ....E....... 419 259-7598
   Toledo *(G-18180)*
Southeast Area Law Enforcement.........E....... 216 475-1234
   Bedford *(G-1339)*
Superior Clay Corp ....D....... 740 922-4122
   Uhrichsville *(G-18492)*
Toledo Elec Jint Apprnticeship...............E....... 419 666-8088
   Rossford *(G-16612)*
Town of Canal Fulton.............................E....... 330 854-9448
   Canal Fulton *(G-2147)*
Union Rural Electric Coop Inc ....E....... 937 642-1826
   Marysville *(G-13657)*
Universal Advertising Assoc ....E....... 513 522-5000
   Cincinnati *(G-4746)*
Village of Antwerp..................................E....... 419 258-7422
   Antwerp *(G-621)*
Waste Management Ohio Inc ....D....... 614 382-6342
   Canal Winchester *(G-2177)*

ASSOCIATIONS: Engineering

Society Plastics Engineers Inc...............C....... 419 287-4898
   Pemberville *(G-15944)*

ASSOCIATIONS: Fraternal

Belmont & Monroe Lodge 6 of................E....... 740 695-2121
   Saint Clairsville *(G-16619)*
Beta RHO House Assoc Kappa ....D....... 513 221-1280
   Cincinnati *(G-3103)*
Bpo Elks of USA.....................................E....... 740 622-0794
   Coshocton *(G-9089)*
Delta Gamma Fraternity ....E....... 614 481-8169
   Upper Arlington *(G-18549)*
Enon Firemans Association....................E....... 937 864-7429
   Enon *(G-10727)*
Fraternal Order Eagles Inc ....E....... 330 477-8059
   Canton *(G-2370)*
Fraternal Order Eagles Inc ....E....... 419 738-2582
   Wapakoneta *(G-18795)*
Fraternal Order Eagles Inc ....E....... 419 332-3961
   Fremont *(G-11200)*
Fraternal Order Eagles Inc ....E....... 440 293-5997
   Andover *(G-612)*
Fraternal Order Eagles Inc ....E....... 614 883-2200
   Grove City *(G-11563)*
Fraternal Order of Eagles ....E....... 937 323-0671
   Springfield *(G-17200)*
Fraternal Order of Police of O................D....... 614 224-5700
   Columbus *(G-7700)*
Hamilton Lodge 93 Benevolent P ....E....... 513 887-4384
   Liberty Twp *(G-12725)*
Knights of Columbus..............................E....... 937 890-2971
   Dayton *(G-9664)*
Knights of Columbus..............................E....... 419 628-2089
   Minster *(G-14665)*
Knights of Columbus..............................D....... 740 382-3671
   Marion *(G-13547)*
Louisville Frternal Order of E ....E....... 330 875-2113
   Louisville *(G-13102)*
Maumee Lodge No 1850 Bnvlt................E....... 419 893-7272
   Maumee *(G-13943)*
Moose International Inc..........................E....... 513 422-6776
   Middletown *(G-14441)*
New Boston Aerie 2271 FOE ....E....... 740 456-0171
   New Boston *(G-15012)*
Order of Unite Commercial Tra...............D....... 614 487-9680
   Columbus *(G-8479)*
Polish American Citizens Club ....E....... 330 253-0496
   Akron *(G-395)*
Port Clinton Bpo Elks Ldge 1718............E....... 419 734-1900
   Port Clinton *(G-16251)*
Portsmouth Lodge 154 B P O E.............E....... 740 353-1013
   Portsmouth *(G-16299)*
Schlee Malt House Condo Assn ....E....... 614 463-1999
   Columbus *(G-8695)*

ASSOCIATIONS: Homeowners

Lake Mhawk Prperty Owners Assn ....E....... 330 863-0000
   Malvern *(G-13253)*
Mills Creek Association..........................E....... 440 327-5336
   North Ridgeville *(G-15471)*
Muirfield Association Inc ....E....... 614 889-0922
   Dublin *(G-10401)*

ASSOCIATIONS: Parent Teacher

Clearmount Elementary School...............E....... 330 497-5640
   Canton *(G-2313)*

Norwich Elementary Pto.........................E....... 614 921-6000
   Hilliard *(G-11938)*

ASSOCIATIONS: Real Estate Management

Al Neyer LLC..D....... 513 271-6400
   Cincinnati *(G-2980)*
American Bulk Commodities Inc.............C....... 330 758-0841
   Youngstown *(G-20103)*
Boyd Property Group LLC......................E....... 614 725-5228
   Columbus *(G-7126)*
Capital Properties MGT Ltd....................E....... 216 991-3057
   Cleveland *(G-5178)*
E M Columbus LLC................................E....... 614 861-3232
   Columbus *(G-7559)*
Eagle Realty Group LLC ....E....... 513 361-7700
   Cincinnati *(G-3528)*
Executive Properties Inc ....E....... 330 376-4037
   Akron *(G-211)*
Fairfield Homes Inc................................E....... 740 653-3583
   Lancaster *(G-12534)*
First Realty Property MGT Ltd...............E....... 440 720-0100
   Mayfield Village *(G-14011)*
Fleetwood Management Inc ....E....... 614 538-1277
   Columbus *(G-7674)*
Forest City Commercial MGT Inc...........C....... 216 621-6060
   Cleveland *(G-5612)*
Forest Cy Residential MGT Inc..............E....... 216 621-6060
   Cleveland *(G-5623)*
G H A Inc..E....... 440 729-2130
   Chesterland *(G-2798)*
G J Goudreau & Co................................E....... 216 351-5233
   Cleveland *(G-5646)*
Hallmark Management Associates ....E....... 216 681-0080
   Cleveland *(G-5722)*
I H S Services Inc..................................E....... 419 224-8811
   Lima *(G-12802)*
Irg Realty Advisors LLC ....E....... 330 659-4060
   Richfield *(G-16513)*
John Dellagnese & Assoc Inc.................E....... 330 668-4000
   Akron *(G-295)*
Kaval-Levine Management Co................E....... 440 944-5402
   Willoughby Hills *(G-19731)*
Kencor Properties Inc............................E....... 513 984-3870
   Cincinnati *(G-3911)*
Kettering Medical Center ....D....... 937 866-2984
   Miamisburg *(G-14311)*
Klingbeil Management Group Co ....E....... 614 220-8900
   Columbus *(G-7997)*
L J F Management Inc ....E....... 513 688-0104
   Blue Ash *(G-1623)*
L O M Inc ....E....... 216 363-6009
   Cleveland *(G-5914)*
Marion Plaza Inc....................................D....... 330 747-2661
   Niles *(G-15295)*
Miller-Vlentine Operations Inc ....E....... 937 293-0900
   Dayton *(G-9750)*
Miller-Vlentine Operations Inc ....A....... 513 771-0900
   Dayton *(G-9751)*
Model Group Inc.....................................E....... 513 559-0048
   Cincinnati *(G-4112)*
Morelia Consultants LLC.......................D....... 513 469-1500
   Cincinnati *(G-4116)*
Multi Builders Inc....................................E....... 216 831-1400
   Cleveland *(G-6088)*
North American Properties Inc...............E....... 513 721-2744
   Cincinnati *(G-4176)*
Oakwood Management Company ....E....... 614 866-8702
   Reynoldsburg *(G-16471)*
Olmsted Residence Corporation ....C....... 440 235-7100
   Olmsted Twp *(G-15680)*
Pache Management Company Inc.........E....... 614 451-9236
   Columbus *(G-8504)*
Paran Management Company Ltd ....E....... 216 921-5663
   Cleveland *(G-6233)*
Pizzuti Inc...E....... 614 280-4000
   Columbus *(G-8547)*
Plaza Properties Inc...............................E....... 614 237-3726
   Columbus *(G-8552)*
Preferred RE Investments LLC..............E....... 614 901-2400
   Westerville *(G-19344)*
Real Property Management Inc ....E....... 614 766-6500
   Dublin *(G-10439)*
Red Brick Property MGT LLC................E....... 513 524-9340
   Oxford *(G-15830)*
Reuben Co ....E....... 419 241-3400
   Toledo *(G-18155)*
Rlj Management Co Inc ....E....... 614 942-2020
   Dublin *(G-8639)*
Rose Community Management LLC ......C....... 917 542-3600
   Independence *(G-12254)*

RPM Midwest LLC................................E....... 513 762-9000
   Cincinnati *(G-4451)*
S & S Real Estate Managers LLC ....D....... 937 256-7000
   Dayton *(G-9283)*
Schottenstein RE Group LLC ....E....... 614 418-8900
   Columbus *(G-8703)*
Schroeder Company..............................E....... 419 473-3139
   Toledo *(G-18175)*
STS Restaurant Management Inc ....E....... 419 246-0730
   Toledo *(G-18205)*
T & R Properties.....................................E....... 614 923-4000
   Dublin *(G-10472)*
Tolson Enterprises Inc ....E....... 419 843-6465
   Toledo *(G-18256)*
Towne Properties Assoc Inc ....E....... 513 489-4059
   Cincinnati *(G-4671)*
Wallick Properties Midwest LLC.............C....... 614 539-9041
   Grove City *(G-11610)*
Wallick Properties Midwest LLC.............A....... 614 863-4640
   New Albany *(G-15010)*
West-Way Management Company.........E....... 440 250-1851
   Westlake *(G-19566)*
Whitehurst Company..............................E....... 419 865-0799
   Maumee *(G-13994)*
Zaremba Group Incorporated ....E....... 216 221-6600
   Cleveland *(G-6779)*
Zaremba Group LLC..............................C....... 216 221-6600
   Lakewood *(G-12504)*

ASSOCIATIONS: Trade

American Jersey Cattle Assn ....E....... 614 861-3636
   Reynoldsburg *(G-16427)*
Buckeye Power Inc ....E....... 614 781-0573
   Columbus *(G-7160)*
Greater Clvland Hlthcare Assn ....D....... 216 696-6900
   Cleveland *(G-5701)*
Gs1 Us Inc ....E....... 609 620-0200
   Dayton *(G-9592)*
New Waterford Fireman.........................E....... 330 457-2363
   New Waterford *(G-15139)*
Ohio Association Realtors Inc ....E....... 614 228-6675
   Columbus *(G-8319)*
Ohio Farm Bur Federation Inc ....D....... 614 249-2400
   Columbus *(G-8345)*
Ohio Rural Electric Coops Inc ....E....... 614 846-5757
   Columbus *(G-8371)*
Precision Metalforming Assn ....E....... 216 241-1482
   Independence *(G-12245)*
United States Trotting Assn ....D....... 614 224-2291
   Westerville *(G-19447)*
Vigilant Global Trade Svcs LLC.............E....... 260 417-1825
   Shaker Heights *(G-16871)*

ATHLETIC CLUB & GYMNASIUMS, MEMBERSHIP

Chagrin Valley Athletic Club ....D....... 440 543-5141
   Chagrin Falls *(G-2712)*
Cincinnati Sports Mall Inc ....D....... 513 527-4000
   Cincinnati *(G-3329)*
Friars Club Inc..D....... 513 488-8777
   Cincinnati *(G-3654)*
Life Time Fitness Inc ....C....... 513 234-0660
   Mason *(G-13732)*
Shadow Valley Tennis & Fitness ....E....... 419 861-3986
   Toledo *(G-18183)*
Young Mens Christian Associat ....E....... 513 731-0115
   Cincinnati *(G-4866)*

ATHLETIC EQPT INSPECTION SVCS

Side Effects Inc......................................E....... 937 704-9696
   Franklin *(G-11165)*

ATHLETIC ORGANIZATION

Center For Health Affairs ....D....... 800 362-2628
   Cleveland *(G-5208)*
Oberlin College ....E....... 440 775-8500
   Oberlin *(G-15655)*
Professnal Glfers Assn of Amer ....E....... 419 882-3197
   Sylvania *(G-17606)*
United Sttes Bowl Congress Inc.............D....... 440 327-0102
   North Ridgeville *(G-15478)*
United Sttes Bowl Congress Inc.............D....... 614 237-3716
   Columbus *(G-8903)*
University of Cincinnati ....C....... 513 556-4603
   Cincinnati *(G-4771)*

ATOMIZERS

Cr Brands Inc ....D...... 513 860-5039
　West Chester (G-19058)

AUCTION SVCS: Livestock

Barnesville Livestock Sales Co ....E...... 740 425-3611
　Barnesville (G-989)
Kidron Auction Inc ....E...... 330 857-2641
　Kidron (G-12442)
Mt Hope Auction Inc ....E...... 330 674-6188
　Mount Hope (G-14866)
Muskingum Livestock Sales Inc ....E...... 740 452-9984
　Zanesville (G-20510)
United Producers Inc ....E...... 937 456-4161
　Eaton (G-10579)

AUCTION SVCS: Motor Vehicle

ABC Detroit/Toledo Auto Auctn ....E...... 419 872-0872
　Perrysburg (G-15971)
Adesa Corporation LLC ....C...... 937 746-5361
　Franklin (G-11148)
Adesa-Ohio Llc ....C...... 330 467-8280
　Northfield (G-15508)
Auction Broadcasting Co LLC ....C...... 419 872-0872
　Perrysburg (G-15972)
Columbus Fair Auto Auction Inc ....A...... 614 497-2000
　Obetz (G-15666)
Copart Inc ....E...... 614 497-1590
　Columbus (G-7437)
Cox Automotive Inc ....C...... 513 874-9310
　West Chester (G-19057)
Cox Automotive Inc ....B...... 614 871-2771
　Grove City (G-11550)
Gallipolis Auto Auction Inc ....E...... 740 446-1576
　Gallipolis (G-11317)
Greater Cleveland Auto Auction ....D...... 216 433-7777
　Cleveland (G-5695)
Montpelier Auto Auction Ohio ....E...... 419 485-1691
　Montpelier (G-14744)
Value Auto Auction LLC ....D...... 740 982-3030
　Crooksville (G-9153)

AUCTIONEERS: Fee Basis

Auction Services Inc ....A...... 614 497-2000
　Obetz (G-15663)
Baker Bnngson Rlty Auctioneers ......E...... 419 547-7777
　Clyde (G-6810)
Kramer & Kramer Inc ....E...... 937 456-1101
　Eaton (G-10563)
Mt Hope Auction Inc ....E...... 330 674-6188
　Mount Hope (G-14866)
Skipco Financial Adjusters ....D...... 330 854-4800
　Canal Fulton (G-2146)
Tri Green Interstate Equipment ....E...... 614 879-7731
　London (G-13008)

AUDIO & VIDEO EQPT, EXC COMMERCIAL

Pioneer Automotive Tech Inc ....C...... 937 746-2293
　Springboro (G-17136)
Tech Products Corporation ....E...... 937 438-1100
　Miamisburg (G-14355)

AUDIO-VISUAL PROGRAM PRODUCTION SVCS

Bkg Holdings LLC ....E...... 614 252-7455
　Columbus (G-7113)
Intgrted Bridge Communications ......E...... 513 381-1380
　Cincinnati (G-3839)
Pagetech Ltd ....D...... 614 238-0518
　Columbus (G-8507)
Ron Foth Retail Inc ....E...... 614 888-7771
　Columbus (G-8646)
Universal Technology Corp ....D...... 937 426-2808
　Beavercreek (G-1216)
Video Works ....D...... 419 865-6800
　Toledo (G-18291)

AUDITING SVCS

City of Wellston ....D...... 740 384-2428
　Wellston (G-18998)
Protiviti Inc ....E...... 216 696-6010
　Cleveland (G-6325)

AUTO & HOME SUPPLY STORES: Auto & Truck Eqpt & Parts

Admiral Truck Parts Inc ....E...... 330 659-6311
　Bath (G-1033)
Advance Auto Parts Inc ....E...... 440 226-3150
　Chardon (G-2738)
Allstate Trk Sls of Estrn OH ....E...... 330 339-5555
　New Philadelphia (G-15080)
Dutro Ford Lincoln-Mercury Inc ....D...... 740 452-6334
　Zanesville (G-20470)
MJ Auto Parts Inc ....E...... 440 205-6272
　Mentor (G-14221)
Pete Baur Buick Gmc Inc ....E...... 440 238-5600
　Cleveland (G-6270)
Stricker Bros Inc ....E...... 513 732-1152
　Batavia (G-1026)

AUTO & HOME SUPPLY STORES: Automotive Access

Cox Automotive Inc ....B...... 614 871-2771
　Grove City (G-11550)
H & H Auto Parts Inc ....E...... 330 494-2975
　Canton (G-2387)
Jim Hayden Inc ....D...... 513 563-8828
　Cincinnati (G-3873)

AUTO & HOME SUPPLY STORES: Automotive parts

Bridgeport Auto Parts Inc ....E...... 740 635-0441
　Bridgeport (G-1860)
Car Parts Warehouse Inc ....E...... 216 281-4500
　Brookpark (G-1937)
Cole-Valley Motor Co ....D...... 330 372-1665
　Warren (G-18835)
Crown Dielectric Inds Inc ....C...... 614 224-5161
　Columbus (G-7467)
Dave Dnnis Chrysler Jeep Dodge ....D...... 937 429-5566
　Beavercreek Township (G-1267)
Four Wheel Drive Hardware LLC .....C...... 330 482-4733
　Columbiana (G-6859)
General Parts Inc ....E...... 614 267-5197
　Columbus (G-7734)
Genuine Parts Company ....B...... 614 766-6865
　Columbus (G-7740)
Greenleaf Ohio LLC ....E...... 330 832-6001
　Massillon (G-13815)
H & H Auto Parts Inc ....D...... 330 456-4778
　Canton (G-2386)
Haasz Automall LLC ....D...... 330 296-2866
　Ravenna (G-16387)
Hahn Automotive Warehouse Inc .....E...... 937 223-1068
　Dayton (G-9597)
Hamilton Automotive Warehouse .....D...... 513 896-4100
　Hamilton (G-11739)
Jegs Automotive Inc ....C...... 614 294-5050
　Delaware (G-10110)
Joseph Russo ....E...... 440 748-2690
　Grafton (G-11441)
K - O - I Warehouse Inc ....E...... 937 323-5585
　Springfield (G-17218)
K-M-S Industries Inc ....E...... 440 243-6680
　Brookpark (G-1948)
Man-Tansky Inc ....E...... 740 454-2512
　Zanesville (G-20499)
Ohio Auto Supply Company ....E...... 330 454-5105
　Canton (G-2478)
Pat Young Service Co Inc ....E...... 216 447-8550
　Cleveland (G-6250)
Pep Boys - Manny Moe & Jack ....E...... 614 864-2092
　Columbus (G-8534)
Santmyer Oil Co Inc ....D...... 330 262-6501
　Wooster (G-19911)
Smyth Automotive Inc ....D...... 513 528-2800
　Cincinnati (G-4543)
Smyth Automotive Inc ....D...... 513 528-0061
　Cincinnati (G-4544)
Snyders Antique Auto Parts Inc ....E...... 330 549-5313
　New Springfield (G-15131)
Stoops Frghtlnr-Qlity Trlr Inc ....E...... 937 236-4092
　Dayton (G-9909)

AUTO & HOME SUPPLY STORES: Batteries, Automotive & Truck

OReilly Automotive Inc ....D...... 330 494-0042
　North Canton (G-15360)
OReilly Automotive Inc ....E...... 419 630-0811
　Bryan (G-2015)
OReilly Automotive Inc ....D...... 330 318-3136
　Boardman (G-1742)

AUTO & HOME SUPPLY STORES: Truck Eqpt & Parts

Bulldawg Holdings LLC ....E...... 419 423-3131
　Findlay (G-11010)
Dales Truck Parts Inc ....E...... 937 766-2551
　Cedarville (G-2632)
Esec Corporation ....E...... 614 875-3732
　Grove City (G-11558)
Helton Enterprises Inc ....E...... 419 423-4180
　Findlay (G-11046)
Heritage Truck Equipment Inc ....E...... 330 699-4491
　Akron (G-262)
Hill Intl Trcks NA LLC ....D...... 330 386-6440
　East Liverpool (G-10522)
Kaffenbarger Truck Eqp Co ....E...... 513 772-6800
　Cincinnati (G-3900)
Palmer Trucks Inc ....E...... 937 235-3318
　Dayton (G-9799)
Perkins Motor Service Ltd ....E...... 440 277-1256
　Lorain (G-13071)
Premier Truck Parts Inc ....E...... 216 642-5000
　Cleveland (G-6302)
Transport Specialists Inc ....E...... 513 771-2220
　Cincinnati (G-4680)
Valley Ford Truck Inc ....D...... 216 524-2400
　Cleveland (G-6683)
Western Branch Diesel Inc ....E...... 330 454-8800
　Canton (G-2585)
Wz Management Inc ....E...... 330 628-4881
　Akron (G-514)

AUTO SPLYS & PARTS, NEW, WHSLE: Exhaust Sys, Mufflers, Etc

P & M Exhaust Systems Whse ....E...... 513 825-2660
　Cincinnati (G-4247)

AUTOMATED TELLER MACHINE NETWORK

PNC Bank-Atm ....E...... 937 865-6800
　Miamisburg (G-14336)

AUTOMATED TELLER MACHINE OR ATM REPAIR SVCS

Atm Solutions Inc ....D...... 513 742-4900
　Cincinnati (G-3061)
Cbord Group Inc ....C...... 330 498-2702
　Uniontown (G-18513)

AUTOMATIC REGULATING CONTROL: Building Svcs Monitoring, Auto

Evokes LLC ....E...... 513 947-8433
　Mason (G-13700)

AUTOMOBILE FINANCE LEASING

BMW Financial Services Na LLC .....E...... 614 718-6900
　Hilliard (G-11882)
BMW Financial Services Na LLC .....C...... 614 718-6900
　Dublin (G-10265)
Ford Motor Company ....E...... 513 573-1101
　Mason (G-13702)
Kempthorn Motors Inc ....E...... 330 452-6511
　Canton (G-2424)
Keybank National Association ....B...... 800 539-2968
　Cleveland (G-5899)
Kings Cove Automotive LLC ....E...... 513 677-0177
　Fairfield (G-10870)
Klaben Leasing and Sales Inc ....D...... 330 673-9971
　Kent (G-12382)
Security Nat Auto Accptnce LLC .....C...... 513 459-8118
　Mason (G-13758)

AUTOMOBILE RECOVERY SVCS

Almost Family Inc ....E...... 513 662-3400
　Cincinnati (G-2993)
OReilly Automotive Inc ....D...... 216 642-7591
　Seven Hills (G-16835)
OReilly Automotive Inc ....D...... 213 332-0427
　Maple Heights (G-13412)
OReilly Automotive Inc ....E...... 330 238-1416
　Alliance (G-551)

Quadax Inc E 330 759-4600
Youngstown *(G-20334)*
Tbn Acquisition LLC D 740 653-2091
Lancaster *(G-12580)*
Venture Plastics Inc E 330 872-6262
Newton Falls *(G-15279)*
West Corporation B 330 574-0510
Niles *(G-15310)*

AUTOMOBILE STORAGE GARAGE

Chillicothe City School Dst E 740 775-2936
Chillicothe *(G-2818)*
United Parcel Service Inc OH C 419 424-9494
Findlay *(G-11095)*

AUTOMOBILES & OTHER MOTOR VEHICLES WHOLESALERS

1106 West Main Inc E 330 673-2122
Kent *(G-12350)*
Abers Garage Inc E 419 281-5500
Ashland *(G-649)*
Akron Auto Auction Inc C 330 724-7708
Coventry Township *(G-9122)*
Baker Vehicle Systems Inc E 330 467-2250
Macedonia *(G-13189)*
Bobb Automotive Inc E 614 853-3000
Columbus *(G-7123)*
Chuck Nicholson Pntc-GMC Trcks E 330 343-7781
Dover *(G-10180)*
Coughlin Chevrolet Inc D 740 964-9191
Pataskala *(G-15922)*
Dave Knapp Ford Lincoln Inc E 937 547-3000
Greenville *(G-11496)*
Donley Ford-Lincoln Inc E 419 281-3673
Ashland *(G-679)*
Dons Automotive Group LLC E 419 337-3010
Wauseon *(G-18951)*
Dons Brooklyn Chevrolet Inc E 216 741-1500
Cleveland *(G-5504)*
Doug Bigelow Chevrolet Inc D 330 644-7500
Akron *(G-198)*
Doug Marine Motors Inc E 740 335-3700
Wshngtn CT Hs *(G-20020)*
Downtown Ford Lincoln Inc D 330 456-2781
Canton *(G-2344)*
Dutro Ford Lincoln-Mercury Inc D 740 452-6334
Zanesville *(G-20470)*
Ed Schmidt Auto Inc C 419 874-4331
Perrysburg *(G-16001)*
Ed Tomko Chryslr Jep Dge Inc E 440 835-5900
Avon Lake *(G-929)*
Gene Stevens Auto & Truck Ctr E 419 429-2000
Findlay *(G-11036)*
George P Ballas Buick GMC Trck D 419 535-1000
Toledo *(G-17913)*
Graham Chevrolet-Cadillac Co D 419 989-4012
Ontario *(G-15690)*
Haydocy Automotive Inc D 614 279-8880
Columbus *(G-7804)*
Hidy Motors Inc D 937 426-9564
Dayton *(G-9272)*
Interstate Truckway Inc E 614 771-1220
Columbus *(G-7919)*
Kempthorn Automall C 330 456-8287
Canton *(G-2423)*
Klaben Lincoln Ford Inc D 330 673-3139
Kent *(G-12383)*
Laria Chevrolet-Buick Inc E 330 925-2015
Rittman *(G-16553)*
McCluskey Chevrolet Inc C 513 761-1111
Cincinnati *(G-4035)*
Medina Management Company LLC D 330 723-3291
Medina *(G-14102)*
Mullinax East LLC D 440 296-3020
Wickliffe *(G-19608)*
National Car Mart III Inc E 216 398-2228
Cleveland *(G-6102)*
Performance Pontc-Oldmbl GM Tr E 330 264-1113
Wooster *(G-19902)*
Rush Truck Centers Ohio Inc D 513 733-8500
Cincinnati *(G-4458)*
Rush Truck Centers Ohio Inc E 419 224-6045
Lima *(G-12872)*
Rush Truck Leasing Inc E 614 876-3500
Columbus *(G-8660)*
Sharpnack Chevrolet Co E 440 967-3144
Vermilion *(G-18716)*
Sims Buick-G M C Truck Inc D 330 372-3500
Warren *(G-18900)*
Slimans Sales & Service Inc E 440 988-4484
Amherst *(G-604)*
South East Chevrolet Co E 440 585-9300
Willoughby Hills *(G-19735)*
Stoops Frghtlnr-Qlity Trlr Inc E 937 236-4092
Dayton *(G-9909)*
Stratton Chevrolet Co E 330 537-3151
Beloit *(G-1432)*
Valley Ford Truck Inc D 216 524-2400
Cleveland *(G-6683)*
Village Motors Inc D 330 674-2055
Millersburg *(G-14626)*
Voss Auto Network Inc E 937 428-2447
Dayton *(G-9976)*
Voss Chevrolet Inc C 937 428-2500
Dayton *(G-9978)*
Voss Dodge E 937 435-7800
Dayton *(G-9979)*
Voss Toyota Inc E 937 427-3700
Beavercreek *(G-1218)*
Walt Sweeney Fleet Sales E 513 932-2717
Lebanon *(G-12657)*
Warner Buick-Nissan Inc E 419 423-7161
Findlay *(G-11099)*
White Family Companies Inc C 937 222-3701
Dayton *(G-9996)*

AUTOMOBILES: Wholesalers

Albert Mike Leasing Inc C 513 563-1400
Cincinnati *(G-2982)*
Beechmont Motors Inc E 513 388-3883
Cincinnati *(G-3089)*
Beechmont Toyota Inc D 513 388-3800
Cincinnati *(G-3092)*
Central Hummr East E 216 514-2700
Cleveland *(G-5212)*
Honda North America Inc E 937 642-5000
Marysville *(G-13625)*
Midwest Motors Inc E 330 758-5800
Youngstown *(G-20286)*
Performance Autoplex LLC D 513 870-5033
Fairfield *(G-10895)*
Stykemain Pntiac-Buick-Gmc Ltd D 419 784-5252
Defiance *(G-10059)*

AUTOMOTIVE & TRUCK GENERAL REPAIR SVC

1st Gear Auto Inc E 216 458-0791
Bedford *(G-1291)*
Abraham Ford LLC E 440 233-7402
Elyria *(G-10592)*
Advantage Ford Lincoln Mercury E 419 334-9751
Fremont *(G-11182)*
Ashtabula Area City School Dst E 440 992-1221
Ashtabula *(G-712)*
Auto Center USA Inc E 513 683-4900
Cincinnati *(G-3066)*
Beechmont Ford Inc C 513 752-6611
Cincinnati *(G-2904)*
Bill Delord Autocenter Inc D 513 932-3000
Lebanon *(G-12592)*
Bob-Boyd Ford Inc D 614 860-0606
Lancaster *(G-12510)*
Bowling Green Lncln-Mrcury Inc E 419 352-2553
Bowling Green *(G-1765)*
Brentlinger Enterprises C 614 889-2571
Dublin *(G-10267)*
Brown Motor Sales Co E 419 531-0151
Toledo *(G-17785)*
Burtons Collision E 513 984-3396
Cincinnati *(G-3154)*
Cain Motors Inc E 330 494-5588
Canton *(G-2280)*
Cascade Group Inc E 330 929-1861
Cuyahoga Falls *(G-9169)*
Central Cadillac Limited D 216 861-5800
Cleveland *(G-5209)*
Chillicothe City School Dst E 740 775-2936
Chillicothe *(G-2818)*
City of Berea E 440 826-5853
Berea *(G-1451)*
Classic International Inc D 440 975-1222
Mentor *(G-14158)*
Cole-Valley Motor Co D 330 372-1665
Warren *(G-18835)*
Columbus SAI Motors LLC E 614 851-3273
Columbus *(G-7383)*
Conrads Tire Service Inc E 216 941-3333
Cleveland *(G-5392)*
Contitech North America Inc E 440 225-5363
Akron *(G-162)*
Coughlin Chevrolet Inc D 740 964-9191
Pataskala *(G-15922)*
County Engineering Office E 419 334-9731
Fremont *(G-11189)*
County Engineers Office E 740 702-3130
Chillicothe *(G-2829)*
County of Lorain D 440 326-5880
Elyria *(G-10615)*
Crestmont Cadillac Corporation E 216 831-5300
Cleveland *(G-5437)*
Dan Tobin Pontiac Buick GMC D 614 889-6300
Columbus *(G-7484)*
Dave Dnnis Chrysler Jeep Dodge D 937 429-5566
Beavercreek Township *(G-1267)*
Dave White Chevrolet Inc C 419 885-4444
Sylvania *(G-17581)*
Dcr Systems LLC E 440 205-9900
Mentor *(G-14167)*
Decosky Motor Holdings Inc E 740 397-9122
Mount Vernon *(G-14892)*
Delaware City School District E 740 363-5901
Delaware *(G-10087)*
Don Wood Bck Oldsmble Pntiac C D 740 593-6641
Athens *(G-783)*
Don Wood Inc D 740 593-6641
Athens *(G-784)*
Donnell Ford-Lincoln E 330 332-0031
Salem *(G-16694)*
Doug Bigelow Chevrolet Inc D 330 644-7500
Akron *(G-198)*
Doug Marine Motors Inc E 740 335-3700
Wshngtn CT Hs *(G-20020)*
Downtheroad Inc E 740 452-4579
Zanesville *(G-20469)*
Downtown Ford Lincoln Inc D 330 456-2781
Canton *(G-2344)*
Dunning Motor Sales Inc E 740 439-4465
Cambridge *(G-2110)*
Dutro Ford Lincoln-Mercury Inc D 740 452-6334
Zanesville *(G-20470)*
Ed Mullinax Ford LLC C 440 984-2431
Amherst *(G-591)*
Ed Schmidt Auto Inc C 419 874-4331
Perrysburg *(G-16001)*
Ed Tomko Chryslr Jep Dge Inc E 440 835-5900
Avon Lake *(G-929)*
Family Ford Lincoln Inc D 740 373-9127
Marietta *(G-13445)*
FCA US LLC E 419 727-2800
Toledo *(G-17881)*
Flagship Services of Ohio Inc D 740 533-1657
Ironton *(G-12289)*
Germain On Scarborough LLC C 614 868-0300
Columbus *(G-7748)*
Giles Marathon Inc E 440 974-8815
Mentor *(G-14180)*
Glenway Automotive Service E 513 921-2117
Cincinnati *(G-3679)*
Goodyear Tire & Rubber Company A 330 796-2121
Akron *(G-243)*
Greenwood Chevrolet Inc C 330 270-1299
Youngstown *(G-20209)*
Greenwoods Hubbard Chevy-Olds E 330 568-4335
Hubbard *(G-12087)*
Greg Ford Sweet Inc E 440 593-7714
North Kingsville *(G-15391)*
Grismer Tire Company E 937 643-2526
Centerville *(G-2678)*
Grogans Towne Chrysler Inc C 419 476-0761
Toledo *(G-17924)*
Guess Motors Inc E 866 890-0522
Carrollton *(G-2622)*
Haydocy Automotive Inc D 614 279-8880
Columbus *(G-7804)*
Hill Intl Trcks NA LLC D 330 386-6440
East Liverpool *(G-10522)*
Hoss Value Cars & Trucks Inc E 937 428-2400
Dayton *(G-9622)*
Irace Inc E 330 836-7247
Akron *(G-283)*
Jake Sweeney Automotive Inc C 513 782-2800
Cincinnati *(G-3859)*
Jeff Wyler Chevrolet Inc B 513 752-3447
Batavia *(G-1018)*
Jerry Haag Motors Inc E 937 402-2090
Hillsboro *(G-11984)*
Jim Brown Chevrolet Inc E 440 255-5511
Mentor *(G-14198)*

Employee Codes: A=Over 500 employees, B=251-500
C=101-250, D=51-100, E=25-50
2018 Harris Ohio
Services Directory
1401

AUTOMOTIVE & TRUCK GENERAL REPAIR SVC

SERVICES SECTION

Company	Col	Phone
Jim Keim Ford	D	614 888-3333
Columbus *(G-7941)*		
Joe Dodge Kidd Inc	E	513 752-1804
Cincinnati *(G-2921)*		
Joseph Chevrolet Oldsmobile Co	C	513 741-6700
Cincinnati *(G-3887)*		
Joseph Russo		440 748-2690
Grafton *(G-11441)*		
Jtekt Auto Tenn Morristown	C	440 835-1000
Westlake *(G-19503)*		
K & M Tire Inc	C	419 695-1061
Delphos *(G-10145)*		
Kempthorn Automall	C	330 456-8287
Canton *(G-2423)*		
Kempthorn Automall	D	800 451-3877
Canton *(G-2422)*		
Kennedy Mint Inc	D	440 572-3222
Cleveland *(G-5895)*		
Kent Automotive Inc		330 678-5520
Kent *(G-12377)*		
Kenworth of Cincinnati Inc	D	513 771-5831
Cincinnati *(G-3916)*		
Kerry Ford Inc	D	513 671-6400
Cincinnati *(G-3918)*		
Kings Toyota Inc	D	513 583-4333
Cincinnati *(G-3928)*		
Klaben Family Dodge Inc	E	330 673-9971
Kent *(G-12381)*		
Krieger Ford Inc	C	614 888-3320
Columbus *(G-8014)*		
Lakewood Chrysler-Plymouth	E	216 521-1000
Brookpark *(G-1950)*		
Lakota Bus Garage		419 986-5558
Kansas *(G-12347)*		
Lane Chevrolet	D	937 426-2313
Beavercreek Township *(G-1273)*		
Lang Chevrolet Co		937 426-2313
Beavercreek Township *(G-1274)*		
Lariche Subaru Inc	D	419 422-1855
Findlay *(G-11056)*		
Lavery Chevrolet-Buick Inc	E	330 823-1100
Alliance *(G-544)*		
Lebanon Chrysler - Plymouth Inc	E	513 932-2717
Lebanon *(G-12620)*		
Lebanon Ford Inc	D	513 932-1010
Lebanon *(G-12621)*		
Lima Auto Mall Inc	D	419 993-6000
Lima *(G-12816)*		
Lima City School District	E	419 996-3450
Lima *(G-12817)*		
Lincoln Mrcury Kings Auto Mall	C	513 683-3800
Cincinnati *(G-3984)*		
Lindsey Accura Inc	E	800 980-8199
Columbus *(G-8070)*		
Lower Great Lakes Kenworth Inc	E	419 874-3511
Perrysburg *(G-16029)*		
Madison Motor Service Inc	E	419 332-0727
Fremont *(G-11211)*		
Man-Tansky Inc	E	740 454-2512
Zanesville *(G-20499)*		
Mark Thomas Ford Inc	E	330 638-1010
Cortland *(G-9077)*		
Martin Chevrolet Inc	E	937 849-1381
New Carlisle *(G-15027)*		
Mathews Dodge Chrysler Jeep	E	740 389-2341
Marion *(G-13563)*		
Mathews Ford Inc	D	740 522-2181
Newark *(G-15202)*		
Mathews Kennedy Ford L-M Inc	D	740 387-3673
Marion *(G-13564)*		
Matia Motors Inc	E	440 365-7311
Elyria *(G-10650)*		
May Jim Auto Sales LLC	E	419 422-9797
Findlay *(G-11063)*		
Medina World Cars Inc	E	330 725-4901
Strongsville *(G-17493)*		
Mike Castrucci Ford	C	513 831-7010
Milford *(G-14541)*		
Monro Inc	D	440 835-2393
Westlake *(G-19517)*		
Montrose Ford Inc	D	330 666-0711
Fairlawn *(G-10966)*		
Morris Cadillac Buick GMC	D	440 327-4181
North Olmsted *(G-15432)*		
Mullinax East LLC	D	440 296-3020
Wickliffe *(G-19608)*		
Nassief Automotive Inc	E	440 997-5151
Austinburg *(G-865)*		
National Auto Experts LLC	E	440 274-5114
Strongsville *(G-17497)*		
Nick Mayer Lincoln-Mercury Inc	E	440 835-3700
Westlake *(G-19521)*		
Northern Automotive Inc	E	614 436-2001
Columbus *(G-8290)*		
Northgate Chrysler Jeep Inc	D	513 385-3900
Cincinnati *(G-4180)*		
Ohio Automobile Club		614 559-0000
Columbus *(G-8320)*		
Oregon Ford Inc	C	419 698-4444
Oregon *(G-15746)*		
OReilly Automotive Inc	E	937 660-3040
Germantown *(G-11399)*		
OReilly Automotive Inc	E	419 324-2077
Toledo *(G-18112)*		
OReilly Automotive Inc	E	740 845-1016
London *(G-13004)*		
OReilly Automotive Inc	E	614 444-5352
Columbus *(G-8480)*		
OReilly Automotive Inc	E	513 731-7700
Cincinnati *(G-4233)*		
OReilly Automotive Inc	E	330 267-4383
Hartville *(G-11828)*		
Palmer Trucks Inc	E	937 235-3318
Dayton *(G-9799)*		
Parrish Tire Company of Akron	E	330 628-6800
Mogadore *(G-14682)*		
Pep Boys - Manny Moe & Jack	E	614 864-2092
Columbus *(G-8534)*		
Pierson Automotive Inc	E	513 424-1881
Middletown *(G-14485)*		
Progrssive Oldsmobile Cadillac	E	330 833-8585
Massillon *(G-13845)*		
Ricart Ford Inc	B	614 836-5321
Groveport *(G-11667)*		
Ron Marhofer Automall Inc	E	330 923-5059
Cuyahoga Falls *(G-9217)*		
Rondy Fleet Services Inc	C	330 745-9016
Barberton *(G-977)*		
Roush Equipment Inc	C	614 882-1535
Westerville *(G-19442)*		
Rush Motor Sales Inc	E	614 471-9980
Columbus *(G-8659)*		
Rush Truck Centers Ohio Inc	D	513 733-8500
Cincinnati *(G-4458)*		
Rush Truck Centers Ohio Inc	E	419 224-6045
Lima *(G-12872)*		
Rush Truck Leasing Inc	E	614 876-3500
Columbus *(G-8660)*		
Schoner Chevrolet Inc	E	330 877-6731
Hartville *(G-11830)*		
Sharpnack Chevrolet Co	E	440 967-3144
Vermilion *(G-18716)*		
Sonic Automotive	D	614 870-8200
Columbus *(G-8748)*		
Specialized Services Inc	E	330 448-4035
Masury *(G-13868)*		
Spires Motors Inc	E	614 771-2345
Hilliard *(G-11953)*		
Spitzer Chevrolet Inc	D	330 467-4141
Northfield *(G-15524)*		
Spitzer Motor City Inc	E	567 307-7119
Ontario *(G-15716)*		
Spurlock Truck Service	E	937 268-6100
Dayton *(G-9900)*		
Stratton Chevrolet Co	E	330 537-3151
Beloit *(G-1432)*		
Sunnyside Toyota Inc	D	440 777-9911
North Olmsted *(G-15446)*		
Surfside Motors Inc	E	419 462-1746
Galion *(G-11306)*		
Tallmadge Board of Education	E	330 633-2215
Tallmadge *(G-17656)*		
Tansky Motors Inc	E	650 322-7069
Logan *(G-12989)*		
Taylor Chevrolet Inc	C	740 653-2091
Lancaster *(G-12579)*		
Trader Buds Westside Dodge	D	614 272-0000
Columbus *(G-8861)*		
Travelcenters of America LLC	D	330 769-2053
Lodi *(G-12966)*		
Trepanier Daniels & Trepanier	D	740 286-1288
Jackson *(G-12319)*		
United Parcel Service Inc OH	C	419 872-0211
Perrysburg *(G-16066)*		
Valentine Buick Gmc Inc	D	937 878-7371
Fairborn *(G-10808)*		
Vin Devers	C	888 847-9535
Sylvania *(G-17626)*		
Volvo BMW Dyton Evans Volkswag	E	937 890-6200
Dayton *(G-9975)*		
Voss Auto Network Inc	E	937 428-2447
Dayton *(G-9976)*		
Voss Toyota Inc	E	937 427-3700
Beavercreek *(G-1218)*		
Wagner Lincoln-Mercury Inc	E	419 435-8131
Carey *(G-2601)*		
Walker Auto Group Inc	D	937 433-4950
Miamisburg *(G-14367)*		
Warner Buick-Nissan Inc	E	419 423-7161
Findlay *(G-11099)*		
Young Truck Sales Inc	E	330 477-6271
Canton *(G-2592)*		
Youngstown-Kenworth Inc	E	330 534-9761
Hubbard *(G-12093)*		
Zanesville Chevrolet Cadillac	E	740 452-3611
Zanesville *(G-20554)*		
Zender Electric	E	419 436-1538
Fostoria *(G-11143)*		
Ziegler Tire and Supply Co	E	513 539-7574
Monroe *(G-14719)*		

AUTOMOTIVE BATTERIES WHOLESALERS

Company	Col	Phone
Hankook Tire America Corp	E	330 896-6199
Uniontown *(G-18523)*		
Harris Battery Company Inc	E	330 874-0205
Bolivar *(G-1748)*		

AUTOMOTIVE BODY SHOP

Company	Col	Phone
American Nat Fleet Svc Inc	D	216 447-6060
Cleveland *(G-5017)*		
Bakers Cllsion Repr Specialist	E	419 524-1350
Mansfield *(G-13263)*		
Bauman Chrysler Jeep Dodge	E	419 332-8291
Fremont *(G-11185)*		
Buddies Inc	E	216 642-3362
Cleveland *(G-5156)*		
Burtons Collision	E	513 984-3396
Cincinnati *(G-3154)*		
Busam Fairfield LLC	E	513 771-8100
Fairfield *(G-10825)*		
Carls Body Shop Inc	E	937 253-5166
Dayton *(G-9383)*		
Cincinnati Collision Center	E	513 984-4445
Blue Ash *(G-1555)*		
Coughlin Chevrolet Inc	E	740 852-1122
London *(G-12995)*		
Dave Dnnis Chrysler Jeep Dodge	D	937 429-5566
Beavercreek Township *(G-1267)*		
Dent Magic	E	614 864-3368
Columbus *(G-7507)*		
Don Tester Ford Lincoln Inc	E	419 668-8233
Norwalk *(G-15570)*		
Eastside Body Shop	E	513 624-1145
Cincinnati *(G-3538)*		
Excalibur Auto Body Inc	E	440 942-5550
Willowick *(G-19739)*		
Jake Sweeney Body Shop	E	513 782-1100
Cincinnati *(G-3860)*		
Jeff Wyler Ft Thomas Inc	D	513 752-7450
Cincinnati *(G-2919)*		
Joyce Buick Inc	E	419 529-3211
Ontario *(G-15696)*		
King Collision Inc	E	330 372-3242
Warren *(G-18870)*		
Kumler Collision Inc	E	740 653-4301
Lancaster *(G-12546)*		
Magic Industries Inc	E	614 759-8422
Columbus *(G-8097)*		
Maines Collision Repr & Bdy Sp	D	937 322-4618
Springfield *(G-17228)*		
Medina World Cars Inc	E	330 725-4901
Strongsville *(G-17493)*		
Mowerys Collision Inc	E	614 274-6072
Columbus *(G-8201)*		
Paul Hrnchar Ford-Mercury Inc	E	330 533-3673
Canfield *(G-2207)*		
Ron Marhofer Automall Inc	B	330 835-6707
Cuyahoga Falls *(G-9216)*		
Ron Marhofer Collision Center	E	330 686-2262
Stow *(G-17391)*		
St Clair Auto Body	E	216 531-7300
Cleveland *(G-6521)*		
Suburban Collision Centers	E	440 243-5533
Berea *(G-1470)*		
Target Auto Body Inc	E	216 391-1942
Cleveland *(G-6570)*		
Three C Body Shop Inc	D	614 274-9700
Columbus *(G-8842)*		
Voss Auto Network Inc	B	937 433-1444
Dayton *(G-9977)*		

SERVICES SECTION

AUTOMOTIVE PARTS, ACCESS & SPLYS

White Family Collision Center .... E 419 885-8885
 Sylvania *(G-17628)*

AUTOMOTIVE BODY, PAINT & INTERIOR REPAIR & MAINTENANCE SVC

Advantage Ford Lincoln Mercury .... E 419 334-9751
 Fremont *(G-11182)*
Arch Abraham Susuki Ltd .... E 440 934-6001
 Elyria *(G-10594)*
Bobbart Industries Inc .... E 419 350-5477
 Sylvania *(G-17576)*
Brown Motor Sales Co .... E 419 531-0151
 Toledo *(G-17785)*
Chesrown Oldsmobile GMC Inc .... E 614 846-3040
 Columbus *(G-7255)*
Coughlin Chevrolet Inc .... D 740 964-9191
 Pataskala *(G-15922)*
Coughlin Chevrolet Toyota Inc .... D 740 366-1381
 Newark *(G-15162)*
Dan Tobin Pontiac Buick GMC .... D 614 889-6300
 Columbus *(G-7484)*
Dave White Chevrolet Inc .... C 419 885-4444
 Sylvania *(G-17581)*
Donnell Ford-Lincoln .... E 330 332-0031
 Salem *(G-16694)*
Doug Bigelow Chevrolet Inc .... D 330 644-7500
 Akron *(G-198)*
Dutro Ford Lincoln-Mercury Inc .... D 740 452-6334
 Zanesville *(G-20470)*
Ed Mullinax Ford LLC .... C 440 984-2431
 Amherst *(G-591)*
Ed Schmidt Auto Inc .... E 419 874-4511
 Perrysburg *(G-16001)*
Family Ford Lincoln Inc .... D 740 373-9127
 Marietta *(G-13445)*
George P Ballas Buick GMC Trck .... E 419 535-1000
 Toledo *(G-17913)*
Grogans Towne Chrysler Inc .... C 419 476-0761
 Toledo *(G-17924)*
Haydocy Automotive Inc .... D 614 279-8880
 Columbus *(G-7804)*
Jake Sweeney Automotive Inc .... C 513 782-2800
 Cincinnati *(G-3859)*
Jeff Wyler Chevrolet Inc .... B 513 752-3447
 Batavia *(G-1018)*
Joe Dodge Kidd Inc .... E 513 752-1804
 Cincinnati *(G-2921)*
Joseph Chevrolet Oldsmobile Co .... C 513 741-6700
 Cincinnati *(G-3887)*
Kerry Ford Inc .... D 513 671-6400
 Cincinnati *(G-3918)*
Lang Chevrolet Co .... D 937 426-2313
 Beavercreek Township *(G-1274)*
Lavery Chevrolet-Buick Inc .... E 330 823-1100
 Alliance *(G-544)*
Leikin Motor Companies Inc .... D 440 946-6900
 Willoughby *(G-19686)*
Lima Auto Mall Inc .... D 419 993-6000
 Lima *(G-12816)*
Mark Thomas Ford Inc .... E 330 638-1010
 Cortland *(G-9077)*
Mathews Kennedy Ford L-M Inc .... D 740 387-3673
 Marion *(G-13564)*
Matia Motors Inc .... E 440 365-7311
 Elyria *(G-10650)*
Mike Castrucci Ford .... C 513 831-7010
 Milford *(G-14541)*
Montrose Ford Inc .... D 330 666-0711
 Fairlawn *(G-10966)*
Mullinax East LLC .... D 440 296-3020
 Wickliffe *(G-19608)*
Oregon Ford Inc .... E 419 698-4444
 Oregon *(G-15746)*
Pierson Automotive Inc .... E 513 424-1881
 Middletown *(G-14485)*
Ron Marhofer Automall Inc .... E 330 923-5059
 Cuyahoga Falls *(G-9217)*
Roush Equipment Inc .... C 614 882-1535
 Westerville *(G-19442)*
Sharpnack Chevrolet Co .... E 440 967-3144
 Vermilion *(G-18716)*
Sonic Automotive-1495 Automall .... E 614 317-4326
 Columbus *(G-8749)*
Sunnyside Toyota Inc .... D 440 777-9911
 North Olmsted *(G-15446)*
Surfside Motors Inc .... E 419 462-1746
 Galion *(G-11306)*
Tansky Motors Inc .... E 650 322-7069
 Logan *(G-12989)*
Walker Auto Group Inc .... D 937 433-4950
 Miamisburg *(G-14367)*
Warner Buick-Nissan Inc .... E 419 423-7161
 Findlay *(G-11099)*

AUTOMOTIVE BRAKE REPAIR SHOPS

Bridgestone Ret Operations LLC .... E 330 929-3391
 Cuyahoga Falls *(G-9167)*
Monro Inc .... D 614 360-3883
 Columbus *(G-8185)*
Monro Muffler Brake Inc .... D 937 999-3202
 Springboro *(G-17130)*

AUTOMOTIVE COLLISION SHOPS

Auto Body North Inc .... E 614 436-3700
 Columbus *(G-7076)*
Downtown Ford Lincoln Inc .... D 330 456-2781
 Canton *(G-2344)*
King Collision .... E 330 729-0525
 Youngstown *(G-20247)*
Lennys Auto Sales Inc .... E 330 848-2993
 Barberton *(G-970)*
Sharpnack Chvrlet Bick Cdillac .... D 419 935-0194
 Willard *(G-19626)*
Tallmadge Collision Center .... E 330 630-2188
 Tallmadge *(G-17657)*
True2form Collision Repair Ctr .... E 330 399-6659
 Warren *(G-18907)*

AUTOMOTIVE CUSTOMIZING SVCS, NONFACTORY BASIS

Auto Additions Inc .... E 614 899-9100
 Westerville *(G-19369)*
Transitworks LLC .... D 330 861-1118
 Akron *(G-480)*

AUTOMOTIVE DEALERS, NEC

Lindsey Accura Inc .... E 800 980-8199
 Columbus *(G-8070)*

AUTOMOTIVE EMISSIONS TESTING SVCS

Air Compliance Testing Inc .... E 216 525-0900
 Cleveland *(G-4972)*
Envirotest Systems Corp .... E 330 963-4464
 Twinsburg *(G-18409)*
Envirotest Systems Corp .... E 330 963-4464
 Berea *(G-1456)*
Envirotest Systems Corp .... E 330 963-4464
 Cleveland *(G-5545)*
Envirotest Systems Corp .... E 330 963-4464
 Kent *(G-12368)*
Envirotest Systems Corp .... E 330 963-4464
 Elyria *(G-10629)*
Envirotest Systems Corp .... E 330 963-4464
 Cleveland *(G-5546)*
Envirotest Systems Corp .... E 330 963-4464
 Chagrin Falls *(G-2716)*
Envirotest Systems Corp .... E 330 963-4464
 Painesville *(G-15855)*
Envirotest Systems Corp .... E 330 963-4464
 Medina *(G-14063)*
Envirotest Systems Corp .... E 330 963-4464
 Chardon *(G-2749)*
Envirotest Systems Corp .... E 330 963-4464
 Amherst *(G-593)*
Envirotest Systems Corp .... E 330 963-4464
 Spencer *(G-17105)*
Envirotest Systems Corp .... E 330 963-4464
 Twinsburg *(G-18410)*

AUTOMOTIVE GLASS REPLACEMENT SHOPS

Advanced Auto Glass Inc .... E 412 373-6675
 Akron *(G-21)*
Belletech Corp .... D 937 599-3774
 Bellefontaine *(G-1378)*
C-Auto Glass Inc .... E 216 351-2193
 Cleveland *(G-5169)*
Mels Auto Glass Inc .... E 513 563-7771
 Cincinnati *(G-4054)*
Pgw Auto Glass LLC .... E 419 993-2421
 Lima *(G-12859)*
Ryans All-Glass Incorporated .... E 513 771-4440
 Cincinnati *(G-4461)*
Safelite Fulfillment Inc .... E 614 781-5449
 Columbus *(G-8670)*
Safelite Fulfillment Inc .... E 216 475-7781
 Cleveland *(G-6435)*
Safelite Glass Corp .... E 614 431-4936
 Worthington *(G-19995)*
Safelite Group Inc .... A 614 210-9000
 Columbus *(G-8672)*
Techna Glass Inc .... E 513 685-3800
 Milford *(G-14566)*
Wiechart Enterprises Inc .... E 419 227-0027
 Lima *(G-12921)*

AUTOMOTIVE LETTERING & PAINTING SVCS

Sharonville Car Wash .... E 513 769-4219
 Cincinnati *(G-4509)*

AUTOMOTIVE PAINT SHOP

American Bulk Commodities Inc .... C 330 758-0841
 Youngstown *(G-20103)*
Decorative Paint Incorporated .... D 419 485-0632
 Montpelier *(G-14743)*
Jim Brown Chevrolet Inc .... E 440 255-5511
 Mentor *(G-14198)*
Merrick Body Shop .... E 440 243-6700
 Berea *(G-1463)*
Precision Coatings Systems .... E 937 642-4727
 Marysville *(G-13645)*
Three C Body Shop Inc .... E 614 885-0900
 Columbus *(G-8843)*

AUTOMOTIVE PARTS, ACCESS & SPLYS

Accel Performance Group LLC .... C 216 658-6413
 Independence *(G-12177)*
Alex Products Inc .... C 419 399-4500
 Paulding *(G-15927)*
Amsted Industries Incorporated .... C 614 836-2323
 Groveport *(G-11622)*
Atlas Industries Inc .... B 419 637-2117
 Tiffin *(G-17671)*
Bobbart Industries Inc .... E 419 350-5477
 Sylvania *(G-17576)*
Buyers Products Company .... C 440 974-8888
 Mentor *(G-14152)*
Comprehensive Logistics Co Inc .... E 330 793-0504
 Youngstown *(G-20158)*
Doug Marine Motors Inc .... E 740 335-3700
 Wshngtn CT Hs *(G-20020)*
Falls Stamping & Welding Co .... C 330 928-1191
 Cuyahoga Falls *(G-9185)*
Federal-Mogul LLC .... C 740 432-2393
 Cambridge *(G-2113)*
Ftech R&D North America Inc .... D 937 339-2777
 Troy *(G-18354)*
Hendrickson International Corp .... D 740 929-5600
 Hebron *(G-11849)*
Hi-Tek Manufacturing Inc .... C 513 459-1094
 Mason *(G-13717)*
Honda of America Mfg Inc .... C 937 644-0724
 Marysville *(G-13626)*
Industry Products Co .... B 937 778-0585
 Piqua *(G-16150)*
Ishikawa Gasket America Inc .... C 419 353-7300
 Bowling Green *(G-1783)*
Jeff Wyler Chevrolet Inc .... B 513 752-3447
 Batavia *(G-1018)*
Joseph Industries Inc .... D 330 528-0091
 Streetsboro *(G-17418)*
Leadec Corp .... E 513 731-3590
 Blue Ash *(G-1627)*
Marmon Highway Tech LLC .... E 330 878-5595
 Dover *(G-10197)*
Ohio Auto Supply Company .... E 330 454-5105
 Canton *(G-2478)*
Parker-Hannifin Corporation .... A 216 531-3000
 Cleveland *(G-6241)*
Pioneer Automotive Tech Inc .... C 937 746-2293
 Springboro *(G-17136)*
Sanoh America Inc .... C 740 392-9200
 Mount Vernon *(G-14922)*
Thyssenkrupp Bilstein Amer Inc .... E 513 881-7600
 West Chester *(G-19162)*
Toledo Molding & Die Inc .... D 419 692-6022
 Delphos *(G-10152)*
Unison Industries LLC .... B 937 426-0621
 Dayton *(G-9285)*
US Tsubaki Power Transm LLC .... C 419 626-4560
 Sandusky *(G-16807)*
Venco Venturo Industries LLC .... E 513 772-8448
 Cincinnati *(G-4806)*

AUTOMOTIVE PARTS, ACCESS & SPLYS — SERVICES SECTION

Western Branch Diesel Inc .... E 330 454-8800
  Canton (G-2585)

AUTOMOTIVE PRDTS: Rubber

Myers Industries Inc .... E 330 253-5592
  Akron (G-348)

AUTOMOTIVE RADIATOR REPAIR SHOPS

Perkins Motor Service Ltd .... E 440 277-1256
  Lorain (G-13071)

AUTOMOTIVE REPAIR SHOPS: Brake Repair

Tuffy Associates Corp .... E 419 865-6900
  Toledo (G-18264)

AUTOMOTIVE REPAIR SHOPS: Diesel Engine Repair

Columbus Diesel Supply Co Inc .... E 614 445-8391
  Reynoldsburg (G-16439)
Cummins Inc .... E 614 771-1000
  Hilliard (G-11894)
Skinner Diesel Services Inc .... E 614 491-8785
  Columbus (G-8741)
W W Williams Company LLC .... E 419 837-5067
  Perrysburg (G-16070)
W W Williams Company LLC .... D 614 228-5000
  Columbus (G-8959)
W W Williams Company LLC .... E 330 225-7751
  Brunswick (G-1995)

AUTOMOTIVE REPAIR SHOPS: Electrical Svcs

Reliability First Corporation .... E 216 503-0600
  Cleveland (G-6371)
Rubini Enterprises Inc .... E 419 729-7010
  Toledo (G-18166)

AUTOMOTIVE REPAIR SHOPS: Engine Repair, Exc Diesel

Columbus Col-Weld Corporation .... E 614 276-5303
  Columbus (G-7341)

AUTOMOTIVE REPAIR SHOPS: Frame & Front End Repair Svcs

Burtons Collision .... E 513 984-3396
  Cincinnati (G-3154)

AUTOMOTIVE REPAIR SHOPS: Frame Repair Shops

Three C Body Shop Inc .... D 614 274-9700
  Columbus (G-8842)

AUTOMOTIVE REPAIR SHOPS: Machine Shop

Carroll Halliday Inc .... E 740 335-1670
  Wshngtn CT Hs (G-20014)
RL Best Company .... E 330 758-8601
  Boardman (G-1744)

AUTOMOTIVE REPAIR SHOPS: Muffler Shop, Sale/Rpr/Installation

Dayton-Dixie Mufflers Inc .... E 419 243-7281
  Toledo (G-17846)
Monro Inc .... D 440 835-2393
  Westlake (G-19517)
Tuffy Associates Corp .... E 419 865-6900
  Toledo (G-18264)

AUTOMOTIVE REPAIR SHOPS: Rebuilding & Retreading Tires

Grismer Tire Company .... E 937 643-2526
  Centerville (G-2678)
K S Bandag Inc .... E 330 264-9237
  Wooster (G-19876)

AUTOMOTIVE REPAIR SHOPS: Tire Recapping

Best One Tire & Svc Lima Inc .... E 419 229-2380
  Lima (G-12746)

Central Ohio Bandag LP .... E 740 454-9728
  Zanesville (G-20460)
H & H Retreading Inc .... D 740 682-7721
  Oak Hill (G-15618)

AUTOMOTIVE REPAIR SHOPS: Trailer Repair

Bbt Fleet Services LLC .... E 419 462-7722
  Mansfield (G-13264)
Capitol City Trailers Inc .... D 614 491-2616
  Obetz (G-15664)
Double A Trailer Sales Inc .... E 419 692-7626
  Delphos (G-10142)
Hans Truck and Trlr Repr Inc .... E 216 581-0046
  Cleveland (G-5724)
Heritage Truck Equipment Inc .... E 330 699-4491
  Akron (G-262)
Jones Truck & Spring Repr Inc .... D 614 443-4619
  Columbus (G-7949)
Mac Trailer Manufacturing Inc .... C 330 823-9900
  Alliance (G-547)
Mac Trailer Service Inc .... E 330 823-9190
  Alliance (G-548)
Marmon Highway Tech LLC .... E 330 878-5595
  Dover (G-10197)
Nelson Manufacturing Company .... D 419 523-5321
  Ottawa (G-15799)
Stoops Frghtlnr-Qlity Trlr Inc .... E 937 236-4092
  Dayton (G-9909)
Transport Services Inc .... E 440 582-4900
  Cleveland (G-6612)

AUTOMOTIVE REPAIR SHOPS: Truck Engine Repair, Exc Indl

Allied Truck Parts Co .... E 330 477-8127
  Canton (G-2234)
Carl E Oeder Sons Sand & Grav .... E 513 494-1555
  Lebanon (G-12594)
Hartwig Transit Inc .... E 513 563-1765
  Cincinnati (G-3740)
Hy-Tek Material Handling Inc .... D 614 497-2500
  Columbus (G-7873)
J D S Leasing Inc .... E 440 236-6575
  Columbia Station (G-6847)
Kaffenbarger Truck Eqp Co .... E 513 772-6800
  Cincinnati (G-3900)
Kirk NationaLease Co .... E 937 498-1151
  Sidney (G-16939)
Loves Travel Stops .... E 419 643-8482
  Beaverdam (G-1290)
Maines Collision Repr & Bdy Sp .... D 937 322-4618
  Springfield (G-17228)
Midway Garage Inc .... E 740 345-0699
  Newark (G-15207)
Mizar Motors Inc .... D 419 729-2400
  Toledo (G-18065)
Newtown Nine Inc .... E 330 376-7741
  Akron (G-351)
Rubini Enterprises Inc .... E 419 729-7010
  Toledo (G-18166)
Scotts Towing Co .... E 419 729-7888
  Toledo (G-18176)
Steubenville Truck Center Inc .... E 740 282-2711
  Steubenville (G-17337)

AUTOMOTIVE REPAIR SHOPS: Turbocharger & Blower Repair

Star Leasing Co .... D 614 278-9999
  Columbus (G-8776)

AUTOMOTIVE REPAIR SHOPS: Wheel Alignment

Speck Sales Incorporated .... E 419 353-8312
  Bowling Green (G-1794)

AUTOMOTIVE REPAIR SVC

Beechmont Motors Inc .... E 513 388-3883
  Cincinnati (G-3089)
Beechmont Toyota Inc .... D 513 388-3800
  Cincinnati (G-3092)
Broad & James Inc .... E 614 231-8697
  Columbus (G-7146)
Coates Car Care Inc .... E 330 652-4180
  Niles (G-15289)
East Manufacturing Corporation .... B 330 325-9921
  Randolph (G-16372)

First Services Inc .... A 513 241-2200
  Cincinnati (G-3619)
First Transit Inc .... B 513 241-2200
  Cincinnati (G-3624)
Fleetpride West Inc .... E 419 243-3161
  Toledo (G-17895)
Fred Martin Nissan LLC .... E 330 644-8888
  Akron (G-229)
Germain Ford LLC .... C 614 889-7777
  Columbus (G-7747)
Goodyear Tire & Rubber Company .... A 330 796-2121
  Akron (G-243)
Haasz Automall LLC .... E 330 296-2866
  Ravenna (G-16387)
Irace Inc .... E 330 836-7247
  Akron (G-283)
Jeff Wyler Chevrolet Inc .... B 513 752-3447
  Batavia (G-1018)
Kings Cove Automotive LLC .... D 513 677-0177
  Fairfield (G-10870)
Montrose Sheffield LLC .... E 440 934-6699
  Sheffield Village (G-16892)
Paul Hrnchar Ford-Mercury Inc .... E 330 533-3673
  Canfield (G-2207)
S&S Car Care Inc .... E 330 494-9535
  Canton (G-2521)
Sanoh America Inc .... C 740 392-9200
  Mount Vernon (G-14922)
Spitzer Chevrolet Inc .... E 330 467-4141
  Northfield (G-15524)
United Garage & Service Corp .... D 216 623-1550
  Cleveland (G-6639)

AUTOMOTIVE REPAIR SVCS, MISCELLANEOUS

County of Stark .... E 330 477-3609
  Massillon (G-13799)
St Marys City Board Education .... E 419 394-1116
  Saint Marys (G-16684)

AUTOMOTIVE RUSTPROOFING & UNDERCOATING SHOPS

Buddies Inc .... E 216 642-3362
  Cleveland (G-5156)
Dave Marshall Inc .... D 937 878-9135
  Fairborn (G-10790)

AUTOMOTIVE SPLYS & PARTS, NEW, WHOL: Auto Servicing Eqpt

Columbus Public School Dst .... C 614 365-5263
  Columbus (G-7376)

AUTOMOTIVE SPLYS & PARTS, NEW, WHOL: Testing Eqpt, Electric

Nu-Di Products Co Inc .... D 216 251-9070
  Cleveland (G-6170)

AUTOMOTIVE SPLYS & PARTS, NEW, WHOLESALE: Bumpers

Durable Corporation .... D 800 537-1603
  Norwalk (G-15571)

AUTOMOTIVE SPLYS & PARTS, NEW, WHOLESALE: Engines/Eng Parts

Auto Aftermarket Concepts .... E 513 942-2535
  Cincinnati (G-3065)
Cadna Rubber Company Inc .... E 901 566-9090
  Fairlawn (G-10940)
Interstate Diesel Service Inc .... C 216 881-0015
  Cleveland (G-5834)
Keihin Thermal Tech Amer Inc .... B 740 869-3000
  Mount Sterling (G-14873)

AUTOMOTIVE SPLYS & PARTS, NEW, WHOLESALE: Seat Covers

Jim Hayden Inc .... D 513 563-8828
  Cincinnati (G-3873)

AUTOMOTIVE SPLYS & PARTS, NEW, WHOLESALE: Splys

Advance Stores Company Inc .... C 740 369-4491
  Delaware (G-10067)

SERVICES SECTION

AUTOMOTIVE SVCS, EXC REPAIR & CARWASHES: Maintenance

Company	Code	Phone
Automotive Distributors Co Inc — Akron (G-85)	E	330 785-7290
Bills Battery Company Inc — Cincinnati (G-3108)	E	513 922-0100
Car Parts Warehouse Inc — Brookpark (G-1937)	E	216 281-4500
Finishmaster Inc — Columbus (G-7657)	D	614 228-4328
General Parts Inc — Columbus (G-7734)	E	614 267-5197
Winston Products LLC — Cleveland (G-6754)	D	440 478-1418

AUTOMOTIVE SPLYS & PARTS, NEW, WHOLESALE: Tools & Eqpt

Company	Code	Phone
Cornwell Quality Tools Company — Wadsworth (G-18751)	E	330 335-2933
Matco Tools Corporation — Stow (G-17382)	B	330 929-4949
Myers Industries Inc — Akron (G-348)	E	330 253-5592

AUTOMOTIVE SPLYS & PARTS, NEW, WHOLESALE: Trailer Parts

Company	Code	Phone
Frontier Tank Center Inc — Richfield (G-16510)	E	330 659-3888
Transport Services Inc — Cleveland (G-6612)	E	440 582-4900

AUTOMOTIVE SPLYS & PARTS, NEW, WHOLESALE: Wheels

Company	Code	Phone
Herbert E Orr Company — Paulding (G-15931)	C	419 399-4866
Rocknstarr Holdings LLC — Youngstown (G-20354)	E	330 509-9086

AUTOMOTIVE SPLYS & PARTS, USED, WHOLESALE

Company	Code	Phone
G-Cor Automotive Corp — Columbus (G-7721)	E	614 443-6735
Greenleaf Ohio LLC — Massillon (G-13815)	E	330 832-6001
Myers Bus Parts and Sups Co — Canfield (G-2202)	E	330 533-2275

AUTOMOTIVE SPLYS & PARTS, USED, WHOLESALE: Dry Cell Batt

Company	Code	Phone
Bob Sumerel Tire Co Inc — Columbus (G-7122)	E	614 527-9700

AUTOMOTIVE SPLYS & PARTS, WHOLESALE, NEC

Company	Code	Phone
Accel Performance Group LLC — Independence (G-12177)	C	216 658-6413
Advance Auto Parts Inc — Chardon (G-2738)	E	440 226-3150
Alex Products Inc — Paulding (G-15927)	C	419 399-4500
Atlas Industries Inc — Tiffin (G-17671)	B	419 637-2117
Automotive Distributors Co Inc — Columbus (G-7077)	D	614 476-1315
Automotive Distributors Co Inc — Cleveland (G-5083)	E	216 398-2014
Bendix Coml Vhcl Systems LLC — Elyria (G-10597)	B	440 329-9000
Bridgeport Auto Parts Inc — Bridgeport (G-1860)	E	740 635-0441
Brookville Roadster Inc — Brookville (G-1961)	E	937 833-4605
Building 8 Inc — Cincinnati (G-3148)	E	513 771-8000
Car Parts Warehouse Inc — Perry (G-15959)	E	440 259-2991
Columbus Diesel Supply Co Inc — Reynoldsburg (G-16439)	E	614 445-8391
Crown Dielectric Inds Inc — Columbus (G-7467)	C	614 224-5161
D-G Custom Chrome LLC — Cincinnati (G-3457)	E	513 531-1881
Dana Heavy Vehicle Systems — Holland (G-12018)	D	419 866-3900
Denso International Amer Inc — Hillsboro (G-11972)	B	937 393-6800
Fayette Parts Service Inc — Steubenville (G-17316)	C	740 282-4547
Four Wheel Drive Hardware LLC — Columbiana (G-6859)	C	330 482-4733
Freudenberg-Nok General Partnr — Milan (G-14494)	B	419 499-2502
G-Cor Automotive Corp — Columbus (G-7721)	E	614 443-6735
General Parts Inc — Brunswick (G-1980)	D	330 220-6500
Genuine Parts Company — Columbus (G-7740)	B	614 766-6865
Greenleaf Auto Recyclers LLC — Massillon (G-13814)	E	330 832-6001
H & H Auto Parts Inc — Canton (G-2386)	D	330 456-4778
H & H Auto Parts Inc — Canton (G-2387)	E	330 494-2975
Hahn Automotive Warehouse Inc — Dayton (G-9597)	E	937 223-1068
Hamilton Automotive Warehouse — Hamilton (G-11738)	D	513 896-4000
Hamilton Automotive Warehouse — Hamilton (G-11739)	D	513 896-4100
Hebco Products Inc — Bucyrus (G-2039)	A	419 562-7987
Hite Parts Exchange Inc — Columbus (G-7842)	E	614 272-5115
Honda Trading America Corp — Marysville (G-13627)	C	937 644-8004
Ieh Auto Parts LLC — Marietta (G-13454)	E	740 373-8327
Ieh Auto Parts LLC — Caldwell (G-2086)	E	740 732-2395
Ieh Auto Parts LLC — Marietta (G-13455)	E	740 373-8151
Jegs Automotive Inc — Delaware (G-10110)	C	614 294-5050
Joseph Russo — Grafton (G-11441)	E	440 748-2690
K - O - I Warehouse Inc — Springfield (G-17218)	E	937 323-5585
K - O - I Warehouse Inc — Cincinnati (G-3896)	E	513 357-2400
Kar Products — Cleveland (G-5884)	A	216 416-7200
Kenton Auto and Truck Wrecking — Kenton (G-12420)	E	419 673-8234
Keystone Automotive Inds Inc — Cincinnati (G-3920)	D	513 961-5500
KOI Enterprises Inc — Cincinnati (G-3939)	E	513 357-2400
McBee Supply Corporation — Cleveland (G-6001)	D	216 881-0015
MJ Auto Parts Inc — Mentor (G-14221)	E	440 205-6272
National Marketshare Group — Cincinnati (G-4140)	E	513 921-0800
Ohashi Technica USA Inc — Sunbury (G-17560)	E	740 965-5115
Ohio Auto Supply Company — Canton (G-2478)	E	330 454-5105
OReilly Automotive Inc — North Canton (G-15360)	D	330 494-0042
OReilly Automotive Inc — Bryan (G-2015)	E	419 630-0811
OReilly Automotive Inc — Boardman (G-1742)	E	330 318-3136
Par International Inc — Obetz (G-15669)	E	614 529-1300
Pat Young Service Co Inc — Cleveland (G-6250)	E	216 447-8550
R L Morrissey & Assoc Inc — Solon (G-17044)	E	440 498 3730
Rubini Enterprises Inc — Toledo (G-18166)	E	419 729-7010
Shiloh Manufacturing LLC — Valley City (G-18624)	E	330 558-2693
Smyth Automotive Inc — Cincinnati (G-4543)	D	513 528-2800
Smyth Automotive Inc — Cincinnati (G-4544)	D	513 528-0061
Smyth Automotive Inc — West Chester (G-19157)	E	513 777-6400
Snyders Antique Auto Parts Inc — New Springfield (G-15131)	E	330 549-5313
Stellar Srkg Acquisition LLC — Seville (G-16847)	E	330 769-8484
Stoddard Imported Cars Inc — Mentor (G-14245)	D	440 951-1040
Thyssenkrupp Bilstein Amer Inc — West Chester (G-19162)	E	513 881-7600
Turbo Parts LLC — Marion (G-13587)	E	740 223-1695
Ventra Salem LLC — Salem (G-16718)	A	330 337-8002
W W Williams Company LLC — Perrysburg (G-16070)	E	419 837-5067
Whites Service Center Inc — Urbana (G-18602)	E	937 653-5279
World Auto Parts Inc — Cleveland (G-6758)	E	216 781-8418

AUTOMOTIVE SPLYS, USED, WHOLESALE & RETAIL

Company	Code	Phone
Lkq Triplettasap Inc — Akron (G-323)	C	330 733-6333
Speedie Auto Salvage Ltd — Dover (G-10215)	E	330 878-9961
Stricker Bros Inc — Batavia (G-1026)	E	513 732-1152

AUTOMOTIVE SPLYS/PART, NEW, WHOL: Spring, Shock Absorb/Strut

Company	Code	Phone
Thyssenkrupp Bilstein Amer Inc — Hamilton (G-11778)	C	513 881-7600

AUTOMOTIVE SPLYS/PARTS, NEW, WHOL: Body Rpr/Paint Shop Splys

Company	Code	Phone
G & C Finishes From The Future — Dayton (G-9567)	E	937 890-3002
Klase Enterprises Inc — Canton (G-2427)	E	330 452-6300

AUTOMOTIVE SVCS, EXC REPAIR & CARWASHES: Customizing

Company	Code	Phone
AGC Automotive Americas — Bellefontaine (G-1375)	D	937 599-3131
Auto Concepts Cincinnatti LLC — Cincinnati (G-3067)	E	513 769-4540
Cresttek LLC — Dublin (G-10313)	E	248 602-2083

AUTOMOTIVE SVCS, EXC REPAIR & CARWASHES: Insp & Diagnostic

Company	Code	Phone
SGS North America Inc — Cincinnati (G-4507)	E	513 674-7048

AUTOMOTIVE SVCS, EXC REPAIR & CARWASHES: Lubrication

Company	Code	Phone
Coates Car Care Inc — Niles (G-15289)	E	330 652-4180
Reladyne LLC — Cincinnati (G-4402)	E	513 489-6000
Yund Inc — Massillon (G-13864)	E	330 837-9358

AUTOMOTIVE SVCS, EXC REPAIR & CARWASHES: Maintenance

Company	Code	Phone
AAA Ohio Auto Club — Worthington (G-19937)	D	614 431-7800
Auto Warehousing Co Inc — Warren (G-18820)	E	330 824-5149
Cintas Corporation No 1 — Mason (G-13678)	A	513 459-1200
Cleveland Pick-A-Part Inc — Columbia Station (G-6843)	E	440 236-5031
Dealer Supply and Eqp Ltd — Toledo (G-17847)	E	419 724-8473
Delphi Automotive Systems LLC — Warren (G-18848)	E	248 724-5953
Eaton Corporation — Beachwood (G-1074)	B	440 523-5000
Fayette Parts Service Inc — Wintersville (G-19810)	C	724 880-3616
First Vehicle Services Inc — Cincinnati (G-3625)	C	513 241-2200
Herrnstein Chrysler Inc — Chillicothe (G-2846)	D	740 773-2203
Industrial Sorting Svcs Inc — Cincinnati (G-3817)	E	513 772-6501
Pete Baur Buick Gmc Inc — Cleveland (G-6270)	E	440 238-5600

AUTOMOTIVE SVCS, EXC REPAIR & CARWASHES: Maintenance

Quest Quality Services LLC .... D 419 704-7407
  Maumee (G-13965)
Sears Roebuck and Co .... C 614 797-2095
  Columbus (G-6906)
Sears Roebuck and Co .... E 937 427-8528
  Beavercreek (G-1207)
Sears Roebuck and Co .... D 419 226-4172
  Lima (G-12874)
Sears Roebuck and Co .... D 614 760-7195
  Dublin (G-10450)
Sears Roebuck and Co .... C 330 652-5128
  Niles (G-15304)
Sears Roebuck and Co .... C 440 846-3595
  Cleveland (G-6459)
Valvoline Instant Oil Change .... E 937 548-0123
  Greenville (G-11522)
Valvoline LLC .... D 513 557-3100
  Cincinnati (G-4802)

AUTOMOTIVE SVCS, EXC REPAIR & CARWASHES: Road Svc

Van Wert County Engineers .... E 419 238-0210
  Van Wert (G-18648)

AUTOMOTIVE SVCS, EXC REPAIR: Carwash, Automatic

Allied Car Wash Inc .... E 513 559-1733
  Cincinnati (G-2990)
Elliott Auto Bath Inc .... E 513 422-3700
  Middletown (G-14425)
Expresso Car Wash Systems Inc .... E 419 866-7099
  Toledo (G-17873)
Falls Supersonic Car Wash Inc .... E 330 928-1657
  Cuyahoga Falls (G-9186)
JKL Development Company .... E 937 390-0358
  Springfield (G-17217)
North Lima Dairy Queen Inc .... E 330 549-3220
  North Lima (G-15406)
Robert Stough Ventures Corp .... E 419 882-4073
  Toledo (G-18162)
Royal Car Wash Inc .... E 513 385-2777
  Cincinnati (G-4448)
Royal Sheen Service Center .... E 330 966-7200
  Canton (G-2517)

AUTOMOTIVE SVCS, EXC REPAIR: Carwash, Self-Service

Coates Car Care Inc .... E 330 652-4180
  Niles (G-15289)

AUTOMOTIVE SVCS, EXC REPAIR: Truck Wash

Blue Beacon of Hubbard Inc .... E 330 534-4419
  Hubbard (G-12082)
Blue Beacon USA LP II .... E 330 534-4419
  Hubbard (G-12083)
Blue Beacon USA LP II .... E 419 643-8146
  Beaverdam (G-1289)
Blue Beacon USA LP II .... E 937 437-5533
  New Paris (G-15075)
Truckomat Corporation .... E 740 467-2818
  Hebron (G-11861)

AUTOMOTIVE SVCS, EXC REPAIR: Washing & Polishing

3 B Ventures LLC .... E 419 236-9461
  Lima (G-12729)
Car Wash .... E 216 662-6289
  Cleveland (G-5179)
Expresso Car Wash Systems Inc .... D 419 536-7540
  Toledo (G-17872)
John Atwood Inc .... E 440 777-4147
  North Olmsted (G-15428)
Johnnys Carwash .... D 513 474-6603
  Cincinnati (G-3879)
Klean A Kar Inc .... E 614 221-3145
  Columbus (G-7996)
Mikes Carwash Inc .... C 513 677-4700
  Loveland (G-13146)
Moo Moo North Hamilton LLC .... E 614 751-9274
  Etna (G-10730)
Mr Magic Carnegie Inc .... E 440 461-7572
  Beachwood (G-1105)
Napoleon Wash-N-Fill Inc .... C 419 422-7216
  Findlay (G-11068)

Red Carpet Car Wash Inc .... E 330 477-5772
  Canton (G-2504)
Sharonville Car Wash .... E 513 769-4219
  Cincinnati (G-4509)
Waterway Gas & Wash Company .... E 330 995-2900
  Aurora (G-864)
Yund Inc .... E 330 837-9358
  Massillon (G-13864)

AUTOMOTIVE SVCS, EXC RPR/CARWASHES: High Perf Auto Rpr/Svc

Chesrown Oldsmobile Cadillac .... E 740 366-7373
  Granville (G-11461)
Steve Austin Auto Group .... E 937 592-3015
  Bellefontaine (G-1399)

AUTOMOTIVE TOWING & WRECKING SVC

Atlas Towing Service .... E 513 451-1854
  Cincinnati (G-3060)
G&M Towing and Recovery LLC .... E 216 271-0581
  Cleveland (G-5649)
Precision Coatings Systems .... E 937 642-4727
  Marysville (G-13645)
Pro-Tow Inc .... E 614 444-8697
  Columbus (G-8564)
Scotts Towing Co .... E 419 729-7888
  Toledo (G-18176)
Star Leasing Co .... D 614 278-9999
  Columbus (G-8776)
World Trck Towing Recovery Inc .... E 330 723-1116
  Seville (G-16848)

AUTOMOTIVE TOWING SVCS

Abers Garage Inc .... E 419 281-5500
  Ashland (G-649)
Arlington Towing Inc .... E 614 488-2006
  Columbus (G-7043)
B & D Auto & Towing Inc .... C 440 237-3737
  North Royalton (G-15481)
Beaverdam Fleet Services Inc .... E 419 643-8880
  Beaverdam (G-1288)
Broad & James Inc .... E 614 231-8697
  Columbus (G-7146)
Charlie Towing Service Inc .... E 440 234-5300
  Berea (G-1450)
Dutys Towing .... E 614 252-3336
  Columbus (G-7553)
Eastland Crane Service Inc .... E 614 868-9750
  Columbus (G-7565)
Eitel Towing Service Inc .... E 614 877-4139
  Orient (G-15760)
Genicon Inc .... E 419 491-4478
  Swanton (G-17565)
Jo Lynn Inc .... D 419 994-3204
  Loudonville (G-13092)
Madison Motor Service Inc .... E 419 332-0727
  Fremont (G-11211)
Maines Collision Repr & Bdy Sp .... D 937 322-4618
  Springfield (G-17228)
Richs Towing & Service Inc .... E 440 234-3435
  Middleburg Heights (G-14385)
Rustys Towing Service Inc .... D 614 491-6288
  Columbus (G-8661)
Sandys Auto & Truck Svc Inc .... D 937 461-4980
  Moraine (G-14823)
Sandys Towing .... E 937 461-4980
  Moraine (G-14824)
Shamrock Towing Inc .... E 614 882-3555
  Westerville (G-19352)
Southwood Auto Sales .... E 330 788-8822
  Youngstown (G-20378)
Sprandel Enterprises Inc .... E 513 777-6622
  West Chester (G-19158)
Spurlock Truck Service .... E 937 268-6100
  Dayton (G-9900)
Steve S Towing and Recovery .... E 513 422-0254
  Middletown (G-14462)

AUTOMOTIVE TRANSMISSION REPAIR SVC

Luk Transmission System LLC .... E 330 464-4184
  Wooster (G-19885)
Ohio Transmission Corporation .... E 614 342-6247
  Columbus (G-8452)
W W Williams Company LLC .... D 614 228-5000
  Columbus (G-8959)
W W Williams Company LLC .... E 330 225-7751
  Brunswick (G-1995)

AUTOMOTIVE UPHOLSTERY SHOPS

Kallas Enterprises Inc .... E 330 253-6893
  Akron (G-300)

AUTOMOTIVE WELDING SVCS

Brown Industrial Inc .... E 937 693-3838
  Botkins (G-1752)
Industry Products Co .... B 937 778-0585
  Piqua (G-16150)
Perkins Motor Service Ltd .... E 440 277-1256
  Lorain (G-13071)
R K Industries Inc .... D 419 523-5001
  Ottawa (G-15804)
Rose City Manufacturing Inc .... D 937 325-5561
  Springfield (G-17268)
Turn-Key Industrial Svcs LLC .... D 614 274-1128
  Columbus (G-8878)

AUTOMOTIVE: Seat Frames, Metal

Alex Products Inc .... E 419 399-4500
  Paulding (G-15927)
Systems Jay LLC Nanogate .... B 419 747-4161
  Mansfield (G-13370)

AVIATION PROPELLER & BLADE REPAIR SVCS

Standrdaero Component Svcs Inc .... A 513 618-9588
  Cincinnati (G-4581)

AVIATION SCHOOL

Jet Mintenance Consulting Corp .... E 937 205-2406
  Wilmington (G-19764)

BABYSITTING BUREAU

Carol Scudere .... E 614 839-4357
  New Albany (G-14979)
Jack & Jill Babysitting Svc .... E 513 731-5261
  Cincinnati (G-3853)

BADGES, WHOLESALE

Raco Industries LLC .... D 513 984-2101
  Blue Ash (G-1672)

BAGS: Plastic

Dayton Industrial Drum Inc .... E 937 253-8933
  Dayton (G-9263)

BAGS: Plastic, Made From Purchased Materials

Ampac Holdings LLC .... A 513 671-1777
  Cincinnati (G-3017)
Atlapac Corp .... D 614 252-2121
  Columbus (G-7067)

BAGS: Shopping, Made From Purchased Materials

Ampac Holdings LLC .... A 513 671-1777
  Cincinnati (G-3017)

BAIL BONDING SVCS

A-1 Bail Bonds Inc .... E 937 372-2400
  Xenia (G-20039)

BAKERIES, COMMERCIAL: On Premises Baking Only

Amish Door Inc .... B 330 359-5464
  Wilmot (G-19797)
Buns of Delaware Inc .... E 740 363-2867
  Delaware (G-10075)
Klosterman Baking Co .... D 513 242-1004
  Cincinnati (G-3933)
Kroger Co .... C 740 335-4030
  Wshngtn CT Hs (G-20028)
Mustard Seed Health Fd Mkt Inc .... E 440 519-3663
  Solon (G-17031)
Schwebel Baking Company .... C 440 248-1500
  Solon (G-17049)
Thurns Bakery & Deli .... E 614 221-9246
  Columbus (G-8844)
White Castle System Inc .... B 614 228-5781
  Columbus (G-8986)

SERVICES SECTION

BAKERIES: On Premises Baking & Consumption

Company	Code	Phone
Aladdins Baking Company Inc	E	216 861-0317
Cleveland (G-4981)		
Buns of Delaware Inc	E	740 363-2867
Delaware (G-10075)		
Mapleside Valley LLC	C	330 225-5576
Brunswick (G-1987)		
Michaels Bakery Inc	E	216 351-7530
Cleveland (G-6048)		
Mocha House Inc	E	330 392-3020
Warren (G-18882)		
Servatii Inc	D	513 271-5040
Cincinnati (G-4500)		
Thurns Bakery & Deli	E	614 221-9246
Columbus (G-8844)		
Troyers Home Pantry	E	330 698-4182
Apple Creek (G-627)		

BAKERY PRDTS: Cookies & crackers

Company	Code	Phone
Norcia Bakery	E	330 454-1077
Canton (G-2474)		

BAKERY PRDTS: Wholesalers

Company	Code	Phone
Aladdins Baking Company Inc	E	216 861-0317
Cleveland (G-4981)		
Alfred Nickles Bakery Inc	E	419 332-6418
Fremont (G-11183)		
Alfred Nickles Bakery Inc	D	330 628-9964
Mogadore (G-14669)		
Bagel Place Inc	E	419 885-1000
Toledo (G-17762)		
Bimbo Bakeries Usa Inc	E	614 868-7565
Columbus (G-7110)		
Bimbo Bakeries Usa Inc	E	740 446-4552
Gallipolis (G-11309)		
Busken Bakery Inc	D	513 871-2114
Cincinnati (G-3157)		
Dutchman Hospitality Group Inc	C	614 873-3414
Plain City (G-16189)		
Interbake Foods LLC	C	614 294-4931
Columbus (G-7913)		
Interbake Foods LLC	A	614 294-4931
Columbus (G-7914)		
Klosterman Baking Co	D	513 242-1004
Cincinnati (G-3933)		
Made From Scratch Inc	E	614 873-3344
Plain City (G-16197)		
Michaels Bakery Inc	E	216 351-7530
Cleveland (G-6048)		
Michaels Gourmet Catering	E	419 698-2988
Toledo (G-18060)		
P&S Bakery Inc	E	330 707-4141
Youngstown (G-20312)		
Skallys Old World Bakery Inc	E	513 931-1411
Cincinnati (G-4537)		
Thurns Bakery & Deli	E	614 221-9246
Columbus (G-8844)		
Troyers Home Pantry	E	330 698-4182
Apple Creek (G-627)		

BAKERY: Wholesale Or Wholesale & Retail Combined

Company	Code	Phone
Calvary Christian Ch of Ohio	E	740 828-9000
Frazeysburg (G-11174)		
Norcia Bakery	E	330 454-1077
Canton (G-2474)		

BAKING PAN GLAZING & CLEANING SVCS

Company	Code	Phone
Cmbb LLC	C	937 652-2151
Urbana (G-18581)		
Russell T Bundy Associates Inc	D	937 652-2151
Urbana (G-18600)		

BALLET PRODUCTION SVCS

Company	Code	Phone
Ballet Metropolitan Inc	C	614 229-4860
Columbus (G-7088)		
Ohio Chamber Ballet	E	330 972-7900
Akron (G-363)		

BANKS: Commercial, NEC

Company	Code	Phone
Croghan Bancshares Inc	D	419 794-9399
Maumee (G-13902)		
Farm Credit Mid-America	E	740 441-9312
Albany (G-519)		
First Merchants Bank	E	614 486-9000
Columbus (G-7666)		
FNB Corporation	D	330 425-1818
Twinsburg (G-18416)		
Huntington Insurance Inc	E	419 429-4627
Findlay (G-11048)		
Huntington National Bank	C	513 762-1860
Cincinnati (G-3799)		
Huntington National Bank	E	330 742-7013
Youngstown (G-20224)		
Huntington National Bank	E	330 343-6611
Dover (G-10193)		
Huntington National Bank	E	740 773-2681
Chillicothe (G-2852)		
Huntington National Bank	E	614 480-4293
Columbus (G-7869)		
Huntington National Bank	E	740 452-8444
Zanesville (G-20489)		
Huntington National Bank	B	614 480-4293
Columbus (G-7870)		
Huntington National Bank	E	740 695-3323
Saint Clairsville (G-16638)		
Huntington National Bank	E	419 226-8200
Lima (G-12801)		
Huntington National Bank	E	216 515-6401
Cleveland (G-5792)		
Huntington National Bank	E	419 782-5050
Defiance (G-10035)		
Jpmorgan Chase Bank Nat Assn	E	614 759-8955
Reynoldsburg (G-16460)		
Jpmorgan Chase Bank Nat Assn	E	740 382-7362
Marion (G-13544)		
Jpmorgan Chase Bank Nat Assn	E	440 277-1038
Lorain (G-13044)		
MB Financial Inc	D	937 283-2027
Wilmington (G-19772)		
PNC Bank National Association	C	330 742-4426
Youngstown (G-20327)		
PNC Bank National Association	C	330 562-9700
Aurora (G-850)		
PNC Bank National Association	C	330 854-0974
Canal Fulton (G-2145)		
Raymond James Fincl Svcs Inc	E	419 586-5121
Celina (G-2661)		
Republic Bank	B	513 793-7666
Blue Ash (G-1680)		
UBS Financial Services Inc	E	440 414-2740
Westlake (G-19558)		
Wesbanco Inc	E	614 208-7298
Columbus (G-8979)		
Westfield Bank Fsb	E	800 368-8930
Westfield Center (G-19453)		

BANKS: Federal Reserve

Company	Code	Phone
Federal Rsrve Bnk of Cleveland	A	216 579-2000
Cleveland (G-5583)		

BANKS: Federal Reserve Branches

Company	Code	Phone
Federal Rsrve Bnk of Cleveland	C	513 721-4787
Cincinnati (G-3599)		

BANKS: Mortgage & Loan

Company	Code	Phone
Amerifirst Financial Corp	D	216 452-5120
Lakewood (G-12470)		
Chase Manhattan Mortgage Corp	A	614 422-6900
Columbus (G-7254)		
Fairway Independent Mrtg Corp	E	614 930-6552
Columbus (G-7632)		
Farm Credit Mid-America	E	740 441-9312
Albany (G-519)		
Fifth Third Bank	D	513 579-5203
Cincinnati (G-3608)		
Fifth Third Bank of Sthrn OH	E	937 840-5353
Hillsboro (G-11974)		
First Day Fincl Federal Cr Un	E	937 222-4546
Dayton (G-9548)		
First Federal Bank of Midwest	E	419 695-1055
Delphos (G-16114)		
First Ohio Banc & Lending Inc	B	216 642-8900
Cleveland (G-5599)		
First Ohio Home Finance Inc	E	937 322-3396
Springfield (G-17199)		
FNB Corporation	D	330 721-7484
Medina (G-14066)		
FNB Corporation	D	330 425-1818
Twinsburg (G-18416)		
Liberty Mortgage Company Inc	E	614 224-4000
Columbus (G-8057)		
M/I Financial LLC	D	614 418-8650
Columbus (G-8094)		
M/I Homes Inc	B	614 418-8000
Columbus (G-8095)		
MB Financial Inc	D	937 283-2027
Wilmington (G-19772)		
National City Mortgage Inc	A	937 910-1200
Miamisburg (G-14325)		
Pgim Inc	E	419 331-6604
Lima (G-12858)		
Precision Funding Corp	E	330 405-1313
Twinsburg (G-18455)		
Sunrise Mortgage Services Inc	D	614 989-5412
Gahanna (G-11271)		
Vinton County Nat Bnk McArthur	E	740 596-2525
Mc Arthur (G-14019)		
Wells Fargo Home Mortgage Inc	E	614 781-8847
Dublin (G-10490)		

BANKS: National Commercial

Company	Code	Phone
Century National Bank	E	800 548-3557
Zanesville (G-20462)		
Champaign National Bank Urbana	E	614 798-1321
Dublin (G-10287)		
Chase Equipment Finance Inc	C	800 678-2601
Columbus (G-6876)		
Citizens Bank National Assn	D	330 580-1913
Canton (G-2310)		
Citizens Nat Bnk of Bluffton	E	419 358-8040
Bluffton (G-1730)		
Citizens Nat Bnk of Bluffton	E	419 224-0400
Lima (G-12753)		
Citizens Nat Bnk Urbana Ohio	E	937 653-1200
Urbana (G-18580)		
Citizens National Bank	E	740 472-1696
Woodsfield (G-19813)		
Civista Bank	E	419 744-3100
Norwalk (G-15564)		
Colonial Banc Corp	E	937 456-5544
Eaton (G-10554)		
Consumers National Bank	E	330 868-7701
Minerva (G-14644)		
Credit First NA	C	216 362-5000
Brookpark (G-1941)		
Croghan Bancshares Inc	D	419 794-9399
Maumee (G-13902)		
Eastern Ohio P-16	E	330 675-7623
Warren (G-18854)		
Fairfield National Bank	E	740 653-7242
Lancaster (G-12538)		
Farmers Nat Bnk of Canfield	C	330 533-3341
Canfield (G-2190)		
Farmers National Bank	D	330 544-7447
Niles (G-15293)		
Farmers National Bank	E	330 682-1010
Orrville (G-15771)		
Farmers National Bank	D	330 682-1030
Orrville (G-15772)		
Fifth Third Bank	C	513 574-4457
Cincinnati (G-3606)		
Fifth Third Bank of NW Ohio	B	419 259-7820
Toledo (G-17887)		
First Capital Bancshares Inc	D	740 775-6777
Chillicothe (G-2839)		
First Citizens Nat Bnk Inc	E	419 294-2351
Upper Sandusky (G-18561)		
First Financial Bancorp	C	513 551-5640
Cincinnati (G-3615)		
First Financial Bank	E	513 979-5800
Cincinnati (G-3616)		
First Nat Bnk of Nelsonville	E	740 753-1941
Nelsonville (G-14963)		
First National Bank Bellevue	E	419 483-7340
Bellevue (G-1410)		
First National Bank of Pandora	E	419 384-3221
Pandora (G-15890)		
First National Bank of Waverly	E	740 947-2136
Waverly (G-18971)		
First National Bank of Waverly	E	740 493-3372
Piketon (G-16114)		
First National Bank PA	E	330 747-0292
Youngstown (G-20189)		
First National Bnk of Dennison	E	740 922-2532
Dennison (G-10163)		
FNB Corporation	E	440 439-2200
Cleveland (G-5610)		
FNB Corporation	D	330 425-1818
Twinsburg (G-18416)		
Futura Banc Corp	D	937 653-1167
Urbana (G-18588)		

Employee Codes: A=Over 500 employees, B=251-500 C=101-250, D=51-100, E=25-50

BANKS: National Commercial

Greenville National Bank .... E 937 548-1114
  Greenville (G-11506)
Huntington Bancshares Inc .... C 614 480-8300
  Columbus (G-7865)
Huntington National Bank .... A 330 996-6300
  Akron (G-273)
Huntington National Bank .... A 330 384-7201
  Akron (G-274)
Huntington National Bank .... E 330 384-7092
  Akron (G-275)
Huntington National Bank .... E 216 621-1717
  Cleveland (G-5791)
Huntington National Bank .... D 614 480-8300
  Columbus (G-7871)
Huntington National Bank .... E 330 343-6611
  Dover (G-10193)
Huntington National Bank .... E 740 452-8444
  Zanesville (G-20489)
Huntington National Bank .... C 513 762-1860
  Cincinnati (G-3799)
Huntington National Bank .... E 740 773-2681
  Chillicothe (G-2852)
Huntington National Bank .... E 419 226-8200
  Lima (G-12801)
Huntington Technology Finance .... B 614 480-5169
  Columbus (G-7872)
Icx Corporation .... E 330 656-3611
  Cleveland (G-5800)
Jpmorgan Chase Bank Nat Assn .... E 614 876-7650
  Hilliard (G-11917)
Jpmorgan Chase Bank Nat Assn .... E 614 248-2410
  Reynoldsburg (G-16461)
Jpmorgan Chase Bank Nat Assn .... E 614 794-7398
  Westerville (G-19413)
Jpmorgan Chase Bank Nat Assn .... E 614 476-1910
  Columbus (G-7952)
Jpmorgan Chase Bank Nat Assn .... E 513 221-1040
  Cincinnati (G-3890)
Jpmorgan Chase Bank Nat Assn .... E 513 826-2317
  Blue Ash (G-1621)
Jpmorgan Chase Bank Nat Assn .... E 419 358-4055
  Bluffton (G-1733)
Jpmorgan Chase Bank Nat Assn .... E 216 781-2127
  Columbus (G-7953)
Jpmorgan Chase Bank Nat Assn .... E 614 248-5391
  Columbus (G-7954)
Jpmorgan Chase Bank Nat Assn .... E 513 985-5120
  Cincinnati (G-3891)
Jpmorgan Chase Bank Nat Assn .... E 513 784-0770
  Cincinnati (G-3892)
Jpmorgan Chase Bank Nat Assn .... A 740 363-8032
  Delaware (G-10112)
Jpmorgan Chase Bank Nat Assn .... E 330 364-7242
  New Philadelphia (G-15104)
Jpmorgan Chase Bank Nat Assn .... E 419 394-2358
  Saint Marys (G-16678)
Jpmorgan Chase Bank Nat Assn .... E 419 294-4944
  Upper Sandusky (G-18562)
Jpmorgan Chase Bank Nat Assn .... E 740 676-2671
  Bellaire (G-1366)
Jpmorgan Chase Bank Nat Assn .... E 330 972-1905
  Cuyahoga Falls (G-9198)
Jpmorgan Chase Bank Nat Assn .... E 513 985-5350
  Milford (G-14529)
Jpmorgan Chase Bank Nat Assn .... E 513 595-6450
  Cincinnati (G-3893)
Jpmorgan Chase Bank Nat Assn .... E 440 442-7800
  Cleveland (G-5873)
Jpmorgan Chase Bank Nat Assn .... E 330 972-1735
  New Franklin (G-15045)
Jpmorgan Chase Bank Nat Assn .... E 330 287-5101
  Wooster (G-19874)
Jpmorgan Chase Bank Nat Assn .... E 330 650-0476
  Hudson (G-12126)
Jpmorgan Chase Bank Nat Assn .... E 440 352-5491
  Perry (G-15961)
Jpmorgan Chase Bank Nat Assn .... E 419 424-7570
  Findlay (G-11052)
Jpmorgan Chase Bank Nat Assn .... A 937 534-8218
  Dayton (G-9646)
Jpmorgan Chase Bank Nat Assn .... E 330 225-1330
  Brunswick (G-1984)
Jpmorgan Chase Bank Nat Assn .... E 330 325-7855
  Randolph (G-16373)
Jpmorgan Chase Bank Nat Assn .... E 330 287-5101
  Wooster (G-19875)
Jpmorgan Chase Bank Nat Assn .... E 419 946-3015
  Mount Gilead (G-14854)
Jpmorgan Chase Bank Nat Assn .... E 419 586-6668
  Celina (G-2648)
Jpmorgan Chase Bank Nat Assn .... B 440 352-5969
  Painesville (G-15859)
Jpmorgan Chase Bank Nat Assn .... E 330 545-2551
  Girard (G-11416)
Jpmorgan Chase Bank Nat Assn .... E 440 286-6111
  Chardon (G-2753)
Jpmorgan Chase Bank Nat Assn .... E 330 972-1915
  Akron (G-298)
Jpmorgan Chase Bank Nat Assn .... E 330 759-1750
  Youngstown (G-20242)
Jpmorgan Chase Bank Nat Assn .... E 419 424-7512
  Findlay (G-11053)
Jpmorgan Chase Bank Nat Assn .... D 614 248-5800
  Westerville (G-19414)
Jpmorgan Chase Bank Nat Assn .... E 614 920-4182
  Canal Winchester (G-2161)
Jpmorgan Chase Bank Nat Assn .... E 614 834-3120
  Pickerington (G-16098)
Jpmorgan Chase Bank Nat Assn .... E 614 853-2999
  Galloway (G-11344)
Jpmorgan Chase Bank Nat Assn .... E 614 248-3315
  Powell (G-16340)
Jpmorgan Chase Bank Nat Assn .... E 740 657-8906
  Lewis Center (G-12690)
Jpmorgan Chase Bank Nat Assn .... E 216 524-0600
  Seven Hills (G-16831)
Jpmorgan Chase Bank Nat Assn .... E 740 374-2263
  Marietta (G-13459)
Jpmorgan Chase Bank Nat Assn .... E 614 248-7505
  Westerville (G-19415)
Jpmorgan Chase Bank Nat Assn .... C 614 248-5800
  Westerville (G-19416)
Jpmorgan Chase Bank Nat Assn .... E 419 739-3600
  Wapakoneta (G-18800)
Jpmorgan Chase Bank Nat Assn .... E 330 722-6626
  Medina (G-14087)
Jpmorgan Chase Bank Nat Assn .... E 614 248-2083
  Columbus (G-7956)
Jpmorgan Chase Bank Nat Assn .... E 216 781-4437
  Cleveland (G-5874)
Jpmorgan Chase Bank Nat Assn .... E 614 759-8955
  Reynoldsburg (G-16460)
Keybanc Capital Markets Inc .... B 800 553-2240
  Cleveland (G-5898)
Keybank National Association .... B 800 539-2968
  Cleveland (G-5899)
Kingston National Bank Inc .... E 740 642-2191
  Kingston (G-12451)
Lcnb National Bank .... D 513 932-1414
  Lebanon (G-12618)
Lcnb National Bank .... D 937 456-5544
  Eaton (G-10565)
Merchants National Bank .... E 937 393-1134
  Hillsboro (G-11987)
Merrill Lynch Business .... E 513 791-5700
  Blue Ash (G-1642)
National City Mortgage .... E 614 401-5030
  Dublin (G-10404)
Northwest Bank .... B 330 342-4018
  Hudson (G-12137)
Pandora Bancshares Inc .... E 419 384-3221
  Pandora (G-15893)
Park National Bank .... C 740 349-8451
  Newark (G-15225)
Park National Bank .... E 614 228-0063
  Columbus (G-8515)
Peoples Bancorp Inc .... E 740 373-3155
  Marietta (G-13484)
Peoples Bank .... E 937 748-0067
  Springboro (G-17134)
Peoples Bank .... E 740 286-6773
  Wellston (G-19005)
Peoples Bank .... C 937 382-1441
  Wilmington (G-19778)
Peoples Bank National Assn .... E 937 746-5733
  Franklin (G-11163)
PNC Banc Corp Ohio .... E 513 651-8738
  Cincinnati (G-4307)
PNC Bank National Association .... C 330 375-8342
  Akron (G-394)
PNC Bank National Association .... E 740 349-8431
  Newark (G-15228)
PNC Bank National Association .... E 419 621-2930
  Sandusky (G-16785)
PNC Bank National Association .... B 419 259-5466
  Toledo (G-18129)
PNC Bank National Association .... C 330 742-4426
  Youngstown (G-20327)
PNC Bank National Association .... C 330 562-9700
  Aurora (G-850)
Riverhills Bank .... E 513 553-6700
  Milford (G-14557)
Second National Bank .... E 937 548-2122
  Greenville (G-11519)
Standing Stone National Bank .... E 740 653-5115
  Lancaster (G-12577)
State Bank and Trust Company .... E 419 485-5521
  Montpelier (G-14748)
The First Central National Bnk .... E 937 663-4186
  Saint Paris (G-16686)
The Liberty Nat Bankof Ada .... E 419 673-1217
  Kenton (G-12424)
United Bank National Assn .... E 419 562-3040
  Bucyrus (G-2049)
US Bank National Association .... A 513 632-4234
  Cincinnati (G-4792)
US Bank National Association .... E 740 353-4151
  Portsmouth (G-16318)
US Bank National Association .... A 513 979-1000
  Cincinnati (G-4793)
US Bank National Association .... E 513 458-2844
  Cincinnati (G-4794)
US Bank National Association .... D 937 873-7845
  Fairborn (G-10807)
US Bank National Association .... E 937 335-8351
  Troy (G-18384)
US Bank National Association .... E 937 498-1131
  Sidney (G-16958)
Wells Fargo Bank National Assn .... D 513 424-6640
  Middletown (G-14470)

BANKS: State Commercial

Andover Bancorp Inc .... E 440 293-7605
  Andover (G-609)
Apple Creek Banking Co (inc) .... E 330 698-2631
  Apple Creek (G-623)
Citizens Bnk of Logan Ohio Inc .... E 740 380-2561
  Logan (G-12970)
Civista Bank .... E 419 744-3100
  Norwalk (G-15564)
CNB Bank .... D 419 562-7040
  Bucyrus (G-2030)
Commercial Svgs Bank Millersbu .... E 330 674-9015
  Millersburg (G-14595)
Consumers Bancorp Inc .... C 330 868-7701
  Minerva (G-14643)
Crogan Colonial Bank .... E 419 483-2541
  Bellevue (G-1407)
CSB Bancorp Inc .... E 330 674-9015
  Millersburg (G-14602)
Farmers Citizens Bank .... E 419 562-7040
  Bucyrus (G-2037)
Farmers National Bank .... D 330 544-7447
  Niles (G-15293)
Federal Home Ln Bnk Cincinnati .... D 513 852-5719
  Cincinnati (G-3597)
First Commonwealth Bank .... E 740 548-3340
  Delaware (G-10094)
First Federal Bank of Midwest .... E 419 695-1055
  Delphos (G-10143)
First Financial Bank .... C 877 322-9530
  Cincinnati (G-3617)
First National Bank PA .... E 330 747-0292
  Youngstown (G-20189)
First State Bank .... E 937 695-0331
  Winchester (G-19801)
Fort Jennings State Bank .... E 419 286-2527
  Fort Jennings (G-11108)
Henry County Bank .... E 419 599-1065
  Napoleon (G-14942)
Huntington National Bank .... E 330 742-7013
  Youngstown (G-20224)
Huntington National Bank .... E 740 695-3323
  Saint Clairsville (G-16638)
Huntington National Bank .... E 419 782-5050
  Defiance (G-10035)
Independence Bank .... E 216 447-1444
  Cleveland (G-5809)
Jpmorgan Chase Bank Nat Assn .... A 614 436-3055
  Columbus (G-6888)
Jpmorgan Chase Bank Nat Assn .... E 614 759-8955
  Reynoldsburg (G-16460)
Keybank National Association .... B 800 539-2968
  Cleveland (G-5899)
North Valley Bank .... E 740 452-7920
  Zanesville (G-20518)
Northwest Ohio Chapter Cfma .... E 419 891-1040
  Maumee (G-13950)
Ohio Valley Bank Company .... C 740 446-2631
  Gallipolis (G-11331)

SERVICES SECTION

BEAUTY SALONS

Ohio Valley Bank Company .... E 740 446-2631		
Gallipolis (G-11333)		
Park National Bank .... C 740 349-8451		
Newark (G-15226)		
Park National Bank .... E 937 324-6800		
Springfield (G-17258)		
Portage Community Bank Inc .... D 330 296-8090		
Ravenna (G-16397)		
Savings Bank .... E 740 474-3191		
Circleville (G-4903)		
The Liberty Nat Bankof Ada .... E 419 673-1217		
Kenton (G-12424)		
The Middlefield Banking Co .... E 440 632-1666		
Middlefield (G-14403)		
The Peoples Bank Co Inc .... E 419 678-2385		
Coldwater (G-6836)		
Unified Bank .... E 740 633-0445		
Martins Ferry (G-13602)		
Union Bank Company .... E 740 387-2265		
Marion (G-13588)		
Wesbanco Inc .... E 740 532-0263		
Ironton (G-12304)		
Wesbanco Bank Inc .... D 740 425-1927		
Barnesville (G-992)		

BANQUET HALL FACILITIES

A Tara Tiffanys Property .... E 330 448-0778
   Brookfield (G-1896)
Assembly Center .... E 800 582-1099
   Monroe (G-14687)
Banquets Unlimited .... E 859 689-4000
   Cincinnati (G-3075)
Brown Derby Roadhouse .... E 330 528-3227
   Hudson (G-12105)
Buffalo Jacks .... E 937 473-2524
   Covington (G-9136)
Buns of Delaware Inc .... E 740 363-2867
   Delaware (G-10075)
Carrie Cerino Restaurants Inc .... C 440 237-3434
   Cleveland (G-5186)
Cheers Chalet .... E 740 654-9036
   Lancaster (G-12516)
City Life Inc .... E 216 523-5899
   Cleveland (G-5246)
City of Beavercreek .... D 937 320-0742
   Beavercreek (G-1161)
City of Centerville .... D 937 438-3585
   Dayton (G-9409)
City of Vandalia .... E 937 890-1300
   Vandalia (G-18674)
Cleveland Metroparks .... C 216 661-6500
   Cleveland (G-5326)
Connor Concepts Inc .... D 937 291-1661
   Dayton (G-9423)
Coshocton Village Inn Suites .... E 740 622-9455
   Coshocton (G-9098)
Davis Catering Inc .... D 513 241-3464
   Cincinnati (G-3464)
De Lucas Place In Park .... D 440 233-7272
   Lorain (G-13035)
Deyor Performing Arts Center .... E 330 744-4269
   Youngstown (G-20168)
Dinos Catering Inc .... E 440 943-1010
   Wickliffe (G-19593)
Farm Inc .... E 513 922-7020
   Cincinnati (G-3592)
Findlay Inn & Conference Ctr .... D 419 422-5682
   Findlay (G-11027)
German Family Society Inc .... E 330 678-8229
   Kent (G-12371)
Grandview Ht Ltd Partnr Ohio .... D 937 766-5519
   Springfield (G-17203)
Guys Party Center .... E 330 724-6373
   Akron (G-249)
Haribol Haribol Ino .... E 330 339-7731
   New Philadelphia (G-15099)
Heatherwoode Golf Course .... C 937 748-3222
   Springboro (G-17122)
Iacominis Papa Joes Inc .... E 330 923-7999
   Akron (G-276)
Kinane Inc .... E 513 459-0177
   Mason (G-13727)
Kitchen Katering Inc .... E 216 481-8080
   Euclid (G-10766)
Kohler Foods Inc .... E 937 291-3600
   Dayton (G-9665)
La Villa Cnference Banquet Ctr .... E 216 265-9305
   Cleveland (G-5915)
Lees Roby Inc .... E 330 872-0983
   Newton Falls (G-15276)

Leos La Piazza Inc .... E 937 339-5553
   Troy (G-18361)
Little Miami River Catering Co .... E 937 848-2464
   Bellbrook (G-1372)
Lorain Party Center .... E 440 282-5599
   Lorain (G-13057)
Mackil Inc .... E 937 833-3310
   Brookville (G-1964)
Makoy Center Inc .... E 614 777-1211
   Hilliard (G-11924)
Mandalay Inc .... E 937 294-6600
   Moraine (G-14799)
Mason Family Resorts LLC .... B 513 339-0141
   Mason (G-13736)
Michaels Inc .... D 440 357-0384
   Mentor (G-14217)
Mocha House Inc .... E 330 392-3020
   Warren (G-18882)
Monaco Palace Inc .... E 614 475-4817
   Newark (G-15210)
Mustard Seed Health Fd Mkt Inc ...... E 440 519-3663
   Solon (G-17031)
New Jersey Aquarium LLC .... D 614 414-7300
   Columbus (G-8273)
Occasions Party Centre .... E 330 882-5113
   New Franklin (G-15046)
Old Barn Out Back Inc .... D 419 999-3989
   Lima (G-12848)
Pines Golf Club .... E 330 684-1414
   Orrville (G-15783)
Raymond Recepton House .... E 614 276-6127
   Columbus (G-8589)
Refectory Restaurant Inc .... E 614 451-9774
   Columbus (G-8602)
Riverside Cmnty Urban Redev .... C 330 929-3000
   Cuyahoga Falls (G-9215)
Roscoe Village Foundation .... D 740 622-2222
   Coshocton (G-9116)
Sam BS Restaurant .... E 419 353-2277
   Bowling Green (G-1793)
Sauder Village .... B 419 446-2541
   Archbold (G-644)
Snpj Recreation Farm .... E 440 256-3423
   Willoughby (G-19715)
Spagnas .... E 740 376-9245
   Marietta (G-13501)
The Oaks Lodge .... E 330 769-2601
   Chippewa Lake (G-2899)
Toris Station .... E 513 829-7815
   Fairfield (G-10915)
Twin Haven Reception Hall .... E 330 425-1616
   Twinsburg (G-18480)
Valley Hospitality Inc .... E 740 374-9660
   Marietta (G-13513)
Villa Milano Inc .... E 614 882-2058
   Columbus (G-8941)
Vulcan Machinery Corporation .... E 330 376-6025
   Akron (G-500)
William Royce Inc .... D 513 771-3361
   Cincinnati (G-4850)
Winking Lizard Inc .... D 330 467-1002
   Peninsula (G-15954)
Winking Lizard Inc .... D 330 220-9944
   Brunswick (G-1998)

BAR

Bass Lake Tavern Inc .... D 440 285-3100
   Chardon (G-2741)
Bpo Elks of USA .... E 740 622-0794
   Coshocton (G-9089)
Brothers Properties Corp .... C 513 381-3000
   Cincinnati (G-3141)
Elms Country Club Inc .... E 330 833-2668
   North Lawrence (G-15392)
Hyatt Corporation .... B 614 463-1234
   Columbus (G-7874)
Louisville Frternal Order of E .... E 330 875-2113
   Louisville (G-13102)
Loyal Oak Golf Course Inc .... E 330 825-2904
   Barberton (G-971)
Mohawk Golf Club .... E 419 447-5876
   Tiffin (G-17687)
OBannon Creek Golf Club .... E 513 683-5657
   Loveland (G-13151)
Springfield Country Club Co .... E 937 399-4215
   Springfield (G-17280)
Waterfront & Associates Inc .... B 859 581-1414
   Cincinnati (G-4824)

BARBER SHOPS

Attractions .... E 740 592-5600
   Athens (G-778)
Head Quarters Inc .... E 440 233-8508
   Lorain (G-13041)
Lucas Metropolitan Hsing Auth .... D 419 259-9457
   Toledo (G-18018)
Mfh Inc .... E 937 435-4701
   Dayton (G-9723)
Ricks Hair Center .... E 330 545-5120
   Girard (G-11425)
Ulta Beauty Inc .... E 513 752-1472
   Cincinnati (G-2937)
Ulta Beauty Inc .... D 419 621-1345
   Sandusky (G-16804)

BARGES BUILDING & REPAIR

McGinnis Inc .... C 740 377-4391
   South Point (G-17092)
McNational Inc .... E 740 377-4391
   South Point (G-17093)
Superior Marine Ways Inc .... C 740 894-6224
   Proctorville (G-16361)

BARS: Concrete Reinforcing, Fabricated Steel

Gateway Concrete Forming Svcs .... D 513 353-2000
   Miamitown (G-14371)
Ohio Bridge Corporation .... C 740 432-6334
   Cambridge (G-2125)
Smith Brothers Erection Inc .... E 740 373-3575
   Marietta (G-13500)

BASKETS, WHOLESALE

Potter Inc .... E 419 636-5624
   Bryan (G-2017)

BATTERY CHARGERS

TL Industries Inc .... C 419 666-8144
   Northwood (G-15547)

BATTERY REPAIR & SVCS

Tri-City Industrial Power Inc .... E 937 866-4099
   Miamisburg (G-14361)

BEADS, WHOLESALE

J L Swaney Inc .... E 740 884-4450
   Chillicothe (G-2855)

BEARINGS & PARTS Ball

Federal-Mogul LLC .... C 740 432-2393
   Cambridge (G-2113)

BEAUTY & BARBER SHOP EQPT

Aluminum Line Products Company ... D 440 835-8880
   Westlake (G-19459)
Carroll Hills Industries Inc .... D 330 627-5524
   Carrollton (G-2614)

BEAUTY CULTURE SCHOOL

Yearwood Corporation .... E 937 223-3572
   Dayton (G-10006)

BEAUTY SALONS

Bajon Salon Montgomery .... E 513 984-8880
   Cincinnati (G-3073)
Calico Court .... E 740 455-2541
   Zanesville (G-20453)
Changes Hair Designers Inc .... E 614 846-6666
   Columbus (G-6875)
Definitions of Design Inc .... E 419 891-0188
   Maumee (G-13906)
Ecotage .... E 513 782-2229
   Cincinnati (G-3544)
Flux A Salon By Hazelton .... E 419 841-5100
   Perrysburg (G-16004)
G E G Enterprises Inc .... E 330 494-9160
   Canton (G-2374)
Head Quarters Inc .... E 440 233-8508
   Lorain (G-13041)
Intl Europa Salon & Spa .... E 216 292-6969
   Cleveland (G-5836)

Employee Codes: A=Over 500 employees, B=251-500
C=101-250, D=51-100, E=25-50

BEAUTY SALONS / SERVICES SECTION

JC Penney Corporation Inc .... B 330 633-7700
   Akron *(G-290)*
Kenneths Hair Salons & Day Sp .... B 614 457-7712
   Columbus *(G-7978)*
Kerr House Inc .... E 419 832-1733
   Grand Rapids *(G-11451)*
Laser Hair Removal Center .... D 937 433-7536
   Dayton *(G-9674)*
Linda Cpers Idntity Hair Dsign .... D 513 791-2555
   Cincinnati *(G-3985)*
Mark Luikart Inc .... E 330 339-9141
   New Philadelphia *(G-15109)*
Mfh Inc .... E 937 435-4701
   Dayton *(G-9723)*
Mfh Inc .... D 937 435-4701
   Dayton *(G-9724)*
Michael Christopher Salon Inc .... E 440 449-0999
   Cleveland *(G-6047)*
Mzf Inc .... E 216 464-3910
   Cleveland *(G-6096)*
Paragon Salons Inc .... E 513 651-4600
   Cincinnati *(G-4250)*
Rometrics Too Hair Nail Gllery .... E 440 808-1391
   Westlake *(G-19543)*
Salon Alexandre Inc .... E 513 207-8406
   West Chester *(G-19227)*
Salon Ware Inc .... E 330 665-2244
   Copley *(G-9062)*
Tanos Salon .... E 216 831-7880
   Cleveland *(G-6569)*
Tara Flaherty .... E 419 565-1334
   Mansfield *(G-13372)*
Ulta Beauty Inc .... C 440 248-5618
   Solon *(G-17062)*
Uptown Hair Studio Inc .... E 937 832-2111
   Englewood *(G-10723)*

BED & BREAKFAST INNS

Alexander House Inc .... E 513 523-4569
   Oxford *(G-15810)*
Bass Lake Tavern Inc .... D 440 285-3100
   Chardon *(G-2741)*
Eastlake Lodging LLC .... E 440 953-8000
   Eastlake *(G-10546)*
Emmett Dan House Ltd Partnr .... E 740 392-6886
   Mount Vernon *(G-14894)*
Riders 1812 Inn .... E 440 354-0922
   Painesville *(G-15878)*
Spread Eagle Tavern Inc .... E 330 223-1583
   Hanoverton *(G-11787)*

BEDDING & BEDSPRINGS STORES

Cinmar LLC .... C 513 603-1000
   West Chester *(G-19040)*

BEDDING, BEDSPREADS, BLANKETS & SHEETS: Comforters & Quilts

Aunties Attic .... E 740 548-5059
   Lewis Center *(G-12669)*

BEER & ALE WHOLESALERS

Cdc Management Co .... C 614 781-0216
   Columbus *(G-7218)*
Dayton Heidelberg Distrg Co .... C 614 308-0400
   Columbus *(G-7494)*
Dayton Heidelberg Distrg Co .... C 419 666-9783
   Perrysburg *(G-15994)*
Donzells Flower & Grdn Ctr Inc .... E 330 724-0550
   Akron *(G-197)*
Glazers Distributors Ohio Inc .... E 440 542-7000
   Solon *(G-17010)*
Southern Glazers Wine and Sp .... D 330 422-9463
   Streetsboro *(G-17430)*
Southern Glzers Dstrs Ohio LLC .... D 614 552-7900
   Columbus *(G-8754)*

BEER & ALE, WHOLESALE: Beer & Other Fermented Malt Liquors

Anheuser-Busch LLC .... C 513 381-3927
   Cincinnati *(G-3031)*
Bellas Co .... E 740 598-4171
   Mingo Junction *(G-14653)*
Beverage Distributors Inc .... C 216 431-1600
   Cleveland *(G-5121)*
Bonbright Distributors Inc .... C 937 222-1001
   Dayton *(G-9363)*
Brown Distributing Inc .... D 740 349-7999
   Newark *(G-15151)*
Cavalier Distributing Company .... D 513 247-9222
   Blue Ash *(G-1552)*
Cbo LLC .... E 740 598-4121
   Mingo Junction *(G-14654)*
Central Beverage Group Ltd .... C 614 294-3555
   Lewis Center *(G-12674)*
City Beverage Company .... E 419 782-7065
   Defiance *(G-10022)*
Columbus Distributing Company .... B 614 846-1000
   Columbus *(G-7346)*
Columbus Distributing Company .... E 740 726-2211
   Waldo *(G-18782)*
Dayton Heidelberg Distrg Co .... C 937 222-8692
   Moraine *(G-14770)*
Dayton Heidelberg Distrg Co .... C 937 220-6450
   Moraine *(G-14772)*
Dayton Heidelberg Distrg Co .... D 513 421-5000
   Cincinnati *(G-3468)*
Dickerson Distributing Company .... D 513 539-8483
   Monroe *(G-14693)*
Goodman Beverage Co Inc .... D 440 787-2255
   Lorain *(G-13040)*
Heritage Beverage Company LLC .... D 440 255-5550
   Mentor *(G-14190)*
Hill Distributing Company .... D 614 276-6533
   Dublin *(G-10361)*
House of La Rose Cleveland .... C 440 746-7500
   Brecksville *(G-1827)*
Jetro Cash and Carry Entps LLC .... D 216 525-0101
   Cleveland *(G-5862)*
K M C Corporation .... E 740 598-4171
   Mingo Junction *(G-14655)*
Knall Beverage Inc .... D 216 252-2500
   Cleveland *(G-5905)*
Litter Distributing Co Inc .... D 740 774-2831
   Chillicothe *(G-2861)*
M & A Distributing Co Inc .... E 440 703-4580
   Solon *(G-17024)*
Matesich Distributing Co .... D 740 349-8686
   Newark *(G-15201)*
Nwo Beverage Inc .... E 419 725-2162
   Northwood *(G-15541)*
Ohio Valley Wine Company .... D 513 771-9370
   Cincinnati *(G-4213)*
R L Lipton Distributing Co .... D 216 475-4150
   Maple Heights *(G-13414)*
Rhinegeist LLC .... D 513 381-1367
   Cincinnati *(G-4414)*
Superior Beverage Company Inc .... D 440 703-4580
   Solon *(G-17057)*
The Maple City Ice Company .... E 419 668-2531
   Norwalk *(G-15594)*
Treu House of Munch Inc .... D 419 666-7770
   Northwood *(G-15549)*
Warsteiner Importers Agency .... E 513 942-9872
   West Chester *(G-19183)*

BEER, WINE & LIQUOR STORES: Beer, Packaged

Dayton Heidelberg Distrg Co .... C 937 220-6450
   Moraine *(G-14772)*

BEER, WINE & LIQUOR STORES: Wine

Iacominis Papa Joes Inc .... D 330 923-7999
   Akron *(G-276)*
Larosas Inc .... A 513 347-5660
   Cincinnati *(G-3962)*

BELTING: Plastic

Polychem Corporation .... D 419 547-1400
   Clyde *(G-6820)*

BELTS: Seat, Automotive & Aircraft

Tk Holdings Inc .... E 937 778-9713
   Piqua *(G-16168)*

BEVERAGE STORES

P-Americas LLC .... D 216 252-7377
   Cleveland *(G-6227)*
Superior Beverage Group Ltd .... C 614 294-3555
   Lewis Center *(G-12706)*
Superior Beverage Group Ltd .... C 440 703-4580
   Solon *(G-17058)*

BEVERAGES, ALCOHOLIC: Near Beer

Georgetown Vineyards Inc .... E 740 435-3222
   Cambridge *(G-2115)*

BEVERAGES, ALCOHOLIC: Wines

Ferrante Wine Farm Inc .... E 440 466-8466
   Geneva *(G-11361)*

BEVERAGES, BEER & ALE, WHOLESALE: Ale

Esber Beverage Company .... E 330 456-4361
   Canton *(G-2360)*
Hanson Distributing Co Inc .... D 419 435-3214
   Fostoria *(G-11130)*

BEVERAGES, NONALCOHOLIC: Bottled & canned soft drinks

Abbott Laboratories .... A 614 624-3191
   Columbus *(G-6924)*
Borden Dairy Co Cincinnati LLC .... C 513 948-8811
   Cincinnati *(G-3127)*
G & J Pepsi-Cola Bottlers Inc .... E 740 774-2148
   Chillicothe *(G-2841)*
P-Americas LLC .... E 419 227-3541
   Lima *(G-12853)*
Pepsi-Cola Metro Btlg Co Inc .... B 330 963-0426
   Twinsburg *(G-18453)*

BEVERAGES, NONALCOHOLIC: Carbonated

G & J Pepsi-Cola Bottlers Inc .... B 740 354-9191
   Franklin Furnace *(G-11171)*
P-Americas LLC .... C 330 746-7652
   Youngstown *(G-20313)*

BEVERAGES, NONALCOHOLIC: Carbonated, Canned & Bottled, Etc

Central Coca-Cola Btlg Co Inc .... C 419 476-6622
   Toledo *(G-17798)*
Coca-Cola Bottling Co Cnsld .... D 937 878-5000
   Dayton *(G-9414)*
G & J Pepsi-Cola Bottlers Inc .... D 740 593-3366
   Athens *(G-788)*

BEVERAGES, NONALCOHOLIC: Flavoring extracts & syrups, nec

Abbott Laboratories .... A 614 624-3191
   Columbus *(G-6924)*
Agrana Fruit Us Inc .... C 937 693-3821
   Anna *(G-616)*

BEVERAGES, NONALCOHOLIC: Soft Drinks, Canned & Bottled, Etc

American Bottling Company .... D 614 237-4201
   Columbus *(G-6985)*
G & J Pepsi-Cola Bottlers Inc .... D 740 452-2721
   Zanesville *(G-20479)*
Pepsi-Cola Metro Btlg Co Inc .... B 937 461-4664
   Dayton *(G-9806)*

BEVERAGES, WINE & DISTILLED ALCOHOLIC, WHOLESALE: Wine

August Food & Wine LLC .... E 513 421-2020
   Cincinnati *(G-3063)*
Bellas Co .... E 740 598-4171
   Mingo Junction *(G-14653)*
Dayton Heidelberg Distrg Co .... C 216 520-2626
   Cleveland *(G-5471)*
Dayton Heidelberg Distrg Co .... D 419 666-9783
   Perrysburg *(G-15995)*
Dayton Heidelberg Distrg Co .... C 614 308-0400
   Columbus *(G-7494)*
Dayton Heidelberg Distrg Co .... C 937 220-6450
   Moraine *(G-14772)*
E & J Gallo Winery .... E 513 381-4050
   Cincinnati *(G-3520)*
Goodman Beverage Co Inc .... D 440 787-2255
   Lorain *(G-13040)*
H Dennert Distributing Corp .... C 513 871-7272
   Cincinnati *(G-3722)*
K M C Corporation .... E 740 598-4171
   Mingo Junction *(G-14655)*

SERVICES SECTION

BLOOD RELATED HEALTH SVCS

M & M Wine Cellar Inc .... E 330 536-6450
  Lowellville *(G-13172)*
Mid-Ohio Wines Inc .... E 440 989-1011
  Lorain *(G-13061)*
Ohio Valley Wine Company .... D 513 771-9370
  Cincinnati *(G-4213)*
R L Lipton Distributing Co .... D 216 475-4150
  Maple Heights *(G-13414)*
Southern Glazers Wine and Sp ...... D 330 422-9463
  Streetsboro *(G-17430)*
Southern Glzers Dstrs Ohio LLC .... D 614 552-7900
  Columbus *(G-8754)*
Superior Beverage Company Inc ... D 440 703-4580
  Solon *(G-17057)*
Vanguard Wines LLC .... D 614 291-3493
  Columbus *(G-8934)*
Vervasi Vineyard & Itln Bistro .... E 330 497-1000
  Canton *(G-2576)*
Vintage Wine Distributor Inc .... E 614 876-2580
  Columbus *(G-8942)*
Wine Trends Inc .... E 216 520-2626
  Independence *(G-12277)*

BEVERAGES, WINE/DISTILLED ALCOH, WHOL: Brandy/Brandy Spirits

Fredericks Wine & Dine .... E 216 581-5299
  Cleveland *(G-5635)*

BIBLE CAMPS

Sheldon Harry E Calvary Camp ..... D 440 593-4381
  Conneaut *(G-9046)*

BICYCLE REPAIR SHOP

Huffy Corporation .... D 937 743-5011
  Springboro *(G-17124)*
Straders Nrthwst Schwinn .... E 614 889-2453
  Columbus *(G-8793)*

BICYCLE SHOPS

Straders Nrthwst Schwinn .... E 614 889-2453
  Columbus *(G-8793)*
Zide Sport Shop of Ohio Inc .... D 740 373-6446
  Marietta *(G-13521)*

BICYCLES, PARTS & ACCESS

Huffy Corporation .... D 937 743-5011
  Springboro *(G-17124)*

BILLIARD & POOL PARLORS

Cloverleaf Bowling Center Inc .... E 216 524-4833
  Cleveland *(G-5366)*

BILLIARD EQPT & SPLYS WHOLESALERS

Dtv Inc .... E 216 226-5465
  Mayfield Heights *(G-14001)*

BILLIARD TABLE REPAIR SVCS

Dtv Inc .... E 216 226-5465
  Mayfield Heights *(G-14001)*

BILLING & BOOKKEEPING SVCS

APS Medical Billing .... D 419 866-1804
  Toledo *(G-17756)*
Billing Connection Inc .... E 740 964-0043
  Reynoldsburg *(G-16430)*
Cbiz Med MGT Professionals Inc .. E 614 771-2222
  Hilliard *(G-11889)*
Cincinnati Medical Billing Svc .... E 513 965-8041
  Cincinnati *(G-3314)*
Compensation Programs of Ohio . E 330 652-9821
  Youngstown *(G-20156)*
Comprehensive Med Data MGT LLC D 614 717 0040
  Powell *(G-16331)*
Doctors Consulting Service .... E 614 793-1980
  Dublin *(G-10322)*
E T Financial Service Inc .... E 937 716-1726
  Trotwood *(G-18346)*
Emergency Medical Svcs Billing ... E 216 664-2598
  Cleveland *(G-5534)*
Healthpro Medical Billing Inc .... D 419 223-2717
  Lima *(G-12796)*
Kennedy Group Enterprises Inc .... E 440 879-0078
  Strongsville *(G-17481)*
MBI Solutions Inc .... C 937 619-4000
  Dayton *(G-9705)*

MD Business Solutions Inc .... E 513 872-4500
  Blue Ash *(G-1637)*
Med3000 Group Inc .... E 937 291-7850
  Miamisburg *(G-14316)*
Medic Management Group LLC .... D 330 670-5316
  Akron *(G-336)*
Medical Account Services Inc .... E 937 297-6072
  Moraine *(G-14803)*
Medical Care PSC Inc .... E 513 281-4400
  Cincinnati *(G-4042)*
Medical Care Reimbursement .... E 513 281-4400
  Cincinnati *(G-4043)*
Midwest Emergency Services LLC E 586 294-2700
  Fairlawn *(G-10965)*
Nationwide Childrens Hospital ...... E 330 253-5200
  Akron *(G-349)*
Northcoast Healthcare MGT Inc ... C 216 591-2000
  Beachwood *(G-1108)*
Ohio Bell Telephone Company ..... A 216 822-3439
  Cleveland *(G-6185)*
Pioneer Physicians Networking .... E 330 633-6601
  Tallmadge *(G-17647)*
Quadax Inc .... E 330 759-4600
  Youngstown *(G-20334)*
Quadax Inc .... C 440 777-6300
  Middleburg Heights *(G-14384)*
Quadax Inc .... E 614 882-1200
  Westerville *(G-19438)*
Radiology Assoc Canton Inc .... E 330 363-2842
  Canton *(G-2503)*
Real Property Management Inc ... E 614 766-6500
  Dublin *(G-10439)*
Sheakley Med MGT Resources LLC D 513 891-1006
  Cincinnati *(G-4512)*
Specialty Medical Services .... E 440 245-8010
  Lorain *(G-13076)*
Superior Med Inc .... E 740 439-8839
  Cambridge *(G-2130)*
Terry J Reppa & Associates .... E 440 888-8533
  Cleveland *(G-6586)*
Village of Byesville .... E 740 685-5901
  Byesville *(G-2072)*

BINDING SVC: Books & Manuals

A-A Blueprint Co Inc .... E 330 794-8803
  Akron *(G-13)*
AGS Custom Graphics Inc .... D 330 963-7770
  Macedonia *(G-13186)*
Bindery & Spc Pressworks Inc ...... D 614 873-4623
  Plain City *(G-16184)*
Consolidated Graphics Group Inc. C 216 881-9191
  Cleveland *(G-5393)*
Copley Ohio Newspapers Inc .... C 330 364-5577
  New Philadelphia *(G-15087)*
D & S Crtive Cmmunications Inc .. D 419 524-6699
  Mansfield *(G-13288)*
Fedex Office & Print Svcs Inc .... E 937 436-0677
  Dayton *(G-9544)*
Hecks Direct Mail & Prtg Svc .... E 419 697-3505
  Toledo *(G-17950)*
Hopewell Industries Inc .... E 740 622-3563
  Coshocton *(G-9107)*
Monco Enterprises Inc .... A 937 461-0034
  Dayton *(G-9754)*
Ohio Laminating & Binding Inc .... E 614 771-4868
  Hilliard *(G-11939)*
Quick Tab II Inc .... D 419 448-6622
  Tiffin *(G-17694)*
R T Industries Inc .... C 937 335-5784
  Troy *(G-18374)*
Repro Acquisition Company LLC . E 216 738-3800
  Cleveland *(G-6378)*
Tj Metzgers Inc .... D 419 861-8611
  Toledo *(G-18219)*
Traxium LLC .... E 330 572-8200
  Stow *(G-17397)*
Youngstown ARC Engraving Co ... E 330 793-2471
  Youngstown *(G-20423)*

BINDING SVC: Pamphlets

Macke Brothers Inc .... D 513 771-7500
  Cincinnati *(G-4008)*

BINGO HALL

David Barber Civic Center .... E 740 498-4383
  Newcomerstown *(G-15266)*
Our Lady Prptual Hlp Cnmty Bngo E 513 742-3200
  Cincinnati *(G-4243)*

BIOFEEDBACK CENTERS

First Call For Help Inc .... E 419 599-1660
  Napoleon *(G-14939)*
Sleep Care Inc .... E 614 901-8989
  Columbus *(G-8743)*

BIOLOGICAL PRDTS: Exc Diagnostic

Bio-Blood Components Inc .... E 614 294-3183
  Columbus *(G-7111)*
EMD Millipore Corporation .... C 513 631-0445
  Norwood *(G-15599)*
Perkinelmer Hlth Sciences Inc .... E 330 825-4525
  Akron *(G-385)*

BIRTH CONTROL CLINIC

Planned Prnthood of Mhning Vly . E 330 788-6506
  Youngstown *(G-20323)*

BLASTING SVC: Sand, Metal Parts

Industrial Mill Maintenance .... E 330 746-1155
  Youngstown *(G-20232)*

BLOCK & BRICK: Sand Lime

R W Sidley Incorporated .... E 440 352-9343
  Painesville *(G-15875)*

BLOCKS: Standard, Concrete Or Cinder

Hanson Aggregates East LLC .... E 740 773-2172
  Chillicothe *(G-2844)*
J P Sand & Gravel Company .... E 614 497-0083
  Lockbourne *(G-12958)*
Koltcz Concrete Block Co .... E 440 232-3630
  Bedford *(G-1315)*
National Lime and Stone Co .... E 614 497-0083
  Lockbourne *(G-12959)*
Quality Block & Supply Inc .... E 330 364-4411
  Mount Eaton *(G-14850)*
Snyder Concrete Products Inc ...... E 937 885-5176
  Moraine *(G-14825)*

BLOOD BANK

Bio-Blood Components Inc .... E 614 294-3183
  Columbus *(G-7111)*
Biolife Plasma Services LP .... E 419 224-0117
  Lima *(G-12748)*
Csl Plasma Inc .... D 937 331-9186
  Dayton *(G-9448)*
Foundation For Communit .... C 937 461-3450
  Dayton *(G-9558)*
Lifeshare Cmnty Blood Svcs Inc ... E 440 322-6159
  Elyria *(G-10643)*
Lifeshare Community Blood Svcs. E 440 322-6573
  Elyria *(G-10644)*

BLOOD DONOR STATIONS

Csl Plasma Inc .... D 330 535-4338
  Akron *(G-181)*

BLOOD RELATED HEALTH SVCS

24 - Seven Home Hlth Care LLC .. E 614 794-0325
  Hilliard *(G-11873)*
Addus Homecare Corporation ...... A 866 684-0385
  Wintersville *(G-19807)*
Atrium Medical Center .... A 937 499-9596
  Middletown *(G-14474)*
Black Stone Cincinnati LLC .... E 937 773-8573
  Piqua *(G-16136)*
Blood Services Cntl Ohio Reg .... C 614 253-7981
  Columbus *(G-7119)*
Cardinal Health Inc .... C 614 473-0786
  Columbus *(G-7192)*
Carespring Health Care MGT LLC E 513 943-4000
  Loveland *(G-13113)*
Central Ohio Poison Center .... E 800 222-1222
  Columbus *(G-7233)*
County of Carroll .... E 330 627-4866
  Carrollton *(G-2615)*
Covenant Home Health Care LLC E 614 465-2017
  Columbus *(G-7452)*
Diverscare Healthcare Svcs Inc .... E 513 867-4100
  Hamilton *(G-11723)*
Engaged Health Care Bus Svcs ... E 614 457-8180
  Columbus *(G-7594)*
First Choice Medical Staffing .... D 513 631-5656
  Cincinnati *(G-3614)*

BLOOD RELATED HEALTH SVCS

H B Magruder Memorial Hospital ....B....... 419 734-4539
  Port Clinton (G-16247)
Health Data MGT Solutions Inc ....D....... 216 595-1232
  Beachwood (G-1084)
Health Partners Western Ohio ....E....... 419 679-5994
  Kenton (G-12419)
Horizon Home Health Care ....E....... 937 264-3155
  Vandalia (G-18686)
Kettering Adventist Healthcare ....E....... 937 401-6306
  Centerville (G-2681)
Kindred Healthcare Inc ....E....... 513 336-0178
  Mason (G-13728)
Kindred Healthcare Inc ....D....... 419 224-1888
  Lima (G-12809)
Maxim Healthcare Services Inc ....D....... 740 522-6094
  Hebron (G-11852)
Maxim Healthcare Services Inc ....D....... 740 772-4100
  Chillicothe (G-2863)
Maxim Healthcare Services Inc ....D....... 216 606-3000
  Independence (G-12233)
Maxim Healthcare Services Inc ....D....... 614 986-3001
  Gahanna (G-11257)
Mercy Health ....E....... 440 988-1009
  Amherst (G-600)
Ohio State University ....E....... 614 257-5200
  Columbus (G-8409)
Peregrine Health Services Inc ....D....... 419 586-4135
  Celina (G-2659)
Philips Healthcare Cleveland ....E....... 440 483-3235
  Highland Heights (G-11870)
Serenity HM Healthcare Svcs LLC ....D....... 937 222-0002
  Dayton (G-9876)
Signature Healthcare LLC ....C....... 330 372-1977
  Warren (G-18899)
Summa Health System ....A....... 330 836-9023
  Akron (G-454)
Taylor Murtis Human Svcs Sys ....C....... 216 283-4400
  Cleveland (G-6572)
Toledo Clinic Inc ....C....... 419 865-3111
  Holland (G-12061)
Unity Health Network LLC ....E....... 330 655-3820
  Hudson (G-12148)
Unity Health Network LLC ....D....... 330 923-5899
  Cuyahoga Falls (G-9229)
Unity Health Network LLC ....D....... 330 633-7782
  Tallmadge (G-17659)
Wheeling Hospital Inc ....D....... 740 676-4623
  Bellaire (G-1368)
Young Mens Christian Associat ....C....... 419 794-7304
  Maumee (G-13996)

BLOWERS & FANS

A A S Amels Sheet Meta L Inc ....E....... 330 793-9326
  Youngstown (G-20094)
Kirk Williams Company Inc ....D....... 614 875-9023
  Grove City (G-11573)
Langdon Inc ....E....... 513 733-5955
  Cincinnati (G-3960)
Ohio Blow Pipe Company ....E....... 216 681-7379
  Cleveland (G-6186)
Pcy Enterprises Inc ....E....... 513 241-5566
  Cincinnati (G-4270)
Tosoh America Inc ....B....... 614 539-8622
  Grove City (G-11606)

BLUEPRINTING SVCS

American Reprographics Co LLC ....E....... 614 224-5149
  Columbus (G-7005)
Cannell Graphics LLC ....E....... 614 781-9760
  Worthington (G-19944)
Franklin Imaging Llc ....E....... 614 885-6894
  Columbus (G-7697)
Key Blue Prints Inc ....D....... 614 228-3285
  Columbus (G-7983)
Profile Digital Printing LLC ....E....... 937 866-4241
  Dayton (G-9835)
Queen City Reprographics ....C....... 513 326-2300
  Cincinnati (G-4371)

BOARDING SCHOOL

Marsh Foundation ....E....... 419 238-1695
  Van Wert (G-18639)
Society of The Transfiguration ....E....... 513 771-7462
  Cincinnati (G-4548)

BOAT BUILDING & REPAIR

Don Wartko Construction Co ....D....... 330 673-5252
  Kent (G-12366)

BOAT DEALERS

Bob Pulte Chevrolet Inc ....E....... 513 932-0303
  Lebanon (G-12593)
S B S Transit Inc ....B....... 440 288-2222
  Lorain (G-13075)

BOAT DEALERS: Motor

Sima Marine Sales Inc ....E....... 440 269-3200
  Willoughby (G-19714)
South Shore Marine Services ....E....... 419 433-5798
  Huron (G-12174)

BOAT REPAIR SVCS

Superior Marine Ways Inc ....C....... 740 894-6224
  Proctorville (G-16361)

BOAT YARD: Boat yards, storage & incidental repair

Containerport Group Inc ....E....... 513 771-0275
  West Chester (G-19049)
Erie Island Resort and Marina ....E....... 419 734-9117
  Warren (G-18856)
Sandusky Harbor Marina Inc ....E....... 419 627-1201
  Sandusky (G-16791)
Tack-Anew Inc ....E....... 419 734-4212
  Port Clinton (G-16257)

BODIES: Truck & Bus

Hendrickson International Corp ....D....... 740 929-5600
  Hebron (G-11849)
Joseph Industries Inc ....D....... 330 528-0091
  Streetsboro (G-17418)
Youngstown-Kenworth Inc ....E....... 330 534-9761
  Hubbard (G-12093)

BOILER & HEATING REPAIR SVCS

Babcock & Wilcox Company ....A....... 330 753-4511
  Barberton (G-955)
Columbs/Worthington Htg AC Inc ....E....... 614 771-5381
  Columbus (G-7325)
Honeywell International Inc ....D....... 216 459-6053
  Cleveland (G-5770)
Nbw Inc ....E....... 216 377-1700
  Cleveland (G-6114)
Rmf Nooter Inc ....D....... 419 727-1970
  Toledo (G-18159)
Smith & Oby Service Co ....E....... 440 735-5322
  Bedford (G-1337)

BOILER REPAIR SHOP

Norris Brothers Co Inc ....C....... 216 771-2233
  Cleveland (G-6137)
Osterfeld Champion Service ....E....... 937 254-8437
  Dayton (G-9795)

BOND & MORTGAGE COMPANIES

Rapid Mortgage Company ....E....... 937 748-8888
  Dayton (G-9842)
Realty Corporation of America ....E....... 216 522-0020
  Cleveland Heights (G-6795)
Residential Finance Corp ....B....... 614 324-4700
  Columbus (G-8619)

BOOK STORES

Barbour Publishing Inc ....E....... 740 922-1321
  Uhrichsville (G-18487)
Friends of The Lib Cyahoga FLS ....C....... 330 928-2117
  Cuyahoga Falls (G-9190)
Mile Inc ....D....... 614 794-2203
  Worthington (G-19978)
Province of St John The Baptis ....D....... 513 241-5615
  Cincinnati (G-4352)
University of Cincinnati ....E....... 513 556-4200
  Cincinnati (G-4767)

BOOK STORES: Religious

Emerge Ministries Inc ....E....... 330 865-8351
  Akron (G-208)

BOOKS, WHOLESALE

Afit Ls Usaf ....E....... 937 255-3636
  Dayton (G-9249)

Alliance Medical Inc ....E....... 800 890-3092
  Dublin (G-10242)
Barbour Publishing Inc ....E....... 740 922-1321
  Uhrichsville (G-18487)
CSS Publishing Co Inc ....E....... 419 227-1818
  Lima (G-12768)
Ed Map Inc ....E....... 740 753-3439
  Nelsonville (G-14962)
H & M Patch Company ....D....... 614 339-8950
  Columbus (G-7788)
Hubbard Company ....E....... 419 784-4455
  Defiance (G-10034)
Indico LLC ....D....... 440 775-7777
  Oberlin (G-15646)
Media Source Inc ....D....... 614 873-7635
  Plain City (G-16199)
Scholastic Book Fairs Inc ....D....... 513 714-1000
  West Chester (G-19146)
Zaner-Bloser Inc ....E....... 614 486-0221
  Columbus (G-9025)

BOTANICAL GARDENS

Cleveland Metroparks ....C....... 216 661-6500
  Cleveland (G-5326)

BOTTLED GAS DEALERS: Propane

Hearthstone Utilities Inc ....D....... 440 974-3770
  Cleveland (G-5744)
Litter Bob Fuel & Heating Co ....E....... 740 773-2196
  Chillicothe (G-2860)
Youngstown Propane Inc ....E....... 330 792-6571
  Youngstown (G-20435)

BOTTLED WATER DELIVERY

K & R Distributors Inc ....E....... 937 864-5495
  Fairborn (G-10799)
Pro-Kleen Industrial Svcs Inc ....E....... 740 689-1886
  Lancaster (G-12566)

BOTTLES: Plastic

Phoenix Technologies Intl LLC ....E....... 419 353-7738
  Bowling Green (G-1789)

BOUTIQUE STORES

Artistic Dance Enterprises ....E....... 614 761-2882
  Columbus (G-7046)

BOWLING CENTERS

Midway Bowling Lanes Inc ....E....... 330 762-7477
  Cuyahoga Falls (G-9210)
Skylane LLC ....E....... 330 527-9999
  Garrettsville (G-11352)
Sortino Management & Dev Co ....E....... 419 626-6761
  Sandusky (G-16796)
Toledo Sports Center Inc ....E....... 419 693-0687
  Toledo (G-18251)
Westgate Lanes Incorporated ....E....... 419 229-3845
  Lima (G-12920)

BOWLING EQPT & SPLY STORES

Chillicothe Bowling Lanes Inc ....E....... 740 773-3300
  Chillicothe (G-2817)

BOWLING EQPT & SPLYS

Done-Rite Bowling Service Co ....E....... 440 232-3280
  Bedford (G-1304)

BOXES & SHOOK: Nailed Wood

Quadco Rehabilitation Center ....B....... 419 682-1011
  Stryker (G-17537)

BOXES: Corrugated

BDS Packaging Inc ....D....... 937 643-0530
  Moraine (G-14752)
Cambridge Packaging Inc ....E....... 740 432-3351
  Cambridge (G-2101)
Westrock CP LLC ....D....... 770 448-2193
  Wshngtn CT Hs (G-20038)

BOXES: Wooden

Lefco Worthington LLC ....E....... 216 432-4422
  Cleveland (G-5931)

SERVICES SECTION

BOYS' CAMPS
Ohio Camp Cherith Inc .... E 330 725-4202
  Medina *(G-14110)*

BOYS' TOWNS
Friars Club Inc .... D 513 488-8777
  Cincinnati *(G-3654)*
Twelve Inc .... E 330 837-3555
  Massillon *(G-13859)*
Village Network .... C 330 264-0650
  Wooster *(G-19922)*

BRAKES & BRAKE PARTS
Hebco Products Inc .... A 419 562-7987
  Bucyrus *(G-2039)*

BRAZING SVCS
Paulo Products Company .... E 440 942-0153
  Willoughby *(G-19703)*

BRICK, STONE & RELATED PRDTS WHOLESALERS
CCI Supply Inc .... C 440 953-0045
  Mentor *(G-14154)*
Hamilton-Parker Company .... D 614 358-7800
  Columbus *(G-7797)*
Kuhlman Corporation .... C 419 897-6000
  Maumee *(G-13934)*
Modern Builders Supply Inc .... D 330 726-7000
  Youngstown *(G-20288)*
Modern Builders Supply Inc .... C 330 729-2690
  Youngstown *(G-20289)*
Modern Builders Supply Inc .... E 419 241-3961
  Toledo *(G-18068)*
Nexgen Enterprises Inc .... C 513 618-0300
  Cincinnati *(G-4162)*
R W Sidley Incorporated .... E 330 793-7374
  Youngstown *(G-20340)*
Sidwell Materials Inc .... C 740 849-2394
  Zanesville *(G-20533)*
Stamm Contracting Co Inc .... E 330 274-8230
  Mantua *(G-13395)*
Stone Coffman Company LLC ..... E 614 861-4668
  Gahanna *(G-11270)*

BRIDAL SHOPS
Emmys Bridal Inc .... E 419 628-7555
  Minster *(G-14661)*

BROACHING MACHINES
Ohio Broach & Machine Company ..... E 440 946-1040
  Willoughby *(G-19699)*

BROADCASTING & COMMS EQPT: Antennas, Transmitting/Comms
Central USA Wireless LLC .... E 513 469-1500
  Cincinnati *(G-3218)*

BROADCASTING STATIONS, RADIO: Educational
Dayton Public School District .... D 937 542-3000
  Dayton *(G-9489)*
Marietta College .... E 740 376-4790
  Marietta *(G-13467)*

BROADCASTING STATIONS, RADIO: Exc Music Format
Ohio University .... E 740 593-1771
  Athens *(G-805)*

BROADCASTING STATIONS, RADIO: Music Format
Ashtabula Broadcasting Station ... E 440 993-2126
  Ashtabula *(G-713)*
CBS Radio Inc .... D 513 699-5105
  Cincinnati *(G-3198)*
Cincinnati Public Radio Inc .... E 513 241-8282
  Cincinnati *(G-3323)*
Cumulus Broadcasting LLC .... D 330 783-1000
  Youngstown *(G-20163)*

D A Peterson Inc .... E 330 821-1111
  Alliance *(G-537)*
Iheartcommunications Inc .... E 419 529-2211
  Mansfield *(G-13311)*
Southeastern Ohio Brdcstg Sys ... E 740 452-5431
  Zanesville *(G-20535)*
Southeastern Ohio TV Sys .... E 740 452-5431
  Zanesville *(G-20536)*

BROADCASTING STATIONS, RADIO: Sports
Fairborn Sftball Offcials Assn .... E 937 902-9920
  Dayton *(G-9538)*

BROADCASTING STATIONS, TELEVISION: Translator Station
Gray Television Group Inc .... D 419 531-1313
  Toledo *(G-17920)*
Ohio State University .... C 614 292-4510
  Columbus *(G-8406)*

BROKERS & DEALERS: Mortgages, Buying & Selling
Equity Resources Inc .... D 513 518-6318
  Cincinnati *(G-3571)*
Southwest Financial Svcs Ltd ...... C 513 621-6699
  Cincinnati *(G-4552)*
The Cadle Company .... C 330 872-0918
  Newton Falls *(G-15278)*
Van Dyk Mortgage Corporation ... E 513 429-2122
  Mason *(G-13777)*

BROKERS & DEALERS: Securities
Citigroup Global Markets Inc .... E 419 842-5383
  Toledo *(G-17806)*
Columbus Metro Federal Cr Un ... E 614 239-0210
  Columbus *(G-7368)*
Corporate Fin Assoc of Clumbus ..... D 614 457-9219
  Columbus *(G-7444)*
Diamond Hill Capital MGT Inc ...... E 614 255-3333
  Columbus *(G-7516)*
Ifs Financial Services Inc .... E 513 362-8000
  Westerville *(G-19410)*
Independence Capital Corp .... E 440 888-7000
  Cleveland *(G-5810)*
Keybanc Capital Markets Inc .... B 800 553-2240
  Cleveland *(G-5898)*
Kidney & Hypertension Con .... E 330 649-9400
  Canton *(G-2425)*
MAI Capital Management LLC .... E 216 920-4913
  Cleveland *(G-5968)*
Merrill Lynch Pierce Fenner .... E 614 225-3197
  Springfield *(G-17243)*
Merrill Lynch Pierce Fenner .... E 330 702-0535
  Canfield *(G-2201)*
Merrill Lynch Pierce Fenner .... E 330 670-2400
  Bath *(G-1034)*
Nationwide Inv Svcs Corp .... D 614 249-7111
  Columbus *(G-8244)*
Ohio Department of Commerce ..... E 614 644-7381
  Columbus *(G-8325)*
Shane Security Services Inc .... D 330 757-4001
  Poland *(G-16226)*
Stonehenge Fincl Holdings Inc .... E 614 246-2500
  Columbus *(G-8791)*
UBS Financial Services Inc .... E 513 792-2146
  Cincinnati *(G-4716)*
UBS Financial Services Inc .... E 614 460-6559
  Columbus *(G-8883)*
UBS Financial Services Inc .... E 513 792-2100
  Cincinnati *(G-4717)*
Valmark Insurance Agency LLC ..... D 330 576-1234
  Akron *(G-492)*
Wells Fargo Clearing Svcs LLC ... E 216 378-2722
  Cleveland *(G-6730)*

BROKERS & DEALERS: Security
Bowers Insurance Agency Inc ..... E 330 638-6146
  Cortland *(G-9073)*
Citigroup Global Markets Inc .... D 860 291-4181
  Beavercreek *(G-1233)*
Citigroup Global Markets Inc .... D 513 579-8300
  Cincinnati *(G-3355)*
Huntington Insurance Inc .... D 614 480-3800
  Columbus *(G-7866)*
Mc Cloy Financial Services .... D 614 457-6233
  Columbus *(G-8133)*

BROKERS, MARINE TRANSPORTATION

Merrill Lynch Pierce Fenner .... E 614 475-2798
  Columbus *(G-8150)*
Merrill Lynch Pierce Fenner .... E 740 452-3681
  Zanesville *(G-20501)*
Merrill Lynch Pierce Fenner .... E 937 847-4000
  Miamisburg *(G-14319)*
Merrill Lynch Pierce Fenner .... D 614 225-3000
  Columbus *(G-8151)*
Merrill Lynch Pierce Fenner .... E 330 670-2400
  Akron *(G-338)*
Merrill Lynch Pierce Fenner .... E 216 363-6500
  Cleveland *(G-6030)*
Merrill Lynch Pierce Fenner .... D 330 670-2400
  Akron *(G-339)*
Merrill Lynch Pierce Fenner .... E 614 825-0350
  Columbus *(G-6895)*
Merrill Lynch Pierce Fenner .... E 216 292-8000
  Cleveland *(G-6031)*
Merrill Lynch Pierce Fenner .... E 330 497-6600
  Canton *(G-2460)*
Merrill Lynch Pierce Fenner .... E 330 655-2312
  Hudson *(G-12132)*
Morgan Stanley .... E 440 835-6750
  Westlake *(G-19518)*
Morgan Stanley & Co LLC .... E 614 798-3100
  Dublin *(G-10400)*
O N Equity Sales Company .... A 513 794-6794
  Montgomery *(G-14728)*
UBS Financial Services Inc .... E 937 428-1300
  Dayton *(G-9942)*
UBS Financial Services Inc .... E 614 442-6240
  Columbus *(G-8884)*
UBS Financial Services Inc .... E 937 223-3141
  Miamisburg *(G-14362)*
Valmark Securities Inc .... E 330 576-1234
  Akron *(G-493)*
Wunderlich Securities Inc .... E 440 646-1400
  Cleveland *(G-6763)*

BROKERS & DEALERS: Stock
Citigroup Global Markets Inc .... E 440 617-2000
  Cleveland *(G-5243)*
Merrill Lynch Pierce Fenner .... E 419 891-2091
  Perrysburg *(G-16032)*
Merrill Lynch Pierce Fenner .... E 330 702-7300
  Canfield *(G-2200)*
Morgan Stanley .... E 216 523-3000
  Cleveland *(G-6076)*
Morgan Stanley .... D 614 473-2086
  Columbus *(G-8188)*
Morgan Stnley Smith Barney LLC ..... E 216 360-4900
  Cleveland *(G-6077)*
Ross Sinclaire & Assoc LLC .... E 513 381-3939
  Cincinnati *(G-4441)*
Sirak Financial Services Inc .... D 330 493-0642
  Canton *(G-2530)*
UBS Financial Services Inc .... D 513 576-5000
  Cincinnati *(G-4715)*
UBS Financial Services Inc .... D 419 318-5525
  Sylvania *(G-17625)*
UBS Financial Services Inc .... E 216 831-3400
  Cleveland *(G-6628)*
Wells Fargo Clearing Svcs LLC ... E 614 764-2040
  Dublin *(G-10489)*
Wells Fargo Clearing Svcs LLC ... E 614 221-8371
  Columbus *(G-8976)*
Wells Fargo Clearing Svcs LLC ... E 419 356-3272
  Toledo *(G-18302)*
Wells Fargo Clearing Svcs LLC ... E 440 835-9250
  Westlake *(G-19565)*
Wells Fargo Clearing Svcs LLC ... E 419 720-9700
  Toledo *(G-18303)*
Wells Fargo Clearing Svcs LLC ... D 216 574-7300
  Cleveland *(G-6731)*

BROKERS' SVCS
Gateway Distribution Inc .... E 513 891-4477
  Cincinnati *(G-3664)*
Knisely Inc .... D 330 343-5812
  Dover *(G-10195)*
Shamrock Companies Inc .... C 440 899-9510
  Westlake *(G-19546)*
Shredded Bedding Corporation ... E 740 893-3567
  Centerburg *(G-2668)*

BROKERS, MARINE TRANSPORTATION
Alpha Freight Systems Inc .... D 800 394-9001
  Hudson *(G-12104)*

Complete Qlty Trnsp Sltons LLC..........E...... 513 914-4882
Cincinnati *(G-3404)*
Containerport Group Inc......................D...... 440 333-1330
Cleveland *(G-5400)*
Covenant Transport Inc........................D...... 423 821-1212
Columbus *(G-7453)*
Kgbo Holdings Inc................................E...... 800 580-3101
West Chester *(G-19101)*
Ringler Feedlots LLC............................E...... 419 253-5300
Marengo *(G-13425)*

BROKERS: Business

Corporate Fin Assoc of Clumbus..........D...... 614 457-9219
Columbus *(G-7444)*

BROKERS: Food

Acosta Inc...D...... 440 498-7370
Solon *(G-16970)*
Advantage Sales & Mktg LLC...............D...... 513 841-0500
Blue Ash *(G-1527)*
Advantage Waypoint LLC.....................E...... 248 919-3144
Twinsburg *(G-18389)*
Atlantic Fish & Distrg Co.......................E...... 330 454-1307
Canton *(G-2248)*
Cantrell Oil Company............................E...... 937 695-8003
Winchester *(G-19800)*
Euclid Fish Company.............................D...... 440 951-6448
Mentor *(G-14172)*
General Mills Inc...................................D...... 513 770-0558
Mason *(G-13706)*
Impact Sales Inc.....................................D...... 937 274-1905
Dayton *(G-9628)*
Kcbs LLC...E...... 513 421-9422
Cincinnati *(G-3903)*
Keystone Foods LLC..............................C...... 419 843-3009
Toledo *(G-17993)*
Mpf Sales and Mktg Group LLC............C...... 513 793-6241
Blue Ash *(G-1647)*
Queensgate Food Group LLC...............D...... 513 721-5503
Cincinnati *(G-4374)*
R G Sellers Company.............................E...... 937 299-1545
Moraine *(G-14819)*
Shaker Valley Foods Inc.........................E...... 216 961-8600
Cleveland *(G-6476)*
Spartannash Company..........................A...... 937 599-1110
Bellefontaine *(G-1397)*
Spartannash Company..........................B...... 419 228-3141
Lima *(G-12880)*
Spartannash Company..........................D...... 513 793-6300
Cincinnati *(G-4556)*
Sygma Network Inc................................C...... 614 771-3801
Columbus *(G-8814)*
Total Wholesale Inc................................E...... 216 361-5757
Cleveland *(G-6605)*
US Foods Inc...C...... 330 963-6789
Twinsburg *(G-18483)*
US Foods Inc...A...... 614 539-7993
West Chester *(G-19240)*
Valley Wholesale Foods Inc...................E...... 740 354-5216
Portsmouth *(G-16320)*
Vendors Supply Inc.................................E...... 513 755-2111
West Chester *(G-19179)*

BROKERS: Loan

Best Reward Credit Union.....................E...... 216 367-8000
Cleveland *(G-5119)*
Board of Dir of Wittenbe........................E...... 937 327-6310
Springfield *(G-17152)*
Caliber Home Loans Inc.........................E...... 937 435-5363
Dayton *(G-9376)*
Clyde-Findlay Area Cr Un Inc...............E...... 419 547-7781
Clyde *(G-6812)*
Columbus Metro Federal Cr Un............E...... 614 239-0210
Columbus *(G-7369)*
Directions Credit Union Inc....................E...... 419 524-7113
Mansfield *(G-13292)*
Firefighters Cmnty Cr Un Inc................E...... 216 621-4644
Cleveland *(G-5587)*
Firelands Federal Credit Union.............E...... 419 483-4180
Bellevue *(G-1409)*
First Merchants Bank..............................E...... 614 486-9000
Columbus *(G-7666)*
Fremont Federal Credit Union...............C...... 419 334-4434
Fremont *(G-11201)*
George W Mc Cloy...................................D...... 614 457-6233
Columbus *(G-7744)*
Guardian Savings Bank...........................E...... 513 942-3535
West Chester *(G-19086)*
Guardian Savings Bank...........................E...... 513 528-8787
Cincinnati *(G-3717)*
Henry County Bank..................................E...... 419 599-1065
Napoleon *(G-14942)*
Manhattan Mortgage Group Ltd............D...... 614 933-8955
Blacklick *(G-1510)*
Nationstar Mortgage LLC........................D...... 614 985-9500
Columbus *(G-8228)*
Osgood State Bank (inc).........................E...... 419 582-2681
Osgood *(G-15792)*
Precision Funding Corp..........................E...... 330 405-1313
Twinsburg *(G-18455)*
Second National Bank.............................E...... 937 548-2122
Greenville *(G-11519)*
Seven Seventeen Credit Un Inc.............C...... 330 372-8100
Warren *(G-18897)*
Seven Seventeen Credit Un Inc.............E...... 330 372-8100
Warren *(G-18898)*
State Bank and Trust Company..............E...... 419 783-8950
Defiance *(G-10058)*
The Peoples Savings and Ln Co............E...... 937 653-1600
Urbana *(G-18601)*

BROKERS: Mortgage, Arranging For Loans

All State Home Mortgage Inc.................D...... 216 261-7700
Euclid *(G-10742)*
American Eagle Mortgage Co LLC.........E...... 440 988-2900
Lorain *(G-13011)*
Commonwealth Financial Svcs..............E...... 440 449-7709
Cleveland *(G-5379)*
Equitable Mortgage Corporation...........E...... 614 764-1232
Columbus *(G-7602)*
Equity Consultants LLC..........................D...... 330 659-7600
Seven Hills *(G-16829)*
Forest City Residential Dev....................E...... 216 621-6060
Cleveland *(G-5621)*
Nations Lending Corporation.................D...... 440 842-4817
Independence *(G-12238)*
Premiere Service Mortgage Corp...........E...... 513 546-9895
West Chester *(G-19130)*
Randall Mortgage Services.....................C...... 614 336-7948
Dublin *(G-10437)*
Real Estate Mortgage Corp....................D...... 440 356-5373
Chagrin Falls *(G-2704)*
Sibcy Cline Mortgage Services..............E...... 513 984-6776
Cincinnati *(G-4524)*
Union Mortgage Services Inc.................E...... 614 457-4815
Columbus *(G-8889)*
Welles Bowen Realty Inc........................D...... 419 535-0011
Toledo *(G-18300)*
William D Taylor Sr Inc...........................D...... 614 653-6683
Etna *(G-10740)*

BROKERS: Printing

Pxp Ohio...E...... 614 575-4242
Reynoldsburg *(G-16473)*
Veritiv Pubg & Print MGT Inc................E...... 330 650-5522
Hudson *(G-12149)*

BROKERS: Security

Charles Schwab & Co Inc........................E...... 330 908-4478
Richfield *(G-16500)*
Charles Schwab Corporation.................E...... 440 617-2301
Westlake *(G-19473)*
Charles Schwab Corporation.................E...... 216 291-9333
Cleveland *(G-5229)*
Deutsche Bank Securities Inc.................E...... 440 237-0188
Broadview Heights *(G-1878)*
Linsalata Capital Partners Fun...............C...... 440 684-1400
Cleveland *(G-5945)*
Merrill Lynch Pierce Fenner...................E...... 513 562-2100
Cincinnati *(G-4080)*
Merrill Lynch Pierce Fenner...................E...... 614 798-4354
Dublin *(G-10395)*
Morgan Stanley..E...... 513 721-2000
Cincinnati *(G-4118)*
Nationwide Life Insur Co Amer...............A...... 800 688-5177
Columbus *(G-8245)*
Raymond James Fincl Svcs Inc.............E...... 513 287-6777
Cincinnati *(G-4388)*
Raymond James Fincl Svcs Inc.............E...... 419 586-5121
Celina *(G-2661)*
Robert W Baird & Co Inc.........................E...... 216 737-7330
Cleveland *(G-6404)*
The Huntington Investment Co..............E...... 614 480-3600
Columbus *(G-8836)*
The Huntington Investment Co..............E...... 513 351-2555
Cincinnati *(G-4643)*
Wells Fargo Clearing Svcs LLC..............E...... 513 241-9900
Cincinnati *(G-4831)*
Westmnster Fncl Securities Inc..............E...... 937 898-5010
Dayton *(G-9995)*

BRONZING SVCS: Baby Shoes

Bron-Shoe Company...............................E...... 614 252-0967
Columbus *(G-7150)*

BROOMS & BRUSHES

Mill Rose Laboratories Inc......................E...... 440 974-6730
Mentor *(G-14219)*
Stephen M Trudick...................................E...... 440 834-1891
Burton *(G-2065)*

BROOMS & BRUSHES: Household Or Indl

Mill-Rose Company..................................C...... 440 255-9171
Mentor *(G-14220)*

BUCKETS: Plastic

Impact Products LLC...............................C...... 419 841-2891
Toledo *(G-17971)*

BUILDING & OFFICE CLEANING SVCS

Ashland Cleaning LLC............................E...... 419 281-1747
Ashland *(G-653)*
Corporate Cleaning Inc...........................E...... 614 203-6051
Columbus *(G-7441)*
High-TEC Industrial Services.................C...... 937 667-1772
Tipp City *(G-17718)*
Image By J & K LLC.................................B...... 888 667-6929
Maumee *(G-13927)*
Living Matters LLC..................................E...... 866 587-8074
Cleveland *(G-5948)*
Seaway Sponge & Chamois Co..............E...... 419 691-4694
Toledo *(G-18177)*

BUILDING & STRUCTURAL WOOD MEMBERS

Carter-Jones Lumber Company.............C...... 330 674-9060
Millersburg *(G-14591)*
Holmes Lumber & Bldg Ctr Inc..............C...... 330 674-9060
Millersburg *(G-14604)*

BUILDING CLEANING & MAINTENANCE SVCS

A 1 Janitorial Cleaning Svc....................E...... 513 932-8003
Lebanon *(G-12585)*
ABM Facility Services Inc.......................E...... 859 767-4393
Cincinnati *(G-2961)*
Absolute Cleaning Services...................D...... 440 542-1742
Solon *(G-16968)*
Advanced Facilities Maint Corp.............E...... 614 389-3495
Columbus *(G-6946)*
Akron Public School Maint Svcs............D...... 330 761-2640
Akron *(G-51)*
Allen-Keith Construction Co..................D...... 330 266-2220
Canton *(G-2231)*
Atlantis Co Inc..D...... 888 807-3272
Cleveland *(G-5078)*
Ats Group LLC..C...... 216 744-5757
Solon *(G-16979)*
Belfor USA Group Inc..............................E...... 513 860-3111
West Chester *(G-19192)*
Butterfield Co Inc......................................D...... 330 832-1282
Massillon *(G-13790)*
C & K Industrial Services Inc..................D...... 216 642-0055
Independence *(G-12192)*
C M S Enterprises Inc..............................E...... 740 653-1940
Lancaster *(G-12512)*
Camco Inc...E...... 740 477-3682
Circleville *(G-4881)*
Caveney Inc..D...... 330 497-4600
North Canton *(G-15328)*
Columbus Public School Dst...................B...... 614 365-5043
Columbus *(G-7378)*
Complete Building Maint LLC................E...... 513 235-7511
Cincinnati *(G-3403)*
County of Cuyahoga................................A...... 216 443-6954
Cleveland *(G-5423)*
Custom Maint...D...... 330 793-2523
Youngstown *(G-20164)*
Dempsey Inc...D...... 330 758-2309
Youngstown *(G-20167)*

SERVICES SECTION

BURGLAR ALARM MAINTENANCE & MONITORING SVCS

Environment Control of Greater ....D....... 614 868-9788
   Columbus *(G-7599)*
Feecorp Industrial Services ....C....... 740 533-1445
   Ironton *(G-12288)*
Green Impressions LLC ....E....... 440 240-8508
   Sheffield Village *(G-16886)*
Harrison Industries Inc ....D....... 740 942-2988
   Cadiz *(G-2077)*
Heco Operations Inc ....E....... 614 888-5700
   Worthington *(G-19962)*
High Power Inc ....E....... 937 667-1772
   Tipp City *(G-17717)*
Hopewell Industries Inc ....C....... 740 622-3563
   Coshocton *(G-9107)*
Inner-Space Cleaning Corp ....C....... 440 646-0701
   Cleveland *(G-5823)*
Inovative Facility Svcs LLC ....B....... 419 861-1710
   Maumee *(G-13928)*
J Rutledge Enterprises Inc ....E....... 502 241-4100
   Cincinnati *(G-3852)*
John O Bostock Jr ....E....... 937 263-8540
   Dayton *(G-9644)*
Kettering City School District ....D....... 937 297-1990
   Dayton *(G-9652)*
Key Center Properties LP ....E....... 216 687-0500
   Cleveland *(G-5897)*
Kleman Services LLC ....E....... 419 339-0871
   Lima *(G-12811)*
Lake Side Building Maintenance ....E....... 216 589-9900
   Cleveland *(G-5919)*
Licking-Knox Goodwill Inds Inc ....D....... 614 235-7675
   Columbus *(G-8058)*
Mrap LLC ....E....... 614 545-3190
   Columbus *(G-8202)*
N Services Inc ....D....... 513 793-2000
   Blue Ash *(G-1651)*
Northpointe Property MGT LLC ....C....... 614 579-9712
   Columbus *(G-8294)*
Promanco Inc ....E....... 740 374-2120
   Marietta *(G-13491)*
Psp Operations Inc ....E....... 614 888-5700
   Worthington *(G-19987)*
Putman Janitorial Service Inc ....E....... 513 942-1900
   West Chester *(G-19222)*
Restoration Resources Inc ....D....... 330 650-4486
   Hudson *(G-12141)*
Richland Newhope Industries ....C....... 419 774-4400
   Mansfield *(G-13358)*
ServiceMaster By Sidwell Inc ....E....... 740 687-1077
   Lancaster *(G-12573)*
ServiceMaster Clean ....E....... 440 349-0979
   Bedford *(G-1335)*
Shining Company ....C....... 614 588-4115
   Columbus *(G-8727)*
Sr Improvements Services LLC ....E....... 567 207-6488
   Vickery *(G-18733)*
Star Inc ....C....... 740 354-1517
   Portsmouth *(G-16314)*
Suburban Maint Contrs Inc ....E....... 440 237-7765
   North Royalton *(G-15504)*
T & L Enterprises Inc ....E....... 440 234-5900
   Berea *(G-1471)*
T N C Construction Inc ....E....... 614 554-5330
   Grove City *(G-11604)*
Trg Maintenance LLC ....A....... 614 891-4850
   Westerville *(G-19356)*
Tri Tech Service Systems Inc ....C....... 937 787-4664
   Somerville *(G-17071)*
Ultimate Building Maintenance ....D....... 330 369-9771
   Warren *(G-18918)*
United Scoto Senior Activities ....E....... 740 354-6672
   Portsmouth *(G-16316)*
University of Cincinnati ....A....... 513 556-6381
   Cincinnati *(G-4761)*
Ward & Werner Co ....C....... 614 885-0741
   Worthington *(G-20006)*
Wheeler Cleaning LLC ....E....... 614 818-0981
   Westerville *(G-19450)*
White Glove Executive Services ....E....... 614 226-2553
   Grove City *(G-11617)*

BUILDING CLEANING SVCS

Ace Building Maintenance LLC ....E....... 614 471-2223
   Columbus *(G-6937)*
Beneficial Building Services ....D....... 330 848-2556
   Akron *(G-97)*
Circle Building Services Inc ....D....... 614 228-6090
   Columbus *(G-7275)*
DCS Sanitation Management Inc ....E....... 513 891-4980
   Cincinnati *(G-3469)*
Guardian Care Services ....E....... 614 436-8500
   Columbus *(G-7782)*
Leadec Corp ....E....... 513 731-3590
   Blue Ash *(G-1627)*
Lucas Building Mainenance LLC ....A....... 740 479-1800
   Ironton *(G-12297)*
MPW Industrial Services Inc ....E....... 440 277-9072
   Lorain *(G-13062)*
Quality Clg Svc of NW Ohio ....E....... 419 335-9105
   Wauseon *(G-18961)*
Stout Lori Cleaning & Such ....E....... 419 637-7644
   Gibsonburg *(G-11404)*
W David Maupin Inc ....E....... 419 389-0458
   Toledo *(G-18294)*

BUILDING COMPONENT CLEANING SVCS

MPW Industrial Services Inc ....D....... 330 454-1898
   Canton *(G-2467)*
Professional Restoration Svc ....E....... 330 825-1803
   Medina *(G-14114)*

BUILDING COMPONENTS: Structural Steel

Frederick Steel Company LLC ....D....... 513 821-6400
   Cincinnati *(G-3646)*
GL Nause Co Inc ....E....... 513 722-9500
   Loveland *(G-13128)*
J&J Precision Machine Ltd ....D....... 330 923-5783
   Cuyahoga Falls *(G-9197)*
Louis Arthur Steel Company ....D....... 440 997-5545
   Geneva *(G-11365)*
Mound Technologies Inc ....E....... 937 748-2937
   Springboro *(G-17131)*
Turn-Key Industrial Svcs LLC ....D....... 614 274-1128
   Columbus *(G-8878)*
Universal Fabg Cnstr Svcs Inc ....D....... 614 274-1128
   Columbus *(G-8905)*
Wernli Realty Inc ....D....... 937 258-7878
   Beavercreek *(G-1262)*

BUILDING INSPECTION SVCS

A2z Field Services LLC ....C....... 614 873-0211
   Plain City *(G-16179)*
Inspection Group Incorporated ....E....... 614 891-3606
   Westerville *(G-19316)*
Quality Control Inspection ....D....... 440 359-1900
   Cleveland *(G-6334)*
Technical Assurance Inc ....E....... 440 953-3147
   Willoughby *(G-19717)*

BUILDING MAINTENANCE SVCS, EXC REPAIRS

Alpha & Omega Bldg Svcs Inc ....D....... 937 229-3536
   Dayton *(G-9320)*
AMF Facility Services Inc ....E....... 800 991-2273
   Dayton *(G-9334)*
Blanchard Valley Health System ....A....... 419 423-4500
   Findlay *(G-10997)*
Butchko Electric Inc ....E....... 440 985-3180
   Amherst *(G-589)*
G J Goudreau & Co ....E....... 216 351-5233
   Cleveland *(G-5646)*
Lima Sheet Metal Machine & Mfg ....E....... 419 229-1161
   Lima *(G-12827)*
Louderback Fmly Invstments Inc ....E....... 937 845-1762
   New Carlisle *(G-15026)*

BUILDING PRDTS & MATERIALS DEALERS

Carter-Jones Companies Inc ....E....... 330 673-6100
   Kent *(G-12354)*
Carter-Jones Lumber Company ....A....... 330 673-6000
   Kent *(G-12356)*
Carter-Jones Lumber Company ....C....... 330 674-9060
   Millersburg *(G-14591)*
CCI Supply Inc ....C....... 440 953-0045
   Mentor *(G-14154)*
Clays Heritage Carpet Inc ....E....... 330 497-1280
   Canton *(G-2312)*
Contract Lumber Inc ....C....... 740 964-3147
   Pataskala *(G-15921)*
Contractors Materials Company ....E....... 513 733-3000
   Cincinnati *(G-3413)*
D C Curry Lumber Company ....E....... 330 264-5223
   Wooster *(G-19860)*
Daniels Lumber Co Inc ....D....... 330 533-2211
   Canfield *(G-2188)*
Dilly Door Co ....E....... 419 782-1181
   Defiance *(G-10028)*
Do It Best Corp ....C....... 330 725-3859
   Medina *(G-14061)*
Famous Enterprises Inc ....E....... 419 478-0343
   Toledo *(G-17879)*
Hamilton-Parker Company ....D....... 614 358-7800
   Columbus *(G-7797)*
Holmes Lumber & Bldg Ctr Inc ....C....... 330 674-9060
   Millersburg *(G-14604)*
Hull Builders Supply Inc ....E....... 440 967-3159
   Vermilion *(G-18710)*
J & B Equipment & Supply Inc ....D....... 419 884-1155
   Mansfield *(G-13314)*
Judy Mills Company Inc ....E....... 513 271-4241
   Cincinnati *(G-3895)*
K M B Inc ....E....... 330 889-3451
   Bristolville *(G-1872)*
Khempco Bldg Sup Co Ltd Partnr ....D....... 740 549-0465
   Delaware *(G-10113)*
Lang Stone Company Inc ....E....... 614 235-4099
   Columbus *(G-8038)*
Lowes Home Centers LLC ....C....... 216 351-4723
   Cleveland *(G-5953)*
Lowes Home Centers LLC ....C....... 419 739-1300
   Wapakoneta *(G-18803)*
Lowes Home Centers LLC ....C....... 440 392-0027
   Mentor *(G-14210)*
Lowes Home Centers LLC ....C....... 330 245-4300
   Akron *(G-329)*
Lowes Home Centers LLC ....C....... 330 965-4500
   Youngstown *(G-20257)*
Lowes Home Centers LLC ....C....... 937 854-8200
   Dayton *(G-9691)*
Mentor Lumber and Supply Co ....C....... 440 255-8814
   Mentor *(G-14214)*
Schneider Home Equipment Co ....E....... 513 522-1200
   Cincinnati *(G-4483)*
Stamm Contracting Co Inc ....E....... 330 274-8230
   Mantua *(G-13395)*
Thomas Do-It Center Inc ....E....... 740 446-2002
   Gallipolis *(G-11339)*

BUILDING SCALES MODELS

3-D Technical Services Company ....E....... 937 746-2901
   Franklin *(G-11147)*

BUILDINGS & COMPONENTS: Prefabricated Metal

Hoge Lumber Company ....E....... 419 753-2263
   New Knoxville *(G-15052)*

BUILDINGS, PREFABRICATED: Wholesalers

Real America Inc ....B....... 216 261-1177
   Cleveland *(G-6357)*

BUILDINGS: Farm & Utility

Morton Buildings Inc ....D....... 419 675-2311
   Kenton *(G-12422)*

BUILDINGS: Prefabricated, Metal

Enclosure Suppliers LLC ....E....... 513 782-3900
   Cincinnati *(G-3555)*

BUILDINGS: Prefabricated, Wood

Morton Buildings Inc ....D....... 419 675-2311
   Kenton *(G-12422)*
Vinyl Design Corporation ....E....... 419 283-4009
   Holland *(G-12067)*

BURGLAR ALARM MAINTENANCE & MONITORING SVCS

Area Wide Protective Inc ....E....... 513 321-9889
   Fairfield *(G-10820)*
Guardian Protection Svcs Inc ....D....... 513 422-5319
   West Chester *(G-19085)*
Habitec Security Inc ....E....... 419 537-6768
   Holland *(G-12025)*
Integrated Protection Svcs Inc ....D....... 513 631-5505
   Cincinnati *(G-3827)*
Johnson Cntrls SEC Sltions LLC ....C....... 330 497-0850
   Canton *(G-2419)*
Johnson Cntrls SEC Sltions LLC ....D....... 440 262-1084
   Brecksville *(G-1830)*
Johnson Cntrls SEC Sltions LLC ....C....... 561 988-3600
   Dublin *(G-10380)*

Employee Codes: A=Over 500 employees, B=251-500
C=101-250, D=51-100, E=25-50

BURGLAR ALARM MAINTENANCE & MONITORING SVCS — SERVICES SECTION

Johnson Cntrls SEC Sltions LLC .... E 419 243-8400
  Maumee *(G-13931)*
Mills Security Alarm Systems .... E 513 921-4600
  Cincinnati *(G-4101)*
Ohio Valley Integration Svcs .... E 937 492-0008
  Sidney *(G-16946)*
Research & Investigation Assoc .... E 419 526-1299
  Mansfield *(G-13355)*
Shiver Security Systems Inc .... E 513 719-4000
  Mason *(G-13760)*
State Alarm Inc .... E 330 726-8111
  Youngstown *(G-20382)*
United States Protective .... E 216 475-8550
  Independence *(G-12271)*
Vector Security Inc .... E 440 466-7233
  Geneva *(G-11372)*
Vector Security Inc .... E 330 726-9841
  Boardman *(G-1745)*

BURIAL VAULTS: Concrete Or Precast Terrazzo

Mack Industries .... C 419 353-7081
  Bowling Green *(G-1785)*

BURLAP WHOLESALERS

Dayton Bag & Burlap Co .... C 937 258-8000
  Dayton *(G-9461)*

BUS BARS: Electrical

Schneider Electric Usa Inc .... D 513 755-5000
  West Chester *(G-19145)*

BUS CHARTER SVC: Local

A T V Inc .... C 614 252-5060
  Columbus *(G-6920)*
Charter Vans Inc .... E 937 898-4043
  Vandalia *(G-18669)*
Croswell of Williamsburg LLC .... E 513 724-2206
  Williamsburg *(G-19631)*
Cusa LI Inc .... C 216 267-8810
  Brookpark *(G-1942)*
Cuyahoga Marketing Service .... E 440 526-5350
  Cleveland *(G-5457)*
Firstgroup America Inc .... D 513 241-2200
  Cincinnati *(G-3626)*
Lakefront Lines Inc .... D 513 829-8290
  Fairfield *(G-10872)*
Lakefront Lines Inc .... C 216 267-8810
  Brookpark *(G-1949)*
Marfre Inc .... C 513 321-3377
  Cincinnati *(G-4021)*
Precious Cargo Transportation .... E 440 564-8039
  Newbury *(G-15260)*
Queen City Transportation LLC .... B 513 941-8700
  Cincinnati *(G-4372)*
S B S Transit Inc .... B 440 288-2222
  Lorain *(G-13075)*
Transit Service Company .... E 330 782-3343
  Youngstown *(G-20390)*

BUS CHARTER SVC: Long-Distance

Buckeye Charter Service Inc .... E 419 222-2455
  Lima *(G-12750)*
Buckeye Charter Service Inc .... E 937 879-3000
  Dayton *(G-9368)*
Croswell of Williamsburg LLC .... E 513 724-2206
  Williamsburg *(G-19631)*
Cusa LI Inc .... C 216 267-8810
  Brookpark *(G-1942)*
Cuyahoga Marketing Service .... E 440 526-5350
  Cleveland *(G-5457)*
Garfield Hts Coach Line Inc .... D 440 232-4550
  Chagrin Falls *(G-2697)*
Greyhound Lines Inc .... E 614 221-0577
  Columbus *(G-7779)*
Hat White Management LLC .... E 800 525-7967
  Akron *(G-257)*
Lakefront Lines Inc .... C 216 267-8810
  Brookpark *(G-1949)*
Lakefront Lines Inc .... E 419 537-0677
  Toledo *(G-18000)*
Lakefront Lines Inc .... E 614 476-1113
  Columbus *(G-8031)*
Pioneer Trails Inc .... E 330 674-1234
  Millersburg *(G-14616)*
Put In Bay Transportation .... E 419 285-4855
  Put In Bay *(G-16370)*
Queen City Transportation LLC .... B 513 941-8700
  Cincinnati *(G-4372)*
S B S Transit Inc .... B 440 288-2222
  Lorain *(G-13075)*
Starforce National Corporation .... C 513 979-3600
  Cincinnati *(G-4586)*
Sutton Motor Coach Tours Inc .... E 330 726-2800
  Youngstown *(G-20386)*
Tesco-Transportion Eqp Sls .... E 419 836-2835
  Oregon *(G-15751)*

BUS TERMINALS & SVC FACILITIES

Lakota Local School District .... C 513 777-2150
  Liberty Township *(G-12722)*
Meigs Local School District .... E 740 742-2990
  Middleport *(G-14408)*
Ottawa County Transit Board .... E 419 898-7433
  Oak Harbor *(G-15615)*

BUSES: Wholesalers

Tesco-Transportion Eqp Sls .... E 419 836-2835
  Oregon *(G-15751)*

BUSHINGS & BEARINGS

McNeil Industries Inc .... E 440 951-7756
  Painesville *(G-15866)*

BUSINESS & SECRETARIAL SCHOOLS

Academy Court Reporting Inc .... E 216 861-3222
  Cleveland *(G-4951)*

BUSINESS ACTIVITIES: Non-Commercial Site

Ability Works Inc .... C 419 626-1048
  Sandusky *(G-16723)*
Adventure Cmbat Operations LLC .... E 330 818-1029
  Canton *(G-2228)*
Boardman Molded Intl LLC .... C 330 788-2400
  Youngstown *(G-20120)*
Boyd Property Group LLC .... E 614 725-5228
  Columbus *(G-7126)*
Burgess & Niple / Heapy Engine .... D 614 459-2050
  Columbus *(G-7170)*
Calvin Lanier .... E 937 952-4221
  Dayton *(G-9377)*
Cardio Partners Inc .... D 614 760-5038
  Dublin *(G-10278)*
Clovvr LLC .... E 740 653-2224
  Columbus *(G-7308)*
Emco Usa LLC .... E 740 588-1722
  Zanesville *(G-20474)*
Evanston Bulldogs Youth Footba .... E 513 254-9500
  Cincinnati *(G-3579)*
Haven Financial Enterprise .... E 800 265-2401
  Cleveland *(G-5732)*
Hochstedler Construction Ltd .... E 740 427-4880
  Gambier *(G-11347)*
Improvedge LLC .... E 614 793-1738
  Powell *(G-16338)*
Industrial Insul Coatings LLC .... E 800 506-1399
  Girard *(G-11414)*
Infoverity LLC .... E 614 327-5173
  Dublin *(G-10375)*
Jacqueline Kumi-Sakyi .... D 740 282-5955
  Steubenville *(G-17322)*
Jason Wilson .... E 937 604-8209
  Tipp City *(G-17720)*
John Stewart Company .... D 513 703-5412
  Cincinnati *(G-3878)*
Jrb Industries LLC .... E 567 825-7022
  Greenville *(G-11511)*
Legacy Industrial Services LLC .... E 606 584-8953
  Ripley *(G-16547)*
Lions Gate SEC Solutions Inc .... E 440 539-8382
  Euclid *(G-10767)*
McConnell Excavating Ltd .... E 440 774-4578
  Oberlin *(G-15649)*
McDonalds 3490 .... E 330 762-7747
  Akron *(G-333)*
Microanalysis Society Inc .... B 614 256-8063
  Hilliard *(G-11934)*
Miencorp Inc .... E 330 978-8511
  Niles *(G-15296)*
Mount Auburn Community Hdo .... D 513 659-4514
  Cincinnati *(G-4124)*
Mroeki Inc .... C 330 318-3926
  Youngstown *(G-20290)*
Mt Washington Care Center Inc .... C 513 231-4561
  Cincinnati *(G-4130)*
P3 Infrastructure Inc .... A 330 686-1129
  Stow *(G-17385)*
Platinum Prestige Property .... E 614 705-2251
  Columbus *(G-8550)*
Pmwi LLC .... D 614 975-5004
  Hilliard *(G-11943)*
Popper & Associates Msrp LLC .... E 614 798-8991
  Dublin *(G-10428)*
Quality Lines Inc .... C 740 815-1165
  Findlay *(G-11078)*
Reliable Polymer Services LP .... E 800 321-0954
  Wadsworth *(G-18769)*
Roy J Miller .... E 330 674-2405
  Millersburg *(G-14619)*
Service Pronet Inc .... E 614 874-4300
  Columbus *(G-8716)*
Shotstop Ballistics LLC .... E 330 686-0020
  Stow *(G-17392)*
Snapblox Hosted Solutions LLC .... E 866 524-7707
  Cincinnati *(G-4545)*
Soundtrack Printing .... C 330 606-7117
  Cuyahoga Falls *(G-9219)*
Tim Mundy .... E 937 862-8686
  Spring Valley *(G-17111)*
Top Tier Soccer LLC .... E 937 903-6114
  Dayton *(G-9932)*
Tri County Tower Service .... E 330 538-9874
  North Jackson *(G-15389)*
Vigilant Global Trade Svcs LLC .... E 260 417-1825
  Shaker Heights *(G-16871)*

BUSINESS FORMS WHOLESALERS

GBS Corp .... C 330 494-5330
  North Canton *(G-15339)*
Optimum System Products Inc .... E 614 885-4464
  Westerville *(G-19433)*
Shamrock Companies Inc .... C 440 899-9510
  Westlake *(G-19546)*

BUSINESS FORMS: Printed, Manifold

Custom Products Corporation .... D 440 528-7100
  Solon *(G-16999)*
Eleet Cryogenics Inc .... E 330 874-4009
  Bolivar *(G-1746)*
GBS Corp .... C 330 494-5330
  North Canton *(G-15339)*

BUSINESS MACHINE REPAIR, ELECTRIC

Blakemans Valley Off Eqp Inc .... E 330 729-1000
  Youngstown *(G-20116)*
Blue Technologies Inc .... E 330 499-9300
  Canton *(G-2266)*
Leppo Inc .... C 330 633-3999
  Tallmadge *(G-17643)*
Modern Office Methods Inc .... D 513 791-0909
  Blue Ash *(G-1644)*
Modern Office Methods Inc .... E 614 891-3693
  Westerville *(G-19426)*
Ohio Business Machines LLC .... E 216 485-2000
  Cleveland *(G-6187)*
Toshiba Amer Bus Solutions Inc .... E 216 642-7555
  Cleveland *(G-6603)*

BUSINESS SUPPORT SVCS

Beheydts Auto Wrecking .... E 330 658-6109
  Doylestown *(G-10223)*
Dennis & Carol Liederbach .... E 256 582-6200
  Northfield *(G-15513)*
Eventions Ltd .... E 216 952-9898
  Cleveland *(G-5556)*
J Cherie LLC .... E 216 453-1051
  Shaker Heights *(G-16862)*
Madison Cnty Lndon Cy Hlth Dst .... E 740 852-3065
  London *(G-12999)*
Notoweega Nation Inc .... D 740 777-1480
  Logan *(G-12986)*
R Square Inc .... E 216 328-2077
  Cleveland *(G-6340)*
Rolling Hocevar & Associa .... E 614 760-8320
  Dublin *(G-10443)*
Streamline Technical Svcs LLC .... D 614 441-7448
  Lockbourne *(G-12961)*

BUSINESS TRAINING SVCS

International Association of .... E 330 628-3012
  Canton *(G-2413)*

SERVICES SECTION
CANDY & CONFECTIONS: Chocolate Covered Dates

BUTTER WHOLESALERS
Hillandale Farms Corporation..............E....... 330 724-3199
  Akron (G-265)

CABINETS: Entertainment
Kraftmaid Trucking Inc......................D....... 440 632-2531
  Middlefield (G-14396)

CABINETS: Entertainment Units, Household, Wood
Progressive Furniture Inc..................E....... 419 446-4500
  Archbold (G-641)

CABINETS: Kitchen, Wood
Brower Products Inc..........................D....... 937 563-1111
  Cincinnati (G-3142)
Carter-Jones Lumber Company..........C....... 330 674-9060
  Millersburg (G-14591)
Hattenbach Company..........................D....... 216 881-5200
  Cleveland (G-5731)
Holmes Lumber & Bldg Ctr Inc............C....... 330 674-9060
  Millersburg (G-14604)
Online Mega Sellers Corp..................D....... 888 384-6468
  Toledo (G-18109)
Riverside Cnstr Svcs Inc.....................E....... 513 723-0900
  Cincinnati (G-4427)

CABINETS: Office, Wood
Hoge Lumber Company.....................E....... 419 753-2263
  New Knoxville (G-15052)

CABINETS: Show, Display, Etc, Wood, Exc Refrigerated
Hattenbach Company..........................D....... 216 881-5200
  Cleveland (G-5731)

CABLE & OTHER PAY TELEVISION DISTRIBUTION
Armstrong Utilities Inc.......................E....... 330 758-6411
  North Lima (G-15396)
ASC of Cincinnati Inc.........................E....... 513 886-7100
  Lebanon (G-12590)
C T Wireless.......................................D....... 937 653-2208
  Urbana (G-18574)
Conneaut Telephone Company..........E....... 440 593-7140
  Conneaut (G-9041)
Ohio News Network...........................D....... 614 460-3700
  Columbus (G-8362)
Verizon Communications Inc.............C....... 440 892-4504
  Westlake (G-19562)

CABLE & PAY TELEVISION SVCS: Closed Circuit
State Alarm Inc...................................E....... 330 726-8111
  Youngstown (G-20382)

CABLE & PAY TELEVISION SVCS: Direct Broadcast Satellite
Dish Network Corporation.................D....... 614 534-2001
  Hilliard (G-11896)
Satcom Service LLC...........................D....... 614 863-6470
  Reynoldsburg (G-16481)

CABLE & PAY TELEVISION SVCS: Multipoint Distribution Sys/MDS
Fulfillment Technologies LLC.............C....... 513 346-3100
  West Chester (G-19203)

CABLE & PAY TV SVCS: Satellite Master Antenna Sys/SMATV
DSI Systems Inc.................................E....... 614 871-1456
  Grove City (G-11557)

CABLE TELEVISION
Chillicothe Telephone Company........C....... 740 772-8200
  Chillicothe (G-2825)
Coaxial Communications of Sout.......D....... 513 797-4400
  Columbus (G-7311)
Comcast Cble Cmmunications LLC....C....... 503 372-9144
  Steubenville (G-17312)
Comcast Corporation..........................D....... 740 633-3437
  Bridgeport (G-1861)
Comcast Corporation..........................D....... 419 586-1458
  Celina (G-2640)
Comcast Spotlight..............................E....... 440 617-2280
  Westlake (G-19478)
Comcast Spotlight Inc.........................B....... 216 575-8016
  Cleveland (G-5373)
Cox Cable Cleveland Area Inc............C....... 216 676-8300
  Cleveland (G-5431)
Cox Communications Inc...................D....... 216 712-4500
  Parma (G-15903)
Cox Communications Inc...................D....... 937 222-5700
  Dayton (G-9442)
Doylestown Communications.............E....... 330 658-7000
  Doylestown (G-10226)
Erie County Cablevision Inc...............E....... 419 627-0800
  Sandusky (G-16753)
Insight Communications of Co...........C....... 614 236-1200
  Columbus (G-7905)
Massillon Cable TV Inc......................D....... 330 833-4134
  Massillon (G-13833)
Spectrum MGT Holdg Co LLC...........E....... 614 481-5408
  Columbus (G-8759)
Spectrum MGT Holdg Co LLC...........D....... 740 455-9705
  Zanesville (G-20537)
Spectrum MGT Holdg Co LLC...........D....... 330 856-2343
  Warren (G-18901)
Spectrum MGT Holdg Co LLC...........D....... 419 386-0040
  Port Clinton (G-16256)
Spectrum MGT Holdg Co LLC...........D....... 740 762-0291
  Chillicothe (G-2888)
Spectrum MGT Holdg Co LLC...........D....... 513 469-1112
  Cincinnati (G-4559)
Spectrum MGT Holdg Co LLC...........E....... 614 344-4159
  Columbus (G-8760)
Spectrum MGT Holdg Co LLC...........D....... 937 552-5760
  Springfield (G-17276)
Spectrum MGT Holdg Co LLC...........D....... 740 200-3385
  Athens (G-812)
Spectrum MGT Holdg Co LLC...........D....... 614 503-4153
  Hilliard (G-11952)
Spectrum MGT Holdg Co LLC...........D....... 440 319-3271
  Ashtabula (G-764)
Spectrum MGT Holdg Co LLC...........E....... 419 775-9292
  Mansfield (G-13366)
Spectrum MGT Holdg Co LLC...........E....... 330 208-9028
  Akron (G-446)
Spectrum MGT Holdg Co LLC...........D....... 937 684-8891
  Dayton (G-9896)
Spectrum MGT Holdg Co LLC...........E....... 740 772-7809
  Lancaster (G-12576)
Spectrum MGT Holdg Co LLC...........D....... 937 294-6800
  Dayton (G-9897)
Spectrum MGT Holdg Co LLC...........D....... 937 306-6082
  Piqua (G-16166)
Time Warner Cable Entps LLC...........A....... 614 255-6289
  Columbus (G-8845)
Time Warner Cable Entps LLC...........D....... 513 489-5000
  Blue Ash (G-1695)
Time Warner Cable Entps LLC...........E....... 614 481-5072
  Columbus (G-8846)
Time Warner Cable Inc........................D....... 614 236-1200
  Columbus (G-8847)
Time Warner Cable Inc........................D....... 440 366-0416
  Elyria (G-10684)
Time Warner Cable Inc........................D....... 419 331-1111
  Lima (G-12899)
Time Warner Cable Inc........................D....... 614 481-5050
  Columbus (G-8848)
Time Warner Cable Inc........................E....... 330 800-3874
  Akron (G-477)
Time Warner Cable Inc........................A....... 614 481 6000
  Columbus (G-8849)
Time Warner Cable Inc........................D....... 330 494-9200
  Canton (G-2562)
Time Warner Cable Inc........................E....... 330 633-9203
  Youngstown (G-20389)
Time Warner Cable Inc........................D....... 513 489-5000
  Blue Ash (G-1697)
Time Warner Cable Inc........................E....... 937 471-1572
  Eaton (G-10577)
Time Warner Cable Inc........................D....... 513 523-6333
  Oxford (G-15831)
Time Warner Cable Inc........................E....... 937 483-5152
  Troy (G-18379)
Time Warner Cable Inc........................D....... 740 345-4329
  Newark (G-15240)
Time Warner Cable Inc........................D....... 937 667-8302
  Tipp City (G-17727)
Time Warner Cable Inc........................D....... 937 492-4145
  Sidney (G-16957)
TSC Television Inc..............................D....... 419 941-6001
  Wapakoneta (G-18811)
USI Cable Corp..................................E....... 937 606-2636
  Piqua (G-16173)

CABLE WIRING SETS: Battery, Internal Combustion Engines
Noco Company...................................B....... 216 464-8131
  Solon (G-17035)

CABLE: Noninsulated
Microplex Inc......................................E....... 330 498-0600
  North Canton (G-15353)

CABS, FOR HIRE: Horse Drawn
Age Line Inc.......................................E....... 216 941-9990
  Cleveland (G-4968)
Total Transportation Trckg Inc............E....... 216 398-6090
  Cleveland (G-6604)

CAFES
Covelli Family Ltd Partnership............E....... 330 856-3176
  Warren (G-18842)
Howley Bread Group Ltd...................D....... 440 808-1600
  Westlake (G-19492)

CAFETERIAS
Westgate Lanes Incorporated.............E....... 419 229-3845
  Lima (G-12920)

CALENDARS, WHOLESALE
Gordon Bernard Company LLC..........E....... 513 248-7600
  Milford (G-14523)

CALIBRATING SVCS, NEC
Raitz Inc..E....... 513 769-1200
  Cincinnati (G-4384)

CAMERA & PHOTOGRAPHIC SPLYS STORES
Click Camera & Video........................E....... 937 435-3072
  Miamisburg (G-14285)
Collins KAO Inc..................................E....... 513 948-9000
  Cincinnati (G-3388)
KAO Collins Inc..................................D....... 513 948-9000
  Cincinnati (G-3901)

CAMPGROUNDS
Big Broth and Big Siste of Cen...........E....... 614 839-2447
  Columbus (G-7106)
Clare-Mar Camp Inc...........................E....... 440 647-3318
  New London (G-15066)
Dayton Tall Timbers Resort................E....... 937 833-3888
  Brookville (G-1962)
Elbe Properties..................................A....... 513 489-1955
  Cincinnati (G-3545)
Real America Inc................................B....... 216 261-1177
  Cleveland (G-6357)

CAMPSITES
Great Miami Valley YMCA..................E....... 513 867-0600
  Hamilton (G-11734)

CANDLES
Gorant Chocolatier LLC......................C....... 330 726-8821
  Boardman (G-1740)

CANDLES: Wholesalers
White Barn Candle Co........................A....... 614 856-6000
  Reynoldsburg (G-16490)

CANDY & CONFECTIONS: Chocolate Covered Dates
Walnut Creek Chocolate Company.....E....... 330 893-2995
  Walnut Creek (G-18785)

CANDY & CONFECTIONS: Cough Drops, Exc Pharmaceutical Preps

Amerisource Health Svcs LLC .... D 614 492-8177
  Columbus *(G-7012)*

CANDY MAKING GOODS & SPLYS, WHOLESALE

Albrecht Inc .... E 513 576-9900
  Milford *(G-14501)*

CANDY, NUT & CONFECTIONERY STORE: Popcorn, Incl Caramel Corn

Drc Holdings Inc .... E 419 230-0188
  Pandora *(G-15889)*

CANDY, NUT & CONFECTIONERY STORES: Candy

Gorant Chocolatier LLC .... C 330 726-8821
  Boardman *(G-1740)*
Robert E McGrath Inc .... E 440 572-7747
  Strongsville *(G-17503)*
Walnut Creek Chocolate Company .... E 330 893-2995
  Walnut Creek *(G-18785)*

CANDY, NUT & CONFECTIONERY STORES: Produced For Direct Sale

Cleveland Soc For The Blind .... C 216 791-8118
  Cleveland *(G-5347)*

CANDY: Chocolate From Cacao Beans

Walnut Creek Chocolate Company .... E 330 893-2995
  Walnut Creek *(G-18785)*

CANNED SPECIALTIES

Abbott Laboratories .... A 614 624-3191
  Columbus *(G-6924)*
Bittersweet Inc .... D 419 875-6986
  Whitehouse *(G-19584)*
Skyline Chili Inc .... C 513 874-1188
  Fairfield *(G-10910)*

CANS: Fiber

Sonoco Products Company .... D 937 429-0040
  Beavercreek Township *(G-1285)*

CANVAS PRDTS

Samsel Rope & Marine Supply Co .... E 216 241-0333
  Cleveland *(G-6442)*

CANVAS PRDTS: Convertible Tops, Car/Boat, Fm Purchased Mtrl

Crown Dielectric Inds Inc .... C 614 224-5161
  Columbus *(G-7467)*

CANVAS PRDTS: Shades, Made From Purchased Materials

Lumenomics Inc .... E 614 798-3500
  Lewis Center *(G-12693)*

CAR LOADING SVCS

Ameripro Logistics LLC .... E 410 375-3469
  Dayton *(G-9333)*

CAR WASH EQPT

Giant Industries Inc .... E 419 531-4600
  Toledo *(G-17915)*

CAR WASHES

Beheydts Auto Wrecking .... E 330 658-6109
  Doylestown *(G-10223)*
Bp .... E 216 731-3826
  Euclid *(G-10745)*
Car Wash Plus Ltd .... E 513 683-4228
  Cincinnati *(G-3175)*
Consumer Foods .... E 440 284-5972
  Elyria *(G-10608)*
Covington Car Wash Inc .... E 513 831-6164
  Milford *(G-14514)*

Four Season Car Wash .... E 330 372-4163
  Warren *(G-18858)*
Henderson Road Rest Systems .... E 614 442-3310
  Columbus *(G-7825)*
J & T Washes Inc .... E 614 486-9093
  Columbus *(G-7930)*
Lawnview Industries Inc .... C 937 653-5217
  Urbana *(G-18593)*
Napoleon Wash-N-Fill Inc .... D 419 592-0851
  Napoleon *(G-14947)*
Sax 5th Ave Car Wash Inc .... E 614 486-9093
  Columbus *(G-8688)*
Susan A Smith Crystal Care .... E 419 747-2666
  Butler *(G-2068)*

CARBON & GRAPHITE PRDTS, NEC

Applied Sciences Inc .... E 937 766-2020
  Cedarville *(G-2631)*
GE Aviation Systems LLC .... B 937 898-5881
  Vandalia *(G-18681)*
Graftech Holdings Inc .... C 216 676-2000
  Independence *(G-12214)*
Mill-Rose Company .... C 440 255-9171
  Mentor *(G-14220)*

CARBON PAPER & INKED RIBBONS

Pubco Corporation .... D 216 881-5300
  Cleveland *(G-6332)*

CARDS: Beveled

Cott Systems Inc .... D 614 847-4405
  Columbus *(G-7449)*

CARNIVAL & AMUSEMENT PARK EQPT WHOLESALERS

Majestic Manufacturing Inc .... E 330 457-2447
  New Waterford *(G-15138)*

CARPET & RUG CLEANING PLANTS

C M S Enterprises Inc .... E 740 653-1940
  Lancaster *(G-12512)*
Farrow Cleaners Co .... E 216 561-2355
  Cleveland *(G-5574)*
Martin Carpet Cleaning Company .... E 614 443-4655
  Columbus *(G-8121)*

CARPET & UPHOLSTERY CLEANING SVCS

Allen-Keith Construction Co .... D 330 266-2220
  Canton *(G-2231)*
Americas Floor Source LLC .... E 216 342-4929
  Bedford Heights *(G-1346)*
Bechtl Bldng Mntnc Crprtn of .... D 330 759-2797
  Youngstown *(G-20111)*
C&C Clean Team Enterprises LLC .... C 513 321-5100
  Cincinnati *(G-3163)*
Icon Environmental Group LLC .... E 513 426-6767
  Milford *(G-14526)*
Image By J & K LLC .... B 888 667-6929
  Maumee *(G-13927)*
New Albany Cleaning Services .... E 614 855-9990
  New Albany *(G-14997)*
Ohio Building Service Inc .... E 513 761-0268
  Cincinnati *(G-4202)*
Springfeld Unfrm-Linen Sup Inc .... D 937 323-5544
  Springfield *(G-17278)*
Sunset Carpet Cleaning .... E 937 836-5531
  Englewood *(G-10721)*
Teasdale Fenton Carpet Cleanin .... D 513 797-0900
  Cincinnati *(G-4628)*
Widmers LLC .... E 513 321-5100
  Cincinnati *(G-4848)*

CARPET & UPHOLSTERY CLEANING SVCS: Carpet/Furniture, On Loc

Arslanian Bros Crpt Rug Clg Co .... E 216 271-6888
  Warrensville Heights *(G-18931)*
Carpet Services Plus Inc .... E 330 458-2409
  Canton *(G-2301)*
Coit Services of Ohio Inc .... D 216 626-0040
  Cleveland *(G-5369)*
Lazar Brothers Inc .... E 440 585-9333
  Wickliffe *(G-19606)*
Merlene Enterprises Inc .... E 440 593-6771
  Conneaut *(G-9044)*

Samron Inc .... E 330 782-6539
  Youngstown *(G-20366)*
Stanley Steemer Intl Inc .... C 614 764-2007
  Dublin *(G-10461)*
Stanley Steemer Intl Inc .... E 419 227-1212
  Lima *(G-12891)*
Stanley Steemer Intl Inc .... E 513 771-0213
  Cincinnati *(G-4582)*
Stanley Steemer Intl Inc .... E 614 652-2241
  Dublin *(G-10462)*
Stanley Steemer Intl Inc .... E 937 431-3205
  Beavercreek Township *(G-1286)*
Stanley Stemer of Akron Canton .... E 330 785-5005
  Coventry Township *(G-9133)*
Velco Inc .... E 513 772-4226
  Cincinnati *(G-4805)*
Wiggins Clg & Crpt Svc Inc .... D 937 279-9080
  Dayton *(G-9998)*

CARPET & UPHOLSTERY CLEANING SVCS: On Customer Premises

D & J Master Clean Inc .... E 614 847-1181
  Columbus *(G-7477)*
Marks Cleaning Service Inc .... E 330 725-5702
  Medina *(G-14094)*

CARTONS: Egg, Molded Pulp, Made From Purchased Materials

Tekni-Plex Inc .... E 419 491-2407
  Holland *(G-12060)*

CASH REGISTERS WHOLESALERS

Business Data Systems Inc .... E 330 633-1221
  Tallmadge *(G-17633)*

CASINO HOTELS & MOTELS

Hollywood Casino Toledo .... D 419 661-5200
  Toledo *(G-17956)*
Horseshoe Cleveland MGT LLC .... E 216 297-4777
  Cleveland *(G-5776)*

CASTINGS: Commercial Investment, Ferrous

B W Grinding Co .... E 419 923-1376
  Lyons *(G-13185)*
Howmet Corporation .... E 800 242-9898
  Newburgh Heights *(G-15251)*

CASTINGS: Die, Aluminum

Akron Foundry Co .... C 330 745-3101
  Akron *(G-40)*
Seilkop Industries Inc .... E 513 761-1035
  Cincinnati *(G-4492)*
Yoder Industries Inc .... C 937 278-5769
  Dayton *(G-10007)*

CASTINGS: Die, Nonferrous

Empire Brass Co .... E 216 431-6565
  Cleveland *(G-5537)*
Yoder Industries Inc .... C 937 278-5769
  Dayton *(G-10007)*

CASTINGS: Machinery, Aluminum

Enprotech Industrial Tech LLC .... C 216 883-3220
  Cleveland *(G-5542)*

CASTINGS: Precision

Akron Foundry Co .... C 330 745-3101
  Akron *(G-40)*

CATALOG & MAIL-ORDER HOUSES

Big Lots Stores Inc .... B 614 278-6800
  Columbus *(G-7107)*
Cornerstone Brands Group Inc .... A 513 603-1000
  West Chester *(G-19053)*

CATALOG SALES

Amerimark Holdings LLC .... B 440 325-2000
  Cleveland *(G-5025)*
Cinmar LLC .... C 513 603-1000
  West Chester *(G-19040)*

SERVICES SECTION

CHEMICALS & ALLIED PRDTS WHOLESALERS, NEC

CATAPULTS

Universal Fabg Cnstr Svcs Inc ....D 614 274-1128
  Columbus *(G-8905)*

CATERERS

A Tara Tiffanys Property ....E 330 448-0778
  Brookfield *(G-1896)*
AVI Food Systems Inc ....C 330 372-6000
  Warren *(G-18827)*
Bagel Place Inc ....E 419 885-1000
  Toledo *(G-17762)*
Black Tie Affair Inc ....E 330 345-8333
  Wooster *(G-19832)*
Davis Catering Inc ....D 513 241-3464
  Cincinnati *(G-3464)*
De Lucas Place In Park ....D 440 233-7272
  Lorain *(G-13035)*
Fredericks Wine & Dine ....E 216 581-5299
  Cleveland *(G-5635)*
Kitchen Katering Inc ....E 216 481-8080
  Euclid *(G-10766)*
Kohler Foods Inc ....E 937 291-3600
  Dayton *(G-9665)*
Little Miami River Catering Co ....E 937 848-2464
  Bellbrook *(G-1372)*
Lmt Enterprises Maumee Inc ....E 419 891-7325
  Maumee *(G-13936)*
Lorain Party Center ....E 440 282-5599
  Lorain *(G-13057)*
Made From Scratch Inc ....E 614 873-3344
  Plain City *(G-16197)*
Michaels Gourmet Catering ....E 419 698-2988
  Toledo *(G-18060)*
Mustard Seed Health Fd Mkt Inc ....E 440 519-3663
  Solon *(G-17031)*
Pine Brook Golf Club Inc ....E 440 748-2939
  Grafton *(G-11443)*
Plaza Inn Foods Inc ....E 937 354-2181
  Mount Victory *(G-14930)*
Sycamore Lake Inc ....C 440 729-9775
  Chesterland *(G-2804)*
Twin Haven Reception Hall ....E 330 425-1616
  Twinsburg *(G-18480)*
Winking Lizard Inc ....D 330 467-1002
  Peninsula *(G-15954)*

CEMENT & CONCRETE RELATED PRDTS & EQPT: Bituminous

Mesa Industries Inc ....D 513 321-2950
  Cincinnati *(G-4081)*

CEMENT ROCK: Crushed & Broken

R W Sidley Incorporated ....E 440 352-9343
  Painesville *(G-15876)*

CEMENT: Hydraulic

Huron Cement Products Company ....E 419 433-4161
  Huron *(G-12166)*

CEMETERIES

Catholic Cemeteries ....E 614 491-2751
  Lockbourne *(G-12946)*
Catholic Diocese of Cleveland ....E 216 267-2850
  Cleveland *(G-5192)*
City of Cleveland ....E 216 348-7210
  Cleveland *(G-5256)*
Stonemor Partners LP ....E 330 491-8001
  Canton *(G-2553)*
Stonemor Partners LP ....E 937 866-4135
  Dayton *(G-9908)*

CEMETERIES: Real Estate Operation

Arlington Memorial Grdns Assn ....E 513 521-7003
  Cincinnati *(G-3047)*
Green Haven Memorial Gardens ....E 330 533-6811
  Canfield *(G-2192)*
Ottawa Hills Memorial Park ....E 419 539-0218
  Ottawa Hills *(G-15806)*
Roman Cthlic Docese Youngstown ....E 330 792-4721
  Youngstown *(G-20356)*
Stonemor Partners LP ....E 330 425-8128
  Twinsburg *(G-18474)*
Sunset Memorial Park Assn ....E 440 777-0450
  North Olmsted *(G-15447)*

CEMETERY ASSOCIATION

Green Lawn Cemetery Assn ....E 614 444-1123
  Columbus *(G-7777)*
Miami Valley Memory Grdns Assn ....E 937 885-7779
  Dayton *(G-9736)*
Spring Grove Cmtry & Arboretum ....D 513 681-7526
  Cincinnati *(G-4563)*
Sunset Hills Cemetery Corp ....E 330 494-2051
  Canton *(G-2555)*
Toledo Memorial Pk & Mausoleum ....E 419 882-7151
  Sylvania *(G-17624)*

CEMETERY MEMORIAL DEALERS

Maza Inc ....E 614 760-0003
  Plain City *(G-16198)*

CENTRAL RESERVE DEPOSITORY: Federal Home Loan Banks

Federal Home Ln Bnk Cincinnati ....A 513 852-7500
  Cincinnati *(G-3596)*

CERAMIC FLOOR & WALL TILE WHOLESALERS

Accco Inc ....E 740 697-2005
  Roseville *(G-16600)*
Clay Burley Products Co ....E 740 452-3633
  Roseville *(G-16601)*

CHAINS: Power Transmission

US Tsubaki Power Transm LLC ....C 419 626-4560
  Sandusky *(G-16807)*

CHAMBERS OF COMMERCE

Canton Reg Cham of Comm Fdn ....E 330 456-7253
  Canton *(G-2296)*
Chamber Commerce New Carlisle ....E 937 845-3911
  New Carlisle *(G-15021)*
Cincinnati USA Rgional Chamber ....D 513 579-3100
  Cincinnati *(G-3334)*
Dayton Area Chamber Commerce ....E 937 226-1444
  Dayton *(G-9459)*
Greater Cleveland Partnership ....D 216 621-3300
  Cleveland *(G-5698)*
Greater Columbus Chmbr Commrce ......E 614 221-1321
  Columbus *(G-7774)*
Ohio Chamber of Commerce Inc ....E 614 228-4201
  Columbus *(G-8321)*
Youngstown-Warren Reg Chamber ....E 330 744-2131
  Youngstown *(G-20436)*

CHARGE ACCOUNT SVCS

Medigistics Inc ....D 614 430-5700
  Columbus *(G-8144)*

CHARTER FLYING SVC

Business Aircraft Group Inc ....D 216 348-1415
  Cleveland *(G-5162)*
Jilco Industries Inc ....E 330 698-0280
  Kidron *(G-12441)*

CHASSIS: Motor Vehicle

Falls Stamping & Welding Co ....C 330 928-1191
  Cuyahoga Falls *(G-9185)*

CHECK CASHING SVCS

Allied Cash Holdings LLC ....D 305 371-3141
  Cincinnati *(G-2991)*
Buckeye Check Cashing Inc ....C 614 798-5900
  Dublin *(G-10271)*
Cashland Financial Svcs Inc ....E 937 253-7842
  Dayton *(G-9387)*
Check N Go of Iowa Inc ....E 563 359-7800
  Cincinnati *(G-3235)*
Checksmart Financial Company ....E 614 798-5900
  Dublin *(G-10289)*
CNG Financial Corporation ....B 513 336-7735
  Cincinnati *(G-3375)*
Community Choice Financial Inc ....D 440 602-9922
  Willoughby *(G-19655)*
Ohio Check Cashers Inc ....E 513 559-0220
  Cincinnati *(G-4203)*
Southwestern PCF Spclty Fin Inc ....E 513 336-7735
  Cincinnati *(G-4555)*

CHECK CLEARING SVCS

Chemical Bank ....D 330 965-5806
  Youngstown *(G-20138)*
Huntington National Bank ....D 614 480-0067
  Columbus *(G-7868)*
Huntington National Bank ....D 614 336-4620
  Dublin *(G-10369)*
Jpmorgan Chase Bank Nat Assn ....E 740 423-4111
  Belpre *(G-1439)*
National Consumer Coop Bnk ....E 937 393-4246
  Hillsboro *(G-11988)*

CHECK VALIDATION SVCS

Security Check LLC ....C 614 944-5788
  Columbus *(G-8710)*

CHEESE WHOLESALERS

Coblentz Distributing Inc ....C 330 852-2888
  Walnut Creek *(G-18784)*
Great Lakes Cheese Co Inc ....B 440 834-2500
  Hiram *(G-12002)*
Lori Holding Co ....E 740 342-3230
  New Lexington *(G-15055)*
Mds Foods Inc ....E 330 879-9780
  Navarre *(G-14955)*
Siemer Distributing Company ....E 740 342-3230
  New Lexington *(G-15063)*
Troyer Cheese Inc ....E 330 893-2479
  Millersburg *(G-14625)*

CHEMICAL CLEANING SVCS

Bleachtech LLC ....E 216 921-1980
  Seville *(G-16838)*
Chemical Solvents Inc ....E 216 741-9310
  Cleveland *(G-5232)*
Hydrochem LLC ....E 330 792-6569
  Youngstown *(G-20226)*

CHEMICAL PROCESSING MACHINERY & EQPT

Guild Associates Inc ....D 614 798-8215
  Dublin *(G-10355)*

CHEMICAL SPLYS FOR FOUNDRIES

Atotech USA Inc ....D 216 398-0550
  Cleveland *(G-5080)*

CHEMICALS & ALLIED PRDTS WHOLESALERS, NEC

Airgas Usa LLC ....E 513 563-8070
  Cincinnati *(G-2979)*
Akrochem Corporation ....E 330 535-2108
  Barberton *(G-949)*
Ashland LLC ....C 614 790-3333
  Dublin *(G-10256)*
Avalon Foodservice Inc ....C 330 854-4551
  Canal Fulton *(G-2140)*
Bleachtech LLC ....E 216 921-1980
  Seville *(G-16838)*
Calvary Industries Inc ....D 513 874-1113
  Fairfield *(G-10828)*
Cimcool Industrial Pdts LLC ....D 888 246-2665
  Cincinnati *(G-3275)*
Dupont Inc ....D 937 268-3411
  Dayton *(G-9509)*
Hillside Maint Sup Co Inc ....E 513 751-4100
  Cincinnati *(G-3767)*
Imcd Us LLC ....E 216 228-8900
  Lakewood *(G-12483)*
Koch Knight LLC ....D 330 488-1651
  East Canton *(G-10504)*
Maines Paper & Food Svc Inc ....E 216 643-7500
  Bedford *(G-1319)*
Rde System Corp ....C 513 933-8000
  Lebanon *(G-12640)*
Rudolph Brothers & Co ....E 614 833-0707
  Canal Winchester *(G-2169)*
Schaaf Drugs LLC ....E 419 879-4327
  Lima *(G-12873)*
Skidmore Sales & Distrg Co Inc ....E 513 755-4200
  West Chester *(G-19156)*
Sunsource Inc ....E 513 941-6200
  Cincinnati *(G-4601)*
T&L Global Management LLC ....D 614 586-0303
  Columbus *(G-8818)*

CHEMICALS & ALLIED PRDTS WHOLESALERS, NEC

The Mau-Sherwood Supply Co .... E 330 405-1200
  Twinsburg (G-18475)
Tricor Industrial Inc .... D 330 264-3299
  Wooster (G-19919)
VWR Chemicals LLC .... E 330 425-2522
  Aurora (G-860)
Wampum Hardware Co .... E 740 685-2585
  Salesville (G-16721)
Zep Inc .... E 440 239-1580
  Cleveland (G-6784)

CHEMICALS & ALLIED PRDTS, WHOL: Chemicals, Swimming Pool/Spa

Rhiel Supply Co Inc .... E 330 799-7777
  Austintown (G-873)

CHEMICALS & ALLIED PRDTS, WHOL: Food Additives/Preservatives

Mitsubshi Intl Fd Ingrdnts Inc .... E 614 652-1111
  Dublin (G-10399)

CHEMICALS & ALLIED PRDTS, WHOL: Gases, Compressed/Liquefied

Matheson Tri-Gas Inc .... E 614 771-1311
  Hilliard (G-11925)

CHEMICALS & ALLIED PRDTS, WHOLESALE: Alkalines & Chlorine

Ashland LLC .... E 614 232-8510
  Columbus (G-7049)
Ashland LLC .... E 614 276-6144
  Columbus (G-7050)
Ashland LLC .... D 216 961-4690
  Cleveland (G-5070)
Ashland LLC .... E 216 883-8200
  Cleveland (G-5071)
Ashland LLC .... D 419 289-9588
  Ashland (G-658)

CHEMICALS & ALLIED PRDTS, WHOLESALE: Anti-Corrosion Prdts

Electro Prime Group LLC .... E 419 476-0100
  Toledo (G-17863)

CHEMICALS & ALLIED PRDTS, WHOLESALE: Caustic Soda

National Colloid Company .... E 740 282-1171
  Steubenville (G-17332)

CHEMICALS & ALLIED PRDTS, WHOLESALE: Chemicals, Indl

Accurate Lubr & Met Wkg Fluids .... E 937 461-9906
  Dayton (G-9305)
Budenheim Usa Inc .... E 614 345-2400
  Columbus (G-7164)
Chemical Services Inc .... E 937 898-5566
  Dayton (G-9401)
Chemical Solvents Inc .... D 216 741-9310
  Cleveland (G-5233)
CL Zimmerman Delaware LLC .... E 513 860-9300
  West Chester (G-19042)
Custom Chemical Solutions .... E 800 291-1057
  Loveland (G-13119)
Eliokem Inc .... D 330 734-1100
  Fairlawn (G-10947)
Galaxy Associates Inc .... E 513 731-6350
  Cincinnati (G-3660)
Lanxess Corporation .... C 440 279-2367
  Chardon (G-2755)
Nexeo Solutions LLC .... E 330 405-0461
  Twinsburg (G-18451)
Palmer Holland Inc .... D 440 686-2300
  North Olmsted (G-15438)
Rwc Inc .... E 614 890-0600
  Westerville (G-19351)
Sea-Land Chemical Co .... D 440 871-7887
  Westlake (G-19545)
Tembec Btlsr Inc .... E 419 244-5856
  Toledo (G-18216)
Tosoh America Inc .... B 614 539-8622
  Grove City (G-11606)
Univar USA Inc .... C 513 714-5264
  West Chester (G-19239)

Univar USA Inc .... E 419 666-7880
  Walbridge (G-18779)
Univar USA Inc .... E 330 425-4330
  Twinsburg (G-18482)
Univar USA Inc .... E 513 870-4050
  Hamilton (G-11783)
Univar USA Inc .... D 440 238-8550
  Strongsville (G-17520)
Young Chemical Co LLC .... E 330 486-4210
  Twinsburg (G-18486)

CHEMICALS & ALLIED PRDTS, WHOLESALE: Chemicals, Indl & Heavy

Harwick Standard Dist Corp .... D 330 798-9300
  Akron (G-255)
Industrial Chemical Corp .... E 330 725-0800
  Medina (G-14079)

CHEMICALS & ALLIED PRDTS, WHOLESALE: Compressed Gas

Airgas Usa LLC .... B 216 642-6600
  Independence (G-12183)
Weiler Welding Company Inc .... D 937 222-8312
  Moraine (G-14835)

CHEMICALS & ALLIED PRDTS, WHOLESALE: Concrete Additives

Sika Corporation .... D 740 387-9224
  Marion (G-13579)

CHEMICALS & ALLIED PRDTS, WHOLESALE: Detergent/Soap

Anatrace Products LLC .... E 419 740-6600
  Maumee (G-13876)
Chemical Solvents Inc .... E 216 741-9310
  Cleveland (G-5232)
Cr Brands Inc .... D 513 860-5039
  West Chester (G-19058)

CHEMICALS & ALLIED PRDTS, WHOLESALE: Detergents

Procter & Gamble Distrg LLC .... B 513 945-7960
  Cincinnati (G-4341)
Procter & Gamble Distrg LLC .... C 937 387-5189
  Union (G-18499)
Procter & Gamble Distrg LLC .... B 513 626-2500
  Blue Ash (G-1667)
Washing Systems LLC .... C 800 272-1974
  Loveland (G-13163)

CHEMICALS & ALLIED PRDTS, WHOLESALE: Dry Ice

D & D Investment Co .... E 614 272-6567
  Columbus (G-7476)

CHEMICALS & ALLIED PRDTS, WHOLESALE: Essential Oils

Cantrell Oil Company .... E 937 695-8003
  Winchester (G-19800)

CHEMICALS & ALLIED PRDTS, WHOLESALE: Glue

Gorilla Glue Company .... E 513 271-3300
  Cincinnati (G-3688)

CHEMICALS & ALLIED PRDTS, WHOLESALE: Oxygen

Americas Best Medical Eqp Co .... E 330 928-0884
  Akron (G-73)
Braden Med Services Inc .... E 740 732-2356
  Caldwell (G-2082)
Medi Home Health Agency Inc .... E 740 266-3977
  Steubenville (G-17329)

CHEMICALS & ALLIED PRDTS, WHOLESALE: Plastics Film

Multi-Plastics Inc .... D 740 548-4894
  Lewis Center (G-12696)

SERVICES SECTION

CHEMICALS & ALLIED PRDTS, WHOLESALE: Plastics Materials, NEC

Alro Steel Corporation .... E 419 720-5300
  Toledo (G-17747)
Inno-Pak LLC .... E 740 363-0090
  Delaware (G-10109)
Thyssenkrupp Materials NA Inc .... E 937 898-7400
  Miamisburg (G-14360)

CHEMICALS & ALLIED PRDTS, WHOLESALE: Plastics Prdts, NEC

Bprex Plastic Packaging Inc .... C 419 423-3271
  Findlay (G-11007)
F B Wright Co Cincinnati .... E 513 874-9100
  West Chester (G-19071)
Polymer Packaging Inc .... D 330 832-2000
  Massillon (G-13844)
Queen City Polymers Inc .... E 513 779-0990
  West Chester (G-19136)
Surreal Entertainment LLC .... E 330 262-5277
  Wooster (G-19918)
Tahoma Enterprises Inc .... D 330 745-9016
  Barberton (G-982)
Tahoma Rubber & Plastics Inc .... D 330 745-9016
  Barberton (G-983)
Wilbert Inc .... D 419 483-2300
  Bellevue (G-1419)

CHEMICALS & ALLIED PRDTS, WHOLESALE: Plastics Sheets & Rods

HP Manufacturing Company Inc .... D 216 361-6500
  Cleveland (G-5788)
Ilpea Industries Inc .... C 330 562-2916
  Aurora (G-842)

CHEMICALS & ALLIED PRDTS, WHOLESALE: Plastics, Basic Shapes

Checker Notions Company Inc .... D 419 893-3636
  Maumee (G-13894)

CHEMICALS & ALLIED PRDTS, WHOLESALE: Resins

Florline Group Inc .... E 330 830-3380
  Massillon (G-13808)
Hexpol Compounding LLC .... C 440 834-4644
  Burton (G-2062)
Polyone Corporation .... D 440 930-1000
  Avon Lake (G-937)

CHEMICALS & ALLIED PRDTS, WHOLESALE: Resins, Plastics

Cannon Group Inc .... E 614 890-0343
  Westerville (G-19375)

CHEMICALS & ALLIED PRDTS, WHOLESALE: Rubber, Synthetic

Mantaline Corporation .... D 330 274-2264
  Mantua (G-13392)

CHEMICALS & ALLIED PRDTS, WHOLESALE: Salts & Polishes, Indl

Cargill Incorporated .... D 440 716-4664
  North Olmsted (G-15411)

CHEMICALS & ALLIED PRDTS, WHOLESALE: Sanitation Preparations

Bonded Chemicals Inc .... E 614 777-9240
  Columbus (G-7124)
Joshen Paper & Packaging Co .... C 216 441-5600
  Cleveland (G-5872)

CHEMICALS & ALLIED PRDTS, WHOLESALE: Sealants

Applied Indus Tech - Dixie Inc .... C 216 426-4000
  Cleveland (G-5054)
Applied Industrial Tech Inc .... B 216 426-4000
  Cleveland (G-5055)
United McGill Corporation .... E 614 829-1200
  Groveport (G-11681)

SERVICES SECTION

CHEMICALS & ALLIED PRDTS, WHOLESALE: Spec Clean/Sanitation

Dawnchem Inc .... E 440 943-3332
Willoughby (G-19658)
Midwest Industrial Supply Inc .... E 800 321-0699
Toledo (G-18061)
Texo International Inc .... D 513 731-6350
Norwood (G-15600)

CHEMICALS & ALLIED PRDTS, WHOLESALE: Syn Resin, Rub/Plastic

Flex Technologies Inc .... E 330 897-6311
Baltic (G-945)
Kraton Polymers US LLC .... B 740 423-7571
Belpre (G-1441)
Phoenix Technologies Intl LLC .... E 419 353-7738
Bowling Green (G-1789)
Polyone Corporation .... D 440 930-1000
North Baltimore (G-15315)

CHEMICALS, AGRICULTURE: Wholesalers

Waterworks America Inc .... C 440 526-4815
Cleveland (G-6724)

CHEMICALS: Agricultural

Scotts Miracle-Gro Company .... B 937 644-0011
Marysville (G-13651)

CHEMICALS: Bleaching Powder, Lime Bleaching Compounds

Bleachtech LLC .... E 216 921-1980
Seville (G-16838)

CHEMICALS: High Purity, Refined From Technical Grade

Heraeus Precious Metals North .... E 937 264-1000
Vandalia (G-18682)

CHEMICALS: Inorganic, NEC

BASF Catalysts LLC .... D 216 360-5005
Cleveland (G-5097)
Borchers Americas Inc .... D 440 899-2950
Westlake (G-19466)
Calvary Industries Inc .... D 513 874-1113
Fairfield (G-10828)
National Colloid Company .... E 740 282-1171
Steubenville (G-17332)
Univar USA Inc .... C 513 714-5264
West Chester (G-19239)

CHEMICALS: Isotopes, Radioactive

Aldrich Chemical .... D 937 859-1808
Miamisburg (G-14269)

CHEMICALS: NEC

Aldrich Chemical .... D 937 859-1808
Miamisburg (G-14269)
Ashland LLC .... C 614 790-3333
Dublin (G-10256)
Borchers Americas Inc .... D 440 899-2950
Westlake (G-19466)
Cargill Incorporated .... C 216 651-7200
Cleveland (G-5184)
Cincinnati - Vulcan Company .... D 513 242-5300
Cincinnati (G-3278)
EMD Millipore Corporation .... C 513 631-0445
Norwood (G-15599)
Flexsys America LP .... D 330 666-4111
Akron (G-227)
Fuchs Lubricants Co .... E 330 963-0400
Twinsburg (G-18419)
Hexpol Compounding LLC .... C 440 834-4644
Burton (G-2062)
Lubrizol Advanced Mtls Inc .... E 440 933-0400
Avon Lake (G-934)
Morton Salt Inc .... C 330 925-3015
Rittman (G-16554)
National Colloid Company .... E 740 282-1171
Steubenville (G-17332)
New Vulco Mfg & Sales Co LLC .... D 513 242-2672
Cincinnati (G-4158)
Noco Company .... B 216 464-8131
Solon (G-17035)

Rhenium Alloys Inc .... D 440 365-7388
North Ridgeville (G-15475)
State Industrial Products Corp .... B 877 747-6986
Cleveland (G-6530)
Teknol Inc .... D 937 264-0190
Dayton (G-9922)
Univar USA Inc .... C 513 714-5264
West Chester (G-19239)

CHEMICALS: Organic, NEC

Alco-Chem Inc .... E 330 253-3535
Akron (G-64)
Aldrich Chemical .... D 937 859-1808
Miamisburg (G-14269)
Borchers Americas Inc .... D 440 899-2950
Westlake (G-19466)
Heraeus Precious Metals North .... E 937 264-1000
Vandalia (G-18682)
National Colloid Company .... E 740 282-1171
Steubenville (G-17332)
Univar USA Inc .... C 513 714-5264
West Chester (G-19239)

CHICKEN SLAUGHTERING & PROCESSING

V H Cooper & Co Inc .... C 419 375-4116
Fort Recovery (G-11120)

CHILD & YOUTH SVCS, NEC

A Better Choice Child Care LLC .... E 614 268-8503
Columbus (G-6919)
Applewood Centers Inc .... B 216 696-6815
Cleveland (G-5050)
Applewood Centers Inc .... D 216 521-6511
Cleveland (G-5051)
Applewood Centers Inc .... E 440 324-1300
Lorain (G-13014)
Applewood Centers Inc .... C 216 741-2241
Cleveland (G-5052)
Board of Delaware County .... D 740 201-3600
Lewis Center (G-12671)
Brook Beech .... C 216 831-2255
Cleveland (G-5144)
Carvaka Inc .... E 513 381-1531
Cincinnati (G-3189)
Catholic Charities Corporation .... E 419 289-1903
Ashland (G-670)
Center For Families & Children .... D 216 432-7200
Cleveland (G-5206)
Child Focus Inc .... E 513 732-8800
Batavia (G-998)
Child Focus Inc .... D 513 752-1555
Cincinnati (G-3243)
Child Focus Inc .... D 937 444-1613
Mount Orab (G-14867)
Childrens Advocacy Center .... E 740 432-6581
Cambridge (G-2104)
Childrens HM of Cncinnati Ohio .... C 513 272-2800
Cincinnati (G-3244)
Childrens Hosp Med Ctr Akron .... E 330 633-2055
Tallmadge (G-17634)
County of Adams .... E 937 544-5067
West Union (G-19277)
County of Allen .... E 419 227-8590
Lima (G-12765)
County of Allen .... E 419 996-7050
Lima (G-12767)
County of Ashtabula .... D 440 998-1811
Ashtabula (G-739)
County of Clark .... B 937 327-1700
Springfield (G-17182)
County of Clinton .... E 937 382-2449
Wilmington (G-19750)
County of Coshocton .... D 740 622-1020
Coshocton (G-9100)
County of Cuyahoga .... A 216 432-2621
Cleveland (G-5427)
County of Hamilton .... E 513 821-6946
Cincinnati (G-3433)
County of Huron .... D 419 663-5437
Norwalk (G-15569)
County of Lake .... E 440 350-4000
Painesville (G-15847)
County of Logan .... E 937 599-7290
Bellefontaine (G-1383)
County of Marion .... E 740 389-2317
Marion (G-13534)
County of Montgomery .... D 937 224-5437
Dayton (G-9438)

CHILD DAY CARE SVCS

County of Tuscarawas .... E 330 343-0099
New Philadelphia (G-15090)
County of Wayne .... E 330 287-5600
Wooster (G-19857)
Crawford County Children Svcs .... E 419 562-1200
Bucyrus (G-2035)
Family & Child Abuse .... E 419 244-3053
Toledo (G-17876)
For Specialized Alternatives .... E 419 695-8010
Delphos (G-10144)
Franklin Cnty Bd Commissioners .... B 614 462-3275
Columbus (G-7685)
Franklin Cnty Bd Commissioners .... B 614 229-7100
Columbus (G-7687)
Grove Cy Chrstn Child Care Ctr .... D 614 875-2551
Grove City (G-11568)
Hancock Job & Family Services .... D 419 424-7022
Findlay (G-11043)
House of New Hope .... E 740 345-5437
Saint Louisville (G-16668)
Juvenile Court Cnty Muskingum .... E 740 453-0351
Zanesville (G-20493)
Lawrence Cnty Bd Dev Dsblities .... E 740 377-2356
South Point (G-17090)
Lighthouse Youth Services Inc .... D 513 221-3350
Cincinnati (G-3982)
Miami County Childrens Svcs Bd .... E 937 335-4103
Troy (G-18364)
National Youth Advocate Progra .... E 740 349-7511
Newark (G-15217)
National Youth Advocate Progra .... E 614 487-8758
Columbus (G-8225)
Ohio Youth Advocate Program Inc .... D 614 252-6927
Columbus (G-8453)
Ohioguidestone .... E 440 234-2006
Berea (G-1467)
Providence House Inc .... E 216 651-5982
Cleveland (G-6326)
Safely Home Inc .... E 440 232-9310
Bedford (G-1334)
Services On Mark Inc .... E 614 846-5400
Worthington (G-19997)
Simply Youth LLC .... D 330 284-2537
Canton (G-2528)
Specialized Alternatives For F .... A 419 695-8010
Delphos (G-10151)
Sylvania Community Svcs Ctr .... E 419 885-2451
Sylvania (G-17618)
University of Cincinnati .... D 513 556-3803
Cincinnati (G-4779)
Wood County Chld Svcs Assn .... D 419 352-7588
Bowling Green (G-1798)
Young Womns Chrstn Assc Canton .... D 330 453-7644
Canton (G-2593)
Youth Advocate Services .... E 614 258-9927
Columbus (G-9022)

CHILD DAY CARE SVCS

A CCS Day Care Centers Inc .... E 513 841-2227
Cincinnati (G-2954)
Abacus Child Care Centers Inc .... E 330 773-4200
Akron (G-14)
Abilities First Foundation .... C 513 423-9496
Middletown (G-14411)
Action For Children Inc .... E 614 224-0222
Columbus (G-6941)
Akron Summit Cmnty Action Agcy .... D 330 733-2290
Akron (G-57)
All About Kids Daycare N .... E 330 494-8700
North Canton (G-15323)
All For Kids Inc .... E 740 435-8050
Cambridge (G-2093)
All My Sons Business Dev Corp .... E 469 461-5000
Cleveland (G-4989)
Angel Care Inc .... E 440 736-7267
Brecksville (G-1812)
Angels On Earth Child Care Co .... E 216 476-8100
Cleveland (G-5036)
Apple Tree Nursery School Inc .... E 419 530-1070
Toledo (G-17755)
Arlitt Child Development Ctr .... D 513 556-3802
Cincinnati (G-3048)
Bay Village City School Dst .... E 440 617-7330
Cleveland (G-5102)
Beavercreek YMCA .... D 937 426-9622
Dayton (G-9351)
Bethlehem Lutheran Ch Parma .... E 440 845-2230
Cleveland (G-5120)
Board Man Frst Untd Methdst Ch .... E 330 758-4527
Youngstown (G-20119)

Employee Codes: A=Over 500 employees, B=251-500
C=101-250, D=51-100, E=25-50

CHILD DAY CARE SVCS — SERVICES SECTION

Bright Horizons Chld Ctrs LLC ..... E 614 566-4847
 Columbus *(G-7138)*
Brunswick City Schools ..... A 330 225-7731
 Brunswick *(G-1969)*
Canton Country Day School ..... E 330 453-8279
 Canton *(G-2286)*
Carol Scudere ..... E 614 839-4357
 New Albany *(G-14979)*
Catholic Social Svc Miami Vly ..... E 937 223-7217
 Dayton *(G-9390)*
Chal-Ron LLC ..... E 216 383-9050
 Cleveland *(G-5225)*
Child Care Resource Center ..... E 216 575-0061
 Cleveland *(G-5236)*
Child Focus Inc ..... D 937 444-1613
 Mount Orab *(G-14867)*
Children First Inc ..... E 614 466-0945
 Columbus *(G-7260)*
Childrens Rehabilitation Ctr ..... E 330 856-2107
 Warren *(G-18833)*
Christian Missionary Alliance ..... E 614 457-4085
 Columbus *(G-7268)*
City of Lakewood ..... E 216 226-0080
 Cleveland *(G-5266)*
Cleveland Child Care Inc ..... E 216 631-3211
 Cleveland *(G-5293)*
Cleveland Mus Schl Settlement ..... C 216 421-5806
 Cleveland *(G-5339)*
Columbus Christian Center Inc ..... E 614 416-9673
 Columbus *(G-7337)*
Columbus Day Care Center ..... E 614 269-8980
 Columbus *(G-7345)*
Columbus Montessori Education ..... E 614 231-3790
 Columbus *(G-7370)*
Consolidated Learning Ctrs Inc ..... C 614 791-0050
 Dublin *(G-10308)*
Council For Economic Opport ..... D 216 696-9077
 Cleveland *(G-5414)*
Council On Rur Svc Prgrams Inc ..... E 937 773-0773
 Piqua *(G-16141)*
County of Athens ..... D 740 592-3061
 Athens *(G-781)*
County of Guernsey ..... E 740 439-5555
 Cambridge *(G-2106)*
County of Mercer ..... D 419 586-2369
 Celina *(G-2643)*
Creative Center For Children ..... E 513 867-1118
 Hamilton *(G-11719)*
Creative Childrens World LLC ..... E 513 336-7799
 Mason *(G-13692)*
Creative Playroom ..... D 216 475-6464
 Cleveland *(G-5433)*
Creative Playrooms Inc ..... E 440 572-9365
 Strongsville *(G-17453)*
Creative Playrooms Inc ..... E 440 349-9111
 Solon *(G-16998)*
Creme De La Creme Colorado Inc ..... E 513 459-4300
 Mason *(G-13693)*
Days of Discovery ..... E 937 862-4465
 Spring Valley *(G-17110)*
Diocese of Toledo ..... E 419 243-7255
 Toledo *(G-17854)*
Dover City Schools ..... D 330 343-8880
 Dover *(G-10184)*
Early Childhood Learning Commu ..... D 614 451-6418
 Columbus *(G-7563)*
East End Neighborhood Hse Assn ..... E 216 791-9378
 Cleveland *(G-5519)*
Elderly Day Care Center ..... E 419 228-2688
 Lima *(G-12773)*
Enrichment Center of Wishing W ..... D 440 237-5000
 Cleveland *(G-5543)*
Epworth Preschool and Daycare ..... E 740 387-1062
 Marion *(G-13538)*
Erie Huron Cac Headstart Inc ..... E 419 663-2623
 Norwalk *(G-15572)*
Family YMCA of LANcstr&fairfld ..... D 740 277-7373
 Lancaster *(G-12541)*
Findlay Y M C A Child Dev ..... E 419 422-3174
 Findlay *(G-11031)*
First Apostolic Church ..... E 419 885-4888
 Toledo *(G-17891)*
First Assembly Child Care ..... E 419 529-6501
 Mansfield *(G-13302)*
First Baptist Day Care Center ..... E 216 371-9394
 Cleveland *(G-5590)*
First Community Church ..... E 614 488-0681
 Columbus *(G-7662)*
First Community Church ..... E 614 488-0681
 Columbus *(G-7663)*

First Fruits Child Dev Ctr I ..... E 216 862-4715
 Euclid *(G-10755)*
Four Oaks Early Intervention ..... E 937 562-6779
 Xenia *(G-20051)*
Frans Child Care-Mansfield ..... C 419 775-2500
 Mansfield *(G-13304)*
Friend-Ship Child Care Ctr LLC ..... E 330 484-2051
 Canton *(G-2372)*
Galion Community Center YMCA ..... E 419 468-7754
 Galion *(G-11297)*
Gearity Early Child Care Ctr ..... E 216 371-7356
 Cleveland *(G-5665)*
Geary Family YMCA Fostria ..... E 419 435-6608
 Fostoria *(G-11128)*
Genesis Healthcare System ..... E 740 453-4959
 Zanesville *(G-20482)*
Gethsemane Lutheran Church ..... E 614 885-4319
 Columbus *(G-7749)*
Goddard School ..... E 513 271-6311
 Cincinnati *(G-3681)*
Grace Baptist Church ..... E 937 652-1133
 Urbana *(G-18589)*
Grace Brthren Ch Columbus Ohio ..... E 614 888-7733
 Westerville *(G-19310)*
Great Expectations D CA Center ..... E 330 782-9500
 Youngstown *(G-20205)*
Great Miami Valley YMCA ..... D 513 887-0001
 Hamilton *(G-11733)*
Great Miami Valley YMCA ..... E 513 892-9622
 Fairfield Township *(G-10930)*
Great Miami Valley YMCA ..... D 513 887-0014
 Hamilton *(G-11735)*
Great Miami Valley YMCA ..... E 513 868-9622
 Hamilton *(G-11736)*
Great Miami Valley YMCA ..... D 513 829-3091
 Hamilton *(G-10854)*
Hardin County Family YMCA ..... E 419 673-6131
 Kenton *(G-12416)*
Health Care Plus ..... E 614 340-7587
 Columbus *(G-6882)*
Highland County Family YMCA ..... E 937 840-9622
 Hillsboro *(G-11978)*
Huber Heights YMCA ..... D 937 236-9622
 Dayton *(G-9623)*
Independence Local Schools ..... E 216 642-5865
 Independence *(G-12219)*
Israel Adath ..... E 513 793-1800
 Cincinnati *(G-3846)*
Just 4 Kidz Childcare ..... E 440 285-2221
 Chardon *(G-2754)*
Kangaroo Pouch Daycare Inc ..... E 440 473-4725
 Cleveland *(G-5881)*
Kids World ..... E 614 473-9229
 Columbus *(G-7988)*
Kidz By Riverside Inc ..... E 330 392-0700
 Warren *(G-18869)*
Kindercare Learning Ctrs LLC ..... E 513 961-3164
 Cincinnati *(G-3926)*
Kindercare Learning Ctrs LLC ..... E 614 759-6622
 Columbus *(G-7989)*
Kingdom Kids Inc ..... E 513 851-6400
 Hamilton *(G-11750)*
Ladan Learning Center ..... E 614 426-4306
 Columbus *(G-8029)*
Lake County YMCA ..... A 440 352-3303
 Painesville *(G-15860)*
Lake County YMCA ..... C 440 946-1160
 Willoughby *(G-19680)*
Lake County YMCA ..... E 440 259-2724
 Perry *(G-15962)*
Lake County YMCA ..... D 440 428-5125
 Madison *(G-13227)*
Lakewood Catholic Academy ..... E 216 521-4352
 Lakewood *(G-12486)*
Lawrence Cnty Bd Dev Dsblities ..... E 740 377-2356
 South Point *(G-17090)*
Le Chaperon Rouge ..... E 440 934-0296
 Avon *(G-905)*
Le Chaperon Rouge Company ..... E 440 899-9477
 Westlake *(G-19509)*
Life Center Adult Day Care ..... E 614 866-7212
 Reynoldsburg *(G-16465)*
Lillian and Betty Ratner Schl ..... E 216 464-0033
 Cleveland *(G-5942)*
Lima Family YMCA ..... E 419 223-6045
 Lima *(G-12821)*
Little Dreamers Big Believers ..... E 614 294-2922
 Columbus *(G-8073)*
Little Lambs Childrens Center ..... E 614 471-9269
 Gahanna *(G-11254)*

Madison Local School District ..... B 419 589-2600
 Mansfield *(G-13326)*
Medcentral Health System ..... E 419 526-8043
 Mansfield *(G-13341)*
Miami Valley Hospital ..... E 937 224-3916
 Dayton *(G-9733)*
Mini University Inc ..... E 513 275-5184
 Oxford *(G-15825)*
Mk Childcare Warsaw Ave LLC ..... E 513 922-6279
 Cincinnati *(G-4107)*
Mlm Childcare LLC ..... E 513 623-8243
 Cincinnati *(G-4109)*
My Place Child Care ..... E 740 349-3505
 Newark *(G-15215)*
N & C Active Learning LLC ..... E 937 545-1342
 Beavercreek *(G-1193)*
Nanaeles Day Care Inc ..... E 216 991-6139
 Cleveland *(G-6099)*
National Benevolent Associatio ..... D 216 476-0333
 Cleveland *(G-6101)*
Nbdc II LLC ..... E 513 681-5439
 Cincinnati *(G-4147)*
Neighborhood House ..... D 614 252-4941
 Columbus *(G-8256)*
New Bgnnngs Assembly of God Ch ..... E 614 497-2658
 Columbus *(G-8271)*
New Dawn Health Care Inc ..... C 330 343-5521
 Dover *(G-10202)*
New Life Christian Center ..... E 740 687-1572
 Lancaster *(G-12561)*
New School Inc ..... E 513 281-7999
 Cincinnati *(G-4157)*
Nicoles Child Care Center ..... D 216 751-6668
 Cleveland *(G-6132)*
Noahs Ark Child Dev Ctr ..... E 513 988-0921
 Trenton *(G-18342)*
Northfield Presbt Ch Day Care ..... E 330 467-4411
 Northfield *(G-15521)*
Northfield Presbt Day Care Ctr ..... E 330 467-4411
 Northfield *(G-15522)*
Northwest Child Development An ..... E 937 559-9565
 Dayton *(G-9776)*
Oak Creek United Church ..... E 937 434-3941
 Dayton *(G-9779)*
Ohio Dept of Job & Fmly Svcs ..... C 614 466-1213
 Columbus *(G-8335)*
Ohio State University ..... D 614 292-4453
 Columbus *(G-8405)*
Ohioguidestone ..... E 440 234-2006
 Berea *(G-1467)*
Our Lady of Bethlehem Schools ..... E 614 459-8285
 Columbus *(G-8499)*
Pike County YMCA ..... E 740 947-8862
 Waverly *(G-18974)*
Precious Angels Lrng Ctr Inc ..... E 440 886-1919
 Cleveland *(G-6294)*
Presbyterian Child Center ..... E 740 852-3190
 London *(G-13006)*
Professional Maint of Columbus ..... B 513 579-1762
 Cincinnati *(G-4343)*
Promedica Health Systems Inc ..... A 567 585-7454
 Toledo *(G-18141)*
R & J Investment Co Inc ..... C 440 934-5204
 Avon *(G-915)*
R L B Inc ..... E 513 793-3758
 Blue Ash *(G-1670)*
Ravenna Assembly of God Inc ..... E 330 297-1493
 Ravenna *(G-16404)*
Robert A Kaufmann Inc ..... E 216 663-1150
 Maple Heights *(G-13415)*
Ross County YMCA ..... D 740 772-4340
 Chillicothe *(G-2882)*
Saint James Day Care Center ..... E 513 662-2287
 Cincinnati *(G-4470)*
Saint Johns Villa ..... E 330 627-4662
 Carrollton *(G-2628)*
Sandusky Area YMCA Foundation ..... E 419 621-9622
 Sandusky *(G-16790)*
Santas Hide Away Hollow Inc ..... E 440 632-5000
 Middlefield *(G-14402)*
Seton Catholic School Hudson ..... E 330 342-4200
 Hudson *(G-12143)*
Sharonville Mthdist Wkdays Nrs ..... E 513 563-8278
 Cincinnati *(G-4510)*
Sisters of Notre D ..... E 419 471-0170
 Toledo *(G-18189)*
Something Special Lrng Ctr Inc ..... E 419 422-1400
 Findlay *(G-11082)*
Springfield Family Y M C A ..... D 937 323-3781
 Springfield *(G-17281)*

SERVICES SECTION

St Marys City Board Education .... D 419 394-2616
Saint Marys *(G-16685)*
St Stephen United Church Chrst .... E 419 624-1814
Sandusky *(G-16797)*
St Stephens Community House .... D 614 294-6347
Columbus *(G-8770)*
St Thomas Episcopal Church .... E 513 831-6908
Terrace Park *(G-17662)*
Success Kidz 24-Hr Enrchmt Ctr .... E 614 419-2276
Columbus *(G-8799)*
Sycamore Board of Education .... D 513 489-3937
Cincinnati *(G-4608)*
Sylvania Community Svcs Ctr .... E 419 885-2451
Sylvania *(G-17618)*
Tiny Tots Day Nursery .... E 330 755-6473
Struthers *(G-17535)*
Trinity Luth Child Care .... E 419 289-2126
Ashland *(G-703)*
Trinity United Methodist Ch .... E 419 224-2909
Lima *(G-12905)*
Troy Christian School .... D 937 339-5692
Troy *(G-18382)*
U C Child Care Center Inc .... E 513 961-2825
Cincinnati *(G-4713)*
Ucc Childrens Center .... E 513 217-5501
Middletown *(G-14488)*
United Rehabilitation Services .... D 937 233-1230
Dayton *(G-9947)*
United States Enrichment Corp .... A 740 897-2457
Piketon *(G-16129)*
University of Akron .... E 330 972-8210
Akron *(G-489)*
Upper Arlington City Schl Dst .... E 614 487-5133
Columbus *(G-8914)*
Vermilion Family YMCA .... E 440 967-4208
Vermilion *(G-18720)*
Wenzler Daycare Learning Ctr .... E 937 435-8200
Dayton *(G-9990)*
West Liberty Care Center Inc .... C 937 465-5065
West Liberty *(G-19264)*
West Ohio Cmnty Action Partnr .... C 419 227-2586
Lima *(G-12919)*
West Ohio Conference of .... E 937 773-5313
Piqua *(G-16175)*
West Shore Child Care Center .... C 440 333-2040
Cleveland *(G-6736)*
Westerville-Worthington Learni .... E 614 891-4105
Westerville *(G-19449)*
Wise Choices In Learning Ltd .... E 440 324-6056
Elyria *(G-10694)*
Worthington United Methdst Ch .... E 614 885-5365
Worthington *(G-20011)*
Wright State University .... E 937 775-4070
Dayton *(G-9290)*
Wsos Child Development Program ..... E 419 334-8511
Fremont *(G-11230)*
Y M C A Central Stark County .... E 330 305-5437
Canton *(G-2590)*
Y M C A Central Stark County .... E 330 875-1611
Louisville *(G-13108)*
Y M C A Central Stark County .... E 330 877-8933
Uniontown *(G-18545)*
Y M C A Central Stark County .... E 330 830-6275
Massillon *(G-13862)*
Y M C A Central Stark County .... E 330 498-4082
Canton *(G-2591)*
Y M C A of Ashland Ohio Inc .... D 419 289-0626
Ashland *(G-709)*
YMCA .... E 330 823-1930
Alliance *(G-566)*
YMCA Inc .... D 330 385-6400
East Liverpool *(G-10536)*
YMCA of Clermont County Inc .... E 513 724-9622
Batavia *(G-1032)*
YMCA of Massillon .... E 330 879-0800
Navarre *(G-14957)*
Young Mens Christian .... C 513 791-5000
Blue Ash *(G-1725)*
Young Mens Christian .... B 513 932-1424
Lebanon *(G-12660)*
Young Mens Christian Assn .... D 740 373-2250
Marietta *(G-13520)*
Young Mens Christian Assn .... E 419 238-0443
Van Wert *(G-18653)*
Young Mens Christian Assoc .... E 330 724-1255
Akron *(G-516)*
Young Mens Christian Assoc .... A 330 376-1335
Akron *(G-517)*
Young Mens Christian Assoc .... D 419 523-5233
Ottawa *(G-15805)*
Young Mens Christian Assoc .... E 937 228-9622
Dayton *(G-10012)*
Young Mens Christian Assoc .... C 937 223-5201
Springboro *(G-17144)*
Young Mens Christian Assoc .... C 614 871-9622
Grove City *(G-11620)*
Young Mens Christian Assoc .... A 937 223-5201
Dayton *(G-10009)*
Young Mens Christian Assoc .... D 330 923-5223
Cuyahoga Falls *(G-9237)*
Young Mens Christian Assoc .... E 330 467-8366
Macedonia *(G-13219)*
Young Mens Christian Assoc .... E 330 784-0408
Akron *(G-515)*
Young Mens Christian Assoc .... C 614 416-9622
Gahanna *(G-11276)*
Young Mens Christian Assoc .... C 740 881-1058
Powell *(G-16355)*
Young Mens Christian Assoc .... C 614 334-9622
Hilliard *(G-11967)*
Young Mens Christian Assoc .... E 937 312-1810
Dayton *(G-10010)*
Young Mens Christian Assoc .... C 614 539-1770
Urbancrest *(G-18609)*
Young Mens Christian Assoc .... D 614 252-3166
Columbus *(G-9019)*
Young Mens Christian Assoc .... E 937 593-9001
Bellefontaine *(G-1401)*
Young Mens Christian Associat .... E 513 731-0115
Cincinnati *(G-4866)*
Young Mens Christian Associat .... C 513 474-1400
Cincinnati *(G-4867)*
Young Mens Christian Associat .... E 419 729-8135
Toledo *(G-18320)*
Young Mens Christian Associat .... D 513 241-9622
Cincinnati *(G-4868)*
Young Mens Christian Associat .... D 513 923-4466
Cincinnati *(G-4869)*
Young Mens Christian Associat .... E 419 474-3995
Toledo *(G-18322)*
Young Mens Christian Associat .... D 419 866-9622
Maumee *(G-13997)*
Young Mens Christian Associat .... C 419 475-3496
Toledo *(G-18323)*
Young Mens Christian Associat .... E 419 691-3523
Oregon *(G-15756)*
Young Mens Christian Mt Vernon ...... D 740 392-9622
Mount Vernon *(G-14927)*
Young MNS Chrstn Assn Clveland .... E 216 521-8400
Lakewood *(G-12502)*
Young MNS Chrstn Assn Clveland .... D 440 842-5200
North Royalton *(G-15507)*
Young MNS Chrstn Assn Clveland .... E 216 731-7454
Cleveland *(G-6774)*
Young MNS Chrstn Assn Clveland .... D 440 285-7543
Chardon *(G-2780)*
Young MNS Chrstn Assn Grter NY .... E 740 392-9622
Mount Vernon *(G-14928)*
Young Womens Christian .... D 419 241-3235
Toledo *(G-18325)*
Young Womens Christian .... D 937 461-5550
Dayton *(G-10013)*
Young Womens Christian .... E 419 238-6639
Van Wert *(G-18654)*
Young Womens Christian Assn .... D 614 224-9121
Columbus *(G-9021)*
Young Womens Christian Assn .... E 330 746-6361
Youngstown *(G-20422)*
Young Womens Christian Associ ..... E 216 881-6878
Cleveland *(G-6776)*
Young Womns Chrstn Assc Canton .. D 330 453-0789
Canton *(G-2594)*
YWCA of Greater Cincinnati .... D 513 241-7090
Cincinnati *(G-4870)*
YWCA Shelter & Housing Network ... E 937 222-6333
Dayton *(G-10014)*

CHILD GUIDANCE SVCS

Child Adlscent Behavioral Hlth .... E 330 454-7917
Canton *(G-2304)*
Child Adlscent Behavioral Hlth .... D 330 433-6075
Canton *(G-2305)*
Comprehensive Cmnty Child Care .... E 513 221-0033
Cincinnati *(G-3405)*
County of Cuyahoga .... E 216 443-5100
Cleveland *(G-5422)*
Mercy Health - St .... E 419 696-7465
Oregon *(G-15741)*
Richland County Child Support .... E 419 774-5700
Mansfield *(G-13356)*

CHINAWARE WHOLESALERS

CHILD RESTRAINT SEATS, AUTOMOTIVE, WHOLESALE

Recaro Child Safety LLC .... E 248 904-1570
Cincinnati *(G-4392)*
TS Tech Americas Inc .... E 740 593-5958
Athens *(G-817)*
TS Tech Americas Inc .... B 614 575-4100
Reynoldsburg *(G-16486)*

CHILDBIRTH PREPARATION CLINIC

Central Ohio Primary Care .... D 614 552-2300
Reynoldsburg *(G-16437)*
Family Birth Center Lima Mem .... E 419 998-4570
Lima *(G-12776)*
Hanger Inc .... E 419 841-9852
Sylvania *(G-17591)*
Kindred Healthcare Inc .... A 937 433-2400
Dayton *(G-9661)*
Medical Specialties Distrs LLC .... E 614 888-7939
Columbus *(G-6894)*
Mercy Health .... E 937 323-4585
Springfield *(G-17235)*
Mercy Health .... E 513 981-5750
Cincinnati *(G-4061)*
Mercy Health .... D 937 653-3445
Urbana *(G-18595)*
Mercy Health .... C 330 746-7211
Youngstown *(G-20282)*
Molina Healthcare Inc .... B 216 606-1400
Independence *(G-12235)*
Primary Cr Ntwrk Prmr Hlth Prt .... E 513 204-5785
Mason *(G-13750)*
Salo Incorporated .... A 740 964-2904
Pataskala *(G-15925)*
Sports Medicine Grant Inc .... E 614 461-8199
Pickerington *(G-16106)*
Wheeling Hospital Inc .... D 740 671-0850
Shadyside *(G-16853)*

CHILDREN'S & INFANTS' CLOTHING STORES

Abercrombie & Fitch Trading Co .... E 614 283-6500
New Albany *(G-14970)*

CHILDREN'S AID SOCIETY

Cleveland Municipal School Dst .... D 216 521-6511
Cleveland *(G-5337)*
Feed Lucas County Children Inc .... D 419 260-1556
Toledo *(G-17885)*
Franklin Cnty Bd Commissioners ...... C 614 275-2571
Columbus *(G-7683)*
Homes For Kids of Ohio Inc .... E 330 544-8005
Niles *(G-15294)*
Prokids Inc .... E 513 281-2000
Cincinnati *(G-4347)*
Scioto County Ohio .... E 740 456-4164
New Boston *(G-15013)*

CHILDREN'S BOARDING HOME

One Way Farm of Fairfield Inc .... E 513 829-3276
Fairfield *(G-10889)*

CHILDREN'S DANCING SCHOOL

Artistic Dance Enterprises .... E 614 761-2882
Columbus *(G-7046)*

CHILDREN'S HOME

Christian Chld HM Ohio Inc .... D 330 345-7949
Wooster *(G-19841)*
County of Richland .... C 419 774-4100
Mansfield *(G-13280)*
County of Wayne .... D 330 345-5340
Wooster *(G-19856)*
Mid-Western Childrens Home .... E 513 877-2141
Pleasant Plain *(G-16215)*
Necco Center .... D 740 534-1386
Pedro *(G-15937)*
Pathway Caring For Children .... D 330 493-0083
Canton *(G-2489)*
Saint Joseph Orphanage .... D 513 741-3100
Cincinnati *(G-4472)*

CHINAWARE WHOLESALERS

Ghp II LLC .... B 740 681-6825
Lancaster *(G-12544)*

CHIROPRACTORS' OFFICES

Name		Phone
Active Chiropractic	E	440 893-8800
Chagrin Falls *(G-2688)*		
Lbi Starbucks DC 3	C	614 415-6363
Columbus *(G-8046)*		

CHOCOLATE, EXC CANDY FROM BEANS: Chips, Powder, Block, Syrup

Name		Phone
Gorant Chocolatier LLC	C	330 726-8821
Boardman *(G-1740)*		
Malleys Candies Inc	E	216 529-6262
Cleveland *(G-5974)*		
Robert E McGrath Inc	E	440 572-7747
Strongsville *(G-17503)*		

CHURCHES

Name		Phone
Epworth Preschool and Daycare	E	740 387-1062
Marion *(G-13538)*		
First Christian Church	E	330 445-2700
Canton *(G-2367)*		
Salvation Army	E	937 528-5100
Dayton *(G-9863)*		

CIGARETTE STORES

Name		Phone
M & R Amusement Services Inc	E	937 525-0404
Springfield *(G-17227)*		

CIRCUIT BOARD REPAIR SVCS

Name		Phone
Mid-Ohio Electric Co	E	614 274-8000
Columbus *(G-8165)*		

CLAIMS ADJUSTING SVCS

Name		Phone
Crawford & Company	E	440 243-8710
Cleveland *(G-5432)*		
S & S Halthcare Strategies Ltd	C	513 772-8866
Cincinnati *(G-4464)*		
Summit Claim Services LLC	D	330 706-9898
New Franklin *(G-15050)*		

CLEANING & DESCALING SVC: Metal Prdts

Name		Phone
Carpe Diem Industries LLC	E	419 358-0129
Bluffton *(G-1729)*		
Carpe Diem Industries LLC	D	419 659-5639
Columbus Grove *(G-9029)*		
Chemical Solvents Inc	E	216 741-9310
Cleveland *(G-5232)*		

CLEANING & DYEING PLANTS, EXC RUGS

Name		Phone
A One Fine Dry Cleaners Inc	D	513 351-2663
Cincinnati *(G-2955)*		
Apc2 Inc	D	513 231-5540
Cincinnati *(G-3033)*		
Caskey Cleaning Co	D	614 443-7448
Columbus *(G-7204)*		
Coit Services of Ohio Inc	D	216 626-0040
Cleveland *(G-5369)*		
Dee Jay Cleaners Inc	E	216 731-7060
Euclid *(G-10750)*		
Dublin Cleaners Inc	D	614 764-9934
Columbus *(G-7548)*		
La France South Inc	E	330 782-1400
Youngstown *(G-20251)*		
Rockwood Dry Cleaners Corp	E	614 471-3700
Gahanna *(G-11265)*		
Rondinelli Company Inc	D	330 726-7643
Youngstown *(G-20358)*		
Widmers LLC	C	513 321-5100
Cincinnati *(G-4848)*		

CLEANING EQPT: Commercial

Name		Phone
MPW Industrial Svcs Group Inc	D	740 927-8790
Hebron *(G-11855)*		

CLEANING EQPT: Floor Washing & Polishing, Commercial

Name		Phone
Image By J & K LLC	B	888 667-6929
Maumee *(G-13927)*		

CLEANING OR POLISHING PREPARATIONS, NEC

Name		Phone
Ohio Auto Supply Company	E	330 454-5105
Canton *(G-2478)*		

CLEANING PRDTS: Specialty

Name		Phone
Rose Products and Services Inc	E	614 443-7647
Columbus *(G-8649)*		

CLEANING SVCS

Name		Phone
Acpx2	E	513 829-2100
Fairfield *(G-10815)*		
Akil Incorporated	E	419 625-0857
Sandusky *(G-16724)*		
Ashland Cleaning LLC	E	419 281-1747
Ashland *(G-654)*		
Calvin Klein Inc	E	330 562-2746
Aurora *(G-833)*		
Corporate Cleaning Inc	E	614 203-6051
Columbus *(G-7441)*		
French Company LLC	D	330 963-4344
Twinsburg *(G-18418)*		
Lance A1 Cleaning Services LLC	D	614 370-0550
Columbus *(G-8035)*		
Liberty Casting Company LLC	E	740 363-1941
Delaware *(G-10116)*		
Med Clean	C	614 207-3317
Columbus *(G-8141)*		
Mid-American Clg Contrs Inc	C	937 859-6222
Dayton *(G-9743)*		
Mispace Inc	E	614 626-2602
Columbus *(G-8179)*		
Oregon Clean Energy Center	E	419 566-9466
Oregon *(G-15745)*		
Premier Cleaning Services Inc	E	513 831-2492
Milford *(G-14555)*		
Steven H Byerly Inc	E	614 882-0092
Columbus *(G-8788)*		

CLEANING SVCS: Industrial Or Commercial

Name		Phone
A B M Inc	E	419 421-2292
Findlay *(G-10988)*		
Ajax Commercial Cleaning Inc	D	330 928-4543
Cuyahoga Falls *(G-9158)*		
Any Domest Work Inc	D	440 845-9911
Cleveland *(G-5045)*		
Blue Chip 2000 Coml Clg Inc	B	513 561-2999
Cincinnati *(G-3119)*		
Carrara Companies Inc	D	330 659-2800
Richfield *(G-16499)*		
Champion Clg Specialists Inc	E	513 871-2333
Cincinnati *(G-3227)*		
Control Cleaning Solutions	E	330 220-3333
Brunswick *(G-1973)*		
Cummins Facility Services LLC	B	740 726-9800
Prospect *(G-16364)*		
Environment Ctrl Beachwood Inc	D	330 405-6201
Twinsburg *(G-18408)*		
Essentialprofile1corp	E	614 805-4794
Columbus *(G-7611)*		
Four Corners Cleaning Inc	E	330 644-0834
Barberton *(G-963)*		
Galaxie Industrial Svcs LLC	E	330 503-2334
Youngstown *(G-20193)*		
Industrial Air Control Inc	D	330 772-6422
Hubbard *(G-12088)*		
Metropolitan Envmtl Svcs Inc	D	614 771-1881
Hilliard *(G-11930)*		
Milford Coml Clg Svcs Inc	E	513 575-5678
Milford *(G-14542)*		
MPW Industrial Services Inc	A	800 827-8790
Hebron *(G-11854)*		
MPW Industrial Services Inc	D	740 774-5251
Chillicothe *(G-2864)*		
MPW Industrial Services Inc	D	937 644-0200
East Liberty *(G-10511)*		
MPW Industrial Svcs Group Inc	D	740 927-8790
Hebron *(G-11855)*		
New Albany Cleaning Services	E	614 855-9990
New Albany *(G-14997)*		
Ohio State University	A	614 292-6158
Columbus *(G-8445)*		
Pinnacle Building Services Inc	C	614 871-6190
Chillicothe *(G-2871)*		
Professional Hse Clg Svcs Inc	E	440 729-7866
Chesterland *(G-2801)*		
R K Hydro-Vac Inc	E	937 773-8600
Piqua *(G-16164)*		
Rde System Corporation	D	513 933-8000
Dayton *(G-9843)*		
Schenker Inc	E	419 491-1055
Swanton *(G-17570)*		
TNT Power Wash Inc	E	614 662-3110
Groveport *(G-11676)*		
TNT Power Wash Inc	E	614 662-3110
Groveport *(G-11677)*		
Toledo Building Services Co	A	419 241-3101
Toledo *(G-18228)*		
Two Men & A Vacuum LLC	D	614 300-7970
Columbus *(G-8881)*		
Vadakin Inc	E	740 373-7518
Marietta *(G-13512)*		
Veolia Es Industrial Svcs Inc	C	937 425-0512
Dayton *(G-9968)*		
Wiggins Clg & Crpt Svc Inc	D	937 279-9080
Dayton *(G-9998)*		

CLEARINGHOUSE ASSOCIATIONS: Bank Or Check

Name		Phone
Nationwide Biweekly ADM Inc	C	937 376-5800
Xenia *(G-20071)*		
Ptc Holdings Inc	B	216 771-6960
Cleveland *(G-6331)*		

CLOTHING & ACCESS, WOMEN, CHILD & INFANT, WHOL: Diapers

Name		Phone
Procter & Gamble Distrg LLC	B	513 626-2500
Blue Ash *(G-1667)*		

CLOTHING & ACCESS, WOMEN, CHILD & INFANT, WHSLE: Sportswear

Name		Phone
Brennan-Eberly Team Sports Inc	E	419 865-8326
Holland *(G-12013)*		

CLOTHING & ACCESS, WOMEN, CHILDREN & INFANT, WHOL: Handbags

Name		Phone
Atrium Buying Corporation	D	740 966-8200
Blacklick *(G-1500)*		
RG Barry Corporation	D	614 864-6400
Pickerington *(G-16105)*		

CLOTHING & ACCESS, WOMEN, CHILDREN & INFANT, WHOL: Uniforms

Name		Phone
Cintas Corporation No 1	A	513 459-1200
Mason *(G-13678)*		
Cintas Corporation No 2	D	937 401-0098
Vandalia *(G-18670)*		
Cintas Sales Corporation	B	513 459-1200
Cincinnati *(G-3353)*		
Lion-Vallen Ltd Partnership	B	937 898-1949
Dayton *(G-9686)*		

CLOTHING & ACCESS, WOMEN, CHILDREN/INFANT, WHOL: Baby Goods

Name		Phone
Toys r Us Inc	E	614 759-7744
Reynoldsburg *(G-16485)*		

CLOTHING & ACCESS: Costumes, Theatrical

Name		Phone
Costume Specialists Inc	E	614 464-2115
Columbus *(G-7448)*		

CLOTHING & ACCESS: Hospital Gowns

Name		Phone
Standard Textile Co Inc	B	513 761-9255
Cincinnati *(G-4579)*		

CLOTHING & FURNISHINGS, MEN'S & BOYS', WHOLESALE: Gloves

Name		Phone
Safety Solutions Inc	D	614 799-9900
Dublin *(G-10446)*		

CLOTHING & FURNISHINGS, MEN'S & BOYS', WHOLESALE: Uniforms

Name		Phone
Cintas Corporation No 1	A	513 459-1200
Mason *(G-13678)*		
Cintas Sales Corporation	B	513 459-1200
Cincinnati *(G-3353)*		
Lion-Vallen Ltd Partnership	B	937 898-1949
Dayton *(G-9686)*		
Standard Textile Co Inc	B	513 761-9255
Cincinnati *(G-4579)*		
Walter F Stephens Jr Inc	E	937 746-0521
Franklin *(G-11167)*		

SERVICES SECTION

CLOTHING & FURNISHINGS, MENS & BOYS, WHOL: Sportswear/Work

Brennan-Eberly Team Sports Inc ....E 419 865-8326
  Holland (G-12013)

CLOTHING & FURNISHINGS, MENS & BOYS, WHOLESALE: Apprl Belts

J Peterman Company LLC ....E 888 647-2555
  Blue Ash (G-1619)

CLOTHING STORES, NEC

Schneider Saddlery LLC ....E 440 543-2700
  Chagrin Falls (G-2733)

CLOTHING STORES: Dancewear

Artistic Dance Enterprises ....E 614 761-2882
  Columbus (G-7046)

CLOTHING STORES: Designer Apparel

K Amalia Enterprises Inc ....D 614 733-3800
  Plain City (G-16195)

CLOTHING STORES: Formal Wear

American Commodore Tu ....D 216 291-4601
  Cleveland (G-5006)
Rondinellis Tuxedo ....E 330 726-7768
  Youngstown (G-20359)

CLOTHING STORES: Lingerie & Corsets, Underwear

Pure Romance LLC ....D 513 248-8656
  Cincinnati (G-4356)

CLOTHING STORES: T-Shirts, Printed, Custom

Soundtrack Printing ....C 330 606-7117
  Cuyahoga Falls (G-9219)
TSC Apparel LLC ....D 513 771-1138
  Cincinnati (G-4703)

CLOTHING/ACCESS, WOMEN, CHILDREN/INFANT, WHOL: Hosp Gowns

Philips Medical Systems Clevel ....B 440 247-2652
  Cleveland (G-6273)

CLOTHING/FURNISHINGS, MEN/BOY, WHOL: Furnishings, Exc Shoes

RG Barry Corporation ....D 614 864-6400
  Pickerington (G-16105)

CLOTHING: Caps, Baseball

Barbs Graffiti Inc ....E 216 881-5550
  Cleveland (G-5094)

CLOTHING: Hospital, Men's

Standard Textile Co Inc ....B 513 761-9255
  Cincinnati (G-4579)

CLOTHING: T-Shirts & Tops, Knit

E Retailing Associates LLC ....D 614 300-5785
  Columbus (G-7561)

CLOTHING: Uniforms & Vestments

Walter F Stephens Jr Inc ....E 937 746-0521
  Franklin (G-11167)

CLOTHING: Uniforms, Ex Athletic, Women's, Misses' & Juniors'

Cintas Corporation ....A 513 459-1200
  Cincinnati (G-3349)
Cintas Corporation ....D 513 631-5750
  Cincinnati (G-3350)
Cintas Corporation No 2 ....D 330 966-7800
  Canton (G-2309)
Standard Textile Co Inc ....B 513 761-9255
  Cincinnati (G-4579)

CLOTHING: Uniforms, Military, Men/Youth, Purchased Materials

Vgs Inc ....C 216 431-7800
  Cleveland (G-6693)

CLOTHING: Uniforms, Work

Cintas Corporation ....D 513 631-5750
  Cincinnati (G-3350)
Cintas Corporation ....A 513 459-1200
  Cincinnati (G-3349)
Cintas Corporation No 2 ....D 330 966-7800
  Canton (G-2309)
Cintas Sales Corporation ....B 513 459-1200
  Cincinnati (G-3353)
Vgs Inc ....C 216 431-7800
  Cleveland (G-6693)

CLUTCHES, EXC VEHICULAR

Logan Clutch Corporation ....E 440 808-4258
  Cleveland (G-5950)

COAL & OTHER MINERALS & ORES WHOLESALERS

Graphel Corporation ....C 513 779-6166
  West Chester (G-19083)
Tosoh America Inc ....B 614 539-8622
  Grove City (G-11606)

COAL MINING SERVICES

American Energy Corporation ....B 740 926-2430
  Beallsville (G-1139)
Buckingham Coal Company LLC ....D 740 767-2907
  Zanesville (G-20452)
Coal Services Inc ....D 740 795-5220
  Powhatan Point (G-16356)
Harrison County Coal Company ....D 740 338-3100
  Saint Clairsville (G-16637)
Ohio Valley Resources Inc ....E 740 795-5220
  Saint Clairsville (G-16649)
Peabody Coal Company ....B 740 450-2420
  Zanesville (G-20524)
Rosebud Mining Company ....E 330 222-2334
  Carrollton (G-2627)
Suncoke Energy Nc ....E 513 727-5571
  Middletown (G-14463)

COAL MINING SVCS: Bituminous, Contract Basis

Ohio Valley Coal Company ....B 740 926-1351
  Saint Clairsville (G-16648)
Ohio Valley Transloading Co ....A 740 795-4967
  Saint Clairsville (G-16650)

COAL MINING: Anthracite

Coal Services Inc ....D 740 795-5220
  Powhatan Point (G-16356)

COAL MINING: Bituminous & Lignite Surface

Daron Coal Company LLC ....C 614 643-0337
  Cadiz (G-2074)
J & D Mining Inc ....E 330 339-4935
  New Philadelphia (G-15103)
Murray American Energy Inc ....A 740 338-3100
  Saint Clairsville (G-16645)

COAL MINING: Bituminous Coal & Lignite-Surface Mining

Coal Services Inc ....D 740 795-5220
  Powhatan Point (G-16356)
Rosebud Mining Company ....E 740 768-2097
  Bergholz (G-1476)

COAL MINING: Bituminous Underground

American Energy Corporation ....B 740 926-2430
  Beallsville (G-1139)
Coal Services Inc ....D 740 795-5220
  Powhatan Point (G-16356)
Murray Kentucky Energy Inc ....B 740 338-3100
  Saint Clairsville (G-16646)
Rosebud Mining Company ....E 740 658-4217
  Freeport (G-11181)

COCKTAIL LOUNGE

Rosebud Mining Company ....E 740 768-2097
  Bergholz (G-1476)
Rosebud Mining Company ....E 740 922-9122
  Uhrichsville (G-18491)
Rosebud Mining Company ....E 330 222-2334
  Carrollton (G-2627)
Western KY Coal Resources LLC ....B 740 338-3100
  Saint Clairsville (G-16660)

COAL MINING: Bituminous, Strip

B&N Coal Inc ....D 740 783-3575
  Dexter City (G-10170)
Oxford Min Cmpany-Kentucky LLC .....C 740 622-6302
  Coshocton (G-9114)
Oxford Mining Company Inc ....D 740 342-7666
  New Lexington (G-15059)
Rosebud Mining Company ....E 740 922-9122
  Uhrichsville (G-18491)
Sands Hill Coal Hauling Co Inc ....C 740 384-4211
  Hamden (G-11688)

COAL MINING: Bituminous, Surface, NEC

Marietta Coal Co ....E 740 695-2197
  Saint Clairsville (G-16643)

COAL MINING: Lignite, Surface, NEC

Nacco Industries Inc ....E 440 229-5151
  Cleveland (G-6098)

COATING SVC: Aluminum, Metal Prdts

SH Bell Company ....E 412 963-9910
  East Liverpool (G-10534)

COATING SVC: Metals & Formed Prdts

Howmet Corporation ....E 800 242-9898
  Newburgh Heights (G-15251)

COATING SVC: Metals, With Plastic Or Resins

Corrotec Inc ....E 937 325-3585
  Springfield (G-17177)
Godfrey & Wing Inc ....E 330 562-1440
  Aurora (G-840)

COATINGS: Epoxy

BASF Construction Chem LLC ....E 216 831-5500
  Cleveland (G-5098)

COCKTAIL LOUNGE

Akron Management Corp ....B 330 644-8441
  Akron (G-48)
Al-Mar Lanes ....E 419 352-4637
  Bowling Green (G-1757)
Avalon Inn Services Inc ....C 330 856-1900
  Warren (G-18824)
Bramarjac Inc ....E 419 884-3434
  Mansfield (G-13268)
Capri Bowling Lanes Inc ....E 937 832-4000
  Dayton (G-9379)
Carrie Cerino Restaurants Inc ....C 440 237-3434
  Cleveland (G-5186)
Chillicothe Bowling Lanes Inc ....E 740 773-3300
  Chillicothe (G-2817)
City Life Inc ....E 216 523-5899
  Cleveland (G-5246)
Columbus Square Bowling Palace ....E 614 895-1122
  Columbus (G-7387)
Corporate Exchange Hotel Assoc ....C 614 890-8600
  Columbus (G-7443)
Eastbury Bowling Center ....E 330 452-3700
  Canton (G-2348)
Holiday Lanes Inc ....E 614 861-1600
  Columbus (G-7846)
Interstate Lanes of Ohio Ltd ....E 419 666-2695
  Rossford (G-16609)
Island Service Company ....C 419 285-3695
  Put In Bay (G-16368)
McPaul Corp ....E 419 447-6313
  Tiffin (G-17684)
Paul A Ertel ....D 216 696-8888
  Cleveland (G-6252)
Pike Run Golf Club Inc ....E 419 538-7000
  Ottawa (G-15803)
Poelking Lanes Inc ....D 937 299-5573
  Dayton (G-9814)

COCKTAIL LOUNGE

R P L Corporation .... C 937 335-0021
  Troy *(G-18373)*
Rainbow Lanes Inc .... E 614 491-7155
  Columbus *(G-8586)*
Riverside Cmnty Urban Redev .... C 330 929-3000
  Cuyahoga Falls *(G-9215)*
Sb Hotel LLC .... E 614 793-2244
  Dublin *(G-10449)*
Stonehedge Enterprises Inc .... E 330 928-2161
  Akron *(G-451)*
The Oaks Lodge .... E 330 769-2601
  Chippewa Lake *(G-2899)*
Town House Motor Lodge Corp .... E 740 452-4511
  Zanesville *(G-20539)*
Victory Lanes Inc .... E 937 323-8684
  Springfield *(G-17292)*
Wedgewood Lanes Inc .... E 330 792-1949
  Youngstown *(G-20410)*

COFFEE SVCS

Filterfresh Coffee Service Inc .... E 513 681-8911
  West Chester *(G-19201)*
K & R Distributors Inc .... E 937 864-5495
  Fairborn *(G-10799)*
Sanese Services Inc .... B 614 436-1234
  Warren *(G-18895)*
Walter Alexander Entps Inc .... E 513 841-1100
  Cincinnati *(G-4823)*

COIN COUNTERS

Garda CL Technical Svcs Inc .... E 937 294-4099
  Moraine *(G-14788)*

COIN-OPERATED LAUNDRY

American Sales Inc .... E 937 253-9520
  Dayton *(G-9254)*
Fox Cleaners Inc .... D 937 276-4171
  Dayton *(G-9559)*

COIN-OPERATED LAUNDRY MACHINE ROUTES

Joseph S Mischell .... E 513 542-9800
  Cincinnati *(G-3888)*

COINS, WHOLESALE

Anderson Press Incorporated .... E 615 370-9922
  Ashland *(G-650)*
United States Commemrtv Art GA ..... E 330 494-5504
  Canton *(G-2571)*

COLD STORAGE MACHINERY WHOLESALERS

D & D Investment Co .... E 614 272-6567
  Columbus *(G-7476)*

COLLECTION AGENCIES

Allied Interstate LLC .... D 715 386-1810
  Columbus *(G-6971)*
Axcess Rcvery Cr Solutions Inc .... E 513 229-6700
  Cincinnati *(G-3070)*
Dfs Corporate Services LLC .... E 614 777-7020
  Hilliard *(G-11895)*
Guardian Water & Power Inc .... D 614 291-3141
  Columbus *(G-7785)*
Head Mercantile Co Inc .... D 440 847-2700
  Westlake *(G-19490)*
Innovtive Cllectn Concepts Inc .... E 513 489-5500
  Blue Ash *(G-1615)*
Jared Galleria of Jewelery .... D 614 476-6532
  Columbus *(G-7935)*
Macys Cr & Customer Svcs Inc .... A 513 398-5221
  Mason *(G-13734)*
Medical Administrators Inc .... E 440 899-2229
  Westlake *(G-19513)*

COLLECTION AGENCY, EXC REAL ESTATE

Apelles LLC .... E 614 899-7322
  Columbus *(G-7028)*
C & S Associates Inc .... E 440 461-9661
  Highland Heights *(G-11868)*
Celco Ltd .... E 330 655-7000
  Hudson *(G-12107)*
Choice Recovery Inc .... D 614 358-9900
  Columbus *(G-7266)*
Controlled Credit Corporation .... E 513 921-2600
  Cincinnati *(G-3414)*
Credit Adjustments Inc .... D 419 782-3709
  Defiance *(G-10024)*
Credit Bur Collectn Svcs Inc .... E 614 223-0688
  Columbus *(G-7458)*
Credit Bur Collectn Svcs Inc .... E 937 496-2577
  Dayton *(G-9444)*
Estate Information Svcs LLC .... D 614 729-1700
  Gahanna *(G-11241)*
Fidelity Properties Inc .... E 330 821-9700
  Alliance *(G-539)*
Finance System of Toledo Inc .... E 419 578-4300
  Toledo *(G-17888)*
First Federal Credit Control .... E 216 360-2000
  Cleveland *(G-5596)*
General Audit Corp .... E 419 993-2900
  Lima *(G-12782)*
General Revenue Corporation .... B 513 469-1472
  Mason *(G-13707)*
HMC Group Inc .... E 440 847-2720
  Westlake *(G-19491)*
Hs Financial Group LLC .... E 440 871-8484
  Westlake *(G-19493)*
JP Recovery Services Inc .... D 440 356-5048
  Rocky River *(G-16583)*
McCarthy Burgess & Wolff Inc .... C 440 735-5100
  Bedford *(G-1321)*
Media Collections Inc .... D 216 831-5626
  Twinsburg *(G-18447)*
Medical Care PSC Inc .... E 513 281-4400
  Cincinnati *(G-4042)*
National Entp Systems Inc .... B 440 542-1360
  Solon *(G-17032)*
Ncs Incorporated .... D 440 684-9455
  Cleveland *(G-6115)*
PRC Medical LLC .... D 330 493-9004
  Cuyahoga Falls *(G-9213)*
Receivable MGT Svcs Corp .... D 330 659-1000
  Richfield *(G-16525)*
Recovery One LLC .... D 614 336-4207
  Columbus *(G-8596)*
Reliant Capital Solutions LLC .... E 614 452-6100
  Gahanna *(G-11264)*
Revenue Assistance Corporation ...... C 216 763-2100
  Cleveland *(G-6387)*
Rossman .... E 614 523-4150
  New Albany *(G-15006)*
Security Check LLC .... E 614 944-5788
  Columbus *(G-8710)*
Tek-Collect Incorporated .... E 614 299-2766
  Columbus *(G-8828)*
United Collection Bureau Inc .... C 419 866-6227
  Toledo *(G-18269)*
United Collection Bureau Inc .... E 419 866-6227
  Maumee *(G-13989)*

COLLEGE, EXC JUNIOR

Baldwin Wallace University .... E 440 826-2285
  Berea *(G-1446)*
Kenyon College .... E 740 427-2202
  Gambier *(G-11348)*
Marietta College .... E 740 376-4790
  Marietta *(G-13467)*
Oberlin College .... C 440 775-8519
  Oberlin *(G-15654)*
University of Toledo .... A 419 383-4000
  Toledo *(G-18279)*
University of Toledo .... A 419 383-3759
  Toledo *(G-18281)*

COLLEGES, UNIVERSITIES & PROFESSIONAL SCHOOLS

Antioch University .... D 937 769-1366
  Yellow Springs *(G-20088)*
Aultman Hospital .... A 330 452-9911
  Canton *(G-2253)*
Cleveland Clinic Lerner Colleg .... D 216 445-3853
  Cleveland *(G-5309)*
Ohio State Univ Wexner Med Ctr ...... A 614 293-7521
  Columbus *(G-8385)*
Ohio State University .... E 614 292-5491
  Columbus *(G-8398)*
Ohio State University .... B 614 292-3238
  Columbus *(G-8427)*
Ohio State University .... D 614 292-4453
  Columbus *(G-8405)*
Ohio State University .... A 614 293-2494
  Columbus *(G-8412)*

SERVICES SECTION

Ohio State University .... C 614 292-6251
  Columbus *(G-8431)*
Ohio State University .... E 614 293-8333
  Columbus *(G-8441)*

COLOR SEPARATION: Photographic & Movie Film

Tj Metzgers Inc .... D 419 861-8611
  Toledo *(G-18219)*

COMBINATION UTILITIES, NEC

City of Lorain .... C 440 204-2500
  Lorain *(G-13024)*
City of Painesville .... B 440 392-5795
  Painesville *(G-15841)*
Jersey Central Pwr & Light Co .... E 330 315-6713
  Fairlawn *(G-10960)*
Ohio Edison Company .... C 740 671-2900
  Shadyside *(G-16851)*
Universal Green Energy Solutio .... E 844 723-7768
  Reynoldsburg *(G-16487)*
University of Cincinnati .... E 513 558-1799
  Cincinnati *(G-4772)*

COMBINED ELEMENTARY & SECONDARY SCHOOLS, PRIVATE

Christian Schools Inc .... D 330 857-7311
  Kidron *(G-12440)*
East Dayton Christian School .... E 937 252-5400
  Dayton *(G-9268)*
Laurel School .... C 216 464-1441
  Cleveland *(G-5928)*
Open Door Christian School .... D 440 322-6386
  Elyria *(G-10666)*

COMMERCIAL & INDL SHELVING WHOLESALERS

Cbf Industries Inc .... E 216 229-9300
  Bedford *(G-1298)*
EBO Inc .... E 216 229-9300
  Bedford *(G-1305)*

COMMERCIAL & OFFICE BUILDINGS RENOVATION & REPAIR

Advanced Intgrted Slutions LLC .... E 313 724-8600
  Blue Ash *(G-1524)*
Airko Inc .... E 440 333-0133
  Cleveland *(G-4978)*
Apex Restoration Contrs Ltd .... E 513 489-1795
  Cincinnati *(G-3035)*
Arnolds Home Improvement LLC ...... E 734 847-9600
  Toledo *(G-17759)*
Belfor USA Group Inc .... E 330 916-6468
  Peninsula *(G-15947)*
Brackett Builders Inc .... E 937 339-7505
  Troy *(G-18350)*
Burge Building Co Inc .... E 440 245-6871
  Lorain *(G-13021)*
Canton Floors Inc .... E 330 492-1121
  Canton *(G-2288)*
CFS Construction Inc .... E 513 559-4500
  Cincinnati *(G-3222)*
Daugherty Construction Inc .... E 216 731-9444
  Euclid *(G-10748)*
Disaster Reconstruction Inc .... E 440 918-1523
  Eastlake *(G-10545)*
Fryman-Kuck General Contrs Inc ...... E 937 274-2892
  Dayton *(G-9564)*
Icon Environmental Group LLC .... E 513 426-6767
  Milford *(G-14526)*
Ingle-Barr Inc .... D 740 702-6117
  Chillicothe *(G-2853)*
James Hunt Construction Co .... E 513 721-0559
  Cincinnati *(G-3861)*
Jeffrey Carr Construction Inc .... E 330 879-5210
  Massillon *(G-13826)*
Jtf Construction Inc .... D 513 860-9835
  Fairfield *(G-10866)*
M-A Building and Maint Co .... E 216 391-5577
  Independence *(G-12231)*
Mattlin Construction Inc .... E 513 598-5402
  Cleves *(G-6804)*
Mc Meechan Construction Co .... E 216 581-9373
  Cleveland *(G-5999)*
Mural & Son Inc .... E 216 267-3322
  Cleveland *(G-6090)*

SERVICES SECTION
COMMUNICATIONS SVCS

Oliver House Rest Complex .... D 419 243-1302
 Toledo *(G-18105)*
Plevniak Construction Inc .... E 330 718-1600
 Youngstown *(G-20324)*
Quality Masonry Company Inc .... E 740 387-6720
 Marion *(G-13573)*
Ram Construction Services of .... D 513 297-1857
 West Chester *(G-19137)*
Residence Artists Inc .... E 440 286-8822
 Chardon *(G-2764)*
Residntial Coml Rnovations Inc .... E 330 815-1476
 Clinton *(G-6807)*
Smb Construction Co Inc .... E 419 269-1473
 Toledo *(G-18191)*
Swartz Enterprises Inc .... E 419 331-1024
 Lima *(G-12895)*
Trisco Systems Incorporated .... C 419 339-9912
 Lima *(G-12906)*
VIP Restoration Inc .... D 216 426-9500
 Cleveland *(G-6699)*
Wingler Construction Corp .... E 614 626-8546
 Columbus *(G-9000)*

COMMERCIAL ART & GRAPHIC DESIGN SVCS

Don Drumm Studios & Gallery .... E 330 253-6840
 Akron *(G-196)*
Exhibitpro Inc .... E 614 885-9541
 New Albany *(G-14985)*
Fx Digital Media Inc .... E 216 241-4040
 Cleveland *(G-5643)*
General Theming Contrs LLC .... C 614 252-6342
 Columbus *(G-7736)*
Graffiti Inc .... D 216 881-5550
 Cleveland *(G-5685)*
Innovtive Crtive Solutions LLC .... E 614 491-9638
 Groveport *(G-11647)*
Mc Sign Company .... C 440 209-6200
 Mentor *(G-14211)*
Northern Ohio Printing Inc .... E 216 398-0000
 Cleveland *(G-6160)*
Sfc Graphics Inc .... E 419 255-1283
 Toledo *(G-18181)*
Visual Art Graphic Services .... E 330 274-2775
 Mantua *(G-13397)*
Whitespace Design Group Inc .... E 330 762-9320
 Akron *(G-510)*
Young Mens Christian .... C 513 791-5000
 Blue Ash *(G-1725)*

COMMERCIAL ART & ILLUSTRATION SVCS

Fisher Design Inc .... E 513 417-8235
 Cincinnati *(G-3630)*
ONeil & Associates Inc .... C 937 865-0800
 Miamisburg *(G-14330)*
Young & Rubicam Inc .... C 513 419-2300
 Cincinnati *(G-4864)*

COMMERCIAL CONTAINERS WHOLESALERS

Kaufman Container Company .... C 216 898-2000
 Cleveland *(G-5887)*

COMMERCIAL EQPT & SPLYS, WHOLESALE: Price Marking

Century Marketing Corporation .... C 419 354-2591
 Bowling Green *(G-1772)*

COMMERCIAL EQPT WHOLESALERS, NEC

Acorn Distributors Inc .... E 614 294-6444
 Columbus *(G-6940)*
AVI Food Systems Inc .... E 740 452-9363
 Zanesville *(G-20445)*
Bakemark USA LLC .... D 513 870-0880
 West Chester *(G-19023)*
Burns Industrial Equipment Inc .... E 330 425-2476
 Macedonia *(G-13191)*
Cleveland Coin Mch Exch Inc .... D 847 842-6310
 Willoughby *(G-19653)*
CMC Daymark Corporation .... C 419 354-2591
 Bowling Green *(G-1773)*
General Data Company Inc .... C 513 752-7978
 Cincinnati *(G-2916)*
Koenig Equipment Inc .... D 937 877-1920
 Tipp City *(G-17721)*

Restaurant Equippers Inc .... E 614 358-6622
 Columbus *(G-8624)*
Shearer Farm Inc .... E 419 465-4622
 Monroeville *(G-14722)*
Sprayworks Equipment Group LLC .... E 330 587-4141
 Canton *(G-2536)*

COMMERCIAL EQPT, WHOLESALE: Bakery Eqpt & Splys

Cmbb LLC .... C 937 652-2151
 Urbana *(G-18581)*
Russell T Bundy Associates Inc .... D 937 652-2151
 Urbana *(G-18600)*

COMMERCIAL EQPT, WHOLESALE: Coffee Brewing Eqpt & Splys

Access Catalog Company LLC .... E 440 572-5377
 Strongsville *(G-17438)*

COMMERCIAL EQPT, WHOLESALE: Comm Cooking & Food Svc Eqpt

Business Data Systems Inc .... E 330 633-1221
 Tallmadge *(G-17633)*
Carroll Manufacturing & Sales .... E 440 937-3900
 Avon *(G-884)*
Harry C Lobalzo & Sons Inc .... E 330 666-6758
 Akron *(G-253)*
Nemco Inc .... D 419 542-7751
 Hicksville *(G-11866)*
Quality Supply Co .... E 937 890-6114
 Cincinnati *(G-4360)*
S S Kemp & Company .... C 216 271-7062
 Cleveland *(G-6428)*
Service Solutions Group LLC .... E 513 772-6600
 Cincinnati *(G-4501)*
Vulcan Feg .... D 937 332-2763
 Troy *(G-18387)*
Wasserstrom Company .... B 614 228-6525
 Columbus *(G-8970)*

COMMERCIAL EQPT, WHOLESALE: Restaurant, NEC

Burkett and Sons Inc .... E 419 242-7377
 Perrysburg *(G-15982)*
Globe Food Equipment Company .... E 937 299-5493
 Moraine *(G-14790)*
ITW Food Equipment Group LLC .... A 937 332-2396
 Troy *(G-18359)*
John H Kappus Co .... E 216 367-6677
 Cleveland *(G-5867)*
N Wasserstrom & Sons Inc .... C 614 228-5550
 Columbus *(G-8212)*
Specialty Equipment Sales Co .... E 216 351-2559
 Brooklyn Heights *(G-1927)*
The Cottingham Paper Co .... E 614 294-6444
 Columbus *(G-8834)*
Trimark Usa LLC .... D 216 271-7700
 Cleveland *(G-6618)*
Zink Foodservice Group .... E 800 492-7400
 Westerville *(G-19359)*

COMMERCIAL EQPT, WHOLESALE: Scales, Exc Laboratory

Brechbuhler Scales Inc .... E 330 458-3060
 Canton *(G-2269)*
Filing Scale Company Inc .... E 330 425-3092
 Twinsburg *(G-18415)*

COMMERCIAL EQPT, WHOLESALE: Teaching Machines, Electronic

Productivity Qulty Systems Inc .... E 937 885-2255
 Dayton *(G-9833)*

COMMERCIAL EQPT, WHOLESALE: Vending Machines, Coin-Operated

Dtv Inc .... E 216 226-5465
 Mayfield Heights *(G-14001)*

COMMERCIAL PHOTOGRAPHIC STUDIO

Childers Photography .... E 937 256-0501
 Dayton *(G-9261)*
Eclipsecorp LLC .... E 614 626-8536
 Columbus *(G-7572)*

Ideal Image Inc .... D 937 832-1660
 Englewood *(G-10709)*

COMMERCIAL PRINTING & NEWSPAPER PUBLISHING COMBINED

Copley Ohio Newspapers Inc .... C 330 364-5577
 New Philadelphia *(G-15087)*
Dispatch Printing Company .... C 740 548-5331
 Lewis Center *(G-12684)*

COMMODITIES SAMPLING SVC

US Protection Service LLC .... D 513 422-7910
 Cincinnati *(G-4796)*

COMMODITY CONTRACT POOL OPERATORS

Roulston Research Corp .... E 216 431-3000
 Cleveland *(G-6414)*

COMMODITY CONTRACTS BROKERS, DEALERS

Merrill Lynch Pierce Fenner .... E 937 847-4000
 Miamisburg *(G-14319)*
Merrill Lynch Pierce Fenner .... D 330 670-2400
 Akron *(G-339)*
Wells Fargo Clearing Svcs LLC .... E 216 574-7300
 Cleveland *(G-6731)*

COMMODITY INVESTORS

Lti Inc .... D 614 278-7777
 Columbus *(G-8085)*

COMMON SAND MINING

Demmy Sand and Gravel LLC .... E 937 325-8840
 Springfield *(G-17189)*
Welch Holdings Inc .... E 513 353-3220
 Cincinnati *(G-4829)*

COMMUNICATIONS CARRIER: Wired

Cosmic Concepts Ltd .... C 614 228-1104
 Columbus *(G-7447)*
Verizon Business Global LLC .... E 614 219-2317
 Hilliard *(G-11963)*
Verizon Select Services Inc .... E 908 559-2054
 North Royalton *(G-15506)*

COMMUNICATIONS EQPT REPAIR & MAINTENANCE

Consolidated Communications .... E 330 896-3905
 Canton *(G-2321)*
Mobilcomm Inc .... D 513 742-5555
 Cincinnati *(G-4110)*
Professional Telecom Svcs .... E 513 232-7700
 Cincinnati *(G-4344)*

COMMUNICATIONS EQPT WHOLESALERS

Clercom Inc .... D 513 724-6101
 Williamsburg *(G-19630)*
Commercial Electronics Inc .... E 740 281-0180
 Newark *(G-15157)*
Communications III Inc .... E 614 901-7720
 Westerville *(G-19390)*
Consolidated Communications .... E 330 896-3905
 Canton *(G-2321)*
Midwest Digital Inc .... D 330 900-4744
 North Canton *(G-15355)*
Quasonix Inc .... E 513 942-1287
 West Chester *(G-19135)*
Sound Com Corporation .... D 440 234-2604
 Berea *(G-1469)*
Winncom Technologies Corp .... E 440 498-9510
 Solon *(G-17068)*

COMMUNICATIONS SVCS

Centre Communications Corp .... E 440 454-3262
 Beavercreek *(G-1232)*
Htp Inc .... E 614 885-1272
 Columbus *(G-6885)*
Stg Communication Services Inc .... E 330 482-0500
 Columbiana *(G-6863)*
University of Cincinnati .... A 513 556-5087
 Cincinnati *(G-4764)*

COMMUNICATIONS SVCS

Wireless Source Entps LLC ....E 419 266-5556
  Bowling Green (G-1797)

COMMUNICATIONS SVCS: Cellular

Aka Wireless Inc ....E 216 213-8040
  Hartville (G-11814)
AT&T Corp ....D 614 798-3898
  Dublin (G-10257)
AT&T Corp ....D 614 539-0165
  Grove City (G-11532)
AT&T Corp ....D 614 575-3044
  Columbus (G-7063)
AT&T Corp ....D 614 851-2400
  Columbus (G-7064)
AT&T Corp ....E 330 505-4200
  Niles (G-15282)
AT&T Inc ....E 937 320-9648
  Beavercreek (G-1227)
AT&T Mobility LLC ....E 614 291-2500
  Columbus (G-7066)
AT&T Mobility LLC ....C 330 565-5000
  Youngstown (G-20106)
AT&T Mobility LLC ....E 440 846-3232
  Strongsville (G-17445)
AT&T Mobility LLC ....E 419 516-0602
  Lima (G-12743)
AT&T Mobility LLC ....E 937 439-4900
  Centerville (G-2674)
AT&T Services Inc ....C 937 456-2330
  Eaton (G-10553)
Cellco Partnership ....B 614 560-2000
  Dublin (G-10281)
Cellco Partnership ....D 330 486-1005
  Twinsburg (G-18398)
Cellco Partnership ....D 614 560-8552
  Lewis Center (G-12673)
Cellco Partnership ....D 513 923-2700
  Cincinnati (G-3202)
Cellco Partnership ....D 614 476-9786
  Columbus (G-7220)
Cellco Partnership ....D 330 764-7380
  Medina (G-14044)
Cellco Partnership ....D 330 823-7758
  Alliance (G-531)
Cellco Partnership ....D 419 333-1009
  Fremont (G-11187)
Cellco Partnership ....D 440 886-5461
  Parma (G-15901)
Cellco Partnership ....D 330 928-4382
  Cuyahoga Falls (G-9170)
Cellco Partnership ....D 419 353-0904
  Bowling Green (G-1771)
Cellco Partnership ....D 740 652-9540
  Lancaster (G-12515)
Cellco Partnership ....D 740 695-3600
  Saint Clairsville (G-16631)
Cellco Partnership ....D 419 784-3800
  Defiance (G-10021)
Cellco Partnership ....D 740 432-7785
  Cambridge (G-2103)
Cellco Partnership ....D 330 376-8275
  Akron (G-126)
Cellco Partnership ....D 513 755-1666
  West Chester (G-19035)
Cellco Partnership ....D 513 697-1190
  Cincinnati (G-3203)
Cellco Partnership ....D 440 934-0576
  Avon (G-885)
Cellco Partnership ....D 419 381-1726
  Toledo (G-17795)
Cellco Partnership ....C 216 765-1444
  Beachwood (G-1061)
Cellco Partnership ....D 440 998-3111
  Ashtabula (G-731)
Cellco Partnership ....D 513 422-3437
  Middletown (G-14477)
Cellco Partnership ....D 740 588-0018
  Zanesville (G-20458)
Cellco Partnership ....E 513 688-1300
  Cincinnati (G-3204)
Cellco Partnership ....E 419 424-2351
  Findlay (G-11011)
Cellco Partnership ....E 419 331-4644
  Lima (G-12752)
Cellco Partnership ....D 419 897-9133
  Maumee (G-13892)
Cellco Partnership ....E 614 759-4400
  Reynoldsburg (G-16434)
Cellco Partnership ....D 419 625-7900
  Sandusky (G-16736)
Cellco Partnership ....E 440 953-1155
  Mentor (G-14155)
Cellco Partnership ....E 440 646-9625
  Cleveland (G-5203)
Cellco Partnership ....E 440 846-8881
  Strongsville (G-17448)
Cellco Partnership ....E 740 397-6609
  Mount Vernon (G-14881)
Cellco Partnership ....E 614 459-7200
  Columbus (G-7221)
Cellco Partnership ....E 937 429-4000
  Beavercreek (G-1158)
Cellco Partnership ....E 513 671-2200
  Cincinnati (G-3205)
Cellco Partnership ....E 513 697-0222
  Cincinnati (G-3206)
Cellco Partnership ....E 330 665-5220
  Fairlawn (G-10941)
Cellco Partnership ....E 419 843-2995
  Toledo (G-17796)
Cellco Partnership ....E 330 493-7979
  Canton (G-2302)
Cellco Partnership ....E 216 573-5880
  Independence (G-12195)
Cellco Partnership ....D 937 578-0022
  Marysville (G-13611)
Cellco Partnership ....D 440 542-9631
  Solon (G-16990)
Cellco Partnership ....D 330 626-0524
  Streetsboro (G-17408)
Cellco Partnership ....D 740 362-2408
  Delaware (G-10077)
Cellco Partnership ....E 440 324-9479
  Elyria (G-10601)
Cellco Partnership ....E 614 793-8989
  Dublin (G-10283)
Cellco Partnership ....D 614 277-2900
  Grove City (G-11544)
Cellco Partnership ....E 740 522-6446
  Newark (G-15155)
Cellco Partnership ....D 330 345-6465
  Wooster (G-19838)
Cellco Partnership ....E 330 722-6622
  Medina (G-14043)
Cellco Partnership ....E 440 984-5200
  Amherst (G-590)
Cellco Partnership ....E 740 450-1525
  Zanesville (G-20459)
Century Tel of Odon Inc ....C 440 244-8544
  Lorain (G-13022)
Nextel Communications Inc ....D 513 891-9200
  Cincinnati (G-4163)
Nextel Communications Inc ....E 614 801-9267
  Grove City (G-11584)
Nextel Partners Operating Corp ....E 330 305-1365
  North Canton (G-15357)
Nextel Partners Operating Corp ....E 419 380-2000
  Toledo (G-18086)
Prime Communications LP ....E 281 240-7800
  Canton (G-2494)
Round Room LLC ....E 440 888-0322
  North Royalton (G-15500)
Sprint Spectrum LP ....E 614 575-5500
  Columbus (G-8765)
Sprint Spectrum LP ....E 614 428-2300
  Columbus (G-8767)
Supermedia LLC ....D 740 369-2391
  Marion (G-13583)
Verizon Communications Inc ....D 419 281-1714
  Ashland (G-705)
Verizon Communications Inc ....C 330 334-1268
  Wadsworth (G-18772)
Verizon Communications Inc ....C 440 892-4504
  Westlake (G-19562)
Verizon Wireless Inc ....D 937 434-2355
  Dayton (G-9969)
Wireless Center Inc ....B 216 503-3777
  Cleveland (G-6755)

COMMUNICATIONS SVCS: Data

A M Communications Ltd ....D 419 528-3051
  Vandalia (G-18655)
Brand Technologies Inc ....E 419 873-6600
  Perrysburg (G-15980)
Calvert Wire & Cable Corp ....E 216 433-7600
  Cleveland (G-5173)
Cellco Partnership ....D 330 308-0549
  New Philadelphia (G-15084)
Cellco Partnership ....D 614 793-8989
  Dublin (G-10282)
Communication Svc For Deaf Inc ....C 937 299-0917
  Moraine (G-14762)
Inet Interactive LLC ....E 513 322-5600
  West Chester (G-19093)
Jay Blue Communications ....E 216 661-2828
  Cleveland (G-5853)
Oovoo LLC ....D 917 515-2074
  Kettering (G-12434)
Springdot Inc ....D 513 542-4000
  Cincinnati (G-4568)
Time Warner Cable Inc ....E 513 354-1100
  Blue Ash (G-1696)
Velocity Grtest Phone Ever Inc ....C 419 868-9983
  Holland (G-12066)
Verizon Communications Inc ....C 419 874-3933
  Perrysburg (G-16069)

COMMUNICATIONS SVCS: Electronic Mail

Maximum Communications Inc ....E 513 489-3414
  Cincinnati (G-4031)

COMMUNICATIONS SVCS: Internet Connectivity Svcs

1 Community ....E 216 923-2272
  Cleveland (G-4917)
4mybenefits Inc ....E 513 891-6648
  Blue Ash (G-1521)
At T Broadband & Intern ....E 614 839-4271
  Columbus (G-7060)
Bluespring Software Inc ....E 513 794-1764
  Blue Ash (G-1547)
Broadvox LLC ....E 216 373-4600
  Cleveland (G-5142)
Buckeye Telesystem Inc ....D 419 724-9898
  Northwood (G-15528)
Community Isp Inc ....E 419 867-6060
  Toledo (G-17824)
Datzap LLC ....E 330 785-2100
  Akron (G-187)
Dct Telecom Group Inc ....E 440 892-0300
  Westlake (G-19482)
Great Lakes Telcom Ltd ....E 330 629-8848
  Youngstown (G-20207)
Intellinet Corporation ....E 216 289-4100
  Cleveland (G-5827)
Intgrted Bridge Communications ....E 513 381-1380
  Cincinnati (G-3839)
Level 3 Telecom LLC ....E 614 255-2000
  Worthington (G-19972)
Level 3 Telecom LLC ....E 234 542-6279
  Akron (G-316)
Level 3 Telecom LLC ....E 513 841-0000
  Cincinnati (G-3970)
Premier System Integrators Inc ....D 513 217-7294
  Middletown (G-14452)
Raco Wireless LLC ....D 513 870-6480
  Blue Ash (G-1673)
Revolution Group Inc ....D 614 212-1111
  Westerville (G-19349)
Skycasters LLC ....E 330 785-2100
  Akron (G-440)
Time Warner Cable Inc ....E 330 800-3874
  Akron (G-477)
TSC Communications Inc ....E 419 739-2200
  Wapakoneta (G-18810)
West Central Ohio Internet ....E 419 229-2645
  Lima (G-12916)

COMMUNICATIONS SVCS: Internet Host Svcs

Advanced Cmpt Connections LLC .....E 419 668-4080
  Norwalk (G-15561)
Connectlink Inc ....E 740 867-5095
  Chesapeake (G-2783)
Construction Biddingcom LLC ....E 440 716-4087
  North Olmsted (G-15418)
Ecommerce Inc ....D 800 861-9394
  Columbus (G-7573)
Infotelecom Holdings LLC ....B 216 373-4811
  Cleveland (G-5821)
Intellinex LLC ....B 216 685-6000
  Independence (G-12220)
Jumplinecom Inc ....E 614 859-1170
  Columbus (G-7959)
Kreative Communication Network ......E 330 743-1612
  Youngstown (G-20249)
Link Iq LLC ....E 859 983-6080
  Dayton (G-9684)

SERVICES SECTION

COMMUNITY ACTION AGENCY

Making Evrlasting Memories LLC .... E 513 864-0100
 Cincinnati *(G-4016)*
Massillon Cable TV Inc .... D 330 833-4134
 Massillon *(G-13833)*
Oxcyon Inc .... E 440 239-3345
 Cleveland *(G-6223)*
Profit Recovery of Ohio .... C 440 243-1743
 Cleveland *(G-6310)*
Roundtable Online Learning LLC .... E 440 220-5252
 Chagrin Falls *(G-2731)*
Tremor LLC .... E 513 983-1100
 Blue Ash *(G-1700)*

COMMUNICATIONS SVCS: Nonvocal Message

Stratacache Inc .... C 937 224-0485
 Dayton *(G-9910)*

COMMUNICATIONS SVCS: Online Svc Providers

Armstrong Utilities Inc .... E 740 894-3886
 South Point *(G-17080)*
C T Wireless .... D 937 653-2208
 Urbana *(G-18574)*
Com Net Inc .... D 419 739-3100
 Wapakoneta *(G-18792)*
F+w Media Inc .... B 513 531-2690
 Blue Ash *(G-1591)*
Primax Marketing Group .... E 513 443-2797
 Cincinnati *(G-4329)*
Suite 224 Internet .... E 440 593-7113
 Conneaut *(G-9047)*

COMMUNICATIONS SVCS: Radio Pager Or Beeper

Twin Comm Inc .... E 740 774-4701
 Marietta *(G-13508)*

COMMUNICATIONS SVCS: Signal Enhancement Network Svcs

Cincinnati Voice and Data .... D 513 683-4127
 Loveland *(G-13115)*
Telcom Construction Svcs Inc .... D 330 239-6900
 Medina *(G-14134)*
Vox Mobile .... E 800 536-9030
 Independence *(G-12274)*

COMMUNICATIONS SVCS: Telegram

AT&T Corp .... A 513 629-5000
 Cincinnati *(G-3054)*

COMMUNICATIONS SVCS: Telephone Or Video

AVI-Spl Employee .... E 937 836-4787
 Englewood *(G-10697)*
Tpusa Inc .... A 614 621-5512
 Columbus *(G-8860)*

COMMUNICATIONS SVCS: Telephone, Broker

J E Davis Corporation .... E 440 377-4700
 Sheffield Village *(G-16887)*
Rxp Ohio LLC .... D 614 937-2844
 Columbus *(G-8663)*

COMMUNICATIONS SVCS: Telephone, Data

AT&T Datacomm LLC .... E 614 223-5799
 Westerville *(G-19368)*
Mvd Communications LLC .... D 513 683-4711
 Mason *(G-13741)*
Quanexus Inc .... E 937 885-7272
 Dayton *(G-9837)*
Swn Communications Inc .... E 877 698-3262
 Dayton *(G-9917)*

COMMUNICATIONS SVCS: Telephone, Local

Alltel Communications Corp .... D 740 349-8551
 Newark *(G-15141)*
Champaign Telephone Company .... E 937 653-4000
 Urbana *(G-18579)*
Chillicothe Telephone Company .... C 740 772-8200
 Chillicothe *(G-2825)*
Chillicothe Telephone Company .... D 740 772-8361
 Chillicothe *(G-2826)*
Conneaut Telephone Company .... E 440 593-7140
 Conneaut *(G-9041)*
Deliass Assets Corp .... E 614 891-0101
 Westerville *(G-19393)*
Doylestown Telephone Company .... E 330 658-2121
 Doylestown *(G-10228)*
Doylestown Telephone Company .... E 330 658-6666
 Doylestown *(G-10229)*
Horizon Telcom Inc .... B 740 772-8200
 Chillicothe *(G-2851)*
Orwell Communications Inc .... E 937 855-6511
 Germantown *(G-11400)*
Quality One Technologies Inc .... E 937 855-6511
 Germantown *(G-11401)*
Verizon North Inc .... E 740 942-2566
 Cadiz *(G-2081)*
Verizon North Inc .... E 419 734-5000
 Port Clinton *(G-16258)*
Verizon North Inc .... E 330 339-7733
 New Philadelphia *(G-15121)*
Verizon Wireless .... E 330 963-1300
 Twinsburg *(G-18484)*
Windstream Ohio LLC .... C 440 329-4000
 Elyria *(G-10693)*
Windstream Western Reserve LLC .... C 330 650-8000
 Hudson *(G-12153)*

COMMUNICATIONS SVCS: Telephone, Local & Long Distance

Alltel Communications Corp .... E 330 656-8000
 Chardon *(G-2739)*
AT&T Corp .... D 937 320-9648
 Beavercreek *(G-1226)*
AT&T Corp .... D 740 455-3042
 Zanesville *(G-20444)*
AT&T Corp .... D 740 549-4546
 Lewis Center *(G-12667)*
AT&T Corp .... D 330 665-3100
 Akron *(G-82)*
AT&T Corp .... D 440 951-5309
 Willoughby *(G-19646)*
AT&T Corp .... C 330 752-7776
 Akron *(G-83)*
AT&T Corp .... D 513 741-1700
 Cincinnati *(G-3053)*
AT&T Corp .... C 216 672-0809
 Cleveland *(G-5075)*
AT&T Corp .... E 330 723-1717
 Medina *(G-14037)*
AT&T Services Inc .... C 937 456-2330
 Eaton *(G-10553)*
Cellco Partnership .... E 330 922-5997
 Stow *(G-17355)*
Communication Options Inc .... E 614 901-7095
 New Albany *(G-14982)*
Ohio Bell Telephone Company .... A 216 822-3439
 Cleveland *(G-6185)*
Round Room LLC .... E 330 880-0660
 Massillon *(G-13851)*
Round Room LLC .... E 937 429-2230
 Beavercreek *(G-1206)*
Sprint Communications Co LP .... E 419 725-2444
 Toledo *(G-18197)*
Sprint Spectrum LP .... E 440 686-2600
 North Olmsted *(G-15445)*
Sprint Spectrum LP .... E 614 575-5500
 Columbus *(G-8765)*
Sprint Spectrum LP .... E 614 793-2500
 Columbus *(G-8766)*
Sprint Spectrum LP .... E 614 428-2300
 Columbus *(G-8767)*
Verizon Business Global LLC .... E 440 457-4049
 North Royalton *(G-15505)*
Verizon Business Global LLC .... E 614 219-2317
 Hilliard *(G-11963)*
Verizon Communications Inc .... C 330 334-1268
 Wadsworth *(G-18772)*
Verizon Communications Inc .... C 440 892-4504
 Westlake *(G-19562)*
Verizon Communications Inc .... E 740 383-0527
 Marion *(G-13594)*
Verizon South Inc .... D 740 354-0544
 Portsmouth *(G-16321)*

COMMUNICATIONS SVCS: Telephone, Long Distance

AT&T Corp .... A 513 629-5000
 Cincinnati *(G-3054)*
First Communications LLC .... E 330 835-2323
 Fairlawn *(G-10953)*
First Communications LLC .... B 330 835-2323
 Fairlawn *(G-10954)*
Marietta College .... E 740 376-4790
 Marietta *(G-13467)*
MCI Communications Svcs Inc .... B 216 265-9953
 Cleveland *(G-6005)*
MCI Communications Svcs Inc .... B 440 635-0418
 Chardon *(G-2757)*
Mitel (delaware) Inc .... E 513 733-8000
 West Chester *(G-19122)*
Png Telecommunications Inc .... D 513 942-7900
 Cincinnati *(G-4311)*
Professional Telecom Svcs .... E 513 232-7700
 Cincinnati *(G-4344)*
Verizon Business Global LLC .... E 330 505-2368
 Niles *(G-15308)*

COMMUNICATIONS SVCS: Television Antenna Construction & Rent

Armstrong Utilities Inc .... E 740 894-3886
 South Point *(G-17080)*

COMMUNITY ACTION AGENCY

Abcd Inc .... E 330 455-6385
 Canton *(G-2223)*
Adams & Brown Counties Economi .... E 937 695-0316
 Winchester *(G-19799)*
Adams & Brown Counties Economi .... C 937 378-6041
 Georgetown *(G-11383)*
Akron Cmnty Svc Ctr Urban Leag .... E 234 542-4141
 Akron *(G-33)*
American Red Cross of Grtr Col .... E 614 253-7981
 Columbus *(G-7004)*
Ashtabula County Commnty Actn .... D 440 997-5957
 Ashtabula *(G-720)*
Clinton County Community Actn .... E 937 382-8365
 Wilmington *(G-19750)*
Clinton County Community Actn .... E 937 382-5624
 Wilmington *(G-19751)*
Community Action Program Corp .... D 740 373-3745
 Marietta *(G-13436)*
Community Action Program Corp .... E 740 373-6016
 Marietta *(G-13437)*
Community Action Program Inc .... D 937 382-0225
 Wilmington *(G-19755)*
Council On Rur Svc Prgrams Inc .... E 937 492-8787
 Sidney *(G-16924)*
Council On Rur Svc Prgrams Inc .... E 937 778-5220
 Piqua *(G-16140)*
Council On Rur Svc Prgrams Inc .... E 937 773-0773
 Piqua *(G-16141)*
County of Montgomery .... D 937 225-4192
 Dayton *(G-9431)*
Hancock Hardin Wyandot Putnam .... C 419 423-3755
 Findlay *(G-11042)*
Hockingthensperry Cmnty Action .... E 740 767-4500
 Glouster *(G-11435)*
Jackson-Vinton Cmnty Action .... E 740 384-3722
 Wellston *(G-19003)*
Leads Inc .... E 740 349-8606
 Newark *(G-15184)*
Lorain County Community Action .... E 440 245-2009
 Lorain *(G-13052)*
Miami Cnty Cmnty Action Cuncil .... E 937 335-7921
 Troy *(G-18363)*
Miami Valley Community Action .... D 937 222-1009
 Dayton *(G-9728)*
Neighborhood Progress Inc .... E 216 830-2770
 Cleveland *(G-6117)*
Northwestrn OH Communty Action .... C 419 784-2150
 Defiance *(G-10051)*
Ohio Citizen Action .... E 216 861-5200
 Cleveland *(G-6189)*
Ohio Hrtland Cmnty Action Comm .... E 740 387-1039
 Marion *(G-13569)*
Ohio Hrtland Cmnty Action Comm .... E 419 468-5121
 Galion *(G-11303)*
Tri-County Community Act .... E 740 385-6812
 Logan *(G-12991)*
West Ohio Cmnty Action Partnr .... C 419 227-2586
 Lima *(G-12919)*

Employee Codes: A=Over 500 employees, B=251-500
C=101-250, D=51-100, E=25-50

COMMUNITY CENTER

Avita Health System..............C....... 419 468-7059
Galion *(G-11290)*
Canton Jewish Community Center.......D....... 330 452-6444
Canton *(G-2291)*
City of Brecksville..............D....... 440 526-4109
Brecksville *(G-1819)*
City of Independence..............E....... 216 524-7373
Cleveland *(G-5264)*
Community Services Inc..............D....... 937 667-8631
Tipp City *(G-17714)*
County of Guernsey..............D....... 740 432-2381
Cambridge *(G-2108)*
Davita Inc..............E....... 440 293-6028
Andover *(G-611)*
Don Bosco Community Center Inc........E....... 816 421-3160
Cleveland *(G-5501)*
East Toledo Family Center..............D....... 419 691-1429
Toledo *(G-17861)*
Economic & Cmnty Dev Inst Inc..............E....... 614 559-0104
Columbus *(G-7575)*
Hudson City Engineering Dept..............E....... 330 342-1770
Hudson *(G-12121)*
Impact Community Action..............D....... 614 252-2799
Columbus *(G-7885)*
Jewish Cmnty Ctr of Toledo..............D....... 419 885-4485
Sylvania *(G-17597)*
Jewish Fdrtion of Grter Dayton..............D....... 937 837-2651
Dayton *(G-9641)*
Mahoning Youngstown Community......D....... 330 747-7921
Youngstown *(G-20268)*
National Mentor Holdings Inc..............A....... 513 221-0175
Cincinnati *(G-4141)*
Salem Community Center Inc..............D....... 330 332-5885
Salem *(G-16712)*
Shaw Jewish Community Center..............C....... 330 867-7850
Akron *(G-437)*
Southern Ohio Medical Center..............A....... 740 354-5000
Portsmouth *(G-16313)*
St Pauls Community Center..............D....... 419 255-5520
Toledo *(G-18200)*
St Stephens Community House..............D....... 614 294-6347
Columbus *(G-8770)*
Taylor Murtis Human Svcs Sys..............D....... 216 281-7192
Cleveland *(G-6574)*
Taylor Murtis Human Svcs Sys..............D....... 216 283-4400
Cleveland *(G-6573)*

COMMUNITY CENTERS: Adult

Area Agency On Aging Planni..............C....... 800 258-7277
Dayton *(G-9343)*
Area Agency On Aging Dst 7 Inc..............C....... 800 582-7277
Rio Grande *(G-16546)*
Area Agency On Aging Dst 7 Inc..............E....... 740 446-7000
Gallipolis *(G-11308)*
Area Office On Aging of Nwstrn..............D....... 419 382-0624
Toledo *(G-17758)*
Ashtabula County Commnty Actn..............D....... 440 593-6441
Conneaut *(G-9037)*
Ashtabula Job and Family Svcs..............C....... 440 994-2020
Ashtabula *(G-725)*
Brown Cnty Snior Ctzen Council..............E....... 937 378-6603
Georgetown *(G-11385)*
Canton Christian Home Inc..............C....... 330 456-0004
Canton *(G-2283)*
Care & Share of Erie Count..............D....... 419 624-1411
Sandusky *(G-16733)*
Central OH Area Agency On Agng..............C....... 614 645-7250
Columbus *(G-7228)*
Cincinnati Area Senior Svcs..............C....... 513 721-4330
Cincinnati *(G-3281)*
City of Bucyrus..............E....... 419 562-3050
Bucyrus *(G-2029)*
City of Canal Winchester..............E....... 614 837-8276
Canal Winchester *(G-2157)*
City of Lakewood..............E....... 216 521-1515
Lakewood *(G-12473)*
City of Parma..............E....... 440 888-4514
Cleveland *(G-5273)*
Clermont Senior Services Inc..............E....... 513 724-1255
Batavia *(G-1004)*
Community Caregivers..............D....... 330 533-3427
Youngstown *(G-20151)*
Crawford County Council On Agi..............E....... 419 562-3050
Bucyrus *(G-2036)*
Cuyahoga County..............D....... 216 420-6750
Cleveland *(G-5450)*
Day Share Ltd..............E....... 513 451-1100
Cincinnati *(G-3467)*
Delhi Township..............D....... 513 922-0060
Cincinnati *(G-3481)*
Direction Home Akron Canton AR..............C....... 330 896-9172
Uniontown *(G-18517)*
Elderly United of Springfield..............D....... 937 323-4948
Springfield *(G-17193)*
Episcopal Retirement Homes Inc..............E....... 513 271-9610
Cincinnati *(G-3567)*
Family Senior Care Inc..............E....... 740 441-1428
Gallipolis *(G-11315)*
Gerlach John J Center For Sen..............E....... 614 566-5858
Columbus *(G-7746)*
Hardin Cnty Cncil On Aging Inc..............E....... 419 673-1102
Kenton *(G-12414)*
Haven Bhavioral Healthcare Inc..............B....... 937 234-0100
Dayton *(G-9601)*
Kettering Recreation Center..............E....... 937 296-2587
Dayton *(G-9657)*
Lake County Council On Aging..............E....... 440 205-8111
Mentor *(G-14203)*
Mercy Health Partners..............B....... 513 451-8900
Cincinnati *(G-4074)*
Miami Valley Community Action..............D....... 937 548-8143
Greenville *(G-11514)*
Middltown Area Senior Citizens..............D....... 513 423-1734
Middletown *(G-14438)*
Mount Carmel Health..............C....... 614 234-8170
Columbus *(G-8197)*
Muskingum Cnty Ctr For Seniors..............E....... 740 454-9761
Zanesville *(G-20504)*
Muskingum County Ohio..............D....... 740 452-0678
Zanesville *(G-20506)*
Northgate Pk Retirement Cmnty..............D....... 513 923-3711
Cincinnati *(G-4181)*
Ohio District 5 Area..............C....... 419 522-5612
Ontario *(G-15707)*
Older Wiser Life Services LLC..............E....... 330 659-2111
Richfield *(G-16522)*
Olmsted Residence Corporation..............C....... 440 235-7100
Olmsted Twp *(G-15680)*
Pickaway County Community Acti..............E....... 740 477-1655
Circleville *(G-4896)*
Pro Seniors Inc..............E....... 513 345-4160
Cincinnati *(G-4338)*
Senior Resource Connection..............C....... 937 223-8246
Dayton *(G-9875)*
Senior Star Management Company..............B....... 513 271-1747
Cincinnati *(G-4497)*
Sourcepoint..............D....... 740 363-6677
Delaware *(G-10128)*
Sycamore Senior Center..............D....... 513 984-1234
Blue Ash *(G-1692)*
Tuscarawas County Commitee..............D....... 330 364-6611
Dover *(G-10217)*
United Scoto Senior Activities..............E....... 740 354-6672
Portsmouth *(G-16316)*
Vantage Aging..............D....... 330 253-4597
Akron *(G-495)*
Vasconcellos Inc..............E....... 513 576-1250
Milford *(G-14573)*
Village of Groveport..............E....... 614 830-2060
Groveport *(G-11684)*
Western Reserve Area Agency..............C....... 216 621-0303
Cleveland *(G-6742)*
Western Reserve Area Agency..............E....... 216 621-0303
Cleveland *(G-6743)*
Wood County Committee On Aging......E....... 419 353-5661
Bowling Green *(G-1799)*

COMMUNITY CENTERS: Youth

Central Ohio Youth For Christ..............E....... 614 732-5260
Columbus *(G-7243)*
Cincinnati Youth Collaborative..............E....... 513 475-4165
Cincinnati *(G-3335)*
Crittenton Family Services..............E....... 614 251-0103
Columbus *(G-7464)*
Directions For Youth Families..............E....... 614 258-8043
Columbus *(G-7520)*
Directions For Youth Families..............E....... 614 694-0203
Columbus *(G-7521)*
Fairborn YMCA..............E....... 937 754-9622
Fairborn *(G-10796)*
Focus On Youth Inc..............E....... 513 644-1030
West Chester *(G-19075)*
KElly Youth Services Inc..............E....... 513 761-0700
Cincinnati *(G-3910)*
Lighthouse Youth Services Inc..............D....... 513 221-1017
Cincinnati *(G-3980)*
Lighthouse Youth Services Inc..............D....... 740 634-3094
Bainbridge *(G-942)*
Lorain Cnty Bys Girls CLB Inc..............E....... 440 775-2582
Lorain *(G-13048)*
Marion Family YMCA..............D....... 740 725-9622
Marion *(G-13556)*
Muskingum County Adult and CHI..............E....... 740 849-2344
Zanesville *(G-20505)*
New Horizon Youth Center Co..............E....... 740 782-0092
Bethesda *(G-1485)*
Sheakley Cente..............E....... 513 487-7106
Cincinnati *(G-4511)*
Young Mens Christian Assn..............C....... 330 744-8411
Youngstown *(G-20421)*
Youth Services Ohio Department..............C....... 419 875-6965
Liberty Center *(G-12716)*

COMMUNITY COLLEGE

Key Career Place..............D....... 216 987-3029
Cleveland *(G-5896)*

COMMUNITY DEVELOPMENT GROUPS

Catholic Chrties Regional Agcy..............D....... 330 744-3320
Youngstown *(G-20134)*
Columbus Urban League Inc..............E....... 614 257-6300
Columbus *(G-7391)*
Community Imprv Corp Nble Cnty..............D....... 740 509-0248
Caldwell *(G-2083)*
East End Community Svcs Corp..............E....... 937 259-1898
Dayton *(G-9514)*
Famicos Foundation..............E....... 216 791-6476
Cleveland *(G-5569)*
Greater Cleveland Food Bnk Inc..............C....... 216 738-2265
Cleveland *(G-5696)*
Guernsey County Cmnty Dev Corp..............E....... 740 439-0020
Cambridge *(G-2117)*
Habitat For Humanity..............E....... 216 429-1299
Cleveland *(G-5718)*
Habitat For Humanity Intl..............E....... 513 721-4483
Cincinnati *(G-3726)*
Karamu House Inc..............E....... 216 795-7070
Cleveland *(G-5885)*
Life Enriching Communities..............E....... 513 719-3510
Loveland *(G-13138)*
Lifeservices Development Corp..............E....... 440 257-3866
Mentor *(G-14209)*
Lutheran Metropolitan Ministry..............C....... 216 658-4638
Cleveland *(G-5960)*
Mobile Meals Inc..............D....... 330 376-7717
Akron *(G-346)*
Montpelier Senior Center..............E....... 419 485-3218
Montpelier *(G-14745)*
Neighborhood Development Svcs..............E....... 330 296-2003
Ravenna *(G-16393)*
Randall R Leab..............E....... 330 689-6263
Ashland *(G-693)*
REM-Ohio Inc..............E....... 440 986-3337
South Amherst *(G-17074)*
Rosemary Center..............E....... 216 481-4823
Euclid *(G-10774)*
Salvation Army..............D....... 800 728-7825
Columbus *(G-8682)*
Senior Independence..............D....... 330 873-3468
Fairlawn *(G-10975)*
Tipp-Monroe Community Svcs Inc..............E....... 937 667-8631
Tipp City *(G-17729)*
United Labor Agency Inc..............C....... 216 664-3446
Cleveland *(G-6641)*
University of Tledo Foundation..............E....... 419 530-7730
Toledo *(G-18276)*
University Settlement Inc..............E....... 216 641-8948
Cleveland *(G-6669)*
Urban League of Greater Southw..............D....... 513 281-9955
Cincinnati *(G-4787)*

COMMUNITY SVCS EMPLOYMENT TRAINING PROGRAM

Community Action..............E....... 740 354-7541
Portsmouth *(G-16271)*
Goodwill Inds Rhbilitation Ctr..............B....... 330 454-9461
Canton *(G-2384)*
Gw Business Solutions LLC..............C....... 740 645-9861
Newark *(G-15172)*
Licking-Knox Goodwill Inds Inc..............D....... 740 345-9861
Newark *(G-15196)*
Marion Cnty Bd Dev Dsabilities..............D....... 740 387-1035
Marion *(G-13554)*
Ohio Dept of Job & Fmly Svcs..............E....... 614 752-9494
Columbus *(G-8334)*
Project Rebuild Inc..............E....... 330 639-1559
Canton *(G-2495)*

SERVICES SECTION

Vocational Guidance Services .... A 216 431-7800
  Cleveland *(G-6708)*

COMMUNITY THEATER PRODUCTION SVCS

Licking County Players Inc .... E 740 349-2287
  Newark *(G-15189)*
The In Cincinnati Playhouse .... D 513 421-3888
  Cincinnati *(G-4644)*
Xenia Area Cmnty Theater Inc .... D 937 372-0516
  Xenia *(G-20085)*

COMMUTATORS: Electronic

Ra Consultants LLC .... E 513 469-6600
  Blue Ash *(G-1671)*

COMPACT DISCS OR CD'S, WHOLESALE

Telarc International Corp .... E 216 464-2313
  Beachwood *(G-1130)*

COMPOST

Kurtz Bros Compost Services .... E 330 864-2621
  Akron *(G-310)*
Werlor Inc .... E 419 784-4285
  Defiance *(G-10063)*

COMPRESSORS, AIR CONDITIONING: Wholesalers

Air Systems of Ohio Inc .... E 216 741-1700
  Brooklyn Heights *(G-1910)*
Best Aire Compressor Service .... D 419 726-0055
  Millbury *(G-14577)*
Diversified Air Systems Inc .... E 330 784-3466
  Akron *(G-194)*

COMPRESSORS: Air & Gas, Including Vacuum Pumps

Finishmaster Inc .... D 614 228-4328
  Columbus *(G-7657)*

COMPRESSORS: Repairing

A P O Holdings Inc .... D 330 650-1330
  Hudson *(G-12100)*
Best Aire Compressor Service .... D 419 726-0055
  Millbury *(G-14577)*
Diversified Air Systems Inc .... E 330 784-3466
  Akron *(G-194)*
National Compressor Svcs LLC .... E 419 868-4980
  Holland *(G-12040)*

COMPRESSORS: Wholesalers

A P O Holdings Inc .... D 330 650-1330
  Hudson *(G-12100)*
Air Systems of Ohio Inc .... E 216 741-1700
  Brooklyn Heights *(G-1910)*
Atlas Machine and Supply Inc .... E 502 584-7262
  West Chester *(G-19190)*
Becker Pumps Corporation .... D 330 928-9966
  Cuyahoga Falls *(G-9165)*
Breathing Air Systems Inc .... E 614 864-1235
  Reynoldsburg *(G-16431)*
General Electric Intl Inc .... E 330 963-2066
  Twinsburg *(G-18422)*
Industrial Air Centers Inc .... E 614 274-9171
  Columbus *(G-7893)*

COMPUTER & COMPUTER SOFTWARE STORES

Computer Helper Publishing .... E 614 939-9094
  Columbus *(G-7417)*
Datavantage Corporation .... B 440 498-4414
  Cleveland *(G-5464)*
Great Lakes Computer Corp .... D 440 937-1100
  Avon *(G-895)*
Harley-Davidson Dlr Systems Inc ..... D 216 573-1393
  Cleveland *(G-5726)*
Micro Center Inc .... B 614 850-3000
  Hilliard *(G-11931)*
Micro Electronics Inc .... D 614 334-1430
  Columbus *(G-8160)*
Microman Inc .... E 614 923-8000
  Dublin *(G-10397)*
Office World Inc .... E 419 991-4694
  Lima *(G-12928)*
Ohio Business Machines LLC .... E 216 485-2000
  Cleveland *(G-6187)*
Resource One Cmpt Systems Inc .... D 614 485-4800
  Worthington *(G-19993)*

COMPUTER & COMPUTER SOFTWARE STORES: Peripheral Eqpt

Cincinnati Bell Techno .... B 513 841-2287
  Cincinnati *(G-3287)*
Personalized Data Corporation .... E 216 289-2200
  Cleveland *(G-6268)*

COMPUTER & COMPUTER SOFTWARE STORES: Personal Computers

Micro Center Online Inc .... C 614 326-8500
  Columbus *(G-8159)*
Micro Electronics Inc .... D 614 850-3500
  Hilliard *(G-11933)*
Micro Electronics Inc .... C 440 449-7000
  Cleveland *(G-6049)*
Micro Electronics Inc .... E 513 782-8500
  Cincinnati *(G-4090)*
Micro Electronics Inc .... B 614 850-3000
  Hilliard *(G-11932)*

COMPUTER & COMPUTER SOFTWARE STORES: Software & Access

Information Builders Inc .... E 513 891-2338
  Montgomery *(G-14726)*
Provantage LLC .... D 330 494-3781
  North Canton *(G-15362)*
S & P Solutions Inc .... C 440 918-9111
  Willoughby Hills *(G-19734)*

COMPUTER & COMPUTER SOFTWARE STORES: Software, Bus/Non-Game

Retalix Inc .... C 937 384-2277
  Miamisburg *(G-14342)*
Stratacache Inc .... C 937 224-0485
  Dayton *(G-9910)*

COMPUTER & DATA PROCESSING EQPT REPAIR & MAINTENANCE

Decisionone Corporation .... E 614 883-0228
  Urbancrest *(G-18604)*
Efix Computer Repair & Svc LLC ..... E 937 985-4447
  Kettering *(G-12429)*
Positive Bus Solutions Inc .... D 513 772-2255
  Cincinnati *(G-4317)*
Realm Technologies LLC .... E 513 297-3095
  Lebanon *(G-12641)*

COMPUTER & OFFICE MACHINE MAINTENANCE & REPAIR

Bpi Infrmtion Systems Ohio Inc .... E 440 717-4112
  Brecksville *(G-1815)*
Bsl - Applied Laser Tech LLC .... E 216 663-8181
  Cleveland *(G-5154)*
Butler County of Ohio .... E 513 887-3418
  Hamilton *(G-11705)*
Cincinnati Copiers Inc .... C 513 769-0606
  Blue Ash *(G-1556)*
Cincinnati Voice and Data .... D 513 683-4127
  Loveland *(G-13115)*
County of Montgomery .... B 937 496-3103
  Dayton *(G-9439)*
CTS Construction Inc .... D 513 489-8290
  Cincinnati *(G-3445)*
Diebold Nixdorf Incorporated .... D 513 870-1400
  Hamilton *(G-11722)*
DMC Technology Group .... E 419 535-2900
  Toledo *(G-17855)*
Enterprise Data Management Inc ..... E 513 791-7272
  Blue Ash *(G-1588)*
Evanhoe & Associates Inc .... E 937 235-2995
  Dayton *(G-9269)*
Government Acquisitions Inc .... E 513 721-8700
  Cincinnati *(G-3689)*
HP Inc .... E 513 983-2817
  Cincinnati *(G-3791)*
Intelligent Information Inc .... E 513 860-4233
  West Chester *(G-19210)*
Northcoast Duplicating Inc .... C 216 573-6681
  Cleveland *(G-6150)*

COMPUTER INTERFACE EQPT: Indl Process

Park Place Technologies LLC .... B 610 544-0571
  Mayfield Heights *(G-14005)*
Park Place Technologies LLC .... C 877 778-8707
  Mayfield Heights *(G-14006)*
Perry Pro Tech Inc .... D 419 228-1360
  Lima *(G-12857)*
Pomeroy It Solutions Sls Inc .... E 440 717-1364
  Brecksville *(G-1842)*
Resource One Cmpt Systems Inc .... D 614 485-4800
  Worthington *(G-19993)*
Sjn Data Center LLC .... E 513 386-7871
  Cincinnati *(G-4534)*
Systems Alternatives Intl .... E 419 891-1100
  Maumee *(G-13985)*
Uptime Corporation .... E 216 661-1655
  Brooklyn Heights *(G-1930)*
Wellington Technologies Inc .... E 440 238-4377
  Westlake *(G-19564)*
Wrg Services Inc .... E 440 942-8650
  Willoughby *(G-19727)*
Xerox Corporation .... D 216 642-7806
  Cleveland *(G-6767)*

COMPUTER DATA ESCROW SVCS

Speedeon Data LLC .... E 440 264-2100
  Cleveland *(G-6519)*

COMPUTER FACILITIES MANAGEMENT SVCS

Ability Network Inc .... E 513 943-8888
  Cincinnati *(G-2901)*
City of Cleveland .... E 216 664-2941
  Cleveland *(G-5252)*
Computer Sciences Corporation .... E 937 904-5113
  Dayton *(G-9262)*
Computer Sciences Corporation .... C 614 801-2343
  Grove City *(G-11548)*
CSRA LLC .... B 937 429-9774
  Beavercreek *(G-1164)*
Dedicated Tech Services Inc .... D 614 309-0059
  Dublin *(G-10317)*
Dyn Marine Services Inc .... E 937 427-2663
  Beavercreek *(G-1170)*
E&I Solutions LLC .... E 937 912-0288
  Beavercreek *(G-1171)*
Evanhoe & Associates Inc .... E 937 235-2995
  Dayton *(G-9269)*
General Electric Company .... C 513 583-3500
  Cincinnati *(G-3669)*
Jjr Solutions LLC .... E 937 912-0288
  Beavercreek *(G-1180)*
Jyg Innovations LLC .... E 937 630-3858
  Dayton *(G-9647)*
Med3000 Group Inc .... E 937 291-7850
  Miamisburg *(G-14316)*
Selecttech Services Corp .... C 937 438-9905
  Centerville *(G-2685)*
Technical Assurance Inc .... E 440 953-3147
  Willoughby *(G-19717)*

COMPUTER GRAPHICS SVCS

Clubessential LLC .... E 800 448-1475
  Blue Ash *(G-1560)*
Great Lakes Publishing Company ..... D 216 771-2833
  Cleveland *(G-5691)*
Hyperquake LLC .... E 513 563-6555
  Cincinnati *(G-3806)*
Interact One Inc .... E 513 469-7042
  Blue Ash *(G-1616)*
International Data MGT Inc .... E 330 869-8500
  Fairlawn *(G-10959)*
Karcher Group Inc .... E 330 493-6141
  North Canton *(G-15348)*
Kuno Creative Group LLC .... E 440 225-4144
  Avon *(G-904)*
Service Pronet Inc .... E 614 874-4300
  Columbus *(G-8716)*
Universal Enterprises Inc .... C 419 529-3500
  Ontario *(G-15718)*

COMPUTER INTERFACE EQPT: Indl Process

Keithley Instruments LLC .... C 440 248-0400
  Solon *(G-17021)*

COMPUTER PERIPHERAL EQPT REPAIR & MAINTENANCE

Ascendtech Inc ....E 216 458-1101
Willoughby *(G-19645)*
Great Lakes Computer Corp ....D 440 937-1100
Avon *(G-895)*
Mt Business Technologies Inc ....C 419 529-6100
Mansfield *(G-13348)*

COMPUTER PERIPHERAL EQPT, NEC

Government Acquisitions Inc ....E 513 721-8700
Cincinnati *(G-3689)*
Parker-Hannifin Corporation ....D 513 831-2340
Milford *(G-14550)*
Systemax Manufacturing Inc ....C 937 368-2300
Dayton *(G-9919)*
Tech Pro Inc ....E 330 923-3546
Akron *(G-473)*

COMPUTER PERIPHERAL EQPT, WHOLESALE

Advanced Cmpt Connections LLC ....E 419 668-4080
Norwalk *(G-15561)*
Advantech Corporation ....D 513 742-8895
Blue Ash *(G-1528)*
Ascendtech Inc ....E 216 458-1101
Willoughby *(G-19645)*
Cincinnati Bell Techno ....D 513 841-6700
Cincinnati *(G-3286)*
Cisco Systems Inc ....D 614 764-4987
Dublin *(G-10293)*
Cranel Incorporated ....D 614 431-8000
Columbus *(G-6879)*
Legrand North America LLC ....B 937 224-0639
Moraine *(G-14798)*
Manatron Inc ....E 937 431-4000
Beavercreek *(G-1252)*
Meyer Hill Lynch Corporation ....E 419 897-9797
Maumee *(G-13947)*
Micro Center Online Inc ....C 614 326-8500
Columbus *(G-8159)*
Micro Electronics Inc ....D 614 334-1430
Columbus *(G-8160)*
Micro Electronics Inc ....B 614 850-3000
Hilliard *(G-11932)*
Micro Electronics Inc ....D 614 850-3500
Hilliard *(G-11933)*
Micro Electronics Inc ....C 440 449-7000
Cleveland *(G-6049)*
Micro Electronics Inc ....C 513 782-8500
Cincinnati *(G-4090)*
Microplex Inc ....E 330 498-0600
North Canton *(G-15353)*
Park Place International LLC ....D 877 991-1991
Chagrin Falls *(G-2728)*

COMPUTER PERIPHERAL EQPT: Decoders

Harris Mackessy & Brennan ....C 614 221-6831
Westerville *(G-19311)*

COMPUTER PROGRAMMING SVCS

Aclara Technologies LLC ....C 440 528-7200
Solon *(G-16969)*
Advanced Prgrm Resources Inc ....E 614 761-9994
Dublin *(G-10234)*
American Systems Cnsulting Inc ....D 614 282-7180
Dublin *(G-10252)*
Btas Inc ....C 937 431-9431
Beavercreek *(G-1155)*
Camgen Ltd ....E 330 204-8636
Canal Winchester *(G-2154)*
Care Information Systems LLC ....D 614 496-4338
Dublin *(G-10279)*
Cengage Learning Inc ....B 513 229-1000
Mason *(G-13674)*
Cimx LLC ....E 513 248-7700
Cincinnati *(G-3276)*
Coleman Professional Svcs Inc ....B 330 673-1347
Kent *(G-12360)*
Command Alkon Incorporated ....D 614 799-0600
Dublin *(G-10302)*
Computer Helper Publishing ....E 614 939-9094
Columbus *(G-7417)*
County of Montgomery ....B 937 496-3103
Dayton *(G-9439)*
Datavantage Corporation ....B 440 498-4414
Cleveland *(G-5464)*
Devcare Solutions Ltd ....E 614 221-2277
Columbus *(G-7511)*
Dexxxon Digital Storage Inc ....E 740 548-7179
Lewis Center *(G-12681)*
Distribution Data Incorporated ....E 216 362-3009
Brookpark *(G-1943)*
DMC Technology Group ....E 419 535-2900
Toledo *(G-17855)*
Drb Systems LLC ....D 330 645-3299
Akron *(G-200)*
Drs Signal Technologies Inc ....E 937 429-7470
Beavercreek *(G-1169)*
Dynamite Technologies LLC ....D 614 538-0095
Columbus *(G-7556)*
Eclipse Blind Systems Inc ....C 330 296-0112
Ravenna *(G-16384)*
Eliassen Group LLC ....E 781 205-8100
Blue Ash *(G-1583)*
Exodus Integrity Service ....D 440 918-0140
Willoughby *(G-19663)*
First Data Gvrnmnt Solutns Inc ....C 513 489-9599
Blue Ash *(G-1595)*
Gb Liquidating Company Inc ....E 513 248-7600
Milford *(G-14520)*
Gracie Plum Investments Inc ....E 740 355-9029
Portsmouth *(G-16282)*
Harley-Dvidson Dlr Systems Inc ....D 216 573-1393
Cleveland *(G-5726)*
Icr Inc ....D 513 900-7007
Mason *(G-13718)*
Indecon Solutions LLC ....E 614 799-1850
Dublin *(G-10374)*
Indigo Group ....E 513 557-8794
Liberty Twp *(G-12726)*
Infor (us) Inc ....B 678 319-8000
Columbus *(G-7896)*
Jyg Innovations LLC ....E 937 630-3858
Dayton *(G-9647)*
Lifecycle Solutions Jv LLC ....D 937 938-1321
Beavercreek *(G-1187)*
Mapsys Inc ....E 614 255-7258
Columbus *(G-8104)*
Office World Inc ....E 419 991-4694
Lima *(G-12928)*
Ohio University ....D 740 593-1000
Athens *(G-804)*
Pegasus Technical Services Inc ....E 513 793-0094
Cincinnati *(G-4274)*
Pillar Technology Group LLC ....D 614 535-7868
Columbus *(G-8544)*
Rainbow Data Systems Inc ....E 937 431-8000
Beavercreek *(G-1202)*
Resource International Inc ....C 614 823-4949
Columbus *(G-8622)*
Roadtrippers Inc ....E 917 688-9887
Cincinnati *(G-4432)*
Sawdey Solution Services Inc ....E 937 490-4060
Beavercreek *(G-1259)*
Scientific Forming Tech Corp ....E 614 451-8330
Columbus *(G-8705)*
Seapine Software Inc ....E 513 754-1655
Mason *(G-13757)*
Seifert & Group Inc ....D 330 833-2700
Massillon *(G-13852)*
Staid Logic LLC ....E 309 807-0575
Columbus *(G-8772)*
Sumaria Systems Inc ....D 937 429-6070
Beavercreek *(G-1210)*
Tata America Intl Corp ....B 513 677-6500
Milford *(G-14565)*
Tech Mahindra (americas) Inc ....D 216 912-2002
Cleveland *(G-6577)*
Triplett & Adams Entps Inc ....D 816 221-1024
New Concord *(G-15039)*
Tyco International MGT Co LLC ....E 888 787-8324
Cincinnati *(G-4712)*
Vediscovery LLC ....E 216 241-3443
Cleveland *(G-6688)*
Ventech Solutions Inc ....D 614 757-1167
Columbus *(G-6909)*
Yashco Systems Inc ....E 614 467-4600
Hilliard *(G-11966)*

COMPUTER PROGRAMMING SVCS: Custom

Critical Business Analysis Inc ....E 419 874-0800
Perrysburg *(G-15991)*
Digiknow Inc ....E 888 482-4455
Cleveland *(G-5483)*
Erp Analysts Inc ....B 614 718-9222
Dublin *(G-10339)*
Evanhoe & Associates Inc ....E 937 235-2995
Dayton *(G-9269)*
Horizon Payroll Services Inc ....B 937 434-8244
Dayton *(G-9621)*
Netsmart Technologies Inc ....D 614 764-0143
Dublin *(G-10407)*
Sordyl & Associates Inc ....E 419 866-6811
Maumee *(G-13979)*
Strategic Data Systems Inc ....E 513 772-7374
Cincinnati *(G-4595)*

COMPUTER RELATED MAINTENANCE SVCS

Arrow Electronics Inc ....D 440 498-6400
Solon *(G-16978)*
Ascendtech Inc ....E 216 458-1101
Willoughby *(G-19645)*
Atos It Solutions and Svcs Inc ....B 513 336-1000
Mason *(G-13665)*
Creek Technologies Company ....C 937 272-4581
Beavercreek *(G-1163)*
Dedicated Tech Services Inc ....D 614 309-0059
Dublin *(G-10317)*
Digital Controls Corporation ....D 513 746-8118
Miamisburg *(G-14297)*
Digital Management Inc ....D 240 223-4800
Mason *(G-13695)*
E&I Solutions LLC ....E 937 912-0288
Beavercreek *(G-1171)*
Echo-Tape LLC ....E 614 892-3246
Columbus *(G-7571)*
Fhc Enterprises LLC ....E 614 271-3513
Columbus *(G-7653)*
Greentree Group Inc ....D 937 490-5500
Dayton *(G-9591)*
Jjr Solutions LLC ....E 937 912-0288
Beavercreek *(G-1180)*
Jyg Innovations LLC ....E 937 630-3858
Dayton *(G-9647)*
Laketec Communications Inc ....E 440 892-2001
North Olmsted *(G-15429)*
Link Iq LLC ....E 859 983-6080
Dayton *(G-9684)*
Plus One Communications LLC ....B 330 255-4500
Akron *(G-393)*
Staid Logic LLC ....E 309 807-0575
Columbus *(G-8772)*
Top Gun Sales Performance Inc ....E 513 770-0870
Mason *(G-13770)*
Vana Solutions LLC ....E 937 242-6399
Beavercreek *(G-1217)*
Ventech Solutions Inc ....D 614 757-1167
Columbus *(G-6909)*
Wolters Kluwer Clinical Drug ....D 330 650-6506
Hudson *(G-12154)*

COMPUTER RELATED SVCS, NEC

Liebert Field Services Inc ....E 614 841-5763
Westerville *(G-19326)*
PC Connection Services ....C 937 382-4800
Wilmington *(G-19777)*

COMPUTER SOFTWARE DEVELOPMENT

Alien Technology LLC ....C 408 782-3900
Miamisburg *(G-14270)*
Astute Inc ....E 614 508-6100
Columbus *(G-7058)*
Auto Des Sys Inc ....E 614 488-7984
Upper Arlington *(G-18548)*
Billback Systems LLC ....E 937 433-1844
Dayton *(G-9358)*
Bluespring Software Inc ....E 513 794-1764
Blue Ash *(G-1547)*
Briteskies LLC ....E 216 369-3600
Cleveland *(G-5140)*
Business Equipment Co Inc ....E 513 948-1500
Cincinnati *(G-3156)*
Cincom Intrnational Operations ....B 513 612-2300
Cincinnati *(G-3342)*
Cintech LLC ....D 513 731-6000
Cincinnati *(G-3354)*
Cloudroute LLC ....E 216 373-4601
Cleveland *(G-5365)*
Clubessential LLC ....E 800 448-1475
Blue Ash *(G-1560)*
Cochin Technologies LLC ....E 440 941-4856
Avon *(G-891)*
Commercial Time Sharing Inc ....E 330 644-3059
Akron *(G-152)*

Comtech Global Inc .....D 614 796-1148
Columbus *(G-7419)*
Connectivity Systems Inc .....E 740 420-5400
Williamsport *(G-19637)*
CT Logistics Inc .....C 216 267-1636
Cleveland *(G-5446)*
Dassault Systemes Simulia Corp .....E 513 275-1430
Mason *(G-13694)*
Dedicated Tech Services Inc .....D 614 309-0059
Dublin *(G-10317)*
Digitek Software Inc .....E 614 764-8875
Lewis Center *(G-12683)*
Diskcopy Duplication Services .....E 440 460-0800
Cleveland *(G-5488)*
Dizer Corp .....E 440 368-0200
Painesville *(G-15851)*
Domin-8 Entp Solutions Inc .....D 513 492-5800
Mason *(G-13697)*
Dotloop LLC .....C 513 257-0550
Cincinnati *(G-3500)*
Einstruction Corporation .....D 330 746-3015
Youngstown *(G-20178)*
Electronic Registry Systems .....E 513 771-7330
Cincinnati *(G-3549)*
Exact Software North Amer LLC .....C 978 539-6186
Dublin *(G-10341)*
Exceptional Innovation Inc .....D 614 901-8899
Westerville *(G-19302)*
Expert Technical Consultants .....E 614 430-9113
Piqua *(G-16143)*
Fastems LLC .....E 513 779-4614
West Chester *(G-19072)*
Flairsoft Ltd .....E 614 888-0700
Columbus *(G-7673)*
Formsoft Group Ltd .....E 937 885-5015
Dayton *(G-9556)*
Gannett Media Tech Intl .....E 513 665-3777
Cincinnati *(G-3661)*
Health Care Dataworks Inc .....D 614 255-5400
Columbus *(G-7809)*
Henry Call Inc .....C 216 433-5609
Cleveland *(G-5749)*
Hyland LLC .....B 440 788-5045
Westlake *(G-19495)*
Ils Technology LLC .....E 800 695-8650
Cleveland *(G-5805)*
Incubit LLC .....D 740 362-1401
Delaware *(G-10108)*
Inet Interactive LLC .....E 513 322-5600
West Chester *(G-19093)*
Infovision 21 Inc .....E 614 761-8844
Dublin *(G-10376)*
Integrated Telehealth Inc .....E 216 373-2221
Hudson *(G-12124)*
Intelligrated Systems Inc .....A 866 936-7300
Mason *(G-13720)*
Intelligrated Systems LLC .....A 513 701-7300
Mason *(G-13721)*
International Technegroup Inc .....D 513 576-3900
Milford *(G-14527)*
Iq Innovations LLC .....E 614 222-0882
Columbus *(G-7921)*
Irth Solutions Inc .....E 614 459-2328
Columbus *(G-7923)*
Isqft Inc .....C 513 645-8004
Cincinnati *(G-3845)*
Keithley Instruments LLC .....C 440 248-0400
Solon *(G-17021)*
Kiwiplan Inc .....E 513 554-1500
Cincinnati *(G-3931)*
Knowledge MGT Interactive Inc .....E 614 224-0664
Columbus *(G-8005)*
Leader Technologies Inc .....E 614 890-1986
Lewis Center *(G-12692)*
Liberty Comm Sftwr Sltions Inc .....E 614 318-5000
Columbus *(G-8056)*
Lisnr Inc .....E 513 322-8400
Cincinnati *(G-3990)*
London Computer Systems Inc .....D 513 583-0840
Loveland *(G-13140)*
Main Sequence Technology Inc .....E 440 946-5214
Mentor On The Lake *(G-14261)*
Marshall Information Svcs LLC .....E 614 430-0355
Columbus *(G-8120)*
Matrix Pointe Software LLC .....E 216 333-1263
Westlake *(G-19512)*
Mede America of Ohio LLC .....A 330 425-3241
Twinsburg *(G-18446)*
Metacarta Incorporated .....E 937 458-0345
Springfield *(G-17244)*
Mirifex Systems LLC .....C 440 891-1210
Sharon Center *(G-16876)*
Morphick Inc .....E 844 506-6774
Blue Ash *(G-1646)*
Mri Software LLC .....C 800 327-8770
Solon *(G-17030)*
MSI International LLC .....E 330 869-6459
Cleveland *(G-6087)*
Netrada North America LLC .....E 866 345-5835
West Chester *(G-19218)*
New Innovations Inc .....E 330 899-9954
Uniontown *(G-18530)*
Noble Technologies Corp .....E 330 287-1530
Wooster *(G-19895)*
Northwods Cnslting Prtners Inc .....C 614 781-7800
Dublin *(G-10410)*
Nsb Retail Systems Inc .....D 614 840-1421
Lewis Center *(G-12698)*
Ntt Data Inc .....D 513 794-1400
Cincinnati *(G-4188)*
Parker-Hannifin Corporation .....D 513 831-2340
Milford *(G-14550)*
Patterson Pope Inc .....D 513 891-4430
Cincinnati *(G-4263)*
Paychex Inc .....D 800 939-2462
Lima *(G-12855)*
Persistent Systems Inc .....E 727 786-0379
Marion *(G-13572)*
Plumbline Solutions Inc .....E 419 581-2963
Findlay *(G-11076)*
Positive Bus Solutions Inc .....D 513 772-2255
Cincinnati *(G-4317)*
Primax Marketing Group .....E 513 443-2797
Cincinnati *(G-4329)*
Productivity Qulty Systems Inc .....E 937 885-2255
Dayton *(G-9833)*
Quest Software Inc .....D 614 336-9223
Dublin *(G-10434)*
Qvidian Corporation .....E 513 631-1155
Blue Ash *(G-1669)*
Retalix Usa Inc .....C 937 384-2277
Miamisburg *(G-14343)*
Rippe & Kingston Systems Inc .....D 513 241-1375
Cincinnati *(G-4421)*
Sadler-Necamp Financial Svcs .....E 513 489-5477
Cincinnati *(G-4466)*
Sanctuary Software Studio Inc .....E 330 666-9690
Fairlawn *(G-10972)*
Sap America Inc .....E 513 762-7630
Cincinnati *(G-4478)*
Shoptech Industrial Sftwr .....D 513 985-9900
Cincinnati *(G-4517)*
Siemens Product Life Mgmt Sftw .....D 513 576-2400
Milford *(G-14562)*
Srinsoft Inc .....E 614 893-6535
Dublin *(G-10459)*
Strategic Insurance Sftwr Inc .....E 614 915-9769
Columbus *(G-8794)*
Sumtotal Systems LLC .....C 352 264-2800
Columbus *(G-8802)*
Sunstorm Games LLC .....E 216 403-4820
Beachwood *(G-1128)*
Systems Evolution Inc .....D 513 459-1992
Cincinnati *(G-4611)*
Thinkware Incorporated .....E 513 598-3300
Cincinnati *(G-4650)*
Timeware Inc .....E 330 963-2700
Twinsburg *(G-18476)*
TOA Technologies Inc .....D 216 360-8106
Beachwood *(G-1131)*
Triad Governmental Systems .....E 937 376-5446
Xenia *(G-20080)*
Virtual Hold Technology LLC .....D 330 660-1181
Akron *(G-498)*
Widepint Intgrted Sltions Corp .....E 614 410-1587
Columbus *(G-8992)*

COMPUTER SOFTWARE DEVELOPMENT & APPLICATIONS

Acadia Solutions Inc .....E 614 505-6135
Dublin *(G-10233)*
Advantage Technology Group .....E 513 563-3560
West Chester *(G-19013)*
Aktion Associates Incorporated .....E 419 893-7001
Maumee *(G-13873)*
Assured Information SEC Inc .....D 937 427-9720
Beavercreek *(G-1148)*
Batch Labs Inc .....D 216 901-9366
Cleveland *(G-5100)*
Camgen Ltd .....D 330 204-8636
Cleveland *(G-5174)*
Cott Systems Inc .....D 614 847-4405
Columbus *(G-7449)*
Crosschx Inc .....D 800 501-3161
Columbus *(G-7465)*
Deemsys Inc .....D 614 322-9928
Gahanna *(G-11239)*
Foresight Corporation .....E 614 791-1600
Dublin *(G-10349)*
Frontier Technology Inc .....E 937 429-3302
Beavercreek Township *(G-1269)*
Fund Evaluation Group LLC .....E 513 977-4400
Cincinnati *(G-3658)*
Gatesair Inc .....E 513 459-3400
Mason *(G-13704)*
Imflux Inc .....E 513 488-1017
Hamilton *(G-11743)*
Inreality LLC .....E 513 218-9603
Cincinnati *(G-3820)*
Jjr Solutions LLC .....E 937 912-0288
Beavercreek *(G-1180)*
Keystone Technology Cons .....E 330 666-6200
Akron *(G-306)*
Kmi Inc .....E 614 326-6304
Columbus *(G-8000)*
Lakeland Foundation .....E 440 525-7094
Willoughby *(G-19683)*
Marxent Labs LLC .....D 937 999-5005
Kettering *(G-12433)*
Maximation LLC .....D 614 526-2260
Columbus *(G-8131)*
Mitosis LLC .....E 937 557-3440
Dayton *(G-9752)*
Raco Wireless LLC .....D 513 870-6480
Blue Ash *(G-1673)*
Saec/Kinetic Vision Inc .....C 513 793-4959
Cincinnati *(G-4467)*
Service Pronet Inc .....E 614 874-4300
Columbus *(G-8716)*
Solutions Through Innovative T .....D 937 320-9994
Beavercreek *(G-1209)*

COMPUTER SOFTWARE SYSTEMS ANALYSIS & DESIGN: Custom

22nd Century Technologies Inc .....D 866 537-9191
Beavercreek *(G-1142)*
Big Red Rooster .....D 614 255-0200
Columbus *(G-7108)*
Cdo Technologies Inc .....D 937 258-0022
Dayton *(G-9260)*
Certified SEC Solutions Inc .....E 216 785-2986
Independence *(G-12196)*
Checkfree Services Corporation .....A 614 564-3000
Dublin *(G-10288)*
Click4care Inc .....D 614 431-3700
Powell *(G-16328)*
Commsys Inc .....E 937 220-4990
Moraine *(G-14761)*
Diversified Systems Inc .....E 614 476-9939
Westerville *(G-19394)*
Edaptive Computing Inc .....D 937 433-0477
Dayton *(G-9520)*
Fascor Inc .....E 513 421-1777
Cincinnati *(G-3593)*
Genomoncology LLC .....E 216 496-4216
Cleveland *(G-5669)*
Gensuite LLC .....D 513 774-1000
Mason *(G-13708)*
Itcube LLC .....D 513 891-7300
Blue Ash *(G-1618)*
Lap Technology LLC .....E 937 415-5794
Dayton *(G-9673)*
Logic Soft Inc .....D 614 884-5544
Dublin *(G-10391)*
Manifest Solutions Corp .....D 614 930-2800
Upper Arlington *(G-18555)*
Odyssey Consulting Services .....C 614 523-4248
Columbus *(G-8314)*
Oeconnection LLC .....C 888 776-5792
Richfield *(G-16519)*
Online Mega Sellers Corp .....D 888 384-6468
Toledo *(G-18109)*
Primatech Inc .....E 614 841-9800
Columbus *(G-8560)*
Systems Alternatives Intl .....E 419 891-1100
Maumee *(G-13985)*
Tridec Technologies LLC .....E 937 938-8160
Huber Heights *(G-12099)*

COMPUTER SOFTWARE SYSTEMS ANALYSIS & DESIGN: Custom

Unicon International Inc .... C 614 861-7070
  Columbus (G-8888)
Wtw Delaware Holdings LLC .... C 216 937-4000
  Cleveland (G-6762)

COMPUTER SOFTWARE WRITERS

Holo Pundits Inc .... E 614 707-5225
  Dublin (G-10364)
Pcms Datafit Inc .... D 513 587-3100
  Cincinnati (G-4269)

COMPUTER SOFTWARE WRITERS: Freelance

Boundless Flight Inc .... E 440 610-3683
  Rocky River (G-16571)

COMPUTER STORAGE DEVICES, NEC

EMC Corporation .... D 513 794-9624
  Blue Ash (G-1584)
EMC Corporation .... E 216 606-2000
  Independence (G-12206)
Teradata Corporation .... B 866 548-8348
  Miamisburg (G-14356)

COMPUTER SYSTEM SELLING SVCS

Infotelecom Holdings LLC .... B 216 373-4811
  Cleveland (G-5821)
Velocity Grtest Phone Ever Inc .... C 419 868-9983
  Holland (G-12066)

COMPUTER SYSTEMS ANALYSIS & DESIGN

Honeywell International Inc .... D 513 745-7200
  Cincinnati (G-3782)
Northrop Grumman Systems Corp .... E 937 429-6450
  Beavercreek (G-1255)
Peerless Technologies Corp .... D 937 490-5000
  Beavercreek Township (G-1279)
Teknobility LLC .... E 216 255-9433
  Medina (G-14133)

COMPUTER TERMINALS

Parker-Hannifin Corporation .... D 513 831-2340
  Milford (G-14550)

COMPUTER TRAINING SCHOOLS

Pomeroy It Solutions Sls Inc .... E 440 717-1364
  Brecksville (G-1842)

COMPUTER-AIDED DESIGN SYSTEMS SVCS

Pegasus Technical Services Inc .... E 513 793-0094
  Cincinnati (G-4274)

COMPUTER-AIDED ENGINEERING SYSTEMS SVCS

Thinkpath Engineering Svcs LLC ...... D 937 291-8374
  Miamisburg (G-14358)
Twism Enterprises LLC .... E 513 800-1098
  Cincinnati (G-4711)

COMPUTERS, NEC

Ascendtech Inc .... E 216 458-1101
  Willoughby (G-19645)
Parker-Hannifin Corporation .... D 513 831-2340
  Milford (G-14550)
Systemax Manufacturing Inc .... C 937 368-2300
  Dayton (G-9919)
Teradata Corporation .... B 866 548-8348
  Miamisburg (G-14356)
Teradata Operations Inc .... D 937 242-4030
  Miamisburg (G-14357)

COMPUTERS, NEC, WHOLESALE

Arrow Globl Asset Dspstion Inc .... D 614 328-4100
  Gahanna (G-11233)
HP Inc .... E 513 983-2817
  Cincinnati (G-3791)
Office World Inc .... E 419 991-4694
  Lima (G-12928)
Pcm Sales Inc .... E 501 342-1000
  Cleveland (G-6255)
Pcm Sales Inc .... C 513 842-3500
  Blue Ash (G-1663)
Pcm Sales Inc .... E 740 548-2222
  Lewis Center (G-12702)
Vecmar Corporation .... E 440 953-1119
  Mentor (G-14254)

COMPUTERS, PERIPHERAL & SOFTWARE, WHOLESALE: Word Processing

Blue Technologies Inc .... E 330 499-9300
  Canton (G-2266)
Gordon Flesch Company Inc .... E 419 884-2031
  Mansfield (G-13305)

COMPUTERS, PERIPHERALS & SOFTWARE, WHOLESALE: Printers

Bsl - Applied Laser Tech LLC .... E 216 663-8181
  Cleveland (G-5154)
Raco Industries LLC .... D 513 984-2101
  Blue Ash (G-1672)

COMPUTERS, PERIPHERALS & SOFTWARE, WHOLESALE: Software

Avid Technologies Inc .... E 330 487-0770
  Twinsburg (G-18395)
Canon Solutions America Inc .... D 937 260-4495
  Miamisburg (G-14278)
Commercial Time Sharing Inc .... E 330 644-3059
  Akron (G-152)
Computer Helper Publishing .... E 614 939-9094
  Columbus (G-7417)
Dolbey Systems Inc .... E 440 392-9900
  Painesville (G-15852)
Enhanced Software Inc .... E 877 805-8388
  Columbus (G-7596)
Environmental Systems Research ..... E 614 933-8698
  Columbus (G-7600)
Exact Software North Amer LLC .... C 978 539-6186
  Dublin (G-10341)
GBS Corp .... E 330 797-2700
  Youngstown (G-20197)
Indico LLC .... D 440 775-7777
  Oberlin (G-15646)
Insight Direct Usa Inc .... E 614 456-0423
  Columbus (G-7906)
Isqft Inc .... C 513 645-8004
  Cincinnati (G-3845)
Kiwiplan Inc .... E 513 554-1500
  Cincinnati (G-3931)
Manatron Sabre Systems and Svc .... D 937 431-4000
  Beavercreek (G-1253)
Mediquant Inc .... D 440 746-2300
  Brecksville (G-1833)
Mitel (delaware) Inc .... E 513 733-8000
  West Chester (G-19122)
Positive Bus Solutions Inc .... E 513 772-2255
  Cincinnati (G-4317)
Quilalea Corporation .... E 330 487-0777
  Richfield (G-16524)
Software Info Systems LLC .... E 513 791-7777
  Cincinnati (G-4550)
Software Solutions Inc .... E 513 932-6667
  Lebanon (G-12648)
Total Loop Inc .... D 888 614-5667
  Uniontown (G-18541)
Transcriptiongear Inc .... E 888 834-2392
  Painesville (G-15882)

COMPUTERS, PERIPHERALS & SOFTWARE, WHOLESALE: Terminals

Business Data Systems Inc .... E 330 633-1221
  Tallmadge (G-17633)

CONCERT MANAGEMENT SVCS

Ovations .... E 216 687-9292
  Cleveland (G-6220)

CONCRETE CURING & HARDENING COMPOUNDS

BASF Construction Chem LLC .... E 216 831-5500
  Cleveland (G-5098)
Sika Corporation .... D 740 387-9224
  Marion (G-13579)

CONCRETE PRDTS

Baxter Burial Vault Service .... E 513 641-1010
  Cincinnati (G-3082)
Hanson Aggregates East LLC .... E 740 773-2172
  Chillicothe (G-2844)
Hanson Concrete Products Ohio ...... E 614 443-4846
  Columbus (G-7800)
Hilltop Basic Resources Inc .... E 513 621-1500
  Cincinnati (G-3768)
Huron Cement Products Company ... E 419 433-4161
  Huron (G-12166)
K M B Inc .... E 330 889-3451
  Bristolville (G-1872)
Lang Stone Company Inc .... D 614 235-4099
  Columbus (G-8038)
Orrville Trucking & Grading Co .... E 330 682-4010
  Orrville (G-15780)
Pawnee Maintenance Inc .... D 740 373-6861
  Marietta (G-13483)
Snyder Concrete Products Inc .... E 937 885-5176
  Moraine (G-14825)
Tri County Concrete Inc .... E 330 425-4464
  Twinsburg (G-18477)

CONCRETE: Asphaltic, Not From Refineries

Shelly Materials Inc .... D 740 246-6315
  Thornville (G-17668)

CONCRETE: Dry Mixture

Smith Concrete Co .... E 740 373-7441
  Dover (G-10214)

CONCRETE: Ready-Mixed

Central Ready Mix LLC .... E 513 402-5001
  Cincinnati (G-3216)
D W Dickey And Son Inc .... E 330 424-1441
  Lisbon (G-12935)
G Big Inc .... E 740 867-5758
  Chesapeake (G-2784)
Hanson Aggregates East LLC .... E 740 773-2172
  Chillicothe (G-2844)
Hanson Aggregates East LLC .... E 937 364-2311
  Hillsboro (G-11976)
Hanson Aggregates East LLC .... E 937 587-2671
  Peebles (G-15939)
Hilltop Basic Resources Inc .... E 513 621-1500
  Cincinnati (G-3768)
Hull Builders Supply Inc .... E 440 967-3159
  Vermilion (G-18710)
Huron Cement Products Company ... E 419 433-4161
  Huron (G-12166)
Joe McClelland Inc .... E 740 452-3036
  Zanesville (G-20492)
K M B Inc .... E 330 889-3451
  Bristolville (G-1872)
Kuhlman Corporation .... C 419 897-6000
  Maumee (G-13934)
Mecco Inc .... E 513 422-3651
  Middletown (G-14434)
National Lime and Stone Co .... E 419 423-3400
  Findlay (G-11069)
Orrville Trucking & Grading Co .... E 330 682-4010
  Orrville (G-15780)
Phillips Companies .... E 937 426-5461
  Beavercreek Township (G-1280)
Phillips Ready Mix Co .... D 937 426-5151
  Beavercreek Township (G-1281)
Quality Block & Supply Inc .... E 330 364-4411
  Mount Eaton (G-14850)
R W Sidley Incorporated .... E 330 793-7374
  Youngstown (G-20340)
Smith Concrete Co .... E 740 373-7441
  Dover (G-10214)
Stamm Contracting Co Inc .... E 330 274-8230
  Mantua (G-13395)
Terminal Ready-Mix Inc .... E 440 288-0181
  Lorain (G-13081)
Tri County Concrete Inc .... E 330 425-4464
  Twinsburg (G-18477)
W G Lockhart Construction Co .... D 330 745-6520
  Akron (G-501)

CONDENSERS: Heat Transfer Eqpt, Evaporative

Hydro-Dyne Inc .... E 330 832-5076
  Massillon (G-13821)

CONES, PYROMETRIC: Earthenware

Orton Edward Jr Crmic Fndation .... E 614 895-2663
  Westerville (G-19339)

CONFECTIONERY PRDTS WHOLESALERS

Albert Guarnieri & Co .... D 330 794-9834
  Akron (G-63)
EBY-Brown Company LLC .... C 937 324-1036
  Springfield (G-17192)
JE Carsten Company .... E 330 794-4440
  Akron (G-291)
Lobby Shoppes Inc .... C 937 324-0002
  Springfield (G-17223)
Novelart Manufacturing Company .... C 513 351-7700
  Cincinnati (G-4187)
The Anter Brothers Company .... E 216 252-4555
  Cleveland (G-6589)
Tiffin Paper Company .... E 419 447-2121
  Tiffin (G-17706)

CONFECTIONS & CANDY

Malleys Candies Inc .... E 216 529-6262
  Cleveland (G-5974)
Nestle Usa Inc .... E 513 576-4930
  Loveland (G-13148)

CONFINEMENT SURVEILLANCE SYS MAINTENANCE & MONITORING SVCS

Macair Aviation LLC .... E 937 347-1302
  Xenia (G-20069)

CONNECTORS: Electronic

Powell Electrical Systems Inc .... D 330 966-1750
  Canton (G-2491)

CONSERVATION PROGRAMS ADMINISTRATION SVCS

City of Cleveland .... E 216 348-7210
  Cleveland (G-5256)
Natural Resources Ohio Dept .... E 419 394-3611
  Saint Marys (G-16680)
Natural Resources Ohio Dept .... D 419 938-5411
  Perrysville (G-16080)
Natural Resources Ohio Dept .... E 614 265-6948
  Columbus (G-8249)
Natural Resources Ohio Dept .... E 614 265-6852
  Columbus (G-8250)
Ohio Dept Natural Resources .... E 740 869-3124
  Mount Sterling (G-14874)

CONSTRUCTION & MINING MACHINERY WHOLESALERS

Advanced Specialty Products .... D 419 882-6528
  Bowling Green (G-1756)
Cope Farm Equipment Inc .... E 330 821-5867
  Alliance (G-536)
E T B Ltd .... E 740 373-6686
  Marietta (G-13443)
Ebony Construction Co .... E 419 841-3455
  Sylvania (G-17585)
Equipment Maintenance Inc .... E 513 353-3518
  Cleves (G-6799)
Findlay Implement Co .... E 419 424-0471
  Findlay (G-11026)
Hartville Hardware Inc .... C 330 877-4690
  Hartville (G-11820)
JD Equipment Inc .... D 740 450-7446
  Zanesville (G-20491)
Koenig Equipment Inc .... D 937 877 1920
  Tipp City (G-17721)
Kuester Implement Company Inc .... E 740 944-1502
  Bloomingdale (G-1517)
Lefeld Implement Inc .... E 419 678-2375
  Coldwater (G-6831)
Mesa Industries Inc .... D 513 321-2950
  Cincinnati (G-4081)
Ohio Machinery Co .... E 330 874-1003
  Bolivar (G-1750)
Shearer Farm Inc .... E 330 345-9023
  Wooster (G-19915)
Shearer Farm Inc .... E 419 465-4622
  Monroeville (G-14722)
Shetlers Sales & Service Inc .... E 330 760-3358
  Copley (G-9064)

Simpson Strong-Tie Company Inc .... C 614 876-8060
  Columbus (G-8737)
Stone Products Inc .... E 800 235-6088
  Canton (G-2552)

CONSTRUCTION EQPT REPAIR SVCS

Hans Truck and Trlr Repr Inc .... E 216 581-0046
  Cleveland (G-5724)
Leppo Inc .... E 330 456-2930
  Canton (G-2434)
Mine Equipment Services LLC .... E 740 936-5427
  Sunbury (G-17558)
Ohio Machinery Co .... E 330 530-9010
  Girard (G-11421)
TNT Equipment Company .... E 614 882-1549
  Columbus (G-8852)
Vermeer Sales & Service Inc .... E 330 723-8383
  Medina (G-14136)

CONSTRUCTION EQPT: Cranes

Terex Utilities Inc .... D 513 539-9770
  Monroe (G-14714)

CONSTRUCTION EQPT: Roofing Eqpt

Dimensional Metals Inc .... D 740 927-3633
  Reynoldsburg (G-16447)

CONSTRUCTION MATERIALS, WHOLESALE: Aggregate

Arrowhead Transport Co .... E 330 638-2900
  Cortland (G-9072)
Bruder Inc .... E 216 791-9800
  Maple Heights (G-13402)
Digeronimo Aggregates LLC .... E 216 524-2950
  Independence (G-12204)
Hanson Aggregates East LLC .... E 937 442-6009
  Winchester (G-19802)
Lafarge North America Inc .... D 419 798-4486
  Marblehead (G-13422)
Martin Marietta Materials Inc .... E 513 829-6446
  Fairfield (G-10875)
Martin Marietta Materials Inc .... E 614 871-6708
  Grove City (G-11579)

CONSTRUCTION MATERIALS, WHOLESALE: Air Ducts, Sheet Metal

American Warming and Vent .... D 419 288-2703
  Bradner (G-1808)

CONSTRUCTION MATERIALS, WHOLESALE: Awnings

Schneider Home Equipment Co .... E 513 522-1200
  Cincinnati (G-4483)

CONSTRUCTION MATERIALS, WHOLESALE: Block, Concrete & Cinder

Allega Recycled Mtls & Sup Co .... E 216 447-0814
  Cleveland (G-4992)
Quality Block & Supply Inc .... E 330 364-4411
  Mount Eaton (G-14850)

CONSTRUCTION MATERIALS, WHOLESALE: Brick, Exc Refractory

Snyder Concrete Products Inc .... E 937 885-5176
  Moraine (G-14825)

CONSTRUCTION MATERIALS, WHOLESALE: Building Stone

C & B Buck Bros Asp Maint LLC .... E 419 536-7325
  Toledo (G-17789)
Lang Stone Company Inc .... D 614 235-4099
  Columbus (G-8038)

CONSTRUCTION MATERIALS, WHOLESALE: Building Stone, Granite

Direct Import Home Decor Inc .... E 216 898-9758
  Cleveland (G-5485)
Indus Trade & Technology LLC .... E 614 527-0257
  Columbus (G-7892)
Jainco International Inc .... C 440 519-0100
  Solon (G-17020)

Justice & Co Inc .... E 330 225-6000
  Medina (G-14088)
Micro Construction LLC .... E 740 862-0751
  Baltimore (G-948)

CONSTRUCTION MATERIALS, WHOLESALE: Building Stone, Marble

Maza Inc .... E 614 760-0003
  Plain City (G-16198)

CONSTRUCTION MATERIALS, WHOLESALE: Building, Exterior

Bennett Supply of Ohio LLC .... E 800 292-5577
  Macedonia (G-13190)
Bluelinx Corporation .... E 330 794-1141
  Akron (G-105)
Boise Cascade Company .... E 740 382-6766
  Marion (G-13525)
Francis-Schulze Co .... E 937 295-3941
  Russia (G-16614)
Hd Supply Inc .... E 614 771-4849
  Groveport (G-11643)
Koch Aluminum Mfg Inc .... E 419 625-5956
  Sandusky (G-16774)
Lowes Home Centers LLC .... C 216 351-4723
  Cleveland (G-5953)
Lowes Home Centers LLC .... C 419 739-1300
  Wapakoneta (G-18803)
Lowes Home Centers LLC .... C 937 235-2920
  Dayton (G-9688)
Lowes Home Centers LLC .... C 740 574-6200
  Wheelersburg (G-19578)
Lowes Home Centers LLC .... C 330 665-9356
  Akron (G-328)
Lowes Home Centers LLC .... C 330 829-2700
  Alliance (G-545)
Lowes Home Centers LLC .... C 937 599-4000
  Bellefontaine (G-1388)
Lowes Home Centers LLC .... C 419 420-7531
  Findlay (G-11057)
Lowes Home Centers LLC .... C 330 832-1901
  Massillon (G-13829)
Lowes Home Centers LLC .... C 513 741-0585
  Cincinnati (G-3996)
Lowes Home Centers LLC .... C 614 433-9957
  Columbus (G-6892)
Lowes Home Centers LLC .... C 740 389-9737
  Marion (G-13549)
Lowes Home Centers LLC .... C 740 450-5500
  Zanesville (G-20497)
Lowes Home Centers LLC .... C 513 598-7050
  Cincinnati (G-3997)
Lowes Home Centers LLC .... C 614 769-9940
  Reynoldsburg (G-16466)
Lowes Home Centers LLC .... C 614 853-6200
  Columbus (G-8079)
Lowes Home Centers LLC .... C 440 937-3500
  Avon (G-906)
Lowes Home Centers LLC .... C 513 445-1000
  South Lebanon (G-17078)
Lowes Home Centers LLC .... B 216 831-2860
  Bedford (G-1318)
Lowes Home Centers LLC .... C 937 327-6000
  Springfield (G-17226)
Lowes Home Centers LLC .... C 419 331-3598
  Lima (G-12832)
Lowes Home Centers LLC .... C 740 681-3464
  Lancaster (G-12551)
Lowes Home Centers LLC .... C 614 659-0530
  Dublin (G-10392)
Lowes Home Centers LLC .... C 614 238-2601
  Columbus (G-8080)
Lowes Home Centers LLC .... C 740 522-0003
  Newark (G-15199)
Lowes Home Centers LLC .... C 740 773-7777
  Chillicothe (G-2862)
Lowes Home Centers LLC .... C 440 998-6555
  Ashtabula (G-752)
Lowes Home Centers LLC .... B 513 753-5094
  Cincinnati (G-2924)
Lowes Home Centers LLC .... C 614 497-6170
  Columbus (G-8081)
Lowes Home Centers LLC .... C 513 731-6127
  Cincinnati (G-3998)
Lowes Home Centers LLC .... C 330 287-2261
  Wooster (G-19884)
Lowes Home Centers LLC .... C 937 339-2544
  Troy (G-18362)

CONSTRUCTION MATERIALS, WHOLESALE: Building, Exterior

Lowes Home Centers LLC ....C....... 440 392-0027
  Mentor (G-14210)
Lowes Home Centers LLC ....C....... 440 942-2759
  Willoughby (G-19688)
Lowes Home Centers LLC ....C....... 740 374-2151
  Marietta (G-13462)
Lowes Home Centers LLC ....C....... 419 874-6758
  Perrysburg (G-16030)
Lowes Home Centers LLC ....C....... 330 626-2980
  Streetsboro (G-17419)
Lowes Home Centers LLC ....C....... 419 389-9464
  Toledo (G-18013)
Lowes Home Centers LLC ....C....... 419 843-9758
  Toledo (G-18014)
Lowes Home Centers LLC ....C....... 614 447-2851
  Columbus (G-8082)
Lowes Home Centers LLC ....C....... 330 245-4300
  Akron (G-329)
Lowes Home Centers LLC ....C....... 513 965-3280
  Milford (G-14532)
Lowes Home Centers LLC ....C....... 330 908-2750
  Northfield (G-15519)
Lowes Home Centers LLC ....C....... 419 470-2491
  Toledo (G-18015)
Lowes Home Centers LLC ....C....... 513 336-9741
  Mason (G-13733)
Lowes Home Centers LLC ....C....... 937 498-8400
  Sidney (G-16941)
Lowes Home Centers LLC ....C....... 740 699-3000
  Saint Clairsville (G-16642)
Lowes Home Centers LLC ....C....... 330 920-9280
  Stow (G-17381)
Lowes Home Centers LLC ....C....... 740 589-3750
  Athens (G-799)
Lowes Home Centers LLC ....C....... 740 393-5350
  Mount Vernon (G-14910)
Lowes Home Centers LLC ....C....... 937 547-2400
  Greenville (G-11513)
Lowes Home Centers LLC ....C....... 330 335-1900
  Wadsworth (G-18763)
Lowes Home Centers LLC ....C....... 937 347-4000
  Xenia (G-20068)
Lowes Home Centers LLC ....C....... 440 239-2630
  Strongsville (G-17485)
Lowes Home Centers LLC ....C....... 513 755-4300
  West Chester (G-19113)
Lowes Home Centers LLC ....C....... 513 671-2093
  Cincinnati (G-3999)
Lowes Home Centers LLC ....C....... 440 331-1027
  Rocky River (G-16585)
Lowes Home Centers LLC ....C....... 330 677-3040
  Kent (G-12384)
Lowes Home Centers LLC ....C....... 419 747-1920
  Ontario (G-15698)
Lowes Home Centers LLC ....C....... 330 339-1936
  New Philadelphia (G-15107)
Lowes Home Centers LLC ....C....... 440 985-5700
  Lorain (G-13058)
Lowes Home Centers LLC ....C....... 419 447-4101
  Tiffin (G-17682)
Lowes Home Centers LLC ....C....... 937 578-4440
  Marysville (G-13632)
Lowes Home Centers LLC ....C....... 440 324-5004
  Elyria (G-10647)
Lowes Home Centers LLC ....C....... 937 438-4900
  Dayton (G-9689)
Lowes Home Centers LLC ....C....... 937 427-1110
  Beavercreek (G-1189)
Lowes Home Centers LLC ....C....... 937 848-5600
  Dayton (G-9690)
Lowes Home Centers LLC ....C....... 614 529-5900
  Hilliard (G-11923)
Lowes Home Centers LLC ....C....... 513 737-3700
  Hamilton (G-11755)
Lowes Home Centers LLC ....C....... 740 894-7120
  South Point (G-17091)
Lowes Home Centers LLC ....C....... 513 727-3900
  Middletown (G-14431)
Lowes Home Centers LLC ....C,...... 419 355-0221
  Fremont (G-11210)
Lowes Home Centers LLC ....C....... 419 624-6000
  Sandusky (G-16777)
Lowes Home Centers LLC ....C....... 419 782-9000
  Defiance (G-10045)
Lowes Home Centers LLC ....C....... 330 609-8000
  Warren (G-18876)
Lowes Home Centers LLC ....C....... 330 965-4500
  Youngstown (G-20257)
Lowes Home Centers LLC ....C....... 937 383-7000
  Wilmington (G-19769)
Lowes Home Centers LLC ....C....... 937 854-8200
  Dayton (G-9691)
Lowes Home Centers LLC ....C....... 330 497-2720
  Canton (G-2440)
Lowes Home Centers LLC ....C....... 740 266-3500
  Steubenville (G-17327)
Lowes Home Centers LLC ....C....... 614 476-7100
  Columbus (G-8083)
Marsh Building Products Inc ....E....... 937 222-3321
  Dayton (G-9700)
Northwest Building Resources ....E....... 419 286-5400
  Fort Jennings (G-11109)
Orrville Trucking & Grading Co ....E....... 330 682-4010
  Orrville (G-15780)
Palmer-Donavin Mfg Co ....D....... 614 277-2777
  Urbancrest (G-18607)
Ply-Trim South Inc ....E....... 330 799-7876
  Youngstown (G-20326)
Schneider Home Equipment Co ....E....... 513 522-1200
  Cincinnati (G-4483)
Style Crest Inc ....B....... 419 332-7369
  Fremont (G-11223)
Usavinyl LLC ....E....... 614 771-4805
  Groveport (G-11682)

CONSTRUCTION MATERIALS, WHOLESALE: Building, Interior

Meyer Decorative Surfaces USA ....E....... 800 776-3900
  Hudson (G-12133)

CONSTRUCTION MATERIALS, WHOLESALE: Ceiling Systems & Prdts

D & S Crtive Cmmunications Inc ....E....... 419 524-4312
  Mansfield (G-13289)
Eger Products Inc ....D....... 513 753-4200
  Amelia (G-580)

CONSTRUCTION MATERIALS, WHOLESALE: Cement

Boral Resources LLC ....D....... 740 622-8042
  Coshocton (G-9088)
Huron Cement Products Company .....E....... 419 433-4161
  Huron (G-12166)

CONSTRUCTION MATERIALS, WHOLESALE: Ceramic, Exc Refractory

Mees Distributors Inc ....E....... 513 541-2311
  Cincinnati (G-4051)

CONSTRUCTION MATERIALS, WHOLESALE: Door Frames

Huttig Building Products Inc ....E....... 614 492-8248
  Obetz (G-15667)
Mae Holding Company ....E....... 513 751-2424
  Cincinnati (G-4011)
Provia Holdings Inc ....C....... 330 852-4711
  Sugarcreek (G-17546)

CONSTRUCTION MATERIALS, WHOLESALE: Doors, Garage

Dayton Door Sales Inc ....E....... 937 253-9181
  Dayton (G-9472)
Dayton Door Sales Inc ....E....... 937 253-9181
  Dayton (G-9471)
Graf and Sons Inc ....E....... 614 481-2020
  Columbus (G-7765)
North Shore Door Co Inc ....E....... 800 783-6112
  Elyria (G-10662)

CONSTRUCTION MATERIALS, WHOLESALE: Drywall Materials

Gms Inc ....E....... 937 222-4444
  Dayton (G-9575)
Hwz Distribution Group LLC ....E....... 513 618-0300
  West Chester (G-19209)
Hwz Distribution Group LLC ....E....... 513 723-1150
  Cincinnati (G-3800)
J & B Equipment & Supply Inc ....D....... 419 884-1155
  Mansfield (G-13314)
L & W Supply Corporation ....E....... 614 276-6391
  Columbus (G-8019)
Meander Tire Company Inc ....E....... 330 750-6155
  Youngstown (G-20278)

Robinson Insulation Co Inc ....E....... 937 323-9599
  Springfield (G-17264)

CONSTRUCTION MATERIALS, WHOLESALE: Eavestroughing, Part/Sply

Apco Industries Inc ....D....... 614 224-2345
  Columbus (G-7027)

CONSTRUCTION MATERIALS, WHOLESALE: Glass

Cleveland Glass Block Inc ....E....... 216 531-6363
  Cleveland (G-5316)
Cleveland Glass Block Inc ....E....... 614 252-5888
  Columbus (G-7299)
Glenny Glass Company ....E....... 513 489-2233
  Milford (G-14522)
Harmon Inc ....E....... 513 645-1550
  West Chester (G-19089)
Medina Glass Block Inc ....E....... 330 239-0239
  Medina (G-14100)
Olde Towne Windows Inc ....E....... 419 626-9613
  Milan (G-14496)

CONSTRUCTION MATERIALS, WHOLESALE: Gravel

Westfall Aggregate & Mtls Inc ....D....... 740 420-9090
  Circleville (G-4907)

CONSTRUCTION MATERIALS, WHOLESALE: Hardboard

Kansas City Hardwood Corp ....E....... 913 621-1975
  Lakewood (G-12484)

CONSTRUCTION MATERIALS, WHOLESALE: Joists

Marysville Steel Inc ....E....... 937 642-5971
  Marysville (G-13636)

CONSTRUCTION MATERIALS, WHOLESALE: Lime, Exc Agricultural

Mid-Ohio Valley Lime Inc ....E....... 740 373-1006
  Marietta (G-13477)

CONSTRUCTION MATERIALS, WHOLESALE: Limestone

Hull Builders Supply Inc ....E....... 440 967-3159
  Vermilion (G-18710)
Pinney Dock & Transport LLC ....E....... 440 964-7186
  Ashtabula (G-760)

CONSTRUCTION MATERIALS, WHOLESALE: Masons' Materials

Koltcz Concrete Block Co ....E....... 440 232-3630
  Bedford (G-1315)

CONSTRUCTION MATERIALS, WHOLESALE: Metal Buildings

Six C Fabrication Inc ....D....... 330 296-5594
  Ravenna (G-16412)

CONSTRUCTION MATERIALS, WHOLESALE: Millwork

Clem Lumber and Distrg Co ....D....... 330 821-2130
  Alliance (G-534)

CONSTRUCTION MATERIALS, WHOLESALE: Molding, All Materials

Toledo Molding & Die Inc ....D....... 419 354-6050
  Bowling Green (G-1795)
Toledo Molding & Die Inc ....D....... 419 692-6022
  Delphos (G-10152)

CONSTRUCTION MATERIALS, WHOLESALE: Pallets, Wood

Millwood Inc ....C....... 440 914-0540
  Solon (G-17028)
Pallet Distributors Inc ....C....... 888 805-9670
  Lakewood (G-12494)

SERVICES SECTION

CONSTRUCTION MATERIALS, WHOLESALE: Particleboard

Litco International Inc .... E 330 539-5433
 Vienna (G-18739)

CONSTRUCTION MATERIALS, WHOLESALE: Prefabricated Structures

Morton Buildings Inc .... D 419 675-2311
 Kenton (G-12422)
Palmer-Donavin Mfg Co .... E 419 692-5000
 Delphos (G-10148)
Will-Burt Company .... B 330 682-7015
 Orrville (G-15789)
Will-Burt Company .... E 330 682-7015
 Orrville (G-15790)

CONSTRUCTION MATERIALS, WHOLESALE: Roof, Asphalt/Sheet Metal

Beacon Sales Acquisition Inc .... C 330 425-3359
 Twinsburg (G-18397)

CONSTRUCTION MATERIALS, WHOLESALE: Roofing & Siding Material

Allied Building Products Corp .... E 216 362-1764
 Cleveland (G-4993)
Allied Building Products Corp .... E 513 784-9090
 Cincinnati (G-2989)
Allied Building Products Corp .... E 614 488-0717
 Columbus (G-6969)
Associated Materials LLC .... E 614 985-4611
 Columbus (G-7055)
Associated Materials LLC .... B 330 929-1811
 Cuyahoga Falls (G-9161)
Associated Materials Group Inc .... E 330 929-1811
 Cuyahoga Falls (G-9162)
Associated Mtls Holdings LLC .... A 330 929-1811
 Cuyahoga Falls (G-9163)
Modern Builders Supply Inc .... E 937 222-2627
 Dayton (G-9753)
Palmer-Donavin Mfg Co .... C 614 486-0975
 Columbus (G-8511)
Willoughby Supply Company .... E 440 942-7939
 Mentor (G-14258)

CONSTRUCTION MATERIALS, WHOLESALE: Sand

Acme Company .... D 330 758-2313
 Poland (G-16219)
Columbus Coal & Lime Co .... E 614 224-9241
 Columbus (G-7340)
Kenmore Construction Co Inc .... C 330 762-8936
 Akron (G-303)
Sylvester Materials Co .... C 419 841-3874
 Sylvania (G-17621)

CONSTRUCTION MATERIALS, WHOLESALE: Septic Tanks

Valicor Environmental Svcs LLC .... D 513 733-4666
 Monroe (G-14717)

CONSTRUCTION MATERIALS, WHOLESALE: Sewer Pipe, Clay

Sewer Rodding Equipment Co .... E 419 991-2065
 Lima (G-12876)

CONSTRUCTION MATERIALS, WHOLESALE: Siding, Exc Wood

Apco Industries Inc .... D 614 224-2345
 Columbus (G-7027)
Norandex Bldg Mtls Dist Inc .... A 330 656-8924
 Hudson (G-12136)
Vinyl Design Corporation .... E 419 283-4009
 Holland (G-12067)

CONSTRUCTION MATERIALS, WHOLESALE: Stone, Crushed Or Broken

Proterra Inc .... E 216 383-8449
 Wickliffe (G-19612)

CONSTRUCTION MATERIALS, WHOLESALE: Trim, Sheet Metal

Dublin Millwork Co Inc .... E 614 889-7776
 Dublin (G-10331)

CONSTRUCTION MATERIALS, WHOLESALE: Veneer

Milestone Ventures LLC .... E 317 908-2093
 Newark (G-15208)
T J Ellis Enterprises Inc .... E 419 999-5026
 Lima (G-12898)

CONSTRUCTION MATERIALS, WHOLESALE: Windows

Allied Building Products Corp .... E 513 784-9090
 Cincinnati (G-2989)
Associated Materials LLC .... B 330 929-1811
 Cuyahoga Falls (G-9161)
Associated Materials Group Inc .... E 330 929-1811
 Cuyahoga Falls (G-9162)
Associated Mtls Holdings LLC .... A 330 929-1811
 Cuyahoga Falls (G-9163)
Gunton Corporation .... C 216 831-2420
 Cleveland (G-5710)
Olde Towne Windows Inc .... E 419 626-9613
 Milan (G-14496)
Pella Corporation .... D 513 948-8480
 Cincinnati (G-4275)
Window Factory of America .... D 440 439-3050
 Bedford (G-1344)

CONSTRUCTION MATLS, WHOL: Lumber, Rough, Dressed/Finished

Acord Rk Lumber Company .... E 740 289-3761
 Piketon (G-16108)
Appalachia Wood Inc .... E 740 596-2551
 Mc Arthur (G-14015)
Appalachian Hardwood Lumber Co .... E 440 232-6767
 Cleveland (G-5049)
Baillie Lumber Co LP .... E 419 462-2000
 Galion (G-11292)
Brenneman Lumber Co .... E 740 397-0573
 Mount Vernon (G-14879)
Carter-Jones Companies Inc .... E 330 673-6100
 Kent (G-12354)
Carter-Jones Lumber Company .... C 330 673-6100
 Kent (G-12355)
Carter-Jones Lumber Company .... A 330 673-6000
 Kent (G-12356)
Eagle Hardwoods Inc .... E 330 339-8838
 Newcomerstown (G-15267)
Gross Lumber Inc .... D 330 683-2055
 Apple Creek (G-625)
Hartzell Hardwoods Inc .... D 937 773-7054
 Piqua (G-16146)
J McCoy Lumber Co Ltd .... E 937 587-3423
 Peebles (G-15940)
Keim Lumber Company .... E 330 893-2251
 Baltic (G-946)
Khempco Bldg Sup Co Ltd Partnr .... E 740 549-0465
 Delaware (G-10113)
Lumberjacks Inc .... E 330 762-2401
 Akron (G-330)
Mentor Lumber and Supply Co .... E 440 255-8814
 Mentor (G-14214)
Muth Lumber Company Inc .... E 740 533-0800
 Ironton (G-12300)
Nilco LLC .... E 888 248-5151
 Hartville (G-11827)
Nilco LLC .... E 330 538-3386
 North Jackson (G-15384)
Paxton Hardwoods LLC .... E 513 984-8200
 Cincinnati (G-4266)
Premier Construction Company .... E 513 874-2611
 Fairfield (G-10896)
Price Woods Products Inc .... E 513 722-1200
 Loveland (G-13153)
Stephen M Trudick .... E 440 834-1891
 Burton (G-2065)
Tri-State Forest Products Inc .... E 937 323-6325
 Springfield (G-17289)
Wappoo Wood Products Inc .... E 937 492-1166
 Sidney (G-16960)

CONSTRUCTION MATLS, WHOLESALE: Soil Erosion Cntrl Fabrics

Efficient Services Ohio Inc .... E 330 627-4440
 Carrollton (G-2619)

CONSTRUCTION MTRLS, WHOL: Exterior Flat Glass, Plate/Window

Anderson Glass Co Inc .... E 614 476-4877
 Columbus (G-7018)
Century Glass Co .... E 216 361-7700
 Cleveland (G-5218)

CONSTRUCTION SAND MINING

J P Sand & Gravel Company .... E 614 497-0083
 Lockbourne (G-12958)
Lakeside Sand & Gravel Inc .... E 330 274-2569
 Mantua (G-13390)
Mecco Inc .... E 513 422-3651
 Middletown (G-14434)
Morrow Gravel Company Inc .... C 513 771-0820
 Cincinnati (G-4120)
National Lime and Stone Co .... E 614 497-0083
 Lockbourne (G-12959)

CONSTRUCTION SITE PREPARATION SVCS

Great Lakes Crushing Ltd .... E 440 944-5500
 Wickliffe (G-19599)
Landscping Rclmtion Spcialists .... E 330 339-4900
 New Philadelphia (G-15106)
Miller Logging Inc .... E 330 279-4721
 Holmesville (G-12074)

CONSTRUCTION: Agricultural Building

Witmers Inc .... E 330 427-2147
 Salem (G-16719)

CONSTRUCTION: Airport Runway

Crp Contracting .... D 614 338-8501
 Columbus (G-7469)
Nas Ventures .... D 614 338-8501
 Columbus (G-8213)

CONSTRUCTION: Apartment Building

Abco Contracting LLC .... E 419 973-4772
 Toledo (G-17739)
Bernard Busson Builder .... E 330 929-4926
 Akron (G-99)
Cooper Woda Companies Inc .... D 614 396-3200
 Columbus (G-7436)
Donald R Kenney & Company .... E 614 540-2404
 Westerville (G-19300)
Etech-Systems LLC .... E 216 221-6600
 Lakewood (G-12477)
Forest City Residential Dev .... E 216 621-6060
 Cleveland (G-5621)
G J Goudreau & Co .... E 216 351-5233
 Cleveland (G-5646)
Homewood Corporation .... C 614 898-7200
 Columbus (G-7857)
K-Y Residential Coml Indus Dev .... D 330 448-4055
 Brookfield (G-1897)
Lemmon & Lemmon Inc .... C 330 497-8686
 North Canton (G-15351)
National Housing Corporation .... E 614 481-8106
 Columbus (G-8220)
Schroeder Company .... E 419 473-3139
 Toledo (G-18175)
Showe Builders Inc .... E 614 481-8106
 Columbus (G-8729)
Snavely Building Company .... E 440 585-9091
 Chagrin Falls (G-2705)
Towne Building Group Inc .... D 513 381-8696
 Cincinnati (G-4666)
Woda Construction Inc .... E 614 396-3200
 Columbus (G-9002)

CONSTRUCTION: Athletic Field

Scg Fields LLC .... E 440 546-1200
 Brecksville (G-1849)
Sports Surfaces Cnstr LLC .... E 440 546-1200
 Brecksville (G-1852)

CONSTRUCTION: Bridge

Company	Code	Phone
A P OHoro Company	D	330 759-9317
Youngstown (G-20095)		
Aecom Energy & Cnstr Inc	B	216 622-2300
Cleveland (G-4962)		
Akil Incorporated	E	419 625-0857
Sandusky (G-16724)		
Armstrong Steel Erectors Inc	E	740 345-4503
Newark (G-15144)		
Becdir Construction Company	E	330 547-2134
Berlin Center (G-1480)		
Brumbaugh Construction Inc	E	937 692-5107
Arcanum (G-629)		
Colas Solutions Inc	E	513 272-5348
Cincinnati (G-3380)		
Complete General Cnstr Co	C	614 258-9515
Columbus (G-7414)		
E S Wagner Company	D	419 691-8651
Oregon (G-15733)		
Eagle Bridge Co	E	937 492-5654
Sidney (G-16930)		
J & J Schlaegel Inc	E	937 652-2045
Urbana (G-18592)		
Kokosing Construction Co Inc	C	614 228-1029
Columbus (G-8007)		
MBC Holdings Inc	A	419 445-1015
Archbold (G-638)		
National Engrg & Contg Co	A	440 238-3331
Cleveland (G-6107)		
Ohio Bridge Corporation	C	740 432-6334
Cambridge (G-2125)		
Prus Construction Company	C	513 321-7774
Cincinnati (G-4354)		
Righter Co Inc	E	614 272-9700
Columbus (G-8629)		
Righter Construction Svcs Inc	E	614 272-9700
Columbus (G-8630)		
Ruhlin Company	C	330 239-2800
Sharon Center (G-16877)		
Sunesis Construction Company	C	513 326-6000
West Chester (G-19161)		
Velotta Company	E	330 239-1211
Sharon Center (G-16880)		
Westpatrick Corp	E	614 875-8200
Columbus (G-8981)		

CONSTRUCTION: Commercial & Institutional Building

Company	Code	Phone
A2 Services LLC	D	440 466-6611
Geneva (G-11358)		
Adena Corporation	C	419 529-4456
Ontario (G-15682)		
Aecom Energy & Cnstr Inc	C	419 698-6277
Oregon (G-15723)		
Boak & Sons Inc	C	330 793-5646
Youngstown (G-20118)		
Cocca Development Ltd	D	330 729-1010
Youngstown (G-20145)		
Colaianni Construction Inc	E	740 769-2362
Dillonvale (G-10173)		
Columbus City Trnsp Div	C	614 645-3182
Columbus (G-7338)		
Combs Interior Specialties Inc	D	937 879-2047
Fairborn (G-10787)		
Corna Kokosing Construction Co	C	614 901-8844
Westerville (G-19392)		
Dynamic Structures Inc	E	330 892-0164
New Waterford (G-15137)		
Fairfield Homes Inc	C	614 873-3533
Plain City (G-16192)		
Fc 1346 LLC	E	330 864-8170
Akron (G-221)		
Ferguson Construction Company	D	937 274-1173
Dayton (G-9545)		
Foti Contracting LLC	C	330 656-3454
Wickliffe (G-19598)		
G III Reitter Walls LLC	E	614 545-4444
Columbus (G-7718)		
G Stephens Inc	E	419 241-5188
Toledo (G-17904)		
Gilbane Building Company	E	614 948-4000
Columbus (G-7750)		
Greystone Group-Avery Ltd	E	216 464-3580
Cleveland (G-5705)		
Kajima International Inc	E	440 544-2600
Cleveland (G-5880)		
Kbj-Summit LLC	D	440 232-3334
Bedford (G-1314)		
L Jack Ruscilli	E	614 876-9484
Columbus (G-8023)		
Luke Theis Enterprises Inc	D	419 422-2040
Findlay (G-11059)		
M & W Construction Entps LLC	E	419 227-2000
Lima (G-12835)		
Ml - De - Con Inc	D	740 532-2277
Ironton (G-12299)		
Miller-Valentine Construction	D	937 293-0900
Dayton (G-9749)		
Mpower Inc	E	614 783-0478
Gahanna (G-11258)		
Nitschke Sampson Dietz Inc	E	614 464-1933
Columbus (G-8281)		
Nordmann Roofing Co Inc	E	419 691-5737
Toledo (G-18089)		
Nyman Construction Inc	E	216 475-7800
Cleveland (G-6173)		
Oberer Development Co	E	937 910-0851
Miamisburg (G-14328)		
Ozanne Construction Co Inc	E	216 696-2876
Cleveland (G-6224)		
Righter Co Inc	E	614 272-9700
Columbus (G-8629)		
Righter Construction Svcs Inc	E	614 272-9700
Columbus (G-8630)		
Rudolph Libbe Inc	B	419 241-5000
Walbridge (G-18777)		
Shelly and Sands Inc	E	740 859-2104
Rayland (G-16418)		
Shelly and Sands Inc	E	614 444-5100
Columbus (G-8725)		
Skanska USA Building Inc	E	513 421-0082
Cincinnati (G-4538)		
Tab Construction Company Inc	E	330 454-5228
Canton (G-2557)		
Tri State Corporation	E	513 763-0215
Cincinnati (G-4683)		
Universal Development MGT Inc	E	330 759-7017
Girard (G-11428)		
VIP Restoration Inc	D	216 426-9500
Cuyahoga Falls (G-9232)		
Whiting-Turner Contracting Co	E	614 459-6515
Worthington (G-20009)		
Whiting-Turner Contracting Co	D	440 449-9200
Cleveland (G-6750)		

CONSTRUCTION: Commercial & Office Building, New

Company	Code	Phone
A & A Wall Systems Inc	E	513 489-0086
Cincinnati (G-2950)		
A P & P Dev & Cnstr Co	D	330 833-8886
Massillon (G-13782)		
AA Boos & Sons Inc	D	419 691-2329
Oregon (G-15721)		
Adolph Johnson & Son Co	E	330 544-8900
Mineral Ridge (G-14635)		
Albert M Higley Company	C	216 404-5783
Cleveland (G-4982)		
Ams Inc	E	513 244-8500
Cincinnati (G-3020)		
Amsdell Construction Inc	C	216 458-0670
Cleveland (G-5031)		
Austin Building and Design Inc	C	440 544-2600
Cleveland (G-5081)		
B & B Contrs & Developers Inc	D	330 270-5020
Youngstown (G-20109)		
Becker Construction Inc	E	937 859-8308
Dayton (G-9352)		
Bogner Construction Company	D	330 262-6730
Wooster (G-19833)		
Brocon Construction Inc	E	614 871-7300
Grove City (G-11538)		
Brumbaugh Construction Inc	E	937 692-5107
Arcanum (G-629)		
Bruns Building & Dev Corp Inc	D	419 925-4095
Saint Henry (G-16665)		
C Tucker Cope & Assoc Inc	E	330 482-4472
Columbiana (G-6854)		
Calvary Contracting Inc	E	937 754-0300
Tipp City (G-17711)		
Camargo Construction Company	E	513 248-1500
Cincinnati (G-3168)		
Cedarwood Construction Company	D	330 836-9971
Akron (G-125)		
Chaney Roofing Maintenance	E	419 639-2761
Clyde (G-6811)		
Cincinnati Coml Contg LLC	E	513 561-6633
Cincinnati (G-3294)		
Cm-Gc LLC	E	513 527-4141
Cincinnati (G-3372)		
Conger Construction Group Inc	E	513 932-1206
Lebanon (G-12597)		
Construction One Inc	E	614 961-1140
Columbus (G-7424)		
Continental RE Companies	C	614 221-1800
Columbus (G-7431)		
Corporate Cleaning Inc	E	614 203-6051
Columbus (G-7441)		
Crapsey & Gillis Contractors	E	513 891-6333
Loveland (G-13117)		
Crock Construction Co	E	740 732-2306
Caldwell (G-2084)		
D & G Focht Construction Co	E	419 732-2412
Port Clinton (G-16243)		
D E Huddleston Inc	E	740 773-2130
Chillicothe (G-2832)		
DAG Construction Co Inc	E	513 542-8597
Cincinnati (G-3459)		
Dan Marchetta Cnstr Co Inc	E	330 668-4800
Akron (G-186)		
Danis Building Construction Co	B	937 228-1225
Miamisburg (G-14291)		
Daytep Inc	E	937 456-5860
Eaton (G-10556)		
Deerfield Construction Co Inc	E	513 984-4096
Loveland (G-13122)		
Desalvo Construction Company	E	330 759-8145
Hubbard (G-12085)		
DKM Construction Inc	E	740 289-3006
Piketon (G-16113)		
Donleys Inc	C	216 524-6800
Cleveland (G-5503)		
Dorsten Industries Inc	E	419 628-2327
Minster (G-14660)		
Douglas Company	E	419 865-8600
Holland (G-12021)		
Dugan & Meyers Construction Co	E	513 891-4300
Blue Ash (G-1579)		
Dugan & Meyers Construction Co	E	614 257-7430
Columbus (G-6880)		
Dugan & Meyers Interests Inc	E	513 891-4300
Blue Ash (G-1580)		
Dunlop and Johnston Inc	E	330 220-2700
Valley City (G-18616)		
Elford Inc	C	614 488-4000
Columbus (G-7588)		
Enterprise Construction Inc	E	440 349-3443
Solon (G-17003)		
Equity Inc	E	614 802-2900
Hilliard (G-11900)		
Ernest Fritsch	E	614 436-5995
Columbus (G-7606)		
Exxcel Project Management LLC	E	614 621-4500
Columbus (G-7624)		
Feick Contractors Inc	E	419 625-3241
Sandusky (G-16756)		
Ferguson Construction Company	C	937 498-2381
Sidney (G-16933)		
Finneytown Contracting Corp	E	513 482-2700
Cincinnati (G-3612)		
Fiorilli Construction Co Inc	E	216 696-5845
Medina (G-14065)		
Fleming Construction Co	E	740 494-2177
Prospect (G-16365)		
Floyd P Bucher & Son Inc	E	419 867-8792
Toledo (G-17898)		
Ford Development Corp	D	513 772-1521
Cincinnati (G-3637)		
Fortney & Weygandt Inc	E	440 716-4000
North Olmsted (G-15422)		
Foti Construction Company LLP	E	440 347-0728
Wickliffe (G-19597)		
Fred Olivieri Construction Co	E	330 494-1007
North Canton (G-15338)		
G J Goudreau & Co	E	216 351-5233
Cleveland (G-5646)		
Gold Star Insulation L P	E	614 221-3241
Columbus (G-7757)		
Gowdy Partners LLC	E	614 488-4424
Columbus (G-7764)		
Grae-Con Construction Inc	D	740 282-6830
Steubenville (G-17321)		
Greater Dayton Cnstr Ltd	D	937 426-3577
Beavercreek (G-1243)		
Gutknecht Construction Company	E	614 532-5410
Columbus (G-7787)		
Hal Homes Inc	E	513 984-5360
Blue Ash (G-1606)		

SERVICES SECTION

CONSTRUCTION: Guardrails, Highway

Hanlin-Rainaldi Construction ....E 614 436-4204
  Columbus *(G-7799)*
Higgins Building Company Inc ....E 740 439-5553
  Cambridge *(G-2120)*
Homan Inc ....E 419 925-4349
  Maria Stein *(G-13428)*
Hughes & Knollman Construction ....D 614 237-6167
  Columbus *(G-7862)*
Ideal Company Inc ....E 937 836-8683
  Clayton *(G-4911)*
Interstate Construction Inc ....E 614 539-1188
  Grove City *(G-11572)*
Ivan Weaver Construction Co ....E 330 695-3461
  Fredericksburg *(G-11177)*
J & F Construction and Dev Inc ....E 419 562-6662
  Bucyrus *(G-2042)*
Jhi Group Inc ....C 419 465-4611
  Monroeville *(G-14721)*
JJO Construction Inc ....E 440 255-1515
  Mentor *(G-14199)*
JKL Construction Inc ....E 513 553-3333
  New Richmond *(G-15128)*
Justice & Business Svcs LLC ....E 740 423-5005
  Belpre *(G-1440)*
Kapp Construction Inc ....E 937 324-0134
  Springfield *(G-17219)*
Kenny Obayashi Joint Venture V ....C 703 969-0611
  Akron *(G-304)*
Knoch Corporation ....D 330 244-1440
  Canton *(G-2428)*
Kokosing Construction Co Inc ....C 614 228-1029
  Columbus *(G-8007)*
Krumroy-Cozad Cnstr Corp ....E 330 376-4136
  Akron *(G-309)*
L Brands Store Dsign Cnstr Inc ....C 614 415-7000
  Columbus *(G-8021)*
Lathrop Company Inc ....E 419 893-7000
  Toledo *(G-18001)*
LEWaro-D&j-A Joint Venture Co ....E 937 443-0000
  Dayton *(G-9678)*
Lm Constrction Trry Lvrini Inc ....E 740 695-9604
  Saint Clairsville *(G-16641)*
Mark-L Inc ....E 614 863-8432
  Gahanna *(G-11256)*
McDonalds Design & Build Inc ....E 419 782-4191
  Defiance *(G-10047)*
McNerney & Son Inc ....E 419 666-0200
  Toledo *(G-18046)*
MCR Services Inc ....E 614 421-0860
  Columbus *(G-8138)*
Messer Construction Co ....D 937 291-1300
  Dayton *(G-9721)*
Messer Construction Co ....D 614 275-0141
  Columbus *(G-8152)*
Mid-Continent Construction Co ....E 440 439-6100
  Oakwood Village *(G-15631)*
Midwest Roofing & Furnace Co ....E 614 252-5241
  Columbus *(G-8172)*
Miles-Mcclellan Cnstr Co Inc ....E 614 487-7744
  Columbus *(G-8173)*
Miller Contracting Group Inc ....E 419 453-3825
  Ottoville *(G-15808)*
Monarch Construction Company ....C 513 351-6900
  Cincinnati *(G-4114)*
Mowry Construction & Engrg Inc ....E 419 289-2262
  Ashland *(G-690)*
Mullett Company ....E 440 564-9000
  Newbury *(G-15259)*
Murphy Contracting Co ....E 330 743-8915
  Youngstown *(G-20292)*
National Housing Corporation ....E 614 481-8106
  Columbus *(G-8220)*
Pepper Cnstr Co Ohio LLC ....E 614 793-4477
  Dublin *(G-10425)*
Peterson Construction Company ....C 419 941-2233
  Wapakoneta *(G-18806)*
Prestige Interiors Inc ....E 330 425-1690
  Twinsburg *(G-18456)*
Property Estate Management LLC .....E 513 684-0418
  Cincinnati *(G-4348)*
QBS Inc ....E 330 821-8801
  Alliance *(G-552)*
Quantum Construction Company ....E 513 351-6903
  Cincinnati *(G-4361)*
R A Hermes Inc ....E 513 251-5200
  Cincinnati *(G-4377)*
R L Fortney Management Inc ....C 440 716-4000
  North Olmsted *(G-15441)*
Ray Fogg Building Methods Inc ....E 216 351-7976
  Cleveland *(G-6354)*

Renier Construction Corp ....E 614 866-4580
  Columbus *(G-8613)*
Retail Renovations Inc ....E 330 334-4501
  Wadsworth *(G-18770)*
Romanelli & Hughes Building Co ....E 614 891-2042
  Westerville *(G-19441)*
Ruhlin Company ....C 330 239-2800
  Sharon Center *(G-16877)*
Ruscilli Construction Co Inc ....D 614 876-9484
  Columbus *(G-8658)*
Schirmer Construction Co ....E 440 716-4900
  North Olmsted *(G-15443)*
Schnippel Construction Inc ....E 937 693-3831
  Botkins *(G-1753)*
Scs Construction Services Inc ....E 513 929-0260
  Cincinnati *(G-4487)*
Season Contractors Inc ....E 440 717-0188
  Broadview Heights *(G-1891)*
Simonson Construction Svcs Inc ....D 419 281-8299
  Ashland *(G-699)*
Site Worx LLC ....D 513 229-0295
  Lebanon *(G-12647)*
Smith Construction Group Inc ....E 937 426-0500
  Beavercreek Township *(G-1284)*
Spieker Company ....E 419 872-7000
  Perrysburg *(G-16062)*
Stanley Miller Construction Co ....E 330 484-2229
  East Sparta *(G-10541)*
Studer-Obringer Inc ....E 419 492-2121
  New Washington *(G-15136)*
Sunrush Construction Co Inc ....E 740 775-1300
  Chillicothe *(G-2889)*
T O J Inc ....E 440 352-1900
  Mentor *(G-14247)*
Tri-Con Incorporated ....E 513 530-9844
  Blue Ash *(G-1701)*
Trubuilt Construction Svcs LLC ....E 614 279-4800
  Columbus *(G-8875)*
Turner Construction Company ....E 216 522-1180
  Cleveland *(G-6623)*
Turner Construction Company ....D 513 363-0883
  Cincinnati *(G-4706)*
Turner Construction Company ....D 614 984-3000
  Columbus *(G-8879)*
Turner Construction Company ....C 513 721-4224
  Cincinnati *(G-4705)*
Tusing Builders Ltd ....E 419 465-3100
  Monroeville *(G-14723)*
Twok General Co ....E 740 417-9195
  Delaware *(G-10131)*
Union Industrial Contractors ....E 440 998-7871
  Ashtabula *(G-765)*
Universal Contracting Corp ....E 513 482-2700
  Cincinnati *(G-4747)*
Van Con Inc ....E 937 890-8400
  Dayton *(G-9962)*
Van Tassel Construction Corp ....E 419 873-0188
  Perrysburg *(G-16068)*
Vig Property Development LLC ....E 888 384-5970
  Cincinnati *(G-4814)*
Weaver Custom Homes Inc ....E 330 264-5444
  Wooster *(G-19927)*
Welty Building Company Ltd ....D 330 867-2400
  Fairlawn *(G-10981)*
West Roofing Systems Inc ....E 800 356-5748
  Lagrange *(G-12462)*
Woodward Construction Inc ....E 513 247-9241
  Blue Ash *(G-1721)*

CONSTRUCTION: Commercial & Office Buildings, Prefabricated

Wenco Inc ....C 937 849-6002
  New Carlisle *(G-15033)*

CONSTRUCTION: Concrete Patio

Architctural Con Solutions Inc ....E 614 940-5399
  Columbus *(G-7038)*

CONSTRUCTION: Condominium

Bob Schmitt Homes Inc ....D 440 327-9495
  North Ridgeville *(G-15455)*
Dixon Builders & Developers ....D 513 887-6400
  West Chester *(G-19066)*
Dugan & Meyers Construction Co ......C 513 891-4300
  Blue Ash *(G-1579)*
Dugan & Meyers Interests Inc ....C 513 891-4300
  Blue Ash *(G-1580)*
Hills Communities Inc ....C 513 984-0300
  Blue Ash *(G-1611)*

Superior Kraft Homes LLC ....D 740 947-7710
  New Boston *(G-15015)*
T O J Inc ....E 440 352-1900
  Mentor *(G-14247)*

CONSTRUCTION: Curb

Charles H Hamilton Co ....D 513 683-2442
  Maineville *(G-13241)*

CONSTRUCTION: Dams, Waterways, Docks & Other Marine

Aecom Energy & Cnstr Inc ....B 216 622-2300
  Cleveland *(G-4962)*
Jacobs Constructors Inc ....D 419 226-1344
  Lima *(G-12806)*
Kokosing Industrial Inc ....B 614 212-5700
  Westerville *(G-19418)*
Sunesis Environmental LLC ....D 513 326-6000
  Fairfield *(G-10912)*

CONSTRUCTION: Drainage System

Ohio Irrigation Lawn Sprinkler ....E 937 432-9911
  Dayton *(G-9786)*

CONSTRUCTION: Electric Power Line

Main Lite Electric Co Inc ....E 330 369-8333
  Warren *(G-18877)*

CONSTRUCTION: Elevated Highway

Fryman-Kuck General Contrs Inc ....E 937 274-2892
  Dayton *(G-9564)*

CONSTRUCTION: Fire Station

Valley View Fire Dept ....E 216 524-7200
  Cleveland *(G-6685)*

CONSTRUCTION: Food Prdts Manufacturing or Packing Plant

Resers Fine Foods Inc ....E 216 231-7112
  Cleveland *(G-6382)*

CONSTRUCTION: Garage

Alpine Structures LLC ....E 330 359-5708
  Dundee *(G-10499)*

CONSTRUCTION: Gas Main

Fishel Company ....C 937 233-2268
  Dayton *(G-9551)*
Majaac Inc ....E 419 636-5678
  Bryan *(G-2010)*

CONSTRUCTION: Golf Course

Buckeye Landscape Service Inc ....D 614 866-0088
  Blacklick *(G-1501)*
M T Golf Course Managment Inc ....E 513 923-1188
  Cincinnati *(G-4006)*
Zinni Golf Co Inc ....E 330 533-7155
  Canfield *(G-2218)*

CONSTRUCTION: Grain Elevator

Agridry LLC ....E 419 459-4399
  Edon *(G-10585)*
Movers and Shuckers LLC ....E 740 263-2164
  Mount Vernon *(G-14915)*

CONSTRUCTION: Greenhouse

Ludy Greenhouse Mfg Corp ....D 800 255-5839
  New Madison *(G-15072)*
Rough Brothers Mfg Inc ....D 513 242-0310
  Cincinnati *(G-4446)*

CONSTRUCTION: Guardrails, Highway

Lake Erie Construction Co ....C 419 668-3302
  Norwalk *(G-15578)*
M P Dory Co ....D 614 444-2138
  Columbus *(G-8093)*
Paul Peterson Company ....E 614 486-4375
  Columbus *(G-8522)*
Pdk Construction Inc ....E 740 992-6451
  Pomeroy *(G-16234)*
Security Fence Group Inc ....E 513 681-3700
  Cincinnati *(G-4489)*

CONSTRUCTION: Heavy

CDM Constructors Inc D 740 947-7500
Waverly *(G-18968)*

Kokosing Construction Co Inc E 440 323-9346
Elyria *(G-10638)*

CONSTRUCTION: Heavy Highway & Street

A P OHoro Company D 330 759-9317
Youngstown *(G-20095)*

Anthony Allega Cement Contr E 216 447-0814
Cleveland *(G-5042)*

Becdir Construction Company E 330 547-2134
Berlin Center *(G-1480)*

Canton Public Works E 330 489-3030
Canton *(G-2295)*

City of Cuyahoga Falls E 330 971-8030
Cuyahoga Falls *(G-9176)*

City of Westerville E 614 901-6500
Westerville *(G-19382)*

Colas Solutions Inc E 513 272-5348
Cincinnati *(G-3380)*

Cook Paving and Cnstr Co E 216 267-7705
Independence *(G-12201)*

County of Delaware D 740 833-2400
Delaware *(G-10083)*

County of Monroe E 740 472-0760
Woodsfield *(G-19814)*

County of Portage D 330 296-6411
Ravenna *(G-16379)*

County of Shelby E 937 498-7244
Sidney *(G-16925)*

Double Z Construction Company D 614 274-9334
Columbus *(G-7542)*

Erie Construction Group Inc E 419 625-7374
Sandusky *(G-16752)*

Franklin Cnty Bd Commissioners C 614 462-3030
Columbus *(G-7682)*

Fred A Nemann Co E 513 467-9400
Cincinnati *(G-3645)*

Hardin County Engineer E 419 673-2232
Kenton *(G-12415)*

LEWaro-D&j-A Joint Venture Co E 937 443-0000
Dayton *(G-9678)*

Northstar Asphalt Inc E 330 497-0936
North Canton *(G-15358)*

Queen City Blacktop Company E 513 251-8400
Cincinnati *(G-4362)*

R D Jergens Contractors Inc D 937 669-9799
Vandalia *(G-18697)*

Samples Chuck-General Contr E 419 586-1434
Celina *(G-2663)*

Shelly Company E 330 425-7861
Twinsburg *(G-18469)*

Smalls Asphalt Paving Inc E 740 427-4096
Gambier *(G-11350)*

Tab Construction Company Inc E 330 454-5228
Canton *(G-2557)*

Township of Copley D 330 666-1853
Copley *(G-9067)*

Tri State Corporation E 513 763-0215
Cincinnati *(G-4683)*

Trucco Construction Co Inc C 740 417-9010
Delaware *(G-10130)*

Unicustom Inc E 513 874-9806
Fairfield *(G-10919)*

W G Lockhart Construction Co D 330 745-6520
Akron *(G-501)*

CONSTRUCTION: Hospital

Messer Construction Co E 513 672-5000
Cincinnati *(G-4082)*

Messer Construction Co D 513 242-1541
Cincinnati *(G-4083)*

CONSTRUCTION: Hotel & Motel, New

Amsdell Construction Inc C 216 458-0670
Cleveland *(G-5031)*

Messer Construction Co D 513 242-1541
Cincinnati *(G-4083)*

CONSTRUCTION: Indl Building & Warehouse

Adolph Johnson & Son Co E 330 544-8900
Mineral Ridge *(G-14635)*

Akron Public Schools B 330 761-1660
Akron *(G-52)*

Al Neyer LLC D 513 271-6400
Cincinnati *(G-2981)*

Allen-Keith Construction Co D 330 266-2220
Canton *(G-2231)*

Bell Hensley Inc E 937 498-1718
Sidney *(G-16915)*

Bilfinger Westcon Inc E 330 818-9734
Canton *(G-2263)*

Boak & Sons Inc C 330 793-5646
Youngstown *(G-20118)*

Chemsteel Construction Company E 440 234-3930
Middleburg Heights *(G-14379)*

Cm-Gc LLC E 513 527-4141
Cincinnati *(G-3372)*

Compak Inc E 419 207-8888
Ashland *(G-675)*

Continental RE Companies C 614 221-1800
Columbus *(G-7431)*

Corna Kokosing Construction Co C 614 901-8844
Westerville *(G-19392)*

DAG Construction Co Inc E 513 542-8597
Cincinnati *(G-3459)*

Danis Building Construction Co B 937 228-1225
Miamisburg *(G-14291)*

Dawn Incorporated E 330 652-7711
Warren *(G-18847)*

Deerfield Construction Co Inc E 513 984-4096
Loveland *(G-13122)*

DKM Construction Inc E 740 289-3006
Piketon *(G-16113)*

Dunlop and Johnston Inc E 330 220-2700
Valley City *(G-18616)*

Dynamic Structures Inc E 330 892-0164
New Waterford *(G-15137)*

Enerfab Inc B 513 641-0500
Cincinnati *(G-3557)*

Hammond Construction Inc D 330 455-7039
Canton *(G-2389)*

Helm and Associates Inc E 419 893-1480
Maumee *(G-13924)*

J & F Construction and Dev Inc E 419 562-6662
Bucyrus *(G-2042)*

Jack Gibson Construction Co D 330 394-5280
Warren *(G-18867)*

Kajima International Inc C 440 544-2600
Cleveland *(G-5880)*

Kapp Construction Inc E 937 324-0134
Springfield *(G-17219)*

Kramer & Feldman Inc E 513 821-7444
Cincinnati *(G-3942)*

Lathrop Company Inc E 419 893-7000
Toledo *(G-18001)*

Lcs Inc E 419 678-8600
Saint Henry *(G-16666)*

Lepi Enterprises Inc D 740 453-2980
Zanesville *(G-20495)*

Lm Constrction Trry Lvrini Inc E 740 695-9604
Saint Clairsville *(G-16641)*

Luke Theis Enterprises Inc D 419 422-2040
Findlay *(G-11059)*

M & W Construction Entps LLC E 419 227-2000
Lima *(G-12835)*

McTech Corp E 216 391-7700
Cleveland *(G-6009)*

Messer Construction Co D 513 242-1541
Cincinnati *(G-4083)*

Mike Coates Cnstr Co Inc C 330 652-0190
Niles *(G-15297)*

Monarch Construction Company C 513 351-6900
Cincinnati *(G-4114)*

Mv Commercial Construction LLC C 937 293-0900
Dayton *(G-9763)*

Nyman Construction Co E 216 475-7800
Cleveland *(G-6173)*

Ors Nasco Inc E 918 781-5300
West Chester *(G-19219)*

Oswald Company Inc E 513 745-4424
Cincinnati *(G-4241)*

Pawnee Maintenance Inc D 740 373-6861
Marietta *(G-13483)*

Pepper Cnstr Co Ohio LLC E 614 793-4477
Dublin *(G-10425)*

Quantum Construction Company E 513 351-6903
Cincinnati *(G-4361)*

Refrigeration Systems Company D 614 263-0913
Columbus *(G-8603)*

Registered Contractors Inc E 440 205-0873
Mentor *(G-14235)*

Righter Construction Svcs Inc E 614 272-9700
Columbus *(G-8630)*

Robertson Cnstr Svcs Inc D 740 929-1000
Heath *(G-11842)*

Rudolph/Libbe Companies Inc A 419 241-5000
Walbridge *(G-18778)*

Skanska USA Building Inc E 513 421-0082
Cincinnati *(G-4538)*

Stamm Contracting Co Inc E 330 274-8230
Mantua *(G-13395)*

Star Builders Inc E 440 986-5951
Amherst *(G-606)*

Steel Warehouse Cleveland LLC E 888 225-3760
Cleveland *(G-6534)*

Structural Building Systems D 330 656-9353
Hudson *(G-12145)*

Studer-Obringer Inc E 419 492-2121
New Washington *(G-15136)*

Technical Assurance Inc E 440 953-3147
Willoughby *(G-19717)*

Tri State Corporation E 513 763-0215
Cincinnati *(G-4683)*

Whiting-Turner Contracting Co D 440 449-9200
Cleveland *(G-6750)*

CONSTRUCTION: Indl Building, Prefabricated

Wenco Inc C 937 849-6002
New Carlisle *(G-15033)*

CONSTRUCTION: Indl Buildings, New, NEC

AA Boos & Sons Inc D 419 691-2329
Oregon *(G-15721)*

Adena Corporation C 419 529-4456
Ontario *(G-15682)*

Aecom Energy & Cnstr Inc B 216 622-2300
Cleveland *(G-4962)*

Albert M Higley Company C 216 404-5783
Cleveland *(G-4982)*

Austin Building and Design Inc C 440 544-2600
Cleveland *(G-5081)*

Ayrshire Inc E 440 286-9507
Chardon *(G-2740)*

B & B Contrs & Developers Inc D 330 270-5020
Youngstown *(G-20109)*

Beem Construction Inc E 937 693-3176
Botkins *(G-1751)*

Ben D Imhoff Inc E 330 683-4498
Orrville *(G-15766)*

Butt Construction Company Inc E 937 426-1313
Dayton *(G-9259)*

C Tucker Cope & Assoc Inc E 330 482-4472
Columbiana *(G-6854)*

Central Ohio Building Co Inc E 614 475-6392
Columbus *(G-7229)*

Chapman Industrial Cnstr Inc D 330 343-1632
Louisville *(G-13095)*

D & G Focht Construction Co E 419 732-2412
Port Clinton *(G-16243)*

D E Huddleston Inc E 740 773-2130
Chillicothe *(G-2832)*

Delventhal Company E 419 244-5570
Millbury *(G-14578)*

Desalvo Construction Company E 330 759-8145
Hubbard *(G-12085)*

Dorsten Industries Inc E 419 628-2327
Minster *(G-14660)*

Dotson Company E 419 877-5176
Whitehouse *(G-19585)*

Dugan & Meyers Construction Co C 513 891-4300
Blue Ash *(G-1579)*

Dugan & Meyers Construction Co E 614 257-7430
Columbus *(G-6880)*

Dugan & Meyers Interests Inc E 513 891-4300
Blue Ash *(G-1580)*

Elford Inc C 614 488-4000
Columbus *(G-7588)*

Equity Inc E 614 802-2900
Hilliard *(G-11900)*

Exxcel Project Management LLC E 614 621-4500
Columbus *(G-7624)*

Ferguson Construction Company C 937 498-2381
Sidney *(G-16933)*

Ferguson Construction Company D 937 274-1173
Dayton *(G-9545)*

Fleming Construction Co E 740 494-2177
Prospect *(G-16365)*

Floyd P Bucher & Son Inc E 419 867-8792
Toledo *(G-17898)*

Fortney & Weygandt Inc E 440 716-4000
North Olmsted *(G-15422)*

Geis Construction Inc D 330 528-3500
Streetsboro *(G-17413)*

SERVICES SECTION

CONSTRUCTION: Railway Roadbed

Head Inc .... E 614 338-8501
  Columbus (G-7808)
Higgins Building Company Inc .... E 740 439-5553
  Cambridge (G-2120)
Hume Supply Inc .... E 419 991-5751
  Lima (G-12800)
Hummel Construction Company .... E 330 274-8584
  Ravenna (G-16388)
Justice & Business Svcs LLC .... E 740 423-5005
  Belpre (G-1440)
Knoch Corporation .... D 330 244-1440
  Canton (G-2428)
Kokosing Construction Co Inc .... C 614 228-1029
  Columbus (G-8007)
McDonalds Design & Build Inc .... E 419 782-4191
  Defiance (G-10047)
McNerney & Son Inc .... E 419 666-0200
  Toledo (G-18046)
Mel Lanzer Co .... E 419 592-2801
  Napoleon (G-14945)
Mid-Continent Construction Co .... E 440 439-6100
  Oakwood Village (G-15631)
Miles-Mcclellan Cnstr Co Inc .... E 614 487-7744
  Columbus (G-8173)
Miller-Valentine Construction .... D 937 293-0900
  Dayton (G-9749)
Mowry Construction & Engrg Inc .... E 419 289-2262
  Ashland (G-690)
Mullett Company .... E 440 564-9000
  Newbury (G-15259)
Murphy Contracting Co .... E 330 743-8915
  Youngstown (G-20292)
Nicolozakes Trckg & Cnstr Inc .... E 740 432-5648
  Cambridge (G-2124)
Norris Brothers Co Inc .... C 216 771-2233
  Cleveland (G-6137)
Palmetto Construction Svcs LLC .... E 614 503-7150
  Columbus (G-8512)
QBS Inc .... E 330 821-8801
  Alliance (G-552)
R G Smith Company .... E 419 524-4778
  Mansfield (G-13352)
Ray Fogg Building Methods Inc .... E 216 351-7976
  Cleveland (G-6354)
Rudolph Libbe Inc .... B 419 241-5000
  Walbridge (G-18777)
Ruhlin Company .... C 330 239-2800
  Sharon Center (G-16877)
Ruscilli Construction Co Inc .... D 614 876-9484
  Columbus (G-8658)
Schirmer Construction Co .... E 440 716-4900
  North Olmsted (G-15443)
Schnippel Construction Inc .... E 937 693-3831
  Botkins (G-1753)
Simmons Brothers Corporation .... E 330 722-1415
  Medina (G-14125)
Spieker Company .... E 419 872-7000
  Perrysburg (G-16062)
Standard Contg & Engrg Inc .... D 440 243-1001
  Brookpark (G-1955)
Stanley Miller Construction Inc .... E 330 484-2229
  East Sparta (G-10541)
Stevens Engineers Constrs Inc .... E 440 277-6207
  Lorain (G-13079)
Sunrush Construction Co Inc .... E 740 775-1300
  Chillicothe (G-2889)
Suresite Consulting Group LLC .... E 216 593-0400
  Beachwood (G-1129)
Testa Enterprises Inc .... E 330 926-9060
  Cuyahoga Falls (G-9225)
Troy Built Building LLC .... D 419 425-1093
  Findlay (G-11094)
Turner Construction Company .... C 513 721-4224
  Cincinnati (G-4705)
TWC Concrete Services LLC .... D 513 771-8192
  Cincinnati (G-4709)
Union Industrial Contractors .... E 440 998-7871
  Ashtabula (G-765)
Universal Contracting Corp .... E 513 482-2700
  Cincinnati (G-4747)
Williams Bros Builders Inc .... E 440 365-3261
  Elyria (G-10692)

CONSTRUCTION: Indl Plant

Babcock & Wilcox Company .... A 330 753-4511
  Barberton (G-955)
ISI Systems Inc .... E 740 942-0050
  Cadiz (G-2078)
Jack Gibson Construction Co .... D 330 394-5280
  Warren (G-18867)
Pae & Associates Inc .... E 937 833-0013
  Dayton (G-9798)
Tri-America Contractors Inc .... E 740 574-0148
  Wheelersburg (G-19582)
Whiting-Turner Contracting Co .... D 440 449-9200
  Cleveland (G-6750)

CONSTRUCTION: Institutional Building

Aecom Energy & Cnstr Inc .... B 216 622-2300
  Cleveland (G-4962)
Ben D Imhoff Inc .... E 330 683-4498
  Orrville (G-15766)
Butt Construction Company Inc .... E 937 426-1313
  Dayton (G-9259)
Central Ohio Building Co Inc .... E 614 475-6392
  Columbus (G-7229)
Head Inc .... E 614 338-8501
  Columbus (G-7808)
J & R Associates .... A 440 250-4080
  Brookpark (G-1947)
Mike Coates Cnstr Co Inc .... C 330 652-0190
  Niles (G-15297)

CONSTRUCTION: Irrigation System

Riepenhoff Landscape Ltd .... E 614 876-4683
  Hilliard (G-11950)

CONSTRUCTION: Land Preparation

Independence Excavating Inc .... E 216 524-1700
  Independence (G-12218)
Jacobs Constructors Inc .... E 513 595-7900
  Cincinnati (G-3854)
Petro Environmental Tech .... E 513 489-6789
  Cincinnati (G-4287)
Schweitzer Construction Co .... E 513 761-4980
  Cincinnati (G-4485)
Todd Alspaugh & Associates .... E 419 476-8126
  Toledo (G-18224)

CONSTRUCTION: Marine

Aquarius Marine LLC .... E 614 875-8200
  Columbus (G-7031)
J Way Leasing Ltd .... E 440 934-1020
  Avon (G-899)
McDermott International Inc .... C 740 687-4292
  Lancaster (G-12554)

CONSTRUCTION: Multi-Family Housing

Al Neyer LLC .... D 513 271-6400
  Cincinnati (G-2981)
Fairfield Homes Inc .... E 740 653-3583
  Lancaster (G-12534)
GCI Construction LLC .... E 216 831-6100
  Beachwood (G-1083)
Iacovetta Builders Inc .... E 614 272-6464
  Columbus (G-7880)
Runyon & Sons Roofing Inc .... D 440 974-6810
  Mentor (G-14238)
Schnippel Construction Inc .... E 937 693-3831
  Botkins (G-1753)

CONSTRUCTION: Multi-family Dwellings, New

Douglas Construction Company .... E 419 865-8600
  Holland (G-12022)
I & M J Gross Company 440 237-1681
  Cleveland (G-5798)
Interstate Construction Inc .... E 614 539-1188
  Grove City (G-11572)
Lifestyle Communities Ltd .... E 614 918-2000
  Columbus (G-8065)
Snavely Development Company .... E 440 585-9091
  Chagrin Falls (G-2706)
Turner Construction Company .... C 513 721-4224
  Cincinnati (G-4705)

CONSTRUCTION: Nonresidential Buildings, Custom

Gem Interiors Inc .... E 513 831-6535
  Milford (G-14521)

CONSTRUCTION: Oil & Gas Line & Compressor Station

A Crano Excavating Inc .... E 330 630-1061
  Akron (G-11)
Don Wartko Construction Co .... D 330 673-5252
  Kent (G-12366)
Six C Fabrication Inc .... D 330 296-5594
  Ravenna (G-16412)

CONSTRUCTION: Oil & Gas Pipeline Construction

Bluefoot Industrial LLC .... E 740 314-5299
  Steubenville (G-17304)
J B Express Inc .... D 740 702-9830
  Chillicothe (G-2854)
Mid-Ohio Contracting Inc .... C 330 343-2925
  Dover (G-10199)
Mid-Ohio Pipeline Company Inc .... E 419 884-3772
  Mansfield (G-13346)
Minnesota Limited LLC .... C 330 343-4612
  Dover (G-10200)
Russell Hawk Enterprises Inc .... E 330 343-4612
  Dover (G-10210)
Southtown Heating & Cooling .... E 937 320-9900
  Moraine (G-14827)
Vallejo Company .... E 216 741-3933
  Cleveland (G-6682)

CONSTRUCTION: Pharmaceutical Manufacturing Plant

Liebel-Flarsheim Company LLC .... C 513 761-2700
  Cincinnati (G-3977)

CONSTRUCTION: Pipeline, NEC

AAA Flexible Pipe Cleaning .... E 216 341-2900
  Cleveland (G-4941)
ABC Piping Co .... E 216 398-4000
  Brooklyn Heights (G-1908)
Aecom Energy & Cnstr Inc .... B 216 622-2300
  Cleveland (G-4962)
Bolt Construction Inc .... D 330 549-0349
  Youngstown (G-20122)
Enviro-Flow Companies Ltd .... E 740 453-7980
  Zanesville (G-20476)
H & W Contractors Inc .... E 330 833-0982
  Massillon (G-13816)
Mannon Pipeline LLC .... E 740 643-1534
  Willow Wood (G-19736)
Miller Pipeline LLC .... B 937 506-8837
  Tipp City (G-17722)
Miller Pipeline LLC .... B 614 777-8377
  Hilliard (G-11936)
Quality Lines Inc .... C 740 815-1165
  Findlay (G-11078)
R & R Pipeline Inc .... D 740 345-3692
  Newark (G-15230)

CONSTRUCTION: Pond

Brunk Excavating Inc .... E 513 360-0308
  Monroe (G-14691)

CONSTRUCTION: Power & Communication Transmission Tower

Broadband Express LLC .... D 419 536-9127
  Toledo (G-17783)
Microwave Leasing Services LLC .... E 614 308-5433
  Columbus (G-8161)

CONSTRUCTION: Power Plant

Babcock & Wilcox Cnstr Co Inc .... D 330 860-6301
  Barberton (G-954)
Enerfab Inc .... B 513 641-0500
  Cincinnati (G-3557)
Siemens Energy Inc .... B 740 393-8897
  Mount Vernon (G-14923)

CONSTRUCTION: Railroad & Subway

E S Wagner Company .... D 419 691-8651
  Oregon (G-15733)

CONSTRUCTION: Railway Roadbed

Amtrac of Ohio Inc .... D 330 683-7206
  Orrville (G-15763)

Employee Codes: A=Over 500 employees, B=251-500
C=101-250, D=51-100, E=25-50

Delta Railroad Cnstr Inc ....D...... 440 992-2997
Ashtabula *(G-741)*
Fritz-Rumer-Cooke Co Inc........E...... 614 444-8844
Columbus *(G-7710)*
Railworks Corporation ....B...... 330 538-2261
North Jackson *(G-15387)*

CONSTRUCTION: Refineries

Toledo Refining Company LLC........C...... 419 698-6600
Oregon *(G-15752)*
W Pol Contracting Inc........E...... 330 325-7177
Ravenna *(G-16415)*

CONSTRUCTION: Religious Building

Midwest Church Cnstr Ltd ....E...... 419 874-0838
Perrysburg *(G-16033)*

CONSTRUCTION: Residential, Nec

Advocate Property Servic ....E...... 330 952-1313
Medina *(G-14032)*
Ahv Development LLC........D...... 614 890-1440
Westerville *(G-19283)*
Asbuilt Construction Ltd........E...... 937 550-4900
Franklin *(G-11149)*
Central Ohio Contractors Inc........D...... 740 369-7700
Delaware *(G-10078)*
Cy Schwieterman Inc........E...... 419 753-2566
Wapakoneta *(G-18794)*
D C Curry Lumber Company........E...... 330 264-5223
Wooster *(G-19860)*
Danis Industrial Cnstr Co........D...... 937 228-1225
Miamisburg *(G-14292)*
Dr Michael J Hulit........E...... 330 863-7173
Malvern *(G-13250)*
Endeavor Construction Ltd........E...... 513 469-1900
Pleasant Plain *(G-16214)*
Equity Central LLC........E...... 614 861-7777
Gahanna *(G-11240)*
Fairfield Homes Inc........C...... 614 873-3533
Plain City *(G-16192)*
G III Reitter Walls LLC ....E...... 614 545-4444
Columbus *(G-7718)*
Greater Dayton Cnstr Ltd........D...... 937 426-3577
Beavercreek *(G-1243)*
Habitat For Humanity Mid Ohio ....E...... 614 422-4828
Columbus *(G-7790)*
Installed Building Pdts Inc........C...... 614 221-3399
Columbus *(G-7908)*
Lake Erie Home Repair........E...... 419 871-0687
Norwalk *(G-15579)*
Mv Residential Cnstr Inc........A...... 513 588-1000
Cincinnati *(G-4133)*
Nitschke Sampson Dietz Inc........E...... 614 464-1933
Columbus *(G-8281)*
Oberer Development Co........E...... 937 910-0851
Miamisburg *(G-14328)*
Oberer Residential Cnstr........C...... 937 278-0851
Miamisburg *(G-14329)*
Otterbein Snior Lfstyle Chices ....B...... 513 933-5400
Lebanon *(G-12636)*
Pivotek LLC ....E...... 513 372-6205
West Chester *(G-19128)*
Property Estate Management LLC ....E...... 513 684-0418
Cincinnati *(G-4348)*
Pulte Homes Inc........E...... 330 239-1587
Medina *(G-14116)*
Rockford Homes Inc........D...... 614 785-0015
Columbus *(G-6905)*
Safeguard Properties MGT LLC........A...... 216 739-2900
Cleveland *(G-6434)*
Strawser Construction Inc ....E...... 614 276-5501
Columbus *(G-8796)*
Topmind/Planex Construction ....E...... 248 719-0474
Middletown *(G-14469)*
Transcon Builders Inc ....E...... 440 439-3400
Cleveland *(G-6609)*
Upgrade Homes ....E...... 614 975-8532
Columbus *(G-8912)*
Wirtzberger Enterprises Corp........E...... 440 428-1901
Madison *(G-13238)*

CONSTRUCTION: Restaurant

Restaurant Specialties Inc ....E...... 614 885-9707
Sunbury *(G-17561)*

CONSTRUCTION: Scaffolding

Kramig Co........E...... 513 761-4010
Cincinnati *(G-3943)*

CONSTRUCTION: School Building

Jack Gibson Construction Co ....D...... 330 394-5280
Warren *(G-18867)*

CONSTRUCTION: Sewer Line

A P OHoro Company........D...... 330 759-9317
Youngstown *(G-20095)*
Adleta Inc........E...... 513 554-1469
Cincinnati *(G-2973)*
Bitzel Excavating Inc ....E...... 330 477-9653
Canton *(G-2265)*
Cook Paving and Cnstr Co........E...... 216 267-7705
Independence *(G-12201)*
Darby Creek Excavating Inc........D...... 740 477-8600
Circleville *(G-4886)*
E S Wagner Company........D...... 419 691-8651
Oregon *(G-15733)*
Fleming Construction Co........E...... 740 494-2177
Prospect *(G-16365)*
George J Igel & Co Inc........A...... 614 445-8421
Columbus *(G-7742)*
H M Miller Construction Co........D...... 330 628-4811
Mogadore *(G-14677)*
Jack Conie & Sons Corp ....D...... 614 291-5931
Columbus *(G-7933)*
Kokosing Construction Co Inc ....C...... 614 228-1029
Columbus *(G-8007)*
Larry Smith Contractors Inc ....E...... 513 367-0218
Cleves *(G-6803)*
Maintenance Unlimited Inc........E...... 440 238-1162
Strongsville *(G-17486)*
Marucci and Gaffney Excvtg Co........E...... 330 743-8170
Youngstown *(G-20273)*
Mike Enyart & Sons Inc ....D...... 740 523-0235
South Point *(G-17095)*
Municpal Cntrs Saling Pdts Inc ....E...... 513 482-3300
Cincinnati *(G-4131)*
National Engrg & Contg Co........A...... 440 238-3331
Cleveland *(G-6107)*
Nerone & Sons Inc........E...... 216 662-2235
Cleveland *(G-6120)*
Rla Investments Inc........E...... 513 554-1470
Cincinnati *(G-4430)*
Todd Alspaugh & Associates........E...... 419 476-8126
Toledo *(G-18224)*
Wenger Excavating Inc........E...... 330 837-4767
Dalton *(G-9244)*
Zemba Bros Inc........E...... 740 452-1880
Zanesville *(G-20561)*

CONSTRUCTION: Shopping Center & Mall

Arbor Construction Co........E...... 216 360-8989
Cleveland *(G-5059)*
Eckinger Construction Company........E...... 330 453-2566
Canton *(G-2350)*
Etech-Systems LLC ....D...... 216 221-6600
Lakewood *(G-12477)*
K-Y Residential Coml Indus Dev ....D...... 330 448-4055
Brookfield *(G-1897)*
R B Development Company Inc........B...... 513 829-8100
Fairfield *(G-10897)*

CONSTRUCTION: Silo, Agricultural

Marietta Silos LLC........E...... 740 373-2822
Marietta *(G-13473)*

CONSTRUCTION: Single-Family Housing

50 X 20 Holding Company Inc........E...... 740 238-4262
Belmont *(G-1428)*
50 X 20 Holding Company Inc........E...... 330 865-4663
Akron *(G-10)*
A-Sons Construction Inc........D...... 614 846-2438
Columbus *(G-6923)*
Alexander and Bebout Inc........D...... 419 238-9567
Van Wert *(G-18626)*
Asplundh Construction Corp........C...... 614 532-5224
Columbus *(G-7052)*
Ayers Service Group LLC ....E...... 419 678-4811
Coldwater *(G-6827)*
Bernard Busson Builder........E...... 330 929-4926
Akron *(G-99)*
Brayman Construction Corp........E...... 740 237-0000
Ironton *(G-12282)*
Brock & Associates Builders........E...... 330 757-7150
Youngstown *(G-20127)*
Buckeye Cmnty Hope Foundation ....C...... 614 942-2014
Columbus *(G-7158)*
Burkhart Trucking Inc........E...... 740 896-2244
Lowell *(G-13168)*
Burkshire Construction Company ....E...... 440 885-9700
Cleveland *(G-5159)*
Cleveland Construction Inc ....E...... 440 255-8000
Mason *(G-13685)*
Columbus Drywall & Insulation........D...... 614 257-0257
Columbus *(G-7347)*
Columbus Drywall Inc ....E...... 614 257-0257
Columbus *(G-7348)*
Combs Interior Specialties Inc ....D...... 937 879-2047
Fairborn *(G-10787)*
Cork Inc........E...... 614 253-8400
Columbus *(G-7440)*
Cy Schwieterman Inc........E...... 419 753-2566
Wapakoneta *(G-18794)*
Denny R King ....E...... 513 917-7968
Hamilton *(G-11721)*
Design Homes & Development Co ....E...... 937 438-3667
Dayton *(G-9499)*
Dominion Homes Inc ....D...... 614 356-5000
Dublin *(G-10323)*
Dublin Building Systems Co........E...... 614 760-5831
Dublin *(G-10325)*
Elite Home Remodeling Inc........E...... 614 785-6700
Columbus *(G-7589)*
Endeavor Construction Ltd........E...... 513 469-1900
Pleasant Plain *(G-16214)*
Environmental Materials LLC ....E...... 330 558-9168
Hinckley *(G-11997)*
Equity Central LLC........E...... 614 861-7777
Gahanna *(G-11240)*
Fetters Construction Inc ....C...... 419 542-0944
Hicksville *(G-11863)*
G Stephens Inc........E...... 419 241-5188
Toledo *(G-17904)*
GCI Construction LLC ....E...... 216 831-6100
Beachwood *(G-1083)*
Goettle Co........D...... 513 825-8100
Cincinnati *(G-3682)*
Great Lakes Companies Inc........C...... 513 554-0720
Cincinnati *(G-3702)*
Great Traditions Homes ....E...... 513 759-7444
West Chester *(G-19084)*
Hochstedler Construction Ltd ....E...... 740 427-4880
Gambier *(G-11347)*
Hoppes Construction LLC ....E...... 580 310-0090
Malvern *(G-13252)*
Investmerica limited ....D...... 216 618-3296
Chagrin Falls *(G-2701)*
J A A Interior & Coml Cnstr........E...... 216 431-7633
Cleveland *(G-5839)*
Kokosing Construction Co Inc ....E...... 440 323-9346
Elyria *(G-10638)*
Lei Cbus LLC........E...... 614 302-8830
Worthington *(G-19971)*
M M Construction........E...... 513 553-0106
Bethel *(G-1483)*
Manufactured Housing Entps Inc........C...... 419 636-4511
Bryan *(G-2011)*
Miller Contracting Group Inc ....E...... 419 453-3825
Ottoville *(G-15808)*
Miracle Renovations........E...... 513 371-0750
Cincinnati *(G-4103)*
Moyer Industries Inc........E...... 937 832-7283
Clayton *(G-4915)*
MPW Construction Services........E...... 440 647-6661
Wellington *(G-18995)*
Nasco Roofing and Cnstr Inc........E...... 330 746-3566
Youngstown *(G-20294)*
New NV Co LLC........C...... 330 896-7611
Uniontown *(G-18531)*
Nhs - Totco Inc ....E...... 419 691-2900
Toledo *(G-18087)*
Northern Style Cnstr LLC........D...... 330 412-9594
Akron *(G-358)*
Nrp Contractors LLC ....E...... 216 475-8900
Cleveland *(G-6166)*
Oberer Development Co........E...... 937 910-0851
Miamisburg *(G-14328)*
Pirhl Contractors LLC........E...... 216 378-9690
Cleveland *(G-6283)*
RE Middleton Cnstr LLC........E...... 513 398-9255
Mason *(G-13753)*
Registered Contractors Inc........E...... 440 205-0873
Mentor *(G-14235)*
Shoupes Constuction........E...... 937 352-6457
Xenia *(G-20076)*
Spartan Construction Co Inc ....E...... 419 389-1854
Toledo *(G-18194)*

Swartz Enterprises Inc ... E ... 419 331-1024
Lima *(G-12895)*

Sws Environmental Services ... E ... 254 629-1718
Findlay *(G-11089)*

Tusing Builders Ltd ... E ... 419 465-3100
Monroeville *(G-14723)*

Two-X Engners Constructers LLC ... E ... 330 995-0592
Aurora *(G-857)*

Vibo Construction Inc ... E ... 614 210-6780
Columbus *(G-8938)*

Zinz Cnstr & Restoration ... E ... 330 332-7939
Youngstown *(G-20438)*

CONSTRUCTION: Single-family Housing, New

50 X 20 Holding Company Inc ... D ... 330 478-4500
Canton *(G-2220)*

A & R Builders Ltd ... E ... 330 893-2111
Millersburg *(G-14583)*

Allan Hunter Construction LLC ... E ... 330 634-9882
Akron *(G-67)*

Bob Schmitt Homes Inc ... D ... 440 327-9495
North Ridgeville *(G-15455)*

Bob Webb Builders Inc ... E ... 740 548-5577
Lewis Center *(G-12672)*

Brady Homes Inc ... E ... 440 937-6255
Avon *(G-880)*

C V Perry & Co ... E ... 614 221-4131
Columbus *(G-7176)*

Cooper Woda Companies Inc ... D ... 614 396-3200
Columbus *(G-7436)*

Crapsey & Gillis Contractors ... E ... 513 891-6333
Loveland *(G-13117)*

Crock Construction Co ... E ... 740 732-2306
Caldwell *(G-2084)*

Dan Marchetta Cnstr Co Inc ... E ... 330 668-4800
Akron *(G-186)*

Daugherty Construction Inc ... E ... 216 731-9444
Euclid *(G-10748)*

David W Milliken ... E ... 740 998-5023
Frankfort *(G-11145)*

Dayton Roof & Remodeling Co ... E ... 937 224-7667
Beavercreek *(G-1167)*

Dixon Builders & Developers ... D ... 513 887-6400
West Chester *(G-19066)*

Dold Homes Inc ... E ... 419 874-2535
Perrysburg *(G-15999)*

Drees Company ... E ... 330 899-9554
Uniontown *(G-18518)*

Duffy Homes Inc ... E ... 614 410-4100
Columbus *(G-7549)*

E A Zicka Co ... E ... 513 451-1440
Cincinnati *(G-3523)*

Enterprise Construction Inc ... E ... 440 349-3443
Solon *(G-17003)*

Etech-Systems LLC ... D ... 216 221-6600
Lakewood *(G-12477)*

Gold Star Insulation L P ... E ... 614 221-3241
Columbus *(G-7757)*

Greater Dayton Cnstr Ltd ... D ... 937 426-3577
Beavercreek *(G-1243)*

H&H Custom Homes LLC ... E ... 419 994-4070
Loudonville *(G-13090)*

Hersh Construction Inc ... E ... 330 877-1515
Hartville *(G-11822)*

HMS Construction & Rental Co ... D ... 330 628-4811
Mogadore *(G-14679)*

Hoge Lumber Company ... E ... 419 753-2263
New Knoxville *(G-15052)*

Ivan Weaver Construction Co ... E ... 330 695-3461
Fredericksburg *(G-11177)*

J W Enterprises Inc ... D ... 740 774-4500
Chillicothe *(G-2856)*

Joshua Investment Company Inc ... E ... 614 428-5555
Columbus *(G-7951)*

K Hovnanian Summit Homes LLC ... E ... 330 454-4048
Canton *(G-2421)*

Kf Construction and Excvtg LLC ... E ... 419 547-7555
Clyde *(G-6817)*

Lemmon & Lemmon Inc ... C ... 330 497-8686
North Canton *(G-15351)*

Luke Theis Enterprises Inc ... D ... 419 422-2040
Findlay *(G-11059)*

Maronda Homes Inc Florida ... D ... 937 472-3907
Eaton *(G-10566)*

Marous Brothers Cnstr Inc ... B ... 440 951-3904
Willoughby *(G-19692)*

Miller Homes of Kidron LLC ... E ... 330 857-0161
Kidron *(G-12444)*

Nicholson Builders Inc ... E ... 614 846-8621
Columbus *(G-8278)*

Nvr Inc ... E ... 440 933-7734
Avon *(G-910)*

Nvr Inc ... E ... 440 584-4200
Kent *(G-12389)*

Nvr Inc ... E ... 440 639-0525
Painesville *(G-15868)*

Nvr Inc ... E ... 513 494-0167
South Lebanon *(G-17079)*

Nvr Inc ... E ... 440 584-4250
Brecksville *(G-1838)*

Oberer Residential Cnstr ... C ... 937 278-0851
Miamisburg *(G-14329)*

P T I Inc ... E ... 419 445-2800
Pettisville *(G-16082)*

Park Group Co of America Inc ... E ... 440 238-9440
Strongsville *(G-17499)*

Petros Homes Inc ... E ... 440 546-9000
Cleveland *(G-6272)*

Phil Wagler Construction Inc ... E ... 330 899-0316
Uniontown *(G-18532)*

R A Hermes Inc ... E ... 513 251-5200
Cincinnati *(G-4377)*

Residence Artists Inc ... E ... 440 286-8822
Chardon *(G-2764)*

Robert C Verbon Inc ... E ... 419 867-6868
Toledo *(G-18160)*

Robert Lucke Homes Inc ... E ... 513 683-3300
Cincinnati *(G-4437)*

Rockford Homes Inc ... D ... 614 785-0015
Columbus *(G-6905)*

Romanelli & Hughes Building Co ... E ... 614 891-2042
Westerville *(G-19441)*

Season Contractors Inc ... E ... 440 717-0188
Broadview Heights *(G-1891)*

Simonson Construction Svcs Inc ... D ... 419 281-8299
Ashland *(G-699)*

Snavely Building Company ... E ... 440 585-9091
Chagrin Falls *(G-2705)*

Snavely Development Company ... E ... 440 585-9091
Chagrin Falls *(G-2706)*

Society Handicapped Citz Medin ... D ... 330 722-1710
Medina *(G-14127)*

Steel Valley Construction Co ... E ... 330 392-8391
Warren *(G-18902)*

Towne Development Group Ltd ... E ... 513 381-8696
Cincinnati *(G-4667)*

Trimat Construction Inc ... E ... 740 388-9515
Bidwell *(G-1496)*

Trinity Home Builders Inc ... E ... 614 889-7830
Columbus *(G-8874)*

Van Con Inc ... E ... 937 890-8400
Dayton *(G-9962)*

Weaver Custom Homes Inc ... E ... 330 264-5444
Wooster *(G-19927)*

Wh Midwest LLC ... C ... 330 896-7611
Uniontown *(G-18543)*

Woda Construction Inc ... E ... 614 396-3200
Columbus *(G-9002)*

CONSTRUCTION: Steel Buildings

Ferrous Metal Transfer ... E ... 216 671-8500
Brooklyn *(G-1906)*

J & J General Maintenance Inc ... E ... 740 533-9729
Ironton *(G-12293)*

Maco Construction Services ... E ... 330 482-4472
Columbiana *(G-6860)*

CONSTRUCTION: Street Sign Installation & Mntnce

A & A Safety Inc ... E ... 513 943-6100
Amelia *(G-571)*

CONSTRUCTION: Street Surfacing & Paving

Barbicas Construction Co ... E ... 330 733-9101
Akron *(G-89)*

Barrett Paving Materials Inc ... C ... 513 271-6200
Middletown *(G-14475)*

Camargo Construction Company ... E ... 513 248-1500
Cincinnati *(G-3168)*

Image Pavement Maintenance ... E ... 937 833-9200
Brookville *(G-1963)*

Lash Paving Inc ... D ... 740 635-4335
Bridgeport *(G-1864)*

Lyndco Inc ... E ... 740 671-9098
Shadyside *(G-16850)*

Maintenance Systems of N Ohio ... E ... 440 323-1291
Elyria *(G-10648)*

Moyer Industries Inc ... E ... 937 832-7283
Clayton *(G-4915)*

Precision Paving Inc ... E ... 419 499-7283
Milan *(G-14498)*

Rack Seven Paving Co Inc ... E ... 513 271-4863
Cincinnati *(G-4382)*

Rick Eplion Paving ... E ... 740 446-3000
Gallipolis *(G-11338)*

S & K Asphalt & Concrete ... E ... 330 848-6284
Akron *(G-422)*

Shelly Company ... E ... 419 396-7641
Carey *(G-2598)*

Shelly Company ... E ... 740 441-1714
Circleville *(G-4904)*

Shelly Company ... D ... 419 422-8854
Findlay *(G-11080)*

Shelly Materials Inc ... E ... 740 666-5841
Ostrander *(G-15794)*

CONSTRUCTION: Svc Station

Duncan Oil Co ... E ... 937 426-5945
Dayton *(G-9267)*

CONSTRUCTION: Swimming Pools

Aquarian Pools Inc ... E ... 513 576-9771
Loveland *(G-13111)*

Buckeye Pool Inc ... E ... 937 434-7916
Dayton *(G-9370)*

Burnett Pools Inc ... E ... 330 372-1725
Cortland *(G-9074)*

High-Tech Pools Inc ... E ... 440 979-5070
North Olmsted *(G-15425)*

Metropolitan Pool Service Co ... E ... 216 741-9451
Parma *(G-15910)*

Ohio Pools & Spas Inc ... E ... 330 494-7755
Canton *(G-2482)*

CONSTRUCTION: Telephone & Communication Line

Fishel Company ... D ... 614 274-8100
Columbus *(G-7667)*

Fishel Company ... D ... 614 850-4400
Columbus *(G-7669)*

Gudenkauf Corporation ... C ... 614 488-1776
Columbus *(G-7786)*

Kenneth G Myers Cnstr Co Inc ... D ... 419 639-2051
Green Springs *(G-11478)*

O C I Construction Co Inc ... E ... 440 338-3166
Novelty *(G-15602)*

Parallel Technologies Inc ... D ... 614 798-9700
Dublin *(G-10421)*

CONSTRUCTION: Tennis Court

C & B Buck Bros Asp Maint LLC ... E ... 419 536-7325
Toledo *(G-17789)*

Image Pavement Maintenance ... E ... 937 833-9200
Brookville *(G-1963)*

CONSTRUCTION: Transmitting Tower, Telecommunication

Dynamic Construction Inc ... D ... 740 927-8898
Pataskala *(G-15923)*

Sky Climber Twr Solutions LLC ... E ... 740 203-3900
Delaware *(G-10127)*

Stg Communication Services Inc ... E ... 330 482-0500
Columbiana *(G-6864)*

Tri County Tower Service ... E ... 330 538-9874
North Jackson *(G-15389)*

CONSTRUCTION: Tunnel

Capitol Tunneling Inc ... E ... 614 444-0255
Columbus *(G-7188)*

K M & M ... C ... 216 651-3333
Cleveland *(G-5879)*

Kassouf Company ... E ... 216 651-3333
Avon *(G-902)*

CONSTRUCTION: Utility Line

Adams-Robinson Enterprises Inc ... C ... 937 274-5318
Dayton *(G-9308)*

Boone Coleman Construction Inc ... E ... 740 858-6661
Portsmouth *(G-16266)*

Ch2m Hill Constructors Inc ... E ... 937 228-4285
Dayton *(G-9395)*

SERVICES

Employee Codes: A=Over 500 employees, B=251-500
C=101-250, D=51-100, E=25-50

2018 Harris Ohio
Services Directory

1443

CONSTRUCTION: Utility Line

Company		Phone
Charles H Hamilton Co	D	513 683-2442
Maineville (G-13241)		
City of Dayton	E	937 333-3725
Dayton (G-9410)		
City of Englewood	E	937 836-2434
Englewood (G-10700)		
County of Clermont	E	513 732-7970
Batavia (G-1007)		
County of Delaware	C	740 833-2240
Delaware (G-10082)		
County of Union	D	937 645-4145
Marysville (G-13614)		
Dave Sugar Excavating LLC	E	330 542-1100
Petersburg (G-16081)		
Ford Development Corp	D	513 772-1521
Cincinnati (G-3637)		
Kokosing Industrial Inc	B	614 212-5700
Westerville (G-19418)		
Nelson Stark Company	C	513 489-0866
Cincinnati (G-4154)		
North Bay Construction Inc	E	440 835-1898
Westlake (G-19522)		
Ots-NJ LLC	D	732 833-0600
Butler (G-2067)		
Schaffer Mark Excvtg & Trcking	D	419 668-5990
Norwalk (G-15592)		
Sunesis Construction Company	C	513 326-6000
West Chester (G-19161)		
Sunesis Environmental LLC	D	513 326-6000
Fairfield (G-10912)		
Thayer Pwr Comm Line Cnstr LLC	E	814 474-1174
Reynoldsburg (G-16483)		
Tribute Contracting & Cons LLC	E	740 451-1010
South Point (G-17098)		

CONSTRUCTION: Warehouse

Company		Phone
Amsdell Construction Inc	C	216 458-0670
Cleveland (G-5031)		
Genco of Lebanon Inc	A	330 837-0561
Massillon (G-13813)		
Koroseal Interior Products LLC	E	855 753-5474
Marietta (G-13461)		

CONSTRUCTION: Waste Disposal Plant

Company		Phone
Apex Environmental LLC	D	740 543-4389
Amsterdam (G-607)		
Uranium Disposition Svcs LLC	C	740 289-3620
Piketon (G-16130)		

CONSTRUCTION: Waste Water & Sewage Treatment Plant

Company		Phone
A P OHoro Company	D	330 759-9317
Youngstown (G-20095)		
Fryman-Kuck General Contrs Inc	E	937 274-2892
Dayton (G-9564)		
Kirk Bros Co Inc	D	419 595-4020
Alvada (G-569)		
Kokosing Construction Co Inc	C	614 228-1029
Columbus (G-8007)		
Peterson Construction Company	C	419 941-2233
Wapakoneta (G-18806)		
Platinum Restoration Inc	E	440 327-0699
Elyria (G-10671)		
Ulliman Schutte Cnstr LLC	B	937 247-0375
Miamisburg (G-14363)		

CONSTRUCTION: Water & Sewer Line

Company		Phone
Fabrizi Trucking & Pav Co Inc	C	330 483-3291
Cleveland (G-5564)		
J & J General Maintenance Inc	E	740 533-9729
Ironton (G-12293)		
Kirk Bros Co Inc	D	419 595-4020
Alvada (G-569)		

CONSTRUCTION: Water Main

Company		Phone
Brock & Sons Inc	E	513 874-4555
Fairfield (G-10824)		
Digioia/Suburban Excvtg LLC	D	440 237-1978
North Royalton (G-15487)		
Inliner American Inc	E	614 529-6440
Hilliard (G-11914)		
Miracle Plumbing & Heating Co	E	330 477-2402
Canton (G-2464)		
Schweitzer Construction Co	E	513 761-4980
Cincinnati (G-4485)		
Underground Utilities Inc	D	419 465-2587
Monroeville (G-14724)		

CONSULTING SVC: Actuarial

Company		Phone
Goodwill Idstrs Grtr Clvlnd L	E	330 339-5746
New Philadelphia (G-15095)		
Wtw Delaware Holdings LLC	C	216 937-4000
Cleveland (G-6762)		

CONSULTING SVC: Business, NEC

Company		Phone
Accenture LLP	C	216 685-1435
Cleveland (G-4953)		
Accenture LLP	C	614 629-2000
Columbus (G-6934)		
Accessrn Inc	D	419 698-1988
Maumee (G-13872)		
Acrt Services Inc	A	330 945-7500
Akron (G-19)		
Actionlink LLC	A	888 737-8757
Akron (G-20)		
American Health Group Inc	D	419 891-1212
Maumee (G-13875)		
Andy Mark Inc	C	513 248-8000
Milford (G-14504)		
Apple Growth Partners Inc	D	330 867-7350
Akron (G-78)		
Ardent Technologies Inc	C	937 312-1345
Dayton (G-9342)		
Ashtabula Cnty Eductl Svc Ctr	D	440 576-4085
Jefferson (G-12328)		
Avantia Inc	E	216 901-9366
Cleveland (G-5085)		
Axiom Product Development LLC	E	513 791-2425
Blue Ash (G-1537)		
B2b Power Partners	E	614 309-6964
Galena (G-11279)		
Bbs & Associates Inc	E	330 665-5227
Akron (G-92)		
Benchmark National Corporation	E	419 660-1100
Bellevue (G-1406)		
Biorx LLC	D	866 442-4679
Cincinnati (G-3109)		
Bkd LLP	D	513 621-8300
Cincinnati (G-3111)		
Bright Horizons Chld Ctrs LLC	E	614 227-0550
Columbus (G-7137)		
Calabresem Racek & Markos Inc	E	216 696-5442
Cleveland (G-5171)		
Capital City Indus Systems LLC	E	614 519-5047
Put In Bay (G-16366)		
Cardinal Maintenance & Svc Co	C	330 252-0282
Akron (G-122)		
Cash Flow Solutions Inc	D	513 524-2320
Oxford (G-15814)		
Cbiz Inc	D	330 644-2044
Uniontown (G-18512)		
Cgh-Global Technologies LLC	E	800 376-0655
Cincinnati (G-3225)		
Check It Out 4 Me LLC	E	513 568-4269
Cincinnati (G-3234)		
Cincinnati Cnslting Consortium	E	513 233-0011
Cincinnati (G-3293)		
Clermont County Gen Hlth Dst	E	513 732-7499
Batavia (G-1001)		
Composite Tech Amer Inc	E	330 562-5201
Cleveland (G-5390)		
Connaissance Consulting LLC	C	614 289-5200
Columbus (G-7421)		
Consultants Collections	E	330 666-6900
Akron (G-161)		
Corporate Ladder Search	E	330 776-4390
Uniontown (G-18515)		
Dan-Ray Construction LLC	E	216 518-8484
Cleveland (G-5462)		
Dancor Inc	E	614 340-2155
Columbus (G-7486)		
Datavantage Corporation	B	440 498-4414
Cleveland (G-5464)		
Dedicated Technologies Inc	E	614 460-3200
Columbus (G-7499)		
Deemsys Inc	D	614 322-9928
Gahanna (G-11239)		
Deloitte & Touche LLP	B	513 784-7100
Cincinnati (G-3482)		
Deloitte Consulting LLP	E	937 223-8821
Dayton (G-9497)		
E Retailing Associates LLC	D	614 300-5785
Columbus (G-7561)		
Educational Solutions Co	E	614 989-4588
Columbus (G-7581)		
Enviroscience Inc	D	330 688-0111
Stow (G-17364)		
Excellence In Motivation Inc	C	763 445-3000
Dayton (G-9533)		
General Electric Company	C	513 583-3626
Mason (G-13705)		
Governan LLC	E	614 761-2400
Columbus (G-7763)		
Gunning & Associates Mktg Inc	E	513 688-1370
Cincinnati (G-3719)		
Halley Consulting Group LLC	E	614 899-7325
Westerville (G-19405)		
Homeland Defense Solutions	E	513 333-7800
Cincinnati (G-3781)		
Humantics Innovative Solutions	E	567 265-5200
Huron (G-12165)		
Image Consulting Services Inc	E	440 951-9919
Cleveland (G-5806)		
Impact Medical Mgt Group	E	440 365-7014
Elyria (G-10636)		
Improvedge LLC	E	614 793-1738
Powell (G-16338)		
Infoverity LLC	E	614 327-5173
Dublin (G-10375)		
Integrated Solutions and	E	513 826-1932
Dayton (G-9632)		
Jennings & Associates	E	740 369-4426
Delaware (G-10111)		
Juice Technologies Inc	E	800 518-5576
Columbus (G-7957)		
Kemper Company	D	440 846-1100
Strongsville (G-17480)		
Kenexis Consulting Corporation	E	614 451-7031
Upper Arlington (G-18553)		
Kennedy Group Enterprises Inc	E	440 879-0078
Strongsville (G-17481)		
Key Office Services	E	419 747-9749
Mansfield (G-13319)		
Ladder Man Inc	E	614 784-1120
Wooster (G-19882)		
Landrum & Brown Incorporated	E	513 530-5333
Blue Ash (G-1625)		
Lateef Elmin Mhammad Inv Group	E	937 450-3388
Springfield (G-17220)		
Legacy Consultant Pharmacy	E	336 760-1670
Bedford (G-1316)		
Lextant Corporation	E	614 228-9711
Columbus (G-8055)		
Mannik & Smith Group Inc	E	419 891-2222
Maumee (G-13938)		
Mary Kelleys Inc	D	614 760-7041
Columbus (G-8122)		
Mediadvertiser Company	E	513 651-0265
Fayetteville (G-10984)		
Nexus Communications Inc	E	740 549-1092
Columbus (G-8276)		
Nugrowth Solutions LLC	E	800 747-9273
Columbus (G-8305)		
Occupational Health Services	E	937 492-7296
Sidney (G-16944)		
Ohio Utilities Protection Svc	D	330 759-0050
Youngstown (G-20310)		
Peq Services + Solutions Inc	E	937 610-4800
Miamisburg (G-14334)		
Ply-Trim Enterprises Inc	E	330 799-7876
Youngstown (G-20325)		
Qwaide Enterprises LLC	E	614 209-0551
New Albany (G-15003)		
Resolvit Resources LLC	E	513 619-5900
Cincinnati (G-4409)		
RJ Runge Company Inc	E	419 740-5781
Port Clinton (G-16253)		
Romitech Inc	E	937 297-9529
Dayton (G-9855)		
Root Inc	D	419 874-0077
Sylvania (G-17612)		
Saloma Intl Co Since 1978	E	440 941-1527
Akron (G-426)		
Scioto Packaging Inc	E	614 491-1500
Columbus (G-8707)		
Seifert & Group Inc	D	330 833-2700
Massillon (G-13852)		
Service Corps Retired Execs	E	330 379-3163
Akron (G-434)		
Sheakley Med MGT Resources LLC	E	513 891-1006
Cincinnati (G-4512)		
Six Disciplines LLC	E	419 424-6647
Findlay (G-11081)		
Smith & English II Inc	E	513 697-9300
Loveland (G-13161)		
Software Support Group Inc	D	216 566-0555
Shaker Heights (G-16866)		

Sordyl & Associates Inc ....E 419 866-6811
Maumee (G-13979)
Status Solutions LLC ....E 866 846-7272
Westerville (G-19354)
Stout Risius Ross LLC ....E 216 685-5000
Cleveland (G-6544)
Summit Solutions Inc ....E 937 291-4333
Dayton (G-9913)
Systems Evolution Inc ....D 513 459-1992
Cincinnati (G-4610)
Techsolve Inc ....D 513 948-2000
Cincinnati (G-4631)
Th Services ....E 740 258-9054
Newark (G-15238)
Tipharah Group Corp ....C 937 430-6266
Dayton (G-9929)
Tipharah Group Corp ....C 937 430-6266
Dayton (G-9930)
Towe & Associates Inc ....E 937 275-0900
West Milton (G-19269)
Tribute Contracting & Cons LLC ....E 740 451-1010
South Point (G-17098)
Truechoicepack Corp ....E 937 630-3832
Mason (G-13775)
Uc Health Llc ....A 513 475-7630
West Chester (G-19168)
US Home Center LLC ....E 614 737-9000
Columbus (G-8924)
Vans Express Inc ....E 216 224-5388
Hinckley (G-12001)
Weber Obrien Ltd ....E 419 885-8338
Sylvania (G-17627)
William Sydney Druen ....E 614 444-7655
Columbus (G-8996)
Wtb Inc ....E 216 298-1895
Cleveland (G-6761)
Yashco Systems Inc ....E 614 467-4600
Hilliard (G-11966)

CONSULTING SVC: Computer

1 Edi Source Inc ....C 440 519-7800
Solon (G-16967)
3sg Corporation ....E 614 761-8394
Dublin (G-10231)
Advanced Prgrm Resources Inc ....E 614 761-9994
Dublin (G-10234)
Advantage Technology Group ....E 513 563-3560
West Chester (G-19013)
American Bus Solutions Inc ....D 614 888-2227
Lewis Center (G-12665)
Attevo Inc ....D 216 928-2800
Beachwood (G-1053)
Baseline Consulting LLC ....D 440 336-5382
Cleveland (G-5096)
Bcg Systems That Work Inc ....E 330 864-4816
Akron (G-93)
Cache Next Generation LLC ....D 614 850-9444
Hilliard (G-11887)
Cgi Technologies Solutions Inc ....D 614 228-2245
Columbus (G-7246)
Cincinnati Bell Inc ....D 513 397-9900
Cincinnati (G-3285)
Cincinnati Bell Techno ....D 513 841-6700
Cincinnati (G-3286)
Cincinnati Bell Techno ....B 513 841-2287
Cincinnati (G-3287)
Cincom Systems Inc ....E 513 389-2344
Cincinnati (G-3344)
Comptech Computer Tech Inc ....E 937 228-2667
Dayton (G-9420)
Datacomm Tech ....E 614 755-5100
Reynoldsburg (G-16444)
Datafield Inc ....C 614 847-9600
Worthington (G-19953)
DMC Technology Group ....E 419 535-2900
Toledo (G-17855)
E2b Teknologies Inc ....E 440 352-4700
Chardon (G-2748)
Einstruction Corporation ....D 330 746-3015
Youngstown (G-20178)
Enterprise Data Management Inc ....E 513 791-7272
Blue Ash (G-1588)
Enterprise Systems Sftwr LLC ....D 419 841-3179
Toledo (G-17868)
Entrust Solutions LLC ....E 614 504-4900
Columbus (G-7597)
Forsythe Solutions Group Inc ....D 513 697-5100
Cincinnati (G-3638)
Franklin Cmpt Svcs Group Inc ....E 614 431-3327
New Albany (G-14986)
Genesis Corp ....E 614 934-1211
Columbus (G-7738)
Girard Technologies Inc ....E 330 783-2495
Youngstown (G-20201)
GP Strategies Corporation ....E 513 583-8810
Mason (G-13710)
Infovision 21 Inc ....E 614 761-8844
Dublin (G-10376)
Integrated Solutions and ....E 513 826-1932
Dayton (G-9632)
International Bus Mchs Corp ....B 917 406-7400
Beavercreek (G-1179)
Itelligence Inc ....D 513 956-2000
Cincinnati (G-3847)
Kristi Britton ....E 614 868-7612
Reynoldsburg (G-16464)
Maxim Technologies Inc ....E 614 457-6325
Hilliard (G-11926)
Mt Business Technologies Inc ....C 419 529-6100
Mansfield (G-13348)
Natural Resources Ohio Dept ....E 614 265-6852
Columbus (G-8250)
Navigtor MGT Prtners Ltd Lblty ....E 614 796-0090
Columbus (G-8251)
Netsmart Technologies Inc ....E 440 942-4040
Solon (G-17033)
Netwave Corporation ....E 614 850-6300
Dublin (G-10408)
Oasis Systems Inc ....E 937 426-1295
Beavercreek Township (G-1277)
Ohio State University ....C 614 292-4843
Columbus (G-8407)
Onx USA LLC ....D 440 569-2300
Cleveland (G-6207)
Prime Prodata Inc ....E 330 497-2578
North Canton (G-15361)
Quanexus Inc ....E 937 885-7272
Dayton (G-9837)
R Dorsey & Company Inc ....E 614 486-8900
Worthington (G-19989)
Rainbow Data Systems Inc ....E 937 431-8000
Beavercreek (G-1202)
Revolution Group Inc ....D 614 212-1111
Westerville (G-19349)
Rippe & Kingston Systems Inc ....D 513 241-1375
Cincinnati (G-4421)
Rockwell Automation Ohio Inc ....D 513 576-6151
Milford (G-14558)
Roundtower Technologies LLC ....D 513 247-7900
Cincinnati (G-4447)
Snapblox Hosted Solutions LLC ....E 866 524-7707
Cincinnati (G-4545)
Sophisticated Systems Inc ....D 614 418-4600
Columbus (G-8750)
Technology Recovery Group Ltd ....D 440 250-9970
Westlake (G-19554)
Techsoft Systems Inc ....E 513 772-5010
Cincinnati (G-4630)
Teksystems Inc ....E 216 606-3600
Independence (G-12265)
Teksystems Inc ....E 513 719-3950
Cincinnati (G-4633)
Telligen Tech Inc ....E 614 934-1554
Columbus (G-8831)
Teradata Operations Inc ....D 937 242-4030
Miamisburg (G-14357)
Unicon International Inc ....C 614 861-7070
Columbus (G-8888)
Vital Resources Inc ....E 440 614-5150
Huron (G-12175)
Vitalyst ....D 216 201-9070
Cleveland (G-6705)
Warnock Tanner & Assoc Inc ....E 419 897-6999
Maumee (G-13993)
Web Yoga Inc ....E 937 428-0000
Dayton (G-9987)
Wolcott Group ....E 330 666-5900
Medina (G-14139)
Zin Technologies Inc ....C 440 625-2200
Middleburg Heights (G-14392)

CONSULTING SVC: Data Processing

American Systems Cnsulting Inc ....D 614 282-7180
Dublin (G-10252)
Definitive Solutions Co Inc ....D 513 719-9100
Cincinnati (G-3479)
Diversified Systems Inc ....E 614 476-9939
Westerville (G-19394)
Illumination Works LLC ....D 937 938-1321
Beavercreek (G-1178)
Indecon Solutions LLC ....E 614 799-1850
Dublin (G-10374)
Interactive Bus Systems Inc ....E 513 984-2205
Cincinnati (G-3832)
Professional Data Resources Inc ....C 513 792-5100
Blue Ash (G-1668)
Qbase LLC ....E 888 458-0345
Beavercreek (G-1201)
S & P Solutions Inc ....C 440 918-9111
Willoughby Hills (G-19734)

CONSULTING SVC: Educational

Barbara S Desalvo Inc ....E 513 729-2111
Cincinnati (G-3077)
Hobsons Inc ....C 513 891-5444
Cincinnati (G-3774)

CONSULTING SVC: Engineering

ACC Automation Co Inc ....E 330 928-3821
Akron (G-15)
Advanced Engrg Solutions Inc ....D 937 743-6900
Springboro (G-17113)
Aecom ....D 330 253-9741
Cleveland (G-4961)
Aecom Global II LLC ....E 937 233-1230
Dayton (G-9311)
Alexander & Associates Co ....C 513 731-7800
Cincinnati (G-2983)
Alphaport Inc ....E 216 619-2400
Cleveland (G-4997)
Alt & Witzig Engineering Inc ....E 513 777-9890
West Chester (G-19018)
Amec Fstr Whlr Envrnmnt Infrst ....E 513 489-6611
Blue Ash (G-1531)
Amg Inc ....E 937 260-4646
Dayton (G-9335)
Avid Technologies Inc ....E 330 487-0770
Twinsburg (G-18395)
Azimuth Corporation ....E 937 256-8571
Beavercreek Township (G-1265)
BBC&m Engineering Inc ....D 614 793-2226
Dublin (G-10259)
Bbs Professional Corporation ....E 614 888-3100
Columbus (G-7095)
Bertec Corporation ....E 614 543-0962
Columbus (G-7102)
Black & Veatch Corporation ....E 614 473-0921
Columbus (G-7115)
Brilligent Solutions Inc ....E 937 879-4148
Fairborn (G-10785)
BSI Engineering LLC ....C 513 201-3100
Cincinnati (G-3145)
Burgess & Niple Inc ....B 502 254-2344
Columbus (G-7169)
Burgess & Niple Inc ....D 440 354-9700
Painesville (G-15837)
Burgess & Niple Inc ....C 513 579-0042
Cincinnati (G-3149)
Cbc Engineers & Associates Ltd ....E 937 428-6150
Dayton (G-9391)
CDM Smith Inc ....E 740 897-2937
Piketon (G-16110)
Cec Combustion Safety LLC ....E 216 749-2992
Brookpark (G-1938)
Ch2m Hill Inc ....D 513 243-5070
Cincinnati (G-3226)
Cha Consulting Inc ....C 216 443-1700
Cleveland (G-5224)
Chemstress Consultant Company ....C 330 535-5591
Akron (G-130)
Choice One Engineering Corp ....E 937 497-0200
Sidney (G-16919)
Circuits & Cables Inc ....E 937 415-2070
Vandalia (G-18671)
Clarkdietrich Engineering Serv ....D 513 870-1100
West Chester (G-19044)
Clear Vision Engineering LLC ....E 419 478-7151
Toledo (G-17816)
Control Concepts & Design Inc ....D 513 771-7271
West Chester (G-19051)
County of Athens ....E 740 593-5514
Athens (G-780)
County of Champaign ....E 937 653-4848
Urbana (G-18584)
CT Consultants Inc ....E 513 791-1700
Blue Ash (G-1573)
Ctl Engineering Inc ....C 614 276-8123
Columbus (G-7474)
Curtiss-Wright Controls ....E 937 252-5601
Fairborn (G-10789)

Employee Codes: A=Over 500 employees, B=251-500
C=101-250, D=51-100, E=25-50
2018 Harris Ohio
Services Directory
1445

Dlz National Inc E 614 888-0040
Columbus *(G-7534)*

Dlz Ohio Inc C 614 888-0040
Columbus *(G-7535)*

Dlz Ohio Inc E 330 923-0401
Akron *(G-195)*

E & A Pedco Services Inc D 513 782-4920
Cincinnati *(G-3519)*

Engineering Design and Testing D 440 239-0362
Cleveland *(G-5541)*

Engisystems Inc D 513 229-8860
Mason *(G-13699)*

Environmental Quality MGT D 513 825-7500
Cincinnati *(G-3562)*

Essig Research Inc E 513 942-7100
West Chester *(G-19198)*

Evans Mechwart Ham B 614 775-4500
New Albany *(G-14984)*

Fishbeck Thmpson Carr Hber Inc E 513 469-2370
Blue Ash *(G-1596)*

Forte Indus Eqp Systems Inc E 513 398-2800
Mason *(G-13703)*

Fosdick & Hilmer Inc D 513 241-5640
Cincinnati *(G-3641)*

Frontier Technology Inc E 937 429-3302
Beavercreek Township *(G-1269)*

Gannett Fleming Inc E 614 794-9424
Westerville *(G-19402)*

Gbc Design Inc E 330 283-6870
Akron *(G-233)*

Global Risk Consultants Corp E 440 746-8861
Brecksville *(G-1825)*

Glowe-Smith Industrial Inc C 330 638-5088
Vienna *(G-18737)*

Hammontree & Associates Ltd E 330 499-8817
Canton *(G-2390)*

Hawa Incorporated E 614 451-1711
Columbus *(G-7803)*

Hntb Corporation E 216 522-1140
Cleveland *(G-5763)*

Hull & Associates Inc E 614 793-8777
Dublin *(G-10367)*

Hull & Associates Inc E 419 385-2018
Toledo *(G-17965)*

HWH Archtcts-Ngnrs-Plnners Inc D 216 875-4000
Cleveland *(G-5794)*

Iet Inc E 419 385-1233
Toledo *(G-17969)*

Ijus LLC D 614 470-9882
Gahanna *(G-11248)*

J R Johnson Engineering Inc E 440 234-9972
Cleveland *(G-5842)*

Jacobs Engineering Group Inc E 513 595-7500
Cincinnati *(G-3855)*

Jacobs Engineering Group Inc D 513 595-7500
Cincinnati *(G-3856)*

Jetson Engineering D 513 965-5999
Cincinnati *(G-3867)*

Jones & Henry Engineers Ltd D 419 473-9611
Toledo *(G-17986)*

Kemron Environmental Svcs Inc D 740 373-4071
Marietta *(G-13460)*

Keuchel & Associates Inc E 330 945-9455
Cuyahoga Falls *(G-9202)*

Kevin Kennedy Associates Inc E 317 536-7000
Columbus *(G-7982)*

Kleingers Group Inc D 614 882-4311
Westerville *(G-19319)*

Kleingers Group Inc D 513 779-7851
West Chester *(G-19103)*

Leidos Engineering LLC D 330 405-9810
Twinsburg *(G-18441)*

Louis Perry & Associates Inc C 330 334-1585
Wadsworth *(G-18762)*

M Consultants LLC D 614 839-4639
Westerville *(G-19421)*

M Retail Engineering Inc E 614 818-2323
Westerville *(G-19422)*

M-E Companies Inc D 614 818-4900
Westerville *(G-19423)*

M-E Companies Inc E 513 942-3141
Cincinnati *(G-4007)*

Macaulay-Brown Inc B 937 426-3421
Beavercreek *(G-1251)*

Majidzadeh Enterprises Inc E 614 823-4949
Columbus *(G-8101)*

Mannik & Smith Group Inc C 419 891-2222
Maumee *(G-13938)*

Mannik & Smith Group Inc E 740 942-4222
Cadiz *(G-2079)*

Maval Industries LLC C 330 405-1600
Twinsburg *(G-18445)*

McGill Smith Punshon Inc E 513 759-0004
Cincinnati *(G-4036)*

Metamateria Partners LLC E 614 340-1690
Columbus *(G-8153)*

Michael Baker Intl Inc C 614 418-1773
Columbus *(G-8158)*

Michael Benza and Assoc Inc E 440 526-4206
Brecksville *(G-1834)*

Middough Inc B 216 367-6000
Cleveland *(G-6054)*

Modern Tech Solutions Inc D 937 426-9025
Beavercreek Township *(G-1275)*

Ms Consultants Inc C 330 744-5321
Youngstown *(G-20291)*

Ms Consultants Inc C 614 898-7100
Columbus *(G-8203)*

Nexus Engineering Group LLC D 216 404-7867
Cleveland *(G-6129)*

On-Power Inc E 513 228-2100
Lebanon *(G-12633)*

Osborn Engineering Company D 216 861-2020
Cleveland *(G-6216)*

P E Systems Inc D 937 258-0141
Dayton *(G-9280)*

Pakteem Technical Services D 513 772-1515
Cincinnati *(G-4248)*

Pegasus Technical Services Inc E 513 793-0094
Cincinnati *(G-4274)*

Peterman Associates Inc E 419 722-9566
Findlay *(G-11074)*

Phoenix Group Holding Co C 937 704-9850
Springboro *(G-17135)*

Pioneer Solutions LLC E 216 383-3400
Euclid *(G-10771)*

Poggemeyer Design Group Inc E 419 748-7438
Mc Clure *(G-14020)*

Power Engineers Incorporated E 513 326-1500
Cincinnati *(G-4318)*

Power Engineers Incorporated E 234 678-9875
Akron *(G-399)*

Power System Engineering Inc E 740 568-9220
Marietta *(G-13490)*

Process Plus LLC C 513 742-7590
Cincinnati *(G-4340)*

Professional Service Inds Inc E 614 876-8000
Columbus *(G-8568)*

Professional Service Inds Inc D 216 447-1335
Cleveland *(G-6309)*

Quality Aero Inc E 614 436-1609
Worthington *(G-19988)*

Quilalea Corporation E 330 487-0777
Richfield *(G-16524)*

Resource International D 513 769-6998
Blue Ash *(G-1682)*

Resource International Inc C 614 823-4949
Columbus *(G-8622)*

River Consulting LLC D 614 797-2480
Columbus *(G-8633)*

Rovisys Company C 330 562-8600
Aurora *(G-854)*

S&Me Inc D 614 793-2226
Dublin *(G-10445)*

Safran Humn Rsrces Support Inc D 513 552-3230
Cincinnati *(G-4468)*

Sandusky County Engr & Hwy Gar E 419 334-9731
Fremont *(G-11219)*

Scheeser Buckley Mayfield LLC E 330 896-4664
Uniontown *(G-18538)*

Schomer Glaus Pyle D 614 210-0751
Columbus *(G-8699)*

Schomer Glaus Pyle B 330 572-2100
Akron *(G-430)*

Schomer Glaus Pyle D 330 645-2131
Coventry Township *(G-9132)*

Schooley Caldwell Associates D 614 628-0300
Columbus *(G-8702)*

Sea Ltd D 614 888-4160
Columbus *(G-8709)*

Sebesta Inc E 216 351-7621
Parma *(G-15915)*

Shaffer Pomeroy Ltd E 419 756-7302
Mansfield *(G-13363)*

Sierra Lobo Inc E 419 332-7101
Fremont *(G-11220)*

Sigma Technologies Ltd E 419 874-9262
Perrysburg *(G-16059)*

Sponseller Group Inc E 419 861-3000
Holland *(G-12056)*

Stilson & Associates Inc E 614 847-0300
Columbus *(G-8789)*

Strand Associates Inc E 614 835-0460
Groveport *(G-11675)*

Stress Engineering Svcs Inc D 513 336-6701
Mason *(G-13764)*

Sumaria Systems Inc D 937 429-6070
Beavercreek *(G-1210)*

Terracon Consultants Inc C 513 321-5816
Cincinnati *(G-4636)*

Terracon Consultants Inc E 614 863-3113
Gahanna *(G-11273)*

Thomas L Miller D 740 374-3041
Marietta *(G-13503)*

Transystems Corporation E 614 433-7800
Columbus *(G-8866)*

Transystems Corporation E 216 861-1780
Cleveland *(G-6614)*

Ttl Associates Inc C 419 241-4556
Toledo *(G-18263)*

Utility Technologies Intl Corp E 614 879-7624
Groveport *(G-11683)*

Varo Engineers Inc E 740 587-2228
Granville *(G-11472)*

W E Quicksall and Assoc Inc E 330 339-6676
New Philadelphia *(G-15122)*

Zin Technologies Inc C 440 625-2200
Middleburg Heights *(G-14392)*

CONSULTING SVC: Executive Placement & Search

Abacus Corporation B 614 367-7000
Reynoldsburg *(G-16423)*

Accountants To You LLC E 513 651-2855
Cincinnati *(G-2965)*

Alexander Mann Solutions Corp B 216 336-6756
Cleveland *(G-4984)*

American Bus Personnel Svcs E 513 770-3300
Mason *(G-13661)*

Backtrack Inc D 440 205-8280
Mentor *(G-14147)*

Chad Downing E 614 532-5127
Columbus *(G-7250)*

Daily Services LLC C 614 431-5100
Columbus *(G-7483)*

Diversity Search Group LLC B 614 352-2988
Columbus *(G-7528)*

Endevis LLc E 419 482-4848
Toledo *(G-17867)*

Everstaff LLC E 877 392-6151
Cleveland *(G-5559)*

Experis Us Inc E 614 223-2300
Columbus *(G-7622)*

Fast Switch Ltd B 614 336-1122
Dublin *(G-10347)*

First Diversity Staffing Group B 937 323-4114
Springfield *(G-17198)*

Global Exec Slutions Group LLC E 330 666-3354
Akron *(G-238)*

Global Tchnical Recruiters Inc E 216 251-9560
Westlake *(G-19486)*

Global Tchnical Recruiters Inc E 440 365-1670
Elyria *(G-10630)*

Jacor LLC A 330 441-4182
Medina *(G-14084)*

Kforce Inc E 216 643-8141
Independence *(G-12222)*

Management Recruiters Intl Inc E 614 252-6200
Columbus *(G-8102)*

Marvel Consultants E 216 292-2855
Cleveland *(G-5989)*

National Staffing Group Ltd E 440 546-0800
Brecksville *(G-1835)*

On Search Partners LLC E 440 318-1006
Solon *(G-17036)*

Pps Holding LLC D 513 985-6400
Cincinnati *(G-4319)*

Psychpros Inc E 513 651-9500
Cincinnati *(G-4355)*

R E Richards Inc E 330 499-1001
Canton *(G-2501)*

Robert Half International Inc D 937 224-7376
Dayton *(G-9854)*

Robert Half International Inc D 330 629-9494
Youngstown *(G-20353)*

Robert Half International Inc D 614 221-1544
Columbus *(G-8641)*

Rvet Operating LLC E 513 683-5020
Loveland *(G-13157)*

SERVICES SECTION

CONSULTING SVC: Management

S & H Risner Inc .... D 937 778-8563
  Piqua *(G-16165)*
Tech Center Inc .... E 330 762-6212
  Akron *(G-472)*
Telecmmnctons Stffing Slutions ... E 614 799-9300
  Dublin *(G-10475)*
Thinkpath Engineering Svcs LLC ... D 937 291-8374
  Miamisburg *(G-14358)*
Trak Staffing Services Inc .... E 513 333-4199
  Cincinnati *(G-4677)*
Vector Technical Inc .... C 440 946-8800
  Willoughby *(G-19722)*
Willory LLC .... E 330 576-5486
  Bath *(G-1037)*
Wjcb LLC .... E 513 631-3200
  Blue Ash *(G-1718)*

CONSULTING SVC: Financial Management

Ameriprise Financial Svcs Inc ..... E 614 934-4057
  Dublin *(G-10253)*
B&F Capital Markets Inc .... E 216 472-2700
  Cleveland *(G-5090)*
Bodine Perry LLC .... E 330 702-8100
  Canfield *(G-2183)*
Boenning & Scattergood Inc .... E 614 336-8851
  Powell *(G-16326)*
Budros Ruhlin & Roe Inc .... E 614 481-6900
  Columbus *(G-7165)*
Chapman & Chapman Inc .... E 440 934-4102
  Avon *(G-887)*
Commercial Debt Cunseling Corp ... D 614 848-9800
  Columbus *(G-7399)*
Consumer Credit Counseling .... E 800 254-4100
  Cleveland *(G-5399)*
Financial Network Group Ltd ...... E 513 469-7500
  Cincinnati *(G-3610)*
General Fncl Tax Cnsulting LLC ... E 888 496-2679
  Cincinnati *(G-2917)*
Kaiser Consulting LLC .... E 614 378-5361
  Powell *(G-16341)*
Kelley Companies .... D 330 668-6100
  Copley *(G-9057)*
Km2 Solutions LLC .... B 610 213-1408
  Columbus *(G-7999)*
Lang Financial Group Inc .... E 513 699-2966
  Blue Ash *(G-1626)*
Lpl Financial Holdings Inc .... E 513 772-2592
  Cincinnati *(G-4001)*
MB Financial Inc .... D 937 283-2027
  Wilmington *(G-19772)*
Mc Cloy Financial Services .... E 614 457-6233
  Columbus *(G-8133)*
Merrill Lynch Pierce Fenner ...... C 513 579-3600
  Cincinnati *(G-4079)*
Merrill Lynch Pierce Fenner ...... D 614 225-3000
  Columbus *(G-8151)*
Merrill Lynch Pierce Fenner ...... E 330 655-2312
  Hudson *(G-12132)*
Neighborhood Development Svcs .... E 330 296-2003
  Ravenna *(G-16393)*
Oppenheimer & Co Inc .... E 513 723-9200
  Cincinnati *(G-4228)*
Pension Corporation America .... E 513 281-3366
  Cincinnati *(G-4277)*
Real Estate Capital Fund LLC ...... E 216 491-3990
  Cleveland *(G-6358)*
Royalton Financial Group .... E 440 582-3020
  Cleveland *(G-6419)*
Savage and Associates Inc .... D 419 731-4441
  Upper Sandusky *(G-18565)*
Support Fincl Resources Inc .... E 800 444-5465
  Centerville *(G-2686)*
Truepoint Inc .... E 513 792-6648
  Blue Ash *(G-1705)*
Weber Obrien Ltd .... E 419 885-8338
  Sylvania *(G-17627)*

CONSULTING SVC: Human Resource

Acloche LLC .... E 888 608-0889
  Columbus *(G-6938)*
Amotec Inc .... E 440 250-4600
  Cleveland *(G-5030)*
Barrett & Associates Inc .... E 330 928-2323
  Cuyahoga Falls *(G-9164)*
Clemans Nelson & Assoc Inc .... E 614 923-7700
  Dublin *(G-10295)*
Devry University Inc .... C 614 251-6969
  Columbus *(G-7515)*
Hr Butler LLC .... E 614 923-2900
  Dublin *(G-10366)*

Institute For Human Services ...... E 614 251-6000
  Columbus *(G-7910)*
Kroger Refill Center .... E 614 333-5017
  Columbus *(G-8016)*
Peoplefacts LLC .... E 800 849-1071
  Maumee *(G-13958)*
Peopleworks Dev of Hr LLC .... E 419 636-4637
  Bryan *(G-2016)*
Sheakley Unicomp Inc .... C 513 771-2277
  Cincinnati *(G-4513)*
Sheakley-Uniservice Inc .... C 513 771-2277
  Cincinnati *(G-4514)*
State of Ohio .... C 614 466-3455
  Columbus *(G-8782)*
Synergy Consulting Group Inc ...... E 330 899-9301
  Uniontown *(G-18540)*

CONSULTING SVC: Management

Accelerant Technologies LLC .... D 419 236-8768
  Genoa *(G-11374)*
Advanced Prgrm Resources Inc ...... E 614 761-9994
  Dublin *(G-10234)*
Armada Ltd .... E 614 505-7256
  Powell *(G-16324)*
AT&T Government Solutions Inc ..... D 937 306-3030
  Beavercreek *(G-1149)*
Atlas Advisors LLC .... E 888 282-0873
  Columbus *(G-7068)*
Attevo Inc .... D 216 928-2800
  Beachwood *(G-1053)*
Aultman Health Foundation .... A 330 682-3010
  Orrville *(G-15765)*
Austin Building and Design Inc .... C 440 544-2600
  Cleveland *(G-5081)*
Azimuth Corporation .... E 937 256-8571
  Beavercreek Township *(G-1265)*
Backoffice Associates LLC .... D 419 660-4600
  Norwalk *(G-15562)*
Baxter Hodell Donnelly Preston .... C 513 271-1634
  Cincinnati *(G-3083)*
Benchmark Technologies Corp .... E 419 843-6691
  Toledo *(G-17769)*
Bionetics Corporation .... E 757 873-0900
  Heath *(G-11835)*
Burke Inc .... C 513 241-5663
  Cincinnati *(G-3150)*
C H Dean Inc .... D 937 222-9531
  Beavercreek *(G-1156)*
Cbiz Inc .... C 216 447-9000
  Cleveland *(G-5196)*
Center For Health Affairs .... D 800 362-2628
  Cleveland *(G-5208)*
Clgt Solutions LLC .... E 740 920-4795
  Granville *(G-11462)*
Commquest Services Inc .... C 330 455-0374
  Canton *(G-2316)*
Comprehensive Logistics Co Inc .... E 330 233-2627
  Avon Lake *(G-927)*
Corbus LLC .... E 937 226-7724
  Dayton *(G-9428)*
Crown Westfalen LLC .... C 614 488-1169
  Columbus *(G-7468)*
Dayton Foundation Inc .... E 937 222-0410
  Dayton *(G-9474)*
Dedicated Tech Services Inc .... D 614 309-0059
  Dublin *(G-10317)*
Deloitte & Touche LLP .... D 937 223-8821
  Dayton *(G-9496)*
Deloitte & Touche LLP .... C 216 589-1300
  Cleveland *(G-5474)*
Deloitte & Touche LLP .... B 513 784-7100
  Cincinnati *(G-3482)*
Deloitte Consulting LLP .... D 937 223-8821
  Dayton *(G-9497)*
Delta Energy LLC .... E 614 761-3603
  Dublin *(G-10318)*
Digital Controls Corporation .... D 513 746-8118
  Miamisburg *(G-14297)*
Diversified Systems Inc .... E 614 476-9939
  Westerville *(G-19394)*
Duke Energy Ohio Inc .... C 513 421-9500
  Cincinnati *(G-3511)*
Duncan Falls Assoc .... D 740 674-7105
  Duncan Falls *(G-10498)*
Enterprise Data Management Inc .... E 513 791-7272
  Blue Ash *(G-1588)*
Financial Design Group Inc .... E 419 843-4737
  Toledo *(G-17889)*
Focus Solutions Inc .... E 513 376-8349
  Cincinnati *(G-3635)*

Forest City Enterprises Inc .... D 216 621-6060
  Cleveland *(G-5613)*
Four Seasons Environmental Inc .... B 513 539-2978
  Monroe *(G-14696)*
Frank Gates Service Company .... B 614 793-8000
  Dublin *(G-10350)*
Garretyson Frm Resolution Grp ..... C 513 794-0400
  Loveland *(G-13127)*
Gbq Consulting LLC .... D 614 221-1120
  Columbus *(G-7731)*
Genesis Corp .... E 614 934-1211
  Columbus *(G-7738)*
GP Strategies Corporation .... E 513 583-8810
  Mason *(G-13710)*
Gray & Pape Inc .... E 513 287-7700
  Cincinnati *(G-3694)*
Greentree Group Inc .... D 937 490-5500
  Dayton *(G-9591)*
H T V Industries Inc .... D 216 514-0060
  Cleveland *(G-5716)*
Halley Consulting Group LLC .... E 614 899-7325
  Westerville *(G-19405)*
Harris Mackessy & Brennan .... C 614 221-6831
  Westerville *(G-19311)*
HDR Engineering Inc .... E 614 839-5770
  Columbus *(G-7807)*
Henry Call Inc .... C 216 433-5609
  Cleveland *(G-5749)*
HJ Ford Associates Inc .... E 937 429-9711
  Beavercreek *(G-1176)*
I T E LLC .... D 513 576-6200
  Loveland *(G-13132)*
Infor (us) Inc .... E 614 781-2325
  Columbus *(G-6886)*
Innovative Technologies Corp .... D 937 252-2145
  Dayton *(G-9275)*
Integra Realty Resources - Cin .... B 513 561-2305
  Cincinnati *(G-3826)*
Integrated Prj Resources LLC ...... E 330 272-0998
  Salem *(G-16701)*
Iron Mountain Info MGT LLC .... C 440 248-0999
  Solon *(G-17019)*
Island Hospitality MGT LLC .... E 614 864-8844
  Columbus *(G-7927)*
J G Martin Inc .... D 216 491-1584
  Cleveland *(G-5841)*
Jersey Central Pwr & Light Co ..... C 330 315-6713
  Fairlawn *(G-10960)*
Jonathon R Johnson & Assoc .... E 216 932-6529
  Cleveland *(G-5870)*
Jyg Innovations LLC .... E 937 630-3858
  Dayton *(G-9647)*
Knowledgeworks Foundation .... D 513 241-1422
  Cincinnati *(G-9337)*
Landrum & Brown Incorporated ...... D 513 530-5333
  Blue Ash *(G-1625)*
Level Seven .... D 216 524-9055
  Independence *(G-12224)*
Managed Technology Svcs LLC .... D 937 247-8915
  Miamisburg *(G-14315)*
McKinsey & Company Inc .... D 216 274-4000
  Cleveland *(G-6007)*
Med-Pass Incorporated .... E 937 438-8884
  Dayton *(G-9711)*
Medco Health Solutions Inc .... A 614 822-2000
  Dublin *(G-10393)*
Medical Account Services Inc ...... E 937 297-6072
  Moraine *(G-14803)*
Merrill Lynch Pierce Fenner .... E 937 847-4000
  Miamisburg *(G-14319)*
Merrill Lynch Pierce Fenner .... D 330 670-2400
  Akron *(G-339)*
Mid-Amrica Cnsulting Group Inc .... D 216 432-6925
  Cleveland *(G-6053)*
Nationwide Rtirement Solutions .... C 614 854-8300
  Dublin *(G-10405)*
Navigtor MGT Prtners Ltd Lblty ... E 614 796-0090
  Columbus *(G-8251)*
Netsmart Technologies Inc .... D 614 764-0143
  Dublin *(G-10407)*
Northwest Country Place Inc .... D 440 488-2700
  Willoughby *(G-19698)*
Ohio Custodial Maintenance .... C 614 443-1232
  Columbus *(G-8323)*
Ohio State University .... E 614 728-8100
  Columbus *(G-8432)*
One10 LLC .... D 763 445-3000
  Dayton *(G-9792)*
OR Colan Associates LLC .... E 440 827-6116
  Cleveland *(G-6210)*

Employee Codes: A=Over 500 employees, B=251-500
C=101-250, D=51-100, E=25-50

Organizational Horizons Inc ....E 614 268-6013
Worthington (G-19981)
Park International Theme Svcs ....E 513 381-6131
Cincinnati (G-4253)
Pcs Cost ....E 216 771-1090
Cleveland (G-6256)
Perduco Group Inc ....E 937 401-0271
Beavercreek (G-1196)
Phoenix Cosmopolitan Group LLC ....E 814 746-4863
Avon (G-914)
Piasans Mill Inc ....E 419 448-0100
Tiffin (G-17693)
Power Management Inc ....E 937 222-2909
Dayton (G-9817)
Professnal Mint Cincinnati Inc ....A 513 579-1161
Cincinnati (G-4345)
Provenitfinance LLC ....E 888 958-1060
Pickerington (G-16103)
Quality Solutions Inc ....E 440 933-9946
Cleveland (G-6335)
Quick Solutions Inc ....C 614 825-8000
Westerville (G-19347)
Rahim Inc ....E 216 621-8977
Cleveland (G-6349)
Redwood Living Inc ....C 216 360-9441
Independence (G-12247)
Residential Hm Assn of Marion ....C 740 387-9999
Marion (G-13575)
Risk International Svcs Inc ....E 216 255-3400
Fairlawn (G-10969)
RMS of Ohio Inc ....B 440 617-6605
Westlake (G-19542)
Rpf Consulting LLC ....E 678 494-8030
Cincinnati (G-4450)
Rse Group Inc ....D 937 596-6167
Jackson Center (G-12325)
Ruralogic Inc ....D 419 630-0500
Beachwood (G-1122)
Sacs Cnslting Training Ctr Inc ....E 330 255-1101
Akron (G-424)
Safelite Solutions LLC ....A 614 210-9000
Columbus (G-8673)
Schrudder Prfmce Group LLC ....E 513 652-7675
West Chester (G-19147)
Signet Management Co Ltd ....C 330 762-9102
Akron (G-438)
Sodexo Inc ....E 330 425-0709
Twinsburg (G-18470)
SSS Consulting Inc ....E 937 259-1200
Dayton (G-9901)
Standard Register Inc ....A 937 221-1000
Dayton (G-9903)
Sun Valley Infosys LLC ....D 937 267-6435
Springfield (G-17283)
Surgere Inc ....E 330 526-7971
North Canton (G-15371)
Tacg LLC ....D 937 203-8201
Beavercreek (G-1212)
Taylor Strategy Partners LLC ....E 614 436-6650
Columbus (G-8825)
Terry J Reppa & Associates ....E 440 888-8533
Cleveland (G-6586)
Towers Watson Pennsylvania Inc ....E 513 345-4200
Cincinnati (G-4665)
Trinity Health Corporation ....E 419 448-3124
Tiffin (G-17707)
University of Dayton ....C 937 255-3141
Dayton (G-9951)
University of Dayton ....C 937 229-3913
Dayton (G-9955)
Vand Corp ....E 216 481-3788
Cleveland (G-6686)
Vediscovery LLC ....E 216 241-3443
Cleveland (G-6688)
Venator Holdings LLC ....D 248 792-9209
Maumee (G-13992)
Viaquest Behavioral Health LLC ....E 614 339-0868
Dublin (G-10482)
William Thomas Group Inc ....D 800 582-3107
Cincinnati (G-4851)
Willowood Care Center ....C 330 225-3156
Brunswick (G-1997)
Workplace Media Inc ....E 440 392-2171
Mentor (G-14260)
Worthington Public Library ....C 614 807-2626
Worthington (G-20010)

CONSULTING SVC: Marketing Management

2060 Digital LLC ....E 513 699-5012
Cincinnati (G-2941)
Advanced Computer Graphics ....E 513 936-5060
Blue Ash (G-1523)
Ake Marketing ....E 440 232-1661
Bedford (G-1293)
Applied Marketing Services ....E 440 716-9962
Westlake (G-19460)
Archway Marketing Services Inc ....C 440 572-0725
Strongsville (G-17444)
Brandmuscle Inc ....C 216 464-4342
Cleveland (G-5133)
Club Life Entertainment LLC ....E 216 831-1134
Beachwood (G-1066)
Coho Creative LLC ....E 513 751-7500
Cincinnati (G-3379)
Communica Inc ....E 419 244-7766
Toledo (G-17823)
Concordia Properties LLC ....E 513 671-0120
Cincinnati (G-3409)
Contract Marketing Inc ....D 440 639-9100
Mentor (G-14162)
Cornerstone Brands Group Inc ....A 513 603-1000
West Chester (G-19053)
D L Ryan Companies LLC ....E 614 436-6558
Westerville (G-19296)
Davis 5 Star Holdings LLC ....E 954 470-8456
Springfield (G-17187)
Direct Options Inc ....E 513 779-4416
West Chester (G-19064)
Dunnhumby Inc ....D 513 579-3400
Cincinnati (G-3514)
Dwight Spencer & Associates ....E 614 488-3123
Columbus (G-7554)
Efficient Collaborative Retail ....D 440 498-0500
Solon (G-17001)
Epipheo Incorporated ....E 888 687-7620
Cincinnati (G-3565)
Fahlgren Inc ....D 614 383-1500
Columbus (G-7629)
Fathom Seo LLC ....D 614 291-8456
Columbus (G-7643)
Fathom Seo LLC ....D 216 525-0510
Cleveland (G-5577)
Frankes Wood Products LLC ....E 937 642-0706
Marysville (G-13620)
Gund Sports Marketing Llc ....E 216 420-2000
Cleveland (G-5709)
Hafenbrack Mktg Cmmnctions Inc ....E 937 424-8950
Dayton (G-9596)
Ilead LLC ....E 440 846-2346
Strongsville (G-17476)
Innerworkings Inc ....E 513 984-9500
Cincinnati (G-3819)
Inquiry Systems Inc ....E 614 464-3800
Columbus (G-7904)
Ipsos-Asi LLC ....D 513 872-4300
Cincinnati (G-3842)
ITM Marketing Inc ....C 740 295-3575
Coshocton (G-9108)
Language Logic ....E 513 241-9112
Cincinnati (G-3961)
Madison Avenue Mktg Group Inc ....E 419 473-9000
Toledo (G-18026)
Mes Inc ....D 740 201-8112
Lewis Center (G-12694)
Mission Pride Inc ....E 216 759-7404
Cleveland Heights (G-6793)
National Yllow Pages Media LLC ....E 216 447-9400
Independence (G-12237)
Nsa Technologies LLC ....C 330 576-4600
Akron (G-359)
Ologie LLC ....D 614 221-1107
Columbus (G-8466)
Parker Marketing Research LLC ....E 513 248-8100
Milford (G-14549)
Pat Henry Group LLC ....E 216 447-0831
Milford (G-14551)
Patientpint Hosp Solutions LLC ....C 513 936-6800
Cincinnati (G-4259)
Patientpint Ntwrk Slutions LLC ....D 513 936-6800
Cincinnati (G-4260)
Patientpoint LLC ....E 513 936-6800
Cincinnati (G-4261)
Peopletomysitecom LLC ....E 800 295-4519
Columbus (G-8533)
Pitmark Services Inc ....E 330 876-2217
Kinsman (G-12454)
Quotient Technology Inc ....E 513 229-8659
Mason (G-13752)
R D D Inc ....C 216 781-5858
Cleveland (G-6339)
R P Marketing Public Relations ....E 419 241-2221
Holland (G-12050)
Resource Ventures Ltd ....D 614 621-2888
Columbus (G-8623)
Revlocal Inc ....D 740 392-9246
Mount Vernon (G-14919)
SBC Advertising Ltd ....C 614 891-7070
Columbus (G-8692)
SCI Direct LLC ....A 330 494-5504
North Canton (G-15366)
Stohen Group LLC ....E 513 448-6288
Mason (G-13763)
Sumner Solutions Inc ....E 513 531-6382
Cincinnati (G-4599)
Universal Marketing Group LLC ....D 419 720-9696
Toledo (G-18275)
Weber Partners Ltd ....E 614 222-6806
Columbus (G-8974)
Young and Associates Inc ....E 330 678-0524
Kent (G-12407)

CONSULTING SVC: New Business Start Up

Dari Pizza Enterprises II Inc ....C 419 534-3000
Maumee (G-13905)
Ingleside Investments Inc ....E 614 221-1025
Columbus (G-7898)

CONSULTING SVC: Online Technology

Blue Chip Consulting Group LLC ....E 216 503-6001
Seven Hills (G-16827)
Cadre Computer Resources Co ....E 513 762-7350
Cincinnati (G-3164)
Cardinal Solutions Group Inc ....D 513 984-6700
Cincinnati (G-3179)
Cgi Technologies Solutions Inc ....C 216 687-1480
Cleveland (G-5222)
Cgi Technologies Solutions Inc ....D 614 880-2200
Columbus (G-6874)
Cisco Systems Inc ....A 937 427-4264
Beavercreek (G-1160)
Comresource Inc ....E 614 221-6348
Columbus (G-7418)
Datalysys LLC ....E 614 495-0260
Dublin (G-10316)
Dayhuff Group LLC ....E 614 854-9999
Worthington (G-19954)
E-Mek Technologies LLC ....D 937 424-3163
Dayton (G-9510)
Entrypoint Consulting LLC ....D 216 674-9070
Cleveland (G-5544)
Enviro It LLC ....E 614 453-0709
Columbus (G-7598)
Estreamz Inc ....E 513 278-7836
Cincinnati (G-3577)
Everest Technologies Inc ....E 614 436-3120
Worthington (G-19958)
Fit Technologies LLC ....E 216 583-0733
Cleveland (G-5601)
Genesis Corp ....D 330 597-4100
Akron (G-235)
Great Nthrn Cnsulting Svcs Inc ....E 614 890-9999
Columbus (G-7771)
Indus Valley Consultants Inc ....C 937 660-4748
Dayton (G-9629)
Information Control Corp ....B 614 523-3070
Columbus (G-7897)
Integrity Information Tech Inc ....E 937 846-1769
New Carlisle (G-15024)
International Association of ....E 330 628-3012
Canton (G-2413)
Intralot Inc ....E 440 268-2900
Strongsville (G-17477)
Intelligence Outsourcing Inc ....D 513 956-2000
Cincinnati (G-3848)
Lan Solutions Inc ....E 513 469-6500
Blue Ash (G-1624)
Lanco Global Systems Inc ....D 937 660-8090
Dayton (G-9672)
Leadership Circle LLC ....E 801 518-2980
Whitehouse (G-19588)
Lightwell Inc ....E 614 310-2700
Dublin (G-10389)
London Computer Systems Inc ....D 513 583-0840
Loveland (G-13140)
Main Sail LLC ....D 216 472-5100
Cleveland (G-5969)
Myca Mltmdia Trning Sltons LLC ....E 513 544-2379
Blue Ash (G-1650)
Nova Technology Solutions LLC ....E 937 426-2596
Beavercreek (G-1194)

SERVICES SECTION

CONSULTING SVCS, BUSINESS: Systems Analysis & Engineering

Optimum Technology Inc .... E 614 785-1110
 Columbus (G-8474)
Pcm Sales Inc .... D 937 885-6444
 Miamisburg (G-14333)
Perceptis LLC .... C 216 458-4122
 Cleveland (G-6264)
Phoenix Systems Group Inc .... E 330 726-6500
 Youngstown (G-20320)
Platinum Technologies .... E 216 926-1080
 Akron (G-392)
Recker Consulting LLC .... D 513 924-5500
 Cincinnati (G-4393)
Regent Systems Inc .... D 937 640-8010
 Dayton (G-9845)
Sjn Data Center LLC .... E 513 386-7871
 Cincinnati (G-4534)
Sogeti USA LLC .... E 614 847-4477
 Westerville (G-19353)
Sogeti USA LLC .... D 937 433-3334
 Dayton (G-9887)
Sogeti USA LLC .... C 937 291-8100
 Miamisburg (G-14351)
Sogeti USA LLC .... E 216 654-2230
 Cleveland (G-6493)
Sogeti USA LLC .... E 513 824-3000
 Blue Ash (G-1689)
Sonit Systems LLC .... E 419 446-2151
 Archbold (G-646)
Strategic Systems Inc .... C 614 717-4774
 Dublin (G-10464)
Vertical Knowledge LLC .... D 216 920-7790
 Chagrin Falls (G-2709)

CONSULTING SVC: Personnel Management

Patrick Mahoney .... E 614 292-5766
 Columbus (G-8521)
Selection MGT Systems Inc .... D 513 522-8764
 Cincinnati (G-4494)

CONSULTING SVC: Productivity Improvement

Productivity Qulty Systems Inc .... E 937 885-2255
 Dayton (G-9833)

CONSULTING SVC: Telecommunications

Acadia Solutions Inc .... E 614 505-6135
 Dublin (G-10233)
American Broadband Telecom Co .... E 419 824-5800
 Toledo (G-17748)
AT&T Corp .... A 216 298-1513
 Cleveland (G-5074)
Communications III Inc .... E 614 901-7720
 Westerville (G-19390)
CTS Construction Inc .... D 513 489-8290
 Cincinnati (G-3445)
Massillon Cable TV Inc .... D 330 833-4134
 Massillon (G-13833)
Neutral Telecom Corporation .... E 440 377-4700
 North Ridgeville (G-15472)
Tangoe Inc .... D 614 842-9918
 Columbus (G-8821)
Turnkey Network Solutions LLC .... E 614 876-9944
 Columbus (G-8880)
Twism Enterprises LLC .... E 513 800-1098
 Cincinnati (G-4711)
Uts Inc .... E 513 332-9000
 Cincinnati (G-4800)

CONSULTING SVCS, BUSINESS: Agricultural

Feg Consulting LLC .... E 412 224-2263
 Blue Ash (G-1592)

CONSULTING SVCS, BUSINESS: City Planning

City of Coshocton .... D 740 622-1763
 Coshocton (G-9090)
Poggemeyer Design Group Inc .... C 419 244-8074
 Bowling Green (G-1791)
Schooley Caldwell Associates .... D 614 628-0300
 Columbus (G-8702)
Toledo Metro Area Cncl Gvrnmnt .... E 419 241-9155
 Toledo (G-18242)

CONSULTING SVCS, BUSINESS: Communications

A M Communications Ltd .... D 419 528-3051
 Galion (G-11289)
Interactive Solutions Intl LLC .... E 513 619-5100
 Cincinnati (G-3833)
Nas Rcrtment Cmmunications LLC ..... C 216 478-0300
 Cleveland (G-6100)
Northeast Ohio Communic .... D 330 399-2700
 Warren (G-18888)
Pro Ed Communications Inc .... E 216 595-7919
 Cleveland (G-6308)

CONSULTING SVCS, BUSINESS: Economic

Miami Valley Regional Plg Comm .... E 937 223-6323
 Dayton (G-9737)
Port Grter Cincinnati Dev Auth .... E 513 621-3000
 Cincinnati (G-4315)
Team NEO .... E 216 363-5400
 Cleveland (G-6576)

CONSULTING SVCS, BUSINESS: Employee Programs Administration

Bravo Wellness LLC .... E 216 658-9500
 Cleveland (G-5134)
Compmanagement Health Systems ..... D 614 766-5223
 Dublin (G-10307)
Employee Benefit Management .... E 614 766-5800
 Dublin (G-10336)
Incentisoft Solutions LLC 877 562-4461
 Cleveland (G-5808)
Klais and Company Inc .... E 330 867-8443
 Fairlawn (G-10963)
Nationwide Rtirement Solutions .... C 614 854-8300
 Dublin (G-10405)
Sequent Inc .... D 614 436-5880
 Columbus (G-6907)
Simplifi Eso LLC .... C 614 635-8679
 Columbus (G-8736)

CONSULTING SVCS, BUSINESS: Energy Conservation

Hoskins International LLC .... E 419 628-6015
 Minster (G-14664)
Nationwide Energy Partners LLC .... E 614 918-2031
 Columbus (G-8240)

CONSULTING SVCS, BUSINESS: Environmental

Acrt Inc .... E 800 622-2562
 Akron (G-18)
Allied Environmental Svcs Inc .... E 419 227-4004
 Lima (G-12739)
Als Group Usa Corp .... E 513 733-5336
 Blue Ash (G-1530)
Arcadis US Inc .... D 419 473-1121
 Toledo (G-17757)
Bjaam Environmental Inc .... E 330 854-5300
 Canal Fulton (G-2141)
Bureau Veritas North Amer Inc .... E 330 252-5100
 Akron (G-119)
CDM SMITH INC .... E 614 847-8340
 Columbus (G-7219)
Clinton-Carvell Inc .... E 614 351-8858
 Columbus (G-7303)
Coact Associates Ltd .... E 866 646-4400
 Toledo (G-17818)
Ecs Holdco Inc .... E 614 433-0170
 Worthington (G-19955)
Emergency Response & Trnng .... E 440 349-2700
 Solon (G-17002)
Envirnmental Resources MGT Inc .... E 216 593-5200
 Beachwood (G-1076)
Envirnmental Resources MGT Inc .... E 513 830-9030
 Blue Ash (G-1589)
Environmental Solutions .... E 513 451-1777
 Cincinnati (G-3563)
Floyd Browne Group Inc .... E 740 363-6792
 Delaware (G-10097)
Grace Consulting Inc .... E 440 647-6672
 Wellington (G-18992)
Hull & Associates Inc .... E 614 793-8777
 Dublin (G-10367)
Hzw Environmental Cons LLC .... E 800 804-8484
 Mentor (G-14194)
Icon Environmental Group LLC .... E 513 426-6767
 Milford (G-14526)
Interdyne Corporation .... E 419 229-8192
 Lima (G-12805)
Kemron Environmental Svcs Inc .... D 740 373-4071
 Marietta (G-13460)
Lawhon and Associates Inc .... E 614 481-8600
 Columbus (G-8044)
On Site Instruments LLC .... E 614 846-1900
 Lewis Center (G-12699)
Orin Group LLC 330 630-3937
 Akron (G-376)
Safety-Kleen Systems Inc .... E 513 563-0931
 Fairfield (G-10902)
Sunpro Inc 330 966-0910
 North Canton (G-15370)
Tetra Tech Inc .... E 513 251-2730
 Cincinnati (G-4638)
Ttl Associates Inc .... E 419 241-4556
 Toledo (G-18263)
Vahalla Company Inc .... E 216 326-2245
 Cleveland (G-6681)

CONSULTING SVCS, BUSINESS: Indl Development Planning

Big Red Rooster .... D 614 255-0200
 Columbus (G-7108)

CONSULTING SVCS, BUSINESS: Lighting

Jones Group Interiors Inc .... E 330 253-9180
 Akron (G-297)

CONSULTING SVCS, BUSINESS: Safety Training Svcs

ABC Fire Inc .... E 440 237-6677
 North Royalton (G-15480)
Alice Training Institute LLC .... D 330 661-0106
 Medina (G-14034)
Kirila Fire Trning Fclties Inc .... E 724 854-5207
 Brookfield (G-1899)
Mission Essntial Personnel LLC .... C 614 416-2345
 New Albany (G-14992)

CONSULTING SVCS, BUSINESS: Sys Engnrg, Exc Computer/Prof

Aecom Global II LLC .... D 419 774-9862
 Delta (G-10155)
Centric Consulting LLC .... D 888 781-7567
 Dayton (G-9394)
Construction Resources Inc .... E 440 248-9800
 Cleveland (G-5397)
Controlsoft Inc .... E 440 443-3900
 Cleveland (G-5404)
Devcare Solutions Ltd .... E 614 221-2277
 Columbus (G-7511)
Ellipse Solutions LLC .... E 937 312-1547
 Dayton (G-9525)
Equity Engineering Group Inc .... D 216 283-9519
 Shaker Heights (G-16860)
Gleaming Systems LLC .... E 614 348-7475
 Lewis Center (G-12686)
Indecon Solutions LLC .... E 614 799-1850
 Dublin (G-10374)
Jyg Innovations LLC .... E 937 630-3858
 Dayton (G-9647)
Peak 10 Inc .... E 513 645-2900
 Hamilton (G-11762)
Primatech Inc .... E 614 841-9800
 Columbus (G-8560)
Sadler-Necamp Financial Svcs .... E 513 489-5477
 Cincinnati (G-4466)
Sawdey Solution Services Inc .... E 937 490-4060
 Beavercreek (G-1259)
Shotstop Ballistics LLC .... E 330 686-0020
 Stow (G-17392)
Sjn Data Center LLC .... E 513 386-7871
 Cincinnati (G-4534)

CONSULTING SVCS, BUSINESS: Systems Analysis & Engineering

Industrial Vibrations Cons .... D 513 932-4678
 Lebanon (G-12612)
Interactive Engineering Corp .... E 330 239-6888
 Medina (G-14082)
Lumenance LLC .... E 319 541-6811
 Columbus (G-8086)

Employee Codes: A=Over 500 employees, B=251-500
C=101-250, D=51-100, E=25-50

CONSULTING SVCS, BUSINESS: Systems Analysis & Engineering

Oracle Systems Corporation ....D....... 216 328-9100
Beachwood *(G-1112)*

CONSULTING SVCS, BUSINESS: Test Development & Evaluation

Benchmark Technologies Corp ....E....... 419 843-6691
Toledo *(G-17769)*

CONSULTING SVCS, BUSINESS: Testing, Educational Or Personnel

Clgt Solutions LLC ....E....... 740 920-4795
Granville *(G-11462)*
Envision Corporation ....D....... 513 772-5437
Cincinnati *(G-3564)*

CONSULTING SVCS, BUSINESS: Traffic

Celebrity Security Inc ....E....... 216 671-6425
Cleveland *(G-5202)*
City of Akron ....E....... 330 375-2851
Akron *(G-141)*
Its Traffic Systems Inc ....D....... 440 892-4500
Westlake *(G-19500)*

CONSULTING SVCS, BUSINESS: Urban Planning & Consulting

Emersion Design LLC ....E....... 513 841-9100
Cincinnati *(G-3553)*
Flavik Village Development ....E....... 216 429-1182
Cleveland *(G-5605)*
Lorain Cnty Elderly Hsing Corp ....D....... 440 288-1600
Lorain *(G-13049)*
Northeast Ohio Areawide ....E....... 216 621-3055
Cleveland *(G-6153)*
Star County Home Consortium ....E....... 330 451-7395
Canton *(G-2538)*
Trumbull Housing Dev Corp ....D....... 330 369-1533
Warren *(G-18912)*

CONSULTING SVCS: Nuclear

Accelerant Technologies LLC ....D....... 419 236-8768
Genoa *(G-11374)*

CONSULTING SVCS: Physics

Central Ohio Primary Care ....E....... 614 882-0708
Westerville *(G-19381)*

CONSULTING SVCS: Psychological

Coleman Professional Svcs Inc ....B....... 330 673-1347
Kent *(G-12360)*
Psychology Consultants Inc ....E....... 330 764-7916
Medina *(G-14115)*

CONSULTING SVCS: Scientific

Centric Consulting LLC ....E....... 513 791-3061
Cincinnati *(G-3219)*
National Valuation Consultants ....E....... 513 929-4100
Cincinnati *(G-4143)*

CONSUMER BUYING SVCS

Best Upon Request Corp Inc ....D....... 513 605-7800
Cincinnati *(G-3102)*

CONSUMER CREDIT REPORTING BUREAU

Cbc Companies Inc ....D....... 614 538-6100
Columbus *(G-7214)*
Cbcinnovis International Inc ....E....... 614 222-4343
Columbus *(G-7215)*
Innovis Data Solutions Inc ....E....... 614 222-4343
Columbus *(G-7903)*

CONSUMER PURCHASING SVCS

Administrative Svcs Ohio Dept ....D....... 614 466-5090
Columbus *(G-6944)*

CONTAINERS: Cargo, Wood

Frankes Wood Products LLC ....E....... 937 642-0706
Marysville *(G-13620)*

CONTAINERS: Corrugated

Buckeye Boxes Inc ....E....... 614 274-8484
Columbus *(G-7156)*

Systems Pack Inc ....E....... 330 467-5729
Macedonia *(G-13211)*

CONTAINERS: Metal

Sabco Industries Inc ....E....... 419 531-5347
Toledo *(G-18169)*
Westrock CP LLC ....D....... 770 448-2193
Wshngtn CT Hs *(G-20038)*

CONTAINERS: Plastic

Hendrickson International Corp ....D....... 740 929-5600
Hebron *(G-11849)*
Ilpea Industries Inc ....C....... 330 562-2916
Aurora *(G-842)*

CONTAINERS: Shipping, Bombs, Metal Plate

Industrial Repair & Mfg Inc ....E....... 419 822-4232
Delta *(G-10159)*

CONTAINERS: Shipping, Wood

Frankes Wood Products LLC ....E....... 937 642-0706
Marysville *(G-13620)*

CONTAINMENT VESSELS: Reactor, Metal Plate

FSRc Tanks Inc ....E....... 234 221-2015
Bolivar *(G-1747)*

CONTRACTOR: Dredging

Metropolitan Envmtl Svcs Inc ....D....... 614 771-1881
Hilliard *(G-11930)*

CONTRACTOR: Framing

Castle Construction Co Inc ....E....... 419 289-1122
Ashland *(G-669)*
Dynamic Structures Inc ....E....... 330 892-0164
New Waterford *(G-15137)*
Metal Framing Enterprises LLC ....E....... 216 433-7080
Cleveland *(G-6032)*
Season Contractors Inc ....E....... 440 717-0188
Broadview Heights *(G-1891)*

CONTRACTOR: Rigging & Scaffolding

AM Industrial Group LLC ....E....... 216 433-7171
Brookpark *(G-1935)*
J R Mead Industrial Contrs ....E....... 614 891-4466
Galena *(G-11284)*
Janson Industries ....D....... 330 455-7029
Canton *(G-2417)*
Sws Equipment Services Inc ....E....... 330 806-2767
Akron *(G-470)*

CONTRACTORS: Access Control System Eqpt

Frontier Security LLC ....E....... 937 247-2824
Miamisburg *(G-14303)*
Northwestern Ohio SEC Systems ....E....... 419 227-1655
Lima *(G-12845)*
Yeck Brothers Company ....E....... 937 294-4000
Moraine *(G-14837)*

CONTRACTORS: Access Flooring System Installation

American Star Painting Co LLC ....E....... 740 373-5634
Marietta *(G-13432)*
Corporate Floors Inc ....E....... 216 475-3232
Cleveland *(G-5409)*
OK Interiors Corp ....C....... 513 742-3278
Cincinnati *(G-4217)*

CONTRACTORS: Acoustical & Ceiling Work

Century Contractors Inc ....E....... 440 232-2626
Cleveland *(G-5215)*
Certanteed Gyps Ciling Mfg Inc ....E....... 800 233-8990
Aurora *(G-835)*
Frank Novak & Sons Inc ....D....... 216 475-2495
Cleveland *(G-5632)*
OK Interiors Corp ....C....... 513 742-3278
Cincinnati *(G-4217)*
Republic/Construction ....E....... 330 747-1510
Youngstown *(G-20348)*

Sports Facility Acoustics Inc ....E....... 440 323-1400
Elyria *(G-10682)*
T and D Interiors Incorporated ....E....... 419 331-4372
Lima *(G-12897)*
Valley Acoustics Inc ....E....... 330 799-1894
Youngstown *(G-20401)*

CONTRACTORS: Acoustical & Insulation Work

Immaculate Interiors ....E....... 440 324-9300
Elyria *(G-10635)*
Omni Fireproofing Co LLC ....D....... 513 870-9115
West Chester *(G-19126)*
R E Kramig & Co Inc ....C....... 513 761-4010
Cincinnati *(G-4378)*

CONTRACTORS: Antenna Installation

Midwest Contracting Inc ....E....... 419 866-4560
Holland *(G-12037)*

CONTRACTORS: Artificial Turf Installation

Motz Group Inc ....E....... 513 533-6452
Cincinnati *(G-4123)*

CONTRACTORS: Asbestos Removal & Encapsulation

AAA Amrican Abatement Asb Corp ....D....... 216 281-9400
Cleveland *(G-4940)*
Allied Environmental Svcs Inc ....E....... 419 227-4004
Lima *(G-12739)*
Cardinal Environmental Svc Inc ....E....... 330 252-0220
Akron *(G-121)*
Central Insulation Systems Inc ....E....... 513 242-0600
Cincinnati *(G-3214)*
Daniel A Terreri & Sons Inc ....E....... 330 538-2950
Youngstown *(G-20165)*
Keen & Cross Envmtl Svcs Inc ....E....... 513 674-1700
Cincinnati *(G-3905)*
Lepi Enterprises Inc ....D....... 740 453-2980
Zanesville *(G-20495)*
Pedersen Insulation Company ....E....... 614 471-3788
Columbus *(G-8529)*
Precision Environmental Co ....B....... 216 642-6040
Independence *(G-12244)*
Priority 1 Construction Svcs ....E....... 513 922-0203
Cincinnati *(G-4332)*

CONTRACTORS: Asphalt

B G Trucking & Construction ....E....... 330 620-8734
Akron *(G-88)*
Barbicas Construction Co ....E....... 330 733-9101
Akron *(G-89)*
Brown County Asphalt Inc ....E....... 937 446-2481
Georgetown *(G-11387)*
Depuy Paving Inc ....E....... 614 272-0256
Columbus *(G-7509)*
Freisthler Paving Inc ....E....... 937 498-4802
Sidney *(G-16935)*
Geddis Paving & Excavating ....E....... 419 536-8501
Toledo *(G-17910)*
George Kuhn Enterprises Inc ....E....... 614 481-8838
Columbus *(G-7743)*
J K Enterprises Inc ....D....... 614 481-8838
Columbus *(G-7931)*
Jennite Co ....E....... 419 531-1791
Toledo *(G-17984)*
Lucas County Asphalt Inc ....E....... 419 476-0705
Toledo *(G-18016)*
Maintenance Systerms of N Ohio ....E....... 440 323-1291
Elyria *(G-10648)*
Miller Yount Paving Inc ....E....... 330 372-4408
Cortland *(G-9079)*
Morrow Gravel Company Inc ....C....... 513 771-0820
Cincinnati *(G-4120)*
Northstar Asphalt Inc ....E....... 330 497-0936
North Canton *(G-15358)*
Ohio Paving & Cnstr Co Inc ....E....... 440 975-8929
Willoughby *(G-19701)*
Pavement Protectors Inc ....E....... 614 875-9989
Grove City *(G-11590)*
Perrin Asphalt Co Inc ....D....... 330 253-1020
Akron *(G-386)*
Premier Asphalt Paving Co Inc ....E....... 440 237-6600
North Royalton *(G-15498)*
Prus Construction Company ....C....... 513 321-7774
Cincinnati *(G-4354)*

SERVICES SECTION

CONTRACTORS: Coating, Caulking & Weather, Water & Fire

Queen City Blacktop Company ....E 513 251-8400
  Cincinnati *(G-4362)*
S & K Asphalt & Concrete ....E 330 848-6284
  Akron *(G-422)*
Sheedy Paving Inc ....E 614 252-2111
  Columbus *(G-8724)*
Smalls Asphalt Paving Inc ....E 740 427-4096
  Gambier *(G-11350)*
Tallmadge Asphalt & Pav Co Inc ....D 330 677-0000
  Kent *(G-12399)*
Tri-Mor Corp ....C 330 963-3101
  Twinsburg *(G-18478)*
Wenger Asphalt Inc ....E 330 837-4767
  Dalton *(G-9243)*

CONTRACTORS: Awning Installation

Apco Aluminum Awning Co ....E 614 334-2726
  Columbus *(G-7026)*

CONTRACTORS: Banking Machine Installation & Svc

Diebold Incorporated ....C 330 588-3619
  Canton *(G-2340)*
Diebold Nixdorf Incorporated ....D 513 870-1400
  Hamilton *(G-11722)*

CONTRACTORS: Bathtub Refinishing

Sayles Company LLC ....E 614 801-0432
  Columbus *(G-8689)*
Thiels Replacement Systems Inc ....D 419 289-6139
  Ashland *(G-701)*

CONTRACTORS: Boiler Maintenance Contractor

Arise Incorporated ....E 440 746-8860
  Brecksville *(G-1814)*
Park Corporation ....B 216 267-4870
  Cleveland *(G-6234)*
Prout Boiler Htg & Wldg Inc ....E 330 744-0293
  Youngstown *(G-20331)*

CONTRACTORS: Boiler Setting

Nbw Inc ....E 216 377-1700
  Cleveland *(G-6114)*

CONTRACTORS: Bricklaying

Duer Construction Co Inc ....D 330 848-9930
  Akron *(G-202)*
Giambrone Masonry Inc ....D 216 475-1200
  Hudson *(G-12118)*
International Masonry Inc ....D 614 469-8338
  Columbus *(G-7917)*
Jess Hauer Masonry Inc ....E 513 521-2178
  Cincinnati *(G-3866)*
Kurzhals Inc ....E 513 941-4624
  Cincinnati *(G-3950)*
Medhurst Mason Contractors Inc ....C 440 543-8885
  Chagrin Falls *(G-2725)*

CONTRACTORS: Bridge Painting

Apbn Inc ....E 724 964-8252
  Campbell *(G-2138)*
Apostolos Group Inc ....D 330 670-9900
  Copley *(G-9052)*
Liberty Maintenance Inc ....D 330 755-7711
  Youngstown *(G-20255)*
Liberty-Alpha III JV ....E 330 755-7711
  Campbell *(G-2139)*
North Star Painting Co Inc ....E 330 743-2333
  Youngstown *(G-20302)*

CONTRACTORS: Building Board-up

Trak-1 Technology Inc ....E 513 204-5530
  Mason *(G-13772)*

CONTRACTORS: Building Eqpt & Machinery Installation

Allied Erct & Dismantling Co ....C 330 744-0808
  Youngstown *(G-20101)*
CTS Construction Inc ....D 513 489-8290
  Cincinnati *(G-3445)*
Nbw Inc ....E 216 377-1700
  Cleveland *(G-6114)*

North Bay Construction Inc ....E 440 835-1898
  Westlake *(G-19522)*
Schindler Elevator Corporation ....E 614 573-2777
  Columbus *(G-8694)*

CONTRACTORS: Building Fireproofing

Northwest Firestop Inc ....E 419 517-4777
  Toledo *(G-18093)*
Omni Fireproofing Co LLC ....D 513 870-9115
  West Chester *(G-19126)*
Thermal Solutions Inc ....D 740 886-2861
  Proctorville *(G-16362)*

CONTRACTORS: Building Sign Installation & Mntnce

Archer Corporation ....E 330 455-9995
  Canton *(G-2244)*
Brilliant Electric Sign Co Ltd ....D 216 741-3800
  Brooklyn Heights *(G-1911)*
Danite Holdings Ltd ....E 614 444-3333
  Columbus *(G-7488)*
Gus Holthaus Signs Inc ....E 513 861-0060
  Cincinnati *(G-3720)*
Identitek Systems Inc ....D 330 832-9844
  Massillon *(G-13822)*
Lighting Maint Harmon Sign ....D 419 841-6658
  Toledo *(G-18006)*
Palazzo Brothers Electric Inc ....E 419 668-1100
  Norwalk *(G-15587)*
United-Maier Signs Inc ....D 513 681-6600
  Cincinnati *(G-4743)*

CONTRACTORS: Building Site Preparation

Ground Penetrating Radar Sys ....E 419 843-9804
  Toledo *(G-17926)*
Rudzik Excavating Inc ....E 330 755-1540
  Struthers *(G-17534)*

CONTRACTORS: Cable Laying

South Shore Cable Cnstr Inc ....D 440 816-0033
  Cleveland *(G-6498)*
Universal Recovery Systems ....D 614 299-0184
  Columbus *(G-8907)*
Wachter Inc ....C 513 777-0701
  West Chester *(G-19243)*

CONTRACTORS: Cable Splicing Svcs

Buckeye Cable Systems Inc ....E 419 724-2539
  Toledo *(G-17787)*

CONTRACTORS: Cable TV Installation

Broadband Express Inc ....E 614 823-6464
  Westerville *(G-19288)*
Broadband Express LLC ....E 513 834-8085
  Cincinnati *(G-3136)*
Broadband Express LLC ....D 419 536-9127
  Toledo *(G-17783)*
Cable TV Services Inc ....C 440 816-0033
  Cleveland *(G-5170)*
Dss Installations Ltd ....E 513 761-7000
  Cincinnati *(G-3505)*
Precision Broadbnd Installatns ....C 614 523-2917
  Westerville *(G-19343)*
Primetech Communications Inc ....E 513 942-6000
  West Chester *(G-19132)*

CONTRACTORS: Caisson Drilling

Parks Drilling Company ....E 614 761-7707
  Dublin *(G-10422)*
Scherzinger Drilling Inc ....E 513 738-2000
  Harrison *(G-11808)*

CONTRACTORS: Carpentry Work

Airko Inc ....E 440 333-0133
  Cleveland *(G-4978)*
Brock & Associates Builders ....E 330 757-7150
  Youngstown *(G-20127)*
Combs Interior Specialties Inc ....D 937 879-2047
  Fairborn *(G-10787)*
Command Roofing Co ....C 937 298-1155
  Moraine *(G-14760)*
Competitive Interiors Inc ....C 330 297-1281
  Ravenna *(G-16378)*
Contract Lumber Inc ....C 740 964-3147
  Pataskala *(G-15921)*

Hgc Construction Co ....D 513 861-8866
  Cincinnati *(G-3759)*
J & B Equipment & Supply Inc ....D 419 884-1155
  Mansfield *(G-13314)*
Marous Brothers Cnstr Inc ....B 440 951-3904
  Willoughby *(G-19692)*
Mjr-Construction Co ....E 216 523-8050
  Cleveland *(G-6071)*
Ohio Builders Resources LLC ....E 614 865-0306
  Westerville *(G-19336)*
Overhead Door Co- Cincinnati ....C 513 346-4000
  West Chester *(G-19127)*
Premier Construction Company ....E 513 874-2611
  Fairfield *(G-10896)*
Riverside Cnstr Svcs Inc ....E 513 723-0900
  Cincinnati *(G-4427)*
Roger Kreps Drywall & Plst Inc ....D 330 726-6090
  Youngstown *(G-20355)*
Valley Acoustics Inc ....E 330 799-1894
  Youngstown *(G-20401)*
Woodpeckers Inc ....E 440 238-1824
  Strongsville *(G-17525)*

CONTRACTORS: Carpentry, Cabinet & Finish Work

Builders Firstsource Inc ....E 937 898-1358
  Vandalia *(G-18665)*
Casegoods Inc ....E 330 825-2461
  Barberton *(G-960)*
Countertop Alternatives Inc ....E 937 254-3334
  Dayton *(G-9430)*
Mammana Custom Woodworking Inc ...E 216 581-9059
  Maple Heights *(G-13410)*
Schlabach Wood Design Inc ....E 330 897-2600
  Baltic *(G-947)*

CONTRACTORS: Carpentry, Cabinet Building & Installation

Forum Manufacturing Inc ....E 937 349-8685
  Milford Center *(G-14576)*

CONTRACTORS: Carpet Laying

Dominguez Inc ....E 513 425-9955
  Middletown *(G-14424)*
Legacy Commercial Flooring Ltd ....B 614 476-1043
  Columbus *(G-8048)*
Patellas Floor Center Inc ....E 330 758-4099
  Youngstown *(G-20316)*
Progressive Flooring Svcs Inc ....E 614 868-9005
  Etna *(G-10738)*
Schoch Tile & Carpet Inc ....E 513 922-3466
  Cincinnati *(G-4484)*

CONTRACTORS: Chimney Construction & Maintenance

Able Company Ltd Partnership ....D 614 444-7663
  Columbus *(G-6926)*
Ray St Clair Roofing Inc ....E 513 874-1234
  Fairfield *(G-10898)*

CONTRACTORS: Closet Organizers, Installation & Design

Ptmj Enterprises ....C 440 543-8000
  Solon *(G-17042)*

CONTRACTORS: Coating, Caulking & Weather, Water & Fire

American Star Painting Co LLC ....E 740 373-5634
  Marietta *(G-13432)*
Capital Fire Protection Co ....E 614 279-9448
  Columbus *(G-7183)*
Central Fire Protection Co Inc ....E 937 322-0713
  Springfield *(G-17158)*
M T Golf Course Managment Inc .....E 513 923-1188
  Cincinnati *(G-4006)*
Midwest Industrial Supply Inc ....E 800 321-0699
  Toledo *(G-18061)*
OCP Contractors Inc ....E 419 865-7168
  Holland *(G-12043)*
Prime Polymers Inc ....E 330 662-4200
  Medina *(G-14113)*
Regency Roofing Companies Inc ....E 330 468-1021
  Macedonia *(G-13208)*

Employee Codes: A=Over 500 employees, B=251-500
C=101-250, D=51-100, E=25-50

CONTRACTORS: Commercial & Office Building

CONTRACTORS: Commercial & Office Building

Company		Phone
Abco Contracting LLC	E	419 973-4772
Toledo (G-17739)		
Al Neyer LLC	D	513 271-6400
Cincinnati (G-2981)		
Alvada Const Inc	C	419 595-4224
Alvada (G-568)		
Berlin Construction Ltd	E	330 893-2003
Millersburg (G-14587)		
Boyas Excavating Inc	E	216 524-3620
Cleveland (G-5131)		
Brenmar Construction Inc	D	740 286-2151
Jackson (G-12307)		
Cattrell Companies Inc	D	740 537-2481
Toronto (G-18336)		
Cleveland Construction Inc	E	440 255-8000
Mentor (G-14159)		
Cleveland Construction Inc	E	740 927-9000
Columbus (G-7298)		
Cleveland Construction Inc	E	440 255-8000
Mason (G-13685)		
Da Vinci Group Inc	E	614 419-2393
Reynoldsburg (G-16442)		
Delventhal Company	E	419 244-5570
Millbury (G-14578)		
Design Homes & Development Co	E	937 438-3667
Dayton (G-9499)		
Dotson Company	E	419 877-5176
Whitehouse (G-19585)		
Dugan & Meyers LLC	C	513 891-4300
Blue Ash (G-1581)		
Early Construction Co	E	740 894-4150
South Point (G-17085)		
Goliath Contracting Ltd	E	614 568-7878
Reynoldsburg (G-16455)		
Hammond Construction Inc	D	330 455-7039
Canton (G-2389)		
J&H Rnfrcing Strl Erectors Inc	C	740 355-0141
Portsmouth (G-16292)		
Kirila Contractors Inc	D	330 448-4055
Brookfield (G-1898)		
Kramer & Feldman Inc	E	513 821-7444
Cincinnati (G-3942)		
Link Construction Group Inc	E	937 292-7774
Bellefontaine (G-1385)		
Mel Lanzer Co	E	419 592-2801
Napoleon (G-14945)		
Muha Construction Inc	E	937 435-0678
Dayton (G-9760)		
Multicon Builders Inc	E	614 241-2070
Columbus (G-8206)		
Multicon Builders Inc	E	614 463-1142
Columbus (G-8207)		
N Cook Inc	E	513 275-9872
Cincinnati (G-4135)		
Ohio Maint & Renovation Inc	E	330 315-3101
Akron (G-367)		
Ohio Technical Services Inc	E	614 372-0829
Columbus (G-8450)		
Oswald Company Inc	E	513 745-4424
Cincinnati (G-4241)		
Palmetto Construction Svcs LLC		614 503-7150
Columbus (G-8512)		
Pivotek LLC	E	513 372-6205
West Chester (G-19128)		
Quandel Construction Group Inc	E	717 657-0909
Westerville (G-19439)		
Reece-Campbell Inc	D	513 542-4600
Cincinnati (G-4397)		
Registered Contractors Inc	E	440 205-0873
Mentor (G-14235)		
Rudolph/Libbe Companies Inc	A	419 241-5000
Walbridge (G-18778)		
Runyon & Sons Roofing Inc	D	440 974-6810
Mentor (G-14238)		
Snavely Building Company	E	440 585-9091
Chagrin Falls (G-2705)		
Stamm Contracting Co Inc	E	330 274-8230
Mantua (G-13395)		
Star Builders Inc	E	440 986-5951
Amherst (G-606)		
Stockmeister Enterprises Inc	E	740 286-1619
Jackson (G-12318)		
T Allen Inc	E	440 234-2366
Berea (G-1472)		
Watertown Steel Company LLC	E	740 749-3512
Waterford (G-18940)		
Williams Bros Builders Inc	E	440 365-3261
Elyria (G-10692)		
Winsupply Inc	D	937 294-5331
Moraine (G-14836)		
Wise Services Inc	E	937 854-0281
Dayton (G-10001)		
Xtreme Contracting Ltd	E	614 568-7030
Reynoldsburg (G-16492)		

CONTRACTORS: Communications Svcs

Company		Phone
Fine-Line Communications Inc	E	330 562-0731
Aurora (G-838)		
Gatesair Inc	E	513 459-3400
Mason (G-13704)		
Legrand North America LLC	B	937 224-0639
Moraine (G-14798)		
Legrand North America LLC	C	937 224-0639
Dayton (G-9676)		
Professional Telecom Svcs	E	513 232-7700
Cincinnati (G-4344)		
Telecom Expertise Inds Inc	D	937 548-5254
Greenville (G-11521)		
Telephone & Cmpt Contrs Inc	E	419 726-8142
Toledo (G-18215)		
US Communications and Elc Inc	D	440 519-0880
Cleveland (G-6676)		

CONTRACTORS: Computer Installation

Company		Phone
Advanced Service Tech LLC	E	937 435-4376
Miamisburg (G-14268)		
Dayton/Cncinnati Tech Svcs LLC	E	513 892-3940
Blue Ash (G-1575)		
Intercnnect Cbling Netwrk Svcs	E	440 891-0465
Berea (G-1461)		
Pomeroy It Solutions Sls Inc	E	440 717-1364
Brecksville (G-1842)		
Staley Inc	E	614 552-2333
Plain City (G-16207)		

CONTRACTORS: Concrete

Company		Phone
21st Century Con Cnstr Inc	E	216 362-0900
Cleveland (G-4925)		
Adleta Inc	E	513 554-1469
Cincinnati (G-2973)		
Aerodynamic Concrete & Cnstr	E	330 906-7477
Akron (G-23)		
Alan Stone Co Inc	E	740 448-1100
Cutler (G-9156)		
Atlas Construction Company	D	614 475-4705
Columbus (G-7070)		
B & D Concrete Footers Inc	E	740 964-2294
Etna (G-10731)		
Baker Concrete Cnstr Inc	A	513 539-4000
Monroe (G-14688)		
Berlin Contractors	E	330 893-2904
Berlin (G-1477)		
Bh Group LLC	D	513 671-3300
West Chester (G-19027)		
Ceco Concrete Cnstr Del LLC	E	734 455-3535
West Chester (G-19034)		
Ceco Concrete Cnstr Del LLC	D	513 874-6953
West Chester (G-19033)		
Cem-Base Inc	E	330 963-3101
Twinsburg (G-18399)		
Concrete Coring Company Inc	E	937 864-7325
Enon (G-10726)		
Cook Paving and Cnstr Co	E	216 267-7705
Independence (G-12201)		
Cornerstone Concrete Cnstr Inc	E	937 442-2805
Sardinia (G-16812)		
Donley Concrete Cutting	D	614 834-0300
Pickerington (G-16094)		
DOT Diamond Core Drilling Inc	E	440 322-6466
Elyria (G-10617)		
Dwyer Concrete Lifting Inc	E	614 501-0998
Groveport (G-11635)		
E&I Construction LLC	E	513 421-2045
Cincinnati (G-3525)		
Elastizell Systems Inc	E	937 298-1313
Moraine (G-14779)		
Engineered Con Structures Corp	E	216 520-2000
Cleveland (G-5540)		
Formwork Services LLC	E	513 539-4000
Monroe (G-14695)		
G Big Inc	E	740 867-5758
Chesapeake (G-2784)		
Gardner Cement Contractors	D	419 389-0768
Toledo (G-17909)		
Gironda Vito & Bros Inc	E	330 630-9399
Akron (G-236)		
H & R Concrete Inc	E	937 885-2910
Dayton (G-9594)		
Hanson Concrete Products Ohio	E	614 443-4846
Columbus (G-7800)		
Hovest Construction	E	419 456-3426
Ottawa (G-15798)		
Ivan Law Inc	E	330 533-5000
Youngstown (G-20238)		
Jostin Construction Inc	E	513 559-9390
Cincinnati (G-3889)		
Keim Concrete LLC	E	330 264-5313
Wooster (G-19877)		
L & I Custom Walls Inc	E	513 683-2045
Loveland (G-13137)		
Lavy Concrete Construction	E	937 606-4754
Covington (G-9137)		
Lithko Contracting LLC	E	513 564-2000
West Chester (G-19110)		
Lithko Contracting LLC	D	513 863-5100
Monroe (G-14703)		
Lockhart Concrete Co	D	330 745-6520
Akron (G-325)		
Mattlin Construction Inc	E	513 598-5402
Cleves (G-6804)		
Milcon Concrete Inc	E	937 339-6274
Troy (G-18366)		
Modern Day Concrete Cnstr	E	513 738-1026
Harrison (G-11806)		
Norris Brothers Co Inc	C	216 771-2233
Cleveland (G-6137)		
Northeast Concrete & Cnstr	E	614 898-5728
Westerville (G-19333)		
Ohio Paving Group LLC	E	216 475-1700
Cleveland (G-6193)		
Platform Cement Inc	E	440 602-9750
Mentor (G-14229)		
Quality Cement Inc	E	216 676-8838
Cleveland (G-6333)		
R W Sidley Incorporated	E	440 352-9343
Painesville (G-15875)		
Shelly and Sands Inc	E	614 444-5100
Columbus (G-8725)		
Shelly and Sands Inc	E	740 453-0721
Zanesville (G-20532)		
Shepherd Excavating Inc	D	614 889-1115
Dublin (G-10452)		
Spano Brothers Cnstr Co	E	330 645-1544
Akron (G-445)		
Spaulding Construction Co Inc	E	330 494-1776
Canton (G-2534)		
Spillman Company	E	614 444-2184
Columbus (G-8762)		
Staarmann Concrete Inc	E	513 756-9191
Hamilton (G-11774)		
Stamm Contracting Co Inc	E	330 274-8230
Mantua (G-13395)		
Standard Contg & Engrg Inc	D	440 243-1001
Brookpark (G-1955)		
Thompson Concrete Ltd	C	740 756-7256
Carroll (G-2609)		
Towne Construction Svcs LLC	C	513 561-3700
Batavia (G-1028)		
Triple Q Foundations Co Inc	E	513 932-3121
Lebanon (G-12654)		
Trucco Construction Co Inc	C	740 417-9010
Delaware (G-10130)		
Tscs Inc	E	419 644-3921
Metamora (G-14266)		
U S A Concrete Specialists	E	330 482-9150
Columbiana (G-6865)		
Vandra Bros Construction Inc	E	440 232-3030
Cleveland (G-6687)		
Wasiniak Construction Inc	D	419 668-8624
Norwalk (G-15596)		

CONTRACTORS: Concrete Pumping

Company		Phone
Akron Concrete Corp	E	330 864-1188
Akron (G-35)		
Foor Concrete Co Inc	D	740 513-4346
Delaware (G-10098)		
H & M Precision Concrete LLC	E	937 547-0012
Greenville (G-11508)		
Newcomer Concrete Services Inc	D	419 668-2789
Norwalk (G-15581)		
North Coast Concrete Inc	E	216 642-1114
Cleveland (G-6139)		
Phillips Companies	E	937 426-5461
Beavercreek Township (G-1280)		
Phillips Ready Mix Co	D	937 426-5151
Beavercreek Township (G-1281)		

SERVICES SECTION

CONTRACTORS: Electrical

Scioto-Darby Concrete Inc ....E....... 614 876-3114
  Hilliard *(G-11951)*
Signature Concrete Inc ....E....... 937 723-8435
  Dayton *(G-9884)*
Williams Concrete Cnstr Co Inc ....E....... 330 745-6388
  Norton *(G-15560)*

CONTRACTORS: Concrete Reinforcement Placing

Midwest Reinforcing Contrs ....E....... 937 390-8998
  Springfield *(G-17248)*

CONTRACTORS: Concrete Repair

Independence Excavating Inc ....E....... 216 524-1700
  Independence *(G-12218)*
Lithko Restoration Tech LLC ....D....... 513 863-5500
  Monroe *(G-14704)*
Lithko Restoration Tech LLC ....E....... 614 221-0711
  Columbus *(G-8072)*
Ohio Con Sawing & Drlg Inc ....E....... 419 841-1330
  Sylvania *(G-17603)*
Ohio Con Sawing & Drlg Inc ....E....... 614 252-1122
  Columbus *(G-8322)*
Prime Polymers Inc ....E....... 330 662-4200
  Medina *(G-14113)*
Suburban Maint & Cnstr Inc ....E....... 440 237-7765
  North Royalton *(G-15503)*

CONTRACTORS: Concrete Structure Coating, Plastic

Paulo Products Company ....E....... 440 942-0153
  Willoughby *(G-19703)*
Perrysburg Rsdntial Seal Cting ....E....... 419 872-7325
  Perrysburg *(G-16043)*
Systems Jay LLC Nanogate ....A....... 419 524-3778
  Mansfield *(G-13369)*

CONTRACTORS: Construction Caulking

American International Cnstr................E....... 440 243-5535
  Berea *(G-1445)*
Angelos Caulking & Sealants Co ....E....... 614 236-1350
  Columbus *(G-7020)*
BASF Construction Chem LLC ....E....... 216 831-5500
  Cleveland *(G-5098)*
Coon Caulking & Sealants Inc ....D....... 330 875-2100
  Louisville *(G-13098)*
Hummel Industries Incorporated ....E....... 513 242-1321
  Cincinnati *(G-3798)*
Terrafirm Construction LLC ....E....... 913 433-2998
  Columbus *(G-8832)*

CONTRACTORS: Construction Site Cleanup

Early Construction Co ....E....... 740 894-5150
  South Point *(G-17085)*
Extreme Detail Clg Cnstr Svcs ....E....... 419 392-3243
  Toledo *(G-17874)*
MRM Construction Inc ....E....... 740 388-0079
  Gallipolis *(G-11329)*

CONTRACTORS: Construction Site Metal Structure Coating

Bogie Industries Inc Ltd ....E....... 330 745-3105
  Akron *(G-106)*
Carpe Diem Industries LLC ....D....... 419 659-5639
  Columbus Grove *(G-9029)*
Carpe Diem Industries LLC ....E....... 419 358-0129
  Bluffton *(G-1729)*
Chemsteel Construction Company ....E....... 440 234-3930
  Middleburg Heights *(G-14379)*
L B Foster Company ....C....... 330 652-1461
  Mineral Ridge *(G-14637)*

CONTRACTORS: Core Drilling & Cutting

Barr Engineering Incorporated ....E....... 614 714-0299
  Columbus *(G-7091)*

CONTRACTORS: Countertop Installation

Countertop Alternatives Inc ....E....... 937 254-3334
  Dayton *(G-9430)*
Modlich Stoneworks Inc ....E....... 614 276-2848
  Columbus *(G-8181)*

CONTRACTORS: Demolition, Building & Other Structures

B & B Wrecking & Excvtg Inc ....E....... 216 429-1700
  Cleveland *(G-5089)*
C & J Contractors Inc ....E....... 216 391-5700
  Cleveland *(G-5167)*
Daniel A Terreri & Sons Inc ....E....... 330 538-2950
  Youngstown *(G-20165)*
Eslich Wrecking Company ....E....... 330 488-8300
  Louisville *(G-13101)*
Independence Excavating Inc ....E....... 216 524-1700
  Independence *(G-12218)*
JS Paris Excavating Inc ....E....... 330 538-3048
  North Jackson *(G-15382)*
Marucci and Gaffney Excvtg Co ....E....... 330 743-8170
  Youngstown *(G-20273)*
Miller Brothers Cnstr Dem LLC ....E....... 513 257-1082
  Oxford *(G-15824)*
ORourke Wrecking Company ....D....... 513 871-1400
  Cincinnati *(G-4235)*
S G Loewendick and Sons Inc ....E....... 614 539-2582
  Grove City *(G-11594)*
Sidwell Materials Inc ....C....... 740 849-2394
  Zanesville *(G-20533)*

CONTRACTORS: Diamond Drilling & Sawing

Curtiss-Wright Flow Control ....D....... 513 735-2538
  Batavia *(G-1008)*
Curtiss-Wright Flow Control ....D....... 513 528-7900
  Cincinnati *(G-2909)*
Safety Grooving & Grinding LP ....E....... 419 592-8666
  Napoleon *(G-14950)*

CONTRACTORS: Directional Oil & Gas Well Drilling Svc

Warren Drilling Co Inc ....C....... 740 783-2775
  Dexter City *(G-10171)*

CONTRACTORS: Drapery Track Installation

Style-Line Incorporated ....E....... 614 291-0600
  Columbus *(G-8798)*

CONTRACTORS: Driveway

American Coatings Corporation ....E....... 614 335-1000
  Plain City *(G-16181)*
Cox Paving Inc ....D....... 937 780-3075
  Wshngtn CT Hs *(G-20018)*
Image Pavement Maintenance ....E....... 937 833-9200
  Brookville *(G-1963)*

CONTRACTORS: Drywall

Anstine Drywall Inc ....E....... 330 784-3867
  Akron *(G-77)*
Apex Interiors Inc ....E....... 330 327-2226
  Avon *(G-875)*
Architectural Intr Restoration ....E....... 216 241-2255
  Cleveland *(G-5065)*
Blackstar Drywall Inc ....E....... 614 242-4242
  Sunbury *(G-17550)*
Cincinnati Drywall Inc ....E....... 513 321-7322
  Cincinnati *(G-3299)*
Clubhouse Pub N Grub ....E....... 440 884-2582
  Cleveland *(G-5368)*
Columbus Drywall & Insulation ....D....... 614 257-0257
  Columbus *(G-7347)*
Columbus Drywall Inc ....E....... 614 257-0257
  Columbus *(G-7348)*
Compass Construction Inc ....D....... 614 761-7800
  Dublin *(G-10305)*
Competitive Interiors Inc ....C....... 330 297-1281
  Ravenna *(G-16376)*
Construction Systems Inc ....E....... 614 252-0708
  Columbus *(G-7425)*
Dayton Walls & Ceilings Inc ....D....... 937 277-0531
  Dayton *(G-9494)*
Fairfield Insul & Drywall Inc ....E....... 740 654-8811
  Lancaster *(G-12536)*
Giorgi of Chesapeake Inc ....E....... 740 256-1724
  Crown City *(G-9155)*
Halker Drywall Inc ....E....... 419 646-3679
  Columbus Grove *(G-9030)*
Hughes & Knollman Construction ....E....... 614 237-6167
  Columbus *(G-7862)*
Integrity Wall & Ceiling Inc ....E....... 419 381-1855
  Toledo *(G-17976)*
Knollman Construction LLC ....C....... 614 841-0130
  Columbus *(G-8004)*
Kreps Ron Drywall & Plst Co ....E....... 330 726-8252
  Youngstown *(G-20250)*
Larry L Minges ....E....... 513 738-4901
  Hamilton *(G-11752)*
M & S Drywall Inc ....E....... 513 738-1510
  Harrison *(G-11805)*
Newark Drywall Inc ....E....... 740 763-3572
  Nashport *(G-14952)*
OCP Contractors Inc ....E....... 419 865-7168
  Holland *(G-12043)*
Porter Drywall Inc ....D....... 614 890-2111
  Westerville *(G-19437)*
Roger Kreps Drywall & Plst Inc ....D....... 330 726-6090
  Youngstown *(G-20355)*
Roricks Inc ....E....... 330 497-6888
  Canton *(G-2516)*
Valley Interior Systems Inc ....E....... 937 890-7319
  Dayton *(G-9961)*
Valley Interior Systems Inc ....B....... 513 961-0400
  Cincinnati *(G-4801)*
Valley Interior Systems Inc ....C....... 614 351-8440
  Columbus *(G-8930)*

CONTRACTORS: Earthmoving

Jack Conie & Sons Corp ....D....... 614 291-5931
  Columbus *(G-7933)*

CONTRACTORS: Electric Power Systems

Dovetail Construction Co Inc ....E....... 740 592-1800
  Cleveland *(G-5508)*

CONTRACTORS: Electrical

Acpi Systems Inc ....E....... 513 738-3840
  Cincinnati *(G-2968)*
AE Electric Inc ....E....... 419 392-8468
  Grand Rapids *(G-11448)*
Aetna Building Maintenance Inc ....B....... 614 476-1818
  Columbus *(G-6953)*
Akron Foundry Co ....E....... 330 745-3101
  Barberton *(G-950)*
Allcan Global Services Inc ....E....... 513 825-1655
  Cincinnati *(G-2987)*
American Electric Power Co Inc ....E....... 740 829-4129
  Conesville *(G-9035)*
American Electric Power Co Inc ....E....... 419 998-5106
  Lima *(G-12740)*
American Electric Power Co Inc ....E....... 614 856-2750
  Columbus *(G-6987)*
American Electric Power Co Inc ....E....... 740 295-3070
  Coshocton *(G-9087)*
AMS Construction Inc ....C....... 513 398-6689
  Maineville *(G-13240)*
AMS Construction Inc ....E....... 513 794-0410
  Loveland *(G-13110)*
Apollo Heating and AC Inc ....E....... 513 271-3600
  Cincinnati *(G-3036)*
Atlas Industrial Contrs LLC ....B....... 614 841-4500
  Columbus *(G-7072)*
Bay Mechanical & Elec Corp ....D....... 440 282-6816
  Lorain *(G-13017)*
Buckeye Cable Systems Inc ....E....... 419 724-2539
  Toledo *(G-17787)*
Cincinnati Voice and Data ....D....... 513 683-4127
  Loveland *(G-13115)*
Colgan-Davis Inc ....E....... 419 893-6116
  Maumee *(G-13895)*
Copp Systems Inc ....E....... 937 228-4188
  Dayton *(G-9427)*
CTS Construction Inc ....D....... 513 489-8290
  Cincinnati *(G-3445)*
Davis H Elliot Cnstr Co Inc ....C....... 937 847-8025
  Miamisburg *(G-14293)*
Dynamic Currents Corp ....E....... 419 861-2036
  Holland *(G-12023)*
Excel Electrical Contractor ....E....... 740 965-3795
  Worthington *(G-19959)*
Fishel Company ....E....... 614 850-4400
  Columbus *(G-7669)*
General Electric Company ....D....... 330 256-5331
  Cuyahoga Falls *(G-9192)*
General Electric Company ....E....... 614 527-1078
  Hilliard *(G-11902)*
General Electric Company ....C....... 513 583-3500
  Cincinnati *(G-3669)*
Helm and Associates Inc ....E....... 419 893-1480
  Maumee *(G-13924)*

Employee Codes: A=Over 500 employees, B=251-500
C=101-250, D=51-100, E=25-50

CONTRACTORS: Electrical

Horizon Mechanical and Elec ....E....... 419 529-2738
   Mansfield (G-13309)
Ies Infrstrcture Solutions LLC 330 830-3500
   Massillon (G-13823)
Industrial Power Systems Inc ....C....... 419 531-3121
   Rossford (G-16608)
Insight Communications of Co ....C....... 614 236-1200
   Columbus (G-7905)
Interstate Fire & SEC Systems ....E....... 330 453-9495
   Canton (G-2414)
John A Becker Co 614 272-8800
   Columbus (G-7942)
Kastle Technologies Co LLC ....E....... 513 360-2901
   Monroe (G-14702)
Kastle Technologies Co LLC ....E....... 614 433-9860
   Columbus (G-7968)
Lake Horry Electric ....D....... 440 808-8791
   Chagrin Falls (G-2702)
Lippincott Plumbing-Heating AC ....E....... 419 222-0856
   Lima (G-12829)
M & L Electric Inc 937 833-5154
   Lewisburg (G-12712)
Nationwide Energy Partners LLC ....E....... 614 918-2031
   Columbus (G-8240)
North Electric Inc ....E....... 216 331-4141
   Cleveland (G-6140)
Northwest Electrical Contg Inc ....E....... 419 865-4757
   Holland (G-12041)
O D Miller Electric Co Inc ....E....... 330 875-1651
   Louisville (G-13103)
Ohio Power Company 888 216-3523
   Canton (G-2483)
Ohio Power Company ....E....... 419 443-4634
   Tiffin (G-17691)
RJ Runge Company Inc ....E....... 419 740-5781
   Port Clinton (G-16253)
Rmf Nooter Inc ....D....... 419 727-1970
   Toledo (G-18159)
Robinson Htg Air-Conditioning ....E....... 513 422-6812
   Middletown (G-14455)
Saturn Electric Inc ....E....... 937 278-2580
   Dayton (G-9868)
Schneder Elc Bldngs Amrcas Inc ....D....... 513 398-9800
   Lebanon (G-12644)
Shawntech Communications Inc ....E....... 937 898-4900
   Miamisburg (G-14350)
Southtown Heating & Cooling ....E....... 937 320-9900
   Moraine (G-14827)
Star Dist & Manufacturring LLC ....D....... 513 860-3573
   West Chester (G-19231)
Sunpro Inc ....D....... 330 966-0910
   North Canton (G-15270)
Superior Group ....C....... 614 488-8035
   Columbus (G-8805)
T & B Electric Ltd ....E....... 740 881-5696
   Ostrander (G-15795)
Timmerman John P Heating AC Co .....E....... 419 229-4015
   Lima (G-12900)
Vaughn Industries LLC ....E....... 740 548-7100
   Lewis Center (G-12710)
Zender Electric ....E....... 419 436-1538
   Fostoria (G-11143)
Zenith Systems LLC ....C....... 216 587-9510
   Cleveland (G-6783)
Zenith Systems LLC ....B....... 216 406-7916
   Atwater (G-823)

CONTRACTORS: Electronic Controls Installation

Controls Inc ....E....... 330 239-4345
   Medina (G-14051)
Delta Electrical Contrs Ltd ....E....... 513 421-7744
   Cincinnati (G-3483)
Industrial Comm & Sound Inc ....E....... 614 276-8123
   Cincinnati (G-3816)

CONTRACTORS: Energy Management Control

Hoskins International LLC ....E....... 419 628-6015
   Minster (G-14664)
Mc Phillips Plbng Htg & AC Co ....E....... 216 481-1400
   Cleveland (G-6000)
Siemens Energy Inc ....B....... 740 393-8897
   Mount Vernon (G-14923)

CONTRACTORS: Epoxy Application

Flow-Liner Systems Ltd ....E....... 800 348-0020
   Zanesville (G-20478)

Ohio Concrete Resurfacing Inc ....E....... 440 786-9100
   Bedford (G-1326)

CONTRACTORS: Erection & Dismantling, Poured Concrete Forms

Ceco Concrete Cnstr Del LLC ....D....... 513 874-6953
   West Chester (G-19033)
Ceco Concrete Cnstr Del LLC ....E....... 734 455-3535
   West Chester (G-19034)
Stachler Concrete Inc ....E....... 419 678-3867
   Saint Henry (G-16667)

CONTRACTORS: Excavating

Allard Excavation LLC ....D....... 740 778-2242
   South Webster (G-17102)
Anderzack-Pitzen Cnstr Inc ....E....... 419 553-7015
   Metamora (G-14265)
Bansal Construction Inc 513 874-5410
   Fairfield (G-10822)
Bontrager Excavating Co Inc ....E....... 330 499-8775
   Uniontown (G-18508)
Boyas Excavating Inc 216 524-3620
   Cleveland (G-5131)
Brunk Excavating Inc 513 360-0308
   Monroe (G-14691)
Burkhart Excavating Inc ....E....... 740 896-3312
   Lowell (G-13167)
C & J Contractors Inc ....E....... 216 391-5700
   Cleveland (G-5167)
Camargo Construction Company ....E....... 513 248-1500
   Cincinnati (G-3168)
Charles F Jergens Cnstr Inc ....E....... 937 233-1830
   Dayton (G-9399)
Charles Jergens Contractor ....E....... 937 233-1830
   Dayton (G-9400)
D B Bentley Inc ....E....... 440 352-8495
   Painesville (G-15849)
Dave Sugar Excavating LLC ....E....... 330 542-1100
   Petersburg (G-16081)
Digioia/Suburban Excvtg LLC ....D....... 440 237-1978
   North Royalton (G-15487)
Don Wartko Construction Co ....D....... 330 673-5252
   Kent (G-12366)
Elite Excavating Company Inc ....E....... 419 683-4200
   Mansfield (G-13297)
Eslich Wrecking Company ....E....... 330 488-8300
   Louisville (G-13101)
Fishel Company ....C....... 937 233-2268
   Dayton (G-9551)
Ford Development Corp ....D....... 513 772-1521
   Cincinnati (G-3637)
Geddis Paving & Excavating ....E....... 419 536-8501
   Toledo (G-17910)
Geotex Construction Svcs Inc ....E....... 614 444-5690
   Columbus (G-7745)
GMC Excavation & Trucking ....E....... 419 468-0121
   Galion (G-11300)
Goettle Holding Company Inc ....C....... 513 825-8100
   Cincinnati (G-3683)
Ground Tech Inc ....E....... 330 270-0700
   Youngstown (G-20210)
H & R Concrete Inc ....E....... 937 885-2910
   Dayton (G-9594)
Hardrock Excavating LLC ....D....... 330 792-9524
   Youngstown (G-20212)
Independence Excavating Inc ....E....... 216 524-1700
   Independence (G-12218)
Indian Nation Inc ....E....... 740 532-6143
   North Canton (G-15345)
John F Gallagher Plumbing Co ....E....... 440 946-4256
   Eastlake (G-10547)
JS Bova Excavating LLC ....E....... 234 254-4040
   Struthers (G-17532)
Kelchner Inc ....C....... 937 704-9890
   Springboro (G-17125)
Law Excavating Inc ....E....... 740 745-3420
   Saint Louisville (G-16669)
Layton Inc ....E....... 740 349-7101
   Newark (G-15182)
Layton Trucking Inc ....E....... 740 366-1447
   Newark (G-15183)
Luburgh Inc ....E....... 740 452-3668
   Zanesville (G-20498)
Menke Bros Construction Co ....E....... 419 286-2086
   Delphos (G-10147)
Metropolitan Envmtl Svcs Inc ....D....... 614 771-1881
   Hilliard (G-11930)
Mike Enyart & Sons Inc ....D....... 740 523-0235
   South Point (G-17095)

Mike George Excavating ....E....... 419 855-4147
   Genoa (G-11382)
Mike Pusateri Excavating Inc ....E....... 330 385-5221
   East Liverpool (G-10525)
Miller Yount Paving Inc ....E....... 330 372-4408
   Cortland (G-9079)
Modern Poured Walls Inc ....E....... 440 647-6661
   Wellington (G-18994)
Nelson Stark Company ....C....... 513 489-0866
   Cincinnati (G-4154)
Ohio Heavy Equipment Lsg LLC ....E....... 513 965-6600
   Fairfield (G-10888)
Osborne Co ....E....... 440 942-7000
   Mentor (G-14226)
Phillips Ready Mix Co ....D....... 937 426-5151
   Beavercreek Township (G-1281)
Rack & Ballauer Excvtg Co Inc ....E....... 513 738-7000
   Hamilton (G-11766)
Ray Bertolini Trucking Co ....E....... 330 867-0666
   Akron (G-405)
Rbm Environmental and Cnstr ....E....... 419 693-5840
   Oregon (G-15748)
S E T Inc ....E....... 330 536-6724
   Lowellville (G-13174)
Schumm Richard A Plbg & Htg ....E....... 419 238-4994
   Van Wert (G-18643)
Siler Excavation Services ....E....... 513 400-8628
   Milford (G-14563)
Sisler Heating & Cooling Inc ....E....... 330 722-7101
   Medina (G-14126)
Spano Brothers Cnstr Co ....E....... 330 645-1544
   Akron (G-445)
Stahlheber & Sons Inc ....E....... 513 726-4446
   Hamilton (G-11775)
Standard Contg & Engrg Inc ....D....... 440 243-1001
   Brookpark (G-1955)
Star-Ex Inc ....E....... 937 473-2397
   Covington (G-9139)
Stonegate Construction Inc ....D....... 740 423-9170
   Belpre (G-1444)
Sws Environmental Services ....E....... 254 629-1718
   Findlay (G-11089)
Todd Alspaugh & Associates ....E....... 419 476-8126
   Toledo (G-18224)
Trimat Construction Inc ....E....... 740 388-9515
   Bidwell (G-1496)
Utter Construction Inc ....C....... 513 876-2246
   Bethel (G-1484)
Vandalia Blacktop Seal Coating ....E....... 937 454-0571
   Dayton (G-9965)

CONTRACTORS: Exterior Concrete Stucco

Reitter Stucco Inc ....E....... 614 291-2212
   Columbus (G-8609)
Reitter Wall Systems Inc ....D....... 614 545-4444
   Columbus (G-8610)

CONTRACTORS: Exterior Painting

Mrap LLC ....E....... 614 545-3190
   Columbus (G-8202)
Reilly Painting Co ....E....... 216 371-8160
   Cleveland Heights (G-6796)
Rl Painting and Mfg Inc ....E....... 937 968-5526
   Union City (G-18503)

CONTRACTORS: Fence Construction

Allied Builders Inc ....E....... 937 226-0311
   Dayton (G-9316)
Deerfield Farms ....E....... 330 584-4715
   Deerfield (G-10018)
Mills Fence Co Inc ....E....... 513 631-0333
   Cincinnati (G-4100)
Security Fence Group Inc ....E....... 513 681-3700
   Cincinnati (G-4489)
Southway Fence Company ....E....... 330 477-5251
   Canton (G-2533)

CONTRACTORS: Fiber Optic Cable Installation

Elect General Contractors Inc ....E....... 740 420-3437
   Circleville (G-4888)
Newcome Corp ....E....... 614 848-5688
   Columbus (G-6897)
Taylor Telecommunications Inc ....D....... 330 628-5501
   Mogadore (G-14685)
Universal Recovery Systems ....D....... 614 299-0184
   Columbus (G-8907)

SERVICES SECTION

CONTRACTORS: Fire Detection & Burglar Alarm Systems

Company	Code	Phone
ABC Fire Inc — North Royalton (G-15480)	E	440 237-6677
D B A Inc — Cincinnati (G-3454)	E	513 541-6600
GA Business Purchaser LLC — Toledo (G-17905)	D	419 255-8400
Gene Ptacek Son Fire Eqp Inc — Cleveland (G-5666)	E	216 651-8300
Gillmore Security Systems Inc — Cleveland (G-5672)	E	440 232-1000
Koorsen Fire & Security Inc — Vandalia (G-18687)	E	937 324-9405
Megacity Fire Protection Inc — Dayton (G-9717)	E	937 335-0775
Paladin Protective Systems Inc — Cleveland (G-6229)	E	216 441-6500
Protech Security Inc — Canton (G-2496)	E	330 499-3555
Research & Investigation Assoc — Mansfield (G-13355)	E	419 526-1299
Simplex Time Recorder LLC — West Chester (G-19154)	E	800 746-7539
Southeast Security Corporation — Sharon Center (G-16879)	E	330 239-4600
State Alarm Inc — Youngstown (G-20382)	E	330 726-8111
Vector Security Inc — Geneva (G-11372)	E	440 466-7233
Vector Security Inc — Boardman (G-1745)	E	330 726-9841

CONTRACTORS: Fire Sprinkler System Installation Svcs

Company	Code	Phone
ABC Fire Inc — North Royalton (G-15480)	E	440 237-6677
Fire Guard LLC — Sunbury (G-17556)	E	740 625-5181
Johnson Controls — West Chester (G-19098)	D	513 874-1227
Johnson Controls — Dublin (G-10381)	D	614 602-2000
Johnson Controls — Dublin (G-10382)	D	614 717-9079
Mac Mechanical Corporation — Cleveland (G-5962)	E	216 531-0444
Vulcan Enterprises Inc — Carey (G-2600)	E	419 396-3535

CONTRACTORS: Floor Laying & Other Floor Work

Company	Code	Phone
Andover Floor Covering — Newbury (G-15254)	E	440 293-5339
Bcf LLC — Miamisburg (G-14274)	E	937 746-0721
Centimark Corporation — Stow (G-17356)	C	330 920-3560
Clays Heritage Carpet Inc — Canton (G-2312)	E	330 497-1280
Cleveland Construction Inc — Mentor (G-14159)	E	440 255-8000
Cleveland Construction Inc — Columbus (G-7298)	E	740 927-9000
Command Carpet — Kent (G-12361)	D	330 673-7404
Company Inc — Cleveland (G-5387)	E	216 431-2334
Done-Rite Bowling Service Co — Bedford (G-1304)	E	440 232-3280
Florline Group Inc — Massillon (G-13808)	E	330 030-3380
JD Music Tile Co — Circleville (G-4892)	E	740 420-9611
Marble Restoration Inc — Maumee (G-13939)	D	419 865-9000
OCP Contractors Inc — Holland (G-12043)	E	419 865-7168
Preferred Acquisition Co LLC — Cleveland (G-6298)	D	216 587-0957
Prime Polymers Inc — Medina (G-14113)	E	330 662-4200
PTX Flooring Inc — Toledo (G-18143)	E	419 726-1775
Regal Carpet Center Inc — Cleveland (G-6366)	E	216 475-1844
Rite Rug Co — Westerville (G-19350)	E	614 882-4322
Rite Rug Co — West Chester (G-19225)	E	513 942-0010
Rite Rug Co — Fairborn (G-10803)	E	937 318-9197
Samron Inc — Youngstown (G-20366)	E	330 782-6539
Stedman Floor Co Inc — Groveport (G-11674)	E	614 836-3190
T and D Interiors Incorporated — Lima (G-12897)	E	419 331-4372
Tremco Incorporated — Beachwood (G-1133)	B	216 292-5000
W R Shepherd Inc — Powell (G-16353)	E	614 889-2896
Weiffenbach Marble & Tile Co — Englewood (G-10724)	E	937 832-7055

CONTRACTORS: Flooring

Company	Code	Phone
Technical Construction Spc — Cuyahoga Falls (G-9224)	E	330 929-1088

CONTRACTORS: Food Concessions

Company	Code	Phone
Lobby Shoppes Inc — Springfield (G-17223)	C	937 324-0002
Swim Incorporated — Worthington (G-20002)	E	614 885-1619

CONTRACTORS: Food Svcs Eqpt Installation

Company	Code	Phone
Kens Beverage Inc — Fairfield (G-10869)	E	513 874-8200

CONTRACTORS: Foundation & Footing

Company	Code	Phone
Arledge Construction Inc — Columbus (G-7041)	E	614 732-4258
Central Ohio Poured Walls Inc — Dublin (G-10285)	E	614 889-0505
Cleveland Concrete Cnstr Inc — Brooklyn Heights (G-1913)	D	216 741-3954
Day Precision Wall Inc — Cleves (G-6798)	E	513 353-2999
Gateway Concrete Forming Svcs — Miamitown (G-14371)	D	513 353-2000
Goettle Holding Company Inc — Cincinnati (G-3683)	C	513 825-8100
Halcomb Concrete Construction — Fairfield (G-10856)	E	513 829-3576
Hayes Concrete Construction — Cincinnati (G-3742)	E	513 648-9400
Hoyer Poured Walls Inc — Marysville (G-13628)	E	937 642-6148
J & D Home Improvement Inc — Reynoldsburg (G-16459)	D	740 927-0722
Lithko Contracting LLC — Plain City (G-16196)	C	614 733-0300
Menke Bros Construction Co — Delphos (G-10147)	E	419 286-2086
Metcon Ltd — Bradford (G-1807)	E	937 447-9200
Modern Poured Walls Inc — Wellington (G-18994)	D	440 647-6661
Sowder Concrete Corporation — Dayton (G-9893)	E	937 890-1633

CONTRACTORS: Foundation Building

Company	Code	Phone
J & D Home Improvement Inc — Reynoldsburg (G-16459)	D	740 927-0722
Mural & Son Inc — Cleveland (G-6090)	E	216 267-3322
Ohio State Home Services Inc — Hilliard (G-11940)	D	614 850-5600

CONTRACTORS: Fountain Installation

Company	Code	Phone
Lawn Management Sprinkler Co — Cincinnati (G-3964)	E	513 272-3808

CONTRACTORS: Garage Doors

Company	Code	Phone
Dortronic Service Inc — Cleveland (G-5506)	E	216 739-3667
Garage Door Systems LLC — West Chester (G-19204)	C	513 321-9600
Graf and Sons Inc — Columbus (G-7765)	E	614 481-2020
Nofziger Door Sales Inc — Wauseon (G-18960)	E	419 337-9900
Overhead Inc — Toledo (G-18113)	E	419 476-7811

CONTRACTORS: Gas Field Svcs, NEC

Company	Code	Phone
Clearfield Ohio Holdings Inc — Waverly (G-18969)	D	740 947-5121
Stingray Pressure Pumping LLC — Belmont (G-1430)	E	405 648-4177

CONTRACTORS: General Electric

Company	Code	Phone
A J Goulder Electric Co — Willoughby (G-19640)	E	440 942-4026
Abbott Electric — Canton (G-2222)	D	330 452-6601
Accurate Electric Cnstr Inc — Reynoldsburg (G-16424)	C	614 863-1844
Aero Electrical Contractors — Canal Winchester (G-2152)	E	614 834-8181
Aey Electric Inc — Youngstown (G-20099)	E	330 792-5745
All Phase Power and Ltg Inc — Sandusky (G-16725)	E	419 624-9640
American Electric Power Co Inc — Columbus (G-6989)	E	614 716-1000
Archiable Electric Company — Cincinnati (G-3043)	D	513 621-1307
Area Energy & Electric Inc — Marysville (G-13606)	E	937 642-0386
Area Energy & Electric Inc — Sidney (G-16913)	C	937 498-4784
Atkins & Stang Inc — Cincinnati (G-3057)	D	513 242-8300
Atlas Electrical Construction — Elyria (G-10595)	E	440 323-5418
B & J Electrical Company Inc — Cincinnati (G-3072)	E	513 351-7100
Bansal Construction Inc — Fairfield (G-10822)	E	513 874-5410
Banta Electrical Contrs Inc — Cleves (G-6797)	D	513 353-4446
BCU Electric Inc — Ashland (G-663)	E	419 281-8944
Beacon Electric Company — Cincinnati (G-3087)	D	513 851-0711
Becdel Controls Incorporated — Niles (G-15284)	E	330 652-1386
Benevento Enterprises Inc — Cleveland (G-5114)	D	216 621-5890
Berwick Electric Company — Canal Winchester (G-2153)	E	614 834-2301
Biz Com Electric Inc — Cincinnati (G-3110)	E	513 961-7200
Bodie Electric Inc — Fostoria (G-11123)	E	419 435-3672
Bp-Ls-Pt Co — Columbus (G-7128)	D	614 841-4500
Brennan Electric LLC — Miamitown (G-14370)	E	513 353-2229
Bryan Electric Inc — Saint Clairsville (G-16630)	E	740 695-9834
Busy Bee Electric Inc — Hooven (G-12076)	E	513 353-3553
Butchko Electric Inc — Amherst (G-589)	E	440 985-3180
Capital City Electric LLC — New Albany (G-14978)	E	614 933-8700
Carey Electric Co — Vandalia (G-18667)	E	937 669-3399
Cattrell Companies Inc — Toronto (G-18336)	D	740 537-2481
Chapel Electric Co LLC — Dayton (G-9397)	E	937 222-2290
Claypool Electric Inc — Lancaster (G-12519)	C	740 653-5683
Cochran Electric Inc — Powell (G-16329)	E	614 847-0035
Commercial Electric Pdts Corp — Cleveland (G-5376)	E	216 241-2886
Converse Electric Inc — Grove City (G-11549)	D	614 808-4377
Corporate Electric Company LLC — Barberton (G-962)	E	330 331-7517
Countryside Electric Inc — Columbus (G-7450)	E	614 478-7960
Craftsman Electric Inc — Cincinnati (G-3437)	D	513 891-4426
D C Minnick Contracting Ltd — Springfield (G-17186)	E	937 322-1012
D E Williams Electric Inc — Chagrin Falls (G-2695)	E	440 543-1222

Employee Codes: A=Over 500 employees, B=251-500, C=101-250, D=51-100, E=25-50

Darana Hybrid Inc ....D 513 785-7540
Hamilton (G-11720)
Davis Pickering & Company Inc ....D 740 373-5896
Marietta (G-13441)
Denier Electric Co Inc ....C 513 738-2641
Harrison (G-11796)
Denier Electric Co Inc ....E 614 338-4664
Grove City (G-11553)
DIA Electric Inc ....E 513 281-0783
Cincinnati (G-3488)
Dillard Electric Inc ....E 937 836-5381
Union (G-18498)
Dynalectric Company ....E 614 529-7500
Columbus (G-7555)
Dynamic Mechanical Systems ....E 513 858-6722
Fairfield (G-10843)
E S I Inc ....D 513 454-3741
West Chester (G-19195)
Eco Engineering Inc ....D 513 985-8300
Cincinnati (G-3543)
Efficient Electric Corp ....E 614 552-0200
Columbus (G-7587)
Electric Connection Inc ....D 614 436-1121
Westerville (G-19397)
Electrical Corp America Inc ....D 440 245-3007
Lorain (G-13038)
Enertech Electrical Inc ....E 330 536-2131
Lowellville (G-13171)
Erb Electric Co ....C 740 633-5055
Bridgeport (G-1862)
Fishel Company ....D 614 274-8100
Columbus (G-7667)
Fowler Electric Co ....D 440 735-2385
Bedford (G-1307)
Frey Electric Inc ....D 513 385-0700
Cincinnati (G-3653)
Garber Electrical Contrs Inc ....D 937 771-5202
Englewood (G-10704)
Gateway Electric Incorporated ....C 216 518-5500
Cleveland (G-5657)
Gem Electric ....E 440 286-6200
Chardon (G-2751)
Gem Industrial Inc ....D 419 467-3287
Walbridge (G-18775)
Goodin Electric Inc ....E 740 522-3113
Newark (G-15171)
Gorjanc Comfort Services Inc ....E 440 449-4411
Cleveland (G-5681)
Harrington Electric Company ....D 216 361-5101
Cleveland (G-5727)
Hatzel & Buehler Inc ....E 740 420-3088
Circleville (G-4889)
Hilscher-Clarke Electric Co ....E 330 452-9806
Canton (G-2400)
Hilscher-Clarke Electric Co ....D 740 622-5557
Coshocton (G-9105)
Indrolect Co ....E 513 821-4788
Cincinnati (G-3815)
Instrmntation Ctrl Systems Inc ....E 513 662-2600
Cincinnati (G-3822)
J & J General Maintenance Inc ....E 740 533-9729
Ironton (G-12293)
J W Didado Electric Inc ....C 330 374-0070
Akron (G-286)
Jess Howard Electric Company ....C 614 864-2167
Blacklick (G-1509)
Jims Electric Inc ....E 440 327-8800
North Ridgeville (G-15465)
Joe Dickey Electric Inc ....D 330 549-3976
North Lima (G-15403)
John H Cooper Elec Contg Co ....E 513 271-5000
Cincinnati (G-3877)
John P Novatny Electric Co ....E 330 630-8900
Akron (G-296)
JZE Electric Inc ....C 440 243-7600
Cleveland (G-5878)
K Ray Holding Co ....E 614 861-4738
Brice (G-1858)
Kal Electric Inc ....E 740 593-8720
Athens (G-796)
Kastle Electric Co LLC ....D 937 254-2681
Moraine (G-14794)
Kastle Electric Company ....C 937 254-2681
Moraine (G-14795)
Kastle Electric Company ....E 513 360-2901
Monroe (G-14701)
Kathman Electric Co Inc ....E 513 353-3365
Cleves (G-6800)
Kenmarc Inc ....E 513 541-2791
Cincinnati (G-3913)
Kidron Electric Inc ....E 330 857-2871
Kidron (G-12443)
Kraft Electrical Contg Inc ....E 513 467-0500
Cincinnati (G-3941)
Kween Industries Inc ....E 513 932-2293
Lebanon (G-12617)
Laibe Electric Co ....D 419 724-8200
Toledo (G-17999)
Lake Erie Electric Inc ....D 440 835-5565
Westlake (G-19507)
Lake Erie Electric Inc ....E 330 724-1241
Akron (G-312)
Lake Erie Electric Inc ....E 419 529-4611
Ontario (G-15697)
Lin R Rogers Elec Contrs Inc ....B 614 876-9336
Hilliard (G-11922)
Lowry Controls Inc ....E 513 583-0182
Loveland (G-13142)
Main Lite Electric Co Inc ....E 330 369-8333
Warren (G-18877)
Mayers Electric Co Inc ....C 513 272-2900
Cincinnati (G-4032)
McClintock Electric Inc ....E 330 264-6380
Wooster (G-19886)
McKeever & Niekamp Elc Inc ....E 937 431-9363
Beavercreek (G-1191)
MDU Resources Group Inc ....E 937 424-2550
Moraine (G-14801)
Miller Cable Company ....D 419 639-2091
Green Springs (G-11479)
Mutual Electric Company ....E 937 254-6211
Dayton (G-9762)
New River Electrical Corp ....E 614 891-1142
Westerville (G-19430)
Ngn Electric Corp ....E 330 923-2777
Brecksville (G-1837)
Northeast Ohio Electric LLC ....B 216 587-9510
Cleveland (G-6155)
Ohio Valley Elec Svcs LLC ....D 513 771-2410
Blue Ash (G-1655)
Osterwisch Company Inc ....D 513 791-3282
Cincinnati (G-4240)
Oyer Electric Inc ....D 740 773-2828
Chillicothe (G-2868)
Palazzo Brothers Electric Inc ....E 419 668-1100
Norwalk (G-15587)
Penn-Ohio Electrical Company ....E 330 448-1234
Masury (G-13867)
Perram Electric Inc ....E 330 239-2661
Wadsworth (G-18768)
Positive Electric Inc ....E 937 428-0606
Dayton (G-9816)
Precision Electrical Services ....E 740 474-4490
Circleville (G-4901)
Proline Electric Inc ....E 740 687-4571
Lancaster (G-12567)
Queen City Electric Inc ....E 513 591-2600
Cincinnati (G-4363)
R & R Wiring Contractors Inc ....E 513 752-6304
Batavia (G-1022)
R J Martin Elec Svcs Inc ....D 216 662-7100
Bedford Heights (G-1358)
Rapier Electric Inc ....D 513 868-9087
Hamilton (G-11767)
Reddy Electric Co ....C 937 372-8205
Xenia (G-20072)
Regent Electric Inc ....D 419 476-8333
Toledo (G-18147)
Reliable Contractors Inc ....D 937 433-0262
Dayton (G-9846)
Reynolds Electric Company Inc ....D 419 228-5448
Lima (G-12868)
Roehrenbeck Electric Inc ....E 614 443-9709
Columbus (G-8644)
Romanoff Electric Inc ....C 614 755-4500
Gahanna (G-11266)
Romanoff Electric Co LLC ....C 419 726-2627
Toledo (G-18164)
Romanoff Electric Co LLC ....D 937 640-7925
Toledo (G-18165)
Royal Electric Cnstr Corp ....E 614 253-6600
Columbus (G-8653)
Ruhl Electric Co ....E 330 823-7230
Alliance (G-559)
S & E Electric Inc ....E 330 425-7866
Twinsburg (G-18465)
Sabroske Electric Inc ....E 419 332-6444
Fremont (G-11218)
Safeway Electric Company Inc ....E 614 443-7672
Columbus (G-8674)
Security Fence Group Inc ....E 513 681-3700
Cincinnati (G-4489)
Servall Electric Company Inc ....E 513 771-5584
Cincinnati (G-4499)
Settle Muter Electric Ltd ....C 614 866-7554
Columbus (G-8718)
Sidney Electric Company ....D 419 222-1109
Sidney (G-16954)
Smink Electric Inc ....E 440 322-5518
Elyria (G-10680)
South Shore Electric Inc ....E 440 366-6289
Elyria (G-10681)
Speelman Electric Inc ....D 330 633-1410
Tallmadge (G-17650)
Studebaker Electric Company ....D 937 890-9510
Dayton (G-9911)
T J Williams Electric Co ....E 513 738-5366
Harrison (G-11809)
Thompson Electric Inc ....C 330 686-2300
Munroe Falls (G-14933)
Transtar Electric Inc ....D 419 385-7573
Toledo (G-18260)
Tri Area Electric Co Inc ....E 330 744-0151
Youngstown (G-20392)
Triec Electrical Services Inc ....E 937 323-3721
Springfield (G-17290)
Unicustom Inc ....E 513 874-9806
Fairfield (G-10919)
United Electric Company Inc ....E 502 459-5242
Cincinnati (G-4732)
Valley Electrical Cnsld Inc ....C 330 539-4044
Girard (G-11429)
Vaughn Industries LLC ....B 419 396-3900
Carey (G-2599)
Vec Inc ....E 330 539-4044
Girard (G-11430)
VIP Electric Company ....E 440 255-0180
Mentor (G-14256)
W W Schaub Electric Co ....E 330 494-3560
Canton (G-2581)
Wachter Inc ....C 513 777-0701
West Chester (G-19243)
Wagner Industrial Electric Inc ....E 937 298-7481
Moraine (G-14833)
Wells Brother Electric Inc ....D 937 394-7559
Anna (G-618)
Westfield Electric Inc ....E 419 862-0078
Gibsonburg (G-11405)
Wood Electric Inc ....D 330 339-7002
New Philadelphia (G-15123)
Woolace Electric Corp ....E 419 428-3161
Stryker (G-17539)
X F Construction Svcs Inc ....E 614 575-2700
Columbus (G-9012)

CONTRACTORS: Glass Tinting, Architectural & Automotive

AGC Automotive Americas ....D 937 599-3131
Bellefontaine (G-1375)

CONTRACTORS: Glass, Glazing & Tinting

A E D Inc ....E 419 661-9999
Northwood (G-15526)
Advanced Auto Glass Inc ....E 412 373-6675
Akron (G-21)
AGC Automotive Americas ....D 937 599-3131
Bellefontaine (G-1375)
Anderson Aluminum Corporation ....D 614 476-4877
Columbus (G-7017)
E J Robinson Glass Co ....E 513 242-9250
Cincinnati (G-3524)
J & B Equipment & Supply Inc ....D 419 884-1155
Mansfield (G-13314)
Lakeland Glass Co ....E 440 277-4527
Lorain (G-13047)
Lorain Glass Co Inc ....D 440 277-6004
Lorain (G-13054)
Medina Glass Block Inc ....E 330 239-0239
Medina (G-14100)
Modern Glass Pnt & Tile Co Inc ....E 740 454-1253
Zanesville (G-20503)
Pioneer Cldding Glzing Systems ....E 216 816-4242
Cleveland (G-6282)
Pioneer Cldding Glzing Systems ....D 513 583-5925
Mason (G-13747)
R C Hemm Glass Shops Inc ....E 937 773-5591
Piqua (G-16163)
Richardson Glass Service Inc ....D 740 366-5090
Newark (G-15232)

SERVICES SECTION

Ryans All-Glass Incorporated .... E 513 771-4440
  Cincinnati *(G-4461)*
Thomas Glass Company Inc .... E 614 268-8611
  Worthington *(G-20003)*
Toledo Glass LLC .... E 419 241-3151
  Toledo *(G-18237)*
United GL & Panl Systems Inc .... E 330 244-9745
  Canton *(G-2568)*
Wiechart Enterprises Inc .... E 419 227-0027
  Lima *(G-12921)*

CONTRACTORS: Gutters & Downspouts

Apco Industries Inc .... D 614 224-2345
  Columbus *(G-7027)*
Durable Slate Co .... E 216 751-0151
  Shaker Heights *(G-16859)*
Leaffilter North LLC .... D 330 655-7950
  Hudson *(G-12131)*
Mid-America Gutters Inc .... E 513 671-4000
  West Chester *(G-19215)*
Mollett Seamless Gutter Co .... E 513 825-0500
  West Chester *(G-19123)*
Thiels Replacement Systems Inc .... D 419 289-6139
  Ashland *(G-701)*

CONTRACTORS: Heating & Air Conditioning

Aggressive Mechanical Inc .... E 614 443-3280
  Columbus *(G-6956)*
Allied Restaurant Svc Ohio Inc .... E 419 589-4759
  Mansfield *(G-13260)*
Area Energy & Electric Inc .... C 937 498-4784
  Sidney *(G-16913)*
Dave Pinkerton .... E 740 477-8888
  Chillicothe *(G-2834)*
Drake State Air .... E 937 472-3740
  Eaton *(G-10557)*
Ellerbrock Heating & AC .... E 419 782-1834
  Defiance *(G-10029)*
Engineering Excellence .... D 972 535-3756
  Blue Ash *(G-1587)*
G Mechanical Inc .... E 614 844-6750
  Columbus *(G-7719)*
Gorjanc Comfort Services Inc .... E 440 449-4411
  Cleveland *(G-5681)*
HEat Ttal Fclty Slutions Inc .... E 740 965-3005
  Galena *(G-11283)*
Horizon Mechanical and Elec .... E 419 529-2738
  Mansfield *(G-13309)*
J Feldkamp Design Build Ltd .... E 513 870-0601
  Fairfield *(G-10864)*
Johnson Controls Inc .... D 614 895-6600
  Westerville *(G-19412)*
Kuempel Service Inc .... E 513 271-6500
  Cincinnati *(G-3948)*
Ohio Fabricators Inc .... E 216 391-2400
  Cleveland *(G-6190)*
R & R Hvac Systems .... E 419 861-0266
  Holland *(G-12048)*
Robinson Htg Air-Conditioning .... E 513 422-6812
  Middletown *(G-14455)*
Schibi Heating & Cooling Corp .... E 513 385-3344
  Cincinnati *(G-4481)*
Service Experts Htg & AC LLC .... E 614 859-6993
  Columbus *(G-8715)*
Service Experts LLC .... E 330 577-3918
  Akron *(G-435)*
Wenger Temperature Control .... E 614 586-4016
  Columbus *(G-8978)*

CONTRACTORS: Heating Systems Repair & Maintenance Svc

American Air Furnace Company .... D 614 876-1702
  Grove City *(G-11528)*
Emcor Fclities Svcs N Amer Inc .... D 614 430-5078
  Columbus *(G-7591)*
Thompson Heating & Cooling .... E 513 242-4450
  Cincinnati *(G-4656)*
Thompson Heating Corporation .... D 513 769-7696
  Cincinnati *(G-4657)*

CONTRACTORS: Highway & Street Construction, General

Aecom Energy & Cnstr Inc .... B 216 622-2300
  Cleveland *(G-4962)*
Alan Stone Company .... D 740 448-1100
  Cutler *(G-9157)*

Beaver Constructors Inc .... D 330 478-2151
  Canton *(G-2261)*
Brock & Sons Inc .... E 513 874-4555
  Fairfield *(G-10824)*
Cincinnati Fill Inc .... E 513 242-7526
  Cincinnati *(G-3304)*
D B Bentley Inc .... E 440 352-8495
  Painesville *(G-15849)*
D G M Inc .... D 740 226-1950
  Beaver *(G-1141)*
Don S Cisle Contractor Inc .... D 513 867-1400
  Hamilton *(G-11724)*
Ferrous Metal Transfer .... E 216 671-8500
  Brooklyn *(G-1906)*
Fryman-Kuck General Contrs Inc .... E 937 274-2892
  Dayton *(G-9564)*
Independence Excavating Inc .... E 216 524-1700
  Independence *(G-12218)*
J A Donadee Corporation .... E 330 533-3305
  Canfield *(G-2197)*
J&B Steel Erectors Inc .... C 513 874-1722
  West Chester *(G-19096)*
K West Group LLC .... C 972 722-3874
  Perrysburg *(G-16022)*
Kenmore Construction Co Inc .... C 330 762-8936
  Akron *(G-303)*
Kenmore Construction Co Inc .... D 330 832-8888
  Massillon *(G-13827)*
Kokosing Construction Co Inc .... C 614 228-1029
  Columbus *(G-8007)*
Kokosing Construction Co Inc .... E 614 228-1029
  Columbus *(G-8008)*
Kokosing Inc .... D 614 212-5700
  Westerville *(G-19417)*
McDaniels Cnstr Corp Inc .... D 614 252-5852
  Columbus *(G-8134)*
Nerone & Sons Inc .... E 216 662-2235
  Cleveland *(G-6120)*
Perk Company Inc .... E 216 391-1444
  Cleveland *(G-6265)*
R B Jergens Contractors Inc .... D 937 669-9799
  Vandalia *(G-18696)*
Ray Bertolini Trucking Co .... E 330 867-0666
  Akron *(G-405)*
Ruhlin Company .... C 330 239-2800
  Sharon Center *(G-16877)*
Schweitzer Construction Co .... E 513 761-4980
  Cincinnati *(G-4485)*
Spieker Company .... E 419 872-7000
  Perrysburg *(G-16062)*
Stonegate Construction Inc .... D 740 423-9170
  Belpre *(G-1444)*
Sunesis Construction Company .... C 513 326-6000
  West Chester *(G-19161)*
Trafftech Inc .... E 216 361-8808
  Cleveland *(G-6608)*
Tucson Inc .... E 330 339-4935
  New Philadelphia *(G-15118)*
Velotta Company .... E 330 239-1211
  Sharon Center *(G-16880)*
Virginia Ohio-West Excvtg Co .... C 740 676-7464
  Shadyside *(G-16852)*
Waltek Inc .... E 614 469-0156
  Columbus *(G-8965)*
Westpatrick Corp .... E 614 875-8200
  Columbus *(G-8981)*

CONTRACTORS: Highway & Street Paving

Akil Incorporated .... E 419 625-0857
  Sandusky *(G-16724)*
Allied Paving Inc .... E 419 666-3100
  Holland *(G-12006)*
Armor Paving & Sealing .... E 614 751-6900
  Reynoldsburg *(G-16429)*
Butler Asphalt Co LLC .... E 937 890-1141
  Vandalia *(G-18666)*
Chemcote Inc .... E 614 792-2683
  Dublin *(G-10290)*
City of Lima .... E 419 221-5165
  Lima *(G-12754)*
City of Norwalk .... E 419 663-6715
  Norwalk *(G-15563)*
Columbus Asphalt Paving Inc .... E 614 759-9800
  Gahanna *(G-11235)*
Cunningham Paving Company .... E 216 581-8600
  Bedford *(G-1302)*
Decorative Paving Company .... E 513 576-1222
  Loveland *(G-13121)*
Ebony Construction Co .... E 419 841-3455
  Sylvania *(G-17585)*

CONTRACTORS: Hydronics Heating

Erie Blacktop Inc .... E 419 625-7374
  Sandusky *(G-16751)*
Fabrizi Trucking & Pav Co Inc .... C 330 483-3291
  Cleveland *(G-5564)*
Hicon Inc .... D 513 242-3612
  Cincinnati *(G-3760)*
J K Meurer Corp .... E 513 831-7500
  Loveland *(G-13135)*
Ken Heiberger Paving Inc .... D 614 837-0290
  Canal Winchester *(G-2162)*
Kirila Contractors Inc .... D 330 448-4055
  Brookfield *(G-1898)*
Kokosing Construction Inc .... A 330 263-4168
  Wooster *(G-19881)*
MBC Holdings Inc .... A 419 445-1015
  Archbold *(G-638)*
Miller Bros Const Inc .... E 419 445-1015
  Archbold *(G-639)*
Neff Paving Ltd .... E 740 453-3063
  Zanesville *(G-20516)*
Premier Asphalt Paving Co Inc .... E 440 237-6600
  North Royalton *(G-15498)*
R T Vernal Paving Inc .... E 330 549-3189
  North Lima *(G-15407)*
Scot Burton Contractors LLC .... E 440 564-1011
  Newbury *(G-15261)*
Shelly and Sands Inc .... E 740 453-6260
  Zanesville *(G-20531)*
Shelly and Sands Inc .... E 614 444-5100
  Columbus *(G-8725)*
Shelly and Sands Inc .... D 419 529-8455
  Ontario *(G-15713)*
Shelly and Sands Inc .... E 740 453-0721
  Zanesville *(G-20532)*
Superior Paving & Materials .... E 330 499-5849
  Canton *(G-2556)*
Terminal Ready-Mix Inc .... E 440 288-0181
  Lorain *(G-13081)*
Vandalia Blacktop Seal Coating .... E 937 454-0571
  Dayton *(G-9965)*

CONTRACTORS: Highway & Street Resurfacing

K & M Construction Company .... C 330 723-3681
  Medina *(G-14089)*
Prime Polymers Inc .... E 330 662-4200
  Medina *(G-14113)*

CONTRACTORS: Home & Office Intrs Finish, Furnish/Remodel

Aic Contracting Inc .... E 513 881-5900
  Cincinnati *(G-2978)*
Lorad LLC .... E 216 265-2862
  Westlake *(G-19511)*
Ram Restoration LLC .... E 937 347-7418
  Dayton *(G-9841)*

CONTRACTORS: Hotel & Motel Renovation

Akron Citicenter Hotel LLC .... D 330 253-8355
  Akron *(G-31)*
Optima 777 LLC .... E 216 771-7700
  Cleveland *(G-6208)*

CONTRACTORS: Hotel, Motel/Multi-Family Home Renovtn/Remodel

Cardinal Builders Inc .... E 614 237-1000
  Columbus *(G-7190)*
CFS Construction Inc .... E 513 559-4500
  Cincinnati *(G-3222)*
Dependble Bldrs Renovators LLC .... E 614 761-8250
  Dublin *(G-10320)*
Patriot Roofing Company Inc .... E 513 469-7663
  Blue Ash *(G-1662)*
Ram Restoration LLC .... E 937 347-7418
  Dayton *(G-9841)*

CONTRACTORS: Hydraulic Eqpt Installation & Svcs

North Bay Construction Inc .... E 440 835-1898
  Westlake *(G-19522)*

CONTRACTORS: Hydronics Heating

Jackson Comfort Systems Inc .... E 330 468-3111
  Northfield *(G-15518)*

Employee Codes: A=Over 500 employees, B=251-500
C=101-250, D=51-100, E=25-50

CONTRACTORS: Hydronics Heating

Ray Esser & Sons Inc .... E 440 324-2018
  Elyria *(G-10673)*

CONTRACTORS: Indl Building Renovation, Remodeling & Repair

Belfor USA Group Inc .... E 330 916-6468
  Peninsula *(G-15947)*
Farrow Cleaners Co .... E 216 561-2355
  Cleveland *(G-5574)*
Fryman-Kuck General Contrs Inc .... E 937 274-2892
  Dayton *(G-9564)*
Grunwell-Cashero Co .... E 419 476-2426
  Toledo *(G-17927)*
Icon Environmental Group LLC ..... E 513 426-6767
  Milford *(G-14526)*
Ingle-Barr Inc .... D 740 702-6117
  Chillicothe *(G-2853)*
Maintenance Unlimited Inc .... E 440 238-1162
  Strongsville *(G-17486)*
Matt Construction Services .... D 216 641-0030
  Cleveland *(G-5994)*
Mc Meechan Construction Co .... E 216 581-9373
  Cleveland *(G-5999)*
McGraw/Kokosing Inc .... B 614 212-5700
  Monroe *(G-14705)*
Miencorp Inc .... E 330 978-8511
  Niles *(G-15296)*
Mural & Son Inc .... E 216 267-3322
  Cleveland *(G-6090)*
Ram Construction Services of ...... D 513 297-1857
  West Chester *(G-19137)*
Reinnovations Contracting Inc ...... E 330 505-9035
  Mineral Ridge *(G-14638)*
Tradesmen Group Inc .... E 614 799-0889
  Plain City *(G-16210)*
Trisco Systems Incorporated .... C 419 339-9912
  Lima *(G-12906)*
Universal Fabg Cnstr Svcs Inc ...... D 614 274-1128
  Columbus *(G-8905)*
Van Tassel Construction Corp ...... E 419 873-0188
  Perrysburg *(G-16068)*
Virginia Ohio-West Excvtg Co .... C 740 676-7464
  Shadyside *(G-16852)*

CONTRACTORS: Insulation Installation, Building

All Construction Services Inc .... E 330 225-1653
  Brunswick *(G-1967)*
Boak & Sons Inc .... C 330 793-5646
  Youngstown *(G-20118)*
Buckholz Wall Systems LLC .... E 614 870-1775
  Hilliard *(G-11886)*
Builder Services Group Inc .... D 614 263-9378
  Columbus *(G-7166)*
Builder Services Group Inc .... E 513 942-2204
  Hamilton *(G-11695)*
Central Insulation Systems Inc ..... E 513 242-0600
  Cincinnati *(G-3214)*
Community Action Comsn Belmont .... E 740 695-0293
  Saint Clairsville *(G-16632)*
Edwards Mooney & Moses .... D 614 351-1439
  Columbus *(G-7582)*
Global Insulation Inc .... E 330 479-3100
  Canton *(G-2381)*
Industrial Insul Coatings LLC .... E 800 506-1399
  Girard *(G-11414)*
Installed Building Pdts II LLC .... D 626 812-6070
  Columbus *(G-7907)*
Installed Building Pdts LLC .... E 614 308-9900
  Columbus *(G-7909)*
Installed Building Pdts LLC .... E 330 798-9640
  Akron *(G-280)*
Installed Building Pdts LLC .... E 419 662-4524
  Northwood *(G-15534)*
Insulating Sales Co Inc .... E 513 742-2600
  Cincinnati *(G-3823)*
Liberty Insulation Co Inc .... D 513 621-0108
  Beavercreek *(G-1186)*
M K Moore & Sons Inc .... E 937 236-1812
  Dayton *(G-9693)*
Pedersen Insulation Company ...... E 614 471-3788
  Columbus *(G-8529)*
Priority 1 Construction Svcs .... E 513 922-0203
  Cincinnati *(G-4332)*
Rak Corrosion Control Inc .... E 440 985-2171
  Amherst *(G-602)*
Robinson Insulation Co Inc .... E 937 323-9599
  Springfield *(G-17264)*
Roofing By Insulation Inc .... E 937 315-5024
  New Carlisle *(G-15030)*
Sandel Corp .... E 614 475-5898
  Gahanna *(G-11267)*
Thermal Solutions Inc .... D 513 742-2836
  Fairfield *(G-10914)*
Thermal Solutions Inc .... D 740 886-2861
  Proctorville *(G-16362)*
Thermo-TEC Insulation Inc .... E 216 663-3842
  Euclid *(G-10779)*
Truteam LLC .... E 513 942-2204
  Hamilton *(G-11779)*
Unified Cnstr Systems Ltd .... E 330 773-2511
  Akron *(G-483)*
United Insulation Co Inc .... E 614 263-9378
  Columbus *(G-8893)*

CONTRACTORS: Kitchen & Bathroom Remodeling

Bathroom Alternatives Inc .... E 937 434-1984
  Dayton *(G-9349)*
Cardinal Builders Inc .... E 614 237-1000
  Columbus *(G-7190)*
Complete Services Inc .... E 513 770-5575
  Mason *(G-13688)*
Erie Construction Mid-West Inc ... E 937 898-4688
  Dayton *(G-9530)*
Hughes Kitchens and Bath LLC ... E 330 455-5269
  Canton *(G-2407)*
Korman Construction Corp .... E 614 274-2170
  Columbus *(G-8011)*

CONTRACTORS: Lighting Conductor Erection

Maxwell Lightning Protection .... E 937 228-7250
  Dayton *(G-9703)*

CONTRACTORS: Lighting Syst

Brush Contractors Inc .... D 614 850-8500
  Columbus *(G-7154)*
Cls Facilities MGT Svcs Inc .... E 440 602-4600
  Mentor *(G-14160)*
Lawn Management Sprinkler Co .... E 513 272-3808
  Cincinnati *(G-3964)*
Lighting Services Inc .... E 330 405-4879
  Twinsburg *(G-18442)*
Quebe Holdings Inc .... D 937 222-2290
  Dayton *(G-9838)*
Wireless Environment LLC .... E 216 455-0192
  Mayfield Village *(G-14014)*

CONTRACTORS: Lightweight Steel Framing Installation

OCP Contractors Inc .... E 419 865-7168
  Holland *(G-12043)*

CONTRACTORS: Machine Rigging & Moving

Advanced Tool & Supply Inc .... E 937 278-7337
  Dayton *(G-9310)*
Atlas Industrial Contrs LLC .... B 614 841-4500
  Columbus *(G-7072)*
Canton Erectors Inc .... E 330 453-7363
  Canton *(G-2287)*
Fenton Rigging & Contg Inc .... C 513 631-5500
  Cincinnati *(G-3602)*
Gardner Contracting Company ..... E 216 881-3800
  Cleveland *(G-5654)*
Hensley Industries Inc .... E 513 769-6666
  Cincinnati *(G-3757)*
Myers Machinery Movers Inc .... E 614 871-5052
  Grove City *(G-11582)*
Piqua Steel Co .... D 937 773-3632
  Piqua *(G-16159)*
Sk Rigging Co Inc .... E 513 771-7766
  Cincinnati *(G-4536)*
Standard Contg & Engrg Inc .... D 440 243-1001
  Brookpark *(G-1955)*

CONTRACTORS: Machinery Dismantling

J R Mead Industrial Contrs .... E 614 891-4466
  Galena *(G-11284)*

CONTRACTORS: Machinery Installation

A and A Mllwright Rigging Svcs ... E 513 396-6212
  Cincinnati *(G-2951)*
Gem Industrial Inc .... D 419 467-3287
  Walbridge *(G-18775)*
Glt Inc .... E 937 395-0508
  Moraine *(G-14791)*
Grubb Construction Inc .... E 419 293-2316
  Mc Comb *(G-14021)*
Hy-Tek Material Handling Inc ...... D 614 497-2500
  Columbus *(G-7873)*
Industrial Power Systems Inc ...... C 419 531-3121
  Rossford *(G-16608)*
Intertec Corporation .... B 419 537-9711
  Toledo *(G-17977)*
Norris Brothers Co Inc .... C 216 771-2233
  Cleveland *(G-6137)*
Spallinger Millwright Svc Co .... E 419 225-5830
  Lima *(G-12879)*
Tesar Industrial Contrs Inc .... E 216 741-8008
  Cleveland *(G-6587)*

CONTRACTORS: Maintenance, Parking Facility Eqpt

Purple Marlin Inc .... E 440 323-1291
  Elyria *(G-10672)*

CONTRACTORS: Marble Installation, Interior

Cleveland Marble Mosaic Co .... C 216 749-2840
  Cleveland *(G-5324)*
Cutting Edge Countertops Inc ..... E 419 873-9500
  Perrysburg *(G-15992)*
T H Winston Company .... E 513 271-2123
  Cincinnati *(G-4613)*

CONTRACTORS: Marble Masonry, Exterior

Cleveland Marble Mosaic Co .... C 216 749-2840
  Cleveland *(G-5324)*

CONTRACTORS: Masonry & Stonework

Albert Freytag Inc .... E 419 628-2018
  Minster *(G-14659)*
Bama Masonry Inc .... E 440 834-4175
  Burton *(G-2060)*
Beaver Constructors Inc .... D 330 478-2151
  Canton *(G-2261)*
Benchmark Masonry Contractors .... D 937 228-1225
  Middletown *(G-14417)*
Buckner and Sons Masonry Inc ... E 614 279-9777
  Columbus *(G-7163)*
Centennial Prsrvtion Group LLC .... E 614 238-0730
  Columbus *(G-7222)*
Crowe Masonry .... E 330 296-5539
  Ravenna *(G-16382)*
Debello Masonry Inc .... E 937 235-2096
  Carlisle *(G-2603)*
Empire Masonry Company Inc .... D 440 230-2800
  North Royalton *(G-15488)*
F B and S Masonry Inc .... E 330 608-3442
  Silver Lake *(G-16962)*
Foti Construction Company LLP .... E 440 347-0728
  Wickliffe *(G-19597)*
Hester Masonry Co Inc .... E 937 890-2283
  Vandalia *(G-18685)*
Hicon Inc .... D 513 242-3612
  Cincinnati *(G-3760)*
Hovest Construction .... E 419 456-3426
  Ottawa *(G-15798)*
Hummel Industries Incorporated ... E 513 242-1321
  Cincinnati *(G-3798)*
Industrial First Inc .... C 216 991-8605
  Bedford *(G-1313)*
J C Masonry Construction Inc ..... E 330 823-9795
  Alliance *(G-542)*
Karst & Sons Inc .... E 614 501-9530
  Reynoldsburg *(G-16462)*
Miter Masonry Contractors .... E 513 821-3334
  Arlington Heights *(G-648)*
OBrien Cut Stone Company .... E 216 663-7800
  Cleveland *(G-6178)*
Pioneer Cldding Glzing Systems ... E 216 816-4242
  Cleveland *(G-6282)*
S A Storer and Sons Company ..... D 419 843-3133
  Sylvania *(G-17614)*
Steven H Byerly Inc .... E 614 882-0092
  Columbus *(G-8788)*
VIP Restoration Inc .... D 216 426-9500
  Cuyahoga Falls *(G-9232)*
Warren Guillard Bricklayers .... E 330 633-3855
  Tallmadge *(G-17660)*

SERVICES SECTION

CONTRACTORS: Oil Sampling Svcs

Wasiniak Construction Inc ....D...... 419 668-8624
  Norwalk *(G-15596)*
Whitaker Masonry Inc ....E...... 330 225-7970
  Brunswick *(G-1996)*
William Kerfoot Masonry Inc ....E...... 330 772-6460
  Burghill *(G-2056)*
Zavarella Brothers Cnstr Co ....E...... 440 232-2243
  Cleveland *(G-6782)*

CONTRACTORS: Mechanical

A J Stockmeister Inc ....E...... 740 286-2106
  Jackson *(G-12305)*
Advanced Mechanical Svcs Inc ....E...... 937 879-7426
  Fairborn *(G-10783)*
Ayers-Sterrett Inc ....E...... 419 238-5480
  Van Wert *(G-18628)*
Ayrshire Inc ....D...... 440 992-0743
  Ashtabula *(G-728)*
Bayes Inc ....E...... 419 661-3933
  Perrysburg *(G-15975)*
Brewer-Garrett Co ....C...... 440 243-3535
  Middleburg Heights *(G-14378)*
Buckeye Mechanical Contg Inc ....E...... 740 282-0089
  Toronto *(G-18334)*
Cahill Corporation ....E...... 330 724-1224
  Uniontown *(G-18510)*
Campbell Inc ....D...... 419 476-4444
  Northwood *(G-15529)*
Cattrell Companies Inc ....D...... 740 537-2481
  Toronto *(G-18336)*
Chemsteel Construction Company .....E...... 440 234-3930
  Middleburg Heights *(G-14379)*
Clearcreek Construction ....E...... 740 420-3568
  Stoutsville *(G-17349)*
Coleman Spohn Corporation ....E...... 216 431-8070
  Cleveland *(G-5370)*
Commercial Hvac Inc ....E...... 513 396-6100
  Cincinnati *(G-3399)*
Complete Mechanical Svcs LLC ....D...... 513 489-3080
  Blue Ash *(G-1565)*
Debra-Kuempel Inc ....D...... 513 271-6500
  Cincinnati *(G-3476)*
Dimech Services Inc ....E...... 419 727-0111
  Toledo *(G-17853)*
Dunbar Mechanical Inc ....D...... 734 856-6601
  Toledo *(G-17859)*
Edwards Electrical & Mech ....E...... 614 485-2003
  Columbus *(G-7584)*
Enerfab Inc ....B...... 513 641-0500
  Cincinnati *(G-3557)*
Energy MGT Specialists Inc ....E...... 216 676-9045
  Cleveland *(G-5539)*
Enervise Incorporated ....C...... 513 761-6000
  Blue Ash *(G-1586)*
Enervise Incorporated ....E...... 614 885-9800
  Columbus *(G-7593)*
Envirnmental Engrg Systems Inc ....E...... 937 228-6492
  Dayton *(G-9527)*
Excellence Alliance Group Inc ....E...... 513 619-4800
  Cincinnati *(G-3585)*
Falls Heating & Cooling Inc ....E...... 330 929-8777
  Cuyahoga Falls *(G-9183)*
Farber Corporation ....E...... 614 294-1626
  Columbus *(G-7637)*
Fowler Electric Co ....D...... 440 735-2385
  Bedford *(G-1307)*
Gem Industrial Inc ....E...... 419 467-3287
  Walbridge *(G-18775)*
Greer & Whitehead Cnstr Inc ....E...... 513 202-1757
  Harrison *(G-11799)*
Guenther Mechanical Inc ....C...... 419 289-6900
  Ashland *(G-681)*
Industrial Power Systems Inc ....C...... 419 531-3121
  Rossford *(G-16608)*
Jarvis Mechanical Constrs Inc ....E...... 513 831-0055
  Milford *(G-14528)*
John F Gallagher Plumbing Co ....E...... 440 946-4256
  Eastlake *(G-10547)*
Julian Speer Co ....D...... 614 261-6331
  Columbus *(G-7958)*
Kirk Williams Company Inc ....D...... 614 875-9023
  Grove City *(G-11573)*
Limbach Company LLC ....C...... 614 299-2175
  Columbus *(G-8067)*
Lochard Inc ....D...... 937 492-8811
  Sidney *(G-16940)*
Marlin Mechanical LLC ....E...... 800 669-2645
  Cleveland *(G-5981)*
Mechancal/Industrial Contg Inc ....E...... 513 489-8282
  Cincinnati *(G-4040)*
Mechanical Cnstr Managers LLC ....C...... 937 274-1987
  Dayton *(G-9709)*
Mechanical Systems Dayton Inc ....D...... 937 254-3235
  Dayton *(G-9277)*
Monroe Mechanical Incorporated ......E...... 513 539-7555
  Monroe *(G-14706)*
Osterfeld Champion Service ....E...... 937 254-8437
  Dayton *(G-9795)*
Perfection Mechanical Svcs Inc ....D...... 513 772-7545
  Cincinnati *(G-4280)*
Premier Rstrtion Mech Svcs LLC ....E...... 513 420-1600
  Middletown *(G-14451)*
Process Construction Inc ....D...... 513 251-2211
  Cincinnati *(G-4339)*
R Kelly Inc ....E...... 513 631-8488
  Cincinnati *(G-4379)*
Regal Plumbing & Heating Co ....E...... 937 492-2894
  Sidney *(G-16949)*
Relmec Mechanical LLC ....C...... 216 391-1030
  Cleveland *(G-6372)*
Rmf Nooter Inc ....D...... 419 727-1970
  Toledo *(G-18159)*
RPC Mechanical Services ....C...... 513 733-1641
  Cincinnati *(G-4449)*
Sauer Group Inc ....C...... 614 853-2500
  Columbus *(G-8685)*
Sauer Incorporated ....D...... 614 853-2500
  Columbus *(G-8686)*
Schmid Mechanical Co ....E...... 614 261-6331
  Columbus *(G-8696)*
Schweizer Dipple Inc ....D...... 440 786-8090
  Cleveland *(G-6451)*
Scioto Services LLc ....E...... 937 644-0888
  Marysville *(G-13649)*
Sexton Industrial Inc ....C...... 513 530-5555
  West Chester *(G-19228)*
Speer Industries Incorporated ....C...... 614 261-6331
  Columbus *(G-8761)*
The Peck-Hannaford Briggs Co ....D...... 513 681-4600
  Cincinnati *(G-4645)*
Trame Mechanical Inc ....E...... 937 258-1000
  Dayton *(G-9936)*
Triton Services Inc ....C...... 513 679-6800
  Mason *(G-13774)*
Vaughn Industries LLC ....B...... 419 396-3900
  Carey *(G-2599)*
Vaughn Industries LLC ....E...... 740 548-7100
  Lewis Center *(G-12710)*
Warner Mechanical Corporation ....E...... 419 332-7116
  Fremont *(G-11229)*
Western Reserve Mechanical Inc ....E...... 330 652-3888
  Niles *(G-15311)*
York-Mahoning Mech Contrs Inc ....D...... 330 788-7011
  Youngstown *(G-20420)*

CONTRACTORS: Millwrights

Hgc Construction Co ....D...... 513 861-8866
  Cincinnati *(G-3759)*
K F T Inc ....D...... 513 241-5910
  Cincinnati *(G-3897)*
Orbit Movers & Erectors Inc ....E...... 937 277-8080
  Dayton *(G-9793)*

CONTRACTORS: Mosaic Work

Midwest Mosaic Inc ....E...... 419 377-3894
  Toledo *(G-18062)*

CONTRACTORS: Multi-Family Home Remodeling

Garland Group Inc ....E...... 614 294-4411
  Columbus *(G-7730)*
Klingbeil Management Group Co ....E...... 614 220-8900
  Columbus *(G-7997)*
Oliver House Rest Complex ....D...... 419 243-1302
  Toledo *(G-18105)*
Residntial Coml Rnovations Inc ....E...... 330 815-1476
  Clinton *(G-6807)*
Rubber City Realty Inc ....D...... 330 745-9034
  Akron *(G-421)*

CONTRACTORS: Nonresidential Building Design & Construction

Hi-Five Development Svcs Inc ....E...... 513 336-9280
  Mason *(G-13716)*
Wenger Temperature Control ....E...... 614 586-4016
  Columbus *(G-8978)*

CONTRACTORS: Nuclear Power Refueling

Bwxt Nclear Oprtions Group Inc ....E...... 216 912-3000
  Cleveland *(G-5166)*

CONTRACTORS: Office Furniture Installation

Corporate Environments of Ohio ....E...... 614 358-3375
  Columbus *(G-7442)*
Jtc Contracting Inc ....E...... 216 635-0745
  Cleveland *(G-5875)*
Lincoln Moving & Storage Co ....D...... 216 741-5500
  Cleveland *(G-5943)*
Modular Systems Technicians ....E...... 216 459-2630
  Cleveland *(G-6072)*
P-N-D Communications Inc ....E...... 419 683-1922
  Crestline *(G-9149)*
Wegman Construction Company ....E...... 513 381-1111
  Cincinnati *(G-4828)*

CONTRACTORS: Oil & Gas Field Fire Fighting Svcs

Cgh-Global Emerg Mngmt Strateg .....E...... 800 376-0655
  Cincinnati *(G-2905)*

CONTRACTORS: Oil & Gas Field Geological Exploration Svcs

New World Energy Resources ....B...... 740 344-4087
  Newark *(G-15218)*

CONTRACTORS: Oil & Gas Field Geophysical Exploration Svcs

Dlz Ohio Inc ....C...... 614 888-0040
  Columbus *(G-7535)*

CONTRACTORS: Oil & Gas Well Drilling Svc

Advent Drilling Inc ....E...... 330 497-2533
  Canton *(G-2227)*
Eclipse Resources - Ohio LLC ....E...... 740 452-4503
  Zanesville *(G-20472)*
J D Drilling Co ....E...... 740 949-2512
  Racine *(G-16371)*
Kilbarger Construction Inc ....C...... 740 385-5531
  Logan *(G-12980)*
Qes Pressure Control LLC ....E...... 724 324-2391
  Lore City *(G-13087)*
Stratagraph Ne Inc ....E...... 740 373-3091
  Marietta *(G-13502)*
Victor McKenzie Drilling Co ....E...... 740 453-0834
  Zanesville *(G-20544)*

CONTRACTORS: Oil & Gas Well Flow Rate Measurement Svcs

Fts International Inc ....A...... 330 754-2375
  East Canton *(G-10503)*

CONTRACTORS: Oil & Gas Well On-Site Foundation Building Svcs

Greer & Whitehead Cnstr Inc ....E...... 513 202-1757
  Harrison *(G-11799)*

CONTRACTORS: Oil & Gas Well Redrilling

Decker Drilling Inc ....E...... 740 749-3939
  Vincent *(G-18743)*

CONTRACTORS: Oil Field Haulage Svcs

Fishburn Tank Truck Service ....D...... 419 253-6031
  Marengo *(G-13424)*

CONTRACTORS: Oil Field Mud Drilling Svcs

Kelchner Inc ....C...... 937 704-9890
  Springboro *(G-17125)*

CONTRACTORS: Oil Field Pipe Testing Svcs

Express Energy Svcs Oper LP ....E...... 740 337-4530
  Toronto *(G-18337)*

CONTRACTORS: Oil Sampling Svcs

Bdi Inc ....B...... 216 642-9100
  Cleveland *(G-5104)*

Employee Codes: A=Over 500 employees, B=251-500
C=101-250, D=51-100, E=25-50

CONTRACTORS: Oil/Gas Field Casing,Tube/Rod Running,Cut/Pull

Varco LP .... E 440 277-8696
  Lorain *(G-13084)*

CONTRACTORS: Oil/Gas Well Construction, Rpr/Dismantling Svcs

Siler Excavation Services .... E 513 400-8628
  Milford *(G-14563)*

CONTRACTORS: On-Site Welding

Burdens Machine & Welding .... E 740 345-9246
  Newark *(G-15153)*
Lefeld Welding & Stl Sups Inc .... E 419 678-2397
  Coldwater *(G-6832)*
Marsam Metalfab Inc .... E 330 405-1520
  Twinsburg *(G-18444)*
Nelson Stud Welding Inc .... E 440 250-9242
  Westlake *(G-19520)*
Quality Fabricated Metals Inc .... E 330 332-7008
  Salem *(G-16707)*
Six C Fabrication Inc .... D 330 296-5594
  Ravenna *(G-16412)*

CONTRACTORS: Ornamental Metal Work

Architectural Metal Erectors .... E 513 242-5106
  Cincinnati *(G-3044)*

CONTRACTORS: Paint & Wallpaper Stripping

Decoating Inc .... E 419 347-9191
  Shelby *(G-16899)*

CONTRACTORS: Painting & Wall Covering

A & A Safety Inc .... E 513 943-6100
  Amelia *(G-571)*
Cummins Building Maint Inc .... D 740 726-9800
  Prospect *(G-16363)*
David W Steinbach Inc .... E 330 497-5959
  Canton *(G-2334)*
National Electro-Coatings Inc .... D 216 898-0080
  Cleveland *(G-6106)*
Performance Painting LLC .... E 440 735-3340
  Oakwood Village *(G-15632)*

CONTRACTORS: Painting, Commercial

American Star Painting Co LLC .... E 740 373-5634
  Marietta *(G-13432)*
August Groh & Sons Inc .... E 513 821-0090
  Cincinnati *(G-3064)*
Dennis Todd Painting Inc .... E 614 879-7952
  West Jefferson *(G-19250)*
Ionno Properties s Corp .... E 330 479-9267
  Dennison *(G-10165)*
Johnson & Fischer Inc .... E 614 276-8868
  Columbus *(G-7943)*
Muha Construction Inc .... E 937 435-0678
  Dayton *(G-9760)*
Painting Company .... C 614 873-1334
  Plain City *(G-16203)*
Preferred Acquisition Co LLC .... D 216 587-0957
  Cleveland *(G-6298)*
South Town Painting Inc .... E 937 847-1600
  Miamisburg *(G-14353)*
Unique Construction Svcs Inc .... E 513 608-1363
  Blue Ash *(G-1711)*
W F Bolin Company Inc .... E 614 276-6397
  Columbus *(G-8958)*
Yerman & Young Painting Inc .... E 330 861-0022
  Barberton *(G-986)*

CONTRACTORS: Painting, Commercial, Exterior

Allstate Painting & Contg Co .... D 330 220-5533
  Brunswick *(G-1968)*
Barbara Gheens Painting Inc .... E 740 949-0405
  Long Bottom *(G-13009)*
Costello Pntg Bldg Restoration .... E 513 321-3326
  Cincinnati *(G-3425)*
Dependable Painting Co .... E 216 431-4470
  Cleveland *(G-5476)*
Mike Morris .... E 330 767-4122
  Brewster *(G-1856)*

CONTRACTORS: Painting, Commercial, Interior

Frank Novak & Sons Inc .... D 216 475-2495
  Cleveland *(G-5632)*
Lou Ritenour Decorators Inc .... D 330 425-3232
  Twinsburg *(G-18443)*
Masterpiece Painting Company .... E 330 395-9900
  Warren *(G-18878)*

CONTRACTORS: Painting, Indl

A B Industrial Coatings .... E 614 228-0383
  Columbus *(G-6918)*
Eagle Industrial Painting LLC .... E 330 866-5965
  Magnolia *(G-13239)*
Flamos Enterprises Inc .... E 330 478-0009
  Canton *(G-2369)*
Gpc Contracting Company .... E 740 264-6060
  Steubenville *(G-17320)*
Industrial Mill Maintenance .... E 330 746-1155
  Youngstown *(G-20232)*
P & W Painting Contractors Inc ...... E 419 698-2209
  Toledo *(G-18115)*
Vimas Painting Company Inc .... E 330 536-2222
  Lowellville *(G-13175)*

CONTRACTORS: Painting, Residential

Cipriano Painting 440 892-1827
  Cleveland *(G-5241)*
Classic Papering & Painting 614 221-0505
  Columbus *(G-7294)*
Commercial Painting Inc 614 298-9963
  Worthington *(G-19949)*
Kendrick-Mollenauer Pntg Co 614 443-7037
  Columbus *(G-7977)*
Lehn Painting Inc .... E 513 732-1515
  Batavia *(G-1019)*
Perry Interiors Inc .... E 513 761-9333
  Batavia *(G-1021)*
Residence Artists Inc .... E 440 286-8822
  Chardon *(G-2764)*

CONTRACTORS: Parking Facility Eqpt Installation

Signature Control Systems LLC ...... E 614 864-2222
  Columbus *(G-8731)*

CONTRACTORS: Parking Lot Maintenance

Camco Inc .... E 740 477-3682
  Circleville *(G-4881)*
Image Pavement Maintenance .... E 937 833-9200
  Brookville *(G-1963)*

CONTRACTORS: Patio & Deck Construction & Repair

Bzak Landscaping Inc .... E 513 831-0907
  Milford *(G-14508)*
Deerfield Farms .... E 330 584-4715
  Deerfield *(G-10018)*
North Branch Nursery Inc .... E 419 287-4679
  Pemberville *(G-15942)*
Olde Towne Windows Inc .... E 419 626-9613
  Milan *(G-14496)*
Services On Deck Inc .... E 513 759-2854
  Liberty Township *(G-12724)*
Shade Tree Cool Living LLC .... E 614 844-5990
  Columbus *(G-8719)*

CONTRACTORS: Pavement Marking

Aero-Mark Inc .... E 330 995-0100
  Streetsboro *(G-17405)*
Kneisel Contracting Corp .... E 513 615-8816
  Cincinnati *(G-3935)*
Mark Dura Inc .... E 330 995-0883
  Aurora *(G-847)*

CONTRACTORS: Pile Driving

Goettle Holding Company Inc .... C 513 825-8100
  Cincinnati *(G-3683)*
Righter Construction Svcs Inc .... E 614 272-9700
  Columbus *(G-8630)*

CONTRACTORS: Pipe & Boiler Insulating

Advanced Industrial Svcs LLC .... D 419 661-8522
  Toledo *(G-17743)*

Alloyd Insulation Co Inc .... E 937 890-7900
  Dayton *(G-9319)*
M K Moore & Sons Inc .... E 937 236-1812
  Dayton *(G-9693)*
Priority III Contracting Inc .... E 513 922-0203
  Cincinnati *(G-4333)*
R E Kramig & Co Inc .... C 513 761-4010
  Cincinnati *(G-4378)*

CONTRACTORS: Pipe Laying

Steelial Wldg Met Fbrction Inc .... E 740 669-5300
  Vinton *(G-18744)*

CONTRACTORS: Plastering, Plain or Ornamental

Cleveland Construction Inc .... E 440 255-8000
  Mentor *(G-14159)*
Cleveland Construction Inc .... E 740 927-9000
  Columbus *(G-7298)*
Lm Constrction Trry Lvrini Inc .... E 740 695-9604
  Saint Clairsville *(G-16641)*
Synthetic Stucco Corporation .... E 513 897-9227
  Waynesville *(G-18987)*
Western Reserve Interiors Inc .... E 216 447-1081
  Cleveland *(G-6745)*

CONTRACTORS: Plumbing

A AAA H Jacks Plumbing Htg Co .... E 440 946-1166
  Wickliffe *(G-19591)*
A Team LLC .... E 216 271-7223
  Cleveland *(G-4936)*
A-1 Advanced Plumbing Inc .... E 614 873-0548
  Plain City *(G-16178)*
ABC Piping Co .... E 216 398-4000
  Brooklyn Heights *(G-1908)*
Adelmos Electric Sewer Clg Co .... E 216 641-2301
  Brooklyn Heights *(G-1909)*
Advance Mechanical Plbg & Htg ..... E 937 879-9405
  Fairborn *(G-10782)*
American Residential Svcs LLC ...... D 216 561-8880
  Cleveland *(G-5020)*
Applied Mechanical Systems Inc .... D 513 825-1800
  Cincinnati *(G-3037)*
ARS Rescue Rooter Inc .... E 440 842-8494
  Cleveland *(G-5068)*
Aztec Plumbing Inc .... E 513 732-3320
  Milford *(G-14506)*
Bay Mechanical & Elec Corp .... D 440 282-6816
  Lorain *(G-13017)*
Bellman Plumbing Inc .... E 440 324-4477
  Elyria *(G-10596)*
Best Plumbing Limited .... E 614 855-1919
  New Albany *(G-14974)*
Blue Chip Plumbing Inc .... E 513 941-4010
  Cincinnati *(G-3120)*
Brady Plumbing & Heating Inc .... E 440 324-4261
  Elyria *(G-10599)*
Bruner Corporation .... C 614 334-9000
  Hilliard *(G-11884)*
Crawford Mechanical Svcs Inc .... D 614 478-9424
  Columbus *(G-7455)*
Dar Plumbing 614 445-8243
  Columbus *(G-7489)*
Diewald & Pope Inc .... E 614 861-6160
  Reynoldsburg *(G-16446)*
Dival Inc .... D 216 831-4200
  Warrensville Heights *(G-18932)*
Dynamic Mechanical Systems .... E 513 858-6722
  Fairfield *(G-10843)*
Eaton Plumbing Inc .... E 614 891-7005
  Westerville *(G-19396)*
Ecoplumbers Inc .... E 614 299-9903
  Hilliard *(G-11899)*
Enviro-Flow Companies Ltd .... E 740 453-7980
  Zanesville *(G-20476)*
Flickinger Piping Company Inc .... E 330 364-4224
  Dover *(G-10189)*
Freeland Contracting Co .... E 614 443-2718
  Columbus *(G-7702)*
Glennco Systems Inc .... E 740 353-4328
  Portsmouth *(G-16280)*
Grabill Plumbing & Heating .... E 330 756-2075
  Beach City *(G-1043)*
Gross Plumbing Incorporated .... E 440 324-9999
  Elyria *(G-10632)*
H & M Plumbing Co .... E 614 491-4880
  Columbus *(G-7789)*
Houston Dick Plbg & Htg Inc .... E 740 763-3961
  Newark *(G-15176)*

SERVICES SECTION

CONTRACTORS: Roofing

J & D Home Improvement Inc .... D 740 927-0722
  Reynoldsburg (G-16459)
Jeff Plumber Inc .... E 330 940-2600
  Akron (G-292)
Ke Gutridge LLC .... C 614 252-0420
  Columbus (G-7969)
Ken Neyer Plumbing Inc .... C 513 353-3311
  Cleves (G-6801)
Komar Plumbing Co .... E 330 758-5073
  Youngstown (G-20248)
Lippincott Plumbing-Heating AC .... E 419 222-0856
  Lima (G-12829)
Mansfield Plumbing Pdts LLC .... E 330 496-2301
  Big Prairie (G-1498)
Marvin W Mielke Inc .... D 330 725-8845
  Medina (G-14095)
Mc Phillips Plbg Htg & AC Co .... E 216 481-1400
  Cleveland (G-6000)
Mechanical Construction Co .... E 740 353-5668
  Portsmouth (G-16295)
Midwestern Plumbing Service .... E 513 753-0050
  Cincinnati (G-4094)
Mj Baumann Co Inc .... D 614 759-7100
  Columbus (G-8180)
Muetzel Plumbing & Heating Co .... D 614 299-7700
  Columbus (G-8205)
Nelson Stark Company .... C 513 489-0866
  Cincinnati (G-4154)
Neptune Plumbing & Heating Co .... D 216 475-9100
  Cleveland (G-6119)
Northern Ohio Plumbing Co .... E 440 951-3370
  Eastlake (G-10550)
Northern Plumbing Systems .... E 513 831-5111
  Goshen (G-11437)
Paramount Plumbing Inc .... E 330 336-1096
  Norton (G-15558)
Perry Kelly Plumbing Inc .... E 513 528-6554
  Cincinnati (G-4282)
Peterman Plumbing and Htg Inc .... E 330 364-4497
  Dover (G-10206)
Pioneer Pipe Inc .... B 740 376-2400
  Marietta (G-13488)
Piper Plumbing Inc .... E 330 274-0160
  Mantua (G-13394)
PNC Mortgage Company .... C 412 762-2000
  Miamisburg (G-14337)
Professional Plumbing Services .... E 740 454-1066
  Zanesville (G-20527)
Queen City Mechanicals Inc .... E 513 353-1430
  Cincinnati (G-4366)
Rapid Plumbing Inc .... D 513 575-1509
  Loveland (G-13154)
River Plumbing Inc .... E 440 934-3720
  Avon (G-916)
Roman Plumbing Company .... D 330 455-5155
  Canton (G-2515)
Ron Johnson Plumbing and Htg .... E 419 433-5365
  Norwalk (G-15591)
Roto-Rooter Development Co .... E 513 762-6690
  Cincinnati (G-4442)
Roto-Rooter Services Company .... D 513 762-6690
  Cincinnati (G-4444)
S&D/Osterfeld Mech Contrs Inc .... E 937 277-1700
  Dayton (G-9862)
Schmid Mechanical Inc .... E 330 264-3633
  Wooster (G-19912)
Slagle Mechanical Contractors .... E 937 492-4151
  Sidney (G-16956)
Standard Plumbing & Heating Co .... D 330 453-5150
  Canton (G-2537)
Steel Valley Construction Co .... E 330 392-8391
  Warren (G-18902)
Steingass Mechanical Contg .... E 330 725-6090
  Medina (G-14129)
Thomas J Dyer Company .... E 513 321-8100
  Cincinnati (G-4653)
U S A Plumbing Company .... E 614 882-6402
  Columbus (G-8882)
Wells Brother Electric Inc .... D 937 394-7559
  Anna (G-618)
West Jefferson Plumbing Htg .... E 614 879-9606
  West Jefferson (G-19256)
Whisler Plumbing & Heating Inc .... E 330 833-2875
  Massillon (G-13861)
Whitt Inc .... E 513 753-7707
  Amelia (G-584)
Wilkes & Company Inc .... E 419 433-2325
  Huron (G-12176)

CONTRACTORS: Pollution Control Eqpt Installation

McGill Airclean LLC .... D 614 829-1200
  Columbus (G-8136)

CONTRACTORS: Post Disaster Renovations

Belfor USA Group Inc .... E 513 860-3111
  West Chester (G-19192)
C M S Enterprises Inc .... E 740 653-1940
  Lancaster (G-12512)
Clarke Contractors Corp .... E 513 285-7844
  West Chester (G-19045)
Design Rstrtion Reconstruction .... E 330 563-0010
  North Canton (G-15332)
Disaster Reconstruction Inc .... E 440 918-1523
  Eastlake (G-10545)
Stanley Stemer of Akron Canton .... E 330 785-5005
  Coventry Township (G-9133)

CONTRACTORS: Power Generating Eqpt Installation

Clopay Corporation .... C 800 282-2260
  Mason (G-13686)

CONTRACTORS: Precast Concrete Struct Framing & Panel Placing

Frameco Inc .... E 216 433-7080
  Cleveland (G-5629)
Vmi Group Inc .... D 330 405-4146
  Macedonia (G-13216)

CONTRACTORS: Prefabricated Window & Door Installation

Advance Door Company .... E 216 883-2424
  Cleveland (G-4957)
Burbank Inc .... E 419 698-3434
  Toledo (G-17788)
Dayton Door Sales Inc .... E 937 253-9181
  Dayton (G-9471)
Dilly Door Co .... E 419 782-1181
  Defiance (G-10028)
Erie Construction Mid-West Inc .... E 419 472-4200
  Toledo (G-17869)
Midwest Curtainwalls Inc .... E 216 641-7900
  Cleveland (G-6060)
OK Interiors Corp .... C 513 742-3278
  Cincinnati (G-4217)
Ray St Clair Roofing Inc .... E 513 874-1234
  Fairfield (G-10898)
Regency Windows Corporation .... D 330 963-4077
  Twinsburg (G-18459)
Ryans All-Glass Incorporated .... E 513 771-4440
  Cincinnati (G-4461)
Thiels Replacement Systems Inc .... D 419 289-6139
  Ashland (G-701)
Williams Bros Roofg Siding Co .... E 937 434-3838
  Dayton (G-9999)
Window Factory of America .... D 440 439-3050
  Bedford (G-1344)

CONTRACTORS: Process Piping

Lucas Plumbing & Heating Inc .... E 440 282-4567
  Lorain (G-13059)
United Group Services Inc .... C 800 633-9690
  West Chester (G-19238)

CONTRACTORS: Refractory or Acid Brick Masonry

Allen Refractories Company .... C 740 927-8000
  Pataskala (G-15920)
Onex Construction Inc .... E 330 995-9015
  Streetsboro (G-17424)

CONTRACTORS: Refrigeration

All Temp Refrigeration Inc .... E 419 692-5016
  Delphos (G-10137)
Dickson Industrial Park Inc .... E 740 377-9162
  South Point (G-17083)
Hattenbach Company .... E 216 881-5200
  Cleveland (G-5731)
Morrison Inc .... E 740 373-5869
  Marietta (G-13478)
North East Mechanical Inc .... E 440 871-7525
  Westlake (G-19523)
Wadsworth Service Inc .... E 419 861-8181
  Middleburg Heights (G-14391)

CONTRACTORS: Resilient Floor Laying

River City Furniture LLC .... D 513 612-7303
  West Chester (G-19141)

CONTRACTORS: Roof Repair

Centimark Corporation .... E 614 536-1960
  Reynoldsburg (G-16435)
Eastside Roofg Restoration Co .... E 513 471-0434
  Cincinnati (G-3539)
Holland Roofing Inc .... E 330 963-0237
  Twinsburg (G-18430)
Ohio & Indiana Roofing .... E 937 339-8768
  Troy (G-18368)
Patriot Roofing Company Inc .... E 513 469-7663
  Blue Ash (G-1662)

CONTRACTORS: Roofing

1st Choice Roofing Company .... E 216 227-7755
  Cleveland (G-4923)
Able Company Ltd Partnership .... D 614 444-7663
  Columbus (G-6926)
Able Roofing LLC .... E 614 444-7663
  Columbus (G-6927)
Advanced Industrial Roofg Inc .... D 330 837-1999
  Massillon (G-13784)
AH Sturgill Roofing Inc .... E 937 254-2955
  Dayton (G-9250)
Architectural Systems Inc .... D 614 873-2057
  Plain City (G-16182)
Atlas Roofing Company .... E 330 467-7683
  Cleveland (G-5079)
Aw Farrell Son Inc .... E 513 334-0715
  Milford (G-14505)
B & B Roofing Inc .... E 740 772-4759
  Chillicothe (G-2815)
Beck Company .... E 216 883-0909
  Cleveland (G-5110)
Bh Group LLC .... D 513 671-3300
  West Chester (G-19028)
Boak & Sons Inc .... C 330 793-5646
  Youngstown (G-20118)
Building Technicians Corp .... E 440 466-1651
  Geneva (G-11359)
Burbank Inc .... E 419 698-3434
  Toledo (G-17788)
Burns & Scalo Roofing Co Inc .... E 740 383-4639
  Marion (G-13527)
Campeon Roofg & Waterproofing .... E 513 271-8972
  Cincinnati (G-3173)
Centimark Corporation .... E 937 704-9909
  Franklin (G-11152)
Chaney Roofing Maintenance .... E 419 639-2761
  Clyde (G-6811)
Chemcote Roofing Company .... D 614 792-2683
  Dublin (G-10291)
Command Roofing Co .... C 937 298-1155
  Moraine (G-14760)
Contract Lumber Inc .... C 740 964-3147
  Pataskala (G-15921)
Cornelius Joel Roofing Inc .... E 513 367-4401
  Harrison (G-11795)
Dahm Brothers Company Inc .... E 937 461-5627
  Dayton (G-9449)
Dalton Roofing Co .... D 513 871-2800
  Cincinnati (G-3460)
Damschroder Roofing Inc .... E 419 332-5000
  Fremont (G-11194)
Daugherty Construction Inc .... E 216 731-9444
  Euclid (G-10748)
Deer Park Roofing Inc .... E 513 891-9151
  Cincinnati (G-3478)
Diamond Roofing Systems LLP .... E 330 856-2500
  Warren (G-18849)
Division 7 Inc .... E 740 965-1970
  Galena (G-11281)
Dun Rite Home Improvement Inc .... E 330 650-5322
  Macedonia (G-13196)
Durable Slate Co .... D 614 299-5522
  Columbus (G-7552)
Feazel Roofing Company .... E 614 898-7663
  Westerville (G-19306)
Fred Christen & Sons Company .... D 419 243-4161
  Toledo (G-17900)

CONTRACTORS: Roofing

Frost Roofing Inc .... D 419 739-2701
  Wapakoneta *(G-18796)*
Harold J Becker Company Inc .... E 614 279-1414
  Beavercreek *(G-1245)*
Hicks Roofing Inc .... E 330 364-7737
  New Philadelphia *(G-15100)*
Hinckley Roofing Inc .... E 330 722-7663
  Medina *(G-14076)*
Holland Roofing Inc .... E 614 430-3724
  Columbus *(G-7847)*
Industrial Energy Systems Inc .... E 216 267-9590
  Cleveland *(G-5816)*
K & W Roofing Inc .... E 740 927-3122
  Etna *(G-10735)*
Kelley Brothers Roofing Inc .... D 513 829-7717
  Fairfield *(G-10868)*
Kerkan Roofing Inc .... D 513 821-0556
  Cincinnati *(G-3917)*
Korman Construction Corp .... E 614 274-2170
  Columbus *(G-8011)*
Meade Construction Inc .... E 740 694-5525
  Lexington *(G-12715)*
Midwest Roofing & Furnace Co .... E 614 252-5241
  Columbus *(G-8172)*
Moisture Guard Corporation .... E 330 928-7200
  Stow *(G-17383)*
Molloy Roofing Company .... E 513 791-7400
  Blue Ash *(G-1645)*
N F Mansuetto & Sons Inc .... E 740 633-7320
  Martins Ferry *(G-13600)*
Nasco Roofing and Cnstr Inc .... E 330 746-3566
  Youngstown *(G-20294)*
Nations Roof of Ohio LLC .... E 937 439-4160
  Springboro *(G-17132)*
Nordmann Roofing Co Inc .... E 419 691-5737
  Toledo *(G-18089)*
Northern Ohio Roofg Shtmtl Inc .... E 440 322-8262
  Elyria *(G-10664)*
Phinney Industrial Roofing .... D 614 308-9000
  Columbus *(G-8542)*
Preferred Roofing Services LLC .... E 216 587-0957
  Cleveland *(G-6301)*
Promanco Inc .... E 740 374-2120
  Marietta *(G-13491)*
R & B Contractors LLC .... E 513 738-0954
  Shandon *(G-16873)*
Ray St Clair Roofing Inc .... E 513 874-1234
  Fairfield *(G-10898)*
Regency Roofing Companies Inc .... E 330 468-1021
  Macedonia *(G-13208)*
Richland Co & Associates Inc .... E 419 782-0141
  Defiance *(G-10054)*
Roofing By Insulation Inc .... E 937 315-5024
  New Carlisle *(G-15030)*
Roth Bros Inc .... C 330 793-5571
  Youngstown *(G-20360)*
Simon Roofing and Shtmtl Corp .... C 330 629-7392
  Youngstown *(G-20376)*
Squires Construction Company .... E 216 252-0300
  Rocky River *(G-16592)*
T & F Systems Inc .... D 216 881-3525
  Cleveland *(G-6563)*
Tecta America Corp .... D 419 447-1716
  Tiffin *(G-17703)*
Tecta America Zero Company LLC .... D 513 541-1848
  Cincinnati *(G-4632)*
Terik Roofing Inc .... E 330 785-0060
  Coventry Township *(G-9134)*
Tremco Incorporated .... B 216 292-5000
  Beachwood *(G-1133)*
Tycor Roofing Inc .... E 330 452-8150
  Canton *(G-2566)*
Valley Roofing LLC .... E 513 831-9444
  Milford *(G-14572)*
Weatherproofing Tech Inc .... D 216 292-5000
  Beachwood *(G-1136)*
Weatherproofing Tech Inc .... A 281 480-7900
  Beachwood *(G-1137)*
West Roofing Systems Inc .... E 800 356-5748
  Lagrange *(G-12462)*
Williams Bros Roofg Siding Co .... E 937 434-3838
  Dayton *(G-9999)*
Wm Kramer and Sons Inc .... D 513 353-1142
  Cleves *(G-6806)*
Wolfes Roofing Inc .... E 419 666-6233
  Walbridge *(G-18781)*

CONTRACTORS: Roofing & Gutter Work

Preferred Roofing Ohio Inc .... E 216 587-0957
  Cleveland *(G-6300)*

CONTRACTORS: Safety & Security Eqpt

Guardian Protection Svcs Inc .... E 330 797-1570
  Youngstown *(G-20211)*
Mills Security Alarm Systems .... E 513 921-4600
  Cincinnati *(G-4101)*
Simplex Time Recorder LLC .... E 513 874-1227
  West Chester *(G-19229)*

CONTRACTORS: Sandblasting Svc, Building Exteriors

Aerco Sandblasting Company .... E 419 224-2464
  Lima *(G-12732)*
Allstate Painting & Contg Co .... D 330 220-5533
  Brunswick *(G-1968)*
Euclid Indus Maint Clg Contrs .... C 216 361-0288
  Cleveland *(G-5553)*
Flamos Enterprises Inc .... E 330 478-0009
  Canton *(G-2369)*
Ionno Properties s Corp .... E 330 479-9267
  Dennison *(G-10165)*
Rak Corrosion Control Inc .... E 440 985-2171
  Amherst *(G-602)*
Universal Fabg Cnstr Svcs Inc .... D 614 274-1128
  Columbus *(G-8905)*

CONTRACTORS: Septic System

Accurate Mechanical Inc .... E 740 654-5898
  Lancaster *(G-12506)*
Mack Industries .... C 419 353-7081
  Bowling Green *(G-1785)*
Nieman Plumbing Inc .... D 513 851-5588
  Cincinnati *(G-4169)*
Zemba Bros Inc .... E 740 452-1880
  Zanesville *(G-20561)*

CONTRACTORS: Sheet Metal Work, NEC

All-Type Welding & Fabrication .... E 440 439-3990
  Cleveland *(G-4991)*
Anchor Metal Processing Inc .... E 216 362-1850
  Cleveland *(G-5035)*
Avon Lake Sheet Metal Co .... E 440 933-3505
  Avon Lake *(G-923)*
Budde Sheet Metal Works Inc .... E 937 224-0868
  Dayton *(G-9372)*
Detmer & Sons Inc .... E 937 879-2373
  Fairborn *(G-10793)*
Dimensional Metals Inc .... D 740 927-3633
  Reynoldsburg *(G-16447)*
Ducts Inc .... E 216 391-2400
  Cleveland *(G-5511)*
Eckstein Roofing Company .... E 513 941-1511
  Cincinnati *(G-3542)*
Franck and Fric Incorporated .... D 216 524-4451
  Cleveland *(G-5631)*
Geauga Mechanical Company .... D 440 285-2000
  Chardon *(G-2750)*
Global Insulation Inc .... D 330 479-3100
  Canton *(G-2381)*
Hickey Metal Fabrication Roofg .... E 330 337-9329
  Salem *(G-16698)*
J A Guy Inc .... E 937 642-3415
  Marysville *(G-13629)*
Kirk & Blum Manufacturing Co .... C 513 458-2600
  Cincinnati *(G-3929)*
Kirk & Blum Manufacturing Co .... E 419 782-9885
  Defiance *(G-10043)*
Mechanical Cnstr Managers LLC .... C 937 274-1987
  Dayton *(G-9709)*
Mechanical Construction Co .... E 740 353-5668
  Portsmouth *(G-16295)*
National Blanking LLC .... E 419 385-0636
  Toledo *(G-18073)*
Ohio Fabricators Inc .... E 216 391-2400
  Cleveland *(G-6190)*
Ontario Mechanical LLC .... E 419 529-2578
  Ontario *(G-15709)*
Pcy Enterprises Inc .... E 513 241-5566
  Cincinnati *(G-4270)*
Quality Electrical & Mech Inc .... E 419 294-3591
  Lima *(G-12865)*
Slagle Mechanical Contractors .... E 937 492-4151
  Sidney *(G-16956)*
Tendon Manufacturing Inc .... E 216 663-3200
  Cleveland *(G-6582)*
York-Mahoning Mech Contrs Inc .... D 330 788-7011
  Youngstown *(G-20420)*

CONTRACTORS: Sheet metal Work, Architectural

Ameridian Specialty Services .... E 513 769-0150
  Cincinnati *(G-3014)*
Giorgi of Chesapeake Inc .... E 740 256-1724
  Crown City *(G-9155)*

CONTRACTORS: Shoring & Underpinning

Boyas Excavating Inc .... E 216 524-3620
  Cleveland *(G-5131)*
Goettle Holding Company Inc .... C 513 825-8100
  Cincinnati *(G-3683)*

CONTRACTORS: Sidewalk

Cioffi & Son Construction .... E 330 794-9448
  Akron *(G-137)*

CONTRACTORS: Siding

Airko Inc .... E 440 333-0133
  Cleveland *(G-4978)*
Cardinal Builders Inc .... E 614 237-1000
  Columbus *(G-7190)*
Champion Opco LLC .... B 513 924-4858
  Cincinnati *(G-3228)*
D&T Installed Siding LLC .... E 614 444-8445
  Columbus *(G-7482)*
Erie Construction Mid-West Inc .... E 419 472-4200
  Toledo *(G-17869)*
Erie Construction Mid-West Inc .... E 937 898-4688
  Dayton *(G-9530)*
Holmes Siding Contractors .... D 330 674-2867
  Millersburg *(G-14605)*
Industrial First Inc .... C 216 991-8605
  Bedford *(G-1313)*
Olde Towne Windows Inc .... E 419 626-9613
  Milan *(G-14496)*
Regency Windows Corporation .... D 330 963-4077
  Twinsburg *(G-18459)*

CONTRACTORS: Single-Family Home Fire Damage Repair

AAA Standard Services Inc .... D 419 535-0274
  Toledo *(G-17737)*
Belfor USA Group Inc .... E 330 916-6468
  Peninsula *(G-15947)*
Davis Paul Restoration Dayton .... E 937 436-3411
  Moraine *(G-14766)*
Farris Enterprises Inc .... E 614 367-9611
  Worthington *(G-19960)*
Farrow Cleaners Inc .... E 216 561-2355
  Cleveland *(G-5574)*
Icon Environmental Group LLC .... E 513 426-6767
  Milford *(G-14526)*
Smb Construction Co Inc .... E 419 269-1473
  Toledo *(G-18191)*

CONTRACTORS: Single-family Home General Remodeling

1522 Hess Street LLC .... E 614 291-6876
  Columbus *(G-6912)*
AAA Home Repair Services .... E 937 748-9988
  Springboro *(G-17112)*
Airko Inc .... E 440 333-0133
  Cleveland *(G-4978)*
Apco Industries Inc .... D 614 224-2345
  Columbus *(G-7027)*
Apex Restoration Contrs Ltd .... E 513 489-1795
  Cincinnati *(G-3035)*
Arnolds Home Improvement LLC .... E 734 847-9600
  Toledo *(G-17759)*
Berlin Construction Ltd .... E 330 893-2003
  Millersburg *(G-14587)*
Brian-Kyles Construction Inc .... E 440 242-0298
  Lorain *(G-13019)*
Burge Building Co Inc .... E 440 245-6871
  Lorain *(G-13021)*
Cardinal Builders Inc .... E 614 237-1000
  Columbus *(G-7190)*
Community Improvement Corp .... E 440 466-4675
  Geneva *(G-11360)*
Craftsmen Restoration LLC 877 442-3424
  Akron *(G-174)*
Disaster Reconstruction Inc .... E 440 918-1523
  Eastlake *(G-10545)*
Dry It Rite LLC .... E 614 295-8135
  Columbus *(G-7546)*

SERVICES SECTION

CONTRACTORS: Underground Utilities

Edrich Supply Co ....E 440 238-9440
 Strongsville *(G-17459)*
Erie Construction Mid-West Inc ....E 937 898-4688
 Dayton *(G-9530)*
Harrison Construction Inc ....E 740 373-7000
 Marietta *(G-13450)*
Hometown Improvement Co ....E 614 846-1060
 Columbus *(G-7853)*
Improve It Home Remodeling Inc ....E 614 297-5121
 Columbus *(G-7886)*
Ingle-Barr Inc ....D 740 702-6117
 Chillicothe *(G-2853)*
J & D Home Improvement Inc ....D 740 927-0722
 Reynoldsburg *(G-16459)*
J Russell Construction ....E 330 633-6462
 Tallmadge *(G-17642)*
Midwest Roofing & Furnace Co ....E 614 252-5241
 Columbus *(G-8172)*
Mural & Son Inc ....E 216 267-3322
 Cleveland *(G-6090)*
Neals Construction Company ....E 513 489-7700
 Cincinnati *(G-4149)*
Nextt Corp ....E 513 813-6398
 Cincinnati *(G-4165)*
Nitschke Sampson Dietz Inc ....E 614 464-1933
 Columbus *(G-8281)*
Nrp Group LLC ....D 216 475-8900
 Cleveland *(G-6167)*
Rubber City Realty Inc ....D 330 745-9034
 Akron *(G-421)*
Squires Construction Company ....E 216 252-0300
 Rocky River *(G-16592)*
Sure Home Improvments LLC ....E 614 586-0610
 Columbus *(G-8811)*
Toth Renovation LLC ....E 614 542-9683
 Columbus *(G-8855)*
Wingler Construction Corp ....E 614 626-8546
 Columbus *(G-9000)*

CONTRACTORS: Skylight Installation

Scs Construction Services Inc ....E 513 929-0260
 Cincinnati *(G-4487)*

CONTRACTORS: Solar Energy Eqpt

Dovetail Construction Co Inc ....E 740 592-1800
 Cleveland *(G-5508)*

CONTRACTORS: Sound Eqpt Installation

Eighth Day Sound Systems Inc ....E 440 995-2647
 Cleveland *(G-5529)*
Live Technologies Holdings Inc ....D 614 278-7777
 Columbus *(G-8074)*

CONTRACTORS: Special Trades, NEC

Brown Contracting & Dev LLC ....E 419 341-3939
 Port Clinton *(G-16238)*
Central Ohio Custom Contg LLC ....E 614 579-4971
 Mount Vernon *(G-14882)*
Multi Cntry SEC Slutions Group ....E 216 973-0291
 Cleveland *(G-6089)*
Toledo Area Insulator Wkrs Jac ....D 419 531-5911
 Toledo *(G-18226)*
Trinity Contracting Inc ....D 614 905-4410
 Columbus *(G-8871)*

CONTRACTORS: Specialized Public Building

Forest City Residential Dev ....E 216 621-6060
 Cleveland *(G-5621)*

CONTRACTORS: Spraying, Nonagricultural

Resource International Inc ....C 614 823-4949
 Columbus *(G-8622)*

CONTRACTORS: Sprinkler System

Eckert Fire Protec ....E 513 948-1030
 Cincinnati *(G-3541)*
Johnson Controls ....C 440 268-1160
 Strongsville *(G-17478)*
Supply Network Inc ....E 614 527-5800
 Columbus *(G-8806)*

CONTRACTORS: Steam Cleaning, Building Exterior

TNT Mobile Powerwash Inc ....E 614 402-7474
 Canal Winchester *(G-2172)*

CONTRACTORS: Stone Masonry

Casagrande Masonry Inc ....E 740 964-0781
 New Albany *(G-14980)*
Lang Masonry Contractors Inc ....D 740 749-3512
 Waterford *(G-18939)*
S P S & Associates Inc ....E 330 283-4267
 Silver Lake *(G-16963)*
Van Ness Stone Inc ....E 440 564-1111
 Newbury *(G-15263)*

CONTRACTORS: Storage Tank Erection, Metal

Columbiana Boiler Company LLC ....E 330 482-3373
 Columbiana *(G-6855)*
Daniel A Terreri & Sons Inc ....E 330 538-2950
 Youngstown *(G-20165)*
FSRc Tanks Inc ....E 234 221-2015
 Bolivar *(G-1747)*
Mid Atlantic Stor Systems Inc ....D 740 335-2019
 Wshngtn CT Hs *(G-20032)*

CONTRACTORS: Store Fixture Installation

Goliath Contracting Ltd ....E 614 568-7878
 Reynoldsburg *(G-16455)*

CONTRACTORS: Structural Iron Work, Structural

Columbus Steel Erectors Inc ....E 614 876-5050
 Columbus *(G-7388)*
Forest City Erectors Inc ....D 330 425-2345
 Twinsburg *(G-18417)*
Foundation Steel LLC ....D 419 402-4241
 Swanton *(G-17564)*
J&H Rnfrcing Strl Erectors Inc ....C 740 355-0141
 Portsmouth *(G-16292)*
Orbit Movers & Erectors Inc ....E 937 277-8080
 Dayton *(G-9793)*
Sofco Erectors Inc ....E 513 771-1600
 Cincinnati *(G-4549)*

CONTRACTORS: Structural Steel Erection

Akron Erectors Inc ....E 330 745-7100
 Akron *(G-39)*
Black Swamp Steel Inc ....E 419 867-8050
 Holland *(G-12010)*
Dublin Building Systems Co ....E 614 760-5831
 Dublin *(G-10325)*
Evers Welding Co Inc ....E 513 385-7352
 Cincinnati *(G-3582)*
Frederick Steel Company LLC ....D 513 821-6400
 Cincinnati *(G-3646)*
GL Nause Co Inc ....E 513 722-9500
 Loveland *(G-13128)*
Henry Gurtzweiler Inc ....D 419 729-3955
 Toledo *(G-17953)*
Hovest Construction ....E 419 456-3426
 Ottawa *(G-15798)*
Industrial First Inc ....C 216 991-8605
 Bedford *(G-1313)*
Kelley Steel Erectors Inc ....E 440 232-1573
 Cleveland *(G-5891)*
Legacy Industrial Services LLC ....E 606 584-8953
 Ripley *(G-16547)*
Marysville Steel Inc ....E 937 642-5971
 Marysville *(G-13636)*
Mason Steel Erecting Inc ....E 440 439-1040
 Cleveland *(G-5992)*
Mohawk RE-Bar Services Inc ....E 440 268-0780
 Strongsville *(G-17495)*
Mound Technologies Inc ....E 937 748-2937
 Springboro *(G-17131)*
Northhend Archtctural Pdts Inc ....E 513 577-7988
 Cincinnati *(G-4179)*
Ontario Mechanical LLC ....E 419 529-2578
 Ontario *(G-15709)*
R&F Erectors Inc ....E 513 574-8273
 Cincinnati *(G-4381)*
Reading Rock Residential LLC ....E 513 874-4770
 West Chester *(G-19223)*
Rittman Inc ....D 330 927-6855
 Rittman *(G-16556)*
Sawyer Steel Erectors Inc ....E 419 867-8050
 Holland *(G-12052)*
Seneca Steel Erectors Inc ....E 740 385-0517
 Logan *(G-12987)*
Smith Brothers Erection Inc ....E 740 373-3575
 Marietta *(G-13500)*

Stein Inc ....D 216 883-4277
 Cleveland *(G-6535)*

CONTRACTORS: Svc Station Eqpt

Empaco Equipment Corporation ....E 330 659-9393
 Richfield *(G-16505)*

CONTRACTORS: Svc Station Eqpt Installation, Maint & Repair

Industrial Fiberglass Spc Inc ....E 937 222-9000
 Dayton *(G-9630)*
X F Construction Svcs Inc ....E 614 575-2700
 Columbus *(G-9012)*

CONTRACTORS: Tile Installation, Ceramic

OCP Contractors Inc ....E 419 865-7168
 Holland *(G-12043)*
Rite Rug Co ....E 614 552-1190
 Reynoldsburg *(G-16478)*
Southwestern Tile and MBL Co ....E 614 464-1257
 Columbus *(G-8757)*
Virginia Tile Company ....E 216 741-8400
 Brooklyn Heights *(G-1931)*

CONTRACTORS: Trenching

Byrnes-Conway Company ....D 513 948-8882
 Cincinnati *(G-3159)*
Maintenance Unlimited Inc ....E 440 238-1162
 Strongsville *(G-17486)*
Mollett Seamless Gutter Co ....E 513 825-0500
 West Chester *(G-19123)*

CONTRACTORS: Tuck Pointing & Restoration

American International Cnstr ....E 440 243-5535
 Berea *(G-1445)*
Harold K Phlips Rstration Inc ....E 614 443-5699
 Columbus *(G-7802)*
Kapton Caulking & Building ....E 440 526-0670
 Cleveland *(G-5883)*
Lencyk Masonry Co Inc ....E 330 729-9780
 Youngstown *(G-20254)*
Platinum Restoration Inc ....E 440 327-0699
 Elyria *(G-10671)*
Technical Construction Spc ....E 330 929-1088
 Cuyahoga Falls *(G-9224)*

CONTRACTORS: Underground Utilities

Amboy Contractors LLc ....D 419 644-2111
 Metamora *(G-14264)*
American Boring Inc ....E 740 969-8000
 Carroll *(G-2607)*
Anderzack-Pitzen Cnstr Inc ....E 419 553-7015
 Metamora *(G-14265)*
Finlaw Construction Inc ....E 330 889-2074
 Bristolville *(G-1871)*
Fishel Company ....C 614 850-9012
 Columbus *(G-7668)*
Geotex Construction Svcs Inc ....E 614 444-5690
 Columbus *(G-7745)*
Gleason Construction Co Inc ....D 419 865-7480
 Holland *(G-12024)*
Great Lakes Crushing Ltd ....E 440 944-5500
 Wickliffe *(G-19599)*
J Daniel & Company Inc ....D 513 575-3100
 Loveland *(G-13134)*
JS Bova Excavating LLC ....E 234 254-4040
 Struthers *(G-17532)*
Ohio Utilities Protection Svc ....D 330 759-0050
 Youngstown *(G-20310)*
Precision Pipeline Svcs LLC ....E 740 652-1679
 Lancaster *(G-12565)*
R D Jergens Contractors Inc ....D 937 669-9799
 Vandalia *(G-18697)*
Terrace Construction Co Inc ....D 216 739-3170
 Cleveland *(G-6585)*
Trucco Construction Co Inc ....C 740 417-9010
 Delaware *(G-10130)*
Usic Locating Services LLC ....E 419 874-9988
 North Baltimore *(G-15316)*
Usic Locating Services LLC ....D 513 554-0456
 Cincinnati *(G-4799)*
Utilicon Corporation ....E 216 391-8500
 Cleveland *(G-6680)*
Woodward Excavating Co ....E 614 866-4384
 Reynoldsburg *(G-16491)*

CONTRACTORS: Ventilation & Duct Work

A A S Amels Sheet Meta L Inc..............E....... 330 793-9326
Youngstown *(G-20094)*
Feldkamp Enterprises Inc..............C....... 513 347-4500
Cincinnati *(G-3600)*
Franck and Fric Incorporated..............D....... 216 524-4451
Cleveland *(G-5631)*
Jacobs Mechanical Co..............C....... 513 681-6800
Cincinnati *(G-3857)*
Sisler Heating & Cooling Inc..............E....... 330 722-7101
Medina *(G-14126)*
TH Martin Inc..............D....... 216 741-2020
Cleveland *(G-6588)*

CONTRACTORS: Wall Covering

Clubhouse Pub N Grub..............E....... 440 884-2582
Cleveland *(G-5368)*

CONTRACTORS: Wall Covering, Commercial

Cleveland Construction Inc..............E....... 440 255-8000
Mason *(G-13685)*

CONTRACTORS: Warm Air Heating & Air Conditioning

A A Astro Service Inc..............D....... 216 459-0363
Cleveland *(G-4928)*
A To Zoff Co Inc..............E....... 330 733-7902
Akron *(G-12)*
Accurate Heating & Cooling..............E....... 740 775-5005
Chillicothe *(G-2807)*
Air Comfort Systems Inc..............E....... 216 587-4125
Cleveland *(G-4971)*
Air Conditioning Entps Inc..............E....... 440 729-0900
Cleveland *(G-4973)*
Air-Temp Climate Control Inc..............E....... 216 579-1552
Cleveland *(G-4974)*
Aire-Tech Inc..............E....... 614 836-5670
Groveport *(G-11621)*
Airtron LP..............D....... 614 274-2345
Columbus *(G-6960)*
Airtron LP..............D....... 513 860-5959
Cincinnati *(G-2902)*
All About Heating Cooling..............E....... 513 621-4620
Cincinnati *(G-2984)*
Apollo Heating and AC Inc..............E....... 513 271-3600
Cincinnati *(G-3036)*
Apple Heating Inc..............E....... 440 997-1212
Barberton *(G-952)*
Arco Heating & AC Co..............E....... 216 663-3211
Solon *(G-16976)*
Ashland Comfort Control Inc..............E....... 419 281-0144
Ashland *(G-656)*
Atlas Capital Services Inc..............D....... 614 294-7373
Columbus *(G-7069)*
Bachmans Inc..............E....... 513 943-5300
Batavia *(G-995)*
Bay Furnace Sheet Metal Co..............E....... 440 871-3777
Westlake *(G-19463)*
Blind & Son LLC..............D....... 330 753-7711
Barberton *(G-959)*
Brennan & Associates Inc..............E....... 216 391-4822
Cleveland *(G-5135)*
Burrier Service Company Inc..............E....... 440 946-6019
Mentor *(G-14151)*
Castle Heating & Air Inc..............E....... 216 696-3940
Solon *(G-16989)*
Century Mech Solutions Inc..............E....... 513 681-5700
Cincinnati *(G-3220)*
Cincinnati Air Conditioning Co..............D....... 513 721-5622
Cincinnati *(G-3279)*
Colonial Heating & Cooling Co..............E....... 614 837-6100
Pickerington *(G-16091)*
Columbs/Worthington Htg AC Inc..............E....... 614 771-5381
Columbus *(G-7325)*
Columbus Heating & Vent Co..............C....... 614 274-1177
Columbus *(G-7357)*
Comfort Systems USA Ohio Inc..............E....... 440 703-1600
Bedford *(G-1300)*
Commercial Comfort Systems Inc..............E....... 419 481-4444
Perrysburg *(G-15988)*
Corcoran and Harnist Htg & AC..............E....... 513 921-2227
Cincinnati *(G-3421)*
Crane Heating & AC Co..............E....... 513 641-4700
Cincinnati *(G-3438)*
Crown Heating & Cooling Inc..............D....... 330 499-4988
Uniontown *(G-18516)*
Custom AC & Htg Co..............D....... 614 552-4822
Gahanna *(G-11238)*
David R White Services Inc..............E....... 740 594-8381
Athens *(G-782)*
Del Monde Inc..............E....... 859 371-7780
Miamisburg *(G-14296)*
Detmer & Sons Inc..............E....... 937 879-2373
Fairborn *(G-10793)*
Dooley Heating and AC LLC..............E....... 614 278-9944
Columbus *(G-7541)*
Drake State Air Systems Inc..............E....... 937 472-0640
Eaton *(G-10558)*
Favret Company..............D....... 614 488-5211
Columbus *(G-7644)*
Fitzenrider Inc..............E....... 419 784-0828
Defiance *(G-10032)*
Geauga Mechanical Company..............D....... 440 285-2000
Chardon *(G-2750)*
Gene Tolliver Corp..............D....... 440 324-7727
Medina *(G-14068)*
General Temperature Ctrl Inc..............E....... 614 837-3888
Canal Winchester *(G-2159)*
Genes Refrigeration Htg & AC..............E....... 330 723-4104
Medina *(G-14069)*
Gilbert Heating & AC..............E....... 419 625-8875
Sandusky *(G-16762)*
Gundlach Sheet Metal Works Inc..............D....... 419 626-4525
Sandusky *(G-16766)*
Gundlach Sheet Metal Works Inc..............E....... 419 734-7351
Port Clinton *(G-16246)*
Haslett Heating & Cooling Inc..............E....... 614 299-2133
Dublin *(G-10358)*
Havsco Inc..............E....... 440 439-8900
Bedford *(G-1310)*
Helm and Associates Inc..............E....... 419 893-1480
Maumee *(G-13924)*
Imperial Heating and Coolg Inc..............D....... 440 498-1788
Solon *(G-17017)*
Inloes Mechanical Inc..............E....... 513 896-9499
Hamilton *(G-11744)*
J A Guy Inc..............E....... 937 642-3415
Marysville *(G-13629)*
J F Bernard Inc..............E....... 330 785-3830
Akron *(G-285)*
J W Geopfert Co Inc..............E....... 330 762-2293
Akron *(G-287)*
Jennings Heating Company Inc..............E....... 330 784-1286
Akron *(G-293)*
Jonle Co Inc..............E....... 513 662-2282
Cincinnati *(G-3885)*
K Company Incorporated..............C....... 330 773-5125
Coventry Township *(G-9127)*
Kessler Heating & Cooling..............E....... 614 837-9961
Canal Winchester *(G-2163)*
Kidron Electric Inc..............E....... 330 857-2871
Kidron *(G-12443)*
Kusan Inc..............E....... 614 262-1818
Columbus *(G-8018)*
Lakes Heating and AC..............E....... 330 644-7811
Coventry Township *(G-9128)*
Langdon Inc..............E....... 513 733-5955
Cincinnati *(G-3960)*
Limbach Company LLC..............E....... 614 299-2175
Columbus *(G-8066)*
Luxury Heating Co..............D....... 440 366-0971
Sheffield Village *(G-16890)*
M&M Heating & Cooling Inc..............D....... 419 243-3005
Toledo *(G-18024)*
McAfee Heating & AC Co Inc..............E....... 937 438-1976
Dayton *(G-9706)*
Metal Masters Inc..............E....... 330 343-3515
Dover *(G-10198)*
Metro Heating and AC Co..............E....... 614 777-1237
Hilliard *(G-11929)*
Midwest Roofing & Furnace Co..............E....... 614 252-5241
Columbus *(G-8172)*
Miracle Plumbing & Heating Co..............E....... 330 477-2402
Canton *(G-2464)*
Noron Inc..............E....... 419 726-2677
Toledo *(G-18092)*
Ogrinc Mechanical Corporation..............E....... 216 765-8010
Cleveland *(G-6183)*
Ohio Heating and Refrigeration..............E....... 614 863-6666
Columbus *(G-8351)*
Osterwisch Company Inc..............D....... 513 791-3282
Cincinnati *(G-4240)*
Overcashier and Horst Htg & AC..............E....... 419 841-3333
Sylvania *(G-17605)*
P K Wadsworth Heating & Coolg..............E....... 440 248-4821
Solon *(G-17037)*
Peck-Hannaford Briggs Svc Corp..............D....... 513 681-1200
Cincinnati *(G-4271)*
Perfection Group Inc..............C....... 513 772-7545
Cincinnati *(G-4279)*
Perfection Services Inc..............E....... 513 772-7545
Cincinnati *(G-4281)*
Pre-Fore Inc..............E....... 740 467-2206
Millersport *(G-14631)*
Quality Electrical & Mech Inc..............E....... 419 294-3591
Lima *(G-12865)*
Recker and Boerger Inc..............D....... 513 942-9663
West Chester *(G-19224)*
Reupert Heating and AC Co Inc..............E....... 513 922-5050
Cincinnati *(G-4410)*
Roth Bros Inc..............C....... 330 793-5571
Youngstown *(G-20360)*
Sals Heating and Cooling Inc..............E....... 216 676-4949
Cleveland *(G-6438)*
Schmids Service Now Inc..............E....... 330 264-2040
Wooster *(G-19913)*
Schneller Heating and AC Co..............E....... 859 341-1200
Cincinnati *(G-2930)*
Schumm Richard A Plbg & Htg..............E....... 419 238-4994
Van Wert *(G-18643)*
Smith & Oby Company..............D....... 440 735-5333
Walton Hills *(G-18791)*
Smith & Oby Service Co..............E....... 440 735-5322
Bedford *(G-1337)*
Smylie One Heating & Cooling..............E....... 440 449-4328
Bedford *(G-1338)*
Superior Mechanical Svcs Inc..............E....... 937 259-0082
Dayton *(G-9284)*
Tanner Heating & AC Inc..............E....... 937 299-2500
Moraine *(G-14829)*
Timmerman John P Heating AC Co..............E....... 419 229-4015
Lima *(G-12900)*
Trane Inc..............E....... 440 946-7823
Mentor *(G-14248)*
Universal Enterprises Inc..............C....... 419 529-3500
Ontario *(G-15718)*
V M Systems Inc..............D....... 419 535-1044
Toledo *(G-18285)*
Volpone Enterprises Inc..............E....... 440 969-1141
Ashtabula *(G-767)*
Waibel Heating Company..............E....... 614 837-7615
Canal Winchester *(G-2176)*
Watkins Mechanical Inc..............E....... 937 748-0220
Springboro *(G-17141)*
Willis One Hour Heating & AC..............D....... 513 752-2512
Cincinnati *(G-2938)*
Wojos Heating & AC Inc..............E....... 419 693-3220
Northwood *(G-15552)*

CONTRACTORS: Water Well Drilling

Collector Wells Intl Inc..............E....... 614 888-6263
Columbus *(G-7320)*
Moodys of Dayton Inc..............E....... 614 443-3898
Miamisburg *(G-14323)*
Patterson-Uti Drilling Co LLC..............E....... 724 239-2812
Saint Clairsville *(G-16652)*

CONTRACTORS: Water Well Servicing

Ohio Drilling Company..............E....... 330 832-1521
Massillon *(G-13842)*

CONTRACTORS: Waterproofing

Adelmos Electric Sewer Clg Co..............E....... 216 641-2301
Brooklyn Heights *(G-1909)*
Basement Systems Ohio Inc..............C....... 330 423-4430
Twinsburg *(G-18396)*
Burbank Inc..............E....... 419 698-3434
Toledo *(G-17788)*
Daniels Basement Waterproofing..............E....... 440 965-4332
Berlin Heights *(G-1481)*
Gem City Waterproofing..............E....... 937 220-6800
Dayton *(G-9569)*
Harold J Becker Company Inc..............E....... 614 279-1414
Beavercreek *(G-1245)*
J & D Home Improvement Inc..............D....... 740 927-0722
Reynoldsburg *(G-16459)*
Jaco Waterproofing LLC..............E....... 513 738-0084
Fairfield *(G-10865)*
Kapton Caulking & Building..............E....... 440 526-0670
Cleveland *(G-5883)*
Mural & Son Inc..............E....... 216 267-3322
Cleveland *(G-6090)*
Ohio State Home Services Inc..............C....... 330 467-1055
Macedonia *(G-13207)*
Ohio State Home Services Inc..............D....... 614 850-5600
Hilliard *(G-11940)*

SERVICES SECTION

CONVALESCENT HOMES

Paul Peterson Company ....E....... 614 486-4375
  Columbus *(G-8522)*
Ram Construction Services ....E....... 440 740-0100
  Broadview Heights *(G-1890)*
Ram Construction Services of ....D....... 513 297-1857
  West Chester *(G-19137)*
Riverfront Diversified Inc ....D....... 513 874-7200
  West Chester *(G-19142)*
Rusk Industries Inc ....D....... 419 841-6055
  Toledo *(G-18168)*
Suburban Maint & Cnstr Inc ....E....... 440 237-7765
  North Royalton *(G-15503)*
U S A Waterproofing Inc ....E....... 330 425-2440
  Twinsburg *(G-18481)*
Unified Cnstr Systems Ltd ....E....... 330 773-2511
  Akron *(G-483)*

CONTRACTORS: Window Treatment Installation

Vwc Liquidation Company LLC ....C....... 330 372-6776
  Warren *(G-18922)*

CONTRACTORS: Windows & Doors

Door Shop & Service Inc ....E....... 614 423-8043
  Westerville *(G-19301)*
Fortune Brands Windows Inc ....B....... 614 532-3500
  Columbus *(G-7681)*
Traichal Construction Company ....E....... 800 255-3667
  Niles *(G-15307)*
Youngstown Automatic Door Co ....E....... 330 747-3135
  Youngstown *(G-20427)*

CONTRACTORS: Wood Floor Installation & Refinishing

Cincinnati Floor Company Inc ....E....... 513 641-4500
  Cincinnati *(G-3305)*
Continental Office Furn Corp ....C....... 614 262-5010
  Columbus *(G-7428)*
Frank Novak & Sons Inc ....D....... 216 475-2495
  Cleveland *(G-5632)*
Hoover & Wells Inc ....C....... 419 691-9220
  Toledo *(G-17959)*
K H F Inc ....E....... 330 928-0694
  Cuyahoga Falls *(G-9200)*
Schumacher & Co Inc ....E....... 859 655-9000
  Milford *(G-14560)*

CONTRACTORS: Wrecking & Demolition

Allgeier & Son Inc ....E....... 513 574-3735
  Cincinnati *(G-2988)*
Allied Erct & Dismantling Co ....C....... 330 744-0808
  Youngstown *(G-20101)*
Aztec Services Group Inc ....D....... 513 541-2002
  Cincinnati *(G-3071)*
Bladecutters Lawn Service Inc ....E....... 937 274-3861
  Dayton *(G-9360)*
Boyas Excavating Inc ....E....... 216 524-3620
  Cleveland *(G-5131)*
Brunk Excavating Inc ....E....... 513 360-0308
  Monroe *(G-14691)*
Charles F Jergens Cnstr Inc ....E....... 937 233-1830
  Dayton *(G-9399)*
Cook Paving and Cnstr Co ....E....... 216 267-7705
  Independence *(G-12201)*
Dave Sugar Excavating LLC ....E....... 330 542-1100
  Petersburg *(G-16081)*
Fluor-Bwxt Portsmouth LLC ....A....... 866 706-6992
  Piketon *(G-16115)*
Mosier Industrial Services ....E....... 419 683-4000
  Crestline *(G-9148)*
Ray Bertolini Trucking Co ....E....... 330 867-0666
  Akron *(C-405)*
Rnw Holdings Inc ....E....... 330 792-0600
  Youngstown *(G-20352)*
Schaffer Mark Excvtg & Trcking ....D....... 419 668-5990
  Norwalk *(G-15592)*
Sunesis Environmental LLC ....D....... 513 326-6000
  Fairfield *(G-10912)*

CONTROL EQPT: Electric

Controls Inc ....E....... 330 239-4345
  Medina *(G-14051)*

CONTROL EQPT: Noise

Tech Products Corporation ....E....... 937 438-1100
  Miamisburg *(G-14355)*

CONTROL PANELS: Electrical

Innovative Controls Corp ....D....... 419 691-6684
  Toledo *(G-17974)*
Instrmntation Ctrl Systems Inc ....E....... 513 662-2600
  Cincinnati *(G-3822)*
Panelmatic Inc ....E....... 330 782-8007
  Youngstown *(G-20315)*
Scott Fetzer Company ....C....... 216 267-9000
  Cleveland *(G-6452)*

CONTROLS & ACCESS: Indl, Electric

Corrotec Inc ....E....... 937 325-3585
  Springfield *(G-17177)*
PMC Systems Limited ....E....... 330 538-2268
  North Jackson *(G-15386)*

CONTROLS: Environmental

Alan Manufacturing Inc ....E....... 330 262-1555
  Wooster *(G-19825)*
Babcock & Wilcox Company ....A....... 330 753-4511
  Barberton *(G-955)*
Cincinnati Air Conditioning Co ....D....... 513 721-5622
  Cincinnati *(G-3279)*
Hunter Defense Tech Inc ....E....... 216 438-6111
  Solon *(G-17016)*
Peco II Inc ....D....... 614 431-0694
  Columbus *(G-8528)*
Pepperl + Fuchs Inc ....C....... 330 425-3555
  Twinsburg *(G-18452)*
Schneder Elc Bldngs Amrcas Inc ....D....... 513 398-9800
  Lebanon *(G-12644)*

CONTROLS: Relay & Ind

Chandler Systems Incorporated ....D....... 888 363-9434
  Ashland *(G-673)*
Command Alkon Incorporated ....D....... 614 799-0600
  Dublin *(G-10302)*
Curtiss-Wright Controls ....E....... 937 252-5601
  Fairborn *(G-10789)*
GE Aviation Systems LLC ....B....... 937 898-5881
  Vandalia *(G-18681)*
Hite Parts Exchange Inc ....E....... 614 272-5115
  Columbus *(G-7842)*
Innovative Controls Corp ....D....... 419 691-6684
  Toledo *(G-17974)*
Peco II Inc ....D....... 614 431-0694
  Columbus *(G-8528)*
Pepperl + Fuchs Inc ....C....... 330 425-3555
  Twinsburg *(G-18452)*
Schneider Electric Usa Inc ....D....... 513 755-5000
  West Chester *(G-19145)*
Stock Fairfield Corporation ....C....... 440 543-6000
  Chagrin Falls *(G-2735)*

CONVALESCENT HOME

ASAP Homecare Inc ....D....... 330 491-0700
  Canton *(G-2246)*
Bel Air Care Center ....D....... 330 821-3939
  Alliance *(G-527)*
Birchaven Village ....E....... 419 424-3000
  Findlay *(G-10995)*
Bmnh Inc ....C....... 937 845-3561
  New Carlisle *(G-15020)*
Brewster Parke Inc ....D....... 330 767-4179
  Brewster *(G-1854)*
Brookdale Senior Living Inc ....E....... 419 756-5599
  Mansfield *(G-13270)*
Brookdale Senior Living Inc ....D....... 330 666-7011
  Akron *(G-114)*
Brookdale Senior Living Inc ....F....... 440 802 4200
  Westlake *(G-19467)*
Brookview Healthcare Ctr ....D....... 419 784-1014
  Defiance *(G-10020)*
Chcc Home Health Care ....E....... 330 759-4069
  Austintown *(G-869)*
Country Club Center Homes Inc ....D....... 330 343-6351
  Dover *(G-10182)*
Dublin Geriatric Care Co LP ....E....... 614 761-1188
  Dublin *(G-10328)*
Elms Retirement Village Inc ....D....... 440 647-2414
  Wellington *(G-18991)*
Gaslite Villa Convalescent Ctr ....E....... 330 494-4500
  Canal Fulton *(G-2143)*
Golden Living LLC ....D....... 419 599-4070
  Napoleon *(G-14941)*
Golden Living LLC ....D....... 419 227-2154
  Lima *(G-12784)*
Golden Living LLC ....D....... 419 394-3308
  Saint Marys *(G-16674)*
Golden Living LLC ....C....... 440 247-4200
  Chagrin Falls *(G-2698)*
Golden Living LLC ....C....... 614 861-6666
  Columbus *(G-7759)*
Golden Living LLC ....C....... 440 256-8100
  Willoughby *(G-19667)*
Golden Living LLC ....C....... 330 297-5781
  Ravenna *(G-16386)*
Golden Living LLC ....C....... 330 762-6486
  Akron *(G-240)*
Golden Living LLC ....D....... 330 335-1558
  Wadsworth *(G-18753)*
Golden Living LLC ....D....... 330 725-3393
  Medina *(G-14071)*
Hcf Management Inc ....D....... 419 435-8112
  Fostoria *(G-11131)*
Heath Nursing Care Center ....C....... 740 522-1171
  Newark *(G-15173)*
Hospice of The Western Reserve ....D....... 440 357-5833
  Mentor *(G-14193)*
Hospice of The Western Reserve ....C....... 216 227-9048
  Cleveland *(G-5781)*
J E F Inc ....D....... 513 921-4130
  Cincinnati *(G-3851)*
Laurel Health Care Company ....C....... 614 885-0408
  Worthington *(G-19969)*
Lcd Home Health Agency LLC ....E....... 513 497-0441
  Hamilton *(G-11753)*
Lima Cnvlscent HM Fndation Inc ....D....... 419 227-5450
  Lima *(G-12818)*
Marymount Health Care Systems ....E....... 216 332-1100
  Cleveland *(G-5990)*
Mennonite Memorial Home Inc ....E....... 419 358-7654
  Bluffton *(G-1735)*
National Church Residences ....C....... 614 451-2151
  Columbus *(G-8215)*
Nentwick Convalescent Home ....C....... 330 385-5001
  East Liverpool *(G-10527)*
Ohio Presbt Retirement Svcs ....C....... 937 415-5666
  Dayton *(G-9789)*
Ohio Valley Manor Inc ....C....... 937 392-4318
  Ripley *(G-16548)*
Provider Services Inc ....D....... 614 888-2021
  Columbus *(G-8575)*
Rae-Ann Enterprises Inc ....C....... 440 249-5092
  Cleveland *(G-6346)*
RMS of Ohio Inc ....E....... 513 841-0990
  Cincinnati *(G-4431)*
Salutary Providers Inc ....C....... 440 964-8446
  Ashtabula *(G-762)*
Senior Care Inc ....E....... 937 291-3211
  Miamisburg *(G-14347)*
Senior Lifestyle Corporation ....D....... 513 777-4457
  West Chester *(G-19150)*
University Hospitals Health ....A....... 440 285-4040
  Chardon *(G-2775)*
Vienna Enterprises Inc ....C....... 937 568-4524
  South Vienna *(G-17101)*
Wedgewood Estates ....E....... 419 756-7400
  Westerville *(G-19358)*
Whetstone Care Center LLC ....C....... 614 457-1100
  Columbus *(G-8985)*
Whetstone Care Center LLC ....C....... 740 474-6036
  Circleville *(G-4908)*
Whispering Hills Care Center ....E....... 740 392-3982
  Mount Vernon *(G-14925)*

CONVALESCENT HOMES

3g Operating Company LLC ....B....... 440 944-9400
  Parma *(G-15897)*
Altenheim Foundation Inc ....E....... 440 238-3361
  Strongsville *(G-17442)*
Altercare of Bucyrus Inc ....C....... 419 562-7644
  Bucyrus *(G-2023)*
Altercare of Mentor Center ....C....... 440 953-4421
  Mentor *(G-14142)*
Altercare of Millersburg ....D....... 330 674-4444
  Millersburg *(G-14584)*
Amberwood Manor ....C....... 330 339-2151
  New Philadelphia *(G-15081)*
American Nursing Care Inc ....D....... 513 576-0262
  Milford *(G-14503)*
American Nursing Care Inc ....D....... 419 228-0888
  Lima *(G-12741)*
Anderson Healthcare Ltd ....D....... 513 474-6200
  Cincinnati *(G-3022)*
Andover Vlg Retirement Cmnty ....C....... 440 293-5416
  Andover *(G-610)*

CONVALESCENT HOMES SERVICES SECTION

Austin Woods Nursing Center ....C.... 330 792-7681
Youngstown *(G-20107)*

Autumn Hills Care Center Inc ....C.... 330 652-2053
Niles *(G-15283)*

Beacon of Light Ltd ....E.... 419 531-9060
Toledo *(G-17765)*

Bellbrook Rhbltion Healthcare ....D.... 937 848-8421
Bellbrook *(G-1370)*

Bethany Nursing Home Inc ....E.... 330 492-7171
Canton *(G-2262)*

Blossom Hills Nursing Home ....D.... 440 635-5567
Huntsburg *(G-12157)*

Braeview Manor Inc ....C.... 216 486-9300
Cleveland *(G-5132)*

Brecksville Leasing Co LLC ....C.... 330 659-6166
Richfield *(G-16498)*

Brenn Field Nursing Center ....C.... 330 683-4075
Orrville *(G-15767)*

Brentwood Life Care Company ....C.... 330 468-2273
Northfield *(G-15511)*

Briar Hl Hlth Care Rsdence Inc ....D.... 440 632-5241
Middlefield *(G-14394)*

Briarfield At Ashley Circle ....C.... 330 793-3010
Youngstown *(G-20125)*

Briarwood Ltd ....D.... 330 688-1828
Stow *(G-17354)*

Brookdale Senior Living Inc ....C.... 937 294-1772
Oakwood *(G-15620)*

Bryden Place Inc ....C.... 614 258-6623
Beachwood *(G-1057)*

Burlington House Inc ....D.... 513 851-7888
Cincinnati *(G-3153)*

Canton Assisted Living ....C.... 330 492-7131
Canton *(G-2282)*

Care One LLC ....C.... 937 236-6707
Dayton *(G-9380)*

Carington Health Systems ....B.... 513 732-6500
Batavia *(G-997)*

Carington Health Systems ....C.... 513 961-8881
Cincinnati *(G-3185)*

Carington Health Systems ....C.... 937 743-2754
Franklin *(G-11151)*

Caritas Inc ....E.... 419 332-2589
Fremont *(G-11186)*

Carlisle Health Care Inc ....E.... 937 746-2662
Carlisle *(G-2602)*

Carriage Inn of Cadiz Inc ....E.... 740 942-8084
Cadiz *(G-2073)*

Carriage Inn of Trotwood Inc ....C.... 937 854-1180
Trotwood *(G-18345)*

Carriage Inn of Trotwood Inc ....D.... 937 277-0505
Dayton *(G-9384)*

Carriage Inn Retirement Cmnty ....C.... 937 278-0404
Dayton *(G-9385)*

Carroll Health Care Center ....C.... 330 627-5501
Carrollton *(G-2613)*

Casto Health Care ....D.... 419 884-6400
Mansfield *(G-13272)*

Catherines Care Center Inc ....D.... 740 282-3605
Steubenville *(G-17309)*

CHS Miami Valley Inc ....E.... 330 204-1040
Sidney *(G-16920)*

Chs-Norwood Inc ....C.... 513 351-7007
Cincinnati *(G-3274)*

Church of God Retirement Cmnty ....C.... 513 422-5600
Middletown *(G-14420)*

Cincinnati Senior Care LLC ....E.... 513 272-0600
Cincinnati *(G-3326)*

City View Nursing & Rehab LLC ....C.... 216 361-1414
Cleveland *(G-5279)*

Clermont Care Inc ....C.... 513 831-1770
Milford *(G-14513)*

Coal Grove Long Term Care Inc ....D.... 740 532-0449
Ironton *(G-12287)*

Columbus Clny For Elderly Care ....C.... 614 891-5055
Westerville *(G-19385)*

Columbus W Hlth Care Co Partnr ....C.... 614 274-4222
Columbus *(G-7393)*

Communi Care Inc ....E.... 419 382-2200
Toledo *(G-17822)*

Communicare Health Svcs Inc ....C.... 937 399-9217
Springfield *(G-17170)*

Community Skilled Health Care ....C.... 330 373-1160
Warren *(G-18837)*

Country Club Center Homes Inc ....D.... 330 343-6351
Dover *(G-10182)*

Country Club Center II Ltd ....C.... 740 397-2350
Mount Vernon *(G-14886)*

Country Court Ltd ....C.... 740 397-4125
Mount Vernon *(G-14887)*

County of Erie ....C.... 419 627-8733
Huron *(G-12164)*

County of Ottawa ....C.... 419 898-6459
Oak Harbor *(G-15607)*

County of Sandusky ....D.... 419 334-2602
Fremont *(G-11191)*

Covenant Care Ohio Inc ....D.... 419 898-5506
Port Clinton *(G-16242)*

Covenant Care Ohio Inc ....D.... 937 526-5570
Versailles *(G-18726)*

Covington Snf Inc ....E.... 330 426-2920
East Palestine *(G-10537)*

Crestmont Nursing Home N Corp ....C.... 216 228-9550
Lakewood *(G-12475)*

Crestmont Nursing Home N Corp ....D.... 216 228-9550
Lakewood *(G-12476)*

Crestview Ridge Nursing ....E.... 937 393-6700
Hillsboro *(G-11971)*

Crystal Care Centers Inc ....E.... 419 281-9595
Ashland *(G-677)*

Crystal Care Centers Inc ....E.... 419 747-2666
Mansfield *(G-13286)*

Crystal Care Centers Inc ....D.... 419 747-2666
Mansfield *(G-13287)*

Crystal Care Ctr of Portsmouth ....E.... 740 354-6619
Portsmouth *(G-16274)*

D James Incorporated ....C.... 513 574-4550
Cincinnati *(G-3456)*

Danridge Nursing Home Inc ....D.... 330 746-5157
Youngstown *(G-20166)*

DMD Management Inc ....E.... 330 405-6040
Twinsburg *(G-18406)*

Doylestown Health Care Center ....C.... 330 658-1533
Doylestown *(G-10227)*

Eaglewood Care Center ....C.... 937 399-7195
Springfield *(G-17191)*

East Carroll Nursing Home ....D.... 330 627-6900
Carrollton *(G-2618)*

East Water Leasing Co LLC ....D.... 419 278-6921
Deshler *(G-10169)*

Eastside Multi Care Inc ....C.... 216 662-3343
Maple Heights *(G-13407)*

Embassy Healthcare Inc ....D.... 513 868-6500
Fairfield *(G-10847)*

Emery Leasing Co LLC ....B.... 216 475-8880
Cleveland *(G-5536)*

Fairport Enterprises Inc ....C.... 330 830-9988
Massillon *(G-13806)*

Falling Leasing Co LLC ....C.... 440 238-1100
Strongsville *(G-17463)*

Falls Village Retirement Cmnty ....D.... 330 945-9797
Cuyahoga Falls *(G-9187)*

Four Seasons Washington LLC ....D.... 740 895-6101
Wshngtn CT Hs *(G-20024)*

Franklin Shcp Inc ....D.... 440 614-0160
Columbus *(G-7698)*

Friendship Vlg of Clmbus Ohio ....D.... 614 890-8287
Columbus *(G-7707)*

Front Leasing Co LLC ....C.... 440 243-4000
Berea *(G-1460)*

Gables At Green Pastures ....C.... 937 642-3893
Marysville *(G-13621)*

Gables Care Center Inc ....C.... 740 937-2900
Hopedale *(G-12078)*

Gallipolis Care LLC ....C.... 740 446-7112
Gallipolis *(G-11318)*

Garden Manor Extended Care Cen ....C.... 513 420-5972
Middletown *(G-14426)*

Gardens At Wapakoneta ....E.... 419 738-0725
Wapakoneta *(G-18797)*

Gaymont Nursing Homes Inc ....D.... 419 668-8258
Norwalk *(G-15576)*

GFS Leasing Inc ....D.... 330 877-2666
Hartville *(G-11818)*

Glendale Place Care Center LLC ....E.... 513 771-1779
Cincinnati *(G-3678)*

Glendora Health Care Center ....D.... 330 264-0912
Wooster *(G-19863)*

Golden Living LLC ....D.... 419 227-2154
Lima *(G-12784)*

Good Shepard Village LLC ....D.... 937 322-1911
Springfield *(G-17202)*

Good Shepherd Home For Aged ....C.... 614 228-5200
Ashland *(G-680)*

Grace Brethren Village Inc ....E.... 937 836-4011
Englewood *(G-10707)*

Greenbrier Senior Living Cmnty ....C.... 440 888-5900
Cleveland *(G-5702)*

Guardian Elder Care LLC ....C.... 330 549-0898
North Lima *(G-15402)*

Hamlet Village In Chagrin FLS ....D.... 216 263-6033
Chagrin Falls *(G-2700)*

Hampton Woods Nursing Ctr Inc ....E.... 330 707-1400
Poland *(G-16224)*

Hanover House Inc ....C.... 330 837-1741
Massillon *(G-13817)*

Harborside Clveland Ltd Partnr ....C.... 440 526-4770
Broadview Heights *(G-1881)*

Hcf Management Inc ....D.... 419 999-2010
Lima *(G-12791)*

Hcf of Bowl Green Care Ctr Inc ....D.... 419 352-7558
Bowling Green *(G-1781)*

Hcf of Court House Inc ....B.... 740 335-9290
Wshngtn CT Hs *(G-20025)*

Hcf of Crestview Inc ....D.... 937 426-5033
Beavercreek *(G-1246)*

Hcf of Fox Run Inc ....D.... 419 424-0832
Findlay *(G-11045)*

Hcf of Piqua Inc ....D.... 937 773-0040
Piqua *(G-16147)*

Hcf of Roselawn Inc ....C.... 419 647-4115
Spencerville *(G-17108)*

Hcf of Shawnee Inc ....D.... 419 999-2055
Lima *(G-12794)*

Hcf of Van Wert Inc ....D.... 419 999-2010
Van Wert *(G-18634)*

Hcf of Wapakoneta Inc ....D.... 419 738-3711
Wapakoneta *(G-18798)*

Hcr Manorcare Med Svcs Fla LLC ....D.... 513 233-0831
Cincinnati *(G-3747)*

Hcr Manorcare Med Svcs Fla LLC ....C.... 419 252-5500
Portsmouth *(G-16283)*

Hcr Manorcare Med Svcs Fla LLC ....C.... 419 531-2127
Toledo *(G-17939)*

Hcr Manorcare Med Svcs Fla LLC ....C.... 330 753-5005
Barberton *(G-965)*

Hcr Manorcare Med Svcs Fla LLC ....C.... 513 561-4111
Cincinnati *(G-3748)*

Hcr Manorcare Med Svcs Fla LLC ....C.... 614 882-1511
Westerville *(G-19407)*

Hcr Manorcare Med Svcs Fla LLC ....D.... 330 668-6889
Akron *(G-259)*

Hcr Manorcare Med Svcs Fla LLC ....C.... 419 252-5500
Toledo *(G-17940)*

Hcr Manorcare Med Svcs Fla LLC ....C.... 216 251-3300
Cleveland *(G-5735)*

Hcr Manorcare Med Svcs Fla LLC ....D.... 440 473-0090
Cleveland *(G-5736)*

Hcr Manorcare Med Svcs Fla LLC ....C.... 216 486-2300
Cleveland *(G-5737)*

Hcr Manorcare Med Svcs Fla LLC ....C.... 937 436-9700
Centerville *(G-2679)*

Hcr Manorcare Med Svcs Fla LLC ....C.... 419 691-3088
Oregon *(G-15738)*

Hcr Manorcare Med Svcs Fla LLC ....E.... 440 808-9275
Westlake *(G-19489)*

Hcr Manorcare Med Svcs Fla LLC ....C.... 513 591-0400
Cincinnati *(G-3749)*

Health Care Rtrement Corp Amer ....C.... 419 252-5500
Toledo *(G-17942)*

Health Care Rtrement Corp Amer ....D.... 740 286-5026
Jackson *(G-12312)*

Health Care Rtrement Corp Amer ....D.... 740 373-8920
Marietta *(G-13452)*

Health Care Rtrement Corp Amer ....C.... 937 429-1106
Dayton *(G-9271)*

Health Care Rtrement Corp Amer ....D.... 614 882-3782
Westerville *(G-19408)*

Health Care Rtrement Corp Amer ....D.... 937 599-5123
Bellefontaine *(G-1384)*

Health Care Rtrement Corp Amer ....D.... 614 464-2273
Columbus *(G-7811)*

Health Care Rtrement Corp Amer ....C.... 937 390-0005
Springfield *(G-17204)*

Health Care Rtrement Corp Amer ....D.... 740 894-3287
South Point *(G-17088)*

Health Care Rtrement Corp Amer ....D.... 937 393-5766
Hillsboro *(G-11977)*

Health Care Rtrement Corp Amer ....D.... 937 773-9346
Piqua *(G-16148)*

Health Care Rtrement Corp Amer ....C.... 937 866-8885
Miamisburg *(G-14306)*

Health Care Rtrement Corp Amer ....C.... 419 878-8523
Waterville *(G-18942)*

Heartlnd-Riverview S Pt OH LLC ....C.... 740 894-3287
South Point *(G-17089)*

Hempstead Manor ....C.... 740 354-8150
Portsmouth *(G-16286)*

Hennis Nursing Home ....C.... 330 364-8849
Dover *(G-10191)*

SERVICES SECTION

CONVENTION & TRADE SHOW SVCS

Highbanks Care Center LLC .... D ... 614 888-2021
  Columbus (G-7833)
Hill Side Plaza .... D ... 216 486-6300
  Cleveland (G-5756)
Hillspring Health Care Center .... E ... 937 748-1100
  Springboro (G-17123)
Hilty Memorial Home Inc .... C ... 419 384-3218
  Pandora (G-15892)
Hooberry Associates Inc .... D ... 330 872-1991
  Newton Falls (G-15274)
Huron Health Care Center Inc .... C ... 419 433-4990
  Huron (G-12167)
Huston Nursing Home .... C ... 740 384-3485
  Hamden (G-11687)
Isabelle Ridgway Care Ctr Inc .... C ... 614 252-4931
  Columbus (G-7926)
Ivy Health Care Inc .... C ... 513 251-2557
  Cincinnati (G-3849)
Jennings Eliza Home Inc .... C ... 216 226-0282
  Cleveland (G-5857)
Jma Healthcare LLC .... C ... 440 439-7976
  Cleveland (G-5865)
Kenwood Ter Hlth Care Ctr Inc .... C ... 513 793-2255
  Cincinnati (G-3915)
Kimes Convalescent Center .... E ... 740 593-3391
  Athens (G-797)
Kindred Nursing Centers E LLC ...... D ... 614 276-8222
  Columbus (G-7991)
Kindred Nursing Centers E LLC ...... C ... 614 837-9666
  Canal Winchester (G-2164)
Kindred Nursing Centers E LLC ...... C ... 314 631-3000
  Pickerington (G-16099)
Kindred Nursing Centers E LLC ...... C ... 502 596-7300
  Logan (G-12981)
King Tree Leasing Co LLC .... D ... 937 278-0723
  Dayton (G-9663)
Kingston Healthcare Company .... C ... 419 289-3859
  Ashland (G-684)
Lancia Nursing Home Inc .... E ... 740 695-4404
  Saint Clairsville (G-16640)
Laurel Healthcare .... C ... 419 782-7879
  Defiance (G-10044)
Levering Management Inc .... D ... 419 756-4747
  Mansfield (G-13323)
Liberty Nrsing Ctr of Jmestown .... D ... 937 675-3311
  Jamestown (G-12327)
Liberty Nrsing Ctr Rvrside LLC .... D ... 513 557-3621
  Cincinnati (G-3975)
Liberty Nursing Center .... E ... 937 836-5143
  Englewood (G-10712)
Life Care Centers America Inc .... C ... 440 365-5200
  Elyria (G-10640)
Life Care Centers America Inc .... C ... 440 871-3030
  Westlake (G-19510)
Life Care Centers America Inc .... D ... 614 889-6320
  Columbus (G-8061)
Lincoln Crawford Nrsg/Rehab CT .... E ... 513 861-2044
  Cincinnati (G-3983)
Lincoln Park Associates II LP .... C ... 937 297-4300
  Dayton (G-9683)
Locust Ridge Nursing Home Inc ...... C ... 937 444-2920
  Williamsburg (G-19633)
Lodge Care Center Inc .... C ... 513 683-9966
  Loveland (G-13139)
Lorantffy Care Center Inc .... D ... 330 666-2631
  Copley (G-9059)
Loveland Health Care Ctr LLC .... C ... 513 605-6000
  Loveland (G-13141)
Lutheran Senior City Inc .... B ... 614 228-5200
  Columbus (G-8089)
Lynnhaven Xii LLC .... C ... 419 756-7111
  Mansfield (G-13325)
Manleys Manor Nursing Home Inc ... C ... 419 424-0402
  Findlay (G-11060)
Manor Care of America Inc .... C ... 330 867-8530
  Akron (G-332)
Manor Care of America Inc .... C ... 330 492-7835
  Canton (G-2445)
Manor Care of America Inc .... C ... 440 779-6900
  North Olmsted (G-15430)
Manor Care of America Inc .... C ... 440 951-5551
  Willoughby (G-19690)
Manor Care of America Inc .... C ... 440 345-9300
  North Royalton (G-15496)
Mansfield Memorial Homes LLC ..... C ... 419 774-5100
  Mansfield (G-13333)
Maple Knoll Communities Inc .... E ... 513 524-7990
  Oxford (G-15817)
Maple Knoll Communities Inc .... B ... 513 782-2400
  Cincinnati (G-4019)

Maplewood Nursing Center Inc .... E ... 740 383-2126
  Marion (G-13550)
Mason Health Care Center .... D ... 513 398-2881
  Mason (G-13737)
Masonic Healthcare Inc .... B ... 937 525-3001
  Springfield (G-17229)
Mayfair Nursing Care Centers .... D ... 614 889-6320
  Columbus (G-8132)
Mayflower Nursing Home Inc .... C ... 330 492-7131
  Canton (G-2452)
McClellan Management Inc .... C ... 419 855-7755
  Genoa (G-11381)
Meadow Wind Hlth Care Ctr Inc ..... C ... 330 833-2026
  Massillon (G-13838)
Medina Meadows .... D ... 330 725-1550
  Medina (G-14103)
Medina Medical Investors Ltd .... C ... 330 483-3131
  Medina (G-14104)
Megco Management Inc .... C ... 330 874-9999
  Bolivar (G-1749)
Mill Manor Nursing Home Inc .... E ... 440 967-6614
  Vermilion (G-18715)
Mt Washington Care Center Inc ...... C ... 513 231-4561
  Cincinnati (G-4130)
Multicare Management Group .... C ... 513 868-6500
  Fairfield (G-10883)
Muskingum County Ohio .... D ... 740 454-1911
  Zanesville (G-20507)
New Albany Care Center LLC .... C ... 614 855-8866
  Columbus (G-8270)
Newark Care Center LLC .... D ... 740 366-2321
  Newark (G-15219)
Newcomerstown Progress Corp ...... C ... 740 498-5165
  Newcomerstown (G-15271)
Nightingale Holdings LLC .... B ... 330 645-0200
  Akron (G-352)
Normandy Manor of Rocky River .... C ... 440 333-5401
  Rocky River (G-16588)
Northpoint Senior Services LLC ...... C ... 740 373-3597
  Marietta (G-13480)
Northpoint Senior Services LLC ...... D ... 513 248-1655
  Milford (G-14545)
Oak Creek Terrace Inc .... C ... 937 439-1454
  Dayton (G-9778)
Oak Health Care Investors .... D ... 740 397-3200
  Mount Vernon (G-14916)
October Enterprises Inc .... C ... 937 456-9535
  Eaton (G-10571)
Ohiohealth Corporation .... A ... 614 788-8860
  Columbus (G-8457)
Omni Manor Inc .... C ... 330 545-1550
  Girard (G-11423)
Omni Manor Inc .... C ... 330 793-5648
  Youngstown (G-20311)
Parkview Manor Inc .... C ... 419 243-5191
  Toledo (G-18119)
Pickaway Manor Inc .... C ... 740 474-5400
  Circleville (G-4899)
Piketon Nursing Center Inc .... D ... 740 289-4074
  Piketon (G-16125)
Pleasant View Nursing Home .... D ... 330 745-6028
  Barberton (G-972)
Progressive Green Meadows LLC ... C ... 330 875-1456
  Louisville (G-13105)
Quaker Heights Nursing HM Inc ..... D ... 513 897-6050
  Waynesville (G-18986)
R & J Investment Co Inc .... C ... 440 934-5204
  Avon (G-915)
Rcr East Inc .... C ... 513 793-2090
  Cincinnati (G-4389)
Rcr East Inc .... C ... 513 231-8292
  Cincinnati (G-4390)
Rivers Bend Health Care LLC .... C ... 740 894-3476
  South Point (G-17097)
Royal Oak Nrsing Rhbltition Ctr ...... D ... 440 884-9191
  Cleveland (G-6417)
Saber Healthcare Group LLC .... E ... 216 292-5706
  Bedford (G-1333)
Sarah Jane Living Center Ltd .... E ... 419 692-6618
  Delphos (G-10150)
Sensi Care 3 .... E ... 440 323-6310
  Elyria (G-10679)
Sisters Od Saint Joseph of SAI .... B ... 216 531-7426
  Euclid (G-10776)
Solon Pnte At Emrald Ridge LLC .... C ... 440 498-3000
  Solon (G-17054)
Springhills LLC .... C ... 937 274-1400
  Dayton (G-9899)
St Catherines Care Centers O .... C ... 419 435-8112
  Fostoria (G-11141)

St Catherines Care Ctr Findlay .... C ... 419 422-3978
  Findlay (G-11084)
Summitt Ohio Leasing Co LLC .... C ... 937 436-2273
  Dayton (G-9914)
Sunbridge Circleville .... E ... 740 477-1695
  Circleville (G-4906)
Swanton Hlth Care Rtrement Ctr .... D ... 419 825-1145
  Swanton (G-17572)
Trinity Healthcare Corporation .... C ... 513 489-2444
  Cincinnati (G-4700)
Uhrichsville Health Care Ctr .... C ... 740 922-2208
  Uhrichsville (G-18494)
United Church Homes Inc .... C ... 513 922-1440
  Cincinnati (G-4730)
United Church Homes Inc .... C ... 330 854-4177
  Canal Fulton (G-2148)
United Church Homes Inc .... C ... 937 426-8481
  Beavercreek (G-1261)
Van Rue Incorporated .... C ... 419 238-0715
  Van Wert (G-18646)
Vancrest Ltd .... C ... 419 695-2871
  Delphos (G-10153)
Vancrest Ltd .... C ... 419 749-2194
  Convoy (G-9050)
Vancrest Ltd .... C ... 937 456-3010
  Eaton (G-10580)
Village Green Healthcare Ctr .... D ... 937 548-1993
  Greenville (G-11523)
Volunters Amer Care Facilities .... C ... 419 447-7151
  Tiffin (G-17708)
Volunters Amer Care Facilities .... C ... 419 334-9521
  Fremont (G-11226)
Vrable Healthcare Inc .... E ... 614 545-5500
  Columbus (G-8954)
Walton Manor Health Care Ctr .... C ... 440 439-4433
  Cleveland (G-6721)
Water Leasing Co LLC .... C ... 440 285-9400
  Chardon (G-2778)
Wessell Generations Inc .... C ... 440 775-1491
  Oberlin (G-15662)
West View Manor Inc .... C ... 330 264-8640
  Wooster (G-19928)
Whetstone Care Center LLC .... C ... 614 875-7700
  Grove City (G-11616)
Whetstone Care Center LLC .... C ... 614 457-1100
  Columbus (G-8985)
Whetstone Care Center LLC .... C ... 740 474-6036
  Circleville (G-4908)
Wickliffe Country Place Ltd .... C ... 440 944-9400
  Wickliffe (G-19616)
Willowood Care Center .... C ... 330 225-3156
  Brunswick (G-1997)
Wood County Ohio .... C ... 419 353-8411
  Bowling Green (G-1802)
Woodland Country Manor Inc .... E ... 513 523-4449
  Somerville (G-17072)
Zandex Inc .... C ... 740 676-8381
  Shadyside (G-16854)
Zandex Health Care Corporation .... C ... 740 454-9747
  Zanesville (G-20553)

CONVENIENCE STORES

Duncan Oil Co .... E ... 937 426-5945
  Dayton (G-9267)
Holland Oil Company .... D ... 330 835-1815
  Akron (G-269)
Ta Operating LLC .... B ... 440 808-9100
  Westlake (G-19553)
Travelcenters America Inc .... A ... 440 808-9100
  Westlake (G-19555)

CONVENTION & TRADE SHOW SVCS

Akron-Summit Convention .... E ... 330 374-7560
  Akron (G-62)
City of North Olmsted .... E ... 440 777-0678
  North Olmsted (G-15417)
Columbus Bride .... D ... 614 888-4567
  Columbus (G-7334)
Convention & Vistors Bureau of ...... E ... 216 875-6603
  Cleveland (G-5405)
Global Spectrum .... D ... 513 419-7300
  Cincinnati (G-3680)
I-X Center Corporation .... C ... 216 265-2675
  Cleveland (G-5799)
Jbjs Acquisitions LLC .... E ... 513 769-0393
  Cincinnati (G-3864)
Miami University .... D ... 513 529-6911
  Oxford (G-15821)
Nexxtshow Exposition Svcs LLC .... E ... 877 836-3131
  Cincinnati (G-4166)

Employee Codes: A=Over 500 employees, B=251-500
C=101-250, D=51-100, E=25-50

CONVENTION & TRADE SHOW SVCS

Wiegands Lake Park Inc .... E 440 338-5795
  Novelty *(G-15604)*

CONVERTERS: Data

Cisco Systems Inc .... A 937 427-4264
  Beavercreek *(G-1160)*

CONVERTERS: Phase Or Rotary, Electrical

Electric Service Co Inc .... E 513 271-6387
  Cincinnati *(G-3547)*

CONVEYOR SYSTEMS: Belt, General Indl Use

Mine Equipment Services LLC .... E 740 936-5427
  Sunbury *(G-17558)*

CONVEYOR SYSTEMS: Robotic

Grob Systems Inc .... C 419 358-9015
  Bluffton *(G-1731)*

CONVEYORS & CONVEYING EQPT

Alba Manufacturing Inc .... D 513 874-0551
  Fairfield *(G-10818)*
Allied Fabricating & Wldg Co .... E 614 751-6664
  Columbus *(G-6970)*
Dillin Engineered Systems Corp ...... E 419 666-6789
  Perrysburg *(G-15998)*
Grasan Equipment Company Inc .... D 419 526-4440
  Mansfield *(G-13306)*
Innovative Controls Corp .... D 419 691-6684
  Toledo *(G-17974)*
Intelligrated Systems Inc .... A 866 936-7300
  Mason *(G-13720)*
Intelligrated Systems LLC .... A 513 701-7300
  Mason *(G-13721)*
Intelligrated Systems Ohio LLC .... A 513 701-7300
  Mason *(G-13722)*
K F T Inc .... D 513 241-5910
  Cincinnati *(G-3897)*
Pfpc Enterprises Inc .... B 513 941-6200
  Cincinnati *(G-4290)*
Power-Pack Conveyor Company .... E 440 975-9955
  Willoughby *(G-19705)*
Siemens Industry Inc .... E 440 526-2770
  Brecksville *(G-1850)*
Stock Fairfield Corporation .... C 440 543-6000
  Chagrin Falls *(G-2735)*

COOKING & FOOD WARMING EQPT: Commercial

High-TEC Industrial Services .... C 937 667-1772
  Tipp City *(G-17718)*
Lima Sheet Metal Machine & Mfg ... E 419 229-1161
  Lima *(G-12827)*

COPPER ORE MINING

Warrenton Copper LLC .... E 636 456-3488
  Cleveland *(G-6723)*

COPY MACHINES WHOLESALERS

Andrew Belmont Sargent .... E 513 769-7800
  Cincinnati *(G-3027)*
Blakemans Valley Off Eqp Inc .... E 330 729-1000
  Youngstown *(G-20116)*
Blue Technologies Inc .... C 216 271-4800
  Cleveland *(G-5126)*
Blue Technologies Inc .... E 330 499-9300
  Canton *(G-2266)*
Canon Solutions America Inc .... D 937 260-4495
  Miamisburg *(G-14278)*
Document Solutions Ohio LLC .... E 614 846-2400
  Columbus *(G-7539)*
Graphic Entps Off Slutions Inc .... D 800 553-6616
  North Canton *(G-15341)*
Meritech Inc .... D 216 459-8333
  Cleveland *(G-6028)*
Mt Business Technologies Inc .... C 419 529-6100
  Mansfield *(G-13348)*
Office Products Toledo Inc .... E 419 865-7001
  Holland *(G-12044)*
Visual Edge Technology Inc .... C 330 494-9694
  Canton *(G-2579)*

CORK PRDTS, FABRICATED, WHOLESALE

RLM Fabricating Inc .... E 419 729-6130
  Toledo *(G-18158)*

CORRECTIONAL FACILITY OPERATIONS

Community Education Ctrs Inc .... B 330 424-4065
  Lisbon *(G-12933)*
Corecivic Inc .... B 330 746-3777
  Youngstown *(G-20162)*
Correction Commission NW Ohio ... C 419 428-3800
  Stryker *(G-17536)*
Franklin Community Base Correc ... D 614 525-4600
  Columbus *(G-7693)*
Licking Muskingum Cmnty Correc.. E 740 349-6980
  Newark *(G-15193)*
Management & Training Corp .... C 801 693-2600
  Conneaut *(G-9043)*
Neocap/Cbcf .... E 330 675-2669
  Warren *(G-18885)*

CORRECTIONAL INSTITUTIONS

Ohio Dept Rhbilitation Corectn .... B 614 274-9000
  Columbus *(G-8336)*

CORRECTIONAL INSTITUTIONS, GOVERNMENT: Detention Center

County of Ross .... E 740 773-4169
  Chillicothe *(G-2830)*

CORRECTIONAL INSTITUTIONS, GOVERNMENT: Prison, government

Youth Services Ohio Department .... C 419 875-6965
  Liberty Center *(G-12716)*

CORRECTIONAL INSTITUTIONS, GOVERNMENT: State

Rehabltation Corectn Ohio Dept ..... D 614 752-0800
  Columbus *(G-8608)*

CORRESPONDENCE SCHOOLS

Zaner-Bloser Inc .... D 614 486-0221
  Columbus *(G-9025)*

CORRUGATED PRDTS: Boxes, Partition, Display Items, Sheet/Pad

Kennedy Mint Inc .... D 440 572-3222
  Cleveland *(G-5895)*

COSMETIC PREPARATIONS

Universal Packg Systems Inc .... B 513 732-2000
  Batavia *(G-1029)*
Universal Packg Systems Inc .... B 513 674-9400
  Cincinnati *(G-4748)*
Universal Packg Systems Inc .... E 513 735-4777
  Batavia *(G-1030)*

COSMETICS & TOILETRIES

Luminex Home Decor .... A 513 563-1113
  Blue Ash *(G-1632)*
Nehemiah Manufacturing Co LLC ... E 513 351-5700
  Cincinnati *(G-4150)*

COSMETICS WHOLESALERS

Cosmax USA Inc Cosmax USA Corp ... E 440 600-5738
  Solon *(G-16996)*

COSMETOLOGIST

Salon Hazelton .... E 419 874-9404
  Perrysburg *(G-16055)*
Soto Salon & Spa .... E 419 872-5555
  Perrysburg *(G-16060)*
Star Beauty Plus LLC .... E 216 662-9750
  Maple Heights *(G-13419)*

COSMETOLOGY & PERSONAL HYGIENE SALONS

Beauty Bar LLC .... E 419 537-5400
  Toledo *(G-17766)*
M C Hair Consultants Inc .... E 234 678-3987
  Cuyahoga Falls *(G-9206)*
Marios International Spa & Ht .... C 330 562-5141
  Aurora *(G-846)*
Mato Inc .... E 440 729-9008
  Chesterland *(G-2799)*
Pure Concept Salon Inc .... E 513 770-2120
  Mason *(G-13751)*
Vlp Inc .... E 330 758-8811
  Youngstown *(G-20407)*

COSMETOLOGY SCHOOL

Creative Images College of B .... E 937 478-7922
  Dayton *(G-9443)*
Nurtur Holdings LLC .... E 614 487-3033
  Loveland *(G-13149)*
Raphaels Schl Buty Culture Inc ...... E 330 782-3395
  Boardman *(G-1743)*

COUNCIL FOR SOCIAL AGENCY

Adams County Senior Citizens .... E 937 544-7459
  West Union *(G-19273)*
ARC Industries Incorporated O .... E 614 836-6050
  Groveport *(G-11624)*
Council On Aging of Southweste .... C 513 721-1025
  Cincinnati *(G-3427)*
Fairfield Cnty Job & Fmly Svcs ...... D 800 450-8845
  Lancaster *(G-12529)*
Fairfield County .... D 740 653-4060
  Lancaster *(G-12531)*
Jewish Edcatn Ctr of Cleveland ..... D 216 371-0446
  Cleveland Heights *(G-6791)*

COUNTERS & COUNTING DEVICES

Aclara Technologies LLC .... C 440 528-7200
  Solon *(G-16969)*
Commercial Electric Pdts Corp .... E 216 241-2886
  Cleveland *(G-5376)*

COUNTRY CLUBS

Alexander J Abernethy .... E 740 432-2107
  Byesville *(G-2069)*
American Golf Corporation .... D 440 286-9544
  Chesterland *(G-2792)*
American Golf Corporation .... D 310 664-4278
  Grove City *(G-11529)*
Athens Golf & Country Club .... E 740 592-1655
  Athens *(G-774)*
Avalon Golf & Country Club .... D 330 539-5008
  Vienna *(G-18735)*
Avon Oaks Country Club .... D 440 892-0660
  Avon *(G-876)*
Beechmont Inc .... D 216 831-9100
  Cleveland *(G-5111)*
Bel-Wood Country Club Inc .... D 513 899-3361
  Morrow *(G-14843)*
Belmont Country Club .... D 419 666-1472
  Perrysburg *(G-15977)*
Belmont Hills Country Club .... D 740 695-2181
  Saint Clairsville *(G-16626)*
Brook Plum Country Club .... D 419 625-5394
  Sandusky *(G-16729)*
Brookside Country Club Inc .... D 330 477-6505
  Canton *(G-2270)*
Brookside Golf & Cntry CLB Co ..... D 614 889-2581
  Columbus *(G-7153)*
Browns Run Country Club .... D 513 423-6291
  Middletown *(G-14419)*
Buckeye Golf Club Co Inc .... E 419 636-6984
  Bryan *(G-2003)*
Camargo Club .... C 513 561-9292
  Cincinnati *(G-3167)*
Cambridge Country Club Company ... D 740 439-2744
  Byesville *(G-2070)*
Catawba-Cleveland Dev Corp .... D 419 797-4424
  Port Clinton *(G-16239)*
Chagrin Valley Country Club Co ..... D 440 248-4310
  Chagrin Falls *(G-2692)*
Chagrin Valley Hunt Club .... D 440 423-4414
  Gates Mills *(G-11356)*
Chillicothe Country Club Co .... D 740 775-0150
  Chillicothe *(G-2819)*
Cincinnati Country Club .... C 513 533-5200
  Cincinnati *(G-3295)*
Cleveland Skating Club .... C 216 791-2800
  Cleveland *(G-5346)*
Clovernook Country Club .... D 513 521-0333
  Cincinnati *(G-3371)*
Club At Hillbrook Inc .... E 440 247-4940
  Chagrin Falls *(G-2694)*

Clubcorp Usa Inc .... E 216 851-2582
Cleveland *(G-5367)*
Coldstream Country Club .... E 513 231-3900
Cincinnati *(G-3381)*
Columbia Hills Country CLB Inc .... E 440 236-5051
Columbia Station *(G-6844)*
Columbus Country Club .... D 614 861-1332
Columbus *(G-7343)*
Country Club Inc .... C 216 831-9200
Cleveland *(G-5417)*
Country Club At Muirfield Vlg .... E 614 764-1714
Dublin *(G-10310)*
Country Club of Hudson .... E 330 650-1188
Hudson *(G-12113)*
Country Club of North .... E 937 374-5000
Xenia *(G-20047)*
County of Perry .... E 740 342-0416
New Lexington *(G-15053)*
Dayton Country Club Company .... D 937 294-3352
Dayton *(G-9467)*
Dry Run Limited Partnership .... E 513 561-9119
Cincinnati *(G-3504)*
Elms Country Club Inc .... E 330 833-2668
North Lawrence *(G-15392)*
Elms of Massillon Inc .... E 330 833-2668
North Lawrence *(G-15393)*
Elyria Country Club Company .... C 440 322-6391
Elyria *(G-10621)*
Fairlawn Country Club Company .... D 330 836-5541
Akron *(G-213)*
Findlay Country Club .... E 419 422-9263
Findlay *(G-11025)*
Five Seasons Spt Cntry CLB Inc .... D 513 842-1188
Cincinnati *(G-3633)*
Five Seasons Spt Cntry CLB Inc .... D 937 848-9200
Dayton *(G-9553)*
Five Seasons Spt Cntry CLB Inc .... D 440 899-4555
Cleveland *(G-5602)*
Four Bridges Country Club Ltd .... D 513 759-4620
Liberty Township *(G-12720)*
Glenmoor Country Club Inc .... C 330 966-3600
Canton *(G-2380)*
Golf Course Maintenance .... D 330 262-9141
Wooster *(G-19864)*
Grove Walnut Country Club Inc .... E 937 253-3109
Dayton *(G-9270)*
Hawthorne Valley Country Club .... D 440 232-1400
Bedford *(G-1311)*
Hyde Park Golf & Country Club .... D 513 321-3721
Cincinnati *(G-3801)*
Inverness Club .... D 419 578-9000
Toledo *(G-17978)*
Kenwood Country Club Inc .... C 513 527-3590
Cincinnati *(G-3914)*
Kettenring Country Club Inc .... E 419 782-2101
Defiance *(G-10042)*
Kirtland Country Club .... E 440 942-4400
Willoughby *(G-19675)*
Kirtland Country Club Company .... D 440 942-4400
Willoughby *(G-19676)*
Lake Front II Inc .... E 330 337-8033
Salem *(G-16703)*
Lakes Golf & Country Club Inc .... E 614 882-2582
Westerville *(G-19320)*
Lakewood Country Club Company .... D 440 871-0400
Cleveland *(G-5922)*
Lenau Park .... E 440 235-2646
Olmsted Twp *(G-15677)*
Losantiville Country Club .... D 513 631-4133
Cincinnati *(G-3994)*
Maketewah Country Club Company .... D 513 242-9333
Cincinnati *(G-4015)*
Marietta Country Club Inc .... E 740 373-7722
Marietta *(G-13468)*
Marion Country Club Company .... E 740 387-0974
Marion *(G-13555)*
Mayfield Sand Ridge Club .... D 216 381-0826
Cleveland *(G-5995)*
Meadowbrook Country Club .... D 937 836-5186
Clayton *(G-4914)*
Medallion Club .... C 614 794-6999
Westerville *(G-19328)*
Miami Valley Golf Club .... D 937 278-7381
Dayton *(G-9730)*
Montgomery Swim & Tennis Club .... E 513 793-6433
Montgomery *(G-14727)*
Moraine Country Club .... E 937 294-6200
Dayton *(G-9756)*
Moundbuilders Country Club Co .... D 740 344-4500
Newark *(G-15213)*
N C R Employee Benefit Assn .... C 937 299-3571
Dayton *(G-9766)*
New Albany Country Club Comm A .... C 614 939-8500
New Albany *(G-14998)*
New Wembley LLC .... E 440 543-8171
Chagrin Falls *(G-2726)*
Oakwood Club Inc .... D 216 381-7755
Cleveland *(G-6174)*
Oxford Country Club Inc .... E 513 524-0801
Oxford *(G-15827)*
Piqua Country Club Holding Co .... E 937 773-7744
Piqua *(G-16156)*
Portage Country Club Company .... D 330 836-8565
Akron *(G-396)*
Progressive Fishing Assn .... D 419 877-9909
Whitehouse *(G-19589)*
Raintree Country Club Inc .... E 330 699-3232
Uniontown *(G-18534)*
Rawiga Country Club Inc .... D 330 336-2220
Seville *(G-16843)*
Shady Hollow Cntry CLB Co Inc .... D 330 832-1581
Massillon *(G-13854)*
Shaker Heights Country Club Co .... C 216 991-3324
Shaker Heights *(G-16865)*
Shawnee Country Club .... D 419 227-7177
Lima *(G-12877)*
Silver Lake Country Club .... D 330 688-6066
Silver Lake *(G-16964)*
Silver Lake Management Corp .... C 330 688-6066
Silver Lake *(G-16965)*
Snow Hill Country Club Inc .... E 937 987-2491
New Vienna *(G-15132)*
Springfield Country Club Co .... E 937 399-4215
Springfield *(G-17280)*
Steubenville Country Club Inc .... D 740 264-0521
Steubenville *(G-17336)*
Sycamore Creek Country Club .... C 937 748-0791
Springboro *(G-17139)*
Sylvania Country Club .... D 419 392-0530
Sylvania *(G-17619)*
Terrace Park Country Club Inc .... D 513 965-4061
Milford *(G-14567)*
Tippecanoe Country Club Inc .... E 330 758-7518
Canfield *(G-2213)*
Toledo Club .... D 419 243-2200
Toledo *(G-18234)*
Troy Country Club Inc .... E 937 335-5691
Troy *(G-18383)*
Turtle Golf Management Ltd .... E 614 882-5920
Westerville *(G-19446)*
Union Country Club .... E 330 343-5544
Dover *(G-10218)*
Walden Company Ltd .... C 330 562-7145
Aurora *(G-862)*
Wedgewood Golf & Country Club .... C 614 793-9600
Powell *(G-16354)*
Western Hills Country Club .... D 513 922-0011
Cincinnati *(G-4842)*
Westwood Country Club Company .... D 440 331-3016
Rocky River *(G-16595)*
Wetherngton Golf Cntry CLB Inc .... D 513 755-2582
West Chester *(G-19185)*
Weymouth Valley Inc .... E 440 498-8888
Solon *(G-17067)*
York Temple Country Club Inc .... E 614 885-5459
Columbus *(G-9015)*
Youngstown Country Club .... D 330 759-1040
Youngstown *(G-20430)*
Zanesville Country Club .... E 740 452-2726
Zanesville *(G-20555)*

COURIER OR MESSENGER SVCS

Dash Logistics Inc .... E 937 382-9110
Wilmington *(G-19760)*
Logistics Inc .... E 419 478-1514
Toledo *(G-18007)*
Reliable Rnners Curier Svc Inc .... E 440 578-1011
Mentor *(G-14236)*
Rush Package Delivery Inc .... E 513 771-7874
Cincinnati *(G-4457)*
Rush Package Delivery Inc .... D 937 297-6182
Dayton *(G-9859)*
Trumbull Special Courier Inc .... E 330 841-0074
Warren *(G-18916)*

COURIER SVCS, AIR: Letter Delivery, Private

Abx Air Inc .... B 937 382-5591
Wilmington *(G-19741)*
Abx Air Inc .... A 937 366-2282
Wilmington *(G-19742)*
Federal Express Corporation .... E 800 463-3339
Lima *(G-12780)*
Federal Express Corporation .... D 800 463-3339
Vandalia *(G-18679)*
Fedex Ground Package Sys Inc .... E 800 463-3339
Richfield *(G-16508)*
United Parcel Service Inc .... D 614 385-9100
Columbus *(G-8895)*

COURIER SVCS, AIR: Package Delivery, Private

Clp Towne Inc .... E 440 234-3324
Brookpark *(G-1940)*
Federal Express Corporation .... E 800 463-3339
Mansfield *(G-13300)*
Federal Express Corporation .... B 614 492-6106
Columbus *(G-7646)*
Federal Express Corporation .... C 800 463-3339
Northwood *(G-15531)*
Federal Express Corporation .... C 800 463-3339
Columbus *(G-7647)*
Federal Express Corporation .... C 800 463-3339
Columbus *(G-7648)*
Federal Express Corporation .... E 800 463-3339
Canton *(G-2365)*
Fedex Ground Package Sys Inc .... E 800 463-3339
Chillicothe *(G-2838)*
Fedex Office & Print Svcs Inc .... E 440 946-6353
Willoughby *(G-19664)*
Prestige Delivery Systems LLC .... D 216 332-8000
Cleveland *(G-6304)*

COURIER SVCS, AIR: Parcel Delivery, Private

Federal Express Corporation .... D 937 898-3474
Vandalia *(G-18680)*

COURIER SVCS: Air

Air Transport Svcs Group Inc .... E 937 382-5591
Wilmington *(G-19743)*
Ames Material Services Inc .... A 937 382-5591
Wilmington *(G-19746)*
Dhl Express (usa) Inc .... E 614 865-8325
Westerville *(G-19297)*
Dhl Express (usa) Inc .... E 800 225-5345
Lockbourne *(G-12949)*
Dhl Express (usa) Inc .... E 440 239-0670
Cleveland *(G-5480)*
Federal Express Corporation .... D 800 463-3339
Miamisburg *(G-14301)*
Fedex Corporation .... E 440 234-0315
Cleveland *(G-5584)*
Fedex Corporation .... E 614 801-0953
Grove City *(G-11559)*
Fedex Freight Corporation .... E 800 979-9232
Chillicothe *(G-2837)*
Garda CL Technical Svcs Inc .... E 937 294-4099
Moraine *(G-14788)*
Lgstx Services Inc .... D 866 931-2337
Wilmington *(G-19766)*
Prime Time Enterprises Inc .... E 440 891-8855
Cleveland *(G-6306)*
United Parcel Service Inc OH .... D 419 222-7399
Lima *(G-12909)*
United Parcel Service Inc OH .... C 330 339-6281
New Philadelphia *(G-15120)*
United Parcel Service Inc OH .... D 419 782-3552
Defiance *(G-10062)*
United States Cargo & Courier .... E 216 325-0483
Cleveland *(G-6646)*

COURIER SVCS: Ground

City Dash Inc .... C 513 562-2000
Cincinnati *(G-3357)*
Clp Towne Inc .... E 440 234-3324
Brookpark *(G-1940)*
Federal Express Corporation .... D 800 463-3339
Miamisburg *(G-14301)*
Federal Express Corporation .... D 937 898-3474
Vandalia *(G-18680)*
Fedex Freight Corporation .... E 800 521-3505
Lima *(G-12781)*
Fedex Ground Package Sys Inc .... B 800 463-3339
Toledo *(G-17884)*
Firelands Security Services .... E 419 627-0562
Sandusky *(G-16759)*
Keller Logistics Group Inc .... D 419 784-4805
Defiance *(G-10039)*

SERVICES

Employee Codes: A=Over 500 employees, B=251-500
C=101-250, D=51-100, E=25-50
2018 Harris Ohio
Services Directory
1469

COURIER SVCS: Ground

Prime Time Enterprises Inc..................E....... 440 891-8855
  Cleveland (G-6306)
Priority Dispatch Inc........................E....... 216 332-9852
  Solon (G-17041)
Robert M Neff Inc..............................D....... 614 444-1562
  Columbus (G-8642)
Rush Package Delivery Inc..............C....... 937 224-7874
  Dayton (G-9858)
SMS Transport LLC.............................E....... 937 813-8897
  Dayton (G-9886)
United Parcel Service Inc OH............C....... 419 424-9494
  Findlay (G-11095)
United Parcel Service Inc OH............C....... 419 872-0211
  Perrysburg (G-16066)
United Parcel Service Inc OH............B....... 740 363-0636
  Delaware (G-10133)
United States Cargo & Courier..........E....... 216 325-0483
  Cleveland (G-6646)
United States Cargo & Courier..........E....... 614 449-2854
  Columbus (G-8900)

COURIER SVCS: Package By Vehicle

City Taxicab & Transfer Co.................E....... 440 992-2156
  Ashtabula (G-734)
Clockwork Logistics Inc........................E....... 216 587-5371
  Garfield Heights (G-11351)
Elite Expediting Corp...........................D....... 614 279-1181
  Worthington (G-19956)
Fed Ex Rob Carpenter.........................E....... 419 260-1889
  Maumee (G-13915)
Federal Express Corporation..............B....... 614 492-6106
  Columbus (G-7646)
Fedex Ground Package Sys Inc..........E....... 330 244-1534
  Canton (G-2366)
Fedex Ground Package Sys Inc..........C....... 800 463-3339
  Richfield (G-16509)
Palmer Express Incorporated...........E....... 440 942-3333
  Willoughby (G-19702)
Prestige Delivery Systems LLC..........D....... 216 332-8000
  Cleveland (G-6304)
Stat Express Delivery LLC..................E....... 614 880-7828
  Worthington (G-20000)
United Parcel Service Inc...................D....... 937 859-2314
  West Carrollton (G-19010)
United Parcel Service Inc...................E....... 800 742-5877
  Chillicothe (G-2892)
United Parcel Service Inc...................E....... 614 431-0600
  Columbus (G-8896)
United Parcel Service Inc...................E....... 440 846-6000
  Strongsville (G-17519)
United Parcel Service Inc OH............C....... 419 747-3080
  Mansfield (G-13380)
United Parcel Service Inc OH............C....... 740 373-0772
  Marietta (G-13511)
United Parcel Service Inc OH............A....... 419 891-6776
  Maumee (G-13990)
United Parcel Service Inc OH............C....... 614 841-7159
  Columbus (G-8897)
United Parcel Service Inc OH............C....... 800 742-5877
  Zanesville (G-20542)
United Parcel Service Inc OH............D....... 419 891-6841
  Toledo (G-18271)
United Parcel Service Inc OH............D....... 419 782-3552
  Defiance (G-10062)
United Parcel Service Inc OH............C....... 937 382-0658
  Wilmington (G-19791)
United Parcel Service Inc OH............C....... 800 742-5877
  Youngstown (G-20399)

COURIER SVCS: Parcel By Vehicle

Centaur Mail Inc..................................E....... 419 887-5857
  Maumee (G-13893)
Fedex Smartpost Inc...........................D....... 800 463-3339
  Grove City (G-11561)
United Parcel Service Inc...................B....... 440 826-2591
  Cleveland (G-6643)
United Parcel Service Inc OH............C....... 513 852-6135
  Cincinnati (G-4736)
United Parcel Service Inc OH............C....... 800 742-5877
  Cleveland (G-6644)
United Parcel Service Inc OH............D....... 419 222-7399
  Lima (G-12909)
United Parcel Service Inc OH............C....... 440 826-4320
  Wooster (G-19921)
United Parcel Service Inc OH............C....... 330 545-0177
  Girard (G-11427)
United Parcel Service Inc OH............D....... 440 275-3301
  Austinburg (G-866)
United Parcel Service Inc OH............C....... 330 339-6281
  New Philadelphia (G-15120)

United Parcel Service Inc OH............C....... 740 598-4293
  Brilliant (G-1870)
United Parcel Service Inc OH............E....... 740 592-4570
  Athens (G-818)
United Parcel Service Inc OH............E....... 740 968-3508
  Saint Clairsville (G-16658)
United Parcel Service Inc OH............C....... 330 478-1007
  Canton (G-2570)
United Parcel Service Inc OH............C....... 419 586-8556
  Celina (G-2665)
United Parcel Service Inc OH............C....... 513 241-5289
  Cincinnati (G-4737)
United Parcel Service Inc OH............C....... 614 383-4580
  Marion (G-13593)
United Parcel Service Inc OH............C....... 513 782-4000
  Cincinnati (G-4738)
United Parcel Service Inc OH............D....... 513 241-5316
  Cincinnati (G-4739)
United Parcel Service Inc OH............C....... 614 272-8500
  Obetz (G-15672)
United Parcel Service Inc OH............D....... 513 863-1681
  Hamilton (G-11781)
United Parcel Service Inc OH............C....... 937 773-4762
  Piqua (G-16170)

COURT REPORTING SVCS

Academy Court Reporting Inc...........E....... 216 861-3222
  Cleveland (G-4951)
Ace-Merit LLC..E....... 513 241-3200
  Cincinnati (G-2967)
Mehler and Hagestrom Inc.................E....... 216 621-4984
  Cleveland (G-6020)
National Service Information..............E....... 740 387-6806
  Marion (G-13567)

COURTS

County of Hamilton..............................C....... 513 552-1200
  Cincinnati (G-3429)
County of Logan....................................E....... 937 599-7252
  Bellefontaine (G-1380)
County of Summit.................................C....... 330 643-2943
  Akron (G-169)
Supreme Court United States............E....... 419 213-5800
  Toledo (G-18212)
Supreme Court United States...........E....... 513 564-7575
  Cincinnati (G-4605)
Supreme Court United States...........E....... 216 357-7300
  Cleveland (G-6558)

COURTS OF LAW: County Government

Butler County of Ohio..........................E....... 513 887-3090
  Hamilton (G-11704)

COURTS OF LAW: Federal

6th Circuit Court..................................E....... 614 719-3100
  Dayton (G-9294)

COURTS OF LAW: Local

Butler County Clerk of Courts.............D....... 513 887-3282
  Hamilton (G-11701)

COURTS OF LAW: State

Supreme Court of Ohio........................E....... 937 898-3996
  Vandalia (G-18700)

COVERS: Automobile Seat

Crown Dielectric Inds Inc....................C....... 614 224-5161
  Columbus (G-7467)

CRANE & AERIAL LIFT SVCS

American Crane Inc.............................E....... 614 496-2268
  Reynoldsburg (G-16426)
Bay Mechanical & Elec Corp...............D....... 440 282-6816
  Lorain (G-13017)
Crane 1 Services Inc...........................E....... 937 704-9900
  Miamisburg (G-14289)
Division 7 Inc..E....... 740 965-1970
  Galena (G-11281)
In Terminal Services Corp...................E....... 216 518-8407
  Maple Heights (G-13409)
Pollock Research & Design Inc..........E....... 330 332-3300
  Salem (G-16706)

SERVICES SECTION

CRANES & MONORAIL SYSTEMS

Emh Inc..E....... 330 220-8600
  Valley City (G-18617)

CRANES: Indl Plant

Hiab USA Inc...D....... 419 482-6000
  Perrysburg (G-16012)

CRANES: Indl Truck

Venturo Manufacturing Inc................E....... 513 772-8448
  Cincinnati (G-4807)

CRANES: Overhead

ACC Automation Co Inc.......................E....... 330 928-3821
  Akron (G-15)

CRANKSHAFTS & CAMSHAFTS: Machining

Atlas Industries Inc.............................B....... 419 637-2117
  Tiffin (G-17671)

CRATING SVCS: Shipping

Kenco Group Inc..................................E....... 614 409-8754
  Groveport (G-11653)

CREATIVE SVCS: Advertisers, Exc Writers

Digital Color Intl LLC............................E....... 330 762-6959
  Akron (G-193)

CREDIT & OTHER FINANCIAL RESPONSIBILITY INSURANCE

Progressive Corporation......................B....... 440 461-5000
  Cleveland (G-6317)

CREDIT AGENCIES: Federal & Federally Sponsored

Columbus Metro Federal Cr Un..........E....... 614 239-0210
  Columbus (G-7368)
Columbus Metro Federal Cr Un..........E....... 614 239-0210
  Columbus (G-7369)

CREDIT AGENCIES: Federal Home Loan Mortgage Corporation

Hanna Holdings Inc.............................E....... 440 971-5600
  North Royalton (G-15492)

CREDIT AGENCIES: National Consumer Cooperative Bank

National Cooperative Bank NA............D....... 937 393-4246
  Hillsboro (G-11989)

CREDIT BUREAUS

Cbc Companies Inc.............................E....... 614 222-4343
  Columbus (G-7213)
Credit Infonet Inc.................................E....... 937 235-2546
  Dayton (G-9445)
Kreller Bus Info Group Inc..................E....... 513 723-8900
  Cincinnati (G-3945)
Open Online LLC...................................E....... 614 481-6999
  Columbus (G-8470)
Pasco Inc..B....... 330 650-0613
  Hudson (G-12138)

CREDIT CARD PROCESSING SVCS

Relentless Recovery Inc.....................D....... 216 621-8333
  Cleveland (G-6370)

CREDIT CARD SVCS

Alliance Data Systems Corp................B....... 614 729-5000
  Westerville (G-19362)
Alliance Data Systems Corp................C....... 614 729-5800
  Reynoldsburg (G-16425)
Banc Certified Merch Svcs LLC..........E....... 614 850-2740
  Hilliard (G-11880)
Citicorp Credit Services Inc..............B....... 212 559-1000
  Columbus (G-7277)
Dfs Corporate Services LLC...............B....... 614 777-7020
  Hilliard (G-11895)
Elder-Beerman Stores Corp................A....... 937 296-2700
  Moraine (G-14780)

SERVICES SECTION

CUSTODIAL SVCS: School, Contract Basis

Heartland Payment Systems LLC..........D....... 513 518-6125
  Loveland (G-13130)
Jpmorgan Chase Bank Nat Assn...........A....... 614 436-3055
  Columbus (G-6888)
Macys Cr & Customer Svcs Inc..............D....... 513 881-9950
  West Chester (G-19114)
Macys Cr & Customer Svcs Inc..............A....... 513 398-5221
  Mason (G-13734)
Npc Group Inc ....A....... 312 627-6000
  Symmes Twp (G-17629)
Solupay Consulting Inc ....D....... 216 535-9016
  Twinsburg (G-18471)
Worldpay Inc ....C....... 513 900-5250
  Symmes Twp (G-17631)

CREDIT INST, SHORT-TERM BUSINESS: Financing Dealers

Lakewood Acceptance Corp ....E....... 216 658-1234
  Cleveland (G-5921)

CREDIT INSTITUTIONS, SHORT-TERM BUS: Buying Install Notes

Sherman Financial Group LLC ....E....... 513 707-3000
  Cincinnati (G-4516)
Unifund Ccr LLC ....D....... 513 489-8877
  Blue Ash (G-1709)
Unifund Corporation ....E....... 513 489-8877
  Blue Ash (G-1710)

CREDIT INSTITUTIONS, SHORT-TERM BUS: Wrkg Capital Finance

Business Backer LLC ....E....... 513 792-6866
  Cincinnati (G-3155)
Preferred Capital Lending Inc ....E....... 216 472-1391
  Cleveland (G-6299)

CREDIT INSTITUTIONS: Personal

Caliber Home Loans Inc ....E....... 937 435-5363
  Dayton (G-9376)
Citizens Capital Markets Inc ....E....... 216 589-0900
  Cleveland (G-5244)
Education Loan Servicing Corp ....D....... 216 706-8130
  Cleveland (G-5527)
Farm Credit Mid-America ....E....... 740 441-9312
  Albany (G-519)
General Revenue Corporation ....B....... 513 469-1472
  Mason (G-13707)
Macys Cr & Customer Svcs Inc ....A....... 513 398-5221
  Mason (G-13734)
PNC Bank National Association ....D....... 440 546-6760
  Brecksville (G-1841)
Security Nat Auto Accptnce LLC ....C....... 513 459-8118
  Mason (G-13758)
Stark Federal Credit Union ....E....... 330 493-8325
  Canton (G-2547)
Student Loan Strategies LLC ....E....... 513 645-5400
  Cincinnati (G-4597)
Tebo Financial Services Inc ....E....... 234 207-2500
  Canton (G-2558)

CREDIT INSTITUTIONS: Short-Term Business

Ally Financial Inc....................................E....... 330 533-7300
  Canfield (G-2182)
General Electric Company ....C....... 440 255-0930
  Mentor (G-14179)
General Electric Company ....E....... 937 534-2000
  Dayton (G-9571)
General Electric Company ....A....... 937 534-6920
  Dayton (G-9570)
Morgan Stanley ....E....... 330 670-4600
  Akron (G-347)
Scott Fetzer Financial Group ....E....... 440 892-3000
  Cleveland (G-6453)

CREDIT INVESTIGATION SVCS

Corps Security Agency Inc ....D....... 513 631-3200
  Blue Ash (G-1568)

CREDIT UNIONS: Federally Chartered

Aur Group Financial Credit Un ....E....... 513 737-0508
  Hamilton (G-11694)
Aurgroup Financial Credit Un ....D....... 513 942-4422
  Fairfield (G-10821)
B F G Federal Credit Union....................D....... 330 374-2990
  Akron (G-87)
Bayer Heritage Federal Cr Un ....C....... 740 929-2015
  Hebron (G-11845)
Best Reward Credit Union......................E....... 216 367-8000
  Cleveland (G-5119)
Bmi Federal Credit Union.......................D....... 614 707-4000
  Dublin (G-10264)
Bmi Federal Credit Union.......................E....... 614 298-8527
  Columbus (G-7120)
Canton School Employees Fed Cr ....E....... 330 452-9801
  Canton (G-2298)
Century Federal Credit Union ....E....... 216 535-3600
  Cleveland (G-5217)
Cincinnati Central Cr Un Inc ....D....... 513 241-2050
  Cincinnati (G-3291)
Cinco Credit Union ....E....... 513 281-9988
  Cincinnati (G-3341)
Cinfed Federal Credit Union ....D....... 513 333-3800
  Cincinnati (G-3348)
Clyde-Findlay Area Cr Un Inc ....E....... 419 547-7781
  Clyde (G-6812)
Columbus Municipal Employees............E....... 614 224-8890
  Columbus (G-7371)
Corporate One Federal Cr Un ....D....... 614 825-9314
  Columbus (G-6878)
Desco Federal Credit Union ....E....... 740 354-7791
  Portsmouth (G-16275)
Dover Phila Federal Credit Un ....D....... 330 364-8874
  Dover (G-10187)
Education First Credit Un Inc ....E....... 614 221-9376
  Columbus (G-7580)
Fairview Hlth Sys Fderal Cr Un ....A....... 216 476-7000
  Cleveland (G-5567)
Firelands Federal Credit Union..............E....... 419 483-4180
  Bellevue (G-1409)
First Day Fincl Federal Cr Un ....E....... 937 222-4546
  Dayton (G-9548)
First Miami Student Credit Un ....E....... 513 529-1251
  Oxford (G-15815)
Fremont Federal Credit Union ....C....... 419 334-4434
  Fremont (G-11201)
Glass City Federal Credit Un ....E....... 419 887-1000
  Maumee (G-13922)
Honda Federal Credit Union ....E....... 937 642-6000
  Marysville (G-13624)
Lima Superior Federal Cr Un ....C....... 419 223-9746
  Lima (G-12828)
Miami University ....E....... 513 529-1251
  Oxford (G-15822)
Midwest Cmnty Federal Cr Un ....E....... 419 782-9856
  Defiance (G-10050)
Ohio Catholic Federal Cr Un ....E....... 216 663-6800
  Cleveland (G-6188)
Ohio Healthcare Federal Cr Un ....E....... 614 737-6034
  Dublin (G-10413)
River Valley Credit Union Inc ....D....... 937 859-1970
  Miamisburg (G-14344)
Saint Francis De Sales Church ....E....... 440 884-2319
  Cleveland (G-6436)
School Employees Lorain County ....E....... 440 324-3400
  Elyria (G-10678)
Sun Federal Credit Union.......................E....... 800 786-0945
  Maumee (G-13981)
Sun Federal Credit Union.......................D....... 419 537-0200
  Toledo (G-18207)
True Core Federal Credit Union..............E....... 740 345-6608
  Newark (G-15241)
Vacationland Federal Credit Un ....E....... 440 967-5155
  Sandusky (G-16808)

CREDIT UNIONS: State Chartered

Aur Group Financial Credit Un ....E....... 513 737-0508
  Hamilton (G-11694)
Cuso Corporation ....D....... 513 984-2876
  Cincinnati (G-3450)
Education First Credit Un Inc ....E....... 614 221-9376
  Columbus (G-7580)
Midusa Credit Union ....E....... 513 420-8640
  Middletown (G-14482)

CREMATORIES

Cremation Service Inc ....E....... 216 861-2334
  Cleveland (G-5435)

CRISIS CENTER

Community Center ....D....... 330 746-7721
  Youngstown (G-20152)
Crisis Intervention & Rcvy Ctr ....D....... 330 455-9407
  Canton (G-2327)
Help Hotline Crisis Center......................E....... 330 747-5111
  Youngstown (G-20216)
Huckleberry House ....D....... 614 294-5553
  Columbus (G-7861)
Sioto Paintsville Mental Hlth..................E....... 740 775-1260
  Chillicothe (G-2885)

CRISIS INTERVENTION CENTERS

Community Counseling Services............E....... 419 468-8211
  Bucyrus (G-2031)
Crisis Intvntn Ctr Stark Cnty ....D....... 330 452-9812
  Canton (G-2328)
Help Line of Dlware Mrrow Cnty ....E....... 740 369-3316
  Delaware (G-10104)
Rape Information & Counseling ....E....... 330 782-3936
  Youngstown (G-20341)
Scioto Pnt Vly Mental Hlth Ctr ....E....... 740 335-6935
  Wshngtn CT Hs (G-20034)

CRUDE PETROLEUM & NATURAL GAS PRODUCTION

AB Resources LLC ....E....... 440 922-1098
  Brecksville (G-1810)
Kenoil Inc ....E....... 330 262-1144
  Wooster (G-19879)

CRUDE PETROLEUM & NATURAL GAS PRODUCTION

City of Lancaster ....E....... 740 687-6670
  Lancaster (G-12518)
Resource America Inc ....E....... 330 896-8510
  Uniontown (G-18536)

CRUDE PETROLEUM PRODUCTION

Alliance Petroleum Corporation ....D....... 330 493-0440
  Canton (G-2233)
Belden & Blake Corporation ....E....... 330 602-5551
  Dover (G-10177)
Chevron Ae Resources LLC ....E....... 330 654-4343
  Deerfield (G-10017)
Gulfport Energy Corporation ....E....... 740 251-0407
  Saint Clairsville (G-16636)
Koch Knight LLC ....D....... 330 488-1651
  East Canton (G-10504)
Resource Energy Inc ....E....... 330 896-8510
  Uniontown (G-18537)
Xto Energy Inc..D....... 740 671-9901
  Bellaire (G-1369)

CRYSTAL GOODS, WHOLESALE

Gia USA Inc ....E....... 216 831-8678
  Cleveland (G-5670)

CUPS: Paper, Made From Purchased Materials

Ricking Paper and Specialty Co ....E....... 513 825-3551
  Cincinnati (G-4418)

CURTAIN & DRAPERY FIXTURES: Poles, Rods & Rollers

Lumenomics Inc......................................E....... 614 798-3500
  Lewis Center (G-12693)

CURTAIN WALLS: Building, Steel

Scs Construction Services Inc ....E....... 513 929-0260
  Cincinnati (G-4487)

CURTAINS: Window, From Purchased Materials

Style-Line Incorporated..........................E....... 614 291-0600
  Columbus (G-8798)

CUSTODIAL SVCS: School, Contract Basis

Logan-Hocking School District ....E....... 740 385-7844
  Logan (G-12985)
Toledo Public Schools.............................D....... 419 243-6422
  Toledo (G-18247)

Employee Codes: A=Over 500 employees, B=251-500
C=101-250, D=51-100, E=25-50

CUSTOMIZING SVCS — SERVICES SECTION

CUSTOMIZING SVCS

1157 Design Concepts LLC ....E....... 937 497-1157
  Sidney (G-16909)

CUSTOMS CLEARANCE OF FREIGHT

Comprehensive Logistics Co Inc ....E....... 800 734-0372
  Youngstown (G-20159)

CUT STONE & STONE PRODUCTS

Brower Products Inc ....D....... 937 563-1111
  Cincinnati (G-3142)
Lang Stone Company Inc ....D....... 614 235-4099
  Columbus (G-8038)
National Lime and Stone Co ....D....... 419 562-0771
  Bucyrus (G-2044)
National Lime and Stone Co ....C....... 419 396-7671
  Carey (G-2596)

CUTLERY

Alliance Knife Inc ....E....... 513 367-9000
  Harrison (G-11789)
Npk Construction Equipment Inc ....D....... 440 232-7900
  Bedford (G-1324)

CYLINDER & ACTUATORS: Fluid Power

Eaton-Aeroquip Llc ....D....... 419 891-7775
  Maumee (G-13907)
Hydraulic Parts Store Inc ....E....... 330 364-6667
  New Philadelphia (G-15102)
Hydraulic Specialists Inc ....E....... 740 922-3343
  Midvale (G-14490)
Robeck Fluid Power Co ....D....... 330 562-1140
  Aurora (G-852)
Steel Eqp Specialists Inc ....D....... 330 823-8260
  Alliance (G-563)
Swagelok Company ....D....... 440 349-5934
  Solon (G-17059)

Convents

Ursuline Convent Sacred Heart ....E....... 419 531-8990
  Toledo (G-18283)

DAIRY PRDTS STORE: Ice Cream, Packaged

Austintown Dairy Inc ....E....... 330 629-6170
  Youngstown (G-20108)
Cleveland Dairy Queen Inc ....C....... 440 946-3690
  Willoughby (G-19654)

DAIRY PRDTS STORES

Discount Drug Mart Inc ....C....... 330 725-2340
  Medina (G-14059)
Hans Rothenbuhler & Son Inc ....E....... 440 632-6000
  Middlefield (G-14395)
J V Hansel Inc ....E....... 330 716-0806
  Warren (G-18866)
S and S Gilardi Inc ....D....... 740 397-2751
  Mount Vernon (G-14921)
Smithfoods Orrville Inc ....E....... 740 389-4643
  Marion (G-13580)
United Dairy Farmers Inc ....C....... 513 396-8700
  Cincinnati (G-4731)
Youngs Jersey Dairy Inc ....B....... 937 325-0629
  Yellow Springs (G-20091)

DAIRY PRDTS WHOLESALERS: Fresh

Auburn Dairy Products Inc ....E....... 614 488-2536
  Columbus (G-7073)
Barkett Fruit Co Inc ....E....... 330 364-6645
  Dover (G-10176)
Borden Dairy Co Cincinnati LLC ....C....... 513 948-8811
  Cincinnati (G-3127)
Euclid Fish Company ....E....... 440 951-6448
  Mentor (G-14172)
Giant Eagle Inc ....E....... 216 292-7000
  Bedford Heights (G-1352)
Hans Rothenbuhler & Son Inc ....E....... 440 632-6000
  Middlefield (G-14395)
Hillcrest Egg & Cheese Co ....D....... 216 361-4625
  Cleveland (G-5757)
Instantwhip Foods Inc ....E....... 330 688-8825
  Stow (G-17375)
Instantwhip-Akron Inc ....E....... 614 488-2536
  Stow (G-17376)
Instantwhip-Columbus Inc ....E....... 614 871-9447
  Grove City (G-11571)

Louis Trauth Dairy LLC ....B....... 859 431-7553
  West Chester (G-19213)
S and S Gilardi Inc ....D....... 740 397-2751
  Mount Vernon (G-14921)
Sysco Cincinnati LLC ....B....... 513 563-6300
  Cincinnati (G-4609)
US Foods Inc ....A....... 614 539-7993
  West Chester (G-19240)
Weaver Bros Inc ....D....... 937 526-3907
  Versailles (G-18731)

DAIRY PRDTS: Butter

Dairy Farmers America Inc ....E....... 330 670-7800
  Medina (G-14057)

DAIRY PRDTS: Cheese

Dairy Farmers America Inc ....E....... 330 670-7800
  Medina (G-14057)

DAIRY PRDTS: Dietary Supplements, Dairy & Non-Dairy Based

Instantwhip-Columbus Inc ....E....... 614 871-9447
  Grove City (G-11571)

DAIRY PRDTS: Frozen Desserts & Novelties

Louis Trauth Dairy LLC ....B....... 859 431-7553
  West Chester (G-19213)
Robert E McGrath Inc ....E....... 440 572-7747
  Strongsville (G-17503)
Springdale Ice Cream Beverage ....E....... 513 699-4984
  Cincinnati (G-4567)
Youngs Jersey Dairy Inc ....B....... 937 325-0629
  Yellow Springs (G-20091)

DAIRY PRDTS: Ice Cream & Ice Milk

United Dairy Farmers Inc ....C....... 513 396-8700
  Cincinnati (G-4731)

DAIRY PRDTS: Milk, Condensed & Evaporated

Hans Rothenbuhler & Son Inc ....E....... 440 632-6000
  Middlefield (G-14395)

DAIRY PRDTS: Milk, Fluid

Dairy Farmers America Inc ....E....... 330 670-7800
  Medina (G-14057)
Louis Trauth Dairy LLC ....B....... 859 431-7553
  West Chester (G-19213)

DAIRY PRDTS: Milk, Processed, Pasteurized, Homogenized/Btld

Borden Dairy Co Cincinnati LLC ....C....... 513 948-8811
  Cincinnati (G-3127)
United Dairy Farmers Inc ....C....... 513 396-8700
  Cincinnati (G-4731)

DAIRY PRDTS: Natural Cheese

Great Lakes Cheese Co Inc ....B....... 440 834-2500
  Hiram (G-12002)
Hans Rothenbuhler & Son Inc ....E....... 440 632-6000
  Middlefield (G-14395)
Miceli Dairy Products Co ....D....... 216 791-6222
  Cleveland (G-6045)

DAIRY PRDTS: Whipped Topping, Exc Frozen Or Dry Mix

Auburn Dairy Products Inc ....E....... 614 488-2536
  Columbus (G-7073)
Instantwhip-Columbus Inc ....E....... 614 871-9447
  Grove City (G-11571)

DANCE HALL OR BALLROOM OPERATION

Eldora Enterprises Inc ....E....... 937 338-3815
  New Weston (G-15140)
Piqua Country Club Holding Co ....E....... 937 773-7744
  Piqua (G-16156)

DANCE HALL SVCS

Applause Talent Presentation ....E....... 513 844-6788
  Hamilton (G-11692)

DANCE INSTRUCTOR & SCHOOL

Truenorth Cultural Arts ....E....... 440 949-5200
  Sheffield Village (G-16895)

DATA ENTRY SVCS

Cache Next Generation LLC ....D....... 614 850-9444
  Hilliard (G-11887)
Coleman Professional Svcs Inc ....C....... 330 628-2275
  Akron (G-151)
Coleman Professional Svcs Inc ....B....... 330 673-1347
  Kent (G-12360)
Lake Data Center Inc ....D....... 440 944-2020
  Wickliffe (G-19605)

DATA PROCESSING & PREPARATION SVCS

Btas Inc ....C....... 937 431-9431
  Beavercreek (G-1155)
Cbc Companies Inc ....D....... 614 538-6100
  Columbus (G-7214)
Central Command Inc ....E....... 330 723-2062
  Columbia Station (G-6842)
City of Cleveland ....D....... 216 664-2430
  Cleveland (G-5254)
Cleveland State University ....E....... 216 687-3786
  Cleveland (G-5348)
Convergys Gvrnment Sltions LLC ....D....... 513 723-7006
  Cincinnati (G-3419)
Datatrak International Inc ....E....... 440 443-0082
  Mayfield Heights (G-14000)
Definitive Solutions Co Inc ....D....... 513 719-9100
  Cincinnati (G-3479)
Eliassen Group LLC ....E....... 781 205-8100
  Blue Ash (G-1583)
Enterprise Data Management Inc ....E....... 513 791-7272
  Blue Ash (G-1588)
Expedata LLC ....E....... 937 439-6767
  Dayton (G-9536)
Gracie Plum Investments Inc ....E....... 740 355-9029
  Portsmouth (G-16282)
Illumination Works LLC ....D....... 937 938-1321
  Beavercreek (G-1178)
Infovision 21 Inc ....E....... 614 761-8844
  Dublin (G-10376)
Lockheed Martin ....A....... 330 796-2800
  Akron (G-326)
Lou-Ray Associates Inc ....E....... 330 220-1999
  Brunswick (G-1986)
Mast Technology Services Inc ....A....... 614 415-7000
  Columbus (G-8126)
Medical Mutual Services LLC ....C....... 440 878-4800
  Strongsville (G-17492)
Mri Software LLC ....C....... 800 327-8770
  Solon (G-17030)
New Pros Communications Inc ....D....... 740 201-0410
  Powell (G-16345)
Racksquared LLC ....E....... 614 737-8812
  Columbus (G-8583)
Rgis LLC ....D....... 248 651-2511
  Reynoldsburg (G-16477)
Sedlak Management Cons Inc ....E....... 216 206-4700
  Cleveland (G-6464)
Sumaria Systems Inc ....D....... 937 429-6070
  Beavercreek (G-1210)
Thinkware Incorporated ....E....... 513 598-3300
  Cincinnati (G-4650)
Vediscovery LLC ....E....... 216 241-3443
  Cleveland (G-6688)

DATA PROCESSING SVCS

1st All File Recovery Usa ....E....... 800 399-7150
  Shaker Heights (G-16855)
Aero Fulfillment Services Corp ....D....... 800 225-7145
  Mason (G-13658)
Alliance Data Systems Corp ....B....... 614 729-4000
  Columbus (G-6968)
Automatic Data Processing Inc ....C....... 216 447-1980
  Cleveland (G-5082)
Automatic Data Processing Inc ....C....... 614 212-4831
  Westerville (G-19370)
Change Healthcare Holdings Inc ....E....... 330 405-0001
  Hudson (G-12108)
Change Healthcare Holdings Inc ....E....... 216 589-5878
  Cleveland (G-5227)
Cincinnati Bell Inc ....D....... 513 397-9900
  Cincinnati (G-3285)
Convergys Corporation ....A....... 513 723-7000
  Cincinnati (G-3417)

SERVICES SECTION
DESIGN SVCS: Computer Integrated Systems

County of Cuyahoga .... C 216 443-8011
  Cleveland *(G-5421)*
Csi Complete Inc .... E 800 343-0641
  Plain City *(G-16186)*
Ctrac Inc .... E 440 572-1000
  Cleveland *(G-5447)*
Data Direction Inc .... E 216 362-5900
  Cleveland *(G-5463)*
Decisionone Corporation 614 883-0228
  Urbancrest *(G-18604)*
Early Express Services Inc .... E 937 223-5801
  Dayton *(G-9511)*
Enterprise Services LLC .... D 740 423-9501
  Belpre *(G-1436)*
Integrated Data Services Inc .... D 937 656-5496
  Dayton *(G-9631)*
Integrated Marketing Tech Inc .... D 330 225-3550
  Brunswick *(G-1982)*
Midwest Tape LLC .... B 419 868-9370
  Holland *(G-12038)*
Northwest Ohio Computer Assn .. D 419 267-5565
  Archbold *(G-640)*
Office World Inc .... E 419 991-4694
  Lima *(G-12928)*
Quadax Inc .... E 614 882-1200
  Westerville *(G-19438)*
Rurbanc Data Services Inc .... D 419 782-2530
  Defiance *(G-10055)*
Sourcelink Ohio LLC .... C 937 885-8000
  Miamisburg *(G-14352)*
Speedeon Data LLC .... E 440 264-2100
  Cleveland *(G-6519)*
Vantiv LLC .... B 877 713-5964
  Symmes Twp *(G-17630)*

DATABASE INFORMATION RETRIEVAL SVCS

Ecommerce LLC .... D 800 861-9394
  Columbus *(G-7574)*
Lexisnexis Group .... C 937 865-6800
  Miamisburg *(G-14314)*
One Source Technology LLC .... E 216 420-1700
  Cleveland *(G-6205)*
Title First Agency Inc .... E 614 224-9207
  Columbus *(G-8850)*

DATING SVCS

Great Southern Video Inc .... E 216 642-8855
  Cleveland *(G-5693)*

DEBT COUNSELING OR ADJUSTMENT SVCS: Individuals

Consumer Credit Coun .... E 614 552-2222
  Gahanna *(G-11237)*

DECORATIVE WOOD & WOODWORK

77 Coach Supply Ltd .... E 330 674-1454
  Millersburg *(G-14582)*
Woodpeckers Inc .... E 440 238-1824
  Strongsville *(G-17525)*

DEGREASING MACHINES

Crowne Group LLC .... D 216 589-0198
  Cleveland *(G-5440)*

DELIVERY SVCS, BY VEHICLE

Blood Courier Inc .... E 216 251-3050
  Cleveland *(G-5123)*
Capitol Express Entps Inc .... D 614 279-2819
  Columbus *(G-7187)*
DD&b Inc .... E 614 577-0550
  Columbus *(G-7496)*
Dyno Nobel Transportation .... E 740 439-5050
  Cambridge *(G-2111)*
Early Express Services Inc .... E 937 223-5801
  Dayton *(G-9511)*
Fedex Ground Package Sys Inc .. C 412 859-2653
  Steubenville *(G-17317)*
Fedex Ground Package Sys Inc .. B 800 463-3339
  Toledo *(G-17884)*
Fedex Ground Package Sys Inc .. D 513 942-4330
  West Chester *(G-19200)*
Hc Transport Inc .... E 513 574-1800
  Cincinnati *(G-3744)*
James Air Cargo Inc .... E 440 243-9095
  Cleveland *(G-5849)*
Masur Trucking Inc .... E 513 860-9600
  Cincinnati *(G-4029)*
Midway Delivery Service .... E 216 391-0700
  Cleveland *(G-6059)*
Prestige Delivery Systems LLC .... E 614 836-8980
  Groveport *(G-11663)*
Priority Dispatch Inc .... E 513 791-3900
  Blue Ash *(G-1665)*
Priority Dispatch Inc .... E 216 332-9852
  Solon *(G-17041)*
Quick Delivery Service Inc .... E 330 453-3709
  Canton *(G-2500)*
R & M Delivery .... E 740 574-2113
  Franklin Furnace *(G-11173)*
Rapid Delivery Service Co Inc ..... E 513 733-0500
  Cincinnati *(G-4385)*
Rush Package Delivery Inc .... D 937 297-6182
  Dayton *(G-9859)*
Thomas Transport Delivery Inc ... E 330 908-3100
  Macedonia *(G-13212)*
Top Dawg Group LLC .... E 216 398-1066
  Brooklyn Heights *(G-1928)*
Total Package Express Inc .... E 513 741-5500
  Cincinnati *(G-4662)*
Wright Brothers Aero Inc .... E 937 454-8475
  Dayton *(G-10004)*

DENTAL EQPT & SPLYS

Dental Ceramics Inc .... E 330 523-5240
  Richfield *(G-16504)*
Dresch Tolson Dental Labs .... D 419 842-6730
  Sylvania *(G-17584)*
United Dental Laboratories .... E 330 253-1810
  Akron *(G-484)*
Wbc Group LLC .... D 866 528-2144
  Hudson *(G-12150)*

DENTAL EQPT & SPLYS WHOLESALERS

Benco Dental Supply Co .... D 513 874-2990
  Cincinnati *(G-3098)*
Benco Dental Supply Co .... D 614 761-1053
  Dublin *(G-10261)*
Dentronix Inc .... E 330 916-7300
  Cuyahoga Falls *(G-9179)*
Henry Schein Inc .... E 440 349-0891
  Cleveland *(G-5750)*
Professional Sales Associates .... E 330 299-7343
  Seville *(G-16842)*

DENTAL EQPT & SPLYS: Orthodontic Appliances

Dentronix Inc .... E 330 916-7300
  Cuyahoga Falls *(G-9179)*

DENTISTS' OFFICES & CLINICS

C Ted Forsberg .... E 440 992-3145
  Ashtabula *(G-730)*
Concorde Therapy Group Inc ...... C 330 493-4210
  Canton *(G-2319)*
Dental One Inc .... E 216 584-1000
  Independence *(G-12203)*
Dental Servics of Ohio Daniel ...... D 614 863-2222
  Reynoldsburg *(G-16445)*
Denture Center .... E 440 964-0542
  Ashtabula *(G-742)*
Dr Michael J Hulit .... E 330 863-7173
  Malvern *(G-13250)*
Health Smile Center .... E 440 992-2700
  Ashtabula *(G-747)*
Lima Dental Assoc Risolvato Lt ... E 419 228-4036
  Lima *(G-12820)*
Martin Ls DDS Ms .... E 513 829-8999
  Fairfield *(G-10874)*
Metro Health Dental Associates .. E 216 778-4982
  Cleveland *(G-6034)*
Metrohealth System .... E 216 957-1500
  Cleveland *(G-6041)*
Ohio State University .... D 614 292-2751
  Columbus *(G-8443)*
R P Cunningham DDS Inc .... E 614 885-2022
  Worthington *(G-19990)*

DEPARTMENT STORES

Centro Properties Group LLC ...... E 440 324-6610
  Elyria *(G-10602)*

DEPARTMENT STORES: Non-Discount

Elder-Beerman Stores Corp .... A 937 296-2700
  Moraine *(G-14780)*

JC Penney Corporation Inc .... B 330 633-7700
  Akron *(G-290)*

DEPARTMENT STORES: Surplus & Salvage

Glen Surplus Sales Inc .... E 419 347-1212
  Shelby *(G-16900)*
Goodwill Inds Centl Ohio Inc .... B 614 294-5181
  Columbus *(G-7760)*
Public Safety Ohio Department ... E 937 335-6209
  Troy *(G-18372)*

DEPOSIT INSURANCE

American Mutl Share Insur Corp .. E 614 764-1900
  Dublin *(G-10251)*
Excess Share Insurance Corp ..... E 614 764-1900
  Dublin *(G-10343)*

DESALTER KITS: Sea Water

Luxfer Magtech Inc .... E 513 772-3066
  Cincinnati *(G-4003)*

DESIGN SVCS, NEC

Bollin & Sons Inc .... E 419 693-6573
  Toledo *(G-17776)*
Cdc Technologies Inc .... D 937 886-9713
  Dayton *(G-9392)*
Controls Inc .... E 330 239-4345
  Medina *(G-14051)*
Elevar Design Group Inc .... E 513 721-0600
  Cincinnati *(G-3550)*
Emersion Design LLC .... E 513 841-9100
  Cincinnati *(G-3553)*
Lindsey Cnstr & Design Inc .... E 330 785-9931
  Akron *(G-321)*
Loth Inc .... E 513 554-4900
  Cincinnati *(G-3995)*
Snl Designs Ltd .... E 440 247-2344
  Chagrin Falls *(G-2707)*

DESIGN SVCS: Commercial & Indl

Design Central Inc .... E 614 890-0202
  Columbus *(G-7510)*
Electrovations Inc .... E 330 274-3558
  Aurora *(G-837)*
Elite Enclosure Company LLC .... E 937 492-3548
  Sidney *(G-16931)*
Hanco International .... D 330 456-9407
  Canton *(G-2392)*
Ies Systems Inc .... E 330 533-6683
  Canfield *(G-2196)*
Military Resources LLC .... E 330 263-1040
  Wooster *(G-19888)*
Military Resources LLC .... D 330 309-9970
  Wooster *(G-19889)*
New Path International LLC .... E 614 410-3974
  Powell *(G-16344)*
North Bay Construction Inc .... E 440 835-1898
  Westlake *(G-19522)*
Polaris Automation Inc .... D 614 431-0170
  Lewis Center *(G-12704)*
Priority Designs Inc .... E 614 337-9979
  Columbus *(G-8561)*
R and J Corporation .... E 440 871-6009
  Westlake *(G-19536)*
Ultra Tech Machinery Inc .... E 330 929-5544
  Cuyahoga Falls *(G-9228)*

DESIGN SVCS: Computer Integrated Systems

Aclara Technologies LLC .... C 440 528-7200
  Solon *(G-16969)*
Advanced Service Tech LLC .... E 937 435-4376
  Miamisburg *(G-14268)*
Afidence Inc .... E 513 234-5822
  Mason *(G-13659)*
Assured Information SEC Inc ...... D 937 427-9720
  Beavercreek *(G-1148)*
Attevo Inc .... D 216 928-2800
  Beachwood *(G-1053)*
Baxter Hodell Donnelly Preston .. C 513 271-1634
  Cincinnati *(G-3083)*
Bpi Infrmtion Systems Ohio Inc ... E 440 717-4112
  Brecksville *(G-1815)*
Cdo Technologies Inc .... D 937 258-0022
  Dayton *(G-9260)*
Cincom Intrnational Operations ... B 513 612-2300
  Cincinnati *(G-3342)*

Employee Codes: A=Over 500 employees, B=251-500
C=101-250, D=51-100, E=25-50

DESIGN SVCS: Computer Integrated Systems

Convergys Corporation .... A 513 723-7000
  Cincinnati (G-3417)
Cott Systems Inc .... D 614 847-4405
  Columbus (G-7449)
Definitive Solutions Co Inc .... D 513 719-9100
  Cincinnati (G-3479)
Document Tech Systems Ltd .... E 330 928-5311
  Cuyahoga Falls (G-9181)
E&I Solutions LLC .... E 937 912-0288
  Beavercreek (G-1171)
Exact Software North Amer LLC .... C 614 410-2600
  Dublin (G-10342)
Matrix Management Solutions .... C 330 470-3700
  Canton (G-2451)
Microman Inc .... E 614 923-8000
  Dublin (G-10397)
Natural Resources Ohio Dept .... E 614 265-6852
  Columbus (G-8250)
Northrop Grumman Technical .... C 937 320-3100
  Beavercreek Township (G-1276)
Ohio State University .... E 614 728-8100
  Columbus (G-8432)
Pcms Datafit Inc .... D 513 587-3100
  Cincinnati (G-4269)
Pomeroy It Solutions Sls Inc .... E 440 717-1364
  Brecksville (G-1842)
Presidio Infrastructure .... E 614 381-1400
  Dublin (G-10429)
Rainbow Data Systems Inc .... E 937 431-8000
  Beavercreek (G-1202)
Reynolds and Reynolds Company .... A 937 485-2000
  Kettering (G-12435)
Rovisys Building Tech LLC .... E 330 954-7600
  Aurora (G-853)
Sgi Matrix LLC .... D 937 438-9033
  Miamisburg (G-14349)
Software Solutions Inc .... E 513 932-6667
  Lebanon (G-12648)
Sogeti USA LLC .... E 614 847-4477
  Westerville (G-19353)
Suite 224 Internet .... E 440 593-7113
  Conneaut (G-9047)
Sumaria Systems Inc .... D 937 429-6070
  Beavercreek (G-1210)
Sytronics Inc .... E 937 431-6100
  Beavercreek (G-1211)
Tata America Intl Corp .... B 513 677-6500
  Milford (G-14565)
Tsi Inc .... E 419 468-1855
  Galion (G-11307)
Wescom Solutions Inc .... E 513 831-1207
  Milford (G-14574)

DETECTIVE & ARMORED CAR SERVICES

Aset Corporation .... E 937 890-8881
  Vandalia (G-18659)
Infinite SEC Solutions LLC .... E 419 720-5678
  Toledo (G-17973)
Pennington International Inc .... E 513 631-2130
  Cincinnati (G-4276)
Safeguard Properties LLC .... A 216 739-2900
  Cleveland (G-6433)
Seven Secured Inc .... E 281 362-2887
  Strongsville (G-17505)
Veteran Security Patrol Co .... E 937 222-7333
  Dayton (G-9971)

DETECTIVE AGENCY

Acrux Investigation Agency .... B 937 842-5780
  Lakeview (G-12467)
Cefaratti Investigation & Prcs .... E 216 696-1161
  Cleveland (G-5201)
Key II Security Inc .... E 937 339-8530
  Troy (G-18360)
Marshall & Associates Inc .... E 513 683-6396
  Loveland (G-13144)

DETECTIVE SVCS

Atlantis Co Inc .... D 888 807-3272
  Cleveland (G-5078)
Securitas SEC Svcs USA Inc .... D 513 639-7615
  Cincinnati (G-4488)

DETOXIFICATION CENTERS, OUTPATIENT

Choices Behavioral Healthcare .... E 216 881-4060
  Cleveland (G-5238)
Ryan Sheridan .... E 330 270-2380
  Youngstown (G-20364)

DIAGNOSTIC SUBSTANCES

Perkinelmer Hlth Sciences Inc .... E 330 825-4525
  Akron (G-385)
Thermo Fisher Scientific Inc .... C 800 871-8909
  Oakwood Village (G-15635)

DICE & DICE CUPS

Container Graphics Corp .... D 419 531-5133
  Toledo (G-17831)

DIES & TOOLS: Special

Acro Tool & Die Company .... D 330 773-5173
  Akron (G-17)
Athens Mold and Machine Inc .... D 740 593-6613
  Akron (G-84)
Custom Machine Inc .... E 419 986-5122
  Tiffin (G-17676)
General Tool Company .... C 513 733-5500
  Cincinnati (G-3675)
Mtd Holdings Inc .... B 330 225-2600
  Valley City (G-18622)
Seilkop Industries Inc .... E 513 761-1035
  Cincinnati (G-4492)
Tipp Machine & Tool Inc .... C 937 890-8428
  Dayton (G-9931)

DIET & WEIGHT REDUCING CENTERS

Diet Center Worldwide Inc .... E 330 665-5861
  Akron (G-192)
Formu3 International Inc .... E 330 668-1461
  Akron (G-228)

DIETICIANS' OFFICES

Dietary Solutions Inc .... E 614 985-6567
  Lewis Center (G-12682)

DIODES: Light Emitting

Ceso Inc .... D 937 435-8584
  Miamisburg (G-14281)

DIRECT SELLING ESTAB: Coffee, Soda/Beer, Etc, Door-To-Door

M & R Amusement Services Inc .... E 937 525-0404
  Springfield (G-17227)

DIRECT SELLING ESTABLISHMENTS: Appliances, House-To-House

Central Repair Service Inc .... E 513 943-0500
  Point Pleasant (G-16218)

DIRECT SELLING ESTABLISHMENTS: Telemarketing

Universal Marketing Group LLC .... D 419 720-9696
  Toledo (G-18275)

DISASTER SVCS

A Team LLC .... E 216 271-7223
  Cleveland (G-4936)
American Red Cross .... D 513 579-3000
  Cincinnati (G-3012)

DISC JOCKEYS

Rock House Entrmt Group Inc .... C 440 232-7625
  Oakwood Village (G-15633)

DISCOUNT DEPARTMENT STORES

Target Stores Inc .... C 614 279-4224
  Columbus (G-8822)
Walmart Inc .... C 937 399-0370
  Springfield (G-17296)
Walmart Inc .... B 740 286-8203
  Jackson (G-12321)

DISINFECTING SVCS

DCS Sanitation Management Inc .... D 513 891-4980
  Cincinnati (G-3469)

DISKETTE DUPLICATING SVCS

Arszman & Lyons   LLC .... E 513 527-4900
  Blue Ash (G-1536)

Evanhoe & Associates Inc .... E 937 235-2995
  Dayton (G-9269)

DISPLAY FIXTURES: Wood

Ptmj Enterprises .... C 440 543-8000
  Solon (G-17042)

DISPLAY ITEMS: Solid Fiber, Made From Purchased Materials

Digital Color Intl LLC .... E 330 762-6959
  Akron (G-193)

DISPLAY LETTERING SVCS

Team Sports LLC .... E 419 865-8326
  Holland (G-12059)

DOCK EQPT & SPLYS, INDL

Tmt Inc .... C 419 592-1041
  Perrysburg (G-16064)

DOCUMENT DESTRUCTION SVC

Cdd LLC .... B 905 829-2794
  Mason (G-13673)
P C Workshop Inc .... D 419 399-4805
  Paulding (G-15932)
Shred-It USA LLC .... E 800 697-4733
  Fairfield (G-10907)
TDS Document Management Ltd .... E 614 367-9633
  Columbus (G-8826)
Weaver Industries Inc .... C 330 745-2400
  Akron (G-508)

DOCUMENT STORAGE SVCS

Allied Infotech Corporation .... D 330 745-8529
  Akron (G-68)
Cintas Corporation No 2 .... D 440 838-8611
  Cleveland (G-5240)

DOMESTIC HELP SVCS

Carol Scudere .... E 614 839-4357
  New Albany (G-14979)
Franklin Cnty Crt Common Pleas .... E 614 525-5775
  Columbus (G-7690)
Larue Enterprises Inc .... E 937 438-5711
  Beavercreek (G-1248)
Maids Home Service of Cincy .... E 513 396-6900
  Cincinnati (G-4013)
Super Shine Inc .... E 513 423-8999
  Middletown (G-14464)

DOMICILIARY CARE FACILITY

Brookdale Deer Park .... D 513 745-7600
  Cincinnati (G-3137)
Judson .... D 216 791-2004
  Cleveland (G-5876)

DOOR & WINDOW REPAIR SVCS

Advance Door Company .... E 216 883-2424
  Cleveland (G-4957)
Dortronic Service Inc .... E 216 739-3667
  Cleveland (G-5506)
Marsh Building Products Inc .... E 937 222-3321
  Dayton (G-9700)
Southern Ohio Door Contrls Inc .... E 513 353-4793
  Miamitown (G-14373)
Thomas Door Controls Inc .... E 614 263-1756
  Columbus (G-8837)

DOORS & WINDOWS WHOLESALERS: All Materials

American Warming and Vent .... D 419 288-2703
  Bradner (G-1808)
Andersen Distribution Inc .... C 937 898-7844
  Dayton (G-9336)
Gorell Enterprises Inc .... B 724 465-1800
  Streetsboro (G-17414)
Mason Structural Steel Inc .... D 440 439-1040
  Walton Hills (G-18790)
Modern Builders Supply Inc .... E 513 531-1000
  Cincinnati (G-4113)
Norandex Bldg Mtls Dist Inc .... A 330 656-8924
  Hudson (G-12136)
Southern Ohio Door Contrls Inc .... E 513 353-4793
  Miamitown (G-14373)

SERVICES SECTION

DRUG STORES

Traichal Construction Company.............E....... 800 255-3667
  Niles *(G-15307)*

DOORS & WINDOWS: Storm, Metal

Champion Opco LLC ....B....... 513 924-4858
  Cincinnati *(G-3228)*

DOORS: Garage, Overhead, Metal

Clopay Corporation ....C....... 800 282-2260
  Mason *(G-13686)*

DOORS: Garage, Overhead, Wood

Clopay Corporation ....C....... 800 282-2260
  Mason *(G-13686)*

DOORS: Glass

Scs Construction Services Inc ....E....... 513 929-0260
  Cincinnati *(G-4487)*

DOORS: Wooden

Khempco Bldg Sup Co Ltd Partnr.........D....... 740 549-0465
  Delaware *(G-10113)*
S R Door Inc ....D....... 740 927-3558
  Hebron *(G-11859)*

DRAFTING SPLYS WHOLESALERS

Key Blue Prints Inc ....D....... 614 228-3285
  Columbus *(G-7983)*
Queen City Reprographics....................C....... 513 326-2300
  Cincinnati *(G-4371)*

DRAFTING SVCS

Seifert Technologies Inc......................D....... 330 833-2700
  Massillon *(G-13853)*

DRAGSTRIP OPERATION

National Hot Rod Association ....C....... 740 928-5706
  Hebron *(G-11858)*

DRAPERIES & CURTAINS

Accent Drapery Co Inc ....E....... 614 488-0741
  Columbus *(G-6933)*
Janson Industries ....D....... 330 455-7029
  Canton *(G-2417)*
Vocational Services Inc ....C....... 216 431-8085
  Cleveland *(G-6709)*

DRAPERIES & DRAPERY FABRICS, COTTON

Lumenomics Inc................................E....... 614 798-3500
  Lewis Center *(G-12693)*

DRAPERIES: Plastic & Textile, From Purchased Materials

Standard Textile Co Inc ....B....... 513 761-9255
  Cincinnati *(G-4579)*

DRAPERY & UPHOLSTERY STORES: Draperies

Accent Drapery Co Inc ....E....... 614 488-0741
  Columbus *(G-6933)*
Farrow Cleaners Co ....E....... 216 561-2355
  Cleveland *(G-5574)*

DRAPES & DRAPERY FABRICS, FROM MANMADE FIBER

Lumenomics Inc................................E....... 614 798-3500
  Lewis Center *(G-12693)*

DRIED FRUITS WHOLESALERS

Ohio Hickory Harvest Brand Pro............E....... 330 644-6266
  Coventry Township *(G-9130)*

DRINKING PLACES: Alcoholic Beverages

A C Management Inc..........................E....... 440 461-9200
  Cleveland *(G-4931)*
B & I Hotel Management LLC...............C....... 330 995-0200
  Aurora *(G-828)*
Best Western Columbus N Hotel ....E....... 614 888-8230
  Columbus *(G-7103)*
Bird Enterprises LLC..........................E....... 330 674-1457
  Millersburg *(G-14589)*
Breezy Point Ltd Partnership................E....... 330 995-0600
  Aurora *(G-831)*
Broad Street Hotel Assoc LP ....D....... 614 861-0321
  Columbus *(G-7147)*
Cambridge Country Club Company.......E....... 740 439-2744
  Byesville *(G-2070)*
Ch Relty Iv/Clmbus Partners LP ....D....... 614 885-3334
  Columbus *(G-7247)*
Claire De Leigh Corp ....E....... 614 459-6575
  Columbus *(G-7289)*
Cleveland Airport Hospitality................D....... 440 871-6000
  Westlake *(G-19476)*
Clubhouse Pub N Grub ....E....... 440 884-2582
  Cleveland *(G-5368)*
Columbus Airport Ltd Partnr ....C....... 614 475-7551
  Columbus *(G-7326)*
Columbus Country Club......................D....... 614 861-1332
  Columbus *(G-7343)*
Commonwealth Hotels LLC ....C....... 614 790-9000
  Dublin *(G-10303)*
Epiqurian Inns ....D....... 614 885-2600
  Worthington *(G-19957)*
Fairlawn Associates Ltd ....C....... 330 867-5000
  Fairlawn *(G-10949)*
Fairlawn Country Club Company ....D....... 330 836-5541
  Akron *(G-213)*
Fat Jacks Pizza II Inc ....E....... 419 227-1813
  Lima *(G-12779)*
Findlay Country Club..........................E....... 419 422-9263
  Findlay *(G-11025)*
First Hotel Associates LP ....D....... 614 228-3800
  Columbus *(G-7665)*
Gallipolis Hospitality Inc ....E....... 740 446-0090
  Gallipolis *(G-11319)*
Grandview Ht Ltd Partnr Ohio ....D....... 937 766-5519
  Springfield *(G-17203)*
Granville Hospitality Llc ....D....... 740 587-3333
  Granville *(G-11466)*
Haiku ....E....... 614 294-8168
  Columbus *(G-7794)*
Hit Portfolio I Misc Trs LLC ....C....... 614 228-1234
  Columbus *(G-7840)*
Lodging Industry Inc ....E....... 440 323-7488
  Sandusky *(G-16776)*
Madison Route 20 LLC ....E....... 440 358-7888
  Painesville *(G-15864)*
Marriott Hotel Services Inc ....C....... 216 252-5333
  Cleveland *(G-5982)*
Mayfield Sand Ridge Club ....D....... 216 381-0826
  Cleveland *(G-5995)*
Medallion Club ....C....... 614 794-6999
  Westerville *(G-19328)*
Natural Resources Ohio Dept...............D....... 419 938-5411
  Perrysville *(G-16080)*
Northeast Cincinnati Hotel LLC ....C....... 513 459-9800
  Mason *(G-13743)*
Ohio State Parks Inc..........................D....... 513 664-3504
  College Corner *(G-6838)*
Ohio State University.........................B....... 614 292-3238
  Columbus *(G-8427)*
Park Hotels & Resorts Inc ....B....... 216 464-5950
  Cleveland *(G-6237)*
Park Raceway Inc ....C....... 419 476-7751
  Dayton *(G-9802)*
Quail Hollow Management Inc ....D....... 440 639-4000
  Painesville *(G-15874)*
Ridgehills Hotel Ltd Partnr..................D....... 440 585-0600
  Wickliffe *(G-19613)*
River Road Hotel Corp ....E....... 614 267-7461
  Columbus *(G-8634)*
S P S Inc...F....... 937 339 7801
  Troy *(G-18378)*
Saw Mill Creek Ltd ....C....... 419 433-3800
  Huron *(G-12170)*
Summit Associates Inc.......................E....... 216 831-3300
  Cleveland *(G-6547)*
Tartan Fields Golf Club Ltd ....D....... 614 792-0900
  Dublin *(G-10473)*
Union Club Company ....D....... 216 621-4230
  Cleveland *(G-6631)*
Westgate Limited Partnership ....E....... 419 535-7070
  Toledo *(G-18307)*
Weymouth Valley Inc ....D....... 440 498-8888
  Solon *(G-17067)*
Wyndham International Inc ....E....... 330 666-9300
  Copley *(G-9069)*
Xanterra Parks & Resorts Inc ....C....... 740 439-2751
  Cambridge *(G-2134)*

DRINKING PLACES: Bars & Lounges

Plaz-Way Inc ....E....... 330 264-9025
  Wooster *(G-19904)*
Rhinegeist LLC ....D....... 513 381-1367
  Cincinnati *(G-4414)*
Valley Hospitality Inc ....E....... 740 374-9660
  Marietta *(G-13513)*

DRINKING PLACES: Tavern

16 Bit Bar ....E....... 513 381-1616
  Cincinnati *(G-2939)*
Cork Enterprises Inc..........................E....... 740 654-1842
  Lancaster *(G-12523)*
Island House Inc ....E....... 419 734-0100
  Port Clinton *(G-16248)*
Mahalls 20 Lanes ....E....... 216 521-3280
  Cleveland *(G-5966)*
Marcus Theatres Corporation ....D....... 614 436-9818
  Columbus *(G-8108)*
Northland Lanes Inc ....E....... 419 224-1961
  Lima *(G-12844)*
Roscoe Village Foundation ....D....... 740 622-2222
  Coshocton *(G-9116)*
Snows Lakeside Tavern ....E....... 513 954-5626
  Cincinnati *(G-4546)*

DRIVE-A-WAY AUTOMOBILE SVCS

Cronins Inc ....E....... 513 851-5900
  Cincinnati *(G-3440)*

DRUG ABUSE COUNSELOR, NONTREATMENT

Hocking College Addc........................E....... 740 541-2221
  Glouster *(G-11434)*

DRUG CLINIC, OUTPATIENT

Amethyst Inc ....D....... 614 242-1284
  Columbus *(G-7014)*
Central Commnty Hlth Brd of Ha ....E....... 513 559-2981
  Cincinnati *(G-3212)*
Clermont Recovery Center Inc ....E....... 513 735-8100
  Batavia *(G-1003)*
Community Action Against Addic ....E....... 216 881-0765
  Cleveland *(G-5382)*

DRUG STORES

Ancillary Medical Investments..............E....... 937 456-5520
  Eaton *(G-10552)*
City of Wooster ....A....... 330 263-8100
  Wooster *(G-19846)*
Columbus Prescr Phrms Inc................C....... 614 294-1600
  Westerville *(G-19389)*
Discount Drug Mart Inc ....C....... 330 725-2340
  Medina *(G-14059)*
Discount Drug Mart Inc ....D....... 330 343-7700
  Dover *(G-10183)*
Garys Pharmacy Inc ....E....... 937 456-5777
  Eaton *(G-10561)*
George W Arensberg Phrm Inc............E....... 740 344-2195
  Newark *(G-15169)*
Giant Eagle Inc ....D....... 330 364-5301
  Dover *(G-10190)*
Guernsey Health Enterprises...............A....... 740 439-3561
  Cambridge *(G-2118)*
Joseph A Girgis MD Inc......................E....... 440 930-6095
  Sheffield Village *(G-16889)*
Kaiser-Wells Inc ....E....... 419 668-7651
  Norwalk *(G-15577)*
Kroger Co ....C....... 937 294-7210
  Dayton *(G-9666)*
Kunkel Pharmaceuticals Inc ....E....... 513 231-1943
  Cincinnati *(G-3949)*
Medical Service Company...................D....... 440 232-3000
  Bedford *(G-1322)*
Omnicare Phrm of Midwest LLC..........D....... 513 719-2600
  Cincinnati *(G-4223)*
Shr Management Resources Corp ....E....... 937 274-1546
  Dayton *(G-9879)*
St Lukes Hospital..............................A....... 419 893-5911
  Maumee *(G-13980)*
Trumbull-Mahoning Med Group............D....... 330 372-8800
  Cortland *(G-9084)*
Walgreen Co ....E....... 937 433-5314
  Dayton *(G-9981)*
Walgreen Co ....E....... 614 236-8622
  Columbus *(G-8961)*

DRUG STORES

SERVICES SECTION

Walgreen Co .... E 330 677-5650
  Kent *(G-12404)*
Walgreen Co .... E 330 745-2674
  Barberton *(G-984)*
Walgreen Co .... E 937 396-1358
  Kettering *(G-12438)*
Walgreen Co .... E 937 781-9561
  Dayton *(G-9982)*
Walgreen Co .... E 330 733-4237
  Akron *(G-503)*
Walgreen Co .... E 937 277-6022
  Dayton *(G-9983)*
Walgreen Co .... E 740 368-9380
  Delaware *(G-10134)*
Walgreen Co .... E 614 336-0431
  Dublin *(G-10487)*
Walgreen Co .... E 937 859-3879
  Miamisburg *(G-14366)*
Walgreen Co .... E 330 928-5444
  Cuyahoga Falls *(G-9235)*
Ziks Family Pharmacy 100 .... E 937 225-9350
  Dayton *(G-10015)*

DRUGS & DRUG PROPRIETARIES, WHOL: Biologicals/Allied Prdts

Columbus Serum Company .... C 614 444-5211
  Columbus *(G-7384)*

DRUGS & DRUG PROPRIETARIES, WHOLESALE

Buderer Drug Company Inc .... E 419 627-2800
  Sandusky *(G-16730)*
F Dohmen Co .... C 614 757-5000
  Dublin *(G-10344)*
MSA Group Inc .... B 614 334-0400
  Columbus *(G-8204)*
Omnicare Phrm of Midwest LLC .... D 513 719-2600
  Cincinnati *(G-4223)*
Pharmed Corporation .... C 440 250-5400
  Westlake *(G-19533)*

DRUGS & DRUG PROPRIETARIES, WHOLESALE: Antiseptics

Beiersdorf Inc .... C 513 682-7300
  West Chester *(G-19191)*

DRUGS & DRUG PROPRIETARIES, WHOLESALE: Biotherapeutics

Imagepace LLC .... B 513 579-9911
  Cincinnati *(G-3809)*

DRUGS & DRUG PROPRIETARIES, WHOLESALE: Blood Plasma

Biolife Plasma Services LP .... D 419 425-8680
  Findlay *(G-10994)*

DRUGS & DRUG PROPRIETARIES, WHOLESALE: Druggists' Sundries

Mimrx Co Inc .... B 614 850-6672
  Columbus *(G-8176)*
Riser Foods Company .... D 216 292-7000
  Bedford Heights *(G-1359)*
Samuels Products Inc .... E 513 891-4456
  Blue Ash *(G-1686)*

DRUGS & DRUG PROPRIETARIES, WHOLESALE: Patent Medicines

Institutional Care Pharmacy .... C 419 447-6216
  Tiffin *(G-17681)*
Teva Womens Health Inc .... C 513 731-9900
  Cincinnati *(G-4639)*

DRUGS & DRUG PROPRIETARIES, WHOLESALE: Pharmaceuticals

Amerisourcebergen Corporation .... C 610 727-7000
  Columbus *(G-7013)*
Amerisourcebergen Corporation .... D 614 497-3665
  Lockbourne *(G-12944)*
Amerisourcebergen Drug Corp .... D 614 409-0741
  Lockbourne *(G-12945)*
Biorx LLC .... D 866 442-4679
  Cincinnati *(G-3109)*
Boehringer Ingelheim USA Corp .... E 440 232-3320
  Bedford *(G-1297)*
Braden Med Services Inc .... E 740 732-2356
  Caldwell *(G-2082)*
Capital Wholesale Drug Company .... D 614 297-8225
  Columbus *(G-7185)*
Cardinal Health Inc .... D 614 497-9552
  Obetz *(G-15665)*
Cardinal Health Inc .... D 614 757-7690
  Columbus *(G-7193)*
Cardinal Health 107 LLC .... C 740 455-2462
  Zanesville *(G-20455)*
Cardinal Health 414 LLC .... E 419 867-1077
  Holland *(G-12014)*
Cardinal Health 414 LLC .... E 937 438-1888
  Moraine *(G-14759)*
Discount Drug Mart Inc .... C 330 725-2340
  Medina *(G-14059)*
Edwards Gem Inc .... D 330 342-8300
  Hudson *(G-12115)*
Evergreen Pharmaceutical LLC .... B 513 719-2600
  Cincinnati *(G-3580)*
Evergreen Phrm Cal Inc .... E 513 719-2600
  Cincinnati *(G-3581)*
Greenfield Hts Oper Group LLC .... E 312 877-1153
  Lima *(G-12787)*
Heartland Healthcare Svcs LLC .... C 419 535-8435
  Toledo *(G-17947)*
Keysource Acquisition LLC .... E 513 469-7881
  Cincinnati *(G-3919)*
Kroger Co .... B 614 898-3200
  Westerville *(G-19419)*
Masters Drug Company Inc .... D 800 982-7922
  Lebanon *(G-12625)*
Masters Pharmaceutical Inc .... C 513 354-2690
  Lebanon *(G-12626)*
Masters Pharmaceutical Inc .... D 800 982-7922
  Lebanon *(G-12627)*
McKesson Corporation .... C 740 636-3500
  Wshngtn CT Hs *(G-20030)*
Medpace Inc .... A 513 579-9911
  Cincinnati *(G-4049)*
Ncs Healthcare of Ohio LLC .... E 330 364-5011
  Dover *(G-10201)*
Neighborcare Inc .... A 513 719-2600
  Cincinnati *(G-4151)*
Omnicare Inc .... C 513 719-2600
  Cincinnati *(G-4220)*
Omnicare Distribution Ctr LLC .... D 419 720-8200
  Cincinnati *(G-4221)*
Orchard Phrm Svcs LLC .... C 330 491-4200
  North Canton *(G-15359)*
Pca-Corrections LLC .... E 614 297-8244
  Columbus *(G-8525)*
Prasco LLC .... D 513 204-1100
  Mason *(G-13748)*
Prescription Supply Inc .... D 419 661-6600
  Northwood *(G-15543)*
Remedi Seniorcare of Ohio LLC .... E 800 232-4239
  Troy *(G-18377)*
River City Pharma .... D 513 870-1680
  Fairfield *(G-10900)*
Robert J Matthews Company .... D 330 834-3000
  Massillon *(G-13849)*
Skilled Care Pharmacy Inc .... C 513 459-7626
  Mason *(G-13762)*
Specialized Pharmacy Svcs LLC .... E 513 719-2600
  Cincinnati *(G-4557)*
Superior Care Pharmacy Inc .... C 513 719-2600
  Cincinnati *(G-4603)*
Triplefin LLC .... D 855 877-5346
  Blue Ash *(G-1703)*
Westhaven Services Co LLC .... B 419 661-2200
  Perrysburg *(G-16073)*

DRUGS & DRUG PROPRIETARIES, WHOLESALE: Vitamins & Minerals

Basic Drugs Inc .... E 937 898-4010
  Vandalia *(G-18662)*
Physicians Weight Ls Ctr Amer .... E 330 666-7952
  Akron *(G-389)*
Raisin Rack Inc .... E 614 882-5886
  Westerville *(G-19440)*
Shaklee Corporation .... C 614 409-2953
  Groveport *(G-11671)*
Suarez Corporation Industries .... D 330 494-4282
  Canton *(G-2554)*
Vitamin Shoppe Inc .... E 440 238-5987
  Strongsville *(G-17522)*

Wbc Group LLC .... D 866 528-2144
  Hudson *(G-12150)*

DRYCLEANING & LAUNDRY SVCS: Commercial & Family

Buckeye Launderer and Clrs LLC .... D 419 592-2941
  Sylvania *(G-17577)*
Dee Jay Cleaners Inc .... E 216 731-7060
  Euclid *(G-10750)*
Economy Linen & Towel Svc Inc .... C 740 454-6888
  Zanesville *(G-20473)*
Evergreen Cooperative Ldry Inc .... E 216 268-3548
  Cleveland *(G-5558)*
George Gardner .... D 419 636-4277
  Bryan *(G-2006)*
Heights Laundry & Dry Cleaning .... E 216 932-9666
  Cleveland Heights *(G-6789)*
Midwest Laundry Inc .... D 513 563-5560
  Cincinnati *(G-4092)*
Ohio Textile Service Inc .... E 740 450-4900
  Zanesville *(G-20520)*

DRYCLEANING PLANTS

Aramark Unf & Career AP LLC .... D 937 223-6667
  Dayton *(G-9340)*
Cintas Corporation No 2 .... D 440 238-5565
  Strongsville *(G-17449)*
Edco Cleaners Inc .... E 330 477-3357
  Canton *(G-2351)*
Farrow Cleaners Co .... E 216 561-2355
  Cleveland *(G-5574)*
Fox Cleaners Inc .... D 937 276-4171
  Dayton *(G-9559)*
George Gardner .... D 419 636-4277
  Bryan *(G-2006)*
Heider Cleaners Inc .... E 937 298-6631
  Dayton *(G-9609)*
Heights Laundry & Dry Cleaning .... E 216 932-9666
  Cleveland Heights *(G-6789)*
Kimmel Cleaners Inc .... D 419 294-1959
  Upper Sandusky *(G-18564)*
Kramer Enterprises Inc .... D 419 422-7924
  Findlay *(G-11055)*
Midwest Laundry Inc .... D 513 563-5560
  Cincinnati *(G-4092)*
Pierce Cleaners Inc .... E 614 888-4225
  Columbus *(G-8543)*
Quality Cleaners of Ohio Inc .... E 330 688-5616
  Stow *(G-17388)*
Rentz Corp .... E 937 434-2774
  Dayton *(G-9848)*
Sunset Carpet Cleaning .... E 937 836-5531
  Englewood *(G-10721)*

DRYCLEANING SVC: Drapery & Curtain

Dutchess Dry Cleaners .... E 330 759-9382
  Youngstown *(G-20174)*
Velco Inc .... E 513 772-4226
  Cincinnati *(G-4805)*

DRYERS & REDRYERS: Indl

Agridry LLC .... E 419 459-4399
  Edon *(G-10585)*

DUCTS: Sheet Metal

Langdon Inc .... E 513 733-5955
  Cincinnati *(G-3960)*
United McGill Corporation .... E 614 829-1200
  Groveport *(G-11681)*

DURABLE GOODS WHOLESALERS, NEC

Roofing Supply Group LLC .... E 614 239-1111
  Columbus *(G-8647)*
U-Haul Neighborhood Dealer -Ce .... E 419 929-3724
  New London *(G-15071)*

DYES & PIGMENTS: Organic

Hexpol Compounding LLC .... C 440 834-4644
  Burton *(G-2062)*

EARTH SCIENCE SVCS

ASC Group Inc .... E 614 268-2514
  Columbus *(G-7048)*
Diproinduca (usa) Limited LLC .... D 330 722-4442
  Medina *(G-14058)*

SERVICES SECTION

Superior Envmtl Sltons SES Inc .... B 513 874-6910
 West Chester *(G-19234)*

EATING PLACES

5901 Pfffer Rd Htels Sites LLC .... D 513 793-4500
 Blue Ash *(G-1522)*
A C Management Inc .... E 440 461-9200
 Cleveland *(G-4931)*
Akron Management Corp .... B 330 644-8441
 Akron *(G-48)*
Americas Best Value Inn .... E 419 626-9890
 Sandusky *(G-16726)*
Avalon Foodservice Inc .... C 330 854-4551
 Canal Fulton *(G-2140)*
AVI Food Systems Inc .... E 740 452-9363
 Zanesville *(G-20445)*
B & I Hotel Management LLC .... C 330 995-0200
 Aurora *(G-828)*
Bel-Wood Country Club Inc .... D 513 899-3361
 Morrow *(G-14843)*
Best Western Columbus N Hotel .... E 614 888-8230
 Columbus *(G-7103)*
Bob Mor Inc .... C 419 485-5555
 Montpelier *(G-14737)*
Brandywine Country Club Inc .... E 330 657-2525
 Peninsula *(G-15948)*
Breezy Point Ltd Partnership .... E 330 995-0600
 Aurora *(G-831)*
Broad Street Hotel Assoc LP .... D 614 861-0321
 Columbus *(G-7147)*
Brothers Properties Corp .... C 513 381-3000
 Cincinnati *(G-3141)*
Buehler Food Markets Inc .... C 330 364-3079
 Dover *(G-10179)*
Buns of Delaware Inc .... E 740 363-2867
 Delaware *(G-10075)*
Buxton Inn Inc .... E 740 587-0001
 Granville *(G-11459)*
Cambridge Country Club Company .... E 740 439-2744
 Byesville *(G-2070)*
Cameron Mitchell Rest LLC .... E 614 621-3663
 Columbus *(G-7180)*
Canter Inn Inc .... E 740 354-7711
 Portsmouth *(G-16267)*
Canterbury Golf Club Inc .... D 216 561-1914
 Cleveland *(G-5177)*
Capri Bowling Lanes Inc .... E 937 832-4000
 Dayton *(G-9379)*
Ch Relty Iv/Clmbus Partners LP .... D 614 885-3334
 Columbus *(G-7247)*
Charter Hotel Group Ltd Partnr .... E 216 772-4538
 Mentor *(G-14156)*
Cheers Chalet .... E 740 654-9036
 Lancaster *(G-12516)*
Chgc Inc .... D 330 225-6122
 Valley City *(G-18614)*
Circling Hills Golf Course .... E 513 367-5858
 Harrison *(G-11794)*
City of Centerville .... D 937 438-3585
 Dayton *(G-9409)*
Cleveland Airport Hospitality .... D 440 871-6000
 Westlake *(G-19476)*
Cleveland Crowne Plaza Airport .... D 440 243-4040
 Cleveland *(G-5311)*
Cleveland Racquet Club Inc .... D 216 831-2155
 Cleveland *(G-5341)*
Cleveland Rest Oper Ltd Partnr .... C 216 328-1121
 Cleveland *(G-5344)*
Clintonville Community Mkt .... E 614 261-3663
 Columbus *(G-7304)*
Clubhouse Pub N Grub .... E 440 884-2582
 Cleveland *(G-5368)*
Columbus Airport Ltd Partnr .... C 014 475-7551
 Columbus *(G-7326)*
Columbus Country Club .... D 614 861-1332
 Columbus *(G-7343)*
Columbus Museum of Art .... D 614 221-6801
 Columbus *(G-7372)*
Commodore Prry Inns Suites LLC .... D 419 732-2645
 Port Clinton *(G-16240)*
Commonwealth Hotels LLC .... C 614 790-9000
 Dublin *(G-10303)*
Corporate Exchange Hotel Assoc .... C 614 890-8600
 Columbus *(G-7443)*
Coshocton Bowling Center .... E 740 622-6332
 Coshocton *(G-9093)*
Country Club of Hudson .... E 330 650-1188
 Hudson *(G-12113)*
Crossgate Lanes Inc .... E 513 891-0310
 Blue Ash *(G-1572)*

Dinos Catering Inc .... E 440 943-1010
 Wickliffe *(G-19593)*
Emmett Dan House Ltd Partnr .... E 740 392-6886
 Mount Vernon *(G-14894)*
Fairlawn Country Club Company .... D 330 836-5541
 Akron *(G-213)*
Farm Inc .... E 513 922-7020
 Cincinnati *(G-3592)*
Ferrante Wine Farm Inc .... E 440 466-8466
 Geneva *(G-11361)*
Findlay Country Club .... E 419 422-9263
 Findlay *(G-11025)*
Findlay Inn & Conference Ctr .... D 419 422-5682
 Findlay *(G-11027)*
First Hotel Associates LP .... D 614 228-3800
 Columbus *(G-7665)*
Fox Den Fairways Inc .... E 330 678-6792
 Stow *(G-17368)*
Fred W Albrecht Grocery Co .... C 330 645-6222
 Coventry Township *(G-9124)*
Gallipolis Hospitality Inc .... E 740 446-0090
 Gallipolis *(G-11319)*
Glenlaurel Inc .... E 740 385-4070
 Rockbridge *(G-16560)*
Golden Lamb .... C 513 932-5065
 Lebanon *(G-12608)*
Grandview Ht Ltd Partnr Ohio .... D 937 766-5519
 Springfield *(G-17203)*
Green Township Hospitality LLC .... B 513 574-6000
 Cincinnati *(G-3712)*
Grizzly Golf Center Inc .... E 513 398-5200
 Mason *(G-13712)*
Guys Party Center .... E 330 724-6373
 Akron *(G-249)*
Haiku .... E 614 294-8168
 Columbus *(G-7794)*
Hauck Hospitality LLC .... D 513 563-8330
 Cincinnati *(G-3741)*
Heritage Golf Club Ltd Partnr .... D 614 777-1690
 Hilliard *(G-11908)*
Hit Portfolio I Misc Trs LLC .... E 216 575-1234
 Cleveland *(G-5760)*
Hit Portfolio I Misc Trs LLC .... C 614 228-1234
 Columbus *(G-7840)*
I-X Center Corporation .... E 216 265-2675
 Cleveland *(G-5799)*
Iacominis Papa Joes Inc .... D 330 923-7999
 Akron *(G-276)*
Ice Land USA Ltd .... E 440 268-2800
 Strongsville *(G-17475)*
Island Service Company .... C 419 285-3695
 Put In Bay *(G-16368)*
Jackson I-94 Ltd Partnership .... E 614 793-2244
 Dublin *(G-10379)*
Kinane Inc .... D 513 459-0177
 Mason *(G-13727)*
Lancaster Country Club .... D 740 654-3535
 Lancaster *(G-12549)*
Madison Route 20 LLC .... E 440 358-7888
 Painesville *(G-15864)*
Mahoning Country Club Inc .... E 330 545-2517
 Girard *(G-11420)*
Maplecrst Asistd Lvg Intl Ordr .... E 419 562-4988
 Bucyrus *(G-2043)*
Mapleside Valley LLC .... C 330 225-5576
 Brunswick *(G-2411)*
Marion Country Club Company .... E 740 387-0974
 Marion *(G-13555)*
Marriott Hotel Services Inc .... C 216 252-5333
 Cleveland *(G-5982)*
Mary Kelleys Inc .... D 614 760-7041
 Columbus *(G-8122)*
Mayfield Sand Ridge Club .... D 216 381-0826
 Cleveland *(G-5995)*
McPaul Corp .... E 419 447-6313
 Tiffin *(G-17684)*
Meadowbrook Country Club .... D 937 836-5186
 Clayton *(G-4913)*
Medallion Club .... C 614 794-6999
 Westerville *(G-19328)*
Mohawk Golf Club .... E 419 447-5876
 Tiffin *(G-17687)*
Monaco Palace Inc .... E 614 475-4817
 Newark *(G-15210)*
N C R Employee Benefit Assn .... E 937 299-3571
 Dayton *(G-9766)*
Natural Resources Ohio Dept .... E 419 938-5411
 Perrysville *(G-16080)*
Northeast Cincinnati Hotel LLC .... C 513 459-9800
 Mason *(G-13743)*

Ohio State Parks Inc .... D 513 664-3504
 College Corner *(G-6838)*
Ohio State University .... B 614 292-3238
 Columbus *(G-8427)*
Park Hotels & Resorts Inc .... B 216 464-5950
 Cleveland *(G-6237)*
Park Raceway Inc .... C 419 476-7751
 Dayton *(G-9802)*
Pike Run Golf Club Inc .... E 419 538-7000
 Ottawa *(G-15803)*
Pines Golf Club .... E 330 684-1414
 Orrville *(G-15783)*
Piqua Country Club Holding Co .... E 937 773-7744
 Piqua *(G-16156)*
Quail Hollow Management Inc .... D 440 639-4000
 Painesville *(G-15874)*
Rcwc Col Inc .... D 614 564-9344
 Columbus *(G-8592)*
Renaissance Corporation .... E 937 526-3672
 Versailles *(G-18729)*
Riders 1812 Inn .... E 440 354-0922
 Painesville *(G-15878)*
Ridgehills Hotel Ltd Partnr .... D 440 585-0600
 Wickliffe *(G-19613)*
Rockwell Springs Trout Club .... E 419 684-7971
 Clyde *(G-6821)*
S & S Management Inc .... E 567 356-4151
 Wapakoneta *(G-18807)*
Saint Johns Villa .... C 330 627-4662
 Carrollton *(G-2628)*
Sanese Services Inc .... B 614 436-1234
 Warren *(G-18895)*
Saw Mill Creek Ltd .... C 419 433-3800
 Huron *(G-12170)*
Sawmill Creek Resort Ltd .... C 419 433-3800
 Huron *(G-12172)*
Seagate Hospitality Group LLC .... E 216 252-7700
 Cleveland *(G-6457)*
Shady Hollow Cntry CLB Co Inc .... D 330 832-1581
 Massillon *(G-13854)*
Shawnee Country Club .... E 419 227-7177
 Lima *(G-12877)*
Silver Lake Country Club .... D 330 688-6066
 Silver Lake *(G-16964)*
Six Continents Hotels Inc .... C 513 563-8330
 Cincinnati *(G-4533)*
Skallys Old World Bakery Inc .... E 513 931-1411
 Cincinnati *(G-4537)*
Sortino Management & Dev Co .... E 419 626-6761
 Sandusky *(G-16796)*
Spread Eagle Tavern Inc .... E 330 223-1583
 Hanoverton *(G-11787)*
Springfield Country Club Co .... E 937 399-4215
 Springfield *(G-17280)*
Stranahan Theatre Trust .... E 419 381-8851
 Toledo *(G-18204)*
Summit Associates Inc .... D 216 831-3300
 Cleveland *(G-6547)*
Ta Operating LLC .... B 440 808-9100
 Westlake *(G-19553)*
Tartan Fields Golf Club Ltd .... D 614 792-0900
 Dublin *(G-10473)*
Tiki Bowling Lanes Inc .... E 740 654-4513
 Lancaster *(G-12581)*
Tippecanoe Country Club Inc .... E 330 758-7518
 Canfield *(G-2213)*
Travelcenters America Inc .... A 440 808-9100
 Westlake *(G-19555)*
Travelcenters of America LLC .... D 330 769-2053
 Lodi *(G-12966)*
Trepanier Daniels & Trepanier .... D 740 286-1288
 Jackson *(G-12319)*
Union Club Company .... D 216 621-4230
 Cleveland *(G-6631)*
United Scoto Senior Activities .... E 740 354-6672
 Portsmouth *(G-16316)*
University of Cincinnati .... A 513 556-6381
 Cincinnati *(G-4761)*
Vermilion Boat Club Inc .... E 440 967-6634
 Vermilion *(G-18719)*
Wadsworth Galaxy Rest Inc .... D 330 334-3663
 Wadsworth *(G-18773)*
Walden Club .... D 330 995-7162
 Aurora *(G-861)*
Walden Company Ltd .... C 330 562-7145
 Aurora *(G-862)*
Weymouth Valley Inc .... E 440 498-8888
 Solon *(G-17067)*
William Royce Inc .... D 513 771-3361
 Cincinnati *(G-4850)*

EATING PLACES

Wyndham International Inc .... C 216 615-7500
  Cleveland *(G-6764)*
Wyndham International Inc .... E 330 666-9300
  Copley *(G-9069)*
Xanterra Parks & Resorts Inc .... C 740 439-2751
  Cambridge *(G-2134)*
York Temple Country Club Inc .... E 614 885-5459
  Columbus *(G-9015)*
Youngstown Country Club .... D 330 759-1040
  Youngstown *(G-20430)*

ECONOMIC PROGRAMS ADMINISTRATION SVCS, NEC

National Weather Service .... E 937 383-0031
  Wilmington *(G-19774)*
National Weather Service .... E 216 265-2370
  Cleveland *(G-6113)*
National Weather Service .... E 419 522-1375
  Mansfield *(G-13349)*
Ohio Department of Commerce .... C 614 728-8400
  Columbus *(G-8326)*

EDUCATIONAL PROGRAM ADMINISTRATION, GOVERNMENT: County

County of Lucas .... D 419 385-6021
  Toledo *(G-17838)*
Cuyahoga County .... D 216 265-3030
  Cleveland *(G-5451)*

EDUCATIONAL PROGRAMS ADMINISTRATION SVCS

County of Hamilton .... C 513 552-1200
  Cincinnati *(G-3429)*
Jacqueline Kumi-Sakyi .... D 740 282-5955
  Steubenville *(G-17322)*
Ohio Department of Education .... E 740 289-2908
  Piketon *(G-16120)*

EDUCATIONAL SVCS

3c Technologies Inc .... D 419 868-8999
  Holland *(G-12005)*
A+ Solutions LLC .... E 216 896-0111
  Beachwood *(G-1044)*
Allen County Eductl Svc Ctr .... D 419 222-1836
  Lima *(G-12734)*
Aset Corporation .... E 937 890-8881
  Vandalia *(G-18659)*
Heartbeats To City Inc .... E 330 452-4524
  Canton *(G-2397)*
Iq Innovations LLC .... E 614 222-0882
  Columbus *(G-7921)*
Knowledgeworks Foundation .... D 513 241-1422
  Cincinnati *(G-3937)*
Lakeland Foundation .... E 440 525-7094
  Willoughby *(G-19683)*
Microanalysis Society Inc .... B 614 256-8063
  Hilliard *(G-11934)*
Osu Nephrology Medical Ctr .... E 614 293-8300
  Columbus *(G-8487)*
Rev1 Ventures .... E 614 487-3700
  Columbus *(G-8627)*
Roundtable Online Learning LLC .... E 440 220-5252
  Chagrin Falls *(G-2731)*
W T C S A Headstart Niles Ctr .... E 330 652-0338
  Niles *(G-15309)*

EDUCATIONAL SVCS, NONDEGREE GRANTING: Continuing Education

Columbus Montessori Education .... E 614 231-3790
  Columbus *(G-7370)*
Deemsys Inc .... D 614 322-9928
  Gahanna *(G-11239)*
Great Oaks Inst Tech Creer Dev .... D 513 771-8840
  Cincinnati *(G-3703)*
Great Oaks Inst Tech Creer Dev .... E 513 771-8840
  Cincinnati *(G-3704)*
Lake Erie Nature & Science Ctr .... E 440 871-2900
  Bay Village *(G-1040)*

EGG WHOLESALERS

Ballas Egg Products Corp .... D 614 453-0386
  Zanesville *(G-20446)*
Barkett Fruit Co Inc .... E 330 364-6645
  Dover *(G-10176)*

C W Egg Products LLC .... E 419 375-5800
  Fort Recovery *(G-11113)*
Cooper Frms Spring Madow Farms ..... E 419 375-4119
  Rossburg *(G-16605)*
Hillandale Farms Inc .... E 740 968-3597
  Flushing *(G-11104)*
Hillandale Farms Corporation .... E 330 724-3199
  Akron *(G-265)*
Hillcrest Egg & Cheese Co .... D 216 361-4625
  Cleveland *(G-5757)*
Ohio Fresh Eggs LLC .... C 740 893-7200
  Croton *(G-9154)*
Ohio Fresh Eggs LLC .... E 937 354-2233
  Mount Victory *(G-14929)*
R W Sauder Inc .... E 330 359-5440
  Winesburg *(G-19806)*

ELECTRIC & OTHER SERVICES COMBINED

City of Columbus .... C 614 645-7627
  Columbus *(G-7278)*
Cliffs Minnesota Minerals Co .... A 216 694-5700
  Cleveland *(G-5361)*
Dayton Power and Light Company .... D 937 549-2641
  Manchester *(G-13255)*
Dayton Power and Light Company .... D 937 331-4123
  Moraine *(G-14774)*
Dayton Power and Light Company .... C 937 224-6000
  Dayton *(G-9264)*
Dayton Power and Light Company .... E 937 331-3032
  Miamisburg *(G-14294)*
Duke Energy Kentucky Inc .... C 704 594-6200
  Cincinnati *(G-3507)*
Duke Energy Ohio Inc .... D 704 382-3853
  Cincinnati *(G-3508)*
Medical Center Co (inc) .... E 216 368-4256
  Cleveland *(G-6014)*
Stockport Mill Country Inn Inc .... E 740 559-2822
  Stockport *(G-17346)*

ELECTRIC FENCE CHARGERS

Agratronix LLC .... E 330 562-2222
  Streetsboro *(G-17406)*

ELECTRIC MOTOR REPAIR SVCS

3-D Service Ltd .... C 330 830-3500
  Massillon *(G-13780)*
Fenton Bros Electric Co .... E 330 343-0093
  New Philadelphia *(G-15094)*
Horner Industrial Services Inc .... E 937 390-6667
  Springfield *(G-17208)*
Kiemle-Hankins Company .... E 419 661-2430
  Perrysburg *(G-16024)*
M & R Electric Motor Svc Inc .... E 937 222-6282
  Dayton *(G-9692)*
Magnetech Industrial Svcs Inc .... C 330 830-3500
  Massillon *(G-13831)*
Matlock Electric Co Inc .... E 513 731-9600
  Cincinnati *(G-4030)*
Mid-Ohio Electric Co .... E 614 274-8000
  Columbus *(G-8165)*
National Electric Coil Inc .... B 614 488-1151
  Columbus *(G-8217)*
Shoemaker Electric Company .... E 614 294-5626
  Columbus *(G-8728)*
Whelco Industrial Ltd .... E 419 873-6134
  Perrysburg *(G-16074)*

ELECTRIC POWER DISTRIBUTION TO CONSUMERS

Adams Rural Electric Coop Inc .... E 937 544-2305
  West Union *(G-19274)*
American Electric Power Co Inc .... E 740 594-1988
  Athens *(G-771)*
American Electric Power Co Inc .... D 614 351-3715
  Columbus *(G-6988)*
American Electric Power Co Inc .... E 740 384-7981
  Wellston *(G-18997)*
American Electric Power Co Inc .... E 330 580-5085
  Canton *(G-2238)*
American Electric Power Co Inc .... E 740 598-4164
  Brilliant *(G-1865)*
American Electric Pwr Svc Corp .... B 614 716-1000
  Columbus *(G-6990)*
Buckeye Rural Elc Coop Inc .... E 740 379-2025
  Patriot *(G-15926)*
Butler Rural Electric Coop .... E 513 867-4400
  Oxford *(G-15812)*

SERVICES SECTION

Carroll Electric Coop Inc .... E 330 627-2116
  Carrollton *(G-2611)*
Cinergy Corp .... A 513 421-9500
  Cincinnati *(G-3346)*
City of Cuyahoga Falls .... E 330 971-8000
  Cuyahoga Falls *(G-9173)*
Cleveland Elc Illuminating Co .... D 440 953-7650
  Painesville *(G-15843)*
Consolidated Electric Coop .... E 740 363-2641
  Delaware *(G-10081)*
Consolidated Electric Coop Inc .... D 419 947-3055
  Mount Gilead *(G-14852)*
Deepwell Energy Services LLC .... C 740 685-2253
  Senecaville *(G-16823)*
Dynegy Washington II LLC .... E 713 507-6400
  Beverly *(G-1490)*
Frontier Power Company .... E 740 622-6755
  Coshocton *(G-9103)*
Guernsy-Muskingum Elc Coop Inc .... E 740 826-7661
  New Concord *(G-15034)*
Hearthstone Utilities Inc .... D 440 974-3770
  Cleveland *(G-5744)*
Holmes-Wayne Electric Coop .... E 330 674-1055
  Millersburg *(G-14606)*
Jersey Central Pwr & Light Co .... A 440 546-8609
  Brecksville *(G-1829)*
Jersey Central Pwr & Light Co .... D 216 479-1132
  Cleveland *(G-5861)*
Licking Rural Electrification .... D 740 892-2071
  Utica *(G-18612)*
Mid-Ohio Energy Cooperative .... E 419 568-5321
  Kenton *(G-12421)*
North Central Elc Coop Inc .... E 800 426-3072
  Attica *(G-822)*
Ohio Edison Company .... C 330 747-2071
  Youngstown *(G-20304)*
Ohio Power Company .... E 330 264-1616
  Wooster *(G-19897)*
Paulding-Putnam Electric Coop .... E 419 399-5015
  Paulding *(G-15935)*
Pennsylvania Power Company .... C 800 720-3600
  Akron *(G-383)*
Pioneer Rural Electric Coop .... D 800 762-0997
  Piqua *(G-16155)*
South Central Power Company .... E 740 474-6045
  Circleville *(G-4905)*
South Central Power Company .... C 740 653-4422
  Lancaster *(G-12575)*
South Central Power Company .... E 614 837-4351
  Canal Winchester *(G-2171)*
South Central Power Company .... E 740 425-4018
  Barnesville *(G-991)*
Toledo Edison Company .... C 800 447-3333
  Akron *(G-478)*
Toledo Edison Company .... D 419 249-5364
  Holland *(G-12062)*
Union Rural Electric Coop Inc .... E 937 642-1826
  Marysville *(G-13657)*

ELECTRIC POWER GENERATION: Fossil Fuel

City of Painesville .... E 440 392-5954
  Painesville *(G-15840)*
Dayton Power and Light Company .... B 937 549-2641
  Aberdeen *(G-2)*
Dayton Power and Light Company .... D 937 549-2641
  Manchester *(G-13255)*
Dynegy Inc .... C 513 467-4900
  North Bend *(G-15318)*

ELECTRIC POWER, COGENERATED

AEP Dresden Plant .... E 740 450-1964
  Dresden *(G-10230)*

ELECTRIC SERVICES

AEP Energy Partners Inc .... E 614 716-1000
  Columbus *(G-6949)*
AEP Power Marketing Inc .... A 614 716-1000
  Columbus *(G-6952)*
American Electric Power Co Inc .... E 419 420-3011
  Findlay *(G-10990)*
American Electric Power Co Inc .... C 330 438-7024
  Canton *(G-2237)*
American Electric Pwr Svc Corp .... E 614 582-1742
  Columbus *(G-6991)*
Appalachian Power Company .... C 614 716-1000
  Columbus *(G-7029)*
Appalachian Power Company .... D 330 438-7102
  Canton *(G-2243)*

SERVICES SECTION — ELECTRICAL APPLIANCES, TELEVISIONS & RADIOS WHOLESALERS

Butterfly Inc .... E 440 892-7777
  Independence (G-12191)
Cardinal Operating Company .... C 740 598-4164
  Brilliant (G-1867)
City of Dublin .... E 614 410-4750
  Dublin (G-10294)
City of Hudson Village .... D 330 650-1052
  Hudson (G-12112)
City of Toledo .... D 419 245-1800
  Toledo (G-17807)
City of Westerville .... E 614 901-6700
  Westerville (G-19383)
Columbus Southern Power Co .... E 614 716-1000
  Columbus (G-7385)
Columbus Southern Power Co .... D 740 829-2378
  Conesville (G-9036)
Dayton Power and Light Company .... D 937 331-4123
  Moraine (G-14774)
Duke Energy Beckjord LLC .... A 513 287-2561
  Cincinnati (G-3506)
Duke Energy Ohio Inc .... D 704 382-3853
  Cincinnati (G-3508)
Duke Energy Ohio Inc .... C 800 544-6900
  Cincinnati (G-3509)
Duke Energy Ohio Inc .... E 513 287-1120
  Cincinnati (G-3510)
Duke Energy Ohio Inc .... C 513 467-5000
  New Richmond (G-15127)
Duquesne Light Company .... C 330 385-6103
  East Liverpool (G-10519)
Firstenergy Corp .... A 800 736-3402
  Akron (G-225)
Firstenergy Nuclear Oper Co .... A 800 646-0400
  Akron (G-226)
Gavin AEP Plant .... E 740 925-3166
  Cheshire (G-2791)
Granger Elc Hancock Cnty LLC .... E 517 371-9765
  Findlay (G-11038)
Great Lakes Energy .... E 440 582-4662
  Broadview Heights (G-1880)
Hancock-Wood Electric Coop Inc .... E 419 257-3241
  North Baltimore (G-15313)
Igs Solar LLC .... E 844 447-7652
  Dublin (G-10373)
Indiana Michigan Power Company .... C 614 716-1000
  Columbus (G-7889)
Jersey Central Pwr & Light Co .... C 800 736-3402
  Akron (G-294)
Jersey Central Pwr & Light Co .... D 440 994-8271
  Ashtabula (G-751)
Jersey Central Pwr & Light Co .... D 419 366-2915
  Sandusky (G-16771)
Jersey Central Pwr & Light Co .... E 330 315-6713
  Fairlawn (G-10960)
Jersey Central Pwr & Light Co .... C 740 537-6308
  Stratton (G-17403)
Jersey Central Pwr & Light Co .... D 440 326-3222
  Elyria (G-10637)
Jersey Central Pwr & Light Co .... D 216 432-6330
  Cleveland (G-5860)
Jersey Central Pwr & Light Co .... D 330 336-9884
  Wadsworth (G-18758)
Jersey Central Pwr & Light Co .... D 440 953-7651
  Painesville (G-15858)
Metropolitan Edison Company .... C 800 736-3402
  Akron (G-342)
National Gas & Oil Corporation .... D 740 344-2102
  Newark (G-15216)
Nisource Inc .... E 614 460-4878
  Columbus (G-8280)
Ohio Edison Company .... C 800 736-3402
  Akron (G-365)
Ohio Edison Company .... C 330 336-9880
  Wadsworth (G-18766)
Ohio Power Company .... C 614 716-1000
  Columbus (G-8366)
Ohio Power Company .... D 740 695-7800
  Saint Clairsville (G-16647)
Pennsylvania Electric Company .... D 800 545-7741
  Akron (G-382)
Public Service Company Okla .... C 614 716-1000
  Columbus (G-8578)

ELECTRIC SVCS, NEC Power Broker

Ohio Valley Electric Corp .... D 740 289-7225
  Piketon (G-16122)

ELECTRIC SVCS, NEC Power Transmission

Cinergy Pwr Gneration Svcs LLC .... A 513 421-9500
  Cincinnati (G-3347)

Ohio Power Company .... E 614 836-2570
  Gahanna (G-11262)

ELECTRIC SVCS, NEC: Power Generation

AEP Generating Company .... A 614 223-1000
  Columbus (G-6951)
American Electric Power Co Inc .... E 740 779-5261
  Chillicothe (G-2814)
American Municipal Power Inc .... C 614 540-1111
  Columbus (G-7002)
Buckeye Power Inc .... B 740 598-6534
  Brilliant (G-1866)
Buckeye Power Inc .... E 614 781-0573
  Columbus (G-7160)
City of Hamilton .... D 513 785-7450
  Hamilton (G-11711)
Cleveland Elc Illuminating Co .... E 800 589-3101
  Akron (G-147)
Dayton Power and Light Company .... C 937 224-6000
  Dayton (G-9264)
Dayton Power and Light Company .... E 937 331-3032
  Miamisburg (G-14294)
DPL Inc .... E 937 331-4063
  Dayton (G-9266)
Echogen Power Systems Del Inc .... E 234 542-4379
  Akron (G-206)
Jersey Central Pwr & Light Co .... D 937 327-1218
  Springfield (G-17216)
NRG Power Midwest LP .... D 440 930-6401
  Avon Lake (G-936)
NRG Power Midwest LP .... D 330 505-4327
  Niles (G-15301)
Ohio Edison Company .... C 740 671-2900
  Shadyside (G-16851)
Ohio Power Company .... D 614 836-2570
  Groveport (G-11660)
Ohio Power Company .... E 614 836-2570
  Columbus (G-8367)
Ohio Valley Electric Corp .... D 740 289-7200
  Piketon (G-16121)
Southwestern Electric Power Co .... C 614 716-1000
  Columbus (G-8756)
Toledo Edison Company .... E 419 321-8488
  Oak Harbor (G-15617)

ELECTRICAL APPARATUS & EQPT WHOLESALERS

Belting Company of Cincinnati .... E 937 498-2104
  Sidney (G-16916)
Best Lighting Products Inc .... D 740 964-0063
  Etna (G-10732)
Bostwick-Braun Company .... D 419 259-3600
  Toledo (G-17778)
Calvert Wire & Cable Corp .... E 216 433-7600
  Cleveland (G-5173)
Communications Supply Corp .... E 330 208-1900
  Cleveland (G-5381)
Dickman Supply Inc .... C 937 492-6166
  Sidney (G-16928)
Dickman Supply Inc .... E 937 492-6166
  Greenville (G-11498)
Dxp Enterprises Inc .... E 513 242-2227
  Cincinnati (G-3517)
Hughes Corporation .... E 440 238-2550
  Strongsville (G-17473)
Johnson Cntrls SEC Sltions LLC .... D 440 262-1084
  Brecksville (G-1830)
Kirk Key Interlock Company LLC .... E 330 833-8223
  North Canton (G-15350)
Laughlin Music & Vending Svc .... E 740 593-7778
  Athens (G-798)
Major Electronix Corp .... E 440 942-0054
  Eastlake (G-10548)
Monarch Electric Service Co .... D 216 433-7800
  Cleveland (G-6073)
New Haven Estates Inc .... E 419 933-2181
  New Haven (G-15051)
Newark Electronics Corporation .... C 330 523-4912
  Richfield (G-16518)
Ohio Rural Electric Coops Inc .... E 614 846-5757
  Columbus (G-8371)
Powell Electrical Systems Inc .... D 330 966-1750
  Canton (G-2491)
Professional Electric Pdts Co .... E 419 269-3790
  Toledo (G-18137)
Rexel Usa Inc .... E 216 778-6400
  Cleveland (G-6388)
Schneider Electric Usa Inc .... D 513 755-5000
  West Chester (G-19145)

Siemens Industry Inc .... D 513 742-5590
  Cincinnati (G-4526)
Simplex Time Recorder LLC .... E 513 874-1227
  West Chester (G-19229)
Thomas Door Controls Inc .... E 614 263-1756
  Columbus (G-8837)
W W Grainger Inc .... C 330 425-8387
  Macedonia (G-13217)
W W Williams Company LLC .... E 419 837-5067
  Perrysburg (G-16070)
Wesco Distribution Inc .... E 937 228-9668
  Dayton (G-9991)
Wolff Bros Supply Inc .... E 419 425-8511
  Findlay (G-11101)
Wolff Bros Supply Inc .... E 330 786-4140
  Akron (G-511)
Wright State University .... A 937 775-3333
  Beavercreek (G-1222)

ELECTRICAL APPLIANCES, TELEVISIONS & RADIOS WHOLESALERS

Lowes Home Centers LLC .... C 216 351-4723
  Cleveland (G-5953)
Lowes Home Centers LLC .... C 419 739-1300
  Wapakoneta (G-18803)
Lowes Home Centers LLC .... C 937 235-2920
  Dayton (G-9688)
Lowes Home Centers LLC .... C 740 574-6200
  Wheelersburg (G-19578)
Lowes Home Centers LLC .... C 330 665-9356
  Akron (G-328)
Lowes Home Centers LLC .... C 330 829-2700
  Alliance (G-545)
Lowes Home Centers LLC .... C 937 599-4000
  Bellefontaine (G-1388)
Lowes Home Centers LLC .... C 419 420-7531
  Findlay (G-11057)
Lowes Home Centers LLC .... C 330 832-1901
  Massillon (G-13829)
Lowes Home Centers LLC .... C 513 741-0585
  Cincinnati (G-3996)
Lowes Home Centers LLC .... C 614 433-9957
  Columbus (G-6892)
Lowes Home Centers LLC .... C 740 389-9737
  Marion (G-13549)
Lowes Home Centers LLC .... C 740 450-5500
  Zanesville (G-20497)
Lowes Home Centers LLC .... C 513 598-7050
  Cincinnati (G-3997)
Lowes Home Centers LLC .... C 614 769-9940
  Reynoldsburg (G-16466)
Lowes Home Centers LLC .... C 614 853-6200
  Columbus (G-8079)
Lowes Home Centers LLC .... C 440 937-3500
  Avon (G-906)
Lowes Home Centers LLC .... C 513 445-1000
  South Lebanon (G-17078)
Lowes Home Centers LLC .... B 216 831-2860
  Bedford (G-1318)
Lowes Home Centers LLC .... C 937 327-6000
  Springfield (G-17226)
Lowes Home Centers LLC .... C 419 331-3598
  Lima (G-12832)
Lowes Home Centers LLC .... C 740 681-3464
  Lancaster (G-12551)
Lowes Home Centers LLC .... C 614 659-0530
  Dublin (G-10392)
Lowes Home Centers LLC .... C 614 238-2601
  Columbus (G-8080)
Lowes Home Centers LLC .... C 740 522-0003
  Newark (G-15199)
Lowes Home Centers LLC .... C 740 773-7777
  Chillicothe (G-2862)
Lowes Home Centers LLC .... C 440 998-6555
  Ashtabula (G-752)
Lowes Home Centers LLC .... B 513 753-5094
  Cincinnati (G-2924)
Lowes Home Centers LLC .... C 614 497-6170
  Columbus (G-8081)
Lowes Home Centers LLC .... C 513 731-6127
  Cincinnati (G-3998)
Lowes Home Centers LLC .... C 330 287-2261
  Wooster (G-19884)
Lowes Home Centers LLC .... C 937 339-2544
  Troy (G-18362)
Lowes Home Centers LLC .... C 440 392-0027
  Mentor (G-14210)
Lowes Home Centers LLC .... C 440 942-2759
  Willoughby (G-19688)

ELECTRICAL APPLIANCES, TELEVISIONS & RADIOS WHOLESALERS

SERVICES SECTION

Lowes Home Centers LLC ....C........ 740 374-2151
  Marietta *(G-13462)*
Lowes Home Centers LLC ....C........ 419 874-6758
  Perrysburg *(G-16030)*
Lowes Home Centers LLC ....C........ 330 626-2980
  Streetsboro *(G-17419)*
Lowes Home Centers LLC ....C........ 419 389-9464
  Toledo *(G-18013)*
Lowes Home Centers LLC ....C........ 419 843-9758
  Toledo *(G-18014)*
Lowes Home Centers LLC ....C........ 614 447-2851
  Columbus *(G-8082)*
Lowes Home Centers LLC ....C........ 330 245-4300
  Akron *(G-329)*
Lowes Home Centers LLC ....C........ 513 965-3280
  Milford *(G-14532)*
Lowes Home Centers LLC ....C........ 330 908-2750
  Northfield *(G-15519)*
Lowes Home Centers LLC ....C........ 419 470-2491
  Toledo *(G-18015)*
Lowes Home Centers LLC ....C........ 513 336-9741
  Mason *(G-13733)*
Lowes Home Centers LLC ....C........ 937 498-8400
  Sidney *(G-16941)*
Lowes Home Centers LLC ....C........ 740 699-3000
  Saint Clairsville *(G-16642)*
Lowes Home Centers LLC ....C........ 330 920-9280
  Stow *(G-17381)*
Lowes Home Centers LLC ....C........ 740 589-3750
  Athens *(G-799)*
Lowes Home Centers LLC ....C........ 740 393-5350
  Mount Vernon *(G-14910)*
Lowes Home Centers LLC ....C........ 937 547-2400
  Greenville *(G-11513)*
Lowes Home Centers LLC ....C........ 330 335-1900
  Wadsworth *(G-18763)*
Lowes Home Centers LLC ....C........ 937 347-4000
  Xenia *(G-20068)*
Lowes Home Centers LLC ....C........ 440 239-2630
  Strongsville *(G-17485)*
Lowes Home Centers LLC ....C........ 513 755-4300
  West Chester *(G-19113)*
Lowes Home Centers LLC ....C........ 513 671-2093
  Cincinnati *(G-3999)*
Lowes Home Centers LLC ....C........ 440 331-1027
  Rocky River *(G-16585)*
Lowes Home Centers LLC ....C........ 330 677-3040
  Kent *(G-12384)*
Lowes Home Centers LLC ....C........ 419 747-1920
  Ontario *(G-15698)*
Lowes Home Centers LLC ....C........ 330 339-1936
  New Philadelphia *(G-15107)*
Lowes Home Centers LLC ....C........ 440 985-5700
  Lorain *(G-13058)*
Lowes Home Centers LLC ....C........ 419 447-4101
  Tiffin *(G-17682)*
Lowes Home Centers LLC ....C........ 937 578-4440
  Marysville *(G-13632)*
Lowes Home Centers LLC ....C........ 937 438-4900
  Dayton *(G-9689)*
Lowes Home Centers LLC ....C........ 937 427-1110
  Beavercreek *(G-1189)*
Lowes Home Centers LLC ....C........ 937 848-5600
  Dayton *(G-9690)*
Lowes Home Centers LLC ....C........ 614 529-5900
  Hilliard *(G-11923)*
Lowes Home Centers LLC ....C........ 513 737-3700
  Hamilton *(G-11755)*
Lowes Home Centers LLC ....C........ 740 894-7120
  South Point *(G-17091)*
Lowes Home Centers LLC ....C........ 513 727-3900
  Middletown *(G-14431)*
Lowes Home Centers LLC ....C........ 419 355-0221
  Fremont *(G-11210)*
Lowes Home Centers LLC ....C........ 419 624-6000
  Sandusky *(G-16777)*
Lowes Home Centers LLC ....C........ 419 782-9000
  Defiance *(G-10045)*
Lowes Home Centers LLC ....C........ 330 609-8000
  Warren *(G-18876)*
Lowes Home Centers LLC ....C........ 330 965-4500
  Youngstown *(G-20257)*
Lowes Home Centers LLC ....C........ 937 383-7000
  Wilmington *(G-19769)*
Lowes Home Centers LLC ....C........ 937 854-8200
  Dayton *(G-9691)*
Lowes Home Centers LLC ....C........ 330 497-2720
  Canton *(G-2440)*
Lowes Home Centers LLC ....C........ 740 266-3500
  Steubenville *(G-17327)*

Lowes Home Centers LLC ....C........ 614 476-7100
  Columbus *(G-8083)*
Mas Inc ....E........ 330 659-3333
  Richfield *(G-16514)*
Mobilcomm Inc ....D........ 513 742-5555
  Cincinnati *(G-4110)*
Panasonic Corp North America ....D........ 513 770-9294
  Mason *(G-13745)*
Panasonic Corp North America ....E........ 201 392-6872
  Troy *(G-18371)*
Pdi Communication Systems Inc ....D........ 937 743-6010
  Springboro *(G-17133)*
RPC Electronics Inc ....E........ 877 522-7927
  Cleveland *(G-6420)*

ELECTRICAL CONSTRUCTION MATERIALS WHOLESALERS

John A Becker Co ....D........ 937 226-1341
  Dayton *(G-9643)*
Johnson Electric Supply Co ....E........ 513 421-3700
  Cincinnati *(G-3882)*
Westfield Electric Inc ....E........ 419 862-0078
  Gibsonburg *(G-11405)*

ELECTRICAL CURRENT CARRYING WIRING DEVICES

GE Aviation Systems LLC ....B........ 937 898-5881
  Vandalia *(G-18681)*
Legrand North America LLC ....B........ 937 224-0639
  Moraine *(G-14798)*
Simpson Strong-Tie Company Inc ....C........ 614 876-8060
  Columbus *(G-8737)*
Watteredge LLC ....D........ 440 933-6110
  Avon Lake *(G-940)*

ELECTRICAL DISCHARGE MACHINING, EDM

Morris Technologies Inc ....C........ 513 733-1611
  Cincinnati *(G-4119)*

ELECTRICAL EQPT & SPLYS

Akron Foundry Co ....E........ 330 745-3101
  Barberton *(G-950)*
Circle Prime Manufacturing ....E........ 330 923-0019
  Cuyahoga Falls *(G-9172)*
Commercial Electric Pdts Corp ....E........ 216 241-2886
  Cleveland *(G-5376)*
Corrpro Companies Inc ....E........ 330 723-5082
  Medina *(G-14052)*
Hannon Company ....D........ 330 456-4728
  Canton *(G-2393)*
Kiemle-Hankins Company ....E........ 419 661-2430
  Perrysburg *(G-16024)*
Kraft Electrical Contg Inc ....E........ 614 836-9300
  Groveport *(G-11655)*
Matlock Electric Co Inc ....E........ 513 731-9600
  Cincinnati *(G-4030)*
Philips Medical Systems Clevel ....B........ 440 247-2652
  Cleveland *(G-6273)*
Powell Electrical Systems Inc ....D........ 330 966-1750
  Canton *(G-2491)*
Riverside Drives Inc ....E........ 216 362-1211
  Cleveland *(G-6399)*
Wesco Distribution Inc ....E........ 419 666-1670
  Northwood *(G-15551)*

ELECTRICAL EQPT FOR ENGINES

Sumitomo Elc Wirg Systems Inc ....E........ 937 642-7579
  Marysville *(G-13653)*

ELECTRICAL EQPT REPAIR & MAINTENANCE

Amko Service Company ....E........ 330 364-8857
  Midvale *(G-14489)*
Ascendtech Inc ....E........ 216 458-1101
  Willoughby *(G-19645)*
Boeing Company ....E........ 740 788-4000
  Newark *(G-15148)*
City of Wadsworth ....E........ 330 334-1581
  Wadsworth *(G-18749)*
Electric Motor Tech LLC ....E........ 513 821-9999
  Cincinnati *(G-3546)*
Enprotech Industrial Tech LLC ....C........ 216 883-3220
  Cleveland *(G-5542)*
Fosbel Inc ....C........ 216 362-3900
  Brookpark *(G-1945)*

General Electric Company ....D........ 216 883-1000
  Cleveland *(G-5667)*
High Line Corporation ....E........ 330 848-8800
  Akron *(G-264)*
J-C-R Tech Inc ....E........ 937 783-2296
  Blanchester *(G-1515)*
Narrow Way Custom Technology ....E........ 937 743-1611
  Carlisle *(G-2605)*
Ohio Machinery Co ....E........ 740 453-0563
  Zanesville *(G-20519)*
Rubber City Machinery Corp ....E........ 330 434-3500
  Akron *(G-419)*
Star Dist & Manufacturring LLC ....D........ 513 860-3573
  West Chester *(G-19231)*
Steel Eqp Specialists Inc ....D........ 330 823-8260
  Alliance *(G-563)*
Terex Utilities Inc ....D........ 513 539-9770
  Monroe *(G-14714)*
Wauseon Machine & Mfg Inc ....D........ 419 337-0940
  Wauseon *(G-18964)*

ELECTRICAL EQPT REPAIR SVCS

Electrical Appl Repr Svc Inc ....E........ 216 459-8700
  Brooklyn Heights *(G-1915)*
Fak Group Inc ....E........ 440 498-8465
  Solon *(G-17006)*
Internash Global Svc Group LLC ....D........ 513 772-0430
  West Chester *(G-19211)*
Kiemle-Hankins Company ....E........ 419 661-2430
  Perrysburg *(G-16024)*
Magnetech Industrial Svcs Inc ....D........ 330 830-3500
  Massillon *(G-13830)*
S D Myers Inc ....C........ 330 630-7000
  Tallmadge *(G-17648)*

ELECTRICAL EQPT REPAIR SVCS: High Voltage

Casey Equipment Corporation ....E........ 330 750-1005
  Struthers *(G-17527)*

ELECTRICAL EQPT: Automotive, NEC

Electra Sound Inc ....D........ 216 433-9600
  Parma *(G-15906)*

ELECTRICAL GOODS, WHOLESALE: Alarms & Signaling Eqpt

Research & Investigation Assoc ....E........ 419 526-1299
  Mansfield *(G-13355)*

ELECTRICAL GOODS, WHOLESALE: Batteries, Storage, Indl

Tri-City Industrial Power Inc ....E........ 937 866-4099
  Miamisburg *(G-14361)*

ELECTRICAL GOODS, WHOLESALE: Boxes & Fittings

Akron Electric Inc ....D........ 330 745-8891
  Akron *(G-37)*
Akron Foundry Co ....C........ 330 745-3101
  Akron *(G-40)*

ELECTRICAL GOODS, WHOLESALE: Burglar Alarm Systems

GA Business Purchaser LLC ....D........ 419 255-8400
  Toledo *(G-17905)*
Interstate Fire & SEC Systems ....E........ 330 453-9495
  Canton *(G-2414)*
Sievers Security Systems Inc ....E........ 216 383-1234
  Cleveland *(G-6481)*
State Alarm Inc ....E........ 330 726-8111
  Youngstown *(G-20382)*

ELECTRICAL GOODS, WHOLESALE: Cable Conduit

Legrand North America LLC ....B........ 937 224-0639
  Moraine *(G-14798)*

ELECTRICAL GOODS, WHOLESALE: Clothes Dryers, Electric & Gas

Super Laundry Inc ....E........ 614 258-5147
  Columbus *(G-8804)*

ELECTRICAL GOODS, WHOLESALE: Connectors

Ladd Distribution LLC ....D...... 937 438-2646
  Kettering (G-12432)

ELECTRICAL GOODS, WHOLESALE: Electrical Appliances, Major

C C Mitchell Supply Company ....E....... 440 526-2040
  Cleveland (G-5168)
Danby Products Inc ....E....... 519 425-8627
  Findlay (G-11020)
Don Walter Kitchen Distrs Inc ....E....... 330 793-9338
  Youngstown (G-20172)
Rieman Arszman Cstm Distrs Inc ....E....... 513 874-5444
  Fairfield (G-10899)

ELECTRICAL GOODS, WHOLESALE: Electronic Parts

Airborn Electronics Inc ....E....... 330 245-2830
  Akron (G-25)
Allied Enterprises Inc ....E....... 440 808-8760
  Westlake (G-19457)
Avnet Inc ....E....... 440 479-3607
  Eastlake (G-10544)
Avnet Inc ....E....... 440 349-7600
  Beachwood (G-1054)
Funai Service Corporation ....E....... 614 409-2600
  Groveport (G-11641)
General Electric Company ....E....... 614 899-8923
  Westerville (G-19403)
Hubbell Power Systems Inc ....D....... 330 335-2361
  Wadsworth (G-18757)
Koehlke Components Inc ....E....... 937 435-5435
  Franklin (G-11160)
Major Electronix Corp ....E....... 440 942-0054
  Eastlake (G-10548)
McM Electronics Inc ....D....... 937 434-0031
  Dayton (G-9708)
Mendelson Electronics Co Inc ....E....... 937 461-3525
  Dayton (G-9718)
Newark Corporation ....B....... 330 523-4457
  Richfield (G-16517)
Newark Electronics Corporation ....C....... 330 523-4912
  Richfield (G-16518)
REM Electronics Supply Co Inc ....E....... 330 373-1300
  Warren (G-18893)
Schuster Electronics Inc ....E....... 330 425-8134
  Twinsburg (G-18468)

ELECTRICAL GOODS, WHOLESALE: Facsimile Or Fax Eqpt

Donnellon Mc Carthy Inc ....E....... 937 299-0200
  Moraine (G-14776)
Gordon Flesch Company Inc ....E....... 419 884-2031
  Mansfield (G-13305)
Ricoh Usa Inc ....D....... 513 984-9898
  Blue Ash (G-1683)
Visual Edge Technology Inc ....C....... 330 494-9694
  Canton (G-2579)

ELECTRICAL GOODS, WHOLESALE: Fire Alarm Systems

Gene Ptacek Son Fire Eqp Inc ....E....... 216 651-8300
  Cleveland (G-5666)

ELECTRICAL GOODS, WHOLESALE: Generators

Buckeye Power Sales Co Inc ....D....... 513 755-2323
  Blacklick (G-1502)
Buckeye Power Sales Co Inc ....E....... 937 346-8322
  Moraine (G-14756)
Western Branch Diesel Inc ....E....... 330 454-8800
  Canton (G-2585)

ELECTRICAL GOODS, WHOLESALE: Household Appliances, NEC

Colonial Sales Inc ....E....... 740 397-4970
  Mount Vernon (G-14883)

ELECTRICAL GOODS, WHOLESALE: Intercommunication Eqpt

Copp Systems Inc ....E....... 937 228-4188
  Dayton (G-9427)

ELECTRICAL GOODS, WHOLESALE: Light Bulbs & Related Splys

Handl-It Inc ....D....... 440 439-9400
  Bedford (G-1309)

ELECTRICAL GOODS, WHOLESALE: Lighting Fittings & Access

Technical Consumer Pdts Inc ....B....... 800 324-1496
  Aurora (G-856)

ELECTRICAL GOODS, WHOLESALE: Lighting Fixtures, Comm & Indl

Cls Facilities MGT Svcs Inc ....E....... 440 602-4600
  Mentor (G-14160)

ELECTRICAL GOODS, WHOLESALE: Mobile telephone Eqpt

Cellco Partnership ....E....... 440 779-1313
  North Olmsted (G-15412)
Shawntech Communications Inc ....E....... 937 898-4900
  Miamisburg (G-14350)

ELECTRICAL GOODS, WHOLESALE: Modems, Computer

Enviro It LLC ....E....... 614 453-0709
  Columbus (G-7598)

ELECTRICAL GOODS, WHOLESALE: Motor Ctrls, Starters & Relays

Winkle Electric Company Inc ....E....... 330 744-5303
  Youngstown (G-20418)

ELECTRICAL GOODS, WHOLESALE: Motors

Ametek Tchnical Indus Pdts Inc ....D....... 330 677-3754
  Kent (G-12352)
Electric Motor Tech LLC ....E....... 513 821-9999
  Cincinnati (G-3546)
Horner Industrial Services Inc ....E....... 937 390-6667
  Springfield (G-17208)
M & R Electric Motor Svc Inc ....E....... 937 222-6282
  Dayton (G-9692)
Matlock Electric Co Inc ....E....... 513 731-9600
  Cincinnati (G-4030)
Mid-Ohio Electric Co ....E....... 614 274-8000
  Columbus (G-8165)
Shoemaker Electric Company ....E....... 614 294-5626
  Columbus (G-8728)
WW Grainger Inc ....E....... 614 276-5231
  Columbus (G-9010)
WW Grainger Inc ....E....... 513 563-7100
  Blue Ash (G-1722)

ELECTRICAL GOODS, WHOLESALE: Paging & Signaling Eqpt

Pager Plus One Inc ....C....... 513 748-3788
  Milford (G-14548)

ELECTRICAL GOODS, WHOLESALE: Radio Parts & Access, NEC

Comproducts Inc ....E....... 614 276-5552
  Columbus (G-7416)
P & R Communications Svc Inc ....E....... 937 222-0861
  Dayton (G-9796)

ELECTRICAL GOODS, WHOLESALE: Security Control Eqpt & Systems

Convergint Technologies LLC ....C....... 513 771-1717
  Cincinnati (G-3416)
Honeywell International Inc ....E....... 614 717-2270
  Columbus (G-7858)
Mace Personal Def & SEC Inc ....E....... 440 424-5321
  Cleveland (G-5964)

ELECTRICAL GOODS, WHOLESALE: Semiconductor Devices

Avnet Inc ....E....... 614 865-1400
  Columbus (G-7078)

ELECTRICAL GOODS, WHOLESALE: Sound Eqpt

Audio-Technica US Inc ....D....... 330 686-2600
  Stow (G-17353)
C A E C Inc ....E....... 614 337-1091
  Columbus (G-7173)
Electra Sound Inc ....D....... 216 433-9600
  Parma (G-15906)

ELECTRICAL GOODS, WHOLESALE: Switchgear

ABB Inc ....E....... 440 585-7804
  Beachwood (G-1045)

ELECTRICAL GOODS, WHOLESALE: Telephone & Telegraphic Eqpt

Acadia Solutions Inc ....E....... 614 505-6135
  Dublin (G-10233)
Acuative Corporation ....D....... 440 202-4500
  Strongsville (G-17439)
AT&T Corp ....E....... 330 505-4200
  Niles (G-15282)
Cellco Partnership ....E....... 330 722-6622
  Medina (G-14043)
E-Cycle LLC ....D....... 614 832-7032
  Hilliard (G-11897)
Wurtec Incorporated ....D....... 419 726-1066
  Toledo (G-18317)

ELECTRICAL GOODS, WHOLESALE: Telephone Eqpt

ABC Appliance Inc ....E....... 419 693-4414
  Oregon (G-15722)
Famous Industries Inc ....E....... 330 535-1811
  Akron (G-219)
Midwest Communications Inc ....D....... 800 229-4756
  North Canton (G-15354)
Mitel (delaware) Inc ....E....... 513 733-8000
  West Chester (G-19122)
Neteam Systems LLC ....E....... 330 523-5100
  Cleveland (G-6121)
Polycom Inc ....E....... 937 245-1853
  Englewood (G-10716)
Pro Oncall Technologies LLC ....D....... 513 489-7660
  Cincinnati (G-4337)
Tele-Solutions Inc ....E....... 330 782-2888
  Youngstown (G-20388)
Teletronic Services Inc ....E....... 216 778-6500
  Strongsville (G-17515)
Warwick Communications Inc ....E....... 216 787-0300
  Broadview Heights (G-1895)

ELECTRICAL GOODS, WHOLESALE: Vacuum Cleaners, Household

Bechtl Bldng Mntnc Crprtn of ....D....... 330 759-2797
  Youngstown (G-20111)
Royal Appliance Mfg Co ....C....... 440 996-2000
  Cleveland (G-6415)

ELECTRICAL GOODS, WHOLESALE: Washing Machines

Whirlpool Corporation ....D....... 419 423-6097
  Findlay (G-11100)
Whirlpool Corporation ....C....... 740 383-7122
  Marion (G-13596)

ELECTRICAL GOODS, WHOLESALE: Wire & Cable

Afc Cable Systems Inc ....D....... 740 435-3340
  Cambridge (G-2092)
Associated Mtls Holdings LLC ....A....... 330 929-1811
  Cuyahoga Falls (G-9163)
Manufactured Assemblies Corp ....D....... 937 898-2060
  Vandalia (G-18688)
Multilink Inc ....C....... 440 366-6966
  Elyria (G-10656)

ELECTRICAL GOODS, WHOLESALE: Wire & Cable

Noco Company .... B 216 464-8131
　Solon *(G-17035)*
Scott Fetzer Company .... C 216 267-9000
　Cleveland *(G-6452)*
Sumitomo Elc Wirg Systems Inc .... E 937 642-7579
　Marysville *(G-13653)*

ELECTRICAL GOODS, WHOLESALE: Wire & Cable, Ctrl & Sig

Signature Control Systems LLC .... E 614 864-2222
　Columbus *(G-8731)*
Winkle Industries Inc .... D 330 823-9730
　Alliance *(G-565)*

ELECTRICAL GOODS, WHOLESALE: Wire & Cable, Electronic

Iewc Corp .... E 440 835-5601
　Westlake *(G-19497)*
Illinois Tool Works Inc .... E 216 292-7161
　Bedford *(G-1312)*
TPC Wire & Cable Corp .... D 800 521-7935
　Macedonia *(G-13213)*

ELECTRICAL HOUSEHOLD APPLIANCE REPAIR

Alco-Chem Inc .... E 330 833-8551
　Canton *(G-2230)*
Central Repair Service Inc .... E 513 943-0500
　Point Pleasant *(G-16218)*
Household Centralized Svc Inc .... E 419 474-5754
　Toledo *(G-17962)*

ELECTRICAL MEASURING INSTRUMENT REPAIR & CALIBRATION SVCS

Instrmntation Ctrl Systems Inc .... E 513 662-2600
　Cincinnati *(G-3822)*
Tegam Inc .... E 440 466-6100
　Geneva *(G-11369)*

ELECTRICAL SPLYS

Accurate Mechanical Inc .... E 740 654-5898
　Lancaster *(G-12506)*
Consolidated Elec Distrs Inc .... E 614 445-8871
　Columbus *(G-7423)*
Dickman Supply Inc .... E 937 492-6166
　Sidney *(G-16929)*
Edison Equipment .... E 614 883-5710
　Columbus *(G-7577)*
Fenton Bros Electric Co .... E 330 343-0093
　New Philadelphia *(G-15094)*
Furbay Electric Supply Co .... D 330 454-3033
　Canton *(G-2373)*
Graybar Electric Company Inc .... E 216 573-6144
　Cleveland *(G-5688)*
Graybar Electric Company Inc .... D 513 719-7400
　Cincinnati *(G-3695)*
Graybar Electric Company Inc .... E 614 486-4391
　Columbus *(G-7770)*
Gross Electric Inc .... E 419 537-1818
　Toledo *(G-17925)*
H Leff Electric Company .... C 216 325-0941
　Cleveland *(G-5715)*
John A Becker Co .... D 513 771-2550
　Cincinnati *(G-3876)*
John A Becker Co .... E 614 272-8800
　Columbus *(G-7942)*
Loeb Electric Company .... D 614 294-6351
　Columbus *(G-8075)*
Mars Electric Company .... D 440 946-2250
　Cleveland *(G-5984)*
McNaughton-McKay Elc Ohio Inc .... D 614 476-2800
　Columbus *(G-8137)*
McNaughton-McKay Elc Ohio Inc .... E 419 422-2984
　Findlay *(G-11064)*
McNaughton-McKay Elc Ohio Inc .... E 419 891-0262
　Maumee *(G-13946)*
Noland Company .... C 937 396-7980
　Moraine *(G-14812)*
Rexel Usa Inc .... D 440 248-3800
　Solon *(G-17047)*
Rexel Usa Inc .... E 419 625-6761
　Sandusky *(G-16789)*
Rexel Usa Inc .... E 614 771-7373
　Hilliard *(G-11949)*
Richards Electric Sup Co Inc .... C 513 242-8800
　Cincinnati *(G-4416)*

Sabroske Electric Inc .... E 419 332-6444
　Fremont *(G-11218)*
Schneider Electric Usa Inc .... E 440 526-9070
　Richfield *(G-16529)*
Wesco Distribution Inc .... E 216 741-0441
　Cleveland *(G-6734)*
Wolff Bros Supply Inc .... E 330 400-5990
　Sandusky *(G-16810)*
Wolff Bros Supply Inc .... E 330 264-5900
　Wooster *(G-19930)*

ELECTRODES: Thermal & Electrolytic

De Nora Tech LLC .... D 440 710-5300
　Painesville *(G-15850)*
Graphel Corporation .... C 513 779-6166
　West Chester *(G-19083)*

ELECTROMEDICAL EQPT

Vieuray Incorporated .... D 440 703-3210
　Oakwood Village *(G-15636)*

ELECTROMETALLURGICAL PRDTS

Rhenium Alloys Inc .... D 440 365-7388
　North Ridgeville *(G-15475)*

ELECTRONIC EQPT REPAIR SVCS

Automation & Control Tech Ltd .... E 419 661-6400
　Perrysburg *(G-15973)*
Electric Service Co Inc .... E 513 271-6387
　Cincinnati *(G-3547)*
Liebert Corporation .... D 614 841-6104
　Columbus *(G-8060)*
Liebert Corporation .... A 614 888-0246
　Columbus *(G-8059)*
Ohio State University .... A 614 292-6158
　Columbus *(G-8445)*
Service Solutions Group LLC .... E 513 772-6600
　Cincinnati *(G-4501)*

ELECTRONIC PARTS & EQPT WHOLESALERS

Access Catalog Company LLC .... E 440 572-5377
　Strongsville *(G-17438)*
Agilysys Inc .... E 440 519-6262
　Solon *(G-16971)*
Arrow Electronics Inc .... D 440 498-3617
　Solon *(G-16977)*
Cincinnati Voice and Data .... D 513 683-4127
　Loveland *(G-13115)*
Exonic Systems LLC .... E 330 315-3100
　Akron *(G-212)*
Fox International Limited Inc .... E 216 454-1001
　Beachwood *(G-1080)*
Graybar Electric Company Inc .... E 216 573-6144
　Cleveland *(G-5688)*
Harris Battery Company Inc .... E 330 874-0205
　Bolivar *(G-1748)*
Hughes Corporation .... E 440 238-2550
　Strongsville *(G-17474)*
Keithley Instruments Intl Corp .... B 440 248-0400
　Cleveland *(G-5889)*
Konica Minolta Business Soluti .... D 440 546-5795
　Broadview Heights *(G-1882)*
Mark Feldstein & Assoc Inc .... E 419 867-9500
　Sylvania *(G-17600)*
Mega Techway Inc .... C 440 605-0700
　Cleveland *(G-6019)*
Mobilcomm Inc .... D 513 742-5555
　Cincinnati *(G-4110)*
Pepperl + Fuchs Inc .... C 330 425-3555
　Twinsburg *(G-18452)*
Western Tradewinds Inc .... E 937 859-4300
　Miamisburg *(G-14368)*
Wholesale House Inc .... D 419 542-1315
　Hicksville *(G-11867)*

ELECTRONIC SHOPPING

Ampersand Group LLC .... E 330 379-0044
　Akron *(G-75)*
E Retailing Associates LLC .... D 614 300-5785
　Columbus *(G-7561)*
Midwest Tape LLC .... B 419 868-9370
　Holland *(G-12038)*

ELEMENTARY & SECONDARY PRIVATE DENOMINATIONAL SCHOOLS

Catholic Diocese of Columbus .... D 614 276-5263
　Columbus *(G-7210)*
Joseph and Florence Mandel .... D 216 464-4055
　Beachwood *(G-1092)*
Our Lady of Bethlehem Schools .... E 614 459-8285
　Columbus *(G-8499)*
Saint Cecilia Church .... E 614 878-5353
　Columbus *(G-8677)*

ELEMENTARY & SECONDARY SCHOOLS, COMBINED CATHOLIC

Troy Christian School .... D 937 339-5692
　Troy *(G-18382)*

ELEMENTARY & SECONDARY SCHOOLS, PRIVATE NEC

Christian Perry Pre School .... E 330 477-7262
　Canton *(G-2307)*
Christian Wooster School .... E 330 345-6436
　Wooster *(G-19842)*
Fairmount Montessori Assn .... E 216 321-7571
　Cleveland *(G-5565)*
First Apostolic Church .... E 419 885-4888
　Toledo *(G-17891)*
Jewish Day Schl Assoc Grtr Clv .... D 216 763-1400
　Pepper Pike *(G-15957)*
New Hope Christian Academy .... E 740 477-6427
　Circleville *(G-4893)*
Nightingale Montessori Inc .... E 937 324-0336
　Springfield *(G-17252)*
Ruffing Montessori School .... E 440 333-2250
　Rocky River *(G-16591)*
Seton Catholic School Hudson .... E 330 342-4200
　Hudson *(G-12143)*
Zion Christian School .... E 330 792-4066
　Youngstown *(G-20439)*

ELEMENTARY & SECONDARY SCHOOLS, PUBLIC

Brunswick City Schools .... A 330 225-7731
　Brunswick *(G-1969)*
Clermont North East School Dst .... E 513 625-8283
　Batavia *(G-1002)*
Cleveland Municipal School Dst .... B 216 838-0000
　Cleveland *(G-5335)*
Cleveland Municipal School Dst .... E 216 838-8700
　Cleveland *(G-5336)*
Dover City Schools .... D 330 343-8880
　Dover *(G-10184)*
Independence Local Schools .... E 216 642-5865
　Independence *(G-12219)*
Kettering City School District .... D 937 499-1770
　Dayton *(G-9653)*
Lakewood City School District .... E 216 529-4400
　Lakewood *(G-12487)*
Madison Local School District .... B 419 589-2600
　Mansfield *(G-13326)*
Northwest Local School Dst .... D 513 923-1000
　Cincinnati *(G-4182)*
St Marys City Board Education .... E 419 394-1116
　Saint Marys *(G-16684)*
St Marys City Board Education .... D 419 394-2616
　Saint Marys *(G-16685)*
Sycamore Board of Education .... D 513 489-3937
　Cincinnati *(G-4608)*

ELEMENTARY & SECONDARY SCHOOLS, SPECIAL EDUCATION

Ashtabula Cnty Eductl Svc Ctr .... D 440 576-4085
　Jefferson *(G-12328)*
Brown Co Ed Service Center .... D 937 378-6118
　Georgetown *(G-11386)*
Positive Education Program .... E 216 227-2730
　Cleveland *(G-6291)*
Positive Education Program .... E 440 471-8200
　Cleveland *(G-6292)*

ELEMENTARY SCHOOLS, CATHOLIC

Cardinal Pacelli School .... B 513 321-1048
　Cincinnati *(G-3178)*
St Pauls Catholic Church .... E 330 724-1263
　Akron *(G-448)*

SERVICES SECTION

ELEMENTARY SCHOOLS, NEC

Goldwood Primary School Pta ....E....... 440 356-6720
  Rocky River *(G-16579)*

ELEMENTARY SCHOOLS, PRIVATE

Canton Country Day School ....E....... 330 453-8279
  Canton *(G-2286)*
Discovery School ....E....... 419 756-8880
  Mansfield *(G-13294)*
Hudson Montessori Association ....E....... 330 650-0424
  Hudson *(G-12122)*
Lillian and Betty Ratner Schl ....E....... 216 464-0033
  Cleveland *(G-5942)*
New School Inc ....E....... 513 281-7999
  Cincinnati *(G-4157)*
Old Trail School ....D....... 330 666-1118
  Bath *(G-1035)*
Pillar of Fire ....E....... 513 542-1212
  Cincinnati *(G-4300)*
Samkel Inc ....E....... 614 491-3270
  Columbus *(G-8683)*
West Side Montessori ....D....... 419 866-1931
  Toledo *(G-18306)*

ELEMENTARY SCHOOLS, PUBLIC

Bay Village City School Dst ....E....... 440 617-7330
  Cleveland *(G-5102)*
Columbus Public School Dst ....E....... 614 365-5456
  Columbus *(G-7377)*
Delaware City School District ....E....... 740 363-5901
  Delaware *(G-10087)*
Kettering City School District ....D....... 937 297-1990
  Dayton *(G-9652)*
Lima City School District ....E....... 419 996-3450
  Lima *(G-12817)*
Lincolnview Local Schools ....C....... 419 968-2226
  Van Wert *(G-18638)*
Logan-Hocking School District ....E....... 740 385-7844
  Logan *(G-12985)*
Upper Arlington City Schl Dst ....E....... 614 487-5133
  Columbus *(G-8914)*

ELEVATOR: Grain, Storage Only

Consolidated Grain & Barge Co ....E....... 513 941-4805
  Cincinnati *(G-3411)*
Consolidated Grain & Barge Co ....D....... 419 785-1941
  Defiance *(G-10023)*
Deerfield Farms Service Inc ....D....... 330 584-4715
  Deerfield *(G-10019)*
Mercer Landmark Inc ....E....... 419 586-7443
  Celina *(G-2655)*

ELEVATORS & EQPT

Otis Elevator Company ....D....... 216 573-2333
  Cleveland *(G-6218)*
Schindler Elevator Corporation ....E....... 419 861-5900
  Holland *(G-12054)*

ELEVATORS WHOLESALERS

Otis Elevator Company ....E....... 614 777-6500
  Columbus *(G-8498)*
Schindler Elevator Corporation ....E....... 614 573-2777
  Columbus *(G-8694)*
Thyssenkrupp Elevator Corp ....E....... 440 717-0080
  Broadview Heights *(G-1893)*
Thyssenkrupp Elevator Corp ....E....... 614 895-8930
  Westerville *(G-19445)*

ELEVATORS: Installation & Conversion

Otis Elevator Company ....D....... 513 531-7888
  Cincinnati *(G-4242)*
Otis Elevator Company ....D....... 216 573-2333
  Cleveland *(G-6218)*
Schindler Elevator Corporation ....C....... 419 867-5100
  Holland *(G-12053)*
Schindler Elevator Corporation ....D....... 216 370-9524
  Cleveland *(G-6447)*
Thyssenkrupp Elevator Corp ....E....... 513 241-6000
  Cincinnati *(G-4659)*
Thyssenkrupp Elevator Corp ....E....... 614 895-8930
  Westerville *(G-19445)*

EMBROIDERING & ART NEEDLEWORK FOR THE TRADE

McCc Sportswear Inc ....E....... 513 583-9210
  West Chester *(G-19214)*

EMBROIDERY ADVERTISING SVCS

Evolution Crtive Solutions LLC ....E....... 513 681-4450
  Cincinnati *(G-3584)*
Screen Works Inc ....E....... 937 264-9111
  Dayton *(G-9870)*

EMERGENCY & RELIEF SVCS

Ansonia Area Emergency Service ....E....... 937 337-2651
  Ansonia *(G-619)*
Cgh-Global Emerg Mngmt Strateg ....E....... 800 376-0655
  Cincinnati *(G-2905)*
Counseling Center Huron County ....E....... 419 663-3737
  Norwalk *(G-15567)*
County of Holmes ....E....... 330 674-1926
  Millersburg *(G-14596)*
County of Mercer ....E....... 419 678-8071
  Coldwater *(G-6828)*
Firelands Regional Health Sys ....E....... 419 663-3737
  Norwalk *(G-15573)*
Mercy Health ....A....... 440 233-1000
  Lorain *(G-13060)*
Oriana House Inc ....D....... 330 996-7730
  Akron *(G-374)*
Saline Township ....E....... 330 532-2195
  Hammondsville *(G-11786)*
Trumball Cnty Fire Chiefs Assn ....D....... 330 675-6602
  Warren *(G-18908)*

EMERGENCY SHELTERS

Battered Womens Shelter ....E....... 330 723-3900
  Medina *(G-14038)*
Battered Womens Shelter ....E....... 330 374-0740
  Akron *(G-91)*
Beatitude House ....E....... 440 992-0265
  Ashtabula *(G-729)*
Choices For Vctims Dom Volence ....E....... 614 224-6617
  Worthington *(G-19947)*
Domestic Violence Project Inc ....E....... 330 445-2000
  Canton *(G-2343)*
Faith Mission Inc ....E....... 614 224-6617
  Columbus *(G-7633)*
Harbor House Inc ....E....... 740 498-7213
  New Philadelphia *(G-15096)*
Homefull ....D....... 937 293-1945
  Dayton *(G-9618)*
Light of Hearts Villa ....D....... 440 232-1991
  Cleveland *(G-5941)*
Tender Mercies Inc ....E....... 513 721-8666
  Cincinnati *(G-4635)*
Tri County Help Center Inc ....E....... 740 695-5441
  Saint Clairsville *(G-16657)*

EMPLOYEE LEASING SVCS

Cbiz Inc ....C....... 216 447-9000
  Cleveland *(G-5196)*
Columbiana Service Company LLC ......D....... 330 482-5511
  Columbiana *(G-6856)*
D C Transportation Service ....C....... 440 237-0900
  North Royalton *(G-15485)*
Diversfied Emplyee Sltions Inc ....B....... 330 764-4125
  Medina *(G-14060)*
Hr Services Inc ....E....... 419 224-2462
  Lima *(G-12799)*
Innovtive Sltons Unlimited LLC ....E....... 740 289-3282
  Piketon *(G-16118)*
JB Management Inc ....D....... 419 841-2596
  Toledo *(G-17983)*
Paradigm Industrial LLC ....E....... 937 224-4415
  Dayton *(G-9801)*
Prueter Enterprises Ltd ....E....... 419 872-5343
  Perrysburg *(G-16046)*
Renhill Stffing Srvces-America ....E....... 419 254-2800
  Perrysburg *(G-16051)*
Sequent Inc ....D....... 614 436-5880
  Columbus *(G-6907)*
Verified Person Inc ....E....... 901 767-6121
  Independence *(G-12272)*

EMPLOYMENT AGENCY SVCS

Abilities First Foundation ....C....... 513 423-9496
  Middletown *(G-14411)*

EMPLOYMENT AGENCY SVCS

Alliance Solutions Group LLC ....E....... 216 525-0100
  Independence *(G-12185)*
Aspen Community Living ....C....... 614 880-6000
  Columbus *(G-7051)*
Atrium Apparel Corporation ....D....... 612 889-0959
  Johnstown *(G-12335)*
Blanchard Valley Industries ....D....... 419 422-6386
  Findlay *(G-11000)*
Bmch Inc ....D....... 216 642-1300
  Independence *(G-12189)*
Brown Medical LLC ....E....... 740 574-8728
  Wheelersburg *(G-19571)*
Cardinalcommerce Corporation ....D....... 877 352-8444
  Mentor *(G-14153)*
Career Cnnctions Staffing Svcs ....E....... 440 471-8210
  Westlake *(G-19469)*
Careworks of Ohio Inc ....B....... 614 792-1085
  Dublin *(G-10280)*
Cleveland Job Corps Center ....E....... 216 541-2500
  Cleveland *(G-5323)*
Cnsld Humacare- Employee MGT ....E....... 513 605-3522
  Cincinnati *(G-3376)*
Comprehensive Health Care Svcs ....C....... 513 245-0100
  Cincinnati *(G-3406)*
Construction Labor Contrs LLC ....D....... 614 932-9937
  Dublin *(G-10309)*
Corporate Ladder Search ....E....... 330 776-4390
  Uniontown *(G-18515)*
County of Guernsey ....D....... 740 432-2381
  Cambridge *(G-2108)*
County of Huron ....D....... 419 668-8126
  Norwalk *(G-15568)*
County of Wayne ....E....... 330 264-5060
  Wooster *(G-19855)*
Csu/Career Services Center ....E....... 216 687-2233
  Cleveland *(G-5445)*
Ctpartners Exec Search Inc ....D....... 216 464-8710
  Beachwood *(G-1069)*
Custom Staffing Inc ....E....... 419 221-3097
  Lima *(G-12770)*
Damascus Staffing LLC ....D....... 513 954-8941
  Maineville *(G-13242)*
Dawson Resources ....B....... 614 274-8900
  Columbus *(G-7492)*
Discover Training Inc ....D....... 614 871-0010
  Grove City *(G-11554)*
E & L Premier Corporation ....C....... 330 836-9901
  Fairlawn *(G-10946)*
Exodus Integrity Service ....D....... 440 918-0140
  Willoughby *(G-19663)*
First Choice Med Staff of Ohio ....D....... 419 521-2700
  Mansfield *(G-13303)*
First Choice Medical Staffing ....B....... 216 521-2222
  Cleveland *(G-5593)*
Future Unlimited Inc ....E....... 330 273-6677
  Brunswick *(G-1979)*
Goodwill Industries Inc ....E....... 330 724-6995
  Akron *(G-241)*
Gus Perdikakis Associates ....D....... 513 583-0900
  Cincinnati *(G-3721)*
Heitmeyer Group LLC ....B....... 614 573-5571
  Westerville *(G-19312)*
HJ Ford Associates Inc ....E....... 937 429-9711
  Beavercreek *(G-1176)*
Horizon Personnel Resources ....C....... 440 585-0031
  Wickliffe *(G-19602)*
Horizons Employment Svcs LLC ....B....... 419 254-9644
  Toledo *(G-17960)*
Hospice of Darke County Inc ....E....... 419 678-4808
  Coldwater *(G-6830)*
Hr Services Inc ....E....... 419 224-2462
  Lima *(G-12799)*
Human Resources Services ....E....... 740 587-3484
  Westerville *(G-19314)*
I-Force LLC ....C....... 614 431-5100
  Columbus *(G-7879)*
Integrity Enterprizes ....E....... 216 289-8801
  Euclid *(G-10764)*
Its Technologies Inc ....D....... 419 842-2100
  Holland *(G-12030)*
Job 1 USA ....D....... 419 255-5005
  Toledo *(G-17985)*
Key Career Place ....D....... 216 987-3029
  Cleveland *(G-5896)*
Kforce Inc ....E....... 614 436-4027
  Columbus *(G-7985)*
Kilgore Group Inc ....E....... 513 684-3721
  Cincinnati *(G-3922)*
Lane Wood Industries ....B....... 419 352-5059
  Bowling Green *(G-1784)*

Licking-Knox Goodwill Inds Inc D 740 397-0051
Mount Vernon *(G-14909)*

Mancan Inc A 440 884-9675
Strongsville *(G-17487)*

Mid Ohio Employment Services E 419 747-5466
Ontario *(G-15703)*

Midwest Emergency Services LLC E 586 294-2700
Fairlawn *(G-10965)*

Murtech Consulting LLC D 216 328-8580
Cleveland *(G-6091)*

Nurses Care Inc E 513 791-0233
Cincinnati *(G-4193)*

Nurses Heart Med Staffing LLC E 614 648-5111
Columbus *(G-8306)*

Ohio Dept of Job & Fmly Svcs D 330 484-5402
Akron *(G-364)*

Ohio State University A 614 293-2494
Columbus *(G-8412)*

Onestaff Inc E 859 815-1345
Cincinnati *(G-4227)*

Pathway Inc E 419 242-7304
Toledo *(G-18122)*

Pearl Interactive Network Inc B 614 258-2943
Columbus *(G-8527)*

Prn Nurse Inc B 614 864-9292
Columbus *(G-8562)*

Professonal Data Resources Inc C 513 792-5100
Blue Ash *(G-1668)*

Promedica Physcn Cntinuum Svcs C 419 824-7200
Sylvania *(G-17608)*

PSI Associates Inc B 330 425-8474
Twinsburg *(G-18457)*

Randstad Technologies LLC D 614 436-0961
Columbus *(G-6903)*

Randstad Technologies LLC D 216 520-0206
Independence *(G-12246)*

Randstad Technologies LP E 614 552-3280
Hilliard *(G-11948)*

Rightthing LLC B 419 420-1830
Findlay *(G-11079)*

Rkpl Inc D 419 224-2121
Lima *(G-12869)*

Rumpf Corporation E 419 255-5005
Toledo *(G-18167)*

Safegard Bckgrund Screning LLC C 216 370-7345
Cleveland *(G-6432)*

Seifert & Group Inc D 330 833-2700
Massillon *(G-13852)*

Tailored Management Services D 614 859-1500
Columbus *(G-8820)*

Telamon Corporation E 937 254-2004
Dayton *(G-9923)*

Tradesmen Services LLC D 440 349-3432
Macedonia *(G-13215)*

Tradesource Inc C 216 801-4944
Parma *(G-15916)*

Work Solutions Group LLC E 440 205-8297
Mentor *(G-14259)*

Wtw Delaware Holdings LLC C 216 937-4000
Cleveland *(G-6762)*

EMPLOYMENT SVCS: Labor Contractors

Advantage Resourcing Amer Inc E 781 472-8900
Cincinnati *(G-2976)*

Alliance Legal Solutions LLC D 216 525-0100
Independence *(G-12184)*

Belflex Staffing Network LLC C 513 488-8588
Cincinnati *(G-3096)*

Mj-6 LLC E 419 517-7725
Toledo *(G-18066)*

Per Diem Nurse Staffing LLT E 419 878-8880
Waterville *(G-18944)*

Robert Half International Inc D 614 602-0505
Dublin *(G-10442)*

Staffmark Investment LLC C 513 651-3600
Cincinnati *(G-4574)*

Stearns Companies LLC E 419 422-0241
Findlay *(G-11085)*

Tradesmen International LLC E 440 349-3432
Macedonia *(G-13214)*

Tradesource Inc C 614 824-3883
Columbus *(G-8862)*

United Steelworkers E 440 244-1358
Lorain *(G-13083)*

EMPLOYMENT SVCS: Nurses' Registry

A-1 Nursing Care Inc C 614 268-3800
Columbus *(G-6922)*

Accentcare Home Health Cal Inc C 740 387-4568
Marion *(G-13522)*

Alternate Solutions First LLC C 937 298-1111
Dayton *(G-9325)*

Assured Health Care Inc E 937 294-2803
Dayton *(G-9346)*

Blanchard Valley Health System D 419 424-3000
Findlay *(G-10998)*

Carestar Inc C 513 618-8300
Cincinnati *(G-3183)*

Childrens Home Care Dayton D 937 641-4663
Dayton *(G-9402)*

Collier Nursing Service Inc C 513 791-4357
Montgomery *(G-14725)*

Community Hlth Prfssionals Inc C 419 238-9223
Van Wert *(G-18630)*

Community Hlth Prfssionals Inc D 419 586-6266
Celina *(G-2642)*

Community Home Care E 330 971-7011
Cuyahoga Falls *(G-9177)*

County of Holmes E 330 674-5035
Millersburg *(G-14597)*

Dedicated Nursing Assoc Inc D 937 886-4559
Miamisburg *(G-14295)*

Dedicated Nursing Assoc Inc E 866 450-5550
Cincinnati *(G-3477)*

Dedicated Nursing Assoc Inc E 877 411-8350
Galloway *(G-11343)*

Dedicated Nursing Assoc Inc E 877 547-9144
Parma *(G-15905)*

Dedicated Nursing Assoc Inc C 888 465-6929
Beavercreek *(G-1237)*

Epilogue Inc D 440 582-5555
North Royalton *(G-15489)*

First Choice Medical Staffing D 419 861-2722
Toledo *(G-17892)*

Firstat Nursing Services D 216 295-1500
Cleveland *(G-5600)*

Health & HM Care Concepts Inc E 740 383-4968
Marion *(G-13542)*

Health Care Plus E 614 340-7587
Columbus *(G-6882)*

Home Care Network Inc D 937 435-1142
Dayton *(G-9613)*

Interim Halthcare Columbus Inc E 330 836-5571
Fairlawn *(G-10958)*

Medi Home Health Agency Inc E 740 266-3977
Steubenville *(G-17329)*

Medical Solutions LLC D 513 936-3468
Blue Ash *(G-1638)*

P E Miller & Assoc D 614 231-4743
Columbus *(G-8502)*

Personal Touch HM Care IPA Inc E 937 456-4447
Eaton *(G-10573)*

Private Practice Nurses Inc E 216 481-1305
Cleveland *(G-6307)*

Prn Health Services Inc D 513 792-2217
Cincinnati *(G-4336)*

St Ritas Medical Center C 419 538-7025
Lima *(G-12887)*

Talemed LLC B 513 774-7300
Loveland *(G-13162)*

Taylors Staffing D 740 446-3305
Pomeroy *(G-16236)*

Ulrich Professional Group E 330 673-9501
Kent *(G-12402)*

Vishnia & Associates Inc D 330 929-5512
Cuyahoga Falls *(G-9233)*

Wise Medical Staffing Inc D 740 775-4108
Chillicothe *(G-2898)*

ENGINEERING HELP SVCS

Belcan LLC A 513 645-1509
West Chester *(G-19026)*

Belcan LLC A 513 891-0972
Blue Ash *(G-1538)*

Belcan LLC A 513 217-4562
Middletown *(G-14416)*

Belcan LLC A 740 393-8888
Mount Vernon *(G-14878)*

Belcan Corporation A 513 985-7777
Blue Ash *(G-1539)*

Belcan Corporation D 513 891-0972
Solon *(G-16983)*

Belcan Corporation A 614 224-6080
Columbus *(G-7099)*

Belcan Svcs Group Ltd Partnr C 513 891-0972
Blue Ash *(G-1541)*

Belcan Svcs Group Ltd Partnr D 937 859-8880
Miamisburg *(G-14275)*

Prestige Technical Svcs Inc E 513 779-6800
West Chester *(G-19131)*

Top Echelon Contracting Inc B 330 454-3508
Canton *(G-2564)*

ENGINEERING SVCS

7nt Enterprises LLC E 937 435-3200
Dayton *(G-9295)*

ABB Inc E 440 585-7804
Beachwood *(G-1045)*

Accelerant Technologies LLC D 419 236-8768
Genoa *(G-11374)*

Adaptive Corporation E 440 257-7460
Hudson *(G-12101)*

Advantage Aerotech Inc E 614 759-8329
Columbus *(G-6947)*

Aecom Energy & Cnstr Inc D 216 523-5600
Cleveland *(G-4965)*

Aecom Global II LLC D 216 523-5600
Cleveland *(G-4966)*

Airgas Usa LLC C 440 232-1590
Cleveland *(G-4977)*

Alfons Haar Inc E 937 560-2031
Springboro *(G-17114)*

American Electric Pwr Svc Corp B 614 716-1000
Columbus *(G-6990)*

American Rock Mechanics Inc E 330 963-0550
Twinsburg *(G-18390)*

Ann Corbett Design Inc E 740 432-2969
Cambridge *(G-2095)*

Aptim Corp E 513 782-4700
Cincinnati *(G-3038)*

Austin Building and Design Inc C 440 544-2600
Cleveland *(G-5081)*

B&N Coal Inc D 740 783-3575
Dexter City *(G-10170)*

Belcan LLC A 513 891-0972
Blue Ash *(G-1538)*

Belcan Corporation C 513 277-3100
Cincinnati *(G-3095)*

Belcan Engineering Group LLC A 513 891-0972
Blue Ash *(G-1540)*

Bendix Coml Vhcl Systems LLC B 440 329-9000
Elyria *(G-10597)*

BHF Incorporated E 740 945-6410
Scio *(G-16816)*

Booz Allen Hamilton Inc E 937 429-5580
Beavercreek *(G-1154)*

Boral Resources LLC D 740 622-8042
Coshocton *(G-9088)*

Bowen Engineering Corporation C 614 536-0273
Columbus *(G-7125)*

Brewer-Garrett Co C 440 243-3535
Middleburg Heights *(G-14378)*

Burgess & Niple / Heapy Engine D 614 459-2050
Columbus *(G-7170)*

Butler County of Ohio D 513 867-5744
Hamilton *(G-11703)*

Ch2m Hill Inc E 614 888-3100
Columbus *(G-7249)*

Ch2m Hill Constructors Inc E 937 228-4285
Dayton *(G-9395)*

Circle Prime Manufacturing E 330 923-0019
Cuyahoga Falls *(G-9172)*

City of Akron D 330 375-2355
Akron *(G-142)*

City of Delphos E 419 695-4010
Delphos *(G-10138)*

City of Sandusky D 419 627-5829
Sandusky *(G-16738)*

City of Toledo D 419 936-2275
Toledo *(G-17813)*

Civil & Environmental Cons Inc E 513 985-0226
Milford *(G-14512)*

Cmta Inc C 502 326-3085
Cincinnati *(G-3373)*

Coal Services Inc D 740 795-5220
Powhatan Point *(G-16356)*

Corrpro Companies Inc E 330 723-5082
Medina *(G-14052)*

County Engineers Office E 740 702-3130
Chillicothe *(G-2829)*

County of Brown E 937 378-6456
Georgetown *(G-11390)*

County of Coshocton E 740 622-2135
Coshocton *(G-9099)*

County of Crawford E 419 562-7731
Bucyrus *(G-2034)*

County of Delaware D 740 833-2400
Delaware *(G-10083)*

County of Erie E 419 627-7710
Sandusky *(G-16749)*

SERVICES SECTION

ENGINEERING SVCS: Acoustical

Company	Code	Phone
County of Fayette	E	740 335-1541
Wshngtn CT Hs (G-20017)		
County of Fulton	E	419 335-3816
Wauseon (G-18949)		
County of Gallia	E	740 446-4009
Gallipolis (G-11313)		
County of Lorain	E	440 326-5884
Elyria (G-10612)		
County of Lucas	D	419 213-2892
Holland (G-12016)		
County of Madison	E	740 852-9404
London (G-12996)		
County of Montgomery	D	937 854-4576
Dayton (G-9433)		
County of Perry	E	740 342-2191
New Lexington (G-15054)		
County of Portage	D	330 296-6411
Ravenna (G-16379)		
County of Richland	E	419 774-5591
Mansfield (G-13283)		
County of Stark	C	330 477-6781
Canton (G-2324)		
County of Summit	C	330 643-2850
Akron (G-170)		
County of Union	E	937 645-3018
Marysville (G-13612)		
County of Washington	E	740 376-7430
Marietta (G-13438)		
County of Wayne	D	330 287-5500
Wooster (G-19858)		
Custom Materials Inc	E	440 543-8284
Chagrin Falls (G-2713)		
Cuyahoga County	A	216 348-3800
Cleveland (G-5453)		
Design Knowledge Company	D	937 320-9244
Beavercreek (G-1168)		
Dizer Corp	E	440 368-0200
Painesville (G-15851)		
Dkmp Consulting Inc	C	614 733-0979
Plain City (G-16187)		
Dlhbowles Inc	B	330 478-2503
Canton (G-2342)		
Dlr Group Inc	D	216 522-1350
Cleveland (G-5495)		
Dlz American Drilling Inc	E	614 888-0040
Columbus (G-7532)		
Dlz Construction Services Inc	E	614 888-0040
Columbus (G-7533)		
Donald E Didion II	E	419 483-2226
Bellevue (G-1408)		
Earl Twinam	E	740 820-2654
Portsmouth (G-16277)		
Early Construction Co	E	740 894-5150
South Point (G-17085)		
Emerson Process MGT Lllp	E	877 468-6384
Columbus (G-6881)		
Emh Inc	E	330 220-8600
Valley City (G-18617)		
Enprotech Industrial Tech LLC	C	216 883-3220
Cleveland (G-5542)		
Fed/Matrix A Joint Venture LLC	E	863 665-6363
Dayton (G-9542)		
Fishel Company	D	614 850-4400
Columbus (G-7669)		
Fishel Company	D	614 274-8100
Columbus (G-7667)		
Futura Design Service Inc	E	937 890-5252
Dayton (G-9565)		
G Herschman Architects Inc	D	216 223-3200
Cleveland (G-5645)		
Garmann/Miller & Assoc Inc	E	419 628-4240
Minster (G-14662)		
GE Aviation Systems LLC	D	937 474-0397
Dayton (G-9568)		
General Electric Intl Inc	C	617 443-3000
Cincinnati (G-3673)		
Global Military Expert Co	E	800 738-9795
Beavercreek (G-1242)		
Greene County	E	937 562-7500
Xenia (G-20054)		
Gus Perdikakis Associates	D	513 583-0900
Cincinnati (G-3721)		
HDR Engineering Inc	E	614 839-5770
Columbus (G-7807)		
Heery International Inc	E	216 781-1313
Cleveland (G-5746)		
Hlg Engineering & Survey Inc	E	614 760-8320
Dublin (G-10363)		
Hokuto USA Inc	E	614 782-6200
Grove City (G-11570)		
Horn Electric Company	E	330 364-7784
Dover (G-10192)		
HP Inc	E	513 983-2817
Cincinnati (G-3791)		
Hunter Defense Tech Inc	E	216 438-6111
Solon (G-17016)		
Hydro-Dyne Inc	E	330 832-5076
Massillon (G-13821)		
Icr Inc	E	513 900-7007
Mason (G-13718)		
Infoscitex Corporation	E	937 429-9008
Beavercreek Township (G-1270)		
Innovative Controls Corp	D	419 691-6684
Toledo (G-17974)		
Innovtve Sltons Unlimited LLC	E	740 289-3282
Piketon (G-16118)		
Innovtve Sltons Unlimited LLC	D	740 289-3282
Piketon (G-16119)		
Jacobs Constructors Inc	E	419 226-1344
Lima (G-12806)		
Jdi Group Inc	D	419 725-7161
Maumee (G-13930)		
Jjr Solutions LLC	E	937 912-0288
Beavercreek (G-1180)		
Jobes Henderson & Assoc Inc	E	740 344-5451
Newark (G-15178)		
Juice Technologies Inc	E	800 518-5576
Columbus (G-7957)		
K&K Technical Group Inc	C	513 202-1300
Harrison (G-11804)		
Kendall Holdings Ltd	E	614 486-4750
Columbus (G-7976)		
Keyw Corporation	E	937 702-9512
Beavercreek (G-1182)		
Knox County Engineer	E	740 397-1590
Mount Vernon (G-14905)		
KZF Bwsc Joint Venture	E	513 621-6211
Cincinnati (G-3951)		
KZF Design Inc	D	513 621-6211
Cincinnati (G-3952)		
L3 Aviation Products Inc	E	614 825-2001
Columbus (G-8025)		
Logan County Engineering Off	E	937 592-2791
Bellefontaine (G-1386)		
Mahoning County	D	330 799-1581
Youngstown (G-20261)		
Manufacturing Services Intl	E	937 299-9922
Dayton (G-9697)		
Matrix Research Inc	E	937 427-8433
Beavercreek (G-1190)		
Metcalf & Eddy Inc	E	216 910-2000
Cleveland (G-6033)		
Micro Industries Corporation	D	740 548-7878
Westerville (G-19424)		
Mistras Group Inc	E	419 836-5904
Millbury (G-14580)		
Mistras Group Inc	D	330 244-1541
North Canton (G-15356)		
Modal Shop Inc	E	513 351-9919
Cincinnati (G-4111)		
Moody-Nolan Inc	C	614 461-4664
Columbus (G-8187)		
Muskingum County Ohio	E	740 453-0381
Zanesville (G-20508)		
Natural Resources Ohio Dept	E	614 265-6948
Columbus (G-8249)		
Neteam Systems LLC	E	330 523-5100
Cleveland (G-6121)		
New Path International LLC	E	614 410-3974
Powell (G-16344)		
Northrop Grumman Technical	C	937 320-3100
Beavercreek Township (G-1276)		
Ohio Blow Pipe Company	E	216 081-7379
Cleveland (G-6186)		
Ohio Structures Inc	E	330 533-0084
Canfield (G-2206)		
Optimetrics Inc	E	937 306-7180
Beavercreek Township (G-1278)		
Peco II Inc	D	614 431-0694
Columbus (G-8528)		
Pmwi LLC	E	614 975-5004
Hilliard (G-11943)		
Polaris Automation Inc	D	614 431-0170
Lewis Center (G-12704)		
Providence Rees Inc	E	614 833-6231
Columbus (G-8573)		
Racaza International LLC	E	614 973-9266
Dublin (G-10436)		
RAD-Con Inc	E	440 871-5720
Lakewood (G-12496)		
RCT Engineering Inc	E	561 684-7534
Beachwood (G-1118)		
Reed Westlake Leskosky Ltd	D	216 522-0449
Cleveland (G-6365)		
Safran Power Usa LLC	C	330 487-2000
Twinsburg (G-18466)		
Seifert & Group Inc	D	330 833-2700
Massillon (G-13852)		
Sgi Matrix LLC	D	937 438-9033
Miamisburg (G-14349)		
Sgt Inc	B	216 433-3982
Cleveland (G-6473)		
Slick Automated Solutions Inc	E	567 247-1080
Ontario (G-15714)		
Society Plastics Engineers Inc	C	419 287-4898
Pemberville (G-15944)		
Stantec Arch & Engrg PC	E	216 454-2150
Cleveland (G-6524)		
Stantec Arch & Engrg PC	E	614 486-4383
Columbus (G-8773)		
Stantec Architecture Inc	E	216 454-2150
Cleveland (G-6525)		
Stantec Consulting Svcs Inc	E	614 210-2000
Dublin (G-10463)		
Stantec Consulting Svcs Inc	E	216 621-2407
Cleveland (G-6527)		
Stantec Consulting Svcs Inc	E	216 454-2150
Cleveland (G-6526)		
Stantec Consulting Svcs Inc	E	513 842-8200
Cincinnati (G-4583)		
Stantec Consulting Svcs Inc	C	614 486-4383
Columbus (G-8774)		
Sumitomo Elc Wirg Systems Inc	E	937 642-7579
Marysville (G-13654)		
Sunpower Inc	D	740 594-2221
Athens (G-813)		
Superior Mechanical Svcs Inc	E	937 259-0082
Dayton (G-9284)		
Technical Assurance Inc	E	440 953-3147
Willoughby (G-19717)		
Technical Consultants Inc	E	513 521-2696
Cincinnati (G-4629)		
Telecom Expertise Inds Inc	D	937 548-5254
Greenville (G-11521)		
Thermal Treatment Center Inc	E	216 881-8100
Cleveland (G-6591)		
Thinkpath Engineering Svcs LLC	D	937 291-8374
Miamisburg (G-14358)		
Transcore Its LLC	E	440 243-2222
Cleveland (G-6610)		
Trumbull County Engineering	D	330 675-2640
Warren (G-18910)		
Tsi Inc	E	419 468-1855
Galion (G-11307)		
Turnkey Network Solutions LLC	E	614 876-9944
Columbus (G-8880)		
U S Army Corps of Engineers	D	740 269-2681
Uhrichsville (G-18493)		
U S Army Corps of Engineers	D	740 767-3527
Glouster (G-11436)		
U S Army Corps of Engineers	D	513 684-3048
Cincinnati (G-4714)		
Universal Technology Corp	D	937 426-2808
Beavercreek (G-1216)		
University of Akron	D	330 972-6008
Akron (G-488)		
University of Cincinnati	E	513 556-3732
Cincinnati (G-4770)		
URS Group Inc	D	216 622-2300
Cleveland (G-6675)		
URS Group Inc	C	614 464-4500
Columbus (G-8921)		
URS Group Inc	D	513 651-3440
Cincinnati (G-4791)		
URS-Smith Group VA Idiq Joint	E	614 464-4500
Columbus (G-8922)		
US Tech Arospc Engrg Corp	D	330 455-1181
Canton (G-2574)		
Usaf Sctt	E	937 257-0228
Dayton (G-9289)		
Varo Engineers Inc	D	513 729-9313
West Chester (G-19178)		
Wastren Advantage Inc	E	970 254-1277
Piketon (G-16132)		
Wilkris Company	E	513 271-9344
Terrace Park (G-17663)		

ENGINEERING SVCS: Acoustical

Company	Code	Phone
L&T Technology Services Ltd	E	732 688-4402
Dublin (G-10384)		

Employee Codes: A=Over 500 employees, B=251-500
C=101-250, D=51-100, E=25-50

ENGINEERING SVCS: Acoustical

Straight 72 Inc .... D 740 943-5730
  Marysville *(G-13652)*

ENGINEERING SVCS: Aviation Or Aeronautical

Boeing Company .... B 937 431-3503
  Wright Patterson Afb *(G-20012)*
GE Aviation Systems LLC .... B 937 898-5881
  Vandalia *(G-18681)*
Honeywell International Inc .... D 937 484-2261
  Urbana *(G-18591)*
Jacobs Technology Inc .... E 937 429-5056
  Beavercreek Township *(G-1271)*
Lockheed Martin Corporation .... C 937 429-0100
  Beavercreek *(G-1188)*
Optis Solutions .... E 513 948-2070
  Cincinnati *(G-4230)*
Quest Global Services-Na Inc .... D 513 648-4900
  Cincinnati *(G-4376)*
Reps Resource LLC .... E 513 874-0500
  West Chester *(G-19138)*
Vantage Partners LLC .... E 216 925-1302
  Brookpark *(G-1957)*

ENGINEERING SVCS: Civil

Barr Engineering Incorporated .... E 614 714-0299
  Columbus *(G-7091)*
Bayer & Becker Inc .... E 513 492-7401
  Mason *(G-13667)*
Bramhall Engrg & Surveying Co .... E 440 934-7878
  Avon *(G-881)*
Brumbaugh Engrg Surveying LLC .... E 937 698-3000
  West Milton *(G-19268)*
Ceso Inc .... D 937 435-8584
  Miamisburg *(G-14281)*
County Engineering Office .... E 419 334-9731
  Fremont *(G-11189)*
County of Hamilton .... D 513 946-4250
  Cincinnati *(G-3430)*
CT Consultants Inc .... C 440 951-9000
  Mentor *(G-14166)*
Design Homes & Development Co .... E 937 438-3667
  Dayton *(G-9499)*
Dj Neff Enterpeises Inc .... E 440 884-3100
  Cleveland *(G-5494)*
Dynamix Engineering Ltd .... D 614 443-1178
  Columbus *(G-7557)*
Dynotec Inc .... E 614 880-7320
  Columbus *(G-7558)*
E P Ferris & Associates Inc .... E 614 299-2999
  Columbus *(G-7560)*
Engineering Associates Inc .... E 330 345-6556
  Wooster *(G-19862)*
Euthenics Inc .... E 440 260-1555
  Strongsville *(G-17462)*
Feller Finch & Associates Inc .... E 419 893-3680
  Maumee *(G-13916)*
Hockaden & Associates Inc .... E 614 252-0993
  Columbus *(G-7843)*
Jack A Hamilton & Assoc Inc .... E 740 968-4947
  Flushing *(G-11105)*
Johnson Mirmiran Thompson Inc .... D 614 714-0270
  Blue Ash *(G-1620)*
Johnson Mirmiran Thompson Inc .... D 614 714-0270
  Cleveland *(G-5869)*
KS Associates Inc .... D 440 365-4730
  Elyria *(G-10639)*
Land Design Consultants .... E 440 255-8463
  Mentor *(G-14207)*
Michael Baker Intl Inc .... C 330 453-3110
  Canton *(G-2461)*
Michael Baker Intl Inc .... E 412 269-6300
  Cleveland *(G-6046)*
Northast Ohio Rgonal Sewer Dst .... D 216 961-2187
  Cleveland *(G-6146)*
Pollock Research & Design Inc .... E 330 332-3300
  Salem *(G-16706)*
Prime Ae Group Inc .... D 614 839-0250
  Columbus *(G-6902)*
Ra Consultants LLC .... E 513 469-6600
  Blue Ash *(G-1671)*
Richard L Bowen & Assoc Inc .... D 216 491-9300
  Cleveland *(G-6391)*
Sands Decker Cps Llc .... E 614 459-6992
  Columbus *(G-8684)*
Schomer Glaus Pyle .... E 216 518-5544
  Cleveland *(G-6449)*
T J Neff Holdings Inc .... E 440 884-3100
  Cleveland *(G-6564)*

Thelen Associates Inc .... E 513 825-4350
  Cincinnati *(G-4648)*
Wade Trim .... E 216 363-0300
  Cleveland *(G-6716)*
Woolpert Inc .... E 614 476-6000
  Columbus *(G-9005)*

ENGINEERING SVCS: Construction & Civil

Alstom Grid LLC .... D 330 688-4061
  Stow *(G-17352)*
Intren Inc .... D 815 482-0651
  Cincinnati *(G-3841)*
Johnson Mirmiran Thompson Inc .... D 614 714-0270
  Columbus *(G-7944)*
L R G Inc .... E 937 890-0510
  Dayton *(G-9668)*
LEWaro-D&j-A Joint Venture Co .... E 937 443-0000
  Dayton *(G-9678)*

ENGINEERING SVCS: Electrical Or Electronic

Acpi Systems Inc .... E 513 738-3840
  Cincinnati *(G-2968)*
Camgen Ltd .... E 330 204-8636
  Canal Winchester *(G-2154)*
Denmark Consultants Inc .... E 513 530-9984
  Blue Ash *(G-1576)*
Electrol Systems Inc .... E 513 942-7777
  Cincinnati *(G-3548)*
Electrovations Inc .... E 330 274-3558
  Aurora *(G-837)*
High Voltage Maintenance Corp .... E 937 278-0811
  Dayton *(G-9611)*
I T E LLC .... D 513 576-6200
  Loveland *(G-13132)*
Karpinski Engineering Inc .... D 216 391-3700
  Cleveland *(G-5886)*
L-3 Cmmncations Nova Engrg Inc .... C 877 282-1168
  Mason *(G-13730)*
Mid-Ohio Electric Co .... E 614 274-8000
  Columbus *(G-8165)*
Nu Waves Ltd .... E 513 360-0800
  Middletown *(G-14444)*
Peters Tschantz & Assoc Inc .... E 330 666-3702
  Akron *(G-388)*
Phantom Technical Services Inc .... E 614 868-9920
  Columbus *(G-8541)*
PMC Systems Limited .... E 330 538-2268
  North Jackson *(G-15386)*
Pyramid Control Systems Inc .... E 513 679-7400
  Cincinnati *(G-4357)*
Stock Fairfield Corporation .... C 440 543-6000
  Chagrin Falls *(G-2735)*
Thermaltech Engineering Inc .... E 513 561-2271
  Cincinnati *(G-4649)*
TL Industries Inc .... C 419 666-8144
  Northwood *(G-15547)*

ENGINEERING SVCS: Fire Protection

Cgh-Global Emerg Mngmt Strateg .... E 800 376-0655
  Cincinnati *(G-2905)*

ENGINEERING SVCS: Heating & Ventilation

Cetek Ltd .... E 216 362-3900
  Cleveland *(G-5220)*

ENGINEERING SVCS: Industrial

Crowne Group LLC .... D 216 589-0198
  Cleveland *(G-5440)*
HJ Ford Associates Inc .... C 937 429-9711
  Beavercreek *(G-1176)*
Industrial Origami Inc .... E 440 260-0000
  Cleveland *(G-5817)*
Jedson Engineering Inc .... D 513 965-5999
  Cincinnati *(G-3865)*
Los Alamos Technical Assoc Inc .... E 614 508-1200
  Westerville *(G-19420)*
Production Design Services Inc .... D 937 866-3377
  Dayton *(G-9832)*
Schneider Elc Systems USA Inc .... E 440 234-3900
  Cleveland *(G-6448)*
Technology House Ltd .... E 440 248-3025
  Streetsboro *(G-17434)*

ENGINEERING SVCS: Machine Tool Design

Hardy Diagnostics .... D 937 550-2768
  Springboro *(G-17121)*

Invotec Engineering Inc .... D 937 886-3232
  Miamisburg *(G-14307)*
Youngstown Plastic Tooling .... E 330 782-7222
  Youngstown *(G-20434)*

ENGINEERING SVCS: Mechanical

Chipmatic Tool & Machine Inc .... D 419 862-2737
  Elmore *(G-10587)*
Dillin Engineered Systems Corp .... E 419 666-6789
  Perrysburg *(G-15998)*
Jdrm Engineering Inc .... E 419 824-2400
  Sylvania *(G-17595)*
Karpinski Engineering Inc .... E 614 430-9820
  Columbus *(G-6891)*
Mechanical Support Svcs Inc .... E 614 777-8808
  Hilliard *(G-11927)*
Morris Technologies Inc .... C 513 733-1611
  Cincinnati *(G-4119)*
R E Warner & Associates Inc .... D 440 835-9400
  Westlake *(G-19537)*
Saec/Kinetic Vision Inc .... C 513 793-4959
  Cincinnati *(G-4467)*
Shotstop Ballistics LLC .... E 330 686-0020
  Stow *(G-17392)*
Techsolve Inc .... D 513 948-2000
  Cincinnati *(G-4631)*
TSS Technologies Inc .... B 513 772-7000
  West Chester *(G-19166)*
Twism Enterprises LLC .... E 513 800-1098
  Cincinnati *(G-4711)*

ENGINEERING SVCS: Mining

Kucera International Inc .... D 440 975-4230
  Willoughby *(G-19678)*

ENGINEERING SVCS: Pollution Control

Neundorfer Inc .... E 440 942-8990
  Willoughby *(G-19697)*

ENGINEERING SVCS: Professional

Brown and Caldwell .... E 614 410-6144
  Dublin *(G-10270)*
Capano & Associates LLC .... E 513 403-6000
  Liberty Township *(G-12717)*
Eaton-Aeroquip Llc .... D 419 891-7775
  Maumee *(G-13907)*
Ms Consultants Inc .... E 216 522-1926
  Cleveland *(G-6086)*
Poggemeyer Design Group Inc .... C 419 244-8074
  Bowling Green *(G-1791)*
Premier Integration .... E 330 545-8690
  Girard *(G-11424)*
Primatech Inc .... E 614 841-9800
  Columbus *(G-8560)*
Strand Associates Inc .... E 513 861-5600
  Cincinnati *(G-4594)*
Thorson Baker & Assoc Inc .... C 330 659-6688
  Richfield *(G-16530)*
URS Group Inc .... D 330 836-9111
  Akron *(G-490)*
Wheaton & Sprague Engineering .... E 330 923-5560
  Stow *(G-17400)*

ENGINEERING SVCS: Sanitary

Aecom Technical Services Inc .... E 937 233-1898
  Batavia *(G-994)*
Arcadis US Inc .... D 330 434-1995
  Akron *(G-80)*
Atc Group Services LLC .... D 513 771-2112
  Cincinnati *(G-3056)*
Johnson Mirmiran Thompson Inc .... D 614 714-0270
  Columbus *(G-7945)*
Macdonald Mott LLC .... E 216 535-3640
  Cleveland *(G-5963)*
Medina County Sanitary .... E 330 273-3610
  Medina *(G-14098)*

ENGINEERING SVCS: Structural

County of Hancock .... E 419 422-7433
  Findlay *(G-11018)*
Emersion Design LLC .... E 513 841-9100
  Cincinnati *(G-3553)*
Ssoe Inc .... E 330 821-7198
  Alliance *(G-560)*
Steven Schaefer Associates Inc .... D 513 542-3300
  Cincinnati *(G-4593)*

SERVICES SECTION

Technical Construction Spc .... E 330 929-1088
Cuyahoga Falls *(G-9224)*
Thp Limited Inc .... D 513 241-3222
Cincinnati *(G-4658)*

ENGINES: Internal Combustion, NEC

Cummins Bridgeway Columbus LLC .... D 614 771-1000
Hilliard *(G-11893)*
Cummins Inc .... E 614 771-1000
Hilliard *(G-11894)*
Western Branch Diesel Inc .... E 330 454-8800
Canton *(G-2585)*

ENGRAVING SVCS

Things Remembered Inc .... C 440 473-2000
Highland Heights *(G-11872)*

ENTERTAINERS

Dayton Metro Chapter .... E 937 294-0192
Dayton *(G-9482)*

ENTERTAINERS & ENTERTAINMENT GROUPS

Adventure Cmbat Operations LLC .... E 330 818-1029
Canton *(G-2228)*
Bird Enterprises LLC .... E 330 674-1457
Millersburg *(G-14589)*
Catholic Diocese of Columbus .... D 614 276-5263
Columbus *(G-7210)*
Columbus Association For The P .... D 614 469-0939
Columbus *(G-7332)*
Henrys King Touring Company .... E 330 628-1886
Mogadore *(G-14678)*
Ingram Entrmt Holdings Inc .... E 419 662-3132
Perrysburg *(G-16017)*
J S P A Inc .... E 407 957-6664
Columbus *(G-7932)*
Muskingum Vly Symphonic Winds .... E 740 826-8095
New Concord *(G-15035)*
Northeast Ohio Dukes .... E 330 360-0968
Warren *(G-18889)*
Nulife Music Group .... E 216 870-3720
Cleveland *(G-6171)*
Philo Band Boosters .... E 740 221-3023
Zanesville *(G-20525)*
Radio Seaway Inc .... E 216 916-6100
Cleveland *(G-6343)*

ENTERTAINMENT PROMOTION SVCS

Playhouse Square Foundation .... B 216 771-4444
Cleveland *(G-6286)*
Theatre Management Corporation .... E 513 723-1180
Cincinnati *(G-4647)*

ENTERTAINMENT SVCS

A To Z Golf Managment Co .... E 937 434-4911
Dayton *(G-9299)*
Cincinnati Circus Company LLC .... D 513 921-5454
Cincinnati *(G-3292)*
Club Life Entertainment LLC .... E 216 831-1134
Beachwood *(G-1066)*
Etc Gameco LLC .... D 614 428-7529
Columbus *(G-7615)*
Food Concepts Intl Inc .... D 513 336-7449
Mason *(G-13701)*
Fountain Square MGT Group LLC .... E 513 621-4400
Cincinnati *(G-3642)*
Rcwc Col Inc .... E 614 564-9344
Columbus *(G-8592)*
Run Jump-N-Play .... E 513 701-7529
Blue Ash *(G-1685)*
Zink Calls .... E 419 732-6171
Port Clinton *(G-16259)*

ENVELOPES

Ampac Holdings LLC .... A 513 671-1777
Cincinnati *(G-3017)*
Envelope Mart of Ohio Inc .... E 440 365-8177
Elyria *(G-10628)*
Pac Worldwide Corporation .... D 800 610-9367
Middletown *(G-14448)*
Western States Envelope Co .... D 419 666-7480
Walbridge *(G-18780)*

ENVELOPES WHOLESALERS

EMI Enterprises Inc .... E 419 666-0012
Northwood *(G-15530)*
Envelope Mart of North E Ohio .... E 440 322-8862
Elyria *(G-10627)*
Envelope Mart of Ohio Inc .... E 440 365-8177
Elyria *(G-10628)*
Pac Worldwide Corporation .... D 800 610-9367
Middletown *(G-14448)*
Western States Envelope Co .... D 419 666-7480
Walbridge *(G-18780)*

ENVIRON QUALITY PROGS ADMIN, GOVT: Sanitary Engineering

Mahoning County .... E 330 793-5514
Youngstown *(G-20260)*

ENVIRON QUALITY PROGS ADMIN, GOVT: Water Control & Quality

City of Lakewood .... E 216 252-4322
Cleveland *(G-5265)*

ENVIRONMENTAL QUALITY PROGS ADMIN, GOVT: Recreational

City of Cleveland .... E 216 621-4231
Cleveland *(G-5253)*
County of Hancock .... E 419 425-7275
Findlay *(G-11019)*

ENVIRONMENTAL QUALITY PROGS ADMIN, GOVT: Waste Mgmt

Poggemeyer Design Group Inc .... E 419 748-7438
Mc Clure *(G-14020)*

ENZYMES

Mp Biomedicals LLC .... C 440 337-1200
Solon *(G-17029)*

EQUIPMENT & VEHICLE FINANCE LEASING COMPANIES

PNC Equipment Finance LLC .... D 513 421-9191
Cincinnati *(G-4310)*
Summit Funding Group Inc .... D 513 489-1222
Mason *(G-13765)*

EQUIPMENT: Rental & Leasing, NEC

All Erection & Crane Rental .... C 216 524-6550
Cleveland *(G-4986)*
All Erection & Crane Rental .... D 216 524-6550
Cleveland *(G-4987)*
All Temp Refrigeration Inc .... E 419 692-5016
Delphos *(G-10137)*
Ayrshire Inc .... D 440 992-0743
Ashtabula *(G-728)*
Baker Equipment and Mtls Ltd .... E 513 422-6697
Monroe *(G-14689)*
Baker Vehicle Systems Inc .... E 330 467-2250
Macedonia *(G-13189)*
Budco Group Inc .... E 513 621-6111
Cincinnati *(G-3146)*
Budget Dumpster LLC .... E 866 284-6164
Westlake *(G-19468)*
De Nora Tech LLC .... D 440 710-5300
Painesville *(G-15850)*
Easton Sales and Rental LLC .... E 440 708-0099
Chagrin Falls *(G-2714)*
Elliott Tool Technologies Ltd .... D 937 253-6133
Dayton *(G-9524)*
Fifth Third Equipment Fin Co .... E 800 972-3030
Cincinnati *(G-3609)*
Filing Scale Company Inc .... E 330 425-3092
Twinsburg *(G-18415)*
Garda CL Great Lakes Inc .... B 561 939-7000
Columbus *(G-7727)*
Gordon Brothers Inc .... E 800 331-7611
Salem *(G-16697)*
Great Lakes Crushing Ltd .... E 440 944-5500
Wickliffe *(G-19599)*
Independence Equipment Lsg Co .... E 216 642-3408
Cleveland *(G-5811)*
J Way Leasing Ltd .... E 440 934-1020
Avon *(G-899)*

EXPLOSIVES, EXC AMMO & FIREWORKS WHOLESALERS

JBK Group Inc .... E 216 901-0000
Cleveland *(G-5854)*
M & L Leasing Co .... E 330 343-8910
Mineral City *(G-14633)*
Mapleview Farms Inc .... E 419 826-3671
Swanton *(G-17567)*
MH Logistics Corp .... E 330 425-2476
Hudson *(G-12134)*
Miami Industrial Trucks Inc .... D 937 293-4194
Moraine *(G-14805)*
Millers Rental and Sls Co Inc .... E 216 642-1447
Cleveland *(G-6067)*
Mitel (delaware) Inc .... E 513 733-8000
West Chester *(G-19122)*
Ohio Machinery Co .... C 419 874-7975
Perrysburg *(G-16036)*
Piqua Steel Co .... D 937 773-3632
Piqua *(G-16159)*
Rent-N-Roll .... D 513 528-6929
Cincinnati *(G-4406)*
Rumpke Waste Inc .... C 937 548-1939
Greenville *(G-11517)*
S and R Leasing .... E 330 276-3061
Millersburg *(G-14620)*
Safety-Kleen Systems Inc .... E 440 992-8665
Ashtabula *(G-761)*
Sunbelt Rentals Inc .... E 216 362-0300
Cleveland *(G-6549)*
Thomas Do-It Center Inc .... E 740 446-2002
Gallipolis *(G-11339)*
Towlift Inc .... C 216 749-6800
Brooklyn Heights *(G-1929)*
U Haul Co of Northwestern Ohio .... E 419 478-1101
Toledo *(G-18266)*
United Rentals North Amer Inc .... E 800 877-3687
Perrysburg *(G-16067)*
Valley Industrial Trucks Inc .... E 330 788-4081
Youngstown *(G-20402)*
Vincent Ltg Systems Co Inc .... E 216 475-7600
Solon *(G-17065)*
Winner Aviation Corporation .... D 330 856-5000
Vienna *(G-18742)*
Yockey Group Inc .... E 513 899-2188
Morrow *(G-14849)*

ETCHING SVC: Metal

Woodrow Manufacturing Co .... E 937 399-9333
Springfield *(G-17300)*

EXCAVATING MACHINERY & EQPT WHOLESALERS

Fabco Inc .... D 419 427-0872
Findlay *(G-11022)*

EXECUTIVE OFFICES: Federal, State & Local

City of Euclid .... E 216 289-2800
Cleveland *(G-5260)*
City of Kent .... D 330 678-8105
Kent *(G-12359)*

EXHIBITORS, ITINERANT, MOTION PICTURE

AMC Entertainment Inc .... E 614 429-0100
Columbus *(G-6984)*
American Multi-Cinema Inc .... D 614 801-9130
Grove City *(G-11530)*
American Multi-Cinema Inc .... E 614 889-0580
Dublin *(G-10250)*
B and D Investment Partnership .... E 937 233-6698
Dayton *(G-9348)*
Carmike Cinemas Inc .... E 740 264-1680
Steubenville *(G-17306)*
Danbarry Linemas Inc .... E 740 779-6115
Chillicothe *(G-2833)*

EXPLOSIVES

Viking Explosives LLC .... E 218 263-8845
Cleveland *(G-6696)*

EXPLOSIVES, EXC AMMO & FIREWORKS WHOLESALERS

D W Dickey and Son Inc .... E 330 424-1441
Lisbon *(G-12935)*
Viking Explosives LLC .... E 218 263-8845
Cleveland *(G-6696)*
Wampum Hardware Co .... E 419 273-2542
Forest *(G-11107)*

Employee Codes: A=Over 500 employees, B=251-500
C=101-250, D=51-100, E=25-50

EXTENDED CARE FACILITY | SERVICES SECTION

EXTENDED CARE FACILITY

Company	Ph	Phone
Arlington Court Nursing Upper Arlington (G-18547)	C	614 545-5502
Broadview Nursing Home Inc Parma (G-15900)	C	216 661-5084
Brookdale Snior Lving Cmmnties Austintown (G-868)	E	330 249-1071
Chillicothe Long Term Care Chillicothe (G-2821)	C	740 773-6161
Country Pointe Skilled Nursing Wooster (G-19853)	E	330 264-7881
Crestview Manor Nursing Home Lancaster (G-12524)	C	740 654-2634
Crestview Manor Nursing Home Lancaster (G-12525)	C	740 654-2634
Ezra Health Care Inc Beachwood (G-1078)	C	440 498-3000
Franklin Boulevard Nursing Hm Cleveland (G-5633)	C	216 651-1600
Golden Years Nursing Home Inc Hamilton (G-11732)	E	513 893-0471
Governors Village LLC Cleveland (G-5682)	E	440 449-8788
Havar Inc Marietta (G-13451)	E	740 373-7175
Hcf of Briarwood Inc Coldwater (G-6829)	B	419 678-2311
Hcr Manorcare Med Svcs Fla LLC Cincinnati (G-3746)	E	513 745-9600
Heritage Park Rehabilita New Paris (G-15078)	E	937 437-2311
House of Loreto Canton (G-2405)	D	330 453-8137
Lakewood Health Care Center Lakewood (G-12490)	C	216 226-3103
Liberty Nursing Home Inc Xenia (G-20067)	D	937 376-2121
Madison Care Inc Madison (G-13230)	D	440 428-1492
Manor Care Inc Toledo (G-18028)	D	419 252-5500
Manor Care of America Inc Chagrin Falls (G-2724)	D	440 543-6766
McKinley Life Care Center LLC Canton (G-2455)	D	330 456-1014
Meigs Center Ltd Middleport (G-14407)	C	740 992-6472
Minerva Elder Care Inc Minerva (G-14648)	E	330 868-4147
Ridge Pleasant Valley Inc Cleveland (G-6395)	C	440 845-0200
Rolling Hlls Rhab Wellness Ctr Brunswick (G-1989)	C	330 225-9121
Ruffing Care Inc Tiffin (G-17696)	D	419 447-4662
Sisters of Charity of Cinc Mount Saint Joseph (G-14872)	C	513 347-5436
Springview Manor Nursing Home Lima (G-12883)	E	419 227-3661
Tri County Extended Care Ctr Fairfield (G-10917)	C	513 829-3555
Weber Health Care Center Inc Wellington (G-18996)	C	440 647-2088
West Park Retirement Community Cincinnati (G-4836)	C	513 451-8900

EXTERMINATING & FUMIGATING SVCS

Company	Ph	Phone
Orkin LLC Columbus (G-8481)	E	614 888-5811
Steve Shaffer Columbus (G-8787)	E	614 276-6355

EYEGLASSES

Company	Ph	Phone
Essilor Laboratories Amer Inc Columbus (G-7613)	E	614 274-0840
Toledo Optical Laboratory Inc Toledo (G-18246)	D	419 248-3384

FABRICS: Broadwoven, Synthetic Manmade Fiber & Silk

Company	Ph	Phone
Owens Corning Sales LLC Granville (G-11471)	B	740 587-3562

FABRICS: Metallized

Company	Ph	Phone
Laserflex Corporation Hilliard (G-11920)	D	614 850-9600

FABRICS: Trimmings

Company	Ph	Phone
Bates Metal Products Inc Port Washington (G-16260)	D	740 498-8371
Brown Cnty Bd Mntal Rtardation Georgetown (G-11384)	E	937 378-4891
Fedex Office & Print Svcs Inc Westerville (G-19400)	E	614 898-0000
General Theming Contrs LLC Columbus (G-7736)	C	614 252-6342
Hunt Products Inc Newburgh Heights (G-15252)	E	440 667-2457
Screen Works Inc Dayton (G-9870)	E	937 264-9111
Tendon Manufacturing Inc Cleveland (G-6582)	E	216 663-3200
Woodrow Manufacturing Co Springfield (G-17300)	E	937 399-9333

FABRICS: Woven, Narrow Cotton, Wool, Silk

Company	Ph	Phone
Keuchel & Associates Inc Cuyahoga Falls (G-9202)	E	330 945-9455
Samsel Rope & Marine Supply Co Cleveland (G-6442)	E	216 241-0333

FACIAL SALONS

Company	Ph	Phone
Phyllis At Madison Cincinnati (G-4295)	E	513 321-1300

FACILITIES SUPPORT SVCS

Company	Ph	Phone
Aramark Facility Services LLC Cleveland (G-5057)	E	216 687-5000
Cuyahoga County Convention Fac Cleveland (G-5455)	D	216 928-1600
Emcor Facilities Services Inc Cincinnati (G-3552)	D	888 846-9462
Facilitysource LLC Columbus (G-7627)	B	614 318-1700
Firstgroup America Inc Cincinnati (G-3626)	D	513 241-2200
Franklin Cnty Bd Commissioners Columbus (G-7684)	C	614 462-3800
Independence of Portage County Ravenna (G-16390)	C	330 296-2851
L B & B Associates Inc Cleveland (G-5913)	E	216 451-2672
MPW Industrial Svcs Group Inc Hebron (G-11855)	D	740 927-8790
North Bay Construction Inc Westlake (G-19522)	E	440 835-1898
Selecttech Services Corp Centerville (G-2685)	C	937 438-9905
Space Management Inc Dayton (G-9894)	E	937 254-6622
Technical Assurance Inc Willoughby (G-19717)	E	440 953-3147
Wastren - Energx Mission Piketon (G-16131)	C	740 897-3724
Wastren Advantage Inc Piketon (G-16132)	E	970 254-1277

FACILITY RENTAL & PARTY PLANNING SVCS

Company	Ph	Phone
Black Tie Affair Inc Wooster (G-19832)	E	330 345-8333
Camargo Rental Center Inc Cincinnati (G-3170)	E	513 271-6510
Fun Day Events LLC Gahanna (G-11242)	E	740 549-9000
Goldfish Swim School Chagrin Falls (G-2718)	E	216 364-9090
Kiddie Party Company LLC Mayfield Heights (G-14003)	E	440 273-7680
Lazer Kraze Galena (G-11286)	E	513 339-1030

FAMILY COUNSELING SVCS

Company	Ph	Phone
Allwell Behavioral Health Svcs Cambridge (G-2094)	E	740 439-4428
Cambridge Counseling Center Zanesville (G-20454)	C	740 450-7790
Center For Families & Children Cleveland (G-5207)	E	216 252-5800
Cincinnati Ctr/Psychoanalysis Cincinnati (G-3296)	E	513 961-8484
Consolidated Care Inc West Liberty (G-19261)	E	937 465-8065
Consolidated Care Inc West Liberty (G-19262)	E	937 465-8065
County of Paulding Paulding (G-15930)	E	419 399-3636
Develpmntal Dsblties Ohio Dept Batavia (G-1010)	C	513 732-9200
Emerge Counseling Service Akron (G-207)	E	330 865-8351
Frs Counseling Inc Hillsboro (G-11975)	E	937 393-0585
Oneeighty Inc Wooster (G-19900)	D	330 263-6021
Southast Cmnty Mental Hlth Ctr Columbus (G-8752)	E	614 444-0800
Summit Cnty Dept Job Fmly Svcs Akron (G-465)	D	330 643-8200
Westark Family Services Inc Massillon (G-13860)	E	330 832-5043

FAMILY OR MARRIAGE COUNSELING

Company	Ph	Phone
Compass Family and Cmnty Svcs Youngstown (G-20153)	E	330 743-9275
Compass Family and Cmnty Svcs Youngstown (G-20154)	D	330 743-9275
Trillium Family Solutions Inc Cuyahoga Falls (G-9227)	D	330 454-7066

FAMILY PLANNING CENTERS

Company	Ph	Phone
Noble Cnty Nble Cnty Cmmsoners Caldwell (G-2088)	E	740 732-4958

FAMILY PLANNING CLINIC

Company	Ph	Phone
Family Planning Center Cambridge (G-2112)	E	740 439-3340
Family Plnning Assoc of Ne Painesville (G-15856)	E	440 352-0608
Fulton County Health Dept Wauseon (G-18956)	E	419 337-6979
Planned Parenthood Association Dayton (G-9811)	E	937 226-0780
Planned Parenthood NW Ohio Inc Toledo (G-18128)	E	419 255-1115
Planned Parenthood of SW OH Cincinnati (G-4302)	E	513 721-7635
Planned Prenthood Greater Ohio Columbus (G-8549)	E	614 224-2235
Planned Prenthood Greater Ohio Akron (G-391)	E	330 535-2671
Planned Prenthood Greater Ohio Bedford Heights (G-1356)	E	216 961-8804
Planned Prenthood Greater Ohio Youngstown (G-20322)	E	330 788-2487

FAMILY SVCS AGENCY

Company	Ph	Phone
Catholic Social Svc Miami Vly Dayton (G-9390)	E	937 223-7217
Commquest Services Inc Canton (G-2316)	C	330 455-0374
Community Action Comm Pike CNT Piketon (G-16112)	C	740 289-2371
Community Action Comm Pike CNT Portsmouth (G-16272)	E	740 961-4011
Community Action Comm Pike CNT Jackson (G-12310)	E	740 286-2826
Community Action Commission Sandusky (G-16745)	D	419 626-6540
County of Geauga Chardon (G-2746)	D	440 564-2246
Couple To Couple Leag Intl Inc Cincinnati (G-3434)	E	513 471-2000
Goodrich Gnnett Nghborhood Ctr Cleveland (G-5678)	E	216 432-1717
Greenleaf Family Center Akron (G-247)	E	330 376-9494
Jewish Family Service of The C Cincinnati (G-3869)	E	513 469-1188
Jewish Family Services Associa Cleveland (G-5863)	E	216 292-3999
Lifespan Incorporated Hamilton (G-11754)	D	513 868-3210
New Horizon Youth Family Ctr Lancaster (G-12560)	E	740 687-0835
Salvation Army Dayton (G-9863)	E	937 528-5100

SERVICES SECTION

FARM & GARDEN MACHINERY WHOLESALERS

Bzak Landscaping Inc ....E 513 831-0907
  Milford *(G-14508)*
Fackler Country Gardens Inc ....E 740 522-3128
  Granville *(G-11465)*
Gardner-Connell LLC ....E 614 456-4000
  Columbus *(G-7729)*
Hull Bros Inc ....E 419 375-2827
  Fort Recovery *(G-11118)*
Krystowski Tractor Sales Inc ....E 440 647-2015
  Wellington *(G-18993)*
Pax Steel Products Inc ....E 419 678-1481
  Coldwater *(G-6834)*
Schmidt Machine Company ....E 419 294-3814
  Upper Sandusky *(G-18566)*
Streacker Tractor Sales Inc ....E 419 422-6973
  Findlay *(G-11087)*
Western Tradewinds Inc ....E 937 859-4300
  Miamisburg *(G-14368)*

FARM MACHINERY REPAIR SVCS

Apple Farm Service Inc ....E 937 526-4851
  Covington *(G-9135)*
Cope Farm Equipment Inc ....E 330 821-5867
  Alliance *(G-536)*
Witmers Inc ....E 330 427-2147
  Salem *(G-16719)*

FARM PRDTS, RAW MATERIAL, WHOLESALE: Tobacco & Tobacco Prdts

Altria Group Distribution Co ....C 804 274-2000
  Mason *(G-13660)*

FARM PRDTS, RAW MATERIALS, WHOLESALE: Farm Animals

Hills Supply Inc ....E 740 477-8994
  Circleville *(G-4890)*

FARM PRDTS, RAW MATERIALS, WHOLESALE: Hides

Inland Products Inc ....E 614 443-3425
  Columbus *(G-7899)*

FARM SPLY STORES

Centerra Co-Op ....E 419 281-2153
  Ashland *(G-672)*

FARM SPLYS WHOLESALERS

A M Leonard Inc ....D 937 773-2694
  Piqua *(G-16133)*
Alabama Farmers Coop Inc ....E 419 655-2289
  Cygnet *(G-9238)*
Andersons Inc ....C 419 893-5050
  Maumee *(G-13879)*
Archbold Elevator Inc ....E 419 445-2451
  Archbold *(G-632)*
Centerra Co-Op ....E 800 362-9598
  Jefferson *(G-12331)*
Champaign Landmark Inc ....E 937 652-2135
  Urbana *(G-18577)*
Gardner-Connell LLC ....E 614 456-4000
  Columbus *(G-7729)*
Jiffy Products America Inc ....E 440 282-2818
  Lorain *(G-13043)*
Phillips Ready Mix Co ....D 937 426-5151
  Beavercreek Township *(G-1281)*
Sunrise Cooperative Inc ....B 937 575-6780
  Piqua *(G-16167)*
Trupointe Cooperative Inc ....B 937 575-6780
  Piqua *(G-16169)*
United States Dept Agriculture ....E 419 626-8439
  Sandusky *(G-16806)*

FARM SPLYS, WHOLESALE: Feed

Cooper Farms Inc ....D 419 375-4116
  Fort Recovery *(G-11115)*
Gerber Feed Service Inc ....E 330 857-4421
  Dalton *(G-9241)*
K M B Inc ....E 330 889-3451
  Bristolville *(G-1872)*
Keynes Bros Inc ....E 740 385-6824
  Logan *(G-12979)*
Premier Feeds LLC ....E 937 584-2411
  Wilmington *(G-19779)*
Purina Animal Nutrition LLC ....E 419 224-2015
  Lima *(G-12863)*
Purina Animal Nutrition LLC ....E 330 682-1951
  Orrville *(G-15784)*
Purina Animal Nutrition LLC ....E 330 879-2158
  Massillon *(G-13846)*
Sunrise Cooperative Inc ....E 937 462-8341
  South Charleston *(G-17077)*
Sunrise Cooperative Inc ....E 937 382-1633
  Wilmington *(G-19789)*

FARM SPLYS, WHOLESALE: Flower & Field Bulbs

Express Seed Company ....D 440 774-2259
  Oberlin *(G-15643)*

FARM SPLYS, WHOLESALE: Garden Splys

Berns Grnhse & Grdn Ctr Inc ....E 513 423-5306
  Middletown *(G-14418)*
Bfg Supply Co Llc ....E 440 834-1883
  Burton *(G-2061)*
Do Cut Sales & Service Inc ....E 330 533-9878
  Warren *(G-18851)*

FARM SPLYS, WHOLESALE: Greenhouse Eqpt & Splys

Mac Kenzie Nursery Supply Inc ....E 440 259-3517
  Perry *(G-15963)*

FARM SPLYS, WHOLESALE: Herbicides

Noxious Vegetation Control Inc ....D 614 486-8994
  Ashville *(G-770)*

FARM SPLYS, WHOLESALE: Seed, Grass

Lesco Inc ....C 216 706-9250
  Cleveland *(G-5936)*

FASTENERS WHOLESALERS

Fastener Corp of America Inc ....E 440 835-5100
  Westlake *(G-19485)*

FASTENERS: Metal

Midwest Motor Supply Co ....C 800 233-1294
  Columbus *(G-8170)*

FASTENERS: Notions, NEC

Midwest Motor Supply Co ....C 800 233-1294
  Columbus *(G-8170)*

FEDERAL SAVINGS & LOAN ASSOCIATIONS

American Savings Bank ....E 740 354-3177
  Portsmouth *(G-16264)*
Belmont Federal Sav & Ln Assn ....E 740 676-1165
  Bellaire *(G-1363)*
Chemical Bank ....E 440 779-0807
  North Olmsted *(G-15414)*
Chemical Bank ....E 513 232-0800
  Cincinnati *(G-3238)*
Chemical Bank ....E 440 926-2191
  Grafton *(G-11440)*
Chemical Bank ....E 330 314-1395
  Poland *(G-16222)*
Chemical Bank ....E 440 323-7451
  Elyria *(G-10603)*
Chemical Bank ....D 330 298-0510
  Ravenna *(G-16376)*
Chemical Bank ....D 330 314-1380
  Youngstown *(G-20139)*
Cheviot Mutual Holding Company ....D 513 661-0457
  Cincinnati *(G-3242)*
Cincinnati Federal ....E 513 574-3025
  Cincinnati *(G-3302)*
Cincinnatus Savings & Loan ....E 513 661-6903
  Cincinnati *(G-3338)*
Citizens Federal Sav & Ln Assn ....E 937 593-0015
  Bellefontaine *(G-1379)*
Fairfield Federal Sav & Ln Assn ....E 740 653-3863
  Lancaster *(G-12533)*
First Fdral Sav Ln Assn Galion ....D 419 468-1518
  Galion *(G-11294)*
First Fdral Sav Ln Assn Lkwood ....C 216 221-7300
  Lakewood *(G-12478)*

FERTILIZER, AGRICULTURAL: Wholesalers

First Fdral Sav Ln Assn Lorain ....D 440 282-6188
  Lorain *(G-13039)*
First Fdral Sav Ln Assn Newark ....E 740 345-3494
  Newark *(G-13041)*
First Fdral Sving Ln Assn Dlta ....E 419 822-3131
  Delta *(G-10158)*
First Federal Bank of Midwest ....E 419 782-5015
  Defiance *(G-10031)*
First Federal Bank of Midwest ....E 419 695-1055
  Delphos *(G-10143)*
First Federal Bank of Midwest ....D 419 855-8326
  Genoa *(G-11376)*
First Federal Bank of Ohio ....D 419 468-1518
  Galion *(G-11295)*
First Federal Cmnty Bnk Assn ....D 330 364-7777
  Dover *(G-10188)*
Greenville Federal ....E 937 548-4158
  Greenville *(G-11504)*
Harrison Building and Ln Assn ....E 513 367-2015
  Harrison *(G-11801)*
Home City Federal Savings Bank ....E 937 390-0470
  Springfield *(G-17205)*
Liberty Capital Inc ....D 937 382-1000
  Wilmington *(G-19767)*
New York Community Bank ....E 440 734-7040
  North Olmsted *(G-15434)*
New York Community Bank ....E 216 741-7333
  Cleveland *(G-6126)*
Peoples Federal Sav & Ln Assn ....E 937 492-6129
  Sidney *(G-16947)*
Talmer Bank and Trust ....E 330 726-3396
  Canfield *(G-2211)*
Third Federal Savings ....B 800 844-7333
  Cleveland *(G-6592)*
Third Federal Savings ....E 440 885-4900
  Cleveland *(G-6593)*
Third Federal Savings ....E 440 716-1865
  North Olmsted *(G-15448)*
Third Federal Savings ....E 440 843-6300
  Cleveland *(G-6594)*
Unity National Bank ....E 937 773-0752
  Piqua *(G-16171)*

FEDERAL SAVINGS BANKS

Century National Bank ....E 740 454-2521
  Zanesville *(G-20461)*
Century National Bank ....E 740 455-7330
  Zanesville *(G-20463)*
Congressional Bank ....E 614 441-9230
  Columbus *(G-7420)*
Guardian Savings Bank ....E 513 942-3535
  West Chester *(G-19086)*
Liberty Savings Bank FSB ....C 937 382-1000
  Wilmington *(G-19768)*
Peoples Bank ....D 740 373-3155
  Marietta *(G-13485)*
Union Savings Bank ....D 937 434-1254
  Dayton *(G-9944)*
Wesbanco Inc ....E 740 532-0263
  Ironton *(G-12304)*

FENCING DEALERS

Able Contracting Group Inc ....E 440 951-0880
  Painesville *(G-15832)*
Mills Fence Co Inc ....E 513 631-0333
  Cincinnati *(G-4100)*
Usavinyl LLC ....E 614 771-4805
  Groveport *(G-11682)*

FENCING: Chain Link

Richards Whl Fence Co Inc ....E 330 773-0423
  Akron *(G-415)*

FERRALLOY ORES, EXC VANADIUM

Rhenium Alloys Inc ....D 440 365-7388
  North Ridgeville *(G-15475)*

FERTILIZER MINERAL MINING

Everris NA Inc ....E 614 726-7100
  Dublin *(G-10340)*

FERTILIZER, AGRICULTURAL: Wholesalers

Andersons Agriculture Group LP ....E 419 893-5050
  Maumee *(G-13881)*
Deerfield Farms Service Inc ....D 330 584-4715
  Deerfield *(G-10019)*

FERTILIZER, AGRICULTURAL: Wholesalers

Hanby Farms Inc .... E 740 763-3554
  Nashport *(G-14951)*
Morral Companies LLC .... E 740 465-3251
  Morral *(G-14842)*
Ohigro Inc .... E 740 726-2429
  Waldo *(G-18783)*
S & D Application LLC .... E 419 288-3660
  Wayne *(G-18978)*
Sunrise Cooperative Inc .... E 937 323-7536
  Springfield *(G-17284)*

FERTILIZERS: NEC

Ohigro Inc .... E 740 726-2429
  Waldo *(G-18783)*

FERTILIZERS: Phosphatic

Andersons Inc .... C 419 893-5050
  Maumee *(G-13879)*

FIBER & FIBER PRDTS: Synthetic Cellulosic

Flexsys America LP .... D 330 666-4111
  Akron *(G-227)*

FIBER OPTICS

Jason Wilson .... E 937 604-8209
  Tipp City *(G-17720)*

FIELD WAREHOUSING SVCS

Frankes Unlimited Inc .... E 937 642-0706
  Marysville *(G-13619)*
Penske Logistics LLC .... E 419 547-2615
  Clyde *(G-6819)*
Truechoicepack Corp .... E 937 630-3832
  Mason *(G-13775)*

FILE FOLDERS

GBS Corp .... C 330 494-5330
  North Canton *(G-15339)*

FILM & SHEET: Unsuppported Plastic

Ampac Holdings LLC .... A 513 671-1777
  Cincinnati *(G-3017)*
General Data Company Inc .... C 513 752-7978
  Cincinnati *(G-2916)*
Industry Products Co .... B 937 778-0585
  Piqua *(G-16150)*
Polyone Corporation .... D 440 930-1000
  Avon Lake *(G-937)*

FILM DEVELOPING & PRINTING SVCS

Marco Photo Service Inc .... D 419 529-9010
  Ontario *(G-15700)*

FILM: Rubber

B D G Wrap-Tite Inc .... D 440 349-5400
  Solon *(G-16981)*

FILTER ELEMENTS: Fluid & Hydraulic Line

Two M Precision Co Inc .... E 440 946-2120
  Willoughby *(G-19719)*

FILTERS

Hunter Defense Tech Inc .... E 216 438-6111
  Solon *(G-17016)*
Swift Filters Inc .... E 440 735-0995
  Oakwood Village *(G-15634)*

FILTERS & SOFTENERS: Water, Household

Enting Water Conditioning Inc .... E 937 294-5100
  Moraine *(G-14781)*

FINANCIAL INVESTMENT ACTIVITIES, NEC: Security Transfer

Flex Fund Inc .... E 614 766-7000
  Dublin *(G-10348)*

FINANCIAL INVESTMENT ADVICE

Ameriprise Financial Svcs Inc .... E 614 934-4057
  Dublin *(G-10253)*
Ameriprise Financial Svcs Inc .... D 614 846-8723
  Worthington *(G-19940)*
Brookdale Senior Living Inc .... D 855 308-2438
  Cincinnati *(G-3138)*
Brown WD General Agency Inc .... D 216 241-5840
  Cleveland *(G-5152)*
Carnegie Capital Asset MGT LLC .... E 216 595-1349
  Cleveland *(G-5185)*
CNG Financial Corp .... A 513 336-7735
  Cincinnati *(G-3374)*
Cw Financial LLC .... B 941 907-9490
  Beachwood *(G-1070)*
Direct Maintenance LLC .... E 330 744-5211
  Youngstown *(G-20169)*
Financial Engines Inc .... E 330 726-3100
  Boardman *(G-1739)*
Ifs Financial Services Inc .... E 513 362-8000
  Westerville *(G-19410)*
Kemba Financial Credit Un Inc .... D 614 235-2395
  Columbus *(G-7973)*
Lang Financial Group Inc .... E 513 699-2966
  Blue Ash *(G-1626)*
Lassiter Corporation .... E 216 391-4800
  Cleveland *(G-5927)*
Merrill Lynch Pierce Fenner .... D 614 225-3152
  Columbus *(G-8149)*
Merrill Lynch Pierce Fenner .... E 216 363-6500
  Cleveland *(G-6030)*
Merrill Lynch Pierce Fenner .... E 937 847-4000
  Miamisburg *(G-14319)*
Merrill Lynch Pierce Fenner .... D 614 225-3000
  Columbus *(G-8151)*
Merrill Lynch Pierce Fenner .... D 330 670-2400
  Akron *(G-339)*
Morgan Stanley .... D 614 473-2086
  Columbus *(G-8188)*
Morgan Stanley .... E 513 721-2000
  Cincinnati *(G-4118)*
Mt Washington Care Center Inc .... C 513 231-4561
  Cincinnati *(G-4130)*
Stepstone Group Real Estate LP .... E 216 522-0330
  Cleveland *(G-6538)*
Sterling Ltd Co .... E 216 464-8850
  Cleveland *(G-6539)*
Stonehenge Capital Company LLC .... E 614 246-2456
  Columbus *(G-8790)*
The Cadle Company .... C 330 872-0918
  Newton Falls *(G-15278)*
Victory Capital Management Inc .... C 216 898-2400
  Brooklyn *(G-1907)*
Westminster Financial Company .... E 937 898-5010
  Dayton *(G-9994)*
William D Taylor Sr Inc .... D 614 653-6683
  Etna *(G-10740)*

FINANCIAL SVCS

1 Financial Corporation .... E 513 936-1400
  Blue Ash *(G-1520)*
6200 Rockside LLC .... D 216 642-8004
  Cleveland *(G-4927)*
Allstate Insurance Company .... E 330 650-2917
  Hudson *(G-12102)*
Ampersand Group LLC .... E 330 379-0044
  Akron *(G-75)*
Banc One Services Corporation .... A 614 248-5800
  Columbus *(G-6869)*
Bdo Usa LLP .... E 513 592-2400
  Cincinnati *(G-3085)*
Business Backer LLC .... E 513 792-6866
  Cincinnati *(G-3155)*
Cbiz Inc .... C 216 447-9000
  Cleveland *(G-5196)*
Cincinnati Financial Corp .... A 513 870-2000
  Fairfield *(G-10833)*
Citizens Financial Svcs Inc .... D 513 385-3200
  Cincinnati *(G-3356)*
Cleveland Clinic Foundation .... B 216 444-5000
  Cleveland *(G-5299)*
Collections Acquisition Co LLC .... C 614 944-5788
  Columbus *(G-7319)*
Credit First National Assn .... B 216 362-5300
  Cleveland *(G-5434)*
E T Financial Service Inc .... E 937 716-1726
  Trotwood *(G-18346)*
Facts Management Company .... E 440 892-4272
  Westlake *(G-19483)*
Fnb Inc .... E 740 922-2532
  Dennison *(G-10164)*
FNB Corporation .... D 330 425-1818
  Twinsburg *(G-18416)*
Gabriel Partners LLC .... E 216 771-2550
  Cleveland *(G-5650)*
Horter Investment MGT LLC .... E 513 984-9933
  Cincinnati *(G-3784)*
Jean R Wagner .... D 614 430-0065
  Westerville *(G-19317)*
Landmark America Inc .... E 330 372-6800
  Warren *(G-18873)*
Liberty Healthshare Inc .... E 855 585-4237
  Canton *(G-2436)*
Nationwide General Insur Co .... D 614 249-7111
  Columbus *(G-8243)*
Netrada North America LLC .... E 866 345-5835
  West Chester *(G-19218)*
Producers Credit Corporation .... E 614 433-2150
  Columbus *(G-8565)*
Reliance Financial Services NA .... E 419 783-8007
  Defiance *(G-10053)*
Resilience Capitl Partners LLC .... A 216 292-0200
  Cleveland *(G-6384)*
Skylight Financial Group LLC .... E 216 621-5680
  Cleveland *(G-6486)*
Sparkbase Inc .... E 216 867-0877
  Cleveland *(G-6514)*
Sterling Buying Group LLC .... E 513 564-9000
  Cincinnati *(G-4589)*
UBS Financial Services Inc .... E 330 655-8319
  Hudson *(G-12147)*
UBS Financial Services Inc .... E 440 414-2740
  Westlake *(G-19558)*
UBS Financial Services Inc .... E 419 624-6800
  Sandusky *(G-16803)*
UBS Financial Services Inc .... E 740 336-7823
  Marietta *(G-13509)*
Unirush LLC .... D 866 766-2229
  Blue Ash *(G-1712)*

FINGERPRINTING SVCS

Donty Horton HM Care Dhhc LLC .... E 513 463-3442
  Cincinnati *(G-3499)*

FIRE ALARM MAINTENANCE & MONITORING SVCS

ABC Fire Inc .... E 440 237-6677
  North Royalton *(G-15480)*
Gene Ptacek Son Fire Eqp Inc .... E 216 651-8300
  Cleveland *(G-5666)*
Gillmore Security Systems Inc .... E 440 232-1000
  Cleveland *(G-5672)*
Koorsen Fire & Security Inc .... E 937 324-9405
  Vandalia *(G-18687)*

FIRE CONTROL EQPT REPAIR SVCS, MILITARY

Fire Foe Corp .... E 330 759-9834
  Girard *(G-11413)*

FIRE EXTINGUISHER SVC

Abco Fire LLC .... E 800 875-7200
  Cincinnati *(G-2960)*
Abco Holdings LLC .... D 216 433-7200
  Cleveland *(G-4946)*
Koorsen Fire & Security Inc .... E 937 324-9405
  Vandalia *(G-18687)*
Megacity Fire Protection Inc .... E 937 335-0775
  Dayton *(G-9717)*

FIRE EXTINGUISHERS, WHOLESALE

3s Incorporated .... E 513 202-5070
  Harrison *(G-11788)*
Gene Ptacek Son Fire Eqp Inc .... E 216 651-8300
  Cleveland *(G-5666)*
Koorsen Fire & Security Inc .... E 614 878-2228
  Columbus *(G-8009)*
Koorsen Fire & Security Inc .... E 614 878-2228
  Columbus *(G-8010)*

FIRE OR BURGLARY RESISTIVE PRDTS

Donald E Didion II .... E 419 483-2226
  Bellevue *(G-1408)*

FIRE PROTECTION EQPT

A-1 Sprinkler Company Inc .... D 937 859-6198
  Miamisburg *(G-14267)*
Action Coupling & Eqp Inc .... D 330 279-4242
  Holmesville *(G-12070)*

SERVICES SECTION

FIRE PROTECTION SVCS: Contracted

AA Fire Protection LLC ....E 440 327-0060
  Elyria (G-10590)
Abco Fire LLC ....D...... 216 433-7200
  Cleveland (G-4945)
Bst & G Joint Fire District ....E 740 965-3841
  Sunbury (G-17551)
City of Solon ....E 440 248-6939
  Solon (G-16992)
City of Wooster ....E 330 263-5266
  Wooster (G-19845)
Colerain Volunteer Fire Co ....E 740 738-0735
  Dillonvale (G-10174)
Greentown Vlntr Fire Dept Inc ....E 330 494-3002
  Uniontown (G-18522)
J Schoen Enterprises Inc ....E 419 536-0970
  Toledo (G-17981)

FIRE PROTECTION, EXC CONTRACT

ADT Security ....D...... 440 397-5751
  Strongsville (G-17440)

FIRE PROTECTION, GOVERNMENT: County

County of Holmes ....E 330 674-1926
  Millersburg (G-14596)

FIRE PROTECTION, GOVERNMENT: Fire Department, Volunteer

Leroy Twp Fire Dept ....E 440 254-4124
  Painesville (G-15863)
Richland Township Fire Dept ....E 740 536-7313
  Rushville (G-16613)

FIRE PROTECTION, GOVERNMENT: Local

City of Whitehall ....E 614 237-5478
  Columbus (G-7286)
City of Willoughby Hills ....E 440 942-7207
  Willoughby Hills (G-19729)
Township of Chester ....E 440 729-9951
  Chesterland (G-2805)

FIREARMS & AMMUNITION, EXC SPORTING, WHOLESALE

Keidel Supply Company Inc ....E 513 351-1600
  Cincinnati (G-3906)
Rk Family Inc ....C 740 389-2674
  Marion (G-13577)
Rk Family Inc ....C 419 355-8230
  Fremont (G-11216)
Rk Family Inc ....B 330 264-5475
  Wooster (G-19907)
Rk Family Inc ....E 513 934-0015
  Lebanon (G-12643)
Vinifera Imports Ltd ....E 440 942-9463
  Mentor (G-14255)
Woodcraft Supply LLC ....E 513 407-8371
  Cincinnati (G-4859)

FIREARMS, EXC SPORTING, WHOLESALE

Southern Ohio Gun Distrs Inc ....E 513 932-8148
  Lebanon (G-12649)

FIREWOOD, WHOLESALE

Bladecutters Lawn Service Inc ....E 937 274-3861
  Dayton (G-9360)

FIREWORKS SHOPS

Miller Fireworks Company Inc ....E 419 865-7329
  Holland (G-12039)

FIREWORKS: Wholesalers

Miller Fireworks Company Inc ....E 419 865-7329
  Holland (G-12039)

FISH & SEAFOOD WHOLESALERS

101 River Inc ....E 440 352-6343
  Grand River (G-11455)
Farm House Food Distrs Inc ....E 216 791-6948
  Cleveland (G-5573)
Omega Sea LLC ....E 440 639-2372
  Painesville (G-15870)
Omegasea Ltd Liability Co ....E 440 639-2372
  Painesville (G-15871)

Sherwood Food Distributors LLC ....B 216 662-6794
  Maple Heights (G-13418)

FISH, PACKAGED FROZEN: Wholesalers

King Kold Inc ....E 937 836-2731
  Englewood (G-10711)
Produce One Inc ....D...... 931 253-4749
  Dayton (G-9831)

FISHING CAMPS

Rockwell Springs Trout Club ....E 419 684-7971
  Clyde (G-6821)

FITTINGS & ASSEMBLIES: Hose & Tube, Hydraulic Or Pneumatic

Ohio Hydraulics Inc ....E 513 771-2590
  Cincinnati (G-4207)

FITTINGS: Pipe

Parker-Hannifin Corporation ....B 937 456-5571
  Eaton (G-10572)
Parker-Hannifin Corporation ....C 614 279-7070
  Columbus (G-8516)
SSP Fittings Corp ....D...... 330 425-4250
  Twinsburg (G-18472)

FLAT GLASS: Construction

S R Door Inc ....D...... 740 927-3558
  Hebron (G-11859)

FLEA MARKET

Ferguson Hills Inc ....D...... 513 539-4497
  Dayton (G-9546)
Hrm Enterprises Inc ....C 330 877-9353
  Hartville (G-11823)
Rainbow Flea Market Inc ....E 614 291-3133
  Columbus (G-8585)
Traders World Inc ....E 513 424-2052
  Monroe (G-14715)

FLIGHT TRAINING SCHOOLS

Abx Air Inc ....B 937 382-5591
  Wilmington (G-19741)

FLOATING DRY DOCKS

Pinney Dock & Transport LLC ....E 440 964-7186
  Ashtabula (G-760)

FLOOR COVERING STORES

Americas Floor Source LLC ....E 216 342-4929
  Bedford Heights (G-1346)
Command Carpet ....D...... 330 673-7404
  Kent (G-12361)
Modern Glass Pnt & Tile Co Inc ....E 740 454-1253
  Zanesville (G-20503)
Rite Rug Co ....E 614 478-3365
  Columbus (G-8632)
Samron Inc ....E 330 782-6539
  Youngstown (G-20366)
Schoch Tile & Carpet Inc ....E 513 922-3466
  Cincinnati (G-4484)

FLOOR COVERING STORES: Carpets

Americas Floor Source LLC ....D...... 614 808-3915
  Columbus (G-7011)
Andover Floor Covering ....E 440 203 5330
  Newbury (G-15254)
Bcf LLC ....E 937 746-0721
  Miamisburg (G-14274)
Clays Heritage Carpet Inc ....E 330 497-1280
  Canton (G-2312)
Farrow Cleaners Co ....E 216 561-2355
  Cleveland (G-5574)
Marble Restoration Inc ....E 419 865-9000
  Maumee (G-13939)
Patellas Floor Center Inc ....E 330 758-4099
  Youngstown (G-20316)
Regal Carpet Center Inc ....E 216 475-1844
  Cleveland (G-6366)
Regency Windows Corporation ....E 330 963-4077
  Twinsburg (G-18459)
Rite Rug Co ....E 937 318-9197
  Fairborn (G-10803)

FLOWERS & FLORISTS' SPLYS WHOLESALERS

Stanley Steemer Intl Inc ....C 614 764-2007
  Dublin (G-10461)

FLOOR COVERING STORES: Floor Tile

JP Flooring Systems Inc ....E 513 346-4300
  West Chester (G-19099)
Justice & Co Inc ....E 330 225-6000
  Medina (G-14088)

FLOOR COVERING: Plastic

Armaly LLC ....E 740 852-3621
  London (G-12992)

FLOOR COVERINGS WHOLESALERS

Americas Floor Source LLC ....D...... 614 808-3915
  Columbus (G-7011)
D & S Crtive Cmmunications Inc ....E 419 524-4312
  Mansfield (G-13289)
Pfpc Enterprises Inc ....B 513 941-6200
  Cincinnati (G-4290)
PTX Flooring Inc ....E 419 726-1775
  Toledo (G-18143)

FLOOR WAXING SVCS

Stanley Stemer of Akron Canton ....E 330 785-5005
  Coventry Township (G-9133)

FLORIST: Flowers, Fresh

Circle S Farms Inc ....E 614 878-9462
  Grove City (G-11546)
Gears Garden Center Inc ....E 513 931-3800
  Cincinnati (G-3665)
Gs Ohio Inc ....D...... 614 885-5350
  Powell (G-16337)
Hirts Greenhouse Inc ....E 440 238-8200
  Strongsville (G-17470)
HJ Benken Flor & Greenhouses ....D...... 513 891-1040
  Cincinnati (G-3772)
Kens Flower Shop Inc ....E 419 841-9590
  Perrysburg (G-16023)
Lowes Greenhouse & Gift Shop ....E 440 543-5123
  Chagrin Falls (G-2722)
Oberers Flowers Inc ....E 937 223-1253
  Dayton (G-9781)
Rosby Brothers Inc ....E 216 351-0850
  Cleveland (G-6411)
Scarffs Nursery Inc ....C 937 845-3130
  New Carlisle (G-15031)
Wickline Landscaping Inc ....E 937 372-0521
  Xenia (G-20083)

FLORIST: Plants, Potted

Maria Gardens Inc ....E 440 238-7637
  Strongsville (G-17489)
Park Cincinnati Board ....D...... 513 421-4086
  Cincinnati (G-4252)

FLORISTS

Buehler Food Markets Inc ....C 330 364-3079
  Dover (G-10179)
Fred W Albrecht Grocery Co ....C 330 645-6222
  Coventry Township (G-9124)
Made From Scratch Inc ....E 614 873-3344
  Plain City (G-16197)
Wilsons Hillview Farm Inc ....E 740 763-2873
  Newark (G-15247)

FLORISTS' SPLYS, WHOLESALE

New Diamond Line Cont Corp ....E 330 644-9993
  Coventry Township (G-9129)

FLOTATION COMPANIES: Securities

Cowen and Company LLC ....E 440 331-3531
  Rocky River (G-16575)

FLOWERS & FLORISTS' SPLYS WHOLESALERS

Cottage Gardens Inc ....D...... 440 259-2900
  Perry (G-15960)
Darice Inc ....C 440 238-9150
  Strongsville (G-17456)
Flowerland Garden Centers ....E 440 439-8636
  Oakwood Village (G-15629)

FLOWERS & FLORISTS' SPLYS WHOLESALERS

Giant Eagle Inc .... D 330 364-5301
  Dover *(G-10190)*
North Branch Nursery Inc .... E 419 287-4679
  Pemberville *(G-15942)*
Scarffs Nursery Inc .... C 937 845-3130
  New Carlisle *(G-15031)*
Schmidt Bros Inc .... E 419 826-3671
  Swanton *(G-17571)*

FLOWERS & NURSERY STOCK, WHOLESALE

August Corso Sons Inc .... C 419 626-0765
  Sandusky *(G-16727)*
Lcn Holdings Inc .... E 440 259-5571
  Madison *(G-13229)*
Mac Kenzie Nursery Supply Inc .... E 440 259-3517
  Perry *(G-15963)*
Petitti Enterprises Inc .... E 440 236-5055
  Columbia Station *(G-6851)*
Rentokil North America Inc .... E 614 837-0099
  Groveport *(G-11666)*

FLOWERS, ARTIFICIAL, WHOLESALE

Flower Factory Inc .... D 614 275-6220
  Columbus *(G-7677)*

FLOWERS, FRESH, WHOLESALE

Claprood Roman J Co .... E 614 221-5515
  Columbus *(G-7290)*
Denver Wholesale Florists Co .... E 419 241-7241
  Toledo *(G-17850)*
Gs Ohio Inc .... D 614 885-5350
  Powell *(G-16337)*
Kens Flower Shop Inc .... E 419 841-9590
  Perrysburg *(G-16023)*
Oberers Flowers Inc .... E 937 223-1253
  Dayton *(G-9781)*

FLUID POWER PUMPS & MOTORS

Aerocontrolex Group Inc .... D 440 352-6182
  Painesville *(G-15833)*
Eaton-Aeroquip Llc .... D 419 891-7775
  Maumee *(G-13907)*
Giant Industries Inc .... E 419 531-4600
  Toledo *(G-17915)*
Hite Parts Exchange Inc .... E 614 272-5115
  Columbus *(G-7842)*
Hydraulic Parts Store Inc .... E 330 364-6667
  New Philadelphia *(G-15102)*
Ingersoll-Rand Company .... E 419 633-6800
  Bryan *(G-2008)*
Pfpc Enterprises Inc .... B 513 941-6200
  Cincinnati *(G-4290)*
Robeck Fluid Power Co .... D 330 562-1140
  Aurora *(G-852)*

FLUID POWER VALVES & HOSE FITTINGS

Alkon Corporation .... D 419 355-9111
  Fremont *(G-11184)*
Eaton-Aeroquip Llc .... D 419 891-7775
  Maumee *(G-13907)*
Hydraulic Parts Store Inc .... E 330 364-6667
  New Philadelphia *(G-15102)*
Parker-Hannifin Corporation .... B 937 456-5571
  Eaton *(G-10572)*
SSP Fittings Corp .... D 330 425-4250
  Twinsburg *(G-18472)*
Superior Products LLC .... D 216 651-9400
  Cleveland *(G-6555)*
Superior Products Llc .... D 216 651-9400
  Cleveland *(G-6554)*

FLUXES

Bluefoot Industrial LLC .... E 740 314-5299
  Steubenville *(G-17304)*

FOAMS & RUBBER, WHOLESALE

Johnson Bros Rubber Co Inc .... D 419 853-4122
  West Salem *(G-19270)*
Johnson Bros Rubber Co Inc .... E 419 752-4814
  Greenwich *(G-11526)*
Tahoma Enterprises Inc .... D 330 745-9016
  Barberton *(G-982)*
Tahoma Rubber & Plastics Inc .... D 330 745-9016
  Barberton *(G-983)*

FOIL & LEAF: Metal

A J Oster Foils LLC .... D 330 823-1700
  Alliance *(G-521)*

FOOD PRDTS, CANNED: Chili

Gold Star Chili Inc .... E 513 231-4541
  Cincinnati *(G-3684)*

FOOD PRDTS, CANNED: Ethnic

Troyer Cheese Inc .... E 330 893-2479
  Millersburg *(G-14625)*

FOOD PRDTS, CANNED: Fruits

Louis Trauth Dairy LLC .... B 859 431-7553
  West Chester *(G-19213)*

FOOD PRDTS, CANNED: Tomatoes

Hirzel Canning Company .... D 419 693-0531
  Northwood *(G-15533)*

FOOD PRDTS, CONFECTIONERY, WHOLESALE: Candy

Gorant Chocolatier LLC .... C 330 726-8821
  Boardman *(G-1740)*
Gummer Wholesale Inc .... D 740 928-0415
  Heath *(G-11838)*
Robert E McGrath Inc .... E 440 572-7747
  Strongsville *(G-17503)*

FOOD PRDTS, CONFECTIONERY, WHOLESALE: Nuts, Salted/Roasted

Ohio Hickory Harvest Brand Pro ...... E 330 644-6266
  Coventry Township *(G-9130)*
Tarrier Foods Corp .... E 614 876-8594
  Columbus *(G-8823)*

FOOD PRDTS, CONFECTIONERY, WHOLESALE: Potato Chips

Jones Potato Chip Co .... E 419 529-9424
  Mansfield *(G-13317)*
S-L Distribution Company Inc .... D 740 676-6932
  Bellaire *(G-1367)*

FOOD PRDTS, CONFECTIONERY, WHOLESALE: Snack Foods

Frito-Lay North America Inc .... D 513 874-0112
  West Chester *(G-19202)*
Frito-Lay North America Inc .... C 216 491-4000
  Cleveland *(G-5642)*
Frito-Lay North America Inc .... E 937 224-8716
  Dayton *(G-9563)*
Frito-Lay North America Inc .... C 614 508-3004
  Columbus *(G-7709)*
Grippo Foods Inc .... E 513 923-1900
  Cincinnati *(G-3714)*
Mike-Sells Potato Chip Co .... E 937 228-9400
  Dayton *(G-9747)*
Shearers Foods LLC .... A 330 834-4030
  Massillon *(G-13855)*

FOOD PRDTS, CONFECTIONERY, WHOLESALE: Syrups, Fountain

Multi-Flow Dispensers Ohio Inc .... D 216 641-0200
  Brooklyn Heights *(G-1921)*

FOOD PRDTS, FISH & SEAFOOD, WHOLESALE: Fresh

Midwest Seafood Inc .... D 937 746-8856
  Springboro *(G-17129)*

FOOD PRDTS, FISH & SEAFOOD, WHOLESALE: Frozen, Unpackaged

Sfd Company LLC .... D 216 662-8000
  Maple Heights *(G-13417)*

FOOD PRDTS, FISH & SEAFOOD, WHOLESALE: Seafood

Ocean Wide Seafood Company .... E 937 610-5740
  Cincinnati *(G-4197)*

SERVICES SECTION

Riser Foods Company .... D 216 292-7000
  Bedford Heights *(G-1359)*
Ritchies Food Distributors Inc .... E 740 443-6303
  Piketon *(G-16127)*

FOOD PRDTS, FROZEN: NEC

King Kold Inc .... E 937 836-2731
  Englewood *(G-10711)*
Skyline Chili Inc .... C 513 874-1188
  Fairfield *(G-10910)*

FOOD PRDTS, FRUITS & VEG, FRESH, WHOL: Banana Ripening Svc

Z Produce Co Inc .... E 614 224-4373
  Columbus *(G-9024)*

FOOD PRDTS, FRUITS & VEGETABLES, FRESH, WHOLESALE

Al Peake & Sons Inc .... E 419 243-9284
  Toledo *(G-17745)*
Anselmo Rssis Premier Prod Ltd ..... E 800 229-5517
  Cleveland *(G-5040)*
Caruso Inc .... C 513 860-9200
  Cincinnati *(G-3188)*
Chariott Foods Inc .... E 419 243-1101
  Toledo *(G-17802)*
Chefs Garden Inc .... C 419 433-4947
  Huron *(G-12162)*
Del Monte Fresh Produce NA Inc .... E 614 527-7398
  Columbus *(G-7503)*
Dole Fresh Vegetables Inc .... C 937 525-4300
  Springfield *(G-17190)*
Farris Produce Inc .... E 330 837-4607
  Massillon *(G-13807)*
Hillcrest Egg & Cheese Co .... E 216 361-4625
  Cleveland *(G-5757)*
Joe Lasita & Sons Inc .... E 513 241-5288
  Cincinnati *(G-3875)*
Midwest Fresh Foods Inc .... E 614 469-1492
  Columbus *(G-8169)*
Miles Farmers Market Inc .... C 440 248-5222
  Solon *(G-17027)*
Pics Produce Inc .... E 513 381-1239
  Cincinnati *(G-4297)*
Powell Company Ltd .... D 419 228-3552
  Lima *(G-12861)*
Produce One Inc .... D 931 253-4749
  Dayton *(G-9831)*
Reinhart Foodservice LLC .... C 513 421-9184
  Cincinnati *(G-4400)*
Sirna & Sons Inc .... C 330 298-2222
  Ravenna *(G-16411)*
Spartannash Company .... D 513 793-6300
  Cincinnati *(G-4556)*

FOOD PRDTS, FRUITS & VEGETABLES, FRESH, WHOLESALE: Potatoes

Mrs Dennis Potato Farm Inc .... E 419 335-2778
  Wauseon *(G-18959)*

FOOD PRDTS, FRUITS & VEGETABLES, FRESH, WHOLESALE: Vegetable

Barkett Fruit Co Inc .... E 330 364-6645
  Dover *(G-10176)*

FOOD PRDTS, FRUITS & VEGETABLES, FRESH, WHOLESALE: Vegetable

Cabbage Inc .... E 440 899-9171
  Sheffield Village *(G-16885)*
Freshway Foods Inc .... C 937 498-4664
  Sidney *(G-16936)*
Greenline Foods Inc .... D 419 354-1149
  Bowling Green *(G-1778)*

FOOD PRDTS, MEAT & MEAT PRDTS, WHOLESALE: Brokers

Tsg-Cincinnati LLC .... D 513 793-6241
  Blue Ash *(G-1707)*

FOOD PRDTS, MEAT & MEAT PRDTS, WHOLESALE: Cured Or Smoked

Smithfield Packaged Meats Corp ..... B 513 782-3805
  Cincinnati *(G-4542)*

SERVICES SECTION

FOOD PRDTS, WHOLESALE: Water, Mineral Or Spring, Bottled

Troyer Cheese Inc .... E 330 893-2479
 Millersburg *(G-14625)*

FOOD PRDTS, MEAT & MEAT PRDTS, WHOLESALE: Fresh

A To Z Portion Ctrl Meats Inc .... E 419 358-2926
 Bluffton *(G-1726)*
Blue Ribbon Meats Inc .... D 216 631-8850
 Cleveland *(G-5124)*
Carles Bratwurst Inc .... E 419 562-7741
 Bucyrus *(G-2028)*
Dutch Creek Foods Inc .... E 330 852-2631
 Sugarcreek *(G-17545)*
Empire Packing Company LP .... D 513 942-5400
 West Chester *(G-19196)*
Giant Eagle Inc .... E 216 292-7000
 Bedford Heights *(G-1352)*
Hillcrest Egg & Cheese Co .... D 216 361-4625
 Cleveland *(G-5757)*
Jetro Cash and Carry Entps LLC .... E 216 525-0101
 Cleveland *(G-5862)*
Kenosha Beef International Ltd .... C 614 771-1330
 Columbus *(G-7979)*
Landes Fresh Meats Inc .... E 937 836-3613
 Clayton *(G-4912)*
Lori Holding Co .... E 740 342-3230
 New Lexington *(G-15055)*
Marshallville Packing Co Inc .... E 330 855-2871
 Marshallville *(G-13597)*
Northern Frozen Foods Inc .... C 440 439-0600
 Cleveland *(G-6158)*
Produce One Inc .... D 931 253-4749
 Dayton *(G-9831)*
Ritchies Food Distributors Inc .... E 740 443-6303
 Piketon *(G-16127)*
S and S Gilardi Inc .... D 740 397-2751
 Mount Vernon *(G-14921)*
Sfd Company LLC .... D 216 662-8000
 Maple Heights *(G-13417)*
Sherwood Food Distributors LLC .... B 216 662-6794
 Maple Heights *(G-13418)*
Siemer Distributing Company .... E 740 342-3230
 New Lexington *(G-15063)*
Spartannash Company .... D 513 793-6300
 Cincinnati *(G-4556)*
Steaks & Such Inc .... E 330 837-9296
 Massillon *(G-13858)*
Tasty Pure Food Company .... E 330 434-8141
 Akron *(G-471)*

FOOD PRDTS, MEAT & MEAT PRDTS, WHOLESALE: Lard

Boars Head Provisions Co Inc .... B 614 662-5300
 Groveport *(G-11625)*

FOOD PRDTS, POULTRY, WHOLESALE: Live/Dressed/Frozen, Unpkgd

Di Feo & Sons Poultry Inc .... E 330 564-8172
 Akron *(G-191)*
Sfd Company LLC .... D 216 662-8000
 Maple Heights *(G-13417)*

FOOD PRDTS, WHOL: Canned Goods, Fruit, Veg, Seafood/Meats

Avalon Foodservice Inc .... C 330 854-4551
 Canal Fulton *(G-2140)*
Food Distributors Inc .... E 740 439-2764
 Cambridge *(G-2114)*
Hillcrest Egg & Cheese Co .... D 216 361-4625
 Cleveland *(G-5757)*
Mattingly Foods Inc .... C 740 454-0136
 Zanesville *(G-20500)*
Northern Frozen Foods Inc .... C 440 439-0600
 Cleveland *(G-6158)*
Peck Distributors Inc .... E 216 587-6814
 Maple Heights *(G-13413)*
Powell Company Ltd .... D 419 228-3552
 Lima *(G-12861)*
Produce One Inc .... D 931 253-4749
 Dayton *(G-9831)*
Ritchies Food Distributors Inc .... E 740 443-6303
 Piketon *(G-16127)*
Z Produce Co Inc .... E 614 224-4373
 Columbus *(G-9024)*

FOOD PRDTS, WHOLESALE: Baking Splys

Bakemark USA LLC .... D 513 870-0880
 West Chester *(G-19023)*
Cassanos Inc .... E 937 294-8400
 Dayton *(G-9388)*

FOOD PRDTS, WHOLESALE: Beverage Concentrates

Flavorfresh Dispensers Inc .... E 216 641-0200
 Brooklyn Heights *(G-1916)*

FOOD PRDTS, WHOLESALE: Beverages, Exc Coffee & Tea

Esber Beverage Company .... E 330 456-4361
 Canton *(G-2360)*
G & J Pepsi-Cola Bottlers Inc .... D 740 593-3366
 Athens *(G-788)*
Knall Beverage Inc .... D 216 252-2500
 Cleveland *(G-5905)*
Louis Trauth Dairy LLC .... B 859 431-7553
 West Chester *(G-19213)*
R L Lipton Distributing LLC .... D 800 321-6553
 Austintown *(G-872)*
Superior Beverage Group Ltd .... D 614 294-3555
 Lewis Center *(G-12706)*
Superior Beverage Group Ltd .... C 440 703-4580
 Solon *(G-17058)*

FOOD PRDTS, WHOLESALE: Chocolate

Walnut Creek Chocolate Company .... E 330 893-2995
 Walnut Creek *(G-18785)*

FOOD PRDTS, WHOLESALE: Coffee & Tea

Spectrum Supportive Services .... C 216 761-2388
 Cleveland *(G-6518)*
Staufs Coffee Roasters II Inc .... E 614 487-6050
 Columbus *(G-8785)*

FOOD PRDTS, WHOLESALE: Coffee, Green Or Roasted

Berardis Fresh Roast Inc .... E 440 582-4303
 North Royalton *(G-15482)*
Coffee Break Corporation .... E 513 841-1100
 Cincinnati *(G-3377)*

FOOD PRDTS, WHOLESALE: Corn

Hanby Farms Inc .... E 740 763-3554
 Nashport *(G-14951)*
Pioneer Hi-Bred Intl Inc .... E 419 748-8051
 Grand Rapids *(G-11452)*

FOOD PRDTS, WHOLESALE: Dried or Canned Foods

Tarrier Foods Corp .... E 614 876-8594
 Columbus *(G-8823)*

FOOD PRDTS, WHOLESALE: Grain Elevators

Archbold Elevator Inc .... E 419 445-2451
 Archbold *(G-632)*
Ardent Mills LLC .... E 614 274-2545
 Columbus *(G-7039)*
Barnets Inc .... E 937 452-3275
 Camden *(G-2136)*
Deerfield Farms Service Inc .... D 330 584-4715
 Deerfield *(G-10019)*
Fort Recovery Equity Inc .... C 419 375-4119
 Fort Recovery *(G-11117)*

FOOD PRDTS, WHOLESALE: Grains

Champaign Landmark Inc .... E 937 652-2135
 Urbana *(G-18577)*
Consolidated Grain & Barge Co .... D 419 785-1941
 Defiance *(G-10023)*
Cooper Hatchery Inc .... C 419 594-3325
 Oakwood *(G-15623)*
Hansen-Mueller Co .... E 419 729-5535
 Toledo *(G-17931)*
Heritage Cooperative Inc .... D 419 294-2371
 West Mansfield *(G-19267)*
Sunrise Cooperative Inc .... B 937 575-6780
 Piqua *(G-16167)*
Trupointe Cooperative Inc .... B 937 575-6780
 Piqua *(G-16169)*

FOOD PRDTS, WHOLESALE: Health

Natural Foods Inc .... E 419 537-1713
 Toledo *(G-18079)*

FOOD PRDTS, WHOLESALE: Juices

M & M Wine Cellar Inc .... E 330 536-6450
 Lowellville *(G-13172)*
Ohio Citrus Juices Inc .... E 614 539-0030
 Grove City *(G-11589)*

FOOD PRDTS, WHOLESALE: Molasses, Indl

Interntional Molasses Corp Ltd .... E 937 276-7980
 Dayton *(G-9635)*

FOOD PRDTS, WHOLESALE: Natural & Organic

Clintonville Community Mkt .... E 614 261-3663
 Columbus *(G-7304)*
Hanson-Faso Sales & Marketing .... E 216 642-4500
 Cleveland *(G-5725)*

FOOD PRDTS, WHOLESALE: Pizza Splys

Ohio Pizza Products Inc .... D 937 294-6969
 Monroe *(G-14707)*
Rdp Foodservice Ltd .... E 614 261-5661
 Columbus *(G-8593)*
Swan Sales .... E 513 422-3100
 Middletown *(G-14465)*
Wasserstrom Company .... E 614 228-6525
 Columbus *(G-8971)*

FOOD PRDTS, WHOLESALE: Salt, Edible

Morton Salt Inc .... C 330 925-3015
 Rittman *(G-16554)*

FOOD PRDTS, WHOLESALE: Sauces

Crowning Food Company .... D 937 323-4699
 Springfield *(G-17185)*

FOOD PRDTS, WHOLESALE: Spaghetti

Osf International Inc .... E 513 942-6620
 Fairfield *(G-10891)*

FOOD PRDTS, WHOLESALE: Specialty

Antonio Sofo Son Importing Co .... C 419 476-4211
 Toledo *(G-17754)*
Atlantic Foods Corp .... D 513 772-3535
 Cincinnati *(G-3058)*
Classic Delight Inc .... E 419 394-7955
 Saint Marys *(G-16671)*
Cleveland Sysco Inc .... A 216 201-3000
 Cleveland *(G-5349)*
Euro Usa Inc .... D 216 714-0500
 Cleveland *(G-5555)*
Leo A Dick & Sons Co .... E 330 452-5010
 Canton *(G-2432)*
National Marketshare Group .... E 513 921-0800
 Cincinnati *(G-4140)*
Sherwood Food Distributors LLC .... B 216 662-6794
 Maple Heights *(G-13418)*
Troyer Cheese Inc .... E 330 893-2479
 Millersburg *(G-14625)*

FOOD PRDTS, WHOLESALE: Starch

G & J Pepsi-Cola Bottlers Inc .... E 740 774-2148
 Chillicothe *(G-2841)*

FOOD PRDTS, WHOLESALE: Water, Mineral Or Spring, Bottled

Distillata Company .... D 216 771-2900
 Cleveland *(G-5489)*
Hill Distributing Company .... D 614 276-6533
 Dublin *(G-10361)*
Magnetic Springs Water Company .... D 614 421-1780
 Columbus *(G-8098)*

FOOD PRDTS, WHOLESALE: Wine Makers' Eqpt & Splys

Wine-Art of Ohio Inc ....E...... 330 678-7733
  Kent *(G-12406)*

FOOD PRDTS: Coffee

Generations Coffee Company LLC ....E...... 440 546-0901
  Brecksville *(G-1824)*

FOOD PRDTS: Dried & Dehydrated Fruits, Vegetables & Soup Mix

Hirzel Canning Company ....D...... 419 693-0531
  Northwood *(G-15533)*

FOOD PRDTS: Eggs, Processed

Ballas Egg Products Corp....................D...... 614 453-0386
  Zanesville *(G-20446)*
Fort Recovery Equity Inc ....C...... 419 375-4119
  Fort Recovery *(G-11117)*
Ohio Fresh Eggs LLC ....C...... 740 893-7200
  Croton *(G-9154)*

FOOD PRDTS: Eggs, Processed, Frozen

Cal-Maine Foods Inc ....E...... 937 968-4874
  Union City *(G-18500)*

FOOD PRDTS: Flour

Ardent Mills LLC ....E...... 614 274-2545
  Columbus *(G-7039)*

FOOD PRDTS: Flour & Other Grain Mill Products

Hansen-Mueller Co ....E...... 419 729-5535
  Toledo *(G-17931)*
Pioneer Hi-Bred Intl Inc ....E...... 419 748-8051
  Grand Rapids *(G-11452)*

FOOD PRDTS: Mixes, Flour

General Mills Inc ....D...... 513 770-0558
  Mason *(G-13706)*

FOOD PRDTS: Potato & Corn Chips & Similar Prdts

Robert E McGrath Inc ....E...... 440 572-7747
  Strongsville *(G-17503)*
Shearers Foods LLC ....A...... 330 834-0030
  Massillon *(G-13855)*

FOOD PRDTS: Potato Chips & Other Potato-Based Snacks

Ballreich Bros Inc ....C...... 419 447-1814
  Tiffin *(G-17672)*
Jones Potato Chip Co ....E...... 419 529-9424
  Mansfield *(G-13317)*
Mike-Sells Potato Chip Co ....E...... 937 228-9400
  Dayton *(G-9747)*

FOOD PRDTS: Poultry, Processed, Frozen

Martin-Brower Company LLC ....B...... 513 773-2301
  West Chester *(G-19118)*

FOOD PRDTS: Preparations

Agrana Fruit Us Inc ....C...... 937 693-3821
  Anna *(G-616)*
Ballreich Bros Inc ....C...... 419 447-1814
  Tiffin *(G-17672)*
Dole Fresh Vegetables Inc ....C...... 937 525-4300
  Springfield *(G-17190)*
Freshway Foods Inc ....C...... 937 498-4664
  Sidney *(G-16936)*
Gold Star Chili Inc ....E...... 513 231-4541
  Cincinnati *(G-3684)*
Hiland Group Incorporated ....D...... 330 499-8404
  Canton *(G-2399)*
Ohio Hickory Harvest Brand Pro ....E...... 330 644-6266
  Coventry Township *(G-9130)*
Tarrier Foods Corp ....E...... 614 876-8594
  Columbus *(G-8823)*

FOOD PRDTS: Salads

Barkett Fruit Co Inc ....E...... 330 364-6645
  Dover *(G-10176)*
Dno Inc ....D...... 614 231-3601
  Columbus *(G-7536)*
Sandridge Food Corporation ....C...... 330 725-8883
  Medina *(G-14123)*

FOOD PRDTS: Sugar

Domino Foods Inc ....D...... 216 432-3222
  Cleveland *(G-5499)*

FOOD PRDTS: Turkey, Processed, NEC

Cooper Hatchery Inc ....C...... 419 594-3325
  Oakwood *(G-15623)*

FOOD PRODUCTS MACHINERY

Harry C Lobalzo & Sons Inc ....E...... 330 666-6758
  Akron *(G-253)*
Innovative Controls Corp ....D...... 419 691-6684
  Toledo *(G-17974)*
ITW Food Equipment Group LLC ....A...... 937 332-2396
  Troy *(G-18359)*
Lima Sheet Metal Machine & Mfg ....E...... 419 229-1161
  Lima *(G-12827)*
N Wasserstrom & Sons Inc ....C...... 614 228-5550
  Columbus *(G-8212)*
R and J Corporation ....E...... 440 871-6009
  Westlake *(G-19536)*
Winston Products LLC ....D...... 440 478-1418
  Cleveland *(G-6754)*
Wolf Machine Company ....C...... 513 791-5194
  Blue Ash *(G-1719)*

FOOD STORES: Convenience, Chain

Convenient Food Mart Inc ....E...... 800 860-4844
  Mentor *(G-14163)*
Lykins Companies Inc ....C...... 513 831-8820
  Milford *(G-14533)*
Travelcenters of America LLC ....D...... 330 769-2053
  Lodi *(G-12966)*
United Dairy Farmers Inc ....C...... 513 396-8700
  Cincinnati *(G-4731)*

FOOD STORES: Convenience, Independent

1st Stop Inc ....E...... 937 695-0318
  Winchester *(G-19798)*

FOOD STORES: Delicatessen

Bagel Place Inc ....E...... 419 885-1000
  Toledo *(G-17762)*
Michaels Bakery Inc ....E...... 216 351-7530
  Cleveland *(G-6048)*
Weilands Fine Meats Inc ....E...... 614 267-9910
  Columbus *(G-8975)*

FOOD STORES: Grocery, Chain

Aldi Inc ....D...... 330 273-7351
  Hinckley *(G-11994)*
Fred W Albrecht Grocery Co ....C...... 330 666-6781
  Akron *(G-230)*
Sack n Save Inc ....E...... 740 382-2464
  Marion *(G-13578)*

FOOD STORES: Grocery, Independent

Buehler Food Markets Inc ....C...... 330 364-3079
  Dover *(G-10179)*
Carfagnas Incorporated ....E...... 614 846-6340
  Columbus *(G-7199)*
Sommers Market LLC ....D...... 330 352-7470
  Hartville *(G-11831)*

FOOD STORES: Supermarket, More Than 100K Sq Ft, Hypermrkt

Walmart Inc ....C...... 937 399-0370
  Springfield *(G-17296)*
Walmart Inc ....B...... 740 286-8203
  Jackson *(G-12321)*

FOOD STORES: Supermarkets

Giant Eagle Inc ....D...... 330 364-5301
  Dover *(G-10190)*

FOOD STORES: Supermarkets, Chain

Giant Eagle Inc ....E...... 216 292-7000
  Bedford Heights *(G-1352)*
Jo Lynn Inc ....D...... 419 994-3204
  Loudonville *(G-13092)*
Kroger Co ....C...... 513 782-3300
  Cincinnati *(G-3946)*
Kroger Co ....C...... 740 335-4030
  Wshngtn CT Hs *(G-20028)*
Kroger Co ....C...... 937 294-7210
  Dayton *(G-9666)*
Kroger Co ....B...... 614 898-3200
  Westerville *(G-19419)*
Kroger Co ....D...... 740 363-4398
  Delaware *(G-10114)*
Kroger Co ....C...... 614 759-2745
  Columbus *(G-8015)*
Kroger Co ....B...... 937 376-7962
  Xenia *(G-20066)*
Kroger Co ....D...... 937 848-5990
  Dayton *(G-9667)*
Riser Foods Company ....D...... 216 292-7000
  Bedford Heights *(G-1359)*
Spartannash Company ....D...... 513 793-6300
  Cincinnati *(G-4556)*

FOOD STORES: Supermarkets, Independent

Farm House Food Distrs Inc ....E...... 216 791-6948
  Cleveland *(G-5573)*
Fisher Foods Marketing Inc ....C...... 330 497-3000
  North Canton *(G-15337)*
Lofinos Inc ....D...... 937 431-1662
  Beavercreek *(G-1250)*
Mary C Enterprises Inc ....D...... 937 253-6169
  Dayton *(G-9701)*

FOOTWEAR, WHOLESALE: Athletic

Brennan-Eberly Team Sports Inc ....E...... 419 865-8326
  Holland *(G-12013)*

FOOTWEAR, WHOLESALE: Shoes

Drew Ventures Inc ....E...... 740 653-4271
  Lancaster *(G-12528)*
Georgia Boot LLC ....D...... 740 753-1951
  Nelsonville *(G-14964)*
Lehigh Outfitters LLC ....C...... 740 753-1951
  Nelsonville *(G-14965)*
Safety Solutions Inc ....D...... 614 799-9900
  Dublin *(G-10446)*

FORGINGS

Edward W Daniel LLC ....E...... 440 647-1960
  Wellington *(G-18990)*
US Tsubaki Power Transm LLC ....C...... 419 626-4560
  Sandusky *(G-16807)*

FORGINGS: Iron & Steel

S&V Industries Inc ....E...... 330 666-1986
  Medina *(G-14121)*

FORGINGS: Nonferrous

Edward W Daniel LLC ....E...... 440 647-1960
  Wellington *(G-18990)*

FORGINGS: Plumbing Fixture, Nonferrous

Mansfield Plumbing Pdts LLC ....A...... 419 938-5211
  Perrysville *(G-16079)*

FORMS: Concrete, Sheet Metal

Efco Corp ....E...... 614 876-1226
  Columbus *(G-7586)*

FOUNDRIES: Aluminum

Akron Foundry Co ....C...... 330 745-3101
  Akron *(G-40)*
Akron Foundry Co ....E...... 330 745-3101
  Barberton *(G-950)*
Aluminum Line Products Company ....D...... 440 835-8880
  Westlake *(G-19459)*
Yoder Industries Inc ....C...... 937 278-5769
  Dayton *(G-10007)*

SERVICES SECTION

FREIGHT TRANSPORTATION ARRANGEMENTS

FOUNDRIES: Brass, Bronze & Copper

Anchor Bronze and Metals Inc ....E........ 440 549-5653
  Cleveland *(G-5033)*
National Bronze Mtls Ohio Inc ....E........ 440 277-1226
  Lorain *(G-13063)*

FOUNDRIES: Nonferrous

Technology House Ltd ....E........ 440 248-3025
  Streetsboro *(G-17434)*
Yoder Industries Inc ....C........ 937 278-5769
  Dayton *(G-10007)*

FOUNDRIES: Steel

B-Tek Scales LLC ....E........ 330 471-8900
  Canton *(G-2259)*
Worthington Industries Inc ....C........ 513 539-9291
  Monroe *(G-14718)*
Worthington Stelpac Systems LLC ....C........ 614 438-3205
  Columbus *(G-9009)*

FOUNDRY MACHINERY & EQPT

Equipment Manufacturers Intl ....E........ 216 651-6700
  Cleveland *(G-5548)*

FRAMES & FRAMING WHOLESALE

Culver Art & Frame Co ....E........ 740 548-6868
  Lewis Center *(G-12679)*
Hobby Lobby Stores Inc ....E........ 330 686-1508
  Stow *(G-17371)*

FRANCHISES, SELLING OR LICENSING

Cassanos Inc ....E........ 937 294-8400
  Dayton *(G-9388)*
Clark Brands LLC ....A........ 330 723-9886
  Medina *(G-14048)*
Convenient Food Mart Inc ....E........ 800 860-4844
  Mentor *(G-14163)*
Covelli Family Ltd Partnership ....E........ 330 856-3176
  Warren *(G-18842)*
Diet Center Worldwide Inc ....E........ 330 665-5861
  Akron *(G-192)*
East of Chicago Pizza Inc ....E........ 419 225-7116
  Lima *(G-12771)*
Epcon Cmmnties Franchising Inc ....D........ 614 761-1010
  Dublin *(G-10337)*
Escape Enterprises Inc ....E........ 614 224-0300
  Columbus *(G-7609)*
Giant Eagle Inc ....E........ 216 292-7000
  Bedford Heights *(G-1352)*
Gold Star Chili Inc ....E........ 513 231-4541
  Cincinnati *(G-3684)*
Gosh Enterprises Inc ....E........ 614 923-4700
  Columbus *(G-7762)*
Howley Bread Group Ltd ....D........ 440 808-1600
  Westlake *(G-19492)*
Larosas Inc ....A........ 513 347-5660
  Cincinnati *(G-3962)*
Marcos Inc ....C........ 419 885-4844
  Toledo *(G-18042)*
McDonalds Corporation ....E........ 614 682-1128
  Columbus *(G-8135)*
Moto Franchise Corporation ....E........ 937 291-1900
  Dayton *(G-9758)*
Ohio Valley Acquisition Inc ....B........ 513 553-0768
  Cincinnati *(G-4211)*
Petland Inc ....D........ 740 775-2464
  Chillicothe *(G-2870)*
Physicians Weight Ls Ctr Amer ....E........ 330 666-7952
  Akron *(G-389)*
Premier Broadcasting Co Inc ....E........ 614 866-0700
  Columbus *(G-8555)*
Red Robin Gourmet Burgers Inc ....D........ 330 305-1080
  Canton *(G-2505)*
ServiceMaster of Defiance Inc ....C........ 419 784-5570
  Defiance *(G-10057)*
Skyline Chili Inc ....C........ 513 874-1188
  Fairfield *(G-10910)*
Stanley Steemer Intl Inc ....C........ 614 764-2007
  Dublin *(G-10461)*
Ta Operating LLC ....E........ 440 808-9100
  Westlake *(G-19553)*
Travelcenters of America LLC ....B........ 724 981-9464
  Westlake *(G-19556)*
Tuffy Associates Corp ....E........ 419 865-6900
  Toledo *(G-18264)*
United Mercantile Corporation ....E........ 513 831-1300
  Milford *(G-14571)*

Wendys Company ....B........ 614 764-3100
  Dublin *(G-10491)*
Wendys Restaurants LLC ....C........ 614 764-3100
  Dublin *(G-10492)*

FREIGHT CAR LOADING & UNLOADING SVCS

Precision Vhcl Solutions LLC ....E........ 513 651-9444
  Cincinnati *(G-4320)*
Specialty Logistics Inc ....E........ 513 421-2041
  Cincinnati *(G-4558)*

FREIGHT CONSOLIDATION SVCS

Dayton Freight Lines Inc ....D........ 937 236-4880
  Dayton *(G-9475)*

FREIGHT FORWARDING ARRANGEMENTS

Blood Courier Inc ....E........ 216 251-3050
  Cleveland *(G-5123)*
C & M Express Logistics Inc ....E........ 440 350-0802
  Painesville *(G-15838)*
Ceva Freight LLC ....E........ 216 898-6765
  Cleveland *(G-5221)*
Ceva Logistics LLC ....B........ 614 482-5000
  Groveport *(G-11628)*
Ceva Logistics US Inc ....E........ 614 482-5107
  Columbus *(G-7245)*
CH Robinson Freight Svcs Ltd ....E........ 440 234-7811
  Cleveland *(G-5223)*
Colonial Courier Service Inc ....E........ 419 891-0922
  Maumee *(G-13897)*
Contech Trckg & Logistics LLC ....D........ 513 645-7000
  West Chester *(G-19050)*
Dhl Supply Chain (usa) ....D........ 614 836-1265
  Groveport *(G-11633)*
Dhl Supply Chain (usa) ....D........ 614 662-9200
  Lockbourne *(G-12951)*
Distribution Data Incorporated ....E........ 216 362-3009
  Brookpark *(G-1943)*
Exel Freight Connect Inc ....D........ 855 393-5378
  Columbus *(G-7619)*
Exel Global Logistics Inc ....E........ 440 243-5900
  Cleveland *(G-5561)*
Exel N Amercn Logistics Inc ....C........ 800 272-1052
  Westerville *(G-19398)*
Expeditors Intl Wash Inc ....E........ 614 492-9840
  Lockbourne *(G-12953)*
Gateway Distribution Inc ....E........ 513 891-4477
  Cincinnati *(G-3664)*
GKN Freight Services Inc ....E........ 419 232-5623
  Van Wert *(G-18633)*
Global Transportation Services ....E........ 614 409-0770
  Reynoldsburg *(G-16454)*
Martin Logistics Inc ....D........ 330 456-8000
  Canton *(G-2450)*
Nippon Express USA Inc ....D........ 614 801-5695
  Grove City *(G-11585)*
Nissin Intl Trnspt USA Inc ....D........ 937 644-2644
  Marysville *(G-13642)*
Noramco Transport Corp ....E........ 513 245-9050
  Cincinnati *(G-4172)*
Norfolk Southern Corporation ....E........ 216 518-8407
  Maple Heights *(G-13411)*
Nutrition Trnsp Svcs LLC ....C........ 937 962-2661
  Lewisburg *(G-12713)*
Overland Xpress LLC ....E........ 513 528-1158
  Cincinnati *(G-4245)*
Roadrunner Trnsp Systems Inc ....E........ 330 920-4101
  Peninsula *(G-15950)*
Ryan Logistics Inc ....E........ 937 642-4158
  Marysville *(G-13648)*
SMS Transport LLC ....E........ 937 813-8897
  Dayton *(G-9886)*
Tazmanian Freight Fwdg Inc ....E........ 216 265-7881
  Middleburg Heights *(G-14387)*
Tier One Distribution LLC ....D........ 937 323-6325
  Springfield *(G-17288)*
Tpg Noramco LLC ....E........ 513 245-9050
  Cincinnati *(G-4676)*
Transfreight Inc ....E........ 937 332-0366
  Troy *(G-18381)*
TV Minority Company Inc ....E........ 937 832-9350
  Englewood *(G-10722)*
USF Holland LLC ....C........ 216 941-4340
  Cleveland *(G-6678)*

FREIGHT FORWARDING ARRANGEMENTS: Domestic

Ardmore Power Logistics LLC ....E........ 216 502-0640
  Westlake *(G-19461)*
Ceva Freight LLC ....D........ 614 482-5100
  Groveport *(G-11627)*
Exel Global Logistics Inc ....E........ 614 409-4500
  Columbus *(G-7620)*
Horizon South Inc ....D........ 800 480-6829
  Cleveland *(G-5775)*
Innovative Logistics Group Inc ....E........ 937 832-9350
  Englewood *(G-10710)*
Krakowski Trucking Inc ....E........ 330 722-7935
  Medina *(G-14092)*

FREIGHT FORWARDING ARRANGEMENTS: Foreign

Elite Transportation Svcs LLC ....E........ 330 769-5830
  Seville *(G-16839)*
Expeditors Intl Wash Inc ....D........ 440 243-9900
  Cleveland *(G-5562)*

FREIGHT HANDLING SVCS: Air

Exel Inc ....B........ 614 865-8500
  Westerville *(G-19305)*
James Air Cargo Inc ....E........ 440 243-9095
  Cleveland *(G-5849)*

FREIGHT TRANSPORTATION ARRANGEMENTS

Airnet Systems Inc ....C........ 614 409-4900
  Columbus *(G-6958)*
Bleckmann USA LLC ....E........ 740 809-2645
  Johnstown *(G-12337)*
CH Robinson Company Inc ....E........ 614 933-5100
  Columbus *(G-7248)*
Containerport Group Inc ....D........ 216 692-3124
  Euclid *(G-10747)*
Cos Express Inc ....D........ 614 276-9000
  Columbus *(G-7446)*
County of Medina ....E........ 330 723-9670
  Medina *(G-14055)*
Craig Transportation Co ....E........ 419 874-7981
  Maumee *(G-13901)*
Dick Lavy Trucking Inc ....C........ 937 448-2104
  Bradford *(G-1806)*
Estes Express Lines Inc ....E........ 330 659-9750
  Richfield *(G-16506)*
Faf Inc ....A........ 800 496-4696
  Groveport *(G-11638)*
Faro Services Inc ....B........ 614 497-1700
  Groveport *(G-11639)*
FCA US LLC ....D........ 419 729-5959
  Toledo *(G-17882)*
Fedex Freight Corporation ....C........ 800 521-3505
  Lima *(G-12781)*
Fedex Freight Corporation ....C........ 800 728-8190
  Northwood *(G-15532)*
Fedex Supply Chain ....C........ 614 491-1518
  Lockbourne *(G-12955)*
Fedex Truckload Brokerage Inc ....E........ 234 310-4090
  Uniontown *(G-18520)*
Globaltranz Enterprises Inc ....C........ 513 745-0138
  Blue Ash *(G-1603)*
Hub City Terminals Inc ....D........ 440 779-2226
  Westlake *(G-19494)*
Hub City Terminals Inc ....E........ 419 217-5200
  Toledo *(G-17964)*
Jarrett Logistics Systems Inc ....C........ 330 682-0099
  Orrville *(G-15775)*
JB Hunt Transport Svcs Inc ....A........ 614 335-6681
  Columbus *(G-7937)*
Keller Logistics Group Inc ....E........ 866 276-9486
  Defiance *(G-10040)*
Lesaint Logistics LLC ....D........ 513 988-0101
  Trenton *(G-18341)*
Logikor LLC ....D........ 513 762-7678
  Cincinnati *(G-3993)*
Mid Ohio Vly Bulk Trnspt Inc ....E........ 740 373-2481
  Marietta *(G-13476)*
Millwood Inc ....E........ 330 393-4400
  Vienna *(G-18740)*
Millwood Natural LLC ....C........ 330 393-4400
  Vienna *(G-18741)*
Moving Solutions Inc ....D........ 440 946-9300
  Mentor *(G-14223)*

Employee Codes: A=Over 500 employees, B=251-500
C=101-250, D=51-100, E=25-50

2018 Harris Ohio
Services Directory

1495

FREIGHT TRANSPORTATION ARRANGEMENTS

Newark Parcel Service Company .... E 614 253-3777
  Columbus *(G-8274)*
Omni Interglobal Inc .... E 216 239-3833
  Cleveland *(G-6202)*
Packship Usa Inc .... D 330 682-7225
  Orrville *(G-15782)*
Ray Hamilton Companies .... E 513 641-5400
  Blue Ash *(G-1676)*
Rehrig Penn Logistics Inc .... E 614 833-2564
  Canal Winchester *(G-2166)*
Rk Express International LLC .... D 513 574-2400
  Cincinnati *(G-4429)*
Roe Transport Inc .... E 937 497-7161
  Sidney *(G-16951)*
Rondy Fleet Services Inc .... C 330 745-9016
  Barberton *(G-977)*
Stack Container Service Inc .... E 216 531-7555
  Euclid *(G-10777)*
Total Quality Logistics LLC .... D 513 831-2600
  Cincinnati *(G-4663)*
Trx Great Plains Inc .... D 855 259-9259
  Cleveland *(G-6620)*
Verst Group Logistics Inc .... E 513 772-2494
  Cincinnati *(G-4810)*
William R Morse .... E 440 352-2600
  Painesville *(G-15887)*
Wnb Group LLC .... E 513 641-5400
  Cincinnati *(G-4855)*
Wright Distribution Centers .... E 419 227-7621
  Lima *(G-12922)*
Xpo Intermodal Inc .... D 614 923-1400
  Dublin *(G-10494)*
Xpo Stacktrain LLC .... E 614 923-1400
  Dublin *(G-10496)*
Yrc Inc .... E 913 344-5174
  Copley *(G-9071)*

FROZEN FRUITS WHOLESALERS

Powell Company Ltd .... D 419 228-3552
  Lima *(G-12861)*

FRUIT & VEGETABLE MARKETS

Circle S Farms Inc .... E 614 878-9462
  Grove City *(G-11546)*
Euclid Fish Company .... D 440 951-6448
  Mentor *(G-14172)*

FRUIT STANDS OR MARKETS

Mapleside Valley LLC .... C 330 225-5576
  Brunswick *(G-1987)*
Miles Farmers Market Inc .... C 440 248-5222
  Solon *(G-17027)*
Vermilion Farm Market .... E 440 967-9666
  Vermilion *(G-18721)*

FRUITS & VEGETABLES WHOLESALERS: Fresh

Bowman Organic Farms Ltd .... E 740 246-3936
  Thornville *(G-17666)*
Circle S Farms Inc .... E 614 878-9462
  Grove City *(G-11546)*
Dno Inc .... D 614 231-3601
  Columbus *(G-7536)*
Giant Eagle Inc .... E 216 292-7000
  Bedford Heights *(G-1352)*
US Foods Inc .... A 614 539-7993
  West Chester *(G-19240)*
Vermilion Farm Market .... E 440 967-9666
  Vermilion *(G-18721)*

FUEL OIL DEALERS

Aim Leasing Company .... D 330 759-0438
  Girard *(G-11407)*
Bazell Oil Co Inc .... E 740 385-5420
  Logan *(G-12968)*
Centerra Co-Op .... E 419 281-2153
  Ashland *(G-672)*
Cincinnati - Vulcan Company .... D 513 242-5300
  Cincinnati *(G-3278)*
Circleville Oil Co .... D 740 474-7568
  Circleville *(G-4882)*
Cuyahoga Landmark Inc .... E 440 238-3900
  Strongsville *(G-17454)*
Duncan Oil Co .... E 937 426-5945
  Dayton *(G-9267)*
Earhart Petroleum Inc .... E 937 335-2928
  Troy *(G-18353)*

Lykins Oil Company .... E 513 831-8820
  Milford *(G-14534)*
New Vulco Mfg & Sales Co LLC .... D 513 242-2672
  Cincinnati *(G-4158)*
Santmyer Oil Co Inc .... D 330 262-6501
  Wooster *(G-19911)*
The Columbia Oil Co .... D 513 868-8700
  Liberty Twp *(G-12728)*
Troutwine Auto Sales Inc .... E 937 692-8373
  Arcanum *(G-631)*
Ull Inc .... E 440 543-5195
  Chagrin Falls *(G-2737)*

FUND RAISING ORGANIZATION, NON-FEE BASIS

Air Frce Museum Foundation Inc .... E 937 258-1218
  Dayton *(G-9253)*
Catholic Charities Corporation .... E 216 939-3713
  Cleveland *(G-5189)*
Catholic Charities Corporation .... E 216 268-4006
  Cleveland *(G-5190)*
Catholic Charities Corporation .... E 419 289-1903
  Ashland *(G-670)*
Catholic Charities Corporation .... E 216 334-2900
  Cleveland *(G-5191)*
Childrens Hospital Foundation .... E 614 355-0888
  Columbus *(G-7262)*
Cincinnati Institute Fine Arts .... E 513 871-2787
  Cincinnati *(G-3312)*
City of Columbus .... D 614 645-3072
  Columbus *(G-7281)*
Cleveland Jewish Federation .... C 216 593-2900
  Cleveland *(G-5322)*
Colonial Senior Services Inc .... E 513 856-8600
  Hamilton *(G-11713)*
Columbus Jewish Federation .... E 614 237-7686
  Columbus *(G-7361)*
Daybreak Inc .... E 937 395-4600
  Dayton *(G-9455)*
Easter Seals Metro Chicago Inc .... E 419 332-3016
  Fremont *(G-11196)*
Fort Hamilton Hosp Foundation .... B 513 867-5492
  Hamilton *(G-11727)*
Greene County Career Center .... E 937 372-6941
  Xenia *(G-20057)*
Interact For Health .... E 513 458-6600
  Cincinnati *(G-3831)*
Medill Elemntary Sch of Volntr .... E 740 687-7352
  Lancaster *(G-12556)*
National Multiple Sclerosis .... E 330 759-9066
  Youngstown *(G-20299)*
Nationwide Childrens Hospital .... C 614 722-2700
  Columbus *(G-8229)*
Orphan Foundation of America .... E 571 203-0270
  Beachwood *(G-1113)*
Playhouse Square Holdg Co LLC .... C 216 771-4444
  Cleveland *(G-6287)*
Sharon Twnship Frfighters Assn .... E 330 239-4992
  Sharon Center *(G-16878)*
United Way Greater Stark Cnty .... E 330 491-0445
  Canton *(G-2573)*
United Way of Summit County .... E 330 762-7601
  Akron *(G-486)*

FUNDRAISING SVCS

Bbs & Associates Inc .... E 330 665-5227
  Akron *(G-92)*
Board of Dir of Wittenbe .... D 937 327-6231
  Springfield *(G-17151)*
Bowling Green State Univ Fdn .... E 419 372-2551
  Bowling Green *(G-1766)*
Chapel HI Chrstn Schl Endwment ...... D 330 929-1901
  Cuyahoga Falls *(G-9171)*
Clovernook Center For The Bli .... C 513 522-3860
  Cincinnati *(G-3370)*
Innovairre Communications LLC .... D 330 869-8500
  Fairlawn *(G-10957)*
Lighthouse Youth Services Inc .... D 513 861-1111
  Cincinnati *(G-3981)*
Miami University .... D 513 529-1230
  Oxford *(G-15823)*
Ohio Presbyterian Rtr Svcs .... E 614 888-7800
  Columbus *(G-8369)*
White Oak Investments Inc .... E 614 491-1000
  Columbus *(G-8987)*

FUNERAL DIRECTOR

Busch Development Corporation .... E 440 842-7800
  Cleveland *(G-5161)*

FUNERAL HOME

Cole Selby Funeral Inc .... E 330 856-4695
  Vienna *(G-18736)*
Cummings and Davis Fnrl HM Inc ...... E 216 541-1111
  Cleveland *(G-5448)*
Davidson Becker Inc .... D 330 755-2111
  Struthers *(G-17530)*
Domajaparo Inc .... E 513 742-3600
  Cincinnati *(G-3497)*
E F Boyd & Son Inc .... E 216 791-0770
  Cleveland *(G-5516)*
Ferfolia Funeral Homes Inc .... E 216 663-4222
  Northfield *(G-15516)*
Keller Ochs Koch Inc .... E 419 332-8288
  Fremont *(G-11208)*
Martin Altmeyer Funeral Home .... E 330 385-3650
  East Liverpool *(G-10524)*
Newcomer Funeral Svc Group Inc ..... B 513 521-1971
  Cincinnati *(G-4160)*
Paul R Young Funeral Homes .... E 513 521-9303
  Cincinnati *(G-4264)*
Rutherford Funeral Home Inc .... E 614 451-0593
  Columbus *(G-8662)*
Spring Grove Funeral Homes Inc .... C 513 681-7526
  Cincinnati *(G-4564)*

FUNERAL HOMES & SVCS

Cremation Service Inc .... E 216 621-6222
  Cleveland *(G-5436)*

FUNGICIDES OR HERBICIDES

Scotts Company LLC .... A 937 644-3729
  Marysville *(G-13650)*

FURNACES & OVENS: Indl

Hannon Company .... D 330 456-4728
  Canton *(G-2393)*
RAD-Con Inc .... E 440 871-5720
  Lakewood *(G-12496)*
United McGill Corporation .... E 614 829-1200
  Groveport *(G-11681)*

FURNACES: Indl, Electric

Ajax Tocco Magnethermic Corp .... C 330 372-8511
  Warren *(G-18815)*

FURNACES: Warm Air, Electric

Columbus Heating & Vent Co .... C 614 274-1177
  Columbus *(G-7357)*

FURNITURE & CABINET STORES: Custom

Professional Laminate Mllwk Inc .... E 513 891-7858
  Milford *(G-14556)*

FURNITURE REFINISHING SVCS

American Signature Inc .... C 614 449-6107
  Columbus *(G-7007)*

FURNITURE REFINISHING SVCS

Soft Touch Wood LLC .... E 330 545-4204
  Girard *(G-11426)*

FURNITURE REPAIR & MAINTENANCE SVCS

Business Furniture LLC .... E 937 293-1010
  Dayton *(G-9375)*
Everybodys Inc .... E 937 293-1010
  Moraine *(G-14782)*

FURNITURE STORES

Beacon Company .... E 330 733-8322
  Akron *(G-95)*
Big Sandy Furniture Inc .... D 740 574-2113
  Franklin Furnace *(G-11169)*
Big Sandy Furniture Inc .... E 740 894-4242
  Chesapeake *(G-2781)*
Big Sandy Furniture Inc .... E 740 354-3193
  Portsmouth *(G-16265)*
Big Sandy Furniture Inc .... E 740 775-4244
  Chillicothe *(G-2816)*
Columbus AAA Corp .... E 614 889-2840
  Dublin *(G-10300)*
Dtv Inc .... E 216 226-5465
  Mayfield Heights *(G-14001)*

SERVICES SECTION

Patterson Pope Inc .... D 513 891-4430
  Cincinnati *(G-4263)*
Workshops of David T Smith .... E 513 932-2472
  Morrow *(G-14848)*

FURNITURE STORES: Office

Cbf Industries Inc .... E 216 229-9300
  Bedford *(G-1298)*
Corporate Environments of Ohio .... E 614 358-3375
  Columbus *(G-7442)*
EBO Inc .... E 216 229-9300
  Bedford *(G-1305)*
Loth Inc .... D 614 487-4000
  Columbus *(G-8077)*
Recycled Systems Furniture Inc .... E 614 880-9110
  Worthington *(G-19991)*
River City Furniture LLC .... D 513 612-7303
  West Chester *(G-19141)*
Thomas W Ruff and Company .... B 800 828-0234
  Columbus *(G-8838)*
Trimble Engineering & Cnstr .... E 937 233-8921
  Dayton *(G-9938)*

FURNITURE STORES: Outdoor & Garden

Harrison Industries Inc .... D 740 942-2988
  Cadiz *(G-2077)*

FURNITURE WHOLESALERS

Big Lots Inc .... E 330 726-0796
  Youngstown *(G-20115)*
Big Lots Stores Inc .... B 614 278-6800
  Columbus *(G-7107)*
Cornerstone Brands Inc .... A 513 603-1000
  West Chester *(G-19052)*
Federated Logistics .... E 937 294-3074
  Moraine *(G-14784)*
Friends Service Co Inc .... D 419 427-1704
  Findlay *(G-11033)*
Indepndence Office Bus Sup Inc .... D 216 398-8880
  Cleveland *(G-5815)*
La-Z-Boy Incorporated .... C 614 478-0898
  Columbus *(G-8026)*
McNerney & Son Inc .... E 419 666-0200
  Toledo *(G-18046)*
Mill Distributors Inc .... D 330 995-9200
  Aurora *(G-848)*
Pottery Barn Inc .... E 216 378-1211
  Cleveland *(G-6293)*
Sauder Woodworking Co .... A 419 446-3828
  Archbold *(G-645)*
Staples Inc .... E 614 472-2014
  Columbus *(G-8775)*
Value City Furniture Inc .... E 330 929-2111
  Cuyahoga Falls *(G-9231)*
Workshops of David T Smith .... E 513 932-2472
  Morrow *(G-14848)*

FURNITURE, MATTRESSES: Wholesalers

Mat Innovative Solutions LLC .... E 216 398-8010
  Independence *(G-12232)*

FURNITURE, OFFICE: Wholesalers

Apg Office Furnishings Inc .... E 216 621-4590
  Cleveland *(G-5048)*
Business Furniture LLC .... E 937 293-1010
  Dayton *(G-9375)*
Cbf Industries Inc .... E 216 229-9300
  Bedford *(G-1298)*
Continental Office Furn Corp .... C 614 262-5010
  Columbus *(G-7428)*
EBO Inc .... E 216 229-9300
  Bedford *(G-1305)*
Everybodys Inc .... E 937 293-1010
  Moraine *(G-14782)*
Jones Group Interiors Inc .... E 330 253-9180
  Akron *(G-297)*
King Business Interiors Inc .... E 614 430-0020
  Columbus *(G-7992)*
Loth Inc .... D 614 487-4000
  Columbus *(G-8077)*
Loth Inc .... D 614 225-1933
  Columbus *(G-8078)*
Office Furniture Resources Inc .... E 216 781-8200
  Cleveland *(G-6180)*
Regency Seating Inc .... E 330 848-3700
  Akron *(G-408)*
S P Richards Company .... E 614 497-2270
  Obetz *(G-15670)*

Seagate Office Products Inc .... E 419 861-6161
  Holland *(G-12055)*
Springfield Business Eqp Co .... E 937 322-3828
  Springfield *(G-17279)*
W B Mason Co Inc .... D 216 267-5000
  Cleveland *(G-6713)*
Wasserstrom Company .... B 614 228-6525
  Columbus *(G-8970)*

FURNITURE, WHOLESALE: Bedsprings

Mantua Manufacturing Co .... C 800 333-8333
  Bedford *(G-1320)*

FURNITURE, WHOLESALE: Filing Units

Central Business Equipment Co .... E 513 891-4430
  Cincinnati *(G-3210)*
Patterson Pope Inc .... D 513 891-4430
  Cincinnati *(G-4263)*

FURNITURE, WHOLESALE: Tables, Occasional

Progressive Furniture Inc .... E 419 446-4500
  Archbold *(G-641)*

FURNITURE: Bed Frames & Headboards, Wood

Progressive Furniture Inc .... E 419 446-4500
  Archbold *(G-641)*

FURNITURE: Frames, Box Springs Or Bedsprings, Metal

Mantua Manufacturing Co .... C 800 333-8333
  Bedford *(G-1320)*

FURNITURE: Household, Upholstered, Exc Wood Or Metal

Bulk Carrier Trnsp Eqp Co .... E 330 339-3333
  New Philadelphia *(G-15083)*

FURNITURE: Household, Wood

Diversified Products & Svcs .... C 740 393-6202
  Mount Vernon *(G-14893)*
Ken Harper .... C 740 439-4452
  Byesville *(G-2071)*
Vocational Services Inc .... C 216 431-8085
  Cleveland *(G-6709)*

FURNITURE: Institutional, Exc Wood

Soft Touch Wood LLC .... E 330 545-4204
  Girard *(G-11426)*
Yanfeng US Automotive .... D 419 662-4905
  Northwood *(G-15553)*

FURNITURE: Mattresses & Foundations

Walter F Stephens Jr Inc .... E 937 746-0521
  Franklin *(G-11167)*

FURNITURE: Office, Exc Wood

Casco Mfg Solutions Inc .... D 513 681-0003
  Cincinnati *(G-3191)*
National Electro-Coatings Inc .... D 216 898-0080
  Cleveland *(G-6106)*
Recycled Systems Furniture Inc .... E 614 880-9110
  Worthington *(G-19991)*

FURNITURE: Office, Wood

National Electro-Coatings Inc .... D 216 898-0080
  Cleveland *(G-6106)*
Symatic Inc .... E 330 225-1510
  Brunswick *(G-1991)*

FURNITURE: Play Pens, Children's, Wood

Western & Southern Lf Insur Co .... A 513 629-1800
  Cincinnati *(G-4839)*

GAMES & TOYS: Child Restraint Seats, Automotive

Recaro Child Safety LLC .... E 248 904-1570
  Cincinnati *(G-4392)*

GARAGE DOOR REPAIR SVCS

Dayton Door Sales Inc .... E 937 253-9181
  Dayton *(G-9471)*
Dayton Door Sales Inc .... E 937 253-9181
  Dayton *(G-9472)*

GARMENT: Pressing & cleaners' agents

C&C Clean Team Enterprises LLC .... C 513 321-5100
  Cincinnati *(G-3163)*

GAS & OIL FIELD EXPLORATION SVCS

Alliance Petroleum Corporation .... D 330 493-0440
  Canton *(G-2233)*
American Envmtl Group Ltd .... B 330 659-5930
  Richfield *(G-16495)*
Bakerwell Inc .... D 614 898-7590
  Westerville *(G-19286)*
Belden & Blake Corporation .... E 330 602-5551
  Dover *(G-10177)*
Chevron Ae Resources LLC .... E 330 654-4343
  Deerfield *(G-10017)*
Husky Marketing and Supply Co .... E 614 210-2300
  Dublin *(G-10370)*
Precision Geophysical Inc .... E 330 674-2198
  Millersburg *(G-14617)*
Range Rsurces - Appalachia LLC .... E 330 866-3301
  Dover *(G-10207)*
Resource America Inc .... E 330 896-8510
  Uniontown *(G-18536)*
Resource Energy Inc .... D 330 896-8510
  Uniontown *(G-18537)*
Triad Energy Corporation .... E 740 374-2940
  Marietta *(G-13505)*
True North Energy LLC .... E 440 442-0060
  Mayfield Heights *(G-14009)*

GAS & OIL FIELD SVCS, NEC

Timothy Sinfield .... E 740 685-3684
  Pleasant City *(G-16213)*

GAS & OTHER COMBINED SVCS

Columbia Gas of Ohio Inc .... D 419 539-6046
  Toledo *(G-17820)*
Dayton Power and Light Company ...... D 937 549-2641
  Manchester *(G-13255)*
Dayton Power and Light Company ...... E 937 331-3032
  Miamisburg *(G-14294)*
Dayton Power and Light Company ...... D 937 331-4123
  Moraine *(G-14774)*
Duke Energy Kentucky Inc .... C 704 594-6200
  Cincinnati *(G-3507)*
G & O Resources Ltd .... D 330 253-2525
  Akron *(G-232)*
Heritage Cooperative Inc .... D 419 294-2371
  West Mansfield *(G-19267)*
National Gas & Oil Corporation .... D 740 344-2102
  Newark *(G-15216)*

GAS FIELD MACHINERY & EQPT

Jet Rubber Company .... E 330 325-1821
  Rootstown *(G-16597)*

GAS PRODUCTION & DISTRIBUTION

True North Energy LLC .... E 614 222-0198
  Columbus *(G-8876)*
Usher Transport Inc .... E 614 875-0528
  Grove City *(G-11607)*

GAS PRODUCTION & DISTRIBUTION: Liq Petroleum, Distrib-Mains

Heritage Cooperative Inc .... D 419 294-2371
  West Mansfield *(G-19267)*

GAS STATIONS

Bp .... E 216 731-3826
  Euclid *(G-10745)*
Buehler Food Markets Inc .... C 330 364-3079
  Dover *(G-10179)*
Free Enterprises Incorporated .... D 330 722-2031
  Medina *(G-14067)*
Holland Oil Company .... D 330 835-1815
  Akron *(G-269)*
Travelcenters of America LLC .... D 330 769-2053
  Lodi *(G-12966)*

GAS STATIONS

Travelcenters of America LLC .... A 440 808-9100
  Westlake (G-19557)
Triumph Energy Corporation .... E 513 367-9900
  Harrison (G-11811)

GAS SYSTEM CONVERSION SVCS

Compliant Healthcare Tech LLC .... E 216 255-9607
  Cleveland (G-5389)

GASES: Acetylene

Delille Oxygen Company .... E 614 444-1177
  Columbus (G-7504)

GASES: Indl

National Gas & Oil Corporation .... D 740 344-2102
  Newark (G-15216)

GASKETS

Industry Products Co .... B 937 778-0585
  Piqua (G-16150)
Ohio Gasket and Shim Co Inc .... E 330 630-0626
  Akron (G-366)

GASKETS & SEALING DEVICES

Federal-Mogul LLC .... C 740 432-2393
  Cambridge (G-2113)
Ishikawa Gasket America Inc .... C 419 353-7300
  Bowling Green (G-1783)

GASOLINE FILLING STATIONS

Calvary Christian Ch of Ohio .... E 740 828-9000
  Frazeysburg (G-11174)
Convenient Food Mart Inc .... E 800 860-4844
  Mentor (G-14163)
Cuyahoga Landmark Inc .... E 440 238-3900
  Strongsville (G-17454)
Earhart Petroleum Inc .... E 937 335-2928
  Troy (G-18353)
Giles Marathon Inc .... E 440 974-8815
  Mentor (G-14180)
Irace Inc .... E 330 836-7247
  Akron (G-283)
Napoleon Wash-N-Fill Inc .... D 419 592-0851
  Napoleon (G-14947)
Sines Inc .... E 440 352-6572
  Painesville (G-15879)
Ta Operating LLC .... B 440 808-9100
  Westlake (G-19553)
Travelcenters America Inc .... A 440 808-9100
  Westlake (G-19555)
True North Energy LLC .... E 440 442-0060
  Mayfield Heights (G-14009)
True North Energy LLC .... E 877 245-9336
  Brecksville (G-1853)
United Dairy Farmers Inc .... C 513 396-8700
  Cincinnati (G-4731)

GASOLINE WHOLESALERS

Cuyahoga Landmark Inc .... E 440 238-3900
  Strongsville (G-17454)
Duncan Oil Co .... E 937 426-5945
  Dayton (G-9267)
Free Enterprises Incorporated .... D 330 722-2031
  Medina (G-14067)
Holland Oil Company .... D 330 835-1815
  Akron (G-269)
Krebs Steve BP Oil Co .... E 513 641-0150
  Cincinnati (G-3944)
Lykins Companies Inc .... C 513 831-8820
  Milford (G-14533)
Lykins Oil Company .... E 513 831-8820
  Milford (G-14534)
Marathon Petroleum Company LP .... B 330 479-5688
  Canton (G-2446)
Marathon Petroleum Company LP .... E 614 274-1125
  Columbus (G-8105)
Marathon Petroleum Company LP .... E 513 932-6007
  Lebanon (G-12624)
Marathon Petroleum Corporation .... B 419 422-2121
  Findlay (G-11061)
Mplx Terminals LLC .... E 440 526-4653
  Cleveland (G-6082)
Mplx Terminals LLC .... B 330 479-5539
  Canton (G-2466)
Mplx Terminals LLC .... E 504 252-8064
  Heath (G-11840)

Nzr Retail of Toledo Inc .... D 419 724-0005
  Toledo (G-18100)
The Columbia Oil Co .... D 513 868-8700
  Liberty Twp (G-12728)
True North Energy LLC .... E 877 245-9336
  Brecksville (G-1853)

GATES: Ornamental Metal

Mound Technologies Inc .... E 937 748-2937
  Springboro (G-17131)

GEARS: Power Transmission, Exc Auto

Forge Industries Inc .... A 330 782-8301
  Youngstown (G-20191)

GENERAL & INDUSTRIAL LOAN INSTITUTIONS

Mtd Acceptance Corp Inc .... B 330 225-2600
  Valley City (G-18621)

GENERAL COUNSELING SVCS

Access Counseling Services LLC .... C 513 649-8008
  Middletown (G-14472)
Adena Health System .... E 740 779-4888
  Chillicothe (G-2812)
Ben El Child Development Ctr .... E 937 465-0010
  Urbana (G-18573)
Bobby Tripodi Foundation Inc .... E 216 524-3787
  Independence (G-12190)
Catholic Charities Corporation .... E 216 939-3713
  Cleveland (G-5189)
Center For Families & Children .... E 440 888-0300
  Cleveland (G-5205)
Clermont Counseling Center .... E 513 345-8555
  Cincinnati (G-3363)
Clermont Counseling Center .... E 513 947-7000
  Amelia (G-579)
Cleveland Center For Etng Dsor .... E 216 765-2535
  Beachwood (G-1064)
Compdrug .... D 614 224-4506
  Columbus (G-7412)
Directions For Youth Families .... E 614 294-2661
  Columbus (G-7522)
Emerge Ministries Inc .... E 330 865-8351
  Akron (G-208)
F R S Connections .... E 937 393-9662
  Hillsboro (G-11973)
Family Life Counseling .... E 419 774-9969
  Mansfield (G-13299)
Friend To Friend Program .... E 216 861-1838
  Cleveland (G-5640)
Marion Area Counseling Ctr .... C 740 387-5210
  Marion (G-13553)
Mental Health & Recovery Ctr .... E 937 383-3031
  Wilmington (G-19773)
Mental Health Services .... E 216 623-6555
  Cleveland (G-6025)
Mercy Health .... E 440 324-0400
  Elyria (G-10652)
Mid-Ohio Psychological Svcs Inc .... E 740 687-0042
  Lancaster (G-12558)
Midwest Behavioral Care Ltd .... E 937 454-0092
  Dayton (G-9744)
North East Ohio Health Svcs .... D 216 831-6466
  Beachwood (G-1107)
Northland Brdg Franklin Cnty .... E 614 846-2588
  Columbus (G-8291)
Pastoral Counseling Svc Summit .... C 330 996-4600
  Akron (G-378)
Pressley Ridge Pryde .... E 513 559-1402
  Cincinnati (G-4325)
Ryan Sheridan .... E 330 270-2380
  Youngstown (G-20364)
Santantonio Diana and Assoc .... E 440 323-5121
  Elyria (G-10677)
Scioto Pnt Vly Mental Hlth Ctr .... C 740 775-1260
  Chillicothe (G-2884)
Southast Cmnty Mental Hlth Ctr .... E 614 293-9613
  Worthington (G-19998)
Syntero Inc .... E 614 889-5722
  Dublin (G-10471)
Talbert House Health .... E 513 541-7577
  Cincinnati (G-4622)
Townhall 2 .... E 330 678-3006
  Kent (G-12400)
Tuscarawas County Help ME Grow .... E 330 339-3493
  New Philadelphia (G-15119)

GENERAL MERCHANDISE, NONDURABLE, WHOLESALE

Aurora Wholesalers LLC .... D 440 248-5200
  Solon (G-16980)
Buy Below Retail Inc .... E 216 292-7805
  Cleveland (G-5165)
Clercom Inc .... D 513 724-6101
  Williamsburg (G-19630)
Hammacher Schlemmer & Co Inc .... C 513 860-4570
  West Chester (G-19088)
Harold Tatman & Sons Entps Inc .... E 740 655-2880
  Kingston (G-12450)
Hays Enterprises Inc .... E 330 299-8639
  Warren (G-18861)
Hi-Way Distributing Corp Amer .... D 330 645-6633
  Coventry Township (G-9125)
ICM Distributing Company Inc .... E 234 212-3030
  Twinsburg (G-18431)
Merchandise Inc .... D 513 353-2200
  Miamitown (G-14372)
Riser Foods Company .... D 216 292-7000
  Bedford Heights (G-1359)
Trademark Global LLC .... D 440 960-6226
  Lorain (G-13082)
X-S Merchandise Inc .... E 216 524-5620
  Independence (G-12278)

GERIATRIC RESIDENTIAL CARE FACILITY

Advanced Geriatric Education & .... E 888 393-9799
  Loveland (G-13109)
College Park Inc .... E 740 623-4607
  Coshocton (G-9091)
Eci Inc .... B 419 986-5566
  Burgoon (G-2057)
First Community Village .... B 614 324-4455
  Columbus (G-7664)
Glen Wesley Inc .... D 614 888-7492
  Columbus (G-7755)
Grace Hospice LLC .... E 440 826-0350
  Cleveland (G-5683)
Hcf Management Inc .... C 419 999-2055
  Lima (G-12792)
Lindley Inn .... E 740 797-9701
  The Plains (G-17665)
Oakleaf Village Ltd .... D 614 431-1739
  Columbus (G-8311)
Sattlerpearson Inc .... E 419 698-3822
  Northwood (G-15544)
United Church Homes Inc .... C 937 426-8481
  Beavercreek (G-1261)
Washington Manor Inc .... E 937 433-3441
  Dayton (G-9984)
West View Manor Inc .... C 330 264-8640
  Wooster (G-19928)
Whitehouse Operator LLC .... D 419 877-5338
  Whitehouse (G-19590)

GERIATRIC SOCIAL SVCS

Adams County Senior Citizens .... E 937 544-7459
  West Union (G-19273)
Aultman Hospital .... A 330 363-6262
  Canton (G-2255)
City of Highland Heights .... D 440 461-2441
  Cleveland (G-5262)
Comforcare Senior Services Inc .... E 513 777-4860
  West Chester (G-19048)
Concordia Care .... D 216 791-3580
  Cleveland (G-5391)
Otterbein Snior Lfstyle Chices .... C 419 394-2366
  Saint Marys (G-16682)

GIFT SHOP

Amish Door Inc .... B 330 359-5464
  Wilmot (G-19797)
Auxiliary St Lukes Hospital .... E 419 893-5911
  Maumee (G-13884)
Bennett Enterprises Inc .... B 419 874-3111
  Perrysburg (G-15978)
Columbus Zoological Park Assn .... C 614 645-3400
  Powell (G-16330)
Dutch Heritage Farms Inc .... E 330 893-3232
  Berlin (G-1478)
Dutchman Hospitality Group Inc .... C 614 873-3414
  Plain City (G-16189)
Golden Lamb .... C 513 932-5065
  Lebanon (G-12608)
Gs Ohio Inc .... D 614 885-5350
  Powell (G-16337)

SERVICES SECTION

H & M Patch Company............................D....... 614 339-8950
   Columbus *(G-7788)*
Hrm Enterprises Inc..............................C....... 330 877-9353
   Hartville *(G-11823)*
Lowes Greenhouse & Gift Shop............E....... 440 543-5123
   Chagrin Falls *(G-2722)*
Mapleside Valley LLC...........................C....... 330 225-5576
   Brunswick *(G-1987)*
Park Cincinnati Board............................D....... 513 421-4086
   Cincinnati *(G-4252)*
Sauder Village...B....... 419 446-2541
   Archbold *(G-644)*
Things Remembered Inc.......................C....... 440 473-2000
   Highland Heights *(G-11872)*
Waterbeds n Stuff Inc...........................E....... 614 871-1171
   Grove City *(G-11612)*
Youngs Jersey Dairy Inc.......................B....... 937 325-0629
   Yellow Springs *(G-20091)*

GIFT WRAPPING SVCS

D H Packaging Co..................................A....... 513 791-2022
   Cincinnati *(G-3455)*

GIFT, NOVELTY & SOUVENIR STORES: Party Favors

J V Hansel Inc..E....... 330 716-0806
   Warren *(G-18866)*

GIFTS & NOVELTIES: Wholesalers

Ameri Interntl Trade Grp Inc................E....... 419 586-6433
   Celina *(G-2634)*
Aunties Attic..E....... 740 548-5059
   Lewis Center *(G-12669)*
Dollar Paradise......................................E....... 216 432-0421
   Cleveland *(G-5498)*
Dwa Mrkting Prmtional Pdts LLC........E....... 216 476-0635
   Strongsville *(G-17457)*
Esc and Company Inc..........................E....... 614 794-0568
   Columbus *(G-7608)*
Flower Factory Inc................................D....... 614 275-6220
   Columbus *(G-7677)*
K & M International Inc.........................D....... 330 425-2550
   Twinsburg *(G-18435)*
M & M Wintergreens Inc......................D....... 216 398-1288
   Cleveland *(G-5961)*
Mark Feldstein & Assoc Inc.................E....... 419 867-9500
   Sylvania *(G-17600)*
Nannicola Wholesale Co......................D....... 330 799-0888
   Youngstown *(G-20293)*
Par International Inc.............................E....... 614 529-1300
   Obetz *(G-15669)*
Waterbeds n Stuff Inc...........................E....... 614 871-1171
   Grove City *(G-11612)*

GIRLS CAMPS

Archdiocese of Cincinnati....................D....... 513 729-1725
   Cincinnati *(G-3041)*
Camp Pinecliff Inc.................................D....... 614 236-5698
   Columbus *(G-7181)*

GLASS FABRICATORS

AGC Automotive Americas..................D....... 937 599-3131
   Bellefontaine *(G-1375)*
Anderson Glass Co Inc........................E....... 614 476-4877
   Columbus *(G-7018)*
Enclosure Suppliers LLC.....................E....... 513 782-3900
   Cincinnati *(G-3555)*
Fuyao Glass America Inc....................C....... 937 496-5777
   Dayton *(G-9566)*
Ghp II LLC..D....... 740 681-6825
   Lancaster *(G-12544)*
Rumpke Transportation Co LLC..........E....... 513 242-4600
   Cincinnati *(G-4454)*

GLASS PRDTS, FROM PURCHASED GLASS: Windshields

Safelite Group Inc.................................A....... 614 210-9000
   Columbus *(G-8672)*

GLASS PRDTS, PRESSED OR BLOWN: Glass Fibers, Textile

Owens Corning Sales LLC...................A....... 419 248-8000
   Toledo *(G-18114)*

GLASS STORES

Cleveland Glass Block Inc...................E....... 216 531-6363
   Cleveland *(G-5316)*
Cleveland Glass Block Inc...................E....... 614 252-5888
   Columbus *(G-7299)*
Lorain Glass Co Inc..............................D....... 440 277-6004
   Lorain *(G-13054)*
Medina Glass Block Inc.......................E....... 330 239-0239
   Medina *(G-14100)*
R C Hemm Glass Shops Inc................E....... 937 773-5591
   Piqua *(G-16163)*

GLASS, AUTOMOTIVE: Wholesalers

Fuyao Glass America Inc....................C....... 937 496-5777
   Dayton *(G-9566)*
Pgw Auto Glass LLC............................E....... 419 993-2421
   Lima *(G-12859)*

GLASS: Fiber

Industrial Fiberglass Spc Inc...............E....... 937 222-9000
   Dayton *(G-9630)*

GLASS: Flat

Schodorf Truck Body & Eqp Co...........E....... 614 228-6793
   Columbus *(G-8698)*

GLASS: Pressed & Blown, NEC

Anderson Glass Co Inc........................E....... 614 476-4877
   Columbus *(G-7018)*
Pgw Auto Glass LLC............................E....... 419 993-2421
   Lima *(G-12859)*

GLASS: Structural

Continental GL Sls & Inv Group..........B....... 614 679-1201
   Powell *(G-16332)*

GLOVES: Work

Chester West Holdings Inc..................C....... 800 647-1900
   Cincinnati *(G-3241)*
Wcm Holdings Inc................................C....... 513 705-2100
   Cincinnati *(G-4826)*

GO-CART DEALERS

Goofy Golf Inc..E....... 419 625-1308
   Sandusky *(G-16764)*

GOLF CARTS: Powered

Kmj Leasing Ltd...................................E....... 614 871-3883
   Orient *(G-15761)*

GOLF CARTS: Wholesalers

Century Equipment Inc........................E....... 419 865-7400
   Toledo *(G-17800)*
Century Equipment Inc........................E....... 216 292-6911
   Cleveland *(G-5216)*

GOLF COURSES: Public

797 Elks Golf Club Inc.........................E....... 937 382-2666
   Wilmington *(G-19740)*
A To Z Golf Managmnt Co...................E....... 937 434-4911
   Dayton *(G-9299)*
Aboutgolf Limited..................................D....... 419 482-9095
   Maumee *(G-13871)*
American Golf Corporation..................E....... 740 965-5122
   Galena *(G-11278)*
Amix Inc..E....... 513 539-7220
   Middletown *(C-14413)*
Aston Oaks Golf Club...........................E....... 513 467-0070
   North Bend *(G-15317)*
Avalon Golf & Country Club................D....... 330 539-5008
   Vienna *(G-18735)*
Avalon Lakes Golf Inc.........................E....... 330 856-8898
   Warren *(G-18825)*
Avon Properties Inc..............................E....... 440 934-6217
   Avon *(G-877)*
Avondale Golf Club...............................E....... 440 934-4398
   Avon *(G-878)*
Bayview Retirees Golf Course.............D....... 419 726-8081
   Toledo *(G-17764)*
Beckett Ridge Country Club................D....... 513 874-2710
   West Chester *(G-19024)*
Black Diamond Golf Course.................E....... 330 674-6110
   Millersburg *(G-14590)*

GOLF COURSES: Public

Blackbrook Country Club Inc..............E....... 440 951-0010
   Mentor *(G-14150)*
Blue Heron Golf Course Inc................E....... 330 722-0227
   Medina *(G-14039)*
Bramarjac Inc...E....... 419 884-3434
   Mansfield *(G-13268)*
Brandywine Country Club Inc............E....... 330 657-2525
   Peninsula *(G-1943)*
Brentwood Golf Club Inc.....................E....... 440 322-9254
   Sheffield Village *(G-16884)*
Bw Enterprises Inc................................E....... 937 568-9660
   South Charleston *(G-17075)*
Cambridge Country Club Company....E....... 740 439-2744
   Byesville *(G-2070)*
Championship Management Co..........E....... 740 524-4653
   Sunbury *(G-17552)*
Chardon Lakes Golf Course Inc.........E....... 440 285-4653
   Chardon *(G-2742)*
Chgc Inc..D....... 330 225-6122
   Valley City *(G-18614)*
Chippewa Golf Corp.............................E....... 330 658-2566
   Doylestown *(G-10224)*
Circling Hills Golf Course....................E....... 513 367-5858
   Harrison *(G-11794)*
City of Akron..E....... 330 864-0020
   Akron *(G-138)*
City of Beavercreek..............................D....... 937 320-0742
   Beavercreek *(G-1161)*
City of Blue Ash...................................E....... 513 745-8577
   Blue Ash *(G-1558)*
City of Cuyahoga Falls........................E....... 330 971-8416
   Cuyahoga Falls *(G-9174)*
City of Miamisburg...............................E....... 937 866-4653
   Miamisburg *(G-14284)*
City of Parma..E....... 440 885-8876
   Cleveland *(G-5272)*
City of Pickerington..............................E....... 614 645-8474
   Pickerington *(G-16089)*
City of Vandalia.....................................E....... 937 890-1300
   Vandalia *(G-18674)*
City of Westlake....................................E....... 440 835-6442
   Westlake *(G-19475)*
City of Willoughby................................E....... 440 953-4280
   Willoughby *(G-19652)*
Cleveland Metroparks..........................D....... 440 526-4285
   Brecksville *(G-1820)*
Cleveland Metroparks..........................D....... 440 232-7184
   Cleveland *(G-5330)*
Cleveland Metroparks..........................E....... 440 331-1070
   Cleveland *(G-5331)*
Columbus Frkln Cnty Pk......................E....... 614 861-3193
   Reynoldsburg *(G-16440)*
Columbus Zoological Park Assn........C....... 614 645-3400
   Powell *(G-16330)*
Creekside Golf Ltd...............................E....... 513 785-2999
   Fairfield Township *(G-10928)*
Creekside Ltd LLC................................D....... 513 583-4977
   Loveland *(G-13118)*
Crooked Tree Golf Course...................E....... 513 398-3933
   Cincinnati *(G-3441)*
Darby Creek Golf Course Inc.............E....... 937 349-7491
   Marysville *(G-13616)*
Dorlon Golf Club....................................E....... 440 236-8234
   Columbia Station *(G-6845)*
E J Links Co The Inc............................E....... 440 235-0501
   Olmsted Twp *(G-15675)*
Emerald Woods Golf Course...............E....... 440 236-8940
   Columbia Station *(G-6846)*
Fox Den Fairways Inc..........................E....... 330 678-6792
   Stow *(G-17368)*
Ganzfair Investment Inc......................E....... 614 792-6630
   Delaware *(G-10100)*
Gc At Stonelick Hills.............................E....... 513 735-4653
   Batavia *(G-1014)*
Golf Club of Dublin LLC......................E....... 614 889-5469
   Dublin *(G-10354)*
Grizzly Golf Center Inc........................B....... 513 398-5200
   Mason *(G-13712)*
Hawkins Markets Inc...........................E....... 330 435-4611
   Creston *(G-9150)*
Heatherwoode Golf Course..................C....... 937 748-3222
   Springboro *(G-17122)*
Heritage Golf Club Ltd Partnr.............D....... 614 777-1690
   Hilliard *(G-11908)*
Hickory Woods Golf Course Inc.........E....... 513 575-3900
   Loveland *(G-13131)*
Homestead Golf Course Inc................E....... 937 698-4876
   Tipp City *(G-17719)*
Indian Ridge Golf Club L L C..............E....... 513 524-4653
   Oxford *(G-15816)*

Joe McClelland Inc.....E..... 740 452-3036
Zanesville *(G-20492)*
Kinsale Golf & Fitnes CLB LLC.....C..... 740 881-6500
Powell *(G-16343)*
Lake Metroparks.....E..... 440 428-3164
Madison *(G-13228)*
Link & Reneissance Inc.....E..... 440 235-0501
Olmsted Twp *(G-15678)*
Links At Windy Knoll LLC.....D..... 937 631-3744
Springfield *(G-17222)*
Locust Hills Golf Inc.....E..... 937 265-5152
Springfield *(G-17224)*
Loyal Oak Golf Course Inc.....E..... 330 825-2904
Barberton *(G-971)*
Madison Route 20 LLC.....E..... 440 358-7888
Painesville *(G-15864)*
Mahoning Country Club Inc.....E..... 330 545-2517
Girard *(G-11420)*
Mayfair Country Club Inc.....D..... 330 699-2209
Uniontown *(G-18528)*
Meadowlake Corporation.....E..... 330 492-2010
Canton *(G-2456)*
Mill Creek Golf Course Corp.....E..... 740 666-7711
Ostrander *(G-15793)*
Mill Creek Metropolitan Park.....D..... 330 740-7112
Youngstown *(G-20287)*
Mohican Hills Golf Club Inc.....E..... 419 368-4700
Jeromesville *(G-12333)*
Moundbuilders Country Club Co.....D..... 740 344-4500
Newark *(G-15213)*
Norwalk Golf Properties Inc.....E..... 419 668-8535
Norwalk *(G-15586)*
Ohio State Parks Inc.....D..... 513 664-3504
College Corner *(G-6838)*
Park Arrowhead Golf Club Inc.....E..... 419 628-2444
Minster *(G-14667)*
Phoenix Golf Links.....E..... 614 539-3636
Grove City *(G-11591)*
Pine Brook Golf Club Inc.....E..... 440 748-2939
Grafton *(G-11443)*
Pine Hills Golf Club Inc.....E..... 330 225-4477
Hinckley *(G-11999)*
Pines Golf Club.....E..... 330 684-1414
Orrville *(G-15783)*
Quail Hollow Management Inc.....D..... 440 639-4000
Painesville *(G-15874)*
River Greens Golf Course Inc.....E..... 740 545-7817
West Lafayette *(G-19259)*
Sable Creek Golf Course Inc.....E..... 330 877-9606
Hartville *(G-11829)*
Scioto Reserve Inc.....D..... 740 881-9082
Powell *(G-16349)*
Scioto Reserve Inc.....D..... 740 881-6500
Powell *(G-16350)*
Shady Hollow Cntry CLB Co Inc.....D..... 330 832-1581
Massillon *(G-13854)*
Shaker Run Golf Club.....D..... 513 727-0007
Lebanon *(G-12645)*
Silver Lake Country Club.....D..... 330 688-6066
Silver Lake *(G-16964)*
Split Rock Golf Club Inc.....E..... 614 877-9755
Orient *(G-15762)*
Spring Hills Golf Club.....E..... 330 825-2439
New Franklin *(G-15047)*
Sugarbush Golf Inc.....E..... 330 527-4202
Garrettsville *(G-11353)*
Tamaron Golf LLC.....D..... 419 474-5067
Toledo *(G-18213)*
TW Recreational Services.....E..... 419 836-1466
Oregon *(G-15754)*
Valley View Golf Club Inc.....E..... 330 928-9034
Cuyahoga Falls *(G-9230)*
Vieira Inc.....E..... 937 599-3221
Bellefontaine *(G-1400)*
Wicked Woods Gulf Club Inc.....E..... 440 564-7960
Newbury *(G-15264)*
Win Tamer Corporation.....E..... 330 637-2881
Cortland *(G-9085)*
Wmvh LLC.....D..... 513 425-7886
Middletown *(G-14471)*
Yankee Run Golf Course.....D..... 330 448-8096
Brookfield *(G-1903)*

GOLF DRIVING RANGES

797 Elks Golf Club Inc.....E..... 937 382-2666
Wilmington *(G-19740)*
Bramarjac Inc.....E..... 419 884-3434
Mansfield *(G-13268)*
Clubcorp Usa Inc.....E..... 330 724-4444
Akron *(G-149)*
Darby Creek Golf Course Inc.....E..... 937 349-7491
Marysville *(G-13616)*
Hamilton County Parks District.....E..... 513 825-3701
Cincinnati *(G-3732)*
Youngs Jersey Dairy Inc.....B..... 937 325-0629
Yellow Springs *(G-20091)*

GOLF EQPT

Golf Galaxy Golfworks Inc.....C..... 740 328-4193
Newark *(G-15170)*

GOLF GOODS & EQPT

797 Elks Golf Club Inc.....E..... 937 382-2666
Wilmington *(G-19740)*
Akron Management Corp.....B..... 330 644-8441
Akron *(G-48)*
Avon Properties Inc.....E..... 440 934-6217
Avon *(G-877)*
Beckett Ridge Country Club.....D..... 513 874-2710
West Chester *(G-19024)*
Bramarjac Inc.....E..... 419 884-3434
Mansfield *(G-13268)*
Darby Creek Golf Course Inc.....E..... 937 349-7491
Marysville *(G-13616)*
Delaware Golf Club Inc.....E..... 740 362-2582
Delaware *(G-10089)*
Fox Den Fairways Inc.....E..... 330 678-6792
Stow *(G-17368)*
Grizzly Golf Center Inc.....B..... 513 398-5200
Mason *(G-13712)*
Lancaster Country Club.....D..... 740 654-3535
Lancaster *(G-12549)*
Links At Windy Knoll LLC.....D..... 937 631-3744
Springfield *(G-17222)*
Loyal Oak Golf Course Inc.....E..... 330 825-2904
Barberton *(G-971)*
OBannon Creek Golf Club.....E..... 513 683-5657
Loveland *(G-13151)*
Park Arrowhead Golf Club Inc.....E..... 419 628-2444
Minster *(G-14667)*
Pine Brook Golf Club Inc.....E..... 440 748-2939
Grafton *(G-11443)*
Tippecanoe Country Club Inc.....E..... 330 758-7518
Canfield *(G-2213)*
Walden Club.....D..... 330 995-7162
Aurora *(G-861)*

GOURMET FOOD STORES

Antonio Sofo Son Importing Co.....C..... 419 476-4211
Toledo *(G-17754)*
Gust Gallucci Co.....E..... 216 881-0045
Cleveland *(G-5711)*
Mustard Seed Health Fd Mkt Inc.....E..... 440 519-3663
Solon *(G-17031)*
Staufs Coffee Roasters II Inc.....E..... 614 487-6050
Columbus *(G-8785)*

GOVERNMENT, EXECUTIVE OFFICES: City & Town Managers' Offices

City of Compassion.....D..... 419 422-7800
Findlay *(G-11013)*
City of Louisville.....D..... 330 875-3321
Louisville *(G-13096)*
City of Oberlin.....E..... 440 775-1531
Oberlin *(G-15640)*
City of Wellston.....D..... 740 384-2428
Wellston *(G-18998)*
Delhi Township.....D..... 513 922-0060
Cincinnati *(G-3481)*
Granger Township.....E..... 330 239-2111
Medina *(G-14072)*
Village of Antwerp.....E..... 419 258-7422
Antwerp *(G-621)*
Village of Coldwater.....D..... 419 678-2685
Coldwater *(G-6837)*
Village of Cuyahoga Heights.....C..... 216 641-7020
Cleveland *(G-6697)*

GOVERNMENT, EXECUTIVE OFFICES: County Supervisor/Exec Office

Alpha Group of Delaware Inc.....D..... 614 222-1855
Columbus *(G-6976)*
Alpha Group of Delaware Inc.....D..... 740 368-5810
Delaware *(G-10069)*
Alpha Group of Delaware Inc.....E..... 740 368-5820
Delaware *(G-10070)*
Butler County of Ohio.....C..... 513 887-3728
Fairfield Township *(G-10926)*
Butler County Bd of Mental RE.....C..... 513 785-2870
Fairfield Township *(G-10927)*
Butler County Board of Develop.....E..... 513 867-5913
Fairfield *(G-10826)*
Clermont County Community Svcs.....E..... 513 732-2277
Batavia *(G-1000)*
County of Athens.....E..... 740 593-5514
Athens *(G-780)*
County of Athens.....D..... 740 592-3061
Athens *(G-781)*
County of Auglaize.....D..... 419 629-2419
New Bremen *(G-15017)*
County of Brown.....E..... 937 378-6104
Georgetown *(G-11391)*
County of Coshocton.....D..... 740 622-1020
Coshocton *(G-9100)*
County of Erie.....D..... 419 433-0617
Milan *(G-14493)*
County of Erie.....C..... 419 627-8733
Huron *(G-12164)*
County of Erie.....C..... 419 626-6781
Sandusky *(G-16748)*
County of Erie.....E..... 419 627-7710
Sandusky *(G-16749)*
County of Gallia.....D..... 740 446-3222
Gallipolis *(G-11311)*
County of Gallia.....E..... 740 446-2665
Gallipolis *(G-11312)*
County of Guernsey.....E..... 740 439-5555
Cambridge *(G-2106)*
County of Holmes.....E..... 330 279-2801
Holmesville *(G-12071)*
County of Holmes.....E..... 330 674-5916
Millersburg *(G-14599)*
County of Holmes.....C..... 330 674-1015
Millersburg *(G-14600)*
County of Holmes.....E..... 330 674-1111
Millersburg *(G-14601)*
County of Huron.....D..... 419 668-8126
Norwalk *(G-15568)*
County of Huron.....D..... 419 663-5437
Norwalk *(G-15569)*
County of Lucas.....C..... 419 213-3000
Toledo *(G-17833)*
County of Lucas.....C..... 419 213-4700
Toledo *(G-17834)*
County of Lucas.....B..... 419 213-8999
Toledo *(G-17835)*
County of Madison.....E..... 740 852-9404
London *(G-12996)*
County of Marion.....D..... 740 387-1035
Marion *(G-13535)*
County of Marion.....E..... 740 387-6688
Marion *(G-13532)*
County of Marion.....E..... 740 389-2317
Marion *(G-13534)*
County of Medina.....E..... 330 723-9553
Medina *(G-14053)*
County of Medina.....D..... 330 995-5243
Medina *(G-14054)*
County of Medina.....E..... 330 723-9670
Medina *(G-14055)*
County of Meigs.....E..... 740 992-2117
Middleport *(G-14406)*
County of Mercer.....E..... 419 586-5106
Celina *(G-2644)*
County of Montgomery.....E..... 937 225-4010
Dayton *(G-9435)*
County of Ottawa.....E..... 419 898-7433
Oak Harbor *(G-15606)*
County of Ottawa.....C..... 419 898-6459
Oak Harbor *(G-15607)*
County of Ottawa.....E..... 419 898-2089
Oak Harbor *(G-15608)*
County of Pickaway.....D..... 740 474-7588
Circleville *(G-4885)*
County of Richland.....E..... 419 774-5676
Mansfield *(G-13278)*
County of Richland.....C..... 419 774-4100
Mansfield *(G-13280)*
County of Richland.....C..... 419 774-5400
Mansfield *(G-13281)*
County of Richland.....E..... 419 774-5591
Mansfield *(G-13283)*
County of Richland.....B..... 419 774-4200
Mansfield *(G-13284)*
County of Sandusky.....C..... 419 334-2602
Fremont *(G-11192)*

SERVICES SECTION

County of Stark .... E 330 477-3609
  Massillon *(G-13799)*
County of Summit .... D 330 643-2300
  Akron *(G-168)*
County of Summit .... C 330 643-2850
  Akron *(G-170)*
County of Trumbull .... D 330 675-2640
  Warren *(G-18840)*
County of Tuscarawas .... E 330 343-0099
  New Philadelphia *(G-15090)*
County of Union .... E 937 645-3018
  Marysville *(G-13612)*
County of Wayne .... D 330 262-1786
  Wooster *(G-19854)*
County of Wayne .... D 330 345-5340
  Wooster *(G-19856)*
County of Williams .... C 419 636-4508
  Bryan *(G-2005)*
Franklin Cnty Bd Commissioners .... C 614 462-3030
  Columbus *(G-7682)*
Jackson-Vinton Cmnty Action .... E 740 384-3722
  Wellston *(G-19003)*
Mahoning County .... D 330 797-2837
  Youngstown *(G-20262)*
Noble Cnty Nble Cnty Cmmsoners ...... E 740 732-4958
  Caldwell *(G-2088)*
North Point Eductl Svc Ctr .... E 440 967-0904
  Huron *(G-12168)*
Oriana House Inc .... A 330 535-8116
  Akron *(G-373)*
R T Industries Inc .... C 937 339-8313
  Troy *(G-18375)*
Scioto County Ohio .... E 740 456-4164
  New Boston *(G-15013)*
Wood County Ohio .... C 419 353-8411
  Bowling Green *(G-1802)*

GOVERNMENT, EXECUTIVE OFFICES: Local

City of Aurora .... D 330 562-8662
  Aurora *(G-836)*

GOVERNMENT, EXECUTIVE OFFICES: Mayors'

City of Akron .... E 330 375-2851
  Akron *(G-141)*
City of Akron .... D 330 375-2355
  Akron *(G-142)*
City of Canal Winchester .... E 614 837-8276
  Canal Winchester *(G-2157)*
City of Cuyahoga Falls .... E 330 971-8416
  Cuyahoga Falls *(G-9174)*
City of Kenton .... E 419 674-4850
  Kenton *(G-12409)*
City of Marion .... D 740 382-1479
  Marion *(G-13531)*
City of New Philadelphia .... E 330 339-2121
  New Philadelphia *(G-15086)*
City of Norwalk .... E 419 663-6715
  Norwalk *(G-15563)*
City of Perrysburg .... E 419 872-8020
  Perrysburg *(G-15987)*
City of Portsmouth .... E 740 353-5419
  Portsmouth *(G-16269)*
City of Sandusky .... E 419 627-5907
  Sandusky *(G-16739)*
City of Toledo .... D 419 245-1800
  Toledo *(G-17807)*
City of Toledo .... A 419 245-1001
  Toledo *(G-17808)*
City of Toledo .... C 419 936-2924
  Toledo *(G-17810)*
City of Wadsworth .... E 330 334-1581
  Wadsworth *(G-18749)*
City of Wilmington .... F 937 382-7001
  Wilmington *(G-19748)*
City of Wooster .... E 330 263-5266
  Wooster *(G-19845)*
City of Youngstown .... E 330 742-8749
  Youngstown *(G-20144)*
Jackson Co Bd of Dd .... D 740 384-7938
  Wellston *(G-19001)*
Township of Copley .... D 330 666-1853
  Copley *(G-9067)*

GOVERNMENT, GENERAL: Administration

Butler County Clerk of Courts .... D 513 887-3282
  Hamilton *(G-11701)*
City of Cleveland .... D 216 664-2430
  Cleveland *(G-5254)*
Employment Relations Board .... E 513 863-0828
  Hamilton *(G-11726)*
Supreme Court of Ohio .... E 614 387-9800
  Cincinnati *(G-8809)*
Workers Compensation Ohio Bur .... A 614 644-6292
  Columbus *(G-9007)*

GOVERNMENT, GENERAL: Administration, County

County of Perry .... E 740 342-0416
  New Lexington *(G-15053)*
County of Tuscarawas .... D 330 339-7791
  New Philadelphia *(G-15091)*

GOVERNMENT, GENERAL: Administration, State

Natural Resources Ohio Dept .... E 614 265-6948
  Columbus *(G-8249)*
Transportation Ohio Department .... E 614 275-1300
  Columbus *(G-8865)*

GOVERNMENT, GENERAL: Supply Agency

Emergency Medical Svcs Billing .... E 216 664-2598
  Cleveland *(G-5534)*

GOVERNMENT, LEGISLATIVE BODIES: County

County of Lucas .... E 419 213-4500
  Toledo *(G-17837)*

GOVERNMENT, LEGISLATIVE BODIES: County Commissioner

County of Clermont .... E 513 732-7661
  Batavia *(G-1006)*

GOVERNMENT, LEGISLATIVE BODIES: Town Council

Town of Canal Fulton .... E 330 854-9448
  Canal Fulton *(G-2147)*

GRADING SVCS

D&M Carter LLC .... E 513 831-8843
  Miamiville *(G-14375)*
Great Lakes Crushing Ltd .... E 440 944-5500
  Wickliffe *(G-19599)*

GRAIN & FIELD BEANS WHOLESALERS

Andersons Inc .... C 419 893-5050
  Maumee *(G-13879)*
Consolidated Grain & Barge Co .... E 513 941-4805
  Cincinnati *(G-3411)*

GRANITE: Crushed & Broken

Martin Marietta Materials Inc .... E 513 701-1140
  West Chester *(G-19117)*

GRANITE: Cut & Shaped

Cutting Edge Countertops Inc .... E 419 873-9500
  Perrysburg *(G-15992)*

GRANTMAKING FOUNDATIONS

Altruism Society Inc .... D 877 283-4001
  Beachwood *(G-1049)*
Golden Endings Golden Ret Resc ...... E 614 486-0773
  Columbus *(G-7758)*
Miami Valley Community Action .... D 937 222-1009
  Dayton *(G-9728)*
Shawnee Weekday Early Lrng Ctr ...... E 419 991-4806
  Lima *(G-12930)*

GRAPHIC ARTS & RELATED DESIGN SVCS

Academy Graphic Comm Inc .... E 216 661-2550
  Cleveland *(G-4952)*
Adcom Group Inc .... E 216 574-9100
  Cleveland *(G-4955)*
Art-American Printing Plates .... E 216 241-4420
  Cleveland *(G-5069)*
Container Graphics Corp .... E 419 531-5133
  Toledo *(G-17831)*
Coyne Graphic Finishing Inc .... E 740 397-6232
  Mount Vernon *(G-14889)*

GROCERIES WHOLESALERS, NEC

Edward Howard & Co .... E 216 781-2400
  Cleveland *(G-5528)*
Evolution Crtive Solutions LLC .... E 513 681-4450
  Cincinnati *(G-3584)*
Fitch Inc .... D 614 885-3453
  Columbus *(G-7670)*
Graphic Publications Inc .... E 330 674-2300
  Millersburg *(G-14603)*
Haney Inc .... D 513 561-1441
  Cincinnati *(G-3735)*
Interbrand Hulefeld Inc .... D 513 421-2210
  Cincinnati *(G-3835)*
Mitosis LLC .... E 937 557-3440
  Dayton *(G-9752)*
Mueller Art Cover & Binding Co .... E 440 238-3303
  Strongsville *(G-17496)*
Northeast Scene Inc .... E 216 241-7550
  Cleveland *(G-6157)*
Real Art Design Group Inc .... E 937 223-9955
  Dayton *(G-9844)*
RGI Inc .... E 513 221-2121
  Cincinnati *(G-4411)*
Suntwist Corp .... D 800 935-3534
  Maple Heights *(G-13420)*
Taylor Made Graphics .... E 440 882-6318
  Cleveland *(G-6571)*
Third Dimension Inc .... E 877 926-3223
  Geneva *(G-11370)*

GRAPHITE MINING SVCS

Graftech Holdings Inc .... C 216 676-2000
  Independence *(G-12214)*

GRAVEL MINING

Fleming Construction Co .... E 740 494-2177
  Prospect *(G-16365)*
Stansley Mineral Resources Inc .... E 419 843-2813
  Sylvania *(G-17617)*
Watson Gravel Inc .... D 513 863-0070
  Hamilton *(G-11784)*

GREASES & INEDIBLE FATS, RENDERED

Inland Products Inc .... E 614 443-3425
  Columbus *(G-7899)*

GREENHOUSES: Prefabricated Metal

Ludy Greenhouse Mfg Corp .... D 800 255-5839
  New Madison *(G-15072)*
Rough Brothers Mfg Inc .... D 513 242-0310
  Cincinnati *(G-4446)*

GREETING CARD SHOPS

AG Interactive Inc .... C 216 889-5000
  Cleveland *(G-4967)*
Garys Pharmacy Inc .... E 937 456-5777
  Eaton *(G-10561)*
Gorant Chocolatier LLC .... E 330 726-8821
  Boardman *(G-1740)*
Mohun Health Care Center .... E 614 416-6132
  Columbus *(G-8182)*

GRINDING SVC: Precision, Commercial Or Indl

Micro Products Co Inc .... D 440 943-0258
  Willoughby Hills *(G-19732)*
Tipp Machine & Tool Inc .... C 937 890-8428
  Dayton *(G-9931)*
Universal Grinding Corporation .... E 216 631-9410
  Cleveland *(G-6648)*

GROCERIES WHOLESALERS, NEC

American Bottling Company .... D 614 237-4201
  Columbus *(G-6985)*
Brothers Trading Co Inc .... C 937 746-1010
  Springboro *(G-17117)*
Central Coca-Cola Btlg Co Inc .... C 419 476-6622
  Toledo *(G-17798)*
Dayton Heidelberg Distrg Co .... C 937 220-6450
  Moraine *(G-14772)*
EBY-Brown Company LLC .... C 937 324-1036
  Springfield *(G-17192)*
Frito-Lay North America Inc .... E 216 491-4000
  Cleveland *(G-5642)*
Frito-Lay North America Inc .... D 419 893-8171
  Maumee *(G-13919)*

G & J Pepsi-Cola Bottlers Inc ....B....... 740 354-9191
Franklin Furnace (G-11171)
G & J Pepsi-Cola Bottlers Inc ....D....... 740 452-2721
Zanesville (G-20479)
Generations Coffee Company LLC ....E....... 440 546-0901
Brecksville (G-1824)
Gordon Food Service Inc ....E....... 419 747-1212
Ontario (G-15689)
Gordon Food Service Inc ....E....... 419 225-8983
Lima (G-12786)
Gordon Food Service Inc ....E....... 440 953-1785
Mentor (G-14181)
Gordon Food Service Inc ....E....... 216 573-4900
Cleveland (G-5680)
Gust Gallucci Co ....E....... 216 881-0045
Cleveland (G-5711)
Hiland Group Incorporated ....D....... 330 499-8404
Canton (G-2399)
Luxfer Magtech Inc ....E....... 513 772-3066
Cincinnati (G-4003)
Maines Paper & Food Svc Inc ....E....... 216 643-7500
Bedford (G-1319)
Norcia Bakery ....E....... 330 454-1077
Canton (G-2474)
P-Americas LLC ....C....... 330 746-7652
Youngstown (G-20313)
Pepsi-Cola Metro Btlg Co Inc................B....... 937 461-4664
Dayton (G-9806)
Pepsi-Cola Metro Btlg Co Inc................B....... 330 963-0426
Twinsburg (G-18453)
Procter & Gamble Distrg LLC ....B....... 513 626-2500
Blue Ash (G-1667)
R L Lipton Distributing Co ....D....... 216 475-4150
Maple Heights (G-13414)
Schwebel Baking Company ....C....... 440 248-1500
Solon (G-17049)
Servatii Inc ....D....... 513 271-5040
Cincinnati (G-4500)
Skidmore Sales & Distrg Co Inc ....E....... 513 755-4200
West Chester (G-19156)
Skyline Chili Inc ....C....... 513 874-1188
Fairfield (G-10910)
Swh Mimis Cafe LLC ....D....... 614 433-0441
Columbus (G-6908)
Sygma Network Inc ....C....... 614 734-2500
Dublin (G-10470)
Sysco Cincinnati LLC ....B....... 513 563-6300
Cincinnati (G-4609)
Tiffin Paper Company ....E....... 419 447-2121
Tiffin (G-17706)
US Foods Inc ....C....... 330 963-6789
Twinsburg (G-18483)
US Foods Inc ....A....... 614 539-7993
West Chester (G-19240)

GROCERIES, GENERAL LINE WHOLESALERS

Albert Guarnieri & Co ....D....... 330 794-9834
Akron (G-63)
Anderson and Dubose Inc ....D....... 440 248-8800
Warren (G-18817)
Brothers Trading Co Inc ....C....... 937 746-1010
Springboro (G-17117)
Chas G Buchy Packing Company ....E....... 800 762-1060
Cincinnati (G-3232)
Circle S Farms Inc..................................E....... 614 878-9462
Grove City (G-11546)
Dwa Mrkting Prmtional Pdts LLC ....E....... 216 476-0635
Strongsville (G-17457)
EBY-Brown Company LLC ....C....... 937 324-1036
Springfield (G-17192)
Food Sample Express LLc ....D....... 330 225-3550
Brunswick (G-1978)
Forths Foods Inc.....................................E....... 740 886-9769
Proctorville (G-16358)
Giant Eagle Inc ....E....... 216 292-7000
Bedford Heights (G-1352)
Greeneview Foods LLC ....E....... 937 675-4161
Jamestown (G-12326)
Gummer Wholesale Inc ....D....... 740 928-0415
Heath (G-11838)
Hillandale Farms Corporation................E....... 330 724-3199
Akron (G-265)
J V Hansel Inc...E....... 330 716-0806
Warren (G-18866)
Jetro Cash and Carry Entps LLC............D....... 216 525-0101
Cleveland (G-5862)
John Zidian Co Inc ....D....... 330 743-6050
Youngstown (G-20240)

Kroger Co ....D....... 740 363-4398
Delaware (G-10114)
Kroger Co ....C....... 614 759-2745
Columbus (G-8015)
Kroger Co ....B....... 937 376-7962
Xenia (G-20066)
Kroger Co ....D....... 937 848-5990
Dayton (G-9667)
Larosas Inc ....A....... 513 347-5660
Cincinnati (G-3962)
Mattingly Foods Inc ....C....... 740 454-0136
Zanesville (G-20500)
Meadowbrook Meat Company Inc.........C....... 614 771-9660
Columbus (G-8140)
Mountain Foods Inc ....E....... 440 286-7177
Chardon (G-2758)
Nestle Usa Inc ....E....... 513 576-4930
Loveland (G-13148)
Novelart Manufacturing Company ....C....... 513 351-7700
Cincinnati (G-4187)
Ovations Food Services LP ....D....... 513 419-7254
Cincinnati (G-4244)
Physicians Weight Ls Ctr Amer.............E....... 330 666-7952
Akron (G-389)
Pollak Distributing Co Inc ....E....... 216 851-9911
Euclid (G-10772)
Restaurant Depot LLC ....E....... 216 525-0101
Cleveland (G-6386)
Ricking Paper and Specialty Co............E....... 513 825-3551
Cincinnati (G-4418)
Riser Foods Company.............................D....... 216 292-7000
Bedford Heights (G-1359)
Sandridge Food Corporation..................C....... 330 725-8883
Medina (G-14123)
Sherwood Food Distributors LLC ....B....... 216 662-6794
Maple Heights (G-13418)
Sommers Market LLC ....D....... 330 352-7470
Hartville (G-11831)
Spartannash Company............................D....... 419 998-2562
Lima (G-12881)
Spartannash Company............................D....... 937 599-1110
Bellefontaine (G-1398)
Sysco Central Ohio Inc...........................B....... 614 272-0658
Columbus (G-8816)
Tasty Pure Food Company......................E....... 330 434-8141
Akron (G-471)
Tusco Grocers Inc....................................D....... 740 922-8721
Dennison (G-10167)
Wrightway Fd Svc Rest Sup Inc ....E....... 419 222-7911
Lima (G-12923)

GROUP DAY CARE CENTER

Agj Kidz LLC ....E....... 937 350-1001
Centerville (G-2669)
Anderson Little...E....... 513 474-7800
Cincinnati (G-3025)
Aultman Hospital ....E....... 330 452-2273
Canton (G-2256)
Bright Horizons Chld Ctrs LLC ....E....... 614 754-7023
Columbus (G-7135)
Bright Horizons Chld Ctrs LLC ....E....... 614 566-9322
Columbus (G-7136)
Bright Horizons Chld Ctrs LLC ....E....... 330 375-7633
Akron (G-111)
Brooksedge Day Care Center ....E....... 614 529-0077
Hilliard (G-11883)
Centerville Child Development...............E....... 937 434-5949
Dayton (G-9393)
Champons In Making Daycare LLC ....E....... 937 728-4886
Wilmington (G-19747)
Child Dev Ctr Jackson Cnty ....E....... 740 286-3995
Jackson (G-12309)
Christian Perry Pre School ....E....... 330 477-7262
Canton (G-2307)
Coleeta Daycare Llc................................E....... 614 310-6465
Columbus (G-7317)
Creative Learning Child Care..................E....... 440 729-9001
Chesterland (G-2794)
Early Learning Tree Chld Ctr ....D....... 937 276-3221
Dayton (G-9512)
Edwards Creative Learning Ctr ....E....... 614 492-8977
Columbus (G-7583)
Epworth United Methodist Ch.................D....... 740 387-1062
Marion (G-13539)
Future Advantage Inc ....E....... 330 686-7707
Stow (G-17369)
Giggles & Wiggles Inc ....E....... 740 574-4536
Wheelersburg (G-19577)
Gingerbread Inc ....E....... 513 793-4122
Blue Ash (G-1601)

Goddard School ....E....... 614 920-9810
Canal Winchester (G-2160)
Hilty Child Care Center...........................E....... 419 384-3220
Pandora (G-15891)
Hopes Drams Childcare Lrng Ctr ....E....... 330 793-8260
Youngstown (G-20220)
Jewish Day Schl Assoc Grtr Clv.............D....... 216 763-1400
Pepper Pike (G-15957)
Jolly Tots Too Inc ....E....... 614 471-0688
Columbus (G-7946)
Kandy Kane Childrens Lrng Ctr ....E....... 330 864-6642
Akron (G-301)
Kare A Lot ....E....... 614 298-8933
Columbus (G-7963)
Kare A Lot Infnt Tddlr Dev Ctr ....E....... 614 481-7532
Columbus (G-7964)
Kiddie Kollege Inc....................................E....... 440 327-5435
North Ridgeville (G-15466)
Kids Ahead Inc ....E....... 330 628-7404
Mogadore (G-14680)
Kids Country ....E....... 330 899-0909
Uniontown (G-18525)
Kids-Play Inc ....E....... 330 896-2400
Uniontown (G-18526)
Kinder Kare Day Nursery ....E....... 740 886-6905
Proctorville (G-16360)
Kindercare Education LLC.....................E....... 513 896-4769
Fairfield Township (G-10933)
Kindercare Education LLC.....................E....... 330 405-5556
Twinsburg (G-18438)
Kindercare Education LLC.....................E....... 440 442-3360
Cleveland (G-5902)
Kindercare Learning Ctrs Inc.................E....... 937 435-2353
Dayton (G-9659)
Kindercare Learning Ctrs Inc.................E....... 614 888-9696
Worthington (G-19966)
Kindercare Learning Ctrs LLC...............E....... 740 549-0264
Lewis Center (G-12691)
Kindercare Learning Ctrs LLC...............E....... 440 442-8067
Cleveland (G-5903)
Kindercare Learning Ctrs LLC...............E....... 614 866-4446
Reynoldsburg (G-16463)
Kindercare Learning Ctrs LLC...............E....... 513 791-4712
Cincinnati (G-3927)
Kindertown Educational Centers ....E....... 859 344-8802
Cleves (G-6802)
Kozmic Korner ....E....... 330 494-4148
Canton (G-2429)
M J J B Ltd..E....... 937 748-4414
Springboro (G-17127)
McKinley Early Childhood Ctr ....E....... 330 454-4800
Canton (G-2454)
McKinley Early Childhood Ctr ....E....... 330 252-2552
Akron (G-334)
Medina Advantage Inc ....E....... 330 723-8697
Medina (G-14096)
Ministerial Day Care-Headstart..............E....... 216 541-7400
Cleveland (G-6068)
Morrow County Child Care Ctr ....D....... 419 946-5007
Mount Gilead (G-14857)
Oberlin Early Childhood Center ....E....... 440 774-8193
Oberlin (G-15657)
Powell Enterprises Inc.............................E....... 614 882-0111
Westerville (G-19342)
Rainbow Station Day Care Inc ....E....... 614 759-8667
Pickerington (G-16104)
Something Special Lrng Ctr Inc ....E....... 419 878-4190
Waterville (G-18945)
Sunny Day Academy LLC ....E....... 614 718-1717
Dublin (G-10465)
Van Wert County Day Care Inc ....E....... 419 238-9918
Van Wert (G-18647)
Wesley Educ Cntr For Chldrn ....E....... 513 569-1840
Cincinnati (G-4834)
West Chester Chrstn Chld ....E....... 513 777-6300
West Chester (G-19184)
Young Services Inc ....E....... 419 704-2009
Toledo (G-18324)

GROUP FOSTER HOME

Akron Summit Cmnty Action Agcy ....C....... 330 572-8532
Akron (G-56)
Commons of Providence.........................D....... 419 624-1171
Sandusky (G-16744)
County of Lorain ....C....... 440 329-5340
Elyria (G-10616)
Help Foundation Inc ....E....... 216 486-5258
Cleveland (G-5748)
Mended Reeds Home..............................E....... 740 533-1883
Ironton (G-12298)

Oasis Thrptic Fster Care Ntwrk ....E 740 698-0340
  Albany *(G-520)*
Rescare ....E 740 867-3051
  Chesapeake *(G-2787)*
Saint Joseph Orphanage ....D 937 643-0398
  Moraine *(G-14822)*

GROUP HOSPITALIZATION PLANS

Anthem Insurance Companies Inc ....E 330 492-2151
  Canton *(G-2242)*
Anthem Insurance Companies Inc ....C 330 783-9800
  Seven Hills *(G-16826)*
Aultcare Corp ....B 330 363-6360
  Canton *(G-2249)*
Kelley Companies ....D 330 668-6100
  Copley *(G-9057)*
Ohio Health Choice Inc ....D 800 554-0027
  Cleveland *(G-6191)*
United Healthcare Ohio Inc ....D 216 694-4080
  Cleveland *(G-6640)*
United Healthcare Ohio Inc ....B 614 410-7000
  Columbus *(G-8891)*

GUARD PROTECTIVE SVCS

Cal Crim Inc ....C 513 563-5500
  Trenton *(G-18340)*
Community Crime Patrol ....E 614 247-1765
  Columbus *(G-7402)*
Darke County Sheriffs Patrol ....D 937 548-3399
  Greenville *(G-11495)*
Highway Patrol ....E 740 354-2888
  Lucasville *(G-13181)*
Metro Safety and Security LLC ....D 614 792-2770
  Columbus *(G-8154)*
National Alliance SEC Agcy Inc ....C 937 387-6517
  Dayton *(G-9768)*
Public Safety Ohio Department ....E 419 768-3955
  Mount Gilead *(G-14863)*
Shane Security Services Inc ....D 330 757-4001
  Poland *(G-16226)*

GUARD SVCS

1st Advnce SEC Invstgtions Inc ....E 937 317-4433
  Dayton *(G-9292)*
American Svcs & Protection LLC ....D 614 884-0177
  Columbus *(G-7009)*
Area Wide Protective Inc ....E 513 321-9889
  Fairfield *(G-10820)*
Bdtk Private Security ....E 937 520-1784
  Dayton *(G-9350)*
Metropolitan Security Svcs Inc ....A 216 298-4076
  Cleveland *(G-6044)*
Metropolitan Security Svcs Inc ....B 330 253-6459
  Akron *(G-343)*
NASA-Trmi Group Inc ....D 937 387-6517
  Dayton *(G-9767)*
Official Investigations Inc ....D 844 263-3424
  Cincinnati *(G-4200)*
Rmi International Inc ....D 937 642-5032
  Marysville *(G-13647)*
Start-Black Servicesjv LLC ....D 740 598-4891
  Mingo Junction *(G-14657)*
Veteran Security Patrol Co ....C 513 381-4482
  Cincinnati *(G-4811)*

GUIDED MISSILES & SPACE VEHICLES

Boeing Company ....A 740 788-4000
  Newark *(G-15147)*

GYMNASTICS INSTRUCTION

Christian Twigs Gymnastics CLB ....E 937 866-8356
  Dayton *(G-9406)*
Cincinnati Gymnastics Academy ....E 513 860-3082
  Fairfield *(G-10834)*
Flytz Gymnastics Inc ....E 330 926-2900
  Cuyahoga Falls *(G-9189)*
Gymnastic World Inc ....E 440 526-2970
  Cleveland *(G-5712)*
Integrity Global Marketing LLC ....D 330 492-9989
  Canton *(G-2412)*
Midwest Gymnstics Cheerleading ....E 614 764-0775
  Dublin *(G-10398)*

HAIRDRESSERS

Alsan Corporation ....D 330 385-3636
  East Liverpool *(G-10514)*

Anthony David Salon & Spa ....E 440 233-8570
  Lorain *(G-13013)*
Anthony Roccos Hair Design ....E 440 646-1925
  Cleveland *(G-5044)*
Attractions ....E 740 592-5600
  Athens *(G-778)*
Bella Capelli Inc ....E 440 899-1225
  Westlake *(G-19465)*
Castilian & Co ....E 937 836-9671
  Englewood *(G-10699)*
Dana Lauren Salon & Spa ....E 440 262-1092
  Broadview Heights *(G-1877)*
David Scott Salon ....E 440 734-7595
  North Olmsted *(G-15419)*
Diane Babiuch ....E 419 867-8837
  Holland *(G-12020)*
Edge Hair Design & Spa ....E 330 477-2300
  Canton *(G-2352)*
Frank Santo LLC ....E 216 831-9374
  Pepper Pike *(G-15955)*
Hair Forum ....E 513 245-0800
  Cincinnati *(G-3729)*
Hair Shoppe Inc ....D 330 497-1651
  Canton *(G-2388)*
Hairy Cactus Salon Inc ....E 513 771-9335
  West Chester *(G-19087)*
Jbj Enterprises Inc ....E 440 992-6051
  Ashtabula *(G-750)*
John Rbrts Hair Studio Spa Inc ....D 216 839-1430
  Cleveland *(G-5868)*
L A Hair Force ....E 419 756-3101
  Mansfield *(G-13321)*
Marios International Spa & Ht ....E 440 845-7373
  Cleveland *(G-5979)*
Michael A Garcia Salon ....E 614 235-1605
  Columbus *(G-8157)*
Mitchells Salon & Day Spa ....B 513 793-0900
  Cincinnati *(G-4104)*
Noggins Hair Design Inc ....E 513 474-4405
  Cincinnati *(G-4171)*
P JS Hair Styling Shoppe ....E 440 333-1244
  Cleveland *(G-6226)*
Paragon Salons Inc. ....E 513 683-6700
  Cincinnati *(G-4251)*
Philip Icuss Jr ....E 740 264-4647
  Steubenville *(G-17333)*
Reflections Hair Studio Inc ....E 330 725-5782
  Medina *(G-14119)*
Salon La ....E 513 784-1700
  Cincinnati *(G-4473)*
Shamas Ltd ....E 419 872-9908
  Perrysburg *(G-16058)*
Sheer Professionals Inc ....E 330 345-8666
  Wooster *(G-19916)*
Tanyas Image LLC ....E 513 386-9981
  Cincinnati *(G-4623)*
Urban Oasis Inc ....E 614 766-9946
  Dublin *(G-10480)*

HALFWAY GROUP HOME, PERSONS WITH SOCIAL OR PERSONAL PROBLEMS

Alvis Inc ....C 614 252-1788
  Columbus *(G-6979)*
Lutheran Home ....D 419 724-1414
  Toledo *(G-18019)*
Midwest Health Services Inc ....C 330 828-0779
  Massillon *(G-13840)*

HALFWAY HOME FOR DELINQUENTS & OFFENDERS

Womens Recovery Center ....E 937 562-2400
  Xenia *(G-20084)*

HAND TOOLS, NEC: Wholesalers

Elliott Tool Technologies Ltd ....D 937 253-6133
  Dayton *(G-9524)*

HANDYMAN SVCS

Handy Hubby ....E 419 754-1150
  Toledo *(G-17930)*
Sr Improvements Services LLC ....E 567 207-6488
  Vickery *(G-18733)*

HANGARS & OTHER AIRCRAFT STORAGE FACILITIES

Winner Aviation Corporation ....D 330 856-5000
  Vienna *(G-18742)*

HARDWARE

Action Coupling & Eqp Inc ....D 330 279-4242
  Holmesville *(G-12070)*
Edward W Daniel LLC ....E 440 647-1960
  Wellington *(G-18990)*
First Francis Company Inc ....E 440 352-8927
  Painesville *(G-15857)*
Gateway Concrete Forming Svcs ....D 513 353-2000
  Miamitown *(G-14371)*
Hebco Products Inc ....A 419 562-7987
  Bucyrus *(G-2039)*
Ohio Hydraulics Inc ....E 513 771-2590
  Cincinnati *(G-4207)*
Samsel Rope & Marine Supply Co ....E 216 241-0333
  Cleveland *(G-6442)*
Summers Acquisition Corp ....E 216 941-7700
  Cleveland *(G-6546)*

HARDWARE & BUILDING PRDTS: Plastic

Associated Materials LLC ....B 330 929-1811
  Cuyahoga Falls *(G-9161)*
Associated Materials Group Inc ....E 330 929-1811
  Cuyahoga Falls *(G-9162)*
Associated Mtls Holdings LLC ....A 330 929-1811
  Cuyahoga Falls *(G-9163)*
Gorell Enterprises Inc ....B 724 465-1800
  Streetsboro *(G-17414)*
Style Crest Enterprises Inc ....D 419 355-8586
  Fremont *(G-11224)*

HARDWARE & EQPT: Stage, Exc Lighting

Janson Industries ....D 330 455-7029
  Canton *(G-2417)*

HARDWARE STORES

Ace Hardware Corporation ....C 440 333-4223
  Rocky River *(G-16568)*
Ace Rental Place ....D 937 642-2891
  Marysville *(G-13605)*
Carter-Jones Lumber Company ....D 330 784-5441
  Akron *(G-123)*
Cornelius Joel Roofing Inc ....E 513 367-4401
  Harrison *(G-11795)*
Daniels Lumber Co Inc ....D 330 533-2211
  Canfield *(G-2188)*
Do Cut Sales & Service Inc ....E 330 533-9878
  Warren *(G-18851)*
Do It Best Corp ....C 330 725-3859
  Medina *(G-14061)*
Famous Enterprises Inc ....E 216 529-1010
  Cleveland *(G-5571)*
Hartville Hardware Inc ....C 330 877-4690
  Hartville *(G-11820)*
Lochard Inc ....D 937 492-8811
  Sidney *(G-16940)*
Matco Tools Corporation ....B 330 929-4949
  Stow *(G-17382)*
Nilco LLC ....E 888 248-5151
  Hartville *(G-11827)*
Thomas Do-It Center Inc ....E 740 446-2002
  Gallipolis *(G-11339)*

HARDWARE STORES: Door Locks & Lock Sets

Bass Security Services Inc ....D 216 755-1200
  Bedford Heights *(G-1347)*

HARDWARE STORES: Pumps & Pumping Eqpt

Best Aire Compressor Service ....D 419 726-0055
  Millbury *(G-14577)*

HARDWARE STORES: Tools

Slaters Inc ....E 740 654-2204
  Lancaster *(G-12574)*
Tool Testing Lab Inc ....E 937 898-5696
  Tipp City *(G-17730)*

HARDWARE WHOLESALERS

HARDWARE WHOLESALERS

Company		Phone
Ace Hardware Corporation	C	440 333-4223
Rocky River *(G-16568)*		
Atlas Bolt & Screw Company LLC	C	419 289-6171
Ashland *(G-660)*		
Barnes Group Inc	E	419 891-9292
Maumee *(G-13885)*		
Do Cut Sales & Service Inc	E	330 533-9878
Warren *(G-18851)*		
F & M Mafco Inc	C	513 367-2151
Harrison *(G-11797)*		
GMI Holdings Inc	D	330 794-0846
Akron *(G-239)*		
Hd Supply Facilities Maint Ltd	E	440 542-9188
Solon *(G-17014)*		
Hillman Companies Inc	D	513 851-4900
Cincinnati *(G-3762)*		
Hillman Companies Inc	B	513 851-4900
Cincinnati *(G-3763)*		
Hillman Companies Inc	E	513 851-4900
Cincinnati *(G-3764)*		
Hillman Group Inc	C	513 851-4900
Cincinnati *(G-3765)*		
Hman Group Holdings Inc	A	513 851-4900
Cincinnati *(G-3773)*		
Khempco Bldg Sup Co Ltd Partnr	D	740 549-0465
Delaware *(G-10113)*		
Mae Holding Company	E	513 751-2424
Cincinnati *(G-4011)*		
Matco Tools Corporation	B	330 929-4949
Stow *(G-17382)*		
Menards Contractor Sales	E	419 726-4029
Toledo *(G-18050)*		
Norwood Hardware & Supply Co	E	513 733-1175
Cincinnati *(G-4185)*		
Ohashi Technica USA Inc	E	740 965-5115
Sunbury *(G-17560)*		
Reitter Stucco Inc	E	614 291-2212
Columbus *(G-8609)*		
Serv-A-Lite Products Inc	C	309 762-7741
(G-4498)		
The Mau-Sherwood Supply Co	E	330 405-1200
Twinsburg *(G-18475)*		
Waxman Industries Inc	C	440 439-1830
Cleveland *(G-6726)*		
Ziegler Bolt & Parts Co	D	330 478-2542
Canton *(G-2595)*		

HARDWARE, WHOLESALE: Bolts

Company		Phone
Hodell-Natco Industries Inc	E	773 472-2305
Cleveland *(G-5765)*		
Mid-State Bolt and Nut Co Inc	E	614 253-8631
Columbus *(G-8166)*		

HARDWARE, WHOLESALE: Builders', NEC

Company		Phone
Akron Hardware Consultants Inc	D	330 644-7167
Akron *(G-47)*		
Bostwick-Braun Company	D	419 259-3600
Toledo *(G-17778)*		
Do It Best Corp	C	330 725-3859
Medina *(G-14061)*		
La Force Inc	D	614 875-2545
Grove City *(G-11574)*		
LE Smith Company	D	419 636-4555
Bryan *(G-2009)*		
Mazzella Holding Company Inc	E	513 772-4466
Cleveland *(G-5997)*		
Midland Hardware Company	E	216 228-7721
Cleveland *(G-6056)*		

HARDWARE, WHOLESALE: Casters & Glides

Company		Phone
Waxman Consumer Pdts Group Inc	D	440 439-1830
Cleveland *(G-6725)*		
Waxman Consumer Pdts Group Inc	D	614 491-0500
Groveport *(G-11686)*		

HARDWARE, WHOLESALE: Garden Tools, Hand

Company		Phone
A M Leonard Inc	D	937 773-2694
Piqua *(G-16133)*		

HARDWARE, WHOLESALE: Nuts

Company		Phone
Facil North America Inc	C	330 487-2500
Twinsburg *(G-18414)*		
Omni Fasteners Inc	E	440 838-1800
Broadview Heights *(G-1888)*		

HARDWARE, WHOLESALE: Power Tools & Access

Company		Phone
Noco Company	B	216 464-8131
Solon *(G-17035)*		
Saw Service and Supply Company	E	216 252-5600
Cleveland *(G-6444)*		
TTI Floor Care North Amer Inc	B	440 996-2000
Solon *(G-17061)*		
WW Grainger Inc	E	614 276-5231
Columbus *(G-9010)*		

HARDWARE, WHOLESALE: Saw Blades

Company		Phone
Country Saw and Knife Inc	E	330 332-1611
Salem *(G-16692)*		

HARDWARE, WHOLESALE: Screws

Company		Phone
Brighton-Best Intl Inc	E	440 238-1350
Strongsville *(G-17447)*		
Kar Products	A	216 416-7200
Cleveland *(G-5884)*		

HARDWARE: Rubber

Company		Phone
Reynolds Industries Inc	E	330 889-9466
West Farmington *(G-19246)*		

HARNESS ASSEMBLIES: Cable & Wire

Company		Phone
Microplex Inc	E	330 498-0600
North Canton *(G-15353)*		

HEAD START CENTER, EXC IN CONJUNCTION WITH SCHOOL

Company		Phone
Butler County Eductl Svc Ctr	E	513 737-2817
Hamilton *(G-11702)*		
Child Care Resources Inc	D	740 454-6251
Zanesville *(G-20464)*		
Child Dvlpmnt Cncl of Frnkln	D	614 221-1709
Columbus *(G-7258)*		
Child Dvlpmnt Cncl of Frnkln	E	614 416-5178
Columbus *(G-7259)*		
Child Focus Inc	D	513 752-1555
Cincinnati *(G-3243)*		
Clinton County Community Actn	E	937 382-5624
Wilmington *(G-19751)*		
Community Action Comsn Belmont	D	740 676-0800
Bellaire *(G-1364)*		
Community Action Comsn Belmont	E	740 695-0293
Saint Clairsville *(G-16632)*		
Corporation For OH Appalachian	E	330 364-8882
New Philadelphia *(G-15089)*		
Coshocton County Head Start	E	740 622-3667
Coshocton *(G-9095)*		
Council of Ecnmc Opprtnts of G	E	216 651-5154
Cleveland *(G-5416)*		
Council On Rur Svc Prgrams Inc	D	937 452-1090
Camden *(G-2137)*		
Council On Rur Svc Prgrams Inc	E	937 492-8787
Sidney *(G-16924)*		
Crossroads Lake County Adole	E	440 358-7370
Painesville *(G-15848)*		
Hamilton County Eductl Svc Ctr	D	513 674-4200
Cincinnati *(G-3731)*		
Harcatus Tri-County Community	D	330 602-5442
New Philadelphia *(G-15098)*		
Hcesc Early Learning Program	C	513 589-3021
Cincinnati *(G-3745)*		
Knox County Head Start Inc	E	740 397-1344
Mount Vernon *(G-14906)*		
Lorain County Community Action	E	440 246-0480
Lorain *(G-13053)*		
Louis Stokes Head Start	E	216 295-0854
Cleveland *(G-5952)*		
Marion Head Start Center	E	740 382-6858
Marion *(G-13561)*		
Miami Vly Child Dev Ctrs Inc	D	937 226-5664
Dayton *(G-9740)*		
Miami Vly Child Dev Ctrs Inc	E	937 228-1644
Dayton *(G-9741)*		
Migrant Head Start	E	937 846-0699
New Carlisle *(G-15028)*		
Pickaway County Community Acti	E	740 474-7411
Circleville *(G-4895)*		
Pike County Head Start Inc	E	740 289-2371
Piketon *(G-16124)*		
Portage Private Industry	D	330 297-7795
Ravenna *(G-16403)*		
Pulaski Head Start	E	419 636-8862
Bryan *(G-2019)*		
Scioto County C A O Headstart	E	740 354-3333
Portsmouth *(G-16306)*		
South-Western City School Dst	D	614 801-8438
Grove City *(G-11599)*		
Spanish American Committee	E	216 961-2100
Cleveland *(G-6513)*		
Stark County Cmnty Action Agcy	E	330 821-5977
Alliance *(G-561)*		
W S O S Community A	E	419 729-8035
Toledo *(G-18295)*		
W S O S Community A	D	419 333-6068
Fremont *(G-11227)*		
W S O S Community A	D	419 334-8511
Fremont *(G-11228)*		

HEALTH & ALLIED SERVICES, NEC

Company		Phone
Baltic Health Care Corp	D	330 897-4311
Baltic *(G-944)*		
Cardinal Healthcare	E	954 202-1883
Columbus *(G-7195)*		
Celtic Healthcare Ne Ohio Inc	E	724 742-4360
Youngstown *(G-20135)*		
Clinic5	E	614 598-9960
Columbus *(G-7301)*		
Consulate Management Co LLC	D	740 259-5536
Lucasville *(G-13177)*		
District Board Health Mahoning	E	330 270-2855
Youngstown *(G-20170)*		
Divine Healthcare Services LLC	E	614 899-6767
Columbus *(G-7529)*		
Franklin County Adamh Board	E	614 224-1057
Columbus *(G-7694)*		
Greater Clvland Hlthcare Assn	D	216 696-6900
Cleveland *(G-5701)*		
Heartspring Home Hlth Care LLC	E	937 531-6920
Dayton *(G-9608)*		
Highpoint Home Healthcare Agcy	E	330 491-1805
Canton *(G-2398)*		
Hyde Park Health Center	E	513 272-0600
Cincinnati *(G-3802)*		
Medical Arts Physician Center	D	216 431-1500
Cleveland *(G-6013)*		
Metro Health System	D	330 669-2249
Smithville *(G-16966)*		
Novus Clinic	E	330 630-9699
Tallmadge *(G-17646)*		
Regensis Stna Training Program	E	614 849-0115
Columbus *(G-8607)*		
Seneca County Ems	C	419 447-0266
Tiffin *(G-17698)*		
Trihealth Hf LLC	E	513 398-3445
Mason *(G-13773)*		
TVC Home Health Care	E	330 755-1110
Youngstown *(G-20396)*		

HEALTH & WELFARE COUNCIL

Company		Phone
City of Columbus	D	614 645-7417
Columbus *(G-7282)*		
Concord	E	614 882-9338
Westerville *(G-19391)*		

HEALTH CLUBS

Company		Phone
Akron General Medical Center	C	330 665-8000
Akron *(G-46)*		
Beechmont Racquet Club Inc	E	513 528-5700
Cincinnati *(G-3091)*		
Champions Gym	E	937 294-8202
Dayton *(G-9396)*		
Fitworks Holding LLC	E	330 688-2329
Stow *(G-17367)*		
Fitworks Holding LLC	E	440 333-4141
Rocky River *(G-16578)*		
Fitworks Holding LLC	E	513 531-1500
Cincinnati *(G-3632)*		
Flexeco Incorporated	E	216 812-3304
Cleveland *(G-5606)*		
Holzer Clinic LLC	E	740 446-5412
Gallipolis *(G-11323)*		
Kinsale Golf & Fitnes CLB LLC	C	740 881-6500
Powell *(G-16343)*		
Life Time Fitness Inc	C	952 229-7158
Dublin *(G-10388)*		
Life Time Fitness Inc	C	614 428-6000
Columbus *(G-8062)*		
New Carlisle Spt & Fitnes Ctr	E	937 846-1000
New Carlisle *(G-15029)*		

SERVICES SECTION

HELP SUPPLY SERVICES

Oid Associates .... E 330 666-3161	Stephen R Saddemi MD .... E 419 578-7200	Samuel Steel Pickling Company .... D 330 963-3777
Akron *(G-370)*	Toledo *(G-18201)*	Twinsburg *(G-18467)*
Southwest General Health Ctr .... D 440 816-4202	Youngstown Ohio Otpatient Svcs .... E 330 884-2020	Thermal Treatment Center Inc .... E 216 881-8100
Cleveland *(G-6502)*	Youngstown *(G-20433)*	Cleveland *(G-6591)*
T O J Inc .... E 440 352-1900		
Mentor *(G-14247)*	## HEALTH SCREENING SVCS	## HEATERS: Room & Wall, Including Radiators
TLC Health Wellness & Fitness .... E 330 527-4852		
Garrettsville *(G-11354)*	Advantage Imaging LLC .... E 216 292-9998	Hunter Defense Tech Inc .... E 216 438-6111
Wyandotte Athletic Club .... E 614 861-6303	Beachwood *(G-1047)*	Solon *(G-17016)*
Columbus *(G-9011)*	Clevelnd Clnc Chagrn Flls Fmly .... E 440 893-9393	
	Chagrin Falls *(G-2693)*	## HEATING & AIR CONDITIONING EQPT & SPLYS WHOLESALERS
## HEALTH FOOD & SUPPLEMENT STORES	Cols Health & Wellness Testing .... E 614 839-2781	
	Westerville *(G-19384)*	Airtron LP .... D 614 274-2345
Cornucopia Inc .... E 216 521-4600	County of Clark 937 390-5600	Columbus *(G-6960)*
Lakewood *(G-12474)*	Springfield *(G-17178)*	Buckeye Heating and AC Sup Inc .... E 216 831-0066
Raisin Rack Inc .... E 614 882-5886	Healing Touch Healthcare .... E 937 610-5555	Bedford Heights *(G-1348)*
Westerville *(G-19440)*	Dayton *(G-9603)*	Copeland Access + Inc .... E 937 498-3802
	Life Line Screening Amer Ltd .... E 216 581-6556	Sidney *(G-16923)*
## HEALTH INSURANCE CARRIERS	Independence *(G-12227)*	Daikin Applied Americas Inc .... E 763 553-5009
	Ohio State University .... D 614 292-0110	Dayton *(G-9450)*
Aultcare Insurance Company .... B 330 363-6360	Columbus *(G-8418)*	Famous Enterprises Inc .... E 419 478-0343
Canton *(G-2250)*	P N P Inc .... D 330 386-1231	Toledo *(G-17879)*
Blue Cross & Blue Shield Mich .... A 330 783-3841	East Liverpool *(G-10532)*	Hamilton-Parker Company .... D 614 358-7800
Youngstown *(G-20117)*	Peregrine Health Services Inc .... D 419 298-2321	Columbus *(G-7797)*
Caresource Management Group Co ...... A 937 224-3300	Edgerton *(G-10584)*	Honeywell International Inc .... E 216 459-6053
Dayton *(G-9381)*	Proactive Occptnal Mdicine Inc .... E 740 574-8728	Cleveland *(G-5770)*
Caresource Management Group Co ...... E 614 221-3370	Wheelersburg *(G-19580)*	Honeywell International Inc .... E 614 717-2270
Hilliard *(G-11888)*	Renaissance Home Health Care .... E 216 662-8702	Columbus *(G-7858)*
Caresource Management Group Co ...... A 937 224-3300	Bedford *(G-1331)*	Lennox Industries Inc .... E 614 871-3017
Dayton *(G-9382)*	Ryan Sheridan .... E 330 270-2380	Grove City *(G-11575)*
Cincinnati Equitable Insur Co .... E 513 621-1826	Youngstown *(G-20364)*	Luxury Heating Co .... D 440 366-0971
Cincinnati *(G-3301)*		Sheffield Village *(G-16890)*
Dawson Companies .... D 440 333-9000	## HEALTH SYSTEMS AGENCY	Monroe Mechanical Incorporated .... E 513 539-7555
Richfield *(G-16503)*		Monroe *(G-14706)*
Farmers New World Lf Insur Co .... C 614 764-9975	City of Portsmouth .... E 740 353-5153	Robertson Heating Sup Co Ohio .... D 800 433-9532
Columbus *(G-7642)*	Portsmouth *(G-16268)*	Alliance *(G-553)*
Hometown Hospital Health Plan .... C 330 834-2200	County of Medina .... D 330 995-5243	Siemens Industry Inc .... D 216 365-7030
Massillon *(G-13820)*	Medina *(G-14054)*	Cleveland *(G-6480)*
Medical Benefits Mutl Lf Insur .... C 740 522-8425	Emeritus Corporation 330 477-5727	Style Crest Inc .... C 419 332-7369
Newark *(G-15204)*	Canton *(G-2353)*	Fremont *(G-11222)*
Summa Insurance Company Inc .... B 800 996-8411	Epilepsy Cntr of Nrthwstrn OH .... D 419 867-5950	Style Crest Inc .... B 419 332-7369
Akron *(G-462)*	Maumee *(G-13911)*	Fremont *(G-11223)*
Superior Dental Care Inc .... E 937 438-0283	Health Partners Western Ohio .... E 419 221-3072	Style Crest Enterprises Inc .... E 419 355-8586
Dayton *(G-9916)*	Lima *(G-12795)*	Fremont *(G-11224)*
	Integrated Services of Appala .... D 740 594-6807	Wadsworth-Slawson Inc .... E 216 391-7263
## HEALTH MAINTENANCE ORGANIZATION: Insurance Only	Athens *(G-794)*	Perrysburg *(G-16072)*
	Licking County Aging Program .... D 740 345-0821	Wolff Bros Supply Inc .... D 330 786-4140
	Newark *(G-15187)*	Akron *(G-511)*
1-888 Ohio Comp LLC .... D 216 426-0646	Occupational Health Link .... E 614 885-0039	Yanfeng US Automotive .... E 419 662-4905
Cleveland *(G-4918)*	Columbus *(G-8312)*	Northwood *(G-15553)*
Aetna Health California Inc .... E 614 933-6000	Pike Cnty Adult Activities Ctr .... E 740 947-7503	
New Albany *(G-14972)*	Waverly *(G-18972)*	## HEATING EQPT & SPLYS
Aetna Life Insurance Company .... E 330 659-8000	Pilot Dogs Incorporated .... E 614 221-6367	
Richfield *(G-16493)*	Columbus *(G-8545)*	Trumbull Manufacturing Inc .... D 330 393-6624
Benefit Services Inc .... D 330 666-0337	Prevent Blindness - Ohio .... E 614 464-2020	Warren *(G-18914)*
Copley *(G-9053)*	Columbus *(G-8558)*	
Cigna Corporation .... C 216 642-1700	Solidarity Health Network Inc .... E 216 831-1220	## HELP SUPPLY SERVICES
Independence *(G-12197)*	Cleveland *(G-6494)*	
Family Health Plan Inc .... C 419 241-6501	Wood County Ohio .... D 419 353-6914	Amerimed Inc .... E 513 942-3670
Toledo *(G-17877)*	Bowling Green *(G-1803)*	West Chester *(G-19019)*
Healthspan Integrated Care .... E 440 937-2350		Ashtabula Stevedore Company .... E 440 964-7186
Avon *(G-897)*	## HEARING TESTING SVCS	Ashtabula *(G-727)*
Healthspan Integrated Care .... E 440 572-1000		Aspen Community Living .... C 614 880-6000
Cleveland *(G-5743)*	Beall Inc .... E 440 974-8719	Columbus *(G-7051)*
Humana Health Plan Ohio Inc .... D 513 784-5200	Mentor *(G-14149)*	Atrium Apparel Corporation 612 889-0959
Cincinnati *(G-3796)*	Cincinnati Speech Hearing Ctr .... E 513 221-0527	Johnstown *(G-12335)*
Humana Inc .... E 330 877-5464	Cincinnati *(G-3328)*	Belflex Staffing Network LLC .... C 513 488-8588
Hartville *(G-11824)*		Cincinnati *(G-3096)*
Humana Inc .... E 216 328-2047	## HEAT TREATING: Metal	CPC Logistics Inc 513 874-5787
Independence *(G-12217)*		Fairfield *(G-10838)*
Humana Inc .... E 614 210-1038	A M Castle & Co .... D 330 425-7000	Edge Plastics Inc .... E 419 522-6696
Dublin *(G-10368)*	Bedford *(G-1292)*	Mansfield *(G-13296)*
Massillon Cmnty Hosp Hlth Plan .... C 330 837-6880	Carpe Diem Industries LLC .... E 419 358-0129	Firstat Nursing Services .... D 216 295-1500
Massillon *(G-13835)*	Bluffton *(G-1729)*	Cleveland *(G-5600)*
Oxford Blazer Company Inc .... E 614 792-2220	Carpe Diem Industries LLC .... D 419 659-5639	Innovtive Sltons Unlimited LLC .... D 740 289-3282
Dublin *(G-10419)*	Columbus Grove *(G-9029)*	Piketon *(G-16119)*
Promedica Health Systems Inc .... A 567 585-7454	Clifton Steel Company .... D 216 662-6111	Medsearch Staffing Service .... E 440 243-6363
Toledo *(G-18141)*	Maple Heights *(G-13403)*	Cleveland *(G-6018)*
Uc Health Llc .... B 513 585-7600	Euclid Heat Treating Co .... D 216 481-8444	MPW Industrial Services Inc .... D 937 644-0200
Cincinnati *(G-4719)*	Euclid *(G-10752)*	East Liberty *(G-10511)*
United Healthcare Ohio Inc .... C 513 603-6200	Gerdau Macsteel Atmosphere Ann .... D 330 478-0314	Nursing Resources Corp .... C 419 333-3000
Blue Ash *(G-1713)*	Canton *(G-2379)*	Maumee *(G-13951)*
Unitedhealth Group Inc .... B 513 603-6200	HI Tecmetal Group Inc .... E 440 373-5101	Ohio Dept of Job & Fmly Svcs .... E 419 334-3891
Cincinnati *(G-4744)*	Wickliffe *(G-19601)*	Fremont *(G-11215)*
	HI Tecmetal Group Inc .... E 440 946-2280	P E Miller & Associates Inc .... D 614 231-4743
## HEALTH PRACTITIONERS' OFFICES, NEC	Willoughby *(G-19602)*	Columbus *(G-8503)*
	Lapham-Hickey Steel Corp .... E 614 443-4881	Professional Transportation .... E 419 661-0576
Central Ohio Sleep Medicine .... E 614 475-6700	Columbus *(G-8039)*	Walbridge *(G-18776)*
Westerville *(G-19292)*	Miller Consolidated Industries .... C 937 294-2681	Rkpl Inc .... D 419 224-2121
Occupational Health Services .... E 937 492-7296	Moraine *(G-14806)*	Lima *(G-12869)*
Sidney *(G-16944)*	Northwind Industries Inc .... E 216 433-0666	
	Cleveland *(G-6163)*	

Employee Codes: A=Over 500 employees, B=251-500
C=101-250, D=51-100, E=25-50

HELP SUPPLY SERVICES

Taylors Staffing .... D 740 446-3305
  Pomeroy *(G-16236)*
Volt Management Corp .... D 513 791-2600
  Cincinnati *(G-4818)*
Yrs Inc .... D 330 665-3906
  Akron *(G-518)*

HELPING HAND SVCS, INCLUDING BIG BROTHER, ETC

Big Broth and Big Siste of Cen .... E 614 839-2447
  Columbus *(G-7106)*
Cleaners Extraordinaire Inc .... D 937 324-8488
  Springfield *(G-17166)*

HIGHWAY & STREET MAINTENANCE SVCS

Able Contracting Group Inc .... E 440 951-0880
  Painesville *(G-15832)*
Ashtabula County Commissioners .... E 440 576-2816
  Jefferson *(G-12329)*
Belmont County of Ohio .... E 740 695-1580
  Saint Clairsville *(G-16625)*
C J & L Construction Inc .... E 513 769-3600
  Cincinnati *(G-3160)*
City of Aurora .... D 330 562-8662
  Aurora *(G-836)*
City of Avon .... E 440 937-5740
  Avon *(G-889)*
City of Brecksville .... E 440 526-1384
  Brecksville *(G-1818)*
City of Euclid .... E 216 289-2800
  Cleveland *(G-5260)*
City of Kent .... D 330 678-8105
  Kent *(G-12359)*
City of North Ridgeville .... E 440 327-8326
  North Ridgeville *(G-15460)*
City of North Royalton .... E 440 582-3002
  Cleveland *(G-5270)*
City of Portsmouth .... E 740 353-5419
  Portsmouth *(G-16269)*
City of Streetsboro .... E 330 626-2856
  Streetsboro *(G-17410)*
City of Willoughby .... D 440 953-4111
  Willoughby *(G-19650)*
County of Clinton .... E 937 382-2078
  Wilmington *(G-19759)*
County of Holmes .... E 330 674-5076
  Millersburg *(G-14598)*
County of Seneca .... E 419 447-3863
  Tiffin *(G-17674)*
County of Summit .... C 330 643-2860
  Akron *(G-171)*
County of Trumbull .... D 330 675-2640
  Warren *(G-18840)*
Eaton Construction Co Inc .... D 740 474-3414
  Circleville *(G-4887)*
George Kuhn Enterprises Inc .... E 614 481-8838
  Columbus *(G-7743)*
J K Enterprises Inc .... D 614 481-8838
  Columbus *(G-7931)*
Ohio Department Transportation .... C 740 363-1251
  Delaware *(G-10119)*
Ohio Department Transportation .... E 937 548-3015
  Greenville *(G-11515)*
Ohio Department Transportation .... E 419 738-4214
  Wapakoneta *(G-18805)*
Ohio Department Transportation .... E 330 533-4351
  Canfield *(G-2205)*
Ohio Tpk & Infrastructure Comm .... E 419 826-4831
  Swanton *(G-17569)*
Ohio Tpk & Infrastructure Comm .... C 440 234-2081
  Berea *(G-1466)*
Springboro Service Center .... E 937 748-0020
  Springboro *(G-17138)*
Transportation Ohio Department .... E 740 773-3191
  Chillicothe *(G-2891)*
Turnpike and Infrastructure Co .... D 330 527-2169
  Windham *(G-19804)*

HIGHWAY BRIDGE OPERATION

Johnson Mirmiran Thompson Inc .... D 614 714-0270
  Columbus *(G-7944)*

HISTORICAL SOCIETY

Anderson Twnship Hstorical Soc .... E 513 231-2114
  Cincinnati *(G-3026)*
Delaware County Historical Soc .... D 740 369-3831
  Delaware *(G-10088)*
National Underground Railroad .... D 513 333-7500
  Cincinnati *(G-4142)*
New London Area Historical Soc .... D 419 929-3674
  New London *(G-15068)*
Western Reserve Historical Soc .... D 216 721-5722
  Cleveland *(G-6744)*

HOBBY, TOY & GAME STORES: Arts & Crafts & Splys

Darice Inc .... C 440 238-9150
  Strongsville *(G-17456)*
Hobby Lobby Stores Inc .... E 330 686-1508
  Stow *(G-17371)*

HOBBY, TOY & GAME STORES: Children's Toys & Games, Exc Dolls

Hobby Lobby Stores Inc .... D 419 861-1862
  Holland *(G-12027)*

HOBBY, TOY & GAME STORES: Toys & Games

Heaven Bound Ascensions .... E 330 633-3288
  Tallmadge *(G-17640)*

HOGS WHOLESALERS

Kalmbach Pork Finishing LLC .... D 419 294-3838
  Upper Sandusky *(G-18563)*
Robert Winner Sons Inc .... E 419 582-4321
  Yorkshire *(G-20092)*
United Producers Inc .... C 614 433-2150
  Columbus *(G-8899)*

HOLDING COMPANIES, NEC

Bleux Holdings LLC .... E 859 414-5060
  Cincinnati *(G-3114)*
Going Home Medical Holding Co .... E 305 340-1034
  Strongsville *(G-17466)*
M J S Holding .... E 614 410-2512
  Columbus *(G-8092)*

HOLDING COMPANIES: Banks

Community Invstors Bancorp Inc .... E 419 562-7055
  Bucyrus *(G-2032)*
Comunibanc Corp .... D 419 599-1065
  Napoleon *(G-14936)*
First Capital Bancshares Inc .... D 740 775-6777
  Chillicothe *(G-2839)*
Genbanc .... E 419 855-8381
  Genoa *(G-11377)*
Greenville National Bancorp .... E 937 548-1114
  Greenville *(G-11505)*
Portage Bancshares Inc .... D 330 296-8090
  Ravenna *(G-16396)*

HOLDING COMPANIES: Investment, Exc Banks

Ampac Holdings LLC .... A 513 671-1777
  Cincinnati *(G-3017)*
Aprecia Pharmaceuticals Co .... C 513 864-4107
  Blue Ash *(G-1534)*
Betco Corporation .... C 419 241-2156
  Bowling Green *(G-1763)*
Che International Group LLC .... E 513 444-2072
  Cincinnati *(G-3233)*
CV Perry Builders .... E 614 221-4131
  Columbus *(G-7475)*
Drt Holdings Inc .... D 937 298-7391
  Dayton *(G-9505)*
Elyria Foundry Holdings LLC .... B 440 322-4657
  Elyria *(G-10622)*
Entelco Corporation .... E 419 872-4620
  Maumee *(G-13910)*
Global Graphene Group Inc .... E 937 331-9884
  Dayton *(G-9573)*
Hman Group Holdings Inc .... A 513 851-4900
  Cincinnati *(G-3773)*
Lion Group Inc .... E 937 898-1949
  Dayton *(G-9685)*
Liqui-Box International Inc .... D 614 888-9280
  Columbus *(G-8071)*
Live Technologies Holdings Inc .... D 614 278-7777
  Columbus *(G-8074)*
Mssl Consolidated Inc .... B 330 766-5510
  Warren *(G-18883)*

SERVICES SECTION

Nationwide Life Insur Co Amer .... A 800 688-5177
  Columbus *(G-8245)*
Nri Global Inc .... E 905 790-2828
  Delta *(G-10162)*
Ocr Services Corporation .... C 513 719-2600
  Cincinnati *(G-4199)*
Pet Food Holdings Inc .... D 419 394-3374
  Saint Marys *(G-16683)*
Pf Holdings LLC .... D 740 549-3558
  Lewis Center *(G-12703)*
Premix Holding Company .... B 330 666-3751
  Fairlawn *(G-10968)*
Qsr Parent Co .... A 330 425-8472
  Twinsburg *(G-18458)*
Savare Corporation 770 517-3749
  Columbus *(G-8687)*
Towne Investment Company LP .... D 513 381-8696
  Cincinnati *(G-4668)*
Vala Holdings Ltd .... C 216 398-2980
  Parma *(G-15918)*
Wasserstrom Holdings Inc .... E 614 228-6525
  Columbus *(G-8972)*

HOLDING COMPANIES: Personal, Exc Banks

A and S Ventures Inc .... E 419 376-3934
  Toledo *(G-17734)*
Amrstrong Distributors Inc .... E 419 483-4840
  Bellevue *(G-1402)*
Caston Holdings LLC .... C 440 871-8697
  Westlake *(G-19471)*
Global Cnsld Holdings Inc .... D 513 703-0965
  Mason *(G-13709)*
Jbo Holding Company .... C 216 367-8787
  Cleveland *(G-5855)*
Select-Arc Inc .... C 937 295-5215
  Fort Loramie *(G-11111)*
Washington Court Hse Holdg LLC .... E 614 873-7733
  Wshngtn CT Hs *(G-20037)*

HOME CENTER STORES

Apco Industries Inc .... D 614 224-2345
  Columbus *(G-7027)*
Builders Firstsource Inc .... E 513 874-9950
  Cincinnati *(G-3147)*
Home Depot USA Inc .... C 614 523-0600
  Columbus *(G-7848)*
Home Depot USA Inc .... C 330 965-4790
  Boardman *(G-1741)*
Home Depot USA Inc .... C 330 497-1810
  Canton *(G-2402)*
Home Depot USA Inc .... C 513 688-1654
  Cincinnati *(G-3778)*
Home Depot USA Inc .... C 330 922-3448
  Cuyahoga Falls *(G-9194)*
Home Depot USA Inc .... C 937 312-9053
  Dayton *(G-9614)*
Home Depot USA Inc .... C 937 312-9076
  Dayton *(G-9615)*
Home Depot USA Inc .... C 216 692-2780
  Euclid *(G-10762)*
Home Depot USA Inc .... C 216 676-9969
  Cleveland *(G-5767)*
Home Depot USA Inc .... C 216 581-6611
  Maple Heights *(G-13408)*
Home Depot USA Inc .... D 937 431-7346
  Beavercreek *(G-1177)*
Home Depot USA Inc .... C 330 245-0280
  Akron *(G-271)*
Home Depot USA Inc .... D 937 837-1551
  Dayton *(G-9616)*
Home Depot USA Inc .... C 216 297-1303
  Cleveland Heights *(G-6790)*
Home Depot USA Inc .... C 513 661-2413
  Cincinnati *(G-3779)*
Home Depot USA Inc .... C 513 887-1450
  Fairfield Township *(G-10931)*
Home Depot USA Inc .... C 419 476-4573
  Toledo *(G-17957)*
Home Depot USA Inc .... C 440 357-0428
  Mentor *(G-14191)*
Home Depot USA Inc .... C 513 631-1705
  Cincinnati *(G-3780)*
Home Depot USA Inc .... C 440 684-1343
  Highland Heights *(G-11869)*
Home Depot USA Inc .... C 419 537-1920
  Toledo *(G-17958)*
Home Depot USA Inc .... C 614 878-9150
  Columbus *(G-7849)*
Home Depot USA Inc .... C 440 826-9092
  Strongsville *(G-17471)*

SERVICES SECTION

HOME FOR THE MENTALLY HANDICAPPED

Home Depot USA Inc .... C 614 939-5036
  Columbus *(G-7850)*
Home Depot USA Inc .... D 440 937-2240
  Avon *(G-898)*
Home Depot USA Inc .... C 614 577-1601
  Reynoldsburg *(G-16458)*
Home Depot USA Inc .... C 330 220-2654
  Brunswick *(G-1981)*
Home Depot USA Inc .... C 419 626-6493
  Sandusky *(G-16768)*
Home Depot USA Inc .... C 614 876-5558
  Hilliard *(G-11911)*
Home Depot USA Inc .... C 440 324-7222
  Elyria *(G-10633)*
Home Depot USA Inc .... C 419 529-0015
  Ontario *(G-15691)*
Home Depot USA Inc .... C 216 251-3091
  Cleveland *(G-5768)*
Lowes Home Centers LLC .... C 937 235-2920
  Dayton *(G-9688)*
Lowes Home Centers LLC .... C 740 574-6200
  Wheelersburg *(G-19578)*
Lowes Home Centers LLC .... C 330 665-9356
  Akron *(G-328)*
Lowes Home Centers LLC .... C 330 829-2700
  Alliance *(G-545)*
Lowes Home Centers LLC .... C 937 599-4000
  Bellefontaine *(G-1388)*
Lowes Home Centers LLC .... C 419 420-7531
  Findlay *(G-11057)*
Lowes Home Centers LLC .... C 330 832-1901
  Massillon *(G-13829)*
Lowes Home Centers LLC .... C 513 741-0585
  Cincinnati *(G-3996)*
Lowes Home Centers LLC .... C 614 433-9957
  Columbus *(G-6892)*
Lowes Home Centers LLC .... C 740 389-9737
  Marion *(G-13549)*
Lowes Home Centers LLC .... C 740 450-5500
  Zanesville *(G-20497)*
Lowes Home Centers LLC .... C 513 598-7050
  Cincinnati *(G-3997)*
Lowes Home Centers LLC .... C 614 769-9940
  Reynoldsburg *(G-16466)*
Lowes Home Centers LLC .... C 614 853-6200
  Columbus *(G-8079)*
Lowes Home Centers LLC .... C 440 937-3500
  Avon *(G-906)*
Lowes Home Centers LLC .... C 513 445-1000
  South Lebanon *(G-17078)*
Lowes Home Centers LLC .... B 216 831-2860
  Bedford *(G-1318)*
Lowes Home Centers LLC .... C 937 327-6000
  Springfield *(G-17226)*
Lowes Home Centers LLC .... C 419 331-3598
  Lima *(G-12832)*
Lowes Home Centers LLC .... C 740 681-3464
  Lancaster *(G-12551)*
Lowes Home Centers LLC .... C 614 659-0530
  Dublin *(G-10392)*
Lowes Home Centers LLC .... C 614 238-2601
  Columbus *(G-8080)*
Lowes Home Centers LLC .... C 740 522-0003
  Newark *(G-15199)*
Lowes Home Centers LLC .... C 740 773-7777
  Chillicothe *(G-2862)*
Lowes Home Centers LLC .... C 440 998-6555
  Ashtabula *(G-752)*
Lowes Home Centers LLC .... B 513 753-5094
  Cincinnati *(G-2924)*
Lowes Home Centers LLC .... C 614 497-6170
  Columbus *(G-8081)*
Lowes Home Centers LLC .... C 513 731-6127
  Cincinnati *(G-3998)*
Lowes Home Centers LLC .... C 330 287-2261
  Wooster *(G-19884)*
Lowes Home Centers LLC .... C 937 339-2544
  Troy *(G-18362)*
Lowes Home Centers LLC .... C 440 942-2759
  Willoughby *(G-19688)*
Lowes Home Centers LLC .... C 740 374-2151
  Marietta *(G-13462)*
Lowes Home Centers LLC .... C 419 874-6758
  Perrysburg *(G-16030)*
Lowes Home Centers LLC .... C 330 626-2980
  Streetsboro *(G-17419)*
Lowes Home Centers LLC .... C 419 389-9464
  Toledo *(G-18013)*
Lowes Home Centers LLC .... C 419 843-9758
  Toledo *(G-18014)*
Lowes Home Centers LLC .... C 614 447-2851
  Columbus *(G-8082)*
Lowes Home Centers LLC .... C 513 965-3280
  Milford *(G-14532)*
Lowes Home Centers LLC .... C 330 908-2750
  Northfield *(G-15519)*
Lowes Home Centers LLC .... C 419 470-2491
  Toledo *(G-18015)*
Lowes Home Centers LLC .... C 513 336-9741
  Mason *(G-13733)*
Lowes Home Centers LLC .... C 937 498-8400
  Sidney *(G-16941)*
Lowes Home Centers LLC .... C 740 699-3000
  Saint Clairsville *(G-16642)*
Lowes Home Centers LLC .... C 330 920-9280
  Stow *(G-17381)*
Lowes Home Centers LLC .... C 740 589-3750
  Athens *(G-799)*
Lowes Home Centers LLC .... C 740 393-5350
  Mount Vernon *(G-14910)*
Lowes Home Centers LLC .... C 937 547-2400
  Greenville *(G-11513)*
Lowes Home Centers LLC .... C 330 335-1900
  Wadsworth *(G-18763)*
Lowes Home Centers LLC .... C 937 347-4000
  Xenia *(G-20068)*
Lowes Home Centers LLC .... C 440 239-2630
  Strongsville *(G-17485)*
Lowes Home Centers LLC .... C 513 755-4300
  West Chester *(G-19113)*
Lowes Home Centers LLC .... C 513 671-2093
  Cincinnati *(G-3999)*
Lowes Home Centers LLC .... C 440 331-1027
  Rocky River *(G-16585)*
Lowes Home Centers LLC .... C 330 677-3040
  Kent *(G-12384)*
Lowes Home Centers LLC .... C 419 747-1920
  Ontario *(G-15698)*
Lowes Home Centers LLC .... C 330 339-1936
  New Philadelphia *(G-15107)*
Lowes Home Centers LLC .... C 440 985-5700
  Lorain *(G-13058)*
Lowes Home Centers LLC .... C 419 447-4101
  Tiffin *(G-17682)*
Lowes Home Centers LLC .... C 937 578-4440
  Marysville *(G-13632)*
Lowes Home Centers LLC .... C 440 324-5004
  Elyria *(G-10647)*
Lowes Home Centers LLC .... C 937 438-4900
  Dayton *(G-9689)*
Lowes Home Centers LLC .... C 937 427-1110
  Beavercreek *(G-1189)*
Lowes Home Centers LLC .... C 937 848-5600
  Dayton *(G-9690)*
Lowes Home Centers LLC .... C 614 529-5900
  Hilliard *(G-11923)*
Lowes Home Centers LLC .... C 513 737-3700
  Hamilton *(G-11755)*
Lowes Home Centers LLC .... C 740 894-7120
  South Point *(G-17091)*
Lowes Home Centers LLC .... C 513 727-3900
  Middletown *(G-14431)*
Lowes Home Centers LLC .... C 419 355-0221
  Fremont *(G-11210)*
Lowes Home Centers LLC .... C 419 624-6000
  Sandusky *(G-16777)*
Lowes Home Centers LLC .... C 419 782-9000
  Defiance *(G-10045)*
Lowes Home Centers LLC .... C 330 609-8000
  Warren *(G-18876)*
Lowes Home Centers LLC .... C 937 383-7000
  Wilmington *(G-19769)*
Lowes Home Centers LLC .... C 330 497-2720
  Canton *(G-2440)*
Lowes Home Centers LLC .... C 740 266-3500
  Steubenville *(G-17327)*
Lowes Home Centers LLC .... C 614 476-7100
  Columbus *(G-8083)*
Menard Inc .... C 937 630-3550
  Miamisburg *(G-14317)*
Menard Inc .... C 513 737-2204
  Fairfield Township *(G-10934)*

HOME FOR THE DESTITUTE

Caracole Inc .... E 513 761-1480
  Cincinnati *(G-3176)*
Volunters of Amer Greater Ohio .... C 614 253-6100
  Columbus *(G-8951)*

HOME FOR THE EMOTIONALLY DISTURBED

Adriel School Inc .... D 937 465-0010
  West Liberty *(G-19260)*
Bellefaire Jewish Chld Bur .... B 216 932-2800
  Shaker Heights *(G-16856)*
Buckeye Ranch Inc .... D 614 384-7700
  Columbus *(G-7161)*
Buckeye Ranch Inc .... B 614 875-2371
  Grove City *(G-11542)*
Community Support Services Inc .... C 330 253-9388
  Akron *(G-157)*
Ohioguidestone .... E 440 234-2006
  Berea *(G-1467)*
United Methodist Childrens .... D 614 885-5020
  Worthington *(G-20004)*

HOME FOR THE MENTALLY HANDICAPPED

Abilities First Foundation .... C 513 423-9496
  Middletown *(G-14411)*
Alternative Residences Two .... C 740 526-0514
  Saint Clairsville *(G-16616)*
Alternative Residences Two .... E 330 453-0200
  Canton *(G-2236)*
Ashtabula County Residential I .... E 440 593-6404
  Conneaut *(G-9038)*
Assoc Dvlpmtly Disabled .... E 614 486-4361
  Westerville *(G-19365)*
Assoc Dvlpmtly Disabled .... E 614 447-0606
  Columbus *(G-7054)*
Bastin Home Inc .... E 513 734-2662
  Bethel *(G-1482)*
Bittersweet Inc .... D 419 875-6986
  Whitehouse *(G-19584)*
Cincinnatis Optimum RES Envir .... C 513 771-2673
  Cincinnati *(G-3337)*
Community Hsing Netwrk Dev Co .... C 614 487-6700
  Columbus *(G-7405)*
Community Living Experiences .... E 614 588-0320
  Columbus *(G-7406)*
County of Auglaize .... D 419 629-2419
  New Bremen *(G-15017)*
County of Holmes .... E 330 279-2801
  Holmesville *(G-12071)*
County of Lorain .... E 440 329-3734
  Elyria *(G-10610)*
Eastwood Residential Living .... E 440 417-0608
  Madison *(G-13223)*
ECHO Residential Support .... E 614 210-0944
  Columbus *(G-7570)*
Erie Residential Living Inc .... E 419 625-0060
  Sandusky *(G-16754)*
Evant .... E 330 920-1517
  Stow *(G-17365)*
Firelands Regional Health Sys .... E 419 448-9440
  Tiffin *(G-17679)*
Franklin County Residential S .... B 614 844-5847
  Columbus *(G-7696)*
G & D Alternative Living Inc .... E 937 446-2803
  Sardinia *(G-16813)*
Hopewell .... E 440 693-4074
  Mesopotamia *(G-14263)*
Horizons Tuscarawas/Carroll .... E 330 262-4183
  Wooster *(G-19869)*
I A R Inc .... E 740 432-3371
  Cambridge *(G-2121)*
Independence of Portage County .... C 330 296-2851
  Ravenna *(G-16390)*
Josina Lott Foundation .... E 419 866-9013
  Toledo *(G-17987)*
McElvain Group Home .... E 419 589-6697
  Mansfield *(G-13336)*
Miami Vly Hsing Oprtunties Inc .... E 937 263-4449
  Dayton *(G-9742)*
Muskingum Residentials Inc .... E 740 453-5350
  Zanesville *(G-20511)*
National Mentor Holdings Inc .... A 419 443-0867
  Fostoria *(G-11135)*
Network Housing 2005 Inc .... D 614 487-6700
  Columbus *(G-8265)*
New Avenues To Independence .... E 888 853-8905
  Ashtabula *(G-756)*
New Nghbors Rsdential Svcs Inc .... E 937 717-5731
  Springfield *(G-17251)*
Ohio Department of Health .... B 419 447-1450
  Tiffin *(G-17690)*
Our Lady of Wayside Inc .... B 440 934-6152
  Avon *(G-911)*
Portage County Board .... E 330 297-6209
  Ravenna *(G-16399)*

Employee Codes: A=Over 500 employees, B=251-500
C=101-250, D=51-100, E=25-50

R T Industries Inc........C....... 937 335-5784
Troy *(G-18374)*
Residential Home For The Devlp........C....... 740 622-9778
Coshocton *(G-9115)*
Residential Home For The Devlp........E....... 740 452-5133
Zanesville *(G-20529)*
Residential Management Systems........E....... 614 880-6014
Worthington *(G-19992)*
Rhc Inc........C....... 513 389-7501
Cincinnati *(G-4413)*
Second Phase Inc........E....... 330 797-9930
Youngstown *(G-20369)*
Society Handicapped Citz Medin........E....... 330 722-1900
Seville *(G-16844)*
Sociey For Handicapped Citizen........C....... 330 725-7041
Seville *(G-16845)*
Tri County Mental Health Svcs........C....... 740 592-3091
Athens *(G-815)*
Wynn-Reeth Inc........E....... 419 639-2094
Green Springs *(G-11481)*

HOME FOR THE MENTALLY RETARDED

Alexson Services Inc........B....... 513 874-0423
Fairfield *(G-10819)*
Anne Grady Corporation........C....... 419 380-8985
Holland *(G-12009)*
Ardmore Inc........C....... 330 535-2601
Akron *(G-81)*
Butler County Bd of Mental RE........E....... 513 785-2815
Hamilton *(G-11700)*
Butler County Bd of Mental RE........C....... 513 785-2870
Fairfield Township *(G-10927)*
Butler County Board of Develop........E....... 513 867-5913
Fairfield *(G-10826)*
Champaign Residential Svcs Inc........A....... 937 653-1320
Urbana *(G-18578)*
Choices In Community Living........C....... 937 898-3655
Dayton *(G-9405)*
Clark County Board of Developm........C....... 937 328-5200
Springfield *(G-17163)*
Community Hbilitation Svcs Inc........E....... 234 334-4288
Akron *(G-155)*
Concepts In Community Living........E....... 740 393-0055
Mount Vernon *(G-14885)*
County of Cuyahoga........C....... 216 241-8230
Cleveland *(G-5424)*
County of Lorain........E....... 440 282-3074
Lorain *(G-13034)*
County of Richland........D....... 419 774-4300
Mansfield *(G-13277)*
Develpmntal Dsblties Ohio Dept........B....... 419 385-0231
Toledo *(G-17851)*
Develpmntal Dsblties Ohio Dept........C....... 330 544-2231
Columbus *(G-7512)*
Eastwood Residential Living........E....... 440 428-1588
Madison *(G-13224)*
Friends of Good Shepherd Manor........D....... 740 289-2861
Lucasville *(G-13179)*
Gateways To Better Living Inc........E....... 330 270-0952
Youngstown *(G-20195)*
Gateways To Better Living Inc........E....... 330 797-1764
Canfield *(G-2191)*
Gateways To Better Living Inc........E....... 330 792-2854
Youngstown *(G-20196)*
Gentlebrook Inc........C....... 330 877-3694
Hartville *(G-11817)*
Hattie Larlham Center For........C....... 330 274-2272
Mantua *(G-13387)*
Hattie Larlham Center For........D....... 330 274-2272
Mantua *(G-13388)*
Manfield Living Center Ltd........E....... 419 512-1711
Mansfield *(G-13328)*
Mount Aloysius Corp........C....... 740 342-3343
New Lexington *(G-15056)*
New Avenues To Independence........D....... 216 481-1907
Cleveland *(G-6122)*
New Avenues To Independence........E....... 216 671-8224
Cleveland *(G-6123)*
Opportunity Homes Inc........E....... 330 424-1411
Lisbon *(G-12941)*
REM-Ohio Inc........E....... 937 335-8267
Troy *(G-18376)*
REM-Ohio Inc........D....... 330 644-9730
Coventry Township *(G-9131)*
REM-Ohio Inc........D....... 614 367-1370
Reynoldsburg *(G-16474)*
Renaissance House Inc........E....... 419 663-1316
Norwalk *(G-15590)*
Residential Hm Assn of Marion........C....... 740 387-9999
Marion *(G-13575)*
Residential Inc........E....... 740 342-4158
New Lexington *(G-15062)*
Sunshine Communities........B....... 419 865-0251
Maumee *(G-13982)*
Toward Independence Inc........E....... 937 376-3996
Xenia *(G-20079)*
Wiley Homes Inc........D....... 419 535-3988
Toledo *(G-18309)*

HOME FOR THE MENTALLY RETARDED, EXC SKILLED OR INTERMEDIATE

Americas Dream Homes LLC........E....... 614 252-7834
Columbus *(G-7010)*
Boyds Kinsman Home Inc........E....... 330 876-5581
Kinsman *(G-12453)*
Brookside Extended Care Center........C....... 513 398-1020
Mason *(G-13669)*
Buckeye Community Services Inc........C....... 740 941-1639
Waverly *(G-18967)*
Columbus Ctr For Humn Svcs Inc........C....... 614 641-2904
Columbus *(G-7344)*
Columbus Ctr For Humn Svcs Inc........E....... 614 245-8180
New Albany *(G-14981)*
Community Concepts Inc........C....... 513 398-8181
Mason *(G-13687)*
Consumer Support Services Inc........B....... 740 788-8257
Newark *(G-15158)*
County of Richland........B....... 419 774-4200
Mansfield *(G-13284)*
County of Wood........B....... 419 686-6951
Portage *(G-16261)*
East Carroll Nursing Home........D....... 330 627-6900
Carrollton *(G-2618)*
Echoing Hills Village Inc........E....... 937 237-7881
Dayton *(G-9519)*
Echoing Hills Village Inc........D....... 440 986-3085
South Amherst *(G-17073)*
Heinzerling Foundation........C....... 614 272-8888
Columbus *(G-7821)*
Heinzerling Foundation........A....... 614 272-2000
Columbus *(G-7822)*
Kingston Healthcare Company........C....... 440 967-1800
Vermilion *(G-18712)*
Minamyer Residential Mr/Dd Svc........E....... 614 802-0190
Columbus *(G-8177)*
On-Call Nursing Inc........D....... 216 577-8890
Lakewood *(G-12493)*
Stewart Lodge Inc........D....... 440 417-1898
Madison *(G-13236)*
United Cerebral Palsy........D....... 216 381-9993
Cleveland *(G-6636)*

HOME FOR THE PHYSICALLY HANDICAPPED

Brighter Horizons Residential........E....... 440 417-1751
Madison *(G-13221)*
County of Hancock........E....... 419 422-6387
Findlay *(G-11016)*

HOME FURNISHINGS WHOLESALERS

American Frame Corporation........E....... 419 893-5595
Maumee *(G-13874)*
Bcf LLC........E....... 937 746-0721
Miamisburg *(G-14274)*
Bostwick-Braun Company........D....... 419 259-3600
Toledo *(G-17778)*
Interdesign Inc........B....... 440 248-0136
Solon *(G-17018)*
Marketing Results Ltd........E....... 614 575-9300
Columbus *(G-8111)*
National Marketshare Group........E....... 513 921-0800
Cincinnati *(G-4140)*
Norwood Hardware & Supply Co........E....... 513 733-1175
Cincinnati *(G-4185)*
Old Time Pottery Inc........D....... 513 825-5211
Cincinnati *(G-4219)*
Old Time Pottery Inc........D....... 440 842-1244
Cleveland *(G-6199)*
Old Time Pottery Inc........D....... 614 337-1258
Columbus *(G-8464)*
Wholesale Decor LLC........E....... 330 587-7100
Hartville *(G-11833)*

HOME HEALTH CARE SVCS

A-1 Nursing Care Inc........C....... 614 268-3800
Columbus *(G-6922)*
Ability Matters LLC........E....... 614 214-9652
Hilliard *(G-11875)*
Above & Beyond Caregivers LLC........E....... 614 478-1700
Columbus *(G-6928)*
Accentcare Home Health Cal Inc........C....... 740 387-4568
Marion *(G-13522)*
Advance Home Care LLC........D....... 614 436-3611
Columbus *(G-6945)*
Advance Home Care LLC........D....... 937 723-6335
Dayton *(G-9309)*
Advantage Home Health Svcs Inc........E....... 330 491-8161
North Canton *(G-15320)*
All About Home Care Svcs LLC........E....... 937 222-2980
Dayton *(G-9315)*
All Heart Home Care LLC........E....... 419 298-0034
Edgerton *(G-10581)*
All Hearts Home Health Care........E....... 440 342-2026
Cleveland *(G-4988)*
Almost Family Inc........E....... 614 457-1900
Columbus *(G-6973)*
Almost Family Inc........E....... 330 724-7545
Akron *(G-69)*
Almost Family Inc........E....... 216 464-0443
Cleveland *(G-4994)*
Alpine Nursing Care........E....... 216 650-6295
Cleveland *(G-4998)*
Alternate Sltions Private Duty........D....... 937 298-1111
Dayton *(G-9324)*
Alternate Solutions First LLC........C....... 937 298-1111
Dayton *(G-9325)*
Alternative Home Care & Stffng........E....... 513 794-0571
Cincinnati *(G-2997)*
Alternative Home Health Care........E....... 513 794-0555
Cincinnati *(G-2998)*
Altimate Care LLC........E....... 614 794-9600
Columbus *(G-6978)*
Amandacare Inc........C....... 614 884-8880
Columbus *(G-6980)*
Amedisys Inc........E....... 740 373-8549
Marietta *(G-13430)*
Amenity Home Health Care LLC........E....... 513 931-3689
Cincinnati *(G-3000)*
American Nursing Care Inc........E....... 513 731-4600
Cincinnati *(G-3009)*
American Nursing Care Inc........E....... 937 438-3844
Dayton *(G-9330)*
American Nursing Care Inc........D....... 419 228-0888
Lima *(G-12741)*
American Nursing Care Inc........D....... 740 452-0569
Zanesville *(G-20442)*
Angel Above Byond Hm Hlth Svcs........E....... 513 553-9955
New Richmond *(G-15124)*
Angels 4 Life LLC........E....... 513 474-5683
Cincinnati *(G-3029)*
Angels In Waiting Home Care........E....... 440 946-0349
Mentor *(G-14144)*
Angels Visiting........D....... 419 298-0034
Edgerton *(G-10582)*
Angmar Medical Holdings Inc........D....... 330 835-9663
Fairlawn *(G-10937)*
Answercare LLC........D....... 855 213-1511
Canton *(G-2241)*
Arcadia Services Inc........D....... 330 869-9520
Akron *(G-79)*
Arcadia Services Inc........D....... 937 912-5800
Beavercreek *(G-1147)*
Area Agency On Aging Planni........C....... 800 258-7277
Dayton *(G-9343)*
Area Office On Aging of Nwstrn........D....... 419 382-0624
Toledo *(G-17758)*
Arlingworth Home Health Inc........E....... 614 659-0961
Dublin *(G-10255)*
Around Clock Home Care........D....... 440 350-2547
Painesville *(G-15835)*
ASAP Homecare Inc........E....... 330 334-7027
Wadsworth *(G-18748)*
ASAP Homecare Inc........D....... 330 263-4733
Wooster *(G-19829)*
Ashtabula Rgional Hm Hlth Svcs........D....... 440 992-4663
Ashtabula *(G-726)*
Assured Health Care Inc........E....... 937 294-2803
Dayton *(G-9346)*
Atrium Health System........A....... 937 499-5606
Middletown *(G-14473)*
B & L Agency LLC........E....... 740 373-8272
Marietta *(G-13434)*
Benjamin Rose Institute........D....... 216 791-8000
Cleveland *(G-5117)*
Bethesda Hospital Association........A....... 740 454-4000
Zanesville *(G-20447)*

SERVICES SECTION

HOME HEALTH CARE SVCS

Beyond The Horizons Home Healt ..... E 608 630-0617
  Columbus *(G-7105)*
Black Stone Cincinnati LLC ..... D 937 424-1370
  Moraine *(G-14754)*
Black Stone Cincinnati LLC ..... E 513 924-1370
  Cincinnati *(G-3112)*
Blanchard Valley Health System ..... D 419 424-3000
  Findlay *(G-10998)*
Braden Med Services Inc ..... E 740 732-2356
  Caldwell *(G-2082)*
Bradley Bay Assisted Living ..... E 440 871-4509
  Bay Village *(G-1038)*
Bridgeshome Health Care ..... E 330 764-1000
  Medina *(G-14040)*
Brightstar Healthcare ..... E 513 321-4688
  Blue Ash *(G-1549)*
Brook Haven Home Health Care ..... E 937 833-6945
  Brookville *(G-1959)*
Brookdale Senior Living Commun ..... E 937 548-6800
  Greenville *(G-11490)*
Brookdale Senior Living Inc ..... E 614 336-3677
  Dublin *(G-10269)*
Brookdale Senior Living Inc ..... E 513 745-9292
  Cincinnati *(G-3139)*
Brookdale Senior Living Inc ..... E 330 262-1615
  Wooster *(G-19835)*
Buckeye Hills-Hck Vly Reg Dev ..... E 740 373-6400
  Reno *(G-16421)*
Buckeye Home Health Care ..... C 513 791-6446
  Blue Ash *(G-1550)*
Buckeye Home Healthcare Inc ..... E 614 776-3372
  Westerville *(G-19373)*
Buckeye Rsdntial Solutions LLC ..... D 330 235-9183
  Ravenna *(G-16374)*
C K of Cincinnati Inc ..... C 513 752-5533
  Cincinnati *(G-3161)*
C R G Health Care Systems ..... E 330 498-8107
  Niles *(G-15285)*
Capital Health Homecare ..... E 740 264-8815
  Steubenville *(G-17305)*
Capital Senior Living Corp ..... C 330 748-4204
  Macedonia *(G-13192)*
Caprice Health Care Inc ..... C 330 965-9200
  North Lima *(G-15400)*
Caregivers Health Network Inc ..... D 513 662-3400
  Cincinnati *(G-3182)*
Carestar Inc ..... C 513 618-8300
  Cincinnati *(G-3183)*
Caring Hands Inc ..... C 330 821-6310
  Alliance *(G-530)*
Caring Hands Home Health Care ..... E 740 532-9020
  Ironton *(G-12285)*
Caring Hearts Home Health Care ..... B 513 339-1237
  Mason *(G-13670)*
Carl Mills ..... D 740 282-2382
  Toronto *(G-18335)*
Central Star ..... C 419 756-9449
  Mansfield *(G-13275)*
Chcc Home Health Care ..... E 330 759-4069
  Austintown *(G-869)*
Chemed Corporation ..... D 513 762-6690
  Cincinnati *(G-3237)*
Chestnut Hill Management Co ..... D 614 855-3700
  Columbus *(G-7256)*
CHI Health At Home ..... D 513 576-0262
  Milford *(G-14509)*
Childrens Home Care Dayton ..... D 937 641-4663
  Dayton *(G-9402)*
Childrens Home Care Group ..... B 330 543-5000
  Akron *(G-134)*
Childrens Homecare Services ..... C 614 355-1100
  Columbus *(G-7261)*
Circle J Home Health Care ..... D 330 482-0877
  Salineville *(G-16722)*
City of Wooster ..... E 330 263-8636
  Wooster *(G-19844)*
Columbus W Hlth Care Co Partnr ..... E 614 274-4005
  Columbus *(G-7392)*
Comfort Healthcare ..... E 216 281-9999
  Cleveland *(G-5375)*
Community Caregivers ..... E 330 725-9800
  Wadsworth *(G-18750)*
Community Concepts Inc ..... C 513 398-8181
  Mason *(G-13687)*
Community Health Systems Inc ..... D 330 841-9011
  Warren *(G-18836)*
Community Home Care ..... E 330 971-7011
  Cuyahoga Falls *(G-9177)*
Companions of Ashland LLC ..... E 419 281-2273
  Ashland *(G-676)*

Compassionate In Home Care ..... E 614 888-5683
  Worthington *(G-19950)*
Comprehensive Health Care Svcs ..... C 513 245-0100
  Cincinnati *(G-3406)*
Concord Hlth Rhabilitation Ctr ..... E 740 574-8441
  Wheelersburg *(G-19575)*
Consumer Support Services Inc ..... C 330 652-8800
  Niles *(G-15290)*
Consumer Support Services Inc ..... B 740 788-8257
  Newark *(G-15158)*
Continued Care Inc ..... E 419 222-2273
  Lima *(G-12759)*
Continuum Home Care Inc ..... E 440 964-3332
  Ashtabula *(G-737)*
Cori Care Inc ..... D 614 848-4357
  Columbus *(G-7439)*
Cottages of Clayton ..... E 937 280-0300
  Dayton *(G-9429)*
County of Knox ..... E 740 392-2200
  Mount Vernon *(G-14888)*
County of Washington ..... E 740 373-2028
  Marietta *(G-13439)*
County of Williams ..... E 419 485-3141
  Montpelier *(G-14742)*
Covington Square Senior APT ..... E 740 623-4603
  Coshocton *(G-9101)*
Crawford Cnty Shared Hlth Svcs ..... E 419 468-7985
  Galion *(G-11293)*
Dacas Nursing Systems Inc ..... C 330 884-2530
  Warren *(G-18846)*
Daugwood Inc ..... E 937 429-9465
  Beavercreek *(G-1165)*
Daynas Homecare LLC ..... E 216 323-0323
  Maple Heights *(G-13405)*
Dayton Hospice Incorporated ..... B 937 256-4490
  Dayton *(G-9479)*
Dayton Hospice Incorporated ..... C 513 422-0300
  Franklin *(G-11153)*
Decahealth Inc ..... D 866 908-3514
  Toledo *(G-17848)*
Diamonds Pearls Hlth Svcs LLC ..... E 216 752-8500
  Cleveland *(G-5482)*
Dillon Holdings LLC ..... C 513 942-5600
  West Chester *(G-19062)*
Discount Drug Mart Inc ..... C 330 725-2340
  Medina *(G-14059)*
Diversified Health Management ..... E 614 338-8888
  Columbus *(G-7527)*
Eldercare Services Inst LLC ..... D 216 791-8000
  Cleveland *(G-5530)*
Ember Home Care ..... B 740 922-6968
  Uhrichsville *(G-18489)*
Emh Regional Homecare Agency ..... E 440 329-7519
  Elyria *(G-10625)*
Enhanced Homecare Medina Inc ..... E 330 952-2331
  Medina *(G-14062)*
Every Child Succeeds ..... C 513 636-2830
  Cincinnati *(G-3583)*
Everyday Homecare ..... E 937 444-1672
  Mount Orab *(G-14868)*
Exclusive Homecare Services ..... D 937 236-6750
  Dayton *(G-9534)*
Fairfield Community Health Ctr ..... E 740 277-6043
  Lancaster *(G-12530)*
Fairhope Hospice and Palliativ ..... D 740 654-7077
  Lancaster *(G-12540)*
Family Senior Care Inc ..... E 740 441-1428
  Gallipolis *(G-11315)*
Family Service of NW Ohio ..... D 419 321-6455
  Toledo *(G-17878)*
Fidelity Health Care ..... B 937 208-6400
  Moraine *(G-14785)*
First Community Hlth Svcs LLC ..... E 937 247-0400
  Dayton *(G-9547)*
First Community Village ..... B 614 324-4455
  Columbus *(G-7664)*
Frencor Inc ..... E 330 332-1203
  Salem *(G-16696)*
Gardens Western Reserve Inc ..... D 330 928-4500
  Cuyahoga Falls *(G-9191)*
Genesis Healthcare System ..... A 740 454-5000
  Zanesville *(G-20481)*
Good Samaritan Hosp Cincinnati ..... E 513 569-6251
  Cincinnati *(G-3685)*
Graceworks Lutheran Services ..... B 937 436-6850
  Dayton *(G-9583)*
Great Lakes Home Hlth Svcs Inc ..... E 888 260-9835
  Toledo *(G-17921)*
Great Lakes Home Hlth Svcs Inc ..... E 888 260-9835
  Akron *(G-245)*

Great Lakes Home Hlth Svcs Inc ..... E 888 260-9835
  Mentor *(G-14184)*
Guardian Angls Home Hlth Svcs ..... D 419 517-7797
  Sylvania *(G-17590)*
Hamilton Homecare Inc ..... E 614 221-0022
  Columbus *(G-7796)*
Hastings Home Health Ctr Inc ..... E 216 898-3300
  Medina *(G-14074)*
Hattie Larlham Community Svcs ..... E 330 274-2272
  Mantua *(G-13389)*
Hcr Manorcare Med Svcs Fla LLC ..... D 513 233-0831
  Cincinnati *(G-3747)*
Health Care Depo of Ohio LLC ..... D 614 776-3333
  Columbus *(G-7810)*
Health Care Facility MGT LLC ..... D 513 489-7100
  Blue Ash *(G-1608)*
Health Care Plus ..... E 614 340-7587
  Columbus *(G-6882)*
Healthcare Circle Inc ..... D 440 331-7347
  Strongsville *(G-17468)*
Healthcare Holdings Inc ..... D 513 530-1600
  Blue Ash *(G-1609)*
Healthlinx Inc ..... E 513 402-2018
  Cincinnati *(G-3754)*
Healthsource of Ohio Inc ..... E 937 981-7707
  Greenfield *(G-11487)*
Heart To Heart Home Health ..... E 330 335-9999
  Wadsworth *(G-18755)*
Heartland Home Care LLC ..... E 614 433-0423
  Columbus *(G-7818)*
Heartland Hospice Services LLC ..... D 614 433-0423
  Columbus *(G-7819)*
Heartland Hospice Services LLC ..... D 740 351-0575
  Portsmouth *(G-16285)*
Heartland Hospice Services LLC ..... D 740 259-0281
  Lucasville *(G-13180)*
Heartland Hospice Services LLC ..... D 419 531-0440
  Perrysburg *(G-16010)*
Heartland Hospice Services LLC ..... D 216 901-1464
  Independence *(G-12216)*
Heartland Hospice Services LLC ..... D 937 299-6980
  Dayton *(G-9607)*
Heavenly Home Health ..... E 740 859-4735
  Rayland *(G-16417)*
Helping Hands Health Care Inc ..... C 513 755-4181
  West Chester *(G-19206)*
Heritage Day Health Centers ..... E 614 451-2151
  Columbus *(G-7830)*
Heritage Health Care Services ..... D 419 222-2404
  Lima *(G-12798)*
Heritage Health Care Services ..... C 419 867-2002
  Maumee *(G-13925)*
Heritage Home Health Care ..... E 440 333-1925
  Rocky River *(G-16580)*
Holy Family Hospice ..... D 440 888-7722
  Parma *(G-15909)*
Home Care Relief Inc ..... D 216 692-2270
  Euclid *(G-10761)*
Home Helpers ..... E 937 393-8600
  Hillsboro *(G-11983)*
Home Helpers In Home Care ..... D 330 455-5440
  Canton *(G-2403)*
Home Instead Senior Care ..... D 330 334-4664
  Wadsworth *(G-18756)*
Home Instead Senior Care ..... E 740 393-2500
  Mount Vernon *(G-14898)*
Home Instead Senior Care ..... D 330 729-1233
  Youngstown *(G-20218)*
Home Instead Senior Care ..... D 614 432-8524
  Upper Arlington *(G-18551)*
Homereach Inc ..... C 614 566-0850
  Worthington *(G-19965)*
Hometech Healthcare Svcs LLC ..... E 216 295-9120
  Cleveland *(G-5769)*
Hope Homes Inc ..... E 330 688-4935
  Stow *(G-17372)*
Horizon HM Hlth Care Agcy LLC ..... E 614 279-2933
  Columbus *(G-7859)*
Hospice Cincinnati Inc ..... E 513 862-1100
  Cincinnati *(G-3785)*
Hospice Cincinnati Inc ..... D 513 891-7700
  Cincinnati *(G-3786)*
Hospice of Genesis Health ..... E 740 454-5381
  Zanesville *(G-20488)*
Hospice of Knox County ..... E 740 397-5188
  Mount Vernon *(G-14899)*
Hospice of Memorial Hospita L ..... E 419 334-6626
  Clyde *(G-6815)*
Hospice of Miami County Inc ..... E 937 335-5191
  Troy *(G-18358)*

Employee Codes: A=Over 500 employees, B=251-500
C=101-250, D=51-100, E=25-50

HOME HEALTH CARE SVCS — SERVICES SECTION

Hospice of North Central Ohio .... E 419 524-9200
  Ontario (G-15692)
Hospice of North Central Ohio .... E 419 281-7107
  Ashland (G-682)
Hospice of Ohio LLC .... D 440 286-2500
  Cleveland (G-5777)
Hospice of The Western Reserve .... D 330 800-2240
  Medina (G-14077)
Hospice of The Western Reserve .... D 440 997-6619
  Ashtabula (G-748)
Hospice of The Western Reserve .... D 800 707-8922
  Cleveland (G-5780)
Huntsey Corporation .... E 614 568-5030
  Westerville (G-19315)
In Home Health LLC .... E 419 531-0440
  Toledo (G-17972)
In Home Health LLC .... E 513 831-5800
  Cincinnati (G-3810)
In Home Health LLC .... E 419 355-9209
  Fremont (G-11207)
Independent Living of Ohio .... E 937 323-8400
  Springfield (G-17211)
Infinity Health Services Inc .... D 440 614-0145
  Westlake (G-19498)
Infusion Partners Inc .... E 513 396-6060
  Cincinnati (G-3818)
Inter Healt Care of Cambr Zane .... E 614 436-9404
  Columbus (G-7912)
Inter Healt Care of Cambr Zane .... E 513 984-1110
  Cincinnati (G-3830)
Interim Halthcare Columbus Inc .... E 614 888-3130
  Gahanna (G-11249)
Interim Halthcare Columbus Inc .... E 330 836-5571
  Fairlawn (G-10958)
Interim Healthcare .... D 740 354-5550
  Portsmouth (G-16291)
Interim Healthcare SE Ohio Inc .... D 740 373-3800
  Marietta (G-13457)
International Healthcare Corp .... E 513 731-3338
  Cincinnati (G-3836)
Jag Healthcare Inc .... A 440 385-4370
  Rocky River (G-16582)
Kaiser-Wells Inc .... E 419 668-7651
  Norwalk (G-15577)
Kindred Healthcare Inc .... C 440 232-1800
  Bedford Heights (G-1355)
Labelle Hmhealth Care Svcs LLC .... D 440 842-3005
  Cleveland (G-5916)
Labelle Hmhealth Care Svcs LLC .... D 740 392-1405
  Mount Vernon (G-14908)
Laurie Ann Home Health Care .... E 330 872-7512
  Newton Falls (G-15275)
Lbs International Inc .... D 614 866-3688
  Pickerington (G-16100)
Liberty Health Care Center Inc .... E 937 296-1550
  Bellbrook (G-1371)
Lifecare Alliance .... C 614 278-3130
  Columbus (G-8063)
Lighthouse Medical Staffing .... D 614 937-6259
  Hilliard (G-11921)
Little Miami Home Care Inc .... E 513 248-8988
  Milford (G-14531)
Living Assistance Services .... D 330 733-1532
  Tallmadge (G-17644)
Loft Services LLC .... E 614 855-2452
  New Albany (G-14991)
Loving Hands Home Care Inc .... E 330 792-7032
  Youngstown (G-20256)
Lutheran Social Services of .... E 614 228-5200
  Worthington (G-19975)
Mahoning Vly Infusioncare Inc .... C 330 759-9487
  Youngstown (G-20266)
Main Street Fmly Medicine LLC .... E 614 253-8537
  Columbus (G-8100)
Majastan Group LLC .... D 216 231-6400
  Cleveland (G-5971)
Manor Care Inc .... D 419 252-5500
  Toledo (G-18028)
Maple Knoll Communities Inc .... B 513 782-2400
  Cincinnati (G-4019)
Maplecrst Asistd Lvg Intl Ordr .... E 419 562-4988
  Bucyrus (G-2043)
Marion General Hosp HM Hlth .... E 740 383-8770
  Marion (G-13558)
Marymount Hospital Inc .... B 216 581-0500
  Cleveland (G-5991)
Mch Services Inc 260 432-9699
  Dayton (G-9707)
Med America Hlth Systems Corp .... A 937 223-6192
  Dayton (G-9710)

Medcentral Health System .... E 419 526-8442
  Mansfield (G-13338)
Medcorp Inc .... D 419 727-7000
  Toledo (G-18047)
Medcorp Inc .... C 419 425-9700
  Findlay (G-11065)
Medi Home Health Agency Inc .... E 740 266-3977
  Steubenville (G-17329)
Medi Home Health Agency Inc .... E 740 441-1779
  Gallipolis (G-11328)
Medlink of Ohio Inc .... B 216 751-5900
  Cleveland (G-6016)
Memorial Hospital .... E 419 547-6419
  Clyde (G-6818)
Menorah Park Center For Senio .... D 330 867-2143
  Cuyahoga Falls (G-9208)
Mercer Cnty Joint Townshp Hosp .... E 419 584-0143
  Celina (G-2653)
Mid Ohio Home Health Ltd .... E 419 529-3883
  Ontario (G-15704)
Mircale Health Care .... C 614 237-7702
  Columbus (G-8178)
Mount Carmel Health .... D 614 234-0100
  Westerville (G-19427)
Mount Crmel Hospice Evrgrn Ctr .... D 614 234-0200
  Columbus (G-8200)
Multicare Home Health Services .... D 216 731-8900
  Euclid (G-10768)
National Church Residences .... E 614 451-2151
  Columbus (G-8216)
National Mentor Holdings Inc .... A 419 443-0867
  Fostoria (G-11135)
National Mentor Holdings Inc .... A 330 835-1468
  Fairlawn (G-10967)
National Mentor Holdings Inc .... A 234 806-5361
  Warren (G-18884)
Nationwide Childrens Hospital .... E 614 355-8300
  Westerville (G-19331)
Nationwide Health MGT LLC .... D 440 888-8888
  Parma (G-15911)
NC Hha Inc .... D 216 593-7750
  Elyria (G-10658)
NCR At Home Health & Wellness .... E 614 451-2151
  Columbus (G-8253)
New Life Hospice Inc .... E 440 934-1458
  Lorain (G-13064)
New Life Hospice Inc .... D 440 934-1458
  Sheffield Village (G-16893)
Nightingale Home Care .... E 614 457-6006
  Columbus (G-8279)
Nightingale Home Healthcare .... E 614 408-0104
  Dublin (G-10409)
Nurses Care Inc .... D 513 424-1141
  Miamisburg (G-14327)
Nurses Care Inc .... E 513 424-1141
  Fairfield (G-10885)
Nursing Resources Corp .... E 419 333-3000
  Maumee (G-13951)
Odyssey Healthcare Inc .... C 614 414-0500
  Gahanna (G-11260)
Ohio North E Hlth Systems Inc .... E 330 747-9551
  Youngstown (G-20308)
Ohio Senior Home Hlth Care LLC .... D 614 470-6070
  Columbus (G-8375)
Ohio Valley Home Care LLC .... E 330 385-2333
  East Liverpool (G-10529)
Ohio Valley Home Health Inc .... E 740 249-4219
  Athens (G-809)
Ohio Valley Home Health Inc .... E 740 441-1393
  Gallipolis (G-11334)
Ohiohealth Corporation .... A 614 788-8860
  Columbus (G-8457)
Omni Park Health Care LLC .... C 216 289-8963
  Euclid (G-10770)
Omnicare Inc .... C 513 719-2600
  Cincinnati (G-4220)
On-Call Nursing Inc .... D 216 577-8890
  Lakewood (G-12493)
Open Arms Health Systems LLC .... E 614 385-8354
  Columbus (G-8469)
Option Care Enterprises Inc .... C 513 576-8400
  Milford (G-14546)
Option Care Infusion Svcs Inc .... E 614 431-6453
  Columbus (G-8475)
Option Care Infusion Svcs Inc .... D 513 576-8400
  Milford (G-14546)
P E Miller & Assoc .... E 614 231-4743
  Columbus (G-8502)
P E Miller & Associates Inc .... E 614 231-4743
  Columbus (G-8503)

Palladium Healthcare LLC .... C 216 644-4383
  Cleveland (G-6230)
Paramount Support Service .... D 740 526-0540
  Saint Clairsville (G-16651)
Parkside Care Corporation .... D 440 286-2273
  Chardon (G-2761)
Passion To Heal Healthcare .... E 216 849-0180
  Cleveland (G-6249)
Paula Jo Moore .... E 330 894-2910
  Kensington (G-12349)
Personal Touch HM Care IPA Inc .... C 216 986-0885
  Cleveland (G-6267)
Personal Touch HM Care IPA Inc .... C 513 868-2272
  Hamilton (G-11763)
Personal Touch HM Care IPA Inc .... E 513 984-9600
  Cincinnati (G-4283)
Personal Touch HM Care IPA Inc .... D 614 227-6952
  Columbus (G-8539)
Personal Touch HM Care IPA Inc .... A 330 263-1112
  Wooster (G-19903)
Phoenix Homes Inc .... E 419 692-2421
  Delphos (G-10149)
Physicians Choice Inc .... E 513 844-1608
  Liberty Twp (G-12727)
Preferred Medical Group Inc .... C 404 403-8310
  Beachwood (G-1115)
Premier Care .... D 614 431-0599
  Worthington (G-19985)
Premier Health Partners .... A 937 499-9596
  Dayton (G-9820)
Premierfirst Home Health Care .... E 614 443-3110
  Columbus (G-8557)
Pressley Ridge Foundation .... E 513 737-0400
  Hamilton (G-11764)
Prime Home Care LLC .... E 419 535-1414
  Toledo (G-18136)
Private HM Care Foundation Inc .... D 513 662-8999
  Cincinnati (G-4335)
Prome Conti Care Serv Corpo .... A 419 885-1715
  Sylvania (G-17607)
Quality Care Nursing Svc Inc .... B 740 377-9095
  South Point (G-17096)
Quantum Health Inc .... D 614 846-4318
  Columbus (G-8581)
R & F Inc .... E 419 868-2909
  Holland (G-12047)
Reflektions Ltd .... E 614 560-6994
  Delaware (G-10123)
REM Corp .... E 740 828-2601
  Frazeysburg (G-11176)
RES-Care Inc .... E 740 782-1476
  Bethesda (G-1486)
RES-Care Inc .... E 440 729-2432
  Chesterland (G-2802)
Rescare Ohio Inc .... E 740 867-4568
  Chesapeake (G-2788)
Right At Home .... D 937 291-2244
  Springboro (G-17137)
Right At Home LLC .... E 614 734-1110
  Columbus (G-6904)
RMS of Ohio Inc .... D 937 291-3622
  Dayton (G-9853)
Ross County Health District .... C 740 775-1114
  Chillicothe (G-2880)
RWS Enterprises LLC .... E 513 598-6770
  Cincinnati (G-4460)
Salo Inc .... D 614 436-9404
  Columbus (G-8679)
Sand Run Supports LLC .... E 330 256-2127
  Fairlawn (G-10973)
Sar Enterprises LLC .... D 419 472-8181
  Toledo (G-18172)
Sdx Home Care Operations LLC .... D 877 692-0345
  Springfield (G-17271)
Senior Care Management Inc .... E 419 578-7000
  Toledo (G-18178)
Senior Independence .... E 330 744-5071
  Youngstown (G-20370)
Senior Independence .... D 330 873-3468
  Fairlawn (G-10975)
Senior Independence Adult .... E 513 539-2697
  Monroe (G-14712)
Senior Select Home Health Care .... E 330 665-4663
  Fairlawn (G-10976)
Signature Health Services LLC .... E 740 522-6017
  Heath (G-11844)
Simone Health Management Inc .... E 614 224-1347
  Columbus (G-8735)
Source Diagnostics LLC .... D 440 542-9481
  Solon (G-17055)

SERVICES SECTION — HOMES FOR THE ELDERLY

Southern Care Inc .... E 419 774-0555
  Ontario (G-15715)
Special Touch Homecare LLC .... E 937 549-1843
  Manchester (G-13256)
St Augustine Towers .... E 216 634-7444
  Cleveland (G-6520)
St Ritas Medical Center .... C 419 538-7025
  Lima (G-12887)
Summa Health Center Lk Medina .... E 330 952-0014
  Medina (G-14130)
Summit Acres Inc .... C 740 732-2364
  Caldwell (G-2089)
Sunshine Homecare .... E 419 207-9900
  Ashland (G-700)
Supportcare Inc .... E 614 889-5837
  Dublin (G-10467)
Supreme Touch Home Health Svcs .... E 614 783-1115
  Columbus (G-8810)
Svh Holdings LLC .... D 844 560-7775
  Columbus (G-8813)
Synergy Homecare South Dayton .... E 937 610-0555
  Dayton (G-9918)
Think-Ability LLC .... E 419 589-2238
  Mansfield (G-13374)
Tk Homecare Llc .... C 419 517-7000
  Toledo (G-18220)
TLC Home Health Care Inc .... E 740 732-5211
  Caldwell (G-2090)
Toledo District Nurses Assn .... C 419 255-0983
  Sylvania (G-17622)
Toledo Hospital .... C 419 291-2273
  Sylvania (G-17623)
Traditions At Stygler Road .... E 614 475-8778
  Columbus (G-8863)
Trusted Homecare Solutions .... E 937 506-7063
  Dayton (G-9940)
Tsk Assisted Living Services .... E 330 297-2000
  Ravenna (G-16414)
Twin Maples Home Health Care .... E 740 596-1022
  McArthur (G-14017)
Uahs Heather Hill Home Health .... E 440 285-5098
  Chardon (G-2772)
Union Hospital Home Hlth Care .... E 330 343-6909
  Dover (G-10221)
United Home Health Services .... D 614 880-8686
  Columbus (G-8892)
Universal Health Care Svcs Inc .... C 614 547-0282
  Columbus (G-8906)
Universal Nursing Services .... E 330 434-7318
  Akron (G-487)
University Hospitals Cleveland .... D 216 844-4663
  Cleveland (G-6661)
University Hospitals He .... B 216 844-4663
  Cleveland (G-6663)
University Mednet .... B 216 383-0100
  Euclid (G-10780)
Ussa Inc .... E 740 354-6672
  Portsmouth (G-16319)
Vancrest Health Care Center .... D 419 264-0700
  Holgate (G-12004)
VIP Homecare Inc .... D 330 929-2838
  Akron (G-497)
Visions Matter LLC .... D 513 934-1934
  Lebanon (G-12656)
Visiting Nurse Associat .... C 513 345-8000
  Cincinnati (G-4815)
Vistacare USA Inc .... E 614 975-3230
  Columbus (G-8946)
Vitas Healthcare Corporation .... D 513 742-6310
  Cincinnati (G-4816)
Vitas Healthcare Corporation .... E 216 706-2100
  Cleveland (G-6706)
Vrable III Inc .... E 740 446-7150
  Bidwell (G-1497)
Western Reserve Area Agency .... C 216 621-0303
  Cleveland (G-6742)
Ziks Family Pharmacy 100 .... E 937 225-9350
  Dayton (G-10015)

HOME IMPROVEMENT & RENOVATION CONTRACTOR AGENCY

Eagle Industries Ohio Inc .... E 513 247-2900
  Fairfield (G-10844)
Longworth Enterprises Inc .... B 513 738-4663
  West Chester (G-19112)
Menard Inc .... B 614 501-1654
  Columbus (G-8146)
Teasdale Fenton Carpet Cleanin .... D 513 797-0900
  Cincinnati (G-4628)

HOMEBUILDERS & OTHER OPERATIVE BUILDERS

American Prservation Bldrs LLC .... D 216 236-2007
  Cleveland (G-5019)
CV Perry Builders .... E 614 221-4131
  Columbus (G-7475)
Dixon Builders & Developers .... D 513 887-6400
  West Chester (G-19066)
Glencoe Restoration Group LLC .... E 330 752-1244
  Akron (G-237)
M/I Homes of Austin LLC .... E 614 418-8000
  Columbus (G-8096)
Mainthia Technologies Inc .... D 216 433-2198
  Cleveland (G-5970)
Multicon Construction Co .... E 614 351-2683
  Columbus (G-8208)
Nvr Inc .... C 513 202-0323
  Harrison (G-11807)
Nvr Inc .... E 937 529-7000
  Dayton (G-9777)

HOMEFURNISHING STORES: Fireplaces & Wood Burning Stoves

Overhead Inc .... E 419 476-7811
  Toledo (G-18113)
Southtown Heating & Cooling .... E 937 320-9900
  Moraine (G-14827)

HOMEFURNISHING STORES: Lighting Fixtures

Gross Electric Inc .... E 419 537-1818
  Toledo (G-17925)
Mars Electric Company .... D 440 946-2250
  Cleveland (G-5984)

HOMEFURNISHING STORES: Metalware

Scs Construction Services Inc .... E 513 929-0260
  Cincinnati (G-4487)

HOMEFURNISHING STORES: Pottery

Workshops of David T Smith .... E 513 932-2472
  Morrow (G-14848)

HOMEFURNISHINGS & SPLYS, WHOLESALE: Decorative

Dwa Mrkting Prmtional Pdts LLC .... E 216 476-0635
  Strongsville (G-17457)
Everfast Inc .... B 216 360-9176
  Cleveland (G-5557)
Luminex Home Decor .... A 513 563-1113
  Blue Ash (G-1632)
Ten Thousand Villages Cleveland .... E 216 575-1058
  Cleveland (G-6580)

HOMEFURNISHINGS, WHOLESALE: Blankets

Mill Distributors Inc .... D 330 995-9200
  Aurora (G-848)

HOMEFURNISHINGS, WHOLESALE: Blinds, Venetian

Style-Line Incorporated .... E 614 291-0600
  Columbus (G-8798)

HOMEFURNISHINGS, WHOLESALE: Carpets

Business Furniture LLC .... E 937 293-1010
  Dayton (G-9375)
Dealers Supply North Inc .... E 614 274-6285
  Lockbourne (G-12948)
Everybodys Inc .... E 937 293-1010
  Moraine (G-14782)
Ohio Valley Flooring Inc .... D 513 271-3434
  Cincinnati (G-4212)
Regal Carpet Center Inc .... E 216 475-1844
  Cleveland (G-6366)
State Crest Carpet & Flooring .... E 440 232-3980
  Bedford (G-1340)

HOMEFURNISHINGS, WHOLESALE: Draperies

Accent Drapery Co Inc .... E 614 488-0741
  Columbus (G-6933)
Lumenomics Inc .... E 614 798-3500
  Lewis Center (G-12693)

HOMEFURNISHINGS, WHOLESALE: Grills, Barbecue

Hayward Distributing Co .... E 614 272-5953
  Columbus (G-7805)

HOMEFURNISHINGS, WHOLESALE: Kitchenware

Famous Distribution Inc .... D 330 762-9621
  Akron (G-215)
G G Marck & Associates Inc .... E 419 478-0900
  Toledo (G-17903)
Pottery Barn Inc .... E 614 478-3154
  Columbus (G-8553)
Walter F Stephens Jr Inc .... E 937 746-0521
  Franklin (G-11167)
World Tableware Inc .... D 419 325-2608
  Toledo (G-18314)

HOMEFURNISHINGS, WHOLESALE: Mirrors/Pictures, Framed/Unframd

Century Glass Co .... E 216 361-7700
  Cleveland (G-5218)

HOMEFURNISHINGS, WHOLESALE: Pottery

Original Hartstone Pottery Inc .... E 740 452-9999
  Zanesville (G-20521)
Workshops of David T Smith .... E 513 932-2472
  Morrow (G-14848)

HOMEFURNISHINGS, WHOLESALE: Rugs

Cinmar LLC .... C 513 603-1000
  West Chester (G-19040)
Rite Rug Co .... E 440 945-4100
  Strongsville (G-17502)

HOMEFURNISHINGS, WHOLESALE: Wood Flooring

JP Flooring Systems Inc .... E 513 346-4300
  West Chester (G-19099)

HOMES FOR THE ELDERLY

Abbewood Limited Partnership .... E 440 366-8980
  Elyria (G-10591)
Aleph Home & Senior Care Inc .... D 216 382-7689
  Cleveland (G-4983)
Aspen Woodside Village .... D 440 439-8666
  Cleveland (G-5072)
Assisted Living Concepts LLC .... E 419 224-6327
  Lima (G-12742)
Berea Lake Towers Inc .... E 440 243-9050
  Berea (G-1448)
Brookdale Senior Living Inc .... D 513 229-3155
  Mason (G-13668)
Brookdale Senior Living Inc .... C 614 794-2499
  Westerville (G-19372)
Brookdale Senior Living Inc .... D 419 422-8657
  Findlay (G-11008)
Browning Mesonic Community .... E 419 878-4055
  Waterville (G-18941)
Caritas Inc .... E 419 332-2589
  Fremont (G-11186)
Carriage Crt Mrysvlle Ltd Prtn .... E 937 642-2202
  Marysville (G-13609)
Clark Memorial Home Assn .... E 937 399-4262
  Springfield (G-17164)
County of Allen .... C 419 221-1103
  Lima (G-12763)
County of Logan .... C 937 592-2901
  Bellefontaine (G-1382)
Eastgate Village .... E 513 753-4400
  Cincinnati (G-2915)
Episcopal Retirement Homes Inc .... E 513 271-9610
  Cincinnati (G-3567)
Episcopal Retirement Homes Inc .... E 513 561-6363
  Cincinnati (G-3568)

Employee Codes: A=Over 500 employees, B=251-500
C=101-250, D=51-100, E=25-50

HOMES FOR THE ELDERLY SERVICES SECTION

Episcopal Retirement Homes Inc ....C 513 871-2090
Cincinnati *(G-3569)*
Evangelical Retirement ....C 937 837-5581
Dayton *(G-9532)*
Fairways ....D 440 943-2050
Wickliffe *(G-19596)*
Friendship Vlg of Clumbus Ohio ....C 614 890-8282
Columbus *(G-7708)*
Glenwood Community Inc ....E 740 376-9555
Marietta *(G-13447)*
Hackensack Meridian Health Inc ....D 513 792-9697
Cincinnati *(G-3727)*
Harrison Co County Home ....E 740 942-3573
Cadiz *(G-2075)*
Inn At Christine Valley ....E 330 270-3347
Youngstown *(G-20236)*
J & R Associates ....A 440 250-4080
Brookpark *(G-1947)*
Kent Ridge At Golden Pond Ltd ....D 330 677-4040
Kent *(G-12378)*
Kingston Healthcare Company ....D 740 389-2311
Marion *(G-13546)*
Lakeside Manor Inc ....E 330 549-2545
North Lima *(G-15404)*
Mason Health Care Center ....D 513 398-2881
Mason *(G-13737)*
New Dawn Health Care Inc ....C 330 343-5521
Dover *(G-10202)*
Oakleaf Toledo Ltd Partnership ....E 419 885-3934
Toledo *(G-18101)*
Ohio Department of Aging ....D 614 466-5500
Columbus *(G-8324)*
Ohio Living ....C 513 681-4230
Cincinnati *(G-4208)*
Ohio Living ....B 440 942-4342
Willoughby *(G-19700)*
Orrvilla Retirement Community ....E 330 683-4455
Orrville *(G-15777)*
Otterbein Homes ....D 513 933-5439
Lebanon *(G-12634)*
Otterbein Snior Lfstyle Chices ....C 513 260-7690
Middletown *(G-14483)*
Otterbein Snior Lfstyle Chices ....B 513 933-5400
Lebanon *(G-12636)*
Otterbein Snior Lfstyle Chices ....C 419 645-5114
Cridersville *(G-9152)*
Otterbein Snior Lfstyle Chices ....E 419 943-4376
Leipsic *(G-12663)*
Paisley House For Aged Women ....E 330 799-9431
Youngstown *(G-20314)*
Paul Dennis ....E 440 746-8600
Brecksville *(G-1839)*
Premier Estates 525 LLC ....D 513 631-6800
Cincinnati *(G-4323)*
Premier Estates 526 LLC ....D 513 922-1440
Cincinnati *(G-4324)*
Pristine Senior Living ....D 513 471-8667
Cincinnati *(G-4334)*
Pristine Snior Lving Englewood ....C 937 836-5143
Englewood *(G-10718)*
SEM Villa Inc ....E 513 831-3262
Loveland *(G-13158)*
Senior Care Inc ....E 937 372-1530
Xenia *(G-20075)*
Senior Care Inc ....E 937 291-3211
Miamisburg *(G-14347)*
Senior Lifestyle Corporation ....D 513 777-4457
West Chester *(G-19150)*
Sisters of Little ....C 513 281-8001
Cincinnati *(G-4532)*
Sisters of Mercy ....E 419 332-8208
Fremont *(G-11221)*
St Luke Lutheran Community ....E 330 868-5600
Minerva *(G-14651)*
Sunrise Senior Living Inc ....E 614 846-6500
Worthington *(G-20001)*
Sunrise Senior Living Inc ....D 440 895-2383
Rocky River *(G-16593)*
Sunrise Senior Living LLC ....E 937 836-9617
Englewood *(G-10720)*
Sunrise Senior Living LLC ....E 614 718-2062
Dublin *(G-10466)*
Sunset House Inc ....C 419 536-4645
Toledo *(G-18210)*
Sunset Rtrment Communities Inc ....D 419 724-1200
Ottawa Hills *(G-15807)*
Terre Forme Enterprises Inc ....E 330 847-6800
Mineral Ridge *(G-14640)*
United Church Homes Inc ....D 740 376-5600
Marietta *(G-13510)*
United Church Homes Inc ....C 513 922-1440
Cincinnati *(G-4730)*
Uvmc Nursing Care Inc ....C 937 667-7500
Tipp City *(G-17731)*
Wesleyan Village ....B 440 284-9000
Elyria *(G-10690)*
Womens Welsh Clubs of America ....D 440 331-0420
Rocky River *(G-16596)*
Zandex Inc ....E 740 452-2087
Zanesville *(G-20547)*

HOSE: Automobile, Rubber

Myers Industries Inc ....E 330 253-5592
Akron *(G-348)*

HOSE: Flexible Metal

First Francis Company Inc ....E 440 352-8927
Painesville *(G-15857)*

HOSES & BELTING: Rubber & Plastic

Allied Fabricating & Wldg Co ....E 614 751-6664
Columbus *(G-6970)*
Contitech North America Inc ....E 440 225-5363
Akron *(G-162)*
Eaton-Aeroquip Llc ....D 419 891-7775
Maumee *(G-13907)*
Goodyear Tire & Rubber Company ....A 330 796-2121
Akron *(G-243)*
Watteredge LLC ....D 440 933-6110
Avon Lake *(G-940)*

HOSPITAL EQPT REPAIR SVCS

Eastern Medical Equipment Co ....E 330 394-5555
Warren *(G-18853)*
Providian Med Field Svc LLC ....E 440 833-0460
Highland Heights *(G-11871)*

HOSPITALS: AMA Approved Residency

Marion General Hospital Inc ....D 740 383-8400
Marion *(G-13559)*
Trinity Hospital Twin City ....B 740 922-2800
Dennison *(G-10166)*

HOSPITALS: Cancer

Arthur G James Cancer Hospital ....E 614 293-3300
Columbus *(G-7045)*
Mercy Health - Springfield C ....E 937 323-5001
Springfield *(G-17241)*
Mercy Health Anderson Hospital ....E 513 624-4025
Cincinnati *(G-4069)*
Metrohealth System ....C 216 957-2100
Cleveland *(G-6043)*
Parma Clinic Cancer Center ....E 440 743-4747
Cleveland *(G-6246)*

HOSPITALS: Children's

Childrens Hosp Med Ctr Akron ....A 330 425-3344
Twinsburg *(G-18400)*
Childrens Hosp Med Ctr Akron ....A 330 308-5432
New Philadelphia *(G-15085)*
Childrens Hosp Med Ctr Akron ....E 330 629-6085
Youngstown *(G-20140)*
Childrens Hosp Med Ctr Akron ....A 330 543-1000
Akron *(G-135)*
Childrens Hosp Med Ctr Akron ....E 330 543-8004
Akron *(G-136)*
Childrens Hosp Med Ctr Akron ....E 330 676-1020
Kent *(G-12357)*
Childrens Hospital ....E 513 636-4051
Cincinnati *(G-3245)*
Childrens Hospital Medical Ctr ....A 513 636-4200
Cincinnati *(G-3249)*
Childrens Hospital Medical Ctr ....A 513 636-6036
Cincinnati *(G-2906)*
Childrens Hospital Medical Ctr ....A 513 636-4200
Cincinnati *(G-3252)*
Childrens Hospital Medical Ctr ....E 513 636-6800
Mason *(G-13676)*
Childrens Medical Ctr Toledo ....A 937 641-3000
Dayton *(G-9403)*
Dayton Childrens Hospital ....A 937 641-3000
Dayton *(G-9464)*
Metrohealth System ....E 216 778-3867
Cleveland *(G-6042)*
Nationwide Childrens Hospital ....C 614 722-2700
Columbus *(G-8229)*
Nationwide Childrens Hospital ....B 614 722-5750
Columbus *(G-8230)*
Nationwide Childrens Hospital ....A 614 722-2000
Columbus *(G-8231)*
Nationwide Childrens Hospital ....B 513 636-6000
Cincinnati *(G-2925)*
Nationwide Childrens Hospital ....E 330 253-5200
Akron *(G-349)*
Nationwide Childrens Hospital ....A 614 722-2000
Columbus *(G-8232)*
Nationwide Childrens Hospital ....E 614 355-8300
Westerville *(G-19331)*
Nationwide Childrens Hospital ....B 614 722-8200
Columbus *(G-8233)*
Nationwide Childrens Hospital ....A 614 864-9216
Pickerington *(G-16102)*
Nationwide Childrens Hospital ....A 614 355-0802
Columbus *(G-8234)*
Nationwide Childrens Hospital ....B 614 355-8100
Columbus *(G-8235)*
Nationwide Childrens Hospital ....B 614 355-9200
Columbus *(G-8236)*
Nationwide Childrens Hospital ....B 614 355-8000
Columbus *(G-8237)*
Shriners Hspitals For Children ....B 513 872-6000
Cincinnati *(G-4519)*
Toledo Childrens Hosp Fdn ....E 419 824-9072
Toledo *(G-18231)*

HOSPITALS: Chronic Disease

Stein Hospice Services Inc ....B 800 625-5269
Sandusky *(G-16800)*
Stein Hospice Services Inc ....D 419 663-3222
Norwalk *(G-15593)*

HOSPITALS: Hospital, Professional Nursing School

Kettering Medical Center ....E 937 298-4331
Kettering *(G-12431)*
Kettering Medical Center ....E 937 384-8750
Dayton *(G-9656)*

HOSPITALS: Medical & Surgical

Acute Care Specialty Hospital ....A 330 363-4860
Canton *(G-2224)*
Adams County Regional Med Ctr ....C 937 386-3001
Seaman *(G-16818)*
Adams County Regional Med Ctr ....D 937 386-3400
Seaman *(G-16819)*
Adena Health System ....C 740 779-7500
Wshngtn CT Hs *(G-20013)*
Ado Health Services Inc ....D 330 629-2888
Youngstown *(G-20097)*
Affiliates In Oral & Maxlofcl ....E 513 829-8080
Fairfield *(G-10817)*
Akron City Hospital Inc ....A 330 253-5046
Akron *(G-32)*
Akron General Medical Center ....C 330 344-1980
Akron *(G-44)*
Akron General Medical Center ....C 330 344-1444
Akron *(G-45)*
Akron General Medical Center ....C 330 665-8000
Akron *(G-46)*
Allen Medical Center ....C 440 986-4000
Oberlin *(G-15638)*
Allianalce Hospitalist Group ....E 330 823-5626
Alliance *(G-523)*
Alliance Citizens Health Assn ....A 330 596-6000
Alliance *(G-524)*
Ashtabula County Medical Ctr ....A 440 997-2262
Ashtabula *(G-722)*
Ashtabula County Medical Ctr ....C 440 997-6960
Ashtabula *(G-723)*
Atrium Medical Center ....E 513 420-5013
Middletown *(G-14414)*
Aultman Hospital ....A 330 452-9911
Canton *(G-2253)*
Aultman Hospital ....B 330 452-9911
Canton *(G-2254)*
Aultman Hospital ....A 330 363-6262
Canton *(G-2255)*
Aultman Hospital ....E 330 452-2273
Canton *(G-2256)*
Aultman North Inc ....E 330 305-6999
Canton *(G-2258)*
Auxiliary Bd Fairview Gen Hosp ....A 216 476-7000
Cleveland *(G-5084)*
Bay Park Community Hospital ....D 419 690-7900
Oregon *(G-15725)*

SERVICES SECTION HOSPITALS: Medical & Surgical

Beavercreek Medical Center.....D..... 937 558-3000
Beavercreek *(G-1152)*
Beavercreek Medical Center.....D..... 937 558-3000
Beavercreek *(G-1153)*
Beckett Springs LLC.....E..... 513 942-9500
West Chester *(G-19025)*
Bellevue Hospital.....B..... 419 483-4040
Bellevue *(G-1404)*
Bellevue Hospital.....B..... 419 547-0074
Bellevue *(G-1405)*
Belmont Bhc Pines Hospital Inc.....C..... 330 759-2700
Youngstown *(G-20113)*
Belmont Community Hospital.....B..... 740 671-1200
Bellaire *(G-1362)*
Bethesda Hospital Inc.....E..... 513 894-8888
Fairfield Township *(G-10924)*
Bethesda Hospital Inc.....A..... 513 569-6100
Cincinnati *(G-3105)*
Bethesda Hospital Inc.....A..... 513 745-1111
Cincinnati *(G-3106)*
Bethesda Hospital Inc.....E..... 513 563-1505
Cincinnati *(G-3107)*
Bethesda Hospital Association.....A..... 740 454-4000
Zanesville *(G-20447)*
Blue Chp Srgcl Ctr Ptns LLC.....D..... 513 561-8900
Cincinnati *(G-3121)*
Bon Secours Health System.....E..... 740 966-3116
Johnstown *(G-12338)*
Bridgeshome Health Care.....E..... 330 764-1000
Medina *(G-14040)*
Brown Memorial Hospital.....B..... 440 593-1131
Conneaut *(G-9040)*
Bucyrus Community Hospital LLC.....D..... 419 562-4677
Bucyrus *(G-2027)*
Caep-Dunlap LLC.....E..... 330 456-2695
Canton *(G-2279)*
Center For Health Affairs.....D..... 800 362-2628
Cleveland *(G-5208)*
Center For Spinal Disorders.....E..... 419 383-4878
Toledo *(G-17797)*
Change Healthcare Tech Enabled.....D..... 614 566-5861
Columbus *(G-7252)*
Charles Mercy Hlth-St Hospita.....D..... 419 696-7200
Oregon *(G-15728)*
Chester West Medical Center.....A..... 513 298-3000
West Chester *(G-19037)*
Childrens Hosp Med Ctr Akron.....A..... 330 308-5432
New Philadelphia *(G-15085)*
Childrens Hospital Medical Ctr.....A..... 513 803-9600
Liberty Township *(G-12719)*
Childrens Hospital Medical Ctr.....A..... 513 636-8778
Cincinnati *(G-3255)*
Christ Hospital.....E..... 513 564-4000
Cincinnati *(G-3260)*
Christ Hospital.....C..... 513 561-7809
Cincinnati *(G-3261)*
Christ Hospital.....B..... 513 272-3448
Cincinnati *(G-3264)*
Christ Hospital Spine Surgery.....E..... 513 619-5899
Cincinnati *(G-3270)*
City Hospital Association.....A..... 330 385-7200
East Liverpool *(G-10517)*
City of Wooster.....A..... 330 263-8100
Wooster *(G-19846)*
Cleveland Clinic Foundation.....A..... 216 636-8335
Cleveland *(G-5296)*
Cleveland Clinic Foundation.....A..... 440 282-6669
Lorain *(G-13025)*
Cleveland Clinic Foundation.....A..... 800 223-2273
Cleveland *(G-5300)*
Cleveland Clinic Foundation.....A..... 216 444-5755
Cleveland *(G-5301)*
Cleveland Clinic Foundation.....A..... 440 327-1050
North Ridgeville *(G-15461)*
Cleveland Clinic Foundation.....A..... 216 448-0116
Beachwood *(G-1065)*
Cleveland Clinic Foundation.....A..... 440 986-4000
Broadview Heights *(G-1874)*
Cleveland Clinic Foundation.....D..... 216 444-5757
Cleveland *(G-5305)*
Cleveland Clinic Foundation.....A..... 216 444-2200
Cleveland *(G-5306)*
Cleveland Clinic Foundation.....E..... 330 287-4930
Wooster *(G-19848)*
Cleveland Clinic Foundation.....D..... 216 444-2820
Cleveland *(G-5297)*
Cleveland Clinic Foundation.....D..... 440 988-5651
Lorain *(G-13026)*
Cleveland Clinic Health System.....E..... 440 449-4500
Cleveland *(G-5307)*
Cleveland Clinic Health System.....E..... 216 692-7555
Cleveland *(G-5308)*
Clevelnd Clnc Hlth Systm East.....E..... 330 287-4830
Wooster *(G-19850)*
Clevelnd Clnc Hlth Systm East.....E..... 330 468-0190
Northfield *(G-15512)*
Clevelnd Clnc Hlth Systm East.....E..... 216 761-3300
Cleveland *(G-5358)*
Clinical Research Center.....D..... 513 636-4412
Cincinnati *(G-3366)*
Clinton Memorial Hospital.....A..... 937 382-6611
Wilmington *(G-19753)*
Columbia-Csa/Hs Greater Canton.....A..... 330 489-1000
Canton *(G-2315)*
Community Health Ptnrs Reg Fou.....A..... 440 960-4000
Lorain *(G-13030)*
Community Hospital of Bedford.....B..... 440 735-3900
Bedford *(G-1301)*
Community Hospital Springfield.....A..... 937 325-0531
Springfield *(G-17171)*
Community Hsptals Wllness Ctrs.....D..... 419 485-3154
Montpelier *(G-14741)*
Community Hsptals Wllness Ctrs.....D..... 419 445-2015
Archbold *(G-635)*
Community Hsptals Wllness Ctrs.....C..... 419 636-1131
Bryan *(G-2004)*
Community Mercy Hlth Partners.....E..... 937 523-6670
Springfield *(G-17175)*
Copc Hospitals.....E..... 614 268-8164
Columbus *(G-7438)*
County of Holmes.....C..... 330 674-1015
Millersburg *(G-14600)*
Dayton Osteopathic Hospital.....A..... 937 762-1629
Dayton *(G-9484)*
Deaconess Hospital of Cincinna.....D..... 513 559-2100
Cincinnati *(G-3472)*
Defiance Hospital Inc.....B..... 419 782-6955
Defiance *(G-10027)*
Delphos Ambulatory Care Center.....E..... 419 692-2662
Delphos *(G-10141)*
Dhsc LLC.....D..... 330 832-8761
Massillon *(G-13800)*
Doctors Hospital Cleveland Inc.....C..... 740 753-7300
Nelsonville *(G-14961)*
Elmwood of Green Springs Ltd.....D..... 419 639-2626
Green Springs *(G-11476)*
Encompass Health Corporation.....E..... 205 970-4869
Springfield *(G-17194)*
Euclid Hospital.....D..... 216 531-9000
Euclid *(G-10753)*
Fairfield Medical Center.....A..... 740 687-8000
Lancaster *(G-12537)*
Fairview Hospital.....E..... 216 476-7000
Cleveland *(G-5568)*
Fairview Hospital.....D..... 440 871-1063
Westlake *(G-19484)*
Fayette County Memorial Hosp.....C..... 740 335-1210
Wshngtn CT Hs *(G-20022)*
Firelands Regional Health Sys.....A..... 419 557-7400
Sandusky *(G-16757)*
Firelands Regional Health Sys.....E..... 419 332-5524
Fremont *(G-11197)*
Fisher-Titus Medical Center.....A..... 419 668-8101
Norwalk *(G-15575)*
Flower Hospital.....A..... 419 824-1444
Sylvania *(G-17588)*
Fort Hamilton Hospital.....D..... 513 867-2000
Hamilton *(G-11728)*
Fulton County Health Center.....C..... 419 335-2017
Wauseon *(G-18953)*
Fulton County Health Center.....A..... 419 335-2015
Wauseon *(G-18955)*
G M A Surgery Inc.....E..... 937 429-7350
Beavercreek *(G-1174)*
Garden II Leasing Co LLC.....D..... 419 381-0037
Toledo *(G-17908)*
Glenmont.....E..... 614 876-0084
Hilliard *(G-11903)*
Good Samaritan Hosp Cincinnati.....E..... 513 569-6251
Cincinnati *(G-3685)*
Good Samaritan Hospital.....E..... 937 224-4646
Dayton *(G-9576)*
Good Samaritan Hospital.....E..... 937 734-2612
Dayton *(G-9578)*
Grace Hospital.....D..... 216 476-2704
Cleveland *(G-5684)*
Grace Hospital.....D..... 216 687-1500
Bedford *(G-1308)*
Grace Hospital.....D..... 216 687-4013
Amherst *(G-595)*
Grady Memorial Hospital.....E..... 740 615-1000
Delaware *(G-10102)*
Greater Dayton Surgery Ctr LLC.....E..... 937 535-2200
Dayton *(G-9589)*
Greenfield Area Medical Ctr.....D..... 937 981-9400
Greenfield *(G-11485)*
Guernsey Health Systems Inc.....A..... 740 439-3561
Cambridge *(G-2119)*
Hardin Memorial Hospital.....E..... 419 673-0761
Kenton *(G-12418)*
Hcl of Dayton Inc.....C..... 937 384-8300
Miamisburg *(G-14305)*
Healthspan Integrated Care.....D..... 216 362-2000
Cleveland *(G-5739)*
Heart Hospital of Dto LLC.....B..... 937 734-8000
Dayton *(G-9606)*
Henry County Hospital Inc.....B..... 419 592-4015
Napoleon *(G-14943)*
Holzer Health System.....E..... 740 446-5060
Gallipolis *(G-11324)*
Holzer Hospital Foundation.....A..... 740 446-5000
Gallipolis *(G-11325)*
Holzer Hospital Foundation.....B..... 740 446-5000
Gallipolis *(G-11326)*
Holzer Medical Ctr - Jackson.....B..... 740 288-4625
Jackson *(G-12313)*
Hometown Hospital Health Plan.....C..... 330 834-2200
Massillon *(G-13820)*
Hometown Urgent Care.....C..... 937 342-9520
Springfield *(G-17206)*
Hospice of Genesis Health.....E..... 740 454-5381
Zanesville *(G-20488)*
Humana Inc.....A..... 330 498-0537
Canton *(G-2408)*
Jewish Hospital LLC.....A..... 513 686-3000
Cincinnati *(G-3871)*
Jewish Hospital Cincinnati Inc.....A..... 513 686-3303
Cincinnati *(G-3872)*
Joel Pomerene Memorial Hosp.....B..... 330 674-1015
Millersburg *(G-14609)*
Joint Township Dst Mem Hosp.....B..... 419 394-3335
Saint Marys *(G-16676)*
Kettering Adventist Healthcare.....D..... 937 534-4651
Moraine *(G-14796)*
Kettering Adventist Healthcare.....D..... 937 878-8644
Fairborn *(G-10800)*
Kettering Medical Center.....D..... 937 702-4000
Beavercreek *(G-1181)*
Kettering Medical Center.....B..... 937 866-0551
Miamisburg *(G-14310)*
Kindred Healthcare Inc.....D..... 937 222-5963
Dayton *(G-9660)*
Kindred Healthcare Inc.....D..... 937 222-5963
Dayton *(G-9662)*
Kindred Hospital Central Ohio.....E..... 419 526-0777
Lima *(G-12810)*
Knox Community Hospital.....A..... 740 393-9000
Mount Vernon *(G-14904)*
Lake Hospital System Inc.....A..... 440 953-9600
Willoughby *(G-19681)*
Lake Hospital System Inc.....A..... 440 632-3024
Middlefield *(G-14397)*
Lakewood Hospital Association.....A..... 216 529-7160
Lakewood *(G-12491)*
Lakewood Hospital Association.....E..... 216 228-5437
Cleveland *(G-5923)*
Licking Memorial Hospital.....A..... 740 348-4137
Newark *(G-15192)*
Life Line Screening.....D..... 216 581-6556
Independence *(G-12226)*
Lima Memorial Hospital.....D..... 419 228-3335
Lima *(G-12824)*
Lima Memorial Hospital La.....B..... 419 738-5151
Wapakoneta *(G-18801)*
Lima Memorial Joint Oper Co.....A..... 419 228-5165
Lima *(G-12825)*
Lodi Community Hospital.....C..... 330 948-1222
Lodi *(G-12964)*
Ltac Investors LLC.....C..... 740 346-2600
Steubenville *(G-17328)*
Lutheran Medical Center.....B..... 216 696-4300
Solon *(G-17023)*
Madison Family Health Corp.....C..... 740 845-7000
London *(G-13000)*
Madison Medical Campus.....E..... 440 428-6800
Madison *(G-13232)*
Manor Care Inc.....D..... 419 252-5500
Toledo *(G-18028)*
Marietta Memorial Hospital.....B..... 740 401-0362
Belpre *(G-1442)*

Employee Codes: A=Over 500 employees, B=251-500
C=101-250, D=51-100, E=25-50
2018 Harris Ohio
Services Directory
1513
SERVICES

HOSPITALS: Medical & Surgical — SERVICES SECTION

Name	Col	Phone
Marietta Memorial Hospital — Marietta (G-13471)	A	740 374-1400
Marietta Memorial Hospital — Marietta (G-13472)	E	740 373-8549
Marion Gen Social Work Dept — Marion (G-13557)	E	740 383-8788
Mary Rutan Hospital — Bellefontaine (G-1390)	A	937 592-4015
Marymount Hospital Inc — Cleveland (G-5991)	B	216 581-0500
Marysvlle Ohio Srgical Ctr LLC — Marysville (G-13638)	D	937 642-6622
Massillon Health System LLC — Massillon (G-13836)	A	330 837-7200
McCullough-Hyde Mem Hosp Inc — Oxford (G-15818)	E	513 523-2111
McCullough-Hyde Mem Hosp Inc — Hamilton (G-11758)	B	513 863-2215
Med America Hlth Systems Corp — Dayton (G-9710)	A	937 223-6192
Medcath Intermediate Holdings — Dayton (G-9712)	B	937 221-8016
Medcentral Health System — Ontario (G-15701)	E	419 526-8900
Medcentral Health System — Mansfield (G-13338)	E	419 526-8442
Medcentral Health System — Mansfield (G-13339)	D	419 526-8000
Medcentral Health System — Mansfield (G-13340)	D	419 526-8970
Medcentral Health System — Crestline (G-9147)	C	419 683-1040
Medcentral Health System — Shelby (G-16901)	E	419 342-5015
Medcentral Health System — Mansfield (G-13341)	E	419 526-8043
Medical Center At Elizabeth Pl — Dayton (G-9713)	C	937 223-6237
Medina Hospital — Medina (G-14101)	E	330 723-3117
Medone Hospital Physicians — Columbus (G-8145)	E	314 255-6900
Memorial Hospital — Fremont (G-11212)	A	419 334-6657
Memorial Hospital — Clyde (G-6818)	E	419 547-6419
Memorial Hospital Union County — Marysville (G-13640)	C	937 644-1001
Mental Health and Addi Serv — Columbus (G-8148)	C	614 752-0333
Mercer Cnty Joint Townshp Hosp — Coldwater (G-6833)	D	419 678-2341
Mercer Cnty Joint Townshp Hosp — Celina (G-2654)	E	419 586-1611
Mercy Franciscan Hosp Mt Airy — Cincinnati (G-4057)	A	513 853-5101
Mercy Frncscan Hosp Wstn Hills — Cincinnati (G-4058)	A	513 389-5000
Mercy Hamilton Hospital — Fairfield (G-10878)	E	513 603-8600
Mercy Health — Youngstown (G-20280)	C	330 729-1372
Mercy Health — Cincinnati (G-4060)	D	513 639-0250
Mercy Health — Cincinnati (G-4062)	C	513 639-2800
Mercy Health — Cincinnati (G-4064)	E	513 639-2800
Mercy Health — Youngstown (G-20281)	E	330 792-7418
Mercy Health — Lorain (G-13060)	A	440 233-1000
Mercy Health - St — Oregon (G-15741)	E	419 696-7465
Mercy Health Anderson Hospital — Cincinnati (G-4067)	A	513 624-4500
Mercy Health Anderson Hospital — Cincinnati (G-4068)	E	513 624-1950
Mercy Health Anderson Hospital — Cincinnati (G-4069)	E	513 624-4025
Mercy Health Cincinnati LLC — Cincinnati (G-4070)	D	513 952-5000
Mercy Health Partners — Cincinnati (G-4071)	D	513 233-2444
Mercy Health Partners — Cincinnati (G-4072)	D	513 389-5000
Mercy Health Partners — Cincinnati (G-4073)	C	513 853-5101
Mercy Health Partners — Blue Ash (G-1641)	D	513 981-5056
Mercy Health Partners — Cincinnati (G-4075)	D	513 686-4800
Mercy Health Sys - Nthrn Reg — Toledo (G-18056)	B	419 251-1359
Mercy Hlth St Vincent Med LLC — Toledo (G-18057)	A	419 251-3232
Mercy Hospital of Defiance — Defiance (G-10048)	C	419 782-8444
Mercy Hospital Tiffin Ohio — Tiffin (G-17686)	B	419 455-7000
Mercy Medical Center — Springfield (G-17242)	A	937 390-5000
Mercy Medical Center Inc — Canton (G-2459)	E	330 489-1000
Mercy Mem Hosp Urbana Ohio — Urbana (G-18596)	B	937 653-5231
Metrohealth Medical Center — Cleveland (G-6036)	A	216 778-7800
Metrohealth System — Cleveland (G-6041)	E	216 957-1500
Metrohealth System — Beachwood (G-1101)	E	216 765-0733
Metrohealth System — Westlake (G-19515)	E	216 957-3200
Metrohealth System — Beachwood (G-1102)	E	216 591-0523
Miami Valley Hospital — Dayton (G-9731)	C	937 436-5200
Miami Valley Hospital — Vandalia (G-18689)	A	937 208-7065
Miami Valley Hospital — Dayton (G-9732)	A	937 208-8000
Morrow County Hospital — Mount Gilead (G-14859)	B	419 949-3085
Morrow County Hospital — Mount Gilead (G-14860)	B	419 947-9127
Mount Carmel East Hospital — Columbus (G-8195)	A	614 234-6000
Mount Carmel Health — Columbus (G-8196)	A	614 234-5000
Mount Carmel Health System — Columbus (G-8198)	A	614 234-6000
Mount Carmel Health System — New Albany (G-14994)	E	614 775-6600
Neuroscience Center Inc — Columbus (G-8269)	D	614 293-8930
New Albany Surgery Center LLC — New Albany (G-15001)	C	614 775-1616
New Lfcare Hspitals Dayton LLC — Miamisburg (G-14326)	B	937 384-8300
Niagara Health Corporation — Columbus (G-8277)	C	614 898-4000
Norwalk Area Hlth Systems Inc — Norwalk (G-15584)	A	419 668-8101
Ohio Osteopathic Hospital Assn — Columbus (G-8365)	E	614 299-2107
Ohio State Univ Wexner Med Ctr — Columbus (G-8384)	E	614 293-8000
Ohio State Univ Wexner Med Ctr — Columbus (G-8386)	C	614 366-3687
Ohio State University — Columbus (G-8393)	A	614 257-3000
Ohio State University — Columbus (G-8395)	C	614 293-8750
Ohio State University — Columbus (G-8437)	E	614 293-8419
Ohio State University — Columbus (G-8440)	E	614 293-8196
Ohio State University — Columbus (G-8441)	E	614 293-8333
Ohio State University — Columbus (G-8442)	A	614 293-8000
Ohiohealth Corporation — Columbus (G-8454)	C	614 566-5456
Ohiohealth Corporation — Dublin (G-10416)	B	614 544-8000
Ohiohealth Corporation — Columbus (G-8455)	C	614 566-2124
Ohiohealth Corporation — Columbus (G-8458)	D	614 566-5977
Ohiohealth Corporation — Columbus (G-8459)	C	614 566-4800
Ohiohealth Corporation — Columbus (G-8457)	A	614 788-8860
Ohiohlth Rverside Methdst Hosp — Columbus (G-8462)	A	614 566-5000
Orrville Hospital Foundation — Orrville (G-15779)	C	330 684-4700
Osu Nephrology Medical Ctr — Columbus (G-8487)	E	614 293-8300
Parma Community General Hosp — Parma (G-15912)	A	440 743-3000
Promedica Health Systems Inc — Toledo (G-18141)	A	567 585-7454
Providence Hospital — Cincinnati (G-4350)	A	513 853-5000
Rchp - Wilmington LLC — Wilmington (G-19781)	D	937 382-6611
Research Institute At Nation — Columbus (G-8617)	C	614 722-2700
Richmond Medical Center — Richmond Heights (G-16542)	B	440 585-6500
Robinson Health System Inc — Ravenna (G-16406)	E	330 678-4100
Robinson Health System Inc — Ravenna (G-16407)	A	330 297-0811
Robinson Health System Inc — Kent (G-12394)	E	330 297-0811
Robinson Memorial Hospital — Streetsboro (G-17428)	E	330 626-3455
Salem Community Hospital — Salem (G-16713)	A	330 332-1551
Samaritan Health Partners — Dayton (G-9865)	A	937 208-8400
Samaritan N Surgery Ctr Ltd — Englewood (G-10719)	E	937 567-6100
Samaritan Regional Health Sys — Ashland (G-697)	E	419 281-1330
Samaritan Regional Health Sys — Ashland (G-698)	B	419 289-0491
Select Medical Corporation — Cleveland (G-6467)	C	216 983-8030
Select Medical Corporation — Akron (G-432)	A	330 761-7500
Select Specialty Hosp Columbus — Columbus (G-8712)	D	614 291-8467
Select Specialty Hospital — Cincinnati (G-4493)	D	513 862-4700
Shelby County Mem Hosp Assn — Sidney (G-16952)	A	937 498-2311
Shelby County Mem Hosp Assn — Sidney (G-16953)	D	937 492-9591
Sheltering Arms Hospital Found — Athens (G-811)	B	740 592-9300
Sister of Mercy of Clerm Count — Batavia (G-1024)	D	513 732-8200
Sisters of Mrcy of Wllard Ohio — Willard (G-19627)	A	419 964-5000
Skilled Nurse Ctr of — Barberton (G-979)	E	330 615-3717
Southern Ohio Medical Center — Portsmouth (G-16311)	A	740 354-5000
Southstern Ohio Rgonal Med Ctr — Cambridge (G-2129)	E	740 439-3561
Southwest Cmnty Hlth Systems — Cleveland (G-6500)	A	440 816-8000
Southwest General Health Ctr — Cleveland (G-6502)	D	440 816-4202
Southwest General Health Ctr — Strongsville (G-17510)	C	440 816-4900
Southwest General Health Ctr — Cleveland (G-6503)	D	440 816-8200
Southwest General Health Ctr — Cleveland (G-6504)	A	440 816-8000
Southwest General Health Ctr — Cleveland (G-6505)	E	440 816-8005
Southwest Healthcare of Brown — Georgetown (G-11398)	D	937 378-7800
Specialty Hosp Cleveland Inc — Cleveland (G-6515)	B	216 592-2830
St Anne Mercy Hospital — Toledo (G-18199)	E	419 407-2663
St John Medical Center — Westlake (G-19550)	D	440 835-8000
St Ritas Medical Center — Lima (G-12885)	A	419 227-3361
St Ritas Medical Center — Glandorf (G-11432)	E	419 538-6288
St Vincent Charity Med Ctr — Cleveland (G-6523)	A	216 861-6200
Steward Northside Med Ctr Inc — Youngstown (G-20383)	E	330 884-1000
Steward Trumbull Mem Hosp Inc — Warren (G-18904)	A	330 841-9011
Summa Health — Barberton (G-980)	D	330 753-3649
Summa Health — Stow (G-17395)	E	330 688-4531
Summa Health — Barberton (G-981)	A	330 615-3000

SERVICES SECTION

HOSPITALS: Rehabilitation, Alcoholism

Summa Health System .... D 330 535-7319
  Akron *(G-453)*
Summa Health System .... E 330 375-3000
  Akron *(G-456)*
Summa Health System .... A 330 334-1504
  Wadsworth *(G-18771)*
Summa Health System .... D 330 375-3584
  Akron *(G-457)*
Summa Health System .... C 330 375-3315
  Akron *(G-458)*
Summa Health System .... E 330 375-3000
  Akron *(G-460)*
Surgery and Gynecology Inc .... E 614 294-1603
  Columbus *(G-8812)*
Sylvania Franciscan Health .... E 419 882-8373
  Maumee *(G-13984)*
Toledo Hospital .... D 419 291-8701
  Toledo *(G-18239)*
Trihealth Evendale Hospital .... C 513 454-2222
  Cincinnati *(G-4692)*
Trinity Health System .... B 740 283-7000
  Steubenville *(G-17342)*
Trinity Health System .... A 740 264-8000
  Steubenville *(G-17340)*
Trinity Health System .... E 740 264-8101
  Steubenville *(G-17341)*
Trinity Hospital Holding Co .... A 740 264-8000
  Steubenville *(G-17343)*
Trinity West .... A 740 264-8000
  Steubenville *(G-17344)*
Tripoint Medical Center .... A 440 375-8100
  Painesville *(G-15883)*
Uc Health Llc .... E 513 584-8600
  Cincinnati *(G-4721)*
Uhhs-Memorial Hosp of Geneva ... C 440 466-1141
  Geneva *(G-11371)*
Union Hospital Association .... D 330 343-3311
  Dover *(G-10219)*
University Hospitals .... B 216 593-5500
  Cleveland *(G-6654)*
University Hospitals .... E 216 536-3020
  Cleveland *(G-6655)*
University Hospitals .... A 440 285-6000
  Chardon *(G-2774)*
University Hospitals .... A 216 767-8900
  Shaker Heights *(G-16869)*
University Hospitals .... A 440 743-3000
  Parma *(G-15917)*
University Hospitals .... E 216 844-6400
  Cleveland *(G-6656)*
University Hospitals Cleveland .... A 216 844-1000
  Cleveland *(G-6659)*
University Hospitals Cleveland .... E 440 205-5755
  Mentor *(G-14252)*
University Hospitals Cleveland .... A 216 844-1000
  Cleveland *(G-6660)*
University Hospitals Cleveland .... D 216 844-4663
  Cleveland *(G-6661)*
University Hospitals Cleveland .... A 216 844-4323
  Shaker Heights *(G-16870)*
University Hospitals Cleveland .... D 216 721-8457
  Beachwood *(G-1135)*
University Hospitals Cleveland .... A 216 844-3528
  Cleveland *(G-6662)*
University Hospitals Health Sy .... E 216 844-4663
  Cleveland *(G-6664)*
University of Cincinnati .... E 513 584-4396
  Cincinnati *(G-4763)*
University of Cincinnati .... E 513 584-1000
  Cincinnati *(G-4778)*
Universty of Cincinnti Medcl C ... E 513 584-1000
  Cincinnati *(G-4785)*
Uvmc Management Corporation ... D 937 440-4000
  Troy *(G-18385)*
VA Medical Center Automated RE ... E 740 772-7118
  Chillicothe *(G-2894)*
Van Wert County Hospital Assn ... A 419 238-2390
  Van Wert *(G-18649)*
Van Wert Medical Services Ltd ... B 419 238-7727
  Van Wert *(G-18651)*
Vibra Healthcare LLC .... D 330 675-5555
  Warren *(G-18921)*
Wayne Healthcare .... B 937 548-1141
  Greenville *(G-11524)*
Wood County Hospital Assoc ..... A 419 354-8900
  Bowling Green *(G-1800)*
Wright Center .... E 216 382-1868
  Cleveland *(G-6760)*
Wyandot Memorial Hospital .... C 419 294-4991
  Upper Sandusky *(G-18570)*

HOSPITALS: Medical School Affiliated With Nursing

Adena Health System .... E 740 779-7201
  Chillicothe *(G-2808)*
Adena Health System .... A 740 779-7360
  Chillicothe *(G-2809)*
Adena Health System .... C 740 420-3000
  Circleville *(G-4877)*
Adena Health System .... C 937 981-9444
  Greenfield *(G-11482)*
Adena Health System .... C 740 779-8995
  Chillicothe *(G-2810)*
Adena Health System .... E 740 779-4801
  Chillicothe *(G-2811)*
Christ Hospital .... B 513 688-1111
  Cincinnati *(G-3262)*
Christ Hospital .... A 513 585-2000
  Cincinnati *(G-3266)*
Community Hlth Ptnr Reg Hlth S ... A 440 960-4000
  Lorain *(G-13031)*
Mentor Surgery Center Ltd .... E 440 205-5725
  Mentor *(G-14215)*
Regency Hospital Toledo LLC .... E 419 318-5700
  Sylvania *(G-17609)*

HOSPITALS: Medical School Affiliated with Residency

Doctors Ohiohealth Corporation ... A 614 544-5424
  Columbus *(G-7537)*
Ohiohealth Corporation .... E 614 566-5414
  Columbus *(G-8460)*

HOSPITALS: Medical School Affiliation

Cleveland Clinic Lerner Colleg .... D 216 445-3853
  Cleveland *(G-5309)*
Ohio State University .... E 614 293-8158
  Columbus *(G-8417)*
Ohio State University .... C 614 292-6251
  Columbus *(G-8431)*
University Hospitals .... B 440 250-2001
  Westlake *(G-19560)*
University of Cincinnati .... E 513 584-7522
  Cincinnati *(G-4756)*
University of Cincinnati .... E 513 584-1000
  Cincinnati *(G-4776)*
University of Toledo .... B 419 383-4229
  Toledo *(G-18282)*

HOSPITALS: Mental Retardation

Astoria Place Columbus LLC ..... D 614 228-5900
  Columbus *(G-7057)*
Blanchard Vly Residential Ctr .... E 419 422-6503
  Findlay *(G-11002)*
Bridges To Independence Inc ..... E 740 375-5533
  Marion *(G-13526)*
CHS-Lake Erie Inc .... C 440 964-8446
  Ashtabula *(G-733)*
Columbus Area .... D 614 251-6561
  Columbus *(G-7328)*
County of Montgomery .... B 937 264-0460
  Dayton *(G-9434)*
County of Perry .... E 740 342-0416
  New Lexington *(G-15053)*
Creative Foundations Inc .... E 614 832-2121
  Mount Vernon *(G-14890)*
Echoing Hills Village Inc .... A 740 327-2311
  Warsaw *(G-18936)*
Gateways To Better Living Inc ... E 330 480-9870
  Youngstown *(G-20194)*
Logan Healthcare Leasing LLC ... D 216 367-1214
  Logan *(G-12984)*
Mental Rtrdation Preble Cnty Bd ... E 937 456-5891
  Eaton *(G-10568)*
Pleasant Hill Leasing LLC .... C 740 289-2394
  Piketon *(G-16126)*
Ridge Murray Prod Ctr Oberlin ... E 440 774-7400
  Oberlin *(G-15660)*
Siffrin Residential Assn .... C 330 799-8932
  Youngstown *(G-20375)*
Union Christel Manor Inc .... D 937 968-6265
  Union City *(G-18505)*
Winchester Place Leasing LLC ... D 614 834-2273
  Canal Winchester *(G-2179)*

HOSPITALS: Mental, Exc For The Mentally Retarded

Adriel School Inc .... D 937 465-0010
  West Liberty *(G-19260)*
Central Commnty Hlth Brd of Ha ... C 513 559-2000
  Cincinnati *(G-3211)*
Central Community .... D 513 559-2000
  Cincinnati *(G-3213)*
Community Mental Healthcare ... E 330 343-1811
  Dover *(G-10181)*
County of Paulding .... E 419 399-3636
  Paulding *(G-15930)*
Eastway Corporation .... C 937 496-2000
  Dayton *(G-9516)*
Eastway Corporation .... A 937 531-7000
  Dayton *(G-9517)*
Mental Hlth Serv For CL & Mad ... E 937 390-7980
  Springfield *(G-17233)*
Mental Hlth Serv For CL & Mad ... C 937 399-9500
  Springfield *(G-17234)*
Mental Hlth Serv For CL & Mad ... E 740 852-6256
  London *(G-13003)*
Rehab Continuum Inc .... E 513 984-8070
  Blue Ash *(G-1679)*
Rescue Incorporated .... E 419 255-9585
  Toledo *(G-18153)*

HOSPITALS: Orthopedic

Crystal Clnic Orthpdic Ctr LLC ... D 330 668-4040
  Akron *(G-179)*
Crystal Clnic Orthpdic Ctr LLC ... D 330 535-3396
  Akron *(G-180)*
Northwest Ohio Orthopedic & Sp ... C 419 427-1984
  Findlay *(G-11071)*
Orthopedic One Inc .... E 614 545-7900
  Columbus *(G-8485)*
Trihealth Os LLC .... D 513 791-6611
  Montgomery *(G-14735)*

HOSPITALS: Professional Nursing School With AMA Residency

Toledo Hospital .... A 419 291-4000
  Toledo *(G-18238)*

HOSPITALS: Psychiatric

Belmont Bhc Pines Hospital Inc ... C 330 759-2700
  Youngstown *(G-20113)*
Bethesda Hospital Association ... A 740 454-4000
  Zanesville *(G-20447)*
Bhc Fox Run Hospital Inc .... C 740 695-2131
  Saint Clairsville *(G-16628)*
Center For Chemical Addictions ... D 513 381-6672
  Cincinnati *(G-3207)*
Develpmntal Dsblties Ohio Dept ... A 740 446-1642
  Gallipolis *(G-11314)*
Develpmntal Dsblties Ohio Dept ... B 614 272-0509
  Columbus *(G-7513)*
Focus Healthcare of Ohio LLC ... E 419 891-9333
  Maumee *(G-13918)*
Heartland Bhavioral Healthcare ... B 330 833-3135
  Massillon *(G-13819)*
Laurelwood Hospital .... B 440 953-3000
  Willoughby *(G-19685)*
Marymount Hospital Inc .... B 216 581-0500
  Cleveland *(G-5991)*
Mental Health and Addi Serv ...... C 419 381-1881
  Toledo *(G-18051)*
Mental Health and Addi Serv ...... B 513 948-3600
  Cincinnati *(G-4055)*
Mental Health and Addi Serv ...... D 614 752-0333
  Columbus *(G-8147)*
Mental Health and Addi Serv ...... B 330 467-7131
  Northfield *(G-15520)*
Mercy Health .... A 440 233-1000
  Lorain *(G-13060)*
Oglethorpe Middlepoint LLC ...... E 419 968-2950
  Middle Point *(G-14377)*
Ohio Hospital For Psychiatry ...... E 877 762-9026
  Columbus *(G-8354)*
Southast Cmnty Mental Hlth Ctr ... E 614 444-0800
  Columbus *(G-8752)*
St Ritas Medical Center .... E 419 226-9067
  Lima *(G-12884)*

HOSPITALS: Rehabilitation, Alcoholism

Center For Chemical Addictions ... D 513 381-6672
  Cincinnati *(G-3207)*

Employee Codes: A=Over 500 employees, B=251-500
C=101-250, D=51-100, E=25-50

2018 Harris Ohio
Services Directory

HOSPITALS: Rehabilitation, Alcoholism

Community Counseling Services .... E 419 468-8211
  Bucyrus *(G-2031)*
Crossroads Center .... C 513 475-5300
  Cincinnati *(G-3442)*
Frs Counseling Inc .... E 937 393-0585
  Hillsboro *(G-11975)*
Health Recovery Services Inc .... C 740 592-6720
  Athens *(G-791)*
Marietta Memorial Hospital .... A 740 374-1400
  Marietta *(G-13471)*
Maryhaven Inc .... C 614 449-1530
  Columbus *(G-8123)*
Maryhaven Inc .... E 937 644-9192
  Marysville *(G-13634)*
McKinley Hall Inc .... E 937 328-5300
  Springfield *(G-17230)*
Morrow County Council On Drugs .... E 419 947-4055
  Mount Gilead *(G-14858)*
Oriana House Inc .... C 216 361-9655
  Cleveland *(G-6214)*
Parkside Behavioral Healthcare .... E 614 471-2552
  Gahanna *(G-11263)*
Select Spclty Hsptal-Akron LLC .... D 330 761-7500
  Akron *(G-433)*
Southast Cmnty Mental Hlth Ctr .... E 614 444-0800
  Columbus *(G-8752)*
Talbert House .... D 513 684-7968
  Cincinnati *(G-4621)*
Transitional Living Inc .... D 513 863-6383
  Fairfield Township *(G-10936)*
Youngstown Committee On Alchol ...... D 330 744-1181
  Youngstown *(G-20429)*

HOSPITALS: Rehabilitation, Drug Addiction

Akron Gen Edwin Shaw Rhbltion .... C 330 375-1300
  Cuyahoga Falls *(G-9159)*
Alcohol Drug Addction & Mental .... E 937 443-0416
  Dayton *(G-9314)*
Behavral Cnnctions WD Cnty Inc .... E 419 352-5387
  Bowling Green *(G-1761)*
Compass Corp For Recovery Svcs ...... D 419 241-8827
  Toledo *(G-17825)*
County of Stark .... E 330 455-6644
  Canton *(G-2325)*
Firelands Regional Health Sys .... E 419 332-5524
  Fremont *(G-11197)*
Glenbeigh Health Sources Inc .... C 440 951-7000
  Rock Creek *(G-16558)*
Glenbeigh Hospital .... E 440 563-3400
  Rock Creek *(G-16559)*
Lorain County Alcohol and Drug .... E 440 989-4900
  Lorain *(G-13051)*
Mental Health & Recovery Ctr .... E 937 383-3031
  Wilmington *(G-19773)*
Oriana House Inc .... D 330 996-7730
  Akron *(G-374)*
Pike Cnty Recovery Council Inc .... E 740 835-8437
  Waverly *(G-18973)*
Recovery Works Healing Ctr LLC .... E 937 384-0580
  West Carrollton *(G-19009)*
Scioto Pnt Vly Mental Hlth Ctr .... E 740 335-6935
  Wshngtn CT Hs *(G-20034)*
Southwest General Health Ctr .... D 440 816-8200
  Cleveland *(G-6503)*
Syntero Inc .... E 614 889-5722
  Dublin *(G-10471)*
Talbert House .... C 513 751-7747
  Cincinnati *(G-4618)*

HOSPITALS: Specialty, NEC

Affiliates In Oral & Maxlofcl .... E 513 829-8080
  Fairfield *(G-10817)*
Affiliates In Oral & Maxlofcl .... E 513 829-8080
  West Chester *(G-19015)*
Anderson Healthcare Ltd .... D 513 474-6200
  Cincinnati *(G-3022)*
Arthur G James Cancer .... A 614 293-4878
  Columbus *(G-7044)*
Aultman Hospital .... A 330 452-9911
  Canton *(G-2253)*
Aultman Hospital .... B 330 452-9911
  Canton *(G-2254)*
Charity Hospice Inc .... E 740 264-2280
  Steubenville *(G-17310)*
Community Care Hospice .... E 937 382-5400
  Wilmington *(G-19756)*
County of Clark .... D 937 390-5615
  Springfield *(G-17180)*
Covenant Care Ohio Inc .... D 937 878-7046
  Fairborn *(G-10788)*
Encompass Health Corporation .... C 513 418-5600
  Cincinnati *(G-3556)*
Greenbrier Senior Living Cmnty .... C 440 888-5900
  Cleveland *(G-5702)*
Hcr Manorcare Med Svcs Fla LLC .... C 614 882-1511
  Westerville *(G-19407)*
HealthSouth .... C 937 424-8200
  Dayton *(G-9605)*
Heart Hospital of Dto LLC .... B 937 734-8000
  Dayton *(G-9606)*
Hospice of Central Ohio .... C 740 344-0311
  Newark *(G-15175)*
Hospice of Middletown .... E 513 424-2273
  Middletown *(G-14428)*
Hospice of Northwest Ohio .... D 419 661-4001
  Toledo *(G-17961)*
Hospice of The Valley Inc .... D 330 788-1992
  Youngstown *(G-20221)*
Hospice of The Western Reserve .... D 330 800-2240
  Medina *(G-14077)*
Liberty Nrsing Ctr Rvrside LLC .... D 513 557-3621
  Cincinnati *(G-3975)*
Lutheran Medical Center .... B 216 696-4300
  Solon *(G-17023)*
Medcath Intermediate Holdings .... B 937 221-8016
  Dayton *(G-9712)*
Mercy Health .... E 419 226-9064
  Lima *(G-12839)*
Newark Sleep Diagnostic Center .... E 740 522-9499
  Newark *(G-15223)*
Nord Center Associates Inc .... E 440 233-7232
  Lorain *(G-13068)*
Ohio State University .... E 614 293-4925
  Columbus *(G-8446)*
Salvation Army .... C 330 773-3331
  Akron *(G-428)*
Stein Hospice Services Inc .... D 419 447-0475
  Sandusky *(G-16798)*
Stein Hospice Services Inc .... D 419 502-0019
  Sandusky *(G-16799)*
Trinity Health Corporation .... B 614 846-5420
  Columbus *(G-8872)*
Twin Oaks Care Center Inc .... E 419 524-1205
  Mansfield *(G-13379)*
University Hospitals Cleveland .... A 216 844-1000
  Cleveland *(G-6660)*
University Hospitals Health .... A 440 285-4040
  Chardon *(G-2775)*
University Mednet .... B 216 383-0100
  Euclid *(G-10780)*
Uvmc Nursing Care Inc .... C 937 473-2075
  Covington *(G-9140)*
Vibra Hosp Mahoning Vly LLC .... D 330 726-5000
  Youngstown *(G-20405)*
Whetstone Care Center LLC .... C 614 875-7700
  Grove City *(G-11616)*

HOSPITALS: Substance Abuse

Cornell Companies Inc .... C 419 747-3322
  Shelby *(G-16898)*
Laurelwood Hospital .... B 440 953-3000
  Willoughby *(G-19685)*
Ohio Department Youth Services .... E 740 881-3337
  Columbus *(G-8332)*
Stella Maris Inc .... E 216 781-0550
  Cleveland *(G-6536)*

HOTEL: Franchised

21c Cincinnati LLC .... D 513 578-6600
  Cincinnati *(G-2942)*
Avalon Inn Services Inc .... C 330 856-1900
  Warren *(G-18824)*
Boulevard Motel Corp .... E 440 234-3131
  Cleveland *(G-5130)*
CER Hotels LLC .... E 330 422-1855
  Streetsboro *(G-17409)*
Chillicothe Motel LLC .... E 740 773-3903
  Chillicothe *(G-2822)*
Columbus Worthington Hospitali .... D 614 885-3334
  Columbus *(G-7394)*
Comfort Inn .... E 740 454-4144
  Zanesville *(G-20466)*
Doubletree Guest Suites Dayton .... D 937 436-2400
  Miamisburg *(G-14298)*
Hardage Hotels I LLC .... E 614 766-7762
  Dublin *(G-10357)*
Hyatt Corporation .... B 614 463-1234
  Columbus *(G-7874)*
Intercontinental Hotels Group .... E 216 707-4100
  Cleveland *(G-5829)*
Lieben Wooster LP .... E 330 390-5722
  Millersburg *(G-14610)*
Mansfield Hotel Partnership .... D 419 529-1000
  Mansfield *(G-13332)*
Msk Hospitality Inc .... E 513 771-0370
  Cincinnati *(G-4127)*
Newark Management Partners LLC ..... D 740 322-6455
  Newark *(G-15220)*
Nf II Cleveland Op Co LLC .... E 216 443-9043
  Cleveland *(G-6130)*
Riverside Cmnty Urban Redev .... D 330 929-3000
  Cuyahoga Falls *(G-9215)*
Rockside Hospitality LLC .... D 216 524-0700
  Independence *(G-12251)*
Sage Hospitality Resources LLC .... D 513 771-2080
  Cincinnati *(G-4469)*
Sojourn Lodging Inc .... E 330 422-1855
  Streetsboro *(G-17429)*
TownePlace Suites By Marriott .... E 419 425-9545
  Findlay *(G-11093)*
TownePlace Suites By Marriott .... E 513 774-0610
  Cincinnati *(G-4673)*
West Montrose Properties .... D 330 867-4013
  Fairlawn *(G-10982)*

HOTELS & MOTELS

1100 Carnegie LP .... D 216 658-6400
  Cleveland *(G-4919)*
50 S Front LLC .... D 614 224-4600
  Columbus *(G-6914)*
506 Phelps Holdings LLC .... E 513 651-1234
  Cincinnati *(G-2946)*
5901 Pfffer Rd Htels Sites LLC .... D 513 793-4500
  Blue Ash *(G-1522)*
631 South Main Street Dev LLC .... D 419 423-0631
  Findlay *(G-10987)*
75 East State LLC .... E 614 365-4500
  Columbus *(G-6916)*
AIR Management Group LLC .... D 330 856-1900
  Warren *(G-18814)*
Airport Core Hotel LLC .... C 614 536-0500
  Columbus *(G-6959)*
AK Group Hotels Inc .... E 937 372-9921
  Xenia *(G-20040)*
Amitel Beachwood Ltd Partnr .... E 216 831-3030
  Cleveland *(G-5027)*
Amitel Limited Partnership .... E 440 234-6688
  Cleveland *(G-5028)*
Amitel Rockside Ltd Partnr .... E 216 520-1450
  Cleveland *(G-5029)*
Ap/Aim Dublin Suites Trs LLC .... D 614 790-9000
  Dublin *(G-10254)*
Apple Gate Operating Co Inc .... E 330 405-4488
  Twinsburg *(G-18392)*
Ashford Trs Lessee LLC .... E 937 436-2400
  Miamisburg *(G-14272)*
At Hospitality LLC .... D 513 527-9962
  Cincinnati *(G-3052)*
Bennett Enterprises Inc .... B 419 874-3111
  Perrysburg *(G-15978)*
Best Western Executive Inn .... E 330 794-1050
  Akron *(G-101)*
Best Wooster Inc .... E 330 264-7750
  Wooster *(G-19831)*
Blue-Kenwood LLC .... E 513 469-6900
  Blue Ash *(G-1546)*
Broad Street Hotel Assoc LP .... D 614 861-0321
  Columbus *(G-7147)*
Brothers Properties Corp .... C 513 381-3000
  Cincinnati *(G-3141)*
Buffalo-Gtb Associates LLC .... E 216 831-3735
  Beachwood *(G-1059)*
Buxton Inn Inc .... E 740 587-0001
  Granville *(G-11459)*
Ca-Mj Hotel Associates Ltd .... D 330 494-6494
  Canton *(G-2278)*
Cambria Green Management LLC ...... E 330 899-1263
  Uniontown *(G-18511)*
Canton Hotel Holdings Inc .... D 330 492-1331
  Canton *(G-2289)*
Canus Hospitality LLC .... E 937 323-8631
  Springfield *(G-17155)*
Carol Burton Management LLC .... E 419 666-5120
  Toledo *(G-17793)*
Cerruti LLC .... E 330 562-0120
  Aurora *(G-834)*
Ch Relty Iv/Clmbus Partners LP .... D 614 885-3334
  Columbus *(G-7247)*
Cherry Valley Lodge .... E 740 788-1200
  Newark *(G-15156)*

SERVICES SECTION

HOUSEHOLD APPLIANCE PARTS: Wholesalers

Cincinnati Netherland Ht LLC .... B 513 421-9100
 Cincinnati *(G-3320)*
Cleveland Airport Hospitality .... D 440 871-6000
 Westlake *(G-19476)*
Cleveland Bchwood Hsptlity LLC .... D 216 464-5950
 Beachwood *(G-1063)*
Cleveland Crowne Plaza Airport .... E 440 243-4040
 Cleveland *(G-5311)*
Cleveland Westlake .... E 440 892-0333
 Westlake *(G-19477)*
Cmp I Blue Ash Owner LLC .... E 513 733-4334
 Blue Ash *(G-1561)*
Cmp I Columbus I Owner LLC .... E 614 764-9393
 Dublin *(G-10297)*
Cmp I Columbus II Owner LLC .... E 614 436-7070
 Columbus *(G-7309)*
Columbus Airport Ltd Partnr .... C 614 475-7551
 Columbus *(G-7326)*
Columbus Easton Hotel LLC .... E 614 414-5000
 Columbus *(G-7350)*
Columbus Easton Hotel LLC .... E 614 383-2005
 Columbus *(G-7351)*
Columbus Hotel Partners .... E 513 891-1066
 Blue Ash *(G-1563)*
Columbus Leasing LLC .... D 614 885-1885
 Columbus *(G-7363)*
Commodore Prry Inns Suites LLC ...... D 419 732-2645
 Port Clinton *(G-16240)*
Commonwealth Hotels LLC .... C 614 790-9000
 Dublin *(G-10303)*
Concord Hamiltonian Rvrfrnt Ho .... D 513 896-6200
 Hamilton *(G-11717)*
Continental GL Sls & Inv Group .... B 614 679-1201
 Powell *(G-16332)*
Corporate Exchange Hotel Assoc .... C 614 890-8600
 Columbus *(G-7443)*
Courtyard By Marriott Dayton .... E 937 220-9060
 Dayton *(G-9441)*
Courtyard Management Corp .... E 216 901-9988
 Cleveland *(G-5430)*
CPX Canton Airport LLC .... C 330 305-0500
 North Canton *(G-15330)*
Crowne Plaza Toledo .... D 419 241-1411
 Toledo *(G-17841)*
DB&p Logistics Inc .... E 614 491-4035
 Columbus *(G-7495)*
Drury Hotels Company LLC .... E 614 221-7008
 Columbus *(G-7545)*
Drury Hotels Company LLC .... E 937 454-5200
 Dayton *(G-9506)*
Drury Hotels Company LLC .... E 513 771-5601
 Cincinnati *(G-3503)*
Drury Hotels Company LLC .... E 614 798-8802
 Grove City *(G-11556)*
Durga Llc .... D 513 771-2080
 Cincinnati *(G-3515)*
Epiqurian Inns .... D 614 885-2600
 Worthington *(G-19957)*
First Hotel Associates LP .... D 614 228-3800
 Columbus *(G-7665)*
Gallipolis Hospitality Inc .... E 740 446-0090
 Gallipolis *(G-11319)*
Gateway Hospitality Group Inc .... C 330 405-9800
 Twinsburg *(G-18420)*
Geeta Hospitality Inc .... E 937 642-3777
 Marysville *(G-13622)*
Glidden House Associates Ltd .... E 216 231-8900
 Cleveland *(G-5674)*
Golden Lamb .... C 513 932-5065
 Lebanon *(G-12608)*
Grand Heritage Hotel Portland .... E 440 734-4477
 North Olmsted *(G-15424)*
Grand View Inn Inc .... D 740 377-4388
 South Point *(G-17086)*
Granville Hospitality Llc .... D 740 587-3333
 Granville *(G-11466)*
Green Township Hospitality LLC .... B 513 574-6000
 Cincinnati *(G-3712)*
Hampton Inn & Suite Inc .... E 440 234-0206
 Middleburg Heights *(G-14382)*
Haribol Haribol Inc .... E 330 339-7731
 New Philadelphia *(G-15099)*
Hauck Hospitality LLC .... D 513 563-8330
 Cincinnati *(G-3741)*
Hdi Ltd .... E 937 224-0800
 Dayton *(G-9602)*
Hilton Garden Inn .... D 614 263-7200
 Columbus *(G-7837)*
Hilton Garden Inn Akron .... E 330 966-4907
 Canton *(G-2401)*

Hilton Garden Inn Beavercreek .... D 937 458-2650
 Dayton *(G-9273)*
Hilton Grdn Inn Clmbus Polaris .... E 614 846-8884
 Columbus *(G-6883)*
Hilton Grdn Inn Columbus Arprt .... D 614 231-2869
 Columbus *(G-7838)*
Hit Portfolio I Hil Trs LLC .... E 614 235-0717
 Dublin *(G-10362)*
Hit Portfolio I Misc Trs LLC .... C 216 575-1234
 Cleveland *(G-5760)*
Hit Portfolio I Misc Trs LLC .... E 614 846-4355
 Columbus *(G-7839)*
Hit Portfolio I Misc Trs LLC .... C 614 228-1234
 Columbus *(G-7840)*
Hit Swn Trs LLC .... E 614 228-3200
 Columbus *(G-7841)*
Honey Run Retreats LLC .... E 330 674-0011
 Millersburg *(G-14607)*
Hoster Hotels LLC .... E 419 931-8900
 Perrysburg *(G-16014)*
Hyatt Regency Columbus .... B 614 463-1234
 Columbus *(G-7875)*
Ihg Management (maryland) LLC ...... C 614 461-4100
 Columbus *(G-7883)*
Independent Hotel Partners LLC .... D 216 524-0700
 Cleveland *(G-5814)*
Integrated CC LLC .... E 216 707-4132
 Cleveland *(G-5825)*
Integrity Hotel Group .... C 937 224-0800
 Dayton *(G-9633)*
Intercntnntal Ht Group Rsurces .... D 216 707-4300
 Cleveland *(G-5828)*
Island Hospitality MGT LLC .... E 614 864-8844
 Columbus *(G-7927)*
Island House Inc .... E 419 734-0100
 Port Clinton *(G-16248)*
Jagi Springhill LLC .... E 216 264-4190
 Independence *(G-12221)*
Janus Hotels and Resorts Inc .... E 513 631-8500
 Lewisburg *(G-12711)*
Kmb Management Services Corp ..... E 330 263-2660
 Wooster *(G-19880)*
Kribha LLC .... E 740 788-8991
 Newark *(G-15180)*
Lancaster Host LLC .... E 740 654-4445
 Lancaster *(G-12550)*
Legacy Village Hospitality LLC .... D 216 382-3350
 Cleveland *(G-5932)*
Levis Commons Hotel LLC .... D 419 873-3573
 Perrysburg *(G-16027)*
Liberty Ctr Lodging Assoc LLC .... E 608 833-4100
 Liberty Township *(G-12723)*
Longaberger Company .... D 740 349-8411
 Newark *(G-15197)*
Lq Management LLC .... E 614 866-6456
 Reynoldsburg *(G-16467)*
Lq Management LLC .... D 513 771-0300
 Cincinnati *(G-4002)*
Lq Management LLC .... E 216 447-1133
 Cleveland *(G-5954)*
Lq Management LLC .... E 216 251-8500
 Cleveland *(G-5955)*
March Investors Ltd .... E 740 373-5353
 Marietta *(G-13463)*
Marios International Spa & Ht .... C 330 562-5141
 Aurora *(G-846)*
Marriott Hotel Services Inc .... C 216 252-5333
 Cleveland *(G-5982)*
Marriott International Inc .... E 330 484-0300
 Canton *(G-2449)*
McPaul Corp .... E 419 447-6313
 Tiffin *(G-17684)*
Meander Inn Inc .... E 330 544-2378
 Youngstown *(G-20276)*
Meander Inn Incorporated .... E 330 544-0660
 Youngstown *(G-20277)*
Moody Nat Cy Dt Clumbus Mt LLC ... D 614 228-3200
 Columbus *(G-8186)*
Moody Nat Cy Willoughby Mt LLC .... E 440 530-1100
 Willoughby *(G-19693)*
Natural Resources Ohio Dept .... E 419 938-5411
 Perrysville *(G-16080)*
Northern Tier Hospitality LLC .... D 570 888-7711
 Westlake *(G-19525)*
Ntk Hotel Group II LLC .... D 614 559-2000
 Columbus *(G-8302)*
Oakwood Hospitality Corp .... E 440 786-1998
 Bedford *(G-1325)*
Oberlin College .... D 440 935-1475
 Oberlin *(G-15656)*

Oh-16 Clvlnd Arprt S Prprty Su .... E 440 243-8785
 Middleburg Heights *(G-14383)*
Ohio State University .... E 614 247-4000
 Columbus *(G-8404)*
Park Hotels & Resorts Inc .... B 216 464-5950
 Cleveland *(G-6237)*
Primary Dayton Innkeepers LLC .... E 937 938-9550
 Dayton *(G-9827)*
R & K Gorby LLC .... E 419 222-0004
 Lima *(G-12866)*
Radisson Hotel Cleve .... E 440 734-5060
 North Olmsted *(G-15442)*
Rama Inc .... E 614 473-9888
 Columbus *(G-8587)*
Renaissance Hotel Operating Co ...... A 216 696-5600
 Cleveland *(G-6374)*
Residence Inn By Marriott Beav .... E 937 427-3914
 Beavercreek *(G-1204)*
River Road Hotel Corp .... E 614 267-7461
 Columbus *(G-8634)*
Rose Gracias .... E 614 785-0001
 Columbus *(G-8648)*
S & S Management Inc .... E 937 235-2000
 Dayton *(G-9861)*
S & S Management Inc .... E 567 356-4151
 Wapakoneta *(G-18807)*
S P S Inc .... E 937 339-7801
 Troy *(G-18378)*
Seagate Hospitality Group LLC .... E 216 252-7700
 Cleveland *(G-6457)*
Select Hotels Group LLC .... E 513 754-0003
 Mason *(G-13759)*
Select Hotels Group LLC .... E 216 328-1060
 Cleveland *(G-6466)*
Select Hotels Group LLC .... E 614 799-1913
 Dublin *(G-10451)*
Shaker House .... D 216 991-6000
 Cleveland *(G-6475)*
Shiv Hotels LLC .... E 740 374-8190
 Marietta *(G-13499)*
Signature Boutique Hotel LP .... E 216 595-0900
 Beachwood *(G-1125)*
Six Continents Hotels Inc .... C 513 563-8330
 Cincinnati *(G-4533)*
Skyline Clvland Rnaissance LLC .... D 216 696-5600
 Cleveland *(G-6487)*
Sonesta Intl Hotels Corp .... C 614 791-8554
 Dublin *(G-10457)*
Sree Hotels LLC .... E 513 354-2430
 Cincinnati *(G-4570)*
Strongsville Lodging Assoc 1 .... C 440 238-8800
 Strongsville *(G-17512)*
Summithotel .... D 513 527-9900
 Cincinnati *(G-4598)*
Synergy Hotels LLC .... E 614 492-9000
 Obetz *(G-15671)*
Toledo Inns Inc .... E 440 243-4040
 Cleveland *(G-6601)*
Valley Hospitality Inc .... E 740 374-9660
 Marietta *(G-13513)*
Visicon Inc .... D 937 879-2696
 Fairborn *(G-10809)*
W2005/Fargo Hotels (pool C) .... E 937 429-5505
 Fairborn *(G-10810)*
Westgate Limited Partnership .... C 419 535-7070
 Toledo *(G-18307)*
Wm Columbus Hotel LLC .... C 614 228-3800
 Columbus *(G-9001)*
Wph Cincinnati LLC .... C 513 771-2080
 Cincinnati *(G-4861)*
Wyndham International Inc .... C 216 615-7500
 Cleveland *(G-6764)*
Zincks Inn .... E 330 803-0000
 Berlin *(G-1479)*

HOTLINE

Battle Bullying Hotline Inc .... D 216 731-1976
 Cleveland *(G-5101)*
Chagrin Valley Dispatch .... E 440 247-7321
 Bedford *(G-1299)*
City of Willoughby Hills .... E 440 942-7207
 Willoughby Hills *(G-19729)*
Option Line .... E 614 586-1380
 Columbus *(G-8476)*

HOUSEHOLD APPLIANCE PARTS: Wholesalers

Dayton Appliance Parts Co .... E 937 224-0487
 Dayton *(G-9458)*

Employee Codes: A=Over 500 employees, B=251-500
C=101-250, D=51-100, E=25-50

HOUSEHOLD APPLIANCE PARTS: Wholesalers

Merc Acquisitions Inc ....E 216 925-5918
   Twinsburg (G-18448)
V and V Appliance Parts Inc ....E 330 743-5144
   Youngstown (G-20400)

HOUSEHOLD APPLIANCE REPAIR SVCS

Sears Roebuck and Co ....E 330 629-7700
   Youngstown (G-20368)
Tracy Refrigeration Inc ....E 419 223-4786
   Lima (G-12902)

HOUSEHOLD APPLIANCE STORES

Appliance Recycl Ctrs Amer Inc ....D 614 876-8771
   Hilliard (G-11878)
Hull Bros Inc ....E 419 375-2827
   Fort Recovery (G-11118)
Lowes Home Centers LLC ....C 216 351-4723
   Cleveland (G-5953)
Lowes Home Centers LLC ....C 419 739-1300
   Wapakoneta (G-18803)
Lowes Home Centers LLC ....C 937 235-2920
   Dayton (G-9688)
Lowes Home Centers LLC ....C 740 574-6200
   Wheelersburg (G-19578)
Lowes Home Centers LLC ....C 330 665-9356
   Akron (G-328)
Lowes Home Centers LLC ....C 330 829-2700
   Alliance (G-545)
Lowes Home Centers LLC ....C 937 599-4000
   Bellefontaine (G-1388)
Lowes Home Centers LLC ....C 419 420-7531
   Findlay (G-11057)
Lowes Home Centers LLC ....C 330 832-1901
   Massillon (G-13829)
Lowes Home Centers LLC ....C 513 741-0585
   Cincinnati (G-3996)
Lowes Home Centers LLC ....C 614 433-9957
   Columbus (G-6892)
Lowes Home Centers LLC ....C 740 389-9737
   Marion (G-13549)
Lowes Home Centers LLC ....C 740 450-5500
   Zanesville (G-20497)
Lowes Home Centers LLC ....C 513 598-7050
   Cincinnati (G-3997)
Lowes Home Centers LLC ....C 614 769-9940
   Reynoldsburg (G-16466)
Lowes Home Centers LLC ....C 614 853-6200
   Columbus (G-8079)
Lowes Home Centers LLC ....C 440 937-3500
   Avon (G-906)
Lowes Home Centers LLC ....C 513 445-1000
   South Lebanon (G-17078)
Lowes Home Centers LLC ....B 216 831-2860
   Bedford (G-1318)
Lowes Home Centers LLC ....C 937 327-6000
   Springfield (G-17226)
Lowes Home Centers LLC ....C 419 331-3598
   Lima (G-12832)
Lowes Home Centers LLC ....C 740 681-3464
   Lancaster (G-12551)
Lowes Home Centers LLC ....C 614 659-0530
   Dublin (G-10392)
Lowes Home Centers LLC ....C 614 238-2601
   Columbus (G-8080)
Lowes Home Centers LLC ....C 740 522-0003
   Newark (G-15199)
Lowes Home Centers LLC ....C 740 773-7777
   Chillicothe (G-2862)
Lowes Home Centers LLC ....C 440 998-6555
   Ashtabula (G-752)
Lowes Home Centers LLC ....B 513 753-5094
   Cincinnati (G-2924)
Lowes Home Centers LLC ....C 614 497-6170
   Columbus (G-8081)
Lowes Home Centers LLC ....C 513 731-6127
   Cincinnati (G-3998)
Lowes Home Centers LLC ....C 330 287-2261
   Wooster (G-19884)
Lowes Home Centers LLC ....C 937 339-2544
   Troy (G-18362)
Lowes Home Centers LLC ....C 440 392-0027
   Mentor (G-14210)
Lowes Home Centers LLC ....C 440 942-2759
   Willoughby (G-19688)
Lowes Home Centers LLC ....C 740 374-2151
   Marietta (G-13462)
Lowes Home Centers LLC ....C 419 874-6758
   Perrysburg (G-16030)
Lowes Home Centers LLC ....C 330 626-2980
   Streetsboro (G-17419)
Lowes Home Centers LLC ....C 419 389-9464
   Toledo (G-18013)
Lowes Home Centers LLC ....C 419 843-9758
   Toledo (G-18014)
Lowes Home Centers LLC ....C 614 447-2851
   Columbus (G-8082)
Lowes Home Centers LLC ....C 330 245-4300
   Akron (G-329)
Lowes Home Centers LLC ....C 513 965-3280
   Milford (G-14532)
Lowes Home Centers LLC ....C 330 908-2750
   Northfield (G-15519)
Lowes Home Centers LLC ....C 419 470-2491
   Toledo (G-18015)
Lowes Home Centers LLC ....C 513 336-9741
   Mason (G-13733)
Lowes Home Centers LLC ....C 937 498-8400
   Sidney (G-16941)
Lowes Home Centers LLC ....C 740 699-3000
   Saint Clairsville (G-16642)
Lowes Home Centers LLC ....C 330 920-9280
   Stow (G-17381)
Lowes Home Centers LLC ....C 740 589-3750
   Athens (G-799)
Lowes Home Centers LLC ....C 740 393-5350
   Mount Vernon (G-14910)
Lowes Home Centers LLC ....C 937 547-2400
   Greenville (G-11513)
Lowes Home Centers LLC ....C 330 335-1900
   Wadsworth (G-18763)
Lowes Home Centers LLC ....C 937 347-4000
   Xenia (G-20068)
Lowes Home Centers LLC ....C 440 239-2630
   Strongsville (G-17485)
Lowes Home Centers LLC ....C 513 755-4300
   West Chester (G-19113)
Lowes Home Centers LLC ....C 513 671-2093
   Cincinnati (G-3999)
Lowes Home Centers LLC ....C 440 331-1027
   Rocky River (G-16585)
Lowes Home Centers LLC ....C 330 677-3040
   Kent (G-12384)
Lowes Home Centers LLC ....C 419 747-1920
   Ontario (G-15698)
Lowes Home Centers LLC ....C 330 339-1936
   New Philadelphia (G-15107)
Lowes Home Centers LLC ....C 440 985-5700
   Lorain (G-13058)
Lowes Home Centers LLC ....C 419 447-4101
   Tiffin (G-17682)
Lowes Home Centers LLC ....C 937 578-4440
   Marysville (G-13632)
Lowes Home Centers LLC ....C 440 324-5004
   Elyria (G-10647)
Lowes Home Centers LLC ....C 937 438-4900
   Dayton (G-9689)
Lowes Home Centers LLC ....C 937 427-1110
   Beavercreek (G-1189)
Lowes Home Centers LLC ....C 937 848-5600
   Dayton (G-9690)
Lowes Home Centers LLC ....C 614 529-5900
   Hilliard (G-11923)
Lowes Home Centers LLC ....C 513 737-3700
   Hamilton (G-11755)
Lowes Home Centers LLC ....C 740 894-7120
   South Point (G-17091)
Lowes Home Centers LLC ....C 513 727-3900
   Middletown (G-14431)
Lowes Home Centers LLC ....C 419 355-0221
   Fremont (G-11210)
Lowes Home Centers LLC ....C 419 624-6000
   Sandusky (G-16777)
Lowes Home Centers LLC ....C 419 782-9000
   Defiance (G-10045)
Lowes Home Centers LLC ....C 330 609-8000
   Warren (G-18876)
Lowes Home Centers LLC ....C 330 965-4500
   Youngstown (G-20257)
Lowes Home Centers LLC ....C 937 383-7000
   Wilmington (G-19769)
Lowes Home Centers LLC ....C 937 854-8200
   Dayton (G-9691)
Lowes Home Centers LLC ....C 330 497-2720
   Canton (G-2440)
Lowes Home Centers LLC ....C 740 266-3500
   Steubenville (G-17327)
Lowes Home Centers LLC ....C 614 476-7100
   Columbus (G-8083)
Sears Roebuck and Co ....E 330 629-7700
   Youngstown (G-20368)

SERVICES SECTION

Staufs Coffee Roasters II Inc ....E 614 487-6050
   Columbus (G-8785)
Tracy Refrigeration Inc ....E 419 223-4786
   Lima (G-12902)

HOUSEHOLD APPLIANCE STORES: Air Cond Rm Units, Self-Contnd

Robertson Htg Sup Aliance Ohio ....C 330 821-9180
   Alliance (G-554)

HOUSEHOLD APPLIANCE STORES: Appliance Parts

Dayton Appliance Parts Co ....E 937 224-0487
   Dayton (G-9458)

HOUSEHOLD APPLIANCE STORES: Electric

Morrison Inc ....E 740 373-5869
   Marietta (G-13478)
Schmids Service Now Inc ....E 330 264-2040
   Wooster (G-19913)
Thompson Heating Corporation ....D 513 769-7696
   Cincinnati (G-4657)

HOUSEHOLD APPLIANCE STORES: Electric Household, Major

Big Sandy Furniture Inc ....E 740 775-4244
   Chillicothe (G-2816)
Recker and Boerger Inc ....D 513 942-9663
   West Chester (G-19224)

HOUSEHOLD APPLIANCE STORES: Gas Appliances

Big Sandy Furniture Inc ....E 740 354-3193
   Portsmouth (G-16265)
Big Sandy Furniture Inc ....D 740 574-2113
   Franklin Furnace (G-11169)

HOUSEHOLD FURNISHINGS, NEC

Casco Mfg Solutions Inc ....D 513 681-0003
   Cincinnati (G-3191)

HOUSEHOLD SEWING MACHINES WHOLESALERS: Electric

Vsm Sewing Inc ....C 440 808-6550
   Westlake (G-19563)

HOUSEKEEPING & MAID SVCS

Carol Scudere ....E 614 839-4357
   New Albany (G-14979)
Larue Enterprises Inc ....E 937 438-5711
   Beavercreek (G-1248)
Molly Maid of Lorain County ....E 440 327-0000
   Elyria (G-10655)
The Maids ....D 440 735-6243
   Bedford Heights (G-1360)

HOUSES: Fraternity & Sorority

Alpha CHI Omega ....E 614 291-3871
   Columbus (G-6974)
Ohio State University ....E 614 294-2635
   Columbus (G-8430)
Sigma CHI Frat ....E 614 297-8783
   Columbus (G-8730)

HOUSES: Lodging, Organization

Air Force US Dept of ....D 937 257-6068
   Dayton (G-9252)
Rockwell Springs Trout Club ....E 419 684-7971
   Clyde (G-6821)

HOUSES: Rooming & Boarding

Lodging First LLC ....E 614 792-2770
   Dublin (G-10390)

HOUSEWARE STORES

Provantage LLC ....D 330 494-3781
   North Canton (G-15362)

SERVICES SECTION

INDL CONTRACTORS: Exhibit Construction

HOUSEWARES, ELECTRIC: Cooking Appliances
Nacco Industries Inc .... E 440 229-5151
  Cleveland *(G-6098)*

HOUSING AUTHORITY OPERATOR
County of Allen .... E 419 228-6065
  Lima *(G-12762)*

HOUSING PROGRAM ADMIN, GOVT: Housing Authority, Nonoperating
Akron Metropolitan Hsing Auth .... C 330 920-1652
  Stow *(G-17350)*

HOUSING PROGRAM ADMINISTRATION, GOVT: Planning & Development
City of Toledo .... D 419 245-1400
  Toledo *(G-17811)*

HOUSING PROGRAMS ADMINISTRATION SVCS
Mount Auburn Community Hdo .... D 513 659-4514
  Cincinnati *(G-4124)*
Trumbull Housing Dev Corp .... D 330 369-1533
  Warren *(G-18912)*

HUMAN RESOURCE, SOCIAL WORK & WELFARE ADMINISTRATION SVCS
Clinton County Dept Jobs/Fmly .... D 937 382-0963
  Wilmington *(G-19752)*
Ohio Department of Aging .... D 614 466-5500
  Columbus *(G-8324)*
Ohio Dept of Job & Fmly Svcs .... D 330 484-5402
  Akron *(G-364)*
Ohio Dept of Job & Fmly Svcs .... C 614 466-1213
  Columbus *(G-8335)*
Ohio Pub Emplyees Rtrement Sys .... B 614 228-8471
  Columbus *(G-8370)*
School Employees Retirement .... C 614 222-5853
  Columbus *(G-8701)*

HUMANE SOCIETIES
Animal Protective League .... E 216 771-4616
  Cleveland *(G-5039)*
Belmont County of Ohio .... E 740 695-4708
  Saint Clairsville *(G-16621)*
City of Brunswick .... C 330 225-9144
  Brunswick *(G-1972)*
Franklin Cnty Bd Commissioners .... E 614 462-4360
  Columbus *(G-7689)*
Hamilton County Society .... E 513 541-6100
  Cincinnati *(G-3733)*
Ohio School Boards Association .... E 614 540-4000
  Columbus *(G-8372)*

HYDRAULIC EQPT REPAIR SVC
Boc Water Hydraulics Inc .... E 330 332-4444
  Salem *(G-16691)*
Dover Hydraulics Inc .... D 330 364-1617
  Dover *(G-10185)*
Hydraulic Specialists Inc .... E 740 922-3343
  Midvale *(G-14490)*
Ohio Machinery Co .... D 330 874-1003
  Bolivar *(G-1750)*
Perkins Motor Service Ltd .... E 440 277-1256
  Lorain *(G-13071)*

ICE
Home City Ice Company .... E 614 836-2877
  Groveport *(G-11644)*
Lori Holding Co .... E 740 342-3230
  New Lexington *(G-15055)*

ICE CREAM & ICES WHOLESALERS
Handels Homemade Ice Cream .... E 330 922-4589
  Cuyahoga Falls *(G-9193)*
United Dairy Farmers Inc .... C 513 396-8700
  Cincinnati *(G-4731)*

ICE WHOLESALERS
Home City Ice Company .... E 614 836-2877
  Groveport *(G-11644)*
Lori Holding Co .... E 740 342-3230
  New Lexington *(G-15055)*
Siemer Distributing Company .... E 740 342-3230
  New Lexington *(G-15063)*

IGNEOUS ROCK: Crushed & Broken
Great Lakes Crushing Ltd .... E 440 944-5500
  Wickliffe *(G-19599)*

INCUBATORS & BROODERS: Farm
Chick Master Incubator Company .... C 330 722-5591
  Medina *(G-14045)*

INDL & PERSONAL SVC PAPER WHOLESALERS
Avalon Foodservice Inc .... C 330 854-4551
  Canal Fulton *(G-2140)*
Buckeye Boxes Inc .... E 614 274-8484
  Columbus *(G-7156)*
Buckeye Paper Co Inc .... E 330 477-5925
  Canton *(G-2272)*
Dawnchem Inc .... E 440 943-3332
  Willoughby *(G-19658)*
Dayton Industrial Drum Inc .... E 937 253-8933
  Dayton *(G-9263)*
Deufol Worldwide Packaging LLC .... D 440 232-1100
  Bedford *(G-1303)*
Deufol Worldwide Packaging LLC .... D 414 967-8000
  Fairfield *(G-10840)*
Food Distributors Inc .... E 740 439-2764
  Cambridge *(G-2114)*
J V Hansel Inc .... E 330 716-0806
  Warren *(G-18866)*
Keystone Foods LLC .... C 419 843-3009
  Toledo *(G-17993)*
M Conley Company .... D 330 456-8243
  Canton *(G-2442)*
Maines Paper & Food Svc Inc .... E 216 643-7500
  Bedford *(G-1319)*
Millcraft Group LLC .... D 216 441-5500
  Cleveland *(G-6063)*
Millcraft Paper Company .... C 216 441-5505
  Cleveland *(G-6064)*
Millcraft Paper Company .... E 614 675-4800
  Columbus *(G-8175)*
Millcraft Paper Company .... E 216 441-5500
  Cleveland *(G-6065)*
Ohio & Michigan Paper Company .... E 419 666-1500
  Perrysburg *(G-16035)*
Peck Distributors Inc .... E 216 587-6814
  Maple Heights *(G-13413)*
Pollak Distributing Co Inc .... E 216 851-9911
  Euclid *(G-10772)*
Ricking Paper and Specialty Co .... E 513 825-3551
  Cincinnati *(G-4418)*
Sysco Cincinnati LLC .... B 513 563-6300
  Cincinnati *(G-4609)*
The Cincinnati Cordage Ppr Co .... E 513 242-3600
  Cincinnati *(G-4640)*
The Cottingham Paper Co .... E 614 294-6444
  Columbus *(G-8834)*
Veritiv Operating Company .... E 614 251-7100
  Columbus *(G-8935)*
Veritiv Operating Company .... E 216 573-7400
  Independence *(G-12273)*
Veritiv Operating Company .... C 513 285-0999
  Fairfield *(G-10922)*

INDL & PERSONAL SVC PAPER, WHOL: Bags, Paper/Disp Plastic
Atlapac Corp .... D 614 252-2121
  Columbus *(G-7067)*
Berk Enterprises Inc .... D 330 369-1192
  Warren *(G-18829)*
Cannon Group Inc .... E 614 890-0343
  Westerville *(G-19375)*
Joshen Paper & Packaging Co .... C 216 441-5600
  Cleveland *(G-5872)*
North American Plas Chem Inc .... E 330 627-2210
  Carrollton *(G-2624)*

INDL & PERSONAL SVC PAPER, WHOL: Boxes, Corrugtd/Solid Fiber
Compass Packaging LLC .... E 330 274-2001
  Mantua *(G-13386)*
Impressive Packaging Inc .... E 419 368-6808
  Hayesville *(G-11834)*
Jit Packaging Aurora Inc .... E 330 562-8080
  Aurora *(G-843)*
Welch Packaging LLC .... E 937 223-3958
  Dayton *(G-9989)*
Westrock CP LLC .... D 770 448-2193
  Wshngtn CT Hs *(G-20038)*

INDL & PERSONAL SVC PAPER, WHOL: Container, Paper/Plastic
I Supply Co .... C 937 878-5240
  Fairborn *(G-10798)*

INDL & PERSONAL SVC PAPER, WHOL: Paper, Wrap/Coarse/Prdts
Alco-Chem Inc .... E 330 833-8551
  Canton *(G-2230)*
Mailender Inc .... D 513 942-5453
  West Chester *(G-19115)*
Millcraft Paper Company .... E 937 222-7829
  Dayton *(G-9748)*
Polymer Packaging Inc .... D 330 832-2000
  Massillon *(G-13844)*
Tiffin Paper Company .... E 419 447-2121
  Tiffin *(G-17706)*

INDL & PERSONAL SVC PAPER, WHOLESALE: Boxes & Containers
Cardinal Container Corporation .... E 614 497-3033
  Columbus *(G-7191)*

INDL & PERSONAL SVC PAPER, WHOLESALE: Disposable
Acorn Distributors Inc .... E 614 294-6444
  Columbus *(G-6940)*

INDL & PERSONAL SVC PAPER, WHOLESALE: Paper Tubes & Cores
Espt Liquidation Inc .... D 330 698-4711
  Apple Creek *(G-624)*
Precision Products Group Inc .... D 330 698-4711
  Apple Creek *(G-626)*
Sonoco Products Company .... D 937 429-0040
  Beavercreek Township *(G-1285)*

INDL & PERSONAL SVC PAPER, WHOLESALE: Patterns, Paper
Millers Textile Services Inc .... D 419 738-3552
  Wapakoneta *(G-18804)*

INDL & PERSONAL SVC PAPER, WHOLESALE: Press Sensitive Tape
Tape Products Company .... D 513 489-8840
  Cincinnati *(G-4624)*

INDL & PERSONAL SVC PAPER, WHOLESALE: Shipping Splys
G R R Inc .... D 800 628-9195
  West Chester *(G-19078)*
Mast Logistics Services Inc .... C 614 415-7500
  Columbus *(G-8125)*
Systems Pack Inc .... E 330 467-5729
  Macedonia *(G-13211)*

INDL & PERSONAL SVC PAPER, WHOLESALE: Towels, Paper
Aci Industries Converting Ltd .... E 740 368-4160
  Delaware *(G-10066)*

INDL CONTRACTORS: Exhibit Construction
Benchmark Craftsman Inc .... E 330 975-4214
  Seville *(G-16837)*

INDL DIAMONDS WHOLESALERS

Chardon Tool & Supply Co Inc ....E 440 286-6440
Chardon *(G-2743)*

INDL EQPT CLEANING SVCS

Industrial Air Control Inc ....D 330 772-6422
Hubbard *(G-12088)*
MPW Container Management Corp ....D 216 362-8400
Cleveland *(G-6083)*
National Heat Exch Clg Corp ....E 330 482-0893
Youngstown *(G-20296)*

INDL EQPT SVCS

3-D Service Ltd ....C 330 830-3500
Massillon *(G-13780)*
Commercial Electric Pdts Corp ....E 216 241-2886
Cleveland *(G-5376)*
Dayton Industrial Drum Inc ....E 937 253-8933
Dayton *(G-9263)*
Eagleburgmann Ke Inc ....E 859 746-0091
Cincinnati *(G-3529)*
Famous Enterprises Inc ....E 330 762-9621
Akron *(G-217)*
Forge Industries Inc ....A 330 782-8301
Youngstown *(G-20191)*
GL Nause Co Inc ....E 513 722-9500
Loveland *(G-13128)*
Graphic Systems Services Inc ....E 937 746-0708
Springboro *(G-17120)*
Grob Systems Inc ....C 419 358-9015
Bluffton *(G-1731)*
Henry P Thompson Company ....E 513 248-3200
Milford *(G-14524)*
Industrial Parts & Service Co ....E 330 966-5025
Canton *(G-2411)*
Industrial Repair & Mfg Inc ....E 419 822-4232
Delta *(G-10159)*
Interstate Lift Trucks Inc ....E 216 328-0970
Cleveland *(G-5835)*
Magnetech Industrial Svcs Inc ....C 330 830-3500
Massillon *(G-13831)*
Miami Industrial Trucks Inc ....D 937 293-4194
Moraine *(G-14805)*
Obr Cooling Towers Inc ....E 419 243-3443
Rossford *(G-16610)*
Primetals Technologies USA LLC ....E 419 929-1554
New London *(G-15070)*
Quintus Technologies LLC ....E 614 891-2732
Lewis Center *(G-12705)*
Raymond Storage Concepts Inc ....E 513 891-7290
Blue Ash *(G-1677)*
Reladyne LLC ....E 513 489-6000
Cincinnati *(G-4402)*
Scott Fetzer Company ....E 440 892-3000
Westlake *(G-19544)*
Ssi Fabricated Inc ....E 513 217-3535
Middletown *(G-14459)*
Team Industrial Services Inc ....E 440 498-9494
Cleveland *(G-6575)*
Towlift Inc ....D 614 851-1001
Columbus *(G-8856)*
Towlift Inc ....E 419 666-1333
Northwood *(G-15548)*
Transforce Inc ....E 513 860-4402
West Chester *(G-19165)*
US Molding Machinery Co Inc ....E 440 918-1701
Willoughby *(G-19721)*
Walker National Inc ....E 614 492-1614
Columbus *(G-8962)*
Winelco Inc ....E 513 755-8050
West Chester *(G-19187)*

INDL GASES WHOLESALERS

Airgas Inc ....B 866 935-3370
Cleveland *(G-4975)*
Airgas Inc ....B 440 632-1758
Middlefield *(G-14393)*
Airgas Merchant Gases LLC ....B 800 242-0105
Cleveland *(G-4976)*
Airgas Safety Inc ....E 513 942-1465
Hamilton *(G-11689)*
Airgas Usa LLC ....D 440 786-2864
Oakwood Village *(G-15625)*

INDL HELP SVCS

Diversified Labor Support LLC ....B 440 234-3090
Cleveland *(G-5492)*

INDL MACHINERY & EQPT WHOLESALERS

ABB Inc ....E 440 585-7804
Beachwood *(G-1045)*
Addisonmckee Inc ....C 513 228-7000
Lebanon *(G-12587)*
Aerocontrolex Group Inc ....D 440 352-6182
Painesville *(G-15833)*
Airgas Usa LLC ....E 513 563-8070
Cincinnati *(G-2979)*
Alkon Corporation ....D 419 355-9111
Fremont *(G-11184)*
Alkon Corporation ....E 614 799-6650
Dublin *(G-10241)*
Ats Systems Oregon Inc ....B 541 738-0932
Lewis Center *(G-12668)*
Best & Donovan N A Inc ....E 513 791-9180
Blue Ash *(G-1542)*
Bevcorp LLC ....D 440 954-3500
Willoughby *(G-19647)*
Bionix Safety Technologies ....E 419 727-0552
Toledo *(G-17773)*
Blastmaster Holdings Usa LLC ....D 877 725-2781
Columbus *(G-7118)*
Bostwick-Braun Company ....D 419 259-3600
Toledo *(G-17778)*
Brown Industrial Inc ....E 937 693-3838
Botkins *(G-1752)*
Cecil I Walker Machinery Co ....E 740 286-7566
Jackson *(G-12308)*
Cinc ....E 419 663-6644
Collins *(G-6839)*
Clarke Power Services Inc ....E 937 684-4402
Huber Heights *(G-12094)*
Columbus Equipment Company ....E 513 771-3922
Cincinnati *(G-3389)*
CPI - Cnstr Polymers Inc ....E 330 861-5200
North Canton *(G-15329)*
Ctm Integration Incorporated ....E 330 332-1800
Salem *(G-16693)*
Dreier & Maller Inc ....E 614 575-0065
Reynoldsburg *(G-16448)*
Dxp Enterprises Inc ....E 513 242-2227
Cincinnati *(G-3517)*
EMI Corp ....D 937 596-5511
Jackson Center *(G-12322)*
Equipment Depot Ohio Inc ....E 513 934-2121
Lebanon *(G-12603)*
Equipment Manufacturers Intl ....E 216 651-6700
Cleveland *(G-5548)*
Esec Corporation ....E 614 875-3732
Grove City *(G-11558)*
Feintool Equipment Corporation ....E 513 791-1118
Blue Ash *(G-1593)*
Freeman Manufacturing & Sup Co ....E 440 934-1902
Avon *(G-893)*
Ged Holdings Inc ....C 330 963-5401
Twinsburg *(G-18421)*
General Electric Company ....E 513 530-7107
Blue Ash *(G-1599)*
Glavin Industries Inc ....E 440 349-0049
Solon *(G-17009)*
Great Lakes Water Treatment ....E 216 464-8292
Cleveland *(G-5692)*
Hannon Company ....D 330 456-4728
Canton *(G-2393)*
Hendrickson International Corp ....D 740 929-5600
Hebron *(G-11849)*
Howden North America Inc ....C 513 874-2400
Fairfield *(G-10861)*
IMS Company ....D 440 543-1615
Chagrin Falls *(G-2720)*
Intelligrated Systems Inc ....A 866 936-7300
Mason *(G-13720)*
Intelligrated Systems Ohio LLC ....A 513 701-7300
Mason *(G-13722)*
Jed Industries Inc ....E 440 639-9973
Grand River *(G-11456)*
Jr Engineering Inc ....C 330 848-0960
Barberton *(G-968)*
Kennametal Inc ....D 216 898-6120
Cleveland *(G-5894)*
Kolbus America Inc ....E 216 931-5100
Cleveland *(G-5908)*
Kyocera SGS Precision Tools ....E 330 688-6667
Munroe Falls *(G-14931)*
Linden Industries Inc ....E 330 928-4064
Cuyahoga Falls *(G-9205)*
Lns America Inc ....D 513 528-5674
Cincinnati *(G-2923)*
Maag Automatik Inc ....E 330 677-2225
Kent *(G-12385)*
Maple Mountain Industries Inc ....C 330 948-2510
Lodi *(G-12965)*
Marcy Industries Company LLC ....E 740 943-2343
Marion *(G-13552)*
MH Logistics Corp ....E 330 425-2476
Hudson *(G-12134)*
Mine Equipment Services LLC ....E 740 936-5427
Sunbury *(G-17558)*
Minerva Welding and Fabg Inc ....E 330 868-7731
Minerva *(G-14649)*
Multi Products Company ....E 330 674-5981
Millersburg *(G-14613)*
Ohio Transmission Corporation ....C 614 342-6247
Columbus *(G-8451)*
Ohio Transmission Corporation ....E 513 539-8411
Middletown *(G-14445)*
Park Corporation ....B 216 267-4870
Cleveland *(G-6234)*
Parker-Hannifin Corporation ....E 216 896-3000
Cleveland *(G-6240)*
Pfpc Enterprises Inc ....B 513 941-6200
Cincinnati *(G-4290)*
Pines Manufacturing Inc ....E 440 835-5553
Westlake *(G-19534)*
Power-Pack Conveyor Company ....E 440 975-9955
Willoughby *(G-19705)*
Primetals Technologies USA LLC ....E 419 929-1554
New London *(G-15070)*
Prospect Mold & Die Company ....D 330 929-3311
Cuyahoga Falls *(G-9214)*
Reid Asset Management Company ....E 216 642-3223
Cleveland *(G-6368)*
Rubber City Machinery Corp ....E 330 434-3500
Akron *(G-419)*
Samuel Strapping Systems Inc ....D 740 522-2500
Heath *(G-11843)*
Select Industries Corp ....E 937 233-9191
Dayton *(G-9874)*
Shawcor Pipe Protection LLC ....E 513 683-7800
Loveland *(G-13159)*
Shearer Farm Inc ....E 440 237-4806
North Royalton *(G-15502)*
Siemens Industry Inc ....E 440 526-2770
Brecksville *(G-1850)*
Stolle Machinery Company LLC ....E 330 493-0444
Canton *(G-2550)*
Stolle Machinery Company LLC ....D 330 453-2015
North Canton *(G-15369)*
Super Systems Inc ....E 513 772-0060
Cincinnati *(G-4602)*
Union Supply Group Inc ....E 614 409-1444
Groveport *(G-11680)*
United Grinding North Amer Inc ....D 937 859-1975
Miamisburg *(G-14364)*
Venturo Manufacturing Inc ....E 513 772-8448
Cincinnati *(G-4807)*
W W Williams Company LLC ....E 330 225-7751
Brunswick *(G-1995)*
W W Williams Company LLC ....E 419 837-5067
Perrysburg *(G-16070)*
Western Tradewinds Inc ....E 937 859-4300
Miamisburg *(G-14368)*
Wilkris Company ....E 513 271-9344
Terrace Park *(G-17663)*
Winelco Inc ....E 513 755-8050
West Chester *(G-19187)*
Woodworkers Outlet ....E 440 286-3942
Chardon *(G-2779)*
Wurtec Incorporated ....D 419 726-1066
Toledo *(G-18317)*
WW Grainger Inc ....E 513 563-7100
Blue Ash *(G-1722)*

INDL MACHINERY REPAIR & MAINTENANCE

A and A Millwright Rigging Svcs ....E 513 396-6212
Cincinnati *(G-2951)*
Ajax Tocco Magnethermic Corp ....C 330 372-8511
Warren *(G-18815)*
Applied Industrial Tech Inc ....B 216 426-4000
Cleveland *(G-5055)*
Cecil I Walker Machinery Co ....E 740 286-7566
Jackson *(G-12308)*
Cleveland Electric Labs Co ....E 800 447-2207
Twinsburg *(G-18401)*
Cleveland Pump Repr & Svcs LLC ....E 330 963-3100
Twinsburg *(G-18402)*
Convergint Technologies LLC ....C 513 771-1717
Cincinnati *(G-3416)*

SERVICES SECTION

INDL SPLYS, WHOLESALE: Fittings

Elmco Engineering Oh Inc .... E 419 238-1100
  Van Wert (G-18632)
Emsco Inc .... E 330 830-7125
  Massillon (G-13803)
Emsco Inc .... E 330 833-5600
  Massillon (G-13804)
Estabrook Corporation .... E 440 234-8566
  Berea (G-1457)
General Plastex Inc .... E 330 745-7775
  Barberton (G-964)
J&J Precision Machine Ltd .... E 330 923-5783
  Cuyahoga Falls (G-9197)
Konecranes Inc .... E 513 755-2800
  West Chester (G-19104)
Laserflex Corporation .... D 614 850-9600
  Hilliard (G-11920)
Lucas Precision LLC .... E 216 451-5588
  Cleveland (G-5957)
Maintenance & Repair Tech Inc .... E 513 422-1198
  Middletown (G-14432)
Mmic Inc .... D 513 697-0445
  Loveland (G-13147)
Monarch Electric Service Co .... D 216 433-7800
  Cleveland (G-6073)
OKL Can Line Inc .... E 513 825-1655
  Cincinnati (G-4218)
Paradigm Industrial LLC .... E 937 224-4415
  Dayton (G-9801)
Patriot Indus Contg Svcs LLC .... E 513 248-8222
  Milford (G-14552)
S & S Inc .... E 216 383-1880
  Cleveland (G-6425)
SMS Technical Services LLC .... E 330 426-4126
  East Palestine (G-10539)
Steel Eqp Specialists Inc .... D 330 823-8260
  Alliance (G-563)
Towlift Inc .... C 216 749-6800
  Brooklyn Heights (G-1929)
Victory Machine and Fab .... E 937 693-3171
  Sidney (G-16959)
Williams Super Service Inc .... E 330 733-7750
  East Sparta (G-10542)
Winkle Industries Inc .... D 330 823-9730
  Alliance (G-565)
Wood Graphics Inc .... E 513 771-6300
  Cincinnati (G-4858)

INDL PROCESS INSTRUMENTS: Controllers, Process Variables

Schneider Electric Usa Inc .... D 513 755-5000
  West Chester (G-19145)

INDL SPLYS WHOLESALERS

3b Holdings Inc .... D 800 791-7124
  Cleveland (G-4926)
Advanced Tool & Supply Inc .... E 937 278-7337
  Dayton (G-9310)
Alkon Corporation .... E 614 799-6650
  Dublin (G-10241)
All Ohio Threaded Rod Co Inc .... E 216 426-1800
  Cleveland (G-4990)
Alro Steel Corporation .... E 419 720-5300
  Toledo (G-17747)
Applied Industrial Tech Inc .... B 216 426-4000
  Cleveland (G-5055)
Applied Mint Sups Slutions LLC .... E 216 456-3600
  Strongsville (G-17443)
Bechtl Bldng Mntnc Crprtn of .... D 330 759-2797
  Youngstown (G-20111)
Brand Energy & Infrastructure .... E 419 324-1305
  Toledo (G-17781)
Ci Disposition Co .... E 216 587-5200
  Brooklyn Heights (G-1912)
Cornwell Quality Tools Company .... D 330 620-2027
  Mogadore (G-14673)
Cornwell Quality Tools Company .... E 330 335-2933
  Wadsworth (G-18751)
Dolin Supply Co .... E 304 529-4171
  South Point (G-17084)
Dynatech Systems Inc .... E 440 365-1774
  Elyria (G-10618)
Eagle Industrial Truck Mfg LLC .... E 734 442-1000
  Swanton (G-17563)
Edward W Daniel LLC .... E 440 647-1960
  Wellington (G-18990)
Ellison Technologies Inc .... E 310 323-2121
  Hamilton (G-11725)
Fcx Performance Inc .... E 614 324-6050
  Columbus (G-7645)

Flodraulic Group Incorporated .... E 614 276-8141
  Columbus (G-7676)
General Factory Sups Co Inc .... E 513 864-6007
  Cincinnati (G-3674)
Ges Graphite Inc .... E 205 838-0820
  Parma (G-15908)
Goss Supply Company .... E 740 454-2571
  Zanesville (G-20483)
Great Lakes Textiles Inc .... E 440 439-1300
  Solon (G-17012)
Hd Supply Facilities Maint Ltd .... E 440 542-9188
  Solon (G-17014)
Kaman Corporation .... E 330 468-1811
  Macedonia (G-13205)
Koi Siferd Hossellman .... E 419 228-1221
  Lima (G-12812)
Lakeside Supply Co .... E 216 941-6800
  Cleveland (G-5920)
Lancaster Commercial Pdts LLC .... E 740 286-5081
  Columbus (G-8032)
Lawrence Industries Inc .... C 216 518-7000
  Cleveland (G-5929)
Liberty Casting Company LLC .... E 740 363-1941
  Delaware (G-10116)
Logan Clutch Corporation .... E 440 808-4258
  Cleveland (G-5950)
Mazzella Holding Company Inc .... D 513 772-4466
  Cleveland (G-5997)
McWane Inc .... B 740 622-6651
  Coshocton (G-9111)
Megacity Fire Protection Inc .... E 937 335-0775
  Dayton (G-9717)
Merchandise Inc .... E 513 353-2200
  Miamitown (G-14372)
Mill-Rose Company .... C 440 255-9171
  Mentor (G-14220)
MRC Global (us) Inc .... E 419 324-0039
  Toledo (G-18071)
MRC Global (us) Inc .... E 513 489-6922
  Cincinnati (G-4126)
New Haven Estates Inc .... E 419 933-2181
  New Haven (G-15051)
Noland Company .... C 937 396-7980
  Moraine (G-14812)
Precision Supply Company Inc .... D 330 225-5530
  Brunswick (G-1988)
Riten Industries .... D 740 335-5353
  Wshngtn CT Hs (G-20033)
Samsel Rope & Marine Supply Co .... E 216 241-0333
  Cleveland (G-6442)
Samuel Strapping Systems Inc .... D 740 522-2500
  Heath (G-11843)
Scioto Services LLc .... E 937 644-0888
  Marysville (G-13649)
Selinsky Force LLC .... C 330 477-4527
  Canton (G-2525)
SSP Fittings Corp .... D 330 425-4250
  Twinsburg (G-18472)
Stark Industrial LLC .... E 330 493-9773
  North Canton (G-15368)
Tricor Industrial Inc .... D 330 264-3299
  Wooster (G-19919)
Tricor Metals .... D 330 264-3299
  Wooster (G-19920)
W W Grainger Inc .... C 330 425-8387
  Macedonia (G-13217)
Watteredge LLC .... D 440 933-6110
  Avon Lake (G-940)
Wesco Distribution Inc .... E 419 666-1670
  Northwood (G-15551)
Wesco Distribution Inc .... E 216 741-0441
  Cleveland (G-6734)
Wesco Distribution Inc .... E 937 228-9668
  Dayton (G-9991)
Winsupply Inc .... D 937 294-5331
  Moraine (G-14836)
Wulco Inc .... D 513 679-2600
  Cincinnati (G-4862)

INDL SPLYS, WHOL: Fasteners, Incl Nuts, Bolts, Screws, Etc

Afc Industries Inc .... E 513 874-7456
  Fairfield (G-10816)
Andre Corporation 574 293-0207
  Mason (G-13662)
Atlas Bolt & Screw Company LLC .... C 419 289-6171
  Ashland (G-660)
Chandler Products LLC .... E 216 481-4400
  Cleveland (G-5226)

Earnest Machine Products Co .... E 440 895-8400
  Rocky River (G-16577)
Facil North America Inc .... C 330 487-2500
  Twinsburg (G-18414)
Great Lakes Fasteners Inc .... E 330 425-4488
  Twinsburg (G-18425)
J & J Entps Westerville Inc .... E 614 898-5997
  Sunbury (G-17557)
L & J Fasteners Inc .... E 614 876-7313
  Hilliard (G-11919)
Mid-State Bolt and Nut Co Inc .... E 614 253-8631
  Columbus (G-8166)
R L Morrissey & Assoc Inc .... E 440 498-3730
  Solon (G-17044)
Stafast Products Inc .... E 440 357-5546
  Painesville (G-15880)
State Industrial Products Corp .... C 216 861-6363
  Cleveland (G-6531)
Supply Technologies LLC .... C 440 947-2100
  Cleveland (G-6556)
Ziegler Bolt & Parts Co .... D 330 478-2542
  Canton (G-2595)

INDL SPLYS, WHOLESALE: Abrasives

American Producers Sup Co Inc .... E 740 373-5050
  Marietta (G-13431)
ARC Abrasives Inc .... D 800 888-4885
  Troy (G-18347)
Buffalo Abrasives Inc .... E 614 891-6450
  Westerville (G-19374)
Mirka USA Inc .... D 330 963-6421
  Twinsburg (G-18449)

INDL SPLYS, WHOLESALE: Adhesives, Tape & Plasters

Gorilla Glue Company .... E 513 271-3300
  Cincinnati (G-3688)

INDL SPLYS, WHOLESALE: Barrels, New Or Reconditioned

Sabco Industries Inc .... E 419 531-5347
  Toledo (G-18169)

INDL SPLYS, WHOLESALE: Bearings

Bearing & Drive Systems Inc .... D 440 846-9700
  Strongsville (G-17446)
Bearing Distributors Inc .... C 216 642-9100
  Cleveland (G-5107)
Bearing Technologies Ltd .... D 440 937-4770
  Avon (G-879)
Belting Company of Cincinnati .... C 513 621-9050
  Cincinnati (G-3097)
Federal-Mogul LLC .... C 740 432-2393
  Cambridge (G-2113)
Forge Industries Inc .... A 330 782-8301
  Youngstown (G-20191)
North Coast Bearings LLC .... E 440 930-7600
  Avon (G-908)

INDL SPLYS, WHOLESALE: Bottler Splys

Tolco Corporation .... D 419 241-1113
  Toledo (G-18225)

INDL SPLYS, WHOLESALE: Drums, New Or Reconditioned

Dayton Industrial Drum Inc .... E 937 253-8933
  Dayton (G-9263)

INDL SPLYS, WHOLESALE: Electric Tools

WW Grainger Inc .... E 614 276-5231
  Columbus (G-9010)

INDL SPLYS, WHOLESALE: Fasteners & Fastening Eqpt

Ors Nasco Inc .... E 918 781-5300
  West Chester (G-19219)

INDL SPLYS, WHOLESALE: Fittings

Faster Inc .... E 419 868-8197
  Maumee (G-13914)
Superior Products LLC .... D 216 651-9400
  Cleveland (G-6555)

INDL SPLYS, WHOLESALE: Fittings

Superior Products Llc .... D 216 651-9400
  Cleveland *(G-6554)*

INDL SPLYS, WHOLESALE: Gaskets

Ishikawa Gasket America Inc .... C 419 353-7300
  Bowling Green *(G-1783)*
Newman International Inc .... D 513 932-7379
  Lebanon *(G-12630)*

INDL SPLYS, WHOLESALE: Gaskets & Seals

Buckeye Rubber & Packing Co .... E 216 464-8900
  Beachwood *(G-1058)*

INDL SPLYS, WHOLESALE: Gears

Apex Gear .... E 614 539-3002
  Grove City *(G-11531)*
Cincinnati Gearing Systems Inc .... D 513 527-8600
  Cincinnati *(G-3306)*

INDL SPLYS, WHOLESALE: Hydraulic & Pneumatic Pistons/Valves

Alkon Corporation .... D 419 355-9111
  Fremont *(G-11184)*
Clippard Instrument Lab Inc .... C 513 521-4261
  Cincinnati *(G-3367)*
Fischer Pump & Valve Company .... E 513 583-4800
  Loveland *(G-13125)*

INDL SPLYS, WHOLESALE: Knives, Indl

Alliance Knife Inc .... E 513 367-9000
  Harrison *(G-11789)*
CB Manufacturing & Sls Co Inc .... D 937 866-5986
  Miamisburg *(G-14279)*

INDL SPLYS, WHOLESALE: Mill Splys

Allied Supply Company Inc .... E 937 224-9833
  Dayton *(G-9317)*
Vallen Distribution Inc .... D 513 942-9100
  West Chester *(G-19177)*

INDL SPLYS, WHOLESALE: Plastic, Pallets

Pallet Distributors Inc .... C 888 805-9670
  Lakewood *(G-12494)*

INDL SPLYS, WHOLESALE: Power Transmission, Eqpt & Apparatus

Binkelman Corporation .... E 419 537-9333
  Toledo *(G-17771)*
Commercial Electric Pdts Corp .... E 216 241-2886
  Cleveland *(G-5376)*
Great Lakes Power Products Inc .... D 440 951-5111
  Mentor *(G-14185)*
Ohio Transmission Corporation .... C 614 342-6247
  Columbus *(G-8451)*
Ohio Transmission Corporation .... E 419 468-7866
  Galion *(G-11304)*

INDL SPLYS, WHOLESALE: Rubber Goods, Mechanical

Advanced Elastomer Systems LP .... C 800 352-7866
  Akron *(G-22)*
Jet Rubber Company .... E 330 325-1821
  Rootstown *(G-16597)*
Mullins International Sls Corp .... D 937 233-4213
  Dayton *(G-9761)*
Summers Acquisition Corp .... E 216 941-7700
  Cleveland *(G-6546)*
Timco Rubber Products Inc .... E 216 267-6242
  Berea *(G-1473)*

INDL SPLYS, WHOLESALE: Seals

Datwyler Sling Sltions USA Inc .... D 937 387-2800
  Vandalia *(G-18676)*
Mc Neal Industries Inc .... E 440 721-0400
  Painesville *(G-15865)*
McNeil Industries Inc .... E 440 951-7756
  Painesville *(G-15866)*
Roger Zatkoff Company .... E 248 478-2400
  Twinsburg *(G-18462)*

INDL SPLYS, WHOLESALE: Signmaker Eqpt & Splys

Sign Source USA Inc .... D 419 224-1130
  Lima *(G-12878)*

INDL SPLYS, WHOLESALE: Tools

B W Grinding Co .... E 419 923-1376
  Lyons *(G-13185)*
File Sharpening Company Inc .... E 937 376-8268
  Xenia *(G-20050)*
H & D Steel Service Inc .... E 440 237-3390
  North Royalton *(G-15491)*
Pennsylvania Tl Sls & Svc Inc .... D 330 758-0845
  Youngstown *(G-20317)*

INDL SPLYS, WHOLESALE: Tools, NEC

Luke Collison .... E 740 969-2283
  Lancaster *(G-12552)*
Lute Supply Inc .... E 740 353-1447
  Portsmouth *(G-16294)*

INDL SPLYS, WHOLESALE: Valves & Fittings

A-T Controls Inc .... E 513 530-5175
  West Chester *(G-19188)*
Brennan Industries Inc .... E 440 248-7088
  Solon *(G-16985)*
Crane Pumps & Systems Inc .... B 937 773-2442
  Piqua *(G-16142)*
Dayton Windustrial Co .... E 937 461-2603
  Dayton *(G-9495)*
Eagle Equipment Corporation .... E 937 746-0510
  Franklin *(G-11154)*
Famous Distribution Inc .... D 330 762-9621
  Akron *(G-215)*
Main Line Supply Co Inc .... E 937 254-6910
  Dayton *(G-9695)*
Ruthman Pump and Engineering .... E 937 783-2411
  Blanchester *(G-1516)*
The Mau-Sherwood Supply Co .... E 330 405-1200
  Twinsburg *(G-18475)*
Victory White Metal Company .... D 216 271-1400
  Cleveland *(G-6694)*

INDL TOOL GRINDING SVCS

Seilkop Industries Inc .... E 513 761-1035
  Cincinnati *(G-4492)*

INDL TRUCK REPAIR SVCS

All Lift Service Company Inc .... E 440 585-1542
  Willoughby *(G-19642)*
Fallsway Equipment Co Inc .... C 330 633-6000
  Akron *(G-214)*
I L T Diversified Mtl Hdlg .... E 419 865-8025
  Holland *(G-12029)*
Sharron Group Inc .... E 614 873-5856
  Plain City *(G-16206)*
Terex Utilities Inc .... E 614 444-7373
  Etna *(G-10739)*
Toyota Industries N Amer Inc .... E 937 237-0976
  Dayton *(G-9935)*

INDOOR PARKING SVCS

ABM Parking Services Inc .... E 330 747-7678
  Youngstown *(G-20096)*

INDUSTRIAL & COMMERCIAL EQPT INSPECTION SVCS

Argus International Inc .... E 513 852-1010
  Cincinnati *(G-3046)*
Cec Combustion Safety LLC .... E 216 749-2992
  Brookpark *(G-1938)*
Ohio Fabricators Inc .... E 216 391-2400
  Cleveland *(G-6190)*
Orbit Industries Inc .... D 440 243-3311
  Cleveland *(G-6211)*
Predictive Service LLC .... D 866 772-6770
  Cleveland *(G-6296)*
Quintus Technologies LLC .... E 614 891-2732
  Lewis Center *(G-12705)*
Reid Asset Management Company ..... E 216 642-3223
  Cleveland *(G-6368)*

INFORMATION BUREAU SVCS

County of Clermont .... E 513 732-7661
  Batavia *(G-1006)*
National Service Information .... E 740 387-6806
  Marion *(G-13567)*
Provato LLC .... E 440 546-0768
  Brecksville *(G-1844)*
Rxoc Information Operations .... E 937 255-1151
  Dayton *(G-9282)*

INFORMATION RETRIEVAL SERVICES

Advant-E Corporation .... D 937 429-4288
  Beavercreek *(G-1145)*
AGS Custom Graphics Inc .... D 330 963-7770
  Macedonia *(G-13186)*
Bluespring Software Inc .... E 513 794-1764
  Blue Ash *(G-1547)*
Cobalt Group Inc .... E 614 876-4013
  Hilliard *(G-11891)*
Com Net Inc .... D 419 739-3100
  Wapakoneta *(G-18792)*
Community Isp Inc .... E 419 867-6060
  Toledo *(G-17824)*
Cyxtera Data Centers Inc .... B 216 986-2742
  Cleveland *(G-5460)*
Hkm Drect Mkt Cmmnications Inc ..... C 216 651-9500
  Cleveland *(G-5762)*
Innovative Technologies Corp .... D 937 252-2145
  Dayton *(G-9275)*
Intellicorp Records Inc .... D 216 450-5200
  Beachwood *(G-1089)*
Medical Mutual Services LLC .... C 440 878-4800
  Strongsville *(G-17492)*
Peoplefacts LLC .... E 800 849-1071
  Maumee *(G-13958)*
Png Telecommunications Inc .... D 513 942-7900
  Cincinnati *(G-4311)*
Relx Inc .... B 937 865-6800
  Miamisburg *(G-14339)*
Repro Acquisition Company LLC .... E 216 738-3800
  Cleveland *(G-6378)*
Salvagedata Recovery LLC .... E 914 600-2434
  Cleveland *(G-6439)*
Security Hut Inc .... C 216 226-0461
  Lakewood *(G-12500)*
Seifert & Group Inc .... D 330 833-2700
  Massillon *(G-13852)*
TSC Communications Inc .... E 419 739-2200
  Wapakoneta *(G-18810)*
Verisk Crime Analytics Inc .... E 614 865-6000
  Worthington *(G-20005)*
Verizon Business Global LLC .... E 614 219-2317
  Hilliard *(G-11963)*
Webmd Health Corp .... E 330 425-3241
  Twinsburg *(G-18485)*

INFORMATION SVCS: Consumer

Action For Children Inc .... E 614 224-0222
  Columbus *(G-6941)*
Child & Elder Care Insights .... E 440 356-2900
  Rocky River *(G-16573)*
Research Associates Inc .... D 440 892-1000
  Cleveland *(G-6381)*

INNS

B & I Hotel Management LLC .... C 330 995-0200
  Aurora *(G-828)*
Bird Enterprises LLC .... E 330 674-1457
  Millersburg *(G-14589)*
Brookdale Senior Living Inc .... D 937 738-7342
  Marysville *(G-13607)*
Chimneys Inn .... E 937 567-7850
  Dayton *(G-9404)*
Drury Hotels Company LLC .... E 614 798-8802
  Dublin *(G-10324)*
Fairlawn Associates Ltd .... C 330 867-5000
  Fairlawn *(G-10949)*
Fmw Rri Opco LLC .... E 614 744-2659
  Columbus *(G-7678)*
Frog & Toad Inc .... E 419 877-1180
  Whitehouse *(G-19586)*
Glenlaurel Inc .... E 740 385-4070
  Rockbridge *(G-16560)*
Hotel 2345 LLC .... E 614 766-7762
  Dublin *(G-10365)*
Indus Airport Hotels I LLC .... D 614 231-2869
  Columbus *(G-7891)*

SERVICES SECTION

Indus Hilliard Hotel LLC ....E...... 614 334-1800
  Hilliard (G-11913)
Inn At Marietta Ltd ....D...... 740 373-9600
  Marietta (G-13456)
Motel Partners LLC ....E...... 740 594-3000
  Athens (G-802)
Pacific Heritg Inn Polaris LLC ....E...... 614 880-9080
  Columbus (G-6899)
Plaza Inn Foods Inc ....E...... 937 354-2181
  Mount Victory (G-14930)
R & H Service Inc ....E...... 330 626-2888
  Streetsboro (G-17427)
Renaissance Corporation ....E...... 937 526-3672
  Versailles (G-18729)
Roce Group LLC ....E...... 330 969-2627
  Stow (G-17390)
Rukh Boardman Properties LLC ....D...... 330 726-5472
  Youngstown (G-20361)
Sar Biren ....E...... 419 865-0407
  Maumee (G-13974)
Stockport Mill Country Inn Inc ....E...... 740 559-2822
  Stockport (G-17346)
Stoney Ridge Inn South Ltd ....D...... 513 539-9247
  Monroe (G-14713)
Tharaldson Hospitality MGT ....E...... 513 947-9402
  Cincinnati (G-2935)
W2005/Fargo Hotels (pool C) ....D...... 614 791-8675
  Dublin (G-10486)

INSPECTION & TESTING SVCS

Acuren Inspection Inc ....E...... 937 228-9729
  Dayton (G-9307)
Benchmark National Corporation ....E...... 419 660-1100
  Bellevue (G-1406)
Catsi Inc ....E...... 740 574-8417
  Wheelersburg (G-19572)
Christ Hospital ....C...... 513 564-1340
  Cincinnati (G-3263)
James Ray Lozier ....E...... 419 884-2656
  Mansfield (G-13316)
Mistras Group Inc ....E...... 419 227-4100
  Lima (G-12841)
National Board of Boiler ....D...... 614 888-8320
  Columbus (G-8214)
Servicelink Field Services LLC ....A...... 440 424-0058
  Solon (G-17050)
Vista Industrial Packaging LLC ....D...... 800 454-6117
  Columbus (G-8945)

INSPECTION SVCS, TRANSPORTATION

Pti Qlity Cntnment Sltions LLC ....D...... 313 304-8677
  Toledo (G-18142)
Pti Qlity Cntnment Sltions LLC ....E...... 330 306-0125
  Warren (G-18892)

INSTRUMENTS, MEASURING & CNTRL: Testing, Abrasion, Etc

Standards Testing Labs Inc ....E...... 330 833-8548
  Massillon (G-13856)

INSTRUMENTS, MEASURING & CONTROLLING: Cable Testing

Multilink Inc ....C...... 440 366-6966
  Elyria (G-10656)

INSTRUMENTS: Analytical

Bionix Safety Technologies ....E...... 419 727-0552
  Toledo (G-17773)
Dentronix Inc ....E...... 330 916-7300
  Cuyahoga Falls (G-9179)
Orton Edward Jr Crmic Fndation ....E...... 614 895-2663
  Westerville (G-19339)
Reid Asset Management Company ....E...... 216 642-3223
  Cleveland (G-6368)
Teledyne Instruments Inc ....E...... 513 229-7000
  Mason (G-13767)
Teledyne Tekmar Company ....E...... 513 229-7000
  Mason (G-13768)

INSTRUMENTS: Eye Examination

Eye Center ....E...... 614 228-3937
  Columbus (G-7625)

INSTRUMENTS: Indl Process Control

ABB Inc ....C...... 440 585-8500
  Cleveland (G-4944)
Airmate Company ....D...... 419 636-3184
  Bryan (G-2000)
Chandler Systems Incorporated ....D...... 888 363-9434
  Ashland (G-673)
Ingersoll-Rand Company ....E...... 419 633-6800
  Bryan (G-2008)
Innovative Controls Corp ....D...... 419 691-6684
  Toledo (G-17974)
Parker-Hannifin Corporation ....A...... 216 531-3000
  Cleveland (G-6241)
Production Design Services Inc ....D...... 937 866-3377
  Dayton (G-9832)
Stock Fairfield Corporation ....C...... 440 543-6000
  Chagrin Falls (G-2735)

INSTRUMENTS: Measurement, Indl Process

Command Alkon Incorporated ....D...... 614 799-0600
  Dublin (G-10302)

INSTRUMENTS: Measuring & Controlling

Aclara Technologies LLC ....C...... 440 528-7200
  Solon (G-16969)
AT&T Government Solutions Inc ....D...... 937 306-3030
  Beavercreek (G-1149)
Bionix Safety Technologies ....E...... 419 727-0552
  Toledo (G-17773)
Matrix Research Inc ....E...... 937 427-8433
  Beavercreek (G-1190)
Super Systems Inc ....E...... 513 772-0060
  Cincinnati (G-4602)
Tech Pro Inc ....E...... 330 923-3546
  Akron (G-473)
Tech Products Corporation ....E...... 937 438-1100
  Miamisburg (G-14355)
Tegam Inc ....E...... 440 466-6100
  Geneva (G-11369)
Teledyne Instruments Inc ....E...... 513 229-7000
  Mason (G-13767)
Teledyne Tekmar Company ....E...... 513 229-7000
  Mason (G-13768)

INSTRUMENTS: Measuring Electricity

Aclara Technologies LLC ....C...... 440 528-7200
  Solon (G-16969)
Hughes Corporation ....E...... 440 238-2550
  Strongsville (G-17473)
Keithley Instruments LLC ....C...... 440 248-0400
  Solon (G-17021)
Orton Edward Jr Crmic Fndation ....E...... 614 895-2663
  Westerville (G-19339)
Tech Pro Inc ....E...... 330 923-3546
  Akron (G-473)

INSTRUMENTS: Measuring, Electrical Energy

Drs Signal Technologies Inc ....E...... 937 429-7470
  Beavercreek (G-1169)

INSTRUMENTS: Medical & Surgical

Applied Medical Technology Inc ....E...... 440 717-4000
  Brecksville (G-1813)
Casco Mfg Solutions Inc ....D...... 513 681-0003
  Cincinnati (G-3191)
Dentronix Inc ....E...... 330 916-7300
  Cuyahoga Falls (G-9179)
General Data Company Inc ....C...... 513 752-7978
  Cincinnati (G-2916)
Morris Technologies Inc ....C...... 513 733-1611
  Cincinnati (G-4119)
Synergy Health North Amer Inc ....D...... 513 398-6406
  Mason (G-13766)
Thermo Fisher Scientific Inc ....C...... 800 871-8909
  Oakwood Village (G-15635)

INSTRUMENTS: Power Measuring, Electrical

TTI Floor Care North Amer Inc ....B...... 440 996-2000
  Solon (G-17061)

INSTRUMENTS: Test, Electrical, Engine

Nu-Di Products Co Inc ....D...... 216 251-9070
  Cleveland (G-6170)

INSTRUMENTS: Test, Electronic & Electric Measurement

Bionix Safety Technologies ....E...... 419 727-0552
  Toledo (G-17773)
Keithley Instruments Intl Corp ....B...... 440 248-0400
  Cleveland (G-5889)
Speelman Electric Inc ....D...... 330 633-1410
  Tallmadge (G-17650)

INSTRUMENTS: Test, Electronic & Electrical Circuits

Hannon Company ....D...... 330 456-4728
  Canton (G-2393)

INSULATION & CUSHIONING FOAM: Polystyrene

Austin Foam Plastics Inc ....E...... 614 921-0824
  Columbus (G-7075)

INSULATION MATERIALS WHOLESALERS

Alpine Insulation I LLC ....A...... 614 221-3399
  Columbus (G-6977)
CCI Supply Inc ....C...... 440 953-0045
  Mentor (G-14154)
Great Lakes Textiles Inc ....E...... 440 439-1300
  Solon (G-17012)
Installed Building Pdts Inc ....C...... 614 221-3399
  Columbus (G-7908)
R E Kramig & Co Inc ....C...... 513 761-4010
  Cincinnati (G-4378)

INSULATION: Fiberglass

Owens Corning Sales LLC ....A...... 419 248-8000
  Toledo (G-18114)

INSULATORS & INSULATION MATERIALS: Electrical

Eger Products Inc ....D...... 513 753-4200
  Amelia (G-580)

INSURANCE AGENCIES & BROKERS

American Modrn Insur Group Inc ....C...... 800 543-2644
  Amelia (G-576)
Gallagher Bassett Services ....E...... 614 764-7616
  Dublin (G-10352)
George W Mc Cloy ....D...... 614 457-6233
  Columbus (G-7744)
MetLife Auto HM Insur Agcy Inc ....A...... 815 266-5301
  Dayton (G-9722)
Metropolitan Life Insur Co ....E...... 440 746-8699
  Broadview Heights (G-1883)
Metropolitan Life Insur Co ....D...... 614 792-1463
  Dublin (G-10396)
New York Life Insurance Co ....C...... 216 520-1345
  Independence (G-12239)
New York Life Insurance Co ....D...... 513 621-9999
  Cincinnati (G-4159)
NI of Ky Inc ....E...... 216 643-7100
  Rocky River (G-16587)
Progressive Casualty Insur Co ....E...... 440 683-8164
  Cleveland (G-6313)
Progressive Corporation ....A...... 800 925-2886
  Cleveland (G-6316)
Rick Allman ....E...... 330 699-1660
  Canton (G-2514)
Seymour & Associates ....E...... 419 517-7079
  Maumee (G-13975)
State Farm General Insur Co ....D...... 740 364-5000
  Newark (G-15235)
State Farm Life Insurance Co ....D...... 937 276-1900
  Dayton (G-9905)
State Farm Mutl Auto Insur Co ....D...... 419 873-0100
  Perrysburg (G-16063)
State Farm Mutl Auto Insur Co ....D...... 216 621-3723
  Cleveland (G-6528)
State Farm Mutl Auto Insur Co ....A...... 614 775-2001
  New Albany (G-15008)
State Farm Mutl Auto Insur Co ....A...... 740 364-5000
  Newark (G-15236)
State Farm Mutl Auto Insur Co ....D...... 216 321-1422
  Cleveland (G-6529)
Uct Property Inc ....E...... 614 228-3276
  Columbus (G-8885)

Employee Codes: A=Over 500 employees, B=251-500
C=101-250, D=51-100, E=25-50

INSURANCE AGENTS, NEC

A A Hammersmith Insurance Inc .... E 330 832-7411
Massillon *(G-13781)*
A-1 General Insurance Agency .... D 216 986-3000
Cleveland *(G-4939)*
AAA Cincinnati Insurance Svc .... E 513 345-5600
Cincinnati *(G-2959)*
AAA Club Alliance Inc .... C 937 427-5884
Beavercreek *(G-1144)*
Aba Insurance Services Inc .... D 800 274-5222
Mayfield Heights *(G-13998)*
Allan Miller Insurance Agency .... E 513 863-2629
Hamilton *(G-11691)*
Allen Gardiner Deroberts .... E 614 221-1500
Columbus *(G-6966)*
Allstate Insurance Company .... E 330 650-2917
Hudson *(G-12102)*
Althans Insurance Agency Inc .... E 440 247-6422
Chagrin Falls *(G-2689)*
American Empire Surplus Lines .... E 513 369-3000
Cincinnati *(G-3002)*
American Family Home Insur Co .... D 513 943-7100
Amelia *(G-573)*
American Fidelity Assurance Co .... A 800 437-1011
Columbus *(G-6992)*
American Highways Insur Agcy .... C 330 659-8900
Richfield *(G-16496)*
American Income Life Insur Co .... D 440 582-0040
Cleveland *(G-5010)*
American Insur Administrators .... E 614 486-5388
Dublin *(G-10248)*
American Security Insurance Co .... E 937 327-7700
Springfield *(G-17147)*
Ameriprise Financial Svcs Inc .... D 614 846-8723
Worthington *(G-19940)*
Archer-Meek-Weiler Agency Inc .... E 614 212-1009
Westerville *(G-19285)*
Art Hauser Insurance Inc .... D 513 745-9200
Cincinnati *(G-3050)*
Auto-Owners Insurance Company .... D 937 432-6740
Miamisburg *(G-14273)*
Auto-Owners Life Insurance Co .... D 419 227-1452
Lima *(G-12744)*
Axa Advisors LLC .... E 513 762-7705
Cincinnati *(G-3069)*
Bowers Insurance Agency Inc .... E 330 638-6146
Cortland *(G-9073)*
Brands Insurance Agency Inc .... E 513 777-7775
West Chester *(G-19031)*
Britton-Gallagher & Assoc Inc .... D 216 658-7100
Cleveland *(G-5141)*
Brooks & Stafford Co .... E 216 696-3000
Cleveland *(G-5147)*
Bruce Klinger .... E 419 473-2270
Toledo *(G-17786)*
Brunswick Companies .... E 330 864-8800
Fairlawn *(G-10939)*
Buren Insurance Group Inc .... E 419 281-8060
Ashland *(G-668)*
Cai/Insurance Agency Inc .... E 513 221-1140
Cincinnati *(G-3165)*
Clark Theders Insurance Agency .... E 513 779-2800
West Chester *(G-19043)*
Cobos Insurance Centre LLC .... E 440 324-3732
Elyria *(G-10606)*
Colonial Lf Accident Insur Co .... B 614 793-8622
Dublin *(G-10299)*
Combined Insurance Co Amer .... D 614 210-6209
Columbus *(G-7396)*
Cornerstone Broker Ins Svcs AG .... E 513 241-7675
Cincinnati *(G-3423)*
Donald P Pipino Company Ltd .... D 330 726-8177
Youngstown *(G-20173)*
Employers Mutual Casualty Co .... D 513 221-6010
Blue Ash *(G-1585)*
Erie Indemnity Company .... D 330 433-6300
Canton *(G-2357)*
Executive Insurance Agency .... E 330 576-1234
Akron *(G-210)*
Explorer Rv Insurance Agcy Inc .... C 330 659-8900
Richfield *(G-16507)*
F W Arnold Agency Co Inc .... E 330 832-1556
Massillon *(G-13805)*
Factory Mutual Insurance Co .... D 513 742-9516
Cincinnati *(G-3588)*
Family Heritg Lf Insur Co Amer .... E 440 922-5200
Broadview Heights *(G-1879)*
Fedeli Group Inc .... D 216 328-8080
Cleveland *(G-5580)*
First Acceptance Corporation .... E 614 237-9700
Columbus *(G-7659)*
Freedom Specialty Insurance Co .... C 614 249-1545
Columbus *(G-7701)*
Galt Enterprises Inc .... E 216 464-6744
Moreland Hills *(G-14839)*
German Mutual Insurance Co .... E 419 599-3993
Napoleon *(G-14940)*
Hanover Insurance Company .... D 614 408-9000
Dublin *(G-10356)*
Hanover Insurance Company .... D 513 829-4555
Fairfield *(G-10857)*
Hartford Fire Insurance Co .... C 216 447-1000
Cleveland *(G-5729)*
Home and Farm Insurance Co .... D 937 778-5000
Piqua *(G-16149)*
Hummel Group Inc .... E 330 683-1050
Orrville *(G-15774)*
Huntington Insurance Inc .... C 419 720-7900
Toledo *(G-17966)*
Huntington Insurance Inc .... E 614 480-3800
Columbus *(G-7866)*
Huntington Insurance Inc .... E 330 430-1300
Canton *(G-2409)*
Huntington Insurance Inc .... E 330 674-2931
Millersburg *(G-14608)*
Hylant Group Inc .... E 513 985-2400
Cincinnati *(G-3805)*
Hylant Group Inc .... E 614 932-1200
Dublin *(G-10371)*
Hylant Group Inc .... C 419 255-1020
Toledo *(G-17968)*
Hylant Group Inc .... D 216 447-1050
Cleveland *(G-5797)*
Hylant-Maclean Inc .... E 614 932-1200
Dublin *(G-10372)*
Jpmorgan Chase Bank Nat Assn .... B 843 679-3653
Columbus *(G-7955)*
Knight Crockett Miller Ins .... E 419 254-2400
Toledo *(G-17996)*
Lang Financial Group Inc .... E 513 699-2966
Blue Ash *(G-1626)*
Lighthouse Insurance Group LLC .... D 216 503-2439
Independence *(G-12228)*
Louieville Title Agncy For Nrt .... D 419 248-4611
Toledo *(G-18010)*
Mc Cloy Financial Services .... D 614 457-6233
Columbus *(G-8133)*
McGohan/Brabender Agency Inc .... D 937 293-1600
Moraine *(G-14800)*
Medical Mutual of Ohio .... D 440 878-4800
Strongsville *(G-17491)*
Medical Mutual of Ohio .... B 216 292-0400
Beachwood *(G-1099)*
Motorists Mutual Insurance Co .... E 440 779-8900
North Olmsted *(G-15433)*
National Auto Care Corporation .... D 800 548-1875
Westerville *(G-19330)*
National General Insurance .... B 212 380-9462
Cleveland *(G-6108)*
Nationwide Corporation .... A 330 452-8705
Canton *(G-2471)*
Nationwide Life Insur Co Amer .... A 800 688-5177
Columbus *(G-8245)*
Nationwide Mutl Fire Insur Co .... E 614 249-7111
Columbus *(G-8246)*
Nationwide Mutual Insurance Co .... A 330 489-5000
Canton *(G-2472)*
Nb and T Insurance Agency Inc .... E 937 393-1985
Hillsboro *(G-11990)*
New England Life Insurance Co .... E 614 457-6233
Columbus *(G-8272)*
Nl of Ky Inc .... E 614 224-0772
Columbus *(G-8283)*
Ohio National Life Assurance .... A 513 794-6100
Montgomery *(G-14731)*
Phelan Insurance Agency Inc .... E 800 843-3069
Versailles *(G-18727)*
Postema Insurance & Investment .... E 419 782-2500
Defiance *(G-10052)*
R L King Insurance Agency .... E 419 255-9947
Holland *(G-12049)*
Rankin & Rankin Inc .... E 740 452-7575
Zanesville *(G-20528)*
Rick Blazing Insurance Agency .... E 513 677-8300
Cincinnati *(G-4417)*
Schauer Group Incorporated .... E 330 453-7721
Canton *(G-2523)*
Schwendeman Agency Inc .... E 740 373-6793
Marietta *(G-13496)*
Seibert-Keck Insurance Agency .... E 330 867-3140
Fairlawn *(G-10974)*
Self-Funded Plans Inc .... E 216 566-1455
Cleveland *(G-6468)*
Selman & Company .... D 440 646-9336
Cleveland *(G-6469)*
State Auto Prperty Cslty Insur .... E 440 842-6200
Strongsville *(G-17511)*
Steele W W Jr Agency Inc .... E 330 453-7721
Canton *(G-2549)*
Stolly Insurance Agency Inc .... E 419 227-2570
Lima *(G-12893)*
Support Insur Systems Agcy Inc .... E 937 434-5700
Centerville *(G-2687)*
Todd Associates Inc .... D 440 461-1101
Beachwood *(G-1132)*
Travelers Property Cslty Corp .... E 513 639-5300
Cincinnati *(G-4682)*
Travelers Property Cslty Corp .... C 216 643-2100
Cleveland *(G-6615)*
United Agencies Inc .... E 216 696-8044
Cleveland *(G-6632)*
UNUM Life Insurance Co Amer .... E 614 807-2500
Columbus *(G-8911)*
Usi Inc .... D 419 243-1191
Toledo *(G-18284)*
Vision Service Plan .... C 614 471-7511
Columbus *(G-8944)*
W P Dolle LLC .... E 513 421-6515
Cincinnati *(G-4821)*
Wabe Maquaw Holdings Inc .... D 419 243-1191
Toledo *(G-18297)*
Wallace & Turner Insurance Inc .... E 937 324-8492
Springfield *(G-17294)*
Western & Southern Lf Insur Co .... E 234 380-4525
Hudson *(G-12151)*
William D Taylor Sr Inc .... D 614 653-6683
Etna *(G-10740)*
Wilmared Inc .... E 513 891-6615
Loveland *(G-13166)*
Zurich American Insurance Co .... E 216 328-9400
Independence *(G-12279)*

INSURANCE BROKERS, NEC

American Risk Services LLC .... E 513 772-3712
Cincinnati *(G-3013)*
AON Consulting Inc .... E 614 436-8100
Columbus *(G-7023)*
AON Consulting Inc .... D 614 847-4670
Columbus *(G-7024)*
AON Consulting Inc .... E 216 621-8100
Cleveland *(G-5046)*
AON Risk Svcs Northeast Inc .... A 216 621-8100
Cleveland *(G-5047)*
Arthur J Gallagher & Co .... E 513 977-3100
Cincinnati *(G-3051)*
Benefit ADM Agcy LLC .... E 614 791-1143
Dublin *(G-10262)*
Employers Select Plan Agcy Inc .... E 216 642-4200
Independence *(G-12208)*
Forge Industries Inc .... A 330 782-8301
Youngstown *(G-20191)*
Hyatt Legal Plans Inc .... D 216 241-0022
Cleveland *(G-5796)*
Insurance Intermediaries Inc .... D 614 846-1111
Columbus *(G-7911)*
Kellison & Co .... D 216 464-5160
Cleveland *(G-5892)*
Marsh & McLennan Agency LLC .... E 513 248-4888
Loveland *(G-13143)*
Marsh & McLennan Agency LLC .... C 937 228-4135
Dayton *(G-9699)*
Marsh USA Inc .... B 216 937-1700
Cleveland *(G-5985)*
Marsh USA Inc .... D 513 287-1600
Cincinnati *(G-4027)*
Marsh USA Inc .... D 614 227-6200
Columbus *(G-8119)*
Marsh USA Inc .... D 216 830-8000
Cleveland *(G-5986)*
Ohio Mutual Insurance Company .... C 419 562-3011
Bucyrus *(G-2046)*
Richfield Financial Group Inc .... E 440 546-4288
Brecksville *(G-1847)*
Stephens-Matthews Mktg Inc .... E 740 984-8011
Beverly *(G-1493)*
Wellington F Roemer Insurance .... E 419 473-0258
Toledo *(G-18301)*

SERVICES SECTION

INSURANCE CARRIERS: Automobile

Company	Code	Phone
American Commerce Insurance Co Columbus (G-6986)	C	614 272-6951
Geico General Insurance Co Cincinnati (G-3666)	B	513 794-3426
Grange Mutual Casualty Company Columbus (G-7769)	A	614 445-2900
Ohio Casualty Insurance Co Hamilton (G-11761)	C	513 867-3000
Ohio Indemnity Company Columbus (G-8355)	E	614 228-1601
Progressive Casualty Insur Co Cleveland (G-6314)	D	440 603-4033
Progressive Select Insur Co Cleveland (G-6322)	A	440 461-5000
Safe Auto Insurance Company Woodsfield (G-19819)	C	740 472-1900
Safe Auto Insurance Group Inc Columbus (G-8669)	D	614 231-0200
Verti Insurance Company Columbus (G-8936)	D	844 448-3784

INSURANCE CARRIERS: Bank Deposit

Company	Code	Phone
American Contrs Indemnity Co Cincinnati (G-3001)	E	513 688-0800

INSURANCE CARRIERS: Direct Accident & Health

Company	Code	Phone
1-888 Ohio Comp LLC Cleveland (G-4918)	D	216 426-0646
American Financial Group Inc Cincinnati (G-3006)	C	513 579-2121
J P Farley Corporation Westlake (G-19501)	E	440 250-4300
James B Oswald Company Medina (G-14085)	E	330 723-3637
Medical Bnfits Admnstrtors Inc Newark (G-15205)	D	740 522-8425
Progressive Casualty Insur Co Mayfield Village (G-14012)	A	440 461-5000
Signature Healthcare LLC Bedford (G-1336)	C	440 232-1800
State Farm Mutl Auto Insur Co New Albany (G-15008)	A	614 775-2001
Transamerica Premier Lf Insur Columbus (G-8864)	E	614 488-5983

INSURANCE CARRIERS: Hospital & Medical

Company	Code	Phone
Amerigroup Ohio Inc Blue Ash (G-1532)	E	513 733-2300
Anthem Insurance Companies Inc Worthington (G-19941)	D	614 438-3542
Aultman Hospital Canton (G-2255)	A	330 363-6262
Clinical Research Center Cincinnati (G-3366)	D	513 636-4412
Close To Home Health Care Ctr Dublin (G-10296)	E	614 932-9013
Community Insurance Company Cincinnati (G-3401)	E	859 282-7888
Custom Design Benefits Inc Cincinnati (G-3451)	E	513 598-2929
Dcp Holding Company Sharonville (G-16881)	D	513 554-1100
Deaconess Associations Inc Cincinnati (G-3471)	B	513 559-2100
Ebso Inc Findlay (G-11021)	E	419 423-3823
Ebso Inc Cleveland (G-5525)	E	440 262-1133
Firelands Regional Health Sys Sandusky (G-16758)	C	419 626-7400
Healthspan Integrated Care Cleveland (G-5740)	E	216 621-5600
Healthspan Integrated Care Cleveland (G-5741)	E	216 524-7377
Healthspan Integrated Care Brewster (G-1855)	E	330 767-3436
Healthspan Integrated Care Twinsburg (G-18428)	E	330 486-2800
Healthspan Integrated Care Hartville (G-11821)	E	330 877-4018
Healthspan Integrated Care Wadsworth (G-18754)	E	330 334-1549
Healthspan Integrated Care Akron (G-261)	E	330 633-8400
Healthspan Integrated Care Lakewood (G-12481)	E	216 362-2277
J P Farley Corporation Westlake (G-19501)	E	440 250-4300
Medical Mutual of Ohio Cleveland (G-6015)	A	216 687-7000
Medical Mutual of Ohio Toledo (G-18049)	B	419 473-7100
Metrohealth System Cleveland (G-6042)	E	216 778-3867
Miami Valley Hospitalist Group Dayton (G-9734)	D	937 208-8394
Molina Healthcare Inc Columbus (G-8183)	A	800 642-4168
Vitamin Shoppe Inc Strongsville (G-17522)	E	440 238-5987

INSURANCE CARRIERS: Life

Company	Code	Phone
21st Century Financial Inc Akron (G-9)	E	330 668-9065
Allstate Insurance Company Hudson (G-12102)	E	330 650-2917
American Financial Group Inc Cincinnati (G-3006)	C	513 579-2121
Ameritas Life Insurance Corp Cincinnati (G-3015)	E	513 595-2334
Bankers Life & Casualty Co Columbus (G-6870)	E	614 987-0590
Cincinnati Life Insurance Co Fairfield (G-10836)	A	513 870-2000
Columbus Financial Gr Columbus (G-6877)	E	614 785-5100
Farmers Group Inc Columbus (G-7638)	C	614 406-2424
Grange Indemnity Insurance Co Columbus (G-7767)	D	614 445-2900
Grange Life Insurance Company Columbus (G-7768)	E	800 445-3030
Guardian Life Insur Co of Amer Cincinnati (G-3716)	E	513 579-1114
Home Loan Financial Corp Coshocton (G-9106)	E	740 622-0444
Howard Hanna Smythe Cramer Medina (G-14078)	D	330 725-4137
Hylant Administrative Services Toledo (G-17967)	E	419 255-1020
J P Farley Corporation Westlake (G-19501)	E	440 250-4300
Kelley Companies Copley (G-9057)	D	330 668-6100
Lafayette Life Insurance Co Cincinnati (G-3958)	E	800 443-8793
Loyal American Life Insur Co	C	800 633-6752
Massachusetts Mutl Lf Insur Co Cincinnati (G-4028)	E	513 579-8555
Massachusetts Mutl Lf Insur Co Cleveland (G-5993)	E	216 592-7359
Motorists Life Insurance Co Columbus (G-8192)	E	614 225-8211
Nationwide Financial Svcs Inc Columbus (G-8242)	C	614 249-7111
Nationwide General Insur Co Columbus (G-8243)	D	614 249-7111
Nationwide Mutual Insurance Co Lewis Center (G-12697)	E	614 430-3047
New York Life Insurance Co Lakewood (G-12492)	D	216 221-1100
Northwestern Mutl Lf Insur Co Columbus (G-8299)	E	614 221-5287
Ohio Pia Service Corporation Gahanna (G-11261)	E	614 552-8000
Penn Mutual Life Insurance Co Akron (G-381)	E	330 668-9065
Progressive Bayside Insur Co Cleveland (G-6312)	B	440 395-4460
Sirak Financial Services Canton (G-2529)	D	330 493-3211
State Farm Mutl Auto Insur Co New Albany (G-15008)	A	614 775-2001
Summa Insurance Company Inc Akron (G-462)	B	800 996-8411
Ulysses Caremark Holding Corp Solon (G-17063)	C	440 542-4214
Voya Financial Inc Columbus (G-8953)	E	614 431-5000
Western & Southern Lf Insur Co Grove City (G-11615)	E	614 277-4800
Western & Southern Lf Insur Co Ontario (G-15720)	E	419 524-1800
Western & Southern Lf Insur Co Cincinnati (G-4839)	A	513 629-1800
Western & Southern Lf Insur Co Hudson (G-12151)	E	234 380-4525

INSURANCE CARRIERS: Pet, Health

Company	Code	Phone
Hartville Group Inc Akron (G-254)	E	330 484-8166
Ohio Farmers Insurance Company Canton (G-2479)	C	330 484-5660

INSURANCE CARRIERS: Property & Casualty

Company	Code	Phone
Affiliated FM Insurance Co North Olmsted (G-15409)	E	216 362-4820
American Financial Group Inc Cincinnati (G-3006)	C	513 579-2121
American Modern Home Insur Co Amelia (G-574)	E	513 943-7100
American Select Insurance Co Westfield Center (G-19451)	A	330 887-0101
American Western Home Insur Co Amelia (G-577)	B	513 943-7100
Central Mutual Insurance Co Van Wert (G-18629)	B	419 238-1010
Cincinnati Financial Corp Fairfield (G-10833)	A	513 870-2000
Farmers Group Inc Columbus (G-7638)	C	614 406-2424
Foremost Insurance Company Independence (G-12212)	E	216 674-7000
Grange Mutual Casualty Company Cincinnati (G-3692)	A	513 671-3722
Great American Insurance Co Cincinnati (G-3697)	A	513 369-5000
Great American Insurance Co Fairfield (G-10853)	D	513 603-2570
Great American Insurance Co Cincinnati (G-3698)	D	513 763-7035
Home and Farm Insurance Co Piqua (G-16149)	D	937 778-5000
James B Oswald Company Medina (G-14085)	E	330 723-3637
Lancer Insurance Company Cleveland (G-5925)	E	440 473-1634
Liberty Mutual Insurance Co Gahanna (G-11253)	E	614 864-4100
Liberty Mutual Insurance Co Westerville (G-19325)	E	614 855-6193
Liberty Mutual Insurance Co Blue Ash (G-1628)	E	513 984-0550
Motorists Mutual Insurance Co Uniontown (G-18529)	E	330 896-9311
National Interstate Corp Richfield (G-16515)	D	330 659-8900
National Interstate Insur Co Richfield (G-16516)	C	330 659-8900
Nationwide General Insur Co Columbus (G-8243)	D	614 249-7111
Ohio Casualty Insurance Co Fairfield (G-10887)	A	800 843-6446
Ohio Farmers Insurance Company Westfield Center (G-19452)	A	800 243-0210
Ohio National Life Insur Co Montgomery (G-14732)	D	513 794-6100
Progressive Agency Inc Cleveland (G-6311)	C	440 461-5000
Progressive Casualty Insur Co Mayfield Village (G-14012)	A	440 461-5000
Progressive Casualty Insur Co Cleveland (G-6313)	E	440 683-8164
Progressive Choice Insur Co Cleveland (G-6315)	A	440 461-5000
Progressive Corporation Cleveland (G-6317)	B	440 461-5000
Progressive Max Insurance Co Youngstown (G-20329)	E	330 533-8733
Progressive Northwestern Insur Cleveland (G-6319)	E	440 461-5000
State Auto Financial Corp Columbus (G-8780)	E	614 464-5000
Wayne Mutual Insurance Co Wooster (G-19924)	E	330 345-8100

INSURANCE CARRIERS: Title

Company	Code	Phone
A R E A Title Agency Inc Toledo (G-17735)	E	419 242-5485
Barristers of Ohio LLC Warren (G-18828)	E	330 898-5600
First Amrcn Cash Advnce SC LLC Akron (G-224)	D	330 644-9144

Employee Codes: A=Over 500 employees, B=251-500
C=101-250, D=51-100, E=25-50

2018 Harris Ohio Services Directory

INSURANCE CARRIERS: Title

Howard Hanna Smythe Cramer ....D....... 330 725-4137
   Medina *(G-14078)*
Mortgage Information Services ....D....... 216 514-7480
   Cleveland *(G-6078)*
Northwest Hts Title Agcy LLC ....E....... 614 451-6313
   Columbus *(G-8296)*
Northwest Ttl Agy of OH MI In ....D....... 419 241-8195
   Toledo *(G-18096)*
Omega Title Agency LLC ....D....... 330 436-0600
   Stow *(G-17384)*
Service Center Title Agency 937 312-3080
   Dayton *(G-9877)*
Southern Title of Ohio Ltd ....E....... 419 525-4600
   Mansfield *(G-13365)*
Sterling Land Title Agency ....E....... 513 755-3700
   West Chester *(G-19160)*
Stewart Advnced Land Title Ltd ....E....... 513 753-2800
   Cincinnati *(G-2933)*

INSURANCE CARRIERS: Worker's Compensation

Amtrust North America Inc ....C....... 216 328-6100
   Cleveland *(G-5032)*
Broadspire Services Inc ....E....... 614 436-8990
   Columbus *(G-7148)*
Occupational Health Link ....E....... 614 885-0039
   Columbus *(G-8312)*
Seven Hills Fireman Assn 216 524-3321
   Seven Hills *(G-16836)*
Workers Compensation Ohio Bur ....A....... 614 644-6292
   Columbus *(G-9007)*

INSURANCE CLAIM ADJUSTERS, NOT EMPLOYED BY INSURANCE COMPANY

Ohic Insurance Company ....D....... 614 221-7777
   Columbus *(G-8315)*
Supreme Court of Ohio ....E....... 614 387-9800
   Columbus *(G-8809)*
York Risk Services Group Inc ....E....... 440 863-2500
   Cleveland *(G-6771)*

INSURANCE CLAIM PROCESSING, EXC MEDICAL

Amtrust North America Inc ....C....... 216 328-6100
   Cleveland *(G-5032)*
Envision Phrm Svcs LLC ....B....... 330 405-8080
   Twinsburg *(G-18411)*
Grange Mutual Casualty Company ....E....... 614 337-4400
   Cleveland *(G-5686)*
Harrington Health Services Inc ....C....... 614 212-7000
   Westerville *(G-19406)*
Infoquest Information Services ....E....... 614 761-3003
   Columbus *(G-7895)*
Safelite Group Inc ....A....... 614 210-9000
   Columbus *(G-8672)*

INSURANCE EDUCATION SVCS

Keybank National Association ....C....... 216 813-0000
   Cleveland *(G-5901)*

INSURANCE INFORMATION & CONSULTING SVCS

Business Admnstrators Cons Inc ....E....... 614 863-8780
   Reynoldsburg *(G-16433)*
Chapman & Chapman Inc ....E....... 440 934-4102
   Avon *(G-887)*
Gallagher Benefit Services Inc ....E....... 216 623-2600
   Cleveland *(G-5652)*
Pasco Inc ....B....... 330 650-0613
   Hudson *(G-12138)*
Paul Moss LLC ....E....... 216 765-1580
   Solon *(G-17038)*

INSURANCE RESEARCH SVCS

Strategic Research Group Inc ....E....... 614 220-8860
   Columbus *(G-8795)*
Ues Metals Group ....E....... 937 255-9340
   Beavercreek *(G-1214)*

INSURANCE: Agents, Brokers & Service

Ability Network Inc ....E....... 513 943-8888
   Cincinnati *(G-2901)*
Advanced Group Corp ....E....... 216 431-8800
   Cleveland *(G-4959)*
AFLAC Incorporated ....C....... 614 410-1696
   Columbus *(G-6954)*
All America Insurance Company ....B....... 419 238-1010
   Van Wert *(G-18627)*
Allan Peace & Associates Inc ....E....... 513 579-1700
   Cincinnati *(G-2986)*
Allstate Insurance Company ....D....... 330 656-6000
   Hudson *(G-12103)*
Alpha Investment Partnership ....D....... 513 621-1826
   Cincinnati *(G-2994)*
Alternative Care Mgt Systems ....E....... 614 761-0035
   Dublin *(G-10243)*
American Gen Lf Insur Co Del ....E....... 513 762-7807
   Cincinnati *(G-3007)*
American Title of Ohio LLC ....E....... 303 868-2250
   Cleveland *(G-5024)*
Anthem Midwest Inc ....A....... 614 433-8350
   Mason *(G-13663)*
Axa Advisors LLC ....D....... 216 621-7715
   Cleveland *(G-5087)*
Brown & Brown of Ohio LLC ....C....... 419 874-1974
   Perrysburg *(G-15981)*
Careworks of Ohio Inc ....B....... 614 792-1085
   Dublin *(G-10280)*
Cincinnati Equitable Insur Co ....E....... 440 349-2210
   Solon *(G-16991)*
Columbus Life Insurance Co ....D....... 513 361-6700
   Cincinnati *(G-3390)*
Compmanagement Inc ....E....... 614 376-5300
   Dublin *(G-10306)*
Corporate Health Benefits ....E....... 740 348-1401
   Newark *(G-15161)*
Corporate Plans Inc ....E....... 440 542-7800
   Solon *(G-16995)*
CSC Insurance Agency Inc ....D....... 614 895-2000
   Westerville *(G-19294)*
Defense Info Systems Agcy ....C....... 614 692-4433
   Columbus *(G-7502)*
Ebso Inc ....E....... 419 423-3823
   Findlay *(G-11021)*
Employee Benefit Management ....E....... 614 766-5800
   Dublin *(G-10336)*
Erie Insurance Exchange ....D....... 614 430-8530
   Columbus *(G-7604)*
Farmers Financial Services ....E....... 937 424-0643
   Beavercreek *(G-1240)*
Farmers Group Inc ....E....... 330 467-6575
   Northfield *(G-15515)*
Farmers Group Inc ....E....... 614 766-6005
   Columbus *(G-7639)*
Farmers Group Inc ....E....... 614 799-3200
   Columbus *(G-7640)*
Farmers Group Inc ....E....... 216 750-4010
   Independence *(G-12211)*
Farmers Insurance of Columbus ....B....... 614 799-3200
   Columbus *(G-7641)*
Farmers New World Lf Insur Co ....C....... 614 764-9975
   Columbus *(G-7642)*
Federal Insurance Company ....E....... 216 687-1700
   Cleveland *(G-5581)*
Federal Insurance Company ....E....... 513 721-0601
   Cincinnati *(G-3598)*
Financial Design Group Inc ....E....... 419 843-4737
   Toledo *(G-17889)*
First Acceptance Corporation ....E....... 937 778-8888
   Piqua *(G-16144)*
First Acceptance Corporation ....E....... 513 741-0811
   Cincinnati *(G-3613)*
First Acceptance Corporation ....E....... 614 492-1446
   Columbus *(G-7660)*
First Acceptance Corporation ....E....... 330 792-7181
   Youngstown *(G-20188)*
First Acceptance Corporation ....E....... 614 853-3344
   Columbus *(G-7661)*
First Defiance Financial Corp ....E....... 419 353-8611
   Bowling Green *(G-1776)*
Great American Advisors Inc ....E....... 513 357-3300
   Cincinnati *(G-3696)*
Guardian Business Services ....E....... 614 416-6090
   Columbus *(G-7781)*
Huntington Insurance Inc ....E....... 216 206-1787
   Cleveland *(G-5790)*
Huntington Insurance Inc ....E....... 330 262-6611
   Wooster *(G-19873)*
Huntington Insurance Inc ....D....... 614 899-8500
   Columbus *(G-7867)*
Huntington Insurance Inc ....E....... 330 337-9933
   Salem *(G-16700)*
International Healthcare Corp ....D....... 513 731-3338
   Cincinnati *(G-3836)*
James B Oswald Company ....E....... 330 723-3637
   Medina *(G-14085)*
Leonard Insur Svcs Agcy Inc ....E....... 330 266-1904
   Canton *(G-2433)*
Licking Memorial Hlth Systems ....A....... 220 564-4000
   Newark *(G-15191)*
Life Insurance Mktg Co Inc ....E....... 330 867-1707
   Akron *(G-318)*
Lincoln Fincl Advisors Corp ....D....... 614 888-6516
   Columbus *(G-8069)*
Luce Smith & Scott Inc ....E....... 440 746-1700
   Brecksville *(G-1832)*
Masters Agency Inc ....E....... 330 805-5985
   Wadsworth *(G-18764)*
Motorists Mutual Insurance Co ....E....... 937 435-5540
   Dayton *(G-9759)*
Nationwide Corporation ....E....... 614 249-7111
   Columbus *(G-8238)*
Nationwide Corporation ....D....... 614 249-4302
   Columbus *(G-8239)*
Nationwide Corporation ....B....... 614 277-5103
   Grove City *(G-11583)*
Nationwide Mutual Insurance Co ....E....... 614 948-4153
   Westerville *(G-19332)*
Nationwide Rtirement Solutions ....C....... 614 854-8300
   Dublin *(G-10405)*
Neace Assoc Insur Agcy of Ohio ....E....... 614 224-0772
   Columbus *(G-8255)*
NI of Ky Inc ....E....... 740 689-9876
   Lancaster *(G-12562)*
Northwestern Mutl Lf Insur Co ....D....... 513 366-3600
   Cincinnati *(G-4183)*
Northwstern Ohio Admnistrators 419 248-2401
   Holland *(G-12042)*
Ohio Indemnity Company ....E....... 614 228-1601
   Columbus *(G-8355)*
Old Rpblic Ttle Nthrn Ohio LLC ....A....... 216 524-5700
   Independence *(G-12242)*
Progressive Casualty Insur Co ....A....... 440 461-5000
   Mayfield Village *(G-14012)*
Progressive Hawaii Insurance C ....C....... 440 461-5000
   Cleveland *(G-6318)*
Progressive Premier Insurance ....C....... 440 461-5000
   Cleveland *(G-6321)*
Prudential Insur Co of Amer ....E....... 513 612-6400
   Cincinnati *(G-4353)*
Prudential Insur Co of Amer ....E....... 330 896-7200
   Uniontown *(G-18533)*
Prudential Insur Co of Amer ....E....... 440 684-4409
   Cleveland *(G-6327)*
Prudential Insur Co of Amer ....E....... 419 893-6227
   Maumee *(G-13962)*
Royalton Financial Group ....E....... 440 582-3020
   Cleveland *(G-6419)*
Safe Auto Insurance Company ....B....... 614 231-0200
   Columbus *(G-8668)*
Safe Auto Insurance Group Inc ....B....... 614 231-0200
   Columbus *(G-8669)*
Sbm Business Services Inc ....E....... 330 396-7000
   Akron *(G-429)*
Sirak-Moore Insurance Agcy Inc ....E....... 330 493-3211
   Canton *(G-2531)*
Smart ....C....... 216 228-9400
   North Olmsted *(G-15444)*
State Automobile Mutl Insur Co ....A....... 833 724-3577
   Columbus *(G-8781)*
Thomas Gentz ....E....... 513 247-7300
   Cincinnati *(G-4652)*
United Insurance Company Amer ....E....... 513 771-6771
   Cincinnati *(G-4733)*
United Insurance Company Amer ....E....... 419 531-4289
   Toledo *(G-18270)*
United Insurance Company Amer ....E....... 216 514-1904
   Beachwood *(G-1134)*
United Ohio Insurance Company ....C....... 419 562-3011
   Bucyrus *(G-2050)*
USI Insurance Services Nat ....E....... 614 228-5565
   Columbus *(G-8927)*
USI Midwest LLC ....C....... 513 852-6300
   Cincinnati *(G-4798)*
Valmark Insurance Agency LLC ....D....... 330 576-1234
   Akron *(G-492)*
Voya Financial Inc ....E....... 614 431-5000
   Columbus *(G-8953)*
Willis of Ohio Inc ....E....... 614 457-7000
   Columbus *(G-8997)*
Workers Compensation Ohio Bur ....A....... 800 644-6292
   Columbus *(G-9006)*
York Risk Services Group Inc ....C....... 866 391-9675
   Dublin *(G-10497)*

SERVICES SECTION

INTERCOMMUNICATIONS SYSTEMS:
Electric

Quasonix Inc .... E 513 942-1287
   West Chester *(G-19135)*

INTERIOR DECORATING SVCS

Flamos Enterprises Inc .... E 330 478-0009
   Canton *(G-2369)*
Karlsberger Companies .... C 614 461-9500
   Columbus *(G-7966)*

INTERIOR DESIGN SVCS, NEC

Dlr Group Inc .... D 216 522-1350
   Cleveland *(G-5495)*
G Herschman Architects Inc .... D 216 223-3200
   Cleveland *(G-5645)*
Interbrand Design Forum Inc .... C 937 439-4400
   Cincinnati *(G-3834)*
Interior Supply Cincinnati LLC .... E 614 424-6611
   Columbus *(G-7915)*
Rdl Architects Inc .... E 216 752-4300
   Cleveland *(G-6356)*
Rite Rug Co .... E 614 478-3365
   Columbus *(G-8632)*
River City Furniture LLC .... D 513 612-7303
   West Chester *(G-19141)*
Vocon Design Inc .... D 216 588-0800
   Cleveland *(G-6710)*

INTERIOR DESIGNING SVCS

Chute Gerdeman Inc .... D 614 469-1001
   Columbus *(G-7271)*
CIP International Inc .... D 513 874-9925
   West Chester *(G-19041)*
Collaborative Inc .... E 419 242-7405
   Toledo *(G-17819)*
E & A Pedco Services Inc .... D 513 782-4920
   Cincinnati *(G-3519)*
Jones Group Interiors Inc .... E 330 253-9180
   Akron *(G-297)*
Michael Schuster Associates .... E 513 241-5666
   Cincinnati *(G-4089)*
Ohio Design Centre .... D 216 831-1245
   Beachwood *(G-1111)*

INTERMEDIATE CARE FACILITY

10 Wilmington Place .... D 937 253-1010
   Dayton *(G-9291)*
A M Mc Gregor Home .... B 216 851-8200
   Cleveland *(G-4933)*
A Provide Care Inc .... C 330 828-2278
   Dalton *(G-9239)*
Advance Care Inc .... D 513 932-1121
   Lebanon *(G-12588)*
Alexson Services Inc .... B 513 874-0423
   Fairfield *(G-10819)*
Algart Health Care Inc .... D 216 631-1550
   Cleveland *(G-4985)*
Alpha Nursing Homes Inc .... C 740 345-9197
   Newark *(G-15142)*
Alpha Nursing Homes Inc .... D 740 622-2074
   Coshocton *(G-9086)*
Altercare Inc .... C 330 335-2555
   Wadsworth *(G-18746)*
Altercare Nobles Pond Inc .... D 330 834-4800
   Canton *(G-2235)*
Alternative Residences Two .... C 740 526-0514
   Saint Clairsville *(G-16616)*
Alternative Residences Two .... E 330 453-0200
   Canton *(G-2236)*
American Retirement Corp .... D 216 291-6140
   Cleveland *(G-5021)*
Amherst Manor Nursing Home .... D 440 988-4415
   Amherst *(G-588)*
Anchor Lodge Nursing Home Inc ..... C 440 244-2019
   Lorain *(G-13012)*
Anne Grady Corporation .... C 419 380-8985
   Holland *(G-12009)*
Apostolic Christian Home Inc .... D 330 927-1010
   Rittman *(G-16550)*
Arbors East LLC .... C 614 575-9003
   Columbus *(G-7033)*
Arlington Care Ctr .... C 740 344-0303
   Newark *(G-15143)*
Arlington Court Nursing .... C 614 545-5502
   Upper Arlington *(G-18547)*

Audrich Inc .... C 419 483-6225
   Bellevue *(G-1403)*
Baptist Home and Center .... C 513 662-5880
   Cincinnati *(G-3076)*
Bel Air Care Center .... D 330 821-3939
   Alliance *(G-527)*
Bittersweet Inc .... D 419 875-6986
   Whitehouse *(G-19584)*
Blossom Hills Nursing Home .... D 440 635-5567
   Huntsburg *(G-12157)*
Braeview Manor Inc .... C 216 486-9300
   Cleveland *(G-5132)*
Brethren Care Inc .... C 419 289-0803
   Ashland *(G-666)*
Brewster Parke Inc .... D 330 767-4179
   Brewster *(G-1854)*
Briarfield At Ashley Circle .... C 330 793-3010
   Youngstown *(G-20125)*
Brook Willow Chrstn Cmmunities ..... C 614 885-3300
   Columbus *(G-7151)*
Brookville Enterprises Inc .... B 937 833-2133
   Brookville *(G-1960)*
Butler County of Ohio .... C 513 887-3728
   Fairfield Township *(G-10926)*
Butler County Board of Develop ...... E 513 867-5913
   Fairfield *(G-10826)*
C R G Health Care Systems .... E 330 498-8107
   Niles *(G-15285)*
Camargo Manor Inc .... D 513 605-3000
   Cincinnati *(G-3169)*
Canton Assisted Living .... C 330 492-7131
   Canton *(G-2282)*
Capital Senior Living Corp .... B 513 829-6200
   Fairfield *(G-10829)*
Caprice Health Care Inc .... C 330 965-9200
   North Lima *(G-15400)*
Cardinal Retirement Village .... E 330 928-7888
   Cuyahoga Falls *(G-9168)*
Carington Health Systems .... C 937 743-2754
   Franklin *(G-11151)*
Carriage Crt Mrysvlle Ltd Prtn .... E 937 642-2202
   Marysville *(G-13609)*
Carroll Golden Age Retreat .... E 330 627-4665
   Carrollton *(G-2612)*
Carroll Health Care Center .... C 330 627-5501
   Carrollton *(G-2613)*
Center Ridge Nursing Home Inc ...... C 440 327-1295
   North Ridgeville *(G-15458)*
Chelmsford Apartments Ltd .... E 419 389-0800
   Toledo *(G-17803)*
Childs Investment Co .... D 330 837-2100
   Massillon *(G-13794)*
Choices In Community Living .... C 937 898-3655
   Dayton *(G-9405)*
Church of God Retirement Cmnty .... C 513 422-5600
   Middletown *(G-14420)*
Columbus Area Integrated Healt ..... D 614 252-0711
   Columbus *(G-7330)*
Commons of Providence .... D 419 624-1171
   Sandusky *(G-16744)*
Communicare Health Svcs Inc .... D 419 394-7611
   Saint Marys *(G-16672)*
Concord Health Care Inc .... C 419 626-5373
   Sandusky *(G-16746)*
Concord Health Care Inc .... E 330 759-2357
   Youngstown *(G-20160)*
Congregate Living of America .... E 937 393-6700
   Hillsboro *(G-11969)*
Congregate Living of America .... D 513 899-2801
   Morrow *(G-14845)*
Consulate Healthcare Inc .... E 419 865-1248
   Maumee *(G-13899)*
Consulate Management Co LLC ..... D 440 237-7966
   Cleveland *(G-5398)*
Country Club Center Homes Inc ..... D 330 343-6351
   Dover *(G-10182)*
Country Club Center II Ltd .... C 740 397-2350
   Mount Vernon *(G-14886)*
Country Club Retirement Center ..... C 740 671-9330
   Bellaire *(G-1365)*
County of Lorain .... C 440 282-3074
   Lorain *(G-13034)*
County of Shelby .... C 937 492-6900
   Sidney *(G-16926)*
County of Wood .... B 419 686-6951
   Portage *(G-16261)*
Covenant Care Ohio Inc .... D 937 878-7046
   Fairborn *(G-10788)*
Cridersville Health Care Ctr .... E 419 645-4468
   Cridersville *(G-9151)*

INTERMEDIATE CARE FACILITY

Crystal Care Centers Inc .... E 419 747-2666
   Mansfield *(G-13286)*
Crystalwood Inc .... D 513 605-1000
   Cincinnati *(G-3443)*
Dayspring Health Care Center .... C 937 864-5800
   Fairborn *(G-10792)*
Deaconess Long Term Care of MI ... A 513 487-3600
   Cincinnati *(G-3474)*
Dearth Management Company .... C 419 253-0144
   Marengo *(G-13423)*
Develpmntal Dsblties Ohio Dept ..... D 740 446-1642
   Gallipolis *(G-11314)*
Develpmntal Dsblties Ohio Dept ..... B 614 272-0509
   Columbus *(G-7513)*
Dover Nursing Center .... D 330 364-4436
   Dover *(G-10186)*
Doylestown Health Care Center ...... C 330 658-1533
   Doylestown *(G-10227)*
Eagle Creek Nursing Center .... E 937 544-5531
   West Union *(G-19278)*
Earley & Ross Ltd .... D 740 634-3301
   Sabina *(G-16615)*
East Galbraith Nursing Home .... C 513 984-5220
   Cincinnati *(G-3532)*
Eastern Star Hm of Cyhoga Cnty .... D 216 761-0170
   Cleveland *(G-5521)*
Ebenezer Road Corp .... C 513 941-0099
   Cincinnati *(G-3540)*
Echoing Hills Village Inc .... D 440 989-1400
   Lorain *(G-13037)*
Edgewood Manor of Wellston .... E 740 384-5611
   Wellston *(G-18999)*
Elms Retirement Village Inc .... D 440 647-2414
   Wellington *(G-18991)*
Elmwood Center Inc .... D 419 639-2626
   Green Springs *(G-11475)*
Fairmont Nursing Home Inc .... D 440 338-8220
   Newbury *(G-15256)*
Falls Village Retirement Cmnty .... D 330 945-9797
   Cuyahoga Falls *(G-9187)*
Filling Memorial Home of Mercy ..... B 419 592-6451
   Napoleon *(G-14938)*
Fisher-Titus Medical Center .... E 419 668-4228
   Norwalk *(G-15574)*
Fisher-Titus Medical Center .... A 419 668-8101
   Norwalk *(G-15575)*
Flower Hospital .... B 419 824-1000
   Sylvania *(G-17587)*
Fort Austin Ltd Partnership .... C 440 892-4200
   Cleveland *(G-5624)*
Foundations Hlth Solutions Inc .... D 440 793-0200
   North Olmsted *(G-15423)*
Franciscan At St Leonard .... B 937 433-0480
   Dayton *(G-9560)*
Friends of Good Shepherd Manor ... D 740 289-2861
   Lucasville *(G-13179)*
Furney Group Home .... E 419 389-0152
   Toledo *(G-17902)*
Garbry Ridge Assisted Living .... E 937 778-9385
   Piqua *(G-16145)*
Gaslite Villa Convalescent Ctr .... D 330 494-4500
   Canal Fulton *(G-2143)*
Gateway Health Care Center .... C 216 486-4949
   Cleveland *(G-5658)*
Gaymont Nursing Homes Inc .... D 419 668-8258
   Norwalk *(G-15576)*
Generation Health & Rehab Cntr .... D 740 344-9465
   Newark *(G-15168)*
Gillette Nursing Home Inc .... D 330 372-1960
   Warren *(G-18860)*
Golden Living LLC .... D 419 227-2154
   Lima *(G-12784)*
Golden Living LLC .... D 419 301-3308
   Saint Marys *(G-16674)*
Golden Living LLC .... C 614 861-6666
   Columbus *(G-7759)*
Golden Living LLC .... C 330 297-5781
   Ravenna *(G-16386)*
Golden Living LLC .... D 330 335-1558
   Wadsworth *(G-18753)*
Good Shepherd Home .... C 419 937-1801
   Fostoria *(G-11129)*
Greens of Lyndhurst The Inc .... C 440 460-1000
   Cleveland *(G-5704)*
Guardian Elde .... D 419 225-9040
   Lima *(G-12788)*
Guernsey Health Systems Inc .... A 740 439-3561
   Cambridge *(G-2119)*
Harborside Sylvania LLC .... D 419 882-1875
   Sylvania *(G-17592)*

Employee Codes: A=Over 500 employees, B=251-500
C=101-250, D=51-100, E=25-50

INTERMEDIATE CARE FACILITY — SERVICES SECTION

Company	Grade	Phone
Hattie Larlham Center For, Mantua (G-13387)	C	330 274-2272
Healthcare Facility MGT LLC, Akron (G-260)	C	330 836-7953
Healthcare Management Cons, Rockford (G-16563)	E	419 363-2193
Heinzerling Foundation, Columbus (G-7821)	C	614 272-8888
Hempstead Manor, Portsmouth (G-16286)	C	740 354-8150
Hennis Nursing Home, Dover (G-10191)	C	330 364-8849
Heritage Park Rehabilita, New Paris (G-15078)	E	937 437-2311
Heritage Professional Services, New Boston (G-15011)	C	740 456-8245
Hill Side Plaza, Cleveland (G-5756)	D	216 486-6300
Home Echo Club Inc, Pickerington (G-16096)	C	614 864-1718
Horn Nursing and Rehab Center, Wooster (G-19870)	D	330 262-2951
Horn Nursing and Rehab Center, Wooster (G-19871)	C	330 345-9050
Humility House, Youngstown (G-20222)	D	330 505-0144
Independence of Portage County, Ravenna (G-16390)	C	330 296-2851
Inn At Lakeview, Groveport (G-11646)	D	614 836-2866
Inn At Marietta Ltd, Marietta (G-13456)	D	740 373-9600
Isabelle Ridgway Care Ctr Inc, Columbus (G-7926)	C	614 252-4931
Jennings Eliza Home Inc, Cleveland (G-5857)	C	216 226-0282
Jennings Ctr For Older Adults, Cleveland (G-5858)	B	216 581-2900
Judson, Cleveland (G-5876)	D	216 791-2004
Kendal At Oberlin, Oberlin (G-15647)	C	440 775-0094
Kindred Healthcare Oper Inc, West Lafayette (G-19258)	D	740 545-6355
Kindred Healthcare Operating, Whitehouse (G-19587)	D	419 877-5338
Kingston Healthcare Company, Sylvania (G-17598)	D	419 824-4200
Lakeside Manor Inc, North Lima (G-15404)	E	330 549-2545
Laurels of Hillsboro, Hillsboro (G-11985)	D	937 393-1925
Levering Management Inc, Delaware (G-10115)	D	740 369-6400
Lexington Court Care Center, Mansfield (G-13324)	D	419 884-2000
Liberty Nursing Center, Englewood (G-10712)	E	937 836-5143
Liberty Nursing Center of Thre, Cincinnati (G-3976)	C	513 941-0787
Liberty Nursing of Willard, Willard (G-19622)	D	419 935-0148
Liberty Residence II, Wadsworth (G-18760)	E	330 334-3262
Life Care Centers America Inc, Valley City (G-18619)	C	330 483-3131
Lifeservices Development Corp, Mentor (G-14209)	E	440 257-3866
Light of Hearts Villa, Cleveland (G-5941)	D	440 232-1991
Lincoln Park Associates II LP, Dayton (G-9683)	C	937 297-4300
Longmeadow Care Center Inc, Ravenna (G-16392)	C	330 297-5781
Luther Home of Mercy, Williston (G-19639)	B	419 836-3918
Lutheran Home, Cleveland (G-5959)	B	440 871-0090
Lutheran Village At Wolf Creek, Holland (G-12033)	C	419 861-2233
Lynnhaven V LLC, Windsor (G-19805)	C	440 272-5600
Main Street Terrace Care Ctr, Lancaster (G-12553)	D	740 653-8767
Manorcare of Willoughby Inc, Toledo (G-18041)	C	419 252-5500
Mansfield Memorial Homes LLC, Mansfield (G-13333)	C	419 774-5100
Maple Knoll Communities Inc, Cincinnati (G-4019)	B	513 782-2400
McClellan Management Inc, Genoa (G-11381)	C	419 855-7755
McV Health Care Facilities, Mason (G-13738)	C	513 398-1486
Mennonite Memorial Home Inc, Bluffton (G-1734)	C	419 358-1015
Mill Manor Nursing Home Inc, Vermilion (G-18715)	E	440 967-6614
Mill Run Care Center LLC, Hilliard (G-11935)	D	614 527-3000
Mount Aloysius Corp, New Lexington (G-15056)	C	740 342-3343
Muskingum County Ohio, Zanesville (G-20507)	D	740 454-1911
Muskingum Residentials Inc, Zanesville (G-20511)	E	740 453-5350
New Dawn Health Care Inc, Dover (G-10202)	C	330 343-5521
New Hope & Horizons, Cincinnati (G-4156)	E	513 761-7999
North Hills Management Company, Zanesville (G-20517)	D	740 450-9999
North Shore Retirement Cmnty, Lakeside (G-12465)	E	419 798-8203
Northpoint Senior Services LLC, Marietta (G-13480)	C	740 373-3597
Northpoint Senior Services LLC, Milford (G-14545)	D	513 248-1655
Norwood Health Care Center LLC, Cincinnati (G-4186)	D	513 351-0153
Oak Health Care Investors, Mount Vernon (G-14916)	D	740 397-3200
October Enterprises Inc, Eaton (G-10571)	C	937 456-9535
Ohio Eastern Star Home, Mount Vernon (G-14917)	C	740 397-1706
Ohio Living, Cincinnati (G-4208)	C	513 681-4230
Ohio Living, Columbus (G-8357)	B	614 224-1651
Ohio Presbt Retirement Svcs, Youngstown (G-20309)	B	330 746-2944
Ohio Presbt Retirement Svcs, Monroe (G-14708)	C	513 539-7391
Ohio Presbt Retirement Svcs, Sidney (G-16945)	B	937 498-2391
Ohio Valley Manor Inc, Ripley (G-16548)	C	937 392-4318
Olmsted Manor Nursing Home, North Olmsted (G-15436)	C	440 250-4080
On-Call Nursing Inc, Lakewood (G-12493)	D	216 577-8890
Orchard Villa Inc, Oregon (G-15744)	C	419 697-4100
Orion Care Services LLC, Cleveland (G-6215)	C	216 752-3600
Otterbein Portage Valley Inc, Pemberville (G-15943)	C	888 749-4950
Otterbein Snior Lfstyle Chices, Lebanon (G-12636)	B	513 933-5400
Palm Crest East Inc, Elyria (G-10668)	E	440 322-0726
Park Creek Rtirement Cmnty Inc, Cleveland (G-6235)	E	440 842-5100
Parkview Manor Inc, Englewood (G-10714)	D	937 296-1550
Parma Care Center Inc, Cleveland (G-6245)	C	216 661-6800
Personacare of Ohio Inc, Painesville (G-15873)	C	440 357-1311
Pickaway Manor Inc, Circleville (G-4899)	C	740 474-5400
Pleasant Lake Nursing Home, Cleveland (G-6289)	B	440 842-2273
Rae-Ann Holdings Inc, Westlake (G-19539)	D	440 871-0500
Raeann Inc, Geneva (G-11368)	D	440 466-5733
Renaissance House Inc, Sandusky (G-16787)	D	419 626-1110
Rescare, Chesapeake (G-2787)	E	740 867-3051
Rescare Ohio Inc, Williamsburg (G-19635)	E	513 724-1177
Residence of Chardon, Chardon (G-2765)	D	440 286-2277
Rest Haven Nursing Home Inc, Greenville (G-11516)	C	937 548-1138
Ridge Pleasant Valley Inc, Cleveland (G-6395)	C	440 845-0200
Ridgewood At Friendship Vlg, Columbus (G-8628)	E	614 890-8285
Rivers Bend Health Care LLC, South Point (G-17097)	D	740 894-3476
Roman Cthlic Docese Youngstown, Louisville (G-13106)	C	330 875-5562
Rose Mary Johanna Grassell, Cleveland (G-6412)	C	216 481-4823
Royal Manor Health Care Inc, Cleveland (G-6416)	E	216 752-3600
Saint Johns Villa, Carrollton (G-2628)	C	330 627-4662
Salutary Providers Inc, Ashtabula (G-762)	C	440 964-8446
Samaritan Care Center & Villa, Medina (G-14122)	D	330 725-4123
Sarah Moore Hlth Care Ctr Inc, Delaware (G-10125)	D	740 362-9641
Sateri Home Inc, Youngstown (G-20367)	D	330 758-8106
Senior Care Inc, Medina (G-14124)	D	330 721-2000
Senior Care Inc, Lima (G-12875)	C	419 516-4788
Sensi Care 3, Elyria (G-10679)	E	440 323-6310
Sisters of Little, Warrensville Heights (G-18934)	C	216 464-1222
Sisters of Little, Cincinnati (G-4532)	C	513 281-8001
Society Handicapped Citz Medin, Seville (G-16844)	E	330 722-1900
Sociey For Handicapped Citizen, Seville (G-16845)	C	330 725-7041
Spring Meadow Extended Care Ce, Holland (G-12057)	D	419 866-6124
Spring Meadow Extended Care Ce, Mansfield (G-13367)	D	419 866-6124
St Augustine Corporation, Lakewood (G-12501)	B	216 939-7600
Stratford Commons Inc, Solon (G-17056)	C	440 914-0900
Summit Acres Inc, Caldwell (G-2089)	C	740 732-2364
Summit Facility Operations LLC, Tallmadge (G-17652)	D	330 633-0555
Sunbridge Healthcare LLC, New Lexington (G-15064)	C	740 342-5161
Sunrise Manor Convalescent Ctr, Amelia (G-583)	D	513 797-5144
Sunset House Inc, Toledo (G-18210)	C	419 536-4645
Sunshine Communities, Maumee (G-13982)	B	419 865-0251
Swanton Hlth Care Rtrement Ctr, Swanton (G-17572)	D	419 825-1145
The Maria-Joseph Center, Dayton (G-9926)	B	937 278-2692
The Villa At Lake MGT Co, Conneaut (G-9048)	D	440 599-1999
Twilight Gardens Healthcare, Norwalk (G-15595)	E	419 668-2086
Twin Maples Nursing Home, Mc Arthur (G-14018)	E	740 596-5955
Twin Pines Retreat Care Center, Stow (G-17398)	E	330 688-5553
Twin Towers, Cincinnati (G-4710)	B	513 853-2000
United Cerebral Palsy, Cleveland (G-6636)	D	216 381-9993
United Church Homes Inc, Fairborn (G-10806)	C	937 878-0262
United Church Homes Inc, Jackson (G-12320)	D	740 286-7551
United Church Homes Inc, Cincinnati (G-4730)	C	513 922-1440
United Church Homes Inc, Beavercreek (G-1261)	C	937 426-8481
United Church Homes Inc, Upper Sandusky (G-18568)	C	419 294-4973
University Hospitals Health, Chardon (G-2775)	A	440 285-4040
University Manor Hlth Care Ctr, Cleveland (G-6665)	C	216 721-1400
Vancare Inc, Vandalia (G-18706)	C	937 898-4202
Vienna Enterprises Inc, South Vienna (G-17101)	E	937 568-4524
Volunters Amer Care Facilities, Lima (G-12911)	C	419 225-9040

SERVICES SECTION

IRON ORES

Walnut Hills Inc .... C 330 852-2457
 Walnut Creek (G-18786)
Washington Manor Inc .... E 937 433-3441
 Dayton (G-9984)
Weber Health Care Center Inc .... C 440 647-2088
 Wellington (G-18996)
Wedgewood Estates .... E 419 756-7400
 Westerville (G-19358)
Wellington Place LLC .... D 440 734-9933
 North Olmsted (G-15450)
Wesley Ridge Inc .... C 614 759-0023
 Reynoldsburg (G-16489)
West Liberty Care Center Inc .... C 937 465-5065
 West Liberty (G-19264)
Western Rsrve Msonic Cmnty Inc .... C 330 721-3000
 Medina (G-14138)
Wexner Heritage Village .... B 614 231-4900
 Columbus (G-8984)
Willow Brook Chrstn Cmmunities .... D 740 369-0048
 Delaware (G-10135)
Windsor House Inc .... C 330 549-9259
 Columbiana (G-6867)
Windsor Medical Center Inc .... C 330 499-8300
 Canton (G-2587)
Woodside Village Care Center .... D 419 947-2015
 Mount Gilead (G-14865)
Zandex Inc .... E 740 695-3281
 Saint Clairsville (G-16662)
Zandex Inc .... E 740 454-1400
 Zanesville (G-20546)
Zandex Inc .... C 740 454-9769
 Zanesville (G-20548)
Zandex Inc .... C 740 695-7233
 Saint Clairsville (G-16663)
Zandex Inc .... C 740 872-0809
 New Concord (G-15040)
Zandex Health Care Corporation .... C 740 452-4636
 Zanesville (G-20550)
Zandex Health Care Corporation .... C 740 454-9769
 Zanesville (G-20551)
Zandex Health Care Corporation .... E 740 454-1400
 Zanesville (G-20552)
Zandex Health Care Corporation .... D 740 454-1400
 Johnstown (G-12345)
Zandex Health Care Corporation .... C 740 454-1400
 New Concord (G-15041)
Zandex Health Care Corporation .... C 740 454-9747
 Zanesville (G-20553)

INTERMEDIATE INVESTMENT BANKS

Lancaster Pollard Mrtg Co LLC .... D 614 224-8800
 Columbus (G-8034)
N C B International Department .... D 216 488-7990
 Cleveland (G-6097)

INVENTORY COMPUTING SVCS

Accurate Inventory and C .... B 800 777-9414
 Columbus (G-6936)
Canton Inventory Service .... E 330 453-1633
 Canton (G-2290)
Huffy Corporation .... D 937 743-5011
 Springboro (G-17124)
Merchant Data Service Inc .... C 937 847-6585
 Miamisburg (G-14318)
Rgis LLC .... D 216 447-1744
 Independence (G-12249)
Rgis LLC .... D 330 799-1566
 Youngstown (G-20351)
Rgis LLC .... D 248 651-2511
 Reynoldsburg (G-16477)
Rgis LLC .... D 330 896-9802
 Akron (G-414)
Rgis LLC .... C 513 772-5990
 Cincinnati (G-4412)

INVESTMENT ADVISORY SVCS

American Money Management Corp .... E 513 579-2592
 Cincinnati (G-3008)
Ameriprise Financial Svcs Inc .... E 330 494-9300
 Akron (G-74)
Bartlett & Co LLC .... D 513 621-4612
 Cincinnati (G-3081)
Centaurus Financial Inc .... D 419 756-9747
 Mansfield (G-13273)
Crestview Partners II Gp LP .... B 216 898-2400
 Brooklyn (G-1905)
Diamond Hill Funds .... E 614 255-3333
 Columbus (G-7517)

Eubel Brady Suttman Asset Mgt .... E 937 291-1223
 Miamisburg (G-14300)
Financial Network Group Ltd .... E 513 469-7500
 Cincinnati (G-3610)
Financial Plnners of Cleveland .... E 440 473-1115
 Cleveland (G-5586)
Fort Wash Inv Advisors Inc .... D 513 361-7600
 Cincinnati (G-3639)
Fund Evaluation Group LLC .... E 513 977-4400
 Cincinnati (G-3658)
Jpmorgan Inv Advisors Inc .... A 614 248-5800
 Columbus (G-6890)
Lancaster Pollard Mrtg Co LLC .... D 614 224-8800
 Columbus (G-8034)
Lincoln Fincl Advisors Corp .... E 216 765-7400
 Beachwood (G-1096)
MAI Capital Management LLC .... D 216 920-4800
 Cleveland (G-5967)
Merrill Lynch Pierce Fenner .... D 740 335-2930
 Wshngtn CT Hs (G-20031)
Oak Associates Ltd .... E 330 666-5263
 Akron (G-360)
Parkwood Corporation .... E 216 875-6500
 Cleveland (G-6244)
Red Capital Partners LLC .... D 614 857-1400
 Columbus (G-8598)
S&P Global Inc .... C 614 835-2444
 Groveport (G-11669)
S&P Global Inc .... C 330 482-9544
 Leetonia (G-12662)
Standard Retirement Svcs Inc .... E 440 808-2724
 Westlake (G-19551)
Stratos Wealth Partners Ltd .... D 440 519-2500
 Beachwood (G-1127)
Summit Financial Strategies .... E 614 885-1115
 Columbus (G-8801)

INVESTMENT BANKERS

Brown Gibbons Lang & Co LLC .... E 216 241-2800
 Cleveland (G-5150)
Cadle Company II Inc .... C 330 872-0918
 Newton Falls (G-15273)
Jpmorgan Chase Bank Nat Assn .... A 614 436-3055
 Columbus (G-6888)
Lancaster Pollard & Co LLC .... E 614 224-8800
 Columbus (G-8033)
McM Capital Partners .... B 216 514-1840
 Beachwood (G-1098)
R B C Apollo Equity Partners .... E 216 875-2626
 Cleveland (G-6338)
Riverside Partners LLC .... E 216 344-1040
 Cleveland (G-6400)

INVESTMENT COUNSELORS

C H Dean Inc .... D 937 222-9531
 Beavercreek (G-1156)
Johnson Trust Co .... C 513 598-8859
 Cincinnati (G-3884)
Mc Cormack Advisors Intl .... E 216 522-1200
 Cleveland (G-5998)
Meeder Asset Management Inc .... D 614 760-2112
 Dublin (G-10394)
Sena Weller Rohs Williams .... E 513 241-6443
 Cincinnati (G-4495)

INVESTMENT FIRM: General Brokerage

Cincinnati Financial Corp .... A 513 870-2000
 Fairfield (G-10833)
Haven Financial Enterprise .... E 800 265-2401
 Cleveland (G-5732)
Hbi Payments Ltd .... D 614 944-5788
 Columbus (G-7806)
Jdel Inc .... E 614 436-2418
 Columbus (G-7938)
Kgbo Holdings Inc .... E 800 580-3101
 Centerville (G-2682)
Morgan Stanley & Co LLC .... E 614 228-0600
 Columbus (G-8189)
Red Capital Markets LLC .... C 614 857-1400
 Columbus (G-8597)
Stateco Financial Services .... D 614 464-5000
 Columbus (G-8784)
Western & Southern Lf Insur Co .... A 513 629-1800
 Cincinnati (G-4839)
Western Southern Mutl Holdg Co .... A 866 832-7719
 Cincinnati (G-4844)
Western Sthern Fincl Group Inc .... A 866 832-7719
 Cincinnati (G-4845)

INVESTMENT FUNDS, NEC

Rockbridge Capital LLC .... E 614 246-2400
 Columbus (G-8643)
Rockwood Equity Partners LLC .... E 216 378-9326
 Cleveland (G-6409)

INVESTMENT FUNDS: Open-Ended

James Advantage Funds .... E 937 426-7640
 Xenia (G-20064)

INVESTMENT OFFICES: Management, Closed-End

National Housing Tr Ltd Partnr .... E 614 451-9929
 Columbus (G-8221)

INVESTMENT OFFICES: Money Market Mutual

Jpmorgan High Yield Fund .... E 614 248-7017
 Columbus (G-6889)

INVESTMENT RESEARCH SVCS

Cleveland Research Company LLC .... E 216 649-7250
 Cleveland (G-5343)
Longbow Research LLC .... D 216 986-0700
 Independence (G-12230)

INVESTORS, NEC

Arthur Middleton Capital Holdn .... C 330 966-3033
 Canton (G-2245)
Blackbird Capital Group LLC .... E 513 762-7890
 Cincinnati (G-3113)
Capital Investment Group Inc .... E 513 241-5090
 Cincinnati (G-3174)
Community Choice Financial Inc .... D 614 798-5900
 Dublin (G-10304)
Ctd Investments LLC .... E 614 570-9949
 Columbus (G-7473)
First Business Fincl Svcs Inc .... E 216 573-3792
 Cleveland (G-5591)
K M Clemens DDS Inc .... E 419 228-4036
 Lima (G-12807)
Natl City Coml Capitol LLC .... E 513 455-9746
 Cincinnati (G-4145)
Newmark & Company RE Inc .... E 216 453-3000
 Cleveland (G-6127)
Rightway Investments LLC .... E 216 854-7697
 Twinsburg (G-18461)
Shancliff Investments Ltd .... C 330 883-5560
 Youngstown (G-20372)
Shields Capital Corporation .... D 216 767-1340
 Beachwood (G-1123)
Superior Street Partners LLC .... D 216 862-0058
 Shaker Heights (G-16868)
The Huntington Investment Co .... D 216 351-2555
 Cincinnati (G-4643)
Weinberg Capital Group Inc .... D 216 503-8307
 Cleveland (G-6728)
Wings Investors Company Ltd .... E 513 241-5800
 Cincinnati (G-4853)

INVESTORS: Real Estate, Exc Property Operators

Jpmorgan Chase Bank Nat Assn .... A 614 436-3055
 Columbus (G-6888)
Klingbeil Capital MGT LLC .... D 614 396-4919
 Worthington (G-19967)
M-E Companies Inc .... D 614 818-4900
 Westerville (G-19423)

IRON ORE MINING

Cleveland-Cliffs Inc .... D 216 694-5700
 Cleveland (G-5357)
Cliffs Minnesota Minerals Co .... A 216 694-5700
 Cleveland (G-5361)
The Cleveland-Cliffs Iron Co .... C 216 694-5700
 Cleveland (G-6590)
Tilden Mining Company LC .... A 216 694-5700
 Cleveland (G-6600)
Wabush Mines Cliffs Mining Co .... A 216 694-5700
 Cleveland (G-6715)

IRON ORES

International Steel Group .... C 330 841-2800
 Warren (G-18865)

Employee Codes: A=Over 500 employees, B=251-500
C=101-250, D=51-100, E=25-50

IRRIGATION SYSTEMS, NEC Water Distribution Or Sply Systems

City of Dayton..................................D....... 937 333-7138
  Dayton (G-9413)

JANITORIAL & CUSTODIAL SVCS

AAA Standard Services Inc................D....... 419 535-0274
  Toledo (G-17737)
ABM Janitorial Services Inc...............C....... 216 861-1199
  Cleveland (G-4948)
ABM Janitorial Services Inc...............C....... 513 731-1418
  Cincinnati (G-2962)
Academic Support Services LLC.........E....... 740 274-6138
  Columbus (G-6930)
Access Cleaning Service Inc...............E....... 937 276-2605
  Dayton (G-9303)
Accomodaire Total Cleaning LLC........E....... 614 367-1347
  Columbus (G-6935)
Aetna Building Maintenance Inc..........B....... 614 476-1818
  Columbus (G-6953)
Aetna Building Maintenance Inc..........C....... 866 238-6201
  Dayton (G-9312)
Akron Area Commercial Cleaning........E....... 330 434-0767
  Akron (G-26)
All Pro Cleaning Services Inc..............D....... 440 519-0055
  Solon (G-16974)
Alpha & Omega Bldg Svcs Inc.............E....... 513 429-5082
  Blue Ash (G-1529)
Alpha & Omega Bldg Svcs Inc.............B....... 937 298-2125
  Dayton (G-9321)
American Maintenance Svcs Inc..........E....... 330 744-3400
  Youngstown (G-20104)
Anchor Cleaning Contractors...............E....... 216 961-7343
  Cleveland (G-5034)
Apex Environmental Svcs LLC.............D....... 513 772-2739
  Cincinnati (G-3034)
Aramark Facility Services LLC.............E....... 216 687-5000
  Cleveland (G-5057)
August Groh & Sons Inc......................E....... 513 821-0090
  Cincinnati (G-3064)
Basol Maintenance Service Inc............D....... 419 422-0946
  Findlay (G-10993)
Bebley Enterprises Inc.........................E....... 419 389-9424
  Toledo (G-17767)
Bechtl Bldng Mntnc Crprtn of...............D....... 330 759-2797
  Youngstown (G-20111)
Bkg Services Inc.................................E....... 614 476-1800
  Columbus (G-7114)
Buckeye Commercial Cleaning............E....... 614 866-4700
  Pickerington (G-16087)
Cardinal Maintenance & Svc Co..........C....... 330 252-0282
  Akron (G-122)
Clean All Services Inc.........................C....... 937 498-4146
  Sidney (G-16921)
Clean Break Inc..................................E....... 330 638-5648
  Warren (G-18834)
Clean Care Inc...................................C....... 419 725-2100
  Toledo (G-17815)
Cleaner Carpet & Jantr Inc..................E....... 513 469-2070
  Mason (G-13684)
CMS Business Services LLC...............D....... 740 687-0577
  Lancaster (G-12520)
Coleman Professional Svcs Inc...........B....... 330 673-1347
  Kent (G-12360)
Commercial Cleaning Solutions...........E....... 937 981-4870
  Greenfield (G-11483)
Crystal Clear Bldg Svcs Inc.................D....... 440 439-2288
  Oakwood Village (G-15628)
Csi International Inc............................A....... 614 781-1571
  Worthington (G-19952)
Cummins Building Maint Inc................D....... 740 726-9800
  Prospect (G-16363)
Custom Cleaning and Maint.................E....... 440 946-7028
  Willoughby (G-19657)
Custom Cleaning Service LLC.............E....... 440 774-1222
  Oberlin (G-15641)
Custom Maid Cleaning Services..........E....... 513 351-6571
  Cincinnati (G-3452)
D & J Master Clean Inc.......................D....... 614 847-1181
  Columbus (G-7477)
Dave & Barb Enterprises Inc...............D....... 513 553-0050
  New Richmond (G-15125)
Dependable Cleaning Contrs..............D....... 440 953-9191
  Willoughby (G-19659)
Dove Building Services Inc..................D....... 614 299-4700
  Columbus (G-7543)
Dublin Coml Property Svcs Inc............E....... 419 732-6732
  Port Clinton (G-16244)

Environment Ctrl of Miami Cnty...........D....... 937 669-9900
  Tipp City (G-17716)
Euclid Indus Maint Clg Contrs..............C....... 216 361-0288
  Cleveland (G-5553)
Executive Management Services.........C....... 419 529-8800
  Ontario (G-15688)
Extreme Detail Clg Cnstr Svcs.............E....... 419 392-3243
  Toledo (G-17874)
Family Entertainment Services............D....... 740 286-8587
  Jackson (G-12311)
Gca Services Group Inc......................   800 422-8760
  Cleveland (G-5661)
General Building Maintenance.............D....... 330 682-2238
  Orrville (G-15773)
General Services Cleaning Co.............E....... 614 840-0562
  Columbus (G-7735)
George Gardner.................................D....... 419 636-4277
  Bryan (G-2006)
Gsf North American Jantr Svc..............C....... 513 733-1451
  West Chester (G-19205)
Heits Building Svcs Cnkd LLC.............D....... 855 464-3487
  Cincinnati (G-3756)
House Calls LLC................................E....... 513 841-9800
  Cincinnati (G-3789)
Ivory Services Inc...............................E....... 216 344-3094
  Cleveland (G-5838)
J B M Cleaning & Supply Co...............E....... 330 837-8805
  Massillon (G-13825)
J V Janitorial Services Inc...................E....... 216 749-1150
  Cleveland (G-5845)
Jancoa Janitorial Services Inc.............B....... 513 351-7200
  Cincinnati (G-3862)
Jani-Source Inc..................................E....... 740 374-6298
  Marietta (G-13458)
Janitorial Services Inc........................B....... 216 341-8601
  Cleveland (G-5851)
Jantech Building Services Inc.............C....... 216 661-6102
  Brooklyn Heights (G-1917)
Jenkins Enterprises LLC.....................E....... 513 752-7896
  Cincinnati (G-2920)
Jordan Kyli Enterprises Inc.................E....... 216 256-3773
  Westlake (G-19502)
Justin L Paulk....................................D....... 513 422-7060
  Middletown (G-14481)
K & L Floormasters LLC.....................E....... 330 493-0869
  Canton (G-2420)
K & M Kleening Service Inc.................D....... 614 737-3750
  Groveport (G-11652)
Kellermyer Bergensons Svcs LLC........D....... 419 867-4300
  Maumee (G-13932)
Kelli Woods Management Inc.............C....... 419 478-1200
  Toledo (G-17992)
Ktm Enterprises Inc............................E....... 937 548-8357
  Greenville (G-11512)
Mapp Building Service LLC.................E....... 513 253-3990
  Blue Ash (G-1633)
Marks Cleaning Service Inc.................E....... 330 725-5702
  Medina (G-14094)
Mathews Josiah.................................E....... 567 204-8818
  Lima (G-12837)
Mid-American Clg Contrs Inc..............C....... 419 429-6222
  Findlay (G-11067)
Mid-American Clg Contrs Inc..............D....... 419 229-3899
  Lima (G-12840)
Mid-American Clg Contrs Inc..............C....... 614 291-7170
  Columbus (G-8163)
Mougianis Industries Inc.....................D....... 740 264-6372
  Steubenville (G-17331)
Nicholas D Starr Inc...........................C....... 419 229-3192
  Lima (G-12843)
North Coast Sales..............................E....... 440 632-0793
  Middlefield (G-14400)
Nortone Service Inc...........................E....... 740 527-2057
  Buckeye Lake (G-2022)
Ohio Building Service Inc....................E....... 513 761-0268
  Cincinnati (G-4202)
Ohio Custodial Maintenance................C....... 614 443-1232
  Columbus (G-8323)
Perry Contract Services Inc................D....... 614 274-4350
  Columbus (G-8537)
Priority Building Services Inc..............D....... 937 233-7030
  Beavercreek Township (G-1282)
Pro Care Janitor Supply......................E....... 937 778-2275
  Piqua (G-16162)
Pro-Touch Inc....................................C....... 614 586-0303
  Columbus (G-8563)
Professional Maint Dayton..................D....... 937 461-5259
  Dayton (G-9834)
Professional Maint of Columbus..........C....... 614 443-6528
  Columbus (G-8567)

Professional Maint of Columbus..........B....... 513 579-1762
  Cincinnati (G-4343)
Professnal Mint Cincinnati Inc.............A....... 513 579-1161
  Cincinnati (G-4345)
Quality Assured Cleaning Inc..............D....... 614 798-1505
  Columbus (G-8580)
Quality Cleaning Systems LLC............E....... 330 567-2050
  Shreve (G-16908)
R T Industries Inc...............................C....... 937 335-5784
  Troy (G-18374)
Rde System Corp...............................C....... 513 933-8000
  Lebanon (G-12640)
Red Carpet Janitorial Service..............B....... 513 242-7575
  Cincinnati (G-4395)
Romaster Corp...................................D....... 330 825-1945
  Norton (G-15559)
Rwk Services Inc................................E....... 440 526-2144
  Cleveland (G-6423)
Saftek Industrial Service Inc................E....... 937 667-1772
  Tipp City (G-17726)
Scioto Services LLc............................E....... 937 644-0888
  Marysville (G-13649)
ServiceMaster By Steinbach................E....... 330 497-5959
  Canton (G-2526)
ServiceMaster of Defiance Inc.............D....... 419 784-5570
  Defiance (G-10057)
Starlight Enterprises Inc......................C....... 330 339-2020
  New Philadelphia (G-15116)
Super Shine Inc..................................E....... 513 423-8999
  Middletown (G-14464)
T&L Global Management LLC.............D....... 614 586-0303
  Columbus (G-8818)
Turn Around Group Inc.......................D....... 330 372-0064
  Warren (G-18917)
Twin Cedars Services Inc...................D....... 513 932-0399
  Lebanon (G-12655)
Wells & Sons Janitorial Svc.................E....... 937 878-4375
  Fairborn (G-10813)
Wj Service Co Inc...............................E....... 330 372-5040
  Warren (G-18928)
York Building Maintenance Inc............C....... 216 398-8100
  Cleveland (G-6770)
Youngstown Window Cleaning Co.......C....... 330 743-3880
  Girard (G-11431)

JANITORIAL EQPT & SPLYS WHOLESALERS

Acorn Distributors Inc.........................E....... 614 294-6444
  Columbus (G-6940)
Airgas Usa LLC..................................B....... 216 642-6600
  Independence (G-12183)
Alco-Chem Inc....................................E....... 330 253-3535
  Akron (G-64)
Alco-Chem Inc....................................E....... 330 833-8551
  Canton (G-2230)
Clean Innovations...............................E....... 614 299-1187
  Columbus (G-7295)
Envirochemical Inc.............................E....... 440 287-2200
  Solon (G-17004)
Friends Service Co Inc.......................D....... 419 427-1704
  Findlay (G-11033)
H P Products Corporation...................D....... 513 683-8553
  Cincinnati (G-3723)
Hillside Maint Sup Co Inc....................E....... 513 751-4100
  Cincinnati (G-3767)
I Supply Co..C....... 937 878-5240
  Fairborn (G-10798)
Impact Products LLC..........................C....... 419 841-2891
  Toledo (G-17971)
M Conley Company.............................D....... 330 456-8243
  Canton (G-2442)
National Marketshare Group................E....... 513 921-0800
  Cincinnati (G-4140)
Phillips Supply Company.....................D....... 513 579-1762
  Cincinnati (G-4292)
Powell Company Ltd..........................D....... 419 228-3552
  Lima (G-12861)
Pro-Touch Inc....................................C....... 614 586-0303
  Columbus (G-8563)
Rhiel Supply Co Inc............................E....... 330 799-7777
  Austintown (G-873)
Rose Products and Services Inc.........E....... 614 443-7647
  Columbus (G-8649)
Seaway Sponge & Chamois Co..........E....... 419 691-4694
  Toledo (G-18177)
ServiceMaster of Defiance Inc.............D....... 419 784-5570
  Defiance (G-10057)
The Cottingham Paper Co..................E....... 614 294-6444
  Columbus (G-8834)

SERVICES SECTION

JEWELRY APPAREL
Marfo Company..................................D....... 614 276-3352
  Columbus (G-8109)

JEWELRY REPAIR SVCS
Sdr Services LLC...............................E....... 513 625-0695
  Goshen (G-11439)

JEWELRY STORES
Equity Diamond Brokers Inc...............E....... 513 793-4760
  Cincinnati (G-3570)

JEWELRY, WHOLESALE
Equity Diamond Brokers Inc...............E....... 513 793-4760
  Cincinnati (G-3570)
Marfo Company..................................D....... 614 276-3352
  Columbus (G-8109)

JOB COUNSELING
Linking Employment Abilities............E....... 216 696-2716
  Cleveland (G-5944)

JOB TRAINING & VOCATIONAL REHABILITATION SVCS
A W S Inc..D....... 216 941-8800
  Cleveland (G-4938)
Abilities First Foundation...................C....... 513 423-9496
  Middletown (G-14411)
Alpha Group of Delaware Inc.............E....... 740 368-5820
  Delaware (G-10070)
Anne Grady Corporation......................E....... 419 867-7501
  Holland (G-12008)
ARC Industries Incorporated O..........B....... 614 836-0700
  Groveport (G-11623)
Butler County of Ohio..........................E....... 513 785-6500
  Hamilton (G-11697)
Cleveland Christian Home Inc............C....... 216 671-0977
  Cleveland (G-5294)
Collins Career Center.........................D....... 740 867-6641
  Chesapeake (G-2782)
County of Geauga...............................D....... 440 564-2246
  Chardon (G-2746)
County of Hancock..............................E....... 419 422-6387
  Findlay (G-11016)
County of Lake....................................A....... 440 350-5100
  Mentor (G-14164)
County of Lake....................................D....... 440 269-2193
  Willoughby (G-19656)
County of Marion.................................D....... 740 387-1035
  Marion (G-13535)
County of Mercer................................D....... 419 586-2369
  Celina (G-2643)
County of Montgomery........................B....... 937 225-4804
  Dayton (G-9436)
County of Stark...................................D....... 330 484-4814
  Canton (G-2322)
Dayton Urban League.........................E....... 937 226-1513
  Dayton (G-9493)
Deepwood Industries Inc....................C....... 440 350-5231
  Mentor (G-14168)
Don Bosco Community Center Inc....D....... 816 421-3160
  Cleveland (G-5500)
Findaway World LLC..........................D....... 440 893-0808
  Solon (G-17007)
Goodwill Idstrs Grtr Clvlnd L...............E....... 440 783-1168
  Strongsville (G-17467)
Goodwill Industries Inc........................E....... 330 724-6995
  Akron (G-241)
Great Oaks Inst Tech Creer Dev........E....... 513 771-8840
  Cincinnati (G-3703)
Great Oaks Inst Tech Creer Dev........E....... 513 771-8840
  Cincinnati (G-3704)
Handson Central Ohio Inc..................E....... 614 221-2455
  Columbus (G-7798)
Hockingthensperry Cmnty Action.......E....... 740 767-4500
  Glouster (G-11435)
Holmes County Board of Dd...............D....... 330 674-8045
  Holmesville (G-12072)
Integrated Services of Appala............D....... 740 594-6807
  Athens (G-794)
Ironton and Lawrence County............B....... 740 532-3534
  Ironton (G-12291)
Joe and Jill Lewis Inc..........................C....... 937 718-8829
  Dayton (G-9642)
Matco Industries Inc...........................E....... 740 852-7054
  London (G-13002)

Mickis Creative Options Inc................E....... 419 526-4254
  Mansfield (G-13344)
Ohio State University..........................D....... 614 685-3192
  Columbus (G-8401)
Pickaway Diversfied Industries...........D....... 740 474-1522
  Circleville (G-4897)
Richland Newhope Industries.............E....... 419 774-4200
  Mansfield (G-13359)
Richland Newhope Industries.............D....... 419 774-4496
  Mansfield (G-13360)
Richland Newhope Industries.............C....... 419 774-4400
  Mansfield (G-13358)
Ridge Murray Prod Ctr Oberlin...........E....... 440 774-7400
  Oberlin (G-15660)
Southeast Diversified Inds..................D....... 740 432-4241
  Cambridge (G-2128)
TAC Industries Inc..............................B....... 937 328-5200
  Springfield (G-17285)
TAC Industries Inc..............................C....... 937 328-5200
  Springfield (G-17286)
United Disability Services Inc.............C....... 330 374-1169
  Akron (G-485)
Vgs Inc...C....... 216 431-7800
  Cleveland (G-6693)
Vision & Vocational Services..............E....... 614 294-5571
  Columbus (G-8943)
Vocational Services Inc......................C....... 216 431-8085
  Cleveland (G-6709)
Waycraft Inc..D....... 419 563-0550
  Bucyrus (G-2051)
Waycraft Inc..D....... 419 562-3321
  Bucyrus (G-2052)
Weaver Industries Inc.........................E....... 330 379-3660
  Akron (G-506)
Weaver Industries Inc.........................C....... 330 666-5114
  Akron (G-507)
Weaver Industries Inc.........................C....... 330 733-2431
  Tallmadge (G-17661)
Wood County Ohio..............................E....... 419 352-5059
  Bowling Green (G-1804)
Zanesville Welfare Organizatio..........B....... 740 450-6060
  Zanesville (G-20559)
Zepf Center...E....... 419 213-5627
  Toledo (G-18330)

JOB TRAINING SVCS
Akron Blind Center & Workshop........D....... 330 253-2555
  Akron (G-29)
American Line Builders Apprent........D....... 937 849-4177
  Medway (G-14140)
Butler County Bd of Mental RE..........C....... 513 785-2870
  Fairfield Township (G-10927)
County of Crawford.............................D....... 419 562-0015
  Bucyrus (G-2033)
County of Holmes...............................E....... 330 674-1111
  Millersburg (G-14601)
Goodwill Inds Centl Ohio Inc..............B....... 614 294-5181
  Columbus (G-7760)
Goodwill Inds Centl Ohio Inc..............E....... 614 274-5296
  Columbus (G-7761)
Goodwill Inds Lorain Cnty Inc............E....... 440 242-2124
  Elyria (G-10631)
GP Strategies Corporation.................E....... 513 583-8810
  Mason (G-13710)
Miami University.................................B....... 513 727-3200
  Middletown (G-14435)
Ohio State University..........................D....... 614 292-4353
  Columbus (G-8410)
Portage Private Industry....................D....... 330 297-7795
  Ravenna (G-16403)
Spanish American Committee............E....... 216 961-2100
  Cleveland (G-6513)
Star Inc...C....... 740 354-1517
  Portsmouth (G-16314)
Step By Step Emplyment Trining......E....... 440 967-9042
  Vermilion (G-18717)
W S O S Community A........................E....... 419 639-2802
  Green Springs (G-11480)
W S O S Community A........................D....... 419 334-8511
  Fremont (G-11228)
W S O S Community A........................D....... 419 333-6068
  Fremont (G-11227)
Workforce Initiative Assn....................E....... 330 433-9675
  Canton (G-2588)

JUICE, FROZEN: Wholesalers
Mattingly Foods Inc............................C....... 740 454-0136
  Zanesville (G-20500)

JUNIOR HIGH SCHOOLS, PUBLIC
Ashland City School District...............E....... 419 289-7967
  Ashland (G-652)

JUNIOR OR SENIOR HIGH SCHOOLS, NEC
Adams Cnty /Ohio Vly Schl Dst..........D....... 937 544-2951
  West Union (G-19271)
Don Bosco Community Center Inc....D....... 816 421-3160
  Cleveland (G-5500)

JUVENILE CORRECTIONAL FACILITIES
Bellmont County.................................E....... 740 695-9750
  Saint Clairsville (G-16618)
County of Richland.............................D....... 419 774-5578
  Mansfield (G-13282)
County of Ross..................................E....... 740 773-4169
  Chillicothe (G-2830)
County of Summit...............................C....... 330 643-2943
  Akron (G-169)
Five County Joint Juvenile Det..........E....... 937 642-1015
  Marysville (G-13618)
Franklin Cnty Bd Commissioners......E....... 614 462-3429
  Columbus (G-7686)
Lighthouse Youth Services Inc..........D....... 740 634-3094
  Bainbridge (G-942)
Multi County Juvenile Det Ctr............E....... 740 652-1525
  Lancaster (G-12559)

JUVENILE CORRECTIONAL HOME
Medina Cnty Jvnile Dtntion Ctr..........E....... 330 764-8408
  Medina (G-14097)
Multi-Cnty Jvnile Attntion Sys............D....... 330 484-6471
  Canton (G-2469)

KEY DUPLICATING SHOP
Hillman Companies Inc......................B....... 513 851-4900
  Cincinnati (G-3764)
Hman Group Holdings Inc..................A....... 513 851-4900
  Cincinnati (G-3773)

KIDNEY DIALYSIS CENTERS
Alomie Dialysis LLC..........................E....... 740 941-1688
  Waverly (G-18965)
Amelia Davita Dialysis Center...........E....... 513 797-0713
  Amelia (G-572)
Barrington Dialysis LLC.....................D....... 740 346-2740
  Steubenville (G-17303)
Basin Dialysis LLC.............................E....... 937 643-2337
  Kettering (G-12427)
Beck Dialysis LLC..............................E....... 513 422-6879
  Middletown (G-14415)
Bio-Mdcal Applcations Ohio Inc.........E....... 937 279-3120
  Trotwood (G-18344)
Bio-Mdcal Applcations Ohio Inc.........E....... 419 874-3447
  Perrysburg (G-15979)
Bio-Mdcal Applcations Ohio Inc.........E....... 330 928-4511
  Cuyahoga Falls (G-9166)
Bio-Mdcal Applcations Ohio Inc.........E....... 330 376-4905
  Akron (G-102)
Bio-Mdcal Applcations Ohio Inc.........E....... 419 774-0180
  Mansfield (G-13266)
Bio-Mdcal Applcations Ohio Inc.........E....... 330 896-6311
  Uniontown (G-18507)
Bio-Mdcal Applcations Ohio Inc.........E....... 614 338-8202
  Columbus (G-7112)
Bio-Mdcal Applications RI Inc............E....... 740 389-4111
  Marion (G-13524)
Cdc of Shaker Heights.......................E....... 216 295-7000
  Cleveland (G-5200)
Centers For Dialysis Care Inc............E....... 216 295-7000
  Shaker Heights (G-16858)
Columbus-Rna-Davita LLC................E....... 614 985-1732
  Columbus (G-7395)
Comm Ltd Care Dialysis Center........E....... 513 784-1800
  Cincinnati (G-3397)
Community Dialysis Center................C....... 216 229-6170
  Cleveland (G-5384)
Community Dialysis Ctr Mentor.........E....... 440 255-5999
  Mentor (G-14161)
Court Dialysis LLC.............................E....... 740 773-3733
  Chillicothe (G-2831)
Crestview Health Care Center...........D....... 740 695-2500
  Saint Clairsville (G-16634)
Davita Healthcare Partners Inc..........E....... 216 961-6498
  Cleveland (G-5469)
Davita Healthcare Partners Inc..........E....... 440 353-0114
  North Ridgeville (G-15462)

Employee Codes: A=Over 500 employees, B=251-500
C=101-250, D=51-100, E=25-50

2018 Harris Ohio
Services Directory

KIDNEY DIALYSIS CENTERS

Davita Inc .... E 513 939-1110
  Fairfield *(G-10839)*
Davita Inc .... E 216 712-4700
  Rocky River *(G-16576)*
Davita Inc .... E 440 891-5645
  Cleveland *(G-5470)*
Davita Inc .... E 740 376-2622
  Marietta *(G-13442)*
Davita Inc .... E 937 456-1174
  Eaton *(G-10555)*
Davita Inc .... E 330 494-2091
  Canton *(G-2335)*
Davita Inc .... E 216 525-0990
  Independence *(G-12202)*
Davita Inc .... E 937 879-0433
  Fairborn *(G-10791)*
Davita Inc .... E 937 426-6475
  Beavercreek *(G-1166)*
Davita Inc .... E 937 435-4030
  Dayton *(G-9452)*
Davita Inc .... E 937 376-1453
  Xenia *(G-20049)*
Davita Inc .... E 513 784-1800
  Cincinnati *(G-3465)*
Davita Inc .... E 740 401-0607
  Belpre *(G-1435)*
Davita Inc .... E 330 335-2300
  Wadsworth *(G-18752)*
Davita Inc .... E 440 251-6237
  Madison *(G-13222)*
Davita Inc .... E 330 733-1861
  Akron *(G-188)*
Davita Inc .... E 419 697-2191
  Oregon *(G-15730)*
Davita Inc .... E 513 624-0400
  Cincinnati *(G-3466)*
Dayton Regional Dialysis Inc .... E 937 898-5526
  Dayton *(G-9490)*
Desoto Dialysis LLC .... E 419 691-1514
  Oregon *(G-15731)*
Dialysis Center of Dayton East .... E 937 252-1867
  Dayton *(G-9500)*
Dialysis Clinic Inc .... D 513 281-0091
  Cincinnati *(G-3489)*
Dialysis Clinic Inc .... E 740 351-0596
  Portsmouth *(G-16276)*
Dialysis Clinic Inc .... E 513 777-0855
  West Chester *(G-19061)*
Dialysis Clinic Inc .... E 740 264-6687
  Steubenville *(G-17314)*
Dialysis Specialists Fairfield .... E 513 863-6331
  Fairfield *(G-10841)*
Dome Dialysis LLC .... E 614 882-1734
  Westerville *(G-19395)*
DSI East .... E 330 733-1861
  Akron *(G-201)*
Dva Healthcare - South .... E 513 347-0444
  Cincinnati *(G-3516)*
Dva Renal Healthcare Inc .... E 740 454-2911
  Zanesville *(G-20471)*
Fort Dialysis LLC .... E 330 837-7730
  Massillon *(G-13809)*
Fresenius Med Care Butler Cty .... E 513 737-1415
  Hamilton *(G-11730)*
Fresenius Med Care Hldings Inc .... E 800 881-5101
  Columbus *(G-7703)*
Fresenius Medical Care Vro LLC .... E 614 875-2349
  Grove City *(G-11564)*
Goza Dialysis LLC .... E 513 738-0276
  Fairfield *(G-10852)*
Greater Columbus Regional .... D 614 228-9114
  Columbus *(G-7775)*
Greenfield Health Systems Corp .... E 419 389-9681
  Toledo *(G-17923)*
Hemodialysis Services Inc .... E 216 378-2691
  Beachwood *(G-1085)*
Heyburn Dialysis LLC .... E 614 876-3610
  Hilliard *(G-11909)*
Innovative Dialysis of Toledo .... E 419 473-9900
  Toledo *(G-17975)*
Isd Renal Inc .... D 330 375-6848
  Akron *(G-284)*
Kidney Center of Bexley LLC .... C 614 231-2200
  Columbus *(G-7987)*
Kidney Center Partnership .... D 330 799-1150
  Youngstown *(G-20244)*
Kidney Group Inc .... E 330 746-1488
  Youngstown *(G-20245)*
Kidney Services W Centl Ohio .... E 419 227-0918
  Lima *(G-12808)*

Kinswa Dialysis LLC .... E 419 332-0310
  Fremont *(G-11209)*
Lakeshore Dialysis LLC .... E 937 278-0516
  Dayton *(G-9670)*
Lory Dialysis LLC .... E 740 522-2955
  Newark *(G-15198)*
Mahoney Dialysis LLC .... E 937 642-0676
  Marysville *(G-13633)*
Manzano Dialysis LLC .... E 937 879-0433
  Fairborn *(G-10802)*
Mesilla Dialysis LLC .... E 937 484-4600
  Urbana *(G-18597)*
Morro Dialysis LLC .... E 937 865-0633
  Miamisburg *(G-14324)*
Mount Carmel E Dialysis Clnc .... E 614 322-0433
  Columbus *(G-8194)*
Ohio Renal Care Group LLC .... D 440 974-3459
  Mentor *(G-14224)*
Pendster Dialysis LLC .... E 937 237-0769
  Huber Heights *(G-12097)*
Renal Life Link Inc .... E 937 383-3338
  Wilmington *(G-19782)*
Seneca Dialysis LLC .... E 419 443-1051
  Tiffin *(G-17700)*
Steele Dialysis LLC .... E 419 462-1028
  Galion *(G-11305)*
Tonka Bay Dialysis LLC .... E 740 375-0849
  Marion *(G-13585)*
Total Renal Care Inc .... E 937 294-6711
  Kettering *(G-12436)*
Total Renal Care Inc .... E 937 252-1867
  Dayton *(G-9933)*
Trinity Health Corporation .... B 614 846-5420
  Columbus *(G-8872)*
Vogel Dialysis LLC .... E 614 834-3564
  Canal Winchester *(G-2175)*
Wakoni Dialysis LLC .... E 937 294-7188
  Moraine *(G-14834)*
Wallowa Dialysis LLC .... E 419 747-4039
  Ontario *(G-15719)*
Wauseon Dialysis LLC .... E 419 335-0695
  Wauseon *(G-18963)*

KINDERGARTEN

Akron Metropolitan Hsing Auth .... C 330 920-1652
  Stow *(G-17350)*
Colonial Senior Services Inc .... C 513 856-8600
  Hamilton *(G-11713)*
Colonial Senior Services Inc .... C 513 867-4006
  Hamilton *(G-11714)*
Hanna Perkins School .... E 216 991-4472
  Shaker Heights *(G-16861)*
J&B Sprafka Enterprises Inc .... E 330 733-4212
  Akron *(G-288)*
Montessori Community School .... E 740 344-9411
  Newark *(G-15211)*
Royal Redeemer Lutheran Church .... E 440 237-7958
  Cleveland *(G-6418)*
Twinbrook Hills Baptist Church .... E 513 863-3107
  Hamilton *(G-11780)*
Whitehall City Schools .... E 614 417-5680
  Columbus *(G-8988)*

KITCHEN CABINET STORES, EXC CUSTOM

Brower Products Inc .... D 937 563-1111
  Cincinnati *(G-3142)*
Creative Products Inc .... E 419 866-5501
  Holland *(G-12017)*
Lumberjacks Inc .... E 330 762-2401
  Akron *(G-330)*
Schlabach Wood Design Inc .... E 330 897-2600
  Baltic *(G-947)*
Thiels Replacement Systems Inc .... D 419 289-6139
  Ashland *(G-701)*

KITCHEN CABINETS WHOLESALERS

Brower Products Inc .... D 937 563-1111
  Cincinnati *(G-3142)*
Clark Son Actn Liquidation Inc .... E 330 837-9710
  Canal Fulton *(G-2142)*
Direct Import Home Decor Inc .... E 216 898-9758
  Cleveland *(G-5485)*
Don Walter Kitchen Distrs Inc .... E 330 793-9338
  Youngstown *(G-20172)*
Keidel Supply Company Inc .... E 513 351-1600
  Cincinnati *(G-3906)*
Lute Supply Inc .... E 740 353-1447
  Portsmouth *(G-16294)*

Professional Laminate Mllwk Inc .... E 513 891-7858
  Milford *(G-14556)*
Sims-Lohman Inc .... E 513 651-3510
  Cincinnati *(G-4529)*

KITCHEN TOOLS & UTENSILS WHOLESALERS

Creative Products Inc .... E 419 866-5501
  Holland *(G-12017)*
Newell Brands Inc .... C 419 662-2225
  Bowling Green *(G-1786)*

KITCHENWARE STORES

Nacco Industries Inc .... E 440 229-5151
  Cleveland *(G-6098)*
Pottery Barn Inc .... E 614 478-3154
  Columbus *(G-8553)*
Wasserstrom Company .... B 614 228-6525
  Columbus *(G-8970)*

KNIVES: Agricultural Or Indl

CB Manufacturing & Sls Co Inc .... D 937 866-5986
  Miamisburg *(G-14279)*

LABELS: Paper, Made From Purchased Materials

CMC Daymark Corporation .... C 419 354-2591
  Bowling Green *(G-1773)*
General Data Company Inc .... C 513 752-7978
  Cincinnati *(G-2916)*

LABOR RESOURCE SVCS

Focus Solutions Inc .... C 513 376-8349
  Cincinnati *(G-3635)*
Integrated Marketing Tech Inc .... E 330 225-3550
  Brunswick *(G-1982)*
Staffmark Holdings Inc .... D 513 651-1111
  Cincinnati *(G-4573)*
Stage Works .... E 513 522-3118
  Cincinnati *(G-4575)*

LABOR UNION

American Federation of Gov .... E 513 861-6047
  Cincinnati *(G-3004)*
Brotherhood of Locomotive Engi .... E 740 345-0978
  Newark *(G-15150)*
Cleveland Teachers Union Inc .... E 216 861-7676
  Cleveland *(G-5351)*
Healthcare and Social .... E 614 461-1199
  Columbus *(G-7812)*
International Chem Wkrs Cr Un .... E 330 926-1444
  Akron *(G-282)*
International Union United Au .... E 216 447-6080
  Cleveland *(G-5832)*
International Union United Au .... D 513 897-4939
  Waynesville *(G-18984)*
International Union United Au .... E 513 563-1252
  Cincinnati *(G-3837)*
International Union United Au .... E 419 893-4677
  Maumee *(G-13929)*
Interntional Assn Firefighters .... E 330 823-5222
  Alliance *(G-541)*
Licking Knox Labor Council .... D 740 345-1765
  Newark *(G-15190)*
Local Union 856 Uaw Bldg Corp .... E 330 733-6231
  Akron *(G-324)*
National Assn Ltr Carriers .... E 419 289-8359
  Ashland *(G-691)*
National Assn Ltr Carriers .... D 419 693-8392
  Northwood *(G-15538)*
Ohio Assn Pub Schl Employees .... E 614 890-4770
  Columbus *(G-8317)*
Ohio Assn Pub Schl Employees .... E 937 253-5100
  Dayton *(G-9279)*
Ohio Assn Pub Schl Employees .... D 330 659-7335
  Richfield *(G-16520)*
Ohio Civil Service Employees A .... D 614 865-4700
  Westerville *(G-19337)*
Ohio Education Association .... E 614 485-6000
  Columbus *(G-8338)*
Ohio Education Association .... D 614 228-4526
  Columbus *(G-8339)*
Ohio Lbrers Frnge Bneft Prgram .... E 614 898-9006
  Westerville *(G-19432)*
Ohio Operating Engineers Apprn .... E 614 487-6531
  Columbus *(G-8363)*

SERVICES SECTION

LABORATORIES: Dental, Crown & Bridge Production

Smart..C...... 216 228-9400
  North Olmsted *(G-15444)*
Union Cnstr Wkrs Hlth Plan..................E...... 419 248-2401
  Holland *(G-12065)*
United Fd & Coml Wkrs Intl Un..............E...... 216 241-2828
  Broadview Heights *(G-1894)*
United Fd Coml Wkrs Local 880.............E...... 216 241-5930
  Cleveland *(G-6638)*
United Food & Commercial Wkr..............E...... 330 452-4850
  Canton *(G-2567)*
United Food Comml Wrkrs Un.................E...... 614 235-3635
  Columbus *(G-8890)*
United Steelworkers.................................E...... 740 772-5988
  Chillicothe *(G-2893)*
United Steelworkers.................................C...... 740 928-0157
  Newark *(G-15242)*
United Steelworkers.................................E...... 440 979-1050
  North Olmsted *(G-15449)*
United Steelworkers.................................E...... 419 238-7980
  Van Wert *(G-18645)*
United Steelworkers.................................E...... 740 633-0899
  Martins Ferry *(G-13603)*
United Steelworkers.................................E...... 440 244-1358
  Lorain *(G-13083)*
United Steelworkers.................................E...... 440 354-2328
  Painesville *(G-15885)*
United Steelworkers.................................E...... 614 272-8609
  Columbus *(G-8902)*
United Steelworkers.................................E...... 740 622-8860
  Coshocton *(G-9120)*
United Steelworkers of America...........C...... 330 493-7721
  Canton *(G-2572)*

LABORATORIES, TESTING: Automobile Proving & Testing Ground

Ohio Department Transportation..........D...... 614 275-1324
  Columbus *(G-8330)*
Transportation Ohio Department...........E...... 614 275-1300
  Columbus *(G-8865)*

LABORATORIES, TESTING: Food

Agrana Fruit Us Inc.................................C...... 937 693-3821
  Anna *(G-616)*
Daymark Food Safety Systems..............C...... 419 353-2458
  Bowling Green *(G-1774)*
Food Safety Net Services Ltd...............E...... 614 274-2070
  Columbus *(G-7680)*
Nestle Usa Inc..D...... 614 526-5300
  Dublin *(G-10406)*

LABORATORIES, TESTING: Hazardous Waste

Aqua Tech Envmtl Labs Inc...................E...... 740 389-5991
  Marion *(G-13523)*
Envirite of Ohio Inc................................E...... 330 456-6238
  Canton *(G-2356)*

LABORATORIES, TESTING: Hydrostatic

US Tubular Products Inc........................D...... 330 832-1734
  North Lawrence *(G-15394)*

LABORATORIES, TESTING: Industrial Sterilization

Isomedix Operations Inc........................E...... 614 836-5757
  Groveport *(G-11648)*
Isomedix Operations Inc........................C...... 440 354-2600
  Mentor *(G-14196)*

LABORATORIES, TESTING: Metallurgical

Ctl Engineering Inc.................................C...... 614 276-8123
  Columbus *(G-7474)*
Element Mtrls Tchnlgy Hntngtn..............E...... 216 643-1208
  Cleveland *(G-5532)*
J T Adams Co Inc....................................E...... 216 641-3290
  Cleveland *(G-5844)*
Metcut Research Associates Inc..........D...... 513 271-5100
  Cincinnati *(G-4084)*

LABORATORIES, TESTING: Pollution

Grace Consulting Inc..............................E...... 440 647-6672
  Wellington *(G-18992)*
Ohio Rver Vly Wtr Snttion Comm..........E...... 513 231-7719
  Cincinnati *(G-4210)*
Shaw Group Inc......................................A...... 937 593-2022
  Bellefontaine *(G-1396)*

LABORATORIES, TESTING: Prdt Certification, Sfty/Performance

Juice Technologies Inc..........................E...... 800 518-5576
  Columbus *(G-7957)*
Tool Testing Lab Inc...............................E...... 937 898-5696
  Tipp City *(G-17730)*

LABORATORIES, TESTING: Product Testing

Bwi North America Inc............................E...... 937 212-2892
  Moraine *(G-14757)*
Cliff North Consultants Inc....................E...... 513 251-4930
  Cincinnati *(G-3364)*
Glowe-Smith Industrial Inc....................C...... 330 638-5088
  Vienna *(G-18737)*
McCloy Engineering LLC.......................E...... 513 984-4112
  Fairfield *(G-10877)*
Smithers Quality Assessments..............E...... 330 762-4231
  Akron *(G-442)*
Smithers Rapra Inc.................................E...... 330 297-1495
  Ravenna *(G-16413)*
Smithers Rapra Inc.................................D...... 330 762-7441
  Akron *(G-443)*
Smithers Tire & Auto Testng TX............E...... 330 762-7441
  Akron *(G-444)*
Standard Laboratories Inc....................E...... 513 422-1088
  Middletown *(G-14460)*
Wallover Enterprises Inc........................E...... 440 238-9250
  Strongsville *(G-17523)*

LABORATORIES, TESTING: Product Testing, Safety/Performance

Bionetics Corporation.............................E...... 757 873-0900
  Heath *(G-11835)*
Chemsultants International Inc..............E...... 440 974-3080
  Mentor *(G-14157)*
Plastic Technologies Inc........................D...... 419 867-5400
  Holland *(G-12046)*
Standards Testing Labs Inc...................E...... 330 833-8548
  Massillon *(G-13856)*

LABORATORIES, TESTING: Soil Analysis

Analytical Pace Services LLC...............E...... 937 832-8242
  Englewood *(G-10696)*
Brookside Laboratories Inc...................E...... 419 977-2766
  New Bremen *(G-15016)*
Testamerica Laboratories Inc...............C...... 800 456-9396
  North Canton *(G-15372)*
Testamerica Laboratories Inc...............E...... 513 733-5700
  Cincinnati *(G-4637)*

LABORATORIES, TESTING: Water

Enviroscience Inc...................................D...... 330 688-0111
  Stow *(G-17364)*
Mobile Analytical Services.....................E...... 614 873-1710
  Plain City *(G-16201)*
MPW Industrial Services Inc.................E...... 740 345-2431
  Newark *(G-15214)*
National Testing Laboratories...............E...... 440 449-2525
  Cleveland *(G-6112)*

LABORATORIES: Biological

Lexamed..E...... 419 693-5307
  Toledo *(G-18004)*
Medpace Inc..A...... 513 366-3220
  Cincinnati *(G-4048)*
Stembanc Inc..E...... 440 332-4279
  Chardon *(G-2770)*

LABORATORIES: Biological Research

Asymmetric Technologies LLC..............E...... 614 725-5310
  Columbus *(G-7059)*
Biosortia Pharmaceuticals Inc..............E...... 614 636-4850
  Dublin *(G-10263)*
Edison Biotechnology Institute..............E...... 740 593-4713
  Athens *(G-786)*
Mp Biomedicals LLC..............................C...... 440 337-1200
  Solon *(G-17029)*
Stembanc Inc..E...... 440 332-4279
  Chardon *(G-2770)*
Taitech Inc...E...... 937 431-1007
  Beavercreek *(G-1260)*

LABORATORIES: Biotechnology

Battelleed...D...... 614 859-6433
  Columbus *(G-7093)*

Charles River Laboratories Inc.............C...... 419 647-4196
  Spencerville *(G-17107)*
Childrens Hospital Medical Ctr.............A...... 513 636-4200
  Cincinnati *(G-3252)*
EMD Millipore Corporation....................C...... 513 631-0445
  Norwood *(G-15599)*
Medpace Inc..A...... 513 579-9911
  Cincinnati *(G-4049)*
Ues Inc...E...... 937 426-6900
  Beavercreek *(G-1213)*

LABORATORIES: Blood Analysis

Cols Health & Wellness Testing............E...... 614 839-2781
  Westerville *(G-19384)*
Laboratory Corporation America..........E...... 614 475-7852
  Columbus *(G-8027)*
Laboratory Corporation America..........E...... 440 838-0404
  Cleveland *(G-5918)*
Ridgepark Medical Associates..............E...... 216 749-8256
  Cleveland *(G-6396)*

LABORATORIES: Commercial Nonphysical Research

AK Steel Corporation..............................C...... 513 425-6541
  Middletown *(G-14412)*
Applied Research Assoc Inc..................E...... 937 873-8166
  Dayton *(G-9339)*
Clinical Research MGT Inc....................B...... 330 278-2343
  Hinckley *(G-11996)*
I T E LLC...D...... 513 576-6200
  Loveland *(G-13132)*
Infocision Management Corp.................B...... 330 544-1400
  Youngstown *(G-20235)*
Integer Holdings Corporation................E...... 216 937-2800
  Cleveland *(G-5824)*
Ipsos-Asi LLC..D...... 513 872-4300
  Cincinnati *(G-3842)*
Marketing Research Svcs Inc...............D...... 513 772-7580
  Cincinnati *(G-4022)*
Ohio State University.............................D...... 614 292-0476
  Columbus *(G-8438)*
Power Management Inc.........................E...... 937 222-2909
  Dayton *(G-9817)*
Sytronics Inc...E...... 937 431-6100
  Beavercreek *(G-1211)*

LABORATORIES: Dental

Classic Dental Labs Inc.........................E...... 614 443-0328
  Columbus *(G-7293)*
Doling & Associates Dental Lab............E...... 937 254-0075
  Dayton *(G-9503)*
Sentage Corporation..............................E...... 937 865-5900
  Miamisburg *(G-14348)*
State Valley Dental Center.....................E...... 330 920-8060
  Cuyahoga Falls *(G-9220)*

LABORATORIES: Dental & Medical X-Ray

Alliance Imaging Inc...............................C...... 330 493-5100
  Canton *(G-2232)*
Berkebile Russell & Associates.............E...... 440 989-4480
  Lorain *(G-13018)*
Dayton Medical Imaging.........................D...... 937 439-0390
  Dayton *(G-9481)*
Medical Imging Diagnostics LLC............E...... 330 726-0322
  Youngstown *(G-20279)*
Mount Carmel Imaging & Therapy.........E...... 614 234-8080
  Columbus *(G-8199)*
Proscan Imaging LLC.............................E...... 513 759-7350
  West Chester *(G-19133)*
Regional Imaging Cons Corp................F...... 330 726-9000
  Youngstown *(G-20343)*
Trident USA Health Svcs LLC...............E...... 614 888-2226
  Columbus *(G-8870)*
X-Ray Industries Inc..............................E...... 216 642-0100
  Cleveland *(G-6766)*

LABORATORIES: Dental, Artificial Teeth Production

Health Smile Center...............................E...... 440 992-2700
  Ashtabula *(G-747)*

LABORATORIES: Dental, Crown & Bridge Production

Dental Ceramics Inc..............................E...... 330 523-5240
  Richfield *(G-16504)*

Dresch Tolson Dental Labs....................D....... 419 842-6730
Sylvania *(G-17584)*
National Dentex LLC..............................E....... 216 671-0577
Cleveland *(G-6105)*
Roe Dental Laboratory Inc....................D....... 216 663-2233
Independence *(G-12252)*

LABORATORIES: Dental, Denture Production

Greater Cincinnati Dental Labs............E....... 513 385-4222
Cincinnati *(G-3708)*
United Dental Laboratories....................E....... 330 253-1810
Akron *(G-484)*

LABORATORIES: Electronic Research

Promerus LLC...E....... 440 922-0300
Brecksville *(G-1843)*
Rambus Inc...E....... 440 397-2549
Brecksville *(G-1845)*
Steiner Eoptics Inc..................................D....... 937 426-2341
Miamisburg *(G-14354)*

LABORATORIES: Environmental Research

ASC Group Inc...E....... 614 268-2514
Columbus *(G-7048)*
Conwed Plas Acquisition V LLC............D....... 440 926-2607
Akron *(G-163)*
Hydrogeologic Inc...................................E....... 330 463-3303
Hudson *(G-12123)*
Terracon Consultants Inc.......................E....... 614 863-3113
Gahanna *(G-11273)*

LABORATORIES: Medical

Arbor View Family Medicine Inc............E....... 740 687-3386
Lancaster *(G-12509)*
Associated Imaging Corporation..........E....... 419 517-0500
Toledo *(G-17760)*
Blossom Nursing & Rehab Center.........C....... 330 337-3033
Salem *(G-16690)*
Brook Haven Home Health Care.............E....... 937 833-6945
Brookville *(G-1959)*
Cellular Technology Limited..................E....... 216 791-5084
Shaker Heights *(G-16857)*
Childrens Hospital Medical Ctr..............E....... 513 636-6400
Fairfield *(G-10830)*
Cleveland Heartlab Inc..........................D....... 866 358-9828
Cleveland *(G-5317)*
Compunet Clinical Labs LLC..................D....... 937 427-2655
Beavercreek *(G-1234)*
Compunet Clinical Labs LLC..................D....... 937 342-0015
Springfield *(G-17176)*
Compunet Clinical Labs LLC..................C....... 937 296-0844
Moraine *(G-14763)*
Compunet Clinical Labs LLC..................B....... 937 208-3555
Dayton *(G-9421)*
Drew Medical Inc....................................E....... 407 363-6700
Hudson *(G-12114)*
Drs Hill & Thomas Co............................E....... 440 944-8887
Cleveland *(G-5509)*
Gloria Gadmack Do................................C....... 216 363-2353
Cleveland *(G-5675)*
Heart To Heart Home Health..................E....... 330 335-9999
Wadsworth *(G-18755)*
Labcare..E....... 330 753-3649
Barberton *(G-969)*
Labone Inc...A....... 513 585-9000
Cincinnati *(G-3955)*
Laboratory Corporation America..........E....... 440 951-6841
Willoughby *(G-19679)*
Laboratory Corporation America..........E....... 440 328-3275
Mansfield *(G-13322)*
Maternohio Clinical Assoicates............E....... 614 457-7660
Columbus *(G-8128)*
Medcentral Workable.............................E....... 419 526-8444
Ontario *(G-15702)*
Mercy Health Youngstown LLC..............A....... 330 729-1420
Youngstown *(G-20283)*
Midwest Ultrasound Inc..........................E....... 513 936-0444
Cincinnati *(G-4093)*
Midwest Ultrasound Inc..........................D....... 513 248-8885
Milford *(G-14540)*
Monroe Family Health Center................E....... 740 472-0757
Woodsfield *(G-19818)*
Mp Biomedicals LLC..............................C....... 440 337-1200
Solon *(G-17029)*
Nationwide Childrens Hospital..............C....... 614 722-2700
Columbus *(G-8229)*
Northeast OH Neighborhood Heal.........C....... 216 231-2323
Cleveland *(G-6152)*
Shared PET Imaging Llc.........................C....... 330 491-0480
Canton *(G-2527)*
St Ritas Medical Center..........................D....... 419 226-9229
Lima *(G-12886)*
Standards Testing Labs Inc....................E....... 330 833-8548
Massillon *(G-13856)*
Summa Health...D....... 330 753-3649
Barberton *(G-980)*
Summa Health...E....... 330 688-4531
Stow *(G-17395)*
Superior Medical Care Inc......................E....... 440 282-7420
Lorain *(G-13080)*
University of Cincinnati..........................E....... 513 558-4444
Cincinnati *(G-4762)*
University of Cincinnati..........................C....... 513 558-5439
Cincinnati *(G-4766)*

LABORATORIES: Medical Pathology

Bayless Pathmark Inc..............................E....... 440 274-2494
Cleveland *(G-5103)*
Consultants Laboratory Medici..............E....... 419 535-9629
Toledo *(G-17830)*
Lima Pathology Associates Labs...........E....... 419 226-9595
Lima *(G-12826)*
Oncodiagnostic Laboratory Inc.............E....... 216 861-5846
Cleveland *(G-6203)*
Osu Pathology Services LLC..................D....... 614 293-5905
Columbus *(G-8489)*
Osu Pathology Services LLC..................B....... 614 247-6461
Columbus *(G-8490)*
Pathology Laboratories Inc....................C....... 419 255-4600
Toledo *(G-18121)*
Vet Path Services Inc..............................E....... 513 469-0777
Mason *(G-13778)*

LABORATORIES: Noncommercial Research

Advantage Aerotech Inc..........................E....... 614 759-8329
Columbus *(G-6947)*
American Cancer Society East..............B....... 888 227-6446
Dublin *(G-10245)*
Benjamin Rose Institute..........................D....... 216 791-8000
Cleveland *(G-5115)*
Dayton Foundation Inc............................E....... 937 222-0410
Dayton *(G-9474)*
Ofeq Institute Inc.....................................E....... 440 943-1497
Wickliffe *(G-19610)*
Ohio Aerospace Institute.........................D....... 440 962-3000
Cleveland *(G-6184)*
Ohio State University..............................D....... 614 292-1681
Columbus *(G-8402)*
Ohio Technical College Inc....................C....... 216 881-1700
Cleveland *(G-6195)*
Ohiohealth Research Institute...............E....... 614 566-4297
Columbus *(G-8461)*
Roholt Vision Institute Inc......................E....... 330 702-8755
Canfield *(G-2208)*
University of Dayton...............................A....... 937 229-2919
Dayton *(G-9952)*

LABORATORIES: Physical Research, Commercial

Alcatel-Lucent USA Inc..........................B....... 614 860-2000
Dublin *(G-10239)*
Alliance Imaging Inc...............................C....... 330 493-5100
Canton *(G-2232)*
Antioch University...................................D....... 937 769-1366
Yellow Springs *(G-20088)*
Applied Research Assoc Inc..................E....... 937 435-1016
Dayton *(G-9338)*
Arthur G James Cancer..........................A....... 614 293-4878
Columbus *(G-7044)*
Azimuth Corporation...............................E....... 937 256-8571
Beavercreek Township *(G-1265)*
BASF Catalysts LLC...............................D....... 216 360-5005
Cleveland *(G-5097)*
Borchers Americas Inc...........................D....... 440 899-2950
Westlake *(G-19466)*
Bridgestone Research LLC....................A....... 330 379-7570
Akron *(G-110)*
Brilligent Solutions Inc...........................E....... 937 879-4148
Fairborn *(G-10785)*
Cast Metals Technology Inc...................E....... 937 968-5460
Union City *(G-18501)*
Chemimage Filter Tech LLC...................E....... 330 686-2829
Stow *(G-17357)*
Circle Prime Manufacturing....................E....... 330 923-0019
Cuyahoga Falls *(G-9172)*
Cleveland F E S Center..........................D....... 216 231-3257
Cleveland *(G-5314)*
Ctl Engineering Inc.................................C....... 614 276-8123
Columbus *(G-7474)*
Curtiss-Wright Controls..........................E....... 937 252-5601
Fairborn *(G-10789)*
Defense Research Assoc Inc..................E....... 937 431-1644
Dayton *(G-9265)*
Edison Welding Institute Inc..................C....... 614 688-5000
Columbus *(G-7578)*
Ensafe Inc...E....... 513 621-7233
West Chester *(G-19068)*
Flexsys America LP...............................D....... 330 666-4111
Akron *(G-227)*
Fram Group Operations LLC..................D....... 419 661-6700
Perrysburg *(G-16005)*
Illumination Research Inc......................E....... 513 774-9531
Mason *(G-13719)*
Keeptryan Inc...D....... 330 319-1866
Akron *(G-302)*
Kemron Environmental Svcs Inc...........D....... 740 373-4071
Marietta *(G-13460)*
Kenmore Research Company.................D....... 330 297-1407
Ravenna *(G-16391)*
Laboratory Corporation America..........A....... 614 336-3993
Dublin *(G-10385)*
Leidos Inc...B....... 937 431-2220
Beavercreek *(G-1185)*
Leidos Technical Services Inc...............D....... 513 672-8400
West Chester *(G-19212)*
Lindner Clinical Trial Center..................E....... 513 585-1777
Cincinnati *(G-3987)*
Lyondell Chemical Company..................D....... 513 530-4000
Cincinnati *(G-4004)*
Midwest Optoelectronics LLC...............C....... 419 724-0565
Toledo *(G-18063)*
Modern Tech Solutions Inc....................D....... 937 426-9025
Beavercreek Township *(G-1275)*
Muskingum Starlight Industries............D....... 740 453-4622
Zanesville *(G-20513)*
Nationwide Childrens Hospital..............C....... 614 722-2700
Columbus *(G-8229)*
Natural Resources Ohio Dept................E....... 614 265-6852
Columbus *(G-8250)*
Nsa Technologies LLC..........................C....... 330 576-4600
Akron *(G-359)*
Omnova Solutions Inc...........................D....... 330 794-6300
Akron *(G-371)*
Owens Corning Sales LLC....................B....... 740 587-3562
Granville *(G-11471)*
Pen Brands LLC.....................................E....... 216 447-1199
Brooklyn Heights *(G-1923)*
Plastic Technologies Inc........................D....... 419 867-5400
Holland *(G-12046)*
Potter Technologies LLC.......................D....... 419 380-8404
Toledo *(G-18131)*
Q Labs LLC..C....... 513 471-1300
Cincinnati *(G-4359)*
Renovo Neural Inc..................................E....... 216 445-4252
Cleveland *(G-6376)*
Rogosin Institute Inc..............................E....... 937 374-3116
Xenia *(G-20074)*
Schneller LLC...D....... 330 673-1299
Kent *(G-12395)*
Sensation Research...............................E....... 513 602-1611
Maineville *(G-13246)*
Sunpower Inc..D....... 740 594-2221
Athens *(G-813)*
Sytronics Inc...E....... 937 431-6100
Beavercreek *(G-1211)*
Wyle Laboratories Inc............................C....... 937 320-2712
Beavercreek *(G-1264)*

LABORATORIES: Testing

Cadx Systems Inc...................................D....... 937 431-1464
Beavercreek *(G-1157)*
Connie Parks...E....... 330 759-8334
Hubbard *(G-12084)*
Ecg Scanning & Medical Svcs...............E....... 888 346-5837
Moraine *(G-14778)*
Laboratory Corporation America..........E....... 937 383-6964
Wilmington *(G-19765)*
Laboratory Corporation America..........E....... 330 865-3624
Akron *(G-311)*
Laboratory Corporation America..........E....... 614 882-6278
Columbus *(G-8028)*
Laboratory Corporation America..........E....... 513 242-6800
Cincinnati *(G-3956)*
Laboratory Corporation America..........E....... 419 281-7100
Ashland *(G-685)*
Laboratory Corporation America..........E....... 937 866-8188
Miamisburg *(G-14313)*

SERVICES SECTION

LABORATORIES (continued)

Laboratory Corporation America .... A 614 336-3993
  Dublin (G-10385)
Laboratory Corporation America .... E 440 884-1591
  Cleveland (G-5917)
Laboratory Corporation America .... E 740 522-2034
  Newark (G-15181)
Laboratory Corporation America .... E 330 686-0194
  Stow (G-17379)
Laboratory of Dermatopathology .... E 937 434-2351
  Dayton (G-9669)
Medical Diagnostic Lab Inc .... D 440 333-1375
  Westlake (G-19514)
Medpace Bioanalytical Labs LLC .... E 513 366-3260
  Cincinnati (G-4050)
Suburban Medical Laboratory .... C 330 929-7992
  Euclid (G-10778)
Triad Group Inc .... D 419 228-8800
  Lima (G-12904)
University of Cincinnati .... D 513 584-5331
  Cincinnati (G-4769)
Zak Enterprises Ltd .... D 216 261-9700
  Euclid (G-10781)

LABORATORIES: Testing

Advanced Testing Lab Inc .... C 513 489-8447
  Blue Ash (G-1525)
Advanced Testing MGT Group Inc .... C 513 489-8447
  Blue Ash (G-1526)
Akzo Nobel Coatings Inc .... C 614 294-3361
  Columbus (G-6962)
Als Group Usa Corp .... E 513 733-5336
  Blue Ash (G-1530)
Als Services Usa Corp .... D 513 582-8277
  West Chester (G-19017)
Als Services Usa Corp .... E 604 998-5311
  Cleveland (G-4999)
Atc Group Services LLC .... D 513 771-2112
  Cincinnati (G-3056)
Balancing Company Inc .... E 937 898-9111
  Vandalia (G-18661)
Barr Engineering Incorporated .... E 614 714-0299
  Columbus (G-7091)
Bayless Pathmark Inc .... E 440 274-2494
  Cleveland (G-5103)
Bowser-Morner Inc .... E 419 691-4800
  Toledo (G-17779)
Cincinnati Sub-Zero Pdts LLC .... C 800 989-7373
  Cincinnati (G-3331)
Clinton-Carvell Inc .... E 614 351-8858
  Columbus (G-7303)
Csa America Inc .... C 216 524-4990
  Cleveland (G-5441)
Csa America Inc .... D 216 524-4990
  Cleveland (G-5442)
Curtiss-Wright Flow Control .... D 513 528-7900
  Cincinnati (G-2910)
Curtiss-Wright Flow Ctrl Corp .... D 513 528-7900
  Cincinnati (G-2911)
Dna Diagnostics Center Inc .... C 513 881-7800
  Fairfield (G-10842)
Electro-Analytical Inc .... E 440 951-3514
  Mentor (G-14171)
Element Cincinnati .... E 513 984-4112
  Fairfield (G-10845)
Element Mtls Tech Cncnnati Inc .... E 513 771-2536
  Fairfield (G-10846)
Emlab P&K LLC .... D 330 497-9396
  North Canton (G-15335)
First Energy Nuclear Oper Co .... D 440 604-9836
  Cleveland (G-5595)
Fram Group Operations LLC .... D 419 661-6700
  Perrysburg (G-16005)
General Electric Company .... E 937 587-2631
  Peebles (G-15938)
Godfrey & Wing Inc .... E 330 562-1440
  Aurora (G-840)
Grl Engineers Inc .... E 216 831-6131
  Solon (G-17013)
High Voltage Maintenance Corp .... E 937 278-0811
  Dayton (G-9611)
Idexx Laboratories Inc .... D 330 629-6076
  Youngstown (G-20229)
Intertek Testing Svcs NA Inc .... E 614 279-8090
  Columbus (G-7920)
Kemron Environmental Svcs Inc .... D 740 373-4071
  Marietta (G-13460)
Kenmore Research Company .... D 330 297-1407
  Ravenna (G-16391)
Laboratory Corporation America .... E 440 205-8299
  Mentor (G-14202)
Landing Gear Test Facility .... E 937 255-5740
  Dayton (G-9276)
Mercy Health .... E 330 841-4406
  Warren (G-18880)
Mistras Group Inc .... E 740 788-9188
  Heath (G-11839)
North Amercn Science Assoc Inc .... C 419 666-9455
  Northwood (G-15539)
Northast Ohio Rgonal Sewer Dst .... C 216 641-6000
  Cleveland (G-6147)
Nsl Analytical Services Inc .... D 216 438-5200
  Cleveland (G-6169)
Nucon International Inc .... E 614 846-5710
  Columbus (G-8303)
Omega Laboratories Inc .... D 330 628-5748
  Mogadore (G-14681)
Pace Analytical Services Inc .... E 614 486-5421
  Dublin (G-10420)
Professional Service Inds Inc .... E 614 876-8000
  Columbus (G-8568)
Q Labs LLC .... C 513 471-1300
  Cincinnati (G-4359)
Reid Asset Management Company .... E 216 642-3223
  Cleveland (G-6368)
Resource International Inc .... C 614 823-4949
  Columbus (G-8622)
Rev1 Ventures .... E 614 487-3700
  Columbus (G-8627)
S D Myers Inc .... C 330 630-7000
  Tallmadge (G-17648)
Sample Machining Inc .... E 937 258-3338
  Dayton (G-9866)
SD Myers LLC .... D 330 630-7000
  Tallmadge (G-17649)
Sensation Research .... E 513 602-1611
  Maineville (G-13246)
Silliker Laboratories Ohio Inc .... E 614 486-0150
  Columbus (G-8732)
Summit Environmental Tech Inc .... E 330 253-8211
  Cuyahoga Falls (G-9222)
US Inspection Services Inc .... E 937 660-9879
  Dayton (G-9958)
US Inspection Services Inc .... E 513 671-7073
  Cincinnati (G-4795)
Wyle Laboratories Inc .... E 937 912-3470
  Beavercreek (G-1224)
X-Ray Industries Inc .... E 216 642-0100
  Cleveland (G-6766)
Yoder Industries Inc .... C 937 278-5769
  Dayton (G-10007)

LABORATORIES: Testing, Assaying

Antech Diagnostics Inc .... E 330 665-4996
  Copley (G-9051)

LABORATORIES: Ultrasound

Amerathon LLC .... B 513 752-7300
  Cincinnati (G-2903)
Mercy Health Youngstown LLC .... A 330 746-7211
  Youngstown (G-20284)
Proscan Imaging LLC .... D 513 281-3400
  Cincinnati (G-4349)
Stork Studios Inc .... E 419 841-7766
  Toledo (G-18203)
Womens Centers-Dayton .... E 937 228-2222
  Dayton (G-10002)

LABORATORY APPARATUS & FURNITURE

Chemsultants International Inc .... E 440 974-3080
  Mentor (G-14157)
Dentronix Inc .... E 330 916-7300
  Cuyahoga Falls (G-9179)
Ies Systems Inc .... E 330 533-6683
  Canfield (G-2196)
Philips Medical Systems Clevel .... B 440 247-2652
  Cleveland (G-6273)
Tech Pro Inc .... E 330 923-3546
  Akron (G-473)
Teledyne Instruments Inc .... E 513 229-7000
  Mason (G-13767)
Teledyne Tekmar Company .... E 513 229-7000
  Mason (G-13768)

LABORATORY EQPT, EXC MEDICAL: Wholesalers

Perkinelmer Hlth Sciences Inc 330 825-4525
  Akron (G-385)
Teledyne Instruments Inc .... E 513 229-7000
  Mason (G-13767)
Teledyne Tekmar Company .... E 513 229-7000
  Mason (G-13768)

LABORATORY EQPT: Clinical Instruments Exc Medical

Cellular Technology Limited .... E 216 791-5084
  Shaker Heights (G-16857)

LABORATORY INSTRUMENT REPAIR SVCS

Tech Pro Inc .... E 330 923-3546
  Akron (G-473)

LADDERS: Metal

Bauer Corporation .... E 800 321-4760
  Wooster (G-19830)

LAMINATED PLASTICS: Plate, Sheet, Rod & Tubes

Applied Medical Technology Inc .... E 440 717-4000
  Brecksville (G-1813)
Ilpea Industries Inc .... C 330 562-2916
  Aurora (G-842)

LAMINATING SVCS

Conversion Tech Intl Inc .... E 419 924-5566
  West Unity (G-19280)
Kent Adhesive Products Co .... D 330 678-1626
  Kent (G-12376)
Ohio Laminating & Binding Inc .... E 614 771-4868
  Hilliard (G-11939)
United Art and Education Inc .... E 800 322-3247
  Dayton (G-9945)

LAND SUBDIVIDERS & DEVELOPERS: Commercial

Al Neyer LLC .... D 513 271-6400
  Cincinnati (G-2981)
C V Perry & Co .... E 614 221-4131
  Columbus (G-7176)
Cardida Corporation .... E 740 439-4359
  Kimbolton (G-12446)
Coral Company .... E 216 932-8822
  Cleveland (G-5408)
Creekside II LLC .... E 614 280-4000
  Columbus (G-7459)
Duke Realty Corporation .... D 513 651-3900
  Mason (G-13698)
Eagle Realty Group LLC .... E 513 361-7700
  Cincinnati (G-3528)
Forest City Washington LLC .... E 202 496-6600
  Cleveland (G-5622)
Goodman Properties Inc .... E 740 264-7781
  Steubenville (G-17318)
Highland Som Development .... E 330 528-3500
  Streetsboro (G-17416)
Laurel Development Corporation .... E 614 794-8800
  Westerville (G-19321)
Mid-Ohio Development Corp .... D 614 836-0606
  Groveport (G-11657)
Multicon Builders Inc .... E 614 241-2070
  Columbus (G-8206)
Multicon Builders Inc .... E 614 463-1142
  Columbus (G-8207)
Oberer Development Co .... E 937 910-0851
  Miamisburg (G-14328)
Ostendorf-Morris Properties 216 001-7200
  Cleveland (G-6217)
Phillips Edison & Company LLC .... E 513 554-1110
  Cincinnati (G-4291)
Req/Jqh Holdings Inc .... D 513 891-1066
  Blue Ash (G-1681)
Robert L Stark Enterprises Inc .... E 216 292-0242
  Cleveland (G-6403)
Slavic Village Development .... E 216 429-1182
  Cleveland (G-6488)
Sommerset Development Ltd .... C 440 286-6194
  Chardon (G-2768)
Southgate Corp .... E 740 522-2151
  Newark (G-15234)
Sunrise Land Co .... E 216 621-6060
  Cleveland (G-6550)
T O J Inc .... E 440 352-1900
  Mentor (G-14247)

Employee Codes: A=Over 500 employees, B=251-500
C=101-250, D=51-100, E=25-50

LAND SUBDIVIDERS & DEVELOPERS: Commercial

The Daimler Group Inc .... E 614 488-4424
  Columbus (G-8835)
Zaremba Group Incorporated .... E 216 221-6600
  Cleveland (G-6779)
Zaremba Group LLC .... C 216 221-6600
  Lakewood (G-12504)

LAND SUBDIVIDERS & DEVELOPERS: Residential

Bob Schmitt Homes Inc .... D 440 327-9495
  North Ridgeville (G-15455)
Breezy Point Ltd Partnership .... C 440 247-3363
  Solon (G-16984)
Columbus Housing Partnr Inc .... D 614 221-8889
  Columbus (G-7360)
Forrer Development Ltd .... E 937 431-6489
  Dayton (G-9557)
Towne Development Group Ltd .... E 513 381-8696
  Cincinnati (G-4667)
Wryneck Development LLC .... E 419 354-2535
  Bowling Green (G-1805)

LAND SUBDIVISION & DEVELOPMENT

Carnegie Management & Dev Corp .... E 440 892-6800
  Westlake (G-19470)
Carter-Jones Companies Inc .... E 330 673-6100
  Kent (G-12354)
Edwards Land Company .... E 614 241-2070
  Columbus (G-7585)
Equity Inc .... E 614 802-2900
  Hilliard (G-11900)
Forest City Enterprises LP .... B 216 621-6060
  Cleveland (G-5614)
Forest Cy Residential MGT Inc .... C 216 621-6060
  Cleveland (G-5623)
George J Igel & Co Inc .... A 614 445-8421
  Columbus (G-7742)
Greystone Group-Avery Ltd .... E 216 464-3580
  Cleveland (G-5705)
Henkle-Schueler & Associates .... E 513 932-6070
  Lebanon (G-12611)
Lha Developments .... E 330 785-3219
  Akron (G-317)
Lt Land Development LLC .... E 937 382-0072
  Wilmington (G-19770)
Magnum Management Corporation .... A 419 627-2334
  Sandusky (G-16778)
Midwestern Plumbing Service .... E 513 753-0050
  Cincinnati (G-4094)
Miller-Vlentine Operations Inc .... E 937 293-0900
  Dayton (G-9750)
Miller-Vlentine Operations Inc .... A 513 771-0900
  Dayton (G-9751)
Mv Residential Development LLC .... E 937 293-0900
  Moraine (G-14810)
Nationwide Rlty Investors Ltd .... E 614 857-2330
  Columbus (G-8248)
Newcomerstown Development Inc .... C 740 498-5165
  Newcomerstown (G-15270)
North American Properties Inc .... E 513 721-2744
  Cincinnati (G-4176)
Piatt Park Ltd Partnership .... D 513 381-8696
  Cincinnati (G-4296)
Pizzuti Builders LLC .... E 614 280-4000
  Columbus (G-8546)
Pizzuti Inc .... E 614 280-4000
  Columbus (G-8547)
Rama Tika Developers LLC .... E 419 806-6446
  Mansfield (G-13353)
Richland Mall Shopping Ctr .... E 419 529-4003
  Mansfield (G-13357)
Robert C Verbon Inc .... E 419 867-6868
  Toledo (G-18160)
Rockford Homes Inc .... D 614 785-0015
  Columbus (G-6905)
Sawyer Realtors .... E 513 423-6521
  Middletown (G-14456)
Seg of Ohio Inc .... E 614 414-7300
  Columbus (G-8711)
Signature Associates Inc .... E 419 244-7505
  Toledo (G-18188)
Soho Development Company .... D 614 207-3261
  Johnstown (G-12342)
TP Mechanical Contractors Inc .... A 513 851-8881
  Cincinnati (G-4675)
TP Mechanical Contractors Inc .... C 614 253-8556
  Columbus (G-8859)
Urban Retail Properties LLC .... E 513 346-4482
  Cincinnati (G-4790)

Visconsi Companies Ltd .... E 216 464-5550
  Cleveland (G-6700)
Wallick Enterprises Inc .... D 614 863-4640
  New Albany (G-15009)
Warren Housing Development .... D 330 369-1533
  Warren (G-18925)
Windsor Companies .... E 740 653-8822
  Lancaster (G-12584)

LANGUAGE SCHOOLS

Cincilingua Inc .... E 513 721-8782
  Cincinnati (G-3277)

LAUNDRIES, EXC POWER & COIN-OPERATED

Central Ohio Medical Textiles .... C 614 453-9274
  Columbus (G-7231)
Clean Living Laundry LLC .... E 513 569-0439
  Cincinnati (G-3362)
Springfeld Unfrm-Linen Sup Inc .... D 937 323-5544
  Springfield (G-17278)

LAUNDRY & DRYCLEANER AGENTS

Apc2 Inc .... E 513 231-5540
  Cincinnati (G-3033)

LAUNDRY & DRYCLEANING SVCS, EXC COIN-OPERATED: Pickup

R & E Joint Venture Inc .... E 614 891-9404
  Westerville (G-19348)

LAUNDRY & GARMENT SVCS, NEC: Accy/Non-Garment Cleaning/Rpr

Van Dyne-Crotty Co .... E 614 684-0048
  Columbus (G-8932)

LAUNDRY & GARMENT SVCS, NEC: Garment Alteration & Repair

Hyo OK Inc .... E 614 876-7644
  Hilliard (G-11912)
Quality Cleaners of Ohio Inc .... E 330 688-5616
  Stow (G-17388)

LAUNDRY & GARMENT SVCS, NEC: Garment Making, Alter & Repair

Pins & Needles Inc .... E 440 243-6400
  Cleveland (G-6281)

LAUNDRY SVC: Mat & Rug Sply

Kimmel Cleaners Inc .... D 419 294-1959
  Upper Sandusky (G-18564)

LAUNDRY SVC: Safety Glove Sply

Brent Industries Inc .... E 419 382-8693
  Toledo (G-17782)

LAUNDRY SVC: Work Clothing Sply

Unifirst Corporation .... E 614 575-9999
  Blacklick (G-1511)

LAUNDRY SVCS: Indl

Aramark Unf & Career AP LLC .... C 614 445-8341
  Columbus (G-7032)
Aramark Unf & Career AP LLC .... C 216 341-7400
  Cleveland (G-5058)
Cintas Corporation .... D 330 821-2220
  Alliance (G-532)
Cintas Corporation No 2 .... D 440 238-5565
  Strongsville (G-17449)
Cintas Corporation No 2 .... D 614 878-7313
  Columbus (G-7274)
Cintas Corporation No 2 .... C 614 860-9152
  Blacklick (G-1504)
Duckworth Enterprises LLC .... E 614 575-2900
  Reynoldsburg (G-16449)
Midwest Laundry Inc .... D 513 563-5560
  Cincinnati (G-4092)
Morgan Services Inc .... E 419 243-2214
  Toledo (G-18070)
Springfeld Unfrm-Linen Sup Inc .... D 937 323-5544
  Springfield (G-17278)

LAWN & GARDEN EQPT

Mtd Holdings Inc .... B 330 225-2600
  Valley City (G-18622)
Power Distributors LLC .... D 614 876-3533
  Columbus (G-8554)
Scotts Company LLC .... A 937 644-3729
  Marysville (G-13650)

LAWN & GARDEN EQPT STORES

Carmichael Equipment Inc .... E 740 446-2412
  Bidwell (G-1494)
Equipment Maintenance Inc .... E 513 353-3518
  Cleves (G-6799)
Hull Bros Inc .... E 419 375-2827
  Fort Recovery (G-11118)
Supers Landscaping Inc .... E 440 775-0027
  Oberlin (G-15661)

LAWN MOWER REPAIR SHOP

Altaquip LLC .... E 513 674-6464
  Harrison (G-11790)
Supers Landscaping Inc .... E 440 775-0027
  Oberlin (G-15661)

LEASING & RENTAL SVCS: Cranes & Aerial Lift Eqpt

A and A Mllwright Rigging Svcs .... E 513 396-6212
  Cincinnati (G-2951)
All Aerials LLC .... E 330 659-9600
  Richfield (G-16494)
American Crane Inc .... E 614 496-2268
  Reynoldsburg (G-16426)
Canton Erectors Inc .... E 330 453-7363
  Canton (G-2287)
Eastland Crane Service Inc .... E 614 868-9750
  Columbus (G-7565)
General Crane Rental LLC .... E 330 908-0001
  Macedonia (G-13198)
Interstate Lift Trucks Inc .... E 216 328-0970
  Cleveland (G-5835)
Jeffers Crane Service Inc .... D 419 693-0421
  Oregon (G-15740)
Kelley Steel Erectors Inc .... D 440 232-1573
  Cleveland (G-5891)
Piqua Steel Co .... D 937 773-3632
  Piqua (G-16159)
United Rentals North Amer Inc .... E 800 877-3687
  Perrysburg (G-16067)

LEASING & RENTAL SVCS: Earth Moving Eqpt

Malavite Excavating Inc .... E 330 484-1274
  East Sparta (G-10540)

LEASING & RENTAL SVCS: Oil Field Eqpt

Eleet Cryogenics Inc .... E 330 874-4009
  Bolivar (G-1746)

LEASING & RENTAL: Computers & Eqpt

Information Builders Inc .... E 513 891-2338
  Montgomery (G-14726)
Pomeroy It Solutions Sls Inc .... E 440 717-1364
  Brecksville (G-1842)

LEASING & RENTAL: Construction & Mining Eqpt

1st Choice LLC .... D 877 564-6658
  Cleveland (G-4922)
Ahern Rentals Inc .... E 440 498-0869
  Solon (G-16972)
All Crane Rental Corp .... D 614 261-1800
  Columbus (G-6964)
All Erection & Crane Rental .... C 216 524-6550
  Cleveland (G-4986)
All Erection & Crane Rental .... D 216 524-6550
  Cleveland (G-4987)
AVI Food Systems Inc .... E 440 255-3468
  Mentor (G-14146)
Bluefoot Industrial LLC .... E 740 314-5299
  Steubenville (G-17304)
Bobcat Enterprises Inc .... C 513 874-8945
  West Chester (G-19030)
Cecil I Walker Machinery Co .... E 740 286-7566
  Jackson (G-12308)

Charles Jergens Contractor..................E 937 233-1830
Dayton *(G-9400)*
Columbus Equipment Company ....E 614 437-0352
Columbus *(G-7352)*
Columbus Equipment Company ....E 614 443-6541
Columbus *(G-7353)*
Dolin Supply Co......................................E 304 529-4171
South Point *(G-17084)*
Efco Corp..E 614 876-1226
Columbus *(G-7586)*
F & M Mafco Inc.......................................C 513 367-2151
Harrison *(G-11797)*
H M Miller Construction Co..................D 330 628-4811
Mogadore *(G-14677)*
Holt Rental Services...............................E 513 771-0515
Cincinnati *(G-3776)*
Indian Nation Inc.....................................E 740 532-6143
North Canton *(G-15345)*
JBK Group Inc..E 216 901-0000
Cleveland *(G-5854)*
Lefeld Welding & Stl Sups Inc ....E 419 678-2397
Coldwater *(G-6832)*
Leppo Inc..E 330 456-2930
Canton *(G-2434)*
Leppo Inc..C 330 633-3999
Tallmadge *(G-17643)*
Miami Industrial Trucks Inc...................E 419 424-0042
Findlay *(G-11066)*
Midwest Equipment Co ....E 216 441-1400
Cleveland *(G-6061)*
Ohio Machinery Co ....E 330 530-9010
Girard *(G-11421)*
Ohio Machinery Co ....C 440 526-6200
Broadview Heights *(G-1886)*
Phillips Ready Mix Co.............................D 937 426-5151
Beavercreek Township *(G-1281)*
Pollock Research & Design Inc ....E 330 332-3300
Salem *(G-16706)*
RELAM Inc..E 440 232-3354
Solon *(G-17046)*
Sommerset Development Ltd ....C 440 286-6194
Chardon *(G-2768)*
Sunbelt Rentals Inc.................................E 216 362-0300
Cleveland *(G-6549)*
TNT Equipment Company.......................E 614 882-1549
Columbus *(G-8852)*
Towlift Inc ....E 419 666-1333
Northwood *(G-15548)*
Trimble Engineering & Cnstr ....E 937 233-8921
Dayton *(G-9938)*

LEASING & RENTAL: Medical Machinery & Eqpt

American Home Health Care Inc ....E 614 237-1133
Columbus *(G-6996)*
Ancillary Medical Investments...............E 937 456-5520
Eaton *(G-10552)*
Apria Healthcare LLC ....E 614 351-5920
Columbus *(G-7030)*
Apria Healthcare LLC ....E 216 485-1180
Cleveland *(G-5056)*
Apria Healthcare LLC ....D 419 471-1919
Maumee *(G-13883)*
Boardman Medical Supply Co ....C 330 545-6700
Girard *(G-11408)*
Braden Med Services Inc ....E 740 732-2356
Caldwell *(G-2082)*
Cornerstone Medical Associates ....E 330 374-0229
Akron *(G-165)*
Fairfield Medical Center ....A 740 687-8000
Lancaster *(G-12537)*
Fortec Medical Inc....................................E 330 463-1265
Hudson *(G-12117)*
Fortec Medical Inc....................................E 513 742-9100
Cincinnati *(G-3640)*
Medic Home Health Care LLC ....E 440 449-7727
Cleveland *(G-6012)*
Medical Service Company.......................D 440 232-3000
Bedford *(G-1322)*
Medical Specialties Distrs LLC..............E 440 232-0320
Oakwood Village *(G-15630)*
Millers Rental and Sls Co Inc.................D 330 753-8600
Akron *(G-345)*
North Ohio Heart Center.........................D 440 204-4000
Lorain *(G-13069)*
Sateri Home Inc..D 330 758-8106
Youngstown *(G-20367)*
Seeley Enterprises Company ....E 440 293-6600
Andover *(G-614)*
Seeley Medical Oxygen Co ....E 440 255-7163
Andover *(G-615)*
St Ritas Medical Center...........................A 419 227-3361
Lima *(G-12885)*
Toledo Medical Equipment Co..............E 419 866-7120
Maumee *(G-13987)*

LEASING & RENTAL: Mobile Home Sites

Mercelina Mobile Home Park ....D 419 586-5407
Celina *(G-2652)*
Park Management Specialist ....D 419 893-4879
Maumee *(G-13956)*

LEASING & RENTAL: Office Machines & Eqpt

Gordon Flesch Company Inc.................E 419 884-2031
Mansfield *(G-13305)*
Modern Office Methods Inc....................D 513 791-0909
Blue Ash *(G-1644)*
Office Products Toledo Inc ....E 419 865-7001
Holland *(G-12044)*
Oscar Rbrtsn Doc Mgmt Svcs ....E 800 991-4611
Blue Ash *(G-1661)*
Ricoh Usa Inc ....D 513 984-9898
Blue Ash *(G-1683)*

LEASING & RENTAL: Other Real Estate Property

Baker Bnngson Rlty Auctioneers...........E 419 547-7777
Clyde *(G-6810)*
Bessemer and Lake Erie RR Co ....C 440 593-1102
Conneaut *(G-9039)*
Catawba-Cleveland Dev Corp ....D 419 797-4424
Port Clinton *(G-16239)*
Cutler Real Estate Inc ....E 614 339-4664
Dublin *(G-10314)*
Darfus..E 740 380-1710
Logan *(G-12971)*
Employers Mutual Casualty Co ....D 513 221-6010
Blue Ash *(G-1585)*
Etb University Properties LLC..............C 440 826-2212
Berea *(G-1458)*
Fairlawn Associates Ltd..........................C 330 867-5000
Fairlawn *(G-10949)*
Hertz Clvland 600 Superior LLC ....E 310 584-8108
Cleveland *(G-5754)*
J & E LLC...E 513 241-0429
Cincinnati *(G-3850)*
Midway Realty Company.........................E 440 324-2404
Elyria *(G-10654)*
Ohio Living ....A 330 638-2420
Cortland *(G-9081)*
Real Living Inc...D 614 560-9942
Powell *(G-16347)*
Realty One Inc...E 440 333-8700
Rocky River *(G-16590)*
Royalton 6001 Ltd.....................................E 216 447-0070
Independence *(G-12256)*
Sami S Rafidi...C 330 799-9508
Youngstown *(G-20365)*
Select Hotels Group LLC........................E 513 754-0003
Mason *(G-13759)*
Stranahan Theatre Trust.........................D 419 381-8851
Toledo *(G-18204)*

LEASING & RENTAL: Trucks, Indl

All Lift Service Company Inc ....E 440 585-1542
Willoughby *(G-19642)*
Bluefoot Industrial LLC...........................E 740 314-5299
Steubenville *(G-17304)*
Bobcat of Dayton Inc...............................E 937 293-3176
Moraine *(G-14755)*
Brennan Industrial Truck Co...................E 419 867 6000
Holland *(G-12012)*
Fallsway Equipment Co Inc ....C 330 633-6000
Akron *(G-214)*
I L T Diversified Mtl Hdlg........................E 419 865-8025
Holland *(G-12029)*
Springfield Cartage LLC.........................D 937 222-2120
Dayton *(G-9898)*

LEASING & RENTAL: Trucks, Without Drivers

E H Schmidt Executive.............................D 419 874-4331
Perrysburg *(G-16000)*
Graham Chevrolet-Cadillac Co..............D 419 989-4012
Ontario *(G-15690)*
Hogan Truck Leasing Inc ....E 513 454-3500
Fairfield *(G-10859)*
Interstate Truckway Inc ....D 513 542-5500
Cincinnati *(G-3838)*
Kempthorn Automall ....C 330 456-8287
Canton *(G-2423)*
Kempthorn Automall ....D 800 451-3877
Canton *(G-2422)*
Krieger Ford Inc..C 614 888-3320
Columbus *(G-8014)*
McCluskey Chevrolet Inc ....C 513 761-1111
Cincinnati *(G-4035)*
Miami Valley Intl Trcks Inc......................D 513 733-8500
Cincinnati *(G-4087)*
Montrose Ford Inc.....................................D 330 666-0711
Fairlawn *(G-10966)*
Northern Management & Leasing..........D 216 676-4600
Cleveland *(G-6159)*
Penske Truck Leasing Co LP..................E 513 771-7701
Cincinnati *(G-4278)*
Predator Trucking Company...................E 330 530-0712
Mc Donald *(G-14024)*
Premier Truck Sls & Rentl Inc.................E 216 642-5000
Cleveland *(G-6303)*
Rouen Chrysler Plymouth Dodge..........E 419 837-6228
Woodville *(G-19824)*
Roush Equipment Inc..............................C 614 882-1535
Westerville *(G-19442)*
Rush Truck Centers Ohio Inc..................D 513 733-8500
Cincinnati *(G-4458)*
Rush Truck Centers Ohio Inc..................E 419 224-6045
Lima *(G-12872)*
Rush Truck Leasing Inc...........................E 614 876-3500
Columbus *(G-8660)*
Schoner Chevrolet Inc.............................E 330 877-6731
Hartville *(G-11830)*
South East Chevrolet Co..........................E 440 585-9300
Willoughby Hills *(G-19735)*
U Haul Co of Northwestern Ohio ....E 419 478-1101
Toledo *(G-18266)*
U-Haul Neighborhood Dealer -Ce ....E 419 929-3724
New London *(G-15071)*
Vin Devers..C 888 847-9535
Sylvania *(G-17626)*
Voss Auto Network Inc............................E 937 428-2447
Dayton *(G-9976)*
White Family Companies Inc ....C 937 222-3701
Dayton *(G-9996)*

LEASING & RENTAL: Utility Trailers & RV's

Brown Gibbons Lang Ltd Ptrship...........E 216 241-2800
Cleveland *(G-5151)*
Ryder Truck Rental Inc............................E 614 846-6780
Columbus *(G-8665)*
U-Haul Neighborhood Dealer -Ce ....E 419 929-3724
New London *(G-15071)*

LEASING: Passenger Car

1106 West Main Inc ....E 330 673-2122
Kent *(G-12350)*
Albert Mike Leasing Inc...........................C 513 563-1400
Cincinnati *(G-2982)*
Auto Center USA Inc.................................E 513 683-4900
Cincinnati *(G-3066)*
Beechmont Ford Inc ....C 513 752-6611
Cincinnati *(G-2904)*
Bob Pulte Chevrolet Inc ....E 513 932-0303
Lebanon *(G-12593)*
Bobb Automotive Inc................................E 614 853-3000
Columbus *(G-7123)*
Brondes All Makes Auto Leasing ....D 419 887-1511
Maumee *(G-13891)*
Brown Motor Sales Co..............................E 419 531-0151
Toledo *(G-17785)*
Budget Rent A Car System Inc ....E 937 898-1396
Vandalia *(G-18664)*
Carcorp Inc...C 877 857-2801
Columbus *(G-7189)*
Chesrown Oldsmobile GMC Inc ....E 614 846-3040
Columbus *(G-7255)*
Chuck Nicholson Inc ....E 330 674-4015
Millersburg *(G-14594)*
City Yellow Cab Company.......................E 330 253-3141
Akron *(G-144)*
Classic Buick Olds Cadillac......................D 440 639-4500
Painesville *(G-15842)*
Clerac LLC..E 440 345-3999
Strongsville *(G-17450)*
Columbus SAI Motors LLC ....E 614 851-3273
Columbus *(G-7383)*
Dave White Chevrolet Inc........................C 419 885-4444
Sylvania *(G-17581)*

SERVICES

Employee Codes: A=Over 500 employees, B=251-500
C=101-250, D=51-100, E=25-50

2018 Harris Ohio
Services Directory

1537

LEASING: Passenger Car

Dunning Motor Sales Inc ....E...... 740 439-4465
  Cambridge (G-2110)
E H Schmidt Executive ....D...... 419 874-4331
  Perrysburg (G-16000)
Ed Schmidt Chevrolet Inc ....D...... 419 897-8600
  Maumee (G-13908)
Ed Tomko Chryslr Jep Dge Inc ......E...... 440 835-5900
  Avon Lake (G-929)
Enterprise Holdings Inc ....E...... 937 879-0023
  Cincinnati (G-3559)
Germain On Scarborough LLC ....C...... 614 868-0300
  Columbus (G-7748)
Graham Chevrolet-Cadillac Co ......D...... 419 989-4012
  Ontario (G-15690)
Greenwoods Hubbard Chevy-Olds ..E...... 330 568-4335
  Hubbard (G-12087)
Grogans Towne Chrysler Inc ....C...... 419 476-0761
  Toledo (G-17924)
Hidy Motors Inc ....D...... 937 426-9564
  Dayton (G-9272)
Jake Sweeney Automotive Inc ....C...... 513 782-2800
  Cincinnati (G-3859)
Jim Brown Chevrolet Inc ....C...... 440 255-5511
  Mentor (G-14197)
Joe Dodge Kidd Inc ....E...... 513 752-1804
  Cincinnati (G-2921)
Kempthorn Automall ....C...... 330 456-8287
  Canton (G-2423)
Kempthorn Automall ....D...... 800 451-3877
  Canton (G-2422)
Kent Automotive Inc ....E...... 330 678-5520
  Kent (G-12377)
Kerns Chevrolet-Buick-Gmc Inc ....E...... 419 586-5131
  Celina (G-2649)
Kerry Ford Inc ....D...... 513 671-6400
  Cincinnati (G-3918)
Kings Toyota Inc ....D...... 513 583-4333
  Cincinnati (G-3928)
Klaben Family Dodge Inc ....E...... 330 673-9971
  Kent (G-12381)
Klaben Lincoln Ford Inc ....D...... 330 673-3139
  Kent (G-12383)
Krieger Ford Inc ....C...... 614 888-3320
  Columbus (G-8014)
Lakewood Chrysler-Plymouth ....E...... 216 521-1000
  Brookpark (G-1950)
Lang Chevrolet Co ....D...... 937 426-2313
  Beavercreek Township (G-1274)
Lariche Subaru Inc ....D...... 419 422-1855
  Findlay (G-11056)
Lavery Chevrolet-Buick Inc ....E...... 330 823-1100
  Alliance (G-544)
Lebanon Chrysler - Plymouth Inc ..C...... 513 932-2717
  Lebanon (G-12620)
Lima Auto Mall Inc ....D...... 419 993-6000
  Lima (G-12816)
Lincoln Mrcury Kings Auto Mall ....C...... 513 683-3800
  Cincinnati (G-3984)
Mathews Dodge Chrysler Jeep ......E...... 740 389-2341
  Marion (G-13563)
Mathews Kennedy Ford L-M Inc ....D...... 740 387-3673
  Marion (G-13564)
Mc Daniel Motor Co (Inc) ....E...... 740 389-2355
  Marion (G-13565)
McCluskey Chevrolet Inc ....C...... 513 761-1111
  Cincinnati (G-4035)
Medina World Cars Inc ....E...... 330 725-4901
  Strongsville (G-17493)
Merrick Chevrolet Co ....D...... 440 878-6700
  Strongsville (G-17494)
Montrose Ford Inc ....D...... 330 666-0711
  Fairlawn (G-10966)
Mullinax Ford North Canton Inc ....C...... 330 238-3206
  Canton (G-2468)
Nick Mayer Lincoln-Mercury Inc ....E...... 440 835-3700
  Westlake (G-19521)
Northgate Chrysler Jeep Inc ....D...... 513 385-3900
  Cincinnati (G-4180)
Oregon Ford Inc ....C...... 419 698-4444
  Oregon (G-15746)
Partners Auto Group Bdford Inc ....D...... 440 439-2323
  Bedford (G-1329)
Ron Marhofer Automall Inc ....E...... 330 923-5059
  Cuyahoga Falls (G-9217)
Rouen Chrysler Plymouth Dodge ..D...... 419 837-6228
  Woodville (G-19824)
Roush Equipment Inc ....C...... 614 882-1535
  Westerville (G-19442)
Saturn of Toledo Inc ....E...... 419 841-9070
  Toledo (G-18173)

Schoner Chevrolet Inc ....E...... 330 877-6731
  Hartville (G-11830)
Sharpnack Chevrolet Co ....E...... 440 967-3144
  Vermilion (G-18716)
Sonic Automotive ....D...... 614 870-8200
  Columbus (G-8748)
Sonic Automotive-1495 Automall ..E...... 614 317-4326
  Columbus (G-8749)
Sorbir Inc ....D...... 440 449-1000
  Cleveland (G-6495)
South East Chevrolet Co ....E...... 440 585-9300
  Willoughby Hills (G-19735)
Spitzer Auto World Amherst ....D...... 440 988-4444
  Amherst (G-605)
Sunnyside Toyota Inc ....D...... 440 777-9911
  North Olmsted (G-15446)
Tansky Motors Inc ....E...... 650 322-7069
  Logan (G-12989)
Team Rahal of Dayton Inc ....E...... 937 438-3800
  Dayton (G-9921)
Tom Ahl Chryslr-Plymouth-Dodge ..C...... 419 227-0202
  Lima (G-12901)
Toyota of Bedford ....D...... 440 439-8600
  Bedford (G-1341)
Van Devere Inc ....D...... 330 253-6137
  Akron (G-494)
Vin Devers ....C...... 888 847-9535
  Sylvania (G-17626)
Yark Automotive Group Inc ....C...... 419 841-7771
  Toledo (G-18319)

LEASING: Railroad Property

Feridean Group Inc ....E...... 614 898-7488
  Westerville (G-19308)

LEASING: Residential Buildings

Birchaven Village ....D...... 419 424-3000
  Findlay (G-10996)
Cincinnati Metro Hsing Auth ....E...... 513 421-8190
  Cincinnati (G-3316)
Cincinnati Metro Hsing Auth ....E...... 513 333-0670
  Cincinnati (G-3317)
Cwb Property Managment Inc ......E...... 614 793-2244
  Dublin (G-10315)
J & R Associates ....A...... 440 250-4080
  Brookpark (G-1947)
Kent Place Housing ....D...... 614 942-2020
  Columbus (G-7981)
L and M Investment Co ....E...... 740 653-3583
  Lancaster (G-12547)
North Park Care Center LLC ....D...... 440 250-4080
  Brookpark (G-1953)
Norwalk Golf Properties Inc ....E...... 419 668-8535
  Norwalk (G-15586)
Original Partners Ltd Partnr ....C...... 513 381-8696
  Cincinnati (G-4234)
Our House Inc ....E...... 440 835-2110
  Westlake (G-19532)
Towne Properties Assoc Inc ....E...... 513 874-3737
  Cincinnati (G-4672)
Westview-Youngstown Ltd ....D...... 330 799-2787
  Youngstown (G-20414)

LEATHER & CUT STOCK WHOLESALERS

Leather Gallery Inc ....E...... 513 312-1722
  Lebanon (G-12619)

LEATHER GOODS, EXC FOOTWEAR, GLOVES, LUGGAGE/BELTING, WHOL

B D G Wrap-Tite Inc ....D...... 440 349-5400
  Solon (G-16981)

LEATHER GOODS: Coin Purses

Hamilton Manufacturing Corp ....E...... 419 867-4858
  Holland (G-12026)

LEATHER, LEATHER GOODS & FURS, WHOLESALE

Millennium Leather LLC ....E...... 201 541-7121
  Mason (G-13740)

LEGAL AID SVCS

Advoctes For Bsic Lgal Eqality ......E...... 419 255-0814
  Toledo (G-17744)

Community Legal Aid Services ......E...... 330 725-1231
  Medina (G-14049)
Community Legal Aid Services ......D...... 330 535-4191
  Akron (G-156)
Legal Aid Society Cincinnati ....D...... 513 241-9400
  Cincinnati (G-3968)
Legal Aid Society of Cleveland ......E...... 216 861-5500
  Cleveland (G-5934)
Legal Aid Society of Columbus ....D...... 614 737-0139
  Columbus (G-8050)
Legal Aid Western Ohio Inc ....D...... 419 724-0030
  Toledo (G-18003)
Litigation Management Inc ....B...... 440 484-2000
  Mayfield Heights (G-14004)
Toledo Legal Aid Society ....E...... 419 720-3048
  Toledo (G-18241)

LEGAL COUNSEL & PROSECUTION: Attorney General's Office

Bricker & Eckler LLP ....C...... 513 870-6700
  Cincinnati (G-3131)

LEGAL COUNSEL & PROSECUTION: County Government

County of Richland ....E...... 419 774-5676
  Mansfield (G-13278)

LEGAL COUNSEL & PROSECUTION: Local Government

City of Columbus ....E...... 614 645-6624
  Columbus (G-7284)

LEGAL COUNSEL & PROSECUTION: Public Prosecutors' Office

County of Portage ....E...... 330 297-3850
  Ravenna (G-16381)

LEGAL OFFICES & SVCS

American Title Services Inc ....E...... 330 652-1609
  Niles (G-15281)
Arthur Middleton Capital Holdn ....E...... 330 966-9000
  North Canton (G-15326)
Baker & Hostetler LLP ....C...... 614 228-1541
  Columbus (G-7086)
Benesch Friedlander Coplan & ....E...... 614 223-9300
  Columbus (G-7100)
Bigmar Inc ....E...... 740 966-5800
  Johnstown (G-12336)
Bolotin Law Offices ....E...... 419 424-9800
  Findlay (G-11006)
Butler County of Ohio ....E...... 513 887-3090
  Hamilton (G-11704)
City of Columbus ....E...... 614 645-6624
  Columbus (G-7284)
City of Lakewood ....C...... 216 529-6170
  Cleveland (G-5267)
Cleveland Metro Bar Assn ....E...... 216 696-3525
  Cleveland (G-5325)
Cleveland Teachers Union Inc ......E...... 216 861-7676
  Cleveland (G-5351)
County of Portage ....E...... 330 297-3850
  Ravenna (G-16381)
Executives Agencies ....E...... 614 466-2980
  Columbus (G-7618)
Fairfield Federal Sav Ln Assn ......E...... 740 653-3863
  Lancaster (G-12533)
Franklin Cnty Bd Commissioners ..C...... 614 462-3194
  Columbus (G-7688)
General Audit Corp ....E...... 419 993-2900
  Lima (G-12782)
Hoglund Chwlkowski Mrozik Pllc ..C...... 330 252-8009
  Akron (G-268)
Jefferson Medical Co ....E...... 216 443-9000
  Cleveland (G-5856)
Lawrence Cnty Hstorical Museum ..E...... 740 532-1222
  Ironton (G-12296)
Lewis Adkins W Jr ....D...... 216 623-0501
  Cleveland (G-5937)
Litigation Support Svcs Inc ....E...... 513 241-5605
  Cincinnati (G-3992)
Marshall & Associates Inc ....E...... 513 683-6396
  Loveland (G-13144)
Morris Schneider Wittstadt LLC ....E...... 440 942-5168
  Willoughby (G-19694)
National Service Information ....E...... 740 387-6806
  Marion (G-13567)

SERVICES SECTION — LEGAL SVCS: General Practice Attorney or Lawyer

Northwest Ttl Agy of OH MI In ....D....... 419 241-8195
  Toledo *(G-18096)*
Ohio Disability Rights Law Pol ....E....... 614 466-7264
  Columbus *(G-8337)*
Ohio State Bar Association ....E....... 614 487-2050
  Columbus *(G-8377)*
Opers Legal Dept ....E....... 614 227-0550
  Columbus *(G-8471)*
Pappas Leah ....E....... 614 621-7007
  Columbus *(G-8514)*
Porter Wrght Morris Arthur LLP ....E....... 513 381-4700
  Cincinnati *(G-4316)*
Recovery One LLC ....D....... 614 336-4207
  Columbus *(G-8596)*
Scott D Phillips ....E....... 513 870-8200
  West Chester *(G-19148)*
Shared Services LLC ....D....... 513 821-4278
  Cincinnati *(G-4508)*
Squire Patton Boggs (us) LLP ....E....... 513 361-1200
  Cincinnati *(G-4569)*
Supreme Court of Ohio ....E....... 937 898-3996
  Vandalia *(G-18700)*
United Scoto Senior Activities ....E....... 740 354-6672
  Portsmouth *(G-16316)*
Zaremba Group Incorporated ....E....... 216 221-6600
  Cleveland *(G-6779)*
Zaremba Group LLC ....C....... 216 221-6600
  Lakewood *(G-12504)*

LEGAL SVCS: Administrative & Government Law

Butler County Clerk of Courts ....D....... 513 887-3282
  Hamilton *(G-11701)*
London City Admin Offices ....D....... 740 852-3243
  London *(G-12997)*
Village of Strasburg ....D....... 330 878-7115
  Strasburg *(G-17402)*

LEGAL SVCS: Bankruptcy Law

Garretson Firm Resolution ....C....... 513 794-0400
  Loveland *(G-13126)*
Law Offices of John D Clunk C........D....... 330 436-0300
  Stow *(G-17380)*

LEGAL SVCS: Criminal Law

Bonezzi Swtzer Mrphy Plito Lpa ......E....... 216 875-2767
  Cleveland *(G-5128)*

LEGAL SVCS: Debt Collection Law

Value Recovery Group Inc ....E....... 614 324-5959
  Columbus *(G-8931)*

LEGAL SVCS: General Practice Attorney or Lawyer

Allen Khnle Stovall Neuman LLP .....E....... 614 221-8500
  Columbus *(G-6967)*
Altick & Corwin Co Lpa ....E....... 937 223-1201
  Dayton *(G-9327)*
American Financial Corporation ......D....... 513 579-2121
  Cincinnati *(G-3005)*
Anspach Meeks Ellenberger LLP .....E....... 614 745-8350
  Columbus *(G-7022)*
Anspach Meeks Ellenberger LLP .....E....... 419 447-6181
  Toledo *(G-17753)*
Anthony Omalley Atty ....E....... 216 479-6100
  Cleveland *(G-5043)*
Auman Mahan & Furry A Legal ....E....... 937 223-6003
  Dayton *(G-9347)*
Bailey Cavalieri LLC ....E....... 614 221-3258
  Columbus *(G-7085)*
Baker & Hostetler LLP ....B....... 216 861-7587
  Cleveland *(G-5091)*
Baker & Hostetler LLP ....B....... 216 621-0200
  Cleveland *(G-5092)*
Baker & Hostetler LLP ....E....... 513 929-3400
  Cincinnati *(G-3074)*
Baker Dblkar Beck Wley Mathews ...E....... 330 499-6000
  Canton *(G-2260)*
Bavan & Associates ....E....... 330 650-0088
  Northfield *(G-15510)*
Bordas & Bordas Pllc ....E....... 740 695-8141
  Saint Clairsville *(G-16629)*
Bricker & Eckler LLP ....C....... 513 870-6700
  Cincinnati *(G-3131)*
Bruce M Allman ....D....... 513 352-6712
  Cincinnati *(G-3143)*

Buckingham Dlttle Brroughs LLC .....D....... 888 811-2825
  Canton *(G-2275)*
Buckingham Dlttle Brroughs LLC .....D....... 330 492-8717
  Canton *(G-2277)*
Burke Manley Lpa ....E....... 513 721-5525
  Cincinnati *(G-3152)*
Butler Cincione and Dicuccio ....E....... 614 221-3151
  Columbus *(G-7172)*
Calfee Halter & Griswold LLP ....B....... 216 831-2732
  Cleveland *(G-5172)*
Calfee Halter & Griswold LLP ....C....... 513 693-4880
  Cincinnati *(G-3166)*
Calfee Halter & Griswold LLP ....E....... 614 621-1500
  Columbus *(G-7177)*
Calfee Halgerr Griswold LLC ....E....... 614 621-7003
  Columbus *(G-7178)*
Chamberlain Hr ....C....... 216 589-9280
  Avon *(G-886)*
City of Marion ....D....... 740 382-1479
  Marion *(G-13531)*
Connor Evans Hafenstein LLP ....E....... 614 464-2025
  Columbus *(G-7422)*
Cors & Bassett LLC ....D....... 513 852-8200
  Cincinnati *(G-3424)*
County of Montgomery ....C....... 937 225-5623
  Dayton *(G-9437)*
County of Ottawa ....C....... 419 898-6459
  Oak Harbor *(G-15607)*
County of Ottawa ....E....... 419 898-2089
  Oak Harbor *(G-15608)*
Dacia R Crum ....D....... 513 698-5000
  Cincinnati *(G-3458)*
Dagger Johnston Miller ....E....... 740 653-6464
  Lancaster *(G-12526)*
Dana & Pariser Attys ....E....... 614 253-1010
  Columbus *(G-7485)*
David L Barth Lwyr ....D....... 513 852-8228
  Cincinnati *(G-3463)*
Douglass & Associates Co Lpa ....E....... 216 362-7777
  Cleveland *(G-5507)*
Duane Morris LLP ....E....... 202 577-3075
  Cleveland *(G-5510)*
Duane Morris LLP ....E....... 937 424-7086
  Columbus *(G-7547)*
Dworken & Bernstein Co Lpa ....E....... 216 861-4211
  Cleveland *(G-5514)*
Dworken & Bernstein Co Lpa ....E....... 440 352-3391
  Painesville *(G-15853)*
Eastman & Smith Ltd ....C....... 419 241-6000
  Toledo *(G-17862)*
Elizabeth H Farbman ....E....... 330 744-5211
  Youngstown *(G-20179)*
Elliott Heller Maas Morrow Lpa ....E....... 330 792-6611
  Youngstown *(G-20180)*
Freeze/Arnold A Freund Legal ....D....... 937 222-2424
  Dayton *(G-9562)*
Friedberg Meyers Roman ....E....... 216 831-0042
  Cleveland *(G-5638)*
Friedman Domiano Smith Co Lpa ...E....... 216 621-0070
  Cleveland *(G-5639)*
Frost Brown Todd LLC ....B....... 513 651-6800
  Cincinnati *(G-3656)*
Frost Brown Todd LLC ....E....... 614 464-1211
  Columbus *(G-7711)*
Fuller & Henry Ltd ....E....... 419 247-2500
  Toledo *(G-17901)*
Gottlieb Johnson Beam Dal P ....E....... 740 452-7555
  Zanesville *(G-20484)*
Hammond Law Group LLC ....E....... 513 381-2011
  Cincinnati *(G-3734)*
Harrington Hoppe Mitchell Ltd ....E....... 330 744-1111
  Youngstown *(G-20213)*
Harris & Burgin ....E....... 513 891-3270
  Blue Ash *(G-1607)*
Hawkins & Co Lpa Ltd ....E....... 216 861-1365
  Cleveland *(G-5733)*
Heller Maas Moro & Magill ....E....... 330 393-6602
  Youngstown *(G-20215)*
Heyman Ralph E Attorney At Law ...D....... 937 449-2820
  Dayton *(G-9610)*
International Paper Compa ....D....... 513 248-6000
  Loveland *(G-13133)*
Jackson Kelly Pllc ....D....... 330 252-9060
  Akron *(G-289)*
James C Sass Atty ....E....... 419 843-3545
  Toledo *(G-17982)*
James L Jacobson ....E....... 937 223-1130
  Dayton *(G-9639)*
Javitch Block LLC ....D....... 216 623-0000
  Columbus *(G-7936)*

Jeffrey W Smith ....E....... 740 532-9000
  Ironton *(G-12294)*
Jones Day Limited Partnership ....C....... 614 469-3939
  Columbus *(G-7947)*
Katz Teller Brant Hild Co Lpa ....D....... 513 721-4532
  Cincinnati *(G-3902)*
Kegler Brown Hl Ritter Co Lpa ....C....... 614 462-5400
  Columbus *(G-7970)*
Kegler Brown Hl Ritter Co Lpa ....D....... 216 586-6650
  Cleveland *(G-5888)*
Kelley & Ferraro LLP ....E....... 216 575-0777
  Cleveland *(G-5890)*
Kenneth Zerrusen ....D....... 330 869-9007
  Fairlawn *(G-10962)*
Kimberly Williford Attorney ....E....... 419 241-1220
  Toledo *(G-17994)*
Kohnen & Patton ....E....... 513 381-0656
  Cincinnati *(G-3938)*
Krugliak Wilkins Grifiyhd & ....E....... 330 364-3472
  New Philadelphia *(G-15105)*
Levine Arnold S Law Offices ....E....... 513 241-6748
  Cincinnati *(G-3973)*
Levy & Associates LLC ....E....... 614 898-5200
  Columbus *(G-8053)*
Lewis P C Jackson ....E....... 216 750-0404
  Independence *(G-12225)*
Loveland & Brosius LLC ....E....... 614 488-4092
  Upper Arlington *(G-18554)*
Magolius Margolius & Assoc Lpa ....D....... 216 621-2034
  Cleveland *(G-5965)*
Maguire & Schneider LLP ....E....... 614 224-1222
  Columbus *(G-8099)*
Mazanec Raskin & Ryder Co Lpa ...D....... 440 248-7906
  Cleveland *(G-5996)*
Micha Ltd ....E....... 740 653-6464
  Lancaster *(G-12557)*
Miller Cnfeld Pddock Stone PLC ....D....... 513 394-5252
  Cincinnati *(G-4096)*
Murray & Murray Co Lpa ....E....... 419 624-3000
  Sandusky *(G-16779)*
Nicola Gudbranson & Cooper LLC ..E....... 216 621-7227
  Cleveland *(G-6131)*
Ohio Northern University ....C....... 419 227-0061
  Lima *(G-12847)*
Peter M Kostoff ....D....... 330 849-6681
  Akron *(G-387)*
Peterj Brodhead ....E....... 216 696-3232
  Cleveland *(G-6271)*
Reese Pyle Drake & Meyer ....E....... 740 345-3431
  Newark *(G-15231)*
Reimer Law Co ....C....... 440 600-5500
  Solon *(G-17045)*
Renner Kenner Grieve Bobak ....E....... 330 376-1242
  Akron *(G-410)*
Rennie & Jonson Montgomery ....E....... 513 241-4722
  Cincinnati *(G-4405)*
Rich Crites & Dittmer LLC ....E....... 614 228-5822
  Dublin *(G-10440)*
Rickerier and Eckler ....E....... 513 870-6565
  West Chester *(G-19140)*
Ritter & Randolph LLC ....E....... 513 381-5700
  Cincinnati *(G-4422)*
Rose & Dobyns An Ohio Partnr ....D....... 937 382-2838
  Wilmington *(G-19784)*
Schimpf Ginocchio Mullins Lpa ....E....... 513 977-5570
  Cincinnati *(G-4482)*
Sebaly Shillito & Dyer Lpa ....E....... 937 222-2500
  Dayton *(G-9871)*
Seeley Svdge Ebert Gourash Lpa ...E....... 216 566-8200
  Cleveland *(G-6465)*
Shindler Neff Holmes Schlag ....E....... 419 243-6281
  Toledo *(G-18184)*
Siegel Siegel J & Jennings Co ....E....... 216 703-1004
  Beachwood *(G-1124)*
Smith Rolfes & Skazdahl Lpa ....E....... 513 579-0080
  Cincinnati *(G-4541)*
Spengler Nathanson PLL ....D....... 419 241-2201
  Toledo *(G-18195)*
Tafaro John ....D....... 513 381-0656
  Cincinnati *(G-4614)*
Thompson Hine LLP ....C....... 614 469-3200
  Columbus *(G-8840)*
Thompson Hine LLP ....C....... 614 469-3200
  Columbus *(G-8841)*
Thompson Hine LLP ....C....... 937 443-6859
  Miamisburg *(G-14359)*
Thos A Lupica ....D....... 419 252-6298
  Toledo *(G-18217)*
Tucker Ellis LLP ....D....... 720 897-4400
  Cleveland *(G-6621)*

Employee Codes: A=Over 500 employees, B=251-500
C=101-250, D=51-100, E=25-50

LEGAL SVCS: General Practice Attorney or Lawyer

Firm		Phone
Tucker Ellis LLP	C	216 592-5000
Cleveland (G-6622)		
Tucker Ellis LLP	D	614 358-9717
Columbus (G-8877)		
Ulmer & Berne LLP	C	513 698-5058
Cincinnati (G-4724)		
Ulmer & Berne LLP	E	614 229-0000
Columbus (G-8886)		
Wegman Hessler Vanderburg	D	216 642-3342
Cleveland (G-6727)		
Weiner Keith D Co L P A Inc	E	216 771-6500
Cleveland (G-6729)		
Weltman Weinberg & Reis Co Lpa	C	513 723-2200
Cincinnati (G-4832)		
Wiles Boyle Burkholder &	D	614 221-5216
Columbus (G-8993)		
Wood & Lamping LLP	E	513 852-6000
Cincinnati (G-4857)		
Young & Alexander Co Lpa	D	937 224-9291
Dayton (G-10008)		
Zeiger Tigges & Little LLP	E	614 365-9900
Columbus (G-9026)		

LEGAL SVCS: General Practice Law Office

Firm		Phone
Agee Clymer Mitchell & Laret	E	614 221-3318
Columbus (G-6955)		
Barkan & Neff Co Lpa	E	614 221-4221
Columbus (G-7090)		
Bieser Greer & Landis LLP	E	937 223-3277
Dayton (G-9355)		
Brennan Manna & Diamond LLC	E	330 253-5060
Akron (G-109)		
Bricker & Eckler LLP	B	614 227-2300
Columbus (G-7134)		
Brouse McDowell Lpa	E	216 830-6830
Cleveland (G-5148)		
Brown and Margolius Co Lpa	E	216 621-2034
Cleveland (G-5149)		
Buckingham Dittle Brroughs LLC	C	330 376-5300
Akron (G-118)		
Buckingham Dittle Brroughs LLC	D	330 492-8717
Canton (G-2276)		
Buckingham Dittle Brroughs LLC	D	216 621-5300
Cleveland (G-5155)		
Carlile Patchen & Murphy LLP	D	614 228-6135
Columbus (G-7200)		
Carpenter Lipps & Leland LLP	E	614 365-4100
Columbus (G-7202)		
Cavitch Familo & Durkin Co Lpa	E	216 621-7860
Cleveland (G-5195)		
Climaco Lefkwtz Peca Wlcox &	D	216 621-8484
Cleveland (G-5363)		
Cohen Todd Kite Stanford LLC	E	513 205-7286
Cincinnati (G-3378)		
Coolidge Law	D	937 223-8177
Dayton (G-9425)		
Coolidge Wall Co LPA	E	937 223-8177
Dayton (G-9426)		
Crabbe Brown & James LLP	E	614 229-4587
Columbus (G-7454)		
Critchfield Crtchfield Johnston	D	330 264-4444
Wooster (G-19859)		
Davis Young A Legal Prof Assn	E	216 348-1700
Cleveland (G-5468)		
Day Ketterer Ltd	D	330 455-0173
Canton (G-2336)		
Dinn Hochman and Potter LLC	E	440 446-1100
Cleveland (G-5484)		
Dinsmore & Shohl LLP	B	513 977-8200
Cincinnati (G-3491)		
E S Gallon & Associates	E	937 586-3100
Moraine (G-14777)		
Elk & Elk Co Lpa	D	800 355-6446
Mayfield Heights (G-14002)		
Ernest V Thomas Jr	E	513 961-5311
Cincinnati (G-3574)		
Faulkner Grmhsen Keister Shenk	E	937 492-1271
Sidney (G-16932)		
Fay Sharpe LLP	E	216 363-9000
Cleveland (G-5578)		
Firm Hahn Law	E	614 221-0240
Columbus (G-7658)		
Flanagan Lberman Hoffman Swaim	E	937 223-5200
Dayton (G-9554)		
Gallagher Gams Pryor Tallan	E	614 228-5151
Columbus (G-7725)		
Gallagher Sharp	C	216 241-5310
Cleveland (G-5653)		
Gallon Takacs Boissoneault & S	D	419 843-2001
Toledo (G-17906)		
Green Haines Sgambati Lpa	E	330 743-5101
Youngstown (G-20208)		
Hahmooeser & Parks	E	330 864-5550
Cleveland (G-5719)		
Hahn Loeser & Parks LLP	C	216 621-0150
Cleveland (G-5720)		
Hermann Cahn & Schneider LLP	E	216 781-5515
Cleveland (G-5751)		
Horenstein Nicho & Blume A L	E	937 224-7200
Dayton (G-9620)		
Ice Miller LLP	D	614 462-2700
Columbus (G-7881)		
Isaac Brant Ledman Teetor LLP	D	614 221-2121
Columbus (G-7924)		
Isaac Wiles Burkholder & Teeto	D	614 221-5216
Columbus (G-7925)		
Jackson Kohrman & Pll Krantz	D	216 696-8700
Cleveland (G-5847)		
Janik LLP	D	440 838-7600
Cleveland (G-5850)		
Javitch Block LLC	E	513 381-3051
Cincinnati (G-3863)		
Javitch Block LLC	C	216 623-0000
Cleveland (G-5852)		
Jones Day Limited Partnership	A	216 586-3939
Cleveland (G-5871)		
Jones Law Group LLC	E	614 545-9998
Columbus (G-7948)		
Joseph R Harrison Company Lpa	E	330 666-6900
Barberton (G-967)		
Kademenos Wisehart Hines	E	419 524-6011
Mansfield (G-13318)		
Keating Muething & Klekamp Pll	B	513 579-6400
Cincinnati (G-3904)		
Kelly Farrish Lpa	E	513 621-8700
Cincinnati (G-3909)		
Kendis & Associates Co Lpa	E	216 579-1818
Cleveland (G-5893)		
Krugliak Wilkins Grifiyhd &	D	330 497-0700
Canton (G-2430)		
Lane Alton & Horst LLC	E	614 228-6885
Columbus (G-8036)		
Larrimer & Larrimer LLC	E	614 221-7548
Columbus (G-8041)		
Laurito & Laurito LLC	E	937 743-4878
Dayton (G-9675)		
Law Offces Rbert A Schrger Lpa	E	614 824-5731
Columbus (G-8043)		
Lerner Sampson & Rothfuss	B	513 241-3100
Cincinnati (G-3969)		
Lewis P C Jackson	E	937 306-6304
Beavercreek (G-1249)		
Lindhorst & Dreidame Co Lpa	D	513 421-6630
Cincinnati (G-3986)		
Littler Mendelson PC	D	216 696-7600
Cleveland (G-5947)		
LLP Ziegler Metzger	E	216 781-5470
Cleveland (G-5949)		
Luper Neidental & Logan A Leg	E	614 221-7663
Columbus (G-8087)		
Lyons Doughty & Veldhuis PC	E	614 229-3888
Columbus (G-8090)		
Manchester Bennett Towers & Ul	E	330 743-1171
Youngstown (G-20271)		
Manley Deas & Kochalski LLC	D	614 220-5611
Columbus (G-8103)		
Mannion & Gray Co LpA	E	216 344-9422
Cleveland (G-5976)		
Marshall & Melhorn LLC	E	419 249-7100
Toledo (G-18043)		
MCDONALD HOPKINS LLC	E	216 348-5400
Cleveland (G-6002)		
Millikin and Fitton Law Firm	E	513 829-6700
Hamilton (G-11759)		
Nadler Nadler & Burdman Co Lpa	E	330 533-6195
Canfield (G-2204)		
Nicholas E Davis	E	937 228-2838
Dayton (G-9773)		
Nurenberg Plevin Heller	D	440 423-0750
Cleveland (G-6172)		
OConnor Acciani & Levy LLC	E	513 241-7111
Cincinnati (G-4198)		
Palmer Volkema Thomas Inc	E	614 221-4400
Columbus (G-8510)		
Pearne & Gordon LLP	E	216 579-1700
Cleveland (G-6257)		
Pickrel Schaeffer Ebeling Lpa	D	937 223-1130
Dayton (G-9809)		
Porter Wrght Morris Arthur LLP	D	216 443-2506
Cleveland (G-6290)		
Porter Wrght Morris Arthur LLP	E	937 449-6810
Dayton (G-9815)		
Rathbone Group LLC	D	800 870-5521
Cleveland (G-6353)		
Reisenfeld & Assoc Lpa LLC	C	513 322-7000
Cincinnati (G-4401)		
Reminger Co LPA	C	216 687-1311
Cleveland (G-6373)		
Reminger Co LPA	E	513 721-1311
Cincinnati (G-4403)		
Rendigs Fry Kiely & Dennis LLP	D	513 381-9200
Cincinnati (G-4404)		
Renner Otto Boiselle & Sklar	E	216 621-1113
Cleveland (G-6375)		
Robbins Kelly Patterson Tucker	E	513 721-3330
Cincinnati (G-4433)		
Roderick Linton Belfance LLP	C	330 434-3000
Akron (G-417)		
Roetzel and Andress A Legal P	C	330 376-2700
Akron (G-418)		
Roetzel and Andress A Legal P	E	216 623-0150
Cleveland (G-6410)		
Shumaker Loop & Kendrick LLP	C	419 241-9000
Toledo (G-18187)		
Spangenberg Shibley Liber LLP	E	216 215-7445
Cleveland (G-6512)		
Stagnaro Saba Patterson Co Lpa	E	513 533-2700
Cincinnati (G-4576)		
Stagnaro Saba Patterson Co Lpa	E	513 533-2700
Cincinnati (G-4577)		
Stark Knoll	E	330 376-3300
Akron (G-450)		
Sweeney Robert E Co Lpa	E	216 696-0606
Cleveland (G-6561)		
Taft Stettinius Hollister LLP	B	513 381-2838
Cincinnati (G-4616)		
Taft Stettinius Hollister LLP	D	614 221-4000
Columbus (G-8819)		
Taft Stettinius Hollister LLP	D	216 241-3141
Cleveland (G-6567)		
Thompson Hine LLP	B	216 566-5500
Cleveland (G-6596)		
Thrasher Dinsmore & Dolan	E	440 285-2242
Chardon (G-2771)		
Ulmer & Berne LLP	B	216 583-7000
Cleveland (G-6630)		
Ulmer & Berne LLP	D	513 698-5000
Cincinnati (G-4723)		
Vorys Sater Seymour Pease LLP	E	216 479-6100
Cleveland (G-6712)		
Walter Haverfield LLP	D	216 781-1212
Cleveland (G-6719)		
Warner Dennehey Marshall	D	216 912-3787
Cleveland (G-6722)		
Weltman Weinberg & Reis Co Lpa	C	216 739-5100
Brooklyn Heights (G-1933)		
Weltman Weinberg & Reis Co Lpa	A	216 685-1000
Cleveland (G-6732)		
Weltman Weinberg & Reis Co Lpa	C	614 801-2600
Grove City (G-11614)		
Weltman Weinberg & Reis Co Lpa	C	216 459-8633
Cleveland (G-6733)		
Wickens Hrzer Pnza Cook Btista	D	440 695-8000
Avon (G-919)		
Wong Margaret W Assoc Co Lpa	E	313 527-9989
Cleveland (G-6757)		
Wood Herron & Evans LLP	D	513 241-2324
Cincinnati (G-4856)		

LEGAL SVCS: Labor & Employment Law

Firm		Phone
Freking Betz	E	513 721-1975
Cincinnati (G-3652)		
Jurus Stanley R Atty At Law	E	614 486-0297
Columbus (G-7960)		
Larrimer & Larrimer LLC	E	419 222-6266
Columbus (G-8040)		
National Labor Relations Board	E	216 522-3716
Cleveland (G-6110)		
Ross Brittain Schonberg Lpa	E	216 447-1551
Independence (G-12255)		
Scott Scriven & Wahoff LLP	E	614 222-8686
Columbus (G-8708)		
Smith Peter Kalail Co Lpa	E	216 503-5055
Independence (G-12261)		
Zashin & Rich Co LPA	E	216 696-4441
Cleveland (G-6781)		

LEGAL SVCS: Real Estate Law

Firm		Phone
Carlisle McNellie Rini Kram	E	216 360-7200
Beachwood (G-1060)		

SERVICES SECTION

LEGAL SVCS: Specialized Law Offices, Attorney

County of Lucas	C	419 213-4700
Toledo *(G-17834)*		
Frantz Ward LLP	C	216 515-1660
Cleveland *(G-5634)*		
OBrien Law Firm Company Lpa	E	216 685-7500
Westlake *(G-19526)*		
Reminger Co LPA	D	419 254-1311
Toledo *(G-18150)*		
Wilmer Cutler Pick Hale Dorr	B	937 395-2100
Dayton *(G-10000)*		

LEGISLATIVE BODIES: Federal, State & Local

County of Auglaize	C	419 738-3816
Wapakoneta *(G-18793)*		

LEGITIMATE LIVE THEATER PRODUCERS

Columbus Association For The P	D	614 469-0939
Columbus *(G-7332)*		
Little Theater Off Broadway	E	614 875-3919
Grove City *(G-11578)*		

LESSORS: Farm Land

Mapleview Farms Inc	E	419 826-3671
Swanton *(G-17567)*		

LESSORS: Landholding Office

James Lafontaine	E	740 474-5052
Circleville *(G-4891)*		
Mwa Enterprises Ltd	E	419 599-3835
Napoleon *(G-14946)*		

LIABILITY INSURANCE

American Commerce Insurance Co	C	614 272-6951
Columbus *(G-6986)*		

LIFE INSURANCE AGENTS

Brown WD General Agency Inc	D	216 241-5840
Cleveland *(G-5152)*		
Carriage Town Chrysler Plymouth	D	740 369-9611
Delaware *(G-10076)*		
Savage and Associates Inc	D	419 475-8665
Toledo *(G-18174)*		
Transamerica Premier Lf Insur	E	216 524-1436
Independence *(G-12269)*		
Union Security Insurance Co	E	513 621-1924
Cincinnati *(G-4727)*		
United American Insurance Co	E	440 265-9200
Strongsville *(G-17518)*		
Western & Southern Lf Insur Co	E	440 324-2626
Elyria *(G-10691)*		
Western & Southern Lf Insur Co	E	330 792-6818
Youngstown *(G-20411)*		
Western & Southern Lf Insur Co	E	330 825-9935
Barberton *(G-985)*		
Western & Southern Lf Insur Co	E	937 435-1964
Dayton *(G-9993)*		
Western & Southern Lf Insur Co	E	740 653-3210
Lancaster *(G-12583)*		
Western & Southern Lf Insur Co	E	513 891-0777
Loveland *(G-13165)*		
Western & Southern Lf Insur Co	E	614 898-1066
Columbus *(G-6910)*		
Western & Southern Lf Insur Co	E	937 773-5303
Piqua *(G-16176)*		
Western & Southern Lf Insur Co	E	937 399-7696
Springfield *(G-17298)*		
Western & Southern Lf Insur Co	E	740 354-2848
Portsmouth *(G-16322)*		
Western & Southern Lf Insur Co	E	937 393-1969
Hillsboro *(G-11992)*		

LIFE INSURANCE CARRIERS

American Income Life Insur Co	D	440 582-0040
Cleveland *(G-5010)*		
Cincinnati Financial Corp	A	513 870-2000
Fairfield *(G-10833)*		
Columbus Life Insurance Co	D	513 361-6700
Cincinnati *(G-3390)*		
Employers Mutual Casualty Co	D	513 221-6010
Blue Ash *(G-1585)*		
Great American Life Insur Co	E	513 357-3300
Cincinnati *(G-3699)*		
Midland-Guardian Co	A	513 943-7100
Amelia *(G-582)*		
Nationwide Mutual Insurance Co	A	614 249-7111
Columbus *(G-8247)*		
Ohio Casualty Insurance Co	A	800 843-6446
Fairfield *(G-10887)*		
Transamerica Premier Lf Insur	E	614 488-5983
Columbus *(G-8864)*		
United American Insurance Co	E	440 265-9200
Strongsville *(G-17518)*		
United Omaha Life Insurance Co	E	216 573-6900
Cleveland *(G-6642)*		

LIFE INSURANCE: Fraternal Organizations

American Mutual Life Assn	E	216 531-1900
Cleveland *(G-5016)*		

LIFE INSURANCE: Mutual Association

Irongate Inc	C	937 433-3300
Centerville *(G-2680)*		
Ohio Nat Mutl Holdings Inc	A	513 794-6100
Montgomery *(G-14729)*		
Ohio National Fincl Svcs Inc	A	513 794-6100
Montgomery *(G-14730)*		
Union Central Life Insur Co	E	866 696-7478
Cincinnati *(G-4726)*		

LIFEGUARD SVC

Cincinnati Pool Management Inc	A	513 777-1444
Cincinnati *(G-3322)*		
Metropolitan Pool Service Co	E	216 741-9451
Parma *(G-15910)*		

LIGHTING EQPT: Motor Vehicle

Federal-Mogul LLC	C	740 432-2393
Cambridge *(G-2113)*		

LIGHTING FIXTURES WHOLESALERS

Capital Lighting Inc	D	614 841-1200
Columbus *(G-6871)*		
GE Lighting Solutions LLC	E	216 266-4800
Cleveland *(G-5663)*		
LSI Industries Inc	C	913 281-1100
Blue Ash *(G-1631)*		
Vincent Ltg Systems Co Inc	E	216 475-7600
Solon *(G-17065)*		

LIGHTING FIXTURES, NEC

GE Lighting Solutions LLC	E	216 266-4800
Cleveland *(G-5663)*		
Will-Burt Company	B	330 682-7015
Orrville *(G-15789)*		

LIGHTING FIXTURES: Indl & Commercial

Best Lighting Products Inc	D	740 964-0063
Etna *(G-10732)*		
LSI Industries Inc	C	913 281-1100
Blue Ash *(G-1631)*		

LIGHTING FIXTURES: Motor Vehicle

Grimes Aerospace Company	B	937 484-2001
Urbana *(G-18590)*		

LIGHTING MAINTENANCE SVC

Ermc II LP	E	513 424-8517
Middletown *(G-14478)*		
Sylvania Lighting Svcs Corp	E	440 742-8208
Solon *(G-17060)*		

LIME

Hanson Aggregates East LLC	E	937 587-2671
Peebles *(G-15939)*		
Hanson Aggregates East LLC	D	419 483-4390
Castalia *(G-2630)*		
National Lime and Stone Co	C	419 396-7671
Carey *(G-2596)*		
Piqua Materials Inc	E	937 773-4824
Piqua *(G-16158)*		
Shelly Materials Inc	E	740 666-5841
Ostrander *(G-15794)*		

LIME ROCK: Ground

National Lime and Stone Co	C	419 396-7671
Carey *(G-2596)*		

LIMESTONE: Crushed & Broken

Acme Company	D	330 758-2313
Poland *(G-16219)*		
Allgeier & Son Inc	E	513 574-3735
Cincinnati *(G-2988)*		
Chesterhill Stone Co	E	740 849-2338
East Fultonham *(G-10505)*		
Hanson Aggregates East LLC	E	937 587-2671
Peebles *(G-15939)*		
Hanson Aggregates East LLC	E	937 364-2311
Hillsboro *(G-11976)*		
Lang Stone Company Inc	D	614 235-4099
Columbus *(G-8038)*		
Martin Marietta Materials Inc	E	513 353-1400
North Bend *(G-15319)*		
Martin Marietta Materials Inc	E	513 701-1140
West Chester *(G-19117)*		
National Lime and Stone Co	E	740 548-4206
Delaware *(G-10117)*		
National Lime and Stone Co	E	419 423-3400
Findlay *(G-11069)*		
National Lime and Stone Co	D	419 562-0771
Bucyrus *(G-2044)*		
Omya Industries Inc	D	513 387-4600
Blue Ash *(G-1657)*		
Shelly Materials Inc	E	740 666-5841
Ostrander *(G-15794)*		
Shelly Materials Inc	D	740 246-6315
Thornville *(G-17668)*		
Sidwell Materials Inc	C	740 849-2394
Zanesville *(G-20533)*		
Stoneco Inc	E	419 393-2555
Oakwood *(G-15624)*		
White Rock Quarry L P	A	419 855-8388
Clay Center *(G-4910)*		

LIMESTONE: Dimension

National Lime and Stone Co	D	419 562-0771
Bucyrus *(G-2044)*		
Stoneco Inc	D	419 422-8854
Findlay *(G-11086)*		

LIMESTONE: Ground

Conag Inc	E	419 394-8870
Saint Marys *(G-16673)*		
Hanson Aggregates East LLC	D	419 483-4390
Castalia *(G-2630)*		
Piqua Materials Inc	E	937 773-4824
Piqua *(G-16158)*		
Piqua Materials Inc	E	513 771-0820
Cincinnati *(G-4301)*		
Wagner Quarries Company	E	419 625-8141
Sandusky *(G-16809)*		

LIMOUSINE SVCS

A1 Mr Limo Inc	E	440 943-5466
Wickliffe *(G-19592)*		
Aladdins Enterprises Inc	E	614 891-3440
Westerville *(G-19361)*		
American Livery Service Inc	E	216 221-9330
Cleveland *(G-5011)*		
Capital Transportation Inc	C	614 258-0400
Columbus *(G-7184)*		
Cleveland Auto Livery Inc	E	216 421-1101
Cleveland *(G-5291)*		
Contract Transport Services	E	216 524-8435
Cleveland *(G-5403)*		
Eastern Horizon Inc	E	614 253-7000
Columbus *(G-7564)*		
Eric Boeppler Fmly Ltd Partnr	D	513 336-0108
Fairfield *(G-10848)*		
Fab Limousines Inc	E	330 792-6700
Youngstown *(G-20184)*		
First Class Limos Inc	E	440 248-1114
Cleveland *(G-5594)*		
Gold Cross Limousine Service	E	330 757-3053
Struthers *(G-17531)*		
Henderson Road Rest Systems	E	614 442-3310
Columbus *(G-7825)*		
Hopkin Arprt Lmsine Shttle Svc	E	216 267-8282
Brookpark *(G-1946)*		
Jls Enterprises Inc	E	513 769-1888
West Chester *(G-19097)*		
Lakefront Lines Inc	E	419 537-0677
Toledo *(G-18000)*		
Northwest Limousine Inc	E	440 322-5804
Elyria *(G-10665)*		

Employee Codes: A=Over 500 employees, B=251-500
C=101-250, D=51-100, E=25-50

LIMOUSINE SVCS

Precious Cargo Transportation .... E 440 564-8039
  Newbury *(G-15260)*
Shima Limousine Services Inc .... E 440 918-6400
  Mentor *(G-14242)*

LINEN SPLY SVC

Aramark Unf & Career AP LLC .... C 216 341-7400
  Cleveland *(G-5058)*
Cintas Corporation No 2 .... E 740 687-6230
  Lancaster *(G-12517)*
Kimmel Cleaners Inc .... D 419 294-1959
  Upper Sandusky *(G-18564)*
Midwest Laundry Inc .... D 513 563-5560
  Cincinnati *(G-4092)*
Morgan Services Inc .... E 419 243-2214
  Toledo *(G-18070)*
Morgan Services Inc .... C 216 241-3107
  Cleveland *(G-6075)*
Morgan Services Inc .... D 937 223-5241
  Dayton *(G-9757)*
Springfeld Unfrm-Linen Sup Inc .... D 937 323-5544
  Springfield *(G-17278)*
Synergy Health North Amer Inc .... D 513 398-6406
  Mason *(G-13766)*
Van Dyne-Crotty Co .... E 440 248-6935
  Solon *(G-17064)*

LINEN SPLY SVC: Towel

Superior Linen & AP Svcs Inc .... D 513 751-1345
  Cincinnati *(G-4604)*

LINEN SPLY SVC: Uniform

Aramark Unf & Career AP LLC .... D 937 223-6667
  Dayton *(G-9340)*
Aramark Unf & Career AP LLC .... C 614 445-8341
  Columbus *(G-7032)*
Barberton Laundry & Cleaning .... E 330 825-6911
  Barberton *(G-958)*
Buckeye Linen Service Inc .... D 740 345-4046
  Newark *(G-15152)*
Cintas Corporation No 1 .... A 513 459-1200
  Mason *(G-13678)*
Cintas Corporation No 2 .... C 419 661-8714
  Perrysburg *(G-15986)*
Cintas Corporation No 2 .... D 440 238-5565
  Strongsville *(G-17449)*
Cintas Corporation No 2 .... D 614 878-7313
  Columbus *(G-7274)*
Cintas Corporation No 2 .... D 440 352-4003
  Painesville *(G-15839)*
Cintas Corporation No 2 .... C 614 860-9152
  Blacklick *(G-1504)*
Cintas Corporation No 2 .... D 937 401-0098
  Vandalia *(G-18670)*
Cintas Corporation No 2 .... C 513 965-0800
  Milford *(G-14511)*
Economy Linen & Towel Svc Inc .... C 740 454-6888
  Zanesville *(G-20473)*
Kramer Enterprises Inc .... D 419 422-7924
  Findlay *(G-11055)*
Millers Textile Services Inc .... D 419 738-3552
  Wapakoneta *(G-18804)*
Millers Textile Services Inc .... E 614 262-1206
  Springfield *(G-17249)*
Paris Cleaners Inc .... C 330 296-3300
  Ravenna *(G-16395)*
Unifirst Corporation .... E 614 575-9999
  Blacklick *(G-1511)*
Unifirst Corporation .... D 937 746-0531
  Franklin *(G-11166)*
Van Dyne-Crotty Co .... E 614 684-0048
  Columbus *(G-8932)*
Van Dyne-Crotty Co .... C 614 491-3903
  Columbus *(G-8933)*

LIQUEFIED PETROLEUM GAS WHOLESALERS

Centerra Co-Op .... E 800 362-9598
  Jefferson *(G-12331)*
Centerra Co-Op .... E 419 281-2153
  Ashland *(G-672)*
Hearthstone Utilities Inc .... D 440 974-3770
  Cleveland *(G-5744)*
Youngstown Propane Inc .... E 330 792-6571
  Youngstown *(G-20435)*

LIQUIDATORS

Midwest Liquidators Inc .... E 614 433-7355
  Worthington *(G-19977)*
Sb Capital Group LLC .... E 516 829-2400
  Columbus *(G-8691)*

LIVESTOCK LOAN COMPANIES

Producers Credit Corporation .... E 614 433-2150
  Columbus *(G-8565)*

LIVESTOCK WHOLESALERS, NEC

Hord Livestock Company Inc .... E 419 562-0277
  Bucyrus *(G-2041)*

LOADS: Electronic

TL Industries Inc .... C 419 666-8144
  Northwood *(G-15547)*

LOGGING

Appalachia Wood Inc .... E 740 596-2551
  Mc Arthur *(G-14015)*
Miller Logging Inc .... E 330 279-4721
  Holmesville *(G-12074)*

LOOSELEAF BINDERS

Mueller Art Cover & Binding Co .... E 440 238-3303
  Strongsville *(G-17496)*

LOTIONS OR CREAMS: Face

Beiersdorf Inc .... C 513 682-7300
  West Chester *(G-19191)*

LUBRICATING OIL & GREASE WHOLESALERS

Accurate Lubr & Met Wkg Fluids .... E 937 461-9906
  Dayton *(G-9305)*
Applied Indus Tech - Dixie Inc .... C 216 426-4000
  Cleveland *(G-5054)*
Blue Star Lubrication Tech LLC .... E 847 285-1888
  Cincinnati *(G-3122)*
Northeast Lubricants Ltd .... C 216 478-0507
  Cleveland *(G-6151)*
Specialty Lubricants Corp .... E 330 425-2567
  Macedonia *(G-13210)*

LUGGAGE & LEATHER GOODS STORES: Leather, Exc Luggage & Shoes

Leather Gallery Inc .... E 513 312-1722
  Lebanon *(G-12619)*

LUMBER & BLDG MATLS DEALER, RET: Garage Doors, Sell/Install

Dayton Door Sales Inc .... E 937 253-9181
  Dayton *(G-9471)*
Dayton Door Sales Inc .... E 937 253-9181
  Dayton *(G-9472)*
Overhead Door Co- Cincinnati .... C 513 346-4000
  West Chester *(G-19127)*
Overhead Inc .... E 419 476-7811
  Toledo *(G-18113)*

LUMBER & BLDG MATRLS DEALERS, RET: Bath Fixtures, Eqpt/Sply

Bathroom Alternatives Inc .... E 937 434-1984
  Dayton *(G-9349)*
Xtreme Contracting Ltd .... E 614 568-7030
  Reynoldsburg *(G-16492)*

LUMBER & BLDG MATRLS DEALERS, RETAIL: Doors, Wood/Metal

Koch Aluminum Mfg Inc .... E 419 625-5956
  Sandusky *(G-16774)*
Nofziger Door Sales Inc .... C 419 337-9900
  Wauseon *(G-18960)*

LUMBER & BLDG MTRLS DEALERS, RET: Planing Mill Prdts/Lumber

Keim Lumber Company .... E 330 893-2251
  Baltic *(G-946)*

LUMBER & BLDG MTRLS DEALERS, RET: Windows, Storm, Wood/Metal

Squires Construction Company .... E 216 252-0300
  Rocky River *(G-16592)*

LUMBER & BUILDING MATERIAL DEALERS, RETAIL: Roofing Material

Cornelius Joel Roofing Inc .... E 513 367-4401
  Harrison *(G-11795)*
Johns Manville Corporation .... D 419 784-7000
  Defiance *(G-10038)*

LUMBER & BUILDING MATERIALS DEALER, RET: Door & Window Prdts

Daugherty Construction Inc .... E 216 731-9444
  Euclid *(G-10748)*
Dun Rite Home Improvement Inc .... E 330 650-5322
  Macedonia *(G-13196)*
Erie Construction Mid-West Inc .... E 937 898-4688
  Dayton *(G-9530)*
Fortune Brands Windows Inc .... B 614 532-3500
  Columbus *(G-7681)*
Garage Door Systems LLC .... C 513 321-9600
  West Chester *(G-19204)*
Olde Towne Windows Inc .... E 419 626-9613
  Milan *(G-14496)*
Window Factory of America .... D 440 439-3050
  Bedford *(G-1344)*

LUMBER & BUILDING MATERIALS DEALER, RET: Masonry Matls/Splys

B G Trucking & Construction .... E 330 620-8734
  Akron *(G-88)*
Koltcz Concrete Block Co .... E 440 232-3630
  Bedford *(G-1315)*
Mack Industries .... C 419 353-7081
  Bowling Green *(G-1785)*
Maza Inc .... E 614 760-0003
  Plain City *(G-16198)*
Stone Coffman Company LLC .... E 614 861-4668
  Gahanna *(G-11270)*

LUMBER & BUILDING MATERIALS DEALERS, RETAIL: Brick

Bruder Inc .... E 216 791-9800
  Maple Heights *(G-13402)*
Columbus Coal & Lime Co .... E 614 224-9241
  Columbus *(G-7340)*

LUMBER & BUILDING MATERIALS DEALERS, RETAIL: Cement

Huron Cement Products Company .... E 419 433-4161
  Huron *(G-12166)*

LUMBER & BUILDING MATERIALS DEALERS, RETAIL: Countertops

Modlich Stoneworks Inc .... E 614 276-2848
  Columbus *(G-8181)*

LUMBER & BUILDING MATERIALS DEALERS, RETAIL: Siding

Marsh Building Products Inc .... E 937 222-3321
  Dayton *(G-9700)*
Regency Windows Corporation .... D 330 963-4077
  Twinsburg *(G-18459)*

LUMBER & BUILDING MATLS DEALERS, RET: Concrete/Cinder Block

Allega Recycled Mtls & Sup Co .... E 216 447-0814
  Cleveland *(G-4992)*

LUMBER & BUILDING MTRLS DEALERS, RET: Insulation Mtrl, Bldg

Alpine Insulation I LLC .... A 614 221-3399
  Columbus *(G-6977)*
Installed Building Pdts Inc .... C 614 221-3399
  Columbus *(G-7908)*
Installed Building Pdts LLC .... E 419 662-4524
  Northwood *(G-15534)*

SERVICES SECTION

MACHINERY & EQPT, INDL, WHOL: Brewery Prdts Mfrg, Commercial

LUMBER: Dimension, Hardwood
J McCoy Lumber Co Ltd .... E 937 587-3423
  Peebles *(G-15940)*
Stephen M Trudick .... E 440 834-1891
  Burton *(G-2065)*

LUMBER: Fiberboard
Frankes Wood Products LLC .... E 937 642-0706
  Marysville *(G-13620)*

LUMBER: Hardwood Dimension & Flooring Mills
Baillie Lumber Co LP .... E 419 462-2000
  Galion *(G-11292)*
Carter-Jones Lumber Company .... C 330 674-9060
  Millersburg *(G-14591)*
Gross Lumber Inc .... E 330 683-2055
  Apple Creek *(G-625)*
Hartzell Hardwoods Inc .... D 937 773-7054
  Piqua *(G-16146)*
Holmes Lumber & Bldg Ctr Inc .... C 330 674-9060
  Millersburg *(G-14604)*
Wappoo Wood Products Inc .... E 937 492-1166
  Sidney *(G-16960)*

LUMBER: Plywood, Hardwood
Sims-Lohman Inc .... E 513 651-3510
  Cincinnati *(G-4529)*
Wappoo Wood Products Inc .... E 937 492-1166
  Sidney *(G-16960)*

LUMBER: Plywood, Softwood
Wappoo Wood Products Inc .... E 937 492-1166
  Sidney *(G-16960)*

LUMBER: Treated
Appalachia Wood Inc .... E 740 596-2551
  Mc Arthur *(G-14015)*

LUNCHROOMS & CAFETERIAS
Dari Pizza Enterprises II Inc .... C 419 534-3000
  Maumee *(G-13905)*

MACHINE PARTS: Stamped Or Pressed Metal
Abbott Tool Inc .... E 419 476-6742
  Toledo *(G-17738)*

MACHINE SHOPS
All-Type Welding & Fabrication .... E 440 439-3990
  Cleveland *(G-4991)*
Jed Industries Inc .... E 440 639-9973
  Grand River *(G-11456)*
Metcut Research Associates Inc ...... D 513 271-5100
  Cincinnati *(G-4084)*
Neff Machinery and Supplies .... E 740 454-0128
  Zanesville *(G-20515)*

MACHINE TOOL ACCESS: Cutting
Container Graphics Corp .... D 419 531-5133
  Toledo *(G-17831)*
Kyocera SGS Precision Tools .... E 330 688-6667
  Munroe Falls *(G-14931)*

MACHINE TOOL ACCESS: Diamond Cutting, For Turning, Etc
Chardon Tool & Supply Co Inc .... E 440 286-6440
  Chardon *(G-2743)*

MACHINE TOOL ACCESS: Drill Bushings, Drilling Jig
Jergens Inc .... B 216 486-5540
  Cleveland *(G-5859)*

MACHINE TOOL ACCESS: Knives, Metalworking
Alliance Knife Inc .... E 513 367-9000
  Harrison *(G-11789)*

MACHINE TOOLS & ACCESS
Imco Carbide Tool Inc .... D 419 661-6313
  Perrysburg *(G-16015)*
Johnson Bros Rubber Co Inc .... E 419 752-4814
  Greenwich *(G-11526)*
Matvest Inc .... E 614 487-8720
  Columbus *(G-8130)*
Ohio Broach & Machine Company .... E 440 946-1040
  Willoughby *(G-19699)*
Production Design Services Inc .... D 937 866-3377
  Dayton *(G-9832)*
Setco Sales Company .... D 513 941-5110
  Cincinnati *(G-4502)*
Stark Industrial LLC .... E 330 493-9773
  North Canton *(G-15368)*

MACHINE TOOLS, METAL CUTTING: Home Workshop
H & D Steel Service Inc .... E 440 237-3390
  North Royalton *(G-15491)*

MACHINE TOOLS, METAL CUTTING: Sawing & Cutoff
AM Industrial Group LLC .... E 216 433-7171
  Brookpark *(G-1935)*
Lawrence Industries Inc .... C 216 518-7000
  Cleveland *(G-5929)*

MACHINE TOOLS, METAL CUTTING: Tool Replacement & Rpr Parts
Cardinal Builders Inc .... E 614 237-1000
  Columbus *(G-7190)*
J-C-R Tech Inc .... E 937 783-2296
  Blanchester *(G-1515)*

MACHINE TOOLS, METAL FORMING: Bending
Addisonmckee Inc .... C 513 228-7000
  Lebanon *(G-12587)*
Pines Manufacturing Inc .... E 440 835-5553
  Westlake *(G-19534)*

MACHINE TOOLS, METAL FORMING: Marking
Monode Marking Products Inc .... E 440 975-8802
  Mentor *(G-14222)*

MACHINE TOOLS, METAL FORMING: Mechanical, Pneumatic Or Hyd
Compass Systems & Sales LLC .... D 330 733-2111
  Norton *(G-15555)*

MACHINE TOOLS: Metal Cutting
Acro Tool & Die Company .... D 330 773-5173
  Akron *(G-17)*
Alliance Knife Inc .... E 513 367-9000
  Harrison *(G-11789)*
Carter Manufacturing Co Inc .... E 513 398-7303
  Mason *(G-13672)*
Elliott Tool Technologies Ltd .... D 937 253-6133
  Dayton *(G-9524)*
J and S Tool Incorporated .... E 216 676-8330
  Cleveland *(G-5840)*

MACHINE TOOLS: Metal Forming
Anderson & Vreeland Inc .... D 419 636-5002
  Bryan *(G-2002)*
Elliott Tool Technologies Ltd .... D 937 253-6133
  Dayton *(G-9524)*
Howmet Corporation .... E 800 242-9898
  Newburgh Heights *(G-15251)*
J and S Tool Incorporated .... E 216 676-8330
  Cleveland *(G-5840)*
Scotts Miracle-Gro Company .... B 937 644-0011
  Marysville *(G-13651)*

MACHINERY & EQPT FINANCE LEASING
Dana Credit Corporation .... D 419 887-3000
  Maumee *(G-13903)*
Ohio Machinery Co .... C 440 526-6200
  Broadview Heights *(G-1886)*

Reynolds and Reynolds Company ... A 937 485-2000
  Kettering *(G-12435)*
Ricoh Usa Inc .... D 513 984-9898
  Blue Ash *(G-1683)*

MACHINERY & EQPT, AGRICULTURAL, WHOL: Farm Eqpt Parts/Splys
Myers Equipment Corporation .... E 330 533-5556
  Canfield *(G-2203)*
Rk Family Inc .... C 513 737-0436
  Hamilton *(G-11770)*

MACHINERY & EQPT, AGRICULTURAL, WHOLESALE: Agricultural, NEC
Apple Farm Service Inc .... E 937 526-4851
  Covington *(G-9135)*
Speck Sales Incorporated .... E 419 353-8312
  Bowling Green *(G-1794)*

MACHINERY & EQPT, AGRICULTURAL, WHOLESALE: Dairy
Roger Shawn Houck .... E 513 933-0563
  Oregonia *(G-15758)*

MACHINERY & EQPT, AGRICULTURAL, WHOLESALE: Farm Implements
Cahall Bros Inc .... E 937 378-4439
  Georgetown *(G-11388)*
Crouse Implement .... E 740 892-2086
  Utica *(G-18611)*
Evolution Ag LLC .... E 740 363-1341
  Plain City *(G-16191)*
Farmers Equipment Inc .... E 419 339-7000
  Lima *(G-12778)*
Farmers Equipment Inc .... E 419 339-7000
  Urbana *(G-18586)*
Homier & Sons Inc .... E 419 596-3965
  Continental *(G-9049)*
Shearer Farm Inc .... E 419 529-6160
  Ontario *(G-15712)*

MACHINERY & EQPT, AGRICULTURAL, WHOLESALE: Landscaping Eqpt
Dta Inc .... E 419 529-2920
  Ontario *(G-15687)*
Kenmar Lawn & Grdn Care Co LLC . E 330 239-2924
  Medina *(G-14091)*

MACHINERY & EQPT, AGRICULTURAL, WHOLESALE: Lawn
Hayward Distributing Co .... E 614 272-5953
  Columbus *(G-7805)*
Lesco Inc .... C 216 706-9250
  Cleveland *(G-5936)*

MACHINERY & EQPT, AGRICULTURAL, WHOLESALE: Lawn & Garden
Bostwick-Braun Company .... D 419 259-3600
  Toledo *(G-17778)*
Buckeye Supply Company .... E 740 452-3641
  Zanesville *(G-20451)*
Ohio Irrigation Lawn Sprinkler .... E 937 432-9911
  Dayton *(G-9786)*

MACHINERY & EQPT, AGRICULTURAL, WHOLESALE: Livestock Eqpt
Coughlin Chevrolet Inc .... E 740 852-1122
  London *(G-12995)*
Fort Recovery Equipment Inc .... E 419 375-1006
  Fort Recovery *(G-11116)*

MACHINERY & EQPT, AGRICULTURAL, WHOLESALE: Tractors
Shearer Farm Inc .... E 440 237-4806
  North Royalton *(G-15502)*

MACHINERY & EQPT, INDL, WHOL: Brewery Prdts Mfrg, Commercial
D M I Distribution Inc .... E 765 584-3234
  Columbus *(G-7481)*

MACHINERY & EQPT, INDL, WHOL: Brewery Prdts Mfrg, Commercial

SERVICES SECTION

Staufs Coffee Roasters II Inc ....E 614 487-6050
  Columbus *(G-8785)*

MACHINERY & EQPT, INDL, WHOL: Controlling Instruments/Access

Innovative Enrgy Solutions LLC ....E 937 228-3044
  Hamilton *(G-11745)*
Modal Shop Inc ....D 513 351-9919
  Cincinnati *(G-4111)*
Rilco Industrial Controls Inc ....E 513 530-0055
  Cincinnati *(G-4420)*

MACHINERY & EQPT, INDL, WHOL: Environ Pollution Cntrl, Air

Questar Solutions LLC ....E 330 966-2070
  North Canton *(G-15363)*

MACHINERY & EQPT, INDL, WHOL: Meters, Consumption Registerng

Neopost USA Inc ....E 440 526-3196
  Brecksville *(G-1836)*

MACHINERY & EQPT, INDL, WHOL: Oil Field Tool Joints, Rebuilt

Ken Miller Supply Inc ....D 330 264-9146
  Wooster *(G-19878)*

MACHINERY & EQPT, INDL, WHOLESALE: Cement Making

Spillman Company ....E 614 444-2184
  Columbus *(G-8762)*

MACHINERY & EQPT, INDL, WHOLESALE: Chemical Process

Aldrich Chemical ....D 937 859-1808
  Miamisburg *(G-14269)*

MACHINERY & EQPT, INDL, WHOLESALE: Conveyor Systems

Alba Manufacturing Inc ....D 513 874-0551
  Fairfield *(G-10818)*
Daifuku America Corporation ....C 614 863-1888
  Reynoldsburg *(G-16443)*
E F Bavis & Associates Inc ....E 513 677-0500
  Maineville *(G-13243)*
Tkf Conveyor Systems LLC ....C 513 621-5260
  Cincinnati *(G-4660)*
Vargo Integrated Systems Inc ....E 614 876-1163
  Hilliard *(G-11962)*

MACHINERY & EQPT, INDL, WHOLESALE: Cranes

Hiab USA Inc ....D 419 482-6000
  Perrysburg *(G-16012)*
Tiffin Loader Crane Company ....D 419 448-8156
  Tiffin *(G-17705)*
Venco Venturo Industries LLC ....E 513 772-8448
  Cincinnati *(G-4806)*

MACHINERY & EQPT, INDL, WHOLESALE: Dairy Prdts Manufacturing

Heritage Equipment Company ....E 614 873-3941
  Plain City *(G-16193)*
Rodem Inc ....E 513 922-6140
  Cincinnati *(G-4439)*

MACHINERY & EQPT, INDL, WHOLESALE: Drilling Bits

Dickman Supply Inc ....C 937 492-6166
  Sidney *(G-16928)*
Dickman Supply Inc ....E 937 492-6166
  Greenville *(G-11498)*

MACHINERY & EQPT, INDL, WHOLESALE: Engines & Parts, Diesel

Clarke Power Services Inc ....D 513 771-2200
  Cincinnati *(G-3360)*
Cummins Bridgeway Columbus LLC ....D 614 771-1000
  Hilliard *(G-11893)*

Cummins Inc ....E 614 771-1000
  Hilliard *(G-11894)*
Detroit Diesel Corporation ....B 330 430-4300
  Canton *(G-2339)*
Fluid Mechanics LLC ....E 216 362-7800
  Avon Lake *(G-930)*
W W Williams Company LLC ....E 330 534-1161
  Hubbard *(G-12092)*
W W Williams Company LLC ....D 800 336-6651
  West Chester *(G-19242)*
Western Branch Diesel Inc ....E 330 454-8800
  Canton *(G-2585)*

MACHINERY & EQPT, INDL, WHOLESALE: Engines, Gasoline

Gardner Inc ....C 614 456-4000
  Columbus *(G-7728)*

MACHINERY & EQPT, INDL, WHOLESALE: Engs & Parts, Air-Cooled

Power Distributors LLC ....D 614 876-3533
  Columbus *(G-8554)*

MACHINERY & EQPT, INDL, WHOLESALE: Fans

Howden American Fan Company ....E 513 874-2400
  Fairfield *(G-10860)*
WW Grainger Inc ....E 614 276-5231
  Columbus *(G-9010)*

MACHINERY & EQPT, INDL, WHOLESALE: Food Manufacturing

R and J Corporation ....E 440 871-6009
  Westlake *(G-19536)*
Sentinel Fluid Controls LLC ....E 419 478-9086
  Toledo *(G-18179)*

MACHINERY & EQPT, INDL, WHOLESALE: Food Product Manufacturng

Bettcher Industries Inc ....C 440 965-4422
  Wakeman *(G-18774)*

MACHINERY & EQPT, INDL, WHOLESALE: Heat Exchange

Sgl Carbon Technic LLC ....E 440 572-3600
  Strongsville *(G-17506)*

MACHINERY & EQPT, INDL, WHOLESALE: Hoists

Pennsylvania TI Sls & Svc Inc ....D 330 758-0845
  Youngstown *(G-20317)*

MACHINERY & EQPT, INDL, WHOLESALE: Hydraulic Systems

Argo-Hytos Inc ....A 419 353-6070
  Bowling Green *(G-1758)*
Bosch Rexroth Corporation ....E 614 527-7400
  Grove City *(G-11535)*
Eaton Corporation ....B 216 523-5000
  Beachwood *(G-1075)*
Eaton Corporation ....B 216 920-2000
  Cleveland *(G-5524)*
Hagglunds Drives Inc ....E 614 527-7400
  Columbus *(G-7793)*
Hydraulic Parts Store Inc ....E 330 364-6667
  New Philadelphia *(G-15102)*
Isaacs Company ....E 513 336-8500
  Mason *(G-13724)*
JWF Technologies Llc ....E 513 769-9611
  Fairfield *(G-10867)*
Kar Products ....E 216 416-7200
  Cleveland *(G-5884)*
Ohio Hydraulics Inc ....E 513 771-2590
  Cincinnati *(G-4207)*
R & M Fluid Power Inc ....E 330 758-2766
  Youngstown *(G-20337)*
Robeck Fluid Power Co ....D 330 562-1140
  Aurora *(G-852)*
Scott Industrial Systems Inc ....D 937 233-8146
  Dayton *(G-9869)*
STS Operating Inc ....E 513 941-6200
  Cincinnati *(G-4596)*

System Seals Inc ....D 440 735-0200
  Cleveland *(G-6562)*
Triad Technologies LLC ....E 937 832-2861
  Vandalia *(G-18701)*

MACHINERY & EQPT, INDL, WHOLESALE: Indl Machine Parts

Double A Trailer Sales Inc ....E 419 692-7626
  Delphos *(G-10142)*

MACHINERY & EQPT, INDL, WHOLESALE: Instruments & Cntrl Eqpt

ABB Inc ....C 440 585-8500
  Cleveland *(G-4944)*
Fcx Performance Inc ....E 614 324-6050
  Columbus *(G-7645)*
Neff Group Distributors Inc ....E 440 835-7010
  Westlake *(G-19519)*
Simco Supply Co ....E 614 253-1999
  Columbus *(G-8733)*
South Shore Controls Inc ....E 440 259-2500
  Perry *(G-15967)*

MACHINERY & EQPT, INDL, WHOLESALE: Lift Trucks & Parts

Crown Equipment Corporation ....A 419 629-2311
  New Bremen *(G-15018)*
Crown Equipment Corporation ....D 419 629-2311
  New Bremen *(G-15019)*
Fastener Industries Inc ....E 440 891-2031
  Berea *(G-1459)*
I L T Diversified Mtl Hdlg ....E 419 865-8025
  Holland *(G-12029)*
Interstate Lift Trucks Inc ....E 216 328-0970
  Cleveland *(G-5835)*
Joseph Industries Inc ....D 330 528-0091
  Streetsboro *(G-17418)*
Newtown Nine Inc ....D 440 781-0623
  Macedonia *(G-13206)*
Towlift Inc ....D 614 851-1001
  Columbus *(G-8856)*
Towlift Inc ....E 419 531-6110
  Toledo *(G-18258)*
Toyota Industries N Amer Inc ....E 937 237-0976
  Dayton *(G-9935)*
Toyota Material Hdlg Ohio Inc ....D 216 328-0970
  Independence *(G-12268)*
Williams Super Service Inc ....E 330 733-7750
  East Sparta *(G-10542)*

MACHINERY & EQPT, INDL, WHOLESALE: Machine Tools & Access

Absolute Machine Tools Inc ....D 440 839-9696
  Lorain *(G-13010)*
Advanced Tool & Supply Inc ....E 937 278-7337
  Dayton *(G-9310)*
AM Industrial Group LLC ....E 216 433-7171
  Brookpark *(G-1935)*
Eurolink Inc ....E 740 392-1549
  Mount Vernon *(G-14895)*
Gosiger Inc ....C 937 228-5174
  Dayton *(G-9581)*
Gosiger Inc ....D 937 228-5174
  Dayton *(G-9582)*
Imco Carbide Tool Inc ....D 419 661-6313
  Perrysburg *(G-16015)*
J and S Tool Incorporated ....E 216 676-8330
  Cleveland *(G-5840)*
Jergens Inc ....B 216 486-5540
  Cleveland *(G-5859)*
Kyocera SGS Precision Tools ....D 330 686-4151
  Cuyahoga Falls *(G-9203)*
Neff Machinery and Supplies ....E 740 454-0128
  Zanesville *(G-20515)*
Ohio Tool Systems Inc ....D 330 659-4181
  Richfield *(G-16521)*
Precision Supply Company Inc ....D 330 225-5530
  Brunswick *(G-1988)*
Salvagnini America Inc ....E 513 874-8284
  Hamilton *(G-11772)*
Wolf Machine Company ....C 513 791-5194
  Blue Ash *(G-1719)*
Yoder Machinery Sales Company ....E 419 865-5555
  Holland *(G-12069)*

2018 Harris Ohio Services Directory

(G-0000) Company's Geographic Section entry number

SERVICES SECTION

MACHINERY, MAILING: Postage Meters

MACHINERY & EQPT, INDL, WHOLESALE: Machine Tools & Metalwork

Ellison Technologies Inc ....E 440 546-1920
Brecksville (G-1823)

MACHINERY & EQPT, INDL, WHOLESALE: Noise Control

Tech Products Corporation ....E 937 438-1100
Miamisburg (G-14355)

MACHINERY & EQPT, INDL, WHOLESALE: Packaging

Alfons Haar Inc ....E 937 560-2031
Springboro (G-17114)
Bollin & Sons Inc ....E 419 693-6573
Toledo (G-17776)
S & S Inc ....E 216 383-1880
Cleveland (G-6425)
Tape Products Company ....D 513 489-8840
Cincinnati (G-4624)
Tripack LLC ....E 859 282-7914
Milford (G-14570)

MACHINERY & EQPT, INDL, WHOLESALE: Paper Manufacturing

Goettsch Int Inc ....E 513 563-6500
Blue Ash (G-1604)
Industrial Maint Svcs Inc ....E 440 729-2068
Chagrin Falls (G-2721)

MACHINERY & EQPT, INDL, WHOLESALE: Petroleum Industry

C H Bradshaw Co ....E 614 871-2087
Grove City (G-11543)

MACHINERY & EQPT, INDL, WHOLESALE: Plastic Prdts Machinery

Nfm/Welding Engineers Inc ....E 330 837-3868
Massillon (G-13841)
Sumitomo Demag Plstc Machinery .....E 440 876-8960
Strongsville (G-17514)

MACHINERY & EQPT, INDL, WHOLESALE: Pneumatic Tools

Tomita USA Inc ....E 614 873-6509
Plain City (G-16209)

MACHINERY & EQPT, INDL, WHOLESALE: Processing & Packaging

Equipment Depot Ohio Inc ....E 513 934-2121
Lebanon (G-12604)
Veritiv Operating Company ....D 216 901-5700
Cleveland (G-6689)

MACHINERY & EQPT, INDL, WHOLESALE: Propane Conversion

KA Bergquist Inc ....E 419 865-4196
Toledo (G-17989)

MACHINERY & EQPT, INDL, WHOLESALE: Recycling

Gateway Products Recycling Inc ....E 216 341-8777
Cleveland (G-5659)
RSR Partners LLC ....B 440 519-1708
Twinsburg (G-18463)

MACHINERY & EQPT, INDL, WHOLESALE: Robots

Remtec Engineering ....E 513 860-4299
Mason (G-13756)

MACHINERY & EQPT, INDL, WHOLESALE: Safety Eqpt

A & A Safety Inc ....E 513 943-6100
Amelia (G-571)
Area Wide Protective Inc ....E 614 272-7840
Columbus (G-7040)
Boler Company ....C 330 445-6728
Canton (G-2267)
Cintas Corporation ....A 513 459-1200
Cincinnati (G-3349)
Cintas Corporation ....D 513 631-5750
Cincinnati (G-3350)
Cintas Corporation No 2 ....A 513 459-1200
Mason (G-13679)
Cintas Corporation No 2 ....A 513 459-1200
Mason (G-13680)
Impact Products LLC ....C 419 841-2891
Toledo (G-17971)
M Conley Company ....D 330 456-8243
Canton (G-2442)
Paul Peterson Company ....E 614 486-4375
Columbus (G-8522)
Safety Solutions Inc ....D 614 799-9900
Dublin (G-10446)
Safety Today Inc ....E 614 409-7200
Grove City (G-11595)
US Safetygear Inc ....E 330 898-1344
Warren (G-18919)

MACHINERY & EQPT, INDL, WHOLESALE: Tanks, Storage

Cleveland Tank & Supply Inc ....E 216 771-8265
Cleveland (G-5350)
Tank Leasing Corp ....E 330 339-3333
New Philadelphia (G-15117)

MACHINERY & EQPT, INDL, WHOLESALE: Trailers, Indl

Quality Trailers of Oh Inc ....E 330 332-9630
Salem (G-16708)

MACHINERY & EQPT, WHOLESALE: Construction & Mining, Ladders

Bauer Corporation ....E 800 321-4760
Wooster (G-19830)
Dover Investments Inc ....E 440 235-5511
Olmsted Falls (G-15673)

MACHINERY & EQPT, WHOLESALE: Construction, Cranes

American Crane Inc ....E 614 496-2268
Reynoldsburg (G-16426)
Reco Equipment Inc ....E 740 619-8071
Belmont (G-1429)

MACHINERY & EQPT, WHOLESALE: Construction, General

Advanced Industrial Svcs LLC ....D 800 846-9094
Toledo (G-17742)
Columbus Equipment Company ....E 614 437-0352
Columbus (G-7352)
Columbus Equipment Company ....E 513 771-3922
Cincinnati (G-3389)
Columbus Equipment Company ....E 330 659-6681
Richfield (G-16502)
Columbus Equipment Company ....E 614 443-6541
Columbus (G-7353)
F & M Mafco Inc ....C 513 367-2151
Harrison (G-11797)
K & M Contracting Ohio Inc ....E 330 759-1090
Girard (G-11418)
Leppo Inc ....C 330 633-3999
Tallmadge (G-17643)
Murphy Tractor & Eqp Co Inc ....E 513 772-3232
Cincinnati (G-4132)
Npk Construction Equipment Inc ....D 440 232-7900
Bedford (G-1324)
Ohio Machinery Co ....C 419 874-7975
Perrysburg (G-16036)
Ohio Machinery Co ....E 740 942-4626
Cadiz (G-2080)
Ohio Machinery Co ....E 330 478-6525
Canton (G-2481)
Ohio Machinery Co ....E 740 453-0563
Zanesville (G-20519)
Ohio Machinery Co ....C 513 771-0515
Cincinnati (G-4209)
Ohio Machinery Co ....B 614 878-2287
Columbus (G-8359)
Ohio Machinery Co ....D 440 526-0520
Broadview Heights (G-1887)
Ohio Machinery Co ....D 937 335-7660
Troy (G-18370)
Ohio Machinery Co ....E 330 530-9010
Girard (G-11421)
Ohio Machinery Co ....C 440 526-6200
Broadview Heights (G-1886)
Southeastern Equipment Co Inc ....C 614 889-1073
Dublin (G-10458)
TNT Equipment Company ....E 614 882-1549
Columbus (G-8852)
Wrench Ltd Company ....D 740 654-5304
Carroll (G-2610)

MACHINERY & EQPT, WHOLESALE: Contractors Materials

American Producers Sup Co Inc ....D 740 373-5050
Marietta (G-13431)
Bobcat Enterprises Inc ....C 513 874-8945
West Chester (G-19030)
Carmichael Equipment Inc ....E 740 446-2412
Bidwell (G-1494)
Cecil I Walker Machinery Co ....E 740 286-7566
Jackson (G-12308)
Richard Goettle Inc ....D 513 825-8100
Cincinnati (G-4415)
Vermeer Sales & Service Inc ....E 330 723-8383
Medina (G-14136)

MACHINERY & EQPT, WHOLESALE: Drilling, Wellpoints

Yoder Drilling and Geothermal ....E 330 852-4342
Sugarcreek (G-17548)

MACHINERY & EQPT, WHOLESALE: Logging

Baker & Sons Equipment Co ....E 740 567-3317
Lewisville (G-12714)

MACHINERY & EQPT, WHOLESALE: Masonry

EZ Grout Corporation Inc ....E 740 962-2024
Malta (G-13249)

MACHINERY & EQPT, WHOLESALE: Oil Field Eqpt

Belden & Blake Corporation ....E 330 602-5551
Dover (G-10177)
Stallion Oilfield Cnstr LLC ....E 330 868-2083
Paris (G-15896)

MACHINERY & EQPT, WHOLESALE: Road Construction & Maintenance

Terry Asphalt Materials Inc ....E 513 874-6192
Hamilton (G-11777)

MACHINERY & EQPT: Electroplating

Corrotec Inc ....E 937 325-3585
Springfield (G-17177)

MACHINERY & EQPT: Farm

Intertec Corporation ....B 419 537-9711
Toledo (G-17977)

MACHINERY & EQPT: Gas Producers, Generators/Other Rltd Eqpt

Applied Marketing Services ....F 440 716 0962
Westlake (G-19460)

MACHINERY BASES

Elite Enclosure Company LLC ....E 937 492-3548
Sidney (G-16931)

MACHINERY CLEANING SVCS

Burch Hydro Inc ....E 740 694-9146
Fredericktown (G-11178)

MACHINERY, MAILING: Postage Meters

Pitney Bowes Inc ....D 203 426-7025
Brecksville (G-1840)
Pitney Bowes Inc ....D 740 374-5535
Marietta (G-13489)

MACHINERY, METALWORKING: Assembly, Including Robotic — SERVICES SECTION

MACHINERY, METALWORKING: Assembly, Including Robotic
Hunter Defense Tech Inc .... E 216 438-6111
Solon *(G-17016)*

MACHINERY, METALWORKING: Cutting & Slitting
Ged Holdings Inc .... C 330 963-5401
Twinsburg *(G-18421)*

MACHINERY, OFFICE: Paper Handling
Symatic Inc .... E 330 225-1510
Brunswick *(G-1991)*

MACHINERY, PACKAGING: Wrapping
Samuel Strapping Systems Inc .... D 740 522-2500
Heath *(G-11843)*

MACHINERY, WOODWORKING: Pattern Makers'
Seilkop Industries Inc .... E 513 761-1035
Cincinnati *(G-4492)*

MACHINERY/EQPT, INDL, WHOL: Cleaning, High Press, Sand/Steam
Contract Sweepers & Eqp Co .... E 614 221-7441
Columbus *(G-7435)*
Tom Langhals .... E 419 659-5629
Columbus Grove *(G-9031)*

MACHINERY: Ammunition & Explosives Loading
Military Resources LLC .... E 330 263-1040
Wooster *(G-19888)*
Military Resources LLC .... D 330 309-9970
Wooster *(G-19889)*

MACHINERY: Assembly, Exc Metalworking
Remtec Engineering .... E 513 860-4299
Mason *(G-13756)*

MACHINERY: Automotive Related
Wauseon Machine & Mfg Inc .... D 419 337-0940
Wauseon *(G-18964)*

MACHINERY: Binding
Baumfolder Corporation .... D 937 492-1281
Sidney *(G-16914)*

MACHINERY: Bottling & Canning
OKL Can Line Inc .... E 513 825-1655
Cincinnati *(G-4218)*

MACHINERY: Construction
Grasan Equipment Company Inc .... D 419 526-4440
Mansfield *(G-13306)*
Kaffenbarger Truck Eqp Co .... E 513 772-6800
Cincinnati *(G-3900)*
Npk Construction Equipment Inc .... D 440 232-7900
Bedford *(G-1324)*
Pubco Corporation .... D 216 881-5300
Cleveland *(G-6332)*

MACHINERY: Custom
Alfons Haar Inc .... E 937 560-2031
Springboro *(G-17114)*
East End Welding Company .... C 330 677-6000
Kent *(G-12367)*
Enprotech Industrial Tech LLC .... C 216 883-3220
Cleveland *(G-5542)*
Interscope Manufacturing Inc .... E 513 423-8866
Middletown *(G-14429)*
Invotec Engineering Inc .... D 937 886-3232
Miamisburg *(G-14307)*
Narrow Way Custom Technology .... E 937 743-1611
Carlisle *(G-2605)*
Sample Machining Inc .... E 937 258-3338
Dayton *(G-9866)*
Steel Eqp Specialists Inc .... D 330 823-8260
Alliance *(G-563)*

MACHINERY: Glassmaking
Ged Holdings Inc .... C 330 963-5401
Twinsburg *(G-18421)*
Intertec Corporation .... B 419 537-9711
Toledo *(G-17977)*
J & S Industrial Mch Pdts Inc .... D 419 691-1380
Toledo *(G-17980)*

MACHINERY: Logging Eqpt
Buck Equipment Inc .... E 614 539-3039
Grove City *(G-11540)*

MACHINERY: Metalworking
Addisonmckee Inc .... C 513 228-7000
Lebanon *(G-12587)*
Ctm Integration Incorporated .... E 330 332-1800
Salem *(G-16693)*
Pines Manufacturing Inc .... E 440 835-5553
Westlake *(G-19534)*
South Shore Controls Inc .... E 440 259-2500
Perry *(G-15967)*

MACHINERY: Mining
Kaffenbarger Truck Eqp Co .... E 513 772-6800
Cincinnati *(G-3900)*
Npk Construction Equipment Inc .... D 440 232-7900
Bedford *(G-1324)*

MACHINERY: Packaging
Ctm Integration Incorporated .... E 330 332-1800
Salem *(G-16693)*
Millwood Inc .... E 330 393-4400
Vienna *(G-18740)*
Millwood Natural LLC .... C 330 393-4400
Vienna *(G-18741)*

MACHINERY: Paper Industry Miscellaneous
Baumfolder Corporation .... D 937 492-1281
Sidney *(G-16914)*

MACHINERY: Plastic Working
Linden Industries Inc .... E 330 928-4064
Cuyahoga Falls *(G-9205)*
Vulcan Machinery Corporation .... E 330 376-6025
Akron *(G-500)*
Youngstown Plastic Tooling .... E 330 782-7222
Youngstown *(G-20434)*

MACHINERY: Printing Presses
Graphic Systems Services Inc .... E 937 746-0708
Springboro *(G-17120)*

MACHINERY: Recycling
Grasan Equipment Company Inc .... D 419 526-4440
Mansfield *(G-13306)*

MACHINERY: Road Construction & Maintenance
Forge Industries Inc .... A 330 782-8301
Youngstown *(G-20191)*
Power-Pack Conveyor Company ..... E 440 975-9955
Willoughby *(G-19705)*

MACHINERY: Rubber Working
Rubber City Machinery Corp .... E 330 434-3500
Akron *(G-419)*

MACHINERY: Textile
Wolf Machine Company .... C 513 791-5194
Blue Ash *(G-1719)*

MACHINERY: Wire Drawing
EZ Grout Corporation Inc .... E 740 962-2024
Malta *(G-13249)*

MAGAZINES, WHOLESALE
Windy Hill Ltd Inc .... D 216 391-4800
Cleveland *(G-6753)*

MAGNETS: Permanent
Walker National Inc .... E 614 492-1614
Columbus *(G-8962)*
Winkle Industries Inc .... D 330 823-9730
Alliance *(G-565)*

MAIL PRESORTING SVCS
Pitney Bowes Presort Svcs Inc .... D 513 860-3607
West Chester *(G-19220)*

MAIL-ORDER HOUSE, NEC
American Frame Corporation .... E 419 893-5595
Maumee *(G-13874)*
Schneider Saddlery LLC .... E 440 543-2700
Chagrin Falls *(G-2733)*

MAIL-ORDER HOUSES: Arts & Crafts Eqpt & Splys
Craft Wholesalers Inc .... C 740 964-6210
Groveport *(G-11630)*

MAIL-ORDER HOUSES: Automotive Splys & Eqpt
Jegs Automotive Inc .... C 614 294-5050
Delaware *(G-10110)*

MAIL-ORDER HOUSES: Books, Exc Book Clubs
Pure Romance LLC .... D 513 248-8656
Cincinnati *(G-4356)*

MAIL-ORDER HOUSES: Cheese
K & R Distributors Inc .... E 937 864-5495
Fairborn *(G-10799)*

MAIL-ORDER HOUSES: Computer Software
Provantage LLC .... D 330 494-3781
North Canton *(G-15362)*

MAIL-ORDER HOUSES: Computers & Peripheral Eqpt
PC Connection Sales Corp .... C 937 382-4800
Wilmington *(G-19776)*
Systemax Manufacturing Inc .... C 937 368-2300
Dayton *(G-9919)*

MAIL-ORDER HOUSES: Educational Splys & Eqpt
Bendon Inc .... D 419 207-3600
Ashland *(G-664)*

MAIL-ORDER HOUSES: Gift Items
H & M Patch Company .... D 614 339-8950
Columbus *(G-7788)*

MAILBOX RENTAL & RELATED SVCS
Ngm Inc .... E 513 821-7363
Cincinnati *(G-4168)*
United Parcel Service Inc .... E 440 243-3344
Middleburg Heights *(G-14389)*
United Parcel Service Inc OH .... B 740 363-0636
Delaware *(G-10133)*
United Parcel Service Inc OH .... B 614 277-3300
Urbancrest *(G-18608)*

MAILING & MESSENGER SVCS
Richardson Printing Corp .... D 740 373-5362
Marietta *(G-13495)*
United Parcel Service Inc OH .... B 216 676-4560
Cleveland *(G-6645)*
United Parcel Service Inc OH .... B 614 870-4111
Columbus *(G-8898)*

MAILING LIST: Brokers
New Pros Communications Inc ...... D 740 201-0410
Powell *(G-16345)*

MAILING LIST: Compilers

Brothers Publishing Co LLC .... E 937 548-3330
  Greenville (G-11491)
Haines & Company Inc .... C 330 494-9111
  North Canton (G-15343)

MAILING SVCS, NEC

Aero Fulfillment Services Corp .... D 800 225-7145
  Mason (G-13658)
Angstrom Graphics Inc Midwest .... E 330 225-8950
  Cleveland (G-5038)
Bindery & Spc Pressworks Inc .... D 614 873-4623
  Plain City (G-16184)
Blue Chip Mailing Services Inc .... E 513 541-4800
  Blue Ash (G-1545)
Bpm Realty Inc .... E 614 221-6811
  Columbus (G-7129)
Case Western Reserve Univ .... E 216 368-2560
  Cleveland (G-5187)
Centurion of Akron Inc .... D 330 645-6699
  Copley (G-9054)
Ctrac Inc .... E 440 572-1000
  Cleveland (G-5447)
Dayton Mailing Services Inc .... E 937 222-5056
  Dayton (G-9480)
Early Express Services Inc .... E 937 223-5801
  Dayton (G-9511)
Fine Line Graphics Corp .... C 614 486-0276
  Columbus (G-7656)
J C Direct Mail Inc .... C 614 836-4848
  Groveport (G-11649)
Literature Fulfillment Svcs .... E 513 774-8600
  Blue Ash (G-1629)
Macke Brothers Inc .... D 513 771-7500
  Cincinnati (G-4008)
Macys Cr & Customer Svcs Inc .... D 513 881-9950
  West Chester (G-19114)
Mail It Corp .... E 419 249-4848
  Toledo (G-18027)
Patented Acquisition Corp .... D 937 353-2299
  Miamisburg (G-14332)
Postal Mail Sort Inc .... E 330 747-1515
  Youngstown (G-20328)
Power Management Inc .... E 937 222-2909
  Dayton (G-9817)
Presort America Ltd .... D 614 836-5120
  Groveport (G-11662)
United Mail LLC .... D 513 482-7429
  Cincinnati (G-4734)
W C National Mailing Corp .... B 614 836-5703
  Groveport (G-11685)
Weekleys Mailing Service Inc .... D 440 234-4325
  Berea (G-1475)

MANAGEMENT CONSULTING SVCS: Administrative

Facilities MGT Solutions LLC .... E 513 639-2230
  Cincinnati (G-3587)
Incentisoft Solutions LLC .... D 877 562-4461
  Cleveland (G-5808)
Klingbeil Management Group Co .... E 614 220-8900
  Columbus (G-7997)
National Administative Svc LLC .... E 614 358-3607
  Dublin (G-10403)
Ride Share Information .... E 513 621-6300
  Cincinnati (G-4419)

MANAGEMENT CONSULTING SVCS: Automation & Robotics

Clear Vision Engineering LLC .... E 419 478-7151
  Toledo (G-17816)
Motion Controls Robotics Inc .... E 419 334-5886
  Fremont (G-11214)
Remtec Automation LLC .... E 877 759-8151
  Mason (G-13755)

MANAGEMENT CONSULTING SVCS: Banking & Finance

Banc Amer Prctice Slutions Inc .... C 614 794-8247
  Westerville (G-19287)
Kings Medical Company .... C 330 653-3968
  Hudson (G-12128)
Nationwide Financial Svcs Inc .... C 614 249-7111
  Columbus (G-8242)
Trinity Credit Counseling Inc .... E 513 769-0621
  Cincinnati (G-4699)

MANAGEMENT CONSULTING SVCS: Business

5me LLC .... E 513 719-1600
  Cincinnati (G-2900)
Accenture LLP .... C 216 685-1435
  Cleveland (G-4953)
Accenture LLP .... C 614 629-2000
  Columbus (G-6934)
Accenture LLP .... D 513 455-1000
  Cincinnati (G-2963)
Accenture LLP .... D 513 651-2444
  Cincinnati (G-2964)
Accurate Inventory and C .... B 800 777-9414
  Columbus (G-6936)
Advocate Solutions LLC .... E 614 444-5144
  Columbus (G-6948)
Arysen Inc .... D 440 230-4400
  Independence (G-12188)
Avatar Management Services .... E 330 963-3900
  Macedonia (G-13187)
Btas Inc .... C 937 431-9431
  Beavercreek (G-1155)
Corporate Fin Assoc of Clumbus .... D 614 457-9219
  Columbus (G-7444)
Dayton Aerospace Inc .... E 937 426-4300
  Beavercreek Township (G-1268)
DE Foxx & Associates Inc .... B 513 621-5522
  Cincinnati (G-3470)
Dental One Inc .... E 216 584-1000
  Independence (G-12203)
Enabling Partners LLC .... E 440 878-9418
  Strongsville (G-17461)
Engaged Health Care Bus Svcs .... E 614 457-8180
  Columbus (G-7594)
Epiphany Management Group LLC .... E 330 706-4056
  Akron (G-209)
Ernst & Young LLP .... C 614 224-5678
  Columbus (G-7607)
Ernst & Young LLP .... C 513 612-1400
  Cincinnati (G-3575)
Excellence Alliance Group Inc .... E 513 619-4800
  Cincinnati (G-3585)
Finit Group LLC .... D 513 793-4648
  Cincinnati (G-3611)
Incubit LLC .... D 740 362-1401
  Delaware (G-10108)
Industry Insights Inc .... E 614 389-2100
  Columbus (G-7894)
Kalypso LP .... D 216 378-4290
  Beachwood (G-1093)
Marsh Berry & Company Inc .... E 440 354-3230
  Beachwood (G-1097)
McKinsey & Company Inc .... E 216 274-4000
  Cleveland (G-6006)
Normandy Group LLC .... E 513 745-0990
  Blue Ash (G-1654)
Orbit Systems Inc .... E 614 504-8011
  Lewis Center (G-12700)
Phoenix Resource Network LLC .... E 800 990-4948
  Cincinnati (G-4294)
Projetech Inc .... E 513 481-4900
  Cincinnati (G-4346)
Racksquared LLC .... E 614 737-8812
  Columbus (G-8583)
Root Inc .... D 419 874-0077
  Sylvania (G-17612)
Scrogginsgrear Inc .... C 513 672-4281
  Cincinnati (G-4486)
Smith & English II Inc .... E 513 697-9300
  Loveland (G-13161)
Smithers Group Inc .... D 330 762-7441
  Akron (G-441)
Smithers Rapra Inc .... D 330 762-7441
  Akron (G-443)
Socius1 LLC .... D 614 280-9880
  Dublin (G-10455)
Solenis LLC .... E 614 336-1101
  Dublin (G-10456)
Versatex LLC .... E 513 639-3119
  Cincinnati (G-4808)

MANAGEMENT CONSULTING SVCS: Business Planning & Organizing

Antero Resources Corporation .... D 740 760-1000
  Marietta (G-13433)
Equity Resources Inc .... D 513 518-6318
  Cincinnati (G-3571)
First Data Gvrnment Sltions LP .... E 513 489-9599
  Blue Ash (G-1594)
Techncal Sltons Spcialists Inc .... E 513 792-8930
  Blue Ash (G-1693)
Total Marketing Resources LLC .... E 330 220-1275
  Brunswick (G-1993)
Tsg Resources Inc .... A 330 498-8200
  North Canton (G-15376)

MANAGEMENT CONSULTING SVCS: Compensation & Benefits Planning

Corporate Plans Inc .... E 440 542-7800
  Solon (G-16995)
Findley Davies Inc .... D 419 255-1360
  Toledo (G-17890)
Group Management Services Inc .... E 330 659-0100
  Richfield (G-16511)
Independent Evaluators Inc .... D 419 872-5650
  Perrysburg (G-16016)
Mercer (us) Inc .... E 513 632-2600
  Cincinnati (G-4056)
Parman Group Inc .... E 513 673-0077
  Columbus (G-8519)
Progressive Entps Holdings Inc .... A 614 794-3300
  Westerville (G-19346)
Rx Options LLC .... D 330 405-8080
  Twinsburg (G-18464)
Stagnaro Saba Patterson Co Lpa .... E 513 533-2700
  Cincinnati (G-4576)
The Sheakley Group Inc .... E 513 771-2277
  Cincinnati (G-4646)
Wtw Delaware Holdings LLC .... C 216 937-4000
  Cleveland (G-6762)

MANAGEMENT CONSULTING SVCS: Construction Project

Critical Business Analysis Inc .... E 419 874-0800
  Perrysburg (G-15991)
G Stephens Inc .... E 419 241-5188
  Toledo (G-17904)
Kettering Adventist Healthcare .... E 513 867-3166
  Liberty Township (G-12721)
LEWaro-D&j-A Joint Venture Co .... E 937 443-0000
  Dayton (G-9678)
Smoot Construction Co Ohio .... E 614 257-0032
  Columbus (G-8747)

MANAGEMENT CONSULTING SVCS: Corporation Organizing

Comex North America Inc .... D 303 307-2100
  Cleveland (G-5374)

MANAGEMENT CONSULTING SVCS: Distribution Channels

Arras Group Inc .... E 216 621-1601
  Cleveland (G-5067)
Trilogy Fulfillment LLC .... E 614 491-0553
  Groveport (G-11678)

MANAGEMENT CONSULTING SVCS: Food & Beverage

AVI Food Systems Inc .... C 330 372-6000
  Warren (G-18827)

MANAGEMENT CONSULTING SVCS: Franchising

Cleveland Dairy Queen Inc .... C 440 946-3690
  Willoughby (G-19654)
Its Financial LLC .... D 937 425-6889
  Beavercrook (C-1247)
Producer Group LLC .... E 440 871-7700
  Rocky River (G-16589)

MANAGEMENT CONSULTING SVCS: General

Career Partners Intl LLC .... A 919 401-4260
  Columbus (G-7198)
Hctec Partners LLC .... D 513 985-6400
  Cincinnati (G-3750)
Murtech Consulting LLC .... D 216 328-8580
  Cleveland (G-6091)
Oncall LLC .... D 513 381-4320
  Cincinnati (G-4225)
Paragon Consulting Inc .... E 440 684-3101
  Cleveland (G-6231)
Paragon Tec Inc .... D 216 361-5555
  Cleveland (G-6232)

MANGEMENT CONSULTING SVCS: General

Pope & Associates Inc .... E 513 671-1277
  Cincinnati *(G-4314)*
Turtle Golf Management Ltd .... E 614 882-5920
  Westerville *(G-19446)*
Xzamcorp .... E 330 629-2218
  Perry *(G-15969)*

MANAGEMENT CONSULTING SVCS: Hospital & Health

Acuity Healthcare LP .... D 740 283-7499
  Steubenville *(G-17302)*
Alps Services Inc .... E 513 671-6300
  Cincinnati *(G-2995)*
Alternative Care Mgt Systems .... E 614 761-0035
  Dublin *(G-10243)*
American Health Group Inc .... D 419 891-1212
  Maumee *(G-13875)*
Beacon of Light Ltd .... E 419 531-9060
  Toledo *(G-17765)*
Chattree and Associates Inc .... D 216 831-1494
  Cleveland *(G-5231)*
East Way Behavioral Hlth Care .... C 937 222-4900
  Dayton *(G-9515)*
Emerald Health Network Inc .... D 216 479-2030
  Fairlawn *(G-10948)*
First Choice Medical Staffing .... E 419 626-9740
  Sandusky *(G-16761)*
Germain & Co Inc .... E 937 885-5827
  Dayton *(G-9572)*
Healthcomp Inc .... D 216 696-6900
  Cleveland *(G-5738)*
Integra Group Inc .... E 513 326-5600
  Cincinnati *(G-3824)*
Malik Punam .... D 513 636-1333
  Cincinnati *(G-4017)*
Med3000 Group Inc .... E 937 291-7850
  Miamisburg *(G-14316)*
Medical Recovery Systems Inc .... D 513 872-7000
  Cincinnati *(G-4044)*
Medisync Midwest Ltd Lblty Co .... D 513 533-1199
  Cincinnati *(G-4047)*
Ohic Insurance Company .... D 614 221-7777
  Columbus *(G-8315)*
Ohiohealth Corporation .... D 614 566-3500
  Columbus *(G-8456)*
Optimal Life Intgrtve Mdcne PA .... E 419 474-3657
  Sylvania *(G-17604)*
Patient Account MGT Svcs LLC .... E 614 575-0044
  Columbus *(G-8520)*
Plus Management Services Inc .... C 419 225-9018
  Lima *(G-12860)*
PSI Supply Chain Solutions LLC .... E 614 389-4717
  Dublin *(G-10432)*
Regent Systems Inc .... D 937 640-8010
  Dayton *(G-9845)*
Spirit Women Health Netwrk LLC .... E 561 544-2004
  Cincinnati *(G-2932)*
Touchstone Group Assoc LLC .... E 513 791-1717
  Cincinnati *(G-4664)*
United Audit Systems Inc .... C 513 723-1122
  Cincinnati *(G-4728)*
University of Cincinnati Phys .... E 513 475-8521
  Cincinnati *(G-4780)*
Vernon F Glaser & Associates .... E 937 298-5536
  Dayton *(G-9970)*
Wellington Group LLC .... E 216 525-2200
  Independence *(G-12275)*

MANAGEMENT CONSULTING SVCS: Industrial & Labor

Mancan Inc .... A 440 884-9675
  Strongsville *(G-17487)*

MANAGEMENT CONSULTING SVCS: Industry Specialist

Brentley Institute Inc .... E 216 225-0087
  Cleveland *(G-5137)*
Carol Scudere .... E 614 839-4357
  New Albany *(G-14979)*
Chemsultants International Inc .... E 440 974-3080
  Mentor *(G-14157)*
Dealers Group Limited .... E 440 352-4970
  Beachwood *(G-1073)*
Dedicated Technologies Inc .... D 614 460-3200
  Columbus *(G-7499)*
Ohio Edison Company .... C 330 740-7754
  Youngstown *(G-20305)*

Protiviti Inc .... E 216 696-6010
  Cleveland *(G-6325)*
Software Answers Inc .... E 440 526-0095
  Brecksville *(G-1851)*
Triad Oil & Gas Engineering .... D 740 374-2940
  Marietta *(G-13506)*

MANAGEMENT CONSULTING SVCS: Information Systems

Affiliated Resource Group Inc .... D 614 889-6555
  Dublin *(G-10236)*
Fusion Alliance LLC .... E 614 852-8000
  Westerville *(G-19309)*
Fusion Alliance LLC .... E 513 563-8444
  Blue Ash *(G-1597)*
Jjr Solutions LLC .... E 937 912-0288
  Beavercreek *(G-1180)*
Kennedy Group Enterprises Inc .... E 440 879-0078
  Strongsville *(G-17481)*
Tek Systems .... D 614 789-6200
  Dublin *(G-10474)*
Vartek Services Inc .... E 937 438-3550
  Dayton *(G-9967)*

MANAGEMENT CONSULTING SVCS: Maintenance

County of Marion .... E 740 382-0624
  Marion *(G-13536)*
Hamilton Parks Conservancy .... E 513 785-7055
  Hamilton *(G-11740)*
Shermco Industries Inc .... D 614 836-8556
  Groveport *(G-11672)*

MANAGEMENT CONSULTING SVCS: Management Engineering

Johnson Mirmiran Thompson Inc .... D 614 714-0270
  Columbus *(G-7944)*
Shotstop Ballistics LLC .... E 330 686-0020
  Stow *(G-17392)*

MANAGEMENT CONSULTING SVCS: Manufacturing

Impact Ceramics LLC .... E 440 554-3624
  Cleveland *(G-5807)*
Midwest Mfg Solutions LLC .... E 513 381-7200
  West Chester *(G-19216)*
Ply-Trim Enterprises Inc .... E 330 799-7876
  Youngstown *(G-20325)*
Techsolve Inc .... D 513 948-2000
  Cincinnati *(G-4631)*

MANAGEMENT CONSULTING SVCS: Merchandising

Merchandising Services Co .... D 866 479-8246
  Blue Ash *(G-1639)*

MANAGEMENT CONSULTING SVCS: New Products & Svcs

Akron Centl Engrv Mold Mch Inc .... E 330 794-8704
  Akron *(G-30)*

MANAGEMENT CONSULTING SVCS: Planning

Aeea LLC .... E 330 497-5304
  Canton *(G-2229)*
Interbrand Design Forum Inc .... C 937 439-4400
  Cincinnati *(G-3834)*
Karlsberger Companies .... C 614 461-9500
  Columbus *(G-7966)*
National City Cmnty Dev Corp .... C 216 575-2000
  Cleveland *(G-6103)*
Ohio-Kentucky-Indiana Regional .... E 513 621-6300
  Cincinnati *(G-4214)*
Retail Forward Inc .... E 614 355-4000
  Columbus *(G-8625)*
Sedlak Management Cons Inc .... E 216 206-4700
  Cleveland *(G-6464)*
Shp Leading Design .... D 513 381-2112
  Cincinnati *(G-4518)*

MANAGEMENT CONSULTING SVCS: Public Utilities

United States Enrichment Corp .... A 740 897-2331
  Piketon *(G-16128)*
United States Enrichment Corp .... A 740 897-2457
  Piketon *(G-16129)*

MANAGEMENT CONSULTING SVCS: Quality Assurance

Benchmark National Corporation .... E 419 660-1100
  Bellevue *(G-1406)*
Safety Resources Company Ohio .... E 330 477-1100
  Canton *(G-2522)*
Smithers Quality Assessments .... E 330 762-4231
  Akron *(G-442)*

MANAGEMENT CONSULTING SVCS: Real Estate

0714 Inc .... E 440 327-2123
  North Ridgeville *(G-15452)*
Chartwell Group LLC .... E 216 360-0009
  Cleveland *(G-5230)*
Classic Real Estate Co .... E 937 393-3416
  Hillsboro *(G-11968)*
Hanna Commercial LLC .... D 216 861-7200
  Cleveland *(G-5723)*
Homelife Companies Inc .... E 740 369-1297
  Delaware *(G-10106)*
Ohio Equities LLC .... E 614 207-1805
  Columbus *(G-8340)*
Signature Associates Inc .... E 419 244-7505
  Toledo *(G-18188)*
Stepstone Group Real Estate LP .... E 216 522-0330
  Cleveland *(G-6538)*
Toni & Marie Bader .... E 937 339-3621
  Troy *(G-18380)*

MANAGEMENT CONSULTING SVCS: Restaurant & Food

Columbus Public School Dst .... E 614 365-5000
  Columbus *(G-7379)*
L and C Soft Serve Inc .... E 330 364-3823
  Dover *(G-10196)*
Thomas and King Inc .... C 614 527-0571
  Hilliard *(G-11958)*
Walgreen Co .... E 216 595-1407
  Cleveland *(G-6718)*

MANAGEMENT CONSULTING SVCS: Retail Trade Consultant

Goodwill Inds of Southern Ohio .... E 740 353-4394
  Portsmouth *(G-16281)*
Harbor Freight Tools Usa Inc .... D 330 479-9852
  Canton *(G-2394)*
Melo International Inc .... B 440 519-0526
  Cleveland *(G-6023)*
Sb Capital Acquisitions LLC .... A 614 443-4080
  Columbus *(G-8690)*

MANAGEMENT CONSULTING SVCS: Training & Development

1st Advnce SEC Invstgtions Inc .... E 937 317-4433
  Dayton *(G-9292)*
Automotive Events Inc .... E 440 356-1383
  Rocky River *(G-16570)*
D L A Training Center .... D 614 692-5986
  Columbus *(G-7480)*
Dayton Digital Media Inc .... E 937 223-8335
  Dayton *(G-9469)*
Fitworks Holding LLC .... B 513 923-9931
  Cincinnati *(G-3631)*
Global Military Expert Co .... E 800 738-9795
  Beavercreek *(G-1242)*
Honda of America Mfg Inc .... C 937 644-0724
  Marysville *(G-13626)*
Miami University .... B 513 727-3200
  Middletown *(G-14435)*

MANAGEMENT CONSULTING SVCS: Transportation

Ardmore Power Logistics LLC .... E 216 502-0640
  Westlake *(G-19461)*

SERVICES SECTION

MANAGEMENT SERVICES

Company	Code	Phone
Comprehensive Logistics Co Inc	E	330 793-0504
Youngstown (G-20158)		
CPC Logistics Inc	D	513 874-5787
Fairfield (G-10838)		
Distribution Data Incorporated	E	216 362-3009
Brookpark (G-1943)		
First Transit Inc	B	513 241-2200
Cincinnati (G-3624)		
Group Transportation Svcs Inc	E	800 689-6255
Hudson (G-12119)		
Interchez Lgistics Systems Inc	E	330 923-5080
Stow (G-17377)		
Jarrett Logistics Systems Inc	C	330 682-0099
Orrville (G-15775)		
Mxd Group Inc	E	614 801-0621
Columbus (G-8210)		
Portage Area Rgonal Trnsp Auth	D	330 678-1287
Kent (G-12391)		
TV Minority Company Inc	E	937 832-9350
Englewood (G-10722)		
Universal Transportation Syste	C	513 829-1287
Fairfield (G-10920)		

MANAGEMENT SERVICES

Company	Code	Phone
Advocare Inc	D	216 514-1451
Cleveland (G-4960)		
Aim Integrated Logistics Inc	B	330 759-0438
Girard (G-11406)		
Allcan Global Services Inc	E	513 825-1655
Cincinnati (G-2987)		
American Med	B	330 762-8999
Akron (G-71)		
Andersen Distribution Inc	C	937 898-7844
Dayton (G-9336)		
Apollo Property Management LLC	E	216 468-0050
Beachwood (G-1051)		
Astro Aluminum Enterprises Inc	E	330 755-1414
Struthers (G-17526)		
Babcock & Wilcox Company	A	330 753-4511
Barberton (G-955)		
Benchmark Technologies Corp	E	419 843-6691
Toledo (G-17769)		
Benjamin Rose Institute	D	216 791-3580
Cleveland (G-5116)		
Bernard Busson Builder	E	330 929-4926
Akron (G-99)		
Bridgepoint Risk MGT LLC	E	419 794-1075
Maumee (G-13890)		
Brown Co Ed Service Center	D	937 378-6118
Georgetown (G-11386)		
Cardinal Health Inc	A	614 757-5000
Dublin (G-10275)		
Cardinal Health Inc	D	614 497-9552
Obetz (G-15665)		
Careworks of Ohio Inc	B	614 792-1085
Dublin (G-10280)		
Cargotec Services USA Inc	D	419 482-6866
Perrysburg (G-15984)		
Cdc Management Co	C	614 781-0216
Columbus (G-7218)		
CFM Religion Pubg Group LLC	E	513 931-4050
Cincinnati (G-3221)		
Clermont North East School Dst	E	513 625-8283
Batavia (G-1002)		
Cleveland Clinic Foundation	A	216 636-8335
Cleveland (G-5296)		
Clk Multi-Family MGT LLC	C	614 891-0011
Columbus (G-7305)		
CMS & Co Management Svcs Inc	E	440 989-5200
Lorain (G-13028)		
Coal Services Inc	D	740 795-5220
Powhatan Point (G-16356)		
Colonial Senior Services Inc	C	513 856-8600
Hamilton (G-11713)		
Colonial Senior Services Inc	C	513 867-4006
Hamilton (G-11714)		
Colonial Senior Services Inc	C	513 844-8004
Hamilton (G-11715)		
Community Mercy Foundation	D	937 328-8134
Springfield (G-11713)		
Comprehensive Managed Care Sys	E	513 533-0021
Cincinnati (G-3407)		
Constellations Enterprise LLC	C	330 740-8208
Youngstown (G-20161)		
Consulate Management Co LLC	A	419 683-3436
Crestline (G-9142)		
Crawford & Company	E	330 652-3296
Warren (G-18843)		
Crescent Park Corporation	C	513 759-7000
West Chester (G-19059)		
Crestwood Mgmt LLC	D	440 484-2400
Cleveland (G-5438)		
Cypress Communications Inc	C	404 965-7248
Cleveland (G-5459)		
Cypress Companies Inc	E	330 849-6500
Akron (G-185)		
Dave Commercial Ground MGT	E	440 237-5394
North Royalton (G-15486)		
Dayton Foundation Inc	E	937 222-0410
Dayton (G-9474)		
Dearth Management Company	C	614 847-1070
Columbus (G-7498)		
Dhl Supply Chain (usa)	D	229 888-0699
Westerville (G-19298)		
Dhl Supply Chain (usa)	E	419 727-4318
Toledo (G-17852)		
Distribution Data Incorporated	E	216 362-3009
Brookpark (G-1943)		
Education Innovations Intl LLC	C	614 339-3676
Dublin (G-10334)		
Eleet Cryogenics Inc	E	330 874-4009
Bolivar (G-1746)		
Erie Indemnity Company	D	330 433-6300
Canton (G-2357)		
Excellence In Motivation Inc	C	763 445-3000
Dayton (G-9533)		
Executive Jet Management Inc	B	513 979-6600
Cincinnati (G-3586)		
Facilities Kahn Management	E	313 202-7607
Dayton (G-9537)		
FC Schwendler LLC	E	330 733-8715
Akron (G-222)		
First Services Inc	A	513 241-2200
Cincinnati (G-3619)		
First Transit Inc	B	513 241-2200
Cincinnati (G-3624)		
Fisher Foods Marketing Inc	C	330 497-3000
North Canton (G-15337)		
Flat Rock Care Center	C	419 483-7330
Flat Rock (G-11103)		
Focus Solutions Inc	C	513 376-8349
Cincinnati (G-3635)		
Folkers Management Corporation	E	513 421-0230
Cincinnati (G-3636)		
Fort Hmltn-Hghes Hlthcare Corp	A	513 867-2000
Hamilton (G-11729)		
Foseco Management Inc	B	440 826-4548
Cleveland (G-5626)		
Franklin & Seidelmann LLC	D	216 255-5700
Beachwood (G-1082)		
French Company LLC	D	330 963-4344
Twinsburg (G-18418)		
Frito-Lay North America Inc	D	419 893-8171
Maumee (G-13919)		
Genesis Technology Partners	E	513 585-5800
Cincinnati (G-3676)		
Gentlebrook Inc	C	330 877-3694
Hartville (G-11817)		
Grote Enterprises LLC	D	513 731-5700
Cincinnati (G-3715)		
Hanger Prosthetics &	E	330 633-9807
Tallmadge (G-17638)		
Hcesc Early Learning Program	C	513 589-3021
Cincinnati (G-3745)		
Heery International Inc	E	216 781-1313
Cleveland (G-5746)		
Helmsman Management Svcs LLC	D	614 478-8282
Columbus (G-7824)		
Hmshost Corporation	E	419 547-8667
Clyde (G-6814)		
Holzer Clinic LLC	A	740 446-5411
Gallipolis (G-11321)		
Hospice of Hamilton	E	513 895-1270
Hamilton (G-11742)		
Ideal Setech LLC	E	419 782-5522
Defiance (G-10036)		
Illinois Tool Works Inc	E	513 891-7474
Blue Ash (G-1614)		
Illumetek Corp	E	330 342-7582
Cuyahoga Falls (G-9195)		
Imflux Corp	E	513 488-1017
Hamilton (G-11743)		
Infinite Shares LLC	E	216 317-1601
Mentor (G-14195)		
Infocision Management Corp	C	937 259-2400
Dayton (G-9274)		
Instantwhip-Columbus Inc	E	614 871-9447
Grove City (G-11571)		
Intergrated Consulting	E	216 214-7547
Bedford Heights (G-1353)		
Investek Management Svcs F/C	E	419 873-1236
Perrysburg (G-16018)		
Island Service Company	C	419 285-3695
Put In Bay (G-16368)		
J A G Black Gold Management Co	D	614 565-3246
Lockbourne (G-12957)		
Jake Sweeney Automotive Inc	C	513 782-2800
Cincinnati (G-3859)		
Juice Technologies Inc	E	800 518-5576
Columbus (G-7957)		
Kappa House Corp of Delta	E	614 487-9461
Upper Arlington (G-18552)		
Klingbeil Capital MGT LLC	D	614 396-4919
Worthington (G-19967)		
Kroger Co	C	513 782-3300
Cincinnati (G-3946)		
Kurtz Bros Compost Services	E	330 864-2621
Akron (G-310)		
Leadec Corp	E	513 731-3590
Blue Ash (G-1627)		
Leatherman Nursing Ctrs Corp	A	330 336-6684
Wadsworth (G-18759)		
Legacy Village Management Off	E	216 382-3871
Cleveland (G-5933)		
Levering Management Inc	C	419 768-2401
Chesterville (G-2806)		
Levering Management Inc	D	740 387-9545
Marion (G-13548)		
Licking-Knox Goodwill Inds Inc	D	740 345-9861
Newark (G-15196)		
Lincolnview Local Schools	C	419 968-2226
Van Wert (G-18638)		
Lutheran Housing Services Inc	E	419 861-4990
Toledo (G-18020)		
M A Folkes Company Inc	E	513 785-4200
Hamilton (G-11756)		
Marsh Berry & Company Inc	E	440 354-3230
Beachwood (G-1097)		
MD Business Solutions Inc	E	513 872-4500
Blue Ash (G-1637)		
Med America Hlth Systems Corp	A	937 223-6192
Dayton (G-9710)		
Michael Baker Intl Inc	C	330 453-3110
Canton (G-2461)		
Michael Baker Intl Inc	E	412 269-6300
Cleveland (G-6046)		
Ministerial Day Care-Headstart	E	216 541-7400
Cleveland (G-6091)		
National Heritg Academies Inc	D	937 223-2889
Dayton (G-9769)		
National Heritg Academies Inc	D	513 251-6000
Cincinnati (G-4138)		
National Heritg Academies Inc	D	419 269-2247
Toledo (G-18076)		
National Heritg Academies Inc	D	513 751-5555
Cincinnati (G-4139)		
National Heritg Academies Inc	D	419 531-3285
Toledo (G-18077)		
National Heritg Academies Inc	D	937 235-5498
Dayton (G-9770)		
National Heritg Academies Inc	D	937 278-6671
Dayton (G-9771)		
National Heritg Academies Inc	D	216 731-0127
Euclid (G-10769)		
National Heritg Academies Inc	D	216 451-1725
Cleveland (G-6109)		
National Heritg Academies Inc	D	330 792-4806
Youngstown (G-20297)		
Nexstep Healthcare LLC	E	216 797-4040
Cleveland (G-6128)		
Niederst Management Ltd	D	440 331-8800
Cleveland (G-6133)		
Northcoast Healthcare MGT Inc	C	216 501-2000
Beachwood (G-1108)		
Northwest Local School Dst	D	330 854-2291
Canal Fulton (G-2144)		
Ohio Department of Education	E	740 289-2908
Piketon (G-16120)		
Omnicare Management Company	A	513 719-1535
Cincinnati (G-4222)		
P I & I Motor Express Inc	C	330 448-4035
Masury (G-13866)		
Parkops Columbus LLC	B	877 499-9155
Columbus (G-8518)		
Pazco Inc	E	216 447-9581
Cleveland (G-6254)		
Perduco Group Inc	E	937 401-0271
Beavercreek (G-1196)		
Pipino Management Company	E	330 629-2261
Youngstown (G-20321)		

Employee Codes: A=Over 500 employees, B=251-500
C=101-250, D=51-100, E=25-50

Pk Management LLC....C....216 472-1870
Richmond Heights (G-16540)
Plus Management Services Inc....C....419 225-9018
Lima (G-12860)
Premier Management Co Inc....E....740 867-2144
Chesapeake (G-2786)
Promedica Health Systems Inc....A....567 585-7454
Toledo (G-18141)
Promedica Physcn Cntinuum Svcs....C....419 824-7200
Sylvania (G-17608)
Resource International Inc....C....614 823-4949
Columbus (G-8622)
Revolution Group Inc....D....614 212-1111
Westerville (G-19349)
Ricco Enterprises Incorporated....E....216 883-7775
Cleveland (G-6389)
Richland Mall Shopping Ctr....E....419 529-4003
Mansfield (G-13357)
Ross Consolidated Corp....D....440 748-5800
Grafton (G-11444)
Safeguard Properties LLC....A....216 739-2900
Cleveland (G-6433)
Salvation Army....D....419 447-2252
Tiffin (G-17697)
Shred-It USA LLC....D....847 288-0377
Fairfield (G-10906)
Signature Inc....C....614 734-0010
Dublin (G-10453)
Skanska USA Building Inc....E....513 421-0082
Cincinnati (G-4538)
Sleep Network Inc....E....419 535-9282
Toledo (G-18190)
Smg Holdings Inc....C....614 827-2500
Columbus (G-8744)
Sperian Protection Usa Inc....D....614 539-5056
Grove City (G-11601)
Ssoe Inc....E....330 821-7198
Alliance (G-560)
Stat Integrated Tech Inc....E....440 286-7663
Chardon (G-2769)
Sterling Medical Corporation....C....513 984-1800
Cincinnati (G-4592)
Sylvania Franciscan Health....E....419 882-8373
Maumee (G-13984)
TAC Industries Inc....B....937 328-5200
Springfield (G-17285)
Trinity Hospital Holding Co....A....740 264-8000
Steubenville (G-17343)
Uc Health Llc....C....513 298-3000
West Chester (G-19170)
Uc Health Llc....E....513 584-8600
Cincinnati (G-4721)
Uc Health Llc....A....513 585-6000
Cincinnati (G-4722)
United Telemanagement Corp....E....937 454-1888
Dayton (G-9948)
University Hospitals....D....216 844-8797
Cleveland (G-6657)
University Hospitals Cleveland....E....216 844-3528
Cleveland (G-6662)
Vance Property Management LLC....D....419 887-1878
Toledo (G-18288)
Verst Group Logistics Inc....E....513 772-2494
Cincinnati (G-4810)
Voc Works Ltd....D....614 760-3515
Dublin (G-10484)
Wayne Street Development LLC....E....740 373-5455
Marietta (G-13519)
Western Management Inc....E....216 941-3333
Cleveland (G-6741)
Wings Investors Company Ltd....E....513 241-5800
Cincinnati (G-4853)

MANAGEMENT SVCS, FACILITIES SUPPORT: Environ Remediation

Alco Inc....E....740 527-2991
Logan (G-12967)
Aztec Services Group Inc....D....513 541-2002
Cincinnati (G-3071)
Environmental Specialists Inc....E....740 788-8134
Newark (G-15165)
Four Seasons Environmental Inc....B....513 539-2978
Monroe (G-14696)
Midwest Environmental Inc....E....419 382-9200
Perrysburg (G-16034)
Southside Envmtl Group LLC....E....330 299-0027
Niles (G-15306)
Sunpro Inc....D....330 966-0910
North Canton (G-15370)

MANAGEMENT SVCS, FACILITIES SUPPORT: Jails, Privately Ops

Correctons Comm Sthastern Ohio....D....740 753-4060
Nelsonville (G-14960)

MANAGEMENT SVCS: Administrative

Arthur Middleton Capital Holdn....E....330 966-9000
North Canton (G-15326)
Aultcomp Inc....E....330 830-4919
Massillon (G-13788)
Bravo Wellness LLC....E....216 658-9500
Cleveland (G-5134)
City of Youngstown....B....330 742-8700
Youngstown (G-20143)
County of Cuyahoga....B....216 443-7181
Cleveland (G-5426)
County of Morrow....E....419 946-2618
Mount Gilead (G-14853)
Educatonal Svc Ctr Lorain Cnty....E....440 244-1659
Elyria (G-10619)
Help Foundation Inc....C....216 432-4810
Euclid (G-10758)
Lineage Logistics LLC....E....937 328-3349
Springfield (G-17221)
McR LLC....D....937 879-5055
Beavercreek (G-1192)
Midwest Tape LLC....B....419 868-9370
Holland (G-12038)
Nationwide General Insur Co....D....614 249-7111
Columbus (G-8243)
Netjets Aviation Inc....E....614 239-5501
Gahanna (G-11259)
Ohio State Univ Res Foundation....C....614 292-3815
Columbus (G-8381)
Parker-Hannifin Intl Corp....B....216 896-3000
Cleveland (G-6242)
Providence Medical Group Inc....D....937 297-8999
Moraine (G-14817)
Rjw Inc....E....216 398-6090
Independence (G-12250)
Salvation Army....C....330 773-3331
Akron (G-428)
Standard Retirement Svcs Inc....E....440 808-2724
Westlake (G-19551)
The Sheakley Group Inc....E....513 771-2277
Cincinnati (G-4646)
Thomas Rosser....C....614 890-2900
Westerville (G-19444)
University of Cincinnati....E....513 556-4200
Cincinnati (G-4767)
University of Cincinnati....C....513 558-4231
Cincinnati (G-4768)
Village of Valley View....C....216 524-6511
Cleveland (G-6698)

MANAGEMENT SVCS: Business

3c Technologies Inc....D....419 868-8999
Holland (G-12005)
American Mechanical Group Inc....E....614 575-3720
Columbus (G-7001)
Camden Management Inc....E....513 383-1635
Cincinnati (G-3171)
Dimensionmark Ltd....E....513 305-3525
West Chester (G-19063)
Early Learning Tree Chld Ctr....D....937 293-7907
Dayton (G-9513)
EDM Management Inc....E....330 726-5790
Youngstown (G-20177)
Hat White Management LLC....E....800 525-7967
Akron (G-257)
Henkel Corporation....E....440 255-8900
Mentor (G-14189)
Integra Ohio Inc....B....513 378-5214
Cincinnati (G-3825)
Jeff Wyler Automotive Fmly Inc....E....513 752-7450
Cincinnati (G-2918)
Kaiser Logistics LLC....D....937 534-0213
Monroe (G-14700)
Kross Acquisition Company LLC....E....513 554-0555
Loveland (G-13136)
Medicount Management Inc....E....513 772-4465
Cincinnati (G-4046)
Ohio Cllbrtive Lrng Sltons Inc....E....216 595-5289
Beachwood (G-1110)
Omnicare Purch Ltd Partner Inc....C....800 990-6664
Cincinnati (G-4224)
Osu Internal Medicine LLC....D....614 293-0080
Dublin (G-10418)
Providence Health Partners LLC....E....937 297-8999
Moraine (G-14816)
Quality Supply Chain Co-Op Inc....E....614 764-3124
Dublin (G-10433)
Rev1 Ventures....E....614 487-3700
Columbus (G-8627)
RMS of Ohio Inc....B....440 617-6605
Westlake (G-19542)
Roundstone Management Ltd....E....440 617-0333
Lakewood (G-12499)
Safran Power Usa LLC....C....330 487-2000
Twinsburg (G-18466)
St George & Co Inc....E....330 733-7528
Akron (G-447)
Viaquest Inc....E....614 889-5837
Dublin (G-10481)
Vora Ventures LLC....C....513 792-5100
Blue Ash (G-1716)
Walnut Ridge Management....D....234 678-3900
Akron (G-504)
Zarcal Zanesville LLC....D....216 226-2132
Lakewood (G-12503)

MANAGEMENT SVCS: Circuit, Motion Picture Theaters

Continntal Mssage Solution Inc....D....614 224-4534
Columbus (G-7434)

MANAGEMENT SVCS: Construction

A-Sons Construction Inc....D....614 846-2438
Columbus (G-6923)
Aecom Global II LLC....D....216 523-5600
Cleveland (G-4966)
Ameridian Specialty Services....E....513 769-0150
Cincinnati (G-3014)
Baxter Hodell Donnelly Preston....C....513 271-1634
Cincinnati (G-3083)
C M M Inc....E....330 656-3820
Hudson (G-12106)
Cedarwood Construction Company....D....330 836-9971
Akron (G-125)
Chemstress Consultant Company....C....330 535-5591
Akron (G-130)
Collins & Assoc Technical Svcs....E....740 574-2320
Wheelersburg (G-19573)
Contech-Gdcg....E....937 426-3577
Beavercreek (G-1235)
Cook Paving and Cnstr Co....E....216 267-7705
Independence (G-12201)
Core Resources Inc....D....513 731-1771
Cincinnati (G-3422)
DE Foxx & Associates Inc....B....513 621-5522
Cincinnati (G-3470)
Eclipse Co LLC....E....440 552-9400
Cleveland (G-5526)
Elford Inc....C....614 488-4000
Columbus (G-7588)
G Stephens Inc....D....614 227-0304
Columbus (G-7720)
Gilbane Building Company....E....614 948-4000
Columbus (G-7750)
Hammond Construction Inc....D....330 455-7039
Canton (G-2389)
Hernandez Cnstr Svcs Inc....E....330 796-0500
Fairlawn (G-10955)
Hills Developers Inc....C....513 984-0300
Blue Ash (G-1612)
Innovative Architectural....E....614 416-0614
Columbus (G-7900)
Jack Gibson Construction Co....D....330 394-5280
Warren (G-18867)
Lathrop Company Inc....E....419 893-7000
Toledo (G-18001)
LEWaro-D&j-A Joint Venture Co....E....937 443-0000
Dayton (G-9678)
McDaniels Cnstr Corp Inc....D....614 252-5852
Columbus (G-8134)
Megen Construction Company Inc....E....513 742-9191
Cincinnati (G-4052)
Quality Control Inspection....D....440 359-1900
Cleveland (G-6334)
Quandel Construction Group Inc....E....717 657-0909
Westerville (G-19439)
Renier Construction Corp....E....614 866-4580
Columbus (G-8613)
Richard L Bowen & Assoc Inc....D....216 491-9300
Cleveland (G-6391)
RJ Runge Company Inc....E....419 740-5781
Port Clinton (G-16253)

SERVICES SECTION

MARINAS

Ruscilli Construction Co Inc .... D ... 614 876-9484
  Columbus *(G-8658)*
Simonson Construction Svcs Inc .... D ... 419 281-8299
  Ashland *(G-699)*
Technical Consultants Inc .... E ... 513 521-2696
  Cincinnati *(G-4629)*
Tradesmen International LLC .... C ... 419 502-9140
  Sandusky *(G-16802)*
Triversity Construction Co LLC .... E ... 513 733-0046
  Cincinnati *(G-4702)*
Ttl Associates Inc .... C ... 419 241-4556
  Toledo *(G-18263)*

MANAGEMENT SVCS: Financial, Business

Bailey Associates .... C ... 614 760-7752
  Columbus *(G-7084)*
Critical Business Analysis Inc .... E ... 419 874-0800
  Perrysburg *(G-15991)*
Dco LLC .... B ... 419 931-9086
  Perrysburg *(G-15996)*
Hill Barth & King LLC .... E ... 330 758-8613
  Canfield *(G-2193)*

MANAGEMENT SVCS: Hospital

Acuity Healthcare LP .... D ... 740 283-7499
  Steubenville *(G-17302)*
Blanchard Valley Health System ...... A ... 419 423-4500
  Findlay *(G-10997)*
Blanchard Valley Health System ...... A ... 419 424-3000
  Findlay *(G-10998)*
Carespring Health Care MGT LLC .... E ... 513 943-4000
  Loveland *(G-13113)*
Carington Health Systems .... E ... 513 682-2700
  Hamilton *(G-11706)*
Cincinnati Health Network Inc .... E ... 513 961-0600
  Cincinnati *(G-3309)*
Clevelan Clinic Hlth Sys W Reg .... B ... 216 518-3444
  Cleveland *(G-5286)*
Clevelan Clinic Hlth Sys W Reg .... A ... 216 476-7000
  Cleveland *(G-5287)*
Clevelan Clinic Hlth Sys W Reg .... E ... 216 476-7606
  Cleveland *(G-5288)*
Clevelan Clinic Hlth Sys W Reg .... D ... 216 476-7007
  Cleveland *(G-5289)*
Communicare Health Svcs Inc .... E ... 513 530-1654
  Blue Ash *(G-1564)*
Community Mercy Foundation .... D ... 937 274-1569
  Dayton *(G-9419)*
Community Mercy Hlth Partners .... C ... 937 653-5432
  Urbana *(G-18583)*
Comprehensive Health Care .... A ... 440 329-7500
  Elyria *(G-10607)*
Corporate Health Dimensions .... E ... 740 775-6119
  Chillicothe *(G-2828)*
Emp Management Group Ltd .... D ... 330 493-4443
  Canton *(G-2355)*
Gcha .... D ... 216 696-6900
  Cleveland *(G-5662)*
Harborside Healthcare Corp .... D ... 937 436-6155
  Dayton *(G-9600)*
Healthscope Benefits Inc .... E ... 614 797-5200
  Westerville *(G-19409)*
Hospice of Southern Ohio .... D ... 740 356-2567
  Portsmouth *(G-16289)*
Hospitalists MGT Group LLC .... A ... 866 464-7497
  Canton *(G-2404)*
Jtd Health Systems Inc .... A ... 419 394-3335
  Saint Marys *(G-16679)*
Kettering Adventist Healthcare .... E ... 937 298-4331
  Dayton *(G-9649)*
Kettering Adventist Healthcare .... E ... 937 395-8816
  Miamisburg *(G-14309)*
Licking Memorial Hlth Systems .... A ... 220 564-4000
  Nowark *(G-15191)*
Mary Rtan Hlth Assn Logan Cnty ..... E ... 937 592-4015
  Bellefontaine *(G-1389)*
Marymount Health Care Systems ..... E ... 216 332-1100
  Cleveland *(G-5990)*
Mercy Franciscan Hosp Mt Airy .... A ... 513 853-5101
  Cincinnati *(G-4057)*
Niagara Health Corporation .... E ... 614 898-4000
  Columbus *(G-8277)*
Permedion Inc .... D ... 614 895-9900
  Westerville *(G-19340)*
Renaissance House Inc .... D ... 419 626-1110
  Sandusky *(G-16787)*
Sterling Medical Corporation .... D ... 513 984-1800
  Cincinnati *(G-4591)*
Trihealth Inc .... E ... 513 929-0020
  Cincinnati *(G-4687)*
Trihealth Inc .... E ... 513 865-1111
  Cincinnati *(G-4688)*
Trihealth Inc .... E ... 513 569-6777
  Cincinnati *(G-4689)*
Trihealth Inc .... E ... 513 891-1627
  Blue Ash *(G-1702)*
Trihealth Inc .... E ... 513 569-6111
  Cincinnati *(G-4690)*
Trihealth Inc .... E ... 513 871-2340
  Cincinnati *(G-4691)*
Trihealth Inc .... C ... 513 985-0900
  Montgomery *(G-14734)*
Trinity Health System .... C ... 740 283-7848
  Steubenville *(G-17339)*
Trinity Health System .... A ... 740 264-8000
  Steubenville *(G-17340)*
Trinity Health System .... E ... 740 264-8101
  Steubenville *(G-17341)*
University Hospitals .... A ... 216 767-8900
  Shaker Heights *(G-16869)*
University Hospitals .... A ... 440 743-3000
  Parma *(G-15917)*
Viaquest Behavioral Health LLC .... E ... 614 339-0868
  Dublin *(G-10482)*

MANAGEMENT SVCS: Hotel Or Motel

American Hospitality Group Inc .... B ... 330 336-6684
  Wadsworth *(G-18747)*
Atlantic Hospitality & MGT LLC .... E ... 216 454-5450
  Beachwood *(G-1052)*
Chu Management Co Inc .... E ... 330 725-4571
  Medina *(G-14047)*
Cmp I Owner-T LLC .... E ... 614 764-9393
  Dublin *(G-10298)*
Cmp I Owner-T LLC .... E ... 614 436-7070
  Columbus *(G-7310)*
Cmp I Owner-T LLC .... E ... 513 733-4334
  Blue Ash *(G-1562)*
Crestline Hotels & Resorts LLC .... E ... 614 846-4355
  Columbus *(G-7460)*
Crestline Hotels & Resorts LLC .... E ... 513 489-3666
  Blue Ash *(G-1571)*
M&C Hotel Interests Inc .... E ... 440 543-1331
  Chagrin Falls *(G-2723)*
MEI Hotels Incorporated .... C ... 216 589-0441
  Cleveland *(G-6021)*
Rama Tika Developers LLC .... E ... 419 806-6446
  Mansfield *(G-13353)*
Rbp Atlanta LLC .... D ... 614 246-2522
  Columbus *(G-8590)*
Regal Hospitality LLC .... E ... 614 436-0004
  Columbus *(G-8605)*
Req/Jqh Holdings Inc .... D ... 513 891-1066
  Blue Ash *(G-1681)*
Select Hotels Group LLC .... E ... 513 754-0003
  Mason *(G-13759)*
Tjm Clmbus LLC Tjm Clumbus LLC ...... D ... 614 885-1885
  Columbus *(G-8851)*

MANAGEMENT SVCS: Nursing & Personal Care Facility

Alternative Home Health Care .... E ... 513 794-0555
  Cincinnati *(G-2998)*
Balanced Care Corporation .... E ... 330 908-1166
  Northfield *(G-15509)*
Balanced Care Corporation .... E ... 937 372-7205
  Xenia *(G-20044)*
Christian Benevolent Assocn .... C ... 513 931-5000
  Cincinnati *(G-3271)*
Deaconess Long Term Care Inc .... D ... 513 861-0400
  Cincinnati *(G-3473)*
DMD Management Inc .... C ... 440 944-9400
  Wickliffe *(G-19594)*
DMD Management Inc .... E ... 216 898-8399
  Cleveland *(G-5496)*
Healthcare Management Cons .... A ... 330 623-2193
  Rockford *(G-16563)*
HRP Capital Inc .... E ... 419 865-3111
  Holland *(G-12028)*
Kerrington Health Systems Inc .... C ... 513 863-0360
  Fairfield Township *(G-10932)*
Kettcor Inc .... B ... 937 458-4949
  Miamisburg *(G-14308)*
Kingston Healthcare Company .... E ... 419 247-2880
  Toledo *(G-17995)*
Laurel Health Care Company .... C ... 614 794-8800
  Westerville *(G-19322)*
Laurel Health Care Company .... C ... 614 888-4553
  Worthington *(G-19968)*
Laurel Health Care Company .... C ... 614 885-0408
  Worthington *(G-19969)*
Nursing Care MGT Amer Inc .... D ... 740 927-9888
  Pataskala *(G-15924)*
Nursing Care MGT Amer Inc .... D ... 513 793-5092
  Cincinnati *(G-4194)*
Nursing Care MGT Amer Inc .... C ... 419 385-3958
  Toledo *(G-18098)*
Omnicare Inc .... C ... 513 719-2600
  Cincinnati *(G-4220)*
Saber Healthcare Group LLC .... E ... 216 292-5706
  Bedford *(G-1333)*
Salem Healthcare MGT LLC .... E ... 330 332-1588
  Salem *(G-16714)*
St Augustine Corporation .... B ... 216 939-7600
  Lakewood *(G-12501)*
Westminster Management Company ....C ... 614 274-5154
  Columbus *(G-8980)*
Windsor House Inc .... E ... 440 834-0544
  Burton *(G-2066)*

MANAGEMENT SVCS: Personnel

Trustaff Management Inc .... A ... 513 272-3999
  Blue Ash *(G-1706)*

MANAGEMENT SVCS: Restaurant

Authentic Food LLC .... E ... 740 369-0377
  Delaware *(G-10073)*
Bistro Off Broadway .... E ... 937 316-5000
  Greenville *(G-11489)*
Bon Appetit Management Co .... E ... 614 823-1880
  Westerville *(G-19371)*
Cameron Mitchell Rest LLC .... E ... 614 621-3663
  Columbus *(G-7180)*
D J- Seve Group Inc .... E ... 614 888-6600
  Lewis Center *(G-12680)*
Das Dutch Kitchen Inc .... D ... 330 683-0530
  Dalton *(G-9240)*
Haiku .... E ... 614 294-8168
  Columbus *(G-7794)*
Kmon Inc .... E ... 419 873-0029
  Maumee *(G-13933)*
T K Edwards LLC .... E ... 614 406-8064
  Columbus *(G-8817)*
V Westaar Inc .... E ... 740 803-2803
  Lewis Center *(G-12709)*
Wadsworth Galaxy Rest Inc .... D ... 330 334-3663
  Wadsworth *(G-18773)*
William Royce Inc .... D ... 513 771-3361
  Cincinnati *(G-4850)*

MANAGERS: Athletes

International Management Group ..... B ... 216 522-1200
  Cleveland *(G-5830)*
International Mdsg Corp .... B ... 216 522-1200
  Cleveland *(G-5831)*

MANPOWER POOLS

Patrick Staffing Inc .... E ... 937 743-5585
  Franklin *(G-11162)*

MANPOWER TRAINING

Esc of Cuyahoga County .... D ... 216 524-3000
  Independence *(G-12210)*
Ohio State University .... D ... 614 292-7788
  Columbus *(G-8413)*
Riverview Industries Inc .... C ... 419 898-5250
  Oak Harbor *(G-15616)*

MANUFACTURED & MOBILE HOME DEALERS

Colonial Sales Inc .... E ... 740 397-4970
  Mount Vernon *(G-14883)*

MANUFACTURING INDUSTRIES, NEC

Ace Assembly Packaging Inc .... E ... 330 866-9117
  Waynesburg *(G-18979)*

MARBLE, BUILDING: Cut & Shaped

Heritage Marble of Ohio Inc .... E ... 614 436-1464
  Columbus *(G-7831)*

MARINAS

Catawba-Cleveland Dev Corp .... D ... 419 797-4424
  Port Clinton *(G-16239)*

Employee Codes: A=Over 500 employees, B=251-500
C=101-250, D=51-100, E=25-50

MARINAS

SERVICES SECTION

Island Service Company .... C 419 285-3695
  Put In Bay *(G-16368)*
S B S Transit Inc .... B 440 288-2222
  Lorain *(G-13075)*
Saw Mill Creek Ltd .... C 419 433-3800
  Huron *(G-12170)*
Sima Marine Sales Inc .... E 440 269-3200
  Willoughby *(G-19714)*
Tappan Lake Marina Inc .... E 740 269-2031
  Scio *(G-16817)*
Vermilion Boat Club Inc .... E 440 967-6634
  Vermilion *(G-18719)*

MARINE CARGO HANDLING SVCS

A-1 Quality Labor Services LLC ...... E 513 678-0724
  Cincinnati *(G-2956)*
Consolidated Grain & Barge Co ...... E 513 941-4805
  Cincinnati *(G-3411)*
Kinder Mrgan Lqds Trminals LLC ..... E 513 841-0500
  Cincinnati *(G-3924)*
Marietta Industrial Entps Inc .... D 740 373-2252
  Marietta *(G-13470)*
McGinnis Inc .... C 740 377-4391
  South Point *(G-17092)*
McGinnis Inc .... E 513 941-8070
  Cincinnati *(G-4037)*
McNational Inc .... C 740 377-4391
  South Point *(G-17093)*
Toledo-Lucas County Port Auth ... E 419 243-8251
  Toledo *(G-18255)*
Toledo-Lucas County Port Auth ... E 419 865-2351
  Swanton *(G-17573)*

MARINE CARGO HANDLING SVCS: Loading & Unloading

Bellaire Harbor Service LLC ...... E 740 676-4305
  Bellaire *(G-1361)*

MARINE CARGO HANDLING SVCS: Marine Terminal

Cincinnati Bulk Terminals LLC ... E 513 621-4800
  Cincinnati *(G-3290)*
Reserve Ftl LLC .... E 440 519-1768
  Twinsburg *(G-18460)*

MARINE SPLYS WHOLESALERS

Mazzella Holding Company Inc ... D 513 772-4466
  Cleveland *(G-5997)*
Norman-Spencer Agency Inc ...... E 937 432-1600
  Dayton *(G-9775)*

MARINE SVC STATIONS

Island Service Company .... C 419 285-3695
  Put In Bay *(G-16368)*

MARKETS: Meat & fish

Euclid Fish Company .... D 440 951-6448
  Mentor *(G-14172)*
Weilands Fine Meats Inc .... E 614 267-9910
  Columbus *(G-8975)*

MARKING DEVICES: Embossing Seals & Hand Stamps

System Seals Inc .... D 440 735-0200
  Cleveland *(G-6562)*

MARKING DEVICES: Screens, Textile Printing

Marathon Mfg & Sup Co .... D 330 343-2656
  New Philadelphia *(G-15108)*

MARRIAGE BUREAU

Cuyahoga County .... D 216 443-8920
  Cleveland *(G-5454)*

MARTIAL ARTS INSTRUCTION

Cincinnati Tae Kwon Do Inc ...... E 513 271-6900
  Cincinnati *(G-3333)*

MASSAGE PARLORS

G E G Enterprises Inc .... E 330 477-3133
  Canton *(G-2375)*

Irish Envy LLC .... E 440 808-8000
  Westlake *(G-19499)*
Mark Luikart Inc .... E 330 339-9141
  New Philadelphia *(G-15109)*
Massage Envy .... E 440 878-0500
  Strongsville *(G-17490)*

MATERIALS HANDLING EQPT WHOLESALERS

Agrinomix LLC .... E 440 774-2981
  Oberlin *(G-15637)*
Andersen & Associates Inc ...... E 330 425-8500
  Twinsburg *(G-18391)*
Bobcat of Dayton Inc .... E 937 293-3176
  Moraine *(G-14755)*
Bohl Crane Inc .... D 419 476-7525
  Toledo *(G-17774)*
Bohl Equipment Company .... D 419 476-7525
  Toledo *(G-17775)*
Brennan Industrial Truck Co ...... E 419 867-6000
  Holland *(G-12012)*
Decker Equipment Company Inc ... E 866 252-4395
  Cleveland *(G-5473)*
Devirsified Material Handling ..... E 419 865-8025
  Holland *(G-12019)*
Equipment Depot Ohio Inc .... E 513 891-0600
  Blue Ash *(G-1590)*
Equipment Depot Ohio Inc .... E 513 539-8464
  Monroe *(G-14694)*
Esec Corporation .... E 330 799-1536
  Youngstown *(G-20181)*
Fairborn Equipment Company Inc ... D 419 209-0760
  Upper Sandusky *(G-18560)*
Federal Machinery & Eqp Co ..... E 800 652-2466
  Cleveland *(G-5582)*
Forte Indus Eqp Systems Inc ..... E 513 398-2800
  Mason *(G-13703)*
Great Lakes Power Products Inc ... D 440 951-5111
  Mentor *(G-14185)*
Hgr Industrial Surplus Inc .... E 216 486-4567
  Euclid *(G-10759)*
Hy-Tek Material Handling Inc .... D 614 497-2500
  Columbus *(G-7873)*
Industrial Parts & Service Co ..... E 330 966-5025
  Canton *(G-2411)*
Intelligrated Systems LLC .... A 513 701-7300
  Mason *(G-13721)*
Iwi Incorporated .... E 440 585-5900
  Wickliffe *(G-19604)*
Kmh Systems Inc .... E 513 469-9400
  Cincinnati *(G-3934)*
McCormick Equipment Co Inc ... E 513 677-8888
  Loveland *(G-13145)*
Mh Equipment Company .... E 937 890-6800
  Dayton *(G-9725)*
Mh Equipment Company .... E 614 871-1571
  Grove City *(G-11580)*
Mh Equipment Company .... D 513 681-2200
  Cincinnati *(G-4085)*
Miami Industrial Trucks Inc .... D 937 293-4194
  Moraine *(G-14805)*
Mid-Ohio Forklifts Inc .... E 330 633-1230
  Akron *(G-344)*
Midlands Millroom Supply Inc .... E 330 453-9100
  Canton *(G-2462)*
Newtown Nine Inc .... E 330 376-7741
  Akron *(G-351)*
R&M Materials Handling Inc ...... E 937 328-5100
  Springfield *(G-17262)*
Raymond Storage Concepts Inc ... E 513 891-7290
  Blue Ash *(G-1677)*
Rde System Corp .... C 513 933-8000
  Lebanon *(G-12640)*
Total Fleet Solutions LLC .... E 419 868-8853
  Holland *(G-12063)*
Towlift Inc .... C 216 749-6800
  Brooklyn Heights *(G-1929)*
Towlift Inc .... E 419 666-1333
  Northwood *(G-15548)*
Toyota Industrial Eqp Dlr .... E 419 865-8025
  Holland *(G-12064)*
Toyota Industries N Amer Inc .... E 513 779-7500
  West Chester *(G-19164)*
Valley Industrial Trucks Inc .... E 330 788-4081
  Youngstown *(G-20402)*
Willis Day Management Inc .... E 419 476-8000
  Toledo *(G-18311)*

MATS OR MATTING, NEC: Rubber

Durable Corporation .... D 800 537-1603
  Norwalk *(G-15571)*

MATS, MATTING & PADS: Auto, Floor, Exc Rubber Or Plastic

Crown Dielectric Inds Inc .... C 614 224-5161
  Columbus *(G-7467)*

MATS, MATTING & PADS: Nonwoven

Durable Corporation .... D 800 537-1603
  Norwalk *(G-15571)*

MEAL DELIVERY PROGRAMS

Casleo Corporation .... E 614 252-6508
  Columbus *(G-7205)*
Clossman Catering Incorporated ... E 513 942-7744
  Hamilton *(G-11712)*
Licking County Aging Program ... D 740 345-0821
  Newark *(G-15187)*
Meals On Wheels-Older Adult Al ... E 740 681-5050
  Lancaster *(G-12555)*
Mid-Ohio Foodbank .... C 614 317-9400
  Grove City *(G-11581)*
Tom Paige Catering Company ... E 216 431-4236
  Cleveland *(G-6602)*
Trinity Action Partnership .... E 937 456-2800
  Eaton *(G-10578)*

MEAT & MEAT PRDTS WHOLESALERS

Carfagnas Incorporated .... E 614 846-6340
  Columbus *(G-7199)*
Fresh Mark Inc .... B 330 832-7491
  Massillon *(G-13812)*
Fresh Mark Inc .... B 330 834-3669
  Massillon *(G-13810)*
Hillandale Farms Corporation .... E 330 724-3199
  Akron *(G-265)*
Meadowbrook Meat Company Inc ... C 614 771-9660
  Columbus *(G-8140)*
Pioneer Packing Co .... E 419 352-5283
  Bowling Green *(G-1790)*
Robert Winner Sons Inc .... E 419 582-4321
  Yorkshire *(G-20092)*
Storer Meat Co Inc .... E 216 621-7538
  Cleveland *(G-6543)*
Tri-State Beef Co Inc .... E 513 579-1722
  Cincinnati *(G-4685)*
Weilands Fine Meats Inc .... E 614 267-9910
  Columbus *(G-8975)*

MEAT CUTTING & PACKING

Empire Packing Company LP .... D 513 942-5400
  West Chester *(G-19196)*
Fresh Mark Inc .... B 330 834-3669
  Massillon *(G-13810)*
King Kold Inc .... E 937 836-2731
  Englewood *(G-10711)*
Marshallville Packing Co Inc ...... E 330 855-2871
  Marshallville *(G-13597)*
Robert Winner Sons Inc .... E 419 582-4321
  Yorkshire *(G-20092)*
Shaker Valley Foods Inc .... E 216 961-8600
  Cleveland *(G-6476)*
Tri-State Beef Co Inc .... E 513 579-1722
  Cincinnati *(G-4685)*

MEAT MARKETS

A To Z Portion Ctrl Meats Inc .... E 419 358-2926
  Bluffton *(G-1726)*
Carles Bratwurst Inc .... E 419 562-7741
  Bucyrus *(G-2028)*
Landes Fresh Meats Inc .... E 937 836-3613
  Clayton *(G-4912)*
Marshallville Packing Co Inc ...... E 330 855-2871
  Marshallville *(G-13597)*
Mary C Enterprises Inc .... D 937 253-6169
  Dayton *(G-9701)*
Rubin Erb .... E 330 852-4423
  Sugarcreek *(G-17547)*
S and S Gilardi Inc .... D 740 397-2751
  Mount Vernon *(G-14921)*
Steaks & Such Inc .... E 330 837-9296
  Massillon *(G-13858)*

SERVICES SECTION

MEAT PRDTS: Cooked Meats, From Purchased Meat

King Kold Inc .... E 937 836-2731
  Englewood (G-10711)

MEAT PRDTS: Frozen

Martin-Brower Company LLC ..... B 513 773-2301
  West Chester (G-19118)

MEAT PRDTS: Pork, From Slaughtered Meat

V H Cooper & Co Inc .... C 419 375-4116
  Fort Recovery (G-11120)

MEAT PRDTS: Prepared Beef Prdts From Purchased Beef

Fresh Mark Inc .... B 330 834-3669
  Massillon (G-13810)

MEAT PROCESSED FROM PURCHASED CARCASSES

A To Z Portion Ctrl Meats Inc ..... E 419 358-2926
  Bluffton (G-1726)
Empire Packing Company LP ..... D 513 942-5400
  West Chester (G-19196)
Fresh Mark Inc .... B 330 832-7491
  Massillon (G-13812)
Kenosha Beef International Ltd .. C 614 771-1330
  Columbus (G-7979)
Marshallville Packing Co Inc ...... E 330 855-2871
  Marshallville (G-13597)
Robert Winner Sons Inc .... E 419 582-4321
  Yorkshire (G-20092)
Tri-State Beef Co Inc .... E 513 579-1722
  Cincinnati (G-4685)
White Castle System Inc .... B 614 228-5781
  Columbus (G-8986)

MEATS, PACKAGED FROZEN: Wholesalers

A To Z Portion Ctrl Meats Inc ..... E 419 358-2926
  Bluffton (G-1726)
Blue Ribbon Meats Inc .... D 216 631-8850
  Cleveland (G-5124)
White Castle System Inc .... B 614 228-5781
  Columbus (G-8986)

MECHANICAL INSTRUMENT REPAIR SVCS

Fdc Machine Repair Inc .... E 216 362-1082
  Parma (G-15907)

MEDIA BUYING AGENCIES

Ctv Media Inc .... E 614 848-5800
  Powell (G-16333)
Elyria-Lorain Broadcasting Co .... E 440 322-3761
  Elyria (G-10624)
Empower Mediamarketing Inc .... C 513 871-7779
  Cincinnati (G-3554)
Harmon Media Group .... E 330 478-5325
  Canton (G-2395)

MEDICAL & HOSPITAL EQPT WHOLESALERS

Americas Best Medical Eqp Co .. E 330 928-0884
  Akron (G-73)
Amerimed Inc .... C 513 942-3670
  West Chester (G-19019)
Assuramed Inc .... E 330 963-6998
  Twinsburg (G-18393)
Biorx LLC .... D 866 442-4679
  Cincinnati (G-3109)
Cardinal Health 100 Inc .... B 614 757-5000
  Dublin (G-10276)
Cardinal Health 200 LLC .... E 440 349-1247
  Cleveland (G-5180)
Cardinal Health 301 LLC .... A 614 757-5000
  Dublin (G-10277)
Cintas Corporation No 2 .... D 513 459-1200
  Mason (G-13681)
Clinical Specialties Inc .... C 614 659-6580
  Columbus (G-7302)
Concordnce Hlthcare Sltons LLC . D 419 455-2153
  Tiffin (G-17673)
CT Medical Electronics Co .... E 440 526-3551
  Broadview Heights (G-1876)
Dermamed Coatings Company LLC . E 330 634-9449
  Tallmadge (G-17637)
Espt Liquidation Inc .... D 330 698-4711
  Apple Creek (G-624)
Institutional Care Pharmacy .... C 419 447-6216
  Tiffin (G-17681)
Lake Erie Med Surgical Sup Inc .. E 734 847-3847
  Holland (G-12032)
McKesson Medical-Surgical Inc .. C 614 539-2600
  Urbancrest (G-18606)
Modern Medical Inc .... C 800 547-3330
  Westerville (G-19329)
Noor Home Health Care .... D 216 320-0803
  Cleveland Heights (G-6794)
O E Meyer Co .... D 419 625-1256
  Sandusky (G-16784)
Ohio State University .... E 614 293-8588
  Columbus (G-8422)
Omnicare Inc .... C 513 719-2600
  Cincinnati (G-4220)
Pharmed Corporation .... C 440 250-5400
  Westlake (G-19533)
Precision Products Group Inc .... D 330 698-4711
  Apple Creek (G-626)
Therapy Support Inc .... D 513 469-6999
  Blue Ash (G-1694)
Wbc Group LLC .... D 866 528-2144
  Hudson (G-12150)
Ziks Family Pharmacy 100 .... E 937 225-9350
  Dayton (G-10015)

MEDICAL & SURGICAL SPLYS: Bandages & Dressings

Beiersdorf Inc .... C 513 682-7300
  West Chester (G-19191)

MEDICAL & SURGICAL SPLYS: Clothing, Fire Resistant & Protect

Chester West Holdings Inc .... C 800 647-1900
  Cincinnati (G-3241)
Wcm Holdings Inc .... C 513 705-2100
  Cincinnati (G-4826)

MEDICAL & SURGICAL SPLYS: Hosiery, Support

Julius Zorn Inc .... D 330 923-4999
  Cuyahoga Falls (G-9199)

MEDICAL CENTERS

Big Run Urgent Care Center ...... E 614 871-7130
  Grove City (G-11534)
Blanchard Vly Rgional Hlth Ctr ... C 419 427-0809
  Findlay (G-11003)
Center For Urologic Health LLC . E 330 375-0924
  Akron (G-128)
Childrens Hospital Medical Ctr ... A 513 636-4200
  Cincinnati (G-3247)
Childrens Hospital Medical Ctr ... A 513 803-9600
  Liberty Township (G-12719)
Cleveland Clinic Foundation ...... B 216 448-4325
  Cleveland (G-5302)
Cleveland Clinic Foundation ...... A 216 636-8335
  Cleveland (G-5296)
Community Health Partners Regi . E 440 960-4000
  Lorain (G-13029)
Dayton Eye Surgery Center .... E 937 431-9531
  Beavercreek (G-1236)
Dignity Health .... C 330 493-4443
  Canton (G-2341)
Eye Inst of Northwestern OH In .. E 419 865 3866
  Toledo (G-17875)
Fauster-Cameron Inc .... B 419 784-1414
  Defiance (G-10030)
Health Care Specialists .... E 740 454-4530
  Zanesville (G-20486)
Hometown Urgent Care .... C 614 263-4400
  Columbus (G-7854)
Hometown Urgent Care .... C 330 505-9400
  Warren (G-18862)
Hometown Urgent Care .... C 614 272-1100
  Columbus (G-7856)
Hometown Urgent Care .... C 330 629-2300
  Youngstown (G-20219)
Hometown Urgent Care .... D 740 363-3133
  Delaware (G-10107)
Hometown Urgent Care .... C 937 252-2000
  Wooster (G-19868)
Hometown Urgent Care .... C 513 831-5900
  Milford (G-14525)
Hometown Urgent Care .... C 937 342-9520
  Springfield (G-17206)
Joseph A Girgis MD Inc .... E 440 930-6095
  Sheffield Village (G-16889)
Kaiser Foundation Hospitals ...... A 800 524-7377
  Cleveland Heights (G-6792)
Kaiser Foundation Hospitals ...... A 800 524-7377
  Brooklyn Heights (G-1919)
Labcare .... E 330 753-3649
  Barberton (G-969)
Lake Hospital System Inc .... A 440 632-3024
  Middlefield (G-14397)
Life Line Screening .... D 216 581-6556
  Independence (G-12226)
Med Center One Streetsboro ..... E 330 626-3455
  Streetsboro (G-17421)
Midwest Cmnty Hlth Assoc Inc .. C 419 633-4034
  Bryan (G-2012)
Miller-Valentine Construction .... D 937 293-0900
  Dayton (G-9749)
Northwest Ohio Urgent Care Inc . E 419 720-7363
  Toledo (G-18095)
Ohio State Univ Wexner Med Ctr . C 614 293-2663
  Columbus (G-8382)
Ohio State Univ Wexner Med Ctr . A 614 227-0562
  Columbus (G-8383)
Ohio State University .... E 614 366-3692
  Columbus (G-8388)
Ohio State University .... A 614 293-3860
  Columbus (G-8403)
Ohio University .... D 740 593-2195
  Athens (G-807)
Osu Emergency Medicine LLC .. D 614 947-3700
  Columbus (G-8486)
Osu Physical Medicine LLC .... E 614 366-6398
  Columbus (G-8491)
Richmond Medical Center .... B 440 585-6500
  Richmond Heights (G-16542)
Riverview Health Institute .... E 937 222-5390
  Dayton (G-9852)
Saras Garden .... E 419 335-7272
  Wauseon (G-18962)
Southwest General Health Ctr ... C 440 816-4900
  Strongsville (G-17510)
St Ritas Medical Center .... E 419 996-5895
  Lima (G-12889)
Stark Cnty Emrgncy Physicians .. E 330 492-7950
  Canton (G-2541)
Superior Med Inc .... E 740 439-8839
  Cambridge (G-2130)
Toledo Hospital .... A 419 291-4000
  Toledo (G-18238)
Tri State Urlogic Svcs PSC Inc .. D 513 841-7400
  Cincinnati (G-4684)
Trinity Hospital Twin City .... B 740 922-2800
  Dennison (G-10166)
Trumbull-Mahoning Med Group .. D 330 372-8800
  Cortland (G-9084)
Uc Health Llc .... C 513 475-7777
  West Chester (G-19171)
Uc Health Llc .... A 513 475-7500
  West Chester (G-19172)
University Suburban Health Ctr .. C 216 382-8920
  Cleveland (G-6670)
Veterans Affairs US Dept .... A 937 268-6511
  Dayton (G-9972)
Veterans Health Administration .. A 202 461-4800
  Chillicothe (G-2895)
Veterans Health Administration .. E 513 861-3100
  Cincinnati (G-4812)
Veterans Health Administration .. A 216 791-3800
  Cleveland (G-6691)

MEDICAL EQPT REPAIR SVCS, NON-ELECTRIC

Equipment MGT Svc & Repr Inc . E 937 383-1052
  Wilmington (G-19761)
Precision Endoscopy Amer Inc .. E 410 527-9598
  Stow (G-17386)
United Technical Support Svcs .. E 330 562-3330
  Aurora (G-859)

MEDICAL FIELD ASSOCIATION

American Ceramic Society .... E 614 890-4700
  Westerville (G-19284)
American Cllege Crdlgy Fndtion .. E 614 442-5950
  Dublin (G-10246)

Employee Codes: A=Over 500 employees, B=251-500
C=101-250, D=51-100, E=25-50

MEDICAL FIELD ASSOCIATION — SERVICES SECTION

American Society For Nondstctv ....E 614 274-6003
  Columbus *(G-7008)*
Breathing Association 614 457-4570
  Columbus *(G-7132)*
Central Hospital Services Inc ....D....... 216 696-6900
  Cleveland *(G-5211)*
Columbus Med Assn Foundation ....E 614 240-7420
  Columbus *(G-7365)*
Dnv GL Healthcare Usa Inc 281 396-1610
  Milford *(G-14517)*
Greater Cleveland Hosp Assn ....D....... 216 696-6900
  Cleveland *(G-5697)*
Ohio State Medical Association ....D....... 614 527-6762
  Dublin *(G-10415)*
Physician Hospital Alliance ....E 937 558-3456
  Miamisburg *(G-14335)*
Wingspan Care Group ....E 216 932-2800
  Shaker Heights *(G-16872)*

MEDICAL HELP SVCS

Arcadia Services Inc ....D....... 330 869-9520
  Akron *(G-79)*
Arcadia Services Inc ....D....... 937 912-5800
  Beavercreek *(G-1147)*
Central Ohio Hospitalists 614 255-6900
  Columbus *(G-7230)*
CHI Health At Home ....E 513 576-0262
  Milford *(G-14510)*
Dedicated Nursing Assoc Inc 866 450-5550
  Cincinnati *(G-3477)*
Dedicated Nursing Assoc Inc ....E 877 411-8350
  Galloway *(G-11343)*
Dedicated Nursing Assoc Inc 877 547-9144
  Parma *(G-15905)*
Dedicated Nursing Assoc Inc ....C 888 465-6929
  Beavercreek *(G-1237)*
Emp Holdings Ltd ....A....... 330 493-4443
  Canton *(G-2354)*
Frontline National LLC ....D....... 513 528-7823
  Milford *(G-14519)*
Heartland Employment Svcs LLC ....A....... 419 252-5500
  Toledo *(G-17945)*
Interim Halthcare Columbus Inc ....E 330 836-5571
  Fairlawn *(G-10958)*
Locum Medical Group LLC ....D....... 216 464-2125
  Independence *(G-12229)*
Medport Inc ....D....... 216 244-6832
  Cleveland *(G-6017)*
Msstaff LLC ....C 419 868-8536
  Toledo *(G-18072)*
Neo-Pet LLC ....E 440 893-9949
  Cleveland *(G-6118)*
Physician Staffing Inc ....B....... 440 542-1950
  Solon *(G-17039)*
Poison Information Center ....E 513 636-5111
  Cincinnati *(G-4313)*
Prn Nurse Inc ....B....... 614 864-9292
  Columbus *(G-8562)*
Quadax Inc ....E 330 759-4600
  Youngstown *(G-20334)*
Salo Inc ....A....... 740 623-2331
  Coshocton *(G-9117)*
Township of Chester ....E 440 729-9951
  Chesterland *(G-2805)*

MEDICAL INSURANCE CLAIM PROCESSING: Contract Or Fee Basis

Central Bnfits Admnstrtors Inc ....D....... 614 797-5200
  Westerville *(G-19377)*
Health Design Plus Inc ....D....... 330 656-1072
  Hudson *(G-12120)*
Optumrx Inc ....A....... 614 794-3300
  Westerville *(G-19338)*
Qualchoice Inc ....B....... 330 656-1231
  Beachwood *(G-1117)*

MEDICAL RESCUE SQUAD

Gratis Ems ....E 937 787-4285
  Gratis *(G-11473)*
Harter Ventures Inc ....D....... 419 224-4075
  Lima *(G-12790)*
Leroy Twp Fire Dept ....E 440 254-4124
  Painesville *(G-15863)*
Metrohealth System ....E 216 957-5000
  Cleveland *(G-6037)*

MEDICAL SVCS ORGANIZATION

Aksm/Genesis Medical Svcs Inc ....E 614 447-0281
  Columbus *(G-6961)*
Athens Medical Associates LLC ....D....... 740 594-8819
  Athens *(G-775)*
Broadspire Services Inc ....E 614 436-8990
  Columbus *(G-7148)*
Community & Rural Health Svcs ....E 419 334-8943
  Fremont *(G-11188)*
Excelas LLC 440 442-7310
  Cleveland *(G-5560)*
F R S Connections ....E 937 393-9662
  Hillsboro *(G-11973)*
First Choice Med Staff of Ohio 330 867-1409
  Fairlawn *(G-10952)*
G and H Management 614 268-2273
  Columbus *(G-7717)*
Good Night Medical Ohio LLC ....E 614 384-7433
  Westerville *(G-19404)*
Hopewell Health Centers Inc ....E 740 596-5249
  Mc Arthur *(G-14016)*
Hopewell Health Centers Inc ....E 740 773-1006
  Chillicothe *(G-2849)*
Hospice of Northwest Ohio ....B....... 419 661-4001
  Perrysburg *(G-16013)*
Joint Emergency Med Svc Inc ....E 937 746-3471
  Franklin *(G-11159)*
Kettering Medical Center ....E 937 298-4331
  Dayton *(G-9654)*
Larlham Care Hattie Group ....D....... 330 274-2272
  Mantua *(G-13391)*
Lifecenter Organ Donor Network ....E 513 558-5555
  Cincinnati *(G-3978)*
Lifestges Smrtan Ctr For Women ....E 937 277-8988
  Dayton *(G-9681)*
Mercy Health ....E 440 324-0400
  Elyria *(G-10652)*
Mount Crmel Hospice Evrgrn Ctr ....D....... 614 234-0200
  Columbus *(G-8200)*
Mutual Health Services Company ....D....... 216 687-7000
  Cleveland *(G-6094)*
Mvhe Inc ....E 937 499-8211
  Dayton *(G-9765)*
Northast Ohio Med Rserve Corps 216 789-6653
  Broadview Heights *(G-1885)*
Northeast OH Neighborhood Heal ....C 216 231-2323
  Cleveland *(G-6152)*
Northeast Ohio Orthopedics ....E 330 856-1070
  Warren *(G-18890)*
Ohio Kepro Inc ....E 216 447-9604
  Seven Hills *(G-16834)*
Ohio State University ....D....... 614 293-8074
  Columbus *(G-8447)*
P C Vpa ....E 440 826-0500
  Cleveland *(G-6225)*
Palestine Chld Relief Fund ....D....... 330 678-2645
  Kent *(G-12390)*
Prosperity Care Service ....E 614 430-8626
  Columbus *(G-8572)*
Spryance Inc 678 808-0600
  Toledo *(G-18198)*
Sterling Medical Associates ....D....... 513 984-1800
  Cincinnati *(G-4590)*
Summacare Inc ....B....... 330 996-8410
  Akron *(G-464)*
Uhhs Westlake Medical Center ....C 440 250-2070
  Westlake *(G-19559)*
Unity I Home Healthcare LLC ....E 740 351-0500
  Portsmouth *(G-16317)*
University Womens Healthcare ....E 937 208-2948
  Dayton *(G-9956)*

MEDICAL TRAINING SERVICES

East Way Behavioral Hlth Care ....C 937 222-4900
  Dayton *(G-9515)*
Hometech Healthcare Svcs LLC ....E 216 295-9120
  Cleveland *(G-5769)*

MEDICAL X-RAY MACHINES & TUBES WHOLESALERS

Alpha Imaging LLC ....D....... 440 953-3800
  Willoughby *(G-19643)*
Riverain Technologies LLC ....E 937 425-6811
  Miamisburg *(G-14345)*

MEDICAL, DENTAL & HOSP EQPT, WHOLESALE: X-ray Film & Splys

Philips Medical Systems Clevel ....B....... 440 247-2652
  Cleveland *(G-6273)*

MEDICAL, DENTAL & HOSPITAL EQPT, WHOL: Dentists' Prof Splys

Perio Inc ....E 614 791-1207
  Dublin *(G-10426)*

MEDICAL, DENTAL & HOSPITAL EQPT, WHOL: Hospital Eqpt & Splys

Jones Metal Products Company ....E 740 545-6341
  West Lafayette *(G-19257)*
Phoenix Resource Network LLC ....E 800 990-4948
  Cincinnati *(G-4294)*

MEDICAL, DENTAL & HOSPITAL EQPT, WHOL: Hosptl Eqpt/Furniture

American Home Health Care Inc ....E 614 237-1133
  Columbus *(G-6996)*
Apria Healthcare LLC ....D....... 419 471-1919
  Maumee *(G-13883)*
Braden Med Services Inc ....E 740 732-2356
  Caldwell *(G-2082)*
Eastern Medical Equipment Co ....E 330 394-5555
  Warren *(G-18853)*
Garys Pharmacy Inc ....E 937 456-5777
  Eaton *(G-10561)*
Pdi Communication Systems Inc ....D....... 937 743-6010
  Springboro *(G-17133)*

MEDICAL, DENTAL & HOSPITAL EQPT, WHOL: Physician Eqpt/Splys

Radebaugh-Fetzer Company ....E 440 878-4700
  Strongsville *(G-17501)*

MEDICAL, DENTAL & HOSPITAL EQPT, WHOL: Surgical Eqpt & Splys

Cardinal Health Inc ....A....... 614 757-5000
  Dublin *(G-10275)*
Cardinal Health Inc ....D....... 614 497-9552
  Obetz *(G-15665)*
Columbus Prescr Phrms Inc ....C 614 294-1600
  Westerville *(G-19389)*
Community Srgl Sply Toms Rvr ....C 216 475-8440
  Cleveland *(G-5386)*
Haag-Streit USA Inc ....E 513 336-7255
  Mason *(G-13713)*
Haag-Streit USA Inc ....C 513 336-7255
  Mason *(G-13714)*
Kunkel Pharmaceuticals Inc ....E 513 231-1943
  Cincinnati *(G-3949)*

MEDICAL, DENTAL & HOSPITAL EQPT, WHOLESALE: Artificial Limbs

Blatchford Inc ....D....... 937 291-3636
  Miamisburg *(G-14276)*
Pel LLC ....E 216 267-5775
  Cleveland *(G-6261)*

MEDICAL, DENTAL & HOSPITAL EQPT, WHOLESALE: Diagnostic, Med

Hitachi Hlthcare Americas Corp ....B....... 330 425-1313
  Twinsburg *(G-18429)*
Thermo Fisher Scientific Inc ....C 800 871-8909
  Oakwood Village *(G-15635)*
Tosoh America Inc ....B....... 614 539-8622
  Grove City *(G-11606)*

MEDICAL, DENTAL & HOSPITAL EQPT, WHOLESALE: Med Eqpt & Splys

Advanced Medical Equipment Inc ....E 937 534-1080
  Kettering *(G-12426)*
Advantage Appliance Services ....C 330 498-8101
  Canton *(G-2226)*
Alliance Medical Inc ....E 800 890-3092
  Dublin *(G-10242)*
Ardus Medical Inc ....D....... 855 592-7387
  Blue Ash *(G-1535)*

SERVICES SECTION — MEMBERSHIP ORGANIZATIONS, CIVIC, SOCIAL/FRAT: Youth Orgs

Company	Code	Phone
Biotech Medical Inc — Canton (G-2264)	A	330 494-5504
Bound Tree Medical LLC — Dublin (G-10266)	D	614 760-5000
Cando Pharmaceutical — Loveland (G-13112)	E	513 354-2694
Cardinal Health 200 LLC — Columbus (G-7194)	C	614 491-0050
Cardio Partners Inc — Dublin (G-10278)	D	614 760-5038
Centura Inc — Cleveland (G-5213)	E	216 593-0226
Community Srgl Sply Toms Rvr — Columbus (G-7411)	C	614 307-2975
Compass Health Brands Corp — Middleburg Heights (G-14380)	C	800 947-1728
Cornerstone Med Svcs Midwest — Blue Ash (G-1566)	E	513 554-0222
Cornerstone Medical Associates — Akron (G-165)	E	330 374-0229
Cornerstone Medical Services — Blue Ash (G-1567)	E	513 554-0222
Demarius Corporation — Dublin (G-10319)	E	760 957-5500
Edwards Gem Inc — Hudson (G-12115)	D	330 342-8300
Ferno-Washington Inc — Wilmington (G-19762)	C	877 733-0911
Frantz Medical Group — Mentor (G-14176)	E	440 974-8522
Fresenius Usa Inc — Oregon (G-15736)	E	419 691-2475
Gulf South Medical Supply Inc — Gahanna (G-11245)	E	614 501-9080
Homereach Inc — Lewis Center (G-12688)	E	614 566-0850
Julius Zorn Inc — Cuyahoga Falls (G-9199)	D	330 923-4999
Keysource Acquisition LLC — Cincinnati (G-3919)	E	513 469-7881
Lima Medical Supplies Inc — Lima (G-12823)	E	419 226-9581
M & R Fredericktown Ltd Inc — Akron (G-331)	E	440 801-1563
Marquis Mobility Inc — Canton (G-2448)	D	330 497-5373
McKesson Medical-Surgical Top — Cincinnati (G-4038)	E	513 985-0525
Medline Diamed LLC — Canton (G-2457)	E	330 484-1450
Medpace Inc — Cincinnati (G-4049)	A	513 579-9911
Mill Rose Laboratories Inc — Mentor (G-14219)	E	440 974-6730
Neighborcare Inc — Cincinnati (G-4151)	A	513 719-2600
Nightngl-Alan Med Eqp Svcs LLC — Blue Ash (G-1653)	E	513 247-8200
Partssource Inc — Aurora (G-849)	C	330 562-9900
PMI Supply Inc — Dublin (G-10427)	D	760 598-1128
Radiometer America Inc — Westlake (G-19538)	E	440 925-2977
Sarnova Inc — Dublin (G-10448)	D	614 760-5000
Seeley Medical Oxygen Co — Andover (G-615)	E	440 255-7163
Seneca Medical LLC — Tiffin (G-17701)	C	419 447-0236
Tri-Anim Health Services Inc — Dublin (G-10477)	E	614 760-5000
United Seating & Mobility LLC — Maumee (G-13991)	E	567 302-4000

MEDICAL, DENTAL & HOSPITAL EQPT, WHOLESALE: Medical Lab

Company	Code	Phone
Sourceone Healthcare Tech Inc — Mentor (G-14244)	C	440 701-1200

MEDICAL, DENTAL & HOSPITAL EQPT, WHOLESALE: Safety

Company	Code	Phone
Safety Today Inc — Grove City (G-11595)	E	614 409-7200

MEDICAL, DENTAL & HOSPITAL EQPT, WHOLESALE: Therapy

Company	Code	Phone
Viewray Incorporated — Oakwood Village (G-15636)	D	440 703-3210

MEDICAL, DENTAL/HOSPITAL EQPT, WHOL: Tech Aids, Handicapped

Company	Code	Phone
Siffrin Residential Assn — Youngstown (G-20375)	C	330 799-8932

MEDICAL, DENTAL/HOSPITAL EQPT, WHOL: Veterinarian Eqpt/Sply

Company	Code	Phone
Butler Animal Health Sup LLC — Dublin (G-10273)	C	614 761-9095
Butler Animal Hlth Holdg LLC — Dublin (G-10274)	E	614 761-9095

MEMBER ORGS, CIVIC, SOCIAL & FRATERNAL: Bars & Restaurants

Company	Code	Phone
Feldys — Cincinnati (G-3601)	D	513 474-2212
S R Restaurant Corp — Cleveland (G-6427)	E	216 781-6784

MEMBERSHIP HOTELS

Company	Code	Phone
Cincinnati Fifth Street Ht LLC — Cincinnati (G-3303)	D	513 579-1234

MEMBERSHIP ORGANIZATIONS, BUSINESS: Community Affairs & Svcs

Company	Code	Phone
Bnai Brith Hillel Fdn At Osu — Columbus (G-7121)	E	614 294-4797
Canton Rgnal Chmber of Cmmerce — Canton (G-2297)	E	330 456-7253
In His Prsence Ministries Intl — Columbus (G-7887)	E	614 516-1812
Oak Harbor Lions Club — Oak Harbor (G-15613)	E	419 898-3828
Saint Mary Parish — Chardon (G-2766)	D	440 285-7051

MEMBERSHIP ORGANIZATIONS, BUSINESS: Contractors' Association

Company	Code	Phone
Builders Exchange Inc — Cleveland (G-5158)	E	216 393-6300
Home Bldrs Assn Grter Cncnnati — Cincinnati (G-3777)	D	513 851-6300

MEMBERSHIP ORGANIZATIONS, BUSINESS: Merchants' Association

Company	Code	Phone
Westfield Belden Village — Canton (G-2586)	E	330 494-5490

MEMBERSHIP ORGANIZATIONS, BUSINESS: Public Utility Assoc

Company	Code	Phone
City of Circleville — Circleville (G-4883)	E	740 477-8255
Hecla Water Association — Ironton (G-12290)	E	740 533-0526
Ohio Utilities Protection Svc — Youngstown (G-20310)	D	330 759-0050
Village of Versailles — Versailles (G-18730)	E	937 526-4191

MEMBERSHIP ORGANIZATIONS, CIVIC, SOCIAL/FRAT: Boy Scout Org

Company	Code	Phone
Boy Scouts of America — Cincinnati (G-3128)	E	513 961-2336
Boys & Girls Club of Toledo — Toledo (G-17780)	E	419 241-4258
Heart of OH Cncl Bsa — Mansfield (G-13308)	E	419 522-8300
Simon Knton Cncil Byscuts Amer — Columbus (G-8734)	D	614 436-7200

MEMBERSHIP ORGANIZATIONS, CIVIC, SOCIAL/FRAT: Rec Assoc

Company	Code	Phone
Bluffton Family Recreation — Bluffton (G-1728)	E	419 358-6978
Geary Family YMCA Fostria — Fostoria (G-11128)	E	419 435-6608
Parks Recreation Division — Dayton (G-9803)	E	937 496-7135
Young Mens Christian Assn — Marietta (G-13520)	D	740 373-2250
Young Mens Christian Assoc — Akron (G-517)	A	330 376-1335
Young Mens Christian Assoc — Ottawa (G-15805)	D	419 523-5233

MEMBERSHIP ORGANIZATIONS, CIVIC, SOCIAL/FRAT: Social Assoc

Company	Code	Phone
Family Motor Coach Assn Inc — Cincinnati (G-3590)	E	513 474-3622
Goodwill Service Guild — Cincinnati (G-3687)	E	513 771-4800
Mercy Health — Fairfield (G-10880)	E	513 870-7008
Natio Assoc For The Advan of — Youngstown (G-20295)	E	330 782-9777
Optimist International — Van Wert (G-18640)	D	419 238-5086
The For National Association — Dayton (G-9925)	E	937 470-1059
YMCA of Ashtabula County Inc — Ashtabula (G-768)	D	440 997-5321

MEMBERSHIP ORGANIZATIONS, CIVIC, SOCIAL/FRAT: Youth Orgs

Company	Code	Phone
Boys & Girls Club of Columbus — Columbus (G-7127)	E	614 221-8830
Cafaro Co — Niles (G-15286)	E	330 652-6980
Central Ohio Youth For Christ — Columbus (G-7243)	E	614 732-5260
Chester West YMCA — Liberty Township (G-12718)	E	513 779-3917
Communities In Schools — Columbus (G-7401)	E	614 268-2472
Community Action Columbiana CT — East Liverpool (G-10518)	E	330 385-7251
County of Cuyahoga — Cleveland (G-5428)	D	216 443-7265
County of Darke — Versailles (G-18725)	E	937 526-4488
Fairborn YMCA — Fairborn (G-10796)	E	937 754-9622
Family YMCA of LANcstr&fairfld — Lancaster (G-12541)	D	740 277-7373
Fayette County Family YMCA — Wshngtn CT Hs (G-20021)	D	740 335-0477
Findlay Y M C A Child Dev — Findlay (G-11031)	E	419 422-3174
Frans Child Care-Mansfield — Mansfield (G-13304)	C	419 775-2500
Friends of Art For Cultural — Columbus (G-7706)	E	614 888-9929
Galion Community Center YMCA — Galion (G-11297)	E	419 468-7754
Great Miami Valley YMCA — Middletown (G-14479)	D	513 217-5501
Great Miami Valley YMCA — Hamilton (G-11733)	D	513 887-0001
Great Miami Valley YMCA — Fairfield Township (G-10930)	C	513 892-9622
Great Miami Valley YMCA — Hamilton (G-11734)	D	513 867-0600
Great Miami Valley YMCA — Hamilton (G-11735)	D	513 887-0014
Great Miami Valley YMCA — Hamilton (G-11736)	D	513 868 0622
Great Miami Valley YMCA — Fairfield (G-10854)	D	513 829-3091
Hardin County Family YMCA — Kenton (G-12416)	E	419 673-6131
Highland County Family YMCA — Hillsboro (G-11978)	E	937 840-9622
Huber Heights YMCA — Dayton (G-9623)	D	937 236-9622
Lake County YMCA — Painesville (G-15860)	A	440 352-3303
Lake County YMCA — Willoughby (G-19680)	C	440 946-1160
Lake County YMCA — Perry (G-15962)	E	440 259-2724
Lake County YMCA — Madison (G-13227)	D	440 428-5125

Employee Codes: A=Over 500 employees, B=251-500, C=101-250, D=51-100, E=25-50

MEMBERSHIP ORGANIZATIONS, CIVIC, SOCIAL/FRAT: Youth Orgs

Marion Family YMCA ....D....... 740 725-9622
  Marion (G-13556)
Miami Co YMCA Child Care.....................E....... 937 778-5241
  Piqua (G-16152)
Orrville Boys and Girls Club ....E....... 330 683-4888
  Orrville (G-15778)
Pike County YMCA ....E....... 740 947-8862
  Waverly (G-18974)
Ross County YMCA ....D....... 740 772-4340
  Chillicothe (G-2882)
Sandusky Area YMCA Foundation ....E....... 419 621-9622
  Sandusky (G-16790)
Sidney-Shelby County YMCA ....E....... 937 492-9134
  Sidney (G-16955)
Springfield Family Y M C A ....D....... 937 323-3781
  Springfield (G-17281)
Springfield Little Tigers Foot ....D....... 330 549-2359
  Youngstown (G-20380)
Sycamore Board of Education..................D....... 513 489-3937
  Cincinnati (G-4608)
Ucc Childrens Center ....E....... 513 217-5501
  Middletown (G-14488)
Vermilion Family YMCA ....E....... 440 967-4208
  Vermilion (G-18720)
Wapakoneta YMCA ....D....... 419 739-9622
  Wapakoneta (G-18812)
Y M C A Central Stark County ....E....... 330 305-5437
  Canton (G-2590)
Y M C A Central Stark County ....E....... 330 875-1611
  Louisville (G-13108)
Y M C A Central Stark County ....E....... 330 877-8933
  Uniontown (G-18545)
Y M C A Central Stark County ....E....... 330 830-6275
  Massillon (G-13862)
Y M C A Central Stark County ....E....... 330 498-4082
  Canton (G-2591)
Y M C A of Ashland Ohio Inc ....D....... 419 289-0626
  Ashland (G-709)
YMCA ....E....... 330 823-1930
  Alliance (G-566)
YMCA Inc ....D....... 330 385-6400
  East Liverpool (G-10536)
YMCA of Clermont County Inc ....E....... 513 724-9622
  Batavia (G-1032)
YMCA of Massillon ....E....... 330 879-0800
  Navarre (G-14957)
YMCA of Sandusky Ohio Inc ....E....... 419 621-9622
  Sandusky (G-16811)
Young Mens Christian ....B....... 513 932-1424
  Lebanon (G-12660)
Young Mens Christian Assn ....E....... 419 332-9622
  Fremont (G-11231)
Young Mens Christian Assn ....C....... 330 744-8411
  Youngstown (G-20421)
Young Mens Christian Assn ....E....... 419 238-0443
  Van Wert (G-18653)
Young Mens Christian Assoc.....................C....... 614 491-0980
  Lockbourne (G-12963)
Young Mens Christian Assoc.....................C....... 614 871-9622
  Grove City (G-11620)
Young Mens Christian Assoc.....................A....... 937 223-5201
  Dayton (G-10009)
Young Mens Christian Assoc.....................D....... 330 923-5223
  Cuyahoga Falls (G-9237)
Young Mens Christian Assoc.....................E....... 330 467-8366
  Macedonia (G-13219)
Young Mens Christian Assoc.....................E....... 330 784-0408
  Akron (G-515)
Young Mens Christian Assoc.....................D....... 740 477-1661
  Circleville (G-4909)
Young Mens Christian Assoc.....................C....... 614 885-4252
  Columbus (G-9017)
Young Mens Christian Assoc.....................E....... 330 724-1255
  Akron (G-516)
Young Mens Christian Assoc.....................E....... 614 416-9622
  Gahanna (G-11276)
Young Mens Christian Assoc.....................C....... 740 881-1058
  Powell (G-16355)
Young Mens Christian Assoc.....................C....... 614 334-9622
  Hilliard (G-11967)
Young Mens Christian Assoc.....................E....... 937 312-1810
  Dayton (G-10010)
Young Mens Christian Assoc.....................E....... 614 539-1770
  Urbancrest (G-18609)
Young Mens Christian Assoc.....................D....... 614 276-8224
  Columbus (G-9018)
Young Mens Christian Assoc.....................D....... 513 932-3756
  Oregonia (G-15759)
Young Mens Christian Assoc.....................D....... 614 252-3166
  Columbus (G-9019)

Young Mens Christian Assoc.....................D....... 937 426-9622
  Dayton (G-10011)
Young Mens Christian Assoc.....................E....... 937 228-9622
  Dayton (G-10012)
Young Mens Christian Assoc.....................C....... 937 223-5201
  Springboro (G-17144)
Young Mens Christian Assoc.....................E....... 937 593-9001
  Bellefontaine (G-1401)
Young Mens Christian Assoc.....................C....... 614 834-9622
  Canal Winchester (G-2181)
Young Mens Christian Assoc.....................D....... 330 264-3131
  Wooster (G-19936)
Young Mens Christian Associat ....E....... 419 729-8135
  Toledo (G-18320)
Young Mens Christian Associat ....B....... 419 475-3496
  Toledo (G-18321)
Young Mens Christian Associat ....D....... 513 521-7112
  Cincinnati (G-4865)
Young Mens Christian Associat ....E....... 513 731-0115
  Cincinnati (G-4866)
Young Mens Christian Associat ....E....... 513 474-1400
  Cincinnati (G-4867)
Young Mens Christian Associat ....D....... 513 241-9622
  Cincinnati (G-4868)
Young Mens Christian Associat ....D....... 513 923-4466
  Cincinnati (G-4869)
Young Mens Christian Associat ....E....... 419 474-3995
  Toledo (G-18322)
Young Mens Christian Associat ....D....... 419 866-9622
  Maumee (G-13997)
Young Mens Christian Associat ....C....... 419 475-3496
  Toledo (G-18323)
Young Mens Christian Associat ....D....... 419 691-3523
  Oregon (G-15756)
Young Mens Christian Mt Vernon.............D....... 740 392-9622
  Mount Vernon (G-14927)
Young Mens Christn Assn Shelby.............E....... 419 347-1312
  Shelby (G-16904)
Young MNS Christn Assn Findlay ....D....... 419 422-4424
  Findlay (G-11102)
Young MNS Chrstn Assn Clveland............E....... 216 521-8400
  Lakewood (G-12502)
Young MNS Chrstn Assn Clveland............E....... 216 941-4654
  Cleveland (G-6773)
Young MNS Chrstn Assn Clveland............D....... 440 842-5200
  North Royalton (G-15507)
Young MNS Chrstn Assn Clveland............E....... 216 731-7454
  Cleveland (G-6774)
Young MNS Chrstn Assn Clveland............D....... 216 382-4300
  Cleveland (G-6775)
Young MNS Chrstn Assn Clveland............D....... 440 285-7543
  Chardon (G-2780)
Young MNS Chrstn Assn Clveland............D....... 440 808-8150
  Westlake (G-19569)
Young MNS Chrstn Assn Grter NY ....D....... 740 392-9622
  Mount Vernon (G-14928)
Young Womens Christian ....D....... 937 461-5550
  Dayton (G-10013)
Young Womens Christian ....E....... 419 238-6639
  Van Wert (G-18654)
Young Womens Christian Assn ....D....... 614 224-9121
  Columbus (G-9021)
Young Womens Christian Assn ....E....... 330 746-6361
  Youngstown (G-20422)
Young Womens Christian Associ ....E....... 216 881-6878
  Cleveland (G-6776)
Young Womns Chrstn Assc Canton...........D....... 330 453-0789
  Canton (G-2594)
Young Womns Chrstn Assc Lima..............E....... 419 241-3230
  Toledo (G-18326)
YWCA of Greater Cincinnati ....D....... 513 241-7090
  Cincinnati (G-4870)
YWCA of Hamilton ....E....... 513 856-9800
  Hamilton (G-11785)
YWCA Shelter & Housing Network............E....... 937 222-6333
  Dayton (G-10014)

MEMBERSHIP ORGANIZATIONS, LABOR UNIONS & SIMILAR: Trade

Amalgamated Transit Union ....E....... 216 861-3350
  Cleveland (G-5001)
Painters District Council 6 ....E....... 440 239-4575
  Cleveland (G-6228)
Painters Local Union 555 ....D....... 740 353-1431
  Portsmouth (G-16297)
United Food and Coml Wkrs ....D....... 937 665-0075
  Dayton (G-9946)
United Steelworkers ....E....... 513 793-0272
  Cincinnati (G-4740)

MEMBERSHIP ORGANIZATIONS, NEC: Amateur Sports Promotion

Sporty Events..E....... 440 342-5046
  Chesterland (G-2803)

MEMBERSHIP ORGANIZATIONS, NEC: Art Council

Eastern Mumee Bay Arts Council ....E....... 419 690-5718
  Oregon (G-15734)

MEMBERSHIP ORGANIZATIONS, NEC: Automobile Owner Association

AAA Allied Group Inc.................................B....... 513 762-3100
  Cincinnati (G-2958)
AAA Club Alliance Inc ....D....... 419 843-1200
  Toledo (G-17736)
AAA Miami Valley ....D....... 937 224-2896
  Dayton (G-9300)
AAA South Central Ohio Inc ....E....... 740 354-5614
  Portsmouth (G-16262)
Akron Automobile Association ....D....... 330 762-0631
  Akron (G-28)
American Motorcycle Assn ....D....... 614 856-1900
  Pickerington (G-16083)
Buckeye Drag Racing Assn LLC ....E....... 419 562-0869
  Bucyrus (G-2025)
Columbus Landmarks Foundation ....E....... 614 221-0227
  Columbus (G-7362)
Massillon Automobile Club ....E....... 330 833-1084
  Massillon (G-13832)
Ohio Automobile Club ....C....... 614 431-7901
  Worthington (G-19980)

MEMBERSHIP ORGANIZATIONS, NEC: Bowling club

United Sttes Bowl Congress Inc................D....... 740 922-3120
  Uhrichsville (G-18495)
United Sttes Bowl Congress Inc................D....... 513 761-3338
  Cincinnati (G-4741)
United Sttes Bowl Congress Inc................D....... 419 531-4058
  Toledo (G-18273)

MEMBERSHIP ORGANIZATIONS, NEC: Charitable

Access Inc ....E....... 330 535-2999
  Akron (G-16)
Akron-Canton Regional Foodbank.............E....... 330 535-6900
  Akron (G-61)
Ardmore Inc ....C....... 330 535-2601
  Akron (G-81)
Athletes In Action Sports ....E....... 937 352-1000
  Xenia (G-20043)
Auxiliary St Lukes Hospital.......................E....... 419 893-5911
  Maumee (G-13884)
Broken Arrow Inc ....E....... 419 562-3480
  Bucyrus (G-2024)
Brunswick Food Pantry Inc.......................E....... 330 225-0395
  Brunswick (G-1970)
Carol A & Ralp V H US B Fdn Tr ....E....... 513 632-4426
  Cincinnati (G-3186)
Cincinnati Health Network Inc ....E....... 513 961-0600
  Cincinnati (G-3309)
Cincinnati Humn Relations Comm ....E....... 513 352-3237
  Cincinnati (G-3310)
City of Compassion ....D....... 419 422-7800
  Findlay (G-11013)
Cliffs Cleveland Foundation ....E....... 216 694-5700
  Cleveland (G-5360)
Community Dev For All People ....E....... 614 445-7342
  Columbus (G-7403)
Conserv For Cyhg Vlly Nat Prk ....D....... 330 657-2909
  Peninsula (G-15949)
Council For Economic Opport....................D....... 216 476-3201
  Cleveland (G-5413)
County of Summit Board of Mntl...............A....... 330 634-8100
  Akron (G-173)
Downtown Akron Partnership Inc ....D....... 330 374-7676
  Akron (G-199)
East Akron Neighborhood Dev ....E....... 330 773-6838
  Akron (G-205)
Elizabeths New Life Center Inc ....E....... 937 226-7414
  Dayton (G-9523)
First Capital Enterprises Inc ....D....... 740 773-2166
  Chillicothe (G-2840)

SERVICES SECTION — MEMBERSHIP ORGANIZATIONS, RELIGIOUS: Presbyterian Church

Gideons International .... E 513 932-2857
  Lebanon *(G-12607)*
Goodwill Inds Centl Ohio Inc .... E 740 439-7000
  Cambridge *(G-2116)*
Granger Township .... E 330 239-2111
  Medina *(G-14072)*
Hadassah Dayton Chapter .... E 937 275-0227
  Dayton *(G-9595)*
Heartbeats To City Inc .... E 330 452-4524
  Canton *(G-2397)*
Knox Community Hosp Foundation .... E 740 393-9814
  Mount Vernon *(G-14903)*
Koinonia Homes Inc .... B 216 588-8777
  Cleveland *(G-5906)*
Kroger Co Foundation .... E 513 762-4000
  Cincinnati *(G-3947)*
Leo Yannenoff Jewish Community .... C 614 231-2731
  Columbus *(G-8052)*
Licking Valley Lions Club .... C 740 763-3733
  Newark *(G-15195)*
Marysville Food Pantry .... E 937 644-3248
  Marysville *(G-13635)*
Nami of Preble County Ohio .... E 937 456-4947
  Eaton *(G-10570)*
Northast Ohio Sstnble Cmmnties .... D 216 410-7698
  Akron *(G-355)*
Ohio Academy of Science .... E 614 488-2228
  Columbus *(G-8316)*
Ohio Federation of Soil and WA .... E 614 784-1900
  Reynoldsburg *(G-16472)*
Ohio School Boards Association .... E 614 540-4000
  Columbus *(G-8373)*
Ottawa County Board M R D D .... E 419 734-6650
  Oak Harbor *(G-15614)*
Parma Community General Hosp .... B 440 743-4280
  Parma *(G-15913)*
Pepper Pike Club Company Inc .... D 216 831-9400
  Cleveland *(G-6263)*
Recovery Center .... E 740 687-4500
  Lancaster *(G-12568)*
Ridgeville Community Choir .... E 419 267-3820
  Ridgeville Corners *(G-16545)*
Ronald McDonald Hse Grtr Cinci .... E 513 636-5591
  Cincinnati *(G-4440)*
Royal Arch Masons of Ohio .... E 419 762-5565
  Napoleon *(G-14949)*
Ruritan .... E 330 542-2308
  New Springfield *(G-15130)*
School Choice Ohio Inc .... E 614 223-1555
  Columbus *(G-8700)*
Seneca RE ADS Ind Fostoria Div .... C 419 435-0729
  Fostoria *(G-11140)*
Team NEO .... E 216 363-5400
  Cleveland *(G-6576)*
Womens Civic Club Grove City .... E 614 871-0145
  Grove City *(G-11618)*
Youngstown Neighborhood Dev .... E 330 480-0423
  Youngstown *(G-20432)*
Zanesville Welfare Organizatio .... B 740 450-6060
  Zanesville *(G-20559)*
Zoo Cincinnati .... D 513 961-0041
  Cincinnati *(G-4873)*

MEMBERSHIP ORGANIZATIONS, NEC: Food Co-Operative

Heights Emergency Food Center .... D 216 381-0707
  Cleveland *(G-5747)*

MEMBERSHIP ORGANIZATIONS, NEC: Historical Club

Dayton Society Natural History .... E 513 932-4421
  Oregonia *(G-15757)*
Niles Historical Society .... D 330 544-2143
  Niles *(G-15299)*

MEMBERSHIP ORGANIZATIONS, NEC: Personal Interest

Affinion Group LLC .... A 614 895-1803
  Westerville *(G-19360)*
Carmen Steering Committee .... E 330 756-2066
  Navarre *(G-14954)*
Ethnic Voice of America .... E 440 845-0922
  Cleveland *(G-5552)*
Frazeysburg Lions Club Inc .... E 740 828-2313
  Frazeysburg *(G-11175)*
Greatr Columbus Conventn & Vis .... E 614 221-6623
  Columbus *(G-7776)*

Shoreby Club Inc .... D 216 851-2587
  Cleveland *(G-6479)*
Sons of Un Vtrans of Civil War .... D 740 992-6144
  Middleport *(G-14409)*
Volunteers of America NW Ohio .... E 419 248-3733
  Toledo *(G-18293)*

MEMBERSHIP ORGANIZATIONS, PROF: Education/Teacher Assoc

Aauw Action Fund Inc .... E 330 833-0520
  Massillon *(G-13783)*
Association For Middle Lvl Edu .... E 614 895-4730
  Westerville *(G-19366)*
Buckeye Assn Schl Admnstrators .... E 614 846-4080
  Columbus *(G-7155)*

MEMBERSHIP ORGANIZATIONS, PROFESSIONAL: Accounting Assoc

Ohio Soc of Crtif Pub Accntnts .... D 614 764-2727
  Columbus *(G-8376)*

MEMBERSHIP ORGANIZATIONS, PROFESSIONAL: Health Association

Alzheimers Disease and .... E 216 721-8457
  Beachwood *(G-1050)*
Columbus Medical Association .... E 614 240-7410
  Columbus *(G-7366)*
Consortium For Hlthy & Immunzd .... D 216 201-2001
  Cleveland *(G-5394)*
Dayton Anthem .... D 937 428-8000
  Dayton *(G-9457)*
Detox Health Care Corp Ohio .... B 513 742-6310
  Cincinnati *(G-3485)*
Ohio Department of Health .... C 614 466-1521
  Columbus *(G-8328)*
Ohio Health Council .... D 614 221-7614
  Columbus *(G-8349)*
Ohio Hospital Association .... D 614 221-7614
  Columbus *(G-8353)*

MEMBERSHIP ORGANIZATIONS, REL: Christian & Reformed Church

Calvary Christian Ch of Ohio .... E 740 828-9000
  Frazeysburg *(G-11174)*

MEMBERSHIP ORGANIZATIONS, REL: Churches, Temples & Shrines

Harrison Ave Assembly of God .... E 513 367-6100
  Harrison *(G-11800)*

MEMBERSHIP ORGANIZATIONS, RELIGIOUS: Apostolic Church

First Apostolic Church .... E 419 885-4888
  Toledo *(G-17891)*

MEMBERSHIP ORGANIZATIONS, RELIGIOUS: Assembly Of God Church

New Bgnnngs Assembly of God Ch .... E 614 497-2658
  Columbus *(G-8271)*
Tri County Assembly of God .... E 513 874-8575
  Fairfield *(G-10916)*

MEMBERSHIP ORGANIZATIONS, RELIGIOUS: Baptist Church

Grace Baptist Church .... E 937 652-1133
  Urbana *(G-18589)*
Twinbrook Hills Baptist Church .... E 513 863-3107
  Hamilton *(G-11780)*

MEMBERSHIP ORGANIZATIONS, RELIGIOUS: Brethren Church

Grace Brthren Ch Columbus Ohio .... E 614 888-7733
  Westerville *(G-19310)*

MEMBERSHIP ORGANIZATIONS, RELIGIOUS: Catholic Church

Catholic Diocese of Cleveland .... E 419 289-7224
  Ashland *(G-671)*
Our Lady of Bethlehem Schools .... E 614 459-8285
  Columbus *(G-8499)*

Saint Francis De Sales Church .... E 440 884-2319
  Cleveland *(G-6436)*
Saint Mary Parish .... D 440 285-7051
  Chardon *(G-2766)*
St Pauls Catholic Church .... E 330 724-1263
  Akron *(G-448)*

MEMBERSHIP ORGANIZATIONS, RELIGIOUS: Church Of Christ

Oak Creek United Church .... E 937 434-3941
  Dayton *(G-9779)*
Pilgrim United Church Christ .... E 513 574-4208
  Cincinnati *(G-4299)*
St Stephen United Church Chrst .... E 419 624-1814
  Sandusky *(G-16797)*

MEMBERSHIP ORGANIZATIONS, RELIGIOUS: Church Of God

Salem Church of God Inc .... E 937 836-6500
  Clayton *(G-4916)*

MEMBERSHIP ORGANIZATIONS, RELIGIOUS: Community Church

First Community Church .... E 614 488-0681
  Columbus *(G-7662)*
First Community Church .... E 740 385-3827
  Logan *(G-12972)*
First Community Church .... E 614 488-0681
  Columbus *(G-7663)*
Oesterlen-Services For Youth .... C 937 399-6101
  Springfield *(G-17254)*

MEMBERSHIP ORGANIZATIONS, RELIGIOUS: Lutheran Church

Bethlehem Lutheran Ch Parma .... E 440 845-2230
  Cleveland *(G-5120)*
Gethsemane Lutheran Church .... E 614 885-4319
  Columbus *(G-7749)*
Royal Redeemer Lutheran Church .... E 440 237-7958
  Cleveland *(G-6418)*
Trinity Luth Child Care .... E 419 289-2126
  Ashland *(G-703)*
Upper Arlington Lutheran Ch .... E 614 451-3736
  Columbus *(G-8915)*

MEMBERSHIP ORGANIZATIONS, RELIGIOUS: Methodist Church

Board Man Frst Untd Methdst Ch .... E 330 758-4527
  Youngstown *(G-20119)*
Epworth United Methodist Ch .... D 740 387-1062
  Marion *(G-13539)*
Sharonville Mthdist Wkdays Nrs .... E 513 563-8278
  Cincinnati *(G-4510)*
United Methodist Community Ctr .... E 330 743-5149
  Youngstown *(G-20398)*
West Ohio Conference of .... E 937 773-5313
  Piqua *(G-16175)*
West Ohio Conference of .... E 614 844-6200
  Worthington *(G-20007)*

MEMBERSHIP ORGANIZATIONS, RELIGIOUS: Nonchurch

Sisters of Charity of Cinc .... D 513 347-5200
  Mount Saint Joseph *(G-14871)*

MEMBERSHIP ORGANIZATIONS, RELIGIOUS: Pentecostal Church

New Life Christian Center .... E 740 687-1572
  Lancaster *(G-12561)*
Ravenna Assembly of God Inc .... E 330 297-1493
  Ravenna *(G-16404)*

MEMBERSHIP ORGANIZATIONS, RELIGIOUS: Presbyterian Church

Lebanon Presbyterian Church .... E 513 932-0369
  Lebanon *(G-12623)*
Wsos Child Development Program .... E 419 334-8511
  Fremont *(G-11230)*

MEMBERSHIP ORGS, BUSINESS: Junior Chamber Of Commerce

MEMBERSHIP ORGS, BUSINESS: Junior Chamber Of Commerce

Barberton Jaycees .... E 330 745-3733
  Barberton *(G-957)*

MEMBERSHIP ORGS, CIVIC, SOCIAL & FRAT: Comm Member Club

Columbus Maennerchor .... E 614 444-3531
  Columbus *(G-7364)*
Jewish Community Center Inc .... D 513 761-7500
  Cincinnati *(G-3868)*
O S U Faculty Club .... E 614 292-2262
  Columbus *(G-8309)*
Tiffin Cmnty YMCA Rcration Ctr .... D 419 447-8711
  Tiffin *(G-17704)*
Young Mens Christian Assoc .... D 937 836-9622
  Englewood *(G-10725)*

MEMBERSHIP ORGS, CIVIC, SOCIAL & FRAT: Dwelling-Related

Catholic Association of The Di .... C 216 641-7575
  Cleveland *(G-5188)*
The For Cincinnati Association .... D 513 744-3344
  Cincinnati *(G-4641)*

MEMBERSHIP ORGS, CIVIC, SOCIAL & FRAT: Girl Scout

Buckeye Trils Girl Scout Cncil .... E 937 275-7601
  Dayton *(G-9371)*
Girl Scouts Lake Erie Council .... E 330 864-9933
  Macedonia *(G-13199)*
Girl Scouts North East Ohio .... D 216 481-1313
  Cleveland *(G-5673)*
Girl Scouts North East Ohio .... E 330 864-9933
  Macedonia *(G-13200)*
Girl Scouts of The US Amer .... C 614 487-8101
  Columbus *(G-7751)*
Girl Scouts of Western Ohio .... E 513 489-1025
  Blue Ash *(G-1602)*
Girl Scuts Appleseed Ridge Inc .... E 419 225-4085
  Lima *(G-12783)*
Girl Scuts Ohios Heartland Inc .... D 614 340-8820
  Columbus *(G-7752)*
Girl Scuts Wstn Ohio Tledo Div .... E 419 243-8216
  Toledo *(G-17916)*
Western Rsrve Girl Scout Cncil .... E 330 864-9933
  Macedonia *(G-13218)*

MEMBERSHIP ORGS, CIVIC, SOCIAL & FRATERNAL: Civic Assoc

Benevolent/Protectv Order Elks .... E 440 357-6943
  Painesville *(G-15836)*
Cleveland Botanical Garden .... E 216 721-1600
  Cleveland *(G-5292)*
Cuyahoga County AG Soc .... E 440 243-0090
  Berea *(G-1454)*
Easter Seals Nothern Ohio Inc .... C 440 324-6600
  Lorain *(G-13036)*
Farmersville Fire Assn Inc .... E 937 696-2863
  Farmersville *(G-10983)*
Greater Cincinnati Cnvntn/Vstr .... E 513 621-2142
  Cincinnati *(G-3707)*
Grove City Community Club .... E 614 875-6074
  Grove City *(G-11567)*
International Un Elev Constrs .... C 614 291-5859
  Columbus *(G-7918)*
Kiwanis International Inc .... E 740 385-5887
  Logan *(G-12982)*
Lima Family YMCA .... E 419 223-6045
  Lima *(G-12821)*
Ohio Masonic Retirement Vlg .... D 937 525-1743
  Springfield *(G-17256)*
Order of Symposiarchs America .... E 740 387-9713
  Marion *(G-13571)*
Urban League of Greater Clevlnd .... E 216 622-0999
  Cleveland *(G-6672)*
Wesley Community Center Inc .... E 937 263-3556
  Dayton *(G-9992)*
YMCA of Massillon .... E 330 837-5116
  Massillon *(G-13863)*

MEMBERSHIP ORGS, CIVIC, SOCIAL & FRATERNAL: Condo Assoc

2444 Mdson Rd Cndo Owners Assn .... E 513 871-0100
  Cincinnati *(G-2943)*
Brandywine Master Assn .... D 419 866-0135
  Maumee *(G-13889)*
Owners Management .... E 440 439-3800
  Cleveland *(G-6222)*
Saxon House Condo .... E 440 333-8675
  Cleveland *(G-6445)*
Three Village Condominium .... E 440 461-1483
  Cleveland *(G-6597)*

MEMBERSHIP ORGS, CIVIC, SOCIAL & FRATERNAL: Protection

Cleveland Municipal School Dst .... E 216 459-4200
  Cleveland *(G-5334)*
Division Drnking Ground Waters .... D 614 644-2752
  Columbus *(G-7530)*
The Nature Conservancy .... E 614 717-2770
  Dublin *(G-10476)*
Western Rsrve Land Conservancy .... E 440 729-9621
  Chagrin Falls *(G-2711)*

MEMBERSHIP ORGS, CIVIC, SOCIAL & FRATERNAL: Singing Society

Cleveland Heights Highschool .... E 216 691-5452
  Cleveland *(G-5318)*

MEMBERSHIP ORGS, CIVIC, SOCIAL & FRATERNAL: University Club

Aerie Frtnrl Order Egles 2875 .... E 419 433-4611
  Huron *(G-12159)*
Beta Theta PI Fraternity .... E 513 523-7591
  Oxford *(G-15811)*
Delta Gamma Fraternity .... E 614 487-5599
  Upper Arlington *(G-18550)*
Gamma PHI Beta Sorority Alpha .... D 937 324-3436
  Springfield *(G-17201)*
Grand Aerie of The Fraternal .... E 614 883-2200
  Grove City *(G-11566)*
International Frat of Del .... D 330 922-5959
  Cuyahoga Falls *(G-9196)*
Kappa Kappa Gamma Foundation .... E 614 228-6515
  Columbus *(G-7962)*
Sigma CHI Frat .... E 614 297-8783
  Columbus *(G-8730)*

MEMBERSHIP ORGS, CIVIC, SOCIAL/FRAT: Business Persons Club

Columbus Club Co .... E 614 224-4131
  Columbus *(G-7339)*

MEMBERSHIP ORGS, CIVIC, SOCIAL/FRAT: Educator's Assoc

Junior Achvment Mhning Vly Inc .... E 330 539-5268
  Girard *(G-11417)*
Ohio State University .... E 614 688-5721
  Columbus *(G-8423)*

MEMBERSHIP ORGS, LABOR UNIONS/SIMILAR: Employees' Assoc

American Federation of State .... E 937 461-9983
  Dayton *(G-9329)*
Humaserve Hr LLC .... E 513 605-3522
  Cincinnati *(G-3797)*

MEMBERSHIP ORGS, RELIGIOUS: Non-Denominational Church

Columbus Christian Center Inc .... E 614 416-9673
  Columbus *(G-7337)*
Haven Rest Ministries Inc .... D 330 535-1563
  Akron *(G-258)*
In His Prsence Ministries Intl .... E 614 516-1812
  Columbus *(G-7887)*
World Harvest Church Inc .... B 614 837-1990
  Canal Winchester *(G-2180)*

MEMBERSHIP SPORTS & RECREATION CLUBS

Alano Club Inc .... D 419 335-6211
  Wauseon *(G-18948)*
Armco Association Park .... E 513 695-3980
  Lebanon *(G-12589)*
Avondale Golf Club .... E 440 934-4398
  Avon *(G-878)*
Cincinnati Sports Mall Inc .... D 513 527-4000
  Cincinnati *(G-3329)*
City of Sylvania .... E 419 885-1167
  Sylvania *(G-17579)*
Cleveland Hts Tigers Youth Spo .... E 216 906-4168
  Cleveland *(G-5319)*
Dayton Toro Motorcycle Club .... D 937 723-9133
  Dayton *(G-9492)*
Fairfield Tempo Club .... E 513 863-2081
  Fairfield *(G-10850)*
Family YMCA of LANcstr&fairfld .... C 740 654-0616
  Lancaster *(G-12542)*
Fitworks Holding LLC .... E 440 333-4141
  Rocky River *(G-16578)*
Ganzfair Investment Inc .... E 614 792-6630
  Delaware *(G-10100)*
General Electric Employees .... E 513 243-2129
  Cincinnati *(G-3672)*
Geneva Area Recreational .... E 440 466-1002
  Geneva *(G-11363)*
German Family Society Inc .... E 330 678-8229
  Kent *(G-12371)*
Grove City Community Club .... E 614 875-6074
  Grove City *(G-11567)*
Heritage Golf Club Ltd Partnr .... D 614 777-1690
  Hilliard *(G-11908)*
Lake Wynoka Prprty Owners Assn ...... E 937 446-3774
  Lake Waynoka *(G-12463)*
Lions Club International Inc .... E 330 424-3490
  Lisbon *(G-12939)*
M&C Hotel Interests Inc .... E 440 543-1331
  Chagrin Falls *(G-2723)*
Marietta Bantam Baseball Leag .... E 740 350-9844
  Marietta *(G-13465)*
Meadowbrook Country Club .... D 937 836-5186
  Clayton *(G-4913)*
Miami Rifle Pistol Club .... E 513 732-9943
  Milford *(G-14539)*
Midwest Gymnstics Cheerleading .... E 614 764-0775
  Dublin *(G-10398)*
National Exchange Club .... E 419 535-3232
  Toledo *(G-18074)*
New Albany Athc Booster CLB .... E 614 413-8325
  New Albany *(G-14996)*
Newlex Classic Riders Inc .... D 740 342-3885
  New Lexington *(G-15058)*
Oberlin College .... C 440 775-8519
  Oberlin *(G-15654)*
Ohio Automobile Club .... E 614 277-1310
  Grove City *(G-11588)*
Ohio Automobile Club .... E 513 870-0951
  West Chester *(G-19124)*
Salt Fork Resort Club Inc .... A 740 498-8116
  Kimbolton *(G-12447)*
Sandusky Rotary Club Charitabl .... E 419 625-1707
  Huron *(G-12169)*
Scioto Reserve Inc .... D 740 881-9082
  Powell *(G-16349)*
Tiffin Cmnty YMCA Rcration Ctr .... D 419 447-8711
  Tiffin *(G-17704)*
Vermilion Family YMCA .... E 440 967-4208
  Vermilion *(G-18720)*
YMCA of Ashtabula County Inc .... D 440 997-5321
  Ashtabula *(G-768)*
Young Mens Christian .... C 513 791-5000
  Blue Ash *(G-1725)*
Young Mens Christian Assn .... E 419 332-9622
  Fremont *(G-11231)*
Young Mens Christian Assn .... C 330 744-8411
  Youngstown *(G-20421)*
Young Mens Christian Assoc .... D 740 477-1661
  Circleville *(G-4909)*
Young Mens Christian Assoc .... E 937 426-9622
  Dayton *(G-10011)*
Young Mens Christian Assoc .... D 330 264-3131
  Wooster *(G-19936)*
Young Mens Christian Assoc .... D 937 836-9622
  Englewood *(G-10725)*
Young Mens Christian Assoc .... E 937 228-9622
  Dayton *(G-10012)*
Young Mens Christian Assoc .... C 937 223-5201
  Springboro *(G-17144)*

SERVICES SECTION

MENTAL HEALTH CLINIC, OUTPATIENT

Company	Code	Phone
Young Mens Christian Assoc	C	614 834-9622
Canal Winchester (G-2181)		
Young Mens Christian Associat	C	419 251-9622
Perrysburg (G-16076)		
Young Mens Christian Associat	D	513 521-7112
Cincinnati (G-4865)		
Young Mens Christian Associat	E	513 731-0115
Cincinnati (G-4866)		
Young Mens Christian Associat	C	513 474-1400
Cincinnati (G-4867)		
Young Mens Christn Assn Shelby	D	419 347-1312
Shelby (G-16904)		
Young MNS Christn Assn Findlay	E	419 422-4424
Findlay (G-11102)		
Young MNS Chrstn Assn Clveland	D	216 382-4300
Cleveland (G-6775)		
Young MNS Chrstn Assn Clveland	E	216 941-4654
Cleveland (G-6773)		

MEN'S & BOYS' CLOTHING STORES

Company	Code	Phone
Abercrombie & Fitch Trading Co	E	614 283-6500
New Albany (G-14970)		
For Women Like Me Inc	E	407 848-7339
Chagrin Falls (G-2696)		
J Peterman Company LLC	E	888 647-2555
Blue Ash (G-1619)		

MEN'S & BOYS' CLOTHING WHOLESALERS, NEC

Company	Code	Phone
Abercrombie & Fitch Trading Co	E	614 283-6500
New Albany (G-14970)		
Chester West Holdings Inc	C	800 647-1900
Cincinnati (G-3241)		
For Women Like Me Inc	E	407 848-7339
Chagrin Falls (G-2696)		
K Amalia Enterprises Inc	E	614 733-3800
Plain City (G-16195)		
Mast Industries Inc	C	614 415-7000
Columbus (G-8124)		
Mast Industries Inc	D	614 856-6000
Reynoldsburg (G-16468)		
McCc Sportswear Inc	E	513 583-9210
West Chester (G-19214)		
MGF Sourcing Us LLC	A	614 904-3300
Columbus (G-8156)		
Rassak LLC	E	513 791-9453
Cincinnati (G-4386)		
Rondinellis Tuxedo	E	330 726-7768
Youngstown (G-20359)		

MEN'S & BOYS' SPORTSWEAR WHOLESALERS

Company	Code	Phone
Barbs Graffiti Inc	D	216 881-5550
Cleveland (G-5093)		
Barbs Graffiti Inc	E	216 881-5550
Cleveland (G-5094)		
Gymnastic World Inc	E	440 526-2970
Cleveland (G-5712)		
Heritage Sportswear Inc	D	740 928-7771
Hebron (G-11850)		
R & A Sports Inc	E	216 289-2254
Euclid (G-10773)		

MENTAL HEALTH CLINIC, OUTPATIENT

Company	Code	Phone
A W S Inc	D	216 941-8800
Cleveland (G-4938)		
A+ Solutions LLC	E	216 896-0111
Beachwood (G-1044)		
Alcohol Drug Addction & Mental	E	937 443-0416
Dayton (G-9314)		
Allwell Behavioral Health Svcs	C	740 454-9766
Zanesville (G-20440)		
Allwell Behavioral Health Svcs	E	740 439-4428
Cambridge (G-2094)		
Alta Care Group Inc	E	330 793-2487
Youngstown (G-20102)		
Alternative Paths Inc	E	330 725-9195
Medina (G-14035)		
Bayshore Counseling Service	E	419 626-9156
Sandusky (G-16728)		
Beacon Health	E	440 354-9924
Mentor (G-14148)		
Behavorial Healthcare	E	740 522-8477
Newark (G-15146)		
Behavral Cnnctions WD Cnty Inc	E	419 352-5387
Bowling Green (G-1762)		
Belmont Bhc Pines Hospital Inc	C	330 759-2700
Youngstown (G-20113)		
Bhc Fox Run Hospital Inc	C	740 695-2131
Saint Clairsville (G-16628)		
Blick Clinic Inc	C	330 762-5425
Akron (G-103)		
Blick Clinic Inc	D	330 762-5425
Akron (G-104)		
Butler Bhavioral Hlth Svcs Inc	E	513 896-7887
Hamilton (G-11698)		
Center 5	D	330 379-5900
Akron (G-127)		
Center For Families & Children	E	216 252-5800
Cleveland (G-5207)		
Center For Individual and Fmly	C	419 522-4357
Mansfield (G-13274)		
Central Ohio Mental Health Ctr	C	740 368-7831
Delaware (G-10079)		
Child Focus Inc	D	513 752-1555
Cincinnati (G-3243)		
Coleman Professional Svcs Inc	B	330 673-1347
Kent (G-12360)		
Coleman Professional Svcs Inc	D	330 296-8313
Ravenna (G-16377)		
Columbus Area	D	614 251-6561
Columbus (G-7328)		
Columbus Area Inc	D	614 252-0711
Columbus (G-7329)		
Columbus Area Integrated Healt	D	614 252-0711
Columbus (G-7330)		
Community Counseling Services	E	419 468-8211
Bucyrus (G-2031)		
Community Counslng Ctr Ashtabu	D	440 998-4210
Ashtabula (G-736)		
Community Solutions Assn	E	330 394-9090
Warren (G-18838)		
Community Support Services Inc	C	330 253-9388
Akron (G-157)		
Community Support Services Inc	D	330 253-9675
Akron (G-158)		
Community Support Services Inc	E	330 733-6203
Akron (G-159)		
Communty Mntl Hlth Ctr	D	513 228-7800
Lebanon (G-12596)		
Compass Community Health	E	740 355-7102
Portsmouth (G-16273)		
Comprehensive Behavioral Hlth	E	330 797-4050
Youngstown (G-20157)		
Comprehensive Counseling Svc	E	513 424-0921
Middletown (G-14422)		
Consolidated Care Inc	E	937 465-8065
West Liberty (G-19262)		
Cornerstone Support Services	D	330 339-7850
New Philadelphia (G-15088)		
Counseling Center Huron County	E	419 663-3737
Norwalk (G-15567)		
Counseling Source Inc	E	513 984-9838
Blue Ash (G-1569)		
County of Allen	E	419 221-1226
Lima (G-12766)		
County of Geauga	C	440 286-6264
Chardon (G-2745)		
County of Hamilton	B	513 598-2965
Cincinnati (G-3431)		
Craig and Frances Lindner Cent	C	513 536-4673
Mason (G-13691)		
Crossroads Lake County Adole	D	440 255-1700
Mentor (G-14165)		
Darke Cnty Mental Hlth Clinic	E	937 548-1635
Greenville (G-11494)		
Day-Mont Bhvoral Hlth Care Inc	D	937 222-8111
Moraine (G-14768)		
East Way Behavioral Hlth Care	E	937 222-4900
Dayton (G-9515)		
Emerge Counseling Service	E	330 865-8351
Akron (G-207)		
Empowered For Excellence	E	567 316-7253
Toledo (G-17866)		
Equitas Health Inc	C	614 299-2437
Columbus (G-7603)		
F R S Connections	E	937 393-9662
Hillsboro (G-11973)		
Family Rsource Ctr NW Ohio Inc	E	419 222-1168
Lima (G-12777)		
Family Rsource Ctr NW Ohio Inc	E	419 422-8616
Findlay (G-11023)		
Firelands Regional Health Sys	E	419 332-5524
Fremont (G-11197)		
Foundtion Behavioral Hlth Svcs	E	419 584-1000
Celina (G-2647)		
Frs Counseling Inc	E	937 393-0585
Hillsboro (G-11975)		
Fulton County Health Center	E	419 337-8661
Wauseon (G-18954)		
Giving Tree Inc	E	419 898-0077
Oak Harbor (G-15610)		
Harbor	D	419 479-3233
Toledo (G-17932)		
Harbor	D	419 241-6191
Toledo (G-17933)		
Harbor	E	800 444-3353
Toledo (G-17934)		
Health Partners Health Clinic	E	937 645-8488
Marysville (G-13623)		
Hopewell Health Centers Inc	E	740 385-6594
Logan (G-12977)		
Integrated Youth Services Inc	E	937 427-3837
Springfield (G-17213)		
Ironton and Lawrence County	B	740 532-3534
Ironton (G-12291)		
Jac-Lin Manor	D	419 994-5700
Loudonville (G-13091)		
Lorain County Board	E	440 329-3734
Elyria (G-10646)		
Lutheran Social	E	419 229-2222
Lima (G-12834)		
Main Place Inc	E	740 345-6246
Newark (G-15200)		
Maumee Valley Guidance Center	E	419 782-8856
Defiance (G-10046)		
Mental Health and Addi Serv	E	740 594-5000
Athens (G-801)		
Mental Health and Addi Serv	C	614 752-0333
Columbus (G-8148)		
Mental Hlth Serv For CL & Mad	E	740 852-6256
London (G-13003)		
Mid-Ohio Psychlogical Svcs Inc	E	740 687-0042
Lancaster (G-12558)		
Midwest Behavioral Care Ltd	E	937 454-0092
Dayton (G-9744)		
Moundbuilders Guidance Ctr Inc	E	740 397-0442
Mount Vernon (G-14913)		
National Mentor Holdings Inc	A	330 491-4331
Youngstown (G-20298)		
Nationwide Childrens Hospital	B	614 355-8000
Columbus (G-8237)		
Norcare Enterprises Inc	B	440 233-7232
Lorain (G-13065)		
Nord Center	E	440 233-7232
Lorain (G-13066)		
Nord Center Associates Inc	C	440 233-7232
Lorain (G-13067)		
North Cntl Mntl Hlth Svcs Inc	D	614 227-6865
Columbus (G-8288)		
North Community Counseling Ctr	E	614 846-2588
Columbus (G-8289)		
Northwest Mental Health Svcs	E	614 457-7876
Columbus (G-8297)		
Portage Path Behavorial Health	D	330 253-3100
Akron (G-397)		
Portage Path Behavorial Health	D	330 762-6110
Akron (G-398)		
Pressley Ridge Foundation	A	513 752-4548
Cincinnati (G-2929)		
Psy-Care Inc	E	330 856-6663
Warren (G-18891)		
Psychlgcal Behavioral Cons LLC	E	216 456-8123
Beachwood (G-1116)		
Ravenwood Mental Health Center	E	440 632-5355
Middlefield (G-14401)		
Ravenwood Mental Hlth Ctr Inc	E	440 285-3568
Chardon (G-2763)		
Samaritan Behavioral Health	E	937 276-8333
Dayton (G-9864)		
Scioto Pnt Vly Mental Hlth Ctr	E	740 335-6935
Wshngtn CT Hs (G-20034)		
Scioto Pnt Vly Mental Hlth Ctr	C	740 775-1260
Chillicothe (G-2884)		
Signature Health Inc	B	440 953-9999
Willoughby (G-19713)		
South Community Inc	C	937 293-8300
Moraine (G-14826)		
South Community Inc	E	937 252-0100
Dayton (G-9889)		
Southeast Cmnty Mental Hlth Ctr	C	614 225-0980
Columbus (G-8751)		
Southeast Cmnty Mental Hlth Ctr	E	614 445-6832
Columbus (G-8753)		
Southeast Cmnty Mental Hlth Ctr	E	614 293-9613
Worthington (G-19998)		

Employee Codes: A=Over 500 employees, B=251-500
C=101-250, D=51-100, E=25-50

2018 Harris Ohio Services Directory

Southast Cmnty Mental Hlth Ctr ....E 614 444-0800
Columbus *(G-8752)*
Southern Ohio Bhvoral Hlth LLC ....E 740 533-0055
Ironton *(G-12303)*
St Aloysius Services Inc ....E 513 482-1745
Cincinnati *(G-4571)*
St Ritas Medical Center ....E 419 226-9067
Lima *(G-12884)*
Stark County Board of Developm ....A 330 477-5200
Canton *(G-2543)*
Syntero Inc ....E 614 889-5722
Dublin *(G-10471)*
Taylor Murtis Human Svcs Sys ....D 216 283-4400
Cleveland *(G-6573)*
Taylor Murtis Human Svcs Sys ....D 216 281-7192
Cleveland *(G-6574)*
Thompkins Child Adlescent Svcs ....D 740 622-4470
Coshocton *(G-9118)*
Tri County Mental Health Svcs ....C 740 592-3091
Athens *(G-815)*
Tri County Mental Health Svcs ....D 740 594-5045
Athens *(G-816)*
Trihealth Inc ....E 513 569-6777
Cincinnati *(G-4689)*
Unison Behavioral Health Group ....D 419 242-9577
Toledo *(G-18267)*
Unison Behavioral Health Group ....C 419 693-0631
Toledo *(G-18268)*
Westwood Behavioral Health Ctr ....E 419 238-3434
Van Wert *(G-18652)*
Woodland Centers Inc ....D 740 446-5500
Gallipolis *(G-11341)*
Zepf Center ....E 419 255-4050
Toledo *(G-18328)*
Zepf Center ....D 419 841-7701
Toledo *(G-18329)*
Zepf Center ....E 419 213-5627
Toledo *(G-18330)*
Zepf Center ....E 419 255-4050
Toledo *(G-18331)*
Zepf Center ....E 419 213-5627
Toledo *(G-18332)*

MENTAL HEALTH PRACTITIONERS' OFFICES

Crisis Intervention & Rcvy Ctr ....D 330 455-9407
Canton *(G-2327)*
Layh & Associates ....E 937 767-9171
Yellow Springs *(G-20090)*
Netcare Corporation ....D 614 274-9500
Columbus *(G-8258)*
Netcare Corporation ....E 614 274-9500
Columbus *(G-8259)*

MERCHANDISING MACHINE OPERATORS: Vending

AVI Food Systems Inc ....C 330 372-6000
Warren *(G-18827)*
AVI Food Systems Inc ....E 740 452-9363
Zanesville *(G-20445)*
Dtv Inc ....E 216 226-5465
Mayfield Heights *(G-14001)*
McKirnan Bros Inc ....E 419 586-2428
Celina *(G-2651)*
S & B Enterprises LLC ....E 740 753-2646
Nelsonville *(G-14967)*

METAL & STEEL PRDTS: Abrasive

Tomson Steel Company ....E 513 420-8600
Middletown *(G-14468)*

METAL COMPONENTS: Prefabricated

Pioneer Cldding Glzing Systems ....E 216 816-4242
Cleveland *(G-6282)*

METAL CUTTING SVCS

Gerdau Macsteel Atmosphere Ann ....D 330 478-0314
Canton *(G-2379)*
Independent Steel Company LLC ....E 330 225-7741
Valley City *(G-18618)*
Laserflex Corporation ....D 614 850-9600
Hilliard *(G-11920)*
Perfect Cut-Off Inc ....E 440 943-0000
Wickliffe *(G-19611)*
Precision Strip Inc ....D 937 667-6255
Tipp City *(G-17725)*
Scot Industries Inc ....E 330 262-7585
Wooster *(G-19914)*

METAL FABRICATORS: Architechtural

A & G Manufacturing Co Inc ....E 419 468-7433
Galion *(G-11288)*
Bauer Corporation ....E 800 321-4760
Wooster *(G-19830)*
Blevins Metal Fabrication Inc ....E 419 522-6082
Mansfield *(G-13267)*
Debra-Kuempel Inc ....D 513 271-6500
Cincinnati *(G-3476)*
GL Nause Co Inc ....E 513 722-9500
Loveland *(G-13128)*
Graber Metal Works Inc ....E 440 237-8422
North Royalton *(G-15490)*
Kajima International Inc ....C 440 544-2600
Cleveland *(G-5880)*
Langdon Inc ....E 513 733-5955
Cincinnati *(G-3960)*
Modern Builders Supply Inc ....C 330 729-2690
Youngstown *(G-20289)*
Security Fence Group Inc ....E 513 681-3700
Cincinnati *(G-4489)*
Spillman Company ....E 614 444-2184
Columbus *(G-8762)*
Triangle Precision Industries ....D 937 299-6776
Dayton *(G-9937)*
Viking Fabricators Inc ....E 740 374-5246
Marietta *(G-13515)*

METAL FABRICATORS: Plate

A A S Amels Sheet Meta L Inc ....E 330 793-9326
Youngstown *(G-20094)*
A & G Manufacturing Co Inc ....E 419 468-7433
Galion *(G-11288)*
A M Castle & Co ....D 330 425-7000
Bedford *(G-1292)*
American Tank & Fabricating Co ....D 216 252-1500
Cleveland *(G-5023)*
Babcock & Wilcox Company ....A 330 753-4511
Barberton *(G-955)*
Bico Akron Inc ....D 330 794-1716
Mogadore *(G-14672)*
Blevins Metal Fabrication Inc ....E 419 522-6082
Mansfield *(G-13267)*
Breitinger Company ....C 419 526-4255
Mansfield *(G-13269)*
C & R Inc ....E 614 497-1130
Groveport *(G-11626)*
Curtiss-Wright Flow Ctrl Corp ....D 513 528-7900
Cincinnati *(G-2911)*
Debra-Kuempel Inc ....D 513 271-6500
Cincinnati *(G-3476)*
Efco Corp ....E 614 876-1226
Columbus *(G-7586)*
General Tool Company ....C 513 733-5500
Cincinnati *(G-3675)*
GL Nause Co Inc ....E 513 722-9500
Loveland *(G-13128)*
Graber Metal Works Inc ....E 440 237-8422
North Royalton *(G-15490)*
Jergens Inc ....B 216 486-5540
Cleveland *(G-5859)*
Kendall Holdings Ltd ....E 614 486-4750
Columbus *(G-7976)*
Kirk & Blum Manufacturing Co ....C 513 458-2600
Cincinnati *(G-3929)*
Kirk & Blum Manufacturing Co ....E 419 782-9885
Defiance *(G-10043)*
Langdon Inc ....E 513 733-5955
Cincinnati *(G-3960)*
Lapham-Hickey Steel Corp ....E 614 443-4881
Columbus *(G-8039)*
Long-Stanton Mfg Company ....E 513 874-8020
West Chester *(G-19111)*
Louis Arthur Steel Company ....D 440 997-5545
Geneva *(G-11365)*
Nbw Inc ....E 216 377-1700
Cleveland *(G-6114)*
Pcy Enterprises Inc ....E 513 241-5566
Cincinnati *(G-4270)*
Pioneer Pipe Inc ....B 740 376-2400
Marietta *(G-13488)*
Prout Boiler Htg & Wldg Inc ....E 330 744-0293
Youngstown *(G-20331)*
Schweizer Dipple Inc ....D 440 786-8090
Cleveland *(G-6451)*
St Lawrence Steel Corporation ....E 330 562-9000
Streetsboro *(G-17431)*
Swagelok Company ....D 440 349-5934
Solon *(G-17059)*
Triangle Precision Industries ....D 937 299-6776
Dayton *(G-9937)*
Viking Fabricators Inc ....E 740 374-5246
Marietta *(G-13515)*
Will-Burt Company ....E 330 682-7015
Orrville *(G-15790)*
Will-Burt Company ....B 330 682-7015
Orrville *(G-15789)*

METAL FABRICATORS: Sheet

A A S Amels Sheet Meta L Inc ....E 330 793-9326
Youngstown *(G-20094)*
A & C Welding Inc ....E 330 762-4777
Peninsula *(G-15946)*
A & G Manufacturing Co Inc ....E 419 468-7433
Galion *(G-11288)*
A M Castle & Co ....D 330 425-7000
Bedford *(G-1292)*
Acro Tool & Die Company ....D 330 773-5173
Akron *(G-17)*
Akron Foundry Co ....E 330 745-3101
Barberton *(G-950)*
Alan Manufacturing Inc ....E 330 262-1555
Wooster *(G-19825)*
Alro Steel Corporation ....E 419 720-5300
Toledo *(G-17747)*
American Frame Corporation ....E 419 893-5595
Maumee *(G-13874)*
Anchor Metal Processing Inc ....E 216 362-1850
Cleveland *(G-5035)*
Avon Lake Sheet Metal Co ....E 440 933-3505
Avon Lake *(G-923)*
Bayloff Stmped Pdts Knsman Inc ....D 330 876-4511
Kinsman *(G-12452)*
Blevins Metal Fabrication Inc ....E 419 522-6082
Mansfield *(G-13267)*
Bogie Industries Inc Ltd ....E 330 745-3105
Akron *(G-106)*
Breitinger Company ....C 419 526-4255
Mansfield *(G-13269)*
Budde Sheet Metal Works Inc ....E 937 224-0868
Dayton *(G-9372)*
C-N-D Industries Inc ....E 330 478-8811
Massillon *(G-13791)*
Dimensional Metals Inc ....D 740 927-3633
Reynoldsburg *(G-16447)*
Ducts Inc ....E 216 391-2400
Cleveland *(G-5511)*
Dynamic Weld Corporation ....E 419 582-2900
Osgood *(G-15791)*
First Francis Company Inc ....E 440 352-8927
Painesville *(G-15857)*
Franck and Fric Incorporated ....D 216 524-4451
Cleveland *(G-5631)*
Gaspar Inc ....D 330 477-2222
Canton *(G-2376)*
General Tool Company ....C 513 733-5500
Cincinnati *(G-3675)*
GL Nause Co Inc ....E 513 722-9500
Loveland *(G-13128)*
Graber Metal Works Inc ....E 440 237-8422
North Royalton *(G-15490)*
Gundlach Sheet Metal Works Inc ....D 419 626-4525
Sandusky *(G-16766)*
Industrial Mill Maintenance ....E 330 746-1155
Youngstown *(G-20232)*
Jacobs Mechanical Co ....C 513 681-6800
Cincinnati *(G-3857)*
Joseph T Ryerson & Son Inc ....D 513 542-5800
Columbus *(G-7950)*
Kirk Williams Company Inc ....D 614 875-9023
Grove City *(G-11573)*
Lima Sheet Metal Machine & Mfg ....E 419 229-1161
Lima *(G-12827)*
Long-Stanton Mfg Company ....E 513 874-8020
West Chester *(G-19111)*
Louis Arthur Steel Company ....D 440 997-5545
Geneva *(G-11365)*
M H EBY Inc ....E 614 879-6901
West Jefferson *(G-19253)*
Marsam Metalfab Inc ....E 330 405-1520
Twinsburg *(G-18444)*
McWane Inc ....B 740 622-6651
Coshocton *(G-9111)*
N Wasserstrom & Sons Inc ....C 614 228-5550
Columbus *(G-8212)*
Norstar Aluminum Molds Inc ....D 440 632-0853
Middlefield *(G-14399)*

SERVICES SECTION

METALS SVC CENTERS & WHOLESALERS: Steel

Northwind Industries Inc ....E...... 216 433-0666
  Cleveland (G-6163)
Ohio Blow Pipe Company ....E...... 216 681-7379
  Cleveland (G-6186)
Ohio Steel Sheet & Plate Inc ....E...... 800 827-2401
  Hubbard (G-12090)
Pcy Enterprises Inc ....E...... 513 241-5566
  Cincinnati (G-4270)
Precision Mtal Fabrication Inc ....D...... 937 235-9261
  Dayton (G-9818)
Precision Steel Services Inc ....D...... 419 476-5702
  Toledo (G-18132)
Precision Welding Corporation ....E...... 216 524-6110
  Cleveland (G-6295)
Schweizer Dipple Inc ....E...... 440 786-8090
  Cleveland (G-6451)
Steelial Wldg Met Fbrction Inc ....E...... 740 669-5300
  Vinton (G-18744)
Tendon Manufacturing Inc ....E...... 216 663-3200
  Cleveland (G-6582)
TL Industries Inc ....C...... 419 666-8144
  Northwood (G-15547)
Triangle Precision Industries ....D...... 937 299-6776
  Dayton (G-9937)
Tricor Industrial Inc ....D...... 330 264-3299
  Wooster (G-19919)
Universal Steel Company ....D...... 216 883-4972
  Cleveland (G-6650)
V M Systems Inc ....E...... 419 535-1044
  Toledo (G-18285)
Will-Burt Company ....B...... 330 682-7015
  Orrville (G-15789)
Ysd Industries Inc ....D...... 330 792-6521
  Youngstown (G-20437)

METAL MINING SVCS

Alloy Metal Exchange LLC ....E...... 216 478-0200
  Bedford Heights (G-1345)
Hopedale Mining LLC ....E...... 740 937-2225
  Hopedale (G-12079)

METAL SERVICE CENTERS & OFFICES

A J Oster Foils LLC ....D...... 330 823-1700
  Alliance (G-521)
A M Castle & Co ....D...... 330 425-7000
  Bedford (G-1292)
Advanced Graphite Machining US ....E...... 216 658-6521
  Parma (G-15898)
Aluminum Line Products Company ....D...... 440 835-8880
  Westlake (G-19459)
American Consolidated Inds Inc ....E...... 216 587-8000
  Cleveland (G-5007)
American Tank & Fabricating Co ....D...... 216 252-1500
  Cleveland (G-5023)
Atlas Bolt & Screw Company LLC ....C...... 419 289-6171
  Ashland (G-660)
Atlas Recycling Inc ....E...... 800 837-1520
  Warren (G-18818)
Boston Retail Products Inc ....D...... 330 744-8100
  Youngstown (G-20123)
Canfield Metal Coating Corp ....D...... 330 702-3876
  Canfield (G-2184)
Chatham Steel Corporation ....E...... 740 377-9310
  South Point (G-17081)
Graber Metal Works Inc ....E...... 440 237-8422
  North Royalton (G-15490)
Mes Inc ....E...... 740 201-8112
  Lewis Center (G-12694)
Modern Welding Co Ohio Inc ....E...... 740 344-9425
  Newark (G-15209)
National Bronze Mtls Ohio Inc ....E...... 440 277-1226
  Lorain (G-13063)
Now Tochnology Stool LLC ....D...... 419 385-0636
  Toledo (G-18084)
Ohio Metal Processing Inc ....E...... 740 286-6457
  Jackson (G-12316)
Ohio Steel Sheet & Plate Inc ....E...... 800 827-2401
  Hubbard (G-12090)
Panacea Products Corporation ....E...... 614 850-7000
  Columbus (G-8513)
Samuel Steel Pickling Company ....D...... 330 963-3777
  Twinsburg (G-18467)
SL Wellspring LLC ....D...... 513 948-2339
  Cincinnati (G-4540)
Symcox Grinding & Steele Co ....E...... 330 678-1080
  Kent (G-12398)
Tricor Industrial Inc ....D...... 330 264-3299
  Wooster (G-19919)
Watteredge LLC ....D...... 440 933-6110
  Avon Lake (G-940)

Worthington Industries Inc ....C...... 513 539-9291
  Monroe (G-14718)
Worthington Stelpac Systems LLC ....C...... 614 438-3205
  Columbus (G-9009)

METAL SLITTING & SHEARING

Laser Craft Inc ....E...... 440 327-4300
  North Ridgeville (G-15467)
Metal Shredders Inc ....E...... 937 866-0777
  Miamisburg (G-14320)
Ohio Metal Processing Inc ....E...... 740 286-6457
  Jackson (G-12316)
Ohio Steel Slitters Inc ....E...... 330 477-6741
  Canton (G-2486)
Ohio-Kentucky Steel Corp ....E...... 937 743-4600
  Franklin (G-11161)
Precision Strip Inc ....C...... 419 628-2343
  Minster (G-14668)
Precision Strip Inc ....D...... 419 661-1100
  Perrysburg (G-16044)
Precision Strip Inc ....E...... 513 423-4166
  Middletown (G-14450)
Samuel Steel Pickling Company ....D...... 330 963-3777
  Twinsburg (G-18467)

METAL STAMPING, FOR THE TRADE

Acro Tool & Die Company ....D...... 330 773-5173
  Akron (G-17)
Andre Corporation ....E...... 574 293-0207
  Mason (G-13662)
Bayloff Stmped Pdts Knsman Inc ....D...... 330 876-4511
  Kinsman (G-12452)
Falls Stamping & Welding Co ....C...... 330 928-1191
  Cuyahoga Falls (G-9185)
Ohio Gasket and Shim Co Inc ....E...... 330 630-0626
  Akron (G-366)
Pentaflex Inc ....E...... 937 325-5551
  Springfield (G-17260)
Supply Technologies LLC ....C...... 440 947-2100
  Cleveland (G-6556)

METAL STAMPINGS: Patterned

Seilkop Industries Inc ....E...... 513 761-1035
  Cincinnati (G-4492)

METALS SVC CENTERS & WHOL: Semifinished Prdts, Iron/Steel

Voestlpine Precision Strip LLC ....D...... 330 220-7800
  Brunswick (G-1994)

METALS SVC CENTERS & WHOL: Structural Shapes, Iron Or Steel

Blackburns Fabrication Inc ....E...... 614 875-0784
  Columbus (G-7117)
Infra-Metals Co ....E...... 740 353-1350
  Portsmouth (G-16290)

METALS SVC CENTERS & WHOLESALERS: Cable, Wire

Radix Wire Co ....D...... 216 731-9191
  Cleveland (G-6345)

METALS SVC CENTERS & WHOLESALERS: Casting, Rough,Iron/Steel

Ferralloy Inc ....E...... 440 250-1900
  Cleveland (G-5585)

METALS SVC CENTERS & WHOLESALERS: Concrete Reinforcing Bars

Contractors Materials Company ....E...... 513 733-3000
  Cincinnati (G-3413)

METALS SVC CENTERS & WHOLESALERS: Copper

Anchor Bronze and Metals Inc ....E...... 440 549-5653
  Cleveland (G-5033)

METALS SVC CENTERS & WHOLESALERS: Ferroalloys

Howmet Corporation ....E...... 800 242-9898
  Newburgh Heights (G-15251)

METALS SVC CENTERS & WHOLESALERS: Ferrous Metals

All Metal Sales Inc ....E...... 440 617-1234
  Westlake (G-19456)

METALS SVC CENTERS & WHOLESALERS: Flat Prdts, Iron Or Steel

H & D Steel Service Inc ....E...... 440 237-3390
  North Royalton (G-15491)
Major Metals Company ....E...... 419 886-4600
  Mansfield (G-13327)
National Metal Trading LLC ....E...... 440 487-9771
  Willoughby (G-19695)

METALS SVC CENTERS & WHOLESALERS: Foundry Prdts

Shells Inc ....D...... 330 808-5558
  Copley (G-9063)

METALS SVC CENTERS & WHOLESALERS: Iron & Steel Prdt, Ferrous

Fpt Cleveland LLC ....C...... 216 441-3800
  Cleveland (G-5628)
Heidtman Steel Products ....A...... 419 691-4646
  Toledo (G-17952)
Joseph T Ryerson & Son Inc ....D...... 513 542-5800
  Columbus (G-7950)

METALS SVC CENTERS & WHOLESALERS: Nonferrous Sheets, Etc

Shadco Inc ....E...... 310 217-8777
  Toronto (G-18338)
Thyssenkrupp Materials NA Inc ....C...... 440 234-7500
  Cleveland (G-6599)

METALS SVC CENTERS & WHOLESALERS: Pipe & Tubing, Steel

Earle M Jorgensen Company ....D...... 330 425-1500
  Twinsburg (G-18407)
L B Industries Inc ....E...... 330 750-1002
  Struthers (G-17533)
McWane Inc ....B...... 740 622-6651
  Coshocton (G-9111)

METALS SVC CENTERS & WHOLESALERS: Plates, Metal

Loveman Steel Corporation ....D...... 440 232-6200
  Bedford (G-1317)

METALS SVC CENTERS & WHOLESALERS: Rope, Wire, Exc Insulated

Mazzella Holding Company Inc ....D...... 513 772-4466
  Cleveland (G-5997)
Samsel Rope & Marine Supply Co ....E...... 216 241-0333
  Cleveland (G-6442)

METALS SVC CENTERS & WHOLESALERS: Sheets, Galvanized/Coated

Witt Glvnzing - Cincinnati Inc ....E...... 513 871-5700
  Cincinnati (G-4854)

METALS SVC CENTERS & WHOLESALERS: Sheets, Metal

Atlas Steel Products Co ....D...... 330 425-1600
  Twinsburg (G-18394)
Majestic Steel Usa Inc ....C...... 440 786-2666
  Cleveland (G-5973)

METALS SVC CENTERS & WHOLESALERS: Stampings, Metal

R L Morrissey & Assoc Inc ....E...... 440 498-3730
  Solon (G-17044)

METALS SVC CENTERS & WHOLESALERS: Steel

Albco Sales Inc ....E...... 330 424-9446
  Lisbon (G-12931)

Employee Codes: A=Over 500 employees, B=251-500
C=101-250, D=51-100, E=25-50

METALS SVC CENTERS & WHOLESALERS: Steel

All Foils Inc .... D 440 572-3645
  Strongsville (G-17441)
Alro Steel Corporation .... E 330 929-4660
  Cuyahoga Falls (G-9160)
Alro Steel Corporation .... E 419 720-5300
  Toledo (G-17747)
Alro Steel Corporation .... E 937 253-6121
  Dayton (G-9323)
American Posts LLC .... E 419 720-0652
  Toledo (G-17751)
Associated Steel Company Inc .... E 216 475-8000
  Cleveland (G-5073)
Avalon Precision Cast Co LLC .... C 216 362-4100
  Brookpark (G-1936)
Benjamin Steel Company Inc .... E 937 233-1212
  Springfield (G-17150)
Benjamin Steel Company Inc .... E 419 229-8045
  Lima (G-12745)
Benjamin Steel Company Inc .... E 419 522-5500
  Mansfield (G-13265)
Bico Akron Inc .... D 330 794-1716
  Mogadore (G-14672)
Central Steel and Wire Company .... C 513 242-2233
  Cincinnati (G-3217)
Chapel Steel Corp .... E 800 570-7674
  Bedford Heights (G-1349)
Cincinnati Steel Products Co .... E 513 871-4444
  Cincinnati (G-3330)
Clifton Steel Company .... D 216 662-6111
  Maple Heights (G-13403)
Clinton Aluminum Dist Inc .... C 330 882-6743
  New Franklin (G-15042)
Cme Acquisitions LLC .... E 216 464-4480
  Twinsburg (G-18403)
Coilplus Inc .... D 614 866-1338
  Columbus (G-7315)
Coilplus Inc .... E 937 322-4455
  Springfield (G-17167)
Coilplus Inc .... D 937 778-8884
  Piqua (G-16139)
Contractors Steel Company .... E 330 425-3050
  Twinsburg (G-18404)
Earle M Jorgensen Company .... E 513 771-3223
  Cincinnati (G-3530)
Efco Corp .... E 614 876-1226
  Columbus (G-7586)
F I L US Inc .... E 440 248-9500
  Solon (G-17005)
Fay Industries Inc .... D 440 572-5030
  Strongsville (G-17464)
Flack Steel LLC .... E 216 456-0700
  Cleveland (G-5603)
Freedom Steel Inc .... E 440 266-6800
  Mentor (G-14177)
Haverhill Coke Company LLC .... D 740 355-9819
  Franklin Furnace (G-11172)
Holub Iron & Steel Company .... E 330 252-5655
  Akron (G-270)
Hynes Industries Inc .... C 330 799-3221
  Youngstown (G-20227)
Independent Steel Company LLC .... E 330 225-7741
  Valley City (G-18618)
Is Acquisition Inc .... E 440 287-0150
  Streetsboro (G-17417)
Jade-Sterling Steel Co Inc .... E 330 425-3141
  Twinsburg (G-18434)
Joseph T Ryerson & Son Inc .... E 513 896-4600
  Hamilton (G-11748)
Kloeckner Metals Corporation .... D 513 769-4000
  Cincinnati (G-3932)
Lapham-Hickey Steel Corp .... E 614 443-4881
  Columbus (G-8039)
Latrobe Spcialty Mtls Dist Inc .... D 330 609-5137
  Vienna (G-18738)
Liberty Steel Products Inc .... E 330 538-2236
  North Jackson (G-15383)
Liberty Steel Products Inc .... C 330 534-7998
  Hubbard (G-12089)
Louis Arthur Steel Company .... D 440 997-5545
  Geneva (G-11365)
Master-Halco Inc .... E 513 869-7600
  Fairfield (G-10876)
Matandy Steel & Metal Pdts LLC .... E 513 844-2277
  Hamilton (G-11757)
Metals USA Crbn Flat Rlled Inc .... D 937 882-6354
  Springfield (G-17245)
Metals USA Crbn Flat Rlled Inc .... C 330 264-8416
  Wooster (G-19887)
Miami Valley Steel Service Inc .... C 937 773-7127
  Piqua (G-16153)

Mid-America Steel Corp .... E 800 282-3466
  Cleveland (G-6052)
Mid-West Materials Inc .... E 440 259-5200
  Perry (G-15965)
Miller Consolidated Industries .... C 937 294-2681
  Moraine (G-14806)
Misa Metals Inc .... D 212 660-6000
  West Chester (G-19120)
Misa Metals Inc .... C 440 892-4944
  Westlake (G-19516)
Monarch Steel Company Inc .... E 216 587-8000
  Cleveland (G-6074)
New Technology Steel LLC .... E 419 385-0636
  Toledo (G-18085)
Northstar Alloys & Machine Co .... E 440 234-3069
  Berea (G-1464)
Olympic Steel Inc .... D 216 292-3800
  Cleveland (G-6200)
Olympic Steel Inc .... D 216 292-3800
  Cleveland (G-6201)
Olympic Steel Inc .... E 440 287-0150
  Streetsboro (G-17423)
Olympic Steel Inc .... C 216 292-3800
  Bedford (G-1327)
Parker Steel International Inc .... E 419 473-2481
  Maumee (G-13957)
Phoenix Corporation .... E 513 727-4763
  Middletown (G-14449)
Phoenix Steel Service Inc .... E 216 332-0600
  Cleveland (G-6276)
Precesion Finning Bending Inc .... E 330 382-9351
  East Liverpool (G-10533)
Precision Steel Services Inc .... D 419 476-5702
  Toledo (G-18132)
Quality Steels Corp .... E 937 294-4133
  Moraine (G-14818)
Riverfront Steel Inc .... D 513 769-9999
  Cincinnati (G-4424)
Samuel Son & Co Inc .... D 419 470-7070
  Toledo (G-18171)
Scot Industries Inc .... E 330 262-7585
  Wooster (G-19914)
Select Steel Inc .... E 330 652-1756
  Niles (G-15305)
Specialty Steel Co Inc .... E 800 321-8500
  Cleveland (G-6516)
St Lawrence Steel Corporation .... E 330 562-9000
  Streetsboro (G-17431)
Stark Metal Sales Inc .... E 330 823-7383
  Alliance (G-562)
Steel Plate LLC .... E 888 894-8818
  Twinsburg (G-18473)
Steelsummit Holdings Inc .... E 513 825-8550
  Cincinnati (G-4588)
Thompson Steel Company Inc .... E 937 236-6940
  Dayton (G-9928)
Thyssenkrupp Materials NA Inc .... D 216 883-8100
  Independence (G-12267)
Tomson Steel Company .... E 513 420-8600
  Middletown (G-14468)
United Performance Metals Inc .... C 513 860-6500
  Hamilton (G-11782)
United Steel Service LLC .... C 330 448-4057
  Brookfield (G-1902)
Universal Steel Company .... D 216 883-4972
  Cleveland (G-6650)
Van Pelt Corporation .... E 513 242-6000
  Cincinnati (G-4803)
Waelzholz North America LLC .... E 216 267-5500
  Cleveland (G-6717)
Westfield Steel Inc .... D 937 322-2414
  Springfield (G-17299)
William Wood .... E 740 543-4052
  Bloomingdale (G-1518)

METALS SVC CENTERS & WHOLESALERS: Strip, Metal

Three D Metals Inc .... D 330 220-0451
  Valley City (G-18625)

METALS SVC CENTERS & WHOLESALERS: Tubing, Metal

Industrial Tube and Steel Corp .... D 330 474-5530
  Kent (G-12374)
Swagelok Company .... D 440 349-5934
  Solon (G-17059)

METALS SVC CNTRS & WHOL: Metal Wires, Ties, Cables/Screening

Tylinter Inc .... D 800 321-6188
  Mentor (G-14251)

METALS SVC CTRS & WHOLESALERS: Aluminum Bars, Rods, Etc

Beck Aluminum Intl LLC .... D 440 684-4848
  Cleveland (G-5108)
Metal Conversions Ltd .... E 419 525-0011
  Mansfield (G-13343)
Timken Corporation .... E 330 471-3378
  North Canton (G-15374)
Tri-State Aluminium Inc .... E 419 666-0100
  Toledo (G-18261)

METALS: Primary Nonferrous, NEC

Aci Industries Ltd .... E 740 368-4160
  Delaware (G-10065)
Rhenium Alloys Inc .... D 440 365-7388
  North Ridgeville (G-15475)

METALWORK: Miscellaneous

Watteredge LLC .... D 440 933-6110
  Avon Lake (G-940)
Will-Burt Company .... E 330 682-7015
  Orrville (G-15790)
Will-Burt Company .... B 330 682-7015
  Orrville (G-15789)

METER READERS: Remote

Bermex Inc .... B 330 945-7500
  Akron (G-98)
Guardian Water & Power Inc .... D 614 291-3141
  Columbus (G-7785)
Matvest Inc .... E 614 487-8720
  Columbus (G-8130)
US Bronco Services Inc .... E 513 829-9880
  Fairfield (G-10921)

MGMT CONSULTING SVCS: Matls, Incl Purch, Handle & Invntry

Global Cnsld Holdings Inc .... D 513 703-0965
  Mason (G-13709)
Lesaint Logistics LLC .... D 513 988-0101
  Trenton (G-18341)
Marketing Indus Solutions Corp .... E 513 703-0965
  Mason (G-13735)
Midwest Motor Supply Co .... C 800 233-1294
  Columbus (G-8170)
Southern Ohio Medical Center .... E 740 356-5000
  Portsmouth (G-16312)
Top Echelon Contracting Inc .... B 330 454-3508
  Canton (G-2564)

MGT SVCS, FACIL SUPPT: Base Maint Or Provide Personnel

City of Xenia .... E 937 376-7260
  Xenia (G-20046)
County of Miami .... E 937 335-1314
  Troy (G-18352)
Greene County .... E 937 562-7800
  Xenia (G-20056)
Henry Call Inc .... E 216 433-5609
  Cleveland (G-5749)

MICROFILM EQPT WHOLESALERS

Schenker Inc .... D 614 257-8365
  Lockbourne (G-12960)

MICROFILM SVCS

High Line Corporation .... E 330 848-8800
  Akron (G-264)

MILK, FLUID: Wholesalers

Austintown Dairy Inc .... E 330 629-6170
  Youngstown (G-20108)

MILLING: Cereal Flour, Exc Rice

Keynes Bros Inc .... E 740 385-6824
  Logan (G-12979)

MILLWORK

Company	Code	Phone
Carter-Jones Lumber Company Millersburg *(G-14591)*	C	330 674-9060
Door Fabrication Services Inc Vandalia *(G-18677)*	E	937 454-9207
Dublin Millwork Co Inc Dublin *(G-10331)*	E	614 889-7776
Holmes Lumber & Bldg Ctr Inc Millersburg *(G-14604)*	C	330 674-9060
Judy Mills Company Inc Cincinnati *(G-3895)*	E	513 271-4241
Riverside Cnstr Svcs Inc Cincinnati *(G-4427)*	E	513 723-0900
Stephen M Trudick Burton *(G-2065)*	E	440 834-1891

MINE & QUARRY SVCS: Nonmetallic Minerals

Company	Code	Phone
M G Q Inc Tiffin *(G-17683)*	E	419 992-4236

MINERALS: Ground or Treated

Company	Code	Phone
Acme Company Poland *(G-16219)*	D	330 758-2313
Edw C Levy Co Delta *(G-10157)*	E	419 822-8286
EMD Millipore Corporation Norwood *(G-15599)*	C	513 631-0445
Pioneer Sands LLC Glenford *(G-11433)*	E	740 659-2241
Pioneer Sands LLC Howard *(G-12081)*	E	740 599-7773

MINIATURE GOLF COURSES

Company	Code	Phone
Goofy Golf II Inc Port Clinton *(G-16245)*	D	419 732-6671
Recreational Golf Inc Loveland *(G-13156)*	E	513 677-0347
Stonehedge Enterprises Inc Akron *(G-451)*	E	330 928-2161
Three D Golf LLC Batavia *(G-1027)*	E	513 732-0295

MINING MACHINES & EQPT: Crushers, Stationary

Company	Code	Phone
Grasan Equipment Company Inc Mansfield *(G-13306)*	D	419 526-4440

MISC FINAN INVEST ACTIVITY: Mutual Fund, Ind Salesperson

Company	Code	Phone
Ameriprise Financial Svcs Inc Worthington *(G-19940)*	D	614 846-8723
Axa Advisors LLC Columbus *(G-7079)*	C	614 985-3015
First Command Fncl Plg Inc Beavercreek *(G-1241)*	E	937 429-4490
Nationwide Fin Inst Dis Agency Columbus *(G-8241)*	D	614 249-6825
Ultimus Fund Solutions LLC Cincinnati *(G-4725)*	E	513 587-3400

MIXTURES & BLOCKS: Asphalt Paving

Company	Code	Phone
Barrett Paving Materials Inc Middletown *(G-14475)*	C	513 271-6200
Hy-Grade Corporation Cleveland *(G-5795)*	E	216 341-7711
Image Pavement Maintenance Brookville *(G-1963)*	E	937 833-9200
Mplx Terminals LLC Canton *(G-2466)*	B	330 479-5539
Shelly and Sands Inc Rayland *(G-16418)*	D	740 859-2104
Sidwell Materials Inc Zanesville *(G-20533)*	C	740 849-2394
Smalls Asphalt Paving Inc Gambier *(G-11350)*	E	740 427-4096
Stoneco Inc Oakwood *(G-15624)*	E	419 393-2555

MOBILE HOME REPAIR SVCS

Company	Code	Phone
Sirpilla Recrtl Vhcl Ctr Inc Akron *(G-439)*	D	330 494-2525

MOBILE HOMES, EXC RECREATIONAL

Company	Code	Phone
Manufactured Housing Entps Inc Bryan *(G-2011)*	C	419 636-4511

MODELS

Company	Code	Phone
Morris Technologies Inc Cincinnati *(G-4119)*	C	513 733-1611

MODELS: General, Exc Toy

Company	Code	Phone
3-D Technical Services Company Franklin *(G-11147)*	E	937 746-2901

MOLDED RUBBER PRDTS

Company	Code	Phone
Datwyler Sling Sltions USA Inc Vandalia *(G-18676)*	D	937 387-2800
Jet Rubber Company Rootstown *(G-16597)*	E	330 325-1821

MOLDING COMPOUNDS

Company	Code	Phone
Flex Technologies Inc Baltic *(G-945)*	E	330 897-6311

MOLDING SAND MINING

Company	Code	Phone
Standex International Corp Cincinnati *(G-4580)*	E	513 871-3777

MOLDS: Indl

Company	Code	Phone
Akron Centl Engrv Mold Mch Inc Akron *(G-30)*	E	330 794-8704

MOLDS: Plastic Working & Foundry

Company	Code	Phone
Eger Products Inc Amelia *(G-580)*	D	513 753-4200
Prospect Mold & Die Company Cuyahoga Falls *(G-9214)*	D	330 929-3311

MONEY ORDER ISSUANCE SVCS

Company	Code	Phone
Sack n Save Inc Marion *(G-13578)*	E	740 382-2464

MONTESSORI CHILD DEVELOPMENT CENTER

Company	Code	Phone
All Around Children Montessori Stow *(G-17351)*	E	330 928-1444
Bay Village Montessori Inc Westlake *(G-19464)*	E	440 871-8773
Brookdale Senior Living Inc Cincinnati *(G-3140)*	D	513 745-7600
Canton Montessori Association Canton *(G-2293)*	E	330 452-0148
Creative Playroom Solon *(G-16997)*	E	440 248-3100
Fairmount Montessori Assn Cleveland *(G-5565)*	E	216 321-7571
Nightingale Montessori Inc Springfield *(G-17252)*	E	937 324-0336
Ruffing Montessori School Rocky River *(G-16591)*	E	440 333-2250
West Side Montessori Toledo *(G-18306)*	D	419 866-1931
Westlake Mntsr Schl & Chld Dv Westlake *(G-19568)*	E	440 835-5858

MOPS: Floor & Dust

Company	Code	Phone
Impact Products LLC Toledo *(G-17971)*	C	419 841-2891

MORTGAGE BANKERS

Company	Code	Phone
American Equity Mortgage Inc Dublin *(G-10247)*	D	800 236-2600
American Midwest Mortgage Corp Cleveland *(G-5014)*	E	440 882-5210
Broadview Mortgage Company Powell *(G-16327)*	E	614 854-7000
Chase Manhattan Mortgage Corp Columbus *(G-7253)*	C	614 422-7982
Fairway Independent Mrtg Corp Harrison *(G-11798)*	E	513 367-6344
First Union Banc Corp Uniontown *(G-18521)*	D	330 896-1222
Firstmerit Mortgage Corp Canton *(G-2368)*	D	330 478-3400
Hallmark Home Mortgage LLC Columbus *(G-7795)*	E	614 568-1960
Home Loan Financial Corp Coshocton *(G-9106)*	E	740 622-0444
Huntington National Bank Cincinnati *(G-3799)*	C	513 762-1860
Huntington National Bank Chillicothe *(G-2852)*	E	740 773-2681
Huntington National Bank Lima *(G-12801)*	E	419 226-8200
Jpmorgan Chase Bank Nat Assn Columbus *(G-6888)*	A	614 436-3055
Lancaster Pollard Mrtg Co LLC Columbus *(G-8034)*	D	614 224-8800
Liberty Capital Services LLC Worthington *(G-19973)*	E	614 505-0620
Mortgage Now Inc Cleveland *(G-6079)*	E	800 245-1050
Nations Lending Corporation Independence *(G-12238)*	D	440 842-4817
Nationstar Mortgage LLC Columbus *(G-8228)*	E	614 985-9500
Northern Ohio Investment Co Sylvania *(G-17601)*	D	419 885-8300
Old Rpblic Ttle Nthrn Ohio LLC Independence *(G-12242)*	A	216 524-5700
Primero Home Loans LLC Dublin *(G-10431)*	E	877 959-2921
Priority Mortgage Corp Worthington *(G-19986)*	E	614 431-1141
Quicken Loans Inc Cleveland *(G-6336)*	E	216 586-8900
Security Savings Mortgage Corp Canton *(G-2524)*	D	330 455-2833
Sibcy Cline Inc West Chester *(G-19152)*	D	513 777-8100
Sirva Mortgage Inc Independence *(G-12258)*	D	800 531-3837
Union Home Mortgage Corp Strongsville *(G-17517)*	E	440 234-4300

MORTGAGE COMPANIES: Urban

Company	Code	Phone
G & G Investment LLC Blue Ash *(G-1598)*	D	513 984-0300

MOTEL

Company	Code	Phone
1st Stop Inc Winchester *(G-19798)*	E	937 695-0318
Alsan Corporation East Liverpool *(G-10514)*	D	330 385-3636
Commodore Resorts Inc Port Clinton *(G-16241)*	E	419 285-3101
Detroit Westfield LLC Akron *(G-190)*	D	330 666-4131
East End Ro Burton Inc Willoughby *(G-19660)*	E	440 942-2742
Econo Lodge Sandusky *(G-16750)*	D	419 627-8000
Elbe Properties Cincinnati *(G-3545)*	A	513 489-1955
Motel 6 Operating LP Columbus *(G-8190)*	E	614 431-2525
Motel Investments Marietta Inc Marietta *(G-13479)*	E	740 374-8190
R P L Corporation Troy *(G-18373)*	E	937 335-0021
Westlake Marriott Westlake *(G-19567)*	E	440 892-6887

MOTION PICTURE & VIDEO DISTRIBUTION

Company	Code	Phone
Technicolor Thomson Group Wilmington *(G-19790)*	C	937 383-6000
Zebo Productions Troy *(G-18388)*	D	937 339-0397

MOTION PICTURE & VIDEO PRODUCTION SVCS

Company	Code	Phone
Fastball Spt Productions LLC Cleveland *(G-5576)*	E	440 746-8000
Province of St John The Baptis Cincinnati *(G-4352)*	D	513 241-5615
Shadoart Productions Inc Columbus *(G-8720)*	E	614 227-6125
Shalom Ministries Intl Inc Plain City *(G-16205)*	E	614 504-6052

MOTION PICTURE DISTRIBUTION SVCS

Technicolor Thomson Group .... C 937 383-6000
Wilmington *(G-19790)*

MOTION PICTURE PRODUCTION & DISTRIBUTION

Mills/James Inc .... C 614 777-9933
Hilliard *(G-11937)*

MOTION PICTURE PRODUCTION & DISTRIBUTION: Television

Estreamz Inc .... E 513 278-7836
Cincinnati *(G-3577)*
Fox Television Stations Inc .... C 216 432-4278
Cleveland *(G-5627)*

MOTION PICTURE PRODUCTION ALLIED SVCS

Mills/James Inc .... C 614 777-9933
Hilliard *(G-11937)*
Signal Productions Inc .... E 323 382-0000
Cleveland *(G-6482)*

MOTOR INN

Dino Persichetti .... E 330 821-9600
Alliance *(G-538)*

MOTOR REBUILDING SVCS, EXC AUTOMOTIVE

Integrated Power Services LLC ..... E 513 863-8816
Hamilton *(G-11746)*

MOTOR SCOOTERS & PARTS

Dco LLC .... B 419 931-9086
Perrysburg *(G-15996)*

MOTOR VEHICLE ASSEMBLY, COMPLETE: Autos, Incl Specialty

Brookville Roadster Inc .... E 937 833-4605
Brookville *(G-1961)*
P C Workshop Inc .... D 419 399-4805
Paulding *(G-15932)*

MOTOR VEHICLE ASSEMBLY, COMPLETE: Fire Department Vehicles

Sutphen Corporation .... C 800 726-7030
Dublin *(G-10468)*

MOTOR VEHICLE DEALERS: Automobiles, New & Used

1106 West Main Inc .... E 330 673-2122
Kent *(G-12350)*
Advantage Ford Lincoln Mercury ... E 419 334-9751
Fremont *(G-11182)*
Affordable Cars & Finance Inc ..... E 440 777-2424
North Olmsted *(G-15410)*
Aladdins Enterprises Inc .... E 614 891-3440
Westerville *(G-19361)*
Allstate Trk Sls of Estrn OH .... E 330 339-5555
New Philadelphia *(G-15080)*
Arch Abraham Susuki Ltd .... E 440 934-6001
Elyria *(G-10594)*
Auto Center USA Inc .... E 513 683-4900
Cincinnati *(G-3066)*
Bauman Chrysler Jeep Dodge ...... E 419 332-8291
Fremont *(G-11185)*
Beechmont Ford Inc .... C 513 752-6611
Cincinnati *(G-2904)*
Beechmont Motors Inc .... E 513 388-3883
Cincinnati *(G-3089)*
Beechmont Toyota Inc .... D 513 388-3800
Cincinnati *(G-3092)*
Bill Delord Autocenter Inc .... D 513 932-3000
Lebanon *(G-12592)*
Bob Pulte Chevrolet Inc .... E 513 932-0303
Lebanon *(G-12593)*
Bob-Boyd Ford Inc .... D 614 860-0606
Lancaster *(G-12510)*
Bobb Automotive Inc .... E 614 853-3000
Columbus *(G-7123)*

Bowling Green Lncln-Mrcury Inc .... E 419 352-2553
Bowling Green *(G-1765)*
Brentlinger Enterprises .... C 614 889-2571
Dublin *(G-10267)*
Busam Fairfield LLC .... E 513 771-8100
Fairfield *(G-10825)*
Cain Motors Inc .... E 330 494-5588
Canton *(G-2280)*
Carcorp Inc .... C 877 857-2801
Columbus *(G-7189)*
Cascade Group Inc .... E 330 929-1861
Cuyahoga Falls *(G-9169)*
Central Cadillac Limited .... D 216 861-5800
Cleveland *(G-5209)*
Chesrown Oldsmobile Cadillac ... E 740 366-7373
Granville *(G-11461)*
Chesrown Oldsmobile GMC Inc ... E 614 846-3040
Dublin *(G-7255)*
Chuck Nicholson Pntc-GMC Trcks ... E 330 343-7781
Dover *(G-10180)*
Classic Buick Olds Cadillac .... D 440 639-4500
Painesville *(G-15842)*
Classic International Inc .... E 440 975-1222
Mentor *(G-14158)*
Cole-Valley Motor Co .... E 330 372-1665
Warren *(G-18835)*
Columbus SAI Motors LLC .... E 614 851-3273
Columbus *(G-7383)*
Coughlin Chevrolet Inc .... E 740 852-1122
London *(G-12995)*
Coughlin Chevrolet Inc .... D 740 964-9191
Pataskala *(G-15922)*
Coughlin Chevrolet Toyota Inc ...... D 740 366-1381
Newark *(G-15162)*
Crestmont Cadillac Corporation ... E 216 831-5300
Cleveland *(G-5437)*
Cronins Inc .... E 513 851-5900
Cincinnati *(G-3440)*
Dan Tobin Pontiac Buick GMC ...... D 614 889-6300
Columbus *(G-7484)*
Dave Dnnis Chrysler Jeep Dodge ... E 937 429-5566
Beavercreek Township *(G-1267)*
Dave Knapp Ford Lincoln Inc .... E 937 547-3000
Greenville *(G-11496)*
Dave White Chevrolet Inc .... C 419 885-4444
Sylvania *(G-17581)*
Decosky Motor Holdings Inc .... E 740 397-9122
Mount Vernon *(G-14892)*
Diane Sauer Chevrolet Inc .... D 330 373-1600
Warren *(G-18850)*
Don Tester Ford Lincoln Inc .... E 419 668-8233
Norwalk *(G-15570)*
Don Wood Bck Oldsmble Pntiac C ... D 740 593-6641
Athens *(G-783)*
Don Wood Inc .... D 740 593-6641
Athens *(G-784)*
Donley Ford-Lincoln Inc .... E 419 281-3673
Ashland *(G-679)*
Donnell Ford-Lincoln .... E 330 332-0031
Salem *(G-16694)*
Dons Automotive Group LLC .... E 419 337-3010
Wauseon *(G-18951)*
Dons Brooklyn Chevrolet Inc .... E 216 741-1500
Cleveland *(G-5504)*
Doug Bigelow Chevrolet Inc .... D 330 644-7500
Akron *(G-198)*
Doug Marine Motors Inc .... E 740 335-3700
Wshngtn CT Hs *(G-20020)*
Downtheroad Inc .... E 740 452-4579
Zanesville *(G-20469)*
Downtown Ford Lincoln Inc .... D 330 456-2781
Canton *(G-2344)*
Dunning Motor Sales Inc .... E 740 439-4465
Cambridge *(G-2110)*
Dutro Ford Lincoln-Mercury Inc ... D 740 452-6334
Zanesville *(G-20470)*
Ed Mullinax Ford LLC .... C 440 984-2431
Amherst *(G-591)*
Ed Schmidt Auto Inc .... E 419 874-4331
Perrysburg *(G-16001)*
Ed Schmidt Chevrolet Inc .... D 419 897-8600
Maumee *(G-13908)*
Ed Tomko Chryslr Jep Dge Inc .... E 440 835-5900
Avon Lake *(G-929)*
Falls Motor City Inc .... E 330 929-3066
Cuyahoga Falls *(G-9184)*
Family Ford Lincoln .... D 740 373-9127
Marietta *(G-13445)*
Fred Martin Nissan LLC .... E 330 644-8888
Akron *(G-229)*

Gene Stevens Auto & Truck Ctr .... E 419 429-2000
Findlay *(G-11036)*
George P Ballas Buick GMC Trck ... D 419 535-1000
Toledo *(G-17913)*
Germain Ford LLC .... C 614 889-7777
Columbus *(G-7747)*
Germain On Scarborough LLC ... C 614 868-0300
Columbus *(G-7748)*
Graham Chevrolet-Cadillac Co ... D 419 989-4012
Ontario *(G-15690)*
Greenwood Chevrolet Inc .... E 330 270-1299
Youngstown *(G-20209)*
Greenwoods Hubbard Chevy-Olds ... E 330 568-4335
Hubbard *(G-12087)*
Greg Ford Sweet Inc .... E 440 593-7714
North Kingsville *(G-15391)*
Grogans Towne Chrysler Inc .... C 419 476-0761
Toledo *(G-17924)*
Guess Motors Inc .... E 866 890-0522
Carrollton *(G-2622)*
Haydocy Automotive Inc .... D 614 279-8880
Columbus *(G-7804)*
Herrnstein Chrysler Inc .... D 740 773-2203
Chillicothe *(G-2846)*
Hidy Motors Inc .... D 937 426-9564
Dayton *(G-9272)*
Hoss Value Cars & Trucks Inc ...... E 937 428-2400
Dayton *(G-9622)*
Jeff Wyler Chevrolet Inc .... B 513 752-3447
Batavia *(G-1018)*
Jerry Haag Motors Inc .... E 937 402-2090
Hillsboro *(G-11984)*
Jim Brown Chevrolet Inc .... C 440 255-5511
Mentor *(G-14197)*
Jim Keim Ford .... D 614 888-3333
Columbus *(G-7941)*
Joe Dodge Kidd Inc .... E 513 752-1804
Cincinnati *(G-2921)*
Joseph Chevrolet Oldsmobile Co ... C 513 741-6700
Cincinnati *(G-3887)*
Joyce Buick Inc .... E 419 529-3211
Ontario *(G-15696)*
Kempthorn Automall .... D 800 451-3877
Canton *(G-2422)*
Kempthorn Automall .... C 330 456-8287
Canton *(G-2423)*
Kent Automotive Inc .... D 330 678-5520
Kent *(G-12377)*
Kerns Chevrolet-Buick-Gmc Inc ... E 419 586-5131
Celina *(G-2649)*
Kerry Ford Inc .... D 513 671-6400
Cincinnati *(G-3918)*
Kings Cove Automotive LLC .... D 513 677-0177
Fairfield *(G-10870)*
Kings Toyota Inc .... D 513 583-4333
Cincinnati *(G-3928)*
Klaben Family Dodge Inc .... E 330 673-9971
Kent *(G-12381)*
Klaben Lincoln Ford Inc .... D 330 673-3139
Kent *(G-12383)*
Krieger Ford Inc .... C 614 888-3320
Columbus *(G-8014)*
Lakewood Chrysler-Plymouth ..... E 216 521-1000
Brookpark *(G-1950)*
Lane Chevrolet .... D 937 426-2313
Beavercreek Township *(G-1273)*
Lang Chevrolet Co .... D 937 426-2313
Beavercreek Township *(G-1274)*
Laria Chevrolet-Buick Inc .... E 330 925-2015
Rittman *(G-16553)*
Lariche Subaru Inc .... D 419 422-1855
Findlay *(G-11056)*
Lavery Chevrolet-Buick Inc .... E 330 823-1100
Alliance *(G-544)*
Lebanon Chrysler - Plymouth Inc ... E 513 932-2717
Lebanon *(G-12620)*
Lebanon Ford Inc .... D 513 932-1010
Lebanon *(G-12621)*
Leikin Motor Companies Inc .... D 440 946-6900
Willoughby *(G-19686)*
Liberty Ford Southwest Inc .... D 440 888-2600
Cleveland *(G-5939)*
Lima Auto Mall Inc .... D 419 993-6000
Lima *(G-12816)*
Lincoln Mrcury Kings Auto Mall ... C 513 683-3800
Cincinnati *(G-3984)*
Lindsey Accura Inc .... E 800 980-8199
Columbus *(G-8070)*
Man-Tansky Inc .... E 740 454-2512
Zanesville *(G-20499)*

Mark Thomas Ford Inc..........E....... 330 638-1010
Cortland *(G-9077)*
Martin Chevrolet Inc..........E....... 937 849-1381
New Carlisle *(G-15027)*
Mathews Dodge Chrysler Jeep..........E....... 740 389-2341
Marion *(G-13563)*
Mathews Ford Inc..........D....... 740 522-2181
Newark *(G-15202)*
Mathews Kennedy Ford L-M Inc..........D....... 740 387-3673
Marion *(G-13564)*
Matia Motors Inc..........E....... 440 365-7311
Elyria *(G-10650)*
Mc Daniel Motor Co (Inc)..........E....... 740 389-2355
Marion *(G-13565)*
McCluskey Chevrolet Inc..........C....... 513 761-1111
Cincinnati *(G-4035)*
Medina World Cars Inc..........E....... 330 725-4901
Strongsville *(G-17493)*
Merrick Body Shop..........E....... 440 243-6700
Berea *(G-1463)*
Merrick Chevrolet Co..........D....... 440 878-6700
Strongsville *(G-17494)*
Mike Castrucci Ford..........C....... 513 831-7010
Milford *(G-14541)*
Montrose Ford Inc..........D....... 330 666-0711
Fairlawn *(G-10966)*
Montrose Sheffield LLC..........E....... 440 934-6699
Sheffield Village *(G-16892)*
Morris Cadillac Buick GMC..........D....... 440 327-4181
North Olmsted *(G-15432)*
Mullinax East LLC..........D....... 440 296-3020
Wickliffe *(G-19608)*
Mullinax Ford North Canton Inc..........C....... 330 238-3206
Canton *(G-2468)*
Nassief Automotive Inc..........E....... 440 997-5151
Austinburg *(G-865)*
Nick Mayer Lincoln-Mercury Inc..........E....... 440 835-3700
Westlake *(G-19521)*
Northern Automotive Inc..........E....... 614 436-2001
Columbus *(G-8290)*
Northgate Chrysler Jeep Inc..........D....... 513 385-3900
Cincinnati *(G-4180)*
Oregon Ford Inc..........C....... 419 698-4444
Oregon *(G-15746)*
Partners Auto Group Bdford Inc..........D....... 440 439-2323
Bedford *(G-1329)*
Paul Hrnchar Ford-Mercury Inc..........E....... 330 533-3673
Canfield *(G-2207)*
Performance Pontc-Oldmbl GM Tr..........E....... 330 264-1113
Wooster *(G-19902)*
Pete Baur Buick Gmc Inc..........E....... 440 238-5600
Cleveland *(G-6270)*
Pierson Automotive Inc..........E....... 513 424-1881
Middletown *(G-14485)*
Progrssive Oldsmobile Cadillac..........E....... 330 833-8585
Massillon *(G-13845)*
Ricart Ford Inc..........B....... 614 836-5321
Groveport *(G-11667)*
Ron Marhofer Automall Inc..........B....... 330 835-6707
Cuyahoga Falls *(G-9216)*
Ron Marhofer Automall Inc..........E....... 330 923-5059
Cuyahoga Falls *(G-9217)*
Rouen Chrysler Plymouth Dodge..........E....... 419 837-6228
Woodville *(G-19824)*
Roush Equipment Inc..........C....... 614 882-1535
Westerville *(G-19442)*
Rush Motor Sales Inc..........E....... 614 471-9980
Columbus *(G-8659)*
Saturn of Toledo Inc..........E....... 419 841-9070
Toledo *(G-18173)*
Schoner Chevrolet Inc..........E....... 330 877-6731
Hartville *(G-11830)*
Sharpnack Chevrolet Co..........E....... 440 967-3144
Vermilion *(G-18716)*
Sharpnack Chvrlet Bick Cdillac..........D....... 419 935-0194
Willard *(G-19626)*
Sims Buick-G M C Truck Inc..........D....... 330 372-3500
Warren *(G-18900)*
Slimans Sales & Service Inc..........E....... 440 988-4484
Amherst *(G-604)*
Sonic Automotive..........D....... 614 870-8200
Columbus *(G-8748)*
Sonic Automotive-1495 Automall..........E....... 614 317-4326
Columbus *(G-8749)*
Sorbir Inc..........D....... 440 449-1000
Cleveland *(G-6495)*
South East Chevrolet Co..........E....... 440 585-9300
Willoughby Hills *(G-19735)*
Spires Motors Inc..........E....... 614 771-2345
Hilliard *(G-11953)*
Spitzer Auto World Amherst..........D....... 440 988-4444
Amherst *(G-605)*
Spitzer Chevrolet Company..........E....... 330 966-9524
Canton *(G-2535)*
Spitzer Chevrolet Inc..........D....... 330 467-4141
Northfield *(G-15524)*
Stoddard Imported Cars Inc..........D....... 440 951-1040
Mentor *(G-14245)*
Stratton Chevrolet Co..........E....... 330 537-3151
Beloit *(G-1432)*
Stykemain Pntiac-Buick-Gmc Ltd..........D....... 419 784-5252
Defiance *(G-10059)*
Sunnyside Toyota Inc..........D....... 440 777-9911
North Olmsted *(G-15446)*
Surfside Motors Inc..........E....... 419 462-1746
Galion *(G-11306)*
Sweeny Walt Pntc GMC Trck Sles..........E....... 513 621-4888
Cincinnati *(G-4607)*
Tansky Motors Inc..........E....... 650 322-7069
Logan *(G-12989)*
Taylor Chevrolet Inc..........C....... 740 653-2091
Lancaster *(G-12579)*
Tbn Acquisition LLC..........D....... 740 653-2091
Lancaster *(G-12580)*
Team Rahal of Dayton Inc..........E....... 937 438-3800
Dayton *(G-9921)*
Tom Ahl Chryslr-Plymouth-Dodge..........C....... 419 227-0202
Lima *(G-12901)*
Toyota of Bedford..........D....... 440 439-8600
Bedford *(G-1341)*
Trader Buds Westside Dodge..........D....... 614 272-0000
Columbus *(G-8861)*
Transitworks LLC..........D....... 330 861-1118
Akron *(G-480)*
Transmerica Svcs Technical Sup..........E....... 740 282-3695
Steubenville *(G-17338)*
Troutwine Auto Sales Inc..........E....... 937 692-8373
Arcanum *(G-631)*
Valentine Buick Gmc Inc..........D....... 937 878-7371
Fairborn *(G-10808)*
Valley Ford Truck Inc..........D....... 216 524-2400
Cleveland *(G-6683)*
Van Devere Inc..........D....... 330 253-6137
Akron *(G-494)*
Village Motors Inc..........D....... 330 674-2055
Millersburg *(G-14626)*
Vin Devers..........C....... 888 847-9535
Sylvania *(G-17626)*
Volvo BMW Dyton Evans Volkswag..........E....... 937 890-6200
Dayton *(G-9975)*
Voss Auto Network Inc..........E....... 937 428-2447
Dayton *(G-9976)*
Voss Chevrolet Inc..........C....... 937 428-2500
Dayton *(G-9978)*
Voss Dodge..........E....... 937 435-7800
Dayton *(G-9979)*
Voss Toyota Inc..........E....... 937 427-3700
Beavercreek *(G-1218)*
Wagner Lincoln-Mercury Inc..........E....... 419 435-8131
Carey *(G-2601)*
Walker Auto Group Inc..........D....... 937 433-4950
Miamisburg *(G-14367)*
Warner Buick-Nissan Inc..........E....... 419 423-7161
Findlay *(G-11099)*
White Family Companies Inc..........C....... 937 222-3701
Dayton *(G-9996)*
Whites Service Center Inc..........E....... 937 653-5279
Urbana *(G-18602)*
Yark Automotive Group Inc..........C....... 419 841-7771
Toledo *(G-18319)*
Young Truck Sales Inc..........E....... 330 477-6271
Canton *(G-2592)*
Zanesville Chevrolet Cadillac..........E....... 740 452-3611
Zanesville *(G-20554)*

MOTOR VEHICLE DEALERS: Cars, Used Only

Afford-A-Car Inc..........E....... 937 235-2700
Tipp City *(G-17710)*
Albert Mike Leasing Inc..........C....... 513 563-1400
Cincinnati *(G-2982)*
Coughlin Chevrolet Inc..........E....... 740 852-1122
London *(G-12995)*
D & D Rv and Auto LLC..........E....... 937 839-4555
West Alexandria *(G-19008)*
Hertz Corporation..........E....... 937 890-2721
Vandalia *(G-18683)*
Kenton Auto and Truck Wrecking..........E....... 419 673-8234
Kenton *(G-12420)*
May Jim Auto Sales LLC..........E....... 419 422-9797
Findlay *(G-11063)*
Merrick Body Shop..........E....... 440 243-6700
Berea *(G-1463)*
Midwest Motors Inc..........E....... 330 758-5800
Youngstown *(G-20286)*
Montpelier Auto Auction Ohio..........C....... 419 485-1691
Montpelier *(G-14744)*
Stricker Bros Inc..........E....... 513 732-1152
Batavia *(G-1026)*
Volunters of Amer Greater Ohio..........C....... 614 253-6100
Columbus *(G-8951)*
Voss Auto Network Inc..........B....... 937 433-1444
Dayton *(G-9977)*

MOTOR VEHICLE DEALERS: Pickups & Vans, Used

Life Star Rescue Inc..........E....... 419 238-2507
Van Wert *(G-18637)*

MOTOR VEHICLE DEALERS: Pickups, New & Used

Palmer Trucks Inc..........E....... 937 235-3318
Dayton *(G-9799)*

MOTOR VEHICLE DEALERS: Trucks, Tractors/Trailers, New & Used

Abers Garage Inc..........E....... 419 281-5500
Ashland *(G-649)*
Allied Truck Parts Co..........E....... 330 477-8127
Canton *(G-2234)*
Benedict Enterprises Inc..........E....... 513 539-9216
Monroe *(G-14690)*
Fallsway Equipment Co Inc..........C....... 330 633-6000
Akron *(G-214)*
Freightlner Trcks of Cncinnati..........E....... 513 772-7171
Cincinnati *(G-3651)*
Hans Truck and Trlr Repr Inc..........E....... 216 581-0046
Cleveland *(G-5724)*
Hill Intl Trcks NA LLC..........D....... 330 386-6440
East Liverpool *(G-10522)*
Mansfield Truck Sales & Svc..........E....... 419 522-9811
Mansfield *(G-13335)*
Mizar Motors Inc..........D....... 419 729-2400
Toledo *(G-18065)*
R & R Inc..........E....... 330 799-1536
Youngstown *(G-20338)*
R & R Truck Sales Inc..........E....... 330 784-5881
Akron *(G-402)*
Rumpke/Kenworth Contract..........D....... 740 774-5111
Chillicothe *(G-2883)*
Steubenville Truck Center Inc..........E....... 740 282-2711
Steubenville *(G-17337)*
Stoops Frghtlnr-Qlity Trlr Inc..........E....... 937 236-4092
Dayton *(G-9909)*
Stoops of Lima Inc..........C....... 419 228-4334
Lima *(G-12894)*
Truck Country Indiana Inc..........C....... 419 228-4334
Lima *(G-12907)*

MOTOR VEHICLE PARTS & ACCESS: Body Components & Frames

Frontier Tank Center Inc..........E....... 330 659-3888
Richfield *(G-16510)*

MOTOR VEHICLE PARTS & ACCESS: Booster Cables, Jump-Start

Noco Company..........B....... 216 464-8131
Solon *(G-17035)*

MOTOR VEHICLE PARTS & ACCESS: Clutches

Westfield Steel Inc..........D....... 937 322-2414
Springfield *(G-17299)*

MOTOR VEHICLE PARTS & ACCESS: Engines & Parts

Fram Group Operations LLC..........D....... 419 661-6700
Perrysburg *(G-16005)*
Hite Parts Exchange Inc..........E....... 614 272-5115
Columbus *(G-7842)*
Keihin Thermal Tech Amer Inc..........B....... 740 869-3000
Mount Sterling *(G-14873)*

Employee Codes: A=Over 500 employees, B=251-500
C=101-250, D=51-100, E=25-50
2018 Harris Ohio
Services Directory
1565

MOTOR VEHICLE PARTS & ACCESS: Fuel Systems & Parts

MOTOR VEHICLE PARTS & ACCESS: Fuel Systems & Parts

Interstate Diesel Service Inc .... C 216 881-0015
  Cleveland (G-5834)

MOTOR VEHICLE PARTS & ACCESS: Mufflers, Exhaust

Faurecia Exhaust Systems LLC .... C 419 727-5000
  Toledo (G-17880)

MOTOR VEHICLE PARTS & ACCESS: Power Steering Eqpt

Maval Industries LLC .... C 330 405-1600
  Twinsburg (G-18445)

MOTOR VEHICLE PARTS & ACCESS: Pumps, Hydraulic Fluid Power

Eaton Corporation .... B 216 523-5000
  Beachwood (G-1075)
Eaton Corporation .... B 216 920-2000
  Cleveland (G-5524)

MOTOR VEHICLE PARTS & ACCESS: Wiring Harness Sets

G S Wiring Systems Inc .... B 419 423-7111
  Findlay (G-11034)
Sumitomo Elc Wirg Systems Inc .... E 937 642-7579
  Marysville (G-13653)

MOTOR VEHICLE RACING & DRIVER SVCS

Brush Creek Motorsports .... E 937 515-1353
  West Union (G-19275)
Team Rahal Inc .... D 614 529-7000
  Hilliard (G-11957)

MOTOR VEHICLE SPLYS & PARTS WHOLESALERS: New

Ace Truck Body Inc .... E 614 871-3100
  Grove City (G-11527)
Aftermarket Parts Company LLC .... D 888 333-6224
  Delaware (G-10068)
Beechmont Ford Inc .... C 513 752-6611
  Cincinnati (G-2904)
Beechmont Motors Inc .... E 513 388-3883
  Cincinnati (G-3089)
Beechmont Toyota Inc .... D 513 388-3800
  Cincinnati (G-3092)
Contitech North America Inc .... E 440 225-5363
  Akron (G-162)
Faurecia Exhaust Systems LLC .... C 419 727-5000
  Toledo (G-17880)
G S Wiring Systems Inc .... B 419 423-7111
  Findlay (G-11034)
General Motors LLC .... C 513 874-0535
  West Chester (G-19080)
General Motors LLC .... C 513 603-6600
  West Chester (G-19081)
GKN Driveline North Amer Inc .... D 419 354-3955
  Bowling Green (G-1777)
Goodyear Tire & Rubber Company ..... A 330 796-2121
  Akron (G-243)
Jr Engineering Inc .... C 330 848-0960
  Barberton (G-968)
Keystone Automotive Inds Inc .... E 330 759-8019
  Girard (G-11419)
Lower Great Lakes Kenworth Inc .... E 419 874-3511
  Perrysburg (G-16029)
Luk-Aftermarket Service Inc .... D 330 273-4383
  Valley City (G-18620)
Mac Trailer Manufacturing Inc .... C 330 823-9900
  Alliance (G-547)
Neff Machinery and Supplies .... E 740 454-0128
  Zanesville (G-20515)
Nk Parts Industries Inc .... E 937 493-4651
  Sidney (G-16943)
Pat Young Service Co Inc .... E 440 891-1550
  Avon (G-912)
Pioneer Automotive Tech Inc .... C 937 746-2293
  Springboro (G-17136)
Shrader Tire & Oil Inc .... E 419 472-2128
  Toledo (G-18186)
Tk Holdings Inc .... E 937 778-9713
  Piqua (G-16168)
Truckomat Corporation .... E 740 467-2818
  Hebron (G-11861)
Western Tradewinds Inc .... E 937 859-4300
  Miamisburg (G-14368)

MOTOR VEHICLE SPLYS & PARTS WHOLESALERS: Used

Advance Auto Parts Inc .... E 440 226-3150
  Chardon (G-2738)
Beheydts Auto Wrecking .... E 330 658-6109
  Doylestown (G-10223)
Dales Truck Parts Inc .... E 937 766-2551
  Cedarville (G-2632)
General Motors LLC .... C 513 603-6600
  West Chester (G-19081)
Mac Trailer Manufacturing Inc .... C 330 823-9900
  Alliance (G-547)
Nk Parts Industries Inc .... E 937 493-4651
  Sidney (G-16943)

MOTOR VEHICLE: Shock Absorbers

Thyssenkrupp Bilstein Amer Inc .... C 513 881-7600
  Hamilton (G-11778)

MOTOR VEHICLES & CAR BODIES

Bobbart Industries Inc .... E 419 350-5477
  Sylvania (G-17576)
Comprehensive Logistics Co Inc .... E 330 793-0504
  Youngstown (G-20158)
Honda of America Mfg Inc .... C 937 644-0724
  Marysville (G-13626)

MOTOR VEHICLES, WHOLESALE: Ambulances

Community Emrgcy Med Svcs Ohio .... C 614 751-6651
  Columbus (G-7404)
Life Star Rescue Inc .... E 419 238-2507
  Van Wert (G-18637)

MOTOR VEHICLES, WHOLESALE: Commercial

Interstate Truckway Inc .... D 513 542-5500
  Cincinnati (G-3838)
Sharron Group Inc .... E 614 873-5856
  Plain City (G-16206)

MOTOR VEHICLES, WHOLESALE: Trailers, Truck, New & Used

Bulk Carrier Trnsp Eqp Co .... E 330 339-3333
  New Philadelphia (G-15083)
Great Dane Columbus Inc .... E 614 876-0666
  Hilliard (G-11904)
Great Dane LLC .... E 614 876-0666
  Hilliard (G-11905)
M H EBY Inc .... E 614 879-6901
  West Jefferson (G-19253)
Mac Manufacturing Inc .... A 330 823-9900
  Alliance (G-546)
Mac Manufacturing Inc .... C 330 829-1680
  Salem (G-16704)
Mac Trailer Manufacturing Inc .... C 330 823-9900
  Alliance (G-547)
Worldwide Equipment Inc .... D 513 563-6363
  Cincinnati (G-4860)

MOTOR VEHICLES, WHOLESALE: Truck bodies

Ace Truck Body Inc .... E 614 871-3100
  Grove City (G-11527)
Brown Industrial Inc .... E 937 693-3838
  Botkins (G-1752)
Buckeye Truck Equipment Inc .... E 614 299-1136
  Columbus (G-7162)
Schodorf Truck Body & Eqp Co .... E 614 228-6793
  Columbus (G-8698)
Venco Venturo Industries LLC .... E 513 772-8448
  Cincinnati (G-4806)

MOTOR VEHICLES, WHOLESALE: Truck tractors

Bulldawg Holdings LLC .... E 419 423-3131
  Findlay (G-11010)
Helton Enterprises Inc .... E 419 423-4180
  Findlay (G-11046)
Peterbilt of Cincinnati .... E 513 772-1740
  Cincinnati (G-4285)
Peterbilt of Northwest Ohio .... E 419 423-3441
  Findlay (G-11073)

MOTOR VEHICLES, WHOLESALE: Trucks, commercial

Bob Sumerel Tire Co Inc .... E 513 792-6600
  Cincinnati (G-3125)
Cerni Motor Sales Inc .... D 330 652-9917
  Youngstown (G-20136)
Esec Corporation .... E 330 799-1536
  Youngstown (G-20181)
Esec Corporation .... E 614 875-3732
  Grove City (G-11558)
Freightliner Trcks of Cncinnati .... E 513 772-7171
  Cincinnati (G-3651)
Fyda Freightliner Youngstown .... D 330 797-0224
  Youngstown (G-20192)
Kenworth of Cincinnati Inc .... D 513 771-5831
  Cincinnati (G-3916)
Liberty Ford Southwest Inc .... D 440 888-2600
  Cleveland (G-5939)
Lower Great Lakes Kenworth Inc .... E 419 874-3511
  Perrysburg (G-16029)
Mansfield Truck Sales & Svc .... E 419 522-9811
  Mansfield (G-13335)
Nollenberger Truck Center .... E 419 837-5996
  Stony Ridge (G-17348)
R & R Inc .... E 330 799-1536
  Youngstown (G-20338)
R & R Truck Sales Inc .... E 330 784-5881
  Akron (G-402)
Stoops of Lima Inc .... E 419 228-4334
  Lima (G-12894)
Tri-State Trailer Sales Inc .... E 412 747-7777
  West Chester (G-19237)
Truck Country Indiana Inc .... C 419 228-4334
  Lima (G-12907)
Whites Service Center Inc .... E 937 653-5279
  Urbana (G-18602)
Youngstown-Kenworth Inc .... E 330 534-9761
  Hubbard (G-12093)

MOTOR VEHICLES, WHOLESALE: Vans, commercial

State Park Motors Inc .... E 740 264-3113
  Steubenville (G-17334)

MOTORCYCLE DEALERS

AD Farrow LLC .... E 614 228-6353
  Columbus (G-6942)
Adventure Harley Davidson .... E 330 343-2295
  Dover (G-10175)
Damarc Inc .... E 330 454-6171
  Canton (G-2333)
Mid-Ohio Harley-Davidson Inc .... E 937 322-3590
  Springfield (G-17247)
Valley Harley Davidson Co .... E 740 695-9591
  Belmont (G-1431)
Wholecycle Inc .... E 330 929-8123
  Peninsula (G-15953)

MOTORCYCLE DEALERS

Carcorp Inc .... C 877 857-2801
  Columbus (G-7189)
Freedom Harley-Davidson Inc .... E 330 494-2453
  Canton (G-2371)
Randy L Fork Inc .... E 419 891-1230
  Maumee (G-13967)
Sonic Automotive-1495 Automall .... E 614 317-4326
  Columbus (G-8749)
South E Harley Davidson Sls Co .... E 440 439-5300
  Cleveland (G-6496)

MOTORCYCLE REPAIR SHOPS

AD Farrow LLC .... E 614 228-6353
  Columbus (G-6942)
Adventure Harley Davidson .... E 330 343-2295
  Dover (G-10175)
Damarc Inc .... E 330 454-6171
  Canton (G-2333)
Freedom Harley-Davidson Inc .... E 330 494-2453
  Canton (G-2371)

Mid-Ohio Harley-Davidson Inc E 937 322-3590
Springfield *(G-17247)*
No Cages Harley-Davidson E 614 764-2453
Plain City *(G-16202)*
Randy L Fork Inc E 419 891-1230
Maumee *(G-13967)*
Valley Harley Davidson Co E 740 695-9591
Belmont *(G-1431)*

MOTORCYCLES: Wholesalers

Ktm North America Inc D 855 215-6360
Amherst *(G-598)*
Wholecycle Inc E 330 929-8123
Peninsula *(G-15953)*

MOTORS: Electric

Ametek Tchnical Indus Pdts Inc D 330 677-3754
Kent *(G-12352)*
Hannon Company D 330 456-4728
Canton *(G-2393)*

MOTORS: Generators

City Machine Technologies Inc E 330 740-8186
Youngstown *(G-20142)*
GE Aviation Systems LLC B 937 898-5881
Vandalia *(G-18681)*
General Electric Company D 216 883-1000
Cleveland *(G-5667)*

MOVIE THEATERS, EXC DRIVE-IN

AMC Entertainment Inc E 614 846-6575
Columbus *(G-6982)*
AMC Entertainment Inc E 614 428-5716
Columbus *(G-6983)*
AMC Entertainment Inc E 216 749-0260
Brooklyn *(G-1904)*
American Multi-Cinema Inc E 216 749-0260
Cleveland *(G-5015)*
American Multi-Cinema Inc E 440 331-2826
Rocky River *(G-16569)*
Cincinnati Museum Center B 513 287-7000
Cincinnati *(G-3319)*
Cinemark Usa Inc E 330 965-2335
Youngstown *(G-20141)*
Cinemark Usa Inc C 216 447-8820
Cleveland *(G-5239)*
Cinemark Usa Inc E 330 908-1005
Macedonia *(G-13193)*
Cinemark Usa Inc E 419 589-7300
Ontario *(G-15685)*
Cinemark Usa Inc E 614 538-0403
Columbus *(G-7272)*
Cinemark Usa Inc E 330 497-9118
Canton *(G-2308)*
Cinemark Usa Inc E 614 527-3773
Hilliard *(G-11890)*
Cinemark Usa Inc E 614 471-7620
Gahanna *(G-11234)*
Cinemark Usa Inc E 330 345-2610
Wooster *(G-19843)*
Cinemark Usa Inc E 614 529-8547
Columbus *(G-7273)*
Drc Holdings Inc E 419 230-0188
Pandora *(G-15889)*
Great Eastern Theatre Company D 419 691-9668
Oregon *(G-15737)*
M E Theaters Inc E 937 596-6424
Jackson Center *(G-12323)*
Marcus Theatres Corporation E 614 759-6500
Pickerington *(G-16101)*
Marcus Theatres Corporation D 614 436-9818
Columbus *(G-8108)*
National Amusements Inc E 513 699-1500
Milford *(G-14544)*
National Amusements Inc E 513 699-1500
Cincinnati *(G-4136)*
National Amusements Inc D 419 215-3095
Maumee *(G-13949)*
Ohio Light Opera D 330 263-2345
Wooster *(G-19896)*
Quincy Amusements Inc E 419 874-2154
Perrysburg *(G-16048)*
Regal Cinemas Inc E 614 853-0850
Columbus *(G-8604)*
Regal Cinemas Inc E 330 723-4416
Medina *(G-14120)*
Regal Cinemas Inc E 440 975-8820
Willoughby *(G-19708)*
Regal Cinemas Inc E 937 431-9418
Beavercreek *(G-1203)*
Regal Cinemas Inc E 440 934-3356
Elyria *(G-10675)*
Regal Cinemas Inc E 330 666-9373
Akron *(G-406)*
Regal Cinemas Inc E 440 871-4546
Westlake *(G-19541)*
Regal Cinemas Inc E 330 758-0503
Youngstown *(G-20342)*
Regal Cinemas Inc E 330 633-7668
Akron *(G-407)*
Regal Cinemas Corporation E 513 770-0713
Mason *(G-13754)*
Regal Cinemas Corporation E 440 720-0500
Richmond Heights *(G-16541)*
Regal Cinemas Inc E 440 891-9845
Cleveland *(G-6367)*
Seminole Theater Co LLC E 440 934-6998
Avon Lake *(G-939)*

MOVING SVC & STORAGE: Local

Bell Moving and Storage Inc E 513 942-7500
Fairfield *(G-10823)*
Brendamour Moving & Stor Inc D 800 354-9715
Cincinnati *(G-3129)*
Corrigan Moving Systems-Ann AR E 419 874-2900
Perrysburg *(G-15989)*
Greater Dayton Mvg & Stor Co E 937 235-0011
Dayton *(G-9586)*
Lewis & Michael Inc E 937 252-6683
Dayton *(G-9679)*
Midfitz Inc E 216 663-8816
Cleveland *(G-6055)*
Mitchell & Sons Moving & Stor E 419 289-3311
Ashland *(G-689)*
Planes Moving & Storage Inc C 513 759-6000
West Chester *(G-19129)*
Rollins Moving and Storage Inc E 937 525-4013
Springfield *(G-17267)*
Security Storage Co Inc D 513 961-2700
Cincinnati *(G-4490)*
Tersher Corporation D 440 439-8383
Strongsville *(G-17516)*
University Moving & Storage Co E 248 615-7000
West Chester *(G-19174)*
Vance Property Management LLC D 419 467-9548
Toledo *(G-18287)*

MOVING SVC: Local

Accelerated Moving & Stor Inc E 614 836-1007
Columbus *(G-6932)*
Continental Office Furn Corp E 614 781-0080
Columbus *(G-7429)*
Corrigan Moving Systems-Ann AR E 419 874-2900
Perrysburg *(G-15989)*
Custom Movers Services Inc E 330 564-0507
Stow *(G-17358)*
E & V Ventures Inc E 330 794-6683
Akron *(G-203)*
Greater Dayton Mvg & Stor Co E 937 235-0011
Dayton *(G-9586)*
Leaders Moving Company E 614 785-9595
Worthington *(G-19970)*
Lewis & Michael Mvg & Stor Co E 614 275-2997
Columbus *(G-8054)*
Nest Tenders Limited D 614 901-1570
Columbus *(G-8257)*
Northcoast Moving Enterprising D 440 943-3900
Wickliffe *(G-19609)*
Two Men & Truck Inc E 419 882-1002
Toledo *(G-10265)*
Wnb Group LLC E 513 641-5400
Cincinnati *(G-4855)*

MOVING SVC: Long-Distance

Accelerated Moving & Stor Inc E 614 836-1007
Columbus *(G-6932)*
American Way Van and Stor Inc E 937 898-7294
Vandalia *(G-18658)*
Awrs LLC E 888 611-2292
Cincinnati *(G-3068)*
Corrigan Moving Systems-Ann AR E 419 874-2900
Perrysburg *(G-15989)*
Dearman Moving & Storage Co E 419 524-3456
Mansfield *(G-13291)*
Exel Holdings (usa) Inc C 614 865-8500
Westerville *(G-19303)*
Greater Dayton Mvg & Stor Co E 937 235-0011
Dayton *(G-9586)*
Lewis & Michael Inc E 937 252-6683
Dayton *(G-9679)*
Locker Moving & Storage Inc E 330 784-0477
Canton *(G-2439)*
Midfitz Inc E 216 663-8816
Cleveland *(G-6055)*
Mitchell & Sons Moving & Stor E 419 289-3311
Ashland *(G-689)*
Mxd Group Inc D 866 711-3129
New Albany *(G-14995)*
New World Van Lines Ohio Inc E 614 836-5720
Groveport *(G-11658)*
Nicholas Carney-Mc Inc E 440 243-8560
Sheffield Village *(G-16894)*
Planes Mvg & Stor Co Columbus D 614 777-9090
Columbus *(G-8548)*
Rollins Moving and Storage Inc E 937 525-4013
Springfield *(G-17267)*
Shetler Moving & Stor of Ohio E 513 755-0700
West Chester *(G-19151)*
Tersher Corporation D 440 439-8383
Strongsville *(G-17516)*
Unpacking Etc E 440 871-0506
Westlake *(G-19561)*
Van Howards Lines Inc E 937 235-0007
Dayton *(G-9963)*
Van Mayberrys & Storage Inc E 937 298-8800
Moraine *(G-14832)*
Van Mills Lines Inc C 440 846-0200
Strongsville *(G-17521)*
Van Stevens Lines Inc E 419 729-8871
Toledo *(G-18286)*

MULTI-SVCS CENTER

Salvation Army D 614 252-7171
Columbus *(G-8681)*
Salvation Army D 859 255-5791
Cincinnati *(G-4474)*
Salvation Army D 800 728-7825
Columbus *(G-8682)*
Skyview Baptist Ranch Inc E 330 674-7511
Millersburg *(G-14622)*

MUSEUMS

Akron Art Museum D 330 376-9185
Akron *(G-27)*
Ark Foundation of Dayton E 937 256-2759
Dayton *(G-9344)*
Belpre Historical Society E 740 423-7588
Belpre *(G-1433)*
Butler Institute of Amercn Art E 330 743-1711
Youngstown *(G-20131)*
Chagrin Falls Historical Soc E 440 247-4695
Chagrin Falls *(G-2691)*
Cincinnati Institute Fine Arts E 513 241-0343
Cincinnati *(G-3313)*
Cincinnati Museum Association C 513 721-5204
Cincinnati *(G-3318)*
Cleveland Hungarian Heritg Soc E 216 523-3900
Cleveland *(G-5320)*
Clevelnd Museum of Natural His D 216 231-4600
Cleveland *(G-5359)*
Dayton Art Institute D 937 223-5277
Dayton *(G-9460)*
Dayton History C 937 293-2841
Dayton *(G-9478)*
Dayton Society Natural History D 937 275-7431
Dayton *(G-9491)*
Dayton Society Natural History E 513 932-4421
Oregonia *(G-15757)*
Franklin County Historical Soc C 614 228-2674
Columbus *(G-7695)*
Great Lakes Mseum of Scnce Env C 216 694-2000
Cleveland *(G-5690)*
Kingwood Center E 419 522-0211
Mansfield *(G-13320)*
Lawrence Cnty Hstorical Museum E 740 532-1222
Ironton *(G-12296)*
Miami University C 513 529-2232
Oxford *(G-15819)*
Miami University C 513 529-8380
Oxford *(G-15820)*
Museum Cntmprary Art Cleveland E 216 421-8671
Cleveland *(G-6092)*
Norhteast Ohio Museum E 330 336-7657
Medina *(G-14107)*
Ohio Historical Society C 614 297-2300
Columbus *(G-8352)*

SERVICES

Employee Codes: A=Over 500 employees, B=251-500
C=101-250, D=51-100, E=25-50
2018 Harris Ohio
Services Directory
1567

MUSEUMS

SERVICES SECTION

Rock and Roll of Fame and Muse.........D....... 216 781-7625
  Cleveland *(G-6406)*
Rthrford B Hayes Prsdntial Ctr................E....... 419 332-2081
  Fremont *(G-11217)*
Salem Historical Soc Museum.................E....... 330 337-6733
  Salem *(G-16715)*
Sauder Village...B....... 419 446-2541
  Archbold *(G-644)*
Stan Hywet Hall and Grdns Inc................D....... 330 836-5533
  Akron *(G-449)*
Stark Cnty Historical Soc Inc....................E....... 330 455-7043
  Canton *(G-2542)*
Taft Museum of Art....................................E....... 513 241-0343
  Cincinnati *(G-4615)*
Toledo Museum of Art...............................C....... 419 255-8000
  Toledo *(G-18244)*
Toledo Science Center...............................E....... 419 244-2674
  Toledo *(G-18248)*
Western Reserve Historical Soc................D....... 330 666-3711
  Bath *(G-1036)*

MUSEUMS & ART GALLERIES

Arts and Exhibitions Intl LLC....................D....... 330 995-9300
  Streetsboro *(G-17407)*
Cincinnati Museum Center........................B....... 513 287-7000
  Cincinnati *(G-3319)*
Greater Andrson Premotes Peace.............E....... 513 588-8391
  Cincinnati *(G-3705)*

MUSIC BROADCASTING SVCS

N Safe Sound Security Inc........................E....... 888 317-7233
  Millersburg *(G-14614)*
National Weather Service..........................E....... 937 383-0031
  Wilmington *(G-19774)*

MUSIC RECORDING PRODUCER

Telarc International Corp..........................E....... 216 464-2313
  Beachwood *(G-1130)*

MUSIC SCHOOLS

Phillis Wheat Association Inc...................E....... 216 391-4443
  Cleveland *(G-6274)*

MUSICAL ENTERTAINERS

Musical Arts Association..........................C....... 216 231-7300
  Cleveland *(G-6093)*

MUSICAL INSTRUMENT PARTS & ACCESS, WHOLESALE

Grover Musical Products Inc....................E....... 216 391-1188
  Cleveland *(G-5708)*

MUSICAL INSTRUMENTS & ACCESS: NEC

Belco Works Inc..B....... 740 695-0500
  Saint Clairsville *(G-16617)*

MUSICIAN

Toledo Swiss Singers................................E....... 419 693-4110
  Oregon *(G-15753)*

MUTUAL ACCIDENT & HEALTH ASSOCIATIONS

Union Central Life Insur Co......................A....... 866 696-7478
  Cincinnati *(G-4726)*

MUTUAL FUND MANAGEMENT

Mutual Shareholder Svcs LLC..................E....... 440 922-0067
  Broadview Heights *(G-1884)*

NAIL SALONS

Attitudes New Inc......................................E....... 330 856-1143
  Warren *(G-18819)*
Bellazio Salon & Day Spa.........................E....... 937 432-6722
  Dayton *(G-9354)*
Brenwood Inc..E....... 740 452-7533
  Zanesville *(G-20449)*
Casals Hair Salon Inc................................E....... 330 533-6766
  Canfield *(G-2185)*
Esbi International Salon............................E....... 330 220-3724
  Brunswick *(G-1977)*
Intrigue Salon & Day Spa..........................E....... 330 493-7003
  Canton *(G-2415)*

Kristie Warner...E....... 330 650-4450
  Hudson *(G-12129)*
Le Nails..E....... 440 846-1866
  Cleveland *(G-5930)*
Reves Salon & Spa....................................E....... 419 885-1140
  Sylvania *(G-17611)*
Walmart Inc...C....... 937 399-0370
  Springfield *(G-17296)*

NATIONAL SECURITY FORCES

Defense Fin & Accounting Svc.................A....... 614 693-6700
  Columbus *(G-7501)*

NATIONAL SECURITY, GOVERNMENT: Air Force

Air Force US Dept of.................................B....... 937 656-2354
  Dayton *(G-9251)*
Air Force US Dept of.................................D....... 937 257-6068
  Dayton *(G-9252)*
Army & Air Force Exchange Svc..............C....... 937 257-2928
  Dayton *(G-9255)*
Army & Air Force Exchange Svc..............A....... 937 257-7736
  Dayton *(G-9256)*
US Dept of the Air Force...........................D....... 937 257-0837
  Dayton *(G-9287)*
US Dept of the Air Force...........................E....... 937 255-5150
  Dayton *(G-9288)*

NATIONAL SECURITY, GOVERNMENT: Army

U S Army Corps of Engineers....................D....... 513 684-3048
  Cincinnati *(G-4714)*

NATIONAL SECURITY, GOVERNMENT: National Guard

National Guard Ohio.................................D....... 614 492-3166
  Columbus *(G-8218)*

NATIONAL SECURITY, GOVERNMENT: Navy

United States Dept of Navy.......................E....... 937 938-3926
  Dayton *(G-9286)*

NATURAL GAS DISTRIBUTION TO CONSUMERS

AEP Energy Services Inc..........................B....... 614 583-2900
  Columbus *(G-6950)*
Bay State Gas Company...........................B....... 614 460-4292
  Columbus *(G-7094)*
Cinergy Corp...A....... 513 421-9500
  Cincinnati *(G-3346)*
City of Lancaster.......................................E....... 740 687-6670
  Lancaster *(G-12518)*
City of Toledo...D....... 419 245-1800
  Toledo *(G-17807)*
Columbia Gas of Ohio Inc........................E....... 614 460-6000
  Columbus *(G-7321)*
Columbia Gas of Ohio Inc........................D....... 440 891-2458
  Cleveland *(G-5372)*
Columbia Gas of Ohio Inc........................E....... 419 435-7725
  Findlay *(G-11015)*
Columbia Gas of Ohio Inc........................C....... 614 481-1000
  Columbus *(G-7322)*
Columbia Gas Transmission LLC.............E....... 937 327-7108
  Springfield *(G-17168)*
Delta Energy LLC.....................................E....... 614 761-3603
  Dublin *(G-10318)*
Duke Energy Ohio Inc...............................D....... 704 382-3853
  Cincinnati *(G-3508)*
East Ohio Gas Company...........................C....... 330 742-8121
  Youngstown *(G-20175)*
East Ohio Gas Company...........................E....... 216 736-6959
  Cleveland *(G-5520)*
East Ohio Gas Company...........................D....... 216 736-6120
  Ashtabula *(G-743)*
East Ohio Gas Company...........................C....... 330 478-1700
  Canton *(G-2347)*
Hearthstone Utilities Inc...........................D....... 440 974-3770
  Cleveland *(G-5744)*
National Gas & Oil Corporation................D....... 740 344-2102
  Newark *(G-15216)*
National Gas & Oil Corporation................E....... 740 454-7252
  Zanesville *(G-20514)*
National Gas Oil Corp...............................E....... 740 348-1243
  Hebron *(G-11857)*
Ohio Gas Company...................................E....... 419 636-1117
  Bryan *(G-2013)*

Stand Energy Corporation.........................E....... 513 621-1113
  Cincinnati *(G-4578)*
Volunteer Energy Services Inc..................E....... 614 856-3128
  Pickerington *(G-16107)*

NATURAL GAS PRODUCTION

Interstate Gas Supply Inc.........................C....... 614 659-5000
  Dublin *(G-10378)*
Williams Partners LP.................................C....... 330 966-3674
  North Canton *(G-15379)*

NATURAL GAS TRANSMISSION

Belden & Blake Corporation.....................E....... 330 602-5551
  Dover *(G-10177)*
Columbia Gas of Ohio Inc........................E....... 740 264-5577
  Steubenville *(G-17311)*
Columbia Gas Transmission LLC.............E....... 614 460-4704
  Columbus *(G-7324)*
Consumers Gas Cooperative.....................E....... 330 682-4144
  Orrville *(G-15768)*
Dominion Energy Transm Inc...................E....... 513 932-5793
  Lebanon *(G-12601)*
Duke Energy Ohio Inc...............................D....... 704 382-3853
  Cincinnati *(G-3508)*
Koch Knight LLC.......................................D....... 330 488-1651
  East Canton *(G-10504)*
National Gas & Oil Corporation................D....... 740 344-2102
  Newark *(G-15216)*
National Gas & Oil Corporation................E....... 740 454-7252
  Zanesville *(G-20514)*
Ohio Gas Company...................................E....... 419 636-3642
  Bryan *(G-2014)*
Texas Eastern Transmission LP................E....... 513 932-1816
  Lebanon *(G-12653)*

NATURAL GAS TRANSMISSION & DISTRIBUTION

ARC Gas & Supply LLC............................E....... 216 341-5882
  Cleveland *(G-5063)*
Aspire Energy of Ohio LLC......................E....... 330 682-7726
  Orrville *(G-15764)*
Columbia Gas Transmission LLC.............E....... 740 432-1612
  Cambridge *(G-2105)*
Columbia Gulf Transmission LLC............E....... 740 746-9105
  Sugar Grove *(G-17540)*
Dayton Power and Light Company...........D....... 937 331-4123
  Moraine *(G-14774)*
East Ohio Gas Company...........................A....... 800 362-7557
  Maple Heights *(G-13406)*
East Ohio Gas Company...........................B....... 330 266-2169
  New Franklin *(G-15044)*
East Ohio Gas Company...........................C....... 330 477-9411
  Canton *(G-2345)*
East Ohio Gas Company...........................D....... 330 499-2501
  Canton *(G-2346)*
East Ohio Gas Company...........................C....... 216 736-6917
  Wickliffe *(G-19595)*
East Ohio Gas Company...........................C....... 330 478-1700
  Canton *(G-2347)*
National Gas & Oil Corporation................E....... 740 454-7252
  Zanesville *(G-20514)*

NATURAL GASOLINE PRODUCTION

Husky Marketing and Supply Co..............E....... 614 210-2300
  Dublin *(G-10370)*

NATURAL RESOURCE PRESERVATION SVCS

City of Toledo...E....... 419 936-2875
  Toledo *(G-17809)*
Miami County Park District......................E....... 937 335-6273
  Troy *(G-18365)*

NAUTICAL & NAVIGATIONAL INSTRUMENT REPAIR SVCS

Inertial Airline Services Inc......................E....... 440 995-6555
  Cleveland *(G-5818)*

NAUTICAL REPAIR SVCS

Riverside Marine Inds Inc.........................D....... 419 729-1621
  Toledo *(G-18157)*

SERVICES SECTION

NEIGHBORHOOD CENTER

Childrens Hospital Medical Ctr..........A...... 513 541-4500
  Cincinnati *(G-3246)*
Friendly Inn Settlement House............E...... 216 431-7656
  Cleveland *(G-5641)*
Gladden Community House...................E...... 614 221-7801
  Columbus *(G-7753)*
Phillis Wheat Association Inc.............E...... 216 391-4443
  Cleveland *(G-6274)*
Seven Hlls Neighborhood Houses........D...... 513 407-5362
  Cincinnati *(G-4505)*

NEIGHBORHOOD DEVELOPMENT GROUP

Gc Neighborhood Ctrs Assoc Inc..........C...... 216 298-4440
  Cleveland *(G-5660)*
Neighborhood Hsg Servs Toledo..........E...... 419 691-2900
  Toledo *(G-18081)*

NEW & USED CAR DEALERS

Albert Mike Leasing Inc.........................C...... 513 563-1400
  Cincinnati *(G-2982)*
Carroll Halliday Inc..............................E...... 740 335-1670
  Wshngtn CT Hs *(G-20014)*
Genicon Inc..E...... 419 491-4478
  Swanton *(G-17565)*
Jake Sweeney Automotive Inc..............C...... 513 782-2800
  Cincinnati *(G-3859)*
Jeff Wyler Automotive Fmly Inc............E...... 513 752-7450
  Cincinnati *(G-2918)*
Nollenberger Truck Center....................E...... 419 837-5996
  Stony Ridge *(G-17348)*

NEWS SYNDICATES

Ohio News Network................................D...... 614 460-3700
  Columbus *(G-8362)*

NEWSPAPERS & PERIODICALS NEWS REPORTING SVCS

Associated Press....................................E...... 614 885-3444
  Columbus *(G-7056)*

NEWSSTAND

Sandusky Register.................................E...... 419 625-5500
  Sandusky *(G-16793)*

NONCURRENT CARRYING WIRING DEVICES

Akron Foundry Co..................................E...... 330 745-3101
  Barberton *(G-950)*
Vertiv Energy Systems Inc....................A...... 440 288-1122
  Lorain *(G-13085)*
Zekelman Industries Inc.......................C...... 740 432-2146
  Cambridge *(G-2135)*

NONMETALLIC MINERALS DEVELOPMENT & TEST BORING SVC

Barr Engineering Incorporated.............E...... 614 714-0299
  Columbus *(G-7091)*

NONMETALLIC MINERALS: Support Activities, Exc Fuels

Aluchem of Jackson Inc.......................E...... 740 286-2455
  Jackson *(G-12306)*

NOTARIES PUBLIC

Official Investigations Inc...................D...... 844 263-3424
  Cincinnati *(G-4200)*

NOVELTIES, PAPER, WHOLESALE

Gummer Wholesale Inc........................D...... 740 928-0415
  Heath *(G-11838)*

NOVELTY SHOPS

Top Tier Soccer LLC..............................E...... 937 903-6114
  Dayton *(G-9932)*

NURSERIES & LAWN & GARDEN SPLY STORE, RET: Lawn/Garden Splys

Garick LLC..E...... 937 462-8350
  South Charleston *(G-17076)*
Gears Garden Center Inc......................E...... 513 931-3800
  Cincinnati *(G-3665)*
McCallisters Landscaping & Sup..........E...... 440 259-3348
  Perry *(G-15964)*
R B Stout Inc..E...... 330 666-8811
  Akron *(G-403)*
Tersigni Cargill Entps LLC...................E...... 330 351-0942
  Stow *(G-17396)*
Thomsons Landscaping.......................E...... 740 374-9353
  Marietta *(G-13504)*

NURSERIES & LAWN & GARDEN SPLY STORES, RETAIL

Lesco Inc..C...... 216 706-9250
  Cleveland *(G-5936)*
Lockes Garden Center Inc....................E...... 440 774-6981
  Oberlin *(G-15648)*
Straders Garden Centers Inc...............C...... 614 889-1314
  Columbus *(G-8792)*

NURSERIES & LAWN & GARDEN SPLY STORES, RETAIL: Fertilizer

Centerra Co-Op......................................E...... 419 281-2153
  Ashland *(G-672)*
Centerra Co-Op......................................E...... 800 362-9598
  Jefferson *(G-12331)*
Heritage Cooperative Inc.....................D...... 419 294-2371
  West Mansfield *(G-19267)*
K M B Inc...E...... 330 889-3451
  Bristolville *(G-1872)*
Ohigro Inc...E...... 740 726-2429
  Waldo *(G-18783)*

NURSERIES & LAWN & GARDEN SPLY STORES, RETAIL: Top Soil

Bladecutters Lawn Service Inc............E...... 937 274-3861
  Dayton *(G-9360)*

NURSERIES & LAWN/GARDEN SPLY STORE, RET: Lawnmowers/Tractors

Do Cut Sales & Service Inc..................E...... 330 533-9878
  Warren *(G-18851)*
Findlay Implement Co...........................E...... 419 424-0471
  Findlay *(G-11026)*
Shearer Farm Inc...................................E...... 440 237-4806
  North Royalton *(G-15502)*
Shetlers Sales & Service Inc................E...... 330 760-3358
  Copley *(G-9064)*
Tri Green Interstate Equipment............E...... 614 879-7731
  London *(G-13008)*
Tuttle Landscaping & Grdn Ctr.............E...... 419 756-7555
  Mansfield *(G-13378)*

NURSERIES & LAWN/GARDEN SPLY STORES, RET: Garden Splys/Tools

Barnes Nursery Inc..............................E...... 800 421-8722
  Huron *(G-12161)*
Berns Grnhse & Grdn Ctr Inc................E...... 513 423-5306
  Middletown *(G-14418)*
Bfg Supply Co Llc.................................E...... 440 834-1883
  Burton *(G-2061)*
Fackler Country Gardens Inc...............E...... 740 522-3128
  Granville *(G-11465)*
Knollwood Florists Inc.........................E...... 937 426-0861
  Beavercreek *(G-1183)*
Natorps Inc...D...... 513 398-4769
  Mason *(G-13742)*

NURSERIES/LAWN/GARDEN SPLY STORES, RET: Hydroponic Eqpt/Sply

Naragon Companies Inc.......................E...... 330 745-7700
  Norton *(G-15556)*

NURSERIES/LAWN/GRDN SPLY STORE, RET: Nursery Stck, Seed/Bulb

Dennis Top Soil & Landscaping...........E...... 419 865-5656
  Toledo *(G-17849)*
Grandmas Gardens Inc.........................E...... 937 885-2973
  Waynesville *(G-18982)*
Oakland Nursery Inc.............................E...... 614 268-3834
  Columbus *(G-8310)*
Seed Consultants Inc...........................E...... 740 333-8644
  Wshngtn CT Hs *(G-20035)*
Wickline Landscaping Inc....................E...... 937 372-0521
  Xenia *(G-20083)*

NURSING & PERSONAL CARE FACILITIES, NEC

NURSERY & GARDEN CENTERS

August Corso Sons Inc.........................C...... 419 626-0765
  Sandusky *(G-16727)*
Bzak Landscaping Inc..........................E...... 513 831-0907
  Milford *(G-14508)*
Dawes Arboretum..................................E...... 740 323-2355
  Newark *(G-15164)*
Greenleaf Landscapes Inc...................D...... 740 373-1639
  Marietta *(G-13449)*
Gs Ohio Inc..D...... 614 885-5350
  Powell *(G-16337)*
HJ Benken Flor & Greenhouses............D...... 513 891-1040
  Cincinnati *(G-3772)*
Kuester Implement Company Inc.........E...... 740 944-1502
  Bloomingdale *(G-1517)*
North Branch Nursery Inc....................E...... 419 287-4679
  Pemberville *(G-15942)*
Norvell Landscaping Inc......................E...... 513 423-9009
  Middletown *(G-14443)*
Scarffs Nursery Inc...............................C...... 937 845-3130
  New Carlisle *(G-15031)*
Siebenthaler Company..........................D...... 937 427-4110
  Dayton *(G-9882)*
Wade & Gatton Nurseries.....................D...... 419 883-3191
  Bellville *(G-1427)*
White Pond Gardens Inc.......................E...... 330 836-2727
  Akron *(G-509)*

NURSERY SCHOOLS

Bedford Church of Nazarene.................E...... 440 232-7440
  Bedford *(G-1294)*
Bowling Green Coop Nurs Schl.............E...... 419 352-8675
  Bowling Green *(G-1764)*
Harrison Ave Assembly of God............E...... 513 367-6100
  Harrison *(G-11800)*
Kindercare Learning Ctrs LLC...............E...... 440 248-5437
  Solon *(G-17022)*
Kindercare Learning Ctrs LLC...............E...... 513 771-8787
  Cincinnati *(G-3925)*
Lebanon Presbyterian Church..............E...... 513 932-0369
  Lebanon *(G-12623)*
Montessori Community School............E...... 740 344-9411
  Newark *(G-15211)*
Nurtury...E...... 330 723-1800
  Medina *(G-14109)*
Play Time Day Nursery Inc...................E...... 513 385-8281
  Cincinnati *(G-4304)*
Scribes & Scrbblr Chld Dev Ctr............E...... 440 884-5437
  Cleveland *(G-6455)*

NURSERY STOCK, WHOLESALE

Beroske Farms & Greenhouse Inc.......E...... 419 826-4547
  Delta *(G-10156)*
C M Brown Nurseries Inc.....................E...... 440 259-5403
  Perry *(G-15958)*
Davis Tree Farm & Nursery Inc............E...... 330 483-3324
  Valley City *(G-18615)*
Dennis Top Soil & Landscaping...........E...... 419 865-5656
  Toledo *(G-17849)*
North Coast Perennials Inc..................E...... 440 428-1277
  Madison *(G-13233)*
Rusty Oak Nursery Ltd.........................E...... 330 225-7704
  Valley City *(G-18623)*
Siebenthaler Company..........................D...... 937 427-4110
  Dayton *(G-9882)*
Thorsens Greenhouse LLC..................E...... 740 363-5069
  Delaware *(G-10129)*
Warner Nurseries Inc............................E...... 440 946-0880
  Madison *(G-13237)*

NURSING & PERSONAL CARE FACILITIES, NEC

Csi Managed Care Inc...........................D...... 440 717-1700
  Brecksville *(G-1822)*
Guardian Elder Care Columbus............D...... 614 868-9306
  Columbus *(G-7783)*
Hampton Woods Nursing Ctr Inc..........E...... 330 707-1400
  Poland *(G-16224)*
Pristine Senior Living of......................D...... 419 935-0148
  Willard *(G-19625)*
Sumner On Ridgewood..........................E...... 330 664-1360
  Copley *(G-9066)*
Windsorwood Place Inc........................E...... 740 623-4600
  Coshocton *(G-9121)*

NURSING CARE FACILITIES: Skilled

10 Wilmington Place D 937 253-1010 Dayton *(G-9291)*
204 W Main Street Oper Co LLC D 419 929-1563 New London *(G-15065)*
5440 Charlesgate Rd Oper LLC D 937 236-6707 Dayton *(G-9293)*
A L K Inc D 740 369-8741 Delaware *(G-10064)*
A Provide Care Inc C 330 828-2278 Dalton *(G-9239)*
Adams County Manor D 937 544-2205 West Union *(G-19272)*
Adena NH LLC E 740 546-3620 Adena *(G-7)*
Advance Care Inc D 513 932-1121 Lebanon *(G-12588)*
Ahf Ohio Inc D 330 725-4123 Medina *(G-14033)*
Ahf Ohio Inc D 740 532-6188 Ironton *(G-12280)*
Ahf Ohio Inc D 614 760-8870 Dublin *(G-10237)*
Ahf Ohio Inc D 937 256-4663 Dayton *(G-9313)*
Ahf/Central States Inc D 615 383-3570 Dublin *(G-10238)*
Alexson Services Inc B 513 874-0423 Fairfield *(G-10819)*
Allen Medical Center C 440 986-4000 Oberlin *(G-15638)*
Alpha Nursing Homes Inc D 740 345-9197 Newark *(G-15142)*
Altercare Inc C 330 335-2555 Wadsworth *(G-18746)*
Altercare Inc E 440 327-5285 North Ridgeville *(G-15454)*
Altercare Nobles Pond Inc D 330 834-4800 Canton *(G-2235)*
Altercare of Louisville Center C 330 875-4224 Louisville *(G-13093)*
Amedisys Inc E 740 373-8549 Marietta *(G-13430)*
American Eagle Hlth Care Svcs C 440 428-5103 Madison *(G-13220)*
American Nursing Care Inc E 513 731-4600 Cincinnati *(G-3009)*
American Nursing Care Inc D 513 245-1500 Cincinnati *(G-3010)*
American Nursing Care Inc E 937 438-3844 Dayton *(G-9330)*
American Nursing Care Inc C 614 847-0555 Zanesville *(G-20441)*
Anchor Lodge Nursing Home Inc C 440 244-2019 Lorain *(G-13012)*
Anna Maria of Aurora Inc C 330 562-6171 Aurora *(G-824)*
Anna Maria of Aurora Inc D 330 562-3120 Aurora *(G-825)*
Apostolic Christian Home Inc D 330 927-1010 Rittman *(G-16550)*
Appalachian Respite Care Ltd D 740 984-4262 Beverly *(G-1487)*
April Enterprises Inc B 937 293-7703 Moraine *(G-14751)*
Arbors East LLC D 614 575-9003 Columbus *(G-7033)*
Arbors West LLC D 614 879-7661 West Jefferson *(G-19247)*
Aristocrat W Nursing Hm Corp C 216 252-7730 Cleveland *(G-5066)*
Arlington Care Ctr C 740 344-0303 Newark *(G-15143)*
Ashley Enterprises LLC D 330 726-5790 Boardman *(G-1737)*
Ashley Place Health Care Inc C 330 793-3010 Youngstown *(G-20105)*
Assisted Living Concepts Inc E 419 586-2484 Celina *(G-2635)*
Assumption Village C 330 549-2434 North Lima *(G-15398)*
Astoria Place of Clyde LLC D 419 547-9595 Clyde *(G-6809)*
Audrich Inc C 419 483-6225 Bellevue *(G-1403)*
Aurora Manor Special Care E 440 424-4000 Aurora *(G-827)*
Autumn Aegis Inc D 440 282-6768 Lorain *(G-13015)*
Balanced Care Corporation E 330 908-1166 Northfield *(G-15509)*
Balanced Care Corporation E 937 372-7205 Xenia *(G-20044)*
Baptist Home and Center C 513 662-5880 Cincinnati *(G-3076)*
Barnesville Healthcare Rehab D 740 425-3648 Barnesville *(G-987)*
Bath Manor Limited Partnership E 330 836-1006 Akron *(G-90)*
Beechwood Home C 513 321-9294 Cincinnati *(G-3093)*
Beechwood Terrace Care Ctr Inc C 513 578-6200 Cincinnati *(G-3094)*
Bel Air Care Center D 330 821-3939 Alliance *(G-527)*
Belmont County Home D 740 695-4925 Saint Clairsville *(G-16620)*
Belmore Leasing Co LLC C 216 268-3600 Cleveland *(G-5113)*
Bentley Leasing Co LLC A 330 337-9503 Salem *(G-16688)*
Best Care Nrsing Rhbltion Ctr C 740 574-2558 Wheelersburg *(G-19570)*
Bethesda Foundation Inc E 513 569-6575 Cincinnati *(G-3104)*
Biorx LLC D 866 442-4679 Cincinnati *(G-3109)*
Birchaven Village D 419 424-3000 Findlay *(G-10996)*
Blossom Nursing & Rehab Center C 330 337-3033 Salem *(G-16690)*
Blue Ash Healthcare Group Inc E 513 793-3362 Cincinnati *(G-3118)*
Bmnh Inc C 937 845-3561 New Carlisle *(G-15020)*
Bradley Road Nursing Home C 440 871-3474 Bay Village *(G-1039)*
Brethren Care Inc C 419 289-0803 Ashland *(G-666)*
Brewster Parke Inc D 330 767-4179 Brewster *(G-1854)*
Broadview NH LLC D 614 337-1066 Columbus *(G-7149)*
Brook Willow Chrstn Cmmunities D 614 885-3300 Columbus *(G-7151)*
Brookview Healthcare Ctr D 419 784-1014 Defiance *(G-10020)*
Brookville Enterprises Inc B 937 833-2133 Brookville *(G-1960)*
Bryant Eliza Village B 216 361-6141 Cleveland *(G-5153)*
Bryant Health Center Inc C 740 532-6188 Ironton *(G-12283)*
Butler County of Ohio C 513 887-3728 Fairfield Township *(G-10926)*
Camargo Manor Inc D 513 605-3000 Cincinnati *(G-3169)*
Cambridge Home Healthcare E 740 432-6191 Cambridge *(G-2099)*
Cambridge NH LLC D 740 432-7717 Cambridge *(G-2100)*
Camillus Villa Inc D 440 236-5091 Columbia Station *(G-6841)*
Canterbury Villa of Alliance D 330 821-1391 Alliance *(G-529)*
Capital Health Services Inc E 937 278-0404 Dayton *(G-9378)*
Caprice Health Care Inc C 330 965-9200 North Lima *(G-15400)*
Careserve C 740 454-4000 Zanesville *(G-20457)*
Careserve Inc C 740 962-3761 McConnelsville *(G-14026)*
Carington Health Systems E 513 682-2700 Hamilton *(G-11706)*
Carriage Court Company Inc E 740 654-4422 Lancaster *(G-12514)*
Carriage House Assisted Living E 740 264-7667 Steubenville *(G-17307)*
Carriage Inn of Steubenville C 740 264-7161 Steubenville *(G-17308)*
Castle Nursing Homes Inc C 330 674-0015 Millersburg *(G-14592)*
Center Ridge Nursing Home Inc C 440 327-1295 North Ridgeville *(G-15458)*
Centerburg Two LLC D 740 625-5774 Centerburg *(G-2666)*
Childs Investment Co E 330 837-2100 Massillon *(G-13794)*
Chillicothe Long Term Care D 513 793-8804 Cincinnati *(G-3256)*
Chillicothe Opco LLC D 740 772-5900 Chillicothe *(G-2823)*
Christian Worthington Vlg Inc E 614 846-6076 Columbus *(G-7269)*
CHS Norwood Inc D 513 242-1360 Cincinnati *(G-3273)*
CHS of Bowerston Oper Co Inc D 937 277-0505 Dayton *(G-9407)*
Clifton Care Center Inc C 513 530-1600 Cincinnati *(G-3365)*
Clime Leasing Co LLC D 614 276-4400 Columbus *(G-7300)*
Clovernook Inc C 513 605-4000 Cincinnati *(G-3369)*
Colonial Manor Health Care Ctr C 419 994-4191 Loudonville *(G-13089)*
Columbus Alzheimers Care Ctr C 614 459-7050 Columbus *(G-7327)*
Communicare Health Svcs Inc D 440 234-0454 Berea *(G-1453)*
Communicare Health Svcs Inc D 330 726-3700 Youngstown *(G-20148)*
Communicare Health Svcs Inc C 877 366-5306 Wintersville *(G-19809)*
Communicare Health Svcs Inc D 330 792-7799 Youngstown *(G-20149)*
Communicare Health Svcs Inc D 330 792-5511 Youngstown *(G-20150)*
Communicare Health Svcs Inc C 330 454-2152 Canton *(G-2318)*
Communicare Health Svcs Inc D 330 630-9780 Tallmadge *(G-17635)*
Communicare Health Svcs Inc D 419 394-7611 Saint Marys *(G-16672)*
Community Hlth Prfssionals Inc E 419 634-7443 Ada *(G-4)*
Community Hospital Springfield A 937 325-0531 Springfield *(G-17171)*
Community Mercy Foundation C 937 278-8211 Dayton *(G-9418)*
Community Mercy Hlth Partners C 937 653-5432 Urbana *(G-18583)*
Concord Health Care Inc E 330 759-2357 Youngstown *(G-20160)*
Concord Hlth Rhabilitation Ctr E 740 574-8441 Wheelersburg *(G-19575)*
Congregate Living of America D 513 899-2801 Morrow *(G-14845)*
Congregate Living of America E 937 393-6700 Hillsboro *(G-11969)*
Consulate Healthcare Inc E 419 865-1248 Maumee *(G-13899)*
Consulate Management Co LLC D 330 837-1001 Massillon *(G-13798)*
Consulate Management Co LLC D 419 886-3922 Bellville *(G-1423)*
Consulate Management Co LLC D 440 237-7966 Cleveland *(G-5398)*
Consulate Management Co LLC C 419 683-3255 Crestline *(G-9143)*
Consulate Management Co LLC D 419 867-7926 Maumee *(G-13900)*
Consulate Management Co LLC D 740 259-2351 Lucasville *(G-13176)*
Continent Hlth Co Cortland LLC E 330 637-7906 Cortland *(G-9075)*
Copley Health Center Inc C 330 666-0980 Copley *(G-9055)*
Coshocton Opco LLC D 740 622-1220 Coshocton *(G-9096)*
Cottingham Retirement Cmnty C 513 563-3600 Cincinnati *(G-3426)*
Country Club Retirement Center C 740 671-9330 Bellaire *(G-1365)*
Country Mdow Fclty Oprtons LLC D 419 886-3922 Bellville *(G-1424)*
Countryview of Sunbury D 740 965-3984 Sunbury *(G-17553)*
County of Allen C 419 221-1103 Lima *(G-12763)*
County of Logan C 937 592-2901 Bellefontaine *(G-1382)*
County of Lucas D 419 385-6021 Toledo *(G-17838)*
County of Marion D 740 389-4624 Marion *(G-13533)*
County of Monroe D 740 472-0144 Woodsfield *(G-19815)*

SERVICES SECTION

NURSING CARE FACILITIES: Skilled

Name	Code	Phone
County of Sandusky	C	419 334-2602
Fremont (G-11192)		
County of Shelby	C	937 492-6900
Sidney (G-16926)		
County of Van Wert	E	419 968-2141
Middle Point (G-14376)		
County of Williams	C	419 636-4508
Bryan (G-2005)		
Covenant Care Ohio Inc	D	419 531-4201
Toledo (G-17840)		
Covenant Care Ohio Inc	D	937 378-0188
Georgetown (G-11392)		
Covenant Care Ohio Inc	D	937 399-5551
Springfield (G-17183)		
Covenant Care Ohio Inc	D	937 878-7046
Fairborn (G-10788)		
Crestline Nursing Home Inc	E	419 683-3255
Crestline (G-9144)		
Crestview Health Care Center	D	740 695-2500
Saint Clairsville (G-16634)		
Cridersville Health Care Ctr	E	419 645-4468
Cridersville (G-9151)		
Crotinger Nursing Home Inc	E	937 968-5284
Union City (G-18502)		
Day Spring Health Care Corp	D	740 984-4262
Beverly (G-1489)		
Dayspring Health Care Center	C	937 864-5800
Fairborn (G-10792)		
Dayton Dmh Inc	C	937 436-2273
Dayton (G-9470)		
Dayton Nwborn Care Spclsts Inc	A	937 641-3329
Dayton (G-9483)		
Deaconess Long Term Care of MI	A	513 487-3600
Cincinnati (G-3474)		
Dearth Management Company	C	419 253-0144
Marengo (G-13423)		
Dearth Management Company	E	740 389-1214
Marion (G-13537)		
Dearth Management Company	C	330 339-3595
New Philadelphia (G-15092)		
Dedicated Nursing Assoc Inc	C	888 465-6929
Beavercreek (G-1237)		
Dedicated Nursing Assoc Inc	E	866 450-5550
Cincinnati (G-3477)		
Dedicated Nursing Assoc Inc	E	877 411-8350
Galloway (G-11343)		
Dedicated Nursing Assoc Inc	E	877 547-9144
Parma (G-15905)		
Delaware Opco LLC	D	502 429-8062
Delaware (G-10090)		
Diverscare Healthcare Svcs Inc	E	937 278-8211
Dayton (G-9502)		
Diverscare Healthcare Svcs Inc	E	513 271-7010
Cincinnati (G-3494)		
Diversicare Leasing Corp	D	615 771-7575
Wheelersburg (G-19576)		
Diversicare of Avon LLC	C	440 937-6201
Cleveland (G-5491)		
Diversicare of Mansfield LLC	D	419 529-6447
Ontario (G-15686)		
DMD Management Inc	A	216 371-3600
Cleveland (G-5497)		
Doctors Hospital Cleveland Inc	C	740 753-7300
Nelsonville (G-14961)		
Dover Nursing Center	D	330 364-4436
Dover (G-10186)		
Drake Center LLC	A	513 418-2500
Cincinnati (G-3501)		
Dublin Geriatric Care Co LP	E	614 761-1188
Dublin (G-10328)		
Eagle Creek Nursing Center	E	937 544-5531
West Union (G-19278)		
East Galbraith Nursing Home	C	513 984-5220
Cincinnati (G-3532)		
Eastern Star Hm of Cyhoga Cnty	D	216 761-0170
Cleveland (G-5521)		
Eastgate Health Care Center	C	513 752-3710
Cincinnati (G-2913)		
Eaton Gardens Rehabilitation A	D	937 456-5537
Eaton (G-10559)		
Ebenezer Road Corp	C	513 941-0099
Cincinnati (G-3540)		
Echoing Hills Village Inc	D	937 854-5151
Dayton (G-9518)		
Echoing Hills Village Inc	D	440 989-1400
Lorain (G-13037)		
Edgewood Manor of Lucasville	C	740 259-5536
Lucasville (G-13178)		
Elms Retirement Village Inc	D	440 647-2414
Wellington (G-18991)		
Embassy Autumnwood MGT LLC	D	330 927-2060
Rittman (G-16552)		
Encore Healthcare LLC	C	330 769-2015
Seville (G-16840)		
Episcopal Retirement Homes Inc	E	513 271-9610
Cincinnati (G-3567)		
Es3 Management Inc	D	440 593-6266
Conneaut (G-9042)		
Euclid Health Care Inc	C	513 561-4105
Cincinnati (G-3578)		
Evangelical Lutheran	D	419 365-5115
Arlington (G-647)		
Fairchild MD Leasing Co LLC	C	330 678-4912
Kent (G-12369)		
Fairhope Hospice and Palliativ	D	740 654-7077
Lancaster (G-12540)		
Fairlawn Opco LLC	D	502 429-8062
Fairlawn (G-10950)		
Fairmont Nursing Home Inc	D	440 338-8220
Newbury (G-15256)		
Feridean Commons LLC	E	614 898-7488
Westerville (G-19307)		
First Community Village	B	614 324-4455
Columbus (G-7664)		
First Louisville Arden LLC	E	419 252-5500
Toledo (G-17893)		
First Richmond Corp	D	937 783-4949
Blanchester (G-1514)		
Five Star Senior Living Inc	D	614 451-6793
Columbus (G-7671)		
Flower Hospital	B	419 824-1000
Sylvania (G-17587)		
Fountainhead Nursing Home Inc	E	740 354-9113
Franklin Furnace (G-11170)		
Franciscan Care Ctr Sylvania	C	419 882-2087
Toledo (G-17899)		
Franciscan Sisters of Chicago	D	440 843-7800
Cleveland (G-5630)		
Friendly Nursing Home Inc	E	937 855-2363
Franklin (G-11155)		
Friends Health Care Assn	C	937 767-7363
Yellow Springs (G-20089)		
Friendship Vlg of Clumbus Ohio	C	614 890-8282
Columbus (G-7708)		
Friendship Vlg of Dublin Ohio	C	614 764-1600
Dublin (G-10351)		
Fulton County Health Center	C	419 335-2017
Wauseon (G-18953)		
Gahanna Health Care Center	E	614 475-7222
Columbus (G-7723)		
Galion Community Hospital	B	419 468-4841
Galion (G-11298)		
Gateway Family House	E	216 531-5400
Euclid (G-10756)		
Gateway Health Care Center	C	216 486-4949
Cleveland (G-5658)		
Generation Health & Rehab Cntr	D	740 344-9465
Newark (G-15168)		
Generation Health Corp	C	614 337-1066
Columbus (G-7737)		
GFS Leasing Inc	D	330 296-6415
Kent (G-12372)		
Gibsonburg Health Llc	C	419 637-2104
Gibsonburg (G-11402)		
Gillette Nursing Home Inc	D	330 372-1960
Warren (G-18860)		
Glen Wesley Inc	D	614 888-7492
Columbus (G-7755)		
Glenn View Manor Inc	C	330 652-9901
Mineral Ridge (G-14636)		
Glenward Inc	C	513 863-3100
Fairfield Township (G-10929)		
Golden Living Inc	D	419 599-4070
Napoleon (G-14941)		
Golden Living LLC	C	330 762-6486
Akron (G-240)		
Golden Living LLC	D	330 725-3393
Medina (G-14071)		
Golden Living LLC	D	419 394-3308
Saint Marys (G-16674)		
Golden Living LLC	C	614 861-6666
Columbus (G-7759)		
Golden Living LLC	C	330 297-5781
Ravenna (G-16386)		
Golden Living LLC	D	330 335-1558
Wadsworth (G-18753)		
Good Shepherd Home	C	419 937-1801
Fostoria (G-11129)		
Graceworks Lutheran Services	A	937 433-2140
Dayton (G-9584)		
Greenbrier Senior Living Cmnty	D	440 888-0400
Cleveland (G-5703)		
Greene Oaks	D	937 352-2800
Xenia (G-20060)		
Greens of Lyndhurst The Inc	C	440 460-1000
Cleveland (G-5704)		
Harborside Clveland Ltd Partnr	D	440 871-5900
Westlake (G-19488)		
Harborside Healthcare Corp	C	419 825-1111
Swanton (G-17566)		
Harborside Healthcare NW Ohio	D	419 636-5071
Bryan (G-2007)		
Harborside Pointe Place LLC	C	419 727-7870
Toledo (G-17935)		
Harborside Sylvania LLC	D	419 882-1875
Sylvania (G-17592)		
Harborside Troy LLC	D	937 335-7161
Troy (G-18356)		
Hcf Management Inc	D	740 289-2394
Piketon (G-16117)		
Hcf Management Inc	C	419 999-2055
Lima (G-12792)		
Hcf of Lima Inc	D	419 999-2010
Lima (G-12793)		
Hcf of Perrysburg Inc	D	419 874-0306
Perrysburg (G-16008)		
Hcr Manor Care Svc Fla III Inc	E	419 252-5500
Toledo (G-17938)		
Hcr Manorcare Med Svcs Fla LLC	D	440 887-1442
North Royalton (G-15494)		
Health Care Opportunities Inc	E	513 932-4861
Lebanon (G-12610)		
Health Care Retirement Corp	B	419 252-5500
Toledo (G-17941)		
Health Care Rtrement Corp Amer	D	419 474-6021
Toledo (G-17943)		
Health Care Rtrement Corp Amer	C	419 562-9907
Bucyrus (G-2038)		
Health Care Rtrement Corp Amer	C	937 298-8084
Dayton (G-9604)		
Health Care Rtrement Corp Amer	D	937 456-5537
Eaton (G-10562)		
Health Care Rtrement Corp Amer	D	740 773-5000
Chillicothe (G-2845)		
Health Care Rtrement Corp Amer	C	740 354-4505
Portsmouth (G-16284)		
Health Care Rtrement Corp Amer	D	440 946-1912
Mentor (G-14188)		
Health Care Rtrement Corp Amer	D	740 635-4600
Bridgeport (G-1863)		
Health Care Rtrement Corp Amer	C	419 874-3578
Perrysburg (G-16009)		
Health Care Rtrement Corp Amer	C	937 548-3141
Greenville (G-11509)		
Health Care Rtrement Corp Amer	E	419 337-3050
Wauseon (G-18958)		
Health Care Rtrement Corp Amer	C	513 751-0880
Cincinnati (G-3751)		
Healthcare Facility MGT LLC	D	419 382-2200
Toledo (G-17944)		
Healthcare Facility MGT LLC	C	330 836-7953
Akron (G-260)		
Heartland Fort Myers Fl LLC	E	419 252-5500
Toledo (G-17946)		
Heath Nursing Care Center	C	740 522-1171
Newark (G-15173)		
Heather Knoll Retirement Vlg	C	330 688-8600
Tallmadge (G-17639)		
Heatherhill Care Communities	E	440 285-4040
Chardon (G-2752)		
Hermenia Inc	D	216 795-5710
Cleveland (G-5752)		
Hgcc of Allentown Inc	C	410 252-5500
Toledo (G-17955)		
Hickory Creek Healthcare	D	419 542-7795
Hicksville (G-11864)		
Hill View Retirement Center	C	740 354-3135
Portsmouth (G-16287)		
Hillandale Healthcare Inc	D	513 777-1400
West Chester (G-19090)		
Home Echo Club Inc	C	614 864-1718
Pickerington (G-16096)		
Home The Friends Inc	C	513 897-6050
Waynesville (G-18983)		
Horizon Health Management LLC	D	513 793-5220
Cincinnati (G-3783)		
Horn Nursing and Rehab Center	D	330 262-2951
Wooster (G-19870)		
Horn Nursing and Rehab Center	C	330 345-9050
Wooster (G-19871)		

Employee Codes: A=Over 500 employees, B=251-500
C=101-250, D=51-100, E=25-50

2018 Harris Ohio
Services Directory

1571

Hospice Cincinnati Inc .... E 513 862-1100
Cincinnati *(G-3785)*
Hospice Cincinnati Inc .... D 513 891-7700
Cincinnati *(G-3786)*
Hospice of Genesis Health .... E 740 454-5381
Zanesville *(G-20488)*
Hospice of North Central Ohio .... E 419 281-7107
Ashland *(G-682)*
Hospice of The Western Reserve .... D 440 951-8692
Mentor *(G-14192)*
Hospice of The Western Reserve .... E 440 787-2080
Lorain *(G-13042)*
Hosser Assisted Living .... E 740 286-8785
Jackson *(G-12314)*
Huffman Health Care Inc .... C 937 476-1000
Dayton *(G-9625)*
Humility House .... D 330 505-0144
Youngstown *(G-20222)*
I Vrable Inc .... C 614 545-5500
Columbus *(G-7878)*
Independence Care Community .... D 419 435-8505
Fostoria *(G-11133)*
Ioof Home of Ohio Inc .... E 937 399-8631
Springfield *(G-17215)*
J W J Investments Inc .... C 419 643-3161
Bluffton *(G-1732)*
Jackson County Hlth Facilities .... D 740 384-0722
Wellston *(G-19002)*
Jacobs Dwelling Nursing Home .... E 740 824-3635
Coshocton *(G-9109)*
Jada Inc .... E 419 512-1713
Mount Vernon *(G-14901)*
Jennings Eliza Senior Care .... A 216 226-5000
Olmsted Twp *(G-15676)*
Jennings Ctr For Older Adults .... B 216 581-2900
Cleveland *(G-5858)*
Jewish Fdrtion of Grter Dayton .... D 937 837-2651
Dayton *(G-9641)*
Jewish Home of Cincinnati .... B 513 754-3100
Mason *(G-13726)*
Jo Lin Health Center Inc .... C 740 532-0860
Ironton *(G-12295)*
Joint Township Dst Mem Hosp .... B 419 394-3335
Saint Marys *(G-16676)*
Judson Care Center Inc .... E 216 292-5706
Cincinnati *(G-3894)*
Karl Hc LLC .... B 614 846-5420
Columbus *(G-7965)*
Kendal At Oberlin .... C 440 775-0094
Oberlin *(G-15647)*
Kindred Healthcare Inc .... D 937 222-5963
Dayton *(G-9660)*
Kindred Healthcare Oper Inc .... D 740 545-6355
West Lafayette *(G-19258)*
Kindred Healthcare Oper Inc .... D 614 882-2490
Columbus *(G-7990)*
Kindred Healthcare Oper Inc .... C 740 387-7537
Marion *(G-13545)*
Kindred Healthcare Oper Inc .... C 740 439-4437
Cambridge *(G-2122)*
Kindred Healthcare Operating .... C 330 762-0901
Akron *(G-307)*
Kindred Healthcare Operating .... D 419 877-5338
Whitehouse *(G-19587)*
Kindred Nursing Centers E LLC .... C 513 932-0105
Lebanon *(G-12615)*
Kindred Nursing Centers E LLC .... C 740 344-0357
Newark *(G-15179)*
Kingston Healthcare Company .... C 937 866-9089
Miamisburg *(G-14312)*
Kingston Healthcare Company .... C 440 967-1800
Vermilion *(G-18712)*
Kingston Rsdnce Perrysburg LLC .... D 419 872-6200
Perrysburg *(G-16025)*
Larchwood Health Group LLC .... E 216 941-6100
Cleveland *(G-5926)*
Laurel Health Care Company .... C 614 888-4553
Worthington *(G-19968)*
Laurel Health Care Company .... C 614 885-0408
Worthington *(G-19969)*
Laurel Hlth Care Battle Creek .... E 614 794-8800
Westerville *(G-19323)*
Laurel Hlth Care of Mt Plasant .... D 614 794-8800
Westerville *(G-19324)*
Laurel Lk Retirement Cmnty Inc .... B 330 650-0681
Hudson *(G-12130)*
Laurels of Hillsboro .... D 937 393-1925
Hillsboro *(G-11985)*
Leader Nuring & Rehabilitation .... C 419 252-5718
Toledo *(G-18002)*
Lebanon Nursing & Rehab Ctr .... D 513 932-1121
Lebanon *(G-12622)*
Levering Management Inc .... D 740 387-9545
Marion *(G-13548)*
Levering Management Inc .... D 740 369-6400
Delaware *(G-10115)*
Lexington Court Care Center .... D 419 884-2000
Mansfield *(G-13324)*
Liberty Nursing of Willard .... D 419 935-0148
Willard *(G-19622)*
Life Care Centers America Inc .... C 330 483-3131
Valley City *(G-18619)*
Lima Cnvlscent HM Fndation Inc .... D 419 227-5450
Lima *(G-12818)*
Livin Care Alter of Kirke Inc .... E 740 927-3209
Kirkersville *(G-12455)*
Living Care Alternatives .... E 740 927-3209
Kirkersville *(G-12456)*
Logan Health Care Center .... C 740 385-2155
Logan *(G-12983)*
Longterm Lodging Inc .... C 614 224-0614
Columbus *(G-8076)*
Loving Care Hospice Inc .... E 740 852-7755
London *(G-12998)*
Lutheran Home .... B 440 871-0090
Cleveland *(G-5959)*
Lutheran Scial Svcs Centl Ohio .... C 419 289-3523
Ashland *(G-686)*
Lutheran Village At Wolf Creek .... C 419 861-2233
Holland *(G-12033)*
Lynnhaven V LLC .... C 440 272-5600
Windsor *(G-19805)*
Madeira Health Care Center .... C 513 561-4105
Cincinnati *(G-4009)*
Main Street Terrace Care Ctr .... D 740 653-8767
Lancaster *(G-12553)*
Mallard Cove Senior Dev LLC .... C 513 772-6655
Cincinnati *(G-4018)*
Manor Care Nursing Center .... E 419 252-5500
Toledo *(G-18029)*
Manor Care of Boynton Beach .... C 419 252-5500
Toledo *(G-18030)*
Manor Care of Kansas Inc .... D 419 252-5500
Toledo *(G-18031)*
Manor Care of North Olmsted .... B 419 252-5500
Toledo *(G-18032)*
Manor Care of Plantation Inc .... C 419 252-5500
Toledo *(G-18033)*
Manor Care of York North Inc .... C 419 252-5500
Toledo *(G-18034)*
Manor Care Wilmington Inc .... E 419 252-5500
Toledo *(G-18035)*
Manor Care York (south) Inc .... C 419 252-5500
Toledo *(G-18036)*
Manor Cr-Mprial Rchmond VA LLC .... D 419 252-5000
Toledo *(G-18037)*
Manorcare Health Services LLC .... E 419 252-5500
Toledo *(G-18038)*
Manorcare Health Svcs VA Inc .... D 419 252-5500
Toledo *(G-18039)*
Manorcare of Kingston Court .... C 419 252-5500
Toledo *(G-18040)*
Manorcare of Willoughby Inc .... C 419 252-5500
Toledo *(G-18041)*
Mansfield Opco LLC .... D 502 429-8062
Mansfield *(G-13334)*
Marietta Center For Health & .... C 740 373-1867
Marietta *(G-13466)*
Marion Manor .... D 740 387-9545
Marion *(G-13562)*
Marymount Hospital Inc .... B 216 581-0500
Cleveland *(G-5991)*
Mc Auley Center .... C 937 653-5432
Urbana *(G-18594)*
McGregor Senior Ind Hsing .... D 216 851-8200
Cleveland *(G-6004)*
McKinley Hall Inc .... E 937 328-5300
Springfield *(G-17230)*
McV Health Care Facilities .... C 513 398-1486
Mason *(G-13738)*
Meadowbrook Manor of Hartford .... D 330 772-5253
Fowler *(G-11144)*
Mennonite Memorial Home Inc .... C 419 358-1015
Bluffton *(G-1734)*
Menorah Park Center For Senio .... A 216 831-6500
Cleveland *(G-6024)*
Mentor Way Nursing & Rehab Cen .... C 440 255-9309
Mentor *(G-14216)*
Mercy Health West Park .... C 513 451-8900
Cincinnati *(G-4076)*
Mercy St Theresa Center Inc .... C 513 271-7010
Cincinnati *(G-4078)*
Merit House LLC .... C 419 478-5131
Toledo *(G-18059)*
Merit Leasing Co LLC .... C 216 261-9592
Cleveland *(G-6027)*
Mff Somerset LLc .... E 216 752-5600
Shaker Heights *(G-16863)*
Mill Creek Nursing .... E 419 468-4046
Galion *(G-11302)*
Mill Run Care Center LLC .... D 614 527-3000
Hilliard *(G-11935)*
Mkjb Inc .... C 513 851-8400
Cincinnati *(G-4108)*
Montefiore Home .... B 216 360-9080
Beachwood *(G-1104)*
Mount Vernon NH LLC .... E 740 392-1099
Mount Vernon *(G-14914)*
Multi-Care Inc .... D 440 352-0788
Painesville *(G-15867)*
Myocare Nursing Home Inc .... C 216 252-7555
Cleveland *(G-6095)*
National Church Residences .... C 614 451-2151
Columbus *(G-8215)*
Ncop LLC .... D 419 599-4070
Napoleon *(G-14948)*
Nentwick Convalescent Home .... C 330 385-5001
East Liverpool *(G-10527)*
New Dawn Health Care Inc .... C 330 343-5521
Dover *(G-10202)*
New Life Hospice Inc .... E 440 934-1458
Lorain *(G-13064)*
New Life Hospice Inc .... D 440 934-1458
Sheffield Village *(G-16893)*
Newark NH LLC .... D 740 345-9197
Newark *(G-15221)*
Northpoint Senior Services LLC .... D 740 369-9614
Delaware *(G-10118)*
Norwalk Area Hlth Systems Inc .... A 419 668-8101
Norwalk *(G-15584)*
Norwood Health Care Center LLC .... D 513 351-0153
Cincinnati *(G-4186)*
Nursing Care MGT Amer Inc .... D 740 927-9888
Pataskala *(G-15924)*
Nursing Care MGT Amer Inc .... D 513 793-5092
Cincinnati *(G-4194)*
Nursing Home Management Inc .... D 440 466-1181
Geneva *(G-11367)*
Oak Grove Manor Inc .... C 419 589-6222
Mansfield *(G-13350)*
Oak Health Care Investors .... E 614 794-8800
Westerville *(G-19335)*
Oaktree LLC .... D 513 598-8000
Cincinnati *(G-4196)*
Ohio Department Veterans Svcs .... A 614 644-0898
Columbus *(G-8331)*
Ohio Eastern Star Home .... C 740 397-1706
Mount Vernon *(G-14917)*
Ohio Living .... B 614 224-1651
Columbus *(G-8357)*
Ohio Living .... C 513 681-4230
Cincinnati *(G-4208)*
Ohio Presbt Retirement Svcs .... B 330 746-2944
Youngstown *(G-20309)*
Ohio Presbt Retirement Svcs .... C 330 867-2150
Akron *(G-368)*
Ohio Presbt Retirement Svcs .... B 937 498-2391
Sidney *(G-16945)*
Ohio Presbt Retirement Svcs .... C 513 539-7391
Monroe *(G-14708)*
Ohio Valley Manor Inc .... C 937 392-4318
Ripley *(G-16548)*
Ohioguidestone .... E 440 234-2006
Berea *(G-1467)*
Olmsted Health and Svc Corp .... B 440 235-7100
Olmsted Twp *(G-15679)*
Olmsted Manor Nursing Home .... C 440 250-4080
North Olmsted *(G-15436)*
Olmsted Mnor Rtrment Cmnty Ltd .... E 440 779-8886
North Olmsted *(G-15437)*
Orchard Villa Inc .... C 419 697-4100
Oregon *(G-15744)*
Orion Care Services LLC .... C 216 752-3600
Cleveland *(G-6215)*
Otterbein Portage Valley Inc .... C 888 749-4950
Pemberville *(G-15943)*
Otterbein Snior Lfstyle Chices .... B 513 933-5400
Lebanon *(G-12636)*
Otterbein Snior Lfstyle Chices .... C 419 645-5114
Cridersville *(G-9152)*

SERVICES SECTION

NURSING CARE FACILITIES: Skilled

Company	Code	Phone
Otterbein Snior Lfstyle Chices — Middletown (G-14483)	C	513 260-7690
Otterbein Snior Lfstyle Chices — Saint Marys (G-16682)	C	419 394-2366
Ovm Investment Group LLC — Ripley (G-16549)	C	937 392-0145
Parkcliffe Development — Toledo (G-18118)	D	419 381-9447
Parkview Manor Inc — Englewood (G-10714)	C	937 296-1550
Parma Care Center Inc — Cleveland (G-6245)	C	216 661-6800
Pebble Creek Cnvlscnt Ctr — Akron (G-379)	C	330 645-0200
Phyllis Wheatley Assn Dev — Cleveland (G-6278)	E	216 391-4443
Pine Hills Continuing Care Ctr — Nelsonville (G-14966)	E	740 753-1931
Pleasant Lake Nursing Home — Cleveland (G-6289)	B	440 842-2273
Pleasant Ridge Care Center Inc — Cincinnati (G-4305)	C	513 631-1310
Premier Estates 521 LLC — Cincinnati (G-4322)	D	765 288-2488
Premier Health Care MGT Inc — Blue Ash (G-1664)	E	248 644-5522
Progressive Park LLC — Cleveland (G-6320)	C	330 434-4514
Quality Care Nursing Svc Inc — South Point (G-17096)	B	740 377-9095
R & F Inc — Holland (G-12047)	E	419 868-2909
Rae-Ann Holdings Inc — Cleveland (G-6347)	D	440 871-5181
Rae-Ann Holdings Inc — Westlake (G-19539)	D	440 871-0500
Rae-Ann Suburban Inc — Westlake (G-19540)	C	440 871-5181
Raeann Inc — Cleveland (G-6348)	E	440 871-5181
Raeann Inc — Geneva (G-11368)	D	440 466-5733
Rapids Nursing Homes Inc — Grand Rapids (G-11453)	E	216 292-5706
Red Carpet Health Care Center — Cambridge (G-2127)	C	740 439-4401
Regency Leasing Co LLC — Columbus (G-8606)	B	614 542-3100
Rescare Ohio Inc — Centerburg (G-2667)	E	740 625-6873
Rest Haven Nursing Home Inc — Greenville (G-11516)	C	937 548-1138
Riverside Care Center LLC — Mc Connelsville (G-14022)	D	740 962-5303
Rocky River Leasing Co LLC — Berea (G-1468)	E	440 243-5688
Roman Cthlic Docese Youngstown — Louisville (G-13106)	C	330 875-5562
Rosary Care Center — Sylvania (G-17613)	D	419 824-3600
Rose Ln Hlth Rhabilitation Inc — Massillon (G-13850)	C	330 833-3174
Rosewood Manor — Yorkville (G-20093)	E	740 859-7673
Rossford Grtric Care Ltd Prtnr — Columbus (G-8651)	C	614 459-0445
Royal Manor Health Care Inc — Cleveland (G-6416)	E	216 752-3600
Royce Leasing Co LLC — Portsmouth (G-16305)	D	740 354-1240
Rwdop LLC — Fairlawn (G-10970)	C	330 666-3776
Saber Healthcare Group LLC — Warren (G-18894)	E	330 369-4672
Saber Healthcare Group LLC — Ravenna (G-16410)	E	330 297-4564
Saber Healthcare Group LLC — Wilmington (G-19786)	E	937 382-1621
Saber Healthcare Group LLC — Brecksville (G-1848)	E	440 546-0643
Saber Healthcare Group LLC — Cincinnati (G-4465)	E	513 631-6800
Saber Healthcare Group LLC — Euclid (G-10775)	E	216 486-5736
Saber Healthcare Group LLC — Cleveland (G-6430)	E	216 795-5710
Saber Healthcare Group LLC — Maple Heights (G-13416)	E	216 662-3343
Saber Healthcare Group LLC — Woodstock (G-19821)	E	937 826-3351
Saber Healthcare Group LLC — Bellevue (G-1418)	E	419 483-6225
Saber Healthcare Group LLC — Cortland (G-9082)	E	330 638-4015
Saber Healthcare Group LLC — Grand Rapids (G-11454)	E	419 484-1111
Saber Healthcare Group LLC — Akron (G-423)	E	216 292-5706
Saber Healthcare Group LLC — Hudson (G-12142)	E	330 650-0436
Salem Community Hospital — Salem (G-16713)	A	330 332-1551
Salutary Providers Inc — Ashtabula (G-762)	C	440 964-8446
Samaritan Care Center & Villa — Medina (G-14122)	D	330 725-4123
Sanctuary At Tuttle Crossing — Dublin (G-10447)	D	614 408-0182
Sanctuary At Wilmington Place — Dayton (G-9867)	E	937 256-4663
Sateri Home Inc — Youngstown (G-20367)	D	330 758-8106
Schoenbrunn Healthcare — New Philadelphia (G-15114)	D	330 339-3595
Schroer Properties Inc — Lancaster (G-12572)	D	740 687-5100
Schroer Properties Inc — North Canton (G-15365)	D	330 498-8200
Schroer Properties Inc — Mentor (G-14239)	C	440 357-7900
Select Spclty Hsptal-Akron LLC — Akron (G-433)	D	330 761-7500
Semma Enterprises Inc — Middletown (G-14457)	C	513 863-7775
Senior Care Inc — Xenia (G-20075)	E	937 372-1530
Senior Care Inc — Miamisburg (G-14347)	E	937 291-3211
Shelby County Mem Hosp Assn — Sidney (G-16953)	D	937 492-9591
Shepherd of The Valley Luthera — Youngstown (G-20373)	E	330 530-4038
Shepherd of The Valley Luthera — Youngstown (G-20374)	C	330 726-9061
Shg Whitehall Holdings LLC — Columbus (G-8726)	C	216 292-5706
Sienna Hills Nursing & Rehab — Adena (G-8)	E	740 546-3013
Singleton Health Care Center — Cleveland (G-6483)	E	216 231-0076
Sisters of Charity of Cinc — Mount Saint Joseph (G-14871)	D	513 347-5200
Sisters of Little — Warrensville Heights (G-18934)	C	216 464-1222
Sisters of Little — Oregon (G-15749)	E	419 698-4331
Slovene Home For The Aged — Cleveland (G-6490)	C	216 486-0268
Snf Wadsworth LLC — Solon (G-17052)	D	330 336-3472
Somerset NH LLC — Somerset (G-17070)	D	740 743-2924
Southbrook Health Care Ctr Inc — Springfield (G-17275)	C	937 322-3436
Sprenger Entrprises Inc — Lorain (G-13078)	D	440 244-2019
Spring Meadow Extended Care Ce — Holland (G-12057)	D	419 866-6124
Springhills LLC — Middletown (G-14487)	D	513 424-9999
St Augustine Corporation — Lakewood (G-12501)	B	216 939-7600
St Edward Home — Fairlawn (G-10977)	C	330 668-2828
Stone Crossing Assisted Living — Canton (G-2551)	C	330 492-7131
Stow Opco LLC — Stow (G-17394)	D	502 429-8062
Streetsboro Opco LLC — Streetsboro (G-17433)	D	502 429-8062
Summit Facility Operations LLC — Tallmadge (G-17652)	D	330 633-0555
Sumner Home For The Aged Inc — Copley (G-9065)	C	330 666-2952
Sun Healthcare Group Inc — Defiance (G-10060)	E	419 784-1450
Sunbrdge Marion Hlth Care Corp — Marion (G-13582)	D	740 389-6306
Sunbridge Care Enterprises Inc — Lancaster (G-12578)	D	740 653-8630
Sunbridge Healthcare LLC — New Lexington (G-15064)	C	740 342-5161
Sunrise Connecticut Avenue Ass — Columbus (G-8803)	E	614 451-6766
Sunrise Senior Living Inc — Dayton (G-9915)	D	937 438-0054
Sunrise Senior Living Inc — Gahanna (G-11272)	E	614 418-9775
Sunrise Senior Living Inc — Rocky River (G-16593)	D	440 895-2383
Sunrise Senior Living Inc — Westlake (G-19552)	D	440 808-0074
Sunrise Senior Living Inc — Cleveland (G-6551)	D	216 751-0930
Sunrise Senior Living Inc — Upper Arlington (G-18556)	D	614 457-3500
Sunrise Senior Living Inc — Worthington (G-20001)	E	614 846-6500
Sunrise Senior Living LLC — Wooster (G-19917)	E	330 262-1615
Sunrise Senior Living LLC — Findlay (G-11088)	E	419 425-3440
Sunrise Senior Living LLC — Cincinnati (G-4600)	E	513 729-5233
Sunrise Senior Living LLC — Cuyahoga Falls (G-9223)	D	330 929-8500
Sunrise Senior Living LLC — Cleveland (G-6552)	E	216 447-8909
Sunrise Senior Living LLC — Hamilton (G-11776)	E	513 893-9000
Swa Inc — Cleveland (G-6560)	C	440 243-7888
Swan Pnte Fclty Operations LLC — Maumee (G-13983)	E	419 867-7926
Tender Nursing Care — Reynoldsburg (G-16482)	E	614 856-3508
The Maria-Joseph Center — Dayton (G-9926)	B	937 278-2692
Thornville NH LLC — Thornville (G-17669)	D	740 246-5253
Tlevay Inc — Toledo (G-18223)	C	419 385-3958
Toledo Opco LLC — Toledo (G-18245)	D	502 429-8062
Traditions At Bath Rd Inc — Cuyahoga Falls (G-9226)	C	330 929-6272
Trilogy Health Services LLC — Willard (G-19628)	D	419 935-6511
Trilogy Healthcare Allen LLC — Bluffton (G-1736)	D	419 643-3161
Trilogy Healthcare Putnam LLC — Kalida (G-12346)	C	419 532-2961
Trilogy Rehab Services LLC — Zanesville (G-20540)	A	740 452-3000
Trinity Health Corporation — Columbus (G-8872)	B	614 846-5420
Triumph Hospital Mansfield — Mansfield (G-13376)	E	419 526-0777
Twilight Gardens Healthcare — Norwalk (G-15595)	E	419 668-2086
Twin Maples Nursing Home — Mc Arthur (G-14018)	E	740 596-5955
Twin Oaks Care Center Inc — Mansfield (G-13379)	E	419 524-1205
U C M Residential Services — Union City (G-18504)	D	937 643-3757
United Church Homes Inc — Marion (G-13592)	D	740 382-4885
United Church Homes Inc — Sandusky (G-16805)	C	419 621-1900
United Church Homes Inc — Fairborn (G-10806)	C	937 878-0262
United Church Homes Inc — Marietta (G-13510)	D	740 376-5600
United Church Homes Inc — Jackson (G-12320)	D	740 286-7551
University Hospitals Health — Chardon (G-2775)	A	440 285-4040
University Manor Hlth Care Ctr — Cleveland (G-6665)	C	216 721-1400
Uvmc Management Corporation — Troy (G-18385)	D	937 440-4000
Uvmc Nursing Care Inc — Troy (G-18386)	C	937 440-7663
Uvmc Nursing Care Inc — Tipp City (G-17731)	C	937 667-7500
Uvmc Nursing Care Inc — Covington (G-9140)	C	937 473-2075
V Clew LLC — Lancaster (G-12582)	E	740 687-2273

Employee Codes: A=Over 500 employees, B=251-500
C=101-250, D=51-100, E=25-50

2018 Harris Ohio Services Directory

V Vrable Inc C 614 545-5500
Columbus *(G-8929)*
Valley Hospice Inc D 740 859-5041
Rayland *(G-16419)*
Valley View Alzhimers Care Ctr D 740 998-2948
Frankfort *(G-11146)*
Vancare Inc C 937 898-4202
Vandalia *(G-18706)*
Vibra Healthcare LLC E 330 726-5050
Youngstown *(G-20404)*
Vienna Enterprises Inc E 937 568-4524
South Vienna *(G-17101)*
Vista Centre D 330 424-5852
Lisbon *(G-12942)*
Volunters Amer Care Facilities C 419 225-9040
Lima *(G-12911)*
Vrable II Inc D 614 545-5502
Columbus *(G-8955)*
Vrable IV Inc D 614 545-5502
Columbus *(G-8956)*
Walnut Hills Inc C 330 852-2457
Walnut Creek *(G-18786)*
Washington Manor Inc E 937 433-3441
Dayton *(G-9984)*
Waterville Care LLC D 419 878-3901
Waterville *(G-18947)*
Waverly Care Center Inc E 740 947-2113
Waverly *(G-18976)*
Wayside Farms Inc D 330 666-7716
Peninsula *(G-15952)*
West Liberty Care Center Inc C 937 465-5065
West Liberty *(G-19264)*
West Side Dtscher Fruen Verein E 440 238-3361
Strongsville *(G-17524)*
Western Hills Care Center C 513 941-0099
Cincinnati *(G-4841)*
Western Rsrve Msonic Cmnty Inc C 330 721-3000
Medina *(G-14138)*
Wexner Heritage Village B 614 231-4900
Columbus *(G-8984)*
Widows Home of Dayton Ohio D 937 252-1661
Dayton *(G-9997)*
Willow Brook Chrstn Cmmunities D 740 369-0048
Delaware *(G-10135)*
Wilmingtn Nursng/Rehab Resdidn D 937 382-1621
Wilmington *(G-19793)*
Windsor House Inc D 330 743-1393
Youngstown *(G-20417)*
Windsor House Inc D 330 482-1375
Columbiana *(G-6866)*
Windsor House Inc C 330 549-9259
Columbiana *(G-6867)*
Windsor House Inc C 330 759-7858
Youngstown *(G-20416)*
Windsor House Inc E 440 834-0544
Burton *(G-2066)*
Windsor Medical Center Inc D 330 499-8300
Canton *(G-2587)*
Womens Welsh Clubs of America D 440 331-0420
Rocky River *(G-16596)*
Woodland Assisted Living Resi E 614 755-7591
Columbus *(G-9004)*
Woodsfield Opco LLC D 502 429-8062
Woodsfield *(G-19820)*
Woodside Village Care Center D 419 947-2015
Mount Gilead *(G-14865)*
Woodstock Care Center Inc E 937 826-3351
Woodstock *(G-19822)*
Wyant Leasing Co LLC B 330 836-7953
Akron *(G-513)*
Xenia East Management Systems D 937 372-4495
Xenia *(G-20086)*
Xenia West Management Systems D 937 372-8081
Xenia *(G-20087)*
Youngstown Area Jwish Fdration D 330 746-1076
Youngstown *(G-20426)*
Zandex Inc E 740 454-1400
Zanesville *(G-20546)*
Zandex Inc C 740 454-9769
Zanesville *(G-20548)*
Zandex Inc C 740 695-7233
Saint Clairsville *(G-16663)*
Zandex Inc D 740 967-1111
Johnstown *(G-12344)*
Zandex Inc D 740 454-6823
Zanesville *(G-20549)*
Zandex Inc C 740 872-0809
New Concord *(G-15040)*
Zandex Health Care Corporation C 740 452-4636
Zanesville *(G-20550)*
Zandex Health Care Corporation C 740 454-9769
Zanesville *(G-20551)*
Zandex Health Care Corporation C 740 695-7233
Saint Clairsville *(G-16664)*
Zandex Health Care Corporation C 740 454-1400
New Concord *(G-15041)*
Zandex Health Care Corporation E 740 454-1400
Zanesville *(G-20552)*
Zanesville NH LLC D 740 452-4351
Zanesville *(G-20557)*

NURSING HOME, EXC SKILLED & INTERMEDIATE CARE FACILITY

Accurate Healthcare Inc E 513 208-6988
West Chester *(G-19189)*
Alpha Nursing Homes Inc D 740 622-2074
Coshocton *(G-9086)*
Antioch Cnnction Canton MI LLC E 614 531-9285
Pickerington *(G-16085)*
Antioch Salem Fields Frederick E 614 531-9285
Pickerington *(G-16086)*
Apostolic Christian Home Inc D 330 927-1010
Rittman *(G-16550)*
Arbors West LLC D 614 879-7661
West Jefferson *(G-19247)*
Blue Ash Healthcare Group Inc E 513 793-3362
Cincinnati *(G-3118)*
Bristol Village Homes E 740 947-2118
Waverly *(G-18966)*
Bryant Health Center Inc C 740 532-6188
Ironton *(G-12283)*
Buckeye Home Health Care E 937 291-3780
Dayton *(G-9369)*
Center Ridge Nursing Home Inc C 440 327-1295
North Ridgeville *(G-15458)*
Columbus Alzheimers Care Ctr C 614 459-7050
Columbus *(G-7327)*
Communicare Health Svcs Inc D 740 264-1155
Steubenville *(G-17313)*
Community Mercy Foundation C 937 390-9000
Springfield *(G-17172)*
Concord Care Center of Toledo D 419 385-6616
Toledo *(G-17829)*
Concord Hlth Rhabilitation Ctr E 740 574-8441
Wheelersburg *(G-19575)*
Consulate Management Co LLC D 740 259-2351
Lucasville *(G-13176)*
Country Acres of Wayne County E 330 698-2031
Wooster *(G-19852)*
Country Club Retirement Center D 440 992-0022
Ashtabula *(G-738)*
Country Club Retirement Center C 740 671-9330
Bellaire *(G-1365)*
Country Meadow Care Center LLC E 419 886-3922
Bellville *(G-1425)*
County of Auglaize C 419 738-3816
Wapakoneta *(G-18793)*
County of Henry E 419 592-8075
Napoleon *(G-14937)*
County of Shelby C 937 492-6900
Sidney *(G-16926)*
County of Wyandot D 419 294-1714
Upper Sandusky *(G-18558)*
Deaconess Long Term Care of MI A 513 487-3600
Cincinnati *(G-3474)*
Dobbins Nursing Home Inc C 513 553-4139
New Richmond *(G-15126)*
East Galbraith Health Care Ctr B 513 984-5220
Cincinnati *(G-3531)*
Elizabeth Scott Inc C 419 865-3002
Maumee *(G-13909)*
Encore Healthcare LLC C 330 769-2015
Seville *(G-16840)*
Evangelical Lutheran D 419 365-5115
Arlington *(G-647)*
First Choice Medical Staffing C 216 521-2222
Cleveland *(G-5592)*
First Community Village B 614 324-4455
Columbus *(G-7664)*
Gillette Associates LP D 330 372-1960
Warren *(G-18859)*
H C F Inc C 740 289-2528
Piketon *(G-16116)*
H C R Corp D 419 472-0076
Toledo *(G-17929)*
Harborside Healthcare NW Ohio C 419 636-5071
Bryan *(G-2007)*
Hardin County Home D 419 673-0961
Kenton *(G-12417)*
Harrison Pavilion E 513 662-5800
Cincinnati *(G-3738)*
Hcf of Findlay Inc D 419 999-2010
Findlay *(G-11044)*
Hcf of Fox Run Inc D 419 424-0832
Findlay *(G-11045)*
Hcf of Washington Inc E 419 999-2010
Wshngtn CT Hs *(G-20026)*
Health Care Opportunities Inc E 513 932-0300
Lebanon *(G-12609)*
Hickory Health Care Inc D 330 762-6486
Akron *(G-263)*
Hospice Tuscarawas County Inc D 330 343-7605
New Philadelphia *(G-15101)*
J W J Investments Inc C 419 643-3161
Bluffton *(G-1732)*
Jacobs Dwelling Nursing Home E 740 824-3635
Coshocton *(G-9109)*
Jennings Ctr For Older Adults B 216 581-2900
Cleveland *(G-5858)*
Kingston Healthcare Company E 419 247-2880
Toledo *(G-17995)*
Lancia Nursing Home Inc E 740 264-7101
Steubenville *(G-17325)*
Laurel Health Care Company D 740 264-5042
Steubenville *(G-17326)*
Levering Management Inc D 740 369-6400
Delaware *(G-10115)*
Levering Management Inc E 419 768-2401
Chesterville *(G-2806)*
Lincoln Park Associates II LP C 937 297-4300
Dayton *(G-9683)*
Maplewood At Bath Creek LLC D 234 208-9872
Cuyahoga Falls *(G-9207)*
Marion Manor D 740 387-9545
Marion *(G-13562)*
Mercer Residential Services E 419 586-4709
Celina *(G-2656)*
Mercy Health West Park C 513 451-8900
Cincinnati *(G-4076)*
Mikouis Enterprise Inc D 330 424-1418
Lisbon *(G-12940)*
Mill Run Care Center LLC D 614 527-3000
Hilliard *(G-11935)*
Mkjb Inc C 513 851-8400
Cincinnati *(G-4108)*
Mohun Health Care Center E 614 416-6132
Columbus *(G-8182)*
New Concord Health Center C 740 826-4135
New Concord *(G-15036)*
Norwood Health Care Center LLC D 513 351-0153
Cincinnati *(G-4186)*
Nursing Care MGT Amer Inc D 740 927-9888
Pataskala *(G-15924)*
Nursing Care MGT Amer Inc D 513 793-5092
Cincinnati *(G-4194)*
Oakhill Manor Care Center C 330 875-5060
Louisville *(G-13104)*
Oakwood Health Care Svcs Inc D 440 439-7976
Cleveland *(G-6175)*
Orchard Villa Inc C 419 697-4100
Oregon *(G-15744)*
Otterbein Snior Lfstyle Chices C 513 260-7690
Middletown *(G-14483)*
Overlook House E 216 795-3550
Cleveland *(G-6221)*
Park Haven Inc E 440 992-9441
Ashtabula *(G-759)*
Partners of City View LLC C 216 361-1414
Cleveland *(G-6247)*
Rae-Ann Holdings Inc D 440 871-0500
Westlake *(G-19539)*
Rae-Ann Holdings Inc D 440 871-5181
Cleveland *(G-6347)*
Regency Park D 330 682-2273
Orrville *(G-15785)*
Regency Park Nursing & Rehab D 330 682-2273
Orrville *(G-15786)*
Residence At Kensington Place C 513 863-4218
Hamilton *(G-11769)*
Roselawn Health Services Corp E 330 823-0618
Alliance *(G-558)*
Samaritan Care Center & Villa D 330 725-4123
Medina *(G-14122)*
Sarah Moore Hlth Care Ctr Inc D 740 362-9641
Delaware *(G-10125)*
Schoenbrunn Healthcare D 330 339-3595
New Philadelphia *(G-15114)*
Serenity Center Inc C 614 891-1111
Columbus *(G-8714)*

SERVICES SECTION

Shiloh Group ....C..... 937 833-2219
  Brookville (G-1966)
Society of The Transfiguration ....E..... 513 771-7462
  Cincinnati (G-4548)
Steubenville Country CLB Manor ....D..... 740 266-6118
  Steubenville (G-17335)
Stratford Commons Inc ....C..... 440 914-0900
  Solon (G-17056)
Summit At Park Hills LLC ....E..... 317 462-8048
  Fairborn (G-10805)
Sunrise Senior Living Inc ....E..... 614 846-6500
  Worthington (G-20001)
Susan A Smith Crystal Care ....E..... 419 747-2666
  Butler (G-2068)
The Villa At Lake MGT Co ....D..... 440 599-1999
  Conneaut (G-9048)
Traditions At Mill Run ....D..... 614 771-0100
  Hilliard (G-11960)
Traditions of Chillicothe ....E..... 740 773-8107
  Chillicothe (G-2890)
Uvmc Nursing Care Inc ....C..... 937 473-2075
  Covington (G-9140)
Windsor House Inc ....C..... 330 759-7858
  Youngstown (G-20416)
Yorkland Health Care Inc ....D..... 614 751-2525
  Columbus (G-9016)
Youngstown Area Jwish Fdration ....D..... 330 746-1076
  Youngstown (G-20426)
Zandex Health Care Corporation ....C..... 740 695-7233
  Saint Clairsville (G-16664)

NUTRITION SVCS

Abbott Laboratories ....A..... 614 624-3191
  Columbus (G-6924)
Ironton and Lawrence County ....E..... 740 532-7855
  Ironton (G-12292)
Ironton and Lawrence County ....B..... 740 532-3534
  Ironton (G-12291)
New Carlisle Spt & Fitnes Ctr ....E..... 937 846-1000
  New Carlisle (G-15029)
Ohio State University ....E..... 614 292-5504
  Columbus (G-8397)
Wright Nutrition Inc ....E..... 614 873-0418
  Plain City (G-16212)

NUTS: Metal

Facil North America Inc ....C..... 330 487-2500
  Twinsburg (G-18414)

OFC/CLINIC OF MED DRS: Special, Phys Or Surgeon, Eye Or ENT

Cei Physicians PSC Inc ....E..... 513 531-2020
  Cincinnati (G-3201)
David M Schneider MD Inc ....E..... 513 752-5700
  Cincinnati (G-2912)
Lca-Vision Inc ....C..... 513 792-9292
  Cincinnati (G-3966)
Northast Ohio Eye Surgeons Inc ....E..... 330 678-0201
  Kent (G-12387)
Ohio Retina Associates Inc ....E..... 330 966-9800
  Canton (G-2484)
Surgicenter Ltd ....E..... 740 522-3937
  Newark (G-15237)
System Optics Laser Vision Ctr ....D..... 330 630-2451
  Tallmadge (G-17654)

OFC/CLINIC OF MED DRS: Specl, Phys Or Surgeon, Occup & Indl

Medcentral Health System ....E..... 419 526-8900
  Ontario (G-15701)
Shapiro Shapiro & Shapiro ....E..... 216 927-2030
  Cleveland (G-6477)
Whole Health Management Inc ....E..... 216 921-8601
  Cleveland (G-6751)

OFC/CLINIC, MED DRS: Specl, Phys Or Surgeon, Infect Disease

Central Ohio Primary Care ....D..... 614 508-0110
  Westerville (G-19380)
Ohio State University ....E..... 614 293-8732
  Columbus (G-8415)

OFCS & CLINICS,MEDICAL DRS: Specl, Physician Or Surgn, ENT

Cincinnati Head and Neck Inc ....E..... 513 232-3277
  Cincinnati (G-3308)
Cleveland Ear Nose Throat Ctr ....E..... 440 550-4179
  Mayfield Heights (G-13999)
Dayton Ear Nose Throat Srgeons ....E..... 937 434-0555
  Dayton (G-9473)
E N T Toledo Inc ....E..... 419 578-7555
  Toledo (G-17860)
ENt and Allergy Health Svcs ....E..... 440 779-1112
  North Olmsted (G-15420)
Ohio Head & Neck Surgeons Inc ....E..... 330 492-2844
  Canton (G-2480)
Richard J Nelson MD ....E..... 419 578-7555
  Maumee (G-13971)
University Otolaryngologists ....E..... 614 273-2241
  Columbus (G-8910)

OFFICE CLEANING OR CHARRING SVCS

Clinton-Carvell Inc ....E..... 614 351-8858
  Columbus (G-7303)
Rcs Enterprises Inc ....D..... 614 337-8520
  Columbus (G-8591)
Scarlet & Gray Cleaning Svc ....C..... 513 661-4483
  Cincinnati (G-4479)
Stb Enterprises ....E..... 330 478-0044
  Canton (G-2548)

OFFICE EQPT & ACCESSORY CUSTOMIZING SVCS

Andrew Belmont Sargent ....E..... 513 769-7800
  Cincinnati (G-3027)
Document Imaging Spcialists LLC ....E..... 614 868-9008
  Columbus (G-7538)
Fusion Interior Services Ltd ....E..... 513 759-4100
  West Chester (G-19077)

OFFICE EQPT WHOLESALERS

American Copy Equipment Inc ....C..... 330 722-9555
  Cleveland (G-5008)
Apg Office Furnishings Inc ....E..... 216 621-4590
  Cleveland (G-5048)
Big Lots Stores Inc ....B..... 614 278-6800
  Columbus (G-7107)
Business Alternatives Inc ....E..... 724 325-2777
  Uniontown (G-18509)
Collaborative Inc ....E..... 419 242-7405
  Toledo (G-17819)
Comdoc Inc ....C..... 330 896-2346
  Uniontown (G-18514)
David Francis Corporation ....C..... 216 524-0900
  Cleveland (G-5466)
Document Imaging Spcialists LLC ....E..... 614 868-9008
  Columbus (G-7538)
Essendant Co ....C..... 330 425-4001
  Twinsburg (G-18412)
Essendant Co ....D..... 614 876-7774
  Columbus (G-7610)
Friends Service Co Inc ....D..... 419 427-1704
  Findlay (G-11033)
Giesecke & Devrient Amer Inc ....C..... 330 425-1515
  Twinsburg (G-18423)
Lorain Cnty Sty Off Eqp Co Inc ....E..... 440 960-7070
  Amherst (G-599)
M T Business Technologies ....E..... 440 933-7682
  Avon Lake (G-935)
Modern Office Methods Inc ....D..... 513 791-0909
  Blue Ash (G-1644)
Office Depot Inc ....E..... 800 463-3768
  Cleveland (G-6179)
Office Products Inc/Cleveland ....E..... 919 754-3700
  Cleveland (G-6181)
Office World Inc ....E..... 419 991-4694
  Lima (G-12928)
Ohio Business Machines LLC ....E..... 216 485-2000
  Cleveland (G-6187)
P-N-D Communications Inc ....E..... 419 683-1922
  Crestline (G-9149)
Perry Pro Tech Inc ....E..... 419 475-9030
  Perrysburg (G-16040)
Perry Pro Tech Inc ....D..... 419 228-1360
  Lima (G-12857)
Springfield Business Eqp Co ....E..... 937 322-3828
  Springfield (G-17279)
Symatic Inc ....E..... 330 225-1510
  Brunswick (G-1991)

OFFICE SPLYS, NEC, WHOLESALE

Viking Office Products Inc ....B..... 513 881-7200
  West Chester (G-19181)
W B Mason Co Inc ....D..... 216 267-5000
  Cleveland (G-6713)
Xerox Corporation ....B..... 513 554-3200
  Blue Ash (G-1724)

OFFICE EQPT, WHOLESALE: Blueprinting

Franklin Imaging Llc ....E..... 614 885-6894
  Columbus (G-7697)

OFFICE EQPT, WHOLESALE: Duplicating Machines

Konica Minolta Business Soluti ....E..... 910 990-5837
  Cleveland (G-5911)
Northcoast Duplicating Inc ....C..... 216 573-6681
  Cleveland (G-6150)

OFFICE EQPT, WHOLESALE: Photocopy Machines

Comdoc Inc ....E..... 330 539-4822
  Girard (G-11410)
Donnellon Mc Carthy Inc ....E..... 937 299-3564
  Moraine (G-14775)
Donnellon Mc Carthy Inc ....E..... 513 681-3200
  Cincinnati (G-3498)
Goodremonts ....E..... 419 476-1492
  Toledo (G-17918)
Gordon Flesch Company Inc ....E..... 419 884-2031
  Mansfield (G-13305)
Graphic Enterprises Inc ....D..... 800 553-6616
  North Canton (G-15340)
Ricoh Usa Inc ....D..... 513 984-9898
  Blue Ash (G-1683)
Ricoh Usa Inc ....D..... 614 310-6500
  Worthington (G-19994)
Ricoh Usa Inc ....D..... 330 523-3900
  Richfield (G-16527)
Xerox Corporation ....D..... 216 642-7806
  Cleveland (G-6767)

OFFICE FURNITURE REPAIR & MAINTENANCE SVCS

Recycled Systems Furniture Inc ....E..... 614 880-9110
  Worthington (G-19991)

OFFICE MANAGEMENT SVCS

North Randall Village ....D..... 216 663-1112
  Cleveland (G-6143)
Outreach Professional Svcs Inc ....D..... 216 472-4094
  Cleveland (G-6219)
Summit Advantage LLC ....D..... 330 835-2453
  Fairlawn (G-10979)

OFFICE SPLY & STATIONERY STORES

Staples Inc ....E..... 740 845-5600
  London (G-13007)
Staples Inc ....E..... 614 472-2014
  Columbus (G-8775)

OFFICE SPLY & STATIONERY STORES: Office Forms & Splys

Hubbard Company ....E..... 419 784-4455
  Defiance (G-10034)
Lorain Cnty Sty Off Eqp Co Inc ....E..... 440 960-7070
  Amherst (G-599)
Office Depot Inc ....E..... 800 463-3768
  Cleveland (C-6179)
OfficeMax North America Inc ....E..... 614 899-6186
  Westerville (G-19431)
Veritiv Operating Company ....E..... 419 243-6100
  Toledo (G-18289)
Viking Office Products Inc ....B..... 513 881-7200
  West Chester (G-19181)

OFFICE SPLY & STATIONERY STORES: School Splys

United Art and Education Inc ....E..... 800 322-3247
  Dayton (G-9945)

OFFICE SPLYS, NEC, WHOLESALE

Essendant Co ....D..... 330 650-9361
  Hudson (G-12116)

Employee Codes: A=Over 500 employees, B=251-500
C=101-250, D=51-100, E=25-50

OFFICE SPLYS, NEC, WHOLESALE

Essendant Co .... C 330 425-4001
  Twinsburg (G-18412)
Essendant Co .... D 513 942-1354
  West Chester (G-19197)
Essendant Co .... D 614 876-7774
  Columbus (G-7610)
OfficeMax North America Inc .... E 330 666-4550
  Akron (G-362)
Powell Company Ltd .... D 419 228-3552
  Lima (G-12861)
Seagate Office Products Inc .... E 419 861-6161
  Holland (G-12055)
Wasserstrom Company .... B 614 228-6525
  Columbus (G-8970)

OFFICES & CLINICS DOCTORS OF MED: Intrnl Med Practitioners

Cardiologist of Clark & Champ .... E 937 323-1404
  Springfield (G-17156)
Central Ohio Primary Care .... E 614 882-0708
  Westerville (G-19381)
David Lee Grossman MD .... E 419 843-8150
  Toledo (G-17844)
Erieside Medical Group .... E 440 918-6270
  Willoughby (G-19662)
Joint Township Dst Mem Hosp .... D 419 394-9959
  Saint Marys (G-16675)
Unity Health Network LLC .... E 330 678-7782
  Kent (G-12403)

OFFICES & CLINICS DRS OF MED: Psychiatrists/Psychoanalysts

Consolidated Care Inc .... E 937 465-8065
  West Liberty (G-19262)

OFFICES & CLINICS HLTH PRACTITNRS: Psychiatric Social Wrkr

Consolidated Care Inc .... E 937 465-8065
  West Liberty (G-19262)
Pastoral Counseling Svc Summit .... C 330 996-4600
  Akron (G-378)

OFFICES & CLINICS OF DENTISTS: Dental Clinic

Cincinnati Dental Services .... E 513 741-7779
  Cincinnati (G-3297)
Hudec Dental Associates Inc .... D 216 485-5788
  Brecksville (G-1828)
Metrohealth Dept of Dentistry .... E 216 778-4739
  Cleveland (G-6035)
Smile Brands Inc .... E 419 627-1255
  Sandusky (G-16795)
State Valley Dental Center .... E 330 920-8060
  Cuyahoga Falls (G-9220)
Stow Dental Group Inc .... E 330 688-6456
  Stow (G-17393)

OFFICES & CLINICS OF DENTISTS: Dental Surgeon

Ohio State University .... E 614 292-5144
  Columbus (G-8420)
Oral & Maxillofacial Surgeons .... E 419 385-5743
  Toledo (G-18110)

OFFICES & CLINICS OF DENTISTS: Dentists' Office

Advance Implant Dentistry Inc .... E 513 271-0821
  Cincinnati (G-2974)
Ashtabula Dental Associates .... E 440 992-3146
  Ashtabula (G-724)
Charles C Smith DDS Inc .... E 937 667-2417
  Tipp City (G-17712)
Chester West Dentistry .... E 330 753-7734
  Akron (G-131)
Cincinnati Dental Services .... E 513 753-6446
  Cincinnati (G-2907)
Cincinnati Dental Services .... E 513 721-8888
  Cincinnati (G-3298)
Cincinnati Dental Services .... E 513 774-8800
  Loveland (G-13114)
Dental Facility .... E 614 292-1472
  Columbus (G-7508)
Dental Health Group PA .... E 330 630-9222
  Akron (G-189)

Dental Health Services .... E 330 864-9090
  Fairlawn (G-10944)
Donald Bowen and Assoc DDS .... E 614 274-0454
  Columbus (G-7540)
Family Dental Team Inc .... E 330 733-7911
  Fairlawn (G-10951)
Family Dentistry Inc .... E 513 932-6991
  Lebanon (G-12605)
Fixari Family Dental Inc .... E 614 866-7445
  Columbus (G-7672)
Hopewell Dental Care .... E 740 522-5000
  Newark (G-15174)
Lawrence M Shell DDS .... E 614 235-3444
  Columbus (G-8045)
Locust Dental Center .... E 330 535-7876
  Akron (G-327)
Lucas & Clark Family Dentistry .... E 937 393-3494
  Hillsboro (G-11986)
Mahoning Valley Dental Service .... E 330 759-1771
  Youngstown (G-20264)
Painesville Dental Group Inc .... E 440 354-2183
  Painesville (G-15872)
Rahn Dental Group Inc .... E 937 435-0324
  Dayton (G-9840)
Raymond A Greiner DDS Inc .... E 440 951-6688
  Mentor (G-14232)
Thomas and Associates .... E 330 494-2111
  Canton (G-2561)
Thomas E Anderson DDS Inc .... E 330 467-6466
  Northfield (G-15525)
US Dental Care/M D Gelender .... E 614 252-3181
  Columbus (G-8923)
Van Buren Dental Associates .... E 937 253-9115
  Kettering (G-12437)

OFFICES & CLINICS OF DENTISTS: Group & Corporate Practice

Chester West Dental Group Inc .... E 513 942-8181
  West Chester (G-19036)

OFFICES & CLINICS OF DENTISTS: Prosthodontist

Association of Prosthodontics .... E 614 885-2022
  Worthington (G-19942)
Ohio State University .... D 614 292-5578
  Columbus (G-8392)
Ohio State University .... D 614 292-1472
  Columbus (G-8439)

OFFICES & CLINICS OF DENTISTS: Specialist, Practitioners

Affiliates In Oral & Maxlofcl .... E 513 829-8080
  West Chester (G-19015)
Equitas Health Inc .... C 614 299-2437
  Columbus (G-7603)

OFFICES & CLINICS OF DOCTORS OF MEDICINE: Allergist

Allergy & Asthma Inc .... E 740 654-8623
  Lancaster (G-12507)
Allergy & Asthma Centre Dayton .... E 937 435-8999
  Centerville (G-2672)
Bernstein Allergy Group Inc .... E 513 931-0775
  Cincinnati (G-3099)

OFFICES & CLINICS OF DOCTORS OF MEDICINE: Anesthesiologist

Anesthesia Associates Inc .... E 440 350-0832
  Painesville (G-15834)
Anesthesiology Assoc of Akron .... E 330 344-6401
  Akron (G-76)
Anesthesiology Consultant Inc .... E 614 566-9983
  Columbus (G-7019)
Anesthesiology Services Netwrk .... E 937 208-6173
  Dayton (G-9337)
Anesthsia Assoc Cincinnati Inc .... D 513 585-0577
  Cincinnati (G-3028)
Bel-Park Anesthesia .... E 330 480-3658
  Youngstown (G-20112)
Cleveland Anesthesia Group .... E 216 901-5706
  Independence (G-12198)
Kettering Anesthesia Assoc Inc .... D 937 298-4331
  Dayton (G-9650)
Kevin C McDonnell MD .... D 330 344-6401
  Akron (G-305)

SERVICES SECTION

Midwest Physcans Ansthsia Svcs .... D 614 884-0641
  Columbus (G-8171)
Russell D Ens Do .... E 330 499-5700
  Canton (G-2520)
Sabry Hospital .... E 216 476-7052
  Cleveland (G-6431)
University Anesthesiologists .... E 216 844-3777
  Cleveland (G-6652)

OFFICES & CLINICS OF DOCTORS OF MEDICINE: Dermatologist

Associates In Dermatology Inc .... E 440 249-0274
  Westlake (G-19462)
Buckeye Drmtlogy Drmthphthlogy .... E 614 389-6331
  Dublin (G-10272)
Buckeye Drmtlogy Drmthphthlogy .... E 614 317-9630
  Grove City (G-11541)
Center For Srgcal Drmtlogy Inc .... D 614 847-4100
  Westerville (G-19289)
Dermatlgists of Southwest Ohio .... E 937 435-2094
  Dayton (G-9498)
H M T Dermatology Inc .... E 330 725-0569
  Medina (G-14073)
Helen M Torok MD .... E 330 722-5477
  Medina (G-14075)
Laser Hair Removal Center .... D 937 433-7536
  Dayton (G-9674)
Patricia A Dickerson MD .... E 937 436-1117
  Dayton (G-9804)
Univ Dermatology .... D 513 475-7630
  Cincinnati (G-4745)
University Dermatology Cons .... E 513 584-4775
  Cincinnati (G-4750)
University Dermatology Cons .... E 513 475-7630
  Cincinnati (G-4751)
Warren Drmatology Allergies PC .... E 330 856-6365
  Warren (G-18924)
Westerville Dermatology Inc .... E 614 895-0400
  Westerville (G-19448)
Wright State Physcans Drmtlogy .... E 937 224-7546
  Beavercreek (G-1221)

OFFICES & CLINICS OF DOCTORS OF MEDICINE: Dispensary

Kindred Healthcare Inc .... D 937 222-5963
  Dayton (G-9660)

OFFICES & CLINICS OF DOCTORS OF MEDICINE: Endocrinologist

Endo-Surgical Center Fla LLC .... B 440 708-0582
  Chagrin Falls (G-2715)
Joslin Diabetes Center Inc .... E 937 401-7575
  Dayton (G-9645)
Reproductive Gynecology Inc .... E 330 452-6010
  Canton (G-2507)

OFFICES & CLINICS OF DOCTORS OF MEDICINE: Gastronomist

Columbus Gstrntrlogy Group Inc .... D 614 457-1213
  Columbus (G-7356)
Consultnts In Gastroenterology .... E 440 386-2250
  Painesville (G-15846)
Dayton Primary & Urgent Care .... E 937 461-0800
  Dayton (G-9487)
Digestive Care Inc .... D 937 320-5050
  Beavercreek (G-1238)
Endoscopy Center of Dayton .... E 937 320-5050
  Beavercreek (G-1239)
Gastrntrlogy Assoc Clvland Inc .... E 216 593-7700
  Cleveland (G-5656)
Gastroenterology Associates .... E 330 493-1480
  Canton (G-2377)
Greater Cincinnati Gastro Assc .... D 513 336-8636
  Cincinnati (G-3709)
North Shore Gstrenterology Inc .... D 440 808-1212
  Westlake (G-19524)
Norwood Endoscopy Center .... E 513 731-5600
  Cincinnati (G-4184)
Nwo Gastroenterology Assoc Inc .... E 419 471-1317
  Toledo (G-18099)
Ohio Gstroenterology Group Inc .... E 614 754-5500
  Columbus (G-8347)
Ohio Gstroenterology Group Inc .... D 614 754-5500
  Columbus (G-8348)
Promedica GI Physicians LLC .... E 419 843-7996
  Toledo (G-18139)

Samaritan Professional Corp..............E....... 419 289-0491
Ashland *(G-696)*

OFFICES & CLINICS OF DOCTORS OF MEDICINE: Group Health Assoc

Primecare Sutheastern Ohio Inc ....E....... 740 454-8551
Zanesville *(G-20526)*

OFFICES & CLINICS OF DOCTORS OF MEDICINE: Gynecologist

Christ Hospital ....E....... 513 564-4000
Cincinnati *(G-3260)*
Findlay Womens Care LLC ....E....... 419 420-0904
Findlay *(G-11030)*
George P Pettit MD Inc ....E....... 740 354-1434
Portsmouth *(G-16279)*
Marietta Gynecologic Assoc ....D....... 740 374-3622
Marietta *(G-13469)*
Maumee Ob Gyn Assoc ....E....... 419 891-6201
Maumee *(G-13945)*
Mercy Health..D....... 419 935-0187
Willard *(G-19623)*
Ob-Gyn Specialists Lima Inc ....E....... 419 227-0610
Lima *(G-12846)*
Obstetrics Gynclogy of Reserve ....E....... 330 666-1166
Akron *(G-361)*
Physicians Surgeons For Women ....E....... 937 323-7340
Springfield *(G-17261)*
Primary Cr Ntwrk Prmr Hlth Prt ....D....... 937 424-9800
Dayton *(G-9826)*
Professionals For Womens Hlth..............E....... 614 268-8800
Columbus *(G-8569)*
Reproductive Gynecology Inc ....E....... 330 375-7722
Akron *(G-411)*
Reserve..E....... 330 666-1166
Akron *(G-413)*
Southwestern Obstetricians & G............E....... 614 875-0444
Grove City *(G-11600)*
Stark County Womens Clinic Inc............D....... 330 493-0313
Canton *(G-2546)*
Sunforest Ob Gyn Associates ....E....... 419 473-6622
Toledo *(G-18208)*
University GYN&ob Cnsltnts Inc ....E....... 614 293-8697
Columbus *(G-8909)*
Womens Care Inc......................................D....... 419 756-6000
Mansfield *(G-13383)*

OFFICES & CLINICS OF DOCTORS OF MEDICINE: Hematologist

Columbus Oncology Associates ....D....... 614 442-3130
Columbus *(G-7375)*
Mahoning Vly Hmtlgy Onclgy Aso ....E....... 330 318-1100
Youngstown *(G-20265)*
Medical Onclgy-Hematology Assn ....E....... 937 223-2183
Dayton *(G-9714)*
Ohio Cancer Specialists ....E....... 419 756-2122
Mansfield *(G-13351)*
Trumbull Mem Hosp Foundation ....A....... 330 841-9376
Warren *(G-18915)*

OFFICES & CLINICS OF DOCTORS OF MEDICINE: Med Insurance Plan

American Para Prof Systems Inc............E....... 513 531-2900
Cincinnati *(G-3011)*
Doctors Ohiohealth Corporation ....A....... 614 544-5424
Columbus *(G-7537)*
Medical Mutual of Ohio ....E....... 614 621-4585
Columbus *(G-8143)*
Ohio State Univ Managed Health............E....... 614 292-8405
Columbus *(G-8380)*

OFFICES & CLINICS OF DOCTORS OF MEDICINE: Nephrologist

Dayton Regional Dialysis Inc...................E....... 937 898-5526
Dayton *(G-9490)*
Kidney & Hypertension Center ....E....... 513 861-0800
Cincinnati *(G-3921)*
Kidney Group Inc.......................................E....... 330 746-1488
Youngstown *(G-20245)*
Riverside Nephrology Assoc Inc ....E....... 614 538-2250
Columbus *(G-8635)*
University of Cincinnati............................E....... 513 558-5471
Cincinnati *(G-4774)*

OFFICES & CLINICS OF DOCTORS OF MEDICINE: Neurologist

Mayfield Clinic Inc....................................D....... 513 221-1100
Cincinnati *(G-4033)*
Neurological Associates Inc ....D....... 614 544-4455
Columbus *(G-8268)*
Neurology Nroscience Assoc Inc............E....... 330 572-1011
Akron *(G-350)*
Nuerocare Center Inc................................D....... 330 494-2917
Canton *(G-2477)*
Nuerological & Sleep Disorders ....E....... 513 721-7533
Cincinnati *(G-4190)*
Orthoneuro ....D....... 614 890-6555
Columbus *(G-8483)*
Riverhills Healthcare Inc ....E....... 513 241-2370
Cincinnati *(G-4425)*
Stark County Neurologists Inc ....D....... 330 494-2097
Canton *(G-2544)*
University Neurology Inc..........................D....... 513 475-8730
Cincinnati *(G-4754)*

OFFICES & CLINICS OF DOCTORS OF MEDICINE: Neurosurgeon

Central Ohio Nrlgical Surgeons...............D....... 614 268-9561
Westerville *(G-19378)*
Chander M Kohli MD Facs Inc ....E....... 330 759-6978
Youngstown *(G-20137)*

OFFICES & CLINICS OF DOCTORS OF MEDICINE: Obstetrician

Alliance For Womens Health ....E....... 419 228-1000
Lima *(G-12738)*
Columbus Obsttrcans Gynclgists............E....... 614 434-2400
Columbus *(G-7374)*
Davue Ob-Gyn Associates Inc ....D....... 937 277-8988
Dayton *(G-9453)*
Greater Cincinnati Ob/Gyn Inc.................E....... 513 245-3103
Cincinnati *(G-3710)*
Marysvlle Obsttrics Gynecology ....E....... 937 644-1244
Marysville *(G-13637)*
Metrohealth System ....D....... 216 778-8446
Cleveland *(G-6040)*
Obstetrics & Gynecology S Inc ....E....... 937 296-0167
Dayton *(G-9782)*
Ohio State University................................ .... 614 293-4997
Columbus *(G-8411)*
Preble County General Hlth Dst ....E....... 937 472-0087
Eaton *(G-10575)*
Primehalth Wns Hlth Specialist................E....... 440 918-4630
Willoughby Hills *(G-19733)*
Progressive Womens Care ....E....... 330 629-8466
Youngstown *(G-20330)*
Seven Hills Obgyn Associates ....E....... 513 922-6666
Cincinnati *(G-4503)*
Seven Hills Womens Health Ctrs.............C....... 513 721-3200
Cincinnati *(G-4504)*
Women Health Partners ....E....... 740 363-9021
Delaware *(G-10136)*

OFFICES & CLINICS OF DOCTORS OF MEDICINE: Oncologist

Dayton Physicians LLC ....D....... 937 280-8400
Dayton *(G-9486)*
Hope Ctr For Cncer Care Warren ....D....... 330 856-8600
Warren *(G-18863)*
Independence Oncology ....E....... 216 524-7979
Cleveland *(G-5812)*
Mercy Hospital Tiffin Ohio ....B....... 419 455-8101
Tiffin *(G-17685)*
Ohio State University................................A....... 614 293-5066
Columbus *(G-8436)*
Ohio State University................................A....... 614 257-3000
Columbus *(G-8393)*
Oncolgy/Hmatology Care Inc PSC ....E....... 513 751-2145
Cincinnati *(G-4226)*
Trihealth Oncology Inst LLC ....E....... 513 451-4033
Cincinnati *(G-4697)*
University Hospitals Cleveland ....E....... 440 205-5755
Mentor *(G-14252)*
US Oncology Inc ....E....... 937 352-2140
Xenia *(G-20082)*

OFFICES & CLINICS OF DOCTORS OF MEDICINE: Ophthalmologist

Assocted Ctract Laser Surgeons ....E....... 419 693-4444
Oregon *(G-15724)*
Aultman North Inc.....................................E....... 330 305-6999
Canton *(G-2258)*
Belmont Eye Clinic Inc ....E....... 330 759-7672
Youngstown *(G-20114)*
Canton Ophthalmology Assoc ....E....... 330 994-1286
Canton *(G-2294)*
Cei Physicians Inc ....B....... 513 984-5133
Blue Ash *(G-1553)*
Cei Physicians PSC Inc ....C....... 513 984-5133
Blue Ash *(G-1554)*
Cei Physicians PSC Inc ....E....... 513 233-2700
Cincinnati *(G-3200)*
Drs Ravin Birndorf Ravin Inc ....E....... 877 852-8463
Toledo *(G-17856)*
Eye Care Associates Inc ....D....... 330 746-7691
Youngstown *(G-20183)*
Eye Centers of Ohio Inc ....E....... 330 966-1111
North Canton *(G-15336)*
Eye Centers of Ohio Inc ....E....... 330 966-1111
Canton *(G-2362)*
Fairview Eye Center Inc............................E....... 440 333-3060
Cleveland *(G-5566)*
Kathleen K Karol MD ....D....... 419 878-7992
Toledo *(G-17991)*
Kunesh Eye Center Inc ....E....... 937 298-1703
Oakwood *(G-15621)*
Northast Ohio Eye Surgeons Inc ....E....... 330 836-8545
Akron *(G-353)*
Northwest Eye Surgeons Inc ....E....... 614 451-7550
Columbus *(G-8295)*
Ohio Eye Alliance......................................E....... 330 823-1680
Alliance *(G-550)*
Ohio Eyecare Specialists Inc ....E....... 937 222-3937
Oakwood *(G-15622)*
Ohio State University................................A....... 614 293-8116
Columbus *(G-8396)*
Ophthalmology Associates of ....E....... 419 865-3866
Maumee *(G-13953)*
Ophthlmic Srgeons Cons of Ohio ....E....... 614 221-7464
Columbus *(G-8472)*
Optivue Inc ....C....... 419 891-1391
Oregon *(G-15743)*
Pajka Eye Center Inc.................................E....... 419 228-7432
Lima *(G-12854)*
Regency Park Eye Associates ....E....... 419 882-0588
Toledo *(G-18146)*
Retina Associate of Cleveland ....E....... 216 831-5700
Beachwood *(G-1119)*
Retina Associate of Cleveland ....E....... 216 221-2878
Lakewood *(G-12498)*
Retina Vitreous Associates ....E....... 419 517-6599
Toledo *(G-18154)*
Robert Wiley MD Inc ....E....... 216 621-3211
Cleveland *(G-6405)*
Signature Optical Inc................................E....... 216 831-6299
Beachwood *(G-1126)*
Southern Ohio Eye Assoc LLC.................E....... 740 773-6347
Chillicothe *(G-2886)*
Spectrum Eye Care Inc ....E....... 419 423-8665
Findlay *(G-11083)*
Summit Opthomology Optical ....E....... 330 864-8060
Akron *(G-468)*
System Optics Csmt Srgcal Arts ....E....... 330 630-9699
Tallmadge *(G-17653)*
TLC Eyecare ....E....... 419 882-2020
Toledo *(G-18222)*
University Ophthalmology Assoc ....E....... 216 382-8022
Cleveland *(G-6666)*
Vision Associates Inc ....D....... 419 578-7598
Toledo *(G-18292)*
Wooster Ophthalmologists Inc ....E....... 330 345-7800
Wooster *(G-19933)*

OFFICES & CLINICS OF DOCTORS OF MEDICINE: Pathologist

County of Montgomery..............................E....... 937 225-4156
Dayton *(G-9440)*

OFFICES & CLINICS OF DOCTORS OF MEDICINE: Pediatrician

Anderson Hills Pediatrics Inc ....D....... 513 232-8100
Cincinnati *(G-3023)*

AP Cchmc .... E 513 636-4200
Cincinnati *(G-3032)*
Central Ohio Primary Care .... E 614 891-9505
Westerville *(G-19290)*
Central Ohio Primary Care .... E 614 834-8042
Canal Winchester *(G-2156)*
Central Ohio Primary Care .... E 614 540-7339
Worthington *(G-19946)*
Child & Adolescent Speciality .... E 937 667-7711
Tipp City *(G-17713)*
Children Medical Group Inc .... E 330 762-9033
Akron *(G-133)*
Childrens Hospital Medical Ctr .... A 513 636-8778
Cincinnati *(G-3254)*
Childrens Physician Inc .... E 330 494-5600
Canton *(G-2306)*
Comprehensive Pediatrics .... E 440 835-8270
Westlake *(G-19479)*
Eastern Hills Pediatric Assoc .... E 513 231-3345
Cincinnati *(G-3536)*
Emerald Pediatrics .... E 614 932-5050
Dublin *(G-10335)*
Healthsource of Ohio Inc .... E 937 392-4381
Georgetown *(G-11395)*
Jon R Dvorak MD .... E 419 872-7700
Perrysburg *(G-16021)*
Kiddie West Pediatric Center .... E 614 276-7733
Columbus *(G-7986)*
Mid-Ohio Pdiatrics Adolescents .... E 614 899-0000
Westerville *(G-19425)*
New Beginnings Pediatrics Inc .... E 419 483-4122
Bellevue *(G-1413)*
Ohio Pediatrics Inc .... E 937 299-2339
Dayton *(G-9787)*
Ohio Pediatrics Inc .... E 937 299-2743
Dayton *(G-9788)*
Pediatric Assoc Cincinnati .... E 513 791-1222
Cincinnati *(G-4272)*
Pediatric Assoc of Fairfield .... E 513 874-9460
Fairfield *(G-10893)*
Pediatric Assoc of Springfield .... D 937 328-2320
Springfield *(G-17259)*
Pediatric Associates Inc .... E 614 501-7337
Columbus *(G-8530)*
Pediatric Associates of Dayton .... E 937 832-7337
Englewood *(G-10715)*
Pediatric Care Inc .... E 513 931-6357
Cincinnati *(G-4273)*
Pediatric Services Inc .... E 440 845-1500
Cleveland *(G-6259)*
Pediatrics Assoc of Mt Carmel .... E 513 752-3650
Cincinnati *(G-2927)*
Pediatrics of Akron Inc .... E 330 253-7753
Akron *(G-380)*
Pediatrics of Lima Inc .... E 419 222-4045
Lima *(G-12856)*
Perrysburg Pediatrics .... E 419 872-7700
Perrysburg *(G-16042)*
Portage Pediatrics .... E 330 297-8824
Ravenna *(G-16401)*
Primary Care Physicians Assn .... E 330 499-9944
Canton *(G-2493)*
Queen City Physicians .... D 513 872-2061
Cincinnati *(G-4368)*
Rocking Horse Chld Hlth Ctr .... E 937 328-7266
Springfield *(G-17265)*
Trihealth G LLC .... D 513 624-5535
Cincinnati *(G-4695)*
University Prmry Care Prctices .... E 440 946-7391
Willoughby *(G-19720)*
West Side Pediatrics Inc .... E 513 922-8200
Cincinnati *(G-4838)*

OFFICES & CLINICS OF DOCTORS OF MEDICINE: Psychiatric Clinic

Osu Psychiatry LLC .... E 614 794-1818
Columbus *(G-8492)*
Psy-Care Inc .... E 330 856-6663
Warren *(G-18891)*
Psychiatric Solutions Inc .... C 440 953-3000
Willoughby *(G-19706)*
Psychiatric Solutions Inc .... C 330 759-2700
Youngstown *(G-20333)*
Psychiatric Solutions Inc .... C 419 891-9333
Maumee *(G-13963)*
Psychiatric Solutions Inc .... C 740 695-2131
Saint Clairsville *(G-16653)*

OFFICES & CLINICS OF DOCTORS OF MEDICINE: Psychiatrist

Rakesh Ranjan MD & Assoc Inc .... E 216 375-9897
Cleveland *(G-6350)*
University of Cincinnati .... D 513 558-7700
Cincinnati *(G-4758)*
University of Toledo .... D 419 534-3770
Toledo *(G-18277)*

OFFICES & CLINICS OF DOCTORS OF MEDICINE: Radiologist

Advocate Radiology Bil .... C 614 210-1885
Powell *(G-16323)*
Akron Radiology Inc .... E 330 375-3043
Akron *(G-53)*
Christ Hospital .... D 513 585-0050
Cincinnati *(G-3265)*
Christ Hospital .... C 513 351-0800
Cincinnati *(G-3268)*
Dayton Medical Imaging .... D 937 439-0390
Dayton *(G-9481)*
Drs Hill & Thomas Co .... E 440 944-8887
Cleveland *(G-5509)*
Franklin & Seidelmann Inc .... E 216 255-5700
Beachwood *(G-1081)*
Mrp Inc .... E 513 965-9700
Milford *(G-14543)*
Nuray Radiologists Inc .... E 513 965-8059
Cincinnati *(G-4191)*
Osu Radiology LLC .... E 614 293-8315
Columbus *(G-8493)*
Premier Radiology Group Inc .... E 937 431-9729
Beavercreek *(G-1198)*
Radiology Physicians Inc .... E 614 717-9840
Delaware *(G-10121)*
Riverside Radiology and .... C 614 340-7747
Columbus *(G-8636)*
Summa Health System .... B 330 864-8060
Akron *(G-461)*
Uc Health Llc .... A 513 475-7458
West Chester *(G-19167)*
University of Toledo .... E 419 383-5322
Toledo *(G-18280)*
University Radiology Assoc .... D 513 475-8760
Cincinnati *(G-4784)*
University Rdlgsts of Clveland .... D 216 844-1700
Cleveland *(G-6668)*
Vanguard Imaging Partners .... D 937 236-4780
Dayton *(G-9966)*

OFFICES & CLINICS OF DOCTORS OF MEDICINE: Surgeon

Affiliates In Oral & Maxlofcl .... E 513 829-8080
West Chester *(G-19015)*
Akron General Health System .... E 330 665-8200
Akron *(G-42)*
Chirst Hospital Surgery Center .... E 513 272-3448
Cincinnati *(G-3257)*
Cincinnati Hand Surgery Cons .... E 513 961-4263
Cincinnati *(G-3307)*
Crystal Clinic Surgery Ctr Inc .... A 330 668-4040
Akron *(G-178)*
Evokes LLC .... E 513 947-8433
Mason *(G-13700)*
Mercy Health .... E 513 686-5392
Cincinnati *(G-4059)*
Neurosurgical Network Inc .... E 419 251-1155
Toledo *(G-18083)*
Northast Srgical Assoc of Ohio .... E 216 643-2780
Independence *(G-12240)*
Nueterra Holdings LLC .... E 614 451-0500
Columbus *(G-8304)*
Oral & Maxillofacial Surgeons .... E 419 471-0300
Toledo *(G-18111)*
Osu Surgery LLC .... E 614 293-8116
Columbus *(G-8495)*
Osu Surgery LLC .... C 614 261-1141
Columbus *(G-8496)*
Premier Health Specialists Inc .... E 937 223-4518
Dayton *(G-9821)*
Provider Physicians Inc .... D 614 755-3000
Columbus *(G-8574)*
Queen City General & Vascular .... E 513 232-8181
Cincinnati *(G-4364)*
Riverhills Healthcare Inc .... E 513 791-6400
Cincinnati *(G-4426)*
Surgery Center Cincinnati LLC .... D 513 947-1130
Cincinnati *(G-2934)*
Surgery Ctr An Ohio Ltd Partnr .... D 440 826-3240
Cleveland *(G-6559)*
Surgical Hosp At Southwoods .... E 330 729-8000
Youngstown *(G-20385)*
Taylor Stn Surgical Ctr Ltd .... D 614 751-4466
Columbus *(G-8824)*
Thomas E Rojewski MD Inc .... E 740 454-0158
Zanesville *(G-20538)*
Uc Health Llc .... A 513 475-8881
West Chester *(G-19169)*
University of Cncnnati Srgeons .... E 513 245-3300
Cincinnati *(G-4782)*
University Surgeons Inc .... E 216 844-3021
Cleveland *(G-6671)*
West Central Ohio Group Ltd .... D 419 224-7586
Lima *(G-12915)*

OFFICES & CLINICS OF DOCTORS OF MEDICINE: Surgeon, Plastic

A Thomas Dalagiannis MD .... E 419 887-7000
Maumee *(G-13870)*
Akron Plastic Surgeons Inc .... E 330 253-9161
Akron *(G-50)*
Lawrence A Cervino MD .... E 330 668-4065
Akron *(G-313)*
Lu-Jean Feng Clinic LLC .... E 216 831-7007
Cleveland *(G-5956)*
Ohio Clinic Aesthc Plstc Srgy .... E 440 808-9315
Westlake *(G-19527)*
Plastic Surgery Group Inc .... E 513 791-4440
Cincinnati *(G-4303)*

OFFICES & CLINICS OF DOCTORS OF MEDICINE: Urologist

Advanced Urology Inc .... E 330 758-9787
Youngstown *(G-20098)*
Bruce R Bracken .... E 513 558-3700
Cincinnati *(G-3144)*
Gem City Urologist Inc .... E 937 832-8400
Englewood *(G-10705)*
Northwest Columbus Urology .... E 937 342-9260
Springfield *(G-17253)*
Parkway Surgery Center Inc .... D 419 531-7860
Toledo *(G-18120)*
Promedica Gnt-Urinary Surgeons .... E 419 531-8558
Toledo *(G-18140)*
South Dyton Urlgcal Asscations .... E 937 294-1489
Dayton *(G-9891)*
Southwest Urology LLC .... E 440 845-0900
Cleveland *(G-6507)*
Uhmg Department of Urologist .... E 216 844-3009
Cleveland *(G-6629)*
Urological Associates Inc .... E 614 221-5189
Columbus *(G-8920)*

OFFICES & CLINICS OF DOCTORS, MEDICINE: Gen & Fam Practice

Adena Pckwy-Ross Fmly Physcans .... E 740 779-4500
Chillicothe *(G-2813)*
Alta Partners LLC .... E 440 808-3654
Westlake *(G-19458)*
Barberton Area Family Practice .... E 330 615-3205
Barberton *(G-956)*
Blanchard Valley Hospital .... E 419 423-4335
Findlay *(G-10999)*
Butler Cnty Cmnty Hlth Cnsrtm .... D 513 454-1460
Hamilton *(G-11699)*
Campolo Michael MD .... E 740 522-7600
Newark *(G-15154)*
Canal Physician Group .... E 330 344-4000
Akron *(G-120)*
Central Ohio Primary Care .... E 614 459-3687
Columbus *(G-7234)*
Chillicothe Family Physicians .... E 740 779-4100
Chillicothe *(G-2820)*
Christ Hospital .... D 513 721-8272
Cincinnati *(G-3259)*
Christ Hospital .... D 513 631-3300
Cincinnati *(G-3267)*
City of Columbus .... E 614 645-1600
Columbus *(G-7280)*
Clevelan Clinic Hlth Sys W Reg .... E 216 476-7606
Cleveland *(G-5288)*
Clinton Memorial Hospital .... E 937 383-3402
Wilmington *(G-19754)*

Corporate Health Dimensions ....E 740 775-6119
Chillicothe *(G-2828)*
Defiance Family Physicians ....E 419 785-3281
Defiance *(G-10026)*
Dennis C McCluskey MD & Assoc ....E 330 628-2686
Mogadore *(G-14675)*
Doctors Hosp Physcn Svcs LLC ....E 330 834-4725
Massillon *(G-13801)*
Dublin Family Care Inc ....E 614 761-2244
Dublin *(G-10327)*
Dunlap Family Physicians Inc ....E 330 684-2015
Orrville *(G-15769)*
Fallen Timbers Fmly Physicians ....D 419 893-3321
Maumee *(G-13913)*
Falls Family Practice Inc ....E 330 923-9585
Cuyahoga Falls *(G-9182)*
Family Health Care Center Inc ....E 614 274-4171
Columbus *(G-7635)*
Family Medical Group ....E 513 389-1400
Cincinnati *(G-3589)*
Family Medicine Center Minerva ....E 330 868-4184
Minerva *(G-14645)*
Family Medicine Stark County ....E 330 499-5600
Canton *(G-2363)*
Family Physician Associates ....E 614 901-2273
Westerville *(G-19399)*
Family Physicians Associates ....E 440 442-3866
Cleveland *(G-5570)*
Family Physicians of Coshocton ....E 740 622-0332
Coshocton *(G-9102)*
Family Physicians of Gahanna ....E 614 471-9654
Columbus *(G-7636)*
Family Practice & Associates ....E 937 399-6650
Springfield *(G-17196)*
Family Practice Ctr Salem Inc ....E 330 332-9961
Salem *(G-16695)*
Flowers Family Practice Inc ....E 614 277-9631
Grove City *(G-11562)*
Frederick C Smith Clinic Inc ....E 740 363-9021
Delaware *(G-10099)*
Generations Family Medicine ....E 614 337-1282
Gahanna *(G-11244)*
Grandview Family Practice ....E 740 258-9267
Columbus *(G-7766)*
Healthsource of Ohio Inc ....E 937 981-7707
Greenfield *(G-11487)*
Hillsboro Health Center Inc ....E 937 393-5781
Hillsboro *(G-11982)*
Holzer Clinic LLC ....E 740 886-9403
Proctorville *(G-16359)*
Hopewell Health Centers Inc ....E 740 596-5249
Mc Arthur *(G-14016)*
Institute/Reproductive Health ....E 513 585-2355
Cincinnati *(G-3821)*
Johnson Adams & Protrouski ....E 419 238-6251
Van Wert *(G-18636)*
Lake County Family Practice ....E 440 352-4880
Mentor *(G-14204)*
Medical Diagnostic Lab Inc ....D 440 333-1375
Westlake *(G-19514)*
Medicine Midwest LLC ....E 937 435-8786
Dayton *(G-9715)*
Mercy Health ....E 419 492-1300
New Washington *(G-15135)*
Mercy Health ....D 513 232-7100
Cincinnati *(G-4063)*
Mercy Health ....E 440 937-4600
Avon *(G-907)*
Metropolitan Family Care Inc ....E 614 237-1067
Reynoldsburg *(G-16469)*
Miamisburg Family Practice ....E 937 866-2494
Miamisburg *(G-14322)*
Midwest Retina Inc ....E 614 233-9500
Zanesville *(G-20502)*
Mill Pond Family Physicians ....E 330 928-3111
Cuyahoga Falls *(G-9211)*
Milltown Family Physicians ....E 330 345-8016
Wooster *(G-19891)*
Neighborhood Health Care Inc ....E 216 281-8945
Cleveland *(G-6116)*
New Horizons Surgery Center ....E 740 375-5854
Marion *(G-13568)*
Oakhill Medical Associates ....E 937 599-1411
West Liberty *(G-19263)*
Portage Family Medicine ....E 330 626-5566
Streetsboro *(G-17426)*
Premier Health Partners ....D 937 526-3235
Versailles *(G-18728)*
Primary Cr Ntwrk Prmr Hlth Prt ....E 513 492-5940
Mason *(G-13749)*
Primary Cr Ntwrk Prmr Hlth Prt ....E 937 278-5854
Dayton *(G-9823)*
Primary Cr Ntwrk Prmr Hlth Prt ....D 937 208-9090
Dayton *(G-9824)*
Primary Cr Ntwrk Prmr Hlth Prt ....E 513 420-5233
Middletown *(G-14486)*
Primary Cr Ntwrk Prmr Hlth Prt ....E 937 226-7085
Dayton *(G-9825)*
Primed ....E 937 435-9013
Dayton *(G-9828)*
Primed Physicians ....E 937 298-8058
Dayton *(G-9829)*
Reading Family Practice ....E 513 563-6934
Cincinnati *(G-4391)*
Reid Physician Associates Inc ....B 937 456-4400
Eaton *(G-10576)*
Richard L Liston MD ....D 937 320-2020
Beavercreek *(G-1258)*
River Road Family Physicians ....E 419 872-7745
Perrysburg *(G-16052)*
Robert Ellis ....E 513 821-0275
Cincinnati *(G-4435)*
Springdale Family Medicine PC ....E 513 771-7213
Cincinnati *(G-4566)*
Summa Health System ....E 330 630-9726
Tallmadge *(G-17651)*
Summa Health System ....D 330 375-3584
Akron *(G-457)*
Superior Medical Care Inc ....E 440 282-7420
Lorain *(G-13080)*
Talmage N Porter MD ....E 937 435-9013
Dayton *(G-9920)*
Terence Isakov MD ....D 440 449-1014
Cleveland *(G-6583)*
Tri County Family Physicians ....E 614 837-6363
Canal Winchester *(G-2173)*
Uc Health Llc ....B 513 584-6999
Mason *(G-13776)*
Uc Health Llc ....A 513 648-9077
Cincinnati *(G-4720)*
University Family Physicians ....E 513 929-0104
Cincinnati *(G-4752)*
University Family Physicians ....D 513 475-7505
Cincinnati *(G-4753)*
University of Cincinnati ....E 513 475-8771
Cincinnati *(G-4759)*
Upper Valley Family Care ....E 937 339-5355
Piqua *(G-16172)*
Van Wert County Hospital Assn ....C 419 232-2077
Van Wert *(G-18650)*
Western Family Physicians ....E 513 853-4900
Cincinnati *(G-4840)*
Westshore Prmry Care Assoc Inc ....D 440 934-0276
Sheffield Village *(G-16896)*
Westside Family Practice Inc ....E 614 878-4541
Columbus *(G-8983)*
Wheeling Hospital Inc ....D 740 695-2090
Saint Clairsville *(G-16661)*
Wilmington Medical Associates ....D 937 382-1616
Wilmington *(G-19795)*

OFFICES & CLINICS OF DRS OF MED: Cardiologist & Vascular

Capitol City Cardiology Inc ....E 614 464-0884
Columbus *(G-7186)*
Cardiac Vsclar Thrcic Surgeons ....E 513 421-3494
Cincinnati *(G-3177)*
Cardiologist Clark & Champaign ....E 937 653-8897
Urbana *(G-18575)*
Cardiology Associates of ....E 740 454-6831
Zanesville *(G-20456)*
Cardiology Consultants Inc ....D 330 454-8076
Canton *(G-2299)*
Cardiology Ctr of Cincinnati ....E 513 745 0800
Cincinnati *(G-3180)*
Cardiology Specialists Inc ....E 330 297-6110
Ravenna *(G-16375)*
Cardiovascular Associates Inc ....E 330 747-6446
Youngstown *(G-20133)*
Cardiovascular Clinic Inc ....D 440 882-0075
Cleveland *(G-5182)*
Cardiovascular Consultants Inc ....D 330 454-8076
Canton *(G-2300)*
Cardiovascular Medicine Assoc ....E 440 816-2708
Cleveland *(G-5183)*
Central Ohio Surgical Assoc ....E 614 222-8000
Columbus *(G-7240)*
Columbus Cardiology Cons Inc ....C 614 224-2281
Columbus *(G-7335)*
Columbus Cardiology Cons Inc ....C 614 224-2281
Columbus *(G-7336)*
Cranley Surgical Associates ....E 513 961-4335
Cincinnati *(G-3439)*
Dayton Cardiology Consultants ....E 937 223-3053
Dayton *(G-9462)*
Dayton Heart Center Inc ....D 937 277-4274
Dayton *(G-9477)*
Greater Cin Cardi Consults In ....E 513 751-4222
Cincinnati *(G-3706)*
Hans Zwart MD & Associates ....E 937 433-4183
Dayton *(G-9599)*
Heart Care ....D 614 533-5000
Gahanna *(G-11246)*
Heart Center of N Eastrn Ohio ....E 330 758-7703
Youngstown *(G-20214)*
Heart Specialists of Ohio ....E 614 538-0527
Columbus *(G-7815)*
Mid-Ohio Heart Clinic Inc ....E 419 524-8151
Mansfield *(G-13345)*
Middltown Crdvscular Assoc Inc ....E 513 217-6400
Middletown *(G-14439)*
Midohio Crdiolgy Vascular Cons ....C 614 262-6772
Columbus *(G-8167)*
Mobile Cardiac Imaging LLC ....E 419 251-3711
Toledo *(G-18067)*
North Ohio Heart Center Inc ....E 440 414-9500
Cleveland *(G-6141)*
North Ohio Heart Center Inc ....E 440 366-3600
Elyria *(G-10660)*
North Ohio Heart Center Inc ....E 440 204-4000
Avon *(G-909)*
North Ohio Heart Center Inc ....E 440 204-4000
Lorain *(G-13070)*
North Ohio Heart Center Inc ....E 440 326-4120
Elyria *(G-10661)*
Northeast Ohio Cardiology Svcs ....E 330 253-8195
Akron *(G-356)*
Northern Ohio Med Spclists LLC ....E 419 625-2841
Sandusky *(G-16783)*
Northwest Ohio Cardiology Cons ....D 419 842-3000
Toledo *(G-18094)*
Ohio Gstroenterology Group Inc ....E 614 221-8355
Columbus *(G-8346)*
Ohio Heart ....E 513 206-1320
Cincinnati *(G-4204)*
Ohio Heart Health Center Inc ....C 513 351-9900
Cincinnati *(G-4206)*
Ohio Institute of Cardiac Care ....E 937 322-1700
Springfield *(G-17255)*
Ohio Medical Group ....E 440 414-9400
Westlake *(G-19528)*
Ohio State University ....A 614 293-4967
Columbus *(G-8444)*
Premier Heart Associates Inc ....E 937 832-2425
Dayton *(G-9822)*
Premier Heart Inc ....E 937 832-2425
Englewood *(G-10717)*
Primed Premier Integrated Med ....C 937 291-6893
Dayton *(G-9830)*
Sagar Satyavolu MD ....E 937 323-1404
Springfield *(G-17269)*
Schuster Cardiology ....E 937 866-0637
Miamisburg *(G-14346)*
Toledo Cardiology Cons Inc ....D 419 251-6183
Toledo *(G-18229)*
Toledo Cardiology Inc ....E 419 479-5690
Toledo *(G-18230)*
West Side Cardiology Assoc ....E 440 333-8600
Cleveland *(G-6737)*
West Side Cardiology Assoc ....E 440 333-8600
Cleveland *(G-6738)*

OFFICES & CLINICS OF DRS OF MED: Clinic, Op by Physicians

Ambulatory Medical Care Inc ....C 513 831-8555
Milford *(G-14502)*
Ashtabula Clinic Inc ....D 440 997-6980
Ashtabula *(G-715)*
Aultman North Canton Med Group ....B 330 433-1200
Canton *(G-2257)*
Axesspointe Cmnty Hlth Ctr Inc ....E 330 724-5471
Akron *(G-86)*
Canton Altman Emrgncy Physcans ....E 330 456-2695
Canton *(G-2281)*
Center For Dlysis Cre of Cnfld ....E 330 702-3040
Canfield *(G-2186)*
Centers For Dialysis Care Inc ....E 216 295-7000
Shaker Heights *(G-16858)*

Employee Codes: A=Over 500 employees, B=251-500
C=101-250, D=51-100, E=25-50
2018 Harris Ohio
Services Directory
1579
SERVICES

OFFICES & CLINICS OF DRS OF MED: Clinic, Op by Physicians

Childrens Hospital Medical Ctr .... A 513 636-4200
  Cincinnati (G-3252)
Christian Community Hlth Svcs .... E 513 381-2247
  Cincinnati (G-3272)
Cleveland Clinic Cole Eye Inst .... E 216 444-4508
  Cleveland (G-5295)
Columbus Neighborhood Health C .... C 614 445-0685
  Columbus (G-7373)
Community Action Comm Pike CNT .... E 740 947-7726
  Waverly (G-18970)
Community Mental Health Svc .... D 740 695-9344
  Saint Clairsville (G-16633)
County of Delaware .... D 740 203-2040
  Delaware (G-10084)
Doctors Urgent Care .... E 419 586-1611
  Celina (G-2646)
Family Hlth Svcs Drke Cnty Inc .... C 937 548-3806
  Greenville (G-11500)
Five Rivers Health Centers .... E 937 734-6841
  Dayton (G-9552)
Fresenius Med Care Hldings Inc .... E 216 267-1451
  Cleveland (G-5637)
Heart Ohio Family Health Ctrs .... E 614 235-5555
  Columbus (G-7814)
Holzer Clinic LLC .... C 304 746-3701
  Gallipolis (G-11320)
Holzer Clinic LLC .... C 740 589-3100
  Athens (G-793)
Holzer Clinic LLC .... E 740 446-5412
  Gallipolis (G-11323)
Hometown Urgent Care .... C 937 372-6012
  Xenia (G-20062)
Jyg Innovations LLC .... E 937 630-3858
  Dayton (G-9647)
Lifecare Fmly Hlth & Dntl Ctr .... E 330 454-2000
  Canton (G-2437)
Margaret B Shipley Child Hlth .... E 330 478-6333
  Canton (G-2447)
Matern Ohio Management Inc .... D 614 457-7660
  Columbus (G-8127)
Medical Assoc Cambridge Inc .... E 740 439-3515
  Cambridge (G-2123)
Mercy Health .... E 330 792-7418
  Youngstown (G-20281)
Mercy Hlth St Vincent Med LLC .... A 419 251-0580
  Toledo (G-18058)
Mercy Medical Center Inc .... D 330 649-4380
  Canton (G-2458)
Mercy Medical Center Inc .... E 330 627-7641
  Carrollton (G-2623)
Monroe Family Health Center .... E 740 472-0757
  Woodsfield (G-19818)
Norwalk Clinic Inc .... E 419 668-4851
  Norwalk (G-15585)
Oberlin Clinic Inc .... C 440 774-7337
  Oberlin (G-15653)
Promedica .... D 419 291-3450
  Maumee (G-13960)
Schoenbrunn Healthcare .... D 330 339-3595
  New Philadelphia (G-15114)
Senior Lifestyle Corporation .... D 513 777-4457
  West Chester (G-19150)
Sister of Mercy of Clerm Count .... D 513 732-8200
  Batavia (G-1024)
Toledo Family Health Center .... D 419 241-1554
  Toledo (G-18236)
Total Renal Care Inc .... E 937 294-6711
  Kettering (G-12436)
University Mednet .... C 440 255-0800
  Mentor (G-14253)
University Mednet .... E 440 285-9079
  Bedford (G-1343)
Veterans Health Administration .... B 740 568-0412
  Marietta (G-13514)
Veterans Health Administration .... B 513 943-3680
  Cincinnati (G-4813)
Veterans Health Administration .... C 614 257-5524
  Columbus (G-8937)
Veterans Health Administration .... B 866 463-0912
  Ashtabula (G-766)
Veterans Health Administration .... B 740 695-9321
  Saint Clairsville (G-16659)
Veterans Health Administration .... D 419 259-2000
  Toledo (G-18290)
Veterans Health Administration .... E 330 740-9200
  Youngstown (G-20403)
Veterans Health Administration .... B 216 939-0699
  Cleveland (G-6692)
Veterans Health Administration .... D 330 489-4600
  Canton (G-2577)

Zepf Center .... E 419 255-4050
  Toledo (G-18331)

OFFICES & CLINICS OF DRS OF MED: Em Med Ctr, Freestanding

Amherst Hospital Association .... C 440 988-6000
  Amherst (G-587)
Emergency Medicine Specialists .... D 937 438-8910
  Dayton (G-9526)
Hometown Urgent Care .... C 937 236-8630
  Dayton (G-9619)
Immediate Health Associates .... E 614 794-0481
  Westerville (G-19411)
Immediate Medical Service Inc .... D 330 823-0400
  Alliance (G-540)
Lake Urgent & Family Med Ctr .... E 440 255-6400
  Mentor (G-14206)
Med -Center/Med Partners .... E 440 349-6400
  Cleveland (G-6011)
Mercy Health Youngstown LLC .... A 330 729-1420
  Youngstown (G-20283)
St Ritas Medical Center .... D 419 227-3361
  Lima (G-12888)
Township of Colerain .... C 513 741-7551
  Cincinnati (G-4674)

OFFICES & CLINICS OF DRS OF MED: Health Maint Org Or HMO

Aultman Health Foundation .... C 330 305-6999
  Canton (G-2251)
Aultman Health Foundation .... E 330 452-9911
  Canton (G-2252)
Blanchard Vly Rgional Hlth Ctr .... C 419 358-9010
  Bluffton (G-1727)
Christ Hospital .... C 513 755-4700
  West Chester (G-19038)
County of Lucas .... C 419 213-4018
  Toledo (G-17836)
Foundations Hlth Solutions Inc .... D 440 793-0200
  North Olmsted (G-15423)
Health Collaborative .... D 513 618-3600
  Cincinnati (G-3753)
Healthspan Integrated Care .... C 216 621-5600
  Cleveland (G-5742)

OFFICES & CLINICS OF DRS OF MED: Physician/Surgeon, Int Med

Associated Specialists .... E 937 208-7272
  Dayton (G-9345)
Avita Health System .... C 419 468-4841
  Galion (G-11291)
Blanchard Valley Medical Assoc .... D 419 424-0380
  Findlay (G-11001)
Canyon Medical Center Inc .... E 614 864-6010
  Columbus (G-7182)
Central Ohio Primary Care .... E 614 473-1300
  Columbus (G-7237)
Central Ohio Primary Care .... E 614 268-8164
  Columbus (G-7238)
Central Ohio Primary Care .... D 614 326-2672
  Westerville (G-19291)
Christ Hospital Corporation .... E 513 347-2300
  Cincinnati (G-3269)
Comprehensive Health Care Inc .... E 419 238-7777
  Van Wert (G-18631)
Dayton Childrens Hospital .... E 937 641-3376
  Dayton (G-9463)
Eastern Hill Internal Medicine .... E 513 232-3500
  Cincinnati (G-3535)
George G Ellis Jr MD .... E 330 965-0832
  Youngstown (G-20199)
Goudy Internal Medicine Inc .... D 419 468-8323
  Galion (G-11301)
Hector A Buch Jr MD .... E 419 227-7399
  Lima (G-12797)
Hickman Cancer Center .... D 419 824-1952
  Sylvania (G-17593)
Internal Mdcine Cons of Clmbus .... E 614 878-6413
  Columbus (G-7916)
Internal Medical Physicians .... E 330 868-3711
  Minerva (G-14647)
Internal Medicine of Akron .... E 330 376-2728
  Akron (G-281)
Markowitz Rosenberg Assoc Drs .... E 440 646-2200
  Cleveland (G-5980)
Mercy Health .... D 937 390-1700
  Springfield (G-17236)

Mercy Health .... E 513 248-0100
  Milford (G-14538)
Mercy Medical Associates .... E 513 686-4840
  Cincinnati (G-4077)
Moyal and Petroff MD .... E 440 461-6477
  Cleveland (G-6081)
Occupational Health Services .... E 937 492-7296
  Sidney (G-16944)
Ohio State University .... A 614 293-8045
  Columbus (G-8390)
Premier Integrated Med Assoc .... D 937 291-6813
  Centerville (G-2684)
Queen City Medical Group .... E 513 528-5600
  Cincinnati (G-4367)
Richard Tomm MD .... D 216 297-3060
  Cleveland (G-6393)
Robert E Kose .... E 419 843-7800
  Maumee (G-13973)
Roger S Palutsis MD .... E 330 821-0201
  Alliance (G-557)
Salem Internal Medicine Assoc .... E 330 332-5232
  Salem (G-16716)
Southwest Internal Medicine .... E 440 816-2777
  Cleveland (G-6506)
Stephen A Rudolph Inc .... E 216 381-1367
  Cleveland (G-6537)
Summa Health System .... C 330 375-3315
  Akron (G-459)
Summit Cnty Internists & Assoc .... E 330 375-3690
  Akron (G-466)
Uc Health Llc .... A 513 475-7880
  Cincinnati (G-4718)
University of Cincinnati .... D 513 475-8524
  Cincinnati (G-4775)
Ushc Physicians Inc .... E 216 382-2036
  Cleveland (G-6679)
Veterinary RFRrl&emer Ctr of .... E 330 665-4996
  Copley (G-9068)

OFFICES & CLINICS OF DRS OF MED: Physician/Surgeon, Phy Med

Barb Linden .... E 440 233-1068
  Lorain (G-13016)
Bucyrus Community Physicians .... D 419 492-2200
  New Washington (G-15133)
Central Ohio Primary Care .... E 614 451-1551
  Columbus (G-7235)
Childrens Hospital Medical Ctr .... A 513 636-4366
  Cincinnati (G-3250)
Geoff Answini .... E 513 792-7800
  Cincinnati (G-3677)
Hernando Zegarra .... E 216 831-5700
  Cleveland (G-5753)
Holzer Clinic LLC .... C 304 744-2300
  Gallipolis (G-11322)
Lasik Plus Vision Center .... D 513 794-9964
  Cincinnati (G-3963)
Medical College of Ohio .... E 419 383-7100
  Toledo (G-18048)
Primary Cr Ntwrk Prmr Hlth Prt .... E 937 890-6644
  Vandalia (G-18693)
Summa Health System .... C 330 252-0095
  Akron (G-455)
Wheeling Hospital Inc .... D 740 633-4765
  Martins Ferry (G-13604)

OFFICES & CLINICS OF DRS OF MED: Specialist/Phy, Fertility

Dayton Ob Gyn .... E 937 439-7550
  Centerville (G-2677)

OFFICES & CLINICS OF DRS OF MEDICINE: Geriatric

P C Vpa .... E 937 293-2133
  Moraine (G-14814)

OFFICES & CLINICS OF DRS OF MEDICINE: Med Clinic, Pri Care

3rd Street Community Clinic .... D 419 522-6191
  Mansfield (G-13257)
Bethesda Hospital Inc .... E 513 563-1505
  Cincinnati (G-3107)
Central Ohio Geriatrics LLC .... E 614 530-4077
  Granville (G-11460)
Dayton Physicians LLC .... C 937 547-0563
  Greenville (G-11497)

SERVICES SECTION

OFFICES & CLINICS OF HEALTH PRACTITIONERS: Physical Therapy

Equitas Health Inc .... C 614 299-2437
  Columbus *(G-7603)*
Hometown Urgent Care .... C 614 472-2880
  Columbus *(G-7855)*
Hometown Urgent Care .... C 937 322-6222
  Springfield *(G-17207)*
Hometown Urgent Care .... C 614 835-0400
  Groveport *(G-11645)*
Ironton and Lawrence County .... B 740 532-3534
  Ironton *(G-12291)*
Lakewood Clveland Fmly Med Ctr .... E 216 227-2162
  Lakewood *(G-12488)*
Luke Immediate Care Center .... E 419 227-2245
  Lima *(G-12833)*
Mercy Health .... E 440 366-5577
  North Ridgeville *(G-15470)*
North Coast Prof Co LLC .... C 419 557-5541
  Sandusky *(G-16782)*
Robinson Memorial Hospital .... E 330 626-3455
  Streetsboro *(G-17428)*

OFFICES & CLINICS OF DRS OF MEDICINE: Med Insurance Assoc

Ohio Health Group LLC .... E 614 566-0010
  Columbus *(G-8350)*

OFFICES & CLINICS OF DRS OF MEDICINE: Physician, Orthopedic

Comprhnsive Care Orthpdics Inc .... E 419 473-9500
  Toledo *(G-17827)*
Far Oaks Orthopedists Inc .... E 937 433-5309
  Dayton *(G-9540)*
Hand Ctr At Orthopaedic Inst .... D 937 298-4417
  Dayton *(G-9598)*
Hand Rehabilitation Associates .... E 330 668-4055
  Akron *(G-251)*
Joint Implant Surgeons Inc .... E 614 221-6331
  New Albany *(G-14990)*
Kolczun & Kolczun Orthopedics .... E 440 985-3113
  Lorain *(G-13046)*
Marysvlle Ohio Srgical Ctr LLC .... A 937 578-4200
  Marysville *(G-13639)*
Northast Ohio Orthpedics Assoc .... E 330 344-1980
  Akron *(G-354)*
Northwest Ohio Orthopedics .... E 419 885-2553
  Sylvania *(G-17602)*
Ohio Orthpd Surgery Inst LLC .... E 614 827-8777
  Columbus *(G-8364)*
Orthoneuro .... E 614 890-6555
  Westerville *(G-19434)*
Orthopaedic & Spine Center At .... E 614 468-0300
  Dublin *(G-10417)*
Orthopaedic Institute Ohio Inc .... D 419 222-6622
  Lima *(G-12851)*
Orthopaedic Offices Inc .... E 513 221-5500
  Blue Ash *(G-1659)*
Orthopdic Spt Mdicine Cons Inc .... E 513 777-7714
  Middletown *(G-14447)*
Orthopedic Assoc of Zanesville .... E 740 454-3273
  Zanesville *(G-20522)*
Orthopedic Associates .... E 937 415-9100
  Centerville *(G-2683)*
Orthopedic Associates Dayton .... E 937 280-4988
  Dayton *(G-9794)*
Orthopedic Associates Inc .... E 440 892-1440
  Westlake *(G-19530)*
Orthopedic Cons Cincinnati .... C 513 733-8894
  Blue Ash *(G-1660)*
Orthopedic Cons Cincinnati .... E 513 753-7488
  Cincinnati *(G-2926)*
Orthopedic Cons Cincinnati .... E 513 232-6677
  Cincinnati *(G-4236)*
Orthopedic Cons Cincinnati .... F 513 246-2500
  Cincinnati *(G-4237)*
Orthopedic Cons Cincinnati .... E 513 347-9999
  Cincinnati *(G-4238)*
Orthopedic Diagnstc Trtmnt Ctr .... E 513 791-6611
  Montgomery *(G-14733)*
Orthopedic Diagnstc Trtmnt Ctr .... E 513 221-4848
  Cincinnati *(G-4239)*
Orthopedic One Inc .... D 614 827-8700
  Columbus *(G-8484)*
Orthorpdics Mltspcialty Netwrk .... E 330 493-1630
  Canton *(G-2487)*
Queen Cy Spt Mdcine Rhbltation .... E 513 561-1111
  Cincinnati *(G-4373)*
Reconstructive Orthopedics .... D 513 793-3933
  Cincinnati *(G-4394)*

River Vly Orthpdics Spt Mdcine .... E 740 687-3346
  Lancaster *(G-12570)*
Spectrum Orthopedics Inc Canton .... E 330 455-5367
  North Canton *(G-15367)*
Summit Hand Center Inc .... E 330 668-4055
  Akron *(G-467)*
Teater Orthopedic Surgeons .... E 330 343-3335
  Dover *(G-10216)*
Unity Health Network LLC .... E 330 626-0549
  Streetsboro *(G-17435)*
University of Cincinnati .... D 513 558-4516
  Cincinnati *(G-4757)*
University Orthopaedic Cnsltnt .... E 513 475-8690
  Cincinnati *(G-4783)*
University Orthpedic Assoc Inc .... E 216 844-1000
  Cleveland *(G-6667)*
Youngstown Orthopaedic Assoc .... E 330 726-1466
  Canfield *(G-2217)*

OFFICES & CLINICS OF DRS OF MEDICINE: Pulmonary

Pulmonary & Medicine Dayton .... E 937 439-3600
  Miamisburg *(G-14338)*
Pulmonary Crtcal Care Spcalist .... E 419 843-7800
  Maumee *(G-13964)*
University of Cincinnati .... E 513 558-4831
  Cincinnati *(G-4777)*

OFFICES & CLINICS OF DRS OF MEDICINE: Rheumatology

Columbus Medical Rheumatology .... E 614 486-5200
  Columbus *(G-7367)*
Crystal Arthritis Center Inc .... E 330 668-4045
  Akron *(G-177)*

OFFICES & CLINICS OF DRS OF MEDICINE: Sports Med

Far Oaks Orthopedists Inc .... E 937 433-5309
  Dayton *(G-9539)*
First Settlement Orthopaedics .... E 740 373-8756
  Marietta *(G-13446)*
Ohio State University .... D 614 293-2222
  Columbus *(G-8433)*
OSu Spt Mdcine Physcians Inc .... E 614 293-3600
  Columbus *(G-8494)*
Sports Care Rehabilitation .... E 419 578-7530
  Toledo *(G-18196)*

OFFICES & CLINICS OF DRS, MED: Specialized Practitioners

Akron Neonatology Inc .... E 330 379-9473
  Akron *(G-49)*
Drs Paul Boyles & Kennedy .... E 614 734-3347
  Columbus *(G-7544)*
Foot & Ankle Care Center .... E 937 492-1211
  Sidney *(G-16934)*

OFFICES & CLINICS OF HEALTH PRACTITIONERS: Coroner

County of Cuyahoga .... D 216 721-5610
  Cleveland *(G-5420)*
County of Hamilton .... E 513 221-4524
  Cincinnati *(G-3432)*

OFFICES & CLINICS OF HEALTH PRACTITIONERS: Nurse & Med Asst

Equitas Health Inc .... C 614 299-2437
  Columbus *(G-7603)*
Inter Healt Care of Cambr Zane .... E 513 984-1110
  Cincinnati *(G-3830)*
Kindred Healthcare Inc .... C 440 232-1800
  Bedford Heights *(G-1355)*
Maxim Healthcare Services Inc .... D 740 772-4100
  Chillicothe *(G-2863)*
Msstaff LLC .... E 419 868-8536
  Toledo *(G-18072)*
Tky Associates LLC .... D 419 535-7777
  Toledo *(G-18221)*

OFFICES & CLINICS OF HEALTH PRACTITIONERS: Nutrition

Herman Bair Enterprise .... E 330 262-4449
  Wooster *(G-19867)*

Mercy Health .... E 937 390-5515
  Springfield *(G-17238)*

OFFICES & CLINICS OF HEALTH PRACTITIONERS: Nutritionist

Central Ohio Nutrition Center .... E 614 864-7225
  Columbus *(G-7232)*
George W Arensberg Phrm Inc .... E 740 344-2195
  Newark *(G-15169)*

OFFICES & CLINICS OF HEALTH PRACTITIONERS: Occu Therapist

Chcc Home Health Care .... E 330 759-4069
  Austintown *(G-869)*
Cincinnati Occupational Therap .... E 513 791-5688
  Blue Ash *(G-1557)*
Hometown Urgent Care .... C 330 629-2300
  Youngstown *(G-20219)*
Hometown Urgent Care .... D 740 363-3133
  Delaware *(G-10107)*
Hometown Urgent Care .... C 937 252-2000
  Wooster *(G-19868)*
Hometown Urgent Care .... C 513 831-5900
  Milford *(G-14525)*
Hometown Urgent Care .... C 937 342-9520
  Springfield *(G-17206)*
Medwork LLC .... D 937 449-0800
  Dayton *(G-9716)*
Ohiohealth Corporation .... A 614 788-8860
  Columbus *(G-8457)*
Samaritan Regional Health Sys .... E 419 281-1330
  Ashland *(G-697)*
Summa Health .... B 330 926-0384
  Cuyahoga Falls *(G-9221)*
Therapy In Motion LLC .... C 216 459-2846
  Independence *(G-12266)*

OFFICES & CLINICS OF HEALTH PRACTITIONERS: Paramedic

Blue Ash Fire Department .... E 513 745-8534
  Blue Ash *(G-1544)*
Cgh-Glbal Operations Logistics .... E 800 376-0655
  Cincinnati *(G-3223)*
Colerain Volunteer Fire Co .... E 740 738-0735
  Dillonvale *(G-10174)*
Lifeteam Ems Inc .... E 330 386-9284
  East Liverpool *(G-10523)*
Sandy Creek Joint Fire Dst .... E 330 868-5193
  Minerva *(G-14650)*

OFFICES & CLINICS OF HEALTH PRACTITIONERS: Physical Therapy

Abilities First Foundation .... C 513 423-9496
  Middletown *(G-14411)*
Amedisys Inc .... E 740 373-8549
  Marietta *(G-13430)*
Atrium Medical Center .... E 513 420-5013
  Middletown *(G-14414)*
Aultman Health Foundation .... B 330 875-6050
  Louisville *(G-13094)*
Carington Health Systems .... C 513 961-8881
  Cincinnati *(G-3185)*
Christ Hospital .... B 513 688-1111
  Cincinnati *(G-3262)*
Concorde Therapy Group Inc .... E 330 478-1752
  Canton *(G-2320)*
Concorde Therapy Group Inc .... E 330 493-4210
  Alliance *(G-535)*
First Settlement Orthopaedics .... E 740 373-8756
  Marietta *(G-13446)*
Health Services Inc .... E 330 837-7678
  Massillon *(G-13818)*
Healthsource Inc .... C 330 278-2781
  Hinckley *(G-11998)*
Hilty Memorial Home Inc .... C 419 384-3218
  Pandora *(G-15892)*
Holzer Clinic LLC .... E 740 886-9403
  Proctorville *(G-16359)*
Jewish Home of Cincinnati .... B 513 754-3100
  Mason *(G-13726)*
Kindred Healthcare Oper Inc .... C 740 387-7537
  Marion *(G-13545)*
Licking Rhabilitation Svcs Inc .... E 740 345-2837
  Newark *(G-15194)*
Medcentral Health System .... C 419 342-5015
  Shelby *(G-16901)*

Employee Codes: A=Over 500 employees, B=251-500
C=101-250, D=51-100, E=25-50

OFFICES & CLINICS OF HEALTH PRACTITIONERS: Physical Therapy

Medcentral Health System ....C...... 419 683-1040
  Crestline *(G-9147)*
Mercy Health ....E...... 937 390-5075
  Springfield *(G-17240)*
Mercy Health ....C...... 440 774-6800
  Oberlin *(G-15652)*
Newcomerstown Progress Corp ....C...... 740 498-5165
  Newcomerstown *(G-15271)*
Nexstep Healthcare LLC ....C...... 216 797-4040
  Cleveland *(G-6128)*
Ohio HI Point Career Center ....E...... 937 599-3010
  Urbana *(G-18598)*
Ohio State University ....A...... 614 366-3692
  Columbus *(G-8388)*
Ohio State University ....A...... 614 257-3000
  Columbus *(G-8393)*
Orthoneuro ....D...... 614 890-6555
  Columbus *(G-8482)*
Prohealth Partners Inc ....E...... 419 491-7150
  Perrysburg *(G-16045)*
Quality Care Nursing Svc Inc ....B...... 740 377-9095
  South Point *(G-17096)*
R & F Inc ....E...... 419 868-2909
  Holland *(G-12047)*
Rehab Center ....E...... 330 297-2770
  Ravenna *(G-16405)*
Rehab Continuum Inc ....E...... 513 984-8070
  Blue Ash *(G-1679)*
Rehabilitation Aquatics ....E...... 419 843-2500
  Toledo *(G-18148)*
Selby General Hospital ....C...... 740 568-2037
  Marietta *(G-13497)*
Society For Rehabilitation ....E...... 440 209-0135
  Mentor *(G-14243)*
Sports Therapy Inc ....E...... 513 671-5841
  Cincinnati *(G-4561)*
Sports Therapy Inc ....E...... 513 531-1698
  Cincinnati *(G-4562)*
Steward Trumbull Mem Hosp Inc ....A...... 330 841-9011
  Warren *(G-18904)*
Total Rhabilitation Specialist ....E...... 440 236-8527
  Columbia Station *(G-6852)*
Trihealth G LLC ....D...... 513 922-1200
  Cincinnati *(G-4696)*
Walnut Hills Physical Therapy ....E...... 614 234-8000
  Columbus *(G-8964)*
Weston Group Inc ....E...... 740 454-2741
  Zanesville *(G-20545)*
Wsb Rehabilitation Svcs Inc ....D...... 330 533-1438
  Canfield *(G-2216)*

OFFICES & CLINICS OF HEALTH PRACTITIONERS: Physiotherapist

Bellefontaine Physical Therapy ....E...... 937 592-1625
  Bellefontaine *(G-1377)*
Concorde Therapy Group Inc ....C...... 330 493-4210
  Canton *(G-2319)*
Concorde Therapy Group Inc ....E...... 330 493-4210
  Louisville *(G-13097)*
Summa Rehab Hospital LLC ....E...... 330 572-7300
  Akron *(G-463)*

OFFICES & CLINICS OF HEALTH PRACTITIONERS: Speech Pathology

United Rehabilitation Services ....D...... 937 233-1230
  Dayton *(G-9947)*

OFFICES & CLINICS OF HEALTH PRACTITIONERS: Speech Therapist

A+ Solutions LLC ....E...... 216 896-0111
  Beachwood *(G-1044)*
Just In Time Care Inc ....E...... 614 985-3555
  Columbus *(G-7961)*

OFFICES & CLINICS OF HEALTH PRACTRS: Clinical Psychologist

Appleseed Cmnty Mntal Hlth Ctr ....E...... 419 281-3716
  Ashland *(G-651)*
Center For Cognitive and Beh ....E...... 614 459-4490
  Columbus *(G-7223)*
Childrens Aid Society ....E...... 216 521-6511
  Cleveland *(G-5237)*
Coleman Professional Svcs Inc ....D...... 330 296-8313
  Ravenna *(G-16377)*
Comprehensive Services Inc ....E...... 614 442-0664
  Columbus *(G-7415)*

Emerge Counseling Service ....E...... 330 865-8351
  Akron *(G-207)*
Midwest Behavioral Care Ltd ....E...... 937 454-0092
  Dayton *(G-9744)*
Ohio State University ....D...... 614 292-6741
  Columbus *(G-8419)*
PSI Associates Inc ....B...... 330 425-8474
  Twinsburg *(G-18457)*
Psycare Inc ....C...... 330 759-2310
  Youngstown *(G-20332)*
Psychiatric Solutions Inc ....C...... 440 953-3000
  Willoughby *(G-19706)*
Reverse Center Clinic ....E...... 419 885-8800
  Sylvania *(G-17610)*
Weinstein Donald Jay PHD ....E...... 216 831-1040
  Painesville *(G-15886)*

OFFICES & CLINICS OF HLTH PRACTITIONERS: Reg/Practical Nurse

Accurate Nurse Staffing ....E...... 419 475-2424
  Toledo *(G-17740)*
American Nursing Care Inc ....D...... 740 452-0569
  Zanesville *(G-20442)*
Around Clock Home Care ....D...... 440 350-2547
  Painesville *(G-15835)*
Medlink of Ohio Inc ....B...... 216 751-5900
  Cleveland *(G-6016)*
Medlink of Ohio Inc ....B...... 330 773-9434
  Akron *(G-337)*
Sisters of Mercy Amer Reg Comm ....D...... 419 696-7203
  Oregon *(G-15750)*
Toledo District Nurses Assn ....C...... 419 255-0983
  Sylvania *(G-17622)*

OFFICES & CLINICS OF OPTOMETRISTS: Group & Corporate

Sight Resource Corporation ....D...... 513 942-4423
  West Chester *(G-19153)*

OFFICES & CLINICS OF OPTOMETRISTS: Specialist, Contact Lens

Shawnee Optical Inc ....D...... 440 997-2020
  Ashtabula *(G-763)*

OFFICES & CLINICS OF OPTOMETRISTS: Specialist, Optometrists

Optivue Inc ....C...... 419 891-1391
  Oregon *(G-15743)*
Ottivue ....D...... 419 693-4444
  Oregon *(G-15747)*
Rinkov Eyecare Center ....E...... 614 224-2414
  Columbus *(G-8631)*
Thomas R Truitt Od ....E...... 937 644-8637
  Marysville *(G-13655)*

OIL & GAS FIELD EQPT: Drill Rigs

Buckeye Companies ....E...... 740 452-3641
  Zanesville *(G-20450)*

OIL FIELD MACHINERY & EQPT

Multi Products Company ....E...... 330 674-5981
  Millersburg *(G-14613)*

OIL FIELD SVCS, NEC

Belden & Blake Corporation ....E...... 330 602-5551
  Dover *(G-10177)*
Stratagraph Ne Inc ....E...... 740 373-3091
  Marietta *(G-13502)*
Tk Gas Services Inc ....E...... 740 826-0303
  New Concord *(G-15038)*

OILS & GREASES: Blended & Compounded

Chemical Solvents Inc ....E...... 216 741-9310
  Cleveland *(G-5232)*
Cincinnati - Vulcan Company ....D...... 513 242-5300
  Cincinnati *(G-3278)*
New Vulco Mfg & Sales Co LLC ....D...... 513 242-2672
  Cincinnati *(G-4158)*
Wallover Enterprises Inc ....E...... 440 238-9250
  Strongsville *(G-17523)*

OILS & GREASES: Lubricating

Borchers Americas Inc ....D...... 440 899-2950
  Westlake *(G-19466)*
Fuchs Lubricants Co ....E...... 330 963-0400
  Twinsburg *(G-18419)*
Perma-Fix of Dayton Inc ....E...... 937 268-6501
  Dayton *(G-9807)*
R and J Corporation ....E...... 440 871-6009
  Westlake *(G-19536)*
State Industrial Products Corp ....B...... 877 747-6986
  Cleveland *(G-6530)*
Triad Energy Corporation ....E...... 740 374-2940
  Marietta *(G-13505)*

OILS: Lubricating

Universal Oil Inc ....E...... 216 771-4300
  Cleveland *(G-6649)*

OLD AGE ASSISTANCE

Artis Senior Living ....E...... 513 229-7450
  Mason *(G-13664)*
Ashland Cnty Council On Aging ....E...... 419 281-1477
  Ashland *(G-655)*
Bluebird Retirement Community ....E...... 740 845-1880
  London *(G-12993)*
Brookdale Senior Living Inc ....E...... 937 864-1500
  Fairborn *(G-10786)*
County of Richland ....E...... 419 774-5894
  Mansfield *(G-13279)*
Danbury Woods of Wooster ....E...... 330 264-0355
  Wooster *(G-19861)*
Foundations Hlth Solutions Inc ....D...... 440 793-0200
  North Olmsted *(G-15423)*
Ganzhorn Suites Inc ....D...... 614 356-9810
  Powell *(G-16336)*
Hcr Manorcare Med Svcs Fla LLC ....D...... 440 887-1442
  North Royalton *(G-15494)*
Hilty Memorial Home Inc ....C...... 419 384-3218
  Pandora *(G-15892)*
Jackson County Board On Aging ....E...... 740 286-2909
  Jackson *(G-12315)*
Meigs County Council On Aging ....E...... 740 992-2161
  Pomeroy *(G-16233)*
Nami of Preble County Ohio ....E...... 937 456-4947
  Eaton *(G-10570)*
Senior Outreach Services ....E...... 216 421-6900
  Cleveland *(G-6470)*
Taylor Corporation ....E...... 419 420-0790
  Findlay *(G-11091)*

OLEFINS

Lyondell Chemical Company ....D...... 513 530-4000
  Cincinnati *(G-4004)*

ON-LINE DATABASE INFORMATION RETRIEVAL SVCS

Acxiom Corporation ....C...... 216 520-3181
  Independence *(G-12179)*
Amaxx Inc ....E...... 614 486-3481
  Dublin *(G-10244)*
Doylestown Communications ....E...... 330 658-7000
  Doylestown *(G-10226)*
Oclc Inc ....A...... 614 764-6000
  Dublin *(G-10412)*
Simplified Logistics LLC ....E...... 440 250-8912
  Westlake *(G-19547)*

OPERATIVE BUILDERS: Condominiums

Douglas Construction Company ....E...... 419 865-8600
  Holland *(G-12022)*
Epcon Cmmnties Franchising Inc ....D...... 614 761-1010
  Dublin *(G-10337)*
Epcon Communities Inc ....D...... 614 761-1010
  Dublin *(G-10338)*

OPERATIVE BUILDERS: Townhouse

Nrp Holdings LLC ....C...... 216 475-8900
  Cleveland *(G-6168)*

OPERATOR TRAINING, COMPUTER

Advanced Service Tech LLC ....E...... 937 435-4376
  Miamisburg *(G-14268)*
Babbage-Simmel & Assoc Inc ....E...... 614 481-6555
  Columbus *(G-7082)*

SERVICES SECTION

OPERATOR: Apartment Buildings

Expert System Applications ....E 440 248-0110
 Beachwood *(G-1077)*
S & P Solutions Inc ....C 440 918-9111
 Willoughby Hills *(G-19734)*

OPERATOR: Apartment Buildings

12000 Edgewater Drive LLC ....D 216 520-1250
 Lakewood *(G-12469)*
A P & P Dev & Cnstr Co ....D 330 833-8886
 Massillon *(G-13782)*
Akron Metropolitan Hsing Auth ....C 330 920-1652
 Stow *(G-17350)*
Alcohol Drug Addiction ....D 330 564-4075
 Akron *(G-65)*
Allen Metropolitan Hsing Auth ....E 419 228-6065
 Lima *(G-12737)*
Alliance Towers LLC ....A 330 823-1063
 Alliance *(G-526)*
Alpha PHI Alpha Homes Inc ....D 330 376-2115
 Akron *(G-70)*
Andrews Apartments Ltd ....C 440 946-3600
 Willoughby *(G-19644)*
Arbor Park Phase Two Assoc ....E 561 998-0700
 Cleveland *(G-5060)*
Arbor Pk Phase Three Assoc LP ....E 561 998-0700
 Cleveland *(G-5061)*
Aspen Management Usa LLC ....E 419 281-3367
 Ashland *(G-659)*
Azalea Alabama Investment LLC ....D 216 520-1250
 Cleveland *(G-5088)*
Barcus Company Inc ....E 614 451-9000
 Columbus *(G-7089)*
Belmont Metro Hsing Auth ....E 740 633-5085
 Martins Ferry *(G-13599)*
Biltmore Apartments Ltd ....D 937 461-9695
 Dayton *(G-9359)*
Brethren Care Inc ....C 419 289-0803
 Ashland *(G-666)*
Brodhead Village Ltd ....D 614 863-4640
 New Albany *(G-14976)*
Buckeye Cmnty Eighty One LP ....E 614 942-2020
 Columbus *(G-7157)*
Buckeye Cmnty Thirty Five LP ....E 614 942-2020
 Akron *(G-116)*
Burton Carol Management ....E 216 464-5130
 Cleveland *(G-5160)*
Cassady Vlg Aprtments Ohio LLC ......D 216 520-1250
 Columbus *(G-7208)*
Chelmsford Apartments Ltd ....E 419 389-0800
 Toledo *(G-17803)*
Cincinnati Metro Hsing Auth ....E 513 421-2642
 Cincinnati *(G-3315)*
Cincinnati Metro Hsing Auth ....E 513 333-0670
 Cincinnati *(G-3317)*
Commons of Providence ....D 419 624-1171
 Sandusky *(G-16744)*
Community Prpts Ohio III LLC ....E 614 253-0984
 Columbus *(G-7407)*
Community Prpts Ohio MGT Svcs ......E 614 253-0984
 Columbus *(G-7408)*
Creative Living Housing Corp ....E 614 421-1226
 Columbus *(G-7457)*
Crestview Manor Nursing Home ....C 740 654-2634
 Lancaster *(G-12524)*
Cwb Property Managment Inc ....E 614 793-2244
 Dublin *(G-10315)*
Ea Vica Co ....E 513 481-3500
 Cincinnati *(G-3526)*
Eaglewood Care Center ....C 937 399-7195
 Springfield *(G-17701)*
Edward Rose Associates Inc ....E 513 752-2727
 Batavia *(G-1012)*
Emerald Dev Ecnomic Netwrk Inc ......D 216 961-9690
 Cleveland *(G-5533)*
Englewood Square Ltd ....E 937 836-4117
 Englewood *(G-10703)*
Equity Residential Properties ....E 216 861-2700
 Cleveland *(G-5549)*
Fairfield Homes Inc ....E 740 653-3583
 Lancaster *(G-12535)*
Fairfield Homes Inc ....C 614 873-4533
 Plain City *(G-16192)*
Fay Limited Partnership ....E 513 542-8333
 Cincinnati *(G-3594)*
Fay Limited Partnership ....E 513 241-1911
 Cincinnati *(G-3595)*
Fieldstone Limited Partnership ....C 937 293-0900
 Moraine *(G-14917)*
Fish Creek Plaza Ltd ....D 330 688-0450
 Stow *(G-17366)*

Forest City Enterprises LP ....B 216 621-6060
 Cleveland *(G-5614)*
FTM Associates LLC ....D 614 846-1834
 Columbus *(G-7712)*
G J Goudreau Operating Co ....E 216 741-7524
 Cleveland *(G-5647)*
Galion East Ohio I LP ....D 216 520-1250
 Galion *(G-11299)*
Garland Group Inc ....E 614 294-4411
 Columbus *(G-7730)*
Giffin Management Group Inc ....E 330 758-4695
 Youngstown *(G-20200)*
Glen Wesley Inc ....D 614 888-7492
 Columbus *(G-7755)*
Gms Management Co Inc Iowa ....E 216 766-6000
 Cleveland *(G-5676)*
Goldberg Companies Inc ....E 216 475-2600
 Cleveland *(G-5677)*
Hcf Management Inc ....D 419 999-2010
 Lima *(G-12791)*
Hcf of Bowling Green Inc ....C 419 352-4694
 Bowling Green *(G-1782)*
Highland Village Ltd Partnr ....D 614 863-4640
 New Albany *(G-14988)*
Hills Property Management Inc ....D 513 984-0300
 Blue Ash *(G-1613)*
Holland Management Inc ....B 330 239-4474
 Sharon Center *(G-16874)*
Horizon House Apartments LLC ....D 740 354-6393
 Portsmouth *(G-16288)*
Huber Investment Corporation ....E 937 233-1122
 Dayton *(G-9624)*
Iacovetta Builders Inc ....E 614 272-6464
 Columbus *(G-7880)*
Indian Hills Senior Community ....E 216 486-7700
 Euclid *(G-10763)*
Interntional Towers I Ohio Ltd ....D 216 520-1250
 Youngstown *(G-20237)*
K & D Enterprises Inc ....E 440 946-3600
 Willoughby *(G-19672)*
K&D Group Inc ....E 440 946-3600
 Willoughby *(G-19673)*
Kingsbury Tower I Ltd ....D 216 795-3950
 Cleveland *(G-5904)*
Klingbeil Multifamilty Fund IV ....D 415 398-0106
 Columbus *(G-7998)*
Kopf Construction Corporation ....D 440 933-0250
 Avon Lake *(G-933)*
Lakewoods II Ltd ....E 937 254-6141
 Dayton *(G-9671)*
Links ....E 937 644-9988
 Marysville *(G-13631)*
Little Bark View Limited ....E 216 520-1250
 Cleveland *(G-5946)*
Marsol Apartments ....E 440 449-5800
 Cleveland *(G-5987)*
Menorah Park Center For Senio ....A 216 831-6500
 Cleveland *(G-6024)*
Mercy Health West Park ....C 513 451-8900
 Cincinnati *(G-4076)*
Miami Cnty Cmnty Action Cuncil ....E 937 335-7921
 Troy *(G-18363)*
Millennia Housing MGT Ltd ....E 216 520-1250
 Cleveland *(G-6066)*
Mrn Limited Partnership ....E 216 589-5631
 Cleveland *(G-6084)*
Murray Guttman ....D 513 984-0300
 Blue Ash *(G-1649)*
National Church Residences ....C 614 451-2151
 Columbus *(G-8215)*
National Housing Corporation ....E 614 481-8106
 Columbus *(G-8220)*
Network Restorations II ....E 614 253-0984
 Columbus *(G-8266)*
Network Restorations III LLC ....E 614 253-0984
 Columbus *(G-8267)*
New Birch Manor I Assoc LLC ....D 330 723-3404
 Medina *(G-14106)*
Notre Dame Academy Apartments .....E 216 707-1590
 Cleveland *(G-6164)*
Npa Associates ....D 614 258-4053
 Beachwood *(G-1109)*
Oak Brook Gardens ....D 440 237-3613
 North Royalton *(G-15497)*
Oberer Development Co ....E 937 910-0851
 Miamisburg *(G-14328)*
Ohio Eastern Star Home ....E 740 397-1706
 Mount Vernon *(G-14917)*
Ohio Presbt Retirement Svcs ....B 330 746-2944
 Youngstown *(G-20309)*

Oliver House Rest Complex ....D 419 243-1302
 Toledo *(G-18105)*
Original Partners Ltd Partnr ....C 513 381-8696
 Cincinnati *(G-4234)*
Otterbein Portage Valley Inc ....C 888 749-4950
 Pemberville *(G-15943)*
Overbrook Park Ltd ....D 740 773-1159
 Chillicothe *(G-2867)*
Owners Management Company ....E 440 439-3800
 Bedford *(G-1328)*
Parklane Manor of Akron Inc ....E 330 724-3315
 Akron *(G-377)*
Paul Dennis ....E 440 746-8600
 Brecksville *(G-1839)*
Phoenix Residential Centers ....D 440 887-6097
 Cleveland *(G-6275)*
Pickaway County Community Acti ......D 740 477-1655
 Circleville *(G-4894)*
Pinewood Place Apartments ....A 419 243-1413
 Toledo *(G-18125)*
Plaza Properties Inc ....E 614 237-3726
 Columbus *(G-8552)*
Pleasant Lake Apartments Ltd ....E 440 845-2694
 Cleveland *(G-6288)*
Power Management Inc ....E 937 222-2909
 Dayton *(G-9817)*
Province Kent OH LLC ....E 330 673-3808
 Kent *(G-12392)*
Rahf IV Kent LLC ....E 216 621-6060
 Kent *(G-12393)*
Real Estate Investors Mgt Inc ....E 614 777-2444
 Columbus *(G-8594)*
Riverside Commons Ltd Partnr ....D 614 863-4640
 Reynoldsburg *(G-16479)*
Sateri Home Inc ....D 330 758-8106
 Youngstown *(G-20367)*
Sh-91 Limited Partnership ....E 330 535-1581
 Akron *(G-436)*
Shaker House ....D 216 991-6000
 Cleveland *(G-6475)*
Sherman Thompson Oh Tc LP ....D 216 520-1250
 Ironton *(G-12302)*
SKW Management LLC ....E 937 382-7938
 Lynchburg *(G-13184)*
Slaters Inc ....E 740 654-2204
 Lancaster *(G-12574)*
Smb Construction Co Inc ....E 419 269-1473
 Toledo *(G-18191)*
Smith Tandy Company ....E 614 224-9255
 Columbus *(G-8746)*
Spruce Bough Homes LLC ....D 614 253-0984
 Columbus *(G-8768)*
St Regis Investment LLC ....E 216 520-1250
 Cleveland *(G-6522)*
Stautberg Family LLC ....E 513 941-5070
 Cincinnati *(G-4587)*
Summerfield Homes LLC ....D 614 253-0984
 Columbus *(G-8800)*
Summit Management Services Inc .....E 330 723-0864
 Medina *(G-14131)*
Superior Apartments ....E 216 861-6405
 Cleveland *(G-6553)*
Tm Wallick Rsdntl Prpts I Ltd ....D 614 863-4640
 Reynoldsburg *(G-16484)*
Towne Properties Asset MGT ....A 513 381-8696
 Cincinnati *(G-4669)*
Towne Properties Assoc Inc ....E 513 874-3737
 Cincinnati *(G-4672)*
Townhomes Management Inc ....E 614 228-3578
 Columbus *(G-8858)*
Transcon Builders Inc ....E 440 439-3400
 Cleveland *(G-6609)*
Tyrone Townhouses PA Inv LLC ....D 216 520-1250
 Cleveland *(G-6624)*
Unite Churc Resid of Oxfor Mis ....E 740 382-4885
 Marion *(G-13590)*
United Church Homes ....D 740 382-4885
 Marion *(G-13591)*
United Church Res of Kenton ....D 740 382-4885
 Kenton *(G-12425)*
United Church Residences of ....D 614 837-2008
 Canal Winchester *(G-2174)*
Universal Development MGT Inc ....E 330 759-7017
 Girard *(G-11428)*
Urbancrest Affrdbl Hsing LLC ....E 614 228-3578
 Columbus *(G-8919)*
Vancrest Apts ....E 419 695-7335
 Delphos *(G-10154)*
Victory Sq Aprtmnts Ltd Partnr ....D 330 455-8035
 Canton *(G-2578)*

Employee Codes: A=Over 500 employees, B=251-500
C=101-250, D=51-100, E=25-50

OPERATOR: Apartment Buildings

Wallace F Ackley Co ....D....... 614 231-3661
  Columbus (G-8963)
Walnut Hills Preservation LP ....D....... 513 281-1288
  Cincinnati (G-4822)
Westview Apartments Ohio LLC ....B....... 216 520-1250
  Youngstown (G-20413)
Whitehurst Company ....E....... 419 865-0799
  Maumee (G-13994)
Zanesville Metro Hsing Auth ....D....... 740 454-9714
  Zanesville (G-20556)
Zepf Housing Corp One Inc ....D....... 419 531-0019
  Toledo (G-18333)

OPERATOR: Nonresidential Buildings

Americas Best Value Inn ....E....... 419 626-9890
  Sandusky (G-16726)
Best Western Columbus N Hotel ....E....... 614 888-8230
  Columbus (G-7103)
Canal Road Partners ....E....... 216 447-0814
  Cleveland (G-5176)
Cavaliers Holdings LLC ....C....... 216 420-2000
  Cleveland (G-5193)
Central Ohio Associates Ltd ....D....... 419 342-2045
  Shelby (G-16897)
Centro Properties Group LLC ....E....... 440 324-6610
  Elyria (G-10602)
Ch Relty Iv/Clmbus Partners LP ....D....... 614 885-3334
  Columbus (G-7247)
Cincinnati Sports Mall Inc ....D....... 513 527-4000
  Cincinnati (G-3329)
City of Cleveland ....E....... 216 621-4231
  Cleveland (G-5253)
Columbian Corporation Mantua ....E....... 330 274-2576
  Mantua (G-13385)
Cornerstone Managed Prpts LLC ....E....... 440 263-7708
  Lorain (G-13033)
Coughlin Holdings Ltd Partnr ....E....... 614 847-1002
  Worthington (G-19951)
Dayton Hcri Place Denver ....E....... 419 247-2800
  Toledo (G-17845)
Emmett Dan House Ltd Partnr ....E....... 740 392-6886
  Mount Vernon (G-14894)
Fairfield Homes Inc ....C....... 614 873-3533
  Plain City (G-16192)
Findlay Inn & Conference Ctr ....E....... 419 422-5682
  Findlay (G-11027)
Forest City Enterprises LP ....B....... 216 621-6060
  Cleveland (G-5614)
Forest City Enterprises LP ....E....... 216 416-3756
  Cleveland (G-5615)
Forest City Enterprises LP ....E....... 440 888-8664
  Cleveland (G-5616)
Forest City Enterprises LP ....E....... 216 416-3780
  Cleveland (G-5617)
Forest City Enterprises LP ....E....... 216 416-3766
  Cleveland (G-5618)
Gardner Inc ....C....... 614 456-4000
  Columbus (G-7728)
Glen Arbors Ltd Partnership ....D....... 937 293-0900
  Moraine (G-14789)
Highland Village Ltd Partnr ....D....... 614 863-4640
  New Albany (G-14988)
Hills Property Management Inc ....D....... 513 984-0300
  Blue Ash (G-1613)
Hit Portfolio I Misc Trs LLC ....E....... 614 228-1234
  Columbus (G-7840)
Holland Management Inc ....B....... 330 239-4474
  Sharon Center (G-16874)
I-X Center Corporation ....C....... 216 265-2675
  Cleveland (G-5799)
King Group Inc ....E....... 216 831-9330
  Beachwood (G-1095)
L Brands Service Company LLC ....D....... 614 415-7000
  Columbus (G-8020)
Ladera Healthcare Company ....E....... 614 459-1313
  Columbus (G-8030)
Laudan Properties LLC ....E....... 234 212-3225
  Twinsburg (G-18439)
Marion Road Enterprises ....C....... 614 228-6525
  Columbus (G-8110)
Matco Properties Inc ....D....... 440 366-5501
  Elyria (G-10649)
McM General Properties Ltd ....E....... 216 851-8000
  Cleveland (G-6008)
Oak Health Care Investor ....E....... 614 794-8400
  Westerville (G-19334)
Park Cincinnati Board ....D....... 513 421-4086
  Cincinnati (G-4252)
Phil Giessler ....E....... 614 888-0307
  Worthington (G-19984)

Polaris Towne Center LLC ....E....... 614 456-0123
  Columbus (G-6901)
Power Management Inc ....E....... 937 222-2909
  Dayton (G-9817)
Primo Properties LLC ....E....... 330 606-6746
  Austintown (G-871)
Pubco Corporation ....D....... 216 881-5300
  Cleveland (G-6332)
Richard E Jacobs Group LLC ....E....... 440 871-4800
  Cleveland (G-6390)
Sanico Inc ....D....... 440 439-5686
  Cleveland (G-6443)
Saw Mill Creek Ltd ....E....... 419 433-3800
  Huron (G-12170)
Smg Holdings Inc ....C....... 614 827-2500
  Columbus (G-8744)
Three M Associates ....D....... 330 674-9646
  Millersburg (G-14624)
Valley Title & Escro Agency ....E....... 330 392-6171
  Warren (G-18920)
Wernli Realty Inc ....D....... 937 258-7878
  Beavercreek (G-1262)
Zvn Properties Inc ....D....... 330 854-5890
  Canal Fulton (G-2149)

OPHTHALMIC GOODS

Steiner Eoptics Inc ....D....... 937 426-2341
  Miamisburg (G-14354)

OPHTHALMIC GOODS WHOLESALERS

Haag-Streit USA Inc ....C....... 513 336-7255
  Mason (G-13714)
Interstate Optical Co ....D....... 419 529-6800
  Ontario (G-15694)
Walmart Inc ....B....... 740 286-8203
  Jackson (G-12321)

OPHTHALMIC GOODS, NEC, WHOLESALE: Lenses

Toledo Optical Laboratory Inc ....D....... 419 248-3384
  Toledo (G-18246)

OPHTHALMIC GOODS: Lenses, Ophthalmic

Volk Optical Inc ....D....... 440 942-6161
  Mentor (G-14257)

OPTICAL GOODS STORES

Big Sandy Furniture Inc ....D....... 740 574-2113
  Franklin Furnace (G-11169)
Pen Brands LLC ....E....... 216 447-1199
  Brooklyn Heights (G-1923)
Shawnee Optical Inc ....D....... 440 997-2020
  Ashtabula (G-763)
Summit Opthomology Optical ....E....... 330 864-8060
  Akron (G-468)

OPTICAL GOODS STORES: Contact Lenses, Prescription

Arlington Contact Lens Svc Inc ....E....... 614 921-9894
  Columbus (G-7042)
James D Egbert Optometrist ....E....... 937 236-1770
  Huber Heights (G-12096)

OPTICAL INSTRUMENTS & LENSES

Volk Optical Inc ....D....... 440 942-6161
  Mentor (G-14257)

OPTICAL SCANNING SVCS

Aurora Imaging Company ....E....... 614 761-1390
  Dublin (G-10258)
Merchant Data Service Inc ....C....... 937 847-6585
  Miamisburg (G-14318)
Record Express LLC ....E....... 513 685-7329
  Batavia (G-1023)

OPTOMETRIC EQPT & SPLYS WHOLESALERS

Sight Resource Corporation ....D....... 513 942-4423
  West Chester (G-19153)
Walman Optical Company ....B....... 419 248-3384
  Toledo (G-18298)

OPTOMETRISTS' OFFICES

James D Egbert Optometrist ....E....... 937 236-1770
  Huber Heights (G-12096)
Ohio Eye Specialists Inc ....E....... 800 948-3937
  Chillicothe (G-2866)
Primary Eyecare Associates ....E....... 937 492-2351
  Sidney (G-16948)
Systems Temoptics Coop Opt Un ....E....... 330 633-4321
  Tallmadge (G-17655)

ORCHESTRAS & BANDS

Blue Water Chamber Orchestra ....E....... 440 781-6215
  Cleveland (G-5127)
Cleveland Phlrmonic Orchestra ....D....... 216 556-1800
  Rocky River (G-16574)
Columbus Symphony Orchestra ....D....... 614 228-9600
  Columbus (G-7389)

ORGAN BANK

Life Connection of Ohio ....E....... 419 893-4891
  Maumee (G-13935)
Life Connection of Ohio Inc ....E....... 937 223-8223
  Dayton (G-9680)
Lifebanc ....D....... 216 752-5433
  Cleveland (G-5940)

ORGANIZATIONS & UNIONS: Labor

C W A Local 4326 ....E....... 937 322-2227
  Springfield (G-17154)
Internatl Un Oper Eng 18 ....E....... 216 432-3131
  Cleveland (G-5833)
Lake County Local Hazmat ....E....... 440 350-5499
  Mentor (G-14205)
Local 911 United Mine Workers ....E....... 740 256-6083
  Gallipolis (G-11327)
Pace International Union ....E....... 419 929-1335
  New London (G-15069)
Pace International Union ....E....... 740 772-2038
  Chillicothe (G-2869)
Pace International Union ....E....... 740 289-2368
  Piketon (G-16123)
U S Dept of Labor Occupational ....E....... 216 447-4194
  Independence (G-12270)

ORGANIZATIONS, NEC

Beachwood Prof Fire Fighters C ....E....... 216 292-1968
  Beachwood (G-1055)

ORGANIZATIONS: Civic & Social

Bowling Green State University ....D....... 419 372-2186
  Bowling Green (G-1768)
Burkhardt Springfield Neighbor ....E....... 937 252-7076
  Dayton (G-9374)
Change Healthcare Tech Enabled ....D....... 614 566-5861
  Columbus (G-7252)
Community Mercy Foundation ....D....... 937 328-7000
  Springfield (G-17174)
Delta Kappa Gamma Society ....E....... 419 586-6016
  Celina (G-2645)
EMs Rams Youth Dev Group Inc ....E....... 216 282-4688
  Cleveland (G-5538)
Goldwood Primary School Pta ....E....... 440 356-6720
  Rocky River (G-16579)
Help Foundation Inc ....E....... 216 289-7710
  Euclid (G-10757)
Highland Relief Organization ....E....... 614 843-5152
  Columbus (G-7834)
Independence Foundation Inc ....C....... 330 296-2851
  Ravenna (G-16389)
Independent Order Odd Fellows ....E....... 740 548-5038
  Lewis Center (G-12689)
Intercity Amateur Rdo CLB Inc ....E....... 419 989-3429
  Ontario (G-15693)
International Assn Lions ....E....... 740 986-6502
  Williamsport (G-19638)
International Ordr of Rnbow Fo ....E....... 419 862-3009
  Elmore (G-10588)
Joey Boyle ....E....... 216 273-8317
  Athens (G-795)
Lenau Park ....E....... 440 235-2646
  Olmsted Twp (G-15677)
Lithuanian World Community ....E....... 513 542-0076
  Cincinnati (G-3991)
Miami County Park District ....E....... 937 335-6273
  Troy (G-18365)
Neighborhood Development Svcs ....E....... 330 296-2003
  Ravenna (G-16393)

SERVICES SECTION

ORGANIZATIONS: Veterans' Membership

New Pittsburgh Fire & Rescue F ....E 330 264-1230
  Wooster (G-19892)
Ohio Rver Vly Wtr Snttion Comm ....E 513 231-7719
  Cincinnati (G-4210)
Salvation Army ....D 216 861-8185
  Cleveland (G-6440)
Salvation Army ....D 419 447-2252
  Tiffin (G-17697)
Seneca County Firemens Assn ....D 419 447-7909
  Tiffin (G-17699)
Seven Hills Fireman Assn ....E 216 524-3321
  Seven Hills (G-16836)
Towards Employment Inc ....E 216 696-5750
  Cleveland (G-6607)
Village of Cuyahoga Heights ....C 216 641-7020
  Cleveland (G-6697)
Whitehall Frmens Bnvlence Fund ......E 614 237-5478
  Columbus (G-8989)
Wolves Club Inc ....E 419 476-4418
  Toledo (G-18313)
York Rite ....E 216 751-1417
  Cleveland (G-6772)
Young Mens Christian ....C 513 791-5000
  Blue Ash (G-1725)
Young Mens Christian Assoc ....E 614 878-7269
  Columbus (G-9020)

ORGANIZATIONS: Educational Research Agency

Cincinnti Educ & RES For Vetrn ....E 513 861-3100
  Cincinnati (G-3339)

ORGANIZATIONS: Medical Research

Arthur G James Cancer ....A 614 293-4878
  Columbus (G-7044)
Childrens Hosp Med Ctr Akron ....E 330 633-2055
  Tallmadge (G-17634)
Childrens Hospital Medical Ctr ....A 513 803-1751
  Cincinnati (G-3248)
Childrens Hospital Medical Ctr ....E 513 636-6100
  Cincinnati (G-3251)
Childrens Hospital Medical Ctr ....A 513 636-4200
  Cincinnati (G-3252)
Childrens Hospital Medical Ctr ....E 513 636-6400
  Fairfield (G-10830)
Childrens Hospital Medical Ctr ....E 513 636-6800
  Mason (G-13676)
Cleveland VA Medical Research ....E 216 791-2300
  Cleveland (G-5353)
Kendle International Inc ....E 513 763-1414
  Cincinnati (G-3912)
Mp Biomedicals LLC ....C 440 337-1200
  Solon (G-17029)
Prologue Research Intl Inc ....D 614 324-1500
  Columbus (G-8570)
Research Institute At Nation ....C 614 722-2700
  Columbus (G-8617)
Rogosin Institute Inc ....E 937 374-3116
  Xenia (G-20074)
United States Dept of Navy ....E 937 938-3926
  Dayton (G-9286)
University Hospitals ....D 216 844-8797
  Cleveland (G-6657)
US Dept of the Air Force ....B 937 255-5150
  Dayton (G-9288)
Wright State University ....E 937 298-4331
  Kettering (G-12439)

ORGANIZATIONS: Noncommercial Social Research

American Institute Research ....B 614 221-8717
  Columbus (G-6997)
Truenorth Cultural Arts ....E 440 949-5200
  Sheffield Village (G-16895)

ORGANIZATIONS: Physical Research, Noncommercial

Applied Optimization Inc ....C 937 431-5100
  Beavercreek (G-1146)
Assured Information SEC Inc ....D 937 427-9720
  Beavercreek (G-1148)
Jjr Solutions LLC ....E 937 912-0288
  Beavercreek (G-1180)
Ohio State University ....B 330 263-3701
  Wooster (G-19899)
Sunpower Inc ....D 740 594-2221
  Athens (G-813)

ORGANIZATIONS: Political

County of Richland ....E 419 774-5676
  Mansfield (G-13278)

ORGANIZATIONS: Political Campaign

Republican State Central Execu ....E 614 228-2481
  Columbus (G-8616)

ORGANIZATIONS: Professional

Akron Council of Engineering ....E 330 535-8835
  Akron (G-36)
American Heart Association Inc ....E 614 848-6676
  Columbus (G-6994)
Balanced Care Corporation ....E 330 908-1166
  Northfield (G-15509)
Center School Association ....D 440 995-7400
  Mayfield Village (G-14010)
Community Shelter Board ....E 614 221-9195
  Columbus (G-7410)
Deaconis Assocation Inc ....D 419 874-9008
  Perrysburg (G-15997)
Dignity Health ....C 330 493-4443
  Canton (G-2341)
Emergency Medical Transport ....D 330 484-4000
  North Canton (G-15334)
Greiner Dental Association ....E 440 255-2600
  Mentor (G-14186)
Health Collaborative ....D 513 618-3600
  Cincinnati (G-3753)
Lakeside Association ....E 419 798-4461
  Lakeside (G-12464)
Monroe County Association For ....E 740 472-1712
  Woodsfield (G-19817)
Mount Carmel Health System ....E 614 898-4000
  Westerville (G-19428)
National Ground Water Assn Inc ....E 614 898-7791
  Westerville (G-19429)
Ohio Association of Foodbanks ....E 614 221-4336
  Columbus (G-8318)
Ohio School Psychologists Assn ....E 614 414-5980
  Columbus (G-8374)
Orthodontic Association ....E 419 523-4014
  Ottawa (G-15801)
Pain Net Inc ....D 614 481-5960
  Columbus (G-8509)
Resident Home Association ....D 937 278-0791
  Dayton (G-9850)
State of Ohio ....E 614 466-3834
  Grove City (G-11602)
Union Hospital Association ....A 330 602-0719
  Dover (G-10220)
Visiting Nurse Association ....E 216 931-1300
  Cleveland (G-6704)
Warren Twnship Vlntr Fire Dept ....E 740 373-2424
  Marietta (G-13517)

ORGANIZATIONS: Religious

Ark Foundation of Dayton ....E 937 256-2759
  Dayton (G-9344)
Bnai Brith Hillel Fdn At Osu ....E 614 294-4797
  Columbus (G-7121)
Camp Pinecliff Inc ....D 614 236-5698
  Columbus (G-7181)
Cincinnati Gymnastics Academy ....E 513 860-3082
  Fairfield (G-10834)
Comfort Inn ....E 740 454-4144
  Zanesville (G-20466)
Community Ambulance Service ....D 740 454-6800
  Zanesville (G-20467)
Cyo & Community Services Inc ....E 330 762-2961
  Akron (G-184)
First Assembly Child Care ....E 419 529-6501
  Mansfield (G-13302)
Heartbeat International Inc ....E 614 885-7577
  Columbus (G-7816)
Mideast Baptist Conference ....E 440 834-8984
  Burton (G-2064)
Ohio State Univ Alumni Assn ....E 614 292-2200
  Columbus (G-8379)
Overlook House ....E 216 795-3550
  Cleveland (G-6221)
Pastoral Care Management Svcs ......E 513 205-1398
  Cincinnati (G-4257)
Pillar of Fire ....E 513 542-1212
  Cincinnati (G-4300)
Ross County YMCA ....D 740 772-4340
  Chillicothe (G-2882)

Saint Cecilia Church ....E 614 878-5353
  Columbus (G-8677)
Salvation Army ....D 216 861-8185
  Cleveland (G-6440)
Sheldon Harry E Calvary Camp ....D 440 593-4381
  Conneaut (G-9046)
Sidney-Shelby County YMCA ....E 937 492-9134
  Sidney (G-16955)
Society of The Transfiguration ....E 513 771-7462
  Cincinnati (G-4548)
United Church Homes Inc ....C 419 294-4973
  Upper Sandusky (G-18568)
Wapakoneta YMCA ....D 419 739-9622
  Wapakoneta (G-18812)
West Side Ecumenical Ministry ....C 216 325-9369
  Cleveland (G-6740)
Windsor Medical Center Inc ....D 330 499-8300
  Canton (G-2587)
Young Mens Christian Assoc ....D 937 836-9622
  Englewood (G-10725)
Young Mens Christian Assoc ....C 614 834-9622
  Canal Winchester (G-2181)
Young MNS Chrstn Assn Clveland .....D 440 808-8150
  Westlake (G-19569)

ORGANIZATIONS: Research Institute

American Heart Assn Ohio Vly ....E 216 791-7500
  Cleveland (G-5009)
American Institute Research ....B 614 310-8982
  Columbus (G-6998)
Applied Research Solutions Inc ....D 937 912-6100
  Beavercreek (G-1225)
Barrett Center For Cancer Prev ....D 513 558-3200
  Cincinnati (G-3080)
Charles River Labs Ashland LLC ....C 419 282-8700
  Ashland (G-674)
Macaulay-Brown Inc ....B 937 426-3421
  Beavercreek (G-1251)
Nationwide Childrens Hospital ....A 614 722-2000
  Columbus (G-8232)
Ohio Seed Improvement Assn ....D 614 889-1136
  Dublin (G-10414)
Ohio State University ....C 614 292-5990
  Columbus (G-8429)
Riverside Research Institute ....D 937 431-3810
  Beavercreek (G-1205)
University of Dayton ....C 937 229-2113
  Dayton (G-9953)
University of Dayton ....B 937 229-3822
  Dayton (G-9954)

ORGANIZATIONS: Scientific Research Agency

Cornerstone Research Group Inc ......C 937 320-1877
  Miamisburg (G-14287)
Universities Space Res Assn ....E 216 368-0750
  Cleveland (G-6651)

ORGANIZATIONS: Veterans' Membership

American Legion ....D 330 488-0119
  East Canton (G-10502)
American Legion ....E 440 834-8621
  Burton (G-2059)
American Legion Post ....D 330 393-9858
  Southington (G-17104)
Amvets Post No 6 Inc ....E 330 833-5935
  Massillon (G-13786)
Commodore Denig Post No 83 ....E 419 625-3274
  Sandusky (G-16743)
Disabled American Veterans ....E 330 875-5795
  Louisville (G-13099)
Disabled American Veterans ....B 419 526-0203
  Mansfield (G-13293)
Disabled American Veterans ....B 330 364-1204
  New Philadelphia (G-15093)
Disabled American Veterans ....B 740 367-7973
  Cheshire (G-2789)
Genoa Legion Post 324 ....E 419 855-7049
  Genoa (G-11379)
Ohio Dept Amvet Svc Foundation ......D 614 431-6990
  Columbus (G-8333)
Veterans Fgn Wars Post 2850 ....E 216 631-2585
  Cleveland (G-6690)
Vietnam Veterans America Inc ....E 330 877-6017
  Hartville (G-11832)

ORPHANAGE

ORPHANAGE
Saint Joseph Orphanage .... D 513 231-5010
  Cincinnati *(G-4471)*

ORTHODONTIST
Orthodontic Associates LLC .... E 419 229-8771
  Lima *(G-12850)*
Osu Orthodontic Clinic .... E 614 292-1058
  Columbus *(G-8488)*
Smile Development Inc .... E 419 882-7187
  Sylvania *(G-17615)*

OUTDOOR PARKING SVCS
Falcon Transport Co .... D 330 793-1345
  Youngstown *(G-20186)*

OUTREACH PROGRAM
Area Agency On Aging Reg 9 Inc .... D 740 439-4478
  Cambridge *(G-2096)*
Beth-El Agape Christian Center .... E 614 445-0674
  Columbus *(G-7104)*
Bryant Eliza Village .... B 216 361-6141
  Cleveland *(G-5153)*
First Community Village .... B 614 324-4455
  Columbus *(G-7664)*
Lutheran Scial Svcs Centl Ohio .... E 419 289-3523
  Worthington *(G-19974)*
Menorah Park Center For Senio .... A 216 831-6500
  Cleveland *(G-6024)*
Ross Cnty Cmmittee For Elderly .... E 740 773-3544
  Chillicothe *(G-2877)*

OXYGEN TENT SVCS
Angels Home Care LLC .... E 419 947-9373
  Mount Gilead *(G-14851)*
Kindred Healthcare Inc .... A 937 433-2400
  Dayton *(G-9661)*

PACKAGE DESIGN SVCS
Austin Foam Plastics Inc .... E 614 921-0824
  Columbus *(G-7075)*
Diversipak Inc .... C 513 321-7884
  Cincinnati *(G-3495)*
Libby Prszyk Kthman Hldngs Inc .... C 513 241-6330
  Cincinnati *(G-3974)*
Marsh Inc .... E 513 421-1234
  Cincinnati *(G-4026)*
Nottingham-Spirk Des .... E 216 800-5782
  Cleveland *(G-6165)*
Univenture Inc .... D 937 645-4600
  Dublin *(G-10478)*

PACKAGED FROZEN FOODS WHOLESALERS, NEC
Anderson and Dubose Inc .... D 440 248-8800
  Warren *(G-18817)*
Avalon Foodservice Inc .... C 330 854-4551
  Canal Fulton *(G-2140)*
Best Express Foods Inc .... D 513 531-2378
  Cincinnati *(G-3101)*
Euclid Fish Company .... D 440 951-6448
  Mentor *(G-14172)*
Food Distributors Inc .... E 740 439-2764
  Cambridge *(G-2114)*
Gordon Food Service Inc .... E 419 747-1212
  Ontario *(G-15689)*
Gordon Food Service Inc .... E 419 225-8983
  Lima *(G-12786)*
Gordon Food Service Inc .... E 216 573-4900
  Cleveland *(G-5680)*
Hillcrest Egg & Cheese Co .... D 216 361-4625
  Cleveland *(G-5757)*
Instantwhip Foods Inc .... E 330 688-8825
  Stow *(G-17375)*
Jetro Cash and Carry Entps LLC .... D 216 525-0101
  Cleveland *(G-5862)*
Koch Meat Co Inc .... B 513 874-3500
  Fairfield *(G-10871)*
Lori Holding Co .... E 740 342-3230
  New Lexington *(G-15055)*
Maines Paper & Food Svc Inc .... E 216 643-7500
  Bedford *(G-1319)*
Northern Frozen Foods Inc .... C 440 439-0600
  Cleveland *(G-6158)*
Peck Distributors Inc .... E 216 587-6814
  Maple Heights *(G-13413)*

Pinata Foods Inc .... E 216 281-8811
  Cleveland *(G-6280)*
Ritchies Food Distributors Inc .... E 740 443-6303
  Piketon *(G-16127)*
Sherwood Food Distributors LLC .... B 216 662-6794
  Maple Heights *(G-13418)*
Smithfoods Orrville Inc .... E 740 389-4643
  Marion *(G-13580)*
Spartannash Company .... D 513 793-6300
  Cincinnati *(G-4556)*
Swd Corporation .... E 419 227-2436
  Lima *(G-12896)*
Sysco Central Ohio Inc .... B 614 272-0658
  Columbus *(G-8816)*
Tasty Pure Food Company .... E 330 434-8141
  Akron *(G-471)*
US Foods Inc .... A 614 539-7993
  West Chester *(G-19240)*
Z Produce Co Inc .... E 614 224-4373
  Columbus *(G-9024)*

PACKAGING & LABELING SVCS
Accel Inc .... C 614 656-1100
  New Albany *(G-14971)*
Ace Assembly Packaging Inc .... E 330 866-9117
  Waynesburg *(G-18979)*
Advanced Specialty Products .... D 419 882-6528
  Bowling Green *(G-1756)*
Alternative Services Inc .... E 419 861-2121
  Holland *(G-12007)*
Avery Dennison Corporation .... C 440 534-6000
  Mentor *(G-14145)*
Baumfolder Corporation .... D 937 492-1281
  Sidney *(G-16914)*
BDS Packaging Inc .... D 937 643-0530
  Moraine *(G-14752)*
Corporate Support Inc .... E 419 221-3838
  Lima *(G-12761)*
Crescent Park Corporation .... C 513 759-7000
  West Chester *(G-19059)*
Custom Pkg & Inspecting Inc .... E 330 399-8961
  Warren *(G-18845)*
Custom Products Corporation .... D 440 528-7100
  Solon *(G-16999)*
Custom-Pak Inc .... D 330 725-0800
  Medina *(G-14056)*
D H Packaging Co .... A 513 791-2022
  Cincinnati *(G-3455)*
Domino Foods Inc .... D 216 432-3222
  Cleveland *(G-5499)*
Express Packaging Ohio Inc .... A 740 498-4700
  Newcomerstown *(G-15268)*
First Choice Packaging Inc .... C 419 333-4100
  Fremont *(G-11198)*
Freudenberg-Nok General Partnr .... B 419 499-2502
  Milan *(G-14494)*
Future Poly Tech Inc .... E 614 942-1209
  Columbus *(G-7716)*
Garda CL Great Lakes Inc .... B 561 939-7000
  Columbus *(G-7727)*
General Electric Company .... A 937 534-6920
  Dayton *(G-9570)*
Hunt Products Inc .... E 440 667-2457
  Newburgh Heights *(G-15252)*
Industrial Chemical Corp .... E 330 725-0800
  Medina *(G-14079)*
J & B Systems Company Inc .... C 513 732-2000
  Batavia *(G-1017)*
Keller Logistics Group Inc .... E 866 276-9486
  Defiance *(G-10040)*
King Tut Logistics LLC .... E 614 538-0509
  Columbus *(G-7994)*
Lawnview Industries Inc .... E 937 653-5217
  Urbana *(G-18593)*
M A Folkes Company Inc .... E 513 785-4200
  Hamilton *(G-11756)*
M P & A Fibers Inc .... E 440 926-1074
  Grafton *(G-11442)*
Metzenbaum Sheltered Inds .... C 440 729-1919
  Chesterland *(G-2800)*
Midwest Tape LLC .... B 419 868-9370
  Holland *(G-12038)*
Miller Products Inc .... E 330 238-4200
  Alliance *(G-549)*
Nelson Packaging Company Inc .... D 419 229-3471
  Lima *(G-12844)*
Ohio Gasket and Shim Co Inc .... E 330 630-0626
  Akron *(G-366)*
Packship Usa Inc .... D 330 682-7225
  Orrville *(G-15782)*

Pactiv LLC .... C 614 777-4019
  Columbus *(G-8506)*
Pactiv LLC .... C 614 771-5400
  Columbus *(G-8505)*
Pak Lab .... E 513 735-4777
  Batavia *(G-1020)*
Pandora Manufacturing Llc .... D 419 384-3241
  Ottawa *(G-15802)*
Printpack Inc .... E 513 891-7886
  Cincinnati *(G-4331)*
Project Packaging Inc .... E 216 451-7878
  Cleveland *(G-6323)*
Raco Industries LLC .... D 513 984-2101
  Blue Ash *(G-1672)*
Richland Newhope Industries .... C 419 774-4400
  Mansfield *(G-13358)*
Sonoco Products Company .... E 513 381-2088
  Blue Ash *(G-1690)*
Sonoco Prtective Solutions Inc .... E 937 890-7628
  Dayton *(G-9888)*
Specialty Lubricants Corp .... E 330 425-2567
  Macedonia *(G-13210)*
Systems Pack Inc .... E 330 467-5729
  Macedonia *(G-13211)*
T W I International Inc .... C 440 439-1830
  Cleveland *(G-6566)*
Tekni-Plex Inc .... E 419 491-2407
  Holland *(G-12060)*
Teva Womens Health Inc .... C 513 731-9900
  Cincinnati *(G-4639)*
Third Dimension Inc .... C 877 926-3223
  Geneva *(G-11370)*
Univenture Inc .... D 937 645-4600
  Dublin *(G-10478)*
Univenture Inc .... E 937 645-4600
  Dublin *(G-10479)*
Universal Packg Systems Inc .... B 513 732-2000
  Batavia *(G-1029)*
Universal Packg Systems Inc .... E 513 735-4777
  Batavia *(G-1030)*
Universal Packg Systems Inc .... B 513 674-9400
  Cincinnati *(G-4748)*
Weaver Industries Inc .... C 330 379-3606
  Akron *(G-505)*
Weaver Industries Inc .... C 330 379-3660
  Akron *(G-506)*
Weaver Industries Inc .... C 330 666-5114
  Akron *(G-507)*
Weaver Industries Inc .... C 330 733-2431
  Tallmadge *(G-17661)*

PACKAGING MATERIALS, INDL: Wholesalers
Mauser Usa LLC .... E 740 397-1762
  Mount Vernon *(G-14912)*
Process Pump & Seal Inc .... E 513 988-7000
  Trenton *(G-18343)*

PACKAGING MATERIALS, WHOLESALE
A-Roo Company LLC .... D 440 238-8850
  Strongsville *(G-17437)*
Avery Dennison Corporation .... C 440 534-6000
  Mentor *(G-14145)*
Berlin Packaging LLC .... E 614 777-6282
  Grove City *(G-11533)*
Cambridge Packaging Inc .... E 740 432-3351
  Cambridge *(G-2101)*
Century Marketing Corporation .... C 419 354-2591
  Bowling Green *(G-1772)*
Custom Products Corporation .... C 440 528-7100
  Solon *(G-16999)*
Diversified Products & Svcs .... C 740 393-6202
  Mount Vernon *(G-14893)*
First 2 Market Products LLC .... E 419 874-5444
  Perrysburg *(G-16003)*
Global-Pak Inc .... E 330 482-1993
  Lisbon *(G-12938)*
Gpax Ltd .... E 614 501-7622
  Reynoldsburg *(G-16456)*
Graham Packaging Holdings Co .... E 419 628-1070
  Minster *(G-14663)*
Graham Packg Plastic Pdts Inc .... C 419 423-3271
  Findlay *(G-11037)*
Impressive Packaging Inc .... E 419 368-6808
  Hayesville *(G-11834)*
Kapstone Container Corporation .... C 330 562-6111
  Aurora *(G-844)*
Pacific MGT Holdings LLC .... E 440 324-3339
  Elyria *(G-10667)*
Packaging & Pads R Us LLC .... E 419 499-2905
  Milan *(G-14497)*

SERVICES SECTION

Pakmark LLC .... E 513 285-1040
  Fairfield *(G-10892)*
Questar Solutions LLC .... E 330 966-2070
  North Canton *(G-15363)*
Red Apple Packaging LLC .... E 513 228-5522
  Lebanon *(G-12642)*
Rrp Packaging .... E 419 666-6119
  Perrysburg *(G-16053)*
S & S Inc .... E 216 383-1880
  Cleveland *(G-6425)*
Samuel Strapping Systems Inc .... D 740 522-2500
  Heath *(G-11843)*
Ship-Paq Inc .... E 513 860-0700
  Fairfield *(G-10905)*
SJS Packaging Group Inc .... E 513 841-1351
  Cincinnati *(G-4535)*
Skybox Packaging LLC .... D 419 525-7209
  Mansfield *(G-13364)*
Star Packaging Inc .... E 614 564-9936
  Columbus *(G-8777)*
Sterling Paper Co .... E 614 443-0303
  Columbus *(G-8786)*
Storopack Inc .... E 513 874-0314
  West Chester *(G-19232)*
Superior Packaging Toledo LLC .... E 419 380-3335
  Toledo *(G-18211)*
Systems Pack Inc .... E 330 467-5729
  Macedonia *(G-13211)*
Third Dimension Inc .... E 877 926-3223
  Geneva *(G-11370)*
US Safetygear Inc .... E 330 898-1344
  Warren *(G-18919)*

PACKAGING MATERIALS: Paper

Bollin & Sons Inc .... E 419 693-6573
  Toledo *(G-17776)*
Custom Products Corporation .... D 440 528-7100
  Solon *(G-16999)*
Hunt Products Inc .... E 440 667-2457
  Newburgh Heights *(G-15252)*
Kapstone Container Corporation .... C 330 562-6111
  Aurora *(G-844)*
Springdot Inc .... D 513 542-4000
  Cincinnati *(G-4568)*
Storopack Inc .... E 513 874-0314
  West Chester *(G-19232)*

PACKAGING MATERIALS: Plastic Film, Coated Or Laminated

Universal Packg Systems Inc .... B 513 732-2000
  Batavia *(G-1029)*
Universal Packg Systems Inc .... B 513 674-9400
  Cincinnati *(G-4748)*
Universal Packg Systems Inc .... E 513 735-4777
  Batavia *(G-1030)*

PACKAGING MATERIALS: Polystyrene Foam

Skybox Packaging LLC .... D 419 525-7209
  Mansfield *(G-13364)*
Storopack Inc .... E 513 874-0314
  West Chester *(G-19232)*
Truechoicepack Corp .... E 937 630-3832
  Mason *(G-13775)*

PACKAGING: Blister Or Bubble Formed, Plastic

Truechoicepack Corp .... E 937 630-3832
  Mason *(G-13775)*

PACKING & CRATING SVC

Bates Metal Products Inc .... D 740 498-8371
  Port Washington *(G-16260)*
Calypso Logistics LLC .... C 614 262-8911
  Columbus *(G-7179)*
Crescent Park Corporation .... C 513 759-7000
  West Chester *(G-19059)*
Deufol Worldwide Packaging LLC .... D 440 232-1100
  Bedford *(G-1303)*
Deufol Worldwide Packaging LLC .... D 414 967-8000
  Fairfield *(G-10840)*
Genpak LLC .... E 614 276-5156
  Columbus *(G-7739)*
Lefco Worthington LLC .... E 216 432-4422
  Cleveland *(G-5931)*
Morral Companies LLC .... E 740 465-3251
  Morral *(G-14842)*
Packship Usa Inc .... D 330 682-7225
  Orrville *(G-15782)*
Southeast Diversified Inds .... D 740 432-4241
  Cambridge *(G-2128)*
Sugar Creek Packing Co .... E 513 551-5255
  Blue Ash *(G-1691)*
Vista Industrial Packaging LLC .... D 800 454-6117
  Columbus *(G-8945)*

PACKING & CRATING SVCS: Containerized Goods For Shipping

Containerport Group Inc .... E 440 333-1330
  Columbus *(G-7426)*

PACKING SVCS: Shipping

Amerisource Health Svcs LLC .... D 614 492-8177
  Columbus *(G-7012)*
Flick Lumber Co Inc .... E 419 468-6278
  Galion *(G-11296)*
Hcg Inc .... E 513 539-9269
  Monroe *(G-14697)*
Inquiry Systems Inc .... E 614 464-3800
  Columbus *(G-7904)*
McNerney & Associates LLC .... E 513 241-9951
  Cincinnati *(G-4039)*
Reynolds Industries Inc .... E 330 889-9466
  West Farmington *(G-19246)*
Star Packaging Inc .... E 614 564-9936
  Columbus *(G-8777)*

PADS: Athletic, Protective

Soccer Centre Owners Ltd .... E 419 893-5425
  Maumee *(G-13978)*

PAGING SVCS

Answering Service Inc .... E 440 473-1200
  Cleveland *(G-5041)*
Maximum Communications Inc .... E 513 489-3414
  Cincinnati *(G-4031)*
TSC Communications Inc .... E 419 739-2200
  Wapakoneta *(G-18810)*

PAINT STORE

Comex North America Inc .... D 303 307-2100
  Cleveland *(G-5374)*
Miller Bros Wallpaper Company .... E 513 231-4470
  Cincinnati *(G-4095)*
Modern Glass Pnt & Tile Co Inc .... E 740 454-1253
  Zanesville *(G-20503)*

PAINTING SVC: Metal Prdts

Carpe Diem Industries LLC .... D 419 659-5639
  Columbus Grove *(G-9029)*
Carpe Diem Industries LLC .... E 419 358-0129
  Bluffton *(G-1729)*
Herbert E Orr Company .... C 419 399-4866
  Paulding *(G-15931)*
Precision Coatings Systems .... E 937 642-4727
  Marysville *(G-13645)*
Tendon Manufacturing Inc .... E 216 663-3200
  Cleveland *(G-6582)*

PAINTS & ADDITIVES

Comex North America Inc .... D 303 307-2100
  Cleveland *(G-5374)*
Continental Products Company .... E 216 531-0710
  Cleveland *(G-5402)*

PAINTS & ALLIED PRODUCTS

Akzo Nobel Coatings Inc .... C 614 294-3361
  Columbus *(G-6962)*
Bollin & Sons Inc .... E 419 693-6573
  Toledo *(G-17776)*
Fuchs Lubricants Co .... E 330 963-0400
  Twinsburg *(G-18419)*
Hexpol Compounding LLC .... C 440 834-4644
  Burton *(G-2062)*
Hoover & Wells Inc .... E 419 691-9220
  Toledo *(G-17959)*
Matrix Sys Auto Finishes LLC .... D 248 668-8135
  Massillon *(G-13837)*
Teknol Inc .... D 937 264-0190
  Dayton *(G-9922)*
Tremco Incorporated .... B 216 292-5000
  Beachwood *(G-1133)*

PAINTS, VARNISHES & SPLYS WHOLESALERS

Carlisle Fluid Tech Inc .... E 419 825-5186
  Toledo *(G-17792)*
Continental Products Company .... E 216 531-0710
  Cleveland *(G-5402)*
Finishmaster Inc .... D 614 228-4328
  Columbus *(G-7657)*
Teknol Inc .... D 937 264-0190
  Dayton *(G-9922)*

PAINTS, VARNISHES & SPLYS, WHOLESALE: Paints

Comex North America Inc .... D 303 307-2100
  Cleveland *(G-5374)*
Matrix Sys Auto Finishes LLC .... D 248 668-8135
  Massillon *(G-13837)*
Miller Bros Wallpaper Company .... E 513 231-4470
  Cincinnati *(G-4095)*
Systems Jay LLC Nanogate .... E 419 747-6639
  Mansfield *(G-13371)*

PALLET REPAIR SVCS

Spartan Supply Co Inc .... E 513 932-6954
  Lebanon *(G-12650)*

PALLETIZERS & DEPALLETIZERS

Intelligrated Systems Ohio LLC .... A 513 701-7300
  Mason *(G-13722)*

PALLETS & SKIDS: Wood

Belco Works Inc .... B 740 695-0500
  Saint Clairsville *(G-16617)*
Brookhill Center Industries .... C 419 876-3932
  Ottawa *(G-15796)*
Ken Harper .... C 740 439-4452
  Byesville *(G-2071)*
Quadco Rehabilitation Center .... B 419 682-1011
  Stryker *(G-17537)*
Quadco Rehabilitation Center .... D 419 445-1950
  Archbold *(G-642)*
Richland Newhope Industries .... C 419 774-4400
  Mansfield *(G-13358)*

PALLETS: Plastic

Myers Industries Inc .... E 330 253-5592
  Akron *(G-348)*

PALLETS: Wooden

Gross Lumber Inc .... E 330 683-2055
  Apple Creek *(G-625)*
Litco International Inc .... E 330 539-5433
  Vienna *(G-18739)*

PANELS: Building, Wood

Premier Construction Company .... E 513 874-2611
  Fairfield *(G-10896)*

PAPER & BOARD: Die-cut

Hunt Products Inc .... E 440 667-2457
  Newburgh Heights *(G-15252)*
Kent Adhesive Products Co .... D 330 678-1626
  Kent *(G-12376)*
Springdot Inc .... D 513 542-4000
  Cincinnati *(G-4568)*

PAPER CONVERTING

Buckeye Paper Co Inc .... E 330 477-5925
  Canton *(G-2272)*
Kent Adhesive Products Co .... D 330 678-1626
  Kent *(G-12376)*
Millcraft Group LLC .... E 216 441-5500
  Cleveland *(G-6063)*

PAPER NAPKINS WHOLESALERS

Procter & Gamble Distrg LLC .... B 513 626-2500
  Blue Ash *(G-1667)*

PAPER PRDTS: Sanitary

Giant Industries Inc .... E 419 531-4600
  Toledo *(G-17915)*

PAPER PRDTS: Towels, Napkins/Tissue Paper, From Purchd Mtrls

Aci Industries Converting Ltd..............E....... 740 368-4160
Delaware *(G-10066)*

PAPER, WHOLESALE: Fine

Catalyst Paper (usa) Inc..........................E....... 937 528-3800
Dayton *(G-9389)*
Millcraft Paper Company..........................E....... 937 222-7829
Dayton *(G-9748)*
Mohawk Fine Papers Inc..........................C....... 440 969-2049
Ashtabula *(G-755)*
Veritiv Pubg & Print MGT Inc....................E....... 330 650-5522
Hudson *(G-12149)*

PAPER, WHOLESALE: Printing

Commerce Paper Company.......................E....... 419 241-9101
Toledo *(G-17821)*
Millcraft Paper Company..........................C....... 216 441-5505
Cleveland *(G-6064)*
Millcraft Paper Company..........................E....... 740 924-9470
Columbus *(G-8174)*
Millcraft Paper Company..........................E....... 614 675-4800
Columbus *(G-8175)*
Millcraft Paper Company..........................E....... 216 441-5500
Cleveland *(G-6065)*
Ohio & Michigan Paper Company..............E....... 419 666-1500
Perrysburg *(G-16035)*
Sterling Paper Co....................................E....... 614 443-0303
Columbus *(G-8786)*
The Cincinnati Cordage Ppr Co..................E....... 513 242-3600
Cincinnati *(G-4640)*

PAPER: Adhesive

Kent Adhesive Products Co.......................D....... 330 678-1626
Kent *(G-12376)*

PAPER: Cloth, Lined, Made From Purchased Materials

Tekni-Plex Inc..E....... 419 491-2407
Holland *(G-12060)*

PAPER: Coated & Laminated, NEC

Bollin & Sons Inc....................................E....... 419 693-6573
Toledo *(G-17776)*
Giesecke & Devrient Amer Inc...................C....... 330 425-1515
Twinsburg *(G-18423)*
Ohio Laminating & Binding Inc..................E....... 614 771-4868
Hilliard *(G-11939)*

PAPER: Wrapping & Packaging

Polymer Packaging Inc.............................D....... 330 832-2000
Massillon *(G-13844)*

PAPERBOARD

Pactiv LLC..C....... 614 771-5400
Columbus *(G-8505)*

PARKING GARAGE

Amherst Exempted Vlg Schools.................E....... 440 988-2633
Amherst *(G-586)*
City of Garfield Heights...........................E....... 216 475-1107
Cleveland *(G-5261)*
City of Parma...D....... 440 885-8983
Cleveland *(G-5271)*
City of Portsmouth..................................E....... 740 353-3459
Portsmouth *(G-16270)*
County of Holmes...................................E....... 330 674-5916
Millersburg *(G-14599)*
Kwik Parking..E....... 419 246-0454
Toledo *(G-17997)*
Ohio Department Transportation...............E....... 330 637-5951
Cortland *(G-9080)*
Park-N-Go Inc..E....... 937 890-7275
Vandalia *(G-18692)*
Parking Company America Inc..................E....... 216 265-0500
Cleveland *(G-6243)*
Parking Company America Inc..................E....... 513 381-2179
Cincinnati *(G-4255)*
Sp Plus Corporation................................D....... 216 444-2255
Cleveland *(G-6508)*
Sp Plus Corporation................................E....... 216 687-0141
Cleveland *(G-6509)*

USA Parking Systems Inc.........................D....... 216 621-9255
Cleveland *(G-6677)*

PARKING LOTS

ABM Parking Services Inc........................E....... 937 461-2113
Dayton *(G-9302)*
ABM Parking Services Inc........................E....... 216 621-6600
Cleveland *(G-4949)*
Central Parking System Inc......................E....... 513 381-2621
Cincinnati *(G-3215)*
Park n Fly Inc..E....... 404 264-1000
Cleveland *(G-6238)*
Park Place Management Inc....................E....... 216 362-1080
Cleveland *(G-6239)*
Parking Company America Inc..................B....... 513 241-0415
Cincinnati *(G-4254)*
Prestige Valet Inc...................................D....... 513 871-4220
Cincinnati *(G-4327)*
Shaias Parking Inc.................................E....... 216 621-0328
Cleveland *(G-6474)*
Sp Plus Corporation................................D....... 216 267-7275
Cleveland *(G-6510)*
Sp Plus Corporation................................D....... 216 267-5030
Cleveland *(G-6511)*

PARKING LOTS & GARAGES

Allpro Parking Ohio LLC...........................E....... 614 221-9696
Columbus *(G-6972)*
Asv Services LLC....................................E....... 216 797-1701
Euclid *(G-10743)*
City of Lakewood...................................D....... 216 941-1116
Cleveland *(G-5268)*
City of New Philadelphia..........................E....... 330 339-2121
New Philadelphia *(G-15086)*
Republic Parking System Inc....................E....... 937 415-0016
Vandalia *(G-18698)*
Sharps Valet Parking..............................E....... 513 863-1777
Fairfield *(G-10904)*
Southwood Auto Sales............................E....... 330 788-8822
Youngstown *(G-20378)*

PAROLE OFFICE

Ohio Dept Rhbilitation Corectn..................B....... 614 274-9000
Columbus *(G-8336)*
Rehabltation Corectn Ohio Dept................D....... 614 752-0800
Columbus *(G-8608)*

PARTITIONS & FIXTURES: Except Wood

3-D Technical Services Company...............E....... 937 746-2901
Franklin *(G-11147)*
HP Manufacturing Company Inc................D....... 216 361-6500
Cleveland *(G-5788)*

PARTITIONS WHOLESALERS

Door Fabrication Services Inc...................E....... 937 454-9207
Vandalia *(G-18677)*
OK Interiors Corp...................................C....... 513 742-3278
Cincinnati *(G-4217)*

PARTITIONS: Wood & Fixtures

Brower Products Inc...............................D....... 937 563-1111
Cincinnati *(G-3142)*
Creative Products Inc.............................E....... 419 866-5501
Holland *(G-12017)*
Diversified Products & Svcs.....................C....... 740 393-6202
Mount Vernon *(G-14893)*
LE Smith Company.................................D....... 419 636-4555
Bryan *(G-2009)*
Symatic Inc...E....... 330 225-1510
Brunswick *(G-1991)*

PARTS: Metal

Clifton Steel Company............................D....... 216 662-6111
Maple Heights *(G-13403)*

PARTY & SPECIAL EVENT PLANNING SVCS

Cec Entertainment Inc............................D....... 937 439-1108
Miamisburg *(G-14280)*
Eventions Ltd..E....... 216 952-9898
Cleveland *(G-4556)*
Excel Decorators Inc..............................E....... 614 522-0056
Columbus *(G-7616)*
Pure Romance LLC................................D....... 513 248-8656
Cincinnati *(G-4356)*

PASSENGER AIRLINE SVCS

American Airlines Inc..............................E....... 937 890-6668
Vandalia *(G-18657)*
Champlain Enterprises LLC......................A....... 440 779-4588
North Olmsted *(G-15413)*
Delta Air Lines Inc..................................D....... 614 239-4440
Columbus *(G-7506)*
Envoy Air Inc...D....... 614 231-4391
Columbus *(G-7601)*
Menzies Aviation (texas) Inc....................E....... 216 362-6565
Cleveland *(G-6026)*
Psa Airlines Inc......................................D....... 937 454-9338
Vandalia *(G-18694)*
Psa Airlines Inc......................................C....... 937 454-1116
Vandalia *(G-18695)*
United Airlines Inc..................................E....... 937 454-2009
Vandalia *(G-18703)*
United Airlines Inc..................................C....... 216 501-4700
Cleveland *(G-6633)*

PATENT OWNERS & LESSORS

Cleveland Rest Oper Ltd Partnr................C....... 216 328-1121
Cleveland *(G-5344)*
Hobby Lobby Stores Inc..........................D....... 419 861-1862
Holland *(G-12027)*
Ohio/Oklahoma Hearst TV Inc..................C....... 513 412-5000
Cincinnati *(G-4216)*

PATIENT MONITORING EQPT WHOLESALERS

Clinical Technology Inc............................E....... 440 526-0160
Brecksville *(G-1821)*

PATROL SVCS: Electric Transmission Or Gas Lines

City of Cleveland....................................E....... 216 664-3922
Cleveland *(G-5258)*

PATTERNS: Indl

Freeman Manufacturing & Sup Co.............E....... 440 934-1902
Avon *(G-893)*
Shells Inc..D....... 330 808-5558
Copley *(G-9063)*

PAYROLL SVCS

Advance Payroll Funding Ltd....................C....... 216 831-8900
Beachwood *(G-1046)*
Ahola Corporation..................................D....... 440 717-7620
Brecksville *(G-1811)*
Chard Snyder & Associates Inc................C....... 513 459-9997
Mason *(G-13675)*
Hr Butler LLC..E....... 614 923-2900
Dublin *(G-10366)*
Humaserve Hr LLC.................................E....... 513 605-3522
Cincinnati *(G-3797)*
Kent State University..............................D....... 330 672-2607
Kent *(G-12379)*
Paychex Inc..E....... 614 781-6143
Worthington *(G-19982)*
Paychex Inc..C....... 330 342-0530
Hudson *(G-12139)*
Paychex Inc..E....... 513 727-9182
Middletown *(G-14484)*
Paychex Inc..D....... 614 210-0400
Dublin *(G-10423)*
Paycom Software Inc..............................A....... 888 678-0796
Cincinnati *(G-4267)*
Paycor Inc..E....... 614 985-6140
Worthington *(G-19983)*
Paycor Inc..E....... 216 447-7913
Cleveland *(G-6253)*
Paycor Inc..C....... 513 381-0505
Cincinnati *(G-4268)*
Payroll Services Unlimited.......................E....... 740 653-9581
Lancaster *(G-12564)*
Sheakley-Uniservice Inc..........................C....... 513 771-2277
Cincinnati *(G-4514)*
Top Echelon Contracting Inc....................B....... 330 454-3508
Canton *(G-2564)*

PENSION & RETIREMENT PLAN CONSULTANTS

Alpha Group Agency Inc..........................E....... 216 520-0440
Cleveland *(G-4996)*

SERVICES SECTION

Cbiz Inc .... D 330 644-2044
  Uniontown *(G-18512)*
Financial Plnners of Cleveland .... E 440 473-1115
  Cleveland *(G-5586)*
Nationwide Financial Svcs Inc .... C 614 249-7111
  Columbus *(G-8242)*
Noble-Davis Consulting Inc .... E 440 519-0850
  Solon *(G-17034)*
Producer Group LLC .... E 440 871-7700
  Rocky River *(G-16589)*
Sirak Financial Services Inc .... D 330 493-0642
  Canton *(G-2530)*
The Sheakley Group Inc .... E 513 771-2277
  Cincinnati *(G-4646)*

PENSION FUNDS

Nationwide Rtirement Solutions .... C 614 854-8300
  Dublin *(G-10405)*
Ohio Pub Emplyees Rtrement Sys ...... B 614 228-8471
  Columbus *(G-8370)*
State Tchers Rtrement Sys Ohio .... C 614 227-4090
  Columbus *(G-8783)*

PERFORMING ARTS CENTER PRODUCTION SVCS

Beck Center For Arts .... C 216 521-2540
  Cleveland *(G-5109)*
Deyor Performing Arts Center .... E 330 744-4269
  Youngstown *(G-20168)*
Playhouse Square Holdg Co LLC .... C 216 771-4444
  Cleveland *(G-6287)*
University of Findlay .... C 419 434-4531
  Findlay *(G-11097)*

PERIODICALS, WHOLESALE

Findaway World LLC .... D 440 893-0808
  Solon *(G-17007)*

PERSONAL APPEARANCE SVCS

Engle Management Group .... D 513 232-9729
  Cincinnati *(G-3558)*
Life Time Fitness Inc .... C 614 428-6000
  Columbus *(G-8062)*
Mercy Health .... D 419 407-3990
  Toledo *(G-18053)*
Mitchells Salon & Day Spa .... C 513 793-0900
  West Chester *(G-19121)*
Ussa Inc .... E 740 354-6672
  Portsmouth *(G-16319)*

PERSONAL CARE FACILITY

Adams County Manor .... D 937 544-2205
  West Union *(G-19272)*
Brown Memorial Home Inc .... D 740 474-6238
  Circleville *(G-4880)*
Carriage Inn of Bowerston Inc .... D 740 269-8001
  Bowerston *(G-1754)*
Childrens Forever Haven Inc .... E 440 652-6749
  North Royalton *(G-15483)*
Co Open Options Inc .... E 513 932-0724
  Lebanon *(G-12595)*
Concord Hlth Rhabilitation Ctr .... E 740 574-8441
  Wheelersburg *(G-19575)*
Cred-Kap Inc .... D 330 755-1466
  Struthers *(G-17529)*
Cypress Hospice LLC .... E 440 973-0250
  Berea *(G-1455)*
Dearth Management Company .... E 740 389-1214
  Marion *(G-13537)*
Dearth Management Company .... C 614 847-1070
  Columbus *(G-7498)*
Dearth Management Company .... C 330 339-3595
  New Philadelphia *(G-15092)*
Elmwood Center Inc .... D 419 639-2581
  Green Springs *(G-11474)*
Emeritus Corporation .... E 330 342-0934
  Stow *(G-17363)*
Emeritus Corporation .... E 614 836-5990
  Groveport *(G-11636)*
Grace Hospice LLC .... C 513 458-5545
  Cincinnati *(G-3690)*
Grace Hospice LLC .... C 937 293-1381
  Moraine *(G-14792)*
Grace Hospice LLC .... C 216 288-7413
  Mentor *(G-14183)*
Hospice of Hope Inc .... D 937 444-4900
  Mount Orab *(G-14869)*

Hospice of Miami Valley LLC .... E 937 458-6028
  Xenia *(G-20063)*
Hospice Southwest Ohio Inc .... D 513 770-0820
  Cincinnati *(G-3787)*
Inn At Univ Vlg MGT Co LLC .... E 330 837-3000
  Massillon *(G-13824)*
Inner City Nursing Home .... C 216 795-1363
  Cleveland *(G-5822)*
Judson Care Center Inc .... E 216 292-5706
  Cincinnati *(G-3894)*
Kindred Nursing Centers E LLC .... C 740 772-5900
  Chillicothe *(G-2857)*
Living Care Altrntves of Utica .... E 740 892-3414
  Utica *(G-18018)*
Lutheran Memorial Home Inc .... D 419 502-5700
  Toledo *(G-18021)*
Mary Scott Nursing Home Inc .... D 937 278-0761
  Dayton *(G-9702)*
Meigs Center Ltd .... C 740 992-6472
  Middleport *(G-14407)*
Mercer Residential Svcs Inc .... D 419 586-4709
  Celina *(G-2657)*
Mercy Health .... E 937 390-9665
  Springfield *(G-17237)*
Perio Inc .... E 614 791-1207
  Dublin *(G-10426)*
Pleasant View Nursing Home .... E 330 848-5028
  Barberton *(G-973)*
Queen City Hospice LLC .... E 513 510-4406
  Cincinnati *(G-4365)*
Singleton Health Care Center .... E 216 231-0076
  Cleveland *(G-6483)*
St Luke Lutheran Community .... D 330 644-3914
  New Franklin *(G-15048)*
St Luke Lutheran Community .... D 330 644-3914
  New Franklin *(G-15049)*
Stein Hospice Services Inc .... E 419 663-3222
  Norwalk *(G-15593)*
Voiers Enterprises Inc .... E 740 259-2838
  Mc Dermott *(G-14023)*
West Park Retirement Community ...... C 513 451-8900
  Cincinnati *(G-4836)*
Zandex Inc .... D 740 967-1111
  Johnstown *(G-12344)*
Zandex Inc .... D 740 454-6823
  Zanesville *(G-20549)*
Zandex Health Care Corporation .... C 740 695-7233
  Saint Clairsville *(G-16664)*
Zusman Community Hospice .... E 614 559-0350
  Columbus *(G-9028)*

PERSONAL CREDIT INSTITUTIONS: Auto Loans, Incl Insurance

Central Credit Corp .... E 614 856-5840
  Reynoldsburg *(G-16436)*

PERSONAL CREDIT INSTITUTIONS: Auto/Consumer Finance Co's

Toyota Motor Credit Corp .... D 513 984-7100
  Blue Ash *(G-1698)*

PERSONAL CREDIT INSTITUTIONS: Consumer Finance Companies

Dfs Corporate Services LLC .... E 614 283-2499
  New Albany *(G-14983)*
Howard Hanna Smythe Cramer .... D 330 725-4137
  Medina *(G-14078)*
Security National Bank & Tr Co .... E 937 324-6800
  Springfield *(G-17272)*
United Consumer Fincl Svcs Co .... C 440 835-3230
  Cleveland *(G-6637)*

PERSONAL CREDIT INSTITUTIONS: Finance Licensed Loan Co's, Sm

Homeland Credit Union Inc .... E 740 775-3331
  Chillicothe *(G-2848)*

PERSONAL CREDIT INSTITUTIONS: Financing, Autos, Furniture

722 Redemption Funding Inc .... E 513 679-8302
  Cincinnati *(G-2948)*
Affordable Cars & Finance Inc .... E 440 777-2424
  North Olmsted *(G-15410)*
Mtd Holdings Inc .... B 330 225-2600
  Valley City *(G-18622)*

PERSONAL CREDIT INSTITUTIONS: Install Sales Finance

General Electric Company .... A 330 433-5163
  Canton *(G-2378)*

PERSONAL DOCUMENT & INFORMATION SVCS

Cintas Document Management LLC .... E 800 914-1960
  Mason *(G-13682)*
Contintnal Mssage Solution Inc .... D 614 224-4534
  Columbus *(G-7434)*
Humility of Mary Info Systems .... D 330 884-6600
  Youngstown *(G-20223)*
Public Safety Ohio Department .... A 614 752-7600
  Columbus *(G-8577)*

PERSONAL FINANCIAL SVCS

Nelson Financial Group .... E 513 686-7800
  Dayton *(G-9278)*
Pccw Teleservices (us) Inc .... A 614 652-6300
  Dublin *(G-10424)*

PERSONAL INVESTIGATION SVCS

Employeescreeniq Inc .... D 216 514-2800
  Independence *(G-12207)*
Human Resource Profile Inc .... E 513 388-4300
  Cincinnati *(G-3795)*
Sterling Infosystems Inc .... E 216 685-7600
  Independence *(G-12262)*
Tricor Emplyment Screening Ltd .... E 800 818-5116
  Berea *(G-1474)*

PERSONAL SHOPPING SVCS

Intelisol Inc .... D 614 409-0052
  Lockbourne *(G-12956)*

PERSONAL SVCS

City of Rocky River .... E 440 356-5630
  Cleveland *(G-5275)*

PERSONAL SVCS, NEC

Cabin Restaurant .... E 330 562-9171
  Aurora *(G-832)*

PEST CONTROL IN STRUCTURES SVCS

All Gone Termite & Pest Ctrl .... E 513 874-7500
  West Chester *(G-19016)*
Central Exterminating Company .... E 216 771-0555
  Cleveland *(G-5210)*
General Pest Control Company .... E 216 252-7140
  Cleveland *(G-5668)*
Rentokil North America Inc .... E 330 797-9090
  Youngstown *(G-20344)*
Rentokil North America Inc .... E 216 328-0700
  Brooklyn Heights *(G-1924)*
Terminix Intl Coml Xenia .... E 513 539-7846
  Middletown *(G-14467)*

PEST CONTROL SVCS

Scotts Miracle-Gro Company .... B 937 644-0011
  Marysville *(G-13651)*
Terminix Intl Co Ltd Partnr .... E 513 942-6670
  Fairfield *(G-10913)*
Terminix Intl Co Ltd Partnr .... E 216 518-1091
  Cleveland *(G-6584)*
Terminix Intl Co Ltd Partnr .... E 419 868-8290
  Maumee *(G-13986)*
Terminix Intl Co Ltd Partnr .... E 513 539-7846
  Middletown *(G-14466)*
Terminix Intl Co Ltd Partnr .... E 978 744-2402
  Canton *(G-2560)*

PESTICIDES WHOLESALERS

Univar Inc .... E 440 510-1259
  Eastlake *(G-10551)*

PET & PET SPLYS STORES

Anark Inc .... E 513 825-7387
  Cincinnati *(G-3021)*
Petsmart Inc .... E 513 336-0365
  Mason *(G-13746)*
Red Dog Pet Resort & Spa .... E 513 733-3647
  Cincinnati *(G-4396)*

Employee Codes: A=Over 500 employees, B=251-500
C=101-250, D=51-100, E=25-50

PET FOOD WHOLESALERS

PET FOOD WHOLESALERS
Butler Animal Hlth Holdg LLC .... E 614 761-9095
  Dublin *(G-10274)*

PET SPLYS
Miraclecorp Products .... D 937 293-9994
  Moraine *(G-14808)*

PET SPLYS WHOLESALERS
Columbus Serum Company .... C 614 444-5211
  Columbus *(G-7384)*
Petland Inc .... D 740 775-2464
  Chillicothe *(G-2870)*
Wolverton Inc .... E 330 220-3320
  Brunswick *(G-1999)*

PETROLEUM & PETROLEUM PRDTS, WHOL Svc Station Splys, Petro
X F Construction Svcs Inc .... E 614 575-2700
  Columbus *(G-9012)*

PETROLEUM & PETROLEUM PRDTS, WHOLESALE Crude Oil
Afm East Archwood Oil Inc .... E 330 786-1000
  Akron *(G-24)*
Bd Oil Gathering Corp .... E 740 374-9355
  Marietta *(G-13435)*
Lyden Oil Company .... E 330 792-1100
  Youngstown *(G-20258)*
Vesco Oil Corporation .... E 614 367-1412
  Blacklick *(G-1512)*

PETROLEUM & PETROLEUM PRDTS, WHOLESALE Diesel Fuel
Hightowers Petroleum Company .... E 513 423-4272
  Middletown *(G-14480)*
Knisely Inc .... D 330 343-5812
  Dover *(G-10195)*

PETROLEUM & PETROLEUM PRDTS, WHOLESALE Fuel Oil
Bazell Oil Co Inc .... E 740 385-5420
  Logan *(G-12968)*
Coolants Plus Inc .... E 513 892-4000
  Hamilton *(G-11718)*
D W Dickey and Son Inc .... E 330 424-1441
  Lisbon *(G-12935)*
Earhart Petroleum Inc .... E 937 335-2928
  Troy *(G-18353)*
Hartland Petroleum LLC .... E 740 452-3115
  Zanesville *(G-20485)*
Santmyer Oil Co Inc .... D 330 262-6501
  Wooster *(G-19911)*
Sines Inc .... E 440 352-6572
  Painesville *(G-15879)*
Troutwine Auto Sales Inc .... E 937 692-8373
  Arcanum *(G-631)*

PETROLEUM & PETROLEUM PRDTS, WHOLESALE Petroleum Brokers
Heartland Petroleum LLC .... E 614 441-4001
  Columbus *(G-7820)*

PETROLEUM & PETROLEUM PRDTS, WHOLESALE: Bulk Stations
Campbell Oil Company .... D 330 833-8555
  Massillon *(G-13792)*
Cincinnati - Vulcan Company .... D 513 242-5300
  Cincinnati *(G-3278)*
Englefield Inc .... D 740 452-2707
  Zanesville *(G-20475)*
New Vulco Mfg & Sales Co LLC .... D 513 242-2672
  Cincinnati *(G-4158)*
Ney Oil Company Inc .... D 419 485-4009
  Montpelier *(G-14746)*
Universal Oil Inc .... E 216 771-4300
  Cleveland *(G-6649)*

PETROLEUM PRDTS WHOLESALERS
Champaign Landmark Inc .... E 937 652-2135
  Urbana *(G-18577)*

Circleville Oil Co .... D 740 474-7568
  Circleville *(G-4882)*
Clay Distributing Co .... E 419 426-3051
  Attica *(G-821)*
Koch Knight LLC .... D 330 488-1651
  East Canton *(G-10504)*
Mplx Terminals LLC .... E 513 451-0485
  Cincinnati *(G-4125)*
Shrader Tire & Oil Inc .... E 419 472-2128
  Toledo *(G-18186)*
Travelcenters of America LLC .... D 330 793-4426
  Youngstown *(G-20391)*
Triumph Energy Corporation .... E 513 367-9900
  Harrison *(G-11811)*
Ull Inc .... E 440 543-5195
  Chagrin Falls *(G-2737)*

PHARMACEUTICAL PREPARATIONS: Proprietary Drug PRDTS
Buderer Drug Company Inc .... E 419 627-2800
  Sandusky *(G-16730)*

PHARMACEUTICALS
Abbott Laboratories .... A 614 624-3191
  Columbus *(G-6924)*
Amerisourcebergen Corporation .... D 614 497-3665
  Lockbourne *(G-12944)*
Bigmar Inc .... E 740 966-5800
  Johnstown *(G-12336)*
Biorx Inc .... D 866 442-4679
  Cincinnati *(G-3109)*
Mp Biomedicals LLC .... C 440 337-1200
  Solon *(G-17029)*
Omnicare Phrm of Midwest LLC .... D 513 719-2600
  Cincinnati *(G-4223)*
River City Pharma .... D 513 870-1680
  Fairfield *(G-10900)*
Teva Womens Health Inc .... E 513 731-9900
  Cincinnati *(G-4639)*

PHARMACEUTICALS: Mail-Order Svc
Catamaran Home Dlvry Ohio Inc .... D 440 930-5520
  Avon Lake *(G-924)*
Edwards Gem Inc .... D 330 342-8300
  Hudson *(G-12115)*
Medco Health Solutions Inc .... A 614 822-2000
  Dublin *(G-10393)*

PHARMACIES & DRUG STORES
Buehler Food Markets Inc .... C 330 364-3079
  Dover *(G-10179)*
Fred W Albrecht Grocery Co .... C 330 645-6222
  Coventry Township *(G-9124)*
Fred W Albrecht Grocery Co .... C 330 666-6781
  Akron *(G-230)*
Institutional Care Pharmacy .... E 419 447-6216
  Tiffin *(G-17681)*
Kroger Co .... C 614 759-2745
  Columbus *(G-8015)*
Marc Glassman Inc .... E 330 995-9246
  Aurora *(G-845)*
Modern Medical Inc .... C 800 547-3330
  Westerville *(G-19329)*
Neighborcare Inc .... A 513 719-2600
  Cincinnati *(G-4151)*
Northeast OH Neighborhood Heal .... C 216 231-2323
  Cleveland *(G-6152)*
Target Stores Inc .... E 614 279-4224
  Columbus *(G-8822)*
Walmart Inc .... B 740 286-8203
  Jackson *(G-12321)*

PHOSPHATES
Scotts Company LLC .... A 937 644-3729
  Marysville *(G-13650)*

PHOTOCOPY MACHINE REPAIR SVCS
Comdoc Inc .... C 330 896-2346
  Uniontown *(G-18514)*
Woodhull LLC .... E 937 294-5311
  Springboro *(G-17143)*
Xerox Corporation .... E 419 418-6500
  Toledo *(G-18318)*
Xerox Corporation .... D 216 642-7806
  Cleveland *(G-6767)*

SERVICES SECTION

PHOTOCOPY MACHINES
Xerox Corporation .... B 513 554-3200
  Blue Ash *(G-1724)*

PHOTOCOPY SPLYS WHOLESALERS
Ricoh Usa Inc .... D 513 984-9898
  Blue Ash *(G-1683)*

PHOTOCOPYING & DUPLICATING SVCS
A-A Blueprint Co Inc .... E 330 794-8803
  Akron *(G-13)*
ARC Document Solutions Inc .... D 216 281-1234
  Cleveland *(G-5062)*
ARC Document Solutions Inc .... E 513 326-2300
  Cincinnati *(G-3040)*
ARC Document Solutions Inc .... E 937 277-7930
  Dayton *(G-9341)*
Fedex Office & Print Svcs Inc .... E 937 436-0677
  Dayton *(G-9544)*
Fedex Office & Print Svcs Inc .... E 614 621-1100
  Columbus *(G-7650)*
Fedex Office & Print Svcs Inc .... E 614 538-1429
  Columbus *(G-7651)*
Fedex Office & Print Svcs Inc .... E 614 898-0000
  Westerville *(G-19400)*
Fedex Office & Print Svcs Inc .... E 216 292-2679
  Beachwood *(G-1079)*
Mike Rennie .... E 513 830-0020
  Dayton *(G-9746)*
Oscar Rbrtsn Doc Mgmt Svcs .... E 800 991-4611
  Blue Ash *(G-1661)*
Ricoh Usa Inc .... D 216 574-9111
  Cleveland *(G-6394)*
Ricoh Usa Inc .... E 330 384-9111
  Akron *(G-416)*
Ricoh Usa Inc .... D 513 984-9898
  Blue Ash *(G-1683)*
TMR Inc .... C 330 220-8564
  Brunswick *(G-1992)*

PHOTOENGRAVING SVC
Youngstown ARC Engraving Co .... E 330 793-2471
  Youngstown *(G-20423)*

PHOTOFINISHING LABORATORIES
Buckeye Prof Imaging Inc .... E 800 433-1292
  Canton *(G-2273)*
Click Camera & Video .... E 937 435-3072
  Miamisburg *(G-14285)*
Digico Imaging Inc .... D 614 239-5200
  Columbus *(G-7519)*
Discount Drug Mart Inc .... E 330 343-7700
  Dover *(G-10183)*
Kroger Co .... C 937 294-7210
  Dayton *(G-9666)*
Solar Imaging LLC .... E 614 626-8536
  Gahanna *(G-11268)*
Target Stores Inc .... C 614 279-4224
  Columbus *(G-8822)*
Walgreen Co .... E 937 433-5314
  Dayton *(G-9981)*
Walgreen Co .... E 614 236-8622
  Columbus *(G-8961)*
Walgreen Co .... E 330 677-5650
  Kent *(G-12404)*
Walgreen Co .... E 330 745-2674
  Barberton *(G-984)*
Walgreen Co .... E 937 396-1358
  Kettering *(G-12438)*
Walgreen Co .... E 937 781-9561
  Dayton *(G-9982)*
Walgreen Co .... E 330 733-4237
  Akron *(G-503)*
Walgreen Co .... E 937 277-6022
  Dayton *(G-9983)*
Walgreen Co .... E 740 368-9380
  Delaware *(G-10134)*
Walgreen Co .... E 614 336-0431
  Dublin *(G-10487)*
Walgreen Co .... E 937 859-3879
  Miamisburg *(G-14366)*
Walgreen Co .... E 330 928-5444
  Cuyahoga Falls *(G-9235)*

PHOTOFINISHING LABORATORIES
Buehler Food Markets Inc .... C 330 364-3079
  Dover *(G-10179)*

Fred W Albrecht Grocery Co..................C....... 330 645-6222
Coventry Township (G-9124)
Fred W Albrecht Grocery Co..................C....... 330 666-6781
Akron (G-230)
Marc Glassman Inc..............................C....... 330 995-9246
Aurora (G-845)

PHOTOGRAMMATIC MAPPING SVCS

Aerocon Photogrammetric Svcs...........E....... 440 946-6277
Willoughby (G-19641)
Kucera International Inc.......................D....... 440 975-4230
Willoughby (G-19678)

PHOTOGRAPH DEVELOPING & RETOUCHING SVCS

Vista Color Imaging Inc.......................E....... 216 651-2830
Brooklyn Heights (G-1932)

PHOTOGRAPHIC EQPT & SPLYS WHOLESALERS

Collins KAO Inc....................................E....... 513 948-9000
Cincinnati (G-3388)
KAO Collins Inc.....................................D....... 513 948-9000
Cincinnati (G-3901)
Technicolor Thomson Group.................C....... 937 383-6000
Wilmington (G-19790)

PHOTOGRAPHY SVCS: Commercial

AG Interactive Inc.................................C....... 216 889-5000
Cleveland (G-4967)
Interphace Phtgrphy Cmmnctions........E....... 254 289-6270
Amelia (G-581)
Marsh Inc..E....... 513 421-1234
Cincinnati (G-4026)
Phantom Photography LLC...................E....... 419 215-8060
Toledo (G-18123)
Queen City Reprographics....................C....... 513 326-2300
Cincinnati (G-4371)
Rapid Mortgage Company....................E....... 937 748-8888
Dayton (G-9842)
Woodard Photographic Inc..................E....... 419 483-3364
Bellevue (G-1420)
Youngstown ARC Engraving Co............E....... 330 793-2471
Youngstown (G-20423)

PHOTOGRAPHY SVCS: Portrait Studios

Pam Johnsonident.................................D....... 419 946-4551
Mount Gilead (G-14861)
Universal Technology Corp...................D....... 937 426-2808
Beavercreek (G-1216)

PHOTOGRAPHY SVCS: School

Lifetouch Nat Schl Studios Inc.............E....... 419 483-8200
Bellevue (G-1412)
Lifetouch Nat Schl Studios Inc.............E....... 330 497-1291
Canton (G-2438)
Lifetouch Nat Schl Studios Inc.............E....... 513 772-2110
Cincinnati (G-3979)
Woodard Photographic Inc..................E....... 419 483-3364
Bellevue (G-1420)

PHOTOGRAPHY SVCS: Still Or Video

Childers Photography...........................E....... 937 256-0501
Dayton (G-9261)
Lifetouch Inc...E....... 419 435-2646
Fostoria (G-11134)
Lifetouch Inc...E....... 937 298-6275
Dayton (G-9682)
Peters Main Street Photography..........E....... 740 852-2731
London (G-13005)
Rapid Mortgage Company....................E....... 937 748-8888
Dayton (G-9842)
Ripcho Studio..E....... 216 631-0664
Cleveland (G-6397)
Royal Color Inc......................................B....... 440 234-1337
Bellevue (G-1417)
Usam Inc...D....... 330 244-8782
Canton (G-2575)

PHOTOGRAPHY: Aerial

Aerocon Photogrammetric Svcs...........E....... 440 946-6277
Willoughby (G-19641)
Kucera International Inc.......................D....... 440 975-4230
Willoughby (G-19678)

PHOTOTYPESETTING SVC

Tj Metzgers Inc.....................................D....... 419 861-8611
Toledo (G-18219)

PHYSICAL EXAMINATION & TESTING SVCS

Brecksvlle Halthcare Group Inc............D....... 440 546-0643
Brecksville (G-1816)
Fairfield Diagnstc Imaging LLC............E....... 740 654-7559
Lancaster (G-12532)
Kettering Medical Center......................E....... 937 299-0099
Dayton (G-9655)
Ohio North E Hlth Systems Inc.............E....... 330 747-9551
Youngstown (G-20308)

PHYSICAL EXAMINATION SVCS, INSURANCE

Alveo Health LLC...................................E....... 513 557-3502
Cincinnati (G-2999)

PHYSICAL FITNESS CENTERS

Amitel Limited Partnership...................E....... 440 234-6688
Cleveland (G-5028)
Avalon Holdings Corporation...............D....... 330 856-8800
Warren (G-18823)
B & I Hotel Management LLC...............C....... 330 995-0200
Aurora (G-828)
Bennett Enterprises Inc........................B....... 419 874-3111
Perrysburg (G-15978)
Best Western Columbus N Hotel..........E....... 614 888-8230
Columbus (G-7103)
Breezy Point Ltd Partnership................E....... 330 995-0600
Aurora (G-831)
Broad Street Hotel Assoc LP................D....... 614 861-0321
Columbus (G-7147)
Canter Inn Inc.......................................E....... 740 354-7711
Portsmouth (G-16267)
Carroll Properties..................................E....... 513 398-8075
Mason (G-13671)
Centerville Fitness Inc..........................E....... 937 291-7990
Centerville (G-2675)
Chalk Box Get Fit LLC...........................E....... 440 992-9619
Ashtabula (G-732)
Chillicothe Motel LLC...........................E....... 740 773-3903
Chillicothe (G-2822)
Chillicothe Racquet Club......................E....... 740 773-4928
Chillicothe (G-2824)
City of Brecksville.................................D....... 440 526-4109
Brecksville (G-1819)
Columbus Country Club.......................D....... 614 861-1332
Columbus (G-7343)
Coshocton Village Inn Suites................E....... 740 622-9455
Coshocton (G-9098)
Emh Regional Medical Center..............D....... 440 988-6800
Avon (G-892)
Family YMCA of LANcstr&fairfld...........C....... 740 654-0616
Lancaster (G-12542)
Family YMCA of LANcstr&fairfld...........D....... 740 277-7373
Lancaster (G-12541)
Findlay Country Club............................E....... 419 422-9263
Findlay (G-11025)
Findlay Y M C A Child Dev.....................E....... 419 422-3174
Findlay (G-11031)
Fitness International LLC.....................E....... 513 298-0134
West Chester (G-19074)
Fitness International LLC.....................E....... 419 482-7740
Maumee (G-13917)
Frans Child Care-Mansfield..................C....... 419 775-2500
Mansfield (G-13304)
Galion Community Center YMCA..........E....... 419 468-7754
Galion (G-11297)
Geeta Hospitality Inc............................E....... 937 642-3777
Marysville (G-13622)
General Electric Company....................E....... 513 243-9404
Cincinnati (G-3670)
Grandview Ht Ltd Partnr Ohio..............D....... 937 766-5519
Springfield (G-17203)
Great Miami Valley YMCA......................D....... 513 887-0001
Hamilton (G-11733)
Great Miami Valley YMCA......................C....... 513 892-9622
Fairfield Township (G-10930)
Great Miami Valley YMCA......................D....... 513 887-0014
Hamilton (G-11735)
Great Miami Valley YMCA......................D....... 513 868-9622
Hamilton (G-11736)
Great Miami Valley YMCA......................D....... 513 829-3091
Fairfield (G-10854)
Grooveryde Cle.....................................E....... 323 595-1701
Cleveland (G-5706)
Hardin County Family YMCA.................E....... 419 673-6131
Kenton (G-12416)
Highland County Family YMCA.............E....... 937 840-9622
Hillsboro (G-11978)
Huber Heights YMCA.............................D....... 937 236-9622
Dayton (G-9623)
Island Hospitality MGT LLC...................E....... 614 864-8844
Columbus (G-7927)
Jto Club Corp..D....... 440 352-1900
Mentor (G-14200)
Kettering Recreation Center.................E....... 937 296-2587
Dayton (G-9657)
Lake County YMCA.................................A....... 440 352-3303
Painesville (G-15860)
Lake County YMCA.................................C....... 440 946-1160
Willoughby (G-19680)
Lake County YMCA.................................E....... 440 259-2724
Perry (G-15962)
Lake County YMCA.................................D....... 440 428-5125
Madison (G-13227)
Lima Family YMCA.................................E....... 419 223-6045
Lima (G-12821)
Mansfield Hotel Partnership.................D....... 419 529-1000
Mansfield (G-13332)
Meadowbrook Country Club.................D....... 937 836-5186
Clayton (G-4913)
Medallion Club......................................C....... 614 794-6999
Westerville (G-19328)
N C R Employee Benefit Assn...............C....... 937 299-3571
Dayton (G-9766)
Ohio State University............................E....... 614 293-2800
Columbus (G-8391)
Ohio State University............................B....... 614 292-3238
Columbus (G-8427)
Pike County YMCA.................................E....... 740 947-8862
Waverly (G-18974)
Queen City Racquet Club LLC................D....... 513 771-2835
Cincinnati (G-4370)
Redefine Enterprises LLC.....................E....... 330 952-2024
Medina (G-14118)
Ross County YMCA.................................D....... 740 772-4340
Chillicothe (G-2882)
S P S Inc..E....... 937 339-7801
Troy (G-18378)
Scioto Reserve Inc................................D....... 740 881-9082
Powell (G-16349)
Select Hotels Group LLC........................E....... 614 799-1913
Dublin (G-10451)
Shady Hollow Cntry CLB Co Inc............D....... 330 832-1581
Massillon (G-13854)
Springfield Family Y M C A....................D....... 937 323-3781
Springfield (G-17281)
Swim Incorporated................................E....... 614 885-1619
Worthington (G-20002)
Sycamore Board of Education..............D....... 513 489-3937
Cincinnati (G-4608)
Synergy Hotels LLC...............................E....... 614 492-9000
Obetz (G-15671)
Tippecanoe Country Club Inc................E....... 330 758-7518
Canfield (G-2213)
Ucc Childrens Center............................E....... 513 217-5501
Middletown (G-14488)
Vermilion Family YMCA.........................E....... 440 967-4208
Vermilion (G-18720)
Washington Twnship Mntgomery.........C....... 937 433-0130
Dayton (G-9986)
Y M C A Central Stark County................E....... 330 305-5437
Canton (G-2590)
Y M C A Central Stark County................E....... 330 875-1611
Louisville (G-13108)
Y M C A Central Stark County................E....... 330 877-8933
Uniontown (G-18545)
Y M C A Central Stark County................E....... 330 830-6275
Massillon (G-13862)
Y M C A Central Stark County................E....... 330 498-4082
Canton (G-2591)
Y M C A of Ashland Ohio Inc..................D....... 419 289-0626
Ashland (G-709)
YMCA...E....... 330 823-1930
Alliance (G-566)
YMCA...D....... 937 653-9622
Urbana (G-18603)
YMCA Inc...D....... 330 385-6400
East Liverpool (G-10536)
YMCA of Clermont County Inc...............E....... 513 724-9622
Batavia (G-1032)
YMCA of Massillon.................................E....... 330 879-0800
Navarre (G-14957)
Young Mens Christian...........................B....... 513 932-1424
Lebanon (G-12660)

Employee Codes: A=Over 500 employees, B=251-500
C=101-250, D=51-100, E=25-50
2018 Harris Ohio
Services Directory
1591

PHYSICAL FITNESS CENTERS

Young Mens Christian Assn.............E....... 419 238-0443
  Van Wert *(G-18653)*
Young Mens Christian Assoc...........C....... 614 871-9622
  Grove City *(G-11620)*
Young Mens Christian Assoc...........A....... 937 223-5201
  Dayton *(G-10009)*
Young Mens Christian Assoc...........D....... 330 923-5223
  Cuyahoga Falls *(G-9237)*
Young Mens Christian Assoc...........E....... 330 467-8366
  Macedonia *(G-13219)*
Young Mens Christian Assoc...........E....... 330 784-0408
  Akron *(G-515)*
Young Mens Christian Assoc...........C....... 614 416-9622
  Gahanna *(G-11276)*
Young Mens Christian Assoc...........C....... 740 881-1058
  Powell *(G-16355)*
Young Mens Christian Assoc...........C....... 614 334-9622
  Hilliard *(G-11967)*
Young Mens Christian Assoc...........E....... 937 312-1810
  Dayton *(G-10010)*
Young Mens Christian Assoc...........E....... 614 539-1770
  Urbancrest *(G-18609)*
Young Mens Christian Assoc...........D....... 614 252-3166
  Columbus *(G-9019)*
Young Mens Christian Assoc...........E....... 937 593-9001
  Bellefontaine *(G-1401)*
Young Mens Christian Assoc...........D....... 740 477-1661
  Circleville *(G-4909)*
Young Mens Christian Assoc...........D....... 330 264-3131
  Wooster *(G-19936)*
Young Mens Christian Assoc...........E....... 937 228-9622
  Dayton *(G-10012)*
Young Mens Christian Assoc...........C....... 937 223-5201
  Springboro *(G-17144)*
Young Mens Christian Assoc...........E....... 614 834-9622
  Canal Winchester *(G-2181)*
Young Mens Christian Associat........E....... 419 729-8135
  Toledo *(G-18320)*
Young Mens Christian Associat........C....... 513 241-9622
  Cincinnati *(G-4868)*
Young Mens Christian Associat........D....... 513 923-4466
  Cincinnati *(G-4869)*
Young Mens Christian Associat........E....... 419 474-3995
  Toledo *(G-18322)*
Young Mens Christian Associat........E....... 419 866-9622
  Maumee *(G-13997)*
Young Mens Christian Associat........C....... 419 475-3496
  Toledo *(G-18323)*
Young Mens Christian Associat........D....... 419 691-3523
  Oregon *(G-15756)*
Young Mens Christian Associat........C....... 513 474-1400
  Cincinnati *(G-4867)*
Young Mens Christian Mt Vernon......D....... 740 392-9622
  Mount Vernon *(G-14927)*
Young Mens Christn Assn Shelby......D....... 419 347-1312
  Shelby *(G-16904)*
Young MNS Christn Assn Findlay......D....... 419 422-4424
  Findlay *(G-11102)*
Young MNS Chrstn Assn Clveland......E....... 216 521-8400
  Lakewood *(G-12502)*
Young MNS Chrstn Assn Clveland......D....... 440 842-5200
  North Royalton *(G-15507)*
Young MNS Chrstn Assn Clveland......E....... 216 731-7454
  Cleveland *(G-6774)*
Young MNS Chrstn Assn Clveland......D....... 440 285-7543
  Chardon *(G-2780)*
Young MNS Chrstn Assn Clveland......D....... 216 382-4300
  Cleveland *(G-6775)*
Young MNS Chrstn Assn Clveland......D....... 440 808-8150
  Westlake *(G-19569)*
Young MNS Chrstn Assn Grter NY....D....... 740 392-9622
  Mount Vernon *(G-14928)*
Young Womens Christian ....E....... 937 461-5550
  Dayton *(G-10013)*
Young Womens Christian ....E....... 419 238-6639
  Van Wert *(G-18654)*
Young Womens Christian Assn.........D....... 614 224-9121
  Columbus *(G-9021)*
Young Womens Christian Assn.........E....... 330 746-6361
  Youngstown *(G-20422)*
Young Womens Christian Associ.......E....... 216 881-6878
  Cleveland *(G-6776)*
Young Womns Chrstn Assc Canton....D....... 330 453-0789
  Canton *(G-2594)*
YWCA of Greater Cincinnati ....D....... 513 241-7090
  Cincinnati *(G-4870)*
YWCA Shelter & Housing Network....E....... 937 222-6333
  Dayton *(G-10014)*

PHYSICAL FITNESS CLUBS WITH TRAINING EQPT

Aussiefit I LLC..E....... 614 755-4400
  Columbus *(G-7074)*
Compel Fitness LLC.................................C....... 216 965-5694
  Cincinnati *(G-3402)*
Fitness International LLC..........................E....... 937 427-0700
  Beavercreek *(G-1173)*
L A Fitness Intl LLC...................................E....... 937 439-2795
  Washington Township *(G-18938)*
Victory Ftnes Ctrs of Columbus..................E....... 614 351-1688
  Columbus *(G-8939)*
W T Sports Inc..E....... 740 654-0035
  Dublin *(G-10485)*

PHYSICIANS' OFFICES & CLINICS: Medical

American Hlth Ntwrk & Fmly PRC................E....... 419 524-2212
  Mansfield *(G-13261)*
Ameripath Cincinnati Inc............................E....... 513 745-8330
  Blue Ash *(G-1533)*
Cardinal Orthopaedic Group Inc.................E....... 614 759-1186
  Columbus *(G-7196)*
Christopher C Kaeding..............................E....... 614 293-3600
  Columbus *(G-7270)*
Cleveland Clinic Foundation.......................E....... 330 287-4930
  Wooster *(G-19848)*
Clyo Internal Medicine Inc........................D....... 937 435-5857
  Centerville *(G-2676)*
Digestive Specialists Inc..........................E....... 937 534-7330
  Dayton *(G-9501)*
Elizabeth Place Holdings LLC....................E....... 323 300-3700
  Dayton *(G-9522)*
Family Physicians Inc...............................E....... 330 494-7099
  Canton *(G-2364)*
Frederick C Smith Clinic Inc......................B....... 740 383-7000
  Marion *(G-13540)*
Health Works Mso Inc...............................E....... 740 368-5366
  Delaware *(G-10103)*
Holzer Clinic LLC......................................A....... 740 446-5411
  Gallipolis *(G-11321)*
HRP Capital Inc.......................................E....... 419 865-3111
  Holland *(G-12028)*
Kettering Adventist Healthcare..................D....... 937 298-3399
  Kettering *(G-12430)*
Medical Arts Physician Center...................D....... 216 431-1500
  Cleveland *(G-6013)*
Medical Group Associates Inc...................E....... 740 283-4773
  Steubenville *(G-17330)*
Midwest Allergy Associates......................E....... 614 846-5944
  Columbus *(G-8168)*
Northeast Family Health Care....................E....... 330 630-2332
  Tallmadge *(G-17645)*
Ob Gyn Associates of Lancaster................E....... 740 653-5088
  Lancaster *(G-12563)*
Obstetrics & Gynecology Assoc.................D....... 513 221-3800
  Fairfield *(G-10886)*
Ohio State University.................................B....... 614 293-8133
  Columbus *(G-8434)*
Osup Community Outreach LLC................E....... 614 685-1542
  Columbus *(G-8497)*
Pioneer Physicians Networking..................E....... 330 633-6601
  Tallmadge *(G-17647)*
Public Safety Ohio Department..................E....... 937 335-6209
  Troy *(G-18372)*
Radiology & Imaging Services...................E....... 330 864-0832
  Akron *(G-404)*
Russell Weisman Jr MD.............................C....... 216 844-3127
  Cleveland *(G-6422)*
Somc Foundation Inc................................D....... 740 356-5000
  Portsmouth *(G-16310)*
South Dayton Acute Care Cons.................E....... 937 433-8990
  Dayton *(G-9890)*
Southwest Family Physicians....................D....... 440 816-2750
  Cleveland *(G-6501)*
Stark Medical Specialties Inc....................E....... 330 837-1111
  Massillon *(G-13857)*
Toledo Clinic Inc......................................B....... 419 473-3561
  Toledo *(G-18232)*
Trihealth G LLC.......................................D....... 513 732-0700
  Cincinnati *(G-4693)*
University Eye Surgeons...........................C....... 614 293-5635
  Columbus *(G-8908)*
Wooster Clinic Inc....................................C....... 330 264-1512
  Wooster *(G-19931)*

PHYSICIANS' OFFICES & CLINICS: Medical doctors

Adrian M Schnall MD................................D....... 216 291-4300
  Cleveland *(G-4956)*
American Health Network Inc....................E....... 614 794-4500
  Columbus *(G-6993)*
American Health Network Inc....................E....... 740 363-5437
  Delaware *(G-10071)*
American Hlth Netwrk Ohio LLC.................D....... 614 794-4500
  Columbus *(G-6995)*
Arlington Contact Lens Svc Inc..................E....... 614 921-9894
  Columbus *(G-7042)*
Ashtabula County Medical Ctr....................C....... 440 997-6960
  Ashtabula *(G-723)*
Belmont Bhc Pines Hospital Inc.................C....... 330 759-2700
  Youngstown *(G-20113)*
Bio-Mdical Applications RI Inc...................E....... 740 389-4111
  Marion *(G-13524)*
Bloomberg Ross MD.................................E....... 740 454-1216
  Zanesville *(G-20448)*
Brian Brocker Dr.......................................E....... 330 747-9215
  Youngstown *(G-20124)*
Cardio Thoracic Surgery...........................E....... 614 293-4509
  Columbus *(G-7197)*
Cardiologist..D....... 440 882-0075
  Cleveland *(G-5181)*
Center For Dagnstc Imaging Inc................C....... 614 841-0800
  Columbus *(G-6872)*
Central Ohio Primary Care.........................D....... 614 818-9550
  Westerville *(G-19379)*
Central Ohio Primary Care.........................E....... 614 442-7550
  Columbus *(G-7239)*
Charles L Maccallum MD Inc.....................E....... 330 655-2161
  Hudson *(G-12109)*
Chester West Dentistry............................E....... 330 753-7734
  Akron *(G-131)*
Childrens Hosp Med Ctr Akron...................E....... 330 543-8004
  Akron *(G-136)*
Childrens Hospital Medical Ctr..................E....... 513 636-6800
  Mason *(G-13676)*
Christ Hospital...C....... 513 561-7809
  Cincinnati *(G-3261)*
Christian Healthcare................................E....... 330 848-1511
  Barberton *(G-961)*
City of Whitehall......................................E....... 614 237-5478
  Columbus *(G-7286)*
Clevelan Clinic Hlth Sys W Reg.................D....... 216 476-7007
  Cleveland *(G-5289)*
Cleveland Clinic Community Onc...............E....... 216 447-9747
  Independence *(G-12199)*
Cleveland Preterm....................................E....... 216 991-4577
  Cleveland *(G-5340)*
Coleman Professional Svcs Inc..................B....... 330 673-1347
  Kent *(G-12360)*
Community Mercy Foundation....................B....... 937 652-3645
  Urbana *(G-18582)*
Compass Community Health......................E....... 740 355-7102
  Portsmouth *(G-16273)*
Comprhensive Cardiologist Cons...............E....... 513 936-9191
  Cincinnati *(G-3408)*
Concorde Therapy Group Inc....................E....... 330 493-4210
  Alliance *(G-535)*
Covenant Care Ohio Inc...........................D....... 937 526-5570
  Versailles *(G-18726)*
Crossroads Lake County Adole..................D....... 440 255-1700
  Mentor *(G-14165)*
Davis Eye Center......................................E....... 330 923-5676
  Cuyahoga Falls *(G-9178)*
Davita Inc...E....... 615 341-6311
  Georgetown *(G-11393)*
Emergency Medical Group Inc....................E....... 419 866-6009
  Toledo *(G-17865)*
Emergency Services Inc............................E....... 614 224-6420
  Columbus *(G-7592)*
Emp Management Group Ltd....................D....... 330 493-4443
  Canton *(G-2355)*
Envision Healthcare Corp..........................A....... 937 534-7330
  Dayton *(G-9528)*
Eric Hasemeier Do...................................E....... 740 594-7979
  Athens *(G-787)*
Eye Center...E....... 614 228-3937
  Columbus *(G-7625)*
Fairview Hospital......................................E....... 216 476-7000
  Cleveland *(G-5568)*
Family Health Partners Inc.......................E....... 419 935-0196
  Willard *(G-19619)*
Family Health Plan Inc..............................C....... 419 241-6501
  Toledo *(G-17877)*
Far Oaks Orthopedists Inc.......................E....... 937 298-0452
  Vandalia *(G-18678)*

SERVICES SECTION

PICTURE FRAMING SVCS, CUSTOM

First Med Urgent & Fmly Ctr .... E 740 756-9238
  Lancaster *(G-12543)*
Fortunefavorsthe Bold LLC .... E 216 469-2845
  Lakewood *(G-12479)*
Good Samaritan Hosp Cincinnati .... E 513 569-6251
  Cincinnati *(G-3685)*
Good Samaritan Hospital .... C 937 276-6784
  Englewood *(G-10706)*
GTE Internet .... D 614 508-6000
  Columbus *(G-7780)*
Gw Sutherland MD .... E 419 578-7200
  Toledo *(G-17928)*
Herzig-Krall Medical Group .... E 513 896-9595
  Fairfield *(G-10858)*
Home Health Connection Inc .... E 614 839-4545
  Worthington *(G-19964)*
Kaiser Foundation Hospitals .... A 440 350-3614
  Concord Township *(G-9032)*
Kaiser Foundation Hospitals .... A 330 633-8400
  Akron *(G-299)*
Kaiser Foundation Hospitals .... A 216 524-7377
  Avon *(G-901)*
Kaiser Foundation Hospitals .... A 216 524-7377
  Brooklyn Heights *(G-1918)*
Kaiser Foundation Hospitals .... A 800 524-7377
  North Canton *(G-15347)*
Kaiser Foundation Hospitals .... A 800 524-7377
  Medina *(G-14090)*
Kaiser Foundation Hospitals .... A 800 524-7377
  Fairlawn *(G-10961)*
Kaiser Foundation Hospitals .... A 800 524-7377
  Mentor *(G-14201)*
Kaiser Foundation Hospitals .... A 800 524-7377
  Kent *(G-12375)*
Kaiser Foundation Hospitals .... A 216 524-7377
  Rocky River *(G-16584)*
Kaiser Foundation Hospitals .... A 216 524-7377
  Strongsville *(G-17479)*
Kaiser Foundation Hospitals .... A 330 486-2800
  Twinsburg *(G-18436)*
Kentucky Heart Institute Inc .... E 740 353-8100
  Portsmouth *(G-16293)*
Lakewood Hospital Association .... E 216 228-5437
  Cleveland *(G-5923)*
Layh & Associates .... E 937 767-9171
  Yellow Springs *(G-20090)*
Lifestges Smrtan Ctr For Women .... E 937 277-8988
  Dayton *(G-9681)*
Luis F Soto MD .... E 330 649-9400
  Canton *(G-2441)*
Lutheran Medical Center .... B 216 696-4300
  Solon *(G-17023)*
Magnum Medical Overseas JV LLC .... D 979 848-8169
  Cincinnati *(G-4012)*
Mammovan Inc .... E 330 726-2064
  Youngstown *(G-20270)*
MBC Cardiologist Inc .... D 937 223-4461
  Dayton *(G-9704)*
Medical Associates of Mid-Ohio .... E 419 289-1331
  Ashland *(G-688)*
Medicine Midwest LLC .... E 513 533-1199
  Cincinnati *(G-4045)*
Mercer Cnty Joint Townshp Hosp .... E 419 586-1611
  Celina *(G-2654)*
Mercy Health .... E 513 829-1700
  Fairfield *(G-10879)*
Mercy Health .... E 440 355-4206
  Lagrange *(G-12460)*
Mercy Health .... E 513 686-8100
  Blue Ash *(G-1640)*
Mercy Health .... E 440 336-2239
  Elyria *(G-10651)*
Mercy Health .... E 440 327-7372
  North Ridgeville *(G-15469)*
Mercy Health .... E 440 775-1881
  Oberlin *(G-15650)*
Mercy Health .... E 440 934-8344
  Sheffield Village *(G-16891)*
Mercy Health .... E 440 967-8713
  Vermilion *(G-18714)*
Mercy Health .... D 513 233-6736
  Cincinnati *(G-4065)*
Mercy Health .... C 419 251-2659
  Toledo *(G-18052)*
Mercy Health .... D 513 585-9600
  Cincinnati *(G-4066)*
Mercy Health .... D 419 475-4666
  Toledo *(G-18054)*
Mercy Health .... E 419 476-2124
  Toledo *(G-18055)*

Mercy Health .... D 419 264-5800
  Holgate *(G-12003)*
Mercy Professional Care .... E 330 832-2280
  Massillon *(G-13839)*
Metro Health System .... D 330 669-2249
  Smithville *(G-16966)*
Mvhe Inc .... E 937 499-8211
  Dayton *(G-9765)*
National Guard Ohio .... D 614 492-3166
  Columbus *(G-8218)*
National Rgstry Emrgncy Mdcl .... E 614 888-4484
  Columbus *(G-8224)*
Nelson & Bold Inc .... E 440 975-1422
  Willoughby *(G-19696)*
Northeast OH Neighborhood Heal ...... C 216 231-2323
  Cleveland *(G-6152)*
Ohio Heart and Vascular .... E 513 206-1800
  Cincinnati *(G-4205)*
Ohio North E Hlth Systems Inc .... E 330 747-9551
  Youngstown *(G-20307)*
Ohio State Univ Wexner Med Ctr .... A 614 293-6255
  Columbus *(G-8387)*
Ohio State Univ Wexner Med Ctr .... A 614 293-7521
  Columbus *(G-8385)*
Ohio State University .... A 614 293-7417
  Columbus *(G-8394)*
Ohio University .... E 740 593-1660
  Athens *(G-808)*
Orthoneuro .... D 614 890-6555
  Columbus *(G-8482)*
Pain Control Consultants Inc .... E 614 430-5727
  Columbus *(G-8508)*
Pain Net Inc .... D 614 481-5960
  Columbus *(G-8509)*
Physicians Care of Marietta .... D 740 373-2519
  Marietta *(G-13487)*
Physicians In Family Practice .... E 440 775-1881
  Oberlin *(G-15658)*
Premier Health Group LLC .... E 937 535-4100
  Dayton *(G-9819)*
Premier Physicians Centers Inc .... E 440 895-5085
  Westlake *(G-19535)*
Primary Care Nursing Services .... D 614 764-0960
  Dublin *(G-10430)*
Primary Cr Ntwrk Prmr Hlth Prt .... E 937 743-5965
  Franklin *(G-11164)*
Primary Eyecare Associates .... E 937 492-2351
  Sidney *(G-16948)*
Promedica Health Systems Inc .... E 419 891-6201
  Maumee *(G-13961)*
Queen City Physicians Ltd .... E 513 791-6992
  Cincinnati *(G-4369)*
R I D Inc .... E 419 251-4790
  Toledo *(G-18145)*
Rehab Continuum Inc .... E 513 984-8070
  Blue Ash *(G-1679)*
Retina Group Inc .... E 614 464-3937
  Columbus *(G-8626)*
Robert E Lubow MD .... E 513 961-8861
  Cincinnati *(G-4434)*
Robert F Arrom Md Inc .... E 513 893-4107
  Fairfield *(G-10901)*
Robinson Health System Inc .... A 330 297-0811
  Ravenna *(G-16407)*
Shawneespring Hlth Cre Cntr RI .... B 513 943-4000
  Loveland *(G-13160)*
Signature Healthcare LLC .... C 440 232-1800
  Bedford *(G-1336)*
Southast Cmnty Mental Hlth Ctr .... C 614 225-0980
  Columbus *(G-8751)*
Southern Ohio Wns Cancer Prj .... D 740 775-7332
  Chillicothe *(G-2887)*
Southwest Ohio Ent Spclsts Inc .... E 937 496-2600
  Dayton *(G-9892)*
Summa Health .... A 330 873-1518
  Akron *(G-452)*
Summa Health System .... E 330 375-3000
  Akron *(G-460)*
Summa Health System .... C 330 375-3315
  Akron *(G-458)*
Thomas L Stover Inc .... E 330 665-8060
  Mogadore *(G-14686)*
Tri County Mental Health Svcs .... C 740 592-3091
  Athens *(G-815)*
Trihealth Inc .... E 513 891-1627
  Blue Ash *(G-1702)*
Trihealth G LLC .... E 513 346-5000
  Cincinnati *(G-4694)*
Trihealth G LLC .... D 513 922-1200
  Cincinnati *(G-4696)*

Trihealth Inc .... C 513 985-0900
  Montgomery *(G-14734)*
Trinity Health System .... B 740 283-7000
  Steubenville *(G-17342)*
Union Hospital Association .... D 330 343-3311
  Dover *(G-10219)*
United Health Network Ltd .... E 330 492-2102
  Canton *(G-2569)*
University Hospitals .... E 216 767-8500
  Cleveland *(G-6658)*
University Hospitals .... A 216 767-8900
  Shaker Heights *(G-16869)*
University Hospitals .... A 440 743-3000
  Parma *(G-15917)*
University Hospitals .... D 216 844-8797
  Cleveland *(G-6657)*
University Hospitals Cleveland .... D 216 721-8457
  Beachwood *(G-1135)*
University Medical Assoc Inc .... C 740 593-0753
  Athens *(G-819)*
University of Cincinnati .... E 513 558-4194
  Cincinnati *(G-4755)*
University of Cincinnati .... B 513 558-1200
  Cincinnati *(G-4760)*
University of Cincinnati Phys .... E 513 475-8000
  West Chester *(G-19175)*
University of Cincinnati Phys .... C 513 475-7934
  Cincinnati *(G-4781)*
University of Toledo .... E 419 383-3556
  Toledo *(G-18278)*
Univesrty of Cincinnti Medcl C .... A 513 475-8000
  Cincinnati *(G-4786)*
Univesrty of Cincinnti Medcl C .... A 513 475-8300
  West Chester *(G-19176)*
US Dept of the Air Force .... D 937 257-0837
  Dayton *(G-9287)*
Volk Optical Inc .... D 440 942-6161
  Mentor *(G-14257)*
West Park Family Physician .... E 419 472-1124
  Toledo *(G-18305)*
Women Physicans of Ob/Gyn Inc .... E 614 734-3340
  Columbus *(G-9003)*
Yeater Alene K MD .... E 740 348-4694
  Newark *(G-15249)*

PHYSICIANS' OFFICES & CLINICS: Osteopathic

Adena Health System .... E 740 779-7201
  Chillicothe *(G-2808)*
Christ Hospital .... C 513 561-7809
  Cincinnati *(G-3261)*
Davis Eye Center .... E 330 923-5676
  Cuyahoga Falls *(G-9178)*
Doctors Hospital Health Center .... E 614 544-0101
  Grove City *(G-11555)*
Eric Hasemeier Do .... E 740 594-7979
  Athens *(G-787)*
Family Practice Center Inc .... E 330 682-3075
  Orrville *(G-15770)*
Grandview Family Practice .... E 740 258-9267
  Columbus *(G-7766)*
Hometown Urgent Care .... C 937 372-6012
  Xenia *(G-20062)*
Internal Mdcine Cons of Clmbus .... E 614 878-6413
  Columbus *(G-7916)*
Medical Surgical Associates .... E 740 522-7600
  Newark *(G-15206)*
Mercy Health .... D 419 264-5800
  Holgate *(G-12003)*
Metro Health System .... D 330 669-2249
  Smithville *(G-16966)*
Michael G Lawley .... E 513 793-3933
  Cincinnati *(G-4088)*
Mount Carmel Health .... E 614 855-4878
  New Albany *(G-14993)*
Physicians In Family Practice .... E 440 775-1881
  Oberlin *(G-15658)*
R I D Inc .... E 419 251-4790
  Toledo *(G-18145)*
Sports Medicine Grant Inc .... D 614 461-8174
  Columbus *(G-8763)*
Ulrich Professional Group .... E 330 673-9501
  Kent *(G-12402)*

PICTURE FRAMING SVCS, CUSTOM

American Frame Corporation .... E 419 893-5595
  Maumee *(G-13874)*

Employee Codes: A=Over 500 employees, B=251-500
C=101-250, D=51-100, E=25-50

PIECE GOODS, NOTIONS & DRY GOODS, WHOL: Textiles, Woven

Welspun Usa Inc .... E 614 945-5100
  Grove City *(G-11613)*

PIECE GOODS, NOTIONS & DRY GOODS, WHOLESALE: Fabrics

Miami Corporation .... E 513 451-6700
  Cincinnati *(G-4086)*

PIECE GOODS, NOTIONS & DRY GOODS, WHOLESALE: Tape, Textile

Great Lakes Textiles Inc .... E 440 439-1300
  Solon *(G-17012)*

PIECE GOODS, NOTIONS/DRY GOODS, WHOL: Drapery Mtrl, Woven

Style-Line Incorporated .... E 614 291-0600
  Columbus *(G-8798)*

PIECE GOODS, NOTIONS/DRY GOODS, WHOL: Sewing Splys/Notions

Checker Notions Company Inc .... D 419 893-3636
  Maumee *(G-13894)*
R S Sewing Inc .... E 330 478-3360
  Canton *(G-2502)*

PILOT SVCS: Aviation

Constant Aviation LLC .... C 800 440-9004
  Cleveland *(G-5396)*
Jet Mintenance Consulting Corp .... E 937 205-2406
  Wilmington *(G-19764)*
Macair Aviation LLC .... E 937 347-1302
  Xenia *(G-20069)*
Netjets Assn Shred Arcft Plots .... D 614 863-2008
  Columbus *(G-8260)*
Waypoint Aviation LLC .... E 800 769-4765
  Cincinnati *(G-4825)*

PIPE & FITTING: Fabrication

Atlas Industrial Contrs LLC .... B 614 841-4500
  Columbus *(G-7072)*
Contractors Steel Company .... E 330 425-3050
  Twinsburg *(G-18404)*
Crest Bending Inc .... E 419 492-2108
  New Washington *(G-15134)*
Elliott Tool Technologies Ltd .... D 937 253-6133
  Dayton *(G-9524)*
Kings Welding and Fabg Inc .... E 330 738-3592
  Mechanicstown *(G-14031)*
Phillips Mfg and Tower Co .... D 419 347-1720
  Shelby *(G-16902)*
Rbm Environmental and Cnstr .... E 419 693-5840
  Oregon *(G-15748)*
Rhenium Alloys Inc .... D 440 365-7388
  North Ridgeville *(G-15475)*
Scot Industries Inc .... E 330 262-7585
  Wooster *(G-19914)*
SSP Fittings Corp .... D 330 425-4250
  Twinsburg *(G-18472)*
Swagelok Company .... D 440 349-5934
  Solon *(G-17059)*
Tri-America Contractors Inc .... E 740 574-0148
  Wheelersburg *(G-19582)*
Unison Industries LLC .... B 937 426-0621
  Dayton *(G-9285)*
United Group Services Inc .... C 800 633-9690
  West Chester *(G-19238)*
Zekelman Industries Inc .... C 740 432-2146
  Cambridge *(G-2135)*

PIPE & FITTINGS: Cast Iron

McWane Inc .... B 740 622-6651
  Coshocton *(G-9111)*

PIPE FITTINGS: Plastic

Lenz Inc .... E 937 277-9364
  Dayton *(G-9677)*

PIPE SECTIONS, FABRICATED FROM PURCHASED PIPE

Kottler Metal Products Co Inc .... E 440 946-7473
  Willoughby *(G-19677)*
Pioneer Pipe Inc .... B 740 376-2400
  Marietta *(G-13488)*

PIPE: Seamless Steel

Zekelman Industries Inc .... E 740 432-2146
  Cambridge *(G-2135)*

PIPELINE & POWER LINE INSPECTION SVCS

Dreier & Maller Inc .... E 614 575-0065
  Reynoldsburg *(G-16448)*

PIPELINE TERMINAL FACILITIES: Independent

Brothers Auto Transport LLC .... E 330 824-0082
  Warren *(G-18831)*
Commercial Warehouse & Cartage .... D 614 409-3901
  Groveport *(G-11629)*
CSX Corporation .... A 614 242-3932
  Columbus *(G-7472)*
CT Logistics Inc .... C 216 267-1636
  Cleveland *(G-5446)*
Dayton Freight Lines Inc .... C 419 589-0350
  Mansfield *(G-13290)*
DSV Solutions LLC .... D 740 989-1200
  Little Hocking *(G-12943)*
Fidelitone Inc .... D 440 260-6523
  Middleburg Heights *(G-14381)*
Hogan Services Inc .... E 614 491-8402
  Columbus *(G-7844)*
Jarrells Moving & Transport Co .... E 330 952-1240
  Medina *(G-14086)*
Lake Local Board of Education .... B 330 877-9383
  Hartville *(G-11826)*
Mkm Distribution Services Inc .... D 330 549-9670
  North Lima *(G-15405)*
Moore Trnspt Tulsa Ltd Lblty .... D 419 726-4499
  Toledo *(G-18069)*
Mwd Logistics Inc .... D 419 522-3510
  Ontario *(G-15705)*
PAm Transportation Svcs Inc .... A 330 270-7900
  North Jackson *(G-15385)*
Schenker Inc .... E 614 662-7217
  Groveport *(G-11670)*
Schroeder Associates Inc .... E 419 258-5075
  Antwerp *(G-620)*
Secure Trnsp Co Ohio LLC .... E 800 856-9994
  Worthington *(G-19996)*
Woodruff Enterprises Inc .... E 937 399-9300
  Springfield *(G-17301)*

PIPELINES, EXC NATURAL GAS: Gasoline, Common Carriers

Integrity Kokosing Pipeline Sv .... C 740 694-6315
  Fredericktown *(G-11180)*

PIPELINES: Crude Petroleum

Bluefoot Industrial LLC .... E 740 314-5299
  Steubenville *(G-17304)*
Marathon Pipe Line LLC .... C 419 422-2121
  Findlay *(G-11062)*
Ohio Oil Gathering Corporation .... E 740 828-2892
  Nashport *(G-14953)*

PIPELINES: Natural Gas

Columbia Gas Transmission LLC .... E 614 460-6000
  Columbus *(G-7323)*
Columbia Gas Transmission LLC .... E 740 397-8242
  Mount Vernon *(G-14884)*
Columbia Gas Transmission LLC .... E 740 892-2552
  Homer *(G-12075)*
Eureka Midstream LLC .... E 740 868-1325
  Marietta *(G-13444)*
Utica East Ohio Midstream LLC .... A 740 431-4168
  Dennison *(G-10163)*

PIPELINES: Refined Petroleum

Buckeye Pipe Line Services Co .... E 419 698-8770
  Oregon *(G-15726)*

Marathon Pipe Line LLC .... C 419 422-2121
  Findlay *(G-11062)*
Three Rivers Energy LLC .... E 740 623-3035
  Coshocton *(G-9119)*

PIPES & TUBES: Steel

Alro Steel Corporation .... E 937 253-6121
  Dayton *(G-9323)*
Benjamin Steel Company Inc .... E 937 233-1212
  Springfield *(G-17150)*
Crest Bending Inc .... E 419 492-2108
  New Washington *(G-15134)*
Major Metals Company .... E 419 886-4600
  Mansfield *(G-13327)*
Phillips Mfg and Tower Co .... D 419 347-1720
  Shelby *(G-16902)*
Unison Industries LLC .... B 937 426-0621
  Dayton *(G-9285)*

PIPES OR FITTINGS: Sewer, Clay

Superior Clay Corp .... D 740 922-4122
  Uhrichsville *(G-18492)*

PISTONS & PISTON RINGS

Federal-Mogul LLC .... C 740 432-2393
  Cambridge *(G-2113)*

PLANETARIUMS

Lake Erie Nature & Science Ctr .... E 440 871-2900
  Bay Village *(G-1040)*

PLANNING & DEVELOPMENT ADMIN, GOVT: Urban & Community, Local

City of Columbus .... D 614 645-8270
  Columbus *(G-7283)*

PLANNING & DEVELOPMENT ADMIN, GOVT: Urban/Community, County

Cuyahoga County .... A 216 348-3800
  Cleveland *(G-5453)*

PLANNING & DEVELOPMENT ADMINISTRATION, GOVT: County Agency

City of Berea .... E 440 826-5853
  Berea *(G-1451)*

PLANT CARE SVCS

Rentokil North America Inc .... E 614 837-0099
  Canal Winchester *(G-2168)*

PLANTING MACHINERY & EQPT WHOLESALERS

Agrinomix LLC .... E 440 774-2981
  Oberlin *(G-15637)*

PLANTS, POTTED, WHOLESALE

Express Seed Company .... D 440 774-2259
  Oberlin *(G-15643)*
Maria Gardens Inc .... E 440 238-7637
  Strongsville *(G-17489)*
Plantscaping Inc .... D 216 367-1200
  Cleveland *(G-6285)*
Rentokil North America Inc .... E 216 739-0200
  Brooklyn Heights *(G-1925)*
Straders Garden Centers Inc .... C 614 889-1314
  Columbus *(G-8792)*

PLAQUES: Picture, Laminated

Lawnview Industries Inc .... C 937 653-5217
  Urbana *(G-18593)*

PLASMAPHEROUS CENTER

Biolife Plasma Services LP .... D 419 425-8680
  Findlay *(G-10994)*
Csl Plasma Inc .... D 614 267-4982
  Columbus *(G-7471)*
Csl Plasma Inc .... D 216 398-0440
  Cleveland *(G-5443)*

PLASTIC COLORING & FINISHING
Ampacet Corporation .... E 513 247-5400
  Cincinnati *(G-3018)*

PLASTIC PRDTS REPAIR SVCS
Integrity Processing LLC .... E 330 285-6937
  Barberton *(G-966)*

PLASTICS FILM & SHEET
Clopay Corporation .... C 800 282-2260
  Mason *(G-13686)*

PLASTICS MATERIAL & RESINS
Flexsys America LP .... D 330 666-4111
  Akron *(G-227)*
Freeman Manufacturing & Sup Co .... E 440 934-1902
  Avon *(G-893)*
Kraton Polymers US LLC .... B 740 423-7571
  Belpre *(G-1441)*
Lubrizol Advanced Mtls Inc .... E 440 933-0400
  Avon Lake *(G-934)*
Polymer Packaging Inc .... D 330 832-2000
  Massillon *(G-13844)*
Tembec Btlsr Inc .... E 419 244-5856
  Toledo *(G-18216)*

PLASTICS MATERIALS, BASIC FORMS & SHAPES WHOLESALERS
Advanced Elastomer Systems LP .... C 800 352-7866
  Akron *(G-22)*
Ampacet Corporation .... E 513 247-5400
  Cincinnati *(G-3018)*
Polymershapes LLC .... E 937 877-1903
  Tipp City *(G-17724)*

PLASTICS PROCESSING
Ball Bounce and Sport Inc .... B 419 289-9310
  Ashland *(G-661)*
HP Manufacturing Company Inc .... D 216 361-6500
  Cleveland *(G-5788)*
Samuel Strapping Systems Inc .... E 740 522-2500
  Heath *(G-11843)*
Tahoma Enterprises Inc .... D 330 745-9016
  Barberton *(G-982)*
Tahoma Rubber & Plastics Inc .... E 330 745-9016
  Barberton *(G-983)*

PLASTICS SHEET: Packing Materials
Kapstone Container Corporation .... C 330 562-6111
  Aurora *(G-844)*

PLASTICS: Cast
S&V Industries Inc .... E 330 666-1986
  Medina *(G-14121)*

PLASTICS: Extruded
Eclipse Blind Systems Inc .... C 330 296-0112
  Ravenna *(G-16384)*

PLASTICS: Injection Molded
Dlhbowles Inc .... B 330 478-2503
  Canton *(G-2342)*
Lancaster Commercial Pdts LLC .... E 740 286-5081
  Columbus *(G-8032)*
Queen City Polymers Inc .... E 513 779-0990
  West Chester *(G-19136)*
US Molding Machinery Co Inc .... E 440 918-1701
  Willoughby *(G-19721)*

PLASTICS: Molded
U S Development Corp .... E 330 673-6900
  Kent *(G-12401)*

PLASTICS: Polystyrene Foam
A K Athletic Equipment Inc .... E 614 920-3069
  Canal Winchester *(G-2151)*
Armaly LLC .... E 740 852-3621
  London *(G-12992)*
Myers Industries Inc .... E 330 253-5592
  Akron *(G-348)*

PLASTICS: Thermoformed
First Choice Packaging Inc .... C 419 333-4100
  Fremont *(G-11198)*

PLATE WORK: For Nuclear Industry
Curtiss-Wright Flow Control .... D 513 735-2538
  Batavia *(G-1008)*
Curtiss-Wright Flow Control .... D 513 528-7900
  Cincinnati *(G-2909)*

PLATES
Amos Media Company .... B 937 498-2111
  Sidney *(G-16912)*
Anderson & Vreeland Inc .... D 419 636-5002
  Bryan *(G-2002)*
Art-American Printing Plates .... E 216 241-4420
  Cleveland *(G-5069)*
Wood Graphics Inc .... E 513 771-6300
  Cincinnati *(G-4858)*

PLATES: Sheet & Strip, Exc Coated Prdts
Major Metals Company .... E 419 886-4600
  Mansfield *(G-13327)*

PLATING & POLISHING SVC
A J Oster Foils LLC .... D 330 823-1700
  Alliance *(G-521)*
D-G Custom Chrome LLC .... D 513 531-1881
  Cincinnati *(G-3457)*
Electro Prime Group LLC .... E 419 476-0100
  Toledo *(G-17863)*
Micro Products Co Inc .... D 440 943-0258
  Willoughby Hills *(G-19732)*
Samuel Steel Pickling Company .... D 330 963-3777
  Twinsburg *(G-18467)*
Scot Industries Inc .... E 330 262-7585
  Wooster *(G-19914)*
Worthington Industries Inc .... C 513 539-9291
  Monroe *(G-14718)*
Yoder Industries Inc .... C 937 278-5769
  Dayton *(G-10007)*

PLATING COMPOUNDS
Pazco Inc .... E 216 447-9581
  Cleveland *(G-6254)*

PLATING SVC: NEC
Bron-Shoe Company .... E 614 252-0967
  Columbus *(G-7150)*

PLEATING & STITCHING SVC
Barbs Graffiti Inc .... E 216 881-5550
  Cleveland *(G-5094)*
Shamrock Companies Inc .... C 440 899-9510
  Westlake *(G-19546)*

PLUMBING & HEATING EQPT & SPLY, WHOLESALE: Hydronic Htg Eqpt
Accurate Mechanical Inc .... E 740 654-5898
  Lancaster *(G-12506)*
Habegger Corporation .... D 513 612-4700
  Cincinnati *(G-3725)*
Industrial Controls Distrs LLC .... E 513 733-5200
  West Chester *(G-19092)*
Morrow Control and Supply Inc .... E 330 452-9791
  Canton *(G-2465)*
Palmer-Donavin Mfg Co .... E 419 692-5000
  Delphos *(G-10148)*
Ssi Fabricated Inc .... E 513 217-3535
  Middletown *(G-14459)*
United Atmtc Htng Spply of Clv .... E 216 621-5571
  Cleveland *(G-6634)*

PLUMBING & HEATING EQPT & SPLYS WHOLESALERS
Famous Distribution Inc .... D 330 762-9621
  Akron *(G-215)*
Famous Distribution Inc .... E 330 434-5194
  Akron *(G-216)*
Famous Enterprises Inc .... E 330 762-9621
  Akron *(G-217)*
Famous II Inc .... D 330 762-9621
  Akron *(G-218)*
Famous Industries Inc .... E 330 535-1811
  Akron *(G-219)*
Famous Industries Inc .... E 330 535-1811
  Akron *(G-220)*
Ferguson Enterprises Inc .... E 513 771-6566
  West Chester *(G-19073)*
Gordon Brothers Inc .... C 800 331-7611
  Salem *(G-16697)*
Habegger Corporation .... E 330 499-4328
  North Canton *(G-15342)*
New Haven Estates Inc .... E 419 933-2181
  New Haven *(G-15051)*
Noland Company .... C 937 396-7980
  Moraine *(G-14812)*
Oatey Supply Chain Svcs Inc .... C 216 267-7100
  Cleveland *(G-6176)*
Rexel Usa Inc .... E 419 625-6761
  Sandusky *(G-16789)*
Robertson Heating Sup Co Ohio .... E 800 433-9532
  Alliance *(G-553)*
The Famous Manufacturing Co .... E 330 762-9621
  Akron *(G-476)*
Trumbull Industries Inc .... E 330 393-6624
  Warren *(G-18913)*
Trumbull Manufacturing Inc .... D 330 393-6624
  Warren *(G-18914)*
Waxman Consumer Pdts Group Inc .... D 440 439-1830
  Cleveland *(G-6725)*
Waxman Industries Inc .... C 440 439-1830
  Cleveland *(G-6726)*
Wolff Bros Supply Inc .... E 330 786-4140
  Akron *(G-511)*

PLUMBING & HEATING EQPT & SPLYS, WHOL: Fireplaces, Prefab
L B Brunk & Sons Inc .... E 330 332-0359
  Salem *(G-16702)*
Mason Structural Steel Inc .... D 440 439-1040
  Walton Hills *(G-18790)*
Reading Rock Residential LLC .... E 513 874-4770
  West Chester *(G-19223)*

PLUMBING & HEATING EQPT & SPLYS, WHOL: Pipe/Fitting, Plastic
Corrosion Fluid Products Corp .... E 248 478-0100
  Columbus *(G-7445)*
Macomb Group Inc .... E 419 666-6899
  Northwood *(G-15536)*

PLUMBING & HEATING EQPT & SPLYS, WHOL: Plumbing Fitting/Sply
Eastway Supplies Inc .... E 614 252-3650
  Columbus *(G-7569)*
Edelman Plumbing Supply Inc .... E 216 591-0150
  Bedford Heights *(G-1351)*
Empire Brass Co .... E 216 431-6565
  Cleveland *(G-5537)*
Famous Enterprises Inc .... E 330 938-6350
  Sebring *(G-16822)*
Ferguson Enterprises Inc .... E 614 876-8555
  Hilliard *(G-11901)*
Hajoca Corporation .... E 216 447-0050
  Cleveland *(G-5721)*
Keidel Supply Company Inc .... E 513 351-1600
  Cincinnati *(G-3906)*
Lakeside Supply Co .... E 216 941-6800
  Cleveland *(G-5920)*
Lute Supply Inc .... E 740 353-1447
  Portsmouth *(G-16294)*
Mansfield Plumbing Pdts LLC .... A 419 938-5211
  Perrysville *(G-16079)*
Maumee Plumbing & Htg Sup Inc ...... E 419 874-7991
  Perrysburg *(G-16031)*
Parker-Hannifin Corporation .... B 937 456-5571
  Eaton *(G-10572)*
Parker-Hannifin Corporation .... C 614 279-7070
  Columbus *(G-8516)*
Pickrel Brothers Inc .... E 937 461-5960
  Dayton *(G-9808)*
Robertson Htg Sup Aliance Ohio .... C 330 821-9180
  Alliance *(G-554)*
Robertson Htg Sup Canton Ohio .... E 330 821-9180
  Alliance *(G-555)*
Robertson Htg Sup Clumbus Ohio ..... C 330 821-9180
  Alliance *(G-556)*
Trumbull Industries Inc .... D 330 799-3333
  Youngstown *(G-20393)*

PLUMBING & HEATING EQPT & SPLYS, WHOL: Plumbing Fitting/Sply — SERVICES SECTION

Waxman Consumer Pdts Group Inc......D...... 614 491-0500
  Groveport (G-11686)
Winsupply Inc...E...... 937 865-0796
  Miamisburg (G-14369)
Winsupply Inc...D...... 937 294-5331
  Moraine (G-14836)
Wolff Bros Supply Inc..................................E...... 419 425-8511
  Findlay (G-11101)
Wolff Bros Supply Inc..................................E...... 330 264-5900
  Wooster (G-19930)
Woodhill Supply Inc.....................................E...... 440 269-1100
  Willoughby (G-19726)
Worly Plumbing Supply Inc........................D...... 614 445-1000
  Columbus (G-9008)
Zekelman Industries Inc..............................C...... 740 432-2146
  Cambridge (G-2135)

PLUMBING & HEATING EQPT & SPLYS, WHOL: Water Purif Eqpt

Chandler Systems Incorporated................D...... 888 363-9434
  Ashland (G-673)
Enting Water Conditioning Inc...................E...... 937 294-5100
  Moraine (G-14781)
Nelsen Corporation......................................E...... 330 745-6000
  Norton (G-15557)
Wayne/Scott Fetzer Company....................C...... 800 237-0987
  Harrison (G-11812)

PLUMBING FIXTURES

Empire Brass Co...E...... 216 431-6565
  Cleveland (G-5537)
Mansfield Plumbing Pdts LLC.....................A...... 419 938-5211
  Perrysville (G-16079)
Trumbull Manufacturing Inc........................D...... 330 393-6624
  Warren (G-18914)
Waxman Industries Inc................................E...... 440 439-1830
  Cleveland (G-6726)
Zekelman Industries Inc..............................C...... 740 432-2146
  Cambridge (G-2135)

PLUMBING FIXTURES: Plastic

Bobbart Industries Inc.................................E...... 419 350-5477
  Sylvania (G-17576)
Mansfield Plumbing Pdts LLC.....................E...... 330 496-2301
  Big Prairie (G-1498)
Mansfield Plumbing Pdts LLC.....................A...... 419 938-5211
  Perrysville (G-16079)

PLUMBING FIXTURES: Vitreous

Mansfield Plumbing Pdts LLC.....................A...... 419 938-5211
  Perrysville (G-16079)

PODIATRISTS' OFFICES

Ankle and Foot Care Center.......................E...... 330 385-2413
  East Liverpool (G-10515)
Center For Foot & Ankle Care....................E...... 513 533-1199
  Cincinnati (G-3208)
Toledo Clinic Inc..C...... 419 381-9977
  Toledo (G-18233)
Unity Health Network LLC..........................E...... 330 626-0549
  Streetsboro (G-17435)

POLICE PROTECTION

ADT Security...D...... 440 397-5751
  Strongsville (G-17440)
City of Toledo...E...... 419 936-2875
  Toledo (G-17809)
Metrohealth System.....................................C...... 216 957-2100
  Cleveland (G-6043)
Metrohealth System.....................................E...... 216 957-5000
  Cleveland (G-6037)

POLICE PROTECTION: Local Government

City of Lakewood...C...... 216 529-6170
  Cleveland (G-5267)

POLICE PROTECTION: Sheriffs' Office

County of Montgomery.................................D...... 937 225-4192
  Dayton (G-9431)

POLICE PROTECTION: State Highway Patrol

Greene County...E...... 937 562-7500
  Xenia (G-20054)
Public Safety Ohio Department..................E...... 937 335-6209
  Troy (G-18372)

POLICYHOLDERS' CONSULTING SVCS

Alex N Sill Company....................................E...... 216 524-9999
  Seven Hills (G-16825)

POLITICAL ACTION COMMITTEES

Republican Headquarters............................E...... 330 343-6131
  Dover (G-10209)

POLYETHYLENE CHLOROSULFONATED RUBBER

Lyondell Chemical Company.......................D...... 513 530-4000
  Cincinnati (G-4004)

POLYVINYLIDENE CHLORIDE RESINS

Great Lakes Textiles Inc..............................E...... 440 439-1300
  Solon (G-17012)

POPCORN & SUPPLIES WHOLESALERS

Poppees Popcorn Inc..................................E...... 440 327-0775
  North Ridgeville (G-15474)

POSTERS, WHOLESALE

Scholastic Book Fairs Inc...........................D...... 513 714-1000
  West Chester (G-19146)

POULTRY & POULTRY PRDTS WHOLESALERS

Borden Dairy Co Cincinnati LLC.................C...... 513 948-8811
  Cincinnati (G-3127)
Euclid Fish Company...................................D...... 440 951-6448
  Mentor (G-14172)
Koch Meat Co Inc..B...... 513 874-3500
  Fairfield (G-10871)
Sysco Cincinnati LLC..................................B...... 513 563-6300
  Cincinnati (G-4609)

POULTRY & SMALL GAME SLAUGHTERING & PROCESSING

Cal-Maine Foods Inc...................................E...... 937 337-9576
  Rossburg (G-16604)
Koch Meat Co Inc..B...... 513 874-3500
  Fairfield (G-10871)
Ohio Fresh Eggs LLC..................................E...... 937 354-2233
  Mount Victory (G-14926)
Weaver Bros Inc..D...... 937 526-3907
  Versailles (G-18731)

POWDER: Metal

Bogie Industries Inc Ltd..............................E...... 330 745-3105
  Akron (G-106)

POWER MOWERS WHOLESALERS

Century Equipment Inc................................E...... 419 865-7400
  Toledo (G-17800)
Century Equipment Inc................................E...... 513 285-1800
  Hamilton (G-11707)
Century Equipment Inc................................E...... 216 292-6911
  Cleveland (G-5216)

POWER SUPPLIES: Transformer, Electronic Type

Electric Service Co Inc................................E...... 513 271-6387
  Cincinnati (G-3547)

POWER TOOL REPAIR SVCS

Saw Service and Supply Company.............E...... 216 252-5600
  Cleveland (G-6444)

POWER TRANSMISSION EQPT WHOLESALERS

ABB Inc..C...... 614 818-6300
  Westerville (G-19282)
Applied Indus Tech - CA LLC.....................B...... 216 426-4000
  Cleveland (G-5053)
Bearing & Drive Systems Inc.....................D...... 440 846-9700
  Strongsville (G-17446)
Belting Company of Cincinnati...................C...... 513 621-9050
  Cincinnati (G-3097)
Riverside Drives Inc...................................E...... 216 362-1211
  Cleveland (G-6399)

Stock Fairfield Corporation.........................C...... 440 543-6000
  Chagrin Falls (G-2735)

POWER TRANSMISSION EQPT: Mechanical

City Machine Technologies Inc...................E...... 330 740-8186
  Youngstown (G-20142)
General Electric Company..........................D...... 216 883-1000
  Cleveland (G-5667)
Hite Parts Exchange Inc.............................E...... 614 272-5115
  Columbus (G-7842)
Western Branch Diesel Inc.........................E...... 330 454-8800
  Canton (G-2585)

POWER TRANSMISSION EQPT: Vehicle

Adelmans Truck Parts Corp.......................E...... 330 456-0206
  Canton (G-2225)

PRACTICAL NURSING SCHOOL

Lcd Home Health Agency LLC....................E...... 513 497-0441
  Hamilton (G-11753)

PRECIPITATORS: Electrostatic

McGill Airclean LLC.....................................D...... 614 829-1200
  Columbus (G-8136)
Neundorfer Inc...E...... 440 942-8990
  Willoughby (G-19697)
United McGill Corporation..........................E...... 614 829-1200
  Groveport (G-11681)

PRESCHOOL CENTERS

1 Amazing Place Co....................................E...... 419 420-0424
  Findlay (G-10986)
A & D Daycare and Learning Ctr...............E...... 937 263-4447
  Dayton (G-9296)
A Better Child Care Corp............................E...... 513 353-5437
  Cincinnati (G-2952)
A Childs Place Nursery School..................D...... 330 493-1333
  Canton (G-2221)
A New Beginning Preschool.......................D...... 216 531-7465
  Cleveland (G-4934)
ABC Child Care & Learning Ctr..................E...... 440 964-8799
  Ashtabula (G-710)
Academy Kids Learning Ctr Inc..................E...... 614 258-5437
  Columbus (G-6931)
Adams Cnty /Ohio Vly Schl Dst..................D...... 937 544-2951
  West Union (G-19271)
Ajm Worthington Inc....................................E...... 614 888-5800
  Worthington (G-19938)
All About Kids..E...... 937 885-7480
  Centerville (G-2671)
Allen County Eductl Svc Ctr.......................D...... 419 222-1836
  Lima (G-12734)
Ashland City School District.......................E...... 419 289-7967
  Ashland (G-652)
Assoc Dvlpmtly Disabled............................E...... 614 447-0606
  Columbus (G-7054)
Bailey & Long Inc..E...... 614 937-9435
  Columbus (G-7083)
Balsara Enterprise Ltd................................E...... 330 497-7000
  Solon (G-16982)
Beavercreek Church of Nazarene..............E...... 937 426-0079
  Beavercreek (G-1151)
Bombeck Family Learning Center..............E...... 937 229-2158
  Dayton (G-9362)
Bright Beginnings.......................................E...... 937 748-2612
  Springboro (G-17116)
Brownstone Private Child Care..................E...... 216 221-1470
  Lakewood (G-12472)
Butler County Bd of Mental RE..................E...... 513 785-2815
  Hamilton (G-11700)
Campbell Family Childcare Inc..................E...... 614 855-4780
  New Albany (G-14977)
Canton City School District........................E...... 330 456-3167
  Canton (G-2284)
Cardinal Pacelli School..............................B...... 513 321-1048
  Cincinnati (G-3178)
Cherished Childrens Early.........................E...... 330 424-4402
  Negley (G-14959)
Childrens Discovery Center.......................E...... 419 861-1060
  Holland (G-12015)
Childtime Childcare Inc.............................E...... 330 723-8697
  Medina (G-14046)
Childvine Inc...E...... 937 748-1260
  Springboro (G-17118)
Chippewa School District...........................E...... 330 658-4868
  Doylestown (G-10225)
Christian Rivertree School........................E...... 330 494-1860
  Massillon (G-13795)

SERVICES SECTION — PRINTING TRADES MACHINERY & EQPT REPAIR SVCS

Christian Schools Inc .... D 330 857-7311
  Kidron *(G-12440)*
Christian Wooster School .... E 330 345-6436
  Wooster *(G-19842)*
Cincinnati Early Learning Ctr .... E 513 961-2690
  Cincinnati *(G-3300)*
Cincinnati Early Learning Ctr .... E 513 367-2129
  Harrison *(G-11793)*
Colerain Dry Rdge Chldcare Ltd ..... E 513 923-4300
  Cincinnati *(G-3387)*
Colonial Senior Services Inc .... C 513 867-4006
  Hamilton *(G-11714)*
Colonial Senior Services Inc .... C 513 856-8600
  Hamilton *(G-11713)*
Columbus Public School Dst .... E 614 365-5456
  Columbus *(G-7377)*
Dakota Girls LLC .... E 614 801-2558
  Grove City *(G-11551)*
Delth Corporation .... E 440 255-7655
  Mentor *(G-14169)*
Discovery School .... E 419 756-8880
  Mansfield *(G-13294)*
Dublin Latchkey Inc .... D 614 793-0871
  Dublin *(G-10329)*
Dublin Learning Academy .... E 614 761-1800
  Dublin *(G-10330)*
Early Childhood Enrichment Ctr ..... E 216 991-9761
  Cleveland *(G-5518)*
Early Learning Tree Chld Ctr .... D 937 293-7907
  Dayton *(G-9513)*
East Dayton Christian School .... E 937 252-5400
  Dayton *(G-9268)*
Ernst Corporation .... E 513 697-6970
  Cincinnati *(G-3576)*
Fairborn St Luke Untd Mthdst .... E 937 878-5042
  Fairborn *(G-10795)*
Family Lrng Ctr At Sentinel .... E 419 448-5079
  Tiffin *(G-17678)*
First Christian Church .... E 330 445-2700
  Canton *(G-2367)*
First School Corp .... E 937 433-3455
  Dayton *(G-9550)*
Flying Colors Public Preschool ...... E 740 349-1629
  Newark *(G-15167)*
For Kids Sake Inc .... E 330 726-6878
  Youngstown *(G-20190)*
Goddard School .... E 513 697-9663
  Loveland *(G-13129)*
Goddard School of Avon .... E 440 934-3300
  Avon *(G-894)*
Goddard School of Twinsburg .... E 330 487-0394
  Twinsburg *(G-18424)*
Golden Key Ctr For Excptnl Chl ..... E 330 493-4400
  Canton *(G-2382)*
Hanna Perkins School .... E 216 991-4472
  Shaker Heights *(G-16861)*
Hewlettco Inc .... E 440 238-4600
  Strongsville *(G-17469)*
Horizon Education Centers .... C 440 779-1930
  North Olmsted *(G-15426)*
Hudson Montessori Association ..... E 330 650-0424
  Hudson *(G-12122)*
Hyde Park Play School .... E 513 631-2095
  Cincinnati *(G-3804)*
Ironton and Lawrence County .... B 740 532-3534
  Ironton *(G-12291)*
J Nan Enterprises LLC .... E 330 653-3766
  Hudson *(G-12125)*
J&B Sprafka Enterprises Inc .... E 330 733-4212
  Akron *(G-288)*
Joseph and Florence Mandel .... D 216 464-4055
  Beachwood *(G-1092)*
Kiddle Korral .... E 419 626-9082
  Sandusky *(G-16773)*
Kids First Learning Centers .... D 440 235-2500
  Olmsted Falls *(G-15674)*
Kids Kastle Day Care .... E 419 586-0903
  Celina *(G-2650)*
Kids R Kids 2 Ohio .... E 513 860-3197
  West Chester *(G-19102)*
Kids R Kids Schools Qulty Lrng ..... E 937 748-1260
  Springboro *(G-17126)*
Kids-Play Inc .... E 330 896-2400
  Canton *(G-2426)*
Kidstown LLC .... E 330 502-4484
  Youngstown *(G-20246)*
Kinder Garden School .... E 513 791-4300
  Blue Ash *(G-1622)*
Kindercare Education LLC .... E 614 337-2035
  Gahanna *(G-11250)*

Krieger Enterprises Inc .... E 513 573-9132
  Mason *(G-13729)*
Lakewood Community Care Center E 216 226-0080
  Lakewood *(G-12489)*
Laurel School .... C 216 464-1441
  Cleveland *(G-5928)*
Learning Tree Childcare Ctr .... E 419 229-5484
  Lima *(G-12927)*
Liberty Bible Academy Assn .... E 513 754-1234
  Mason *(G-13731)*
Logan Housing Corp Inc .... D 937 592-2009
  Bellefontaine *(G-1387)*
Louisville Child Care Center .... E 330 875-4303
  Uniontown *(G-18527)*
Madison Local School District .... E 440 428-5111
  Madison *(G-13231)*
Merry Moppets Early Learning .... E 614 529-1730
  Hilliard *(G-11928)*
Miami Valley Family Care Ctr .... E 937 268-0336
  Dayton *(G-9729)*
Miami Valley School .... E 937 434-4444
  Dayton *(G-9738)*
Miami Vly Child Dev Ctrs Inc .... C 937 325-2559
  Springfield *(G-17246)*
Mini University Inc .... C 937 426-1414
  Beavercreek *(G-1254)*
New Hope Christian Academy .... E 740 477-6427
  Circleville *(G-4893)*
Nichalex Inc .... E 330 726-1422
  Youngstown *(G-20300)*
Noahs Ark Child Care Inc .... E 330 325-7236
  Rootstown *(G-16599)*
Noahs Ark Creative Care .... E 740 323-3664
  Newark *(G-15224)*
Noahs Ark Learning Center .... E 740 965-1668
  Sunbury *(G-17559)*
Nobel Learning Center .... E 740 732-4722
  Caldwell *(G-2087)*
North Broadway Childrens Ctr .... E 614 262-6222
  Columbus *(G-8287)*
Northside Baptst Child Dev Ctr ...... E 513 932-5642
  Lebanon *(G-12631)*
Northwest Local School Dst .... D 513 923-1000
  Cincinnati *(G-4182)*
Notre Dame College of Ohio .... E 440 279-1127
  Chardon *(G-2760)*
Old Trail School .... D 330 666-1118
  Bath *(G-1035)*
Open Door Christian School .... D 440 322-6386
  Elyria *(G-10666)*
Ourday At Messiah Preschool .... E 614 882-4416
  Westerville *(G-19435)*
Oxford Blazer Company Inc .... E 614 792-2220
  Dublin *(G-10419)*
P J & R J Connection Inc .... E 513 398-2777
  Mason *(G-13744)*
Paulding Exempted Vlg Schl Dst .... C 419 594-3309
  Paulding *(G-15934)*
Pilgrim United Church Christ .... E 513 574-4208
  Cincinnati *(G-4299)*
Playtime Preschool LLC .... E 614 975-1005
  Columbus *(G-8551)*
Pride -N- Joy Preschool Inc .... E 740 522-3338
  Newark *(G-15229)*
Primrose School At Golf Vlg .... E 740 881-5830
  Powell *(G-16346)*
Primrose School At Polaris .... E 614 899-2588
  Westerville *(G-19345)*
Primrose School of Symmes .... E 513 697-6970
  Cincinnati *(G-4330)*
Ready Set Grow .... E 614 855-5100
  New Albany *(G-15005)*
Rockport United Methodist Ch .... E 440 331-9434
  Cleveland *(G-6407)*
Royal Redeemer Lutheran Church . E 440 237-7958
  Cleveland *(G-6418)*
Saint Cecilia Church .... E 614 878-5353
  Columbus *(G-8677)*
Salem Church of God Inc .... E 937 836-6500
  Clayton *(G-4916)*
Samkel Inc .... E 614 491-3270
  Columbus *(G-8683)*
Smoky Row Childrens Center .... E 614 766-2122
  Powell *(G-16352)*
Southside Learning & Dev Ctr .... E 614 444-1529
  Columbus *(G-8755)*
St Pauls Catholic Church .... E 330 724-1263
  Akron *(G-448)*
T L C Child Development Center ... E 330 655-2797
  Hudson *(G-12146)*

T M C Systems LLC .... E 440 740-1234
  Broadview Heights *(G-1892)*
Tri County Assembly of God .... E 513 874-8575
  Fairfield *(G-10916)*
Twinbrook Hills Baptist Church ...... E 513 863-3107
  Hamilton *(G-11780)*
Upper Arlington Lutheran Ch .... E 614 451-3736
  Columbus *(G-8915)*
Valentour Education Inc .... E 937 434-5949
  Dayton *(G-9960)*
Wee Care Daycare .... E 330 856-1313
  Warren *(G-18926)*
Wee Care Learning Center .... E 937 454-9363
  Dayton *(G-9988)*
Whitehall City Schools .... E 614 417-5680
  Columbus *(G-8988)*
Willoughby Montessori Day Schl ... E 440 942-5602
  Willoughby *(G-19725)*
Zion Christian School .... E 330 792-4066
  Youngstown *(G-20439)*

PRESSED FIBER & MOLDED PULP PRDTS, EXC FOOD PRDTS

Vista Industrial Packaging LLC ...... D 800 454-6117
  Columbus *(G-8945)*

PRINTED CIRCUIT BOARDS

Circle Prime Manufacturing .... E 330 923-0019
  Cuyahoga Falls *(G-9172)*
Interactive Engineering Corp .... E 330 239-6888
  Medina *(G-14082)*
Metzenbaum Sheltered Inds .... C 440 729-1919
  Chesterland *(G-2800)*

PRINTERS' SVCS: Folding, Collating, Etc

Bookmasters Inc .... C 419 281-1802
  Ashland *(G-665)*
Document Concepts Inc .... E 330 575-5685
  North Canton *(G-15333)*
Patented Acquisition Corp .... D 937 353-2299
  Miamisburg *(G-14332)*
Printing Services .... E 440 708-1999
  Chagrin Falls *(G-2729)*

PRINTING & WRITING PAPER WHOLESALERS

Millcraft Group LLC .... D 216 441-5500
  Cleveland *(G-6063)*
OfficeMax Contract Inc .... D 216 898-2400
  Cleveland *(G-6182)*
Veritiv Operating Company .... E 419 243-6100
  Toledo *(G-18289)*

PRINTING MACHINERY

Anderson & Vreeland Inc .... D 419 636-5002
  Bryan *(G-2002)*
Wood Graphics Inc .... E 513 771-6300
  Cincinnati *(G-4858)*

PRINTING MACHINERY, EQPT & SPLYS: Wholesalers

Anderson & Vreeland Inc .... D 419 636-5002
  Bryan *(G-2002)*
Esko-Graphics Inc .... D 937 454-1721
  Miamisburg *(G-14299)*
General Data Company Inc .... C 513 752-7978
  Cincinnati *(G-2916)*
Heidelberg USA Inc .... E 937 492-1281
  Sidney *(G-16938)*
Hirsch International Holdings .... D 513 733-4111
  Cincinnati *(G-3769)*
Monode Marking Products Inc .... E 440 975-8802
  Mentor *(G-14222)*

PRINTING TRADES MACHINERY & EQPT REPAIR SVCS

Hall Contracting Services Inc .... D 440 930-0050
  Avon Lake *(G-932)*
Industrial Maint Svcs Inc .... E 440 729-2068
  Chagrin Falls *(G-2721)*

Employee Codes: A=Over 500 employees, B=251-500
C=101-250, D=51-100, E=25-50

PRINTING, COMMERCIAL: Labels & Seals, NEC — SERVICES SECTION

PRINTING, COMMERCIAL: Labels & Seals, NEC
- Century Marketing Corporation .... C 419 354-2591
  Bowling Green *(G-1772)*

PRINTING, COMMERCIAL: Screen
- Glavin Industries Inc .... E 440 349-0049
  Solon *(G-17009)*
- Innovtive Crtive Solutions LLC .... E 614 491-9638
  Groveport *(G-11647)*
- Kaufman Container Company .... C 216 898-2000
  Cleveland *(G-5887)*

PRINTING, LITHOGRAPHIC: Calendars
- Novelty Advertising Co Inc .... E 740 622-3113
  Coshocton *(G-9113)*

PRINTING, LITHOGRAPHIC: Forms & Cards, Business
- Optimum System Products Inc .... E 614 885-4464
  Westerville *(G-19433)*

PRINTING, LITHOGRAPHIC: Forms, Business
- Quick Tab II Inc .... D 419 448-6622
  Tiffin *(G-17694)*

PRINTING, LITHOGRAPHIC: Offset & photolithographic printing
- Hecks Direct Mail & Prtg Svc .... E 419 661-6028
  Toledo *(G-17951)*
- Kennedy Mint Inc .... D 440 572-3222
  Cleveland *(G-5895)*
- Power Management Inc .... E 937 222-2909
  Dayton *(G-9817)*

PRINTING, LITHOGRAPHIC: On Metal
- Queen City Reprographics .... C 513 326-2300
  Cincinnati *(G-4371)*

PRINTING: Books
- Hubbard Company .... E 419 784-4455
  Defiance *(G-10034)*

PRINTING: Commercial, NEC
- Advanced Specialty Products .... D 419 882-6528
  Bowling Green *(G-1756)*
- Aero Fulfillment Services Corp .... D 800 225-7145
  Mason *(G-13658)*
- AGS Custom Graphics Inc .... D 330 963-7770
  Macedonia *(G-13186)*
- Bindery & Spc Pressworks Inc .... D 614 873-4623
  Plain City *(G-16184)*
- Bollin & Sons Inc .... E 419 693-6573
  Toledo *(G-17776)*
- Consolidated Graphics Group Inc .... C 216 881-9191
  Cleveland *(G-5393)*
- Custom Products Corporation .... D 440 528-7100
  Solon *(G-16999)*
- Dayton Mailing Services Inc .... E 937 222-5056
  Dayton *(G-9480)*
- Evolution Crtive Solutions LLC .... E 513 681-4450
  Cincinnati *(G-3584)*
- Fedex Office & Print Svcs Inc .... E 614 898-0000
  Westerville *(G-19400)*
- Gb Liquidating Company Inc .... E 513 248-7600
  Milford *(G-14520)*
- GBS Corp .... C 330 494-5430
  North Canton *(G-15339)*
- General Data Company Inc .... C 513 752-7978
  Cincinnati *(G-2916)*
- General Theming Contrs LLC .... C 614 252-6342
  Columbus *(G-7736)*
- Haines & Company Inc .... C 330 494-9111
  North Canton *(G-15343)*
- Hecks Direct Mail & Prtg Svc .... E 419 697-3505
  Toledo *(G-17950)*
- Hkm Drect Mkt Cmmnications Inc .... C 216 651-9500
  Cleveland *(G-5762)*
- Profile Digital Printing LLC .... E 937 866-4241
  Dayton *(G-9835)*
- Springdot Inc .... D 513 542-4000
  Cincinnati *(G-4568)*
- Tj Metzgers Inc .... D 419 861-8611
  Toledo *(G-18219)*
- Youngstown ARC Engraving Co .... E 330 793-2471
  Youngstown *(G-20423)*

PRINTING: Flexographic
- Samuels Products Inc .... E 513 891-4456
  Blue Ash *(G-1686)*

PRINTING: Gravure, Color
- Fx Digital Media Inc .... E 216 241-4040
  Cleveland *(G-5643)*

PRINTING: Gravure, Rotogravure
- Shamrock Companies Inc .... C 440 899-9510
  Westlake *(G-19546)*

PRINTING: Laser
- Marketing Comm Resource Inc .... D 440 484-3010
  Willoughby *(G-19691)*

PRINTING: Letterpress
- A-A Blueprint Co Inc .... E 330 794-8803
  Akron *(G-13)*
- Exact Software North Amer LLC .... C 978 539-6186
  Dublin *(G-10341)*
- Traxium LLC .... E 330 572-8200
  Stow *(G-17397)*

PRINTING: Lithographic
- Bookmasters Inc .... C 419 281-1802
  Ashland *(G-665)*
- Century Marketing Corporation .... C 419 354-2591
  Bowling Green *(G-1772)*
- D & S Crtive Cmmunications Inc .... D 419 524-6699
  Mansfield *(G-13288)*
- Digital Color Intl LLC .... E 330 762-6959
  Akron *(G-193)*
- Directconnectgroup Ltd .... A 216 281-2866
  Cleveland *(G-5486)*
- Edwards Electrical & Mech .... E 614 485-2003
  Columbus *(G-7584)*
- Gb Liquidating Company Inc .... E 513 248-7600
  Milford *(G-14520)*
- Gordon Bernard Company LLC .... E 513 248-7600
  Milford *(G-14523)*
- Haines & Company Inc .... C 330 494-9111
  North Canton *(G-15343)*
- Hkm Drect Mkt Cmmnications Inc .... C 216 651-9500
  Cleveland *(G-5762)*
- Mc Sign Company .... C 440 209-6200
  Mentor *(G-14211)*
- McNerney & Associates LLC .... E 513 241-9951
  Cincinnati *(G-4039)*
- Printing Services .... E 440 708-1999
  Chagrin Falls *(G-2729)*
- Profile Digital Printing LLC .... E 937 866-4241
  Dayton *(G-9835)*
- Province of St John The Baptis .... D 513 241-5615
  Cincinnati *(G-4352)*
- Quad/Graphics Inc .... C 614 276-4800
  Columbus *(G-8579)*
- Richardson Printing Corp .... D 740 373-5362
  Marietta *(G-13495)*
- Sandusky Newspapers Inc .... C 419 625-5500
  Sandusky *(G-16792)*
- Sourcelink Ohio LLC .... C 937 885-8000
  Miamisburg *(G-14352)*
- Visual Art Graphic Services .... E 330 274-2775
  Mantua *(G-13397)*
- Woodrow Manufacturing Co .... E 937 399-9333
  Springfield *(G-17300)*
- Youngstown ARC Engraving Co .... E 330 793-2471
  Youngstown *(G-20423)*

PRINTING: Offset
- A-A Blueprint Co Inc .... E 330 794-8803
  Akron *(G-13)*
- Academy Graphic Comm Inc .... E 216 661-2550
  Cleveland *(G-4952)*
- AGS Custom Graphics Inc .... D 330 963-7770
  Macedonia *(G-13186)*
- Angstrom Graphics Inc Midwest .... B 216 271-5300
  Cleveland *(G-5037)*
- Bindery & Spc Pressworks Inc .... D 614 873-4623
  Plain City *(G-16184)*
- Bpm Realty Inc .... E 614 221-6811
  Columbus *(G-7129)*
- Consolidated Graphics Group Inc .... C 216 881-9191
  Cleveland *(G-5393)*
- Copley Ohio Newspapers Inc .... C 330 364-5577
  New Philadelphia *(G-15087)*
- Fine Line Graphics Corp .... C 614 486-0276
  Columbus *(G-7656)*
- Galaxy Balloons Incorporated .... C 216 476-3360
  Cleveland *(G-5651)*
- Hecks Direct Mail & Prtg Svc .... E 419 697-3505
  Toledo *(G-17950)*
- Hubbard Company .... E 419 784-4455
  Defiance *(G-10034)*
- Repro Acquisition Company LLC .... E 216 738-3800
  Cleveland *(G-6378)*
- Springdot Inc .... D 513 542-4000
  Cincinnati *(G-4568)*
- Tj Metzgers Inc .... D 419 861-8611
  Toledo *(G-18219)*
- Traxium LLC .... E 330 572-8200
  Stow *(G-17397)*

PRINTING: Photolithographic
- Friends Service Co Inc .... D 419 427-1704
  Findlay *(G-11033)*

PRINTING: Screen, Fabric
- R & A Sports Inc .... E 216 289-2254
  Euclid *(G-10773)*

PRINTING: Screen, Manmade Fiber & Silk, Broadwoven Fabric
- Evolution Crtive Solutions LLC .... E 513 681-4450
  Cincinnati *(G-3584)*

PRIVATE INVESTIGATOR SVCS
- Belayusa Corporation .... E 614 878-8200
  Columbus *(G-7098)*
- Celebrity Security Inc .... E 216 671-6425
  Cleveland *(G-5202)*
- Cooperate Screening Services .... C 440 816-0500
  Cleveland *(G-5407)*
- Corporate Screening Svcs Inc .... D 440 816-0500
  Cleveland *(G-5410)*
- D B A Inc .... E 513 541-6600
  Cincinnati *(G-3454)*
- Info Trak Incorporated .... E 419 747-9296
  Mansfield *(G-13312)*
- Jefferson Invstgtors Scurities .... D 740 283-3681
  Steubenville *(G-17323)*
- Kreller Bus Info Group Inc .... E 513 723-8900
  Cincinnati *(G-3945)*
- Security Hut Inc .... C 216 226-0461
  Lakewood *(G-12500)*
- Sterling Infosystems Inc .... E 216 685-7600
  Independence *(G-12262)*

PROBATION OFFICE
- 6th Circuit Court .... E 614 719-3100
  Columbus *(G-6915)*
- 6th Circuit Court .... E 614 719-3100
  Dayton *(G-9294)*
- County of Cuyahoga .... A 419 399-8260
  Paulding *(G-15929)*
- County of Erie .... C 419 626-6781
  Sandusky *(G-16748)*
- County of Lorain .... E 440 326-4700
  Elyria *(G-10611)*
- County of Summit .... D 330 643-2300
  Akron *(G-168)*
- County of Tuscarawas .... D 330 339-7791
  New Philadelphia *(G-15091)*
- Supreme Court United States .... E 419 213-5800
  Toledo *(G-18212)*
- Supreme Court United States .... D 614 719-3107
  Columbus *(G-8808)*
- Supreme Court United States .... E 513 564-7575
  Cincinnati *(G-4605)*
- Supreme Court United States .... E 216 357-7300
  Cleveland *(G-6558)*
- Wood County Ohio .... C 419 354-9201
  Bowling Green *(G-1801)*

PRODUCT STERILIZATION SVCS
- Steriltek Inc .... E 615 627-0241
  Painesville *(G-15881)*

SERVICES SECTION
PUBLIC HEALTH PROGRAMS ADMINISTRATION SVCS

PROFESSIONAL DANCE SCHOOLS
Ballet Metropolitan Inc .... C 614 229-4860
Columbus *(G-7088)*

PROFESSIONAL EQPT & SPLYS, WHOLESALE: Analytical Instruments
Pts Prfssnal Technical Svc Inc .... D 513 642-0111
West Chester *(G-19134)*
Testamerica Laboratories Inc .... D 937 294-6856
Moraine *(G-14830)*

PROFESSIONAL EQPT & SPLYS, WHOLESALE: Bank
Diebold Incorporated .... C 330 588-3619
Canton *(G-2340)*
Diebold Nixdorf Incorporated .... D 513 870-1400
Hamilton *(G-11722)*
Hamilton Safe Products Co Inc .... E 614 268-5530
Hilliard *(G-11906)*
Panini North America Inc .... E 937 291-2195
Dayton *(G-9800)*

PROFESSIONAL EQPT & SPLYS, WHOLESALE: Engineers', NEC
Franklin Imaging Llc .... E 614 885-6894
Columbus *(G-7697)*
S&V Industries Inc .... E 330 666-1986
Medina *(G-14121)*
US Tsubaki Power Transm LLC .... C 419 626-4560
Sandusky *(G-16807)*

PROFESSIONAL EQPT & SPLYS, WHOLESALE: Optical Goods
Champion Optical Network .... E 216 831-1800
Beachwood *(G-1062)*
Essilor Laboratories Amer Inc .... E 614 274-0840
Columbus *(G-7613)*
Shawnee Optical Inc .... D 440 997-2020
Ashtabula *(G-763)*

PROFESSIONAL EQPT & SPLYS, WHOLESALE: Precision Tools
Monarch Steel Company Inc .... E 216 587-8000
Cleveland *(G-6074)*

PROFESSIONAL SCHOOLS
Cleveland Municipal School Dst .... D 216 459-4200
Cleveland *(G-5334)*

PROFESSIONAL STANDARDS REVIEW BOARDS
Chesapeake Research Review LLC ...... E 410 884-2900
Cincinnati *(G-3240)*
Schulman Assocs Instl Review .... C 513 761-4100
Blue Ash *(G-1687)*
William I Notz .... E 614 292-3154
Columbus *(G-8995)*

PROFILE SHAPES: Unsupported Plastics
Alkon Corporation .... E 614 799-6650
Dublin *(G-10241)*
Bobbart Industries Inc .... E 419 350-5477
Sylvania *(G-17576)*
HP Manufacturing Company Inc .... D 216 361-6500
Cleveland *(G-5788)*

PROGRAM ADMINISTRATION, GOVERNMENT: Social & Human Resources
County of Cuyahoga .... D 216 443-7265
Cleveland *(G-5428)*
Cuyahoga County .... D 216 420-6750
Cleveland *(G-5450)*
Cuyahoga County .... D 216 443-8920
Cleveland *(G-5454)*

PROGRAM ADMINISTRATION, GOVERNMENT: Social & Manpower, State
Ohio Dept of Job & Fmly Svcs .... E 419 334-3891
Fremont *(G-11215)*

Ohio Dept of Job & Fmly Svcs .... E 614 752-9494
Columbus *(G-8334)*
Ohio Rehabilitation Svcs Comm .... E 330 643-3080
Akron *(G-369)*

PROGRAM ADMINISTRATION, GOVT: Social & Manpower, County
County of Cuyahoga .... E 216 443-5100
Cleveland *(G-5422)*
County of Cuyahoga .... D 216 681-4433
Cleveland *(G-5425)*
Cuyahoga County .... A 216 431-4500
Cleveland *(G-5452)*

PROMOTION SVCS
Fast Traxx Promotions LLC .... E 740 767-3740
Millfield *(G-14632)*
Marsh Inc .... E 513 421-1234
Cincinnati *(G-4026)*
Midway Mall Merchants Assoc .... E 440 244-1245
Elyria *(G-10653)*
Quotient Technology Inc .... E 513 229-8659
Mason *(G-13752)*

PROOFREADING SVCS
Robert Erney .... E 312 788-9005
Brookpark *(G-1954)*

PROPERTY & CASUALTY INSURANCE AGENTS
Cincinnati Financial Corp .... A 513 870-2000
Fairfield *(G-10833)*
McGowan & Company Inc .... D 800 545-1538
Cleveland *(G-6003)*
National Interstate Corp .... D 330 659-8900
Richfield *(G-16515)*
Ohio Farmers Insurance Company ..... A 800 243-0210
Westfield Center *(G-19452)*
Ohio Farmers Insurance Company ..... C 330 484-5660
Canton *(G-2479)*
Ohio Farmers Insurance Company ..... D 614 848-6174
Columbus *(G-6898)*
Schiff John J & Thomas R & Co .... E 513 870-2580
Fairfield *(G-10903)*
Westfield Services Inc .... E 614 796-7700
Columbus *(G-6911)*

PROPERTY DAMAGE INSURANCE
Carrara Companies Inc .... D 330 659-2800
Richfield *(G-16499)*
Century Surety Company .... E 614 895-2000
Westerville *(G-19293)*
Factory Mutual Insurance Co .... C 440 779-0651
North Olmsted *(G-15421)*
Ohio Fair Plan Undwrt Assn .... E 614 839-6446
Columbus *(G-8344)*
Personal Service Insurance Co .... B 800 282-9416
Columbus *(G-8538)*
Platinum Restoration Contrs .... E 440 327-0699
Elyria *(G-10670)*

PUBLIC FINANCE, TAX/MONETARY POLICY OFFICES, GOVT: Taxation
Gilmore Jasion Mahler Ltd .... E 419 794-2000
Maumee *(G-13921)*

PUBLIC FINANCE, TAXATION & MONETARY POLICY OFFICES
City of Cleveland .... E 216 664-2620
Cleveland *(G-5255)*
Ohio Department of Commerce .... E 614 644-7381
Columbus *(G-8325)*

PUBLIC HEALTH PROGRAM ADMIN, GOVT: Health Statistics Ctr
County of Cuyahoga .... C 216 443-8011
Cleveland *(G-5421)*
County of Cuyahoga .... A 216 443-6954
Cleveland *(G-5423)*

PUBLIC HEALTH PROGRAM ADMIN, GOVT: Mental Health Agency
County of Carroll .... E 330 627-7651
Carrollton *(G-2616)*
County of Cuyahoga .... C 216 241-8230
Cleveland *(G-5424)*
County of Hamilton .... B 513 742-1576
Cincinnati *(G-3428)*
County of Hamilton .... B 513 598-2965
Cincinnati *(G-3431)*
County of Paulding .... E 419 399-3636
Paulding *(G-15930)*
County of Stark .... D 330 484-4814
Canton *(G-2322)*
Mental Health and Addi Serv .... C 419 381-1881
Toledo *(G-18051)*
Mental Health and Addi Serv .... B 513 948-3600
Cincinnati *(G-4055)*
Mental Health and Addi Serv .... D 614 752-0333
Columbus *(G-8147)*
Mental Health and Addi Serv .... B 330 467-7131
Northfield *(G-15520)*

PUBLIC HEALTH PROGRAM ADMINISTRATION, GOVERNMENT: County
Clermont County Gen Hlth Dst .... E 513 732-7499
Batavia *(G-1001)*
County of Clark .... D 937 390-5615
Springfield *(G-17180)*
County of Cuyahoga .... D 216 721-5610
Cleveland *(G-5420)*
County of Holmes .... E 330 674-5035
Millersburg *(G-14597)*
County of Knox .... E 740 392-2200
Mount Vernon *(G-14888)*
County of Summit .... A 330 634-8193
Tallmadge *(G-17636)*
County of Union .... D 937 645-6733
Marysville *(G-13613)*
County of Williams .... E 419 485-3141
Montpelier *(G-14742)*
Wood County Ohio .... D 419 353-6914
Bowling Green *(G-1803)*

PUBLIC HEALTH PROGRAM ADMINISTRATION, GOVERNMENT: Local
City of Columbus .... D 614 645-7417
Columbus *(G-7282)*

PUBLIC HEALTH PROGRAM ADMINISTRATION, GOVERNMENT: State
Mental Health and Addi Serv .... E 740 594-5000
Athens *(G-801)*

PUBLIC HEALTH PROGRAM ADMINISTRATION, GOVT: Cancer Detection
Kindred Healthcare Inc .... A 937 433-2400
Dayton *(G-9661)*

PUBLIC HEALTH PROGRAM ADMINISTRATION, GOVT: Child Health
Champaign Cnty Board of Dd .... C 937 653-5217
Urbana *(G-18576)*
County of Cuyahoga .... A 216 432-2621
Cleveland *(G-5427)*

PUBLIC HEALTH PROGRAMS ADMINISTRATION SVCS
Alcohol Drug Addiction .... D 330 564-4075
Akron *(G-65)*
Angmar Medical Holdings Inc .... D 330 835-9663
Fairlawn *(G-10937)*
Buckeye Home Health Care .... C 513 791-6446
Blue Ash *(G-1550)*
City of Columbus .... E 614 645-1600
Columbus *(G-7280)*
City of Columbus .... D 614 645-3072
Columbus *(G-7281)*
County of Hamilton .... E 513 821-6946
Cincinnati *(G-3433)*
Develpmntal Dsblties Ohio Dept .... A 740 446-1642
Gallipolis *(G-11314)*

Employee Codes: A=Over 500 employees, B=251-500
C=101-250, D=51-100, E=25-50

PUBLIC HEALTH PROGRAMS ADMINISTRATION SVCS

Develpmntal Dsblties Ohio Dept ....B....... 419 385-0231
  Toledo (G-17851)
Develpmntal Dsblties Ohio Dept ....C....... 330 544-2231
  Columbus (G-7512)
Develpmntal Dsblties Ohio Dept ....B....... 614 272-0509
  Columbus (G-7513)
Develpmntal Dsblties Ohio Dept ....C....... 937 233-8108
  Columbus (G-7514)
Develpmntal Dsblties Ohio Dept ....C....... 513 732-9200
  Batavia (G-1010)
Fulton County Health Dept ....E....... 419 337-6979
  Wauseon (G-18956)
Mental Health and Addi Serv ....C....... 614 752-0333
  Columbus (G-8148)
Noor Home Health Care ....D....... 216 320-0803
  Cleveland Heights (G-6794)
Ohio Department of Health ....D....... 937 285-6250
  Dayton (G-9784)
Ohio Department of Health ....B....... 419 447-1450
  Tiffin (G-17690)
Ohio Department of Health ....C....... 614 466-1521
  Columbus (G-8328)
Ohio Department of Health ....A....... 614 438-1255
  Columbus (G-8329)
Opportunities For Ohioans ....E....... 513 852-3260
  Cincinnati (G-4229)
Royal Health Services LLC ....E....... 614 826-1316
  Columbus (G-8654)

PUBLIC LIBRARY

Worthington Public Library ....C....... 614 807-2626
  Worthington (G-20010)

PUBLIC ORDER & SAFETY ACTIVITIES, NEC

ADT Security ....D....... 440 397-5751
  Strongsville (G-17440)

PUBLIC ORDER & SAFETY OFFICES, GOVERNMENT: County

County of Cuyahoga ....D....... 216 475-7066
  Cleveland (G-5419)

PUBLIC ORDER & SAFETY OFFICES, GOVT: Emergency Mgmt Office

City of Cleveland ....B....... 216 664-2555
  Cleveland (G-5249)

PUBLIC RELATIONS & PUBLICITY SVCS

Dix & Eaton Incorporated ....E....... 216 241-0405
  Cleveland (G-5493)
Domestic Relations ....E....... 937 225-4063
  Dayton (G-9504)
Edward Howard & Co ....E....... 216 781-2400
  Cleveland (G-5528)
Fahlgren Inc ....D....... 614 383-1500
  Columbus (G-7629)
Paul Werth Associates Inc ....E....... 614 224-8114
  Columbus (G-8524)
Roman/Peshoff Inc ....E....... 419 241-2221
  Holland (G-12051)
SBC Advertising Ltd ....C....... 614 891-7070
  Columbus (G-8692)
United States Trotting Assn ....D....... 614 224-2291
  Columbus (G-8901)
Ver-A-Fast Corp ....E....... 440 331-0250
  Rocky River (G-16594)

PUBLIC RELATIONS SVCS

Babbage-Simmel & Assoc Inc ....E....... 614 481-6555
  Columbus (G-7082)
City of Cleveland Heights ....E....... 216 291-2323
  Cleveland Heights (G-6787)
Code One Communications Inc ....E....... 614 338-0321
  Columbus (G-7313)
County of Guernsey ....D....... 800 307-8422
  Cambridge (G-2107)
County of Logan ....E....... 937 599-7252
  Bellefontaine (G-1380)
Forwith Logistics LLC ....E....... 513 386-8310
  Milford (G-14518)
L Brands Service Company LLC ....D....... 614 415-7000
  Columbus (G-8020)
Marcus Thomas Llc ....D....... 330 793-3000
  Youngstown (G-20272)
Ohio State University ....E....... 614 293-3737
  Columbus (G-8424)

Whitespace Design Group Inc ....E....... 330 762-9320
  Akron (G-510)

PUBLIC WELFARE CENTER

Belmont County of Ohio ....E....... 740 695-3813
  Saint Clairsville (G-16623)
County of Brown ....E....... 937 378-6104
  Georgetown (G-11391)
County of Clark ....C....... 937 327-1700
  Springfield (G-17179)
County of Geauga ....D....... 440 285-9141
  Chardon (G-2747)
County of Huron ....D....... 419 668-8126
  Norwalk (G-15568)
County of Marion ....E....... 740 387-6688
  Marion (G-13532)
Dayton Urban League ....E....... 937 226-1513
  Dayton (G-9493)
Greene County ....C....... 937 562-6000
  Xenia (G-20055)
Stark Cnty Dept Job Fmly Svcs ....B....... 330 451-8400
  Canton (G-2540)
Vantage Aging ....A....... 440 324-3588
  Elyria (G-10686)

PUBLISHERS: Book

Bookmasters Inc ....C....... 419 281-1802
  Ashland (G-665)
Hubbard Company ....E....... 419 784-4455
  Defiance (G-10034)
Precision Metalforming Assn ....E....... 216 241-1482
  Independence (G-12245)
Province of St John The Baptis ....D....... 513 241-5615
  Cincinnati (G-4352)
Zaner-Bloser Inc ....E....... 614 486-0221
  Columbus (G-9025)

PUBLISHERS: Books, No Printing

Asm International ....D....... 440 338-5151
  Novelty (G-15601)
Bendon Inc ....D....... 419 207-3600
  Ashland (G-664)
CSS Publishing Co Inc ....E....... 419 227-1818
  Lima (G-12768)
F+w Media Inc ....B....... 513 531-2690
  Blue Ash (G-1591)
Golf Galaxy Golfworks Inc ....C....... 740 328-4193
  Newark (G-15170)
Relx Inc ....E....... 937 865-6800
  Miamisburg (G-14340)
Wolters Kluwer Clinical Drug ....D....... 330 650-6506
  Hudson (G-12154)

PUBLISHERS: Magazines, No Printing

Amos Media Company ....B....... 937 498-2111
  Sidney (G-16912)
CFM Religion Pubg Group LLC ....E....... 513 931-4050
  Cincinnati (G-3221)
F+w Media Inc ....B....... 513 531-2690
  Blue Ash (G-1591)
Great Lakes Publishing Company ....E....... 216 771-2833
  Cleveland (G-5691)
Province of St John The Baptis ....D....... 513 241-5615
  Cincinnati (G-4352)

PUBLISHERS: Miscellaneous

Amos Media Company ....B....... 937 498-2111
  Sidney (G-16912)
AT&T Corp ....A....... 614 223-8236
  Columbus (G-7062)
Gb Liquidating Company Inc ....E....... 513 248-7600
  Milford (G-14520)
Gordon Bernard Company LLC ....E....... 513 248-7600
  Milford (G-14523)
L M Berry and Company ....A....... 937 296-2121
  Moraine (G-14797)
Lexisnexis Group ....C....... 937 865-6800
  Miamisburg (G-14314)
Province of St John The Baptis ....D....... 513 241-5615
  Cincinnati (G-4352)

PUBLISHERS: Music, Sheet

Lorenz Corporation ....D....... 937 228-6118
  Dayton (G-9687)

PUBLISHERS: Newspaper

B G News ....E....... 419 372-2601
  Bowling Green (G-1759)
Franklin Communications Inc ....D....... 614 459-9769
  Columbus (G-7692)
Iheartcommunications Inc ....E....... 419 223-2060
  Lima (G-12803)
Northeast Scene Inc ....E....... 216 241-7550
  Cleveland (G-6157)
Ohio News Network ....D....... 614 460-3700
  Columbus (G-8362)
Sandusky Newspapers Inc ....C....... 419 625-5500
  Sandusky (G-16792)

PUBLISHERS: Newspapers, No Printing

American City Bus Journals Inc ....E....... 937 528-4400
  Dayton (G-9328)
Brothers Publishing Co LLC ....E....... 937 548-3330
  Greenville (G-11491)
Crain Communications Inc ....D....... 330 836-9180
  Akron (G-175)

PUBLISHERS: Periodical, With Printing

American Ceramic Society ....E....... 614 890-4700
  Westerville (G-19284)

PUBLISHERS: Periodicals, Magazines

AGS Custom Graphics Inc ....D....... 330 963-7770
  Macedonia (G-13186)
Crain Communications Inc ....D....... 330 836-9180
  Akron (G-175)

PUBLISHERS: Periodicals, No Printing

Agri Communicators Inc ....E....... 614 273-0465
  Columbus (G-6957)
Asm International ....D....... 440 338-5151
  Novelty (G-15601)
C & S Associates Inc ....E....... 440 461-9661
  Highland Heights (G-11868)
Columbus Bride ....D....... 614 888-4567
  Columbus (G-7334)
Graphic Publications Inc ....E....... 330 674-2300
  Millersburg (G-14603)
Lorenz Corporation ....D....... 937 228-6118
  Dayton (G-9687)
Northeast Scene Inc ....E....... 216 241-7550
  Cleveland (G-6157)

PUBLISHERS: Technical Manuals

ONeil & Associates Inc ....C....... 937 865-0800
  Miamisburg (G-14330)

PUBLISHERS: Telephone & Other Directory

B G News ....E....... 419 372-2601
  Bowling Green (G-1759)

PUBLISHERS: Trade journals, No Printing

Relx Inc ....E....... 937 865-6800
  Miamisburg (G-14340)

PUBLISHING & BROADCASTING: Internet Only

Deemsys Inc ....D....... 614 322-9928
  Gahanna (G-11239)

PUBLISHING & PRINTING: Books

McGraw-Hill School Education H ....B....... 419 207-7400
  Ashland (G-687)
World Harvest Church Inc ....B....... 614 837-1990
  Canal Winchester (G-2180)

PUBLISHING & PRINTING: Directories, NEC

Haines & Company Inc ....C....... 330 494-9111
  North Canton (G-15343)

PUBLISHING & PRINTING: Magazines: publishing & printing

Family Motor Coach Assn Inc ....E....... 513 474-3622
  Cincinnati (G-3590)

SERVICES SECTION

PUBLISHING & PRINTING: Newsletters, Business Svc
Quality Solutions Inc .... E 440 933-9946
  Cleveland (G-6335)

PUBLISHING & PRINTING: Newspapers
Amos Media Company .... B 937 498-2111
  Sidney (G-16912)

PUBLISHING & PRINTING: Trade Journals
Ohio Association Realtors Inc .... E 614 228-6675
  Columbus (G-8319)

PULP MILLS
Rumpke Transportation Co LLC .... C 513 242-4600
  Cincinnati (G-4454)
Waste Parchment Inc .... E 330 674-6868
  Millersburg (G-14627)

PUMPS
Eaton-Aeroquip Llc .... D 419 891-7775
  Maumee (G-13907)
General Electric Company .... D 216 883-1000
  Cleveland (G-5667)
Giant Industries Inc .... E 419 531-4600
  Toledo (G-17915)
Ingersoll-Rand Company .... E 419 633-6800
  Bryan (G-2008)
Tolco Corporation .... D 419 241-1113
  Toledo (G-18225)

PUMPS & PARTS: Indl
Cima Inc .... E 513 682-5900
  Fairfield (G-10831)

PUMPS & PUMPING EQPT REPAIR SVCS
Compak Inc .... E 419 207-8888
  Ashland (G-675)

PUMPS & PUMPING EQPT WHOLESALERS
Buckeye Supply Company .... E 740 452-3641
  Zanesville (G-20451)
Corrosion Fluid Products Corp .... E 248 478-0100
  Columbus (G-7445)
Estabrook Corporation .... E 440 234-8566
  Berea (G-1457)
Fischer Pump & Valve Company .... E 513 583-4800
  Loveland (G-13125)
Giant Industries Inc .... E 419 531-4600
  Toledo (G-17915)
Graco Ohio Inc .... D 330 494-1313
  Canton (G-2385)
Henry P Thompson Company .... E 513 248-3200
  Milford (G-14524)
Ohio Transmission Corporation .... E 419 468-7866
  Galion (G-11304)
Process Pump & Seal Inc .... E 513 988-7000
  Trenton (G-18343)

PUMPS: Domestic, Water Or Sump
Wayne/Scott Fetzer Company .... C 800 237-0987
  Harrison (G-11812)

PUMPS: Measuring & Dispensing
Tolco Corporation .... D 419 241-1113
  Toledo (G-18225)

PUMPS: Oil Well & Field
General Electric Intl Inc .... E 330 963-2066
  Twinsburg (G-18422)

PURCHASING SVCS
City of Cleveland .... E 216 664-2620
  Cleveland (G-5255)
Neighborcare Inc .... A 513 719-2600
  Cincinnati (G-4151)

RACE TRACK OPERATION
Raceway Foods Inc .... E 513 932-2457
  Lebanon (G-12639)
Stonehedge Enterprises Inc .... E 330 928-2161
  Akron (G-451)

RACETRACKS: Auto
Columbus Motor Speedway Inc .... D 614 491-1047
  Grove City (G-11547)
Eldora Enterprises Inc .... E 937 338-3815
  New Weston (G-15140)
Fast Traxx Promotions LLC .... E 740 767-3740
  Millfield (G-14632)
Kil Kare Inc .... D 937 429-2961
  Xenia (G-20065)
Portsmouth Raceway Park Inc .... E 740 354-3278
  Portsmouth (G-16301)

RACETRACKS: Horse
Park Raceway Inc .... C 419 476-7751
  Dayton (G-9802)
Pnk (ohio) LLC .... A 513 232-8000
  Cincinnati (G-4312)
River Downs Turf Club Inc .... E 513 232-8000
  Cincinnati (G-4423)
Scioto Downs Inc .... A 614 295-4700
  Columbus (G-8706)
Thistledown Inc .... C 216 662-8600
  Cleveland (G-6595)

RACKS: Display
Bates Metal Products Inc .... D 740 498-8371
  Port Washington (G-16260)

RADIO & TELEVISION COMMUNICATIONS EQUIPMENT
Gatesair Inc .... E 513 459-3400
  Mason (G-13704)
Jason Wilson .... E 937 604-8209
  Tipp City (G-17720)

RADIO & TELEVISION OR TV ANNOUNCING SVCS
Dispatch Productions Inc .... D 614 460-3700
  Columbus (G-7525)

RADIO & TELEVISION REPAIR
Office World Inc .... E 419 991-4694
  Lima (G-12928)

RADIO BROADCASTING & COMMUNICATIONS EQPT
Circle Prime Manufacturing .... E 330 923-0019
  Cuyahoga Falls (G-9172)

RADIO BROADCASTING STATIONS
Alpha Media LLC .... E 937 294-5858
  Dayton (G-9322)
Bonneville International Corp .... D 513 699-5102
  Cincinnati (G-3126)
Bowling Green State University .... D 419 372-8657
  Bowling Green (G-1767)
CBS Corporation .... C 513 749-1035
  Cincinnati (G-3197)
CBS Radio Inc .... E 216 861-0100
  Cleveland (G-5199)
Cd1025 .... E 614 221-9923
  Columbus (G-7217)
City Casters .... E 937 224-1137
  Dayton (G-9408)
Cumulus Broadcasting LLC .... E 850 243-7676
  Cincinnati (G-3447)
Cumulus Media Inc .... D 419 725-5700
  Toledo (G-17842)
Cumulus Media Inc .... D 513 241-9898
  Cincinnati (G-3448)
Cumulus Media Inc .... D 419 240-1000
  Toledo (G-17843)
Educational and Community Rdo .... E 513 724-3939
  Batavia (G-1011)
Elyria-Lorain Broadcasting Co .... E 440 322-3761
  Elyria (G-10623)
Family Stations Inc .... E 330 783-9986
  Youngstown (G-20187)
Findlay Publishing Company .... E 419 422-4545
  Findlay (G-11028)
Franklin Communications Inc .... E 614 451-2191
  Columbus (G-7691)
Franklin Communications Inc .... E 614 459-9769
  Columbus (G-7692)

RADIO BROADCASTING STATIONS

Gap Radio Broadcasting LLC .... E 440 992-9700
  Ashtabula (G-744)
Hubbard Radio Cincinnati LLC .... D 513 699-5102
  Cincinnati (G-3794)
Iheartcommunications Inc .... E 419 625-1010
  Sandusky (G-16770)
Iheartcommunications Inc .... E 937 224-1137
  Dayton (G-9626)
Iheartcommunications Inc .... D 614 486-6101
  Columbus (G-7882)
Iheartcommunications Inc .... C 937 224-1137
  Dayton (G-9627)
Iheartcommunications Inc .... C 216 520-2600
  Cleveland (G-5803)
Iheartcommunications Inc .... E 419 289-2605
  Ashland (G-683)
Iheartcommunications Inc .... E 330 965-0057
  Youngstown (G-20230)
Iheartcommunications Inc .... C 216 409-9673
  Cleveland (G-5804)
Iheartcommunications Inc .... D 419 782-9336
  Defiance (G-10037)
Iheartcommunications Inc .... E 419 223-2060
  Lima (G-12803)
Ingleside Investments Inc .... E 614 221-1025
  Columbus (G-7898)
Johnny Appleseed Broadcasting .... E 419 529-5900
  Ontario (G-15695)
Kent State University .... E 330 672-3114
  Kent (G-12380)
Maverick Media .... E 419 331-1600
  Lima (G-12838)
Media-Com Inc .... E 330 673-2323
  Kent (G-12386)
North American Broadcasting .... D 614 481-7800
  Columbus (G-8286)
Ohio State University .... C 614 292-4510
  Columbus (G-8406)
Ohio University .... E 740 593-1771
  Athens (G-806)
Pillar of Fire .... E 513 542-1212
  Cincinnati (G-4300)
Public Broadcasting Found NW .... D 419 380-4600
  Toledo (G-18144)
Radio Promotions .... C 513 381-5000
  Cincinnati (G-4383)
Radio Seaway Inc .... E 216 916-6100
  Cleveland (G-6343)
Radiohio Incorporated .... D 614 460-3850
  Columbus (G-8584)
Rubber City Radio Group .... D 330 869-9800
  Akron (G-420)
Saga Communications Neng Inc .... D 614 451-2191
  Columbus (G-8675)
Salem Media Group Inc .... D 216 901-0921
  Cleveland (G-6437)
Sandusky Newspapers Inc .... C 419 625-5500
  Sandusky (G-16792)
Sunrise Television Corp .... E 419 244-2197
  Toledo (G-18209)
Urban One Inc .... D 216 579-1111
  Cleveland (G-6673)
Urban One Inc .... E 513 749-1009
  Cincinnati (G-4788)
Urban One Inc .... E 614 487-1444
  Columbus (G-8918)
Urban One Inc .... D 216 861-0100
  Cleveland (G-6674)
Urban One Inc .... E 513 679-6000
  Cincinnati (G-4789)
W H O T Inc .... D 330 783-1000
  Youngstown (G-20408)
W K H R Radio .... E 440 708-0915
  Bainbridge (G-943)
W M V O 1300 AM .... E 740 397-1000
  Mount Vernon (G-14924)
Weol .... E 440 236-9283
  Elyria (G-10688)
Wqio 93q Request .... E 740 392-9370
  Mount Vernon (G-14926)
Wqmx Love Fund .... D 330 869-9800
  Akron (G-512)
Wrwk 1065 .... E 419 725-5700
  Toledo (G-18315)
Wzrx .... E 419 223-2060
  Lima (G-12924)
Xavier University .... E 513 745-3335
  Cincinnati (G-4863)

Employee Codes: A=Over 500 employees, B=251-500
C=101-250, D=51-100, E=25-50

2018 Harris Ohio Services Directory

RADIO COMMUNICATIONS: Airborne Eqpt

RADIO COMMUNICATIONS: Airborne Eqpt
Quasonix Inc .... E 513 942-1287
  West Chester (G-19135)

RADIO COMMUNICATIONS: Carrier Eqpt
L-3 Cmmncations Nova Engrg Inc .... C 877 282-1168
  Mason (G-13730)

RADIO REPAIR & INSTALLATION SVCS
Comproducts Inc .... E 614 276-5552
  Columbus (G-7416)

RADIO REPAIR SHOP, NEC
P & R Communications Svc Inc .... E 937 222-0861
  Dayton (G-9796)
Staley Technologies Inc .... E 330 339-2898
  New Philadelphia (G-15115)

RADIO, TELEVISION & CONSUMER ELECTRONICS STORES: Eqpt, NEC
Audio-Technica US Inc .... D 330 686-2600
  Stow (G-17353)

RADIO, TV & CONSUMER ELEC STORES: Automotive Sound Eqpt
C A E C Inc .... E 614 337-1091
  Columbus (G-7173)
Electra Sound Inc .... D 216 433-9600
  Parma (G-15906)
Hi-Way Distributing Corp Amer .... D 330 645-6633
  Coventry Township (G-9125)
Jim Hayden Inc .... D 513 563-8828
  Cincinnati (G-3873)

RADIO, TV & CONSUMER ELEC STORES: High Fidelity Stereo Eqpt
ABC Appliance Inc .... E 419 693-4414
  Oregon (G-15722)

RADIO, TV/CONSUMER ELEC STORES: Antennas, Satellite Dish
Dss Installations Ltd .... E 513 761-7000
  Cincinnati (G-3505)

RADIOS WHOLESALERS
W W W M .... E 419 240-1055
  Toledo (G-18296)

RAILROAD CAR CUSTOMIZING SVCS
Consolidated Rail Corporation .... D 440 786-3014
  Macedonia (G-13194)
Transco Railway Products Inc .... E 419 726-3383
  Toledo (G-18259)

RAILROAD CAR RENTING & LEASING SVCS
Andersons Inc .... C 419 893-5050
  Maumee (G-13879)
Djj Holding Corporation .... C 513 621-8770
  Cincinnati (G-3496)

RAILROAD CAR REPAIR SVCS
Andersons Inc .... C 419 893-5050
  Maumee (G-13879)
Jk-Co LLC .... E 419 422-5240
  Findlay (G-11051)
R W Godbey Railroad Services .... E 513 651-3800
  Cincinnati (G-4380)

RAILROAD CARGO LOADING & UNLOADING SVCS
Ahoy Transport LLC .... E 740 596-0536
  Creola (G-9141)
All American Trnsp Svcs LLC .... E 419 589-7433
  Ontario (G-15684)
Alstom Signaling Operation LLC .... B 513 552-6485
  Cincinnati (G-2996)
American Linehaul Corporation .... E 614 409-8568
  Columbus (G-7000)
Ashtabula Chemical Corp .... E 440 998-0100
  Ashtabula (G-714)
Coldliner Express Inc .... E 614 570-0836
  Columbus (G-7316)
Great Lakes Cold Logistics .... E 216 520-0930
  Independence (G-12215)
Hoc Transport Company .... E 330 630-0100
  Akron (G-267)
Hometech Healthcare Svcs LLC .... E 216 295-9120
  Cleveland (G-5769)
Kettering City School District .... D 937 499-1770
  Dayton (G-9653)
Meda-Care Transportation Inc .... E 513 521-4799
  Cincinnati (G-4041)
Midwest Trmnals Tledo Intl Inc .... E 419 698-8171
  Toledo (G-18064)
Movers and Shuckers LLC .... E 740 263-2164
  Mount Vernon (G-14915)
Multi Flow Transport Inc .... E 216 641-0200
  Brooklyn Heights (G-1920)
Nye F A & Sons Enterprises .... E 419 986-5400
  Tiffin (G-17689)
Ohio State University .... E 614 292-6122
  Columbus (G-8426)
Parsec Inc .... E 513 621-6111
  Cincinnati (G-4256)
Universal Transportation Syste .... E 513 539-9491
  Monroe (G-14716)
Water Transport LLC .... E 740 937-2199
  Hopedale (G-12080)
Wmk Inc .... E 630 782-1900
  Richfield (G-16533)
World Trck Towing Recovery Inc .... E 330 723-1116
  Seville (G-16848)

RAILROAD EQPT
Amsted Industries Incorporated .... C 614 836-2323
  Groveport (G-11622)
Buck Equipment Inc .... E 614 539-3039
  Grove City (G-11540)
Johnson Bros Rubber Co Inc .... E 419 752-4814
  Greenwich (G-11526)
L B Foster Company .... E 330 652-1461
  Mineral Ridge (G-14637)

RAILROAD EQPT & SPLYS WHOLESALERS
A & K Railroad Materials Inc .... E 419 537-9470
  Toledo (G-17733)
Amsted Industries Incorporated .... C 614 836-2323
  Groveport (G-11622)
Buck Equipment Inc .... E 614 539-3039
  Grove City (G-11540)
Djj Holding Corporation .... C 513 621-8770
  Cincinnati (G-3496)
Ysd Industries Inc .... D 330 792-6521
  Youngstown (G-20437)

RAILROAD EQPT: Cars, Rebuilt
Jk-Co LLC .... E 419 422-5240
  Findlay (G-11051)

RAILROAD FREIGHT AGENCY
Norfolk Southern Corporation .... D 740 535-4102
  Mingo Junction (G-14656)

RAILROAD MAINTENANCE & REPAIR SVCS
Andersons Inc .... E 419 891-6634
  Maumee (G-13878)
Tmt Inc .... C 419 592-1041
  Perrysburg (G-16064)

RAILROAD SWITCHING & TERMINAL SVCS
Ashland Railway Inc .... E 419 525-2822
  Mansfield (G-13262)
National Railroad Pass Corp .... E 419 246-0159
  Toledo (G-18078)
Norfolk Southern Corporation .... D 740 535-4102
  Mingo Junction (G-14656)

RAILROADS: Long Haul
Ann Arbor Railroad Inc .... E 419 726-4181
  Toledo (G-17752)
Ashland Railway Inc .... E 419 525-2822
  Mansfield (G-13262)
Cleveland Harbor Belt RR LLC .... E 440 746-0801
  Solon (G-16993)
Cleveland Works Railway Co .... D 216 429-7267
  Cleveland (G-5355)
Cliffs Resources Inc .... C 216 694-5700
  Cleveland (G-5362)
Columbus & Ohio River RR Co .... D 740 622-8092
  Coshocton (G-9092)
CSX Corporation .... C 419 225-4121
  Lima (G-12769)
CSX Transportation Inc .... C 419 933-5027
  Willard (G-19618)
CSX Transportation Inc .... E 440 992-0871
  Ashtabula (G-740)
CSX Transportation Inc .... E 513 369-5514
  Cincinnati (G-3444)
CSX Transportation Inc .... E 937 642-2221
  Marysville (G-13615)
CSX Transportation Inc .... E 419 257-1225
  North Baltimore (G-15312)
CSX Transportation Inc .... E 513 422-2031
  Middletown (G-14423)
CSX Transportation Inc .... D 419 697-2323
  Oregon (G-15729)
Illinois & Midland RR Inc .... E 217 670-1242
  Columbus (G-7884)
Indiana & Ohio Central RR .... C 740 385-3127
  Logan (G-12978)
Indiana & Ohio Rail Corp .... E 513 860-1000
  Cincinnati (G-3813)
Indiana & Ohio Rail Corp .... E 419 229-1010
  Lima (G-12804)
Indiana & Ohio Railway Company .... D 513 860-1000
  Cincinnati (G-3814)
Nimishillen & Tuscarawas LLC .... E 330 438-5821
  Canton (G-2473)
Norfolk Southern Corporation .... D 419 436-2408
  Fostoria (G-11136)
Norfolk Southern Corporation .... E 614 251-2684
  Columbus (G-8284)
Norfolk Southern Corporation .... E 419 381-5505
  Toledo (G-18090)
Norfolk Southern Corporation .... D 419 254-1562
  Toledo (G-18091)
Norfolk Southern Corporation .... E 440 992-2274
  Ashtabula (G-757)
Norfolk Southern Corporation .... D 440 992-2215
  Ashtabula (G-758)
Norfolk Southern Corporation .... E 513 271-0972
  Cincinnati (G-4173)
Norfolk Southern Corporation .... E 216 362-6087
  Cleveland (G-6134)
Norfolk Southern Corporation .... E 419 529-4574
  Ontario (G-15706)
Norfolk Southern Corporation .... C 419 483-1423
  Bellevue (G-1414)
Norfolk Southern Corporation .... E 419 485-3510
  Montpelier (G-14747)
Norfolk Southern Corporation .... E 216 362-6087
  Cleveland (G-6135)
Norfolk Southern Corporation .... E 419 626-4323
  Sandusky (G-16781)
Norfolk Southern Corporation .... D 740 353-4529
  Portsmouth (G-16296)
Norfolk Southern Corporation .... E 937 297-5420
  Moraine (G-14813)
Norfolk Southern Corporation .... E 513 977-3246
  Cincinnati (G-4174)
Norfolk Southern Railway Co .... D 440 439-1827
  Bedford (G-1323)
Republic N&T Railroad Inc .... C 330 438-5826
  Canton (G-2508)
Trans-Continental Systems Inc .... E 513 769-4774
  Cincinnati (G-4678)
Wheeling & Lake Erie Rlwy Co .... B 330 767-3401
  Brewster (G-1857)

REAL ESTATE AGENCIES & BROKERS
Allen Est Mangement Ltd .... E 419 526-6505
  Mansfield (G-13259)
Altobelli Realestate .... E 330 652-0200
  Niles (G-15280)
Best Realty Inc .... E 513 932-3948
  Lebanon (G-12591)
Big Hill Realty Corp .... D 937 426-4420
  Beavercreek (G-1229)
C V Perry & Co .... E 614 221-4131
  Columbus (G-7176)
Chartwell Group LLC .... E 216 360-0009
  Cleveland (G-5230)
Classic Real Estate Co .... E 937 393-3416
  Hillsboro (G-11968)
Coldwell Banker .... E 513 321-9944
  Cincinnati (G-3382)

SERVICES SECTION

REAL ESTATE AGENCIES: Residential

Continental Realty Ltd .... E 614 221-6260
   Columbus *(G-7432)*
Cutler Real Estate .... D 330 733-7575
   Ravenna *(G-16383)*
Cutler Real Estate .... D 330 492-7230
   Canton *(G-2332)*
Cutler Real Estate Inc .... E 614 339-4664
   Dublin *(G-10314)*
Ddr Corp .... E 216 755-5547
   Canton *(G-2337)*
Deed Realty Co .... E 330 225-5220
   Brunswick *(G-1974)*
Di Salle Real Estate Co .... E 419 885-4475
   Sylvania *(G-17582)*
Equity Central LLC .... E 614 861-7777
   Gahanna *(G-11240)*
Flex Realty .... E 419 841-6208
   Toledo *(G-17896)*
Garland Group Inc .... E 614 294-4411
   Columbus *(G-7730)*
Hanna Holdings Inc .... E 440 971-5600
   North Royalton *(G-15492)*
Hanna Holdings Inc .... D 330 707-1000
   Poland *(G-16225)*
Her Inc .... E 614 239-7400
   Columbus *(G-7828)*
Her Inc .... C 614 889-7400
   Dublin *(G-10359)*
Howard Hanna Smythe Cramer ..... E 440 237-8888
   North Royalton *(G-15495)*
Howard Hanna Smythe Cramer ..... E 330 345-2244
   Wooster *(G-19872)*
Howard Hanna Smythe Cramer ..... E 440 248-3000
   Solon *(G-17015)*
Howard Hanna Smythe Cramer ..... E 216 831-0210
   Beachwood *(G-1086)*
Howard Hanna Smythe Cramer ..... D 216 447-4477
   Akron *(G-272)*
Howard Hanna Smythe Cramer ..... E 330 468-6833
   Macedonia *(G-13202)*
Howard Hanna Smythe Cramer ..... D 330 725-4137
   Medina *(G-14078)*
Howard Hanna Smythe Cramer ..... E 440 835-2800
   Cleveland *(G-5783)*
Howard Hanna Smythe Cramer ..... E 440 282-8002
   Amherst *(G-597)*
Howard Hanna Smythe Cramer ..... E 330 686-1166
   Stow *(G-17374)*
Howard Hanna Smythe Cramer ..... D 216 831-9310
   Pepper Pike *(G-15956)*
Howard Hanna Smythe Cramer ..... E 330 896-3333
   Uniontown *(G-18524)*
Jacobs Real Estate Services .... E 216 514-9830
   Beachwood *(G-1090)*
Joseph Schmidt Realty Inc .... E 330 225-6688
   Brunswick *(G-1983)*
Kramer & Kramer Inc .... E 937 456-1101
   Eaton *(G-10563)*
Lakeside Realty LLC .... E 330 793-4200
   Youngstown *(G-20252)*
Lee & Associates Inc .... E 614 923-3300
   Dublin *(G-10386)*
Lenz Inc .... E 937 277-9364
   Dayton *(G-9677)*
Lewis Price Realty Co .... E 330 856-1911
   Warren *(G-18875)*
Mendelson Realty Ltd .... E 937 461-3525
   Dayton *(G-9719)*
Mike Sikora Realty Inc .... E 440 255-7777
   Mentor *(G-14218)*
National Realty Services Inc .... E 614 798-0971
   Columbus *(G-8222)*
Noneman Real Estate Company .... E 419 531-4020
   Toledo *(G-18088)*
NOR Corp .... C 440 300-0099
   Elyria *(G-10659)*
Ohio Equities LLC .... D 614 469-0058
   Columbus *(G-8341)*
Phil Giessler .... E 614 888-0307
   Worthington *(G-19984)*
Phillips Edison & Company LLC .... E 513 554-1110
   Cincinnati *(G-4291)*
Randolph and Associates RE .... E 614 269-8418
   Columbus *(G-8588)*
Real Estate Capital Fund LLC .... E 216 491-3990
   Cleveland *(G-6358)*
Real Estate Showcase .... E 740 389-2000
   Marion *(G-13574)*
Real Living Title Agency Ltd .... E 440 974-7810
   Painesville *(G-15877)*
Realty One Inc .... E 330 686-1166
   Stow *(G-17389)*
Realty One Inc .... E 216 221-6585
   Lakewood *(G-12497)*
Realty One Inc .... D 440 526-2900
   Brecksville *(G-1846)*
Realty One Inc .... E 330 896-5225
   Uniontown *(G-18535)*
Realty One Inc .... E 440 365-8392
   Elyria *(G-10674)*
Residential One Realty Inc .... E 614 436-9830
   Columbus *(G-8620)*
Robert F Lindsay Co .... D 419 476-6221
   Toledo *(G-18161)*
Rubber City Realty Inc .... E 330 745-9034
   Akron *(G-421)*
Rybac Inc .... E 614 228-3578
   Columbus *(G-8664)*
Sibcy Cline Inc .... E 937 610-3404
   Dayton *(G-9881)*
Sibcy Cline Inc .... D 513 829-0044
   Fairfield *(G-10909)*
Sibcy Cline Inc .... D 513 777-8100
   West Chester *(G-19152)*
Sibcy Cline Inc .... E 513 793-2700
   Cincinnati *(G-4522)*
Sibcy Cline Inc .... E 513 931-7700
   Cincinnati *(G-4523)*
Star One Holdings Inc .... E 513 300-6663
   Cincinnati *(G-4585)*
Steve Brown .... D 937 436-2700
   Dayton *(G-9907)*
Stouffer Realty Inc .... E 330 835-4900
   Fairlawn *(G-10978)*
Sweda Sweda Associates Inc .... E 419 433-4841
   Avon *(G-917)*
Townhomes Management Inc .... E 614 228-3578
   Columbus *(G-8858)*
TSS Real Estate Ltd .... C 513 772-7000
   Cincinnati *(G-4704)*
U S Associates Realty Inc .... E 216 663-3400
   Cleveland *(G-6625)*
West Shell Gale Schnetzer .... E 513 683-3833
   Loveland *(G-13164)*
Williams Homes LLC .... E 419 472-1005
   Toledo *(G-18310)*
Zaremba LLC .... D 216 221-6600
   Cleveland *(G-6780)*

REAL ESTATE AGENCIES: Buying

Cutler and Associates Inc .... E 330 493-9323
   Canton *(G-2331)*
Mrap LLC .... E 614 545-3190
   Columbus *(G-8202)*
Sawmill Road Management Co LLC ... E ... 937 342-9071
   Springfield *(G-17270)*

REAL ESTATE AGENCIES: Commercial

Adena Commercial LLC .... E 614 436-9800
   Columbus *(G-6868)*
Bellwether Entp RE Capitl LLC ...... E 216 820-4500
   Cleveland *(G-5112)*
Bre Ddr Parker Pavilions LLC .... E 216 755-6451
   Beachwood *(G-1056)*
Carnegie Companies Inc .... E 440 232-2300
   Solon *(G-16987)*
Cassidy Trley Coml RE Svcs Inc .... E 513 771-2580
   Cincinnati *(G-3192)*
Cbre Inc .... D 513 369-1300
   Cincinnati *(G-3196)*
Cbre Inc .... E 216 687-1800
   Cleveland *(G-5198)*
Cbre Inc .... E 614 419-7429
   Blacklick *(G-1503)*
Cbre Inc .... D 614 438-5488
   Columbus *(G-7216)*
Cushman & Wakefield Inc .... E 937 222-7884
   Moraine *(G-14765)*
Eastgate Professional Off Pk V ...... E 513 943-0050
   Cincinnati *(G-2914)*
Ellis Richard CB Reichle Klein .... E 419 861-1100
   Toledo *(G-17864)*
Giammarco Properties LLC .... E 419 885-4844
   Toledo *(G-17914)*
Hadler Realty Company .... E 614 457-6650
   Columbus *(G-7791)*
J S N Holdings .... E 216 447-0070
   Cleveland *(G-5843)*
Knoxbi Company LLC .... E 440 892-6800
   Westlake *(G-19506)*
Marcus Mllchap RE Inv Svcs Inc .... E 614 360-9800
   Columbus *(G-8107)*
Midland Atlantic Prpts LLC .... E 513 792-5000
   Cincinnati *(G-4091)*
Mv Land Development Company .... B 937 293-0900
   Dayton *(G-9764)*
Northpointe Plaza .... D 614 744-2229
   Columbus *(G-8293)*
Signature Associates Inc .... E 419 244-7505
   Toledo *(G-18188)*
West Shell Commercial Inc .... D 513 721-4200
   Cincinnati *(G-4837)*

REAL ESTATE AGENCIES: Leasing & Rentals

Blossom Hill Elderly Housing L ...... D 330 385-4310
   East Liverpool *(G-10516)*
Coffman Family Partnership .... E 614 864-5400
   Columbus *(G-7314)*
Ducru Spe LLC .... E 937 228-2224
   Dayton *(G-9507)*
Inc/Ballew A Head Joint Ventr .... D 614 338-5801
   Columbus *(G-7888)*
Lt Land Development LLC .... E 937 382-0072
   Wilmington *(G-19770)*
Nwd Arena District II LLC .... E 614 857-2330
   Columbus *(G-8308)*
Pfh Partners LLC .... E 513 241-5800
   Cincinnati *(G-4289)*
Triad PII .... E 740 374-2940
   Marietta *(G-13507)*
Triangle Office Park LLC .... E 513 563-7555
   Cincinnati *(G-4686)*

REAL ESTATE AGENCIES: Multiple Listing Svc

Sweeney Team Inc .... E 513 241-3400
   Cincinnati *(G-4606)*

REAL ESTATE AGENCIES: Rental

Brg Realty Group LLC .... C 513 936-5960
   Cincinnati *(G-3130)*
Green Springs Residential Ltd .... C 419 639-2581
   Green Springs *(G-11477)*
Neyer Real Estate MGT LLC .... E 513 618-6000
   Cincinnati *(G-4167)*
Tom Properties LLC .... D 614 781-0055
   Columbus *(G-8853)*
Valley View Place .... C 740 454-7720
   Zanesville *(G-20543)*
Village Communities LLC .... C 614 540-2400
   Westerville *(G-19357)*

REAL ESTATE AGENCIES: Residential

1440 Corporation Inc .... E 513 424-2421
   Middletown *(G-14410)*
AA Green Realty Inc .... E 419 352-5331
   Bowling Green *(G-1755)*
Baur Leo Century 21 Realty .... E 440 585-2300
   Willowick *(G-19737)*
Beyond 2000 Realty Inc .... E 440 842-7200
   Cleveland *(G-5122)*
Big Hill Realty Corp .... C 937 435-1177
   Dayton *(G-9356)*
Big Hill Realty Corp .... E 937 429-2200
   Beavercreek *(G-1230)*
Capital Partners Realty LLC .... E 614 888-1000
   Worthington *(G-19945)*
Carleton Realty Inc .... E 740 653-5200
   Lancaster *(G-12513)*
Century 21 Elite Performance .... E 937 438-8221
   Spring Valloy *(C-17109)*
Century 21 Trammell Odonnell ..... D 440 888-6800
   Cleveland *(G-5214)*
Century 21-Joe Walker & Assoc .... E 614 899-1400
   Columbus *(G-6873)*
Coldwell Banker First Place RE ..... D 330 726-8161
   Poland *(G-16223)*
Coldwell Banker King Thompson ... E 614 759-0808
   Pickerington *(G-16090)*
Coldwell Banker West Shell .... E 513 829-4000
   West Chester *(G-19046)*
Coldwell Banker West Shell .... D 513 922-9400
   Cincinnati *(G-3383)*
Coldwell Banker West Shell .... E 513 385-9300
   Cincinnati *(G-3384)*
Coldwell Banker West Shell .... D 513 777-7900
   West Chester *(G-19047)*

REAL ESTATE AGENCIES: Residential

Company	Location	Col	Phone
Coldwell Banker West Shell	Cincinnati (G-3385)	E	513 271-7200
Coldwell Bnkr Hritg Rltors LLC	Dayton (G-9415)	E	937 304-8500
Coldwell Bnkr Hritg Rltors LLC	Springboro (G-17119)	E	937 748-5500
Coldwell Bnkr Hritg Rltors LLC	Dayton (G-9416)	E	937 434-7600
Coldwell Bnkr Hritg Rltors LLC	Beavercreek Township (G-1266)	E	937 426-6060
Coldwell Bnkr Hritg Rltors LLC	Dayton (G-9417)	E	937 439-4500
Coldwell Bnkr Hritg Rltors LLC	Vandalia (G-18675)	E	937 890-2200
Comey & Shepherd LLC	Cincinnati (G-3391)	E	513 489-2100
Comey & Shepherd LLC	Cincinnati (G-3392)	C	513 561-5800
Comey & Shepherd LLC	Cincinnati (G-3393)	E	513 321-4343
Comey & Shepherd LLC	Cincinnati (G-3394)	E	513 231-2800
Comey & Shepherd LLC	Cincinnati (G-3395)	E	513 891-4444
Cutler Real Estate	Fairlawn (G-10943)	C	330 836-9141
Danberry Co	Maumee (G-13904)	D	419 866-8888
David Campbell	Dayton (G-9451)	E	937 266-7064
Five & Company Realty Inc	Findlay (G-11032)	E	419 423-8004
Geneva Chervenic Realty Inc	Stow (G-17370)	D	330 686-8400
Hanna Holdings Inc	Avon (G-896)	E	440 933-6195
Henkle-Schueler & Associates	Lebanon (G-12611)	E	513 932-6070
Her Inc	Columbus (G-7826)	E	614 240-7400
Her Inc	Columbus (G-7827)	E	614 221-7400
Her Inc	Worthington (G-19963)	D	614 888-7400
Her Inc	Hilliard (G-11907)	E	614 771-7400
Hoeting Inc	Cincinnati (G-3775)	D	513 451-4800
Howard Hanna Smythe Cramer	Cleveland (G-5782)	C	216 447-4477
Howard Hanna Smythe Cramer	Rocky River (G-16581)	E	440 333-6500
Howard Hanna Smythe Cramer	Willoughby (G-19671)	E	440 516-4444
Howard Hanna Smythe Cramer	Beachwood (G-1087)	E	216 751-8550
Hunter Realty Inc	Cleveland (G-5789)	E	216 831-2911
Hunter Realty Inc	Geneva (G-11364)	E	440 466-9177
Irongate Inc	Centerville (G-2680)	C	937 433-3300
J W Enterprises Inc	Chillicothe (G-2856)	D	740 774-4500
Jordan Realtors Inc	Cincinnati (G-3886)	E	513 791-0281
Joseph Walker Inc	Columbus (G-6887)	E	614 895-3840
Karam & Simon Realty Inc	Cuyahoga Falls (G-9201)	E	330 929-0707
Keller Williams Advisors LLC	Cincinnati (G-3907)	E	513 766-9200
Keller Williams Advisory Rlty	Cincinnati (G-3908)	E	513 372-6500
Keller Williams Classic Pro	Columbus (G-7972)	E	614 451-8500
Keller Williams Rlty M Walker	Stow (G-17378)	E	330 571-2020
Key Realty Ltd	Holland (G-12031)	C	419 270-7445
Lucien Realty	Cleveland (G-5958)	D	440 331-8500
Mall Realty Inc	Dayton (G-9696)	E	937 866-3700
Maryann McEowen	Cortland (G-9078)	D	330 638-6351
Mc Mahon Realestate Co	Newark (G-15203)	E	740 344-2250
Miller-Vintine Partners Ltd Lc	Cincinnati (G-4098)	E	513 588-1000
Murwood Real Estate Group LLC	Beachwood (G-1106)	E	216 839-5500
Noakes Rooney Rlty & Assoc Co	Findlay (G-11070)	E	419 423-4861
North Wood Realty	Youngstown (G-20303)	C	330 423-0837
North Wood Realty	Warren (G-18886)	E	330 856-3915
Nrt Commercial Utah LLC	Columbus (G-8301)	D	614 239-0808
Nrt Commercial Utah LLC	Dublin (G-10411)	E	614 889-0808
Platinum RE Professionals LLC	Willoughby (G-19704)	E	440 942-2100
Prudential Calhoon Co Realtors	Hilliard (G-11945)	E	614 777-1000
Prudential Lucien Realty	Lakewood (G-12495)	E	216 226-4673
Prudential Select Properties	Mentor (G-14230)	D	440 255-1111
Prudential Welsh Realty	Mentor (G-14231)	E	440 974-3100
Re/Max	Beavercreek (G-1257)	E	937 477-4997
Re/Max Consultant Group	New Albany (G-15004)	D	614 855-2822
RE/Max Experts Realty	Dover (G-10208)	E	330 364-7355
RE/Max Real Estate Experts	Mentor (G-14233)	E	440 255-6505
Real Estate II Inc	Springfield (G-17263)	E	937 390-3119
Realty One Inc	North Royalton (G-15499)	D	440 888-8600
Remax Homesource	Willoughby (G-19709)	E	440 951-2500
REO Network Inc	Marietta (G-13494)	E	740 374-8900
Roediger Realty Inc	Springfield (G-17266)	E	937 322-0352
Rolls Realty	Powell (G-16348)	E	614 792-5662
Saxton Real Estate Co	Grove City (G-11596)	D	614 875-2327
Sibcy Cline Inc	Cincinnati (G-2931)	E	513 752-4000
Sibcy Cline Inc	Cincinnati (G-4520)	D	513 793-2121
Sibcy Cline Inc	Fairfield (G-10908)	E	513 385-3330
Sibcy Cline Inc	Cincinnati (G-4521)	D	513 984-4100
Sibcy Cline Inc	Mason (G-13761)	D	513 677-1830
Sibcy Cline Inc	Beavercreek (G-1208)	E	937 429-2101
Sibcy Cline Inc	Lebanon (G-12646)	D	513 932-6334
Star One Holdings Inc	Cincinnati (G-4584)	E	513 474-9100
Star One Holdings Inc	West Chester (G-19159)	E	513 779-9500
Sue Smedley	Springfield (G-17282)	E	937 399-5155
Sweeney Team Inc	Lebanon (G-12651)	E	513 934-0700
Tiger 2010 LLC	North Canton (G-15373)	E	330 236-5100
Tom Baier & Assoc Inc	Canton (G-2563)	E	330 497-3115
Ward Realestate Inc	Ashland (G-707)	E	419 281-2000
Welles Bowen Realty Inc	Toledo (G-18300)	D	419 535-0011
Western Reserve Realty LLC	Chagrin Falls (G-2710)	E	440 247-3707
Wilbur Realty Inc	Kent (G-12405)	E	330 673-5883
William Zamarelli Realtors	Warren (G-18927)	E	330 856-2299
Y Town Realty Inc	Youngstown (G-20419)	E	330 743-8844
Yocum Realty Company	Lima (G-12925)	E	419 222-3040

REAL ESTATE AGENCIES: Selling

Company	Location	Col	Phone
Plus Realty Cincinnati Inc	Milford (G-14554)	E	513 575-4500
Realty One Inc	Mentor (G-14234)	C	440 951-2123
Richard H Freyhof	Urbana (G-18599)	E	937 653-5837

REAL ESTATE AGENTS & MANAGERS

Company	Location	Col	Phone
0714 Inc	North Ridgeville (G-15452)	E	440 327-2123
2780 Airport Drive LLC	Cincinnati (G-2944)	E	513 563-7555
36 E Seventh LLC	Cincinnati (G-2945)	E	513 699-2279
Abco Contracting LLC	Toledo (G-17739)	E	419 973-4772
Allen Metro Hsing MGT Dev Corp	Lima (G-12736)	E	419 228-6065
American Title Services Inc	Niles (G-15281)	E	330 652-1609
Amsdell Construction Inc	Cleveland (G-5031)	C	216 458-0670
Arena Management Holdings LLC	Cincinnati (G-3045)	A	513 421-4111
Blue Ash Distribution Ctr LLC	Cincinnati (G-3117)	E	513 699-2279
Brookdale Senior Living Inc	Grove City (G-11539)	D	614 277-1200
Buckeye Cmnty Twenty Six LP	Columbus (G-7159)	E	614 942-2020
Capital Senior Living	Rocky River (G-16572)	E	440 356-5444
Cincinnati Coml Contg LLC	Cincinnati (G-3294)	E	513 561-6633
Cleveland Real Estate Partners	Cleveland (G-5342)	E	216 623-1600
Communicare Health Svcs Inc	Montpelier (G-14740)	D	419 485-8307
Communicare Health Svcs Inc	Youngstown (G-20149)	D	330 792-7799
Communicare Health Svcs Inc	Saint Marys (G-16672)	D	419 394-7611
Communicare Health Svcs Inc	Canton (G-2317)	E	330 454-6508
Communicare Health Svcs Inc	Youngstown (G-20150)	D	330 792-5511
Communicare Health Svcs Inc	Canton (G-2318)	C	330 454-2152
Communicare Health Svcs Inc	Tallmadge (G-17635)	D	330 630-9780
Connor Group A RE Inv Firm LLC	Miamisburg (G-14286)	B	937 434-3095
Crawford Hoying Ltd	Dublin (G-10312)	C	614 335-2020
Croxton Realty Company	Canton (G-2330)	E	330 492-1697
Cushman & Wakefield Inc	Norwood (G-15598)	E	513 631-1121
Cutler and Associates Inc	Akron (G-182)	D	330 896-1680
Cutler and Associates Inc	Stow (G-17359)	E	330 688-2100
Cutler Real Estate	North Canton (G-15331)	D	330 499-9922
Cutler Real Estate	Stow (G-17360)	E	330 688-2100
Cutler Real Estate	Akron (G-183)	E	330 644-0644
Cwb Property Managment Inc	Dublin (G-10315)	E	614 793-2244
Darfus	Logan (G-12971)	E	740 380-1710
Dari Pizza Enterprises II Inc	Maumee (G-13905)	C	419 534-3000
Design Homes & Development Co	Dayton (G-9499)	E	937 438-3667
Duke Realty Corporation	Mason (G-13698)	D	513 651-3900
E A Zicka Co	Cincinnati (G-3523)	E	513 451-1440
Eaton Group GMAC Real Estate	Warren (G-18855)	E	330 726-9999
Echoing Hills Village Inc	Warsaw (G-18936)	A	740 327-2311
Elden Properties Ltd Partnr	Vermilion (G-18709)	E	440 967-0521
Essex Healthcare Corporation	Columbus (G-7612)	E	614 416-0600
Fairfield Homes Inc	Plain City (G-16192)	C	614 873-3533
Fay Limited Partnership	Cincinnati (G-3595)	E	513 241-1911
Fc Continental Landlord LLC	Cleveland (G-5579)	A	216 621-6060

2018 Harris Ohio Services Directory

(G-0000) Company's Geographic Section entry number

REAL ESTATE OPERATORS, EXC DEVELOPERS: Auditorium & Hall

Company	Code	Phone
Fujiyama International Inc	E	614 891-2224
Columbus (G-7713)		
Gideon	D	800 395-6014
Cleveland (G-5671)		
Goldberg Companies Inc	E	440 944-8656
Willoughby Hills (G-19730)		
Greentown Center LLC	D	937 490-4990
Beavercreek (G-1244)		
Greystone Group-Avery Ltd	E	216 464-3580
Cleveland (G-5705)		
Her Inc	E	614 878-4734
Columbus (G-7829)		
Her Inc	D	614 864-7400
Pickerington (G-16095)		
Her Inc	C	614 890-7400
Westerville (G-19313)		
Hmshost Corporation	C	419 547-8667
Clyde (G-6814)		
Home Town Realtors LLC	D	937 890-9111
Dayton (G-9617)		
Homelife Companies Inc	E	740 369-1297
Delaware (G-10106)		
Howard Hanna Smythe Cramer	E	800 656-7356
Canfield (G-2195)		
Howard Hanna Smythe Cramer	E	440 248-3380
Cleveland (G-5784)		
Howard Hanna Smythe Cramer	D	330 562-6188
Aurora (G-841)		
Howard Hanna Smythe Cramer	E	440 428-1818
Madison (G-13225)		
Howard Hanna Smythe Cramer	E	330 493-6555
Canton (G-2406)		
Howard Hanna Smythe Cramer	E	440 526-1800
Cleveland (G-5785)		
Hunt Club LLC	E	419 885-4647
Sylvania (G-17594)		
Integra Cncinnati/Columbus Inc	E	614 764-8040
Dublin (G-10377)		
Investek Realty LLC	E	419 873-1236
Perrysburg (G-16019)		
Irongate Inc	E	937 298-6000
Dayton (G-9637)		
Irongate Inc	D	937 432-3432
Dayton (G-9638)		
Jobar Enterprise Inc	E	216 561-5184
Cleveland (G-5866)		
Jones Lang Lsalle Americas Inc	E	216 447-5276
Brecksville (G-1831)		
Kwik Parking	E	419 246-0454
Toledo (G-17997)		
Linn Street Holdings LLC	E	513 699-8825
Cincinnati (G-3988)		
Longwood Phase One Assoc LP	E	561 998-0700
Cleveland (G-5951)		
Meadowbrook Mall Company	E	330 747-2661
Youngstown (G-20275)		
Midwest Liquidators Inc	E	614 433-7355
Worthington (G-19977)		
Miller-Valentine Partners Ltd	E	513 588-1000
Cincinnati (G-4097)		
Mri Software LLC	C	800 327-8770
Solon (G-17030)		
National Church Residences	C	614 451-2151
Columbus (G-8215)		
Nationwide Mutual Insurance Co	A	614 249-7111
Columbus (G-8247)		
Neighborhood Properties Inc	E	419 473-2604
Toledo (G-18082)		
Newmark & Company RE Inc	E	216 453-3000
Cleveland (G-6127)		
Nisbet Corporation	C	513 563-1111
Cincinnati (G-4170)		
Normandy Office Associates	D	513 381-8696
Cincinnati (G-4175)		
North Star Realty Incorporated	E	513 737-1700
Fairfield (G-10884)		
Oak Brook Gardens	D	440 237-3613
North Royalton (G-15497)		
Oberer Residential Cnstr	C	937 278-0851
Miamisburg (G-14329)		
One Lincoln Park	D	937 298-0594
Dayton (G-9791)		
Owners Management Company	E	440 439-3800
Bedford (G-1328)		
Petros Homes Inc	E	440 546-9000
Cleveland (G-6272)		
Port Lawrence Title and Tr Co	E	419 244-4605
Toledo (G-18130)		
Premier Prpts Centl Ohio Inc	E	614 755-4275
Columbus (G-8556)		
R A Hermes Inc	E	513 251-5200
Cincinnati (G-4377)		
Real Living Inc	D	614 560-9942
Powell (G-16347)		
Realty One Inc	D	440 238-1400
Cleveland (G-6359)		
Realty One Inc	E	440 333-8700
Rocky River (G-16590)		
Realty One Inc	E	330 562-2277
Aurora (G-851)		
Realty One Inc	E	330 262-7200
Wooster (G-19906)		
Realty One Inc	D	440 282-8002
Amherst (G-603)		
Realty One Inc	E	440 835-6500
Bay Village (G-1041)		
Residential Hm Assn of Marion	C	740 387-9999
Marion (G-13575)		
Richland Mall Shopping Ctr	E	419 529-4003
Mansfield (G-13357)		
Ron Neff Real Estate	E	740 773-4670
Chillicothe (G-2876)		
Sami S Rafidi	C	330 799-9508
Youngstown (G-20365)		
Sawyer Realtors	E	513 423-6521
Middletown (G-14456)		
Siena Springs II	E	513 639-2800
Dayton (G-9883)		
Skye Development Company LLC	E	216 223-0160
Cleveland (G-6485)		
Springcar Company LLC	E	440 892-6800
Westlake (G-19549)		
Sterling Heights Gsa Prpts Ltd	E	419 609-7000
Sandusky (G-16801)		
Towne Properties Assoc Inc	E	513 874-3737
Cincinnati (G-4672)		
U S Title Agency Inc	E	216 621-1424
Cleveland (G-6627)		
Ufcw 75 Real Estate Corp	D	937 677-0075
Dayton (G-9943)		
United Management Inc	E	513 936-8568
Cincinnati (G-4735)		
University Circle Incorporated	E	216 791-3900
Cleveland (G-6653)		
Visconsi Companies Ltd	E	216 464-5550
Cleveland (G-6700)		
Washington Square Apartments	E	740 349-8353
Newark (G-15244)		
Zaremba Zanesville LLC	E	216 221-6600
Lakewood (G-12505)		

REAL ESTATE APPRAISERS

Company	Code	Phone
Al-Mar Lanes	E	419 352-4637
Bowling Green (G-1757)		
Appraisal Research Corporation	C	419 423-3582
Findlay (G-10991)		
Baker Bnngson Rlty Auctioneers	E	419 547-7777
Clyde (G-6810)		
Calabresem Racek & Markos Inc	E	216 696-5442
Cleveland (G-5171)		
Manatron Sabre Systems and Svc	D	937 431-4000
Beavercreek (G-1253)		
Martin + WD Apprisal Group Ltd	E	419 241-4998
Toledo (G-18044)		
Mortgage Information Services	D	216 514-7480
Cleveland (G-6078)		
Stickelman Schneider Assoc LLC	E	513 475-6000
Fairborn (G-10804)		

REAL ESTATE AUCTION

Company	Code	Phone
Butler County of Ohio	D	513 887-3154
Hamilton (G-11696)		

REAL ESTATE ESCROW AGENCIES

Company	Code	Phone
Real Living Title Agency Ltd	D	614 459-7400
Columbus (G-8595)		
Resource Title Agency Inc	D	216 520-0050
Cleveland (G-6385)		
Resource Title Nat Agcy Inc	D	216 520-0050
Independence (G-12248)		

REAL ESTATE INVESTMENT TRUSTS

Company	Code	Phone
Ddr Corp	E	614 785-6445
Columbus (G-7497)		
Ddr Corp	C	216 755-5500
Beachwood (G-1071)		
Ddr Tucson Spectrum I LLC	E	216 755-5500
Beachwood (G-1072)		
Forest City Realty Trust Inc	E	216 621-6060
Cleveland (G-5620)		
Investmerica limited	D	216 618-3296
Chagrin Falls (G-2701)		
Morelia Consultants LLC	E	513 469-1500
Cincinnati (G-4116)		
Moskowitz Family Ltd	C	513 729-2300
Cincinnati (G-4122)		
Washington Prime Group LP	A	614 621-9000
Columbus (G-8968)		

REAL ESTATE MANAGERS: Cemetery

Company	Code	Phone
City of Willoughby	B	440 953-4111
Willoughby (G-19651)		

REAL ESTATE MANAGERS: Condominium

Company	Code	Phone
Brookwood Management Company	E	330 497-6565
Canton (G-2271)		
Hidden Lake Condominiums	D	614 488-1131
Columbus (G-7832)		

REAL ESTATE MANAGERS: Cooperative Apartment

Company	Code	Phone
Erhal Inc	E	513 272-5555
Cincinnati (G-3572)		
Waldon Management Corp	E	330 792-7688
Youngstown (G-20409)		

REAL ESTATE OPERATORS, EXC DEVEL: Prprty, Auditorium/Theater

Company	Code	Phone
Ohio State University	A	614 688-3939
Columbus (G-8389)		

REAL ESTATE OPERATORS, EXC DEVEL: Theater Bldg, Owner & Op

Company	Code	Phone
Columbus Association For The P	A	614 469-1045
Columbus (G-7331)		

REAL ESTATE OPERATORS, EXC DEVELOPERS: Apartment Hotel

Company	Code	Phone
D & S Properties	E	614 224-6663
Columbus (G-7478)		
E A Zicka Co	E	513 451-1440
Cincinnati (G-3523)		
Forest City Properties LLC	C	216 621-6060
Cleveland (G-5619)		
Intown Suites Management Inc	E	937 433-9038
Dayton (G-9636)		
Islander Company	E	440 243-0593
Cleveland (G-5837)		
L S C Service Corp	E	216 521-7260
Lakewood (G-12485)		
Oakwood Management Company	E	740 774-3570
Chillicothe (G-2865)		
Olentangy Village Associates	E	614 515-4680
Columbus (G-8465)		
Washington Square Apartments	E	740 349-8353
Newark (G-15244)		

REAL ESTATE OPERATORS, EXC DEVELOPERS: Auditorium & Hall

Company	Code	Phone
Assembly Center	E	800 582-1099
Monroe (G-14687)		
Catholic Diocese of Cleveland	E	419 289-7224
Ashland (G-671)		
Dayton Hara Arena Conf Exhibtn	E	937 278-4776
Dayton (G-9476)		
Hall Nazareth Inc	D	419 832-2900
Grand Rapids (G-11449)		
Makoy Center Inc	E	614 777-1211
Hilliard (G-11924)		
Musical Arts Association	C	216 231-7300
Cleveland (G-6093)		
Rootstown Township	E	330 296-8240
Ravenna (G-16409)		
Stranahan Theatre Trust	D	419 381-8851
Toledo (G-18204)		
Waterfront & Associates Inc	B	859 581-1414
Cincinnati (G-4824)		

Employee Codes: A=Over 500 employees, B=251-500
C=101-250, D=51-100, E=25-50

REAL ESTATE OPERATORS, EXC DEVELOPERS: Bank Building

Keybank National Association ....E 216 689-8481
Cleveland *(G-5900)*

REAL ESTATE OPERATORS, EXC DEVELOPERS: Commercial/Indl Bldg

127 PS Fee Owner LLC ....D 216 520-1250
Cleveland *(G-4920)*
Ad Investments LLC ....E 614 857-2340
Columbus *(G-6943)*
American Maritime Officers ....E 419 255-3940
Toledo *(G-17749)*
Anderson Jeffery R RE Inc ....E 513 241-5800
Cincinnati *(G-3024)*
Ashtabula Chemical Corp ....E 440 998-0100
Ashtabula *(G-714)*
Barcus Company Inc ....E 614 451-9000
Columbus *(G-7089)*
C M Limited ....E 614 888-4567
Columbus *(G-7174)*
Campbell Construction Inc ....D 330 262-5186
Wooster *(G-19836)*
Cararo Co Inc ....E 330 652-6980
Niles *(G-15287)*
Carew Realty Inc ....E 513 241-3888
Cincinnati *(G-3184)*
Carnegie Management & Dev Corp ....E 440 892-6800
Westlake *(G-19470)*
Casto Communities Cnstr Ltd ....B 614 228-8545
Columbus *(G-7209)*
Cincinnatian Hotel ....C 513 381-3000
Cincinnati *(G-3336)*
Coldwell Bnkr Hritg Rltors LLC ....E 937 434-7600
Dayton *(G-9416)*
Compco Land Company ....D 330 482-0200
Youngstown *(G-20155)*
Continental Properties ....B 614 221-1800
Columbus *(G-7430)*
Court Stret Center Associates ....E 513 241-0415
Cincinnati *(G-3435)*
Daniel Maury Construction Co ....E 513 984-4096
Loveland *(G-13120)*
Duke Realty Corporation ....D 614 932-6000
Dublin *(G-10333)*
Equity Residential Properties ....E 216 861-2700
Cleveland *(G-5549)*
F H Bonn ....E 937 323-7024
Springfield *(G-17195)*
Fairlawn Associates Ltd ....C 330 867-5000
Fairlawn *(G-10949)*
Garland/Dbs Inc ....C 216 641-7500
Cleveland *(G-5655)*
Gms Management Co Inc Iowa ....E 216 766-6000
Cleveland *(G-5676)*
Goldberg Companies Inc ....E 440 944-8656
Willoughby Hills *(G-19730)*
Goldberg Companies Inc ....E 216 475-2600
Cleveland *(G-5677)*
Goodall Properties Ltd ....E 513 621-5522
Cincinnati *(G-3686)*
Graham Investment Co ....D 740 382-0902
Marion *(G-13541)*
Greater Clumbus Convention Ctr ....C 614 827-2500
Columbus *(G-7773)*
Hadler-Zimmerman Inc ....E 614 457-6650
Columbus *(G-7792)*
Hoty Enterprises Inc ....E 419 609-7000
Sandusky *(G-16769)*
Islander Company ....E 440 243-0593
Cleveland *(G-5837)*
Jacobs Real Estate Services ....E 216 514-9830
Beachwood *(G-1090)*
Jade Investments ....E 330 425-3141
Twinsburg *(G-18433)*
Judy Mills Company Inc ....E 513 271-4241
Cincinnati *(G-3895)*
Jvc Sports Corp ....E 330 726-1757
Youngstown *(G-20243)*
King James Group IV Ltd ....E 440 250-1851
Westlake *(G-19504)*
King James Park Ltd ....E 440 835-1100
Westlake *(G-19505)*
Kohr Royer Griffith Dev Co LLC ....E 614 228-2471
Columbus *(G-8006)*
L and M Investment Co ....E 740 653-3583
Lancaster *(G-12547)*
Lewis Price Realty Co ....E 330 856-1911
Warren *(G-18875)*
Lmt Enterprises Maumee Inc ....E 419 891-7325
Maumee *(G-13936)*
M & L Leasing Co ....E 330 343-8910
Mineral City *(G-14633)*
Majestic Steel Properties Inc ....D 440 786-2666
Cleveland *(G-5972)*
Manleys Manor Nursing Home Inc ....C 419 424-0402
Findlay *(G-11060)*
Meadowbrook Mall Company ....E 330 747-2661
Youngstown *(G-20275)*
MEI Hotels Incorporated ....C 216 589-0441
Cleveland *(G-6021)*
Mendelson Realty Ltd ....E 937 461-3525
Dayton *(G-9719)*
Mid-Ohio Development Corp ....D 614 836-0606
Groveport *(G-11657)*
Miller-Valentine Partners ....C 937 293-0900
Moraine *(G-14807)*
Olentangy Village Associates ....E 614 515-4680
Columbus *(G-8465)*
Oliver House Rest Complex ....D 419 243-1302
Toledo *(G-18105)*
Park Corporation ....B 216 267-4870
Cleveland *(G-6234)*
PNC Banc Corp Ohio ....E 513 651-8738
Cincinnati *(G-4307)*
Reed Hartman Corporate Center ....E 513 984-3030
Blue Ash *(G-1678)*
Ricco Enterprises Incorporated ....E 216 883-7775
Cleveland *(G-6389)*
Robinson Investments Ltd ....E 937 593-1849
Bellefontaine *(G-1393)*
Rockside Center Ltd ....E 216 447-0070
Cleveland *(G-6408)*
Roemer Land Investment Co ....E 419 475-5151
Toledo *(G-18163)*
Rose Properties Inc ....E 216 881-6000
Cleveland *(G-6413)*
Southwest Associates ....C 440 243-7888
Cleveland *(G-6499)*
Ted Graham ....E 740 223-3509
Marion *(G-13584)*
The C-Z Company ....E 740 432-6334
Cambridge *(G-2131)*
Thompson Hall & Jordan Fnrl HM ....E 513 761-8881
Cincinnati *(G-4655)*
Traders World Inc ....E 513 424-2052
Monroe *(G-14715)*
U S Development Corp ....E 330 673-6900
Kent *(G-12401)*
United Fd Coml Wkrs Local 880 ....E 216 241-5930
Cleveland *(G-6638)*
Universal Veneer Mill Corp ....C 740 522-1147
Newark *(G-15243)*
Visconsi Management Inc ....E 216 464-5550
Cleveland *(G-6701)*
Waldon Management Corp ....E 330 792-7688
Youngstown *(G-20409)*
Washington PRI ....C 614 621-9000
Columbus *(G-8967)*
Weston Inc ....E 440 349-9000
Cleveland *(G-6748)*
White & Chambers Partnership ....E 740 594-8381
Athens *(G-820)*
Whitford Woods Co Inc ....E 440 693-4344
Middlefield *(G-14405)*
Wickliffe Associates Partnr ....E 440 585-3505
Wickliffe *(G-19615)*
Willis Day Management Inc ....E 419 476-8000
Toledo *(G-18311)*
Willis Day Storage Co ....E 419 470-6255
Toledo *(G-18312)*
Zucker Building Company ....D 216 861-7114
Cleveland *(G-6785)*

REAL ESTATE OPERATORS, EXC DEVELOPERS: Property, Retail

Friedman Management Company ....D 614 224-2424
Columbus *(G-7705)*
Washington Prime Group Inc ....D 614 621-9000
Columbus *(G-8969)*

REAL ESTATE OPERATORS, EXC DEVELOPERS: Residential Hotel

Aurora Hotel Partners LLC ....E 330 562-0767
Aurora *(G-826)*
Northeast Cincinnati Hotel LLC ....C 513 459-9800
Mason *(G-13743)*
Westgate Limited Partnership ....C 419 535-7070
Toledo *(G-18307)*

REAL ESTATE OPERATORS, EXC DEVELOPERS: Retirement Hotel

Atria Senior Living Group Inc ....E 513 923-3711
Cincinnati *(G-3062)*
Baptist Home and Center ....C 513 662-5880
Cincinnati *(G-3076)*
Brookdale Lving Cmmunities Inc ....E 330 666-4545
Akron *(G-113)*
Brookdale Senior Living Inc ....D 937 203-8596
Beavercreek Township *(G-1287)*
Brookdale Senior Living Inc ....E 216 321-6331
Cleveland *(G-5145)*
Brookdale Senior Living Inc ....D 330 723-5825
Medina *(G-14041)*
Cardinal Retirement Village ....E 330 928-7888
Cuyahoga Falls *(G-9168)*
Claremont Retirement Village ....D 614 761-2011
Columbus *(G-7291)*
Community Mercy Foundation ....C 937 390-9000
Springfield *(G-17172)*
Copeland Oaks ....B 330 938-1050
Sebring *(G-16820)*
Creative Living Inc ....E 614 421-1131
Columbus *(G-7456)*
Ebenezer Road Corp ....C 513 941-0099
Cincinnati *(G-3540)*
Eci Inc ....B 419 986-5566
Burgoon *(G-2057)*
Episcopal Retirement Homes ....D 513 271-9610
Cincinnati *(G-3566)*
Fort Austin Ltd Partnership ....C 440 892-4200
Cleveland *(G-5624)*
Gemini Properties ....E 419 531-9211
Toledo *(G-17911)*
Gemini Properties ....E 614 764-2800
Dublin *(G-10353)*
Harvest Facility Holdings LP ....E 419 472-7115
Toledo *(G-17937)*
Harvest Facility Holdings LP ....E 440 268-9555
Cleveland *(G-5730)*
Hilltop Village ....E 216 261-8383
Cleveland *(G-5758)*
Judson ....D 216 791-2004
Cleveland *(G-5876)*
Kensington Place Inc ....E 614 252-5276
Columbus *(G-7980)*
Kettering Medical Center ....D 937 866-2984
Miamisburg *(G-14311)*
Menorah Park Center For Senio ....E 216 831-6515
Beachwood *(G-1100)*
Mulberry Garden A L S ....E 330 630-3980
Munroe Falls *(G-14932)*
Neighborhood Properties Inc ....E 419 473-2604
Toledo *(G-18082)*
Northwesterly Ltd ....E 216 228-2266
Cleveland *(G-6162)*
Oakleaf Toledo Ltd Partnership ....E 419 885-3934
Toledo *(G-18101)*
Ohio Living ....B 614 224-1651
Columbus *(G-8357)*
Olmsted Mnor Rtrment Cmnty Ltd ....E 440 779-8886
North Olmsted *(G-15437)*
One Lincoln Park ....D 937 298-0594
Dayton *(G-9791)*
Orrvilla Inc ....E 330 683-4455
Orrville *(G-15776)*
Saint Edward Housing Corp ....E 330 668-2828
Fairlawn *(G-10971)*
Senior Lifestyle Corporation ....D 513 777-4457
West Chester *(G-19150)*
Senior Lifestyle Evergreen Ltd ....C 513 948-2308
Cincinnati *(G-4496)*
Shepherd of The Valley Luthera ....E 330 726-7110
Poland *(G-16227)*
South Franklin Circle ....C 440 247-1300
Chagrin Falls *(G-2734)*
Sunpoint Senior Living Hamlet ....E 440 247-4200
Chagrin Falls *(G-2708)*
Sunset Rtrment Communities Inc ....D 419 724-1200
Ottawa Hills *(G-15807)*
Twin Towers ....B 513 853-2000
Cincinnati *(G-4710)*
Wallick Construction Co ....E 937 399-7009
Springfield *(G-17295)*
Westlake Village Inc ....C 440 892-4200
Cleveland *(G-6747)*

SERVICES SECTION

Windsorwood Place Inc .... E 740 623-4600
  Coshocton *(G-9121)*

REAL ESTATE OPERATORS, EXC DEVELOPERS: Shopping Ctr

Easton Town Center LLC .... C 614 337-2560
  Columbus *(G-7568)*
Mall Park Southern .... D 330 758-4511
  Youngstown *(G-20269)*

REAL ESTATE OPERATORS, EXC DEVELOPERS: Shopping Ctr, Commnty

Chapel Hill Management Inc .... D 330 633-7100
  Akron *(G-129)*
Raf Celina LLC .... E 216 464-6626
  Celina *(G-2660)*

REAL ESTATE OPS, EXC DEVELOPER: Residential Bldg, 4 Or Less

Huber Investment Corporation .... E 937 233-1122
  Dayton *(G-9624)*
Rv Properties LLC .... E 330 928-7888
  Cuyahoga Falls *(G-9218)*

REALTY INVESTMENT TRUSTS

845 Yard Street LLC .... D 614 857-2330
  Columbus *(G-6917)*
Washington Prime Group Inc .... D 614 621-9000
  Columbus *(G-8969)*
Welltower Inc .... E 419 247-2800
  Toledo *(G-18304)*

RECLAIMED RUBBER: Reworked By Manufacturing Process

Tahoma Enterprises Inc .... D 330 745-9016
  Barberton *(G-982)*
Tahoma Rubber & Plastics Inc .... D 330 745-9016
  Barberton *(G-983)*

RECOVERY SVCS: Solvents

Safety-Kleen Systems Inc .... D 740 929-3532
  Hebron *(G-11860)*

RECREATIONAL & SPORTING CAMPS

Columbus Frkln Cnty Pk .... E 614 891-0700
  Westerville *(G-19388)*
Community Services Inc .... D 937 667-8631
  Tipp City *(G-17714)*
Echoing Hills Village Inc .... D 740 594-3541
  Athens *(G-785)*
Echoing Hills Village Inc .... A 740 327-2311
  Warsaw *(G-18936)*
Echoing Hills Village Inc .... D 937 854-5151
  Dayton *(G-9518)*
Echoing Hills Village Inc .... E 937 237-7881
  Dayton *(G-9519)*
Echoing Hills Village Inc .... D 440 989-1400
  Lorain *(G-13037)*
Echoing Hills Village Inc .... D 440 986-3085
  South Amherst *(G-17073)*
First Community Church .... E 740 385-3827
  Logan *(G-12972)*
Mideast Baptist Conference .... E 440 834-8984
  Burton *(G-2064)*
Midwest Gymnstics Cheerleading .... E 614 764-0775
  Dublin *(G-10398)*
Procamps Inc .... E 513 745-5855
  Blue Ash *(G-1666)*
Salvation Army .... D 330 735-2671
  Carrollton *(G-2629)*
Young Mens Christian Assoc .... C 614 885-4252
  Columbus *(G-9017)*

RECREATIONAL CAMPS

Ohio F F A Camps Inc .... E 330 627-2208
  Carrollton *(G-2625)*
West Ohio Conference of .... E 614 844-6200
  Worthington *(G-20007)*

RECREATIONAL DAY CAMPS

J&B Sprafka Enterprises Inc .... E 330 733-4212
  Akron *(G-288)*

RECREATIONAL SPORTING EQPT REPAIR SVCS

All American Sports Corp .... A 440 366-8225
  North Ridgeville *(G-15453)*
Capitol Varsity Sports Inc .... E 513 523-4126
  Oxford *(G-15813)*

RECREATIONAL VEHICLE DEALERS

Clare-Mar Camp Inc .... E 440 647-3318
  New London *(G-15066)*
D & D Rv and Auto LLC .... E 937 839-4555
  West Alexandria *(G-19008)*
L B Brunk & Sons Inc .... E 330 332-0359
  Salem *(G-16702)*
Surfside Motors Inc .... E 419 462-1746
  Galion *(G-11306)*

RECREATIONAL VEHICLE PARKS

Parks Recreation Athens .... E 740 592-0046
  Athens *(G-810)*

RECREATIONAL VEHICLE PARKS & CAMPGROUNDS

Muskingum Wtrshed Cnsrvncy Dst .. E 330 343-6780
  Mineral City *(G-14634)*
Natural Resources Ohio Dept .... E 419 394-3611
  Saint Marys *(G-16680)*

RECYCLABLE SCRAP & WASTE MATERIALS WHOLESALERS

Aci Industries Ltd .... E 740 368-4160
  Delaware *(G-10065)*
Ascendtech Inc .... E 216 458-1101
  Willoughby *(G-19645)*
Associated Paper Stock Inc .... E 330 549-5311
  North Lima *(G-15397)*
Crispin Iron & Metal Co LLC .... E 740 616-6213
  Granville *(G-11464)*
Imperial Alum - Minerva LLC .... D 330 868-7765
  Minerva *(G-14646)*
Lkq Corporation .... E 614 575-8200
  Groveport *(G-11656)*
Lkq Corporation .... E 330 733-6333
  Akron *(G-322)*
Mauser Usa LLC .... E 740 397-1762
  Mount Vernon *(G-14911)*
Midwest Iron and Metal Co .... D 937 222-5992
  Dayton *(G-9745)*
Montgomery Iron & Paper Co Inc .... D 937 222-4059
  Dayton *(G-9755)*
Omnisource LLC .... E 419 227-3411
  Lima *(G-12849)*
PSC Metals Inc .... E 330 455-0212
  Canton *(G-2497)*
Rnw Holdings Inc .... E 330 792-0600
  Youngstown *(G-20352)*
Shredded Bedding Corporation .... E 740 893-3567
  Centerburg *(G-2668)*
Tms International LLC .... E 419 747-5500
  Mansfield *(G-13375)*

REFERRAL SVCS, PERSONAL & SOCIAL PROBLEMS

Caracole Inc .... E 513 761-1480
  Cincinnati *(G-3176)*
Clinton County Board of .... E 937 382-7519
  Wilmington *(G-19749)*
Info Line Inc .... E 330 252-8064
  Akron *(C-277)*
Pregnancy Care of Cincinnati .... E 513 487-7777
  Cincinnati *(G-4321)*

REFINERS & SMELTERS: Aluminum

Imco Recycling of Ohio LLC .... C 740 922-2373
  Uhrichsville *(G-18490)*

REFINERS & SMELTERS: Lead, Secondary

Victory White Metal Company .... E 216 271-7200
  Cleveland *(G-6695)*

REFINERS & SMELTERS: Nonferrous Metal

A J Oster Foils LLC .... D 330 823-1700
  Alliance *(G-521)*

REFRIGERATION REPAIR SVCS

Aci Industries Ltd .... E 740 368-4160
  Delaware *(G-10065)*
City Scrap & Salvage Co .... E 330 753-5051
  Akron *(G-143)*
Fpt Cleveland LLC .... C 216 441-3800
  Cleveland *(G-5628)*
Franklin Iron & Metal Corp .... C 937 253-8184
  Dayton *(G-9561)*
Garden Street Iron & Metal .... E 513 853-3700
  Cincinnati *(G-3662)*
I H Schlezinger Inc .... E 614 252-1188
  Columbus *(G-7877)*
Metal Shredders Inc .... E 937 866-0777
  Miamisburg *(G-14320)*
Metalico Akron Inc .... E 330 376-1400
  Akron *(G-340)*
Midwest Iron and Metal Co .... D 937 222-5992
  Dayton *(G-9745)*
Moskowitz Bros Inc .... E 513 242-2100
  Cincinnati *(G-4121)*
National Bronze Mtls Ohio Inc .... E 440 277-1226
  Lorain *(G-13063)*
R L S Corporation .... E 740 773-1440
  Chillicothe *(G-2872)*
Rnw Holdings Inc .... E 330 792-0600
  Youngstown *(G-20352)*
Rumpke Transportation Co LLC ...... C 513 242-4600
  Cincinnati *(G-4454)*
Thyssenkrupp Materials NA Inc ...... D 216 883-8100
  Independence *(G-12267)*
W R G Inc .... E 216 351-8494
  Cleveland *(G-6714)*

REFINING: Petroleum

Aecom Energy & Cnstr Inc .... C 419 698-6277
  Oregon *(G-15723)*
Koch Knight LLC .... D 330 488-1651
  East Canton *(G-10504)*
Marathon Petroleum Corporation .... B 419 422-2121
  Findlay *(G-11061)*

REFRACTORIES: Nonclay

Martin Marietta Materials Inc .... E 513 701-1140
  West Chester *(G-19117)*

REFRACTORY MATERIALS WHOLESALERS

Allen Refractories Company .... C 740 927-8000
  Pataskala *(G-15920)*

REFRIGERATION & HEATING EQUIPMENT

A A S Amels Sheet Meta L Inc .... E 330 793-9326
  Youngstown *(G-20094)*
Anatrace Products LLC .... E 419 740-6600
  Maumee *(G-13876)*

REFRIGERATION EQPT & SPLYS WHOLESALERS

Allied Supply Company Inc .... E 937 224-9833
  Dayton *(G-9317)*
Buckeye Heating and AC Sup Inc ... E 216 831-0066
  Bedford Heights *(G-1348)*
Controls Center Inc .... D 513 772-2665
  Cincinnati *(G-3415)*
Gordon Brothers Inc .... E 800 331-7611
  Salem *(G-16697)*
WW Grainger Inc .... E 614 276-5231
  Columbus *(G-9010)*

REFRIGERATION EQPT & SPLYS, WHOL: Refrig Units, Motor Veh

Scotts Towing Co .... E 419 729-7888
  Toledo *(G-18176)*

REFRIGERATION EQPT & SPLYS, WHOLESALE: Commercial Eqpt

Hattenbach Company .... D 216 881-5200
  Cleveland *(G-5731)*

REFRIGERATION REPAIR SVCS

Dickson Industrial Park Inc .... E 740 377-9162
  South Point *(G-17083)*
Refrigeration Systems Company ..... D 614 263-0913
  Columbus *(G-8603)*

REFRIGERATION REPAIR SVCS

Roto-Rooter Services Company .... D 513 541-3840
　Cincinnati *(G-4445)*
Transport Specialists Inc .... E 513 771-2220
　Cincinnati *(G-4680)*

REFRIGERATION SVC & REPAIR

Electrical Appl Repr Svc Inc .... E 216 459-8700
　Brooklyn Heights *(G-1915)*
Gardiner Service Company .... C 440 248-3400
　Solon *(G-17008)*
Honeywell International Inc .... D 216 459-6053
　Cleveland *(G-5770)*

REFUGEE SVCS

Community Refugee & Immigration ... D 614 235-5747
　Columbus *(G-7409)*

REFUSE SYSTEMS

Boral Resources LLC .... D 740 622-8042
　Coshocton *(G-9088)*
City of Elyria .... D 440 366-2211
　Elyria *(G-10604)*
City of Lakewood .... E 216 252-4322
　Cleveland *(G-5265)*
City of Perrysburg .... E 419 872-8020
　Perrysburg *(G-15987)*
Clean Harbors Envmtl Svcs Inc .... E 513 681-6242
　Cincinnati *(G-3361)*
County of Portage .... D 330 297-3670
　Ravenna *(G-16380)*
Metalico Akron Inc .... E 330 376-1400
　Akron *(G-340)*
R & R Sanitation Inc .... E 330 325-2311
　Mogadore *(G-14683)*
Republic Services Inc .... E 216 741-4013
　Cleveland *(G-6379)*
Republic Services Inc .... E 937 492-3470
　Sidney *(G-16950)*
Rls Disposal Company Inc .... E 740 773-1440
　Chillicothe *(G-2875)*
Rumpke Waste Inc .... E 937 548-1939
　Greenville *(G-11517)*
Safety-Kleen Systems Inc .... D 740 929-3532
　Hebron *(G-11860)*
T C Rumpke Waste Collection .... E 513 385-7627
　Cincinnati *(G-4612)*
Waste Management Ohio Inc .... D 440 201-1235
　Solon *(G-17066)*
Waste Management Ohio Inc .... D 800 356-5235
　Chillicothe *(G-2896)*
Waste Management Ohio Inc .... E 866 797-9018
　North Jackson *(G-15390)*
Waste Management Ohio Inc .... E 440 286-7116
　Chardon *(G-2777)*
Waste Management Ohio Inc .... E 740 345-1212
　Newark *(G-15245)*
Waste Management Ohio Inc .... E 614 833-5290
　Canal Winchester *(G-2178)*
Waste Management Ohio Inc .... E 440 285-6767
　Geneva *(G-11373)*
Waste Management Ohio Inc .... E 419 221-2029
　Lima *(G-12914)*

REGULATION & ADMIN, GOVT: Public Svc Commission, Exc Transp

City of Westerville .... E 614 901-6500
　Westerville *(G-19382)*

REGULATION & ADMINISTRATION, GOVT: Transp Dept, Nonoperating

City of Hamilton .... E 513 785-7551
　Hamilton *(G-11709)*

REGULATORS: Power

Liebert Corporation .... A 614 888-0246
　Columbus *(G-8059)*

REHABILITATION CENTER, OUTPATIENT TREATMENT

Accelerated Health Systems LLC ..... D 614 334-5135
　Hilliard *(G-11876)*
Audrich Inc .... C 419 483-6225
　Bellevue *(G-1403)*
Aurora Manor Special Care .... E 440 424-4000
　Aurora *(G-827)*

Brecksvlle Hlthcare Group Inc .... D 440 546-0643
　Brecksville *(G-1816)*
Cancer Ntwk of W Cent .... E 419 226-9085
　Lima *(G-12751)*
Childrens Rehabilitation Ctr .... E 330 856-2107
　Warren *(G-18833)*
Concept Rehab Inc .... D 419 843-6002
　Toledo *(G-17828)*
Cora Health Services Inc .... E 419 221-3004
　Lima *(G-12760)*
Country Meadow Care Center LLC ... E 419 886-3922
　Bellville *(G-1425)*
County of Carroll .... E 330 627-7651
　Carrollton *(G-2616)*
Easter Seal Society of .... D 330 743-1168
　Youngstown *(G-20176)*
Education Alternatives .... D 216 332-9360
　Brookpark *(G-1944)*
Hcf of Roselawn Inc .... C 419 647-4115
　Spencerville *(G-17108)*
Heartland Rhblitation Svcs Inc .... D 419 537-0764
　Toledo *(G-17949)*
Heartlnd-Riverview S Pt OH LLC ..... C 740 894-3287
　South Point *(G-17089)*
Hill Manor 1 Inc .... E 740 972-3227
　Columbus *(G-7836)*
Kindred Healthcare Oper Inc .... D 740 545-6355
　West Lafayette *(G-19258)*
Kindred Healthcare Oper Inc .... C 740 387-7537
　Marion *(G-13545)*
Kindred Nursing Centers E LLC .... E 502 596-7300
　Logan *(G-12981)*
Lorain County Alcohol and Drug .... E 440 989-4900
　Lorain *(G-13051)*
Manor Care of Kansas Inc .... D 419 252-5500
　Toledo *(G-18031)*
Marca Terrace Widows .... D 937 252-1661
　Dayton *(G-9698)*
Marietta Center For Health & .... C 740 373-1867
　Marietta *(G-13466)*
Medcentral Health System .... C 419 683-1040
　Crestline *(G-9147)*
Meigs Center Ltd .... C 740 992-6472
　Middleport *(G-14407)*
Metrohealth System .... D 216 778-8446
　Cleveland *(G-6040)*
Midwest Rehab Inc .... D 419 238-3405
　Ada *(G-6)*
Ohio State University .... A 614 257-3000
　Columbus *(G-8393)*
Opportunities For Ohioans .... E 513 852-3260
　Cincinnati *(G-4229)*
Peak Performance Center Inc .... E 440 838-5600
　Broadview Heights *(G-1889)*
Portage Physical Therapists .... D 330 297-9020
　Ravenna *(G-16402)*
Recovery Center .... E 740 687-4500
　Lancaster *(G-12568)*
Rehab Center .... E 330 297-2770
　Ravenna *(G-16405)*
Rehab Medical Inc .... C 513 381-3740
　Cincinnati *(G-4398)*
Rehabcare Group MGT Svcs Inc ..... E 740 779-6732
　Chillicothe *(G-2874)*
Rehabcare Group MGT Svcs Inc ..... D 740 356-6160
　Portsmouth *(G-16303)*
Rehabltition Ctr At Mrietta Mem .... D 740 374-1407
　Marietta *(G-13493)*
Society For Rehabilitation .... E 440 209-0135
　Mentor *(G-14243)*
St Ritas Medical Center .... E 419 228-1535
　Lima *(G-12890)*
Summit Acres Inc .... C 740 732-2364
　Caldwell *(G-2089)*
Sunbrdge Marion Hlth Care Corp ..... D 740 389-6306
　Marion *(G-13582)*
Therapeutic Riding Center Inc .... E 440 708-0013
　Chagrin Falls *(G-2736)*
Theratrust .... E 740 345-7688
　Newark *(G-15239)*
Trihealth G LLC .... E 513 346-5000
　Cincinnati *(G-4694)*
Ultimate Rehab Ltd .... D 513 563-8777
　Blue Ash *(G-1708)*
United Rehabilitation Services .... E 937 233-1230
　Dayton *(G-9947)*
Wsb Rehabilitation Svcs Inc .... A 330 847-7819
　Warren *(G-18929)*

REHABILITATION CTR, RESIDENTIAL WITH HEALTH CARE INCIDENTAL

Amedisys Inc .... E 740 373-8549
　Marietta *(G-13430)*
Cherry St Mission Ministries .... E 419 242-5141
　Toledo *(G-17804)*
City Mission .... E 216 431-3510
　Cleveland *(G-5247)*
Compdrug .... D 614 224-4506
　Columbus *(G-7412)*
Comprehensive Addiction Svc Sy ..... E 419 241-8827
　Toledo *(G-17826)*
Crestview Health Care Center .... D 740 695-2500
　Saint Clairsville *(G-16634)*
Foundations Hlth Solutions Inc .... D 440 793-0200
　North Olmsted *(G-15423)*
Harbor .... D 419 241-6191
　Toledo *(G-17933)*
Health Recovery Services Inc .... C 740 592-6720
　Athens *(G-791)*
Hitchcock Center For Women Inc .... E 216 421-0662
　Cleveland *(G-5761)*
Interval Brotherhood Homes .... D 330 644-4095
　Coventry Township *(G-9126)*
Jo Lin Health Center Inc .... C 740 532-0860
　Ironton *(G-12295)*
Kendal At Granville .... C 740 321-0400
　Granville *(G-11467)*
New Directions Inc .... D 216 591-0324
　Cleveland *(G-6124)*
Rchp - Wilmington LLC .... D 937 382-6611
　Wilmington *(G-19781)*
Rose Mary Johanna Grassell .... E 216 481-4823
　Cleveland *(G-6412)*
Toledo Hospital .... C 419 291-2273
　Sylvania *(G-17623)*
United Cerebral Palsy .... E 216 791-8363
　Cleveland *(G-6635)*
United Cerebral Palsy .... D 216 381-9993
　Cleveland *(G-6636)*
United Cerebral Palsy Gr Cinc .... E 513 221-4606
　Cincinnati *(G-4729)*

REHABILITATION SVCS

A Renewed Mind .... D 419 214-0606
　Perrysburg *(G-15970)*
A W S Inc .... E 216 486-0600
　Euclid *(G-10741)*
Adena NH LLC .... E 740 546-3620
　Adena *(G-7)*
Akron General Medical Center .... D 330 344-6000
　Akron *(G-43)*
Arbor Rehabilitation & Healtcr .... B 440 423-0206
　Gates Mills *(G-11355)*
Beeghly Oaks Operating LLC .... C 330 884-2300
　Boardman *(G-1738)*
Brookdale Place Wooster LLC .... E 330 262-1615
　Wooster *(G-19834)*
Carriage Inn of Cadiz Inc .... E 740 942-8084
　Cadiz *(G-2073)*
City Mission .... E 216 431-3510
　Cleveland *(G-5247)*
Clark County Board of Developm ..... E 937 328-2675
　Springfield *(G-17161)*
Clovernook Center For The Bli .... C 513 522-3860
　Cincinnati *(G-3370)*
Community Drug Board Inc .... D 330 996-5114
　Akron *(G-154)*
Diverscare Healthcare Svcs Inc .... E 937 278-8211
　Dayton *(G-9502)*
Goodwill Inds Rhbilitation Ctr .... C 740 264-6000
　Steubenville *(G-17319)*
Goodwill Inds Rhbilitation Ctr .... B 330 454-9461
　Canton *(G-2384)*
Happy Hearts School .... C 440 224-2157
　Ashtabula *(G-746)*
Harrison Pavilion .... E 513 662-5800
　Cincinnati *(G-3738)*
Hcf Management Inc .... C 740 289-2394
　Piketon *(G-16117)*
Hcf of Roselawn Inc .... C 419 647-4115
　Spencerville *(G-17108)*
Hearing Spch Deaf Ctr Grtr Cnc ...... E 513 221-0527
　Cincinnati *(G-3755)*
James Powers .... E 614 566-9397
　Columbus *(G-7934)*
Kindred Healthcare Inc .... D 216 593-2200
　Beachwood *(G-1094)*

SERVICES SECTION

RENTAL SVCS: Business Machine & Electronic Eqpt

Kingston Rsdnce Perrysburg LLC .... D 419 872-6200
  Perrysburg *(G-16025)*
Liberty Nursing Center of Thre .... C 513 941-0787
  Cincinnati *(G-3976)*
Miami Vly Jvnile Rhblttion Ctr .... E 937 562-4000
  Xenia *(G-20070)*
Muskingum Vly Nrsing Rhblttion .... D 740 984-4262
  Beverly *(G-1492)*
Oaks of West Kettering Inc .... C 937 293-1152
  Dayton *(G-9780)*
Ohio Department of Health .... A 614 438-1255
  Columbus *(G-8329)*
Ohio State University .... A 614 366-3692
  Columbus *(G-8388)*
Rehab Resources .... E 513 474-4123
  Cincinnati *(G-4399)*
River Rock Rehabilitation .... E 740 382-4035
  Marion *(G-13576)*
Southeastern Rehabilitation .... E 740 679-2111
  Salesville *(G-16720)*
Talbert House .... E 513 541-0127
  Cincinnati *(G-4617)*
Talbert House .... D 513 872-5863
  Cincinnati *(G-4620)*
Trihealth Rehabilitation Hosp .... C 513 601-0500
  Cincinnati *(G-4698)*

REINSURANCE CARRIERS: Accident & Health

American Modern Home Svc Co .... E 513 943-7100
  Amelia *(G-575)*
Employers Mutual Casualty Co .... D 513 221-6010
  Blue Ash *(G-1585)*

REINSURANCE CARRIERS: Surety

Progressive Casualty Insur Co .... A 440 461-5000
  Mayfield Village *(G-14012)*
State Automobile Mutl Insur Co .... A 833 724-3577
  Columbus *(G-8781)*

RELOCATION SVCS

Dwellworks LLC .... D 216 682-4200
  Cleveland *(G-5513)*
Sirva Inc .... E 216 606-4000
  Independence *(G-12257)*
Sirva Relocation LLC .... B 216 606-4000
  Independence *(G-12259)*
Wegman Construction Company .... E 513 381-1111
  Cincinnati *(G-4828)*

REMOTE DATABASE INFORMATION RETRIEVAL SVCS

Mirifex Systems LLC .... C 440 891-1210
  Sharon Center *(G-16876)*

RENT-A-CAR SVCS

Avis Administration .... D 937 898-2581
  Vandalia *(G-18660)*
Budget Rent A Car System Inc .... D 216 267-2080
  Cleveland *(G-5157)*
Cartemp USA Inc .... C 440 715-1000
  Solon *(G-16988)*
Clerac LLC .... E 440 345-3999
  Strongsville *(G-17450)*
Crawford Group Inc .... D 419 873-7360
  Perrysburg *(G-15990)*
Dealers Group Limited .... E 440 352-4970
  Beachwood *(G-1073)*
Enterprise Holdings Inc .... D 614 866-1480
  Reynoldsburg *(G-16451)*
Enterprise Holdings Inc .... E 937 879-0023
  Cincinnati *(G-3559)*
Falls Motor City Inc .... E 330 929-3066
  Cuyahoga Falls *(G-9184)*
Geo Byers Sons Holding Inc .... E 614 239-1084
  Columbus *(G-7741)*
George P Ballas Buick GMC Trck .... D 419 535-1000
  Toledo *(G-17913)*
Hertz Corporation .... D 216 267-8900
  Cleveland *(G-5755)*
Hertz Corporation .... E 513 533-3161
  Cincinnati *(G-3758)*
Hertz Corporation .... E 937 890-2721
  Vandalia *(G-18683)*
Hertz Corporation .... D 937 898-5806
  Vandalia *(G-18684)*

National Rental (us) Inc .... E 937 890-0100
  Vandalia *(G-18690)*
National Rental (us) Inc .... E 614 239-3270
  Columbus *(G-8223)*
Precision Coatings Systems .... E 937 642-4727
  Marysville *(G-13645)*
Rental Concepts Inc .... E 216 525-3870
  Cleveland *(G-6377)*
Schoner Chevrolet Inc .... D 330 877-6731
  Hartville *(G-11830)*
Thrifty Rent-A-Car System Inc .... E 440 842-1660
  Cleveland *(G-6598)*
U Save Auto Rental .... E 330 925-2015
  Rittman *(G-16557)*

RENTAL CENTERS: Furniture

Aarons Inc .... E 330 823-1879
  Alliance *(G-522)*
Aarons Inc .... E 216 251-4500
  Cleveland *(G-4943)*
Aarons Inc .... E 330 385-7201
  East Liverpool *(G-10513)*
Aarons Inc .... E 937 778-3577
  Piqua *(G-16134)*
Aarons Inc .... E 216 587-2745
  Maple Heights *(G-13398)*
Beacon Company .... E 330 733-8322
  Akron *(G-95)*
Cort Business Services Corp .... D 513 759-8181
  West Chester *(G-19054)*

RENTAL CENTERS: General

Quality Supply & Rental Inc .... E 740 286-7517
  Jackson *(G-12317)*

RENTAL CENTERS: Party & Banquet Eqpt & Splys

A B C Rental Center East Inc .... E 216 475-8240
  Cleveland *(G-4929)*
All Occasions Event Rental .... E 513 563-0600
  Cincinnati *(G-2985)*
Camargo Rental Center Inc .... E 513 271-6510
  Cincinnati *(G-3170)*
Columbus AAA Corp .... E 614 889-2840
  Dublin *(G-10300)*
Jbjs Acquisitions LLC .... E 513 769-0393
  Cincinnati *(G-3864)*
Made From Scratch Inc .... E 614 873-3344
  Plain City *(G-16197)*
Maloney & Associates Inc .... E 330 479-7084
  Canton *(G-2443)*
Prime Time Party Rental Inc .... E 937 296-9262
  Moraine *(G-14815)*

RENTAL CENTERS: Tools

Black Swamp Equipment LLC .... E 419 445-0030
  Archbold *(G-633)*
Bnd Rentals Inc .... E 937 898-5061
  Vandalia *(G-18663)*
Chase Phipps .... E 330 754-0467
  Canton *(G-2303)*
Home Depot USA Inc .... C 614 523-0600
  Columbus *(G-7848)*
Home Depot USA Inc .... C 330 965-4790
  Boardman *(G-1741)*
Home Depot USA Inc .... C 330 497-1810
  Canton *(G-2402)*
Home Depot USA Inc .... C 513 688-1654
  Cincinnati *(G-3778)*
Home Depot USA Inc .... C 330 922-3448
  Cuyahoga Falls *(C-9194)*
Home Depot USA Inc .... C 937 312-9053
  Dayton *(G-9614)*
Home Depot USA Inc .... C 937 312-9076
  Dayton *(G-9615)*
Home Depot USA Inc .... C 216 692-2780
  Euclid *(G-10762)*
Home Depot USA Inc .... C 216 676-9969
  Cleveland *(G-5767)*
Home Depot USA Inc .... C 216 581-6611
  Maple Heights *(G-13408)*
Home Depot USA Inc .... C 937 431-7346
  Beavercreek *(G-1177)*
Home Depot USA Inc .... C 330 245-0280
  Akron *(G-271)*
Home Depot USA Inc .... C 937 837-1551
  Dayton *(G-9616)*

Home Depot USA Inc .... C 216 297-1303
  Cleveland Heights *(G-6790)*
Home Depot USA Inc .... C 513 661-2413
  Cincinnati *(G-3779)*
Home Depot USA Inc .... C 513 887-1450
  Fairfield Township *(G-10931)*
Home Depot USA Inc .... C 419 476-4573
  Toledo *(G-17957)*
Home Depot USA Inc .... C 440 357-0428
  Mentor *(G-14191)*
Home Depot USA Inc .... C 513 631-1705
  Cincinnati *(G-3780)*
Home Depot USA Inc .... C 440 684-1343
  Highland Heights *(G-11869)*
Home Depot USA Inc .... C 419 537-1920
  Toledo *(G-17958)*
Home Depot USA Inc .... C 614 878-9150
  Columbus *(G-7849)*
Home Depot USA Inc .... C 440 826-9092
  Strongsville *(G-17471)*
Home Depot USA Inc .... C 614 939-5036
  Columbus *(G-7850)*
Home Depot USA Inc .... D 440 937-2240
  Avon *(G-898)*
Home Depot USA Inc .... C 614 577-1601
  Reynoldsburg *(G-16458)*
Home Depot USA Inc .... C 330 220-2654
  Brunswick *(G-1981)*
Home Depot USA Inc .... C 419 626-6493
  Sandusky *(G-16768)*
Home Depot USA Inc .... C 614 876-5558
  Hilliard *(G-11911)*
Home Depot USA Inc .... C 440 324-7222
  Elyria *(G-10633)*
Home Depot USA Inc .... C 419 529-0015
  Ontario *(G-15691)*
Home Depot USA Inc .... C 216 251-3091
  Cleveland *(G-5768)*

RENTAL SVCS: Aircraft

Flight Options LLC .... C 216 261-3500
  Cleveland *(G-5608)*
Netjets Inc .... E 614 239-5500
  Columbus *(G-8261)*

RENTAL SVCS: Appliance

Rent-A-Center Inc .... D 330 337-1107
  Salem *(G-16710)*
Rent-A-Center Inc .... D 419 382-8585
  Toledo *(G-18151)*

RENTAL SVCS: Audio-Visual Eqpt & Sply

Bkg Holdings LLC .... E 614 252-7455
  Columbus *(G-7113)*
Cleveland Corporate Svcs Inc .... C 216 397-1492
  Cleveland *(G-5310)*
Colortone Audio Visual .... E 216 928-1530
  Cleveland *(G-5371)*
Csr Colortone Staging Rentals .... E 440 914-9500
  Cleveland *(G-5444)*
Live Technologies Holdings Inc .... D 614 278-7777
  Columbus *(G-8074)*
Northeast Projections Inc .... E 330 375-9444
  Cleveland *(G-6156)*
Prestige Audio Visual Inc .... D 513 641-1600
  Cincinnati *(G-4326)*
Rentech Solutions Inc .... D 216 398-1111
  Willoughby *(G-19710)*

RENTAL SVCS: Beach & Water Sports Eqpt

Ohio Dept Natural Resources .... E 740 869-3124
  Mount Sterling *(G-14874)*
Paul A Ertel .... D 216 696-8888
  Cleveland *(G-6252)*
Stockport Mill Country Inn Inc .... E 740 559-2822
  Stockport *(G-17346)*

RENTAL SVCS: Bicycle

Island Bike Rental Inc .... E 419 285-2016
  Put In Bay *(G-16367)*

RENTAL SVCS: Business Machine & Electronic Eqpt

Comdoc Inc .... C 330 896-2346
  Uniontown *(G-18514)*
David Francis Corporation .... C 216 524-0900
  Cleveland *(G-5466)*

Employee Codes: A=Over 500 employees, B=251-500
C=101-250, D=51-100, E=25-50

RENTAL SVCS: Business Machine & Electronic Eqpt

Diane Sauer Chevrolet Inc .... D 330 373-1600
  Warren *(G-18850)*
Pitney Bowes Inc .... D 203 426-7025
  Brecksville *(G-1840)*
Pitney Bowes Inc .... D 740 374-5535
  Marietta *(G-13489)*
Setiawan Associates LLC .... E 614 285-5815
  Columbus *(G-8717)*

RENTAL SVCS: Clothing

Barberton Laundry & Cleaning .... E 330 825-6911
  Barberton *(G-958)*
Emmys Bridal Inc .... E 419 628-7555
  Minster *(G-14661)*

RENTAL SVCS: Costume

Costume Specialists Inc .... E 614 464-2115
  Columbus *(G-7448)*

RENTAL SVCS: Dress Suit

American Commodore Tu .... D 216 291-4601
  Cleveland *(G-5006)*

RENTAL SVCS: Electronic Eqpt, Exc Computers

Fern Exposition Services LLC .... E 513 621-6111
  Cincinnati *(G-3603)*
Modal Shop Inc .... D 513 351-9919
  Cincinnati *(G-4111)*
Warwick Communications Inc .... E 216 787-0300
  Broadview Heights *(G-1895)*

RENTAL SVCS: Golf Cart, Power

South E Harley Davidson Sls Co .... E 440 439-5300
  Cleveland *(G-6496)*

RENTAL SVCS: Home Cleaning & Maintenance Eqpt

Equipment Depot Ohio Inc .... E 513 934-2121
  Lebanon *(G-12604)*
Stout Lori Cleaning & Such .... E 419 637-7644
  Gibsonburg *(G-11404)*
Two Men & A Vacuum LLC .... D 614 300-7970
  Columbus *(G-8881)*

RENTAL SVCS: Invalid Splys

Americas Best Medical Eqp Co .... E 330 928-0884
  Akron *(G-73)*
Pharmerica Long-Term Care Inc .... E 330 425-4450
  Twinsburg *(G-18454)*

RENTAL SVCS: Mobile Communication Eqpt

Mobilcomm Inc .... D 513 742-5555
  Cincinnati *(G-4110)*

RENTAL SVCS: Office Facilities & Secretarial Svcs

Renaissance Hotel Operating Co .... A 216 696-5600
  Cleveland *(G-6374)*

RENTAL SVCS: Oil Eqpt

Grady Rentals LLC .... E 330 627-2022
  Carrollton *(G-2621)*

RENTAL SVCS: Recreational Vehicle

D & D Rv and Auto LLC .... E 937 839-4555
  West Alexandria *(G-19008)*

RENTAL SVCS: Sound & Lighting Eqpt

HEat Ttal Fclty Slutions Inc .... E 740 965-3005
  Galena *(G-11283)*

RENTAL SVCS: Sporting Goods, NEC

Dicks Sporting Goods Inc .... E 740 522-5555
  Heath *(G-11836)*
Dicks Sporting Goods Inc .... E 614 472-4250
  Columbus *(G-7518)*

RENTAL SVCS: Stores & Yards Eqpt

Ace Rental Place .... D 937 642-2891
  Marysville *(G-13605)*
E T B Ltd .... E 740 373-6686
  Marietta *(G-13443)*

RENTAL SVCS: Television

Countryside Rentals Inc .... E 740 634-2666
  Bainbridge *(G-941)*

RENTAL SVCS: Tent & Tarpaulin

Advanced Tenting Solutions .... E 216 291-3300
  Newbury *(G-15253)*
Baker Bnngson Rlty Auctioneers .... E 419 547-7777
  Clyde *(G-6810)*
ONeil Awning and Tent Inc .... D 614 837-6352
  Canal Winchester *(G-2165)*

RENTAL SVCS: Trailer

A Duie Pyle Inc .... D 330 342-7750
  Streetsboro *(G-17404)*
Ample Trailer Leasing & Sales .... E 513 563-2550
  Cincinnati *(G-3019)*
Benedict Enterprises Inc .... E 513 539-9216
  Monroe *(G-14690)*
E & J Trailer Leasing Inc .... E 513 563-7366
  Cincinnati *(G-3521)*
E & J Trailer Sales & Service .... E 513 563-2550
  Cincinnati *(G-3522)*
Eleet Cryogenics Inc .... E 330 874-4009
  Bolivar *(G-1746)*
Ryder Truck Rental Inc .... E 513 772-0223
  Cincinnati *(G-4463)*
Transport Services Inc .... E 440 582-4900
  Cleveland *(G-6612)*
U Haul Co of Northwestern Ohio .... E 419 478-1101
  Toledo *(G-18266)*

RENTAL SVCS: Tuxedo

Rondinelli Company Inc .... D 330 726-7643
  Youngstown *(G-20358)*
Rondinellis Tuxedo .... E 330 726-7768
  Youngstown *(G-20359)*

RENTAL SVCS: Vending Machine

Advance Vending Corp .... E 216 587-9500
  Cleveland *(G-4958)*
Cuyahoga Vending Co Inc .... D 216 663-1457
  Maple Heights *(G-13404)*
Multi-Flow Dispensers Ohio Inc .... D 216 641-0200
  Brooklyn Heights *(G-1921)*

RENTAL SVCS: Video Disk/Tape, To The General Public

Emerge Ministries Inc .... E 330 865-8351
  Akron *(G-208)*
Family Video Movie Club Inc .... E 937 846-1021
  New Carlisle *(G-15023)*

RENTAL SVCS: Work Zone Traffic Eqpt, Flags, Cones, Etc

A & A Safety Inc .... E 513 943-6100
  Amelia *(G-571)*
American Roadway Logistics Inc .... E 330 659-2003
  Richfield *(G-16497)*
Paul Peterson Company .... E 614 486-4375
  Columbus *(G-8522)*
Paul Peterson Safety Div Inc .... E 614 486-4375
  Columbus *(G-8523)*

RENTAL: Passenger Car

Afford-A-Car Inc .... E 937 235-2700
  Tipp City *(G-17710)*
Budget Rent A Car System Inc .... E 937 898-1396
  Vandalia *(G-18664)*
Carroll Halliday Inc .... E 740 335-1670
  Wshngtn CT Hs *(G-20014)*
Crawford Group Inc .... D 330 665-5432
  Akron *(G-176)*
Edison Local School District .... E 740 543-4011
  Amsterdam *(G-608)*
Leikin Motor Companies Inc .... D 440 946-6900
  Willoughby *(G-19686)*
Lincoln Mrcury Kings Auto Mall .... C 513 683-3800
  Cincinnati *(G-3984)*
Schmidt Daily Rental Inc .... D 419 874-4331
  Perrysburg *(G-16057)*
Spitzer Chevrolet Company .... E 330 966-9524
  Canton *(G-2535)*
Sweeny Walt Pntc GMC Trck Sles .... E 513 621-4888
  Cincinnati *(G-4607)*
Taylor Chevrolet Inc .... C 740 653-2091
  Lancaster *(G-12579)*

RENTAL: Portable Toilet

Miller & Co Portable Toil Svcs .... E 330 453-9472
  Canton *(G-2463)*
Pro-Kleen Industrial Svcs Inc .... E 740 689-1886
  Lancaster *(G-12566)*
Rumpke Transportation Co LLC .... E 937 461-0004
  Dayton *(G-9856)*
Superr-Spdie Portable Svcs Inc .... E 330 733-9000
  Akron *(G-469)*
Waids Rainbow Rental Inc .... E 216 524-3736
  Akron *(G-502)*
Waste Management Ohio Inc .... D 800 343-6047
  Fairborn *(G-10811)*

RENTAL: Trucks, With Drivers

Aim Integrated Logistics Inc .... B 330 759-0438
  Girard *(G-11406)*
Aim Leasing Company .... D 330 759-0438
  Girard *(G-11407)*
Hirzel Transfer Co .... E 419 287-3288
  Pemberville *(G-15941)*
J M Towning Inc .... E 614 876-7335
  Hilliard *(G-11915)*
T R L Inc .... C 330 448-4071
  Brookfield *(G-1901)*

RENTAL: Video Tape & Disc

Mile Inc .... D 614 794-2203
  Worthington *(G-19978)*

REPOSSESSION SVCS

G Robert Toney & Assoc Inc .... E 954 791-9601
  Cleveland *(G-5648)*
Interscope Manufacturing Inc .... E 513 423-8866
  Middletown *(G-14429)*
Millennium Cpitl Recovery Corp .... E 330 528-1450
  Hudson *(G-12135)*

REPRODUCTION SVCS: Video Tape Or Disk

Click Camera & Video .... E 937 435-3072
  Miamisburg *(G-14285)*
Litigation Support Svcs Inc .... E 513 241-5605
  Cincinnati *(G-3992)*
Technicolor Thomson Group .... C 937 383-6000
  Wilmington *(G-19790)*

RESEARCH & DEVELOPMENT SVCS, COMMERCIAL: Engineering Lab

Applied Research Assoc Inc .... E 937 873-8166
  Dayton *(G-9339)*
Morris Technologies Inc .... C 513 733-1611
  Cincinnati *(G-4119)*
Quest Global Services-Na Inc .... D 513 563-8855
  Cincinnati *(G-4375)*
Quest Global Services-Na Inc .... D 513 648-4900
  Cincinnati *(G-4376)*
Zin Technologies Inc .... C 440 625-2200
  Middleburg Heights *(G-14392)*

RESEARCH, DEV & TESTING SVCS, COMM: Chem Lab, Exc Testing

Guild Associates Inc .... D 614 798-8215
  Dublin *(G-10355)*
Heraeus Precious Metals North .... E 937 264-1000
  Vandalia *(G-18682)*
Ohio State University .... E 614 688-8220
  Columbus *(G-8425)*
U S Laboratories Inc .... E 440 248-1223
  Cleveland *(G-6626)*

RESEARCH, DEVELOPMENT & TEST SVCS, COMM: Business Analysis

- Scanner Applications LLC .... E 513 248-5588
  Milford (G-14559)

RESEARCH, DEVELOPMENT & TEST SVCS, COMM: Cmptr Hardware Dev

- Aktion Associates Incorporated .... E 419 893-7001
  Maumee (G-13873)

RESEARCH, DEVELOPMENT & TEST SVCS, COMM: Research, Exc Lab

- Alphamicron Inc .... E 330 676-0648
  Kent (G-12351)
- Division of Geological Survey .... E 614 265-6576
  Columbus (G-7531)
- Dwight Spencer & Associates .... E 614 488-3123
  Columbus (G-7554)
- Ohio State University .... E 614 292-9404
  Columbus (G-8435)

RESEARCH, DEVELOPMENT & TESTING SVCS, COMM: Agricultural

- Champaign Premium Grn Growers ...... E 937 826-3003
  Milford Center (G-14575)
- Ohio State University .... A 330 263-3700
  Wooster (G-19898)
- Ohio State University .... E 330 263-3725
  Canton (G-2485)

RESEARCH, DEVELOPMENT & TESTING SVCS, COMM: Bus Economic Sve

- Illumination Research Inc .... E 513 774-9531
  Mason (G-13719)

RESEARCH, DEVELOPMENT & TESTING SVCS, COMM: Natural Resource

- Work Connections Intl LLC .... E 419 448-4655
  Tiffin (G-17709)

RESEARCH, DEVELOPMENT & TESTING SVCS, COMM: Research Lab

- Akron Rubber Dev Lab Inc .... D 330 794-6600
  Akron (G-54)
- American Showa Inc .... E 740 965-4040
  Sunbury (G-17549)
- Applied Sciences Inc .... E 937 766-2020
  Cedarville (G-2631)
- First Energy Nuclear Oper Co .... D 440 604-9836
  Cleveland (G-5595)
- PPG Architectural Finishes Inc .... B 440 826-5100
  Strongsville (G-17500)

RESEARCH, DEVELOPMENT & TESTING SVCS, COMM: Sociological

- Klein Associates Inc .... E 937 873-8166
  Fairborn (G-10801)

RESEARCH, DEVELOPMENT & TESTING SVCS, COMMERCIAL: Business

- Business Research Services .... E 216 831-5200
  Cleveland (G-5163)
- Lindner Clinical Trial Center .... E 513 585-1777
  Cincinnati (G-3987)
- Rebiz LLC .... E 844 467-3249
  Cleveland (G-6360)

RESEARCH, DEVELOPMENT & TESTING SVCS, COMMERCIAL: Economic

- Mahoning Youngstown Community ..... E 330 747-5661
  Youngstown (G-20267)
- Mahoning Youngstown Community ..... D 330 747-7921
  Youngstown (G-20268)
- Ohio State University .... D 614 442-7300
  Columbus (G-8414)

RESEARCH, DEVELOPMENT & TESTING SVCS, COMMERCIAL: Education

- Canton Med Educatn Foundation .... E 330 363-6783
  Canton (G-2292)
- Ohio State University .... D 740 376-7431
  Marietta (G-13481)
- Ohio State University .... D 740 593-2657
  Athens (G-803)
- Ohio State University .... D 614 292-4353
  Columbus (G-8410)
- Ohio State University .... D 614 292-5491
  Columbus (G-8398)
- University of Cincinnati .... E 513 556-4054
  Cincinnati (G-4765)

RESEARCH, DEVELOPMENT & TESTING SVCS, COMMERCIAL: Energy

- Lg Fuel Cell Systems Inc .... E 330 491-4800
  Canton (G-2435)
- Phycal Inc .... E 440 460-2477
  Cleveland (G-6277)

RESEARCH, DEVELOPMENT & TESTING SVCS, COMMERCIAL: Food

- R & D Nestle Center Inc .... C 937 642-7015
  Marysville (G-13646)

RESEARCH, DEVELOPMENT & TESTING SVCS, COMMERCIAL: Medical

- Applied Medical Technology Inc .... E 440 717-4000
  Brecksville (G-1813)
- Center For Eating Disorders .... E 614 896-8222
  Columbus (G-7225)
- Clinical Research MGT Inc .... B 330 278-2343
  Hinckley (G-11996)
- Concord Biosciences LLC .... D 440 357-3200
  Painesville (G-15845)
- Inc Research LLC .... C 513 381-5550
  Cincinnati (G-3812)
- North Amercn Science Assoc Inc .... C 419 666-9455
  Northwood (G-15539)
- North Amercn Science Assoc Inc .... C 419 666-9455
  Northwood (G-15540)

RESEARCH, DEVELOPMENT & TESTING SVCS, COMMERCIAL: Physical

- Atk Space Systems Inc .... E 937 490-4121
  Beavercreek (G-1228)
- Battelle Memorial Institute .... A 614 424-6424
  Columbus (G-7092)
- Battelle Memorial Institute .... E 937 254-0880
  Dayton (G-9257)
- Battelle Memorial Institute .... B 614 424-5435
  West Jefferson (G-19248)
- Battelle Memorial Institute .... C 614 424-5435
  West Jefferson (G-19249)
- Charles Rver Labs Clveland Inc .... D 216 332-1665
  Cleveland (G-5228)
- Ftech R&D North America Inc .... D 937 339-2777
  Troy (G-18354)
- Leidos Inc .... E 330 405-9810
  Twinsburg (G-18440)
- Lubrizol Advanced Mtls Inc .... E 440 933-0400
  Avon Lake (G-934)
- Olon Ricerca Bioscience LLC .... D 440 357-3300
  Painesville (G-15869)
- Velocys Inc .... D 614 733-3300
  Plain City (G-16211)

RESEARCH, DVLPT & TEST SVCS, COMM: Mkt Analysis or Research

- 8451 LLC .... C 513 632-1020
  Cincinnati (G-2949)
- Assistnce In Mktg Columbus Inc .... E 614 583-2100
  Columbus (G-7053)
- Azg Inc .... D 419 724-3000
  Perrysburg (G-15974)
- Burke Inc .... D 513 576-5700
  Milford (G-14507)
- Burke Inc .... E 513 241-5663
  Cincinnati (G-3150)
- Convergys Cstmer MGT Group Inc ...... B 513 723-6104
  Cincinnati (G-3418)
- Creative Marketing Enterprises .... D 419 867-4444
  Sylvania (G-17580)
- Curator Video LLC .... E 513 842-6605
  Blue Ash (G-1574)
- Deskey Associates Inc .... D 513 721-6800
  Cincinnati (G-3484)
- Directions Research Inc .... C 513 651-2990
  Cincinnati (G-3493)
- Douglas Webb & Associates .... D 614 873-9830
  Plain City (G-16188)
- Fields Marketing Research Inc .... D 513 821-6266
  Cincinnati (G-3604)
- Freedonia Publishing LLC .... D 440 684-9600
  Cleveland (G-5636)
- Friedman-Swift Associates Inc .... D 513 772-9200
  Cincinnati (G-3655)
- Gfk Custom Research LLC .... C 513 562-1507
  Blue Ash (G-1600)
- Great Lakes Mktg Assoc Inc .... E 419 534-4700
  Toledo (G-17922)
- Honda R&D Americas Inc .... E 937 644-0439
  Raymond (G-16420)
- Intelliq Health .... D 513 489-8838
  Cincinnati (G-3829)
- Ipsos-Insight LLC .... C 513 552-1100
  Cincinnati (G-3843)
- Leidos Inc .... B 937 431-2220
  Beavercreek (G-1185)
- Maritzcx Research LLC .... B 419 725-4000
  Maumee (G-13941)
- Market Inquiry Llc .... E 513 794-1088
  Blue Ash (G-1634)
- Marketing Research Svcs Inc .... D 513 579-1555
  Cincinnati (G-4023)
- Marketvision Research Inc .... E 513 603-6340
  West Chester (G-19116)
- Marketvision Research Inc .... D 513 791-3100
  Blue Ash (G-1635)
- Nielsen Consumer Insights Inc .... D 513 489-9000
  Blue Ash (G-1652)
- Northrop Grumman Technical .... C 937 320-3100
  Beavercreek Township (G-1276)
- Opinions Ltd .... E 440 893-0300
  Chagrin Falls (G-2703)
- Orc International Inc .... D 513 579-1555
  Cincinnati (G-4231)
- Osborn Marketing Research Corp .... E 440 871-1047
  Westlake (G-19531)
- Q Fact Marketing Research Inc .... C 513 891-2271
  Cincinnati (G-4358)
- Quality Solutions Inc .... E 440 933-9946
  Cleveland (G-6335)
- Ritter & Associates Inc .... E 419 535-5757
  Maumee (G-13972)
- SSS Consulting Inc .... E 937 259-1200
  Dayton (G-9901)
- Strategic Consumer Research .... E 216 261-0308
  Mentor On The Lake (G-14262)
- Tns North America Inc .... D 513 621-7887
  Cincinnati (G-4661)
- Various Views Research Inc .... D 513 489-9000
  Blue Ash (G-1715)
- Wolf Sensory Inc .... E 513 891-9100
  Blue Ash (G-1720)

RESEARCH, DVLPT & TESTING SVCS, COMM: Mkt, Bus & Economic

- Bionetics Corporation .... E 757 873-0900
  Heath (G-11835)
- National Rgstry Emrgncy Mdcl .... E 614 888-4484
  Columbus (G-8224)

RESEARCH, DVLPT & TESTING SVCS, COMM: Survey, Mktg

- Orc International Inc .... E 419 893-0029
  Maumee (G-13954)

RESIDENTIAL CARE FOR CHILDREN

- Nickolas Rsidential Trtmnt Ctr .... E 937 496-7100
  Dayton (G-9774)

RESIDENTIAL CARE FOR THE HANDICAPPED

- Ability Ctr of Greater Toledo .... E 419 517-7123
  Sylvania (G-17575)
- Donty Horton HM Care Dhhc LLC .... E 513 463-3442
  Cincinnati (G-3499)

Flat Rock Care Center .... C 419 483-7330
Flat Rock *(G-11103)*
New England Rms Inc .... E 401 384-6759
Worthington *(G-19979)*
Pine Ridge Pine Vllg Resdntl H .... E 513 724-3460
Williamsburg *(G-19634)*
Residential Management Systems .... E 419 222-8806
Lima *(G-12867)*
Residential Management Systems .... D 419 255-6060
Maumee *(G-13969)*
St Vincent Family Centers .... C 614 252-0731
Columbus *(G-8771)*
Stonewood Residential Inc .... E 216 267-9777
Cleveland *(G-6542)*

RESIDENTIAL MENTAL HEALTH & SUBSTANCE ABUSE FACILITIES

A&L Home Care & Training Ctr .... C 740 886-7623
Proctorville *(G-16357)*
Ahf Ohio Inc .... D 330 725-4123
Medina *(G-14033)*
Ahf Ohio Inc .... D 614 760-8870
Dublin *(G-10237)*
Ahf Ohio Inc .... D 937 256-4663
Dayton *(G-9313)*
American Nursing Care Inc .... C 614 847-0555
Zanesville *(G-20441)*
American Retirement Corp .... D 216 321-6331
Cleveland *(G-5022)*
Arbors At Clide Asssted Living .... E 419 547-7746
Clyde *(G-6808)*
Archdiocese of Cincinnati .... E 513 231-5010
Cincinnati *(G-3042)*
Broadway Care Ctr Mple Hts LLC .... E 216 662-0551
Maple Heights *(G-13401)*
Capital Senior Living Corp .... C 419 874-2564
Perrysburg *(G-15983)*
Capital Senior Living Corp .... C 216 289-9800
Richmond Heights *(G-16536)*
Cardinal Retirement Village .... E 330 928-7888
Cuyahoga Falls *(G-9168)*
Carriage Court Company Inc .... E 740 654-4422
Lancaster *(G-12514)*
Childrens Cmprhensive Svcs Inc .... D 419 589-5511
Mansfield *(G-13276)*
Choices For Vctims Dom Volence .... D 614 258-6080
Columbus *(G-7267)*
Church of God Retirement Cmnty .... C 513 422-5600
Middletown *(G-14420)*
Cleveland Christian Home Inc .... C 216 671-0977
Cleveland *(G-5294)*
Cleveland Municipal School Dst .... C 216 459-9818
Cleveland *(G-5338)*
Close To Home III .... E 740 534-1100
Ironton *(G-12286)*
Cornell Companies Inc .... C 419 747-3322
Shelby *(G-16898)*
County of Hancock .... D 419 424-7050
Findlay *(G-11017)*
Crossroads Center .... C 513 475-5300
Cincinnati *(G-3442)*
Crystalwood Inc .... D 513 605-1000
Cincinnati *(G-3443)*
D-R Training Center & Workshop .... C 419 289-0470
Ashland *(G-678)*
Deaconess Long Term Care of MI .... A 513 487-3600
Cincinnati *(G-3474)*
Domestic Violence Project Inc .... E 330 445-2000
Canton *(G-2343)*
Drake Development Inc .... D 513 418-4370
Cincinnati *(G-3502)*
Echoing Hills Village Inc .... D 740 594-3541
Athens *(G-785)*
Echoing Hills Village Inc .... A 740 327-2311
Warsaw *(G-18936)*
Embracing Autism Inc .... E 614 559-0077
Columbus *(G-7590)*
Emeritus Corporation .... D 440 201-9200
Cleveland *(G-5535)*
Emeritus Corporation .... E 440 269-8600
Willoughby *(G-19661)*
Extended Family Concepts Inc .... E 330 966-2555
Canton *(G-2361)*
First Mental Retardation Corp .... E 937 262-3077
Dayton *(G-9549)*
Friedman Vlg Retirement Cmnty .... E 419 443-1540
Tiffin *(G-17680)*
Furney Group Home .... E 419 389-0152
Toledo *(G-17902)*
Garden Manor Extended Care Cen .... C 513 420-5972
Middletown *(G-14426)*
Gerspacher Companies .... E 330 725-1596
Medina *(G-14070)*
Greenbrier Senior Living Cmnty .... D 440 888-0400
Cleveland *(G-5703)*
Harmony Home Care Inc .... E 440 243-1332
North Royalton *(G-15493)*
Havar Inc .... D 740 594-3533
Athens *(G-790)*
Heinzerling Foundation .... A 614 272-2000
Columbus *(G-7822)*
Hill Manor 1 Inc .... E 740 972-3227
Columbus *(G-7836)*
Judson .... D 216 791-2555
Cleveland *(G-5877)*
Kingston Healthcare Company .... D 419 824-4200
Sylvania *(G-17598)*
Larchwood Health Group LLC .... E 216 941-6100
Cleveland *(G-5926)*
Lutheran Village At Wolf Creek .... C 419 861-2233
Holland *(G-12033)*
Maple Knoll Communities Inc .... E 513 524-7990
Oxford *(G-15817)*
Mulberry Garden A L S .... E 330 630-3980
Munroe Falls *(G-14932)*
National Benevolent Associatio .... D 216 476-0333
Cleveland *(G-6101)*
National Mentor Inc .... E 216 525-1885
Cleveland *(G-6111)*
Newark Resident Homes Inc .... D 740 345-7231
Newark *(G-15222)*
North Cntl Mntal Hlth Svcs Inc .... D 614 227-6865
Columbus *(G-8288)*
North Hills Management Company .... D 740 450-9999
Zanesville *(G-20517)*
Oesterlen-Services For Youth .... C 937 399-6101
Springfield *(G-17254)*
Otterbein Snior Lfstyle Chices .... C 419 394-2366
Saint Marys *(G-16682)*
Parkcliffe Development .... D 419 381-9447
Toledo *(G-18118)*
Providence House Inc .... E 216 651-5982
Cleveland *(G-6326)*
Rehabltion Ctr At Mrietta Mem .... D 740 374-1407
Marietta *(G-13493)*
Rescue Incorporated .... C 419 255-9585
Toledo *(G-18153)*
Saint Johns Villa .... C 330 627-4662
Carrollton *(G-2628)*
Second Mental Retardation .... E 937 262-3077
Dayton *(G-9872)*
Select Spclty Hsptal-Akron LLC .... D 330 761-7500
Akron *(G-433)*
Shalom House Inc .... E 614 239-1999
Columbus *(G-8722)*
Shurmer Place At Altenheim .... E 440 238-9001
Strongsville *(G-17509)*
Society For Handicapped Citzns .... E 937 746-4201
Carlisle *(G-2606)*
Southast Cmnty Mental Hlth Ctr .... C 614 225-0980
Columbus *(G-8751)*
St Edward Home .... C 330 668-2828
Fairlawn *(G-10977)*
Stone Gardens .... D 216 292-0070
Cleveland *(G-6541)*
Style Crest Inc .... B 419 332-7369
Fremont *(G-11223)*
Summerville Senior Living Inc .... D 440 354-5499
Mentor *(G-14246)*
Sunrise Senior Living Inc .... E 614 418-9775
Gahanna *(G-11272)*
Sunrise Senior Living LLC .... E 330 707-1313
Poland *(G-16228)*
Sunrise Senior Living LLC .... E 330 262-1615
Wooster *(G-19917)*
Sunrise Senior Living LLC .... E 419 425-3440
Findlay *(G-11088)*
Sunrise Senior Living LLC .... E 216 447-8909
Cleveland *(G-6552)*
Traditions At Bath Rd Inc .... C 330 929-6272
Cuyahoga Falls *(G-9226)*
Trilogy Health Services LLC .... D 419 935-6511
Willard *(G-19628)*
Wallick Construction Co .... E 937 399-7009
Springfield *(G-17295)*
Wesleyan Senior Living .... D 440 284-9000
Elyria *(G-10689)*
Widows Home of Dayton Ohio .... D 937 252-1661
Dayton *(G-9997)*
Wood County Chld Svcs Assn .... D 419 352-7588
Bowling Green *(G-1798)*
Zandex Health Care Corporation .... C 740 454-1400
New Concord *(G-15041)*

RESIDENTIAL MENTALLY HANDICAPPED FACILITIES

599 W Main Corporation .... E 440 466-5901
Geneva *(G-11357)*
Angels 4 Life LLC .... E 513 474-5683
Cincinnati *(G-3029)*
Beeghly Oaks Operating LLC .... C 330 884-2300
Boardman *(G-1738)*
Boyds Kinsman Home Inc .... E 330 876-5581
Kinsman *(G-12453)*
Center For Eating Disorders .... E 614 896-8222
Columbus *(G-7225)*
Childrens Forever Haven Inc .... E 440 250-9182
Westlake *(G-19474)*
Community Assisted Living Inc .... E 740 653-2575
Lancaster *(G-12522)*
County of Montgomery .... B 937 264-0460
Dayton *(G-9434)*
Elmwood Center Inc .... D 419 447-6885
Tiffin *(G-17677)*
Foundations .... D 937 437-2311
New Paris *(G-15077)*
Harbor .... E 800 444-3353
Toledo *(G-17934)*
Leeda Services Inc .... E 330 392-6006
Warren *(G-18874)*
Lucas County Board of Developm .... D 419 380-4000
Toledo *(G-18017)*
Mental Health Service .... E 937 399-9500
Springfield *(G-17232)*
Miami Valley Hsing Assn I Inc .... E 937 263-4449
Dayton *(G-9735)*
North Point Eductl Svc Ctr .... E 440 967-0904
Huron *(G-12168)*
Places Inc .... D 937 461-4300
Dayton *(G-9810)*
Protem Homecare LLC .... E 216 663-8188
Cleveland *(G-6324)*
RES-Care Inc .... E 740 526-0285
Saint Clairsville *(G-16655)*
RES-Care Inc .... E 513 858-4550
West Chester *(G-19139)*
RES-Care Inc .... E 740 968-0181
Flushing *(G-11106)*
RES-Care Inc .... E 330 627-7552
Carrollton *(G-2626)*
RES-Care Inc .... E 740 941-1178
Waverly *(G-18975)*
RES-Care Inc .... E 419 435-6620
Fostoria *(G-11138)*
RES-Care Inc .... D 740 446-7549
Gallipolis *(G-11337)*
RES-Care Inc .... E 330 453-4144
Canton *(G-2510)*
Residential Concepts Inc .... E 513 724-6067
Williamsburg *(G-19636)*
St Joseph Infant Maternity Hm .... C 513 563-2520
Cincinnati *(G-4572)*
Supportcare Inc .... C 216 446-2650
Independence *(G-12263)*
Triad Residential .... E 419 482-0711
Maumee *(G-13988)*
Vista Centre .... D 330 424-5852
Lisbon *(G-12942)*
Voca of Ohio .... E 419 435-5836
Fostoria *(G-11142)*
Warren County Board Devlpmntal .... E 513 925-1813
Lebanon *(G-12658)*
Willglo Services Inc .... E 614 443-3020
Columbus *(G-8994)*

RESIDENTIAL REMODELERS

Dun Rite Home Improvement Inc .... E 330 650-5322
Macedonia *(G-13196)*
Hays & Sons Construction Inc .... E 513 671-9110
Cincinnati *(G-3743)*
Menard Inc .... C 937 630-3550
Miamisburg *(G-14317)*
Menard Inc .... C 513 737-2204
Fairfield Township *(G-10934)*
Ohio Builders Resources LLC .... E 614 865-0306
Westerville *(G-19336)*
Ram Restoration LLC .... E 937 347-7418
Dayton *(G-9841)*

SERVICES SECTION

Residntial Coml Rnovations Inc .... E 330 815-1476
  Clinton *(G-6807)*
Runyon & Sons Roofing Inc .... D 440 974-6810
  Mentor *(G-14238)*
US Home Center LLC .... E 614 737-9000
  Columbus *(G-8924)*

RESINS: Custom Compound Purchased

Flex Technologies Inc .... E 330 897-6311
  Baltic *(G-945)*
Freeman Manufacturing & Sup Co .... E 440 934-1902
  Avon *(G-893)*
Hexpol Compounding LLC .... C 440 834-4644
  Burton *(G-2062)*
Polyone Corporation .... D 440 930-1000
  Avon Lake *(G-937)*
Polyone Corporation .... D 440 930-1000
  North Baltimore *(G-15315)*

RESORT HOTEL: Franchised

Aurora Hotel Partners LLC .... E 330 562-0767
  Aurora *(G-826)*
Columbus Hotel Partnership LLC .... D 614 890-8600
  Columbus *(G-7359)*
Fh TCH .... E 614 781-1645
  Powell *(G-16334)*
Seal Mayfield LLC .... E 440 684-4100
  Mayfield Heights *(G-14007)*

RESORT HOTELS

Cardida Corporation .... E 740 439-4359
  Kimbolton *(G-12446)*
Cedar Point Park LLC .... D 419 627-2500
  Sandusky *(G-16735)*
Clp Gw Sandusky Tenant LP .... B 419 609-6000
  Sandusky *(G-16741)*
Coshocton Village Inn Suites .... E 740 622-9455
  Coshocton *(G-9098)*
Crefiii Waramaug .... D 937 322-3600
  Springfield *(G-17184)*
Findlay Inn & Conference Ctr .... D 419 422-5682
  Findlay *(G-11027)*
Great Bear Lodge Sandusky LLC .... B 419 609-6000
  Sandusky *(G-16765)*
Hide-A-Way Hills Club .... E 740 746-9589
  Sugar Grove *(G-17541)*
Home2 By Hilton .... E 513 422-3454
  West Chester *(G-19091)*
Hopkins Partners .... C 216 267-1500
  Cleveland *(G-5772)*
Hotel 50 S Front Opco LP .... D 614 228-4600
  Columbus *(G-7860)*
Lmn Development LLC .... D 419 433-7200
  Sandusky *(G-16775)*
Olshan Hotel Management Inc .... E 614 416-8000
  Columbus *(G-8468)*
Qh Management Company LLC .... D 440 497-1100
  Concord Twp *(G-9034)*
Radius Hospitality MGT LLC .... D 330 735-2211
  Sherrodsville *(G-16906)*
Salt Fork Resort Club Inc .... A 740 498-8116
  Kimbolton *(G-12447)*
Sawmill Creek Resort Ltd .... C 419 433-3800
  Huron *(G-12172)*
South Beach Resort .... E 419 798-4900
  Lakeside Marblehead *(G-12466)*
Xanterra Parks & Resorts Inc .... C 740 439-2751
  Cambridge *(G-2134)*
Xanterra Parks & Resorts Inc .... E 419 836-1466
  Oregon *(G-15755)*
Xanterra Parks & Resorts Inc .... C 740 869-2020
  Mount Sterling *(G-14876)*
Xanterra Parks & Resorts Inc .... D 440 564-9144
  Newbury *(G-15265)*

RESPIRATORY THERAPY CLINIC

Genesis Respiratory Svcs Inc .... D 740 354-4363
  Portsmouth *(G-16278)*

REST HOME, WITH HEALTH CARE INCIDENTAL

Autumn Health Care Inc .... E 740 366-2321
  Newark *(G-15145)*
Benjamin Rose Institute .... D 216 791-3580
  Cleveland *(G-5116)*
Bradley Bay Assisted Living .... E 440 871-4509
  Bay Village *(G-1038)*

C Micah Rand Inc .... C 513 605-2000
  Cincinnati *(G-3162)*
Copeland Oaks .... B 330 938-6126
  Sebring *(G-16821)*
County of Medina .... E 330 723-9553
  Medina *(G-14053)*
Laurel Lk Retirement Cmnty Inc .... B 330 650-0681
  Hudson *(G-12130)*
Ohio Living .... E 614 888-7800
  Columbus *(G-8358)*
Ohio Presbt Retirement Svcs .... E 513 539-7391
  Monroe *(G-14708)*
Primrose Rtrment Cmmnities LLC .... E 419 224-1200
  Lima *(G-12862)*
Roman Cthlic Docese Youngstown .... C 330 875-5562
  Louisville *(G-13106)*
Ursuline Convent Sacred Heart .... E 419 531-8990
  Toledo *(G-18283)*

RESTAURANT EQPT REPAIR SVCS

Cov-Ro Inc .... E 330 856-3176
  Warren *(G-18841)*
Harry C Lobalzo & Sons Inc .... E 330 666-6758
  Akron *(G-253)*
Kens Beverage Inc .... E 513 874-8200
  Fairfield *(G-10869)*

RESTAURANTS: Fast Food

Escape Enterprises Inc .... E 614 224-0300
  Columbus *(G-7609)*
Marcus Theatres Corporation .... D 614 436-9818
  Columbus *(G-8108)*
Winking Lizard Inc .... D 330 220-9944
  Brunswick *(G-1998)*

RESTAURANTS:Full Svc, American

Aurora Hotel Partners LLC .... E 330 562-0767
  Aurora *(G-826)*
Bass Lake Tavern Inc .... D 440 285-3100
  Chardon *(G-2741)*
Beverly Hills Inn La Llc .... E 859 494-9151
  Aberdeen *(G-1)*
City Life Inc .... C 216 523-5899
  Cleveland *(G-5246)*
Concord Dayton Hotel II LLC .... D 937 223-1000
  Dayton *(G-9422)*
Connor Concepts Inc .... E 937 291-1661
  Dayton *(G-9423)*
Cork Enterprises Inc .... E 740 654-1842
  Lancaster *(G-12523)*
Crefiii Waramaug .... D 937 322-3600
  Springfield *(G-17184)*
Durga Llc .... D 513 771-2080
  Cincinnati *(G-3515)*
Elms Country Club Inc .... E 330 833-2668
  North Lawrence *(G-15392)*
Epiqurian Inns .... D 614 885-2600
  Worthington *(G-19957)*
Henderson Road Rest Systems .... E 614 442-3310
  Columbus *(G-7825)*
Hrm Enterprises Inc .... E 330 877-9353
  Hartville *(G-11823)*
Mackil Inc .... E 937 833-3310
  Brookville *(G-1964)*
Oberlin College .... D 440 935-1475
  Oberlin *(G-15656)*
Paul A Ertel .... D 216 696-8888
  Cleveland *(G-6252)*
River Road Hotel Corp .... E 614 267-7461
  Columbus *(G-8634)*
Robert C Verbon Inc .... E 419 867-6868
  Toledo *(G-18160)*
Sam BS Restaurant .... E 419 353-2277
  Bowling Green *(G-1793)*
Stockport Mill Country Inn Inc .... E 740 559-2822
  Stockport *(G-17346)*
Town House Motor Lodge Corp .... E 740 452-4511
  Zanesville *(G-20539)*
Travelcenters of America LLC .... A 440 808-9100
  Westlake *(G-19557)*

RESTAURANTS:Full Svc, Diner

Hyatt Corporation .... B 614 463-1234
  Columbus *(G-7874)*

RESTAURANTS:Full Svc, Ethnic Food

Tappan Lake Marina Inc .... E 740 269-2031
  Scio *(G-16817)*

RESTAURANTS:Full Svc, Family

Bistro Off Broadway .... E 937 316-5000
  Greenville *(G-11489)*
Buffalo Jacks .... E 937 473-2524
  Covington *(G-9136)*
Mason Family Resorts LLC .... B 513 339-0141
  Mason *(G-13736)*
R P L Corporation .... C 937 335-0021
  Troy *(G-18373)*
Sb Hotel LLC .... E 614 793-2244
  Dublin *(G-10449)*
Valley Hospitality Inc .... E 740 374-9660
  Marietta *(G-13513)*

RESTAURANTS:Full Svc, Family, Chain

Bennett Enterprises Inc .... B 419 874-3111
  Perrysburg *(G-15978)*
Dino Persichetti .... E 330 821-9600
  Alliance *(G-538)*
Fairlawn Associates Ltd .... C 330 867-5000
  Fairlawn *(G-10949)*
Island House Inc .... E 419 734-0100
  Port Clinton *(G-16248)*
Red Robin Gourmet Burgers Inc .... D 330 305-1080
  Canton *(G-2505)*
Roscoe Village Foundation .... D 740 622-2222
  Coshocton *(G-9116)*
Skylane LLC .... E 330 527-9999
  Garrettsville *(G-11352)*
Skyline Chili Inc .... C 513 874-1188
  Fairfield *(G-10910)*

RESTAURANTS:Full Svc, Family, Independent

AK Group Hotels Inc .... E 937 372-9921
  Xenia *(G-20040)*
Alsan Corporation .... D 330 385-3636
  East Liverpool *(G-10514)*
Amish Door Inc .... B 330 359-5464
  Wilmot *(G-19797)*
Bird Enterprises LLC .... E 330 674-1457
  Millersburg *(G-14589)*
Cherry Valley Lodge .... E 740 788-1200
  Newark *(G-15156)*
Detroit Westfield LLC .... D 330 666-4131
  Akron *(G-190)*
Granville Hospitality Llc .... D 740 587-3333
  Granville *(G-11466)*
Lees Roby Inc .... E 330 872-0983
  Newton Falls *(G-15276)*
Louisville Frternal Order of E .... E 330 875-2113
  Louisville *(G-13102)*
Moundbuilders Country Club Co .... D 740 344-4500
  Newark *(G-15213)*
Old Barn Out Back Inc .... D 419 999-3989
  Lima *(G-12848)*
Riverside Cmnty Urban Redev .... C 330 929-3000
  Cuyahoga Falls *(G-9215)*
Sauder Village .... B 419 446-2541
  Archbold *(G-644)*
Shoreby Club Inc .... C 216 851-2587
  Cleveland *(G-6479)*
The Oaks Lodge .... E 330 769-2601
  Chippewa Lake *(G-2899)*

RESTAURANTS:Full Svc, French

Refectory Restaurant Inc .... E 614 451-9774
  Columbus *(G-8602)*

RESTAURANTS:Full Svc, Italian

Cabin Restaurant .... E 330 562-9171
  Aurora *(G-832)*
Carrie Cerino Restaurants Inc .... C 440 237-3434
  Cleveland *(G-5186)*
Dutchman Hospitality Group Inc .... C 614 873-3414
  Plain City *(G-16189)*
Leos La Piazza Inc .... E 937 339-5553
  Troy *(G-18361)*
Marios International Spa & Ht .... C 330 562-5141
  Aurora *(G-846)*
Spagnas .... E 740 376-9245
  Marietta *(G-13501)*

RESTAURANTS:Full Svc, Mexican

Food Concepts Intl Inc .... D 513 336-7449
  Mason *(G-13701)*

RESTAURANTS:Full Svc, Seafood

James Lafontaine.................................E....... 740 474-5052
Circleville (G-4891)

RESTAURANTS:Full Svc, Steak

Brown Derby Roadhouse.....................E....... 330 528-3227
Hudson (G-12105)

RESTAURANTS:Full Svc, Steak & Barbecue

101 River Inc...E....... 440 352-6343
Grand River (G-11455)

RESTAURANTS:Limited Svc, Box Lunch Stand

Sand Ridge Golf Club............................D....... 440 285-8088
Chardon (G-2767)

RESTAURANTS:Limited Svc, Carry-Out Only, Exc Pizza

Tony Packos Toledo LLC......................D....... 419 691-6054
Toledo (G-18257)

RESTAURANTS:Limited Svc, Chicken

Travelcenters of America LLC...............B....... 724 981-9464
Westlake (G-19556)

RESTAURANTS:Limited Svc, Coffee Shop

Mocha House Inc..................................E....... 330 392-3020
Warren (G-18882)

RESTAURANTS:Limited Svc, Fast-Food, Chain

D J- Seve Group Inc..............................E....... 614 888-6600
Lewis Center (G-12680)
McDonalds Corporation.........................E....... 614 682-1128
Columbus (G-8135)
Pam Johnsonident.................................D....... 419 946-4551
Mount Gilead (G-14861)
Wendys Company..................................B....... 614 764-3100
Dublin (G-10491)
Wendys Restaurants LLC....................C....... 614 764-3100
Dublin (G-10492)
White Castle System Inc......................B....... 614 228-5781
Columbus (G-8986)

RESTAURANTS:Limited Svc, Fast-Food, Independent

McDonalds 3490....................................E....... 330 762-7747
Akron (G-333)
Skateworld Inc......................................E....... 937 294-4032
Dayton (G-9885)

RESTAURANTS:Limited Svc, Grill

Gosh Enterprises Inc............................E....... 614 923-4700
Columbus (G-7762)
OBannon Creek Golf Club.....................E....... 513 683-5657
Loveland (G-13151)
Rivals Sports Grille LLC.......................E....... 216 267-0005
Middleburg Heights (G-14386)
Waterfront & Associates Inc................B....... 859 581-1414
Cincinnati (G-4824)

RESTAURANTS:Limited Svc, Ice Cream Stands Or Dairy Bars

Cleveland Dairy Queen Inc....................C....... 440 946-3690
Willoughby (G-19654)
North Lima Dairy Queen Inc.................E....... 330 549-3220
North Lima (G-15406)
Strike Zone Inc.....................................D....... 440 235-4420
Olmsted Twp (G-15681)
Youngs Jersey Dairy Inc......................B....... 937 325-0629
Yellow Springs (G-20091)

RESTAURANTS:Limited Svc, Lunch Counter

Bpo Elks of USA....................................E....... 740 622-0794
Coshocton (G-9089)

RESTAURANTS:Limited Svc, Pizza

Claire De Leigh Corp............................E....... 614 459-6575
Columbus (G-7289)

Georgetown Vineyards Inc....................E....... 740 435-3222
Cambridge (G-2115)
Premier Broadcasting Co Inc................E....... 614 866-0700
Columbus (G-8555)

RESTAURANTS:Limited Svc, Pizzeria, Chain

Cassanos Inc..E....... 937 294-8400
Dayton (G-9388)
Cec Entertainment Inc.........................D....... 937 439-1108
Miamisburg (G-14280)
East of Chicago Pizza Inc.....................E....... 419 225-7116
Lima (G-12771)
Larosas Inc...A....... 513 347-5660
Cincinnati (G-3962)
Marcos Inc..C....... 419 885-4844
Toledo (G-18042)

RESTAURANTS:Limited Svc, Pizzeria, Independent

Fat Jacks Pizza II Inc............................E....... 419 227-1813
Lima (G-12779)

RESTAURANTS:Ltd Svc, Ice Cream, Soft Drink/Fountain Stands

David W Milliken....................................E....... 740 998-5023
Frankfort (G-11145)

RESTROOM CLEANING SVCS

Corporate Cleaning Inc.........................E....... 614 203-6051
Columbus (G-7441)
Image By J & K LLC..............................B....... 888 667-6929
Maumee (G-13927)
Living Matters LLC................................E....... 866 587-8074
Cleveland (G-5948)

RETAIL BAKERY: Bagels

Bagel Place Inc....................................E....... 419 885-1000
Toledo (G-17762)

RETAIL BAKERY: Bread

Busken Bakery Inc................................D....... 513 871-2114
Cincinnati (G-3157)
Covelli Family Ltd Partnership..............E....... 330 856-3176
Warren (G-18842)
Norcia Bakery.......................................E....... 330 454-1077
Canton (G-2474)
Schwebel Baking Company...................C....... 440 248-1500
Solon (G-17049)

RETAIL FIREPLACE STORES

Youngstown Propane Inc......................E....... 330 792-6571
Youngstown (G-20435)

RETAIL LUMBER YARDS

Asplundh Tree Expert Co......................B....... 740 435-4300
Cambridge (G-2097)
Carter-Jones Lumber Company...........C....... 330 673-6100
Kent (G-12355)
Carter-Jones Lumber Company...........D....... 330 784-5441
Akron (G-123)
Fifth Avenue Lumber Co.......................E....... 614 294-0068
Columbus (G-7654)
Gms Inc...E....... 937 222-4444
Dayton (G-9575)
Hwz Distribution Group LLC................E....... 513 723-1150
Cincinnati (G-3800)

RETAIL STORES: Alarm Signal Systems

Guardian Protection Svcs Inc..............E....... 330 797-1570
Youngstown (G-20211)
Northwestern Ohio SEC Systems........E....... 419 227-1655
Lima (G-12845)
Research & Investigation Assoc..........E....... 419 526-1299
Mansfield (G-13355)
State Alarm Inc....................................E....... 330 726-8111
Youngstown (G-20382)

RETAIL STORES: Alcoholic Beverage Making Eqpt & Splys

Gene Ptacek Son Fire Eqp Inc.............E....... 216 651-8300
Cleveland (G-5666)

RETAIL STORES: Audio-Visual Eqpt & Splys

Cleveland Corporate Svcs Inc..............C....... 216 397-1492
Cleveland (G-5310)
Findaway World LLC.............................D....... 440 893-0808
Solon (G-17007)

RETAIL STORES: Business Machines & Eqpt

Blakemans Valley Off Eqp Inc..............E....... 330 729-1000
Youngstown (G-20116)
Business Alternatives Inc....................E....... 724 325-2777
Uniontown (G-18509)
Cincinnati Copiers Inc..........................C....... 513 769-0606
Blue Ash (G-1556)
Modern Office Methods Inc..................E....... 614 891-3693
Westerville (G-19426)
Toshiba Amer Bus Solutions Inc.........E....... 216 642-7555
Cleveland (G-6603)

RETAIL STORES: Christmas Lights & Decorations

Donzells Flower & Grdn Ctr Inc...........E....... 330 724-0550
Akron (G-197)
McCoy Landscape Services Inc..........E....... 740 375-2730
Marion (G-13566)

RETAIL STORES: Communication Eqpt

Cellco Partnership................................D....... 330 345-6465
Wooster (G-19838)
Mobilcomm Inc......................................D....... 513 742-5555
Cincinnati (G-4110)
Professional Telecom Svcs..................E....... 513 232-7700
Cincinnati (G-4344)
Shawntech Communications Inc.........E....... 937 898-4900
Miamisburg (G-14350)

RETAIL STORES: Concrete Prdts, Precast

J B M Cleaning & Supply Co.................E....... 330 837-8805
Massillon (G-13825)

RETAIL STORES: Educational Aids & Electronic Training Mat

Bendon Inc..D....... 419 207-3600
Ashland (G-664)

RETAIL STORES: Electronic Parts & Eqpt

Ctd Investments LLC............................E....... 614 570-9949
Columbus (G-7473)
Mendelson Electronics Co Inc.............E....... 937 461-3525
Dayton (G-9718)

RETAIL STORES: Farm Eqpt & Splys

Carmichael Equipment Inc...................E....... 740 446-2412
Bidwell (G-1494)
Cope Farm Equipment Inc...................E....... 330 821-5867
Alliance (G-536)
Hull Bros Inc...E....... 419 375-2827
Fort Recovery (G-11118)
JD Equipment Inc.................................D....... 740 450-7446
Zanesville (G-20491)
JD Equipment Inc.................................D....... 614 527-8800
New Albany (G-14989)
Krystowski Tractor Sales Inc..............E....... 440 647-2015
Wellington (G-18993)
Streacker Tractor Sales Inc................E....... 419 422-6973
Findlay (G-11087)
Witmers Inc..E....... 330 427-2147
Salem (G-16719)

RETAIL STORES: Farm Machinery, NEC

Homan Inc...E....... 419 925-4349
Maria Stein (G-13428)
Kuester Implement Company Inc........E....... 740 944-1502
Bloomingdale (G-1517)
Lefeld Implement Inc...........................E....... 419 678-2375
Coldwater (G-6831)
Shearer Farm Inc.................................E....... 419 529-6160
Ontario (G-15712)

RETAIL STORES: Fiberglass Materials, Exc Insulation

Romitech Inc..E....... 937 297-9529
Dayton (G-9855)

SERVICES SECTION

RETAIL STORES: Fire Extinguishers

Johnson Controls .... D 614 602-2000
  Dublin *(G-10381)*
Koorsen Fire & Security Inc .... E 937 324-9405
  Vandalia *(G-18687)*

RETAIL STORES: Hair Care Prdts

G E G Enterprises Inc .... E 330 477-3133
  Canton *(G-2375)*
Mark Luikart Inc .... E 330 339-9141
  New Philadelphia *(G-15109)*
Salon Hazelton .... E 419 874-9404
  Perrysburg *(G-16055)*

RETAIL STORES: Hearing Aids

Nelson & Bold Inc .... E 440 975-1422
  Willoughby *(G-19696)*
United Rehabilitation Services .... D 937 233-1230
  Dayton *(G-9947)*
University Otolaryngologists .... E 614 273-2241
  Columbus *(G-8910)*

RETAIL STORES: Hospital Eqpt & Splys

Boardman Medical Supply Co .... C 330 545-6700
  Girard *(G-11408)*
Community Mercy Foundation .... D 937 328-8134
  Springfield *(G-17173)*
Garys Pharmacy Inc .... E 937 456-5777
  Eaton *(G-10561)*
Health Services Inc .... E 330 837-7678
  Massillon *(G-13818)*
Millers Rental and Sls Co Inc .... D 330 753-8600
  Akron *(G-345)*

RETAIL STORES: Ice

D & D Investment Co .... E 614 272-6567
  Columbus *(G-7476)*
Home City Ice Company .... E 614 836-2877
  Groveport *(G-11644)*

RETAIL STORES: Incontinent Care Prdts

Edwards Gem Inc .... D 330 342-8300
  Hudson *(G-12115)*

RETAIL STORES: Medical Apparatus & Splys

Advanced Medical Equipment Inc .... E 937 534-1080
  Kettering *(G-12426)*
American Home Health Care Inc .... E 614 237-1133
  Columbus *(G-6996)*
Amerimed Inc .... E 513 942-3670
  West Chester *(G-19019)*
Apria Healthcare LLC .... E 216 485-1180
  Cleveland *(G-5056)*
Fairfield Medical Center .... A 740 687-8000
  Lancaster *(G-12537)*
Genesis Respiratory Svcs Inc .... E 740 354-4363
  Portsmouth *(G-16278)*
Modern Medical Inc .... C 800 547-3330
  Westerville *(G-19329)*
Sarnova Inc .... D 614 760-5000
  Dublin *(G-10448)*
Sateri Home Inc .... D 330 758-8106
  Youngstown *(G-20367)*
Seeley Enterprises Company .... E 440 293-6600
  Andover *(G-614)*
Toledo Medical Equipment Co .... E 419 866-7120
  Maumee *(G-13987)*
University Mednet .... B 216 383-0100
  Euclid *(G-10780)*

RETAIL STORES: Mobile Telephones & Eqpt

Aka Wireless Inc .... E 216 213-8040
  Hartville *(G-11814)*
Cellco Partnership .... E 440 953-1155
  Mentor *(G-14155)*
Cellco Partnership .... E 440 646-9625
  Cleveland *(G-5203)*
Cellco Partnership .... E 440 846-8881
  Strongsville *(G-17448)*
Cellco Partnership .... E 740 397-6609
  Mount Vernon *(G-14881)*
Cellco Partnership .... E 614 459-7200
  Columbus *(G-7221)*
Cellco Partnership .... E 937 429-4000
  Beavercreek *(G-1158)*
Cellco Partnership .... E 513 671-2200
  Cincinnati *(G-3205)*
Cellco Partnership .... E 513 697-0222
  Cincinnati *(G-3206)*
Cellco Partnership .... E 740 522-6446
  Newark *(G-15155)*
Commercial Electronics Inc .... E 740 281-0180
  Newark *(G-15157)*
Magic Industries Inc .... E 614 759-8422
  Columbus *(G-8097)*

RETAIL STORES: Orthopedic & Prosthesis Applications

Blatchford Inc .... D 937 291-3636
  Miamisburg *(G-14276)*
Hanger Prosthetics & .... E 330 633-9807
  Tallmadge *(G-17638)*
Unity Health Network LLC .... E 330 626-0549
  Streetsboro *(G-17435)*

RETAIL STORES: Pet Food

Petsmart Inc .... E 513 752-8463
  Cincinnati *(G-2928)*
Petsmart Inc .... E 937 236-1335
  Huber Heights *(G-12098)*
Petsmart Inc .... D 614 418-9389
  Columbus *(G-8540)*
Petsmart Inc .... E 330 922-4114
  Cuyahoga Falls *(G-9212)*
Petsmart Inc .... E 330 629-2479
  Youngstown *(G-20318)*
Petsmart Inc .... E 330 544-1499
  Niles *(G-15303)*
Petsmart Inc .... E 614 497-3001
  Groveport *(G-11661)*
Petsmart Inc .... E 440 974-1100
  Mentor *(G-14228)*

RETAIL STORES: Pet Splys

Miraclecorp Products .... D 937 293-9994
  Moraine *(G-14808)*
Petsmart Inc .... E 513 248-4954
  Milford *(G-14553)*

RETAIL STORES: Photocopy Machines

ABC Appliance Inc .... E 419 693-4414
  Oregon *(G-15722)*
Donnellon Mc Carthy Inc .... E 937 299-0200
  Moraine *(G-14776)*
Woodhull LLC .... E 937 294-5311
  Springboro *(G-17143)*

RETAIL STORES: Picture Frames, Ready Made

Darice Inc .... C 440 238-9150
  Strongsville *(G-17456)*

RETAIL STORES: Plumbing & Heating Splys

Ferguson Enterprises Inc .... E 614 876-8555
  Hilliard *(G-11901)*
Gross Plumbing Incorporated .... E 440 324-9999
  Elyria *(G-10632)*
Horizon Mechanical and Elec .... E 419 529-2738
  Mansfield *(G-13309)*
Robertson Htg Sup Aliance Ohio .... C 330 821-9180
  Alliance *(G-554)*
Southtown Heating & Cooling .... E 937 320-9900
  Moraine *(G-14827)*

RETAIL STORES: Police Splys

Walter F Stephens Jr Inc .... E 937 746-0521
  Franklin *(G-11167)*

RETAIL STORES: Religious Goods

Christian Aid Ministries .... E 330 893-2428
  Millersburg *(G-14593)*

RETAIL STORES: Safety Splys & Eqpt

Area Wide Protective Inc .... E 614 272-7840
  Columbus *(G-7040)*
Paul Peterson Safety Div Inc .... E 614 486-4375
  Columbus *(G-8523)*

RETAIL STORES: Telephone & Communication Eqpt

Cellco Partnership .... E 419 843-2995
  Toledo *(G-17796)*
Cellco Partnership .... E 440 779-1313
  North Olmsted *(G-15412)*
High Line Corporation .... E 330 848-8800
  Akron *(G-264)*
Maximum Communications Inc .... E 513 489-3414
  Cincinnati *(G-4031)*

RETAIL STORES: Telephone Eqpt & Systems

C T Wireless .... D 937 653-2208
  Urbana *(G-18574)*
Cellco Partnership .... D 419 333-1009
  Fremont *(G-11187)*
Cellco Partnership .... E 419 424-2351
  Findlay *(G-11011)*
Cellco Partnership .... D 419 897-9133
  Maumee *(G-13892)*
Cellco Partnership .... E 330 493-7979
  Canton *(G-2302)*
Cellco Partnership .... E 216 573-5880
  Independence *(G-12195)*
Cellco Partnership .... E 614 793-8989
  Dublin *(G-10283)*
Chillicothe Telephone Company .... D 740 772-8361
  Chillicothe *(G-2826)*
Spectrum Networks Inc .... E 513 697-2000
  Cincinnati *(G-4560)*
Twin Comm Inc .... E 740 774-4701
  Marietta *(G-13508)*

RETAIL STORES: Theatrical Eqpt & Splys

Vincent Ltg Systems Co Inc .... E 216 475-7600
  Solon *(G-17065)*

RETAIL STORES: Tropical Fish

RMS Aquaculture Inc .... E 216 433-1340
  Cleveland *(G-6401)*

RETAIL STORES: Typewriters & Business Machines

Perry Pro Tech Inc .... D 419 228-1360
  Lima *(G-12857)*

RETAIL STORES: Water Purification Eqpt

Enting Water Conditioning Inc .... E 937 294-5100
  Moraine *(G-14781)*
Gordon Brothers Inc .... E 800 331-7611
  Salem *(G-16697)*
Great Lakes Water Treatment .... E 216 464-8292
  Cleveland *(G-5692)*

RETAIL STORES: Welding Splys

Albright Welding Supply Co Inc .... E 330 264-2021
  Wooster *(G-19826)*

RETIREMENT COMMUNITIES WITH NURSING

American Retirement Corp .... D 216 291-6140
  Cleveland *(G-5021)*
Berea Lk Twers Rtirement Cmnty .... E 440 243-9050
  Berea *(G-1449)*
Briarwood Ltd .... D 330 688-1828
  Stow *(G-17354)*
Brookdale Lving Cmmunities Inc .... E 937 399-1216
  Springfield *(G-17153)*
Brookdale Senior Living Commun .... E 330 829-0180
  Alliance *(G-528)*
Brookdale Senior Living Commun .... E 937 203-8443
  Beavercreek *(G-1231)*
Brookdale Senior Living Commun .... E 937 548-6800
  Greenville *(G-11490)*
Brookdale Snior Lving Cmmnties .... E 740 366-0005
  Newark *(G-15149)*
Brookdale Snior Lving Cmmnties .... E 937 832-8500
  Englewood *(G-10698)*
Brookdale Snior Lving Cmmnties .... E 419 354-5300
  Bowling Green *(G-1770)*
Brookdale Snior Lving Cmmnties .... E 740 681-9903
  Lancaster *(G-12511)*
Brookdale Snior Lving Cmmnties .... E 419 423-4440
  Findlay *(G-11009)*

Employee Codes: A=Over 500 employees, B=251-500
C=101-250, D=51-100, E=25-50

RETIREMENT COMMUNITIES WITH NURSING

Brookdale Snior Lving Cmmnties .... E 330 249-1071
  Austintown *(G-868)*
Brookdale Snior Lving Cmmnties .... E 419 756-5599
  Mansfield *(G-13271)*
Brookdale Snior Lving Cmmnties .... E 937 773-0500
  Piqua *(G-16137)*
Brookdale Snior Lving Cmmnties .... E 330 793-0085
  Youngstown *(G-20128)*
Burchwood Care Center .... E 513 868-3300
  Fairfield Township *(G-10925)*
Capital Senior Living .... E 440 356-5444
  Rocky River *(G-16572)*
Carroll Golden Age Retreat .... E 330 627-4665
  Carrollton *(G-2612)*
Countryview Assistant Living .... E 740 489-5351
  Lore City *(G-13086)*
Crystal Care Centers Inc .... D 419 747-2666
  Mansfield *(G-13287)*
Crystalwood Inc .... D 513 605-1000
  Cincinnati *(G-3443)*
Friendship Vlg of Dublin Ohio .... C 614 764-1600
  Dublin *(G-10351)*
Gardens Western Reserve Inc .... D 330 342-9100
  Streetsboro *(G-17412)*
Guernsey Health Enterprises .... A 740 439-3561
  Cambridge *(G-2118)*
Hamlet Village In Chagrin FLS .... D 440 247-4200
  Chagrin Falls *(G-2699)*
Hospice of North Central Ohio .... E 419 281-7107
  Ashland *(G-682)*
Inn At Hillenvale Ltd .... D 740 392-8245
  Mount Vernon *(G-14900)*
Judson Palmer Home Corp .... E 419 422-9656
  Findlay *(G-11054)*
Koinonia Homes Inc .... D 216 351-5361
  Cleveland *(G-5907)*
Lutheran Memorial Home Inc .... D 419 502-5700
  Toledo *(G-18021)*
Lutheran Village At Wolf Creek .... C 419 861-2233
  Holland *(G-12033)*
McV Health Care Facilities .... E 513 398-1486
  Mason *(G-13738)*
Medina Medical Investors Ltd .... C 330 483-3131
  Medina *(G-14104)*
Miami Valley Urgent Care .... E 937 252-2000
  Dayton *(G-9739)*
Minford Retirement Center LLC .... E 740 820-2821
  Minford *(G-14652)*
Mt Healthy Christian Home Inc .... C 513 931-5000
  Cincinnati *(G-4128)*
North Park Retirement Cmnty .... E 216 267-0555
  Cleveland *(G-6142)*
Ohio Presbt Retirement Svcs .... B 937 498-2391
  Sidney *(G-16945)*
Olmsted Manor Retirement Prpts .... E 440 250-4080
  Westlake *(G-19529)*
Otterbein Lebanon .... E 513 933-5465
  Lebanon *(G-12635)*
Red Carpet Health Care Center .... C 740 439-4401
  Cambridge *(G-2127)*
Rest Haven Nursing Home Inc .... C 937 548-1138
  Greenville *(G-11516)*
Royalton Senior Living Inc .... E 440 582-4111
  North Royalton *(G-15501)*
Sunrise Senior Living Inc .... D 614 457-3500
  Upper Arlington *(G-18556)*
Valley View Alzhimers Care Ctr .... D 740 998-2948
  Frankfort *(G-11146)*
Victorian Oaks LLC .... E 740 432-2262
  Cambridge *(G-2133)*
Western Rsrve Msonic Cmnty Inc .... C 330 721-3000
  Medina *(G-14138)*
Williamsburg of Cincinnati Mgt .... E 513 948-2308
  Cincinnati *(G-4852)*
Zandex Health Care Corporation .... E 740 454-1400
  Zanesville *(G-20552)*
Zandex Health Care Corporation .... D 740 454-1400
  Johnstown *(G-12345)*
Zandex Health Care Corporation .... C 740 454-9747
  Zanesville *(G-20553)*

REUPHOLSTERY & FURNITURE REPAIR

OfficeMax North America Inc .... E 614 899-6186
  Westerville *(G-19431)*

RIDING APPAREL STORES

Schneider Saddlery LLC .... E 440 543-2700
  Chagrin Falls *(G-2733)*

RIDING STABLES

Foxridge Farms Corp .... E 740 965-1369
  Galena *(G-11282)*
Therapeutic Riding Center Inc .... E 440 708-0013
  Chagrin Falls *(G-2736)*
Valley Riding .... E 216 267-2525
  Cleveland *(G-6684)*

ROBOTS: Assembly Line

Advanced Design Industries Inc .... E 440 277-4141
  Sheffield Village *(G-16883)*
Ats Systems Oregon Inc .... B 541 738-0932
  Lewis Center *(G-12668)*
Production Design Services Inc .... D 937 866-3377
  Dayton *(G-9832)*

RODS: Steel & Iron, Made In Steel Mills

American Posts LLC .... E 419 720-0652
  Toledo *(G-17751)*

ROLL FORMED SHAPES: Custom

Hynes Industries Inc .... C 330 799-3221
  Youngstown *(G-20227)*
Ontario Mechanical LLC .... E 419 529-2578
  Ontario *(G-15709)*

ROLLING MILL MACHINERY

Addisonmckee Inc .... C 513 228-7000
  Lebanon *(G-12587)*
Enprotech Industrial Tech LLC .... C 216 883-3220
  Cleveland *(G-5542)*
Kottler Metal Products Co Inc .... E 440 946-7473
  Willoughby *(G-19677)*
Park Corporation .... B 216 267-4870
  Cleveland *(G-6234)*
Pines Manufacturing Inc .... E 440 835-5553
  Westlake *(G-19534)*
Steel Eqp Specialists Inc .... D 330 823-8260
  Alliance *(G-563)*
Wauseon Machine & Mfg Inc .... D 419 337-0940
  Wauseon *(G-18964)*

ROOFING MATERIALS: Asphalt

Garland/Dbs Inc .... C 216 641-7500
  Cleveland *(G-5655)*
Tremco Incorporated .... B 216 292-5000
  Beachwood *(G-1133)*

ROOFING MATERIALS: Sheet Metal

Interstate Contractors LLC .... E 513 372-5393
  Mason *(G-13723)*
Oatey Supply Chain Svcs Inc .... C 216 267-7100
  Cleveland *(G-6176)*

ROOMING & BOARDING HOUSES: Dormitory, Commercially Operated

A M Management Inc .... E 937 426-6500
  Beavercreek *(G-1143)*

RUBBER

Flexsys America LP .... D 330 666-4111
  Akron *(G-227)*
Kraton Polymers US LLC .... B 740 423-7571
  Belpre *(G-1441)*
Mondo Polymer Technologies Inc .... E 740 376-9396
  Reno *(G-16422)*

RUBBER PRDTS: Mechanical

Datwyler Sling Sltions USA Inc .... E 937 387-2800
  Vandalia *(G-18676)*
Frankes Wood Products LLC .... E 937 642-0706
  Marysville *(G-13620)*
Johnson Bros Rubber Co Inc .... D 419 853-4122
  West Salem *(G-19270)*
Mantaline Corporation .... D 330 274-2264
  Mantua *(G-13392)*
Midlands Millroom Supply Inc .... E 330 453-9100
  Canton *(G-2462)*

RUBBER PRDTS: Reclaimed

Flexsys America LP .... D 330 666-4111
  Akron *(G-227)*

SERVICES SECTION

Lanxess Corporation .... C 440 279-2367
  Chardon *(G-2755)*

RUBBER, CRUDE, WHOLESALE

Two Happy Frogs Incorporated .... E 330 633-1666
  Tallmadge *(G-17658)*

SADDLERY STORES

Schneider Saddlery LLC .... E 440 543-2700
  Chagrin Falls *(G-2733)*

SAFETY EQPT & SPLYS WHOLESALERS

ABC Fire Inc .... E 440 237-6677
  North Royalton *(G-15480)*
Abco Fire LLC .... E 800 875-7200
  Cincinnati *(G-2960)*
Abco Holdings LLC .... D 216 433-7200
  Cleveland *(G-4946)*
Chester West Holdings Inc .... C 800 647-1900
  Cincinnati *(G-3241)*
Safety Today Inc .... E 614 409-7200
  Grove City *(G-11595)*
Union Tank Car Company .... C 419 864-7216
  Marion *(G-13589)*
Wcm Holdings Inc .... C 513 705-2100
  Cincinnati *(G-4826)*

SAFETY INSPECTION SVCS

Flight Services & Systems Inc .... C 216 328-0090
  Cleveland *(G-5609)*

SALES PROMOTION SVCS

Automotive Events Inc .... E 440 356-1383
  Rocky River *(G-16570)*
Campbell Sales Company .... E 513 697-2900
  Cincinnati *(G-3172)*
D L Ryan Companies LLC .... E 614 436-6558
  Westerville *(G-19296)*
Krajewski Corp .... E 740 522-2000
  Granville *(G-11468)*
Nugrowth Solutions LLC .... E 800 747-9273
  Columbus *(G-8305)*
RA Staff Company Inc .... E 440 891-9900
  Cleveland *(G-6342)*

SALT MINING: Common

Cargill Incorporated .... C 216 651-7200
  Cleveland *(G-5184)*

SAND & GRAVEL

Barrett Paving Materials Inc .... E 513 271-6200
  Middletown *(G-14475)*
FML Resin LLC .... E 440 214-3200
  Chesterland *(G-2796)*
FML Terminal Logistics LLC .... D 440 214-3200
  Chesterland *(G-2797)*
Hanson Aggregates East LLC .... E 740 773-2172
  Chillicothe *(G-2844)*
Hilltop Basic Resources Inc .... E 513 621-1500
  Cincinnati *(G-3768)*
Joe McClelland Inc .... E 740 452-3036
  Zanesville *(G-20492)*
Kenmore Construction Co Inc .... E 330 832-8888
  Massillon *(G-13827)*
Martin Marietta Materials Inc .... C 513 701-1140
  West Chester *(G-19117)*
National Lime and Stone Co .... C 419 396-7671
  Carey *(G-2596)*
Oeder Carl E Sons Sand & Grav .... E 513 494-1238
  Lebanon *(G-12632)*
Phillips Ready Mix Co .... D 937 426-5151
  Beavercreek Township *(G-1281)*
Pioneer Sands LLC .... E 740 599-7773
  Howard *(G-12081)*
Rjw Trucking Company Ltd .... E 740 363-5343
  Delaware *(G-10124)*
Shelly and Sands Inc .... E 740 453-0721
  Zanesville *(G-20532)*
Shelly Materials Inc .... D 740 246-6315
  Thornville *(G-17668)*
Smith Concrete Co .... E 740 373-7441
  Dover *(G-10214)*
Tri County Concrete Inc .... E 330 425-4464
  Twinsburg *(G-18477)*

SERVICES SECTION

SAND MINING

Carl E Oeder Sons Sand & Grav ....E...... 513 494-1555
  Lebanon *(G-12594)*
Central Ready Mix LLC ....E...... 513 402-5001
  Cincinnati *(G-3216)*
Osborne Materials Company ....E...... 440 357-7026
  Grand River *(G-11457)*
Small Sand & Gravel Inc ....E...... 740 427-3130
  Gambier *(G-11349)*

SAND: Hygrade

Fairmount Minerals LLC ....C...... 269 926-9450
  Chesterland *(G-2795)*
Pioneer Sands LLC ....E...... 740 659-2241
  Glenford *(G-11433)*
Pioneer Sands LLC ....E...... 740 599-7773
  Howard *(G-12081)*

SANDBLASTING SVC: Building Exterior

Feecorp Corporation ....E...... 614 837-3010
  Canal Winchester *(G-2158)*
Industrial Waste Control Inc ....D...... 330 270-9900
  Youngstown *(G-20233)*
Mc Fadden Construction Inc ....E...... 419 668-4165
  Norwalk *(G-15580)*
Mike Morris ....E...... 330 767-4122
  Brewster *(G-1856)*
Mrap LLC ....E...... 614 545-3190
  Columbus *(G-8202)*
Northpointe Property MGT LLC ....C...... 614 579-9712
  Columbus *(G-8294)*

SANDSTONE: Dimension

Irg Operating LLC ....E...... 440 963-4008
  Vermilion *(G-18711)*

SANITARY SVC, NEC

City of Lima ....B...... 419 221-5294
  Lima *(G-12755)*
City of Toledo ....C...... 419 936-2924
  Toledo *(G-17810)*
Cuyahoga County Sani Engrg Svc ....C...... 216 443-8211
  Cleveland *(G-5456)*
Northast Ohio Rgonal Sewer Dst ....C...... 216 881-6600
  Cleveland *(G-6144)*
Northast Ohio Rgonal Sewer Dst ....C...... 216 641-3200
  Cleveland *(G-6145)*
Wastren Advantage Inc ....E...... 970 254-1277
  Piketon *(G-16132)*

SANITARY SVCS: Disease Control

Digestive Disease Consultants ....E...... 330 225-6468
  Brunswick *(G-1975)*
Ohio State University ....E...... 614 293-8732
  Columbus *(G-8421)*

SANITARY SVCS: Environmental Cleanup

AST Environmental Inc ....E...... 937 743-0002
  Springboro *(G-17115)*
Chemtron Corporation ....E...... 440 937-6348
  Avon *(G-888)*
Diproinduca (usa) Limited LLC ....D...... 330 722-4442
  Medina *(G-14058)*
Environment Control of Greater ....D...... 614 868-9788
  Columbus *(G-7599)*
Interdyne Corporation ....E...... 419 229-8192
  Lima *(G-12805)*
Los Alamos Technical Assoc Inc ....E...... 614 508-1200
  Westerville *(G-19420)*
Samsel Rope & Marine Supply Co ....E...... 216 241-0333
  Cleveland *(G-6442)*
Superior Envmtl Solutions LLC ....B...... 513 874-8355
  West Chester *(G-19235)*

SANITARY SVCS: Hazardous Waste, Collection & Disposal

Avalon Holdings Corporation ....D...... 330 856-8800
  Warren *(G-18823)*
Clean Harbors Envmtl Svcs Inc ....D...... 216 429-2402
  Cleveland *(G-5283)*
Clean Harbors Envmtl Svcs Inc ....D...... 216 429-2401
  Cleveland *(G-5284)*
Clean Harbors Envmtl Svcs Inc ....E...... 740 929-3532
  Hebron *(G-11846)*

Envirosafe Services of Ohio ....E...... 419 698-3500
  Oregon *(G-15735)*
Hydrochem LLC ....E...... 216 861-3949
  Youngstown *(G-20225)*
Stericycle Inc ....E...... 419 729-1934
  Toledo *(G-18202)*
Triad Transport Inc ....E...... 614 491-9497
  Columbus *(G-8868)*
Waste Management Ohio Inc ....E...... 419 547-7791
  Vickery *(G-18734)*

SANITARY SVCS: Incinerator, Operation Of

County of Montgomery ....E...... 937 781-3046
  Moraine *(G-14764)*
Ross Consolidated Corp ....D...... 440 748-5800
  Grafton *(G-11444)*
Ross Incineration Services Inc ....C...... 440 366-2000
  Grafton *(G-11445)*

SANITARY SVCS: Medical Waste Disposal

Browning-Ferris Industries LLC ....D...... 330 393-0385
  Warren *(G-18832)*
Stericycle Inc ....D...... 330 393-0370
  Warren *(G-18903)*
Stericycle Inc ....E...... 513 539-6213
  Middletown *(G-14461)*

SANITARY SVCS: Nonhazardous Waste Disposal Sites

Lafarge North America Inc ....E...... 330 393-5656
  Warren *(G-18872)*

SANITARY SVCS: Oil Spill Cleanup

Cousins Waste Control LLC ....D...... 419 726-1500
  Toledo *(G-17839)*

SANITARY SVCS: Refuse Collection & Disposal Svcs

Allied Waste Systems Inc ....E...... 937 268-8110
  Dayton *(G-9318)*
BFI Waste Services LLC ....C...... 800 437-1123
  Salem *(G-16689)*
Browning-Ferris Industries LLC ....E...... 440 786-9390
  Solon *(G-16986)*
Builders Trash Service ....E...... 614 444-7060
  Columbus *(G-7167)*
Cecos International Inc ....E...... 513 724-6114
  Williamsburg *(G-19629)*
Central Ohio Contractors Inc ....D...... 740 369-7700
  Delaware *(G-10078)*
Industrial Waste Control Inc ....D...... 330 270-9900
  Youngstown *(G-20233)*
Republic Services Inc ....E...... 330 536-8013
  Lowellville *(G-13173)*
Republic Services Inc ....E...... 419 626-2454
  Sandusky *(G-16788)*
Republic Services Inc ....D...... 216 741-4013
  Cleveland *(G-6380)*
Republic Services Inc ....E...... 440 458-5191
  Elyria *(G-10676)*
Republic Services Inc ....E...... 330 830-9050
  Massillon *(G-13847)*
Republic Services Inc ....E...... 330 793-7676
  Youngstown *(G-20347)*
Republic Services Inc ....E...... 440 774-4060
  Oberlin *(G-15659)*
Republic Services Inc ....E...... 513 554-0237
  Cincinnati *(G-4407)*
Republic Services Inc ....E...... 937 268-8110
  Dayton *(G-9849)*
Republic Services Inc ....D...... 740 969-4487
  Columbus *(G-8615)*
Republic Services Inc ....E...... 800 247-3644
  Massillon *(G-13848)*
Republic Services Inc ....E...... 800 331-0988
  Gallipolis *(G-11336)*
Republic Services Inc ....E...... 419 396-3581
  Carey *(G-2597)*
Republic Services Inc ....E...... 419 635-2367
  Port Clinton *(G-16252)*
Rumpke Transportation Co LLC ....E...... 937 461-0004
  Dayton *(G-9856)*
Rumpke Waste Inc ....D...... 937 378-4126
  Georgetown *(G-11397)*
Waste Management Ohio Inc ....C...... 800 343-6047
  Fairborn *(G-10812)*

SANITARY SVCS: Rubbish Collection & Disposal

Big O Refuse Inc ....E...... 740 344-7544
  Granville *(G-11458)*
Republic Services Inc ....E...... 614 308-3000
  Columbus *(G-8614)*
Republic Services Inc ....E...... 419 726-9465
  Toledo *(G-18152)*
Sidwell Materials Inc ....C...... 740 849-2394
  Zanesville *(G-20533)*
Waste Management Ohio Inc ....D...... 866 409-4671
  Northwood *(G-15550)*

SANITARY SVCS: Sanitary Landfill, Operation Of

American Landfill Inc ....E...... 330 866-3265
  Waynesburg *(G-18980)*
Browning-Ferris Inds of Ohio ....D...... 330 536-8013
  Lowellville *(G-13170)*
Browning-Ferris Industries Inc ....E...... 513 899-2942
  Morrow *(G-14844)*
Central Ohio Contractors Inc ....D...... 614 539-2579
  Grove City *(G-11545)*
County of Erie ....D...... 419 433-0617
  Milan *(G-14493)*
Republic Services Inc ....E...... 937 593-3566
  Bellefontaine *(G-1392)*
Republic Services Inc ....E...... 419 925-4592
  Celina *(G-2662)*
Republic Services Inc ....E...... 330 793-7676
  Youngstown *(G-20345)*
Republic Services Inc ....E...... 330 793-7676
  Youngstown *(G-20346)*
Republic Services Inc ....E...... 419 636-5109
  Bryan *(G-2020)*
Rumpke Sanitary Landfill Inc ....C...... 513 851-0122
  Cincinnati *(G-4453)*
Solid Waste Auth Centl Ohio ....C...... 614 871-5100
  Grove City *(G-11598)*
Spring Grove Rsrce Rcovery Inc ....D...... 513 681-6242
  Cincinnati *(G-4565)*

SANITARY SVCS: Sewage Treatment Facility

City of Canton ....E...... 330 489-3080
  Canton *(G-2311)*
City of Xenia ....E...... 937 376-7271
  Xenia *(G-20045)*

SANITARY SVCS: Toxic Or Hazardous Waste Cleanup

Petro Environmental Tech ....E...... 513 489-6789
  Cincinnati *(G-4287)*

SANITARY SVCS: Waste Materials, Disposal At Sea

Waste Management Ohio Inc ....E...... 800 910-2831
  Wooster *(G-19923)*

SANITARY SVCS: Waste Materials, Recycling

Allied Waste Industries LLC ....E...... 440 774-3100
  Oberlin *(G-15639)*
Appliance Recycl Ctrs Amer Inc ....D...... 614 876-8771
  Hilliard *(G-11878)*
Athens-Hcking Cnty Recycl Ctrs ....E...... 740 797-4208
  Athens *(G-777)*
B & B Plastics Recyclers Inc ....C...... 614 409-2880
  Columbus *(G-7081)*
Caraustar Industries Inc ....E...... 937 298-9969
  Moraine *(G-14758)*
Chemtron Corporation ....E...... 440 937-6348
  Avon *(G-888)*
City of Cleveland Heights ....E...... 216 691-7300
  Cleveland *(G-5259)*
Clm Pallet Recycling Inc ....D...... 614 272-5761
  Columbus *(G-7306)*
Eco Global Corp ....E...... 419 363-2681
  Rockford *(G-16561)*
Envirite of Ohio Inc ....E...... 330 456-6238
  Canton *(G-2356)*
Environmental Enterprises Inc ....D...... 513 541-1823
  Cincinnati *(G-3561)*
Envision Waste Services LLC ....D...... 216 831-1818
  Cleveland *(G-5547)*
Fpt Cleveland LLC ....C...... 216 441-3800
  Cleveland *(G-5628)*

Employee Codes: A=Over 500 employees, B=251-500
C=101-250, D=51-100, E=25-50

SANITARY SVCS: Waste Materials, Recycling

Fultz & Son Inc .... E 419 547-9365
  Clyde *(G-6813)*
Garden Street Iron & Metal .... E 513 853-3700
  Cincinnati *(G-3662)*
Gateway Products Recycling Inc .... E 216 341-8777
  Cleveland *(G-5659)*
General Environmental MGT LLC .... D 216 621-3694
  Chagrin Falls *(G-2717)*
Global Scrap Management Inc .... E 513 576-6600
  Batavia *(G-1015)*
Grasan Equipment Company Inc .... D 419 526-4440
  Mansfield *(G-13306)*
Greenstar Mid-America LLC .... E 330 784-1167
  Akron *(G-248)*
Hpj Industries Inc .... D 419 278-1000
  North Baltimore *(G-15314)*
Imco Recycling of Ohio LLC .... C 740 922-2373
  Uhrichsville *(G-18490)*
In-Plas Recycling Inc .... E 513 541-9800
  Cincinnati *(G-3811)*
Interstate Shredding LLC .... E 330 545-5477
  Girard *(G-11415)*
Liberty Tire Recycling LLC .... E 614 871-8097
  Grove City *(G-11576)*
Milliron Recycling Inc .... D 419 747-6522
  Mansfield *(G-13347)*
Mondo Polymer Technologies Inc ...... E 740 376-9396
  Reno *(G-16422)*
Novotec Recycling LLC .... E 614 231-8326
  Columbus *(G-8300)*
Nucor Corporation .... E 407 855-2990
  Cincinnati *(G-4189)*
OK Industries Inc .... E 419 435-2361
  Fostoria *(G-11137)*
Perma-Fix of Dayton Inc .... E 937 268-6501
  Dayton *(G-9807)*
Pinnacle Recycling LLC .... E 330 745-3700
  Akron *(G-390)*
Plastic Recycling Tech Inc .... E 937 615-9286
  Piqua *(G-16161)*
Plastic Recycling Tech Inc .... E 419 238-9395
  Van Wert *(G-18641)*
Polychem Corporation .... D 419 547-1400
  Clyde *(G-6820)*
Recycling Services Inc .... E 419 381-7762
  Maumee *(G-13968)*
Royal Paper Stock Company Inc .... E 513 870-5780
  West Chester *(G-19226)*
Rpg Inc .... D 419 289-2757
  Ashland *(G-695)*
Rumpke Cnsld Companies Inc .... C 513 738-0800
  Hamilton *(G-11771)*
Rumpke Transportation Co LLC .... C 513 242-4600
  Cincinnati *(G-4454)*
Rumpke Waste Inc .... D 513 242-4401
  Cincinnati *(G-4456)*
Rumpke Waste Inc .... D 740 474-9790
  Circleville *(G-4902)*
Shredded Bedding Corporation .... E 740 893-3567
  Centerburg *(G-2668)*
Veolia Es Tchncal Slutions LLC .... D 937 859-6101
  Miamisburg *(G-14365)*
Vexor Technology Inc .... E 330 721-9773
  Medina *(G-14137)*
Waste Parchment Inc .... E 330 674-6868
  Millersburg *(G-14627)*
Wws Associates Inc .... C 513 761-5333
  Blue Ash *(G-1723)*

SANITATION CHEMICALS & CLEANING AGENTS

Alco-Chem Inc .... E 330 253-3535
  Akron *(G-64)*
Cincinnati - Vulcan Company .... D 513 242-5300
  Cincinnati *(G-3278)*
EMD Millipore Corporation .... C 513 631-0445
  Norwood *(G-15599)*
Fuchs Lubricants Co .... E 330 963-0400
  Twinsburg *(G-18419)*
National Colloid Company .... E 740 282-1171
  Steubenville *(G-17332)*
New Vulco Mfg & Sales Co LLC .... D 513 242-2672
  Cincinnati *(G-4158)*
State Industrial Products Corp .... B 877 747-6986
  Cleveland *(G-6530)*
Tolco Corporation .... D 419 241-1113
  Toledo *(G-18225)*
Tremco Incorporated .... B 216 292-5000
  Beachwood *(G-1133)*

Univar USA Inc .... C 513 714-5264
  West Chester *(G-19239)*

SATELLITES: Communications

Great Lakes Telcom Ltd .... E 330 629-8848
  Youngstown *(G-20207)*

SAVINGS & LOAN ASSOCIATIONS, NOT FEDERALLY CHARTERED

Geauga Savings Bank .... E 440 564-9441
  Newbury *(G-15257)*
Harrison Building and Ln Assn .... E 513 367-2015
  Harrison *(G-11801)*
Home Savings Bank .... D 330 499-1900
  North Canton *(G-15344)*
Huntington National Bank .... E 740 335-3771
  Wshngtn CT Hs *(G-20027)*
Mechanics Bank .... E 419 524-0831
  Mansfield *(G-13337)*
The Peoples Savings and Ln Co .... E 937 653-1600
  Urbana *(G-18601)*
Union Savings Bank .... D 937 434-1254
  Dayton *(G-9944)*
Wesbanco Bank Inc .... E 513 741-5766
  Cincinnati *(G-4833)*

SAVINGS INSTITUTIONS: Federally Chartered

Eagle Financial Bancorp Inc .... E 513 574-0700
  Cincinnati *(G-3527)*
First Defiance Financial Corp .... E 419 353-8611
  Bowling Green *(G-1776)*
First Financial Bancorp .... C 513 551-5640
  Cincinnati *(G-3615)*
Guardian Savings Bank .... E 513 528-8787
  Cincinnati *(G-3717)*
Wayne Savings Bancshares Inc .... C 330 264-5767
  Wooster *(G-19925)*
Wayne Savings Community Bank ...... C 330 264-5767
  Wooster *(G-19926)*

SAW BLADES

Dynatech Systems Inc .... E 440 365-1774
  Elyria *(G-10618)*
J and S Tool Incorporated .... E 216 676-8330
  Cleveland *(G-5840)*

SAWING & PLANING MILLS

Appalachia Wood Inc .... E 740 596-2551
  Mc Arthur *(G-14015)*
Baillie Lumber Co LP .... E 419 462-2000
  Galion *(G-11292)*
Gross Lumber Inc .... E 330 683-2055
  Apple Creek *(G-625)*
Hartzell Hardwoods Inc .... D 937 773-7054
  Piqua *(G-16146)*
Sawmill Road Management Co LLC .. E 937 342-9071
  Springfield *(G-17270)*
Stephen M Trudick .... E 440 834-1891
  Burton *(G-2065)*
Wappoo Wood Products Inc .... E 937 492-1166
  Sidney *(G-16960)*

SCAFFOLDING WHOLESALERS

Safway Services LLC .... E 513 860-2626
  West Chester *(G-19144)*

SCALE REPAIR SVCS

Brechbuhler Scales Inc .... E 330 458-3060
  Canton *(G-2269)*
Filing Scale Company Inc .... E 330 425-3092
  Twinsburg *(G-18415)*

SCHOOL BUS SVC

Akron School Trnsp Svcs .... D 330 761-1390
  Akron *(G-55)*
Anthony Wayne Local Schools .... D 419 877-0451
  Whitehouse *(G-19583)*
Beachwood City Schools .... E 216 464-6609
  Cleveland *(G-5106)*
Benton-Carroll-Salem .... E 419 898-6214
  Oak Harbor *(G-15605)*
Berea B O E Trnsp Dept .... E 216 898-8300
  Berea *(G-1447)*

Boardman School Bus Garage .... D 330 726-3425
  Youngstown *(G-20121)*
Canton City School District .... D 330 456-6710
  Canton *(G-2285)*
Chillicothe City School Dst .... E 740 775-2936
  Chillicothe *(G-2818)*
Clark Shawnee Schl Transprtn .... E 937 328-5382
  Springfield *(G-17165)*
Cleveland Municipal School Dst .... B 216 634-7005
  Cleveland *(G-5332)*
Cleveland Municipal School Dst .... B 216 432-4600
  Cleveland *(G-5333)*
Dublin City Schools .... C 614 764-5926
  Dublin *(G-10326)*
First Group Investment Partnr .... D 513 241-2200
  Cincinnati *(G-3618)*
First Student Inc .... D 513 531-6888
  Cincinnati *(G-3620)*
First Student Inc .... E 937 645-0201
  Marysville *(G-13617)*
First Student Inc .... E 513 761-6100
  Cincinnati *(G-3621)*
First Student Inc .... B 513 761-5136
  Cincinnati *(G-3622)*
First Student Inc .... E 419 382-9915
  Toledo *(G-17894)*
First Student Inc .... E 513 241-2200
  Cincinnati *(G-3623)*
Firstgroup America Inc .... D 513 241-2200
  Cincinnati *(G-3626)*
Firstgroup America Inc .... B 513 419-8611
  Cincinnati *(G-3627)*
Firstgroup America Inc .... D 513 241-2200
  Cincinnati *(G-3628)*
Firstgroup Usa Inc .... B 513 241-2200
  Cincinnati *(G-3629)*
Gahanna-Jefferson Pub Schl Dst .... D 614 751-7581
  Columbus *(G-7724)*
Geneva Area City School Dst .... E 440 466-2684
  Geneva *(G-11362)*
Lakota Local School District .... C 513 777-2150
  Liberty Township *(G-12722)*
Lima City School District .... E 419 996-3450
  Lima *(G-12817)*
Mahoning County .... D 330 797-2837
  Youngstown *(G-20262)*
Marfre Inc .... C 513 321-3377
  Cincinnati *(G-4021)*
Massillon City School Bus Gar .... E 330 830-1849
  Massillon *(G-13834)*
Mentor Exempted Vlg Schl Dst .... C 440 974-5260
  Mentor *(G-14212)*
Miamisburg City School Dst .... E 937 866-1283
  Miamisburg *(G-14321)*
Middletown School Vhcl Svc Ctr .... D 513 420-4568
  Middletown *(G-14437)*
New Albany Plain Loc SC Transp ...... E 614 855-2033
  New Albany *(G-15000)*
North Canton City School Dst .... D 330 497-5615
  Canton *(G-2475)*
Northmont Service Center .... D 937 832-5050
  Englewood *(G-10713)*
Ontario Local School District .... E 419 529-3814
  Ontario *(G-15708)*
Palmer Express Incorporated .... E 440 942-3333
  Willoughby *(G-19702)*
Pauls Bus Service Inc .... E 513 851-5089
  Cincinnati *(G-4265)*
Perry Transportation Dept .... E 440 259-3005
  Perry *(G-15966)*
Perrysburg Board of Education .... E 419 874-3127
  Perrysburg *(G-16041)*
Peterman .... E 513 722-2229
  Goshen *(G-11438)*
Peterman .... E 513 539-0324
  Monroe *(G-14709)*
Petermann Ltd .... D 330 653-3323
  Hudson *(G-12140)*
Petermann Northeast LLC .... A 513 351-7383
  Cincinnati *(G-4286)*
Queen City Transportation LLC .... B 513 941-8700
  Cincinnati *(G-4372)*
S B S Transit Inc .... B 440 288-2222
  Lorain *(G-13075)*
S C Wooster Bus Garage .... E 330 264-4060
  Wooster *(G-19910)*
SC Madison Bus Garage .... D 419 589-3373
  Mansfield *(G-13362)*
Streetsboro Board Education .... E 330 626-4909
  Streetsboro *(G-17432)*

SERVICES SECTION

Suburban Transportation Co Inc..............E....... 440 846-9291
  Brunswick *(G-1990)*
Vermilion Board of Education..................E....... 440 204-1700
  Vermilion *(G-18718)*
Washington Local Schools.......................D....... 419 473-8356
  Toledo *(G-18299)*

SCHOOL FOR PHYSICALLY HANDICAPPED, NEC

North Point Eductl Svc Ctr..........................E....... 440 967-0904
  Huron *(G-12168)*

SCHOOL FOR RETARDED, NEC

Abilities First Foundation........................C....... 513 423-9496
  Middletown *(G-14411)*
D-R Training Center & Workshop...............C....... 419 289-0470
  Ashland *(G-678)*
Mental Rtrdtion Preble Cnty Bd..................D....... 937 456-5891
  Eaton *(G-10568)*
Whetstone Industries Inc..........................E....... 419 947-9222
  Mount Gilead *(G-14864)*

SCHOOL SPLYS, EXC BOOKS: Wholesalers

Euclid City Schools..................................D....... 216 261-2900
  Euclid *(G-10751)*
ICM Distributing Company Inc..................E....... 234 212-3030
  Twinsburg *(G-18431)*
Lorenz Corporation..................................D....... 937 228-6118
  Dayton *(G-9687)*
Zaner-Bloser Inc......................................D....... 614 486-0221
  Columbus *(G-9025)*

SCHOOLS & EDUCATIONAL SVCS, NEC

Key Career Place......................................D....... 216 987-3029
  Cleveland *(G-5896)*

SCHOOLS: Elementary & Secondary

Educatonal Svc Ctr Lorain Cnty..................E....... 440 244-1659
  Elyria *(G-10619)*
First School Corp......................................E....... 937 433-3455
  Dayton *(G-9550)*
Flying Colors Public Preschool....................E....... 740 349-1629
  Newark *(G-15167)*
Grace Baptist Church................................E....... 937 652-1133
  Urbana *(G-18589)*
Harrison Ave Assembly of God....................E....... 513 367-6100
  Harrison *(G-11800)*
Interval Brotherhood Homes.......................D....... 330 644-4095
  Coventry Township *(G-9126)*
Medill Elemntary Sch of Volntr..................E....... 740 687-7352
  Lancaster *(G-12556)*
Miami Valley School..................................E....... 937 434-4444
  Dayton *(G-9738)*
Northwest Local School Dst........................D....... 330 854-2291
  Canal Fulton *(G-2144)*
Northwest Ohio Computer Assn...................D....... 419 267-5565
  Archbold *(G-640)*
Ohio School Psychologists Assn..................E....... 614 414-5980
  Columbus *(G-8374)*
Ohio University..D....... 740 593-2195
  Athens *(G-807)*
Paulding Exempted Vlg Schl Dst.................C....... 419 594-3309
  Paulding *(G-15934)*
Ravenna Assembly of God Inc....................E....... 330 297-1493
  Ravenna *(G-16404)*
Young Services Inc....................................E....... 419 704-2009
  Toledo *(G-18324)*

SCHOOLS: Vocational, NEC

Great Oaks Inst Tech Creer Dev..................D....... 513 771-8840
  Cincinnati *(G-3703)*
Great Oaks Inst Tech Creer Dev..................E....... 513 771-8840
  Cincinnati *(G-3704)*

SCRAP & WASTE MATERIALS, WHOLESALE: Auto Wrecking For Scrap

Diver Steel City Auto Crushers..................E....... 330 744-5083
  Youngstown *(G-20171)*
Kenton Auto and Truck Wrecking................E....... 419 673-8234
  Kenton *(G-12420)*

SCRAP & WASTE MATERIALS, WHOLESALE: Ferrous Metal

Agmet LLC..E....... 440 439-7400
  Cleveland *(G-4969)*
Agmet LLC..E....... 216 662-6939
  Maple Heights *(G-13399)*
Allen County Recyclers Inc.........................E....... 419 223-5010
  Lima *(G-12735)*
Byer Steel Recycling Inc...........................E....... 513 948-0300
  Cincinnati *(G-3158)*
City Scrap & Salvage Co............................E....... 330 753-5051
  Akron *(G-143)*
Cohen Electronics Inc...............................D....... 513 425-6911
  Middletown *(G-14421)*
Djj Holding Corporation............................C....... 513 621-8770
  Cincinnati *(G-3496)*
Fpt Cleveland LLC....................................C....... 216 441-3800
  Cleveland *(G-5628)*
Franklin Iron & Metal Corp........................C....... 937 253-8184
  Dayton *(G-9561)*
Harry Rock & Company...............................E....... 330 644-3748
  Cleveland *(G-5728)*
Holub Iron & Steel Company......................E....... 330 252-5655
  Akron *(G-270)*
I H Schlezinger Inc..................................E....... 614 252-1188
  Columbus *(G-7877)*
Metal Management Ohio Inc......................E....... 419 782-7791
  Defiance *(G-10049)*
Metalico Akron Inc...................................E....... 330 376-1400
  Akron *(G-340)*
Moskowitz Bros Inc...................................E....... 513 242-2100
  Cincinnati *(G-4121)*
Niles Iron & Metal Company LLC................E....... 330 652-2262
  Niles *(G-15300)*
Omnisource LLC..D....... 419 537-1631
  Toledo *(G-18107)*
Omnisource LLC..E....... 419 394-3351
  Saint Marys *(G-16681)*
Omnisource LLC..C....... 419 537-9400
  Toledo *(G-18108)*
PSC Metals - Wooster LLC.........................D....... 330 264-8956
  Wooster *(G-19905)*
Reserve Ftl LLC..E....... 773 721-8740
  Canton *(G-2512)*
River Recycling Entps Ltd........................E....... 216 459-2100
  Cleveland *(G-6398)*
Unico Alloys & Metals Inc........................D....... 614 299-0545
  Columbus *(G-8887)*
Wall St Recycling LLC..............................E....... 330 296-8657
  Ravenna *(G-16416)*
Wilmington Iron and Met Co Inc................E....... 937 382-3867
  Wilmington *(G-19794)*

SCRAP & WASTE MATERIALS, WHOLESALE: Junk & Scrap

Slesnick Iron & Metal Co.........................E....... 330 453-8475
  Canton *(G-2532)*

SCRAP & WASTE MATERIALS, WHOLESALE: Metal

Diproinduca (usa) Limited LLC..................D....... 330 722-4442
  Medina *(G-14058)*
G-Cor Automotive Corp.............................E....... 614 443-6735
  Columbus *(G-7721)*
I-Tran Inc...E....... 330 659-0801
  Richfield *(G-16512)*
Jasar Recycling Inc................................D....... 864 233-5421
  East Palestine *(G-10538)*
PSC Metals Inc..E....... 614 299-4175
  Columbus *(G-8570)*
PSC Metals Inc..D....... 234 208-2331
  Barberton *(G-974)*
PSC Metals Inc..E....... 330 794-8300
  Barberton *(G-975)*
PSC Metals Inc..E....... 330 745-4437
  Barberton *(G-976)*
PSC Metals Inc..E....... 330 484-7610
  Canton *(G-2498)*
PSC Metals Inc..E....... 216 341-3400
  Cleveland *(G-6329)*
R L S Corporation....................................E....... 740 773-1440
  Chillicothe *(G-2872)*
Scrap Yard LLC.......................................E....... 216 271-5825
  Cleveland *(G-6454)*

SCRAP & WASTE MATERIALS, WHOLESALE: Nonferrous Metals Scrap

Legend Smelting and Recycl Inc................D....... 740 928-0139
  Hebron *(G-11851)*
M & M Metals International Inc................E....... 513 221-4411
  Cincinnati *(G-4005)*
Miles Alloy Inc......................................E....... 216 245-8893
  Cleveland *(G-6062)*
Muskingum Iron & Metal Co......................E....... 740 452-9351
  Zanesville *(G-20509)*
Quantum Metals Inc................................E....... 513 573-0144
  Lebanon *(G-12638)*
W R G Inc...E....... 216 351-8494
  Cleveland *(G-6714)*

SCRAP & WASTE MATERIALS, WHOLESALE: Oil

Heritage Envmtl Svcs LLC........................E....... 419 729-1321
  Toledo *(G-17954)*

SCRAP & WASTE MATERIALS, WHOLESALE: Paper

Hamilton Scrap Processors.......................E....... 513 863-3474
  Hamilton *(G-11741)*
Royal Paper Stock Company Inc................D....... 614 851-4714
  Columbus *(G-8655)*

SCRAP & WASTE MATERIALS, WHOLESALE: Rags

Intex Supply Company.............................E....... 216 535-4300
  Richmond Heights *(G-16539)*

SCRAP & WASTE MATERIALS, WHOLESALE: Rubber Scrap

Frankes Wood Products LLC.....................E....... 937 642-0706
  Marysville *(G-13620)*

SCRAP STEEL CUTTING

Geneva Liberty Steel Ltd........................E....... 330 740-0103
  Youngstown *(G-20198)*
Toledo Shredding LLC.............................E....... 419 698-1153
  Toledo *(G-18249)*

SCREW MACHINE PRDTS

Hebco Products Inc................................A....... 419 562-7987
  Bucyrus *(G-2039)*
Superior Products Llc............................D....... 216 651-9400
  Cleveland *(G-6554)*

SEALANTS

Teknol Inc...D....... 937 264-0190
  Dayton *(G-9922)*
Tremco Incorporated..............................B....... 216 292-5000
  Beachwood *(G-1133)*

SEALING COMPOUNDS: Sealing, synthetic rubber or plastic

Technical Rubber Company Inc................B....... 740 967-9015
  Johnstown *(G-12343)*

SEARCH & NAVIGATION SYSTEMS

Boeing Company....................................E....... 740 788-4000
  Newark *(G-15148)*
Grimes Aerospace Company.....................B....... 937 484-2001
  Urbana *(G-18590)*

SEARCH & RESCUE SVCS

Richland Township Fire Dept..................E....... 740 536-7313
  Rushville *(G-16613)*

SEAT BELTS: Automobile & Aircraft

Tk Holdings Inc...................................E....... 937 778-9713
  Piqua *(G-16168)*

SECRETARIAL SVCS

Chase Transcriptions Inc......................E....... 330 650-0539
  Hudson *(G-12110)*

Employee Codes: A=Over 500 employees, B=251-500
C=101-250, D=51-100, E=25-50

SECURE STORAGE SVC: Document

Company		Phone
Briar-Gate Realty Inc	E	614 299-2122
Grove City (G-11536)		
Briar-Gate Realty Inc	D	614 299-2121
Grove City (G-11537)		
High Line Corporation	E	330 848-8800
Akron (G-264)		
Infostore LLC	E	216 749-4636
Cleveland (G-5820)		
Iron Mountain Incorporated	D	513 874-3535
West Chester (G-19094)		
Iron Mountain Info MGT LLC	E	513 942-7300
Hamilton (G-11747)		
Iron Mountain Info MGT LLC	C	440 248-0999
Solon (G-17019)		
Iron Mountain Info MGT LLC	E	513 247-2183
Blue Ash (G-1617)		
Ray Hamilton Companies	E	513 641-5400
Blue Ash (G-1676)		

SECURE STORAGE SVC: Household & Furniture

Company		Phone
Andreas Furniture Company	E	330 852-2494
Sugarcreek (G-17543)		
Great Value Storage	E	614 848-8420
Columbus (G-7772)		
Iron Mountain Incorporated	D	614 801-0151
Urbancrest (G-18605)		

SECURITY GUARD SVCS

Company		Phone
1st Choice Security Inc	C	513 381-6789
Cincinnati (G-2940)		
All Secured Security Svcs LLC	E	614 861-0482
Columbus (G-6965)		
Allied Security LLC	B	513 771-3776
Cincinnati (G-2992)		
Alliedbarton Security Svcs LLC	C	614 225-9061
Worthington (G-19939)		
Alliedbarton Security Svcs LLC	C	419 874-9005
Rossford (G-16606)		
Alpha Security LLC	D	330 406-2181
Poland (G-16220)		
Anderson Security Inc	D	937 294-1478
Moraine (G-14749)		
Andy Frain Services Inc	B	419 897-7909
Maumee (G-13882)		
Awp Inc	A	330 677-7401
North Canton (G-15327)		
Buckeye Protective Service	B	330 456-2671
Canton (G-2274)		
Corps Security Agency Inc	D	513 631-3200
Blue Ash (G-1568)		
Danson Inc	C	513 948-0066
Cincinnati (G-3462)		
Deacon 10	D	216 731-4000
Euclid (G-10749)		
Dusk To Dawn Protective Svcs	E	330 837-9992
Massillon (G-13802)		
Elite Isg	E	937 668-6858
Dayton (G-9521)		
Firelands Security Services	E	419 627-0562
Sandusky (G-16759)		
G4s Secure Solutions (usa)	C	513 874-0941
Cincinnati (G-3659)		
Guardsmark LLC	C	513 851-5523
Cincinnati (G-3718)		
Guardsmark LLC	E	419 229-9300
Lima (G-12789)		
Job 1 USA	D	419 255-5005
Toledo (G-17985)		
McKeen Security Inc	D	740 699-1301
Saint Clairsville (G-16644)		
Merchants Scrty Srvc of Dayton	B	937 256-9373
Dayton (G-9720)		
Moonlight Security Inc	D	937 252-1600
Moraine (G-14809)		
Ohio Entertainment Security	D	937 325-7216
South Vienna (G-17100)		
Ohio Support Services Corp	C	614 443-0291
Columbus (G-8448)		
Patrol Urban Services LLC	E	614 620-4672
Westerville (G-19436)		
Pls Protective Services	E	513 521-3581
Cincinnati (G-4306)		
R C Enterprises Inc	D	330 782-2111
Youngstown (G-20339)		
R-Cap Security LLC	C	216 761-6355
Cleveland (G-6341)		
Rumpf Corporation	E	419 255-5005
Toledo (G-18167)		
Ryno 24 Inc	E	440 946-7700
Willoughby (G-19711)		
Sam-Tom Inc	C	216 426-7752
Cleveland (G-6441)		
Securitas SEC Svcs USA Inc	C	216 431-3139
Cleveland (G-6461)		
Securitas SEC Svcs USA Inc	C	614 871-6051
Grove City (G-11597)		
Securitas SEC Svcs USA Inc	A	440 887-6800
Cleveland (G-6462)		
Securitas SEC Svcs USA Inc	C	216 503-2021
Cleveland (G-6463)		
Shield Security Service	E	330 650-2001
Hudson (G-12144)		
St Moritz Security Svcs Inc	D	330 270-5922
Youngstown (G-20381)		
St Moritz Security Svcs Inc	E	614 351-8798
Worthington (G-19999)		
Tenable Protective Svcs Inc	A	216 361-0002
Cleveland (G-6581)		
Tenable Protective Svcs Inc	A	513 741-3560
Cincinnati (G-4634)		
US Protection Service LLC	D	513 422-7910
Cincinnati (G-4796)		
US Security Associates Inc	C	513 381-7033
Cincinnati (G-4797)		
US Security Associates Inc	C	937 454-9035
Vandalia (G-18705)		
US Security Holdings Inc	D	614 488-6110
Columbus (G-8925)		
Whittguard Security Services	C	440 288-7233
Avon (G-918)		
Willo Security Inc	C	614 481-9456
Columbus (G-8998)		
Willo Security Inc	E	440 953-9191
Willoughby (G-19723)		

SECURITY PROTECTIVE DEVICES MAINTENANCE & MONITORING SVCS

Company		Phone
Johnson Cntrls SEC Sltions LLC	E	513 277-4966
Cincinnati (G-3880)		
Securitas Electronic SEC Inc	D	855 331-0359
Uniontown (G-18539)		
Securitas SEC Svcs USA Inc	C	937 224-7432
Dayton (G-9873)		
Security Investments LLC	E	614 441-4601
Westerville (G-19443)		

SECURITY SYSTEMS SERVICES

Company		Phone
ADT Security	D	440 397-5751
Strongsville (G-17440)		
American Svcs & Protection LLC	D	614 884-0177
Columbus (G-7009)		
Anderson Security Inc	D	937 294-1478
Moraine (G-14749)		
Bass Security Services Inc	D	216 755-1200
Bedford Heights (G-1347)		
Brawnstone Security LLC	D	330 800-9006
Canton (G-2268)		
Brentley Institute Inc	E	216 225-0087
Cleveland (G-5137)		
Bureau Workers Compensation	E	614 466-5109
Pickerington (G-16088)		
D B A Inc	E	513 541-6600
Cincinnati (G-3454)		
Electra Sound Inc	C	216 433-1050
Cleveland (G-5531)		
G4s Secure Solutions (usa)	C	614 322-5100
Columbus (G-7722)		
GA Business Purchaser LLC	D	419 255-8400
Toledo (G-17905)		
Guardian Protection Svcs Inc	D	330 797-1570
Youngstown (G-20211)		
Henley & Assoc SEC Group LLC	E	614 378-3727
Blacklick (G-1507)		
Honeywell International Inc	E	614 717-2270
Columbus (G-7858)		
Jenne Inc	C	440 835-0040
Avon (G-900)		
Kst Security Inc	E	614 878-2228
Columbus (G-8017)		
Metro Safety and Security LLC	D	614 792-2770
Columbus (G-8154)		
Northwestern Ohio SEC Systems	E	419 227-1655
Lima (G-12845)		
OGara Group Inc	D	513 338-0660
Cincinnati (G-4201)		
Protech Security Inc	E	330 499-3555
Canton (G-2496)		
Safe-N-Sound Security Inc	D	330 491-1148
Millersburg (G-14621)		
Safeguard Properties LLC	A	216 739-2900
Cleveland (G-6433)		
Securestate LLC	E	216 927-0115
Cleveland (G-6460)		
Surmount Solutions Group LLC	E	937 842-5780
Lakeview (G-12468)		
Universal Green Energy Solutio	E	844 723-7768
Reynoldsburg (G-16487)		
Vigilant Defense	E	513 309-0672
West Chester (G-19180)		
Whitestone Group Inc	B	614 501-7007
Columbus (G-8990)		
Wj Service Co Inc	E	330 372-5040
Warren (G-18928)		
Xentry Systems Integration LLC	E	614 452-7300
Columbus (G-9013)		

SECURITY UNDERWRITERS

Company		Phone
Old Rpblic Ttle Nthrn Ohio LLC	A	216 524-5700
Independence (G-12242)		

SELF-HELP GROUP HOME

Company		Phone
Madison House Inc	E	740 845-0145
London (G-13001)		
Rescare Ohio Inc	E	330 479-9841
Canton (G-2511)		
Rescare Ohio Inc	E	513 724-1177
Williamsburg (G-19635)		
Rescare Ohio Inc	D	513 829-8992
Hamilton (G-11768)		

SELF-HELP ORGANIZATION, NEC

Company		Phone
Positive Education Program	E	216 227-2730
Cleveland (G-6291)		
Substance Abuse Services Inc	E	419 243-7274
Toledo (G-18206)		

SELF-PROPELLED AIRCRAFT DEALER

Company		Phone
Lane Aviation Corporation	C	614 237-3747
Columbus (G-8037)		
McKinley Air Transport Inc	E	330 497-6956
Canton (G-2453)		

SEMICONDUCTOR CIRCUIT NETWORKS

Company		Phone
Micro Industries Corporation	D	740 548-7878
Westerville (G-19424)		

SEMICONDUCTORS & RELATED DEVICES

Company		Phone
CPC Logistics Inc	D	513 874-5787
Fairfield (G-10838)		
Pepperl + Fuchs Inc	C	330 425-3555
Twinsburg (G-18452)		

SENIOR HIGH SCHOOLS, PUBLIC

Company		Phone
Ashtabula Area City School Dst	E	440 992-1221
Ashtabula (G-712)		
Edison Local School District	E	740 543-4011
Amsterdam (G-608)		

SEPTIC TANK CLEANING SVCS

Company		Phone
Pro-Kleen Industrial Svcs Inc	E	740 689-1886
Lancaster (G-12566)		

SERVICE STATION EQPT REPAIR SVCS

Company		Phone
Petro-Com Corp	E	440 327-6900
North Ridgeville (G-15473)		

SERVICES, NEC

Company		Phone
Chp AP Shared Services	E	513 981-6704
Cincinnati (G-3258)		
Linemaster Services LLC	E	614 507-9945
Grove City (G-11577)		
Mid Ohio Emergency Svcs LLC	E	614 566-5070
Columbus (G-8162)		
Moon Co-Op Services	D	513 523-3990
Oxford (G-15826)		
P & D Removal Service	E	513 226-7687
Cincinnati (G-4246)		

SERVICES SECTION

SETTLEMENT HOUSE

Deepwood Industries Inc ....C....... 440 350-5231
  Mentor *(G-14168)*

SEWAGE & WATER TREATMENT EQPT

De Nora Tech LLC ....D....... 440 710-5300
  Painesville *(G-15850)*
Flow-Liner Systems Ltd ....E....... 800 348-0020
  Zanesville *(G-20478)*

SEWAGE FACILITIES

Belmont County of Ohio ....E....... 740 695-3144
  Saint Clairsville *(G-16622)*
City of Akron ....E....... 330 375-2666
  Akron *(G-140)*
City of Avon Lake ....E....... 440 933-6226
  Avon Lake *(G-925)*
City of Columbus ....D....... 614 645-3248
  Lockbourne *(G-12947)*
City of Dayton ....D....... 937 333-1837
  Dayton *(G-9411)*
City of Findlay ....E....... 419 424-7179
  Findlay *(G-11014)*
City of Hamilton ....E....... 513 785-7551
  Hamilton *(G-11709)*
City of Hamilton ....E....... 513 868-5971
  Hamilton *(G-11710)*
City of Kent ....D....... 330 678-8105
  Kent *(G-12359)*
City of Lima ....E....... 419 221-5175
  Lima *(G-12756)*
City of Lorain ....C....... 440 204-2500
  Lorain *(G-13024)*
City of Sandusky ....E....... 419 627-5906
  Sandusky *(G-16737)*
City of Sandusky ....E....... 419 627-5907
  Sandusky *(G-16739)*
City of Toledo ....C....... 419 936-2924
  Toledo *(G-17810)*
City of Toledo ....E....... 419 245-1800
  Toledo *(G-17807)*
City of Westerville ....E....... 614 901-6500
  Westerville *(G-19382)*
City of Zanesville ....E....... 740 455-0641
  Zanesville *(G-20465)*
Clermont Cnty Wtr Rsurces Dept ...D....... 513 732-7970
  Batavia *(G-999)*
County of Lorain ....D....... 440 329-5584
  Elyria *(G-10609)*
County of Stark ....A....... 330 451-2303
  Canton *(G-2323)*
County of Warren ....D....... 513 925-1377
  Lebanon *(G-12600)*
New Lexington City of ....E....... 740 342-1633
  New Lexington *(G-15057)*
Northast Ohio Rgonal Sewer Dst ..C....... 216 641-6000
  Cleveland *(G-6147)*
Northast Ohio Rgonal Sewer Dst ..D....... 216 531-4892
  Cleveland *(G-6148)*
Northast Ohio Rgonal Sewer Dst ..C....... 216 641-3200
  Cleveland *(G-6145)*
Northwestern Water & Sewer Dst ..E....... 419 354-9090
  Bowling Green *(G-1787)*

SEWER CLEANING & RODDING SVC

AAA Pipe Cleaning Corporation ....C....... 216 341-2900
  Cleveland *(G-4942)*
Adelmos Electric Sewer Clg Co .....E....... 216 641-2301
  Brooklyn Heights *(G-1909)*
American Residential Svcs LLC ....E....... 888 762-7752
  Columbus *(G-7006)*
Chemed Corporation ....D....... 513 762-6690
  Cincinnati *(G-3237)*
Drcler & Maller Inc ....E....... 614 575-0065
  Reynoldsburg *(G-16448)*
J and J Environmental Inc ....E....... 513 398-4521
  Mason *(G-13725)*
Mr Rooter Plumbing Corporation ...E....... 419 625-4444
  Independence *(G-12236)*
Nurotoco Massachusetts Inc ....C....... 513 762-6690
  Cincinnati *(G-4192)*
Roto-Rooter Development Co ....D....... 513 762-6690
  Cincinnati *(G-4442)*
Roto-Rooter Group Inc ....C....... 513 762-6690
  Cincinnati *(G-4443)*
Roto-Rooter Services Company .....E....... 614 238-8006
  Columbus *(G-8652)*

Roto-Rooter Services Company .....D....... 513 762-6690
  Cincinnati *(G-4444)*
Roto-Rooter Services Company .....D....... 513 541-3840
  Cincinnati *(G-4445)*
Roto-Rooter Services Company .....E....... 216 429-1928
  Solon *(G-17048)*
Tfh-Eb Inc ....D....... 614 253-7246
  Columbus *(G-8833)*

SEWING CONTRACTORS

Piqua Industrial Cut & Sew ....E....... 937 773-7397
  Piqua *(G-16157)*

SEWING MACHINE STORES

Pins & Needles Inc ....E....... 440 243-6400
  Cleveland *(G-6281)*

SEWING, NEEDLEWORK & PIECE GOODS STORE: Quilting Matls/Splys

Checker Notions Company Inc ......D....... 419 893-3636
  Maumee *(G-13894)*

SEWING, NEEDLEWORK & PIECE GOODS STORES: Knitting Splys

Pins & Needles Inc ....E....... 440 243-6400
  Cleveland *(G-6281)*

SHAPES & PILINGS, STRUCTURAL: Steel

Brenmar Construction Inc ....D....... 740 286-2151
  Jackson *(G-12307)*

SHEET METAL SPECIALTIES, EXC STAMPED

Allied Fabricating & Wldg Co ....E....... 614 751-6664
  Columbus *(G-6970)*
C & R Inc ....E....... 614 497-1130
  Groveport *(G-11626)*
Kirk & Blum Manufacturing Co ......C....... 513 458-2600
  Cincinnati *(G-3929)*
Kirk & Blum Manufacturing Co ......E....... 419 782-9885
  Defiance *(G-10043)*

SHEETING: Laminated Plastic

Schneller LLC ....D....... 330 673-1299
  Kent *(G-12395)*

SHELTERED WORKSHOPS

Ability Works Inc ....C....... 419 626-1048
  Sandusky *(G-16723)*
Alpha Group of Delaware Inc ....D....... 614 222-1855
  Columbus *(G-6976)*
Alpha Group of Delaware Inc ....D....... 740 368-5810
  Delaware *(G-10069)*
Angeline Industries Inc ....D....... 419 294-4488
  Upper Sandusky *(G-18557)*
ARC Industries Incorporated O .....C....... 614 479-2500
  Columbus *(G-7034)*
ARC Industries Incorporated O .....B....... 614 436-4800
  Columbus *(G-7035)*
ARC Industries Incorporated O .....B....... 614 864-2406
  Columbus *(G-7036)*
ARC Industries Incorporated O .....D....... 614 267-1207
  Columbus *(G-7037)*
Atco Inc ....C....... 740 592-6659
  Athens *(G-773)*
Belco Works Inc ....B....... 740 695-0500
  Saint Clairsville *(G-16617)*
Brookhill Center Industries ....E....... 419 876-3932
  Ottawa *(G-15796)*
Brown Cnty Bd Mntal Rtardation ...E....... 937 378-4891
  Georgetown *(G-11384)*
Capabilities Inc ....E....... 419 394-0003
  Saint Marys *(G-16670)*
Carroll Hills Industries Inc ....D....... 330 627-5524
  Carrollton *(G-2614)*
Cincinnati Assn For The Blind ......C....... 513 221-8558
  Cincinnati *(G-3282)*
CLI Incorporated ....C....... 419 668-8840
  Norwalk *(G-15566)*
County of Hamilton ....B....... 513 742-1576
  Cincinnati *(G-3428)*
County of Sandusky ....D....... 419 637-2243
  Fremont *(G-11190)*
County of Seneca ....D....... 419 435-0729
  Fostoria *(G-11125)*

SHELTERED WORKSHOPS

Cuyahoga County ....D....... 216 265-3030
  Cleveland *(G-5451)*
D-R Training Center & Workshop ..C....... 419 289-0470
  Ashland *(G-678)*
Easter Seals Tristate LLC ....D....... 513 281-2316
  Cincinnati *(G-3533)*
Employment Development Inc ......C....... 330 424-7711
  Lisbon *(G-12936)*
Fairfield Industries Inc ....C....... 740 652-7230
  Carroll *(G-2608)*
Fairhaven Sheltered Workshop .....C....... 330 652-1116
  Niles *(G-15291)*
Fairhaven Sheltered Workshop .....C....... 330 847-7275
  Warren *(G-18857)*
Fairhaven Sheltered Workshop .....C....... 330 505-3644
  Niles *(G-15292)*
First Capital Enterprises Inc ....D....... 740 773-2166
  Chillicothe *(G-2840)*
Gallco Inc ....D....... 740 446-3775
  Gallipolis *(G-11316)*
Goodwill Inds of S Centl Ohio ....D....... 740 702-4000
  Chillicothe *(G-2843)*
Goodwill Industries ....E....... 330 264-1300
  Wooster *(G-19865)*
Greene Inc ....D....... 937 562-4200
  Xenia *(G-20058)*
Harco Industries Inc ....E....... 419 674-4159
  Kenton *(G-12413)*
Harrison Industries Inc ....D....... 740 942-2988
  Cadiz *(G-2077)*
Hocking Valley Industries Inc ....D....... 740 385-2118
  Logan *(G-12975)*
Hopewell Industries Inc ....C....... 740 622-3563
  Coshocton *(G-9107)*
Hunter Defense Tech Inc ....E....... 216 438-6111
  Solon *(G-17016)*
J-Vac Industries Inc ....D....... 740 384-2155
  Wellston *(G-19000)*
Ken Harper ....C....... 740 439-4452
  Byesville *(G-2071)*
Knox New Hope Industries Inc .....C....... 740 397-4601
  Mount Vernon *(G-14907)*
Licco Inc ....C....... 740 522-8345
  Newark *(G-15185)*
Lorain County Board ....E....... 440 329-3734
  Elyria *(G-10646)*
Lott Industries Incorporated ....B....... 419 476-2516
  Toledo *(G-18008)*
Lott Industries Incorporated ....B....... 419 891-5215
  Maumee *(G-13937)*
Lott Industries Incorporated ....B....... 419 534-4980
  Toledo *(G-18009)*
Lynn Hope Industries Inc ....D....... 330 674-8045
  Holmesville *(G-12073)*
Marca Industries Inc ....E....... 740 387-1035
  Marion *(G-13551)*
Marion Goodwill Industries ....E....... 740 387-7023
  Marion *(G-13560)*
Medina County Sheltered Inds ......B....... 330 334-4491
  Wadsworth *(G-18765)*
Meigs Industries Inc ....E....... 740 992-6681
  Syracuse *(G-17632)*
Metzenbaum Sheltered Inds ....C....... 440 729-1919
  Chesterland *(G-2800)*
Monco Enterprises Inc ....A....... 937 461-0034
  Dayton *(G-9754)*
Muskingum Starlight Industries ....D....... 740 453-4622
  Zanesville *(G-20512)*
Nick Amster Inc ....C....... 330 264-9667
  Wooster *(G-19893)*
Portage Industries Inc ....C....... 330 296-2839
  Ravenna *(G-16400)*
Production Services Unlimited .....D....... 513 695-1658
  Lebanon *(G-12637)*
R T Industries Inc ....C....... 937 339-8313
  Troy *(G-18375)*
R T Industries Inc ....C....... 937 335-5784
  Troy *(G-18374)*
Ross Training Center Inc ....D....... 937 592-0025
  Bellefontaine *(G-1394)*
RTC Industries Inc ....E....... 937 592-0534
  Bellefontaine *(G-1395)*
Sandco Industries ....C....... 419 334-9090
  Clyde *(G-6822)*
Stark County Board of Developm ..A....... 330 477-5200
  Canton *(G-2543)*
Starlight Enterprises Inc ....C....... 330 339-2020
  New Philadelphia *(G-15116)*
Tri-State Industries Inc ....C....... 740 532-0406
  Coal Grove *(G-6826)*

Employee Codes: A=Over 500 employees, B=251-500
C=101-250, D=51-100, E=25-50

2018 Harris Ohio
Services Directory

SHELTERED WORKSHOPS

U-Co Industries Inc ....D...... 937 644-3021
  Marysville (G-13656)
Wasco Inc ....E...... 740 373-3418
  Marietta (G-13518)
Zanesvlle Welfre Orgnztn/Goodw ....D...... 740 450-6060
  Zanesville (G-20560)

SHELVING: Office & Store, Exc Wood

Panacea Products Corporation ....E...... 614 850-7000
  Columbus (G-8513)

SHIMS: Metal

Ohio Gasket and Shim Co Inc ....E...... 330 630-0626
  Akron (G-366)

SHIPBUILDING & REPAIR

Great Lakes Group ....C...... 216 621-4854
  Cleveland (G-5689)
Tack-Anew Inc ....E...... 419 734-4212
  Port Clinton (G-16257)

SHIPPING AGENTS

Garys Pharmacy Inc ....E...... 937 456-5777
  Eaton (G-10561)
Innovel Solutions Inc ....D...... 614 878-2092
  Columbus (G-7901)
Innovel Solutions Inc ....A...... 614 492-5304
  Columbus (G-7902)
Tersher Corporation ....D...... 440 439-8383
  Strongsville (G-17516)
World Shipping Inc ....E...... 440 356-7676
  Cleveland (G-6759)
Xpo Intermodal Solutions Inc ....A...... 614 923-1400
  Dublin (G-10495)

SHOE STORES

Elder-Beerman Stores Corp ....A...... 937 296-2700
  Moraine (G-14780)

SHOE STORES: Men's

Cov-Ro Inc ....E...... 330 856-3176
  Warren (G-18841)
Lehigh Outfitters LLC ....C...... 740 753-1951
  Nelsonville (G-14965)

SHOES & BOOTS WHOLESALERS

M & R Fredericktown Ltd Inc ....E...... 440 801-1563
  Akron (G-331)
RG Barry Corporation ....D...... 614 864-6400
  Pickerington (G-16105)

SHOES: Men's

Georgia Boot LLC ....D...... 740 753-1951
  Nelsonville (G-14964)

SHOES: Plastic Or Rubber

Georgia Boot LLC ....D...... 740 753-1951
  Nelsonville (G-14964)

SHOES: Women's

Georgia Boot LLC ....D...... 740 753-1951
  Nelsonville (G-14964)

SHOPPING CART REPAIR SVCS

Hays Enterprises Inc ....E...... 330 299-8639
  Warren (G-18861)
Omni Cart Services Inc ....E...... 440 205-8363
  Mentor (G-14225)

SHOPPING CENTERS & MALLS

Cbl & Associates Prpts Inc ....E...... 513 424-8517
  Middletown (G-14476)
Easton Town Center II LLC ....D...... 614 416-7000
  Columbus (G-7567)
First Interstate Properties ....E...... 216 381-2900
  Cleveland (G-5598)
Forest City Properties LLC ....C...... 216 621-6060
  Cleveland (G-5619)
Glemsure Realty Trust ....E...... 740 522-6620
  Heath (G-11837)
Goodman Properties Inc ....E...... 740 264-7781
  Steubenville (G-17318)

Kingsmason Properties Ltd ....E...... 513 932-6010
  Lebanon (G-12616)
Lima Mall Inc ....E...... 419 331-6255
  Lima (G-12822)
Lofinos Inc ....D...... 937 431-1662
  Beavercreek (G-1250)
Mills Corporation ....E...... 513 671-2882
  Cincinnati (G-4099)
Quincy Mall Inc ....E...... 614 228-5331
  Columbus (G-8582)
Schottenstein Realty LLC ....E...... 614 445-8461
  Columbus (G-8704)
Simon Property Group ....E...... 614 717-9300
  Dublin (G-10454)
United Management Inc ....D...... 614 228-5331
  Columbus (G-8894)
Zaremba LLC ....D...... 216 221-6600
  Cleveland (G-6780)

SIDING: Plastic

Style Crest Inc ....B...... 419 332-7369
  Fremont (G-11223)

SIGN PAINTING & LETTERING SHOP

General Theming Contrs LLC ....C...... 614 252-6342
  Columbus (G-7736)
Ray Meyer Sign Company Inc ....E...... 513 984-5446
  Loveland (G-13155)
Toledo Sign Company Inc ....E...... 419 244-4444
  Toledo (G-18250)

SIGNALS: Traffic Control, Electric

Area Wide Protective Inc ....E...... 513 321-9889
  Fairfield (G-10820)
Paul Peterson Company ....E...... 614 486-4375
  Columbus (G-8522)
Security Fence Group Inc ....E...... 513 681-3700
  Cincinnati (G-4489)

SIGNS & ADVERTISING SPECIALTIES

A & A Safety Inc ....E...... 513 943-6100
  Amelia (G-571)
Archer Corporation ....E...... 330 455-9995
  Canton (G-2244)
Bates Metal Products Inc ....D...... 740 498-8371
  Port Washington (G-16260)
Belco Works Inc ....B...... 740 695-0500
  Saint Clairsville (G-16617)
Brown Cnty Bd Mntal Rtardation ....E...... 937 378-4891
  Georgetown (G-11384)
Galaxy Balloons Incorporated ....C...... 216 476-3360
  Cleveland (G-5651)
Glavin Industries Inc ....E...... 440 349-0049
  Solon (G-17009)
HP Manufacturing Company Inc ....D...... 216 361-6500
  Cleveland (G-5788)
Identitek Systems Inc ....D...... 330 832-9844
  Massillon (G-13822)
Orange Barrel Media LLC ....E...... 614 294-4898
  Columbus (G-8477)
Sabco Industries Inc ....E...... 419 531-5347
  Toledo (G-18169)
Screen Works Inc ....E...... 937 264-9111
  Dayton (G-9870)
Sign America Incorporated ....E...... 740 765-5555
  Richmond (G-16535)
Sign Source USA Inc ....D...... 419 224-1130
  Lima (G-12878)

SIGNS & ADVERTISING SPECIALTIES: Signs

Kessler Sign Company ....E...... 740 453-0668
  Zanesville (G-20494)
Paul Peterson Safety Div Inc ....E...... 614 486-4375
  Columbus (G-8523)

SIGNS & ADVERTSG SPECIALTIES: Displays/Cutouts Window/Lobby

BDS Packaging Inc ....D...... 937 643-0530
  Moraine (G-14752)
Benchmark Craftsman Inc ....E...... 330 975-4214
  Seville (G-16837)

SIGNS, ELECTRICAL: Wholesalers

Sign America Incorporated ....E...... 740 765-5555
  Richmond (G-16535)

SIGNS, EXC ELECTRIC, WHOLESALE

Dualite Sales & Service Inc ....C...... 513 724-7100
  Williamsburg (G-19632)

SIGNS: Electrical

Brilliant Electric Sign Co Ltd ....D...... 216 741-3800
  Brooklyn Heights (G-1911)
Danite Holdings Ltd ....E...... 614 444-3333
  Columbus (G-7488)
Gus Holthaus Signs Inc ....E...... 513 861-0060
  Cincinnati (G-3720)
Mc Sign Company ....C...... 440 209-6200
  Mentor (G-14211)
United-Maier Signs Inc ....D...... 513 681-6600
  Cincinnati (G-4743)

SILK SCREEN DESIGN SVCS

Galaxy Balloons Incorporated ....C...... 216 476-3360
  Cleveland (G-5651)
Screen Works Inc ....E...... 937 264-9111
  Dayton (G-9870)
Woodrow Manufacturing Co ....E...... 937 399-9333
  Springfield (G-17300)

SKATING RINKS: Roller

Edgewood Skate Arena ....E...... 419 331-0647
  Lima (G-12772)
Ohio Skate Inc ....E...... 419 476-2808
  Toledo (G-18103)
Skate Town U S A ....E...... 513 874-9855
  West Chester (G-19155)
Skateworld Inc ....E...... 937 294-4032
  Dayton (G-9885)
United Skates America Inc ....E...... 440 944-5300
  Wickliffe (G-19614)

SKI LODGE

Sycamore Lake Inc ....C...... 440 729-9775
  Chesterland (G-2804)

SKILL TRAINING CENTER

Capano & Associates LLC ....E...... 513 403-6000
  Liberty Township (G-12717)

SNACK & NONALCOHOLIC BEVERAGE BARS

Chillicothe Bowling Lanes Inc ....E...... 740 773-3300
  Chillicothe (G-2817)
Freeway Lanes Bowl Group LLC ....E...... 440 946-5131
  Mentor (G-14178)
Holiday Lanes Inc ....E...... 614 861-1600
  Columbus (G-7846)
Loyal Oak Golf Course Inc ....E...... 330 825-2904
  Barberton (G-971)
Plaz-Way Inc ....E...... 330 264-9025
  Wooster (G-19904)
Roseland Lanes Inc ....D...... 440 439-0097
  Bedford (G-1332)
Stonehedge Enterprises Inc ....E...... 330 928-2161
  Akron (G-451)

SNOW PLOWING SVCS

Bauer Lawn Maintenance Inc ....E...... 419 893-5296
  Maumee (G-13886)
Bladecutters Lawn Service Inc ....E...... 937 274-3861
  Dayton (G-9360)
Brunk Excavating Inc ....E...... 513 360-0308
  Monroe (G-14691)
C & B Buck Bros Asp Maint LLC ....E...... 419 536-7325
  Toledo (G-17789)
Dun Rite Home Improvement Inc ....E...... 330 650-5322
  Macedonia (G-13196)
Green Impressions LLC ....E...... 440 240-8508
  Sheffield Village (G-16886)
Greenscapes Landscape Company ....D...... 614 837-1869
  Columbus (G-7778)
H A M Landscaping Inc ....E...... 216 663-6666
  Cleveland (G-5714)
Mc Clurg & Creamer Inc ....E...... 419 866-7080
  Holland (G-12036)
Ohio Irrigation Lawn Sprinkler ....E...... 937 432-9911
  Dayton (G-9786)
Paramount Lawn Service Inc ....E...... 513 984-5200
  Loveland (G-13152)

SERVICES SECTION

SOCIAL SVCS, HANDICAPPED

Schill Landscaping and Lawn CA ....D....... 440 327-3030
  North Ridgeville *(G-15477)*
Spellacys Turf-Lawn Inc ....E....... 740 965-5508
  Galena *(G-11287)*
Supers Landscaping Inc ....E....... 440 775-0027
  Oberlin *(G-15661)*
T L C Landscaping Inc..............................E....... 440 248-4852
  Cleveland *(G-6565)*
T O J Inc..E....... 440 352-1900
  Mentor *(G-14247)*
Warstler Brothers Landscaping ....E....... 330 492-9500
  Canton *(G-2582)*
Yardmaster of Columbus Inc ....E....... 614 863-4510
  Blacklick *(G-1513)*
Z Snow Removal Inc ....E....... 513 683-7719
  Maineville *(G-13248)*

SOAPS & DETERGENTS

Cincinnati - Vulcan Company ....D....... 513 242-5300
  Cincinnati *(G-3278)*
Cr Brands Inc ....D....... 513 860-5039
  West Chester *(G-19058)*
New Vulco Mfg & Sales Co LLC............D....... 513 242-2672
  Cincinnati *(G-4158)*
Washing Systems LLC ....C....... 800 272-1974
  Loveland *(G-13163)*

SOCIAL CHANGE ASSOCIATION

Community Action Columbiana CT........D....... 330 424-7221
  Lisbon *(G-12932)*
Community Re-Entry Inc ....E....... 216 696-2717
  Cleveland *(G-5385)*
Provider Services Inc ....D....... 614 888-2021
  Columbus *(G-8575)*

SOCIAL CLUBS

Akron Womans City Club Inc..................E....... 330 762-6261
  Akron *(G-59)*
Hide-A-Way Hills Club ....E....... 740 746-9589
  Sugar Grove *(G-17541)*
Leo Yannenoff Jewish Community ....C....... 614 231-2731
  Columbus *(G-8052)*
Minature Society Cincinnati ....D....... 513 931-9708
  Cincinnati *(G-4102)*
Toledo Club ....D....... 419 243-2200
  Toledo *(G-18234)*
Tusco Imaa Chapter No 602 ....E....... 330 878-7369
  Strasburg *(G-17401)*
Union Club Company ....D....... 216 621-4230
  Cleveland *(G-6631)*
University Club Inc ....E....... 513 721-2600
  Cincinnati *(G-4749)*
Youngstown Club......................................E....... 330 744-3111
  Youngstown *(G-20428)*

SOCIAL SERVICES INFORMATION EXCHANGE

City of Warrensville Heights ....E....... 216 587-1230
  Cleveland *(G-5277)*
Greene Cnty Chld Svc Brd Frbrn.............D....... 937 878-1415
  Xenia *(G-20052)*
Lifeline Systems Company ....E....... 330 762-5627
  Akron *(G-319)*
Med Assist Prgram of Info Line ....E....... 330 762-0609
  Akron *(G-335)*

SOCIAL SERVICES, NEC

Columbus Surgical Center LLP ....E....... 614 932-9503
  Dublin *(G-10301)*
GE Reuter Stokes....................................D....... 216 749-6332
  Cleveland *(G-5664)*
Jackson Co Bd of Dd ....D....... 740 384-7938
  Wellston *(G-19001)*
Neighborhood Health Care Inc ....E....... 513 221-4949
  Cincinnati *(G-4152)*
Shafer Confession ....E....... 419 399-4662
  Paulding *(G-15936)*
St Jude Social Concern Hot....................D....... 440 365-7971
  Elyria *(G-10683)*
W T C S A Headstart Niles Ctr................E....... 330 652-0338
  Niles *(G-15209)*

SOCIAL SVCS CENTER

Aids Tskfrce Grter Clvland Inc................E....... 216 357-3131
  Cleveland *(G-4970)*
American Cancer Society East................E....... 800 227-2345
  Cleveland *(G-5005)*

American National Red Cross ....C....... 419 382-2707
  Toledo *(G-17750)*
American Red Cross ....E....... 937 376-3111
  Xenia *(G-20041)*
Ashtabula County Community ....C....... 440 997-1721
  Ashtabula *(G-721)*
Bridgeway Inc...B....... 216 688-4114
  Cleveland *(G-5138)*
Catholic Charities Corporation ....B....... 330 723-9615
  Medina *(G-14042)*
Catholic Charities of Southwst.................E....... 937 325-8715
  Springfield *(G-17157)*
Catholic Charities of SW Ohio ....D....... 513 241-7745
  Cincinnati *(G-3194)*
Catholic Diocese of Columbus ....E....... 614 221-5891
  Columbus *(G-7211)*
Catholic Social Services Inc ....D....... 614 221-5891
  Columbus *(G-7212)*
Central Cmnty Hse of Columbus ....E....... 614 253-7267
  Columbus *(G-7227)*
Childrens Hunger Alliance ....D....... 614 341-7700
  Columbus *(G-7263)*
Cleveland Christian Home Inc ....E....... 216 671-0977
  Cleveland *(G-5294)*
Commu Act Comm of Fayette Cnty.........D....... 740 335-7282
  Wshngtn CT Hs *(G-20016)*
Community Action ....E....... 740 354-7541
  Portsmouth *(G-16271)*
Community Action Comsn Belmont.........E....... 740 695-0293
  Saint Clairsville *(G-16632)*
Community Action Program Comm ....E....... 740 653-1711
  Lancaster *(G-12521)*
Community Action-Wayne/Medina ....D....... 330 264-8677
  Wooster *(G-19851)*
Consumer Support Services Inc ....D....... 740 522-5464
  Newark *(G-15159)*
County of Allen ....C....... 419 228-2120
  Lima *(G-12764)*
County of Lorain ....E....... 440 329-3734
  Elyria *(G-10610)*
County of Lorain ....D....... 440 284-1830
  Elyria *(G-10613)*
County of Meigs ....E....... 740 992-2117
  Middleport *(G-14406)*
County of Richland ....C....... 419 774-5400
  Mansfield *(G-13281)*
County of Warren ....E....... 513 695-1420
  Lebanon *(G-12598)*
County of Washington..............................D....... 740 373-5513
  Marietta *(G-13440)*
Creative Foundations Inc ....E....... 740 362-5102
  Delaware *(G-10085)*
East End Community Svcs Corp ....E....... 937 259-1898
  Dayton *(G-9514)*
East End Neighborhood Hse Assn ....E....... 216 791-9378
  Cleveland *(G-5519)*
Easter Seals Center ....D....... 614 228-5523
  Hilliard *(G-11898)*
Fairborn Fish ....E....... 937 879-1313
  Fairborn *(G-10794)*
Faith Mission Inc.......................................E....... 614 224-6617
  Columbus *(G-7634)*
Family Service..E....... 513 381-6300
  Cincinnati *(G-3591)*
Family Service Association ....E....... 937 222-9481
  Moraine *(G-14783)*
Family Service of NW Ohio ....D....... 419 321-6455
  Toledo *(G-17878)*
Free Store/Food Bank Inc ....E....... 513 482-4526
  Cincinnati *(G-3648)*
Fulton County Senior Center ....E....... 419 337-9299
  Wauseon *(G-18957)*
Furniture Bank Central Ohio ....E....... 614 272-9544
  Columbus *(G-7715)*
G M N Tri Cnty Communty Action ....C....... 740 732-2388
  Caldwell *(G-2085)*
Godman Guild ....E....... 614 294-5476
  Columbus *(G-7756)*
Grace Resurrection Association ....E....... 937 548-2595
  Greenville *(G-11503)*
Greater Cincinnati Behavioral ....B....... 513 354-7000
  Walnut Hills *(G-18787)*
Greater Cincinnati Behavioral ....D....... 513 755-2203
  Walnut Hills *(G-18788)*
Greene Cnty Combined Hlth Dst..............D....... 937 374-5600
  Xenia *(G-20053)*
Handson Central Ohio Inc ....E....... 614 221-2255
  Columbus *(G-7798)*
Harcatus Tri-County Community ....E....... 740 922-0933
  New Philadelphia *(G-15097)*

Highlnd Cnty Commnty Action or ....E....... 937 393-3060
  Hillsboro *(G-11981)*
Hockingthensperry Cmnty Action ....E....... 740 385-6813
  Logan *(G-12976)*
Homeless Families Foundation ....E....... 614 461-9427
  Columbus *(G-7852)*
Inside Out ....E....... 937 525-7880
  Springfield *(G-17212)*
Jewish Community Ctr Cleveland ....C....... 216 831-0700
  Beachwood *(G-1091)*
Jewish Family Services ....E....... 614 231-1890
  Columbus *(G-7940)*
Jewish Family Services Associa ....E....... 216 292-3999
  Cleveland *(G-5864)*
Jewish Fderation of Cincinnati.................E....... 513 985-1500
  Cincinnati *(G-3870)*
Kno-Ho-Co- Ashland Community A ....C....... 740 622-9801
  Coshocton *(G-9110)*
Living In Family Environment ....D....... 614 475-5305
  Gahanna *(G-11255)*
Miami Valley Community Action ....E....... 937 456-2800
  Eaton *(G-10569)*
National Youth Advocate Progra ....D....... 614 252-6927
  Columbus *(G-8226)*
Nick Amster Inc..D....... 330 264-9667
  Wooster *(G-19894)*
Ohioguidestone...C....... 440 260-8900
  Cleveland *(G-6197)*
Pathway Inc ....E....... 419 242-7304
  Toledo *(G-18122)*
Pathways of Central Ohio ....E....... 740 345-6166
  Newark *(G-15227)*
Personal & Fmly Counseling Svc ....E....... 330 343-8171
  New Philadelphia *(G-15111)*
Pickaway County Community Acti ....D....... 740 477-1655
  Circleville *(G-4894)*
Pickaway County Community Acti ....E....... 740 474-7411
  Circleville *(G-4895)*
Pump House Ministries ....E....... 419 207-3900
  Ashland *(G-692)*
Rescue Mission of Mahoning Val ....E....... 330 744-5485
  Youngstown *(G-20349)*
Rescue Mission of Mahoning Val ....E....... 330 744-5485
  Youngstown *(G-20350)*
Santa Maria Community Svcs Inc ....E....... 513 557-2720
  Cincinnati *(G-4477)*
Spanish American Committee ....E....... 216 961-2100
  Cleveland *(G-6513)*
St Vincent Family Centers.......................C....... 614 252-0731
  Columbus *(G-8771)*
Support To At Risk Teens........................E....... 216 696-5507
  Cleveland *(G-6557)*
Tasc of Northwest Ohio Inc ....E....... 419 242-9955
  Toledo *(G-18214)*
The Foodbank Inc ....E....... 937 461-0265
  Dayton *(G-9924)*
Trumbull County One Stop ....D....... 330 675-2000
  Warren *(G-18911)*
Ussa Inc ....E....... 740 354-6672
  Portsmouth *(G-16319)*
Volunters of Amer Greater Ohio ....D....... 216 541-9000
  Cleveland *(G-6711)*
Volunters of Amer Greater Ohio ....C....... 614 253-6100
  Columbus *(G-8951)*
Volunters of Amer Greater Ohio ....E....... 614 263-9134
  Columbus *(G-8952)*
West Ohio Cmnty Action Partnr ....C....... 419 227-2586
  Lima *(G-12918)*
West Side Community House ....E....... 216 771-7297
  Cleveland *(G-6739)*
WoodInds Srving Centl Ohio Inc ....E....... 740 349-7051
  Newark *(G-15248)*
Youngstown Area Jwish Fdration ....C....... 330 746-3251
  Youngstown *(G-20425)*
Youngstown Neighborhood Dev ....E....... 330 480-0423
  Youngstown *(G-20432)*

SOCIAL SVCS, HANDICAPPED

Achievement Ctrs For Children...............D....... 216 292-9700
  Cleveland *(G-4954)*
Alexson Services Inc................................E....... 614 889-5837
  Dublin *(G-10240)*
ARC Industries Incorporated O ....B....... 614 836-0700
  Groveport *(G-11623)*
Board Mental Retardation Dvlpm ....E....... 740 472-1712
  Woodsfield *(G-19812)*
Bridges To Independence Inc ....C....... 740 362-1996
  Delaware *(G-10074)*
Broken Arrow Inc ....E....... 419 562-3480
  Bucyrus *(G-2024)*

SOCIAL SVCS, HANDICAPPED

Company	Code	Phone
Catholic Residential Service	E	513 784-0400
Cincinnati (G-3195)		
Champaign Residential Services	E	614 481-5550
Columbus (G-7251)		
Columbus Spech Hearing Ctr Cpd	D	614 263-5151
Columbus (G-7386)		
County of Union	D	937 645-6733
Marysville (G-13613)		
Free Store/Food Bank Inc	E	513 241-1064
Cincinnati (G-3649)		
Freestore/Foodbank	E	513 482-4500
Cincinnati (G-3650)		
Licking County Board of Mrdd	C	740 349-6588
Newark (G-15188)		
Matco Industries Inc	E	740 852-7054
London (G-13002)		
Murray Ridge Production Center	B	440 329-3734
Elyria (G-10657)		
Opportunities For Ohioans	E	614 438-1200
Columbus (G-8473)		
Outreach Cmnty Living Svcs Inc	E	330 263-0862
Wooster (G-19901)		
Pickaway Diversified	E	740 474-1522
Circleville (G-4898)		
Portage County Board	D	330 678-2400
Ravenna (G-16398)		
Sechkar Company	E	740 385-8900
Nelsonville (G-14968)		
Self Reliance Inc	E	937 525-0809
Springfield (G-17273)		
Siffrin Residential Assn	C	330 799-8932
Youngstown (G-20375)		
Society For Handicapped Citzns	E	937 746-4201
Carlisle (G-2606)		
United Disability Services Inc	C	330 374-1169
Akron (G-485)		
Upreach LLC	B	614 442-7702
Columbus (G-8917)		
Whetstone Industries Inc	E	419 947-9222
Mount Gilead (G-14864)		

SOCIAL SVCS: Individual & Family

Company	Code	Phone
Ability Works Inc	C	419 626-1048
Sandusky (G-16723)		
Absolute Care Management Llc	E	614 846-8053
Columbus (G-6929)		
Achievement Ctrs For Children	E	440 250-2520
Westlake (G-19454)		
Action For Children Inc	E	614 224-0222
Columbus (G-6941)		
Akron General Foundation	E	330 344-6888
Akron (G-41)		
All Star Training Club	E	330 352-5602
Akron (G-779)		
Allwell Behavioral Health Svcs	C	740 454-9766
Zanesville (G-20440)		
Alternative Paths Inc	E	330 725-9195
Medina (G-14035)		
American National Red Cross	D	216 303-5476
Parma (G-15899)		
American National Red Cross	D	330 535-6131
Akron (G-72)		
American Red Cross	E	937 222-0124
Dayton (G-9332)		
Archdiocese of Cincinnati	E	937 323-6507
Springfield (G-17148)		
Ashtabula Community Counseling	D	440 998-6032
Ashtabula (G-716)		
Ashtabula County Commnty Actn	D	440 576-6911
Jefferson (G-12330)		
Assisted Living Concepts Inc	E	740 450-2744
Zanesville (G-20443)		
Assoc Dvlpmtly Disabled	E	614 486-4361
Westerville (G-19365)		
Avalon Foodservice Inc	C	330 854-4551
Canal Fulton (G-2140)		
Beavercreek YMCA	D	937 426-9622
Dayton (G-9351)		
Behavioral Treatments	E	614 558-1968
Hilliard (G-11881)		
Behavral Cnnctions WD Cnty Inc	E	419 872-2419
Perrysburg (G-15976)		
Bellefaire Jewish Chld Bur	B	216 932-2800
Shaker Heights (G-16856)		
Belmont County of Ohio	D	740 695-0460
Saint Clairsville (G-16624)		
Benjamin Rose Institute	E	216 791-8000
Cleveland (G-5117)		
Benjamin Rose Institute	D	216 791-3580
Cleveland (G-5116)		
Biomat Usa Inc	E	419 531-3332
Toledo (G-17772)		
Blick Clinic Inc	C	330 762-5425
Akron (G-103)		
Box 21 Rescue Squad Inc	E	937 223-2821
Dayton (G-9365)		
Brenn Field Nursing Center	C	330 683-4075
Orrville (G-15767)		
Butler County of Ohio	C	513 887-3728
Fairfield Township (G-10926)		
Casto Health Care	D	419 884-6400
Mansfield (G-13272)		
Catholic Charities Corporation	E	216 268-4006
Cleveland (G-5190)		
Center For Cognitv Behav Psych	E	614 459-4490
Columbus (G-7224)		
Center For Families & Children	E	216 932-9497
Cleveland Heights (G-6786)		
Center For Individual and Fmly	C	419 522-4357
Mansfield (G-13274)		
Champaign Cnty Board of Dd	E	937 653-5217
Urbana (G-18576)		
Childrens Cmprhensive Svcs Inc	D	419 589-5511
Mansfield (G-13276)		
Childrens Homecare Services	E	614 355-1100
Columbus (G-7261)		
Choices For Vctims Dom Volence	D	614 258-6080
Columbus (G-7267)		
Christian Aid Ministries	E	330 893-2428
Millersburg (G-14593)		
Christian Chld HM Ohio Inc	D	330 345-7949
Wooster (G-19841)		
Cincysmiles Foundation Inc	E	513 621-0248
Cincinnati (G-3345)		
Circle Health Services	E	216 721-4010
Cleveland (G-5242)		
City Gospel Mission	E	513 241-5525
Cincinnati (G-3358)		
Clermont County Community Svcs	E	513 732-2277
Batavia (G-1000)		
Columbus Foundation	E	614 251-4000
Columbus (G-7354)		
Community Action Program Corp	E	740 373-6016
Marietta (G-13437)		
Community Solutions Assn	E	330 394-9090
Warren (G-18838)		
Concord	E	614 882-9338
Westerville (G-19391)		
Consumer Support Services Inc	B	740 788-8257
Newark (G-15158)		
Consumer Support Services Inc	D	330 764-4785
Medina (G-14050)		
Corporation For OH Appalachian	E	740 594-8499
Cheshire (G-2790)		
Council For Economic Opport	D	216 696-9077
Cleveland (G-5414)		
Council On Aging of Southweste	C	513 721-1025
Cincinnati (G-3427)		
Council On Rur Svc Prgrams Inc	E	937 773-0773
Piqua (G-16141)		
County of Clark	B	937 327-1700
Springfield (G-17181)		
County of Columbiana	C	330 424-1386
Lisbon (G-12934)		
County of Cuyahoga	D	216 681-4433
Cleveland (G-5425)		
County of Darke	E	937 526-4488
Versailles (G-18725)		
County of Guernsey	E	740 439-6681
Cambridge (G-2109)		
County of Hamilton	B	513 742-1576
Cincinnati (G-3428)		
County of Highland	E	937 393-4278
Hillsboro (G-11970)		
County of Holmes	E	330 674-1111
Millersburg (G-14601)		
County of Lake	D	440 269-2193
Willoughby (G-19656)		
County of Lucas	E	419 213-3000
Toledo (G-17833)		
County of Lucas	B	419 213-8999
Toledo (G-17835)		
County of Mercer	E	419 586-5106
Celina (G-2644)		
County of Montgomery	B	937 224-5437
Dayton (G-9432)		
County of Montgomery	B	937 225-4804
Dayton (G-9436)		
County of Ottawa	E	419 898-2089
Oak Harbor (G-15608)		
County of Pickaway	D	740 474-7588
Circleville (G-4885)		
County of Richland	C	419 774-4100
Mansfield (G-13280)		
County of Summit	B	330 643-7217
Akron (G-172)		
County of Summit	A	330 634-8193
Tallmadge (G-17636)		
Creative Diversified Services	E	937 376-7810
Xenia (G-20048)		
Crossroads Lake County Adole	D	440 255-1700
Mentor (G-14165)		
Cuyahoga County	A	216 431-4500
Cleveland (G-5452)		
Cyo & Community Services Inc	E	330 762-2961
Akron (G-184)		
Defiance Cnty Bd Commissioners	E	419 782-3233
Defiance (G-10025)		
Developmental Disabilities	E	513 732-7000
Batavia (G-1009)		
Developmental Disabilities	D	513 732-7015
Owensville (G-15809)		
Develpmntal Dsblties Ohio Dept	C	937 233-8108
Columbus (G-7514)		
Don Bosco Community Center Inc	D	816 421-3160
Cleveland (G-5500)		
Easter Seal Society of	D	330 743-1168
Youngstown (G-20176)		
Easter Seals Tristate	C	513 985-0515
Blue Ash (G-1582)		
Easter Seals Tristate LLC	C	513 475-6791
Cincinnati (G-3534)		
Eastway Corporation	C	937 496-2000
Dayton (G-9516)		
Echoing Hills Village Inc	A	740 327-2311
Warsaw (G-18936)		
Equitas Health Inc	C	614 299-2437
Columbus (G-7603)		
Equitas Health Inc	E	937 461-2437
Dayton (G-9529)		
Family Cmnty Svcs Portage Cnty	C	330 297-0078
Ravenna (G-16385)		
Family YMCA of LANcstr&fairfld	D	740 277-7373
Lancaster (G-12541)		
Fayette Progressive Industries	E	740 335-7453
Wshngtn CT Hs (G-20023)		
Findlay Y M C A Child Dev	E	419 422-3174
Findlay (G-11031)		
Frans Child Care-Mansfield	C	419 775-2500
Mansfield (G-13304)		
Galion Community Center YMCA	E	419 468-7754
Galion (G-11297)		
Gallia-Meigs Community Action	E	740 367-7341
Cheshire (G-2790)		
Girl Scuts Appleseed Ridge Inc	E	419 225-4085
Lima (G-12783)		
Golden String Inc	E	330 503-3894
Youngstown (G-20203)		
Good Smaritan Netwrk Ross Cnty	E	740 774-6303
Chillicothe (G-2842)		
Goodwill Inds of S Centl Ohio	D	740 702-4000
Chillicothe (G-2843)		
Goodwill Industries Inc	E	330 724-6995
Akron (G-241)		
Goodwill Industries of Erie	D	419 355-1579
Fremont (G-11204)		
Goodwill Industries of Erie	E	419 625-4744
Sandusky (G-16763)		
Goodwill Industries of Erie	D	419 334-7566
Fremont (G-11205)		
Graceworks Lutheran Services	C	937 433-2110
Dayton (G-9585)		
Great Miami Valley YMCA	D	513 887-0001
Hamilton (G-11733)		
Great Miami Valley YMCA	C	513 892-9622
Fairfield Township (G-10930)		
Great Miami Valley YMCA	D	513 887-0014
Hamilton (G-11735)		
Great Miami Valley YMCA	D	513 868-9622
Hamilton (G-11736)		
Great Miami Valley YMCA	D	513 829-3091
Fairfield (G-10854)		
Greater Cleveland Food Bnk Inc	E	216 738-2265
Cleveland (G-5696)		
Hardin County Family YMCA	E	419 673-6131
Kenton (G-12416)		
Hattie Larlham Center For	C	330 274-2272
Mantua (G-13387)		
Havar Inc	D	740 594-3533
Athens (G-790)		

SERVICES SECTION
SOCIAL SVCS: Individual & Family

Organization	Code	Phone
Haven Rest Ministries Inc	D	330 535-1563
Akron (G-258)		
Healing Hrts Cunseling Ctr Inc	E	419 528-5993
Mansfield (G-13307)		
Heap Home Energy Assistance	D	419 626-6540
Sandusky (G-16767)		
Highland County Family YMCA	E	937 840-9622
Hillsboro (G-11978)		
Hockingthensperry Cmnty Action	E	740 767-4500
Glouster (G-11435)		
Home Instead Senior Care	D	330 334-4664
Wadsworth (G-18756)		
Hospice of Knox County	E	740 397-5188
Mount Vernon (G-14899)		
Hospice of The Valley Inc	D	330 788-1992
Youngstown (G-20221)		
Hospice of The Western Reserve	D	440 997-6619
Ashtabula (G-748)		
Huber Heights YMCA	D	937 236-9622
Dayton (G-9623)		
Inn At Medina Limited LLC	D	330 723-0110
Medina (G-14080)		
Integrated Services of Appala	D	740 594-6807
Athens (G-794)		
Interfaith Hosptlty Ntwrk of W	D	513 934-5250
Lebanon (G-12613)		
Joint Township Dst Mem Hosp	D	419 394-9992
Saint Marys (G-16677)		
Lake County YMCA	A	440 352-3303
Painesville (G-15860)		
Lake County YMCA	C	440 946-1160
Willoughby (G-19680)		
Lake County YMCA	E	440 259-2724
Perry (G-15962)		
Lake County YMCA	D	440 428-5125
Madison (G-13227)		
Leads Inc	E	740 349-8606
Newark (G-15184)		
Licco Inc	C	740 522-8345
Newark (G-15185)		
Lifecare Hospice	E	330 264-4899
Wooster (G-19883)		
Lifecare Hospice	D	330 336-6595
Wadsworth (G-18761)		
Lima Family YMCA	E	419 223-6045
Lima (G-12821)		
Lyman W Liggins Urban Affairs	D	419 385-2532
Toledo (G-18023)		
Maco Inc	E	740 472-5445
Woodsfield (G-19816)		
Mahoning County	D	330 797-2837
Youngstown (G-20262)		
Mahoning Youngstown Community	E	330 747-5661
Youngstown (G-20267)		
Marsh Foundation	E	419 238-1695
Van Wert (G-18639)		
Masco Inc	E	330 797-2904
Youngstown (G-20274)		
Miami Valley Community Action	D	937 222-1009
Dayton (G-9728)		
Miracle Spirtl Retrst Orgnsizn	E	216 324-4287
Cleveland (G-6070)		
Mobile Meals of Salem Inc	E	330 332-2160
Salem (G-16705)		
Mound Builders Guidance Center	D	740 522-2828
Newark (G-15212)		
Mt Washington Care Center Inc	C	513 231-4561
Cincinnati (G-4130)		
National Exchange Club Foundat	E	419 535-3232
Toledo (G-18075)		
Neighborhood House	D	614 252-4941
Columbus (G-8256)		
Northwest Mental Health Svcs	E	614 457-7876
Columbus (G-8297)		
Northwestrn OH Community Action	C	419 784-2150
Defiance (G-10051)		
Ohio Department of Health	B	330 792-2397
Austintown (G-870)		
Ohio Department of Health	B	614 645-3621
Columbus (G-8327)		
Ohio Department of Health	E	937 285-6250
Dayton (G-9784)		
Ohio Dept of Job & Fmly Svcs	C	614 466-1213
Columbus (G-8335)		
Ohio Hrtland Cmnty Action Comm	E	419 468-5121
Galion (G-11303)		
Operation Thank You	E	513 899-3134
Morrow (G-14846)		
Pastoral Care Management Svcs	E	513 205-1398
Cincinnati (G-4257)		
Pathway 2 Hope Inc	E	866 491-3040
Cincinnati (G-4258)		
Pike County YMCA	E	740 947-8862
Waverly (G-18974)		
Planned Parenthood Association	E	937 226-0780
Dayton (G-9811)		
Portsmouth Metro Hsing Auth	E	740 354-4547
Portsmouth (G-16300)		
Private Duty Services Inc	C	419 238-3714
Van Wert (G-18642)		
Rocking Horse Chld Hlth Ctr	E	937 328-7266
Springfield (G-17265)		
Ross County Children Svcs Ctr	D	740 773-2651
Chillicothe (G-2878)		
Ross County Community	E	740 702-7222
Chillicothe (G-2879)		
Ross County YMCA	D	740 772-4340
Chillicothe (G-2882)		
Salvation Army	D	513 762-5600
Cincinnati (G-4475)		
Salvation Army	D	216 861-8185
Cleveland (G-6440)		
Sateri Home Inc	D	330 758-8106
Youngstown (G-20367)		
Seamans Services	E	216 621-4107
Cleveland (G-6458)		
Sickle Cell Awaremess Grp	E	513 281-4450
Cincinnati (G-4525)		
Sidney-Shelby County YMCA	E	937 492-9134
Sidney (G-16955)		
Society of St Vincent De Paul	E	513 421-2273
Cincinnati (G-4547)		
Society St Vincent De Paul Cle	D	216 696-6525
Cleveland (G-6492)		
Southstern Ohio Rgional Fd Ctr	E	740 385-6813
Logan (G-12988)		
Specialized Alternatives For F	C	216 295-7239
Shaker Heights (G-16867)		
Springfield Family Y M C A	D	937 323-3781
Springfield (G-17281)		
St Joseph Infant Maternity Hm	E	513 563-2520
Cincinnati (G-4572)		
St Vincent De Paul Scl Svs	D	937 222-7349
Dayton (G-9902)		
Sunshine Communities	B	419 865-0251
Maumee (G-13982)		
Sycamore Board of Education	D	513 489-3937
Cincinnati (G-4608)		
Tasc of Southeast Ohio	E	740 594-2276
Athens (G-814)		
Tcn Behavioral Health Svcs Inc	C	937 376-8700
Xenia (G-20077)		
Transformation Network	E	419 207-1188
Ashland (G-702)		
Tri-County Community Act	E	740 385-6812
Logan (G-12991)		
Twelve Inc	E	330 837-3555
Massillon (G-13859)		
Ucc Childrens Center	E	513 217-5501
Middletown (G-14488)		
United Rehabilitation Services	D	937 233-1230
Dayton (G-9947)		
United Way Greater Cincinnati	E	513 762-7100
Cincinnati (G-4742)		
United Way of Greater Toledo	D	419 254-4742
Toledo (G-18274)		
United Way of The Greater Dayt	E	937 225-3060
Dayton (G-9949)		
Vermilion Family YMCA	E	440 967-4208
Vermilion (G-18720)		
Volunteers of America NW Ohio	E	419 248-3733
Toledo (G-18293)		
Volunters of Amer Greater Ohio	E	614 861-8551
Columbus (G-8949)		
Volunters of Amer Greater Ohio	C	614 372-3120
Columbus (G-8950)		
Volunters of Amer Greater Ohio	E	419 524-5013
Mansfield (G-13382)		
Volunters of America Cntl Ohio	D	614 801-1655
Grove City (G-11609)		
W S O S Community A	D	419 333-6068
Fremont (G-11227)		
West Ohio Cmnty Action Partnr	C	419 227-2586
Lima (G-12919)		
West Side Ecumenical Ministry	C	216 325-9369
Cleveland (G-6740)		
Y M C A Central Stark County	E	330 305-5437
Canton (G-2590)		
Y M C A Central Stark County	E	330 875-1611
Louisville (G-13108)		
Y M C A Central Stark County	E	330 877-8933
Uniontown (G-18545)		
Y M C A Central Stark County	E	330 830-6275
Massillon (G-13862)		
Y M C A Central Stark County	E	330 498-4082
Canton (G-2591)		
Y M C A of Ashland Ohio Inc	D	419 289-0626
Ashland (G-709)		
YMCA	D	937 653-9622
Urbana (G-18603)		
YMCA	D	330 823-1930
Alliance (G-566)		
YMCA Inc	D	330 385-6400
East Liverpool (G-10536)		
YMCA of Clermont County Inc	E	513 724-9622
Batavia (G-1032)		
YMCA of Massillon	E	330 879-0800
Navarre (G-14957)		
Young Mens Christian	B	513 932-1424
Lebanon (G-12660)		
Young Mens Christian Assn	E	419 332-9622
Fremont (G-11231)		
Young Mens Christian Assn	E	419 238-0443
Van Wert (G-18653)		
Young Mens Christian Assoc	C	614 885-4252
Columbus (G-9017)		
Young Mens Christian Assoc	C	614 276-8224
Columbus (G-9018)		
Young Mens Christian Assoc	C	614 834-9622
Canal Winchester (G-2181)		
Young Mens Christian Assoc	C	614 871-9622
Grove City (G-11620)		
Young Mens Christian Assoc	A	937 223-5201
Dayton (G-10009)		
Young Mens Christian Assoc	D	330 923-5223
Cuyahoga Falls (G-9237)		
Young Mens Christian Assoc	E	330 467-8366
Macedonia (G-13219)		
Young Mens Christian Assoc	E	330 784-0408
Akron (G-515)		
Young Mens Christian Assoc	C	614 416-9622
Gahanna (G-11276)		
Young Mens Christian Assoc	C	740 881-1058
Powell (G-16355)		
Young Mens Christian Assoc	C	614 334-9622
Hilliard (G-11967)		
Young Mens Christian Assoc	E	937 312-1810
Dayton (G-10010)		
Young Mens Christian Assoc	E	614 539-1770
Urbancrest (G-18609)		
Young Mens Christian Assoc	C	614 252-3166
Columbus (G-9019)		
Young Mens Christian Assoc	C	937 223-5201
Springboro (G-17144)		
Young Mens Christian Assoc	E	937 593-9001
Bellefontaine (G-1401)		
Young Mens Christian Associat	E	419 729-8135
Toledo (G-18320)		
Young Mens Christian Associat	D	513 241-9622
Cincinnati (G-4868)		
Young Mens Christian Associat	D	513 923-4466
Cincinnati (G-4869)		
Young Mens Christian Associat	E	419 474-3995
Toledo (G-18322)		
Young Mens Christian Associat	D	419 866-9622
Maumee (G-13997)		
Young Mens Christian Associat	C	419 475-3496
Toledo (G-18323)		
Young Mens Christian Associat	E	419 691-3523
Oregon (G-15756)		
Young Mens Christian Mt Vernon	D	740 392-9622
Mount Vernon (G-14927)		
Young MNS Chrstn Assn Clveland	E	216 941-4651
Cleveland (G-6773)		
Young MNS Chrstn Assn Clveland	D	440 808-8150
Westlake (G-19569)		
Young MNS Chrstn Assn Clveland	E	216 521-8400
Lakewood (G-12502)		
Young MNS Chrstn Assn Clveland	D	440 842-5200
North Royalton (G-15507)		
Young MNS Chrstn Assn Clveland	E	216 731-7454
Cleveland (G-6774)		
Young MNS Chrstn Assn Clveland	D	440 285-7543
Chardon (G-2780)		
Young MNS Chrstn Assn Grter NY	D	740 392-9622
Mount Vernon (G-14928)		
Young Womens Christian	D	419 241-3235
Toledo (G-18325)		
Young Womens Christian	D	937 461-5550
Dayton (G-10013)		

Employee Codes: A=Over 500 employees, B=251-500
C=101-250, D=51-100, E=25-50

SOCIAL SVCS: Individual & Family

Young Womens Christian .... E 419 238-6639
  Van Wert (G-18654)
Young Womens Christian Assn .... D 614 224-9121
  Columbus (G-9021)
Young Womens Christian Assn .... E 330 746-6361
  Youngstown (G-20422)
Young Womens Christian Associ .... E 216 881-6878
  Cleveland (G-6776)
Young Womns Chrstn Assc Canton ..... D 330 453-0789
  Canton (G-2594)
Youngstown Area Jwish Fdration .... D 330 746-1076
  Youngstown (G-20426)
Youngstown Committee On Alchol ..... D 330 744-1181
  Youngstown (G-20429)
Youth Mntrng & At Rsk Intrvntn .... E 216 324-2451
  Richmond Heights (G-16543)
YWCA of Greater Cincinnati .... D 513 241-7090
  Cincinnati (G-4870)
YWCA Shelter & Housing Network ..... E 937 222-6333
  Dayton (G-10014)

SOCIAL WORKER

Four County Family Center .... E 800 693-6000
  Wauseon (G-18952)
Mental Hlth Serv For CL & Mad .... E 937 390-7980
  Springfield (G-17233)
Preble County Council On Aging .... E 937 456-4947
  Eaton (G-10574)

SOFT DRINKS WHOLESALERS

Akron Coca-Cola Bottling Co .... A 330 784-2653
  Akron (G-34)
Bellas Co .... E 740 598-4171
  Mingo Junction (G-14653)
Buckeye Distributing Inc .... C 440 526-6668
  Broadview Heights (G-1873)
Coca-Cola Bottling Co Cnsld .... D 937 878-5000
  Dayton (G-9414)
P-Americas LLC .... E 419 227-3541
  Lima (G-12853)
P-Americas LLC .... D 216 252-7377
  Cleveland (G-6227)
Pepsi-Cola Metro Btlg Co Inc .... E 330 336-3553
  Wadsworth (G-18767)
Pepsi-Cola Metro Btlg Co Inc .... E 440 323-5524
  Elyria (G-10669)

SOFTWARE PUBLISHERS: Application

Advanced Prgrm Resources Inc .... E 614 761-9994
  Dublin (G-10234)
Advant-E Corporation .... D 937 429-4288
  Beavercreek (G-1145)
Delta Media Group Inc .... E 330 493-0350
  Canton (G-2338)
Gracie Plum Investments Inc .... E 740 355-9029
  Portsmouth (G-16282)
Hyland Software Inc .... A 440 788-5000
  Westlake (G-19496)
Microsoft Corporation .... E 614 719-5900
  Columbus (G-6896)
Microsoft Corporation .... E 216 986-1440
  Cleveland (G-6050)
Microsoft Corporation .... E 513 339-2800
  Mason (G-13739)
Mim Software Inc .... E 216 896-9798
  Beachwood (G-1103)
Preemptive Solutions LLC .... E 440 443-7200
  Cleveland (G-6297)
Rivals Sports Grille LLC .... E 216 267-0005
  Middleburg Heights (G-14386)
Sanctuary Software Studio Inc .... E 330 666-9690
  Fairlawn (G-10972)
Software Solutions Inc .... E 513 932-6667
  Lebanon (G-12648)

SOFTWARE PUBLISHERS: Business & Professional

Agile Global Solutions Inc .... E 916 655-7745
  Independence (G-12182)
Air Force US Dept of .... B 937 656-2354
  Dayton (G-9251)
Cincom Systems Inc .... C 513 459-1470
  Mason (G-13677)
Clinicl Otcms Mngmnt Syst LLC .... D 330 650-9900
  Broadview Heights (G-1875)
Infoaccessnet LLC .... E 216 328-0100
  Cleveland (G-5819)

Mapsys Inc .... E 614 255-7258
  Columbus (G-8104)
Netsmart Technologies Inc .... E 440 942-4040
  Solon (G-17033)
Nextmed Systems Inc .... E 216 674-0511
  Cincinnati (G-4164)
Ohio Cllbrtive Lrng Sltons Inc .... E 216 595-5289
  Beachwood (G-1110)
Onx USA LLC .... D 440 569-2300
  Cleveland (G-6207)
Oracle Corporation .... C 513 826-5632
  Beavercreek (G-1195)
Parallel Technologies Inc .... D 614 798-9700
  Dublin (G-10421)
Tmw Systems Inc .... C 216 831-6606
  Mayfield Heights (G-14008)
Turning Technologies LLC .... C 330 746-3015
  Youngstown (G-20395)
Workspeed Management LLC .... E 917 369-9025
  Solon (G-17069)
Zipscene LLC .... D 513 201-5174
  Cincinnati (G-4872)

SOFTWARE PUBLISHERS: Education

Flypaper Studio Inc .... E 602 801-2208
  Cincinnati (G-3634)
Skillsoft Corporation .... D 216 524-5200
  Independence (G-12260)

SOFTWARE PUBLISHERS: Home Entertainment

Estreamz Inc .... E 513 278-7836
  Cincinnati (G-3577)
Triplett & Adams Entps Inc .... D 816 221-1024
  New Concord (G-15039)

SOFTWARE PUBLISHERS: NEC

Auto Des Sys Inc .... E 614 488-7984
  Upper Arlington (G-18548)
Besttransportcom Inc .... E 614 888-2378
  Worthington (G-19943)
Cimx LLC .... E 513 248-7700
  Cincinnati (G-3276)
Citynet Ohio LLC .... E 614 364-7881
  Columbus (G-7287)
Creative Microsystems Inc .... D 937 836-4499
  Englewood (G-10701)
Dakota Software Corporation .... D 216 765-7100
  Cleveland (G-5461)
Datatrak International Inc .... E 440 443-0082
  Mayfield Heights (G-14000)
Digital Controls Corporation .... D 513 746-8118
  Miamisburg (G-14297)
Drb Systems LLC .... D 330 645-3299
  Akron (G-200)
Edict Systems Inc .... E 937 429-4288
  Beavercreek (G-1172)
Einstruction Corporation .... D 330 746-3015
  Youngstown (G-20178)
EMC Corporation .... D 513 794-9624
  Blue Ash (G-1584)
EMC Corporation .... E 216 606-2000
  Independence (G-12206)
Esko-Graphics Inc .... D 937 454-1721
  Miamisburg (G-14299)
Exact Software North Amer LLC .... C 978 539-6186
  Dublin (G-10341)
Explorys Inc .... D 216 767-4700
  Cleveland (G-5563)
Finastra USA Corporation .... E 937 435-2335
  Miamisburg (G-14302)
Flexnova Inc .... E 216 288-6961
  Cleveland (G-5607)
Foundation Software Inc .... D 330 220-8383
  Strongsville (G-17465)
Honeywell International Inc .... D 513 745-7200
  Cincinnati (G-3782)
Hyland LLC .... B 440 788-5045
  Westlake (G-19495)
Juniper Networks Inc .... D 614 932-1432
  Dublin (G-10383)
Matrix Management Solutions .... C 330 470-3700
  Canton (G-2451)
Open Text Inc .... E 614 658-3588
  Hilliard (G-11941)
Oracle Systems Corporation .... E 513 826-6000
  Blue Ash (G-1658)
Patrick J Burke & Co .... E 513 455-8200
  Cincinnati (G-4262)

Peco II Inc .... D 614 431-0694
  Columbus (G-8528)
Retalix Inc .... C 937 384-2277
  Miamisburg (G-14342)
Revolution Group Inc .... D 614 212-1111
  Westerville (G-19349)
Seapine Software Inc .... E 513 754-1655
  Mason (G-13757)
Sigmatek Systems LLC .... D 513 674-0005
  Cincinnati (G-4527)
Software Management Group .... E 513 618-2165
  Cincinnati (G-4551)
Starwin Industries Inc .... E 937 293-8568
  Dayton (G-9904)
Symantec Corporation .... D 216 643-6700
  Independence (G-12264)
Tata America Intl Corp .... B 513 677-6500
  Milford (G-14565)
Teradata Corporation .... B 866 548-8348
  Miamisburg (G-14356)
Thinkware Incorporated .... E 513 598-3300
  Cincinnati (G-4650)
To Scale Software LLC .... E 513 253-0053
  Mason (G-13769)
Triad Governmental Systems .... E 937 376-5446
  Xenia (G-20080)
Virtual Hold Technology LLC .... D 330 666-1181
  Akron (G-498)

SOFTWARE PUBLISHERS: Publisher's

Exponentia US Inc .... E 614 944-5103
  Columbus (G-7623)
Nsa Technologies LLC .... C 330 576-4600
  Akron (G-359)

SOFTWARE TRAINING, COMPUTER

Critical Business Analysis Inc .... E 419 874-0800
  Perrysburg (G-15991)

SOLDERS

Victory White Metal Company .... D 216 271-1400
  Cleveland (G-6694)

SORORITY HOUSES

Alpha Epsilon PHI .... E 614 294-5243
  Columbus (G-6975)
CHI Omega Sorority .... E 937 325-9323
  Springfield (G-17159)

SOUND EFFECTS & MUSIC PRODUCTION: Motion Picture

Live Technologies Holdings Inc .... D 614 278-7777
  Columbus (G-8074)

SOUND RECORDING STUDIOS

Recording Workshop .... E 740 663-1000
  Chillicothe (G-2873)

SOYBEAN PRDTS

Pioneer Hi-Bred Intl Inc .... E 419 748-8051
  Grand Rapids (G-11452)
Schlessman Seed Co .... E 419 499-2572
  Milan (G-14499)

SPACE RESEARCH & TECHNOLOGY, GOVERNMENT: Federal

Keeptryan Inc .... D 330 319-1866
  Akron (G-302)

SPACE VEHICLE EQPT

Curtiss-Wright Controls .... E 937 252-5601
  Fairborn (G-10789)
General Electric Company .... B 513 977-1500
  Cincinnati (G-3667)
Grimes Aerospace Company .... B 937 484-2001
  Urbana (G-18590)
Sunpower Inc .... D 740 594-2221
  Athens (G-813)

SPARK PLUGS: Internal Combustion Engines

Fram Group Operations LLC .... D 419 661-6700
  Perrysburg (G-16005)

SERVICES SECTION

SPORTING & RECREATIONAL GOODS & SPLYS WHOLESALERS

SPAS

Company	Code	Phone
Alsan Corporation	D	330 385-3636
East Liverpool *(G-10514)*		
Changes Hair Designers Inc	E	614 846-6666
Columbus *(G-6875)*		
Jbentley Studio & Spa LLC	D	614 790-8828
Powell *(G-16339)*		
Kerr House Inc	E	419 832-1733
Grand Rapids *(G-11451)*		
Kristie Warner	E	330 650-4450
Hudson *(G-12129)*		
Marios International Spa & Ht	C	330 562-5141
Aurora *(G-846)*		
Mitchells Salon & Day Spa	B	513 793-0900
Cincinnati *(G-4104)*		
Mitchells Salon & Day Spa	D	513 731-0600
Cincinnati *(G-4106)*		
Paragon Salons Inc	E	513 574-7610
Cincinnati *(G-4249)*		
Spa Fitness Centers Inc	E	419 476-6018
Toledo *(G-18193)*		
Tuscany Spa Salon	E	513 489-8872
Cincinnati *(G-4708)*		
Uptown Hair Studio Inc	E	937 832-2111
Englewood *(G-10723)*		

SPECIAL EDUCATION SCHOOLS, PRIVATE

Company	Code	Phone
Adriel School Inc	D	937 465-0010
West Liberty *(G-19260)*		
Education Alternatives	D	216 332-9360
Brookpark *(G-1944)*		
Muskingum Starlight Industries	D	740 453-4622
Zanesville *(G-20513)*		
Oesterlen-Services For Youth	C	937 399-6101
Springfield *(G-17254)*		

SPECIAL EDUCATION SCHOOLS, PUBLIC

Company	Code	Phone
Belmont County of Ohio	D	740 695-0460
Saint Clairsville *(G-16624)*		

SPECIAL EVENTS DECORATION SVCS

Company	Code	Phone
Camargo Rental Center Inc	E	513 271-6510
Cincinnati *(G-3170)*		
Convivo Network LLC	E	216 631-9000
Cleveland *(G-5406)*		

SPECIALIZED LIBRARIES

Company	Code	Phone
Western Reserve Historical Soc	D	216 721-5722
Cleveland *(G-6744)*		

SPECIALTY FOOD STORES: Coffee

Company	Code	Phone
Generations Coffee Company LLC	E	440 546-0901
Brecksville *(G-1824)*		

SPECIALTY FOOD STORES: Eggs & Poultry

Company	Code	Phone
Di Feo & Sons Poultry Inc	E	330 564-8172
Akron *(G-191)*		

SPECIALTY FOOD STORES: Health & Dietetic Food

Company	Code	Phone
Garys Pharmacy Inc	E	937 456-5777
Eaton *(G-10561)*		

SPECIALTY FOOD STORES: Juices, Fruit Or Vegetable

Company	Code	Phone
M & M Wine Cellar Inc	E	330 536-6450
Lowellville *(G-13172)*		

SPECIALTY OUTPATIENT CLINICS, NEC

Company	Code	Phone
Akron General Medical Center	C	330 665-8000
Akron *(G-46)*		
American Kidney Stone MGT Ltd	E	800 637-5188
Columbus *(G-6999)*		
Anazao Community Partners	E	330 264-9597
Wooster *(G-19828)*		
Appleseed Cmnty Mntal Hlth Ctr	E	419 281-3716
Ashland *(G-651)*		
Best Care Nrsng Rhbltttion Ctr	C	740 574-2558
Wheelersburg *(G-19570)*		
Bridgeway Inc	B	216 688-4114
Cleveland *(G-5138)*		
Caprice Health Care Inc	C	330 965-9200
North Lima *(G-15400)*		
Center For Chemical Addictions	D	513 381-6672
Cincinnati *(G-3207)*		
Central Commnty Hlth Brd of Ha	C	513 559-2000
Cincinnati *(G-3211)*		
CHI Health At Home	E	513 576-0262
Milford *(G-14510)*		
Childrens Hospital Medical Ctr	E	513 636-6100
Cincinnati *(G-3251)*		
Childrens Hospital Medical Ctr	E	513 636-6800
Mason *(G-13676)*		
Christ Hospital Spine Surgery	E	513 619-5899
Cincinnati *(G-3270)*		
Cleveland Clinic Foundation	D	440 988-5651
Lorain *(G-13026)*		
Clevelnd Clnc Hlth Systm East	E	330 287-4830
Wooster *(G-19850)*		
Clevelnd Clnc Hlth Systm East	E	330 468-0190
Northfield *(G-15512)*		
Clinton County Board of	E	937 382-7519
Wilmington *(G-19749)*		
Clinton Memorial Hospital	E	937 383-3402
Wilmington *(G-19754)*		
Community Assesment and Treatm	D	216 441-0200
Cleveland *(G-5383)*		
Community Health Centers Ohio	D	216 831-1494
Beachwood *(G-1067)*		
Community Mental Health Svc	D	740 695-9344
Saint Clairsville *(G-16633)*		
Comprehensive Addiction Svc Sy	D	419 241-8827
Toledo *(G-17826)*		
Consumer Advocacy Model	E	937 222-2400
Dayton *(G-9424)*		
Crossroads Center	E	513 475-5300
Cincinnati *(G-3442)*		
Eastway Corporation	C	937 531-7000
Dayton *(G-9517)*		
Fairfld Ctr For Disablts & CER	E	740 653-1186
Lancaster *(G-12539)*		
HCA Holdings Inc	D	440 826-3240
Cleveland *(G-5734)*		
Healthsource of Ohio Inc	E	513 707-1997
Batavia *(G-1016)*		
Healthsource of Ohio Inc	E	937 981-7707
Greenfield *(G-11487)*		
Hope Ctr For Cncer Care Warren	D	330 856-8600
Warren *(G-18863)*		
Hospice of Darke County Inc	E	419 678-4808
Coldwater *(G-6830)*		
Mahoning Vly Hmtlgy Onclgy Aso	E	330 318-1100
Youngstown *(G-20265)*		
Marion Area Counseling Ctr	C	740 387-5210
Marion *(G-13553)*		
McKinley Hall Inc	E	937 328-5300
Springfield *(G-17230)*		
Medcentral Health System	E	419 526-8442
Mansfield *(G-13338)*		
Mercy Healthplexm LLC	E	513 870-7101
Fairfield *(G-10881)*		
Mercy Medical Center Inc	E	330 627-7641
Carrollton *(G-2623)*		
Met Group	E	330 864-1916
Fairlawn *(G-10964)*		
Metrohealth System	E	216 957-5000
Cleveland *(G-6037)*		
Neighborhood Health Asso	D	419 720-7883
Toledo *(G-18080)*		
Neighborhood House	E	614 252-4941
Columbus *(G-8256)*		
North East Ohio Health Svcs	E	216 831-6466
Beachwood *(G-1107)*		
Northpoint Senior Services LLC	D	740 369-9614
Delaware *(G-10118)*		
Odyssey Healthcare Inc	E	937 298-2800
Dayton *(G-9783)*		
Ohio Heart Institute Inc	E	330 747-6446
Youngstown *(G-20306)*		
Oral & Maxillofacial Surgeons	E	419 385-5743
Toledo *(G-18110)*		
Pain Management Associates Inc	E	937 252-2000
Dayton *(G-9281)*		
Plastic Surgery Group Inc	E	513 791-4440
Cincinnati *(G-4303)*		
Positive Education Program	E	440 471-8200
Cleveland *(G-6292)*		
Pregnancy Care of Cincinnati	E	513 487-7777
Cincinnati *(G-4321)*		
Rescue Incorporated	C	419 255-9585
Toledo *(G-18153)*		
Reynolds Road Surgical Ctr LLC	D	419 578-7500
Toledo *(G-18156)*		
Robinson Health System Inc	E	330 678-4100
Ravenna *(G-16406)*		
Shr Management Resources Corp	E	937 274-1546
Dayton *(G-9879)*		
Southwoods Surgical Hospital	E	330 729-8000
Youngstown *(G-20379)*		
Springfield Rgnal Otpatient Ctr	E	937 390-8310
Springfield *(G-17277)*		
St Vincent Family Centers	C	614 252-0731
Columbus *(G-8771)*		
Summa Health System	E	330 375-3315
Akron *(G-458)*		
Surgicenter of Mansfield	E	419 774-9410
Mansfield *(G-13368)*		
Tcn Behavioral Health Svcs Inc	E	937 376-8700
Xenia *(G-20077)*		
United Disability Services Inc	C	330 374-1169
Akron *(G-485)*		
Univ Dermatology	D	513 475-7630
Cincinnati *(G-4745)*		
University Mednet	E	440 255-0800
Mentor *(G-14253)*		
University of Cincinnati	C	513 584-3200
Cincinnati *(G-4773)*		
University Radiology Assoc	E	513 475-8760
Cincinnati *(G-4784)*		
Upper Arlington Surgery Center	E	614 442-6515
Columbus *(G-8916)*		
Wendt-Bristol Health Services	E	614 403-9966
Columbus *(G-8977)*		
West End Health Center Inc	E	513 621-2726
Cincinnati *(G-4835)*		
Wood County Chld Svcs Assn	D	419 352-7588
Bowling Green *(G-1798)*		

SPECULATIVE BUILDERS: Multi-Family Housing

Company	Code	Phone
Bernard Busson Builder	E	330 929-4926
Akron *(G-99)*		

SPECULATIVE BUILDERS: Single-Family Housing

Company	Code	Phone
Dold Homes Inc	E	419 874-2535
Perrysburg *(G-15999)*		
Duffy Homes Inc	E	614 410-4100
Columbus *(G-7549)*		
M/I Homes Inc	B	614 418-8000
Columbus *(G-8095)*		
Phil Wagler Construction Inc	E	330 899-0316
Uniontown *(G-18532)*		
Plus Realty Cincinnati Inc	E	513 575-4500
Milford *(G-14554)*		
Weaver Custom Homes Inc	E	330 264-5444
Wooster *(G-19927)*		
Zicka Walker Builders Ltd	E	513 247-3500
Cincinnati *(G-4871)*		

SPEECH DEFECT CLINIC

Company	Code	Phone
Cincinnati Speech Hearing Ctr	E	513 221-0527
Cincinnati *(G-3328)*		
Youngstown Hearing Speech Ctr	E	330 726-8391
Youngstown *(G-20431)*		

SPEED CHANGERS

Company	Code	Phone
Great Lakes Power Products Inc	D	440 951-5111
Mentor *(G-14185)*		

SPICE & HERB STORES

Company	Code	Phone
Gold Star Chili Inc	E	513 231-4541
Cincinnati *(G-3684)*		

SPONGES, ANIMAL, WHOLESALE

Company	Code	Phone
Armaly LLC	E	740 852-3621
London *(G-12992)*		

SPORTING & ATHLETIC GOODS: Basketball Eqpt & Splys, NEC

Company	Code	Phone
Huffy Corporation	D	937 743-5011
Springboro *(G-17124)*		

SPORTING & RECREATIONAL GOODS & SPLYS WHOLESALERS

Company	Code	Phone
4th and Goal Distribution LLC	E	440 212-0769
Burbank *(G-2054)*		

Employee Codes: A=Over 500 employees, B=251-500 C=101-250, D=51-100, E=25-50

SPORTING & RECREATIONAL GOODS & SPLYS WHOLESALERS

AB Marketing LLC .... E 513 385-6158
   Fairfield *(G-10814)*
Air Venturi Ltd .... D 216 292-2570
   Solon *(G-16973)*
Brennan-Eberly Team Sports Inc .... E 419 865-8326
   Holland *(G-12013)*
Coachs Sports Corner Inc .... E 419 609-3737
   Sandusky *(G-16742)*
Dwa Mrkting Prmtional Pdts LLC .... E 216 476-0635
   Strongsville *(G-17457)*
Kohlmyer Sporting Goods Inc .... E 440 277-8296
   Lorain *(G-13045)*
Mc Gregor Family Enterprises .... E 513 583-0040
   Cincinnati *(G-4034)*
R & A Sports Inc .... E 216 289-2254
   Euclid *(G-10773)*
Schneider Saddlery LLC .... E 440 543-2700
   Chagrin Falls *(G-2733)*
Willow and Cane LLC .... E 609 280-1150
   Springboro *(G-17142)*
Zebec of North America Inc .... E 513 829-5533
   Fairfield *(G-10923)*
Zide Sport Shop of Ohio Inc .... D 740 373-6446
   Marietta *(G-13521)*

SPORTING & RECREATIONAL GOODS, WHOL: Water Slides, Rec Park

Cherry Valley Lodge .... E 740 788-1200
   Newark *(G-15156)*
Durga Llc .... D 513 771-2080
   Cincinnati *(G-3515)*
Lmn Development LLC .... D 419 433-7200
   Sandusky *(G-16775)*

SPORTING & RECREATIONAL GOODS, WHOLESALE: Athletic Goods

Riddell Inc .... E 440 366-8225
   North Ridgeville *(G-15476)*

SPORTING & RECREATIONAL GOODS, WHOLESALE: Boat Access & Part

Miami Corporation .... E 513 451-6700
   Cincinnati *(G-4086)*

SPORTING & RECREATIONAL GOODS, WHOLESALE: Bowling

Beaver-Vu Bowl .... E 937 426-6771
   Beavercreek *(G-1150)*
Done-Rite Bowling Service Co .... E 440 232-3280
   Bedford *(G-1304)*
Micnan Inc .... E 330 920-6200
   Cuyahoga Falls *(G-9209)*

SPORTING & RECREATIONAL GOODS, WHOLESALE: Fitness

21st Century Health Spa Inc .... E 419 476-5585
   Toledo *(G-17732)*
Ball Bounce and Sport Inc .... B 419 289-9310
   Ashland *(G-661)*
Suarez Corporation Industries .... D 330 494-4282
   Canton *(G-2554)*

SPORTING & RECREATIONAL GOODS, WHOLESALE: Golf

Golf Galaxy Golfworks Inc .... C 740 328-4193
   Newark *(G-15170)*

SPORTING & RECREATIONAL GOODS, WHOLESALE: Gymnasium

A K Athletic Equipment Inc .... E 614 920-3069
   Canal Winchester *(G-2151)*

SPORTING & RECREATIONAL GOODS, WHOLESALE: Hunting

Weston Brands LLC .... E 216 901-6801
   Independence *(G-12276)*

SPORTING FIREARMS WHOLESALERS

Acusport Corporation .... C 937 593-7010
   Bellefontaine *(G-1374)*

SPORTING GOODS

Galaxy Balloons Incorporated .... C 216 476-3360
   Cleveland *(G-5651)*
Mc Alarney Pool Spas and Billd .... E 740 373-6698
   Marietta *(G-13474)*
Zebec of North America Inc .... E 513 829-5533
   Fairfield *(G-10923)*

SPORTING GOODS STORES, NEC

Al-Mar Lanes .... E 419 352-4637
   Bowling Green *(G-1757)*
Bigelow Corporation .... E 937 339-3315
   Troy *(G-18349)*
Cambridge Country Club Company ..... E 740 439-2744
   Byesville *(G-2070)*
Coachs Sports Corner Inc .... E 419 609-3737
   Sandusky *(G-16742)*
Columbus Country Club .... D 614 861-1332
   Columbus *(G-7343)*
Emerald Woods Golf Course .... E 440 236-8940
   Columbia Station *(G-6846)*
Hawthorne Valley Country Club .... D 440 232-1400
   Bedford *(G-1311)*
Heritage Golf Club Ltd Partnr .... D 614 777-1690
   Hilliard *(G-11908)*
Kohlmyer Sporting Goods Inc .... E 440 277-8296
   Lorain *(G-13045)*
Madison Route 20 LLC .... E 440 358-7888
   Painesville *(G-15864)*
Mahoning Country Club Inc .... E 330 545-2517
   Girard *(G-11420)*
Mayfield Sand Ridge Club .... D 216 381-0826
   Cleveland *(G-5995)*
Mc Gregor Family Enterprises .... E 513 583-0040
   Cincinnati *(G-4034)*
Meadowlake Corporation .... E 330 492-2010
   Canton *(G-2456)*
Medallion Club .... C 614 794-6999
   Westerville *(G-19328)*
Moundbuilders Country Club Co .... E 740 344-4500
   Newark *(G-15213)*
Pines Golf Club .... E 330 684-1414
   Orrville *(G-15783)*
Quail Hollow Management Inc .... D 440 639-4000
   Painesville *(G-15874)*
Sand Ridge Golf Club .... D 440 285-8088
   Chardon *(G-2767)*
Shady Hollow Cntry CLB Co Inc .... D 330 832-1581
   Massillon *(G-13854)*
Silver Lake Country Club .... D 330 688-6066
   Silver Lake *(G-16964)*
Springfield Country Club Co .... E 937 399-4215
   Springfield *(G-17280)*
Tartan Fields Golf Club Ltd .... D 614 792-0900
   Dublin *(G-10473)*
Yankee Run Golf Course .... D 330 448-8096
   Brookfield *(G-1903)*
Youngstown Country Club .... D 330 759-1040
   Youngstown *(G-20430)*

SPORTING GOODS STORES: Firearms

Pyramyd Air Ltd .... E 216 896-0893
   Solon *(G-17043)*

SPORTING GOODS STORES: Gymnasium Eqpt, NEC

Chalk Box Get Fit LLC .... E 440 992-9619
   Ashtabula *(G-732)*

SPORTING GOODS STORES: Pool & Billiard Tables

Burnett Pools Inc .... E 330 372-1725
   Cortland *(G-9074)*

SPORTING GOODS STORES: Skating Eqpt

Ohio Skate Inc .... E 419 476-2808
   Toledo *(G-18103)*

SPORTING GOODS STORES: Specialty Sport Splys, NEC

Capitol Varsity Sports Inc .... E 513 523-4126
   Oxford *(G-15813)*

SPORTING GOODS STORES: Tennis Goods & Eqpt

Tennis Unlimited Inc .... E 330 928-8763
   Akron *(G-474)*

SPORTS APPAREL STORES

Chalk Box Get Fit LLC .... E 440 992-9619
   Ashtabula *(G-732)*
Dicks Sporting Goods Inc .... E 740 522-5555
   Heath *(G-11836)*
Dicks Sporting Goods Inc .... E 614 472-4250
   Columbus *(G-7518)*
Gymnastic World Inc .... E 440 526-2970
   Cleveland *(G-5712)*

SPORTS CLUBS, MANAGERS & PROMOTERS

Ap23 Sports Complex LLC .... E 614 452-0760
   Columbus *(G-7025)*
Five Seasons Spt Cntry CLB Inc .... D 937 848-9200
   Dayton *(G-9553)*
Windwood Swim & Tennis Club .... E 513 777-2552
   West Chester *(G-19186)*

SPORTS TEAMS & CLUBS: Baseball

Alliance Hot Stove Baseball L .... E 330 823-7034
   Alliance *(G-525)*
Cascia LLC .... E 440 975-8085
   Willoughby *(G-19648)*
Cincinnati Reds LLC .... C 513 765-7000
   Cincinnati *(G-3324)*
Cincinnati Reds LLC .... D 513 765-7923
   Cincinnati *(G-3325)*
Cleveland Indians Baseball Com .... D 216 420-4487
   Cleveland *(G-5321)*
Dayton Prof Basbal CLB LLC .... E 937 228-2287
   Dayton *(G-9488)*
Palisdes Bsbal A Cal Ltd Prtnr .... C 330 505-0000
   Niles *(G-15302)*
Toledo Mud Hens Basbal CLB Inc .... D 419 725-4367
   Toledo *(G-18243)*

SPORTS TEAMS & CLUBS: Basketball

Cavaliers Holdings LLC .... C 216 420-2000
   Cleveland *(G-5193)*

SPORTS TEAMS & CLUBS: Football

Cincinnati Bengals Inc .... E 513 621-3550
   Cincinnati *(G-3289)*
Cleveland Browns Football LLC .... C 440 891-5000
   Berea *(G-1452)*
National Football Museum Inc .... E 330 456-8207
   Canton *(G-2470)*
Ohio High School Football Coac .... E 419 673-1286
   Etna *(G-10737)*

SPORTS TEAMS & CLUBS: Ice Hockey

Colhoc Limited Partnership .... C 614 246-4625
   Columbus *(G-7318)*

SPORTS TEAMS & CLUBS: Soccer

Columbus Team Soccer LLC .... E 614 447-1301
   Columbus *(G-7390)*
Wall2wall Soccer LLC .... E 513 573-9898
   Mason *(G-13779)*

SPRAYS: Self-Defense

Mace Personal Def & SEC Inc .... E 440 424-5321
   Cleveland *(G-5964)*

SPRINGS: Steel

Hendrickson International Corp .... D 740 929-5600
   Hebron *(G-11849)*

SPRINGS: Wire

Barnes Group Inc .... E 419 891-9292
   Maumee *(G-13885)*

SPRINKLING SYSTEMS: Fire Control

Fire Foe Corp .... E 330 759-9834
   Girard *(G-11413)*

SERVICES SECTION

STADIUM EVENT OPERATOR SERVICES

Phoenix .... D 513 721-8901
  Cincinnati *(G-4293)*

STAFFING, EMPLOYMENT PLACEMENT

56 Plus Management LLC .... E 937 323-4114
  Springfield *(G-17145)*
Adecco Usa Inc .... E 419 720-0111
  Toledo *(G-17741)*
Advantage Rn LLC .... D 866 301-4045
  West Chester *(G-19012)*
Allcan Global Services Inc .... E 513 825-1655
  Cincinnati *(G-2987)*
Berns Oneill SEC & Safety LLC .... E 330 374-9133
  Akron *(G-100)*
Custom Halthcare Proffessional .... E 216 381-1010
  Cleveland *(G-5449)*
Dawson Resources .... E 614 255-1400
  Columbus *(G-7491)*
Dedicated Technologies Inc .... D 614 460-3200
  Columbus *(G-7499)*
Employment Network .... E 440 324-5244
  Elyria *(G-10626)*
Gallery Holdings LLC .... D 773 693-6220
  Independence *(G-12213)*
Professional Contract Systems .... C 513 469-8800
  Cincinnati *(G-4342)*
Reserves Network Inc .... E 440 779-1400
  Cleveland *(G-6383)*
Robert Half International Inc .... D 513 563-0770
  Blue Ash *(G-1684)*
Robert Half International Inc .... D 614 221-8326
  Columbus *(G-8640)*
Robert Half International Inc .... D 513 621-8367
  Cincinnati *(G-4436)*
Siffrin Residential Assn .... E 330 799-8932
  Youngstown *(G-20375)*
Staffmark Holdings Inc .... D 513 651-1111
  Cincinnati *(G-4573)*
Taylor Strategy Partners LLC .... E 614 436-6650
  Columbus *(G-8825)*
Wood County Ohio .... E 419 352-5059
  Bowling Green *(G-1804)*
Youth Opportunities Unlimited .... E 216 566-5445
  Cleveland *(G-6777)*

STAINLESS STEEL

Latrobe Spcialty Mtls Dist Inc .... D 330 609-5137
  Vienna *(G-18738)*

STAMPINGS: Automotive

Falls Stamping & Welding Co .... C 330 928-1191
  Cuyahoga Falls *(G-9185)*
Honda of America Mfg Inc .... C 937 644-0724
  Marysville *(G-13626)*
R K Industries Inc .... D 419 523-5001
  Ottawa *(G-15804)*

STAMPINGS: Metal

Bates Metal Products Inc .... D 740 498-8371
  Port Washington *(G-16260)*
Breitinger Company .... C 419 526-4255
  Mansfield *(G-13269)*
Long-Stanton Mfg Company .... E 513 874-8020
  West Chester *(G-19111)*
Matco Tools Corporation .... B 330 929-4949
  Stow *(G-17382)*
Mid-America Steel Corp .... E 800 282-3466
  Cleveland *(G-6052)*
Mtd Holdings Inc .... B 330 225-2600
  Valley City *(G-18622)*
Northwind Industries Inc .... E 216 433-0666
  Cleveland *(G-6163)*
Quality Fabricated Metals Inc .... E 330 332-7008
  Salem *(G-16707)*
Scott Fetzer Company .... C 216 267-9000
  Cleveland *(G-6452)*

STATE CREDIT UNIONS, NOT FEDERALLY CHARTERED

Advantage Credit Union Inc .... E 419 529-5603
  Ontario *(G-15683)*
Atomic Credit Union Inc .... E 740 289-5060
  Piketon *(G-16109)*
Buckeye State Credit Union .... D 330 253-9197
  Akron *(G-117)*
C E S Credit Union Inc .... E 561 203-5443
  Loudonville *(G-13088)*
C E S Credit Union Inc .... E 740 397-1136
  Mount Vernon *(G-14880)*
C E S Credit Union Inc .... E 740 892-3323
  Utica *(G-18610)*
Chaco Credit Union Inc .... E 513 785-3500
  Hamilton *(G-11708)*
Credit Union of Ohio Inc .... E 614 487-6650
  Hilliard *(G-11892)*
Day Air Credit Union Inc .... E 937 643-2160
  Dayton *(G-9454)*
Day-Met Credit Union Inc .... E 937 236-2562
  Moraine *(G-14767)*
Directions Credit Union Inc .... E 419 720-4769
  Sylvania *(G-17583)*
Directions Credit Union Inc .... E 419 524-7113
  Mansfield *(G-13292)*
Erie Shores Credit Union Inc .... E 419 897-8110
  Maumee *(G-13912)*
Firefighters Cmnty Cr Un Inc .... E 216 621-4644
  Cleveland *(G-5587)*
General Electric Credit Union .... E 513 243-4328
  Cincinnati *(G-3671)*
Greater Cincinnati Credit Un .... E 513 559-1234
  Mason *(G-13711)*
Hancock Federal Credit Union .... E 419 420-0338
  Findlay *(G-11041)*
Homeland Credit Union Inc .... D 740 775-3024
  Chillicothe *(G-2847)*
Homeland Credit Union Inc .... E 740 775-3331
  Chillicothe *(G-2848)*
Kemba Credit Union Inc .... C 513 762-5070
  West Chester *(G-19100)*
Kemba Financial Credit Un Inc .... E 614 853-9774
  Columbus *(G-7974)*
Kemba Financial Credit Union .... D 614 235-2395
  Columbus *(G-7975)*
Lima Superior Federal Cr Un .... E 419 738-4512
  Wapakoneta *(G-18802)*
Midusa Credit Union .... E 513 420-8640
  Middletown *(G-14440)*
Ohio Educational Credit Union .... E 216 621-6296
  Seven Hills *(G-16833)*
Pse Credit Union Inc .... E 440 843-8300
  Cleveland *(G-6330)*
Seven Seventeen Credit Un Inc .... E 330 372-8100
  Warren *(G-18897)*
Seven Seventeen Credit Un Inc .... E 330 372-8100
  Warren *(G-18898)*
Sun Federal Credit Union .... D 419 537-0200
  Toledo *(G-18207)*
Taleris Credit Union Inc .... E 216 739-2300
  Cleveland *(G-6568)*
Telhio Credit Union Inc .... E 614 221-3233
  Columbus *(G-8829)*
Telhio Credit Union Inc .... E 614 221-3233
  Columbus *(G-8830)*
Universal 1 Credit Union Inc .... D 800 762-9555
  Dayton *(G-9950)*
Wright-Patt Credit Union Inc .... B 937 912-7000
  Beavercreek *(G-1223)*

STATE SAVINGS BANKS, NOT FEDERALLY CHARTERED

Belmont Savings Bank .... E 740 695-0140
  Saint Clairsville *(G-16627)*
Farmers Savings Bank .... E 330 648-2441
  Spencer *(G-17106)*
Fort Jennings State Bank .... E 419 286-2527
  Fort Jennings *(G-11108)*
Hometown Bank .... E 330 673-9827
  Kent *(G-12373)*
Resolute Bank .... D 419 868-1750
  Maumee *(G-13970)*
United Community Fincl Corp .... C 330 742-0500
  Youngstown *(G-20397)*

STATIONARY & OFFICE SPLYS, WHOL: Computer/Photocopying Splys

Canon Solutions America Inc .... E 216 750-2980
  Independence *(G-12194)*
Dexxxon Digital Storage Inc .... E 740 548-7179
  Lewis Center *(G-12681)*
Med-Pass Incorporated .... E 937 438-8884
  Dayton *(G-9711)*

STATIONARY & OFFICE SPLYS, WHOLESALE: Laser Printer Splys

Electronic Printing Pdts Inc .... E 330 689-3930
  Stow *(G-17362)*

STATIONARY & OFFICE SPLYS, WHOLESALE: Stationery

Business Stationery LLC .... D 216 514-1192
  Cleveland *(G-5164)*
Ohio & Michigan Paper Company ...... E 419 666-1500
  Perrysburg *(G-16035)*

STATIONERY & OFFICE SPLYS WHOLESALERS

AW Faber-Castell Usa Inc .... D 216 643-4660
  Cleveland *(G-5086)*
Essendant Inc .... D 330 425-4001
  Twinsburg *(G-18413)*
Friends Service Co Inc .... D 419 427-1704
  Findlay *(G-11033)*
Indepndence Office Bus Sup Inc .... D 216 398-8880
  Cleveland *(G-5815)*
Pfg Ventures LP .... D 216 520-8400
  Independence *(G-12243)*
Quick Tab II Inc .... D 419 448-6622
  Tiffin *(G-17694)*
S P Richards Company .... E 614 497-2270
  Obetz *(G-15670)*
Signal Office Supply Inc .... E 513 821-2280
  Cincinnati *(G-4528)*
Staples Inc .... E 740 845-5600
  London *(G-13007)*
W B Mason Co Inc .... D 216 267-5000
  Cleveland *(G-6713)*

STEAM HEATING SYSTEMS SPLY SVCS

Akron Energy Systems LLC .... D 330 374-0600
  Akron *(G-38)*

STEAM SPLY SYSTEMS SVCS INCLUDING GEOTHERMAL

Cleveland Thermal LLC .... E 216 241-3636
  Cleveland *(G-5352)*

STEAM, HEAT & AIR CONDITIONING DISTRIBUTION SVC

Brewer-Garrett Co .... C 440 243-3535
  Middleburg Heights *(G-14378)*
Honeywell International Inc .... D 216 459-6053
  Cleveland *(G-5770)*
Medical Center Co (inc) .... E 216 368-4256
  Cleveland *(G-6014)*

STEEL FABRICATORS

A & G Manufacturing Co Inc .... E 419 468-7433
  Galion *(G-11288)*
Albert Freytag Inc .... E 419 628-2018
  Minster *(G-14659)*
Allied Fabricating & Wldg Co .... E 614 751-6664
  Columbus *(G-6970)*
Alro Steel Corporation .... E 937 253-6121
  Dayton *(G-9323)*
Ameridian Specialty Services .... E 513 769-0150
  Cincinnati *(G-3014)*
Arctech Fabricating Inc .... E 937 525-9353
  Springfield *(G-17149)*
Bauer Corporation .... E 800 321-4760
  Wooster *(G-19830)*
Blackburns Fabrication Inc .... E 614 875-0784
  Columbus *(G-7117)*
Blevins Metal Fabrication Inc .... E 419 522-6082
  Mansfield *(G-13267)*
Breitinger Company .... C 419 526-4255
  Mansfield *(G-13269)*
Buck Equipment Inc .... E 614 539-3039
  Grove City *(G-11540)*
C-N-D Industries Inc .... E 330 478-8811
  Massillon *(G-13791)*
Clifton Steel Company .... D 216 662-6111
  Maple Heights *(G-13403)*
Continental GL Sls & Inv Group .... E 614 679-1201
  Powell *(G-16332)*
County of Lake .... D 440 269-2193
  Willoughby *(G-19656)*

Curtiss-Wright Flow Control..................D....... 513 528-7900
Cincinnati *(G-2910)*
Debra-Kuempel Inc..................D....... 513 271-6500
Cincinnati *(G-3476)*
Emh Inc..................E....... 330 220-8600
Valley City *(G-18617)*
Evers Welding Co Inc..................E....... 513 385-7352
Cincinnati *(G-3582)*
Franck and Fric Incorporated..................D....... 216 524-4451
Cleveland *(G-5631)*
George Steel Fabricating Inc..................E....... 513 932-2887
Lebanon *(G-12606)*
Graber Metal Works Inc..................E....... 440 237-8422
North Royalton *(G-15490)*
Hanson Concrete Products Ohio..................E....... 614 443-4846
Columbus *(G-7800)*
Hynes Industries Inc..................C....... 330 799-3221
Youngstown *(G-20227)*
Industrial Mill Maintenance..................E....... 330 746-1155
Youngstown *(G-20232)*
Kings Welding and Fabg Inc..................E....... 330 738-3592
Mechanicstown *(G-14031)*
Kottler Metal Products Co Inc..................E....... 440 946-7473
Willoughby *(G-19677)*
Langdon Inc..................E....... 513 733-5955
Cincinnati *(G-3960)*
Lapham-Hickey Steel Corp..................E....... 614 443-4881
Columbus *(G-8039)*
Laserflex Corporation..................D....... 614 850-9600
Hilliard *(G-11920)*
Lefeld Welding & Stl Sups Inc..................E....... 419 678-2397
Coldwater *(G-6832)*
Marsam Metalfab Inc..................E....... 330 405-1520
Twinsburg *(G-18444)*
Marysville Steel Inc..................E....... 937 642-5971
Marysville *(G-13636)*
Mason Structural Steel Inc..................D....... 440 439-1040
Walton Hills *(G-18790)*
McWane Inc..................B....... 740 622-6651
Coshocton *(G-9111)*
Northwind Industries Inc..................E....... 216 433-0666
Cleveland *(G-6163)*
Ohio Structures Inc..................E....... 330 533-0084
Canfield *(G-2206)*
Pcy Enterprises Inc..................E....... 513 241-5566
Cincinnati *(G-4270)*
Pioneer Pipe Inc..................B....... 740 376-2400
Marietta *(G-13488)*
Precision Steel Services Inc..................D....... 419 476-5702
Toledo *(G-18132)*
Precision Welding Corporation..................E....... 216 524-6110
Cleveland *(G-6295)*
Rbm Environmental and Cnstr..................E....... 419 693-5840
Oregon *(G-15748)*
Rittman Inc..................D....... 330 927-6855
Rittman *(G-16556)*
St Lawrence Steel Corporation..................E....... 330 562-9000
Streetsboro *(G-17431)*
Steel Eqp Specialists Inc..................D....... 330 823-8260
Alliance *(G-563)*
Steelial Wldg Met Fbrction Inc..................E....... 740 669-5300
Vinton *(G-18744)*
Tri-America Contractors Inc..................E....... 740 574-0148
Wheelersburg *(G-19582)*
Triangle Precision Industries..................D....... 937 299-6776
Dayton *(G-9937)*
Viking Fabricators Inc..................E....... 740 374-5246
Marietta *(G-13515)*
Wauseon Machine & Mfg Inc..................D....... 419 337-0940
Wauseon *(G-18964)*
Worthington Industries Inc..................C....... 513 539-9291
Monroe *(G-14718)*
Ysd Industries Inc..................D....... 330 792-6521
Youngstown *(G-20437)*

STEEL MILLS

Alba Manufacturing Inc..................D....... 513 874-0551
Fairfield *(G-10818)*
Alro Steel Corporation..................E....... 937 253-6121
Dayton *(G-9323)*
Benjamin Steel Company Inc..................E....... 937 233-1212
Springfield *(G-17150)*
C & R Inc..................E....... 614 497-1130
Groveport *(G-11626)*
Contractors Steel Company..................E....... 330 425-3050
Twinsburg *(G-18404)*
Franklin Iron & Metal Corp..................C....... 937 253-8184
Dayton *(G-9561)*
Garden Street Iron & Metal..................E....... 513 853-3700
Cincinnati *(G-3662)*
International Steel Group..................C....... 330 841-2800
Warren *(G-18865)*
Lapham-Hickey Steel Corp..................E....... 614 443-4881
Columbus *(G-8039)*
McWane Inc..................B....... 740 622-6651
Coshocton *(G-9111)*
Metals USA Crbn Flat Rlled Inc..................C....... 330 264-8416
Wooster *(G-19887)*
Metals USA Crbn Flat Rlled Inc..................D....... 937 882-6354
Springfield *(G-17245)*
Mid-America Steel Corp..................E....... 800 282-3466
Cleveland *(G-6052)*
Pioneer Pipe Inc..................B....... 740 376-2400
Marietta *(G-13488)*
Precision Strip Inc..................D....... 937 667-6255
Tipp City *(G-17725)*
Samuel Steel Pickling Company..................D....... 330 963-3777
Twinsburg *(G-18467)*
Worthington Industries Inc..................C....... 513 539-9291
Monroe *(G-14718)*
Zekelman Industries Inc..................C....... 740 432-2146
Cambridge *(G-2135)*

STEEL, COLD-ROLLED: Flat Bright, From Purchased Hot-Rolled

Geneva Liberty Steel Ltd..................E....... 330 740-0103
Youngstown *(G-20198)*

STEEL, COLD-ROLLED: Sheet Or Strip, From Own Hot-Rolled

Matandy Steel & Metal Pdts LLC..................D....... 513 844-2277
Hamilton *(G-11757)*

STEEL, HOT-ROLLED: Sheet Or Strip

Ohio Steel Sheet & Plate Inc..................E....... 800 827-2401
Hubbard *(G-12090)*

STEEL: Cold-Rolled

All Ohio Threaded Rod Co Inc..................E....... 216 426-1800
Cleveland *(G-4990)*
Alro Steel Corporation..................E....... 937 253-6121
Dayton *(G-9323)*
Benjamin Steel Company Inc..................E....... 937 233-1212
Springfield *(G-17150)*
Independent Steel Company LLC..................E....... 330 225-7741
Valley City *(G-18618)*
Mid-America Steel Corp..................E....... 800 282-3466
Cleveland *(G-6052)*

STITCHING SVCS: Custom

Blue Chip Mailing Services Inc..................E....... 513 541-4800
Blue Ash *(G-1545)*

STONE: Dimension, NEC

Heritage Marble of Ohio Inc..................E....... 614 436-1464
Columbus *(G-7831)*

STONE: Quarrying & Processing, Own Stone Prdts

Hanson Aggregates East LLC..................E....... 937 364-2311
Hillsboro *(G-11976)*

STONEWARE PRDTS: Pottery

Clay Burley Products Co..................E....... 740 452-3633
Roseville *(G-16601)*

STORE FIXTURES, EXC REFRIGERATED: Wholesalers

Hubert Company LLC..................B....... 513 367-8600
Harrison *(G-11802)*
Takkt America Holding Inc..................C....... 513 367-8600
Harrison *(G-11810)*

STORE FIXTURES: Wood

CIP International Inc..................D....... 513 874-9925
West Chester *(G-19041)*

STORES: Auto & Home Supply

Abraham Ford LLC..................E....... 440 233-7402
Elyria *(G-10592)*
Albert Mike Leasing Inc..................C....... 513 563-1400
Cincinnati *(G-2982)*
Beechmont Ford Inc..................C....... 513 752-6611
Cincinnati *(G-2904)*
Brown Motor Sales Co..................E....... 419 531-0151
Toledo *(G-17785)*
Cascade Group Inc..................E....... 330 929-1861
Cuyahoga Falls *(G-9169)*
Chesrown Oldsmobile GMC Inc..................E....... 614 846-3040
Columbus *(G-7255)*
Contitech North America Inc..................E....... 440 225-5363
Akron *(G-162)*
Coughlin Chevrolet Inc..................D....... 740 964-9191
Pataskala *(G-15922)*
Coughlin Chevrolet Toyota Inc..................D....... 740 366-1381
Newark *(G-15162)*
Cronins Inc..................E....... 513 851-5900
Cincinnati *(G-3440)*
Dave Knapp Ford Lincoln Inc..................E....... 937 547-3000
Greenville *(G-11496)*
Doug Marine Motors Inc..................E....... 740 335-3700
Wshngtn CT Hs *(G-20020)*
Ed Schmidt Auto Inc..................C....... 419 874-4331
Perrysburg *(G-16001)*
G & C Finishes From The Future..................E....... 937 890-3002
Dayton *(G-9567)*
Germain On Scarborough LLC..................C....... 614 868-0300
Columbus *(G-7748)*
Haydocy Automotive Inc..................D....... 614 279-8880
Columbus *(G-7804)*
Jerry Haag Motors Inc..................E....... 937 402-2090
Hillsboro *(G-11984)*
Joe Dodge Kidd Inc..................E....... 513 752-1804
Cincinnati *(G-2921)*
Kent Automotive Inc..................E....... 330 678-5520
Kent *(G-12377)*
Kerry Ford Inc..................D....... 513 671-6400
Cincinnati *(G-3918)*
KOI Enterprises Inc..................D....... 513 357-2400
Cincinnati *(G-3939)*
Lebanon Chrysler - Plymuth Inc..................E....... 513 932-2717
Lebanon *(G-12620)*
Leikin Motor Companies Inc..................D....... 440 946-6900
Willoughby *(G-19686)*
Matia Motors Inc..................E....... 440 365-7311
Elyria *(G-10650)*
Medina World Cars Inc..................E....... 330 725-4901
Strongsville *(G-17493)*
Northgate Chrysler Jeep Inc..................D....... 513 385-3900
Cincinnati *(G-4180)*
Rush Truck Centers Ohio Inc..................D....... 513 733-8500
Cincinnati *(G-4458)*
Rush Truck Centers Ohio Inc..................E....... 419 224-6045
Lima *(G-12872)*
Rush Truck Leasing Inc..................E....... 614 876-3500
Columbus *(G-8660)*
Sonic Automotive..................D....... 614 870-8200
Columbus *(G-8748)*
Sunnyside Toyota Inc..................D....... 440 777-9911
North Olmsted *(G-15446)*
Tansky Motors Inc..................E....... 650 322-7069
Logan *(G-12989)*
Voss Toyota Inc..................E....... 937 427-3700
Beavercreek *(G-1218)*
Walker Auto Group Inc..................D....... 937 433-4950
Miamisburg *(G-14367)*

STUDIOS: Artists & Artists' Studios

American National Red Cross..................D....... 216 431-3152
Cleveland *(G-5018)*
Bob Sumerel Tire Co Inc..................E....... 513 528-1900
Cincinnati *(G-3123)*
Bob Sumerel Tire Co Inc..................E....... 513 598-2300
Cincinnati *(G-3124)*
County of Logan..................E....... 937 599-4221
Bellefontaine *(G-1381)*
Daily Services LLC..................C....... 740 326-6130
Mount Vernon *(G-14891)*
Lighthouse Youth Services Inc..................D....... 513 861-1111
Cincinnati *(G-3981)*
Pcm Inc..................E....... 614 854-1399
Lewis Center *(G-12701)*
Quantech Services Inc..................C....... 937 490-8461
Beavercreek Township *(G-1283)*
Vantage Aging..................A....... 330 785-9770
Akron *(G-496)*

STUDIOS: Sculptor's

Don Drumm Studios & Gallery..................E....... 330 253-6840
Akron *(G-196)*

SERVICES SECTION
SVC ESTABLISHMENT EQPT, WHOLESALE: Firefighting Eqpt

STUDS & JOISTS: Sheet Metal
Matandy Steel & Metal Pdts LLC .... D 513 844-2277
  Hamilton *(G-11757)*

SUB-LESSORS: Real Estate
Schottenstein Realty LLC .... E 614 445-8461
  Columbus *(G-8704)*

SUBSCRIPTION FULFILLMENT SVCS: Magazine, Newspaper, Etc
Ebsco Industries Inc .... B 330 478-0281
  Canton *(G-2349)*
Inquiry Systems Inc .... E 614 464-3800
  Columbus *(G-7904)*

SUBSTANCE ABUSE CLINICS, OUTPATIENT
Christian Chld HM Ohio Inc .... D 330 345-7949
  Wooster *(G-19841)*
Community Behavioral Hlth Inc .... C 513 887-8500
  Hamilton *(G-11716)*
Community Drug Board Inc .... D 330 315-5590
  Akron *(G-153)*
County of Cuyahoga .... E 216 443-7035
  Cleveland *(G-5418)*
Family Recovery Center Inc .... E 330 424-1468
  Lisbon *(G-12937)*
HHC Ohio Inc .... E 440 953-3000
  Willoughby *(G-19668)*
Legacy Freedom Treatment Ctr .... E 614 741-2100
  Columbus *(G-8049)*
Lorain County Alcohol and Drug .... D 440 246-0109
  Lorain *(G-13050)*
Meridian Healthcare .... D 330 797-0070
  Youngstown *(G-20285)*
Philio Inc .... E 419 531-5544
  Toledo *(G-18124)*
Project C U R E Inc .... E 937 262-3500
  Dayton *(G-9836)*
Recovery Resources .... E 216 431-4131
  Cleveland *(G-6361)*
Recovery Resources .... D 216 431-4131
  Cleveland *(G-6362)*

SUBSTANCE ABUSE COUNSELING
Anazao Community Partners .... E 330 264-9597
  Wooster *(G-19828)*
Community Drug Board Inc .... D 330 315-5590
  Akron *(G-153)*
Hispanc Urbn Mnrty Alchlsm DRG .... E 216 398-2333
  Cleveland *(G-5759)*
Oriana House Inc .... E 216 881-5440
  Cleveland *(G-6213)*
Quest Recovery Prevention Svcs .... C 330 453-8252
  Canton *(G-2499)*
Talbert House .... E 513 541-1184
  Cincinnati *(G-4619)*
Talbert House .... D 513 933-9304
  Lebanon *(G-12652)*

SUMMER CAMPS, EXC DAY & SPORTS INSTRUCTIONAL
Camp Patmos Inc .... E 419 746-2214
  Kelleys Island *(G-12348)*
Classroom Antics Inc .... E 800 595-3776
  North Royalton *(G-15484)*
Friars Club Inc .... D 513 488-8777
  Cincinnati *(G-3654)*
Scribes & Scrbblr Chld Dev Ctr .... E 440 884-5437
  Cleveland *(G-6455)*
Skyview Baptist Ranch Inc .... E 330 674-7511
  Millersburg *(G-14622)*
Young Mens Christian Assoc .... D 513 932-3756
  Oregonia *(G-15759)*

SUPERMARKETS & OTHER GROCERY STORES
Discount Drug Mart Inc .... C 330 725-2340
  Medina *(G-14059)*
Forths Foods Inc .... E 740 886-9769
  Proctorville *(G-16358)*
Fred W Albrecht Grocery Co .... C 330 645-6222
  Coventry Township *(G-9124)*
Heights Emergency Food Center .... D 216 381-0707
  Cleveland *(G-5747)*

J V Hansel Inc .... E 330 716-0806
  Warren *(G-18866)*
Yund Inc .... E 330 837-9358
  Massillon *(G-13864)*

SURGICAL APPLIANCES & SPLYS
Cardinal Health Inc .... A 614 757-5000
  Dublin *(G-10275)*
Dentronix Inc .... E 330 916-7300
  Cuyahoga Falls *(G-9179)*
Doling & Associates Dental Lab .... E 937 254-0075
  Dayton *(G-9503)*
Jones Metal Products Company .... E 740 545-6341
  West Lafayette *(G-19257)*
Philips Medical Systems Clevel .... B 440 247-2652
  Cleveland *(G-6273)*

SURGICAL EQPT: See Also Instruments
Mill-Rose Company .... C 440 255-9171
  Mentor *(G-14220)*

SURGICAL INSTRUMENT REPAIR SVCS
Mobile Instr Svc & Repr Inc .... C 937 592-5025
  Bellefontaine *(G-1391)*

SURVEYING & MAPPING: Land Parcels
7nt Enterprises LLC .... E 937 435-3200
  Dayton *(G-9295)*
American Electric Pwr Svc Corp .... B 614 716-1000
  Columbus *(G-6990)*
ASC Group Inc .... E 614 268-2514
  Columbus *(G-7048)*
Barr Engineering Incorporated .... E 614 714-0299
  Columbus *(G-7091)*
Bayer & Becker Inc .... E 513 492-7297
  Mason *(G-13666)*
Bayer & Becker Inc .... E 513 492-7401
  Mason *(G-13667)*
Bramhall Engrg & Surveying Co .... E 440 934-7878
  Avon *(G-881)*
Choice One Engineering Corp .... E 937 497-0200
  Sidney *(G-16919)*
CT Consultants Inc .... C 440 951-9000
  Mentor *(G-14166)*
CT Consultants Inc .... E 513 791-1700
  Blue Ash *(G-1573)*
Ctl Engineering Inc .... C 614 276-8123
  Columbus *(G-7474)*
Dj Neff Enterpeises Inc .... E 440 884-3100
  Cleveland *(G-5494)*
Dlz Ohio Inc .... C 614 888-0040
  Columbus *(G-7535)*
E P Ferris & Associates Inc .... E 614 299-2999
  Columbus *(G-7560)*
Evans Mechwart Ham .... B 614 775-4500
  New Albany *(G-14984)*
Feller Finch & Associates Inc .... E 419 893-3680
  Maumee *(G-13916)*
Ground Penetrating Radar Sys .... E 419 843-9804
  Toledo *(G-17926)*
Hammontree & Associates Ltd .... E 330 499-8817
  Canton *(G-2390)*
Jack A Hamilton & Assoc Inc .... E 740 968-4947
  Flushing *(G-11105)*
Jobes Henderson & Assoc Inc .... E 740 344-5451
  Newark *(G-15178)*
Kleingers Group Inc .... D 513 779-7851
  West Chester *(G-19103)*
KS Associates Inc .... D 440 365-4730
  Elyria *(G-10639)*
Kucera International Inc .... E 440 975-4230
  Willoughby *(G-19678)*
Land Design Consultants .... E 440 255-8463
  Mentor *(G-14207)*
McGill Smith Punshon Inc .... E 513 759-0004
  Cincinnati *(G-4036)*
McSteen & Associates Inc .... E 440 585-9800
  Wickliffe *(G-19607)*
Peterman Associates Inc .... E 419 722-9566
  Findlay *(G-11074)*
Poggemeyer Design Group Inc .... E 419 748-7438
  Mc Clure *(G-14020)*
Poggemeyer Design Group Inc .... E 419 244-8074
  Bowling Green *(G-1791)*
R E Warner & Associates Inc .... D 440 835-9400
  Westlake *(G-19537)*
Resource International Inc .... E 614 823-4949
  Columbus *(G-8622)*

Sands Decker Cps Llc .... E 614 459-6992
  Columbus *(G-8684)*
T J Neff Holdings Inc .... E 440 884-3100
  Cleveland *(G-6564)*
Usic Locating Services LLC .... C 330 733-9393
  Akron *(G-491)*
Wade Trim .... E 216 363-0300
  Cleveland *(G-6716)*

SVC ESTABLISHMENT EQPT & SPLYS WHOLESALERS
Century Equipment Inc .... E 513 285-1800
  Hamilton *(G-11707)*
H & H Green LLC .... E 419 674-4152
  Kenton *(G-12412)*
Lute Supply Inc .... E 740 353-1447
  Portsmouth *(G-16294)*
Mark Humrichouser .... E 614 324-5231
  Westerville *(G-19327)*
Rde System Corp .... C 513 933-8000
  Lebanon *(G-12640)*
Sally Beauty Supply LLC .... C 937 548-7684
  Greenville *(G-11518)*
Sally Beauty Supply LLC .... C 614 278-1691
  Columbus *(G-8678)*

SVC ESTABLISHMENT EQPT, WHOL: Cleaning & Maint Eqpt & Splys
Dawnchem Inc .... E 440 943-3332
  Willoughby *(G-19658)*
Hd Supply Facilities Maint Ltd .... E 440 542-9188
  Solon *(G-17014)*
Mansfield City Building Maint .... E 419 755-9698
  Mansfield *(G-13330)*
Mapp Building Service LLC .... E 513 253-3990
  Blue Ash *(G-1633)*
Mougianis Industries Inc .... D 740 264-6372
  Steubenville *(G-17331)*

SVC ESTABLISHMENT EQPT, WHOL: Concrete Burial Vaults & Boxes
Baxter Burial Vault Service .... E 513 641-1010
  Cincinnati *(G-3082)*

SVC ESTABLISHMENT EQPT, WHOL: Laundry/Dry Cleaning Eqpt/Sply
Norm Sharlotte Inc .... E 336 788-7705
  New Albany *(G-15002)*

SVC ESTABLISHMENT EQPT, WHOLESALE : Barber Shop Eqpt & Splys
Fredrics Corporation .... C 513 874-2226
  West Chester *(G-19076)*

SVC ESTABLISHMENT EQPT, WHOLESALE: Beauty Parlor Eqpt & Sply
MSA Group Inc .... B 614 334-0400
  Columbus *(G-8204)*
North Central Sales Inc .... E 216 481-2418
  Cleveland *(G-6138)*
Perio Inc .... E 614 791-1207
  Dublin *(G-10426)*
Salon Success Intl LLC .... E 330 468-0476
  Macedonia *(G-13209)*
Salon Ware Inc .... E 330 665-2244
  Copley *(G-9062)*

SVC ESTABLISHMENT EQPT, WHOLESALE: Firefighting Eqpt
A-1 Sprinkler Company Inc .... D 937 859-6198
  Miamisburg *(G-14267)*
Action Coupling & Eqp Inc .... D 330 279-4242
  Holmesville *(G-12070)*
Brakefire Incorporated .... E 330 535-4343
  Akron *(G-107)*
Finley Fire Equipment Co .... D 740 962-4328
  McConnelsville *(G-14027)*
Fox International Limited Inc .... E 216 454-1001
  Beachwood *(G-1080)*
Sutphen Corporation .... C 800 726-7030
  Dublin *(G-10468)*

Employee Codes: A=Over 500 employees, B=251-500
C=101-250, D=51-100, E=25-50

SVC ESTABLISHMENT EQPT, WHOLESALE: Laundry Eqpt & Splys

SVC ESTABLISHMENT EQPT, WHOLESALE: Laundry Eqpt & Splys

American Sales Inc .... E 937 253-9520
  Dayton *(G-9254)*
Laughlin Music & Vending Svc .... E 740 593-7778
  Athens *(G-798)*

SVC ESTABLISHMENT EQPT, WHOLESALE: Locksmith Eqpt & Splys

Anixter Inc .... E 513 881-4600
  West Chester *(G-19021)*

SVC ESTABLISHMENT EQPT, WHOLESALE: Restaurant Splys

Commercial Parts & Ser .... D 614 221-0057
  Columbus *(G-7400)*
Martin-Brower Company LLC .... B 513 773-2301
  West Chester *(G-19118)*
Rdp Foodservice Ltd .... D 614 261-5661
  Columbus *(G-8593)*
Wasserstrom Company .... B 614 228-6525
  Columbus *(G-8970)*

SVC ESTABLISHMENT EQPT, WHOLESALE: Vending Machines & Splys

Cleveland Coin Mch Exch Inc .... D 847 842-6310
  Willoughby *(G-19653)*
Shaffer Distributing Company .... D 614 421-6800
  Columbus *(G-8721)*

SWIMMING INSTRUCTION

Goldfish Swim School .... E 216 364-9090
  Chagrin Falls *(G-2718)*

SWIMMING POOL & HOT TUB CLEANING & MAINTENANCE SVCS

Buckeye Pool Inc .... E 937 434-7916
  Dayton *(G-9370)*
Hastings Water Works Inc .... E 440 832-7700
  Brecksville *(G-1826)*
Marcums Don Pool Care Inc .... E 513 561-7050
  Cincinnati *(G-4020)*
Metropolitan Pool Service Co .... E 216 741-9451
  Parma *(G-15910)*

SWIMMING POOL SPLY STORES

Burnett Pools Inc .... E 330 372-1725
  Cortland *(G-9074)*
Marcums Don Pool Care Inc .... E 513 561-7050
  Cincinnati *(G-4020)*
Metropolitan Pool Service Co .... E 216 741-9451
  Parma *(G-15910)*

SWIMMING POOLS, EQPT & SPLYS: Wholesalers

Competitor Swim Products Inc .... D 800 888-7946
  Columbus *(G-7413)*
Emsco .... E 440 238-2100
  Strongsville *(G-17460)*
Mc Alarney Pool Spas and Blld .... E 740 373-6698
  Marietta *(G-13474)*
Metropolitan Pool Service Co .... E 216 741-9451
  Parma *(G-15910)*

SWITCHGEAR & SWITCHBOARD APPARATUS

General Electric Company .... D 216 883-1000
  Cleveland *(G-5667)*
Schneider Electric Usa Inc .... D 513 755-5000
  West Chester *(G-19145)*

SYMPHONY ORCHESTRA

Cincinnati Symphony Orchestra .... C 513 621-1919
  Cincinnati *(G-3332)*
Dayton Performing Arts Aliance .... D 937 224-3521
  Dayton *(G-9485)*
Greater Akron Musical Assn .... D 330 535-8131
  Akron *(G-246)*
Southeastern Ohio Symphony Orc .... E 740 826-8197
  New Concord *(G-15037)*

SYNAGOGUES

Israel Adath .... E 513 793-1800
  Cincinnati *(G-3846)*

SYRUPS, DRINK

Central Coca-Cola Btlg Co Inc .... C 419 476-6622
  Toledo *(G-17798)*
Slush Puppie .... D 513 771-0940
  West Chester *(G-19230)*

SYSTEMS ENGINEERING: Computer Related

Devcare Solutions Ltd .... E 614 221-2277
  Columbus *(G-7511)*
Leidos Inc .... B 858 826-6000
  Columbus *(G-8051)*
Telligen Tech Inc .... E 614 934-1554
  Columbus *(G-8831)*
Ventech Solutions Inc .... D 614 757-1167
  Columbus *(G-6909)*

SYSTEMS INTEGRATION SVCS

Advanced Prgrm Resources Inc .... E 614 761-9994
  Dublin *(G-10234)*
Axia Consulting Inc .... D 614 675-4050
  Columbus *(G-7080)*
Cdw Technologies LLC .... D 513 677-4100
  Cincinnati *(G-3199)*
Commercial Time Sharing Inc .... E 330 644-3059
  Akron *(G-152)*
Commsys Inc .... E 937 220-4990
  Moraine *(G-14761)*
Computers Universal Inc .... C 614 543-0473
  Beavercreek *(G-1162)*
Creative Microsystems Inc .... E 937 836-4499
  Englewood *(G-10701)*
Datascan Field Services LLC .... E 440 914-7300
  Solon *(G-17000)*
Dyncorp .... C 513 942-6500
  West Chester *(G-19067)*
Dyncorp .... D 513 569-7415
  Cincinnati *(G-3518)*
Integrted Prcision Systems Inc .... E 330 963-0064
  Twinsburg *(G-18432)*
Jaekle Group Inc .... E 330 405-9353
  Macedonia *(G-13204)*
Matrix Technologies Inc .... D 419 897-7200
  Maumee *(G-13942)*
Millenium Control Systems LLC .... E 440 510-0050
  Eastlake *(G-10549)*
Northern Datacomm Corp .... E 330 665-0344
  Akron *(G-357)*
Sterling Buying Group LLC .... E 513 564-9000
  Cincinnati *(G-4589)*
Systemax Manufacturing Inc .... C 937 368-2300
  Dayton *(G-9919)*
Tyco International MGT Co LLC .... E 888 787-8324
  Cincinnati *(G-4712)*

SYSTEMS INTEGRATION SVCS: Local Area Network

Acadia Solutions Inc .... E 614 505-6135
  Dublin *(G-10233)*
Cisco Systems Inc .... C 330 523-2000
  Richfield *(G-16501)*
Dedicated Tech Services Inc .... D 614 309-0059
  Dublin *(G-10317)*
Expert System Applications .... E 440 248-0110
  Beachwood *(G-1077)*
HP Inc .... E 440 234-7022
  Cleveland *(G-5787)*
Juniper Networks Inc .... D 614 932-1432
  Columbus *(G-10383)*
Manifest Solutions Corp .... E 614 930-2800
  Upper Arlington *(G-18555)*
United Technical Support Svcs .... D 330 562-3330
  Aurora *(G-858)*

SYSTEMS INTEGRATION SVCS: Office Computer Automation

Presidio Infrastructure .... D 419 241-8303
  Toledo *(G-18134)*
Security Investments LLC .... D 614 441-4601
  Westerville *(G-19443)*

SYSTEMS SOFTWARE DEVELOPMENT SVCS

Aisling Enterprises LLC .... E 937 203-1757
  Centerville *(G-2670)*
Brandmuscle Inc .... C 216 464-4342
  Cleveland *(G-5133)*
Cincinnati Bell Inc .... D 513 397-9900
  Cincinnati *(G-3285)*
Cincom Systems Inc .... B 513 612-2300
  Cincinnati *(G-3343)*
Courtview Justice Solutions .... E 330 497-0033
  Canton *(G-2326)*
Deemsys Inc .... D 614 322-9928
  Gahanna *(G-11239)*
Drb Systems LLC .... D 330 645-3299
  Akron *(G-200)*
Easy2 Technologies Inc .... E 216 479-0482
  Cleveland *(G-5523)*
ID Networks Inc .... E 440 992-0062
  Ashtabula *(G-749)*
Infor (us) Inc .... B 678 319-8000
  Columbus *(G-7896)*
Infor (us) Inc .... D 614 781-2325
  Columbus *(G-6886)*
Knotice LLC .... D 800 801-4194
  Akron *(G-308)*
Mid-Amrica Cnsulting Group Inc .... D 216 432-6925
  Cleveland *(G-6053)*
Online Mega Sellers Corp .... D 888 384-6468
  Toledo *(G-18109)*
Robots and Pencils LP .... D 587 350-4095
  Beachwood *(G-1120)*
Rockwell Automation Ohio Inc .... D 513 576-6151
  Milford *(G-14558)*
Siemens PLM Software .... E 513 576-2400
  Milford *(G-14561)*
Soaring Eagle Inc .... E 330 385-5579
  East Liverpool *(G-10535)*
Talx Corporation .... E 614 527-9404
  Hilliard *(G-11956)*
Tour De Force Crm Inc .... E 419 425-4800
  Findlay *(G-11092)*

TABULATING SVCS

Personalized Data Corporation .... E 216 289-2200
  Cleveland *(G-6268)*

TAGS & LABELS: Paper

Century Marketing Corporation .... C 419 354-2591
  Bowling Green *(G-1772)*

TANK & BOILER CLEANING SVCS

C & W Tank Cleaning Company .... D 419 691-1995
  Oregon *(G-15727)*
Rbm Environmental and Cnstr .... E 419 693-5840
  Oregon *(G-15748)*

TANK REPAIR & CLEANING SVCS

Amko Service Company .... E 330 364-8857
  Midvale *(G-14489)*
Ohio Hydraulics Inc .... E 513 771-2590
  Cincinnati *(G-4207)*
Sabco Industries Inc .... E 419 531-5347
  Toledo *(G-18169)*

TANK REPAIR SVCS

C H Bradshaw Co .... E 614 871-2087
  Grove City *(G-11543)*
Corrotec Inc .... E 937 325-3585
  Springfield *(G-17177)*
Frontier Tank Center Inc .... E 330 659-3888
  Richfield *(G-16510)*

TANKS: Cryogenic, Metal

Amko Service Company .... E 330 364-8857
  Midvale *(G-14489)*
Eleet Cryogenics Inc .... E 330 874-4009
  Bolivar *(G-1746)*

TANKS: Lined, Metal

Modern Welding Co Ohio Inc .... E 740 344-9425
  Newark *(G-15209)*

TANKS: Standard Or Custom Fabricated, Metal Plate

Enerfab Inc ... B ... 513 641-0500
Cincinnati *(G-3557)*
Gaspar Inc ... D ... 330 477-2222
Canton *(G-2376)*

TANNING SALONS

Attractions ... E ... 740 592-5600
Athens *(G-778)*
Diane Babiuch ... E ... 419 867-8837
Holland *(G-12020)*
Noggins Hair Design Inc ... E ... 513 474-4405
Cincinnati *(G-4171)*
Super Tan ... E ... 330 722-2799
Medina *(G-14132)*

TAPES: Pressure Sensitive

Beiersdorf Inc ... C ... 513 682-7300
West Chester *(G-19191)*

TAX RETURN PREPARATION SVCS

Barnes Wendling Cpas Inc ... E ... 216 566-9000
Cleveland *(G-5095)*
Colonial Banc Corp ... E ... 937 456-5544
Eaton *(G-10554)*
Damon Tax Service ... E ... 513 574-9087
Cincinnati *(G-3461)*
Delaneys Tax Accunting Svc Ltd ... E ... 513 248-2829
Milford *(G-14516)*
Deloitte & Touche LLP ... B ... 513 784-7100
Cincinnati *(G-3482)*
Dw Together LLC ... E ... 330 225-8200
Brunswick *(G-1976)*
E T Financial Service Inc ... E ... 937 716-1726
Trotwood *(G-18346)*
H & R Block ... E ... 419 352-9467
Bowling Green *(G-1779)*
H & R Block Inc ... E ... 330 345-1040
Wooster *(G-19866)*
H & R Block Inc ... E ... 216 271-7108
Cleveland *(G-5713)*
H & R Block Inc ... E ... 513 868-1818
Hamilton *(G-11737)*
H&R Block Inc ... E ... 330 773-0412
Akron *(G-250)*
H&R Block Inc ... E ... 440 282-4288
Amherst *(G-596)*
H&R Block Inc ... E ... 216 861-1185
Cleveland *(G-5717)*
Hometown Urgent Care ... C ... 330 629-2300
Youngstown *(G-20219)*
Hometown Urgent Care ... D ... 740 363-3133
Delaware *(G-10107)*
Hometown Urgent Care ... C ... 937 252-2000
Wooster *(G-19868)*
Jennings & Associates ... E ... 740 369-4426
Delaware *(G-10111)*
Liberty Tax Inc ... E ... 614 853-1090
Galloway *(G-11345)*
Phillip Mc Guire ... E ... 740 482-2701
Nevada *(G-14969)*
Skoda Minotti Holdings LLC ... E ... 440 449-6800
Cleveland *(G-6484)*
Village of Coldwater ... D ... 419 678-2685
Coldwater *(G-6837)*

TAXI CABS

Americab Inc ... E ... 216 429-1134
Cleveland *(G-5002)*
City Taxicab & Transfer Co ... E ... 440 992-2156
Ashtabula *(G-734)*
City Yellow Cab Company ... E ... 330 253-3141
Akron *(G-144)*
Columbus Green Cabs Inc ... E ... 614 444-4444
Columbus *(G-7355)*
Independent Radio Taxi Inc ... E ... 330 746-8844
Youngstown *(G-20231)*
Knox Area Transit ... E ... 740 392-7433
Mount Vernon *(G-14902)*
Pickaway County Community Acti ... D ... 740 477-1655
Circleville *(G-4894)*
Shamrock Taxi Ltd ... E ... 614 263-8294
Columbus *(G-8723)*
United Garage & Service Corp ... D ... 216 623-1550
Cleveland *(G-6639)*
Westlake Cab Service ... D ... 440 331-5000
Cleveland *(G-6746)*
Yellow Cab Co of Cleveland ... D ... 216 623-1500
Cleveland *(G-6769)*

TECHNICAL & TRADE SCHOOLS, NEC

Recording Workshop ... E ... 740 663-1000
Chillicothe *(G-2873)*

TECHNICAL INSTITUTE

Cleveland Municipal School Dst ... D ... 216 459-4200
Cleveland *(G-5334)*

TECHNICAL MANUAL PREPARATION SVCS

ONeil & Associates Inc ... C ... 937 865-0800
Miamisburg *(G-14330)*

TECHNICAL WRITING SVCS

Thinkpath Engineering Svcs LLC ... D ... 937 291-8374
Miamisburg *(G-14358)*

TELECOMMUNICATION EQPT REPAIR SVCS, EXC TELEPHONES

AT&T Corp ... A ... 614 223-8236
Columbus *(G-7062)*
Centurylink Inc ... A ... 614 215-4223
Dublin *(G-10286)*
Jersey Central Pwr & Light Co ... E ... 419 321-7207
Oak Harbor *(G-15611)*
Vertiv Energy Systems Inc ... A ... 440 288-1122
Lorain *(G-13085)*

TELECOMMUNICATION SYSTEMS & EQPT

DTE Inc ... E ... 419 522-3428
Mansfield *(G-13295)*
Mitel (delaware) Inc ... E ... 513 733-8000
West Chester *(G-19122)*
Peco II Inc ... D ... 614 431-0694
Columbus *(G-8528)*
Vertiv Energy Systems Inc ... A ... 440 288-1122
Lorain *(G-13085)*

TELECOMMUNICATIONS CARRIERS & SVCS: Wired

AT&T Corp ... D ... 330 337-3505
Salem *(G-16687)*
AT&T Corp ... D ... 614 223-5318
Westerville *(G-19367)*
AT&T Corp ... C ... 614 271-8911
Powell *(G-16325)*
AT&T Corp ... D ... 614 223-6513
Columbus *(G-7061)*
AT&T Corp ... C ... 937 372-9945
Xenia *(G-20042)*
AT&T Corp ... D ... 614 337-3902
Columbus *(G-7065)*
AT&T Corp ... A ... 614 223-8236
Columbus *(G-7062)*
AT&T Mobility LLC ... E ... 614 291-2500
Columbus *(G-7066)*
Cass Information Systems Inc ... E ... 614 839-4503
Columbus *(G-7206)*
Cellco Partnership ... E ... 440 984-5200
Amherst *(G-590)*
Cellco Partnership ... C ... 937 498-2371
Sidney *(G-16918)*
Cellco Partnership ... E ... 740 450-1525
Zanesville *(G-20459)*
Cincinnati Bell Inc ... D ... 513 397-9900
Cincinnati *(G-3285)*
Cincinnati Bell Tele Co LLC ... C ... 513 565-9402
Cincinnati *(G-3288)*
Cinciti Bl Etd Trts LLC ... D ... 513 397-0963
Cincinnati *(G-3340)*
Connect Call Global LLC ... E ... 513 348-1800
Mason *(G-13689)*
Cox Ohio Telcom LLC ... D ... 216 535-3500
Parma *(G-15904)*
Cypress Communications Inc ... C ... 404 965-7248
Cleveland *(G-5459)*
Echo 24 Inc ... E ... 740 964-7081
Reynoldsburg *(G-16450)*
Fte Networks Inc ... D ... 502 657-3500
Cincinnati *(G-3657)*
Kraft Electrical Contg Inc ... E ... 614 836-9300
Groveport *(G-11655)*
Kraftmaid Trucking Inc ... D ... 440 632-2531
Middlefield *(G-14396)*
Level 3 Communications Inc ... E ... 330 256-8999
Akron *(G-315)*
Level 3 Telecom LLC ... E ... 513 841-0000
Cincinnati *(G-3971)*
Level 3 Telecom LLC ... E ... 513 682-7806
West Chester *(G-19107)*
Level 3 Telecom LLC ... E ... 513 682-7806
West Chester *(G-19108)*
Level 3 Telecom LLC ... E ... 513 682-7806
West Chester *(G-19109)*
Level 3 Telecom LLC ... E ... 513 841-0000
Cincinnati *(G-3972)*
Morelia Group LLC ... E ... 513 469-1500
Cincinnati *(G-4117)*
Ohio State University ... E ... 614 292-6291
Columbus *(G-8416)*
Pearl Interactive Network Inc ... B ... 614 258-2943
Columbus *(G-8527)*
Qwest Corporation ... D ... 614 793-9258
Dublin *(G-10435)*
Rxp Wireless LLC ... E ... 330 264-1500
Wooster *(G-19909)*
Spectrum Networks Inc ... E ... 513 697-2000
Cincinnati *(G-4560)*
Telemaxx Communications LLC ... E ... 216 371-8800
Cleveland *(G-6578)*
TSC Television Inc ... D ... 419 941-6001
Wapakoneta *(G-18811)*
TW Telecom Inc ... E ... 234 542-6279
Akron *(G-482)*
United Telephone Company Ohio ... B ... 419 227-1660
Lima *(G-12910)*
Verizon Bus Netwrk Svcs Inc ... E ... 513 897-1501
Waynesville *(G-18988)*
Verizon New York Inc ... C ... 740 383-0411
Marion *(G-13595)*
Verizon North Inc ... D ... 937 382-6961
Wilmington *(G-19792)*
Vox Mobile ... E ... 800 536-9030
Independence *(G-12274)*
Windstream Ohio LLC ... D ... 330 650-8436
Hudson *(G-12152)*
Xo Communications LLC ... E ... 216 619-3200
Cleveland *(G-6768)*

TELECOMMUNICATIONS CARRIERS & SVCS: Wireless

Alltel Communications Corp ... D ... 740 349-8551
Newark *(G-15141)*
AT&T Corp ... A ... 513 629-5000
Cincinnati *(G-3054)*
AT&T Mobility LLC ... E ... 216 382-0825
Cleveland *(G-5076)*
AT&T Mobility LLC ... E ... 513 381-6800
Cincinnati *(G-3055)*
Horizon Pcs Inc ... C ... 740 772-8200
Chillicothe *(G-2850)*
Verizon New York Inc ... E ... 330 364-0508
Dover *(G-10222)*

TELEMARKETING BUREAUS

Alorica Customer Care Inc ... A ... 216 525-3311
Cleveland *(G-4995)*
American Publishers LLC ... D ... 419 626-0623
Huron *(G-12160)*
Ameridial Inc ... B ... 800 445-7128
Canton *(G-2240)*
Ameridial Inc ... D ... 330 479-8044
North Canton *(G-15324)*
Ameridial Inc ... B ... 330 497-4888
North Canton *(G-15325)*
Ameridial Inc ... D ... 330 339-7222
New Philadelphia *(G-15082)*
Ameridial Inc ... D ... 330 868-2000
Minerva *(G-14641)*
Convergys Cstmer MGT Group Inc ... B ... 513 723-6104
Cincinnati *(G-3418)*
Dialamerica Marketing Inc ... C ... 330 836-5293
Fairlawn *(G-10945)*
Dialamerica Marketing Inc ... C ... 440 234-4410
Cleveland *(G-5481)*
Douglas Webb & Associates ... D ... 614 873-9830
Plain City *(G-16188)*
Fox International Limited Inc ... E ... 216 454-1001
Beachwood *(G-1080)*

Employee Codes: A=Over 500 employees, B=251-500
C=101-250, D=51-100, E=25-50

2018 Harris Ohio
Services Directory

1633

SERVICES

Incept Corporation......C...... 330 649-8000
Canton *(G-2410)*
Infocision Management Corp......B...... 330 668-1411
Akron *(G-278)*
Infocision Management Corp......B...... 330 726-0872
Youngstown *(G-20234)*
Infocision Management Corp......D...... 419 529-8685
Mansfield *(G-13313)*
Infocision Management Corp......C...... 330 668-6615
Akron *(G-279)*
Infocision Management Corp......B...... 330 544-1400
Youngstown *(G-20235)*
Pccw Teleservices (us) Inc......A...... 614 652-6300
Dublin *(G-10424)*
R D D Inc......C...... 216 781-5858
Cleveland *(G-6339)*
Rdi Corporation......D...... 513 524-3320
Oxford *(G-15829)*
S&P Data Ohio LLC......B...... 216 965-0018
Cleveland *(G-6429)*
Startek Inc......C...... 419 528-7801
Ontario *(G-15717)*
Summit Advantage LLC......D...... 330 835-2453
Fairlawn *(G-10979)*
Telinx Solutions LLC......E...... 330 819-0657
Medina *(G-14135)*
Tpusa Inc......B...... 330 374-1232
Akron *(G-479)*
Triplefin LLC......E...... 513 794-9870
Blue Ash *(G-1704)*

TELEPHONE ANSWERING SVCS

Academy Answering Service Inc......E...... 440 442-8500
Cleveland *(G-4950)*
Answering Service Inc......E...... 440 473-1200
Cleveland *(G-5041)*
Carol Reese......E...... 513 347-0252
Cincinnati *(G-3187)*
Continental Business Services......E...... 614 224-4534
Columbus *(G-7427)*
Maximum Communications Inc......E...... 513 489-3414
Cincinnati *(G-4031)*
Perceptionist Inc......E...... 614 384-7500
Columbus *(G-8535)*
Telemessaging Services Inc......E...... 440 845-5400
Cleveland *(G-6579)*
Twin Comm Inc......E...... 740 774-4701
Marietta *(G-13508)*

TELEPHONE COUNSELING SVCS

Southast Cmnty Mental Hlth Ctr......E...... 614 445-6832
Columbus *(G-8753)*

TELEPHONE EQPT INSTALLATION

Chapel-Romanoff Tech LLC......E...... 937 222-9840
Dayton *(G-9398)*
Mitel (delaware) Inc......E...... 513 733-8000
West Chester *(G-19122)*
Rei Telecom Inc......E...... 614 255-3100
Canal Winchester *(G-2167)*
Tele-Solutions Inc......E...... 330 782-2888
Youngstown *(G-20388)*

TELEPHONE EQPT: NEC

Commercial Electric Pdts Corp......E...... 216 241-2886
Cleveland *(G-5376)*

TELEPHONE SET REPAIR SVCS

Cellco Partnership......E...... 440 779-1313
North Olmsted *(G-15412)*
DTE Inc......E...... 419 522-3428
Mansfield *(G-13295)*
Mmi-Cpr LLC......E...... 216 674-0645
Independence *(G-12234)*
Professional Telecom Svcs......E...... 513 232-7700
Cincinnati *(G-4344)*

TELEPHONE SVCS

Citigroup Inc......B...... 740 548-0594
Delaware *(G-10080)*
Pathway House LLC......E...... 872 223-9797
Cleveland *(G-6251)*
Republic Telcom Worldwide LLC......D...... 330 244-8285
North Canton *(G-15364)*
Republic Telcom Worldwide LLC......C...... 330 966-4586
Canton *(G-2509)*

Spectrum Networks Inc......E...... 513 697-2000
Cincinnati *(G-4560)*
Toms Installation Co Inc......E...... 419 584-1218
Celina *(G-2664)*

TELEVISION BROADCASTING & COMMUNICATIONS EQPT

Pdi Communication Systems Inc......D...... 937 743-6010
Springboro *(G-17133)*

TELEVISION BROADCASTING STATIONS

Barrington Toledo LLC......E...... 419 535-0024
Toledo *(G-17763)*
Bowling Green State University......E...... 419 372-2700
Bowling Green *(G-1769)*
Dispatch Printing Company......A...... 614 461-5000
Columbus *(G-7524)*
Dispatch Printing Company......C...... 740 548-5331
Lewis Center *(G-12684)*
Fox Television Stations Inc......C...... 216 432-4278
Cleveland *(G-5627)*
Greater Cincinnati TV Educ Fnd......D...... 513 381-4033
Cincinnati *(G-3711)*
Greater Dayton Public TV......D...... 937 220-1600
Dayton *(G-9587)*
Ideastream......C...... 216 916-6100
Cleveland *(G-5801)*
Iheartcommunications Inc......B...... 513 763-5500
Cincinnati *(G-3807)*
Iheartcommunications Inc......C...... 216 520-2600
Cleveland *(G-5803)*
Johnny Appleseed Broadcasting......E...... 419 529-5900
Ontario *(G-15695)*
Lima Communications Corp......D...... 419 228-8835
Lima *(G-12819)*
Miami Valley Broadcasting Corp......C...... 937 259-2111
Dayton *(G-9727)*
New Wrld Cmmunications of Ohio......C...... 216 432-4041
Cleveland *(G-6125)*
Nexstar Broadcasting Inc......C...... 614 263-4444
Columbus *(G-8275)*
Nexstar Broadcasting Inc......D...... 937 293-2101
Moraine *(G-14811)*
Northastern Eductl TV Ohio Inc......E...... 330 677-4549
Kent *(G-12388)*
Ohio News Network......D...... 216 367-7493
Cleveland *(G-6192)*
Ohio University......E...... 740 593-1771
Athens *(G-805)*
Ohio University......E...... 740 593-1771
Athens *(G-806)*
Ohio/Oklahoma Hearst TV Inc......C...... 513 412-5000
Cincinnati *(G-4215)*
Ohio/Oklahoma Hearst TV Inc......C...... 513 412-5000
Cincinnati *(G-4216)*
Public Broadcasting Found NW......D...... 419 380-4600
Toledo *(G-18144)*
Raycom Media Inc......C...... 216 367-7300
Cleveland *(G-6355)*
Raycom Media Inc......C...... 513 421-1919
Cincinnati *(G-4387)*
Sinclair Broadcast Group Inc......E...... 513 641-4400
Cincinnati *(G-4530)*
Sinclair Broadcast Group Inc......D...... 513 641-4400
Cincinnati *(G-4531)*
Sinclair Media II Inc......C...... 614 481-6666
Columbus *(G-8738)*
Sinclair Media II Inc......C...... 614 481-6666
Columbus *(G-8739)*
Sinclair Media II Inc......D...... 614 481-6666
Columbus *(G-8740)*
Southeastern Ohio TV Sys......E...... 740 452-5431
Zanesville *(G-20536)*
Sunrise Television Corp......C...... 937 293-2101
Moraine *(G-14828)*
Sunrise Television Corp......D...... 740 282-9999
Mingo Junction *(G-14658)*
Sunrise Television Corp......E...... 419 244-2197
Toledo *(G-18209)*
Thinktv Network......E...... 937 220-1600
Dayton *(G-9927)*
Toledo Television Investors LP......D...... 419 535-0024
Toledo *(G-18252)*
Vindicator Printing Company......D...... 330 744-8611
Youngstown *(G-20406)*
W B N X T V 55......E...... 330 922-5500
Cuyahoga Falls *(G-9234)*
W L W T T V 5......C...... 513 412-5000
Cincinnati *(G-4820)*

Wbns Tv Inc......C...... 614 460-3700
Columbus *(G-8973)*
Wfmj Television Inc......C...... 330 744-8611
Youngstown *(G-20415)*
Wfts......C...... 216 431-5555
Cleveland *(G-6749)*
Wfts......C...... 513 721-9900
Cincinnati *(G-4847)*
Winston Brdcstg Netwrk Inc......E...... 330 928-5711
Cuyahoga Falls *(G-9236)*
Wkyc-Tv Inc......C...... 216 344-3300
Cleveland *(G-6756)*
Wupw LLC......E...... 419 244-3600
Toledo *(G-18316)*
Wwst Corporation LLC......A...... 330 264-5122
Wooster *(G-19935)*

TELEVISION FILM PRODUCTION SVCS

For Women Like Me Inc......E...... 407 848-7339
Cleveland *(G-5611)*
For Women Like Me Inc......E...... 407 848-7339
Chagrin Falls *(G-2696)*
Greater Cincinnati TV Educ Fnd......D...... 513 381-4033
Cincinnati *(G-3711)*

TELEVISION REPAIR SHOP

Electra Sound Inc......C...... 216 433-1050
Cleveland *(G-5531)*
Electra Sound Inc......D...... 216 433-9600
Parma *(G-15906)*
Household Centralized Svc Inc......E...... 419 474-5754
Toledo *(G-17962)*
Sunrise Television Corp......D...... 740 282-9999
Mingo Junction *(G-14658)*

TEMPORARY HELP SVCS

A B S Temps Inc......E...... 937 252-9888
Dayton *(G-9297)*
Acloche LLC......E...... 888 608-0889
Columbus *(G-6938)*
Act I Temporaries Findlay Inc......B...... 419 423-0713
Findlay *(G-10989)*
Ado Staffing Inc......E...... 419 222-8395
Lima *(G-12731)*
Aerotek Inc......E...... 330 517-7330
Uniontown *(G-18506)*
Aerotek Inc......E...... 216 573-5520
Independence *(G-12181)*
Alliance Solutions Group LLC......E...... 216 525-0100
Independence *(G-12185)*
Alternate Solutions Healthcare......D...... 937 299-1111
Dayton *(G-9326)*
Area Temps Inc......A...... 216 227-8200
Lakewood *(G-12471)*
Area Temps Inc......E...... 216 781-5350
Independence *(G-12187)*
Area Temps Inc......A...... 216 518-2000
Maple Heights *(G-13400)*
Belcan Svcs Group Ltd Partnr......C...... 937 586-5053
Dayton *(G-9353)*
Callos Resource LLC......E...... 330 788-3033
Youngstown *(G-20132)*
Cima Inc......E...... 513 682-5900
Fairfield *(G-10831)*
Custom Staffing Inc......E...... 419 221-3097
Lima *(G-12770)*
Dawson Resources......E...... 614 255-1400
Columbus *(G-7491)*
Doepker Group Inc......E...... 419 355-1409
Fremont *(G-11195)*
E & L Premier Corporation......C...... 330 836-9901
Fairlawn *(G-10946)*
Emily Management Inc......D...... 440 354-6713
Painesville *(G-15854)*
Everstaff LLC......E...... 440 992-0238
Mentor *(G-14173)*
Flex Temp Employment Services......C...... 419 355-9675
Fremont *(G-11199)*
Future Unlimited Inc......E...... 330 273-6677
Brunswick *(G-1979)*
Health Carousel LLC......C...... 866 665-4544
Cincinnati *(G-3752)*
Heiser Staffing Services LLC......E...... 614 800-4188
Columbus *(G-7823)*
Horizon Personnel Resources......C...... 440 585-0031
Wickliffe *(G-19602)*
Inter Healt Care of North OH I......D...... 740 453-5130
Zanesville *(G-20490)*

SERVICES SECTION

Inter Healt Care of North OH I .... E 419 422-5328
  Findlay (G-11050)
Interim Halthcare Columbus Inc .... A 740 349-8700
  Newark (G-15177)
Interim Healthcare of Dayton .... B 937 291-5330
  Dayton (G-9634)
Its Technologies Inc .... D 419 842-2100
  Holland (G-12030)
Job 1 USA .... D 419 255-5005
  Toledo (G-17985)
Kilgore Group Inc .... E 513 684-3721
  Cincinnati (G-3922)
Lee Personnel Inc .... E 513 744-6780
  Cincinnati (G-3967)
Medlink of Ohio Inc .... B 330 773-9434
  Akron (G-337)
Minute Men Inc .... D 216 426-2225
  Cleveland (G-6069)
Pontoon Solutions Inc .... D 855 881-1533
  Maumee (G-13959)
Preferred Temporary Services .... E 330 494-5502
  Canton (G-2492)
Production Design Services Inc .... D 937 866-3377
  Dayton (G-9832)
Ran Temps Inc .... E 216 991-5500
  Cleveland (G-6352)
Randstad Professionals Us LLC .... E 419 893-2400
  Maumee (G-13966)
Randstad Professionals Us LLC .... E 513 792-6658
  Blue Ash (G-1674)
Randstad Professionals Us LP .... E 513 791-8600
  Blue Ash (G-1675)
Reserves Network Inc .... E 440 779-1400
  Cleveland (G-6383)
Robert Half International Inc .... E 216 621-4253
  Cleveland (G-6402)
Rumpf Corporation .... E 419 255-5005
  Toledo (G-18167)
Select Staffing .... D 513 247-9772
  West Chester (G-19149)
Sfn Group Inc .... E 419 727-4104
  Toledo (G-18182)
Spherion of Lima Inc .... A 419 224-8367
  Lima (G-12882)
Tradesmen International LLC .... D 513 771-1115
  Blue Ash (G-1699)
Trueblue Inc .... E 740 282-1079
  Steubenville (G-17345)
Wayne Industries Inc .... E 937 548-6025
  Greenville (G-11525)

TEN PIN CENTERS

Al-Mar Lanes .... E 419 352-4637
  Bowling Green (G-1757)
AMF Bowling Centers Inc .... E 330 725-4548
  Medina (G-14036)
AMF Bowling Centers Inc .... E 614 889-0880
  Columbus (G-7015)
Beaver-Vu Bowl .... E 937 426-6771
  Beavercreek (G-1150)
Big Western Operating Co Inc .... E 614 274-1169
  Columbus (G-7109)
Bigelow Corporation .... E 937 339-3315
  Troy (G-18349)
Bowlmor AMF Corp .... E 440 327-1190
  North Ridgeville (G-15456)
Brookpark Freeway Lanes LLC .... E 216 267-2150
  Cleveland (G-5146)
Capri Bowling Lanes Inc .... E 937 832-4000
  Dayton (G-9379)
Cherry Grove Sports Center .... E 513 232-7199
  Cincinnati (G-3239)
Chillicothe Bowling Lanes Inc .... E 740 773-3300
  Chillicothe (G-2817)
Cloverleaf Bowling Center Inc .... E 216 524-4833
  Cleveland (G-5366)
Columbus Square Bowling Palace .... E 614 895-1122
  Columbus (G-7387)
Coshocton Bowling Center .... E 740 622-6332
  Coshocton (G-9093)
Crossgate Lanes Inc .... E 513 891-0310
  Blue Ash (G-1572)
East Mentor Recreation Inc .... E 440 354-2000
  Mentor (G-14170)
Eastbury Bowling Center .... E 330 452-3700
  Canton (G-2348)
Eastland Lanes Inc .... E 614 868-9866
  Columbus (G-7566)
Freeway Lanes Bowl Group LLC .... E 440 946-5131
  Mentor (G-14178)

Holiday Lanes Inc .... E 614 861-1600
  Columbus (G-7846)
Interstate Lanes of Ohio Ltd .... E 419 666-2695
  Rossford (G-16609)
Madison Bowl Inc .... E 513 271-2700
  Cincinnati (G-4010)
Mahalls 20 Lanes .... E 216 521-3280
  Cleveland (G-5966)
Northland Lanes Inc .... E 419 224-1961
  Lima (G-12844)
Olmsted Lanes Inc .... E 440 777-6363
  North Olmsted (G-15435)
Park Centre Lanes Inc .... E 330 499-0555
  Canton (G-2488)
Plaz-Way Inc .... E 330 264-9025
  Wooster (G-19904)
Poelking Bowling Centers .... E 937 435-3855
  Dayton (G-9813)
Poelking Lanes Inc .... D 937 299-5573
  Dayton (G-9814)
Rainbow Lanes Inc .... E 614 491-7155
  Columbus (G-8586)
Rebman Recreation Inc .... D 440 282-6761
  Lorain (G-13074)
Roseland Lanes Inc .... D 440 439-0097
  Bedford (G-1332)
Sequoia Pro Bowl .... E 614 885-7043
  Columbus (G-8713)
Stonehedge Enterprises Inc .... E 330 928-2161
  Akron (G-451)
Suburban Gala Lanes Inc .... E 419 468-7488
  Bucyrus (G-2047)
Thompson Capri Lanes Inc .... E 614 888-3159
  Columbus (G-8839)
Tiki Bowling Lanes Inc .... E 740 654-4513
  Lancaster (G-12581)
Victory Lanes Inc .... E 937 323-8684
  Springfield (G-17292)
Wedgewood Lanes Inc .... E 330 792-1949
  Youngstown (G-20410)

TENANT SCREENING SVCS

Acxiom Info SEC Svcs Inc .... B 216 685-7600
  Independence (G-12180)

TERMITE CONTROL SVCS

Ohio Exterminating Co Inc .... E 614 294-6311
  Columbus (G-8343)
Scherzinger Corp .... D 513 531-7848
  Cincinnati (G-4480)

TEST BORING, METAL MINING

Hahs Factory Outlet .... E 330 405-4227
  Twinsburg (G-18426)

TESTERS: Gas, Exc Indl Process

Compliant Healthcare Tech LLC .... E 216 255-9607
  Cleveland (G-5389)

TESTING SVCS

Cliff North Consultants Inc .... E 513 251-4930
  Cincinnati (G-3364)
Keyw Corporation .... E 937 702-9512
  Beavercreek (G-1182)
Orton Edward Jr Crmic Fndation .... E 614 895-2663
  Westerville (G-19339)
Smithers Quality Assessments .... E 330 762-4231
  Akron (G-442)
Solar Testing Laboratories Inc .... C 216 741-7007
  Brooklyn Heights (G-1926)
South Central Ohio Eductl Ctr .... E 740 456-0517
  New Boston (G-15014)
SSS Consulting Inc .... E 937 259-1200
  Dayton (G-9901)

TEXTILE & APPAREL SVCS

Affinity Specialty Apparel Inc .... D 866 548-8434
  Fairborn (G-10784)
Nucentury Textile Services LLC .... D 419 241-2267
  Toledo (G-18097)

THEATER COMPANIES

Cincinnati Opera Association .... E 513 768-5500
  Cincinnati (G-3321)
Cincinnati Shakespeare Company .... E 513 381-2273
  Cincinnati (G-3327)

THEATRICAL PRODUCERS & SVCS

City of Cleveland .... D 216 664-6800
  Cleveland (G-5257)
Funny Bone Comedy Club & Cafe .... E 614 471-5653
  Columbus (G-7714)
International Management Group .... B 216 522-1200
  Cleveland (G-5830)
Interntonal Aliance Thea Stage .... E 440 734-4883
  North Olmsted (G-15427)
Ohio Light Opera .... D 330 263-2345
  Wooster (G-19896)
Rock and Roll of Fame and Muse .... D 216 781-7625
  Cleveland (G-6406)
Stranahan Theatre Trust .... D 419 381-8851
  Toledo (G-18204)

THERMOCOUPLES: Indl Process

Cleveland Electric Labs Co .... E 800 447-2207
  Twinsburg (G-18401)

THERMOPLASTIC MATERIALS

Polyone Corporation .... D 440 930-1000
  Avon Lake (G-937)

TICKET OFFICES & AGENCIES: Theatrical

Events On Top .... E 330 757-3786
  Youngstown (G-20182)

TICKET OFFICES & AGENCIES: Travel

Delta Air Lines Inc .... E 216 265-2400
  Cleveland (G-5475)

TIRE & TUBE REPAIR MATERIALS, WHOLESALE

Myers Industries Inc .... E 330 253-5592
  Akron (G-348)
Technical Rubber Company Inc .... B 740 967-9015
  Johnstown (G-12343)

TIRE CORD & FABRIC

ARC Abrasives Inc .... D 800 888-4885
  Troy (G-18347)

TIRE DEALERS

Best One Tire & Svc Lima Inc .... E 419 229-2380
  Lima (G-12746)
Bob Sumerel Tire Co Inc .... E 937 235-0062
  Dayton (G-9361)
Bridgestone Ret Operations LLC .... E 330 929-3391
  Cuyahoga Falls (G-9167)
Conrads Tire Service Inc .... E 216 941-3333
  Cleveland (G-5392)
Dayton Marshall Tire Sales Co .... E 937 293-8330
  Moraine (G-14773)
Grismer Tire Company .... E 937 643-2526
  Centerville (G-2678)
K & M Tire Inc .... C 419 695-1061
  Delphos (G-10145)
Millersburg Tire Service Inc .... E 330 674-1085
  Millersburg (G-14612)
Monro Inc .... D 440 835-2393
  Westlake (G-19517)
North Gateway Tire Co Inc .... E 330 725-8473
  Medina (G-14108)
QT Equipment Company .... E 330 724-3055
  Akron (G-401)
Sines Inc .... E 440 352-6572
  Painesville (G-15879)
Speck Sales Incorporated .... E 419 353-8312
  Bowling Green (G-1794)
Tire Centers LLC .... E 419 287-3227
  Pemberville (G-15945)
Ziegler Tire and Supply Co .... E 330 353-1499
  Massillon (G-13865)

TIRE RECAPPING & RETREADING

Belle Tire .... E 440 735-0800
  Bedford (G-1296)
Bob Sumerel Tire Co Inc .... E 937 235-0062
  Dayton (G-9361)
Bob Sumerel Tire Co Inc .... E 614 527-9700
  Columbus (G-7122)
Bridgestone Ret Operations LLC .... E 513 367-7888
  Harrison (G-11792)

Employee Codes: A=Over 500 employees, B=251-500 ·
C=101-250, D=51-100, E=25-50

2018 Harris Ohio
Services Directory

TIRE RECAPPING & RETREADING

Bridgestone Ret Operations LLC .... E 513 522-2525
  Cincinnati *(G-3132)*
Bridgestone Ret Operations LLC .... E 513 741-9701
  Cincinnati *(G-3133)*
Bridgestone Ret Operations LLC .... E 419 691-7111
  Northwood *(G-15527)*
Bridgestone Ret Operations LLC .... E 513 271-7100
  Cincinnati *(G-3134)*
Bridgestone Ret Operations LLC .... E 419 586-1600
  Celina *(G-2636)*
Goodyear Tire & Rubber Company .... E 440 735-9910
  Walton Hills *(G-18789)*
Goodyear Tire & Rubber Company .... E 614 871-1881
  Grove City *(G-11565)*
Goodyear Tire & Rubber Company .... A 330 796-2121
  Akron *(G-243)*
Tire Centers LLC .... E 419 287-3227
  Pemberville *(G-15945)*

TIRE SUNDRIES OR REPAIR MATERIALS: Rubber

Technical Rubber Company Inc .... B 740 967-9015
  Johnstown *(G-12343)*

TIRES & INNER TUBES

Contitech North America Inc .... E 440 225-5363
  Akron *(G-162)*
Goodyear Tire & Rubber Company .... A 330 796-2121
  Akron *(G-243)*

TIRES & TUBES WHOLESALERS

American Kenda Rbr Indus Ltd .... E 866 536-3287
  Reynoldsburg *(G-16428)*
Bob Sumerel Tire Co Inc .... E 614 527-9700
  Columbus *(G-7122)*
Dealer Tire LLC .... B 216 432-0088
  Cleveland *(G-5472)*
Joseph Russo .... E 440 748-2690
  Grafton *(G-11441)*
Rush Truck Centers Ohio Inc .... D 513 733-8500
  Cincinnati *(G-4458)*
Rush Truck Centers Ohio Inc .... E 419 224-6045
  Lima *(G-12872)*
Rush Truck Leasing Inc .... E 614 876-3500
  Columbus *(G-8660)*
Shrader Tire & Oil Inc .... E 419 472-2128
  Toledo *(G-18186)*
Tire Waste Transport Inc .... B 419 363-2681
  Rockford *(G-16564)*
W D Tire Warehouse Inc .... E 614 461-8944
  Columbus *(G-8957)*

TIRES & TUBES, WHOLESALE: Automotive

Belle Tire Distributors Inc .... E 419 473-1393
  Toledo *(G-17768)*
Bob Sumerel Tire Co Inc .... E 513 792-6600
  Cincinnati *(G-3125)*
Capital Tire Inc .... E 419 241-5111
  Toledo *(G-17790)*
Capital Tire Inc .... E 419 865-7151
  Toledo *(G-17791)*
Conrads Tire Service Inc .... E 216 941-3333
  Cleveland *(G-5392)*
Dayton Marshall Tire Sales Co .... E 937 293-8330
  Moraine *(G-14773)*
Grismer Tire Company .... E 937 643-2526
  Centerville *(G-2678)*
Hankook Tire America Corp .... E 330 896-6199
  Uniontown *(G-18523)*
K & M Tire Inc .... C 419 695-1061
  Delphos *(G-10145)*
K & M Tire Inc .... E 419 695-1060
  Delphos *(G-10146)*
Malone Warehouse Tire Inc .... E 740 592-2893
  Athens *(G-800)*
Millersburg Tire Service Inc .... E 330 674-1085
  Millersburg *(G-14612)*
North Gateway Tire Co Inc .... E 330 725-8473
  Medina *(G-14108)*
Reville Tire Co .... D 330 468-1900
  Northfield *(G-15523)*
Speck Sales Incorporated .... E 419 353-8312
  Bowling Green *(G-1794)*
Stoney Hollow Tire Inc .... D 740 635-5200
  Martins Ferry *(G-13601)*

TIRES & TUBES, WHOLESALE: Truck

Best One Tire & Svc Lima Inc .... E 419 229-2380
  Lima *(G-12746)*
Central Ohio Bandag LP .... E 740 454-9728
  Zanesville *(G-20460)*
Ziegler Tire and Supply Co .... E 330 353-1499
  Massillon *(G-13865)*

TITLE & TRUST COMPANIES

A R E A Title Agency Inc .... E 419 242-5485
  Toledo *(G-17735)*
Chicago Title Insurance Co .... E 216 241-6045
  Cleveland *(G-5234)*
Commerce Title Agcy Youngstown .... E 330 743-1171
  Youngstown *(G-20147)*
First Fincl Title Agcy of Ohio .... E 216 664-1920
  Cleveland *(G-5597)*
Intitle Agency Inc .... D 513 241-8780
  Cincinnati *(G-3840)*
Lakeside Title Escrow Agcy Inc .... E 216 503-5600
  Westlake *(G-19508)*
Landsel Title Agency Inc .... E 614 337-1928
  Gahanna *(G-11252)*
Lawyers Title Company .... E 330 376-0000
  Akron *(G-314)*
Security Title Guarantee Agcy .... C 513 651-3393
  Cincinnati *(G-4491)*
Talon Title Agency LLC .... E 614 818-0500
  Westerville *(G-19355)*
Valley Title & Escrow Agency .... E 440 632-9833
  Middlefield *(G-14404)*

TITLE ABSTRACT & SETTLEMENT OFFICES

American Title Services Inc .... E 330 652-1609
  Niles *(G-15281)*
County of Delaware .... D 740 657-3945
  Lewis Center *(G-12678)*

TITLE INSURANCE AGENTS

Accurate Group Holdings Inc .... D 216 520-1740
  Independence *(G-12178)*
Louisvlle Title Agcy For NW OH .... D 419 248-4611
  Toledo *(G-18011)*
Nations Title Agency of Ohio .... E 614 839-3848
  Columbus *(G-8227)*

TITLE INSURANCE: Guarantee Of Titles

Entitle Direct Group Inc .... C 216 236-7800
  Independence *(G-12209)*

TITLE INSURANCE: Real Estate

Accurate Group Holdings Inc .... D 216 520-1740
  Independence *(G-12178)*
Chicago Title Insurance Co .... D 330 873-9393
  Akron *(G-132)*
Fidelity National Fincl Inc .... E 614 865-1562
  Westerville *(G-19401)*
First American Equity Ln Svcs .... C 800 221-8683
  Cleveland *(G-5588)*
First American Title Insur Co .... E 216 241-1278
  Cleveland *(G-5589)*
First American Title Insur Co .... E 419 625-8505
  Sandusky *(G-16760)*
First American Title Insur Co .... E 740 450-0006
  South Zanesville *(G-17103)*
Landsel Title Agency Inc .... E 614 337-1928
  Gahanna *(G-11252)*
Lawyers Title Cincinnati Inc .... D 513 421-1313
  Cincinnati *(G-3965)*
Lawyers Title Company .... E 330 376-0000
  Akron *(G-314)*
Midland Title Security Inc .... D 216 241-6045
  Cleveland *(G-6057)*
Ohio Real Title Agency LLC .... E 216 373-9900
  Cleveland *(G-6194)*
Port Lawrence Title and Tr Co .... E 419 244-4605
  Toledo *(G-18130)*
Resource Title Agency Inc .... D 216 520-0050
  Cleveland *(G-6385)*
Resource Title Nat Agcy Inc .... D 216 520-0050
  Independence *(G-12248)*
Search 2 Close Columbus Ltd .... E 614 389-5353
  Powell *(G-16351)*
Sterling Land Title Agency .... E 937 438-2000
  Dayton *(G-9906)*
Stewart Title Company .... E 440 520-7130
  Willoughby *(G-19716)*

SERVICES SECTION

Title First Agency Inc .... E 614 224-9207
  Columbus *(G-8850)*
U S Title Agency Inc .... E 216 621-1424
  Cleveland *(G-6627)*
Valmer Land Title Agency .... E 614 860-0005
  Reynoldsburg *(G-16488)*
Valmer Land Title Agency .... E 614 875-7001
  Grove City *(G-11608)*

TITLE SEARCH COMPANIES

Real Living Title Agency Ltd .... D 614 459-7400
  Columbus *(G-8595)*
Weston Inc .... E 440 349-9000
  Cleveland *(G-6748)*

TOBACCO & PRDTS, WHOLESALE: Cigarettes

Core-Mark Ohio .... C 650 589-9445
  Solon *(G-16994)*
Dittman-Adams Company .... E 513 870-7530
  West Chester *(G-19065)*
EBY-Brown Company LLC .... C 937 324-1036
  Springfield *(G-17192)*
Gummer Wholesale Inc .... D 740 928-0415
  Heath *(G-11838)*
JE Carsten Company .... E 330 794-4440
  Akron *(G-291)*

TOBACCO & TOBACCO PRDTS WHOLESALERS

Albert Guarnieri & Co .... D 330 794-9834
  Akron *(G-63)*
Jetro Cash and Carry Entps LLC .... D 216 525-0101
  Cleveland *(G-5862)*
K M C Corporation .... E 740 598-4171
  Mingo Junction *(G-14655)*
McKirnan Bros Inc .... E 419 586-2428
  Celina *(G-2651)*
Novelart Manufacturing Company .... C 513 351-7700
  Cincinnati *(G-4187)*
Swd Corporation .... E 419 227-2436
  Lima *(G-12896)*
The Anter Brothers Company .... E 216 252-4555
  Cleveland *(G-6589)*

TOILETRIES, COSMETICS & PERFUME STORES

Big Sandy Furniture Inc .... D 740 574-2113
  Franklin Furnace *(G-11169)*
Kenneths Hair Salons & Day Sp .... B 614 457-7712
  Columbus *(G-7978)*

TOILETRIES, WHOLESALE: Hair Preparations

G E G Enterprises Inc .... E 330 477-3133
  Canton *(G-2375)*
ICM Distributing Company Inc .... E 234 212-3030
  Twinsburg *(G-18431)*

TOILETRIES, WHOLESALE: Razor Blades

American Cutting Edge Inc .... C 937 438-2390
  Centerville *(G-2673)*

TOILETRIES, WHOLESALE: Toiletries

Nehemiah Manufacturing Co LLC .... E 513 351-5700
  Cincinnati *(G-4150)*
Walter F Stephens Jr Inc .... E 937 746-0521
  Franklin *(G-11167)*

TOILETS, PORTABLE, WHOLESALE

Superr-Spdie Portable Svcs Inc .... E 330 733-9000
  Akron *(G-469)*

TOLL BRIDGE OPERATIONS

Magnum Management Corporation .... A 419 627-2334
  Sandusky *(G-16778)*

TOLL ROAD OPERATIONS

Ohio Tpk & Infrastructure Comm .... C 440 234-2081
  Berea *(G-1465)*

SERVICES SECTION

TRANSPORTATION AGENTS & BROKERS

TOOL REPAIR SVCS
Lawrence Industries Inc .... C 216 518-7000
  Cleveland *(G-5929)*
Pennsylvania Tl Sls & Svc Inc .... D 330 758-0845
  Youngstown *(G-20317)*

TOOLS: Hand
Acme Company .... D 330 758-2313
  Poland *(G-16219)*
Alliance Knife Inc .... E 513 367-9000
  Harrison *(G-11789)*
Cornwell Quality Tools Company .... D 330 628-2627
  Mogadore *(G-14673)*
File Sharpening Company Inc .... E 937 376-8268
  Xenia *(G-20050)*
J and S Tool Incorporated .... E 216 676-8330
  Cleveland *(G-5840)*
Matco Tools Corporation .... B 330 929-4949
  Stow *(G-17382)*
Myers Industries Inc .... D 440 632-0230
  Middlefield *(G-14398)*
Sewer Rodding Equipment Co .... E 419 991-2065
  Lima *(G-12876)*

TOOLS: Hand, Plumbers'
Calvin Lanier .... E 937 952-4221
  Dayton *(G-9377)*

TOOLS: Hand, Power
Huron Cement Products Company .... E 419 433-4161
  Huron *(G-12166)*
Ingersoll-Rand Company .... E 419 633-6800
  Bryan *(G-2008)*
Npk Construction Equipment Inc .... D 440 232-7900
  Bedford *(G-1324)*
Sewer Rodding Equipment Co .... E 419 991-2065
  Lima *(G-12876)*
Wolf Machine Company .... C 513 791-5194
  Blue Ash *(G-1719)*

TOUR OPERATORS
Tours of Black Heritage Inc .... D 440 247-2737
  Cleveland *(G-6606)*

TOURIST INFORMATION BUREAU
Dayton Cvb .... E 937 226-8211
  Dayton *(G-9468)*

TOURIST LODGINGS
Sauder Haritage Inn .... E 419 445-6408
  Archbold *(G-643)*
TW Recreational Services Inc .... E 440 564-9144
  Newbury *(G-15262)*

TOWELS: Fabric & Nonwoven, Made From Purchased Materials
Lawnview Industries Inc .... C 937 653-5217
  Urbana *(G-18593)*

TOWERS: Cooling, Sheet Metal
Obr Cooling Towers Inc .... E 419 243-3443
  Rossford *(G-16610)*

TOWING & TUGBOAT SVC
A M & O Towing Inc .... E 330 385-0639
  Negley *(G-14958)*

TOWING SVCS: Marine
Great Lakes Group .... C 216 621-4854
  Cleveland *(G-5689)*

TOYS
AW Faber-Castell Usa Inc .... D 216 643-4660
  Cleveland *(G-5086)*

TOYS & HOBBY GOODS & SPLYS, WHOLESALE: Arts/Crafts Eqpt/Sply
AW Faber-Castell Usa Inc .... D 216 643-4660
  Cleveland *(G-5086)*
Craft Wholesalers Inc .... C 740 964-6210
  Groveport *(G-11630)*
Flower Factory Inc .... D 614 275-6220
  Columbus *(G-7677)*
K & K Interiors Inc .... D 419 627-0039
  Sandusky *(G-16772)*
Lamrite West Inc .... E 440 268-0634
  Strongsville *(G-17484)*

TOYS & HOBBY GOODS & SPLYS, WHOLESALE: Balloons, Novelty
Galaxy Balloons Incorporated .... C 216 476-3360
  Cleveland *(G-5651)*

TOYS & HOBBY GOODS & SPLYS, WHOLESALE: Bingo Games & Splys
Lancaster Bingo Company Inc .... D 740 681-4759
  Lancaster *(G-12548)*
Nannicola Wholesale Co .... D 330 799-0888
  Youngstown *(G-20293)*

TOYS & HOBBY GOODS & SPLYS, WHOLESALE: Educational Toys
Bendon Inc .... D 419 207-3600
  Ashland *(G-664)*

TOYS & HOBBY GOODS & SPLYS, WHOLESALE: Toys & Games
Closeout Distribution Inc .... A 614 278-6800
  Columbus *(G-7307)*
R and G Enterprises of Ohio .... E 440 845-6870
  Cleveland *(G-6337)*

TOYS & HOBBY GOODS & SPLYS, WHOLESALE: Toys, NEC
Ball Bounce and Sport Inc .... E 419 759-3838
  Dunkirk *(G-10501)*
Ball Bounce and Sport Inc .... B 419 289-9310
  Ashland *(G-661)*
Ball Bounce and Sport Inc .... E 419 289-9310
  Ashland *(G-662)*
ICM Distributing Company Inc .... E 234 212-3030
  Twinsburg *(G-18431)*
K & M International Inc .... D 330 425-2550
  Twinsburg *(G-18435)*
National Marketshare Group .... E 513 921-0800
  Cincinnati *(G-4140)*
Pyramyd Air Ltd .... E 216 896-0893
  Solon *(G-17043)*

TOYS & HOBBY GOODS & SPLYS, WHOLESALE: Video Games
Mas Inc .... E 330 659-3333
  Richfield *(G-16514)*

TOYS, HOBBY GOODS & SPLYS WHOLESALERS
Anderson Press Incorporated .... E 615 370-9922
  Ashland *(G-650)*
Ball Bounce and Sport Inc .... E 614 662-5381
  Columbus *(G-7087)*
Dwa Mrktng Prmtional Pdts LLC .... E 216 476-0635
  Strongsville *(G-17457)*
Lamrite West Inc .... C 440 238-7318
  Strongsville *(G-17482)*
Neil Kravitz Group Sales Inc .... E 513 961-8697
  Cincinnati *(G 4163)*

TRADE SHOW ARRANGEMENT SVCS
Affinity Disp Expositions Inc .... C 513 771-2339
  Cincinnati *(G-2977)*
Definitive Solutions Co Inc .... D 513 719-9100
  Cincinnati *(G-3479)*
Exhibitpro Inc .... E 614 885-9541
  New Albany *(G-14985)*
Relx Inc .... E 937 865-6800
  Miamisburg *(G-14340)*

TRAFFIC CONTROL FLAGGING SVCS
Traffic Ctrl Safety Svcs LLC .... E 330 904-2732
  Alliance *(G-564)*

TRAILERS & PARTS: Truck & Semi's
Mac Manufacturing Inc .... A 330 823-9900
  Alliance *(G-546)*
Mac Manufacturing Inc .... C 330 829-1680
  Salem *(G-16704)*
Mac Trailer Manufacturing Inc .... C 330 823-9900
  Alliance *(G-547)*

TRAILERS & TRAILER EQPT
Interstate Truckway Inc .... E 614 771-1220
  Columbus *(G-7919)*

TRAILERS: Bodies
East Manufacturing Corporation .... B 330 325-9921
  Randolph *(G-16372)*

TRAILERS: Semitrailers, Truck Tractors
Nelson Manufacturing Company .... D 419 523-5321
  Ottawa *(G-15799)*

TRAINING SCHOOL FOR DELINQUENTS
County of Hamilton .... C 513 552-1200
  Cincinnati *(G-3429)*
Healthy Life HM Healthcare LLC .... E 614 865-3368
  Columbus *(G-7813)*

TRANS PROG REG & ADMIN, GOVT: Motor Vehicle Licensing & Insp
Butler County Clerk of Courts .... D 513 887-3282
  Hamilton *(G-11701)*
Public Safety Ohio Department .... A 614 752-7600
  Columbus *(G-8577)*

TRANSFORMERS: Electric
Schneider Electric Usa Inc .... D 513 755-5000
  West Chester *(G-19145)*

TRANSFORMERS: Furnace, Electric
Ajax Tocco Magnethermic Corp .... C 330 372-8511
  Warren *(G-18815)*

TRANSFORMERS: Power Related
Fishel Company .... D 614 850-4400
  Columbus *(G-7669)*
General Electric Company .... D 216 883-1000
  Cleveland *(G-5667)*
Hannon Company .... D 330 456-4728
  Canton *(G-2393)*
Matlock Electric Co Inc .... E 513 731-9600
  Cincinnati *(G-4030)*

TRANSLATION & INTERPRETATION SVCS
Advanced Translation/Cnsltng .... E 440 716-0820
  Westlake *(G-19455)*
Ceiba Enterprises Incorporated .... C 614 818-3220
  Westerville *(G-19376)*
Cincilingua Inc .... E 513 721-8782
  Cincinnati *(G-3277)*
Clgt Solutions LLC .... E 740 920-4795
  Granville *(G-11462)*
Conversa Language Center Inc .... E 513 651-5679
  Cincinnati *(G-3420)*
Mission Essntial Personnel LLC .... C 614 416-2345
  New Albany *(G-14992)*
Vocalink Inc .... B 937 223-1415
  Dayton *(G-9974)*

TRANSPORTATION AGENTS & BROKERS
ABF Freight System Inc .... C 419 525-0118
  Mansfield *(G-13258)*
Action Engneered Logistics LLC .... D 513 681-7900
  Cincinnati *(G-2970)*
Bnsf Logistics LLC .... E 937 526-3141
  Versailles *(G-18723)*
Bolt Express LLC .... C 419 729-6698
  Toledo *(G-17777)*
Commercial Traffic Company .... C 216 267-2000
  Cleveland *(G-5377)*
Commercial Traffic Company .... C 216 267-2000
  Cleveland *(G-5378)*
Freshway Foods Inc .... C 937 498-4664
  Sidney *(G-16937)*

Employee Codes: A=Over 500 employees, B=251-500
C=101-250, D=51-100, E=25-50

TRANSPORTATION AGENTS & BROKERS

SERVICES SECTION

Haid Acquisitions LLC ....D....... 513 941-8700
  Cincinnati *(G-3728)*
J B Express Inc ....D....... 740 702-9830
  Chillicothe *(G-2854)*
Ploger Transportation LLC ....E....... 419 465-2100
  Bellevue *(G-1415)*
Reliable Trnsp Solutions LLC ....E....... 937 378-2700
  Georgetown *(G-11396)*
Shoreline Transportation Inc ....C....... 440 878-2000
  Strongsville *(G-17508)*
Triple T Transport Inc ....D....... 740 657-3244
  Lewis Center *(G-12707)*
United Parcel Service Inc OH ....B....... 740 363-0636
  Delaware *(G-10133)*

TRANSPORTATION ARRANGEMENT SVCS, PASSENGER: Carpool/Vanpool

Daugwood Inc ....E....... 937 429-9465
  Beavercreek *(G-1165)*
Rush Expediting Inc ....E....... 937 885-0894
  Dayton *(G-9857)*

TRANSPORTATION ARRANGEMENT SVCS, PASSENGER: Tours, Conducted

Newport Walking Tours LLC ....E....... 859 951-8560
  Cincinnati *(G-4161)*
Trolley Tours of Cleveland ....E....... 216 771-4484
  Cleveland *(G-6619)*

TRANSPORTATION ARRANGEMNT SVCS, PASS: Travel Tour Pkgs, Whol

Keeptryan Inc ....D....... 330 319-1866
  Akron *(G-302)*

TRANSPORTATION BROKERS: Truck

Ace Doran Hauling & Rigging Co ....E....... 513 681-7900
  Cincinnati *(G-2966)*
Advance Trnsp Systems Inc ....E....... 513 818-4311
  Cincinnati *(G-2975)*
Ameri-Line Inc ....E....... 440 316-4500
  Columbia Station *(G-6840)*
American Marine Express Inc ....E....... 216 268-3005
  Cleveland *(G-5012)*
Burd Brothers Inc ....E....... 513 708-7787
  Dayton *(G-9373)*
Colonial Courier Service Inc ....E....... 419 891-0922
  Maumee *(G-13896)*
Esj Carrier Corporation ....E....... 513 728-7388
  Fairfield *(G-10849)*
Freedom Enterprises Inc ....E....... 419 675-1192
  Kenton *(G-12411)*
Garner Trucking Inc ....C....... 419 422-5742
  Findlay *(G-11035)*
Integrity Ex Logistics LLC ....C....... 888 374-5138
  Cincinnati *(G-3828)*
J Rayl Transport Inc ....E....... 330 940-1668
  Euclid *(G-10765)*
Kgbo Holdings Inc ....E....... 513 831-2600
  Cincinnati *(G-2922)*
Nationwide Transport Llc ....E....... 513 554-0203
  Cincinnati *(G-4144)*
Ohio Transport Inc ....E....... 216 741-8000
  Cleveland *(G-6196)*
Pride Transportation Inc ....E....... 419 424-2145
  Findlay *(G-11077)*
RDF Trucking Corporation ....D....... 440 282-9060
  Lorain *(G-13073)*
Schneider Nat Carriers Inc ....E....... 740 362-6910
  Delaware *(G-10126)*
Total Package Express Inc ....E....... 513 741-5500
  Cincinnati *(G-4662)*
Total Quality Logistics LLC ....E....... 513 831-2600
  Milford *(G-14568)*
Total Quality Logistics LLC ....C....... 513 831-2600
  Milford *(G-14569)*
Total Quality Logistics LLC ....C....... 513 831-2600
  Cincinnati *(G-2936)*

TRANSPORTATION EPQT & SPLYS, WHOL: Aircraft Engs/Eng Parts

Aim Mro Holdings Inc ....D....... 513 831-2938
  Miamiville *(G-14374)*

TRANSPORTATION EPQT & SPLYS, WHOLESALE: Acft/Space Vehicle

Keeptryan Inc ....D....... 330 319-1866
  Akron *(G-302)*

TRANSPORTATION EPQT & SPLYS, WHOLESALE: Nav Eqpt & Splys

Star Dynamics Corporation ....D....... 614 334-4510
  Hilliard *(G-11954)*

TRANSPORTATION EPQT & SPLYS, WHOLESALE: Tanks & Tank Compnts

Eleet Cryogenics Inc ....E....... 330 874-4009
  Bolivar *(G-1746)*

TRANSPORTATION EQPT & SPLYS WHOLESALERS, NEC

Greenfield Products Inc ....D....... 937 981-2696
  Greenfield *(G-11486)*
Roe Transport Inc ....E....... 937 497-7161
  Sidney *(G-16951)*
Schuster Electronics Inc ....E....... 330 425-8134
  Twinsburg *(G-18468)*

TRANSPORTATION EQUIPMENT, NEC

Cleveland Wheels ....D....... 440 937-6211
  Avon *(G-890)*

TRANSPORTATION INSPECTION SVCS

Argus International Inc ....E....... 513 852-1010
  Cincinnati *(G-3046)*

TRANSPORTATION PROG REG & ADMIN, GOVT: Bureau, Public Roads

Transportation Ohio Department ....E....... 740 773-3191
  Chillicothe *(G-2891)*

TRANSPORTATION PROGRAM REGULATION & ADMIN GOVT: Local

City of Lima ....E....... 419 221-5165
  Lima *(G-12754)*

TRANSPORTATION PROGRAM REGULATION & ADMIN, GOVT: Federal

National Railroad Pass Corp ....E....... 419 246-0159
  Toledo *(G-18078)*

TRANSPORTATION PROGRAMS REGULATION & ADMINISTRATION SVCS

Ohio Department Transportation ....C....... 740 363-1251
  Delaware *(G-10119)*
Ohio Department Transportation ....E....... 937 548-3015
  Greenville *(G-11515)*
Ohio Department Transportation ....E....... 419 738-4214
  Wapakoneta *(G-18805)*
Ohio Department Transportation ....D....... 614 275-1324
  Columbus *(G-8330)*
Ohio Department Transportation ....E....... 330 533-4351
  Canfield *(G-2205)*
Ohio Department Transportation ....E....... 330 637-5951
  Cortland *(G-9080)*
Ohio Tpk & Infrastructure Comm ....E....... 419 826-4831
  Swanton *(G-17569)*
Ohio Tpk & Infrastructure Comm ....E....... 440 234-2081
  Berea *(G-1466)*
Turnpike and Infrastructure Co ....D....... 330 527-2169
  Windham *(G-19804)*

TRANSPORTATION SVCS, NEC

Access Home Care LLC ....E....... 937 224-9991
  Dayton *(G-9304)*
Euclid SC Transportation ....D....... 216 797-7600
  Cleveland *(G-5554)*
Genox Transportation Inc ....E....... 419 837-2023
  Perrysburg *(G-16006)*
Jti Transportation Inc ....E....... 419 661-9360
  Stony Ridge *(G-17347)*
Marietta Transfer Company ....E....... 740 896-3565
  Lowell *(G-13169)*

Mikesell Transportation Broker ....E....... 937 996-5731
  Arcanum *(G-630)*
Niese Transport Inc ....E....... 419 523-4400
  Ottawa *(G-15800)*
OH St Trans Dist 02 Outpost ....E....... 419 693-8870
  Northwood *(G-15542)*

TRANSPORTATION SVCS, WATER: Boat Cleaning

Ship Shape Marine Inc ....E....... 419 734-1554
  Port Clinton *(G-16255)*
South Shore Marine Services ....E....... 419 433-5798
  Huron *(G-12174)*

TRANSPORTATION SVCS, WATER: Canal Barge Operations

Consolidated Grain & Barge Co ....E....... 513 941-4805
  Cincinnati *(G-3411)*

TRANSPORTATION SVCS, WATER: Cleaning

MPW Industrial Water Svcs Inc ....C....... 800 827-8790
  Hebron *(G-11856)*

TRANSPORTATION SVCS: Airport

Charter Vans Inc ....E....... 937 898-4043
  Vandalia *(G-18669)*
City of Wilmington ....E....... 937 382-7961
  Wilmington *(G-19748)*
Park-N-Go Inc ....E....... 937 890-7275
  Vandalia *(G-18692)*

TRANSPORTATION SVCS: Airport Limousine, Scheduled Svcs

Hopkins Airport Limousine Svc ....C....... 216 267-8810
  Cleveland *(G-5771)*

TRANSPORTATION SVCS: Airport, Regular Route

Sutton Motor Coach Tours Inc ....E....... 330 726-2800
  Youngstown *(G-20386)*

TRANSPORTATION SVCS: Bus Line Operations

Allen Cnty Regional Trnst Auth ....E....... 419 222-2782
  Lima *(G-12733)*
Central Ohio Transit Authority ....C....... 614 275-5800
  Columbus *(G-7241)*
Central Ohio Transit Authority ....A....... 614 275-5800
  Columbus *(G-7242)*
Greater Dyton Rgnal Trnst Auth ....D....... 937 425-8310
  Dayton *(G-9590)*
Southwest OH Trans Auth ....A....... 513 621-4455
  Cincinnati *(G-4553)*
Southwest OH Trans Auth ....A....... 513 632-7511
  Cincinnati *(G-4554)*
Toledo Area Rgional Trnst Auth ....D....... 419 243-7433
  Toledo *(G-18227)*
Western Reserve Transit Auth ....D....... 330 744-8431
  Youngstown *(G-20412)*

TRANSPORTATION SVCS: Bus Line, Interstate

Greyhound Lines Inc ....E....... 513 421-7442
  Cincinnati *(G-3713)*
Muskingum Coach Company ....E....... 740 622-2545
  Coshocton *(G-9112)*

TRANSPORTATION SVCS: Maint Facilities, Vehicle Passenger

City of Willoughby ....E....... 440 942-0215
  Willoughby *(G-19649)*
Washington Local Schools ....D....... 419 473-8356
  Toledo *(G-18299)*

TRANSPORTATION SVCS: Maintenance Facilities, Buses

Hans Truck and Trlr Repr Inc ....E....... 216 581-0046
  Cleveland *(G-5724)*
Reynoldsburg City Schools ....E....... 614 501-1041
  Reynoldsburg *(G-16475)*

SERVICES SECTION

TRAVEL CLUBS

TRANSPORTATION SVCS: Railroad Terminals
Rail Logistics Inc ....D 440 933-6500
  Avon Lake *(G-938)*

TRANSPORTATION SVCS: Railroad, Passenger
Greater Cleveland ....A 216 566-5107
  Cleveland *(G-5694)*

TRANSPORTATION SVCS: Railroads, Interurban
CSX Transportation Inc ....E 614 898-3651
  Westerville *(G-19295)*
Illinois Central Railroad Co ....E 419 726-6028
  Toledo *(G-17970)*

TRANSPORTATION SVCS: Rental, Local
Direct Expediting LLC ....E 513 459-0100
  Mason *(G-13696)*
Universal Work and Power LLC ....E 513 981-1111
  Blue Ash *(G-1714)*

TRANSPORTATION SVCS: Vanpool Operation
Seneca-Crawford Area Trnsp ....E 419 937-2428
  Tiffin *(G-17702)*

TRANSPORTATION: Air, Nonscheduled Passenger
Lane Aviation Corporation ....C 614 237-3747
  Columbus *(G-8037)*
Ohio Medical Trnsp Inc ....E 937 747-3540
  Marysville *(G-13643)*

TRANSPORTATION: Air, Nonscheduled, NEC
Airnet Systems Inc ....C 614 409-4900
  Columbus *(G-6958)*
Netjets Sales Inc ....C 614 239-5500
  Columbus *(G-8264)*
Options Flight Support Inc ....C 216 261-3500
  Cleveland *(G-6209)*
Panther II Transportation Inc ....C 800 685-0657
  Medina *(G-14111)*

TRANSPORTATION: Air, Scheduled Freight
Federal Express Corporation ....B 614 492-6106
  Columbus *(G-7646)*
Flight Express Inc ....D 305 379-8686
  Columbus *(G-7675)*
United Parcel Service Inc OH ....B 740 363-0636
  Delaware *(G-10133)*

TRANSPORTATION: Air, Scheduled Passenger
American Airlines Inc ....E 216 898-1347
  Cleveland *(G-5004)*
City of Dayton ....C 937 454-8200
  Vandalia *(G-18672)*
Distribution and Trnsp Svc Inc ....E 937 295-3343
  Fort Loramie *(G-11110)*
Executive Jet Management Inc ....B 513 979-6600
  Cincinnati *(G-3586)*
Lane Aviation Corporation ....C 614 237-3747
  Columbus *(G-8037)*

TRANSPORTATION: Bus Transit Systems
Atlantic Greyhound Lines ....E 513 721-4450
  Cincinnati *(G-3059)*
First Transit Inc ....D 513 732-1206
  Batavia *(G-1013)*
Firstgroup America Inc ....D 513 241-2200
  Cincinnati *(G-3626)*
Greater Dayton Rta ....A 937 425-8400
  Dayton *(G-9588)*
Greyhound Lines Inc ....B 614 221-0577
  Columbus *(G-7779)*
Laidlaw Transit Services Inc ....E 513 241-2200
  Cincinnati *(G-3959)*
Precious Cargo Transportation ....E 440 564-8039
  Newbury *(G-15260)*

Stark Area Regional Trnst Auth ....C 330 477-2782
  Canton *(G-2539)*

TRANSPORTATION: Bus Transit Systems
Columbus Public School Dst ....C 614 365-6542
  Columbus *(G-7380)*
First Transit Inc ....D 937 652-4175
  Urbana *(G-18587)*
Metro Regional Transit Auth ....B 330 762-0341
  Akron *(G-341)*
Mv Transportation Inc ....D 740 681-5086
  Cincinnati *(G-4134)*

TRANSPORTATION: Deep Sea Foreign Freight
APL Logistics Ltd ....C 440 930-2822
  Avon Lake *(G-921)*
Toula Industries Ltd LLC ....C 937 689-1818
  Dayton *(G-9934)*

TRANSPORTATION: Deep Sea Passenger
AAA Allied Group Inc ....D 513 228-0866
  Lebanon *(G-12586)*

TRANSPORTATION: Great Lakes Domestic Freight
The Interlake Steamship Co ....E 440 260-6900
  Middleburg Heights *(G-14388)*

TRANSPORTATION: Local Passenger, NEC
Above & Beyond Caregivers LLC ....E 614 478-1700
  Columbus *(G-6928)*
Asv Services LLC ....E 216 797-1701
  Euclid *(G-10743)*
Catholic Charities of SW Ohio ....D 513 241-7745
  Cincinnati *(G-3194)*
City of Lakewood ....E 216 521-1288
  Cleveland *(G-5269)*
Clark County Board of Developm ....D 937 328-5240
  Springfield *(G-17162)*
Cloverleaf Transport Co ....E 419 599-5015
  Napoleon *(G-14935)*
County of Ottawa ....E 419 898-7433
  Oak Harbor *(G-15606)*
Cremation Service Inc ....E 216 861-2334
  Cleveland *(G-5435)*
Critical Life Inc ....E 419 525-0502
  Mansfield *(G-13285)*
Cusa LI Inc ....C 216 267-8810
  Brookpark *(G-1942)*
Donty Horton HM Care Dhhc LLC ....E 513 463-3442
  Cincinnati *(G-3499)*
Firstgroup America Inc ....D 513 241-2200
  Cincinnati *(G-3626)*
Firstgroup America Inc ....D 513 241-2200
  Cincinnati *(G-3628)*
Greater Cleveland Regional ....C 216 781-1110
  Cleveland *(G-5700)*
Guernsey Health Systems Inc ....A 740 439-3561
  Cambridge *(G-2119)*
Intercoastal Trnsp Systems ....D 513 829-1287
  Fairfield *(G-10862)*
Lakefront Lines Inc ....C 216 267-8810
  Brookpark *(G-1949)*
Lakefront Lines Inc ....E 614 476-1113
  Columbus *(G-8031)*
Lakefront Lines Inc ....D 513 829-8290
  Fairfield *(G-10872)*
Liberty Ems Services LLC ....E 216 630-6626
  Cleveland *(G-5938)*
Mahoning County ....D 330 797-2837
  Youngstown *(G-20262)*
Medical Transport Systems Inc ....D 330 837-9818
  North Canton *(G-15352)*
Medpro LLC ....D 937 336-5586
  Eaton *(G-10567)*
Muskingum County Ohio ....D 740 452-0678
  Zanesville *(G-20506)*
Mycity Transporatation Co ....E 216 591-1900
  Shaker Heights *(G-16864)*
National Express Transit Corp ....D 513 322-6214
  Cincinnati *(G-4137)*
Pickaway County Community Acti ....D 740 477-1655
  Circleville *(G-4894)*
Professional Transportation ....E 419 661-0576
  Walbridge *(G-18776)*

Senior Outreach Services ....E 216 421-6900
  Cleveland *(G-6470)*
United Scoto Senior Activities ....E 740 354-6672
  Portsmouth *(G-16316)*
Youngstown Area Jwish Fdration ....D 330 746-1076
  Youngstown *(G-20426)*

TRANSPORTATION: Passenger Ferries
Kelleys Isle Ferry Boat Lines ....E 419 798-9763
  Marblehead *(G-13421)*
Miller Boat Line Inc ....D 419 285-2421
  Put In Bay *(G-16369)*

TRANSPORTATION: Transit Systems, NEC
Anthony Wayne Local Schools ....D 419 877-0451
  Whitehouse *(G-19583)*
City of North Olmsted ....E 440 777-8000
  North Olmsted *(G-15415)*
City Taxicab & Transfer Co ....E 440 992-2156
  Ashtabula *(G-734)*
First Group Investment Partnr ....D 513 241-2200
  Cincinnati *(G-3618)*
Firstgroup America Inc ....D 513 241-2200
  Cincinnati *(G-3626)*
Firstgroup America Inc ....D 513 241-2200
  Cincinnati *(G-3628)*
Firstgroup Usa Inc ....B 513 241-2200
  Cincinnati *(G-3629)*
Greater Cleveland Regional ....D 216 575-3932
  Cleveland *(G-5699)*
Intercoastal Trnsp Systems ....D 513 829-1287
  Fairfield *(G-10862)*
Ironton and Lawrence County ....B 740 532-3534
  Ironton *(G-12291)*
Ironton and Lawrence County ....E 740 532-7855
  Ironton *(G-12292)*
Laketran ....C 440 350-1000
  Painesville *(G-15862)*
Led Transportation ....E 330 484-2772
  Canton *(G-2431)*
Lifecare Ambulance Inc ....E 440 323-6111
  Elyria *(G-10642)*
Mv Transportation Inc ....E 419 627-0740
  Sandusky *(G-16780)*
Norfolk Southern Corporation ....E 740 574-8491
  Wheelersburg *(G-19579)*
Pickaway County Community Acti ....D 740 477-1655
  Circleville *(G-4894)*
Southeast Area Transit ....E 740 454-8574
  Zanesville *(G-20534)*
Stark Area Regional Trnst Auth ....C 330 477-2782
  Canton *(G-2539)*
United Scoto Senior Activities ....E 740 354-6672
  Portsmouth *(G-16316)*
Universal Transportation Syste ....C 513 829-1287
  Fairfield *(G-10920)*
Universal Transportation Syste ....E 513 539-9491
  Monroe *(G-14716)*
Universal Work and Power LLC ....E 513 981-1111
  Blue Ash *(G-1714)*

TRAVEL AGENCIES
AAA Allied Group Inc ....E 419 228-1022
  Lima *(G-12730)*
AAA Allied Group Inc ....B 513 762-3100
  Cincinnati *(G-2958)*
AAA Miami Valley ....D 937 224-2896
  Dayton *(G-9300)*
AAA Shelby County Motor Club ....E 937 492-3167
  Sidney *(G-16910)*
Avalon Holdings Corporation ....D 330 856-8800
  Warren *(G-18823)*
Croswell of Williamsburg LLC ....D 800 782-8747
  Dayton *(G-9446)*
Maritz Travel Company ....B 660 626-1501
  Maumee *(G-13940)*
Muskingum Coach Company ....E 740 622-2545
  Coshocton *(G-9112)*
Pier n Port Travel Inc ....E 513 841-9900
  Cincinnati *(G-4298)*
Professional Travel Inc ....D 440 734-8800
  North Olmsted *(G-15439)*
Travel Authority ....E 513 272-2887
  Cincinnati *(G-4681)*

TRAVEL CLUBS
Loves Travel Stops ....D 419 837-0071
  Perrysburg *(G-16028)*

Employee Codes: A=Over 500 employees, B=251-500
C=101-250, D=51-100, E=25-50

Loves Travel Stops.....E..... 937 325-2961
Springfield *(G-17225)*

TRAVEL TRAILER DEALERS

Sirpilla Recrtl Vhcl Ctr Inc.....D..... 330 494-2525
Akron *(G-439)*
Sonic Automotive-1495 Automall.....E..... 614 317-4326
Columbus *(G-8749)*

TRAVEL TRAILERS & CAMPERS

Capitol City Trailers Inc.....D..... 614 491-2616
Obetz *(G-15664)*

TRAVELER ACCOMMODATIONS, NEC

1460 Ninth St Assoc Ltd Partnr.....E..... 216 241-6600
Cleveland *(G-4921)*
16644 Snow Rd LLC.....E..... 216 676-5200
Brookpark *(G-1934)*
5 Star Hotel Management IV LP.....D..... 614 431-1819
Columbus *(G-6913)*
6300 Sharonville Assoc LLC.....C..... 513 489-3636
Cincinnati *(G-2947)*
A C Management Inc.....E..... 440 461-9200
Cleveland *(G-4931)*
Akron Inn Limited Partnership.....E..... 330 336-7692
Wadsworth *(G-18745)*
Alliance Hospitality.....E..... 330 505-2173
Youngstown *(G-20100)*
Alliance Hospitality Inc.....E..... 440 951-7333
Mentor *(G-14141)*
American Prprty-Mnagement Corp.....D..... 330 454-5000
Canton *(G-2239)*
Americas Best Value Inn.....E..... 419 626-9890
Sandusky *(G-16726)*
Amish Door Inc.....B..... 330 359-5464
Wilmot *(G-19797)*
Amitel Mentor Ltd Partnership.....E..... 440 392-0800
Mentor *(G-14143)*
Ap/Aim Indpndnce Sites Trs LLC.....D..... 216 986-9900
Independence *(G-12186)*
Army & Air Force Exchange Svc.....C..... 937 257-2928
Dayton *(G-9255)*
Arvind Sagar Inc.....E..... 614 428-8800
Columbus *(G-7047)*
Athens OH 1013 LLC.....E..... 740 589-5839
Athens *(G-776)*
Avalon Resort and Spa LLC.....D..... 330 856-1900
Warren *(G-18826)*
Awe Hospitality Group LLC.....C..... 330 888-8836
Macedonia *(G-13188)*
Bellville Hotel Company.....E..... 419 886-7000
Bellville *(G-1421)*
Bennett Enterprises Inc.....E..... 419 893-1004
Maumee *(G-13887)*
Best Western Columbus N Hotel.....E..... 614 888-8230
Columbus *(G-7103)*
Beverly Hills Inn La Llc.....E..... 859 494-9151
Aberdeen *(G-1)*
Bindu Associates LLC.....E..... 440 324-0099
Elyria *(G-10598)*
Black Sapphire C Columbus Univ.....D..... 614 297-9912
Columbus *(G-7116)*
Bob Mor Inc.....C..... 419 485-5555
Montpelier *(G-14737)*
Brice Hotel Inc.....D..... 614 864-1280
Reynoldsburg *(G-16432)*
Cabin Restaurant.....E..... 330 562-9171
Aurora *(G-832)*
Cafaro Peachcreek Co Ltd.....D..... 419 625-6280
Sandusky *(G-16731)*
Cambridge Associates Ltd.....E..... 740 432-7313
Cambridge *(G-2098)*
Cambridge Property Investors.....E..... 740 432-7313
Cambridge *(G-2102)*
Canter Inn Inc.....E..... 740 354-7711
Portsmouth *(G-16267)*
Carlisle Hotels Inc.....E..... 614 851-5599
Columbus *(G-7201)*
Carlson Hotels Ltd Partnership.....D..... 740 386-5451
Marion *(G-13528)*
Carroll Properties.....E..... 513 398-8075
Mason *(G-13671)*
Ceres Enterprises LLC.....D..... 440 617-9385
Westlake *(G-19472)*
Charter Hotel Group Ltd Partnr.....E..... 216 772-4538
Mentor *(G-14156)*
Choice Hotels Intl Inc.....D..... 330 656-1252
Hudson *(G-12111)*
Chu Airport Inn Inc.....E..... 216 267-5100
Brookpark *(G-1939)*
Claire De Leigh Corp.....E..... 614 459-6575
Columbus *(G-7289)*
Clermont Hills Co LLC.....D..... 513 752-4400
Cincinnati *(G-2908)*
Cleveland East Hotel LLC.....D..... 216 378-9191
Cleveland *(G-5312)*
Cleveland S Hospitality LLC.....E..... 216 447-1300
Cleveland *(G-5345)*
Clinic Care Inc.....D..... 216 707-4200
Cleveland *(G-5364)*
Columbia Properties Lima LLC.....D..... 419 222-0004
Lima *(G-12757)*
Columbus Concord Ltd Partnr.....D..... 614 228-3200
Columbus *(G-7342)*
Columbus Easton Hotel LLC.....E..... 614 414-1000
Columbus *(G-7349)*
Columbus Hospitality.....E..... 614 461-2648
Columbus *(G-7358)*
Columbus Oh-16 Airport Gahanna.....E..... 614 501-4770
Gahanna *(G-11236)*
Comfort Inn Northeast.....E..... 513 683-9700
Cincinnati *(G-3396)*
Comfort Inns.....E..... 614 885-4084
Columbus *(G-7398)*
Commonwealth Hotels LLC.....D..... 216 524-5814
Cleveland *(G-5380)*
Concord Dayton Hotel II LLC.....D..... 937 223-1000
Dayton *(G-9422)*
Concord Testa Hotel Assoc LLC.....D..... 330 252-9228
Akron *(G-160)*
Continental/Olentangy Ht LLC.....D..... 614 297-9912
Columbus *(G-7433)*
Cork Enterprises Inc.....E..... 740 654-1842
Lancaster *(G-12523)*
Courtyard By Marriott.....E..... 216 765-1900
Cleveland *(G-5429)*
Courtyard By Marriott.....E..... 513 341-4140
West Chester *(G-19055)*
Courtyard By Marriott.....E..... 440 871-3756
Westlake *(G-19481)*
Courtyard By Marriott.....D..... 937 433-3131
Miamisburg *(G-14288)*
Courtyard By Marriott Rossford.....E..... 419 872-5636
Rossford *(G-16607)*
Courtyard Management Corp.....E..... 614 475-8530
Columbus *(G-7451)*
CPX Carrollton Es LLC.....E..... 330 627-1200
Carrollton *(G-2617)*
Cs Hotels Limited Partnership.....D..... 614 771-8999
Columbus *(G-7470)*
Cumberland Gap LLC.....E..... 513 681-9300
Cincinnati *(G-3446)*
Cwb Property Managment Inc.....E..... 614 793-2244
Dublin *(G-10315)*
Days Inn.....E..... 740 695-0100
Saint Clairsville *(G-16635)*
Dayton Choa.....E..... 937 278-4871
Dayton *(G-9465)*
Dayton Hotels LLC.....E..... 937 832-2222
Englewood *(G-10702)*
Dbp Enterprises LLC.....E..... 740 513-2399
Sunbury *(G-17554)*
Donlen Inc.....D..... 216 961-6767
Cleveland *(G-5502)*
Dure Investments LLC.....E..... 419 697-7800
Oregon *(G-15732)*
Edmond Hotel Investors LLC.....D..... 614 891-2900
Columbus *(G-7579)*
Elden Motels LP.....D..... 440 967-8770
Vermilion *(G-18708)*
Fairfeld Inn Stes Clmbus Arprt.....E..... 614 237-2100
Columbus *(G-7630)*
Fairfield Inn.....D..... 614 267-1111
Columbus *(G-7631)*
Falcon Plaza LLC.....E..... 419 352-4671
Bowling Green *(G-1775)*
First Hospitality Company LLC.....E..... 614 864-4555
Reynoldsburg *(G-16452)*
First Hotel Management LLC.....E..... 614 864-1280
Reynoldsburg *(G-16453)*
Goodnight Inn Inc.....E..... 419 334-9551
Fremont *(G-11203)*
Grandview Ht Ltd Partnr Ohio.....D..... 937 766-5519
Springfield *(G-17203)*
Hampton Inns LLC.....E..... 330 492-0151
Canton *(G-2391)*
Hampton Inns LLC.....E..... 330 422-0500
Streetsboro *(G-17415)*
He Hari Inc.....D..... 614 436-0700
Worthington *(G-19961)*
He Hari Inc.....D..... 614 846-6600
Lewis Center *(G-12687)*
Hilton Polaris.....D..... 614 885-1600
Columbus *(G-6884)*
Hit Portfolio I Misc Trs LLC.....C..... 513 241-3575
Cincinnati *(G-3770)*
Hmshost Corporation.....C..... 419 547-8667
Clyde *(G-6814)*
Holiday Inn.....E..... 419 691-8800
Oregon *(G-15739)*
Holiday Inn Express.....E..... 419 332-7700
Fremont *(G-11206)*
Holiday Inn Express.....E..... 937 424-5757
Dayton *(G-9612)*
Holiday Inn Express.....E..... 614 447-1212
Columbus *(G-7845)*
Holiday Inn of Englewood.....D..... 937 832-1234
Englewood *(G-10708)*
Host Cincinnati Hotel LLC.....C..... 513 621-7700
Cincinnati *(G-3788)*
Hotel Stow LP.....E..... 330 945-9722
Stow *(G-17373)*
Howard Johnson.....D..... 513 825-3129
Cincinnati *(G-3790)*
Hst Lessee Cincinnati LLC.....C..... 513 852-2702
Cincinnati *(G-3793)*
IA Urban Htels Bchwood Trs LLC.....D..... 216 765-8066
Beachwood *(G-1088)*
Indus Airport Hotel II LLC.....D..... 614 235-0717
Columbus *(G-7890)*
Inn At Wickliffe LLC.....E..... 440 585-0600
Wickliffe *(G-19603)*
Jackson I-94 Ltd Partnership.....E..... 614 793-2244
Dublin *(G-10379)*
Jagi Clveland Independence LLC.....C..... 216 524-8050
Cleveland *(G-5848)*
Jagi Juno LLC.....E..... 513 489-1955
Cincinnati *(G-3858)*
Johnson Howard International.....E..... 513 825-3129
Cincinnati *(G-3883)*
Kenyon College.....E..... 740 427-2202
Gambier *(G-11348)*
Lawnfield Properties LLC.....E..... 440 974-3572
Mentor *(G-14208)*
Liberty Ashtabula Holdings.....E..... 330 872-6000
Newton Falls *(G-15277)*
Lodging Industry Inc.....E..... 440 323-7488
Sandusky *(G-16776)*
Lodging Industry Inc.....E..... 419 732-2929
Port Clinton *(G-16250)*
Lodging Industry Inc.....E..... 440 324-3911
Elyria *(G-10645)*
M&C Hotel Interests Inc.....E..... 937 778-8100
Piqua *(G-16151)*
Mansfield Hotel Partnership.....E..... 419 529-2100
Mansfield *(G-13331)*
Marcus Hotels Inc.....E..... 614 228-3800
Columbus *(G-8106)*
Marriott.....E..... 440 542-2375
Solon *(G-17026)*
Marriott International Inc.....C..... 614 861-1400
Columbus *(G-8112)*
Marriott International Inc.....C..... 513 487-3800
Cincinnati *(G-4025)*
Marriott International Inc.....B..... 216 696-9200
Cleveland *(G-5983)*
Marriott International Inc.....B..... 614 228-5050
Columbus *(G-8113)*
Marriott International Inc.....E..... 614 436-7070
Columbus *(G-8114)*
Marriott International Inc.....C..... 614 475-8530
Columbus *(G-8115)*
Marriott International Inc.....C..... 614 864-8844
Columbus *(G-8116)*
Marriott International Inc.....C..... 614 222-2610
Columbus *(G-8117)*
Marriott International Inc.....E..... 614 885-0799
Columbus *(G-8118)*
Marriott International Inc.....E..... 330 666-4811
Copley *(G-9060)*
Marriott International Inc.....C..... 419 866-1001
Holland *(G-12035)*
Marriott International Inc.....E..... 440 716-9977
North Olmsted *(G-15431)*
Marriott International Inc.....C..... 513 530-5060
Blue Ash *(G-1636)*
Mason Family Resorts LLC.....B..... 513 339-0141
Mason *(G-13736)*

SERVICES SECTION

TRUCK GENERAL REPAIR SVC

Maumee Lodging Enterprises ....D....... 419 865-1380
  Maumee *(G-13944)*
Meander Hospitality Group Inc ....E 330 702-0226
  Canfield *(G-2199)*
Meander Hsptality Group II LLC ....E 330 422-0500
  Streetsboro *(G-17420)*
Middletown Innkeepers Inc ....E 513 942-3440
  Fairfield *(G-10882)*
Moti Corporation ....E 440 734-4500
  Cleveland *(G-6080)*
Mrn-Newgar Hotel Ltd ....E 216 443-1000
  Cleveland *(G-6085)*
N P Motel System Inc ....E 330 339-7731
  New Philadelphia *(G-15110)*
Norstar Aluminum Molds Inc ....D 440 632-0853
  Middlefield *(G-14399)*
Northeast Cincinnati Hotel LLC ....C 513 459-9800
  Mason *(G-13743)*
Northland Hotel Inc ....E 614 885-1601
  Columbus *(G-8292)*
Northtown Square Ltd Partnr ....E 419 691-8911
  Oregon *(G-15742)*
Ohio Inns Inc ....E 937 440-9303
  Troy *(G-18369)*
Ohio State University ....B 614 292-3238
  Columbus *(G-8427)*
Olshan Hotel Management Inc ....E 614 414-1000
  Columbus *(G-8467)*
Oxford Hospitality Group Inc ....E 513 524-0114
  Oxford *(G-15828)*
Paradise Hospitality Inc ....C 419 255-6190
  Toledo *(G-18116)*
Park Hotels & Resorts Inc ....C 216 447-0020
  Cleveland *(G-6236)*
Park Hotels & Resorts Inc ....E 937 436-2400
  Miamisburg *(G-14331)*
Park Inn ....E 419 241-3000
  Toledo *(G-18117)*
Parkins Incorporated ....E 614 334-1800
  Hilliard *(G-11942)*
Peitro Properties Ltd Partnr ....E 216 328-7777
  Cleveland *(G-6260)*
PH Fairborn Ht Owner 2800 LLC ......D 937 426-7800
  Beavercreek *(G-1197)*
Pinecraft Land Holdings LLC ....E 330 390-5722
  Millersburg *(G-14615)*
Polaris Innkeepers Inc ....E 614 568-0770
  Westerville *(G-19341)*
Quail Hollow Management Inc ....D 440 639-4000
  Painesville *(G-15874)*
R & Y Holding ....E 419 353-3464
  Bowling Green *(G-1792)*
Radisson Hotel Cleveland Gtwy ....D 216 377-9000
  Cleveland *(G-6344)*
Red Roof Inns Inc ....A 614 744-2600
  Columbus *(G-8600)*
Red Roof Inns Inc ....E 614 224-6539
  Columbus *(G-8601)*
Red Roof Inns Inc ....E 440 892-7920
  Cleveland *(G-6363)*
Red Roof Inns Inc ....E 740 695-4057
  Saint Clairsville *(G-16654)*
Red Roof Inns Inc ....E 440 243-5166
  Cleveland *(G-6364)*
Renthotel Dayton LLC ....D 937 461-4700
  Dayton *(G-9847)*
Req/Jqh Holdings Inc ....D 937 432-0000
  Miamisburg *(G-14341)*
Residence Inn ....E 614 222-2610
  Columbus *(G-8618)*
Richfield Banquet & Confer ....E 330 659-6151
  Richfield *(G-16526)*
Ridgehills Hotel Ltd Partnr ....D 440 585 0600
  Wickliffe *(G-19613)*
Riverview Hotel LLC ....E 614 268-8700
  Columbus *(G-8637)*
Rlj III - Em Clmbus Lessee LLC ....D 614 890-8600
  Columbus *(G-8638)*
Roschmans Restaurant ADM ....E 419 225-8300
  Lima *(G-12871)*
Rossford Hospitality Group Inc ....E 419 874-2345
  Rossford *(G-16611)*
Rukh-Jagi Holdings LLC ....D 330 494-2770
  Canton *(G-2518)*
S & S Management Inc ....E 937 382-5858
  Wilmington *(G-19785)*
Sadguru Krupa LLC ....E 330 644-2111
  Akron *(G-425)*
Saw Mill Creek Ltd ....C 419 433-3800
  Huron *(G-12170)*

Sb Hotel LLC ....E 614 793-2244
  Dublin *(G-10449)*
SDC Unvrsity Cir Developer LLC ......D 216 791-5333
  Cleveland *(G-6456)*
SM Double Tree Hotel Lake ....E 216 241-5100
  Cleveland *(G-6491)*
Solon Lodging Associates LLC ....E 440 248-9600
  Solon *(G-17053)*
Somnus Corporation ....E 740 695-3961
  Saint Clairsville *(G-16656)*
Son-Rise Hotels Inc ....E 330 769-4949
  Seville *(G-16846)*
Sortino Management & Dev Co ....E 419 626-6761
  Sandusky *(G-16796)*
Star Group Ltd ....E 614 428-8678
  Gahanna *(G-11269)*
Starwood Hotels & Resorts ....C 614 345-9291
  Columbus *(G-8778)*
Starwood Hotels & Resorts ....E 614 888-8230
  Columbus *(G-8779)*
Sterling Lodging LLC ....E 419 879-4000
  Lima *(G-12892)*
Stoney Lodge Inc ....D 419 837-6409
  Millbury *(G-14581)*
Strang Corporation ....E 216 961-6767
  Cleveland *(G-6545)*
Summit Associates Inc ....D 216 831-3300
  Cleveland *(G-6547)*
Summit Hotel Trs 144 LLC ....E 216 443-9043
  Cleveland *(G-6548)*
Town House Motor Lodge Corp ....E 740 452-4511
  Zanesville *(G-20539)*
Town Inn Co LLC ....D 614 221-3281
  Columbus *(G-8857)*
Tramz Hotels LLC ....D 440 975-9922
  Willoughby *(G-19718)*
Travelcenters of America LLC ....D 330 769-2053
  Lodi *(G-12966)*
Union Centre Hotel LLC ....C 513 874-7335
  West Chester *(G-19173)*
United Hsptality Solutions LLC ....A 800 238-0487
  Buffalo *(G-2053)*
Uph Holdings LLC ....D 614 447-9777
  Columbus *(G-8913)*
Valleyview Management Co Inc ....E 419 886-4000
  Bellville *(G-1426)*
Vjp Hospitality Ltd ....E 614 475-8383
  Columbus *(G-8948)*
W & H Realty Inc ....E 513 891-1066
  Blue Ash *(G-1717)*
W2005/Fargo Hotels (pool C) ....E 937 890-6112
  Dayton *(G-9980)*
W2005/Fargo Hotels (pool C) ....E 937 322-2200
  Springfield *(G-17293)*
Westpost Columbus LLC ....D 614 885-1885
  Columbus *(G-8982)*
Willoughby Lodging LLC ....E 440 530-1100
  Willoughby *(G-19724)*
Winegardner & Hammons Inc ....C 614 791-1000
  Dublin *(G-10493)*
Wright Executive Ht Ltd Partnr ....C 937 283-3200
  Wilmington *(G-19796)*
Wright Executive Ht Ltd Partnr ....E 937 426-7800
  Beavercreek *(G-1219)*
Wright Executive Ht Ltd Partnr ....E 937 429-0600
  Beavercreek *(G-1220)*
Wyndham International Inc ....E 330 666-9300
  Copley *(G-9069)*

TRAVELERS' CHECK ISSUANCE SVCS

Jpmorgan Chase Bank Nat Assn ....A 614 436-3055
  Columbus *(G-6888)*

TROPHIES, NEC

Lawnview Industries Inc ....C 937 653-5217
  Urbana *(G-18593)*

TROPHY & PLAQUE STORES

Sporty Events ....E 440 342-5046
  Chesterland *(G-2803)*

TRUCK & BUS BODIES: Ambulance

Life Star Rescue Inc ....E 419 238-2507
  Van Wert *(G-18637)*

TRUCK & BUS BODIES: Truck, Motor Vehicle

Brown Industrial Inc ....E 937 693-3838
  Botkins *(G-1752)*

Kaffenbarger Truck Eqp Co ....C 937 845-3804
  New Carlisle *(G-15025)*
Schodorf Truck Body & Eqp Co ....E 614 228-6793
  Columbus *(G-8698)*
Venco Venturo Industries LLC ....E 513 772-8448
  Cincinnati *(G-4806)*

TRUCK & BUS BODIES: Utility Truck

QT Equipment Company ....E 330 724-3055
  Akron *(G-401)*

TRUCK & FREIGHT TERMINALS & SUPPORT ACTIVITIES

Chieftain Trucking & Excav Inc ....E 216 485-8034
  Cleveland *(G-5235)*
Dayton Freight Lines Inc ....D 937 236-4880
  Dayton *(G-9475)*
Disttech LLC ....D 800 321-3143
  Cleveland *(G-5490)*
Eab Truck Service ....D 216 525-0020
  Cleveland *(G-5517)*
Fedex Freight Corporation ....E 877 661-8956
  Mentor *(G-14175)*
Ground Effects LLC ....E 440 565-5925
  Westlake *(G-19487)*
PAm Transportation Svcs Inc ....D 419 935-9501
  Willard *(G-19624)*
Pitt-Ohio Express LLC ....B 216 433-9000
  Cleveland *(G-6284)*
Short Freight Lines Inc ....E 419 729-1691
  Toledo *(G-18185)*
Slay Transportation Co Inc ....C 740 865-2910
  Sardis *(G-16815)*
Stover Transportation Inc ....E 614 777-4184
  Hilliard *(G-11955)*
STS Logistics Inc ....E 419 294-1498
  Upper Sandusky *(G-18567)*
Xpo Logistics Freight Inc ....C 614 876-7100
  Columbus *(G-9014)*
Xpo Logistics Freight Inc ....D 330 896-7300
  Uniontown *(G-18544)*
Yrc Inc ....D 614 878-9281
  Columbus *(G-9023)*

TRUCK BODIES: Body Parts

Kaffenbarger Truck Eqp Co ....E 513 772-6800
  Cincinnati *(G-3900)*

TRUCK BODY SHOP

QT Equipment Company ....E 330 724-3055
  Akron *(G-401)*
Skinner Diesel Services Inc ....E 614 491-8785
  Columbus *(G-8741)*

TRUCK DRIVER SVCS

A Jacobs Inc ....E 614 774-6757
  Hilliard *(G-11874)*
Aldo Peraza ....D 614 804-0403
  Columbus *(G-6963)*
American Bulk Commodities Inc ....C 330 758-0841
  Youngstown *(G-20103)*
Buckeye Leasing Inc ....E 330 758-0841
  Youngstown *(G-20130)*
Hogan Truck Leasing Inc ....E 513 454-3500
  Fairfield *(G-10859)*
Industrial Repair & Mfg Inc ....E 419 822-4232
  Delta *(G-10159)*
Professional Drivers GA Inc ....E 614 529-8282
  Columbus *(G-8566)*
S & B Trucking Inc ....E 614 554-4090
  Hubbard *(G-12091)*
Transportation Unlimited Inc ....A 216 426-0088
  Cleveland *(G-6613)*
Tsl Ltd ....A 419 843-3200
  Toledo *(G-18262)*

TRUCK GENERAL REPAIR SVC

Abers Garage Inc ....E 419 281-5500
  Ashland *(G-649)*
Aim Leasing Company ....D 330 759-0438
  Girard *(G-11407)*
Allstate Trk Sls of Estrn OH ....E 330 339-5555
  New Philadelphia *(G-15080)*
American Nat Fleet Svc Inc ....D 216 447-6060
  Cleveland *(G-5017)*
Beaverdam Fleet Services Inc ....E 419 643-8880
  Beaverdam *(G-1288)*

Employee Codes: A=Over 500 employees, B=251-500
C=101-250, D=51-100, E=25-50

TRUCK GENERAL REPAIR SVC

Benedict Enterprises Inc .... E 513 539-9216
  Monroe *(G-14690)*
City of Toledo .... D 419 936-2507
  Toledo *(G-17812)*
Commercial Truck & Trailer .... E 330 545-9717
  Girard *(G-11411)*
Dickinson Fleet Services LLC .... E 513 772-3629
  Cincinnati *(G-3490)*
Fyda Freightliner Youngstown .... D 330 797-0224
  Youngstown *(G-20192)*
Mansfield Truck Sales & Svc .... E 419 522-9811
  Mansfield *(G-13335)*
Midwest Trailer Sales & Svc .... E 513 772-2818
  West Chester *(G-19119)*
Navistar Intl Trnsp Corp .... C 937 390-4242
  Springfield *(G-17250)*
Peterbilt of Cincinnati .... E 513 772-1740
  Cincinnati *(G-4285)*
PGT Trucking Inc .... E 419 943-3437
  Leipsic *(G-12664)*
R & R Inc .... E 330 799-1536
  Youngstown *(G-20338)*
Rebman Truck Service Inc .... E 419 589-8161
  Mansfield *(G-13354)*
Stoops Frghtlnr-Qlity Trlr Inc .... E 937 236-4092
  Dayton *(G-9909)*
Ta Operating LLC .... B 440 808-9100
  Westlake *(G-19553)*
Ted Ruck Co Inc .... E 419 738-2613
  Wapakoneta *(G-18808)*
Travelcenters America Inc .... A 440 808-9100
  Westlake *(G-19555)*
Travelcenters of America LLC .... A 440 808-9100
  Westlake *(G-19557)*
W W Williams Company LLC .... E 614 527-9400
  Hilliard *(G-11965)*
Workforce Services Inc .... E 330 484-2566
  Canton *(G-2589)*

TRUCK PAINTING & LETTERING SVCS

Palmer Trucks Inc .... E 937 235-3318
  Dayton *(G-9799)*

TRUCK PARTS & ACCESSORIES: Wholesalers

Adelmans Truck Parts Corp .... E 330 456-0206
  Canton *(G-2225)*
Admiral Truck Parts Inc .... E 330 659-6311
  Bath *(G-1033)*
All Lift Service Company Inc .... E 440 585-1542
  Willoughby *(G-19642)*
Allied Truck Parts Co .... E 330 477-8127
  Canton *(G-2234)*
Better Brake Parts Inc .... E 419 227-0685
  Lima *(G-12747)*
Buyers Products Company .... C 440 974-8888
  Mentor *(G-14152)*
Commercial Truck & Trailer .... E 330 545-9717
  Girard *(G-11411)*
Cross Truck Equipment Co Inc .... E 330 477-8151
  Canton *(G-2329)*
East Manufacturing Corporation ..... B 330 325-9921
  Randolph *(G-16372)*
GTM Service Inc .... E 440 944-5099
  Wickliffe *(G-19600)*
Hy-Tek Material Handling Inc .... D 614 497-2500
  Columbus *(G-7873)*
Kaffenbarger Truck Eqp Co .... C 937 845-3804
  New Carlisle *(G-15025)*
Kenworth of Cincinnati Inc .... D 513 771-5831
  Cincinnati *(G-3916)*
Ohio Automotive Supply Co .... E 419 422-1655
  Findlay *(G-11072)*
Perkins Motor Service Ltd .... E 440 277-1256
  Lorain *(G-13071)*
Peterbilt of Cincinnati .... E 513 772-1740
  Cincinnati *(G-4285)*
Power Train Components Inc .... D 419 636-4430
  Bryan *(G-2018)*
Premier Truck Parts Inc .... E 216 642-5000
  Cleveland *(G-6302)*
R & R Inc .... E 330 799-1536
  Youngstown *(G-20338)*
Valley Ford Truck Inc .... D 216 524-2400
  Cleveland *(G-6683)*
W W Williams Company LLC .... D 419 837-5067
  Perrysburg *(G-16071)*
Wz Management Inc .... E 330 628-4881
  Akron *(G-514)*

Young Truck Sales Inc .... E 330 477-6271
  Canton *(G-2592)*
Youngstown-Kenworth Inc .... E 330 534-9761
  Hubbard *(G-12093)*

TRUCK STOPS

Trepanier Daniels & Trepanier .... D 740 286-1288
  Jackson *(G-12319)*

TRUCKING & HAULING SVCS: Animal & Farm Prdt

Store & Haul Inc .... E 419 238-4284
  Van Wert *(G-18644)*

TRUCKING & HAULING SVCS: Baggage Transfer Svcs

Veyance Industrial Svcs Inc .... C 307 682-7855
  Fairlawn *(G-10980)*

TRUCKING & HAULING SVCS: Building Materials

Home Run Inc .... E 800 543-9198
  Xenia *(G-20061)*

TRUCKING & HAULING SVCS: Coal, Local

Iddings Trucking Inc .... C 740 568-1780
  Marietta *(G-13453)*
Robert Neff & Son Inc .... E 740 454-0128
  Zanesville *(G-20530)*

TRUCKING & HAULING SVCS: Contract Basis

A L Smith Trucking Inc .... E 937 526-3651
  Versailles *(G-18722)*
A&R Logistics Inc .... D 614 444-4111
  Columbus *(G-6921)*
ABF Freight System Inc .... D 440 843-4600
  Cleveland *(G-4947)*
ABF Freight System Inc .... E 614 294-3537
  Columbus *(G-6925)*
ABF Freight System Inc .... E 937 236-2210
  Dayton *(G-9301)*
ABF Freight System Inc .... E 513 779-7888
  West Chester *(G-19011)*
ABF Freight System Inc .... E 330 549-3800
  North Lima *(G-15395)*
AG Trucking Inc .... E 937 497-7770
  Sidney *(G-16911)*
All Industrial Group Inc .... E 216 441-2000
  Newburgh Heights *(G-15250)*
Alpha Freight Systems Inc .... D 800 394-9001
  Hudson *(G-12104)*
Ameri-Line Inc .... E 440 316-4500
  Columbia Station *(G-6840)*
Arctic Express Inc .... C 614 876-4008
  Hilliard *(G-11879)*
Arms Trucking Co Inc .... E 800 362-1343
  Huntsburg *(G-12156)*
As Logistics Inc .... D 513 863-4627
  Hamilton *(G-11693)*
Awl Transport Inc .... E 330 899-3444
  Mantua *(G-13384)*
B D Transportation Inc .... E 937 773-9280
  Piqua *(G-16135)*
Besl Transfer Co .... E 513 242-3456
  Cincinnati *(G-3100)*
Blatt Trucking Co Inc .... E 419 898-0002
  Rocky Ridge *(G-16566)*
Bowling Transportation Inc .... D 419 436-9590
  Fostoria *(G-11124)*
Buckeye Waste Industries Inc .... E 330 645-9900
  Coventry Township *(G-9123)*
Bulk Transit Corporation .... E 614 873-4632
  Plain City *(G-16185)*
Bulk Transit Corporation .... E 937 497-9573
  Sidney *(G-16917)*
Bulkmatic Transport Company ...... E 614 497-2372
  Columbus *(G-7168)*
Burd Brothers Inc .... D 800 538-2873
  Batavia *(G-996)*
C&K Trucking LLC .... E 440 657-5249
  Elyria *(G-10600)*
Carry Transport Inc .... E 937 236-0026
  Dayton *(G-9386)*

Cavins Trucking & Garage LLC ...... E 419 661-9947
  Perrysburg *(G-15985)*
Chambers Leasing Systems .... E 937 547-9777
  Greenville *(G-11492)*
Cimarron Express Inc .... D 419 855-7713
  Genoa *(G-11375)*
Clark Trucking Inc .... C 937 642-0335
  East Liberty *(G-10508)*
Classic Carriers Inc .... E 937 604-8118
  Versailles *(G-18724)*
Cowen Truck Line Inc .... D 419 938-3401
  Perrysburg *(G-16078)*
Crw Inc .... D 330 264-3785
  Shreve *(G-16907)*
D L Belknap Trucking Inc .... D 330 868-7766
  Paris *(G-15895)*
Dayton Freight Lines Inc .... E 330 346-0750
  Kent *(G-12364)*
Dedicated Transport LLC .... C 216 641-2500
  Brooklyn Heights *(G-1914)*
Dick Lavy Trucking Inc .... C 937 448-2104
  Bradford *(G-1806)*
Dingledine Trucking Company ...... E 937 652-3454
  Urbana *(G-18585)*
Dlc Transport Inc .... E 740 282-1763
  Steubenville *(G-17315)*
Drew Ag-Transport Inc .... D 937 548-3200
  Greenville *(G-11499)*
Durbin Trucking Inc .... E 419 334-2422
  Oak Harbor *(G-15609)*
Dworkin Inc .... E 216 271-5318
  Cleveland *(G-5515)*
Erie Trucking Inc .... E 419 625-7374
  Sandusky *(G-16755)*
Estes Express Lines Inc .... D 937 237-7536
  Huber Heights *(G-12095)*
Estes Express Lines Inc .... D 419 522-2641
  Mansfield *(G-13298)*
Estes Express Lines Inc .... D 513 779-9581
  West Chester *(G-19070)*
Estes Express Lines Inc .... E 740 401-0410
  Belpre *(G-1437)*
F S T Express Inc .... D 614 529-7900
  Columbus *(G-7626)*
Fedex Freight Corporation .... E 877 661-8956
  Mentor *(G-14175)*
Fedex Ground Package Sys Inc ..... C 614 863-8000
  Columbus *(G-7649)*
Fedex Ground Package Sys Inc ..... B 800 463-3339
  Grove City *(G-11560)*
Fetter and Son LLC .... E 740 465-2961
  Morral *(G-14840)*
Fetter Son Farms Ltd Lblty Co .... E 740 465-2961
  Morral *(G-14841)*
Five Star Trucking Inc .... E 440 953-9300
  Willoughby *(G-19665)*
Foodliner Inc .... E 563 451-1047
  Dayton *(G-9555)*
Fraley & Schilling Inc .... C 740 598-4118
  Brilliant *(G-1868)*
G & S Transfer Inc .... E 330 673-3899
  Kent *(G-12370)*
Garner Trucking Inc .... C 419 422-5742
  Findlay *(G-11035)*
Globe Trucking Inc .... D 419 727-8307
  Toledo *(G-17917)*
Guenther & Sons Inc .... E 513 738-1448
  Ross *(G-16603)*
Harris Distributing Co .... E 513 541-4222
  Cincinnati *(G-3737)*
Hillsboro Transportation Co .... E 513 772-9223
  Cincinnati *(G-3766)*
Hilltrux Tank Lines Inc .... E 330 538-3700
  North Jackson *(G-15381)*
Hoosier Express Inc .... E 419 436-9590
  Fostoria *(G-11132)*
Hyway Trucking Company .... D 419 423-7145
  Findlay *(G-11049)*
J & J Carriers LLC .... E 614 447-2615
  Columbus *(G-7929)*
J M T Cartage Inc .... E 330 478-2430
  Canton *(G-2416)*
J P Jenks Inc .... E 440 428-4500
  Madison *(G-13226)*
J P Transportation Company .... E 513 424-6978
  Middletown *(G-14430)*
K & L Trucking Inc .... E 419 822-3836
  Delta *(G-10160)*
K-Limited Carrier Ltd .... C 419 269-0002
  Toledo *(G-17988)*

SERVICES SECTION

TRUCKING & HAULING SVCS: Heavy, NEC

Kaplan Trucking Company .... D 216 341-3322
  Cleveland *(G-5882)*
Klingshirn & Sons Trucking .... E 937 338-5000
  Burkettsville *(G-2058)*
Kmj Leasing Ltd .... E 614 871-3883
  Orient *(G-15761)*
Knight-Swift Trnsp Hldings Inc .... D 614 274-5204
  Columbus *(G-8003)*
Kuntzman Trucking Inc .... E 330 821-9160
  Alliance *(G-543)*
L V Trucking Inc .... E 614 275-4994
  Columbus *(G-8024)*
La King Trucking Inc .... E 419 225-9039
  Lima *(G-12813)*
Liquid Transport Corp .... E 513 769-4777
  Cincinnati *(G-3989)*
Lt Trucking Inc .... E 440 997-5528
  Ashtabula *(G-754)*
Lyden Company .... E 419 868-6800
  Toledo *(G-18022)*
Mast Trucking Inc .... D 330 674-8913
  Millersburg *(G-14611)*
McMullen Transportation LLC .... E 937 981-4455
  Greenfield *(G-11488)*
Miami Valley Bekins Inc .... E 937 278-4296
  Dayton *(G-9726)*
Mid State Systems Inc .... D 740 928-1115
  Hebron *(G-11853)*
Millis Transfer Inc .... E 513 863-0222
  Hamilton *(G-11760)*
Moeller Trucking Inc .... D 419 925-4799
  Maria Stein *(G-13429)*
Motor Carrier Service Inc .... C 419 693-6207
  Northwood *(G-15537)*
Nationwide Truck Brokers Inc .... E 937 335-9229
  Troy *(G-18367)*
Neighborhood Logistics Co Inc .... E 440 466-0020
  Geneva *(G-11366)*
Old Dominion Freight Line Inc .... E 937 235-1596
  Dayton *(G-9790)*
Old Dominion Freight Line Inc .... E 216 641-5566
  Cleveland *(G-6198)*
Otis Wright & Sons Inc .... E 419 227-4400
  Lima *(G-12852)*
P & D Transportation Inc .... C 740 454-1221
  Zanesville *(G-20523)*
Penske Logistics LLC .... D 216 765-5475
  Beachwood *(G-1114)*
PGT Trucking Inc .... E 419 943-3437
  Leipsic *(G-12664)*
Piqua Transfer & Storage Co .... D 937 773-3743
  Piqua *(G-16160)*
Pitt-Ohio Express LLC .... C 419 726-6523
  Toledo *(G-18126)*
Pitt-Ohio Express LLC .... D 513 860-3424
  West Chester *(G-19221)*
Pros Freight Corporation .... E 440 543-7555
  Chagrin Falls *(G-2730)*
R & L Carriers Inc .... E 419 874-5976
  Perrysburg *(G-16050)*
R K Campf Corp .... E 330 332-7089
  Salem *(G-16709)*
Robert G Owen Trucking Inc .... E 330 756-1013
  Navarre *(G-14956)*
Robert M Neff Inc .... D 614 444-1562
  Columbus *(G-8642)*
Roeder Cartage Company Inc .... D 419 221-1600
  Lima *(G-12870)*
Ron Burge Trucking Inc .... E 330 624-5373
  Burbank *(G-2055)*
Ross Transportation Svcs Inc .... C 440 748-5900
  Grafton *(G-11446)*
S & T Truck and Auto Svc Inc .... E 614 272 8163
  Columbus *(G-8667)*
Saia Motor Freight Line LLC .... E 419 726-9761
  Toledo *(G-18170)*
Saia Motor Freight Line LLC .... E 330 659-4277
  Richfield *(G-16528)*
Saia Motor Freight Line LLC .... D 614 870-8778
  Columbus *(G-8676)*
Scheiderer Transport Inc .... D 614 873-5103
  Plain City *(G-16204)*
Schindewolf Express Inc .... E 937 585-5919
  De Graff *(G-10016)*
Sewell Motor Express Co .... E 937 382-3847
  Wilmington *(G-19787)*
SMS Transport LLC .... E 937 813-8897
  Dayton *(G-9886)*
Spader Freight Services Inc .... E 419 547-1117
  Clyde *(G-6824)*

Superior Bulk Logistics Inc .... E 513 874-3440
  West Chester *(G-19233)*
Thomas E Keller Trucking Inc .... C 419 784-4805
  Defiance *(G-10061)*
Thomas Trucking Inc .... E 513 731-8411
  Cincinnati *(G-4654)*
Titan Transfer Inc .... D 513 458-4233
  West Chester *(G-19163)*
Trans-States Express Inc .... E 513 679-7100
  Cincinnati *(G-4679)*
Transport Corp America Inc .... E 330 538-3328
  North Jackson *(G-15388)*
U S Xpress Inc .... E 937 328-4100
  Springfield *(G-17291)*
U S Xpress Inc .... E 740 363-0700
  Delaware *(G-10132)*
U S Xpress Inc .... E 740 452-4153
  Zanesville *(G-20541)*
UPS Ground Freight Inc .... C 330 659-6693
  Richfield *(G-16531)*
UPS Ground Freight Inc .... E 937 236-4700
  Dayton *(G-9957)*
Valley Transportation Inc .... C 419 289-6200
  Ashland *(G-704)*
Venezia Transport Service Inc .... E 330 542-9735
  New Middletown *(G-15074)*
Vision Express Inc .... E 740 922-8848
  Uhrichsville *(G-18496)*
Vitran Express Inc .... D 216 426-8584
  Cleveland *(G-6707)*
Ward Trucking LLC .... E 330 659-6658
  Richfield *(G-16532)*
Ward Trucking LLC .... E 614 275-3800
  Columbus *(G-8966)*
Werner Enterprises Inc .... E 937 325-5403
  Springfield *(G-17297)*
Xpo Logistics Freight Inc .... C 513 870-0044
  West Chester *(G-19244)*
Xpo Logistics Freight Inc .... E 419 499-8888
  Milan *(G-14500)*
Xpo Logistics Freight Inc .... C 216 433-1000
  Parma *(G-15919)*
Xpo Logistics Freight Inc .... E 740 894-3859
  South Point *(G-17099)*
Xpo Logistics Freight Inc .... C 330 824-2242
  Warren *(G-18930)*
Xpo Logistics Freight Inc .... E 419 294-5728
  Upper Sandusky *(G-18572)*
Xpo Logistics Freight Inc .... D 419 666-3022
  Perrysburg *(G-16075)*
Xpo Logistics Freight Inc .... D 330 896-7300
  Uniontown *(G-18544)*
Xpo Logistics Freight Inc .... E 937 492-3899
  Sidney *(G-16961)*
Yowell Transportation Svc Inc .... E 937 294-5933
  Moraine *(G-14838)*
Yrc Inc .... D 330 659-4151
  Richfield *(G-16534)*
Yrc Inc .... B 419 729-0631
  Toledo *(G-18327)*
Yrc Inc .... C 330 665-0274
  Copley *(G-9070)*

TRUCKING & HAULING SVCS: Draying, Local, Without Storage

Containerport Group Inc .... D 216 692-3124
  Euclid *(G-10747)*
Stack Container Service Inc .... D 216 531-7555
  Euclid *(G-10777)*

TRUCKING & HAULING SVCS: Furniture Moving & Storage, Local

Accelerated Moving & Stor Inc .... E 614 836-1007
  Columbus *(G-6932)*
Leaders Moving Company .... E 614 785-9595
  Worthington *(G-19970)*
Moving Solutions Inc .... D 440 946-9300
  Mentor *(G-14223)*
Nicholas Carney-Mc Inc .... D 330 792-5460
  Youngstown *(G-20301)*
River City Furniture LLC .... D 513 612-7303
  West Chester *(G-19141)*
Shetler Moving & Stor of Ohio .... E 513 755-0700
  West Chester *(G-19151)*
Unpacking Etc .... E 440 871-0506
  Westlake *(G-19561)*

TRUCKING & HAULING SVCS: Furniture, Local W/out Storage

River City Furniture LLC .... D 513 612-7303
  West Chester *(G-19141)*

TRUCKING & HAULING SVCS: Garbage, Collect/Transport Only

BFI Waste Services LLC .... E 800 437-1123
  Salem *(G-16689)*
City of Marion .... D 740 382-1479
  Marion *(G-13531)*
Fultz & Son Inc .... E 419 547-9365
  Clyde *(G-6813)*
R & R Sanitation Inc .... E 330 325-2311
  Mogadore *(G-14683)*
Universal Disposal Inc .... E 440 286-3153
  Chardon *(G-2773)*
Werlor Inc .... E 419 784-4285
  Defiance *(G-10063)*

TRUCKING & HAULING SVCS: Haulage & Cartage, Light, Local

Arrowhead Transport Co .... E 330 638-2900
  Cortland *(G-9072)*
Brookside Holdings LLC .... E 419 224-7019
  Lima *(G-12749)*
Burch Hydro Inc .... E 740 694-9146
  Fredericktown *(G-11178)*
Burch Hydro Trucking Inc .... E 740 694-9146
  Fredericktown *(G-11179)*
Containerport Group Inc .... E 440 333-1330
  Columbus *(G-7426)*
J M T Cartage Inc .... E 330 478-2430
  Canton *(G-2416)*
Montgomery Trucking Company .... E 740 384-2138
  Wellston *(G-19004)*
Nicolozakes Trckg & Cnstr Inc .... E 740 432-5648
  Cambridge *(G-2124)*
Varney Dispatch Inc .... E 513 682-4200
  Cincinnati *(G-4804)*
William Hafer Drayage Inc .... E 513 771-5000
  Cincinnati *(G-4849)*

TRUCKING & HAULING SVCS: Hazardous Waste

American Waste MGT Svcs Inc .... E 330 856-8800
  Warren *(G-18816)*
Cousins Waste Control LLC .... D 419 726-1500
  Toledo *(G-17839)*
Tfh-Eb Inc .... D 614 253-7246
  Columbus *(G-8833)*
Trans Vac Inc .... E 419 229-8192
  Lima *(G-12903)*

TRUCKING & HAULING SVCS: Heavy Machinery, Local

Back In Black Co .... E 419 425-5555
  Findlay *(G-10992)*
Bob Miller Rigging Inc .... E 419 422-7477
  Findlay *(G-11005)*
Tesar Industrial Contrs Inc .... E 216 741-8008
  Cleveland *(G-6587)*

TRUCKING & HAULING SVCS: Heavy, NEC

B & T Express Inc .... D 330 549-0000
  North Lima *(G-15399)*
Cooper Brothers Trucking LLC .... F 330 784-1717
  Akron *(G-164)*
Diamond Heavy Haul Inc .... E 330 677-8061
  Kent *(G-12365)*
Estes Express Lines Inc .... D 440 327-3884
  North Ridgeville *(G-15463)*
Falcon Transport Co .... C 330 793-1345
  Youngstown *(G-20185)*
Ferrous Metal Transfer .... E 216 671-8500
  Brooklyn *(G-1906)*
Golden Hawk Transportation Co .... D 419 683-3304
  Crestline *(G-9146)*
Homan Transportation Inc .... D 419 465-2626
  Monroeville *(G-14720)*
Iddings Trucking Inc .... E 740 568-1780
  Marietta *(G-13453)*
Knight Transportation Inc .... D 614 308-4900
  Columbus *(G-8002)*

Employee Codes: A=Over 500 employees, B=251-500
C=101-250, D=51-100, E=25-50

TRUCKING & HAULING SVCS: Heavy, NEC

L O G Transportation Inc .... E 440 891-0850
   Berea *(G-1462)*
Mizar Motors Inc .... D 419 729-2400
   Toledo *(G-18065)*
Pitt-Ohio Express LLC .... C 614 801-1064
   Grove City *(G-11592)*
R & J Trucking Inc .... D 740 374-3050
   Marietta *(G-13492)*
Richard Wolfe Trucking Inc .... E 740 392-2445
   Mount Vernon *(G-14920)*
Saro Truck Dispatch Inc .... E 419 873-1358
   Perrysburg *(G-16056)*

TRUCKING & HAULING SVCS: Liquid Petroleum, Exc Local

Advantage Tank Lines Inc .... C 330 427-1010
   Leetonia *(G-12661)*
Autumn Industries Inc .... E 330 372-5002
   Warren *(G-18821)*
Lykins Transportation Inc .... D 513 831-8820
   Milford *(G-14535)*
Ohio Oil Gathering Corporation ...... E 740 828-2892
   Nashport *(G-14953)*

TRUCKING & HAULING SVCS: Liquid, Local

Autumn Industries Inc .... E 330 372-5002
   Warren *(G-18821)*
Bobs Moraine Trucking Inc .... E 937 746-8420
   Franklin *(G-11150)*
Drasc Enterprises Inc .... E 330 852-3254
   Sugarcreek *(G-17544)*
Sidle Transit Service Inc .... E 330 683-2807
   Orrville *(G-15787)*

TRUCKING & HAULING SVCS: Live Poultry

Wendel Poultry Service Inc .... E 419 375-2439
   Fort Recovery *(G-11121)*

TRUCKING & HAULING SVCS: Lumber & Timber

Ferrous Metal Transfer 216 671-8500
   Brooklyn *(G-1906)*

TRUCKING & HAULING SVCS: Machinery, Heavy

Gardner Contracting Company .... E 216 881-3800
   Cleveland *(G-5654)*
Miller Transfer and Rigging Co .... E 330 325-2521
   Rootstown *(G-16598)*
Myers Machinery Movers Inc .... E 614 871-5052
   Grove City *(G-11582)*
Nicolozakes Trckg & Cnstr Inc .... E 740 432-5648
   Cambridge *(G-2124)*
Tesar Industrial Contrs Inc .... E 216 741-8008
   Cleveland *(G-6587)*
Tfi Transportation Inc .... E 330 332-4655
   Salem *(G-16717)*

TRUCKING & HAULING SVCS: Mail Carriers, Contract

44444 LLC .... E 330 502-2023
   Austintown *(G-867)*
G & S Transfer Inc 330 673-3899
   Kent *(G-12370)*
Robert M Neff Inc .... D 614 444-1562
   Columbus *(G-8642)*
Rood Trucking Company Inc .... C 330 652-3519
   Mineral Ridge *(G-14639)*
T&T Enterprises of Ohio Inc .... E 513 942-1141
   West Chester *(G-19236)*
Ted Ruck Co Inc 419 738-2613
   Wapakoneta *(G-18808)*

TRUCKING & HAULING SVCS: Petroleum, Local

Certified Oil Inc .... D 614 421-7500
   Columbus *(G-7244)*
Hilltrux Tank Lines Inc .... E 330 965-1103
   Youngstown *(G-20217)*
Santmyer Oil Co Inc .... D 330 262-6501
   Wooster *(G-19911)*

TRUCKING & HAULING SVCS: Safe Moving, Local

Ray Hamilton Companies .... E 513 641-5400
   Blue Ash *(G-1676)*

TRUCKING & HAULING SVCS: Trailer/Container On Flat Car

American Power LLC .... E 937 235-0418
   Dayton *(G-9331)*

TRUCKING, AUTOMOBILE CARRIER

Akron Centl Engrv Mold Mch Inc .... E 330 794-8704
   Akron *(G-30)*
Cassens Transport Company .... C 937 644-8886
   Marysville *(G-13610)*
Cassens Transport Company .... C 419 727-0520
   Toledo *(G-17794)*
Cowan Systems LLC .... E 330 963-8483
   Twinsburg *(G-18405)*
CRST International Inc .... D 740 599-0008
   Danville *(G-9245)*
Express Twing Recovery Svc Inc .... E 513 881-1900
   West Chester *(G-19199)*
Jack Cooper Transport Co Inc .... C 440 949-2044
   Sheffield Village *(G-16888)*
New England Motor Freight Inc ..... D 513 782-0017
   Cincinnati *(G-4155)*
Ohio Auto Delivery Inc .... E 614 277-1445
   Grove City *(G-11587)*
Quality Carriers Inc .... E 419 222-6800
   Lima *(G-12864)*
R & L Transfer Inc .... D 330 743-3609
   Youngstown *(G-20336)*
United Road Services Inc .... D 419 837-2703
   Toledo *(G-18272)*

TRUCKING, DUMP

Aci Const Co Inc .... E 419 595-4284
   Alvada *(G-567)*
Alan Woods Trucking Inc .... E 513 738-3314
   Hamilton *(G-11690)*
Berner Trucking .... E 419 476-0207
   Toledo *(G-17770)*
Berner Trucking Inc .... C 330 343-5812
   Dover *(G-10178)*
Burkhart Trucking Inc .... E 740 896-2244
   Lowell *(G-13168)*
Carl E Oeder Sons Sand & Grav ..... E 513 494-1555
   Lebanon *(G-12594)*
Coshocton Trucking South Inc ...... C 740 622-1311
   Coshocton *(G-9097)*
D & V Trucking Inc .... E 330 482-9440
   Columbiana *(G-6857)*
Daves Sand & Stone Inc .... E 419 445-9256
   Wauseon *(G-18950)*
Edw C Levy Co .... E 419 822-8286
   Delta *(G-10157)*
Forrest Trucking Company .... E 614 879-8642
   West Jefferson *(G-19252)*
James H Alvis Trucking Inc .... E 513 623-8121
   Harrison *(G-11803)*
K R Drenth Trucking Inc .... E 708 983-6340
   Cincinnati *(G-3898)*
Mikes Trucking Ltd .... E 614 879-8808
   Galloway *(G-11346)*
Monesi Trucking & Eqp Repr Inc .... E 614 921-9183
   Columbus *(G-8184)*
R & J Trucking Inc .... E 800 262-9365
   Youngstown *(G-20335)*
R & J Trucking Inc .... D 330 758-0841
   Shelby *(G-16903)*
R & J Trucking Inc .... D 740 374-3050
   Marietta *(G-13492)*
R & J Trucking Inc .... D 440 960-1508
   Lorain *(G-13072)*
R & J Trucking Inc .... E 419 837-9937
   Perrysburg *(G-16049)*
R E Watson Inc .... E 513 863-0070
   Hamilton *(G-11765)*
Sebastiani Trucking Inc .... D 330 286-0059
   Paris *(G-2210)*
Strawser Equipment & Lsg Inc ...... D 614 444-2521
   Columbus *(G-8797)*
Zeiter Trucking Inc .... E 419 668-2229
   Norwalk *(G-15597)*

TRUCKING, REFRIGERATED: Long-Distance

Continental Express Inc .... B 937 497-2100
   Sidney *(G-16922)*
Crete Carrier Corporation .... C 614 853-4500
   Columbus *(G-7461)*
Montgomery Trucking Company .... E 740 384-2138
   Wellston *(G-19004)*
P C C Refrigerated Ex Inc .... E 614 754-8929
   Columbus *(G-8501)*
T & L Transport Inc .... E 330 674-0655
   Millersburg *(G-14623)*

TRUCKING: Except Local

1st Carrier Corp .... D 740 477-2587
   Circleville *(G-4875)*
A C Leasing Company .... E 513 771-3676
   Cincinnati *(G-2953)*
Advantage Tank Lines Inc .... E 330 491-0474
   North Canton *(G-15321)*
All Pro Freight Systems Inc .... D 440 934-2222
   Avon *(G-874)*
B & H Industries Inc .... E 419 485-8373
   Montpelier *(G-14736)*
Bantam Leasing Inc .... E 513 734-6696
   Amelia *(G-578)*
Barnets Inc .... E 937 452-3275
   Camden *(G-2136)*
Bell Moving and Storage Inc .... E 513 942-7500
   Fairfield *(G-10823)*
Berlin Transportaion LLC .... E 330 674-3395
   Millersburg *(G-14588)*
Bestway Transport Co .... E 419 687-2000
   Plymouth *(G-16216)*
Black Horse Carriers Inc .... C 330 225-2250
   Hinckley *(G-11995)*
Blb Transport Inc .... E 740 474-1341
   Circleville *(G-4879)*
Brendamour Moving & Stor Inc .... D 800 354-9715
   Cincinnati *(G-3129)*
Brent Burris Trucking LLC .... E 419 759-2020
   Ada *(G-3)*
Brookside Holdings LLC .... E 419 925-4457
   Maria Stein *(G-13427)*
Bryan Truck Line Inc .... D 419 485-8373
   Montpelier *(G-14739)*
Building Systems Trnsp Co .... C 740 852-9700
   London *(G-12994)*
BWC Trucking Company Inc .... E 740 532-5188
   Ironton *(G-12284)*
By-Line Transit Inc .... E 937 642-2500
   Marysville *(G-13608)*
Carrier Industries Inc .... B 614 851-6363
   Columbus *(G-7203)*
Century Lines Inc .... E 216 271-0700
   Cleveland *(G-5219)*
Ceva Logistics US Inc .... E 937 578-1160
   East Liberty *(G-10507)*
Circle S Transport Inc .... E 614 207-2184
   Columbus *(G-7276)*
Clayton Weaver Trucking Inc .... E 513 896-6932
   Fairfield *(G-10837)*
Cle Transportation Company .... D 567 805-4008
   Norwalk *(G-15565)*
Cleveland Express Trckg Co Inc .... D 216 348-0922
   Cleveland *(G-5313)*
Clopay Transportation Company .. D 513 381-4800
   Cincinnati *(G-3368)*
Clp Towne Inc 440 234-3324
   Brookpark *(G-1940)*
Competitive Transportation .... E 419 529-5300
   Bellville *(G-1422)*
Concept Freight Service Inc .... E 330 784-1134
   New Franklin *(G-15043)*
Containerport Group Inc .... E 440 333-1330
   Columbus *(G-7426)*
Containerport Group Inc .... E 216 341-4800
   Cleveland *(G-5401)*
Contract Freighters Inc .... A 614 577-0447
   Reynoldsburg *(G-16441)*
Cotter Moving & Storage Co .... E 330 535-5115
   Akron *(G-167)*
Cowan Systems LLC .... C 513 769-4774
   Cincinnati *(G-3436)*
Cowan Systems LLC .... C 513 721-6444
   West Chester *(G-19056)*
Coy Brothers Inc .... E 330 533-6864
   Canfield *(G-2187)*
Craig Transportation Co .... E 419 874-7981
   Maumee *(G-13901)*

Crescent Park Corporation....C...... 513 759-7000
West Chester *(G-19059)*
Dart Trucking Company Inc....E...... 330 549-0994
North Lima *(G-15401)*
Daves Sand & Stone Inc....E...... 419 445-9256
Wauseon *(G-18950)*
Davidson Trucking Inc....E...... 419 288-2318
Bradner *(G-1809)*
Dayton Freight Lines Inc....E...... 419 661-8600
Perrysburg *(G-15993)*
Dayton Freight Lines Inc....E...... 614 860-1080
Columbus *(G-7493)*
Dedicated Logistics Inc....D...... 513 275-1135
West Chester *(G-19060)*
Dhl Supply Chain (usa)....E...... 614 492-6614
Lockbourne *(G-12950)*
Dhl Supply Chain (usa)....E...... 513 942-1575
Cincinnati *(G-3487)*
Dill-Elam Inc....E...... 513 575-0017
Loveland *(G-13123)*
Direct Express Delivery Svc....E...... 513 541-0600
Cincinnati *(G-3492)*
Dist-Trans Inc....C...... 614 497-1660
Columbus *(G-7526)*
Distribution and Trnsp Svc Inc....E...... 937 295-3343
Fort Loramie *(G-11110)*
Disttech LLC....D...... 800 321-3143
Cleveland *(G-5490)*
Drasc Enterprises Inc....E...... 330 852-3254
Sugarcreek *(G-17544)*
Elmco Trucking Inc....E...... 419 983-2010
Bloomville *(G-1519)*
Excel Trucking LLC....E...... 614 826-1988
Columbus *(G-7617)*
Exel Inc....B...... 614 865-8500
Westerville *(G-19305)*
Falcon Transport Co....D...... 330 793-1345
Youngstown *(G-20186)*
FANTON Logistics Inc....D...... 216 341-2400
Cleveland *(G-5572)*
Federal Express Corporation....B...... 614 492-6106
Columbus *(G-7646)*
Fedex Custom Critical Inc....B...... 234 310-4090
Uniontown *(G-18519)*
Fedex Freight Corporation....E...... 419 729-1755
Toledo *(G-17883)*
Fedex Freight Corporation....D...... 800 344-6448
West Jefferson *(G-19251)*
Fedex Freight Corporation....E...... 800 354-9489
Zanesville *(G-20477)*
Fedex Ground Package Sys Inc....D...... 513 942-4330
West Chester *(G-19200)*
First Group Investment Partnr....D...... 513 241-2200
Cincinnati *(G-3618)*
Firstenterprises Inc....B...... 740 369-5100
Delaware *(G-10096)*
Firstgroup Usa Inc....B...... 513 241-2200
Cincinnati *(G-3629)*
Foster Sales & Delivery Inc....D...... 740 245-0200
Bidwell *(G-1495)*
Garber Ag Freight Inc....E...... 937 548-8400
Greenville *(G-11501)*
General Transport Incorporated....E...... 330 786-3400
Akron *(G-234)*
Glm Transport Inc....E...... 419 363-2041
Rockford *(G-16562)*
Global Workplace Solutions LLC....D...... 513 759-6000
West Chester *(G-19082)*
GMC Excavation & Trucking....E...... 419 468-0121
Galion *(G-11300)*
Great Lakes Cartage Company....D...... 330 702-1930
Youngstown *(G-20206)*
Green Lines Transportation Inc....E...... 330 863-2111
Malvern *(G-13251)*
H O C J Inc....E...... 614 539-4601
Grove City *(G-11569)*
Harbor Freight Tools Usa Inc....D...... 513 598-4897
Cincinnati *(G-3736)*
Harte-Hanks Trnsp Svcs....D...... 513 458-7600
Cincinnati *(G-3739)*
Hillandale Farms Trnsp....D...... 740 893-2232
Johnstown *(G-12341)*
Home Moving & Storage Co Inc....E...... 614 445-6377
Columbus *(G-7851)*
Horizon Freight System Inc....E...... 216 341-3322
Cleveland *(G-5773)*
Horizon Freight System Inc....E...... 216 341-7410
Cleveland *(G-5774)*
Hs Express LLC....D...... 419 729-2400
Toledo *(G-17963)*
HTI - Hall Trucking Inc....E...... 419 423-9555
Findlay *(G-11047)*
Integres Global Logistics Inc....D...... 866 347-2101
Medina *(G-14081)*
J & B Leasing Inc of Ohio....E...... 419 269-1440
Toledo *(G-17979)*
J B Hunt Transport Inc....C...... 440 786-8436
Bedford Heights *(G-1354)*
J B Hunt Transport Inc....C...... 419 547-2777
Clyde *(G-6816)*
J T Express Inc....E...... 513 727-8185
Monroe *(G-14699)*
J-Trac Inc....E...... 419 524-3456
Mansfield *(G-13315)*
Jaro Transportation Svcs Inc....D...... 330 393-5659
Warren *(G-18868)*
Jarrells Moving & Transport Co....D...... 330 764-4333
Seville *(G-16841)*
JB Hunt Transport Svcs Inc....A...... 614 335-6681
Columbus *(G-7937)*
Jet Express Inc....D...... 937 274-7033
Dayton *(G-9640)*
K & P Trucking LLC....D...... 419 935-8646
Willard *(G-19621)*
Kenan Advantage Group Inc....C...... 877 999-2524
North Canton *(G-15349)*
Keystone Freight Corp....E...... 614 542-0320
Columbus *(G-7984)*
KF Express LLC....E...... 614 258-8858
Powell *(G-16342)*
Kllee Trucking Inc....D...... 740 867-6454
Chesapeake *(G-2785)*
Kuhnle Brothers Inc....C...... 440 564-7168
Newbury *(G-15258)*
L A King Trucking Inc....E...... 419 727-9398
Toledo *(G-17998)*
L J Navy Trucking Company....E...... 614 754-8929
Columbus *(G-8022)*
Lincoln Moving & Storage Co....D...... 216 741-5500
Cleveland *(G-5943)*
LT Harnett Trucking Inc....E...... 440 997-5528
Ashtabula *(G-753)*
Lykins Companies Inc....C...... 513 831-8820
Milford *(G-14533)*
M & B Trucking Express Corp....E...... 440 236-8820
Columbia Station *(G-6848)*
Maines Collision Repr & Bdy Sp....D...... 937 322-4618
Springfield *(G-17228)*
Mansfield Whsng & Dist Inc....C...... 419 522-3510
Ontario *(G-15699)*
Martin Trnsp Systems Inc....D...... 419 726-1348
Toledo *(G-18045)*
Material Suppliers Inc....E...... 419 298-2440
Edgerton *(G-10583)*
Merchants 5 Star Ltd....D...... 740 373-0313
Marietta *(G-13475)*
Miarer Transportation Inc....E...... 419 665-2334
Gibsonburg *(G-11403)*
Midwest Logistics Systems....B...... 419 584-1414
Celina *(G-2658)*
Murray Leasing Inc....C...... 330 386-4757
East Liverpool *(G-10526)*
National Highway Equipment Co....D...... 614 459-4900
Columbus *(G-8219)*
National Trnsp Solutions Inc....D...... 330 405-2660
Twinsburg *(G-18450)*
Nicholas Carney-Mc Inc....D...... 330 792-5460
Youngstown *(G-20301)*
Nick Strimbu Inc....D...... 330 448-4046
Brookfield *(G-1900)*
Nick Strimbu Inc....D...... 330 448-4046
Dover *(G-10203)*
Noramco Transport Corp....E...... 513 245-9050
Cincinnati *(G-4172)*
Oeder Carl E Sons Sand & Grav....E...... 513 494-1238
Lebanon *(G-12632)*
Ohio Carriers Corp....D...... 330 878-5311
Dover *(G-10204)*
OMI Transportation Inc....E...... 419 241-8711
Toledo *(G-18106)*
One Way Express Incorporated....E...... 440 439-9182
Cleveland *(G-6206)*
Osborne Trucking Company....D...... 513 874-2090
Fairfield *(G-10890)*
P & D Transportation Inc....E...... 614 577-1130
Columbus *(G-8500)*
P I & I Motor Express Inc....C...... 330 448-4035
Masury *(G-13866)*
PAm Transportation Svcs Inc....D...... 419 935-9501
Willard *(G-19624)*
Panther II Transportation Inc....C...... 800 685-0657
Medina *(G-14111)*
Panther Premium Logistics Inc....B...... 800 685-0657
Medina *(G-14112)*
Peak Transportation Inc....D...... 419 874-5201
Perrysburg *(G-16038)*
Penske Logistics LLC....D...... 330 626-7623
Streetsboro *(G-17425)*
Peoples Services Inc....E...... 330 453-3709
Canton *(G-2490)*
Pitt-Ohio Express LLC....B...... 216 433-9000
Cleveland *(G-6284)*
Planes Moving & Storage Inc....C...... 513 759-6000
West Chester *(G-19129)*
Platinum Express Inc....D...... 937 235-9540
Dayton *(G-9812)*
Predator Trucking Company....E...... 419 849-2601
Woodville *(G-19823)*
Premium Trnsp Logistics LLC....E...... 419 861-3430
Toledo *(G-18133)*
Pride Transportation Inc....E...... 419 424-2145
Findlay *(G-11077)*
R & L Transfer Inc....C...... 216 531-3324
Norwalk *(G-15589)*
R & L Transfer Inc....C...... 330 482-5800
Columbiana *(G-6862)*
R & S Lines Inc....E...... 419 682-7807
Stryker *(G-17538)*
R E Watson Inc....E...... 513 863-0070
Hamilton *(G-11765)*
R+I Pramount Trnsp Systems Inc....B...... 937 382-1494
Wilmington *(G-19780)*
Ray Bertolini Trucking Co....E...... 330 867-0666
Akron *(G-405)*
Rising Sun Express LLC....D...... 937 596-6167
Jackson Center *(G-12324)*
Rjw Inc....E...... 216 398-6090
Independence *(G-12250)*
RL Trucking Inc....C...... 419 732-4177
Port Clinton *(G-16254)*
Robert Neff & Son Inc....E...... 740 454-0128
Zanesville *(G-20530)*
Rood Trucking Company Inc....C...... 330 652-3519
Mineral Ridge *(G-14639)*
Rose Transport Inc....E...... 614 864-4004
Reynoldsburg *(G-16480)*
Roseville Motor Express Inc....E...... 614 921-2121
Columbus *(G-8650)*
Rrr Express LLC....C...... 800 723-3424
West Chester *(G-19143)*
Rt80 Express Inc....E...... 330 706-0900
Barberton *(G-978)*
Sanfrey Freight Services Inc....E...... 330 372-1883
Warren *(G-18896)*
Schneider Nat Carriers Inc....E...... 740 362-6910
Delaware *(G-10126)*
Schneider National Inc....B...... 419 673-0254
Kenton *(G-12423)*
Schroeder Associates Inc....E...... 419 258-5075
Antwerp *(G-620)*
Security Storage Co Inc....D...... 513 961-2700
Cincinnati *(G-4490)*
Shippers Consolidated Dist....E...... 216 579-9303
Cleveland *(G-6478)*
Shoreline Transportation Inc....C...... 440 878-2000
Strongsville *(G-17508)*
Short Freight Lines Inc....E...... 419 729-1691
Toledo *(G-18185)*
Slay Transportation Co Inc....C...... 740 865-2910
Sardis *(G-16815)*
Smith Trucking Inc....E...... 419 841-8676
Sylvania *(G-17616)*
Spader Freight Carriers Inc....D...... 419 547-1117
Clyde *(G-6823)*
State-Wide Express Inc....D...... 216 676-4600
Cleveland *(G-6532)*
STC Transporation Inc....E...... 216 441-6217
Cleveland *(G-6533)*
Style Crest Transport Inc....D...... 419 332-7369
Fremont *(G-11225)*
Swx Enterprises Inc....E...... 216 676-4600
Brookpark *(G-1956)*
Thoman Weil Moving & Stor Co....E...... 513 251-5000
Cincinnati *(G-4651)*
Three-D Transport Inc....E...... 419 924-5368
West Unity *(G-19281)*
Thyssenkrupp Logistics Inc....D...... 419 662-1800
Northwood *(G-15545)*
Tkx Logistics....E...... 419 662-1800
Northwood *(G-15546)*

Employee Codes: A=Over 500 employees, B=251-500
C=101-250, D=51-100, E=25-50

2018 Harris Ohio
Services Directory

1645

SERVICES

Total Package Express Inc ....E 513 741-5500
Cincinnati *(G-4662)*
Tpg Noramco LLC ....E 513 245-9050
Cincinnati *(G-4676)*
Transportation Unlimited Inc ....A 216 426-0088
Cleveland *(G-6613)*
Triad Transport Inc ....E 614 491-9497
Columbus *(G-8868)*
Trio Trucking Inc ....E 513 679-7100
Cincinnati *(G-4701)*
Triple Ladys Agency Inc ....E 330 274-1100
Mantua *(G-13396)*
UPS Ground Freight Inc ....E 330 448-0440
Masury *(G-13869)*
US Expediting Logistics LLC ....E 937 235-1014
Vandalia *(G-18704)*
USF Holland LLC ....C 937 233-7600
Dayton *(G-9959)*
USF Holland LLC ....C 216 941-4340
Cleveland *(G-6678)*
Vance Road Enterprises Inc ....E 937 268-6953
Dayton *(G-9964)*
W L Logan Trucking Company ....C 330 478-1404
Canton *(G-2580)*
Wannemacher Enterprises Inc ....D 419 225-9060
Lima *(G-12912)*
William R Morse ....E 440 352-2600
Painesville *(G-15887)*
World Shipping Inc ....E 440 356-7676
Cleveland *(G-6759)*
Xpo Cnw Inc ....C 440 716-8971
North Olmsted *(G-15451)*
Xpo Logistics Freight Inc ....C 614 876-7100
Columbus *(G-9014)*
Yrc Inc ....D 614 878-9281
Columbus *(G-9023)*
Zipline Logistics LLC ....D 888 469-4754
Columbus *(G-9027)*
Zone Transportation Co ....D 440 324-3544
Elyria *(G-10695)*

TRUCKING: Local, With Storage

A C Leasing Company ....E 513 771-3676
Cincinnati *(G-2953)*
A Plus Expediting & Logistics ....E 937 424-0220
Dayton *(G-9298)*
Abco Contracting LLC ....E 419 973-4772
Toledo *(G-17739)*
All My Sons Moving & Storge of ....E 614 405-7202
Hilliard *(G-11877)*
All Pro Freight Systems Inc ....D 440 934-2222
Avon *(G-874)*
Arms Trucking Co Inc ....E 800 362-1343
Huntsburg *(G-12156)*
Atlas Home Moving & Storage ....E 614 445-8831
Columbus *(G-7071)*
Bridge Logistics Inc ....E 513 874-7444
West Chester *(G-19193)*
Circle T Logistics Inc ....E 740 262-5096
Marion *(G-13530)*
Clark Trucking Inc ....C 937 642-0335
East Liberty *(G-10508)*
Cleveland Express Trckg Co Inc ....D 216 348-0922
Cleveland *(G-5313)*
Containerport Group Inc ....E 216 341-4800
Cleveland *(G-5401)*
County of Hancock ....E 419 422-7433
Findlay *(G-11018)*
Dhl Supply Chain (usa) ....E 419 727-4318
Toledo *(G-17852)*
Distribution and Trnsp Svc Inc ....E 937 295-3343
Fort Loramie *(G-11110)*
Essential Freight Systems Inc ....D 330 468-5898
Northfield *(G-15514)*
Getgo Transportation Co LLC ....E 419 666-6850
Millbury *(G-14579)*
Henderson Trucking Inc ....E 740 369-6100
Delaware *(G-10105)*
J-Trac Inc ....E 419 524-3456
Mansfield *(G-13315)*
King Tut Logistics LLC ....E 614 538-0509
Columbus *(G-7994)*
Lincoln Moving & Storage Co ....D 216 741-5500
Cleveland *(G-5943)*
Locker Moving & Storage Inc ....E 330 784-0477
Canton *(G-2439)*
M G Q Inc ....E 419 992-4236
Tiffin *(G-17683)*
Mano Logistics LLC ....E 330 454-1307
Canton *(G-2444)*
Marietta Industrial Entps Inc ....D 740 373-2252
Marietta *(G-13470)*
Miami Valley Bekins Inc ....E 937 278-4296
Dayton *(G-9726)*
Mxd Group Inc ....D 866 711-3129
New Albany *(G-14995)*
Neighborhood Logistics Co Inc ....E 440 466-0020
Geneva *(G-11366)*
Picklesimer Trucking Inc ....E 937 642-1091
Marysville *(G-13644)*
Piqua Transfer & Storage Co ....D 937 773-3743
Piqua *(G-16160)*
Planes Mvg & Stor Co Columbus ....D 614 777-9090
Columbus *(G-8548)*
Proterra Inc ....E 216 383-8449
Wickliffe *(G-19612)*
R K Campf Corp ....E 330 332-7089
Salem *(G-16709)*
Ray Hamilton Companies ....E 513 641-5400
Blue Ash *(G-1676)*
Rmb Enterprises Inc ....D 513 539-3431
Middletown *(G-14454)*
Shippers Consolidated Dist ....E 216 579-9303
Cleveland *(G-6478)*
Shoreline Express Inc ....E 440 878-3750
Strongsville *(G-17507)*
Smithfoods Trucking Inc ....E 330 684-6502
Orrville *(G-15788)*
Spartan Whse & Dist Co Inc ....D 614 497-1777
Columbus *(G-8758)*
Spears Transf & Expediting Inc ....E 937 275-2443
Dayton *(G-9895)*
State-Wide Express Inc ....D 216 676-4600
Cleveland *(G-6532)*
Taylor Distributing Company ....D 513 771-1850
Cincinnati *(G-4626)*
Thoman Weil Moving & Stor Co ....E 513 251-5000
Cincinnati *(G-4651)*
Tri Modal Service Inc ....E 614 876-6325
Columbus *(G-8867)*
Van Howards Lines Inc ....E 937 235-0007
Dayton *(G-9963)*
Van Mayberrys & Storage Inc ....E 937 298-8800
Moraine *(G-14832)*
Van Mills Lines Inc ....C 440 846-0200
Strongsville *(G-17521)*
Van Stevens Lines Inc ....E 419 729-8871
Toledo *(G-18286)*
William R Morse ....E 440 352-2600
Painesville *(G-15887)*
Willis Day Management Inc ....E 419 476-8000
Toledo *(G-18311)*
Wnb Group LLC ....E 513 641-5400
Cincinnati *(G-4855)*
Wooster Motor Ways Inc ....C 330 264-9557
Wooster *(G-19932)*
Yowell Transportation Svc Inc ....D 937 294-5933
Moraine *(G-14838)*

TRUCKING: Local, Without Storage

1st Carrier Corp ....D 740 477-2587
Circleville *(G-4875)*
A L Smith Trucking Inc ....E 937 526-3651
Versailles *(G-18722)*
Advantage Tank Lines Inc ....C 330 427-1010
Leetonia *(G-12661)*
AG Trucking Inc ....E 937 497-7770
Sidney *(G-16911)*
Allan Hunter Construction LLC ....E 330 634-9882
Akron *(G-67)*
American Bulk Commodities Inc ....C 330 758-0841
Youngstown *(G-20103)*
Atlantic Coastal Trucking ....C 201 438-6500
Delaware *(G-10072)*
B & H Industries Inc ....E 419 485-8373
Montpelier *(G-14736)*
B & L Transport Inc ....E 866 848-2888
Millersburg *(G-14586)*
B D Transportation Inc ....E 937 773-9280
Piqua *(G-16135)*
Bell Moving and Storage Inc ....E 513 942-7500
Fairfield *(G-10823)*
Besl Transfer Co ....E 513 242-3456
Cincinnati *(G-3100)*
Big Blue Trucking Inc ....E 330 372-1421
Warren *(G-18830)*
Blatt Trucking Co Inc ....E 419 898-0002
Rocky Ridge *(G-16566)*
Blb Transport Inc ....E 740 474-1341
Circleville *(G-4879)*
Bowling Transportation Inc ....D 419 436-9590
Fostoria *(G-11124)*
Brookside Holdings LLC ....E 419 925-4457
Maria Stein *(G-13427)*
Browning-Ferris Industries LLC ....D 330 393-0385
Warren *(G-18832)*
Bryan Truck Line Inc ....D 419 485-8373
Montpelier *(G-14739)*
Building Systems Trnsp Co ....C 740 852-9700
London *(G-12994)*
C & G Transportation Inc ....E 419 288-2653
Wayne *(G-18977)*
C-Z Trucking Co ....D 330 758-2313
Poland *(G-16221)*
Carrier Industries Inc ....B 614 851-6363
Columbus *(G-7203)*
Century Lines Inc ....E 216 271-0700
Cleveland *(G-5219)*
Chambers Leasing Systems Corp ....E 419 726-9747
Toledo *(G-17801)*
Chapin Logistics Inc ....E 440 327-1360
North Ridgeville *(G-15459)*
Charles D McIntosh Trckg Inc ....E 937 378-3803
Georgetown *(G-11389)*
Cheeseman LLC ....B 419 375-4132
Fort Recovery *(G-11114)*
Circle S Transport Inc ....E 614 207-2184
Columbus *(G-7276)*
City Dash Inc ....C 513 562-2000
Cincinnati *(G-3357)*
Clary Trucking Inc ....E 740 702-4242
Chillicothe *(G-2827)*
Clayton Weaver Trucking Inc ....E 513 896-6932
Fairfield *(G-10837)*
Clp Towne Inc ....E 440 234-3324
Brookpark *(G-1940)*
Competitive Transportation ....E 419 529-5300
Bellville *(G-1422)*
Continental Express Inc ....B 937 497-2100
Sidney *(G-16922)*
Continental Transport Inc ....E 513 360-2960
Monroe *(G-14692)*
Cotter Moving & Storage Co ....E 330 535-5115
Akron *(G-167)*
Cowen Truck Line Inc ....D 419 938-3401
Perrysville *(G-16078)*
D&D Trucking and Services Inc ....E 419 692-3205
Delphos *(G-10140)*
Dale Ross Trucking Inc ....E 937 981-2168
Greenfield *(G-11484)*
Davidson Trucking Inc ....E 419 288-2318
Bradner *(G-1809)*
Dedicated Logistics Inc ....D 513 275-1135
West Chester *(G-19060)*
Dedicated Transport LLC ....C 216 641-2500
Brooklyn Heights *(G-1914)*
Dill-Elam Inc ....E 513 575-0017
Loveland *(G-13123)*
Dingledine Trucking Company ....E 937 652-3454
Urbana *(G-18585)*
Disttech LLC ....D 800 321-3143
Cleveland *(G-5490)*
DOT Smith LLC ....E 740 245-5105
Thurman *(G-17670)*
Ed Wilson & Son Trucking Inc ....E 330 549-9287
New Springfield *(G-15129)*
Emory Rothenbuhler & Sons ....E 740 458-1432
Beallsville *(G-1140)*
Falcon Transport Co ....D 330 793-1345
Youngstown *(G-20186)*
Federal Express Corporation ....C 800 463-3339
Bedford *(G-1306)*
Fedex Freight Inc ....D 330 645-0879
Akron *(G-223)*
Fedex Freight Corporation ....E 800 354-9489
Zanesville *(G-20477)*
Fedex Ground Package Sys Inc ....B 800 463-3339
Grove City *(G-11560)*
Findlay Truck Line Inc ....D 419 422-1945
Findlay *(G-11029)*
First Group Investment Partnr ....D 513 241-2200
Cincinnati *(G-3618)*
Firstgroup Usa Inc ....B 513 241-2200
Cincinnati *(G-3629)*
Five Star Trucking Inc ....E 440 953-9300
Willoughby *(G-19665)*
Fraley & Schilling Inc ....C 740 598-4118
Brilliant *(G-1868)*
Garber Ag Freight Inc ....E 937 548-8400
Greenville *(G-11501)*

SERVICES SECTION

TRUCKING: Local, Without Storage

Company	Code	Phone
Garner Trucking Inc	C	419 422-5742
Findlay (G-11035)		
Glm Transport Inc	E	419 363-2041
Rockford (G-16562)		
GMC Excavation & Trucking	E	419 468-0121
Galion (G-11300)		
Golden Hawk Inc	D	419 683-3304
Crestline (G-9145)		
Great Lakes Cartage Company		330 702-1930
Youngstown (G-20206)		
H & W Holdings LLC	E	800 826-3560
South Point (G-17087)		
H L C Trucking Inc	D	740 676-6181
Shadyside (G-16849)		
H T I Express	E	419 423-9555
Findlay (G-11039)		
Heartland Express Inc	C	614 870-8628
Columbus (G-7817)		
Henderson Trucking Inc	E	740 369-6100
Delaware (G-10105)		
Henderson Turf Farm Inc	E	937 748-1559
Franklin (G-11158)		
Home Run Inc	E	800 543-9198
Xenia (G-20061)		
Hyway Trucking Company	D	419 423-7145
Findlay (G-11049)		
Imperial Express Inc	E	937 399-9400
Springfield (G-17210)		
Innovative Logistics Svcs Inc	D	330 468-6422
Northfield (G-15517)		
Integrity Ex Logistics LLC	C	888 374-5138
Cincinnati (G-3828)		
International Truck & Eng Corp	A	937 390-4045
Springfield (G-17214)		
J P Jenks Inc	E	440 428-4500
Madison (G-13226)		
J P Transportation Company	E	513 424-6978
Middletown (G-14430)		
J T Express Inc	E	513 727-8185
Monroe (G-14699)		
J-Trac Inc	E	419 524-3456
Mansfield (G-13315)		
Jet Express Inc	D	937 274-7033
Dayton (G-9640)		
John Brown Trucking Inc	E	330 758-0841
Youngstown (G-20239)		
Kace Logistics LLC	E	419 273-3388
Toledo (G-17990)		
Kenan Advantage Group Inc	C	877 999-2524
North Canton (G-15349)		
KF Express LLC	E	614 258-8858
Powell (G-16342)		
Klingshirn & Sons Trucking	E	937 338-5000
Burkettsville (G-2058)		
KMu Trucking & Excvtg Inc	E	440 934-1008
Avon (G-903)		
Knight Transportation Inc	D	614 308-4900
Columbus (G-8002)		
Ktib Inc	E	330 722-7935
Medina (G-14093)		
Kuhnle Brothers Inc	C	440 564-7168
Newbury (G-15258)		
Kuntzman Trucking Inc	E	330 821-9160
Alliance (G-543)		
L V Trucking Inc	E	614 275-4994
Columbus (G-8024)		
Lairson Trucking LLC	E	513 894-0452
Hamilton (G-11751)		
Lesaint Logistics Inc	C	513 874-3900
West Chester (G-19105)		
Locker Moving & Storage Inc	E	330 784-0477
Canton (G-2439)		
LT Harnett Trucking Inc	E	440 997-5520
Ashtabula (G-753)		
M C Trucking Company LLC	E	937 584-2486
Wilmington (G-19771)		
Mail Contractors America Inc	C	513 769-5967
Cincinnati (G-4014)		
Martin Trnsp Systems Inc	D	419 726-1348
Toledo (G-18045)		
Mid America Trucking Company	E	216 447-0814
Cleveland (G-6051)		
Midwest Logistics Systems	B	419 584-1414
Celina (G-2658)		
Moeller Trucking Inc	D	419 925-4799
Maria Stein (G-13429)		
Murray Leasing Inc	C	330 386-4757
East Liverpool (G-10526)		
Myers Machinery Movers Inc	E	614 871-5052
Grove City (G-11582)		
National Highway Equipment Co	D	614 459-4900
Columbus (G-8219)		
National Trnsp Solutions Inc	D	330 405-2660
Twinsburg (G-18450)		
Nb Trucking Inc	E	740 335-9331
Washington Court Hou (G-18937)		
Neighborhood Logistics Co Inc	E	440 466-0020
Geneva (G-11366)		
Nicholas Carney-Mc Inc	D	330 792-5460
Youngstown (G-20301)		
Northcutt Trucking Inc	E	440 458-5139
Elyria (G-10663)		
Ohio Oil Gathering Corporation	E	740 828-2892
Nashport (G-14953)		
Ohio Transport Corporation	D	513 539-0576
Middletown (G-14446)		
One Way Express Incorporated	E	440 439-9182
Cleveland (G-6206)		
Otis Wright & Sons Inc	E	419 227-4400
Lima (G-12852)		
P & D Transportation Inc	E	614 577-1130
Columbus (G-8500)		
P I & I Motor Express Inc	C	330 448-4035
Masury (G-13866)		
Panther II Transportation Inc	C	800 685-0657
Medina (G-14111)		
Panther Premium Logistics Inc	B	800 685-0657
Medina (G-14112)		
Peak Transportation Inc	D	419 874-5201
Perrysburg (G-16038)		
Peoples Services Inc	E	330 453-3709
Canton (G-2490)		
PGT Trucking Inc	E	419 943-3437
Leipsic (G-12664)		
Pierceton Trucking Co Inc	E	740 446-0114
Gallipolis (G-11335)		
Pitt-Ohio Express LLC	D	419 729-8173
Toledo (G-18127)		
Pitt-Ohio Express LLC	D	513 860-3424
West Chester (G-19221)		
Pitt-Ohio Express LLC	B	216 433-9000
Cleveland (G-6284)		
Powers Equipment	E	740 746-8220
Sugar Grove (G-17542)		
Pride Transportation Inc	E	419 424-2145
Findlay (G-11077)		
Proline Xpress Inc	E	440 777-8120
North Olmsted (G-15440)		
R & L Transfer Inc	C	216 531-3324
Norwalk (G-15589)		
R & L Transfer Inc	C	330 482-5800
Columbiana (G-6862)		
Ramos Trucking Corporation	E	216 781-0770
Cleveland (G-6351)		
Rands Trucking Inc	E	740 397-1144
Mount Vernon (G-14918)		
Ray Bertolini Trucking Co	E	330 867-0666
Akron (G-405)		
Reis Trucking Inc	E	513 353-1960
Cleves (G-6805)		
Reliable Appl Installation Inc	E	614 246-6840
Columbus (G-8612)		
Reliable Appl Installation Inc	D	330 784-7474
Akron (G-409)		
Republic Services Inc	E	513 771-4200
Cincinnati (G-4408)		
Rick Kuntz Trucking Inc	E	330 296-9311
Windham (G-19803)		
Ricketts Excavating Inc	E	740 687-0338
Lancaster (G-12569)		
Rising Sun Express LLC	D	937 596-6167
Jackson Center (G-12324)		
Rjw Trucking Company Ltd	E	740 363-5343
Delaware (G-10124)		
Rmx Freight Systems Inc	E	740 849-2374
Roseville (G-16602)		
Ron Carrocce Trucking Company	C	330 758-0841
Youngstown (G-20357)		
Ross Consolidated Corp	D	440 748-5800
Grafton (G-11444)		
Rt80 Express Inc	E	330 706-0900
Barberton (G-978)		
Rumpke Waste Inc	D	937 378-4126
Georgetown (G-11397)		
Rumpke Waste Inc	D	513 242-4401
Cincinnati (G-4456)		
Rumpke Waste Inc	C	937 548-1939
Greenville (G-11517)		
S B Morabito Trucking Inc	D	216 441-3070
Cleveland (G-6426)		
Sanfrey Freight Services Inc	E	330 372-1883
Warren (G-18896)		
Schindewolf Express Inc	D	937 585-5919
De Graff (G-10016)		
Schroeder Associates Inc	E	419 258-5075
Antwerp (G-620)		
SDS Earth Moving Inc	E	330 358-2132
Diamond (G-10172)		
Sewell Motor Express Co	D	937 382-3847
Wilmington (G-19787)		
Shoreline Transportation Inc	C	440 878-2000
Strongsville (G-17508)		
Slay Transportation Co Inc	C	740 865-2910
Sardis (G-16815)		
Spears Transf & Expediting Inc	E	937 275-2443
Dayton (G-9895)		
Spring Grove Rsrce Rcovery Inc	D	513 681-6242
Cincinnati (G-4565)		
State-Wide Express Inc	E	216 676-4600
Cleveland (G-6532)		
Style Crest Transport Inc	E	419 332-7369
Fremont (G-11225)		
Su-Jon Enterprises	E	330 372-1100
Warren (G-18905)		
Sylvester Materials Co	E	419 841-3874
Sylvania (G-17621)		
Todd A Ruck Inc	E	614 527-9927
Hilliard (G-11959)		
Trans-States Express Inc	C	513 679-7100
Cincinnati (G-4679)		
Transmerica Svcs Technical Sup	E	740 282-3695
Steubenville (G-17338)		
Transportation Unlimited Inc	A	216 426-0088
Cleveland (G-6613)		
Tricont Trucking Company	C	614 527-7398
Columbus (G-8869)		
Trio Trucking Inc	E	513 679-7100
Cincinnati (G-4701)		
Triple Ladys Agency Inc	E	330 274-1100
Mantua (G-13396)		
Tsm Logistics LLC	E	419 234-6074
Rockford (G-16565)		
TV Minority Company Inc	E	937 226-1559
Dayton (G-9941)		
U-Haul Neighborhood Dealer -Ce	E	419 929-3724
New London (G-15071)		
UPS Ground Freight Inc	C	330 659-6693
Richfield (G-16531)		
UPS Ground Freight Inc	E	937 236-4700
Dayton (G-9957)		
USF Holland Inc	D	740 441-1200
Gallipolis (G-11340)		
USF Holland LLC	C	937 233-7600
Dayton (G-9959)		
USF Holland LLC	C	513 874-8960
West Chester (G-19241)		
USF Holland LLC	C	614 529-9300
Columbus (G-8926)		
USF Holland LLC	C	216 941-4340
Cleveland (G-6678)		
Vallejo Company	E	216 741-3933
Cleveland (G-6682)		
Van Howards Lines Inc	E	937 235-0007
Dayton (G-9963)		
Van Mills Lines Inc	C	440 846-0200
Strongsville (G-17521)		
Vexor Technology Inc	E	330 721-9773
Medina (G-14137)		
Vin Devers		888 847-9535
Sylvania (G-17626)		
Vision Express Inc	E	740 922-8848
Uhrichsville (G-18496)		
Vitran Express Inc	C	614 870-2255
Columbus (G-8947)		
W L Logan Trucking Company	C	330 478-1404
Canton (G-2580)		
Wannemacher Enterprises Inc	E	419 225-9060
Lima (G-12912)		
Waste Management Ohio Inc	D	440 201-1235
Solon (G-17066)		
Waste Management Ohio Inc	D	800 343-6047
Fairborn (G-10811)		
Waste Management Ohio Inc	E	440 286-7116
Chardon (G-2777)		
Waste Management Ohio Inc	C	800 343-6047
Fairborn (G-10812)		
Westhafer Trucking Inc	E	330 698-3030
Apple Creek (G-628)		
Wooster Motor Ways Inc	C	330 264-9557
Wooster (G-19932)		

Employee Codes: A=Over 500 employees, B=251-500
C=101-250, D=51-100, E=25-50

TRUCKING: Local, Without Storage

Xpo Logistics Freight Inc ..... E 937 898-9808
  Dayton (G-10005)
Xpo Logistics Freight Inc ..... E 937 364-2361
  Hillsboro (G-11993)
Xpo Logistics Freight Inc ..... E 740 922-5614
  Uhrichsville (G-18497)
Xpo Logistics Freight Inc ..... C 513 870-0044
  West Chester (G-19244)
Xpo Logistics Freight Inc ..... C 216 433-1000
  Parma (G-15919)
Xpo Logistics Freight Inc ..... C 614 876-7100
  Columbus (G-9014)
Xpo Logistics Freight Inc ..... D 330 896-7300
  Uniontown (G-18544)
Yrc Inc ..... D 330 659-4151
  Richfield (G-16534)
Yrc Inc ..... B 419 729-0631
  Toledo (G-18327)
Zemba Bros Inc ..... E 740 452-1880
  Zanesville (G-20561)
Zone Transportation Co ..... D 440 324-3544
  Elyria (G-10695)

TRUCKING: Long-Distance, Less Than Truckload

City Dash Inc ..... C 513 562-2000
  Cincinnati (G-3357)
Dayton Freight Lines Inc ..... D 937 236-4880
  Dayton (G-9475)
Estes Express Lines Inc ..... E 614 275-6000
  Columbus (G-7614)
Estes Express Lines Inc ..... E 419 531-1500
  Toledo (G-17871)
Fedex Freight Inc ..... D 330 645-0879
  Akron (G-223)
Fedex Freight Inc ..... C 937 233-4826
  Dayton (G-9543)
Fedex Freight Corporation ..... E 800 390-0159
  Mansfield (G-13301)
Fedex Freight Corporation ..... E 800 521-3505
  Lima (G-12781)
Fedex Freight Corporation ..... C 800 728-8190
  Northwood (G-15532)
Franklin Specialty Trnspt Inc ..... D 614 529-7900
  Columbus (G-7699)
Old Dominion Freight Line Inc ..... E 330 545-8628
  Girard (G-11422)
Old Dominion Freight Line Inc ..... C 513 771-1486
  West Chester (G-19125)
Old Dominion Freight Line Inc ..... E 419 726-4032
  Toledo (G-18104)
Old Dominion Freight Line Inc ..... B 614 491-3903
  Columbus (G-8463)
Partnership LLC ..... E 440 471-8310
  Cleveland (G-6248)
USF Holland Inc ..... D 740 441-1200
  Gallipolis (G-11340)
USF Holland LLC ..... C 513 874-8960
  West Chester (G-19241)
USF Holland LLC ..... D 419 354-6633
  Bowling Green (G-1796)
USF Holland LLC ..... C 614 529-9300
  Columbus (G-8926)
USF Holland LLC ..... C 330 549-2917
  North Lima (G-15408)
Vitran Express Inc ..... E 513 771-4894
  West Chester (G-19182)
Yrc Inc ..... C 513 874-9320
  West Chester (G-19245)

TRUCKS & TRACTORS: Industrial

Eagle Industrial Truck Mfg LLC ..... E 734 442-1000
  Swanton (G-17563)
Forte Indus Eqp Systems Inc ..... E 513 398-2800
  Mason (G-13703)
General Electric Company ..... B 513 977-1500
  Cincinnati (G-3667)
Pollock Research & Design Inc ..... E 330 332-3300
  Salem (G-16706)
Stock Fairfield Corporation ..... C 440 543-6000
  Chagrin Falls (G-2735)
Transco Railway Products Inc ..... E 419 726-3383
  Toledo (G-18259)
Youngstown-Kenworth Inc ..... E 330 534-9761
  Hubbard (G-12093)

TRUCKS, INDL: Wholesalers

All Lift Service Company Inc ..... E 440 585-1542
  Willoughby (G-19642)

Cross Truck Equipment Co Inc ..... E 330 477-8151
  Canton (G-2329)
Fallsway Equipment Co Inc ..... C 330 633-6000
  Akron (G-214)
Rumpke/Kenworth Contract ..... D 740 774-5111
  Chillicothe (G-2883)

TRUSSES: Wood, Floor

Khempco Bldg Sup Co Ltd Partnr ..... D 740 549-0465
  Delaware (G-10113)

TRUSSES: Wood, Roof

Buckeye Components LLC ..... E 330 482-5163
  Columbiana (G-6853)
Thomas Do-It Center Inc ..... E 740 446-2002
  Gallipolis (G-11339)

TRUST COMPANIES: National With Deposits, Commercial

Farmers National Bank ..... D 330 385-9200
  East Liverpool (G-10521)
Fifth Third Bank ..... C 440 984-2402
  Amherst (G-594)
First-Knox National Bank ..... C 740 399-5500
  Mount Vernon (G-14897)
Huntington National Bank ..... E 216 515-6401
  Cleveland (G-5792)
Lcnb National Bank ..... E 740 775-6777
  Chillicothe (G-2859)
Lorain National Bank ..... C 440 244-6000
  Lorain (G-13056)
Peoples Nat Bnk of New Lxngton ..... E 740 342-5111
  New Lexington (G-15060)
PNC Bank National Association ..... B 513 721-2500
  Cincinnati (G-4308)
PNC Bank National Association ..... E 513 455-9522
  Cincinnati (G-4309)
Security National Bank & Tr Co ..... C 740 426-6384
  Newark (G-15233)
Security National Bank & Tr Co ..... C 937 324-6800
  Springfield (G-17272)

TRUST COMPANIES: State Accepting Deposits, Commercial

Buckeye Community Bank ..... E 440 233-8800
  Lorain (G-13020)
Citizens Bank Company ..... E 740 984-2381
  Beverly (G-1488)
Citizens Bank of Ashville Ohio ..... E 740 983-2511
  Ashville (G-769)
Civista Bank ..... D 419 625-4121
  Sandusky (G-16740)
Croghan Colonial Bank ..... E 419 332-7301
  Fremont (G-11193)
Farmers & Merchants State Bank ..... C 419 446-2501
  Archbold (G-636)
Farmers Bank & Savings Co Inc ..... E 740 992-0088
  Pomeroy (G-16232)
Fifth Third Bancorp ..... D 800 972-3030
  Cincinnati (G-3605)
Fifth Third Bank ..... A 513 579-5203
  Cincinnati (G-3607)
Fifth Third Bank ..... E 419 259-7820
  Toledo (G-17886)
Fifth Third Bank ..... D 330 686-0511
  Cuyahoga Falls (G-9188)
Fifth Third Bank of Sthrn OH ..... E 937 840-5353
  Hillsboro (G-11974)
Fifth Third Bnk of Columbus OH ..... A 614 744-7553
  Columbus (G-7655)
First Commonwealth Bank ..... E 740 369-0048
  Delaware (G-10095)
First Commonwealth Bank ..... E 614 336-2280
  Powell (G-16335)
First Commonwealth Bank ..... C 740 657-7000
  Lewis Center (G-12685)
Genoa Banking Company ..... E 419 855-8381
  Genoa (G-11378)
Heartland Bank ..... E 614 337-4600
  Gahanna (G-11247)
Hicksville Bank Inc ..... E 419 542-7726
  Hicksville (G-11865)
Hocking Vly Bnk of Athens Co ..... E 740 592-4441
  Athens (G-792)
Killbuck Savings Bank Co Inc ..... E 330 276-4881
  Killbuck (G-12445)

Minster Bank ..... E 419 628-2351
  Minster (G-14666)
North Side Bank and Trust Co ..... D 513 542-7800
  Cincinnati (G-4177)
North Side Bank and Trust Co ..... E 513 533-8000
  Cincinnati (G-4178)
Ohio Valley Bank Company ..... D 740 446-2168
  Gallipolis (G-11330)
Ohio Valley Bank Company ..... E 740 446-1646
  Gallipolis (G-11332)
Old Fort Banking Company ..... D 419 447-4790
  Tiffin (G-17692)
Osgood State Bank (inc) ..... E 419 582-2681
  Osgood (G-15792)
Peoples Banking and Trust Co ..... C 740 373-3155
  Marietta (G-13486)
Peoples Banking and Trust Co ..... E 740 439-2767
  Cambridge (G-2126)
Richland Trust Company ..... D 419 525-8700
  Mansfield (G-13361)
Richwood Banking Co ..... E 740 943-2317
  Richwood (G-16544)
Sb Financial Group Inc ..... C 419 783-8950
  Defiance (G-10056)
State Bank and Trust Company ..... E 419 783-8950
  Defiance (G-10058)
State Bank and Trust Company ..... E 419 485-5521
  Montpelier (G-14748)
The Cortland Sav & Bnkg Co ..... D 330 637-8040
  Cortland (G-9083)
The Peoples Bank Co Inc ..... E 419 678-2385
  Coldwater (G-6835)
Vinton County Nat Bnk McArthur ..... E 740 596-2525
  Mc Arthur (G-14019)

TRUST MANAGEMENT SVCS: Charitable

Cleveland Foundation ..... D 216 861-3810
  Cleveland (G-5315)

TRUST MANAGEMENT SVCS: Personal Investment

Charles V Francis Trust ..... E 513 528-5600
  Cincinnati (G-3230)

TUBE & TUBING FABRICATORS

Benjamin Steel Company Inc ..... E 937 233-1212
  Springfield (G-17150)
Parker-Hannifin Corporation ..... B 937 456-5571
  Eaton (G-10572)
US Tubular Products Inc ..... D 330 832-1734
  North Lawrence (G-15394)

TUBES: Steel & Iron

Crest Bending Inc ..... E 419 492-2108
  New Washington (G-15134)
Phillips Mfg and Tower Co ..... D 419 347-1720
  Shelby (G-16902)

TUBING: Flexible, Metallic

Wayne Trail Technologies Inc ..... D 937 295-2120
  Fort Loramie (G-11112)

TUBING: Plastic

Alkon Corporation ..... D 419 355-9111
  Fremont (G-11184)
Dlhbowles Inc ..... B 330 478-2503
  Canton (G-2342)

TUGBOAT SVCS

Shelly Materials Inc ..... D 740 246-6315
  Thornville (G-17668)

TUNGSTEN MILL PRDTS

Rhenium Alloys Inc ..... D 440 365-7388
  North Ridgeville (G-15475)

TURBINES & TURBINE GENERATOR SETS

Pfpc Enterprises Inc ..... B 513 941-6200
  Cincinnati (G-4290)
Siemens Energy Inc ..... B 740 393-8897
  Mount Vernon (G-14923)

SERVICES SECTION   UNIVERSITY

TURBINES: Gas, Mechanical Drive
On-Power Inc .... E 513 228-2100
  Lebanon *(G-12633)*

TURNKEY VENDORS: Computer Systems
Manatron Inc .... E 937 431-4000
  Beavercreek *(G-1252)*
Ranac Computer Corporation .... E 317 844-0141
  Moraine *(G-14820)*

TYPESETTING SVC
A-A Blueprint Co Inc .... E 330 794-8803
  Akron *(G-13)*
Advanced Translation/Cnsltng .... E 440 716-0820
  Westlake *(G-19455)*
AGS Custom Graphics Inc .... D 330 963-7770
  Macedonia *(G-13186)*
Bindery & Spc Pressworks Inc .... D 614 873-4623
  Plain City *(G-16184)*
Bookmasters Inc .... C 419 281-1802
  Ashland *(G-665)*
Brothers Publishing Co LLC .... E 937 548-3330
  Greenville *(G-11491)*
Consoldated Graphics Group Inc .... C 216 881-9191
  Cleveland *(G-5393)*
Copley Ohio Newspapers Inc .... C 330 364-5577
  New Philadelphia *(G-15087)*
D & S Crtive Cmmunications Inc .... D 419 524-6699
  Mansfield *(G-13288)*
Fedex Office & Print Svcs Inc .... E 937 436-0677
  Dayton *(G-9544)*
Fedex Office & Print Svcs Inc .... E 614 621-1100
  Columbus *(G-7650)*
Hecks Direct Mail & Prtg Svc .... E 419 697-3505
  Toledo *(G-17950)*
Hkm Drect Mkt Cmmnications Inc ...... C 216 651-9500
  Cleveland *(G-5762)*
Quad/Graphics Inc .... C 614 276-4800
  Columbus *(G-8579)*
Quick Tab II Inc .... D 419 448-6622
  Tiffin *(G-17694)*
Youngstown ARC Engraving Co .... E 330 793-2471
  Youngstown *(G-20423)*

TYPESETTING SVC: Computer
Wolters Kluwer Clinical Drug .... D 330 650-6506
  Hudson *(G-12154)*

UNIFORM SPLY SVCS: Indl
Aramark Unf & Career AP LLC .... D 513 533-1000
  Cincinnati *(G-3039)*
Aramark Unf & Career AP LLC .... D 937 223-6667
  Dayton *(G-9340)*
Cintas Corporation .... A 513 459-1200
  Cincinnati *(G-3349)*
Cintas Corporation .... E 513 671-7717
  Cincinnati *(G-3351)*
Cintas Corporation .... D 513 631-5750
  Cincinnati *(G-3350)*
Cintas Corporation No 2 .... D 440 746-7777
  Girard *(G-11409)*
Cintas Corporation No 2 .... D 440 746-7777
  Brecksville *(G-1817)*
Cintas Corporation No 2 .... E 513 965-0800
  Milford *(G-14511)*
Cintas Corporation No 2 .... D 330 966-7800
  Canton *(G-2309)*
Cintas R US Inc .... A 513 459-1200
  Cincinnati *(G-3352)*
Cintas Sales Corporation .... B 513 459-1200
  Cincinnati *(G-3353)*
Cintas-Rus LP .... E 513 459-1200
  Mason *(G-13683)*
G&K Services Inc .... D 937 873-4500
  Fairborn *(G-10797)*
Morgan Services Inc .... C 216 241-3107
  Cleveland *(G-6075)*
Rentwear Inc .... D 330 535-2301
  Canton *(G-2506)*
Runt Ware & Sanitary Service .... E 330 494-5776
  Canton *(G-2519)*
Unifirst Corporation .... D 937 746-0531
  Franklin *(G-11166)*
Van Dyne-Crotty Co .... E 614 684-0048
  Columbus *(G-8932)*
Van Dyne-Crotty Co .... C 614 491-3903
  Columbus *(G-8933)*

Van Dyne-Crotty Co .... E 440 248-6935
  Solon *(G-17064)*

UNIFORM STORES
Affinity Specialty Apparel Inc .... D 866 548-8434
  Fairborn *(G-10784)*

UNISEX HAIR SALONS
Best Cuts Inc .... E 440 884-6300
  Cleveland *(G-5118)*
Beverly Hills Inn La Llc 859 494-9151
  Aberdeen *(G-1)*
Collins Salon Inc .... E 513 683-1700
  Loveland *(G-13116)*
Cookie Cutters Haircutters 614 522-0220
  Pickerington *(G-16093)*
Englefield Inc .... D 740 323-2077
  Thornville *(G-17667)*
G E G Enterprises Inc .... E 330 477-3133
  Canton *(G-2375)*
Image Engineering Inc .... E 513 541-8544
  Cincinnati *(G-3808)*
Jbentley Studio & Spa LLC .... D 614 790-8828
  Powell *(G-16339)*
Legrand Services Inc .... E 740 682-6046
  Oak Hill *(G-15619)*
Merle-Holden Enterprises Inc .... E 216 661-6887
  Cleveland *(G-6029)*
Mitchells Salon & Day Spa .... E 513 772-3200
  Cincinnati *(G-4105)*
Mitchells Salon & Day Spa .... D 513 731-0600
  Cincinnati *(G-4106)*
PS Lifestyle LLC .... A 440 600-1595
  Cleveland *(G-6328)*
R L O Inc .... E 937 620-9998
  Dayton *(G-9839)*
Salon Communication Services 614 233-8500
  Columbus *(G-8680)*
Z A F Inc .... E 216 291-1234
  Cleveland *(G-6778)*

UNITED FUND COUNCILS
United Rehabilitation Services .... D 937 233-1230
  Dayton *(G-9947)*
United Way Central Ohio Inc .... D 614 227-2700
  Columbus *(G-8904)*
United Way Greater Cleveland .... C 216 436-2100
  Cleveland *(G-6647)*
United Way of The Greater Dayt .... E 937 225-3060
  Dayton *(G-9949)*

UNIVERSITY
Board of Dir of Wittenbe .... E 937 327-6310
  Springfield *(G-17152)*
Bowling Green State University .... D 419 372-2186
  Bowling Green *(G-1768)*
Bowling Green State University .... D 419 372-8657
  Bowling Green *(G-1767)*
Bowling Green State University .... E 419 372-2700
  Bowling Green *(G-1769)*
Case Western Reserve Univ .... E 216 368-2560
  Cleveland *(G-5187)*
Cleveland State University .... E 216 687-3786
  Cleveland *(G-5348)*
Devry University Inc .... C 614 251-6969
  Columbus *(G-7515)*
Kent State University .... D 330 672-2607
  Kent *(G-12379)*
Kent State University 330 672-3114
  Kent *(G-12380)*
Miami University .... B 513 727-3200
  Middletown *(G-14435)*
Miami University .... D 513 529-6911
  Oxford *(G-15821)*
Miami University .... E 513 529-1251
  Oxford *(G-15822)*
Miami University .... D 513 529-1230
  Oxford *(G-15823)*
Oberlin College .... E 440 775-8500
  Oberlin *(G-15655)*
Ohio State Univ Wexner Med Ctr .... A 614 293-6255
  Columbus *(G-8387)*
Ohio State University .... C 614 292-4843
  Columbus *(G-8407)*
Ohio State University .... E 330 263-3725
  Canton *(G-2485)*
Ohio State University 614 688-5721
  Columbus *(G-8423)*

Ohio State University .... A 614 688-3939
  Columbus *(G-8389)*
Ohio State University .... E 614 293-2800
  Columbus *(G-8391)*
Ohio State University .... D 614 292-5578
  Columbus *(G-8392)*
Ohio State University .... A 614 293-7417
  Columbus *(G-8394)*
Ohio State University .... C 614 293-8750
  Columbus *(G-8395)*
Ohio State University .... A 330 263-3700
  Wooster *(G-19898)*
Ohio State University .... E 614 292-5504
  Columbus *(G-8397)*
Ohio State University .... D 740 376-7431
  Marietta *(G-13481)*
Ohio State University .... E 614 292-4139
  Columbus *(G-8399)*
Ohio State University .... E 614 292-2624
  Columbus *(G-8400)*
Ohio State University .... D 614 685-3192
  Columbus *(G-8401)*
Ohio State University .... E 614 292-1681
  Columbus *(G-8402)*
Ohio State University .... D 740 593-2657
  Athens *(G-803)*
Ohio State University .... A 614 293-3860
  Columbus *(G-8403)*
Ohio State University .... E 614 247-4000
  Columbus *(G-8404)*
Ohio State University .... B 330 263-3701
  Wooster *(G-19899)*
Ohio State University 614 257-5200
  Columbus *(G-8409)*
Ohio State University .... E 614 293-4997
  Columbus *(G-8411)*
Ohio State University 614 292-7788
  Columbus *(G-8413)*
Ohio State University .... D 614 442-7300
  Columbus *(G-8414)*
Ohio State University .... E 614 293-8732
  Columbus *(G-8415)*
Ohio State University .... E 614 292-6291
  Columbus *(G-8416)*
Ohio State University .... E 614 293-8158
  Columbus *(G-8417)*
Ohio State University .... D 614 292-0110
  Columbus *(G-8418)*
Ohio State University .... D 614 292-6741
  Columbus *(G-8419)*
Ohio State University .... E 614 292-5144
  Columbus *(G-8420)*
Ohio State University .... E 614 293-8732
  Columbus *(G-8421)*
Ohio State University .... E 614 293-8588
  Columbus *(G-8422)*
Ohio State University .... E 614 293-3737
  Columbus *(G-8424)*
Ohio State University .... E 614 293-6122
  Columbus *(G-8426)*
Ohio State University .... C 614 292-6661
  Columbus *(G-8428)*
Ohio State University .... C 614 292-5990
  Columbus *(G-8429)*
Ohio State University .... E 614 294-2635
  Columbus *(G-8430)*
Ohio State University .... D 614 293-2222
  Columbus *(G-8433)*
Ohio State University .... B 614 293-8133
  Columbus *(G-8434)*
Ohio State University .... E 614 292-9404
  Columbus *(G-8435)*
Ohio State University .... A 614 293-5066
  Columbus *(G-8436)*
Ohio State University .... E 614 293-8419
  Columbus *(G-8437)*
Ohio State University .... D 614 292-1472
  Columbus *(G-8439)*
Ohio State University .... E 614 293-8196
  Columbus *(G-8440)*
Ohio State University .... A 614 293-8000
  Columbus *(G-8442)*
Ohio State University .... D 614 292-2751
  Columbus *(G-8443)*
Ohio State University .... E 614 293-4925
  Columbus *(G-8446)*
Ohio University .... D 740 593-1000
  Athens *(G-804)*
Ohio University .... E 740 593-1660
  Athens *(G-808)*

Employee Codes: A=Over 500 employees, B=251-500
C=101-250, D=51-100, E=25-50

University Hospitals ....B 440 250-2001
Westlake (G-19560)
University of Akron ....D 330 972-6008
Akron (G-488)
University of Akron ....E 330 972-8210
Akron (G-489)
University of Cincinnati ....A 513 556-6381
Cincinnati (G-4761)
University of Cincinnati ....E 513 556-4054
Cincinnati (G-4765)
University of Cincinnati ....E 513 556-3732
Cincinnati (G-4770)
University of Cincinnati ....E 513 558-4194
Cincinnati (G-4755)
University of Cincinnati ....E 513 584-7522
Cincinnati (G-4756)
University of Cincinnati ....E 513 475-8771
Cincinnati (G-4759)
University of Cincinnati ....B 513 558-1200
Cincinnati (G-4760)
University of Cincinnati ....E 513 558-4444
Cincinnati (G-4762)
University of Cincinnati ....E 513 584-4396
Cincinnati (G-4763)
University of Cincinnati ....A 513 556-5087
Cincinnati (G-4764)
University of Cincinnati ....C 513 558-5439
Cincinnati (G-4766)
University of Cincinnati ....C 513 558-4231
Cincinnati (G-4768)
University of Cincinnati ....D 513 584-5331
Cincinnati (G-4769)
University of Cincinnati ....C 513 556-4603
Cincinnati (G-4771)
University of Cincinnati ....D 513 558-1799
Cincinnati (G-4772)
University of Cincinnati ....C 513 584-3200
Cincinnati (G-4773)
University of Cincinnati ....E 513 558-5471
Cincinnati (G-4774)
University of Cincinnati ....E 513 584-1000
Cincinnati (G-4776)
University of Cincinnati ....E 513 558-4831
Cincinnati (G-4777)
University of Cincinnati ....E 513 584-1000
Cincinnati (G-4778)
University of Cincinnati ....D 513 556-3803
Cincinnati (G-4779)
University of Dayton ....A 937 229-2919
Dayton (G-9952)
University of Dayton ....C 937 255-3141
Dayton (G-9951)
University of Dayton ....C 937 229-2113
Dayton (G-9953)
University of Dayton ....B 937 229-3822
Dayton (G-9954)
University of Dayton ....C 937 229-3913
Dayton (G-9955)
University of Toledo ....B 419 383-4229
Toledo (G-18282)
University of Toledo ....D 419 534-3770
Toledo (G-18277)
University of Toledo ....E 419 383-3556
Toledo (G-18278)
University of Toledo ....E 419 383-5322
Toledo (G-18280)
Wright State University ....E 937 298-4331
Kettering (G-12439)
Wright State University ....A 937 775-3333
Beavercreek (G-1222)
Xavier University ....E 513 745-3335
Cincinnati (G-4863)

UPHOLSTERY WORK SVCS

Casco Mfg Solutions Inc ....D 513 681-0003
Cincinnati (G-3191)

URANIUM ORE MINING, NEC

Centrus Energy Corp ....C 740 897-2457
Piketon (G-16111)

USED CAR DEALERS

Abraham Ford LLC ....E 440 233-7402
Elyria (G-10592)
Akron Auto Auction Inc ....C 330 724-7708
Coventry Township (G-9122)
Arch Abraham Susuki Ltd ....E 440 934-6001
Elyria (G-10594)
Auto Center USA Inc ....E 513 683-4900
Cincinnati (G-3066)
Brown Motor Sales Co ....E 419 531-0151
Toledo (G-17785)
Cain Motors Inc ....E 330 494-5588
Canton (G-2280)
Carcorp Inc ....C 877 857-2801
Columbus (G-7189)
Cascade Group Inc ....E 330 929-1861
Cuyahoga Falls (G-9169)
Central Cadillac Limited ....D 216 861-5800
Cleveland (G-5209)
Chesrown Oldsmobile GMC Inc ....E 614 846-3040
Columbus (G-7255)
Chuck Nicholson Pntc-GMC Trcks ....E 330 343-7781
Dover (G-10180)
Columbus Fair Auto Auction Inc ....A 614 497-2000
Obetz (G-15666)
Columbus SAI Motors LLC ....E 614 851-3273
Columbus (G-7383)
Coughlin Chevrolet Toyota Inc ....D 740 366-1381
Newark (G-15162)
Dan Tobin Pontiac Buick GMC ....D 614 889-6300
Columbus (G-7484)
Dave White Chevrolet Inc ....C 419 885-4444
Sylvania (G-17581)
Don Wood Inc ....D 740 593-6641
Athens (G-784)
Donnell Ford-Lincoln ....E 330 332-0031
Salem (G-16694)
Dons Automotive Group LLC ....E 419 337-3010
Wauseon (G-18951)
Doug Bigelow Chevrolet Inc ....D 330 644-7500
Akron (G-198)
Ed Mullinax Ford LLC ....C 440 984-2431
Amherst (G-591)
Ed Schmidt Auto Inc ....C 419 874-4331
Perrysburg (G-16001)
Gene Stevens Auto & Truck Ctr ....E 419 429-2000
Findlay (G-11036)
George P Ballas Buick GMC Trck ....D 419 535-1000
Toledo (G-17913)
Graham Chevrolet-Cadillac Co ....D 419 989-4012
Ontario (G-15690)
Greenwood Chevrolet Inc ....C 330 270-1299
Youngstown (G-20209)
Grogans Towne Chrysler Inc ....C 419 476-0761
Toledo (G-17924)
Jake Sweeney Automotive Inc ....C 513 782-2800
Cincinnati (G-3859)
Jim Keim Ford ....D 614 888-3333
Columbus (G-7941)
Joseph Chevrolet Oldsmobile Co ....C 513 741-6700
Cincinnati (G-3887)
Kempthorn Automall ....D 800 451-3877
Canton (G-2422)
Kempthorn Automall ....C 330 456-8287
Canton (G-2423)
Kent Automotive Inc ....E 330 678-5520
Kent (G-12377)
Kerns Chevrolet-Buick-Gmc Inc ....E 419 586-5131
Celina (G-2649)
Lang Chevrolet Co ....D 937 426-2313
Beavercreek Township (G-1274)
Laria Chevrolet-Buick Inc ....E 330 925-2015
Rittman (G-16553)
Lariche Subaru Inc ....D 419 422-1855
Findlay (G-11056)
Lavery Chevrolet-Buick Inc ....E 330 823-1100
Alliance (G-544)
Lebanon Chrysler - Plymuth Inc ....E 513 932-2717
Lebanon (G-12620)
Lebanon Ford Inc ....D 513 932-1010
Lebanon (G-12621)
Leikin Motor Companies Inc ....D 440 946-6900
Willoughby (G-19686)
Lincoln Mrcury Kings Auto Mall ....C 513 683-3800
Cincinnati (G-3984)
Lkq Triplettasap Inc ....C 330 733-6333
Akron (G-323)
Mark Thomas Ford Inc ....E 330 638-1010
Cortland (G-9077)
McCluskey Chevrolet Inc ....C 513 761-1111
Cincinnati (G-4035)
Mike Castrucci Ford ....C 513 831-7010
Milford (G-14541)
Montrose Ford Inc ....D 330 666-0711
Fairlawn (G-10966)
Mullinax East LLC ....D 440 296-3020
Wickliffe (G-19608)
Mullinax Ford North Canton Inc ....C 330 238-3206
Canton (G-2468)
Northern Automotive Inc ....E 614 436-2001
Columbus (G-8290)
Progrssive Oldsmobile Cadillac ....E 330 833-8585
Massillon (G-13845)
Rouen Chrysler Plymouth Dodge ....E 419 837-6228
Woodville (G-19824)
Roush Equipment Inc ....C 614 882-1535
Westerville (G-19442)
Schoner Chevrolet Inc ....E 330 877-6731
Hartville (G-11830)
Sharpnack Chevrolet Co ....E 440 967-3144
Vermilion (G-18716)
Skipco Financial Adjusters ....D 330 854-4800
Canal Fulton (G-2146)
Sonic Automotive ....D 614 870-8200
Columbus (G-8748)
Sonic Automotive-1495 Automall ....E 614 317-4326
Columbus (G-8749)
Spitzer Auto World Amherst ....D 440 988-4444
Amherst (G-605)
Spitzer Chevrolet Inc ....D 330 467-4141
Northfield (G-15524)
Sunnyside Toyota Inc ....D 440 777-9911
North Olmsted (G-15446)
Surfside Motors Inc ....E 419 462-1746
Galion (G-11306)
Tansky Motors Inc ....E 650 322-7069
Logan (G-12989)
Toyota of Bedford ....D 440 439-8600
Bedford (G-1341)
Village Motors Inc ....D 330 674-2055
Millersburg (G-14626)
Vin Devers ....C 888 847-9535
Sylvania (G-17626)
Voss Auto Network Inc ....E 937 428-2447
Dayton (G-9976)
Voss Chevrolet Inc ....C 937 428-2500
Dayton (G-9978)
Voss Dodge ....E 937 435-7800
Dayton (G-9979)
Voss Toyota Inc ....E 937 427-3700
Beavercreek (G-1218)
Wagner Lincoln-Mercury Inc ....E 419 435-8131
Carey (G-2601)
Walker Auto Group Inc ....D 937 433-4950
Miamisburg (G-14367)
Warner Buick-Nissan Inc ....E 419 423-7161
Findlay (G-11099)

USED CLOTHING STORES

Goodwill Inds NW Ohio Inc ....D 419 255-0070
Toledo (G-17919)
Goodwill Industries of Erie ....E 419 625-4744
Sandusky (G-16763)
Society St Vincent De Paul Cle ....D 216 696-6525
Cleveland (G-6492)
Volunters of Amer Greater Ohio ....C 614 253-6100
Columbus (G-8951)

USED MERCHANDISE STORES

Blanchard Valley Hospital ....E 419 423-4335
Findlay (G-10999)
Goodwill Inds Centl Ohio Inc ....E 740 439-7000
Cambridge (G-2116)
Goodwill Inds of Ashtabula ....C 440 964-3565
Ashtabula (G-745)
Goodwill Industries ....E 330 264-1300
Wooster (G-19865)
Gw Business Solutions LLC ....C 740 645-9861
Newark (G-15172)
Licking-Knox Goodwill Inds Inc ....D 740 345-9861
Newark (G-15196)
Mc Gregor Family Enterprises ....E 513 583-0040
Cincinnati (G-4034)
Salvation Army ....D 419 447-2252
Tiffin (G-17697)
Salvation Army ....C 330 773-3331
Akron (G-428)
Zanesvlle Welfre Orgnztn/Goodw ....D 740 450-6060
Zanesville (G-20560)

USED MERCHANDISE STORES: Clothing & Shoes

Youngstown Area ....C 330 759-7921
Youngstown (G-20424)

SERVICES SECTION

USED MERCHANDISE STORES: Furniture
Cort Business Services Corp ....D....... 513 759-8181
  West Chester (G-19054)
Marion Goodwill Industries ....E....... 740 387-4023
  Marion (G-13560)

USHER SVC
Dedicated Tech Services Inc............D....... 614 309-0059
  Dublin (G-10317)

UTILITIES REGULATION & ADMINISTRATION
City of Columbus ....C....... 614 645-7627
  Columbus (G-7278)

VACATION LODGES
Das Dutch Village Inn ....D....... 330 482-5050
  Columbiana (G-6858)
Ohio State Parks Inc ....D....... 513 664-3504
  College Corner (G-6838)

VACUUM CLEANER STORES
ABC Appliance Inc ....E....... 419 693-4414
  Oregon (G-15722)

VACUUM CLEANERS: Household
Stanley Steemer Intl Inc ....C....... 614 764-2007
  Dublin (G-10461)

VALET PARKING SVCS
Parking Solutions Inc ....A....... 614 469-7000
  Columbus (G-8517)

VALUE-ADDED RESELLERS: Computer Systems
Cameo Solutions Inc ....E....... 513 645-4220
  West Chester (G-19032)
Dayton/Cncinnati Tech Svcs LLC......E....... 513 892-3940
  Blue Ash (G-1575)
Evanhoe & Associates Inc ....E....... 937 235-2995
  Dayton (G-9269)
Netsmart Technologies Inc ....D....... 614 764-0143
  Dublin (G-10407)
Rolta Advizex Technologies LLC........E....... 216 901-1818
  Independence (G-12253)
Warnock Tanner & Assoc Inc ....E....... 419 897-6999
  Maumee (G-13993)

VALVE REPAIR SVCS, INDL
Keaney Investment Group LLC ....E....... 937 263-6429
  Dayton (G-9648)

VALVES & PIPE FITTINGS
Crane Pumps & Systems Inc ....B....... 937 773-2442
  Piqua (G-16142)
Edward W Daniel LLC ....E....... 440 647-1960
  Wellington (G-18990)
Fcx Performance Inc ....E....... 614 324-6050
  Columbus (G-7645)
Robeck Fluid Power Co ....D....... 330 562-1140
  Aurora (G-852)
Ruthman Pump and Engineering .....E....... 937 783-2411
  Blanchester (G-1516)
Superior Products LLC ....E....... 216 651-9400
  Cleveland (G-6555)
Superior Products Llc ....D....... 216 651-9400
  Cleveland (G-6554)
Swagelok Company ....E....... 440 349-5934
  Solon (G-17059)
Waxman Industries Inc ....C....... 440 439-1830
  Cleveland (G-6726)

VALVES: Aerosol, Metal
Accurate Mechanical Inc ....E....... 740 654-5898
  Lancaster (G-12506)
J Feldkamp Design Build Ltd...........E....... 513 870-0601
  Fairfield (G-10864)

VALVES: Aircraft, Hydraulic
Aerocontrolex Group Inc ....D....... 440 352-6182
  Painesville (G-15833)

VALVES: Indl
Alkon Corporation ....E....... 614 799-6650
  Dublin (G-10241)
Curtiss-Wright Flow Control ....D....... 513 735-2538
  Batavia (G-1008)
Curtiss-Wright Flow Control ....D....... 513 528-7900
  Cincinnati (G-2909)
Curtiss-Wright Flow Control ....D....... 513 528-7900
  Cincinnati (G-2910)
Ruthman Pump and Engineering .....E....... 937 783-2411
  Blanchester (G-1516)
Waxman Industries Inc ....C....... 440 439-1830
  Cleveland (G-6726)

VALVES: Nuclear Power Plant, Ferrous
Alkon Corporation ....D....... 419 355-9111
  Fremont (G-11184)

VARIETY STORE MERCHANDISE, WHOLESALE
Glen Surplus Sales Inc ....E....... 419 347-1212
  Shelby (G-16900)
Glow Industries Inc ....D....... 419 872-4772
  Perrysburg (G-16007)

VARIETY STORES
Big Lots Stores Inc ....B....... 614 278-6800
  Columbus (G-7107)
Discount Drug Mart Inc ....D....... 330 725-2340
  Medina (G-14059)
Dollar Paradise ....E....... 216 432-0421
  Cleveland (G-5498)
Glow Industries Inc ....D....... 419 872-4772
  Perrysburg (G-16007)
Marc Glassman Inc ....C....... 330 995-9246
  Aurora (G-845)
Trepanier Daniels & Trepanier ....D....... 740 286-1288
  Jackson (G-12319)

VEGETABLE STANDS OR MARKETS
A Brown & Sons Nursery ....E....... 937 836-5826
  Brookville (G-1958)

VEHICLES: All Terrain
Wholecycle Inc ....E....... 330 929-8123
  Peninsula (G-15953)

VENDING MACHINE OPERATORS: Beverage
Coffee Break Corporation ....E....... 513 841-1100
  Cincinnati (G-3377)

VENDING MACHINE OPERATORS: Food
Sanese Services Inc ....B....... 614 436-1234
  Warren (G-18895)
Walter Alexander Entps Inc ....E....... 513 841-1100
  Cincinnati (G-4823)

VENDING MACHINE OPERATORS: Sandwich & Hot Food
Laughlin Music & Vending Svc.........E....... 740 593-7778
  Athens (G-798)

VENDING MACHINE REPAIR SVCS
Enterprise Vending Inc ....E....... 513 772-1373
  Cincinnati (G-3560)
Serex Corporation ....E....... 330 726-6062
  Youngstown (G-20371)

VENDING MACHINES & PARTS
Giant Industries Inc ....E....... 419 531-4600
  Toledo (G-17915)

VENTILATING EQPT: Metal
Famous Industries Inc ....E....... 330 535-1811
  Akron (G-219)

VENTURE CAPITAL COMPANIES
Rev1 Ventures ....E....... 614 487-3700
  Columbus (G-8627)

VESSELS: Process, Indl, Metal Plate
Columbiana Boiler Company LLC.....E....... 330 482-3373
  Columbiana (G-6855)

VETERANS AFFAIRS ADMINISTRATION SVCS
Veterans Affairs US Dept..................A....... 937 268-6511
  Dayton (G-9972)
Veterans Health Administration........A....... 513 861-3100
  Cincinnati (G-4812)
Veterans Health Administration........E....... 330 740-9200
  Youngstown (G-20403)

VETERANS' AFFAIRS ADMINISTRATION, GOVERNMENT: Federal
Veterans Health Administration........B....... 740 568-0412
  Marietta (G-13514)
Veterans Health Administration........A....... 202 461-4800
  Chillicothe (G-2895)
Veterans Health Administration........B....... 513 943-3680
  Cincinnati (G-4813)
Veterans Health Administration........A....... 216 791-3800
  Cleveland (G-6691)
Veterans Health Administration........C....... 614 257-5524
  Columbus (G-8937)
Veterans Health Administration........B....... 866 463-0912
  Ashtabula (G-766)
Veterans Health Administration........B....... 740 695-9321
  Saint Clairsville (G-16659)
Veterans Health Administration........D....... 419 259-2000
  Toledo (G-18290)
Veterans Health Administration........B....... 216 939-0699
  Cleveland (G-6692)
Veterans Health Administration........D....... 330 489-4600
  Canton (G-2577)

VETERINARY PRDTS: Instruments & Apparatus
Suarez Corporation Industries ....D....... 330 494-4282
  Canton (G-2554)

VIDEO & AUDIO EQPT, WHOLESALE
Live Technologies Holdings Inc ......D....... 614 278-7777
  Columbus (G-8074)
Merchandise Inc..............................D....... 513 353-2200
  Miamitown (G-14372)

VIDEO PRODUCTION SVCS
Madison Avenue Mktg Group Inc ....E....... 419 473-9000
  Toledo (G-18026)
Mitosis LLC......................................E....... 937 557-3440
  Dayton (G-9752)

VIDEO REPAIR SVCS
K M T Service ....E....... 614 777-7770
  Hilliard (G-11918)

VIDEO TAPE PRODUCTION SVCS
Video Duplication Services Inc........E....... 614 871-3827
  Columbus (G-8940)
World Harvest Church Inc ....E....... 614 837-1990
  Canal Winchester (G-2180)

VIDEO TAPE WHOLESALERS, RECORDED
Midwest Tape LLC...........................B....... 419 868-9370
  Holland (G-12038)

VINYL RESINS, NEC
Polyone Corporation ....D....... 440 930-1000
  North Baltimore (G-15315)

VISITING NURSE
A Touch of Grace Inc ....D....... 740 397-7971
  Mount Vernon (G-14877)
Accentcare Home Health Cal Inc....C....... 740 474-7826
  Circleville (G-4876)
Acute Care Homenursing Service ...E....... 216 271-9100
  Warren (G-18813)
Advantage Home Health Care..........D....... 800 636-2330
  Portsmouth (G-16263)
Alternacare Home Health Inc ....E....... 740 689-1589
  Lancaster (G-12508)

VISITING NURSE — SERVICES SECTION

Company	Code	Phone
Amber Home Care LLC — Columbus (G-6981)	E	614 523-0668
Angels Touch Nursing Care — Cincinnati (G-3030)	E	513 661-4111
Appalachian Community Visi — Athens (G-772)	D	740 594-8226
Apria Healthcare LLC — Miamisburg (G-14271)	E	937 291-2842
B H C Services Inc — Euclid (G-10744)	A	216 289-5300
Bracor Inc — Euclid (G-10746)		216 289-5300
Care Connection of Cincinnati — Cincinnati (G-3181)	D	513 842-1101
Choice Healthcare Limited — Beavercreek (G-1159)		937 254-6220
Clearpath HM Hlth Hospice LLC — Akron (G-145)	D	330 784-2162
Colt Enterprises Inc — Maumee (G-13898)	E	567 336-6062
Comfort Keepers — Lima (G-12758)	E	419 229-1031
Comfort Keepers — Painesville (G-15844)		440 721-0100
Comfort Keepers Inc — Springfield (G-17169)		937 322-6288
Committed To Care Inc — Cincinnati (G-3400)	E	513 245-1190
Community Choice Home Care — Wheelersburg (G-19574)	E	740 574-9900
Community Hlth Prfssionals Inc — Ada (G-4)		419 634-7443
Community Hlth Prfssionals Inc — Archbold (G-634)		419 445-5128
Community Hlth Prfssionals Inc — Van Wert (G-18630)	C	419 238-9223
Community Hlth Prfssionals Inc — Paulding (G-15928)	E	419 399-4708
Community Hlth Prfssionals Inc — Lima (G-12926)	E	419 991-1822
Community Hlth Prfssionals Inc — Celina (G-2641)	E	419 586-1999
Community Hlth Prfssionals Inc — Celina (G-2642)	D	419 586-6266
Community Hlth Prfssionals Inc — Delphos (G-10139)	E	419 695-8101
Constance Care Home Hlth Care — Circleville (G-4884)	D	740 477-6360
Diane Vishnia Rn and Assoc — Cuyahoga Falls (G-9180)	D	330 929-1113
EJq Home Health Care Inc — Elyria (G-10620)	D	440 323-7004
Ember Complete Care — Uhrichsville (G-18488)	C	740 922-6888
Enhanced Home Health Care LLC — Columbus (G-7595)	D	614 433-7266
Excel Health Services LLC — Delaware (G-10093)	D	614 794-0006
Family Nursing Services Inc — Chillicothe (G-2836)	E	740 775-5463
Genesis Caregivers — Zanesville (G-20480)	C	740 454-1370
Hanson Services Inc — Lakewood (G-12480)	C	216 226-5425
Healing Hands Home Health Ltd — Logan (G-12973)	E	740 385-0710
Health Services Coshocton Cnty — Coshocton (G-9104)	E	740 622-7311
Hillebrand Home Health Inc — Cincinnati (G-3761)		513 598-6648
Home Care Advantage — Salem (G-16699)	D	330 337-4663
Home Care Network Inc — Dayton (G-9613)		937 435-1142
Homecare Mtters HM Hlth Hspice — Bucyrus (G-2040)	D	419 562-2001
Hospice Care Ohio — Fairlawn (G-10956)		330 665-1455
Hospice Caring Way — Van Wert (G-18635)	D	419 238-9223
Hospice of The Western Reserve — Cleveland (G-5778)	D	800 707-8921
Intervention For Peace Inc — Medina (G-14083)		330 725-1298
Karopa Incorporate — Hamilton (G-11749)	E	513 860-1616
Loving Family Home Care Inc — Toledo (G-18012)	D	888 469-2178
Marietta Memorial Hospital — Marietta (G-13472)	E	740 373-8549
Northeast Professional Hm Care — Canton (G-2476)	E	330 966-2311
Nurse Medicinal Healthcare Svcs — Grove City (G-11586)	D	614 801-1300
Ohio Home Health Care Inc — Dayton (G-9785)	E	937 853-0271
Ohio Valley Home Hlth Svcs Inc — East Liverpool (G-10530)	E	330 385-2333
Ohioans Home Health Care Inc — Perrysburg (G-16037)	D	419 843-4422
Personal Touch HM Care IPA Inc — Eaton (G-10573)	E	937 456-4447
Primary Care Nursing Services — Dublin (G-10430)	D	614 764-0960
Prime Home Care LLC — Maineville (G-13245)	E	513 340-4183
Private Duty Services Inc — Van Wert (G-18642)	C	419 238-3714
Pro Health Care Services Ltd — Groveport (G-11664)	E	614 856-9111
Quality Life Providers LLC — Hilliard (G-11946)	E	614 527-9999
Robinson Visitn Nrs Asoc/Hospc — Ravenna (G-16408)		330 297-8899
Salem Area Vsiting Nurse Assoc — Salem (G-16711)	E	330 332-9986
Selective Networking Inc — Wheelersburg (G-19581)	D	740 574-2682
Ssth LLC — Columbus (G-8769)	D	614 884-0793
Tky Associates LLC — Toledo (G-18221)	D	419 535-7777
Tri County Visitng Nrs Prvt — Wapakoneta (G-18809)	E	419 738-7430
TVC Home Health Care — Youngstown (G-20396)	E	330 755-1110
Vishnia & Associates Inc — Cuyahoga Falls (G-9233)	D	330 929-5512
Visiting Nrse Assn of Clveland — Ashland (G-706)	B	419 281-2480
Visiting Nrse Assn of Clveland — Mansfield (G-13381)	E	419 522-4969
Visiting Nrse Assn of Clveland — Cleveland (G-6702)	B	216 931-1400
Visiting Nrse Assn of Mid-Ohio — Cleveland (G-6703)	E	216 931-1300
Visiting Nurse Service Inc — Akron (G-499)	B	330 745-1601
Visiting Nurse Service Inc — Chardon (G-2776)	E	440 286-9461

VISUAL COMMUNICATIONS SYSTEMS

Company	Code	Phone
Findaway World LLC — Solon (G-17007)	D	440 893-0808

VITAMINS: Pharmaceutical Preparations

Company	Code	Phone
Vitamin Shoppe Inc — Strongsville (G-17522)	E	440 238-5987

VOCATIONAL OR TECHNICAL SCHOOLS, PUBLIC

Company	Code	Phone
Great Oaks Inst Tech Creer Dev — Cincinnati (G-3703)	D	513 771-8840

VOCATIONAL REHABILITATION AGENCY

Company	Code	Phone
A W S Inc — Euclid (G-10741)	E	216 486-0600
Ash Craft Industries Inc — Ashtabula (G-711)	C	440 224-2177
Center of Voctnl Altrntvs Mntl — Columbus (G-7226)	D	614 294-7117
Community Support Services Inc — Akron (G-157)	C	330 253-9388
Cornucopia Inc — Lakewood (G-12474)		216 521-4600
County of Cuyahoga — Cleveland (G-5419)	D	216 475-7066
Creative Learning Workshop — Warren (G-18844)	E	330 393-5929
Creative Learning Workshop — New Paris (G-15076)	E	937 437-0146
Easter Seals Tristate — Blue Ash (G-1582)	C	513 985-0515
Food For Good Thought Inc — Columbus (G-7679)	E	614 447-0424
Goodwill Ester Seals Miami Vly — Dayton (G-9579)	C	937 461-4800
Goodwill Idstrs Grtr Clvlnd L — Hartville (G-11819)	E	330 877-7921
Goodwill Idstrs Grtr Clvlnd L — Cleveland (G-5679)	E	216 581-6320
Goodwill Idstrs Grtr Clvlnd L — Canton (G-2383)		330 454-9461
Goodwill Inds Centl Ohio Inc — Marietta (G-13448)	D	740 373-1304
Goodwill Inds Centl Ohio Inc — Cambridge (G-2116)	E	740 439-7000
Goodwill Inds NW Ohio Inc — Toledo (G-17919)	D	419 255-0070
Goodwill Inds of Ashtabula — Ashtabula (G-745)	C	440 964-3565
Goodwill Industries of Akron — Akron (G-242)		330 724-6995
Goodwill Industries of Lima — Lima (G-12785)	D	419 228-4821
Jewish Family Services — Columbus (G-7940)	D	614 231-1890
L & M Products Inc — Eaton (G-10564)	C	937 456-7141
Marimor Industries Inc — Lima (G-12836)	C	419 221-1226
Murray Ridge Production Center — Elyria (G-10657)	B	440 329-3734
Ohio Rehabilitation Svcs Comm — Akron (G-369)	E	330 643-3080
Perco Inc — New Lexington (G-15061)	D	740 342-5156
Quadco Rehabilitation Center — Stryker (G-17537)	B	419 682-1011
Quadco Rehabilitation Center — Archbold (G-642)	D	419 445-1950
Richcreek Bailey Rehabilitatio — Mentor (G-14237)	E	440 527-8610
Spectrum Supportive Services — Cleveland (G-6517)	E	216 875-0460
Spectrum Supportive Services — Cleveland (G-6518)	C	216 761-2388
United Cerebral Palsy — Cleveland (G-6635)	C	216 791-8363
Voc Works Ltd — Dublin (G-10484)	D	614 760-3515
Youngstown Area — Youngstown (G-20424)	C	330 759-7921

VOCATIONAL TRAINING AGENCY

Company	Code	Phone
A W S Inc — Rocky River (G-16567)	C	440 333-1791
A W S Inc — Cleveland (G-4937)	B	216 749-0356
County of Hardin — Kenton (G-12410)	E	419 674-4158
Vocational Guidance Services — Elyria (G-10687)	E	440 322-1123

WALL COVERINGS WHOLESALERS

Company	Code	Phone
Fashion Wallcoverings Inc — Cleveland (G-5575)	D	216 432-1600

WALLS: Curtain, Metal

Company	Code	Phone
Midwest Curtainwalls Inc — Cleveland (G-6060)	D	216 641-7900

WAREHOUSING & STORAGE FACILITIES, NEC

Company	Code	Phone
Atrium Apparel Corporation — Johnstown (G-12335)	D	612 889-0959
Ballreich Bros Inc — Tiffin (G-17672)	C	419 447-1814
Comprehensive Logistics Co Inc — Youngstown (G-20158)	E	330 793-0504
Distribution and Trnsp Svc Inc — Fort Loramie (G-11110)	E	937 295-3343
Eddie Bauer LLC — Columbus (G-7576)	E	614 278-9281
Exel Holdings (usa) Inc — Westerville (G-19303)	C	614 865-8500
General Motors LLC — West Chester (G-19081)	C	513 603-6600
Honda Logistics North Amer Inc — East Liberty (G-10509)	A	937 642-0335
Interstate Warehousing VA LLC — Fairfield (G-10863)	D	513 874-6500
Iron Mountain Info MGT LLC — Cincinnati (G-3844)	E	513 297-3268

SERVICES SECTION

WAREHOUSING & STORAGE: General

Company	Code	Phone
Iron Mountain Info MGT LLC	E	513 297-1906
West Chester *(G-19095)*		
Iron Mountain Info MGT LLC	E	614 840-9321
Columbus *(G-7922)*		
Jacobson Warehouse Company Inc	C	614 314-1091
Obetz *(G-15668)*		
Kitchen Collection LLC	E	740 773-9150
Chillicothe *(G-2858)*		
Kuhlman Corporation	C	419 897-6000
Maumee *(G-13934)*		
Lefco Worthington LLC	E	216 432-4422
Cleveland *(G-5931)*		
Locker Moving & Storage Inc	E	330 784-0477
Canton *(G-2439)*		
Midwest Express Inc	A	937 642-0335
East Liberty *(G-10510)*		
Nex Transport Inc	C	937 645-3761
East Liberty *(G-10512)*		
Odw Logistics Inc	B	614 549-5000
Columbus *(G-8313)*		
PC Connection Inc	C	937 382-4800
Wilmington *(G-19775)*		
Radial South LP	C	678 584-4047
Groveport *(G-11665)*		
SH Bell Company	E	412 963-9910
East Liverpool *(G-10534)*		
Ship Shape Marine Inc	E	419 734-1554
Port Clinton *(G-16255)*		
Target Corporation	C	513 671-8603
Cincinnati *(G-4625)*		
Target Corporation	B	614 801-6700
West Jefferson *(G-19255)*		
Vista Industrial Packaging LLC	D	800 454-6117
Columbus *(G-8945)*		
Warren City Board Education	E	330 841-2265
Warren *(G-18923)*		
Wooster Motor Ways Inc	C	330 264-9557
Wooster *(G-19932)*		

WAREHOUSING & STORAGE, REFRIGERATED: Cold Storage Or Refrig

Company	Code	Phone
Americold Logistics LLC	D	330 834-1742
Massillon *(G-13785)*		
Cloverleaf Cold Storage Co	E	330 833-9870
Massillon *(G-13797)*		
D & D Investment Co	E	614 272-6567
Columbus *(G-7476)*		
Fresh Mark Inc	B	330 833-9870
Massillon *(G-13811)*		
Gorbett Enterprises of Solon	E	440 248-3950
Solon *(G-17011)*		
Interstate Warehousing VA LLC	D	513 874-6500
Fairfield *(G-10863)*		
RLR Investments LLC	D	937 382-1494
Wilmington *(G-19783)*		

WAREHOUSING & STORAGE, REFRIGERATED: Frozen Or Refrig Goods

Company	Code	Phone
Exel N Amercn Logistics Inc	C	937 854-7900
Dayton *(G-9535)*		

WAREHOUSING & STORAGE: Automobile, Dead Storage

Company	Code	Phone
Auto Warehousing Co Inc	E	419 727-1534
Toledo *(G-17761)*		

WAREHOUSING & STORAGE: General

Company	Code	Phone
A Duie Pyle Inc	D	330 342-7750
Streetsboro *(C-17404)*		
Aero Fulfillment Services Corp	D	800 225-7145
Mason *(G-13658)*		
Aero Fulfillment Services Corp	D	513 874-4112
West Chester *(G-19014)*		
Albring Vending Company	E	419 726-8059
Toledo *(G-17746)*		
Andersons Inc	C	419 891-6479
Maumee *(G-13877)*		
Andersons Inc		419 893-5050
Maumee *(G-13880)*		
Arett Sales Corp	D	937 552-2005
Troy *(G-18348)*		
Asw Global LLC	D	330 733-6291
Mogadore *(G-14670)*		
Asw Global LLC	D	330 899-1003
Canton *(G-2247)*		
Asw Global LLC		330 798-5184
Mogadore *(G-14671)*		
Building Systems Trnsp Co	C	740 852-9700
London *(G-12994)*		
Burd Brothers Inc	D	800 538-2873
Batavia *(G-996)*		
Calypso Logistics LLC	C	614 262-8911
Columbus *(G-7179)*		
Central Equity Investments Inc	E	937 454-1270
Vandalia *(G-18668)*		
Childrens Hospital Medical Ctr	A	513 636-4200
Cincinnati *(G-3253)*		
Cloverleaf Cold Storage Co	C	419 599-5015
Napoleon *(G-14934)*		
Comprehensive Logistics Co Inc	E	800 734-0372
Youngstown *(G-20159)*		
Containerport Group Inc	E	216 341-4800
Cleveland *(G-5401)*		
Cotter Mdse Stor of Ohio	E	330 773-9177
Akron *(G-166)*		
Crescent Park Corporation	E	513 759-7000
West Chester *(G-19059)*		
Dhl Supply Chain (usa)	E	419 727-4318
Toledo *(G-17852)*		
Dhl Supply Chain (usa)	D	513 482-6015
Cincinnati *(G-3486)*		
Dhl Supply Chain (usa)	D	740 929-2113
Hebron *(G-11848)*		
Dhl Supply Chain (usa)	E	614 662-9247
Groveport *(G-11634)*		
Dhl Supply Chain (usa)	E	513 942-1575
Cincinnati *(G-3487)*		
Dhl Supply Chain (usa)	E	513 745-7445
Blue Ash *(G-1578)*		
Dolgencorp LLC	A	740 588-5700
Zanesville *(G-20468)*		
Doylestown Telephone Company	E	330 658-6666
Doylestown *(G-10229)*		
Efco Corp	E	614 876-1226
Columbus *(G-7586)*		
Exel Inc	D	419 996-7703
Lima *(G-12774)*		
Exel Inc	E	419 226-5500
Lima *(G-12775)*		
Exel Inc	E	614 865-8294
Westerville *(G-19304)*		
Exel Inc	D	740 927-1762
Etna *(G-10734)*		
Exel Inc	B	614 865-8500
Westerville *(G-19305)*		
Faro Services Inc	B	614 497-1700
Groveport *(G-11639)*		
Fedex Sup Chain Dist Sys Inc	C	614 277-3970
Groveport *(G-11640)*		
First Group Investment Partnr	E	513 241-2200
Cincinnati *(G-3618)*		
Firstgroup Usa Inc	B	513 241-2200
Cincinnati *(G-3629)*		
Frito-Lay North America Inc	E	330 786-6000
Akron *(G-231)*		
G & J Pepsi-Cola Bottlers Inc	D	740 593-3366
Athens *(G-788)*		
G & J Pepsi-Cola Bottlers Inc	E	937 393-5744
Wilmington *(G-19763)*		
Getgo Transportation Co LLC	E	419 666-6850
Millbury *(G-14579)*		
H & O Distribution Inc	E	513 874-2090
Fairfield *(G-10855)*		
Handl-It Inc	C	330 468-0734
Macedonia *(G-13201)*		
Hyperlogistics Group Inc	E	614 497-0800
Columbus *(G-7876)*		
J-Trac Inc	E	419 524-3456
Mansfield *(G-13315)*		
Keller Warehousing & Dist LLC	C	419 784-4805
Defiance *(G-10041)*		
Lesaint Logistics LLC	E	513 874-3900
West Chester *(G-19106)*		
Lewis & Michael Inc	E	937 252-6683
Dayton *(G-9679)*		
Liberty Insulation Co Inc	E	513 621-0108
Milford *(G-14530)*		
Mansfield Whsng & Dist Inc	C	419 522-3510
Ontario *(G-15699)*		
McM Electronics Inc	D	937 434-0031
Dayton *(G-9708)*		
Mid-Ohio Development Corp	D	614 836-0606
Groveport *(G-11657)*		
Mxd Group Inc	E	614 801-0621
Columbus *(G-8210)*		
Nifco America Corporation	C	614 836-8733
Groveport *(G-11659)*		
North Coast Logistics Inc	E	216 362-7159
Brookpark *(G-1952)*		
Odw Logistics Inc	B	614 549-5000
Columbus *(G-8313)*		
Osborne Trucking Company	D	513 874-2090
Fairfield *(G-10890)*		
Parker-Hannifin Corporation	D	419 878-7000
Waterville *(G-18943)*		
Peoples Cartage Inc	E	330 833-8571
Massillon *(G-13843)*		
Peoples Services Inc	E	330 453-3709
Canton *(G-2490)*		
Piqua Steel Co	D	937 773-3632
Piqua *(G-16159)*		
Restaurant Equippers Inc	E	614 358-6622
Columbus *(G-8624)*		
South E Harley Davidson Sls Co	E	440 439-3013
Cleveland *(G-6497)*		
Surface Combustion Inc	E	419 878-8444
Waterville *(G-18946)*		
Sygma Network Inc	B	614 734-2500
Dublin *(G-10469)*		
Synnex Corporation	E	614 539-6995
Grove City *(G-11603)*		
Taylor Warehouse Corporation	E	513 771-2956
Cincinnati *(G-4627)*		
Terminal Warehouse Inc	D	330 773-2056
Akron *(G-475)*		
The Maple City Ice Company	E	419 747-4777
Mansfield *(G-13373)*		
Total Warehousing Services	D	419 562-2878
Bucyrus *(G-2048)*		
Triple Ladys Agency Inc	E	330 274-1100
Mantua *(G-13396)*		
TRT Management Corporation	E	419 661-1233
Perrysburg *(G-16065)*		
Whirlpool Corporation	C	419 547-2610
Clyde *(G-6825)*		
Willis Day Management Inc	E	419 476-8000
Toledo *(G-18311)*		
Willis Day Storage Co	E	419 470-6255
Toledo *(G-18312)*		
Wright Distribution Centers	E	419 227-7621
Lima *(G-12922)*		

WAREHOUSING & STORAGE: General

Company	Code	Phone
A1 Quality Labor Svc	E	513 353-0173
Cincinnati *(G-2957)*		
Akron Porcelain & Plastics Co	E	330 745-2159
Barberton *(G-951)*		
Aldi Inc	D	330 273-7351
Hinckley *(G-11994)*		
All Pro Freight Systems Inc	D	440 934-2222
Avon *(G-874)*		
AM Industrial Group LLC	E	216 267-6783
Cleveland *(G-5000)*		
Andersen Distribution Inc	C	937 898-7844
Dayton *(G-9336)*		
Atotech USA Inc	D	216 398-0550
Cleveland *(G-5080)*		
Bartram & Sons Groceries	E	740 532-5216
Ironton *(G-12281)*		
Basista Furniture Inc	E	216 398-5900
Cleveland *(G-5099)*		
BDS Inc	E	513 921-8441
Cincinnati *(G-3086)*		
Big Sandy Distribution Inc	C	740 574-2113
Franklin Furnace *(G-11168)*		
Big Sandy Furniture Inc	D	740 574-2113
Franklin Furnace *(G-11169)*		
Big Sandy Furniture Inc	E	740 354-3193
Portsmouth *(G-16265)*		
Big Sandy Furniture Inc	E	740 775-4244
Chillicothe *(G-2816)*		
Big Sandy Furniture Inc	E	740 894-4242
Chesapeake *(G-2781)*		
Briar-Gate Realty Inc	E	614 299-2121
Columbus *(G-7133)*		
Caterpillar Inc	D	614 834-2400
Canal Winchester *(G-2155)*		
Comprehensive Logistics Co Inc	E	330 233-0805
Parma *(G-15902)*		
Comprehensive Logistics Co Inc	E	440 934-0870
Lorain *(G-13032)*		
Cotter Moving & Storage Co	E	330 535-5115
Akron *(G-167)*		
D M I Distribution Inc	E	765 584-3234
Columbus *(G-7481)*		
Daikin Applied Americas Inc	E	763 553-5009
Dayton *(G-9450)*		

Employee Codes: A=Over 500 employees, B=251-500
C=101-250, D=51-100, E=25-50

Daniel Logistics Inc D 614 367-9442
Columbus *(G-7487)*

Dayton Heidelberg Distrg Co C 419 666-9783
Perrysburg *(G-15994)*

Dedicated Logistics Inc D 513 275-1135
West Chester *(G-19060)*

Dhl Supply Chain (usa) D 614 895-1959
Westerville *(G-19299)*

DSC Logistics Inc D 847 390-6800
Toledo *(G-17857)*

E and P Warehouse Services Ltd E 330 898-4800
Warren *(G-18852)*

Enterprise Vending Inc E 513 772-1373
Cincinnati *(G-3560)*

Essilor of America Inc C 614 492-0888
Groveport *(G-11637)*

Exel Inc E 614 670-6473
Lockbourne *(G-12952)*

Federal Express Corporation B 614 492-6106
Columbus *(G-7646)*

Fedex Supply Chain B 412 820-3700
Lockbourne *(G-12954)*

Fremont Logistics LLC D 419 333-0669
Fremont *(G-11202)*

Fuchs Lubricants Co E 330 963-0400
Twinsburg *(G-18419)*

Fusion Ceramics Inc E 330 627-5821
Carrollton *(G-2620)*

G & S Metal Products Co Inc C 216 831-2388
Cleveland *(G-5644)*

General Motors LLC C 513 874-0535
West Chester *(G-19080)*

GMI Holdings Inc D 330 794-0846
Akron *(G-239)*

Goodwill Ester Seals Miami Vly B 937 461-4800
Dayton *(G-9580)*

Graham Investment Co D 740 382-0902
Marion *(G-13541)*

Graybar Electric Company Inc E 330 799-3220
Youngstown *(G-20204)*

Great Value Storage E 614 848-8420
Columbus *(G-7772)*

Home Depot USA Inc D 513 360-1100
Monroe *(G-14698)*

Ieh Auto Parts LLC E 216 351-2560
Cleveland *(G-5802)*

Ingersoll-Rand Company E 419 633-6800
Bryan *(G-2008)*

Inter Distr Svcs of Cleve E 330 468-4949
Macedonia *(G-13203)*

J B Express Inc D 740 702-9830
Chillicothe *(G-2854)*

Jacobson Warehouse Company Inc E 614 409-0003
Groveport *(G-11650)*

Jacobson Warehouse Company Inc D 614 497-6300
Groveport *(G-11651)*

King Tut Logistics LLC E 614 538-0509
Columbus *(G-7994)*

Kmart Corporation B 614 836-5000
Groveport *(G-11654)*

Kmart Corporation A 330 372-6688
Warren *(G-18871)*

Kuehne + Nagel Inc E 419 635-4051
Port Clinton *(G-16249)*

Kyocera SGS Precision Tools E 330 922-1953
Cuyahoga Falls *(G-9204)*

Lakota Local School District C 513 777-2150
Liberty Township *(G-12722)*

Lesaint Logistics Inc C 513 874-3900
West Chester *(G-19105)*

Lesaint Logistics LLC D 513 988-0101
Trenton *(G-18341)*

Locker Moving & Storage Inc E 330 784-0477
Canton *(G-2439)*

Lowes Home Centers LLC C 419 429-5700
Findlay *(G-11058)*

Lowes Home Centers LLC E 740 636-2100
Wshngtn CT Hs *(G-20029)*

M A Folkes Company Inc E 513 785-4200
Hamilton *(G-11756)*

Malleys Candies Inc E 216 529-6262
Cleveland *(G-5974)*

Marc Glassman Inc C 216 265-7700
Cleveland *(G-5977)*

Menlo Logistics Inc D 740 963-1154
Etna *(G-10736)*

Micro Electronics Inc D 614 334-1430
Columbus *(G-8160)*

Mid-Ohio Mechanical Inc E 740 587-3362
Granville *(G-11470)*

Midwest Trmnals Tledo Intl Inc E 419 698-8171
Toledo *(G-18064)*

Ohio Desk Co E 216 623-0600
Brooklyn Heights *(G-1922)*

P-Americas LLC C 330 746-7652
Youngstown *(G-20313)*

Parker-Hannifin Corporation A 216 531-3000
Cleveland *(G-6241)*

PC Connection Sales Corp C 937 382-4800
Wilmington *(G-19776)*

Pepsi-Cola Metro Btlg Co Inc E 330 336-3553
Wadsworth *(G-18767)*

Pepsi-Cola Metro Btlg Co Inc E 440 323-5524
Elyria *(G-10669)*

Prime Time Enterprises Inc E 440 891-8855
Cleveland *(G-6306)*

Restaurant Depot LLC E 216 525-0101
Cleveland *(G-6386)*

Roppe Holding Company E 419 435-9335
Fostoria *(G-11139)*

RR Donnelley & Sons Company E 614 539-5527
Grove City *(G-11593)*

Safelite Fulfillment Inc E 614 781-5449
Columbus *(G-8670)*

Safelite Fulfillment Inc E 216 475-7781
Cleveland *(G-6435)*

Sally Beauty Supply LLC C 937 548-7684
Greenville *(G-11518)*

Sally Beauty Supply LLC C 614 278-1691
Columbus *(G-8678)*

SH Bell Company E 412 963-9910
East Liverpool *(G-10534)*

Springs Window Fashions LLC D 614 492-6770
Groveport *(G-11673)*

Terminal Warehouse Inc E 330 453-3709
Canton *(G-2559)*

The C-Z Company E 740 432-6334
Cambridge *(G-2131)*

Tmarzetti Company C 614 277-3577
Grove City *(G-11605)*

Top Dawg Group LLC E 216 398-1066
Brooklyn Heights *(G-1928)*

Twist Inc E 937 675-9581
Xenia *(G-20081)*

Utility Trailer Mfg Co E 513 436-2600
Batavia *(G-1031)*

Verst Group Logistics Inc C 513 782-1725
Cincinnati *(G-4809)*

Verst Group Logistics Inc E 513 772-2494
Cincinnati *(G-4810)*

Victory White Metal Company E 216 271-7200
Cleveland *(G-6695)*

W W Williams Company LLC E 614 228-5000
Columbus *(G-8960)*

Walmart Inc B 937 843-3681
Belle Center *(G-1373)*

Walmart Inc A 740 636-5400
Wshngtn CT Hs *(G-20036)*

Walmart Inc A 614 871-7094
Grove City *(G-11611)*

Walmart Inc B 740 765-5700
Wintersville *(G-19811)*

Walmart Inc B 614 409-5500
Lockbourne *(G-12962)*

Warehouse Services Group Llc E 419 868-6400
Holland *(G-12068)*

Westway Trml Cincinnati LLC E 513 921-8441
Cincinnati *(G-4846)*

WAREHOUSING & STORAGE: Liquid

BDS Inc E 513 921-8441
Cincinnati *(G-3086)*

WAREHOUSING & STORAGE: Miniwarehouse

Public Storage E 216 220-7978
Bedford Heights *(G-1357)*

WAREHOUSING & STORAGE: Refrigerated

Cloverleaf Cold Storage Co C 419 599-5015
Napoleon *(G-14934)*

Crescent Park Corporation C 513 759-7000
West Chester *(G-19059)*

Woodruff Enterprises Inc E 937 399-9300
Springfield *(G-17301)*

WAREHOUSING & STORAGE: Self Storage

Al-Mar Lanes E 419 352-4637
Bowling Green *(G-1757)*

Compass Self Storage LLC E 216 458-0670
Cleveland *(G-5388)*

Fulfillment Technologies LLC C 513 346-3100
West Chester *(G-19203)*

Kenco Group Inc E 614 409-8754
Groveport *(G-11653)*

Oatey Supply Chain Svcs Inc E 216 267-7100
Cleveland *(G-6177)*

WARM AIR HEATING & AC EQPT & SPLYS, WHOLESALE Air Filters

Swift Filters Inc E 440 735-0995
Oakwood Village *(G-15634)*

WARM AIR HEATING & AC EQPT & SPLYS, WHOLESALE Furnaces

Famous Distribution Inc E 330 434-5194
Akron *(G-216)*

Famous Distribution Inc D 330 762-9621
Akron *(G-215)*

WARM AIR HEATING & AC EQPT & SPLYS, WHOLESALE Furnaces, Elec

Famous II Inc D 330 762-9621
Akron *(G-218)*

The Famous Manufacturing Co E 330 762-9621
Akron *(G-476)*

WARM AIR HEATING/AC EQPT/SPLYS, WHOL Warm Air Htg Eqpt/Splys

Allied Supply Company Inc E 937 224-9833
Dayton *(G-9317)*

Famous Enterprises Inc E 330 762-9621
Akron *(G-217)*

Famous Enterprises Inc E 216 529-1010
Cleveland *(G-5571)*

Habegger Corporation E 513 853-6644
Cincinnati *(G-3724)*

Lakeside Supply Co E 216 941-6800
Cleveland *(G-5920)*

OEM Parts Outlet E 419 472-2237
Toledo *(G-18102)*

Slawson Equipment Co Inc E 216 391-7263
Cleveland *(G-6489)*

WW Grainger Inc E 614 276-5231
Columbus *(G-9010)*

WARM AIR HEATING/AC EQPT/SPLYS, WHOL: Ventilating Eqpt/Sply

American Hood Systems Inc E 440 365-4567
Elyria *(G-10593)*

WARRANTY INSURANCE: Automobile

Dimension Service Corporation C 614 226-7455
Dublin *(G-10321)*

Heritage Wrranty Insur Rrg Inc D 800 753-5236
Dublin *(G-10360)*

WASHERS: Metal

Andre Corporation E 574 293-0207
Mason *(G-13662)*

Atlas Bolt & Screw Company LLC C 419 289-6171
Ashland *(G-660)*

WASTE CLEANING SVCS

Bedford Heights City Waste E 440 439-5343
Bedford *(G-1295)*

WATCH REPAIR SVCS

Cox Paving Inc D 937 780-3075
Wshngtn CT Hs *(G-20018)*

WATCHES & PARTS, WHOLESALE

Toledo Jewelers Supply Co E 419 241-4181
Toledo *(G-18240)*

SERVICES SECTION

WELDING REPAIR SVC

WATER SOFTENER SVCS

Chardon Laboratories Inc .... E 614 860-1000
  Reynoldsburg (G-16438)
Clearwater Services Inc .... D 330 836-4946
  Akron (G-146)
Cwm Envronmental Cleveland LLC ... E 216 663-0808
  Cleveland (G-5458)
Empire One LLC .... E 330 628-9310
  Mogadore (G-14676)
Hague Water Conditioning Inc .... E 614 482-8121
  Groveport (G-11642)

WATER SOFTENING WHOLESALERS

Hague Water Conditioning Inc .... E 614 482-8121
  Groveport (G-11642)

WATER SPLY: Irrigation

City of Westerville .... E 614 901-6500
  Westerville (G-19382)
Pentair Rsdntial Fltration LLC .... E 440 286-4116
  Chardon (G-2762)

WATER SUPPLY

Aqua Ohio Inc .... E 330 832-5764
  Massillon (G-13787)
Aqua Pennsylvania Inc .... E 614 882-6586
  Westerville (G-19364)
Belmont County of Ohio .... E 740 695-3144
  Saint Clairsville (G-16622)
City Alliance Water Sewer Dst .... E 330 823-5216
  Alliance (G-533)
City of Akron .... E 330 678-0077
  Kent (G-12358)
City of Akron .... C 330 375-2420
  Akron (G-139)
City of Avon Lake .... E 440 933-6226
  Avon Lake (G-925)
City of Celina .... E 419 586-2451
  Celina (G-2639)
City of Cleveland .... E 216 664-3121
  Cleveland (G-5251)
City of Cleveland Heights .... E 216 291-5995
  Cleveland Heights (G-6788)
City of Columbus .... E 614 645-7490
  Columbus (G-7279)
City of Columbus .... E 614 645-8297
  Columbus (G-7285)
City of Columbus .... D 614 645-8270
  Columbus (G-7283)
City of Cuyahoga Falls .... E 330 971-8130
  Cuyahoga Falls (G-9175)
City of Dayton .... C 937 333-6070
  Dayton (G-9412)
City of Dayton .... E 937 333-3725
  Dayton (G-9410)
City of Huron .... D 419 433-5000
  Huron (G-12163)
City of Lorain .... E 440 288-0281
  Lorain (G-13023)
City of Lorain .... C 440 204-2500
  Lorain (G-13024)
City of Massillon .... E 330 833-3304
  Massillon (G-13796)
City of Toledo .... D 419 245-1800
  Toledo (G-17807)
City of Troy .... E 937 335-1914
  Troy (G-18351)
City of Westerville .... F 614 901-6500
  Westerville (G-19382)
City of Youngstown .... E 330 742-8749
  Youngstown (G-20144)
Clearwater Services Inc .... D 330 836-4946
  Akron (G-146)
Cleveland Water Department .... A 216 664-3168
  Cleveland (G-5354)
County of Licking .... E 740 967-5951
  Johnstown (G-12339)
County of Warren .... D 513 925-1377
  Lebanon (G-12600)
Del-Co Water Company Inc .... C 740 548-7746
  Delaware (G-10086)
East Liverpool Water Dept .... E 330 385-8812
  East Liverpool (G-10520)
Employment Relations Board .... E 513 863-0828
  Hamilton (G-11726)
Highland County Water Co Inc .... E 937 393-4281
  Hillsboro (G-11980)

Medical Center Co (inc) .... E 216 368-4256
  Cleveland (G-6014)
New Lexington City of .... E 740 342-1633
  New Lexington (G-15057)
Northern Ohio Rural Water .... E 419 668-7213
  Norwalk (G-15582)
Northwestern Water & Sewer Dst ...... E 419 354-9090
  Bowling Green (G-1787)
Ohio-American Water Co Inc .... E 740 382-3993
  Marion (G-13570)
Ross County Water Company Inc ..... E 740 774-4117
  Chillicothe (G-2881)
Rural Lorain County Water Auth .... D 440 355-5121
  Lagrange (G-12461)
Scioto County Region Wtr Dst 1 .... E 740 259-2301
  Lucasville (G-13182)
Syracuse Water Dept .... E 740 992-7777
  Pomeroy (G-16255)
Toledo Cy Pub Utlity Wtr Distr .... C 419 936-2506
  Toledo (G-18235)
Victory White Metal Company .... E 216 271-7200
  Cleveland (G-6695)

WATER: Distilled

Distillata Company .... D 216 771-2900
  Cleveland (G-5489)

WATERBEDS & ACCESS STORES

Waterbeds n Stuff Inc .... E 614 871-1171
  Grove City (G-11612)

WEATHER FORECASTING SVCS

National Weather Service .... E 937 383-0031
  Wilmington (G-19774)
National Weather Service .... E 216 265-2370
  Cleveland (G-6113)
National Weather Service .... E 419 522-1375
  Mansfield (G-13349)

WEDDING CHAPEL: Privately Operated

Delaware Golf Club Inc .... E 740 362-2582
  Delaware (G-10089)
Hall Nazareth Inc .... D 419 832-2900
  Grand Rapids (G-11449)

WELDING EQPT

Select-Arc Inc .... C 937 295-5215
  Fort Loramie (G-11111)

WELDING EQPT & SPLYS WHOLESALERS

Airgas Usa LLC .... B 216 642-6600
  Independence (G-12183)
Albright Welding Supply Co Inc .... E 330 264-2021
  Wooster (G-19826)
Daihen Inc .... E 937 667-0800
  Tipp City (G-17715)
Lefeld Welding & Stl Sups Inc .... E 419 678-2397
  Coldwater (G-6832)
Matheson Tri-Gas Inc .... E 614 771-1311
  Hilliard (G-11925)
O E Meyer Co .... D 419 625-1256
  Sandusky (G-16784)
Praxair Distribution Inc .... E 330 376-2242
  Akron (G-400)
Taylor - Winfield Corporation .... D 330 797-0300
  Youngstown (G-20387)
Weiler Welding Company Inc .... D 937 222-8312
  Moraine (G-14835)
Weld Plus Inc .... E 513 941-4411
  Cincinnati (G-4830)

WELDING REPAIR SVC

A & C Welding Inc .... E 330 762-4777
  Peninsula (G-15946)
A & G Manufacturing Co Inc .... E 419 468-7433
  Galion (G-11288)
Abbott Tool Inc .... E 419 476-6742
  Toledo (G-17738)
All-Type Welding & Fabrication .... E 440 439-3990
  Cleveland (G-4991)
Allied Fabricating & Wldg Co .... E 614 751-6664
  Columbus (G-6970)
Arctech Fabricating Inc .... E 937 525-9353
  Springfield (G-17149)
Athens Mold and Machine Inc .... D 740 593-6613
  Akron (G-84)

Bayloff Stmped Pdts Knsman Inc ...... D 330 876-4511
  Kinsman (G-12452)
Blevins Metal Fabrication Inc .... E 419 522-6082
  Mansfield (G-13267)
Breitinger Company .... C 419 526-4255
  Mansfield (G-13269)
C & R Inc .... E 614 497-1130
  Groveport (G-11626)
C-N-D Industries Inc .... E 330 478-8811
  Massillon (G-13791)
Carter Manufacturing Co Inc .... E 513 398-7303
  Mason (G-13672)
Chipmatic Tool & Machine Inc .... D 419 862-2737
  Elmore (G-10587)
Compton Metal Products Inc .... E 937 382-2403
  Wilmington (G-19757)
Creative Mold and Machine Inc .... E 440 338-5146
  Newbury (G-15255)
Crest Bending Inc .... E 419 492-2108
  New Washington (G-15134)
Custom Machine Inc .... E 419 986-5122
  Tiffin (G-17676)
Dynamic Weld Corporation .... E 419 582-2900
  Osgood (G-15791)
East End Welding Company .... C 330 677-6000
  Kent (G-12367)
Falls Stamping & Welding Co .... C 330 928-1191
  Cuyahoga Falls (G-9185)
Fosbel Inc .... E 216 362-3900
  Brookpark (G-1945)
Fosbel Holding Inc .... E 216 362-3900
  Cleveland (G-5625)
Gaspar Inc .... D 330 477-2222
  Canton (G-2376)
General Tool Company .... C 513 733-5500
  Cincinnati (G-3675)
George Steel Fabricating Inc .... E 513 932-2887
  Lebanon (G-12606)
Glenridge Machine Co .... E 440 975-1055
  Willoughby (G-19666)
Habco Tool and Dev Co Inc .... E 440 946-5546
  Mentor (G-14187)
HI Tecmetal Group Inc .... E 440 373-5101
  Wickliffe (G-19601)
HI Tecmetal Group Inc .... E 440 946-2280
  Willoughby (G-19669)
Hi-Tek Manufacturing Inc .... C 513 459-1094
  Mason (G-13717)
Hobart Bros Stick Electrode .... C 937 332-5375
  Troy (G-18357)
J & S Industrial Mch Pdts Inc .... D 419 691-1380
  Toledo (G-17980)
Jerl Machine Inc .... D 419 873-0270
  Perrysburg (G-16020)
JMw Welding and Mfg .... E 330 484-2428
  Canton (G-2418)
K-M-S Industries Inc .... E 440 243-6680
  Brookpark (G-1948)
Kings Welding and Fabg Inc .... E 330 738-3592
  Mechanicstown (G-14031)
Kottler Metal Products Co Inc .... E 440 946-7473
  Willoughby (G-19677)
L B Industries Inc .... E 330 750-1002
  Struthers (G-17533)
Laserflex Corporation .... D 614 850-9600
  Hilliard (G-11920)
Liberty Casting Company LLC .... E 740 363-1941
  Delaware (G-10116)
Lima Sheet Metal Machine & Mfg ..... E 419 229-1161
  Lima (G-12827)
Long-Stanton Mfg Company .... E 513 874-8020
  West Chester (G-19111)
Majestic Tool and Machine Inc .... E 440 248-5058
  Solon (G-17025)
Marsam Metalfab Inc .... E 330 405-1520
  Twinsburg (G-18444)
Meta Manufacturing Corporation .... E 513 793-6382
  Blue Ash (G-1643)
Norman Noble Inc .... C 216 761-2133
  Cleveland (G-6136)
Northwind Industries Inc .... E 216 433-0666
  Cleveland (G-6163)
Ohio Hydraulics Inc .... E 513 771-2590
  Cincinnati (G-4207)
Ohio State University .... E 614 292-4139
  Columbus (G-8399)
Pentaflex Inc .... C 937 325-5551
  Springfield (G-17260)
Phillips Mfg and Tower Co .... D 419 347-1720
  Shelby (G-16902)

Employee Codes: A=Over 500 employees, B=251-500
C=101-250, D=51-100, E=25-50

WELDING REPAIR SVC — SERVICES SECTION

Precision Mtal Fabrication Inc .... D 937 235-9261
  Dayton (G-9818)
Precision Welding Corporation .... E 216 524-6110
  Cleveland (G-6295)
Prout Boiler Htg & Wldg Inc .... E 330 744-0293
  Youngstown (G-20331)
Quality Welding Inc .... E 419 483-6067
  Bellevue (G-1416)
Rbm Environmental and Cnstr .... E 419 693-5840
  Oregon (G-15748)
Schmidt Machine Company .... E 419 294-3814
  Upper Sandusky (G-18566)
Steubenville Truck Center Inc .... E 740 282-2711
  Steubenville (G-17337)
Systems Jay LLC Nanogate .... B 419 747-4161
  Mansfield (G-13370)
Tendon Manufacturing Inc .... E 216 663-3200
  Cleveland (G-6582)
Triangle Precision Industries .... D 937 299-6776
  Dayton (G-9937)
Two M Precision Co Inc .... E 440 946-2120
  Willoughby (G-19719)
Valley Machine Tool Co Inc .... E 513 899-2737
  Morrow (G-14847)
Viking Fabricators Inc .... E 740 374-5246
  Marietta (G-13515)
Wayne Trail Technologies Inc .... D 937 295-2120
  Fort Loramie (G-11112)

WELDING SPLYS, EXC GASES: Wholesalers

Albright Welding Supply Co Inc .... E 330 264-2021
  Wooster (G-19826)
Delille Oxygen Company .... E 614 444-1777
  Columbus (G-7504)
F & M Mafco Inc .... C 513 367-2151
  Harrison (G-11797)

WELDMENTS

Loveman Steel Corporation .... D 440 232-6200
  Bedford (G-1317)

WELFARE PENSIONS

County of Seneca .... D 419 447-5011
  Tiffin (G-17675)

WHEELBARROWS

Huffy Corporation .... D 937 743-5011
  Springboro (G-17124)

WHEELS

Rocknstarr Holdings LLC .... E 330 509-9086
  Youngstown (G-20354)

WHEELS & BRAKE SHOES: Railroad, Cast Iron

Amsted Industries Incorporated .... C 614 836-2323
  Groveport (G-11622)

WINDOW & DOOR FRAMES

Midwest Curtainwalls Inc .... D 216 641-7900
  Cleveland (G-6060)

WINDOW CLEANING SVCS

Aetna Building Maintenance Inc .... D 937 324-5711
  Springfield (G-17146)
Ajax Cleaning Contractors Co .... D 216 881-8484
  Cleveland (G-4980)
Clearview Cleaning Contractors .... E 216 621-6688
  Cleveland (G-5285)
E Wynn Inc .... E 614 444-5288
  Columbus (G-7562)
H & B Window Cleaning Inc .... E 440 934-6158
  Avon Lake (G-931)
Ohio Window Cleaning Inc .... D 937 877-0832
  Tipp City (G-17723)

WINDOW FRAMES & SASHES: Plastic

Champion Opco LLC .... B 513 924-4858
  Cincinnati (G-3228)

WINDOW FRAMES, MOLDING & TRIM: Vinyl

Modern Builders Supply Inc .... C 330 729-2690
  Youngstown (G-20289)

Owens Corning Sales LLC .... A 419 248-8000
  Toledo (G-18114)
Vinyl Design Corporation .... E 419 283-4009
  Holland (G-12067)

WINE & DISTILLED ALCOHOLIC BEVERAGES WHOLESALERS

Dayton Heidelberg Distrg Co .... C 419 666-9783
  Perrysburg (G-15994)
Esber Beverage Company .... E 330 456-4361
  Canton (G-2360)
Glazers Distributors Ohio Inc .... E 440 542-7000
  Solon (G-17010)
M & A Distributing Co Inc .... E 440 703-4580
  Solon (G-17024)
M & A Distributing Co Inc .... D 614 294-3555
  Columbus (G-8091)

WINE CELLARS, BONDED: Wine, Blended

Georgetown Vineyards Inc .... E 740 435-3222
  Cambridge (G-2115)

WIRE & WIRE PRDTS

Dolin Supply Co 304 529-4171
  South Point (G-17084)
Efco Corp .... E 614 876-1226
  Columbus (G-7586)
Gateway Concrete Forming Svcs .... D 513 353-2000
  Miamitown (G-14371)
Panacea Products Corporation .... E 614 850-7000
  Columbus (G-8513)
Schweizer Dipple Inc .... D 440 786-8090
  Cleveland (G-6451)

WIRE FENCING & ACCESS WHOLESALERS

Agratronix LLC .... E 330 562-2222
  Streetsboro (G-17406)
Mills Fence Co Inc .... E 513 631-0333
  Cincinnati (G-4100)
Richards Whl Fence Co Inc .... E 330 773-0423
  Akron (G-415)
Security Fence Group Inc .... E 513 681-3700
  Cincinnati (G-4489)

WIRE MATERIALS: Steel

Bayloff Stmped Pdts Knsman Inc .... D 330 876-4511
  Kinsman (G-12452)
File Sharpening Company Inc .... E 937 376-8268
  Xenia (G-20050)
Master-Halco Inc .... E 513 869-7600
  Fairfield (G-10876)
Noco Company .... B 216 464-8131
  Solon (G-17035)

WIRE WINDING OF PURCHASED WIRE

Providence Rees Inc .... E 614 833-6231
  Columbus (G-8573)

WIRE, FLAT: Strip, Cold-Rolled, Exc From Hot-Rolled Mills

Hynes Industries Inc .... C 330 799-3221
  Youngstown (G-20227)

WIRE: Nonferrous

Electrovations Inc .... E 330 274-3558
  Aurora (G-837)
Legrand North America LLC .... B 937 224-0639
  Moraine (G-14798)
Radix Wire Co .... D 216 731-9191
  Cleveland (G-6345)
Scott Fetzer Company .... C 216 267-9000
  Cleveland (G-6452)

WOMEN'S & CHILDREN'S CLOTHING WHOLESALERS, NEC

Abercrombie & Fitch Trading Co .... E 614 283-6500
  New Albany (G-14970)
Cheek-O Inc .... E 513 942-4880
  Cincinnati (G-3236)
Chester West Holdings Inc .... C 800 647-1900
  Cincinnati (G-3241)
Classic Imports Inc .... E 330 262-5277
  Wooster (G-19847)

For Women Like Me Inc .... E 407 848-7339
  Chagrin Falls (G-2696)
J Peterman Company LLC .... E 888 647-2555
  Blue Ash (G-1619)
Mast Industries Inc .... C 614 415-7000
  Columbus (G-8124)
Mast Industries Inc .... D 614 856-6000
  Reynoldsburg (G-16468)
McCc Sportswear Inc .... E 513 583-9210
  West Chester (G-19214)
MGF Sourcing Us LLC .... A 614 904-3300
  Columbus (G-8156)
Rassak LLC .... E 513 791-9453
  Cincinnati (G-4386)

WOMEN'S & GIRLS' SPORTSWEAR WHOLESALERS

Barbs Graffiti Inc .... D 216 881-5550
  Cleveland (G-5093)
Barbs Graffiti Inc .... E 216 881-5550
  Cleveland (G-5094)
Gymnastic World Inc .... E 440 526-2970
  Cleveland (G-5712)
Heritage Sportswear Inc .... D 740 928-7771
  Hebron (G-11850)
R & A Sports Inc .... E 216 289-2254
  Euclid (G-10773)
TSC Apparel LLC .... D 513 771-1138
  Cincinnati (G-4703)

WOMEN'S CLOTHING STORES

Abercrombie & Fitch Trading Co .... E 614 283-6500
  New Albany (G-14970)
For Women Like Me Inc .... E 407 848-7339
  Chagrin Falls (G-2696)
J Cherie LLC .... E 216 453-1051
  Shaker Heights (G-16862)
J Peterman Company LLC .... E 888 647-2555
  Blue Ash (G-1619)

WOOD & WOOD BY-PRDTS, WHOLESALE

77 Coach Supply Ltd .... E 330 674-1454
  Millersburg (G-14582)
Earth n Wood Products Inc .... E 330 644-1858
  Akron (G-204)
Gross Lumber Inc .... E 330 683-2055
  Apple Creek (G-625)
Premium Beverage Supply Ltd .... E 614 777-1007
  Hilliard (G-11944)

WOOD CHIPS, PRODUCED AT THE MILL

Miller Logging Inc .... E 330 279-4721
  Holmesville (G-12074)

WOOD PRDTS: Moldings, Unfinished & Prefinished

J McCoy Lumber Co Ltd .... E 937 587-3423
  Peebles (G-15940)

WOOD PRDTS: Mulch, Wood & Bark

Scotts Company LLC .... A 937 644-3729
  Marysville (G-13650)

WOOD PRDTS: Survey Stakes

Lawnview Industries Inc .... C 937 653-5217
  Urbana (G-18593)

WOODWORK & TRIM: Interior & Ornamental

LE Smith Company .... D 419 636-4555
  Bryan (G-2009)

WORK EXPERIENCE CENTER

Mary Hmmond Adult Actvties Ctr .... D 740 962-4200
  McConnelsville (G-14028)
Trumbull Cmnty Action Program .... E 330 393-2507
  Warren (G-18909)

X-RAY EQPT & TUBES

Philips Medical Systems Clevel .... B 440 247-2652
  Cleveland (G-6273)

X-RAY EQPT REPAIR SVCS

Alpha Imaging LLC .... D 440 953-3800
   Willoughby *(G-19643)*

YACHT CLUBS

Atwood Yacht Club Inc .... E 330 735-2135
   Sherrodsville *(G-16905)*
Blennerhassett Yacht Club Inc .... E 740 423-9062
   Belpre *(G-1434)*
Buckeye Lake Yacht Club Inc .... E 740 929-4466
   Buckeye Lake *(G-2021)*
Cleveland Yachting Club Inc .... D 440 333-1155
   Cleveland *(G-5356)*
Mentor Lagoons Yacht Club Inc .... D 440 205-3625
   Mentor *(G-14213)*
Wildwood Yacht Club Inc .... D 216 531-9052
   Cleveland *(G-6752)*

YOUTH CAMPS

Family YMCA of LANcstr&fairfld .... D 740 277-7373
   Lancaster *(G-12541)*
Findlay Y M C A Child Dev .... E 419 422-3174
   Findlay *(G-11031)*
Galion Community Center YMCA .... E 419 468-7754
   Galion *(G-11297)*
Great Miami Valley YMCA .... D 513 887-0001
   Hamilton *(G-11733)*
Great Miami Valley YMCA .... C 513 892-9622
   Fairfield Township *(G-10930)*
Great Miami Valley YMCA .... D 513 887-0014
   Hamilton *(G-11735)*
Great Miami Valley YMCA .... D 513 868-9622
   Hamilton *(G-11736)*
Great Miami Valley YMCA .... D 513 829-3091
   Fairfield *(G-10854)*
Hardin County Family YMCA .... E 419 673-6131
   Kenton *(G-12416)*
Highland County Family YMCA .... E 937 840-9622
   Hillsboro *(G-11978)*
Huber Heights YMCA .... D 937 236-9622
   Dayton *(G-9623)*
Lake County YMCA .... A 440 352-3303
   Painesville *(G-15860)*
Lake County YMCA .... C 440 946-1160
   Willoughby *(G-19680)*
Lake County YMCA .... E 440 259-2724
   Perry *(G-15962)*
Lake County YMCA .... D 440 428-5125
   Madison *(G-13227)*
Pike County YMCA .... E 740 947-8862
   Waverly *(G-18974)*
Red Oak Camp .... E 440 256-0716
   Willoughby *(G-19707)*
Springfield Family Y M C A .... D 937 323-3781
   Springfield *(G-17281)*
Sycamore Board of Education .... D 513 489-3937
   Cincinnati *(G-4608)*

Ucc Childrens Center .... E 513 217-5501
   Middletown *(G-14488)*
Y M C A Central Stark County .... E 330 305-5437
   Canton *(G-2590)*
Y M C A Central Stark County .... E 330 875-1611
   Louisville *(G-13108)*
Y M C A Central Stark County .... E 330 877-8933
   Uniontown *(G-18545)*
Y M C A Central Stark County .... E 330 830-6275
   Massillon *(G-13862)*
Y M C A Central Stark County .... E 330 498-4082
   Canton *(G-2591)*
Y M C A of Ashland Ohio Inc .... D 419 289-0626
   Ashland *(G-709)*
YMCA .... E 330 823-1930
   Alliance *(G-566)*
YMCA Inc .... D 330 385-6400
   East Liverpool *(G-10536)*
YMCA of Clermont County Inc .... E 513 724-9622
   Batavia *(G-1032)*
YMCA of Massillon .... E 330 879-0800
   Navarre *(G-14957)*
Young Mens Christian .... B 513 932-1424
   Lebanon *(G-12660)*
Young Mens Christian Assn .... E 419 238-0443
   Van Wert *(G-18653)*
Young Mens Christian Assoc .... C 614 871-9622
   Grove City *(G-11620)*
Young Mens Christian Assoc .... A 937 223-5201
   Dayton *(G-10009)*
Young Mens Christian Assoc .... D 330 923-5223
   Cuyahoga Falls *(G-9237)*
Young Mens Christian Assoc .... E 330 467-8366
   Macedonia *(G-13219)*
Young Mens Christian Assoc .... E 330 784-0408
   Akron *(G-515)*
Young Mens Christian Assoc .... C 614 416-9622
   Gahanna *(G-11276)*
Young Mens Christian Assoc .... C 740 881-1058
   Powell *(G-16355)*
Young Mens Christian Assoc .... C 614 334-9622
   Hilliard *(G-11967)*
Young Mens Christian Assoc .... E 937 312-1810
   Dayton *(G-10010)*
Young Mens Christian Assoc .... E 614 539-1770
   Urbancrest *(G-18609)*
Young Mens Christian Assoc .... D 614 252-3166
   Columbus *(G-9019)*
Young Mens Christian Assoc .... E 937 593-9001
   Bellefontaine *(G-1401)*
Young Mens Christian Associat .... E 419 729-8135
   Toledo *(G-18320)*
Young Mens Christian Associat .... D 513 241-9622
   Cincinnati *(G-4868)*
Young Mens Christian Associat .... D 513 923-4466
   Cincinnati *(G-4869)*
Young Mens Christian Associat .... E 419 474-3995
   Toledo *(G-18322)*
Young Mens Christian Associat .... D 419 866-9622
   Maumee *(G-13997)*

Young Mens Christian Associat .... C 419 475-3496
   Toledo *(G-18323)*
Young Mens Christian Associat .... D 419 691-3523
   Oregon *(G-15756)*
Young Mens Christian Mt Vernon .... D 740 392-9622
   Mount Vernon *(G-14927)*
Young MNS Chrstn Assn Clveland ...... E 216 521-8400
   Lakewood *(G-12502)*
Young MNS Chrstn Assn Clveland ...... D 440 842-5200
   North Royalton *(G-15507)*
Young MNS Chrstn Assn Clveland ...... E 216 731-7454
   Cleveland *(G-6774)*
Young MNS Chrstn Assn Clveland ...... D 440 285-7543
   Chardon *(G-2780)*
Young MNS Chrstn Assn Grter NY ...... D 740 392-9622
   Mount Vernon *(G-14928)*
Young Womens Christian .... D 419 241-3235
   Toledo *(G-18325)*
Young Womens Christian .... D 937 461-5550
   Dayton *(G-10013)*
Young Womens Christian .... E 419 238-6639
   Van Wert *(G-18654)*
Young Womens Christian Assn .... D 614 224-9121
   Columbus *(G-9021)*
Young Womens Christian Assn .... E 330 746-6361
   Youngstown *(G-20422)*
Young Womens Christian Associ .... E 216 881-6878
   Cleveland *(G-6776)*
Young Womns Chrstn Assc Canton .... D 330 453-0789
   Canton *(G-2594)*
YWCA of Greater Cincinnati .... D 513 241-7090
   Cincinnati *(G-4870)*
YWCA Shelter & Housing Network ..... E 937 222-6333
   Dayton *(G-10014)*

YOUTH SELF-HELP AGENCY

Help ME Grow .... E 419 738-4773
   Wapakoneta *(G-18799)*

ZOOLOGICAL GARDEN, NONCOMMERCIAL

Akron Zoological Park .... E 330 375-2550
   Akron *(G-60)*
Animal Mgt Svcs Ohio Inc .... E 248 398-6533
   Port Clinton *(G-16237)*
Columbus Zoological Park Assn .... C 614 645-3400
   Powell *(G-16330)*
Toledo Zoological Society .... B 419 385-4040
   Toledo *(G-18254)*
Zoological Society Cincinnati .... B 513 281-4700
   Cincinnati *(G-4874)*

ZOOS & BOTANICAL GARDENS

Cleveland Metroparks .... C 216 661-6500
   Cleveland *(G-5329)*
Park Cincinnati Board .... D 513 421-4086
   Cincinnati *(G-4252)*
Stan Hywet Hall and Grdns Inc .... D 330 836-5533
   Akron *(G-449)*

Employee Codes: A=Over 500 employees, C=101-250, D=51-100, E=25-50

SERVICES SECTION

X-RAY EQPT REPAIR SVCS

Alpha Imaging LLC ....D...... 440 953-3800
Willoughby *(G-19643)*

YACHT CLUBS

Atwood Yacht Club Inc ....E...... 330 735-2135
Sherrodsville *(G-16905)*
Blennerhassett Yacht Club Inc ....E...... 740 423-9062
Belpre *(G-1434)*
Buckeye Lake Yacht Club Inc ....E...... 740 929-4466
Buckeye Lake *(G-2021)*
Cleveland Yachting Club Inc ....D...... 440 333-1155
Cleveland *(G-5356)*
Mentor Lagoons Yacht Club Inc ....D...... 440 205-3625
Mentor *(G-14213)*
Wildwood Yacht Club Inc ....D...... 216 531-9052
Cleveland *(G-6752)*

YOUTH CAMPS

Family YMCA of LANcstr&fairfld ....D...... 740 277-7373
Lancaster *(G-12541)*
Findlay Y M C A Child Dev ....E...... 419 422-3174
Findlay *(G-11031)*
Galion Community Center YMCA ....E...... 419 468-7754
Galion *(G-11297)*
Great Miami Valley YMCA ....D...... 513 887-0001
Hamilton *(G-11733)*
Great Miami Valley YMCA ....C...... 513 892-9622
Fairfield Township *(G-10930)*
Great Miami Valley YMCA ....D...... 513 887-0014
Hamilton *(G-11735)*
Great Miami Valley YMCA ....D...... 513 868-9622
Hamilton *(G-11736)*
Great Miami Valley YMCA ....D...... 513 829-3091
Fairfield *(G-10854)*
Hardin County Family YMCA ....E...... 419 673-6131
Kenton *(G-12416)*
Highland County Family YMCA ....E...... 937 840-9622
Hillsboro *(G-11978)*
Huber Heights YMCA ....D...... 937 236-9622
Dayton *(G-9623)*
Lake County YMCA ....A...... 440 352-3303
Painesville *(G-15860)*
Lake County YMCA ....C...... 440 946-1160
Willoughby *(G-19680)*
Lake County YMCA ....E...... 440 259-2724
Perry *(G-15962)*
Lake County YMCA ....D...... 440 428-5125
Madison *(G-13227)*
Pike County YMCA ....E...... 740 947-8862
Waverly *(G-18974)*
Red Oak Camp ....E...... 440 256-0716
Willoughby *(G-19707)*
Springfield Family Y M C A ....D...... 937 323-3781
Springfield *(G-17281)*
Sycamore Board of Education ....D...... 513 489-3937
Cincinnati *(G-4608)*
Ucc Childrens Center ....E...... 513 217-5501
Middletown *(G-14488)*
Y M C A Central Stark County ....E...... 330 305-5437
Canton *(G-2590)*
Y M C A Central Stark County ....E...... 330 875-1611
Louisville *(G-13108)*
Y M C A Central Stark County ....E...... 330 877-8933
Uniontown *(G-18545)*
Y M C A Central Stark County ....E...... 330 830-6275
Massillon *(G-13862)*
Y M C A Central Stark County ....E...... 330 498-4082
Canton *(G-2591)*
Y M C A of Ashland Ohio Inc ....D...... 419 289-0626
Ashland *(G-709)*
YMCA ....E...... 330 823-1930
Alliance *(G-566)*
YMCA Inc ....D...... 330 385-6400
East Liverpool *(G-10536)*
YMCA of Clermont County Inc ....E...... 513 724-9622
Batavia *(G-1032)*
YMCA of Massillon ....E...... 330 879-0800
Navarre *(G-14957)*
Young Mens Christian ....B...... 513 932-1424
Lebanon *(G-12660)*
Young Mens Christian Assn ....E...... 419 238-0443
Van Wert *(G-18653)*
Young Mens Christian Assoc ....C...... 614 871-9622
Grove City *(G-11620)*
Young Mens Christian Assoc ....A...... 937 223-5201
Dayton *(G-10009)*
Young Mens Christian Assoc ....D...... 330 923-5223
Cuyahoga Falls *(G-9237)*
Young Mens Christian Assoc ....E...... 330 467-8366
Macedonia *(G-13219)*
Young Mens Christian Assoc ....E...... 330 784-0408
Akron *(G-515)*
Young Mens Christian Assoc ....C...... 614 416-9622
Gahanna *(G-11276)*
Young Mens Christian Assoc ....C...... 740 881-1058
Powell *(G-16355)*
Young Mens Christian Assoc ....C...... 614 334-9622
Hilliard *(G-11967)*
Young Mens Christian Assoc ....E...... 937 312-1810
Dayton *(G-10010)*
Young Mens Christian Assoc ....E...... 614 539-1770
Urbancrest *(G-18609)*
Young Mens Christian Assoc ....D...... 614 252-3166
Columbus *(G-9019)*
Young Mens Christian Assoc ....E...... 937 593-9001
Bellefontaine *(G-1401)*
Young Mens Christian Associat ....E...... 419 729-8135
Toledo *(G-18320)*
Young Mens Christian Associat ....D...... 513 241-9622
Cincinnati *(G-4868)*
Young Mens Christian Associat ....D...... 513 923-4466
Cincinnati *(G-4869)*
Young Mens Christian Associat ....E...... 419 474-3995
Toledo *(G-18322)*
Young Mens Christian Associat ....E...... 419 866-9622
Maumee *(G-13997)*
Young Mens Christian Associat ....C...... 419 475-3496
Toledo *(G-18323)*
Young Mens Christian Associat ....D...... 419 691-3523
Oregon *(G-15756)*
Young Mens Christian Mt Vernon ....D...... 740 392-9622
Mount Vernon *(G-14927)*
Young MNS Chrstn Assn Clveland ....E...... 216 521-8400
Lakewood *(G-12502)*
Young MNS Chrstn Assn Clveland ....D...... 440 842-5200
North Royalton *(G-15507)*
Young MNS Chrstn Assn Clveland ....E...... 216 731-7454
Cleveland *(G-6774)*
Young MNS Chrstn Assn Clveland ....D...... 440 285-7543
Chardon *(G-2780)*
Young MNS Chrstn Assn Grter NY ....D...... 740 392-9622
Mount Vernon *(G-14928)*
Young Womens Christian ....D...... 419 241-3235
Toledo *(G-18325)*
Young Womens Christian ....D...... 937 461-5550
Dayton *(G-10013)*
Young Womens Christian ....E...... 419 238-6639
Van Wert *(G-18654)*
Young Womens Christian Assn ....D...... 614 224-9121
Columbus *(G-9021)*
Young Womens Christian Assn ....E...... 330 746-6361
Youngstown *(G-20422)*
Young Womens Christian Associ ....E...... 216 881-6878
Cleveland *(G-6776)*
Young Womns Chrstn Assc Canton ....D...... 330 453-0789
Canton *(G-2594)*
YWCA of Greater Cincinnati ....D...... 513 241-7090
Cincinnati *(G-4870)*
YWCA Shelter & Housing Network ....E...... 937 222-6333
Dayton *(G-10014)*

YOUTH SELF-HELP AGENCY

Help ME Grow ....E...... 419 738-4773
Wapakoneta *(G-18799)*

ZOOLOGICAL GARDEN, NONCOMMERCIAL

Akron Zoological Park ....E...... 330 375-2550
Akron *(G-60)*
Animal Mgt Svcs Ohio Inc ....E...... 248 398-6533
Port Clinton *(G-16237)*
Columbus Zoological Park Assn ....C...... 614 645-3400
Powell *(G-16330)*
Toledo Zoological Society ....B...... 419 385-4040
Toledo *(G-18254)*
Zoological Society Cincinnati ....B...... 513 281-4700
Cincinnati *(G-4874)*

ZOOS & BOTANICAL GARDENS

Cleveland Metroparks ....C...... 216 661-6500
Cleveland *(G-5329)*
Park Cincinnati Board ....D...... 513 421-4086
Cincinnati *(G-4252)*
Stan Hywet Hall and Grdns Inc ....D...... 330 836-5533
Akron *(G-449)*